2015
Third Edition

Profiles
of
North Carolina &
South Carolina

A UNIVERSAL REFERENCE BOOK

Grey House
Publishing

PUBLISHER: Leslie Mackenzie
EDITORIAL DIRECTOR: Laura Mars
EDITOR: David Garoogian
MARKETING DIRECTOR: Jessica Moody

Grey House Publishing, Inc.
4919 Route 22
Amenia, NY 12501
518.789.8700
FAX 845.373.6390
www.greyhouse.com
e-mail: books @greyhouse.com

ISBN: 978-1-61925-138-0

Table of Contents

PART II: SOUTH CAROLINA

Introduction

This is the third edition of *Profiles of North Carolina & South Carolina—Facts, Figures & Statistics for 1,358 Populated Places in North Carolina & South Carolina.* As with the other titles in our *State Profiles* series, it was built with content from Grey House Publishing's award-winning *Profiles of America*—a 4-volume compilation of data on more than 43,000 places in the United States. We have updated and included the North Carolina and South Carolina chapters from *Profiles of America,* and added several new chapters of demographic information and ranking sections, so that *Profiles of North Carolina & South Carolina* is the most comprehensive portrait of the states of North Carolina & South Carolina ever published.

Profiles of North Carolina & South Carolina provides data on all populated communities and counties in the states for which the US Census provides individual statistics. This edition also includes profiles of 226 unincorporated places based on US Census data by zip code.

This premier reference work includes seven major sections that cover everything from **Education** to **Ethnic Backgrounds** to **Climate**. All sections include **Comparative Statistics** or **Rankings**. **About North Carolina** and **About South Carolina** at the front of each section, are comprised of detailed narrative and colorful photos and maps. Here is an overview of each section:

1. About North Carolina and About South Carolina
These NEW 4-color sections gives the researcher a real sense of each state and its history. They include a Photo Gallery, and comprehensive sections on History and Government, Land and Natural Resources, Energy, and Demographic Maps. With charts and maps, these 97 pages help to anchor the researcher to the states, both physically and politically.

2. Profiles
These sections, organized by county, give detailed profiles of 1,358 places plus 146 counties, based on Census 2010 and data from the American Community Survey. We have added current government statistics and original research, so that these profiles pull together statistical and descriptive information on every Census-recognized place in each state. Major fields of information include:

Geography	*Housing*	*Education*	*Religion*
Ancestry	*Transportation*	*Population*	*Climate*
Economy	*Industry*	*Health*	

NEW categories to this edition include data on public and private health insurance, language spoken at home, people with disabilities and veterans. In addition to place profiles, this section includes a **Place Name Index.**

3. Comparative Statistics
These sections include tables that compare North and South Carolina's 100 largest communities by dozens of data points.

4. Community Rankings
These NEW sections include tables that rank the top and bottom 150 communities with population over 2,500, in dozens of categories.

5. Education
These sections begin with an **Educational State Profile,** summarizing number of schools, students, diplomas granted and educational dollars spent. Following the state profile are **School District Rankings** on 16 topics ranging from *Teacher/Student Ratios* to *High School Drop-Out Rates.* Following these rankings are statewide *National Assessment of Educational Progress (NAEP)* results and information about school and district performance from each state's Department of Education.

6. Ancestry and Ethnicity

These sections provide a detailed look at the ancestral, Hispanic and racial makeup of North Carolina's and South Carolina's 200+ ethnic categories. Profiles are included for each state and for all counties and places with 50,000 or more residents. In the ranking section, data is displayed three ways: 1) by number, based on all places regardless of population; 2) by percent, based on all places regardless of population; 3) by percent, based on places with populations of 50,000 or more. You will discover, for example, that the city of Mount Holly, NC has the greatest number of people reporting Jordanian ancestry in the state (205), and that 53.1% of the population of Riverview, SC are of German ancestry.

7. Climate

These sections include a State Summary, three colorful maps and profiles of both National and Cooperative Weather Stations. In addition, you'll find Weather Station Rankings, such as Dunn 4 NW and Hamlet in North Carolina reporting the highest annual extreme maximum temperature at 108° F.

These sections also include Significant Storm Event data from 2000-2009. Here you will learn that an ice storm caused $100 million in property damage in northwest South Carolina in December 2002 and that an F2 tornado was responsible for 3 deaths and 29 injuries in Pender County, NC in August 2004.

Note: The extensive **User Guide** that follows this introduction is segmented into four sections and examines, in some detail, each data field in the individual profiles and comparative sections for all chapters. It provides sources for all data points and statistical definitions as necessary.

User Guide

Places Covered In North Carolina

All 100 counties.

552 incorporated municipalities. Comprised of 454 towns, 77 cities, and 21 villages.

185 Census Designated Places (CDP). The U.S. Bureau of the Census defines a CDP as "a statistical entity, defined for each decennial census according to Census Bureau guidelines, comprising a densely settled concentration of population that is not within an incorporated place, but is locally identified by a name. CDPs are delineated cooperatively by state and local officials and the Census Bureau, following Census Bureau guidelines.

162 unincorporated communities. The communities included have statistics for their ZIP Code Tabulation Area (ZCTA) available from the Census Bureau. They are referred to as "postal areas." "Postal areas" can span multiple ZCTAs. A ZCTA is a statistical entity developed by the Census Bureau to approximate the delivery area for a US Postal Service 5-digit or 3-digit ZIP Code in the US and Puerto Rico. A ZCTA is an aggregation of census blocks that have the same predominant ZIP Code associated with the mailing addresses in the Census Bureau's Master Address File. Thus, the Postal Service's delivery areas have been adjusted to encompass whole census blocks so that the Census Bureau can tabulate census data for the ZCTAs. ZCTAs do not include all ZIP Codes used for mail delivery and therefore do not precisely depict the area within which mail deliveries associated with that ZIP Code occur. Additionally, some areas that are known by a unique name, although they are part of a larger incorporated place, are also included as "postal areas."

Places Covered In South Carolina

All 46 counties.

270 incorporated municipalities. Comprised of 201 towns and 69 cities.

125 Census Designated Places (CDP). The U.S. Bureau of the Census defines a CDP as "a statistical entity, defined for each decennial census according to Census Bureau guidelines, comprising a densely settled concentration of population that is not within an incorporated place, but is locally identified by a name. CDPs are delineated cooperatively by state and local officials and the Census Bureau, following Census Bureau guidelines.

64 unincorporated communities. The communities included have statistics for their ZIP Code Tabulation Area (ZCTA) available from the Census Bureau. They are referred to as "postal areas." "Postal areas" can span multiple ZCTAs. A ZCTA is a statistical entity developed by the Census Bureau to approximate the delivery area for a US Postal Service 5-digit or 3-digit ZIP Code in the US and Puerto Rico. A ZCTA is an aggregation of census blocks that have the same predominant ZIP Code associated with the mailing addresses in the Census Bureau's Master Address File. Thus, the Postal Service's delivery areas have been adjusted to encompass whole census blocks so that the Census Bureau can tabulate census data for the ZCTAs. ZCTAs do not include all ZIP Codes used for mail delivery and therefore do not precisely depict the area within which mail deliveries associated with that ZIP Code occur. Additionally, some areas that are known by a unique name, although they are part of a larger incorporated place, are also included as "postal areas."

For a more in-depth discussion of geographic areas, please refer to the Census Bureau's Geographic Areas Reference Manual at http://www.census.gov/geo/www/garm.html.

IMPORTANT NOTES

- Since the last decennial census, the U.S. Census replaced the long-form sample with the American Community Survey (ACS), which uses a series of monthly samples to produce annually updated estimates for the same areas. ACS estimates are based on data from a sample of housing units (3.54 million in 2013) and people in the population, not the full population. ACS sampling error (uncertainty of data) is greater for those areas with smaller populations. In an effort to provide the most accurate data, *Profiles of Michigan* reports ACS data for counties and communities with populations of 2,500 or more. The profiles for these places (2,500 or more population) also include data from Census 2010, including: population; population growth; population density; race; Hispanic origin; average household size; median age; age under 18; age 65 and over; males per 100 females; homeownership rate; homeowner vacancy rate; and rental vacancy rate. Profiles for counties and communities with 2,500 or less population show data from the Census 2010 only.

- *Profiles of North Carolina & South Carolina* uses the term "community" to refer to all places except counties. The term "county" is used to refer to counties and county-equivalents. All places are defined as of the 2010 Census.

- If a community spans multiple counties, the community will be shown in the county that contains its largest population.

- In each community profile, only school districts that have schools that are physically located within the community are shown. In addition, statistics for each school district cover the entire district, regardless of the physical location of the schools within the district.

- Special care should be taken when interpreting certain statistics for communities containing large colleges or universities. College students were counted as residents of the area in which they were living while attending college (as they have been since the 1950 census). One effect this may have is skewing the figures for population, income, housing, and educational attainment.

- Some information (e.g. income) is available for both counties and individual communities. Other information is available for just counties (e.g. election results), or just individual communities (e.g. local newspapers). Refer to the "Data Explanation and Sources" section for a complete listing.

- Some statistical information is available only for larger communities. In addition, the larger places are more apt to have services such as newspapers, airports, school districts, etc.

- For the most complete information on any community, users should also check the entry for the county in which the community is located. In addition, more information and services will be listed under the larger places in the county.

Data Explanation and Sources: County Profiles

PHYSICAL AND GEOGRAPHICAL CHARACTERISTICS

Physical Location: Describes the physical location of the county. *Source: Columbia University Press, The Columbia Gazetteer of North America and original research.*

Land and Water Area: Land and water area in square miles. *Source: U.S. Census Bureau, Census 2010*

Latitude and Longitude: Latitude and longitude in degrees. *Source: U.S. Census Bureau, Census 2010*

Time Zone: Lists the time zone. *Source: Original research*

Year Organized: Year the county government was organized. *Source: National Association of Counties*

County Seat: Lists the county seat. If a county has more than one seat, then both are listed. *Source: National Association of Counties*

Metropolitan Area: Indicates the metropolitan area the county is located in. Also lists all the component counties of that metropolitan area. The Office of Management and Budget (OMB) defines metropolitan and micropolitan statistical areas. The most current definitions are as of February 2013. *Source: U.S. Census Bureau*

Climate: Includes all weather stations located within the county. Indicates the station name and elevation as well as the monthly average high and low temperatures, average precipitation, and average snowfall. The period of record is generally 1980-2009, however, certain weather stations contain averages going back as far as 1900. *Source: Grey House Publishing, Weather America: A Thirty-Year Summary of Statistical Weather Data and Rankings, 2010*

POPULATION

Population: 2010 figures are a 100% count of population. *Source: U.S. Census Bureau, Census 2010*

Population Growth: The increase or decrease in population between 2000 and 2010. *Source: U.S. Census Bureau, Census 2000, Census 2010*

Population Density: Total 2010 population divided by the land area in square miles. *Source: U.S. Census Bureau, U.S. Census Bureau, Census 2010*

Race/Hispanic Origin: Figures include the U.S. Census Bureau categories of White alone; Black/African American alone; Asian alone; American Indian/Alaska Native alone; Native Hawaiian/Other Pacific Islander alone; two or more races; and Hispanic of any race. Alone refers to the fact that these figures are not in combination with any other race. *Source: U.S. Census Bureau, Census 2010*

The concept of race, as used by the Census Bureau, reflects self-identification by people according to the race or races with which they most closely identify. These categories are socio-political constructs and should not be interpreted as being scientific or anthropological in nature. Furthermore, the race categories include both racial and national-origin groups.

- **White.** A person having origins in any of the original peoples of Europe, the Middle East, or North Africa. It includes people who indicated their race(s) as "White" or reported entries such as Irish, German, Italian, Lebanese, Arab, Moroccan, or Caucasian.
- **Black/African American.** A person having origins in any of the Black racial groups of Africa. It includes people who indicated their race(s) as "Black, African Am., or Negro" or reported entries such as African American, Kenyan, Nigerian, or Haitian.
- **Asian.** A person having origins in any of the original peoples of the Far East, Southeast Asia, or the Indian subcontinent, including, for example, Cambodia, China, India, Japan, Korea, Malaysia, Pakistan, the Philippine Islands, Thailand, and Vietnam. It includes people who indicated their race(s) as "Asian" or reported entries such as "Asian Indian," "Chinese," "Filipino," "Korean," "Japanese," "Vietnamese," and "Other Asian" or provided other detailed Asian responses.
- **American Indian/Alaska Native.** A person having origins in any of the original peoples of North and South America (including Central America) and who maintains tribal affiliation or community attachment. This category includes people who indicated their race(s) as "American Indian or Alaska Native" or

reported their enrolled or principal tribe, such as Navajo, Blackfeet, Inupiat, Yup'ik, or Central American Indian groups or South American Indian groups.

- **Native Hawaiian/Other Pacific Islander.** A person having origins in any of the original peoples of Hawaii, Guam, Samoa, or other Pacific Islands. It includes people who indicated their race(s) as "Pacific Islander" or reported entries such as "Native Hawaiian," "Guamanian or Chamorro," "Samoan," and "Other Pacific Islander" or provided other detailed Pacific Islander responses..

- **Two or More Races.** People may choose to provide two or more races either by checking two or more race response check boxes, by providing multiple responses, or by some combination of check boxes and other responses. The race response categories shown on the questionnaire are collapsed into the five minimum race groups identified by OMB, and the Census Bureau's "Some Other Race" category.

- **Hispanic.** The data on the Hispanic or Latino population were derived from answers to a question that was asked of all people. The terms "Spanish," "Hispanic origin," and "Latino" are used interchangeably. Some respondents identify with all three terms while others may identify with only one of these three specific terms. Hispanics or Latinos who identify with the terms "Spanish," "Hispanic," or "Latino" are those who classify themselves in one of the specific Spanish, Hispanic, or Latino categories listed on the questionnaire ("Mexican," "Puerto Rican," or "Cuban") as well as those who indicate that they are "other Spanish/Hispanic/Latino." People who do not identify with one of the specific origins listed on the questionnaire but indicate that they are "other Spanish/Hispanic/Latino" are those whose origins are from Spain, the Spanish-speaking countries of Central or South America, the Dominican Republic, or people identifying themselves generally as Spanish, Spanish-American, Hispanic, Hispano, Latino, and so on. All write-in responses to the "other Spanish/Hispanic/Latino" category were coded. Origin can be viewed as the heritage, nationality group, lineage, or country of birth of the person or the person's parents or ancestors before their arrival in the United States. People who identify their origin as Spanish, Hispanic, or Latino may be of any race.

Average Household Size: Number of persons in the average household. *Source: U.S. Census Bureau, Census 2010*

Median Age: Median age of the population. *Source: U.S. Census Bureau, Census 2010*

Age Under 18: Percent of the total population under 18 years old. *Source: U.S. Census Bureau, Census 2010*

Age 65 and Over: Percent of the total population age 65 and over. *Source: U.S. Census Bureau, Census 2010*

Males per 100 Females: Number of males per 100 females. *Source: U.S. Census Bureau, Census 2010*

Marital Status: Percentage of population never married, now married, separated, widowed, or divorced. *Source: U.S. Census Bureau, American Community Survey, 2009-2013 Five-Year Estimates*

The marital status classification refers to the status at the time of enumeration. Data on marital status are tabulated only for the population 15 years old and over. Each person was asked whether they were "Now married," "Widowed," "Separated," "Divorced," or "Never married." Couples who live together (for example, people in common-law marriages) were able to report the marital status they considered to be the most appropriate.

- **Never married.** Never married includes all people who have never been married, including people whose only marriage(s) was annulled.

- **Now married.** All people whose current marriage has not ended by widowhood or divorce. This category includes people defined as "separated."

- **Separated.** Includes people legally separated or otherwise absent from their spouse because of marital discord. Those without a final divorce decree are classified as "separated." This category also includes people who have been deserted or who have parted because they no longer want to live together, but who have not obtained a divorce.

- **Widowed.** This category includes widows and widowers who have not remarried.

- **Divorced.** This category includes people who are legally divorced and who have not remarried.

Foreign Born: Percentage of population who were not U.S. citizens at birth. Foreign-born people are those who indicated they were either a U.S. citizen by naturalization or they were not a citizen of the United States. *Source: U.S. Census Bureau, American Community Survey, 2009-2013 Five-Year Estimates*

Speak English Only: Percent of population that reported speaking only English at home. *Source: U.S. Census Bureau, American Community Survey, 2009-2013 Five-Year Estimates*

With Disability: Percent of the civilian noninstitutionalized population that reported having a disability. Disability status is determined from from six types of difficulty: vision, hearing, cognitive, ambulatory, self-care, and independent living. For children under 5 years old, hearing and vision difficulty are used to determine disability status. For children between the ages of 5 and 14, disability status is determined from hearing, vision, cognitive, ambulatory, and self-care difficulties. For people aged 15 years and older, they are considered to have a disability if they have difficulty with any one of the six difficulty types. *Source: U.S. Census Bureau, American Community Survey, 2009-2013 Five-Year Estimates*

Veterans: Percent of the civilian population 18 years and over who have served (even for a short time), but are not currently serving, on active duty in the U.S. Army, Navy, Air Force, Marine Corps, or the Coast Guard, or who served in the U.S. Merchant Marine during World War II. People who served in the National Guard or Reserves are classified as veterans only if they were ever called or ordered to active duty, not counting the 4-6 months for initial training or yearly summer camps. All other civilians are classified as nonveterans. Note: While it is possible for 17 year olds to be veterans of the Armed Forces, ACS data products are restricted to the population 18 years and older. *Source: U.S. Census Bureau, American Community Survey, 2009-2013 Five-Year Estimates*

Ancestry: Largest ancestry groups reported (up to five). The data includes persons who report multiple ancestries. For example, if a person reported being Irish and Italian, they would be included in both categories. Thus, the sum of the percentages may be greater than 100%. *Source: U.S. Census Bureau, American Community Survey, 2009-2013 Five-Year Estimates*

The data represent self-classification by people according to the ancestry group or groups with which they most closely identify. Ancestry refers to a person's ethnic origin or descent, "roots," heritage, or the place of birth of the person, the person's parents, or their ancestors before their arrival in the United States. Some ethnic identities, such as Egyptian or Polish, can be traced to geographic areas outside the United States, while other ethnicities such as Pennsylvania German or Cajun evolved in the United States.

The ancestry question was intended to provide data for groups that were not included in the Hispanic origin and race questions. Therefore, although data on all groups are collected, the ancestry data shown in these tabulations are for non-Hispanic and non-race groups. *See* Race/Hispanic Origin for information on Hispanic and race groups.

RELIGION

Religion: Lists the largest religious groups (up to six) based on the number of adherents divided by the population of the county. Adherents are defined as "all members, including full members, their children and the estimated number of other regular participants who are not considered as communicant, confirmed or full members." *Source: American Religious Bodies, 2010 U.S. Religion Census: Religious Congregations & Membership Study*

ECONOMY

Unemployment Rate: Unemployment rate as of October 2014. Includes all civilians age 16 or over who were unemployed and looking for work. *Source: U.S. Department of Labor, Bureau of Labor Statistics, Local Area Unemployment Statistics*

Leading Industries: Lists the three largest industries (excluding government) based on the number of employees. *Source: U.S. Census Bureau, County Business Patterns 2012*

Farms: The total number of farms and the total acreage they occupy. *Source: U.S. Department of Agriculture, National Agricultural Statistics Service, 2012 Census of Agriculture*

Company Size: The numbers of companies at various employee headcounts. Includes private employers only. *Source: U.S. Census Bureau, County Business Patterns 2012*

- **Employ 1,000 or more persons.** The numbers of companies that employ 1,000 or more persons.
- **Employ 500-999 persons.** The numbers of companies that employ 500 to 999 persons.
- **Employ 100-499 persons.** The numbers of companies that employ 100 to 499 persons.
- **Employ 1-99 persons.** The numbers of companies that employ 1 to 99 persons.

Business Ownership: Number of businesses that are majority-owned by women or various minority groups. *Source: U.S. Census Bureau, 2007 Economic Census, Survey of Business Owners: Black-Owned Firms, 2007 (latest statistics available at time of publication)*

- **Women-Owned.** Number of businesses that are majority-owned by a woman. Majority ownership is defined as having 51 percent or more of the stock or equity in the business.
- **Black-Owned.** Number of businesses that are majority-owned by a Black or African-American person(s). Majority ownership is defined as having 51 percent or more of the stock or equity in the business. Black or African American is defined as a person having origins in any of the black racial groups of Africa, including those who consider themselves to be "Haitian."
- **Hispanic-Owned.** Number of businesses that are majority-owned by a person(s) of Hispanic or Latino origin. Majority ownership is defined as having 51 percent or more of the stock or equity in the business. Hispanic or Latino origin is defined as a person of Cuban, Mexican, Puerto Rican, South or Central American, or other Spanish culture or origin, regardless of race.
- **Asian-Owned.** Number of businesses that are majority-owned by an Asian person(s). Majority ownership is defined as having 51 percent or more of the stock or equity in the business.

EMPLOYMENT

Employment by Occupation: Percentage of the employed civilian population 16 years and over in management, professional, service, sales, farming, construction, and production occupations. *Source: U.S. Census Bureau, American Community Survey, 2009-2013 Five-Year Estimates*

- Management, business, and financial occupations include:
    Management occupations
    Business and financial operations occupations

- Computer, engineering, and science occupations include:
    Computer and mathematical occupations
    Architecture and engineering occupations
    Life, physical, and social science occupations

- Education, legal, community service, arts, and media occupations include:
    Community and social service occupations
    Legal occupations
    Education, training, and library occupations
    Arts, design, entertainment, sports, and media occupations

- Healthcare practitioners and technical occupations include:
    Health diagnosing and treating practitioners and other technical occupations
    Health technologists and technicians

- Service occupations include:
    Healthcare support occupations
    Protective service occupations:
        Fire fighting and prevention, and other protective service workers including supervisors
        Law enforcement workers including supervisors
    Food preparation and serving related occupations
    Building and grounds cleaning and maintenance occupations
    Personal care and service occupations

- Sales and office occupations include:
    Sales and related occupations
    Office and administrative support occupations

- Natural resources, construction, and maintenance occupations include:
    Farming, fishing, and forestry occupations
    Construction and extraction occupations
    Installation, maintenance, and repair occupations

- Production, transportation, and material moving occupations include:
    Production occupations
    Transportation occupations
    Material moving occupations

INCOME

Per Capita Income: Per capita income is the mean income computed for every man, woman, and child in a particular group. It is derived by dividing the total income of a particular group by the total population in that group. Per capita income is rounded to the nearest whole dollar. *Source: U.S. Census Bureau, American Community Survey, 2009-2013 Five-Year Estimates*

Median Household Income: Includes the income of the householder and all other individuals 15 years old and over in the household, whether they are related to the householder or not. The median divides the income distribution into two equal parts: one-half of the cases falling below the median income and one-half above the median. For households, the median income is based on the distribution of the total number of households including those with no income. Median income for households is computed on the basis of a standard distribution and is rounded to the nearest whole dollar. *Source: U.S. Census Bureau, American Community Survey, 2009-2013 Five-Year Estimates*

Average Household Income: Average household income is obtained by dividing total household income by the total number of households. *Source: U.S. Census Bureau, American Community Survey, 2009-2013 Five-Year Estimates*

Percent of Households with Income of $100,000 or more: Percent of households with income of $100,000 or more. *Source: U.S. Census Bureau, American Community Survey, 2009-2013 Five-Year Estimates*

Poverty Rate: Percentage of population with income below the poverty level. Based on individuals for whom poverty status is determined. Poverty status was determined for all people except institutionalized people, people in military group quarters, people in college dormitories, and unrelated individuals under 15 years old. *Source: U.S. Census Bureau, American Community Survey, 2009-2013 Five-Year Estimates*

EDUCATIONAL ATTAINMENT

Figures show the percent of population age 25 and over with the following levels of educational attainment. *Source: U.S. Census Bureau, American Community Survey, 2009-2013 Five-Year Estimates*

- **High school diploma or higher.** Includes people whose highest degree is a high school diploma or its equivalent (GED), people who attended college but did not receive a degree, and people who received a college, university, or professional degree.
- **Bachelor's degree or higher.** Includes people who received a bachelor's, master's, doctorate, or professional degree.
- **Graduate/professional degree or higher.** Includes people who received a master's, doctorate, or professional degree.

HOUSING

Homeownership Rate: Percentage of housing units that are owner-occupied. *Source: U.S. Census Bureau, Census 2010*

Median Home Value: Median value in dollars of all owner-occupied housing units as reported by the owner. *Source: U.S. Census Bureau, American Community Survey, 2009-2013 Five-Year Estimates*

Median Year Structure Built: Year structure built refers to when the building was first constructed, not when it was remodeled, added to, or converted. For mobile homes, houseboats, RVs, etc, the manufacturer's model year was assumed to be the year built. The data relate to the number of units built during the specified periods that were still in existence at the time of enumeration. *Source: U.S. Census Bureau, American Community Survey, 2009-2013 Five-Year Estimates*

Homeowner Vacancy Rate: Proportion of the homeowner inventory that is vacant "for sale." It is computed by dividing the number of vacant units "for sale only" by the sum of the owner-occupied units, vacant units that are "for sale only," and vacant units that have been sold but not yet occupied, and then multiplying by 100. This measure is rounded to the nearest tenth. *Source: U.S. Census Bureau, Census 2010*

Median Gross Rent: Median monthly gross rent in dollars on specified renter-occupied and specified vacant-for-rent units. Specified renter-occupied and specified vacant-for-rent units exclude 1-family houses on 10 acres or more. Gross rent is the contract rent plus the estimated average monthly cost of utilities (electricity, gas, and water and sewer) and fuels (oil, coal, kerosene, wood, etc.) if these are paid by the renter (or paid for the renter by someone else). Gross rent is intended to eliminate differentials that result from varying practices with respect to the inclusion of

utilities and fuels as part of the rental payment. Contract rent is the monthly rent agreed to or contracted for, regardless of any furnishings, utilities, fees, meals, or services that may be included. For vacant units, it is the monthly rent asked for the rental unit at the time of enumeration. *Source: U.S. Census Bureau, American Community Survey, 2009-2013 Five-Year Estimates*

Rental Vacancy Rate: Proportion of the rental inventory that is vacant "for rent." It is computed by dividing the number of vacant units "for rent" by the sum of the renter-occupied units, vacant units that are "for rent," and vacant units that have been rented but not yet occupied, and then multiplying by 100. This measure is rounded to the nearest tenth. *Source: U.S. Census Bureau, Census 2010*

VITAL STATISTICS

Birth Rate: Estimated number of births per 10,000 population in 2013. *Source: U.S. Census Bureau, Annual Components of Population Change, July 1, 2010 - July 1, 2013*

Death Rate: Estimated number of deaths per 10,000 population in 2013. *Source: U.S. Census Bureau, Annual Components of Population Change, July 1, 2010 - July 1, 2013*

Age-adjusted Cancer Mortality Rate: Number of age-adjusted deaths from cancer per 100,000 population in 2011. Cancer is defined as International Classification of Disease (ICD) codes C00–D48.9 Neoplasms. *Source: Centers for Disease Control, CDC Wonder, 2011*

Age-adjusted death rates are weighted averages of the age-specific death rates, where the weights represent a fixed population by age. They are used because the rates of almost all causes of death vary by age. Age adjustment is a technique for "removing" the effects of age from crude rates, so as to allow meaningful comparisons across populations with different underlying age structures. For example, comparing the crude rate of heart disease in Virginia to that of California is misleading, because the relatively older population in Virginia will lead to a higher crude death rate, even if the age-specific rates of heart disease in Virginia and California are the same. For such a comparison, age-adjusted rates would be preferable. Age-adjusted rates should be viewed as relative indexes rather than as direct or actual measures of mortality risk.

Death rates based on counts of twenty or less (≤ 20) are flagged as "Unreliable". Death rates based on fewer than three years of data for counties with populations of less than 100,000 in the 2000 Census counts, are also flagged as "Unreliable" if the number of deaths is five or less (≤ 5).

HEALTH INSURANCE

Health insurance coverage in the ACS and other Census Bureau surveys define coverage to include plans and programs that provide comprehensive health coverage. Plans that provide insurance for specific conditions or situations such as cancer and long-term care policies are not considered coverage. Likewise, other types of insurance like dental, vision, life, and disability insurance are not considered health insurance coverage.

For reporting purposes, the Census Bureau broadly classifies health insurance coverage as private health insurance or public coverage. Private health insurance is a plan provided through an employer or union, a plan purchased by an individual from a private company, or TRICARE or other military health care. Public health coverage includes the federal programs Medicare, Medicaid, and VA Health Care (provided through the Department of Veterans Affairs); the Children's Health Insurance Program (CHIP); and individual state health plans. The types of health insurance are not mutually exclusive; people may be covered by more than one at the same time. People who had no reported health coverage, or those whose only health coverage was Indian Health Service, were considered uninsured. *Source: U.S. Census Bureau, American Community Survey, 2009-2013 Five-Year Estimates*

- **Have Insurance:** Percent of the civilian noninstitutionalized population with any type of comprehensive health insurance.
- **Have Private Insurance.** Percent of the civilian noninstitutionalized population with private health insurance. A person may report that they have both public and private health insurance, thus, the sum of the percentages may be greater than 100%.
- **Have Public Insurance.** Percent of the civilian noninstitutionalized population with public health insurance. A person may report that they have both public and private health insurance, thus, the sum of the percentages may be greater than 100%.
- **Do Not Have Insurance.** Percent of the civilian noninstitutionalized population with no health insurance.
- **Children Under 18 With No Insurance.** Percent of the civilian noninstitutionalized population under age 18 with no health insurance.

HEALTH CARE

Number of physicians, hospital beds and hospital admission per 10,000 population. *Source: Area Resource File (ARF) 2012-2013. U.S. Department of Health and Human Services, Health Resources and Services Administration, Bureau of Health Professions, Rockville, MD.*

- **Number of Physicians.** The number of active, non-federal physicians (MDs and DOs) per 10,000 population in 2011.
- **Number of Hospital Beds.** The number of hospital beds per 10,000 population in 2010.
- **Number of Hospital Admissions.** The number of hospital admissions per 10,000 population in 2010.

AIR QUALITY INDEX

The percentage of days in 2013 the AQI fell into the Good (0-50), Moderate (51-100), Unhealthy for Sensitive Groups (101-150), Unhealthy (151-200), Very Unhealthy (201-300), and Hazardous (300+) ranges. If a range does not appear, its value is zero. Data covers January 2013 through December 2013. *Source: AirData: Access to Air Pollution Data, U.S. Environmental Protection Agency, Office of Air and Radiation*

The AQI is an index for reporting daily air quality. It tells you how clean or polluted your air is, and what associated health concerns you should be aware of. The AQI focuses on health effects that can happen within a few hours or days after breathing polluted air. EPA uses the AQI for five major air pollutants regulated by the Clean Air Act: ground-level ozone, particulate matter, carbon monoxide, sulfur dioxide, and nitrogen dioxide. For each of these pollutants, EPA has established national air quality standards to protect against harmful health effects.

The AQI runs from 0 to 500. The higher the AQI value, the greater the level of air pollution and the greater the health danger. For example, an AQI value of 50 represents good air quality and little potential to affect public health, while an AQI value over 300 represents hazardous air quality. An AQI value of 100 generally corresponds to the national air quality standard for the pollutant, which is the level EPA has set to protect public health. So, AQI values below 100 are generally thought of as satisfactory. When AQI values are above 100, air quality is considered to be unhealthy—at first for certain sensitive groups of people, then for everyone as AQI values get higher. Each category corresponds to a different level of health concern. For example, when the AQI for a pollutant is between 51 and 100, the health concern is "Moderate." Here are the six levels of health concern and what they mean:

- "Good" The AQI value for your community is between 0 and 50. Air quality is considered satisfactory and air pollution poses little or no risk.
- "Moderate" The AQI for your community is between 51 and 100. Air quality is acceptable; however, for some pollutants there may be a moderate health concern for a very small number of individuals. For example, people who are unusually sensitive to ozone may experience respiratory symptoms.
- "Unhealthy for Sensitive Groups" Certain groups of people are particularly sensitive to the harmful effects of certain air pollutants. This means they are likely to be affected at lower levels than the general public. For example, children and adults who are active outdoors and people with respiratory disease are at greater risk from exposure to ozone, while people with heart disease are at greater risk from carbon monoxide. Some people may be sensitive to more than one pollutant. When AQI values are between 101 and 150, members of sensitive groups may experience health effects. The general public is not likely to be affected when the AQI is in this range.
- "Unhealthy" AQI values are between 151 and 200. Everyone may begin to experience health effects. Members of sensitive groups may experience more serious health effects.
- "Very Unhealthy" AQI values between 201 and 300 trigger a health alert, meaning everyone may experience more serious health effects.
- "Hazardous" AQI values over 300 trigger health warnings of emergency conditions. The entire population is more likely to be affected.

TRANSPORTATION

Commute to Work: Percentage of workers 16 years old and over that use the following means of transportation to commute to work: car; public transportation; walk; work from home. The means of transportation data for some areas may show workers using modes of public transportation that are not available in those areas (e.g. subway or elevated riders in a metropolitan area where there actually is no subway or elevated service). This result is largely due to people who worked during the reference week at a location that was different from their usual place of work (such as people away from home on business in an area where subway service was available) and people who used more than one

means of transportation each day but whose principal means was unavailable where they lived (e.g. residents of non-metropolitan areas who drove to the fringe of a metropolitan area and took the commuter railroad most of the distance to work). *Source: U.S. Census Bureau, American Community Survey, 2009-2013 Five-Year Estimates*

Median Travel Time to Work: Median travel time to work for workers 16 years old and over. Travel time to work refers to the total number of minutes that it usually took the person to get from home to work each day during the reference week. The elapsed time includes time spent waiting for public transportation, picking up passengers in carpools, and time spent in other activities related to getting to work. *Source: U.S. Census Bureau, American Community Survey, 2009-2013 Five-Year Estimates*

PRESIDENTIAL ELECTION

2012 Presidential election results. *Source: Dave Leip's Atlas of U.S. Presidential Elections*

NATIONAL AND STATE PARKS

Lists National/State parks located in the area. *Source: U.S. Geological Survey, Geographic Names Information System*

ADDITIONAL INFORMATION CONTACTS

General telephone number and website address (if available) of local government.

Data Explanation and Sources: Community Profiles

PHYSICAL AND GEOGRAPHICAL CHARACTERISTICS

Place Type: Lists the type of place (city, town, village, borough, Census-Designated Place (CDP), township, charter township, plantation, gore, district, grant, location, purchase, municipality, reservation, unorganized territory, or unincorporated postal area). *Source: U.S. Census Bureau, Census 2010 and U.S. Postal Service, City State File*

ZCTA: *This only appears within unincorporated postal areas.* The statistics that follow cover the corresponding ZIP Code Tabulation Area (ZCTA). A ZCTA is a statistical entity developed by the Census Bureau to approximate the delivery area for a US Postal Service 5-digit or 3-digit ZIP Code in the US and Puerto Rico. A ZCTA is an aggregation of census blocks that have the same predominant ZIP Code associated with the mailing addresses in the Census Bureau's Master Address File. Thus, the Postal Service's delivery areas have been adjusted to encompass whole census blocks so that the Census Bureau can tabulate census data for the ZCTAs. ZCTAs do not include all ZIP Codes used for mail delivery and therefore do not precisely depict the area within which mail deliveries associated with that ZIP Code occur. Additionally, some areas that are known by a unique name, although they are part of a larger incorporated place, are also included as "postal areas."

Land and Water Area: Land and water area in square miles. *Source: U.S. Census Bureau, Census 2010*

Latitude and Longitude: Latitude and longitude in degrees. *Source: U.S. Census Bureau, Census 2010.*

Elevation: Elevation in feet. *Source: U.S. Geological Survey, Geographic Names Information System (GNIS)*

HISTORY

Historical information. *Source: Columbia University Press, The Columbia Gazetteer of North America; Original research*

POPULATION

Population: 2010 figures are a 100% count of population. *Source: U.S. Census Bureau, Census 2010*

Population Growth: The increase or decrease in population between 2000 and 2010. *Source: U.S. Census Bureau, Census 2000, Census 2010*

Population Density: Total 2010 population divided by the land area in square miles. *Source: U.S. Census Bureau, U.S. Census Bureau, Census 2010*

Race/Hispanic Origin: Figures include the U.S. Census Bureau categories of White alone; Black/African American alone; Asian alone; American Indian/Alaska Native alone; Native Hawaiian/Other Pacific Islander alone; two or more races; and Hispanic of any race. Alone refers to the fact that these figures are not in combination with any other race. *Source: U.S. Census Bureau, Census 2010*

The concept of race, as used by the Census Bureau, reflects self-identification by people according to the race or races with which they most closely identify. These categories are socio-political constructs and should not be interpreted as being scientific or anthropological in nature. Furthermore, the race categories include both racial and national-origin groups.

- **White.** A person having origins in any of the original peoples of Europe, the Middle East, or North Africa. It includes people who indicated their race(s) as "White" or reported entries such as Irish, German, Italian, Lebanese, Arab, Moroccan, or Caucasian.
- **Black/African American.** A person having origins in any of the Black racial groups of Africa. It includes people who indicated their race(s) as "Black, African Am., or Negro" or reported entries such as African American, Kenyan, Nigerian, or Haitian.
- **Asian.** A person having origins in any of the original peoples of the Far East, Southeast Asia, or the Indian subcontinent, including, for example, Cambodia, China, India, Japan, Korea, Malaysia, Pakistan, the Philippine Islands, Thailand, and Vietnam. It includes people who indicated their race(s) as "Asian" or reported entries such as "Asian Indian," "Chinese," "Filipino," "Korean," "Japanese," "Vietnamese," and "Other Asian" or provided other detailed Asian responses.
- **American Indian/Alaska Native.** A person having origins in any of the original peoples of North and South America (including Central America) and who maintains tribal affiliation or community attachment.

This category includes people who indicated their race(s) as "American Indian or Alaska Native" or reported their enrolled or principal tribe, such as Navajo, Blackfeet, Inupiat, Yup'ik, or Central American Indian groups or South American Indian groups.

- **Native Hawaiian/Other Pacific Islander.** A person having origins in any of the original peoples of Hawaii, Guam, Samoa, or other Pacific Islands. It includes people who indicated their race(s) as "Pacific Islander" or reported entries such as "Native Hawaiian," "Guamanian or Chamorro," "Samoan," and "Other Pacific Islander" or provided other detailed Pacific Islander responses..

- **Two or More Races.** People may choose to provide two or more races either by checking two or more race response check boxes, by providing multiple responses, or by some combination of check boxes and other responses. The race response categories shown on the questionnaire are collapsed into the five minimum race groups identified by OMB, and the Census Bureau's "Some Other Race" category.

- **Hispanic.** The data on the Hispanic or Latino population were derived from answers to a question that was asked of all people. The terms "Spanish," "Hispanic origin," and "Latino" are used interchangeably. Some respondents identify with all three terms while others may identify with only one of these three specific terms. Hispanics or Latinos who identify with the terms "Spanish," "Hispanic," or "Latino" are those who classify themselves in one of the specific Spanish, Hispanic, or Latino categories listed on the questionnaire ("Mexican," "Puerto Rican," or "Cuban") as well as those who indicate that they are "other Spanish/Hispanic/Latino." People who do not identify with one of the specific origins listed on the questionnaire but indicate that they are "other Spanish/Hispanic/Latino" are those whose origins are from Spain, the Spanish-speaking countries of Central or South America, the Dominican Republic, or people identifying themselves generally as Spanish, Spanish-American, Hispanic, Hispano, Latino, and so on. All write-in responses to the "other Spanish/Hispanic/Latino" category were coded. Origin can be viewed as the heritage, nationality group, lineage, or country of birth of the person or the person's parents or ancestors before their arrival in the United States. People who identify their origin as Spanish, Hispanic, or Latino may be of any race.

Average Household Size: Number of persons in the average household. *Source: U.S. Census Bureau, Census 2010*

Median Age: Median age of the population. *Source: U.S. Census Bureau, Census 2010*

Age Under 18: Percent of the total population under 18 years old. *Source: U.S. Census Bureau, Census 2010*

Age 65 and Over: Percent of the total population age 65 and over. *Source: U.S. Census Bureau, Census 2010*

Males per 100 Females: Number of males per 100 females. *Source: U.S. Census Bureau, Census 2010*

Marital Status: Percentage of population never married, now married, separated, widowed, or divorced. *Source: U.S. Census Bureau, American Community Survey, 2009-2013 Five-Year Estimates*

The marital status classification refers to the status at the time of enumeration. Data on marital status are tabulated only for the population 15 years old and over. Each person was asked whether they were "Now married," "Widowed," "Separated," "Divorced," or "Never married." Couples who live together (for example, people in common-law marriages) were able to report the marital status they considered to be the most appropriate.

- **Never married.** Never married includes all people who have never been married, including people whose only marriage(s) was annulled.
- **Now married.** All people whose current marriage has not ended by widowhood or divorce. This category includes people defined as "separated."
- **Separated.** Includes people legally separated or otherwise absent from their spouse because of marital discord. Those without a final divorce decree are classified as "separated." This category also includes people who have been deserted or who have parted because they no longer want to live together, but who have not obtained a divorce.
- **Widowed.** This category includes widows and widowers who have not remarried.
- **Divorced.** This category includes people who are legally divorced and who have not remarried.

Foreign Born: Percentage of population who were not U.S. citizens at birth. Foreign-born people are those who indicated they were either a U.S. citizen by naturalization or they were not a citizen of the United States. *Source: U.S. Census Bureau, American Community Survey, 2009-2013 Five-Year Estimates*

Speak English Only: Percent of population that reported speaking only English at home. *Source: U.S. Census Bureau, American Community Survey, 2009-2013 Five-Year Estimates*

With Disability: Percent of the civilian noninstitutionalized population that reported having a disability. Disability status is determined from from six types of difficulty: vision, hearing, cognitive, ambulatory, self-care, and independent living. For children under 5 years old, hearing and vision difficulty are used to determine disability status. For children between the ages of 5 and 14, disability status is determined from hearing, vision, cognitive, ambulatory, and self-care difficulties. For people aged 15 years and older, they are considered to have a disability if they have difficulty with any one of the six difficulty types. *Source: U.S. Census Bureau, American Community Survey, 2009-2013 Five-Year Estimates*

Veterans: Percent of the civilian population 18 years and over who have served (even for a short time), but are not currently serving, on active duty in the U.S. Army, Navy, Air Force, Marine Corps, or the Coast Guard, or who served in the U.S. Merchant Marine during World War II. People who served in the National Guard or Reserves are classified as veterans only if they were ever called or ordered to active duty, not counting the 4-6 months for initial training or yearly summer camps. All other civilians are classified as nonveterans. Note: While it is possible for 17 year olds to be veterans of the Armed Forces, ACS data products are restricted to the population 18 years and older. *Source: U.S. Census Bureau, American Community Survey, 2009-2013 Five-Year Estimates*

Ancestry: Largest ancestry groups reported (up to five). The data includes persons who report multiple ancestries. For example, if a person reported being Irish and Italian, they would be included in both categories. Thus, the sum of the percentages may be greater than 100%. *Source: U.S. Census Bureau, American Community Survey, 2009-2013 Five-Year Estimates*

The data represent self-classification by people according to the ancestry group or groups with which they most closely identify. Ancestry refers to a person's ethnic origin or descent, "roots," heritage, or the place of birth of the person, the person's parents, or their ancestors before their arrival in the United States. Some ethnic identities, such as Egyptian or Polish, can be traced to geographic areas outside the United States, while other ethnicities such as Pennsylvania German or Cajun evolved in the United States.

The ancestry question was intended to provide data for groups that were not included in the Hispanic origin and race questions. Therefore, although data on all groups are collected, the ancestry data shown in these tabulations are for non-Hispanic and non-race groups. *See* Race/Hispanic Origin for information on Hispanic and race groups.

EMPLOYMENT

Employment by Occupation: Percentage of the employed civilian population 16 years and over in management, professional, service, sales, farming, construction, and production occupations. *Source: U.S. Census Bureau, American Community Survey, 2009-2013 Five-Year Estimates*

- Management, business, and financial occupations include:
    Management occupations
    Business and financial operations occupations

- Computer, engineering, and science occupations include:
    Computer and mathematical occupations
    Architecture and engineering occupations
    Life, physical, and social science occupations

- Education, legal, community service, arts, and media occupations include:
    Community and social service occupations
    Legal occupations
    Education, training, and library occupations
    Arts, design, entertainment, sports, and media occupations

- Healthcare practitioners and technical occupations include:
    Health diagnosing and treating practitioners and other technical occupations
    Health technologists and technicians

- Service occupations include:
    Healthcare support occupations
    Protective service occupations:
        Fire fighting and prevention, and other protective service workers including supervisors
        Law enforcement workers including supervisors
    Food preparation and serving related occupations
    Building and grounds cleaning and maintenance occupations
    Personal care and service occupations

- Sales and office occupations include:
  Sales and related occupations
  Office and administrative support occupations

- Natural resources, construction, and maintenance occupations include:
  Farming, fishing, and forestry occupations
  Construction and extraction occupations
  Installation, maintenance, and repair occupations

- Production, transportation, and material moving occupations include:
  Production occupations
  Transportation occupations
  Material moving occupations

INCOME

Per Capita Income: Per capita income is the mean income computed for every man, woman, and child in a particular group. It is derived by dividing the total income of a particular group by the total population in that group. Per capita income is rounded to the nearest whole dollar. *Source: U.S. Census Bureau, American Community Survey, 2009-2013 Five-Year Estimates*

Median Household Income: Includes the income of the householder and all other individuals 15 years old and over in the household, whether they are related to the householder or not. The median divides the income distribution into two equal parts: one-half of the cases falling below the median income and one-half above the median. For households, the median income is based on the distribution of the total number of households including those with no income. Median income for households is computed on the basis of a standard distribution and is rounded to the nearest whole dollar. *Source: U.S. Census Bureau, American Community Survey, 2009-2013 Five-Year Estimates*

Average Household Income: Average household income is obtained by dividing total household income by the total number of households. *Source: U.S. Census Bureau, American Community Survey, 2009-2013 Five-Year Estimates*

Percent of Households with Income of $100,000 or more: Percent of households with income of $100,000 or more. *Source: U.S. Census Bureau, American Community Survey, 2009-2013 Five-Year Estimates*

Poverty Rate: Percentage of population with income below the poverty level. Based on individuals for whom poverty status is determined. Poverty status was determined for all people except institutionalized people, people in military group quarters, people in college dormitories, and unrelated individuals under 15 years old. *Source: U.S. Census Bureau, American Community Survey, 2009-2013 Five-Year Estimates*

EDUCATIONAL ATTAINMENT

Figures show the percent of population age 25 and over with the following levels of educational attainment. *Source: U.S. Census Bureau, American Community Survey, 2009-2013 Five-Year Estimates*

- **High school diploma or higher.** Includes people whose highest degree is a high school diploma or its equivalent (GED), people who attended college but did not receive a degree, and people who received a college, university, or professional degree.
- **Bachelor's degree or higher.** Includes people who received a bachelor's, master's, doctorate, or professional degree.
- **Graduate/professional degree or higher.** Includes people who received a master's, doctorate, or professional degree.

SCHOOL DISTRICTS

Lists the name of each school district, the grade range (PK=pre-kindergarten; KG=kindergarten), the student enrollment, and the district headquarters' phone number. In each community profile, only school districts that have schools that are physically located within the community are shown. In addition, statistics for each school district cover the entire district, regardless of the physical location of the schools within the district. *Source: U.S. Department of Education, National Center for Educational Statistics, Directory of Public Elementary and Secondary Education Agencies, 2012-13*

COLLEGES

Four-year Colleges: Lists the name of each four-year college, the type of institution (private or public; for-profit or non-profit; religious affiliation; historically black), the total estimated student enrollment in 2013, the general telephone number, and the annual tuition and fees for full-time, first-time undergraduate students (in-state and out-of-state). *Source: U.S. Department of Education, National Center for Educational Statistics, IPEDS College Data, 2013-14*

Two-year Colleges: Lists the name of each two-year college, the type of institution (private or public; for-profit or non-profit; religious affiliation; historically black), the total estimated student enrollment in 2013, the general telephone number, and the annual tuition and fees for full-time, first-time undergraduate students (in-state and out-of-state). *Source: U.S. Department of Education, National Center for Educational Statistics, IPEDS College Data, 2013-14*

Vocational/Technical Schools: Lists the name of each vocational/technical school, the type of institution (private or public; for-profit or non-profit; religious affiliation; historically black), the total estimated student enrollment in 2013, the general telephone number, and the annual tuition and fees for full-time students. *Source: U.S. Department of Education, National Center for Educational Statistics, IPEDS College Data, 2013-14*

HOUSING

Homeownership Rate: Percentage of housing units that are owner-occupied. *Source: U.S. Census Bureau, Census 2010*

Median Home Value: Median value in dollars of all owner-occupied housing units as reported by the owner. *Source: U.S. Census Bureau, American Community Survey, 2009-2013 Five-Year Estimates*

Median Year Structure Built: Year structure built refers to when the building was first constructed, not when it was remodeled, added to, or converted. For mobile homes, houseboats, RVs, etc, the manufacturer's model year was assumed to be the year built. The data relate to the number of units built during the specified periods that were still in existence at the time of enumeration. *Source: U.S. Census Bureau, American Community Survey, 2009-2013 Five-Year Estimates*

Homeowner Vacancy Rate: Proportion of the homeowner inventory that is vacant "for sale." It is computed by dividing the number of vacant units "for sale only" by the sum of the owner-occupied units, vacant units that are "for sale only," and vacant units that have been sold but not yet occupied, and then multiplying by 100. This measure is rounded to the nearest tenth. *Source: U.S. Census Bureau, Census 2010*

Median Gross Rent: Median monthly gross rent in dollars on specified renter-occupied and specified vacant-for-rent units. Specified renter-occupied and specified vacant-for-rent units exclude 1-family houses on 10 acres or more. Gross rent is the contract rent plus the estimated average monthly cost of utilities (electricity, gas, and water and sewer) and fuels (oil, coal, kerosene, wood, etc.) if these are paid by the renter (or paid for the renter by someone else). Gross rent is intended to eliminate differentials that result from varying practices with respect to the inclusion of utilities and fuels as part of the rental payment. Contract rent is the monthly rent agreed to or contracted for, regardless of any furnishings, utilities, fees, meals, or services that may be included. For vacant units, it is the monthly rent asked for the rental unit at the time of enumeration. *Source: U.S. Census Bureau, American Community Survey, 2009-2013 Five-Year Estimates*

Rental Vacancy Rate: Proportion of the rental inventory that is vacant "for rent." It is computed by dividing the number of vacant units "for rent" by the sum of the renter-occupied units, vacant units that are "for rent," and vacant units that have been rented but not yet occupied, and then multiplying by 100. This measure is rounded to the nearest tenth. *Source: U.S. Census Bureau, Census 2010*

HEALTH INSURANCE

Health insurance coverage in the ACS and other Census Bureau surveys define coverage to include plans and programs that provide comprehensive health coverage. Plans that provide insurance for specific conditions or situations such as cancer and long-term care policies are not considered coverage. Likewise, other types of insurance like dental, vision, life, and disability insurance are not considered health insurance coverage.

For reporting purposes, the Census Bureau broadly classifies health insurance coverage as private health insurance or public coverage. Private health insurance is a plan provided through an employer or union, a plan purchased by an individual from a private company, or TRICARE or other military health care. Public health coverage includes the federal programs Medicare, Medicaid, and VA Health Care (provided through the Department of Veterans Affairs); the Children's Health Insurance Program (CHIP); and individual state health plans. The types of health insurance are not

mutually exclusive; people may be covered by more than one at the same time. People who had no reported health coverage, or those whose only health coverage was Indian Health Service, were considered uninsured. *Source: U.S. Census Bureau, American Community Survey, 2009-2013 Five-Year Estimates*

- **Have Insurance:** Percent of the civilian noninstitutionalized population with any type of comprehensive health insurance.
- **Have Private Insurance.** Percent of the civilian noninstitutionalized population with private health insurance. A person may report that they have both public and private health insurance, thus, the sum of the percentages may be greater than 100%.
- **Have Public Insurance.** Percent of the civilian noninstitutionalized population with public health insurance. A person may report that they have both public and private health insurance, thus, the sum of the percentages may be greater than 100%.
- **Do Not Have Insurance.** Percent of the civilian noninstitutionalized population with no health insurance.
- **Children Under 18 With No Insurance.** Percent of the civilian noninstitutionalized population under age 18 with no health insurance.

HOSPITALS

Lists the hospital name and the number of licensed beds. *Source: Grey House Publishing, The Comparative Guide to American Hospitals, 2014*

NEWSPAPERS

List of daily and weekly newspapers with circulation figures. *Source: Gebbie Press, 2015 All-In-One Media Directory*

SAFETY

Violent Crime Rate: Number of violent crimes reported per 10,000 population. Violent crimes include murder, forcible rape, robbery, and aggravated assault. *Source: Federal Bureau of Investigation, Uniform Crime Reports 2013*

Property Crime Rate: Number of property crimes reported per 10,000 population. Property crimes include burglary, larceny-theft, and motor vehicle theft. *Source: Federal Bureau of Investigation, Uniform Crime Reports 2013*

TRANSPORTATION

Commute to Work: Percentage of workers 16 years old and over that use the following means of transportation to commute to work: car; public transportation; walk; work from home. The means of transportation data for some areas may show workers using modes of public transportation that are not available in those areas (e.g. subway or elevated riders in a metropolitan area where there actually is no subway or elevated service). This result is largely due to people who worked during the reference week at a location that was different from their usual place of work (such as people away from home on business in an area where subway service was available) and people who used more than one means of transportation each day but whose principal means was unavailable where they lived (e.g. residents of non-metropolitan areas who drove to the fringe of a metropolitan area and took the commuter railroad most of the distance to work). *Source: U.S. Census Bureau, American Community Survey, 2009-2013 Five-Year Estimates*

Median Travel Time to Work: Median travel time to work for workers 16 years old and over. Travel time to work refers to the total number of minutes that it usually took the person to get from home to work each day during the reference week. The elapsed time includes time spent waiting for public transportation, picking up passengers in carpools, and time spent in other activities related to getting to work. *Source: U.S. Census Bureau, American Community Survey, 2009-2013 Five-Year Estimates*

Amtrak: Indicates if Amtrak rail or bus service is available. Please note that the cities being served continually change. *Source: National Railroad Passenger Corporation, Amtrak National Timetable, 2015*

AIRPORTS

Lists the local airport(s) along with type of service and hub size. *Source: U.S. Department of Transportation, Bureau of Transportation Statistics*

ADDITIONAL INFORMATION CONTACTS

General telephone number and website address (if available) of local government.

User Guide: Education Section

School District Rankings

Number of Schools: Total number of schools in the district. *Source: U.S. Department of Education, National Center for Education Statistics, Common Core of Data, Public Elementary/Secondary School Universe Survey: School Year 2011-2012.*

Number of Teachers: Teachers are defined as individuals who provide instruction to pre-kindergarten, kindergarten, grades 1 through 12, or ungraded classes, or individuals who teach in an environment other than a classroom setting, and who maintain daily student attendance records. Numbers reported are full-time equivalents (FTE). *Source: U.S. Department of Education, National Center for Education Statistics, Common Core of Data, Local Education Agency (School District) Universe Survey: School Year 2011-2012.*

Number of Students: A student is an individual for whom instruction is provided in an elementary or secondary education program that is not an adult education program and is under the jurisdiction of a school, school system, or other education institution. *Sources: U.S. Department of Education, National Center for Education Statistics, Common Core of Data, Local Education Agency (School District) Universe Survey: School Year 2011-2012 and Public Elementary/Secondary School Universe Survey: School Year 2011-2012*

Individual Education Program (IEP) Students: A written instructional plan for students with disabilities designated as special education students under IDEA-Part B. The written instructional plan includes a statement of present levels of educational performance of a child; statement of annual goals, including short-term instructional objectives; statement of specific educational services to be provided and the extent to which the child will be able to participate in regular educational programs; the projected date for initiation and anticipated duration of services; the appropriate objectives, criteria and evaluation procedures; and the schedules for determining, on at least an annual basis, whether instructional objectives are being achieved. *Source: U.S. Department of Education, National Center for Education Statistics, Common Core of Data, Local Education Agency (School District) Universe Survey: School Year 2011-2012*

English Language Learner (ELL) Students: Formerly referred to as Limited English Proficient (LEP). Students being served in appropriate programs of language assistance (e.g., English as a Second Language, High Intensity Language Training, bilingual education). Does not include pupils enrolled in a class to learn a language other than English. Also Limited-English-Proficient students are individuals who were not born in the United States or whose native language is a language other than English; or individuals who come from environments where a language other than English is dominant; or individuals who are American Indians and Alaskan Natives and who come from environments where a language other than English has had a significant impact on their level of English language proficiency; and who, by reason thereof, have sufficient difficulty speaking, reading, writing, or understanding the English language, to deny such individuals the opportunity to learn successfully in classrooms where the language of instruction is English or to participate fully in our society. *Source: U.S. Department of Education, National Center for Education Statistics, Common Core of Data, Local Education Agency (School District) Universe Survey: School Year 2011-2012*

Students Eligible for Free Lunch Program: The free lunch program is defined as a program under the National School Lunch Act that provides cash subsidies for free lunches to students based on family size and income criteria. *Source: U.S. Department of Education, National Center for Education Statistics, Common Core of Data, Public Elementary/Secondary School Universe Survey: School Year 2011-2012*

Students Eligible for Reduced-Price Lunch Program: A student who is eligible to participate in the Reduced-Price Lunch Program under the National School Lunch Act. *Source: U.S. Department of Education, National Center for Education Statistics, Common Core of Data, Public Elementary/Secondary School Universe Survey: School Year 2011-2012*

Student/Teacher Ratio: The number of students divided by the number of teachers (FTE). See Number of Students and Number of Teachers above for for information.

Student/Librarian Ratio: The number of students divided by the number of library and media support staff. Library and media support staff are defined as staff members who render other professional library and media services; also includes library aides and those involved in library/media support. Their duties include selecting, preparing, caring for, and making available to instructional staff, equipment, films, filmstrips, transparencies, tapes, TV programs, and similar materials maintained separately or as part of an instructional materials center. Also included are activities in the audio-visual center, TV studio, related-work-study areas, and services provided by audio-visual personnel.

Numbers are based on full-time equivalents. *Source: U.S. Department of Education, National Center for Education Statistics, Common Core of Data, Local Education Agency (School District) Universe Survey: School Year 2011-2012.*

Student/Counselor Ratio: The number of students divided by the number of guidance counselors. Guidance counselors are professional staff assigned specific duties and school time for any of the following activities in an elementary or secondary setting: counseling with students and parents; consulting with other staff members on learning problems; evaluating student abilities; assisting students in making educational and career choices; assisting students in personal and social development; providing referral assistance; and/or working with other staff members in planning and conducting guidance programs for students. The state applies its own standards in apportioning the aggregate of guidance counselors/directors into the elementary and secondary level components. Numbers reported are full-time equivalents. *Source: U.S. Department of Education, National Center for Education Statistics, Common Core of Data, Local Education Agency (School District) Universe Survey: School Year 2011-2012.*

Current Spending per Student: Expenditure for Instruction, Support Services, and Other Elementary/Secondary Programs. Includes salaries, employee benefits, purchased services, and supplies, as well as payments made by states on behalf of school districts. Also includes transfers made by school districts into their own retirement system. Excludes expenditure for Non-Elementary/Secondary Programs, debt service, capital outlay, and transfers to other governments or school districts. This item is formally called "Current Expenditures for Public Elementary/Secondary Education."

Instruction: Includes payments from all funds for salaries, employee benefits, supplies, materials, and contractual services for elementary/secondary instruction. It excludes capital outlay, debt service, and interfund transfers for elementary/secondary instruction. Instruction covers regular, special, and vocational programs offered in both the regular school year and summer school. It excludes instructional support activities as well as adult education and community services. Instruction salaries includes salaries for teachers and teacher aides and assistants.

Support Services: Relates to support services functions (series 2000) defined in Financial Accounting for Local and State School Systems (National Center for Education Statistics 2000). Includes payments from all funds for salaries, employee benefits, supplies, materials, and contractual services. It excludes capital outlay, debt service, and interfund transfers. It includes expenditure for the following functions:

- Business/Central/Other Support Services
- General Administration
- Instructional Staff Support
- Operation and Maintenance
- Pupil Support Services
- Pupil Transportation Services
- School Administration
- Nonspecified Support Services

Values shown are dollars per pupil per year. They were calculated by dividing the total dollar amounts by the fall membership. Fall membership is comprised of the total student enrollment on October 1 (or the closest school day to October 1) for all grade levels (including prekindergarten and kindergarten) and ungraded pupils. Membership includes students both present and absent on the measurement day. *Source: U.S. Department of Education, National Center for Education Statistics, Common Core of Data, School District Finance Survey (F-33), Fiscal Year 2011.*

Drop-out Rate: A dropout is a student who was enrolled in school at some time during the previous school year; was not enrolled at the beginning of the current school year; has not graduated from high school or completed a state or district approved educational program; and does not meet any of the following exclusionary conditions: has transferred to another public school district, private school, or state- or district-approved educational program; is temporarily absent due to suspension or school-approved illness; or has died. The values shown cover grades 9 through 12. *Note: Drop-out rates are no longer available to the general public disaggregated by grade, race/ethnicity, and gender at the school district level. Beginning with the 2005–06 school year the CCD is reporting dropout data aggregated from the local education agency (district) level to the state level. This allows data users to compare event dropout rates across states, regions, and other jurisdictions. Source: U.S. Department of Education, National Center for Education Statistics, Common Core of Data, Local Education Agency (School District) Universe Survey Dropout and Completion Data, 2008-2009; U.S. Department of Education, National Center for Education Statistics, Common Core of Data, State Dropout and Completion Data File, 2009-2010*

Average Freshman Graduation Rate (AFGR): The AFGR is the number of regular diploma recipients in a given year divided by the average of the membership in grades 8, 9, and 10, reported 5, 4, and 3 years earlier, respectively. For example, the denominator of the 2008–09 AFGR is the average of the 8th-grade membership in 2004–05, 9th-grade membership in 2005–06, and 10th-grade membership in 2006–07. Ungraded students are prorated into

these grades. Averaging these three grades provides an estimate of the number of first-time freshmen in the class of 2005–06 freshmen in order to estimate the on-time graduation rate for 2008–09.

Caution in interpreting the AFGR. Although the AFGR was selected as the best of the available alternatives, several factors make it fall short of a true on-time graduation rate. First, the AFGR does not take into account any imbalances in the number of students moving in and out of the nation or individual states over the high school years. As a result, the averaged freshman class is at best an approximation of the actual number of freshmen, where differences in the rates of transfers, retention, and dropping out in the three grades affect the average. Second, by including all graduates in a specific year, the graduates may include students who repeated a grade in high school or completed high school early and thus are not on-time graduates in that year. *Source: U.S. Department of Education, National Center for Education Statistics, Common Core of Data, Local Education Agency (School District) Universe Survey Dropout and Completion Data, 2008-2009; U.S. Department of Education, National Center for Education Statistics, Common Core of Data, State Dropout and Completion Data File, 2009-2010*

Number of Diploma Recipients: A student who has received a diploma during the previous school year or subsequent summer school. This category includes regular diploma recipients and other diploma recipients. A High School Diploma is a formal document certifying the successful completion of a secondary school program prescribed by the state education agency or other appropriate body. *Note: Diploma counts are no longer available to the general public disaggregated by grade, race/ethnicity, and gender at the school district level. Source: U.S. Department of Education, National Center for Education Statistics, Common Core of Data, Local Education Agency (School District) Universe Survey Dropout and Completion Data, 2008-2009; U.S. Department of Education, National Center for Education Statistics, Common Core of Data, State Dropout and Completion Data File, 2009-2010*

Note: n/a indicates data not available.

State Educational Profile

Please refer to the District Rankings section in the front of this User Guide for an explanation of data for all items except for the following:

Average Salary: The average salary for classroom teachers in 2013-2014. *Source: National Education Association, Rankings & Estimates: Rankings of the States 2013 and Estimates of School Statistics 2014*

College Entrance Exam Scores:

Scholastic Aptitude Test (SAT). *Note: Data covers all students during the 2013 school year. The College Board strongly discourages the comparison or ranking of states on the basis of SAT scores alone. Source: The College Board*

American College Testing Program (ACT). *Note: Data covers all students during the 2013 school year. Source: ACT, 2013 ACT National and State Scores*

National Assessment of Educational Progress (NAEP)

The National Assessment of Educational Progress (NAEP), also known as "the Nation's Report Card," is the only nationally representative and continuing assessment of what America's students know and can do in various subject areas. As a result of the "No Child Left Behind" legislation, all states are required to participate in NAEP.

For more information, visit the U.S. Department of Education, National Center for Education Statistics at http://nces.ed.gov/nationsreportcard.

User Guide: Ancestry and Ethnicity Section

Places Covered

The ancestry and ethnicity profile section of this book covers the state and all counties and places with populations of 50,000 or more. Places included fall into one of the following categories:

Incorporated Places. Depending on the state, places are incorporated as either cities, towns, villages, boroughs, municipalities, independent cities, or corporations. A few municipalities have a form of government combined with another entity (e.g. county) and are listed as special cities or consolidated, unified, or metropolitan governments.

Census Designated Places (CDP). The U.S. Census Bureau defines a CDP as "a statistical entity," defined for each decennial census according to Census Bureau guidelines, comprising a densely settled concentration of population that is not within an incorporated place, but is locally identified by a name. CDPs are delineated cooperatively by state and local officials and the Census Bureau, following Census Bureau guidelines.

Minor Civil Divisions (called charter townships, districts, gores, grants, locations, plantations, purchases, reservations, towns, townships, and unorganized territories) for the states where the Census Bureau has determined that they serve as general-purpose governments. Those states are Connecticut, Maine, Massachusetts, Michigan, Minnesota, New Hampshire, New Jersey, New York, Pennsylvania, Rhode Island, Vermont, and Wisconsin. In some states incorporated municipalities are part of minor civil divisions and in some states they are independent of them.

Note: Several states have incorporated municipalities and minor civil divisions in the same county with the same name. Those communities are given separate entries (e.g. Burlington, New Jersey, in Burlington County will be listed under both the city and township of Burlington). A few states have Census Designated Places and minor civil divisions in the same county with the same name. Those communities are given separate entries (e.g. Bridgewater, Massachusetts, in Plymouth County will be listed under both the CDP and town of Bridgewater).

Source of Data

The ethnicities shown in this book were compiled from two different sources. Data for Race and Hispanic Origin was taken from Census 2010 Summary File 1 (SF1) while Ancestry data was taken from the American Community Survey (ACS) 2006-2010 Five-Year Estimate. The distinction is important because SF1 contains 100-percent data, which is the information compiled from the questions asked of all people and about every housing unit. ACS estimates are compiled from a sampling of households. The 2006-2010 Five-Year Estimate is based on data collected from January 1, 2006 to December 31, 2010.

The American Community Survey (ACS) is a relatively new survey conducted by the U.S. Census Bureau. It uses a series of monthly samples to produce annually updated data for the same small areas (census tracts and block groups) formerly surveyed via the decennial census long-form sample. While some version of this survey has been in the field since 1999, it was not fully implemented in terms of coverage until 2006. In 2005 it was expanded to cover all counties in the country and the 1-in-40 households sampling rate was first applied. The full implementation of the (household) sampling strategy for ACS entails having the survey mailed to about 250,000 households nationwide every month of every year and was begun in January 2005. In January 2006 sampling of group quarters was added to complete the sample as planned. In any given year about 2.5% (1 in 40) of U.S. households will receive the survey. Over any 5-year period about 1 in 8 households should receive the survey (as compared to about 1 in 6 that received the census long form in the 2000 census). Since receiving the survey is not the same as responding to it, the Bureau has adopted a strategy of sampling for non-response, resulting in something closer to 1 in 11 households actually participating in the survey over any 5-year period. For more information about the American Community Survey visit http://www.census.gov/acs/www.

Ancestry

Ancestry refers to a person's ethnic origin, heritage, descent, or "roots," which may reflect their place of birth or that of previous generations of their family. Some ethnic identities, such as "Egyptian" or "Polish" can be traced to geographic areas outside the United States, while other ethnicities such as "Pennsylvania German" or "Cajun" evolved in the United States.

The intent of the ancestry question in the ACS was not to measure the degree of attachment the respondent had to a particular ethnicity, but simply to establish that the respondent had a connection to and self-identified with a particular

ethnic group. For example, a response of "Irish" might reflect total involvement in an Irish community or only a memory of ancestors several generations removed from the respondent.

The Census Bureau coded the responses into a numeric representation of over 1,000 categories. Responses initially were processed through an automated coding system; then, those that were not automatically assigned a code were coded by individuals trained in coding ancestry responses. The code list reflects the results of the Census Bureau's own research and consultations with many ethnic experts. Many decisions were made to determine the classification of responses. These decisions affected the grouping of the tabulated data. For example, the "Indonesian" category includes the responses of "Indonesian," "Celebesian," "Moluccan," and a number of other responses.

Ancestries Covered

Afghan	Palestinian	French, ex. Basque	Scottish
African, Sub-Saharan	Syrian	French Canadian	Serbian
African	Other Arab	German	Slavic
Cape Verdean	Armenian	German Russian	Slovak
Ethiopian	Assyrian/Chaldean/Syriac	Greek	Slovene
Ghanaian	Australian	Guyanese	Soviet Union
Kenyan	Austrian	Hungarian	Swedish
Liberian	Basque	Icelander	Swiss
Nigerian	Belgian	Iranian	Turkish
Senegalese	Brazilian	Irish	Ukrainian
Sierra Leonean	British	Israeli	Welsh
Somalian	Bulgarian	Italian	West Indian, ex.
South African	Cajun	Latvian	Hispanic
Sudanese	Canadian	Lithuanian	Bahamian
Ugandan	Carpatho Rusyn	Luxemburger	Barbadian
Zimbabwean	Celtic	Macedonian	Belizean
Other Sub-Saharan African	Croatian	Maltese	Bermudan
Albanian	Cypriot	New Zealander	British West Indian
Alsatian	Czech	Northern European	Dutch West Indian
American	Czechoslovakian	Norwegian	Haitian
Arab	Danish	Pennsylvania German	Jamaican
Arab	Dutch	Polish	Trinidadian/
Egyptian	Eastern European	Portuguese	Tobagonian
Iraqi	English	Romanian	U.S. Virgin Islander
Jordanian	Estonian	Russian	West Indian
Lebanese	European	Scandinavian	Other West Indian
Moroccan	Finnish	Scotch-Irish	Yugoslavian

The ancestry question allowed respondents to report one or more ancestry groups. Generally, only the first two responses reported were coded. If a response was in terms of a dual ancestry, for example, "Irish English," the person was assigned two codes, in this case one for Irish and another for English. However, in certain cases, multiple responses such as "French Canadian," "Scotch-Irish," "Greek Cypriot," and "Black Dutch" were assigned a single code reflecting their status as unique groups. If a person reported one of these unique groups in addition to another group, for example, "Scotch-Irish English," resulting in three terms, that person received one code for the unique group (Scotch-Irish) and another one for the remaining group (English). If a person reported "English Irish French," only English and Irish were coded. If there were more than two ancestries listed and one of the ancestries was a part of another, such as "German Bavarian Hawaiian," the responses were coded using the more detailed groups (Bavarian and Hawaiian).

The Census Bureau accepted "American" as a unique ethnicity if it was given alone or with one other ancestry. There were some groups such as "American Indian," "Mexican American," and "African American" that were coded and identified separately.

The ancestry question is asked for every person in the American Community Survey, regardless of age, place of birth, Hispanic origin, or race.

Although some people consider religious affiliation a component of ethnic identity, the ancestry question was not designed to collect any information concerning religion. Thus, if a religion was given as an answer to the ancestry question, it was listed in the "Other groups" category which is not shown in this book.

Ancestry should not be confused with a person's place of birth, although a person's place of birth and ancestry may be the same.

Hispanic Origin

The data on the Hispanic or Latino population were derived from answers to a Census 2010 question that was asked of all people. The terms "Spanish," "Hispanic origin," and "Latino" are used interchangeably. Some respondents identify with all three terms while others may identify with only one of these three specific terms. Hispanics or Latinos who identify with the terms "Spanish," "Hispanic," or "Latino" are those who classify themselves in one of the specific Spanish, Hispanic, or Latino categories listed on the questionnaire ("Mexican," "Puerto Rican," or "Cuban") as well as those who indicate that they are "other Spanish/Hispanic/Latino." People who do not identify with one of the specific origins listed on the questionnaire but indicate that they are "other Spanish/Hispanic/Latino" are those whose origins are from Spain, the Spanish-speaking countries of Central or South America, the Dominican Republic, or people identifying themselves generally as Spanish, Spanish-American, Hispanic, Hispano, Latino, and so on. All write-in responses to the "other Spanish/Hispanic/Latino" category were coded.

Hispanic Origins Covered

Hispanic or Latino	Salvadoran	Argentinean	Uruguayan
Central American, ex. Mexican	Other Central American	Bolivian	Venezuelan
Costa Rican	Cuban	Chilean	Other South American
Guatemalan	Dominican Republic	Colombian	Other Hispanic or Latino
Honduran	Mexican	Ecuadorian	
Nicaraguan	Puerto Rican	Paraguayan	
Panamanian	South American	Peruvian	

Origin can be viewed as the heritage, nationality group, lineage, or country of birth of the person or the person's parents or ancestors before their arrival in the United States. People who identify their origin as Hispanic, Latino, or Spanish may be of any race.

Ethnicities Based on Race

The data on race were derived from answers to the Census 2010 question on race that was asked of individuals in the United States. The Census Bureau collects racial data in accordance with guidelines provided by the U.S. Office of Management and Budget (OMB), and these data are based on self-identification.

The racial categories included in the census questionnaire generally reflect a social definition of race recognized in this country and not an attempt to define race biologically, anthropologically, or genetically. In addition, it is recognized that the categories of the race item include racial and national origin or sociocultural groups. People may choose to report more than one race to indicate their racial mixture, such as "American Indian" and "White." People who identify their origin as Hispanic, Latino, or Spanish may be of any race.

Racial Groups Covered

African-American/Black	Crow	Spanish American Indian	Korean
Not Hispanic	Delaware	Tlingit-Haida *(Alaska Native)*	Laotian
Hispanic	Hopi	Tohono O'Odham	Malaysian
American Indian/Alaska Native	Houma	Tsimshian *(Alaska Native)*	Nepalese
Not Hispanic	Inupiat *(Alaska Native)*	Ute	Pakistani
Hispanic	Iroquois	Yakama	Sri Lankan
Alaska Athabascan *(Ala. Nat.)*	Kiowa	Yaqui	Taiwanese
Aleut *(Alaska Native)*	Lumbee	Yuman	Thai
Apache	Menominee	Yup'ik *(Alaska Native)*	Vietnamese
Arapaho	Mexican American Indian	**Asian**	**Hawaii Native/Pacific Islander**
Blackfeet	Navajo	*Not Hispanic*	*Not Hispanic*
Canadian/French Am. Indian	Osage	*Hispanic*	*Hispanic*
Central American Indian	Ottawa	Bangladeshi	Fijian
Cherokee	Paiute	Bhutanese	Guamanian/Chamorro
Cheyenne	Pima	Burmese	Marshallese
Chickasaw	Potawatomi	Cambodian	Native Hawaiian
Chippewa	Pueblo	Chinese, ex. Taiwanese	Samoan
Choctaw	Puget Sound Salish	Filipino	Tongan
Colville	Seminole	Hmong	**White**
Comanche	Shoshone	Indian	*Not Hispanic*
Cree	Sioux	Indonesian	*Hispanic*
Creek	South American Indian	Japanese	

African American or Black: A person having origins in any of the Black racial groups of Africa. It includes people who indicated their race(s) as "Black, African Am., or Negro" or reported entries such as African American, Kenyan, Nigerian, or Haitian.

American Indian or Alaska Native: A person having origins in any of the original peoples of North and South America (including Central America) and who maintains tribal affiliation or community attachment. This category includes people who indicated their race(s) as "American Indian or Alaska Native" or reported their enrolled or principal tribe, such as Navajo, Blackfeet, Inupiat, Yup'ik, or Central American Indian groups or South American Indian groups.

Asian: A person having origins in any of the original peoples of the Far East, Southeast Asia, or the Indian subcontinent, including, for example, Cambodia, China, India, Japan, Korea, Malaysia, Pakistan, the Philippine Islands, Thailand, and Vietnam. It includes people who indicated their race(s) as "Asian" or reported entries such as "Asian Indian," "Chinese," "Filipino," "Korean," "Japanese," "Vietnamese," and "Other Asian" or provided other detailed Asian responses.

Native Hawaiian or Other Pacific Islander: A person having origins in any of the original peoples of Hawaii, Guam, Samoa, or other Pacific Islands. It includes people who indicated their race(s) as "Pacific Islander" or reported entries such as "Native Hawaiian," "Guamanian or Chamorro," "Samoan," and "Other Pacific Islander" or provided other detailed Pacific Islander responses.

White: A person having origins in any of the original peoples of Europe, the Middle East, or North Africa. It includes people who indicated their race(s) as "White" or reported entries such as Irish, German, Italian, Lebanese, Arab, Moroccan, or Caucasian.

Profiles

Each profile shows the name of the place, the county (if a place spans more than one county, the county that holds the majority of the population is shown), and the 2010 population (based on 100-percent data from Census 2010 Summary File 1). The rest of each profile is comprised of all 218 ethnicities grouped into three sections: ancestry; Hispanic origin; and race.

Column one displays the ancestry/Hispanic origin/race name, column two displays the number of people reporting each ancestry/Hispanic origin/race, and column three is the percent of the total population reporting each ancestry/Hispanic origin/race. The population figure shown is used to calculate the value in the "%" column for ethnicities based on race and Hispanic origin. The 2006-2010 estimated population figure from the American Community Survey (not shown) is used to calculate the value in the "%" column for all other ancestries.

For ethnicities in the ancestries group, the value in the "Number" column includes multiple ancestries reported. For example, if a person reported a multiple ancestry such as "French Danish," that response was counted twice in the tabulations, once in the French category and again in the Danish category. Thus, the sum of the counts is not the total population but the total of all responses. Numbers in parentheses indicate the number of people reporting a single ancestry. People reporting a single ancestry includes all people who reported only one ethnic group such as "German." Also included in this category are people with only a multiple-term response such as "Scotch-Irish" who are assigned a single code because they represent one distinct group. For example, the count for German would be interpreted as "The number of people who reported that German was their only ancestry."

For ethnicities based on Hispanic origin, the value in the "Number" column represents the number of people who reported being Mexican, Puerto Rican, Cuban or other Spanish/Hispanic/ Latino (all written-in responses were coded). All ethnicities based on Hispanic origin can be of any race.

For ethnicities based on race data the value in the "Number" column represents the total number of people who reported each category alone or in combination with one or more other race categories. This number represents the maximum number of people reporting and therefore the individual race categories may add up to more than the total population because people may be included in more than one category. The figures in parentheses show the number of people that reported that particular ethnicity alone, not in combination with any other race. For example, in Alabama, the entry for Korean shows 8,320 in parentheses and 10,624 in the "Number" column. This means that 8,320 people reported being Korean alone and 10,624 people reported being Korean alone or in combination with one or more other races.

Rankings

In the rankings section, each ethnicity has three tables. The first table shows the top 10 places sorted by ethnic population (based on all places, regardless of total population), the second table shows the top 10 places sorted by percent of the total population (based on all places, regardless of total population), the third table shows the top 10 places sorted by percent of the total population (based on places with total population of 50,000 or more).

Within each table, column one displays the place name, the state, and the county (if a place spans more than one county, the county that holds the majority of the population is shown). Column one in the first table displays the state only. Column two displays the number of people reporting each ancestry (includes people reporting multiple ancestries), Hispanic origin, or race (alone or in combination with any other race). Column three is the percent of the total population reporting each ancestry, Hispanic origin or race. For tables representing ethnicities based on race or Hispanic origin, the 100-percent population figure from SF1 is used to calculate the value in the "%" column. For all other ancestries, the 2006-2010 five-year estimated population figure from the American Community Survey is used to calculate the value in the "%" column.

Alphabetical Ethnicity Cross-Reference Guide

Afghan *see* Ancestry–Afghan
African *see* Ancestry–African, Sub-Saharan: African
African-American *see* Race–African-American/Black
African-American: Hispanic *see* Race–African-American/Black: Hispanic
African-American: Not Hispanic *see* Race–African-American/Black: Not Hispanic
Alaska Athabascan *see* Race–Alaska Native: Alaska Athabascan
Alaska Native *see* Race–American Indian/Alaska Native
Alaska Native: Hispanic *see* Race–American Indian/Alaska Native: Hispanic
Alaska Native: Not Hispanic *see* Race–American Indian/Alaska Native: Not Hispanic
Albanian *see* Ancestry–Albanian
Aleut *see* Race–Alaska Native: Aleut
Alsatian *see* Ancestry–Alsatian
American *see* Ancestry–American
American Indian *see* Race–American Indian/Alaska Native
American Indian: Hispanic *see* Race–American Indian/Alaska Native: Hispanic
American Indian: Not Hispanic *see* Race–American Indian/Alaska Native: Not Hispanic
Apache *see* Race–American Indian: Apache
Arab *see* Ancestry–Arab: Arab
Arab: Other *see* Ancestry–Arab: Other
Arapaho *see* Race–American Indian: Arapaho
Argentinean *see* Hispanic Origin–South American: Argentinean
Armenian *see* Ancestry–Armenian
Asian *see* Race–Asian
Asian Indian *see* Race–Asian: Indian
Asian: Hispanic *see* Race–Asian: Hispanic
Asian: Not Hispanic *see* Race–Asian: Not Hispanic
Assyrian *see* Ancestry–Assyrian/Chaldean/Syriac
Australian *see* Ancestry–Australian
Austrian *see* Ancestry–Austrian
Bahamian *see* Ancestry–West Indian: Bahamian, except Hispanic
Bangladeshi *see* Race–Asian: Bangladeshi
Barbadian *see* Ancestry–West Indian: Barbadian, except Hispanic
Basque *see* Ancestry–Basque
Belgian *see* Ancestry–Belgian
Belizean *see* Ancestry–West Indian: Belizean, except Hispanic
Bermudan *see* Ancestry–West Indian: Bermudan, except Hispanic
Bhutanese *see* Race–Asian: Bhutanese
Black *see* Race–African-American/Black
Black: Hispanic *see* Race–African-American/Black: Hispanic
Black: Not Hispanic *see* Race–African-American/Black: Not Hispanic
Blackfeet *see* Race–American Indian: Blackfeet
Bolivian *see* Hispanic Origin–South American: Bolivian
Brazilian *see* Ancestry–Brazilian
British *see* Ancestry–British

British West Indian *see* Ancestry–West Indian: British West Indian, except Hispanic
Bulgarian *see* Ancestry–Bulgarian
Burmese *see* Race–Asian: Burmese
Cajun *see* Ancestry–Cajun
Cambodian *see* Race–Asian: Cambodian
Canadian *see* Ancestry–Canadian
Canadian/French American Indian *see* Race–American Indian: Canadian/French American Indian
Cape Verdean *see* Ancestry–African, Sub-Saharan: Cape Verdean
Carpatho Rusyn *see* Ancestry–Carpatho Rusyn
Celtic *see* Ancestry–Celtic
Central American *see* Hispanic Origin–Central American, except Mexican
Central American Indian *see* Race–American Indian: Central American Indian
Central American: Other *see* Hispanic Origin–Central American: Other Central American
Chaldean *see* Ancestry–Assyrian/Chaldean/Syriac
Chamorro *see* Race–Hawaii Native/Pacific Islander: Guamanian or Chamorro
Cherokee *see* Race–American Indian: Cherokee
Cheyenne *see* Race–American Indian: Cheyenne
Chickasaw *see* Race–American Indian: Chickasaw
Chilean *see* Hispanic Origin–South American: Chilean
Chinese (except Taiwanese) *see* Race–Asian: Chinese, except Taiwanese
Chippewa *see* Race–American Indian: Chippewa
Choctaw *see* Race–American Indian: Choctaw
Colombian *see* Hispanic Origin–South American: Colombian
Colville *see* Race–American Indian: Colville
Comanche *see* Race–American Indian: Comanche
Costa Rican *see* Hispanic Origin–Central American: Costa Rican
Cree *see* Race–American Indian: Cree
Creek *see* Race–American Indian: Creek
Croatian *see* Ancestry–Croatian
Crow *see* Race–American Indian: Crow
Cuban *see* Hispanic Origin–Cuban
Cypriot *see* Ancestry–Cypriot
Czech *see* Ancestry–Czech
Czechoslovakian *see* Ancestry–Czechoslovakian
Danish *see* Ancestry–Danish
Delaware *see* Race–American Indian: Delaware
Dominican Republic *see* Hispanic Origin–Dominican Republic
Dutch *see* Ancestry–Dutch
Dutch West Indian *see* Ancestry–West Indian: Dutch West Indian, except Hispanic
Eastern European *see* Ancestry–Eastern European
Ecuadorian *see* Hispanic Origin–South American: Ecuadorian
Egyptian *see* Ancestry–Arab: Egyptian
English *see* Ancestry–English
Eskimo *see* Race–Alaska Native: Inupiat
Estonian *see* Ancestry–Estonian
Ethiopian *see* Ancestry–African, Sub-Saharan: Ethiopian
European *see* Ancestry–European
Fijian *see* Race–Hawaii Native/Pacific Islander: Fijian
Filipino *see* Race–Asian: Filipino
Finnish *see* Ancestry–Finnish
French (except Basque) *see* Ancestry–French, except Basque
French Canadian *see* Ancestry–French Canadian
German *see* Ancestry–German
German Russian *see* Ancestry–German Russian
Ghanaian *see* Ancestry–African, Sub-Saharan: Ghanaian
Greek *see* Ancestry–Greek
Guamanian *see* Race–Hawaii Native/Pacific Islander: Guamanian or Chamorro
Guatemalan *see* Hispanic Origin–Central American: Guatemalan
Guyanese *see* Ancestry–Guyanese
Haitian *see* Ancestry–West Indian: Haitian, except Hispanic
Hawaii Native *see* Race–Hawaii Native/Pacific Islander
Hawaii Native: Hispanic *see* Race–Hawaii Native/Pacific Islander: Hispanic

Hawaii Native: Not Hispanic *see* Race–Hawaii Native/Pacific Islander: Not Hispanic
Hispanic or Latino: *see* Hispanic Origin–Hispanic or Latino (of any race)
Hispanic or Latino: Other *see* Hispanic Origin–Other Hispanic or Latino
Hmong *see* Race–Asian: Hmong
Honduran *see* Hispanic Origin–Central American: Honduran
Hopi *see* Race–American Indian: Hopi
Houma *see* Race–American Indian: Houma
Hungarian *see* Ancestry–Hungarian
Icelander *see* Ancestry–Icelander
Indonesian *see* Race–Asian: Indonesian
Inupiat *see* Race–Alaska Native: Inupiat
Iranian *see* Ancestry–Iranian
Iraqi *see* Ancestry–Arab: Iraqi
Irish *see* Ancestry–Irish
Iroquois *see* Race–American Indian: Iroquois
Israeli *see* Ancestry–Israeli
Italian *see* Ancestry–Italian
Jamaican *see* Ancestry–West Indian: Jamaican, except Hispanic
Japanese *see* Race–Asian: Japanese
Jordanian *see* Ancestry–Arab: Jordanian
Kenyan *see* Ancestry–African, Sub-Saharan: Kenyan
Kiowa *see* Race–American Indian: Kiowa
Korean *see* Race–Asian: Korean
Laotian *see* Race–Asian: Laotian
Latvian *see* Ancestry–Latvian
Lebanese *see* Ancestry–Arab: Lebanese
Liberian *see* Ancestry–African, Sub-Saharan: Liberian
Lithuanian *see* Ancestry–Lithuanian
Lumbee *see* Race–American Indian: Lumbee
Luxemburger *see* Ancestry–Luxemburger
Macedonian *see* Ancestry–Macedonian
Malaysian *see* Race–Asian: Malaysian
Maltese *see* Ancestry–Maltese
Marshallese *see* Race–Hawaii Native/Pacific Islander: Marshallese
Menominee *see* Race–American Indian: Menominee
Mexican *see* Hispanic Origin–Mexican
Mexican American Indian *see* Race–American Indian: Mexican American Indian
Moroccan *see* Ancestry–Arab: Moroccan
Native Hawaiian *see* Race–Hawaii Native/Pacific Islander: Native Hawaiian
Navajo *see* Race–American Indian: Navajo
Nepalese *see* Race–Asian: Nepalese
New Zealander *see* Ancestry–New Zealander
Nicaraguan *see* Hispanic Origin–Central American: Nicaraguan
Nigerian *see* Ancestry–African, Sub-Saharan: Nigerian
Northern European *see* Ancestry–Northern European
Norwegian *see* Ancestry–Norwegian
Osage *see* Race–American Indian: Osage
Ottawa *see* Race–American Indian: Ottawa
Pacific Islander *see* Race–Hawaii Native/Pacific Islander
Pacific Islander: Hispanic *see* Race–Hawaii Native/Pacific Islander: Hispanic
Pacific Islander: Not Hispanic *see* Race–Hawaii Native/Pacific Islander: Not Hispanic
Paiute *see* Race–American Indian: Paiute
Pakistani *see* Race–Asian: Pakistani
Palestinian *see* Ancestry–Arab: Palestinian
Panamanian *see* Hispanic Origin–Central American: Panamanian
Paraguayan *see* Hispanic Origin–South American: Paraguayan
Pennsylvania German *see* Ancestry–Pennsylvania German
Peruvian *see* Hispanic Origin–South American: Peruvian
Pima *see* Race–American Indian: Pima
Polish *see* Ancestry–Polish
Portuguese *see* Ancestry–Portuguese
Potawatomi *see* Race–American Indian: Potawatomi

Pueblo *see* Race–American Indian: Pueblo
Puerto Rican *see* Hispanic Origin–Puerto Rican
Puget Sound Salish *see* Race–American Indian: Puget Sound Salish
Romanian *see* Ancestry–Romanian
Russian *see* Ancestry–Russian
Salvadoran *see* Hispanic Origin–Central American: Salvadoran
Samoan *see* Race–Hawaii Native/Pacific Islander: Samoan
Scandinavian *see* Ancestry–Scandinavian
Scotch-Irish *see* Ancestry–Scotch-Irish
Scottish *see* Ancestry–Scottish
Seminole *see* Race–American Indian: Seminole
Senegalese *see* Ancestry–African, Sub-Saharan: Senegalese
Serbian *see* Ancestry–Serbian
Shoshone *see* Race–American Indian: Shoshone
Sierra Leonean *see* Ancestry–African, Sub-Saharan: Sierra Leonean
Sioux *see* Race–American Indian: Sioux
Slavic *see* Ancestry–Slavic
Slovak *see* Ancestry–Slovak
Slovene *see* Ancestry–Slovene
Somalian *see* Ancestry–African, Sub-Saharan: Somalian
South African *see* Ancestry–African, Sub-Saharan: South African
South American *see* Hispanic Origin–South American
South American Indian *see* Race–American Indian: South American Indian
South American: Other *see* Hispanic Origin–South American: Other South American
Soviet Union *see* Ancestry–Soviet Union
Spanish American Indian *see* Race–American Indian: Spanish American Indian
Sri Lankan *see* Race–Asian: Sri Lankan
Sub-Saharan African *see* Ancestry–African, Sub-Saharan
Sub-Saharan African: Other *see* Ancestry–African, Sub-Saharan: Other
Sudanese *see* Ancestry–African, Sub-Saharan: Sudanese
Swedish *see* Ancestry–Swedish
Swiss *see* Ancestry–Swiss
Syriac *see* Ancestry–Assyrian/Chaldean/Syriac
Syrian *see* Ancestry–Arab: Syrian
Taiwanese *see* Race–Asian: Taiwanese
Thai *see* Race–Asian: Thai
Tlingit-Haida *see* Race–Alaska Native: Tlingit-Haida
Tohono O'Odham *see* Race–American Indian: Tohono O'Odham
Tongan *see* Race–Hawaii Native/Pacific Islander: Tongan
Trinidadian and Tobagonian *see* Ancestry–West Indian: Trinidadian and Tobagonian, except Hispanic
Tsimshian *see* Race–Alaska Native: Tsimshian
Turkish *see* Ancestry–Turkish
U.S. Virgin Islander *see* Ancestry–West Indian: U.S. Virgin Islander, except Hispanic
Ugandan *see* Ancestry–African, Sub-Saharan: Ugandan
Ukrainian *see* Ancestry–Ukrainian
Uruguayan *see* Hispanic Origin–South American: Uruguayan
Ute *see* Race–American Indian: Ute
Venezuelan *see* Hispanic Origin–South American: Venezuelan
Vietnamese *see* Race–Asian: Vietnamese
Welsh *see* Ancestry–Welsh
West Indian *see* Ancestry–West Indian: West Indian, except Hispanic
West Indian (except Hispanic) *see* Ancestry–West Indian, except Hispanic
West Indian: Other *see* Ancestry–West Indian: Other, except Hispanic
White *see* Race–White
White: Hispanic *see* Race–White: Hispanic
White: Not Hispanic *see* Race–White: Not Hispanic
Yakama *see* Race–American Indian: Yakama
Yaqui *see* Race–American Indian: Yaqui
Yugoslavian *see* Ancestry–Yugoslavian
Yuman *see* Race–American Indian: Yuman
Yup'ik *see* Race–Alaska Native: Yup'ik
Zimbabwean *see* Ancestry–African, Sub-Saharan: Zimbabwean

User Guide: Climate Section

SOURCES OF THE DATA

The National Climactic Data Center (NCDC) has two main classes or types of weather stations; first-order stations which are staffed by professional meteorologists and cooperative stations which are staffed by volunteers. All National Weather Service (NWS) stations included in this book are first-order stations.

The data in the climate section is compiled from several sources. The majority comes from the original NCDC computer tapes (DSI-3220 Summary of Month Cooperative). This data was used to create the entire table for each cooperative station and part of each National Weather Service station. The remainder of the data for each NWS station comes from the International Station Meteorological Climate Summary, Version 4.0, September 1996, which is also available from the NCDC.

Storm events come from the NCDC Storm Events Database which is accessible over the Internet at https://www.ncdc.noaa.gov/stormevents.

WEATHER STATION TABLES

The weather station tables are grouped by type (National Weather Service and Cooperative) and then arranged alphabetically. The station name is almost always a place name, and is shown here just as it appears in NCDC data. The station name is followed by the county in which the station is located (or by county equivalent name), the elevation of the station (at the time beginning of the thirty year period) and the latitude and longitude.

The National Weather Service Station tables contain 32 data elements which were compiled from two different sources, the International Station Meteorological Climate Summary (ISMCS) and NCDC DSI-3220 data tapes. The following 13 elements are from the ISMCS: maximum precipitation, minimum precipitation, maximum snowfall, maximum 24-hour snowfall, thunderstorm days, foggy days, predominant sky cover, relative humidity (morning and afternoon), dewpoint, wind speed and direction, and maximum wind gust. The remaining 19 elements come from the DSI-3220 data tapes. The period of record (POR) for data from the DSI-3220 data tapes is 1980-2009. The POR for ISMCS data varies from station to station and appears in a note below each station.

The Cooperative Station tables contain 19 data elements which were all compiled from the DSI-3220 data tapes with a POR of 1980-2009.

WEATHER ELEMENTS (NWS AND COOPERATIVE STATIONS)

The following elements were compiled by the editor from the NCDC DSI-3220 data tapes using a period of record of 1980-2009.

The average temperatures (maximum, minimum, and mean) are the average (see Methodology below) of those temperatures for all available values for a given month. For example, for a given station the average maximum temperature for July is the arithmetic average of all available maximum July temperatures for that station. (Maximum means the highest recorded temperature, minimum means the lowest recorded temperature, and mean means an arithmetic average temperature.)

The extreme maximum temperature is the highest temperature recorded in each month over the period 1980-2009. The extreme minimum temperature is the lowest temperature recorded in each month over the same time period. The extreme maximum daily precipitation is the largest amount of precipitation recorded over a 24-hour period in each month from 1980-2009. The maximum snow depth is the maximum snow depth recorded in each month over the period 1980-2009.

The days for maximum temperature and minimum temperature are the average number of days those criteria were met for all available instances. The symbol $\geq$ means greater than or equal to, the symbol $\leq$ means less than or equal to. For example, for a given station, the number of days the maximum temperature was greater than or equal to 90°F in July, is just an arithmetic average of the number of days in all the available Julys for that station.

Heating and cooling degree days are based on the median temperature for a given day and its variance from 65°F. For example, for a given station if the day's high temperature was 50°F and the day's low temperature was 30°F, the median (midpoint) temperature was 40°F. 40°F is 25 degrees below 65°F, hence on this day there would be 25 heating degree days. This also applies for cooling degree days. For example, for a given station if the day's high temperature was 80°F and the day's low temperature was 70°F, the median (midpoint) temperature was 75°F. 75°F is 10 degrees above 65°F, hence on this day there would be 10 cooling degree days. All heating and/or cooling degree

days in a month are summed for the month giving respective totals for each element for that month. These sums for a given month for a given station over the past thirty years are again summed and then arithmetically averaged. It should be noted that the heating and cooling degree days do not cancel each other out. It is possible to have both for a given station in the same month.

Precipitation data is computed the same as heating and cooling degree days. Mean precipitation and mean snowfall are arithmetic averages of cumulative totals for the month. All available values for the thirty year period for a given month for a given station are summed and then divided by the number of values. The same is true for days of greater than or equal to 0.1", 0.5",and 1.0" of precipitation, and days of greater than or equal to 1.0" of snow depth on the ground. The word trace appears for precipitation and snowfall amounts that are too small to measure.

Finally, remember that all values presented in the tables and the rankings are averages, maximums, or minimums of available data (see Methodology below) for that specific data element for the last thirty years (1980-2009).

WEATHER ELEMENTS (NWS STATIONS ONLY)

The following elements were taken directly from the International Station Meteorological Climate Summary. The periods of records vary per station and are noted at the bottom of each table.

Maximum precipitation, minimum precipitation, maximum snowfall, maximum snow depth, maximum 24-hour snowfall, thunderstorm days, foggy days, relative humidity (morning and afternoon), dewpoint, prevailing wind speed and direction, and maximum wind gust are all self-explanatory.

The word trace appears for precipitation and snowfall amounts that are too small to measure.

Predominant sky cover contains four possible entries: CLR (clear); SCT (scattered); BRK (broken); and OVR (overcast).

INCLUSION CRITERIA—HOW STATIONS WERE SELECTED

The basic criteria is that a station must have data for temperature, precipitation, heating and cooling degree days of sufficient quantity in order to create a meaningful average. More specifically, the definition of sufficiency here has two parts. First, there must be 22 values for a given data element, and second, ten of the nineteen elements included in the table must pass this sufficiency test. For example, in regard to mean maximum temperature (the first element on every data table), a given station needs to have a value for every month of at least 22 of the last thirty years in order to meet the criteria, and, in addition, every station included must have at least ten of the nineteen elements with at least this minimal level of completeness in order to fulfill the criteria. We then removed stations that were geographically close together, giving preference to stations with better data quality.

METHODOLOGY

The following discussion applies only to data compiled from the NCDC DSI-3220 data tapes and excludes weather elements that are extreme maximums or minimums.

The data is based on an arithmetic average of all available data for a specific data element at a given station. For example, the average maximum daily high temperature during July for any given station was abstracted from NCDC source tapes for the thirty Julys, starting in July, 1980 and ending in July, 2009. These thirty figures were then summed and divided by thirty to produce an arithmetic average. As might be expected, there were not thirty values for every data element on every table. For a variety of reasons, NCDC data is sometimes incomplete. Thus the following standards were established.

For those data elements where there were 26-30 values, the data was taken to be essentially complete and an average was computed. For data elements where there were 22-25 values, the data was taken as being partly complete but still valid enough to use to compute an average. Such averages are shown in **bold italic** type to indicate that there was less than 26 values. For the few data elements where there were not even 22 values, no average was computed and 'na' appears in the space. If any of the twelve months for a given data element reported a value of 'na', no annual average was computed and the annual average was reported as 'na' as well.

Thus the basic computational methodology used is designed to provide an arithmetic average. Because of this, such a pure arithmetic average is somewhat different from the special type of average (called a "normal") which NCDC procedures produces and appears in federal publications.

Perhaps the best outline of the contrasting normalization methodology is found in the following paragraph (which appears as part of an NCDC technical document titled, CLIM81 1961-1990 NORMALS TD-9641 prepared by Lewis France of NCDC in May, 1992):

Normals have been defined as the arithmetic mean of a climatological element computed over a long time period. International agreements eventually led to the decision that the appropriate time period would be three consecutive decades (Guttman, 1989). The data record should be consistent (have no changes in location, instruments, observation practices, etc.; these are identified here as "exposure changes") and have no missing values so a normal will reflect the actual average climatic conditions. If any significant exposure changes have occurred, the data record is said to be "inhomogeneous," and the normal may not reflect a true climatic average. Such data need to be adjusted to remove the nonclimatic inhomogeneities. The resulting (adjusted) record is then said to be "homogeneous." If no exposure changes have occurred at a station, the normal is calculated simply by averaging the appropriate 30 values from the 1961-1990 record.

In the main, there are two "inhomogeneities" that NCDC is correcting for with normalization: adjusting for variances in time of day of observation (at the so-called First Order stations data is based on midnight to midnight observation times and this practice is not necessarily followed at cooperative stations which are staffed by volunteers), and second, estimating data that is either missing or incongruent.

The editors had some concerns regarding the comparative results of the two methodologies. Would our methodology produce strikingly different results than NCDC's? To allay concerns, results of the two processes were compared for the time period normalized results are available (1971-2000). In short, what was found was that the answer to this question is no. Never the less, users should be aware that because of both the time period covered (1980-2009) and the methodology used, data is not compatible with data from other sources.

POTENTIAL CAUTIONS

First, as with any statistical reference work of this type, users need to be aware of the source of the data. The information here comes from NOAA, and it is the most comprehensive and reliable core data available. Although it is the best, it is not perfect. Most weather stations are staffed by volunteers, times of observation sometimes vary, stations occasionally are moved (especially over a thirty year period), equipment is changed or upgraded, and all of these factors affect the uniformity of the data. The editors do not attempt to correct for these factors, and this data is not intended for either climatologists or atmospheric scientists. Users with concerns about data collection and reporting protocols are both referred to NCDC technical documentation.

Second, users need to be aware of the methodology here which is described above. Although this methodology has produced fully satisfactory results, it is not directly compatible with other methodologies, hence variances in the results published here and those which appear in other publications will doubtlessly arise.

Third, is the trap of that informal logical fallacy known as "hasty generalization," and its corollaries. This may involve presuming the future will be like the past (specifically, next year will be an average year), or it may involve misunderstanding the limitations of an arithmetic average, but more interestingly, it may involve those mistakes made most innocently by generalizing informally on too broad a basis. As weather is highly localized, the data should be taken in that context. A weather station collects data about climatic conditions at that spot, and that spot may or may not be an effective paradigm for an entire town or area.

North Carolina

About North Carolina

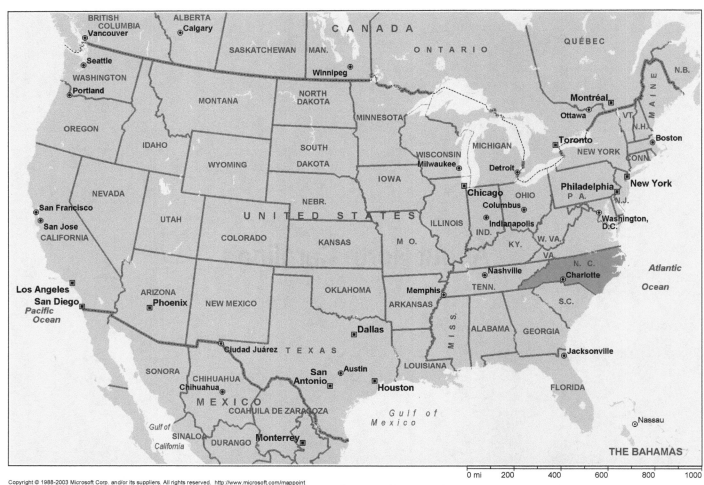

Governor . . . . **Patrick Lloyd "Pat" McCrory (R)**
Lt Governor . . . . **Dan Forest (R)**
State Capital . . . . Raleigh
Date of Statehood . . . . November 21, 1789 (12th state)
Before Statehood. . . . . Province of North Carolina
State Nicknames . . . . Old North State; Tar Heel State
Largest City. . . . . Charlotte
Demonym . . . . North Carolinian
Highest Point. . . . . Mount Mitchell (6,684 feet)
Lowest Point. . . . . Atlantic Ocean (sea level)
Time Zone. . . . . Eastern

State Art Medium . . . . Clay
State Blue Berry . . . . Blueberry *(Genus Vaccinium)*
State Beverage . . . . Milk
State Bird . . . . Cardinal *(Cardinalis cardinalis)*
State Butterfly. . . . . Eastern Tiger Swallowtail *(Papilio glaucus)*
State Carnivorous Plant. . . . Venus Flytrap *(Dionaea muscipula)*
State Colors. . . . . Red and Blue
State Christmas Tree . . . . . Fraser Fir *(Abies fraseri)*
State Dog. . . . . Plott Hound *(Canis lupus familiaris)*
State Flower . . . . Flowering Dogwood *(Cornus Florida)*
State Folk Art . . . . Whirligigs (created by Vollis Simpson)
State Folk Dance. . . . . Clogging
State Fossil . . . . Fossilized teeth of the megalodon shark
State Freshwater Trout . . . . Southern Appalachian Brook Trout *(Salvelinus fontinalis)*
State Frog . . . . Pine Barrens Tree Frog *(Hyla andersonii)*
State Fruit . . . . Scuppernong Grape *(Genus Vitis)*
State Historical Boat . . . . . Shad Boat
State Horse . . . . Colonial Spanish Mustang *(Equus ferus caballus)*
State Insect . . . . Honeybee *(Apis millifera)*
State Mammal. . . . . Grey Squirrel *(Sciurus carolinensis)*
State Marsupial . . . . Virginia Opossum *(Didelphis virginiana)*
State Mineral. . . . . Gold *(Aurum)*
State Motto . . . . "To be, rather than to seem" *("Esse quam videri")*
State Popular Dance . . . . . . Shagging
State Precious Stone . . . . . . Emerald
State Red Berry. . . . . Strawberry *(Genus Fragaria)*
State Reptile . . . . Eastern Box Turtle *(Terrapene carolina)*
State Rock. . . . . Granite
State Salamander. . . . . Marbled Salamander *(Ambystoma opacum)*
State Saltwater Fish. . . . . . . Channel Bass or Red Drum *(Sciaenops ocellatus)*
State Shell . . . . Scotch Bonnet *(Semicassis granulata)*
State Song . . . . The Old North State (words by William Gaston, music by Mrs. E. E. Randolph)
State Sport. . . . . Stock Car Racing
State Tree . . . . Pine *(Genus Pinus)*
State Vegetable . . . . Sweet Potato *(Ipomoea batatas)*
State Wildflower. . . . . Carolina Lily *(Lilium michauxii)*

Charlotte, pictured top, is nicknamed the Queen City, in honor of Charlotte of Mecklenburg-Strelitz, queen consort of Great Britain. It is the largest city in North Carolina and the second largest in the Southeast, behind Jacksonville, Florida, and home to the 23rd busiest airport in the world. The bottom photograph shows a tobacco crop, which has always been an important part of the economy of the state, which ranks first in tobacco production.

The Blue Ridge Mountains, pictured here, is part of the Appalachian Mountain range. The mountains are noted for their bluish haze, attributed to its trees that release isoprene into the atmosphere. The Blue Ridge includes Shenandoah National Park in the north and the Great Smoky Mountains National Park in the south.

Pictured top is the North Carolina State Capitol, located in Raleigh. Completed in 1840, it was built in the Greek Revival style, and was declared a National Monument in 1973. The bottom photograph shows the shoreline of Cape Hattaras, a bend in Hatteras Island, one of the long, thin barrier islands that make up the state's Outer Banks, and the highest risk area for hurricanes and tropical storms along the entire U.S. Eastern seaboard.

History of North Carolina

Pre-Colonial History

The earliest discovered human settlements in what eventually became North Carolina are found at the Hardaway Site near the town of Badin in the south-central part of the state. Radiocarbon dating of the site has not been possible. But, based on other dating methods, such as rock strata and the existence of Dalton-type spear points, the site has been dated to approximately 8000 B.C.E., or 10,000 years old.

Spearpoints of the Dalton type continued to change and evolve slowly for the next 7000 years, suggesting a continuity of culture for most of that time. During this time, settlement was scattered and likely existed solely on the hunter-gatherer level. Toward the end of this period, there is evidence of settled agriculture, such as plant domestication and the development of pottery.

From 1000 B.C.E. until the time of European settlement, the time period is known as the "Woodland period". Permanent villages, based on settled agriculture, were developed throughout the present-day state. By about 800 C.E., towns were fortified throughout the Piedmont region, suggesting the existence of organized tribal warfare. An important site of this late-Woodland period is the Town Creek Indian Mound, an archaeologically rich site occupied from about 1100 to 1450 C.E. by the Pee Dee culture of the Mississippian tradition.

Earliest European Explorations

The earliest exploration of North Carolina by a European expedition is likely that of Giovanni da Verrazzano in 1524. An Italian from Florence, Verrazzano was hired by French merchants in order to procure a sea route to bring silk to the city of Lyon. With the tacit support of King Francis I, Verrazzano sailed west on January 1, 1524 aboard his ship La Dauphine ahead of a flotilla that numbered three ships. The expedition made landfall at Cape Fear, and Verrazzano reported of his explorations to the King of France,

> "The seashore is completely covered with fine sand [15 feet] deep, which rises in the shape of small hills about fifty paces wide... Nearby we could see a stretch of country much higher than the sandy shore, with many beautiful fields and planes[sic] full of great forests, some sparse and some dense; and the trees have so many colors, and are so beautiful and delightful that they defy description."

Verrazzano continued north along the Outer Banks, making periodic explorations as he sought a route further west towards China. When he viewed the Albemarle and Pamlico Sounds opposite the Outer Banks, he believed them to be the Pacific Ocean; his reports of such helped fuel the belief that the westward route to Asia was much closer than previously believed.

Just two years later, in 1526, a group of Spanish colonists from Hispaniola led by Lucas Vázquez de Ayllón landed at the mouth of a river they called the "Rio Jordan", which may have been the Cape Fear River. The party consisted of 500 men and women, their slaves, and horses. One of their ships wrecked off the shore, and valuable supplies were lost; this coupled with illness and rebellion doomed the colony. Ayllón died on October 18, 1526 and the 150 or so survivors of that first year abandoned the colony and attempted to return to Hispaniola. Later explorers reported finding their remains along the coast; as the dead were cast off during the return trip.

Hernando de Soto first explored west-central North Carolina during his 1539-1540 expedition. His first encounter with a native settlement in North Carolina may have been at Guaquilli near modern Hickory. In 1567, Captain Juan Pardo led an expedition from Santa Elena at Parris Island, South Carolina, then the capital of the Spanish colony in the Southeast, into the interior of North Carolina, largely following De Soto's earlier route. His journey was ordered to claim the area as a Spanish colony, pacify and convert the natives, as well as establish another route to protect silver mines in Mexico (the Spanish did not realize the distances involved). Pardo went toward the northwest to be able to get food supplies from natives.

Pardo and his team made a winter base at Joara (near Morganton, in Burke County), which he renamed Cuenca. They built Fort San Juan and left 30 men, while Pardo traveled further, establishing five other forts. In 1567, Pardo's expedition established a mission called Salamanca in what is now Rowan County. Pardo returned by a different route to Santa Elena. After 18 months, in the spring of 1568, natives killed all the soldiers and burned the six forts, including the one at Fort San Juan. The Spanish never returned to the interior to press their colonial claim, but this marked the first European attempt at colonization of the interior. Translation in the 1980s of a journal by Pardo's scribe Bandera have confirmed the expedition and settlement. Archaeological finds at Joara indicate that it was a Mississippian culture settlement and also indicate Spanish settlement at Fort San Juan in 1567-1568. Joara was the largest mound builder settlement in the region. Records of Hernando de Soto's expedition attested to his meeting with them in 1540.

British Colonization

The earliest English attempt at colonization in North America was Roanoke Colony of 1584-1587, the famed "Lost Colony" of Sir Walter Raleigh. The colony was established at Roanoke Island in the Croatan Sound on the leeward side of the Outer Banks. The first attempt at a settlement consisted of 100 or so men led by Ralph Lane. They built a fort, and waited for supplies from a second voyage. While waiting for supplies to return, Lane and his men antagonized the local Croatan peoples, killing several of them in armed skirmishes. The interactions were not all negative, as the local people did teach the colonists some survival skills, such as the construction of dugout canoes.

When the relief was long in coming, the colonists began to give up hope; after a chance encounter with Sir Francis Drake, the colonists elected to accept transport back to England with him. When the supply ships did arrive, only a few days later, they found the colony abandoned. The ship's captain, Richard Grenville, left a small force of 15 men to hold the fort and supplies and wait for a new stock of colonists.

In 1587 a third ship arrived carrying 110 men, 17 women, and 9 children, some of whom had been part of the first group of colonists that had earlier abandoned Roanoke. This group was led by John White. Among them was a pregnant woman; she gave birth to the first English subject born in North America, Virginia Dare. The colonists found the remains of the garrison left behind, likely killed by the Croatan who had been so antagonized by Lane's aggressiveness. White had intended to pick up the remains of the garrison, abandon Roanoke Island, and settle in the Chesapeake Bay. White's Portuguese pilot, Simon Fernandez, refused to carry on further; rather than risk mutiny, White agreed to resettle the former colony.

The Spanish War prevented any further contact between the colony and England until a 1590 expedition, which found no remains of any colonists, just an abandoned colony and the letters "CROATOAN" carved into a tree, and "CRO" carved into another. Despite many investigations, no one knows what happened to the colony. Historians widely believe that the colonists died of starvation and illness; they do not support the myth of their being taken in and assimilated by Native Americans.

Development of North Carolina Colony
The Province of North Carolina developed differently from South Carolina almost from the beginning. The Spanish experienced trouble colonizing North Carolina because it had a dangerous coastline, a lack of ports, and few inland rivers by which to navigate. In the 1650s and 1660s, settlers (mostly English) moved south from Virginia, in addition to runaway servants and fur trappers. They settled chiefly in the Albemarle borderlands region.

In 1665, the Crown issued a second charter to resolve territorial questions. As early as 1689, the Carolina proprietors named a separate deputy-governor for the region of the colony that lay to the north and east of Cape Fear. The division of the colony into North and South was completed at a meeting of the Lords Proprietors held at Craven House in London on December 7, 1710, although the same proprietors continued to control both colonies. The first colonial Governor of North Carolina was Edward Hyde who served from 1711 until 1712. North Carolina became a crown colony in 1729. Smallpox took a heavy toll in the region among Native Americans, who had no immunity to the disease, which had become endemic in Asia and Europe. The 1738

epidemic was said to have killed one-half of the Cherokee, with other tribes of the area suffering equally. Historians estimate there were about 5,000 settlers in 1700 and 11,000 in 1715.

While the voluntary settlers were mostly British, some had brought Africans as laborers; most were enslaved. In the ensuing years, the settlers imported and purchased more slaves to develop plantations in the lowland areas, and the African proportion of the population rose rapidly. A colony at New Bern was composed of Swiss and German settlers. In the late eighteenth century, more German immigrants migrated south after entry into Pennsylvania.

By 1712, the term "North Carolina" was in common use. In 1728, the dividing line between North Carolina and Virginia was surveyed. In 1730, the population in North Carolina was 30,000. By 1729, the Crown bought out seven of the eight original proprietors and made the region a royal colony. John Carteret, 2nd Earl Granville refused to sell; in 1744 he received rights to the vast Granville Tract, constituting the northern half of North Carolina.

Bath the oldest town in North Carolina was the first nominal capital from 1705 until 1722, when Edenton took over the role, but the colony had no permanent institutions of government until their establishment at the new capital New Bern in 1743. Raleigh became capital of North Carolina in 1792.

Immigration from North
The colony grew rapidly from a population of 100,000 in 1752 to 200,000 in 1765. By 1760, enslaved Africans constituted one-quarter of the population and were concentrated along the coast.

In the late eighteenth century, the tide of immigration to North Carolina from Virginia and Pennsylvania began to swell. The Scots-Irish (Ulster Protestants) from what is today Northern Ireland were the largest immigrant group from the British Isles to the colonies before the Revolution. In total, English indentured servants, who arrived mostly in the seventeenth and eighteenth centuries, comprised the majority of English settlers prior to the Revolution. On the eve of the American Revolution, North Carolina was the fastest-growing British colony in North America. The small family farms of the Piedmont contrasted sharply with the plantation economy of the coastal region, where wealthy planters had established a slave society, growing tobacco and rice with slave labor.

Differences in the settlement patterns of eastern and western North Carolina, or the low country and uplands, affected the political, economic, and social life of the state from the eighteenth until the twentieth century. The Tidewater in eastern North Carolina was settled chiefly by immigrants from rural England and the Scottish Highlands. The upcountry of western North Carolina was settled chiefly by Scots-Irish, English and German Protestants, the so-called "cohee". During the Revolutionary War, the English and Highland Scots of eastern North Carolina tended to remain loyal to the British Crown, because of longstanding business and personal connections with Great Britain. The English, Welsh, Scots-Irish and German settlers of western North Carolina tended to favor American independence from Britain.

With no cities and very few towns or villages, the colony was rural and thinly populated. Local taverns provided multiple services ranging from strong drink, beds for travelers, and meeting rooms for politicians and businessmen. In a world sharply divided along lines of ethnicity, gender, race, and class, the tavern keepers' rum proved a solvent that mixed together all sorts of locals, as well as travelers. The increasing variety of drinks on offer, and the emergence of private clubs meeting in the taverns, showed that genteel culture was spreading from London to the periphery of the English world.

The courthouse was usually the most imposing building in a county. Jails were often an important part of the courthouse but were sometimes built separately. Some county governments built tobacco warehouses to provide a common service for their most important export crop.

Slaves
In the early years the line between white indentured servants and African laborers was vague, as some Africans also arrived under indenture, before more were transported as slaves. Some Africans were allowed to earn their freedom before slavery became a lifelong racial caste. Most of the free colored families found in North Carolina

in the censuses of 1790-1810 were descended from unions or marriages between free white women and enslaved or free African or African-American men in colonial Virginia. Because the mothers were free, their children were born free. Such mixed-race families migrated along with their European-American neighbors into the frontier of North Carolina. As the flow of indentured laborers slackened because of improving economic conditions in Britain, the colony was short on labor and imported more slaves. It followed Virginia in increasing its controls on slavery, which became a racial caste of the foreign Africans.

The economy's growth and prosperity was based on slave labor, devoted first to the production of tobacco. The oppressive and brutal experiences of slaves and poor whites led to their using escape, violent resistance, and theft of food and other goods in order to survive.

Politics
In the late 1760s, tensions between Piedmont farmers and coastal planters developed into the Regulator movement. With specie scarce, many inland farmers found themselves unable to pay their taxes and resented the consequent seizure of their property. Local sheriffs sometimes kept taxes for their own gain and sometimes charged twice for the same tax. Governor William Tryon's conspicuous consumption in the construction of a new governor's mansion at New Bern fueled the resentment of yeoman farmers. As the western districts were under-represented in the colonial legislature, the farmers could not obtain redress by legislative means. The frustrated farmers took to arms and closed the court in Hillsborough, North Carolina. Tryon sent troops to the region and defeated the Regulators at the Battle of Alamance in May 1771.

New Nation

American Revolution
The demand for independence came from local grassroots organizations called "Committees of Safety". The First Continental Congress had urged their creation in 1774. By 1775 they had become counter-governments that gradually replaced royal authority and took control of local governments. They regulated the economy, politics, morality, and militia of their individual communities, but many local feuds were played out under ostensibly political affiliations. After December 1776 they came under the control of a more powerful central authority, the Council of Safety.

In the spring of 1776, North Carolinians, meeting in the fourth of their Provincial Congresses, drafted the Halifax Resolves, a set of resolutions that empowered the state's delegates to the Second Continental Congress to concur in a declaration of independence from Great Britain. In July 1776, the new state became part of the new nation, the United States of America.

In 1775 the Patriots easily expelled the Royal governor and suppressed the Loyalists. In November 1776, elected representatives gathered in Halifax to write a new state constitution, which remained in effect until 1835. One of the most prominent Loyalists was John Legett, a rich planter in Bladen County. He organized and led one of the few loyalist brigades in the South (the North Carolina Volunteers, later known as the Royal North Carolina Regiment). After the war, Colonel Legett and some of his men moved to Nova Scotia; the British gave them free land grants in County Harbour as compensation for their losses in the colony. The great majority of Loyalists remained in North Carolina and became citizens of the new nation.

Local militia units proved important in the guerrilla war of 1780-81. Soldiers who enlisted in George Washington's Continental Army fought in numerous battles up and down the land.

Struggling with a weak tax base, state officials used impressment to seize food and supplies needed for the war effort, paying the farmers with promissory notes. To raise soldiers, state officials tried a draft law. Both policies created significant discontent that undermined support for the new nation. The state's large German population, concentrated in the central counties, tried to remain neutral; the Moravians were pacifist because of strong religious beliefs, while Lutheran and Reformed Germans were passively neutral. All peace groups paid triple taxes in lieu of military service.

The British were punctual in paying their regulars and their Loyalist forces, American soldiers went month after month in threadbare uniforms with no pay and scanty supplies. Belatedly, the state tried to make amends. After 1780 soldiers received cash bounties, a slave "or the value thereof," clothing, food, and land (after 1782 they received from 640 to 1,200 acres depending on rank). Since the money supply, based on the Continental currency was subject to high inflation and loss of value, state officials valued compensation in relation to gold and silver.

Military Campaigns of 1780-81
After 1780 the British tried to rouse and arm the Loyalists, believing they were numerous enough to make a difference. The result was fierce guerrilla warfare between units of Patriots and Loyalists. Often the opportunity was seized to settle private grudges and feuds. A major American victory took place at King's Mountain along the North Carolina-South Carolina border. On October 7, 1780 a force of 1000 mountain men from western North Carolina (including what is today part of Tennessee) overwhelmed a force of some 1000 Loyalist and British troops led by Major Patrick Ferguson. The victory essentially ended British efforts to recruit more Loyalists.

The road to American victory at Yorktown led through North Carolina. As the British army moved north toward Virginia, the Southern Division of the Continental Army and local militia prepared to meet them. Following General Daniel Morgan's victory over the British under Banastre Tarleton at the Battle of Cowpens on January 17, 1781, the southern commander Nathanael Greene led British Lord Charles Cornwallis across the heartland of North Carolina, and away from Cornwallis's base of supply in Charleston, South Carolina. This campaign is known as "The Race to the Dan" or "The Race for the River."

Generals Greene and Cornwallis finally met at the Battle of Guilford Courthouse in present-day Greensboro on March 15, 1781. Although the British troops held the field at the end of the battle, their casualties at the hands of the numerically superior Continental Army were crippling. Cornwallis has a poor strategic plan which had failed in holding his heavily garrisoned positions in South Carolina and Georgia, and had failed to subdue North Carolina. By contrast, Greene used a more flexible adaptive approach that negated the British advantages and built an adequate logistical foundation for the American campaigns. Greene's defensive operations provided his forces the opportunity to later seize the strategic offensive from Comwallis and eventually reclaim the Carolinas. The weakened Cornwallis headed to the Virginia coastline to be rescued by the Royal Navy. Continental forces repulsed the Navy and Cornwallis, surrounded by American and French units, surrendered to George Washington, effectively ending the fighting.

By 1786, the population of North Carolina had increased to 350,000.

Early Republic
The United States Constitution drafted in 1787 was controversial in North Carolina. Delegate meetings at Hillsboro in July 1788 initially voted to reject it for anti-federalist reasons. They were persuaded to change their minds partly by the strenuous efforts of James Iredell and William Davies[disambiguation needed] and partly by the prospect of a Bill of Rights. Meanwhile, residents in the wealthy northeastern part of the state, who generally supported the proposed Constitution, threatened to secede if the rest of the state did not fall into line. A second ratifying convention was held in Fayetteville in November 1789, and on November 21, North Carolina became the 12th state to ratify the U.S. Constitution.

North Carolina adopted a new state constitution in 1835. One of the major changes was the introduction of direct election of the governor, for a term of two years; prior to 1835, the legislature elected the governor for a term of one year. North Carolina's current capitol building was completed in 1840.

Transportation
In mid-century, the state's rural and commercial areas were connected by the construction of a 129-mile (208 km) wooden plank road, known as a "farmer's railroad", from Fayetteville in the east to Bethania (northwest of Winston-Salem).

On October 25, 1836 construction began on the Wilmington and Raleigh Railroad to connect the port city of Wilmington with the state capital of Raleigh. In 1849 the North Carolina Railroad was created by act of the

legislature to extend that railroad west to Greensboro, High Point, and Charlotte. During the Civil War the Wilmington-to-Raleigh stretch of the railroad would be vital to the Confederate war effort; supplies shipped into Wilmington would be moved by rail through Raleigh to the Confederate capital of Richmond, Virginia.

Rural Life
During the antebellum period, North Carolina was an overwhelmingly rural state, even by Southern standards. In 1860 only one North Carolina town, the port city of Wilmington, had a population of more than 10,000. Raleigh, the state capital, had barely more than 5,000 residents.

The majority of white families comprised the Plain Folk of the Old South, or "yeoman farmers." They owned their own small farms, and occasionally had a slave or two. Most of their efforts were to build up the farm, and feed their families, with a little surplus sold on the market in order to pay taxes and buy necessities.

Plantations, Slavery and Free Blacks
After the Revolution, Quakers and Mennonites worked to persuade slaveholders to free their slaves. Some were inspired by their efforts and the revolutionary ideals to arrange for manumission of their slaves. The number of free people of color in the state rose markedly in the first couple of decades after the Revolution. Most of the free people of color in the censuses of 1790-1810 were descended from African Americans who became free in colonial Virginia, the children of unions and marriages between white women and African men. These descendants migrated to the frontier during the late eighteenth century along with white neighbors. Free people of color also became concentrated in the eastern coastal plain, especially at port cities such as Wilmington and New Bern, where they could get a variety of jobs and had more freedom in the cities. Restrictions increased beginning in the 1820s; movement by free people of color between counties was prohibited. Additional restrictions against their movements in 1830 under a quarantine act. Free mariners of color on visiting ships were prohibited from having contact with any blacks in the state, in violation of United States treaties. In 1835 free people of color lost the right to vote, following white fears aroused after Nat Turner's Slave Rebellion in 1831. By 1860, there were 30,463 free people of color who lived in the state but could not vote.

Most of North Carolina's slave owners and large plantations were located in the eastern portion of the state. Although its plantation system was smaller and less cohesive than those of Virginia, Georgia or South Carolina, significant numbers of planters were concentrated in the counties around the port cities of Wilmington and Edenton, as well as in the piedmont around the cities of Raleigh, Charlotte and Durham. Planters owning large estates wielded significant political and socio-economic power in antebellum North Carolina, placing their interests above those of the generally non-slave holding "yeoman" farmers of the western part of the state.

While slaveholding was less concentrated in North Carolina than in some Southern states, according to the 1860 census, more than 330,000 people, or 33% of the population of 992,622, were enslaved African Americans. They lived and worked chiefly on plantations in the eastern Tidewater and the upland areas of the Piedmont.

Civil War to 1900

Civil War
In 1860, North Carolina was a slave state, in which about one-third of the population of 992,622 were enslaved African Americans. This was a smaller proportion than many Southern states. In addition, the state had just over 30,000 Free Negroes. there were relatively few large plantations or old aristocratic families. North Carolina was reluctant to secede from the Union when it became clear that Republican Abraham Lincoln had won the presidential election. With the attack on Fort Sumter in April 1861, in Lincoln's call for troops to march to South Carolina, the unionist element virtually collapsed in both of the state, and North Carolina joined the Confederacy.

North Carolina was the site of few battles, but it provided at least 125,000 troops to the Confederacy- far more than any other state. Approximately 40,000 of those troops never returned home, dying of disease, battlefield wounds, and starvation. North Carolina also supplied about 15,000 Union troops. Confederate troops from all parts of North Carolina served in virtually all the major battles of the Army of Northern Virginia, the Confederacy's most famous army. The largest battle fought in North Carolina was at Bentonville, which was a

futile attempt by Confederate General Joseph Johnston to slow Union General William Tecumseh Sherman's advance through the Carolinas in the spring of 1865. In April 1865 after losing the Battle of Morrisville, Johnston surrendered to Sherman at Bennett Place, in what is today Durham, North Carolina. This was the next to last major Confederate Army to surrender. North Carolina's port city of Wilmington was the last major Confederate port for blockade runners; it fell in the spring of 1865 after the nearby Second Battle of Fort Fisher.

Elected in 1862, Governor Zebulon Baird Vance tried to maintain state autonomy against Confederate President Jefferson Davis.

The Union's naval blockade of Southern ports and the breakdown of the Confederate transportation system took a heavy toll on North Carolina residents, as did the runaway inflation of the war years. In the spring of 1863, there were food riots in North Carolina as town dwellers found it hard to buy food. On the other hand, blockade runners brought prosperity several port cities, until they were shut down by the Union Navy in 1864-65.

Even after secession, some North Carolinians refused to support the Confederacy. This was particularly true of non-slave-owning farmers in the state's mountains and western Piedmont region. Some of these farmers remained neutral during the war, while some covertly supported the Union cause during the conflict. Approximately 2,000 white North Carolinians from western North Carolina enlisted in the Union Army and fought for the North in the war. In addition, black men rapidly volunteered to fill two Union regiments raised in the coastal areas of the state that were occupied by Union forces in 1862 and 1863.

Reconstruction Era

During Reconstruction, many African-American leaders arose from people free before the war, men who had escaped to the North and decided to return, and educated migrants from the North who wanted to help in the postwar years. Many who had been in the North had gained some education before their return. In general, however, illiteracy was a problem shared in the early postwar years by most African Americans and about one-third of the whites in the state.

A number of white northerners migrated to North Carolina to work and invest. While feelings in the state were high against carpetbaggers, of the 133 persons at the constitutional convention, only 18 were Northern carpetbaggers and 15 were African American. North Carolina was readmitted to the Union in 1868, after ratifying a new state constitution. It included provisions to establish public education for the first time, prohibit slavery, and adopt universal suffrage. It also provided for public welfare institutions for the first time: orphanages, public charities and a penitentiary. The legislature ratified the Fourteenth Amendment to the U.S. Constitution.

In 1870 the Democratic Party regained power in the state. Governor William W. Holden had used civil powers and spoken out to try to combat the Ku Klux Klan's increasing violence, which was used to suppress black and Republican voting. Conservatives accused him of being head of the Union League, believing in social equality between the races, and practicing political corruption. But, when the legislature voted to impeach him, it charged him only with using and paying troops to put down insurrection (Ku Klux Klan activity) in the state. Holden was impeached and turned over his duties to Lieutenant Governor Tod R. Caldwell on December 20, 1870. The trial began on January 30, 1871, and lasted nearly three months. On March 22, the North Carolina Senate found Holden guilty and ordered him removed from office.

After the national Ku Klux Klan Act of 1871 went into effect in an effort to reduce violence in the South, the U.S. Attorney General, Amos T. Akerman, vigorously prosecuted Klan members in North Carolina. During the late 1870s, there was renewed violence in the Piedmont area, where whites tried to suppress minority black voting in elections. Beginning in 1875, the Red Shirts, a paramilitary group, openly worked for the Democrats to suppress black voting.

Post-Reconstruction and Disfranchisement

As in other Southern states, after white Democrats regained power, they worked to re-establish white supremacy politically and socially. Paramilitary groups such as the Red Shirts beginning in 1875 worked openly to disrupt black political meetings, intimidate leaders and directly challenge voters in campaigns and elections, especially in the Piedmont area. They sometimes physically attacked black voters and community leaders.

Despite this, in the 1880s, black officeholders were at a peak in local offices, where much business was done, as they were elected from black-majority districts. White Democrats regained power on the state level.

Post-Civil War racial politics encouraged efforts to divide and co-opt groups. In the drive to regain power, Democrats supported an effort by state representative Harold McMillan to create separate school districts in 1885 for "Croatan Indians" to gain their support. Of mixed race and claiming Native American heritage, the families had been classified as free people of color in the antebellum years and did not want to send their children to public school classes with former slaves. After having voted with the Republicans, they switched to the Democrats. (In 1913 the group changed their name to "Cherokee Indians of Robeson County", "Siouan Indians of Lumber River" in 1934-1935, and were given limited recognition as Indians by the U.S. Congress as Lumbee in 1956. The Lumbee are one of several Native American tribes that have been officially recognized by the state in the 21st century.)

In 1894 after years of agricultural problems in the state, an interracial coalition of Republicans and Populists won a majority of seats in the state legislature and elected as governor, Republican Daniel L. Russell, the Fusionist candidate. That year North Carolina's 2nd congressional district elected George Henry White, an educated African-American attorney, as its third black representative to Congress since the Civil War.

White Democrats worked to break up the biracial coalition, and reduce voting by blacks and poor whites. In 1896 North Carolina passed a statute that made voter registration more complicated and reduced the number of blacks on voter registration rolls.

In 1898, in an election characterized by violence, fraud and intimidation of black voters by Red Shirts, white Democrats regained control of the state legislature. Two days after the election, a small group of whites in Wilmington implemented their plan to take over the city government if the Democrats were not elected, although the mayor and a majority of city council were white. The cadre led 1500 whites against the black newspaper and neighborhood in what is known as the Wilmington Insurrection of 1898; the mob and other whites killed up to 90 blacks. The cadre forced the resignation of Republican officeholders, including the white mayor, and mostly white aldermen, and ran them out of town. They replaced them with their own slate and that day elected Alfred M. Waddell as mayor. This was the most notorious coup d'etat in United States history.

In 1899 the Democrat-dominated state legislature ratified a new constitution with a suffrage amendment, whose requirements for poll taxes, literacy tests, lengthier residency, and similar mechanisms disfranchised most blacks and many poor whites. Illiterate whites were protected by a grandfather clause, so that if a father or grandfather had voted in 1860 (when all voters were white), his sons or grandsons did not have to pass the literacy test of 1899. This grandfather clause excluded all blacks, as free people of color had lost the franchise in 1835. The US Supreme Court ruled in 1915 that such grandfather clauses were unconstitutional. Every voter had to pay the poll tax until it was abolished by the state in 1920.

Congressman White, an African-American Republican, said after passage of this constitution, "I cannot live in North Carolina and be a man and be treated as a man." He had been re-elected in 1898, but the next year announced his decision not to seek a third term, saying he would leave the state instead. He moved his law practice to Washington, DC and later to Philadelphia in the free state of Pennsylvania, where he founded a commercial bank.

By 1904, black voter turnout had been utterly reduced in North Carolina. Contemporary accounts estimated that 75,000 black male citizens lost the vote. In 1900 blacks numbered 630,207 citizens, about 33% of the state's total population and were unable to elect representatives.

With control of the legislature, white Democrats passed Jim Crow laws establishing racial segregation in public facilities and transportation. African Americans worked for more than 60 years to regain full power to exercise the suffrage and other constitutional rights of citizens. Without the ability to vote, they were excluded from juries and lost all chance at local offices: sheriffs, justices of the peace, jurors, county commissioners and school board members, which were the active site of government around the start of the 20th century. Suppression of the black vote and re-establishment of white supremacy suppressed knowledge of what had been a thriving

black middle class in the state. The Republicans were no longer competitive in state politics, although they had strength in the mountain districts.

20th Century

Reacting to segregation, disfranchisement in 1899, and difficulties in agriculture in the early twentieth century, tens of thousands of African Americans left the state (and hundreds of thousands began to leave the rest of the South) for the North and Midwest - for better opportunities in the Great Migration; in its first wave, from 1910-1940, one and a half million African Americans left the South. They went to Washington, Baltimore, and Philadelphia; and sometimes further north, to industrial cities where there was work, usually taking the trains to connecting cities.

On December 17, 1903, the Wright brothers made the first successful airplane flight at Kitty Hawk, North Carolina. In the early 20th century, North Carolina launched both a major education initiative and a major road-building initiative to enhance the state's economy. The educational initiative was launched by Governor Charles Aycock in 1901. Supposedly, North Carolina built one school per day while Aycock was in office. In addition, North Carolina was helped in the 1920s and 1930s by the Julius Rosenwald Fund, which contributed matching funds to local communities for the construction of thousands of schools for African Americans in rural areas throughout the South. Black parents organized to raise the money, and donated land and labor to build improved schools for their children.

World War I

By 1917-1919 because of disfranchisement of African Americans and establishment of a one-party state, North Carolina Democrats held powerful, senior positions in Congress, holding two of 23 major committee chairmanships in the Senate and four of 18 in the House, as well as the post of House majority leader. White Southerners controlled a block of votes and important chairmanships in Congress because, although they had disfranchised the entire black population of the South, they had not lost any congressional apportionment. With the delegation under control of the Democrats, they exercised party discipline. Their members gained seniority by being re-elected for many years. During the early decades of the 20th century, the Congressional delegation gained the construction of several major U.S. military installations, notably Fort Bragg, in North Carolina. President Woodrow Wilson, a fellow Democrat from the South who was elected due to the suppression of the Republican Party in the South, remained highly popular during World War I and was generally supported by the North Carolina delegation.

During the war, the decrepit ship building industry was revived by large-scale federal contracts landed with Congressional help. Nine new shipyards opened in North Carolina to build ships under contracts from the Emergency Fleet Corporation. Four steamships were made of concrete, but most were made of wood or steel. Thousands of workers rushed to high-paying jobs, as the managers found a shortage of highly skilled mechanics, as well as a housing shortage. Although unions were weak, labor unrest and managerial inexperience caused the delays. The shipyards closed at the end of the war.

The North Carolina Woman's Committee was established as a state agency during the war, headed by Laura Holmes Reilly of Charlotte. Inspired by ideals of the Progressive Movement, it registered women for many volunteer services, promoted increased food production and the elimination of wasteful cooking practices, helped maintain social services, worked to bolster morale of white and black soldiers, improved public health and public schools, and encouraged black participation in its programs. Members helped cope with the devastating Spanish flu epidemic that struck worldwide in late 1918, with very high fatalities. The committee was generally successful in reaching middle-class white and black women. It was handicapped by the condescension of male lawmakers, limited funding, and tepid responses from women on the farms and working-class districts.

The state's road-building initiative began in the 1920s, after the automobile became a popular mode of transportation.

Great Depression and World War II
The state's farmers were badly hurt in the early years of the Great Depression, but benefited greatly by the New Deal programs, especially the tobacco program which guaranteed a steady flow of relatively high income to farmers, and the cotton program, which raised the prices farmers received for their crops (The cotton program caused a rise in prices of cotton goods for consumers during the Depression). The textile industry in the Piedmont region continued to attract cotton mills relocating from the North, where unions had been effective in gaining better wages and conditions.

Prosperity largely returned during World War II. This state supplied the armed forces with more textiles than any other state in the nation. Remote mountain places joined the national economy and had their first taste of prosperity. Hundreds of thousands of young men and a few hundred young women entered the military from this state.

Political scientist V. O. Key analyzed the state political culture in depth in the late 1940s, and concluded it was exceptional in the South for its "progressive outlook and action in many phases of life", especially in the realm of industrial development, commitment to public education, and a moderate-pattern segregation that was relatively free of the rigid racism found in the Deep South.

Education and the Economy
North Carolina invested heavily in its system of higher education, and also became known for its excellent universities. Three major institutions compose the state's Research Triangle: the University of North Carolina at Chapel Hill (chartered in 1789 and greatly expanded from the 1930s on), North Carolina State University, and Duke University (rechartered in 1924).

Conditions of the public elementary and high schools were not as noteworthy. In the 1960s Governor Terry Sanford, a racial moderate, called for more spending on the schools, but Sanford's program featured regressive taxation that fell disproportionately on the workers. In the 1970s Governor James B. Hunt Jr., another racial moderate, championed educational reform.

Reformers have stressed the central role of education in the modernization of the state and economic growth. They have also aggressively pursued economic development, attracting out-of-state, and international corporations with special tax deals and infrastructure development. In the late 20th century, Charlotte became the nation's number two banking center, after New York.

Civil Rights Movement
In 1931, the Negro Voters League was formed in Raleigh to press for voter registration. The city had an educated and politically sophisticated black middle class; by 1946 the League had succeeded in registering 7,000 black voters, an achievement in the segregated South, since North Carolina had essentially disfranchised blacks with provisions of a new constitution in 1899, excluding them from the political system and strengthening its system of white supremacy and Jim Crow.

The work of racial desegregation and enforcement of constitutional civil rights for African Americans continued throughout the state. In the first half of the 20th century, other African Americans voted with their feet, moving in the Great Migration from rural areas to northern and midwestern cities where there were industrial jobs.

During World War II, Durham's Black newspaper, Carolina Times, edited by Louis Austin, took the lead in promoting the "Double V" strategy among civil rights activists. The strategy was to energize blacks to fight victory abroad against the Germans and Japanese, while fighting for victory at home against white supremacy and racial oppression. Activists demanded an end to racial inequality in education, politics, economics, and the armed forces.

In 1960 nearly 25% of the state residents were African American: 1,114,907 citizens who had been living without their constitutional rights. African-American college students began the sit-in at the Woolworth's lunch counter in Greensboro on February 1, 1960, sparking a wave of copycat sit-ins across the American South. They continued the Greensboro sit-in sporadically for several months until, on July 25, African Americans were at last allowed to eat at Woolworth's. Integration of public facilities followed.

Together with continued activism in states throughout the South and raising awareness throughout the country, African Americans' moral leadership gained the passage of the federal Civil Rights Act of 1964 and the Voting Rights Act of 1965 under President Lyndon B. Johnson. Throughout the state, African Americans began to participate fully in political life. In October 1973, Clarence Lightner was elected mayor of Raleigh, making history as the first popularly elected mayor of the city, the first African American to be elected mayor, and the first African American to be elected mayor in a white-majority city of the South. In 1992 the state elected its first African-American congressman since George Henry White in 1898.

In 1979 North Carolina ended the state eugenics program. Since 1929, the state Eugenics Board had deemed thousands of individuals "feeble minded" and had them forcibly sterilized. In 2011 the state legislature debated whether the estimated 2,900 living victims of North Carolina's sterilization regime would be compensated for the harm inflicted upon them by the state. The victims of the program were disproportionately minorities and the poor.

Recent Changes

In 1971, North Carolina ratified its third state constitution. A 1997 amendment to this constitution granted the governor veto power over most legislation. The majority of state residents began to support Republican national candidates in elections starting in 1968 with Richard M. Nixon.

During the last 25 years, North Carolina's population has increased as its economy has grown, especially in finance and knowledge-based industries, attracting people from the North and Midwest. The number of workers in agriculture has declined sharply because of mechanization, and the textile industry has steadily declined because of globalization and movement of jobs in this industry out of the country. Most of the growth in jobs and residents has taken place in metropolitan areas of the Piedmont, in Charlotte, Raleigh-Durham, Greensboro.
Source: Wikipedia, "History of North Carolina," June 23, 2015

Timeline of North Carolina History

Ancient times
The Eastern half of the state was underwater, and giant megalodon sharks roamed the waters.

On land, there were wooly mammoths and mastodons. Archaeologists believe the first Native Americans crossed into the New World from Siberia some 12,000 to 10,000 years ago.

Prior to 1500
Approximately 30 Native American tribes are scattered across North Carolina. Chief among these are the Cherokee, the Catawba, the Tuscarora, and the Croatans. Native Americans build the Town Creek Indian Mound.

1524
Giovanni de Varrazano is the first European to visit North Carolina.

1540
Spanish explorer Hernando de Soto explores the southwestern part of the state in search of gold.

1584-1585
Sir Walter Raleigh sends several shiploads of people to establish the New World's first English colony on North Carolina's Roanoke Island.

1586
The colonists are forced to return to England due to hardships.

1587
July 2: John White establishes a second English colony at Roanoke.

August 18: Virginia Dare is born, becoming the first English child christened on American soil.

August 22: White returns to England for more supplies.

1590
White returns to Roanoke to find that the settlers have all disappeared. The word "CROATOAN" is found carved into a tree. The fate of "The Lost Colony" remains one of the state's most enduring mysteries.

1655
Nathaniel Batts becomes the first European man to permanently settle in North Carolina.

1705
Bath, the first town in North Carolina, is built.

1711-1713
The Tuscarora War between Native Americans and European settlers. After two years of fighting a number of military expeditions, the Tuscarora ended the war, marking the last significant effort by eastern Indians to stop the wave of white settlers crowding them out of their land.

1718
Blackbeard the pirate is killed off the North Carolina coast.

1767-1770
Tryon Palace is built in New Bern, becoming North Carolina's colonial capitol building.

1774
The women of Edenton, led by Penelope Barker, take on British rule by putting down their tea cups in what becomes known as the Edenton Tea Party.

1776
February 27: The Battle of Moores Creek Bridge is the first battle of the American Revolution to be fought in North Carolina.

April 12: North Carolina becomes the first state to vote in favor of independence.

1789
November 21: North Carolina becomes the 12th state of the United States of America.

December 11: The University of North Carolina is chartered, becoming the first public school in the United States.

1794
The capital of North Carolina, which had previously been located in New Bern, is moved to Raleigh.

1799
The first gold nugget is found in the United States at Reed Gold Mine in Cabarrus County.

Early 1800s
North Carolina becomes known as the "Rip Van Winkle" state because it makes so little progress that it appears to be asleep.

1804
The "Walton War" is fought between residents of Georgia and North Carolina.

1828
North Carolina Native Andrew Jackson becomes the 7th president of the United States.

1830s
The U. S. government forces Cherokee Indians from their homes in what becomes known as the "Trail of Tears." Many Cherokee hide in the mountains of North Carolina.

1831
Workmen attempting to fireproof the roof of the State Capitol ironically end up setting the building aflame.

1836
After years of having governors elected by the state senate, Edward B. Dudley becomes the first popularly elected governor of North Carolina.

1840
The first public schools open in North Carolina, based on a plan that had been drafted in 1817.

The new State Capitol is completed.

1845
James Polk becomes the 11th president of the United States.

1853
The first North Carolina State Fair is held.

1861
May 20: North Carolina leaves the Union. Instead of voting to secede from the United States, as other states did, North Carolina voted to "undo" the act that had brought it into the United States.

1861-1865
The United States Civil War. Some 40,000 North Carolinians are killed over the course of the war.

1865
March 19-21: The Battle of Bentonville becomes the bloodiest battle fought in North Carolina. The Confederates are defeated by Union troops.

April 26: A large number of Confederates surrender at Bennett Place, outside of Durham, North Carolina.

May 6: The last Confederate troops in North Carolina surrender.

April 15: Andrew Johnson becomes the 17th president of the United States.

1866
Tuscarora Indian Henry Berry Lowrie leads a revolt in Robeson County, becoming a folk hero to many Native Americans. Six years later, he mysteriously disappears.

1868
July 4: North Carolina is readmitted to the Union.

1877
The last federal reoccupation troops leave North Carolina.

The North Carolina Department of Agriculture is created.

1878
A Cherokee reservation is formed in Western North Carolina, providing protection for those Native Americans who lived in that area.

Late 1800s
The textile and furniture industries grow rapidly in North Carolina.

1897
The first bill to give women the right to vote in North Carolina is proposed, but is sent to a committee on insane asylums and is never passed.

1903
The Wright brothers make man's first successful flight at Kitty Hawk, North Carolina.

1917
The United States enters World War I.

1918
Fort Bragg is established.

1920
The 19th Amendment to the United States Constitution passes, giving women the right to vote across the country, including in North Carolina.

1920s
Tobacco becomes an important crop in North Carolina.

1929
The Great Depression begins.

1941
The United States enters World War II.

1943
Pembroke State College for Indians (now UNC-Pembroke) becomes the nation's first public four-year college for Native Americans.

1954
Hurricane Hazel, one of the most destructive hurricanes in state history, batters the Carolina coast.

1959
Research Triangle Park opens in between Raleigh, Durham and Chapel Hill, ushering in an era of high-tech growth in North Carolina.

1950s-1960s
The Civil Rights Movement.

1960
Governor Terry Sanford starts his "Go Forward" program to improve education in North Carolina.

February 1: The first ever sit-in occurs in Greensboro, North Carolina, to protest segregation at a lunch counter. Within days, sit-ins are occurring across the state.

1960s
The North Carolina Fund, established by Governor Sanford, works to end poverty in North Carolina and becomes a model for programs across the nation.

1965-1973
Vietnam War.

1989
Hurricane Hugo strikes North Carolina, reaching as far inland as Charlotte, and doing major damage.

1993
The Smart Start program to improve school readiness begins. The program is looked upon as a national model.

1994
The Raleigh-Durham area of North Carolina is ranked as the best place to live in the United States.

1996
Hurricane Fran strikes North Carolina, causing massive damage across the state.

Governor Jim Hunt is re-elected to a record 4th term.

Elaine F. Marshall becomes the first female to be elected Secretary of State in North Carolina.

1999
Hurricane Floyd slams into North Carolina, bringing with it flood waters that devastate many areas in the eastern part of the state.

2003
Police arrested Olympic bombing suspect, Eric Robert Rudolph, in Murphy.

2005
State legislature voted implementation of state lottery.

2006
North Carolina Hurricanes won hockey's Stanley Cup

2009
Seven people in North Carolina charged with plotting terror attacks in foreign countries, including Israel and Jordan.

2010
Duke University won NCAA Championship.

2011
Huricane Irene made landfall in North Carolina.

2012
Charlotte hosts Democratic National Convention.

2015
North Carolina AME church shooting massacre suspect Dylan Roof was arrested during a traffic stop in Shelby.
Source: North Carolina Secretary of State; Original research

An Introduction to North Carolina State Government

Organization

North Carolina state government contains three branches: legislative, judicial and executive.

The Legislative Branch

The legislative arm of the state is the North Carolina General Assembly. They enact general and local laws that promote the best interests of the state, and establish rules and regulations governing the conduct of the people.

North Carolina Legislative Building

Like the federal government and almost all the other states (Nebraska being the only exception), North Carolina has a bicameral legislature, consisting of two houses: the Senate and the House of Representatives. The legislature meets annually; the so-called "Long Session" occurs in odd numbered years, while the "Short Session" occurs in even numbered years. Occasionally, in the case of a special need, the Governor may call a Special Session of the General Assembly after they have adjourned for the year.

Senate

The Senate has 50 members. Elections for all 50 seats are held every two years. The Lieutenant Governor is the President of the Senate; however, his/her main duty is to cast a deciding vote in the case of a tie. At the beginning of each biennium, the Senate chooses a President pro Tempore, who presides in the absence of the Lieutenant Governor. The most important duty of the President pro Tempore is to appoint the members to the various standing committees in the Senate.

House of Representatives

The House of Representatives has 120 members. Elections for all 120 seats are held every 2 years. At the beginning of each session, the members of the House choose a Speaker, who presides over the business of the House. In extraordinary cases, such as in the 2003-04 biennium, when the house was evenly divided between the two political parties, co-Speakers may be chosen. As in the Senate, the most important duty of the Speaker is to appoint the members to the various standing committees.

Law Making

Much of the work of the General Assembly is done by standing committees. These committees consider the bills introduced into the two houses, hold hearings, make such changes and amendments as they think necessary, and report their findings back to their respective chambers. If the report on the final version of the bill is favorable, it comes up for debate on the floor of the House or Senate. After final passage in one chamber, the bill is then sent to the other chamber, where the same events occur. A bill passed by both houses is then sent to the Governor, who may either veto the bill, or sign it into law.

The Judicial Branch

Article IV of the North Carolina Constitution establishes the General Court of Justice, which "shall constitute a unified judicial system for purposes of jurisdiction, operation, and administration, and shall consist of an Appellate Division, a Superior Court Division, and a District Court Division." The Constitution also states that the "General Assembly shall have no power to deprive the judicial department of any power or jurisdiction that rightfully pertains to it as a co-ordinate department of the government, nor shall it establish or authorize any courts other than as permitted by this Article."

Appellate Division

The Appellate Division consists of the Supreme Court and the Court of Appeals.

North Carolina Supreme Court

The Supreme Court is the state's highest court. This court has a chief justice and six associate justices, elected to eight-year terms, who hear oral arguments in cases appealed from lower courts. The Supreme Court considers

errors in legal procedures or in judicial interpretation of the law. Its case load consists primarily of cases involving questions of constitutional law, legal questions of major significance, and appeals from convictions imposing death sentences in first-degree murder cases.

North Carolina Court of Appeals

The 15-judge Court of Appeals, created in 1967, is North Carolina's intermediate appellate court. Like the Supreme Court, the Court of Appeals decides only questions of law. It hears a majority of the appeals originating from the state's trial courts. Judges of the Court of Appeals are elected by popular statewide vote for eight-year terms. A Chief Judge for the Court is designated by the Chief Justice of the Supreme Court. Cases are heard by panels of three judges, with the Chief Judge responsible for assigning members of the Court to the five panels.

Superior Courts

The Superior Courts are the general jurisdiction trial courts for the state. All felony criminal cases, civil cases involving more than $10,000 and misdemeanor, and infraction appeals from District Court are tried in Superior Court. A jury of 12 hears the criminal cases. In the civil cases, juries are often waived. The Superior Court is divided into eight divisions and 46 districts across the state. Judges are elected to 8 year terms, and rotate every six months between the districts within their division.

District Courts

The District Courts handle the vast majority of the trial level cases. They have exclusive jurisdiction over civil cases involving less than $10,000, almost all misdemeanors, probable cause hearings in felony cases, juvenile proceedings, mental health hospital commitments, and domestic relations cases. As of 2006, North Carolina had 41 district court districts, and 239 district court judges, elected to four-year terms.

Administrative Office of the Courts

All North Carolina courts, at whatever level, are overseen by the Administrative Office of the Courts (AOC). The basic responsibility of the AOC is to maintain an effective and efficient court system, supporting the courts through technology, personnel, financial, legal, research and purchasing services. The AOC prepares and administers the court system's budget and currently employs more than 400 people.

The Executive Branch

In a move to greatly reduce the number of agencies that had developed in North Carolina government, the Executive Organization Acts of 1971 and 1973 grouped all of the agencies of the Executive Branch into departments plus the Office of the Governor and the Office of the Lieutenant Governor. Since that time, agencies have been renamed and reorganized numerous times. Effective January 1, 2012, the Departments of Correction, Crime Control and Public Safety, and Juvenile Justice and Delinquency were merged into one Department of Public Safety.

Ten members of the executive branch are popularly elected. This includes the Governor, the Lieutenant Governor, the Secretary of State, the State Treasurer, and the State Auditor. The departments of the executive branch that have elected department heads are Agriculture, Insurance, Justice, Labor, and Public Instruction. The remaining department heads are appointed by the governor.

State Agencies

At the time of the Executive Reorganization Acts, there were over 200 independent agencies in state government. Most of these agencies still exist as subdivisions of the executive departments. The location of some agencies may not be obvious--the Division of Veterans Affairs, for instance, is in the Department of Administration. The State Government Portal provides a comprehensive list of state agencies and subdivisions.

In addition to the executive departments, there are three independent executive agencies as well as over 50 licensing boards that provide regulatory control for specific occupations. With the exception of the Office of Administrative Hearings, most of the board members are appointed by the Governor; however, some boards are

made up of members chosen by multiple parties, including the Governor, the Lieutenant Governor, both houses of the General Assembly, and even Council of State members.

Office of Administrative Hearings

The Office of Administrative Hearings is a quasi-judicial agency that adjudicates administrative law cases (that is, cases in which a plaintiff challenges the application—or lack of application—of a particular agency rule), as well as publishing the NC Administrative Code. The Chief Administrative Law Judge, who serves as Director of the OAH and chooses other Administrative Law Judges, is appointed by the Chief Justice of the NC Supreme Court.

Office of the State Controller

The State Controller is the state's Chief Financial Officer, charged with insuring that State appropriations are expended, accounted for, and reported consistently. The State Controller is appointed by the Governor with the approval of the General Assembly.

State Board of Elections

The State Board of Elections administers the election process and deals with all matters of campaign finance disclosure. Members of the Board are chosen by the Governor.

Source: http://ncpedia.org, June 17, 2015

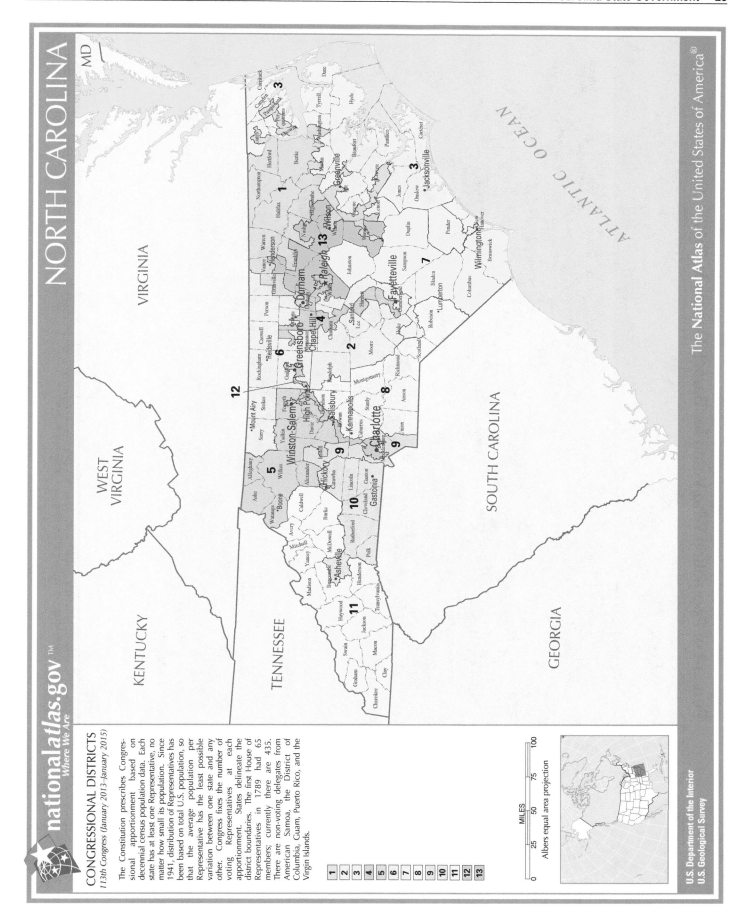

NORTH CAROLINA

nationalatlas.gov™
Where We Are

CONGRESSIONAL DISTRICTS
113th Congress (January 2013–January 2015)

The Constitution prescribes Congressional apportionment based on decennial census population data. Each state has at least one Representative, no matter how small its population. Since 1941, distribution of Representatives has been based on total U.S. population, so that the average population per Representative has the least possible variation between one state and any other. Congress fixes the number of voting Representatives at each apportionment. States delineate the district boundaries. The first House of Representatives in 1789 had 65 members; currently there are 435. There are non-voting delegates from American Samoa, the District of Columbia, Guam, Puerto Rico, and the Virgin Islands.

The National Atlas of the United States of America®

U.S. Department of the Interior
U.S. Geological Survey

MILES
0   25   50   75   100
Albers equal area projection

Percent of Population Who Voted for Barack Obama in 2012

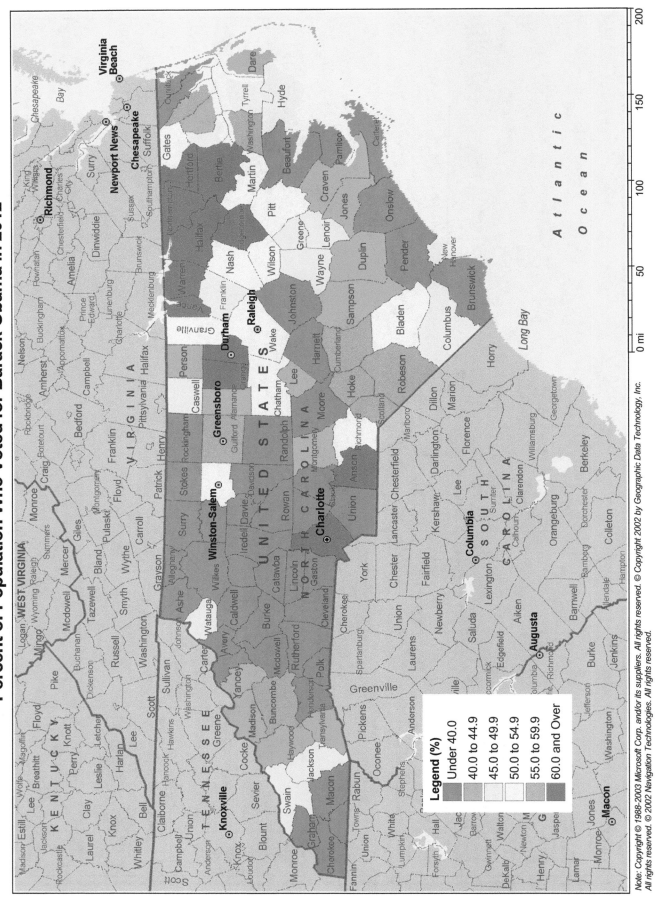

Legend (%)
- Under 40.0
- 40.0 to 44.9
- 45.0 to 49.9
- 50.0 to 54.9
- 55.0 to 59.9
- 60.0 and Over

NORTH CAROLINA - Core Based Statistical Areas (CBSAs) and Counties

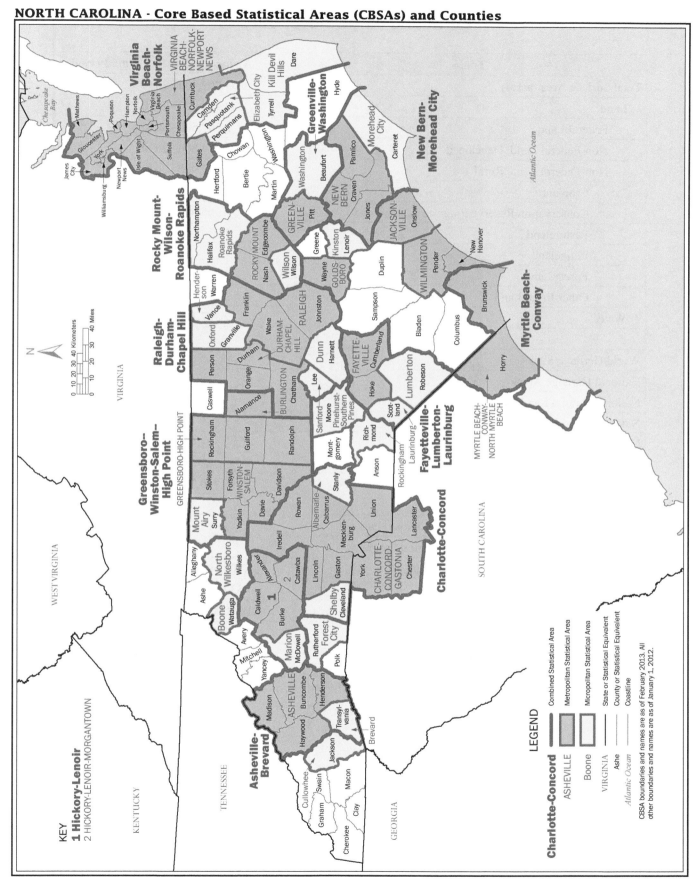

Land and Natural Resources

Topic	Value	Time Period
Total Surface Area (acres)	33,709,300	2010
Land	30,922,200	2010
Federal Land	2,507,500	2010
Non-Federal Land, Developed	4,774,800	2010
Non-Federal Land, Rural	23,639,900	2010
Cropland	5,151,100	2010
Conservation Reserve Program (CRP) Land	65,900	2010
Pastureland	1,914,500	2010
Rangeland	0	2010
Forest Land	15,545,200	2010
Other Rural Land	963,200	2010
Water	2,787,100	2010
World Heritage Sites	1	FY Ending 9/30/2014
National Heritage Areas	2	FY Ending 9/30/2014
National Natural Landmarks	13	FY Ending 9/30/2014
National Historic Landmarks	38	FY Ending 9/30/2014
National Register of Historic Places Listings	2,880	FY Ending 9/30/2014
National Parks	10	FY Ending 9/30/2014
Visitors to National Parks	16,710,759	FY Ending 9/30/2014
Archeological Sites in National Parks	554	FY Ending 9/30/2014
Threatened and Endangered Species in National Parks	23	FY Ending 9/30/2014
Places Recorded by Heritage Documentation Programs	568	FY Ending 9/30/2014
Economic Benefit from National Park Tourism	$1,102,600,000	FY Ending 9/30/2014
Historic Preservation Grants	$37,070,099	Since 1969
Historic Rehabilitation Projects Stimulated by Tax Incentives	$1,250,304,011	Since 1995
Land & Water Conservation Fund Grants	$81,573,910	Since 1965
Acres Transferred by Federal Lands to Local Parks	250	Since 1948

Sources: *United States Department of Agriculture, Natural Resources Conservation Service, National Resources Inventory; U.S. Department of the Interior, National Park Service, State Profiles*

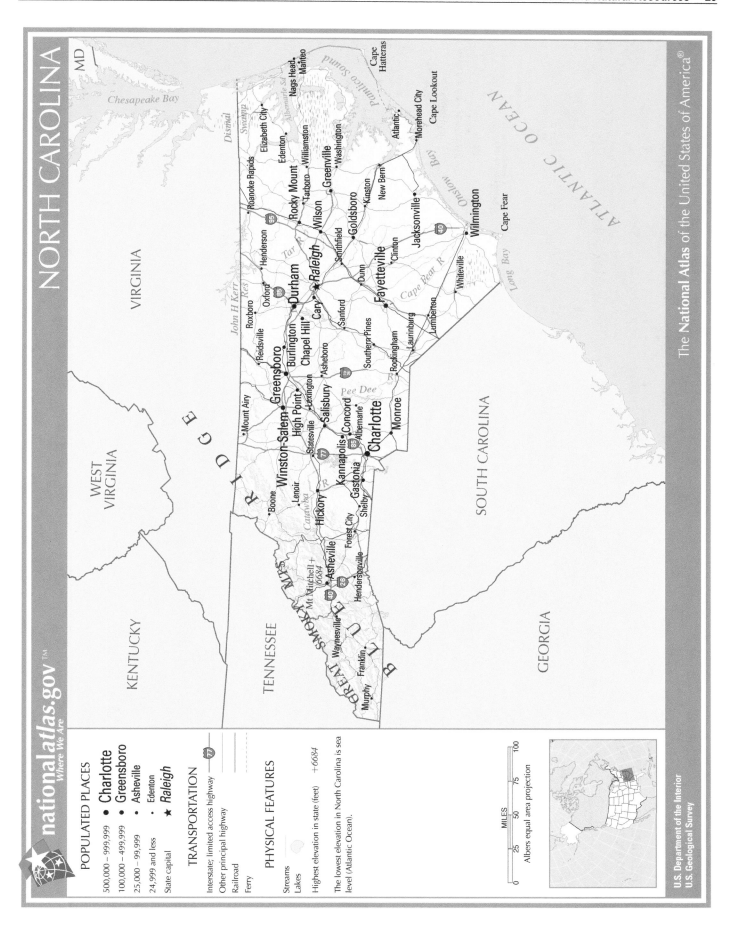

NORTH CAROLINA

POPULATED PLACES

500,000 – 999,999   ● Charlotte
100,000 – 499,999   ● Greensboro
25,000 – 99,999   ● Asheville
24,999 and less   · Edenton
State capital   ★ Raleigh

TRANSPORTATION

Interstate; limited access highway   55
Other principal highway
Railroad
Ferry

PHYSICAL FEATURES

Streams
Lakes
Highest elevation in state (feet)   +6684

The lowest elevation in North Carolina is sea
level (Atlantic Ocean).

MILES
0   25   50   75   100
Albers equal area projection

MD
Chesapeake Bay
VIRGINIA
WEST VIRGINIA
KENTUCKY
TENNESSEE
GEORGIA
SOUTH CAROLINA
ATLANTIC OCEAN

Dismal Swamp
Albemarle Sd
Pamlico Sound
Cape Hatteras
Cape Lookout
Morehead City
Atlantic
Onslow Bay
Cape Fear
Long Bay

BLUE RIDGE
GREAT SMOKY MTS.

Mt Mitchell +6684

Elizabeth City
Nags Head
Manteo
Edenton
Williamston
Washington
Greenville
Roanoke Rapids
Rocky Mount
Tarboro
Wilson
Goldsboro
Kinston
New Bern
Henderson
Oxford
Roxboro
Durham
Raleigh
Cary
Smithfield
Clinton
Jacksonville
Wilmington
Whiteville
Dunn
Fayetteville
Sanford
Southern Pines
Rockingham
Laurinburg
Lumberton
Reidsville
Burlington
Chapel Hill
Greensboro
High Point
Lexington
Asheboro
Winston-Salem
Salisbury
Concord
Albemarle
Monroe
Charlotte
Kannapolis
Gastonia
Statesville
Mount Airy
Boone
Lenoir
Hickory
Shelby
Forest City
Hendersonville
Asheville
Waynesville
Franklin
Murphy

Tar R
Pee Dee
Cape Fear R
Catawba
John H Kerr Res

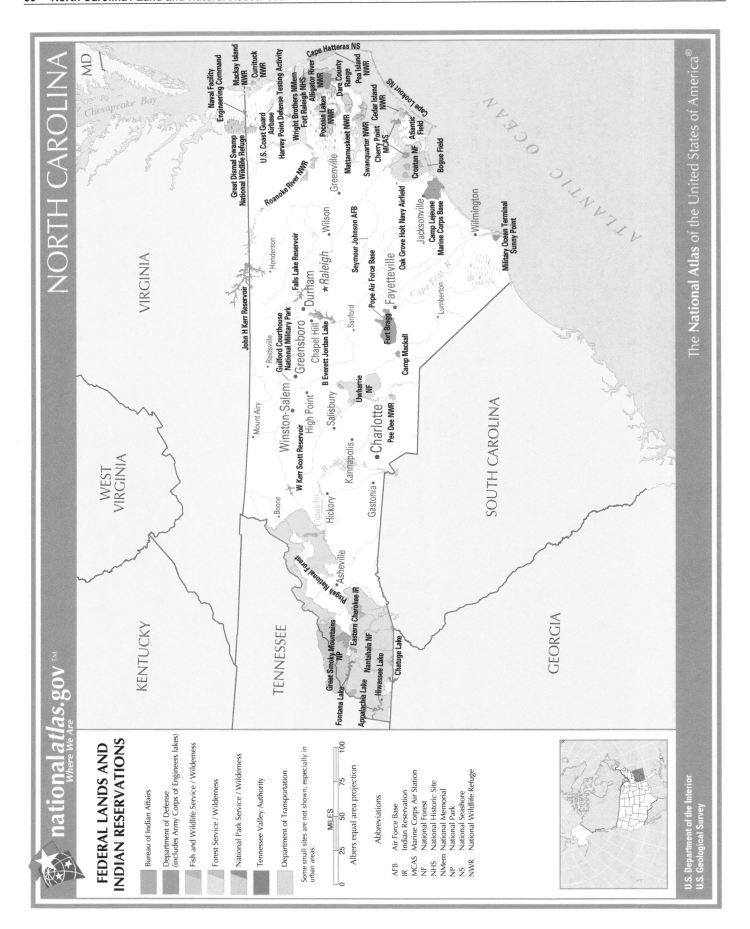

NORTH CAROLINA

FEDERAL LANDS AND
INDIAN RESERVATIONS

Bureau of Indian Affairs

Department of Defense
(includes Army Corps of Engineers lakes)

Fish and Wildlife Service / Wilderness

Forest Service / Wilderness

National Park Service / Wilderness

Tennessee Valley Authority

Department of Transportation

Some small sites are not shown, especially in
urban areas.

MILES

0   25   50   75   100

Albers equal area projection

Abbreviations

AFB   Air Force Base
IR   Indian Reservation
MCAS   Marine Corps Air Station
NF   National Forest
NHS   National Historic Site
NMem   National Memorial
NP   National Park
NS   National Seashore
NWR   National Wildlife Refuge

nationalatlas.gov™
Where We Are

The National Atlas of the United States of America®

U.S. Department of the Interior
U.S. Geological Survey

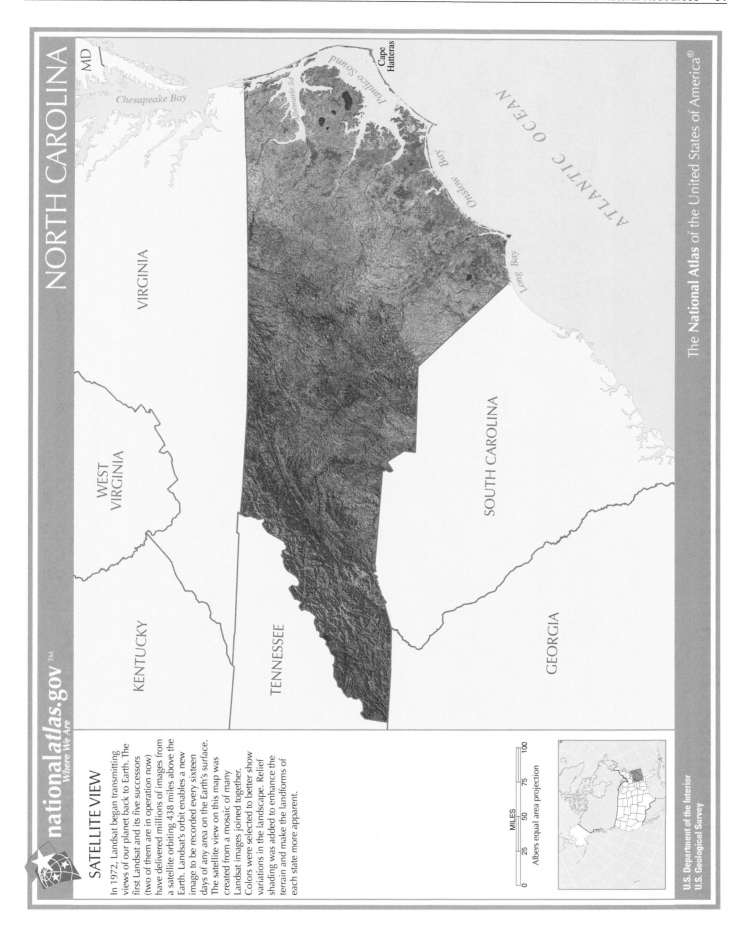

NORTH CAROLINA

SATELLITE VIEW

In 1972, Landsat began transmitting views of our planet back to Earth. The first Landsat and its five successors (two of them are in operation now) have delivered millions of images from a satellite orbiting 438 miles above the Earth. Landsat's orbit enables a new image to be recorded every sixteen days of any area on the Earth's surface. The satellite view on this map was created from a mosaic of many Landsat images joined together. Colors were selected to better show variations in the landscape. Relief shading was added to enhance the terrain and make the landforms of each state more apparent.

MD

Chesapeake Bay

VIRGINIA

WEST VIRGINIA

KENTUCKY

TENNESSEE

SOUTH CAROLINA

GEORGIA

Albemarle Sd.

Pamlico Sound

Cape Hatteras

Onslow Bay

Long Bay

ATLANTIC OCEAN

The National Atlas of the United States of America ®

MILES
0   25   50   75   100
Albers equal area projection

U.S. Department of the Interior
U.S. Geological Survey

Economic Losses from Hazard Events, 1960-2009

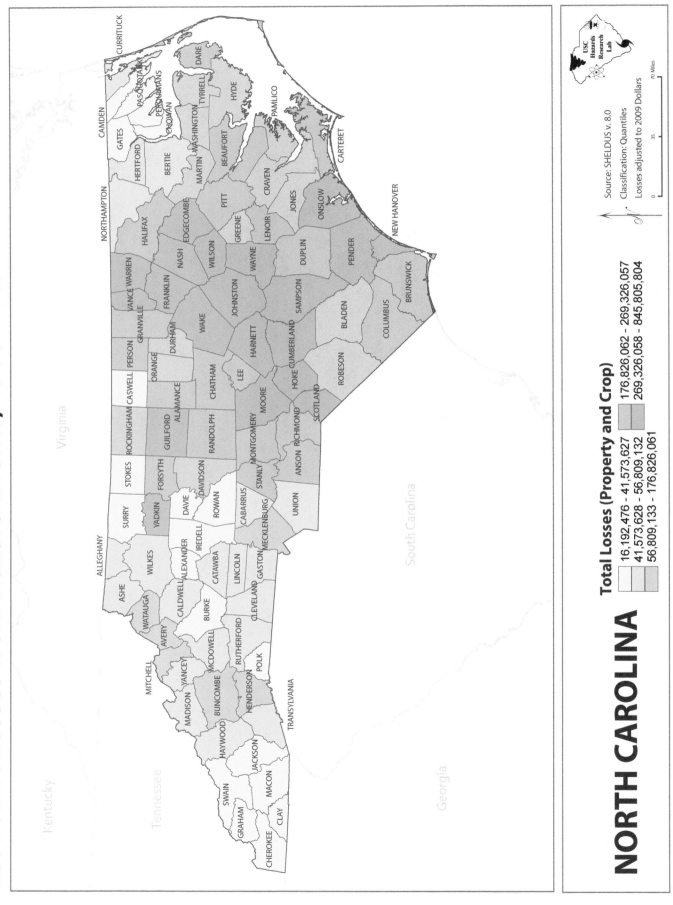

NORTH CAROLINA

Source: SHELDUS v. 8.0
Classification: Quantiles
Losses adjusted to 2009 Dollars

USC Hazards Research Lab

0   35   70 Miles

Total Losses (Property and Crop)

16,192,476 - 41,573,627
41,573,628 - 56,809,132
56,809,133 - 176,826,061
176,826,062 - 269,326,057
269,326,058 - 845,805,804

NORTH CAROLINA

Hazard Losses
1960-2009

Distribution of Losses by Hazard Type
(in 2009 USD million)

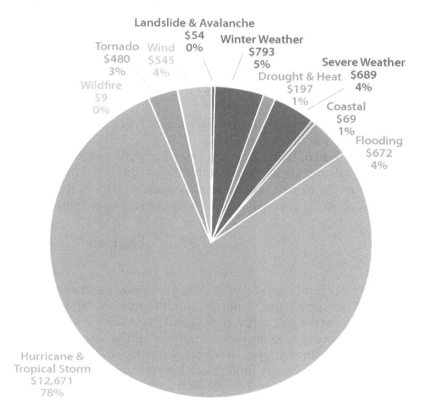

Landslide & Avalanche
$54
0%

Winter Weather
$793
5%

Severe Weather
$689
4%

Drought & Heat
$197
1%

Coastal
$69
1%

Flooding
$672
4%

Tornado
$480
3%

Wind
$545
4%

Wildfire
$9
0%

Hurricane &
Tropical Storm
$12,671
78%

Distribution of Hazard Events
(number of events)

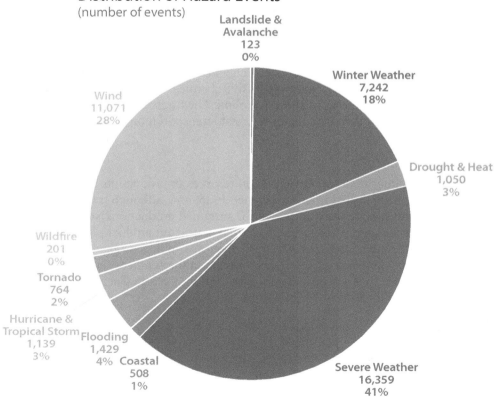

Landslide &
Avalanche
123
0%

Winter Weather
7,242
18%

Drought & Heat
1,050
3%

Wind
11,071
28%

Wildfire
201
0%

Tornado
764
2%

Hurricane &
Tropical Storm
1,139
3%

Flooding
1,429
4%

Coastal
508
1%

Severe Weather
16,359
41%

North Carolina Energy Profile

Quick Facts

- The Dixie Pipeline transports propane from Texas, Louisiana, and Mississippi to customers throughout the Southeast and terminates in Apex, North Carolina.
- Of the 737 public and private-access biodiesel fueling stations nationwide, more than 18% are in North Carolina.
- North Carolina ranked sixth in the nation in net electricity generation from nuclear power in 2014, producing 5.1% of the nation's total.
- More than a third of North Carolina's net electricity generation—38.7% in 2014—comes from coal shipped by rail and truck, primarily from West Virginia, Kentucky, and Pennsylvania.
- In 2014, 6.6% of North Carolina's utility-scale net electricity generation came from renewable energy resources, all of the generation came from conventional hydroelectric power, biomass, and solar energy.

Analysis

Overview

North Carolina rises from sea level at its Atlantic Ocean coastline to the highest peak east of the Mississippi River. The mild climate attracts visitors to North Carolina's varied terrain, which ranges from the barrier islands of the Outer Banks in the east across the Coastal Plain and the Piedmont region to the heavily forested spine of the Appalachian Mountains in the west. Nearly 19 million acres of woodland cover about three-fifths of North Carolina, providing both employment for approximately 67,500 people working in the state's forestry products industry and biomass for energy production. Rivers flowing through the mountainous western part of the state and through the Piedmont region provide hydroelectric power to many communities. Offshore winds along the coast could provide more energy for electricity generation. North Carolina no longer has any fossil fuel production, although assessment of possible shale gas and coalbed methane resources continues. In addition to its natural resources, North Carolina is one of the leading nuclear power producing states in the nation.

Total energy consumption per person in North Carolina is in the bottom third of all states in the nation. The state has a strong agricultural base and is a leading producer of hogs, poultry, and tobacco. North Carolina's key industries include aerospace and aviation, defense, auto manufacturing, biotechnology and pharmaceuticals, green and sustainable energy, financial services, software and information technology, paper and wood products, and textiles. Tobacco products, chemicals, and computers and electronics are the state's leading manufactured products. The energy-intensive chemical industry accounts for one-third of the gross domestic product from manufacturing in North Carolina. The transportation sector is the largest consumer of energy in the state, in part because of the major interstate transportation corridors and aviation hubs located in North Carolina.

Petroleum

North Carolina does not have any crude oil reserves or production. More than 100 exploratory oil and natural gas wells have been drilled in the state since 1925, and, although traces of oil and natural gas were found in a few of these wells, none were sufficient for sustained production. North Carolina does not have any petroleum refineries or crude oil pipelines. There are two petroleum product pipelines that pass through the state, both of which originate on the Gulf Coast. A third pipeline supplies propane from refineries in Texas, Louisiana, and Mississippi to customers in seven states throughout the southeast before traveling across North Carolina on its way to its terminal in Apex, just southwest of Raleigh, North Carolina. Petroleum product imports also arrive in North Carolina at the Port of Wilmington.

Most of the petroleum consumed in North Carolina is used by the transportation sector. North Carolina allows the use of conventional motor gasoline in most of the state. In the summer months, North Carolina requires the use of motor gasoline formulated to reduce emissions that contribute to ozone formation in several of its more densely populated counties. North Carolina's motor gasoline tax is among the highest in the nation.

Natural Gas

North Carolina does not have any natural gas reserves or production. Although no commercial quantities of natural gas have been found in North Carolina, shales and coalbeds in the geologic basins that are located in the center of the state may contain natural gas. The North Carolina Mining and Energy Commission has created a regulatory program for the management of oil and natural gas exploration and development in the state, including the use of horizontal drilling and hydraulic fracturing. The Atlantic Outer Continental Shelf off North Carolina's coast is also believed to have natural gas resource potential. After being restricted for 25 years, leasing in federal waters off North Carolina's coast has been proposed in federal leasing plans for 2017-22.

Increased natural gas use by power generators is driving demand. Three major interstate natural gas pipelines supply North Carolina with natural gas from the south and from the west. Planned pipeline additions would link the state to shale gas production from the Marcellus Shale and the Utica Shale to the north. The electric power sector has overtaken the industrial sector as the state's largest natural gas-consuming sector. The industrial sector led the state in natural gas consumption until 2012 when the electric power sector became the largest user for the first time. The residential sector is the third-largest user of natural gas in the state. About one-fourth of North Carolina households use natural gas for home heating.

Coal

The Deep River coalfield in central North Carolina is the only area in the state known to have coal. Bituminous coal was produced from this field intermittently from 1854 to 1953. Production in the Deep River area ended because the remaining coal is deeply buried, and the coalbeds are broken by many faults. It is estimated that more than 110 million tons of steam coal and coking coal exist in that area, but, because of the faulting, less than half of the coal might ever be mined. Peat, a precursor in the creation of coal, is a fossil fuel of the lowest grade. Fuel-grade peat deposits cover more than a half million acres in coastal North Carolina. Total reserves are about 500 million tons of moisture-free peat. Even though peat can be used as a heat source, peat produced in North Carolina has only been used in agricultural products.

The electric power sector uses almost all of the coal consumed in North Carolina. Most of the coal delivered to North Carolina's electric power generators is shipped by rail and truck from about six states east of the Mississippi River, primarily West Virginia, Kentucky, and Pennsylvania. Coal imports also arrive in North Carolina by ship through the Wilmington Customs District.

Electricity

Before 2010, coal-fired power plants provided more than half of the electricity generated in North Carolina. There was a more than threefold increase in natural gas use for power generation between 2010 and 2014 as electric utilities added natural gas-fired power plants and as natural gas became less expensive relative to coal. By 2014, coal-fired power plants provided less than two-fifths of the electricity generated in North Carolina. Coal and natural gas together still consistently account for approximately three-fifths of the state's net electricity generation. Coal remains the primary fuel for electricity generation in North Carolina followed by nuclear power, which provides about one-third of the state's net generation. North Carolina is one of the nation's top producers of electricity from nuclear power. Conventional hydroelectric power and biomass provide almost all of North Carolina's remaining net electricity generation.

Even though North Carolina is among the top 10 electricity-generating states in the nation, it is a net recipient of interstate transfers of electricity. The residential sector has the largest share of retail sales of electricity in North Carolina. Three-fifths of all households in the state use electricity for home heating, and, because of the hot and humid summers, almost all of the households in the state have air conditioning as well.

Renewable Energy

Hydroelectric dams are the major source of electricity generation from renewable resources in North Carolina. Most of the approximately 70 hydroelectric dams that are monitored by the North Carolina Land Quality Section of the Division of Energy, Mineral, and Land Resources are privately owned including those owned by electric utilities. However, seven hydroelectric dams on the Hiwassee River and the Little Tennessee River in western North Carolina are federally owned and administered by the Tennessee Valley Authority. Three other hydroelectric dams are owned by local governments.

Biomass and solar energy provide additional electricity generation in North Carolina. Although much of North Carolina's generation from biomass comes from wood and wood waste and from municipal solid waste and landfill gas, the state also has abundant biomass resources from agricultural and animal waste. A small but increasing amount of electricity is generated from solar energy. Facilities in North Carolina installed 397 megawatts of solar capacity in 2014, the second-largest amount of any state. The state has the fourth-largest installed solar capacity in the nation. Biomass and solar resources together supply almost 3% of North Carolina's utility-scale net electricity generation. When hydroelectric power is included, renewable resources fuel almost 7% of the state's total net electricity generation.

North Carolina has targeted biofuels in the state's strategic planning. There are six biodiesel plants and one ethanol plant in the state. Biodiesel, a blend of petroleum diesel and bio-based fuel, is sold at refueling stations across North Carolina. Most of the biodiesel stations in the state are private-access stations used for government or private fleets only. An 85% ethanol and 15% gasoline mixture, E85, is sold at about two dozen refueling stations in North Carolina, and more than half of those refueling stations are private-access.

In August 2007, North Carolina became the first state in the southeast to adopt a Renewable Energy and Energy Efficiency Portfolio Standard (REPS). The REPS requires investor-owned electric utilities in North Carolina to meet 12.5% of their retail electricity sales through renewable energy resources or energy efficiency measures by 2021. Rural electric cooperatives and municipal electric suppliers must source 10% of retail electric sales from renewable supplies by 2018. Sales of electricity generated from solar energy are required to reach 0.2% by 2020 for investor-owned utilities. Additionally, the REPS sets statewide targets for energy recovery and electricity derived from swine waste and from poultry waste.

Source: U.S. Energy Information Administration, State Profile and Energy Estimates, June 18, 2015

Population

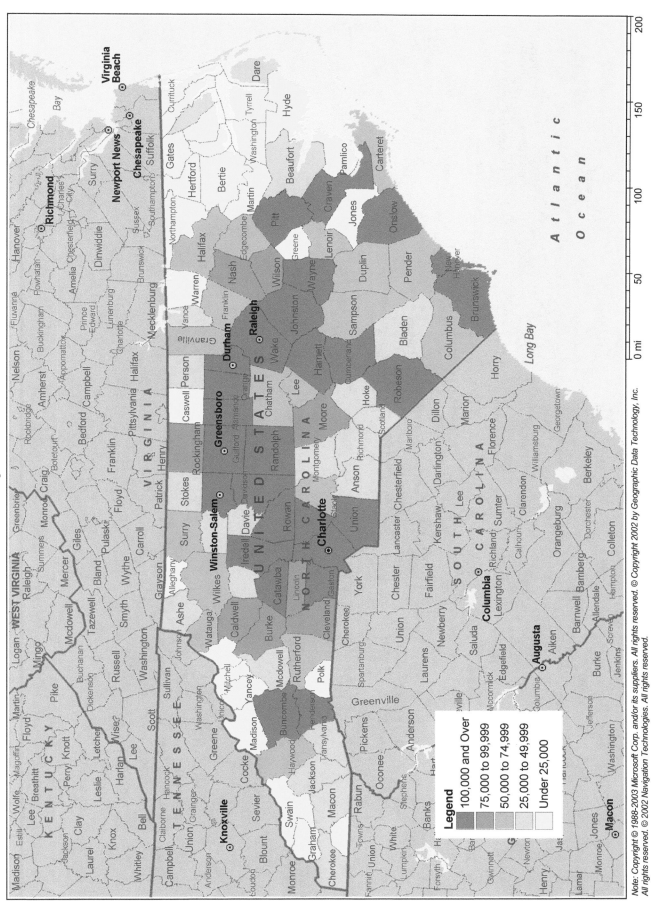

Legend

- 100,000 and Over
- 75,000 to 99,999
- 50,000 to 74,999
- 25,000 to 49,999
- Under 25,000

Percent White

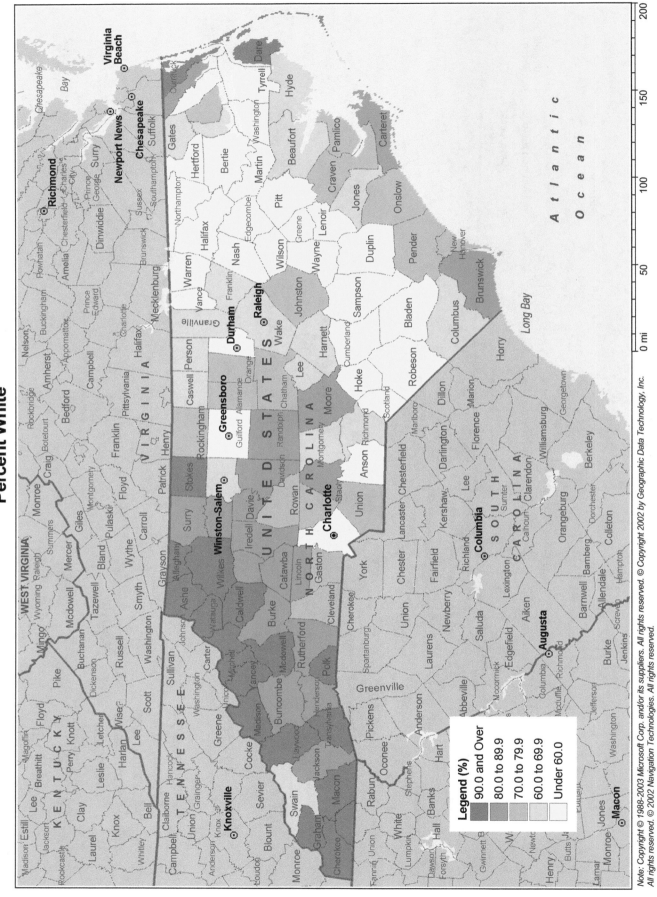

Legend (%)
- 90.0 and Over
- 80.0 to 89.9
- 70.0 to 79.9
- 60.0 to 69.9
- Under 60.0

Percent Black

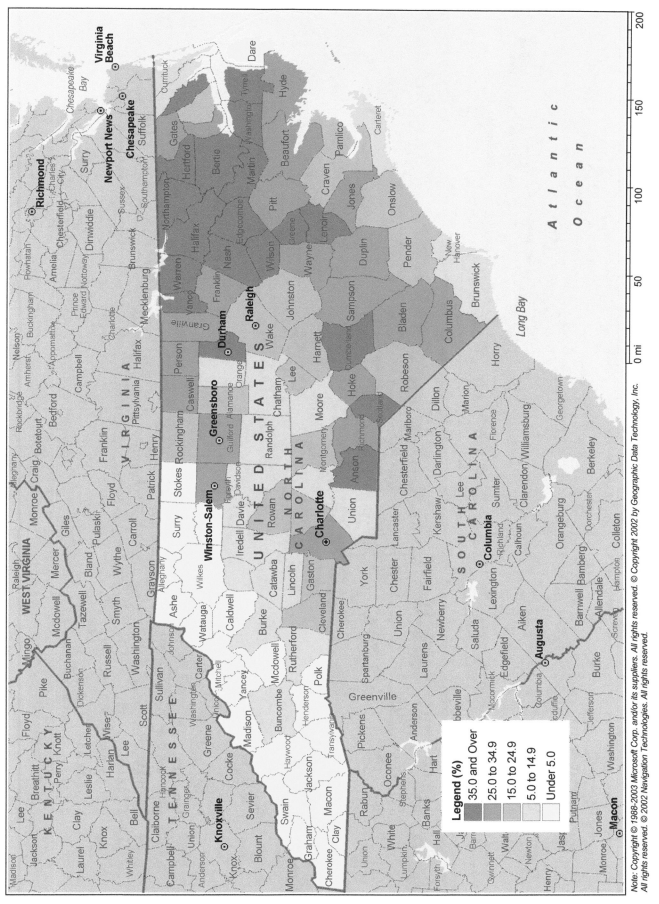

Legend (%)
- 35.0 and Over
- 25.0 to 34.9
- 15.0 to 24.9
- 5.0 to 14.9
- Under 5.0

Percent Asian

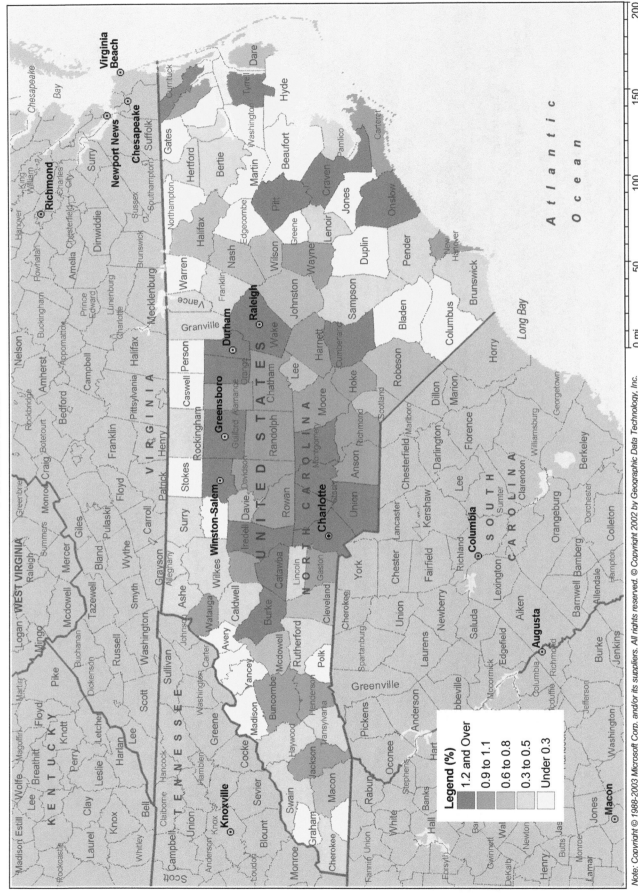

Legend (%)
- 1.2 and Over
- 0.9 to 1.1
- 0.6 to 0.8
- 0.3 to 0.5
- Under 0.3

Percent Hispanic

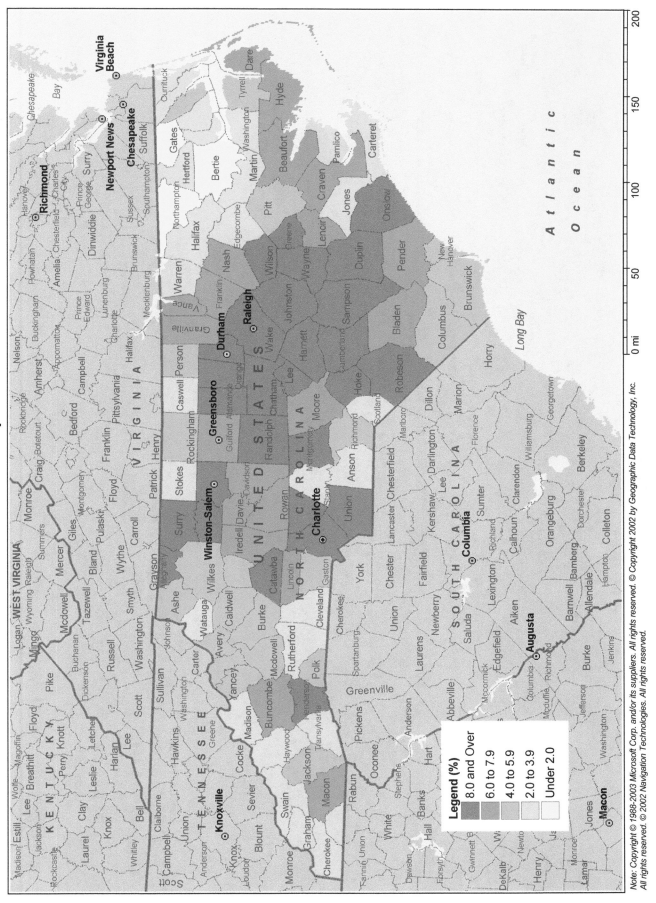

Legend (%)
- 8.0 and Over
- 6.0 to 7.9
- 4.0 to 5.9
- 2.0 to 3.9
- Under 2.0

Median Age

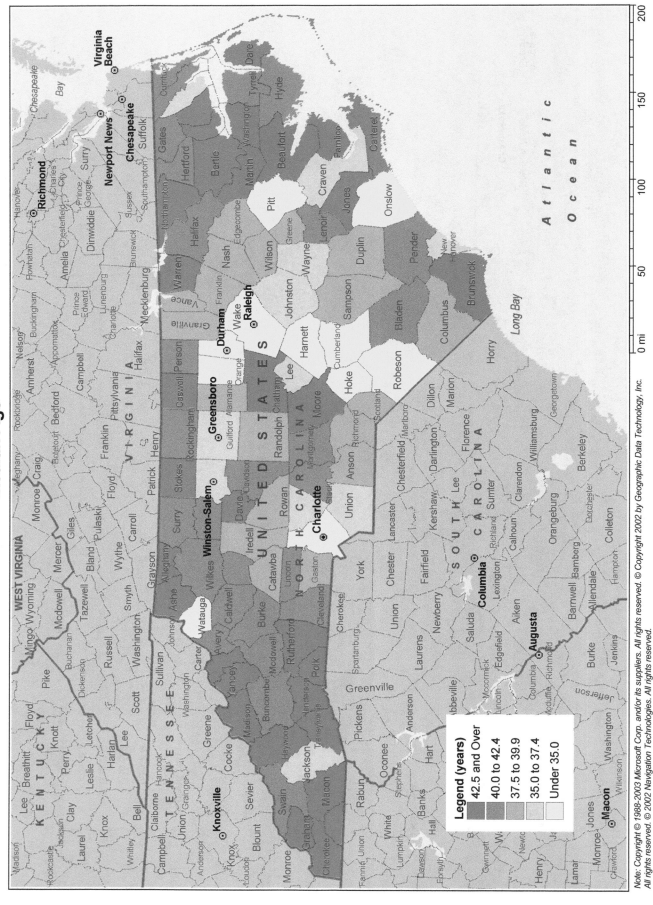

Legend (years)
- 42.5 and Over
- 40.0 to 42.4
- 37.5 to 39.9
- 35.0 to 37.4
- Under 35.0

Median Household Income

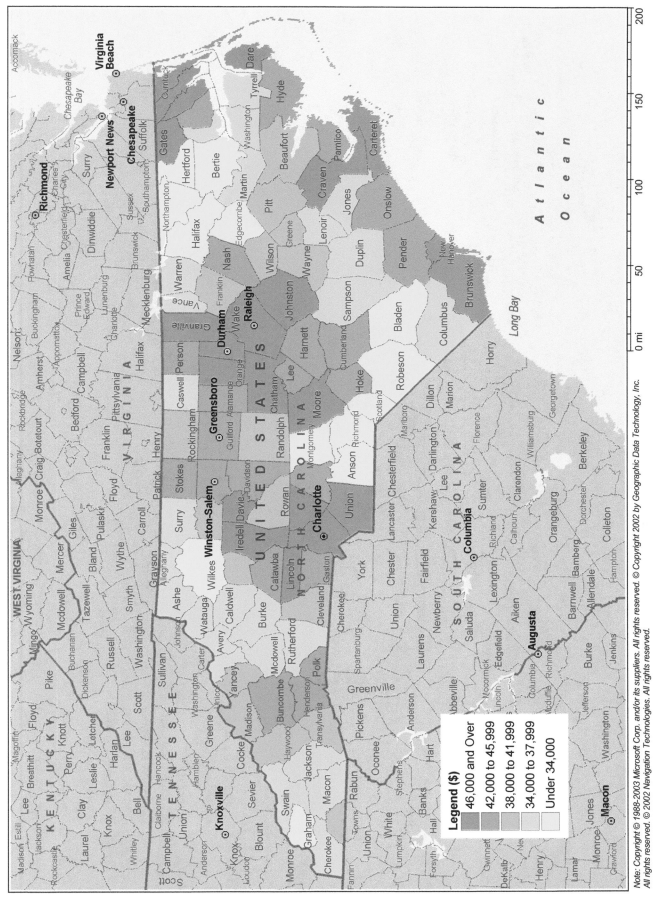

Legend ($)

- 46,000 and Over
- 42,000 to 45,999
- 38,000 to 41,999
- 34,000 to 37,999
- Under 34,000

Median Home Value

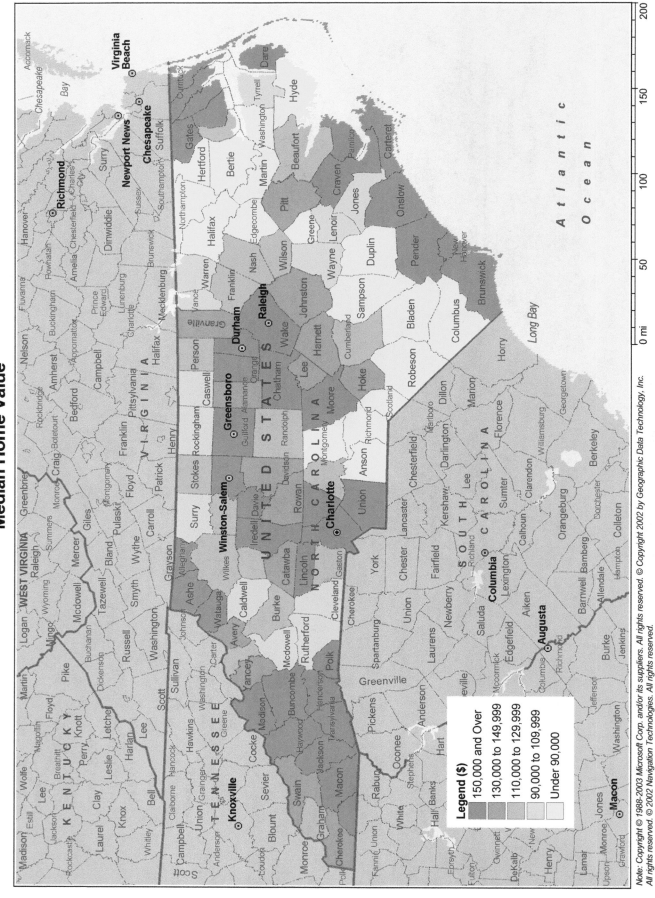

Legend ($)

- 150,000 and Over
- 130,000 to 149,999
- 110,000 to 129,999
- 90,000 to 109,999
- Under 90,000

High School Graduates*

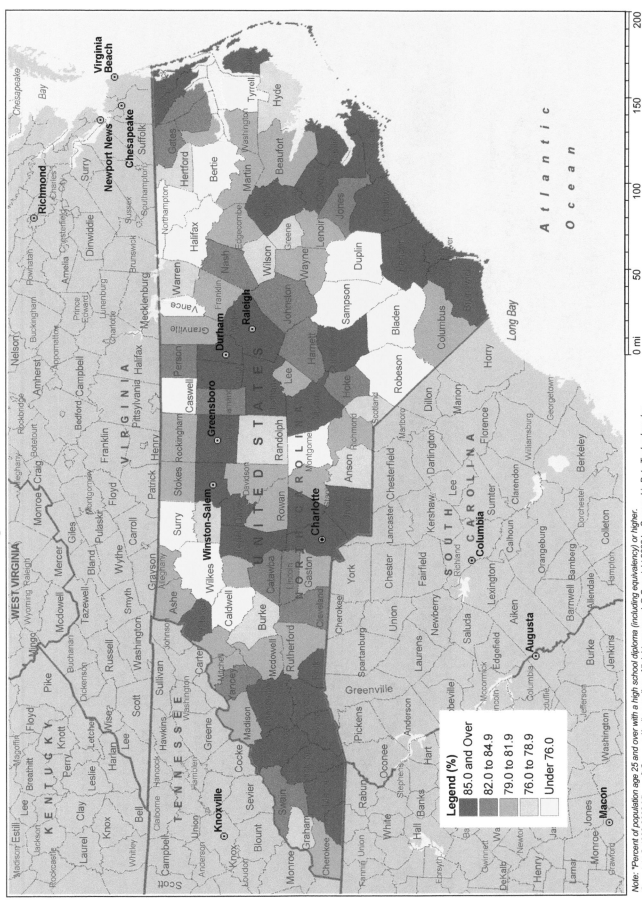

Legend (%)

- 85.0 and Over
- 82.0 to 84.9
- 79.0 to 81.9
- 76.0 to 78.9
- Under 76.0

College Graduates*

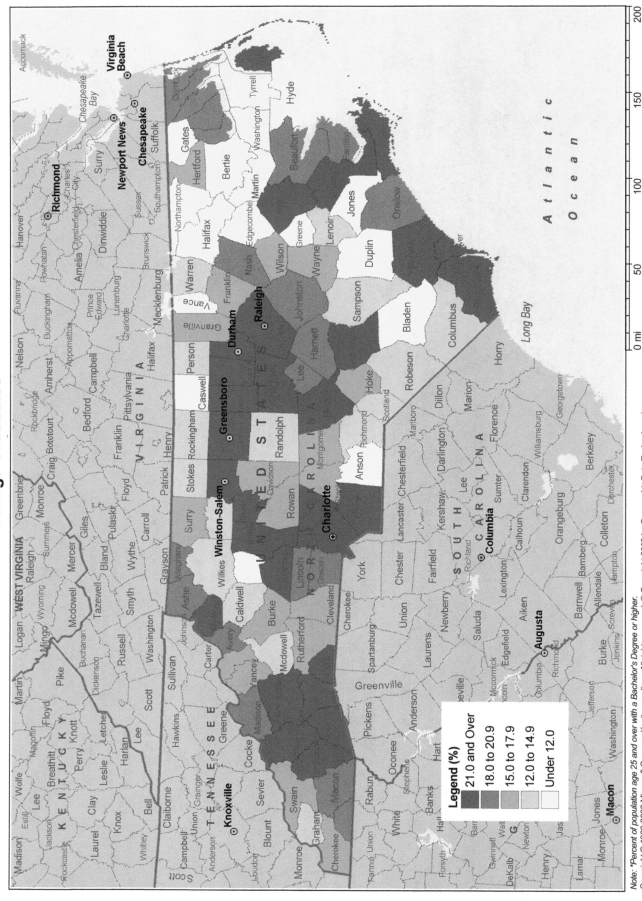

Legend (%)
- 21.0 and Over
- 18.0 to 20.9
- 15.0 to 17.9
- 12.0 to 14.9
- Under 12.0

Note: *Percent of population age 25 and over with a Bachelor's Degree or higher.
Copyright © 1988-2003 Microsoft Corp. and/or its suppliers. All rights reserved. © Copyright 2002 by Geographic Data Technology, Inc.
All rights reserved. © 2002 Navigation Technologies. All rights reserved.

Profiles

Alamance County

Located in north central North Carolina; crossed by the Haw River. Covers a land area of 423.943 square miles, a water area of 10.794 square miles, and is located in the Eastern Time Zone at 36.04° N. Lat., 79.40° W. Long. The county was founded in 1848. County seat is Graham.

Alamance County is part of the Burlington, NC Metropolitan Statistical Area. The entire metro area includes: Alamance County, NC

Weather Station: Burlington Fire Stn #5   Elevation: 660 feet

	Jan	Feb	Mar	Apr	May	Jun	Jul	Aug	Sep	Oct	Nov	Dec
High	50	54	62	72	79	87	90	89	82	72	63	53
Low	29	31	37	46	54	64	68	66	59	47	38	31
Precip	3.3	3.1	4.2	3.5	3.4	4.0	4.6	4.0	3.8	3.3	3.2	3.1
Snow	1.5	1.0	0.2	tr	0.0	0.0	0.0	0.0	0.0	0.0	0.0	tr

High and Low temperatures in degrees Fahrenheit; Precipitation and Snow in inches

Population: 151,131; Growth (since 2000): 15.5%; Density: 356.5 persons per square mile; Race: 71.1% White, 18.8% Black/African American, 1.2% Asian, 0.7% American Indian/Alaska Native, 0.0% Native Hawaiian/Other Pacific Islander, 2.1% two or more races, 11.0% Hispanic of any race; Average household size: 2.45; Median age: 38.7; Age under 18: 23.5%; Age 65 and over: 14.6%; Males per 100 females: 90.7; Marriage status: 29.0% never married, 53.0% now married, 3.1% separated, 7.0% widowed, 11.0% divorced; Foreign born: 7.6%; Speak English only: 88.2%; With disability: 13.9%; Veterans: 9.2%; Ancestry: 11.2% American, 10.8% German, 10.1% English, 7.2% Irish, 3.4% Scotch-Irish

Religion: Six largest groups: 11.2% Baptist, 9.6% Methodist/Pietist, 7.5% Non-denominational Protestant, 6.1% Presbyterian-Reformed, 2.0% Catholicism, 2.0% Pentecostal

Economy: Unemployment rate: 5.5%; Leading industries: 19.5% retail trade; 11.9% health care and social assistance; 10.3% other services (except public administration); Farms: 732 totaling 83,551 acres; Company size: 2 employ 1,000 or more persons, 5 employ 500 to 999 persons, 63 employ 100 to 499 persons, 3,095 employ less than 100 persons; Business ownership: 3,012 women-owned, 967 Black-owned, n/a Hispanic-owned, 256 Asian-owned

Employment: 12.6% management, business, and financial, 4.4% computer, engineering, and science, 9.1% education, legal, community service, arts, and media, 5.6% healthcare practitioners, 16.8% service, 24.9% sales and office, 10.3% natural resources, construction, and maintenance, 16.2% production, transportation, and material moving

Income: Per capita: $23,166; Median household: $43,043; Average household: $57,240; Households with income of $100,000 or more: 14.1%; Poverty rate: 18.3%

Educational Attainment: High school diploma or higher: 83.0%; Bachelor's degree or higher: 21.7%; Graduate/professional degree or higher: 6.7%

Housing: Homeownership rate: 66.8%; Median home value: $137,000; Median year structure built: 1981; Homeowner vacancy rate: 2.9%; Median gross rent: $731 per month; Rental vacancy rate: 11.2%

Vital Statistics: Birth rate: 109.7 per 10,000 population; Death rate: 97.4 per 10,000 population; Age-adjusted cancer mortality rate: 173.1 deaths per 100,000 population

Health Insurance: 83.4% have insurance; 62.8% have private insurance; 32.2% have public insurance; 16.6% do not have insurance; 6.5% of children under 18 do not have insurance

Health Care: Physicians: 14.3 per 10,000 population; Hospital beds: 14.3 per 10,000 population; Hospital admissions: 801.4 per 10,000 population

Air Quality Index: 87.3% good, 12.7% moderate, 0.0% unhealthy for sensitive individuals, 0.0% unhealthy (percent of days)

Transportation: Commute: 93.9% car, 0.2% public transportation, 1.2% walk, 3.7% work from home; Median travel time to work: 23.3 minutes

Presidential Election: 42.6% Obama, 56.3% Romney (2012)

Additional Information Contacts

Alamance Government . . . . (336) 228-1312
 http://www.alamance-nc.com

Alamance County Communities

ALAMANCE (village). Covers a land area of 0.755 square miles and a water area of 0.005 square miles. Located at 36.03° N. Lat; 79.49° W. Long. Elevation is 554 feet.

Population: 951; Growth (since 2000): 206.8%; Density: 1,260.3 persons per square mile; Race: 94.8% White, 2.9% Black/African American, 1.1%

Asian, 0.2% American Indian/Alaska Native, 0.0% Native Hawaiian/Other Pacific Islander, 0.4% Two or more races, 1.3% Hispanic of any race; Average household size: 2.61; Median age: 40.2; Age under 18: 24.2%; Age 65 and over: 12.5%; Males per 100 females: 95.7

Housing: Homeownership rate: 89.6%; Homeowner vacancy rate: 2.4%; Rental vacancy rate: 25.5%

ALTAMAHAW (CDP). Covers a land area of 1.358 square miles and a water area of 0.036 square miles. Located at 36.19° N. Lat; 79.51° W. Long. Elevation is 633 feet.

Population: 347; Growth (since 2000): n/a; Density: 255.5 persons per square mile; Race: 93.7% White, 3.2% Black/African American, 0.0% Asian, 0.0% American Indian/Alaska Native, 0.0% Native Hawaiian/Other Pacific Islander, 0.6% Two or more races, 4.0% Hispanic of any race; Average household size: 2.38; Median age: 43.3; Age under 18: 23.3%; Age 65 and over: 16.7%; Males per 100 females: 80.7

Housing: Homeownership rate: 75.4%; Homeowner vacancy rate: 5.8%; Rental vacancy rate: 5.3%

BURLINGTON (city). Covers a land area of 25.169 square miles and a water area of 0.207 square miles. Located at 36.08° N. Lat; 79.46° W. Long. Elevation is 650 feet.

History: In 1855, when the first train was run through, the settlement later to become Burlington was known as Company Shops. The name was changed in 1887.

Population: 49,963; Growth (since 2000): 11.2%; Density: 1,985.1 persons per square mile; Race: 57.6% White, 28.0% Black/African American, 2.1% Asian, 0.7% American Indian/Alaska Native, 0.1% Native Hawaiian/Other Pacific Islander, 2.4% Two or more races, 16.0% Hispanic of any race; Average household size: 2.38; Median age: 38.3; Age under 18: 24.2%; Age 65 and over: 15.7%; Males per 100 females: 88.0; Marriage status: 30.7% never married, 48.3% now married, 3.9% separated, 7.3% widowed, 13.7% divorced; Foreign born: 8.9%; Speak English only: 86.0%; With disability: 15.8%; Veterans: 9.4%; Ancestry: 9.8% English, 9.5% German, 8.5% American, 5.2% Irish, 3.1% Scotch-Irish

Employment: 12.3% management, business, and financial, 4.5% computer, engineering, and science, 9.2% education, legal, community service, arts, and media, 5.4% healthcare practitioners, 18.8% service, 24.7% sales and office, 7.3% natural resources, construction, and maintenance, 17.7% production, transportation, and material moving

Income: Per capita: $23,127; Median household: $36,858; Average household: $52,983; Households with income of $100,000 or more: 11.8%; Poverty rate: 21.9%

Educational Attainment: High school diploma or higher: 82.7%; Bachelor's degree or higher: 24.0%; Graduate/professional degree or higher: 7.1%

School District(s)
Alamance-Burlington Schools (PK-12)
 2012-13 Enrollment: 22,872 . . . . (336) 570-6060
Clover Garden (KG-12)
 2012-13 Enrollment: 498 . . . . (336) 586-9440

Housing: Homeownership rate: 55.3%; Median home value: $126,100; Median year structure built: 1973; Homeowner vacancy rate: 4.1%; Median gross rent: $728 per month; Rental vacancy rate: 12.6%

Health Insurance: 82.8% have insurance; 57.4% have private insurance; 38.1% have public insurance; 17.2% do not have insurance; 6.2% of children under 18 do not have insurance

Hospitals: Alamance Regional Medical Center (298 beds)

Safety: Violent crime rate: 70.4 per 10,000 population; Property crime rate: 512.6 per 10,000 population

Newspapers: Rock Creek Record (weekly circulation 16000); Times-News (daily circulation 24900)

Transportation: Commute: 94.2% car, 0.6% public transportation, 0.9% walk, 3.3% work from home; Median travel time to work: 21.1 minutes; Amtrak: Train service available.

Airports: Burlington-Alamance Regional (general aviation)

Additional Information Contacts
City of Burlington . . . . (336) 570-1444
 http://www.ci.burlington.nc.us

ELON (town). Covers a land area of 3.885 square miles and a water area of 0.048 square miles. Located at 36.10° N. Lat; 79.51° W. Long. Elevation is 705 feet.

History: Elon (formerly known as Elon College) is a town in Alamance County, North Carolina. When Elon College became Elon University, the town changed its name officially to Elon.

Population: 9,419; Growth (since 2000): n/a; Density: 2,424.4 persons per square mile; Race: 86.7% White, 8.5% Black/African American, 2.0% Asian, 0.1% American Indian/Alaska Native, 0.0% Native Hawaiian/Other Pacific Islander, 1.6% Two or more races, 2.6% Hispanic of any race; Average household size: 2.35; Median age: 21.8; Age under 18: 10.5%; Age 65 and over: 16.4%; Males per 100 females: 77.1; Marriage status: 56.4% never married, 33.2% now married, 1.5% separated, 7.5% widowed, 2.9% divorced; Foreign born: 3.7%; Speak English only: 93.2%; With disability: 10.7%; Veterans: 6.1%; Ancestry: 15.1% German, 8.8% English, 7.9% American, 7.6% Irish, 6.4% Italian

Employment: 20.3% management, business, and financial, 4.8% computer, engineering, and science, 13.6% education, legal, community service, arts, and media, 6.7% healthcare practitioners, 16.0% service, 29.7% sales and office, 3.2% natural resources, construction, and maintenance, 5.8% production, transportation, and material moving

Income: Per capita: $22,138; Median household: $45,538; Average household: $70,374; Households with income of $100,000 or more: 23.8%; Poverty rate: 19.4%

Educational Attainment: High school diploma or higher: 90.9%; Bachelor's degree or higher: 35.8%; Graduate/professional degree or higher: 10.0%

School District(s)
Alamance-Burlington Schools (PK-12)
    2012-13 Enrollment: 22,872 . . . . (336) 570-6060

Four-year College(s)
Elon University (Private, Not-for-profit)
    Fall 2013 Enrollment: 6,305 . . . . (336) 278-2000
    2013-14 Tuition: In-state $30,149; Out-of-state $30,149

Housing: Homeownership rate: 51.4%; Median home value: $198,300; Median year structure built: 1988; Homeowner vacancy rate: 2.3%; Median gross rent: $1,209 per month; Rental vacancy rate: 8.3%

Health Insurance: 92.3% have insurance; 83.2% have private insurance; 21.5% have public insurance; 7.7% do not have insurance; 0.0% of children under 18 do not have insurance

Safety: Violent crime rate: 2.1 per 10,000 population; Property crime rate: 88.3 per 10,000 population

Transportation: Commute: 84.2% car, 0.7% public transportation, 7.1% walk, 5.1% work from home; Median travel time to work: 20.4 minutes

Additional Information Contacts
Town of Elon . . . . (336) 584-3601
    http://www.elonnc.com

GLEN RAVEN (CDP). Covers a land area of 3.518 square miles and a water area of 0.081 square miles. Located at 36.13° N. Lat; 79.46° W. Long. Elevation is 699 feet.

Population: 2,750; Growth (since 2000): 0.0%; Density: 781.7 persons per square mile; Race: 78.7% White, 12.5% Black/African American, 0.6% Asian, 0.6% American Indian/Alaska Native, 0.0% Native Hawaiian/Other Pacific Islander, 2.1% Two or more races, 12.4% Hispanic of any race; Average household size: 2.64; Median age: 37.3; Age under 18: 26.0%; Age 65 and over: 12.4%; Males per 100 females: 89.9; Marriage status: 26.6% never married, 59.5% now married, 0.4% separated, 7.2% widowed, 6.6% divorced; Foreign born: 9.5%; Speak English only: 80.1%; With disability: 14.6%; Veterans: 8.3%; Ancestry: 22.9% German, 13.5% American, 11.0% Irish, 10.6% English, 7.3% Ukrainian

Employment: 13.0% management, business, and financial, 3.6% computer, engineering, and science, 9.4% education, legal, community service, arts, and media, 6.4% healthcare practitioners, 25.6% service, 14.6% sales and office, 13.3% natural resources, construction, and maintenance, 14.0% production, transportation, and material moving

Income: Per capita: $20,904; Median household: $46,830; Average household: $57,044; Households with income of $100,000 or more: 14.7%; Poverty rate: 10.7%

Educational Attainment: High school diploma or higher: 84.1%; Bachelor's degree or higher: 31.6%; Graduate/professional degree or higher: 11.3%

Housing: Homeownership rate: 75.3%; Median home value: $123,500; Median year structure built: 1991; Homeowner vacancy rate: 3.4%; Median gross rent: $644 per month; Rental vacancy rate: 8.2%

Health Insurance: 84.4% have insurance; 60.7% have private insurance; 30.7% have public insurance; 15.6% do not have insurance; 0.0% of children under 18 do not have insurance

Transportation: Commute: 94.1% car, 0.0% public transportation, 0.0% walk, 4.1% work from home; Median travel time to work: 23.4 minutes

GRAHAM (city). County seat. Covers a land area of 9.618 square miles and a water area of 0.065 square miles. Located at 36.06° N. Lat; 79.39° W. Long. Elevation is 636 feet.

History: Graham was established in 1849 and named for William A. Graham, governor of North Carolina (1845-1849). Most of the early settlers were of German ancestry.

Population: 14,153; Growth (since 2000): 10.3%; Density: 1,471.6 persons per square mile; Race: 62.9% White, 22.8% Black/African American, 1.3% Asian, 1.2% American Indian/Alaska Native, 0.0% Native Hawaiian/Other Pacific Islander, 2.4% Two or more races, 15.7% Hispanic of any race; Average household size: 2.40; Median age: 37.5; Age under 18: 25.2%; Age 65 and over: 14.6%; Males per 100 females: 88.0; Marriage status: 28.7% never married, 49.6% now married, 4.7% separated, 8.7% widowed, 12.9% divorced; Foreign born: 11.2%; Speak English only: 80.9%; With disability: 13.3%; Veterans: 10.9%; Ancestry: 10.7% American, 8.9% German, 8.5% English, 5.3% Irish, 4.4% Scotch-Irish

Employment: 9.9% management, business, and financial, 2.3% computer, engineering, and science, 9.1% education, legal, community service, arts, and media, 4.4% healthcare practitioners, 16.3% service, 27.8% sales and office, 10.5% natural resources, construction, and maintenance, 19.5% production, transportation, and material moving

Income: Per capita: $19,243; Median household: $38,975; Average household: $47,057; Households with income of $100,000 or more: 10.3%; Poverty rate: 24.3%

Educational Attainment: High school diploma or higher: 80.0%; Bachelor's degree or higher: 18.5%; Graduate/professional degree or higher: 5.6%

School District(s)
Alamance-Burlington Schools (PK-12)
    2012-13 Enrollment: 22,872 . . . . (336) 570-6060
River Mill Academy (KG-12)
    2012-13 Enrollment: 596 . . . . (336) 229-0909

Two-year College(s)
Alamance Community College (Public)
    Fall 2013 Enrollment: 4,161 . . . . (336) 578-2002
    2013-14 Tuition: In-state $2,175; Out-of-state $7,935

Housing: Homeownership rate: 58.1%; Median home value: $125,700; Median year structure built: 1976; Homeowner vacancy rate: 3.8%; Median gross rent: $698 per month; Rental vacancy rate: 13.7%

Health Insurance: 77.1% have insurance; 54.6% have private insurance; 33.9% have public insurance; 22.9% do not have insurance; 12.9% of children under 18 do not have insurance

Safety: Violent crime rate: 52.6 per 10,000 population; Property crime rate: 406.4 per 10,000 population

Newspapers: Alamance News (weekly circulation 6500)

Transportation: Commute: 96.2% car, 0.0% public transportation, 0.4% walk, 2.4% work from home; Median travel time to work: 20.5 minutes

Additional Information Contacts
City of Graham . . . . (336) 570-6700
    http://www.cityofgraham.com

GREEN LEVEL (town). Covers a land area of 1.353 square miles and a water area of 0.002 square miles. Located at 36.12° N. Lat; 79.35° W. Long. Elevation is 607 feet.

Population: 2,100; Growth (since 2000): 2.8%; Density: 1,552.4 persons per square mile; Race: 21.6% White, 55.0% Black/African American, 0.0% Asian, 2.1% American Indian/Alaska Native, 0.0% Native Hawaiian/Other Pacific Islander, 1.8% Two or more races, 31.0% Hispanic of any race; Average household size: 2.70; Median age: 35.4; Age under 18: 28.9%; Age 65 and over: 12.2%; Males per 100 females: 92.3

Housing: Homeownership rate: 69.6%; Homeowner vacancy rate: 2.3%; Rental vacancy rate: 19.1%

HAW RIVER (town). Covers a land area of 2.801 square miles and a water area of 0.039 square miles. Located at 36.09° N. Lat; 79.36° W. Long. Elevation is 568 feet.

History: Haw River was named for its bordering stream in a region once roamed by the Haw people. Adam Trollinger, a German immigrant, settled here in 1747. The village was known for many years as Trollinger's Ford.

Population: 2,298; Growth (since 2000): 20.4%; Density: 820.4 persons per square mile; Race: 75.9% White, 9.3% Black/African American, 0.9% Asian, 0.4% American Indian/Alaska Native, 0.0% Native Hawaiian/Other Pacific Islander, 2.0% Two or more races, 16.1% Hispanic of any race; Average household size: 2.49; Median age: 38.5; Age under 18: 24.7%; Age 65 and over: 14.7%; Males per 100 females: 94.1

School District(s)

Alamance-Burlington Schools (PK-12)
    2012-13 Enrollment: 22,872 . . . . (336) 570-6060

Housing: Homeownership rate: 74.4%; Homeowner vacancy rate: 2.9%; Rental vacancy rate: 13.5%

Safety: Violent crime rate: 38.4 per 10,000 population; Property crime rate: 213.3 per 10,000 population

MEBANE (city). Covers a land area of 8.357 square miles and a water area of 0.115 square miles. Located at 36.09° N. Lat; 79.27° W. Long. Elevation is 676 feet.

History: Mebane was founded in 1854 by Frank Mebane. The White Furniture Company plant, the first furniture company in North Carolina, was opened in 1881.

Population: 11,393; Growth (since 2000): 56.4%; Density: 1,363.3 persons per square mile; Race: 73.5% White, 20.4% Black/African American, 1.2% Asian, 0.5% American Indian/Alaska Native, 0.1% Native Hawaiian/Other Pacific Islander, 2.6% Two or more races, 6.0% Hispanic of any race; Average household size: 2.41; Median age: 35.8; Age under 18: 26.6%; Age 65 and over: 10.8%; Males per 100 females: 85.9; Marriage status: 27.9% never married, 56.5% now married, 3.7% separated, 5.3% widowed, 10.3% divorced; Foreign born: 5.7%; Speak English only: 93.1%; With disability: 9.7%; Veterans: 8.9%; Ancestry: 14.5% German, 13.7% English, 10.1% Irish, 9.0% American, 4.5% French

Employment: 14.3% management, business, and financial, 7.1% computer, engineering, and science, 14.0% education, legal, community service, arts, and media, 8.3% healthcare practitioners, 15.5% service, 23.1% sales and office, 10.2% natural resources, construction, and maintenance, 7.5% production, transportation, and material moving

Income: Per capita: $27,795; Median household: $55,246; Average household: $65,594; Households with income of $100,000 or more: 19.7%; Poverty rate: 13.4%

Educational Attainment: High school diploma or higher: 91.0%; Bachelor's degree or higher: 32.4%; Graduate/professional degree or higher: 12.9%

School District(s)

Alamance-Burlington Schools (PK-12)
    2012-13 Enrollment: 22,872 . . . . (336) 570-6060
Caswell County Schools (PK-12)
    2012-13 Enrollment: 2,874 . . . . (336) 694-4116

Housing: Homeownership rate: 61.5%; Median home value: $163,500; Median year structure built: 1993; Homeowner vacancy rate: 3.2%; Median gross rent: $800 per month; Rental vacancy rate: 5.4%

Health Insurance: 89.1% have insurance; 75.8% have private insurance; 24.0% have public insurance; 10.9% do not have insurance; 4.8% of children under 18 do not have insurance

Safety: Violent crime rate: 34.3 per 10,000 population; Property crime rate: 543.1 per 10,000 population

Newspapers: Mebane Enterprise (weekly circulation 2400)

Transportation: Commute: 94.9% car, 0.0% public transportation, 0.9% walk, 3.6% work from home; Median travel time to work: 24.0 minutes

Additional Information Contacts

City of Mebane . . . . (919) 563-5901
    http://www.cityofmebane.com/newsite

OSSIPEE (town). Covers a land area of 0.606 square miles and a water area of 0.017 square miles. Located at 36.17° N. Lat; 79.52° W. Long. Elevation is 617 feet.

Population: 543; Growth (since 2000): n/a; Density: 896.0 persons per square mile; Race: 85.1% White, 10.5% Black/African American, 0.2% Asian, 0.0% American Indian/Alaska Native, 0.0% Native Hawaiian/Other Pacific Islander, 1.5% Two or more races, 3.9% Hispanic of any race;

Average household size: 2.51; Median age: 40.4; Age under 18: 23.2%; Age 65 and over: 12.9%; Males per 100 females: 96.7

Housing: Homeownership rate: 73.2%; Homeowner vacancy rate: 3.0%; Rental vacancy rate: 34.1%

SAXAPAHAW (CDP). Covers a land area of 5.185 square miles and a water area of 0.332 square miles. Located at 35.96° N. Lat; 79.32° W. Long. Elevation is 440 feet.

Population: 1,648; Growth (since 2000): 16.2%; Density: 317.9 persons per square mile; Race: 78.7% White, 11.7% Black/African American, 0.1% Asian, 0.5% American Indian/Alaska Native, 0.0% Native Hawaiian/Other Pacific Islander, 1.9% Two or more races, 13.3% Hispanic of any race; Average household size: 2.38; Median age: 36.6; Age under 18: 22.0%; Age 65 and over: 10.3%; Males per 100 females: 98.3

School District(s)

The Hawbridge School (06-12)
    2012-13 Enrollment: 177 . . . . (336) 376-1122

Housing: Homeownership rate: 70.5%; Homeowner vacancy rate: 1.4%; Rental vacancy rate: 7.7%

SNOW CAMP (unincorporated postal area)

ZCTA: 27349

    Covers a land area of 60.970 square miles and a water area of 0.705 square miles. Located at 35.90° N. Lat; 79.42° W. Long. Elevation is 600 feet.

Population: 5,511; Growth (since 2000): 11.9%; Density: 90.4 persons per square mile; Race: 91.6% White, 5.0% Black/African American, 0.5% Asian, 0.2% American Indian/Alaska Native, 0.0% Native Hawaiian/Other Pacific Islander, 1.3% Two or more races, 3.8% Hispanic of any race; Average household size: 2.54; Median age: 40.9; Age under 18: 23.6%; Age 65 and over: 12.8%; Males per 100 females: 98.7; Marriage status: 23.3% never married, 62.0% now married, 0.8% separated, 4.7% widowed, 10.0% divorced; Foreign born: 1.4%; Speak English only: 94.0%; With disability: 13.5%; Veterans: 9.6%; Ancestry: 13.7% English, 11.2% American, 11.0% Irish, 10.6% German, 4.6% Scotch-Irish

Employment: 12.5% management, business, and financial, 1.8% computer, engineering, and science, 4.3% education, legal, community service, arts, and media, 5.0% healthcare practitioners, 15.6% service, 27.0% sales and office, 13.0% natural resources, construction, and maintenance, 20.8% production, transportation, and material moving

Income: Per capita: $21,744; Median household: $48,831; Average household: $56,438; Households with income of $100,000 or more: 10.4%; Poverty rate: 9.6%

Educational Attainment: High school diploma or higher: 78.6%; Bachelor's degree or higher: 13.8%; Graduate/professional degree or higher: 3.6%

School District(s)

Alamance-Burlington Schools (PK-12)
    2012-13 Enrollment: 22,872 . . . . (336) 570-6060

Housing: Homeownership rate: 84.6%; Median home value: $117,200; Median year structure built: 1988; Homeowner vacancy rate: 2.2%; Median gross rent: $446 per month; Rental vacancy rate: 9.0%

Health Insurance: 87.4% have insurance; 69.7% have private insurance; 27.8% have public insurance; 12.6% do not have insurance; 0.3% of children under 18 do not have insurance

Transportation: Commute: 91.5% car, 0.0% public transportation, 1.4% walk, 4.7% work from home; Median travel time to work: 28.0 minutes

SWEPSONVILLE (town). Covers a land area of 1.405 square miles and a water area of 0.082 square miles. Located at 36.03° N. Lat; 79.35° W. Long. Elevation is 522 feet.

Population: 1,154; Growth (since 2000): 25.2%; Density: 821.4 persons per square mile; Race: 90.8% White, 4.8% Black/African American, 0.8% Asian, 0.1% American Indian/Alaska Native, 0.0% Native Hawaiian/Other Pacific Islander, 2.7% Two or more races, 4.4% Hispanic of any race; Average household size: 2.46; Median age: 43.2; Age under 18: 21.1%; Age 65 and over: 16.1%; Males per 100 females: 94.9

Housing: Homeownership rate: 79.1%; Homeowner vacancy rate: 2.3%; Rental vacancy rate: 11.6%

WOODLAWN (CDP). Covers a land area of 3.436 square miles and a water area of 0.243 square miles. Located at 36.12° N. Lat; 79.29° W. Long. Elevation is 604 feet.
Population: 900; Growth (since 2000): -14.4%; Density: 261.9 persons per square mile; Race: 75.0% White, 18.6% Black/African American, 0.3% Asian, 0.8% American Indian/Alaska Native, 0.0% Native Hawaiian/Other Pacific Islander, 2.4% Two or more races, 4.2% Hispanic of any race; Average household size: 2.49; Median age: 44.8; Age under 18: 22.1%; Age 65 and over: 16.0%; Males per 100 females: 92.7
Housing: Homeownership rate: 86.9%; Homeowner vacancy rate: 1.2%; Rental vacancy rate: 11.3%

Alexander County

Located in west central North Carolina; bounded on the south by the Catawba River. Covers a land area of 259.994 square miles, a water area of 3.656 square miles, and is located in the Eastern Time Zone at 35.92° N. Lat., 81.18° W. Long. The county was founded in 1850. County seat is Taylorsville.

Alexander County is part of the Hickory-Lenoir-Morganton, NC Metropolitan Statistical Area. The entire metro area includes: Alexander County, NC; Burke County, NC; Caldwell County, NC; Catawba County, NC

Population: 37,198; Growth (since 2000): 10.7%; Density: 143.1 persons per square mile; Race: 89.6% White, 5.5% Black/African American, 1.0% Asian, 0.3% American Indian/Alaska Native, 0.0% Native Hawaiian/Other Pacific Islander, 1.4% two or more races, 4.3% Hispanic of any race; Average household size: 2.50; Median age: 40.8; Age under 18: 22.7%; Age 65 and over: 15.1%; Males per 100 females: 102.4; Marriage status: 24.6% never married, 57.7% now married, 2.4% separated, 7.2% widowed, 10.5% divorced; Foreign born: 2.6%; Speak English only: 95.0%; With disability: 16.2%; Veterans: 8.7%; Ancestry: 16.2% American, 16.0% German, 9.6% Irish, 8.3% English, 3.2% Scottish
Religion: Six largest groups: 40.0% Baptist, 7.5% Lutheran, 5.8% Methodist/Pietist, 1.8% Non-denominational Protestant, 1.5% Presbyterian-Reformed, 0.5% Pentecostal
Economy: Unemployment rate: 4.7%; Leading industries: 16.3% other services (except public administration); 15.1% retail trade; 12.8% construction; Farms: 603 totaling 58,668 acres; Company size: 0 employ 1,000 or more persons, 1 employs 500 to 999 persons, 12 employ 100 to 499 persons, 557 employ less than 100 persons; Business ownership: 643 women-owned, n/a Black-owned, n/a Hispanic-owned, n/a Asian-owned
Employment: 10.4% management, business, and financial, 2.0% computer, engineering, and science, 7.3% education, legal, community service, arts, and media, 4.6% healthcare practitioners, 14.9% service, 20.7% sales and office, 11.6% natural resources, construction, and maintenance, 28.4% production, transportation, and material moving
Income: Per capita: $20,440; Median household: $40,637; Average household: $51,821; Households with income of $100,000 or more: 10.0%; Poverty rate: 17.2%
Educational Attainment: High school diploma or higher: 79.3%; Bachelor's degree or higher: 11.7%; Graduate/professional degree or higher: 3.9%
Housing: Homeownership rate: 77.5%; Median home value: $121,300; Median year structure built: 1981; Homeowner vacancy rate: 1.6%; Median gross rent: $579 per month; Rental vacancy rate: 10.1%
Vital Statistics: Birth rate: 88.5 per 10,000 population; Death rate: 90.2 per 10,000 population; Age-adjusted cancer mortality rate: 177.6 deaths per 100,000 population
Health Insurance: 84.9% have insurance; 62.0% have private insurance; 36.4% have public insurance; 15.1% do not have insurance; 5.3% of children under 18 do not have insurance
Health Care: Physicians: 3.5 per 10,000 population; Hospital beds: 0.0 per 10,000 population; Hospital admissions: 0.0 per 10,000 population
Air Quality Index: 96.7% good, 3.3% moderate, 0.0% unhealthy for sensitive individuals, 0.0% unhealthy (percent of days)
Transportation: Commute: 96.0% car, 0.1% public transportation, 0.7% walk, 2.7% work from home; Median travel time to work: 24.3 minutes
Presidential Election: 26.8% Obama, 71.3% Romney (2012)
Additional Information Contacts
Alexander Government . . . . (828) 632-1199
    http://www.alexandercountync.gov

Alexander County Communities

BETHLEHEM (CDP). Covers a land area of 7.625 square miles and a water area of 1.256 square miles. Located at 35.82° N. Lat; 81.30° W. Long. Elevation is 1,129 feet.
Population: 4,214; Growth (since 2000): 13.5%; Density: 552.7 persons per square mile; Race: 96.6% White, 0.7% Black/African American, 0.9% Asian, 0.2% American Indian/Alaska Native, 0.0% Native Hawaiian/Other Pacific Islander, 1.2% Two or more races, 2.0% Hispanic of any race; Average household size: 2.43; Median age: 45.5; Age under 18: 20.4%; Age 65 and over: 17.5%; Males per 100 females: 94.1; Marriage status: 22.7% never married, 62.3% now married, 2.5% separated, 5.5% widowed, 9.4% divorced; Foreign born: 2.5%; Speak English only: 95.5%; With disability: 14.1%; Veterans: 11.6%; Ancestry: 22.7% American, 18.8% German, 10.0% Irish, 7.9% English, 3.9% Polish
Employment: 17.1% management, business, and financial, 1.4% computer, engineering, and science, 10.4% education, legal, community service, arts, and media, 6.6% healthcare practitioners, 15.7% service, 13.0% sales and office, 15.9% natural resources, construction, and maintenance, 19.9% production, transportation, and material moving
Income: Per capita: $25,337; Median household: $56,638; Average household: $62,860; Households with income of $100,000 or more: 15.7%; Poverty rate: 10.9%
Educational Attainment: High school diploma or higher: 89.9%; Bachelor's degree or higher: 32.2%; Graduate/professional degree or higher: 10.2%
Housing: Homeownership rate: 86.8%; Median home value: $163,600; Median year structure built: 1985; Homeowner vacancy rate: 2.4%; Median gross rent: $574 per month; Rental vacancy rate: 13.2%
Health Insurance: 86.7% have insurance; 76.4% have private insurance; 25.9% have public insurance; 13.3% do not have insurance; 1.4% of children under 18 do not have insurance
Transportation: Commute: 96.6% car, 0.0% public transportation, 0.0% walk, 3.4% work from home; Median travel time to work: 24.0 minutes

HIDDENITE (CDP). Covers a land area of 1.590 square miles and a water area of 0.005 square miles. Located at 35.91° N. Lat; 81.08° W. Long. Elevation is 1,158 feet.
Population: 536; Growth (since 2000): n/a; Density: 337.2 persons per square mile; Race: 93.8% White, 0.4% Black/African American, 0.0% Asian, 0.0% American Indian/Alaska Native, 0.0% Native Hawaiian/Other Pacific Islander, 0.9% Two or more races, 6.9% Hispanic of any race; Average household size: 2.33; Median age: 43.3; Age under 18: 20.9%; Age 65 and over: 17.7%; Males per 100 females: 100.0
School District(s)
Alexander County Schools (PK-12)
    2012-13 Enrollment: 5,385 . . . . (828) 632-7001
Housing: Homeownership rate: 73.4%; Homeowner vacancy rate: 1.1%; Rental vacancy rate: 11.4%

STONY POINT (CDP). Covers a land area of 2.978 square miles and a water area of 0.009 square miles. Located at 35.87° N. Lat; 81.05° W. Long. Elevation is 1,060 feet.
History: Stony Point is known for the first emerald mine in the United States. The first gem was found in 1875.
Population: 1,317; Growth (since 2000): -4.6%; Density: 442.2 persons per square mile; Race: 88.2% White, 4.4% Black/African American, 0.7% Asian, 0.2% American Indian/Alaska Native, 0.0% Native Hawaiian/Other Pacific Islander, 2.1% Two or more races, 6.8% Hispanic of any race; Average household size: 2.55; Median age: 38.4; Age under 18: 26.0%; Age 65 and over: 15.1%; Males per 100 females: 97.2
School District(s)
Alexander County Schools (PK-12)
    2012-13 Enrollment: 5,385 . . . . (828) 632-7001
Housing: Homeownership rate: 67.8%; Homeowner vacancy rate: 2.7%; Rental vacancy rate: 10.2%

TAYLORSVILLE (town). County seat. Covers a land area of 2.368 square miles and a water area of 0.004 square miles. Located at 35.92° N. Lat; 81.18° W. Long. Elevation is 1,237 feet.
History: Taylorsville was incorporated in 1887.
Population: 2,098; Growth (since 2000): 16.6%; Density: 886.1 persons per square mile; Race: 80.8% White, 13.0% Black/African American, 1.3% Asian, 0.1% American Indian/Alaska Native, 0.0% Native Hawaiian/Other

Pacific Islander, 2.0% Two or more races, 6.3% Hispanic of any race; Average household size: 2.19; Median age: 43.5; Age under 18: 21.8%; Age 65 and over: 25.0%; Males per 100 females: 82.6

School District(s)
Alexander County Schools (PK-12)
   2012-13 Enrollment: 5,385 . . . . (828) 632-7001
Housing: Homeownership rate: 50.8%; Homeowner vacancy rate: 5.9%; Rental vacancy rate: 12.8%
Safety: Violent crime rate: 19.4 per 10,000 population; Property crime rate: 986.9 per 10,000 population
Newspapers: Taylorsville Times (weekly circulation 7200)
Additional Information Contacts
Town of Taylorsville. . . . . (828) 632-2218
   http://www.taylorsvillenc.com

Alleghany County

Located in northwestern North Carolina, in the Blue Ridge; bounded on the north by Virginia. Covers a land area of 235.059 square miles, a water area of 1.488 square miles, and is located in the Eastern Time Zone at 36.49° N. Lat., 81.13° W. Long. The county was founded in 1859. County seat is Sparta.

Population: 11,155; Growth (since 2000): 4.5%; Density: 47.5 persons per square mile; Race: 92.2% White, 1.3% Black/African American, 0.5% Asian, 0.2% American Indian/Alaska Native, 0.0% Native Hawaiian/Other Pacific Islander, 1.1% two or more races, 9.0% Hispanic of any race; Average household size: 2.31; Median age: 45.9; Age under 18: 20.0%; Age 65 and over: 20.7%; Males per 100 females: 98.4; Marriage status: 20.4% never married, 63.1% now married, 2.7% separated, 8.2% widowed, 8.3% divorced; Foreign born: 6.0%; Speak English only: 92.0%; With disability: 17.3%; Veterans: 8.8%; Ancestry: 37.0% American, 12.4% English, 8.4% Irish, 7.0% German, 5.8% Scotch-Irish
Religion: Six largest groups: 22.5% Baptist, 6.3% Methodist/Pietist, 5.1% Non-denominational Protestant, 2.1% European Free-Church, 1.1% Catholicism, 1.1% Pentecostal
Economy: Unemployment rate: 5.9%; Leading industries: 18.5% construction; 16.5% retail trade; 10.8% health care and social assistance; Farms: 567 totaling 90,926 acres; Company size: 0 employ 1,000 or more persons, 0 employ 500 to 999 persons, 2 employ 100 to 499 persons, 247 employ less than 100 persons; Business ownership: 377 women-owned, n/a Black-owned, n/a Hispanic-owned, n/a Asian-owned
Employment: 11.8% management, business, and financial, 3.6% computer, engineering, and science, 9.6% education, legal, community service, arts, and media, 3.7% healthcare practitioners, 16.5% service, 22.0% sales and office, 17.7% natural resources, construction, and maintenance, 14.9% production, transportation, and material moving
Income: Per capita: $19,510; Median household: $35,170; Average household: $44,754; Households with income of $100,000 or more: 7.9%; Poverty rate: 19.8%
Educational Attainment: High school diploma or higher: 79.4%; Bachelor's degree or higher: 18.3%; Graduate/professional degree or higher: 5.2%
Housing: Homeownership rate: 74.9%; Median home value: $156,100; Median year structure built: 1980; Homeowner vacancy rate: 4.6%; Median gross rent: $552 per month; Rental vacancy rate: 14.8%
Vital Statistics: Birth rate: 74.0 per 10,000 population; Death rate: 107.0 per 10,000 population; Age-adjusted cancer mortality rate: 179.5 deaths per 100,000 population
Health Insurance: 80.2% have insurance; 57.0% have private insurance; 40.4% have public insurance; 19.8% do not have insurance; 10.7% of children under 18 do not have insurance
Health Care: Physicians: 11.8 per 10,000 population; Hospital beds: 22.6 per 10,000 population; Hospital admissions: 641.3 per 10,000 population
Transportation: Commute: 92.2% car, 0.0% public transportation, 1.4% walk, 5.3% work from home; Median travel time to work: 27.3 minutes
Presidential Election: 31.2% Obama, 66.9% Romney (2012)
Additional Information Contacts
Alleghany Government . . . . (336) 372-4179
   http://www.alleghanycounty-nc.gov

Alleghany County Communities

ENNICE (unincorporated postal area)
ZCTA: 28623
   Covers a land area of 28.587 square miles and a water area of 0.179 square miles. Located at 36.53° N. Lat; 80.97° W. Long. Elevation is 2,543 feet.
   Population: 1,653; Growth (since 2000): 0.7%; Density: 57.8 persons per square mile; Race: 90.2% White, 0.7% Black/African American, 0.1% Asian, 0.0% American Indian/Alaska Native, 0.0% Native Hawaiian/Other Pacific Islander, 1.4% Two or more races, 12.6% Hispanic of any race; Average household size: 2.42; Median age: 42.4; Age under 18: 21.8%; Age 65 and over: 16.5%; Males per 100 females: 103.3

School District(s)
Alleghany County Schools (PK-12)
   2012-13 Enrollment: 1,507 . . . . (336) 372-4345
   Housing: Homeownership rate: 76.8%; Homeowner vacancy rate: 3.5%; Rental vacancy rate: 16.2%

GLADE VALLEY (unincorporated postal area)
ZCTA: 28627
   Covers a land area of 20.054 square miles and a water area of 0.058 square miles. Located at 36.46° N. Lat; 81.00° W. Long. Elevation is 2,762 feet.
   Population: 1,152; Growth (since 2000): -18.0%; Density: 57.4 persons per square mile; Race: 96.1% White, 0.3% Black/African American, 0.9% Asian, 0.1% American Indian/Alaska Native, 0.0% Native Hawaiian/Other Pacific Islander, 1.3% Two or more races, 3.6% Hispanic of any race; Average household size: 2.34; Median age: 44.0; Age under 18: 22.2%; Age 65 and over: 20.1%; Males per 100 females: 106.5
   Housing: Homeownership rate: 76.7%; Homeowner vacancy rate: 3.0%; Rental vacancy rate: 23.2%

LAUREL SPRINGS (unincorporated postal area)
ZCTA: 28644
   Covers a land area of 68.415 square miles and a water area of 0.297 square miles. Located at 36.43° N. Lat; 81.28° W. Long. Elevation is 2,749 feet.
   Population: 1,494; Growth (since 2000): 1.1%; Density: 21.8 persons per square mile; Race: 95.5% White, 0.3% Black/African American, 0.4% Asian, 0.2% American Indian/Alaska Native, 0.0% Native Hawaiian/Other Pacific Islander, 0.3% Two or more races, 5.6% Hispanic of any race; Average household size: 2.24; Median age: 48.9; Age under 18: 15.9%; Age 65 and over: 22.5%; Males per 100 females: 100.8
   Housing: Homeownership rate: 81.6%; Homeowner vacancy rate: 4.4%; Rental vacancy rate: 14.1%

PINEY CREEK (unincorporated postal area)
ZCTA: 28663
   Covers a land area of 17.478 square miles and a water area of 0.257 square miles. Located at 36.53° N. Lat; 81.31° W. Long. Elevation is 2,759 feet.
   Population: 614; Growth (since 2000): 5.9%; Density: 35.1 persons per square mile; Race: 98.0% White, 1.3% Black/African American, 0.0% Asian, 0.3% American Indian/Alaska Native, 0.0% Native Hawaiian/Other Pacific Islander, 0.2% Two or more races, 7.8% Hispanic of any race; Average household size: 2.29; Median age: 49.9; Age under 18: 17.1%; Age 65 and over: 20.2%; Males per 100 females: 96.8

School District(s)
Alleghany County Schools (PK-12)
   2012-13 Enrollment: 1,507 . . . . (336) 372-4345
   Housing: Homeownership rate: 86.6%; Homeowner vacancy rate: 9.3%; Rental vacancy rate: 12.2%

ROARING GAP (unincorporated postal area)
ZCTA: 28668
   Covers a land area of 13.072 square miles and a water area of 0.094 square miles. Located at 36.41° N. Lat; 80.99° W. Long. Elevation is 2,877 feet.

Population: 300; Growth (since 2000): 111.3%; Density: 23.0 persons per square mile; Race: 97.0% White, 0.3% Black/African American, 0.3% Asian, 0.0% American Indian/Alaska Native, 0.0% Native Hawaiian/Other Pacific Islander, 0.3% Two or more races, 2.3% Hispanic of any race; Average household size: 2.16; Median age: 56.4; Age under 18: 13.7%; Age 65 and over: 30.0%; Males per 100 females: 94.8
Housing: Homeownership rate: 80.5%; Homeowner vacancy rate: 15.8%; Rental vacancy rate: 52.5%

SPARTA (town). County seat. Covers a land area of 2.398 square miles and a water area of 0.008 square miles. Located at 36.50° N. Lat; 81.12° W. Long. Elevation is 2,930 feet.
Population: 1,770; Growth (since 2000): -2.6%; Density: 738.1 persons per square mile; Race: 85.5% White, 2.7% Black/African American, 1.0% Asian, 1.0% American Indian/Alaska Native, 0.2% Native Hawaiian/Other Pacific Islander, 1.5% Two or more races, 14.7% Hispanic of any race; Average household size: 2.13; Median age: 43.3; Age under 18: 21.2%; Age 65 and over: 23.8%; Males per 100 females: 86.1
School District(s)
Alleghany County Schools (PK-12)
    2012-13 Enrollment: 1,507 . . . . (336) 372-4345
Housing: Homeownership rate: 51.8%; Homeowner vacancy rate: 6.2%; Rental vacancy rate: 13.5%
Hospitals: Alleghany County Memorial Hospital (25 beds)
Safety: Violent crime rate: 52.2 per 10,000 population; Property crime rate: 226.2 per 10,000 population
Newspapers: Alleghany News (weekly circulation 4100)

Anson County

Located in southern North Carolina; bounded on the south by South Carolina, on the east by the Pee Dee River, and on the north by Rocky River. Covers a land area of 531.451 square miles, a water area of 5.642 square miles, and is located in the Eastern Time Zone at 34.97° N. Lat., 80.11° W. Long. The county was founded in 1749. County seat is Wadesboro.

Weather Station: Wadesboro										Elevation: 479 feet	
	Jan	Feb	Mar	Apr	May	Jun	Jul	Aug	Sep	Oct	Nov	Dec
High	52	56	64	73	80	87	91	89	83	74	65	55
Low	32	34	41	49	58	66	70	69	62	50	42	34
Precip	4.0	3.5	4.2	3.0	2.9	4.2	4.9	4.6	4.0	3.9	3.3	3.2
Snow	1.6	0.9	0.3	0.0	0.0	0.0	0.0	0.0	0.0	0.0	tr	0.1

High and Low temperatures in degrees Fahrenheit; Precipitation and Snow in inches

Population: 26,948; Growth (since 2000): 6.6%; Density: 50.7 persons per square mile; Race: 47.2% White, 48.6% Black/African American, 1.1% Asian, 0.6% American Indian/Alaska Native, 0.0% Native Hawaiian/Other Pacific Islander, 1.3% two or more races, 3.0% Hispanic of any race; Average household size: 2.51; Median age: 39.5; Age under 18: 22.1%; Age 65 and over: 14.3%; Males per 100 females: 108.4; Marriage status: 36.1% never married, 43.8% now married, 3.5% separated, 8.1% widowed, 12.0% divorced; Foreign born: 3.0%; Speak English only: 95.1%; With disability: 19.2%; Veterans: 9.6%; Ancestry: 7.3% American, 6.9% Irish, 6.6% German, 5.0% English, 2.4% Scotch-Irish
Religion: Six largest groups: 25.8% Baptist, 18.1% Methodist/Pietist, 3.7% Non-denominational Protestant, 2.1% Pentecostal, 0.9% Presbyterian-Reformed, 0.5% Episcopalianism/Anglicanism
Economy: Unemployment rate: 7.1%; Leading industries: 19.1% retail trade; 12.3% health care and social assistance; 12.3% other services (except public administration); Farms: 429 totaling 83,601 acres; Company size: 0 employ 1,000 or more persons, 0 employ 500 to 999 persons, 11 employs 100 to 499 persons, 371 employs less than 100 persons; Business ownership: 425 women-owned, 394 Black-owned, n/a Hispanic-owned, n/a Asian-owned
Employment: 7.2% management, business, and financial, 1.8% computer, engineering, and science, 8.4% education, legal, community service, arts, and media, 4.7% healthcare practitioners, 20.2% service, 18.8% sales and office, 12.2% natural resources, construction, and maintenance, 26.8% production, transportation, and material moving
Income: Per capita: $16,752; Median household: $33,870; Average household: $44,526; Households with income of $100,000 or more: 7.2%; Poverty rate: 24.2%

Educational Attainment: High school diploma or higher: 76.3%; Bachelor's degree or higher: 10.2%; Graduate/professional degree or higher: 3.7%
Housing: Homeownership rate: 68.7%; Median home value: $79,400; Median year structure built: 1973; Homeowner vacancy rate: 3.5%; Median gross rent: $661 per month; Rental vacancy rate: 12.7%
Vital Statistics: Birth rate: 100.9 per 10,000 population; Death rate: 100.9 per 10,000 population; Age-adjusted cancer mortality rate: 199.6 deaths per 100,000 population
Health Insurance: 80.5% have insurance; 54.7% have private insurance; 38.5% have public insurance; 19.5% do not have insurance; 6.3% of children under 18 do not have insurance
Health Care: Physicians: 6.5 per 10,000 population; Hospital beds: 47.1 per 10,000 population; Hospital admissions: 334.8 per 10,000 population
Transportation: Commute: 96.0% car, 0.4% public transportation, 1.0% walk, 2.0% work from home; Median travel time to work: 24.8 minutes
Presidential Election: 62.4% Obama, 37.0% Romney (2012)
National and State Parks: Pee Dee National Wildlife Refuge
Additional Information Contacts
Anson Government . . . . (704) 904-3321
   http://www.co.anson.nc.us

Anson County Communities

ANSONVILLE (town). Covers a land area of 1.471 square miles and a water area of 0 square miles. Located at 35.10° N. Lat; 80.11° W. Long. Elevation is 331 feet.
History: Ansonville was founded as a summer settlement in 1844 by a group of planters from the lower Pee Dee River, seeking higher ground to escape malaria.
Population: 631; Growth (since 2000): -0.8%; Density: 428.8 persons per square mile; Race: 26.9% White, 70.5% Black/African American, 0.8% Asian, 0.0% American Indian/Alaska Native, 0.0% Native Hawaiian/Other Pacific Islander, 0.6% Two or more races, 2.5% Hispanic of any race; Average household size: 2.52; Median age: 42.3; Age under 18: 22.3%; Age 65 and over: 15.5%; Males per 100 females: 93.0
School District(s)
Anson County Schools (PK-12)
    2012-13 Enrollment: 3,651 . . . . (704) 694-4417
Housing: Homeownership rate: 72.8%; Homeowner vacancy rate: 2.6%; Rental vacancy rate: 27.8%

LILESVILLE (town). Covers a land area of 0.993 square miles and a water area of 0 square miles. Located at 34.97° N. Lat; 79.98° W. Long. Elevation is 499 feet.
Population: 536; Growth (since 2000): 16.8%; Density: 539.7 persons per square mile; Race: 47.9% White, 49.4% Black/African American, 0.2% Asian, 0.2% American Indian/Alaska Native, 0.0% Native Hawaiian/Other Pacific Islander, 1.5% Two or more races, 0.7% Hispanic of any race; Average household size: 2.55; Median age: 40.0; Age under 18: 25.2%; Age 65 and over: 16.2%; Males per 100 females: 92.1
School District(s)
Anson County Schools (PK-12)
    2012-13 Enrollment: 3,651 . . . . (704) 694-4417
Housing: Homeownership rate: 76.2%; Homeowner vacancy rate: 0.0%; Rental vacancy rate: 10.7%

MCFARLAN (town). Covers a land area of 0.920 square miles and a water area of 0 square miles. Located at 34.81° N. Lat; 79.98° W. Long. Elevation is 305 feet.
History: McFarlan was settled by Scots-Irish.
Population: 117; Growth (since 2000): 31.5%; Density: 127.2 persons per square mile; Race: 63.2% White, 23.1% Black/African American, 0.0% Asian, 0.9% American Indian/Alaska Native, 0.0% Native Hawaiian/Other Pacific Islander, 0.0% Two or more races, 18.8% Hispanic of any race; Average household size: 2.79; Median age: 40.2; Age under 18: 31.6%; Age 65 and over: 18.8%; Males per 100 females: 88.7
Housing: Homeownership rate: 83.3%; Homeowner vacancy rate: 0.0%; Rental vacancy rate: 12.5%

MORVEN (town). Covers a land area of 1.027 square miles and a water area of 0 square miles. Located at 34.86° N. Lat; 80.00° W. Long. Elevation is 358 feet.
History: Old Morven began about 1800 when William Covington built a tavern at a junction on a stagecoach route.

Population: 511; Growth (since 2000): -11.7%; Density: 497.5 persons per square mile; Race: 19.8% White, 74.6% Black/African American, 0.0% Asian, 0.4% American Indian/Alaska Native, 0.0% Native Hawaiian/Other Pacific Islander, 3.1% Two or more races, 2.9% Hispanic of any race; Average household size: 2.47; Median age: 41.9; Age under 18: 24.5%; Age 65 and over: 16.4%; Males per 100 females: 79.3

School District(s)

Anson County Schools (PK-12)

    2012-13 Enrollment: 3,651 . . . . (704) 694-4417

Housing: Homeownership rate: 64.3%; Homeowner vacancy rate: 2.9%; Rental vacancy rate: 13.6%

PEACHLAND (town). Covers a land area of 1.008 square miles and a water area of 0 square miles. Located at 34.99° N. Lat; 80.27° W. Long. Elevation is 446 feet.

Population: 437; Growth (since 2000): -21.1%; Density: 433.5 persons per square mile; Race: 62.2% White, 34.1% Black/African American, 0.2% Asian, 0.5% American Indian/Alaska Native, 0.0% Native Hawaiian/Other Pacific Islander, 2.1% Two or more races, 0.9% Hispanic of any race; Average household size: 2.41; Median age: 42.2; Age under 18: 22.7%; Age 65 and over: 17.4%; Males per 100 females: 109.1

School District(s)

Anson County Schools (PK-12)

    2012-13 Enrollment: 3,651 . . . . (704) 694-4417

Housing: Homeownership rate: 70.8%; Homeowner vacancy rate: 3.0%; Rental vacancy rate: 14.5%

POLKTON (town). Covers a land area of 3.182 square miles and a water area of 0 square miles. Located at 35.00° N. Lat; 80.20° W. Long. Elevation is 325 feet.

Population: 3,375; Growth (since 2000): 182.4%; Density: 1,060.8 persons per square mile; Race: 33.7% White, 61.0% Black/African American, 0.6% Asian, 1.6% American Indian/Alaska Native, 0.0% Native Hawaiian/Other Pacific Islander, 0.9% Two or more races, 8.2% Hispanic of any race; Average household size: 2.69; Median age: 34.5; Age under 18: 10.3%; Age 65 and over: 4.3%; Males per 100 females: 420.8; Marriage status: 54.4% never married, 26.1% now married, 4.8% separated, 4.4% widowed, 15.0% divorced; Foreign born: 4.5%; Speak English only: 94.1%; With disability: 16.2%; Veterans: 4.6%; Ancestry: 6.7% German, 5.3% Irish, 3.0% English, 2.0% Scotch-Irish, 1.6% American

Employment: 5.3% management, business, and financial, 1.4% computer, engineering, and science, 10.7% education, legal, community service, arts, and media, 7.4% healthcare practitioners, 34.8% service, 13.1% sales and office, 2.9% natural resources, construction, and maintenance, 24.4% production, transportation, and material moving

Income: Per capita: $5,854; Median household: $32,396; Average household: $41,666; Households with income of $100,000 or more: 4.4%; Poverty rate: 23.7%

Educational Attainment: High school diploma or higher: 66.7%; Bachelor's degree or higher: 3.0%; Graduate/professional degree or higher: 1.5%

School District(s)

Anson County Schools (PK-12)

    2012-13 Enrollment: 3,651 . . . . (704) 694-4417

Two-year College(s)

South Piedmont Community College (Public)

    Fall 2013 Enrollment: 2,776 . . . . (704) 272-5300

    2013-14 Tuition: In-state $2,429; Out-of-state $8,581

Housing: Homeownership rate: 46.4%; Median home value: $76,200; Median year structure built: 1978; Homeowner vacancy rate: 4.2%; Median gross rent: $675 per month; Rental vacancy rate: 12.2%

Health Insurance: 81.4% have insurance; 45.9% have private insurance; 43.7% have public insurance; 18.6% do not have insurance; 1.1% of children under 18 do not have insurance

Transportation: Commute: 97.6% car, 0.0% public transportation, 1.0% walk, 1.4% work from home; Median travel time to work: 28.1 minutes

---

WADESBORO (town). County seat. Covers a land area of 6.309 square miles and a water area of 0.013 square miles. Located at 34.96° N. Lat; 80.07° W. Long. Elevation is 512 feet.

History: The site of Wadesboro was the gift of Captain Patrick Boggan, son of the Lord of Castle Finn, who came from Ireland before the Revolutionary War.

Population: 5,813; Growth (since 2000): 63.7%; Density: 921.5 persons per square mile; Race: 35.6% White, 60.7% Black/African American, 1.4% Asian, 0.2% American Indian/Alaska Native, 0.0% Native Hawaiian/Other Pacific Islander, 1.3% Two or more races, 1.8% Hispanic of any race; Average household size: 2.40; Median age: 39.8; Age under 18: 24.6%; Age 65 and over: 19.0%; Males per 100 females: 81.9; Marriage status: 34.8% never married, 41.5% now married, 4.2% separated, 11.8% widowed, 11.8% divorced; Foreign born: 4.1%; Speak English only: 93.3%; With disability: 21.5%; Veterans: 13.0%; Ancestry: 7.6% Irish, 5.8% American, 5.4% English, 5.0% German, 3.0% Scotch-Irish

Employment: 4.5% management, business, and financial, 1.5% computer, engineering, and science, 7.0% education, legal, community service, arts, and media, 7.0% healthcare practitioners, 25.6% service, 21.5% sales and office, 4.9% natural resources, construction, and maintenance, 28.0% production, transportation, and material moving

Income: Per capita: $17,295; Median household: $30,967; Average household: $41,409; Households with income of $100,000 or more: 5.9%; Poverty rate: 26.1%

Educational Attainment: High school diploma or higher: 80.7%; Bachelor's degree or higher: 12.2%; Graduate/professional degree or higher: 4.0%

School District(s)

Anson County Schools (PK-12)

    2012-13 Enrollment: 3,651 . . . . (704) 694-4417

Housing: Homeownership rate: 52.2%; Median home value: $90,200; Median year structure built: 1962; Homeowner vacancy rate: 4.3%; Median gross rent: $691 per month; Rental vacancy rate: 10.7%

Health Insurance: 78.0% have insurance; 47.3% have private insurance; 44.5% have public insurance; 22.0% do not have insurance; 4.2% of children under 18 do not have insurance

Hospitals: Anson Community Hospital (125 beds)

Safety: Violent crime rate: 141.0 per 10,000 population; Property crime rate: 682.2 per 10,000 population

Newspapers: Anson Record (weekly circulation 1900)

Transportation: Commute: 91.3% car, 2.2% public transportation, 2.2% walk, 2.9% work from home; Median travel time to work: 22.9 minutes

Additional Information Contacts

Town of Wadesboro . . . . (704) 694-5171

    http://www.cityofwadesboro.org

Ashe County

Located in northwestern North Carolina, in the Blue Ridge; bounded on the north by Virginia, and on the west by Tennessee. Covers a land area of 426.135 square miles, a water area of 3.134 square miles, and is located in the Eastern Time Zone at 36.44° N. Lat., 81.50° W. Long. The county was founded in 1799. County seat is Jefferson.

Weather Station: Jefferson 2 E   Elevation: 2,770 feet

	Jan	Feb	Mar	Apr	May	Jun	Jul	Aug	Sep	Oct	Nov	Dec
High	43	46	54	63	71	78	81	80	74	65	56	47
Low	22	24	30	37	45	54	58	57	50	38	30	24
Precip	3.7	3.5	4.1	3.9	4.2	3.9	4.6	4.0	3.8	2.9	3.8	3.4
Snow	4.2	3.9	3.0	0.4	0.0	0.0	0.0	0.0	0.0	tr	0.2	2.8

High and Low temperatures in degrees Fahrenheit; Precipitation and Snow in inches

Weather Station: Transou   Elevation: 2,875 feet

	Jan	Feb	Mar	Apr	May	Jun	Jul	Aug	Sep	Oct	Nov	Dec
High	43	46	54	63	70	77	80	79	73	64	55	45
Low	21	24	29	37	45	53	57	56	49	38	30	23
Precip	4.1	3.8	4.8	4.6	4.7	5.2	5.0	4.8	5.0	4.1	5.0	3.8
Snow	8.3	6.4	3.7	1.6	0.0	0.0	0.0	0.0	0.0	tr	0.7	3.5

High and Low temperatures in degrees Fahrenheit; Precipitation and Snow in inches

Population: 27,281; Growth (since 2000): 11.9%; Density: 64.0 persons per square mile; Race: 95.5% White, 0.6% Black/African American, 0.4% Asian, 0.2% American Indian/Alaska Native, 0.0% Native Hawaiian/Other Pacific Islander, 1.0% two or more races, 4.8% Hispanic of any race; Average household size: 2.29; Median age: 45.5; Age under 18: 19.4%; Age 65 and over: 20.2%; Males per 100 females: 97.8; Marriage status: 19.2% never married, 60.9% now married, 2.1% separated, 7.8% widowed, 12.1% divorced; Foreign born: 4.2%; Speak English only: 95.4%; With disability: 16.3%; Veterans: 10.6%; Ancestry: 35.6% American, 10.4% English, 10.1% German, 8.2% Irish, 4.5% Scotch-Irish

Religion: Six largest groups: 33.4% Baptist, 8.0% Methodist/Pietist, 2.2% Catholicism, 1.8% Presbyterian-Reformed, 1.1% Non-denominational Protestant, 0.4% Pentecostal

Economy: Unemployment rate: 6.3%; Leading industries: 19.6% retail trade; 17.0% construction; 10.9% other services (except public administration); Farms: 1,140 totaling 112,462 acres; Company size: 0 employ 1,000 or more persons, 0 employ 500 to 999 persons, 9 employ 100 to 499 persons, 531 employs less than 100 persons; Business ownership: n/a women-owned, n/a Black-owned, n/a Hispanic-owned, n/a Asian-owned

Employment: 10.8% management, business, and financial, 1.6% computer, engineering, and science, 11.2% education, legal, community service, arts, and media, 3.8% healthcare practitioners, 17.1% service, 22.3% sales and office, 16.3% natural resources, construction, and maintenance, 16.9% production, transportation, and material moving

Income: Per capita: $20,838; Median household: $35,951; Average household: $47,902; Households with income of $100,000 or more: 9.0%; Poverty rate: 21.1%

Educational Attainment: High school diploma or higher: 81.4%; Bachelor's degree or higher: 19.5%; Graduate/professional degree or higher: 5.9%

Housing: Homeownership rate: 77.9%; Median home value: $150,900; Median year structure built: 1982; Homeowner vacancy rate: 2.8%; Median gross rent: $644 per month; Rental vacancy rate: 11.9%

Vital Statistics: Birth rate: 86.2 per 10,000 population; Death rate: 118.6 per 10,000 population; Age-adjusted cancer mortality rate: 180.8 deaths per 100,000 population

Health Insurance: 81.9% have insurance; 58.7% have private insurance; 39.3% have public insurance; 18.1% do not have insurance; 5.0% of children under 18 do not have insurance

Health Care: Physicians: 8.1 per 10,000 population; Hospital beds: 31.3 per 10,000 population; Hospital admissions: 582.0 per 10,000 population

Transportation: Commute: 94.8% car, 0.2% public transportation, 0.9% walk, 3.7% work from home; Median travel time to work: 26.6 minutes

Presidential Election: 32.6% Obama, 65.4% Romney (2012)

National and State Parks: Mount Jefferson State Park; New River State Park

Additional Information Contacts

Ashe Government . . . . (336) 846-5501
    http://www.ashecountygov.com

Ashe County Communities

CRESTON (unincorporated postal area)

ZCTA: 28615

Covers a land area of 66.582 square miles and a water area of 0.228 square miles. Located at 36.46° N. Lat; 81.67° W. Long. Elevation is 2,858 feet.

Population: 1,876; Growth (since 2000): -5.6%; Density: 28.2 persons per square mile; Race: 96.5% White, 0.3% Black/African American, 0.6% Asian, 0.4% American Indian/Alaska Native, 0.0% Native Hawaiian/Other Pacific Islander, 1.6% Two or more races, 2.4% Hispanic of any race; Average household size: 2.28; Median age: 48.3; Age under 18: 18.8%; Age 65 and over: 21.4%; Males per 100 females: 101.9

Housing: Homeownership rate: 83.6%; Homeowner vacancy rate: 1.1%; Rental vacancy rate: 8.1%

CRUMPLER (unincorporated postal area)

ZCTA: 28617

Covers a land area of 34.504 square miles and a water area of 0.391 square miles. Located at 36.48° N. Lat; 81.36° W. Long. Elevation is 2,556 feet.

Population: 2,261; Growth (since 2000): -2.2%; Density: 65.5 persons per square mile; Race: 93.5% White, 0.9% Black/African American, 0.2% Asian, 0.4% American Indian/Alaska Native, 0.1% Native Hawaiian/Other Pacific Islander, 0.9% Two or more races, 8.3% Hispanic of any race; Average household size: 2.35; Median age: 42.6; Age under 18: 21.1%; Age 65 and over: 17.8%; Males per 100 females: 97.6

Housing: Homeownership rate: 77.0%; Homeowner vacancy rate: 0.7%; Rental vacancy rate: 7.6%

FLEETWOOD (unincorporated postal area)

ZCTA: 28626

Covers a land area of 32.219 square miles and a water area of 0.263 square miles. Located at 36.29° N. Lat; 81.52° W. Long. Elevation is 2,874 feet.

Population: 2,714; Growth (since 2000): 49.3%; Density: 84.2 persons per square mile; Race: 96.0% White, 0.4% Black/African American, 0.3% Asian, 0.1% American Indian/Alaska Native, 0.1% Native Hawaiian/Other Pacific Islander, 1.6% Two or more races, 4.2% Hispanic of any race; Average household size: 2.39; Median age: 41.1; Age under 18: 19.9%; Age 65 and over: 13.8%; Males per 100 females: 101.3; Marriage status: 11.7% never married, 73.7% now married, 0.0% separated, 7.4% widowed, 7.2% divorced; Foreign born: 2.1%; Speak English only: 98.1%; With disability: 15.7%; Veterans: 14.8%; Ancestry: 24.6% American, 12.1% English, 9.9% German, 9.2% Irish, 5.4% Scottish

Employment: 13.7% management, business, and financial, 1.2% computer, engineering, and science, 15.4% education, legal, community service, arts, and media, 9.8% healthcare practitioners, 13.7% service, 21.8% sales and office, 15.9% natural resources, construction, and maintenance, 8.7% production, transportation, and material moving

Income: Per capita: $25,983; Median household: $51,974; Average household: $58,545; Households with income of $100,000 or more: 13.1%; Poverty rate: 14.9%

Educational Attainment: High school diploma or higher: 92.0%; Bachelor's degree or higher: 32.0%; Graduate/professional degree or higher: 11.0%

Housing: Homeownership rate: 81.7%; Median home value: $219,500; Median year structure built: 1986; Homeowner vacancy rate: 4.1%; Median gross rent: $950 per month; Rental vacancy rate: 13.0%

Health Insurance: 89.7% have insurance; 71.1% have private insurance; 32.0% have public insurance; 10.3% do not have insurance; 0.0% of children under 18 do not have insurance

Transportation: Commute: 94.7% car, 0.0% public transportation, 0.6% walk, 4.7% work from home; Median travel time to work: 29.1 minutes

GLENDALE SPRINGS (unincorporated postal area)

ZCTA: 28629

Covers a land area of 2.381 square miles and a water area of 0.004 square miles. Located at 36.35° N. Lat; 81.37° W. Long. Elevation is 3,074 feet.

Population: 75; Growth (since 2000): 41.5%; Density: 31.5 persons per square mile; Race: 98.7% White, 0.0% Black/African American, 0.0% Asian, 1.3% American Indian/Alaska Native, 0.0% Native Hawaiian/Other Pacific Islander, 0.0% Two or more races, 0.0% Hispanic of any race; Average household size: 2.34; Median age: 43.8; Age under 18: 21.3%; Age 65 and over: 16.0%; Males per 100 females: 87.5

Housing: Homeownership rate: 90.7%; Homeowner vacancy rate: 0.0%; Rental vacancy rate: 50.0%

GRASSY CREEK (unincorporated postal area)

ZCTA: 28631

Covers a land area of 24.945 square miles and a water area of 0.226 square miles. Located at 36.55° N. Lat; 81.41° W. Long. Elevation is 2,654 feet.

Population: 637; Growth (since 2000): 24.7%; Density: 25.5 persons per square mile; Race: 96.2% White, 0.2% Black/African American, 1.4% Asian, 0.0% American Indian/Alaska Native, 0.0% Native Hawaiian/Other Pacific Islander, 0.2% Two or more races, 7.5% Hispanic of any race; Average household size: 2.21; Median age: 47.9; Age under 18: 18.1%; Age 65 and over: 18.5%; Males per 100 females: 110.9

Housing: Homeownership rate: 84.9%; Homeowner vacancy rate: 2.0%; Rental vacancy rate: 4.3%

JEFFERSON (town). County seat. Covers a land area of 2.066 square miles and a water area of 0.004 square miles. Located at 36.42° N. Lat; 81.47° W. Long. Elevation is 2,920 feet.

History: Jefferson was founded in 1800 and named for Thomas Jefferson.

Population: 1,611; Growth (since 2000): 13.3%; Density: 779.6 persons per square mile; Race: 90.6% White, 1.2% Black/African American, 1.1% Asian, 0.1% American Indian/Alaska Native, 0.0% Native Hawaiian/Other Pacific Islander, 0.9% Two or more races, 9.1% Hispanic of any race;

Average household size: 2.12; Median age: 45.3; Age under 18: 17.9%; Age 65 and over: 29.2%; Males per 100 females: 82.7

School District(s)

Ashe County Schools (PK-12)
  2012-13 Enrollment: 3,316 . . . . (336) 246-7175
Housing: Homeownership rate: 50.3%; Homeowner vacancy rate: 6.0%; Rental vacancy rate: 6.0%
Hospitals: Ashe Memorial Hospital
Airports: Ashe County (general aviation)

LANSING (town). Covers a land area of 0.328 square miles and a water area of 0.007 square miles. Located at 36.50° N. Lat; 81.51° W. Long. Elevation is 2,654 feet.
Population: 158; Growth (since 2000): 4.6%; Density: 482.1 persons per square mile; Race: 94.3% White, 1.3% Black/African American, 0.0% Asian, 0.0% American Indian/Alaska Native, 0.6% Native Hawaiian/Other Pacific Islander, 3.2% Two or more races, 0.6% Hispanic of any race; Average household size: 2.26; Median age: 41.0; Age under 18: 19.6%; Age 65 and over: 15.2%; Males per 100 females: 92.7
Housing: Homeownership rate: 62.9%; Homeowner vacancy rate: 0.0%; Rental vacancy rate: 3.7%

TODD (unincorporated postal area)
ZCTA: 28684
  Covers a land area of 52.804 square miles and a water area of 0.238 square miles. Located at 36.34° N. Lat; 81.61° W. Long. Elevation is 2,982 feet.
Population: 2,141; Growth (since 2000): -0.8%; Density: 40.5 persons per square mile; Race: 97.5% White, 0.3% Black/African American, 0.3% Asian, 0.1% American Indian/Alaska Native, 0.0% Native Hawaiian/Other Pacific Islander, 1.2% Two or more races, 1.9% Hispanic of any race; Average household size: 2.37; Median age: 44.9; Age under 18: 20.6%; Age 65 and over: 18.0%; Males per 100 females: 95.9
Housing: Homeownership rate: 84.1%; Homeowner vacancy rate: 3.5%; Rental vacancy rate: 15.8%

WARRENSVILLE (unincorporated postal area)
ZCTA: 28693
  Covers a land area of 25.791 square miles and a water area of 0.198 square miles. Located at 36.47° N. Lat; 81.56° W. Long. Elevation is 2,697 feet.
Population: 1,700; Growth (since 2000): -4.6%; Density: 65.9 persons per square mile; Race: 96.2% White, 0.4% Black/African American, 0.2% Asian, 0.2% American Indian/Alaska Native, 0.0% Native Hawaiian/Other Pacific Islander, 1.3% Two or more races, 3.9% Hispanic of any race; Average household size: 2.36; Median age: 46.0; Age under 18: 21.4%; Age 65 and over: 19.9%; Males per 100 females: 105.3

School District(s)

Ashe County Schools (PK-12)
  2012-13 Enrollment: 3,316 . . . . (336) 246-7175
Housing: Homeownership rate: 83.2%; Homeowner vacancy rate: 0.8%; Rental vacancy rate: 4.0%

WEST JEFFERSON (town). Covers a land area of 2.083 square miles and a water area of 0.002 square miles. Located at 36.39° N. Lat; 81.49° W. Long. Elevation is 2,976 feet.
Population: 1,299; Growth (since 2000): 20.2%; Density: 623.6 persons per square mile; Race: 92.9% White, 0.8% Black/African American, 1.0% Asian, 0.2% American Indian/Alaska Native, 0.0% Native Hawaiian/Other Pacific Islander, 1.7% Two or more races, 7.0% Hispanic of any race; Average household size: 2.06; Median age: 43.9; Age under 18: 18.6%; Age 65 and over: 23.4%; Males per 100 females: 93.3

School District(s)

Ashe County Schools (PK-12)
  2012-13 Enrollment: 3,316 . . . . (336) 246-7175
Housing: Homeownership rate: 48.5%; Homeowner vacancy rate: 2.5%; Rental vacancy rate: 13.8%
Newspapers: Jefferson Post (weekly circulation 6000)
Additional Information Contacts
Town of West Jefferson . . . . (336) 246-3551
  http://www.townofwj.com

Avery County

Located in northwestern North Carolina, in the Blue Ridge; bounded on the west by Tennessee; in Pisgah National Forest. Covers a land area of 247.087 square miles, a water area of 0.142 square miles, and is located in the Eastern Time Zone at 36.07° N. Lat., 81.92° W. Long. The county was founded in 1911. County seat is Newland.

Weather Station: Grandfather Mountain   Elevation: 5,299 feet

	Jan	Feb	Mar	Apr	May	Jun	Jul	Aug	Sep	Oct	Nov	Dec
High	36	38	45	53	61	67	70	69	63	55	47	39
Low	21	23	29	37	46	54	57	57	51	41	33	24
Precip	4.5	4.5	5.4	5.2	5.6	6.4	5.9	5.6	6.0	4.3	4.5	4.3
Snow	14.7	13.6	9.8	6.0	0.5	0.0	0.0	0.0	tr	0.4	2.8	9.2

High and Low temperatures in degrees Fahrenheit; Precipitation and Snow in inches

Population: 17,797; Growth (since 2000): 3.7%; Density: 72.0 persons per square mile; Race: 91.9% White, 4.0% Black/African American, 0.3% Asian, 0.4% American Indian/Alaska Native, 0.0% Native Hawaiian/Other Pacific Islander, 0.8% two or more races, 4.5% Hispanic of any race; Average household size: 2.31; Median age: 42.3; Age under 18: 17.2%; Age 65 and over: 17.4%; Males per 100 females: 119.5; Marriage status: 27.1% never married, 55.1% now married, 1.8% separated, 6.3% widowed, 11.5% divorced; Foreign born: 3.4%; Speak English only: 94.0%; With disability: 19.4%; Veterans: 9.6%; Ancestry: 16.8% German, 14.0% English, 12.5% American, 10.6% Irish, 7.3% Scottish
Religion: Six largest groups: 27.7% Baptist, 5.4% Presbyterian-Reformed, 3.6% Catholicism, 2.4% Lutheran, 1.1% Methodist/Pietist, 1.0% Adventist
Economy: Unemployment rate: 5.7%; Leading industries: 16.4% construction; 16.2% retail trade; 11.5% accommodation and food services; Farms: 483 totaling 28,224 acres; Company size: 0 employ 1,000 or more persons, 0 employ 500 to 999 persons, 5 employ 100 to 499 persons, 508 employ less than 100 persons; Business ownership: 415 women-owned, n/a Black-owned, n/a Hispanic-owned, n/a Asian-owned
Employment: 10.2% management, business, and financial, 1.9% computer, engineering, and science, 11.1% education, legal, community service, arts, and media, 3.5% healthcare practitioners, 22.6% service, 23.5% sales and office, 15.2% natural resources, construction, and maintenance, 12.0% production, transportation, and material moving
Income: Per capita: $21,598; Median household: $36,969; Average household: $53,710; Households with income of $100,000 or more: 10.6%; Poverty rate: 18.0%
Educational Attainment: High school diploma or higher: 81.5%; Bachelor's degree or higher: 20.4%; Graduate/professional degree or higher: 7.1%
Housing: Homeownership rate: 76.5%; Median home value: $140,800; Median year structure built: 1983; Homeowner vacancy rate: 4.5%; Median gross rent: $675 per month; Rental vacancy rate: 22.1%
Vital Statistics: Birth rate: 77.3 per 10,000 population; Death rate: 110.1 per 10,000 population; Age-adjusted cancer mortality rate: 143.3 deaths per 100,000 population
Health Insurance: 79.7% have insurance; 57.9% have private insurance; 35.3% have public insurance; 20.3% do not have insurance; 7.6% of children under 18 do not have insurance
Health Care: Physicians: 12.5 per 10,000 population; Hospital beds: 19.7 per 10,000 population; Hospital admissions: 1,214.8 per 10,000 population
Air Quality Index: 97.8% good, 2.2% moderate, 0.0% unhealthy for sensitive individuals, 0.0% unhealthy (percent of days)
Transportation: Commute: 90.8% car, 0.0% public transportation, 2.3% walk, 6.0% work from home; Median travel time to work: 22.1 minutes
Presidential Election: 24.3% Obama, 74.3% Romney (2012)
Additional Information Contacts
Avery Government . . . . (828) 733-8201
  http://www.averycountync.gov

Avery County Communities

BANNER ELK (town). Covers a land area of 1.887 square miles and a water area of 0 square miles. Located at 36.16° N. Lat; 81.87° W. Long. Elevation is 3,701 feet.
Population: 1,028; Growth (since 2000): 26.8%; Density: 544.9 persons per square mile; Race: 89.0% White, 5.4% Black/African American, 1.5% Asian, 0.1% American Indian/Alaska Native, 0.1% Native Hawaiian/Other Pacific Islander, 1.6% Two or more races, 5.6% Hispanic of any race; Average household size: 2.25; Median age: 22.0; Age under 18: 11.8%; Age 65 and over: 11.6%; Males per 100 females: 89.7

School District(s)
Avery County Schools (PK-12)
  2012-13 Enrollment: 2,245 . . . . (828) 733-6006
Grandfather Academy (01-12)
  2012-13 Enrollment: 34 . . . . (828) 897-4563
Four-year College(s)
Lees-McRae College (Private, Not-for-profit, Presbyterian Church (USA))
  Fall 2013 Enrollment: 890 . . . . (828) 898-5241
  2013-14 Tuition: In-state $24,150; Out-of-state $24,150
Housing: Homeownership rate: 52.3%; Homeowner vacancy rate: 26.8%; Rental vacancy rate: 14.0%
Safety: Violent crime rate: 17.9 per 10,000 population; Property crime rate: 214.9 per 10,000 population
Additional Information Contacts
Town of Banner Elk . . . . (828) 898-5398
  http://www.townofbannerelk.org

CROSSNORE (town). Covers a land area of 0.448 square miles and a water area of 0 square miles. Located at 36.02° N. Lat; 81.93° W. Long. Elevation is 3,383 feet.
Population: 192; Growth (since 2000): -20.7%; Density: 428.8 persons per square mile; Race: 85.9% White, 9.4% Black/African American, 1.0% Asian, 0.5% American Indian/Alaska Native, 0.0% Native Hawaiian/Other Pacific Islander, 1.6% Two or more races, 4.2% Hispanic of any race; Average household size: 2.19; Median age: 27.0; Age under 18: 40.6%; Age 65 and over: 14.1%; Males per 100 females: 82.9
School District(s)
Avery County Schools (PK-12)
  2012-13 Enrollment: 2,245 . . . . (828) 733-6006
Crossnore Academy (KG-12)
  2012-13 Enrollment: 91 . . . . (828) 733-5241
Housing: Homeownership rate: 81.5%; Homeowner vacancy rate: 6.4%; Rental vacancy rate: 23.1%

ELK PARK (town). Covers a land area of 0.691 square miles and a water area of 0 square miles. Located at 36.16° N. Lat; 81.98° W. Long. Elevation is 3,156 feet.
History: Appalachian Trail passes to West on state line.
Population: 452; Growth (since 2000): -1.5%; Density: 654.5 persons per square mile; Race: 92.7% White, 0.2% Black/African American, 0.0% Asian, 1.3% American Indian/Alaska Native, 0.0% Native Hawaiian/Other Pacific Islander, 2.2% Two or more races, 8.8% Hispanic of any race; Average household size: 2.18; Median age: 44.9; Age under 18: 20.1%; Age 65 and over: 17.9%; Males per 100 females: 116.3
School District(s)
Avery County Schools (PK-12)
  2012-13 Enrollment: 2,245 . . . . (828) 733-6006
Housing: Homeownership rate: 67.2%; Homeowner vacancy rate: 1.4%; Rental vacancy rate: 20.0%

GRANDFATHER (village). Covers a land area of 1.484 square miles and a water area of 0.042 square miles. Located at 36.09° N. Lat; 81.85° W. Long. Elevation is 3,907 feet.
Population: 25; Growth (since 2000): -65.8%; Density: 16.9 persons per square mile; Race: 100.0% White, 0.0% Black/African American, 0.0% Asian, 0.0% American Indian/Alaska Native, 0.0% Native Hawaiian/Other Pacific Islander, 0.0% Two or more races, 0.0% Hispanic of any race; Average household size: 1.67; Median age: 71.5; Age under 18: 0.0%; Age 65 and over: 60.0%; Males per 100 females: 78.6
Housing: Homeownership rate: 100.0%; Homeowner vacancy rate: 0.0%; Rental vacancy rate: 0.0%

LINVILLE (unincorporated postal area)
ZCTA: 28646
  Covers a land area of 21.608 square miles and a water area of 0.055 square miles. Located at 36.07° N. Lat; 81.85° W. Long. Elevation is 3,665 feet.
  Population: 342; Growth (since 2000): 48.7%; Density: 15.8 persons per square mile; Race: 95.3% White, 0.0% Black/African American, 0.6% Asian, 0.3% American Indian/Alaska Native, 0.0% Native Hawaiian/Other Pacific Islander, 3.8% Two or more races, 2.9% Hispanic of any race; Average household size: 2.19; Median age: 46.0; Age under 18: 21.9%; Age 65 and over: 21.3%; Males per 100 females: 95.4

Housing: Homeownership rate: 75.6%; Homeowner vacancy rate: 4.1%; Rental vacancy rate: 7.3%
Hospitals: Charles A Cannon Jr Memorial Hospital (70 beds)

MINNEAPOLIS (unincorporated postal area)
ZCTA: 28652
  Covers a land area of 0.081 square miles and a water area of 0 square miles. Located at 36.10° N. Lat; 81.99° W. Long. Elevation is 3,186 feet.
  Population: 46; Growth (since 2000): n/a; Density: 570.5 persons per square mile; Race: 100.0% White, 0.0% Black/African American, 0.0% Asian, 0.0% American Indian/Alaska Native, 0.0% Native Hawaiian/Other Pacific Islander, 0.0% Two or more races, 0.0% Hispanic of any race; Average household size: 2.30; Median age: 49.5; Age under 18: 13.0%; Age 65 and over: 17.4%; Males per 100 females: 100.0
  Housing: Homeownership rate: 90.0%; Homeowner vacancy rate: 5.3%; Rental vacancy rate: 71.4%

NEWLAND (town). County seat. Covers a land area of 0.748 square miles and a water area of 0 square miles. Located at 36.09° N. Lat; 81.93° W. Long. Elevation is 3,612 feet.
Population: 698; Growth (since 2000): -0.9%; Density: 933.4 persons per square mile; Race: 88.8% White, 0.9% Black/African American, 0.4% Asian, 0.9% American Indian/Alaska Native, 0.6% Native Hawaiian/Other Pacific Islander, 0.9% Two or more races, 10.2% Hispanic of any race; Average household size: 2.15; Median age: 40.5; Age under 18: 21.1%; Age 65 and over: 18.9%; Males per 100 females: 94.4
School District(s)
Avery County Schools (PK-12)
  2012-13 Enrollment: 2,245 . . . . (828) 733-6006
Housing: Homeownership rate: 59.0%; Homeowner vacancy rate: 1.6%; Rental vacancy rate: 9.9%
Safety: Violent crime rate: 29.3 per 10,000 population; Property crime rate: 380.7 per 10,000 population
Newspapers: Avery Post (weekly circulation 5000)

PINEOLA (unincorporated postal area)
ZCTA: 28662
  Covers a land area of 1.788 square miles and a water area of 0 square miles. Located at 36.02° N. Lat; 81.90° W. Long. Elevation is 3,550 feet.
  Population: 140; Growth (since 2000): 159.3%; Density: 78.3 persons per square mile; Race: 91.4% White, 0.0% Black/African American, 0.0% Asian, 0.0% American Indian/Alaska Native, 0.0% Native Hawaiian/Other Pacific Islander, 0.0% Two or more races, 14.3% Hispanic of any race; Average household size: 2.41; Median age: 38.5; Age under 18: 20.0%; Age 65 and over: 21.4%; Males per 100 females: 112.1
  Housing: Homeownership rate: 53.4%; Homeowner vacancy rate: 0.0%; Rental vacancy rate: 25.0%

SUGAR MOUNTAIN (village). Covers a land area of 2.455 square miles and a water area of 0 square miles. Located at 36.13° N. Lat; 81.86° W. Long. Elevation is 4,400 feet.
Population: 198; Growth (since 2000): -12.4%; Density: 80.7 persons per square mile; Race: 90.4% White, 2.0% Black/African American, 0.0% Asian, 3.0% American Indian/Alaska Native, 0.0% Native Hawaiian/Other Pacific Islander, 1.0% Two or more races, 4.0% Hispanic of any race; Average household size: 2.11; Median age: 37.3; Age under 18: 16.2%; Age 65 and over: 16.2%; Males per 100 females: 127.6
Housing: Homeownership rate: 68.1%; Homeowner vacancy rate: 18.8%; Rental vacancy rate: 69.7%

Beaufort County

Located in eastern North Carolina, on the Atlantic coast. Covers a land area of 827.192 square miles, a water area of 131.023 square miles, and is located in the Eastern Time Zone at 35.48° N. Lat., 76.84° W. Long. The county was founded in 1705. County seat is Washington.

Beaufort County is part of the Washington, NC Micropolitan Statistical Area. The entire metro area includes: Beaufort County, NC

Weather Station: Aurora 6 N — Elevation: 20 feet

	Jan	Feb	Mar	Apr	May	Jun	Jul	Aug	Sep	Oct	Nov	Dec
High	53	56	62	72	79	86	89	87	82	73	65	56
Low	34	37	42	51	59	68	72	71	66	55	46	38
Precip	3.9	3.1	4.1	3.3	3.9	4.9	5.6	6.3	4.6	3.4	3.0	3.3
Snow	0.3	0.1	tr	0.0	0.0	0.0	0.0	0.0	0.0	0.0	0.0	tr

High and Low temperatures in degrees Fahrenheit; Precipitation and Snow in inches

Weather Station: Belhaven 5 SE — Elevation: 7 feet

	Jan	Feb	Mar	Apr	May	Jun	Jul	Aug	Sep	Oct	Nov	Dec
High	52	56	63	71	79	86	88	87	82	74	65	56
Low	33	35	41	50	58	67	71	69	64	52	44	36
Precip	3.8	2.9	4.2	3.2	3.8	5.0	6.1	6.3	4.5	2.5	3.2	3.0
Snow	0.7	0.6	0.9	0.2	0.0	0.0	0.0	0.0	0.0	0.0	0.0	0.6

High and Low temperatures in degrees Fahrenheit; Precipitation and Snow in inches

Population: 47,759; Growth (since 2000): 6.2%; Density: 57.7 persons per square mile; Race: 68.2% White, 25.6% Black/African American, 0.3% Asian, 0.4% American Indian/Alaska Native, 0.0% Native Hawaiian/Other Pacific Islander, 1.3% two or more races, 6.6% Hispanic of any race; Average household size: 2.37; Median age: 43.8; Age under 18: 22.0%; Age 65 and over: 18.4%; Males per 100 females: 93.0; Marriage status: 24.0% never married, 56.3% now married, 3.2% separated, 8.1% widowed, 11.6% divorced; Foreign born: 4.6%; Speak English only: 93.8%; With disability: 18.5%; Veterans: 10.7%; Ancestry: 12.2% English, 10.9% American, 7.5% Irish, 6.7% German, 1.7% Italian
Religion: Six largest groups: 29.2% Baptist, 8.7% Methodist/Pietist, 4.2% Pentecostal, 3.9% Non-denominational Protestant, 2.7% Episcopalianism/Anglicanism, 2.1% Catholicism
Economy: Unemployment rate: 6.6%; Leading industries: 17.3% retail trade; 11.9% other services (except public administration); 10.8% health care and social assistance; Farms: 364 totaling 148,286 acres; Company size: 1 employs 1,000 or more persons, 1 employs 500 to 999 persons, 15 employ 100 to 499 persons, 1,077 employ less than 100 persons; Business ownership: 1,285 women-owned, n/a Black-owned, n/a Hispanic-owned, n/a Asian-owned
Employment: 10.5% management, business, and financial, 2.8% computer, engineering, and science, 8.5% education, legal, community service, arts, and media, 8.8% healthcare practitioners, 19.7% service, 20.1% sales and office, 15.8% natural resources, construction, and maintenance, 13.8% production, transportation, and material moving
Income: Per capita: $21,636; Median household: $40,429; Average household: $51,449; Households with income of $100,000 or more: 11.1%; Poverty rate: 21.0%
Educational Attainment: High school diploma or higher: 81.7%; Bachelor's degree or higher: 18.3%; Graduate/professional degree or higher: 7.0%
Housing: Homeownership rate: 71.1%; Median home value: $117,000; Median year structure built: 1979; Homeowner vacancy rate: 3.2%; Median gross rent: $656 per month; Rental vacancy rate: 7.6%
Vital Statistics: Birth rate: 102.6 per 10,000 population; Death rate: 116.7 per 10,000 population; Age-adjusted cancer mortality rate: 195.4 deaths per 100,000 population
Health Insurance: 82.1% have insurance; 56.5% have private insurance; 40.9% have public insurance; 17.9% do not have insurance; 11.1% of children under 18 do not have insurance
Health Care: Physicians: 11.8 per 10,000 population; Hospital beds: 27.3 per 10,000 population; Hospital admissions: 869.8 per 10,000 population
Air Quality Index: 100.0% good, 0.0% moderate, 0.0% unhealthy for sensitive individuals, 0.0% unhealthy (percent of days)
Transportation: Commute: 94.2% car, 0.3% public transportation, 1.8% walk, 2.3% work from home; Median travel time to work: 24.5 minutes
Presidential Election: 39.9% Obama, 59.2% Romney (2012)
National and State Parks: Goose Creek State Park
Additional Information Contacts
Beaufort Government . . . . (843) 225-2000
  http://www.co.beaufort.nc.us

Beaufort County Communities

AURORA (town). Covers a land area of 0.928 square miles and a water area of 0.099 square miles. Located at 35.30° N. Lat; 76.79° W. Long. Elevation is 3 feet.
History: Aurora Fossil Museum.
Population: 520; Growth (since 2000): -10.8%; Density: 560.2 persons per square mile; Race: 52.1% White, 42.7% Black/African American, 0.0%

Asian, 0.6% American Indian/Alaska Native, 0.2% Native Hawaiian/Other Pacific Islander, 3.3% Two or more races, 2.9% Hispanic of any race; Average household size: 2.16; Median age: 44.7; Age under 18: 22.7%; Age 65 and over: 20.2%; Males per 100 females: 82.5
School District(s)
Beaufort County Schools (PK-12)
  2012-13 Enrollment: 7,255 . . . . (252) 946-6593
Housing: Homeownership rate: 54.8%; Homeowner vacancy rate: 2.9%; Rental vacancy rate: 17.4%

BATH (town). Covers a land area of 0.358 square miles and a water area of 0.560 square miles. Located at 35.47° N. Lat; 76.81° W. Long. Elevation is 13 feet.
History: Bath is one of the oldest towns in North Carolina, and was at one time the capital of the Province. Colonists settled here as early as 1690. The town was the seat of old Bath County, named for the Earl of Bath, one of the Lords Proprietors. In 1738, when Bath County was divided, the town became the seat of Beaufort County.
Population: 249; Growth (since 2000): -9.5%; Density: 695.1 persons per square mile; Race: 97.6% White, 0.8% Black/African American, 0.0% Asian, 0.0% American Indian/Alaska Native, 0.0% Native Hawaiian/Other Pacific Islander, 1.6% Two or more races, 1.2% Hispanic of any race; Average household size: 1.99; Median age: 56.8; Age under 18: 9.2%; Age 65 and over: 30.5%; Males per 100 females: 87.2
School District(s)
Beaufort County Schools (PK-12)
  2012-13 Enrollment: 7,255 . . . . (252) 946-6593
Housing: Homeownership rate: 88.8%; Homeowner vacancy rate: 5.1%; Rental vacancy rate: 6.7%

BAYVIEW (CDP). Covers a land area of 1.058 square miles and a water area of 0 square miles. Located at 35.44° N. Lat; 76.79° W. Long. Elevation is 7 feet.
Population: 346; Growth (since 2000): n/a; Density: 327.1 persons per square mile; Race: 92.2% White, 6.1% Black/African American, 0.0% Asian, 0.0% American Indian/Alaska Native, 0.0% Native Hawaiian/Other Pacific Islander, 1.2% Two or more races, 0.6% Hispanic of any race; Average household size: 2.20; Median age: 51.0; Age under 18: 16.5%; Age 65 and over: 26.6%; Males per 100 females: 109.7
Housing: Homeownership rate: 82.2%; Homeowner vacancy rate: 0.0%; Rental vacancy rate: 0.0%

BELHAVEN (town). Covers a land area of 1.590 square miles and a water area of 0.499 square miles. Located at 35.54° N. Lat; 76.62° W. Long. Elevation is 4 feet.
Population: 1,688; Growth (since 2000): -14.2%; Density: 1,061.8 persons per square mile; Race: 39.0% White, 55.3% Black/African American, 0.5% Asian, 1.2% American Indian/Alaska Native, 0.0% Native Hawaiian/Other Pacific Islander, 1.7% Two or more races, 5.0% Hispanic of any race; Average household size: 2.22; Median age: 45.8; Age under 18: 22.5%; Age 65 and over: 19.7%; Males per 100 females: 81.1
Housing: Homeownership rate: 57.7%; Homeowner vacancy rate: 11.1%; Rental vacancy rate: 4.9%
Hospitals: Vidant Pungo Hospital (49 beds)
Safety: Violent crime rate: 12.3 per 10,000 population; Property crime rate: 215.5 per 10,000 population
Newspapers: Beaufort-Hyde News (weekly circulation 3500)

BLOUNTS CREEK (unincorporated postal area)
ZCTA: 27814
  Covers a land area of 63.865 square miles and a water area of 14.565 square miles. Located at 35.40° N. Lat; 76.92° W. Long. Elevation is 33 feet.
Population: 1,676; Growth (since 2000): 9.5%; Density: 26.2 persons per square mile; Race: 69.3% White, 28.1% Black/African American, 0.7% Asian, 0.3% American Indian/Alaska Native, 0.0% Native Hawaiian/Other Pacific Islander, 1.1% Two or more races, 1.8% Hispanic of any race; Average household size: 2.25; Median age: 49.9; Age under 18: 17.8%; Age 65 and over: 19.6%; Males per 100 females: 98.8
Housing: Homeownership rate: 85.4%; Homeowner vacancy rate: 3.9%; Rental vacancy rate: 3.4%

CHOCOWINITY (town). Covers a land area of 1.007 square miles and a water area of 0 square miles. Located at 35.51° N. Lat; 77.10° W. Long. Elevation is 39 feet.

Population: 820; Growth (since 2000): 11.9%; Density: 814.2 persons per square mile; Race: 57.8% White, 37.4% Black/African American, 0.6% Asian, 0.5% American Indian/Alaska Native, 0.0% Native Hawaiian/Other Pacific Islander, 2.2% Two or more races, 3.0% Hispanic of any race; Average household size: 2.31; Median age: 42.6; Age under 18: 21.7%; Age 65 and over: 17.4%; Males per 100 females: 84.7

School District(s)

Beaufort County Schools (PK-12)
 2012-13 Enrollment: 7,255 . . . . (252) 946-6593
Housing: Homeownership rate: 51.2%; Homeowner vacancy rate: 2.2%; Rental vacancy rate: 9.5%

EDWARD (unincorporated postal area)

ZCTA: 27821
 Covers a land area of 6.503 square miles and a water area of 0.099 square miles. Located at 35.32° N. Lat; 76.87° W. Long. Elevation is 30 feet.
 Population: 358; Growth (since 2000): -16.6%; Density: 55.1 persons per square mile; Race: 26.5% White, 71.2% Black/African American, 0.0% Asian, 0.0% American Indian/Alaska Native, 0.0% Native Hawaiian/Other Pacific Islander, 2.0% Two or more races, 0.3% Hispanic of any race; Average household size: 2.40; Median age: 43.8; Age under 18: 24.6%; Age 65 and over: 16.2%; Males per 100 females: 90.4
 Housing: Homeownership rate: 65.7%; Homeowner vacancy rate: 1.0%; Rental vacancy rate: 12.1%

PANTEGO (town). Covers a land area of 0.803 square miles and a water area of 0 square miles. Located at 35.59° N. Lat; 76.66° W. Long. Elevation is 3 feet.

Population: 179; Growth (since 2000): 5.3%; Density: 223.0 persons per square mile; Race: 72.1% White, 20.7% Black/African American, 0.0% Asian, 6.7% American Indian/Alaska Native, 0.0% Native Hawaiian/Other Pacific Islander, 0.6% Two or more races, 8.9% Hispanic of any race; Average household size: 2.49; Median age: 43.3; Age under 18: 21.8%; Age 65 and over: 17.3%; Males per 100 females: 118.3
Housing: Homeownership rate: 75.0%; Homeowner vacancy rate: 1.8%; Rental vacancy rate: 0.0%

PINETOWN (CDP). Covers a land area of 1.009 square miles and a water area of 0 square miles. Located at 35.61° N. Lat; 76.86° W. Long. Elevation is 39 feet.

Population: 155; Growth (since 2000): n/a; Density: 153.6 persons per square mile; Race: 97.4% White, 0.0% Black/African American, 0.0% Asian, 0.0% American Indian/Alaska Native, 0.0% Native Hawaiian/Other Pacific Islander, 0.0% Two or more races, 7.1% Hispanic of any race; Average household size: 2.35; Median age: 39.3; Age under 18: 23.2%; Age 65 and over: 12.3%; Males per 100 females: 103.9

School District(s)

Beaufort County Schools (PK-12)
 2012-13 Enrollment: 7,255 . . . . (252) 946-6593
Housing: Homeownership rate: 80.3%; Homeowner vacancy rate: 8.6%; Rental vacancy rate: 0.0%

RIVER ROAD (CDP). Covers a land area of 7.110 square miles and a water area of 0 square miles. Located at 35.51° N. Lat; 76.99° W. Long. Elevation is 13 feet.

Population: 4,394; Growth (since 2000): 7.3%; Density: 618.0 persons per square mile; Race: 60.5% White, 22.7% Black/African American, 0.1% Asian, 1.0% American Indian/Alaska Native, 0.2% Native Hawaiian/Other Pacific Islander, 1.0% Two or more races, 19.9% Hispanic of any race; Average household size: 2.45; Median age: 40.5; Age under 18: 24.0%; Age 65 and over: 15.8%; Males per 100 females: 99.3; Marriage status: 22.0% never married, 61.2% now married, 2.0% separated, 6.0% widowed, 10.7% divorced; Foreign born: 20.4%; Speak English only: 77.0%; With disability: 11.6%; Veterans: 9.9%; Ancestry: 11.6% American, 10.4% English, 7.3% German, 4.4% Irish, 2.0% African
Employment: 8.0% management, business, and financial, 1.3% computer, engineering, and science, 10.5% education, legal, community service, arts, and media, 8.8% healthcare practitioners, 22.3% service, 17.5% sales and office, 21.0% natural resources, construction, and maintenance, 10.5% production, transportation, and material moving

Income: Per capita: $25,357; Median household: $42,061; Average household: $58,256; Households with income of $100,000 or more: 11.8%; Poverty rate: 24.8%
Educational Attainment: High school diploma or higher: 78.2%; Bachelor's degree or higher: 24.2%; Graduate/professional degree or higher: 8.2%
Housing: Homeownership rate: 74.7%; Median home value: $145,800; Median year structure built: 1977; Homeowner vacancy rate: 2.7%; Median gross rent: $701 per month; Rental vacancy rate: 10.7%
Health Insurance: 77.6% have insurance; 54.3% have private insurance; 35.9% have public insurance; 22.4% do not have insurance; 11.6% of children under 18 do not have insurance
Transportation: Commute: 98.1% car, 0.0% public transportation, 0.5% walk, 1.4% work from home; Median travel time to work: 22.5 minutes

WASHINGTON (city). County seat. Covers a land area of 8.188 square miles and a water area of 0.835 square miles. Located at 35.56° N. Lat; 77.05° W. Long. Elevation is 7 feet.

History: In 1771, the General Assembly authorized James Bonner to establish a town at the Forks of the Tar River, which Colonel Bonner later named Washington, in honor of his commander in chief. The George Washington Bicentennial Commission established the fact that of the 422 cities and towns in the nation named for George Washington, this town was the first. Earliest recorded mention of the place as Washington is in an order of the council of safety at Hailfax dated October 1, 1776.
Population: 9,744; Growth (since 2000): 1.7%; Density: 1,190.0 persons per square mile; Race: 49.0% White, 45.5% Black/African American, 0.5% Asian, 0.2% American Indian/Alaska Native, 0.1% Native Hawaiian/Other Pacific Islander, 1.5% Two or more races, 5.5% Hispanic of any race; Average household size: 2.23; Median age: 41.6; Age under 18: 22.5%; Age 65 and over: 18.7%; Males per 100 females: 79.9; Marriage status: 30.2% never married, 41.3% now married, 3.5% separated, 12.7% widowed, 15.8% divorced; Foreign born: 2.6%; Speak English only: 96.5%; With disability: 21.1%; Veterans: 8.9%; Ancestry: 12.1% English, 6.0% American, 5.7% Irish, 5.1% German, 1.7% Italian
Employment: 9.3% management, business, and financial, 2.2% computer, engineering, and science, 14.3% education, legal, community service, arts, and media, 9.9% healthcare practitioners, 24.8% service, 18.2% sales and office, 9.8% natural resources, construction, and maintenance, 11.5% production, transportation, and material moving
Income: Per capita: $17,982; Median household: $30,479; Average household: $40,260; Households with income of $100,000 or more: 6.9%; Poverty rate: 30.5%
Educational Attainment: High school diploma or higher: 80.3%; Bachelor's degree or higher: 23.5%; Graduate/professional degree or higher: 10.3%

School District(s)

Beaufort County Schools (PK-12)
 2012-13 Enrollment: 7,255 . . . . (252) 946-6593
Washington Montessori (KG-08)
 2012-13 Enrollment: 310 . . . . (252) 946-1977

Two-year College(s)

Beaufort County Community College (Public)
 Fall 2013 Enrollment: 2,019 . . . . (252) 946-6194
 2013-14 Tuition: In-state $2,352; Out-of-state $8,496
Housing: Homeownership rate: 47.9%; Median home value: $159,900; Median year structure built: 1973; Homeowner vacancy rate: 7.4%; Median gross rent: $624 per month; Rental vacancy rate: 5.5%
Health Insurance: 85.1% have insurance; 49.0% have private insurance; 49.6% have public insurance; 14.9% do not have insurance; 4.2% of children under 18 do not have insurance
Hospitals: Vidant Beaufort Hospital
Newspapers: Washington Daily News (daily circulation 8800)
Transportation: Commute: 93.5% car, 0.0% public transportation, 2.6% walk, 1.6% work from home; Median travel time to work: 21.8 minutes
Airports: Warren Field (general aviation)
Additional Information Contacts
City of Washington . . . . (252) 975-9300
 http://www.ci.washington.nc.us

WASHINGTON PARK (town). Covers a land area of 0.264 square miles and a water area of 0 square miles. Located at 35.53° N. Lat; 77.03° W. Long. Elevation is 7 feet.

Population: 451; Growth (since 2000): 2.5%; Density: 1,707.7 persons per square mile; Race: 96.7% White, 2.7% Black/African American, 0.0%

Asian, 0.4% American Indian/Alaska Native, 0.0% Native Hawaiian/Other Pacific Islander, 0.2% Two or more races, 1.1% Hispanic of any race; Average household size: 2.31; Median age: 44.3; Age under 18: 26.4%; Age 65 and over: 21.3%; Males per 100 females: 81.9
Housing: Homeownership rate: 84.1%; Homeowner vacancy rate: 3.5%; Rental vacancy rate: 13.9%

Bertie County

Located in northeastern North Carolina; on the coastal plain, bounded on the south and southwest by the Roanoke River, and on the east by the Chowan River and Albemarle Sound. Covers a land area of 699.270 square miles, a water area of 41.979 square miles, and is located in the Eastern Time Zone at 36.06° N. Lat., 76.96° W. Long. The county was founded in 1722. County seat is Windsor.

Weather Station: Lewiston — Elevation: 49 feet

	Jan	Feb	Mar	Apr	May	Jun	Jul	Aug	Sep	Oct	Nov	Dec
High	51	55	63	73	80	87	90	89	83	74	64	55
Low	31	33	39	48	56	65	69	67	61	50	41	34
Precip	3.4	3.1	3.7	3.0	3.3	4.3	5.3	5.0	5.2	3.1	2.9	3.2
Snow	0.6	0.8	0.7	0.0	0.0	0.0	0.0	0.0	0.0	0.0	tr	tr

High and Low temperatures in degrees Fahrenheit; Precipitation and Snow in inches

Population: 21,282; Growth (since 2000): 7.6%; Density: 30.4 persons per square mile; Race: 35.2% White, 62.5% Black/African American, 0.5% Asian, 0.5% American Indian/Alaska Native, 0.0% Native Hawaiian/Other Pacific Islander, 0.9% two or more races, 1.3% Hispanic of any race; Average household size: 2.39; Median age: 42.9; Age under 18: 20.8%; Age 65 and over: 17.2%; Males per 100 females: 98.0; Marriage status: 34.0% never married, 45.2% now married, 4.6% separated, 8.7% widowed, 12.1% divorced; Foreign born: 1.0%; Speak English only: 97.9%; With disability: 20.0%; Veterans: 7.2%; Ancestry: 8.4% American, 5.8% English, 2.8% Irish, 1.8% German, 0.5% Scotch-Irish
Religion: Six largest groups: 25.0% Baptist, 7.2% Pentecostal, 2.2% Non-denominational Protestant, 1.9% Methodist/Pietist, 1.0% Episcopalianism/Anglicanism, 0.4% Catholicism
Economy: Unemployment rate: 7.7%; Leading industries: 21.8% other services (except public administration); 18.0% health care and social assistance; 15.8% retail trade; Farms: 325 totaling 146,754 acres; Company size: 1 employs 1,000 or more persons, 0 employ 500 to 999 persons, 3 employ 100 to 499 persons, 312 employ less than 100 persons; Business ownership: n/a women-owned, 388 Black-owned, n/a Hispanic-owned, n/a Asian-owned
Employment: 9.4% management, business, and financial, 0.8% computer, engineering, and science, 6.2% education, legal, community service, arts, and media, 5.8% healthcare practitioners, 22.9% service, 16.3% sales and office, 14.5% natural resources, construction, and maintenance, 24.1% production, transportation, and material moving
Income: Per capita: $17,096; Median household: $30,768; Average household: $43,889; Households with income of $100,000 or more: 9.1%; Poverty rate: 23.4%
Educational Attainment: High school diploma or higher: 72.6%; Bachelor's degree or higher: 10.6%; Graduate/professional degree or higher: 2.6%
Housing: Homeownership rate: 72.9%; Median home value: $79,100; Median year structure built: 1976; Homeowner vacancy rate: 1.3%; Median gross rent: $586 per month; Rental vacancy rate: 11.5%
Vital Statistics: Birth rate: 93.9 per 10,000 population; Death rate: 120.4 per 10,000 population; Age-adjusted cancer mortality rate: 170.2 deaths per 100,000 population
Health Insurance: 83.7% have insurance; 50.8% have private insurance; 46.6% have public insurance; 16.3% do not have insurance; 4.5% of children under 18 do not have insurance
Health Care: Physicians: 4.4 per 10,000 population; Hospital beds: 2.9 per 10,000 population; Hospital admissions: 215.4 per 10,000 population
Transportation: Commute: 94.2% car, 0.5% public transportation, 2.0% walk, 2.5% work from home; Median travel time to work: 26.2 minutes
Presidential Election: 65.7% Obama, 33.9% Romney (2012)
Additional Information Contacts
Bertie Government . . . . (252) 794-5300
  http://www.co.bertie.nc.us

Bertie County Communities

ASKEWVILLE (town). Covers a land area of 0.489 square miles and a water area of 0 square miles. Located at 36.11° N. Lat; 76.94° W. Long. Elevation is 62 feet.
Population: 241; Growth (since 2000): 33.9%; Density: 492.8 persons per square mile; Race: 95.9% White, 2.9% Black/African American, 0.4% Asian, 0.0% American Indian/Alaska Native, 0.0% Native Hawaiian/Other Pacific Islander, 0.8% Two or more races, 0.0% Hispanic of any race; Average household size: 2.41; Median age: 43.4; Age under 18: 22.4%; Age 65 and over: 18.7%; Males per 100 females: 104.2
Housing: Homeownership rate: 80.0%; Homeowner vacancy rate: 0.0%; Rental vacancy rate: 13.0%

AULANDER (town). Covers a land area of 1.477 square miles and a water area of 0 square miles. Located at 36.23° N. Lat; 77.11° W. Long. Elevation is 66 feet.
Population: 895; Growth (since 2000): 0.8%; Density: 605.9 persons per square mile; Race: 43.7% White, 55.0% Black/African American, 0.1% Asian, 0.1% American Indian/Alaska Native, 0.0% Native Hawaiian/Other Pacific Islander, 1.1% Two or more races, 0.6% Hispanic of any race; Average household size: 2.35; Median age: 42.5; Age under 18: 23.4%; Age 65 and over: 17.8%; Males per 100 females: 81.5
School District(s)
Bertie County Schools (PK-12)
  2012-13 Enrollment: 2,850 . . . . (252) 794-6060
Housing: Homeownership rate: 63.3%; Homeowner vacancy rate: 3.2%; Rental vacancy rate: 3.5%
Safety: Violent crime rate: 11.7 per 10,000 population; Property crime rate: 245.0 per 10,000 population

COLERAIN (town). Covers a land area of 0.263 square miles and a water area of 0 square miles. Located at 36.20° N. Lat; 76.77° W. Long. Elevation is 59 feet.
Population: 204; Growth (since 2000): -7.7%; Density: 776.0 persons per square mile; Race: 90.2% White, 6.4% Black/African American, 0.0% Asian, 0.0% American Indian/Alaska Native, 0.0% Native Hawaiian/Other Pacific Islander, 0.5% Two or more races, 4.9% Hispanic of any race; Average household size: 2.29; Median age: 49.0; Age under 18: 19.6%; Age 65 and over: 24.5%; Males per 100 females: 98.1
School District(s)
Bertie County Schools (PK-12)
  2012-13 Enrollment: 2,850 . . . . (252) 794-6060
Housing: Homeownership rate: 79.7%; Homeowner vacancy rate: 2.7%; Rental vacancy rate: 25.0%

KELFORD (town). Covers a land area of 0.482 square miles and a water area of 0 square miles. Located at 36.18° N. Lat; 77.22° W. Long. Elevation is 92 feet.
Population: 251; Growth (since 2000): 2.4%; Density: 520.5 persons per square mile; Race: 23.1% White, 75.7% Black/African American, 0.0% Asian, 0.0% American Indian/Alaska Native, 0.0% Native Hawaiian/Other Pacific Islander, 1.2% Two or more races, 0.0% Hispanic of any race; Average household size: 2.56; Median age: 39.3; Age under 18: 23.5%; Age 65 and over: 18.3%; Males per 100 females: 87.3
Housing: Homeownership rate: 70.4%; Homeowner vacancy rate: 4.2%; Rental vacancy rate: 25.0%

LEWISTON WOODVILLE (town). Covers a land area of 1.956 square miles and a water area of 0.013 square miles. Located at 36.11° N. Lat; 77.18° W. Long. Elevation is 75 feet.
Population: 549; Growth (since 2000): -10.4%; Density: 280.7 persons per square mile; Race: 14.0% White, 81.6% Black/African American, 1.3% Asian, 0.5% American Indian/Alaska Native, 1.1% Native Hawaiian/Other Pacific Islander, 0.4% Two or more races, 2.0% Hispanic of any race; Average household size: 2.50; Median age: 36.9; Age under 18: 29.7%; Age 65 and over: 11.3%; Males per 100 females: 80.6
School District(s)
Bertie County Schools (PK-12)
  2012-13 Enrollment: 2,850 . . . . (252) 794-6060
Housing: Homeownership rate: 65.4%; Homeowner vacancy rate: 5.3%; Rental vacancy rate: 9.5%

MERRY HILL (unincorporated postal area)

ZCTA: 27957

Covers a land area of 42.495 square miles and a water area of 10.157 square miles. Located at 36.07° N. Lat; 76.76° W. Long. Elevation is 36 feet.

Population: 1,356; Growth (since 2000): 26.3%; Density: 31.9 persons per square mile; Race: 54.9% White, 44.3% Black/African American, 0.1% Asian, 0.1% American Indian/Alaska Native, 0.0% Native Hawaiian/Other Pacific Islander, 0.4% Two or more races, 0.3% Hispanic of any race; Average household size: 2.34; Median age: 48.4; Age under 18: 17.5%; Age 65 and over: 20.5%; Males per 100 females: 93.4

Housing: Homeownership rate: 81.9%; Homeowner vacancy rate: 1.6%; Rental vacancy rate: 12.5%

POWELLSVILLE (town). Covers a land area of 0.357 square miles and a water area of 0 square miles. Located at 36.23° N. Lat; 76.93° W. Long. Elevation is 66 feet.

Population: 276; Growth (since 2000): 6.6%; Density: 773.8 persons per square mile; Race: 37.3% White, 59.4% Black/African American, 0.0% Asian, 1.1% American Indian/Alaska Native, 0.0% Native Hawaiian/Other Pacific Islander, 0.0% Two or more races, 3.6% Hispanic of any race; Average household size: 2.11; Median age: 47.1; Age under 18: 19.2%; Age 65 and over: 21.4%; Males per 100 females: 75.8

Housing: Homeownership rate: 71.8%; Homeowner vacancy rate: 1.1%; Rental vacancy rate: 11.9%

ROXOBEL (town). Covers a land area of 1.043 square miles and a water area of 0 square miles. Located at 36.20° N. Lat; 77.24° W. Long. Elevation is 92 feet.

Population: 240; Growth (since 2000): -8.7%; Density: 230.1 persons per square mile; Race: 54.2% White, 45.8% Black/African American, 0.0% Asian, 0.0% American Indian/Alaska Native, 0.0% Native Hawaiian/Other Pacific Islander, 0.0% Two or more races, 0.4% Hispanic of any race; Average household size: 2.16; Median age: 50.0; Age under 18: 17.5%; Age 65 and over: 22.5%; Males per 100 females: 98.3

Housing: Homeownership rate: 72.9%; Homeowner vacancy rate: 1.2%; Rental vacancy rate: 11.8%

WINDSOR (town). County seat. Covers a land area of 2.833 square miles and a water area of 0 square miles. Located at 35.99° N. Lat; 76.94° W. Long. Elevation is 7 feet.

History: Windsor, on the Chasie River, was a port of entry before the Civil War. The three main streets were named King, Queen, and York, and the cross streets were named for the various Lords Proprietors, according to the plan drawn in England. Windsor became the seat of Bertie County in 1750.

Population: 3,630; Growth (since 2000): 59.0%; Density: 1,281.3 persons per square mile; Race: 32.8% White, 62.6% Black/African American, 2.0% Asian, 0.7% American Indian/Alaska Native, 0.0% Native Hawaiian/Other Pacific Islander, 1.8% Two or more races, 1.1% Hispanic of any race; Average household size: 2.29; Median age: 38.6; Age under 18: 15.3%; Age 65 and over: 16.5%; Males per 100 females: 145.8; Marriage status: 38.5% never married, 38.8% now married, 4.6% separated, 9.0% widowed, 13.8% divorced; Foreign born: 1.5%; Speak English only: 96.6%; With disability: 23.7%; Veterans: 7.0%; Ancestry: 6.4% American, 5.3% English, 4.9% Irish, 1.4% German, 1.0% European

Employment: 9.1% management, business, and financial, 1.3% computer, engineering, and science, 7.7% education, legal, community service, arts, and media, 9.0% healthcare practitioners, 21.2% service, 14.7% sales and office, 8.0% natural resources, construction, and maintenance, 28.8% production, transportation, and material moving

Income: Per capita: $16,054; Median household: $27,284; Average household: $45,066; Households with income of $100,000 or more: 11.0%; Poverty rate: 25.4%

Educational Attainment: High school diploma or higher: 67.7%; Bachelor's degree or higher: 15.8%; Graduate/professional degree or higher: 5.3%

School District(s)

Bertie County Schools (PK-12)

2012-13 Enrollment: 2,850 . . . . (252) 794-6060

Housing: Homeownership rate: 61.2%; Median home value: $87,400; Median year structure built: 1966; Homeowner vacancy rate: 1.6%; Median gross rent: $489 per month; Rental vacancy rate: 6.2%

Health Insurance: 86.4% have insurance; 51.1% have private insurance; 50.2% have public insurance; 13.6% do not have insurance; 1.4% of children under 18 do not have insurance

Hospitals: Vidant Bertie Hospital (15 beds)

Safety: Violent crime rate: 28.1 per 10,000 population; Property crime rate: 145.9 per 10,000 population

Newspapers: Bertie Ledger Advance (weekly circulation 4500)

Transportation: Commute: 96.2% car, 0.0% public transportation, 1.7% walk, 1.0% work from home; Median travel time to work: 23.8 minutes

Bladen County

Located in southeastern North Carolina, on the coastal plain; bounded on the east by the South River; crossed by the Cape Fear River. Covers a land area of 874.328 square miles, a water area of 12.830 square miles, and is located in the Eastern Time Zone at 34.59° N. Lat., 78.54° W. Long. The county was founded in 1734. County seat is Elizabethtown.

Population: 35,190; Growth (since 2000): 9.0%; Density: 40.2 persons per square mile; Race: 56.3% White, 34.9% Black/African American, 0.2% Asian, 2.1% American Indian/Alaska Native, 0.0% Native Hawaiian/Other Pacific Islander, 1.5% two or more races, 7.1% Hispanic of any race; Average household size: 2.40; Median age: 41.3; Age under 18: 23.1%; Age 65 and over: 15.6%; Males per 100 females: 92.3; Marriage status: 31.3% never married, 49.8% now married, 4.4% separated, 9.5% widowed, 9.4% divorced; Foreign born: 4.6%; Speak English only: 93.6%; With disability: 21.4%; Veterans: 8.0%; Ancestry: 14.9% American, 6.7% English, 4.9% Irish, 3.2% Scotch-Irish, 3.1% German

Religion: Six largest groups: 27.0% Baptist, 20.4% Methodist/Pietist, 1.8% Presbyterian-Reformed, 1.8% Pentecostal, 1.3% Non-denominational Protestant, 0.7% Adventist

Economy: Unemployment rate: 8.2%; Leading industries: 17.7% retail trade; 13.1% other services (except public administration); 11.1% health care and social assistance; Farms: 492 totaling 117,323 acres; Company size: 1 employs 1,000 or more persons, 0 employ 500 to 999 persons, 7 employ 100 to 499 persons, 505 employ less than 100 persons; Business ownership: 662 women-owned, n/a Black-owned, n/a Hispanic-owned, n/a Asian-owned

Employment: 10.2% management, business, and financial, 1.5% computer, engineering, and science, 9.4% education, legal, community service, arts, and media, 4.7% healthcare practitioners, 16.4% service, 17.7% sales and office, 19.6% natural resources, construction, and maintenance, 20.4% production, transportation, and material moving

Income: Per capita: $19,154; Median household: $30,164; Average household: $45,090; Households with income of $100,000 or more: 7.9%; Poverty rate: 25.8%

Educational Attainment: High school diploma or higher: 74.7%; Bachelor's degree or higher: 10.5%; Graduate/professional degree or higher: 2.9%

Housing: Homeownership rate: 72.4%; Median home value: $81,800; Median year structure built: 1981; Homeowner vacancy rate: 1.2%; Median gross rent: $593 per month; Rental vacancy rate: 11.6%

Vital Statistics: Birth rate: 97.9 per 10,000 population; Death rate: 118.2 per 10,000 population; Age-adjusted cancer mortality rate: 146.3 deaths per 100,000 population

Health Insurance: 81.6% have insurance; 50.7% have private insurance; 43.7% have public insurance, 18.4% do not have insurance; 10.6% of children under 18 do not have insurance

Health Care: Physicians: 3.7 per 10,000 population; Hospital beds: 7.4 per 10,000 population; Hospital admissions: 265.0 per 10,000 population

Transportation: Commute: 95.4% car, 0.2% public transportation, 2.0% walk, 2.3% work from home; Median travel time to work: 25.5 minutes

Presidential Election: 50.5% Obama, 48.6% Romney (2012)

National and State Parks: Bay Tree Lake State Park; Bladen Lakes State Forest; Jones Lake State Park; Singletary Lake State Park

Additional Information Contacts

Bladen Government . . . . (910) 872-6330
   http://www.bladeninfo.org

Bladen County Communities

BLADENBORO (town). Covers a land area of 2.215 square miles and a water area of 0 square miles. Located at 34.54° N. Lat; 78.79° W. Long. Elevation is 105 feet.
Population: 1,750; Growth (since 2000): 1.9%; Density: 790.0 persons per square mile; Race: 73.2% White, 23.5% Black/African American, 0.4% Asian, 1.0% American Indian/Alaska Native, 0.0% Native Hawaiian/Other Pacific Islander, 1.4% Two or more races, 2.1% Hispanic of any race; Average household size: 2.19; Median age: 40.7; Age under 18: 26.2%; Age 65 and over: 18.3%; Males per 100 females: 78.0
School District(s)
Bladen County Schools (PK-12)
 2012-13 Enrollment: 5,233 . . . . (910) 862-4136
Housing: Homeownership rate: 55.7%; Homeowner vacancy rate: 1.5%; Rental vacancy rate: 10.7%

BUTTERS (CDP). Covers a land area of 1.313 square miles and a water area of 0.009 square miles. Located at 34.56° N. Lat; 78.84° W. Long. Elevation is 115 feet.
Population: 294; Growth (since 2000): 12.6%; Density: 223.9 persons per square mile; Race: 93.5% White, 4.4% Black/African American, 0.0% Asian, 0.0% American Indian/Alaska Native, 0.0% Native Hawaiian/Other Pacific Islander, 0.7% Two or more races, 2.7% Hispanic of any race; Average household size: 2.43; Median age: 41.6; Age under 18: 21.4%; Age 65 and over: 12.6%; Males per 100 females: 79.3
Housing: Homeownership rate: 80.2%; Homeowner vacancy rate: 1.0%; Rental vacancy rate: 3.7%

CLARKTON (town). Covers a land area of 1.244 square miles and a water area of 0.007 square miles. Located at 34.49° N. Lat; 78.66° W. Long. Elevation is 95 feet.
History: Settled c.1760.
Population: 837; Growth (since 2000): 18.7%; Density: 672.7 persons per square mile; Race: 48.0% White, 44.4% Black/African American, 0.2% Asian, 1.2% American Indian/Alaska Native, 0.1% Native Hawaiian/Other Pacific Islander, 2.4% Two or more races, 5.1% Hispanic of any race; Average household size: 2.53; Median age: 38.8; Age under 18: 25.3%; Age 65 and over: 13.7%; Males per 100 females: 83.6
School District(s)
Bladen County Schools (PK-12)
 2012-13 Enrollment: 5,233 . . . . (910) 862-4136
Housing: Homeownership rate: 57.8%; Homeowner vacancy rate: 4.0%; Rental vacancy rate: 11.2%

COUNCIL (unincorporated postal area)
ZCTA: 28434
 Covers a land area of 80.862 square miles and a water area of 0.687 square miles. Located at 34.47° N. Lat; 78.47° W. Long. Elevation is 69 feet.
 Population: 1,329; Growth (since 2000): -23.8%; Density: 16.4 persons per square mile; Race: 32.2% White, 53.5% Black/African American, 0.0% Asian, 12.1% American Indian/Alaska Native, 0.0% Native Hawaiian/Other Pacific Islander, 1.4% Two or more races, 1.2% Hispanic of any race; Average household size: 2.22; Median age: 48.3; Age under 18: 18.0%; Age 65 and over: 19.8%; Males per 100 females: 91.8
 Housing: Homeownership rate: 82.6%; Homeowner vacancy rate: 0.2%; Rental vacancy rate: 5.0%

DUBLIN (town). Covers a land area of 0.435 square miles and a water area of 0 square miles. Located at 34.66° N. Lat; 78.72° W. Long. Elevation is 131 feet.
Population: 338; Growth (since 2000): 35.2%; Density: 776.7 persons per square mile; Race: 66.9% White, 19.5% Black/African American, 0.0% Asian, 1.5% American Indian/Alaska Native, 0.0% Native Hawaiian/Other Pacific Islander, 3.0% Two or more races, 10.9% Hispanic of any race; Average household size: 2.58; Median age: 38.8; Age under 18: 28.1%; Age 65 and over: 16.0%; Males per 100 females: 94.3
School District(s)
Bladen County Schools (PK-12)
 2012-13 Enrollment: 5,233 . . . . (910) 862-4136

Two-year College(s)
Bladen Community College (Public)
 Fall 2013 Enrollment: 1,199 . . . . (910) 879-5500
 2013-14 Tuition: In-state $2,361; Out-of-state $8,505
Housing: Homeownership rate: 62.6%; Homeowner vacancy rate: 0.0%; Rental vacancy rate: 3.8%

EAST ARCADIA (town). Covers a land area of 2.182 square miles and a water area of 0 square miles. Located at 34.38° N. Lat; 78.32° W. Long. Elevation is 59 feet.
Population: 487; Growth (since 2000): -7.1%; Density: 223.2 persons per square mile; Race: 4.3% White, 90.1% Black/African American, 0.0% Asian, 2.1% American Indian/Alaska Native, 0.0% Native Hawaiian/Other Pacific Islander, 3.5% Two or more races, 1.8% Hispanic of any race; Average household size: 2.56; Median age: 38.1; Age under 18: 27.5%; Age 65 and over: 13.6%; Males per 100 females: 82.4
Housing: Homeownership rate: 66.9%; Homeowner vacancy rate: 0.0%; Rental vacancy rate: 1.6%

ELIZABETHTOWN (town). County seat. Covers a land area of 4.648 square miles and a water area of 0.034 square miles. Located at 34.62° N. Lat; 78.61° W. Long. Elevation is 108 feet.
History: Elizabethtown was settled by Scottish, English, and Irish soon after the county had been formed in 1734, and in 1773 it was named for Queen Elizabeth.
Population: 3,583; Growth (since 2000): -3.1%; Density: 770.9 persons per square mile; Race: 43.7% White, 51.0% Black/African American, 0.7% Asian, 0.5% American Indian/Alaska Native, 0.0% Native Hawaiian/Other Pacific Islander, 1.6% Two or more races, 4.1% Hispanic of any race; Average household size: 2.09; Median age: 44.8; Age under 18: 20.7%; Age 65 and over: 21.5%; Males per 100 females: 80.2; Marriage status: 39.2% never married, 32.7% now married, 3.8% separated, 17.0% widowed, 11.1% divorced; Foreign born: 8.0%; Speak English only: 92.2%; With disability: 22.5%; Veterans: 5.3%; Ancestry: 10.3% American, 7.8% Irish, 6.1% English, 5.2% German, 2.4% Scottish
Employment: 8.1% management, business, and financial, 1.3% computer, engineering, and science, 11.5% education, legal, community service, arts, and media, 6.7% healthcare practitioners, 20.1% service, 21.0% sales and office, 22.9% natural resources, construction, and maintenance, 8.4% production, transportation, and material moving
Income: Per capita: $18,265; Median household: $20,698; Average household: $39,631; Households with income of $100,000 or more: 6.5%; Poverty rate: 39.3%
Educational Attainment: High school diploma or higher: 77.5%; Bachelor's degree or higher: 17.0%; Graduate/professional degree or higher: 3.2%
School District(s)
Bladen County Schools (PK-12)
 2012-13 Enrollment: 5,233 . . . . (910) 862-4136
Housing: Homeownership rate: 50.0%; Median home value: $93,900; Median year structure built: 1979; Homeowner vacancy rate: 2.2%; Median gross rent: $335 per month; Rental vacancy rate: 13.0%
Health Insurance: 86.3% have insurance; 51.9% have private insurance; 48.6% have public insurance; 13.7% do not have insurance; 0.0% of children under 18 do not have insurance
Hospitals: Cape Fear Valley - Bladen County Hospital (35 beds)
Newspapers: Bladen Journal (weekly circulation 4800)
Transportation: Commute: 100.0% car, 0.0% public transportation, 0.0% walk, 0.0% work from home; Median travel time to work: 24.8 minutes
Airports: Curtis L Brown Jr Field (general aviation)
Additional Information Contacts
Town of Elizabethtown . . . . (910) 862-2066
 http://www.elizabethtownnc.org

KELLY (CDP). Covers a land area of 11.592 square miles and a water area of 0 square miles. Located at 34.46° N. Lat; 78.31° W. Long. Elevation is 26 feet.
Population: 544; Growth (since 2000): 19.8%; Density: 46.9 persons per square mile; Race: 54.0% White, 43.0% Black/African American, 0.0% Asian, 0.9% American Indian/Alaska Native, 0.0% Native Hawaiian/Other Pacific Islander, 1.3% Two or more races, 2.2% Hispanic of any race; Average household size: 2.05; Median age: 48.8; Age under 18: 18.6%; Age 65 and over: 18.2%; Males per 100 females: 100.0
Housing: Homeownership rate: 79.7%; Homeowner vacancy rate: 1.4%; Rental vacancy rate: 8.2%

TAR HEEL (town). Covers a land area of 0.172 square miles and a water area of 0 square miles. Located at 34.73° N. Lat; 78.79° W. Long. Elevation is 128 feet.
Population: 117; Growth (since 2000): 67.1%; Density: 679.4 persons per square mile; Race: 91.5% White, 0.0% Black/African American, 0.0% Asian, 1.7% American Indian/Alaska Native, 0.0% Native Hawaiian/Other Pacific Islander, 1.7% Two or more races, 5.1% Hispanic of any race; Average household size: 1.95; Median age: 54.3; Age under 18: 11.1%; Age 65 and over: 23.1%; Males per 100 females: 88.7
School District(s)
Bladen County Schools (PK-12)
   2012-13 Enrollment: 5,233 . . . . (910) 862-4136
Housing: Homeownership rate: 73.4%; Homeowner vacancy rate: 0.0%; Rental vacancy rate: 5.9%

WHITE LAKE (town). Covers a land area of 0.984 square miles and a water area of 1.640 square miles. Located at 34.65° N. Lat; 78.49° W. Long. Elevation is 69 feet.
Population: 802; Growth (since 2000): 51.6%; Density: 815.2 persons per square mile; Race: 86.8% White, 5.2% Black/African American, 0.4% Asian, 0.5% American Indian/Alaska Native, 0.0% Native Hawaiian/Other Pacific Islander, 1.0% Two or more races, 8.7% Hispanic of any race; Average household size: 2.28; Median age: 44.7; Age under 18: 19.3%; Age 65 and over: 17.2%; Males per 100 females: 101.5
Housing: Homeownership rate: 65.5%; Homeowner vacancy rate: 9.4%; Rental vacancy rate: 15.7%

WHITE OAK (CDP). Covers a land area of 5.108 square miles and a water area of 0 square miles. Located at 34.74° N. Lat; 78.72° W. Long. Elevation is 56 feet.
Population: 338; Growth (since 2000): 11.2%; Density: 66.2 persons per square mile; Race: 58.3% White, 31.7% Black/African American, 0.0% Asian, 0.3% American Indian/Alaska Native, 0.0% Native Hawaiian/Other Pacific Islander, 0.6% Two or more races, 10.7% Hispanic of any race; Average household size: 2.52; Median age: 40.9; Age under 18: 24.9%; Age 65 and over: 13.0%; Males per 100 females: 87.8
Housing: Homeownership rate: 83.6%; Homeowner vacancy rate: 4.2%; Rental vacancy rate: 24.1%

Brunswick County

Located in southeastern North Carolina; bounded on the east by the Cape Fear River, on the south by the Atlantic Ocean, on the southwest by South Carolina, and on the west by the Waccamaw River; includes Smith Island. Covers a land area of 846.973 square miles, a water area of 202.851 square miles, and is located in the Eastern Time Zone at 34.04° N. Lat., 78.23° W. Long. The county was founded in 1764. County seat is Bolivia.

Brunswick County is part of the Myrtle Beach-Conway-North Myrtle Beach, SC-NC Metropolitan Statistical Area. The entire metro area includes: Brunswick County, NC; Horry County, SC

Weather Station: Longwood											Elevation: 40 feet	
	Jan	Feb	Mar	Apr	May	Jun	Jul	Aug	Sep	Oct	Nov	Dec
High	56	60	66	74	81	86	89	88	83	76	68	59
Low	33	35	40	48	56	66	70	69	62	51	42	35
Precip	4.0	3.5	4.1	3.1	3.4	5.0	5.6	7.0	6.8	3.7	3.3	3.8
Snow	0.2	0.1	0.7	0.0	0.0	0.0	0.0	0.0	0.0	0.0	0.0	0.7

High and Low temperatures in degrees Fahrenheit; Precipitation and Snow in inches

Weather Station: Southport 5 N											Elevation: 20 feet	
	Jan	Feb	Mar	Apr	May	Jun	Jul	Aug	Sep	Oct	Nov	Dec
High	57	59	66	73	80	86	89	88	84	76	69	60
Low	33	36	42	50	58	67	72	70	64	52	44	36
Precip	4.2	3.7	4.3	2.9	3.6	4.4	5.9	6.9	8.4	4.2	3.6	4.0
Snow	tr	0.0	0.3	0.0	0.0	0.0	0.0	0.0	0.0	0.0	0.0	0.5

High and Low temperatures in degrees Fahrenheit; Precipitation and Snow in inches

Population: 107,431; Growth (since 2000): 46.9%; Density: 126.8 persons per square mile; Race: 83.0% White, 11.4% Black/African American, 0.5% Asian, 0.7% American Indian/Alaska Native, 0.0% Native Hawaiian/Other Pacific Islander, 1.8% two or more races, 5.2% Hispanic of any race; Average household size: 2.30; Median age: 47.4; Age under 18: 18.8%; Age 65 and over: 21.4%; Males per 100 females: 96.1; Marriage status: 19.9% never married, 61.3% now married, 3.0% separated, 7.3% widowed, 11.4% divorced; Foreign born: 4.2%; Speak English only: 93.7%;

With disability: 16.1%; Veterans: 14.9%; Ancestry: 14.0% American, 13.9% German, 13.6% Irish, 12.4% English, 5.6% Italian
Religion: Six largest groups: 13.7% Baptist, 8.1% Methodist/Pietist, 5.4% Catholicism, 3.0% Non-denominational Protestant, 1.4% Presbyterian-Reformed, 1.0% Latter-day Saints
Economy: Unemployment rate: 6.0%; Leading industries: 16.4% retail trade; 12.8% construction; 12.1% accommodation and food services; Farms: 254 totaling 45,442 acres; Company size: 0 employ 1,000 or more persons, 1 employs 500 to 999 persons, 28 employ 100 to 499 persons, 2,207 employ less than 100 persons; Business ownership: 3,373 women-owned, 572 Black-owned, 265 Hispanic-owned, 136 Asian-owned
Employment: 12.5% management, business, and financial, 2.9% computer, engineering, and science, 9.0% education, legal, community service, arts, and media, 6.0% healthcare practitioners, 20.4% service, 24.6% sales and office, 12.9% natural resources, construction, and maintenance, 11.6% production, transportation, and material moving
Income: Per capita: $26,839; Median household: $46,438; Average household: $61,517; Households with income of $100,000 or more: 16.1%; Poverty rate: 16.6%
Educational Attainment: High school diploma or higher: 86.3%; Bachelor's degree or higher: 25.1%; Graduate/professional degree or higher: 8.7%
Housing: Homeownership rate: 77.2%; Median home value: $186,600; Median year structure built: 1994; Homeowner vacancy rate: 5.7%; Median gross rent: $860 per month; Rental vacancy rate: 22.7%
Vital Statistics: Birth rate: 88.0 per 10,000 population; Death rate: 105.4 per 10,000 population; Age-adjusted cancer mortality rate: 182.8 deaths per 100,000 population
Health Insurance: 84.5% have insurance; 63.5% have private insurance; 40.8% have public insurance; 15.5% do not have insurance; 7.6% of children under 18 do not have insurance
Health Care: Physicians: 8.3 per 10,000 population; Hospital beds: 12.9 per 10,000 population; Hospital admissions: 411.2 per 10,000 population
Transportation: Commute: 92.4% car, 0.5% public transportation, 1.0% walk, 4.5% work from home; Median travel time to work: 23.3 minutes
Presidential Election: 38.4% Obama, 60.6% Romney (2012)
National and State Parks: Brunswick Town State Historic Site
Additional Information Contacts
Brunswick Government . . . . (910) 253-2000
   http://www.brunsco.net

Brunswick County Communities

ASH (unincorporated postal area)
ZCTA: 28420
   Covers a land area of 140.452 square miles and a water area of 0.278 square miles. Located at 34.07° N. Lat; 78.48° W. Long. Elevation is 49 feet.
Population: 3,886; Growth (since 2000): 5.8%; Density: 27.7 persons per square mile; Race: 78.2% White, 10.8% Black/African American, 0.1% Asian, 1.1% American Indian/Alaska Native, 0.0% Native Hawaiian/Other Pacific Islander, 1.6% Two or more races, 12.1% Hispanic of any race; Average household size: 2.58; Median age: 38.5; Age under 18: 26.2%; Age 65 and over: 13.7%; Males per 100 females: 101.0; Marriage status: 22.1% never married, 64.6% now married, 5.4% separated, 8.9% widowed, 4.5% divorced; Foreign born: 7.8%; Speak English only: 86.1%; With disability: 17.9%; Veterans: 5.9%; Ancestry: 32.0% American, 10.3% German, 8.2% English, 7.2% Irish, 1.4% British
Employment: 5.1% management, business, and financial, 2.5% computer, engineering, and science, 9.1% education, legal, community service, arts, and media, 4.5% healthcare practitioners, 30.8% service, 18.9% sales and office, 19.8% natural resources, construction, and maintenance, 9.3% production, transportation, and material moving
Income: Per capita: $17,604; Median household: $35,061; Average household: $44,510; Households with income of $100,000 or more: 7.6%; Poverty rate: 14.7%
Educational Attainment: High school diploma or higher: 74.9%; Bachelor's degree or higher: 9.7%; Graduate/professional degree or higher: 0.4%
School District(s)
Brunswick County Schools (PK-12)
   2012-13 Enrollment: 12,436 . . . . (910) 253-2900
Housing: Homeownership rate: 74.7%; Median home value: $100,200; Median year structure built: 1988; Homeowner vacancy rate: 1.6%; Median gross rent: $756 per month; Rental vacancy rate: 11.7%

Health Insurance: 78.0% have insurance; 50.8% have private insurance; 39.5% have public insurance; 22.0% do not have insurance; 3.1% of children under 18 do not have insurance
Transportation: Commute: 93.4% car, 0.0% public transportation, 0.0% walk, 0.6% work from home; Median travel time to work: 28.3 minutes

BALD HEAD ISLAND (village). Covers a land area of 3.867 square miles and a water area of 1.905 square miles. Located at 33.86° N. Lat; 77.99° W. Long. Elevation is 10 feet.
Population: 158; Growth (since 2000): -8.7%; Density: 40.9 persons per square mile; Race: 93.7% White, 0.0% Black/African American, 2.5% Asian, 1.3% American Indian/Alaska Native, 0.0% Native Hawaiian/Other Pacific Islander, 1.3% Two or more races, 3.2% Hispanic of any race; Average household size: 1.90; Median age: 64.0; Age under 18: 0.6%; Age 65 and over: 43.7%; Males per 100 females: 105.2
Housing: Homeownership rate: 93.9%; Homeowner vacancy rate: 9.2%; Rental vacancy rate: 78.6%
Additional Information Contacts
Village of Bald Head Island . . . . (910) 457-9700
  http://www.villagebhi.org

BELVILLE (town). Covers a land area of 1.653 square miles and a water area of 0.193 square miles. Located at 34.22° N. Lat; 78.00° W. Long. Elevation is 3 feet.
Population: 1,936; Growth (since 2000): 579.3%; Density: 1,171.5 persons per square mile; Race: 77.1% White, 17.3% Black/African American, 1.0% Asian, 0.4% American Indian/Alaska Native, 0.1% Native Hawaiian/Other Pacific Islander, 2.1% Two or more races, 4.9% Hispanic of any race; Average household size: 2.60; Median age: 35.0; Age under 18: 26.5%; Age 65 and over: 8.3%; Males per 100 females: 99.6
Housing: Homeownership rate: 85.9%; Homeowner vacancy rate: 3.2%; Rental vacancy rate: 6.3%

BOILING SPRING LAKES (city). Covers a land area of 23.292 square miles and a water area of 0.697 square miles. Located at 34.04° N. Lat; 78.07° W. Long. Elevation is 52 feet.
History: Orton Plantation Gardens and Brunswick Town State Historic Site to Northeast.
Population: 5,372; Growth (since 2000): 80.8%; Density: 230.6 persons per square mile; Race: 92.0% White, 4.2% Black/African American, 0.5% Asian, 0.4% American Indian/Alaska Native, 0.1% Native Hawaiian/Other Pacific Islander, 1.9% Two or more races, 2.7% Hispanic of any race; Average household size: 2.53; Median age: 41.2; Age under 18: 23.2%; Age 65 and over: 13.9%; Males per 100 females: 97.3; Marriage status: 23.5% never married, 56.6% now married, 2.0% separated, 8.8% widowed, 11.2% divorced; Foreign born: 2.5%; Speak English only: 98.2%; With disability: 14.8%; Veterans: 19.4%; Ancestry: 21.4% German, 17.8% Irish, 12.8% American, 12.6% English, 8.8% Scottish
Employment: 15.8% management, business, and financial, 2.3% computer, engineering, and science, 8.1% education, legal, community service, arts, and media, 2.5% healthcare practitioners, 25.2% service, 17.9% sales and office, 14.2% natural resources, construction, and maintenance, 14.2% production, transportation, and material moving
Income: Per capita: $22,058; Median household: $43,504; Average household: $49,942; Households with income of $100,000 or more: 8.4%; Poverty rate: 13.6%
Educational Attainment: High school diploma or higher: 91.2%; Bachelor's degree or higher: 17.8%; Graduate/professional degree or higher: 5.1%
Housing: Homeownership rate: 82.3%; Median home value: $170,900; Median year structure built: 1998; Homeowner vacancy rate: 4.1%; Median gross rent: $944 per month; Rental vacancy rate: 8.7%
Health Insurance: 84.7% have insurance; 68.7% have private insurance; 32.0% have public insurance; 15.3% do not have insurance; 6.0% of children under 18 do not have insurance
Safety: Violent crime rate: 18.0 per 10,000 population; Property crime rate: 176.7 per 10,000 population
Transportation: Commute: 97.1% car, 0.0% public transportation, 0.0% walk, 2.1% work from home; Median travel time to work: 25.7 minutes
Additional Information Contacts
City of Boiling Spring Lakes . . . . (910) 845-2614
  http://www.boilingspringlakes.com

BOLIVIA (town). County seat. Covers a land area of 0.636 square miles and a water area of 0 square miles. Located at 34.07° N. Lat; 78.15° W. Long. Elevation is 39 feet.
Population: 143; Growth (since 2000): -3.4%; Density: 224.7 persons per square mile; Race: 88.8% White, 8.4% Black/African American, 0.0% Asian, 0.0% American Indian/Alaska Native, 0.0% Native Hawaiian/Other Pacific Islander, 2.8% Two or more races, 0.0% Hispanic of any race; Average household size: 2.38; Median age: 46.2; Age under 18: 21.7%; Age 65 and over: 23.8%; Males per 100 females: 107.2
School District(s)
Brunswick County Schools (PK-12)
  2012-13 Enrollment: 12,436 . . . . (910) 253-2900
Two-year College(s)
Brunswick Community College (Public)
  Fall 2013 Enrollment: 1,809 . . . . (910) 755-7300
  2013-14 Tuition: In-state $2,388; Out-of-state $8,532
Housing: Homeownership rate: 75.0%; Homeowner vacancy rate: 0.0%; Rental vacancy rate: 11.8%

CALABASH (town). Covers a land area of 3.335 square miles and a water area of 0.341 square miles. Located at 33.90° N. Lat; 78.56° W. Long. Elevation is 49 feet.
Population: 1,786; Growth (since 2000): 151.2%; Density: 535.6 persons per square mile; Race: 86.3% White, 5.9% Black/African American, 0.0% Asian, 0.4% American Indian/Alaska Native, 0.1% Native Hawaiian/Other Pacific Islander, 1.6% Two or more races, 14.5% Hispanic of any race; Average household size: 2.09; Median age: 50.8; Age under 18: 16.2%; Age 65 and over: 29.9%; Males per 100 females: 100.0
Housing: Homeownership rate: 70.3%; Homeowner vacancy rate: 3.8%; Rental vacancy rate: 10.5%
Additional Information Contacts
Town of Calabash . . . . (910) 579-6747
  http://townofcalabash.net

CAROLINA SHORES (town). Covers a land area of 2.556 square miles and a water area of 0.004 square miles. Located at 33.91° N. Lat; 78.57° W. Long. Elevation is 46 feet.
Population: 3,048; Growth (since 2000): 105.7%; Density: 1,192.3 persons per square mile; Race: 95.9% White, 1.6% Black/African American, 0.5% Asian, 0.3% American Indian/Alaska Native, 0.1% Native Hawaiian/Other Pacific Islander, 0.9% Two or more races, 2.1% Hispanic of any race; Average household size: 1.96; Median age: 64.9; Age under 18: 7.2%; Age 65 and over: 49.6%; Males per 100 females: 87.8; Marriage status: 8.3% never married, 65.3% now married, 2.1% separated, 12.9% widowed, 13.5% divorced; Foreign born: 2.6%; Speak English only: 94.1%; With disability: 20.4%; Veterans: 27.9%; Ancestry: 24.6% Irish, 23.2% German, 18.0% Italian, 15.3% English, 5.8% Polish
Employment: 13.5% management, business, and financial, 0.0% computer, engineering, and science, 5.2% education, legal, community service, arts, and media, 13.1% healthcare practitioners, 17.6% service, 36.7% sales and office, 12.3% natural resources, construction, and maintenance, 1.5% production, transportation, and material moving
Income: Per capita: $28,716; Median household: $49,497; Average household: $53,314; Households with income of $100,000 or more: 11.8%; Poverty rate: 9.2%
Educational Attainment: High school diploma or higher: 94.0%; Bachelor's degree or higher: 21.0%; Graduate/professional degree or higher: 9.3%
Housing: Homeownership rate: 91.2%; Median home value: $201,300; Median year structure built: 1997; Homeowner vacancy rate: 6.3%; Median gross rent: $1,116 per month; Rental vacancy rate: 9.2%
Health Insurance: 92.1% have insurance; 80.2% have private insurance; 55.3% have public insurance; 7.9% do not have insurance; 9.7% of children under 18 do not have insurance
Transportation: Commute: 92.0% car, 0.0% public transportation, 3.0% walk, 5.0% work from home; Median travel time to work: 23.7 minutes

CASWELL BEACH (town). Covers a land area of 2.930 square miles and a water area of 1.115 square miles. Located at 33.91° N. Lat; 78.05° W. Long. Elevation is 13 feet.
History: Formerly Fort Caswell.
Population: 398; Growth (since 2000): 7.6%; Density: 135.9 persons per square mile; Race: 97.2% White, 0.0% Black/African American, 0.8% Asian, 0.5% American Indian/Alaska Native, 0.0% Native Hawaiian/Other Pacific Islander, 0.3% Two or more races, 1.8% Hispanic of any race;

Average household size: 1.90; Median age: 63.0; Age under 18: 6.0%; Age 65 and over: 43.0%; Males per 100 females: 85.1
Housing: Homeownership rate: 91.9%; Homeowner vacancy rate: 3.5%; Rental vacancy rate: 76.1%
Additional Information Contacts
Town of Caswell Beach........................... (910) 278-5471
  http://www.caswellbeach.org

HOLDEN BEACH (town). Covers a land area of 2.710 square miles and a water area of 0.708 square miles. Located at 33.91° N. Lat; 78.32° W. Long. Elevation is 3 feet.
Population: 575; Growth (since 2000): -26.9%; Density: 212.2 persons per square mile; Race: 96.9% White, 0.9% Black/African American, 0.0% Asian, 0.2% American Indian/Alaska Native, 0.0% Native Hawaiian/Other Pacific Islander, 0.7% Two or more races, 2.4% Hispanic of any race; Average household size: 1.94; Median age: 62.1; Age under 18: 6.4%; Age 65 and over: 39.3%; Males per 100 females: 93.6
Housing: Homeownership rate: 84.2%; Homeowner vacancy rate: 6.7%; Rental vacancy rate: 85.5%
Additional Information Contacts
Town of Holden Beach .... (910) 842-6488
  http://www.hbtownhall.com

LELAND (town). Covers a land area of 19.781 square miles and a water area of 0.091 square miles. Located at 34.19° N. Lat; 78.01° W. Long. Elevation is 23 feet.
Population: 13,527; Growth (since 2000): 598.0%; Density: 683.8 persons per square mile; Race: 83.9% White, 10.0% Black/African American, 1.5% Asian, 0.6% American Indian/Alaska Native, 0.0% Native Hawaiian/Other Pacific Islander, 2.0% Two or more races, 4.9% Hispanic of any race; Average household size: 2.32; Median age: 38.9; Age under 18: 20.4%; Age 65 and over: 15.0%; Males per 100 females: 93.2; Marriage status: 18.8% never married, 65.3% now married, 2.6% separated, 3.8% widowed, 12.1% divorced; Foreign born: 5.7%; Speak English only: 90.9%; With disability: 11.6%; Veterans: 12.9%; Ancestry: 14.8% German, 14.1% American, 13.4% Irish, 10.7% English, 7.3% Italian
Employment: 17.0% management, business, and financial, 6.0% computer, engineering, and science, 10.9% education, legal, community service, arts, and media, 8.6% healthcare practitioners, 12.7% service, 23.1% sales and office, 9.7% natural resources, construction, and maintenance, 12.1% production, transportation, and material moving
Income: Per capita: $32,228; Median household: $64,471; Average household: $74,818; Households with income of $100,000 or more: 26.3%; Poverty rate: 9.0%
Educational Attainment: High school diploma or higher: 92.8%; Bachelor's degree or higher: 41.0%; Graduate/professional degree or higher: 14.8%
School District(s)
Brunswick County Schools (PK-12)
  2012-13 Enrollment: 12,436 .... (910) 253-2900
Charter Day School (KG-08)
  2012-13 Enrollment: 924......................... (910) 655-1214
Housing: Homeownership rate: 76.4%; Median home value: $197,600; Median year structure built: 2004; Homeowner vacancy rate: 4.0%; Median gross rent: $957 per month; Rental vacancy rate: 10.2%
Health Insurance: 87.3% have insurance; 74.5% have private insurance; 25.9% have public insurance; 12.7% do not have insurance; 4.6% of children under 18 do not have insurance
Safety: Violent crime rate: 15.4 per 10,000 population; Property crime rate: 252.3 per 10,000 population
Transportation: Commute: 92.2% car, 0.0% public transportation, 0.0% walk, 5.0% work from home; Median travel time to work: 23.7 minutes
Additional Information Contacts
Town of Leland .... (910) 371-0148
  http://townofleland.com

LONGWOOD (unincorporated postal area)
ZCTA: 28452
  Covers a land area of 5.821 square miles and a water area of 0.002 square miles. Located at 33.99° N. Lat; 78.55° W. Long. Elevation is 46 feet.
  Population: 694; Growth (since 2000): 92.8%; Density: 119.2 persons per square mile; Race: 43.7% White, 53.3% Black/African American, 0.0% Asian, 0.7% American Indian/Alaska Native, 0.0% Native Hawaiian/Other Pacific Islander, 1.0% Two or more races, 3.0%

Hispanic of any race; Average household size: 2.63; Median age: 38.3; Age under 18: 26.7%; Age 65 and over: 10.7%; Males per 100 females: 89.1
  Housing: Homeownership rate: 78.4%; Homeowner vacancy rate: 1.0%; Rental vacancy rate: 9.5%

NAVASSA (town). Covers a land area of 13.339 square miles and a water area of 0.484 square miles. Located at 34.28° N. Lat; 78.04° W. Long. Elevation is 20 feet.
Population: 1,505; Growth (since 2000): 214.2%; Density: 112.8 persons per square mile; Race: 27.1% White, 63.6% Black/African American, 0.1% Asian, 0.5% American Indian/Alaska Native, 0.0% Native Hawaiian/Other Pacific Islander, 3.8% Two or more races, 10.0% Hispanic of any race; Average household size: 2.64; Median age: 36.0; Age under 18: 25.4%; Age 65 and over: 11.6%; Males per 100 females: 100.7
Housing: Homeownership rate: 77.0%; Homeowner vacancy rate: 1.6%; Rental vacancy rate: 20.6%

NORTHWEST (city). Covers a land area of 7.010 square miles and a water area of 0 square miles. Located at 34.31° N. Lat; 78.15° W. Long. Elevation is 59 feet.
Population: 735; Growth (since 2000): 9.5%; Density: 104.8 persons per square mile; Race: 29.9% White, 66.7% Black/African American, 0.3% Asian, 0.0% American Indian/Alaska Native, 0.0% Native Hawaiian/Other Pacific Islander, 1.5% Two or more races, 3.3% Hispanic of any race; Average household size: 2.55; Median age: 43.1; Age under 18: 23.5%; Age 65 and over: 15.4%; Males per 100 females: 96.5
Housing: Homeownership rate: 75.7%; Homeowner vacancy rate: 1.3%; Rental vacancy rate: 10.3%

OAK ISLAND (town). Covers a land area of 18.516 square miles and a water area of 1.397 square miles. Located at 33.93° N. Lat; 78.08° W. Long. Elevation is 7 feet.
Population: 6,783; Growth (since 2000): 3.2%; Density: 366.3 persons per square mile; Race: 96.7% White, 0.6% Black/African American, 0.3% Asian, 0.6% American Indian/Alaska Native, 0.0% Native Hawaiian/Other Pacific Islander, 1.2% Two or more races, 1.4% Hispanic of any race; Average household size: 2.10; Median age: 52.6; Age under 18: 13.8%; Age 65 and over: 24.5%; Males per 100 females: 96.3; Marriage status: 17.9% never married, 56.7% now married, 3.5% separated, 8.7% widowed, 16.8% divorced; Foreign born: 2.8%; Speak English only: 97.2%; With disability: 14.4%; Veterans: 14.0%; Ancestry: 16.8% American, 15.9% Irish, 14.5% English, 12.4% German, 6.9% French
Employment: 16.3% management, business, and financial, 3.4% computer, engineering, and science, 11.1% education, legal, community service, arts, and media, 8.4% healthcare practitioners, 19.8% service, 22.4% sales and office, 11.7% natural resources, construction, and maintenance, 7.0% production, transportation, and material moving
Income: Per capita: $30,208; Median household: $47,369; Average household: $61,036; Households with income of $100,000 or more: 15.6%; Poverty rate: 8.9%
Educational Attainment: High school diploma or higher: 92.4%; Bachelor's degree or higher: 31.7%; Graduate/professional degree or higher: 11.9%
Housing: Homeownership rate: 70.7%; Median home value: $243,200; Median year structure built: 1988; Homeowner vacancy rate: 12.0%; Median gross rent: $954 per month; Rental vacancy rate: 27.1%
Health Insurance: 80.3% have insurance; 66.1% have private insurance; 39.9% have public insurance; 19.7% do not have insurance; 9.0% of children under 18 do not have insurance
Safety: Violent crime rate: 38.2 per 10,000 population; Property crime rate: 358.2 per 10,000 population
Transportation: Commute: 92.6% car, 1.3% public transportation, 0.6% walk, 2.2% work from home; Median travel time to work: 26.9 minutes
Additional Information Contacts
Town of Oak Island .... (910) 278-5011
  http://www.oakislandnc.com

OCEAN ISLE BEACH (town). Covers a land area of 3.386 square miles and a water area of 1.142 square miles. Located at 33.90° N. Lat; 78.44° W. Long. Elevation is 3 feet.
Population: 550; Growth (since 2000): 29.1%; Density: 162.4 persons per square mile; Race: 96.2% White, 0.2% Black/African American, 1.3% Asian, 0.0% American Indian/Alaska Native, 0.0% Native Hawaiian/Other Pacific Islander, 0.7% Two or more races, 3.5% Hispanic of any race;

Average household size: 1.97; Median age: 58.9; Age under 18: 9.5%; Age 65 and over: 32.0%; Males per 100 females: 105.2
Housing: Homeownership rate: 87.5%; Homeowner vacancy rate: 10.1%; Rental vacancy rate: 89.8%
Additional Information Contacts
Town of Ocean Isle Beach . . . . (910) 579-2166
  http://www.oibgov.com

SAINT JAMES (town). Covers a land area of 8.259 square miles and a water area of 0.038 square miles. Located at 33.95° N. Lat; 78.11° W. Long. Elevation is 10 feet.
Population: 3,165; Growth (since 2000): 293.7%; Density: 383.2 persons per square mile; Race: 97.8% White, 1.0% Black/African American, 0.6% Asian, 0.1% American Indian/Alaska Native, 0.0% Native Hawaiian/Other Pacific Islander, 0.3% Two or more races, 0.9% Hispanic of any race; Average household size: 2.01; Median age: 65.0; Age under 18: 2.5%; Age 65 and over: 49.8%; Males per 100 females: 96.7; Marriage status: 2.5% never married, 89.7% now married, 0.0% separated, 4.9% widowed, 2.9% divorced; Foreign born: 7.1%; Speak English only: 94.6%; With disability: 14.8%; Veterans: 20.0%; Ancestry: 25.1% German, 23.4% Irish, 19.3% English, 8.9% American, 6.2% Italian
Employment: 21.3% management, business, and financial, 2.1% computer, engineering, and science, 8.5% education, legal, community service, arts, and media, 6.4% healthcare practitioners, 9.8% service, 44.2% sales and office, 3.7% natural resources, construction, and maintenance, 4.2% production, transportation, and material moving
Income: Per capita: $67,955; Median household: $85,857; Average household: $132,391; Households with income of $100,000 or more: 43.0%; Poverty rate: 1.0%
Educational Attainment: High school diploma or higher: 97.1%; Bachelor's degree or higher: 55.9%; Graduate/professional degree or higher: 22.5%
Housing: Homeownership rate: 95.7%; Median home value: $450,000; Median year structure built: 2002; Homeowner vacancy rate: 4.0%; Median gross rent: $1,588 per month; Rental vacancy rate: 35.5%
Health Insurance: 98.7% have insurance; 90.5% have private insurance; 55.5% have public insurance; 1.3% do not have insurance; 0.0% of children under 18 do not have insurance
Transportation: Commute: 72.2% car, 0.0% public transportation, 11.7% walk, 16.2% work from home; Median travel time to work: 19.8 minutes

SANDY CREEK (town). Covers a land area of 1.265 square miles and a water area of 0 square miles. Located at 34.28° N. Lat; 78.15° W. Long. Elevation is 36 feet.
Population: 260; Growth (since 2000): 5.7%; Density: 205.6 persons per square mile; Race: 90.0% White, 5.0% Black/African American, 0.8% Asian, 0.4% American Indian/Alaska Native, 0.0% Native Hawaiian/Other Pacific Islander, 3.1% Two or more races, 1.2% Hispanic of any race; Average household size: 2.83; Median age: 37.3; Age under 18: 26.5%; Age 65 and over: 6.9%; Males per 100 females: 111.4
Housing: Homeownership rate: 81.6%; Homeowner vacancy rate: 1.3%; Rental vacancy rate: 5.6%

SHALLOTTE (town). Covers a land area of 9.289 square miles and a water area of 0.068 square miles. Located at 33.97° N. Lat; 78.38° W. Long. Elevation is 16 feet.
History: In 1729, the settlement now known as Shallotte was called Shelote.
Population: 3,675; Growth (since 2000): 166.1%; Density: 395.6 persons per square mile; Race: 85.2% White, 9.3% Black/African American, 1.3% Asian, 0.6% American Indian/Alaska Native, 0.1% Native Hawaiian/Other Pacific Islander, 1.6% Two or more races, 4.8% Hispanic of any race; Average household size: 2.24; Median age: 43.9; Age under 18: 20.6%; Age 65 and over: 22.4%; Males per 100 females: 85.9; Marriage status: 20.9% never married, 58.1% now married, 1.7% separated, 10.5% widowed, 10.5% divorced; Foreign born: 1.9%; Speak English only: 98.3%; With disability: 18.3%; Veterans: 14.1%; Ancestry: 18.5% American, 11.8% English, 10.9% Irish, 10.5% German, 6.6% Italian
Employment: 5.8% management, business, and financial, 2.3% computer, engineering, and science, 2.9% education, legal, community service, arts, and media, 15.0% healthcare practitioners, 31.1% service, 26.2% sales and office, 0.7% natural resources, construction, and maintenance, 16.0% production, transportation, and material moving

Income: Per capita: $23,899; Median household: $44,815; Average household: $57,670; Households with income of $100,000 or more: 21.0%; Poverty rate: 12.6%
Educational Attainment: High school diploma or higher: 88.2%; Bachelor's degree or higher: 24.9%; Graduate/professional degree or higher: 7.0%
School District(s)
Brunswick County Schools (PK-12)
  2012-13 Enrollment: 12,436 . . . . (910) 253-2900
Housing: Homeownership rate: 59.9%; Median home value: $193,700; Median year structure built: 2001; Homeowner vacancy rate: 9.2%; Median gross rent: $866 per month; Rental vacancy rate: 8.1%
Health Insurance: 89.7% have insurance; 69.9% have private insurance; 34.4% have public insurance; 10.3% do not have insurance; 3.0% of children under 18 do not have insurance
Safety: Violent crime rate: 52.1 per 10,000 population; Property crime rate: 547.3 per 10,000 population
Newspapers: Brunswick Beacon (weekly circulation 17000); Brunswick Co. News (weekly circulation 8000)
Transportation: Commute: 95.5% car, 0.7% public transportation, 0.7% walk, 2.6% work from home; Median travel time to work: 18.6 minutes

SOUTHPORT (city). Covers a land area of 3.751 square miles and a water area of 0.027 square miles. Located at 33.92° N. Lat; 78.03° W. Long. Elevation is 16 feet.
History: Southport was founded by Benjamin Smith (later to be governor of North Carolina in 1810-1811) in 1792, and was called Smithville. The present name was adopted in 1889.
Population: 2,833; Growth (since 2000): 20.5%; Density: 755.3 persons per square mile; Race: 82.2% White, 15.4% Black/African American, 0.1% Asian, 0.1% American Indian/Alaska Native, 0.0% Native Hawaiian/Other Pacific Islander, 1.3% Two or more races, 2.9% Hispanic of any race; Average household size: 2.04; Median age: 55.9; Age under 18: 14.0%; Age 65 and over: 31.2%; Males per 100 females: 86.3; Marriage status: 17.4% never married, 49.3% now married, 7.7% separated, 13.7% widowed, 19.6% divorced; Foreign born: 1.4%; Speak English only: 97.4%; With disability: 22.1%; Veterans: 16.9%; Ancestry: 20.0% Irish, 19.1% German, 19.0% English, 11.1% American, 6.3% Scottish
Employment: 12.9% management, business, and financial, 1.2% computer, engineering, and science, 19.5% education, legal, community service, arts, and media, 3.8% healthcare practitioners, 13.1% service, 26.2% sales and office, 6.3% natural resources, construction, and maintenance, 17.0% production, transportation, and material moving
Income: Per capita: $26,583; Median household: $40,647; Average household: $53,485; Households with income of $100,000 or more: 14.8%; Poverty rate: 23.0%
Educational Attainment: High school diploma or higher: 87.0%; Bachelor's degree or higher: 36.7%; Graduate/professional degree or higher: 15.7%
School District(s)
Brunswick County Schools (PK-12)
  2012-13 Enrollment: 12,436 . . . . (910) 253-2900
Housing: Homeownership rate: 67.7%; Median home value: $245,800; Median year structure built: 1987; Homeowner vacancy rate: 10.2%; Median gross rent: $1,020 per month; Rental vacancy rate: 18.0%
Health Insurance: 88.0% have insurance; 60.1% have private insurance; 48.9% have public insurance; 12.0% do not have insurance; 0.0% of children under 18 do not have insurance
Hospitals: J Arthur Dosher Memorial Hospital (64 beds)
Newspapers: State Port Pilot (weekly circulation 7800)
Transportation: Commute: 85.4% car, 4.7% public transportation, 3.4% walk, 5.2% work from home; Median travel time to work: 18.3 minutes
Airports: Cape Fear Regional Jetport/Howie Franklin Field (general aviation)
Additional Information Contacts
City of Southport . . . . (910) 457-5574
  http://www.cityofsouthport.com

SUNSET BEACH (town). Covers a land area of 6.447 square miles and a water area of 0.897 square miles. Located at 33.89° N. Lat; 78.51° W. Long. Elevation is 12 feet.
Population: 3,572; Growth (since 2000): 95.8%; Density: 554.0 persons per square mile; Race: 96.8% White, 0.8% Black/African American, 0.6% Asian, 0.4% American Indian/Alaska Native, 0.0% Native Hawaiian/Other Pacific Islander, 0.8% Two or more races, 1.9% Hispanic of any race;

Average household size: 1.91; Median age: 64.0; Age under 18: 6.3%; Age 65 and over: 46.4%; Males per 100 females: 91.7; Marriage status: 7.7% never married, 80.1% now married, 1.3% separated, 5.9% widowed, 6.4% divorced; Foreign born: 3.3%; Speak English only: 96.9%; With disability: 12.4%; Veterans: 24.9%; Ancestry: 19.6% Irish, 18.8% English, 15.0% German, 14.8% American, 9.6% Italian
Employment: 19.8% management, business, and financial, 0.7% computer, engineering, and science, 11.7% education, legal, community service, arts, and media, 4.8% healthcare practitioners, 22.0% service, 29.7% sales and office, 7.3% natural resources, construction, and maintenance, 4.1% production, transportation, and material moving
Income: Per capita: $42,655; Median household: $54,900; Average household: $83,587; Households with income of $100,000 or more: 25.8%; Poverty rate: 13.2%
Educational Attainment: High school diploma or higher: 92.1%; Bachelor's degree or higher: 45.2%; Graduate/professional degree or higher: 13.4%
Housing: Homeownership rate: 88.3%; Median home value: $273,100; Median year structure built: 1995; Homeowner vacancy rate: 7.7%; Median gross rent: $779 per month; Rental vacancy rate: 73.9%
Health Insurance: 94.9% have insurance; 74.3% have private insurance; 64.6% have public insurance; 5.1% do not have insurance; 0.0% of children under 18 do not have insurance
Safety: Violent crime rate: 2.7 per 10,000 population; Property crime rate: 264.4 per 10,000 population
Transportation: Commute: 73.1% car, 0.0% public transportation, 0.8% walk, 16.6% work from home; Median travel time to work: 19.0 minutes
Additional Information Contacts
Town of Sunset Beach . . . . (910) 579-6297
    http://sunsetbeachnc.gov

SUPPLY (unincorporated postal area)
ZCTA: 28462
    Covers a land area of 93.391 square miles and a water area of 2.457 square miles. Located at 34.03° N. Lat; 78.29° W. Long. Elevation is 26 feet.
    Population: 11,680; Growth (since 2000): 18.9%; Density: 125.1 persons per square mile; Race: 84.3% White, 11.4% Black/African American, 0.2% Asian, 1.0% American Indian/Alaska Native, 0.0% Native Hawaiian/Other Pacific Islander, 1.6% Two or more races, 3.9% Hispanic of any race; Average household size: 2.28; Median age: 48.2; Age under 18: 18.9%; Age 65 and over: 21.7%; Males per 100 females: 95.7; Marriage status: 20.6% never married, 61.9% now married, 2.3% separated, 6.9% widowed, 10.6% divorced; Foreign born: 2.1%; Speak English only: 96.8%; With disability: 19.3%; Veterans: 14.9%; Ancestry: 18.0% American, 14.3% Irish, 11.9% German, 11.9% English, 3.8% French
    Employment: 11.3% management, business, and financial, 1.7% computer, engineering, and science, 5.5% education, legal, community service, arts, and media, 4.8% healthcare practitioners, 16.8% service, 30.8% sales and office, 17.8% natural resources, construction, and maintenance, 11.4% production, transportation, and material moving
    Income: Per capita: $25,045; Median household: $35,497; Average household: $54,209; Households with income of $100,000 or more: 8.5%; Poverty rate: 20.5%
    Educational Attainment: High school diploma or higher: 80.1%; Bachelor's degree or higher: 16.0%; Graduate/professional degree or higher: 5.0%
School District(s)
Brunswick County Schools (PK-12)
    2012-13 Enrollment: 12,436 . . . . (910) 253-2900
    Housing: Homeownership rate: 77.3%; Median home value: $156,200; Median year structure built: 1989; Homeowner vacancy rate: 8.1%; Median gross rent: $660 per month; Rental vacancy rate: 24.6%
    Health Insurance: 82.9% have insurance; 57.8% have private insurance; 45.3% have public insurance; 17.1% do not have insurance; 7.0% of children under 18 do not have insurance
Hospitals: Novant Health Brunswick Medical Center (60 beds)
    Transportation: Commute: 90.5% car, 0.0% public transportation, 1.5% walk, 6.5% work from home; Median travel time to work: 25.2 minutes

VARNAMTOWN (town). Covers a land area of 0.907 square miles and a water area of 0.061 square miles. Located at 33.95° N. Lat; 78.23° W. Long. Elevation is 26 feet.
Population: 541; Growth (since 2000): 12.5%; Density: 596.6 persons per square mile; Race: 97.6% White, 0.9% Black/African American, 0.0% Asian, 0.0% American Indian/Alaska Native, 0.0% Native Hawaiian/Other Pacific Islander, 0.6% Two or more races, 1.5% Hispanic of any race; Average household size: 2.39; Median age: 47.8; Age under 18: 17.7%; Age 65 and over: 23.5%; Males per 100 females: 103.4
Housing: Homeownership rate: 88.1%; Homeowner vacancy rate: 0.0%; Rental vacancy rate: 12.9%

WINNABOW (unincorporated postal area)
ZCTA: 28479
    Covers a land area of 91.326 square miles and a water area of 13.646 square miles. Located at 34.10° N. Lat; 78.02° W. Long. Elevation is 26 feet.
    Population: 4,903; Growth (since 2000): 70.9%; Density: 53.7 persons per square mile; Race: 83.0% White, 12.2% Black/African American, 0.8% Asian, 0.7% American Indian/Alaska Native, 0.0% Native Hawaiian/Other Pacific Islander, 2.1% Two or more races, 2.9% Hispanic of any race; Average household size: 2.44; Median age: 41.3; Age under 18: 21.7%; Age 65 and over: 16.3%; Males per 100 females: 98.0; Marriage status: 19.3% never married, 68.0% now married, 4.7% separated, 5.3% widowed, 7.5% divorced; Foreign born: 1.7%; Speak English only: 96.2%; With disability: 10.6%; Veterans: 10.7%; Ancestry: 18.5% American, 12.8% German, 12.5% Irish, 9.1% English, 6.2% Italian
    Employment: 13.2% management, business, and financial, 10.1% computer, engineering, and science, 8.6% education, legal, community service, arts, and media, 1.8% healthcare practitioners, 12.2% service, 27.9% sales and office, 10.7% natural resources, construction, and maintenance, 15.5% production, transportation, and material moving
    Income: Per capita: $23,481; Median household: $52,003; Average household: $61,504; Households with income of $100,000 or more: 15.6%; Poverty rate: 15.5%
    Educational Attainment: High school diploma or higher: 89.0%; Bachelor's degree or higher: 24.9%; Graduate/professional degree or higher: 4.0%
School District(s)
Brunswick County Schools (PK-12)
    2012-13 Enrollment: 12,436 . . . . (910) 253-2900
    Housing: Homeownership rate: 76.0%; Median home value: $181,400; Median year structure built: 1999; Homeowner vacancy rate: 3.4%; Median gross rent: $732 per month; Rental vacancy rate: 10.0%
    Health Insurance: 90.6% have insurance; 69.9% have private insurance; 33.0% have public insurance; 9.4% do not have insurance; 5.3% of children under 18 do not have insurance
    Transportation: Commute: 96.2% car, 0.0% public transportation, 0.6% walk, 0.4% work from home; Median travel time to work: 25.2 minutes

Buncombe County

Located in western North Carolina, in the Blue Ridge; includes the Black Mountains and Pisgah National Forest in the east; crossed by the French Broad River. Covers a land area of 656.672 square miles, a water area of 3.469 square miles, and is located in the Eastern Time Zone at 35.61° N. Lat., 82.53° W. Long. The county was founded in 1792. County seat is Asheville.

Buncombe County is part of the Asheville, NC Metropolitan Statistical Area. The entire metro area includes: Buncombe County, NC; Haywood County, NC; Henderson County, NC; Madison County, NC

Weather Station: Asheville   Elevation: 2,240 feet

	Jan	Feb	Mar	Apr	May	Jun	Jul	Aug	Sep	Oct	Nov	Dec
High	47	50	58	67	75	82	85	84	77	68	58	49
Low	28	31	37	45	53	61	64	64	57	46	38	31
Precip	2.8	3.1	3.4	3.1	3.3	3.4	3.3	3.4	3.3	2.2	2.9	2.7
Snow	4.1	2.7	2.1	1.1	tr	tr	0.0	0.0	0.0	tr	0.4	2.2

High and Low temperatures in degrees Fahrenheit; Precipitation and Snow in inches

Weather Station: Asheville Regional Arpt   Elevation: 2,140 feet

	Jan	Feb	Mar	Apr	May	Jun	Jul	Aug	Sep	Oct	Nov	Dec
High	48	51	59	68	75	81	84	83	77	68	59	50
Low	27	29	36	43	51	59	64	63	56	45	36	29
Precip	3.6	3.7	4.0	3.4	3.7	4.8	4.3	4.4	3.9	2.9	3.6	3.6
Snow	4.1	2.5	2.1	0.8	tr	tr	tr	tr	0.0	tr	0.1	1.6

High and Low temperatures in degrees Fahrenheit; Precipitation and Snow in inches

Weather Station: Bent Creek   Elevation: 2,109 feet

	Jan	Feb	Mar	Apr	May	Jun	Jul	Aug	Sep	Oct	Nov	Dec
High	48	52	60	69	76	82	84	83	78	69	59	50
Low	26	28	34	41	50	58	62	61	55	44	35	28
Precip	3.8	3.8	4.6	3.8	3.8	4.5	4.5	4.0	4.5	3.0	4.1	3.4
Snow	2.5	1.4	1.1	0.5	0.0	0.0	0.0	0.0	0.0	tr	0.0	0.4

High and Low temperatures in degrees Fahrenheit; Precipitation and Snow in inches

Weather Station: Black Mountain 2 W   Elevation: 2,290 feet

	Jan	Feb	Mar	Apr	May	Jun	Jul	Aug	Sep	Oct	Nov	Dec
High	49	52	60	68	75	81	84	83	77	69	60	51
Low	26	29	34	41	49	57	61	61	54	44	35	28
Precip	3.5	3.6	4.1	3.8	4.1	4.6	3.8	3.9	4.4	3.1	3.6	3.4
Snow	2.6	2.0	1.2	0.6	0.0	0.0	0.0	0.0	0.0	0.0	0.1	1.5

High and Low temperatures in degrees Fahrenheit; Precipitation and Snow in inches

Weather Station: Swannanoa 2 SSE   Elevation: 4,319 feet

	Jan	Feb	Mar	Apr	May	Jun	Jul	Aug	Sep	Oct	Nov	Dec
High	41	44	52	61	68	73	76	75	69	61	52	44
Low	24	27	32	41	49	56	60	59	53	44	35	27
Precip	4.1	4.0	4.6	4.1	3.8	4.7	4.6	4.7	4.6	3.4	4.1	3.5
Snow	7.6	6.3	5.1	3.8	0.5	0.0	0.0	0.0	0.0	0.1	1.1	4.5

High and Low temperatures in degrees Fahrenheit; Precipitation and Snow in inches

Population: 238,318; Growth (since 2000): 15.5%; Density: 362.9 persons per square mile; Race: 87.4% White, 6.4% Black/African American, 1.0% Asian, 0.4% American Indian/Alaska Native, 0.1% Native Hawaiian/Other Pacific Islander, 2.1% two or more races, 6.0% Hispanic of any race; Average household size: 2.30; Median age: 40.6; Age under 18: 20.5%; Age 65 and over: 16.0%; Males per 100 females: 92.9; Marriage status: 28.9% never married, 50.9% now married, 2.9% separated, 7.1% widowed, 13.1% divorced; Foreign born: 5.7%; Speak English only: 92.6%; With disability: 13.8%; Veterans: 10.6%; Ancestry: 15.5% American, 14.0% German, 14.0% English, 13.1% Irish, 4.8% Scotch-Irish

Religion: Six largest groups: 26.5% Baptist, 6.4% Methodist/Pietist, 4.2% Non-denominational Protestant, 3.8% Catholicism, 3.1% Presbyterian-Reformed, 1.5% Pentecostal

Economy: Unemployment rate: 4.0%; Leading industries: 15.4% retail trade; 11.9% professional, scientific, and technical services; 11.5% health care and social assistance; Farms: 1,060 totaling 71,480 acres; Company size: 2 employ 1,000 or more persons, 10 employ 500 to 999 persons, 133 employ 100 to 499 persons, 7,183 employ less than 100 persons; Business ownership: 8,246 women-owned, 517 Black-owned, 401 Hispanic-owned, 381 Asian-owned

Employment: 13.0% management, business, and financial, 4.4% computer, engineering, and science, 12.9% education, legal, community service, arts, and media, 7.3% healthcare practitioners, 20.0% service, 24.4% sales and office, 8.0% natural resources, construction, and maintenance, 10.0% production, transportation, and material moving

Income: Per capita: $26,159; Median household: $44,713; Average household: $60,714; Households with income of $100,000 or more: 16.0%; Poverty rate: 17.1%

Educational Attainment: High school diploma or higher: 89.0%; Bachelor's degree or higher: 33.8%; Graduate/professional degree or higher: 12.2%

Housing: Homeownership rate: 65.7%; Median home value: $191,200; Median year structure built: 1982; Homeowner vacancy rate: 3.0%; Median gross rent: $806 per month; Rental vacancy rate: 8.9%

Vital Statistics: Birth rate: 103.5 per 10,000 population; Death rate: 97.1 per 10,000 population; Age-adjusted cancer mortality rate: 171.8 deaths per 100,000 population

Health Insurance: 83.4% have insurance; 62.8% have private insurance; 33.6% have public insurance; 16.6% do not have insurance; 6.8% of children under 18 do not have insurance

Health Care: Physicians: 39.8 per 10,000 population; Hospital beds: 51.1 per 10,000 population; Hospital admissions: 1,972.1 per 10,000 population

Air Quality Index: 87.4% good, 12.6% moderate, 0.0% unhealthy for sensitive individuals, 0.0% unhealthy (percent of days)

Transportation: Commute: 89.5% car, 0.7% public transportation, 2.4% walk, 6.2% work from home; Median travel time to work: 20.6 minutes
Presidential Election: 55.2% Obama, 42.9% Romney (2012)
National and State Parks: Pisgah National Forest
Additional Information Contacts
Buncombe Government . . . . (828) 250-4100
  http://www.buncombecounty.org

Buncombe County Communities

ALEXANDER (unincorporated postal area)
ZCTA: 28701

Covers a land area of 17.859 square miles and a water area of 0.480 square miles. Located at 35.71° N. Lat; 82.64° W. Long. Elevation is 1,913 feet.

Population: 3,635; Growth (since 2000): 16.9%; Density: 203.5 persons per square mile; Race: 94.7% White, 0.9% Black/African American, 0.3% Asian, 0.4% American Indian/Alaska Native, 0.1% Native Hawaiian/Other Pacific Islander, 1.5% Two or more races, 3.6% Hispanic of any race; Average household size: 2.52; Median age: 41.6; Age under 18: 22.3%; Age 65 and over: 14.9%; Males per 100 females: 93.1; Marriage status: 21.1% never married, 61.5% now married, 3.8% separated, 8.3% widowed, 9.1% divorced; Foreign born: 1.7%; Speak English only: 96.6%; With disability: 16.3%; Veterans: 10.6%; Ancestry: 15.7% English, 15.3% American, 14.2% Irish, 12.6% German, 4.6% French Canadian

Employment: 16.9% management, business, and financial, 4.3% computer, engineering, and science, 7.7% education, legal, community service, arts, and media, 6.3% healthcare practitioners, 15.6% service, 27.2% sales and office, 9.4% natural resources, construction, and maintenance, 12.6% production, transportation, and material moving

Income: Per capita: $23,281; Median household: $51,027; Average household: $60,586; Households with income of $100,000 or more: 15.3%; Poverty rate: 9.8%

Educational Attainment: High school diploma or higher: 90.0%; Bachelor's degree or higher: 17.8%; Graduate/professional degree or higher: 5.0%

Housing: Homeownership rate: 83.1%; Median home value: $188,900; Median year structure built: 1987; Homeowner vacancy rate: 2.1%; Median gross rent: $648 per month; Rental vacancy rate: 9.5%

Health Insurance: 83.0% have insurance; 58.6% have private insurance; 36.2% have public insurance; 17.0% do not have insurance; 9.9% of children under 18 do not have insurance

Transportation: Commute: 95.1% car, 0.0% public transportation, 0.0% walk, 4.9% work from home; Median travel time to work: 28.4 minutes

ARDEN (unincorporated postal area)
ZCTA: 28704

Covers a land area of 32.945 square miles and a water area of 0.728 square miles. Located at 35.46° N. Lat; 82.58° W. Long. Elevation is 2,218 feet.

Population: 18,821; Growth (since 2000): 27.3%; Density: 571.3 persons per square mile; Race: 84.8% White, 6.3% Black/African American, 2.2% Asian, 0.3% American Indian/Alaska Native, 0.1% Native Hawaiian/Other Pacific Islander, 2.2% Two or more races, 9.8% Hispanic of any race; Average household size: 2.39; Median age: 39.3; Age under 18: 24.3%; Age 65 and over: 13.3%; Males per 100 females: 93.0; Marriage status: 28.0% never married, 53.8% now married, 1.7% separated, 6.4% widowed, 11.8% divorced; Foreign born: 11.8%; Speak English only: 85.9%; With disability: 12.3%; Veterans: 11.1%; Ancestry: 16.2% Irish, 13.7% German, 12.1% American, 11.5% English, 5.1% Italian

Employment: 13.1% management, business, and financial, 6.2% computer, engineering, and science, 11.1% education, legal, community service, arts, and media, 6.6% healthcare practitioners, 20.4% service, 25.0% sales and office, 7.8% natural resources, construction, and maintenance, 9.7% production, transportation, and material moving

Income: Per capita: $29,725; Median household: $60,077; Average household: $74,148; Households with income of $100,000 or more: 21.9%; Poverty rate: 13.5%

Educational Attainment: High school diploma or higher: 91.2%; Bachelor's degree or higher: 36.7%; Graduate/professional degree or higher: 13.5%

School District(s)

Buncombe County Schools (PK-12)
2012-13 Enrollment: 25,824 . . . . (828) 232-4160
Housing: Homeownership rate: 65.3%; Median home value: $198,800;
Median year structure built: 1991; Homeowner vacancy rate: 3.4%;
Median gross rent: $862 per month; Rental vacancy rate: 8.4%
Health Insurance: 85.2% have insurance; 68.9% have private
insurance; 27.0% have public insurance; 14.8% do not have insurance;
7.8% of children under 18 do not have insurance
Transportation: Commute: 94.9% car, 0.2% public transportation, 0.4%
walk, 3.5% work from home; Median travel time to work: 19.5 minutes

ASHEVILLE (city). County seat. Covers a land area of 44.933 square
miles and a water area of 0.299 square miles. Located at 35.57° N. Lat;
82.55° W. Long. Elevation is 2,129 feet.
History: The site of Asheville was a part of the Cherokee hunting ground.
In 1794, John Burton laid out a town tract of 21 acres for the county seat
and named it Morristown in honor of Robert Morris, who helped finance the
American Revolution. Three years later when the settlement was
incorporated it was renamed in honor of Samuel Ashe, governor of North
Carolina (1795-1798).
Population: 83,393; Growth (since 2000): 21.1%; Density: 1,855.9
persons per square mile; Race: 79.3% White, 13.4% Black/African
American, 1.4% Asian, 0.3% American Indian/Alaska Native, 0.2% Native
Hawaiian/Other Pacific Islander, 2.6% Two or more races, 6.5% Hispanic
of any race; Average household size: 2.12; Median age: 38.2; Age under
18: 18.5%; Age 65 and over: 16.3%; Males per 100 females: 89.2;
Marriage status: 35.9% never married, 41.6% now married, 3.4%
separated, 7.6% widowed, 14.9% divorced; Foreign born: 6.9%; Speak
English only: 91.0%; With disability: 13.1%; Veterans: 9.7%; Ancestry:
14.4% German, 14.3% English, 12.5% Irish, 11.7% American, 4.2%
Scotch-Irish
Employment: 13.8% management, business, and financial, 4.9%
computer, engineering, and science, 14.9% education, legal, community
service, arts, and media, 8.1% healthcare practitioners, 21.2% service,
22.8% sales and office, 5.9% natural resources, construction, and
maintenance, 8.5% production, transportation, and material moving
Income: Per capita: $26,912; Median household: $42,016; Average
household: $58,863; Households with income of $100,000 or more: 15.4%;
Poverty rate: 20.0%
Educational Attainment: High school diploma or higher: 90.2%;
Bachelor's degree or higher: 43.3%; Graduate/professional degree or
higher: 15.9%

School District(s)

Asheville City Schools (KG-12)
2012-13 Enrollment: 4,195 . . . . (828) 350-7000
Buncombe County Schools (PK-12)
2012-13 Enrollment: 25,824 . . . . (828) 232-4160
Evergreen Community Charter (KG-08)
2012-13 Enrollment: 407 . . . . (828) 298-2173
Francine Delany New School (KG-08)
2012-13 Enrollment: 162 . . . . (828) 236-9441

Four-year College(s)

Daoist Traditions College of Chinese Medical Arts (Private, For-profit)
Fall 2013 Enrollment: 78 . . . . (828) 225-3993
South College-Asheville (Private, For-profit)
Fall 2013 Enrollment: 256 . . . . (828) 398-2500
2013-14 Tuition: In-state $18,675; Out-of-state $18,675
University of North Carolina at Asheville (Public)
Fall 2013 Enrollment: 3,784 . . . . (828) 251-6600
2013-14 Tuition: In-state $6,241; Out-of-state $20,063

Two-year College(s)

Asheville-Buncombe Technical Community College (Public)
Fall 2013 Enrollment: 8,092 . . . . (828) 254-1921
2013-14 Tuition: In-state $2,003; Out-of-state $7,119

Vocational/Technical School(s)

Carolina College of Hair Design (Private, For-profit)
Fall 2013 Enrollment: 59 . . . . (828) 253-2875
2013-14 Tuition: $9,620
Center for Massage & Natural Health (Private, For-profit)
Fall 2013 Enrollment: 58 . . . . (828) 658-0814
2013-14 Tuition: $5,900
Housing: Homeownership rate: 50.4%; Median home value: $196,300;
Median year structure built: 1972; Homeowner vacancy rate: 3.7%; Median
gross rent: $839 per month; Rental vacancy rate: 7.2%

Health Insurance: 82.3% have insurance; 61.0% have private insurance;
33.4% have public insurance; 17.7% do not have insurance; 6.5% of
children under 18 do not have insurance
Hospitals: Asheville - Oteen VA Medical Center; Memorial Mission
Hospital & Asheville Surgery Center (800 beds)
Newspapers: Asheville Citizen-Times (daily circulation 34000); Mountain
Xpress (weekly circulation 28000); Pisgah Mountain News (weekly
circulation 14000); Tribune Papers (weekly circulation 25000)
Transportation: Commute: 84.4% car, 1.6% public transportation, 4.1%
walk, 8.2% work from home; Median travel time to work: 17.8 minutes
Airports: Asheville Regional (primary service/non-hub)
Additional Information Contacts
City of Asheville . . . . (828) 251-1122
http://www.ashevillenc.gov

AVERY CREEK (CDP). Covers a land area of 1.730 square miles
and a water area of 0 square miles. Located at 35.47° N. Lat; 82.57° W.
Long. Elevation is 2,198 feet.
Population: 1,950; Growth (since 2000): 38.8%; Density: 1,127.4 persons
per square mile; Race: 89.2% White, 3.1% Black/African American, 4.1%
Asian, 0.4% American Indian/Alaska Native, 0.0% Native Hawaiian/Other
Pacific Islander, 2.4% Two or more races, 4.4% Hispanic of any race;
Average household size: 2.61; Median age: 39.0; Age under 18: 26.9%;
Age 65 and over: 11.0%; Males per 100 females: 92.1
Housing: Homeownership rate: 84.0%; Homeowner vacancy rate: 4.4%;
Rental vacancy rate: 4.0%

BARNARDSVILLE (unincorporated postal area)
ZCTA: 28709
Covers a land area of 52.777 square miles and a water area of 0.005
square miles. Located at 35.77° N. Lat; 82.38° W. Long. Elevation is
2,201 feet.
Population: 2,225; Growth (since 2000): 35.1%; Density: 42.2 persons
per square mile; Race: 97.6% White, 0.0% Black/African American,
0.1% Asian, 0.1% American Indian/Alaska Native, 0.0% Native
Hawaiian/Other Pacific Islander, 1.4% Two or more races, 1.2%
Hispanic of any race; Average household size: 2.40; Median age: 45.6;
Age under 18: 20.0%; Age 65 and over: 17.5%; Males per 100 females:
96.4

School District(s)

Buncombe County Schools (PK-12)
2012-13 Enrollment: 25,824 . . . . (828) 232-4160
Housing: Homeownership rate: 74.1%; Homeowner vacancy rate:
2.0%; Rental vacancy rate: 6.9%

BENT CREEK (CDP). Covers a land area of 2.210 square miles and
a water area of 0.008 square miles. Located at 35.51° N. Lat; 82.62° W.
Long. Elevation is 2,201 feet.
Population: 1,287; Growth (since 2000): -7.3%; Density: 582.4 persons
per square mile; Race: 95.6% White, 0.3% Black/African American, 0.9%
Asian, 0.7% American Indian/Alaska Native, 0.0% Native Hawaiian/Other
Pacific Islander, 0.6% Two or more races, 2.9% Hispanic of any race;
Average household size: 2.36; Median age: 43.2; Age under 18: 19.8%;
Age 65 and over: 19.3%; Males per 100 females: 101.1
Housing: Homeownership rate: 80.1%; Homeowner vacancy rate: 0.7%;
Rental vacancy rate: 6.1%

BILTMORE FOREST (town). Covers a land area of 2.911 square
miles and a water area of 0.002 square miles. Located at 35.53° N. Lat;
82.54° W. Long. Elevation is 2,274 feet.
History: Vanderbilt country estate here. Biltmore Homespun Shops (est.
1901 by Mrs. Vanderbilt) keep alive the arts of dyeing, spinning, and
hand-weaving wool into cloth. Biltmore Mansion and Estate on French
Bound River to West.
Population: 1,343; Growth (since 2000): -6.7%; Density: 461.3 persons
per square mile; Race: 98.4% White, 0.4% Black/African American, 0.3%
Asian, 0.0% American Indian/Alaska Native, 0.0% Native Hawaiian/Other
Pacific Islander, 0.8% Two or more races, 1.0% Hispanic of any race;
Average household size: 2.39; Median age: 54.1; Age under 18: 21.7%;
Age 65 and over: 29.2%; Males per 100 females: 96.6
Housing: Homeownership rate: 92.7%; Homeowner vacancy rate: 4.7%;
Rental vacancy rate: 8.9%
Safety: Violent crime rate: 0.0 per 10,000 population; Property crime rate:
93.3 per 10,000 population

Additional Information Contacts

Town of Biltmore Forest . . . . (828) 274-0824
http://www.biltmoreforesttownhall.homestead.com

BLACK MOUNTAIN (town).
Covers a land area of 6.702 square miles and a water area of 0.016 square miles. Located at 35.62° N. Lat; 82.33° W. Long. Elevation is 2,398 feet.

History: Named for the old train stop at the Black Mountain Depot, the town is located at the southern end of the Black Mountain range of the Blue Ridge Mountains in the Southern Appalachians. The first recorded inhabitants of the area were the Cherokee. A road was built through the area in 1850 and a railroad followed in 1879.

Population: 7,848; Growth (since 2000): 4.5%; Density: 1,171.0 persons per square mile; Race: 90.0% White, 6.0% Black/African American, 0.6% Asian, 0.3% American Indian/Alaska Native, 0.0% Native Hawaiian/Other Pacific Islander, 2.3% Two or more races, 2.5% Hispanic of any race; Average household size: 2.13; Median age: 47.7; Age under 18: 18.3%; Age 65 and over: 22.7%; Males per 100 females: 83.7; Marriage status: 23.4% never married, 53.7% now married, 6.0% separated, 9.4% widowed, 13.4% divorced; Foreign born: 1.7%; Speak English only: 96.6%; With disability: 18.8%; Veterans: 13.0%; Ancestry: 16.1% German, 15.1% American, 14.2% English, 13.1% Irish, 5.0% Scotch-Irish

Employment: 12.5% management, business, and financial, 2.1% computer, engineering, and science, 14.1% education, legal, community service, arts, and media, 5.1% healthcare practitioners, 22.4% service, 20.5% sales and office, 7.7% natural resources, construction, and maintenance, 15.6% production, transportation, and material moving

Income: Per capita: $22,822; Median household: $40,185; Average household: $50,955; Households with income of $100,000 or more: 13.1%; Poverty rate: 18.2%

Educational Attainment: High school diploma or higher: 87.4%; Bachelor's degree or higher: 30.3%; Graduate/professional degree or higher: 9.8%

School District(s)
Buncombe County Schools (PK-12)
2012-13 Enrollment: 25,824 . . . . (828) 232-4160

Housing: Homeownership rate: 64.0%; Median home value: $171,600; Median year structure built: 1973; Homeowner vacancy rate: 2.9%; Median gross rent: $786 per month; Rental vacancy rate: 9.2%

Health Insurance: 78.9% have insurance; 54.1% have private insurance; 40.7% have public insurance; 21.1% do not have insurance; 7.3% of children under 18 do not have insurance

Safety: Violent crime rate: 8.7 per 10,000 population; Property crime rate: 147.3 per 10,000 population

Newspapers: Black Mountain News (weekly circulation 3200)

Transportation: Commute: 85.4% car, 0.0% public transportation, 2.8% walk, 8.8% work from home; Median travel time to work: 18.9 minutes

Additional Information Contacts

Town of Black Mountain . . . . (828) 669-2300
http://www.townofblackmountain.org/admin.htm

CANDLER (unincorporated postal area)
ZCTA: 28715

Covers a land area of 77.888 square miles and a water area of 0.146 square miles. Located at 35.51° N. Lat; 82.71° W. Long. Elevation is 2,123 feet.

Population: 24,582; Growth (since 2000): 10.5%; Density: 315.6 persons per square mile; Race: 93.4% White, 1.5% Black/African American, 0.6% Asian, 0.5% American Indian/Alaska Native, 0.0% Native Hawaiian/Other Pacific Islander, 1.6% Two or more races, 5.1% Hispanic of any race; Average household size: 2.45; Median age: 40.2; Age under 18: 23.1%; Age 65 and over: 14.8%; Males per 100 females: 96.3; Marriage status: 22.7% never married, 58.6% now married, 2.5% separated, 6.2% widowed, 12.5% divorced; Foreign born: 6.5%; Speak English only: 90.7%; With disability: 15.8%; Veterans: 10.4%; Ancestry: 20.5% American, 11.7% Irish, 11.1% English, 10.7% German, 4.4% Scotch-Irish

Employment: 9.4% management, business, and financial, 4.2% computer, engineering, and science, 9.7% education, legal, community service, arts, and media, 6.5% healthcare practitioners, 21.3% service, 23.0% sales and office, 12.9% natural resources, construction, and maintenance, 12.9% production, transportation, and material moving

Income: Per capita: $23,600; Median household: $43,690; Average household: $56,138; Households with income of $100,000 or more: 12.5%; Poverty rate: 18.8%

Educational Attainment: High school diploma or higher: 84.5%; Bachelor's degree or higher: 19.0%; Graduate/professional degree or higher: 5.5%

School District(s)
Buncombe County Schools (PK-12)
2012-13 Enrollment: 25,824 . . . . (828) 232-4160

Housing: Homeownership rate: 75.9%; Median home value: $161,900; Median year structure built: 1986; Homeowner vacancy rate: 2.5%; Median gross rent: $721 per month; Rental vacancy rate: 12.3%

Health Insurance: 82.0% have insurance; 59.4% have private insurance; 35.8% have public insurance; 18.0% do not have insurance; 8.5% of children under 18 do not have insurance

Transportation: Commute: 95.9% car, 0.1% public transportation, 0.6% walk, 3.1% work from home; Median travel time to work: 22.6 minutes

---

FAIRVIEW (CDP).
Covers a land area of 6.221 square miles and a water area of 0 square miles. Located at 35.52° N. Lat; 82.40° W. Long. Elevation is 2,224 feet.

Population: 2,678; Growth (since 2000): 7.3%; Density: 430.5 persons per square mile; Race: 94.5% White, 1.2% Black/African American, 0.4% Asian, 0.3% American Indian/Alaska Native, 0.0% Native Hawaiian/Other Pacific Islander, 2.3% Two or more races, 2.7% Hispanic of any race; Average household size: 2.50; Median age: 43.2; Age under 18: 22.5%; Age 65 and over: 14.6%; Males per 100 females: 93.1; Marriage status: 27.0% never married, 60.5% now married, 0.9% separated, 2.2% widowed, 10.3% divorced; Foreign born: 9.6%; Speak English only: 91.9%; With disability: 6.9%; Veterans: 12.4%; Ancestry: 20.4% German, 12.9% Irish, 12.5% English, 10.6% Scotch-Irish, 9.5% French

Employment: 7.2% management, business, and financial, 3.3% computer, engineering, and science, 10.9% education, legal, community service, arts, and media, 6.0% healthcare practitioners, 25.8% service, 24.2% sales and office, 12.3% natural resources, construction, and maintenance, 10.3% production, transportation, and material moving

Income: Per capita: $26,815; Median household: $53,556; Average household: $64,832; Households with income of $100,000 or more: 18.4%; Poverty rate: 3.3%

Educational Attainment: High school diploma or higher: 94.4%; Bachelor's degree or higher: 33.9%; Graduate/professional degree or higher: 13.3%

School District(s)
Buncombe County Schools (PK-12)
2012-13 Enrollment: 25,824 . . . . (828) 232-4160

Housing: Homeownership rate: 80.3%; Median home value: $268,300; Median year structure built: 1991; Homeowner vacancy rate: 2.3%; Median gross rent: $492 per month; Rental vacancy rate: 10.7%

Health Insurance: 78.9% have insurance; 63.1% have private insurance; 33.0% have public insurance; 21.1% do not have insurance; 8.1% of children under 18 do not have insurance

Transportation: Commute: 94.6% car, 0.0% public transportation, 0.0% walk, 5.4% work from home; Median travel time to work: 20.9 minutes

---

LEICESTER (unincorporated postal area)
ZCTA: 28748

Covers a land area of 84.571 square miles and a water area of 0 square miles. Located at 35.65° N. Lat; 82.76° W. Long. Elevation is 2,087 feet.

Population: 11,334; Growth (since 2000): 18.6%; Density: 134.0 persons per square mile; Race: 94.9% White, 1.2% Black/African American, 0.7% Asian, 0.6% American Indian/Alaska Native, 0.0% Native Hawaiian/Other Pacific Islander, 1.3% Two or more races, 3.9% Hispanic of any race; Average household size: 2.51; Median age: 41.0; Age under 18: 22.7%; Age 65 and over: 14.4%; Males per 100 females: 98.1; Marriage status: 29.2% never married, 55.3% now married, 1.7% separated, 5.9% widowed, 9.7% divorced; Foreign born: 2.8%; Speak English only: 96.9%; With disability: 17.1%; Veterans: 10.1%; Ancestry: 22.2% American, 12.6% Irish, 11.3% German, 10.6% English, 3.3% Italian

Employment: 12.2% management, business, and financial, 1.2% computer, engineering, and science, 5.1% education, legal, community service, arts, and media, 7.3% healthcare practitioners, 18.1% service, 27.2% sales and office, 15.4% natural resources, construction, and maintenance, 13.4% production, transportation, and material moving

Income: Per capita: $20,928; Median household: $40,781; Average household: $50,159; Households with income of $100,000 or more: 8.4%; Poverty rate: 16.8%

Educational Attainment: High school diploma or higher: 83.1%; Bachelor's degree or higher: 11.9%; Graduate/professional degree or higher: 3.5%

School District(s)
Buncombe County Schools (PK-12)
    2012-13 Enrollment: 25,824 . . . . (828) 232-4160
Housing: Homeownership rate: 79.2%; Median home value: $153,400; Median year structure built: 1987; Homeowner vacancy rate: 2.1%; Median gross rent: $714 per month; Rental vacancy rate: 11.0%
Health Insurance: 82.0% have insurance; 54.9% have private insurance; 38.8% have public insurance; 18.0% do not have insurance; 4.7% of children under 18 do not have insurance
Transportation: Commute: 96.3% car, 0.0% public transportation, 0.8% walk, 2.6% work from home; Median travel time to work: 26.8 minutes

MONTREAT (town).
Covers a land area of 2.729 square miles and a water area of 0.003 square miles. Located at 35.65° N. Lat; 82.30° W. Long. Elevation is 2,602 feet.
History: Montreat was founded as an assembly grounds for the Presbyterian Church in the United States.
Population: 723; Growth (since 2000): 14.8%; Density: 265.0 persons per square mile; Race: 91.3% White, 5.1% Black/African American, 0.7% Asian, 0.0% American Indian/Alaska Native, 0.1% Native Hawaiian/Other Pacific Islander, 1.4% Two or more races, 2.8% Hispanic of any race; Average household size: 2.04; Median age: 24.2; Age under 18: 4.7%; Age 65 and over: 26.7%; Males per 100 females: 89.3
Four-year College(s)
Montreat College (Private, Not-for-profit, Presbyterian Church (USA))
    Fall 2013 Enrollment: 926 . . . . (828) 669-8012
    2013-14 Tuition: In-state $23,520; Out-of-state $23,520
Housing: Homeownership rate: 80.6%; Homeowner vacancy rate: 4.1%; Rental vacancy rate: 32.8%
Additional Information Contacts
Town of Montreat . . . . (828) 669-3810
    http://www.townofmontreat.org

ROYAL PINES (CDP).
Covers a land area of 2.714 square miles and a water area of 0.004 square miles. Located at 35.48° N. Lat; 82.50° W. Long. Elevation is 2,274 feet.
History: Before the arrival of Europeans, the land where Royal Pines now exists lay within the boundaries of the Cherokee Nation. In 1540, Spanish explorer Hernando de Soto came to the area, bringing the first European visitors in addition to European diseases which seriously depleted the native population. The area was used as an open hunting ground until the middle of the 19th century.
Population: 4,272; Growth (since 2000): -19.9%; Density: 1,574.1 persons per square mile; Race: 91.9% White, 4.4% Black/African American, 1.2% Asian, 0.2% American Indian/Alaska Native, 0.0% Native Hawaiian/Other Pacific Islander, 1.7% Two or more races, 1.8% Hispanic of any race; Average household size: 2.43; Median age: 45.3; Age under 18: 20.9%; Age 65 and over: 15.4%; Males per 100 females: 94.8; Marriage status: 24.4% never married, 59.9% now married, 0.7% separated, 4.1% widowed, 11.7% divorced; Foreign born: 3.5%; Speak English only: 96.2%; With disability: 8.9%; Veterans: 12.0%; Ancestry: 14.8% English, 12.0% German, 12.0% Irish, 11.5% French, 10.3% American
Employment: 14.6% management, business, and financial, 8.0% computer, engineering, and science, 11.6% education, legal, community service, arts, and media, 9.2% healthcare practitioners, 21.8% service, 28.8% sales and office, 2.0% natural resources, construction, and maintenance, 3.9% production, transportation, and material moving
Income: Per capita: $34,416; Median household: $69,088; Average household: $89,158; Households with income of $100,000 or more: 28.2%; Poverty rate: 4.9%
Educational Attainment: High school diploma or higher: 97.7%; Bachelor's degree or higher: 46.4%; Graduate/professional degree or higher: 18.6%
Housing: Homeownership rate: 82.5%; Median home value: $201,600; Median year structure built: 1979; Homeowner vacancy rate: 2.0%; Median gross rent: $951 per month; Rental vacancy rate: 8.3%
Health Insurance: 93.2% have insurance; 83.8% have private insurance; 22.8% have public insurance; 6.8% do not have insurance; 4.8% of children under 18 do not have insurance
Transportation: Commute: 93.7% car, 0.0% public transportation, 0.5% walk, 5.8% work from home; Median travel time to work: 17.9 minutes

SWANNANOA (CDP).
Covers a land area of 6.399 square miles and a water area of 0.034 square miles. Located at 35.60° N. Lat; 82.39° W. Long. Elevation is 2,198 feet.
History: Nearby is Swannanoa Railroad tunnel (1,800 feet long; completed 1879). Seat of Warren Wilson College.
Population: 4,576; Growth (since 2000): 10.7%; Density: 715.1 persons per square mile; Race: 87.8% White, 4.7% Black/African American, 1.3% Asian, 0.7% American Indian/Alaska Native, 0.0% Native Hawaiian/Other Pacific Islander, 2.9% Two or more races, 8.9% Hispanic of any race; Average household size: 2.44; Median age: 38.2; Age under 18: 22.7%; Age 65 and over: 12.6%; Males per 100 females: 94.4; Marriage status: 31.7% never married, 48.6% now married, 2.9% separated, 4.7% widowed, 15.0% divorced; Foreign born: 4.6%; Speak English only: 95.4%; With disability: 20.1%; Veterans: 10.9%; Ancestry: 26.1% American, 15.2% German, 13.7% Irish, 9.2% English, 7.6% Scotch-Irish
Employment: 10.7% management, business, and financial, 4.6% computer, engineering, and science, 7.1% education, legal, community service, arts, and media, 4.2% healthcare practitioners, 27.2% service, 22.1% sales and office, 13.5% natural resources, construction, and maintenance, 10.5% production, transportation, and material moving
Income: Per capita: $19,996; Median household: $37,676; Average household: $46,903; Households with income of $100,000 or more: 6.8%; Poverty rate: 22.9%
Educational Attainment: High school diploma or higher: 84.3%; Bachelor's degree or higher: 14.2%; Graduate/professional degree or higher: 4.6%
School District(s)
Artspace Charter (KG-08)
    2012-13 Enrollment: 382 . . . . (828) 298-2787
Buncombe County Schools (PK-12)
    2012-13 Enrollment: 25,824 . . . . (828) 232-4160
Nc Dept of Juvenile Justice (KG-12)
    2012-13 Enrollment: n/a . . . . (919) 733-3388
Four-year College(s)
Warren Wilson College (Private, Not-for-profit)
    Fall 2013 Enrollment: 893 . . . . (828) 298-3325
    2013-14 Tuition: In-state $29,540; Out-of-state $29,540
Housing: Homeownership rate: 70.4%; Median home value: $129,900; Median year structure built: 1978; Homeowner vacancy rate: 1.2%; Median gross rent: $709 per month; Rental vacancy rate: 9.2%
Health Insurance: 78.1% have insurance; 56.8% have private insurance; 29.8% have public insurance; 21.9% do not have insurance; 9.9% of children under 18 do not have insurance
Transportation: Commute: 93.1% car, 0.0% public transportation, 0.8% walk, 4.4% work from home; Median travel time to work: 19.3 minutes

WEAVERVILLE (town).
Covers a land area of 3.435 square miles and a water area of 0.008 square miles. Located at 35.70° N. Lat; 82.56° W. Long. Elevation is 2,178 feet.
Population: 3,120; Growth (since 2000): 29.1%; Density: 908.4 persons per square mile; Race: 95.2% White, 0.9% Black/African American, 0.4% Asian, 0.0% American Indian/Alaska Native, 0.3% Native Hawaiian/Other Pacific Islander, 2.7% Two or more races, 2.1% Hispanic of any race; Average household size: 2.13; Median age: 51.4; Age under 18: 17.4%; Age 65 and over: 27.7%; Males per 100 females: 82.0; Marriage status: 20.1% never married, 62.0% now married, 2.3% separated, 8.1% widowed, 9.8% divorced; Foreign born: 4.0%; Speak English only: 96.9%; With disability: 8.8%; Veterans: 12.3%; Ancestry: 26.3% American, 19.9% German, 17.5% English, 12.5% Irish, 8.1% Scottish
Employment: 18.7% management, business, and financial, 6.5% computer, engineering, and science, 17.0% education, legal, community service, arts, and media, 6.4% healthcare practitioners, 13.8% service, 28.8% sales and office, 3.6% natural resources, construction, and maintenance, 5.2% production, transportation, and material moving
Income: Per capita: $30,231; Median household: $54,700; Average household: $72,313; Households with income of $100,000 or more: 22.7%; Poverty rate: 4.6%
Educational Attainment: High school diploma or higher: 96.1%; Bachelor's degree or higher: 44.7%; Graduate/professional degree or higher: 18.6%
School District(s)
Buncombe County Schools (PK-12)
    2012-13 Enrollment: 25,824 . . . . (828) 232-4160

Housing: Homeownership rate: 74.3%; Median home value: $238,600; Median year structure built: 1985; Homeowner vacancy rate: 2.7%; Median gross rent: $871 per month; Rental vacancy rate: 6.9%
Health Insurance: 89.7% have insurance; 76.0% have private insurance; 35.9% have public insurance; 10.3% do not have insurance; 3.2% of children under 18 do not have insurance
Safety: Violent crime rate: 7.9 per 10,000 population; Property crime rate: 506.0 per 10,000 population
Transportation: Commute: 89.6% car, 0.0% public transportation, 2.4% walk, 7.4% work from home; Median travel time to work: 19.0 minutes
Additional Information Contacts
Town of Weaverville . . . . (828) 645-7116
  http://www.weavervillenc.org

WOODFIN (town). Covers a land area of 8.788 square miles and a water area of 0.411 square miles. Located at 35.65° N. Lat; 82.59° W. Long. Elevation is 2,116 feet.
Population: 6,123; Growth (since 2000): 93.6%; Density: 696.7 persons per square mile; Race: 87.3% White, 4.9% Black/African American, 0.9% Asian, 0.6% American Indian/Alaska Native, 0.0% Native Hawaiian/Other Pacific Islander, 2.5% Two or more races, 8.7% Hispanic of any race; Average household size: 2.31; Median age: 36.6; Age under 18: 18.7%; Age 65 and over: 13.5%; Males per 100 females: 115.5; Marriage status: 38.8% never married, 39.9% now married, 2.9% separated, 8.6% widowed, 12.7% divorced; Foreign born: 7.9%; Speak English only: 89.4%; With disability: 16.6%; Veterans: 5.8%; Ancestry: 17.7% American, 16.1% Irish, 15.3% German, 8.0% English, 4.0% Scotch-Irish
Employment: 10.2% management, business, and financial, 3.0% computer, engineering, and science, 13.0% education, legal, community service, arts, and media, 3.7% healthcare practitioners, 24.7% service, 28.6% sales and office, 8.1% natural resources, construction, and maintenance, 8.7% production, transportation, and material moving
Income: Per capita: $19,562; Median household: $36,102; Average household: $49,217; Households with income of $100,000 or more: 8.8%; Poverty rate: 23.1%
Educational Attainment: High school diploma or higher: 86.1%; Bachelor's degree or higher: 24.5%; Graduate/professional degree or higher: 8.2%
Housing: Homeownership rate: 52.9%; Median home value: $147,000; Median year structure built: 1976; Homeowner vacancy rate: 4.3%; Median gross rent: $801 per month; Rental vacancy rate: 11.4%
Health Insurance: 77.3% have insurance; 52.3% have private insurance; 38.7% have public insurance; 22.7% do not have insurance; 13.6% of children under 18 do not have insurance
Safety: Violent crime rate: 27.5 per 10,000 population; Property crime rate: 178.1 per 10,000 population
Transportation: Commute: 89.2% car, 0.0% public transportation, 0.4% walk, 6.8% work from home; Median travel time to work: 17.7 minutes
Additional Information Contacts
Town of Woodfin . . . . (828) 253-4887
  http://www.woodfin-nc.gov

Burke County

Located in west central North Carolina, in a piedmont area; includes part of Pisgah National Forest. Covers a land area of 507.099 square miles, a water area of 7.976 square miles, and is located in the Eastern Time Zone at 35.75° N. Lat., 81.71° W. Long. The county was founded in 1777. County seat is Morganton.

Burke County is part of the Hickory-Lenoir-Morganton, NC Metropolitan Statistical Area. The entire metro area includes: Alexander County, NC; Burke County, NC; Caldwell County, NC; Catawba County, NC

Weather Station: Hickory Regional Arpt										Elevation: 1,143 feet		
	Jan	Feb	Mar	Apr	May	Jun	Jul	Aug	Sep	Oct	Nov	Dec
High	49	53	61	70	78	85	88	86	80	70	61	51
Low	30	32	39	47	55	64	68	67	60	48	39	32
Precip	3.6	3.6	4.4	3.8	3.7	4.2	4.4	4.2	3.8	3.4	3.5	3.7
Snow	na	na	na	na	na	na	na	na	na	na	na	na

High and Low temperatures in degrees Fahrenheit; Precipitation and Snow in inches

Weather Station: Morganton										Elevation: 1,160 feet		
	Jan	Feb	Mar	Apr	May	Jun	Jul	Aug	Sep	Oct	Nov	Dec
High	51	55	63	72	79	86	89	88	81	72	62	52
Low	27	29	35	44	52	61	65	64	57	45	35	29
Precip	4.0	3.9	4.5	3.8	3.7	4.9	4.1	4.2	4.1	3.5	3.7	4.0
Snow	1.3	1.1	1.1	0.1	0.0	0.0	0.0	0.0	0.0	0.0	tr	0.3

High and Low temperatures in degrees Fahrenheit; Precipitation and Snow in inches

Population: 90,912; Growth (since 2000): 2.0%; Density: 179.3 persons per square mile; Race: 84.4% White, 6.6% Black/African American, 3.5% Asian, 0.4% American Indian/Alaska Native, 0.3% Native Hawaiian/Other Pacific Islander, 1.8% two or more races, 5.1% Hispanic of any race; Average household size: 2.45; Median age: 41.2; Age under 18: 22.2%; Age 65 and over: 16.1%; Males per 100 females: 100.1; Marriage status: 28.6% never married, 51.6% now married, 3.1% separated, 8.3% widowed, 11.5% divorced; Foreign born: 5.1%; Speak English only: 91.2%; With disability: 19.2%; Veterans: 9.0%; Ancestry: 21.1% American, 16.4% German, 12.5% Irish, 8.5% English, 4.0% Scottish
Religion: Six largest groups: 39.8% Baptist, 9.7% Methodist/Pietist, 2.4% Non-denominational Protestant, 2.2% Pentecostal, 1.9% Presbyterian-Reformed, 0.9% Holiness
Economy: Unemployment rate: 6.3%; Leading industries: 17.8% retail trade; 14.2% other services (except public administration); 12.8% health care and social assistance; Farms: 486 totaling 34,387 acres; Company size: 0 employ 1,000 or more persons, 3 employ 500 to 999 persons, 35 employ 100 to 499 persons, 1,429 employ less than 100 persons; Business ownership: 1,611 women-owned, 292 Black-owned, n/a Hispanic-owned, n/a Asian-owned
Employment: 9.6% management, business, and financial, 2.3% computer, engineering, and science, 9.2% education, legal, community service, arts, and media, 7.1% healthcare practitioners, 21.4% service, 20.5% sales and office, 9.4% natural resources, construction, and maintenance, 20.4% production, transportation, and material moving
Income: Per capita: $19,701; Median household: $37,263; Average household: $49,263; Households with income of $100,000 or more: 9.3%; Poverty rate: 20.0%
Educational Attainment: High school diploma or higher: 76.7%; Bachelor's degree or higher: 16.6%; Graduate/professional degree or higher: 6.1%
Housing: Homeownership rate: 72.3%; Median home value: $110,900; Median year structure built: 1976; Homeowner vacancy rate: 2.4%; Median gross rent: $605 per month; Rental vacancy rate: 13.4%
Vital Statistics: Birth rate: 94.5 per 10,000 population; Death rate: 106.6 per 10,000 population; Age-adjusted cancer mortality rate: 197.6 deaths per 100,000 population
Health Insurance: 83.3% have insurance; 57.5% have private insurance; 38.4% have public insurance; 16.7% do not have insurance; 5.2% of children under 18 do not have insurance
Health Care: Physicians: 17.5 per 10,000 population; Hospital beds: 83.9 per 10,000 population; Hospital admissions: 1,717.6 per 10,000 population
Transportation: Commute: 93.7% car, 0.1% public transportation, 1.7% walk, 3.8% work from home; Median travel time to work: 21.2 minutes
Presidential Election: 37.5% Obama, 60.9% Romney (2012)
National and State Parks: Lake James State Park; South Mountains State Park
Additional Information Contacts
Burke Government . . . . (828) 439-4340
  http://www.co.burke.nc.us

Burke County Communities

CONNELLY SPRINGS (town). Covers a land area of 4.990 square miles and a water area of 0 square miles. Located at 35.75° N. Lat; 81.50° W. Long. Elevation is 1,175 feet.
History: Connelly Springs once attracted visitors to its appealing mineral waters.
Population: 1,669; Growth (since 2000): -8.0%; Density: 334.4 persons per square mile; Race: 89.6% White, 1.4% Black/African American, 7.0% Asian, 0.1% American Indian/Alaska Native, 0.0% Native Hawaiian/Other Pacific Islander, 0.7% Two or more races, 2.2% Hispanic of any race; Average household size: 2.56; Median age: 42.8; Age under 18: 22.7%; Age 65 and over: 17.3%; Males per 100 females: 98.5
School District(s)
Burke County Schools (PK-12)
  2012-13 Enrollment: 13,343 . . . . (828) 439-4311

Housing: Homeownership rate: 77.2%; Homeowner vacancy rate: 0.8%; Rental vacancy rate: 16.9%

DREXEL (town). Covers a land area of 1.364 square miles and a water area of 0 square miles. Located at 35.76° N. Lat; 81.61° W. Long. Elevation is 1,194 feet.
Population: 1,858; Growth (since 2000): -4.1%; Density: 1,362.6 persons per square mile; Race: 86.8% White, 3.3% Black/African American, 4.4% Asian, 0.6% American Indian/Alaska Native, 0.2% Native Hawaiian/Other Pacific Islander, 1.1% Two or more races, 4.9% Hispanic of any race; Average household size: 2.32; Median age: 43.6; Age under 18: 20.9%; Age 65 and over: 21.4%; Males per 100 females: 86.5
School District(s)
Burke County Schools (PK-12)
    2012-13 Enrollment: 13,343 . . . . (828) 439-4311
Housing: Homeownership rate: 68.2%; Homeowner vacancy rate: 2.1%; Rental vacancy rate: 14.8%
Safety: Violent crime rate: 0.0 per 10,000 population; Property crime rate: 123.5 per 10,000 population

---

GLEN ALPINE (town). Covers a land area of 2.147 square miles and a water area of 0 square miles. Located at 35.73° N. Lat; 81.78° W. Long. Elevation is 1,214 feet.
Population: 1,517; Growth (since 2000): 39.2%; Density: 706.6 persons per square mile; Race: 87.9% White, 3.2% Black/African American, 5.8% Asian, 0.2% American Indian/Alaska Native, 0.0% Native Hawaiian/Other Pacific Islander, 2.0% Two or more races, 2.2% Hispanic of any race; Average household size: 2.47; Median age: 39.6; Age under 18: 22.8%; Age 65 and over: 16.8%; Males per 100 females: 92.3
Housing: Homeownership rate: 77.2%; Homeowner vacancy rate: 3.3%; Rental vacancy rate: 5.4%

HILDEBRAN (town). Covers a land area of 2.873 square miles and a water area of 0 square miles. Located at 35.72° N. Lat; 81.42° W. Long. Elevation is 1,165 feet.
Population: 2,023; Growth (since 2000): 37.4%; Density: 704.2 persons per square mile; Race: 91.8% White, 1.6% Black/African American, 3.7% Asian, 0.4% American Indian/Alaska Native, 0.0% Native Hawaiian/Other Pacific Islander, 0.9% Two or more races, 2.4% Hispanic of any race; Average household size: 2.51; Median age: 42.0; Age under 18: 20.9%; Age 65 and over: 19.7%; Males per 100 females: 94.5
School District(s)
Burke County Schools (PK-12)
    2012-13 Enrollment: 13,343 . . . . (828) 439-4311
Housing: Homeownership rate: 70.2%; Homeowner vacancy rate: 1.9%; Rental vacancy rate: 4.7%

ICARD (CDP). Covers a land area of 3.826 square miles and a water area of 0.010 square miles. Located at 35.73° N. Lat; 81.46° W. Long. Elevation is 1,188 feet.
Population: 2,664; Growth (since 2000): -2.6%; Density: 696.3 persons per square mile; Race: 93.0% White, 0.5% Black/African American, 2.7% Asian, 0.0% American Indian/Alaska Native, 0.0% Native Hawaiian/Other Pacific Islander, 0.6% Two or more races, 4.0% Hispanic of any race; Average household size: 2.44; Median age: 42.1; Age under 18: 21.5%; Age 65 and over: 17.2%; Males per 100 females: 95.3; Marriage status: 24.5% never married, 51.0% now married, 2.1% separated, 9.6% widowed, 15.0% divorced; Foreign born: 3.9%; Speak English only: 93.1%; With disability: 19.0%; Veterans: 7.4%; Ancestry: 30.7% American, 17.4% Irish, 16.9% German, 6.6% English, 5.0% Scottish
Employment: 7.7% management, business, and financial, 3.7% computer, engineering, and science, 13.3% education, legal, community service, arts, and media, 0.7% healthcare practitioners, 29.1% service, 19.2% sales and office, 0.3% natural resources, construction, and maintenance, 25.9% production, transportation, and material moving
Income: Per capita: $16,214; Median household: $35,386; Average household: $43,162; Households with income of $100,000 or more: 3.7%; Poverty rate: 21.5%
Educational Attainment: High school diploma or higher: 69.4%; Bachelor's degree or higher: 10.2%; Graduate/professional degree or higher: 4.1%
School District(s)
Burke County Schools (PK-12)
    2012-13 Enrollment: 13,343 . . . . (828) 439-4311

Housing: Homeownership rate: 72.1%; Median home value: $86,200; Median year structure built: 1976; Homeowner vacancy rate: 1.7%; Median gross rent: $607 per month; Rental vacancy rate: 19.2%
Health Insurance: 71.6% have insurance; 49.2% have private insurance; 32.5% have public insurance; 28.4% do not have insurance; 5.6% of children under 18 do not have insurance
Transportation: Commute: 93.0% car, 0.0% public transportation, 7.0% walk, 0.0% work from home; Median travel time to work: 20.0 minutes

---

LINVILLE FALLS (unincorporated postal area)
ZCTA: 28647
    Covers a land area of 6.043 square miles and a water area of 0 square miles. Located at 35.94° N. Lat; 81.97° W. Long. Elevation is 3,350 feet.
    Population: 89; Growth (since 2000): n/a; Density: 14.7 persons per square mile; Race: 95.5% White, 0.0% Black/African American, 0.0% Asian, 0.0% American Indian/Alaska Native, 0.0% Native Hawaiian/Other Pacific Islander, 0.0% Two or more races, 4.5% Hispanic of any race; Average household size: 2.54; Median age: 49.8; Age under 18: 19.1%; Age 65 and over: 15.7%; Males per 100 females: 85.4
    Housing: Homeownership rate: 91.5%; Homeowner vacancy rate: 0.0%; Rental vacancy rate: 50.0%

MORGANTON (city). County seat. Covers a land area of 19.153 square miles and a water area of 0 square miles. Located at 35.74° N. Lat; 81.70° W. Long. Elevation is 1,155 feet.
History: Morganton was first called Morganborough for General Daniel Morgan, a Revolutionary soldier.
Population: 16,918; Growth (since 2000): -2.3%; Density: 883.3 persons per square mile; Race: 70.1% White, 12.2% Black/African American, 2.4% Asian, 0.9% American Indian/Alaska Native, 1.5% Native Hawaiian/Other Pacific Islander, 2.9% Two or more races, 16.4% Hispanic of any race; Average household size: 2.36; Median age: 39.7; Age under 18: 22.6%; Age 65 and over: 18.2%; Males per 100 females: 95.4; Marriage status: 34.1% never married, 42.3% now married, 3.3% separated, 9.4% widowed, 14.1% divorced; Foreign born: 11.3%; Speak English only: 82.3%; With disability: 21.8%; Veterans: 10.2%; Ancestry: 13.9% American, 12.9% German, 8.1% Irish, 7.9% English, 5.4% Scottish
Employment: 11.1% management, business, and financial, 1.7% computer, engineering, and science, 12.2% education, legal, community service, arts, and media, 7.3% healthcare practitioners, 24.6% service, 19.4% sales and office, 7.5% natural resources, construction, and maintenance, 16.1% production, transportation, and material moving
Income: Per capita: $20,070; Median household: $31,083; Average household: $47,327; Households with income of $100,000 or more: 11.3%; Poverty rate: 27.9%
Educational Attainment: High school diploma or higher: 74.6%; Bachelor's degree or higher: 22.7%; Graduate/professional degree or higher: 9.0%
School District(s)
Burke County Schools (PK-12)
    2012-13 Enrollment: 13,343 . . . . (828) 439-4311
Deaf and Blind Schools (PK-12)
    2012-13 Enrollment: 177 . . . . (919) 733-6382
Nc Health and Human Resources (KG-12)
    2012-13 Enrollment: n/a . . . . (919) 855-4430
The New Dimensions School (KG-06)
    2012-13 Enrollment: 195 . . . . (828) 437-5753
Two-year College(s)
Western Piedmont Community College (Public)
    Fall 2013 Enrollment: 2,352 . . . . (828) 438-6000
    2013-14 Tuition: In-state $2,326; Out-of-state $8,508
Housing: Homeownership rate: 54.5%; Median home value: $130,000; Median year structure built: 1966; Homeowner vacancy rate: 3.8%; Median gross rent: $640 per month; Rental vacancy rate: 12.6%
Health Insurance: 81.2% have insurance; 50.6% have private insurance; 43.9% have public insurance; 18.8% do not have insurance; 3.4% of children under 18 do not have insurance
Hospitals: CMC - Blue Ridge (269 beds)
Safety: Violent crime rate: 27.9 per 10,000 population; Property crime rate: 291.4 per 10,000 population
Newspapers: News Herald (daily circulation 10700); News Herald (weekly circulation 7800)
Transportation: Commute: 91.4% car, 0.1% public transportation, 3.6% walk, 2.2% work from home; Median travel time to work: 16.7 minutes

Additional Information Contacts
City of Morganton . . . . (828) 437-8863
   http://www.ci.morganton.nc.us

RHODHISS (town). Covers a land area of 1.184 square miles and a water area of 0.074 square miles. Located at 35.77° N. Lat; 81.43° W. Long. Elevation is 958 feet.
Population: 1,070; Growth (since 2000): 192.3%; Density: 903.7 persons per square mile; Race: 92.8% White, 0.8% Black/African American, 1.6% Asian, 0.1% American Indian/Alaska Native, 0.3% Native Hawaiian/Other Pacific Islander, 1.6% Two or more races, 4.6% Hispanic of any race; Average household size: 2.58; Median age: 40.2; Age under 18: 22.3%; Age 65 and over: 13.9%; Males per 100 females: 97.8
Housing: Homeownership rate: 76.1%; Homeowner vacancy rate: 4.0%; Rental vacancy rate: 8.2%

RUTHERFORD COLLEGE (town). Covers a land area of 2.261 square miles and a water area of 0 square miles. Located at 35.75° N. Lat; 81.53° W. Long. Elevation is 1,207 feet.
Population: 1,341; Growth (since 2000): 3.7%; Density: 593.0 persons per square mile; Race: 96.4% White, 0.4% Black/African American, 2.5% Asian, 0.0% American Indian/Alaska Native, 0.0% Native Hawaiian/Other Pacific Islander, 0.6% Two or more races, 0.4% Hispanic of any race; Average household size: 2.33; Median age: 45.5; Age under 18: 20.2%; Age 65 and over: 17.4%; Males per 100 females: 98.1
School District(s)
Burke County Schools (PK-12)
   2012-13 Enrollment: 13,343 . . . . (828) 439-4311
Housing: Homeownership rate: 75.5%; Homeowner vacancy rate: 0.9%; Rental vacancy rate: 5.3%

SALEM (CDP). Covers a land area of 4.286 square miles and a water area of 0 square miles. Located at 35.70° N. Lat; 81.70° W. Long. Elevation is 1,217 feet.
Population: 2,218; Growth (since 2000): -24.1%; Density: 517.5 persons per square mile; Race: 93.6% White, 1.2% Black/African American, 0.5% Asian, 0.2% American Indian/Alaska Native, 0.0% Native Hawaiian/Other Pacific Islander, 1.6% Two or more races, 4.2% Hispanic of any race; Average household size: 2.34; Median age: 44.3; Age under 18: 20.6%; Age 65 and over: 19.3%; Males per 100 females: 96.3
Housing: Homeownership rate: 77.3%; Homeowner vacancy rate: 1.7%; Rental vacancy rate: 16.0%

VALDESE (town). Covers a land area of 7.715 square miles and a water area of 0.013 square miles. Located at 35.76° N. Lat; 81.57° W. Long. Elevation is 1,207 feet.
History: Valdese was settled in 1893 by a colony of 50 families from the Cottian Alps of northern Italy. They called themselves Waldensians for the 12th-century reformer, Peter Waldo.
Population: 4,490; Growth (since 2000): 0.1%; Density: 582.0 persons per square mile; Race: 92.7% White, 1.3% Black/African American, 3.1% Asian, 0.1% American Indian/Alaska Native, 0.2% Native Hawaiian/Other Pacific Islander, 1.5% Two or more races, 2.6% Hispanic of any race; Average household size: 2.28; Median age: 43.5; Age under 18: 22.0%; Age 65 and over: 20.0%; Males per 100 females: 80.8; Marriage status: 22.1% never married, 50.1% now married, 2.4% separated, 18.1% widowed, 9.7% divorced; Foreign born: 3.9%; Speak English only: 93.1%; With disability: 22.7%; Veterans: 10.7%; Ancestry: 22.5% American, 18.9% German, 14.0% Irish, 11.8% English, 7.4% Italian
Employment: 9.1% management, business, and financial, 2.7% computer, engineering, and science, 10.9% education, legal, community service, arts, and media, 3.5% healthcare practitioners, 25.9% service, 18.9% sales and office, 6.8% natural resources, construction, and maintenance, 22.1% production, transportation, and material moving
Income: Per capita: $21,841; Median household: $34,025; Average household: $48,145; Households with income of $100,000 or more: 10.5%; Poverty rate: 15.1%
Educational Attainment: High school diploma or higher: 81.6%; Bachelor's degree or higher: 24.8%; Graduate/professional degree or higher: 11.8%
School District(s)
Burke County Schools (PK-12)
   2012-13 Enrollment: 13,343 . . . . (828) 439-4311

Housing: Homeownership rate: 66.2%; Median home value: $120,600; Median year structure built: 1965; Homeowner vacancy rate: 3.5%; Median gross rent: $356 per month; Rental vacancy rate: 12.3%
Health Insurance: 88.7% have insurance; 64.4% have private insurance; 44.7% have public insurance; 11.3% do not have insurance; 1.6% of children under 18 do not have insurance
Safety: Violent crime rate: 4.5 per 10,000 population; Property crime rate: 153.6 per 10,000 population
Transportation: Commute: 84.7% car, 0.0% public transportation, 4.4% walk, 10.8% work from home; Median travel time to work: 21.2 minutes
Additional Information Contacts
Town of Valdese . . . . (828) 879-2120
   http://www.ci.valdese.nc.us

Cabarrus County

Located in south central North Carolina; piedmont region, drained by the Rocky River. Covers a land area of 361.749 square miles, a water area of 2.715 square miles, and is located in the Eastern Time Zone at 35.39° N. Lat., 80.55° W. Long. The county was founded in 1792. County seat is Concord.

Cabarrus County is part of the Charlotte-Concord-Gastonia, NC-SC Metropolitan Statistical Area. The entire metro area includes: Cabarrus County, NC; Gaston County, NC; Iredell County, NC; Lincoln County, NC; Mecklenburg County, NC; Rowan County, NC; Union County, NC; Chester County, SC; Lancaster County, SC; York County, SC

Weather Station: Concord									Elevation: 689 feet			
	Jan	Feb	Mar	Apr	May	Jun	Jul	Aug	Sep	Oct	Nov	Dec
High	51	56	63	73	80	87	90	89	83	73	63	54
Low	29	31	38	46	55	65	69	68	60	48	38	31
Precip	3.6	3.3	4.3	3.6	3.5	4.3	5.1	4.0	3.9	3.8	3.4	3.2
Snow	1.7	1.4	0.7	tr	0.0	0.0	0.0	0.0	0.0	0.0	tr	0.2

High and Low temperatures in degrees Fahrenheit; Precipitation and Snow in inches

Population: 178,011; Growth (since 2000): 35.8%; Density: 492.1 persons per square mile; Race: 75.4% White, 15.3% Black/African American, 2.0% Asian, 0.4% American Indian/Alaska Native, 0.0% Native Hawaiian/Other Pacific Islander, 2.1% two or more races, 9.4% Hispanic of any race; Average household size: 2.69; Median age: 36.7; Age under 18: 27.4%; Age 65 and over: 11.3%; Males per 100 females: 95.5; Marriage status: 26.6% never married, 58.2% now married, 2.6% separated, 5.2% widowed, 10.1% divorced; Foreign born: 7.6%; Speak English only: 89.4%; With disability: 9.8%; Veterans: 9.4%; Ancestry: 14.4% German, 10.3% American, 9.4% Irish, 8.0% English, 3.6% Italian
Religion: Six largest groups: 17.8% Baptist, 11.2% Methodist/Pietist, 6.8% Pentecostal, 6.6% Non-denominational Protestant, 3.3% Presbyterian-Reformed, 2.8% Lutheran
Economy: Unemployment rate: 5.0%; Leading industries: 18.0% retail trade; 11.8% construction; 11.0% other services (except public administration); Farms: 589 totaling 66,241 acres; Company size: 1 employs 1,000 or more persons, 3 employ 500 to 999 persons, 74 employ 100 to 499 persons, 3,836 employ less than 100 persons; Business ownership: 3,581 women-owned, 977 Black-owned, 370 Hispanic-owned, n/a Asian-owned
Employment: 15.8% management, business, and financial, 5.3% computer, engineering, and science, 10.4% education, legal, community service, arts, and media, 5.4% healthcare practitioners, 16.4% service, 24.9% sales and office, 9.8% natural resources, construction, and maintenance, 12.1% production, transportation, and material moving
Income: Per capita: $25,247; Median household: $53,551; Average household: $68,882; Households with income of $100,000 or more: 20.8%; Poverty rate: 13.2%
Educational Attainment: High school diploma or higher: 86.4%; Bachelor's degree or higher: 25.1%; Graduate/professional degree or higher: 7.7%
Housing: Homeownership rate: 73.7%; Median home value: $167,800; Median year structure built: 1990; Homeowner vacancy rate: 2.5%; Median gross rent: $794 per month; Rental vacancy rate: 12.1%
Vital Statistics: Birth rate: 123.0 per 10,000 population; Death rate: 75.3 per 10,000 population; Age-adjusted cancer mortality rate: 179.3 deaths per 100,000 population
Health Insurance: 84.4% have insurance; 67.8% have private insurance; 26.2% have public insurance; 15.6% do not have insurance; 5.9% of children under 18 do not have insurance

Health Care: Physicians: 22.6 per 10,000 population; Hospital beds: 24.8 per 10,000 population; Hospital admissions: 1,229.1 per 10,000 population
Transportation: Commute: 93.7% car, 0.4% public transportation, 0.7% walk, 4.5% work from home; Median travel time to work: 26.4 minutes
Presidential Election: 39.2% Obama, 59.4% Romney (2012)
Additional Information Contacts
Cabarrus Government. . . . . (704) 920-2000
http://www.cabarruscounty.us

Cabarrus County Communities

CONCORD (city). County seat. Covers a land area of 60.267 square miles and a water area of 0.036 square miles. Located at 35.39° N. Lat; 80.64° W. Long. Elevation is 705 feet.
History: Named for the harmonious settlement of a dispute over the site for the town. Concord was so called because two factions, disagreeing over the place for the county seat of Cabarrus County, finally reached a harmonious settlement at the spot.
Population: 79,066; Growth (since 2000): 41.2%; Density: 1,311.9 persons per square mile; Race: 70.4% White, 17.8% Black/African American, 2.6% Asian, 0.3% American Indian/Alaska Native, 0.1% Native Hawaiian/Other Pacific Islander, 2.3% Two or more races, 12.3% Hispanic of any race; Average household size: 2.68; Median age: 34.9; Age under 18: 28.4%; Age 65 and over: 10.6%; Males per 100 females: 93.1; Marriage status: 28.1% never married, 55.9% now married, 2.4% separated, 5.0% widowed, 11.1% divorced; Foreign born: 10.1%; Speak English only: 86.8%; With disability: 9.2%; Veterans: 9.0%; Ancestry: 13.6% German, 10.2% Irish, 8.8% American, 8.0% English, 4.7% Italian
Employment: 17.5% management, business, and financial, 5.7% computer, engineering, and science, 9.9% education, legal, community service, arts, and media, 6.0% healthcare practitioners, 16.0% service, 25.3% sales and office, 8.7% natural resources, construction, and maintenance, 10.8% production, transportation, and material moving
Income: Per capita: $25,897; Median household: $53,337; Average household: $70,842; Households with income of $100,000 or more: 22.6%; Poverty rate: 12.6%
Educational Attainment: High school diploma or higher: 86.3%; Bachelor's degree or higher: 27.8%; Graduate/professional degree or higher: 8.3%

School District(s)
Cabarrus County Schools (PK-12)
    2012-13 Enrollment: 30,418 . . . . (704) 262-6123
Nc Dept of Juvenile Justice (KG-12)
    2012-13 Enrollment: n/a . . . . (919) 733-3388
Four-year College(s)
Cabarrus College of Health Sciences (Private, Not-for-profit)
    Fall 2013 Enrollment: 451 . . . . (704) 403-1555
    2013-14 Tuition: In-state $11,330; Out-of-state $11,330
Vocational/Technical School(s)
Empire Beauty School-Concord (Private, For-profit)
    Fall 2013 Enrollment: 123 . . . . (800) 920-4593
    2013-14 Tuition: $18,360
Housing: Homeownership rate: 67.8%; Median home value: $168,300; Median year structure built: 1992; Homeowner vacancy rate: 2.8%; Median gross rent: $806 per month; Rental vacancy rate: 11.8%
Health Insurance: 83.6% have insurance; 67.4% have private insurance; 25.5% have public insurance; 16.4% do not have insurance; 6.5% of children under 18 do not have insurance
Hospitals: Carolinas Medical Center - Northeast (457 beds)
Safety: Violent crime rate: 14.7 per 10,000 population; Property crime rate: 307.5 per 10,000 population
Newspapers: Concord Standard (weekly circulation 18000); Independent Tribune (daily circulation 17200)
Transportation: Commute: 93.6% car, 0.6% public transportation, 0.5% walk, 4.4% work from home; Median travel time to work: 25.7 minutes
Airports: Concord Regional (primary service/non-hub)
Additional Information Contacts
City of Concord . . . . (704) 920-5555
http://www.ci.concord.nc.us

HARRISBURG (town). Covers a land area of 9.051 square miles and a water area of 0 square miles. Located at 35.32° N. Lat; 80.65° W. Long. Elevation is 630 feet.
Population: 11,526; Growth (since 2000): 156.5%; Density: 1,273.4 persons per square mile; Race: 75.8% White, 16.4% Black/African

American, 4.5% Asian, 0.5% American Indian/Alaska Native, 0.0% Native Hawaiian/Other Pacific Islander, 2.0% Two or more races, 3.7% Hispanic of any race; Average household size: 2.87; Median age: 37.3; Age under 18: 30.4%; Age 65 and over: 9.2%; Males per 100 females: 95.9; Marriage status: 23.3% never married, 66.9% now married, 1.3% separated, 2.6% widowed, 7.2% divorced; Foreign born: 6.4%; Speak English only: 91.3%; With disability: 5.5%; Veterans: 8.7%; Ancestry: 12.2% Irish, 11.6% German, 10.7% American, 9.0% English, 3.7% Italian
Employment: 23.3% management, business, and financial, 7.2% computer, engineering, and science, 13.0% education, legal, community service, arts, and media, 3.3% healthcare practitioners, 12.9% service, 26.8% sales and office, 6.6% natural resources, construction, and maintenance, 6.9% production, transportation, and material moving
Income: Per capita: $28,537; Median household: $81,808; Average household: $88,458; Households with income of $100,000 or more: 32.5%; Poverty rate: 6.2%
Educational Attainment: High school diploma or higher: 96.2%; Bachelor's degree or higher: 39.9%; Graduate/professional degree or higher: 14.9%

School District(s)
Cabarrus County Schools (PK-12)
    2012-13 Enrollment: 30,418 . . . . (704) 262-6123
Carolina International (KG-10)
    2012-13 Enrollment: 564 . . . . (704) 455-3847
Housing: Homeownership rate: 90.9%; Median home value: $222,100; Median year structure built: 2001; Homeowner vacancy rate: 2.2%; Median gross rent: $1,086 per month; Rental vacancy rate: 6.4%
Health Insurance: 89.7% have insurance; 80.2% have private insurance; 15.5% have public insurance; 10.3% do not have insurance; 7.8% of children under 18 do not have insurance
Transportation: Commute: 93.3% car, 0.5% public transportation, 0.0% walk, 6.2% work from home; Median travel time to work: 24.5 minutes
Additional Information Contacts
Town of Harrisburg . . . . (704) 455-5614
http://www.harrisburgnc.org

KANNAPOLIS (city). Covers a land area of 31.939 square miles and a water area of 0.563 square miles. Located at 35.48° N. Lat; 80.64° W. Long. Elevation is 801 feet.
History: Named for James William Cannon, an early resident and founder of Cannon Mills. Kannopolis was built on a 600-acre tract of abandoned land in 1906 by J.W. Cannon, Sr., founder of Cannon Mills. The Cannon Mills factory started in 1877, producing rough cotton yarn and cloth. Towels were manufactured beginning in 1898. Cannon Mills later became the largest producer of household textiles in the world.
Population: 42,625; Growth (since 2000): 15.5%; Density: 1,334.6 persons per square mile; Race: 68.5% White, 20.3% Black/African American, 1.1% Asian, 0.3% American Indian/Alaska Native, 0.0% Native Hawaiian/Other Pacific Islander, 2.4% Two or more races, 12.1% Hispanic of any race; Average household size: 2.58; Median age: 35.6; Age under 18: 26.8%; Age 65 and over: 13.1%; Males per 100 females: 92.0; Marriage status: 29.8% never married, 51.6% now married, 4.0% separated, 6.8% widowed, 11.8% divorced; Foreign born: 7.1%; Speak English only: 88.2%; With disability: 12.4%; Veterans: 9.6%; Ancestry: 10.9% German, 9.4% American, 6.8% Irish, 5.8% English, 2.3% Scotch-Irish
Employment: 10.4% management, business, and financial, 3.9% computer, engineering, and science, 10.2% education, legal, community service, arts, and media, 4.4% healthcare practitioners, 20.9% service, 25.5% sales and office, 10.6% natural resources, construction, and maintenance, 14.1% production, transportation, and material moving
Income: Per capita: $20,482; Median household: $39,275; Average household: $52,272; Households with income of $100,000 or more: 10.2%; Poverty rate: 20.8%
Educational Attainment: High school diploma or higher: 79.0%; Bachelor's degree or higher: 17.5%; Graduate/professional degree or higher: 5.5%

School District(s)
Cabarrus County Schools (PK-12)
    2012-13 Enrollment: 30,418 . . . . (704) 262-6123
Kannapolis City Schools (PK-12)
    2012-13 Enrollment: 5,511 . . . . (704) 938-1131
Housing: Homeownership rate: 62.8%; Median home value: $127,700; Median year structure built: 1972; Homeowner vacancy rate: 3.6%; Median gross rent: $754 per month; Rental vacancy rate: 14.2%

Health Insurance: 79.7% have insurance; 54.6% have private insurance; 34.4% have public insurance; 20.3% do not have insurance; 7.1% of children under 18 do not have insurance

Safety: Violent crime rate: 19.7 per 10,000 population; Property crime rate: 207.7 per 10,000 population

Newspapers: Kannapolis Citizen (weekly circulation 6500)

Transportation: Commute: 94.8% car, 0.4% public transportation, 1.6% walk, 2.4% work from home; Median travel time to work: 24.5 minutes; Amtrak: Train service available.

Additional Information Contacts
City of Kannapolis . . . . (704) 920-4300
   http://www.cityofkannapolis.com

MIDLAND (town). Covers a land area of 9.984 square miles and a water area of 0 square miles. Located at 35.24° N. Lat; 80.52° W. Long. Elevation is 502 feet.

Population: 3,073; Growth (since 2000): n/a; Density: 307.8 persons per square mile; Race: 89.9% White, 6.2% Black/African American, 0.9% Asian, 0.3% American Indian/Alaska Native, 0.0% Native Hawaiian/Other Pacific Islander, 1.8% Two or more races, 3.5% Hispanic of any race; Average household size: 2.58; Median age: 40.3; Age under 18: 23.1%; Age 65 and over: 13.7%; Males per 100 females: 98.4; Marriage status: 27.2% never married, 57.2% now married, 3.7% separated, 6.4% widowed, 9.2% divorced; Foreign born: 0.0%; Speak English only: 98.2%; With disability: 5.8%; Veterans: 10.8%; Ancestry: 22.5% German, 14.4% English, 13.2% American, 7.3% Scotch-Irish, 4.4% French

Employment: 9.4% management, business, and financial, 2.2% computer, engineering, and science, 2.6% education, legal, community service, arts, and media, 3.5% healthcare practitioners, 24.1% service, 25.2% sales and office, 13.1% natural resources, construction, and maintenance, 20.0% production, transportation, and material moving

Income: Per capita: $23,253; Median household: $52,888; Average household: $57,846; Households with income of $100,000 or more: 14.0%; Poverty rate: 6.1%

Educational Attainment: High school diploma or higher: 85.4%; Bachelor's degree or higher: 11.2%; Graduate/professional degree or higher: 2.0%

School District(s)
Cabarrus County Schools (PK-12)
   2012-13 Enrollment: 30,418 . . . . (704) 262-6123
Housing: Homeownership rate: 81.1%; Median home value: $169,400; Median year structure built: 1985; Homeowner vacancy rate: 1.5%; Median gross rent: $779 per month; Rental vacancy rate: 7.7%

Health Insurance: 84.2% have insurance; 66.8% have private insurance; 30.8% have public insurance; 15.8% do not have insurance; 1.3% of children under 18 do not have insurance

Transportation: Commute: 97.0% car, 0.0% public transportation, 0.0% walk, 3.0% work from home; Median travel time to work: 31.6 minutes

MOUNT PLEASANT (town). Covers a land area of 3.339 square miles and a water area of 0 square miles. Located at 35.41° N. Lat; 80.43° W. Long. Elevation is 627 feet.

Population: 1,652; Growth (since 2000): 31.2%; Density: 494.8 persons per square mile; Race: 94.3% White, 4.0% Black/African American, 0.7% Asian, 0.1% American Indian/Alaska Native, 0.0% Native Hawaiian/Other Pacific Islander, 0.4% Two or more races, 1.8% Hispanic of any race; Average household size: 2.56; Median age: 40.4; Age under 18: 25.4%; Age 65 and over: 15.1%; Males per 100 females: 91.2

School District(s)
Cabarrus County Schools (PK-12)
   2012-13 Enrollment: 30,418 . . . . (704) 262-6123
Housing: Homeownership rate: 69.2%; Homeowner vacancy rate: 2.9%; Rental vacancy rate: 12.7%

Caldwell County

Located in west central North Carolina; drained by the Catawba and Yadkin Rivers. Covers a land area of 471.566 square miles, a water area of 2.747 square miles, and is located in the Eastern Time Zone at 35.96° N. Lat., 81.53° W. Long. The county was founded in 1841. County seat is Lenoir.

Caldwell County is part of the Hickory-Lenoir-Morganton, NC Metropolitan Statistical Area. The entire metro area includes: Alexander County, NC; Burke County, NC; Caldwell County, NC; Catawba County, NC

Weather Station: Lenoir									Elevation: 1,200 feet			
	Jan	Feb	Mar	Apr	May	Jun	Jul	Aug	Sep	Oct	Nov	Dec
High	50	54	62	71	78	85	88	87	81	72	62	53
Low	27	30	36	45	53	62	66	65	58	46	37	29
Precip	3.5	3.6	4.3	4.1	4.2	4.4	4.6	4.0	4.2	3.4	3.2	3.5
Snow	2.3	1.2	1.1	0.1	0.0	0.0	0.0	0.0	0.0	0.0	tr	0.5

High and Low temperatures in degrees Fahrenheit; Precipitation and Snow in inches

Population: 83,029; Growth (since 2000): 7.3%; Density: 176.1 persons per square mile; Race: 90.2% White, 4.9% Black/African American, 0.5% Asian, 0.3% American Indian/Alaska Native, 0.0% Native Hawaiian/Other Pacific Islander, 1.5% two or more races, 4.6% Hispanic of any race; Average household size: 2.46; Median age: 41.3; Age under 18: 22.6%; Age 65 and over: 15.4%; Males per 100 females: 96.8; Marriage status: 24.1% never married, 54.7% now married, 4.0% separated, 7.7% widowed, 13.6% divorced; Foreign born: 2.7%; Speak English only: 95.3%; With disability: 18.0%; Veterans: 8.7%; Ancestry: 18.9% American, 13.1% German, 10.1% Irish, 9.5% English, 3.0% Scotch-Irish

Religion: Six largest groups: 41.8% Baptist, 6.9% Methodist/Pietist, 2.4% Non-denominational Protestant, 2.2% Pentecostal, 1.4% Presbyterian-Reformed, 1.3% Lutheran

Economy: Unemployment rate: 6.3%; Leading industries: 19.1% retail trade; 12.7% other services (except public administration); 10.0% health care and social assistance; Farms: 411 totaling 32,057 acres; Company size: 0 employ 1,000 or more persons, 2 employ 500 to 999 persons, 21 employs 100 to 499 persons, 1,316 employ less than 100 persons; Business ownership: 1,582 women-owned, 119 Black-owned, n/a Hispanic-owned, n/a Asian-owned

Employment: 7.9% management, business, and financial, 2.0% computer, engineering, and science, 8.3% education, legal, community service, arts, and media, 5.5% healthcare practitioners, 16.0% service, 23.4% sales and office, 11.6% natural resources, construction, and maintenance, 25.4% production, transportation, and material moving

Income: Per capita: $19,228; Median household: $34,357; Average household: $47,430; Households with income of $100,000 or more: 7.8%; Poverty rate: 19.5%

Educational Attainment: High school diploma or higher: 75.7%; Bachelor's degree or higher: 12.5%; Graduate/professional degree or higher: 3.8%

Housing: Homeownership rate: 72.0%; Median home value: $105,800; Median year structure built: 1978; Homeowner vacancy rate: 1.9%; Median gross rent: $611 per month; Rental vacancy rate: 10.4%

Vital Statistics: Birth rate: 96.0 per 10,000 population; Death rate: 105.0 per 10,000 population; Age-adjusted cancer mortality rate: 187.8 deaths per 100,000 population

Health Insurance: 82.8% have insurance; 58.5% have private insurance; 36.6% have public insurance; 17.2% do not have insurance; 6.4% of children under 18 do not have insurance

Health Care: Physicians: 8.8 per 10,000 population; Hospital beds: 9.0 per 10,000 population; Hospital admissions: 439.2 per 10,000 population

Air Quality Index: 98.9% good, 1.1% moderate, 0.0% unhealthy for sensitive individuals, 0.0% unhealthy (percent of days)

Transportation: Commute: 94.5% car, 0.0% public transportation, 1.1% walk, 2.9% work from home; Median travel time to work: 23.3 minutes

Presidential Election: 31.4% Obama, 66.9% Romney (2012)

Additional Information Contacts
Caldwell Government . . . . (828) 757-1325
   http://www.caldwellcountync.org

Caldwell County Communities

CAJAH'S MOUNTAIN (town). Covers a land area of 3.386 square miles and a water area of 0 square miles. Located at 35.85° N. Lat; 81.54° W. Long. Elevation is 1,312 feet.

Population: 2,823; Growth (since 2000): 5.2%; Density: 833.8 persons per square mile; Race: 95.5% White, 1.6% Black/African American, 0.7% Asian, 0.3% American Indian/Alaska Native, 0.0% Native Hawaiian/Other Pacific Islander, 0.9% Two or more races, 3.1% Hispanic of any race; Average household size: 2.47; Median age: 42.7; Age under 18: 21.6%; Age 65 and over: 18.4%; Males per 100 females: 92.3; Marriage status: 16.3% never married, 62.9% now married, 2.8% separated, 7.5% widowed, 13.3% divorced; Foreign born: 0.4%; Speak English only: 99.5%; With disability: 18.7%; Veterans: 10.2%; Ancestry: 22.5% American, 15.1% Irish, 14.9% German, 5.9% English, 4.7% Dutch

Employment: 7.4% management, business, and financial, 1.8% computer, engineering, and science, 9.0% education, legal, community service, arts, and media, 4.1% healthcare practitioners, 12.3% service, 28.1% sales and office, 11.3% natural resources, construction, and maintenance, 25.9% production, transportation, and material moving
Income: Per capita: $19,623; Median household: $43,625; Average household: $49,279; Households with income of $100,000 or more: 7.8%; Poverty rate: 10.0%
Educational Attainment: High school diploma or higher: 75.4%; Bachelor's degree or higher: 12.9%; Graduate/professional degree or higher: 4.5%
Housing: Homeownership rate: 73.4%; Median home value: $115,100; Median year structure built: 1974; Homeowner vacancy rate: 1.5%; Median gross rent: $533 per month; Rental vacancy rate: 6.2%
Health Insurance: 86.4% have insurance; 69.1% have private insurance; 30.8% have public insurance; 13.6% do not have insurance; 1.0% of children under 18 do not have insurance
Transportation: Commute: 98.7% car, 0.0% public transportation, 0.3% walk, 0.9% work from home; Median travel time to work: 24.8 minutes

CEDAR ROCK (village).
Covers a land area of 1.169 square miles and a water area of 0 square miles. Located at 35.94° N. Lat; 81.46° W. Long. Elevation is 1,188 feet.
Population: 300; Growth (since 2000): -4.8%; Density: 256.7 persons per square mile; Race: 99.7% White, 0.0% Black/African American, 0.0% Asian, 0.0% American Indian/Alaska Native, 0.0% Native Hawaiian/Other Pacific Islander, 0.0% Two or more races, 1.7% Hispanic of any race; Average household size: 2.26; Median age: 57.8; Age under 18: 13.0%; Age 65 and over: 31.0%; Males per 100 females: 114.3
Housing: Homeownership rate: 97.8%; Homeowner vacancy rate: 0.8%; Rental vacancy rate: 0.0%

COLLETTSVILLE (unincorporated postal area)
ZCTA: 28611
Covers a land area of 74.403 square miles and a water area of 0 square miles. Located at 36.01° N. Lat; 81.74° W. Long. Elevation is 1,096 feet.
Population: 885; Growth (since 2000): 51.5%; Density: 11.9 persons per square mile; Race: 95.6% White, 1.7% Black/African American, 0.9% Asian, 0.7% American Indian/Alaska Native, 0.1% Native Hawaiian/Other Pacific Islander, 0.5% Two or more races, 2.4% Hispanic of any race; Average household size: 2.32; Median age: 45.4; Age under 18: 19.5%; Age 65 and over: 15.3%; Males per 100 females: 107.7

School District(s)
Caldwell County Schools (PK-12)
    2012-13 Enrollment: 12,386 . . . . (828) 728-8407
Housing: Homeownership rate: 82.4%; Homeowner vacancy rate: 2.8%; Rental vacancy rate: 23.0%

GAMEWELL (town).
Covers a land area of 8.117 square miles and a water area of 0 square miles. Located at 35.86° N. Lat; 81.60° W. Long. Elevation is 1,070 feet.
Population: 4,051; Growth (since 2000): 11.2%; Density: 499.1 persons per square mile; Race: 89.5% White, 5.3% Black/African American, 0.2% Asian, 0.0% American Indian/Alaska Native, 0.0% Native Hawaiian/Other Pacific Islander, 1.8% Two or more races, 4.5% Hispanic of any race; Average household size: 2.51; Median age: 41.5; Age under 18: 22.4%; Age 65 and over: 15.4%; Males per 100 females: 99.5; Marriage status: 24.5% never married, 50.9% now married, 3.9% separated, 8.6% widowed, 16.0% divorced; Foreign born: 1.4%; Speak English only: 93.1%; With disability: 16.9%; Veterans: 6.8%; Ancestry: 14.8% American, 12.0% German, 9.6% Irish, 8.3% English, 3.4% Italian
Employment: 4.1% management, business, and financial, 5.6% computer, engineering, and science, 5.1% education, legal, community service, arts, and media, 0.9% healthcare practitioners, 18.9% service, 14.6% sales and office, 20.2% natural resources, construction, and maintenance, 30.5% production, transportation, and material moving
Income: Per capita: $16,138; Median household: $29,976; Average household: $36,821; Households with income of $100,000 or more: 2.8%; Poverty rate: 13.4%
Educational Attainment: High school diploma or higher: 75.4%; Bachelor's degree or higher: 9.3%; Graduate/professional degree or higher: 1.8%

Housing: Homeownership rate: 73.6%; Median home value: $110,100; Median year structure built: 1977; Homeowner vacancy rate: 1.2%; Median gross rent: $606 per month; Rental vacancy rate: 9.7%
Health Insurance: 74.6% have insurance; 49.9% have private insurance; 39.7% have public insurance; 25.4% do not have insurance; 24.0% of children under 18 do not have insurance
Transportation: Commute: 94.4% car, 0.0% public transportation, 0.0% walk, 0.0% work from home; Median travel time to work: 20.9 minutes
Additional Information Contacts
Town of Gamewell. . . . . (828) 754-1991
    http://www.main.nc.us/townofgamewell

GRANITE FALLS (town).
Covers a land area of 5.196 square miles and a water area of 0.044 square miles. Located at 35.80° N. Lat; 81.42° W. Long. Elevation is 1,194 feet.
Population: 4,722; Growth (since 2000): 2.4%; Density: 908.8 persons per square mile; Race: 93.5% White, 1.7% Black/African American, 0.7% Asian, 0.2% American Indian/Alaska Native, 0.0% Native Hawaiian/Other Pacific Islander, 1.5% Two or more races, 5.2% Hispanic of any race; Average household size: 2.48; Median age: 38.9; Age under 18: 24.7%; Age 65 and over: 14.1%; Males per 100 females: 91.6; Marriage status: 25.6% never married, 51.3% now married, 2.0% separated, 8.5% widowed, 14.6% divorced; Foreign born: 4.0%; Speak English only: 93.3%; With disability: 12.6%; Veterans: 7.9%; Ancestry: 21.3% American, 19.6% German, 6.5% English, 6.3% Irish, 4.1% Scotch-Irish
Employment: 13.9% management, business, and financial, 0.9% computer, engineering, and science, 9.5% education, legal, community service, arts, and media, 7.4% healthcare practitioners, 19.3% service, 28.0% sales and office, 4.6% natural resources, construction, and maintenance, 16.5% production, transportation, and material moving
Income: Per capita: $19,508; Median household: $42,917; Average household: $50,314; Households with income of $100,000 or more: 7.4%; Poverty rate: 17.7%
Educational Attainment: High school diploma or higher: 81.6%; Bachelor's degree or higher: 14.4%; Graduate/professional degree or higher: 3.8%

School District(s)
Caldwell County Schools (PK-12)
    2012-13 Enrollment: 12,386 . . . . (828) 728-8407
Housing: Homeownership rate: 65.2%; Median home value: $121,700; Median year structure built: 1982; Homeowner vacancy rate: 2.4%; Median gross rent: $580 per month; Rental vacancy rate: 10.6%
Health Insurance: 80.4% have insurance; 58.5% have private insurance; 29.2% have public insurance; 19.6% do not have insurance; 19.5% of children under 18 do not have insurance
Safety: Violent crime rate: 19.4 per 10,000 population; Property crime rate: 624.1 per 10,000 population
Transportation: Commute: 90.4% car, 0.6% public transportation, 0.9% walk, 6.3% work from home; Median travel time to work: 19.6 minutes
Additional Information Contacts
Town of Granite Falls . . . . (828) 396-3131
    http://www.granitefallsnc.com

HUDSON (town).
Covers a land area of 3.728 square miles and a water area of 0 square miles. Located at 35.85° N. Lat; 81.49° W. Long. Elevation is 1,260 feet.
Population: 3,776; Growth (since 2000): 22.7%; Density: 1,013.0 persons per square mile; Race: 93.5% White, 1.9% Black/African American, 0.2% Asian, 0.3% American Indian/Alaska Native, 0.1% Native Hawaiian/Other Pacific Islander, 1.1% Two or more races, 5.8% Hispanic of any race; Average household size: 2.40; Median age: 40.1; Age under 18: 23.1%; Age 65 and over: 17.3%; Males per 100 females: 93.1; Marriage status: 27.2% never married, 56.4% now married, 1.9% separated, 6.4% widowed, 10.1% divorced; Foreign born: 1.5%; Speak English only: 99.2%; With disability: 15.3%; Veterans: 12.5%; Ancestry: 17.2% German, 14.3% American, 12.6% English, 10.1% Scotch-Irish, 6.2% Irish
Employment: 7.3% management, business, and financial, 1.9% computer, engineering, and science, 9.0% education, legal, community service, arts, and media, 9.1% healthcare practitioners, 18.6% service, 33.7% sales and office, 6.6% natural resources, construction, and maintenance, 13.7% production, transportation, and material moving
Income: Per capita: $27,513; Median household: $48,036; Average household: $72,139; Households with income of $100,000 or more: 17.4%; Poverty rate: 11.8%

Educational Attainment: High school diploma or higher: 87.0%; Bachelor's degree or higher: 16.9%; Graduate/professional degree or higher: 10.4%

School District(s)
Caldwell County Schools (PK-12)
    2012-13 Enrollment: 12,386 . . . . (828) 728-8407

Two-year College(s)
Caldwell Community College and Technical Institute (Public)
    Fall 2013 Enrollment: 3,933 . . . . (828) 726-2200
    2013-14 Tuition: In-state $2,364; Out-of-state $8,508

Housing: Homeownership rate: 70.3%; Median home value: $125,000; Median year structure built: 1976; Homeowner vacancy rate: 2.0%; Median gross rent: $607 per month; Rental vacancy rate: 6.8%

Health Insurance: 90.1% have insurance; 68.9% have private insurance; 36.7% have public insurance; 9.9% do not have insurance; 6.7% of children under 18 do not have insurance

Safety: Violent crime rate: 8.1 per 10,000 population; Property crime rate: 344.1 per 10,000 population

Transportation: Commute: 98.9% car, 0.0% public transportation, 0.0% walk, 0.5% work from home; Median travel time to work: 24.5 minutes

Additional Information Contacts
Town of Hudson . . . . (603) 886-6000
    http://www.hudsonnh.gov

LENOIR (city). County seat. Covers a land area of 19.640 square miles and a water area of 0 square miles. Located at 35.91° N. Lat; 81.53° W. Long. Elevation is 1,171 feet.

History: Lenoir was named for General William Lenoir.

Population: 18,228; Growth (since 2000): 8.5%; Density: 928.1 persons per square mile; Race: 78.4% White, 12.7% Black/African American, 0.9% Asian, 0.4% American Indian/Alaska Native, 0.1% Native Hawaiian/Other Pacific Islander, 2.4% Two or more races, 9.0% Hispanic of any race; Average household size: 2.32; Median age: 41.5; Age under 18: 22.8%; Age 65 and over: 18.5%; Males per 100 females: 90.8; Marriage status: 26.0% never married, 46.6% now married, 4.8% separated, 9.8% widowed, 17.5% divorced; Foreign born: 6.1%; Speak English only: 89.4%; With disability: 19.5%; Veterans: 9.0%; Ancestry: 14.3% American, 11.1% German, 9.6% English, 8.6% Irish, 2.6% Scotch-Irish

Employment: 9.4% management, business, and financial, 2.5% computer, engineering, and science, 9.0% education, legal, community service, arts, and media, 5.3% healthcare practitioners, 16.6% service, 24.3% sales and office, 7.6% natural resources, construction, and maintenance, 25.4% production, transportation, and material moving

Income: Per capita: $17,655; Median household: $28,715; Average household: $42,281; Households with income of $100,000 or more: 6.7%; Poverty rate: 24.6%

Educational Attainment: High school diploma or higher: 74.9%; Bachelor's degree or higher: 14.8%; Graduate/professional degree or higher: 4.9%

School District(s)
Caldwell County Schools (PK-12)
    2012-13 Enrollment: 12,386 . . . . (828) 728-8407

Housing: Homeownership rate: 59.3%; Median home value: $105,300; Median year structure built: 1972; Homeowner vacancy rate: 2.8%; Median gross rent: $577 per month; Rental vacancy rate: 10.1%

Health Insurance: 82.7% have insurance; 54.9% have private insurance; 40.6% have public insurance; 17.3% do not have insurance; 4.0% of children under 18 do not have insurance

Hospitals: Caldwell Memorial Hospital (110 beds)

Newspapers: News-Topic (daily circulation 8700)

Transportation: Commute: 95.4% car, 0.0% public transportation, 0.9% walk, 3.0% work from home; Median travel time to work: 20.4 minutes

Airports: Foothills Regional (general aviation)

Additional Information Contacts
City of Lenoir . . . . (828) 757-2200
    http://www.cityoflenoir.com

NORTHLAKES (CDP). Covers a land area of 1.497 square miles and a water area of 0.404 square miles. Located at 35.78° N. Lat; 81.37° W. Long. Elevation is 932 feet.

Population: 1,534; Growth (since 2000): 10.4%; Density: 1,024.9 persons per square mile; Race: 96.9% White, 0.7% Black/African American, 1.2% Asian, 0.1% American Indian/Alaska Native, 0.0% Native Hawaiian/Other Pacific Islander, 0.8% Two or more races, 1.9% Hispanic of any race;

Average household size: 2.54; Median age: 45.9; Age under 18: 20.7%; Age 65 and over: 13.5%; Males per 100 females: 101.0

Housing: Homeownership rate: 92.9%; Homeowner vacancy rate: 2.1%; Rental vacancy rate: 6.5%

SAWMILLS (town). Covers a land area of 6.618 square miles and a water area of 0.006 square miles. Located at 35.82° N. Lat; 81.48° W. Long. Elevation is 1,234 feet.

Population: 5,240; Growth (since 2000): 6.5%; Density: 791.8 persons per square mile; Race: 94.1% White, 0.9% Black/African American, 0.2% Asian, 0.3% American Indian/Alaska Native, 0.0% Native Hawaiian/Other Pacific Islander, 1.6% Two or more races, 5.2% Hispanic of any race; Average household size: 2.53; Median age: 39.5; Age under 18: 23.5%; Age 65 and over: 13.3%; Males per 100 females: 99.5; Marriage status: 24.9% never married, 55.6% now married, 3.6% separated, 6.1% widowed, 13.4% divorced; Foreign born: 3.3%; Speak English only: 98.9%; With disability: 18.5%; Veterans: 8.1%; Ancestry: 21.5% American, 17.6% Irish, 13.3% German, 10.1% English, 4.4% Scotch-Irish

Employment: 3.5% management, business, and financial, 1.9% computer, engineering, and science, 14.1% education, legal, community service, arts, and media, 5.0% healthcare practitioners, 11.3% service, 19.2% sales and office, 15.7% natural resources, construction, and maintenance, 29.2% production, transportation, and material moving

Income: Per capita: $18,002; Median household: $38,608; Average household: $48,405; Households with income of $100,000 or more: 9.8%; Poverty rate: 20.8%

Educational Attainment: High school diploma or higher: 73.1%; Bachelor's degree or higher: 9.3%; Graduate/professional degree or higher: 3.7%

Housing: Homeownership rate: 65.2%; Median home value: $96,800; Median year structure built: 1983; Homeowner vacancy rate: 1.0%; Median gross rent: $605 per month; Rental vacancy rate: 12.6%

Health Insurance: 82.2% have insurance; 62.4% have private insurance; 32.7% have public insurance; 17.8% do not have insurance; 6.0% of children under 18 do not have insurance

Transportation: Commute: 89.8% car, 0.0% public transportation, 1.6% walk, 6.0% work from home; Median travel time to work: 23.8 minutes

Additional Information Contacts
Town of Sawmills . . . . (828) 396-7903
    http://www.caldwellcochamber.org

Camden County

Located in northeastern North Carolina; bounded on the north by Virginia, on the southeast by the North River Estuary, and on the south by Albemarle Sound. Covers a land area of 240.556 square miles, a water area of 69.658 square miles, and is located in the Eastern Time Zone at 36.34° N. Lat., 76.16° W. Long. The county was founded in 1777. County seat is Camden.

Camden County is part of the Elizabeth City, NC Micropolitan Statistical Area. The entire metro area includes: Camden County, NC; Pasquotank County, NC; Perquimans County, NC

Population: 9,980; Growth (since 2000): 45.0%; Density: 41.5 persons per square mile; Race: 82.1% White, 13.2% Black/African American, 1.5% Asian, 0.3% American Indian/Alaska Native, 0.1% Native Hawaiian/Other Pacific Islander, 2.1% two or more races, 2.2% Hispanic of any race; Average household size: 2.71; Median age: 40.1; Age under 18: 25.6%; Age 65 and over: 12.9%; Males per 100 females: 100.6; Marriage status: 25.1% never married, 60.3% now married, 1.7% separated, 6.7% widowed, 7.8% divorced; Foreign born: 3.1%; Speak English only: 95.6%; With disability: 15.4%; Veterans: 14.7%; Ancestry: 17.4% American, 15.2% Irish, 12.8% English, 11.9% German, 2.9% Italian

Religion: Three largest groups: 16.3% Baptist, 10.9% Methodist/Pietist, 6.5% Pentecostal

Economy: Unemployment rate: 5.5%; Leading industries: 17.1% construction; 16.2% other services (except public administration); 15.3% retail trade; Farms: 60 totaling 49,310 acres; Company size: 0 employ 1,000 or more persons, 0 employ 500 to 999 persons, 0 employ 100 to 499 persons, 111 employs less than 100 persons; Business ownership: n/a women-owned, n/a Black-owned, n/a Hispanic-owned, n/a Asian-owned

Employment: 14.9% management, business, and financial, 8.2% computer, engineering, and science, 8.6% education, legal, community service, arts, and media, 5.7% healthcare practitioners, 18.0% service,

21.9% sales and office, 15.1% natural resources, construction, and maintenance, 7.5% production, transportation, and material moving
Income: Per capita: $25,620; Median household: $56,607; Average household: $68,190; Households with income of $100,000 or more: 20.7%; Poverty rate: 6.0%
Educational Attainment: High school diploma or higher: 86.3%; Bachelor's degree or higher: 18.8%; Graduate/professional degree or higher: 5.7%
Housing: Homeownership rate: 82.1%; Median home value: $220,200; Median year structure built: 1990; Homeowner vacancy rate: 2.4%; Median gross rent: $1,030 per month; Rental vacancy rate: 12.4%
Vital Statistics: Birth rate: 83.4 per 10,000 population; Death rate: 46.1 per 10,000 population; Age-adjusted cancer mortality rate: Unreliable deaths per 100,000 population
Health Insurance: 90.2% have insurance; 74.3% have private insurance; 30.8% have public insurance; 9.8% do not have insurance; 2.3% of children under 18 do not have insurance
Health Care: Physicians: 7.0 per 10,000 population; Hospital beds: 0.0 per 10,000 population; Hospital admissions: 0.0 per 10,000 population
Transportation: Commute: 96.7% car, 0.7% public transportation, 0.0% walk, 1.7% work from home; Median travel time to work: 34.7 minutes
Presidential Election: 32.1% Obama, 66.1% Romney (2012)
National and State Parks: Dismal Swamp State Park
Additional Information Contacts
Camden Government . . . . (252) 338-1919
    http://www.camdencountync.gov

Camden County Communities

CAMDEN (CDP). County seat. Covers a land area of 1.579 square miles and a water area of 0.008 square miles. Located at 36.33° N. Lat; 76.17° W. Long. Elevation is 10 feet.
Population: 599; Growth (since 2000): n/a; Density: 379.4 persons per square mile; Race: 84.3% White, 8.7% Black/African American, 1.3% Asian, 0.7% American Indian/Alaska Native, 0.0% Native Hawaiian/Other Pacific Islander, 3.5% Two or more races, 3.8% Hispanic of any race; Average household size: 2.27; Median age: 41.2; Age under 18: 23.0%; Age 65 and over: 15.7%; Males per 100 females: 99.0
School District(s)
Camden County Schools (PK-12)
    2012-13 Enrollment: 1,929 . . . . (252) 335-0831
Housing: Homeownership rate: 56.4%; Homeowner vacancy rate: 1.3%; Rental vacancy rate: 12.1%

SHAWBORO (unincorporated postal area)
ZCTA: 27973
    Covers a land area of 37.636 square miles and a water area of 0.060 square miles. Located at 36.37° N. Lat; 76.06° W. Long..
    Population: 1,323; Growth (since 2000): 35.1%; Density: 35.2 persons per square mile; Race: 89.7% White, 4.8% Black/African American, 0.5% Asian, 0.5% American Indian/Alaska Native, 0.0% Native Hawaiian/Other Pacific Islander, 1.7% Two or more races, 4.6% Hispanic of any race; Average household size: 2.70; Median age: 39.9; Age under 18: 24.8%; Age 65 and over: 13.1%; Males per 100 females: 95.1
    Housing: Homeownership rate: 79.8%; Homeowner vacancy rate: 2.0%; Rental vacancy rate: 6.5%

SHILOH (unincorporated postal area)
ZCTA: 27974
    Covers a land area of 45.884 square miles and a water area of 25.596 square miles. Located at 36.24° N. Lat; 75.99° W. Long. Elevation is 7 feet.
    Population: 1,285; Growth (since 2000): 8.3%; Density: 28.0 persons per square mile; Race: 85.1% White, 7.5% Black/African American, 5.1% Asian, 0.5% American Indian/Alaska Native, 0.1% Native Hawaiian/Other Pacific Islander, 0.9% Two or more races, 1.2% Hispanic of any race; Average household size: 2.60; Median age: 44.2; Age under 18: 21.2%; Age 65 and over: 16.7%; Males per 100 females: 98.3
    Housing: Homeownership rate: 77.7%; Homeowner vacancy rate: 3.0%; Rental vacancy rate: 11.3%

SOUTH MILLS (CDP). Covers a land area of 1.792 square miles and a water area of 0 square miles. Located at 36.44° N. Lat; 76.33° W. Long. Elevation is 13 feet.
Population: 454; Growth (since 2000): n/a; Density: 253.3 persons per square mile; Race: 74.9% White, 16.3% Black/African American, 2.4% Asian, 0.9% American Indian/Alaska Native, 0.0% Native Hawaiian/Other Pacific Islander, 3.3% Two or more races, 2.4% Hispanic of any race; Average household size: 2.65; Median age: 41.0; Age under 18: 23.8%; Age 65 and over: 19.4%; Males per 100 females: 98.3
Housing: Homeownership rate: 78.4%; Homeowner vacancy rate: 0.7%; Rental vacancy rate: 21.3%

Carteret County

Located in eastern North Carolina, on the Atlantic coast; bounded on the south by Onslow Bay, on the east by Raleigh Bay, and on the northeast by the Neuse River and Pamlico Sound; includes part of Croatan National Forest. Covers a land area of 506.251 square miles, a water area of 834.374 square miles, and is located in the Eastern Time Zone at 34.86° N. Lat., 76.53° W. Long. The county was founded in 1722. County seat is Beaufort.

Carteret County is part of the Morehead City, NC Micropolitan Statistical Area. The entire metro area includes: Carteret County, NC

Weather Station: Cedar Island — Elevation: 7 feet

	Jan	Feb	Mar	Apr	May	Jun	Jul	Aug	Sep	Oct	Nov	Dec
High	54	57	64	73	80	86	90	88	83	74	66	57
Low	37	39	45	53	60	68	72	71	67	57	48	40
Precip	4.6	3.4	4.5	3.5	3.9	4.1	6.2	7.3	6.1	4.7	4.0	4.4
Snow	1.1	0.2	0.6	tr	0.0	0.0	0.0	0.0	0.0	0.0	tr	0.6

High and Low temperatures in degrees Fahrenheit; Precipitation and Snow in inches

Weather Station: Morehead City 2 WNW — Elevation: 9 feet

	Jan	Feb	Mar	Apr	May	Jun	Jul	Aug	Sep	Oct	Nov	Dec
High	56	59	64	71	78	84	88	87	83	76	68	60
Low	36	38	43	51	60	69	73	71	66	56	47	39
Precip	4.6	3.8	4.3	3.3	4.6	4.4	6.1	7.5	7.1	4.7	4.5	4.4
Snow	0.3	0.1	0.7	0.0	0.0	0.0	0.0	0.0	0.0	0.0	0.0	tr

High and Low temperatures in degrees Fahrenheit; Precipitation and Snow in inches

Population: 66,469; Growth (since 2000): 11.9%; Density: 131.3 persons per square mile; Race: 89.3% White, 6.1% Black/African American, 0.9% Asian, 0.5% American Indian/Alaska Native, 0.1% Native Hawaiian/Other Pacific Islander, 2.0% two or more races, 3.4% Hispanic of any race; Average household size: 2.27; Median age: 45.8; Age under 18: 18.9%; Age 65 and over: 19.0%; Males per 100 females: 97.6; Marriage status: 23.1% never married, 56.3% now married, 3.2% separated, 7.4% widowed, 13.1% divorced; Foreign born: 3.4%; Speak English only: 95.3%; With disability: 18.1%; Veterans: 16.9%; Ancestry: 19.7% English, 14.3% German, 13.2% Irish, 12.8% American, 4.3% Italian
Religion: Six largest groups: 16.2% Baptist, 10.8% Methodist/Pietist, 4.9% Pentecostal, 3.5% Catholicism, 3.0% Non-denominational Protestant, 1.6% Latter-day Saints
Economy: Unemployment rate: 5.2%; Leading industries: 19.1% retail trade; 12.1% construction; 12.0% accommodation and food services; Farms: 125 totaling 62,836 acres; Company size: 0 employ 1,000 or more persons, 1 employs 500 to 999 persons, 13 employ 100 to 499 persons, 1,913 employ less than 100 persons; Business ownership: 1,743 women-owned, 86 Black-owned, n/a Hispanic-owned, 128 Asian-owned
Employment: 13.6% management, business, and financial, 3.2% computer, engineering, and science, 10.4% education, legal, community service, arts, and media, 6.0% healthcare practitioners, 18.9% service, 23.6% sales and office, 14.0% natural resources, construction, and maintenance, 10.1% production, transportation, and material moving
Income: Per capita: $27,496; Median household: $46,534; Average household: $61,663; Households with income of $100,000 or more: 15.3%; Poverty rate: 14.4%
Educational Attainment: High school diploma or higher: 88.3%; Bachelor's degree or higher: 23.9%; Graduate/professional degree or higher: 7.7%
Housing: Homeownership rate: 71.4%; Median home value: $199,200; Median year structure built: 1985; Homeowner vacancy rate: 3.9%; Median gross rent: $759 per month; Rental vacancy rate: 17.3%

Vital Statistics: Birth rate: 91.6 per 10,000 population; Death rate: 111.5 per 10,000 population; Age-adjusted cancer mortality rate: 190.8 deaths per 100,000 population

Health Insurance: 83.9% have insurance; 65.8% have private insurance; 36.9% have public insurance; 16.1% do not have insurance; 7.6% of children under 18 do not have insurance

Health Care: Physicians: 19.9 per 10,000 population; Hospital beds: 30.9 per 10,000 population; Hospital admissions: 961.6 per 10,000 population

Air Quality Index: 98.0% good, 2.0% moderate, 0.0% unhealthy for sensitive individuals, 0.0% unhealthy (percent of days)

Transportation: Commute: 91.4% car, 0.6% public transportation, 2.1% walk, 4.1% work from home; Median travel time to work: 23.5 minutes

Presidential Election: 29.0% Obama, 69.8% Romney (2012)

National and State Parks: Cape Lookout National Seashore; Cedar Island National Wildlife Refuge; Fort Macon State Park; Rachael Carson National Estuarine Sanctuary

Additional Information Contacts

Carteret Government............................ (252) 728-8450
  http://www.carteretcountygov.org

Carteret County Communities

ATLANTIC (CDP). Covers a land area of 0.918 square miles and a water area of 0.019 square miles. Located at 34.88° N. Lat; 76.34° W. Long. Elevation is 16 feet.

Population: 543; Growth (since 2000): n/a; Density: 591.7 persons per square mile; Race: 98.2% White, 0.0% Black/African American, 0.0% Asian, 0.0% American Indian/Alaska Native, 0.0% Native Hawaiian/Other Pacific Islander, 0.6% Two or more races, 1.8% Hispanic of any race; Average household size: 2.07; Median age: 52.2; Age under 18: 12.9%; Age 65 and over: 26.0%; Males per 100 females: 109.7

School District(s)

Carteret County Public Schools (PK-12)
  2012-13 Enrollment: 8,701 .... (252) 728-4583

Housing: Homeownership rate: 80.2%; Homeowner vacancy rate: 9.5%; Rental vacancy rate: 22.1%

ATLANTIC BEACH (town). Covers a land area of 2.326 square miles and a water area of 0.344 square miles. Located at 34.70° N. Lat; 76.74° W. Long. Elevation is 10 feet.

History: Just East Fort Macon State Park, with fort built c.1826-1835, restored 1936.

Population: 1,495; Growth (since 2000): -16.1%; Density: 642.9 persons per square mile; Race: 94.4% White, 0.7% Black/African American, 0.9% Asian, 0.5% American Indian/Alaska Native, 0.1% Native Hawaiian/Other Pacific Islander, 2.1% Two or more races, 1.5% Hispanic of any race; Average household size: 1.78; Median age: 50.0; Age under 18: 10.2%; Age 65 and over: 19.7%; Males per 100 females: 115.1

Housing: Homeownership rate: 51.1%; Homeowner vacancy rate: 9.3%; Rental vacancy rate: 12.0%

Safety: Violent crime rate: 100.6 per 10,000 population; Property crime rate: 811.5 per 10,000 population

Additional Information Contacts

Town of Atlantic Beach .... (252) 726-2121
  http://www.atlanticbeach-nc.com

BEAUFORT (town). County seat. Covers a land area of 4.620 square miles and a water area of 0.997 square miles. Located at 34.73° N. Lat; 76.65° W. Long. Elevation is 10 feet.

History: Beaufort was first known as Fishtown. The village was laid out in 1722 as Beaufort, honoring Henry, Duke of Beaufort. Settlers are believed to have arrived as early as 1709. They were French, English, Scottish, Irish, German, and Swedish.

Population: 4,039; Growth (since 2000): 7.1%; Density: 874.2 persons per square mile; Race: 79.0% White, 17.0% Black/African American, 0.7% Asian, 0.2% American Indian/Alaska Native, 0.0% Native Hawaiian/Other Pacific Islander, 2.4% Two or more races, 2.6% Hispanic of any race; Average household size: 1.95; Median age: 46.8; Age under 18: 16.1%; Age 65 and over: 20.7%; Males per 100 females: 90.2; Marriage status: 37.1% never married, 37.3% now married, 3.0% separated, 7.3% widowed, 18.3% divorced; Foreign born: 4.6%; Speak English only: 95.9%; With disability: 17.5%; Veterans: 10.9%; Ancestry: 18.9% English, 13.8% American, 12.0% Irish, 6.1% German, 3.5% French

Employment: 16.6% management, business, and financial, 6.8% computer, engineering, and science, 10.4% education, legal, community service, arts, and media, 2.7% healthcare practitioners, 27.4% service, 20.8% sales and office, 9.7% natural resources, construction, and maintenance, 5.7% production, transportation, and material moving

Income: Per capita: $21,202; Median household: $28,644; Average household: $42,067; Households with income of $100,000 or more: 8.4%; Poverty rate: 32.4%

Educational Attainment: High school diploma or higher: 83.0%; Bachelor's degree or higher: 24.0%; Graduate/professional degree or higher: 11.9%

School District(s)

Carteret County Public Schools (PK-12)
  2012-13 Enrollment: 8,701 .... (252) 728-4583
Tiller School (KG-05)
  2012-13 Enrollment: 189...................... (252) 728-1995

Housing: Homeownership rate: 47.8%; Median home value: $196,500; Median year structure built: 1972; Homeowner vacancy rate: 7.1%; Median gross rent: $602 per month; Rental vacancy rate: 7.8%

Health Insurance: 88.1% have insurance; 57.0% have private insurance; 48.4% have public insurance; 11.9% do not have insurance; 0.0% of children under 18 do not have insurance

Safety: Violent crime rate: 39.0 per 10,000 population; Property crime rate: 411.5 per 10,000 population

Transportation: Commute: 80.5% car, 1.7% public transportation, 3.6% walk, 6.2% work from home; Median travel time to work: 22.1 minutes

Airports: Michael J. Smith Field (general aviation)

Additional Information Contacts

Town of Beaufort.............................. (252) 728-2141
  http://www.beaufortnc.org

BOGUE (town). Covers a land area of 2.765 square miles and a water area of 0.239 square miles. Located at 34.69° N. Lat; 77.03° W. Long. Elevation is 23 feet.

Population: 684; Growth (since 2000): 15.9%; Density: 247.3 persons per square mile; Race: 92.8% White, 2.2% Black/African American, 0.6% Asian, 0.1% American Indian/Alaska Native, 0.0% Native Hawaiian/Other Pacific Islander, 1.8% Two or more races, 5.3% Hispanic of any race; Average household size: 2.60; Median age: 44.4; Age under 18: 22.5%; Age 65 and over: 15.9%; Males per 100 females: 103.0

Housing: Homeownership rate: 78.7%; Homeowner vacancy rate: 3.7%; Rental vacancy rate: 3.4%

BROAD CREEK (CDP). Covers a land area of 3.107 square miles and a water area of 0.011 square miles. Located at 34.74° N. Lat; 76.92° W. Long. Elevation is 10 feet.

Population: 2,334; Growth (since 2000): n/a; Density: 751.3 persons per square mile; Race: 92.5% White, 2.0% Black/African American, 0.3% Asian, 0.8% American Indian/Alaska Native, 0.1% Native Hawaiian/Other Pacific Islander, 2.9% Two or more races, 3.6% Hispanic of any race; Average household size: 2.60; Median age: 39.9; Age under 18: 24.2%; Age 65 and over: 12.4%; Males per 100 females: 101.4

Housing: Homeownership rate: 79.2%; Homeowner vacancy rate: 1.9%; Rental vacancy rate: 8.3%

CAPE CARTERET (town). Covers a land area of 2.486 square miles and a water area of 0.188 square miles. Located at 34.69° N. Lat; 77.06° W. Long. Elevation is 16 feet.

Population: 1,917; Growth (since 2000): 57.9%; Density: 771.1 persons per square mile; Race: 95.3% White, 1.1% Black/African American, 1.8% Asian, 0.6% American Indian/Alaska Native, 0.1% Native Hawaiian/Other Pacific Islander, 0.9% Two or more races, 1.6% Hispanic of any race; Average household size: 2.39; Median age: 48.8; Age under 18: 20.0%; Age 65 and over: 23.9%; Males per 100 females: 96.6

School District(s)

Carteret County Public Schools (PK-12)
  2012-13 Enrollment: 8,701 .... (252) 728-4583

Housing: Homeownership rate: 84.6%; Homeowner vacancy rate: 3.5%; Rental vacancy rate: 7.5%

Safety: Violent crime rate: 0.0 per 10,000 population; Property crime rate: 103.7 per 10,000 population

CEDAR ISLAND (unincorporated postal area)

ZCTA: 28520

Covers a land area of 22.003 square miles and a water area of 50.734 square miles. Located at 34.99° N. Lat; 76.32° W. Long. Elevation is 3 feet.

Population: 327; Growth (since 2000): -0.3%; Density: 14.9 persons per square mile; Race: 99.7% White, 0.0% Black/African American, 0.3% Asian, 0.0% American Indian/Alaska Native, 0.0% Native Hawaiian/Other Pacific Islander, 0.0% Two or more races, 1.8% Hispanic of any race; Average household size: 2.34; Median age: 44.8; Age under 18: 23.2%; Age 65 and over: 21.4%; Males per 100 females: 103.1

Housing: Homeownership rate: 85.7%; Homeowner vacancy rate: 8.4%; Rental vacancy rate: 13.0%

CEDAR POINT (town). Covers a land area of 2.199 square miles and a water area of 0.005 square miles. Located at 34.69° N. Lat; 77.08° W. Long. Elevation is 20 feet.

Population: 1,279; Growth (since 2000): 37.7%; Density: 581.7 persons per square mile; Race: 93.4% White, 1.2% Black/African American, 0.9% Asian, 0.8% American Indian/Alaska Native, 0.0% Native Hawaiian/Other Pacific Islander, 2.3% Two or more races, 2.7% Hispanic of any race; Average household size: 2.30; Median age: 45.8; Age under 18: 21.4%; Age 65 and over: 17.8%; Males per 100 females: 95.6

Housing: Homeownership rate: 74.7%; Homeowner vacancy rate: 2.8%; Rental vacancy rate: 10.8%

DAVIS (CDP). Covers a land area of 2.180 square miles and a water area of 0.013 square miles. Located at 34.79° N. Lat; 76.47° W. Long. Elevation is 3 feet.

Population: 422; Growth (since 2000): n/a; Density: 193.6 persons per square mile; Race: 98.6% White, 0.0% Black/African American, 0.2% Asian, 0.2% American Indian/Alaska Native, 0.0% Native Hawaiian/Other Pacific Islander, 0.7% Two or more races, 0.2% Hispanic of any race; Average household size: 2.23; Median age: 47.4; Age under 18: 17.1%; Age 65 and over: 25.1%; Males per 100 females: 86.7

Housing: Homeownership rate: 83.0%; Homeowner vacancy rate: 2.4%; Rental vacancy rate: 3.0%

EMERALD ISLE (town). Covers a land area of 4.990 square miles and a water area of 0.085 square miles. Located at 34.66° N. Lat; 77.03° W. Long. Elevation is 10 feet.

History: Flying over the area, appearing as a solid green gem in the middle of a sea of sparkling water, a developer looked down from the heavens and said, "This Place Shall be Known as Emerald Isle.

Population: 3,655; Growth (since 2000): 4.8%; Density: 732.4 persons per square mile; Race: 96.7% White, 0.6% Black/African American, 0.8% Asian, 0.2% American Indian/Alaska Native, 0.2% Native Hawaiian/Other Pacific Islander, 1.0% Two or more races, 2.0% Hispanic of any race; Average household size: 2.11; Median age: 52.2; Age under 18: 14.6%; Age 65 and over: 25.8%; Males per 100 females: 103.5; Marriage status: 17.9% never married, 69.2% now married, 2.3% separated, 5.9% widowed, 7.0% divorced; Foreign born: 1.8%; Speak English only: 95.9%; With disability: 14.5%; Veterans: 19.1%; Ancestry: 17.9% American, 16.9% English, 15.2% German, 8.6% Irish, 7.5% Italian

Employment: 26.6% management, business, and financial, 6.7% computer, engineering, and science, 9.9% education, legal, community service, arts, and media, 8.0% healthcare practitioners, 14.7% service, 25.4% sales and office, 4.9% natural resources, construction, and maintenance, 3.8% production, transportation, and material moving

Income: Per capita: $38,813; Median household: $54,201; Average household: $78,312; Households with income of $100,000 or more: 27.7%; Poverty rate: 6.3%

Educational Attainment: High school diploma or higher: 95.8%; Bachelor's degree or higher: 46.5%; Graduate/professional degree or higher: 15.9%

Housing: Homeownership rate: 72.2%; Median home value: $390,600; Median year structure built: 1988; Homeowner vacancy rate: 6.6%; Median gross rent: $1,261 per month; Rental vacancy rate: 65.5%

Health Insurance: 90.7% have insurance; 83.5% have private insurance; 33.7% have public insurance; 9.3% do not have insurance; 0.0% of children under 18 do not have insurance

Safety: Violent crime rate: 32.7 per 10,000 population; Property crime rate: 654.1 per 10,000 population

Transportation: Commute: 84.7% car, 0.0% public transportation, 2.1% walk, 10.2% work from home; Median travel time to work: 23.4 minutes

Additional Information Contacts

Town of Emerald Isle . . . . (252) 354-3424
    http://www.emeraldisle-nc.org

GLOUCESTER (CDP). Covers a land area of 1.436 square miles and a water area of 0.014 square miles. Located at 34.73° N. Lat; 76.54° W. Long. Elevation is 7 feet.

Population: 537; Growth (since 2000): n/a; Density: 374.0 persons per square mile; Race: 98.3% White, 0.0% Black/African American, 0.4% Asian, 0.2% American Indian/Alaska Native, 0.0% Native Hawaiian/Other Pacific Islander, 0.9% Two or more races, 0.7% Hispanic of any race; Average household size: 2.29; Median age: 44.0; Age under 18: 18.1%; Age 65 and over: 14.5%; Males per 100 females: 92.5

Housing: Homeownership rate: 81.2%; Homeowner vacancy rate: 5.0%; Rental vacancy rate: 13.5%

HARKERS ISLAND (CDP). Covers a land area of 2.241 square miles and a water area of 1.607 square miles. Located at 34.70° N. Lat; 76.56° W. Long. Elevation is 10 feet.

Population: 1,207; Growth (since 2000): -20.9%; Density: 538.5 persons per square mile; Race: 98.5% White, 0.0% Black/African American, 0.2% Asian, 0.2% American Indian/Alaska Native, 0.0% Native Hawaiian/Other Pacific Islander, 1.0% Two or more races, 0.1% Hispanic of any race; Average household size: 2.27; Median age: 53.8; Age under 18: 12.6%; Age 65 and over: 26.4%; Males per 100 females: 98.5

School District(s)

Carteret County Public Schools (PK-12)
    2012-13 Enrollment: 8,701 . . . . (252) 728-4583

Housing: Homeownership rate: 80.9%; Homeowner vacancy rate: 6.3%; Rental vacancy rate: 19.8%

INDIAN BEACH (town). Covers a land area of 0.560 square miles and a water area of 0.916 square miles. Located at 34.69° N. Lat; 76.90° W. Long. Elevation is 7 feet.

Population: 112; Growth (since 2000): 17.9%; Density: 200.0 persons per square mile; Race: 97.3% White, 0.9% Black/African American, 0.9% Asian, 0.0% American Indian/Alaska Native, 0.0% Native Hawaiian/Other Pacific Islander, 0.9% Two or more races, 0.0% Hispanic of any race; Average household size: 1.70; Median age: 59.7; Age under 18: 3.6%; Age 65 and over: 35.7%; Males per 100 females: 103.6

Housing: Homeownership rate: 90.9%; Homeowner vacancy rate: 19.8%; Rental vacancy rate: 89.2%

Safety: Violent crime rate: 0.0 per 10,000 population; Property crime rate: 1,052.6 per 10,000 population

MARSHALLBERG (CDP). Covers a land area of 0.637 square miles and a water area of 0.006 square miles. Located at 34.73° N. Lat; 76.51° W. Long. Elevation is 3 feet.

Population: 403; Growth (since 2000): n/a; Density: 632.7 persons per square mile; Race: 97.8% White, 0.0% Black/African American, 1.5% Asian, 0.0% American Indian/Alaska Native, 0.0% Native Hawaiian/Other Pacific Islander, 0.7% Two or more races, 0.2% Hispanic of any race; Average household size: 2.00; Median age: 53.1; Age under 18: 12.9%; Age 65 and over: 24.6%; Males per 100 females: 112.1

Housing: Homeownership rate: 79.7%; Homeowner vacancy rate: 5.3%; Rental vacancy rate: 2.4%

MOREHEAD CITY (town). Covers a land area of 6.851 square miles and a water area of 1.665 square miles. Located at 34.73° N. Lat; 76.74° W. Long. Elevation is 16 feet.

History: Morehead City was founded in 1857 by John Motley Morehead, governor of North Carolina (1841-1845), as a land speculation enterprise. Members of the crews of several British vessels, trapped in the harbor by a Federal blockade, settled here.

Population: 8,661; Growth (since 2000): 12.6%; Density: 1,264.2 persons per square mile; Race: 82.0% White, 10.7% Black/African American, 1.6% Asian, 0.5% American Indian/Alaska Native, 0.2% Native Hawaiian/Other Pacific Islander, 2.5% Two or more races, 6.9% Hispanic of any race; Average household size: 2.06; Median age: 42.4; Age under 18: 19.4%; Age 65 and over: 19.3%; Males per 100 females: 87.0; Marriage status: 24.8% never married, 47.7% now married, 3.7% separated, 9.8% widowed, 17.6% divorced; Foreign born: 5.4%; Speak English only: 94.1%; With disability: 19.5%; Veterans: 15.1%; Ancestry: 15.6% English, 13.8% American, 11.7% Irish, 9.8% German, 4.3% Scotch-Irish

Employment: 17.0% management, business, and financial, 2.8% computer, engineering, and science, 9.9% education, legal, community service, arts, and media, 5.9% healthcare practitioners, 21.1% service, 23.1% sales and office, 8.8% natural resources, construction, and maintenance, 11.5% production, transportation, and material moving

Income: Per capita: $26,548; Median household: $35,982; Average household: $54,974; Households with income of $100,000 or more: 12.7%; Poverty rate: 22.0%

Educational Attainment: High school diploma or higher: 89.5%; Bachelor's degree or higher: 27.5%; Graduate/professional degree or higher: 7.4%

School District(s)

Cape Lookout Marine Sci High (09-12)
    2012-13 Enrollment: 70. . . . . (252) 726-1601
Carteret County Public Schools (PK-12)
    2012-13 Enrollment: 8,701 . . . . (252) 728-4583

Two-year College(s)

Carteret Community College (Public)
    Fall 2013 Enrollment: 1,524 . . . . (252) 222-6000
    2013-14 Tuition: In-state $2,658; Out-of-state $7,266

Housing: Homeownership rate: 50.3%; Median home value: $191,300; Median year structure built: 1981; Homeowner vacancy rate: 4.3%; Median gross rent: $649 per month; Rental vacancy rate: 7.2%

Health Insurance: 78.3% have insurance; 57.0% have private insurance; 39.3% have public insurance; 21.7% do not have insurance; 8.6% of children under 18 do not have insurance

Hospitals: Carteret General Hospital (117 beds)

Safety: Violent crime rate: 62.2 per 10,000 population; Property crime rate: 576.5 per 10,000 population

Newspapers: Carteret County News Times (weekly circulation 11000)

Transportation: Commute: 90.4% car, 0.6% public transportation, 4.3% walk, 2.7% work from home; Median travel time to work: 16.5 minutes; Amtrak: Bus service available.

Additional Information Contacts

Town of Morehead City . . . . (252) 726-6848
    http://www.townofmorehead.com

NEWPORT (town).

Covers a land area of 7.672 square miles and a water area of 0.066 square miles. Located at 34.77° N. Lat; 76.88° W. Long. Elevation is 20 feet.

Population: 4,150; Growth (since 2000): 23.9%; Density: 541.0 persons per square mile; Race: 81.7% White, 11.3% Black/African American, 1.7% Asian, 0.5% American Indian/Alaska Native, 0.1% Native Hawaiian/Other Pacific Islander, 3.2% Two or more races, 4.7% Hispanic of any race; Average household size: 2.38; Median age: 38.9; Age under 18: 21.6%; Age 65 and over: 14.6%; Males per 100 females: 102.2; Marriage status: 30.7% never married, 47.5% now married, 4.9% separated, 7.4% widowed, 14.4% divorced; Foreign born: 4.4%; Speak English only: 94.2%; With disability: 20.3%; Veterans: 23.9%; Ancestry: 14.3% American, 13.7% English, 13.4% Irish, 10.8% German, 3.6% Italian

Employment: 5.8% management, business, and financial, 6.6% computer, engineering, and science, 9.8% education, legal, community service, arts, and media, 3.9% healthcare practitioners, 23.0% service, 19.2% sales and office, 23.8% natural resources, construction, and maintenance, 8.0% production, transportation, and material moving

Income: Per capita: $21,020; Median household: $41,842; Average household: $51,138; Households with income of $100,000 or more: 5.7%; Poverty rate: 10.9%

Educational Attainment: High school diploma or higher: 84.7%; Bachelor's degree or higher: 9.2%; Graduate/professional degree or higher: 2.7%

School District(s)

Carteret County Public Schools (PK-12)
    2012-13 Enrollment: 8,701 . . . . (252) 728-4583

Housing: Homeownership rate: 61.7%; Median home value: $158,700; Median year structure built: 1985; Homeowner vacancy rate: 3.2%; Median gross rent: $842 per month; Rental vacancy rate: 6.5%

Health Insurance: 83.3% have insurance; 73.0% have private insurance; 27.9% have public insurance; 16.7% do not have insurance; 8.1% of children under 18 do not have insurance

Safety: Violent crime rate: 16.7 per 10,000 population; Property crime rate: 253.2 per 10,000 population

Transportation: Commute: 95.2% car, 0.0% public transportation, 1.7% walk, 2.1% work from home; Median travel time to work: 21.9 minutes

Additional Information Contacts

Town of Newport . . . . (262) 223-4749
    http://www.townofnewport.com

PELETIER (town).

Covers a land area of 3.619 square miles and a water area of 0.057 square miles. Located at 34.73° N. Lat; 77.07° W. Long. Elevation is 30 feet.

Population: 644; Growth (since 2000): 32.2%; Density: 178.0 persons per square mile; Race: 92.2% White, 1.2% Black/African American, 0.5% Asian, 0.6% American Indian/Alaska Native, 0.5% Native Hawaiian/Other Pacific Islander, 1.7% Two or more races, 6.1% Hispanic of any race; Average household size: 2.26; Median age: 44.8; Age under 18: 19.3%; Age 65 and over: 17.7%; Males per 100 females: 110.5

Housing: Homeownership rate: 65.2%; Homeowner vacancy rate: 5.1%; Rental vacancy rate: 10.0%

PINE KNOLL SHORES (town).

Covers a land area of 2.224 square miles and a water area of 0.319 square miles. Located at 34.70° N. Lat; 76.83° W. Long. Elevation is 10 feet.

Population: 1,339; Growth (since 2000): -12.1%; Density: 602.2 persons per square mile; Race: 96.3% White, 0.7% Black/African American, 1.0% Asian, 0.1% American Indian/Alaska Native, 0.2% Native Hawaiian/Other Pacific Islander, 1.0% Two or more races, 1.0% Hispanic of any race; Average household size: 2.04; Median age: 62.1; Age under 18: 10.0%; Age 65 and over: 42.7%; Males per 100 females: 95.8

Housing: Homeownership rate: 89.3%; Homeowner vacancy rate: 5.9%; Rental vacancy rate: 15.7%

Safety: Violent crime rate: 0.0 per 10,000 population; Property crime rate: 223.2 per 10,000 population

Additional Information Contacts

Town of Pine Knoll Shores . . . . (252) 247-4353
    http://www.townofpks.com

SALTER PATH (unincorporated postal area)

ZCTA: 28575

Covers a land area of 0.601 square miles and a water area of 4.764 square miles. Located at 34.71° N. Lat; 76.88° W. Long. Elevation is 10 feet.

Population: 316; Growth (since 2000): 135.8%; Density: 525.5 persons per square mile; Race: 99.4% White, 0.0% Black/African American, 0.3% Asian, 0.0% American Indian/Alaska Native, 0.0% Native Hawaiian/Other Pacific Islander, 0.3% Two or more races, 0.0% Hispanic of any race; Average household size: 2.04; Median age: 54.7; Age under 18: 10.1%; Age 65 and over: 29.1%; Males per 100 females: 105.2

Housing: Homeownership rate: 79.2%; Homeowner vacancy rate: 14.1%; Rental vacancy rate: 66.0%

SEALEVEL (unincorporated postal area)

ZCTA: 28577

Covers a land area of 2.645 square miles and a water area of 5.534 square miles. Located at 34.86° N. Lat; 76.37° W. Long. Elevation is 3 feet.

Population: 522; Growth (since 2000): 13.2%; Density: 197.4 persons per square mile; Race: 99.2% White, 0.6% Black/African American, 0.0% Asian, 0.0% American Indian/Alaska Native, 0.0% Native Hawaiian/Other Pacific Islander, 0.2% Two or more races, 0.6% Hispanic of any race; Average household size: 1.96; Median age: 63.3; Age under 18: 10.3%; Age 65 and over: 47.3%; Males per 100 females: 100.8

Housing: Homeownership rate: 64.2%; Homeowner vacancy rate: 0.0%; Rental vacancy rate: 35.8%

SMYRNA (unincorporated postal area)

ZCTA: 28579

Covers a land area of 3.826 square miles and a water area of 3.102 square miles. Located at 34.76° N. Lat; 76.51° W. Long. Elevation is 3 feet.

Population: 622; Growth (since 2000): 59.5%; Density: 162.6 persons per square mile; Race: 98.4% White, 0.3% Black/African American, 0.2% Asian, 0.0% American Indian/Alaska Native, 0.0% Native Hawaiian/Other Pacific Islander, 1.0% Two or more races, 1.8% Hispanic of any race; Average household size: 2.38; Median age: 48.6; Age under 18: 17.0%; Age 65 and over: 19.3%; Males per 100 females: 90.8

School District(s)

Carteret County Public Schools (PK-12)
    2012-13 Enrollment: 8,701 . . . . (252) 728-4583

Housing: Homeownership rate: 86.5%; Homeowner vacancy rate: 2.6%; Rental vacancy rate: 5.4%

STACY (unincorporated postal area)
ZCTA: 28581

Covers a land area of 8.779 square miles and a water area of 6.220 square miles. Located at 34.84° N. Lat; 76.44° W. Long. Elevation is 3 feet.

Population: 214; Growth (since 2000): 3.9%; Density: 24.4 persons per square mile; Race: 94.9% White, 0.0% Black/African American, 0.0% Asian, 0.0% American Indian/Alaska Native, 0.0% Native Hawaiian/Other Pacific Islander, 1.4% Two or more races, 4.7% Hispanic of any race; Average household size: 2.25; Median age: 50.0; Age under 18: 17.8%; Age 65 and over: 21.5%; Males per 100 females: 114.0

Housing: Homeownership rate: 78.9%; Homeowner vacancy rate: 3.8%; Rental vacancy rate: 0.0%

WILLISTON (unincorporated postal area)
ZCTA: 28589

Covers a land area of 10.858 square miles and a water area of 0.949 square miles. Located at 34.81° N. Lat; 76.51° W. Long. Elevation is 3 feet.

Population: 180; Growth (since 2000): -39.2%; Density: 16.6 persons per square mile; Race: 100.0% White, 0.0% Black/African American, 0.0% Asian, 0.0% American Indian/Alaska Native, 0.0% Native Hawaiian/Other Pacific Islander, 0.0% Two or more races, 0.6% Hispanic of any race; Average household size: 2.09; Median age: 49.6; Age under 18: 11.1%; Age 65 and over: 20.0%; Males per 100 females: 102.2

Housing: Homeownership rate: 86.1%; Homeowner vacancy rate: 0.0%; Rental vacancy rate: 0.0%

Caswell County

Located in northern North Carolina, in a piedmont area; bounded on the north by Virginia. Covers a land area of 424.922 square miles, a water area of 3.330 square miles, and is located in the Eastern Time Zone at 36.39° N. Lat., 79.33° W. Long. The county was founded in 1777. County seat is Yanceyville.

Population: 23,719; Growth (since 2000): 0.9%; Density: 55.8 persons per square mile; Race: 62.5% White, 33.8% Black/African American, 0.3% Asian, 0.4% American Indian/Alaska Native, 0.0% Native Hawaiian/Other Pacific Islander, 1.6% two or more races, 3.1% Hispanic of any race; Average household size: 2.43; Median age: 43.6; Age under 18: 20.6%; Age 65 and over: 15.8%; Males per 100 females: 103.7; Marriage status: 27.6% never married, 53.8% now married, 4.5% separated, 8.7% widowed, 9.9% divorced; Foreign born: 1.7%; Speak English only: 96.8%; With disability: 21.2%; Veterans: 7.7%; Ancestry: 10.5% American, 9.7% English, 8.5% Irish, 4.6% German, 2.0% Scottish

Religion: Six largest groups: 15.5% Baptist, 9.7% Methodist/Pietist, 4.2% Non-denominational Protestant, 2.0% Presbyterian-Reformed, 0.3% Pentecostal, 0.1% Episcopalianism/Anglicanism

Economy: Unemployment rate: 5.9%; Leading industries: 19.9% retail trade; 18.3% other services (except public administration); 11.8% health care and social assistance; Farms: 543 totaling 97,060 acres; Company size: 0 employ 1,000 or more persons, 0 employ 500 to 999 persons, 1 employs 100 to 499 persons, 245 employ less than 100 persons; Business ownership: 371 women-owned, n/a Black-owned, n/a Hispanic-owned, n/a Asian-owned

Employment: 8.7% management, business, and financial, 1.4% computer, engineering, and science, 7.5% education, legal, community service, arts, and media, 6.1% healthcare practitioners, 18.9% service, 23.9% sales and office, 11.9% natural resources, construction, and maintenance, 21.5% production, transportation, and material moving

Income: Per capita: $17,975; Median household: $35,315; Average household: $44,954; Households with income of $100,000 or more: 7.7%; Poverty rate: 22.6%

Educational Attainment: High school diploma or higher: 73.2%; Bachelor's degree or higher: 9.0%; Graduate/professional degree or higher: 3.2%

Housing: Homeownership rate: 76.0%; Median home value: $98,900; Median year structure built: 1976; Homeowner vacancy rate: 1.9%; Median gross rent: $592 per month; Rental vacancy rate: 10.5%

Vital Statistics: Birth rate: 96.2 per 10,000 population; Death rate: 108.7 per 10,000 population; Age-adjusted cancer mortality rate: 185.1 deaths per 100,000 population

Health Insurance: 85.2% have insurance; 57.3% have private insurance; 43.2% have public insurance; 14.8% do not have insurance; 5.8% of children under 18 do not have insurance

Health Care: Physicians: 2.2 per 10,000 population; Hospital beds: 0.0 per 10,000 population; Hospital admissions: 0.0 per 10,000 population

Air Quality Index: 74.5% good, 25.5% moderate, 0.0% unhealthy for sensitive individuals, 0.0% unhealthy (percent of days)

Transportation: Commute: 96.7% car, 0.1% public transportation, 1.2% walk, 1.1% work from home; Median travel time to work: 32.5 minutes

Presidential Election: 48.2% Obama, 50.9% Romney (2012)

Additional Information Contacts

Caswell Government . . . . (336) 694-4193
　http://www.caswellcountync.gov

Caswell County Communities

BLANCH (unincorporated postal area)
ZCTA: 27212

Covers a land area of 48.436 square miles and a water area of 0.129 square miles. Located at 36.48° N. Lat; 79.28° W. Long. Elevation is 384 feet.

Population: 2,580; Growth (since 2000): 77.2%; Density: 53.3 persons per square mile; Race: 48.9% White, 47.0% Black/African American, 0.2% Asian, 0.8% American Indian/Alaska Native, 0.1% Native Hawaiian/Other Pacific Islander, 1.4% Two or more races, 3.9% Hispanic of any race; Average household size: 2.44; Median age: 39.2; Age under 18: 12.1%; Age 65 and over: 10.5%; Males per 100 females: 230.3; Marriage status: 42.6% never married, 34.5% now married, 4.9% separated, 7.7% widowed, 15.2% divorced; Foreign born: 4.1%; Speak English only: 92.1%; With disability: 15.5%; Veterans: 6.6%; Ancestry: 6.8% English, 5.6% American, 5.1% Irish, 2.8% German, 2.4% Scotch-Irish

Employment: 5.1% management, business, and financial, 5.9% computer, engineering, and science, 18.8% education, legal, community service, arts, and media, 4.8% healthcare practitioners, 12.6% service, 21.9% sales and office, 10.7% natural resources, construction, and maintenance, 20.2% production, transportation, and material moving

Income: Per capita: $13,207; Median household: $32,727; Average household: $41,382; Households with income of $100,000 or more: 6.4%; Poverty rate: 24.2%

Educational Attainment: High school diploma or higher: 70.2%; Bachelor's degree or higher: 11.4%; Graduate/professional degree or higher: 6.2%

Housing: Homeownership rate: 79.1%; Median home value: $98,400; Median year structure built: 1973; Homeowner vacancy rate: 2.3%; Median gross rent: $616 per month; Rental vacancy rate: 9.9%

Health Insurance: 84.5% have insurance; 55.0% have private insurance; 52.8% have public insurance; 15.5% do not have insurance; 3.8% of children under 18 do not have insurance

Transportation: Commute: 94.8% car, 0.0% public transportation, 2.9% walk, 0.0% work from home; Median travel time to work: 32.7 minutes

LEASBURG (unincorporated postal area)
ZCTA: 27291

Covers a land area of 50.745 square miles and a water area of 1.728 square miles. Located at 36.42° N. Lat; 79.17° W. Long. Elevation is 607 feet.

Population: 1,662; Growth (since 2000): -14.4%; Density: 32.8 persons per square mile; Race: 74.3% White, 23.0% Black/African American, 0.2% Asian, 0.0% American Indian/Alaska Native, 0.0% Native Hawaiian/Other Pacific Islander, 1.1% Two or more races, 3.5% Hispanic of any race; Average household size: 2.36; Median age: 46.7; Age under 18: 19.6%; Age 65 and over: 18.2%; Males per 100 females: 104.9

Housing: Homeownership rate: 81.9%; Homeowner vacancy rate: 3.7%; Rental vacancy rate: 15.9%

MILTON (town). Covers a land area of 0.387 square miles and a water area of <.001 square miles. Located at 36.54° N. Lat; 79.21° W. Long. Elevation is 469 feet.

History: Milton was founded in 1728 and long noted for its horse races.

Population: 166; Growth (since 2000): 25.8%; Density: 429.4 persons per square mile; Race: 51.2% White, 46.4% Black/African American, 0.0% Asian, 0.0% American Indian/Alaska Native, 0.0% Native Hawaiian/Other Pacific Islander, 2.4% Two or more races, 0.0% Hispanic of any race; Average household size: 2.13; Median age: 51.0; Age under 18: 19.3%; Age 65 and over: 22.9%; Males per 100 females: 80.4
Housing: Homeownership rate: 70.5%; Homeowner vacancy rate: 6.7%; Rental vacancy rate: 22.6%

PELHAM (unincorporated postal area)
ZCTA: 27311
Covers a land area of 46.238 square miles and a water area of 0.070 square miles. Located at 36.48° N. Lat; 79.47° W. Long. Elevation is 738 feet.
Population: 3,402; Growth (since 2000): -11.2%; Density: 73.6 persons per square mile; Race: 68.6% White, 28.3% Black/African American, 0.1% Asian, 0.2% American Indian/Alaska Native, 0.0% Native Hawaiian/Other Pacific Islander, 1.7% Two or more races, 2.3% Hispanic of any race; Average household size: 2.39; Median age: 44.4; Age under 18: 22.4%; Age 65 and over: 16.2%; Males per 100 females: 91.8; Marriage status: 19.0% never married, 63.0% now married, 4.8% separated, 5.6% widowed, 12.4% divorced; Foreign born: 0.1%; Speak English only: 99.3%; With disability: 19.5%; Veterans: 7.9%; Ancestry: 13.0% American, 8.5% Irish, 6.9% German, 6.9% English, 2.1% Scotch-Irish
Employment: 10.2% management, business, and financial, 1.5% computer, engineering, and science, 5.6% education, legal, community service, arts, and media, 14.9% healthcare practitioners, 18.7% service, 15.4% sales and office, 9.3% natural resources, construction, and maintenance, 24.3% production, transportation, and material moving
Income: Per capita: $18,734; Median household: $37,213; Average household: $45,923; Households with income of $100,000 or more: 9.9%; Poverty rate: 23.8%
Educational Attainment: High school diploma or higher: 80.3%; Bachelor's degree or higher: 6.7%; Graduate/professional degree or higher: 0.9%
Housing: Homeownership rate: 75.4%; Median home value: $94,600; Median year structure built: 1980; Homeowner vacancy rate: 2.0%; Median gross rent: $597 per month; Rental vacancy rate: 9.3%
Health Insurance: 85.5% have insurance; 53.7% have private insurance; 43.8% have public insurance; 14.5% do not have insurance; 6.8% of children under 18 do not have insurance
Transportation: Commute: 98.0% car, 0.0% public transportation, 1.3% walk, 0.0% work from home; Median travel time to work: 31.2 minutes

---

PROSPECT HILL (unincorporated postal area)
ZCTA: 27314
Covers a land area of 25.940 square miles and a water area of 0.724 square miles. Located at 36.31° N. Lat; 79.20° W. Long. Elevation is 705 feet.
Population: 1,051; Growth (since 2000): 57.3%; Density: 40.5 persons per square mile; Race: 84.7% White, 11.3% Black/African American, 0.1% Asian, 0.3% American Indian/Alaska Native, 0.0% Native Hawaiian/Other Pacific Islander, 1.0% Two or more races, 3.3% Hispanic of any race; Average household size: 2.41; Median age: 45.2; Age under 18: 19.9%; Age 65 and over: 15.0%; Males per 100 females: 104.9
Housing: Homeownership rate: 79.7%; Homeowner vacancy rate: 2.3%; Rental vacancy rate: 10.1%

PROVIDENCE (unincorporated postal area)
ZCTA: 27315
Covers a land area of 26.353 square miles and a water area of 0.131 square miles. Located at 36.51° N. Lat; 79.40° W. Long. Elevation is 554 feet.
Population: 2,243; Growth (since 2000): 41.3%; Density: 85.1 persons per square mile; Race: 87.4% White, 7.8% Black/African American, 0.8% Asian, 0.4% American Indian/Alaska Native, 0.0% Native Hawaiian/Other Pacific Islander, 1.9% Two or more races, 3.9% Hispanic of any race; Average household size: 2.40; Median age: 44.3; Age under 18: 21.6%; Age 65 and over: 17.2%; Males per 100 females: 97.1
School District(s)
Caswell County Schools (PK-12)
    2012-13 Enrollment: 2,874 . . . . (336) 694-4116

Housing: Homeownership rate: 79.0%; Homeowner vacancy rate: 1.7%; Rental vacancy rate: 8.0%

YANCEYVILLE (town). County seat. Covers a land area of 5.523 square miles and a water area of 0.032 square miles. Located at 36.41° N. Lat; 79.34° W. Long. Elevation is 607 feet.
History: Until 1810 the community was known as Caswell County Courthouse, for Richard Caswell, first constitutional governor. When incorporated, Yanceyvill was named for Bartlett Yancey (1785-1828), a native of Caswell County who served four years in Congress.
Population: 2,039; Growth (since 2000): -2.5%; Density: 369.2 persons per square mile; Race: 39.2% White, 54.4% Black/African American, 0.4% Asian, 0.5% American Indian/Alaska Native, 0.1% Native Hawaiian/Other Pacific Islander, 3.7% Two or more races, 3.6% Hispanic of any race; Average household size: 2.14; Median age: 39.8; Age under 18: 17.7%; Age 65 and over: 17.3%; Males per 100 females: 124.8
School District(s)
Caswell County Schools (PK-12)
    2012-13 Enrollment: 2,874 . . . . (336) 694-4116
Housing: Homeownership rate: 41.0%; Homeowner vacancy rate: 2.2%; Rental vacancy rate: 9.2%
Newspapers: Caswell Messenger (weekly circulation 4800)

Catawba County

Located in west central North Carolina, in the piedmont area; bounded on the east and north by the Catawba River. Covers a land area of 398.721 square miles, a water area of 14.694 square miles, and is located in the Eastern Time Zone at 35.66° N. Lat., 81.21° W. Long. The county was founded in 1842. County seat is Newton.

Catawba County is part of the Hickory-Lenoir-Morganton, NC Metropolitan Statistical Area. The entire metro area includes: Alexander County, NC; Burke County, NC; Caldwell County, NC; Catawba County, NC

Population: 154,358; Growth (since 2000): 8.9%; Density: 387.1 persons per square mile; Race: 81.7% White, 8.4% Black/African American, 3.5% Asian, 0.3% American Indian/Alaska Native, 0.0% Native Hawaiian/Other Pacific Islander, 1.9% two or more races, 8.4% Hispanic of any race; Average household size: 2.50; Median age: 39.6; Age under 18: 23.8%; Age 65 and over: 14.1%; Males per 100 females: 96.0; Marriage status: 27.0% never married, 53.7% now married, 3.0% separated, 7.4% widowed, 11.9% divorced; Foreign born: 7.1%; Speak English only: 89.1%; With disability: 12.9%; Veterans: 9.3%; Ancestry: 17.2% German, 13.4% American, 9.2% Irish, 9.1% English, 2.6% Scotch-Irish
Religion: Six largest groups: 21.6% Baptist, 12.9% Methodist/Pietist, 9.9% Lutheran, 3.4% Presbyterian-Reformed, 3.4% Pentecostal, 3.0% Non-denominational Protestant
Economy: Unemployment rate: 5.7%; Leading industries: 17.4% retail trade; 10.2% other services (except public administration); 10.1% manufacturing; Farms: 698 totaling 67,098 acres; Company size: 3 employ 1,000 or more persons, 10 employ 500 to 999 persons, 126 employ 100 to 499 persons, 3,947 employ less than 100 persons; Business ownership: 3,787 women-owned, n/a Black-owned, n/a Hispanic-owned, 267 Asian-owned
Employment: 13.5% management, business, and financial, 3.1% computer, engineering, and science, 9.0% education, legal, community service, arts, and media, 5.7% healthcare practitioners, 15.7% service, 23.6% sales and office, 7.8% natural resources, construction, and maintenance, 21.7% production, transportation, and material moving
Income: Per capita: $23,232; Median household: $44,332; Average household: $59,226; Households with income of $100,000 or more: 14.0%; Poverty rate: 15.2%
Educational Attainment: High school diploma or higher: 82.3%; Bachelor's degree or higher: 21.0%; Graduate/professional degree or higher: 6.6%
Housing: Homeownership rate: 70.4%; Median home value: $133,000; Median year structure built: 1981; Homeowner vacancy rate: 2.6%; Median gross rent: $674 per month; Rental vacancy rate: 11.2%
Vital Statistics: Birth rate: 115.2 per 10,000 population; Death rate: 99.6 per 10,000 population; Age-adjusted cancer mortality rate: 171.1 deaths per 100,000 population
Health Insurance: 84.1% have insurance; 64.4% have private insurance; 31.2% have public insurance; 15.9% do not have insurance; 5.8% of children under 18 do not have insurance

Health Care: Physicians: 23.0 per 10,000 population; Hospital beds: 33.7 per 10,000 population; Hospital admissions: 1,439.3 per 10,000 population
Air Quality Index: 83.8% good, 16.2% moderate, 0.0% unhealthy for sensitive individuals, 0.0% unhealthy (percent of days)
Transportation: Commute: 94.5% car, 0.2% public transportation, 0.8% walk, 3.5% work from home; Median travel time to work: 22.4 minutes
Presidential Election: 34.6% Obama, 64.0% Romney (2012)
Additional Information Contacts
Catawba Government . . . . (828) 465-8200
  http://www.catawbacountync.gov

Catawba County Communities

BROOKFORD (town). Covers a land area of 0.603 square miles and a water area of 0.019 square miles. Located at 35.70° N. Lat; 81.34° W. Long. Elevation is 938 feet.
Population: 382; Growth (since 2000): -12.0%; Density: 633.7 persons per square mile; Race: 86.4% White, 7.6% Black/African American, 2.4% Asian, 0.3% American Indian/Alaska Native, 0.0% Native Hawaiian/Other Pacific Islander, 1.0% Two or more races, 3.4% Hispanic of any race; Average household size: 2.10; Median age: 46.3; Age under 18: 16.2%; Age 65 and over: 18.8%; Males per 100 females: 92.0
Housing: Homeownership rate: 48.4%; Homeowner vacancy rate: 5.3%; Rental vacancy rate: 6.9%

CATAWBA (town). Covers a land area of 3.929 square miles and a water area of 0.064 square miles. Located at 35.71° N. Lat; 81.07° W. Long. Elevation is 869 feet.
History: Murrays Mill Historic District.
Population: 603; Growth (since 2000): -13.6%; Density: 153.5 persons per square mile; Race: 71.3% White, 21.6% Black/African American, 1.0% Asian, 0.7% American Indian/Alaska Native, 0.0% Native Hawaiian/Other Pacific Islander, 1.5% Two or more races, 6.5% Hispanic of any race; Average household size: 2.40; Median age: 46.2; Age under 18: 18.6%; Age 65 and over: 21.6%; Males per 100 females: 95.8
School District(s)
Catawba County Schools (PK-12)
  2012-13 Enrollment: 17,256 . . . . (828) 464-8333
Housing: Homeownership rate: 76.5%; Homeowner vacancy rate: 2.5%; Rental vacancy rate: 17.8%
Safety: Violent crime rate: 33.1 per 10,000 population; Property crime rate: 214.9 per 10,000 population

CLAREMONT (city). Covers a land area of 2.724 square miles and a water area of 0.001 square miles. Located at 35.71° N. Lat; 81.15° W. Long. Elevation is 981 feet.
Population: 1,352; Growth (since 2000): 30.3%; Density: 496.4 persons per square mile; Race: 93.2% White, 1.8% Black/African American, 1.2% Asian, 0.1% American Indian/Alaska Native, 0.0% Native Hawaiian/Other Pacific Islander, 1.8% Two or more races, 3.6% Hispanic of any race; Average household size: 2.31; Median age: 40.2; Age under 18: 22.2%; Age 65 and over: 14.5%; Males per 100 females: 95.7
School District(s)
Catawba County Schools (PK-12)
  2012-13 Enrollment: 17,256 . . . . (828) 464-8333
Housing: Homeownership rate: 75.5%; Homeowner vacancy rate: 3.1%; Rental vacancy rate: 12.3%
Safety: Violent crime rate: 51.7 per 10,000 population; Property crime rate: 243.5 per 10,000 population
Additional Information Contacts
City of Claremont . . . . (909) 624-1681
  http://www.cityofclaremont.org

CONOVER (city). Covers a land area of 10.895 square miles and a water area of 0.030 square miles. Located at 35.72° N. Lat; 81.22° W. Long. Elevation is 1,056 feet.
Population: 8,165; Growth (since 2000): 23.6%; Density: 749.4 persons per square mile; Race: 78.1% White, 9.2% Black/African American, 4.2% Asian, 0.2% American Indian/Alaska Native, 0.0% Native Hawaiian/Other Pacific Islander, 2.5% Two or more races, 12.2% Hispanic of any race; Average household size: 2.39; Median age: 39.8; Age under 18: 23.2%; Age 65 and over: 17.0%; Males per 100 females: 89.7; Marriage status: 24.6% never married, 54.8% now married, 2.6% separated, 6.6% widowed, 14.0% divorced; Foreign born: 10.9%; Speak English only:

83.0%; With disability: 14.1%; Veterans: 12.6%; Ancestry: 15.6% German, 11.5% American, 7.1% Irish, 5.3% English, 3.8% Italian
Employment: 15.4% management, business, and financial, 3.5% computer, engineering, and science, 7.3% education, legal, community service, arts, and media, 6.6% healthcare practitioners, 13.8% service, 23.2% sales and office, 5.2% natural resources, construction, and maintenance, 25.0% production, transportation, and material moving
Income: Per capita: $22,327; Median household: $42,038; Average household: $54,753; Households with income of $100,000 or more: 12.6%; Poverty rate: 17.2%
Educational Attainment: High school diploma or higher: 87.1%; Bachelor's degree or higher: 21.6%; Graduate/professional degree or higher: 6.6%
School District(s)
Catawba County Schools (PK-12)
  2012-13 Enrollment: 17,256 . . . . (828) 464-8333
Newton Conover City Schools (PK-12)
  2012-13 Enrollment: 3,025 . . . . (828) 464-3191
Housing: Homeownership rate: 67.6%; Median home value: $134,000; Median year structure built: 1978; Homeowner vacancy rate: 2.6%; Median gross rent: $627 per month; Rental vacancy rate: 8.4%
Health Insurance: 84.3% have insurance; 60.4% have private insurance; 36.6% have public insurance; 15.7% do not have insurance; 4.5% of children under 18 do not have insurance
Transportation: Commute: 95.1% car, 0.0% public transportation, 0.0% walk, 3.5% work from home; Median travel time to work: 16.4 minutes
Additional Information Contacts
City of Conover . . . . (828) 464-1191
  http://www.conovernc.gov

HICKORY (city). Covers a land area of 29.708 square miles and a water area of 0.093 square miles. Located at 35.74° N. Lat; 81.32° W. Long. Elevation is 1,148 feet.
History: Hickory has been called Hickory Tavern, Hickory Station, and the City of Hickory. The making of hickory wagons began here in 1880.
Population: 40,010; Growth (since 2000): 7.5%; Density: 1,346.8 persons per square mile; Race: 74.9% White, 14.3% Black/African American, 3.2% Asian, 0.3% American Indian/Alaska Native, 0.0% Native Hawaiian/Other Pacific Islander, 2.2% Two or more races, 11.4% Hispanic of any race; Average household size: 2.33; Median age: 37.7; Age under 18: 23.6%; Age 65 and over: 14.3%; Males per 100 females: 91.1; Marriage status: 34.9% never married, 44.4% now married, 3.0% separated, 8.0% widowed, 12.7% divorced; Foreign born: 9.7%; Speak English only: 86.7%; With disability: 11.6%; Veterans: 7.5%; Ancestry: 15.9% German, 11.6% English, 10.0% Irish, 8.3% American, 3.1% Scotch-Irish
Employment: 15.8% management, business, and financial, 3.9% computer, engineering, and science, 10.5% education, legal, community service, arts, and media, 6.7% healthcare practitioners, 19.1% service, 22.4% sales and office, 5.6% natural resources, construction, and maintenance, 16.0% production, transportation, and material moving
Income: Per capita: $25,310; Median household: $39,176; Average household: $61,807; Households with income of $100,000 or more: 17.6%; Poverty rate: 19.3%
Educational Attainment: High school diploma or higher: 84.1%; Bachelor's degree or higher: 31.0%; Graduate/professional degree or higher: 10.2%
School District(s)
Burke County Schools (PK-12)
  2012-13 Enrollment: 13,343 . . . . (828) 439-4311
Catawba County Schools (PK-12)
  2012-13 Enrollment: 17,256 . . . . (828) 464-8333
Hickory City Schools (PK-12)
  2012-13 Enrollment: 4,449 . . . . (828) 322-2855
Four-year College(s)
Lenoir-Rhyne University (Private, Not-for-profit, Evangelical Lutheran Church)
  Fall 2013 Enrollment: 1,898 . . . . (828) 328-1741
  2013-14 Tuition: In-state $29,310; Out-of-state $29,310
Two-year College(s)
Catawba Valley Community College (Public)
  Fall 2013 Enrollment: 4,561 . . . . (828) 327-7000
  2013-14 Tuition: In-state $2,485; Out-of-state $8,531
Housing: Homeownership rate: 54.1%; Median home value: $158,100; Median year structure built: 1980; Homeowner vacancy rate: 3.8%; Median gross rent: $661 per month; Rental vacancy rate: 13.1%

Health Insurance: 80.7% have insurance; 61.3% have private insurance; 29.2% have public insurance; 19.3% do not have insurance; 7.6% of children under 18 do not have insurance
Hospitals: Catawba Valley Medical Center (213 beds); Frye Regional Medical Center (355 beds)
Safety: Violent crime rate: 41.6 per 10,000 population; Property crime rate: 550.5 per 10,000 population
Newspapers: Focus Newspaper (weekly circulation 38000); Hickory Daily Record (daily circulation 21000)
Transportation: Commute: 94.2% car, 0.1% public transportation, 1.3% walk, 3.0% work from home; Median travel time to work: 18.3 minutes
Airports: Hickory Regional (general aviation)
Additional Information Contacts
City of Hickory . . . . (828) 323-7400
  http://www.ci.hickory.nc.us

LAKE NORMAN OF CATAWBA (CDP). Covers a land area of 23.838 square miles and a water area of 8.530 square miles. Located at 35.60° N. Lat; 80.98° W. Long. Elevation is 814 feet.

Population: 7,411; Growth (since 2000): 56.2%; Density: 310.9 persons per square mile; Race: 95.0% White, 2.5% Black/African American, 0.7% Asian, 0.2% American Indian/Alaska Native, 0.0% Native Hawaiian/Other Pacific Islander, 1.2% Two or more races, 2.0% Hispanic of any race; Average household size: 2.43; Median age: 46.5; Age under 18: 19.8%; Age 65 and over: 15.7%; Males per 100 females: 99.1; Marriage status: 15.6% never married, 71.5% now married, 2.7% separated, 5.0% widowed, 7.8% divorced; Foreign born: 1.8%; Speak English only: 97.7%; With disability: 9.9%; Veterans: 11.5%; Ancestry: 22.0% German, 16.3% English, 10.6% American, 10.6% Irish, 7.6% Italian
Employment: 21.9% management, business, and financial, 3.2% computer, engineering, and science, 10.0% education, legal, community service, arts, and media, 2.6% healthcare practitioners, 9.1% service, 31.1% sales and office, 9.9% natural resources, construction, and maintenance, 12.1% production, transportation, and material moving
Income: Per capita: $36,348; Median household: $65,015; Average household: $88,369; Households with income of $100,000 or more: 28.4%; Poverty rate: 3.1%
Educational Attainment: High school diploma or higher: 91.5%; Bachelor's degree or higher: 36.1%; Graduate/professional degree or higher: 11.0%
Housing: Homeownership rate: 85.7%; Median home value: $352,800; Median year structure built: 1991; Homeowner vacancy rate: 3.2%; Median gross rent: $1,019 per month; Rental vacancy rate: 10.1%
Health Insurance: 93.7% have insurance; 86.5% have private insurance; 25.0% have public insurance; 6.3% do not have insurance; 6.0% of children under 18 do not have insurance
Transportation: Commute: 86.1% car, 1.1% public transportation, 0.3% walk, 10.9% work from home; Median travel time to work: 38.2 minutes

LONG VIEW (town). Covers a land area of 3.937 square miles and a water area of 0.010 square miles. Located at 35.72° N. Lat; 81.39° W. Long. Elevation is 1,155 feet.

Population: 4,871; Growth (since 2000): 3.2%; Density: 1,237.3 persons per square mile; Race: 74.5% White, 11.4% Black/African American, 5.0% Asian, 0.4% American Indian/Alaska Native, 0.0% Native Hawaiian/Other Pacific Islander, 3.0% Two or more races, 10.6% Hispanic of any race; Average household size: 2.36; Median age: 38.8; Age under 18: 22.3%; Age 65 and over: 15.8%; Males per 100 females: 96.6; Marriage status: 27.5% never married, 50.9% now married, 6.0% separated, 10.1% widowed, 11.5% divorced; Foreign born: 7.0%; Speak English only: 87.9%; With disability: 15.0%; Veterans: 10.0%; Ancestry: 15.3% German, 13.9% American, 8.7% Irish, 5.2% English, 1.7% Russian
Employment: 9.0% management, business, and financial, 0.5% computer, engineering, and science, 1.9% education, legal, community service, arts, and media, 3.5% healthcare practitioners, 9.2% service, 25.5% sales and office, 8.2% natural resources, construction, and maintenance, 42.3% production, transportation, and material moving
Income: Per capita: $15,565; Median household: $29,705; Average household: $36,542; Households with income of $100,000 or more: 3.9%; Poverty rate: 24.4%
Educational Attainment: High school diploma or higher: 71.7%; Bachelor's degree or higher: 6.1%; Graduate/professional degree or higher: 2.0%

Housing: Homeownership rate: 58.6%; Median home value: $87,100; Median year structure built: 1959; Homeowner vacancy rate: 4.1%; Median gross rent: $665 per month; Rental vacancy rate: 8.4%
Health Insurance: 82.7% have insurance; 52.3% have private insurance; 44.4% have public insurance; 17.3% do not have insurance; 6.5% of children under 18 do not have insurance
Safety: Violent crime rate: 51.4 per 10,000 population; Property crime rate: 532.2 per 10,000 population
Transportation: Commute: 94.3% car, 0.0% public transportation, 0.6% walk, 1.9% work from home; Median travel time to work: 19.4 minutes
Additional Information Contacts
Town of Long View . . . . (828) 332-3921
  http://www.ci.longview.nc.us

MAIDEN (town). Covers a land area of 5.524 square miles and a water area of 0.068 square miles. Located at 35.59° N. Lat; 81.22° W. Long. Elevation is 899 feet.

Population: 3,310; Growth (since 2000): 0.9%; Density: 599.2 persons per square mile; Race: 83.6% White, 11.3% Black/African American, 1.3% Asian, 0.5% American Indian/Alaska Native, 0.0% Native Hawaiian/Other Pacific Islander, 1.5% Two or more races, 6.2% Hispanic of any race; Average household size: 2.50; Median age: 37.9; Age under 18: 22.9%; Age 65 and over: 13.8%; Males per 100 females: 105.6; Marriage status: 28.2% never married, 49.4% now married, 3.8% separated, 7.5% widowed, 15.0% divorced; Foreign born: 3.5%; Speak English only: 94.1%; With disability: 14.8%; Veterans: 9.3%; Ancestry: 21.2% American, 18.1% German, 7.5% English, 4.3% Irish, 1.7% Scottish
Employment: 12.9% management, business, and financial, 1.5% computer, engineering, and science, 4.6% education, legal, community service, arts, and media, 4.1% healthcare practitioners, 14.8% service, 24.1% sales and office, 14.8% natural resources, construction, and maintenance, 23.1% production, transportation, and material moving
Income: Per capita: $18,199; Median household: $39,442; Average household: $44,546; Households with income of $100,000 or more: 2.0%; Poverty rate: 19.6%
Educational Attainment: High school diploma or higher: 73.6%; Bachelor's degree or higher: 6.5%; Graduate/professional degree or higher: 2.5%

School District(s)
Catawba County Schools (PK-12)
  2012-13 Enrollment: 17,256 . . . . (828) 464-8333
Housing: Homeownership rate: 73.4%; Median home value: $100,600; Median year structure built: 1969; Homeowner vacancy rate: 2.5%; Median gross rent: $760 per month; Rental vacancy rate: 12.6%
Health Insurance: 84.3% have insurance; 59.7% have private insurance; 35.8% have public insurance; 15.7% do not have insurance; 7.3% of children under 18 do not have insurance
Safety: Violent crime rate: 24.0 per 10,000 population; Property crime rate: 296.7 per 10,000 population
Transportation: Commute: 94.3% car, 0.0% public transportation, 3.2% walk, 1.1% work from home; Median travel time to work: 28.6 minutes
Additional Information Contacts
Town of Maiden . . . . (828) 464-3112
  http://www.maidennc.com

MOUNTAIN VIEW (CDP). Covers a land area of 4.625 square miles and a water area of 0.010 square miles. Located at 35.68° N. Lat; 81.37° W. Long. Elevation is 1,102 feet.

Population: 3,552; Growth (since 2000): -5.7%; Density: 767.9 persons per square mile; Race: 85.8% White, 8.1% Black/African American, 2.7% Asian, 0.2% American Indian/Alaska Native, 0.1% Native Hawaiian/Other Pacific Islander, 1.5% Two or more races, 4.2% Hispanic of any race; Average household size: 2.60; Median age: 41.1; Age under 18: 23.2%; Age 65 and over: 12.5%; Males per 100 females: 95.7; Marriage status: 25.7% never married, 55.7% now married, 1.4% separated, 6.3% widowed, 12.3% divorced; Foreign born: 3.1%; Speak English only: 94.0%; With disability: 12.1%; Veterans: 14.9%; Ancestry: 20.1% American, 17.3% German, 12.0% English, 10.4% Irish, 4.7% Dutch
Employment: 9.7% management, business, and financial, 7.1% computer, engineering, and science, 11.0% education, legal, community service, arts, and media, 6.3% healthcare practitioners, 12.1% service, 30.0% sales and office, 2.5% natural resources, construction, and maintenance, 21.3% production, transportation, and material moving

Income: Per capita: $22,560; Median household: $48,796; Average household: $55,066; Households with income of $100,000 or more: 11.9%; Poverty rate: 5.4%
Educational Attainment: High school diploma or higher: 86.7%; Bachelor's degree or higher: 20.6%; Graduate/professional degree or higher: 4.7%
Housing: Homeownership rate: 84.0%; Median home value: $126,900; Median year structure built: 1978; Homeowner vacancy rate: 1.7%; Median gross rent: $692 per month; Rental vacancy rate: 7.1%
Health Insurance: 83.4% have insurance; 67.1% have private insurance; 33.6% have public insurance; 16.6% do not have insurance; 8.9% of children under 18 do not have insurance
Transportation: Commute: 96.6% car, 0.0% public transportation, 0.0% walk, 0.6% work from home; Median travel time to work: 21.7 minutes

NEWTON (city). County seat. Covers a land area of 13.770 square miles and a water area of 0.052 square miles. Located at 35.66° N. Lat; 81.23° W. Long. Elevation is 1,007 feet.
History: County Historical Museum. Settled mid-18th century.
Population: 12,968; Growth (since 2000): 3.2%; Density: 941.8 persons per square mile; Race: 73.7% White, 13.9% Black/African American, 3.3% Asian, 0.4% American Indian/Alaska Native, 0.0% Native Hawaiian/Other Pacific Islander, 2.6% Two or more races, 12.9% Hispanic of any race; Average household size: 2.45; Median age: 38.1; Age under 18: 24.2%; Age 65 and over: 15.9%; Males per 100 females: 91.4; Marriage status: 33.0% never married, 44.7% now married, 3.7% separated, 10.0% widowed, 12.3% divorced; Foreign born: 10.1%; Speak English only: 83.8%; With disability: 19.1%; Veterans: 8.6%; Ancestry: 13.3% German, 12.1% American, 9.8% Irish, 7.4% English, 2.6% Italian
Employment: 13.0% management, business, and financial, 2.0% computer, engineering, and science, 7.7% education, legal, community service, arts, and media, 3.5% healthcare practitioners, 20.7% service, 22.0% sales and office, 6.7% natural resources, construction, and maintenance, 24.4% production, transportation, and material moving
Income: Per capita: $16,720; Median household: $32,062; Average household: $41,579; Households with income of $100,000 or more: 6.8%; Poverty rate: 23.6%
Educational Attainment: High school diploma or higher: 76.9%; Bachelor's degree or higher: 16.0%; Graduate/professional degree or higher: 4.0%
School District(s)
Catawba County Schools (PK-12)
    2012-13 Enrollment: 17,256 . . . . (828) 464-8333
Newton Conover City Schools (PK-12)
    2012-13 Enrollment: 3,025 . . . . (828) 464-3191
Housing: Homeownership rate: 58.4%; Median home value: $109,600; Median year structure built: 1971; Homeowner vacancy rate: 3.5%; Median gross rent: $674 per month; Rental vacancy rate: 9.5%
Health Insurance: 79.9% have insurance; 53.3% have private insurance; 40.2% have public insurance; 20.1% do not have insurance; 7.5% of children under 18 do not have insurance
Safety: Violent crime rate: 40.8 per 10,000 population; Property crime rate: 339.8 per 10,000 population
Newspapers: Observer-News-Enterprise (daily circulation 2300)
Transportation: Commute: 97.0% car, 0.2% public transportation, 0.0% walk, 2.1% work from home; Median travel time to work: 19.7 minutes
Additional Information Contacts
City of Newton . . . . (828) 695-4300
    http://www.newtonnc.gov

SAINT STEPHENS (CDP). Covers a land area of 9.504 square miles and a water area of 0.406 square miles. Located at 35.76° N. Lat; 81.27° W. Long. Elevation is 1,119 feet.
Population: 8,759; Growth (since 2000): -7.2%; Density: 921.7 persons per square mile; Race: 82.8% White, 4.2% Black/African American, 4.4% Asian, 0.3% American Indian/Alaska Native, 0.1% Native Hawaiian/Other Pacific Islander, 2.2% Two or more races, 10.3% Hispanic of any race; Average household size: 2.61; Median age: 40.5; Age under 18: 24.4%; Age 65 and over: 15.9%; Males per 100 females: 97.1; Marriage status: 22.6% never married, 55.9% now married, 1.8% separated, 9.1% widowed, 12.4% divorced; Foreign born: 9.5%; Speak English only: 84.4%; With disability: 11.6%; Veterans: 11.9%; Ancestry: 15.2% German, 13.4% American, 9.7% English, 7.6% Irish, 3.4% Scottish
Employment: 8.9% management, business, and financial, 3.3% computer, engineering, and science, 10.3% education, legal, community service, arts,

and media, 6.1% healthcare practitioners, 18.8% service, 20.0% sales and office, 8.5% natural resources, construction, and maintenance, 24.1% production, transportation, and material moving
Income: Per capita: $24,243; Median household: $45,945; Average household: $63,751; Households with income of $100,000 or more: 14.8%; Poverty rate: 12.5%
Educational Attainment: High school diploma or higher: 80.2%; Bachelor's degree or higher: 13.1%; Graduate/professional degree or higher: 3.6%
Housing: Homeownership rate: 79.0%; Median home value: $124,100; Median year structure built: 1977; Homeowner vacancy rate: 1.8%; Median gross rent: $647 per month; Rental vacancy rate: 19.6%
Health Insurance: 87.7% have insurance; 69.6% have private insurance; 30.1% have public insurance; 12.3% do not have insurance; 3.1% of children under 18 do not have insurance
Transportation: Commute: 92.6% car, 0.0% public transportation, 0.9% walk, 4.9% work from home; Median travel time to work: 18.6 minutes

SHERRILLS FORD (unincorporated postal area)
ZCTA: 28673
    Covers a land area of 25.407 square miles and a water area of 4.717 square miles. Located at 35.62° N. Lat; 80.99° W. Long. Elevation is 896 feet.
Population: 5,919; Growth (since 2000): 42.5%; Density: 233.0 persons per square mile; Race: 93.4% White, 4.2% Black/African American, 0.7% Asian, 0.1% American Indian/Alaska Native, 0.1% Native Hawaiian/Other Pacific Islander, 1.1% Two or more races, 1.9% Hispanic of any race; Average household size: 2.44; Median age: 45.1; Age under 18: 21.2%; Age 65 and over: 14.8%; Males per 100 females: 99.1; Marriage status: 17.7% never married, 69.3% now married, 3.7% separated, 2.7% widowed, 10.3% divorced; Foreign born: 1.8%; Speak English only: 98.3%; With disability: 9.5%; Veterans: 9.3%; Ancestry: 22.4% German, 12.9% English, 11.8% American, 10.2% Irish, 8.4% Italian
Employment: 21.8% management, business, and financial, 2.9% computer, engineering, and science, 12.1% education, legal, community service, arts, and media, 2.7% healthcare practitioners, 10.6% service, 27.5% sales and office, 9.3% natural resources, construction, and maintenance, 13.1% production, transportation, and material moving
Income: Per capita: $32,335; Median household: $61,741; Average household: $82,032; Households with income of $100,000 or more: 24.6%; Poverty rate: 3.8%
Educational Attainment: High school diploma or higher: 91.1%; Bachelor's degree or higher: 30.7%; Graduate/professional degree or higher: 8.6%
School District(s)
Catawba County Schools (PK-12)
    2012-13 Enrollment: 17,256 . . . . (828) 464-8333
Housing: Homeownership rate: 85.6%; Median home value: $267,200; Median year structure built: 1989; Homeowner vacancy rate: 2.3%; Median gross rent: $1,044 per month; Rental vacancy rate: 13.1%
Health Insurance: 90.4% have insurance; 80.1% have private insurance; 24.9% have public insurance; 9.6% do not have insurance; 9.9% of children under 18 do not have insurance
Transportation: Commute: 87.9% car, 0.6% public transportation, 0.9% walk, 9.0% work from home; Median travel time to work: 36.1 minutes

TERRELL (unincorporated postal area)
ZCTA: 28682
    Covers a land area of 3.247 square miles and a water area of 2.995 square miles. Located at 35.59° N. Lat; 80.97° W. Long. Elevation is 850 feet.
Population: 1,129; Growth (since 2000): 31.3%; Density: 347.7 persons per square mile; Race: 95.4% White, 1.6% Black/African American, 0.6% Asian, 0.3% American Indian/Alaska Native, 0.0% Native Hawaiian/Other Pacific Islander, 1.2% Two or more races, 2.5% Hispanic of any race; Average household size: 2.35; Median age: 49.6; Age under 18: 16.8%; Age 65 and over: 20.0%; Males per 100 females: 96.3
Housing: Homeownership rate: 81.7%; Homeowner vacancy rate: 3.0%; Rental vacancy rate: 10.0%

Chatham County

Located in central North Carolina, in a piedmont area; drained by the Deep and Haw Rivers. Covers a land area of 682.185 square miles, a water area of 27.646 square miles, and is located in the Eastern Time Zone at 35.70° N. Lat., 79.25° W. Long. The county was founded in 1842. County seat is Pittsboro.

Chatham County is part of the Durham-Chapel Hill, NC Metropolitan Statistical Area. The entire metro area includes: Chatham County, NC; Durham County, NC; Orange County, NC; Person County, NC

Weather Station: Siler City 2 N   Elevation: 609 feet

	Jan	Feb	Mar	Apr	May	Jun	Jul	Aug	Sep	Oct	Nov	Dec
High	50	54	62	71	78	85	88	87	81	71	62	53
Low	29	31	38	46	55	64	68	66	59	47	39	32
Precip	3.9	3.4	4.6	3.5	3.9	3.9	4.6	4.3	4.1	3.9	3.6	3.2
Snow	1.2	0.7	0.4	tr	0.0	0.0	0.0	0.0	0.0	0.0	0.0	0.1

High and Low temperatures in degrees Fahrenheit; Precipitation and Snow in inches

Population: 63,505; Growth (since 2000): 28.7%; Density: 93.1 persons per square mile; Race: 76.0% White, 13.2% Black/African American, 1.1% Asian, 0.5% American Indian/Alaska Native, 0.0% Native Hawaiian/Other Pacific Islander, 1.9% two or more races, 13.0% Hispanic of any race; Average household size: 2.43; Median age: 43.6; Age under 18: 21.8%; Age 65 and over: 18.3%; Males per 100 females: 93.3; Marriage status: 22.3% never married, 61.4% now married, 2.1% separated, 6.6% widowed, 9.7% divorced; Foreign born: 10.0%; Speak English only: 85.1%; With disability: 12.1%; Veterans: 10.9%; Ancestry: 13.3% English, 12.3% German, 9.6% American, 9.3% Irish, 3.1% Italian
Religion: Six largest groups: 21.1% Baptist, 13.2% Methodist/Pietist, 1.7% Non-denominational Protestant, 1.7% Catholicism, 1.5% Presbyterian-Reformed, 1.1% Pentecostal
Economy: Unemployment rate: 3.8%; Leading industries: 13.9% retail trade; 13.4% construction; 11.3% professional, scientific, and technical services; Farms: 1,138 totaling 111,778 acres; Company size: 0 employ 1,000 or more persons, 0 employ 500 to 999 persons, 16 employ 100 to 499 persons, 1,254 employ less than 100 persons; Business ownership: 1,573 women-owned, n/a Black-owned, n/a Hispanic-owned, n/a Asian-owned
Employment: 15.9% management, business, and financial; 6.0% computer, engineering, and science; 12.5% education, legal, community service, arts, and media; 6.6% healthcare practitioners; 16.5% service; 19.9% sales and office; 9.9% natural resources, construction, and maintenance; 12.7% production, transportation, and material moving
Income: Per capita: $31,175; Median household: $57,091; Average household: $76,475; Households with income of $100,000 or more: 24.2%; Poverty rate: 12.4%
Educational Attainment: High school diploma or higher: 85.8%; Bachelor's degree or higher: 36.4%; Graduate/professional degree or higher: 16.7%
Housing: Homeownership rate: 77.4%; Median home value: $211,400; Median year structure built: 1990; Homeowner vacancy rate: 2.3%; Median gross rent: $774 per month; Rental vacancy rate: 9.2%
Vital Statistics: Birth rate: 89.9 per 10,000 population; Death rate: 96.1 per 10,000 population; Age-adjusted cancer mortality rate: 176.7 deaths per 100,000 population
Health Insurance: 85.4% have insurance; 67.9% have private insurance; 33.6% have public insurance; 14.6% do not have insurance; 6.8% of children under 18 do not have insurance
Health Care: Physicians: 57.1 per 10,000 population; Hospital beds: 3.8 per 10,000 population; Hospital admissions: 104.7 per 10,000 population
Air Quality Index: 96.2% good, 3.8% moderate, 0.0% unhealthy for sensitive individuals, 0.0% unhealthy (percent of days)
Transportation: Commute: 87.6% car, 0.8% public transportation, 2.0% walk, 7.4% work from home; Median travel time to work: 26.6 minutes
Presidential Election: 51.8% Obama, 47.0% Romney (2012)
National and State Parks: Jordan Lake State Recreation Area; Research Triangle State Park
Additional Information Contacts
Chatham Government . . . . (912) 652-7271
   http://www.chathamnc.org

Chatham County Communities

BEAR CREEK (unincorporated postal area)
ZCTA: 27207
   Covers a land area of 84.967 square miles and a water area of 0.266 square miles. Located at 35.61° N. Lat; 79.39° W. Long. Elevation is 463 feet.
Population: 3,795; Growth (since 2000): -0.4%; Density: 44.7 persons per square mile; Race: 81.9% White, 14.0% Black/African American, 0.3% Asian, 0.6% American Indian/Alaska Native, 0.0% Native Hawaiian/Other Pacific Islander, 1.7% Two or more races, 5.0% Hispanic of any race; Average household size: 2.49; Median age: 43.4; Age under 18: 21.0%; Age 65 and over: 17.1%; Males per 100 females: 93.8; Marriage status: 22.6% never married, 61.2% now married, 0.9% separated, 5.4% widowed, 10.8% divorced; Foreign born: 1.3%; Speak English only: 97.1%; With disability: 14.5%; Veterans: 13.0%; Ancestry: 15.2% American, 9.5% English, 8.8% German, 4.4% Irish, 3.1% Scottish
Employment: 16.6% management, business, and financial, 2.6% computer, engineering, and science, 8.0% education, legal, community service, arts, and media, 4.9% healthcare practitioners, 29.9% service, 19.0% sales and office, 6.6% natural resources, construction, and maintenance, 12.5% production, transportation, and material moving
Income: Per capita: $25,992; Median household: $46,866; Average household: $63,407; Households with income of $100,000 or more: 21.1%; Poverty rate: 14.0%
Educational Attainment: High school diploma or higher: 84.2%; Bachelor's degree or higher: 17.2%; Graduate/professional degree or higher: 9.1%
School District(s)
Chatham County Schools (PK-12)
   2012-13 Enrollment: 8,454 . . . . (919) 542-3626
   Housing: Homeownership rate: 82.5%; Median home value: $120,400; Median year structure built: 1978; Homeowner vacancy rate: 1.6%; Median gross rent: $905 per month; Rental vacancy rate: 7.6%
   Health Insurance: 84.2% have insurance; 67.8% have private insurance; 30.5% have public insurance; 15.8% do not have insurance; 16.3% of children under 18 do not have insurance
   Transportation: Commute: 91.5% car, 0.0% public transportation, 0.8% walk, 6.4% work from home; Median travel time to work: 29.4 minutes

BENNETT (CDP). Covers a land area of 3.207 square miles and a water area of 0.016 square miles. Located at 35.58° N. Lat; 79.53° W. Long. Elevation is 495 feet.
Population: 282; Growth (since 2000): n/a; Density: 87.9 persons per square mile; Race: 92.2% White, 3.2% Black/African American, 2.5% Asian, 0.4% American Indian/Alaska Native, 0.0% Native Hawaiian/Other Pacific Islander, 1.8% Two or more races, 0.0% Hispanic of any race; Average household size: 2.33; Median age: 44.6; Age under 18: 19.5%; Age 65 and over: 23.0%; Males per 100 females: 89.3
School District(s)
Chatham County Schools (PK-12)
   2012-13 Enrollment: 8,454 . . . . (919) 542-3626
Housing: Homeownership rate: 89.3%; Homeowner vacancy rate: 1.8%; Rental vacancy rate: 7.1%

FEARRINGTON VILLAGE (CDP). Covers a land area of 1.784 square miles and a water area of 0.006 square miles. Located at 35.80° N. Lat; 79.08° W. Long. Elevation is 459 feet.
Population: 2,339; Growth (since 2000): n/a; Density: 1,310.9 persons per square mile; Race: 97.8% White, 0.9% Black/African American, 0.6% Asian, 0.0% American Indian/Alaska Native, 0.0% Native Hawaiian/Other Pacific Islander, 0.5% Two or more races, 1.1% Hispanic of any race; Average household size: 1.68; Median age: 72.3; Age under 18: 3.1%; Age 65 and over: 72.0%; Males per 100 females: 71.7
Housing: Homeownership rate: 80.9%; Homeowner vacancy rate: 3.6%; Rental vacancy rate: 3.0%

GOLDSTON (town). Covers a land area of 0.787 square miles and a water area of 0.005 square miles. Located at 35.59° N. Lat; 79.33° W. Long. Elevation is 420 feet.
Population: 268; Growth (since 2000): -16.0%; Density: 340.7 persons per square mile; Race: 91.4% White, 5.6% Black/African American, 0.4% Asian, 0.0% American Indian/Alaska Native, 0.0% Native Hawaiian/Other

Pacific Islander, 2.2% Two or more races, 3.4% Hispanic of any race; Average household size: 2.21; Median age: 49.0; Age under 18: 17.9%; Age 65 and over: 19.8%; Males per 100 females: 82.3

School District(s)
Chatham County Schools (PK-12)
    2012-13 Enrollment: 8,454 . . . . (919) 542-3626
Housing: Homeownership rate: 80.2%; Homeowner vacancy rate: 2.0%; Rental vacancy rate: 20.0%

GULF (CDP). Covers a land area of 0.910 square miles and a water area of 0.011 square miles. Located at 35.56° N. Lat; 79.28° W. Long. Elevation is 272 feet.
Population: 144; Growth (since 2000): n/a; Density: 158.2 persons per square mile; Race: 96.5% White, 3.5% Black/African American, 0.0% Asian, 0.0% American Indian/Alaska Native, 0.0% Native Hawaiian/Other Pacific Islander, 0.0% Two or more races, 0.0% Hispanic of any race; Average household size: 2.36; Median age: 42.5; Age under 18: 17.4%; Age 65 and over: 18.1%; Males per 100 females: 100.0
Housing: Homeownership rate: 83.6%; Homeowner vacancy rate: 3.7%; Rental vacancy rate: 9.1%

MONCURE (CDP). Covers a land area of 4.715 square miles and a water area of 0.228 square miles. Located at 35.63° N. Lat; 79.07° W. Long. Elevation is 217 feet.
Population: 711; Growth (since 2000): n/a; Density: 150.8 persons per square mile; Race: 54.1% White, 36.6% Black/African American, 0.3% Asian, 0.4% American Indian/Alaska Native, 0.0% Native Hawaiian/Other Pacific Islander, 1.7% Two or more races, 9.6% Hispanic of any race; Average household size: 2.42; Median age: 42.7; Age under 18: 22.1%; Age 65 and over: 13.4%; Males per 100 females: 106.1

School District(s)
Chatham County Schools (PK-12)
    2012-13 Enrollment: 8,454 . . . . (919) 542-3626
Housing: Homeownership rate: 77.9%; Homeowner vacancy rate: 1.7%; Rental vacancy rate: 17.7%

PITTSBORO (town). County seat. Covers a land area of 4.138 square miles and a water area of 0.036 square miles. Located at 35.73° N. Lat; 79.17° W. Long. Elevation is 407 feet.
History: Pittsboro was named for William Pitt, champion of Colonial rights in the British Parliament. The town was settled in 1771 by planters of the Cape Fear region, attracted by its pleasant summer climate.
Population: 3,743; Growth (since 2000): 68.1%; Density: 904.6 persons per square mile; Race: 72.2% White, 19.5% Black/African American, 1.8% Asian, 0.3% American Indian/Alaska Native, 0.0% Native Hawaiian/Other Pacific Islander, 2.4% Two or more races, 8.9% Hispanic of any race; Average household size: 2.28; Median age: 41.4; Age under 18: 20.7%; Age 65 and over: 19.7%; Males per 100 females: 83.7; Marriage status: 30.8% never married, 43.0% now married, 3.8% separated, 9.3% widowed, 16.9% divorced; Foreign born: 8.9%; Speak English only: 84.7%; With disability: 15.5%; Veterans: 11.8%; Ancestry: 12.2% German, 12.2% Irish, 12.0% English, 6.2% French, 5.4% Dutch
Employment: 14.5% management, business, and financial, 10.3% computer, engineering, and science, 21.9% education, legal, community service, arts, and media, 14.9% healthcare practitioners, 13.1% service, 9.6% sales and office, 6.0% natural resources, construction, and maintenance, 9.6% production, transportation, and material moving
Income: Per capita: $27,626; Median household: $53,105; Average household: $65,281; Households with income of $100,000 or more: 13.9%; Poverty rate: 23.1%
Educational Attainment: High school diploma or higher: 84.5%; Bachelor's degree or higher: 39.7%; Graduate/professional degree or higher: 16.2%

School District(s)
Chatham County Schools (PK-12)
    2012-13 Enrollment: 8,454 . . . . (919) 542-3626
Housing: Homeownership rate: 69.6%; Median home value: $203,700; Median year structure built: 1987; Homeowner vacancy rate: 2.7%; Median gross rent: $813 per month; Rental vacancy rate: 7.0%
Health Insurance: 86.5% have insurance; 63.9% have private insurance; 29.9% have public insurance; 13.5% do not have insurance; 5.4% of children under 18 do not have insurance
Safety: Violent crime rate: 40.7 per 10,000 population; Property crime rate: 233.9 per 10,000 population

Transportation: Commute: 89.0% car, 1.7% public transportation, 1.5% walk, 2.7% work from home; Median travel time to work: 28.3 minutes
Additional Information Contacts
Town of Pittsboro . . . . (317) 892-3326
    http://www.pittsboronc.org

SILER CITY (town). Covers a land area of 6.001 square miles and a water area of 0.022 square miles. Located at 35.72° N. Lat; 79.46° W. Long. Elevation is 607 feet.
History: The first settlement at Siler City, a stop on the stage road, was called Silers Crossroads.
Population: 7,887; Growth (since 2000): 13.2%; Density: 1,314.2 persons per square mile; Race: 44.0% White, 19.1% Black/African American, 0.4% Asian, 1.7% American Indian/Alaska Native, 0.2% Native Hawaiian/Other Pacific Islander, 3.4% Two or more races, 49.8% Hispanic of any race; Average household size: 2.94; Median age: 31.1; Age under 18: 29.8%; Age 65 and over: 12.1%; Males per 100 females: 96.5; Marriage status: 37.8% never married, 46.5% now married, 2.8% separated, 5.5% widowed, 10.2% divorced; Foreign born: 32.2%; Speak English only: 54.0%; With disability: 9.7%; Veterans: 4.8%; Ancestry: 7.7% American, 3.6% German, 3.6% Irish, 3.2% English, 1.6% Scotch-Irish
Employment: 4.8% management, business, and financial, 2.1% computer, engineering, and science, 8.0% education, legal, community service, arts, and media, 1.3% healthcare practitioners, 20.4% service, 14.9% sales and office, 10.1% natural resources, construction, and maintenance, 38.4% production, transportation, and material moving
Income: Per capita: $14,234; Median household: $30,676; Average household: $39,910; Households with income of $100,000 or more: 3.5%; Poverty rate: 22.2%
Educational Attainment: High school diploma or higher: 62.8%; Bachelor's degree or higher: 14.4%; Graduate/professional degree or higher: 7.4%

School District(s)
Chatham Charter (KG-08)
    2012-13 Enrollment: 328 . . . . (919) 742-4550
Chatham County Schools (PK-12)
    2012-13 Enrollment: 8,454 . . . . (919) 542-3626
Vocational/Technical School(s)
Body Therapy Institute (Private, For-profit)
    Fall 2013 Enrollment: 64 . . . . (919) 663-3111
    2013-14 Tuition: $14,350
Housing: Homeownership rate: 54.1%; Median home value: $95,700; Median year structure built: 1973; Homeowner vacancy rate: 3.3%; Median gross rent: $667 per month; Rental vacancy rate: 8.1%
Health Insurance: 66.8% have insurance; 34.9% have private insurance; 41.4% have public insurance; 33.2% do not have insurance; 14.0% of children under 18 do not have insurance
Hospitals: Chatham Hospital (68 beds)
Safety: Violent crime rate: 32.8 per 10,000 population; Property crime rate: 394.3 per 10,000 population
Newspapers: Chatham News Publishing (weekly circulation 9000)
Transportation: Commute: 96.0% car, 0.9% public transportation, 0.7% walk, 1.0% work from home; Median travel time to work: 24.6 minutes
Additional Information Contacts
Town of Siler City . . . . (919) 742-4731
    http://www.silercity.org

Cherokee County

Located in western North Carolina, partly in the Blue Ridge; bounded on the south by Georgia, and on the west and northwest by Tennessee; includes Nantahala National Forest. Covers a land area of 455.426 square miles, a water area of 11.298 square miles, and is located in the Eastern Time Zone at 35.14° N. Lat., 84.06° W. Long. The county was founded in 1839. County seat is Murphy.

Weather Station: Andrews   Elevation: 1,750 feet

	Jan	Feb	Mar	Apr	May	Jun	Jul	Aug	Sep	Oct	Nov	Dec
High	49	54	61	70	76	83	86	85	80	71	61	52
Low	24	28	34	40	49	58	62	61	54	42	34	27
Precip	6.3	6.1	6.4	5.0	5.5	5.6	5.0	5.6	4.9	3.4	5.5	5.7
Snow	2.7	2.3	1.3	0.4	0.0	0.0	0.0	0.0	0.0	tr	tr	0.4

High and Low temperatures in degrees Fahrenheit; Precipitation and Snow in inches

Weather Station: Murphy 2 NE   Elevation: 1,640 feet

	Jan	Feb	Mar	Apr	May	Jun	Jul	Aug	Sep	Oct	Nov	Dec
High	49	53	61	70	77	83	86	86	80	71	62	52
Low	26	28	34	41	50	59	63	62	56	44	35	28
Precip	5.3	5.1	5.2	4.4	5.0	4.9	5.0	4.3	4.5	3.2	4.8	4.9
Snow	1.9	1.3	0.7	tr	0.0	0.0	0.0	0.0	0.0	tr	0.1	0.7

High and Low temperatures in degrees Fahrenheit; Precipitation and Snow in inches

Population: 27,444; Growth (since 2000): 12.9%; Density: 60.3 persons per square mile; Race: 93.6% White, 1.3% Black/African American, 0.5% Asian, 1.3% American Indian/Alaska Native, 0.0% Native Hawaiian/Other Pacific Islander, 2.5% two or more races, 2.5% Hispanic of any race; Average household size: 2.30; Median age: 48.1; Age under 18: 19.3%; Age 65 and over: 22.9%; Males per 100 females: 94.6; Marriage status: 20.4% never married, 59.3% now married, 3.1% separated, 8.8% widowed, 11.5% divorced; Foreign born: 2.7%; Speak English only: 95.8%; With disability: 18.9%; Veterans: 12.4%; Ancestry: 13.7% American, 13.5% Irish, 11.4% German, 11.0% English, 5.7% Scottish
Religion: Six largest groups: 27.7% Baptist, 6.8% Methodist/Pietist, 3.7% Catholicism, 1.9% Pentecostal, 1.8% Non-denominational Protestant, 1.2% Latter-day Saints
Economy: Unemployment rate: 7.3%; Leading industries: 22.1% retail trade; 13.1% health care and social assistance; 13.0% construction; Farms: 255 totaling 21,453 acres; Company size: 0 employ 1,000 or more persons, 1 employs 500 to 999 persons, 8 employ 100 to 499 persons, 585 employ less than 100 persons; Business ownership: 787 women-owned, 27 Black-owned, n/a Hispanic-owned, n/a Asian-owned
Employment: 9.4% management, business, and financial, 2.8% computer, engineering, and science, 7.8% education, legal, community service, arts, and media, 7.7% healthcare practitioners, 16.8% service, 26.4% sales and office, 14.3% natural resources, construction, and maintenance, 14.7% production, transportation, and material moving
Income: Per capita: $18,340; Median household: $34,432; Average household: $43,248; Households with income of $100,000 or more: 6.4%; Poverty rate: 17.9%
Educational Attainment: High school diploma or higher: 81.9%; Bachelor's degree or higher: 16.7%; Graduate/professional degree or higher: 5.8%
Housing: Homeownership rate: 79.8%; Median home value: $145,000; Median year structure built: 1989; Homeowner vacancy rate: 5.5%; Median gross rent: $589 per month; Rental vacancy rate: 13.3%
Vital Statistics: Birth rate: 82.7 per 10,000 population; Death rate: 116.8 per 10,000 population; Age-adjusted cancer mortality rate: 175.5 deaths per 100,000 population
Health Insurance: 79.7% have insurance; 52.0% have private insurance; 43.8% have public insurance; 20.3% do not have insurance; 13.2% of children under 18 do not have insurance
Health Care: Physicians: 10.0 per 10,000 population; Hospital beds: 70.3 per 10,000 population; Hospital admissions: 937.3 per 10,000 population
Transportation: Commute: 94.7% car, 0.3% public transportation, 2.2% walk, 2.1% work from home; Median travel time to work: 22.3 minutes
Presidential Election: 26.3% Obama, 72.1% Romney (2012)
Additional Information Contacts
Cherokee Government . . . . (828) 837-5527
    http://www.cherokeecounty-nc.gov

Cherokee County Communities

ANDREWS (town). Covers a land area of 1.633 square miles and a water area of 0 square miles. Located at 35.20° N. Lat; 83.83° W. Long. Elevation is 1,778 feet.
Population: 1,781; Growth (since 2000): 11.2%; Density: 1,090.3 persons per square mile; Race: 88.8% White, 1.3% Black/African American, 0.1% Asian, 1.1% American Indian/Alaska Native, 0.0% Native Hawaiian/Other Pacific Islander, 4.9% Two or more races, 7.5% Hispanic of any race; Average household size: 2.19; Median age: 42.9; Age under 18: 22.9%; Age 65 and over: 20.9%; Males per 100 females: 84.4
School District(s)
Cherokee County Schools (PK-12)
    2012-13 Enrollment: 3,548 . . . . (828) 837-2722
Housing: Homeownership rate: 59.8%; Homeowner vacancy rate: 2.3%; Rental vacancy rate: 16.3%
Newspapers: Andrews Journal (weekly circulation 2800)
Airports: Western Carolina Regional (general aviation)

MARBLE (CDP). Covers a land area of 1.096 square miles and a water area of 0 square miles. Located at 35.18° N. Lat; 83.93° W. Long. Elevation is 1,680 feet.
Population: 321; Growth (since 2000): n/a; Density: 292.8 persons per square mile; Race: 96.9% White, 0.0% Black/African American, 0.0% Asian, 1.9% American Indian/Alaska Native, 0.0% Native Hawaiian/Other Pacific Islander, 1.2% Two or more races, 0.6% Hispanic of any race; Average household size: 2.43; Median age: 44.9; Age under 18: 25.5%; Age 65 and over: 25.5%; Males per 100 females: 101.9
School District(s)
Cherokee County Schools (PK-12)
    2012-13 Enrollment: 3,548 . . . . (828) 837-2722
Housing: Homeownership rate: 73.5%; Homeowner vacancy rate: 6.7%; Rental vacancy rate: 14.6%

MURPHY (town). County seat. Covers a land area of 2.397 square miles and a water area of 0.241 square miles. Located at 35.09° N. Lat; 84.03° W. Long. Elevation is 1,594 feet.
History: Murphy was first established as a trading post about 1830. It was then known as Huntersville for its founder, Colonel A.R.S. Hunter. The town was renamed in honor of Archibald D. Murphey, statesman and champion of popular education. The difference in spelling is the result of a typographical error.
Population: 1,627; Growth (since 2000): 3.8%; Density: 678.8 persons per square mile; Race: 87.6% White, 4.1% Black/African American, 2.1% Asian, 2.5% American Indian/Alaska Native, 0.0% Native Hawaiian/Other Pacific Islander, 2.4% Two or more races, 4.2% Hispanic of any race; Average household size: 2.12; Median age: 41.5; Age under 18: 19.4%; Age 65 and over: 19.5%; Males per 100 females: 92.1
School District(s)
Cherokee County Schools (PK-12)
    2012-13 Enrollment: 3,548 . . . . (828) 837-2722
The Learning Center (KG-08)
    2012-13 Enrollment: 187 . . . . (828) 835-7240
Two-year College(s)
Tri-County Community College (Public)
    Fall 2013 Enrollment: 1,412 . . . . (828) 837-6810
    2013-14 Tuition: In-state $2,346; Out-of-state $8,490
Housing: Homeownership rate: 50.7%; Homeowner vacancy rate: 5.0%; Rental vacancy rate: 8.2%
Hospitals: Murphy Medical Center (184 beds)
Safety: Violent crime rate: 81.7 per 10,000 population; Property crime rate: 772.6 per 10,000 population
Newspapers: Cherokee Scout (weekly circulation 9000); WNC Sentinel (weekly circulation 5000)

Chowan County

Located in northeastern North Carolina; in a coastal plains area, bounded on the west by the Chowan River, and on the south by Albemarle Sound. Covers a land area of 172.473 square miles, a water area of 60.825 square miles, and is located in the Eastern Time Zone at 36.13° N. Lat., 76.60° W. Long. The county was founded in 1672. County seat is Edenton.

Weather Station: Edenton   Elevation: 20 feet

	Jan	Feb	Mar	Apr	May	Jun	Jul	Aug	Sep	Oct	Nov	Dec
High	52	56	64	72	79	86	89	87	82	73	64	55
Low	33	35	40	49	58	66	71	69	63	52	44	36
Precip	3.6	3.1	4.1	3.1	3.7	4.6	5.5	5.6	4.7	3.3	3.2	2.9
Snow	0.9	1.0	0.8	0.1	0.0	0.0	0.0	0.0	0.0	0.0	0.0	0.6

High and Low temperatures in degrees Fahrenheit; Precipitation and Snow in inches

Population: 14,793; Growth (since 2000): 1.8%; Density: 85.8 persons per square mile; Race: 62.0% White, 34.3% Black/African American, 0.4% Asian, 0.3% American Indian/Alaska Native, 0.0% Native Hawaiian/Other Pacific Islander, 1.2% two or more races, 3.2% Hispanic of any race; Average household size: 2.40; Median age: 44.8; Age under 18: 22.4%; Age 65 and over: 19.7%; Males per 100 females: 90.6; Marriage status: 26.5% never married, 53.0% now married, 4.6% separated, 11.4% widowed, 9.1% divorced; Foreign born: 4.4%; Speak English only: 95.9%; With disability: 17.2%; Veterans: 10.7%; Ancestry: 11.1% English, 10.1% American, 6.8% German, 5.8% Irish, 2.6% Italian
Religion: Six largest groups: 22.0% Baptist, 10.4% Methodist/Pietist, 5.2% Episcopalianism/Anglicanism, 3.7% Catholicism, 3.6% Pentecostal, 1.6% Latter-day Saints

Economy: Unemployment rate: 7.0%; Leading industries: 16.4% health care and social assistance; 15.6% retail trade; 11.1% construction; Farms: 141 totaling 58,146 acres; Company size: 0 employ 1,000 or more persons, 0 employ 500 to 999 persons, 4 employ 100 to 499 persons, 367 employ less than 100 persons; Business ownership: n/a women-owned, n/a Black-owned, n/a Hispanic-owned, n/a Asian-owned
Employment: 15.8% management, business, and financial, 4.3% computer, engineering, and science, 12.0% education, legal, community service, arts, and media, 3.6% healthcare practitioners, 16.8% service, 22.0% sales and office, 10.5% natural resources, construction, and maintenance, 15.1% production, transportation, and material moving
Income: Per capita: $19,240; Median household: $34,420; Average household: $47,006; Households with income of $100,000 or more: 10.5%; Poverty rate: 29.0%
Educational Attainment: High school diploma or higher: 79.7%; Bachelor's degree or higher: 20.1%; Graduate/professional degree or higher: 7.7%
Housing: Homeownership rate: 69.2%; Median home value: $129,100; Median year structure built: 1975; Homeowner vacancy rate: 3.2%; Median gross rent: $743 per month; Rental vacancy rate: 8.9%
Vital Statistics: Birth rate: 113.4 per 10,000 population; Death rate: 119.5 per 10,000 population; Age-adjusted cancer mortality rate: 206.5 deaths per 100,000 population
Health Insurance: 84.0% have insurance; 55.9% have private insurance; 43.0% have public insurance; 16.0% do not have insurance; 7.0% of children under 18 do not have insurance
Health Care: Physicians: 17.0 per 10,000 population; Hospital beds: 45.3 per 10,000 population; Hospital admissions: 1,247.8 per 10,000 population
Transportation: Commute: 95.1% car, 0.2% public transportation, 1.9% walk, 1.5% work from home; Median travel time to work: 26.6 minutes
Presidential Election: 47.4% Obama, 51.8% Romney (2012)
Additional Information Contacts
Chowan Government . . . . (252) 482-8431
    http://www.chowancounty-nc.gov

Chowan County Communities

EDENTON (town). County seat. Covers a land area of 5.370 square miles and a water area of 0.198 square miles. Located at 36.06° N. Lat; 76.60° W. Long. Elevation is 10 feet.
History: In 1622 John Pory, secretary of the Virginia Colony, explored the rich bottom lands of the Chowan River in the area now known as Edenton. By 1658, settlers had come down from Jamestown. In 1710 the Edenton settlement was a borough of some importance, virtual capital of the Colony, and the governor's residence. The place was incorporated in 1722 as Edenton in honor of Governor Charles Eden, who had just died. In time, the seat of government moved to a "more sentrical" location. Two early shipyards did a thriving business, and shad and herring fisheries were a chief occupation. Cotton, corn, soybeans, tobacco, cantaloupes, watermelons, and peanuts have been major crops.
Population: 5,004; Growth (since 2000): -7.2%; Density: 931.8 persons per square mile; Race: 40.8% White, 54.8% Black/African American, 0.5% Asian, 0.1% American Indian/Alaska Native, 0.0% Native Hawaiian/Other Pacific Islander, 1.3% Two or more races, 3.4% Hispanic of any race; Average household size: 2.29; Median age: 43.1; Age under 18: 24.3%; Age 65 and over: 21.3%; Males per 100 females: 80.8; Marriage status: 31.8% never married, 42.6% now married, 6.2% separated, 14.0% widowed, 11.5% divorced; Foreign born: 1.6%; Speak English only: 98.5%; With disability: 16.1%; Veterans: 8.7%; Ancestry: 7.4% English, 6.1% American, 4.3% Irish, 3.6% German, 1.8% Scottish
Employment: 16.9% management, business, and financial, 1.6% computer, engineering, and science, 11.0% education, legal, community service, arts, and media, 1.8% healthcare practitioners, 19.2% service, 24.4% sales and office, 7.8% natural resources, construction, and maintenance, 17.4% production, transportation, and material moving
Income: Per capita: $14,911; Median household: $24,396; Average household: $36,748; Households with income of $100,000 or more: 6.2%; Poverty rate: 44.9%
Educational Attainment: High school diploma or higher: 74.5%; Bachelor's degree or higher: 20.7%; Graduate/professional degree or higher: 9.7%
School District(s)
Edenton/chowan Schools (PK-12)
    2012-13 Enrollment: 2,311 . . . . (252) 482-4436

Housing: Homeownership rate: 48.5%; Median home value: $111,100; Median year structure built: 1961; Homeowner vacancy rate: 5.4%; Median gross rent: $649 per month; Rental vacancy rate: 9.2%
Health Insurance: 85.9% have insurance; 45.1% have private insurance; 55.1% have public insurance; 14.1% do not have insurance; 0.0% of children under 18 do not have insurance
Hospitals: Vidant Chowan Hospital (111 beds)
Safety: Violent crime rate: 78.1 per 10,000 population; Property crime rate: 462.6 per 10,000 population
Newspapers: The Chowan Herald (weekly circulation 4000)
Transportation: Commute: 86.7% car, 0.0% public transportation, 6.7% walk, 2.9% work from home; Median travel time to work: 23.4 minutes
Airports: Northeastern Regional (general aviation)
Additional Information Contacts
Town of Edenton . . . . (252) 482-3400
    http://www.townofedenton.com

TYNER (unincorporated postal area)
ZCTA: 27980
    Covers a land area of 51.649 square miles and a water area of 0.089 square miles. Located at 36.25° N. Lat; 76.62° W. Long..
    Population: 2,182; Growth (since 2000): -2.5%; Density: 42.2 persons per square mile; Race: 69.6% White, 25.0% Black/African American, 0.4% Asian, 0.4% American Indian/Alaska Native, 0.2% Native Hawaiian/Other Pacific Islander, 1.8% Two or more races, 4.9% Hispanic of any race; Average household size: 2.56; Median age: 41.6; Age under 18: 23.3%; Age 65 and over: 16.4%; Males per 100 females: 99.8
School District(s)
Edenton/chowan Schools (PK-12)
    2012-13 Enrollment: 2,311 . . . . (252) 482-4436
    Housing: Homeownership rate: 78.6%; Homeowner vacancy rate: 2.0%; Rental vacancy rate: 8.1%

Clay County

Located in western North Carolina; mountainous area, bounded on the south by Georgia, and on the northeast by the Nantahala River; includes part of Nantahala National Forest. Covers a land area of 214.751 square miles, a water area of 5.878 square miles, and is located in the Eastern Time Zone at 35.05° N. Lat., 83.75° W. Long. The county was founded in 1861. County seat is Hayesville.
Population: 10,587; Growth (since 2000): 20.6%; Density: 49.3 persons per square mile; Race: 96.6% White, 0.6% Black/African American, 0.2% Asian, 0.3% American Indian/Alaska Native, 0.0% Native Hawaiian/Other Pacific Islander, 1.4% two or more races, 2.4% Hispanic of any race; Average household size: 2.25; Median age: 49.6; Age under 18: 18.7%; Age 65 and over: 23.6%; Males per 100 females: 97.4; Marriage status: 16.5% never married, 63.3% now married, 4.0% separated, 9.4% widowed, 10.8% divorced; Foreign born: 3.4%; Speak English only: 97.5%; With disability: 14.4%; Veterans: 15.9%; Ancestry: 18.0% American, 14.9% English, 12.5% Irish, 11.9% German, 6.0% Scottish
Religion: Six largest groups: 69.8% Baptist, 8.5% Methodist/Pietist, 6.6% Catholicism, 3.7% Pentecostal, 2.9% Non-denominational Protestant, 2.4% Episcopalianism/Anglicanism
Economy: Unemployment rate: 5.0%; Leading industries: 21.4% construction; 21.4% retail trade; 11.7% other services (except public administration); Farms: 154 totaling 11,752 acres; Company size: 0 employ 1,000 or more persons, 0 employ 500 to 999 persons, 1 employs 100 to 499 persons, 205 employ less than 100 persons; Business ownership: n/a women-owned, n/a Black-owned, n/a Hispanic-owned, n/a Asian-owned
Employment: 10.6% management, business, and financial, 3.7% computer, engineering, and science, 12.2% education, legal, community service, arts, and media, 3.1% healthcare practitioners, 18.0% service, 29.3% sales and office, 11.9% natural resources, construction, and maintenance, 11.3% production, transportation, and material moving
Income: Per capita: $22,081; Median household: $38,828; Average household: $50,277; Households with income of $100,000 or more: 11.4%; Poverty rate: 24.3%
Educational Attainment: High school diploma or higher: 86.9%; Bachelor's degree or higher: 20.6%; Graduate/professional degree or higher: 9.8%

Housing: Homeownership rate: 78.8%; Median home value: $154,700; Median year structure built: 1986; Homeowner vacancy rate: 5.6%; Median gross rent: $615 per month; Rental vacancy rate: 17.1%

Vital Statistics: Birth rate: 71.8 per 10,000 population; Death rate: 129.4 per 10,000 population; Age-adjusted cancer mortality rate: 165.2 deaths per 100,000 population

Health Insurance: 76.3% have insurance; 54.1% have private insurance; 40.8% have public insurance; 23.7% do not have insurance; 16.7% of children under 18 do not have insurance

Health Care: Physicians: 7.5 per 10,000 population; Hospital beds: 0.0 per 10,000 population; Hospital admissions: 0.0 per 10,000 population

Transportation: Commute: 95.2% car, 0.0% public transportation, 1.4% walk, 2.1% work from home; Median travel time to work: 20.5 minutes

Presidential Election: 28.0% Obama, 70.4% Romney (2012)

Additional Information Contacts

Clay Government . . . . (828) 389-0089
  http://www.clayconc.com

Clay County Communities

BRASSTOWN (unincorporated postal area)

ZCTA: 28902

Covers a land area of 22.678 square miles and a water area of 0.048 square miles. Located at 35.02° N. Lat; 83.96° W. Long. Elevation is 1,604 feet.

Population: 1,373; Growth (since 2000): 74.2%; Density: 60.5 persons per square mile; Race: 96.1% White, 0.9% Black/African American, 0.4% Asian, 0.4% American Indian/Alaska Native, 0.0% Native Hawaiian/Other Pacific Islander, 1.4% Two or more races, 2.8% Hispanic of any race; Average household size: 2.33; Median age: 47.5; Age under 18: 19.4%; Age 65 and over: 19.6%; Males per 100 females: 97.8

Housing: Homeownership rate: 86.4%; Homeowner vacancy rate: 5.9%; Rental vacancy rate: 16.2%

HAYESVILLE (town). County seat. Covers a land area of 0.467 square miles and a water area of 0 square miles. Located at 35.05° N. Lat; 83.82° W. Long. Elevation is 1,890 feet.

History: Hayesville was named for George W. Hayes, who represented the district in the legislature.

Population: 311; Growth (since 2000): 4.7%; Density: 666.6 persons per square mile; Race: 97.4% White, 0.0% Black/African American, 0.0% Asian, 1.0% American Indian/Alaska Native, 0.0% Native Hawaiian/Other Pacific Islander, 0.6% Two or more races, 2.3% Hispanic of any race; Average household size: 2.05; Median age: 45.8; Age under 18: 20.9%; Age 65 and over: 22.2%; Males per 100 females: 89.6

School District(s)

Clay County Schools (PK-12)

2012-13 Enrollment: 1,388 . . . . (828) 389-8513

Housing: Homeownership rate: 57.9%; Homeowner vacancy rate: 6.5%; Rental vacancy rate: 17.3%

Newspapers: Clay County Progress (weekly circulation 3700); Smoky Mountain Sentinel (weekly circulation 24000)

WARNE (unincorporated postal area)

ZCTA: 28909

Covers a land area of 9.832 square miles and a water area of 0 square miles. Located at 35.00° N. Lat; 83.90° W. Long. Elevation is 1,736 feet.

Population: 1,030; Growth (since 2000): 79.8%; Density: 104.8 persons per square mile; Race: 95.9% White, 0.6% Black/African American, 0.5% Asian, 0.3% American Indian/Alaska Native, 0.0% Native Hawaiian/Other Pacific Islander, 2.6% Two or more races, 1.7% Hispanic of any race; Average household size: 2.35; Median age: 47.5; Age under 18: 21.1%; Age 65 and over: 20.1%; Males per 100 females: 94.3

Housing: Homeownership rate: 82.2%; Homeowner vacancy rate: 5.1%; Rental vacancy rate: 17.0%

Cleveland County

Located in southwestern North Carolina; bounded on the south by South Carolina; drained by the Broad River. Covers a land area of 464.252 square miles, a water area of 3.999 square miles, and is located in the Eastern Time Zone at 35.33° N. Lat., 81.56° W. Long. The county was founded in 1841. County seat is Shelby.

Cleveland County is part of the Shelby, NC Micropolitan Statistical Area. The entire metro area includes: Cleveland County, NC

Weather Station: Shelby 2 NNE   Elevation: 919 feet

	Jan	Feb	Mar	Apr	May	Jun	Jul	Aug	Sep	Oct	Nov	Dec
High	51	55	63	72	79	86	89	88	81	72	63	53
Low	29	31	38	46	54	63	66	66	58	46	38	31
Precip	3.7	3.5	4.5	3.5	4.2	4.2	4.2	4.4	3.7	3.7	3.8	3.9
Snow	2.7	1.3	1.0	tr	0.0	0.0	0.0	0.0	0.0	0.0	0.1	0.3

High and Low temperatures in degrees Fahrenheit; Precipitation and Snow in inches

Population: 98,078; Growth (since 2000): 1.9%; Density: 211.3 persons per square mile; Race: 75.6% White, 20.7% Black/African American, 0.8% Asian, 0.2% American Indian/Alaska Native, 0.0% Native Hawaiian/Other Pacific Islander, 1.5% two or more races, 2.8% Hispanic of any race; Average household size: 2.49; Median age: 40.3; Age under 18: 23.4%; Age 65 and over: 15.0%; Males per 100 females: 93.2; Marriage status: 27.5% never married, 54.4% now married, 4.2% separated, 7.4% widowed, 10.7% divorced; Foreign born: 2.4%; Speak English only: 96.0%; With disability: 15.9%; Veterans: 9.1%; Ancestry: 27.7% American, 9.0% German, 7.2% English, 6.5% Irish, 2.7% Scotch-Irish

Religion: Six largest groups: 41.5% Baptist, 8.9% Methodist/Pietist, 3.9% Non-denominational Protestant, 1.8% Presbyterian-Reformed, 1.6% Pentecostal, 1.0% Holiness

Economy: Unemployment rate: 5.9%; Leading industries: 19.1% retail trade; 15.1% other services (except public administration); 11.8% health care and social assistance; Farms: 1,036 totaling 116,651 acres; Company size: 2 employ 1,000 or more persons, 2 employ 500 to 999 persons, 34 employ 100 to 499 persons, 1,897 employ less than 100 persons; Business ownership: 1,799 women-owned, 607 Black-owned, 155 Hispanic-owned, 112 Asian-owned

Employment: 9.5% management, business, and financial, 2.3% computer, engineering, and science, 9.9% education, legal, community service, arts, and media, 6.0% healthcare practitioners, 19.2% service, 25.2% sales and office, 8.7% natural resources, construction, and maintenance, 19.3% production, transportation, and material moving

Income: Per capita: $20,062; Median household: $38,989; Average household: $50,235; Households with income of $100,000 or more: 10.2%; Poverty rate: 19.3%

Educational Attainment: High school diploma or higher: 82.0%; Bachelor's degree or higher: 16.3%; Graduate/professional degree or higher: 5.6%

Housing: Homeownership rate: 68.8%; Median home value: $106,100; Median year structure built: 1977; Homeowner vacancy rate: 2.3%; Median gross rent: $642 per month; Rental vacancy rate: 13.3%

Vital Statistics: Birth rate: 111.4 per 10,000 population; Death rate: 117.1 per 10,000 population; Age-adjusted cancer mortality rate: 206.9 deaths per 100,000 population

Health Insurance: 84.2% have insurance; 58.9% have private insurance; 37.5% have public insurance; 15.8% do not have insurance; 4.8% of children under 18 do not have insurance

Health Care: Physicians: 12.8 per 10,000 population; Hospital beds: 49.9 per 10,000 population; Hospital admissions: 1,236.5 per 10,000 population

Transportation: Commute: 94.7% car, 0.4% public transportation, 2.0% walk, 2.3% work from home; Median travel time to work: 23.5 minutes

Presidential Election: 39.4% Obama, 59.5% Romney (2012)

Additional Information Contacts

Cleveland Government . . . . (704) 484-4900
  http://www.clevelandcounty.com

Cleveland County Communities

BELWOOD (town). Covers a land area of 12.300 square miles and a water area of 0.006 square miles. Located at 35.48° N. Lat; 81.53° W. Long. Elevation is 1,020 feet.

Population: 950; Growth (since 2000): -1.2%; Density: 77.2 persons per square mile; Race: 94.3% White, 2.4% Black/African American, 0.3% Asian, 0.9% American Indian/Alaska Native, 0.0% Native Hawaiian/Other Pacific Islander, 1.1% Two or more races, 4.1% Hispanic of any race; Average household size: 2.51; Median age: 41.3; Age under 18: 23.5%; Age 65 and over: 16.1%; Males per 100 females: 100.0

Housing: Homeownership rate: 75.4%; Homeowner vacancy rate: 1.7%; Rental vacancy rate: 7.9%

BOILING SPRINGS (town). Covers a land area of 4.453 square miles and a water area of 0 square miles. Located at 35.25° N. Lat; 81.66° W. Long. Elevation is 883 feet.

History: Seat of Gardner-Webb University.

Population: 4,647; Growth (since 2000): 20.2%; Density: 1,043.6 persons per square mile; Race: 86.1% White, 11.3% Black/African American, 0.4% Asian, 0.2% American Indian/Alaska Native, 0.0% Native Hawaiian/Other Pacific Islander, 1.5% Two or more races, 2.0% Hispanic of any race; Average household size: 2.58; Median age: 24.4; Age under 18: 20.3%; Age 65 and over: 8.6%; Males per 100 females: 89.5; Marriage status: 46.4% never married, 41.3% now married, 0.7% separated, 5.5% widowed, 6.7% divorced; Foreign born: 3.2%; Speak English only: 96.4%; With disability: 11.1%; Veterans: 5.4%; Ancestry: 17.2% American, 16.3% German, 9.8% English, 9.7% Irish, 3.7% Scotch-Irish

Employment: 8.0% management, business, and financial, 4.0% computer, engineering, and science, 29.7% education, legal, community service, arts, and media, 10.5% healthcare practitioners, 7.2% service, 29.4% sales and office, 4.7% natural resources, construction, and maintenance, 6.4% production, transportation, and material moving

Income: Per capita: $22,627; Median household: $61,875; Average household: $80,629; Households with income of $100,000 or more: 27.5%; Poverty rate: 8.6%

Educational Attainment: High school diploma or higher: 89.8%; Bachelor's degree or higher: 49.0%; Graduate/professional degree or higher: 24.8%

Four-year College(s)

Gardner-Webb University (Private, Not-for-profit, Southern Baptist)
    Fall 2013 Enrollment: 4,656 . . . . (704) 406-2361
    2013-14 Tuition: In-state $25,830; Out-of-state $25,830

Housing: Homeownership rate: 73.6%; Median home value: $151,700; Median year structure built: 1992; Homeowner vacancy rate: 2.0%; Median gross rent: $651 per month; Rental vacancy rate: 9.5%

Health Insurance: 90.5% have insurance; 77.2% have private insurance; 21.0% have public insurance; 9.5% do not have insurance; 0.0% of children under 18 do not have insurance

Transportation: Commute: 85.5% car, 1.0% public transportation, 10.5% walk, 3.0% work from home; Median travel time to work: 21.7 minutes

Additional Information Contacts

Town of Boiling Springs . . . . (704) 434-9419
    http://www.boilingspringsnc.net

CASAR (town). Covers a land area of 1.750 square miles and a water area of 0 square miles. Located at 35.51° N. Lat; 81.62° W. Long. Elevation is 1,135 feet.

Population: 297; Growth (since 2000): -3.6%; Density: 169.7 persons per square mile; Race: 98.0% White, 0.0% Black/African American, 0.0% Asian, 0.3% American Indian/Alaska Native, 0.0% Native Hawaiian/Other Pacific Islander, 1.7% Two or more races, 3.4% Hispanic of any race; Average household size: 2.38; Median age: 41.4; Age under 18: 24.9%; Age 65 and over: 20.5%; Males per 100 females: 91.6

School District(s)

Cleveland County Schools (PK-12)
    2012-13 Enrollment: 15,951 . . . . (704) 476-8000

Housing: Homeownership rate: 80.8%; Homeowner vacancy rate: 1.9%; Rental vacancy rate: 16.7%

EARL (town). Covers a land area of 0.861 square miles and a water area of 0 square miles. Located at 35.20° N. Lat; 81.53° W. Long. Elevation is 833 feet.

Population: 260; Growth (since 2000): 11.1%; Density: 301.9 persons per square mile; Race: 91.2% White, 8.1% Black/African American, 0.4% Asian, 0.0% American Indian/Alaska Native, 0.0% Native Hawaiian/Other Pacific Islander, 0.0% Two or more races, 0.4% Hispanic of any race; Average household size: 2.43; Median age: 41.3; Age under 18: 23.1%; Age 65 and over: 13.1%; Males per 100 females: 88.4

Housing: Homeownership rate: 73.8%; Homeowner vacancy rate: 0.0%; Rental vacancy rate: 11.8%

FALLSTON (town). Covers a land area of 2.161 square miles and a water area of 0.005 square miles. Located at 35.43° N. Lat; 81.50° W. Long. Elevation is 1,024 feet.

Population: 607; Growth (since 2000): 0.7%; Density: 280.9 persons per square mile; Race: 92.8% White, 5.1% Black/African American, 0.0% Asian, 0.0% American Indian/Alaska Native, 0.0% Native Hawaiian/Other Pacific Islander, 1.5% Two or more races, 0.7% Hispanic of any race;

Average household size: 2.56; Median age: 37.9; Age under 18: 24.4%; Age 65 and over: 16.0%; Males per 100 females: 90.3

School District(s)

Cleveland County Schools (PK-12)
    2012-13 Enrollment: 15,951 . . . . (704) 476-8000

Housing: Homeownership rate: 74.3%; Homeowner vacancy rate: 3.3%; Rental vacancy rate: 6.0%

GROVER (town). Covers a land area of 0.961 square miles and a water area of 0.029 square miles. Located at 35.17° N. Lat; 81.45° W. Long. Elevation is 860 feet.

History: Kings Mountain National Military Park (S.C.) to Southeast.

Population: 708; Growth (since 2000): 1.4%; Density: 736.9 persons per square mile; Race: 79.9% White, 11.9% Black/African American, 2.1% Asian, 1.0% American Indian/Alaska Native, 0.0% Native Hawaiian/Other Pacific Islander, 4.4% Two or more races, 4.5% Hispanic of any race; Average household size: 2.67; Median age: 36.1; Age under 18: 26.4%; Age 65 and over: 11.9%; Males per 100 females: 97.2

School District(s)

Cleveland County Schools (PK-12)
    2012-13 Enrollment: 15,951 . . . . (704) 476-8000

Housing: Homeownership rate: 66.5%; Homeowner vacancy rate: 2.7%; Rental vacancy rate: 25.8%

KINGS MOUNTAIN (city). Covers a land area of 12.322 square miles and a water area of 0.249 square miles. Located at 35.24° N. Lat; 81.35° W. Long. Elevation is 1,007 feet.

History: Kings Mt. National Military Park (South Carolina) 8 miles to south southwest. Incorporated 1874.

Population: 10,296; Growth (since 2000): 6.2%; Density: 835.6 persons per square mile; Race: 73.0% White, 22.5% Black/African American, 1.6% Asian, 0.2% American Indian/Alaska Native, 0.0% Native Hawaiian/Other Pacific Islander, 1.7% Two or more races, 2.6% Hispanic of any race; Average household size: 2.44; Median age: 40.6; Age under 18: 24.7%; Age 65 and over: 17.3%; Males per 100 females: 85.5; Marriage status: 28.2% never married, 51.1% now married, 6.8% separated, 8.5% widowed, 12.2% divorced; Foreign born: 1.0%; Speak English only: 97.9%; With disability: 21.4%; Veterans: 10.1%; Ancestry: 29.3% American, 12.3% German, 8.1% Irish, 6.1% English, 3.6% Scotch-Irish

Employment: 8.8% management, business, and financial, 1.5% computer, engineering, and science, 7.5% education, legal, community service, arts, and media, 5.2% healthcare practitioners, 17.6% service, 30.0% sales and office, 9.3% natural resources, construction, and maintenance, 20.1% production, transportation, and material moving

Income: Per capita: $19,448; Median household: $33,701; Average household: $47,021; Households with income of $100,000 or more: 8.5%; Poverty rate: 23.6%

Educational Attainment: High school diploma or higher: 82.4%; Bachelor's degree or higher: 13.2%; Graduate/professional degree or higher: 4.0%

School District(s)

Cleveland County Schools (PK-12)
    2012-13 Enrollment: 15,951 . . . . (704) 476-8000

Housing: Homeownership rate: 59.3%; Median home value: $105,700; Median year structure built: 1971; Homeowner vacancy rate: 2.6%; Median gross rent: $606 per month; Rental vacancy rate: 9.4%

Health Insurance: 82.7% have insurance; 53.8% have private insurance; 40.5% have public insurance; 17.3% do not have insurance; 2.2% of children under 18 do not have insurance

Hospitals: Kings Mountain Hospital (102 beds)

Newspapers: Kings Mtn. Herald (weekly circulation 5300)

Transportation: Commute: 95.4% car, 0.0% public transportation, 1.5% walk, 2.9% work from home; Median travel time to work: 22.6 minutes

Additional Information Contacts

City of Kings Mountain . . . . (704) 734-0333
    http://www.cityofkm.com

KINGSTOWN (town). Covers a land area of 1.760 square miles and a water area of 0 square miles. Located at 35.36° N. Lat; 81.62° W. Long. Elevation is 925 feet.

Population: 681; Growth (since 2000): -19.4%; Density: 386.8 persons per square mile; Race: 8.1% White, 89.1% Black/African American, 0.9% Asian, 0.1% American Indian/Alaska Native, 0.0% Native Hawaiian/Other Pacific Islander, 1.0% Two or more races, 1.0% Hispanic of any race;

Average household size: 2.69; Median age: 39.3; Age under 18: 26.6%; Age 65 and over: 15.9%; Males per 100 females: 89.7
Housing: Homeownership rate: 72.4%; Homeowner vacancy rate: 1.6%; Rental vacancy rate: 4.1%

LATTIMORE (town). Covers a land area of 1.025 square miles and a water area of 0 square miles. Located at 35.32° N. Lat; 81.66° W. Long. Elevation is 932 feet.
Population: 488; Growth (since 2000): 16.5%; Density: 476.0 persons per square mile; Race: 94.7% White, 3.1% Black/African American, 0.6% Asian, 0.0% American Indian/Alaska Native, 0.0% Native Hawaiian/Other Pacific Islander, 0.8% Two or more races, 3.1% Hispanic of any race; Average household size: 2.68; Median age: 23.2; Age under 18: 20.7%; Age 65 and over: 9.4%; Males per 100 females: 103.3
Housing: Homeownership rate: 78.2%; Homeowner vacancy rate: 6.3%; Rental vacancy rate: 17.1%

LAWNDALE (town). Covers a land area of 0.805 square miles and a water area of 0.053 square miles. Located at 35.41° N. Lat; 81.56° W. Long. Elevation is 846 feet.
Population: 606; Growth (since 2000): -5.6%; Density: 753.1 persons per square mile; Race: 79.2% White, 15.3% Black/African American, 0.2% Asian, 0.0% American Indian/Alaska Native, 0.0% Native Hawaiian/Other Pacific Islander, 2.1% Two or more races, 4.8% Hispanic of any race; Average household size: 2.47; Median age: 42.1; Age under 18: 25.2%; Age 65 and over: 18.3%; Males per 100 females: 98.7
School District(s)
Cleveland County Schools (PK-12)
    2012-13 Enrollment: 15,951 . . . . (704) 476-8000
Housing: Homeownership rate: 68.6%; Homeowner vacancy rate: 4.0%; Rental vacancy rate: 13.5%

LIGHT OAK (CDP). Covers a land area of 1.437 square miles and a water area of 0 square miles. Located at 35.29° N. Lat; 81.48° W. Long. Elevation is 820 feet.
Population: 691; Growth (since 2000): -11.3%; Density: 480.8 persons per square mile; Race: 26.2% White, 73.2% Black/African American, 0.0% Asian, 0.3% American Indian/Alaska Native, 0.0% Native Hawaiian/Other Pacific Islander, 0.0% Two or more races, 1.9% Hispanic of any race; Average household size: 2.46; Median age: 45.9; Age under 18: 19.2%; Age 65 and over: 19.0%; Males per 100 females: 103.8
Housing: Homeownership rate: 69.4%; Homeowner vacancy rate: 2.5%; Rental vacancy rate: 18.9%

MOORESBORO (town). Covers a land area of 1.767 square miles and a water area of 0 square miles. Located at 35.30° N. Lat; 81.70° W. Long. Elevation is 892 feet.
Population: 311; Growth (since 2000): -1.0%; Density: 176.0 persons per square mile; Race: 81.0% White, 16.7% Black/African American, 0.3% Asian, 0.6% American Indian/Alaska Native, 0.0% Native Hawaiian/Other Pacific Islander, 1.0% Two or more races, 1.0% Hispanic of any race; Average household size: 2.43; Median age: 42.8; Age under 18: 23.5%; Age 65 and over: 16.1%; Males per 100 females: 87.3
School District(s)
Thomas Jefferson Class Academy (KG-12)
    2012-13 Enrollment: 1,199 . . . . (828) 657-9998
Housing: Homeownership rate: 67.2%; Homeowner vacancy rate: 2.2%; Rental vacancy rate: 17.6%

PATTERSON SPRINGS (town). Covers a land area of 0.910 square miles and a water area of 0 square miles. Located at 35.23° N. Lat; 81.52° W. Long. Elevation is 899 feet.
Population: 622; Growth (since 2000): 0.3%; Density: 683.4 persons per square mile; Race: 87.1% White, 8.7% Black/African American, 0.3% Asian, 0.0% American Indian/Alaska Native, 0.0% Native Hawaiian/Other Pacific Islander, 3.1% Two or more races, 2.4% Hispanic of any race; Average household size: 2.50; Median age: 35.6; Age under 18: 26.5%; Age 65 and over: 10.3%; Males per 100 females: 98.1
Housing: Homeownership rate: 57.0%; Homeowner vacancy rate: 0.0%; Rental vacancy rate: 12.3%

POLKVILLE (city). Covers a land area of 1.856 square miles and a water area of 0 square miles. Located at 35.42° N. Lat; 81.64° W. Long. Elevation is 1,073 feet.
Population: 545; Growth (since 2000): 1.9%; Density: 293.6 persons per square mile; Race: 96.5% White, 1.7% Black/African American, 0.2% Asian, 0.0% American Indian/Alaska Native, 0.2% Native Hawaiian/Other Pacific Islander, 1.5% Two or more races, 3.9% Hispanic of any race; Average household size: 2.36; Median age: 41.8; Age under 18: 21.3%; Age 65 and over: 18.3%; Males per 100 females: 94.6
Housing: Homeownership rate: 66.6%; Homeowner vacancy rate: 1.9%; Rental vacancy rate: 17.0%

SHELBY (city). County seat. Covers a land area of 21.076 square miles and a water area of 0.035 square miles. Located at 35.29° N. Lat; 81.54° W. Long. Elevation is 860 feet.
History: Shelby was named for General Isaac Shelby, leader at the Battle of Kings Mountain.
Population: 20,323; Growth (since 2000): 4.3%; Density: 964.3 persons per square mile; Race: 54.7% White, 41.3% Black/African American, 0.8% Asian, 0.4% American Indian/Alaska Native, 0.0% Native Hawaiian/Other Pacific Islander, 1.7% Two or more races, 3.1% Hispanic of any race; Average household size: 2.32; Median age: 41.4; Age under 18: 23.5%; Age 65 and over: 17.7%; Males per 100 females: 86.3; Marriage status: 35.7% never married, 44.9% now married, 3.3% separated, 9.1% widowed, 10.2% divorced; Foreign born: 3.8%; Speak English only: 94.6%; With disability: 16.4%; Veterans: 10.4%; Ancestry: 18.2% American, 7.7% German, 7.4% English, 4.6% Irish, 3.0% Scotch-Irish
Employment: 12.8% management, business, and financial, 2.2% computer, engineering, and science, 13.3% education, legal, community service, arts, and media, 6.3% healthcare practitioners, 21.3% service, 23.8% sales and office, 3.1% natural resources, construction, and maintenance, 17.1% production, transportation, and material moving
Income: Per capita: $19,793; Median household: $32,070; Average household: $47,374; Households with income of $100,000 or more: 10.5%; Poverty rate: 29.1%
Educational Attainment: High school diploma or higher: 86.0%; Bachelor's degree or higher: 21.0%; Graduate/professional degree or higher: 7.6%
School District(s)
Cleveland County Schools (PK-12)
    2012-13 Enrollment: 15,951 . . . . (704) 476-8000
Two-year College(s)
Cleveland Community College (Public)
    Fall 2013 Enrollment: 3,371 . . . . (704) 669-6000
    2013-14 Tuition: In-state $2,302; Out-of-state $8,446
Housing: Homeownership rate: 52.9%; Median home value: $118,100; Median year structure built: 1969; Homeowner vacancy rate: 5.0%; Median gross rent: $669 per month; Rental vacancy rate: 15.1%
Health Insurance: 83.1% have insurance; 51.9% have private insurance; 44.6% have public insurance; 16.9% do not have insurance; 8.0% of children under 18 do not have insurance
Hospitals: Cleveland Regional Medical Center (241 beds)
Safety: Violent crime rate: 61.7 per 10,000 population; Property crime rate: 334.6 per 10,000 population
Newspapers: Shelby Star (daily circulation 14200)
Transportation: Commute: 94.1% car, 0.6% public transportation, 3.0% walk, 1.6% work from home; Median travel time to work: 19.0 minutes
Airports: Shelby-Cleveland County Regional (general aviation)
Additional Information Contacts
City of Shelby . . . . (704) 484-6800
    http://cityofshelby.com

WACO (town). Covers a land area of 0.786 square miles and a water area of 0.005 square miles. Located at 35.36° N. Lat; 81.43° W. Long. Elevation is 915 feet.
Population: 321; Growth (since 2000): -2.1%; Density: 408.4 persons per square mile; Race: 79.1% White, 19.6% Black/African American, 0.0% Asian, 0.0% American Indian/Alaska Native, 0.0% Native Hawaiian/Other Pacific Islander, 0.3% Two or more races, 1.2% Hispanic of any race; Average household size: 2.53; Median age: 43.4; Age under 18: 18.7%; Age 65 and over: 14.3%; Males per 100 females: 100.6
Housing: Homeownership rate: 77.2%; Homeowner vacancy rate: 0.0%; Rental vacancy rate: 6.1%

Columbus County

Located in southeastern North Carolina; swampy area bounded on the southwest by South Carolina, and on the northwest by the Lumber River. Covers a land area of 937.293 square miles, a water area of 16.347 square miles, and is located in the Eastern Time Zone at 34.26° N. Lat., 78.64° W. Long. The county was founded in 1808. County seat is Whiteville.

Weather Station: Whiteville 7 NW   Elevation: 89 feet

	Jan	Feb	Mar	Apr	May	Jun	Jul	Aug	Sep	Oct	Nov	Dec
High	55	59	66	75	82	88	91	89	84	75	68	58
Low	32	34	40	48	57	66	69	68	62	50	41	34
Precip	3.8	3.3	4.0	3.1	4.2	4.4	5.6	5.6	5.3	3.1	2.9	3.1
Snow	0.6	0.5	0.5	tr	0.0	0.0	0.0	0.0	0.0	0.0	0.0	0.5

High and Low temperatures in degrees Fahrenheit; Precipitation and Snow in inches

Population: 58,098; Growth (since 2000): 6.1%; Density: 62.0 persons per square mile; Race: 61.5% White, 30.5% Black/African American, 0.3% Asian, 3.2% American Indian/Alaska Native, 0.0% Native Hawaiian/Other Pacific Islander, 1.5% two or more races, 4.6% Hispanic of any race; Average household size: 2.45; Median age: 39.8; Age under 18: 23.3%; Age 65 and over: 15.2%; Males per 100 females: 98.0; Marriage status: 30.4% never married, 49.2% now married, 3.9% separated, 8.5% widowed, 11.9% divorced; Foreign born: 3.0%; Speak English only: 94.2%; With disability: 20.3%; Veterans: 9.1%; Ancestry: 28.1% American, 6.9% English, 4.5% Irish, 3.6% German, 2.0% Scotch-Irish
Religion: Six largest groups: 37.7% Baptist, 9.4% Methodist/Pietist, 3.4% Pentecostal, 2.8% Non-denominational Protestant, 1.8% Catholicism, 0.9% Presbyterian-Reformed
Economy: Unemployment rate: 7.4%; Leading industries: 20.7% retail trade; 16.0% health care and social assistance; 9.7% other services (except public administration); Farms: 731 totaling 159,227 acres; Company size: 0 employ 1,000 or more persons, 2 employ 500 to 999 persons, 12 employ 100 to 499 persons, 1,023 employ less than 100 persons; Business ownership: 1,224 women-owned, n/a Black-owned, 82 Hispanic-owned, n/a Asian-owned
Employment: 8.8% management, business, and financial, 1.2% computer, engineering, and science, 10.5% education, legal, community service, arts, and media, 6.6% healthcare practitioners, 22.8% service, 24.0% sales and office, 12.2% natural resources, construction, and maintenance, 14.0% production, transportation, and material moving
Income: Per capita: $19,275; Median household: $35,761; Average household: $48,994; Households with income of $100,000 or more: 10.8%; Poverty rate: 25.0%
Educational Attainment: High school diploma or higher: 79.2%; Bachelor's degree or higher: 12.2%; Graduate/professional degree or higher: 4.0%
Housing: Homeownership rate: 71.1%; Median home value: $84,500; Median year structure built: 1978; Homeowner vacancy rate: 1.6%; Median gross rent: $584 per month; Rental vacancy rate: 11.4%
Vital Statistics: Birth rate: 111.4 per 10,000 population; Death rate: 116.3 per 10,000 population; Age-adjusted cancer mortality rate: 196.7 deaths per 100,000 population
Health Insurance: 79.2% have insurance; 49.9% have private insurance; 42.1% have public insurance; 20.8% do not have insurance; 12.9% of children under 18 do not have insurance
Health Care: Physicians: 8.7 per 10,000 population; Hospital beds: 18.5 per 10,000 population; Hospital admissions: 915.2 per 10,000 population
Transportation: Commute: 96.2% car, 0.2% public transportation, 1.2% walk, 1.9% work from home; Median travel time to work: 24.0 minutes
Presidential Election: 45.6% Obama, 53.4% Romney (2012)
National and State Parks: Lake Waccamaw State Park
Additional Information Contacts
Columbus Government . . . . (910) 640-6630
  http://www.columbusco.org

Columbus County Communities

BOARDMAN (town). Covers a land area of 3.071 square miles and a water area of 0.022 square miles. Located at 34.43° N. Lat; 78.94° W. Long. Elevation is 89 feet.
Population: 157; Growth (since 2000): -22.3%; Density: 51.1 persons per square mile; Race: 66.2% White, 33.8% Black/African American, 0.0% Asian, 0.0% American Indian/Alaska Native, 0.0% Native Hawaiian/Other Pacific Islander, 0.0% Two or more races, 0.0% Hispanic of any race;

Average household size: 2.21; Median age: 50.2; Age under 18: 17.8%; Age 65 and over: 28.0%; Males per 100 females: 67.0
Housing: Homeownership rate: 76.1%; Homeowner vacancy rate: 0.0%; Rental vacancy rate: 10.0%

BOLTON (town). Covers a land area of 3.753 square miles and a water area of 0 square miles. Located at 34.32° N. Lat; 78.40° W. Long. Elevation is 66 feet.
Population: 691; Growth (since 2000): 39.9%; Density: 184.1 persons per square mile; Race: 23.6% White, 69.2% Black/African American, 0.0% Asian, 3.2% American Indian/Alaska Native, 0.0% Native Hawaiian/Other Pacific Islander, 2.5% Two or more races, 2.9% Hispanic of any race; Average household size: 2.60; Median age: 40.6; Age under 18: 25.2%; Age 65 and over: 16.4%; Males per 100 females: 98.0
Housing: Homeownership rate: 73.7%; Homeowner vacancy rate: 2.0%; Rental vacancy rate: 10.3%

BRUNSWICK (town). Covers a land area of 0.421 square miles and a water area of 0 square miles. Located at 34.28° N. Lat; 78.70° W. Long. Elevation is 79 feet.
Population: 1,119; Growth (since 2000): 210.8%; Density: 2,658.2 persons per square mile; Race: 34.6% White, 56.3% Black/African American, 0.4% Asian, 3.4% American Indian/Alaska Native, 0.1% Native Hawaiian/Other Pacific Islander, 2.2% Two or more races, 5.5% Hispanic of any race; Average household size: 2.56; Median age: 36.5; Age under 18: 10.9%; Age 65 and over: 6.2%; Males per 100 females: 401.8
Housing: Homeownership rate: 53.3%; Homeowner vacancy rate: 2.2%; Rental vacancy rate: 10.0%

CERRO GORDO (town). Covers a land area of 0.750 square miles and a water area of 0 square miles. Located at 34.32° N. Lat; 78.93° W. Long. Elevation is 89 feet.
Population: 207; Growth (since 2000): -15.2%; Density: 276.0 persons per square mile; Race: 79.2% White, 10.6% Black/African American, 0.0% Asian, 5.8% American Indian/Alaska Native, 0.0% Native Hawaiian/Other Pacific Islander, 2.4% Two or more races, 2.9% Hispanic of any race; Average household size: 2.65; Median age: 38.3; Age under 18: 26.6%; Age 65 and over: 15.9%; Males per 100 females: 88.2
School District(s)
Columbus County Schools (PK-12)
    2012-13 Enrollment: 6,558 . . . . (910) 642-5168
Housing: Homeownership rate: 82.1%; Homeowner vacancy rate: 0.0%; Rental vacancy rate: 33.3%

CHADBOURN (town). Covers a land area of 2.634 square miles and a water area of 0 square miles. Located at 34.32° N. Lat; 78.83° W. Long. Elevation is 105 feet.
Population: 1,856; Growth (since 2000): -12.8%; Density: 704.7 persons per square mile; Race: 38.2% White, 56.9% Black/African American, 0.3% Asian, 2.2% American Indian/Alaska Native, 0.0% Native Hawaiian/Other Pacific Islander, 1.5% Two or more races, 2.6% Hispanic of any race; Average household size: 2.28; Median age: 39.5; Age under 18: 26.6%; Age 65 and over: 16.9%; Males per 100 females: 79.2
School District(s)
Columbus County Schools (PK-12)
    2012-13 Enrollment: 6,558 . . . . (910) 642-5168
Housing: Homeownership rate: 53.2%; Homeowner vacancy rate: 0.9%; Rental vacancy rate: 10.5%
Safety: Violent crime rate: 147.1 per 10,000 population; Property crime rate: 1,242.5 per 10,000 population
Newspapers: News Times (weekly circulation 8400)

CLARENDON (unincorporated postal area)
ZCTA: 28432
    Covers a land area of 35.278 square miles and a water area of 0.174 square miles. Located at 34.17° N. Lat; 78.76° W. Long. Elevation is 105 feet.
    Population: 1,968; Growth (since 2000): 18.9%; Density: 55.8 persons per square mile; Race: 90.0% White, 7.1% Black/African American, 0.1% Asian, 0.6% American Indian/Alaska Native, 0.0% Native Hawaiian/Other Pacific Islander, 1.3% Two or more races, 2.1% Hispanic of any race; Average household size: 2.56; Median age: 38.8; Age under 18: 25.3%; Age 65 and over: 14.2%; Males per 100 females: 91.3

Housing: Homeownership rate: 79.4%; Homeowner vacancy rate: 1.1%; Rental vacancy rate: 16.4%

DELCO (CDP). Covers a land area of 1.515 square miles and a water area of 0 square miles. Located at 34.32° N. Lat; 78.23° W. Long. Elevation is 46 feet.
Population: 348; Growth (since 2000): n/a; Density: 229.6 persons per square mile; Race: 86.2% White, 6.0% Black/African American, 0.0% Asian, 2.0% American Indian/Alaska Native, 0.0% Native Hawaiian/Other Pacific Islander, 4.9% Two or more races, 1.7% Hispanic of any race; Average household size: 2.43; Median age: 43.3; Age under 18: 25.0%; Age 65 and over: 16.4%; Males per 100 females: 87.1
School District(s)
Columbus County Schools (PK-12)
    2012-13 Enrollment: 6,558 . . . . (910) 642-5168
Housing: Homeownership rate: 83.3%; Homeowner vacancy rate: 1.7%; Rental vacancy rate: 11.1%

EVERGREEN (CDP). Covers a land area of 3.856 square miles and a water area of 0 square miles. Located at 34.41° N. Lat; 78.91° W. Long. Elevation is 46 feet.
Population: 420; Growth (since 2000): n/a; Density: 108.9 persons per square mile; Race: 51.4% White, 47.4% Black/African American, 0.0% Asian, 0.0% American Indian/Alaska Native, 0.0% Native Hawaiian/Other Pacific Islander, 0.5% Two or more races, 0.7% Hispanic of any race; Average household size: 2.58; Median age: 43.0; Age under 18: 25.2%; Age 65 and over: 14.0%; Males per 100 females: 79.5
School District(s)
Columbus County Schools (PK-12)
    2012-13 Enrollment: 6,558 . . . . (910) 642-5168
Housing: Homeownership rate: 73.6%; Homeowner vacancy rate: 4.0%; Rental vacancy rate: 10.4%

FAIR BLUFF (town). Covers a land area of 2.145 square miles and a water area of 0 square miles. Located at 34.31° N. Lat; 79.03° W. Long. Elevation is 62 feet.
Population: 951; Growth (since 2000): -19.5%; Density: 443.4 persons per square mile; Race: 33.5% White, 63.6% Black/African American, 0.0% Asian, 0.5% American Indian/Alaska Native, 0.0% Native Hawaiian/Other Pacific Islander, 0.7% Two or more races, 2.1% Hispanic of any race; Average household size: 2.18; Median age: 46.8; Age under 18: 18.9%; Age 65 and over: 18.9%; Males per 100 females: 86.8
Housing: Homeownership rate: 64.9%; Homeowner vacancy rate: 3.4%; Rental vacancy rate: 12.9%

HALLSBORO (CDP). Covers a land area of 3.264 square miles and a water area of 0 square miles. Located at 34.32° N. Lat; 78.59° W. Long. Elevation is 59 feet.
Population: 465; Growth (since 2000): n/a; Density: 142.4 persons per square mile; Race: 37.4% White, 57.0% Black/African American, 0.4% Asian, 1.5% American Indian/Alaska Native, 0.0% Native Hawaiian/Other Pacific Islander, 1.7% Two or more races, 3.2% Hispanic of any race; Average household size: 2.34; Median age: 43.3; Age under 18: 21.3%; Age 65 and over: 20.6%; Males per 100 females: 99.6
School District(s)
Columbus County Schools (PK-12)
    2012-13 Enrollment: 6,558 . . . . (910) 642-5168
Housing: Homeownership rate: 73.9%; Homeowner vacancy rate: 1.3%; Rental vacancy rate: 8.8%

LAKE WACCAMAW (town). Covers a land area of 3.514 square miles and a water area of 0.006 square miles. Located at 34.32° N. Lat; 78.52° W. Long. Elevation is 59 feet.
Population: 1,480; Growth (since 2000): 4.9%; Density: 421.1 persons per square mile; Race: 80.9% White, 13.4% Black/African American, 0.1% Asian, 3.9% American Indian/Alaska Native, 0.0% Native Hawaiian/Other Pacific Islander, 1.3% Two or more races, 1.2% Hispanic of any race; Average household size: 2.23; Median age: 48.4; Age under 18: 19.8%; Age 65 and over: 23.5%; Males per 100 females: 94.0
School District(s)
Columbus County Schools (PK-12)
    2012-13 Enrollment: 6,558 . . . . (910) 642-5168
Housing: Homeownership rate: 75.1%; Homeowner vacancy rate: 4.9%; Rental vacancy rate: 11.1%

Additional Information Contacts
Town of Lake Waccamaw . . . . (910) 646-3700
    http://www.lakewaccamaw.com

NAKINA (unincorporated postal area)
ZCTA: 28455
    Covers a land area of 76.343 square miles and a water area of 0.059 square miles. Located at 34.11° N. Lat; 78.63° W. Long. Elevation is 46 feet.
Population: 2,117; Growth (since 2000): 18.3%; Density: 27.7 persons per square mile; Race: 80.5% White, 7.0% Black/African American, 0.0% Asian, 0.4% American Indian/Alaska Native, 0.0% Native Hawaiian/Other Pacific Islander, 0.8% Two or more races, 14.6% Hispanic of any race; Average household size: 2.54; Median age: 38.0; Age under 18: 25.9%; Age 65 and over: 15.4%; Males per 100 females: 96.0
School District(s)
Columbus County Schools (PK-12)
    2012-13 Enrollment: 6,558 . . . . (910) 642-5168
Housing: Homeownership rate: 75.1%; Homeowner vacancy rate: 1.3%; Rental vacancy rate: 13.7%

RIEGELWOOD (CDP). Covers a land area of 3.122 square miles and a water area of 0.282 square miles. Located at 34.34° N. Lat; 78.22° W. Long. Elevation is 36 feet.
Population: 579; Growth (since 2000): n/a; Density: 185.5 persons per square mile; Race: 70.8% White, 24.9% Black/African American, 0.0% Asian, 1.2% American Indian/Alaska Native, 0.0% Native Hawaiian/Other Pacific Islander, 2.8% Two or more races, 5.4% Hispanic of any race; Average household size: 2.44; Median age: 41.6; Age under 18: 23.1%; Age 65 and over: 18.3%; Males per 100 females: 93.0
School District(s)
Bladen County Schools (PK-12)
    2012-13 Enrollment: 5,233 . . . . (910) 862-4136
Columbus County Schools (PK-12)
    2012-13 Enrollment: 6,558 . . . . (910) 642-5168
Housing: Homeownership rate: 85.6%; Homeowner vacancy rate: 1.0%; Rental vacancy rate: 10.5%

SANDYFIELD (town). Covers a land area of 3.447 square miles and a water area of 0.009 square miles. Located at 34.37° N. Lat; 78.30° W. Long. Elevation is 39 feet.
Population: 447; Growth (since 2000): 31.5%; Density: 129.7 persons per square mile; Race: 15.0% White, 81.2% Black/African American, 0.0% Asian, 1.3% American Indian/Alaska Native, 0.0% Native Hawaiian/Other Pacific Islander, 1.3% Two or more races, 1.8% Hispanic of any race; Average household size: 2.73; Median age: 34.4; Age under 18: 27.5%; Age 65 and over: 11.9%; Males per 100 females: 99.6
Housing: Homeownership rate: 81.1%; Homeowner vacancy rate: 0.0%; Rental vacancy rate: 16.2%

TABOR CITY (town). Covers a land area of 3.175 square miles and a water area of 0 square miles. Located at 34.15° N. Lat; 78.87° W. Long. Elevation is 102 feet.
Population: 2,511; Growth (since 2000): 0.1%; Density: 790.9 persons per square mile; Race: 59.2% White, 36.2% Black/African American, 0.2% Asian, 1.1% American Indian/Alaska Native, 0.0% Native Hawaiian/Other Pacific Islander, 1.8% Two or more races, 2.3% Hispanic of any race; Average household size: 2.24; Median age: 44.0; Age under 18: 21.6%; Age 65 and over: 19.4%; Males per 100 females: 84.6; Marriage status: 28.2% never married, 41.7% now married, 7.0% separated, 13.2% widowed, 16.9% divorced; Foreign born: 0.7%; Speak English only: 98.9%; With disability: 30.4%; Veterans: 9.6%; Ancestry: 28.5% American, 6.8% English, 5.5% Irish, 3.9% German, 2.9% Scotch-Irish
Employment: 6.9% management, business, and financial, 0.6% computer, engineering, and science, 15.6% education, legal, community service, arts, and media, 6.8% healthcare practitioners, 28.4% service, 24.5% sales and office, 5.3% natural resources, construction, and maintenance, 12.0% production, transportation, and material moving
Income: Per capita: $18,663; Median household: $20,048; Average household: $40,893; Households with income of $100,000 or more: 12.6%; Poverty rate: 35.8%
Educational Attainment: High school diploma or higher: 76.3%; Bachelor's degree or higher: 19.1%; Graduate/professional degree or higher: 8.1%

School District(s)
Columbus County Schools (PK-12)
  2012-13 Enrollment: 6,558 . . . . (910) 642-5168
Housing: Homeownership rate: 55.1%; Median home value: $82,100; Median year structure built: 1970; Homeowner vacancy rate: 4.4%; Median gross rent: $543 per month; Rental vacancy rate: 7.6%
Health Insurance: 80.0% have insurance; 42.7% have private insurance; 50.0% have public insurance; 20.0% do not have insurance; 12.1% of children under 18 do not have insurance
Safety: Violent crime rate: 55.4 per 10,000 population; Property crime rate: 380.4 per 10,000 population
Newspapers: Tabor-Loris Tribune (weekly circulation 3000)
Transportation: Commute: 95.3% car, 0.8% public transportation, 0.6% walk, 2.3% work from home; Median travel time to work: 20.3 minutes

WHITEVILLE (city). County seat. Covers a land area of 5.463 square miles and a water area of 0 square miles. Located at 34.33° N. Lat; 78.70° W. Long. Elevation is 98 feet.

History: Whiteville was founded in 1810. Some contend that the name commemorates John White, associated with the Lost Colony, but it probably honors John B. White, member of the general assembly of 1809, whose family deeded the land for the first courthouse.
Population: 5,394; Growth (since 2000): 4.8%; Density: 987.4 persons per square mile; Race: 53.2% White, 41.0% Black/African American, 0.8% Asian, 1.3% American Indian/Alaska Native, 0.1% Native Hawaiian/Other Pacific Islander, 1.7% Two or more races, 3.3% Hispanic of any race; Average household size: 2.14; Median age: 41.4; Age under 18: 22.0%; Age 65 and over: 19.7%; Males per 100 females: 80.8; Marriage status: 33.0% never married, 36.1% now married, 5.6% separated, 11.6% widowed, 19.3% divorced; Foreign born: 4.9%; Speak English only: 91.3%; With disability: 20.6%; Veterans: 9.2%; Ancestry: 15.9% American, 9.7% English, 6.7% German, 5.4% Irish, 2.6% Scotch-Irish
Employment: 5.2% management, business, and financial, 0.8% computer, engineering, and science, 12.1% education, legal, community service, arts, and media, 9.6% healthcare practitioners, 20.4% service, 37.4% sales and office, 6.3% natural resources, construction, and maintenance, 8.3% production, transportation, and material moving
Income: Per capita: $21,209; Median household: $25,722; Average household: $43,480; Households with income of $100,000 or more: 5.4%; Poverty rate: 37.7%
Educational Attainment: High school diploma or higher: 76.5%; Bachelor's degree or higher: 16.7%; Graduate/professional degree or higher: 6.1%
School District(s)
Columbus Charter School (KG-06)
  2012-13 Enrollment: 735 . . . . (910) 641-4042
Columbus County Schools (PK-12)
  2012-13 Enrollment: 6,558 . . . . (910) 642-5168
Whiteville City Schools (PK-12)
  2012-13 Enrollment: 2,317 . . . . (910) 642-4116
Two-year College(s)
Southeastern Community College (Public)
  Fall 2013 Enrollment: 1,402 . . . . (910) 642-7141
  2013-14 Tuition: In-state $2,416; Out-of-state $8,561
Housing: Homeownership rate: 46.5%; Median home value: $94,200; Median year structure built: 1972; Homeowner vacancy rate: 3.4%; Median gross rent: $561 per month; Rental vacancy rate: 10.6%
Health Insurance: 80.5% have insurance; 46.3% have private insurance; 50.4% have public insurance; 19.5% do not have insurance; 2.5% of children under 18 do not have insurance
Hospitals: Columbus Regional Healthcare System (154 beds)
Safety: Violent crime rate: 177.5 per 10,000 population; Property crime rate: 1,143.4 per 10,000 population
Newspapers: The News Reporter (weekly circulation 10500)
Transportation: Commute: 97.7% car, 0.0% public transportation, 0.0% walk, 0.5% work from home; Median travel time to work: 14.3 minutes
Additional Information Contacts
City of Whiteville . . . . (910) 642-8046
  http://www.whitevillecity.com

Craven County

Located in eastern North Carolina; drained by the Neuse and Trent Rivers; includes part of Croatan National Forest. Covers a land area of 708.958 square miles, a water area of 65.204 square miles, and is located in the Eastern Time Zone at 35.12° N. Lat., 77.08° W. Long. The county was founded in 1712. County seat is New Bern.

Craven County is part of the New Bern, NC Metropolitan Statistical Area. The entire metro area includes: Craven County, NC; Jones County, NC; Pamlico County, NC

Weather Station: New Bern Craven Co Reg Arpt   Elevation: 16 feet

	Jan	Feb	Mar	Apr	May	Jun	Jul	Aug	Sep	Oct	Nov	Dec
High	54	58	65	73	80	87	89	88	83	75	67	58
Low	34	36	42	50	59	67	72	71	65	53	44	36
Precip	3.9	3.5	4.6	3.3	4.2	4.4	6.4	6.7	5.2	3.3	3.5	3.5
Snow	na	na	na	na	na	na	na	na	na	na	na	na

High and Low temperatures in degrees Fahrenheit; Precipitation and Snow in inches

Population: 103,505; Growth (since 2000): 13.2%; Density: 146.0 persons per square mile; Race: 70.0% White, 22.4% Black/African American, 2.0% Asian, 0.5% American Indian/Alaska Native, 0.1% Native Hawaiian/Other Pacific Islander, 2.7% two or more races, 6.1% Hispanic of any race; Average household size: 2.45; Median age: 36.2; Age under 18: 23.4%; Age 65 and over: 15.3%; Males per 100 females: 99.0; Marriage status: 25.9% never married, 57.8% now married, 3.6% separated, 6.3% widowed, 10.0% divorced; Foreign born: 4.7%; Speak English only: 92.3%; With disability: 17.7%; Veterans: 17.9%; Ancestry: 13.3% German, 13.2% English, 12.8% Irish, 8.4% American, 4.3% Italian
Religion: Six largest groups: 16.1% Baptist, 11.8% Methodist/Pietist, 6.2% Catholicism, 4.6% Non-denominational Protestant, 2.4% Pentecostal, 2.1% Presbyterian-Reformed
Economy: Unemployment rate: 6.4%; Leading industries: 18.0% retail trade; 11.0% health care and social assistance; 10.9% other services (except public administration); Farms: 256 totaling 70,632 acres; Company size: 1 employs 1,000 or more persons, 3 employ 500 to 999 persons, 28 employ 100 to 499 persons, 2,150 employ less than 100 persons; Business ownership: 2,290 women-owned, n/a Black-owned, 172 Hispanic-owned, 177 Asian-owned
Employment: 9.8% management, business, and financial, 3.5% computer, engineering, and science, 10.0% education, legal, community service, arts, and media, 6.6% healthcare practitioners, 21.1% service, 22.7% sales and office, 13.2% natural resources, construction, and maintenance, 12.9% production, transportation, and material moving
Income: Per capita: $24,260; Median household: $47,141; Average household: $59,612; Households with income of $100,000 or more: 14.7%; Poverty rate: 16.6%
Educational Attainment: High school diploma or higher: 87.2%; Bachelor's degree or higher: 21.0%; Graduate/professional degree or higher: 6.7%
Housing: Homeownership rate: 65.4%; Median home value: $152,400; Median year structure built: 1985; Homeowner vacancy rate: 3.0%; Median gross rent: $870 per month; Rental vacancy rate: 9.6%
Vital Statistics: Birth rate: 153.0 per 10,000 population; Death rate: 92.2 per 10,000 population; Age-adjusted cancer mortality rate: 201.4 deaths per 100,000 population
Health Insurance: 85.0% have insurance; 65.3% have private insurance; 36.8% have public insurance; 15.0% do not have insurance; 5.6% of children under 18 do not have insurance
Health Care: Physicians: 21.4 per 10,000 population; Hospital beds: 33.4 per 10,000 population; Hospital admissions: 1,386.4 per 10,000 population
Transportation: Commute: 91.1% car, 0.2% public transportation, 2.8% walk, 3.7% work from home; Median travel time to work: 21.0 minutes
Presidential Election: 40.6% Obama, 58.3% Romney (2012)
National and State Parks: Croatan National Forest
Additional Information Contacts
Craven Government . . . . (252) 636-6600
  http://www.cravencountync.gov

Craven County Communities

BRICES CREEK (CDP). Covers a land area of 7.844 square miles and a water area of 0.491 square miles. Located at 35.04° N. Lat; 77.08° W. Long. Elevation is 26 feet.

Population: 3,073; Growth (since 2000): 49.2%; Density: 391.8 persons per square mile; Race: 88.7% White, 8.6% Black/African American, 0.7% Asian, 0.0% American Indian/Alaska Native, 0.0% Native Hawaiian/Other Pacific Islander, 1.9% Two or more races, 1.5% Hispanic of any race; Average household size: 2.77; Median age: 41.9; Age under 18: 27.6%; Age 65 and over: 13.1%; Males per 100 females: 96.1; Marriage status:

15.0% never married, 78.3% now married, 2.6% separated, 4.3% widowed, 2.4% divorced; Foreign born: 2.0%; Speak English only: 94.0%; With disability: 16.1%; Veterans: 21.0%; Ancestry: 27.5% German, 15.9% Irish, 15.1% English, 7.3% Italian, 6.2% Dutch

Employment: 11.6% management, business, and financial, 5.7% computer, engineering, and science, 19.2% education, legal, community service, arts, and media, 10.2% healthcare practitioners, 7.5% service, 23.8% sales and office, 6.6% natural resources, construction, and maintenance, 15.4% production, transportation, and material moving

Income: Per capita: $33,613; Median household: $79,821; Average household: $88,768; Households with income of $100,000 or more: 35.9%; Poverty rate: 0.6%

Educational Attainment: High school diploma or higher: 97.1%; Bachelor's degree or higher: 37.6%; Graduate/professional degree or higher: 15.4%

Housing: Homeownership rate: 90.6%; Median home value: $246,700; Median year structure built: 1995; Homeowner vacancy rate: 3.0%; Median gross rent: $1,054 per month; Rental vacancy rate: 4.5%

Health Insurance: 96.6% have insurance; 89.5% have private insurance; 23.6% have public insurance; 3.4% do not have insurance; 1.5% of children under 18 do not have insurance

Transportation: Commute: 97.8% car, 0.0% public transportation, 0.0% walk, 2.2% work from home; Median travel time to work: 28.6 minutes

BRIDGETON (town). Covers a land area of 1.525 square miles and a water area of 0.004 square miles. Located at 35.13° N. Lat; 77.01° W. Long. Elevation is 7 feet.

Population: 454; Growth (since 2000): 38.4%; Density: 297.6 persons per square mile; Race: 81.5% White, 11.9% Black/African American, 0.2% Asian, 0.4% American Indian/Alaska Native, 0.2% Native Hawaiian/Other Pacific Islander, 4.4% Two or more races, 4.6% Hispanic of any race; Average household size: 2.25; Median age: 44.0; Age under 18: 20.0%; Age 65 and over: 18.1%; Males per 100 females: 81.6

Housing: Homeownership rate: 55.0%; Homeowner vacancy rate: 3.4%; Rental vacancy rate: 9.0%

Additional Information Contacts
Town of Bridgeton . . . . (207) 647-8786
   http://bridgtonmaine.org

CHERRY POINT (unincorporated postal area)
ZCTA: 28533
   Covers a land area of 0.444 square miles and a water area of 0 square miles. Located at 34.90° N. Lat; 76.90° W. Long..
   Population: 2,952; Growth (since 2000): n/a; Density: 6,643.0 persons per square mile; Race: 78.1% White, 10.7% Black/African American, 2.0% Asian, 0.7% American Indian/Alaska Native, 0.3% Native Hawaiian/Other Pacific Islander, 2.7% Two or more races, 15.0% Hispanic of any race; Average household size: 0.00; Median age: 21.9; Age under 18: 0.0%; Age 65 and over: 0.0%; Males per 100 females: ***.*; Marriage status: 82.7% never married, 14.1% now married, 1.8% separated, 0.0% widowed, 3.2% divorced; Foreign born: 6.1%; Speak English only: 88.6%; With disability: 0.0%; Veterans: 50.0%; Ancestry: 23.4% German, 23.1% Irish, 8.2% English, 7.8% French, 6.1% Italian

   Employment: 0.0% management, business, and financial, 0.0% computer, engineering, and science, 50.0% education, legal, community service, arts, and media, 0.0% healthcare practitioners, 0.0% service, 0.0% sales and office, 0.0% natural resources, construction, and maintenance, 50.0% production, transportation, and material moving

   Income: Per capita: $26,659; Median household: n/a; Average household: n/a; Households with income of $100,000 or more: n/a; Poverty rate: n/a

   Educational Attainment: High school diploma or higher: 100.0%; Bachelor's degree or higher: 10.9%; Graduate/professional degree or higher: 1.7%

   Housing: Homeownership rate: n/a; Median home value: n/a; Median year structure built: n/a; Homeowner vacancy rate: 0.0%; Median gross rent: n/a per month; Rental vacancy rate: 0.0%

   Health Insurance: 0.0% have insurance; 0.0% have private insurance; 0.0% have public insurance; 0.0% do not have insurance; 0.0% of children under 18 do not have insurance

   Transportation: Commute: 74.2% car, 0.3% public transportation, 17.4% walk, 5.8% work from home; Median travel time to work: 8.1 minutes

Airports: Cherry Point MCAS /Cunningham Field/ (general aviation)

COVE CITY (town). Covers a land area of 0.638 square miles and a water area of 0 square miles. Located at 35.19° N. Lat; 77.32° W. Long. Elevation is 46 feet.

Population: 399; Growth (since 2000): -7.9%; Density: 625.7 persons per square mile; Race: 53.1% White, 43.9% Black/African American, 0.0% Asian, 0.5% American Indian/Alaska Native, 0.0% Native Hawaiian/Other Pacific Islander, 1.5% Two or more races, 2.3% Hispanic of any race; Average household size: 2.35; Median age: 47.8; Age under 18: 16.8%; Age 65 and over: 22.1%; Males per 100 females: 95.6

School District(s)
Craven County Schools (PK-12)
   2012-13 Enrollment: 15,028 . . . . (252) 514-6300
Housing: Homeownership rate: 74.7%; Homeowner vacancy rate: 0.8%; Rental vacancy rate: 14.8%

DOVER (town). Covers a land area of 0.954 square miles and a water area of 0 square miles. Located at 35.22° N. Lat; 77.43° W. Long. Elevation is 62 feet.

Population: 401; Growth (since 2000): -9.5%; Density: 420.5 persons per square mile; Race: 43.4% White, 55.4% Black/African American, 0.0% Asian, 0.7% American Indian/Alaska Native, 0.0% Native Hawaiian/Other Pacific Islander, 0.5% Two or more races, 0.0% Hispanic of any race; Average household size: 2.32; Median age: 40.1; Age under 18: 24.4%; Age 65 and over: 20.0%; Males per 100 females: 78.2

Housing: Homeownership rate: 76.3%; Homeowner vacancy rate: 0.0%; Rental vacancy rate: 10.9%

ERNUL (unincorporated postal area)
ZCTA: 28527
   Covers a land area of 55.566 square miles and a water area of 0.176 square miles. Located at 35.26° N. Lat; 77.03° W. Long. Elevation is 23 feet.
   Population: 1,140; Growth (since 2000): 21.5%; Density: 20.5 persons per square mile; Race: 88.4% White, 8.3% Black/African American, 0.0% Asian, 0.6% American Indian/Alaska Native, 0.0% Native Hawaiian/Other Pacific Islander, 1.1% Two or more races, 3.6% Hispanic of any race; Average household size: 2.50; Median age: 42.3; Age under 18: 21.6%; Age 65 and over: 12.3%; Males per 100 females: 105.4

   Housing: Homeownership rate: 86.2%; Homeowner vacancy rate: 2.0%; Rental vacancy rate: 3.1%

FAIRFIELD HARBOUR (CDP). Covers a land area of 2.878 square miles and a water area of 1.247 square miles. Located at 35.07° N. Lat; 76.96° W. Long. Elevation is 7 feet.

Population: 2,952; Growth (since 2000): 48.9%; Density: 1,025.5 persons per square mile; Race: 94.5% White, 3.5% Black/African American, 0.5% Asian, 0.1% American Indian/Alaska Native, 0.0% Native Hawaiian/Other Pacific Islander, 0.8% Two or more races, 1.8% Hispanic of any race; Average household size: 2.02; Median age: 63.5; Age under 18: 9.6%; Age 65 and over: 45.9%; Males per 100 females: 94.7; Marriage status: 8.9% never married, 80.3% now married, 1.0% separated, 7.2% widowed, 3.5% divorced; Foreign born: 4.2%; Speak English only: 93.9%; With disability: 17.0%; Veterans: 26.5%; Ancestry: 26.1% German, 22.0% English, 18.8% Irish, 6.0% American, 5.0% Italian

Employment: 16.6% management, business, and financial, 8.2% computer, engineering, and science, 17.0% education, legal, community service, arts, and media, 16.2% healthcare practitioners, 6.8% service, 15.5% sales and office, 12.6% natural resources, construction, and maintenance, 7.1% production, transportation, and material moving

Income: Per capita: $34,939; Median household: $64,563; Average household: $71,758; Households with income of $100,000 or more: 19.0%; Poverty rate: 2.1%

Educational Attainment: High school diploma or higher: 99.0%; Bachelor's degree or higher: 50.4%; Graduate/professional degree or higher: 19.4%

Housing: Homeownership rate: 87.2%; Median home value: $224,900; Median year structure built: 1990; Homeowner vacancy rate: 3.7%; Median gross rent: $1,170 per month; Rental vacancy rate: 20.6%

Health Insurance: 94.0% have insurance; 77.7% have private insurance; 56.9% have public insurance; 6.0% do not have insurance; 15.9% of children under 18 do not have insurance

Transportation: Commute: 78.6% car, 0.0% public transportation, 1.9% walk, 19.5% work from home; Median travel time to work: 35.0 minutes

HAVELOCK (city).

Covers a land area of 16.848 square miles and a water area of 0.804 square miles. Located at 34.91° N. Lat; 76.90° W. Long. Elevation is 23 feet.

Population: 20,735; Growth (since 2000): -7.6%; Density: 1,230.7 persons per square mile; Race: 70.0% White, 17.4% Black/African American, 2.9% Asian, 0.7% American Indian/Alaska Native, 0.3% Native Hawaiian/Other Pacific Islander, 4.7% Two or more races, 11.6% Hispanic of any race; Average household size: 2.76; Median age: 23.5; Age under 18: 27.0%; Age 65 and over: 4.2%; Males per 100 females: 121.4; Marriage status: 32.0% never married, 57.3% now married, 3.3% separated, 2.1% widowed, 8.6% divorced; Foreign born: 6.1%; Speak English only: 88.6%; With disability: 12.1%; Veterans: 29.0%; Ancestry: 19.6% German, 16.6% Irish, 9.5% English, 5.9% Italian, 4.3% American
Employment: 6.7% management, business, and financial, 4.0% computer, engineering, and science, 6.1% education, legal, community service, arts, and media, 6.3% healthcare practitioners, 21.4% service, 27.1% sales and office, 18.0% natural resources, construction, and maintenance, 10.3% production, transportation, and material moving
Income: Per capita: $20,596; Median household: $43,461; Average household: $51,527; Households with income of $100,000 or more: 10.4%; Poverty rate: 18.2%
Educational Attainment: High school diploma or higher: 94.4%; Bachelor's degree or higher: 12.5%; Graduate/professional degree or higher: 2.8%

School District(s)
Craven County Schools (PK-12)
    2012-13 Enrollment: 15,028 . . . . (252) 514-6300
Housing: Homeownership rate: 42.9%; Median home value: $137,600; Median year structure built: 1984; Homeowner vacancy rate: 2.2%; Median gross rent: $1,041 per month; Rental vacancy rate: 5.9%
Health Insurance: 85.7% have insurance; 71.7% have private insurance; 24.1% have public insurance; 14.3% do not have insurance; 4.9% of children under 18 do not have insurance
Safety: Violent crime rate: 21.2 per 10,000 population; Property crime rate: 243.2 per 10,000 population
Newspapers: Havelock News (weekly circulation 2600)
Transportation: Commute: 85.6% car, 0.6% public transportation, 6.3% walk, 2.7% work from home; Median travel time to work: 16.6 minutes; Amtrak: Bus service available.
Additional Information Contacts
City of Havelock . . . . (252) 444-6400
    http://www.cityofhavelock.com

JAMES CITY (CDP).

Covers a land area of 7.587 square miles and a water area of 6.292 square miles. Located at 35.06° N. Lat; 77.01° W. Long. Elevation is 13 feet.

History: James City was settled in 1862 by residents from New Bern, when that town was occupied by Union forces during the Civil War. The property belonged to Colonel James Bryan, and the settlement was named for him.
Population: 5,899; Growth (since 2000): 8.8%; Density: 777.5 persons per square mile; Race: 79.9% White, 13.5% Black/African American, 1.1% Asian, 0.4% American Indian/Alaska Native, 0.1% Native Hawaiian/Other Pacific Islander, 2.4% Two or more races, 5.9% Hispanic of any race; Average household size: 2.42; Median age: 40.6; Age under 18: 22.3%; Age 65 and over: 16.5%; Males per 100 females: 97.0; Marriage status: 21.9% never married, 61.3% now married, 2.5% separated, 7.1% widowed, 9.7% divorced; Foreign born: 1.9%; Speak English only: 96.8%; With disability: 16.3%; Veterans: 20.0%; Ancestry: 14.9% English, 12.8% American, 10.8% German, 10.1% Irish, 7.1% Italian
Employment: 8.9% management, business, and financial, 3.0% computer, engineering, and science, 8.2% education, legal, community service, arts, and media, 7.7% healthcare practitioners, 22.8% service, 23.4% sales and office, 11.1% natural resources, construction, and maintenance, 14.8% production, transportation, and material moving
Income: Per capita: $31,734; Median household: $49,735; Average household: $79,549; Households with income of $100,000 or more: 15.7%; Poverty rate: 11.7%
Educational Attainment: High school diploma or higher: 88.0%; Bachelor's degree or higher: 17.8%; Graduate/professional degree or higher: 2.3%
Housing: Homeownership rate: 73.2%; Median home value: $152,300; Median year structure built: 1988; Homeowner vacancy rate: 2.2%; Median gross rent: $945 per month; Rental vacancy rate: 11.0%

Health Insurance: 84.5% have insurance; 68.6% have private insurance; 31.5% have public insurance; 15.5% do not have insurance; 4.3% of children under 18 do not have insurance
Transportation: Commute: 90.7% car, 0.0% public transportation, 0.4% walk, 6.3% work from home; Median travel time to work: 18.3 minutes

NEUSE FOREST (CDP).

Covers a land area of 3.160 square miles and a water area of 0.020 square miles. Located at 34.96° N. Lat; 76.94° W. Long. Elevation is 30 feet.

Population: 2,005; Growth (since 2000): 40.6%; Density: 634.5 persons per square mile; Race: 86.0% White, 6.6% Black/African American, 2.9% Asian, 0.1% American Indian/Alaska Native, 0.2% Native Hawaiian/Other Pacific Islander, 3.2% Two or more races, 5.4% Hispanic of any race; Average household size: 2.60; Median age: 41.0; Age under 18: 24.2%; Age 65 and over: 16.3%; Males per 100 females: 98.5
Housing: Homeownership rate: 81.9%; Homeowner vacancy rate: 2.9%; Rental vacancy rate: 7.3%

NEW BERN (city).

County seat. Covers a land area of 28.230 square miles and a water area of 1.445 square miles. Located at 35.09° N. Lat; 77.07° W. Long. Elevation is 10 feet.

History: The first settlers of New Bern were survivors of an expedition of 650 German Palatines, Protestants expelled from Baden and Bavaria. The town was laid out with the principal streets in the form of a cross, one running northwest from the rivers' junction and one from river to river. The town was named for Switzerland's capital, Bern.
Population: 29,524; Growth (since 2000): 27.7%; Density: 1,045.9 persons per square mile; Race: 57.9% White, 33.2% Black/African American, 3.6% Asian, 0.4% American Indian/Alaska Native, 0.1% Native Hawaiian/Other Pacific Islander, 2.4% Two or more races, 5.8% Hispanic of any race; Average household size: 2.25; Median age: 38.8; Age under 18: 22.8%; Age 65 and over: 17.9%; Males per 100 females: 87.5; Marriage status: 28.9% never married, 50.3% now married, 5.0% separated, 8.9% widowed, 12.0% divorced; Foreign born: 6.4%; Speak English only: 89.8%; With disability: 18.7%; Veterans: 13.9%; Ancestry: 12.2% English, 10.9% Irish, 9.7% German, 6.5% American, 3.7% Scotch-Irish
Employment: 10.2% management, business, and financial, 3.4% computer, engineering, and science, 12.6% education, legal, community service, arts, and media, 6.4% healthcare practitioners, 23.9% service, 20.4% sales and office, 10.6% natural resources, construction, and maintenance, 12.6% production, transportation, and material moving
Income: Per capita: $22,555; Median household: $37,493; Average household: $51,503; Households with income of $100,000 or more: 12.7%; Poverty rate: 24.5%
Educational Attainment: High school diploma or higher: 83.6%; Bachelor's degree or higher: 25.0%; Graduate/professional degree or higher: 8.7%

School District(s)
Craven County Schools (PK-12)
    2012-13 Enrollment: 15,028 . . . . (252) 514-6300
Two-year College(s)
Craven Community College (Public)
    Fall 2013 Enrollment: 3,376 . . . . (252) 638-7200
    2013-14 Tuition: In-state $1,832; Out-of-state $6,440
Housing: Homeownership rate: 54.1%; Median home value: $149,000; Median year structure built: 1982; Homeowner vacancy rate: 5.3%; Median gross rent: $830 per month; Rental vacancy rate: 10.4%
Health Insurance: 83.8% have insurance; 56.5% have private insurance; 43.6% have public insurance; 16.2% do not have insurance; 5.0% of children under 18 do not have insurance
Hospitals: Carolina East Medical Center (350 beds)
Safety: Violent crime rate: 39.3 per 10,000 population; Property crime rate: 513.5 per 10,000 population
Newspapers: Sun Journal (daily circulation 14600)
Transportation: Commute: 92.8% car, 0.0% public transportation, 3.1% walk, 2.7% work from home; Median travel time to work: 19.3 minutes; Amtrak: Bus service available.
Airports: Coastal Carolina Regional (primary service/non-hub)
Additional Information Contacts
City of New Bern . . . . (252) 636-4000
    http://www.ci.new-bern.nc.us

RIVER BEND (town). Covers a land area of 2.509 square miles and a water area of 0.243 square miles. Located at 35.07° N. Lat; 77.15° W. Long. Elevation is 13 feet.

Population: 3,119; Growth (since 2000): 6.7%; Density: 1,243.3 persons per square mile; Race: 88.2% White, 8.6% Black/African American, 1.0% Asian, 0.4% American Indian/Alaska Native, 0.1% Native Hawaiian/Other Pacific Islander, 1.3% Two or more races, 2.6% Hispanic of any race; Average household size: 2.08; Median age: 56.8; Age under 18: 13.5%; Age 65 and over: 37.3%; Males per 100 females: 90.9; Marriage status: 17.0% never married, 67.1% now married, 4.6% separated, 7.4% widowed, 8.5% divorced; Foreign born: 7.0%; Speak English only: 93.0%; With disability: 19.9%; Veterans: 24.3%; Ancestry: 20.6% Irish, 20.0% German, 18.2% American, 13.2% English, 5.2% French

Employment: 8.0% management, business, and financial, 4.6% computer, engineering, and science, 12.1% education, legal, community service, arts, and media, 7.5% healthcare practitioners, 18.9% service, 22.8% sales and office, 15.9% natural resources, construction, and maintenance, 10.1% production, transportation, and material moving

Income: Per capita: $28,656; Median household: $51,964; Average household: $65,166; Households with income of $100,000 or more: 11.0%; Poverty rate: 7.2%

Educational Attainment: High school diploma or higher: 95.0%; Bachelor's degree or higher: 28.2%; Graduate/professional degree or higher: 6.3%

Housing: Homeownership rate: 79.7%; Median home value: $193,400; Median year structure built: 1983; Homeowner vacancy rate: 4.1%; Median gross rent: $831 per month; Rental vacancy rate: 11.8%

Health Insurance: 89.4% have insurance; 75.0% have private insurance; 49.3% have public insurance; 10.6% do not have insurance; 10.1% of children under 18 do not have insurance

Safety: Violent crime rate: 0.0 per 10,000 population; Property crime rate: 119.7 per 10,000 population

Transportation: Commute: 90.4% car, 1.0% public transportation, 0.0% walk, 2.6% work from home; Median travel time to work: 21.2 minutes

Additional Information Contacts

Town of River Bend . . . . (252) 638-3870
    http://www.riverbendnc.org

TRENT WOODS (town). Covers a land area of 2.951 square miles and a water area of 0.481 square miles. Located at 35.08° N. Lat; 77.09° W. Long. Elevation is 13 feet.

History: The ladies of the community had suggested that as the southern boundary was the Trent River with its beautiful wooded shore line, so the new town should be called Trent Woods. On June 19, 1959, the charter was approved. Trent Woods was now a town.

Population: 4,155; Growth (since 2000): -0.9%; Density: 1,408.0 persons per square mile; Race: 96.1% White, 1.9% Black/African American, 0.6% Asian, 0.2% American Indian/Alaska Native, 0.0% Native Hawaiian/Other Pacific Islander, 1.0% Two or more races, 1.4% Hispanic of any race; Average household size: 2.41; Median age: 50.2; Age under 18: 20.6%; Age 65 and over: 24.1%; Males per 100 females: 88.9; Marriage status: 15.3% never married, 67.5% now married, 1.1% separated, 7.7% widowed, 9.5% divorced; Foreign born: 1.3%; Speak English only: 98.1%; With disability: 12.8%; Veterans: 19.3%; Ancestry: 33.4% English, 15.4% German, 11.7% Irish, 9.4% American, 4.4% European

Employment: 17.2% management, business, and financial, 9.4% computer, engineering, and science, 17.0% education, legal, community service, arts, and media, 9.1% healthcare practitioners, 19.5% service, 22.5% sales and office, 4.0% natural resources, construction, and maintenance, 1.3% production, transportation, and material moving

Income: Per capita: $43,982; Median household: $85,554; Average household: $99,482; Households with income of $100,000 or more: 33.6%; Poverty rate: 3.3%

Educational Attainment: High school diploma or higher: 98.6%; Bachelor's degree or higher: 48.9%; Graduate/professional degree or higher: 15.1%

Housing: Homeownership rate: 89.2%; Median home value: $228,300; Median year structure built: 1975; Homeowner vacancy rate: 2.5%; Median gross rent: $675 per month; Rental vacancy rate: 5.0%

Health Insurance: 95.0% have insurance; 90.8% have private insurance; 32.8% have public insurance; 5.0% do not·have insurance; 2.2% of children under 18 do not have insurance

Safety: Violent crime rate: 7.1 per 10,000 population; Property crime rate: 125.3 per 10,000 population

Transportation: Commute: 94.2% car, 0.0% public transportation, 0.0% walk, 5.8% work from home; Median travel time to work: 18.2 minutes

VANCEBORO (town). Covers a land area of 1.714 square miles and a water area of 0 square miles. Located at 35.30° N. Lat; 77.16° W. Long. Elevation is 23 feet.

Population: 1,005; Growth (since 2000): 11.9%; Density: 586.3 persons per square mile; Race: 65.1% White, 30.0% Black/African American, 0.0% Asian, 0.6% American Indian/Alaska Native, 0.0% Native Hawaiian/Other Pacific Islander, 3.8% Two or more races, 2.6% Hispanic of any race; Average household size: 2.61; Median age: 31.1; Age under 18: 32.7%; Age 65 and over: 11.5%; Males per 100 females: 74.5

School District(s)

Craven County Schools (PK-12)
    2012-13 Enrollment: 15,028 . . . . (252) 514-6300

Housing: Homeownership rate: 55.6%; Homeowner vacancy rate: 2.3%; Rental vacancy rate: 6.6%

Safety: Violent crime rate: 19.7 per 10,000 population; Property crime rate: 502.5 per 10,000 population

Cumberland County

Located in south central North Carolina; drained by the Cape Fear and South Rivers. Covers a land area of 652.315 square miles, a water area of 6.052 square miles, and is located in the Eastern Time Zone at 35.05° N. Lat., 78.83° W. Long. The county was founded in 1754. County seat is Fayetteville.

Cumberland County is part of the Fayetteville, NC Metropolitan Statistical Area. The entire metro area includes: Cumberland County, NC; Hoke County, NC

Weather Station: Fayetteville   Elevation: 96 feet

	Jan	Feb	Mar	Apr	May	Jun	Jul	Aug	Sep	Oct	Nov	Dec
High	53	56	64	73	80	87	90	88	83	73	65	56
Low	31	33	39	47	56	66	70	69	62	50	40	33
Precip	3.5	3.1	4.0	3.2	3.2	4.5	5.4	5.3	4.5	3.3	3.0	3.1
Snow	0.4	tr	0.2	0.0	0.0	0.0	0.0	0.0	0.0	0.0	tr	0.0

High and Low temperatures in degrees Fahrenheit; Precipitation and Snow in inches

Population: 319,431; Growth (since 2000): 5.4%; Density: 489.7 persons per square mile; Race: 51.4% White, 36.7% Black/African American, 2.2% Asian, 1.6% American Indian/Alaska Native, 0.4% Native Hawaiian/Other Pacific Islander, 4.6% two or more races, 9.5% Hispanic of any race; Average household size: 2.53; Median age: 31.0; Age under 18: 26.8%; Age 65 and over: 9.5%; Males per 100 females: 93.5; Marriage status: 30.9% never married, 51.6% now married, 3.6% separated, 5.5% widowed, 12.1% divorced; Foreign born: 5.6%; Speak English only: 89.0%; With disability: 13.9%; Veterans: 20.3%; Ancestry: 10.1% German, 8.5% Irish, 6.4% American, 6.0% English, 3.0% Italian

Religion: Six largest groups: 15.0% Baptist, 11.4% Non-denominational Protestant, 6.5% Methodist/Pietist, 5.4% Pentecostal, 2.8% Catholicism, 2.2% Presbyterian-Reformed

Economy: Unemployment rate: 6.6%; Leading industries: 18.3% retail trade; 13.5% health care and social assistance; 11.5% other services (except public administration); Farms: 389 totaling 82,317 acres; Company size: 6 employ 1,000 or more persons, 8 employ 500 to 999 persons, 101 employs 100 to 499 persons, 5,634 employ less than 100 persons; Business ownership: 6,493 women-owned, 4,678 Black-owned, 519 Hispanic-owned, 1,152 Asian-owned

Employment: 10.9% management, business, and financial, 2.8% computer, engineering, and science, 12.6% education, legal, community service, arts, and media, 6.6% healthcare practitioners, 20.3% service, 25.9% sales and office, 8.8% natural resources, construction, and maintenance, 12.0% production, transportation, and material moving

Income: Per capita: $23,067; Median household: $45,231; Average household: $58,134; Households with income of $100,000 or more: 14.2%; Poverty rate: 17.0%

Educational Attainment: High school diploma or higher: 89.2%; Bachelor's degree or higher: 22.7%; Graduate/professional degree or higher: 7.8%

Housing: Homeownership rate: 55.9%; Median home value: $128,700; Median year structure built: 1985; Homeowner vacancy rate: 2.8%; Median gross rent: $853 per month; Rental vacancy rate: 10.5%

Vital Statistics: Birth rate: 174.5 per 10,000 population; Death rate: 71.7 per 10,000 population; Age-adjusted cancer mortality rate: 194.5 deaths per 100,000 population
Health Insurance: 85.7% have insurance; 66.0% have private insurance; 33.0% have public insurance; 14.3% do not have insurance; 6.2% of children under 18 do not have insurance
Health Care: Physicians: 19.6 per 10,000 population; Hospital beds: 31.2 per 10,000 population; Hospital admissions: 1,466.8 per 10,000 population
Air Quality Index: 84.8% good, 15.2% moderate, 0.0% unhealthy for sensitive individuals, 0.0% unhealthy (percent of days)
Transportation: Commute: 91.8% car, 0.6% public transportation, 3.5% walk, 2.9% work from home; Median travel time to work: 21.5 minutes
Presidential Election: 59.4% Obama, 39.7% Romney (2012)
National and State Parks: Bushy Lake State Natural Area
Additional Information Contacts
Cumberland Government . . . . (910) 321-6852
    http://www.co.cumberland.nc.us

Cumberland County Communities

EASTOVER (town). Covers a land area of 11.328 square miles and a water area of 0.009 square miles. Located at 35.10° N. Lat; 78.79° W. Long. Elevation is 95 feet.
Population: 3,628; Growth (since 2000): 163.7%; Density: 320.3 persons per square mile; Race: 74.9% White, 19.2% Black/African American, 0.9% Asian, 1.9% American Indian/Alaska Native, 0.1% Native Hawaiian/Other Pacific Islander, 1.8% Two or more races, 3.0% Hispanic of any race; Average household size: 2.40; Median age: 44.9; Age under 18: 21.1%; Age 65 and over: 18.4%; Males per 100 females: 91.9; Marriage status: 23.5% never married, 59.8% now married, 2.6% separated, 7.1% widowed, 9.7% divorced; Foreign born: 4.7%; Speak English only: 96.8%; With disability: 18.4%; Veterans: 15.8%; Ancestry: 13.1% English, 12.7% American, 7.7% German, 5.9% Irish, 5.1% European
Employment: 12.5% management, business, and financial, 7.4% computer, engineering, and science, 11.2% education, legal, community service, arts, and media, 8.8% healthcare practitioners, 13.3% service, 21.6% sales and office, 8.8% natural resources, construction, and maintenance, 16.3% production, transportation, and material moving
Income: Per capita: $28,108; Median household: $42,639; Average household: $66,998; Households with income of $100,000 or more: 18.0%; Poverty rate: 8.8%
Educational Attainment: High school diploma or higher: 86.4%; Bachelor's degree or higher: 22.0%; Graduate/professional degree or higher: 8.2%
Housing: Homeownership rate: 74.4%; Median home value: $156,900; Median year structure built: 1986; Homeowner vacancy rate: 3.1%; Median gross rent: $719 per month; Rental vacancy rate: 6.0%
Health Insurance: 89.3% have insurance; 73.4% have private insurance; 33.0% have public insurance; 10.7% do not have insurance; 0.0% of children under 18 do not have insurance
Transportation: Commute: 95.9% car, 0.0% public transportation, 2.1% walk, 2.0% work from home; Median travel time to work: 24.1 minutes

FALCON (town). Covers a land area of 1.210 square miles and a water area of <.001 square miles. Located at 35.19° N. Lat; 78.65° W. Long. Elevation is 141 feet.
Population: 258; Growth (since 2000): -21.3%; Density: 213.2 persons per square mile; Race: 73.6% White, 14.3% Black/African American, 0.0% Asian, 0.8% American Indian/Alaska Native, 0.0% Native Hawaiian/Other Pacific Islander, 4.7% Two or more races, 14.0% Hispanic of any race; Average household size: 2.73; Median age: 27.0; Age under 18: 36.8%; Age 65 and over: 12.4%; Males per 100 females: 101.6
Housing: Homeownership rate: 75.6%; Homeowner vacancy rate: 4.7%; Rental vacancy rate: 14.3%

FAYETTEVILLE (city). County seat. Covers a land area of 145.845 square miles and a water area of 1.864 square miles. Located at 35.09° N. Lat; 78.98° W. Long. Elevation is 102 feet.
History: Fayetteville dates from 1739, when Scots led by Colonel McAllister settled Campbelltown. In 1746, a group of expatriated Scots established a grist mill and village at Cross Creek, a mile northwest of Campbelltown. The preponderance of Scottish population made the town a center of Tory influence. In 1783 the settlements of Campbelltown and Cross Creek united and were incorporated. Having shifted their allegiance, the citizens named the place Fayetteville, the first community so honoring

the Marquis de Lafayette. Fayetteville served as the state capital from 1789 to 1793. River and railroad commerce and trade were important to the town in its early days.
Population: 200,564; Growth (since 2000): 65.7%; Density: 1,375.2 persons per square mile; Race: 45.7% White, 41.9% Black/African American, 2.6% Asian, 1.1% American Indian/Alaska Native, 0.4% Native Hawaiian/Other Pacific Islander, 4.9% Two or more races, 10.1% Hispanic of any race; Average household size: 2.45; Median age: 29.9; Age under 18: 25.8%; Age 65 and over: 9.7%; Males per 100 females: 93.6; Marriage status: 32.6% never married, 49.5% now married, 3.8% separated, 5.3% widowed, 12.6% divorced; Foreign born: 6.0%; Speak English only: 88.0%; With disability: 13.6%; Veterans: 22.0%; Ancestry: 10.4% German, 7.9% Irish, 5.4% English, 4.7% American, 2.8% Italian
Employment: 11.0% management, business, and financial, 2.7% computer, engineering, and science, 13.2% education, legal, community service, arts, and media, 7.0% healthcare practitioners, 21.3% service, 26.5% sales and office, 7.5% natural resources, construction, and maintenance, 10.8% production, transportation, and material moving
Income: Per capita: $23,409; Median household: $44,900; Average household: $57,392; Households with income of $100,000 or more: 13.4%; Poverty rate: 17.6%
Educational Attainment: High school diploma or higher: 90.8%; Bachelor's degree or higher: 24.7%; Graduate/professional degree or higher: 8.3%

School District(s)
Alpha Academy (KG-08)
    2012-13 Enrollment: 463. . . . . (910) 223-7711
Cumberland County Schools (PK-12)
    2012-13 Enrollment: 52,925 . . . . (910) 678-2300
Nc Dept of Juvenile Justice (KG-12)
    2012-13 Enrollment: n/a . . . . (919) 733-3388
Four-year College(s)
Carolina College of Biblical Studies (Private, Not-for-profit)
    Fall 2013 Enrollment: 113 . . . . (910) 323-5614
    2013-14 Tuition: In-state $4,725; Out-of-state $4,725
Fayetteville State University (Public, Historically black)
    Fall 2013 Enrollment: 6,179 . . . . (910) 672-1111
    2013-14 Tuition: In-state $4,605; Out-of-state $15,401
Grace College of Divinity (Private, Not-for-profit, Other Protestant)
    Fall 2013 Enrollment: 110 . . . . (910) 221-2224
    2013-14 Tuition: In-state $3,520; Out-of-state $3,520
Methodist University (Private, Not-for-profit, United Methodist)
    Fall 2013 Enrollment: 2,463 . . . . (910) 630-7000
    2013-14 Tuition: In-state $27,830; Out-of-state $27,830
Two-year College(s)
Fayetteville Technical Community College (Public)
    Fall 2013 Enrollment: 12,398 . . . . (910) 678-8400
    2013-14 Tuition: In-state $2,378; Out-of-state $8,522
Miller-Motte College-Fayetteville (Private, For-profit)
    Fall 2013 Enrollment: 734 . . . . (910) 354-1900
    2013-14 Tuition: In-state $10,737; Out-of-state $10,737
Vocational/Technical School(s)
Fayetteville Beauty College (Private, For-profit)
    Fall 2013 Enrollment: 47 . . . . (910) 487-3006
    2013-14 Tuition: $9,750
Paul Mitchell the School-Fayetteville (Private, For-profit)
    Fall 2013 Enrollment: 189 . . . . (910) 485-6310
    2013-14 Tuition: $10,900
Housing: Homeownership rate: 50.3%; Median home value: $125,800; Median year structure built: 1982; Homeowner vacancy rate: 3.3%; Median gross rent: $869 per month; Rental vacancy rate: 10.5%
Health Insurance: 85.9% have insurance; 66.2% have private insurance; 33.9% have public insurance; 14.1% do not have insurance; 5.5% of children under 18 do not have insurance
Hospitals: Cape Fear Valley Medical Center (616 beds); Fayetteville NC VA Medical Center (159 beds)
Safety: Violent crime rate: 57.8 per 10,000 population; Property crime rate: 605.4 per 10,000 population
Newspapers: Fayetteville Observer (daily circulation 50800)
Transportation: Commute: 90.0% car, 0.8% public transportation, 5.0% walk, 3.1% work from home; Median travel time to work: 19.7 minutes; Amtrak: Train service available.
Airports: Fayetteville Regional/Grannis Field (primary service/non-hub); Pope AAF (general aviation)

Additional Information Contacts
City of Fayetteville. . . . . (910) 433-1992
   http://www.ci.fayetteville.nc.us

FORT BRAGG (unincorporated postal area)
ZCTA: 28307
   Covers a land area of 11.697 square miles and a water area of 0.014 square miles. Located at 35.14° N. Lat; 78.98° W. Long..

Population: 17,631; Growth (since 2000): -44.5%; Density: 1,507.3 persons per square mile; Race: 65.5% White, 16.6% Black/African American, 2.0% Asian, 1.2% American Indian/Alaska Native, 1.0% Native Hawaiian/Other Pacific Islander, 8.0% Two or more races, 18.6% Hispanic of any race; Average household size: 3.28; Median age: 21.8; Age under 18: 40.6%; Age 65 and over: 0.1%; Males per 100 females: 106.4; Marriage status: 21.6% never married, 73.0% now married, 1.4% separated, 0.2% widowed, 5.2% divorced; Foreign born: 3.8%; Speak English only: 84.1%; With disability: 4.1%; Veterans: 15.4%; Ancestry: 15.1% German, 14.8% Irish, 5.6% Italian, 5.5% English, 4.8% American

Employment: 7.2% management, business, and financial, 1.3% computer, engineering, and science, 14.9% education, legal, community service, arts, and media, 8.6% healthcare practitioners, 28.0% service, 27.9% sales and office, 3.4% natural resources, construction, and maintenance, 8.7% production, transportation, and material moving

Income: Per capita: $15,706; Median household: $41,460; Average household: $48,082; Households with income of $100,000 or more: 5.9%; Poverty rate: 13.7%

Educational Attainment: High school diploma or higher: 96.8%; Bachelor's degree or higher: 20.8%; Graduate/professional degree or higher: 6.1%

School District(s)
Cumberland County Schools (PK-12)
   2012-13 Enrollment: 52,925 . . . . (910) 678-2300

Housing: Homeownership rate: 0.7%; Median home value: n/a; Median year structure built: 1984; Homeowner vacancy rate: 2.9%; Median gross rent: $1,157 per month; Rental vacancy rate: 7.5%

Health Insurance: 96.3% have insurance; 93.6% have private insurance; 5.7% have public insurance; 3.7% do not have insurance; 2.1% of children under 18 do not have insurance

Transportation: Commute: 78.1% car, 0.9% public transportation, 14.0% walk, 5.2% work from home; Median travel time to work: 11.4 minutes

ZCTA: 28310
   Covers a land area of 4.539 square miles and a water area of 0.021 square miles. Located at 35.16° N. Lat; 79.04° W. Long..

Population: 3,459; Growth (since 2000): n/a; Density: 762.1 persons per square mile; Race: 76.0% White, 12.0% Black/African American, 2.2% Asian, 1.2% American Indian/Alaska Native, 0.3% Native Hawaiian/Other Pacific Islander, 3.6% Two or more races, 14.0% Hispanic of any race; Average household size: 0.00; Median age: 22.3; Age under 18: 0.0%; Age 65 and over: 0.0%; Males per 100 females: ***.*; Marriage status: 80.1% never married, 14.3% now married, 0.6% separated, 0.4% widowed, 5.2% divorced; Foreign born: 4.2%; Speak English only: 87.4%; With disability: 0.0%; Veterans: 82.1%; Ancestry: 22.6% German, 18.6% Irish, 9.4% English, 6.1% Italian, 3.5% Scottish

Employment: 0.0% management, business, and financial, 0.0% computer, engineering, and science, 0.0% education, legal, community service, arts, and media, 0.0% healthcare practitioners, 0.0% service, 100.0% sales and office, 0.0% natural resources, construction, and maintenance, 0.0% production, transportation, and material moving

Income: Per capita: $28,063; Median household: n/a; Average household: n/a; Households with income of $100,000 or more: n/a; Poverty rate: n/a

Educational Attainment: High school diploma or higher: 100.0%; Bachelor's degree or higher: 16.4%; Graduate/professional degree or higher: 7.1%

Housing: Homeownership rate: n/a; Median home value: n/a; Median year structure built: n/a; Homeowner vacancy rate: 0.0%; Median gross rent: n/a per month; Rental vacancy rate: 0.0%

Health Insurance: 0.0% have insurance; 0.0% have private insurance; 0.0% have public insurance; 0.0% do not have insurance; 0.0% of children under 18 do not have insurance

Transportation: Commute: 35.4% car, 1.8% public transportation, 44.9% walk, 17.4% work from home; Median travel time to work: 6.4 minutes

GODWIN (town).
Covers a land area of 0.517 square miles and a water area of <.001 square miles. Located at 35.21° N. Lat; 78.68° W. Long. Elevation is 154 feet.

History: Averasboro State Historical Site to North.

Population: 139; Growth (since 2000): 24.1%; Density: 269.0 persons per square mile; Race: 70.5% White, 27.3% Black/African American, 0.7% Asian, 0.0% American Indian/Alaska Native, 0.0% Native Hawaiian/Other Pacific Islander, 1.4% Two or more races, 0.0% Hispanic of any race; Average household size: 2.57; Median age: 43.8; Age under 18: 20.1%; Age 65 and over: 18.0%; Males per 100 females: 73.8

Housing: Homeownership rate: 77.7%; Homeowner vacancy rate: 2.3%; Rental vacancy rate: 7.7%

HOPE MILLS (town).
Covers a land area of 6.942 square miles and a water area of 0.099 square miles. Located at 34.97° N. Lat; 78.95° W. Long. Elevation is 112 feet.

Population: 15,176; Growth (since 2000): 35.1%; Density: 2,186.0 persons per square mile; Race: 61.9% White, 26.5% Black/African American, 1.8% Asian, 1.9% American Indian/Alaska Native, 0.3% Native Hawaiian/Other Pacific Islander, 4.6% Two or more races, 10.0% Hispanic of any race; Average household size: 2.68; Median age: 31.9; Age under 18: 30.5%; Age 65 and over: 7.5%; Males per 100 females: 85.1; Marriage status: 26.8% never married, 53.5% now married, 3.2% separated, 6.5% widowed, 13.2% divorced; Foreign born: 5.9%; Speak English only: 87.4%; With disability: 13.2%; Veterans: 18.0%; Ancestry: 9.7% Irish, 8.6% American, 7.4% German, 5.9% English, 4.1% Italian

Employment: 12.0% management, business, and financial, 2.2% computer, engineering, and science, 14.8% education, legal, community service, arts, and media, 5.6% healthcare practitioners, 17.9% service, 26.9% sales and office, 7.2% natural resources, construction, and maintenance, 13.4% production, transportation, and material moving

Income: Per capita: $22,913; Median household: $51,442; Average household: $62,030; Households with income of $100,000 or more: 15.6%; Poverty rate: 15.6%

Educational Attainment: High school diploma or higher: 89.0%; Bachelor's degree or higher: 19.6%; Graduate/professional degree or higher: 6.0%

School District(s)
Cumberland County Schools (PK-12)
   2012-13 Enrollment: 52,925 . . . . (910) 678-2300

Housing: Homeownership rate: 63.4%; Median home value: $130,500; Median year structure built: 1992; Homeowner vacancy rate: 2.2%; Median gross rent: $791 per month; Rental vacancy rate: 8.6%

Health Insurance: 88.8% have insurance; 64.2% have private insurance; 34.9% have public insurance; 11.2% do not have insurance; 5.2% of children under 18 do not have insurance

Safety: Violent crime rate: 47.1 per 10,000 population; Property crime rate: 663.7 per 10,000 population

Newspapers: The Sandspur (weekly circulation 25000)

Transportation: Commute: 95.9% car, 0.0% public transportation, 1.1% walk, 0.8% work from home; Median travel time to work: 24.7 minutes

Additional Information Contacts
Town of Hope Mills . . . . (910) 423-4314
   http://townofhopemills.com

LINDEN (town).
Covers a land area of 0.506 square miles and a water area of 0 square miles. Located at 35.25° N. Lat; 78.75° W. Long. Elevation is 118 feet.

Population: 130; Growth (since 2000): 2.4%; Density: 257.2 persons per square mile; Race: 76.9% White, 12.3% Black/African American, 0.8% Asian, 3.1% American Indian/Alaska Native, 0.0% Native Hawaiian/Other Pacific Islander, 1.5% Two or more races, 5.4% Hispanic of any race; Average household size: 2.32; Median age: 49.7; Age under 18: 15.4%; Age 65 and over: 20.8%; Males per 100 females: 85.7

School District(s)
Cumberland County Schools (PK-12)
   2012-13 Enrollment: 52,925 . . . . (910) 678-2300

Housing: Homeownership rate: 76.8%; Homeowner vacancy rate: 0.0%; Rental vacancy rate: 0.0%

POPE ARMY AIRFIELD (unincorporated postal area)
ZCTA: 28308
   Covers a land area of 3.704 square miles and a water area of 0.015 square miles. Located at 35.17° N. Lat; 79.02° W. Long..

Population: 405; Growth (since 2000): n/a; Density: 109.3 persons per square mile; Race: 75.6% White, 14.6% Black/African American, 3.0% Asian, 0.7% American Indian/Alaska Native, 0.0% Native Hawaiian/Other Pacific Islander, 4.0% Two or more races, 9.1% Hispanic of any race; Average household size: 2.75; Median age: 21.8; Age under 18: 6.4%; Age 65 and over: 0.0%; Males per 100 females: 271.6

Housing: Homeownership rate: n/a; Homeowner vacancy rate: 0.0%; Rental vacancy rate: 17.6%

SPRING LAKE (town). Covers a land area of 23.059 square miles and a water area of 0.204 square miles. Located at 35.18° N. Lat; 78.99° W. Long. Elevation is 276 feet.

Population: 11,964; Growth (since 2000): 47.7%; Density: 518.8 persons per square mile; Race: 47.2% White, 36.3% Black/African American, 3.0% Asian, 1.1% American Indian/Alaska Native, 0.5% Native Hawaiian/Other Pacific Islander, 6.9% Two or more races, 15.4% Hispanic of any race; Average household size: 2.65; Median age: 24.9; Age under 18: 31.2%; Age 65 and over: 4.8%; Males per 100 females: 104.0; Marriage status: 28.1% never married, 59.0% now married, 4.4% separated, 1.6% widowed, 11.2% divorced; Foreign born: 5.6%; Speak English only: 86.6%; With disability: 9.5%; Veterans: 18.6%; Ancestry: 9.8% Irish, 9.5% German, 6.4% Italian, 4.8% American, 4.0% English

Employment: 8.2% management, business, and financial, 0.4% computer, engineering, and science, 8.8% education, legal, community service, arts, and media, 6.6% healthcare practitioners, 33.3% service, 27.9% sales and office, 4.0% natural resources, construction, and maintenance, 10.7% production, transportation, and material moving

Income: Per capita: $15,852; Median household: $36,538; Average household: $42,142; Households with income of $100,000 or more: 2.8%; Poverty rate: 23.4%

Educational Attainment: High school diploma or higher: 90.2%; Bachelor's degree or higher: 16.1%; Graduate/professional degree or higher: 5.2%

School District(s)
Cumberland County Schools (PK-12)
    2012-13 Enrollment: 52,925 . . . . (910) 678-2300
Harnett County Schools (PK-12)
    2012-13 Enrollment: 20,569 . . . . (910) 893-8151
Housing: Homeownership rate: 24.7%; Median home value: $92,900; Median year structure built: 1988; Homeowner vacancy rate: 3.1%; Median gross rent: $995 per month; Rental vacancy rate: 12.8%

Health Insurance: 85.5% have insurance; 66.8% have private insurance; 26.8% have public insurance; 14.5% do not have insurance; 5.0% of children under 18 do not have insurance

Transportation: Commute: 90.7% car, 0.4% public transportation, 4.9% walk, 2.8% work from home; Median travel time to work: 17.8 minutes

Additional Information Contacts
Town of Spring Lake . . . . (910) 436-0241
    http://www.spring-lake.org

STEDMAN (town). Covers a land area of 2.081 square miles and a water area of <.001 square miles. Located at 35.01° N. Lat; 78.70° W. Long. Elevation is 125 feet.

Population: 1,028; Growth (since 2000): 54.8%; Density: 493.9 persons per square mile; Race: 83.2% White, 11.7% Black/African American, 0.7% Asian, 1.1% American Indian/Alaska Native, 0.2% Native Hawaiian/Other Pacific Islander, 2.2% Two or more races, 3.2% Hispanic of any race; Average household size: 2.54; Median age: 35.9; Age under 18: 26.4%; Age 65 and over: 11.1%; Males per 100 females: 98.8

School District(s)
Cumberland County Schools (PK-12)
    2012-13 Enrollment: 52,925 . . . . (910) 678-2300
Housing: Homeownership rate: 74.5%; Homeowner vacancy rate: 3.8%; Rental vacancy rate: 7.2%

VANDER (CDP). Covers a land area of 3.748 square miles and a water area of 0.008 square miles. Located at 35.04° N. Lat; 78.79° W. Long. Elevation is 125 feet.

Population: 1,146; Growth (since 2000): -4.8%; Density: 305.7 persons per square mile; Race: 64.0% White, 27.1% Black/African American, 0.9% Asian, 3.6% American Indian/Alaska Native, 0.0% Native Hawaiian/Other Pacific Islander, 2.9% Two or more races, 4.4% Hispanic of any race; Average household size: 2.25; Median age: 44.1; Age under 18: 20.1%; Age 65 and over: 17.3%; Males per 100 females: 84.2

Housing: Homeownership rate: 64.7%; Homeowner vacancy rate: 2.1%; Rental vacancy rate: 9.1%

WADE (town). Covers a land area of 1.785 square miles and a water area of 0.010 square miles. Located at 35.16° N. Lat; 78.74° W. Long. Elevation is 138 feet.

Population: 556; Growth (since 2000): 15.8%; Density: 311.4 persons per square mile; Race: 74.6% White, 20.9% Black/African American, 1.3% Asian, 0.7% American Indian/Alaska Native, 0.0% Native Hawaiian/Other Pacific Islander, 2.3% Two or more races, 3.2% Hispanic of any race; Average household size: 2.47; Median age: 42.0; Age under 18: 23.6%; Age 65 and over: 15.5%; Males per 100 females: 89.1

School District(s)
Cumberland County Schools (PK-12)
    2012-13 Enrollment: 52,925 . . . . (910) 678-2300
Housing: Homeownership rate: 70.7%; Homeowner vacancy rate: 1.2%; Rental vacancy rate: 17.3%

Currituck County

Located in northeastern North Carolina; bounded on the north by Virginia, on the east by the Atlantic Ocean, on the south by Albemarle Sound, and on the southwest by the North River. Covers a land area of 261.852 square miles, a water area of 264.740 square miles, and is located in the Eastern Time Zone at 36.37° N. Lat., 75.94° W. Long. The county was founded in 1672. County seat is Currituck.

Currituck County is part of the Virginia Beach-Norfolk-Newport News, VA-NC Metropolitan Statistical Area. The entire metro area includes: Currituck County, NC; Gates County, NC; Gloucester County, VA; Isle of Wight County, VA; James City County, VA; Mathews County, VA; York County, VA; Chesapeake city, VA; Hampton city, VA; Newport News city, VA; Norfolk city, VA; Poquoson city, VA; Portsmouth city, VA; Suffolk city, VA; Virginia Beach city, VA; Williamsburg city, VA

Population: 23,547; Growth (since 2000): 29.5%; Density: 89.9 persons per square mile; Race: 90.3% White, 5.8% Black/African American, 0.6% Asian, 0.5% American Indian/Alaska Native, 0.0% Native Hawaiian/Other Pacific Islander, 1.8% two or more races, 3.0% Hispanic of any race; Average household size: 2.64; Median age: 41.3; Age under 18: 23.7%; Age 65 and over: 12.9%; Males per 100 females: 98.2; Marriage status: 21.3% never married, 61.9% now married, 3.0% separated, 6.3% widowed, 10.6% divorced; Foreign born: 3.1%; Speak English only: 96.0%; With disability: 12.3%; Veterans: 14.8%; Ancestry: 16.4% American, 15.5% German, 13.2% Irish, 13.2% English, 6.7% Italian

Religion: Six largest groups: 17.0% Baptist, 8.5% Methodist/Pietist, 1.8% Pentecostal, 1.2% Catholicism, 1.1% Non-denominational Protestant, 0.2% Episcopalianism/Anglicanism

Economy: Unemployment rate: 4.5%; Leading industries: 21.5% retail trade; 13.6% construction; 11.8% accommodation and food services; Farms: 82 totaling 35,356 acres; Company size: 0 employ 1,000 or more persons, 0 employ 500 to 999 persons, 3 employ 100 to 499 persons, 591 employs less than 100 persons; Business ownership: 692 women-owned, n/a Black-owned, n/a Hispanic-owned, n/a Asian-owned

Employment: 12.5% management, business, and financial, 3.3% computer, engineering, and science, 7.8% education, legal, community service, arts, and media, 3.6% healthcare practitioners, 16.6% service, 27.3% sales and office, 17.2% natural resources, construction, and maintenance, 11.7% production, transportation, and material moving

Income: Per capita: $25,854; Median household: $57,159; Average household: $67,597; Households with income of $100,000 or more: 20.7%; Poverty rate: 9.8%

Educational Attainment: High school diploma or higher: 85.0%; Bachelor's degree or higher: 18.4%; Graduate/professional degree or higher: 4.9%

Housing: Homeownership rate: 80.6%; Median home value: $223,800; Median year structure built: 1992; Homeowner vacancy rate: 4.1%; Median gross rent: $986 per month; Rental vacancy rate: 12.6%

Vital Statistics: Birth rate: 95.5 per 10,000 population; Death rate: 82.0 per 10,000 population; Age-adjusted cancer mortality rate: 254.0 deaths per 100,000 population

Health Insurance: 81.0% have insurance; 69.7% have private insurance; 23.8% have public insurance; 19.0% do not have insurance; 14.8% of children under 18 do not have insurance

Health Care: Physicians: 4.1 per 10,000 population; Hospital beds: 0.0 per 10,000 population; Hospital admissions: 0.0 per 10,000 population
Transportation: Commute: 95.0% car, 0.3% public transportation, 0.5% walk, 3.2% work from home; Median travel time to work: 33.9 minutes
Presidential Election: 31.5% Obama, 66.3% Romney (2012)
National and State Parks: Mackay Island National Wildlife Refuge
Additional Information Contacts
Currituck Government . . . . (252) 232-2075
   http://www.co.currituck.nc.us

Currituck County Communities

AYDLETT (unincorporated postal area)
ZCTA: 27916
   Covers a land area of 7.754 square miles and a water area of 0 square miles. Located at 36.32° N. Lat; 75.92° W. Long. Elevation is 13 feet.
   Population: 747; Growth (since 2000): 69.4%; Density: 96.3 persons per square mile; Race: 96.0% White, 1.6% Black/African American, 0.8% Asian, 0.4% American Indian/Alaska Native, 0.0% Native Hawaiian/Other Pacific Islander, 0.5% Two or more races, 1.3% Hispanic of any race; Average household size: 2.62; Median age: 43.4; Age under 18: 22.4%; Age 65 and over: 14.1%; Males per 100 females: 91.0
   Housing: Homeownership rate: 82.1%; Homeowner vacancy rate: 4.9%; Rental vacancy rate: 7.3%

BARCO (unincorporated postal area)
ZCTA: 27917
   Covers a land area of 20.115 square miles and a water area of 4.133 square miles. Located at 36.36° N. Lat; 76.00° W. Long. Elevation is 10 feet.
   Population: 833; Growth (since 2000): -5.4%; Density: 41.4 persons per square mile; Race: 74.5% White, 19.2% Black/African American, 0.7% Asian, 0.8% American Indian/Alaska Native, 0.1% Native Hawaiian/Other Pacific Islander, 2.0% Two or more races, 6.2% Hispanic of any race; Average household size: 2.64; Median age: 40.7; Age under 18: 24.2%; Age 65 and over: 18.7%; Males per 100 females: 92.4
School District(s)
Currituck County Schools (PK-12)
   2012-13 Enrollment: 3,916 . . . . (252) 232-2223
   Housing: Homeownership rate: 59.6%; Homeowner vacancy rate: 1.7%; Rental vacancy rate: 16.5%

COINJOCK (CDP). Covers a land area of 0.840 square miles and a water area of 0.031 square miles. Located at 36.35° N. Lat; 75.95° W. Long. Elevation is 3 feet.
Population: 335; Growth (since 2000): n/a; Density: 399.0 persons per square mile; Race: 90.4% White, 2.1% Black/African American, 0.0% Asian, 0.0% American Indian/Alaska Native, 0.3% Native Hawaiian/Other Pacific Islander, 3.3% Two or more races, 4.5% Hispanic of any race; Average household size: 2.39; Median age: 42.8; Age under 18: 20.6%; Age 65 and over: 14.3%; Males per 100 females: 104.3
Housing: Homeownership rate: 64.3%; Homeowner vacancy rate: 3.1%; Rental vacancy rate: 26.5%

COROLLA (unincorporated postal area)
ZCTA: 27927
   Covers a land area of 26.625 square miles and a water area of 43.509 square miles. Located at 36.34° N. Lat; 75.85° W. Long. Elevation is 7 feet.
   Population: 542; Growth (since 2000): -16.4%; Density: 20.4 persons per square mile; Race: 96.7% White, 1.8% Black/African American, 0.7% Asian, 0.2% American Indian/Alaska Native, 0.0% Native Hawaiian/Other Pacific Islander, 0.4% Two or more races, 1.5% Hispanic of any race; Average household size: 1.91; Median age: 56.2; Age under 18: 5.0%; Age 65 and over: 25.8%; Males per 100 females: 103.8
School District(s)
Waters Edge Village School
   2012-13 Enrollment: 15. . . . . (252) 455-9449
   Housing: Homeownership rate: 80.6%; Homeowner vacancy rate: 12.4%; Rental vacancy rate: 45.9%

CURRITUCK (unincorporated postal area)
ZCTA: 27929
   Covers a land area of 5.926 square miles and a water area of 6.546 square miles. Located at 36.44° N. Lat; 75.99° W. Long. Elevation is 7 feet.
   Population: 1,166; Growth (since 2000): 62.8%; Density: 196.8 persons per square mile; Race: 96.9% White, 0.3% Black/African American, 0.5% Asian, 0.1% American Indian/Alaska Native, 0.0% Native Hawaiian/Other Pacific Islander, 1.1% Two or more races, 2.0% Hispanic of any race; Average household size: 2.49; Median age: 48.6; Age under 18: 18.0%; Age 65 and over: 18.6%; Males per 100 females: 99.0
School District(s)
Currituck County Schools (PK-12)
   2012-13 Enrollment: 3,916 . . . . (252) 232-2223
   Housing: Homeownership rate: 88.0%; Homeowner vacancy rate: 3.0%; Rental vacancy rate: 12.5%
Airports: Currituck County Regional (general aviation)

GRANDY (unincorporated postal area)
ZCTA: 27939
   Covers a land area of 6.610 square miles and a water area of 10.222 square miles. Located at 36.24° N. Lat; 75.84° W. Long. Elevation is 13 feet.
   Population: 2,361; Growth (since 2000): 39.7%; Density: 357.2 persons per square mile; Race: 92.7% White, 3.4% Black/African American, 0.5% Asian, 0.3% American Indian/Alaska Native, 0.0% Native Hawaiian/Other Pacific Islander, 1.7% Two or more races, 2.9% Hispanic of any race; Average household size: 2.47; Median age: 41.5; Age under 18: 23.5%; Age 65 and over: 16.3%; Males per 100 females: 103.0
   Housing: Homeownership rate: 73.8%; Homeowner vacancy rate: 9.1%; Rental vacancy rate: 5.3%

HARBINGER (unincorporated postal area)
ZCTA: 27941
   Covers a land area of 3.150 square miles and a water area of 0 square miles. Located at 36.10° N. Lat; 75.82° W. Long. Elevation is 13 feet.
   Population: 536; Growth (since 2000): 516.1%; Density: 170.2 persons per square mile; Race: 95.7% White, 2.6% Black/African American, 0.0% Asian, 0.7% American Indian/Alaska Native, 0.0% Native Hawaiian/Other Pacific Islander, 0.9% Two or more races, 1.7% Hispanic of any race; Average household size: 2.43; Median age: 47.3; Age under 18: 17.9%; Age 65 and over: 16.8%; Males per 100 females: 106.9
   Housing: Homeownership rate: 81.0%; Homeowner vacancy rate: 4.2%; Rental vacancy rate: 2.3%

JARVISBURG (unincorporated postal area)
ZCTA: 27947
   Covers a land area of 12.070 square miles and a water area of 1.418 square miles. Located at 36.19° N. Lat; 75.88° W. Long. Elevation is 13 feet.
   Population: 1,230; Growth (since 2000): 103.6%; Density: 101.9 persons per square mile; Race: 86.3% White, 8.8% Black/African American, 0.3% Asian, 1.1% American Indian/Alaska Native, 0.0% Native Hawaiian/Other Pacific Islander, 2.4% Two or more races, 2.8% Hispanic of any race; Average household size: 2.58; Median age: 43.1; Age under 18: 20.2%; Age 65 and over: 13.8%; Males per 100 females: 97.1
School District(s)
Currituck County Schools (PK-12)
   2012-13 Enrollment: 3,916 . . . . (252) 232-2223
   Housing: Homeownership rate: 77.3%; Homeowner vacancy rate: 6.5%; Rental vacancy rate: 11.5%

KNOTTS ISLAND (unincorporated postal area)
ZCTA: 27950
   Covers a land area of 29.885 square miles and a water area of 22.011 square miles. Located at 36.51° N. Lat; 76.00° W. Long. Elevation is 10 feet.
   Population: 2,006; Growth (since 2000): 9.9%; Density: 67.1 persons per square mile; Race: 97.3% White, 0.2% Black/African American, 0.8% Asian, 0.2% American Indian/Alaska Native, 0.0% Native Hawaiian/Other Pacific Islander, 1.4% Two or more races, 1.2%

Hispanic of any race; Average household size: 2.49; Median age: 44.4; Age under 18: 20.8%; Age 65 and over: 12.2%; Males per 100 females: 99.2

School District(s)

Currituck County Schools (PK-12)

2012-13 Enrollment: 3,916 . . . . (252) 232-2223

Housing: Homeownership rate: 81.3%; Homeowner vacancy rate: 1.9%; Rental vacancy rate: 9.5%

MAPLE (unincorporated postal area)

ZCTA: 27956

Covers a land area of 4.645 square miles and a water area of 0.012 square miles. Located at 36.40° N. Lat; 76.00° W. Long. Elevation is 3 feet.

Population: 340; Growth (since 2000): -30.9%; Density: 73.2 persons per square mile; Race: 96.2% White, 3.2% Black/African American, 0.0% Asian, 0.0% American Indian/Alaska Native, 0.0% Native Hawaiian/Other Pacific Islander, 0.6% Two or more races, 2.1% Hispanic of any race; Average household size: 2.70; Median age: 38.0; Age under 18: 23.2%; Age 65 and over: 13.8%; Males per 100 females: 115.2

Housing: Homeownership rate: 82.2%; Homeowner vacancy rate: 2.1%; Rental vacancy rate: 16.7%

MOYOCK (CDP). Covers a land area of 10.494 square miles and a water area of 0.037 square miles. Located at 36.50° N. Lat; 76.17° W. Long. Elevation is 7 feet.

Population: 3,759; Growth (since 2000): n/a; Density: 358.2 persons per square mile; Race: 88.5% White, 6.9% Black/African American, 1.2% Asian, 0.4% American Indian/Alaska Native, 0.2% Native Hawaiian/Other Pacific Islander, 2.0% Two or more races, 3.6% Hispanic of any race; Average household size: 3.10; Median age: 37.0; Age under 18: 30.1%; Age 65 and over: 8.0%; Males per 100 females: 92.5; Marriage status: 19.3% never married, 63.4% now married, 1.9% separated, 7.6% widowed, 9.6% divorced; Foreign born: 4.1%; Speak English only: 97.8%; With disability: 9.7%; Veterans: 19.4%; Ancestry: 28.5% American, 18.0% German, 13.5% Irish, 12.8% English, 6.5% Polish

Employment: 14.8% management, business, and financial, 5.3% computer, engineering, and science, 13.6% education, legal, community service, arts, and media, 3.5% healthcare practitioners, 12.8% service, 23.1% sales and office, 16.5% natural resources, construction, and maintenance, 10.3% production, transportation, and material moving

Income: Per capita: $26,362; Median household: $81,528; Average household: $78,486; Households with income of $100,000 or more: 28.8%; Poverty rate: 3.0%

Educational Attainment: High school diploma or higher: 87.0%; Bachelor's degree or higher: 17.4%; Graduate/professional degree or higher: 4.6%

School District(s)

Currituck County Schools (PK-12)

2012-13 Enrollment: 3,916 . . . . (252) 232-2223

Housing: Homeownership rate: 91.0%; Median home value: $261,700; Median year structure built: 1995; Homeowner vacancy rate: 2.6%; Median gross rent: $1,375 per month; Rental vacancy rate: 11.7%

Health Insurance: 91.2% have insurance; 86.2% have private insurance; 16.2% have public insurance; 8.8% do not have insurance; 4.4% of children under 18 do not have insurance

Transportation: Commute: 94.1% car, 0.0% public transportation, 1.1% walk, 4.9% work from home; Median travel time to work: 31.8 minutes

POINT HARBOR (unincorporated postal area)

ZCTA: 27964

Covers a land area of 1.476 square miles and a water area of 3.728 square miles. Located at 36.08° N. Lat; 75.81° W. Long. Elevation is 7 feet.

Population: 545; Growth (since 2000): -11.8%; Density: 369.1 persons per square mile; Race: 94.1% White, 3.1% Black/African American, 0.0% Asian, 0.0% American Indian/Alaska Native, 0.0% Native Hawaiian/Other Pacific Islander, 2.4% Two or more races, 5.7% Hispanic of any race; Average household size: 2.28; Median age: 45.3; Age under 18: 19.8%; Age 65 and over: 20.6%; Males per 100 females: 87.3

Housing: Homeownership rate: 74.1%; Homeowner vacancy rate: 2.1%; Rental vacancy rate: 0.0%

POPLAR BRANCH (unincorporated postal area)

ZCTA: 27965

Covers a land area of 16.100 square miles and a water area of 11.842 square miles. Located at 36.27° N. Lat; 75.93° W. Long. Elevation is 13 feet.

Population: 527; Growth (since 2000): -2.0%; Density: 32.7 persons per square mile; Race: 89.9% White, 7.6% Black/African American, 0.0% Asian, 0.2% American Indian/Alaska Native, 0.0% Native Hawaiian/Other Pacific Islander, 1.9% Two or more races, 2.3% Hispanic of any race; Average household size: 2.33; Median age: 44.4; Age under 18: 17.8%; Age 65 and over: 17.3%; Males per 100 females: 99.6

School District(s)

Currituck County Schools (PK-12)

2012-13 Enrollment: 3,916 . . . . (252) 232-2223

Housing: Homeownership rate: 75.7%; Homeowner vacancy rate: 2.8%; Rental vacancy rate: 32.1%

POWELLS POINT (unincorporated postal area)

ZCTA: 27966

Covers a land area of 10.227 square miles and a water area of 16.932 square miles. Located at 36.15° N. Lat; 75.80° W. Long. Elevation is 10 feet.

Population: 1,052; Growth (since 2000): -24.3%; Density: 102.9 persons per square mile; Race: 82.8% White, 13.8% Black/African American, 0.3% Asian, 0.1% American Indian/Alaska Native, 0.0% Native Hawaiian/Other Pacific Islander, 1.8% Two or more races, 2.0% Hispanic of any race; Average household size: 2.52; Median age: 39.4; Age under 18: 23.2%; Age 65 and over: 11.0%; Males per 100 females: 94.8

Housing: Homeownership rate: 62.1%; Homeowner vacancy rate: 7.1%; Rental vacancy rate: 6.5%

Dare County

Located in northeastern North Carolina; tidewater area bounded on the east by the Atlantic Ocean, on the north by Albemarle Sound, and on the west by the Alligator River; includes Roanoke Island and Cape Hatteras. Covers a land area of 383.420 square miles, a water area of 1,179.144 square miles, and is located in the Eastern Time Zone at 35.61° N. Lat., 75.77° W. Long. The county was founded in 1870. County seat is Manteo.

Dare County is part of the Kill Devil Hills, NC Micropolitan Statistical Area. The entire metro area includes: Dare County, NC; Tyrrell County, NC

Weather Station: Cape Hatteras NWS Bldg										Elevation: 9 feet		
	Jan	Feb	Mar	Apr	May	Jun	Jul	Aug	Sep	Oct	Nov	Dec
High	53	54	60	67	75	82	86	85	81	73	65	57
Low	39	40	45	53	61	69	74	73	69	60	51	43
Precip	5.3	3.9	4.8	3.7	3.5	4.1	4.9	6.7	6.0	5.4	5.1	4.3
Snow	na	na	na	na	na	na	na	na	na	na	na	na

High and Low temperatures in degrees Fahrenheit; Precipitation and Snow in inches

Weather Station: Manteo Airport										Elevation: 13 feet		
	Jan	Feb	Mar	Apr	May	Jun	Jul	Aug	Sep	Oct	Nov	Dec
High	52	54	60	69	76	83	87	86	81	72	64	56
Low	36	37	43	51	59	69	73	72	68	58	49	40
Precip	4.1	3.0	4.5	3.4	4.1	5.0	5.1	6.0	4.5	3.5	3.7	3.7
Snow	0.5	0.7	0.0	tr	0.0	0.0	0.0	0.0	0.0	0.0	0.0	0.4

High and Low temperatures in degrees Fahrenheit; Precipitation and Snow in inches

Population: 33,920; Growth (since 2000): 13.2%; Density: 88.5 persons per square mile; Race: 92.3% White, 2.5% Black/African American, 0.6% Asian, 0.4% American Indian/Alaska Native, 0.0% Native Hawaiian/Other Pacific Islander, 1.8% two or more races, 6.5% Hispanic of any race; Average household size: 2.36; Median age: 43.6; Age under 18: 20.0%; Age 65 and over: 15.2%; Males per 100 females: 100.0; Marriage status: 24.1% never married, 56.6% now married, 3.8% separated, 6.5% widowed, 12.8% divorced; Foreign born: 5.9%; Speak English only: 92.5%; With disability: 14.3%; Veterans: 11.4%; Ancestry: 20.4% English, 18.5% Irish, 18.0% German, 12.1% American, 5.4% Italian

Religion: Six largest groups: 15.6% Methodist/Pietist, 5.2% Catholicism, 3.9% Baptist, 3.8% Pentecostal, 3.5% Non-denominational Protestant, 2.3% Episcopalianism/Anglicanism

Economy: Unemployment rate: 5.0%; Leading industries: 22.6% retail trade; 17.2% accommodation and food services; 12.4% construction;

Farms: 9 totaling n/a acres; Company size: 0 employ 1,000 or more persons, 0 employ 500 to 999 persons, 8 employ 100 to 499 persons, 1,870 employ less than 100 persons; Business ownership: 1,581 women-owned, n/a Black-owned, n/a Hispanic-owned, 52 Asian-owned
Employment: 17.8% management, business, and financial, 2.6% computer, engineering, and science, 8.5% education, legal, community service, arts, and media, 3.1% healthcare practitioners, 20.0% service, 25.9% sales and office, 15.2% natural resources, construction, and maintenance, 7.0% production, transportation, and material moving
Income: Per capita: $30,529; Median household: $55,481; Average household: $70,145; Households with income of $100,000 or more: 19.4%; Poverty rate: 8.8%
Educational Attainment: High school diploma or higher: 91.5%; Bachelor's degree or higher: 30.6%; Graduate/professional degree or higher: 9.1%
Housing: Homeownership rate: 70.6%; Median home value: $293,900; Median year structure built: 1987; Homeowner vacancy rate: 3.9%; Median gross rent: $998 per month; Rental vacancy rate: 44.6%
Vital Statistics: Birth rate: 103.7 per 10,000 population; Death rate: 82.5 per 10,000 population; Age-adjusted cancer mortality rate: 152.9 deaths per 100,000 population
Health Insurance: 80.0% have insurance; 66.1% have private insurance; 27.4% have public insurance; 20.0% do not have insurance; 12.4% of children under 18 do not have insurance
Health Care: Physicians: 15.9 per 10,000 population; Hospital beds: 17.8 per 10,000 population; Hospital admissions: 487.7 per 10,000 population
Transportation: Commute: 90.2% car, 0.0% public transportation, 0.6% walk, 6.5% work from home; Median travel time to work: 19.0 minutes
Presidential Election: 41.1% Obama, 57.0% Romney (2012)
National and State Parks: Alligator River National Wildlife Refuge; Cape Hatteras National Seashore; Fort Raleigh National Historic Site; Jockey's Ridge State Park; National Park Service Headquarters; Pea Island National Wildlife Refuge; Wright Brothers National Memorial; Wright Brothers National Memorial Visitor Center
Additional Information Contacts
Dare Government . . . . (252) 475-5000
  http://www.co.dare.nc.us

Dare County Communities

AVON (CDP). Covers a land area of 2.356 square miles and a water area of 0.055 square miles. Located at 35.35° N. Lat; 75.51° W. Long. Elevation is 3 feet.
Population: 776; Growth (since 2000): n/a; Density: 329.4 persons per square mile; Race: 98.2% White, 0.1% Black/African American, 0.0% Asian, 0.1% American Indian/Alaska Native, 0.1% Native Hawaiian/Other Pacific Islander, 0.6% Two or more races, 7.5% Hispanic of any race; Average household size: 2.16; Median age: 50.1; Age under 18: 13.5%; Age 65 and over: 21.3%; Males per 100 females: 106.9
Housing: Homeownership rate: 78.6%; Homeowner vacancy rate: 6.0%; Rental vacancy rate: 91.7%

BUXTON (CDP). Covers a land area of 2.962 square miles and a water area of 0.024 square miles. Located at 35.26° N. Lat; 75.54° W. Long. Elevation is 10 feet.
Population: 1,273; Growth (since 2000): n/a; Density: 429.8 persons per square mile; Race: 94.7% White, 0.5% Black/African American, 0.0% Asian, 0.2% American Indian/Alaska Native, 0.0% Native Hawaiian/Other Pacific Islander, 1.3% Two or more races, 11.5% Hispanic of any race; Average household size: 2.49; Median age: 39.8; Age under 18: 22.6%; Age 65 and over: 12.2%; Males per 100 females: 105.7
School District(s)
Dare County Schools (PK-12)
  2012-13 Enrollment: 5,088 . . . . (252) 480-8888
Housing: Homeownership rate: 66.4%; Homeowner vacancy rate: 1.4%; Rental vacancy rate: 25.4%

DUCK (town). Covers a land area of 2.416 square miles and a water area of 1.302 square miles. Located at 36.18° N. Lat; 75.75° W. Long. Elevation is 13 feet.
Population: 369; Growth (since 2000): n/a; Density: 152.7 persons per square mile; Race: 96.2% White, 0.0% Black/African American, 1.1% Asian, 0.3% American Indian/Alaska Native, 0.0% Native Hawaiian/Other Pacific Islander, 0.8% Two or more races, 2.7% Hispanic of any race;

Average household size: 1.95; Median age: 58.6; Age under 18: 10.8%; Age 65 and over: 35.5%; Males per 100 females: 99.5
Housing: Homeownership rate: 80.9%; Homeowner vacancy rate: 4.9%; Rental vacancy rate: 27.8%
Safety: Violent crime rate: 26.7 per 10,000 population; Property crime rate: 986.7 per 10,000 population

FRISCO (CDP). Covers a land area of 0.752 square miles and a water area of 0.026 square miles. Located at 35.23° N. Lat; 75.63° W. Long. Elevation is 3 feet.
Population: 200; Growth (since 2000): n/a; Density: 266.1 persons per square mile; Race: 98.5% White, 0.0% Black/African American, 0.5% Asian, 0.0% American Indian/Alaska Native, 0.0% Native Hawaiian/Other Pacific Islander, 1.0% Two or more races, 1.0% Hispanic of any race; Average household size: 2.02; Median age: 50.0; Age under 18: 10.0%; Age 65 and over: 16.5%; Males per 100 females: 106.2
Housing: Homeownership rate: 66.7%; Homeowner vacancy rate: 1.5%; Rental vacancy rate: 15.0%

HATTERAS (CDP). Covers a land area of 1.574 square miles and a water area of 0.110 square miles. Located at 35.22° N. Lat; 75.69° W. Long.
Population: 504; Growth (since 2000): n/a; Density: 320.1 persons per square mile; Race: 98.2% White, 0.2% Black/African American, 0.0% Asian, 0.0% American Indian/Alaska Native, 0.0% Native Hawaiian/Other Pacific Islander, 1.6% Two or more races, 2.8% Hispanic of any race; Average household size: 2.22; Median age: 46.8; Age under 18: 15.9%; Age 65 and over: 14.7%; Males per 100 females: 104.0
Housing: Homeownership rate: 71.5%; Homeowner vacancy rate: 6.4%; Rental vacancy rate: 45.8%

KILL DEVIL HILLS (town). Covers a land area of 5.618 square miles and a water area of 0.056 square miles. Located at 36.02° N. Lat; 75.67° W. Long. Elevation is 7 feet.
History: Site of Wright Brothers' flight experiments (1900-1903). Wright Brothers National Memorial to West.
Population: 6,683; Growth (since 2000): 13.3%; Density: 1,189.6 persons per square mile; Race: 89.8% White, 1.2% Black/African American, 1.4% Asian, 0.5% American Indian/Alaska Native, 0.1% Native Hawaiian/Other Pacific Islander, 2.1% Two or more races, 9.1% Hispanic of any race; Average household size: 2.37; Median age: 37.8; Age under 18: 20.4%; Age 65 and over: 9.4%; Males per 100 females: 106.6; Marriage status: 31.7% never married, 43.0% now married, 3.5% separated, 6.3% widowed, 19.0% divorced; Foreign born: 6.4%; Speak English only: 92.3%; With disability: 11.9%; Veterans: 9.4%; Ancestry: 24.4% German, 19.9% Irish, 17.7% English, 7.5% American, 6.3% Polish
Employment: 18.2% management, business, and financial, 2.2% computer, engineering, and science, 11.5% education, legal, community service, arts, and media, 3.2% healthcare practitioners, 21.7% service, 27.4% sales and office, 13.1% natural resources, construction, and maintenance, 2.7% production, transportation, and material moving
Income: Per capita: $29,721; Median household: $55,170; Average household: $63,867; Households with income of $100,000 or more: 17.3%; Poverty rate: 6.2%
Educational Attainment: High school diploma or higher: 96.1%; Bachelor's degree or higher: 34.3%; Graduate/professional degree or higher: 7.5%
School District(s)
Dare County Schools (PK-12)
  2012-13 Enrollment: 5,088 . . . . (252) 480-8888
Housing: Homeownership rate: 61.4%; Median home value: $260,900; Median year structure built: 1983; Homeowner vacancy rate: 4.7%; Median gross rent: $1,055 per month; Rental vacancy rate: 11.0%
Health Insurance: 76.4% have insurance; 66.7% have private insurance; 18.6% have public insurance; 23.6% do not have insurance; 7.5% of children under 18 do not have insurance
Safety: Violent crime rate: 61.1 per 10,000 population; Property crime rate: 462.9 per 10,000 population
Transportation: Commute: 92.2% car, 0.0% public transportation, 0.5% walk, 5.5% work from home; Median travel time to work: 21.5 minutes
Additional Information Contacts
Town of Kill Devil Hills . . . . (262) 449-5300
  http://www.kdhnc.com

KITTY HAWK (town). Covers a land area of 8.114 square miles and a water area of 0.166 square miles. Located at 36.07° N. Lat; 75.72° W. Long. Elevation is 7 feet.

History: Kitty Hawk may have been named for the mosquito hawks that swarmed here at certain seasons. It also may have from the cry of the wild goose. A map prepared in 1729 designates the place as Chickahauk. Kitty Hawk is most noted today as the site of Orville and Wilbur Wright's glider experiments around 1900, which led to the invention of the airplane.

Population: 3,272; Growth (since 2000): 9.4%; Density: 403.3 persons per square mile; Race: 96.3% White, 1.1% Black/African American, 0.8% Asian, 0.2% American Indian/Alaska Native, 0.1% Native Hawaiian/Other Pacific Islander, 1.1% Two or more races, 2.9% Hispanic of any race; Average household size: 2.31; Median age: 45.4; Age under 18: 18.7%; Age 65 and over: 14.9%; Males per 100 females: 97.6; Marriage status: 21.5% never married, 55.5% now married, 7.8% separated, 6.6% widowed, 16.4% divorced; Foreign born: 3.7%; Speak English only: 97.8%; With disability: 11.8%; Veterans: 9.3%; Ancestry: 23.7% English, 20.8% Irish, 17.2% German, 16.2% American, 7.9% Italian

Employment: 17.6% management, business, and financial, 4.9% computer, engineering, and science, 9.0% education, legal, community service, arts, and media, 0.9% healthcare practitioners, 12.3% service, 33.3% sales and office, 16.3% natural resources, construction, and maintenance, 5.7% production, transportation, and material moving

Income: Per capita: $33,265; Median household: $52,109; Average household: $71,980; Households with income of $100,000 or more: 19.4%; Poverty rate: 7.2%

Educational Attainment: High school diploma or higher: 95.2%; Bachelor's degree or higher: 28.2%; Graduate/professional degree or higher: 7.0%

School District(s)
Dare County Schools (PK-12)
    2012-13 Enrollment: 5,088 . . . . (252) 480-8888

Housing: Homeownership rate: 74.5%; Median home value: $321,100; Median year structure built: 1987; Homeowner vacancy rate: 3.1%; Median gross rent: $1,098 per month; Rental vacancy rate: 37.4%

Health Insurance: 81.5% have insurance; 69.4% have private insurance; 24.3% have public insurance; 18.5% do not have insurance; 16.3% of children under 18 do not have insurance

Safety: Violent crime rate: 9.0 per 10,000 population; Property crime rate: 403.2 per 10,000 population

Transportation: Commute: 90.6% car, 0.0% public transportation, 0.0% walk, 8.0% work from home; Median travel time to work: 15.8 minutes

Additional Information Contacts
Town of Kitty Hawk . . . . (252) 261-3552
    http://www.townofkittyhawk.org

MANNS HARBOR (CDP). Covers a land area of 4.077 square miles and a water area of 0.020 square miles. Located at 35.90° N. Lat; 75.78° W. Long. Elevation is 3 feet.

Population: 821; Growth (since 2000): n/a; Density: 201.4 persons per square mile; Race: 89.2% White, 0.7% Black/African American, 0.5% Asian, 0.5% American Indian/Alaska Native, 0.0% Native Hawaiian/Other Pacific Islander, 2.1% Two or more races, 12.4% Hispanic of any race; Average household size: 2.55; Median age: 40.4; Age under 18: 21.7%; Age 65 and over: 14.7%; Males per 100 females: 103.7

Housing: Homeownership rate: 58.7%; Homeowner vacancy rate: 2.6%; Rental vacancy rate: 11.3%

MANTEO (town). County seat. Covers a land area of 1.919 square miles and a water area of 0.061 square miles. Located at 35.90° N. Lat; 75.65° W. Long. Elevation is 7 feet.

History: Manteo was named for the Native American, Manteo.

Population: 1,434; Growth (since 2000): 36.3%; Density: 747.2 persons per square mile; Race: 84.7% White, 8.4% Black/African American, 0.3% Asian, 0.8% American Indian/Alaska Native, 0.0% Native Hawaiian/Other Pacific Islander, 3.0% Two or more races, 9.0% Hispanic of any race; Average household size: 2.11; Median age: 42.8; Age under 18: 20.9%; Age 65 and over: 17.0%; Males per 100 females: 83.1

School District(s)
Dare County Schools (PK-12)
    2012-13 Enrollment: 5,088 . . . . (252) 480-8888

Housing: Homeownership rate: 49.8%; Homeowner vacancy rate: 3.7%; Rental vacancy rate: 14.3%

Safety: Violent crime rate: 51.7 per 10,000 population; Property crime rate: 510.0 per 10,000 population

Newspapers: Coastland Times (weekly circulation 9000)
Airports: Dare County Regional (general aviation)
Additional Information Contacts
Town of Manteo . . . . (252) 473-2133
    http://www.townofmanteo.com

NAGS HEAD (town). Covers a land area of 6.582 square miles and a water area of 0.077 square miles. Located at 35.95° N. Lat; 75.63° W. Long. Elevation is 7 feet.

History: One explanation for the name Nags Head says that in the early days of the settlement, "land pirates" deliberately sought to wreck ships. On a stormy night a lantern was tied to the neck of an old nag, which was then ridden along the beach. Mistaking the light for a beacon, ships were lured to the treacherous reefs, there to be boarded and looted by the wily shoremen. Nags Head became a resort in the early 1800's.

Population: 2,757; Growth (since 2000): 2.1%; Density: 418.9 persons per square mile; Race: 94.6% White, 1.6% Black/African American, 0.3% Asian, 0.5% American Indian/Alaska Native, 0.0% Native Hawaiian/Other Pacific Islander, 1.5% Two or more races, 3.2% Hispanic of any race; Average household size: 2.19; Median age: 46.8; Age under 18: 16.9%; Age 65 and over: 16.8%; Males per 100 females: 98.9; Marriage status: 22.9% never married, 54.5% now married, 1.5% separated, 7.2% widowed, 15.4% divorced; Foreign born: 4.7%; Speak English only: 90.2%; With disability: 14.2%; Veterans: 13.0%; Ancestry: 22.4% English, 19.0% German, 16.4% Irish, 9.0% American, 7.7% Scottish

Employment: 27.0% management, business, and financial, 0.7% computer, engineering, and science, 7.6% education, legal, community service, arts, and media, 7.7% healthcare practitioners, 22.0% service, 17.6% sales and office, 16.3% natural resources, construction, and maintenance, 1.3% production, transportation, and material moving

Income: Per capita: $36,959; Median household: $52,355; Average household: $79,089; Households with income of $100,000 or more: 20.3%; Poverty rate: 6.1%

Educational Attainment: High school diploma or higher: 96.8%; Bachelor's degree or higher: 38.6%; Graduate/professional degree or higher: 13.5%

School District(s)
Dare County Schools (PK-12)
    2012-13 Enrollment: 5,088 . . . . (252) 480-8888

Housing: Homeownership rate: 67.6%; Median home value: $326,200; Median year structure built: 1987; Homeowner vacancy rate: 9.2%; Median gross rent: $1,005 per month; Rental vacancy rate: 71.4%

Health Insurance: 86.4% have insurance; 73.9% have private insurance; 20.9% have public insurance; 13.6% do not have insurance; 0.0% of children under 18 do not have insurance

Hospitals: The Outer Banks Hospital (19 beds)
Newspapers: Outer Banks Sentinel (weekly circulation 10000)
Transportation: Commute: 83.6% car, 0.0% public transportation, 0.3% walk, 13.1% work from home; Median travel time to work: 16.4 minutes
Additional Information Contacts
Town of Nags Head . . . . (252) 441-5508
    http://www.townofnagshead.net

RODANTHE (CDP). Covers a land area of 1.091 square miles and a water area of 0.010 square miles. Located at 35.59° N. Lat; 75.47° W. Long. Elevation is 3 feet.

Population: 261; Growth (since 2000): n/a; Density: 239.2 persons per square mile; Race: 96.2% White, 0.8% Black/African American, 0.4% Asian, 0.8% American Indian/Alaska Native, 0.8% Native Hawaiian/Other Pacific Islander, 1.1% Two or more races, 1.5% Hispanic of any race; Average household size: 2.21; Median age: 42.5; Age under 18: 17.6%; Age 65 and over: 15.3%; Males per 100 females: 125.0

Housing: Homeownership rate: 61.8%; Homeowner vacancy rate: 10.8%; Rental vacancy rate: 85.5%

SALVO (CDP). Covers a land area of 0.968 square miles and a water area of 0.010 square miles. Located at 35.55° N. Lat; 75.47° W. Long. Elevation is 3 feet.

Population: 229; Growth (since 2000): n/a; Density: 236.5 persons per square mile; Race: 96.9% White, 1.3% Black/African American, 0.4% Asian, 0.0% American Indian/Alaska Native, 0.0% Native Hawaiian/Other Pacific Islander, 1.3% Two or more races, 3.1% Hispanic of any race; Average household size: 2.16; Median age: 48.2; Age under 18: 14.8%; Age 65 and over: 19.7%; Males per 100 females: 108.2

Housing: Homeownership rate: 59.4%; Homeowner vacancy rate: 7.4%; Rental vacancy rate: 87.1%

SOUTHERN SHORES (town).
Covers a land area of 3.947 square miles and a water area of 0.204 square miles. Located at 36.12° N. Lat; 75.73° W. Long. Elevation is 16 feet.

Population: 2,714; Growth (since 2000): 23.3%; Density: 687.5 persons per square mile; Race: 97.8% White, 0.3% Black/African American, 0.6% Asian, 0.1% American Indian/Alaska Native, 0.0% Native Hawaiian/Other Pacific Islander, 1.1% Two or more races, 1.5% Hispanic of any race; Average household size: 2.34; Median age: 54.2; Age under 18: 16.7%; Age 65 and over: 27.5%; Males per 100 females: 94.0; Marriage status: 19.4% never married, 65.0% now married, 1.3% separated, 6.6% widowed, 8.9% divorced; Foreign born: 3.2%; Speak English only: 95.5%; With disability: 10.5%; Veterans: 12.9%; Ancestry: 22.5% English, 16.2% German, 15.6% Irish, 11.3% Italian, 10.7% American

Employment: 24.3% management, business, and financial, 3.1% computer, engineering, and science, 6.5% education, legal, community service, arts, and media, 3.5% healthcare practitioners, 24.2% service, 27.4% sales and office, 6.6% natural resources, construction, and maintenance, 4.4% production, transportation, and material moving
Income: Per capita: $38,760; Median household: $81,184; Average household: $92,907; Households with income of $100,000 or more: 35.6%; Poverty rate: 3.0%
Educational Attainment: High school diploma or higher: 97.0%; Bachelor's degree or higher: 49.3%; Graduate/professional degree or higher: 17.3%
Housing: Homeownership rate: 89.3%; Median home value: $455,200; Median year structure built: 1987; Homeowner vacancy rate: 2.6%; Median gross rent: $1,646 per month; Rental vacancy rate: 10.6%
Health Insurance: 87.1% have insurance; 79.4% have private insurance; 31.9% have public insurance; 12.9% do not have insurance; 19.5% of children under 18 do not have insurance
Safety: Violent crime rate: 3.6 per 10,000 population; Property crime rate: 204.9 per 10,000 population
Transportation: Commute: 88.9% car, 0.0% public transportation, 0.5% walk, 9.0% work from home; Median travel time to work: 23.1 minutes
Additional Information Contacts
Town of Southern Shores . . . . (252) 261-2394
  http://www.southernshores.org

STUMPY POINT (unincorporated postal area)
ZCTA: 27978
  Covers a land area of 16.070 square miles and a water area of 6.782 square miles. Located at 35.73° N. Lat; 75.74° W. Long. Elevation is 3 feet.
  Population: 225; Growth (since 2000): n/a; Density: 14.0 persons per square mile; Race: 98.7% White, 0.0% Black/African American, 0.0% Asian, 0.0% American Indian/Alaska Native, 0.0% Native Hawaiian/Other Pacific Islander, 1.3% Two or more races, 0.0% Hispanic of any race; Average household size: 2.56; Median age: 50.2; Age under 18: 20.9%; Age 65 and over: 21.3%; Males per 100 females: 89.1
  Housing: Homeownership rate: 76.1%; Homeowner vacancy rate: 2.9%; Rental vacancy rate: 30.0%

WANCHESE (CDP).
Covers a land area of 4.670 square miles and a water area of 0.819 square miles. Located at 35.84° N. Lat; 75.64° W. Long. Elevation is 7 feet.
Population: 1,642; Growth (since 2000): 7.5%; Density: 351.6 persons per square mile; Race: 95.9% White, 0.2% Black/African American, 0.2% Asian, 0.2% American Indian/Alaska Native, 0.0% Native Hawaiian/Other Pacific Islander, 1.5% Two or more races, 4.4% Hispanic of any race; Average household size: 2.41; Median age: 40.9; Age under 18: 22.5%; Age 65 and over: 14.6%; Males per 100 females: 95.5
Housing: Homeownership rate: 69.7%; Homeowner vacancy rate: 1.5%; Rental vacancy rate: 12.7%

WAVES (CDP).
Covers a land area of 0.551 square miles and a water area of <.001 square miles. Located at 35.57° N. Lat; 75.47° W. Long. Elevation is 3 feet.
Population: 134; Growth (since 2000): n/a; Density: 243.0 persons per square mile; Race: 94.0% White, 0.0% Black/African American, 0.0% Asian, 0.0% American Indian/Alaska Native, 0.0% Native Hawaiian/Other Pacific Islander, 3.0% Two or more races, 4.5% Hispanic of any race;

Average household size: 2.31; Median age: 43.5; Age under 18: 19.4%; Age 65 and over: 21.6%; Males per 100 females: 106.2
Housing: Homeownership rate: 77.6%; Homeowner vacancy rate: 4.2%; Rental vacancy rate: 93.8%

Davidson County

Located in central North Carolina; piedmont area, bounded on the west by the Yadkin River. Covers a land area of 552.675 square miles, a water area of 14.343 square miles, and is located in the Eastern Time Zone at 35.80° N. Lat., 80.21° W. Long. The county was founded in 1822. County seat is Lexington.

Davidson County is part of the Winston-Salem, NC Metropolitan Statistical Area. The entire metro area includes: Davidson County, NC; Davie County, NC; Forsyth County, NC; Stokes County, NC; Yadkin County, NC

Weather Station: Lexington   Elevation: 759 feet

	Jan	Feb	Mar	Apr	May	Jun	Jul	Aug	Sep	Oct	Nov	Dec
High	50	55	63	73	80	86	89	88	82	72	62	53
Low	28	31	37	45	54	63	67	66	59	47	38	30
Precip	3.6	3.6	4.1	3.8	3.2	4.1	4.0	4.0	3.9	3.3	3.5	3.2
Snow	2.4	1.4	0.7	tr	0.0	0.0	0.0	0.0	0.0	0.0	tr	0.4

High and Low temperatures in degrees Fahrenheit; Precipitation and Snow in inches

Population: 162,878; Growth (since 2000): 10.6%; Density: 294.7 persons per square mile; Race: 84.3% White, 8.9% Black/African American, 1.2% Asian, 0.5% American Indian/Alaska Native, 0.0% Native Hawaiian/Other Pacific Islander, 1.5% two or more races, 6.4% Hispanic of any race; Average household size: 2.50; Median age: 40.3; Age under 18: 23.9%; Age 65 and over: 14.4%; Males per 100 females: 96.0; Marriage status: 24.0% never married, 57.1% now married, 3.0% separated, 6.9% widowed, 12.0% divorced; Foreign born: 4.6%; Speak English only: 92.4%; With disability: 15.8%; Veterans: 9.4%; Ancestry: 16.5% German, 12.4% American, 9.2% Irish, 9.2% English, 2.3% Scottish
Religion: Six largest groups: 12.8% Methodist/Pietist, 12.5% Baptist, 4.8% Non-denominational Protestant, 3.5% Presbyterian-Reformed, 1.7% Holiness, 1.5% Lutheran
Economy: Unemployment rate: 5.7%; Leading industries: 16.8% retail trade; 12.0% other services (except public administration); 11.5% construction; Farms: 1,062 totaling 87,310 acres; Company size: 1 employs 1,000 or more persons, 4 employ 500 to 999 persons, 51 employs 100 to 499 persons, 2,720 employ less than 100 persons; Business ownership: 3,417 women-owned, 433 Black-owned, n/a Hispanic-owned, n/a Asian-owned
Employment: 10.4% management, business, and financial, 3.1% computer, engineering, and science, 8.8% education, legal, community service, arts, and media, 5.5% healthcare practitioners, 16.1% service, 25.2% sales and office, 10.1% natural resources, construction, and maintenance, 20.6% production, transportation, and material moving
Income: Per capita: $22,549; Median household: $43,083; Average household: $55,811; Households with income of $100,000 or more: 12.9%; Poverty rate: 16.3%
Educational Attainment: High school diploma or higher: 80.4%; Bachelor's degree or higher: 17.6%; Graduate/professional degree or higher: 5.0%
Housing: Homeownership rate: 72.5%; Median home value: $134,000; Median year structure built: 1982; Homeowner vacancy rate: 2.3%; Median gross rent: $637 per month; Rental vacancy rate: 13.2%
Vital Statistics: Birth rate: 104.5 per 10,000 population; Death rate: 98.5 per 10,000 population; Age-adjusted cancer mortality rate: 183.1 deaths per 100,000 population
Health Insurance: 84.6% have insurance; 62.2% have private insurance; 34.2% have public insurance; 15.4% do not have insurance; 5.5% of children under 18 do not have insurance
Health Care: Physicians: 5.6 per 10,000 population; Hospital beds: 10.4 per 10,000 population; Hospital admissions: 469.0 per 10,000 population
Air Quality Index: 72.8% good, 27.2% moderate, 0.0% unhealthy for sensitive individuals, 0.0% unhealthy (percent of days)
Transportation: Commute: 95.5% car, 0.2% public transportation, 1.1% walk, 2.4% work from home; Median travel time to work: 23.7 minutes
Presidential Election: 29.1% Obama, 69.6% Romney (2012)
National and State Parks: Daniel Boone State Park
Additional Information Contacts
Davidson Government . . . . (336) 242-2000
  http://www.co.davidson.nc.us

Davidson County Communities

DENTON (town). Covers a land area of 1.979 square miles and a water area of 0.006 square miles. Located at 35.64° N. Lat; 80.11° W. Long. Elevation is 699 feet.
Population: 1,636; Growth (since 2000): 12.8%; Density: 826.5 persons per square mile; Race: 98.4% White, 0.1% Black/African American, 0.0% Asian, 0.1% American Indian/Alaska Native, 0.0% Native Hawaiian/Other Pacific Islander, 1.0% Two or more races, 1.0% Hispanic of any race; Average household size: 2.41; Median age: 39.8; Age under 18: 23.5%; Age 65 and over: 14.7%; Males per 100 females: 91.8

School District(s)
Davidson County Schools (PK-12)
    2012-13 Enrollment: 20,259 . . . . (336) 249-8181
Housing: Homeownership rate: 61.0%; Homeowner vacancy rate: 3.5%; Rental vacancy rate: 14.0%
Newspapers: Denton Orator (weekly circulation 2800)

LEXINGTON (city). County seat. Covers a land area of 17.978 square miles and a water area of 0 square miles. Located at 35.80° N. Lat; 80.27° W. Long. Elevation is 807 feet.
History: Lexington was settled in 1775 and later named for the Revolutionary battle site. Lexington became the county seat in 1824.
Population: 18,931; Growth (since 2000): -5.1%; Density: 1,053.0 persons per square mile; Race: 54.7% White, 28.4% Black/African American, 2.9% Asian, 0.7% American Indian/Alaska Native, 0.0% Native Hawaiian/Other Pacific Islander, 2.6% Two or more races, 16.3% Hispanic of any race; Average household size: 2.44; Median age: 37.4; Age under 18: 24.6%; Age 65 and over: 15.1%; Males per 100 females: 92.8; Marriage status: 32.0% never married, 46.8% now married, 5.6% separated, 7.7% widowed, 13.6% divorced; Foreign born: 9.9%; Speak English only: 81.5%; With disability: 20.3%; Veterans: 8.8%; Ancestry: 11.3% German, 8.5% Irish, 7.9% English, 6.6% American, 1.6% Scotch-Irish
Employment: 5.2% management, business, and financial, 2.0% computer, engineering, and science, 8.5% education, legal, community service, arts, and media, 2.6% healthcare practitioners, 23.4% service, 19.8% sales and office, 8.8% natural resources, construction, and maintenance, 29.6% production, transportation, and material moving
Income: Per capita: $16,330; Median household: $28,793; Average household: $40,105; Households with income of $100,000 or more: 5.1%; Poverty rate: 26.5%
Educational Attainment: High school diploma or higher: 70.7%; Bachelor's degree or higher: 12.2%; Graduate/professional degree or higher: 4.0%

School District(s)
Davidson County Schools (PK-12)
    2012-13 Enrollment: 20,259 . . . . (336) 249-8181
Lexington City Schools (PK-12)
    2012-13 Enrollment: 3,203 . . . . (336) 242-1527
Housing: Homeownership rate: 47.6%; Median home value: $100,300; Median year structure built: 1964; Homeowner vacancy rate: 4.7%; Median gross rent: $635 per month; Rental vacancy rate: 18.8%
Health Insurance: 77.6% have insurance; 39.7% have private insurance; 48.4% have public insurance; 22.4% do not have insurance; 5.8% of children under 18 do not have insurance
Hospitals: Lexington Memorial Hospital (94 beds)
Safety: Violent crime rate: 44.9 per 10,000 population; Property crime rate: 335.8 per 10,000 population
Newspapers: The Dispatch (daily circulation 10700)
Transportation: Commute: 93.5% car, 0.9% public transportation, 3.2% walk, 1.2% work from home; Median travel time to work: 22.7 minutes; Amtrak: Train service available.
Airports: Davidson County (general aviation)
Additional Information Contacts
City of Lexington . . . . (336) 243-2489
    http://www.lexingtonnc.net

LINWOOD (unincorporated postal area)
ZCTA: 27299
    Covers a land area of 27.523 square miles and a water area of 1.533 square miles. Located at 35.75° N. Lat; 80.39° W. Long. Elevation is 656 feet.
    Population: 5,190; Growth (since 2000): 24.9%; Density: 188.6 persons per square mile; Race: 91.2% White, 2.3% Black/African American,

0.8% Asian, 0.6% American Indian/Alaska Native, 0.0% Native Hawaiian/Other Pacific Islander, 1.4% Two or more races, 6.9% Hispanic of any race; Average household size: 2.67; Median age: 36.5; Age under 18: 26.8%; Age 65 and over: 10.0%; Males per 100 females: 101.6; Marriage status: 21.7% never married, 59.7% now married, 2.4% separated, 5.3% widowed, 13.2% divorced; Foreign born: 2.3%; Speak English only: 94.2%; With disability: 19.0%; Veterans: 9.5%; Ancestry: 18.7% German, 15.6% Irish, 10.3% American, 3.5% English, 2.6% Dutch
Employment: 5.6% management, business, and financial, 0.4% computer, engineering, and science, 1.6% education, legal, community service, arts, and media, 4.1% healthcare practitioners, 23.5% service, 21.9% sales and office, 13.2% natural resources, construction, and maintenance, 29.6% production, transportation, and material moving
Income: Per capita: $18,531; Median household: $41,875; Average household: $45,752; Households with income of $100,000 or more: 2.9%; Poverty rate: 9.4%
Educational Attainment: High school diploma or higher: 79.3%; Bachelor's degree or higher: 7.0%; Graduate/professional degree or higher: 0.3%
Housing: Homeownership rate: 74.2%; Median home value: $109,100; Median year structure built: 1991; Homeowner vacancy rate: 3.0%; Median gross rent: $606 per month; Rental vacancy rate: 16.9%
Health Insurance: 77.2% have insurance; 52.7% have private insurance; 33.2% have public insurance; 22.8% do not have insurance; 2.9% of children under 18 do not have insurance
Transportation: Commute: 92.3% car, 1.1% public transportation, 0.4% walk, 4.6% work from home; Median travel time to work: 25.6 minutes

MIDWAY (town). Covers a land area of 7.668 square miles and a water area of 0 square miles. Located at 35.97° N. Lat; 80.22° W. Long. Elevation is 902 feet.
Population: 4,679; Growth (since 2000): n/a; Density: 610.2 persons per square mile; Race: 88.2% White, 8.2% Black/African American, 0.5% Asian, 0.4% American Indian/Alaska Native, 0.1% Native Hawaiian/Other Pacific Islander, 0.9% Two or more races, 3.5% Hispanic of any race; Average household size: 2.51; Median age: 42.5; Age under 18: 21.9%; Age 65 and over: 16.1%; Males per 100 females: 97.5; Marriage status: 19.4% never married, 63.4% now married, 3.2% separated, 8.3% widowed, 8.8% divorced; Foreign born: 0.6%; Speak English only: 99.3%; With disability: 14.8%; Veterans: 11.0%; Ancestry: 28.8% German, 18.3% Irish, 11.6% American, 10.8% English, 4.7% Dutch
Employment: 14.0% management, business, and financial, 4.6% computer, engineering, and science, 7.6% education, legal, community service, arts, and media, 8.2% healthcare practitioners, 16.0% service, 31.6% sales and office, 9.4% natural resources, construction, and maintenance, 8.6% production, transportation, and material moving
Income: Per capita: $26,537; Median household: $45,313; Average household: $59,774; Households with income of $100,000 or more: 13.9%; Poverty rate: 10.3%
Educational Attainment: High school diploma or higher: 83.5%; Bachelor's degree or higher: 20.9%; Graduate/professional degree or higher: 8.3%
Housing: Homeownership rate: 82.7%; Median home value: $160,800; Median year structure built: 1983; Homeowner vacancy rate: 1.1%; Median gross rent: $566 per month; Rental vacancy rate: 9.0%
Health Insurance: 92.4% have insurance; 77.5% have private insurance; 32.5% have public insurance; 7.6% do not have insurance; 1.3% of children under 18 do not have insurance
Transportation: Commute: 95.1% car, 0.0% public transportation, 0.0% walk, 3.3% work from home; Median travel time to work: 21.3 minutes

SOUTHMONT (CDP). Covers a land area of 4.561 square miles and a water area of 0.010 square miles. Located at 35.65° N. Lat; 80.27° W. Long. Elevation is 679 feet.
Population: 1,470; Growth (since 2000): n/a; Density: 322.3 persons per square mile; Race: 92.5% White, 4.0% Black/African American, 0.4% Asian, 0.4% American Indian/Alaska Native, 0.1% Native Hawaiian/Other Pacific Islander, 1.8% Two or more races, 1.8% Hispanic of any race; Average household size: 2.48; Median age: 43.2; Age under 18: 22.3%; Age 65 and over: 14.1%; Males per 100 females: 107.0
Housing: Homeownership rate: 83.5%; Homeowner vacancy rate: 3.8%; Rental vacancy rate: 6.7%

THOMASVILLE (city). Covers a land area of 16.767 square miles and a water area of 0.012 square miles. Located at 35.88° N. Lat; 80.08° W. Long. Elevation is 850 feet.

History: North Carolina Vietnam Veterans Memorial. The Big Chair, 18 foot symbol of town's furniture industry. Incorporated 1854.

Population: 26,757; Growth (since 2000): 35.2%; Density: 1,595.8 persons per square mile; Race: 68.3% White, 19.6% Black/African American, 1.1% Asian, 0.7% American Indian/Alaska Native, 0.0% Native Hawaiian/Other Pacific Islander, 2.1% Two or more races, 14.4% Hispanic of any race; Average household size: 2.50; Median age: 36.2; Age under 18: 26.5%; Age 65 and over: 13.9%; Males per 100 females: 91.2; Marriage status: 30.2% never married, 44.6% now married, 2.9% separated, 9.6% widowed, 15.5% divorced; Foreign born: 8.4%; Speak English only: 85.6%; With disability: 14.7%; Veterans: 8.7%; Ancestry: 9.2% German, 8.7% American, 7.6% English, 7.5% Irish, 1.7% Scottish

Employment: 5.0% management, business, and financial, 3.1% computer, engineering, and science, 7.4% education, legal, community service, arts, and media, 4.4% healthcare practitioners, 18.0% service, 28.9% sales and office, 5.9% natural resources, construction, and maintenance, 27.3% production, transportation, and material moving

Income: Per capita: $17,382; Median household: $33,560; Average household: $43,132; Households with income of $100,000 or more: 5.7%; Poverty rate: 27.8%

Educational Attainment: High school diploma or higher: 78.3%; Bachelor's degree or higher: 13.2%; Graduate/professional degree or higher: 2.7%

School District(s)
Davidson County Schools (PK-12)
    2012-13 Enrollment: 20,259 . . . . (336) 249-8181
Thomasville City Schools (PK-12)
    2012-13 Enrollment: 2,526 . . . . (336) 474-4200

Two-year College(s)
Davidson County Community College (Public)
    Fall 2013 Enrollment: 4,073 . . . . (336) 249-8186
    2013-14 Tuition: In-state $1,866; Out-of-state $6,474

Housing: Homeownership rate: 57.8%; Median home value: $105,100; Median year structure built: 1976; Homeowner vacancy rate: 3.3%; Median gross rent: $593 per month; Rental vacancy rate: 13.0%

Health Insurance: 81.2% have insurance; 53.3% have private insurance; 39.5% have public insurance; 18.8% do not have insurance; 4.6% of children under 18 do not have insurance

Hospitals: Novant Health Thomasville Medical Center (81 beds)

Safety: Violent crime rate: 43.5 per 10,000 population; Property crime rate: 408.0 per 10,000 population

Transportation: Commute: 94.6% car, 0.1% public transportation, 2.2% walk, 2.0% work from home; Median travel time to work: 20.1 minutes

Additional Information Contacts
City of Thomasville . . . . (229) 227-7001
    http://www.ci.thomasville.nc.us

TYRO (CDP). Covers a land area of 12.850 square miles and a water area of 0 square miles. Located at 35.80° N. Lat; 80.38° W. Long. Elevation is 823 feet.

Population: 3,879; Growth (since 2000): n/a; Density: 301.9 persons per square mile; Race: 93.5% White, 1.5% Black/African American, 0.5% Asian, 0.5% American Indian/Alaska Native, 0.0% Native Hawaiian/Other Pacific Islander, 1.4% Two or more races, 4.6% Hispanic of any race; Average household size: 2.68; Median age: 37.6; Age under 18: 26.5%; Age 65 and over: 10.6%; Males per 100 females: 104.8; Marriage status: 26.3% never married, 57.6% now married, 1.9% separated, 2.6% widowed, 13.5% divorced; Foreign born: 6.7%; Speak English only: 87.4%; With disability: 12.9%; Veterans: 10.6%; Ancestry: 14.8% American, 13.2% German, 8.3% Irish, 7.8% English, 3.0% Russian

Employment: 3.4% management, business, and financial, 0.0% computer, engineering, and science, 5.4% education, legal, community service, arts, and media, 3.7% healthcare practitioners, 21.9% service, 30.8% sales and office, 17.7% natural resources, construction, and maintenance, 17.1% production, transportation, and material moving

Income: Per capita: $18,545; Median household: $46,034; Average household: $46,828; Households with income of $100,000 or more: 7.4%; Poverty rate: 12.6%

Educational Attainment: High school diploma or higher: 80.6%; Bachelor's degree or higher: 11.2%; Graduate/professional degree or higher: 1.5%

Housing: Homeownership rate: 77.3%; Median home value: $142,100; Median year structure built: 1984; Homeowner vacancy rate: 2.2%; Median gross rent: $633 per month; Rental vacancy rate: 12.2%

Health Insurance: 73.5% have insurance; 46.5% have private insurance; 34.5% have public insurance; 26.5% do not have insurance; 13.6% of children under 18 do not have insurance

Transportation: Commute: 95.2% car, 0.0% public transportation, 0.0% walk, 3.9% work from home; Median travel time to work: 23.2 minutes

WALLBURG (town). Covers a land area of 5.576 square miles and a water area of 0 square miles. Located at 36.01° N. Lat; 80.17° W. Long. Elevation is 919 feet.

Population: 3,047; Growth (since 2000): n/a; Density: 546.5 persons per square mile; Race: 94.9% White, 0.9% Black/African American, 0.8% Asian, 0.5% American Indian/Alaska Native, 0.0% Native Hawaiian/Other Pacific Islander, 1.1% Two or more races, 3.1% Hispanic of any race; Average household size: 2.66; Median age: 41.5; Age under 18: 24.6%; Age 65 and over: 13.4%; Males per 100 females: 100.5; Marriage status: 18.8% never married, 70.3% now married, 4.3% separated, 4.9% widowed, 5.9% divorced; Foreign born: 1.5%; Speak English only: 98.6%; With disability: 14.0%; Veterans: 9.5%; Ancestry: 26.5% German, 14.6% American, 13.3% Irish, 10.7% English, 4.8% Dutch

Employment: 8.7% management, business, and financial, 4.8% computer, engineering, and science, 9.7% education, legal, community service, arts, and media, 8.7% healthcare practitioners, 11.2% service, 30.7% sales and office, 10.9% natural resources, construction, and maintenance, 15.3% production, transportation, and material moving

Income: Per capita: $26,972; Median household: $61,447; Average household: $65,277; Households with income of $100,000 or more: 14.9%; Poverty rate: 7.3%

Educational Attainment: High school diploma or higher: 87.8%; Bachelor's degree or higher: 16.2%; Graduate/professional degree or higher: 3.0%

Housing: Homeownership rate: 87.5%; Median home value: $161,500; Median year structure built: 1981; Homeowner vacancy rate: 1.1%; Median gross rent: $465 per month; Rental vacancy rate: 7.7%

Health Insurance: 91.5% have insurance; 82.9% have private insurance; 21.1% have public insurance; 8.5% do not have insurance; 5.2% of children under 18 do not have insurance

Transportation: Commute: 98.9% car, 0.0% public transportation, 0.0% walk, 1.1% work from home; Median travel time to work: 23.3 minutes

WELCOME (CDP). Covers a land area of 9.313 square miles and a water area of 0 square miles. Located at 35.91° N. Lat; 80.25° W. Long. Elevation is 866 feet.

Population: 4,162; Growth (since 2000): 17.6%; Density: 446.9 persons per square mile; Race: 92.2% White, 3.7% Black/African American, 1.4% Asian, 0.2% American Indian/Alaska Native, 0.0% Native Hawaiian/Other Pacific Islander, 1.1% Two or more races, 3.6% Hispanic of any race; Average household size: 2.43; Median age: 41.7; Age under 18: 22.7%; Age 65 and over: 15.0%; Males per 100 females: 93.5; Marriage status: 22.4% never married, 61.2% now married, 1.9% separated, 7.1% widowed, 9.4% divorced; Foreign born: 5.9%; Speak English only: 89.6%; With disability: 11.2%; Veterans: 7.5%; Ancestry: 19.5% German, 17.1% American, 8.2% Irish, 7.4% English, 3.7% Scotch-Irish

Employment: 7.1% management, business, and financial, 5.6% computer, engineering, and science, 9.5% education, legal, community service, arts, and media, 5.1% healthcare practitioners, 15.8% service, 19.9% sales and office, 14.6% natural resources, construction, and maintenance, 22.3% production, transportation, and material moving

Income: Per capita: $27,028; Median household: $50,500; Average household: $71,670; Households with income of $100,000 or more: 20.7%; Poverty rate: 11.2%

Educational Attainment: High school diploma or higher: 85.2%; Bachelor's degree or higher: 16.4%; Graduate/professional degree or higher: 2.3%

Housing: Homeownership rate: 74.3%; Median home value: $146,200; Median year structure built: 1982; Homeowner vacancy rate: 1.6%; Median gross rent: $681 per month; Rental vacancy rate: 11.0%

Health Insurance: 80.6% have insurance; 63.5% have private insurance; 30.0% have public insurance; 19.4% do not have insurance; 15.2% of children under 18 do not have insurance

Transportation: Commute: 94.6% car, 0.0% public transportation, 3.7% walk, 1.7% work from home; Median travel time to work: 25.4 minutes

Davie County

Located in central North Carolina; in piedmont area, bounded on the east by the Yadkin River, and on the southwest by the South Yadkin River. Covers a land area of 264.105 square miles, a water area of 2.983 square miles, and is located in the Eastern Time Zone at 35.93° N. Lat., 80.54° W. Long. The county was founded in 1836. County seat is Mocksville.

Davie County is part of the Winston-Salem, NC Metropolitan Statistical Area. The entire metro area includes: Davidson County, NC; Davie County, NC; Forsyth County, NC; Stokes County, NC; Yadkin County, NC

Weather Station: Mocksville 5 SE — Elevation: 801 feet

	Jan	Feb	Mar	Apr	May	Jun	Jul	Aug	Sep	Oct	Nov	Dec
High	51	55	63	72	79	86	89	88	82	72	63	53
Low	26	28	35	43	52	61	65	64	57	45	36	28
Precip	3.3	3.3	4.1	3.7	3.4	4.0	4.0	3.8	3.8	3.6	3.2	3.5
Snow	1.8	1.5	0.7	tr	0.0	0.0	0.0	0.0	0.0	0.0	0.1	0.6

High and Low temperatures in degrees Fahrenheit; Precipitation and Snow in inches

Population: 41,240; Growth (since 2000): 18.4%; Density: 156.1 persons per square mile; Race: 87.5% White, 6.3% Black/African American, 0.6% Asian, 0.4% American Indian/Alaska Native, 0.0% Native Hawaiian/Other Pacific Islander, 1.7% two or more races, 6.1% Hispanic of any race; Average household size: 2.52; Median age: 42.5; Age under 18: 23.6%; Age 65 and over: 16.6%; Males per 100 females: 95.4; Marriage status: 21.1% never married, 61.3% now married, 2.0% separated, 7.4% widowed, 10.1% divorced; Foreign born: 4.2%; Speak English only: 92.6%; With disability: 13.3%; Veterans: 10.8%; Ancestry: 22.5% American, 13.2% German, 12.4% English, 8.6% Irish, 3.4% Scotch-Irish
Religion: Six largest groups: 18.9% Methodist/Pietist, 15.0% Baptist, 8.1% Non-denominational Protestant, 2.6% Catholicism, 2.5% Presbyterian-Reformed, 1.8% Pentecostal
Economy: Unemployment rate: 4.7%; Leading industries: 14.1% retail trade; 13.9% construction; 11.4% other services (except public administration); Farms: 640 totaling 59,618 acres; Company size: 0 employ 1,000 or more persons, 0 employ 500 to 999 persons, 9 employ 100 to 499 persons, 783 employ less than 100 persons; Business ownership: 1,060 women-owned, n/a Black-owned, n/a Hispanic-owned, n/a Asian-owned
Employment: 13.3% management, business, and financial, 3.1% computer, engineering, and science, 10.7% education, legal, community service, arts, and media, 7.2% healthcare practitioners, 15.7% service, 24.3% sales and office, 9.2% natural resources, construction, and maintenance, 16.6% production, transportation, and material moving
Income: Per capita: $26,319; Median household: $50,139; Average household: $65,969; Households with income of $100,000 or more: 18.0%; Poverty rate: 13.4%
Educational Attainment: High school diploma or higher: 85.4%; Bachelor's degree or higher: 24.9%; Graduate/professional degree or higher: 8.5%
Housing: Homeownership rate: 81.2%; Median home value: $162,100; Median year structure built: 1986; Homeowner vacancy rate: 2.7%; Median gross rent: $682 per month; Rental vacancy rate: 11.6%
Vital Statistics: Birth rate: 90.5 per 10,000 population; Death rate: 83.5 per 10,000 population; Age-adjusted cancer mortality rate: 164.2 deaths per 100,000 population
Health Insurance: 87.1% have insurance; 69.1% have private insurance; 32.0% have public insurance; 12.9% do not have insurance; 7.6% of children under 18 do not have insurance
Health Care: Physicians: 13.8 per 10,000 population; Hospital beds: 6.0 per 10,000 population; Hospital admissions: 68.9 per 10,000 population
Air Quality Index: 97.7% good, 2.3% moderate, 0.0% unhealthy for sensitive individuals, 0.0% unhealthy (percent of days)
Transportation: Commute: 93.9% car, 0.5% public transportation, 0.9% walk, 3.9% work from home; Median travel time to work: 25.9 minutes
Presidential Election: 27.7% Obama, 71.1% Romney (2012)
Additional Information Contacts
Davie Government . . . . (336) 751-5513
    http://www.co.davie.nc.us

Davie County Communities

ADVANCE (CDP). Covers a land area of 7.161 square miles and a water area of 0.069 square miles. Located at 35.95° N. Lat; 80.39° W. Long. Elevation is 823 feet.
Population: 1,138; Growth (since 2000): n/a; Density: 158.9 persons per square mile; Race: 94.5% White, 2.2% Black/African American, 0.1% Asian, 0.9% American Indian/Alaska Native, 0.0% Native Hawaiian/Other Pacific Islander, 2.0% Two or more races, 1.9% Hispanic of any race; Average household size: 2.47; Median age: 45.3; Age under 18: 22.2%; Age 65 and over: 16.4%; Males per 100 females: 105.4
School District(s)
Davie County Schools (PK-12)
    2012-13 Enrollment: 6,676 . . . . (336) 751-5921
Housing: Homeownership rate: 82.0%; Homeowner vacancy rate: 3.5%; Rental vacancy rate: 10.8%

BERMUDA RUN (town). Covers a land area of 1.654 square miles and a water area of 0.052 square miles. Located at 36.00° N. Lat; 80.42° W. Long. Elevation is 804 feet.
Population: 1,725; Growth (since 2000): 20.5%; Density: 1,042.9 persons per square mile; Race: 95.7% White, 1.7% Black/African American, 1.3% Asian, 0.2% American Indian/Alaska Native, 0.1% Native Hawaiian/Other Pacific Islander, 1.0% Two or more races, 0.8% Hispanic of any race; Average household size: 1.92; Median age: 65.1; Age under 18: 8.6%; Age 65 and over: 50.3%; Males per 100 females: 82.9
Housing: Homeownership rate: 92.6%; Homeowner vacancy rate: 9.2%; Rental vacancy rate: 10.8%

COOLEEMEE (town). Covers a land area of 0.756 square miles and a water area of 0.019 square miles. Located at 35.81° N. Lat; 80.56° W. Long. Elevation is 715 feet.
Population: 960; Growth (since 2000): 6.1%; Density: 1,269.4 persons per square mile; Race: 81.3% White, 8.3% Black/African American, 0.2% Asian, 0.8% American Indian/Alaska Native, 0.0% Native Hawaiian/Other Pacific Islander, 3.3% Two or more races, 7.7% Hispanic of any race; Average household size: 2.58; Median age: 39.5; Age under 18: 26.0%; Age 65 and over: 14.8%; Males per 100 females: 90.1
School District(s)
Davie County Schools (PK-12)
    2012-13 Enrollment: 6,676 . . . . (336) 751-5921
Housing: Homeownership rate: 72.0%; Homeowner vacancy rate: 4.5%; Rental vacancy rate: 21.3%

MOCKSVILLE (town). County seat. Covers a land area of 7.536 square miles and a water area of 0.013 square miles. Located at 35.90° N. Lat; 80.56° W. Long. Elevation is 860 feet.
History: The region around Mocksville was settled between 1740 and 1750 by Scottish, Irish, and English settlers, and sometime later by Germans from the neighboring Moravian Wachovia.
Population: 5,051; Growth (since 2000): 20.9%; Density: 670.2 persons per square mile; Race: 73.9% White, 14.6% Black/African American, 0.8% Asian, 0.6% American Indian/Alaska Native, 0.0% Native Hawaiian/Other Pacific Islander, 3.4% Two or more races, 12.0% Hispanic of any race; Average household size: 2.48; Median age: 39.4; Age under 18: 24.9%; Age 65 and over: 18.3%; Males per 100 females: 82.3; Marriage status: 34.1% never married, 46.7% now married, 3.7% separated, 7.9% widowed, 11.3% divorced; Foreign born: 7.1%; Speak English only: 90.4%; With disability: 18.1%; Veterans: 7.7%; Ancestry: 14.4% American, 14.0% German, 13.4% English, 5.7% Irish, 4.3% Scottish
Employment: 8.3% management, business, and financial, 4.7% computer, engineering, and science, 12.0% education, legal, community service, arts, and media, 4.3% healthcare practitioners, 25.2% service, 23.7% sales and office, 4.9% natural resources, construction, and maintenance, 16.9% production, transportation, and material moving
Income: Per capita: $21,807; Median household: $40,553; Average household: $52,428; Households with income of $100,000 or more: 12.6%; Poverty rate: 18.7%
Educational Attainment: High school diploma or higher: 78.9%; Bachelor's degree or higher: 23.4%; Graduate/professional degree or higher: 7.4%
School District(s)
Davie County Schools (PK-12)
    2012-13 Enrollment: 6,676 . . . . (336) 751-5921

Housing: Homeownership rate: 66.3%; Median home value: $144,500; Median year structure built: 1987; Homeowner vacancy rate: 3.9%; Median gross rent: $617 per month; Rental vacancy rate: 10.2%
Health Insurance: 85.5% have insurance; 60.3% have private insurance; 39.6% have public insurance; 14.5% do not have insurance; 2.7% of children under 18 do not have insurance
Hospitals: Davie County Hospital (81 beds)
Safety: Violent crime rate: 21.6 per 10,000 population; Property crime rate: 435.6 per 10,000 population
Newspapers: Davie County Enterprise (weekly circulation 9100)
Transportation: Commute: 93.6% car, 0.0% public transportation, 2.3% walk, 3.3% work from home; Median travel time to work: 22.4 minutes
Additional Information Contacts
Town of Mocksville . . . . (336) 753-6700
  http://www.mocksville.org

Duplin County

Located in eastern North Carolina; partly swampy coastal plain area, drained by the Northeast Cape Fear River. Covers a land area of 816.219 square miles, a water area of 5.455 square miles, and is located in the Eastern Time Zone at 34.93° N. Lat., 77.93° W. Long. The county was founded in 1749. County seat is Kenansville.

Weather Station: Warsaw 5 E											Elevation: 109 feet	
	Jan	Feb	Mar	Apr	May	Jun	Jul	Aug	Sep	Oct	Nov	Dec
High	55	58	66	74	81	88	91	89	84	75	66	57
Low	33	35	40	48	56	65	69	68	62	51	43	34
Precip	3.3	3.1	3.9	3.1	3.7	4.3	6.4	5.7	5.4	3.5	3.2	3.3
Snow	1.1	0.4	0.0	0.0	0.0	0.0	0.0	0.0	0.0	0.0	0.0	0.7

High and Low temperatures in degrees Fahrenheit; Precipitation and Snow in inches

Population: 58,505; Growth (since 2000): 19.2%; Density: 71.7 persons per square mile; Race: 57.2% White, 25.3% Black/African American, 0.3% Asian, 0.5% American Indian/Alaska Native, 0.1% Native Hawaiian/Other Pacific Islander, 1.6% two or more races, 20.6% Hispanic of any race; Average household size: 2.57; Median age: 37.8; Age under 18: 25.4%; Age 65 and over: 14.2%; Males per 100 females: 96.7; Marriage status: 31.0% never married, 51.4% now married, 3.7% separated, 7.8% widowed, 9.8% divorced; Foreign born: 12.7%; Speak English only: 81.0%; With disability: 16.2%; Veterans: 9.4%; Ancestry: 12.5% American, 7.1% Irish, 7.0% English, 4.4% German, 2.0% Scottish
Religion: Six largest groups: 15.9% Baptist, 7.3% Methodist/Pietist, 2.9% Presbyterian-Reformed, 2.6% Pentecostal, 1.8% Non-denominational Protestant, 0.5% Catholicism
Economy: Unemployment rate: 6.0%; Leading industries: 21.2% retail trade; 12.5% other services (except public administration); 12.4% health care and social assistance; Farms: 940 totaling 230,925 acres; Company size: 1 employs 1,000 or more persons, 3 employ 500 to 999 persons, 11 employs 100 to 499 persons, 831 employs less than 100 persons; Business ownership: 1,053 women-owned, 453 Black-owned, 115 Hispanic-owned, n/a Asian-owned
Employment: 8.9% management, business, and financial, 2.1% computer, engineering, and science, 8.7% education, legal, community service, arts, and media, 4.3% healthcare practitioners, 16.8% service, 16.9% sales and office, 20.0% natural resources, construction, and maintenance, 22.2% production, transportation, and material moving
Income: Per capita: $17,122; Median household: $34,433; Average household: $45,057; Households with income of $100,000 or more: 6.3%; Poverty rate: 26.3%
Educational Attainment: High school diploma or higher: 71.4%; Bachelor's degree or higher: 10.4%; Graduate/professional degree or higher: 3.1%
Housing: Homeownership rate: 69.1%; Median home value: $87,600; Median year structure built: 1982; Homeowner vacancy rate: 1.7%; Median gross rent: $586 per month; Rental vacancy rate: 10.7%
Vital Statistics: Birth rate: 128.7 per 10,000 population; Death rate: 83.5 per 10,000 population; Age-adjusted cancer mortality rate: 155.0 deaths per 100,000 population
Health Insurance: 76.0% have insurance; 50.1% have private insurance; 37.9% have public insurance; 24.0% do not have insurance; 10.9% of children under 18 do not have insurance
Health Care: Physicians: 4.7 per 10,000 population; Hospital beds: 12.4 per 10,000 population; Hospital admissions: 556.9 per 10,000 population

Air Quality Index: 76.6% good, 23.4% moderate, 0.0% unhealthy for sensitive individuals, 0.0% unhealthy (percent of days)
Transportation: Commute: 94.1% car, 0.2% public transportation, 2.3% walk, 2.5% work from home; Median travel time to work: 23.8 minutes
Presidential Election: 43.8% Obama, 55.6% Romney (2012)
Additional Information Contacts
Duplin Government . . . . (910) 296-2104
  http://www.duplincountync.com

Duplin County Communities

ALBERTSON (unincorporated postal area)
ZCTA: 28508
  Covers a land area of 35.311 square miles and a water area of 0.236 square miles. Located at 35.10° N. Lat; 77.82° W. Long. Elevation is 144 feet.
  Population: 2,737; Growth (since 2000): 54.5%; Density: 77.5 persons per square mile; Race: 58.0% White, 4.3% Black/African American, 0.1% Asian, 0.3% American Indian/Alaska Native, 0.0% Native Hawaiian/Other Pacific Islander, 1.9% Two or more races, 46.3% Hispanic of any race; Average household size: 3.06; Median age: 29.3; Age under 18: 32.2%; Age 65 and over: 8.5%; Males per 100 females: 104.9; Marriage status: 34.7% never married, 48.8% now married, 3.9% separated, 7.6% widowed, 8.9% divorced; Foreign born: 19.0%; Speak English only: 67.7%; With disability: 8.9%; Veterans: 11.0%; Ancestry: 18.1% Irish, 11.1% German, 8.4% American, 4.9% Scottish, 3.5% English
  Employment: 5.8% management, business, and financial, 0.0% computer, engineering, and science, 11.5% education, legal, community service, arts, and media, 4.2% healthcare practitioners, 18.6% service, 10.6% sales and office, 14.4% natural resources, construction, and maintenance, 34.9% production, transportation, and material moving
  Income: Per capita: $18,884; Median household: $47,713; Average household: $56,146; Households with income of $100,000 or more: 9.7%; Poverty rate: 32.9%
  Educational Attainment: High school diploma or higher: 73.8%; Bachelor's degree or higher: 14.8%; Graduate/professional degree or higher: 5.1%
School District(s)
Duplin County Schools (PK-12)
  2012-13 Enrollment: 9,514 . . . . (910) 296-1521
  Housing: Homeownership rate: 75.0%; Median home value: $75,100; Median year structure built: 1984; Homeowner vacancy rate: 1.3%; Median gross rent: $626 per month; Rental vacancy rate: 15.2%
  Health Insurance: 66.8% have insurance; 48.9% have private insurance; 27.8% have public insurance; 33.2% do not have insurance; 19.0% of children under 18 do not have insurance
  Transportation: Commute: 95.5% car, 0.0% public transportation, 2.9% walk, 1.6% work from home; Median travel time to work: 28.6 minutes

BEULAVILLE (town). Covers a land area of 1.518 square miles and a water area of 0.001 square miles. Located at 34.92° N. Lat; 77.77° W. Long. Elevation is 85 feet.
Population: 1,296; Growth (since 2000): 21.5%; Density: 853.7 persons per square mile; Race: 69.7% White, 23.3% Black/African American, 0.5% Asian, 0.2% American Indian/Alaska Native, 0.1% Native Hawaiian/Other Pacific Islander, 1.3% Two or more races, 6.5% Hispanic of any race; Average household size: 2.14; Median age: 45.2; Age under 18: 20.9%; Age 65 and over: 24.4%; Males per 100 females: 73.7
School District(s)
Duplin County Schools (PK-12)
  2012-13 Enrollment: 9,514 . . . . (910) 296-1521
Housing: Homeownership rate: 49.1%; Homeowner vacancy rate: 2.3%; Rental vacancy rate: 6.1%
Safety: Violent crime rate: 59.4 per 10,000 population; Property crime rate: 445.8 per 10,000 population

CALYPSO (town). Covers a land area of 0.987 square miles and a water area of 0.002 square miles. Located at 35.15° N. Lat; 78.10° W. Long. Elevation is 161 feet.
Population: 538; Growth (since 2000): 31.2%; Density: 545.1 persons per square mile; Race: 54.8% White, 19.3% Black/African American, 0.0% Asian, 0.4% American Indian/Alaska Native, 0.7% Native Hawaiian/Other Pacific Islander, 3.3% Two or more races, 26.0% Hispanic of any race;

Average household size: 2.61; Median age: 38.6; Age under 18: 23.0%; Age 65 and over: 15.2%; Males per 100 females: 92.1

School District(s)

Duplin County Schools (PK-12)
    2012-13 Enrollment: 9,514 . . . . (910) 296-1521
Housing: Homeownership rate: 68.3%; Homeowner vacancy rate: 0.7%; Rental vacancy rate: 15.6%

CHINQUAPIN (unincorporated postal area)

ZCTA: 28521
    Covers a land area of 41.932 square miles and a water area of 0.109 square miles. Located at 34.82° N. Lat; 77.74° W. Long. Elevation is 39 feet.
    Population: 2,287; Growth (since 2000): 16.4%; Density: 54.5 persons per square mile; Race: 82.2% White, 13.1% Black/African American, 0.1% Asian, 0.3% American Indian/Alaska Native, 0.0% Native Hawaiian/Other Pacific Islander, 1.0% Two or more races, 5.6% Hispanic of any race; Average household size: 2.42; Median age: 42.1; Age under 18: 21.7%; Age 65 and over: 17.6%; Males per 100 females: 98.2

School District(s)

Duplin County Schools (PK-12)
    2012-13 Enrollment: 9,514 . . . . (910) 296-1521
    Housing: Homeownership rate: 78.3%; Homeowner vacancy rate: 0.4%; Rental vacancy rate: 5.9%

FAISON (town).

Covers a land area of 0.784 square miles and a water area of 0 square miles. Located at 35.12° N. Lat; 78.14° W. Long. Elevation is 161 feet.
Population: 961; Growth (since 2000): 29.2%; Density: 1,225.7 persons per square mile; Race: 52.4% White, 12.9% Black/African American, 0.1% Asian, 0.2% American Indian/Alaska Native, 0.0% Native Hawaiian/Other Pacific Islander, 3.2% Two or more races, 38.5% Hispanic of any race; Average household size: 2.59; Median age: 34.4; Age under 18: 27.9%; Age 65 and over: 11.0%; Males per 100 females: 101.5

School District(s)

Sampson County Schools (PK-12)
    2012-13 Enrollment: 8,835 . . . . (910) 592-1401
Housing: Homeownership rate: 50.2%; Homeowner vacancy rate: 2.6%; Rental vacancy rate: 9.9%

GREENEVERS (town).

Covers a land area of 1.569 square miles and a water area of 0 square miles. Located at 34.83° N. Lat; 77.92° W. Long. Elevation is 59 feet.
Population: 634; Growth (since 2000): 13.2%; Density: 404.2 persons per square mile; Race: 8.5% White, 81.9% Black/African American, 0.2% Asian, 0.0% American Indian/Alaska Native, 0.0% Native Hawaiian/Other Pacific Islander, 1.6% Two or more races, 8.7% Hispanic of any race; Average household size: 2.56; Median age: 34.3; Age under 18: 27.6%; Age 65 and over: 12.5%; Males per 100 females: 83.8
Housing: Homeownership rate: 62.0%; Homeowner vacancy rate: 1.3%; Rental vacancy rate: 11.5%

KENANSVILLE (town).

County seat. Covers a land area of 2.120 square miles and a water area of 0 square miles. Located at 34.96° N. Lat; 77.97° W. Long. Elevation is 125 feet.
History: Kenansville was named for the family of Colonel James Kenan, who in 1765 led a force of volunteers from Kenansville to Brunswick to oppose enforcement of the Stamp Act.
Population: 855; Growth (since 2000): -25.6%; Density: 403.2 persons per square mile; Race: 57.9% White, 37.8% Black/African American, 1.1% Asian, 0.6% American Indian/Alaska Native, 0.0% Native Hawaiian/Other Pacific Islander, 1.3% Two or more races, 3.9% Hispanic of any race; Average household size: 1.90; Median age: 50.3; Age under 18: 15.7%; Age 65 and over: 27.5%; Males per 100 females: 81.9

School District(s)

Duplin County Schools (PK-12)
    2012-13 Enrollment: 9,514 . . . . (910) 296-1521

Two-year College(s)

James Sprunt Community College (Public)
    Fall 2013 Enrollment: 1,291 . . . . (910) 296-2400
    2013-14 Tuition: In-state $2,358; Out-of-state $8,502
Housing: Homeownership rate: 48.8%; Homeowner vacancy rate: 5.2%; Rental vacancy rate: 6.2%
Hospitals: Vidant Duplin Hospital (89 beds)

Safety: Violent crime rate: 56.5 per 10,000 population; Property crime rate: 316.4 per 10,000 population
Newspapers: Duplin Times (weekly circulation 17000)
Airports: Duplin County (general aviation)

MAGNOLIA (town).

Covers a land area of 1.020 square miles and a water area of 0.001 square miles. Located at 34.90° N. Lat; 78.05° W. Long. Elevation is 138 feet.
Population: 939; Growth (since 2000): 0.8%; Density: 920.3 persons per square mile; Race: 34.3% White, 33.7% Black/African American, 0.3% Asian, 0.9% American Indian/Alaska Native, 0.2% Native Hawaiian/Other Pacific Islander, 1.8% Two or more races, 40.3% Hispanic of any race; Average household size: 2.74; Median age: 31.7; Age under 18: 31.3%; Age 65 and over: 12.1%; Males per 100 females: 103.7
Housing: Homeownership rate: 48.5%; Homeowner vacancy rate: 2.9%; Rental vacancy rate: 9.3%

POTTERS HILL (CDP).

Covers a land area of 5.346 square miles and a water area of <.001 square miles. Located at 34.96° N. Lat; 77.70° W. Long. Elevation is 92 feet.
Population: 481; Growth (since 2000): n/a; Density: 90.0 persons per square mile; Race: 97.1% White, 0.0% Black/African American, 0.0% Asian, 0.0% American Indian/Alaska Native, 0.0% Native Hawaiian/Other Pacific Islander, 1.5% Two or more races, 2.7% Hispanic of any race; Average household size: 2.33; Median age: 43.9; Age under 18: 17.9%; Age 65 and over: 16.4%; Males per 100 females: 95.5
Housing: Homeownership rate: 80.6%; Homeowner vacancy rate: 0.0%; Rental vacancy rate: 14.9%

ROSE HILL (town).

Covers a land area of 1.436 square miles and a water area of 0 square miles. Located at 34.83° N. Lat; 78.03° W. Long. Elevation is 98 feet.
Population: 1,626; Growth (since 2000): 22.3%; Density: 1,132.2 persons per square mile; Race: 51.4% White, 31.4% Black/African American, 0.5% Asian, 0.2% American Indian/Alaska Native, 0.1% Native Hawaiian/Other Pacific Islander, 1.4% Two or more races, 20.8% Hispanic of any race; Average household size: 2.46; Median age: 40.5; Age under 18: 24.3%; Age 65 and over: 17.5%; Males per 100 females: 90.8

School District(s)

Duplin County Schools (PK-12)
    2012-13 Enrollment: 9,514 . . . . (910) 296-1521
Housing: Homeownership rate: 61.6%; Homeowner vacancy rate: 2.6%; Rental vacancy rate: 7.3%
Safety: Violent crime rate: 47.4 per 10,000 population; Property crime rate: 266.7 per 10,000 population

TEACHEY (town).

Covers a land area of 0.928 square miles and a water area of 0 square miles. Located at 34.77° N. Lat; 78.01° W. Long. Elevation is 69 feet.
Population: 376; Growth (since 2000): 53.5%; Density: 405.2 persons per square mile; Race: 44.9% White, 41.5% Black/African American, 3.5% Asian, 0.3% American Indian/Alaska Native, 0.0% Native Hawaiian/Other Pacific Islander, 0.3% Two or more races, 18.4% Hispanic of any race; Average household size: 2.61; Median age: 33.0; Age under 18: 25.5%; Age 65 and over: 11.4%; Males per 100 females: 91.8

School District(s)

Duplin County Schools (PK-12)
    2012-13 Enrollment: 9,514 . . . . (910) 296-1521
Housing: Homeownership rate: 75.0%; Homeowner vacancy rate: 6.1%; Rental vacancy rate: 7.5%

WALLACE (town).

Covers a land area of 3.066 square miles and a water area of 0 square miles. Located at 34.74° N. Lat; 77.99° W. Long. Elevation is 49 feet.
Population: 3,880; Growth (since 2000): 16.0%; Density: 1,265.5 persons per square mile; Race: 52.0% White, 26.0% Black/African American, 0.2% Asian, 0.4% American Indian/Alaska Native, 0.1% Native Hawaiian/Other Pacific Islander, 1.4% Two or more races, 25.5% Hispanic of any race; Average household size: 2.35; Median age: 40.9; Age under 18: 23.6%; Age 65 and over: 20.8%; Males per 100 females: 84.4; Marriage status: 32.6% never married, 49.5% now married, 5.1% separated, 7.2% widowed, 10.7% divorced; Foreign born: 18.8%; Speak English only: 76.1%; With disability: 12.7%; Veterans: 12.4%; Ancestry: 14.2% American, 5.7% Irish, 4.6% English, 4.4% Pennsylvania German, 4.0% European

Employment: 5.5% management, business, and financial, 0.9% computer, engineering, and science, 5.4% education, legal, community service, arts, and media, 0.0% healthcare practitioners, 18.9% service, 21.5% sales and office, 31.6% natural resources, construction, and maintenance, 16.2% production, transportation, and material moving
Income: Per capita: $17,787; Median household: $39,136; Average household: $44,422; Households with income of $100,000 or more: 9.6%; Poverty rate: 18.6%
Educational Attainment: High school diploma or higher: 67.8%; Bachelor's degree or higher: 13.2%; Graduate/professional degree or higher: 2.7%

School District(s)
Duplin County Schools (PK-12)
    2012-13 Enrollment: 9,514 . . . . (910) 296-1521
Housing: Homeownership rate: 52.5%; Median home value: $115,800; Median year structure built: 1973; Homeowner vacancy rate: 4.7%; Median gross rent: $565 per month; Rental vacancy rate: 7.5%
Health Insurance: 71.2% have insurance; 49.4% have private insurance; 34.2% have public insurance; 28.8% do not have insurance; 3.2% of children under 18 do not have insurance
Safety: Violent crime rate: 32.4 per 10,000 population; Property crime rate: 440.8 per 10,000 population
Newspapers: Pender Chronicle (weekly circulation 6000)
Transportation: Commute: 86.7% car, 0.0% public transportation, 8.8% walk, 3.2% work from home; Median travel time to work: 20.6 minutes
Additional Information Contacts
Town of Wallace . . . . (910) 285-4136
    http://www.townofwallace.com

WARSAW (town).
Covers a land area of 3.053 square miles and a water area of 0.001 square miles. Located at 35.00° N. Lat; 78.09° W. Long. Elevation is 154 feet.
Population: 3,054; Growth (since 2000): 0.1%; Density: 1,000.3 persons per square mile; Race: 33.5% White, 53.0% Black/African American, 0.3% Asian, 0.4% American Indian/Alaska Native, 0.2% Native Hawaiian/Other Pacific Islander, 1.2% Two or more races, 16.9% Hispanic of any race; Average household size: 2.39; Median age: 38.4; Age under 18: 25.4%; Age 65 and over: 17.3%; Males per 100 females: 82.4; Marriage status: 32.3% never married, 39.1% now married, 8.1% separated, 17.9% widowed, 10.6% divorced; Foreign born: 9.3%; Speak English only: 83.9%; With disability: 21.0%; Veterans: 8.2%; Ancestry: 5.0% Irish, 3.9% American, 2.2% English, 1.8% German, 1.5% Scotch-Irish
Employment: 15.6% management, business, and financial, 0.3% computer, engineering, and science, 3.8% education, legal, community service, arts, and media, 1.3% healthcare practitioners, 24.1% service, 10.4% sales and office, 9.5% natural resources, construction, and maintenance, 34.9% production, transportation, and material moving
Income: Per capita: $14,713; Median household: $22,861; Average household: $30,275; Households with income of $100,000 or more: 3.5%; Poverty rate: 37.6%
Educational Attainment: High school diploma or higher: 70.6%; Bachelor's degree or higher: 10.8%; Graduate/professional degree or higher: 2.1%

School District(s)
Duplin County Schools (PK-12)
    2012-13 Enrollment: 9,514 . . . . (910) 296-1521
Housing: Homeownership rate: 46.8%; Median home value: $75,100; Median year structure built: 1973; Homeowner vacancy rate: 3.3%; Median gross rent: $458 per month; Rental vacancy rate: 8.2%
Health Insurance: 76.9% have insurance; 44.1% have private insurance; 46.0% have public insurance; 23.1% do not have insurance; 7.3% of children under 18 do not have insurance
Safety: Violent crime rate: 44.1 per 10,000 population; Property crime rate: 375.2 per 10,000 population
Transportation: Commute: 93.2% car, 0.0% public transportation, 3.5% walk, 1.6% work from home; Median travel time to work: 22.6 minutes
Additional Information Contacts
Town of Warsaw . . . . (910) 293-7814
    http://www.townofwarsawnc.com

Durham County

Located in north central North Carolina; piedmont area, drained by the headstreams of the Neuse River. Covers a land area of 285.975 square miles, a water area of 11.891 square miles, and is located in the Eastern Time Zone at 36.04° N. Lat., 78.88° W. Long. The county was founded in 1881. County seat is Durham.

Durham County is part of the Durham-Chapel Hill, NC Metropolitan Statistical Area. The entire metro area includes: Chatham County, NC; Durham County, NC; Orange County, NC; Person County, NC

Weather Station: Durham   Elevation: 399 feet

	Jan	Feb	Mar	Apr	May	Jun	Jul	Aug	Sep	Oct	Nov	Dec
High	na	54	62	na	78	85	89	88	81	71	62	53
Low	28	29	36	45	54	64	68	67	59	46	37	30
Precip	3.8	3.4	4.8	3.5	3.9	4.4	4.2	4.8	3.9	3.8	3.5	3.4
Snow	1.4	0.6	0.8	tr	0.0	0.0	0.0	0.0	0.0	0.0	0.0	0.1

High and Low temperatures in degrees Fahrenheit; Precipitation and Snow in inches

Population: 267,587; Growth (since 2000): 19.8%; Density: 935.7 persons per square mile; Race: 46.4% White, 38.0% Black/African American, 4.6% Asian, 0.5% American Indian/Alaska Native, 0.1% Native Hawaiian/Other Pacific Islander, 2.6% two or more races, 13.5% Hispanic of any race; Average household size: 2.35; Median age: 33.2; Age under 18: 22.5%; Age 65 and over: 9.8%; Males per 100 females: 91.2; Marriage status: 39.3% never married, 45.8% now married, 2.8% separated, 4.8% widowed, 10.2% divorced; Foreign born: 13.9%; Speak English only: 80.6%; With disability: 10.4%; Veterans: 7.0%; Ancestry: 8.8% English, 8.1% German, 6.1% Irish, 5.4% American, 2.8% Italian
Religion: Six largest groups: 14.1% Baptist, 8.0% Non-denominational Protestant, 5.4% Methodist/Pietist, 3.9% Catholicism, 2.7% Presbyterian-Reformed, 1.7% Pentecostal
Economy: Unemployment rate: 4.8%; Leading industries: 16.7% professional, scientific, and technical services; 14.1% retail trade; 11.7% health care and social assistance; Farms: 232 totaling 20,854 acres; Company size: 19 employ 1,000 or more persons, 8 employ 500 to 999 persons, 189 employ 100 to 499 persons, 6,497 employ less than 100 persons; Business ownership: 7,504 women-owned, 5,441 Black-owned, 808 Hispanic-owned, 907 Asian-owned
Employment: 14.8% management, business, and financial, 9.8% computer, engineering, and science, 15.2% education, legal, community service, arts, and media, 9.4% healthcare practitioners, 16.8% service, 19.6% sales and office, 7.4% natural resources, construction, and maintenance, 6.9% production, transportation, and material moving
Income: Per capita: $29,347; Median household: $51,853; Average household: $71,615; Households with income of $100,000 or more: 22.1%; Poverty rate: 18.5%
Educational Attainment: High school diploma or higher: 86.9%; Bachelor's degree or higher: 45.1%; Graduate/professional degree or higher: 20.5%
Housing: Homeownership rate: 54.3%; Median home value: $180,600; Median year structure built: 1986; Homeowner vacancy rate: 3.1%; Median gross rent: $859 per month; Rental vacancy rate: 10.2%
Vital Statistics: Birth rate: 148.7 per 10,000 population; Death rate: 62.4 per 10,000 population; Age-adjusted cancer mortality rate: 191.4 deaths per 100,000 population
Health Insurance: 83.6% have insurance; 66.5% have private insurance; 26.0% have public insurance; 16.4% do not have insurance; 8.3% of children under 18 do not have insurance
Health Care: Physicians: 92.0 per 10,000 population; Hospital beds: 48.1 per 10,000 population; Hospital admissions: 2,288.5 per 10,000 population
Air Quality Index: 85.5% good, 14.5% moderate, 0.0% unhealthy for sensitive individuals, 0.0% unhealthy (percent of days)
Transportation: Commute: 87.2% car, 3.6% public transportation, 2.9% walk, 4.4% work from home; Median travel time to work: 21.5 minutes
Presidential Election: 75.8% Obama, 23.0% Romney (2012)
Additional Information Contacts
Durham Government . . . . (919) 560-0000
    http://www.co.durham.nc.us

Durham County Communities

BAHAMA (unincorporated postal area)
ZCTA: 27503
    Covers a land area of 36.469 square miles and a water area of 1.362 square miles. Located at 36.15° N. Lat; 78.88° W. Long. Elevation is 512 feet.
    Population: 3,471; Growth (since 2000): 5.1%; Density: 95.2 persons per square mile; Race: 84.8% White, 11.5% Black/African American, 0.9% Asian, 0.4% American Indian/Alaska Native, 0.0% Native

Hawaiian/Other Pacific Islander, 1.2% Two or more races, 2.1% Hispanic of any race; Average household size: 2.48; Median age: 45.6; Age under 18: 21.7%; Age 65 and over: 13.1%; Males per 100 females: 99.5; Marriage status: 37.9% never married, 47.0% now married, 3.4% separated, 2.9% widowed, 12.3% divorced; Foreign born: 4.5%; Speak English only: 87.1%; With disability: 11.6%; Veterans: 11.8%; Ancestry: 14.8% English, 9.9% American, 8.4% German, 6.7% Irish, 2.8% Italian
Employment: 17.4% management, business, and financial, 7.9% computer, engineering, and science, 11.4% education, legal, community service, arts, and media, 12.4% healthcare practitioners, 9.7% service, 26.4% sales and office, 9.8% natural resources, construction, and maintenance, 4.9% production, transportation, and material moving
Income: Per capita: $30,769; Median household: $89,180; Average household: $146,509; Households with income of $100,000 or more: 41.3%; Poverty rate: 5.1%
Educational Attainment: High school diploma or higher: 86.1%; Bachelor's degree or higher: 21.1%; Graduate/professional degree or higher: 11.6%

School District(s)
Durham Public Schools (PK-12)
    2012-13 Enrollment: 33,079 . . . . (919) 560-2000
Housing: Homeownership rate: 85.0%; Median home value: $269,400; Median year structure built: 1980; Homeowner vacancy rate: 1.7%; Median gross rent: $844 per month; Rental vacancy rate: 5.0%
Health Insurance: 91.2% have insurance; 85.3% have private insurance; 19.4% have public insurance; 8.8% do not have insurance; 17.1% of children under 18 do not have insurance
Transportation: Commute: 97.6% car, 0.0% public transportation, 0.0% walk, 2.4% work from home; Median travel time to work: 26.5 minutes

DURHAM (city). County seat. Covers a land area of 107.370 square miles and a water area of 0.910 square miles. Located at 35.98° N. Lat; 78.91° W. Long. Elevation is 400 feet.
History: Durham is new by North Carolina reckoning, dating from the 1850's when a settlement known as Prattsburg grew up around wheat and corn mills serving the farmers. Construction of the North Carolina Railroad in the mid-1850's gave some impetus to growth. William Pratt, a major landowner, refused to give a right-of-way or land for a station. Dr. Bartlett Durham offered four acres about two miles west of Prattsburg and the station was named for him. The railroad detoured around Prattsburg and the Pratt property. The town of Durham was incorporated in 1867, and when Durham County was created from Orange and Wake in 1881, it was made the seat. The rise of the tobacconists marked the beginning of the town's industrial life. As early as 1858 Robert F. Morris was producing tobacco. By 1911, Durham was established as the world's tobacco capital. James B. Duke did with tobacco what Rockefeller did with oil and Carnegie with steel. He became adept at trade. After amassing a fortune, he provided the means for establishing Duke University, for which he left a sizable endowment.
Population: 228,330; Growth (since 2000): 22.1%; Density: 2,126.6 persons per square mile; Race: 42.5% White, 41.0% Black/African American, 5.1% Asian, 0.5% American Indian/Alaska Native, 0.1% Native Hawaiian/Other Pacific Islander, 2.7% Two or more races, 14.2% Hispanic of any race; Average household size: 2.34; Median age: 32.1; Age under 18: 22.7%; Age 65 and over: 8.8%; Males per 100 females: 90.6; Marriage status: 41.5% never married, 43.6% now married, 2.9% separated, 4.7% widowed, 10.2% divorced; Foreign born: 14.6%; Speak English only: 79.8%; With disability: 10.4%; Veterans: 6.4%; Ancestry: 7.7% English, 7.6% German, 5.6% Irish, 4.6% American, 2.8% Italian
Employment: 14.4% management, business, and financial, 10.0% computer, engineering, and science, 15.6% education, legal, community service, arts, and media, 9.6% healthcare practitioners, 17.5% service, 19.2% sales and office, 6.9% natural resources, construction, and maintenance, 6.7% production, transportation, and material moving
Income: Per capita: $28,565; Median household: $49,160; Average household: $68,732; Households with income of $100,000 or more: 20.8%; Poverty rate: 20.0%
Educational Attainment: High school diploma or higher: 86.6%; Bachelor's degree or higher: 46.8%; Graduate/professional degree or higher: 21.8%

School District(s)
Carter Community Charter (KG-08)
    2012-13 Enrollment: 289. . . . . (919) 797-2340
Central Park School for Child (KG-05)
    2012-13 Enrollment: 299. . . . . (919) 682-1200

Durham Public Schools (PK-12)
    2012-13 Enrollment: 33,079 . . . . (919) 560-2000
Global Scholars Academy (KG-04)
    2012-13 Enrollment: 135. . . . . (919) 682-5903
Healthy Start Academy (KG-08)
    2012-13 Enrollment: 411. . . . . (919) 956-5599
Kestrel Heights Sch (06-12)
    2012-13 Enrollment: 1,010 . . . . (919) 484-1300
Maureen Joy Charter (KG-08)
    2012-13 Enrollment: 373. . . . . (919) 493-6056
Nc Health and Human Resources (KG-12)
    2012-13 Enrollment: n/a . . . . (919) 855-4430
Research Triangle Charter (KG-08)
    2012-13 Enrollment: 651. . . . . (919) 957-7108
Research Triangle High School
    2012-13 Enrollment: 146. . . . . (919) 998-6757
Voyager Academy (03-10)
    2012-13 Enrollment: 1,257 . . . . (919) 433-3301

Four-year College(s)
Apex School of Theology (Private, Not-for-profit, Interdenominational)
    Fall 2013 Enrollment: 767. . . . . (919) 572-1625
    2013-14 Tuition: In-state $4,900; Out-of-state $4,900
Duke University (Private, Not-for-profit, United Methodist)
    Fall 2013 Enrollment: 15,467 . . . . (919) 684-8111
    2013-14 Tuition: In-state $45,376; Out-of-state $45,376
ITT Technical Institute-Durham (Private, For-profit)
    Fall 2013 Enrollment: 168. . . . . (919) 401-1400
    2013-14 Tuition: In-state $18,048; Out-of-state $18,048
North Carolina Central University (Public, Historically black)
    Fall 2013 Enrollment: 8,093 . . . . (919) 530-6100
    2013-14 Tuition: In-state $5,526; Out-of-state $16,099
The Art Institute of Raleigh-Durham (Private, For-profit)
    Fall 2013 Enrollment: 781. . . . . (919) 317-3051
    2013-14 Tuition: In-state $17,128; Out-of-state $17,128

Two-year College(s)
Durham Technical Community College (Public)
    Fall 2013 Enrollment: 5,605 . . . . (919) 536-7200
    2013-14 Tuition: In-state $1,840; Out-of-state $6,388
Watts School of Nursing (Private, Not-for-profit)
    Fall 2013 Enrollment: 138. . . . . (919) 470-7348

Vocational/Technical School(s)
CET-Durham (Private, Not-for-profit)
    Fall 2013 Enrollment: 134. . . . . (408) 287-7924
    2013-14 Tuition: $7,958
Durham Beauty Academy (Private, For-profit)
    Fall 2013 Enrollment: 70. . . . . (919) 493-9557
    2013-14 Tuition: $18,100
Park West Barber School (Private, For-profit)
    Fall 2013 Enrollment: 175. . . . . (919) 688-2914
    2013-14 Tuition: $15,735
Regency Beauty Institute-Durham (Private, For-profit)
    Fall 2013 Enrollment: 54. . . . . (800) 787-6456
    2013-14 Tuition: $16,200
The Hair Design School-Durham (Private, For-profit)
    Fall 2013 Enrollment: 65. . . . . (800) 920-4593
    2013-14 Tuition: $15,750
Housing: Homeownership rate: 49.8%; Median home value: $180,500; Median year structure built: 1986; Homeowner vacancy rate: 3.2%; Median gross rent: $852 per month; Rental vacancy rate: 10.4%
Health Insurance: 82.9% have insurance; 65.1% have private insurance; 25.9% have public insurance; 17.1% do not have insurance; 7.6% of children under 18 do not have insurance
Hospitals: Duke Regional Hospital (369 beds); Duke University Hospital (1019 beds); Durham VA Medical Center (232 beds); North Carolina Specialty Hospital (14 beds)
Newspapers: Herald-Sun (daily circulation 39200); Indy Week (weekly circulation 45000)
Transportation: Commute: 86.5% car, 3.9% public transportation, 3.2% walk, 4.3% work from home; Median travel time to work: 21.1 minutes; Amtrak: Train service available.
Additional Information Contacts
City of Durham . . . . (919) 560-1200
    http://www.ci.durham.nc.us

GORMAN (CDP). Covers a land area of 2.878 square miles and a water area of 0.055 square miles. Located at 36.04° N. Lat; 78.81° W. Long. Elevation is 364 feet.

Population: 1,011; Growth (since 2000): 0.9%; Density: 351.3 persons per square mile; Race: 61.0% White, 13.5% Black/African American, 0.6% Asian, 0.5% American Indian/Alaska Native, 0.0% Native Hawaiian/Other Pacific Islander, 1.7% Two or more races, 26.3% Hispanic of any race; Average household size: 2.50; Median age: 38.9; Age under 18: 23.3%; Age 65 and over: 15.9%; Males per 100 females: 101.8

Housing: Homeownership rate: 72.1%; Homeowner vacancy rate: 3.6%; Rental vacancy rate: 4.2%

ROUGEMONT (CDP). Covers a land area of 6.280 square miles and a water area of 0.079 square miles. Located at 36.21° N. Lat; 78.91° W. Long. Elevation is 561 feet.

Population: 978; Growth (since 2000): n/a; Density: 155.7 persons per square mile; Race: 78.8% White, 16.0% Black/African American, 0.2% Asian, 0.4% American Indian/Alaska Native, 0.0% Native Hawaiian/Other Pacific Islander, 3.7% Two or more races, 4.1% Hispanic of any race; Average household size: 2.37; Median age: 48.9; Age under 18: 17.3%; Age 65 and over: 18.4%; Males per 100 females: 103.3

Housing: Homeownership rate: 85.0%; Homeowner vacancy rate: 1.7%; Rental vacancy rate: 4.6%

Edgecombe County

Located in east central North Carolina; in coastal plains area, bounded on the north by Fishing Creek; crossed by the Tar River. Covers a land area of 505.336 square miles, a water area of 1.314 square miles, and is located in the Eastern Time Zone at 35.92° N. Lat., 77.60° W. Long. The county was founded in 1735. County seat is Tarboro.

Edgecombe County is part of the Rocky Mount, NC Metropolitan Statistical Area. The entire metro area includes: Edgecombe County, NC; Nash County, NC

Weather Station: Tarboro 1 S										Elevation: 35 feet		
	Jan	Feb	Mar	Apr	May	Jun	Jul	Aug	Sep	Oct	Nov	Dec
High	52	55	63	73	80	87	90	88	83	73	64	55
Low	29	32	38	46	55	65	69	67	61	49	40	32
Precip	3.6	3.3	3.9	3.2	3.3	3.9	4.7	5.0	4.3	3.0	2.9	3.0
Snow	1.8	1.6	1.1	tr	0.0	0.0	0.0	0.0	0.0	0.0	tr	0.8

High and Low temperatures in degrees Fahrenheit; Precipitation and Snow in inches

Population: 56,552; Growth (since 2000): 1.7%; Density: 111.9 persons per square mile; Race: 38.8% White, 57.4% Black/African American, 0.2% Asian, 0.3% American Indian/Alaska Native, 0.0% Native Hawaiian/Other Pacific Islander, 1.0% two or more races, 3.7% Hispanic of any race; Average household size: 2.54; Median age: 39.6; Age under 18: 24.5%; Age 65 and over: 14.3%; Males per 100 females: 86.6; Marriage status: 34.5% never married, 47.3% now married, 5.5% separated, 8.0% widowed, 10.3% divorced; Foreign born: 2.5%; Speak English only: 96.1%; With disability: 17.8%; Veterans: 9.2%; Ancestry: 9.0% American, 6.8% English, 4.0% Irish, 3.2% European, 2.6% German

Religion: Six largest groups: 14.0% Non-denominational Protestant, 14.0% Baptist, 4.5% Pentecostal, 3.5% Methodist/Pietist, 1.5% Presbyterian-Reformed, 0.9% Episcopalianism/Anglicanism

Economy: Unemployment rate: 10.2%; Leading industries: 18.2% retail trade; 13.7% other services (except public administration); 13.6% health care and social assistance; Farms: 272 totaling 126,635 acres; Company size: 1 employs 1,000 or more persons, 2 employ 500 to 999 persons, 18 employ 100 to 499 persons, 752 employ less than 100 persons; Business ownership: 1,178 women-owned, 1,010 Black-owned, n/a Hispanic-owned, n/a Asian-owned

Employment: 8.6% management, business, and financial, 1.6% computer, engineering, and science, 7.2% education, legal, community service, arts, and media, 4.5% healthcare practitioners, 21.1% service, 22.9% sales and office, 10.8% natural resources, construction, and maintenance, 23.3% production, transportation, and material moving

Income: Per capita: $16,971; Median household: $33,960; Average household: $43,639; Households with income of $100,000 or more: 7.1%; Poverty rate: 25.2%

Educational Attainment: High school diploma or higher: 79.5%; Bachelor's degree or higher: 10.5%; Graduate/professional degree or higher: 2.6%

Housing: Homeownership rate: 62.1%; Median home value: $80,600; Median year structure built: 1978; Homeowner vacancy rate: 2.1%; Median gross rent: $646 per month; Rental vacancy rate: 11.9%

Vital Statistics: Birth rate: 119.3 per 10,000 population; Death rate: 106.3 per 10,000 population; Age-adjusted cancer mortality rate: 212.6 deaths per 100,000 population

Health Insurance: 81.7% have insurance; 51.6% have private insurance; 44.0% have public insurance; 18.3% do not have insurance; 7.9% of children under 18 do not have insurance

Health Care: Physicians: 5.7 per 10,000 population; Hospital beds: 20.9 per 10,000 population; Hospital admissions: 776.4 per 10,000 population

Air Quality Index: 87.0% good, 13.0% moderate, 0.0% unhealthy for sensitive individuals, 0.0% unhealthy (percent of days)

Transportation: Commute: 94.7% car, 0.5% public transportation, 1.3% walk, 2.0% work from home; Median travel time to work: 21.6 minutes

Presidential Election: 67.9% Obama, 31.7% Romney (2012)

Additional Information Contacts

Edgecombe Government . . . . (252) 641-4112
    http://www.edgecombecountync.gov

Edgecombe County Communities

CONETOE (town). Covers a land area of 0.360 square miles and a water area of 0 square miles. Located at 35.82° N. Lat; 77.46° W. Long. Elevation is 49 feet.

Population: 294; Growth (since 2000): -19.5%; Density: 817.7 persons per square mile; Race: 22.1% White, 75.9% Black/African American, 0.0% Asian, 0.3% American Indian/Alaska Native, 0.0% Native Hawaiian/Other Pacific Islander, 1.7% Two or more races, 1.7% Hispanic of any race; Average household size: 2.49; Median age: 43.8; Age under 18: 22.1%; Age 65 and over: 18.0%; Males per 100 females: 94.7

Housing: Homeownership rate: 76.3%; Homeowner vacancy rate: 0.0%; Rental vacancy rate: 20.0%

LEGGETT (town). Covers a land area of 0.699 square miles and a water area of 0 square miles. Located at 35.99° N. Lat; 77.58° W. Long. Elevation is 59 feet.

Population: 60; Growth (since 2000): -22.1%; Density: 85.9 persons per square mile; Race: 66.7% White, 28.3% Black/African American, 0.0% Asian, 0.0% American Indian/Alaska Native, 0.0% Native Hawaiian/Other Pacific Islander, 5.0% Two or more races, 0.0% Hispanic of any race; Average household size: 2.50; Median age: 51.0; Age under 18: 15.0%; Age 65 and over: 20.0%; Males per 100 females: 114.3

Housing: Homeownership rate: 75.0%; Homeowner vacancy rate: 0.0%; Rental vacancy rate: 0.0%

MACCLESFIELD (town). Covers a land area of 0.518 square miles and a water area of 0.007 square miles. Located at 35.75° N. Lat; 77.67° W. Long. Elevation is 95 feet.

Population: 471; Growth (since 2000): 2.8%; Density: 910.1 persons per square mile; Race: 78.8% White, 14.0% Black/African American, 1.9% Asian, 0.0% American Indian/Alaska Native, 0.0% Native Hawaiian/Other Pacific Islander, 3.0% Two or more races, 2.8% Hispanic of any race; Average household size: 2.16; Median age: 46.4; Age under 18: 18.0%; Age 65 and over: 20.8%; Males per 100 females: 86.2

Housing: Homeownership rate: 65.1%; Homeowner vacancy rate: 2.0%; Rental vacancy rate: 15.6%

PINETOPS (town). Covers a land area of 1.003 square miles and a water area of 0 square miles. Located at 35.79° N. Lat; 77.64° W. Long. Elevation is 102 feet.

Population: 1,374; Growth (since 2000): -3.2%; Density: 1,369.3 persons per square mile; Race: 34.2% White, 65.2% Black/African American, 0.0% Asian, 0.2% American Indian/Alaska Native, 0.0% Native Hawaiian/Other Pacific Islander, 0.4% Two or more races, 0.3% Hispanic of any race; Average household size: 2.41; Median age: 41.2; Age under 18: 24.9%; Age 65 and over: 15.5%; Males per 100 females: 84.2

School District(s)

Edgecombe County Schools (PK-12)

    2012-13 Enrollment: 6,866 . . . . (252) 641-2600

Housing: Homeownership rate: 50.0%; Homeowner vacancy rate: 2.7%; Rental vacancy rate: 11.8%

PRINCEVILLE (town). Covers a land area of 1.513 square miles and a water area of 0.011 square miles. Located at 35.89° N. Lat; 77.53° W. Long. Elevation is 26 feet.

History: Princeville was chartered in 1885.

Population: 2,082; Growth (since 2000): 121.5%; Density: 1,376.0 persons per square mile; Race: 2.6% White, 96.3% Black/African American, 0.0% Asian, 0.0% American Indian/Alaska Native, 0.0% Native Hawaiian/Other Pacific Islander, 0.3% Two or more races, 0.8% Hispanic of any race; Average household size: 2.69; Median age: 36.9; Age under 18: 27.2%; Age 65 and over: 11.6%; Males per 100 females: 77.9

Housing: Homeownership rate: 58.7%; Homeowner vacancy rate: 2.1%; Rental vacancy rate: 5.0%

SPEED (town). Covers a land area of 0.283 square miles and a water area of 0 square miles. Located at 35.97° N. Lat; 77.44° W. Long. Elevation is 56 feet.

Population: 80; Growth (since 2000): 14.3%; Density: 282.6 persons per square mile; Race: 33.8% White, 66.3% Black/African American, 0.0% Asian, 0.0% American Indian/Alaska Native, 0.0% Native Hawaiian/Other Pacific Islander, 0.0% Two or more races, 0.0% Hispanic of any race; Average household size: 2.29; Median age: 47.7; Age under 18: 26.2%; Age 65 and over: 17.5%; Males per 100 females: 81.8

Housing: Homeownership rate: 74.3%; Homeowner vacancy rate: 0.0%; Rental vacancy rate: 0.0%

TARBORO (town). County seat. Covers a land area of 11.133 square miles and a water area of 0.037 square miles. Located at 35.91° N. Lat; 77.56° W. Long. Elevation is 43 feet.

History: Tarboro was laid out in 1760 on or near the site of an earlier Tar Burror, established by people of English descent from Virginia. Tarboro was one of several towns that played host to North Carolina's itinerant legislature in its early days.

Population: 11,415; Growth (since 2000): 2.5%; Density: 1,025.3 persons per square mile; Race: 47.2% White, 48.4% Black/African American, 0.5% Asian, 0.1% American Indian/Alaska Native, 0.1% Native Hawaiian/Other Pacific Islander, 0.8% Two or more races, 4.9% Hispanic of any race; Average household size: 2.35; Median age: 42.3; Age under 18: 22.8%; Age 65 and over: 19.1%; Males per 100 females: 84.1; Marriage status: 34.9% never married, 44.6% now married, 6.1% separated, 10.7% widowed, 9.7% divorced; Foreign born: 4.7%; Speak English only: 94.1%; With disability: 17.8%; Veterans: 9.9%; Ancestry: 12.3% American, 7.3% English, 4.3% Irish, 2.4% German, 2.3% European

Employment: 14.0% management, business, and financial, 1.0% computer, engineering, and science, 11.6% education, legal, community service, arts, and media, 7.6% healthcare practitioners, 20.0% service, 22.4% sales and office, 7.5% natural resources, construction, and maintenance, 15.9% production, transportation, and material moving

Income: Per capita: $19,180; Median household: $34,366; Average household: $47,229; Households with income of $100,000 or more: 9.9%; Poverty rate: 17.6%

Educational Attainment: High school diploma or higher: 78.3%; Bachelor's degree or higher: 16.9%; Graduate/professional degree or higher: 5.0%

School District(s)
Edgecombe County Schools (PK-12)
    2012-13 Enrollment: 6,866 . . . . (252) 641-2600
North East Carolina Preparatory Story
    2012-13 Enrollment: 386 . . . . (252) 641-0464
Two-year College(s)
Edgecombe Community College (Public)
    Fall 2013 Enrollment: 2,808 . . . . (252) 823-5166
    2013-14 Tuition: In-state $2,280; Out-of-state $8,420

Housing: Homeownership rate: 54.5%; Median home value: $94,700; Median year structure built: 1972; Homeowner vacancy rate: 2.8%; Median gross rent: $647 per month; Rental vacancy rate: 7.3%

Health Insurance: 80.3% have insurance; 51.1% have private insurance; 45.2% have public insurance; 19.7% do not have insurance; 4.8% of children under 18 do not have insurance

Hospitals: Vidant Edgecombe Hospital

Safety: Violent crime rate: 46.9 per 10,000 population; Property crime rate: 411.6 per 10,000 population

Newspapers: Daily Southerner (daily circulation 3700)

Transportation: Commute: 94.8% car, 0.0% public transportation, 1.4% walk, 2.6% work from home; Median travel time to work: 19.4 minutes

Additional Information Contacts
Town of Tarboro . . . . (252) 641-4200
    http://www.tarboro-nc.com

WHITAKERS (town). Covers a land area of 0.821 square miles and a water area of 0 square miles. Located at 36.11° N. Lat; 77.71° W. Long. Elevation is 128 feet.

History: Whitakers was named for Richard and Elizabeth Carey Whitaker, who settled here in 1740.

Population: 744; Growth (since 2000): -6.9%; Density: 906.7 persons per square mile; Race: 25.5% White, 70.2% Black/African American, 0.5% Asian, 0.3% American Indian/Alaska Native, 0.0% Native Hawaiian/Other Pacific Islander, 2.4% Two or more races, 2.0% Hispanic of any race; Average household size: 2.33; Median age: 45.3; Age under 18: 20.3%; Age 65 and over: 19.8%; Males per 100 females: 86.5

School District(s)
Nash-Rocky Mount Schools (PK-12)
    2012-13 Enrollment: 16,770 . . . . (252) 459-5220

Housing: Homeownership rate: 67.7%; Homeowner vacancy rate: 3.1%; Rental vacancy rate: 12.0%

Safety: Violent crime rate: 81.2 per 10,000 population; Property crime rate: 446.5 per 10,000 population

Forsyth County

Located in north central North Carolina; piedmont area, bounded on the west by the Yadkin River. Covers a land area of 408.148 square miles, a water area of 4.549 square miles, and is located in the Eastern Time Zone at 36.13° N. Lat., 80.26° W. Long. The county was founded in 1849. County seat is Winston-Salem.

Forsyth County is part of the Winston-Salem, NC Metropolitan Statistical Area. The entire metro area includes: Davidson County, NC; Davie County, NC; Forsyth County, NC; Stokes County, NC; Yadkin County, NC

Population: 350,670; Growth (since 2000): 14.6%; Density: 859.2 persons per square mile; Race: 62.3% White, 26.0% Black/African American, 1.9% Asian, 0.4% American Indian/Alaska Native, 0.1% Native Hawaiian/Other Pacific Islander, 2.2% two or more races, 11.9% Hispanic of any race; Average household size: 2.41; Median age: 37.2; Age under 18: 24.4%; Age 65 and over: 13.0%; Males per 100 females: 90.3; Marriage status: 32.8% never married, 50.1% now married, 2.8% separated, 6.4% widowed, 10.7% divorced; Foreign born: 9.2%; Speak English only: 85.9%; With disability: 10.4%; Veterans: 9.4%; Ancestry: 10.8% German, 10.7% English, 7.7% American, 7.7% Irish, 2.6% Scottish

Religion: Six largest groups: 15.8% Baptist, 12.8% Methodist/Pietist, 10.2% Non-denominational Protestant, 4.0% Catholicism, 2.9% Pentecostal, 2.6% Presbyterian-Reformed

Economy: Unemployment rate: 5.2%; Leading industries: 16.5% retail trade; 11.5% professional, scientific, and technical services; 10.0% other services (except public administration); Farms: 662 totaling 40,467 acres; Company size: 8 employ 1,000 or more persons, 14 employ 500 to 999 persons, 223 employ 100 to 499 persons, 7,918 employ less than 100 persons; Business ownership: 7,674 women-owned, 3,783 Black-owned, 884 Hispanic-owned, 587 Asian-owned

Employment: 14.3% management, business, and financial, 5.1% computer, engineering, and science, 12.1% education, legal, community service, arts, and media, 8.0% healthcare practitioners, 18.1% service, 23.2% sales and office, 7.2% natural resources, construction, and maintenance, 12.1% production, transportation, and material moving

Income: Per capita: $26,541; Median household: $45,724; Average household: $65,578; Households with income of $100,000 or more: 17.7%; Poverty rate: 18.6%

Educational Attainment: High school diploma or higher: 87.0%; Bachelor's degree or higher: 31.9%; Graduate/professional degree or higher: 11.1%

Housing: Homeownership rate: 63.9%; Median home value: $150,600; Median year structure built: 1978; Homeowner vacancy rate: 3.1%; Median gross rent: $714 per month; Rental vacancy rate: 12.6%

Vital Statistics: Birth rate: 127.4 per 10,000 population; Death rate: 82.4 per 10,000 population; Age-adjusted cancer mortality rate: 194.1 deaths per 100,000 population

Health Insurance: 84.3% have insurance; 65.7% have private insurance; 29.7% have public insurance; 15.7% do not have insurance; 7.3% of children under 18 do not have insurance

Health Care: Physicians: 54.4 per 10,000 population; Hospital beds: 48.1 per 10,000 population; Hospital admissions: 2,351.2 per 10,000 population
Air Quality Index: 76.4% good, 23.3% moderate, 0.3% unhealthy for sensitive individuals, 0.0% unhealthy (percent of days)
Transportation: Commute: 91.9% car, 1.1% public transportation, 1.4% walk, 4.0% work from home; Median travel time to work: 20.6 minutes
Presidential Election: 53.0% Obama, 45.8% Romney (2012)
Additional Information Contacts
Forsyth Government . . . . (336) 727-2797
    http://www.co.forsyth.nc.us

Forsyth County Communities

BELEWS CREEK (unincorporated postal area)
ZCTA: 27009
Covers a land area of 15.786 square miles and a water area of 1.730 square miles. Located at 36.23° N. Lat; 80.08° W. Long. Elevation is 869 feet.
Population: 2,647; Growth (since 2000): 19.7%; Density: 167.7 persons per square mile; Race: 90.5% White, 7.1% Black/African American, 0.3% Asian, 0.6% American Indian/Alaska Native, 0.1% Native Hawaiian/Other Pacific Islander, 0.8% Two or more races, 2.7% Hispanic of any race; Average household size: 2.57; Median age: 40.7; Age under 18: 23.7%; Age 65 and over: 11.0%; Males per 100 females: 101.0; Marriage status: 21.9% never married, 63.1% now married, 2.4% separated, 7.1% widowed, 7.9% divorced; Foreign born: 0.3%; Speak English only: 99.0%; With disability: 14.7%; Veterans: 13.1%; Ancestry: 21.2% American, 9.2% German, 7.5% Irish, 6.9% English, 6.8% Scottish
Employment: 15.1% management, business, and financial, 5.3% computer, engineering, and science, 7.8% education, legal, community service, arts, and media, 12.4% healthcare practitioners, 12.0% service, 28.6% sales and office, 13.0% natural resources, construction, and maintenance, 5.8% production, transportation, and material moving
Income: Per capita: $25,705; Median household: $55,068; Average household: $66,047; Households with income of $100,000 or more: 14.7%; Poverty rate: 7.2%
Educational Attainment: High school diploma or higher: 85.1%; Bachelor's degree or higher: 22.3%; Graduate/professional degree or higher: 5.2%
Housing: Homeownership rate: 89.8%; Median home value: $164,300; Median year structure built: 1993; Homeowner vacancy rate: 1.9%; Median gross rent: $547 per month; Rental vacancy rate: 0.9%
Health Insurance: 92.6% have insurance; 80.7% have private insurance; 23.5% have public insurance; 7.4% do not have insurance; 0.0% of children under 18 do not have insurance
Transportation: Commute: 97.4% car, 0.0% public transportation, 0.0% walk, 2.6% work from home; Median travel time to work: 28.8 minutes

BETHANIA (town). Covers a land area of 0.687 square miles and a water area of 0.006 square miles. Located at 36.18° N. Lat; 80.33° W. Long. Elevation is 817 feet.
Population: 328; Growth (since 2000): -7.3%; Density: 477.4 persons per square mile; Race: 88.1% White, 8.2% Black/African American, 0.0% Asian, 0.0% American Indian/Alaska Native, 0.0% Native Hawaiian/Other Pacific Islander, 2.4% Two or more races, 3.4% Hispanic of any race; Average household size: 2.12; Median age: 51.3; Age under 18: 12.2%; Age 65 and over: 21.0%; Males per 100 females: 94.1
Housing: Homeownership rate: 81.3%; Homeowner vacancy rate: 1.6%; Rental vacancy rate: 6.1%

CLEMMONS (village). Covers a land area of 11.810 square miles and a water area of 0.209 square miles. Located at 36.03° N. Lat; 80.39° W. Long. Elevation is 840 feet.
History: Clemmons was founded in pre-Revolutionary days by Peter Clemmons.
Population: 18,627; Growth (since 2000): 34.7%; Density: 1,577.3 persons per square mile; Race: 83.2% White, 6.7% Black/African American, 3.7% Asian, 0.3% American Indian/Alaska Native, 0.0% Native Hawaiian/Other Pacific Islander, 1.5% Two or more races, 8.4% Hispanic of any race; Average household size: 2.52; Median age: 40.6; Age under 18: 26.5%; Age 65 and over: 14.6%; Males per 100 females: 91.1; Marriage status: 22.2% never married, 62.5% now married, 2.5% separated, 5.4% widowed, 10.0% divorced; Foreign born: 10.0%; Speak English only: 85.2%; With disability: 7.2%; Veterans: 11.2%; Ancestry:

17.4% German, 14.7% English, 12.6% Irish, 10.4% American, 5.0% Scottish
Employment: 19.0% management, business, and financial, 7.7% computer, engineering, and science, 13.7% education, legal, community service, arts, and media, 9.6% healthcare practitioners, 15.1% service, 21.3% sales and office, 5.0% natural resources, construction, and maintenance, 8.6% production, transportation, and material moving
Income: Per capita: $32,955; Median household: $64,118; Average household: $83,678; Households with income of $100,000 or more: 30.3%; Poverty rate: 7.9%
Educational Attainment: High school diploma or higher: 93.7%; Bachelor's degree or higher: 43.8%; Graduate/professional degree or higher: 13.6%
School District(s)
Forsyth County Schools (PK-12)
    2012-13 Enrollment: 53,881 . . . . (336) 727-2816
Housing: Homeownership rate: 77.9%; Median home value: $206,300; Median year structure built: 1991; Homeowner vacancy rate: 2.9%; Median gross rent: $820 per month; Rental vacancy rate: 20.0%
Health Insurance: 89.3% have insurance; 79.5% have private insurance; 22.7% have public insurance; 10.7% do not have insurance; 5.4% of children under 18 do not have insurance
Newspapers: Clemmons Courier (weekly circulation 2100)
Transportation: Commute: 94.0% car, 0.1% public transportation, 0.9% walk, 4.6% work from home; Median travel time to work: 20.9 minutes
Additional Information Contacts
Village of Clemmons . . . . (336) 345-2929
    http://www.clemmons.org

GERMANTON (CDP). Covers a land area of 1.754 square miles and a water area of 0.016 square miles. Located at 36.26° N. Lat; 80.24° W. Long.
Population: 827; Growth (since 2000): n/a; Density: 471.4 persons per square mile; Race: 94.3% White, 4.0% Black/African American, 0.2% Asian, 0.1% American Indian/Alaska Native, 0.0% Native Hawaiian/Other Pacific Islander, 0.4% Two or more races, 1.9% Hispanic of any race; Average household size: 2.30; Median age: 47.8; Age under 18: 19.0%; Age 65 and over: 20.0%; Males per 100 females: 94.6
School District(s)
Stokes County Schools (PK-12)
    2012-13 Enrollment: 6,904 . . . . (336) 593-8146
Housing: Homeownership rate: 87.8%; Homeowner vacancy rate: 1.9%; Rental vacancy rate: 4.2%

KERNERSVILLE (town). Covers a land area of 17.322 square miles and a water area of 0.110 square miles. Located at 36.11° N. Lat; 80.09° W. Long. Elevation is 1,010 feet.
History: Kernersville was settled by families of German extraction about 1770. According to tradition, about 1756 Caleb Story bought the 400-acre town site outright at the rate of a gallon of rum for 100 acres.
Population: 23,123; Growth (since 2000): 35.0%; Density: 1,334.9 persons per square mile; Race: 77.8% White, 12.6% Black/African American, 1.9% Asian, 0.5% American Indian/Alaska Native, 0.0% Native Hawaiian/Other Pacific Islander, 2.3% Two or more races, 9.7% Hispanic of any race; Average household size: 2.29; Median age: 38.5; Age under 18: 23.7%; Age 65 and over: 13.1%; Males per 100 females: 88.4; Marriage status: 23.6% never married, 56.8% now married, 3.4% separated, 6.8% widowed, 12.8% divorced; Foreign born: 7.1%; Speak English only: 89.6%; With disability: 11.0%; Veterans: 10.9%; Ancestry: 12.6% English, 11.2% German, 9.4% American, 8.7% Irish, 2.4% Scotch-Irish
Employment: 17.7% management, business, and financial, 6.5% computer, engineering, and science, 9.2% education, legal, community service, arts, and media, 6.9% healthcare practitioners, 16.9% service, 26.2% sales and office, 5.7% natural resources, construction, and maintenance, 11.0% production, transportation, and material moving
Income: Per capita: $27,714; Median household: $50,032; Average household: $64,919; Households with income of $100,000 or more: 19.8%; Poverty rate: 13.5%
Educational Attainment: High school diploma or higher: 90.6%; Bachelor's degree or higher: 29.9%; Graduate/professional degree or higher: 9.3%
School District(s)
Forsyth County Schools (PK-12)
    2012-13 Enrollment: 53,881 . . . . (336) 727-2816

Housing: Homeownership rate: 57.2%; Median home value: $174,500; Median year structure built: 1989; Homeowner vacancy rate: 2.7%; Median gross rent: $720 per month; Rental vacancy rate: 11.6%
Health Insurance: 87.4% have insurance; 73.3% have private insurance; 25.6% have public insurance; 12.6% do not have insurance; 6.5% of children under 18 do not have insurance
Safety: Violent crime rate: 36.5 per 10,000 population; Property crime rate: 430.5 per 10,000 population
Newspapers: Kernersville News (weekly circulation 27000)
Transportation: Commute: 93.9% car, 0.0% public transportation, 1.2% walk, 4.0% work from home; Median travel time to work: 21.8 minutes
Additional Information Contacts
Town of Kernersville . . . . (336) 996-3177
    http://toknc.com

LEWISVILLE (town). Covers a land area of 13.969 square miles and a water area of 0.225 square miles. Located at 36.11° N. Lat; 80.42° W. Long. Elevation is 974 feet.
History: Lewisville officially incorporated in 1991 and today is one of the fastest growing communities in Forsyth County with almost 13,000 residents. In 1974, a little league team from Lewisville won the North Carolina state championship and finished third in the South Regional Tournament in St. Petersburg, Florida.
Population: 12,639; Growth (since 2000): 43.2%; Density: 904.8 persons per square mile; Race: 90.3% White, 5.0% Black/African American, 1.7% Asian, 0.3% American Indian/Alaska Native, 0.0% Native Hawaiian/Other Pacific Islander, 1.6% Two or more races, 3.4% Hispanic of any race; Average household size: 2.56; Median age: 43.4; Age under 18: 25.0%; Age 65 and over: 12.7%; Males per 100 females: 94.3; Marriage status: 21.4% never married, 63.3% now married, 1.4% separated, 5.4% widowed, 9.9% divorced; Foreign born: 4.1%; Speak English only: 94.6%; With disability: 8.9%; Veterans: 12.1%; Ancestry: 15.6% English, 14.7% Irish, 13.3% German, 12.7% American, 5.1% Italian
Employment: 20.5% management, business, and financial, 8.3% computer, engineering, and science, 15.3% education, legal, community service, arts, and media, 9.5% healthcare practitioners, 12.7% service, 22.1% sales and office, 4.5% natural resources, construction, and maintenance, 7.0% production, transportation, and material moving
Income: Per capita: $34,550; Median household: $72,825; Average household: $89,424; Households with income of $100,000 or more: 29.9%; Poverty rate: 8.9%
Educational Attainment: High school diploma or higher: 92.7%; Bachelor's degree or higher: 38.1%; Graduate/professional degree or higher: 12.8%
School District(s)
Forsyth County Schools (PK-12)
    2012-13 Enrollment: 53,881 . . . . (336) 727-2816
Housing: Homeownership rate: 86.4%; Median home value: $186,100; Median year structure built: 1984; Homeowner vacancy rate: 1.8%; Median gross rent: $815 per month; Rental vacancy rate: 15.1%
Health Insurance: 93.5% have insurance; 82.9% have private insurance; 22.4% have public insurance; 6.5% do not have insurance; 0.0% of children under 18 do not have insurance
Transportation: Commute: 91.8% car, 0.0% public transportation, 0.2% walk, 7.8% work from home; Median travel time to work: 22.7 minutes
Additional Information Contacts
Town of Lewisville . . . . (336) 945-5558
    http://www.lewisvillenc.net

PFAFFTOWN (unincorporated postal area)
ZCTA: 27040
    Covers a land area of 26.694 square miles and a water area of 0.353 square miles. Located at 36.17° N. Lat; 80.39° W. Long. Elevation is 817 feet.
    Population: 10,893; Growth (since 2000): 13.9%; Density: 408.1 persons per square mile; Race: 86.5% White, 8.9% Black/African American, 1.0% Asian, 0.4% American Indian/Alaska Native, 0.0% Native Hawaiian/Other Pacific Islander, 1.6% Two or more races, 3.7% Hispanic of any race; Average household size: 2.52; Median age: 44.6; Age under 18: 23.3%; Age 65 and over: 16.0%; Males per 100 females: 95.1; Marriage status: 25.2% never married, 58.1% now married, 1.9% separated, 6.7% widowed, 10.0% divorced; Foreign born: 4.7%; Speak English only: 93.4%; With disability: 10.2%; Veterans: 11.9%; Ancestry: 18.9% German, 14.2% Irish, 13.5% English, 12.9% American, 5.0% Italian

Employment: 14.8% management, business, and financial, 7.2% computer, engineering, and science, 12.2% education, legal, community service, arts, and media, 9.9% healthcare practitioners, 16.6% service, 23.2% sales and office, 8.9% natural resources, construction, and maintenance, 7.2% production, transportation, and material moving
Income: Per capita: $29,005; Median household: $62,197; Average household: $77,743; Households with income of $100,000 or more: 23.9%; Poverty rate: 10.7%
Educational Attainment: High school diploma or higher: 92.5%; Bachelor's degree or higher: 32.7%; Graduate/professional degree or higher: 12.8%
School District(s)
Forsyth County Schools (PK-12)
    2012-13 Enrollment: 53,881 . . . . (336) 727-2816
Housing: Homeownership rate: 88.9%; Median home value: $165,700; Median year structure built: 1981; Homeowner vacancy rate: 2.2%; Median gross rent: $689 per month; Rental vacancy rate: 11.0%
Health Insurance: 90.8% have insurance; 78.9% have private insurance; 24.7% have public insurance; 9.2% do not have insurance; 4.5% of children under 18 do not have insurance
Transportation: Commute: 92.9% car, 0.4% public transportation, 0.2% walk, 6.0% work from home; Median travel time to work: 21.7 minutes

RURAL HALL (town). Covers a land area of 2.852 square miles and a water area of 0.009 square miles. Located at 36.22° N. Lat; 80.30° W. Long. Elevation is 1,010 feet.
Population: 2,937; Growth (since 2000): 19.2%; Density: 1,029.8 persons per square mile; Race: 72.8% White, 15.9% Black/African American, 0.5% Asian, 0.2% American Indian/Alaska Native, 0.1% Native Hawaiian/Other Pacific Islander, 2.4% Two or more races, 13.5% Hispanic of any race; Average household size: 2.35; Median age: 38.2; Age under 18: 24.3%; Age 65 and over: 14.9%; Males per 100 females: 91.1; Marriage status: 20.9% never married, 58.7% now married, 3.5% separated, 7.8% widowed, 12.6% divorced; Foreign born: 6.9%; Speak English only: 90.5%; With disability: 12.3%; Veterans: 12.2%; Ancestry: 12.1% American, 10.2% German, 9.6% English, 5.0% Scottish, 3.4% Irish
Employment: 5.9% management, business, and financial, 3.1% computer, engineering, and science, 13.2% education, legal, community service, arts, and media, 4.4% healthcare practitioners, 21.3% service, 24.8% sales and office, 9.3% natural resources, construction, and maintenance, 18.0% production, transportation, and material moving
Income: Per capita: $28,787; Median household: $46,522; Average household: $59,747; Households with income of $100,000 or more: 18.6%; Poverty rate: 8.5%
Educational Attainment: High school diploma or higher: 87.1%; Bachelor's degree or higher: 19.5%; Graduate/professional degree or higher: 6.9%
School District(s)
Forsyth County Schools (PK-12)
    2012-13 Enrollment: 53,881 . . . . (336) 727-2816
Housing: Homeownership rate: 62.1%; Median home value: $134,900; Median year structure built: 1978; Homeowner vacancy rate: 3.1%; Median gross rent: $587 per month; Rental vacancy rate: 19.7%
Health Insurance: 88.6% have insurance; 78.0% have private insurance; 27.0% have public insurance; 11.4% do not have insurance; 4.4% of children under 18 do not have insurance
Transportation: Commute: 94.7% car, 0.0% public transportation, 0.8% walk, 2.3% work from home; Median travel time to work: 20.1 minutes

TOBACCOVILLE (village). Covers a land area of 7.650 square miles and a water area of 0.028 square miles. Located at 36.23° N. Lat; 80.36° W. Long. Elevation is 1,017 feet.
Population: 2,441; Growth (since 2000): 10.5%; Density: 319.1 persons per square mile; Race: 92.0% White, 6.2% Black/African American, 0.3% Asian, 0.5% American Indian/Alaska Native, 0.0% Native Hawaiian/Other Pacific Islander, 0.6% Two or more races, 2.0% Hispanic of any race; Average household size: 2.37; Median age: 45.9; Age under 18: 19.5%; Age 65 and over: 17.0%; Males per 100 females: 101.7
School District(s)
Forsyth County Schools (PK-12)
    2012-13 Enrollment: 53,881 . . . . (336) 727-2816
Housing: Homeownership rate: 83.4%; Homeowner vacancy rate: 1.8%; Rental vacancy rate: 6.5%

WALKERTOWN (town). Covers a land area of 6.587 square miles and a water area of 0.020 square miles. Located at 36.17° N. Lat; 80.15° W. Long. Elevation is 991 feet.

Population: 4,675; Growth (since 2000): 16.6%; Density: 709.7 persons per square mile; Race: 76.9% White, 17.5% Black/African American, 0.6% Asian, 0.3% American Indian/Alaska Native, 0.1% Native Hawaiian/Other Pacific Islander, 1.4% Two or more races, 5.6% Hispanic of any race; Average household size: 2.44; Median age: 42.6; Age under 18: 22.4%; Age 65 and over: 16.3%; Males per 100 females: 91.6; Marriage status: 28.4% never married, 50.1% now married, 3.4% separated, 9.4% widowed, 12.1% divorced; Foreign born: 0.5%; Speak English only: 95.5%; With disability: 11.3%; Veterans: 12.5%; Ancestry: 13.5% German, 13.0% American, 8.8% English, 7.2% Irish, 2.1% Italian

Employment: 9.7% management, business, and financial, 2.8% computer, engineering, and science, 14.8% education, legal, community service, arts, and media, 3.9% healthcare practitioners, 12.5% service, 24.2% sales and office, 16.2% natural resources, construction, and maintenance, 16.0% production, transportation, and material moving

Income: Per capita: $26,629; Median household: $45,388; Average household: $60,900; Households with income of $100,000 or more: 12.1%; Poverty rate: 12.2%

Educational Attainment: High school diploma or higher: 83.7%; Bachelor's degree or higher: 17.0%; Graduate/professional degree or higher: 3.1%

School District(s)
Forsyth County Schools (PK-12)
    2012-13 Enrollment: 53,881 . . . . (336) 727-2816

Housing: Homeownership rate: 78.6%; Median home value: $117,900; Median year structure built: 1977; Homeowner vacancy rate: 2.5%; Median gross rent: $645 per month; Rental vacancy rate: 9.6%

Health Insurance: 85.8% have insurance; 68.7% have private insurance; 36.5% have public insurance; 14.2% do not have insurance; 2.3% of children under 18 do not have insurance

Transportation: Commute: 95.7% car, 1.3% public transportation, 0.1% walk, 2.9% work from home; Median travel time to work: 23.6 minutes

Additional Information Contacts
Town of Walkertown . . . . (919) 435-9400
    http://www.wakeforestnc.gov

WINSTON-SALEM (city). County seat. Covers a land area of 132.449 square miles and a water area of 1.247 square miles. Located at 36.10° N. Lat; 80.26° W. Long. Elevation is 912 feet.

History: The two towns, Winston and Salem, became one municipality in 1913. The town's history began in 1753, when a small party of Moravians from Bethlehem, Pennsylvania, arrived and bought a large tract of land. The area was first called "der Wachau" and later Anglicized to "Wachovia." The first settlement was called "Bethabara," a few miles from the present Winston-Salem. A site in the center of the Wachovia tract was chosen to be Salem, or "peace," and a small settlement began there in 1766. In 1849, when Forsyth County was formed, land was sold for a courthouse site just north of Salem. The community was later named for Major Joseph Winston of Kings Mountain fame. Salem was incorporated by the assembly of 1856-1857; Winston by the assembly of 1859.

Population: 229,617; Growth (since 2000): 23.6%; Density: 1,733.6 persons per square mile; Race: 51.2% White, 34.7% Black/African American, 2.0% Asian, 0.4% American Indian/Alaska Native, 0.1% Native Hawaiian/Other Pacific Islander, 2.4% Two or more races, 14.7% Hispanic of any race; Average household size: 2.38; Median age: 34.6; Age under 18: 24.6%; Age 65 and over: 12.5%; Males per 100 females: 88.6; Marriage status: 38.4% never married, 44.1% now married, 3.0% separated, 6.7% widowed, 10.8% divorced; Foreign born: 11.2%; Speak English only: 82.9%; With disability: 10.6%; Veterans: 8.5%; Ancestry: 9.6% English, 8.8% German, 6.5% Irish, 5.1% American, 2.4% Italian

Employment: 13.2% management, business, and financial, 4.3% computer, engineering, and science, 12.6% education, legal, community service, arts, and media, 8.3% healthcare practitioners, 19.5% service, 22.6% sales and office, 7.2% natural resources, construction, and maintenance, 12.2% production, transportation, and material moving

Income: Per capita: $24,858; Median household: $40,148; Average household: $61,113; Households with income of $100,000 or more: 15.4%; Poverty rate: 23.2%

Educational Attainment: High school diploma or higher: 85.0%; Bachelor's degree or higher: 32.6%; Graduate/professional degree or higher: 12.2%

School District(s)
Arts Based Elementary (KG-05)
    2012-13 Enrollment: 372 . . . . (336) 748-4116
Carter G Woodson School (KG-12)
    2012-13 Enrollment: 485 . . . . (336) 723-6838
Davidson County Schools (PK-12)
    2012-13 Enrollment: 20,259 . . . . (336) 249-8181
Forsyth Academies (KG-08)
    2012-13 Enrollment: 710 . . . . (336) 922-1121
Forsyth County Schools (PK-12)
    2012-13 Enrollment: 53,881 . . . . (336) 727-2816
Quality Education Academy (PK-12)
    2012-13 Enrollment: 424 . . . . (336) 744-7138
The Steam Academy of Winston Salem (05-08)
    2012-13 Enrollment: 102 . . . . (336) 748-3838

Four-year College(s)
Carolina Christian College (Private, Not-for-profit, Churches of Christ)
    Fall 2013 Enrollment: 53 . . . . (336) 744-0900
    2013-14 Tuition: In-state $4,025; Out-of-state $4,025
Piedmont International University (Private, Not-for-profit, Baptist)
    Fall 2013 Enrollment: 384 . . . . (336) 725-8344
    2013-14 Tuition: In-state $12,455; Out-of-state $12,455
Salem College (Private, Not-for-profit, Moravian Church)
    Fall 2013 Enrollment: 1,187 . . . . (336) 721-2600
    2013-14 Tuition: In-state $24,566; Out-of-state $24,566
University of North Carolina School of the Arts (Public)
    Fall 2013 Enrollment: 912 . . . . (336) 770-3399
    2013-14 Tuition: In-state $8,271; Out-of-state $21,416
Wake Forest University (Private, Not-for-profit)
    Fall 2013 Enrollment: 7,602 . . . . (336) 758-5000
    2013-14 Tuition: In-state $44,742; Out-of-state $44,742
Winston-Salem State University (Public, Historically black)
    Fall 2013 Enrollment: 5,399 . . . . (336) 750-2000
    2013-14 Tuition: In-state $5,468; Out-of-state $14,281

Two-year College(s)
Forsyth Technical Community College (Public)
    Fall 2013 Enrollment: 9,528 . . . . (336) 723-0371
    2013-14 Tuition: In-state $1,962; Out-of-state $6,546

Vocational/Technical School(s)
Regency Beauty Institute-Winston-Salem (Private, For-profit)
    Fall 2013 Enrollment: 97 . . . . (800) 787-6456
    2013-14 Tuition: $16,200
The Hair Design School-Winston-Salem (Private, For-profit)
    Fall 2013 Enrollment: 121 . . . . (800) 920-4593
    2013-14 Tuition: $15,750
Winston Salem Barber School (Private, For-profit)
    Fall 2013 Enrollment: 60 . . . . (336) 724-1459
    2013-14 Tuition: $7,675

Housing: Homeownership rate: 56.3%; Median home value: $140,400; Median year structure built: 1974; Homeowner vacancy rate: 3.7%; Median gross rent: $706 per month; Rental vacancy rate: 12.5%

Health Insurance: 82.0% have insurance; 60.6% have private insurance; 31.8% have public insurance; 18.0% do not have insurance; 7.9% of children under 18 do not have insurance

Hospitals: North Carolina Baptist Hospital (1238 beds); Novant Health Forsyth Medical Center (921 beds); Novant Health Park Hospital (22 beds)

Safety: Violent crime rate: 60.5 per 10,000 population; Property crime rate: 545.1 per 10,000 population

Newspapers: Winston-Salem Journal (daily circulation 82200)

Transportation: Commute: 90.7% car, 1.7% public transportation, 1.9% walk, 3.7% work from home; Median travel time to work: 19.2 minutes; Amtrak: Train and bus service available.

Airports: Smith Reynolds (general aviation)

Additional Information Contacts
City of Winston Salem . . . . (336) 727-8000
    http://cityofws.org

Franklin County

Located in north central North Carolina; coastal plains area, drained by the Tar River. Covers a land area of 491.682 square miles, a water area of 2.816 square miles, and is located in the Eastern Time Zone at 36.09° N. Lat., 78.28° W. Long. The county was founded in 1779. County seat is Louisburg.

Franklin County is part of the Raleigh, NC Metropolitan Statistical Area. The entire metro area includes: Franklin County, NC; Johnston County, NC; Wake County, NC

Weather Station: Louisburg   Elevation: 259 feet

	Jan	Feb	Mar	Apr	May	Jun	Jul	Aug	Sep	Oct	Nov	Dec
High	51	55	63	72	79	87	90	88	82	73	64	54
Low	26	27	34	43	51	61	65	63	57	44	35	28
Precip	3.6	3.1	4.3	3.2	3.8	3.9	4.6	5.3	4.2	3.5	3.2	3.1
Snow	1.4	0.4	0.2	tr	0.0	0.0	0.0	0.0	0.0	0.0	tr	0.2

High and Low temperatures in degrees Fahrenheit; Precipitation and Snow in inches

Population: 60,619; Growth (since 2000): 28.3%; Density: 123.3 persons per square mile; Race: 66.0% White, 26.7% Black/African American, 0.5% Asian, 0.5% American Indian/Alaska Native, 0.0% Native Hawaiian/Other Pacific Islander, 1.8% two or more races, 7.9% Hispanic of any race; Average household size: 2.56; Median age: 39.1; Age under 18: 24.5%; Age 65 and over: 12.7%; Males per 100 females: 99.1; Marriage status: 26.4% never married, 58.4% now married, 3.1% separated, 6.2% widowed, 9.0% divorced; Foreign born: 4.6%; Speak English only: 92.1%; With disability: 14.0%; Veterans: 9.2%; Ancestry: 17.9% American, 10.7% English, 10.3% Irish, 8.6% German, 3.6% Italian
Religion: Six largest groups: 21.0% Baptist, 10.3% Non-denominational Protestant, 3.2% Methodist/Pietist, 1.4% Pentecostal, 1.0% Presbyterian-Reformed, 0.9% Catholicism
Economy: Unemployment rate: 5.1%; Leading industries: 18.4% construction; 13.9% retail trade; 12.3% other services (except public administration); Farms: 542 totaling 116,889 acres; Company size: 0 employ 1,000 or more persons, 1 employs 500 to 999 persons, 13 employ 100 to 499 persons, 915 employ less than 100 persons; Business ownership: 1,275 women-owned, 510 Black-owned, 124 Hispanic-owned, n/a Asian-owned
Employment: 13.2% management, business, and financial, 4.3% computer, engineering, and science, 7.8% education, legal, community service, arts, and media, 6.2% healthcare practitioners, 15.7% service, 25.1% sales and office, 13.2% natural resources, construction, and maintenance, 14.5% production, transportation, and material moving
Income: Per capita: $21,399; Median household: $41,696; Average household: $54,997; Households with income of $100,000 or more: 13.8%; Poverty rate: 16.1%
Educational Attainment: High school diploma or higher: 81.2%; Bachelor's degree or higher: 17.1%; Graduate/professional degree or higher: 5.1%
Housing: Homeownership rate: 74.0%; Median home value: $123,300; Median year structure built: 1991; Homeowner vacancy rate: 2.4%; Median gross rent: $702 per month; Rental vacancy rate: 7.6%
Vital Statistics: Birth rate: 105.2 per 10,000 population; Death rate: 84.6 per 10,000 population; Age-adjusted cancer mortality rate: 186.1 deaths per 100,000 population
Health Insurance: 82.5% have insurance; 60.9% have private insurance; 32.5% have public insurance; 17.5% do not have insurance; 7.3% of children under 18 do not have insurance
Health Care: Physicians: 3.4 per 10,000 population; Hospital beds: 11.4 per 10,000 population; Hospital admissions: 195.8 per 10,000 population
Air Quality Index: 97.6% good, 2.4% moderate, 0.0% unhealthy for sensitive individuals, 0.0% unhealthy (percent of days)
Transportation: Commute: 92.8% car, 0.3% public transportation, 1.7% walk, 4.3% work from home; Median travel time to work: 30.2 minutes
Presidential Election: 47.3% Obama, 51.4% Romney (2012)
Additional Information Contacts
Franklin Government. . . . . (919) 496-5994
  http://www.co.franklin.nc.us

Franklin County Communities

BUNN (town). Covers a land area of 0.540 square miles and a water area of 0 square miles. Located at 35.96° N. Lat; 78.25° W. Long. Elevation is 279 feet.
Population: 344; Growth (since 2000): -3.6%; Density: 637.5 persons per square mile; Race: 66.6% White, 28.2% Black/African American, 0.0% Asian, 0.6% American Indian/Alaska Native, 0.0% Native Hawaiian/Other Pacific Islander, 2.6% Two or more races, 10.2% Hispanic of any race; Average household size: 2.19; Median age: 48.0; Age under 18: 20.6%; Age 65 and over: 17.4%; Males per 100 females: 79.2

Franklin County Schools (PK-12)
  2012-13 Enrollment: 8,685 . . . . (919) 496-2600
Housing: Homeownership rate: 47.8%; Homeowner vacancy rate: 1.3%; Rental vacancy rate: 21.9%
Safety: Violent crime rate: 57.1 per 10,000 population; Property crime rate: 628.6 per 10,000 population

CENTERVILLE (town). Covers a land area of 0.282 square miles and a water area of 0.002 square miles. Located at 36.19° N. Lat; 78.11° W. Long. Elevation is 322 feet.
Population: 89; Growth (since 2000): -10.1%; Density: 315.4 persons per square mile; Race: 93.3% White, 3.4% Black/African American, 0.0% Asian, 0.0% American Indian/Alaska Native, 0.0% Native Hawaiian/Other Pacific Islander, 0.0% Two or more races, 4.5% Hispanic of any race; Average household size: 2.47; Median age: 41.5; Age under 18: 18.0%; Age 65 and over: 16.9%; Males per 100 females: 122.5
Housing: Homeownership rate: 72.2%; Homeowner vacancy rate: 3.7%; Rental vacancy rate: 23.1%

FRANKLINTON (town). Covers a land area of 1.603 square miles and a water area of 0 square miles. Located at 36.10° N. Lat; 78.45° W. Long. Elevation is 410 feet.
Population: 2,023; Growth (since 2000): 15.9%; Density: 1,262.3 persons per square mile; Race: 55.8% White, 40.8% Black/African American, 0.2% Asian, 0.1% American Indian/Alaska Native, 0.0% Native Hawaiian/Other Pacific Islander, 2.3% Two or more races, 4.1% Hispanic of any race; Average household size: 2.31; Median age: 41.4; Age under 18: 22.0%; Age 65 and over: 18.5%; Males per 100 females: 84.4

Franklin County Schools (PK-12)
  2012-13 Enrollment: 8,685 . . . . (919) 496-2600
Granville County Schools (PK-12)
  2012-13 Enrollment: 8,655 . . . . (919) 693-4613
Housing: Homeownership rate: 63.1%; Homeowner vacancy rate: 4.1%; Rental vacancy rate: 6.9%
Safety: Violent crime rate: 34.0 per 10,000 population; Property crime rate: 466.0 per 10,000 population

LAKE ROYALE (CDP). Covers a land area of 6.466 square miles and a water area of 0.539 square miles. Located at 35.96° N. Lat; 78.19° W. Long.
Population: 2,506; Growth (since 2000): 3,640.3%; Density: 387.5 persons per square mile; Race: 82.1% White, 14.5% Black/African American, 0.5% Asian, 0.7% American Indian/Alaska Native, 0.0% Native Hawaiian/Other Pacific Islander, 1.6% Two or more races, 2.3% Hispanic of any race; Average household size: 2.35; Median age: 45.0; Age under 18: 20.9%; Age 65 and over: 16.0%; Males per 100 females: 101.9; Marriage status: 19.4% never married, 70.0% now married, 0.7% separated, 2.6% widowed, 8.0% divorced; Foreign born: 3.7%; Speak English only: 94.5%; With disability: 8.9%; Veterans: 14.9%; Ancestry: 15.8% Irish, 12.7% German, 10.9% English, 9.4% American, 7.9% French
Employment: 23.8% management, business, and financial, 6.5% computer, engineering, and science, 7.5% education, legal, community service, arts, and media, 9.0% healthcare practitioners, 4.6% service, 23.9% sales and office, 1.6% natural resources, construction, and maintenance, 23.1% production, transportation, and material moving
Income: Per capita: $25,752; Median household: $44,019; Average household: $64,262; Households with income of $100,000 or more: 20.5%; Poverty rate: 6.3%
Educational Attainment: High school diploma or higher: 95.2%; Bachelor's degree or higher: 30.9%; Graduate/professional degree or higher: 11.6%
Housing: Homeownership rate: 84.1%; Median home value: $165,100; Median year structure built: 1998; Homeowner vacancy rate: 6.3%; Median gross rent: $1,317 per month; Rental vacancy rate: 7.5%
Health Insurance: 90.1% have insurance; 70.6% have private insurance; 39.1% have public insurance; 9.9% do not have insurance; 10.1% of children under 18 do not have insurance
Transportation: Commute: 89.2% car, 0.0% public transportation, 3.7% walk, 7.1% work from home; Median travel time to work: 36.2 minutes

LOUISBURG (town). County seat. Covers a land area of 2.708 square miles and a water area of 0.004 square miles. Located at 36.10° N. Lat; 78.30° W. Long. Elevation is 220 feet.

History: Louisburg was first settled in 1758, and in 1764 was named in commemoration of the capture by American forces of the French fortress at Louisburg, Nova Scotia.

Population: 3,359; Growth (since 2000): 8.0%; Density: 1,240.5 persons per square mile; Race: 47.3% White, 46.9% Black/African American, 0.9% Asian, 0.3% American Indian/Alaska Native, 0.0% Native Hawaiian/Other Pacific Islander, 1.7% Two or more races, 5.5% Hispanic of any race; Average household size: 2.17; Median age: 38.2; Age under 18: 18.0%; Age 65 and over: 21.4%; Males per 100 females: 89.8; Marriage status: 37.0% never married, 37.1% now married, 0.8% separated, 19.1% widowed, 6.8% divorced; Foreign born: 4.4%; Speak English only: 93.1%; With disability: 20.5%; Veterans: 9.1%; Ancestry: 21.8% American, 16.4% English, 3.8% German, 2.8% Scottish, 2.2% Irish

Employment: 7.2% management, business, and financial, 0.5% computer, engineering, and science, 18.3% education, legal, community service, arts, and media, 11.1% healthcare practitioners, 13.5% service, 28.0% sales and office, 7.0% natural resources, construction, and maintenance, 14.4% production, transportation, and material moving

Income: Per capita: $18,529; Median household: $27,325; Average household: $46,798; Households with income of $100,000 or more: 7.8%; Poverty rate: 23.7%

Educational Attainment: High school diploma or higher: 81.2%; Bachelor's degree or higher: 31.2%; Graduate/professional degree or higher: 14.1%

School District(s)
Crosscreek Charter (KG-08)
    2012-13 Enrollment: 181 . . . . (919) 497-3198
Franklin County Schools (PK-12)
    2012-13 Enrollment: 8,685 . . . . (919) 496-2600

Two-year College(s)
Louisburg College (Private, Not-for-profit, United Methodist)
    Fall 2013 Enrollment: 678 . . . . (919) 496-2521
    2013-14 Tuition: In-state $15,540; Out-of-state $15,540

Housing: Homeownership rate: 42.7%; Median home value: $115,500; Median year structure built: 1971; Homeowner vacancy rate: 4.7%; Median gross rent: $676 per month; Rental vacancy rate: 5.5%

Health Insurance: 86.5% have insurance; 67.2% have private insurance; 34.3% have public insurance; 13.5% do not have insurance; 0.0% of children under 18 do not have insurance

Hospitals: Novant Health Franklin Medical Center (85 beds)

Safety: Violent crime rate: 32.1 per 10,000 population; Property crime rate: 297.7 per 10,000 population

Newspapers: Franklin Times (weekly circulation 9200)

Transportation: Commute: 92.1% car, 0.0% public transportation, 7.9% walk, 0.0% work from home; Median travel time to work: 22.6 minutes

Airports: Triangle North Executive (general aviation)

Additional Information Contacts
Town of Louisburg . . . . (919) 496-5994
    http://townoflouisburg.com

YOUNGSVILLE (town). Covers a land area of 1.617 square miles and a water area of 0.007 square miles. Located at 36.03° N. Lat; 78.48° W. Long. Elevation is 466 feet.

Population: 1,157; Growth (since 2000): 77.7%; Density: 715.4 persons per square mile; Race: 69.3% White, 25.1% Black/African American, 0.8% Asian, 0.3% American Indian/Alaska Native, 0.0% Native Hawaiian/Other Pacific Islander, 1.6% Two or more races, 4.8% Hispanic of any race; Average household size: 2.22; Median age: 32.5; Age under 18: 25.0%; Age 65 and over: 8.8%; Males per 100 females: 92.5

School District(s)
Franklin County Schools (PK-12)
    2012-13 Enrollment: 8,685 . . . . (919) 496-2600

Housing: Homeownership rate: 38.9%; Homeowner vacancy rate: 7.7%; Rental vacancy rate: 3.6%

Gaston County

Located in southern North Carolina; in piedmont area, bounded on the south by South Carolina, and on the east by the Catawba River; drained by the South Fork of the Catawba River. Covers a land area of 356.027 square miles, a water area of 8.075 square miles, and is located in the Eastern Time Zone at 35.29° N. Lat., 81.18° W. Long. The county was founded in 1846. County seat is Gastonia.

Gaston County is part of the Charlotte-Concord-Gastonia, NC-SC Metropolitan Statistical Area. The entire metro area includes: Cabarrus County, NC; Gaston County, NC; Iredell County, NC; Lincoln County, NC; Mecklenburg County, NC; Rowan County, NC; Union County, NC; Chester County, SC; Lancaster County, SC; York County, SC

Weather Station: Gastonia   Elevation: 700 feet

	Jan	Feb	Mar	Apr	May	Jun	Jul	Aug	Sep	Oct	Nov	Dec
High	52	56	64	73	80	87	90	89	82	73	64	54
Low	31	33	40	48	57	66	69	69	62	50	41	33
Precip	3.6	3.4	3.8	2.9	3.1	3.8	3.3	4.5	3.7	3.7	3.0	3.2
Snow	0.5	0.2	0.0	0.0	0.0	0.0	0.0	0.0	0.0	0.0	0.0	tr

High and Low temperatures in degrees Fahrenheit; Precipitation and Snow in inches

Population: 206,086; Growth (since 2000): 8.3%; Density: 578.8 persons per square mile; Race: 78.2% White, 15.3% Black/African American, 1.2% Asian, 0.4% American Indian/Alaska Native, 0.0% Native Hawaiian/Other Pacific Islander, 1.8% two or more races, 5.9% Hispanic of any race; Average household size: 2.54; Median age: 38.9; Age under 18: 23.9%; Age 65 and over: 13.2%; Males per 100 females: 93.7; Marriage status: 27.7% never married, 53.1% now married, 3.8% separated, 7.4% widowed, 11.8% divorced; Foreign born: 5.0%; Speak English only: 92.6%; With disability: 16.1%; Veterans: 9.8%; Ancestry: 14.9% American, 12.1% German, 9.9% Irish, 8.0% English, 3.8% Scotch-Irish

Religion: Six largest groups: 30.4% Baptist, 6.9% Methodist/Pietist, 5.5% Pentecostal, 4.5% Non-denominational Protestant, 3.6% Presbyterian-Reformed, 2.0% Catholicism

Economy: Unemployment rate: 5.8%; Leading industries: 16.4% retail trade; 13.7% other services (except public administration); 12.1% health care and social assistance; Farms: 520 totaling 41,923 acres; Company size: 3 employ 1,000 or more persons, 4 employ 500 to 999 persons, 90 employ 100 to 499 persons, 3,796 employ less than 100 persons; Business ownership: 4,285 women-owned, n/a Black-owned, n/a Hispanic-owned, 347 Asian-owned

Employment: 11.6% management, business, and financial, 3.4% computer, engineering, and science, 9.0% education, legal, community service, arts, and media, 5.2% healthcare practitioners, 17.1% service, 25.4% sales and office, 9.8% natural resources, construction, and maintenance, 18.6% production, transportation, and material moving

Income: Per capita: $22,658; Median household: $42,017; Average household: $57,285; Households with income of $100,000 or more: 13.9%; Poverty rate: 17.9%

Educational Attainment: High school diploma or higher: 81.0%; Bachelor's degree or higher: 18.0%; Graduate/professional degree or higher: 5.2%

Housing: Homeownership rate: 67.4%; Median home value: $123,600; Median year structure built: 1978; Homeowner vacancy rate: 2.8%; Median gross rent: $714 per month; Rental vacancy rate: 11.7%

Vital Statistics: Birth rate: 121.6 per 10,000 population; Death rate: 102.9 per 10,000 population; Age-adjusted cancer mortality rate: 204.3 deaths per 100,000 population

Health Insurance: 82.4% have insurance; 59.8% have private insurance; 33.6% have public insurance; 17.6% do not have insurance; 9.6% of children under 18 do not have insurance

Health Care: Physicians: 17.0 per 10,000 population; Hospital beds: 19.0 per 10,000 population; Hospital admissions: 1,113.4 per 10,000 population

Air Quality Index: 89.0% good, 11.0% moderate, 0.0% unhealthy for sensitive individuals, 0.0% unhealthy (percent of days)

Transportation: Commute: 95.5% car, 0.5% public transportation, 0.8% walk, 2.6% work from home; Median travel time to work: 24.4 minutes

Presidential Election: 36.7% Obama, 62.0% Romney (2012)

National and State Parks: Crowders Mountain State Park

Additional Information Contacts
Gaston Government . . . . (704) 866-3100
    http://www.gastongov.com

Gaston County Communities

ALEXIS (unincorporated postal area)
ZCTA: 28006
    Covers a land area of 5.358 square miles and a water area of 0.007 square miles. Located at 35.41° N. Lat; 81.09° W. Long. Elevation is 873 feet.

Population: 1,130; Growth (since 2000): 98.9%; Density: 210.9 persons per square mile; Race: 95.8% White, 1.2% Black/African American, 0.2% Asian, 0.9% American Indian/Alaska Native, 0.0% Native Hawaiian/Other Pacific Islander, 1.8% Two or more races, 0.6% Hispanic of any race; Average household size: 2.46; Median age: 42.5; Age under 18: 20.8%; Age 65 and over: 15.2%; Males per 100 females: 92.2
Housing: Homeownership rate: 80.2%; Homeowner vacancy rate: 1.9%; Rental vacancy rate: 13.2%

BELMONT (city). Covers a land area of 9.934 square miles and a water area of 0.175 square miles. Located at 35.23° N. Lat; 81.04° W. Long. Elevation is 682 feet.
History: Seat of Belmont Abbey College. Monastery and Cathedral (completed 1894).
Population: 10,076; Growth (since 2000): 15.7%; Density: 1,014.3 persons per square mile; Race: 83.6% White, 8.9% Black/African American, 4.1% Asian, 0.3% American Indian/Alaska Native, 0.2% Native Hawaiian/Other Pacific Islander, 1.6% Two or more races, 3.5% Hispanic of any race; Average household size: 2.47; Median age: 37.0; Age under 18: 23.1%; Age 65 and over: 10.9%; Males per 100 females: 94.1; Marriage status: 29.4% never married, 52.0% now married, 3.2% separated, 5.9% widowed, 12.7% divorced; Foreign born: 5.6%; Speak English only: 93.0%; With disability: 13.5%; Veterans: 9.5%; Ancestry: 16.8% German, 14.2% Irish, 13.4% American, 11.6% English, 5.8% Scotch-Irish
Employment: 17.9% management, business, and financial, 3.8% computer, engineering, and science, 14.8% education, legal, community service, arts, and media, 7.1% healthcare practitioners, 15.7% service, 25.7% sales and office, 4.8% natural resources, construction, and maintenance, 10.2% production, transportation, and material moving
Income: Per capita: $33,624; Median household: $54,091; Average household: $82,435; Households with income of $100,000 or more: 25.0%; Poverty rate: 9.2%
Educational Attainment: High school diploma or higher: 86.9%; Bachelor's degree or higher: 33.9%; Graduate/professional degree or higher: 13.4%

School District(s)
Gaston County Schools (PK-12)
    2012-13 Enrollment: 31,804 . . . . (704) 866-6100
Four-year College(s)
Belmont Abbey College (Private, Not-for-profit, Roman Catholic)
    Fall 2013 Enrollment: 1,647 . . . . (704) 461-6700
    2013-14 Tuition: In-state $18,500; Out-of-state $18,500
Housing: Homeownership rate: 70.6%; Median home value: $152,800; Median year structure built: 1980; Homeowner vacancy rate: 3.9%; Median gross rent: $741 per month; Rental vacancy rate: 10.5%
Health Insurance: 86.9% have insurance; 74.5% have private insurance; 24.2% have public insurance; 13.1% do not have insurance; 6.6% of children under 18 do not have insurance
Newspapers: Banner News (weekly circulation 3000)
Transportation: Commute: 91.7% car, 0.2% public transportation, 2.2% walk, 5.3% work from home; Median travel time to work: 22.0 minutes
Additional Information Contacts
City of Belmont . . . . (650) 637-2999
    http://www.belmont.gov

BESSEMER CITY (city). Covers a land area of 4.790 square miles and a water area of 0.038 square miles. Located at 35.28° N. Lat; 81.29° W. Long. Elevation is 902 feet.
History: Bessemer City is a small suburban city in Gaston County, North Carolina is named for Sir Henry Bessemer who created the Bessemer process for smelting iron. Bessemer City was founded on land purchased from the Ormand family, near the Sloan-Washington-Ormand Iron Furnace. Ironically, it was the Bessemer Process that made Bessemer City's early iron smelting industry obsolete.
Population: 5,340; Growth (since 2000): 4.3%; Density: 1,114.9 persons per square mile; Race: 79.6% White, 14.4% Black/African American, 0.7% Asian, 0.4% American Indian/Alaska Native, 0.0% Native Hawaiian/Other Pacific Islander, 1.9% Two or more races, 5.1% Hispanic of any race; Average household size: 2.58; Median age: 37.0; Age under 18: 25.7%; Age 65 and over: 13.0%; Males per 100 females: 95.0; Marriage status: 28.6% never married, 44.9% now married, 3.9% separated, 10.6% widowed, 15.9% divorced; Foreign born: 1.4%; Speak English only: 95.2%;

With disability: 18.0%; Veterans: 12.5%; Ancestry: 22.0% American, 14.2% German, 10.6% Irish, 7.2% English, 3.7% Scotch-Irish
Employment: 4.2% management, business, and financial, 3.7% computer, engineering, and science, 6.7% education, legal, community service, arts, and media, 2.7% healthcare practitioners, 21.9% service, 18.6% sales and office, 12.2% natural resources, construction, and maintenance, 29.9% production, transportation, and material moving
Income: Per capita: $16,118; Median household: $34,482; Average household: $41,664; Households with income of $100,000 or more: 6.5%; Poverty rate: 22.2%
Educational Attainment: High school diploma or higher: 79.7%; Bachelor's degree or higher: 6.3%; Graduate/professional degree or higher: 1.5%

School District(s)
Gaston County Schools (PK-12)
    2012-13 Enrollment: 31,804 . . . . (704) 866-6100
Housing: Homeownership rate: 61.7%; Median home value: $95,000; Median year structure built: 1969; Homeowner vacancy rate: 3.5%; Median gross rent: $743 per month; Rental vacancy rate: 14.2%
Health Insurance: 75.7% have insurance; 50.4% have private insurance; 35.3% have public insurance; 24.3% do not have insurance; 27.8% of children under 18 do not have insurance
Transportation: Commute: 98.4% car, 0.0% public transportation, 0.0% walk, 1.6% work from home; Median travel time to work: 20.7 minutes
Additional Information Contacts
City of Bessemer City . . . . (704) 629-5542
    http://bessemercity.com

CHERRYVILLE (city). Covers a land area of 5.492 square miles and a water area of 0.012 square miles. Located at 35.38° N. Lat; 81.38° W. Long. Elevation is 978 feet.
History: Incorporated 1889.
Population: 5,760; Growth (since 2000): 7.4%; Density: 1,048.9 persons per square mile; Race: 85.1% White, 10.3% Black/African American, 0.7% Asian, 0.2% American Indian/Alaska Native, 0.0% Native Hawaiian/Other Pacific Islander, 1.6% Two or more races, 3.7% Hispanic of any race; Average household size: 2.40; Median age: 41.7; Age under 18: 22.8%; Age 65 and over: 19.2%; Males per 100 females: 89.8; Marriage status: 24.7% never married, 53.1% now married, 1.9% separated, 11.4% widowed, 10.8% divorced; Foreign born: 2.1%; Speak English only: 95.9%; With disability: 15.2%; Veterans: 8.9%; Ancestry: 17.0% American, 16.3% German, 9.9% English, 9.3% Irish, 4.5% Scotch-Irish
Employment: 9.1% management, business, and financial, 3.3% computer, engineering, and science, 12.5% education, legal, community service, arts, and media, 8.5% healthcare practitioners, 13.2% service, 27.7% sales and office, 8.8% natural resources, construction, and maintenance, 16.9% production, transportation, and material moving
Income: Per capita: $23,445; Median household: $42,656; Average household: $55,618; Households with income of $100,000 or more: 17.4%; Poverty rate: 11.1%
Educational Attainment: High school diploma or higher: 80.4%; Bachelor's degree or higher: 19.4%; Graduate/professional degree or higher: 8.4%

School District(s)
Gaston County Schools (PK-12)
    2012-13 Enrollment: 31,804 . . . . (704) 866-6100
Housing: Homeownership rate: 70.4%; Median home value: $104,300; Median year structure built: 1963; Homeowner vacancy rate: 3.2%; Median gross rent: $690 per month; Rental vacancy rate: 12.4%
Health Insurance: 86.6% have insurance; 67.7% have private insurance; 30.9% have public insurance; 13.4% do not have insurance; 4.9% of children under 18 do not have insurance
Safety: Violent crime rate: 30.9 per 10,000 population; Property crime rate: 321.4 per 10,000 population
Newspapers: Cherryville Eagle (weekly circulation 2800)
Transportation: Commute: 96.4% car, 0.0% public transportation, 2.1% walk, 0.7% work from home; Median travel time to work: 24.0 minutes
Additional Information Contacts
City of Cherryville . . . . (704) 435-1700
    http://www.cityofcherryville.com

CRAMERTON (town). Covers a land area of 3.684 square miles and a water area of 0.299 square miles. Located at 35.24° N. Lat; 81.07° W. Long. Elevation is 610 feet.

Population: 4,165; Growth (since 2000): 40.0%; Density: 1,130.5 persons per square mile; Race: 91.1% White, 4.2% Black/African American, 2.2% Asian, 0.6% American Indian/Alaska Native, 0.0% Native Hawaiian/Other Pacific Islander, 1.5% Two or more races, 1.3% Hispanic of any race; Average household size: 2.44; Median age: 40.1; Age under 18: 23.7%; Age 65 and over: 13.2%; Males per 100 females: 85.5; Marriage status: 22.6% never married, 57.8% now married, 4.8% separated, 5.9% widowed, 13.7% divorced; Foreign born: 7.0%; Speak English only: 88.9%; With disability: 10.6%; Veterans: 13.8%; Ancestry: 21.4% American, 13.4% German, 11.3% Irish, 9.4% English, 8.3% Scottish
Employment: 17.4% management, business, and financial, 2.2% computer, engineering, and science, 9.9% education, legal, community service, arts, and media, 10.9% healthcare practitioners, 12.8% service, 26.0% sales and office, 12.5% natural resources, construction, and maintenance, 8.4% production, transportation, and material moving
Income: Per capita: $32,434; Median household: $68,500; Average household: $77,042; Households with income of $100,000 or more: 23.5%; Poverty rate: 6.6%
Educational Attainment: High school diploma or higher: 89.8%; Bachelor's degree or higher: 34.7%; Graduate/professional degree or higher: 10.0%

School District(s)
Gaston County Schools (PK-12)
    2012-13 Enrollment: 31,804 . . . . (704) 866-6100
Housing: Homeownership rate: 76.6%; Median home value: $165,500; Median year structure built: 1991; Homeowner vacancy rate: 3.7%; Median gross rent: $830 per month; Rental vacancy rate: 11.4%
Health Insurance: 90.9% have insurance; 78.1% have private insurance; 20.6% have public insurance; 9.1% do not have insurance; 2.2% of children under 18 do not have insurance
Transportation: Commute: 95.1% car, 0.0% public transportation, 0.4% walk, 3.7% work from home; Median travel time to work: 23.9 minutes
Additional Information Contacts
Town of Cramerton . . . . (704) 824-4337
    http://www.cramerton.org

DALLAS (town). Covers a land area of 2.908 square miles and a water area of <.001 square miles. Located at 35.32° N. Lat; 81.18° W. Long. Elevation is 794 feet.

History: Dallas was the seat of Gaston County from 1846 to 1911.
Population: 4,488; Growth (since 2000): 31.9%; Density: 1,543.1 persons per square mile; Race: 76.4% White, 15.9% Black/African American, 0.6% Asian, 0.4% American Indian/Alaska Native, 0.0% Native Hawaiian/Other Pacific Islander, 1.8% Two or more races, 8.0% Hispanic of any race; Average household size: 2.50; Median age: 34.9; Age under 18: 26.0%; Age 65 and over: 12.1%; Males per 100 females: 91.1; Marriage status: 33.3% never married, 47.6% now married, 3.4% separated, 7.3% widowed, 11.8% divorced; Foreign born: 3.5%; Speak English only: 94.2%; With disability: 13.5%; Veterans: 11.7%; Ancestry: 14.9% American, 9.0% Irish, 8.2% German, 5.8% English, 4.3% Scotch-Irish
Employment: 11.6% management, business, and financial, 1.7% computer, engineering, and science, 4.7% education, legal, community service, arts, and media, 5.2% healthcare practitioners, 21.7% service, 27.5% sales and office, 8.9% natural resources, construction, and maintenance, 18.7% production, transportation, and material moving
Income: Per capita: $20,117; Median household: $33,424; Average household: $47,036; Households with income of $100,000 or more: 8.2%; Poverty rate: 13.7%
Educational Attainment: High school diploma or higher: 86.0%; Bachelor's degree or higher: 16.0%; Graduate/professional degree or higher: 3.1%

School District(s)
Gaston County Schools (PK-12)
    2012-13 Enrollment: 31,804 . . . . (704) 866-6100
Nc Dept of Juvenile Justice (KG-12)
    2012-13 Enrollment: n/a . . . . (919) 733-3388
Two-year College(s)
Gaston College (Public)
    Fall 2013 Enrollment: 5,977 . . . . (704) 922-6200
    2013-14 Tuition: In-state $2,560; Out-of-state $8,704

Housing: Homeownership rate: 57.6%; Median home value: $123,500; Median year structure built: 1980; Homeowner vacancy rate: 3.6%; Median gross rent: $635 per month; Rental vacancy rate: 11.3%
Health Insurance: 78.2% have insurance; 58.6% have private insurance; 30.2% have public insurance; 21.8% do not have insurance; 11.5% of children under 18 do not have insurance
Transportation: Commute: 93.5% car, 0.0% public transportation, 5.4% walk, 0.5% work from home; Median travel time to work: 22.7 minutes
Additional Information Contacts
Town of Dallas. . . . . (704) 922-3176
    http://www.dallasnc.net

GASTONIA (city). County seat. Covers a land area of 50.504 square miles and a water area of 0.226 square miles. Located at 35.25° N. Lat; 81.18° W. Long. Elevation is 804 feet.

History: Gastonia was named for Judge William Gaston.
Population: 71,741; Growth (since 2000): 8.2%; Density: 1,420.5 persons per square mile; Race: 63.0% White, 27.8% Black/African American, 1.3% Asian, 0.4% American Indian/Alaska Native, 0.0% Native Hawaiian/Other Pacific Islander, 2.2% Two or more races, 9.6% Hispanic of any race; Average household size: 2.52; Median age: 38.0; Age under 18: 24.7%; Age 65 and over: 13.6%; Males per 100 females: 89.6; Marriage status: 34.3% never married, 47.6% now married, 3.8% separated, 7.1% widowed, 11.0% divorced; Foreign born: 7.9%; Speak English only: 88.8%; With disability: 14.7%; Veterans: 8.6%; Ancestry: 9.0% German, 8.2% American, 8.0% English, 7.9% Irish, 3.6% Scotch-Irish
Employment: 11.5% management, business, and financial, 3.1% computer, engineering, and science, 9.9% education, legal, community service, arts, and media, 4.7% healthcare practitioners, 18.1% service, 24.4% sales and office, 7.7% natural resources, construction, and maintenance, 20.7% production, transportation, and material moving
Income: Per capita: $21,531; Median household: $40,053; Average household: $56,109; Households with income of $100,000 or more: 13.1%; Poverty rate: 22.3%
Educational Attainment: High school diploma or higher: 80.6%; Bachelor's degree or higher: 21.6%; Graduate/professional degree or higher: 6.5%

School District(s)
Gaston County Schools (PK-12)
    2012-13 Enrollment: 31,804 . . . . (704) 866-6100
Piedmont Community Charter (KG-12)
    2012-13 Enrollment: 1,203 . . . . (704) 853-2428
Vocational/Technical School(s)
Paul Mitchell the School-Gastonia (Private, For-profit)
    Fall 2013 Enrollment: 386 . . . . (704) 864-8723
    2013-14 Tuition: $17,625
Housing: Homeownership rate: 56.3%; Median home value: $135,900; Median year structure built: 1975; Homeowner vacancy rate: 3.6%; Median gross rent: $754 per month; Rental vacancy rate: 11.7%
Health Insurance: 81.4% have insurance; 55.9% have private insurance; 35.7% have public insurance; 18.6% do not have insurance; 9.8% of children under 18 do not have insurance
Hospitals: Caromont Regional Medical Center (435 beds)
Safety: Violent crime rate: 69.8 per 10,000 population; Property crime rate: 529.2 per 10,000 population
Newspapers: Gaston Gazette (daily circulation 29300)
Transportation: Commute: 95.3% car, 0.9% public transportation, 0.9% walk, 2.4% work from home; Median travel time to work: 23.7 minutes; Amtrak: Train service available.
Additional Information Contacts
City of Gastonia. . . . . (704) 866-6720
    http://www.cityofgastonia.com

HIGH SHOALS (city). Covers a land area of 2.595 square miles and a water area of 0.056 square miles. Located at 35.39° N. Lat; 81.20° W. Long. Elevation is 771 feet.

Population: 696; Growth (since 2000): -4.5%; Density: 268.2 persons per square mile; Race: 85.9% White, 7.3% Black/African American, 0.3% Asian, 1.4% American Indian/Alaska Native, 0.0% Native Hawaiian/Other Pacific Islander, 3.2% Two or more races, 4.2% Hispanic of any race; Average household size: 2.59; Median age: 37.0; Age under 18: 26.0%; Age 65 and over: 11.2%; Males per 100 females: 89.1
Housing: Homeownership rate: 62.1%; Homeowner vacancy rate: 2.9%; Rental vacancy rate: 8.7%

LOWELL (city). Covers a land area of 2.661 square miles and a water area of 0.005 square miles. Located at 35.27° N. Lat; 81.10° W. Long. Elevation is 784 feet.

Population: 3,526; Growth (since 2000): 32.5%; Density: 1,325.0 persons per square mile; Race: 85.9% White, 8.7% Black/African American, 1.0% Asian, 0.5% American Indian/Alaska Native, 0.1% Native Hawaiian/Other Pacific Islander, 1.2% Two or more races, 5.7% Hispanic of any race; Average household size: 2.50; Median age: 37.4; Age under 18: 23.7%; Age 65 and over: 13.6%; Males per 100 females: 88.3; Marriage status: 23.0% never married, 51.7% now married, 4.2% separated, 9.8% widowed, 15.4% divorced; Foreign born: 9.3%; Speak English only: 87.3%; With disability: 18.8%; Veterans: 6.3%; Ancestry: 20.5% American, 11.6% German, 8.7% English, 8.1% Irish, 4.0% Dutch

Employment: 11.8% management, business, and financial, 4.3% computer, engineering, and science, 9.2% education, legal, community service, arts, and media, 3.3% healthcare practitioners, 14.2% service, 20.4% sales and office, 6.9% natural resources, construction, and maintenance, 30.0% production, transportation, and material moving

Income: Per capita: $24,410; Median household: $41,607; Average household: $57,699; Households with income of $100,000 or more: 13.2%; Poverty rate: 12.8%

Educational Attainment: High school diploma or higher: 83.0%; Bachelor's degree or higher: 13.5%; Graduate/professional degree or higher: 5.2%

School District(s)
Gaston County Schools (PK-12)
    2012-13 Enrollment: 31,804 . . . . (704) 866-6100

Housing: Homeownership rate: 69.5%; Median home value: $111,900; Median year structure built: 1970; Homeowner vacancy rate: 2.3%; Median gross rent: $691 per month; Rental vacancy rate: 8.1%

Health Insurance: 72.8% have insurance; 58.0% have private insurance; 25.1% have public insurance; 27.2% do not have insurance; 12.8% of children under 18 do not have insurance

Transportation: Commute: 91.2% car, 1.9% public transportation, 0.8% walk, 3.3% work from home; Median travel time to work: 25.9 minutes

Additional Information Contacts
City of Lowell . . . . (704) 824-3518
    http://www.lowellnc.com

MCADENVILLE (town). Covers a land area of 1.387 square miles and a water area of 0.063 square miles. Located at 35.27° N. Lat; 81.08° W. Long. Elevation is 591 feet.

Population: 651; Growth (since 2000): 5.2%; Density: 469.3 persons per square mile; Race: 89.2% White, 2.2% Black/African American, 0.9% Asian, 1.5% American Indian/Alaska Native, 0.2% Native Hawaiian/Other Pacific Islander, 2.2% Two or more races, 5.7% Hispanic of any race; Average household size: 2.58; Median age: 40.5; Age under 18: 22.4%; Age 65 and over: 15.2%; Males per 100 females: 93.8

School District(s)
Gaston County Schools (PK-12)
    2012-13 Enrollment: 31,804 . . . . (704) 866-6100

Housing: Homeownership rate: 69.8%; Homeowner vacancy rate: 1.1%; Rental vacancy rate: 5.0%

MOUNT HOLLY (city). Covers a land area of 9.788 square miles and a water area of 0.197 square miles. Located at 35.31° N. Lat; 81.02° W. Long. Elevation is 614 feet.

History: Mount Holly was built on a tract described in an old Armstrong grant from George II, and transferred to George Rutledge in 1754. Pennsylvania Dutch were destined to play an important part in the development of the town and county. Holly trees on the creek bank suggested the town's name.

Population: 13,656; Growth (since 2000): 42.0%; Density: 1,395.2 persons per square mile; Race: 80.4% White, 12.7% Black/African American, 2.4% Asian, 0.4% American Indian/Alaska Native, 0.1% Native Hawaiian/Other Pacific Islander, 1.6% Two or more races, 5.5% Hispanic of any race; Average household size: 2.49; Median age: 36.2; Age under 18: 25.0%; Age 65 and over: 10.0%; Males per 100 females: 95.4; Marriage status: 26.0% never married, 55.5% now married, 3.9% separated, 5.7% widowed, 12.8% divorced; Foreign born: 7.0%; Speak English only: 90.7%; With disability: 13.3%; Veterans: 9.9%; Ancestry: 15.6% American, 14.6% German, 7.2% Irish, 6.1% English, 4.0% Scottish

Employment: 14.7% management, business, and financial, 4.7% computer, engineering, and science, 9.6% education, legal, community service, arts, and media, 5.1% healthcare practitioners, 14.8% service,

25.3% sales and office, 8.8% natural resources, construction, and maintenance, 17.0% production, transportation, and material moving

Income: Per capita: $27,459; Median household: $49,351; Average household: $66,586; Households with income of $100,000 or more: 20.0%; Poverty rate: 13.9%

Educational Attainment: High school diploma or higher: 85.1%; Bachelor's degree or higher: 24.7%; Graduate/professional degree or higher: 5.6%

School District(s)
Gaston County Schools (PK-12)
    2012-13 Enrollment: 31,804 . . . . (704) 866-6100
Mountain Island Charter (KG-07)
    2012-13 Enrollment: 814 . . . . (704) 827-8840

Housing: Homeownership rate: 66.5%; Median home value: $155,800; Median year structure built: 1988; Homeowner vacancy rate: 3.2%; Median gross rent: $708 per month; Rental vacancy rate: 6.7%

Health Insurance: 84.6% have insurance; 67.9% have private insurance; 27.6% have public insurance; 15.4% do not have insurance; 7.5% of children under 18 do not have insurance

Safety: Violent crime rate: 26.1 per 10,000 population; Property crime rate: 186.8 per 10,000 population

Transportation: Commute: 97.1% car, 0.6% public transportation, 0.2% walk, 1.8% work from home; Median travel time to work: 24.7 minutes

Additional Information Contacts
City of Mount Holly . . . . (704) 827-3931
    http://www.ci.mount-holly.nc.us

RANLO (town). Covers a land area of 1.713 square miles and a water area of 0.002 square miles. Located at 35.29° N. Lat; 81.13° W. Long. Elevation is 797 feet.

Population: 3,434; Growth (since 2000): 56.2%; Density: 2,004.3 persons per square mile; Race: 75.1% White, 15.9% Black/African American, 1.8% Asian, 0.8% American Indian/Alaska Native, 0.0% Native Hawaiian/Other Pacific Islander, 2.3% Two or more races, 7.3% Hispanic of any race; Average household size: 2.71; Median age: 34.9; Age under 18: 26.2%; Age 65 and over: 10.4%; Males per 100 females: 95.3; Marriage status: 26.5% never married, 51.5% now married, 2.7% separated, 7.2% widowed, 14.8% divorced; Foreign born: 5.3%; Speak English only: 89.0%; With disability: 18.7%; Veterans: 9.8%; Ancestry: 16.9% American, 10.3% English, 8.6% German, 8.4% Irish, 5.9% Scottish

Employment: 6.2% management, business, and financial, 5.4% computer, engineering, and science, 9.2% education, legal, community service, arts, and media, 5.0% healthcare practitioners, 22.8% service, 24.0% sales and office, 8.0% natural resources, construction, and maintenance, 19.5% production, transportation, and material moving

Income: Per capita: $19,051; Median household: $41,042; Average household: $46,081; Households with income of $100,000 or more: 4.8%; Poverty rate: 10.8%

Educational Attainment: High school diploma or higher: 78.3%; Bachelor's degree or higher: 15.8%; Graduate/professional degree or higher: 4.6%

Housing: Homeownership rate: 76.1%; Median home value: $103,400; Median year structure built: 1974; Homeowner vacancy rate: 2.3%; Median gross rent: $658 per month; Rental vacancy rate: 9.8%

Health Insurance: 81.1% have insurance; 59.0% have private insurance; 33.9% have public insurance; 18.9% do not have insurance; 11.9% of children under 18 do not have insurance

Transportation: Commute: 97.7% car, 0.5% public transportation, 0.0% walk, 1.1% work from home; Median travel time to work: 25.5 minutes

SPENCER MOUNTAIN (town). Covers a land area of 0.488 square miles and a water area of 0.053 square miles. Located at 35.31° N. Lat; 81.11° W. Long. Elevation is 669 feet.

Population: 37; Growth (since 2000): -27.5%; Density: 75.8 persons per square mile; Race: 73.0% White, 0.0% Black/African American, 0.0% Asian, 0.0% American Indian/Alaska Native, 0.0% Native Hawaiian/Other Pacific Islander, 2.7% Two or more races, 24.3% Hispanic of any race; Average household size: 4.63; Median age: 20.8; Age under 18: 43.2%; Age 65 and over: 8.1%; Males per 100 females: 76.2

Housing: Homeownership rate: 12.5%; Homeowner vacancy rate: 0.0%; Rental vacancy rate: 0.0%

STANLEY (town). Covers a land area of 2.683 square miles and a water area of 0.015 square miles. Located at 35.36° N. Lat; 81.09° W. Long. Elevation is 840 feet.

History: Stanley became an industrial town when a cotton mill was established in 1891. Upon completion of the old Carolina Central Railroad from Charlotte in 1862, the town, then called Brevard Station, became a concentration point for Confederate soldiers from surrounding counties.

Population: 3,556; Growth (since 2000): 16.5%; Density: 1,325.4 persons per square mile; Race: 87.6% White, 9.7% Black/African American, 0.4% Asian, 0.4% American Indian/Alaska Native, 0.0% Native Hawaiian/Other Pacific Islander, 1.3% Two or more races, 1.6% Hispanic of any race; Average household size: 2.52; Median age: 38.7; Age under 18: 24.8%; Age 65 and over: 15.8%; Males per 100 females: 86.1; Marriage status: 24.0% never married, 55.1% now married, 2.9% separated, 12.2% widowed, 8.7% divorced; Foreign born: 0.3%; Speak English only: 98.1%; With disability: 26.0%; Veterans: 11.0%; Ancestry: 24.1% American, 15.0% German, 9.8% Irish, 9.4% English, 5.9% Scottish

Employment: 14.5% management, business, and financial, 3.1% computer, engineering, and science, 8.1% education, legal, community service, arts, and media, 6.4% healthcare practitioners, 22.5% service, 26.5% sales and office, 4.3% natural resources, construction, and maintenance, 14.7% production, transportation, and material moving

Income: Per capita: $27,398; Median household: $34,434; Average household: $63,229; Households with income of $100,000 or more: 9.4%; Poverty rate: 15.2%

Educational Attainment: High school diploma or higher: 73.2%; Bachelor's degree or higher: 15.5%; Graduate/professional degree or higher: 5.1%

School District(s)

Gaston County Schools (PK-12)
    2012-13 Enrollment: 31,804 . . . . (704) 866-6100

Housing: Homeownership rate: 67.0%; Median home value: $113,000; Median year structure built: 1973; Homeowner vacancy rate: 2.8%; Median gross rent: $698 per month; Rental vacancy rate: 11.8%

Health Insurance: 87.6% have insurance; 62.6% have private insurance; 38.9% have public insurance; 12.4% do not have insurance; 17.9% of children under 18 do not have insurance

Safety: Violent crime rate: 13.9 per 10,000 population; Property crime rate: 386.2 per 10,000 population

Transportation: Commute: 97.1% car, 0.0% public transportation, 1.3% walk, 1.2% work from home; Median travel time to work: 22.3 minutes

Additional Information Contacts

Town of Stanley. . . . . (704) 263-4779
   http://townofstanley.org

Gates County

Located in northeastern North Carolina; coastal plains area, bounded on the north by Virginia, and on the south by the Chowan River; includes Dismal Swamp in the east. Covers a land area of 340.445 square miles, a water area of 5.243 square miles, and is located in the Eastern Time Zone at 36.44° N. Lat., 76.70° W. Long. The county was founded in 1778. County seat is Gatesville.

Gates County is part of the Virginia Beach-Norfolk-Newport News, VA-NC Metropolitan Statistical Area. The entire metro area includes: Currituck County, NC; Gates County, NC; Gloucester County, VA; Isle of Wight County, VA; James City County, VA; Mathews County, VA; York County, VA; Chesapeake city, VA; Hampton city, VA; Newport News city, VA; Norfolk city, VA; Poquoson city, VA; Portsmouth city, VA; Suffolk city, VA; Virginia Beach city, VA; Williamsburg city, VA

Population: 12,197; Growth (since 2000): 16.0%; Density: 35.8 persons per square mile; Race: 63.7% White, 33.2% Black/African American, 0.1% Asian, 0.5% American Indian/Alaska Native, 0.1% Native Hawaiian/Other Pacific Islander, 1.8% two or more races, 1.4% Hispanic of any race; Average household size: 2.60; Median age: 42.0; Age under 18: 23.8%; Age 65 and over: 15.0%; Males per 100 females: 95.6; Marriage status: 26.9% never married, 56.0% now married, 2.5% separated, 7.2% widowed, 9.9% divorced; Foreign born: 1.0%; Speak English only: 98.5%; With disability: 16.1%; Veterans: 12.3%; Ancestry: 22.4% American, 10.1% English, 5.9% Irish, 5.7% German, 2.1% Scottish

Religion: Six largest groups: 36.1% Baptist, 9.1% Methodist/Pietist, 3.3% Non-denominational Protestant, 2.1% Pentecostal, 1.6% Presbyterian-Reformed, 0.5% Episcopalianism/Anglicanism

Economy: Unemployment rate: 6.0%; Leading industries: 19.7% retail trade; 16.5% other services (except public administration); 10.2% health care and social assistance; Farms: 182 totaling 63,291 acres; Company size: 0 employ 1,000 or more persons, 0 employ 500 to 999 persons, 0 employ 100 to 499 persons, 127 employ less than 100 persons; Business ownership: n/a women-owned, n/a Black-owned, n/a Hispanic-owned, n/a Asian-owned

Employment: 9.0% management, business, and financial, 2.7% computer, engineering, and science, 7.4% education, legal, community service, arts, and media, 7.4% healthcare practitioners, 15.2% service, 23.1% sales and office, 18.7% natural resources, construction, and maintenance, 16.5% production, transportation, and material moving

Income: Per capita: $21,187; Median household: $46,592; Average household: $54,917; Households with income of $100,000 or more: 14.1%; Poverty rate: 19.6%

Educational Attainment: High school diploma or higher: 83.3%; Bachelor's degree or higher: 11.6%; Graduate/professional degree or higher: 3.0%

Housing: Homeownership rate: 81.6%; Median home value: $150,200; Median year structure built: 1984; Homeowner vacancy rate: 1.7%; Median gross rent: $803 per month; Rental vacancy rate: 6.6%

Vital Statistics: Birth rate: 88.4 per 10,000 population; Death rate: 100.4 per 10,000 population; Age-adjusted cancer mortality rate: 127.8 deaths per 100,000 population

Health Insurance: 88.1% have insurance; 61.6% have private insurance; 38.3% have public insurance; 11.9% do not have insurance; 1.9% of children under 18 do not have insurance

Health Care: Physicians: 0.8 per 10,000 population; Hospital beds: 0.0 per 10,000 population; Hospital admissions: 0.0 per 10,000 population

Transportation: Commute: 95.4% car, 0.0% public transportation, 0.7% walk, 1.6% work from home; Median travel time to work: 36.6 minutes

Presidential Election: 51.6% Obama, 47.6% Romney (2012)

National and State Parks: Merchants Millpond State Park

Additional Information Contacts

Gates Government . . . . (252) 357-2411
   http://www.gatescounty.govoffice2.com

Gates County Communities

CORAPEAKE (unincorporated postal area)
ZCTA: 27926
   Covers a land area of 35.755 square miles and a water area of 0.005 square miles. Located at 36.51° N. Lat; 76.60° W. Long. Elevation is 46 feet.
   Population: 1,915; Growth (since 2000): 16.0%; Density: 53.6 persons per square mile; Race: 75.0% White, 22.0% Black/African American, 0.2% Asian, 0.3% American Indian/Alaska Native, 0.0% Native Hawaiian/Other Pacific Islander, 1.3% Two or more races, 2.5% Hispanic of any race; Average household size: 2.68; Median age: 42.0; Age under 18: 25.0%; Age 65 and over: 13.8%; Males per 100 females: 96.6
   Housing: Homeownership rate: 84.7%; Homeowner vacancy rate: 1.0%; Rental vacancy rate: 4.3%

EURE (unincorporated postal area)
ZCTA: 27935
   Covers a land area of 59.963 square miles and a water area of 1.978 square miles. Located at 36.43° N. Lat; 76.87° W. Long. Elevation is 20 feet.
   Population: 1,698; Growth (since 2000): 11.8%; Density: 28.3 persons per square mile; Race: 78.8% White, 19.2% Black/African American, 0.1% Asian, 0.3% American Indian/Alaska Native, 0.0% Native Hawaiian/Other Pacific Islander, 1.4% Two or more races, 0.7% Hispanic of any race; Average household size: 2.51; Median age: 41.5; Age under 18: 23.6%; Age 65 and over: 14.4%; Males per 100 females: 96.3
   Housing: Homeownership rate: 76.3%; Homeowner vacancy rate: 1.7%; Rental vacancy rate: 8.5%

GATES (unincorporated postal area)
ZCTA: 27937
   Covers a land area of 84.417 square miles and a water area of 0.599 square miles. Located at 36.50° N. Lat; 76.78° W. Long. Elevation is 69 feet.

Population: 4,333; Growth (since 2000): 40.7%; Density: 51.3 persons per square mile; Race: 57.6% White, 37.6% Black/African American, 0.2% Asian, 1.0% American Indian/Alaska Native, 0.0% Native Hawaiian/Other Pacific Islander, 2.7% Two or more races, 1.4% Hispanic of any race; Average household size: 2.74; Median age: 40.1; Age under 18: 25.5%; Age 65 and over: 11.8%; Males per 100 females: 96.2; Marriage status: 30.6% never married, 55.3% now married, 3.4% separated, 6.1% widowed, 8.0% divorced; Foreign born: 1.3%; Speak English only: 97.1%; With disability: 14.2%; Veterans: 11.3%; Ancestry: 14.2% American, 7.7% English, 4.3% Irish, 3.8% German, 3.3% Scottish

Employment: 9.7% management, business, and financial, 1.7% computer, engineering, and science, 3.9% education, legal, community service, arts, and media, 3.2% healthcare practitioners, 16.9% service, 26.4% sales and office, 21.2% natural resources, construction, and maintenance, 17.0% production, transportation, and material moving

Income: Per capita: $19,613; Median household: $45,099; Average household: $53,624; Households with income of $100,000 or more: 13.0%; Poverty rate: 18.1%

Educational Attainment: High school diploma or higher: 84.8%; Bachelor's degree or higher: 6.9%; Graduate/professional degree or higher: 1.0%

School District(s)
Gates County Schools (PK-12)
    2012-13 Enrollment: 1,787 . . . . (252) 357-1113
Housing: Homeownership rate: 83.2%; Median home value: $159,900; Median year structure built: 1989; Homeowner vacancy rate: 2.4%; Median gross rent: $922 per month; Rental vacancy rate: 8.5%
Health Insurance: 85.1% have insurance; 58.7% have private insurance; 35.9% have public insurance; 14.9% do not have insurance; 0.8% of children under 18 do not have insurance
Transportation: Commute: 98.0% car, 0.0% public transportation, 0.0% walk, 0.0% work from home; Median travel time to work: 40.3 minutes

GATESVILLE (town). County seat. Covers a land area of 0.404
square miles and a water area of 0 square miles. Located at 36.41° N. Lat; 76.76° W. Long. Elevation is 23 feet.
History: Gatesville was named in 1780 for Revolutionary General Horatio Gates.
Population: 321; Growth (since 2000): 14.2%; Density: 795.0 persons per square mile; Race: 78.5% White, 20.6% Black/African American, 0.0% Asian, 0.0% American Indian/Alaska Native, 0.0% Native Hawaiian/Other Pacific Islander, 0.9% Two or more races, 0.0% Hispanic of any race; Average household size: 2.31; Median age: 46.6; Age under 18: 19.9%; Age 65 and over: 17.8%; Males per 100 females: 94.5
School District(s)
Gates County Schools (PK-12)
    2012-13 Enrollment: 1,787 . . . . (252) 357-1113
Housing: Homeownership rate: 77.0%; Homeowner vacancy rate: 0.9%; Rental vacancy rate: 13.5%
Newspapers: Gates County Index (weekly circulation 2700)

HOBBSVILLE (unincorporated postal area)
ZCTA: 27946
    Covers a land area of 42.694 square miles and a water area of <.001 square miles. Located at 36.36° N. Lat; 76.60° W. Long. Elevation is 39 feet.
    Population: 1,207; Growth (since 2000): -3.9%; Density: 28.3 persons per square mile; Race: 76.2% White, 20.9% Black/African American, 0.0% Asian, 0.2% American Indian/Alaska Native, 0.4% Native Hawaiian/Other Pacific Islander, 2.2% Two or more races, 0.7% Hispanic of any race; Average household size: 2.42; Median age: 45.0; Age under 18: 20.2%; Age 65 and over: 18.9%; Males per 100 females: 89.2
    Housing: Homeownership rate: 84.8%; Homeowner vacancy rate: 1.4%; Rental vacancy rate: 3.7%

SUNBURY (CDP). Covers a land area of 2.451 square miles and a
water area of 0 square miles. Located at 36.45° N. Lat; 76.61° W. Long. Elevation is 33 feet.
Population: 289; Growth (since 2000): n/a; Density: 117.9 persons per square mile; Race: 83.0% White, 13.8% Black/African American, 0.3% Asian, 0.3% American Indian/Alaska Native, 0.0% Native Hawaiian/Other Pacific Islander, 2.1% Two or more races, 4.5% Hispanic of any race;

Average household size: 2.24; Median age: 40.9; Age under 18: 18.7%; Age 65 and over: 17.6%; Males per 100 females: 102.1
School District(s)
Gates County Schools (PK-12)
    2012-13 Enrollment: 1,787 . . . . (252) 357-1113
Housing: Homeownership rate: 76.0%; Homeowner vacancy rate: 2.9%; Rental vacancy rate: 8.6%

Graham County

Located in western North Carolina; bounded on the west by Tennessee, on the east by the Nantahala River, and on the north by the Little Tennessee River; drained by the Cheoah River; includes the Unicoi and Snowbird Mountains, and Nantahala National Forest. Covers a land area of 292.079 square miles, a water area of 9.586 square miles, and is located in the Eastern Time Zone at 35.35° N. Lat., 83.83° W. Long. The county was founded in 1872. County seat is Robbinsville.

Weather Station: Tapoco   Elevation: 1,109 feet

	Jan	Feb	Mar	Apr	May	Jun	Jul	Aug	Sep	Oct	Nov	Dec
High	50	54	63	72	78	84	87	87	81	71	61	52
Low	29	32	37	44	52	59	63	62	57	46	38	32
Precip	4.9	4.9	5.1	4.3	5.2	5.3	5.3	3.7	3.8	2.7	4.4	4.9
Snow	0.8	1.3	0.2	0.3	0.0	0.0	0.0	0.0	0.0	0.0	tr	0.1

High and Low temperatures in degrees Fahrenheit; Precipitation and Snow in inches

Population: 8,861; Growth (since 2000): 10.9%; Density: 30.3 persons per square mile; Race: 90.3% White, 0.2% Black/African American, 0.3% Asian, 6.4% American Indian/Alaska Native, 0.0% Native Hawaiian/Other Pacific Islander, 1.7% two or more races, 2.2% Hispanic of any race; Average household size: 2.37; Median age: 44.3; Age under 18: 21.6%; Age 65 and over: 19.7%; Males per 100 females: 97.2; Marriage status: 20.0% never married, 61.5% now married, 2.1% separated, 8.5% widowed, 10.0% divorced; Foreign born: 1.8%; Speak English only: 95.9%; With disability: 12.0%; Veterans: 9.4%; Ancestry: 15.1% English, 11.3% Irish, 9.7% American, 5.4% German, 4.1% Scotch-Irish
Religion: Six largest groups: 31.3% Baptist, 2.8% Methodist/Pietist, 0.7% Catholicism, 0.7% Non-denominational Protestant, 0.3% Episcopalianism/Anglicanism, 0.1% Pentecostal
Economy: Unemployment rate: 11.2%; Leading industries: 20.2% retail trade; 17.9% construction; 13.1% accommodation and food services; Farms: 107 totaling 6,837 acres; Company size: 0 employ 1,000 or more persons, 0 employ 500 to 999 persons, 2 employ 100 to 499 persons, 166 employ less than 100 persons; Business ownership: 451 women-owned, n/a Black-owned, n/a Hispanic-owned, n/a Asian-owned
Employment: 8.6% management, business, and financial, 1.1% computer, engineering, and science, 8.8% education, legal, community service, arts, and media, 6.0% healthcare practitioners, 18.0% service, 21.1% sales and office, 17.3% natural resources, construction, and maintenance, 19.0% production, transportation, and material moving
Income: Per capita: $19,780; Median household: $33,903; Average household: $47,331; Households with income of $100,000 or more: 9.4%; Poverty rate: 21.1%
Educational Attainment: High school diploma or higher: 78.6%; Bachelor's degree or higher: 14.4%; Graduate/professional degree or higher: 4.2%
Housing: Homeownership rate: 80.2%; Median home value: $125,700; Median year structure built: 1985; Homeowner vacancy rate: 3.2%; Median gross rent: $549 per month; Rental vacancy rate: 20.4%
Vital Statistics: Birth rate: 105.3 per 10,000 population; Death rate: 111.0 per 10,000 population; Age-adjusted cancer mortality rate: Unreliable deaths per 100,000 population
Health Insurance: 76.7% have insurance; 49.0% have private insurance; 38.9% have public insurance; 23.3% do not have insurance; 13.9% of children under 18 do not have insurance
Health Care: Physicians: 3.4 per 10,000 population; Hospital beds: 0.0 per 10,000 population; Hospital admissions: 0.0 per 10,000 population
Air Quality Index: 93.5% good, 6.5% moderate, 0.0% unhealthy for sensitive individuals, 0.0% unhealthy (percent of days)
Transportation: Commute: 95.9% car, 0.0% public transportation, 1.3% walk, 2.8% work from home; Median travel time to work: 19.7 minutes
Presidential Election: 28.4% Obama, 69.7% Romney (2012)
Additional Information Contacts
Graham Government. . . . . (928) 428-2828
    http://www.grahamcounty.org

Graham County Communities

FONTANA DAM (unincorporated postal area)
ZCTA: 28733
Covers a land area of 7.755 square miles and a water area of 0.776 square miles. Located at 35.43° N. Lat; 83.82° W. Long..
Population: 21; Growth (since 2000): -22.2%; Density: 2.7 persons per square mile; Race: 100.0% White, 0.0% Black/African American, 0.0% Asian, 0.0% American Indian/Alaska Native, 0.0% Native Hawaiian/Other Pacific Islander, 0.0% Two or more races, 0.0% Hispanic of any race; Average household size: 1.91; Median age: 58.5; Age under 18: 0.0%; Age 65 and over: 42.9%; Males per 100 females: 110.0
Housing: Homeownership rate: 45.5%; Homeowner vacancy rate: 0.0%; Rental vacancy rate: 14.3%

LAKE SANTEETLAH (town). Covers a land area of 0.194 square miles and a water area of <.001 square miles. Located at 35.36° N. Lat; 83.87° W. Long. Elevation is 1,985 feet.
Population: 45; Growth (since 2000): n/a; Density: 231.6 persons per square mile; Race: 91.1% White, 0.0% Black/African American, 0.0% Asian, 2.2% American Indian/Alaska Native, 0.0% Native Hawaiian/Other Pacific Islander, 0.0% Two or more races, 8.9% Hispanic of any race; Average household size: 1.73; Median age: 69.5; Age under 18: 13.3%; Age 65 and over: 53.3%; Males per 100 females: 104.5
Housing: Homeownership rate: 80.7%; Homeowner vacancy rate: 4.3%; Rental vacancy rate: 0.0%

ROBBINSVILLE (town). County seat. Covers a land area of 0.458 square miles and a water area of 0.006 square miles. Located at 35.32° N. Lat; 83.81° W. Long. Elevation is 2,047 feet.
History: Robbinsville is nearer to the capitals of six other states than to its own. Lumbering has been a principal activity.
Population: 620; Growth (since 2000): -17.0%; Density: 1,352.3 persons per square mile; Race: 84.7% White, 0.0% Black/African American, 1.0% Asian, 3.4% American Indian/Alaska Native, 0.3% Native Hawaiian/Other Pacific Islander, 1.3% Two or more races, 11.9% Hispanic of any race; Average household size: 2.17; Median age: 39.3; Age under 18: 22.6%; Age 65 and over: 22.1%; Males per 100 females: 98.1
School District(s)
Graham County Schools (PK-12)
2012-13 Enrollment: 1,244 . . . . (828) 479-9820
Housing: Homeownership rate: 53.8%; Homeowner vacancy rate: 1.9%; Rental vacancy rate: 28.6%
Newspapers: The Graham Star (weekly circulation 3500)

Granville County

Located in northern North Carolina; piedmont area, bounded on the north by Virginia; drained by the Tar River. Covers a land area of 531.570 square miles, a water area of 4.929 square miles, and is located in the Eastern Time Zone at 36.30° N. Lat., 78.66° W. Long. The county was founded in 1746. County seat is Oxford.

Granville County is part of the Oxford, NC Micropolitan Statistical Area. The entire metro area includes: Granville County, NC

Population: 59,916; Growth (since 2000): 23.5%; Density: 112.7 persons per square mile; Race: 60.4% White, 32.8% Black/African American, 0.5% Asian, 0.6% American Indian/Alaska Native, 0.1% Native Hawaiian/Other Pacific Islander, 1.7% two or more races, 7.5% Hispanic of any race; Average household size: 2.57; Median age: 39.8; Age under 18: 22.3%; Age 65 and over: 12.4%; Males per 100 females: 114.7; Marriage status: 32.5% never married, 50.8% now married, 4.1% separated, 6.3% widowed, 10.4% divorced; Foreign born: 4.0%; Speak English only: 92.9%; With disability: 19.2%; Veterans: 10.8%; Ancestry: 19.2% American, 10.3% English, 5.9% German, 5.2% Irish, 1.9% Scottish
Religion: Six largest groups: 21.1% Baptist, 12.7% Non-denominational Protestant, 4.9% Methodist/Pietist, 1.0% Pentecostal, 1.0% Catholicism, 0.9% Presbyterian-Reformed
Economy: Unemployment rate: 6.0%; Leading industries: 15.7% retail trade; 14.1% other services (except public administration); 11.5% construction; Farms: 589 totaling 100,822 acres; Company size: 1 employs 1,000 or more persons, 1 employs 500 to 999 persons, 20 employ 100 to

499 persons, 810 employ less than 100 persons; Business ownership: 1,004 women-owned, 694 Black-owned, n/a Hispanic-owned, n/a Asian-owned
Employment: 13.1% management, business, and financial, 4.7% computer, engineering, and science, 8.1% education, legal, community service, arts, and media, 8.0% healthcare practitioners, 14.4% service, 23.8% sales and office, 10.8% natural resources, construction, and maintenance, 17.2% production, transportation, and material moving
Income: Per capita: $22,295; Median household: $49,852; Average household: $59,984; Households with income of $100,000 or more: 16.5%; Poverty rate: 15.4%
Educational Attainment: High school diploma or higher: 81.1%; Bachelor's degree or higher: 16.4%; Graduate/professional degree or higher: 4.6%
Housing: Homeownership rate: 73.5%; Median home value: $137,100; Median year structure built: 1989; Homeowner vacancy rate: 2.3%; Median gross rent: $739 per month; Rental vacancy rate: 9.1%
Vital Statistics: Birth rate: 96.3 per 10,000 population; Death rate: 87.7 per 10,000 population; Age-adjusted cancer mortality rate: 202.6 deaths per 100,000 population
Health Insurance: 86.9% have insurance; 65.9% have private insurance; 32.9% have public insurance; 13.1% do not have insurance; 3.8% of children under 18 do not have insurance
Health Care: Physicians: 9.0 per 10,000 population; Hospital beds: 179.9 per 10,000 population; Hospital admissions: 1,030.4 per 10,000 population
Air Quality Index: 96.7% good, 3.3% moderate, 0.0% unhealthy for sensitive individuals, 0.0% unhealthy (percent of days)
Transportation: Commute: 94.7% car, 0.0% public transportation, 1.0% walk, 3.9% work from home; Median travel time to work: 27.6 minutes
Presidential Election: 51.8% Obama, 47.2% Romney (2012)
Additional Information Contacts
Granville Government . . . . (919) 693-5240
http://granvillenc.govoffice2.com

Granville County Communities

BULLOCK (unincorporated postal area)
ZCTA: 27507
Covers a land area of 47.667 square miles and a water area of 0.798 square miles. Located at 36.51° N. Lat; 78.57° W. Long. Elevation is 427 feet.
Population: 1,929; Growth (since 2000): 11.4%; Density: 40.5 persons per square mile; Race: 68.6% White, 26.2% Black/African American, 0.1% Asian, 0.3% American Indian/Alaska Native, 0.0% Native Hawaiian/Other Pacific Islander, 2.0% Two or more races, 4.1% Hispanic of any race; Average household size: 2.65; Median age: 43.1; Age under 18: 24.6%; Age 65 and over: 15.3%; Males per 100 females: 94.8
Housing: Homeownership rate: 81.9%; Homeowner vacancy rate: 2.1%; Rental vacancy rate: 6.3%

BUTNER (town). Covers a land area of 13.930 square miles and a water area of 0.025 square miles. Located at 36.13° N. Lat; 78.75° W. Long. Elevation is 371 feet.
History: Butner is a town in Granville County, North Carolina, the former site of the U.S. Army's Camp Butner, named for Major General Henry W. Butner (1875-1937), a North Carolina native. The area around Butner has several state and federal correctional institutions.
Population: 7,591; Growth (since 2000): 31.1%; Density: 544.9 persons per square mile; Race: 59.5% White, 30.1% Black/African American, 0.9% Asian, 0.7% American Indian/Alaska Native, 0.0% Native Hawaiian/Other Pacific Islander, 2.3% Two or more races, 14.7% Hispanic of any race; Average household size: 2.56; Median age: 36.9; Age under 18: 26.0%; Age 65 and over: 10.4%; Males per 100 females: 97.3; Marriage status: 35.3% never married, 48.8% now married, 4.2% separated, 6.2% widowed, 9.6% divorced; Foreign born: 4.5%; Speak English only: 88.9%; With disability: 20.9%; Veterans: 12.8%; Ancestry: 13.6% American, 9.5% English, 6.5% German, 5.2% Irish, 2.0% Scotch-Irish
Employment: 5.3% management, business, and financial, 7.3% computer, engineering, and science, 4.8% education, legal, community service, arts, and media, 10.2% healthcare practitioners, 20.0% service, 26.7% sales and office, 13.0% natural resources, construction, and maintenance, 12.7% production, transportation, and material moving

Income: Per capita: $20,530; Median household: $46,681; Average household: $54,361; Households with income of $100,000 or more: 12.7%; Poverty rate: 15.1%

Educational Attainment: High school diploma or higher: 79.6%; Bachelor's degree or higher: 9.6%; Graduate/professional degree or higher: 3.9%

School District(s)

Granville County Schools (PK-12)
    2012-13 Enrollment: 8,655 . . . . (919) 693-4613
Nc Dept of Juvenile Justice (KG-12)
    2012-13 Enrollment: n/a . . . . (919) 733-3388
Nc Health and Human Resources (KG-12)
    2012-13 Enrollment: n/a . . . . (919) 855-4430

Housing: Homeownership rate: 67.5%; Median home value: $128,800; Median year structure built: 1991; Homeowner vacancy rate: 2.1%; Median gross rent: $807 per month; Rental vacancy rate: 11.6%

Health Insurance: 86.5% have insurance; 57.6% have private insurance; 41.5% have public insurance; 13.5% do not have insurance; 4.9% of children under 18 do not have insurance

Safety: Violent crime rate: 26.1 per 10,000 population; Property crime rate: 297.6 per 10,000 population

Transportation: Commute: 95.4% car, 0.0% public transportation, 0.4% walk, 3.9% work from home; Median travel time to work: 23.8 minutes

CREEDMOOR (city). Covers a land area of 4.581 square miles and a water area of 0.224 square miles. Located at 36.13° N. Lat; 78.68° W. Long. Elevation is 371 feet.

Population: 4,124; Growth (since 2000): 84.8%; Density: 900.2 persons per square mile; Race: 59.6% White, 35.2% Black/African American, 0.8% Asian, 0.6% American Indian/Alaska Native, 0.1% Native Hawaiian/Other Pacific Islander, 2.1% Two or more races, 5.0% Hispanic of any race; Average household size: 2.64; Median age: 36.6; Age under 18: 27.3%; Age 65 and over: 10.5%; Males per 100 females: 91.8; Marriage status: 36.0% never married, 49.1% now married, 6.1% separated, 4.6% widowed, 10.3% divorced; Foreign born: 3.1%; Speak English only: 97.5%; With disability: 18.7%; Veterans: 15.7%; Ancestry: 18.2% American, 9.9% German, 8.6% English, 4.5% Scottish, 3.5% African

Employment: 10.0% management, business, and financial, 5.4% computer, engineering, and science, 6.9% education, legal, community service, arts, and media, 8.5% healthcare practitioners, 19.1% service, 25.5% sales and office, 5.5% natural resources, construction, and maintenance, 18.9% production, transportation, and material moving

Income: Per capita: $21,542; Median household: $51,406; Average household: $61,369; Households with income of $100,000 or more: 16.6%; Poverty rate: 12.7%

Educational Attainment: High school diploma or higher: 91.4%; Bachelor's degree or higher: 19.2%; Graduate/professional degree or higher: 5.4%

School District(s)

Granville County Schools (PK-12)
    2012-13 Enrollment: 8,655 . . . . (919) 693-4613

Housing: Homeownership rate: 73.9%; Median home value: $153,600; Median year structure built: 1998; Homeowner vacancy rate: 2.9%; Median gross rent: $888 per month; Rental vacancy rate: 11.7%

Health Insurance: 85.2% have insurance; 71.5% have private insurance; 23.8% have public insurance; 14.8% do not have insurance; 12.5% of children under 18 do not have insurance

Safety: Violent crime rate: 23.5 per 10,000 population; Property crime rate: 199.8 per 10,000 population

Newspapers: Butner-Creedmoor News (weekly circulation 5300)

Transportation: Commute: 99.2% car, 0.0% public transportation, 0.0% walk, 0.8% work from home; Median travel time to work: 24.7 minutes

Additional Information Contacts
City of Creedmoor. . . . . (919) 528-3332
    http://www.cityofcreedmoor.org

OXFORD (city). County seat. Covers a land area of 6.048 square miles and a water area of 0.004 square miles. Located at 36.32° N. Lat; 78.59° W. Long. Elevation is 482 feet.

History: Oxford was founded in 1764 when Bute County was formed from Granville and the seat of Granville was moved to Samuel Benton's plantation, called Oxford.

Population: 8,461; Growth (since 2000): 1.5%; Density: 1,398.9 persons per square mile; Race: 38.6% White, 55.6% Black/African American, 1.1% Asian, 0.4% American Indian/Alaska Native, 0.0% Native Hawaiian/Other

Pacific Islander, 1.8% Two or more races, 4.8% Hispanic of any race; Average household size: 2.36; Median age: 41.4; Age under 18: 23.4%; Age 65 and over: 19.4%; Males per 100 females: 79.4; Marriage status: 35.4% never married, 43.0% now married, 6.9% separated, 9.3% widowed, 12.4% divorced; Foreign born: 2.9%; Speak English only: 95.1%; With disability: 23.4%; Veterans: 8.4%; Ancestry: 14.9% American, 8.4% English, 4.5% Irish, 4.1% German, 1.6% Italian

Employment: 11.1% management, business, and financial, 3.3% computer, engineering, and science, 12.1% education, legal, community service, arts, and media, 10.7% healthcare practitioners, 16.8% service, 25.5% sales and office, 4.1% natural resources, construction, and maintenance, 16.4% production, transportation, and material moving

Income: Per capita: $21,306; Median household: $34,018; Average household: $51,375; Households with income of $100,000 or more: 10.8%; Poverty rate: 23.5%

Educational Attainment: High school diploma or higher: 81.7%; Bachelor's degree or higher: 18.3%; Graduate/professional degree or higher: 7.7%

School District(s)

Granville County Schools (PK-12)
    2012-13 Enrollment: 8,655 . . . . (919) 693-4613

Housing: Homeownership rate: 49.4%; Median home value: $126,000; Median year structure built: 1969; Homeowner vacancy rate: 3.6%; Median gross rent: $754 per month; Rental vacancy rate: 7.8%

Health Insurance: 86.8% have insurance; 58.4% have private insurance; 41.0% have public insurance; 13.2% do not have insurance; 3.8% of children under 18 do not have insurance

Hospitals: Granville Health Systems (142 beds)

Safety: Violent crime rate: 99.9 per 10,000 population; Property crime rate: 666.9 per 10,000 population

Newspapers: Oxford Public Ledger (weekly circulation 13000)

Transportation: Commute: 90.9% car, 0.0% public transportation, 5.7% walk, 3.0% work from home; Median travel time to work: 20.7 minutes

Airports: Henderson-Oxford (general aviation)

Additional Information Contacts
City of Oxford . . . . (919) 603-1100
    http://www.oxfordnc.org

STEM (town). Covers a land area of 1.511 square miles and a water area of 0.001 square miles. Located at 36.20° N. Lat; 78.72° W. Long. Elevation is 472 feet.

Population: 463; Growth (since 2000): 102.2%; Density: 306.3 persons per square mile; Race: 83.6% White, 8.2% Black/African American, 0.4% Asian, 0.6% American Indian/Alaska Native, 0.0% Native Hawaiian/Other Pacific Islander, 3.7% Two or more races, 6.7% Hispanic of any race; Average household size: 2.39; Median age: 32.8; Age under 18: 25.3%; Age 65 and over: 8.2%; Males per 100 females: 97.9

School District(s)

Granville County Schools (PK-12)
    2012-13 Enrollment: 8,655 . . . . (919) 693-4613

Housing: Homeownership rate: 81.4%; Homeowner vacancy rate: 6.5%; Rental vacancy rate: 10.0%

STOVALL (town). Covers a land area of 1.047 square miles and a water area of 0 square miles. Located at 36.45° N. Lat; 78.57° W. Long. Elevation is 476 feet.

Population: 418; Growth (since 2000): 11.2%; Density: 399.4 persons per square mile; Race: 54.5% White, 41.4% Black/African American, 0.2% Asian, 0.2% American Indian/Alaska Native, 0.0% Native Hawaiian/Other Pacific Islander, 1.2% Two or more races, 3.8% Hispanic of any race; Average household size: 2.46; Median age: 41.5; Age under 18: 24.6%; Age 65 and over: 19.6%; Males per 100 females: 96.2

School District(s)

Granville County Schools (PK-12)
    2012-13 Enrollment: 8,655 . . . . (919) 693-4613

Housing: Homeownership rate: 68.8%; Homeowner vacancy rate: 1.7%; Rental vacancy rate: 7.0%

Greene County

Located in east central North Carolina; coastal plains area, drained by Contentnea Creek. Covers a land area of 265.928 square miles, a water area of 0.472 square miles, and is located in the Eastern Time Zone at

35.48° N. Lat., 77.68° W. Long. The county was founded in 1791. County seat is Snow Hill.

Population: 21,362; Growth (since 2000): 12.6%; Density: 80.3 persons per square mile; Race: 50.8% White, 37.3% Black/African American, 0.3% Asian, 0.7% American Indian/Alaska Native, 0.0% Native Hawaiian/Other Pacific Islander, 1.5% two or more races, 14.3% Hispanic of any race; Average household size: 2.60; Median age: 37.7; Age under 18: 23.2%; Age 65 and over: 12.5%; Males per 100 females: 115.7; Marriage status: 33.0% never married, 49.5% now married, 4.7% separated, 7.7% widowed, 9.8% divorced; Foreign born: 8.2%; Speak English only: 84.7%; With disability: 16.1%; Veterans: 9.0%; Ancestry: 12.4% English, 8.9% American, 5.0% Irish, 3.7% German, 2.6% African

Religion: Six largest groups: 10.2% Baptist, 10.0% Methodist/Pietist, 5.1% Non-denominational Protestant, 1.3% Pentecostal, 0.4% Presbyterian-Reformed, 0.0% Other Groups

Economy: Unemployment rate: 5.1%; Leading industries: 17.9% retail trade; 17.9% health care and social assistance; 14.3% construction; Farms: 260 totaling 101,189 acres; Company size: 0 employ 1,000 or more persons, 0 employ 500 to 999 persons, 1 employs 100 to 499 persons, 250 employ less than 100 persons; Business ownership: n/a women-owned, n/a Black-owned, n/a Hispanic-owned, n/a Asian-owned

Employment: 9.0% management, business, and financial, 1.7% computer, engineering, and science, 6.3% education, legal, community service, arts, and media, 6.4% healthcare practitioners, 23.4% service, 22.2% sales and office, 15.5% natural resources, construction, and maintenance, 15.5% production, transportation, and material moving

Income: Per capita: $18,441; Median household: $40,853; Average household: $51,186; Households with income of $100,000 or more: 10.4%; Poverty rate: 23.3%

Educational Attainment: High school diploma or higher: 76.0%; Bachelor's degree or higher: 11.6%; Graduate/professional degree or higher: 3.0%

Housing: Homeownership rate: 69.5%; Median home value: $88,500; Median year structure built: 1982; Homeowner vacancy rate: 1.4%; Median gross rent: $608 per month; Rental vacancy rate: 8.0%

Vital Statistics: Birth rate: 99.8 per 10,000 population; Death rate: 87.6 per 10,000 population; Age-adjusted cancer mortality rate: 211.4 deaths per 100,000 population

Health Insurance: 81.9% have insurance; 57.0% have private insurance; 36.8% have public insurance; 18.1% do not have insurance; 12.1% of children under 18 do not have insurance

Health Care: Physicians: 0.9 per 10,000 population; Hospital beds: 0.0 per 10,000 population; Hospital admissions: 0.0 per 10,000 population

Transportation: Commute: 95.7% car, 0.4% public transportation, 0.7% walk, 2.0% work from home; Median travel time to work: 23.5 minutes

Presidential Election: 45.9% Obama, 53.6% Romney (2012)

Additional Information Contacts
Greene Government . . . . (252) 747-3446
  http://www.co.greene.nc.us

Greene County Communities

HOOKERTON (town). Covers a land area of 0.325 square miles and a water area of 0 square miles. Located at 35.42° N. Lat; 77.59° W. Long. Elevation is 56 feet.

Population: 409; Growth (since 2000): -12.4%; Density: 1,258.3 persons per square mile; Race: 48.2% White, 37.4% Black/African American, 1.2% Asian, 0.2% American Indian/Alaska Native, 0.0% Native Hawaiian/Other Pacific Islander, 1.0% Two or more races, 13.4% Hispanic of any race; Average household size: 2.32; Median age: 39.8; Age under 18: 22.5%; Age 65 and over: 18.8%; Males per 100 females: 82.6

Housing: Homeownership rate: 60.8%; Homeowner vacancy rate: 0.9%; Rental vacancy rate: 2.8%

MAURY (CDP). Covers a land area of 1.053 square miles and a water area of 0 square miles. Located at 35.48° N. Lat; 77.59° W. Long. Elevation is 79 feet.

Population: 1,685; Growth (since 2000): n/a; Density: 1,600.5 persons per square mile; Race: 43.6% White, 50.4% Black/African American, 0.4% Asian, 0.8% American Indian/Alaska Native, 0.1% Native Hawaiian/Other Pacific Islander, 0.7% Two or more races, 11.5% Hispanic of any race; Average household size: 2.53; Median age: 37.7; Age under 18: 8.7%; Age 65 and over: 6.4%; Males per 100 females: 428.2

Housing: Homeownership rate: 56.3%; Homeowner vacancy rate: 1.5%; Rental vacancy rate: 2.9%

SNOW HILL (town). County seat. Covers a land area of 1.550 square miles and a water area of 0 square miles. Located at 35.45° N. Lat; 77.68° W. Long. Elevation is 89 feet.

History: Snow Hill was founded in 1799 but not incorporated until 1855.

Population: 1,595; Growth (since 2000): 5.4%; Density: 1,029.2 persons per square mile; Race: 38.2% White, 52.9% Black/African American, 1.1% Asian, 0.2% American Indian/Alaska Native, 0.0% Native Hawaiian/Other Pacific Islander, 1.1% Two or more races, 8.7% Hispanic of any race; Average household size: 2.21; Median age: 41.9; Age under 18: 21.7%; Age 65 and over: 18.2%; Males per 100 females: 77.4

School District(s)
Greene County Schools (PK-12)
  2012-13 Enrollment: 3,307 . . . . (252) 747-3425

Housing: Homeownership rate: 53.1%; Homeowner vacancy rate: 2.6%; Rental vacancy rate: 5.9%

Safety: Violent crime rate: 69.1 per 10,000 population; Property crime rate: 376.9 per 10,000 population

Newspapers: The Standard Laconic (weekly circulation 3500)

WALSTONBURG (town). Covers a land area of 0.407 square miles and a water area of 0 square miles. Located at 35.60° N. Lat; 77.70° W. Long. Elevation is 112 feet.

Population: 219; Growth (since 2000): -2.2%; Density: 538.2 persons per square mile; Race: 67.1% White, 30.1% Black/African American, 0.0% Asian, 0.5% American Indian/Alaska Native, 0.0% Native Hawaiian/Other Pacific Islander, 0.0% Two or more races, 4.6% Hispanic of any race; Average household size: 2.43; Median age: 40.8; Age under 18: 21.9%; Age 65 and over: 15.1%; Males per 100 females: 110.6

Housing: Homeownership rate: 80.0%; Homeowner vacancy rate: 6.4%; Rental vacancy rate: 25.0%

Guilford County

Located in north central North Carolina; piedmont area, drained by the Haw and Deep Rivers. Covers a land area of 645.704 square miles, a water area of 11.924 square miles, and is located in the Eastern Time Zone at 36.08° N. Lat., 79.79° W. Long. The county was founded in 1770. County seat is Greensboro.

Guilford County is part of the Greensboro-High Point, NC Metropolitan Statistical Area. The entire metro area includes: Guilford County, NC; Randolph County, NC; Rockingham County, NC

Weather Station: Greensboro-High Pt-Winston Salem								Elevation: 896 feet			
	Jan	Feb	Mar	Apr	May	Jun	Jul	Aug	Sep	Oct	Nov	Dec
High	48	52	61	70	77	84	88	86	79	70	61	51
Low	29	32	38	47	55	64	68	67	60	48	39	31
Precip	3.0	2.9	3.7	3.6	3.4	3.8	4.3	3.8	4.1	3.1	3.2	2.9
Snow	3.3	2.5	1.1	tr	tr	tr	tr	tr	0.0	0.0	0.1	0.7

High and Low temperatures in degrees Fahrenheit; Precipitation and Snow in inches

Weather Station: High Point								Elevation: 899 feet			
	Jan	Feb	Mar	Apr	May	Jun	Jul	Aug	Sep	Oct	Nov	Dec
High	51	55	63	73	80	86	89	88	82	72	63	53
Low	30	32	39	47	55	64	67	66	59	48	40	32
Precip	3.5	3.4	4.2	3.8	3.5	3.9	4.5	4.3	3.9	3.4	3.5	3.4
Snow	1.4	1.4	0.4	tr	0.0	0.0	0.0	0.0	0.0	0.0	tr	0.3

High and Low temperatures in degrees Fahrenheit; Precipitation and Snow in inches

Population: 488,406; Growth (since 2000): 16.0%; Density: 756.4 persons per square mile; Race: 57.0% White, 32.5% Black/African American, 3.9% Asian, 0.5% American Indian/Alaska Native, 0.0% Native Hawaiian/Other Pacific Islander, 2.3% two or more races, 7.1% Hispanic of any race; Average household size: 2.41; Median age: 36.3; Age under 18: 23.4%; Age 65 and over: 12.3%; Males per 100 females: 90.8; Marriage status: 35.7% never married, 48.1% now married, 2.9% separated, 5.8% widowed, 10.4% divorced; Foreign born: 9.7%; Speak English only: 87.5%; With disability: 10.6%; Veterans: 8.3%; Ancestry: 9.2% English, 9.1% German, 7.6% American, 6.7% Irish, 2.6% Italian

Religion: Six largest groups: 11.9% Baptist, 10.2% Methodist/Pietist, 8.8% Non-denominational Protestant, 4.0% Presbyterian-Reformed, 3.6% Catholicism, 2.6% Pentecostal

Economy: Unemployment rate: 5.8%; Leading industries: 14.0% retail trade; 10.9% professional, scientific, and technical services; 9.9% health care and social assistance; Farms: 962 totaling 90,750 acres; Company size: 15 employ 1,000 or more persons, 28 employ 500 to 999 persons,

349 employ 100 to 499 persons, 12,741 employs less than 100 persons; Business ownership: 13,221 women-owned, 7,562 Black-owned, 1,341 Hispanic-owned, 1,886 Asian-owned

Employment: 15.3% management, business, and financial, 4.3% computer, engineering, and science, 11.2% education, legal, community service, arts, and media, 5.5% healthcare practitioners, 17.0% service, 27.0% sales and office, 6.9% natural resources, construction, and maintenance, 13.0% production, transportation, and material moving

Income: Per capita: $26,461; Median household: $45,431; Average household: $65,044; Households with income of $100,000 or more: 17.9%; Poverty rate: 18.1%

Educational Attainment: High school diploma or higher: 87.9%; Bachelor's degree or higher: 33.2%; Graduate/professional degree or higher: 11.0%

Housing: Homeownership rate: 60.8%; Median home value: $156,000; Median year structure built: 1982; Homeowner vacancy rate: 3.0%; Median gross rent: $747 per month; Rental vacancy rate: 11.8%

Vital Statistics: Birth rate: 119.7 per 10,000 population; Death rate: 79.3 per 10,000 population; Age-adjusted cancer mortality rate: 162.7 deaths per 100,000 population

Health Insurance: 83.7% have insurance; 64.8% have private insurance; 28.5% have public insurance; 16.3% do not have insurance; 8.1% of children under 18 do not have insurance

Health Care: Physicians: 24.8 per 10,000 population; Hospital beds: 31.0 per 10,000 population; Hospital admissions: 1,307.3 per 10,000 population

Air Quality Index: 82.0% good, 18.0% moderate, 0.0% unhealthy for sensitive individuals, 0.0% unhealthy (percent of days)

Transportation: Commute: 91.3% car, 1.5% public transportation, 1.6% walk, 4.4% work from home; Median travel time to work: 21.1 minutes

Presidential Election: 57.7% Obama, 41.2% Romney (2012)

National and State Parks: Guilford Courthouse National Military Park

Additional Information Contacts

Guilford Government . . . . (336) 641-3383
http://countyweb.co.guilford.nc.us

Guilford County Communities

BROWNS SUMMIT (unincorporated postal area)
ZCTA: 27214

Covers a land area of 48.075 square miles and a water area of 2.355 square miles. Located at 36.21° N. Lat; 79.67° W. Long. Elevation is 804 feet.

Population: 10,294; Growth (since 2000): 64.5%; Density: 214.1 persons per square mile; Race: 59.1% White, 33.9% Black/African American, 0.6% Asian, 0.5% American Indian/Alaska Native, 0.0% Native Hawaiian/Other Pacific Islander, 2.2% Two or more races, 7.0% Hispanic of any race; Average household size: 2.68; Median age: 36.6; Age under 18: 27.4%; Age 65 and over: 10.4%; Males per 100 females: 95.7; Marriage status: 24.9% never married, 62.0% now married, 2.3% separated, 4.7% widowed, 8.4% divorced; Foreign born: 6.7%; Speak English only: 90.7%; With disability: 7.8%; Veterans: 8.3%; Ancestry: 9.9% American, 7.8% German, 6.0% English, 5.0% Irish, 2.5% European

Employment: 12.0% management, business, and financial, 8.7% computer, engineering, and science, 10.1% education, legal, community service, arts, and media, 3.5% healthcare practitioners, 12.6% service, 29.5% sales and office, 12.3% natural resources, construction, and maintenance, 11.2% production, transportation, and material moving

Income: Per capita: $22,146; Median household: $49,688; Average household: $61,384; Households with income of $100,000 or more: 16.1%; Poverty rate: 17.4%

Educational Attainment: High school diploma or higher: 88.9%; Bachelor's degree or higher: 24.8%; Graduate/professional degree or higher: 6.1%

School District(s)
Guilford County Schools (PK-12)
2012-13 Enrollment: 74,161 . . . . (336) 370-8100

Housing: Homeownership rate: 79.5%; Median home value: $166,000; Median year structure built: 1992; Homeowner vacancy rate: 2.0%; Median gross rent: $790 per month; Rental vacancy rate: 11.3%

Health Insurance: 82.5% have insurance; 62.1% have private insurance; 30.0% have public insurance; 17.5% do not have insurance; 5.8% of children under 18 do not have insurance

Transportation: Commute: 93.6% car, 0.0% public transportation, 1.4% walk, 4.7% work from home; Median travel time to work: 24.4 minutes

COLFAX (unincorporated postal area)
ZCTA: 27235

Covers a land area of 13.555 square miles and a water area of 0.038 square miles. Located at 36.09° N. Lat; 80.01° W. Long. Elevation is 965 feet.

Population: 4,136; Growth (since 2000): 75.7%; Density: 305.1 persons per square mile; Race: 90.8% White, 3.7% Black/African American, 3.4% Asian, 0.5% American Indian/Alaska Native, 0.0% Native Hawaiian/Other Pacific Islander, 1.2% Two or more races, 3.0% Hispanic of any race; Average household size: 2.42; Median age: 45.5; Age under 18: 22.8%; Age 65 and over: 23.5%; Males per 100 females: 87.5; Marriage status: 21.4% never married, 64.5% now married, 0.2% separated, 8.8% widowed, 5.2% divorced; Foreign born: 3.7%; Speak English only: 94.6%; With disability: 11.1%; Veterans: 12.1%; Ancestry: 19.0% English, 15.2% American, 14.7% German, 14.7% Irish, 6.8% Scotch-Irish

Employment: 22.0% management, business, and financial, 8.6% computer, engineering, and science, 5.5% education, legal, community service, arts, and media, 4.6% healthcare practitioners, 9.4% service, 26.1% sales and office, 13.5% natural resources, construction, and maintenance, 10.3% production, transportation, and material moving

Income: Per capita: $34,150; Median household: $71,439; Average household: $86,782; Households with income of $100,000 or more: 33.2%; Poverty rate: 3.7%

Educational Attainment: High school diploma or higher: 94.9%; Bachelor's degree or higher: 37.3%; Graduate/professional degree or higher: 11.0%

School District(s)
Guilford County Schools (PK-12)
2012-13 Enrollment: 74,161 . . . . (336) 370-8100

Housing: Homeownership rate: 74.9%; Median home value: $255,800; Median year structure built: 1996; Homeowner vacancy rate: 2.5%; Median gross rent: $2,000+ per month; Rental vacancy rate: 10.0%

Health Insurance: 91.6% have insurance; 82.9% have private insurance; 29.9% have public insurance; 8.4% do not have insurance; 2.4% of children under 18 do not have insurance

Transportation: Commute: 88.2% car, 0.0% public transportation, 1.0% walk, 9.5% work from home; Median travel time to work: 17.7 minutes

FOREST OAKS (CDP). Covers a land area of 4.847 square miles and a water area of 0.106 square miles. Located at 35.99° N. Lat; 79.71° W. Long. Elevation is 761 feet.

Population: 3,890; Growth (since 2000): 20.0%; Density: 802.5 persons per square mile; Race: 81.5% White, 15.2% Black/African American, 0.7% Asian, 0.3% American Indian/Alaska Native, 0.0% Native Hawaiian/Other Pacific Islander, 1.4% Two or more races, 2.0% Hispanic of any race; Average household size: 2.58; Median age: 46.8; Age under 18: 22.1%; Age 65 and over: 19.1%; Males per 100 females: 96.5; Marriage status: 21.9% never married, 68.3% now married, 1.0% separated, 4.0% widowed, 5.8% divorced; Foreign born: 1.7%; Speak English only: 97.9%; With disability: 9.2%; Veterans: 13.2%; Ancestry: 20.7% English, 14.7% American, 9.9% German, 6.0% Irish, 4.3% Italian

Employment: 18.7% management, business, and financial, 6.8% computer, engineering, and science, 11.5% education, legal, community service, arts, and media, 5.2% healthcare practitioners, 12.1% service, 27.2% sales and office, 7.3% natural resources, construction, and maintenance, 11.3% production, transportation, and material moving

Income: Per capita: $32,942; Median household: $79,069; Average household: $85,005; Households with income of $100,000 or more: 31.2%; Poverty rate: 11.2%

Educational Attainment: High school diploma or higher: 93.8%; Bachelor's degree or higher: 42.1%; Graduate/professional degree or higher: 13.0%

Housing: Homeownership rate: 94.7%; Median home value: $204,200; Median year structure built: 1978; Homeowner vacancy rate: 1.9%; Median gross rent: n/a per month; Rental vacancy rate: 4.8%

Health Insurance: 98.4% have insurance; 83.7% have private insurance; 27.8% have public insurance; 1.6% do not have insurance; 0.0% of children under 18 do not have insurance

Transportation: Commute: 90.9% car, 0.0% public transportation, 0.7% walk, 7.7% work from home; Median travel time to work: 25.0 minutes

GIBSONVILLE (town). Covers a land area of 3.495 square miles and a water area of 0.010 square miles. Located at 36.10° N. Lat; 79.54° W. Long. Elevation is 718 feet.

Population: 6,410; Growth (since 2000): 46.6%; Density: 1,834.1 persons per square mile; Race: 79.4% White, 14.6% Black/African American, 1.1% Asian, 0.2% American Indian/Alaska Native, 0.1% Native Hawaiian/Other Pacific Islander, 1.5% Two or more races, 5.9% Hispanic of any race; Average household size: 2.47; Median age: 38.4; Age under 18: 25.2%; Age 65 and over: 11.5%; Males per 100 females: 86.0; Marriage status: 21.4% never married, 59.7% now married, 1.9% separated, 5.2% widowed, 13.8% divorced; Foreign born: 3.8%; Speak English only: 92.9%; With disability: 8.8%; Veterans: 8.3%; Ancestry: 14.1% American, 12.7% German, 9.8% Irish, 6.6% English, 3.5% Scotch-Irish

Employment: 15.8% management, business, and financial, 5.4% computer, engineering, and science, 9.7% education, legal, community service, arts, and media, 9.9% healthcare practitioners, 10.9% service, 25.6% sales and office, 9.6% natural resources, construction, and maintenance, 13.1% production, transportation, and material moving

Income: Per capita: $26,421; Median household: $57,391; Average household: $65,624; Households with income of $100,000 or more: 19.7%; Poverty rate: 8.1%

Educational Attainment: High school diploma or higher: 91.2%; Bachelor's degree or higher: 32.5%; Graduate/professional degree or higher: 14.7%

School District(s)

Guilford County Schools (PK-12)
  2012-13 Enrollment: 74,161 . . . . (336) 370-8100

Housing: Homeownership rate: 76.5%; Median home value: $159,500; Median year structure built: 1989; Homeowner vacancy rate: 2.2%; Median gross rent: $629 per month; Rental vacancy rate: 12.9%

Health Insurance: 88.9% have insurance; 78.2% have private insurance; 23.4% have public insurance; 11.1% do not have insurance; 5.0% of children under 18 do not have insurance

Safety: Violent crime rate: 4.5 per 10,000 population; Property crime rate: 171.9 per 10,000 population

Transportation: Commute: 98.7% car, 0.1% public transportation, 0.0% walk, 1.3% work from home; Median travel time to work: 23.3 minutes

Additional Information Contacts

Town of Gibsonville . . . . (336) 449-4144
  http://www.gibsonville.net

GREENSBORO (city). County seat. Covers a land area of 126.515 square miles and a water area of 5.286 square miles. Located at 36.10° N. Lat; 79.83° W. Long. Elevation is 827 feet.

History: The earliest settlers around Greensboro were Quakers, Germans, and Scots-Irish freeholders, whose zeal for religious, economic, and political freedom dotted the region with churches, wrested prosperity from the wilderness, and helped win independence from the British Crown. The city occupies part of the original grant in 1749 from John Carteret, Earl of Granville, to the Nottingham Company for settlement of a colony of Scots-Irish Presbyterians. A German colony and two groups of Quakers also settled at the same time nearby. In 1808, the General Assembly authorized the commissioners to purchase and lay off a tract of 42 acres in the geographic center of the county. The new town was named Greensboro, in honor of General Nathanael Greene, leader of the Colonial forces at Guilford Courthouse.

Population: 269,666; Growth (since 2000): 20.4%; Density: 2,131.5 persons per square mile; Race: 48.4% White, 40.6% Black/African American, 4.0% Asian, 0.5% American Indian/Alaska Native, 0.1% Native Hawaiian/Other Pacific Islander, 2.6% Two or more races, 7.5% Hispanic of any race; Average household size: 2.31; Median age: 33.4; Age under 18: 22.7%; Age 65 and over: 11.5%; Males per 100 females: 88.7; Marriage status: 41.2% never married, 42.1% now married, 3.0% separated, 5.8% widowed, 10.8% divorced; Foreign born: 10.7%; Speak English only: 86.3%; With disability: 9.9%; Veterans: 7.6%; Ancestry: 8.1% English, 7.6% German, 5.8% Irish, 5.4% American, 2.5% Scotch-Irish

Employment: 14.1% management, business, and financial, 4.1% computer, engineering, and science, 12.0% education, legal, community service, arts, and media, 5.7% healthcare practitioners, 18.0% service, 27.3% sales and office, 6.4% natural resources, construction, and maintenance, 12.5% production, transportation, and material moving

Income: Per capita: $25,861; Median household: $41,120; Average household: $61,440; Households with income of $100,000 or more: 15.2%; Poverty rate: 20.3%

Educational Attainment: High school diploma or higher: 87.7%; Bachelor's degree or higher: 35.7%; Graduate/professional degree or higher: 12.3%

School District(s)

Cornerstone Charter Academy
  2012-13 Enrollment: 519 . . . . (336) 482-3855
Greensboro Academy (KG-08)
  2012-13 Enrollment: 721 . . . . (336) 286-8404
Guilford County Schools (PK-12)
  2012-13 Enrollment: 74,161 . . . . (336) 370-8100
Guilford Preparatory (KG-08)
  2012-13 Enrollment: 217 . . . . (336) 954-1344
Triad Math and Science Academy (KG-09)
  2012-13 Enrollment: 599 . . . . (336) 621-0061
Two Rivers Community (KG-08)
  2012-13 Enrollment: 178 . . . . (828) 262-5411

Four-year College(s)

Bennett College (Private, Not-for-profit, Historically black, United Methodist)
  Fall 2013 Enrollment: 680 . . . . (336) 517-2100
  2013-14 Tuition: In-state $17,355; Out-of-state $17,355
Greensboro College (Private, Not-for-profit, United Methodist)
  Fall 2013 Enrollment: 1,012 . . . . (336) 272-7102
  2013-14 Tuition: In-state $26,306; Out-of-state $26,306
Guilford College (Private, Not-for-profit, Friends)
  Fall 2013 Enrollment: 2,302 . . . . (336) 316-2000
  2013-14 Tuition: In-state $32,470; Out-of-state $32,470
North Carolina A & T State University (Public, Historically black)
  Fall 2013 Enrollment: 10,561 . . . . (336) 334-7500
  2013-14 Tuition: In-state $5,422; Out-of-state $16,503
University of North Carolina at Greensboro (Public)
  Fall 2013 Enrollment: 18,074 . . . . (336) 334-5000
  2013-14 Tuition: In-state $6,382; Out-of-state $20,180

Two-year College(s)

Virginia College-Greensboro (Private, For-profit)
  Fall 2013 Enrollment: 468 . . . . (336) 398-5400
  2013-14 Tuition: In-state $13,140; Out-of-state $13,140

Vocational/Technical School(s)

Brookstone College-Greensboro (Private, For-profit)
  Fall 2013 Enrollment: 154 . . . . (336) 668-2627
  2013-14 Tuition: $19,400
Empire Beauty School-West Greensboro (Private, For-profit)
  Fall 2013 Enrollment: 111 . . . . (800) 920-4593
  2013-14 Tuition: $18,000
Leons Beauty School Inc (Private, For-profit)
  Fall 2013 Enrollment: 143 . . . . (336) 274-4601
  2013-14 Tuition: $6,700
The Hair Design School-E Greensboro (Private, For-profit)
  Fall 2013 Enrollment: 151 . . . . (800) 920-4593
  2013-14 Tuition: $15,750

Housing: Homeownership rate: 52.5%; Median home value: $147,400; Median year structure built: 1981; Homeowner vacancy rate: 3.4%; Median gross rent: $742 per month; Rental vacancy rate: 11.9%

Health Insurance: 82.6% have insurance; 63.1% have private insurance; 28.6% have public insurance; 17.4% do not have insurance; 7.5% of children under 18 do not have insurance

Hospitals: The Moses H Cone Memorial Hospital (536 beds)

Safety: Violent crime rate: 51.9 per 10,000 population; Property crime rate: 413.0 per 10,000 population

Newspapers: News & Record (daily circulation 85500); Rhinoceros Times (weekly circulation 48000)

Transportation: Commute: 90.7% car, 1.9% public transportation, 2.0% walk, 3.8% work from home; Median travel time to work: 20.1 minutes; Amtrak: Train service available.

Airports: Piedmont Triad International (primary service/small hub); Southeast Greensboro (general aviation)

Additional Information Contacts

City of Greensboro . . . . (336) 373-2489
  http://www.greensboro-nc.gov

HIGH POINT (city). Covers a land area of 53.803 square miles and a water area of 1.643 square miles. Located at 35.99° N. Lat; 79.99° W. Long. Elevation is 922 feet.

History: High Point was laid out in 1853, when the state-built North Carolina & Midland Railroad was brought through. Named because it was

the highest point on the railroad line between Goldsboro and Charlotte, the new village became an important trading center with completion in 1854 of the plank road between Salem and Fayetteville. High Point was incorporated in 1859 and soon became the trading center of neighboring farm communities. In 1888, furniture manufacturers were attracted by the abundance of hardwood timber available, and the quiet country town changed into an industrial center.

Population: 104,371; Growth (since 2000): 21.6%; Density: 1,939.9 persons per square mile; Race: 53.6% White, 33.0% Black/African American, 6.1% Asian, 0.6% American Indian/Alaska Native, 0.0% Native Hawaiian/Other Pacific Islander, 2.3% Two or more races, 8.5% Hispanic of any race; Average household size: 2.46; Median age: 35.8; Age under 18: 25.2%; Age 65 and over: 12.0%; Males per 100 females: 88.5; Marriage status: 35.5% never married, 46.6% now married, 3.8% separated, 6.3% widowed, 11.5% divorced; Foreign born: 12.1%; Speak English only: 85.0%; With disability: 12.4%; Veterans: 7.9%; Ancestry: 9.1% German, 7.8% English, 7.0% Irish, 6.2% American, 3.2% Italian
Employment: 13.9% management, business, and financial, 4.1% computer, engineering, and science, 10.2% education, legal, community service, arts, and media, 4.7% healthcare practitioners, 18.2% service, 27.6% sales and office, 5.4% natural resources, construction, and maintenance, 15.9% production, transportation, and material moving
Income: Per capita: $22,940; Median household: $43,083; Average household: $57,190; Households with income of $100,000 or more: 15.4%; Poverty rate: 21.4%
Educational Attainment: High school diploma or higher: 85.7%; Bachelor's degree or higher: 28.9%; Graduate/professional degree or higher: 8.6%

School District(s)

Guilford County Schools (PK-12)
    2012-13 Enrollment: 74,161 . . . . (336) 370-8100
Phoenix Academy Inc (KG-05)
    2012-13 Enrollment: 318 . . . . (336) 869-0079
Randolph County Schools (PK-12)
    2012-13 Enrollment: 18,628 . . . . (336) 318-6100

Four-year College(s)

High Point University (Private, Not-for-profit, United Methodist)
    Fall 2013 Enrollment: 4,199 . . . . (336) 841-9000
    2013-14 Tuition: In-state $30,715; Out-of-state $30,715
ITT Technical Institute-High Point (Private, For-profit)
    Fall 2013 Enrollment: 451 . . . . (336) 819-5900
    2013-14 Tuition: In-state $18,048; Out-of-state $18,048
Laurel University (Private, Not-for-profit)
    Fall 2013 Enrollment: 610 . . . . (336) 887-3000
    2013-14 Tuition: In-state $8,890; Out-of-state $8,890
South University-High Point (Private, For-profit)
    Fall 2013 Enrollment: 249 . . . . (336) 812-7200
    2013-14 Tuition: In-state $16,360; Out-of-state $16,360

Vocational/Technical School(s)

Health And Style Institute (Private, For-profit)
    Fall 2013 Enrollment: 179 . . . . (336) 885-3452
    2013-14 Tuition: $17,875
Regina's College of Beauty-High Point (Private, For-profit)
    Fall 2013 Enrollment: 59 . . . . (336) 885-3336
    2013-14 Tuition: $17,495
Housing: Homeownership rate: 57.1%; Median home value: $146,200; Median year structure built: 1983; Homeowner vacancy rate: 4.0%; Median gross rent: $762 per month; Rental vacancy rate: 12.1%
Health Insurance: 81.0% have insurance; 58.3% have private insurance; 31.5% have public insurance; 19.0% do not have insurance; 11.4% of children under 18 do not have insurance
Hospitals: High Point Regional Hospital (400 beds)
Safety: Violent crime rate: 51.8 per 10,000 population; Property crime rate: 418.5 per 10,000 population
Newspapers: High Point Enterprise (daily circulation 21200); Thomasville Times (weekly circulation 5800)
Transportation: Commute: 91.7% car, 1.8% public transportation, 1.6% walk, 3.9% work from home; Median travel time to work: 20.1 minutes; Amtrak: Train service available.
Additional Information Contacts
City of High Point . . . . (336) 998-3446
    http://www.high-point.net

JAMESTOWN (town). Covers a land area of 2.897 square miles and a water area of 0 square miles. Located at 36.00° N. Lat; 79.94° W. Long. Elevation is 794 feet.
History: Old Jamestown was settled by Quakers in 1757. The village was named for James Mendenhall, a Pennsylvania Quaker who came to North Carolina in 1759.
Population: 3,382; Growth (since 2000): 9.5%; Density: 1,167.2 persons per square mile; Race: 80.6% White, 13.6% Black/African American, 2.5% Asian, 0.4% American Indian/Alaska Native, 0.1% Native Hawaiian/Other Pacific Islander, 1.6% Two or more races, 3.2% Hispanic of any race; Average household size: 2.45; Median age: 45.3; Age under 18: 22.7%; Age 65 and over: 16.9%; Males per 100 females: 93.3; Marriage status: 24.8% never married, 56.7% now married, 1.5% separated, 7.2% widowed, 11.3% divorced; Foreign born: 9.9%; Speak English only: 87.7%; With disability: 10.3%; Veterans: 10.8%; Ancestry: 15.9% German, 15.4% English, 10.9% American, 9.3% Irish, 4.7% Italian
Employment: 21.9% management, business, and financial, 4.0% computer, engineering, and science, 11.0% education, legal, community service, arts, and media, 4.1% healthcare practitioners, 10.3% service, 32.7% sales and office, 4.1% natural resources, construction, and maintenance, 11.8% production, transportation, and material moving
Income: Per capita: $38,344; Median household: $77,261; Average household: $101,664; Households with income of $100,000 or more: 33.9%; Poverty rate: 8.1%
Educational Attainment: High school diploma or higher: 93.0%; Bachelor's degree or higher: 44.0%; Graduate/professional degree or higher: 11.6%

School District(s)

Guilford County Schools (PK-12)
    2012-13 Enrollment: 74,161 . . . . (336) 370-8100
The College Preparatory and Leadership Academy
    2012-13 Enrollment: 112 . . . . (336) 264-5573

Two-year College(s)

Guilford Technical Community College (Public)
    Fall 2013 Enrollment: 13,656 . . . . (336) 334-4822
    2013-14 Tuition: In-state $2,462; Out-of-state $8,606
Housing: Homeownership rate: 78.9%; Median home value: $212,100; Median year structure built: 1983; Homeowner vacancy rate: 3.1%; Median gross rent: $939 per month; Rental vacancy rate: 11.4%
Health Insurance: 88.2% have insurance; 78.5% have private insurance; 27.3% have public insurance; 11.8% do not have insurance; 3.6% of children under 18 do not have insurance
Newspapers: Jamestown News (weekly circulation 2800)
Transportation: Commute: 95.0% car, 0.0% public transportation, 0.6% walk, 4.4% work from home; Median travel time to work: 19.7 minutes
Additional Information Contacts
Town of Jamestown . . . . (336) 454-1138
    http://www.jamestown-nc.us

JULIAN (unincorporated postal area)
ZCTA: 27283
    Covers a land area of 26.335 square miles and a water area of 0.226 square miles. Located at 35.95° N. Lat; 79.64° W. Long. Elevation is 764 feet.
    Population: 3,141; Growth (since 2000): 10.2%; Density: 119.3 persons per square mile; Race: 93.8% White, 3.1% Black/African American, 0.5% Asian, 0.4% American Indian/Alaska Native, 0.2% Native Hawaiian/Other Pacific Islander, 1.1% Two or more races, 2.3% Hispanic of any race; Average household size: 2.43; Median age: 44.7; Age under 18: 20.5%; Age 65 and over: 16.7%; Males per 100 females: 103.2; Marriage status: 14.0% never married, 72.1% now married, 1.2% separated, 2.7% widowed, 11.2% divorced; Foreign born: 1.9%; Speak English only: 96.2%; With disability: 8.8%; Veterans: 11.6%; Ancestry: 17.0% American, 15.1% German, 12.2% English, 6.5% Irish, 3.9% Italian
    Employment: 18.3% management, business, and financial, 5.0% computer, engineering, and science, 9.5% education, legal, community service, arts, and media, 4.4% healthcare practitioners, 10.2% service, 19.6% sales and office, 18.1% natural resources, construction, and maintenance, 14.9% production, transportation, and material moving
    Income: Per capita: $27,215; Median household: $52,015; Average household: $66,245; Households with income of $100,000 or more: 21.0%; Poverty rate: 7.5%

Educational Attainment: High school diploma or higher: 88.5%; Bachelor's degree or higher: 21.2%; Graduate/professional degree or higher: 7.2%
Housing: Homeownership rate: 85.8%; Median home value: $164,300; Median year structure built: 1983; Homeowner vacancy rate: 0.9%; Median gross rent: $646 per month; Rental vacancy rate: 8.0%
Health Insurance: 87.0% have insurance; 73.4% have private insurance; 26.0% have public insurance; 13.0% do not have insurance; 2.2% of children under 18 do not have insurance
Transportation: Commute: 95.3% car, 0.0% public transportation, 0.0% walk, 4.2% work from home; Median travel time to work: 27.4 minutes

MCLEANSVILLE (CDP). Covers a land area of 6.177 square miles and a water area of 0.077 square miles. Located at 36.10° N. Lat; 79.65° W. Long. Elevation is 761 feet.

Population: 1,021; Growth (since 2000): -5.5%; Density: 165.3 persons per square mile; Race: 93.7% White, 4.2% Black/African American, 0.6% Asian, 0.2% American Indian/Alaska Native, 0.0% Native Hawaiian/Other Pacific Islander, 0.7% Two or more races, 3.3% Hispanic of any race; Average household size: 2.33; Median age: 47.0; Age under 18: 18.2%; Age 65 and over: 20.8%; Males per 100 females: 97.1

School District(s)
Guilford County Schools (PK-12)
    2012-13 Enrollment: 74,161 . . . . (336) 370-8100
Housing: Homeownership rate: 77.6%; Homeowner vacancy rate: 0.6%; Rental vacancy rate: 16.2%

OAK RIDGE (town). Covers a land area of 15.377 square miles and a water area of 0.142 square miles. Located at 36.17° N. Lat; 79.99° W. Long. Elevation is 938 feet.

History: The Oak Ridge Military Institute was founded in Oak Ridge in 1852.
Population: 6,185; Growth (since 2000): 55.1%; Density: 402.2 persons per square mile; Race: 88.9% White, 5.2% Black/African American, 3.4% Asian, 0.4% American Indian/Alaska Native, 0.0% Native Hawaiian/Other Pacific Islander, 1.0% Two or more races, 3.0% Hispanic of any race; Average household size: 2.94; Median age: 41.8; Age under 18: 29.9%; Age 65 and over: 8.6%; Males per 100 females: 101.1; Marriage status: 18.9% never married, 70.2% now married, 1.5% separated, 3.9% widowed, 7.0% divorced; Foreign born: 8.2%; Speak English only: 91.3%; With disability: 7.6%; Veterans: 10.1%; Ancestry: 14.4% English, 13.8% German, 10.3% American, 7.9% Irish, 7.1% Italian
Employment: 29.4% management, business, and financial, 10.0% computer, engineering, and science, 10.7% education, legal, community service, arts, and media, 6.0% healthcare practitioners, 11.9% service, 25.1% sales and office, 3.3% natural resources, construction, and maintenance, 3.6% production, transportation, and material moving
Income: Per capita: $40,794; Median household: $100,208; Average household: $115,981; Households with income of $100,000 or more: 50.2%; Poverty rate: 3.0%
Educational Attainment: High school diploma or higher: 97.1%; Bachelor's degree or higher: 50.9%; Graduate/professional degree or higher: 21.5%

School District(s)
Guilford County Schools (PK-12)
    2012-13 Enrollment: 74,161 . . . . (336) 370-8100
Housing: Homeownership rate: 92.1%; Median home value: $333,700; Median year structure built: 1997; Homeowner vacancy rate: 2.5%; Median gross rent: $740 per month; Rental vacancy rate: 8.8%
Health Insurance: 94.6% have insurance; 90.6% have private insurance; 11.1% have public insurance; 5.4% do not have insurance; 1.9% of children under 18 do not have insurance
Newspapers: Northwest Observer (weekly circulation 13000)
Transportation: Commute: 91.8% car, 0.0% public transportation, 0.7% walk, 6.9% work from home; Median travel time to work: 24.6 minutes
Additional Information Contacts
Town of Oak Ridge . . . . (336) 644-7009
    http://www.oakridgenc.com

PLEASANT GARDEN (town). Covers a land area of 15.269 square miles and a water area of 0.124 square miles. Located at 35.96° N. Lat; 79.76° W. Long. Elevation is 856 feet.

Population: 4,489; Growth (since 2000): -4.8%; Density: 294.0 persons per square mile; Race: 83.0% White, 10.7% Black/African American, 0.7% Asian, 0.6% American Indian/Alaska Native, 0.0% Native Hawaiian/Other

Pacific Islander, 1.7% Two or more races, 4.7% Hispanic of any race; Average household size: 2.58; Median age: 45.6; Age under 18: 21.2%; Age 65 and over: 18.8%; Males per 100 females: 94.2; Marriage status: 24.0% never married, 62.0% now married, 1.9% separated, 6.6% widowed, 7.5% divorced; Foreign born: 1.7%; Speak English only: 94.3%; With disability: 11.9%; Veterans: 11.6%; Ancestry: 13.9% English, 12.0% American, 11.0% German, 10.1% Irish, 7.3% Scotch-Irish
Employment: 15.2% management, business, and financial, 4.8% computer, engineering, and science, 6.4% education, legal, community service, arts, and media, 7.0% healthcare practitioners, 7.8% service, 31.3% sales and office, 11.1% natural resources, construction, and maintenance, 16.4% production, transportation, and material moving
Income: Per capita: $28,602; Median household: $63,276; Average household: $77,610; Households with income of $100,000 or more: 27.1%; Poverty rate: 16.5%
Educational Attainment: High school diploma or higher: 89.9%; Bachelor's degree or higher: 19.7%; Graduate/professional degree or higher: 5.9%

School District(s)
Guilford County Schools (PK-12)
    2012-13 Enrollment: 74,161 . . . . (336) 370-8100
Housing: Homeownership rate: 84.2%; Median home value: $149,700; Median year structure built: 1976; Homeowner vacancy rate: 1.8%; Median gross rent: $851 per month; Rental vacancy rate: 8.6%
Health Insurance: 89.2% have insurance; 68.6% have private insurance; 34.5% have public insurance; 10.8% do not have insurance; 6.2% of children under 18 do not have insurance
Transportation: Commute: 90.1% car, 0.0% public transportation, 0.4% walk, 8.5% work from home; Median travel time to work: 27.7 minutes
Additional Information Contacts
Town of Pleasant Garden . . . . (336) 674-3002
    http://www.pleasantgarden.net

SEDALIA (town). Covers a land area of 2.088 square miles and a water area of 0.006 square miles. Located at 36.08° N. Lat; 79.62° W. Long. Elevation is 702 feet.

Population: 623; Growth (since 2000): 0.8%; Density: 298.4 persons per square mile; Race: 20.9% White, 76.1% Black/African American, 0.2% Asian, 0.3% American Indian/Alaska Native, 0.0% Native Hawaiian/Other Pacific Islander, 2.4% Two or more races, 1.8% Hispanic of any race; Average household size: 2.48; Median age: 47.5; Age under 18: 17.7%; Age 65 and over: 20.1%; Males per 100 females: 97.2

School District(s)
Guilford County Schools (PK-12)
    2012-13 Enrollment: 74,161 . . . . (336) 370-8100
Housing: Homeownership rate: 90.4%; Homeowner vacancy rate: 3.0%; Rental vacancy rate: 24.2%

STOKESDALE (town). Covers a land area of 19.245 square miles and a water area of 0.158 square miles. Located at 36.23° N. Lat; 79.98° W. Long. Elevation is 955 feet.

History: Stokesdale was named for John Stokes, a Revolutionary figure.
Population: 5,047; Growth (since 2000): 54.5%; Density: 262.3 persons per square mile; Race: 90.9% White, 4.7% Black/African American, 1.4% Asian, 0.4% American Indian/Alaska Native, 0.0% Native Hawaiian/Other Pacific Islander, 1.3% Two or more races, 3.5% Hispanic of any race; Average household size: 2.73; Median age: 39.9; Age under 18: 27.3%; Age 65 and over: 11.3%; Males per 100 females: 99.7; Marriage status: 24.4% never married, 64.4% now married, 4.2% separated, 4.4% widowed, 6.9% divorced; Foreign born: 3.6%; Speak English only: 93.3%; With disability: 7.6%; Veterans: 7.0%; Ancestry: 18.5% American, 15.8% German, 11.1% English, 10.1% Irish, 3.1% Italian
Employment: 20.4% management, business, and financial, 5.1% computer, engineering, and science, 13.0% education, legal, community service, arts, and media, 7.2% healthcare practitioners, 14.2% service, 21.6% sales and office, 8.9% natural resources, construction, and maintenance, 9.7% production, transportation, and material moving
Income: Per capita: $30,591; Median household: $76,976; Average household: $88,651; Households with income of $100,000 or more: 33.6%; Poverty rate: 11.0%
Educational Attainment: High school diploma or higher: 93.0%; Bachelor's degree or higher: 34.2%; Graduate/professional degree or higher: 12.8%

School District(s)

Guilford County Schools (PK-12)

    2012-13 Enrollment: 74,161 . . . . (336) 370-8100

Housing: Homeownership rate: 84.9%; Median home value: $196,500; Median year structure built: 1996; Homeowner vacancy rate: 2.3%; Median gross rent: $714 per month; Rental vacancy rate: 10.4%

Health Insurance: 86.7% have insurance; 78.5% have private insurance; 15.1% have public insurance; 13.3% do not have insurance; 18.5% of children under 18 do not have insurance

Transportation: Commute: 91.9% car, 0.0% public transportation, 0.6% walk, 6.5% work from home; Median travel time to work: 25.6 minutes

Additional Information Contacts

Town of Stokesdale . . . . (336) 643-4011

    http://www.stokesdale.org

SUMMERFIELD (town). Covers a land area of 26.557 square miles and a water area of 0.294 square miles. Located at 36.20° N. Lat; 79.90° W. Long. Elevation is 906 feet.

History: Summerfield was originally called Bruce's Crossroads for Charles Bruce who owned the site, but in 1812 it was named Summerfield in honor of a visiting evangelist.

Population: 10,232; Growth (since 2000): 45.8%; Density: 385.3 persons per square mile; Race: 89.9% White, 4.4% Black/African American, 2.2% Asian, 0.4% American Indian/Alaska Native, 0.0% Native Hawaiian/Other Pacific Islander, 1.5% Two or more races, 4.3% Hispanic of any race; Average household size: 2.89; Median age: 42.1; Age under 18: 28.9%; Age 65 and over: 9.5%; Males per 100 females: 101.0; Marriage status: 18.5% never married, 68.7% now married, 1.1% separated, 4.9% widowed, 7.9% divorced; Foreign born: 5.3%; Speak English only: 93.0%; With disability: 8.1%; Veterans: 8.7%; Ancestry: 18.7% German, 15.7% English, 14.9% American, 9.4% Irish, 4.2% Italian

Employment: 30.2% management, business, and financial, 4.3% computer, engineering, and science, 12.8% education, legal, community service, arts, and media, 6.8% healthcare practitioners, 9.1% service, 24.8% sales and office, 6.4% natural resources, construction, and maintenance, 5.6% production, transportation, and material moving

Income: Per capita: $45,508; Median household: $98,438; Average household: $124,136; Households with income of $100,000 or more: 49.8%; Poverty rate: 4.5%

Educational Attainment: High school diploma or higher: 94.0%; Bachelor's degree or higher: 51.8%; Graduate/professional degree or higher: 19.0%

School District(s)

Guilford County Schools (PK-12)

    2012-13 Enrollment: 74,161 . . . . (336) 370-8100

Housing: Homeownership rate: 91.2%; Median home value: $331,000; Median year structure built: 1996; Homeowner vacancy rate: 2.0%; Median gross rent: $1,571 per month; Rental vacancy rate: 8.3%

Health Insurance: 94.9% have insurance; 87.1% have private insurance; 16.5% have public insurance; 5.1% do not have insurance; 5.9% of children under 18 do not have insurance

Transportation: Commute: 91.1% car, 0.0% public transportation, 0.4% walk, 7.4% work from home; Median travel time to work: 27.5 minutes

Additional Information Contacts

Town of Summerfield . . . . (336) 643-8655

    http://www.summerfield-nc.com

WHITSETT (town). Covers a land area of 2.631 square miles and a water area of 0.028 square miles. Located at 36.08° N. Lat; 79.57° W. Long. Elevation is 679 feet.

Population: 590; Growth (since 2000): -14.0%; Density: 224.2 persons per square mile; Race: 91.0% White, 6.8% Black/African American, 0.0% Asian, 0.0% American Indian/Alaska Native, 0.0% Native Hawaiian/Other Pacific Islander, 0.3% Two or more races, 2.9% Hispanic of any race; Average household size: 2.30; Median age: 49.0; Age under 18: 15.8%; Age 65 and over: 20.5%; Males per 100 females: 94.7

Housing: Homeownership rate: 80.0%; Homeowner vacancy rate: 1.9%; Rental vacancy rate: 5.5%

Halifax County

Located in northeastern North Carolina; piedmont area, bounded on the north and east by the Roanoke River, and on the south by Fishing Creek. Covers a land area of 724.086 square miles, a water area of 7.093 square miles, and is located in the Eastern Time Zone at 36.25° N. Lat., 77.64° W. Long. The county was founded in 1758. County seat is Halifax.

Halifax County is part of the Roanoke Rapids, NC Micropolitan Statistical Area. The entire metro area includes: Halifax County, NC; Northampton County, NC

Weather Station: Roanoke Rapids   Elevation: 209 feet

	Jan	Feb	Mar	Apr	May	Jun	Jul	Aug	Sep	Oct	Nov	Dec
High	49	52	60	70	78	86	90	88	82	72	62	52
Low	29	31	37	45	54	64	68	67	60	48	39	32
Precip	3.6	3.0	4.1	3.6	3.6	4.0	4.7	4.6	4.3	3.3	3.5	3.3
Snow	0.2	0.6	0.1	0.0	0.0	0.0	0.0	0.0	0.0	0.0	0.0	0.0

High and Low temperatures in degrees Fahrenheit; Precipitation and Snow in inches

Population: 54,691; Growth (since 2000): -4.7%; Density: 75.5 persons per square mile; Race: 40.0% White, 53.2% Black/African American, 0.7% Asian, 3.8% American Indian/Alaska Native, 0.0% Native Hawaiian/Other Pacific Islander, 1.2% two or more races, 2.1% Hispanic of any race; Average household size: 2.42; Median age: 41.7; Age under 18: 23.1%; Age 65 and over: 16.2%; Males per 100 females: 91.5; Marriage status: 33.8% never married, 44.6% now married, 4.6% separated, 9.9% widowed, 11.7% divorced; Foreign born: 1.7%; Speak English only: 97.4%; With disability: 23.6%; Veterans: 8.4%; Ancestry: 8.9% English, 9.0% American, 5.5% Irish, 4.1% German, 1.1% Scotch-Irish

Religion: Six largest groups: 26.3% Baptist, 7.9% Methodist/Pietist, 7.4% Non-denominational Protestant, 3.0% Pentecostal, 0.8% Catholicism, 0.7% Episcopalianism/Anglicanism

Economy: Unemployment rate: 8.5%; Leading industries: 24.1% retail trade; 12.9% health care and social assistance; 12.5% other services (except public administration); Farms: 341 totaling 195,896 acres; Company size: 0 employ 1,000 or more persons, 1 employs 500 to 999 persons, 14 employ 100 to 499 persons, 982 employ less than 100 persons; Business ownership: 894 women-owned, 796 Black-owned, n/a Hispanic-owned, n/a Asian-owned

Employment: 9.8% management, business, and financial, 2.6% computer, engineering, and science, 8.1% education, legal, community service, arts, and media, 5.4% healthcare practitioners, 19.9% service, 24.7% sales and office, 9.3% natural resources, construction, and maintenance, 20.2% production, transportation, and material moving

Income: Per capita: $17,937; Median household: $32,329; Average household: $44,406; Households with income of $100,000 or more: 8.7%; Poverty rate: 27.4%

Educational Attainment: High school diploma or higher: 75.8%; Bachelor's degree or higher: 11.8%; Graduate/professional degree or higher: 4.0%

Housing: Homeownership rate: 64.1%; Median home value: $86,100; Median year structure built: 1975; Homeowner vacancy rate: 1.9%; Median gross rent: $647 per month; Rental vacancy rate: 8.8%

Vital Statistics: Birth rate: 108.1 per 10,000 population; Death rate: 128.3 per 10,000 population; Age-adjusted cancer mortality rate: 208.1 deaths per 100,000 population

Health Insurance: 84.5% have insurance; 50.4% have private insurance; 47.6% have public insurance; 15.5% do not have insurance; 5.9% of children under 18 do not have insurance

Health Care: Physicians: 12.2 per 10,000 population; Hospital beds: 40.0 per 10,000 population; Hospital admissions: 1,282.8 per 10,000 population

Transportation: Commute: 95.1% car, 0.3% public transportation, 1.5% walk, 2.0% work from home; Median travel time to work: 21.9 minutes

Presidential Election: 65.7% Obama, 33.7% Romney (2012)

National and State Parks: Medoc Mountain State Park

Additional Information Contacts

Halifax Government . . . . (252) 583-1131

    http://www.halifaxnc.com

Halifax County Communities

ENFIELD (town). Covers a land area of 1.218 square miles and a water area of 0 square miles. Located at 36.18° N. Lat; 77.67° W. Long. Elevation is 105 feet.

History: Enfield is the oldest town in Halifax County. Enfield was known as Huckleberry Swamp and was the seat of Edgecombe County from 1745 until 1758.

Population: 2,532; Growth (since 2000): 7.9%; Density: 2,078.8 persons per square mile; Race: 11.8% White, 87.5% Black/African American, 0.2% Asian, 0.2% American Indian/Alaska Native, 0.0% Native Hawaiian/Other

Pacific Islander, 0.3% Two or more races, 0.6% Hispanic of any race; Average household size: 2.61; Median age: 40.0; Age under 18: 25.7%; Age 65 and over: 15.5%; Males per 100 females: 77.4; Marriage status: 47.2% never married, 31.6% now married, 6.8% separated, 11.4% widowed, 9.8% divorced; Foreign born: 0.0%; Speak English only: 99.8%; With disability: 27.3%; Veterans: 3.6%; Ancestry: 7.9% American, 4.4% English, 2.5% German, 0.8% Scottish, 0.3% African

Employment: 6.4% management, business, and financial, 0.5% computer, engineering, and science, 14.7% education, legal, community service, arts, and media, 3.4% healthcare practitioners, 17.3% service, 15.7% sales and office, 9.9% natural resources, construction, and maintenance, 32.2% production, transportation, and material moving

Income: Per capita: $11,706; Median household: $22,157; Average household: $29,960; Households with income of $100,000 or more: 2.3%; Poverty rate: 45.4%

Educational Attainment: High school diploma or higher: 63.0%; Bachelor's degree or higher: 8.9%; Graduate/professional degree or higher: 1.7%

School District(s)
Halifax County Schools (PK-12)
    2012-13 Enrollment: 3,638 . . . . (252) 583-5111
Housing: Homeownership rate: 46.6%; Median home value: $73,600; Median year structure built: 1960; Homeowner vacancy rate: 2.8%; Median gross rent: $661 per month; Rental vacancy rate: 7.5%
Health Insurance: 83.8% have insurance; 33.5% have private insurance; 61.1% have public insurance; 16.2% do not have insurance; 0.0% of children under 18 do not have insurance
Safety: Violent crime rate: 72.4 per 10,000 population; Property crime rate: 482.9 per 10,000 population
Transportation: Commute: 91.6% car, 0.0% public transportation, 5.7% walk, 1.3% work from home; Median travel time to work: 23.3 minutes

HALIFAX (town). County seat. Covers a land area of 0.457 square miles and a water area of 0 square miles. Located at 36.33° N. Lat; 77.59° W. Long. Elevation is 125 feet.
History: Halifax was the scene of North Carolina's first constitutional convention. As early as 1723 settlers were established in the region, and when the county was set up in 1757, it was named for the second Earl of Halifax. In 1758 Halifax succeeded the older Enfield as the county seat. In 1760 Halifax was made a borough.
Population: 234; Growth (since 2000): -32.0%; Density: 512.3 persons per square mile; Race: 67.1% White, 32.1% Black/African American, 0.0% Asian, 0.0% American Indian/Alaska Native, 0.0% Native Hawaiian/Other Pacific Islander, 0.0% Two or more races, 0.4% Hispanic of any race; Average household size: 2.16; Median age: 43.0; Age under 18: 22.2%; Age 65 and over: 17.9%; Males per 100 females: 69.6
School District(s)
Halifax County Schools (PK-12)
    2012-13 Enrollment: 3,638 . . . . (252) 583-5111
Weldon City Schools (PK-12)
    2012-13 Enrollment: 1,079 . . . . (252) 536-4821
Housing: Homeownership rate: 72.8%; Homeowner vacancy rate: 3.8%; Rental vacancy rate: 6.7%

HOBGOOD (town). Covers a land area of 1.033 square miles and a water area of 0 square miles. Located at 36.03° N. Lat; 77.39° W. Long. Elevation is 92 feet.
Population: 348; Growth (since 2000): -13.9%; Density: 337.0 persons per square mile; Race: 47.7% White, 50.0% Black/African American, 0.0% Asian, 0.0% American Indian/Alaska Native, 0.0% Native Hawaiian/Other Pacific Islander, 0.6% Two or more races, 4.0% Hispanic of any race; Average household size: 2.25; Median age: 50.5; Age under 18: 16.1%; Age 65 and over: 22.7%; Males per 100 females: 96.6
Housing: Homeownership rate: 63.9%; Homeowner vacancy rate: 3.8%; Rental vacancy rate: 6.7%

HOLLISTER (CDP). Covers a land area of 3.980 square miles and a water area of 0.007 square miles. Located at 36.26° N. Lat; 77.94° W. Long. Elevation is 246 feet.
Population: 674; Growth (since 2000): n/a; Density: 169.4 persons per square mile; Race: 3.3% White, 23.7% Black/African American, 0.0% Asian, 70.5% American Indian/Alaska Native, 0.0% Native Hawaiian/Other Pacific Islander, 2.1% Two or more races, 3.3% Hispanic of any race; Average household size: 2.38; Median age: 40.7; Age under 18: 22.6%; Age 65 and over: 15.1%; Males per 100 females: 100.0

School District(s)
Halifax County Schools (PK-12)
    2012-13 Enrollment: 3,638 . . . . (252) 583-5111
Haliwa-Saponi Tribal School (KG-12)
    2012-13 Enrollment: 170. . . . . (252) 257-5853
Housing: Homeownership rate: 66.4%; Homeowner vacancy rate: 0.5%; Rental vacancy rate: 4.9%

LITTLETON (town). Covers a land area of 0.961 square miles and a water area of <.001 square miles. Located at 36.43° N. Lat; 77.91° W. Long. Elevation is 387 feet.
History: Littleton was founded before the Revolutionary War and named for William P. Little, whose parents built Mosby Hall in 1774.
Population: 674; Growth (since 2000): -2.6%; Density: 701.3 persons per square mile; Race: 48.4% White, 47.0% Black/African American, 0.4% Asian, 1.2% American Indian/Alaska Native, 0.4% Native Hawaiian/Other Pacific Islander, 1.0% Two or more races, 1.2% Hispanic of any race; Average household size: 2.06; Median age: 48.3; Age under 18: 20.0%; Age 65 and over: 23.4%; Males per 100 females: 70.6
School District(s)
Halifax County Schools (PK-12)
    2012-13 Enrollment: 3,638 . . . . (252) 583-5111
Housing: Homeownership rate: 57.8%; Homeowner vacancy rate: 2.6%; Rental vacancy rate: 6.1%
Newspapers: Lake Gaston Gazette (weekly circulation 2700); Littleton Observer (weekly circulation 3000)

ROANOKE RAPIDS (city). Covers a land area of 9.946 square miles and a water area of 0.036 square miles. Located at 36.45° N. Lat; 77.65° W. Long. Elevation is 157 feet.
History: Roanoke Rapids was founded in 1893 by John Armstrong Chaloner, a New York industrialist seeking a site for cotton mills. It was first called Great Falls.
Population: 15,754; Growth (since 2000): -7.1%; Density: 1,584.0 persons per square mile; Race: 63.6% White, 31.2% Black/African American, 1.7% Asian, 0.6% American Indian/Alaska Native, 0.0% Native Hawaiian/Other Pacific Islander, 1.3% Two or more races, 3.2% Hispanic of any race; Average household size: 2.42; Median age: 37.9; Age under 18: 26.3%; Age 65 and over: 14.8%; Males per 100 females: 84.8; Marriage status: 29.4% never married, 49.5% now married, 4.2% separated, 10.0% widowed, 11.2% divorced; Foreign born: 1.5%; Speak English only: 96.4%; With disability: 19.0%; Veterans: 8.4%; Ancestry: 15.7% English, 10.3% American, 7.9% Irish, 5.0% German, 2.3% Italian
Employment: 12.8% management, business, and financial, 3.4% computer, engineering, and science, 10.3% education, legal, community service, arts, and media, 7.9% healthcare practitioners, 15.7% service, 26.9% sales and office, 9.4% natural resources, construction, and maintenance, 13.6% production, transportation, and material moving
Income: Per capita: $19,178; Median household: $34,975; Average household: $47,452; Households with income of $100,000 or more: 11.8%; Poverty rate: 25.6%
Educational Attainment: High school diploma or higher: 79.8%; Bachelor's degree or higher: 18.7%; Graduate/professional degree or higher: 7.0%
School District(s)
Halifax County Schools (PK-12)
    2012-13 Enrollment: 3,638 . . . . (252) 583-5111
Roanoke Rapids City Schools (PK-12)
    2012-13 Enrollment: 3,165 . . . . (252) 519-7100
Housing: Homeownership rate: 53.3%; Median home value: $112,100; Median year structure built: 1966; Homeowner vacancy rate: 2.4%; Median gross rent: $660 per month; Rental vacancy rate: 8.2%
Health Insurance: 86.4% have insurance; 56.5% have private insurance; 42.1% have public insurance; 13.6% do not have insurance; 6.2% of children under 18 do not have insurance
Hospitals: Halifax Regional Medical Center (206 beds)
Safety: Violent crime rate: 58.7 per 10,000 population; Property crime rate: 630.5 per 10,000 population
Newspapers: The Daily Herald (daily circulation 11200)
Transportation: Commute: 93.9% car, 0.2% public transportation, 2.0% walk, 3.1% work from home; Median travel time to work: 16.9 minutes
Airports: Halifax-Northampton Regional (general aviation)
Additional Information Contacts
City of Roanoke Rapids. . . . . (252) 533-2876
    http://www.roanokerapidsnc.com

SCOTLAND NECK (town). Covers a land area of 1.188 square miles and a water area of 0 square miles. Located at 36.13° N. Lat; 77.42° W. Long. Elevation is 98 feet.
History: Scotland Neck, on a fertile neck of land in a bend of the Roanoke River, was settled in 1722 by a colony of Scottish Highlanders from Virginia.
Population: 2,059; Growth (since 2000): -12.8%; Density: 1,733.3 persons per square mile; Race: 30.8% White, 68.3% Black/African American, 0.1% Asian, 0.0% American Indian/Alaska Native, 0.0% Native Hawaiian/Other Pacific Islander, 0.2% Two or more races, 1.6% Hispanic of any race; Average household size: 2.22; Median age: 47.3; Age under 18: 20.0%; Age 65 and over: 23.3%; Males per 100 females: 85.7
School District(s)
Halifax County Schools (PK-12)
    2012-13 Enrollment: 3,638 . . . . (252) 583-5111
Housing: Homeownership rate: 51.0%; Homeowner vacancy rate: 4.0%; Rental vacancy rate: 12.3%
Hospitals: Our Community Hospital
Safety: Violent crime rate: 59.4 per 10,000 population; Property crime rate: 351.3 per 10,000 population
Newspapers: Commonwealth Progress (weekly circulation 3000)

SOUTH ROSEMARY (CDP). Covers a land area of 6.119 square miles and a water area of 0.006 square miles. Located at 36.45° N. Lat; 77.70° W. Long. Elevation is 223 feet.
Population: 2,836; Growth (since 2000): -0.2%; Density: 463.4 persons per square mile; Race: 41.8% White, 55.3% Black/African American, 0.4% Asian, 0.8% American Indian/Alaska Native, 0.0% Native Hawaiian/Other Pacific Islander, 1.1% Two or more races, 1.4% Hispanic of any race; Average household size: 2.37; Median age: 41.7; Age under 18: 22.5%; Age 65 and over: 15.6%; Males per 100 females: 92.1; Marriage status: 32.2% never married, 41.0% now married, 7.8% separated, 14.4% widowed, 12.5% divorced; Foreign born: 0.0%; Speak English only: 98.8%; With disability: 26.8%; Veterans: 7.4%; Ancestry: 9.4% German, 7.9% American, 7.5% Irish, 7.1% English, 1.1% Welsh
Employment: 6.2% management, business, and financial, 2.8% computer, engineering, and science, 7.5% education, legal, community service, arts, and media, 3.7% healthcare practitioners, 33.8% service, 18.1% sales and office, 11.2% natural resources, construction, and maintenance, 16.7% production, transportation, and material moving
Income: Per capita: $14,963; Median household: $27,813; Average household: $33,987; Households with income of $100,000 or more: 1.8%; Poverty rate: 31.5%
Educational Attainment: High school diploma or higher: 76.7%; Bachelor's degree or higher: 4.4%; Graduate/professional degree or higher: 2.1%
Housing: Homeownership rate: 65.7%; Median home value: $64,400; Median year structure built: 1971; Homeowner vacancy rate: 1.5%; Median gross rent: $640 per month; Rental vacancy rate: 4.9%
Health Insurance: 84.0% have insurance; 42.5% have private insurance; 55.5% have public insurance; 16.0% do not have insurance; 8.1% of children under 18 do not have insurance
Transportation: Commute: 97.6% car, 1.2% public transportation, 1.3% walk, 0.0% work from home; Median travel time to work: 19.0 minutes

SOUTH WELDON (CDP). Covers a land area of 0.435 square miles and a water area of 0 square miles. Located at 36.41° N. Lat; 77.60° W. Long. Elevation is 92 feet.
Population: 705; Growth (since 2000): -50.1%; Density: 1,619.1 persons per square mile; Race: 14.9% White, 78.7% Black/African American, 0.1% Asian, 1.1% American Indian/Alaska Native, 0.0% Native Hawaiian/Other Pacific Islander, 1.8% Two or more races, 5.1% Hispanic of any race; Average household size: 2.93; Median age: 25.3; Age under 18: 36.3%; Age 65 and over: 8.5%; Males per 100 females: 85.5
Housing: Homeownership rate: 29.1%; Homeowner vacancy rate: 6.6%; Rental vacancy rate: 8.6%

WELDON (town). Covers a land area of 2.844 square miles and a water area of 0 square miles. Located at 36.42° N. Lat; 77.61° W. Long. Elevation is 72 feet.
History: Weldon began to assume importance after railroad links from Virginia had been built in 1834. When these terminals were connected with Wilmington in 1840, the 161.5-mile stretch was described as the longest railroad in the world.

Population: 1,655; Growth (since 2000): 20.5%; Density: 582.0 persons per square mile; Race: 25.4% White, 70.7% Black/African American, 0.4% Asian, 0.3% American Indian/Alaska Native, 0.0% Native Hawaiian/Other Pacific Islander, 2.8% Two or more races, 1.1% Hispanic of any race; Average household size: 2.47; Median age: 46.2; Age under 18: 21.8%; Age 65 and over: 22.0%; Males per 100 females: 78.1
School District(s)
Johnston County Schools (PK-12)
    2012-13 Enrollment: 33,711 . . . . (919) 934-6031
Weldon City Schools (PK-12)
    2012-13 Enrollment: 1,079 . . . . (252) 536-4821
Two-year College(s)
Halifax Community College (Public)
    Fall 2013 Enrollment: 1,353 . . . . (252) 536-4221
    2013-14 Tuition: In-state $2,345; Out-of-state $8,549
Housing: Homeownership rate: 60.0%; Homeowner vacancy rate: 2.5%; Rental vacancy rate: 9.7%
Safety: Violent crime rate: 24.7 per 10,000 population; Property crime rate: 431.8 per 10,000 population

Harnett County

Located in central North Carolina; bounded on the southeast by the Little River; drained by the Cape Fear River. Covers a land area of 594.987 square miles, a water area of 6.317 square miles, and is located in the Eastern Time Zone at 35.37° N. Lat., 78.87° W. Long. The county was founded in 1855. County seat is Lillington.

Harnett County is part of the Dunn, NC Micropolitan Statistical Area. The entire metro area includes: Harnett County, NC

Weather Station: Dunn 4 NW   Elevation: 200 feet

	Jan	Feb	Mar	Apr	May	Jun	Jul	Aug	Sep	Oct	Nov	Dec
High	52	56	64	73	80	87	90	88	82	73	64	55
Low	30	33	39	47	56	65	69	68	61	49	39	32
Precip	3.5	3.3	4.0	3.3	3.5	4.6	6.3	5.4	4.2	3.2	3.1	3.3
Snow	1.1	0.5	0.4	0.0	0.0	0.0	0.0	0.0	0.0	0.0	0.0	0.3

High and Low temperatures in degrees Fahrenheit; Precipitation and Snow in inches

Population: 114,678; Growth (since 2000): 26.0%; Density: 192.7 persons per square mile; Race: 68.3% White, 20.9% Black/African American, 0.9% Asian, 1.2% American Indian/Alaska Native, 0.1% Native Hawaiian/Other Pacific Islander, 3.1% two or more races, 10.8% Hispanic of any race; Average household size: 2.68; Median age: 33.5; Age under 18: 27.8%; Age 65 and over: 10.4%; Males per 100 females: 96.1; Marriage status: 28.9% never married, 54.4% now married, 3.3% separated, 5.9% widowed, 10.8% divorced; Foreign born: 5.6%; Speak English only: 89.0%; With disability: 13.5%; Veterans: 13.7%; Ancestry: 11.4% American, 9.3% German, 8.8% Irish, 8.6% English, 3.1% Scotch-Irish
Religion: Six largest groups: 16.2% Baptist, 6.3% Methodist/Pietist, 3.9% Non-denominational Protestant, 3.4% Pentecostal, 2.6% Presbyterian-Reformed, 0.8% Catholicism
Economy: Unemployment rate: 6.3%; Leading industries: 16.8% retail trade; 15.2% construction; 10.9% health care and social assistance; Farms: 797 totaling 119,775 acres; Company size: 1 employs 1,000 or more persons, 2 employ 500 to 999 persons, 11 employs 100 to 499 persons, 1,579 employ less than 100 persons; Business ownership: 1,959 women-owned, 649 Black-owned, 128 Hispanic-owned, n/a Asian-owned
Employment: 11.7% management, business, and financial, 3.9% computer, engineering, and science, 10.3% education, legal, community service, arts, and media, 4.4% healthcare practitioners, 18.4% service, 24.6% sales and office, 12.4% natural resources, construction, and maintenance, 14.2% production, transportation, and material moving
Income: Per capita: $20,310; Median household: $44,625; Average household: $56,266; Households with income of $100,000 or more: 14.2%; Poverty rate: 17.2%
Educational Attainment: High school diploma or higher: 84.4%; Bachelor's degree or higher: 18.5%; Graduate/professional degree or higher: 5.7%
Housing: Homeownership rate: 66.9%; Median home value: $132,600; Median year structure built: 1990; Homeowner vacancy rate: 2.9%; Median gross rent: $756 per month; Rental vacancy rate: 11.5%
Vital Statistics: Birth rate: 142.0 per 10,000 population; Death rate: 74.4 per 10,000 population; Age-adjusted cancer mortality rate: 177.5 deaths per 100,000 population

Health Insurance: 84.4% have insurance; 64.7% have private insurance; 30.4% have public insurance; 15.6% do not have insurance; 6.5% of children under 18 do not have insurance
Health Care: Physicians: 6.3 per 10,000 population; Hospital beds: 7.5 per 10,000 population; Hospital admissions: 542.4 per 10,000 population
Transportation: Commute: 94.3% car, 0.2% public transportation, 1.2% walk, 3.1% work from home; Median travel time to work: 28.3 minutes
Presidential Election: 39.7% Obama, 59.1% Romney (2012)
National and State Parks: Raven Rock State Park
Additional Information Contacts
Harnett Government . . . . (910) 893-7555
    http://www.harnett.org

Harnett County Communities

ANGIER (town). Covers a land area of 2.908 square miles and a water area of 0.035 square miles. Located at 35.51° N. Lat; 78.74° W. Long. Elevation is 292 feet.
Population: 4,350; Growth (since 2000): 27.2%; Density: 1,496.0 persons per square mile; Race: 61.7% White, 21.7% Black/African American, 0.6% Asian, 0.8% American Indian/Alaska Native, 0.0% Native Hawaiian/Other Pacific Islander, 2.1% Two or more races, 20.3% Hispanic of any race; Average household size: 2.58; Median age: 34.3; Age under 18: 27.7%; Age 65 and over: 12.8%; Males per 100 females: 89.8; Marriage status: 27.0% never married, 50.5% now married, 5.9% separated, 7.4% widowed, 15.1% divorced; Foreign born: 9.8%; Speak English only: 88.3%; With disability: 14.8%; Veterans: 8.9%; Ancestry: 13.4% American, 11.8% English, 8.8% Irish, 7.5% German, 2.7% Italian
Employment: 10.0% management, business, and financial, 5.8% computer, engineering, and science, 10.4% education, legal, community service, arts, and media, 6.9% healthcare practitioners, 9.3% service, 32.9% sales and office, 14.3% natural resources, construction, and maintenance, 10.3% production, transportation, and material moving
Income: Per capita: $20,974; Median household: $35,265; Average household: $48,092; Households with income of $100,000 or more: 11.3%; Poverty rate: 14.4%
Educational Attainment: High school diploma or higher: 85.3%; Bachelor's degree or higher: 13.8%; Graduate/professional degree or higher: 3.7%
School District(s)
Harnett County Schools (PK-12)
    2012-13 Enrollment: 20,569 . . . . (910) 893-8151
Johnston County Schools (PK-12)
    2012-13 Enrollment: 33,711 . . . . (919) 934-6031
Housing: Homeownership rate: 55.7%; Median home value: $134,200; Median year structure built: 1982; Homeowner vacancy rate: 6.1%; Median gross rent: $741 per month; Rental vacancy rate: 7.0%
Health Insurance: 84.8% have insurance; 63.9% have private insurance; 35.5% have public insurance; 15.2% do not have insurance; 7.7% of children under 18 do not have insurance
Newspapers: Angier Independent (weekly circulation 2500)
Transportation: Commute: 91.3% car, 0.0% public transportation, 0.3% walk, 6.3% work from home; Median travel time to work: 33.3 minutes
Additional Information Contacts
Town of Angier . . . . (910) 893-9111
    http://www.angier.org

BUIES CREEK (CDP). Covers a land area of 2.291 square miles and a water area of 0.006 square miles. Located at 35.41° N. Lat; 78.73° W. Long. Elevation is 207 feet.
History: Buies Creek was established on a creek by the same name. The creek was named for the Buie family, early Scottish settlers who came to the area in 1746 after the Battle of Culloden.
Population: 2,942; Growth (since 2000): 32.8%; Density: 1,284.3 persons per square mile; Race: 78.3% White, 14.8% Black/African American, 2.2% Asian, 0.7% American Indian/Alaska Native, 0.0% Native Hawaiian/Other Pacific Islander, 2.2% Two or more races, 3.6% Hispanic of any race; Average household size: 2.07; Median age: 20.9; Age under 18: 5.5%; Age 65 and over: 4.5%; Males per 100 females: 81.4; Marriage status: 87.1% never married, 9.1% now married, 0.0% separated, 1.8% widowed, 2.0% divorced; Foreign born: 7.6%; Speak English only: 88.4%; With disability: 5.2%; Veterans: 4.2%; Ancestry: 12.3% American, 12.1% English, 11.9% German, 9.6% Scottish, 6.3% Irish
Employment: 6.3% management, business, and financial, 6.3% computer, engineering, and science, 20.1% education, legal, community service, arts,

and media, 8.5% healthcare practitioners, 30.0% service, 23.9% sales and office, 0.0% natural resources, construction, and maintenance, 5.0% production, transportation, and material moving
Income: Per capita: $6,828; Median household: $23,955; Average household: $30,194; Households with income of $100,000 or more: n/a; Poverty rate: 34.0%
Educational Attainment: High school diploma or higher: 97.9%; Bachelor's degree or higher: 55.6%; Graduate/professional degree or higher: 24.1%
School District(s)
Harnett County Schools (PK-12)
    2012-13 Enrollment: 20,569 . . . . (910) 893-8151
Four-year College(s)
Campbell University (Private, Not-for-profit, Baptist)
    Fall 2013 Enrollment: 6,122 . . . . (910) 893-1200
    2013-14 Tuition: In-state $26,240; Out-of-state $26,240
Housing: Homeownership rate: 35.0%; Median home value: $94,200; Median year structure built: 1993; Homeowner vacancy rate: 3.8%; Median gross rent: $814 per month; Rental vacancy rate: 21.0%
Health Insurance: 94.5% have insurance; 89.1% have private insurance; 9.8% have public insurance; 5.5% do not have insurance; 0.0% of children under 18 do not have insurance
Transportation: Commute: 77.2% car, 0.0% public transportation, 13.1% walk, 7.4% work from home; Median travel time to work: 23.5 minutes

BUNNLEVEL (CDP). Covers a land area of 7.559 square miles and a water area of 0.033 square miles. Located at 35.31° N. Lat; 78.76° W. Long. Elevation is 141 feet.
Population: 552; Growth (since 2000): n/a; Density: 73.0 persons per square mile; Race: 50.4% White, 40.9% Black/African American, 0.0% Asian, 2.2% American Indian/Alaska Native, 0.2% Native Hawaiian/Other Pacific Islander, 4.3% Two or more races, 3.3% Hispanic of any race; Average household size: 2.52; Median age: 42.0; Age under 18: 23.0%; Age 65 and over: 14.7%; Males per 100 females: 95.1
School District(s)
Harnett County Schools (PK-12)
    2012-13 Enrollment: 20,569 . . . . (910) 893-8151
Housing: Homeownership rate: 67.2%; Homeowner vacancy rate: 2.6%; Rental vacancy rate: 6.5%

COATS (town). Covers a land area of 1.434 square miles and a water area of 0 square miles. Located at 35.41° N. Lat; 78.67° W. Long. Elevation is 308 feet.
Population: 2,112; Growth (since 2000): 14.5%; Density: 1,473.2 persons per square mile; Race: 72.3% White, 12.2% Black/African American, 0.2% Asian, 0.9% American Indian/Alaska Native, 0.0% Native Hawaiian/Other Pacific Islander, 2.9% Two or more races, 16.4% Hispanic of any race; Average household size: 2.52; Median age: 34.2; Age under 18: 24.6%; Age 65 and over: 12.7%; Males per 100 females: 99.8
School District(s)
Harnett County Schools (PK-12)
    2012-13 Enrollment: 20,569 . . . . (910) 893-8151
Housing: Homeownership rate: 55.5%; Homeowner vacancy rate: 3.7%; Rental vacancy rate: 8.8%
Safety: Violent crime rate: 17.3 per 10,000 population; Property crime rate: 414.2 per 10,000 population

DUNN (city). Covers a land area of 6.473 square miles and a water area of 0 square miles. Located at 35.31° N. Lat; 78.61° W. Long. Elevation is 207 feet.
History: Dunn was founded by descendants of early English and Scottish settlers.
Population: 9,263; Growth (since 2000): 0.7%; Density: 1,431.0 persons per square mile; Race: 50.2% White, 42.5% Black/African American, 0.8% Asian, 1.0% American Indian/Alaska Native, 0.1% Native Hawaiian/Other Pacific Islander, 2.2% Two or more races, 5.3% Hispanic of any race; Average household size: 2.29; Median age: 41.0; Age under 18: 23.7%; Age 65 and over: 18.8%; Males per 100 females: 82.8; Marriage status: 34.7% never married, 41.5% now married, 3.8% separated, 11.2% widowed, 12.6% divorced; Foreign born: 5.1%; Speak English only: 91.9%; With disability: 19.9%; Veterans: 9.3%; Ancestry: 9.9% American, 7.7% English, 5.4% African, 5.2% Irish, 2.4% Scottish
Employment: 10.7% management, business, and financial, 1.0% computer, engineering, and science, 11.7% education, legal, community service, arts, and media, 4.7% healthcare practitioners, 24.2% service,

25.9% sales and office, 9.1% natural resources, construction, and maintenance, 12.7% production, transportation, and material moving
Income: Per capita: $18,830; Median household: $29,399; Average household: $44,635; Households with income of $100,000 or more: 8.7%; Poverty rate: 27.6%
Educational Attainment: High school diploma or higher: 78.5%; Bachelor's degree or higher: 17.2%; Graduate/professional degree or higher: 5.5%
School District(s)
Harnett County Schools (PK-12)
    2012-13 Enrollment: 20,569 . . . . (910) 893-8151
Sampson County Schools (PK-12)
    2012-13 Enrollment: 8,835 . . . . (910) 592-1401
Four-year College(s)
Heritage Bible College (Private, Not-for-profit, Other Protestant)
    Fall 2013 Enrollment: 67 . . . . (800) 297-6351
    2013-14 Tuition: In-state $7,730; Out-of-state $7,730
Housing: Homeownership rate: 51.6%; Median home value: $107,500; Median year structure built: 1973; Homeowner vacancy rate: 2.6%; Median gross rent: $619 per month; Rental vacancy rate: 8.2%
Health Insurance: 78.6% have insurance; 47.1% have private insurance; 44.2% have public insurance; 21.4% do not have insurance; 10.6% of children under 18 do not have insurance
Hospitals: Betsy Johnson Regional Hospital (101 beds)
Newspapers: Daily Record (daily circulation 8600)
Transportation: Commute: 92.2% car, 0.8% public transportation, 1.9% walk, 3.7% work from home; Median travel time to work: 20.4 minutes
Additional Information Contacts
City of Dunn. . . . . (910) 230-3500
    http://www.dunn-nc.org

ERWIN (town). Covers a land area of 4.190 square miles and a water area of 0.039 square miles. Located at 35.32° N. Lat; 78.67° W. Long. Elevation is 190 feet.
History: Averasboro Battleground State Historical Site to South.
Population: 4,405; Growth (since 2000): -2.9%; Density: 1,051.2 persons per square mile; Race: 74.0% White, 17.3% Black/African American, 0.3% Asian, 0.9% American Indian/Alaska Native, 0.0% Native Hawaiian/Other Pacific Islander, 2.6% Two or more races, 7.4% Hispanic of any race; Average household size: 2.43; Median age: 40.1; Age under 18: 23.5%; Age 65 and over: 17.5%; Males per 100 females: 89.9; Marriage status: 25.0% never married, 49.8% now married, 3.8% separated, 12.6% widowed, 12.7% divorced; Foreign born: 3.0%; Speak English only: 92.6%; With disability: 19.6%; Veterans: 10.6%; Ancestry: 14.4% American, 9.6% English, 7.9% Irish, 5.1% German, 4.1% Scotch-Irish
Employment: 11.0% management, business, and financial, 2.8% computer, engineering, and science, 12.5% education, legal, community service, arts, and media, 6.0% healthcare practitioners, 19.0% service, 26.3% sales and office, 11.0% natural resources, construction, and maintenance, 11.3% production, transportation, and material moving
Income: Per capita: $19,969; Median household: $35,542; Average household: $49,945; Households with income of $100,000 or more: 9.8%; Poverty rate: 17.6%
Educational Attainment: High school diploma or higher: 81.4%; Bachelor's degree or higher: 16.1%; Graduate/professional degree or higher: 4.6%
School District(s)
Harnett County Schools (PK-12)
    2012-13 Enrollment: 20,569 . . . . (910) 893-8151
Housing: Homeownership rate: 67.2%; Median home value: $87,600; Median year structure built: 1960; Homeowner vacancy rate: 2.9%; Median gross rent: $699 per month; Rental vacancy rate: 9.3%
Health Insurance: 84.5% have insurance; 58.5% have private insurance; 39.8% have public insurance; 15.5% do not have insurance; 9.0% of children under 18 do not have insurance
Safety: Violent crime rate: 19.5 per 10,000 population; Property crime rate: 313.9 per 10,000 population
Transportation: Commute: 96.1% car, 0.3% public transportation, 0.5% walk, 2.5% work from home; Median travel time to work: 25.4 minutes
Airports: Harnett Regional Jetport (general aviation)
Additional Information Contacts
Town of Erwin . . . . (910) 897-5543
    http://www.erwinny.org

LILLINGTON (town). County seat. Covers a land area of 4.560 square miles and a water area of 0.031 square miles. Located at 35.40° N. Lat; 78.81° W. Long. Elevation is 194 feet.
History: Lillington was named for Revolutionary Colonel Alexander Lillington.
Population: 3,194; Growth (since 2000): 9.6%; Density: 700.5 persons per square mile; Race: 53.5% White, 39.8% Black/African American, 0.9% Asian, 0.9% American Indian/Alaska Native, 0.3% Native Hawaiian/Other Pacific Islander, 1.6% Two or more races, 8.8% Hispanic of any race; Average household size: 2.12; Median age: 39.6; Age under 18: 15.1%; Age 65 and over: 13.6%; Males per 100 females: 145.5; Marriage status: 36.9% never married, 31.3% now married, 4.5% separated, 9.9% widowed, 21.8% divorced; Foreign born: 6.2%; Speak English only: 90.3%; With disability: 19.3%; Veterans: 11.8%; Ancestry: 15.2% American, 7.8% Irish, 6.3% English, 5.8% German, 2.9% Scottish
Employment: 13.4% management, business, and financial, 1.5% computer, engineering, and science, 15.6% education, legal, community service, arts, and media, 3.6% healthcare practitioners, 21.1% service, 19.3% sales and office, 7.0% natural resources, construction, and maintenance, 18.6% production, transportation, and material moving
Income: Per capita: $13,065; Median household: $29,554; Average household: $40,852; Households with income of $100,000 or more: 6.4%; Poverty rate: 25.3%
Educational Attainment: High school diploma or higher: 76.0%; Bachelor's degree or higher: 12.9%; Graduate/professional degree or higher: 4.1%
School District(s)
Harnett County Schools (PK-12)
    2012-13 Enrollment: 20,569 . . . . (910) 893-8151
Housing: Homeownership rate: 42.6%; Median home value: $112,200; Median year structure built: 1972; Homeowner vacancy rate: 7.2%; Median gross rent: $611 per month; Rental vacancy rate: 8.0%
Health Insurance: 84.6% have insurance; 53.2% have private insurance; 46.0% have public insurance; 15.4% do not have insurance; 6.7% of children under 18 do not have insurance
Newspapers: Harnett County News (weekly circulation 3000)
Transportation: Commute: 95.5% car, 0.2% public transportation, 2.6% walk, 0.4% work from home; Median travel time to work: 23.8 minutes
Additional Information Contacts
Town of Lillington . . . . (910) 893-2654
    http://lillingtonnc.com

MAMERS (CDP). Covers a land area of 6.042 square miles and a water area of 0.009 square miles. Located at 35.41° N. Lat; 78.94° W. Long. Elevation is 325 feet.
Population: 826; Growth (since 2000): n/a; Density: 136.7 persons per square mile; Race: 91.5% White, 2.9% Black/African American, 0.5% Asian, 1.9% American Indian/Alaska Native, 0.2% Native Hawaiian/Other Pacific Islander, 1.0% Two or more races, 7.3% Hispanic of any race; Average household size: 2.56; Median age: 38.0; Age under 18: 27.7%; Age 65 and over: 13.4%; Males per 100 females: 105.5
School District(s)
Harnett County Schools (PK-12)
    2012-13 Enrollment: 20,569 . . . . (910) 893-8151
Housing: Homeownership rate: 78.8%; Homeowner vacancy rate: 1.6%; Rental vacancy rate: 13.4%

Haywood County

Located in western North Carolina, partly in the Blue Ridge; bounded on the northwest by Tennessee and the Great Smoky Mountains; drained by Pigeon River. Covers a land area of 553.692 square miles, a water area of 0.933 square miles, and is located in the Eastern Time Zone at 35.56° N. Lat., 82.97° W. Long. The county was founded in 1808. County seat is Waynesville.

Haywood County is part of the Asheville, NC Metropolitan Statistical Area. The entire metro area includes: Buncombe County, NC; Haywood County, NC; Henderson County, NC; Madison County, NC

Weather Station: Waterville 2   Elevation: 1,439 feet

	Jan	Feb	Mar	Apr	May	Jun	Jul	Aug	Sep	Oct	Nov	Dec
High	48	52	61	70	77	83	86	85	79	69	60	50
Low	29	31	38	45	53	61	65	64	58	47	38	31
Precip	3.8	3.9	4.4	4.1	4.9	5.8	5.8	4.3	3.7	2.3	3.2	3.6
Snow	0.9	1.0	1.2	0.9	0.0	0.0	0.0	0.0	0.0	0.0	0.1	0.6

High and Low temperatures in degrees Fahrenheit; Precipitation and Snow in inches

Weather Station: Waynesville 1 E   Elevation: 2,658 feet

	Jan	Feb	Mar	Apr	May	Jun	Jul	Aug	Sep	Oct	Nov	Dec
High	49	52	60	68	75	81	84	83	77	69	60	52
Low	24	26	32	39	47	55	59	58	52	40	32	26
Precip	4.3	4.4	4.6	3.8	4.4	4.0	3.7	4.2	4.0	2.7	3.7	4.0
Snow	4.4	3.1	2.4	1.2	0.2	0.0	0.0	0.0	0.0	tr	0.4	1.8

High and Low temperatures in degrees Fahrenheit; Precipitation and Snow in inches

Population: 59,036; Growth (since 2000): 9.3%; Density: 106.6 persons per square mile; Race: 95.5% White, 1.1% Black/African American, 0.4% Asian, 0.5% American Indian/Alaska Native, 0.0% Native Hawaiian/Other Pacific Islander, 1.1% two or more races, 3.4% Hispanic of any race; Average household size: 2.28; Median age: 45.6; Age under 18: 19.5%; Age 65 and over: 21.0%; Males per 100 females: 93.3; Marriage status: 19.8% never married, 60.3% now married, 2.6% separated, 7.6% widowed, 12.3% divorced; Foreign born: 2.6%; Speak English only: 96.5%; With disability: 15.5%; Veterans: 12.9%; Ancestry: 30.9% American, 13.2% German, 11.2% Irish, 10.5% English, 6.1% Scotch-Irish

Religion: Six largest groups: 45.9% Baptist, 15.1% Methodist/Pietist, 3.6% Non-denominational Protestant, 2.1% Catholicism, 1.2% Pentecostal, 0.9% Holiness

Economy: Unemployment rate: 4.4%; Leading industries: 18.6% retail trade; 13.1% construction; 12.7% other services (except public administration); Farms: 597 totaling 48,975 acres; Company size: 0 employ 1,000 or more persons, 1 employs 500 to 999 persons, 14 employ 100 to 499 persons, 1,359 employ less than 100 persons; Business ownership: 1,454 women-owned, n/a Black-owned, n/a Hispanic-owned, 49 Asian-owned

Employment: 10.6% management, business, and financial, 3.0% computer, engineering, and science, 10.6% education, legal, community service, arts, and media, 7.3% healthcare practitioners, 19.5% service, 23.7% sales and office, 12.3% natural resources, construction, and maintenance, 13.1% production, transportation, and material moving

Income: Per capita: $24,536; Median household: $41,557; Average household: $54,746; Households with income of $100,000 or more: 13.0%; Poverty rate: 16.6%

Educational Attainment: High school diploma or higher: 86.1%; Bachelor's degree or higher: 23.1%; Graduate/professional degree or higher: 8.0%

Housing: Homeownership rate: 74.1%; Median home value: $156,900; Median year structure built: 1979; Homeowner vacancy rate: 3.7%; Median gross rent: $713 per month; Rental vacancy rate: 15.3%

Vital Statistics: Birth rate: 95.3 per 10,000 population; Death rate: 115.9 per 10,000 population; Age-adjusted cancer mortality rate: 179.6 deaths per 100,000 population

Health Insurance: 83.2% have insurance; 60.8% have private insurance; 40.0% have public insurance; 16.8% do not have insurance; 9.4% of children under 18 do not have insurance

Health Care: Physicians: 18.7 per 10,000 population; Hospital beds: 24.9 per 10,000 population; Hospital admissions: 1,076.0 per 10,000 population

Air Quality Index: 88.5% good, 11.5% moderate, 0.0% unhealthy for sensitive individuals, 0.0% unhealthy (percent of days)

Transportation: Commute: 92.9% car, 0.4% public transportation, 1.6% walk, 4.0% work from home; Median travel time to work: 22.9 minutes

Presidential Election: 42.3% Obama, 55.9% Romney (2012)

Additional Information Contacts
Haywood Government . . . . (828) 452-7305
    http://www.haywoodnc.net

Haywood County Communities

CANTON (town). Covers a land area of 3.775 square miles and a water area of 0 square miles. Located at 35.54° N. Lat; 82.85° W. Long. Elevation is 2,615 feet.

History: Canton has been known for its pulp and paper mills.

Population: 4,227; Growth (since 2000): 4.9%; Density: 1,119.7 persons per square mile; Race: 93.6% White, 1.8% Black/African American, 0.1% Asian, 0.7% American Indian/Alaska Native, 0.0% Native Hawaiian/Other Pacific Islander, 1.7% Two or more races, 5.0% Hispanic of any race; Average household size: 2.32; Median age: 40.9; Age under 18: 21.8%; Age 65 and over: 19.8%; Males per 100 females: 91.8; Marriage status: 27.2% never married, 52.4% now married, 1.1% separated, 10.1% widowed, 10.3% divorced; Foreign born: 4.4%; Speak English only: 95.1%; With disability: 9.9%; Veterans: 11.6%; Ancestry: 25.8% American, 15.6% German, 14.1% Irish, 12.0% English, 6.3% Scottish

Employment: 12.3% management, business, and financial, 2.1% computer, engineering, and science, 10.1% education, legal, community service, arts, and media, 5.0% healthcare practitioners, 25.5% service, 22.1% sales and office, 5.6% natural resources, construction, and maintenance, 17.4% production, transportation, and material moving

Income: Per capita: $20,571; Median household: $36,150; Average household: $46,165; Households with income of $100,000 or more: 11.3%; Poverty rate: 15.9%

Educational Attainment: High school diploma or higher: 83.1%; Bachelor's degree or higher: 17.7%; Graduate/professional degree or higher: 7.2%

School District(s)
Haywood County Schools (PK-12)
    2012-13 Enrollment: 7,633 . . . . (828) 456-2400

Housing: Homeownership rate: 68.2%; Median home value: $130,700; Median year structure built: 1954; Homeowner vacancy rate: 3.1%; Median gross rent: $694 per month; Rental vacancy rate: 11.0%

Health Insurance: 76.7% have insurance; 54.8% have private insurance; 38.5% have public insurance; 23.3% do not have insurance; 8.5% of children under 18 do not have insurance

Safety: Violent crime rate: 55.2 per 10,000 population; Property crime rate: 629.2 per 10,000 population

Transportation: Commute: 92.2% car, 2.4% public transportation, 1.6% walk, 3.2% work from home; Median travel time to work: 24.3 minutes

Additional Information Contacts
Town of Canton . . . . (828) 648-2363
    http://www.cantonnc.com

CLYDE (town). Covers a land area of 0.880 square miles and a water area of 0 square miles. Located at 35.53° N. Lat; 82.91° W. Long. Elevation is 2,533 feet.

Population: 1,223; Growth (since 2000): -7.6%; Density: 1,390.1 persons per square mile; Race: 94.8% White, 2.0% Black/African American, 0.4% Asian, 0.8% American Indian/Alaska Native, 0.0% Native Hawaiian/Other Pacific Islander, 0.7% Two or more races, 3.0% Hispanic of any race; Average household size: 2.24; Median age: 38.3; Age under 18: 24.8%; Age 65 and over: 16.4%; Males per 100 females: 91.4

School District(s)
Haywood County Schools (PK-12)
    2012-13 Enrollment: 7,633 . . . . (828) 456-2400

Two-year College(s)
Haywood Community College (Public)
    Fall 2013 Enrollment: 2,290 . . . . (828) 627-2821
    2013-14 Tuition: In-state $2,394; Out-of-state $8,538

Housing: Homeownership rate: 61.1%; Homeowner vacancy rate: 4.3%; Rental vacancy rate: 7.8%

Hospitals: Medwest Haywood (200 beds)

LAKE JUNALUSKA (CDP). Covers a land area of 5.335 square miles and a water area of 0.312 square miles. Located at 35.53° N. Lat; 82.97° W. Long. Elevation is 2,552 feet.

Population: 2,734; Growth (since 2000): 2.2%; Density: 512.5 persons per square mile; Race: 97.8% White, 0.3% Black/African American, 0.3% Asian, 0.5% American Indian/Alaska Native, 0.0% Native Hawaiian/Other Pacific Islander, 0.5% Two or more races, 1.7% Hispanic of any race; Average household size: 2.13; Median age: 52.9; Age under 18: 15.9%; Age 65 and over: 31.3%; Males per 100 females: 87.8; Marriage status: 19.7% never married, 67.2% now married, 2.1% separated, 6.0% widowed, 7.0% divorced; Foreign born: 1.3%; Speak English only: 96.2%; With disability: 8.7%; Veterans: 7.2%; Ancestry: 21.7% American, 17.8% German, 13.6% English, 8.7% Scotch-Irish, 7.7% Scottish

Employment: 13.8% management, business, and financial, 1.8% computer, engineering, and science, 20.9% education, legal, community service, arts, and media, 3.3% healthcare practitioners, 13.3% service, 29.9% sales and office, 9.4% natural resources, construction, and maintenance, 7.6% production, transportation, and material moving

Income: Per capita: $37,953; Median household: $73,804; Average household: $78,633; Households with income of $100,000 or more: 29.9%; Poverty rate: 4.8%

Educational Attainment: High school diploma or higher: 94.5%; Bachelor's degree or higher: 47.5%; Graduate/professional degree or higher: 20.2%

Housing: Homeownership rate: 78.9%; Median home value: $251,400; Median year structure built: 1977; Homeowner vacancy rate: 4.5%; Median gross rent: $744 per month; Rental vacancy rate: 31.2%

Health Insurance: 90.4% have insurance; 81.8% have private insurance; 35.6% have public insurance; 9.6% do not have insurance; 0.0% of children under 18 do not have insurance

Transportation: Commute: 94.8% car, 0.0% public transportation, 1.6% walk, 3.6% work from home; Median travel time to work: 14.3 minutes

---

MAGGIE VALLEY (town). Covers a land area of 3.176 square miles and a water area of 0 square miles. Located at 35.53° N. Lat; 83.06° W. Long. Elevation is 3,012 feet.

Population: 1,150; Growth (since 2000): 89.5%; Density: 362.0 persons per square mile; Race: 92.6% White, 0.6% Black/African American, 1.8% Asian, 0.8% American Indian/Alaska Native, 0.0% Native Hawaiian/Other Pacific Islander, 1.0% Two or more races, 5.3% Hispanic of any race; Average household size: 2.09; Median age: 53.3; Age under 18: 15.4%; Age 65 and over: 26.6%; Males per 100 females: 90.1

Housing: Homeownership rate: 74.4%; Homeowner vacancy rate: 12.4%; Rental vacancy rate: 40.9%

WAYNESVILLE (town). County seat. Covers a land area of 8.924 square miles and a water area of 0 square miles. Located at 35.49° N. Lat; 83.00° W. Long. Elevation is 2,746 feet.

History: Waynesville was named for "Mad Anthony" Wayne, the Revolutionary General. Colonel Robert Love gave the land for the public square, courthouse, jail, cemetery, and several churches. The region was settled by officers and soldiers who had received land grants in the years following the Revolution.

Population: 9,869; Growth (since 2000): 6.9%; Density: 1,105.9 persons per square mile; Race: 92.4% White, 2.4% Black/African American, 0.4% Asian, 0.6% American Indian/Alaska Native, 0.1% Native Hawaiian/Other Pacific Islander, 1.3% Two or more races, 5.7% Hispanic of any race; Average household size: 2.11; Median age: 46.7; Age under 18: 17.8%; Age 65 and over: 24.6%; Males per 100 females: 87.4; Marriage status: 22.9% never married, 50.3% now married, 3.3% separated, 10.8% widowed, 16.0% divorced; Foreign born: 4.8%; Speak English only: 94.9%; With disability: 19.2%; Veterans: 13.6%; Ancestry: 30.0% American, 14.3% German, 11.1% Irish, 8.5% English, 5.8% Scotch-Irish

Employment: 10.1% management, business, and financial, 1.8% computer, engineering, and science, 11.7% education, legal, community service, arts, and media, 10.9% healthcare practitioners, 23.2% service, 25.7% sales and office, 8.6% natural resources, construction, and maintenance, 8.1% production, transportation, and material moving

Income: Per capita: $24,725; Median household: $36,485; Average household: $50,692; Households with income of $100,000 or more: 9.2%; Poverty rate: 20.3%

Educational Attainment: High school diploma or higher: 80.9%; Bachelor's degree or higher: 23.4%; Graduate/professional degree or higher: 8.2%

School District(s)

Haywood County Schools (PK-12)

    2012-13 Enrollment: 7,633 . . . . (828) 456-2400

Housing: Homeownership rate: 57.7%; Median home value: $148,300; Median year structure built: 1970; Homeowner vacancy rate: 4.6%; Median gross rent: $756 per month; Rental vacancy rate: 13.1%

Health Insurance: 79.4% have insurance; 51.7% have private insurance; 43.1% have public insurance; 20.6% do not have insurance; 14.7% of children under 18 do not have insurance

Newspapers: Haywood County News (weekly circulation 19000); Smoky Mountain News (weekly circulation 16000); The Mountaineer (weekly circulation 13000)

Transportation: Commute: 93.5% car, 0.3% public transportation, 0.7% walk, 4.2% work from home; Median travel time to work: 18.0 minutes

Additional Information Contacts

Town of Waynesville . . . . (828) 456-9033
  http://www.townofwaynesville.org

WEST CANTON (CDP). Covers a land area of 1.371 square miles and a water area of 0 square miles. Located at 35.54° N. Lat; 82.87° W. Long. Elevation is 2,726 feet.

Population: 1,247; Growth (since 2000): 7.9%; Density: 909.2 persons per square mile; Race: 97.8% White, 0.5% Black/African American, 0.1% Asian, 0.4% American Indian/Alaska Native, 0.0% Native Hawaiian/Other Pacific Islander, 0.4% Two or more races, 1.4% Hispanic of any race; Average household size: 2.44; Median age: 42.6; Age under 18: 20.9%; Age 65 and over: 18.6%; Males per 100 females: 93.0

Housing: Homeownership rate: 76.5%; Homeowner vacancy rate: 0.5%; Rental vacancy rate: 4.7%

Henderson County

Located in western North Carolina, partly in the Blue Ridge; bounded on the south by South Carolina; drained by the French Broad and Broad Rivers; partly in Pisgah National Forest. Covers a land area of 373.068 square miles, a water area of 2.163 square miles, and is located in the Eastern Time Zone at 35.34° N. Lat., 82.48° W. Long. The county was founded in 1838. County seat is Hendersonville.

Henderson County is part of the Asheville, NC Metropolitan Statistical Area. The entire metro area includes: Buncombe County, NC; Haywood County, NC; Henderson County, NC; Madison County, NC

Weather Station: Fletcher 3 W										Elevation: 2,069 feet		
	Jan	Feb	Mar	Apr	May	Jun	Jul	Aug	Sep	Oct	Nov	Dec
High	47	51	58	67	75	81	84	84	77	68	59	50
Low	24	27	33	40	49	57	61	60	53	41	33	26
Precip	4.0	4.0	4.5	3.7	4.0	5.2	4.7	4.8	4.3	3.2	3.9	3.9
Snow	3.2	2.0	1.4	0.5	tr	0.0	0.0	0.0	0.0	tr	tr	1.0

High and Low temperatures in degrees Fahrenheit; Precipitation and Snow in inches

Weather Station: Hendersonville 1 NE										Elevation: 2,160 feet		
	Jan	Feb	Mar	Apr	May	Jun	Jul	Aug	Sep	Oct	Nov	Dec
High	49	52	60	69	75	82	85	84	77	68	60	51
Low	28	30	36	44	52	60	65	64	57	46	37	30
Precip	4.5	4.4	5.2	4.1	4.0	5.1	5.0	5.3	4.7	3.4	4.5	4.5
Snow	3.0	1.7	1.6	0.4	0.0	0.0	0.0	0.0	0.0	0.0	0.1	0.7

High and Low temperatures in degrees Fahrenheit; Precipitation and Snow in inches

Population: 106,740; Growth (since 2000): 19.7%; Density: 286.1 persons per square mile; Race: 88.9% White, 3.0% Black/African American, 1.0% Asian, 0.4% American Indian/Alaska Native, 0.2% Native Hawaiian/Other Pacific Islander, 1.9% two or more races, 9.8% Hispanic of any race; Average household size: 2.32; Median age: 45.4; Age under 18: 20.6%; Age 65 and over: 22.4%; Males per 100 females: 93.4; Marriage status: 20.4% never married, 60.6% now married, 2.3% separated, 8.3% widowed, 10.7% divorced; Foreign born: 7.7%; Speak English only: 89.4%; With disability: 16.0%; Veterans: 13.3%; Ancestry: 16.1% English, 14.0% German, 13.2% Irish, 13.1% American, 4.8% Scotch-Irish

Religion: Six largest groups: 24.7% Baptist, 5.5% Methodist/Pietist, 4.1% Catholicism, 3.5% Presbyterian-Reformed, 2.6% Non-denominational Protestant, 2.0% Adventist

Economy: Unemployment rate: 4.1%; Leading industries: 16.0% retail trade; 12.7% construction; 11.5% health care and social assistance; Farms: 468 totaling 35,752 acres; Company size: 0 employ 1,000 or more persons, 4 employ 500 to 999 persons, 42 employ 100 to 499 persons, 2,501 employs less than 100 persons; Business ownership: 2,677 women-owned, 176 Black-owned, 386 Hispanic-owned, n/a Asian-owned

Employment: 13.8% management, business, and financial, 3.3% computer, engineering, and science, 9.8% education, legal, community service, arts, and media, 7.7% healthcare practitioners, 17.3% service, 23.5% sales and office, 11.1% natural resources, construction, and maintenance, 13.5% production, transportation, and material moving

Income: Per capita: $25,670; Median household: $44,815; Average household: $59,839; Households with income of $100,000 or more: 15.0%; Poverty rate: 14.1%

Educational Attainment: High school diploma or higher: 87.5%; Bachelor's degree or higher: 27.7%; Graduate/professional degree or higher: 10.2%

Housing: Homeownership rate: 75.1%; Median home value: $185,500; Median year structure built: 1986; Homeowner vacancy rate: 3.6%; Median gross rent: $732 per month; Rental vacancy rate: 12.3%

Vital Statistics: Birth rate: 96.5 per 10,000 population; Death rate: 117.2 per 10,000 population; Age-adjusted cancer mortality rate: 163.5 deaths per 100,000 population

Health Insurance: 82.8% have insurance; 63.2% have private insurance; 38.5% have public insurance; 17.2% do not have insurance; 9.9% of children under 18 do not have insurance

Health Care: Physicians: 21.8 per 10,000 population; Hospital beds: 24.1 per 10,000 population; Hospital admissions: 1,067.7 per 10,000 population

Transportation: Commute: 92.1% car, 0.1% public transportation, 1.8% walk, 5.0% work from home; Median travel time to work: 21.6 minutes

Presidential Election: 35.6% Obama, 63.0% Romney (2012)

National and State Parks: Carl Sandburg Home National Historic Site

Additional Information Contacts

Henderson Government . . . . (828) 697-4808
http://www.hendersoncountync.org

Henderson County Communities

BALFOUR (CDP). Covers a land area of 1.785 square miles and a water area of 0.011 square miles. Located at 35.35° N. Lat; 82.49° W. Long. Elevation is 2,119 feet.

Population: 1,187; Growth (since 2000): -1.1%; Density: 664.8 persons per square mile; Race: 87.0% White, 3.2% Black/African American, 1.3% Asian, 0.3% American Indian/Alaska Native, 0.5% Native Hawaiian/Other Pacific Islander, 2.0% Two or more races, 12.0% Hispanic of any race; Average household size: 2.44; Median age: 39.7; Age under 18: 22.5%; Age 65 and over: 15.6%; Males per 100 females: 91.1

Housing: Homeownership rate: 77.4%; Homeowner vacancy rate: 3.1%; Rental vacancy rate: 24.7%

BARKER HEIGHTS (CDP). Covers a land area of 1.014 square miles and a water area of 0.001 square miles. Located at 35.31° N. Lat; 82.44° W. Long. Elevation is 2,123 feet.

Population: 1,254; Growth (since 2000): 1.4%; Density: 1,237.2 persons per square mile; Race: 70.7% White, 4.8% Black/African American, 0.5% Asian, 1.2% American Indian/Alaska Native, 0.3% Native Hawaiian/Other Pacific Islander, 2.2% Two or more races, 36.4% Hispanic of any race; Average household size: 2.69; Median age: 31.9; Age under 18: 28.9%; Age 65 and over: 12.8%; Males per 100 females: 100.0

Housing: Homeownership rate: 64.4%; Homeowner vacancy rate: 3.2%; Rental vacancy rate: 11.2%

DANA (CDP). Covers a land area of 8.905 square miles and a water area of 0.023 square miles. Located at 35.32° N. Lat; 82.36° W. Long. Elevation is 2,251 feet.

Population: 3,329; Growth (since 2000): n/a; Density: 373.8 persons per square mile; Race: 85.5% White, 1.1% Black/African American, 0.7% Asian, 0.4% American Indian/Alaska Native, 0.1% Native Hawaiian/Other Pacific Islander, 2.6% Two or more races, 19.8% Hispanic of any race; Average household size: 2.63; Median age: 36.6; Age under 18: 26.6%; Age 65 and over: 13.0%; Males per 100 females: 100.8; Marriage status: 19.7% never married, 70.3% now married, 5.9% separated, 7.1% widowed, 2.8% divorced; Foreign born: 5.4%; Speak English only: 85.2%; With disability: 11.9%; Veterans: 13.1%; Ancestry: 19.0% English, 15.4% German, 8.9% Irish, 7.4% American, 5.8% Scottish

Employment: 10.3% management, business, and financial, 5.5% computer, engineering, and science, 12.0% education, legal, community service, arts, and media, 9.0% healthcare practitioners, 17.8% service, 20.3% sales and office, 12.0% natural resources, construction, and maintenance, 13.1% production, transportation, and material moving

Income: Per capita: $18,963; Median household: $41,600; Average household: $47,587; Households with income of $100,000 or more: 7.1%; Poverty rate: 26.2%

Educational Attainment: High school diploma or higher: 87.9%; Bachelor's degree or higher: 17.2%; Graduate/professional degree or higher: 9.7%

School District(s)

Henderson County Schools (PK-12)
2012-13 Enrollment: 13,564 . . . . (828) 697-4733

Housing: Homeownership rate: 75.8%; Median home value: $149,400; Median year structure built: 1990; Homeowner vacancy rate: 3.0%; Median gross rent: $726 per month; Rental vacancy rate: 11.5%

Health Insurance: 65.2% have insurance; 51.5% have private insurance; 23.3% have public insurance; 34.8% do not have insurance; 31.5% of children under 18 do not have insurance

Transportation: Commute: 97.0% car, 0.0% public transportation, 3.0% walk, 0.0% work from home; Median travel time to work: 19.4 minutes

EAST FLAT ROCK (CDP). Covers a land area of 4.291 square miles and a water area of 0.012 square miles. Located at 35.28° N. Lat; 82.42° W. Long. Elevation is 2,208 feet.

Population: 4,995; Growth (since 2000): 20.3%; Density: 1,164.1 persons per square mile; Race: 80.6% White, 4.1% Black/African American, 0.7% Asian, 0.4% American Indian/Alaska Native, 0.4% Native Hawaiian/Other Pacific Islander, 3.2% Two or more races, 22.4% Hispanic of any race; Average household size: 2.49; Median age: 37.6; Age under 18: 24.2%; Age 65 and over: 15.4%; Males per 100 females: 97.3; Marriage status: 27.9% never married, 46.5% now married, 3.3% separated, 8.6% widowed, 17.1% divorced; Foreign born: 16.9%; Speak English only: 72.4%; With disability: 26.6%; Veterans: 5.9%; Ancestry: 16.8% American, 8.8% English, 8.7% Irish, 8.2% German, 2.9% French

Employment: 6.8% management, business, and financial, 0.9% computer, engineering, and science, 8.8% education, legal, community service, arts, and media, 6.9% healthcare practitioners, 22.4% service, 16.9% sales and office, 22.7% natural resources, construction, and maintenance, 14.6% production, transportation, and material moving

Income: Per capita: $16,621; Median household: $25,906; Average household: $37,470; Households with income of $100,000 or more: 2.9%; Poverty rate: 32.9%

Educational Attainment: High school diploma or higher: 80.0%; Bachelor's degree or higher: 15.0%; Graduate/professional degree or higher: 4.1%

School District(s)

Henderson County Schools (PK-12)
2012-13 Enrollment: 13,564 . . . . (828) 697-4733

Housing: Homeownership rate: 67.4%; Median home value: $112,300; Median year structure built: 1981; Homeowner vacancy rate: 2.5%; Median gross rent: $717 per month; Rental vacancy rate: 14.5%

Health Insurance: 68.9% have insurance; 41.8% have private insurance; 37.8% have public insurance; 31.1% do not have insurance; 2.3% of children under 18 do not have insurance

Transportation: Commute: 84.3% car, 0.0% public transportation, 6.1% walk, 8.3% work from home; Median travel time to work: 24.6 minutes

EDNEYVILLE (CDP). Covers a land area of 10.739 square miles and a water area of 0.009 square miles. Located at 35.40° N. Lat; 82.33° W. Long. Elevation is 2,244 feet.

Population: 2,367; Growth (since 2000): n/a; Density: 220.4 persons per square mile; Race: 83.4% White, 3.5% Black/African American, 0.3% Asian, 0.8% American Indian/Alaska Native, 0.0% Native Hawaiian/Other Pacific Islander, 2.2% Two or more races, 18.7% Hispanic of any race; Average household size: 2.69; Median age: 35.3; Age under 18: 27.5%; Age 65 and over: 12.8%; Males per 100 females: 100.1

Housing: Homeownership rate: 68.6%; Homeowner vacancy rate: 2.7%; Rental vacancy rate: 12.3%

ETOWAH (CDP). Covers a land area of 17.534 square miles and a water area of 0.212 square miles. Located at 35.30° N. Lat; 82.59° W. Long. Elevation is 2,106 feet.

History: Etowah is a census-designated place (CDP) in Henderson County, North Carolina.

Population: 6,944; Growth (since 2000): 151.0%; Density: 396.0 persons per square mile; Race: 93.4% White, 1.1% Black/African American, 0.9% Asian, 0.2% American Indian/Alaska Native, 0.0% Native Hawaiian/Other Pacific Islander, 1.8% Two or more races, 5.4% Hispanic of any race; Average household size: 2.30; Median age: 50.7; Age under 18: 18.6%; Age 65 and over: 28.4%; Males per 100 females: 96.8; Marriage status: 17.5% never married, 66.7% now married, 2.4% separated, 6.7% widowed, 9.1% divorced; Foreign born: 4.1%; Speak English only: 97.3%; With disability: 13.7%; Veterans: 16.9%; Ancestry: 21.7% English, 15.4% German, 12.6% American, 11.4% Irish, 4.3% Scottish

Employment: 8.5% management, business, and financial, 4.1% computer, engineering, and science, 9.3% education, legal, community service, arts, and media, 4.3% healthcare practitioners, 21.0% service, 21.5% sales and office, 17.2% natural resources, construction, and maintenance, 14.0% production, transportation, and material moving

Income: Per capita: $25,974; Median household: $45,660; Average household: $58,754; Households with income of $100,000 or more: 12.5%; Poverty rate: 6.5%

Educational Attainment: High school diploma or higher: 95.5%; Bachelor's degree or higher: 28.2%; Graduate/professional degree or higher: 13.1%

School District(s)
Henderson County Schools (PK-12)
    2012-13 Enrollment: 13,564 . . . . (828) 697-4733
Housing: Homeownership rate: 87.4%; Median home value: $180,200; Median year structure built: 1989; Homeowner vacancy rate: 4.1%; Median gross rent: $1,079 per month; Rental vacancy rate: 10.6%
Health Insurance: 85.0% have insurance; 72.8% have private insurance; 35.4% have public insurance; 15.0% do not have insurance; 11.4% of children under 18 do not have insurance
Transportation: Commute: 94.5% car, 0.0% public transportation, 1.6% walk, 1.3% work from home; Median travel time to work: 21.5 minutes

FLAT ROCK (village).
Covers a land area of 8.111 square miles and a water area of 0.129 square miles. Located at 35.26° N. Lat; 82.46° W. Long. Elevation is 2,205 feet.
History: Flat Rock is said to have been the first summer resort in western North Carolina, "discovered" by residents of the South Carolina and Georgia lowlands seeking a moderate summer climate. About 1812 a land company purchased an extensive tract and launched the first real estate boom in this part of the state.
Population: 3,114; Growth (since 2000): 21.4%; Density: 383.9 persons per square mile; Race: 98.2% White, 0.4% Black/African American, 0.4% Asian, 0.2% American Indian/Alaska Native, 0.0% Native Hawaiian/Other Pacific Islander, 0.8% Two or more races, 1.2% Hispanic of any race; Average household size: 2.06; Median age: 64.0; Age under 18: 10.1%; Age 65 and over: 47.7%; Males per 100 females: 92.5; Marriage status: 11.8% never married, 75.8% now married, 0.0% separated, 6.6% widowed, 5.7% divorced; Foreign born: 4.0%; Speak English only: 96.3%; With disability: 13.0%; Veterans: 19.2%; Ancestry: 24.8% English, 20.8% Irish, 15.6% German, 6.3% Italian, 5.9% American
Employment: 13.3% management, business, and financial, 4.4% computer, engineering, and science, 17.2% education, legal, community service, arts, and media, 11.2% healthcare practitioners, 19.4% service, 22.9% sales and office, 3.6% natural resources, construction, and maintenance, 8.1% production, transportation, and material moving
Income: Per capita: $43,782; Median household: $72,276; Average household: $97,663; Households with income of $100,000 or more: 36.9%; Poverty rate: 6.4%
Educational Attainment: High school diploma or higher: 98.4%; Bachelor's degree or higher: 59.4%; Graduate/professional degree or higher: 20.9%

School District(s)
Henderson County Schools (PK-12)
    2012-13 Enrollment: 13,564 . . . . (828) 697-4733
Two-year College(s)
Blue Ridge Community College (Public)
    Fall 2013 Enrollment: 2,324 . . . . (828) 694-1700
    2013-14 Tuition: In-state $2,373; Out-of-state $8,517
Housing: Homeownership rate: 91.2%; Median home value: $389,600; Median year structure built: 1990; Homeowner vacancy rate: 5.2%; Median gross rent: $983 per month; Rental vacancy rate: 36.1%
Health Insurance: 93.3% have insurance; 81.7% have private insurance; 46.7% have public insurance; 6.7% do not have insurance; 10.1% of children under 18 do not have insurance
Transportation: Commute: 87.5% car, 0.8% public transportation, 1.6% walk, 8.0% work from home; Median travel time to work: 20.8 minutes

FLETCHER (town).
Covers a land area of 6.411 square miles and a water area of 0.077 square miles. Located at 35.43° N. Lat; 82.51° W. Long. Elevation is 2,116 feet.
Population: 7,187; Growth (since 2000): 71.7%; Density: 1,121.0 persons per square mile; Race: 88.3% White, 4.1% Black/African American, 3.1% Asian, 0.5% American Indian/Alaska Native, 0.1% Native Hawaiian/Other Pacific Islander, 2.0% Two or more races, 4.8% Hispanic of any race; Average household size: 2.36; Median age: 39.2; Age under 18: 23.7%; Age 65 and over: 13.9%; Males per 100 females: 88.5; Marriage status: 24.8% never married, 53.4% now married, 3.2% separated, 8.2% widowed, 13.5% divorced; Foreign born: 4.3%; Speak English only: 95.3%; With disability: 9.9%; Veterans: 9.8%; Ancestry: 19.4% English, 18.1% American, 17.7% Irish, 10.8% German, 5.0% Scottish
Employment: 16.9% management, business, and financial, 3.8% computer, engineering, and science, 13.2% education, legal, community

service, arts, and media, 9.6% healthcare practitioners, 16.2% service, 24.1% sales and office, 3.8% natural resources, construction, and maintenance, 12.3% production, transportation, and material moving
Income: Per capita: $25,374; Median household: $44,684; Average household: $58,319; Households with income of $100,000 or more: 14.9%; Poverty rate: 7.6%
Educational Attainment: High school diploma or higher: 89.9%; Bachelor's degree or higher: 29.3%; Graduate/professional degree or higher: 8.9%

School District(s)
Buncombe County Schools (PK-12)
    2012-13 Enrollment: 25,824 . . . . (828) 232-4160
Henderson County Schools (PK-12)
    2012-13 Enrollment: 13,564 . . . . (828) 697-4733
Housing: Homeownership rate: 81.3%; Median home value: $178,100; Median year structure built: 1995; Homeowner vacancy rate: 3.3%; Median gross rent: $743 per month; Rental vacancy rate: 6.0%
Health Insurance: 88.1% have insurance; 69.7% have private insurance; 29.9% have public insurance; 11.9% do not have insurance; 5.5% of children under 18 do not have insurance
Safety: Violent crime rate: 9.6 per 10,000 population; Property crime rate: 200.8 per 10,000 population
Transportation: Commute: 92.6% car, 0.0% public transportation, 0.0% walk, 5.1% work from home; Median travel time to work: 19.2 minutes
Additional Information Contacts
Town of Fletcher . . . . (828) 687-3985
    http://www.fletchernc.org

FRUITLAND (CDP).
Covers a land area of 8.026 square miles and a water area of 0.029 square miles. Located at 35.40° N. Lat; 82.42° W. Long. Elevation is 2,215 feet.
Population: 2,031; Growth (since 2000): n/a; Density: 253.1 persons per square mile; Race: 93.2% White, 1.0% Black/African American, 0.2% Asian, 0.5% American Indian/Alaska Native, 0.6% Native Hawaiian/Other Pacific Islander, 2.2% Two or more races, 10.8% Hispanic of any race; Average household size: 2.30; Median age: 42.4; Age under 18: 21.1%; Age 65 and over: 18.0%; Males per 100 females: 101.3
Housing: Homeownership rate: 75.7%; Homeowner vacancy rate: 3.1%; Rental vacancy rate: 13.5%

GERTON (CDP).
Covers a land area of 3.794 square miles and a water area of 0 square miles. Located at 35.48° N. Lat; 82.35° W. Long. Elevation is 2,671 feet.
Population: 254; Growth (since 2000): n/a; Density: 66.9 persons per square mile; Race: 95.3% White, 2.0% Black/African American, 0.4% Asian, 1.2% American Indian/Alaska Native, 0.0% Native Hawaiian/Other Pacific Islander, 0.8% Two or more races, 0.4% Hispanic of any race; Average household size: 1.95; Median age: 47.8; Age under 18: 17.3%; Age 65 and over: 22.8%; Males per 100 females: 96.9
Housing: Homeownership rate: 73.8%; Homeowner vacancy rate: 8.6%; Rental vacancy rate: 20.9%

HENDERSONVILLE (city).
County seat. Covers a land area of 6.940 square miles and a water area of 0.028 square miles. Located at 35.32° N. Lat; 82.46° W. Long. Elevation is 2,159 feet.
History: Hendersonville is the seat of Henderson County, formed in 1838. Town and county were named for Leonard Henderson (1772-1833), Chief Justice of the North Carolina Supreme Court.
Population: 13,137; Growth (since 2000): 26.1%; Density: 1,892.9 persons per square mile; Race: 79.7% White, 9.2% Black/African American, 1.2% Asian, 0.4% American Indian/Alaska Native, 0.3% Native Hawaiian/Other Pacific Islander, 2.2% Two or more races, 13.5% Hispanic of any race; Average household size: 1.96; Median age: 48.7; Age under 18: 17.8%; Age 65 and over: 30.2%; Males per 100 females: 80.9; Marriage status: 23.7% never married, 48.1% now married, 2.6% separated, 14.0% widowed, 14.3% divorced; Foreign born: 9.6%; Speak English only: 87.3%; With disability: 20.8%; Veterans: 13.4%; Ancestry: 12.2% German, 12.2% Irish, 11.3% English, 10.7% American, 5.3% Scotch-Irish
Employment: 13.7% management, business, and financial, 2.3% computer, engineering, and science, 12.2% education, legal, community service, arts, and media, 6.1% healthcare practitioners, 18.2% service, 25.4% sales and office, 10.2% natural resources, construction, and maintenance, 12.0% production, transportation, and material moving

Income: Per capita: $21,210; Median household: $37,060; Average household: $47,415; Households with income of $100,000 or more: 7.3%; Poverty rate: 26.0%
Educational Attainment: High school diploma or higher: 83.3%; Bachelor's degree or higher: 29.8%; Graduate/professional degree or higher: 11.2%

School District(s)
Henderson County Schools (PK-12)
    2012-13 Enrollment: 13,564 . . . . (828) 697-4733
The Mountain Community Sch (KG-08)
    2012-13 Enrollment: 180. . . . . (828) 696-8480
Housing: Homeownership rate: 47.8%; Median home value: $164,300; Median year structure built: 1981; Homeowner vacancy rate: 6.4%; Median gross rent: $712 per month; Rental vacancy rate: 11.0%
Health Insurance: 81.7% have insurance; 52.5% have private insurance; 51.9% have public insurance; 18.3% do not have insurance; 12.1% of children under 18 do not have insurance
Hospitals: Margaret R Pardee Memorial Hospital (282 beds); Park Ridge Health (103 beds)
Safety: Violent crime rate: 39.7 per 10,000 population; Property crime rate: 637.1 per 10,000 population
Newspapers: Hendersonville Tribune (weekly circulation 8000); Times-News (daily circulation 18600)
Transportation: Commute: 89.7% car, 0.2% public transportation, 6.1% walk, 3.4% work from home; Median travel time to work: 16.6 minutes
Additional Information Contacts
City of Hendersonville . . . . (828) 697-3000
    http://www.cityofhendersonville.org

HOOPERS CREEK (CDP).
Covers a land area of 6.967 square miles and a water area of 0.012 square miles. Located at 35.44° N. Lat; 82.44° W. Long. Elevation is 2,159 feet.
Population: 1,056; Growth (since 2000): n/a; Density: 151.6 persons per square mile; Race: 96.4% White, 0.5% Black/African American, 0.3% Asian, 0.5% American Indian/Alaska Native, 0.0% Native Hawaiian/Other Pacific Islander, 2.0% Two or more races, 2.1% Hispanic of any race; Average household size: 2.42; Median age: 41.4; Age under 18: 22.2%; Age 65 and over: 13.9%; Males per 100 females: 95.6
Housing: Homeownership rate: 81.7%; Homeowner vacancy rate: 0.6%; Rental vacancy rate: 4.8%

HORSE SHOE (CDP).
Covers a land area of 7.460 square miles and a water area of 0.112 square miles. Located at 35.33° N. Lat; 82.56° W. Long. Elevation is 2,090 feet.
Population: 2,351; Growth (since 2000): n/a; Density: 315.1 persons per square mile; Race: 96.2% White, 0.8% Black/African American, 0.2% Asian, 0.7% American Indian/Alaska Native, 0.1% Native Hawaiian/Other Pacific Islander, 1.0% Two or more races, 2.7% Hispanic of any race; Average household size: 2.50; Median age: 48.1; Age under 18: 20.6%; Age 65 and over: 20.2%; Males per 100 females: 95.3
School District(s)
Henderson County Schools (PK-12)
    2012-13 Enrollment: 13,564 . . . . (828) 697-4733
Housing: Homeownership rate: 87.4%; Homeowner vacancy rate: 2.2%; Rental vacancy rate: 9.2%

LAUREL PARK (town).
Covers a land area of 2.795 square miles and a water area of 0.022 square miles. Located at 35.31° N. Lat; 82.51° W. Long. Elevation is 2,369 feet.
Population: 2,180; Growth (since 2000): 18.8%; Density: 780.1 persons per square mile; Race: 96.2% White, 1.6% Black/African American, 0.3% Asian, 0.1% American Indian/Alaska Native, 0.1% Native Hawaiian/Other Pacific Islander, 0.9% Two or more races, 2.6% Hispanic of any race; Average household size: 1.92; Median age: 61.6; Age under 18: 12.2%; Age 65 and over: 42.4%; Males per 100 females: 79.3
Housing: Homeownership rate: 78.9%; Homeowner vacancy rate: 7.0%; Rental vacancy rate: 19.9%
Safety: Violent crime rate: 4.5 per 10,000 population; Property crime rate: 107.0 per 10,000 population

MILLS RIVER (town).
Covers a land area of 22.386 square miles and a water area of 0.166 square miles. Located at 35.38° N. Lat; 82.59° W. Long. Elevation is 2,096 feet.
Population: 6,802; Growth (since 2000): n/a; Density: 303.8 persons per square mile; Race: 94.7% White, 1.7% Black/African American, 0.7%

Asian, 0.3% American Indian/Alaska Native, 0.0% Native Hawaiian/Other Pacific Islander, 1.4% Two or more races, 3.9% Hispanic of any race; Average household size: 2.42; Median age: 45.7; Age under 18: 20.8%; Age 65 and over: 17.4%; Males per 100 females: 95.2; Marriage status: 21.3% never married, 63.1% now married, 2.6% separated, 7.1% widowed, 8.6% divorced; Foreign born: 5.2%; Speak English only: 94.1%; With disability: 12.8%; Veterans: 13.7%; Ancestry: 20.2% English, 17.7% German, 17.0% Irish, 15.2% American, 7.6% Scotch-Irish
Employment: 20.2% management, business, and financial, 3.3% computer, engineering, and science, 6.8% education, legal, community service, arts, and media, 9.6% healthcare practitioners, 22.2% service, 20.2% sales and office, 3.9% natural resources, construction, and maintenance, 13.8% production, transportation, and material moving
Income: Per capita: $29,391; Median household: $58,566; Average household: $69,695; Households with income of $100,000 or more: 24.0%; Poverty rate: 7.0%
Educational Attainment: High school diploma or higher: 92.3%; Bachelor's degree or higher: 29.3%; Graduate/professional degree or higher: 13.4%
Housing: Homeownership rate: 83.5%; Median home value: $224,700; Median year structure built: 1989; Homeowner vacancy rate: 2.9%; Median gross rent: $667 per month; Rental vacancy rate: 8.4%
Health Insurance: 91.6% have insurance; 79.0% have private insurance; 32.0% have public insurance; 8.4% do not have insurance; 0.0% of children under 18 do not have insurance
Transportation: Commute: 89.4% car, 0.0% public transportation, 0.3% walk, 10.0% work from home; Median travel time to work: 20.3 minutes

MOUNTAIN HOME (CDP).
Covers a land area of 3.769 square miles and a water area of 0.022 square miles. Located at 35.37° N. Lat; 82.50° W. Long. Elevation is 2,129 feet.
Population: 3,622; Growth (since 2000): 67.0%; Density: 960.9 persons per square mile; Race: 89.6% White, 3.1% Black/African American, 1.4% Asian, 0.7% American Indian/Alaska Native, 0.7% Native Hawaiian/Other Pacific Islander, 1.8% Two or more races, 8.6% Hispanic of any race; Average household size: 2.44; Median age: 46.3; Age under 18: 20.6%; Age 65 and over: 23.8%; Males per 100 females: 94.2; Marriage status: 24.4% never married, 61.9% now married, 1.0% separated, 7.5% widowed, 6.2% divorced; Foreign born: 8.8%; Speak English only: 90.6%; With disability: 18.9%; Veterans: 13.9%; Ancestry: 22.5% German, 15.8% American, 12.6% English, 8.8% Scotch-Irish, 7.0% Irish
Employment: 11.5% management, business, and financial, 2.3% computer, engineering, and science, 7.2% education, legal, community service, arts, and media, 13.4% healthcare practitioners, 18.4% service, 24.5% sales and office, 3.8% natural resources, construction, and maintenance, 18.9% production, transportation, and material moving
Income: Per capita: $22,320; Median household: $33,269; Average household: $52,963; Households with income of $100,000 or more: 14.5%; Poverty rate: 17.0%
Educational Attainment: High school diploma or higher: 89.2%; Bachelor's degree or higher: 27.2%; Graduate/professional degree or higher: 9.1%
Housing: Homeownership rate: 72.3%; Median home value: $188,200; Median year structure built: 1983; Homeowner vacancy rate: 2.9%; Median gross rent: $871 per month; Rental vacancy rate: 11.9%
Health Insurance: 87.9% have insurance; 63.6% have private insurance; 43.3% have public insurance; 12.1% do not have insurance; 3.5% of children under 18 do not have insurance
Transportation: Commute: 94.4% car, 0.1% public transportation, 0.0% walk, 4.3% work from home; Median travel time to work: 21.8 minutes

VALLEY HILL (CDP).
Covers a land area of 2.319 square miles and a water area of 0.060 square miles. Located at 35.29° N. Lat; 82.49° W. Long. Elevation is 2,182 feet.
Population: 2,070; Growth (since 2000): -3.1%; Density: 892.6 persons per square mile; Race: 91.7% White, 2.2% Black/African American, 0.9% Asian, 0.1% American Indian/Alaska Native, 0.0% Native Hawaiian/Other Pacific Islander, 1.7% Two or more races, 7.1% Hispanic of any race; Average household size: 2.15; Median age: 48.6; Age under 18: 16.2%; Age 65 and over: 23.9%; Males per 100 females: 91.7
Housing: Homeownership rate: 76.5%; Homeowner vacancy rate: 3.7%; Rental vacancy rate: 16.0%

ZIRCONIA (unincorporated postal area)

ZCTA: 28790

Covers a land area of 41.878 square miles and a water area of 0.275 square miles. Located at 35.21° N. Lat; 82.51° W. Long. Elevation is 2,185 feet.

Population: 3,205; Growth (since 2000): 26.5%; Density: 76.5 persons per square mile; Race: 96.1% White, 0.2% Black/African American, 0.2% Asian, 0.4% American Indian/Alaska Native, 0.0% Native Hawaiian/Other Pacific Islander, 1.2% Two or more races, 3.2% Hispanic of any race; Average household size: 2.50; Median age: 42.0; Age under 18: 22.0%; Age 65 and over: 15.6%; Males per 100 females: 102.5; Marriage status: 18.2% never married, 66.1% now married, 2.3% separated, 4.6% widowed, 11.1% divorced; Foreign born: 1.5%; Speak English only: 98.9%; With disability: 12.4%; Veterans: 11.0%; Ancestry: 18.4% American, 18.3% English, 18.1% Irish, 9.3% German, 3.4% Scottish

Employment: 16.4% management, business, and financial, 1.9% computer, engineering, and science, 8.2% education, legal, community service, arts, and media, 8.1% healthcare practitioners, 13.4% service, 27.0% sales and office, 12.0% natural resources, construction, and maintenance, 13.0% production, transportation, and material moving

Income: Per capita: $23,077; Median household: $48,246; Average household: $59,913; Households with income of $100,000 or more: 13.7%; Poverty rate: 15.9%

Educational Attainment: High school diploma or higher: 85.6%; Bachelor's degree or higher: 22.3%; Graduate/professional degree or higher: 5.3%

Housing: Homeownership rate: 82.1%; Median home value: $179,300; Median year structure built: 1987; Homeowner vacancy rate: 3.3%; Median gross rent: $815 per month; Rental vacancy rate: 18.7%

Health Insurance: 83.9% have insurance; 65.0% have private insurance; 31.2% have public insurance; 16.1% do not have insurance; 17.1% of children under 18 do not have insurance

Transportation: Commute: 95.0% car, 0.0% public transportation, 0.0% walk, 5.0% work from home; Median travel time to work: 26.0 minutes

Hertford County

Located in northeastern North Carolina; bounded on the north by Virginia, and on the east by the Chowan River; coastal plains and tidewater area, drained by the Meherrin River. Covers a land area of 353.060 square miles, a water area of 7.294 square miles, and is located in the Eastern Time Zone at 36.36° N. Lat., 76.98° W. Long. The county was founded in 1759. County seat is Winton.

Population: 24,669; Growth (since 2000): 9.2%; Density: 69.9 persons per square mile; Race: 35.6% White, 60.5% Black/African American, 0.5% Asian, 1.1% American Indian/Alaska Native, 0.0% Native Hawaiian/Other Pacific Islander, 1.2% two or more races, 2.6% Hispanic of any race; Average household size: 2.40; Median age: 41.0; Age under 18: 21.1%; Age 65 and over: 15.8%; Males per 100 females: 95.7; Marriage status: 37.3% never married, 45.3% now married, 5.6% separated, 8.2% widowed, 9.3% divorced; Foreign born: 4.2%; Speak English only: 94.3%; With disability: 22.4%; Veterans: 8.8%; Ancestry: 7.5% American, 6.7% English, 3.3% Irish, 2.5% German, 1.7% Scottish

Religion: Six largest groups: 24.4% Baptist, 3.5% Pentecostal, 3.5% Methodist/Pietist, 2.1% Non-denominational Protestant, 0.6% Episcopalianism/Anglicanism, 0.6% Adventist

Economy: Unemployment rate: 6.7%; Leading industries: 20.8% retail trade; 16.2% health care and social assistance; 14.6% other services (except public administration); Farms: 162 totaling 83,042 acres; Company size: 0 employ 1,000 or more persons, 1 employs 500 to 999 persons, 7 employ 100 to 499 persons, 493 employ less than 100 persons; Business ownership: n/a women-owned, n/a Black-owned, n/a Hispanic-owned, n/a Asian-owned

Employment: 9.7% management, business, and financial, 0.9% computer, engineering, and science, 14.5% education, legal, community service, arts, and media, 6.1% healthcare practitioners, 22.1% service, 20.6% sales and office, 7.2% natural resources, construction, and maintenance, 18.9% production, transportation, and material moving

Income: Per capita: $17,863; Median household: $33,406; Average household: $47,528; Households with income of $100,000 or more: 9.4%; Poverty rate: 26.0%

Educational Attainment: High school diploma or higher: 77.5%; Bachelor's degree or higher: 15.4%; Graduate/professional degree or higher: 5.8%

Housing: Homeownership rate: 67.0%; Median home value: $84,200; Median year structure built: 1974; Homeowner vacancy rate: 2.1%; Median gross rent: $634 per month; Rental vacancy rate: 9.6%

Vital Statistics: Birth rate: 96.2 per 10,000 population; Death rate: 108.1 per 10,000 population; Age-adjusted cancer mortality rate: 211.5 deaths per 100,000 population

Health Insurance: 85.7% have insurance; 53.7% have private insurance; 44.8% have public insurance; 14.3% do not have insurance; 3.7% of children under 18 do not have insurance

Health Care: Physicians: 12.7 per 10,000 population; Hospital beds: 42.0 per 10,000 population; Hospital admissions: 2,135.1 per 10,000 population

Transportation: Commute: 95.9% car, 0.8% public transportation, 2.1% walk, 0.6% work from home; Median travel time to work: 23.8 minutes

Presidential Election: 71.8% Obama, 27.6% Romney (2012)

Additional Information Contacts

Hertford Government . . . . (252) 358-7805
  http://www.hertfordcountync.gov

Hertford County Communities

AHOSKIE (town). Covers a land area of 4.306 square miles and a water area of 0 square miles. Located at 36.28° N. Lat; 76.99° W. Long. Elevation is 46 feet.

Population: 5,039; Growth (since 2000): 11.4%; Density: 1,170.2 persons per square mile; Race: 28.5% White, 66.6% Black/African American, 1.3% Asian, 1.5% American Indian/Alaska Native, 0.0% Native Hawaiian/Other Pacific Islander, 1.1% Two or more races, 1.6% Hispanic of any race; Average household size: 2.35; Median age: 39.5; Age under 18: 25.7%; Age 65 and over: 19.8%; Males per 100 females: 77.1; Marriage status: 37.0% never married, 39.8% now married, 5.7% separated, 12.9% widowed, 10.3% divorced; Foreign born: 2.7%; Speak English only: 96.5%; With disability: 22.8%; Veterans: 8.3%; Ancestry: 6.6% American, 5.5% English, 3.5% Irish, 2.3% German, 2.0% African

Employment: 7.9% management, business, and financial, 1.3% computer, engineering, and science, 13.5% education, legal, community service, arts, and media, 7.5% healthcare practitioners, 21.5% service, 21.1% sales and office, 6.5% natural resources, construction, and maintenance, 20.7% production, transportation, and material moving

Income: Per capita: $17,493; Median household: $27,000; Average household: $41,302; Households with income of $100,000 or more: 8.1%; Poverty rate: 31.4%

Educational Attainment: High school diploma or higher: 71.7%; Bachelor's degree or higher: 17.0%; Graduate/professional degree or higher: 6.2%

School District(s)

Hertford County Schools (PK-12)
  2012-13 Enrollment: 3,172 . . . . (252) 358-1761

Two-year College(s)

Roanoke-Chowan Community College (Public)
  Fall 2013 Enrollment: 933 . . . . (252) 862-1200
  2013-14 Tuition: In-state $2,389; Out-of-state $8,533

Housing: Homeownership rate: 44.1%; Median home value: $90,900; Median year structure built: 1968; Homeowner vacancy rate: 4.4%; Median gross rent: $635 per month; Rental vacancy rate: 8.0%

Health Insurance: 83.3% have insurance; 47.4% have private insurance; 49.7% have public insurance; 16.7% do not have insurance; 11.8% of children under 18 do not have insurance

Hospitals: Vidant Roanoke Chowan Hospital (105 beds)

Newspapers: Roanoke News Herald (weekly circulation 6300)

Transportation: Commute: 94.2% car, 1.5% public transportation, 2.4% walk, 0.9% work from home; Median travel time to work: 19.7 minutes

Additional Information Contacts

Town of Ahoskie . . . . (252) 332-5146
  http://www.ahoskie-nc.org

COFIELD (village). Covers a land area of 3.141 square miles and a water area of 0 square miles. Located at 36.36° N. Lat; 76.91° W. Long. Elevation is 39 feet.

Population: 413; Growth (since 2000): 19.0%; Density: 131.5 persons per square mile; Race: 7.7% White, 82.1% Black/African American, 0.0% Asian, 5.1% American Indian/Alaska Native, 0.0% Native Hawaiian/Other Pacific Islander, 1.9% Two or more races, 3.4% Hispanic of any race; Average household size: 2.31; Median age: 43.1; Age under 18: 22.5%; Age 65 and over: 15.3%; Males per 100 females: 67.2

Housing: Homeownership rate: 63.6%; Homeowner vacancy rate: 3.4%; Rental vacancy rate: 9.7%

COMO (town). Covers a land area of 3.145 square miles and a water area of 0.010 square miles. Located at 36.50° N. Lat; 77.00° W. Long. Elevation is 75 feet.
Population: 91; Growth (since 2000): 16.7%; Density: 28.9 persons per square mile; Race: 87.9% White, 7.7% Black/African American, 0.0% Asian, 0.0% American Indian/Alaska Native, 0.0% Native Hawaiian/Other Pacific Islander, 4.4% Two or more races, 1.1% Hispanic of any race; Average household size: 2.22; Median age: 42.5; Age under 18: 18.7%; Age 65 and over: 14.3%; Males per 100 females: 111.6
Housing: Homeownership rate: 75.6%; Homeowner vacancy rate: 0.0%; Rental vacancy rate: 0.0%

HARRELLSVILLE (town). Covers a land area of 0.290 square miles and a water area of 0 square miles. Located at 36.30° N. Lat; 76.79° W. Long. Elevation is 62 feet.
Population: 106; Growth (since 2000): 3.9%; Density: 365.3 persons per square mile; Race: 76.4% White, 23.6% Black/African American, 0.0% Asian, 0.0% American Indian/Alaska Native, 0.0% Native Hawaiian/Other Pacific Islander, 0.0% Two or more races, 0.0% Hispanic of any race; Average household size: 2.30; Median age: 46.5; Age under 18: 22.6%; Age 65 and over: 20.8%; Males per 100 females: 86.0
Housing: Homeownership rate: 69.5%; Homeowner vacancy rate: 5.9%; Rental vacancy rate: 0.0%

MURFREESBORO (town). Covers a land area of 2.239 square miles and a water area of 0.052 square miles. Located at 36.44° N. Lat; 77.10° W. Long. Elevation is 82 feet.
History: In 1787, William Murfree gave land surrounding Murfrees Landing for the establishment of the town of Murfreesboro.
Population: 2,835; Growth (since 2000): 38.6%; Density: 1,266.0 persons per square mile; Race: 44.9% White, 50.9% Black/African American, 1.0% Asian, 0.2% American Indian/Alaska Native, 0.0% Native Hawaiian/Other Pacific Islander, 1.4% Two or more races, 2.9% Hispanic of any race; Average household size: 2.17; Median age: 27.5; Age under 18: 16.6%; Age 65 and over: 15.3%; Males per 100 females: 89.0; Marriage status: 51.8% never married, 35.6% now married, 2.7% separated, 7.0% widowed, 5.6% divorced; Foreign born: 1.8%; Speak English only: 97.5%; With disability: 20.8%; Veterans: 10.1%; Ancestry: 11.1% English, 7.3% German, 6.4% American, 4.5% Irish, 3.9% Scottish
Employment: 6.8% management, business, and financial, 1.8% computer, engineering, and science, 26.9% education, legal, community service, arts, and media, 3.0% healthcare practitioners, 19.7% service, 29.7% sales and office, 2.0% natural resources, construction, and maintenance, 10.1% production, transportation, and material moving
Income: Per capita: $21,194; Median household: $41,154; Average household: $55,784; Households with income of $100,000 or more: 14.0%; Poverty rate: 20.1%
Educational Attainment: High school diploma or higher: 89.6%; Bachelor's degree or higher: 31.9%; Graduate/professional degree or higher: 15.8%
School District(s)
Hertford County Schools (PK-12)
    2012-13 Enrollment: 3,172 . . . . (252) 358-1761
Four-year College(s)
Chowan University (Private, Not-for-profit, Southern Baptist)
    Fall 2013 Enrollment: 1,367 . . . . (252) 398-6500
    2013-14 Tuition: In-state $22,510; Out-of-state $22,510
Housing: Homeownership rate: 54.9%; Median home value: $116,100; Median year structure built: 1967; Homeowner vacancy rate: 2.7%; Median gross rent: $527 per month; Rental vacancy rate: 8.8%
Health Insurance: 89.1% have insurance; 61.5% have private insurance; 36.3% have public insurance; 10.9% do not have insurance; 1.4% of children under 18 do not have insurance
Safety: Violent crime rate: 24.9 per 10,000 population; Property crime rate: 260.1 per 10,000 population
Transportation: Commute: 90.9% car, 0.0% public transportation, 7.6% walk, 0.4% work from home; Median travel time to work: 24.6 minutes

WINTON (town). County seat. Covers a land area of 0.817 square miles and a water area of 0.043 square miles. Located at 36.39° N. Lat; 76.93° W. Long. Elevation is 43 feet.
History: Winton was incorporated in 1754 and named for the DeWinton family of England.
Population: 769; Growth (since 2000): -19.6%; Density: 940.7 persons per square mile; Race: 25.9% White, 70.1% Black/African American, 0.0% Asian, 2.3% American Indian/Alaska Native, 0.0% Native Hawaiian/Other Pacific Islander, 1.4% Two or more races, 1.2% Hispanic of any race; Average household size: 2.14; Median age: 42.2; Age under 18: 19.6%; Age 65 and over: 17.8%; Males per 100 females: 88.0
School District(s)
Hertford County Schools (PK-12)
    2012-13 Enrollment: 3,172 . . . . (252) 358-1761
Housing: Homeownership rate: 53.5%; Homeowner vacancy rate: 2.7%; Rental vacancy rate: 11.0%

Hoke County

Located in south central North Carolina, in sand-hills area; bounded on the southwest by the Lumber River. Covers a land area of 390.744 square miles, a water area of 1.552 square miles, and is located in the Eastern Time Zone at 35.02° N. Lat., 79.24° W. Long. The county was founded in 1911. County seat is Raeford.

Hoke County is part of the Fayetteville, NC Metropolitan Statistical Area. The entire metro area includes: Cumberland County, NC; Hoke County, NC

Population: 46,952; Growth (since 2000): 39.5%; Density: 120.2 persons per square mile; Race: 45.3% White, 33.5% Black/African American, 1.0% Asian, 9.6% American Indian/Alaska Native, 0.2% Native Hawaiian/Other Pacific Islander, 4.5% two or more races, 12.4% Hispanic of any race; Average household size: 2.80; Median age: 30.9; Age under 18: 30.2%; Age 65 and over: 7.4%; Males per 100 females: 95.0; Marriage status: 30.4% never married, 54.1% now married, 4.3% separated, 5.5% widowed, 10.0% divorced; Foreign born: 5.7%; Speak English only: 87.3%; With disability: 13.7%; Veterans: 14.8%; Ancestry: 11.3% American, 6.3% Irish, 6.2% German, 4.4% English, 2.3% Italian
Religion: Six largest groups: 8.3% Baptist, 4.6% Non-denominational Protestant, 4.4% Methodist/Pietist, 1.8% Presbyterian-Reformed, 1.6% Catholicism, 1.6% Pentecostal
Economy: Unemployment rate: 5.9%; Leading industries: 19.4% retail trade; 16.1% health care and social assistance; 12.9% other services (except public administration); Farms: 202 totaling 58,588 acres; Company size: 1 employs 1,000 or more persons, 0 employ 500 to 999 persons, 4 employ 100 to 499 persons, 398 employ less than 100 persons; Business ownership: n/a women-owned, n/a Black-owned, 62 Hispanic-owned, 40 Asian-owned
Employment: 9.0% management, business, and financial, 2.3% computer, engineering, and science, 12.5% education, legal, community service, arts, and media, 5.1% healthcare practitioners, 22.0% service, 23.6% sales and office, 10.4% natural resources, construction, and maintenance, 15.1% production, transportation, and material moving
Income: Per capita: $18,761; Median household: $45,489; Average household: $54,209; Households with income of $100,000 or more: 11.9%; Poverty rate: 22.9%
Educational Attainment: High school diploma or higher: 84.0%; Bachelor's degree or higher: 17.2%; Graduate/professional degree or higher: 4.7%
Housing: Homeownership rate: 70.6%; Median home value: $141,300; Median year structure built: 1995; Homeowner vacancy rate: 3.8%; Median gross rent: $781 per month; Rental vacancy rate: 9.9%
Vital Statistics: Birth rate: 187.8 per 10,000 population; Death rate: 54.9 per 10,000 population; Age-adjusted cancer mortality rate: 190.6 deaths per 100,000 population
Health Insurance: 84.4% have insurance; 58.7% have private insurance; 35.2% have public insurance; 15.6% do not have insurance; 4.2% of children under 18 do not have insurance
Health Care: Physicians: 1.2 per 10,000 population; Hospital beds: 0.0 per 10,000 population; Hospital admissions: 0.0 per 10,000 population
Transportation: Commute: 93.6% car, 0.6% public transportation, 1.7% walk, 1.5% work from home; Median travel time to work: 25.3 minutes
Presidential Election: 59.0% Obama, 39.9% Romney (2012)

Additional Information Contacts
Hoke Government . . . . (910) 875-8751
  http://www.hokecounty.org

Hoke County Communities

ASHLEY HEIGHTS (CDP). Covers a land area of 2.221 square miles and a water area of 0 square miles. Located at 35.09° N. Lat; 79.37° W. Long. Elevation is 436 feet.
Population: 380; Growth (since 2000): 11.4%; Density: 171.1 persons per square mile; Race: 56.8% White, 21.8% Black/African American, 0.0% Asian, 12.6% American Indian/Alaska Native, 0.0% Native Hawaiian/Other Pacific Islander, 4.7% Two or more races, 9.5% Hispanic of any race; Average household size: 2.68; Median age: 38.6; Age under 18: 25.3%; Age 65 and over: 11.1%; Males per 100 females: 100.0
Housing: Homeownership rate: 78.2%; Homeowner vacancy rate: 1.8%; Rental vacancy rate: 8.8%

BOWMORE (CDP). Covers a land area of 3.315 square miles and a water area of 0 square miles. Located at 34.94° N. Lat; 79.30° W. Long. Elevation is 259 feet.
Population: 103; Growth (since 2000): -29.0%; Density: 31.1 persons per square mile; Race: 19.4% White, 54.4% Black/African American, 0.0% Asian, 25.2% American Indian/Alaska Native, 0.0% Native Hawaiian/Other Pacific Islander, 1.0% Two or more races, 0.0% Hispanic of any race; Average household size: 2.71; Median age: 40.5; Age under 18: 21.4%; Age 65 and over: 13.6%; Males per 100 females: 80.7
Housing: Homeownership rate: 65.8%; Homeowner vacancy rate: 3.8%; Rental vacancy rate: 7.1%

DUNDARRACH (CDP). Covers a land area of 1.316 square miles and a water area of 0 square miles. Located at 34.92° N. Lat; 79.16° W. Long. Elevation is 223 feet.
Population: 41; Growth (since 2000): -33.9%; Density: 31.1 persons per square mile; Race: 78.0% White, 14.6% Black/African American, 0.0% Asian, 7.3% American Indian/Alaska Native, 0.0% Native Hawaiian/Other Pacific Islander, 0.0% Two or more races, 0.0% Hispanic of any race; Average household size: 2.28; Median age: 51.5; Age under 18: 12.2%; Age 65 and over: 22.0%; Males per 100 females: 95.2
Housing: Homeownership rate: 72.2%; Homeowner vacancy rate: 0.0%; Rental vacancy rate: 0.0%

FIVE POINTS (CDP). Covers a land area of 8.280 square miles and a water area of 0 square miles. Located at 35.02° N. Lat; 79.35° W. Long. Elevation is 348 feet.
Population: 689; Growth (since 2000): 125.2%; Density: 83.2 persons per square mile; Race: 57.0% White, 30.3% Black/African American, 1.0% Asian, 3.0% American Indian/Alaska Native, 0.0% Native Hawaiian/Other Pacific Islander, 5.7% Two or more races, 7.5% Hispanic of any race; Average household size: 2.82; Median age: 38.0; Age under 18: 27.4%; Age 65 and over: 11.8%; Males per 100 females: 99.7
Housing: Homeownership rate: 86.1%; Homeowner vacancy rate: 4.1%; Rental vacancy rate: 18.6%

RAEFORD (city). County seat. Covers a land area of 4.249 square miles and a water area of 0.023 square miles. Located at 34.98° N. Lat; 79.23° W. Long. Elevation is 262 feet.
Population: 4,611; Growth (since 2000): 36.2%; Density: 1,085.1 persons per square mile; Race: 43.6% White, 41.1% Black/African American, 1.0% Asian, 4.3% American Indian/Alaska Native, 0.1% Native Hawaiian/Other Pacific Islander, 3.7% Two or more races, 9.6% Hispanic of any race; Average household size: 2.38; Median age: 39.4; Age under 18: 23.8%; Age 65 and over: 17.1%; Males per 100 females: 88.3; Marriage status: 32.1% never married, 45.9% now married, 6.8% separated, 9.2% widowed, 12.8% divorced; Foreign born: 4.4%; Speak English only: 92.7%; With disability: 10.8%; Veterans: 11.7%; Ancestry: 8.2% American, 3.9% German, 3.4% English, 2.2% Scotch-Irish, 2.1% Irish
Employment: 6.4% management, business, and financial, 3.9% computer, engineering, and science, 22.8% education, legal, community service, arts, and media, 3.5% healthcare practitioners, 19.8% service, 20.0% sales and office, 9.3% natural resources, construction, and maintenance, 14.3% production, transportation, and material moving
Income: Per capita: $19,098; Median household: $26,596; Average household: $48,909; Households with income of $100,000 or more: 13.0%; Poverty rate: 34.3%

Educational Attainment: High school diploma or higher: 79.4%; Bachelor's degree or higher: 23.4%; Graduate/professional degree or higher: 4.9%

School District(s)
Hoke County Schools (PK-12)
  2012-13 Enrollment: 8,404 . . . . (910) 875-4106
Housing: Homeownership rate: 55.7%; Median home value: $124,400; Median year structure built: 1977; Homeowner vacancy rate: 2.7%; Median gross rent: $557 per month; Rental vacancy rate: 6.2%
Health Insurance: 86.1% have insurance; 49.3% have private insurance; 47.8% have public insurance; 13.9% do not have insurance; 8.0% of children under 18 do not have insurance
Safety: Violent crime rate: 59.3 per 10,000 population; Property crime rate: 525.1 per 10,000 population
Newspapers: The News-Journal (weekly circulation 4500)
Transportation: Commute: 94.0% car, 1.0% public transportation, 0.3% walk, 0.9% work from home; Median travel time to work: 20.2 minutes
Additional Information Contacts
City of Raeford . . . . (910) 875-8161
  http://www.raeford.org

ROCKFISH (CDP). Covers a land area of 4.952 square miles and a water area of 0.095 square miles. Located at 34.99° N. Lat; 79.07° W. Long. Elevation is 217 feet.
Population: 3,298; Growth (since 2000): 40.2%; Density: 666.0 persons per square mile; Race: 67.9% White, 20.2% Black/African American, 1.2% Asian, 1.7% American Indian/Alaska Native, 0.5% Native Hawaiian/Other Pacific Islander, 5.1% Two or more races, 11.6% Hispanic of any race; Average household size: 2.76; Median age: 29.6; Age under 18: 31.1%; Age 65 and over: 4.9%; Males per 100 females: 96.3; Marriage status: 21.8% never married, 65.5% now married, 2.0% separated, 0.7% widowed, 12.0% divorced; Foreign born: 7.9%; Speak English only: 83.6%; With disability: 10.3%; Veterans: 23.8%; Ancestry: 18.5% American, 12.5% Irish, 9.7% English, 9.2% German, 3.3% French
Employment: 9.4% management, business, and financial, 1.2% computer, engineering, and science, 7.2% education, legal, community service, arts, and media, 6.2% healthcare practitioners, 26.3% service, 32.5% sales and office, 8.9% natural resources, construction, and maintenance, 8.3% production, transportation, and material moving
Income: Per capita: $22,044; Median household: $62,083; Average household: $67,010; Households with income of $100,000 or more: 16.0%; Poverty rate: 5.6%
Educational Attainment: High school diploma or higher: 94.0%; Bachelor's degree or higher: 16.4%; Graduate/professional degree or higher: 3.5%
Housing: Homeownership rate: 77.3%; Median home value: $162,700; Median year structure built: 1998; Homeowner vacancy rate: 3.0%; Median gross rent: $1,133 per month; Rental vacancy rate: 3.8%
Health Insurance: 91.1% have insurance; 72.9% have private insurance; 29.5% have public insurance; 8.9% do not have insurance; 4.9% of children under 18 do not have insurance
Transportation: Commute: 93.8% car, 0.0% public transportation, 3.8% walk, 1.3% work from home; Median travel time to work: 27.0 minutes

SILVER CITY (CDP). Covers a land area of 1.493 square miles and a water area of 0 square miles. Located at 35.00° N. Lat; 79.23° W. Long. Elevation is 249 feet.
Population: 882; Growth (since 2000): -23.0%; Density: 590.6 persons per square mile; Race: 4.0% White, 89.8% Black/African American, 0.1% Asian, 1.0% American Indian/Alaska Native, 0.0% Native Hawaiian/Other Pacific Islander, 3.3% Two or more races, 2.0% Hispanic of any race; Average household size: 2.51; Median age: 45.4; Age under 18: 20.2%; Age 65 and over: 17.5%; Males per 100 females: 90.1
Housing: Homeownership rate: 67.2%; Homeowner vacancy rate: 1.3%; Rental vacancy rate: 8.5%

Hyde County

Located in eastern North Carolina; tidewater area, bounded on the south by Pamlico Sound; includes Ocracoke Island and Mattamuskeet Lake. Covers a land area of 612.700 square miles, a water area of 811.326 square miles, and is located in the Eastern Time Zone at 35.41° N. Lat., 76.15° W. Long. The county was founded in 1705. County seat is Swan Quarter.

Population: 5,810; Growth (since 2000): -0.3%; Density: 9.5 persons per square mile; Race: 64.0% White, 31.6% Black/African American, 0.3% Asian, 0.5% American Indian/Alaska Native, 0.0% Native Hawaiian/Other Pacific Islander, 1.2% two or more races, 7.1% Hispanic of any race; Average household size: 2.35; Median age: 41.2; Age under 18: 18.5%; Age 65 and over: 15.1%; Males per 100 females: 124.8; Marriage status: 39.3% never married, 44.3% now married, 3.1% separated, 6.9% widowed, 9.4% divorced; Foreign born: 2.8%; Speak English only: 94.7%; With disability: 18.0%; Veterans: 5.7%; Ancestry: 14.2% English, 9.5% Irish, 7.3% German, 5.4% American, 2.1% Scotch-Irish

Religion: Six largest groups: 9.6% Methodist/Pietist, 3.7% Baptist, 2.3% Episcopalianism/Anglicanism, 2.0% Pentecostal, 0.8% Presbyterian-Reformed, 0.0% Other Groups

Economy: Unemployment rate: 5.4%; Leading industries: 23.5% retail trade; 17.3% accommodation and food services; 12.3% construction; Farms: 158 totaling 107,559 acres; Company size: 0 employ 1,000 or more persons, 0 employ 500 to 999 persons, 0 employ 100 to 499 persons, 162 employ less than 100 persons; Business ownership: n/a women-owned, n/a Black-owned, n/a Hispanic-owned, n/a Asian-owned

Employment: 13.2% management, business, and financial, 0.8% computer, engineering, and science, 8.3% education, legal, community service, arts, and media, 3.0% healthcare practitioners, 22.7% service, 24.7% sales and office, 10.0% natural resources, construction, and maintenance, 17.4% production, transportation, and material moving

Income: Per capita: $18,408; Median household: $42,279; Average household: $47,759; Households with income of $100,000 or more: 5.9%; Poverty rate: 25.6%

Educational Attainment: High school diploma or higher: 78.8%; Bachelor's degree or higher: 10.7%; Graduate/professional degree or higher: 0.9%

Housing: Homeownership rate: 73.5%; Median home value: $76,400; Median year structure built: 1979; Homeowner vacancy rate: 1.9%; Median gross rent: $692 per month; Rental vacancy rate: 41.7%

Vital Statistics: Birth rate: 90.9 per 10,000 population; Death rate: 64.7 per 10,000 population; Age-adjusted cancer mortality rate: Unreliable deaths per 100,000 population

Health Insurance: 77.5% have insurance; 47.9% have private insurance; 41.1% have public insurance; 22.5% do not have insurance; 29.8% of children under 18 do not have insurance

Health Care: Physicians: 1.7 per 10,000 population; Hospital beds: 0.0 per 10,000 population; Hospital admissions: 0.0 per 10,000 population

Air Quality Index: 95.7% good, 4.3% moderate, 0.0% unhealthy for sensitive individuals, 0.0% unhealthy (percent of days)

Transportation: Commute: 83.2% car, 0.6% public transportation, 8.9% walk, 0.2% work from home; Median travel time to work: 19.9 minutes

Presidential Election: 48.8% Obama, 50.1% Romney (2012)

National and State Parks: Mattamuskeet National Wildlife Refuge; Pungo National Wildlife Refuge; Swanquarter National Wildlife Refuge

Additional Information Contacts
Hyde Government . . . . (252) 926-1147
  http://www.hydecountync.gov

Hyde County Communities

ENGELHARD (CDP). Covers a land area of 3.216 square miles and a water area of 0 square miles. Located at 35.51° N. Lat; 76.01° W. Long.
Population: 445; Growth (since 2000): n/a; Density: 138.4 persons per square mile; Race: 53.9% White, 41.3% Black/African American, 0.2% Asian, 0.0% American Indian/Alaska Native, 0.0% Native Hawaiian/Other Pacific Islander, 2.5% Two or more races, 9.7% Hispanic of any race; Average household size: 2.73; Median age: 40.5; Age under 18: 24.7%; Age 65 and over: 15.1%; Males per 100 females: 90.2
Housing: Homeownership rate: 62.5%; Homeowner vacancy rate: 4.6%; Rental vacancy rate: 13.9%

FAIRFIELD (CDP). Covers a land area of 7.037 square miles and a water area of 0 square miles. Located at 35.55° N. Lat; 76.23° W. Long. Elevation is 3 feet.
Population: 258; Growth (since 2000): n/a; Density: 36.7 persons per square mile; Race: 56.6% White, 43.4% Black/African American, 0.0% Asian, 0.0% American Indian/Alaska Native, 0.0% Native Hawaiian/Other Pacific Islander, 0.0% Two or more races, 0.0% Hispanic of any race; Average household size: 2.39; Median age: 48.0; Age under 18: 20.9%; Age 65 and over: 20.5%; Males per 100 females: 96.9

Housing: Homeownership rate: 84.9%; Homeowner vacancy rate: 1.1%; Rental vacancy rate: 0.0%

OCRACOKE (CDP). Covers a land area of 8.602 square miles and a water area of 1.018 square miles. Located at 35.07° N. Lat; 76.00° W. Long. Elevation is 3 feet.
Population: 948; Growth (since 2000): 23.3%; Density: 110.2 persons per square mile; Race: 95.6% White, 1.6% Black/African American, 0.2% Asian, 0.4% American Indian/Alaska Native, 0.0% Native Hawaiian/Other Pacific Islander, 0.6% Two or more races, 19.1% Hispanic of any race; Average household size: 2.25; Median age: 38.2; Age under 18: 20.8%; Age 65 and over: 12.8%; Males per 100 females: 98.3
School District(s)
Hyde County Schools (PK-12)
  2012-13 Enrollment: 600 . . . . (252) 926-3281
Housing: Homeownership rate: 64.1%; Homeowner vacancy rate: 4.3%; Rental vacancy rate: 69.9%

SCRANTON (unincorporated postal area)
ZCTA: 27875
  Covers a land area of 55.140 square miles and a water area of 38.093 square miles. Located at 35.46° N. Lat; 76.50° W. Long..
  Population: 517; Growth (since 2000): -10.9%; Density: 9.4 persons per square mile; Race: 62.9% White, 35.2% Black/African American, 0.0% Asian, 0.0% American Indian/Alaska Native, 0.0% Native Hawaiian/Other Pacific Islander, 1.0% Two or more races, 0.8% Hispanic of any race; Average household size: 2.39; Median age: 48.4; Age under 18: 17.0%; Age 65 and over: 15.3%; Males per 100 females: 90.1
  Housing: Homeownership rate: 87.0%; Homeowner vacancy rate: 3.1%; Rental vacancy rate: 12.5%

SWAN QUARTER (CDP). County seat. Covers a land area of 3.950 square miles and a water area of 0.004 square miles. Located at 35.41° N. Lat; 76.32° W. Long.
Population: 324; Growth (since 2000): n/a; Density: 82.0 persons per square mile; Race: 64.5% White, 27.5% Black/African American, 0.0% Asian, 0.0% American Indian/Alaska Native, 0.0% Native Hawaiian/Other Pacific Islander, 3.4% Two or more races, 7.4% Hispanic of any race; Average household size: 2.15; Median age: 49.0; Age under 18: 19.1%; Age 65 and over: 17.9%; Males per 100 females: 98.8
School District(s)
Hyde County Schools (PK-12)
  2012-13 Enrollment: 600 . . . . (252) 926-3281
Housing: Homeownership rate: 72.2%; Homeowner vacancy rate: 1.8%; Rental vacancy rate: 4.5%

SWANQUARTER (unincorporated postal area)
ZCTA: 27885
  Covers a land area of 124.606 square miles and a water area of 41.926 square miles. Located at 35.39° N. Lat; 76.27° W. Long. Elevation is 3 feet.
  Population: 984; Growth (since 2000): -19.9%; Density: 7.9 persons per square mile; Race: 66.7% White, 29.7% Black/African American, 0.1% Asian, 0.0% American Indian/Alaska Native, 0.0% Native Hawaiian/Other Pacific Islander, 2.0% Two or more races, 7.0% Hispanic of any race; Average household size: 2.21; Median age: 50.3; Age under 18: 17.0%; Age 65 and over: 23.5%; Males per 100 females: 93.3
  Housing: Homeownership rate: 74.6%; Homeowner vacancy rate: 0.9%; Rental vacancy rate: 10.1%

Iredell County

Located in west central North Carolina; piedmont area, bounded on the southwest by the Catawba River; drained by tributaries of the Yadkin River. Covers a land area of 573.833 square miles, a water area of 23.069 square miles, and is located in the Eastern Time Zone at 35.81° N. Lat., 80.87° W. Long. The county was founded in 1788. County seat is Statesville.

Iredell County is part of the Charlotte-Concord-Gastonia, NC-SC Metropolitan Statistical Area. The entire metro area includes: Cabarrus County, NC; Gaston County, NC; Iredell County, NC; Lincoln County, NC;

Mecklenburg County, NC; Rowan County, NC; Union County, NC; Chester County, SC; Lancaster County, SC; York County, SC

Weather Station: Statesville 2 NNE   Elevation: 950 feet

	Jan	Feb	Mar	Apr	May	Jun	Jul	Aug	Sep	Oct	Nov	Dec
High	50	55	63	72	79	86	89	87	81	71	62	52
Low	27	29	36	44	53	62	66	65	58	46	36	29
Precip	3.4	3.3	4.2	3.6	3.4	4.3	4.1	3.8	3.7	3.4	3.4	3.6
Snow	2.2	1.2	0.6	0.0	0.0	0.0	0.0	0.0	0.0	0.0	tr	0.4

High and Low temperatures in degrees Fahrenheit; Precipitation and Snow in inches

Population: 159,437; Growth (since 2000): 30.0%; Density: 277.8 persons per square mile; Race: 80.7% White, 11.9% Black/African American, 1.8% Asian, 0.3% American Indian/Alaska Native, 0.0% Native Hawaiian/Other Pacific Islander, 1.8% two or more races, 6.8% Hispanic of any race; Average household size: 2.58; Median age: 38.9; Age under 18: 25.5%; Age 65 and over: 12.8%; Males per 100 females: 97.0; Marriage status: 26.3% never married, 57.7% now married, 3.1% separated, 5.7% widowed, 10.3% divorced; Foreign born: 5.7%; Speak English only: 91.4%; With disability: 12.0%; Veterans: 9.2%; Ancestry: 14.9% German, 12.9% American, 11.1% Irish, 9.5% English, 4.0% Scotch-Irish
Religion: Six largest groups: 18.8% Baptist, 11.1% Methodist/Pietist, 6.1% Non-denominational Protestant, 5.5% Catholicism, 3.8% Presbyterian-Reformed, 1.7% Pentecostal
Economy: Unemployment rate: 5.2%; Leading industries: 14.4% retail trade; 10.9% construction; 10.8% health care and social assistance; Farms: 1,203 totaling 152,385 acres; Company size: 2 employ 1,000 or more persons, 3 employ 500 to 999 persons, 71 employs 100 to 499 persons, 4,211 employs less than 100 persons; Business ownership: 3,786 women-owned, 756 Black-owned, n/a Hispanic-owned, 180 Asian-owned
Employment: 14.5% management, business, and financial, 4.2% computer, engineering, and science, 8.4% education, legal, community service, arts, and media, 5.9% healthcare practitioners, 15.4% service, 23.3% sales and office, 10.3% natural resources, construction, and maintenance, 17.9% production, transportation, and material moving
Income: Per capita: $26,467; Median household: $50,329; Average household: $69,338; Households with income of $100,000 or more: 19.3%; Poverty rate: 13.8%
Educational Attainment: High school diploma or higher: 85.9%; Bachelor's degree or higher: 23.9%; Graduate/professional degree or higher: 7.3%
Housing: Homeownership rate: 73.1%; Median home value: $166,700; Median year structure built: 1990; Homeowner vacancy rate: 2.9%; Median gross rent: $787 per month; Rental vacancy rate: 13.1%
Vital Statistics: Birth rate: 105.8 per 10,000 population; Death rate: 86.7 per 10,000 population; Age-adjusted cancer mortality rate: 185.0 deaths per 100,000 population
Health Insurance: 84.8% have insurance; 67.4% have private insurance; 28.2% have public insurance; 15.2% do not have insurance; 6.8% of children under 18 do not have insurance
Health Care: Physicians: 20.5 per 10,000 population; Hospital beds: 26.9 per 10,000 population; Hospital admissions: 1,254.3 per 10,000 population
Transportation: Commute: 93.2% car, 0.3% public transportation, 0.9% walk, 4.1% work from home; Median travel time to work: 24.4 minutes
Presidential Election: 34.1% Obama, 64.6% Romney (2012)
National and State Parks: Duke Powder State Park
Additional Information Contacts
Iredell Government . . . . (704) 878-3000
  http://www.co.iredell.nc.us

Iredell County Communities

HARMONY (town). Covers a land area of 1.357 square miles and a water area of 0.005 square miles. Located at 35.96° N. Lat; 80.77° W. Long. Elevation is 984 feet.
History: Harmony grew up around the old Harmony Mills Campground, where "protracted meetings" were held annually for many years by members of various churches.
Population: 531; Growth (since 2000): 1.0%; Density: 391.4 persons per square mile; Race: 88.5% White, 5.5% Black/African American, 0.0% Asian, 1.3% American Indian/Alaska Native, 0.0% Native Hawaiian/Other Pacific Islander, 0.8% Two or more races, 9.8% Hispanic of any race; Average household size: 2.58; Median age: 40.4; Age under 18: 25.0%; Age 65 and over: 14.9%; Males per 100 females: 100.4

Iredell-Statesville Schools (PK-12)
  2012-13 Enrollment: 21,400 . . . . (704) 872-8931
Housing: Homeownership rate: 72.9%; Homeowner vacancy rate: 2.6%; Rental vacancy rate: 15.2%

LOVE VALLEY (town). Covers a land area of 0.619 square miles and a water area of 0.002 square miles. Located at 35.99° N. Lat; 80.99° W. Long. Elevation is 1,165 feet.
Population: 90; Growth (since 2000): 200.0%; Density: 145.4 persons per square mile; Race: 87.8% White, 0.0% Black/African American, 0.0% Asian, 0.0% American Indian/Alaska Native, 0.0% Native Hawaiian/Other Pacific Islander, 3.3% Two or more races, 10.0% Hispanic of any race; Average household size: 1.91; Median age: 49.8; Age under 18: 14.4%; Age 65 and over: 15.6%; Males per 100 females: 91.5
Housing: Homeownership rate: 61.7%; Homeowner vacancy rate: 6.5%; Rental vacancy rate: 0.0%

MOORESVILLE (town). Covers a land area of 20.932 square miles and a water area of 0.051 square miles. Located at 35.59° N. Lat; 80.82° W. Long. Elevation is 909 feet.
History: Mooresville was established in 1868.
Population: 32,711; Growth (since 2000): 73.8%; Density: 1,562.7 persons per square mile; Race: 80.2% White, 10.9% Black/African American, 3.3% Asian, 0.5% American Indian/Alaska Native, 0.0% Native Hawaiian/Other Pacific Islander, 2.4% Two or more races, 6.9% Hispanic of any race; Average household size: 2.61; Median age: 34.2; Age under 18: 28.4%; Age 65 and over: 9.8%; Males per 100 females: 94.3; Marriage status: 28.7% never married, 56.0% now married, 2.3% separated, 4.9% widowed, 10.4% divorced; Foreign born: 7.4%; Speak English only: 90.0%; With disability: 7.8%; Veterans: 8.0%; Ancestry: 16.2% German, 12.5% Irish, 9.4% English, 8.3% American, 5.7% Italian
Employment: 16.2% management, business, and financial, 6.7% computer, engineering, and science, 8.3% education, legal, community service, arts, and media, 6.4% healthcare practitioners, 20.0% service, 24.4% sales and office, 8.2% natural resources, construction, and maintenance, 9.9% production, transportation, and material moving
Income: Per capita: $26,392; Median household: $61,003; Average household: $71,324; Households with income of $100,000 or more: 25.3%; Poverty rate: 9.9%
Educational Attainment: High school diploma or higher: 90.6%; Bachelor's degree or higher: 29.0%; Graduate/professional degree or higher: 7.7%

Iredell-Statesville Schools (PK-12)
  2012-13 Enrollment: 21,400 . . . . (704) 872-8931
Mooresville City Schools (PK-12)
  2012-13 Enrollment: 5,873 . . . . (704) 658-2530
Pine Lake Preparatory (KG-12)
  2012-13 Enrollment: 1,599 . . . . (704) 237-5300
NASCAR Technical Institute (Private, For-profit)
  Fall 2013 Enrollment: 1,510 . . . . (704) 658-1950
Pinnacle Institute of Cosmetology (Private, For-profit)
  Fall 2013 Enrollment: 78 . . . . (704) 235-0185
  2013-14 Tuition: $16,200
Housing: Homeownership rate: 64.0%; Median home value: $186,500; Median year structure built: 1997; Homeowner vacancy rate: 3.5%; Median gross rent: $862 per month; Rental vacancy rate: 12.8%
Health Insurance: 85.7% have insurance; 74.7% have private insurance; 18.5% have public insurance; 14.3% do not have insurance; 4.5% of children under 18 do not have insurance
Hospitals: Lake Norman Regional Medical Center (117 beds)
Safety: Violent crime rate: 22.9 per 10,000 population; Property crime rate: 415.4 per 10,000 population
Newspapers: Mooresville Tribune (weekly circulation 5600)
Transportation: Commute: 90.6% car, 0.7% public transportation, 1.1% walk, 4.7% work from home; Median travel time to work: 25.3 minutes
Additional Information Contacts
Town of Mooresville . . . . (704) 663-3800
  http://www.ci.mooresville.nc.us

OLIN (unincorporated postal area)
ZCTA: 28660
  Covers a land area of 31.966 square miles and a water area of 0.238 square miles. Located at 35.97° N. Lat; 80.86° W. Long. Elevation is 912 feet.
  Population: 2,249; Growth (since 2000): 42.5%; Density: 70.4 persons per square mile; Race: 84.5% White, 5.6% Black/African American, 0.1% Asian, 0.8% American Indian/Alaska Native, 0.0% Native Hawaiian/Other Pacific Islander, 0.8% Two or more races, 11.1% Hispanic of any race; Average household size: 2.65; Median age: 38.6; Age under 18: 25.0%; Age 65 and over: 13.1%; Males per 100 females: 98.9
                     School District(s)
Iredell-Statesville Schools (PK-12)
  2012-13 Enrollment: 21,400 . . . . (704) 872-8931
  Housing: Homeownership rate: 79.0%; Homeowner vacancy rate: 2.5%; Rental vacancy rate: 8.2%

STATESVILLE (city). County seat. Covers a land area of 24.253 square miles and a water area of 0.116 square miles. Located at 35.78° N. Lat; 80.87° W. Long. Elevation is 912 feet.
History: The area of Statesville was settled around 1750 and called Fourth Creek. Statesville was founded on the site in 1789.
Population: 24,532; Growth (since 2000): 5.2%; Density: 1,011.5 persons per square mile; Race: 54.8% White, 34.5% Black/African American, 1.9% Asian, 0.3% American Indian/Alaska Native, 0.0% Native Hawaiian/Other Pacific Islander, 2.4% Two or more races, 10.9% Hispanic of any race; Average household size: 2.38; Median age: 37.8; Age under 18: 24.6%; Age 65 and over: 15.9%; Males per 100 females: 88.9; Marriage status: 34.4% never married, 45.1% now married, 4.2% separated, 7.4% widowed, 13.0% divorced; Foreign born: 8.4%; Speak English only: 87.5%; With disability: 13.9%; Veterans: 9.6%; Ancestry: 10.3% German, 8.5% Irish, 8.1% American, 7.8% English, 3.7% Scotch-Irish
Employment: 8.5% management, business, and financial, 2.9% computer, engineering, and science, 10.4% education, legal, community service, arts, and media, 7.2% healthcare practitioners, 13.6% service, 25.5% sales and office, 8.1% natural resources, construction, and maintenance, 23.9% production, transportation, and material moving
Income: Per capita: $20,803; Median household: $32,331; Average household: $51,842; Households with income of $100,000 or more: 9.7%; Poverty rate: 29.4%
Educational Attainment: High school diploma or higher: 80.6%; Bachelor's degree or higher: 20.5%; Graduate/professional degree or higher: 7.9%
                     School District(s)
American Renaissance Middle (KG-08)
  2012-13 Enrollment: 524. . . . . (704) 878-6009
Iredell-Statesville Schools (PK-12)
  2012-13 Enrollment: 21,400 . . . . (704) 872-8931
Success Institute Charter (KG-08)
  2012-13 Enrollment: 103. . . . . (704) 881-0441
                     Two-year College(s)
Mitchell Community College (Public)
  Fall 2013 Enrollment: 3,514 . . . . (704) 878-3200
  2013-14 Tuition: In-state $2,391; Out-of-state $8,535
Housing: Homeownership rate: 52.3%; Median home value: $133,500; Median year structure built: 1971; Homeowner vacancy rate: 5.3%; Median gross rent: $716 per month; Rental vacancy rate: 14.6%
Health Insurance: 81.1% have insurance; 52.9% have private insurance; 39.7% have public insurance; 18.9% do not have insurance; 6.7% of children under 18 do not have insurance
Hospitals: Davis Regional Medical Center (131 beds); Iredell Memorial Hospital (247 beds)
Safety: Violent crime rate: 74.2 per 10,000 population; Property crime rate: 662.7 per 10,000 population
Newspapers: Statesville Record & Landmark (daily circulation 14500)
Transportation: Commute: 94.5% car, 0.0% public transportation, 1.3% walk, 1.5% work from home; Median travel time to work: 19.5 minutes
Airports: Statesville Regional (general aviation)
Additional Information Contacts
City of Statesville. . . . . (704) 878-3583
  http://www.ci.statesville.nc.us

TROUTMAN (town). Covers a land area of 5.358 square miles and a water area of 0.027 square miles. Located at 35.69° N. Lat; 80.89° W. Long. Elevation is 938 feet.
Population: 2,383; Growth (since 2000): 49.7%; Density: 444.7 persons per square mile; Race: 73.3% White, 21.6% Black/African American, 0.9% Asian, 0.3% American Indian/Alaska Native, 0.0% Native Hawaiian/Other Pacific Islander, 2.6% Two or more races, 4.8% Hispanic of any race; Average household size: 2.63; Median age: 37.0; Age under 18: 26.8%; Age 65 and over: 13.1%; Males per 100 females: 95.3
                     School District(s)
Iredell-Statesville Schools (PK-12)
  2012-13 Enrollment: 21,400 . . . . (704) 872-8931
Housing: Homeownership rate: 76.7%; Homeowner vacancy rate: 3.1%; Rental vacancy rate: 15.9%
Safety: Violent crime rate: 24.5 per 10,000 population; Property crime rate: 245.3 per 10,000 population

UNION GROVE (unincorporated postal area)
ZCTA: 28689
  Covers a land area of 44.675 square miles and a water area of 0.168 square miles. Located at 36.04° N. Lat; 80.94° W. Long. Elevation is 1,119 feet.
  Population: 1,712; Growth (since 2000): -1.7%; Density: 38.3 persons per square mile; Race: 94.2% White, 0.2% Black/African American, 0.2% Asian, 0.1% American Indian/Alaska Native, 0.0% Native Hawaiian/Other Pacific Islander, 0.9% Two or more races, 6.0% Hispanic of any race; Average household size: 2.50; Median age: 44.4; Age under 18: 22.4%; Age 65 and over: 14.7%; Males per 100 females: 109.0
                     School District(s)
Iredell-Statesville Schools (PK-12)
  2012-13 Enrollment: 21,400 . . . . (704) 872-8931
  Housing: Homeownership rate: 80.8%; Homeowner vacancy rate: 1.6%; Rental vacancy rate: 16.8%

Jackson County

Located in western North Carolina, partly in the Blue Ridge; bounded on the south by South Carolina; drained by the Tuckasegee River; includes the Balsam and Cowee Mountains, and is part of Nantahala National Forest. Covers a land area of 490.755 square miles, a water area of 3.790 square miles, and is located in the Eastern Time Zone at 35.29° N. Lat., 83.13° W. Long. The county was founded in 1851. County seat is Sylva.

Jackson County is part of the Cullowhee, NC Micropolitan Statistical Area. The entire metro area includes: Jackson County, NC

Weather Station: Cullowhee										Elevation: 2,191 feet	
	Jan	Feb	Mar	Apr	May	Jun	Jul	Aug	Sep	Oct	Nov	Dec
High	49	53	62	70	77	82	85	84	79	70	61	51
Low	26	29	35	42	50	58	62	62	55	44	35	29
Precip	4.5	4.5	4.7	3.9	4.5	4.6	4.5	4.1	4.2	3.0	4.2	4.3
Snow	2.5	1.5	1.1	tr	0.0	0.0	0.0	0.0	0.0	0.1	0.0	1.0

High and Low temperatures in degrees Fahrenheit; Precipitation and Snow in inches

Population: 40,271; Growth (since 2000): 21.6%; Density: 82.1 persons per square mile; Race: 83.2% White, 1.8% Black/African American, 0.9% Asian, 9.4% American Indian/Alaska Native, 0.0% Native Hawaiian/Other Pacific Islander, 1.9% two or more races, 5.1% Hispanic of any race; Average household size: 2.23; Median age: 36.3; Age under 18: 17.7%; Age 65 and over: 15.1%; Males per 100 females: 99.1; Marriage status: 35.7% never married, 47.9% now married, 2.7% separated, 5.5% widowed, 10.9% divorced; Foreign born: 4.6%; Speak English only: 91.6%; With disability: 14.4%; Veterans: 9.4%; Ancestry: 32.3% American, 10.3% German, 9.7% Irish, 7.5% English, 5.5% Scotch-Irish
Religion: Six largest groups: 28.5% Baptist, 7.0% Methodist/Pietist, 3.3% Non-denominational Protestant, 2.0% Episcopalianism/Anglicanism, 1.3% Latter-day Saints, 1.1% Pentecostal
Economy: Unemployment rate: 4.3%; Leading industries: 16.7% retail trade; 16.1% construction; 11.1% accommodation and food services; Farms: 245 totaling 16,201 acres; Company size: 1 employs 1,000 or more persons, 1 employs 500 to 999 persons, 7 employ 100 to 499 persons, 927 employ less than 100 persons; Business ownership: 810 women-owned, n/a Black-owned, n/a Hispanic-owned, n/a Asian-owned

Employment: 10.6% management, business, and financial, 3.0% computer, engineering, and science, 11.9% education, legal, community service, arts, and media, 4.6% healthcare practitioners, 32.6% service, 18.9% sales and office, 12.3% natural resources, construction, and maintenance, 6.2% production, transportation, and material moving
Income: Per capita: $21,014; Median household: $36,951; Average household: $51,042; Households with income of $100,000 or more: 10.0%; Poverty rate: 21.8%
Educational Attainment: High school diploma or higher: 85.0%; Bachelor's degree or higher: 27.9%; Graduate/professional degree or higher: 11.1%
Housing: Homeownership rate: 64.6%; Median home value: $172,800; Median year structure built: 1986; Homeowner vacancy rate: 4.5%; Median gross rent: $636 per month; Rental vacancy rate: 12.2%
Vital Statistics: Birth rate: 91.9 per 10,000 population; Death rate: 75.0 per 10,000 population; Age-adjusted cancer mortality rate: 162.5 deaths per 100,000 population
Health Insurance: 81.4% have insurance; 63.3% have private insurance; 30.6% have public insurance; 18.6% do not have insurance; 12.2% of children under 18 do not have insurance
Health Care: Physicians: 17.5 per 10,000 population; Hospital beds: 27.6 per 10,000 population; Hospital admissions: 1,064.4 per 10,000 population
Air Quality Index: 91.7% good, 7.9% moderate, 0.4% unhealthy for sensitive individuals, 0.0% unhealthy (percent of days)
Transportation: Commute: 91.8% car, 0.1% public transportation, 4.3% walk, 2.6% work from home; Median travel time to work: 19.7 minutes
Presidential Election: 48.5% Obama, 49.4% Romney (2012)
National and State Parks: Whiteside Mountain National Recreation Trail
Additional Information Contacts
Jackson Government . . . . (541) 774-6029
  http://www.jacksonnc.org

Jackson County Communities

BALSAM (unincorporated postal area)
ZCTA: 28707
Covers a land area of 11.016 square miles and a water area of 0 square miles. Located at 35.40° N. Lat; 83.07° W. Long. Elevation is 3,304 feet.
Population: 94; Growth (since 2000): 91.8%; Density: 8.5 persons per square mile; Race: 100.0% White, 0.0% Black/African American, 0.0% Asian, 0.0% American Indian/Alaska Native, 0.0% Native Hawaiian/Other Pacific Islander, 0.0% Two or more races, 0.0% Hispanic of any race; Average household size: 1.96; Median age: 58.7; Age under 18: 8.5%; Age 65 and over: 33.0%; Males per 100 females: 95.8
Housing: Homeownership rate: 91.7%; Homeowner vacancy rate: 13.5%; Rental vacancy rate: 20.0%

CASHIERS (CDP).
Covers a land area of 1.067 square miles and a water area of 0 square miles. Located at 35.11° N. Lat; 83.10° W. Long. Elevation is 3,484 feet.
Population: 157; Growth (since 2000): -19.9%; Density: 147.2 persons per square mile; Race: 87.3% White, 5.7% Black/African American, 0.6% Asian, 0.0% American Indian/Alaska Native, 0.0% Native Hawaiian/Other Pacific Islander, 0.6% Two or more races, 7.6% Hispanic of any race; Average household size: 2.04; Median age: 51.6; Age under 18: 14.6%; Age 65 and over: 21.7%; Males per 100 females: 93.8
School District(s)
Jackson County Schools (PK-12)
  2012-13 Enrollment: 3,662 . . . . (828) 586-2311
Summit Charter (KG-08)
  2012-13 Enrollment: 196. . . . . (828) 743-5755
Housing: Homeownership rate: 68.9%; Homeowner vacancy rate: 11.3%; Rental vacancy rate: 17.2%
Newspapers: Crossroads Chronicle (weekly circulation 3000)

CHEROKEE (CDP).
Covers a land area of 12.061 square miles and a water area of 0 square miles. Located at 35.49° N. Lat; 83.30° W. Long.
Population: 2,138; Growth (since 2000): n/a; Density: 177.3 persons per square mile; Race: 14.5% White, 0.5% Black/African American, 1.1% Asian, 76.1% American Indian/Alaska Native, 0.0% Native Hawaiian/Other Pacific Islander, 6.6% Two or more races, 5.3% Hispanic of any race; Average household size: 2.53; Median age: 33.6; Age under 18: 27.7%; Age 65 and over: 11.4%; Males per 100 females: 92.6

Housing: Homeownership rate: 69.2%; Homeowner vacancy rate: 0.2%; Rental vacancy rate: 15.5%
Hospitals: Cherokee Indian Hospital Authority (32 beds)

CULLOWHEE (CDP).
Covers a land area of 3.505 square miles and a water area of 0 square miles. Located at 35.31° N. Lat; 83.18° W. Long. Elevation is 2,116 feet.
History: Cullowhee a corruption of the Cherokee "Gualiyi," meaning "place of the spring salad."
Population: 6,228; Growth (since 2000): 74.0%; Density: 1,777.1 persons per square mile; Race: 85.8% White, 7.1% Black/African American, 1.2% Asian, 0.7% American Indian/Alaska Native, 0.0% Native Hawaiian/Other Pacific Islander, 1.7% Two or more races, 5.1% Hispanic of any race; Average household size: 1.70; Median age: 21.0; Age under 18: 4.1%; Age 65 and over: 3.8%; Males per 100 females: 105.0; Marriage status: 84.7% never married, 10.3% now married, 2.3% separated, 1.6% widowed, 3.4% divorced; Foreign born: 1.9%; Speak English only: 94.1%; With disability: 8.0%; Veterans: 2.2%; Ancestry: 39.7% American, 13.7% German, 11.2% Irish, 5.1% English, 4.7% Scotch-Irish
Employment: 7.2% management, business, and financial, 2.1% computer, engineering, and science, 14.9% education, legal, community service, arts, and media, 2.2% healthcare practitioners, 34.3% service, 27.6% sales and office, 11.5% natural resources, construction, and maintenance, 0.2% production, transportation, and material moving
Income: Per capita: $7,436; Median household: $17,778; Average household: $26,249; Households with income of $100,000 or more: 3.9%; Poverty rate: 53.7%
Educational Attainment: High school diploma or higher: 86.6%; Bachelor's degree or higher: 38.7%; Graduate/professional degree or higher: 20.7%
School District(s)
Jackson County Schools (PK-12)
  2012-13 Enrollment: 3,662 . . . . (828) 586-2311
Four-year College(s)
Western Carolina University (Public)
  Fall 2013 Enrollment: 10,107 . . . . (828) 227-7100
  2013-14 Tuition: In-state $6,265; Out-of-state $15,862
Housing: Homeownership rate: 12.0%; Median home value: $164,600; Median year structure built: 1988; Homeowner vacancy rate: 1.4%; Median gross rent: $554 per month; Rental vacancy rate: 7.6%
Health Insurance: 88.3% have insurance; 83.5% have private insurance; 9.0% have public insurance; 11.7% do not have insurance; 21.7% of children under 18 do not have insurance
Transportation: Commute: 72.5% car, 0.0% public transportation, 25.4% walk, 2.2% work from home; Median travel time to work: 16.2 minutes

DILLSBORO (town).
Covers a land area of 0.477 square miles and a water area of 0 square miles. Located at 35.37° N. Lat; 83.25° W. Long. Elevation is 1,991 feet.
Population: 232; Growth (since 2000): 13.2%; Density: 486.6 persons per square mile; Race: 97.0% White, 0.4% Black/African American, 0.0% Asian, 0.4% American Indian/Alaska Native, 0.0% Native Hawaiian/Other Pacific Islander, 2.2% Two or more races, 5.2% Hispanic of any race; Average household size: 1.97; Median age: 47.5; Age under 18: 16.4%; Age 65 and over: 21.6%; Males per 100 females: 75.8
Housing: Homeownership rate: 48.3%; Homeowner vacancy rate: 1.7%; Rental vacancy rate: 6.2%

FOREST HILLS (village).
Covers a land area of 0.496 square miles and a water area of 0 square miles. Located at 35.30° N. Lat; 83.20° W. Long. Elevation is 2,290 feet.
Population: 365; Growth (since 2000): 10.6%; Density: 736.4 persons per square mile; Race: 92.1% White, 4.1% Black/African American, 0.8% Asian, 0.5% American Indian/Alaska Native, 0.0% Native Hawaiian/Other Pacific Islander, 1.1% Two or more races, 4.9% Hispanic of any race; Average household size: 1.82; Median age: 43.9; Age under 18: 9.9%; Age 65 and over: 22.7%; Males per 100 females: 114.7
Housing: Homeownership rate: 42.8%; Homeowner vacancy rate: 2.2%; Rental vacancy rate: 7.3%

GLENVILLE (CDP).
Covers a land area of 1.338 square miles and a water area of 0.006 square miles. Located at 35.17° N. Lat; 83.13° W. Long. Elevation is 3,599 feet.
Population: 110; Growth (since 2000): n/a; Density: 82.2 persons per square mile; Race: 94.5% White, 0.0% Black/African American, 0.0%

Asian, 0.0% American Indian/Alaska Native, 0.0% Native Hawaiian/Other Pacific Islander, 0.0% Two or more races, 12.7% Hispanic of any race; Average household size: 1.83; Median age: 55.3; Age under 18: 6.4%; Age 65 and over: 30.0%; Males per 100 females: 115.7
Housing: Homeownership rate: 66.7%; Homeowner vacancy rate: 29.8%; Rental vacancy rate: 13.0%

SAPPHIRE (unincorporated postal area)
ZCTA: 28774
Covers a land area of 45.308 square miles and a water area of 0.186 square miles. Located at 35.09° N. Lat; 83.00° W. Long..
Population: 1,013; Growth (since 2000): 29.0%; Density: 22.4 persons per square mile; Race: 95.1% White, 1.0% Black/African American, 0.2% Asian, 0.5% American Indian/Alaska Native, 0.0% Native Hawaiian/Other Pacific Islander, 0.6% Two or more races, 4.6% Hispanic of any race; Average household size: 2.09; Median age: 56.8; Age under 18: 13.3%; Age 65 and over: 30.8%; Males per 100 females: 100.2
Housing: Homeownership rate: 82.3%; Homeowner vacancy rate: 13.2%; Rental vacancy rate: 19.4%

SYLVA (town). County seat. Covers a land area of 3.191 square miles and a water area of 0 square miles. Located at 35.38° N. Lat; 83.22° W. Long. Elevation is 2,044 feet.
History: Sylva is named for William Sylva, a native of Denmark and an early settler. A paperboard plant and tannery were Sylva's first industry.
Population: 2,588; Growth (since 2000): 6.3%; Density: 811.0 persons per square mile; Race: 85.8% White, 2.7% Black/African American, 1.8% Asian, 2.8% American Indian/Alaska Native, 0.0% Native Hawaiian/Other Pacific Islander, 1.7% Two or more races, 9.0% Hispanic of any race; Average household size: 2.17; Median age: 36.4; Age under 18: 20.1%; Age 65 and over: 17.6%; Males per 100 females: 93.3; Marriage status: 29.5% never married, 46.8% now married, 7.3% separated, 10.2% widowed, 13.4% divorced; Foreign born: 6.4%; Speak English only: 87.4%; With disability: 16.5%; Veterans: 7.1%; Ancestry: 36.2% American, 12.5% Irish, 7.3% English, 6.8% German, 6.4% Scotch-Irish
Employment: 7.7% management, business, and financial, 5.6% computer, engineering, and science, 9.6% education, legal, community service, arts, and media, 4.6% healthcare practitioners, 37.8% service, 20.3% sales and office, 7.0% natural resources, construction, and maintenance, 7.5% production, transportation, and material moving
Income: Per capita: $19,460; Median household: $31,745; Average household: $39,092; Households with income of $100,000 or more: 5.5%; Poverty rate: 20.0%
Educational Attainment: High school diploma or higher: 81.5%; Bachelor's degree or higher: 28.9%; Graduate/professional degree or higher: 12.5%
School District(s)
Jackson County Schools (PK-12)
    2012-13 Enrollment: 3,662 . . . . (828) 586-2311
Two-year College(s)
Southwestern Community College (Public)
    Fall 2013 Enrollment: 2,242 . . . . (828) 339-4000
    2013-14 Tuition: In-state $2,086; Out-of-state $7,462
Housing: Homeownership rate: 49.0%; Median home value: $129,300; Median year structure built: 1969; Homeowner vacancy rate: 3.4%; Median gross rent: $734 per month; Rental vacancy rate: 10.6%
Health Insurance: 81.8% have insurance; 59.1% have private insurance; 34.3% have public insurance; 18.2% do not have insurance; 1.1% of children under 18 do not have insurance
Hospitals: Medwest Harris (86 beds)
Safety: Violent crime rate: 76.5 per 10,000 population; Property crime rate: 670.6 per 10,000 population
Newspapers: Sylva Herald & Ruralite (weekly circulation 6400)
Transportation: Commute: 88.9% car, 1.6% public transportation, 4.5% walk, 2.5% work from home; Median travel time to work: 19.5 minutes
Additional Information Contacts
Town of Sylva . . . . (828) 586-2719
    http://www.townofsylva.org

TUCKASEGEE (unincorporated postal area)
ZCTA: 28783
Covers a land area of 64.196 square miles and a water area of 1.154 square miles. Located at 35.26° N. Lat; 83.01° W. Long. Elevation is 2,165 feet.

Population: 1,593; Growth (since 2000): 31.1%; Density: 24.8 persons per square mile; Race: 85.9% White, 0.6% Black/African American, 0.3% Asian, 1.8% American Indian/Alaska Native, 0.2% Native Hawaiian/Other Pacific Islander, 1.1% Two or more races, 13.4% Hispanic of any race; Average household size: 2.41; Median age: 42.6; Age under 18: 22.6%; Age 65 and over: 16.4%; Males per 100 females: 117.3
Housing: Homeownership rate: 70.8%; Homeowner vacancy rate: 4.3%; Rental vacancy rate: 13.0%

WEBSTER (town). Covers a land area of 0.996 square miles and a water area of 0 square miles. Located at 35.35° N. Lat; 83.22° W. Long. Elevation is 2,152 feet.
Population: 363; Growth (since 2000): -25.3%; Density: 364.4 persons per square mile; Race: 94.8% White, 1.7% Black/African American, 0.0% Asian, 0.6% American Indian/Alaska Native, 0.0% Native Hawaiian/Other Pacific Islander, 2.5% Two or more races, 1.7% Hispanic of any race; Average household size: 2.31; Median age: 38.7; Age under 18: 24.5%; Age 65 and over: 11.8%; Males per 100 females: 90.1
Housing: Homeownership rate: 65.6%; Homeowner vacancy rate: 3.7%; Rental vacancy rate: 0.0%

WHITTIER (unincorporated postal area)
ZCTA: 28789
Covers a land area of 57.032 square miles and a water area of 0.075 square miles. Located at 35.41° N. Lat; 83.32° W. Long..
Population: 5,097; Growth (since 2000): 1.6%; Density: 89.4 persons per square mile; Race: 81.9% White, 0.5% Black/African American, 0.7% Asian, 12.5% American Indian/Alaska Native, 0.0% Native Hawaiian/Other Pacific Islander, 3.5% Two or more races, 3.2% Hispanic of any race; Average household size: 2.30; Median age: 44.2; Age under 18: 19.8%; Age 65 and over: 17.1%; Males per 100 females: 94.5; Marriage status: 19.0% never married, 55.7% now married, 3.5% separated, 11.8% widowed, 13.5% divorced; Foreign born: 1.2%; Speak English only: 98.4%; With disability: 16.5%; Veterans: 15.0%; Ancestry: 34.1% American, 9.2% German, 7.0% Irish, 5.7% English, 5.3% Scotch-Irish
Employment: 6.9% management, business, and financial, 2.1% computer, engineering, and science, 15.0% education, legal, community service, arts, and media, 6.5% healthcare practitioners, 32.9% service, 18.0% sales and office, 13.0% natural resources, construction, and maintenance, 5.5% production, transportation, and material moving
Income: Per capita: $20,931; Median household: $39,060; Average household: $46,076; Households with income of $100,000 or more: 6.1%; Poverty rate: 20.0%
Educational Attainment: High school diploma or higher: 87.2%; Bachelor's degree or higher: 23.8%; Graduate/professional degree or higher: 10.6%
School District(s)
Jackson County Schools (PK-12)
    2012-13 Enrollment: 3,662 . . . . (828) 586-2311
Swain County Schools (PK-12)
    2012-13 Enrollment: 2,081 . . . . (828) 488-3129
Housing: Homeownership rate: 74.9%; Median home value: $159,500; Median year structure built: 1984; Homeowner vacancy rate: 3.5%; Median gross rent: $637 per month; Rental vacancy rate: 20.1%
Health Insurance: 86.4% have insurance; 65.8% have private insurance; 37.6% have public insurance; 13.6% do not have insurance; 21.6% of children under 18 do not have insurance
Transportation: Commute: 96.4% car, 0.0% public transportation, 1.0% walk, 2.5% work from home; Median travel time to work: 19.4 minutes

Johnston County

Located in central North Carolina; coastal plains area, drained by the Neuse River. Covers a land area of 791.299 square miles, a water area of 4.205 square miles, and is located in the Eastern Time Zone at 35.51° N. Lat., 78.37° W. Long. The county was founded in 1746. County seat is Smithfield.

Johnston County is part of the Raleigh, NC Metropolitan Statistical Area. The entire metro area includes: Franklin County, NC; Johnston County, NC; Wake County, NC

Weather Station: Clayton Wtp — Elevation: 299 feet

	Jan	Feb	Mar	Apr	May	Jun	Jul	Aug	Sep	Oct	Nov	Dec
High	51	na	63	72	80	87	89	88	82	73	64	54
Low	29	31	38	47	56	65	69	69	61	49	40	32
Precip	3.8	3.3	4.3	3.2	3.3	4.0	5.0	5.2	4.4	3.2	3.3	3.3
Snow	1.5	0.7	0.4	tr	0.0	0.0	0.0	0.0	0.0	0.0	tr	0.1

High and Low temperatures in degrees Fahrenheit; Precipitation and Snow in inches

Weather Station: Smithfield — Elevation: 149 feet

	Jan	Feb	Mar	Apr	May	Jun	Jul	Aug	Sep	Oct	Nov	Dec
High	52	56	64	73	80	87	90	88	82	73	64	55
Low	30	33	38	46	54	64	68	66	60	48	39	32
Precip	3.6	3.3	4.3	3.4	4.0	4.5	5.6	5.0	4.4	3.1	3.1	3.0
Snow	0.5	0.6	0.6	0.0	0.0	0.0	0.0	0.0	0.0	0.0	0.0	0.2

High and Low temperatures in degrees Fahrenheit; Precipitation and Snow in inches

Population: 168,878; Growth (since 2000): 38.5%; Density: 213.4 persons per square mile; Race: 74.2% White, 15.1% Black/African American, 0.6% Asian, 0.6% American Indian/Alaska Native, 0.0% Native Hawaiian/Other Pacific Islander, 2.0% two or more races, 12.9% Hispanic of any race; Average household size: 2.70; Median age: 36.3; Age under 18: 27.8%; Age 65 and over: 10.2%; Males per 100 females: 97.0; Marriage status: 25.0% never married, 58.7% now married, 3.7% separated, 5.8% widowed, 10.5% divorced; Foreign born: 7.6%; Speak English only: 87.9%; With disability: 12.2%; Veterans: 10.2%; Ancestry: 19.3% American, 10.8% English, 9.2% Irish, 8.7% German, 3.0% Italian

Religion: Six largest groups: 15.6% Baptist, 6.0% Methodist/Pietist, 5.2% Non-denominational Protestant, 4.0% Pentecostal, 2.5% Catholicism, 1.5% Presbyterian-Reformed

Economy: Unemployment rate: 4.9%; Leading industries: 18.2% retail trade; 15.5% construction; 10.5% other services (except public administration); Farms: 1,175 totaling 194,827 acres; Company size: 2 employ 1,000 or more persons, 2 employ 500 to 999 persons, 46 employ 100 to 499 persons, 2,956 employ less than 100 persons; Business ownership: 3,810 women-owned, 1,229 Black-owned, n/a Hispanic-owned, 220 Asian-owned

Employment: 14.2% management, business, and financial; 4.7% computer, engineering, and science, 10.1% education, legal, community service, arts, and media, 4.5% healthcare practitioners, 15.8% service, 24.8% sales and office, 13.0% natural resources, construction, and maintenance, 12.9% production, transportation, and material moving

Income: Per capita: $22,410; Median household: $49,711; Average household: $61,150; Households with income of $100,000 or more: 17.1%; Poverty rate: 17.2%

Educational Attainment: High school diploma or higher: 83.2%; Bachelor's degree or higher: 20.4%; Graduate/professional degree or higher: 5.1%

Housing: Homeownership rate: 73.2%; Median home value: $141,200; Median year structure built: 1992; Homeowner vacancy rate: 2.4%; Median gross rent: $778 per month; Rental vacancy rate: 9.7%

Vital Statistics: Birth rate: 126.5 per 10,000 population; Death rate: 71.1 per 10,000 population; Age-adjusted cancer mortality rate: 188.4 deaths per 100,000 population

Health Insurance: 83.1% have insurance; 62.9% have private insurance; 29.8% have public insurance; 16.9% do not have insurance; 7.4% of children under 18 do not have insurance

Health Care: Physicians: 5.1 per 10,000 population; Hospital beds: 8.5 per 10,000 population; Hospital admissions: 501.3 per 10,000 population

Air Quality Index: 93.1% good, 6.9% moderate, 0.0% unhealthy for sensitive individuals, 0.0% unhealthy (percent of days)

Transportation: Commute: 93.9% car, 0.2% public transportation, 0.6% walk, 3.8% work from home; Median travel time to work: 28.7 minutes

Presidential Election: 35.6% Obama, 63.1% Romney (2012)

Additional Information Contacts
Johnston Government . . . . (919) 989-5100
  http://www.johnstonnc.com

Johnston County Communities

ARCHER LODGE (town).
Covers a land area of 9.278 square miles and a water area of 0.027 square miles. Located at 35.68° N. Lat; 78.37° W. Long. Elevation is 338 feet.

Population: 4,292; Growth (since 2000): n/a; Density: 462.6 persons per square mile; Race: 81.0% White, 8.8% Black/African American, 0.3% Asian, 0.6% American Indian/Alaska Native, 0.0% Native Hawaiian/Other Pacific Islander, 2.1% Two or more races, 12.2% Hispanic of any race;

Average household size: 2.89; Median age: 34.1; Age under 18: 30.9%; Age 65 and over: 5.4%; Males per 100 females: 97.0; Marriage status: 24.8% never married, 67.2% now married, 2.8% separated, 1.0% widowed, 7.0% divorced; Foreign born: 10.1%; Speak English only: 82.4%; With disability: 6.9%; Veterans: 10.6%; Ancestry: 15.0% Irish, 12.0% German, 11.5% English, 11.4% American, 3.8% Scotch-Irish

Employment: 15.4% management, business, and financial, 5.3% computer, engineering, and science, 11.2% education, legal, community service, arts, and media, 5.4% healthcare practitioners, 17.8% service, 17.4% sales and office, 13.1% natural resources, construction, and maintenance, 14.5% production, transportation, and material moving

Income: Per capita: $27,375; Median household: $68,154; Average household: $77,599; Households with income of $100,000 or more: 31.7%; Poverty rate: 5.8%

Educational Attainment: High school diploma or higher: 89.0%; Bachelor's degree or higher: 22.1%; Graduate/professional degree or higher: 3.6%

Housing: Homeownership rate: 87.2%; Median home value: $149,400; Median year structure built: 1996; Homeowner vacancy rate: 1.4%; Median gross rent: $724 per month; Rental vacancy rate: 2.5%

Health Insurance: 80.7% have insurance; 72.9% have private insurance; 13.2% have public insurance; 19.3% do not have insurance; 6.2% of children under 18 do not have insurance

Transportation: Commute: 91.8% car, 1.0% public transportation, 0.0% walk, 6.2% work from home; Median travel time to work: 30.0 minutes

BENSON (town).
Covers a land area of 2.785 square miles and a water area of 0.005 square miles. Located at 35.39° N. Lat; 78.54° W. Long. Elevation is 243 feet.

History: Settled 1779; incorporated 1887.

Population: 3,311; Growth (since 2000): 13.3%; Density: 1,189.0 persons per square mile; Race: 60.2% White, 26.6% Black/African American, 0.5% Asian, 0.4% American Indian/Alaska Native, 0.0% Native Hawaiian/Other Pacific Islander, 2.3% Two or more races, 14.0% Hispanic of any race; Average household size: 2.42; Median age: 37.9; Age under 18: 25.7%; Age 65 and over: 17.5%; Males per 100 females: 82.7; Marriage status: 36.1% never married, 41.7% now married, 6.2% separated, 9.2% widowed, 12.9% divorced; Foreign born: 9.2%; Speak English only: 77.5%; With disability: 16.9%; Veterans: 9.5%; Ancestry: 12.4% American, 4.8% English, 4.5% Scotch-Irish, 3.1% Scottish, 2.3% African

Employment: 10.6% management, business, and financial, 0.0% computer, engineering, and science, 21.6% education, legal, community service, arts, and media, 4.9% healthcare practitioners, 24.5% service, 14.7% sales and office, 12.5% natural resources, construction, and maintenance, 11.2% production, transportation, and material moving

Income: Per capita: $16,027; Median household: $23,750; Average household: $42,341; Households with income of $100,000 or more: 5.5%; Poverty rate: 46.3%

Educational Attainment: High school diploma or higher: 71.2%; Bachelor's degree or higher: 23.1%; Graduate/professional degree or higher: 5.4%

School District(s)
Johnston County Schools (PK-12)
  2012-13 Enrollment: 33,711 . . . . (919) 934-6031
Housing: Homeownership rate: 47.3%; Median home value: $105,600; Median year structure built: 1972; Homeowner vacancy rate: 5.6%; Median gross rent: $513 per month; Rental vacancy rate: 13.0%

Health Insurance: 75.2% have insurance; 39.0% have private insurance; 49.3% have public insurance; 24.8% do not have insurance; 4.0% of children under 18 do not have insurance

Safety: Violent crime rate: 86.9 per 10,000 population; Property crime rate: 576.5 per 10,000 population

Newspapers: News in Review (weekly circulation 4500)

Transportation: Commute: 95.9% car, 0.0% public transportation, 1.8% walk, 2.3% work from home; Median travel time to work: 20.8 minutes

Additional Information Contacts
Town of Benson . . . . (919) 894-3553
  http://www.townofbenson.com

CLAYTON (town).
Covers a land area of 13.511 square miles and a water area of 0.022 square miles. Located at 35.67° N. Long. Elevation is 341 feet.

History: Atkinson's Mill, established 1757, to East.

Population: 16,116; Growth (since 2000): 131.1%; Density: 1,192.8 persons per square mile; Race: 69.5% White, 21.8% Black/African

American, 1.4% Asian, 0.4% American Indian/Alaska Native, 0.0% Native Hawaiian/Other Pacific Islander, 2.1% Two or more races, 10.7% Hispanic of any race; Average household size: 2.65; Median age: 33.4; Age under 18: 30.9%; Age 65 and over: 8.5%; Males per 100 females: 90.6; Marriage status: 24.6% never married, 56.3% now married, 4.0% separated, 6.4% widowed, 12.7% divorced; Foreign born: 5.5%; Speak English only: 90.9%; With disability: 8.7%; Veterans: 10.0%; Ancestry: 13.5% German, 12.6% English, 10.2% Irish, 10.1% American, 4.5% Italian
Employment: 14.1% management, business, and financial, 7.3% computer, engineering, and science, 14.2% education, legal, community service, arts, and media, 6.8% healthcare practitioners, 11.1% service, 25.8% sales and office, 12.3% natural resources, construction, and maintenance, 8.5% production, transportation, and material moving
Income: Per capita: $26,985; Median household: $57,456; Average household: $69,552; Households with income of $100,000 or more: 19.7%; Poverty rate: 12.4%
Educational Attainment: High school diploma or higher: 92.1%; Bachelor's degree or higher: 31.3%; Graduate/professional degree or higher: 8.1%

School District(s)
Johnston County Schools (PK-12)
    2012-13 Enrollment: 33,711 . . . . (919) 934-6031
Housing: Homeownership rate: 65.5%; Median home value: $152,600; Median year structure built: 2000; Homeowner vacancy rate: 4.6%; Median gross rent: $971 per month; Rental vacancy rate: 9.8%
Health Insurance: 85.8% have insurance; 74.6% have private insurance; 18.6% have public insurance; 14.2% do not have insurance; 8.2% of children under 18 do not have insurance
Safety: Violent crime rate: 16.2 per 10,000 population; Property crime rate: 238.5 per 10,000 population
Newspapers: Clayton News-Star (weekly circulation 5200)
Transportation: Commute: 97.8% car, 0.0% public transportation, 0.2% walk, 1.9% work from home; Median travel time to work: 28.4 minutes
Additional Information Contacts
Town of Clayton . . . . (919) 553-6352
    http://townofclaytonnc.org

FOUR OAKS (town).
Covers a land area of 1.623 square miles and a water area of 0.007 square miles. Located at 35.45° N. Lat; 78.42° W. Long. Elevation is 197 feet.
Population: 1,921; Growth (since 2000): 34.9%; Density: 1,183.6 persons per square mile; Race: 69.8% White, 17.5% Black/African American, 0.2% Asian, 0.9% American Indian/Alaska Native, 0.0% Native Hawaiian/Other Pacific Islander, 3.0% Two or more races, 14.1% Hispanic of any race; Average household size: 2.37; Median age: 37.6; Age under 18: 26.2%; Age 65 and over: 14.8%; Males per 100 females: 87.6

School District(s)
Johnston County Schools (PK-12)
    2012-13 Enrollment: 33,711 . . . . (919) 934-6031
Housing: Homeownership rate: 54.4%; Homeowner vacancy rate: 3.1%; Rental vacancy rate: 6.1%

KENLY (town).
Covers a land area of 1.617 square miles and a water area of 0.003 square miles. Located at 35.60° N. Lat; 78.13° W. Long. Elevation is 194 feet.
History: Tobacco Farm Life Museum of North Carolina is here.
Population: 1,339; Growth (since 2000): -14.7%; Density: 827.9 persons per square mile; Race: 58.5% White, 35.3% Black/African American, 0.7% Asian, 0.7% American Indian/Alaska Native, 0.0% Native Hawaiian/Other Pacific Islander, 0.8% Two or more races, 8.1% Hispanic of any race; Average household size: 2.35; Median age: 41.0; Age under 18: 23.7%; Age 65 and over: 16.2%; Males per 100 females: 89.9

School District(s)
Johnston County Schools (PK-12)
    2012-13 Enrollment: 33,711 . . . . (919) 934-6031
Housing: Homeownership rate: 49.4%; Homeowner vacancy rate: 2.4%; Rental vacancy rate: 19.8%
Newspapers: Kenly News (weekly circulation 3000)

MICRO (town).
Covers a land area of 0.384 square miles and a water area of 0 square miles. Located at 35.56° N. Lat; 78.20° W. Long. Elevation is 187 feet.
Population: 441; Growth (since 2000): -2.9%; Density: 1,147.3 persons per square mile; Race: 78.2% White, 12.5% Black/African American, 0.2% Asian, 0.0% American Indian/Alaska Native, 0.0% Native Hawaiian/Other

Pacific Islander, 0.7% Two or more races, 9.5% Hispanic of any race; Average household size: 2.35; Median age: 37.6; Age under 18: 27.2%; Age 65 and over: 23.8%; Males per 100 females: 76.4

School District(s)
Johnston County Schools (PK-12)
    2012-13 Enrollment: 33,711 . . . . (919) 934-6031
Housing: Homeownership rate: 51.1%; Homeowner vacancy rate: 3.0%; Rental vacancy rate: 7.1%

PINE LEVEL (town).
Covers a land area of 1.632 square miles and a water area of 0 square miles. Located at 35.50° N. Lat; 78.25° W. Long. Elevation is 167 feet.
Population: 1,700; Growth (since 2000): 29.5%; Density: 1,041.7 persons per square mile; Race: 73.2% White, 15.2% Black/African American, 0.1% Asian, 0.7% American Indian/Alaska Native, 0.0% Native Hawaiian/Other Pacific Islander, 1.6% Two or more races, 12.9% Hispanic of any race; Average household size: 2.43; Median age: 35.8; Age under 18: 26.9%; Age 65 and over: 13.1%; Males per 100 females: 87.6

School District(s)
Johnston County Schools (PK-12)
    2012-13 Enrollment: 33,711 . . . . (919) 934-6031
Housing: Homeownership rate: 63.7%; Homeowner vacancy rate: 1.8%; Rental vacancy rate: 8.6%

PRINCETON (town).
Covers a land area of 1.036 square miles and a water area of 0 square miles. Located at 35.47° N. Lat; 78.16° W. Long. Elevation is 151 feet.
History: Princeton was incorporated in 1873, when its name was changed from Boone Level.
Population: 1,194; Growth (since 2000): 12.0%; Density: 1,152.3 persons per square mile; Race: 67.2% White, 25.5% Black/African American, 0.9% Asian, 0.8% American Indian/Alaska Native, 0.0% Native Hawaiian/Other Pacific Islander, 1.7% Two or more races, 5.9% Hispanic of any race; Average household size: 2.38; Median age: 38.4; Age under 18: 26.0%; Age 65 and over: 17.3%; Males per 100 females: 76.6

School District(s)
Johnston County Schools (PK-12)
    2012-13 Enrollment: 33,711 . . . . (919) 934-6031
Housing: Homeownership rate: 51.4%; Homeowner vacancy rate: 2.6%; Rental vacancy rate: 6.8%
Newspapers: News Leader (weekly circulation 1800)

SELMA (town).
Covers a land area of 4.848 square miles and a water area of <.001 square miles. Located at 35.54° N. Lat; 78.29° W. Long. Elevation is 174 feet.
Population: 6,073; Growth (since 2000): 2.7%; Density: 1,252.8 persons per square mile; Race: 38.8% White, 37.2% Black/African American, 0.2% Asian, 0.5% American Indian/Alaska Native, 0.1% Native Hawaiian/Other Pacific Islander, 2.9% Two or more races, 34.8% Hispanic of any race; Average household size: 2.74; Median age: 31.8; Age under 18: 29.8%; Age 65 and over: 10.6%; Males per 100 females: 92.9; Marriage status: 41.0% never married, 37.2% now married, 6.1% separated, 7.3% widowed, 14.5% divorced; Foreign born: 30.5%; Speak English only: 61.3%; With disability: 16.8%; Veterans: 8.0%; Ancestry: 8.7% American, 4.0% English, 3.1% German, 1.7% Italian, 1.4% African
Employment: 2.8% management, business, and financial, 0.0% computer, engineering, and science, 10.1% education, legal, community service, arts, and media, 2.0% healthcare practitioners, 25.9% service, 15.8% sales and office, 26.9% natural resources, construction, and maintenance, 16.6% production, transportation, and material moving
Income: Per capita: $11,836; Median household: $19,793; Average household: $27,873; Households with income of $100,000 or more: 1.1%; Poverty rate: 43.8%
Educational Attainment: High school diploma or higher: 64.0%; Bachelor's degree or higher: 7.7%; Graduate/professional degree or higher: 2.8%

School District(s)
Johnston County Schools (PK-12)
    2012-13 Enrollment: 33,711 . . . . (919) 934-6031
Neuse Charter School (KG-08)
    2012-13 Enrollment: 647 . . . . (919) 938-1077
Housing: Homeownership rate: 38.8%; Median home value: $79,500; Median year structure built: 1974; Homeowner vacancy rate: 4.4%; Median gross rent: $683 per month; Rental vacancy rate: 16.3%

Health Insurance: 63.8% have insurance; 26.8% have private insurance; 46.3% have public insurance; 36.2% do not have insurance; 15.7% of children under 18 do not have insurance
Safety: Violent crime rate: 61.1 per 10,000 population; Property crime rate: 466.5 per 10,000 population
Newspapers: Selma News (weekly circulation 5000)
Transportation: Commute: 85.0% car, 0.4% public transportation, 0.6% walk, 2.7% work from home; Median travel time to work: 36.5 minutes; Amtrak: Train service available.
Additional Information Contacts
Town of Selma . . . . (919) 965-9841
    http://www.selma-nc.com

SMITHFIELD (town). County seat. Covers a land area of 12.121 square miles and a water area of 0.014 square miles. Located at 35.52° N. Lat; 78.35° W. Long. Elevation is 148 feet.
History: Founded in 1770, Smithfield was named for Colonel John Smith (1687-1777), an early settler from Virginia who was a delegate to the Halifax convention and who owned the land on which the town was built.
Population: 10,966; Growth (since 2000): -4.7%; Density: 904.7 persons per square mile; Race: 56.9% White, 27.2% Black/African American, 0.8% Asian, 0.5% American Indian/Alaska Native, 0.1% Native Hawaiian/Other Pacific Islander, 1.9% Two or more races, 19.3% Hispanic of any race; Average household size: 2.35; Median age: 41.6; Age under 18: 22.5%; Age 65 and over: 20.8%; Males per 100 females: 86.3; Marriage status: 27.3% never married, 45.7% now married, 5.3% separated, 13.5% widowed, 13.5% divorced; Foreign born: 7.3%; Speak English only: 88.2%; With disability: 19.9%; Veterans: 8.1%; Ancestry: 21.0% American, 12.4% English, 4.9% Irish, 2.4% German, 2.2% Scotch-Irish
Employment: 12.6% management, business, and financial, 2.0% computer, engineering, and science, 9.7% education, legal, community service, arts, and media, 4.7% healthcare practitioners, 19.9% service, 20.8% sales and office, 11.7% natural resources, construction, and maintenance, 18.6% production, transportation, and material moving
Income: Per capita: $18,647; Median household: $31,947; Average household: $46,313; Households with income of $100,000 or more: 10.3%; Poverty rate: 28.4%
Educational Attainment: High school diploma or higher: 77.0%; Bachelor's degree or higher: 19.4%; Graduate/professional degree or higher: 6.4%

School District(s)

Johnston County Schools (PK-12)
    2012-13 Enrollment: 33,711 . . . . (919) 934-6031

Two-year College(s)

Johnston Community College (Public)
    Fall 2013 Enrollment: 4,235 . . . . (919) 934-3051
    2013-14 Tuition: In-state $2,385; Out-of-state $8,529
Housing: Homeownership rate: 51.2%; Median home value: $133,100; Median year structure built: 1972; Homeowner vacancy rate: 2.7%; Median gross rent: $694 per month; Rental vacancy rate: 8.5%
Health Insurance: 81.2% have insurance; 47.3% have private insurance; 48.3% have public insurance; 18.8% do not have insurance; 4.1% of children under 18 do not have insurance
Hospitals: Johnston Memorial Hospital (175 beds)
Safety: Violent crime rate: 62.0 per 10,000 population; Property crime rate: 586.0 per 10,000 population
Newspapers: The Herald (weekly circulation 36500)
Transportation: Commute: 94.0% car, 0.1% public transportation, 0.7% walk, 2.9% work from home; Median travel time to work: 22.5 minutes
Additional Information Contacts
Town of Smithfield. . . . . (919) 934-2116
    http://www.smithfield-nc.com

WILSON'S MILLS (town). Covers a land area of 4.504 square miles and a water area of 0.007 square miles. Located at 35.59° N. Lat; 78.36° W. Long. Elevation is 230 feet.
Population: 2,277; Growth (since 2000): 76.4%; Density: 505.5 persons per square mile; Race: 57.0% White, 30.7% Black/African American, 0.4% Asian, 0.7% American Indian/Alaska Native, 0.0% Native Hawaiian/Other Pacific Islander, 2.2% Two or more races, 18.7% Hispanic of any race; Average household size: 3.03; Median age: 30.4; Age under 18: 32.7%; Age 65 and over: 6.3%; Males per 100 females: 94.4

School District(s)

Johnston County Schools (PK-12)
    2012-13 Enrollment: 33,711 . . . . (919) 934-6031

Housing: Homeownership rate: 71.6%; Homeowner vacancy rate: 2.9%; Rental vacancy rate: 7.3%
Safety: Violent crime rate: 12.6 per 10,000 population; Property crime rate: 134.8 per 10,000 population

Jones County

Located in eastern North Carolina; tidewater area, drained by the Trent River; includes part of Croatan National Forest and Whiteoak Swamp. Covers a land area of 470.708 square miles, a water area of 2.507 square miles, and is located in the Eastern Time Zone at 35.03° N. Lat., 77.36° W. Long. The county was founded in 1778. County seat is Trenton.

Jones County is part of the New Bern, NC Metropolitan Statistical Area. The entire metro area includes: Craven County, NC; Jones County, NC; Pamlico County, NC

Population: 10,153; Growth (since 2000): -2.2%; Density: 21.6 persons per square mile; Race: 63.0% White, 32.4% Black/African American, 0.3% Asian, 0.6% American Indian/Alaska Native, 0.0% Native Hawaiian/Other Pacific Islander, 1.9% two or more races, 3.9% Hispanic of any race; Average household size: 2.41; Median age: 44.1; Age under 18: 21.7%; Age 65 and over: 17.3%; Males per 100 females: 92.7; Marriage status: 25.5% never married, 53.0% now married, 4.1% separated, 9.3% widowed, 12.2% divorced; Foreign born: 4.0%; Speak English only: 94.9%; With disability: 24.6%; Veterans: 13.3%; Ancestry: 14.2% English, 10.8% Irish, 10.5% American, 9.2% German, 2.4% French
Religion: Six largest groups: 13.6% Methodist/Pietist, 13.6% Baptist, 7.5% Non-denominational Protestant, 1.8% Pentecostal, 1.5% Presbyterian-Reformed, 0.1% Episcopalianism/Anglicanism
Economy: Unemployment rate: 6.7%; Leading industries: 19.0% retail trade; 16.8% construction; 10.9% health care and social assistance; Farms: 170 totaling 59,367 acres; Company size: 0 employ 1,000 or more persons, 0 employ 500 to 999 persons, 0 employ 100 to 499 persons, 137 employ less than 100 persons; Business ownership: n/a women-owned, n/a Black-owned, n/a Hispanic-owned, n/a Asian-owned
Employment: 10.6% management, business, and financial, 2.1% computer, engineering, and science, 12.1% education, legal, community service, arts, and media, 3.5% healthcare practitioners, 19.5% service, 19.2% sales and office, 15.3% natural resources, construction, and maintenance, 17.6% production, transportation, and material moving
Income: Per capita: $20,105; Median household: $36,213; Average household: $47,031; Households with income of $100,000 or more: 9.3%; Poverty rate: 16.7%
Educational Attainment: High school diploma or higher: 83.8%; Bachelor's degree or higher: 11.1%; Graduate/professional degree or higher: 3.9%
Housing: Homeownership rate: 74.9%; Median home value: $97,600; Median year structure built: 1980; Homeowner vacancy rate: 1.8%; Median gross rent: $637 per month; Rental vacancy rate: 8.0%
Vital Statistics: Birth rate: 106.7 per 10,000 population; Death rate: 118.5 per 10,000 population; Age-adjusted cancer mortality rate: 254.3 deaths per 100,000 population
Health Insurance: 82.1% have insurance; 56.2% have private insurance; 42.6% have public insurance; 17.9% do not have insurance; 4.7% of children under 18 do not have insurance
Health Care: Physicians: 9.7 per 10,000 population; Hospital beds: 0.0 per 10,000 population; Hospital admissions: 0.0 per 10,000 population
Transportation: Commute: 88.5% car, 0.9% public transportation, 3.2% walk, 4.7% work from home; Median travel time to work: 26.8 minutes
Presidential Election: 45.0% Obama, 54.2% Romney (2012)
Additional Information Contacts
Jones Government . . . . (252) 448-1315
    http://www.co.jones.nc.us

Jones County Communities

MAYSVILLE (town). Covers a land area of 0.701 square miles and a water area of 0 square miles. Located at 34.90° N. Lat; 77.23° W. Long. Elevation is 39 feet.
Population: 1,019; Growth (since 2000): 1.7%; Density: 1,453.6 persons per square mile; Race: 45.2% White, 48.8% Black/African American, 0.7% Asian, 0.7% American Indian/Alaska Native, 0.0% Native Hawaiian/Other Pacific Islander, 3.3% Two or more races, 4.7% Hispanic of any race;

Average household size: 2.48; Median age: 32.1; Age under 18: 25.1%; Age 65 and over: 11.3%; Males per 100 females: 90.5

School District(s)

Jones County Schools (PK-12)

    2012-13 Enrollment: 1,232 . . . . (252) 448-2531

Onslow County Schools (PK-12)

    2012-13 Enrollment: 25,533 . . . . (910) 455-2211

Housing: Homeownership rate: 64.3%; Homeowner vacancy rate: 4.0%; Rental vacancy rate: 5.8%

POLLOCKSVILLE (town). Covers a land area of 0.302 square miles and a water area of 0.014 square miles. Located at 35.01° N. Lat; 77.22° W. Long. Elevation is 16 feet.

History: Pollocksville was named for Colonel Thomas Pollock, a major landowner and proprietary governor of North Carolina (1712-1714, 1722). In Colonial days the town was surrounded by plantations.

Population: 311; Growth (since 2000): 15.6%; Density: 1,030.9 persons per square mile; Race: 68.5% White, 28.6% Black/African American, 0.0% Asian, 1.3% American Indian/Alaska Native, 0.0% Native Hawaiian/Other Pacific Islander, 1.0% Two or more races, 1.0% Hispanic of any race; Average household size: 2.24; Median age: 45.3; Age under 18: 22.2%; Age 65 and over: 20.9%; Males per 100 females: 80.8

School District(s)

Jones County Schools (PK-12)

    2012-13 Enrollment: 1,232 . . . . (252) 448-2531

Housing: Homeownership rate: 63.3%; Homeowner vacancy rate: 4.3%; Rental vacancy rate: 12.1%

TRENTON (town). County seat. Covers a land area of 0.216 square miles and a water area of 0.002 square miles. Located at 35.06° N. Lat; 77.36° W. Long. Elevation is 13 feet.

History: Trenton was built around Brock Mill Pond. The mill began operation before the Civil War.

Population: 287; Growth (since 2000): 39.3%; Density: 1,331.4 persons per square mile; Race: 51.9% White, 36.6% Black/African American, 0.0% Asian, 1.0% American Indian/Alaska Native, 0.0% Native Hawaiian/Other Pacific Islander, 5.9% Two or more races, 7.0% Hispanic of any race; Average household size: 2.43; Median age: 44.4; Age under 18: 21.6%; Age 65 and over: 21.3%; Males per 100 females: 115.8

School District(s)

Jones County Schools (PK-12)

    2012-13 Enrollment: 1,232 . . . . (252) 448-2531

Housing: Homeownership rate: 80.1%; Homeowner vacancy rate: 6.3%; Rental vacancy rate: 11.1%

Lee County

Located in central North Carolina; piedmont and sand-hill area, bounded on the north by Cape Fear and Deep Rivers. Covers a land area of 254.959 square miles, a water area of 4.084 square miles, and is located in the Eastern Time Zone at 35.48° N. Lat., 79.17° W. Long. The county was founded in 1907. County seat is Sanford.

Lee County is part of the Sanford, NC Micropolitan Statistical Area. The entire metro area includes: Lee County, NC

Weather Station: Sanford 8 NE										Elevation: 262 feet	
	Jan	Feb	Mar	Apr	May	Jun	Jul	Aug	Sep	Oct	Nov	Dec
High	53	57	66	75	81	88	91	89	83	74	64	55
Low	29	32	38	45	54	63	67	66	59	47	38	31
Precip	3.8	3.4	4.1	2.9	3.5	4.7	5.0	4.6	4.2	3.7	3.3	3.0
Snow	1.3	0.5	0.4	tr	0.0	0.0	0.0	0.0	0.0	0.0	tr	0.2

High and Low temperatures in degrees Fahrenheit; Precipitation and Snow in inches

Population: 57,866; Growth (since 2000): 18.0%; Density: 227.0 persons per square mile; Race: 66.9% White, 20.0% Black/African American, 0.8% Asian, 0.7% American Indian/Alaska Native, 0.0% Native Hawaiian/Other Pacific Islander, 2.4% two or more races, 18.3% Hispanic of any race; Average household size: 2.58; Median age: 37.4; Age under 18: 25.7%; Age 65 and over: 13.7%; Males per 100 females: 95.5; Marriage status: 30.0% never married, 52.4% now married, 2.7% separated, 7.4% widowed, 10.2% divorced; Foreign born: 11.3%; Speak English only: 81.7%; With disability: 14.0%; Veterans: 10.9%; Ancestry: 10.9% American, 10.0% English, 7.7% German, 7.0% Irish, 3.3% Scotch-Irish

Religion: Six largest groups: 14.1% Baptist, 11.6% Methodist/Pietist, 9.4% Non-denominational Protestant, 5.9% Catholicism, 5.2% Presbyterian-Reformed, 2.5% Pentecostal

Economy: Unemployment rate: 7.5%; Leading industries: 18.5% retail trade; 12.6% health care and social assistance; 12.3% other services (except public administration); Farms: 246 totaling 39,081 acres; Company size: 2 employ 1,000 or more persons, 6 employ 500 to 999 persons, 29 employ 100 to 499 persons, 1,228 employ less than 100 persons; Business ownership: 1,090 women-owned, 390 Black-owned, n/a Hispanic-owned, 63 Asian-owned

Employment: 10.9% management, business, and financial; 3.9% computer, engineering, and science, 9.6% education, legal, community service, arts, and media, 4.3% healthcare practitioners, 18.5% service, 23.6% sales and office, 10.3% natural resources, construction, and maintenance, 18.9% production, transportation, and material moving

Income: Per capita: $21,449; Median household: $44,819; Average household: $56,700; Households with income of $100,000 or more: 13.5%; Poverty rate: 18.9%

Educational Attainment: High school diploma or higher: 80.2%; Bachelor's degree or higher: 20.2%; Graduate/professional degree or higher: 5.5%

Housing: Homeownership rate: 66.6%; Median home value: $131,300; Median year structure built: 1983; Homeowner vacancy rate: 2.7%; Median gross rent: $686 per month; Rental vacancy rate: 8.3%

Vital Statistics: Birth rate: 138.4 per 10,000 population; Death rate: 82.0 per 10,000 population; Age-adjusted cancer mortality rate: 222.4 deaths per 100,000 population

Health Insurance: 81.0% have insurance; 60.9% have private insurance; 32.1% have public insurance; 19.0% do not have insurance; 6.9% of children under 18 do not have insurance

Health Care: Physicians: 12.9 per 10,000 population; Hospital beds: 19.8 per 10,000 population; Hospital admissions: 929.2 per 10,000 population

Air Quality Index: 100.0% good, 0.0% moderate, 0.0% unhealthy for sensitive individuals, 0.0% unhealthy (percent of days)

Transportation: Commute: 95.1% car, 0.2% public transportation, 0.9% walk, 2.4% work from home; Median travel time to work: 23.4 minutes

Presidential Election: 44.6% Obama, 54.3% Romney (2012)

Additional Information Contacts

Lee Government . . . . (919) 718-4600

    http://www.leecountync.gov

Lee County Communities

BROADWAY (town). Covers a land area of 1.295 square miles and a water area of 0.034 square miles. Located at 35.46° N. Lat; 79.05° W. Long. Elevation is 472 feet.

Population: 1,229; Growth (since 2000): 21.1%; Density: 948.9 persons per square mile; Race: 78.8% White, 10.2% Black/African American, 1.1% Asian, 1.4% American Indian/Alaska Native, 0.1% Native Hawaiian/Other Pacific Islander, 1.7% Two or more races, 9.9% Hispanic of any race; Average household size: 2.45; Median age: 43.3; Age under 18: 22.9%; Age 65 and over: 18.2%; Males per 100 females: 85.4

School District(s)

Lee County Schools (PK-12)

    2012-13 Enrollment: 9,994 . . . . (919) 774-6226

Housing: Homeownership rate: 80.0%; Homeowner vacancy rate: 2.7%; Rental vacancy rate: 3.8%

SANFORD (city). County seat. Covers a land area of 26.786 square miles and a water area of 0.254 square miles. Located at 35.48° N. Lat; 79.18° W. Long. Elevation is 358 feet.

History: Incorporated 1874.

Population: 28,094; Growth (since 2000): 21.0%; Density: 1,048.8 persons per square mile; Race: 55.2% White, 27.6% Black/African American, 1.1% Asian, 0.8% American Indian/Alaska Native, 0.0% Native Hawaiian/Other Pacific Islander, 2.8% Two or more races, 25.6% Hispanic of any race; Average household size: 2.60; Median age: 33.3; Age under 18: 28.0%; Age 65 and over: 11.7%; Males per 100 females: 94.2; Marriage status: 35.3% never married, 46.8% now married, 3.4% separated, 8.0% widowed, 9.9% divorced; Foreign born: 14.5%; Speak English only: 76.7%; With disability: 14.0%; Veterans: 9.5%; Ancestry: 8.9% American, 8.7% English, 6.9% German, 6.0% Irish, 2.9% Scotch-Irish

Employment: 11.4% management, business, and financial; 3.8% computer, engineering, and science, 9.6% education, legal, community

service, arts, and media, 4.8% healthcare practitioners, 19.9% service, 22.8% sales and office, 9.1% natural resources, construction, and maintenance, 18.5% production, transportation, and material moving
Income: Per capita: $20,497; Median household: $43,234; Average household: $55,844; Households with income of $100,000 or more: 14.9%; Poverty rate: 22.9%
Educational Attainment: High school diploma or higher: 75.5%; Bachelor's degree or higher: 22.2%; Graduate/professional degree or higher: 6.4%

School District(s)
Harnett County Schools (PK-12)
   2012-13 Enrollment: 20,569 . . . . (910) 893-8151
Lee County Schools (PK-12)
   2012-13 Enrollment: 9,994 . . . . (919) 774-6226

Two-year College(s)
Central Carolina Community College (Public)
   Fall 2013 Enrollment: 4,728 . . . . (919) 775-5401
   2013-14 Tuition: In-state $2,216; Out-of-state $8,360
Housing: Homeownership rate: 52.6%; Median home value: $138,100; Median year structure built: 1978; Homeowner vacancy rate: 3.3%; Median gross rent: $673 per month; Rental vacancy rate: 7.8%
Health Insurance: 78.3% have insurance; 55.4% have private insurance; 33.3% have public insurance; 21.7% do not have insurance; 6.9% of children under 18 do not have insurance
Hospitals: Central Carolina Hospital (137 beds)
Newspapers: Sanford Herald (daily circulation 9200)
Transportation: Commute: 94.5% car, 0.3% public transportation, 1.5% walk, 1.4% work from home; Median travel time to work: 22.5 minutes
Airports: Raleigh Exec Jetport at Sanford-Lee County (general aviation)
Additional Information Contacts
City of Sanford. . . . . (919) 775-8202
   http://www.sanfordnc.net

Lenoir County

Located in east central North Carolina; coastal plains area, drained by the Neuse River. Covers a land area of 400.591 square miles, a water area of 2.227 square miles, and is located in the Eastern Time Zone at 35.24° N. Lat., 77.64° W. Long. The county was founded in 1791. County seat is Kinston.

Lenoir County is part of the Kinston, NC Micropolitan Statistical Area. The entire metro area includes: Lenoir County, NC

Weather Station: Kinston 5 SE										Elevation: 55 feet		
	Jan	Feb	Mar	Apr	May	Jun	Jul	Aug	Sep	Oct	Nov	Dec
High	53	56	64	73	80	87	90	88	83	74	65	56
Low	31	33	39	47	56	64	68	67	61	49	41	33
Precip	3.8	3.3	4.0	3.4	3.9	5.1	5.8	5.5	5.2	3.5	3.2	3.5
Snow	0.4	0.5	0.6	0.0	0.0	0.0	0.0	0.0	0.0	0.0	tr	0.3

High and Low temperatures in degrees Fahrenheit; Precipitation and Snow in inches

Weather Station: Kinston Ag Research										Elevation: 60 feet		
	Jan	Feb	Mar	Apr	May	Jun	Jul	Aug	Sep	Oct	Nov	Dec
High	55	59	67	75	82	88	91	89	84	76	68	58
Low	34	36	42	49	58	66	70	69	63	52	44	37
Precip	3.7	3.2	3.9	3.2	3.7	4.8	5.5	5.1	5.5	3.3	3.1	3.1
Snow	0.1	tr	0.2	0.0	0.0	0.0	0.0	0.0	0.0	0.0	0.0	0.3

High and Low temperatures in degrees Fahrenheit; Precipitation and Snow in inches

Population: 59,495; Growth (since 2000): -0.3%; Density: 148.5 persons per square mile; Race: 53.4% White, 40.5% Black/African American, 0.4% Asian, 0.4% American Indian/Alaska Native, 0.1% Native Hawaiian/Other Pacific Islander, 1.3% two or more races, 6.6% Hispanic of any race; Average household size: 2.39; Median age: 41.0; Age under 18: 24.1%; Age 65 and over: 16.0%; Males per 100 females: 91.3; Marriage status: 30.8% never married, 49.1% now married, 5.3% separated, 9.1% widowed, 11.0% divorced; Foreign born: 3.7%; Speak English only: 93.3%; With disability: 20.5%; Veterans: 9.7%; Ancestry: 12.4% American, 10.6% English, 7.1% Irish, 6.0% African, 4.6% German
Religion: Six largest groups: 19.5% Baptist, 12.8% Non-denominational Protestant, 7.9% Methodist/Pietist, 5.9% Pentecostal, 2.5% Latter-day Saints, 2.1% Buddhism
Economy: Unemployment rate: 6.5%; Leading industries: 19.2% retail trade; 13.8% health care and social assistance; 11.9% other services (except public administration); Farms: 401 totaling 122,104 acres;

Company size: 1 employs 1,000 or more persons, 3 employ 500 to 999 persons, 26 employ 100 to 499 persons, 1,234 employ less than 100 persons; Business ownership: 959 women-owned, n/a Black-owned, n/a Hispanic-owned, n/a Asian-owned
Employment: 10.7% management, business, and financial, 2.8% computer, engineering, and science, 8.9% education, legal, community service, arts, and media, 5.0% healthcare practitioners, 22.5% service, 19.8% sales and office, 12.3% natural resources, construction, and maintenance, 18.0% production, transportation, and material moving
Income: Per capita: $19,760; Median household: $35,770; Average household: $47,589; Households with income of $100,000 or more: 8.9%; Poverty rate: 23.7%
Educational Attainment: High school diploma or higher: 79.0%; Bachelor's degree or higher: 14.0%; Graduate/professional degree or higher: 4.0%
Housing: Homeownership rate: 62.3%; Median home value: $94,200; Median year structure built: 1974; Homeowner vacancy rate: 2.3%; Median gross rent: $642 per month; Rental vacancy rate: 9.7%
Vital Statistics: Birth rate: 110.5 per 10,000 population; Death rate: 123.4 per 10,000 population; Age-adjusted cancer mortality rate: 184.7 deaths per 100,000 population
Health Insurance: 81.0% have insurance; 52.6% have private insurance; 42.2% have public insurance; 19.0% do not have insurance; 6.7% of children under 18 do not have insurance
Health Care: Physicians: 13.0 per 10,000 population; Hospital beds: 176.1 per 10,000 population; Hospital admissions: 1,327.6 per 10,000 population
Air Quality Index: 93.1% good, 6.9% moderate, 0.0% unhealthy for sensitive individuals, 0.0% unhealthy (percent of days)
Transportation: Commute: 94.1% car, 1.0% public transportation, 2.0% walk, 2.5% work from home; Median travel time to work: 22.1 minutes
Presidential Election: 49.0% Obama, 50.5% Romney (2012)
National and State Parks: Caswell-Newse State Historic Site
Additional Information Contacts
Lenoir Government . . . . (252) 559-6450
   http://www.co.lenoir.nc.us

Lenoir County Communities

DEEP RUN (unincorporated postal area)
ZCTA: 28525
   Covers a land area of 44.422 square miles and a water area of 0.165 square miles. Located at 35.13° N. Lat; 77.69° W. Long. Elevation is 102 feet.
   Population: 3,132; Growth (since 2000): 3.9%; Density: 70.5 persons per square mile; Race: 80.5% White, 8.6% Black/African American, 0.1% Asian, 0.8% American Indian/Alaska Native, 0.2% Native Hawaiian/Other Pacific Islander, 1.8% Two or more races, 12.4% Hispanic of any race; Average household size: 2.65; Median age: 38.6; Age under 18: 23.9%; Age 65 and over: 13.4%; Males per 100 females: 97.6; Marriage status: 21.0% never married, 66.7% now married, 3.4% separated, 4.2% widowed, 8.1% divorced; Foreign born: 2.6%; Speak English only: 89.9%; With disability: 20.2%; Veterans: 9.1%; Ancestry: 19.3% American, 17.0% English, 8.5% German, 5.6% Irish, 4.9% Italian
   Employment: 9.3% management, business, and financial, 3.3% computer, engineering, and science, 9.1% education, legal, community service, arts, and media, 8.8% healthcare practitioners, 22.1% service, 19.6% sales and office, 20.1% natural resources, construction, and maintenance, 7.7% production, transportation, and material moving
   Income: Per capita: $19,670; Median household: $54,227; Average household: $55,156; Households with income of $100,000 or more: 10.0%; Poverty rate: 19.9%
   Educational Attainment: High school diploma or higher: 75.2%; Bachelor's degree or higher: 9.0%; Graduate/professional degree or higher: 2.8%

School District(s)
Lenoir County Public Schools (PK-12)
   2012-13 Enrollment: 9,343 . . . . (252) 527-1109
   Housing: Homeownership rate: 73.6%; Median home value: $110,400; Median year structure built: 1980; Homeowner vacancy rate: 1.7%; Median gross rent: $614 per month; Rental vacancy rate: 11.6%
   Health Insurance: 80.1% have insurance; 53.0% have private insurance; 35.0% have public insurance; 19.9% do not have insurance; 3.7% of children under 18 do not have insurance
   Transportation: Commute: 94.8% car, 0.0% public transportation, 2.8% walk, 2.5% work from home; Median travel time to work: 30.6 minutes

JACKSON HEIGHTS (CDP). Covers a land area of 1.439 square miles and a water area of 0 square miles. Located at 35.22° N. Lat; 77.63° W. Long.

Population: 1,141; Growth (since 2000): n/a; Density: 793.1 persons per square mile; Race: 75.2% White, 20.2% Black/African American, 0.0% Asian, 0.2% American Indian/Alaska Native, 0.0% Native Hawaiian/Other Pacific Islander, 1.2% Two or more races, 6.8% Hispanic of any race; Average household size: 2.49; Median age: 41.3; Age under 18: 22.2%; Age 65 and over: 19.1%; Males per 100 females: 91.8
Housing: Homeownership rate: 76.4%; Homeowner vacancy rate: 1.1%; Rental vacancy rate: 12.9%

KINSTON (city). County seat. Covers a land area of 18.360 square miles and a water area of 0.164 square miles. Located at 35.28° N. Lat; 77.59° W. Long. Elevation is 43 feet.

History: The site of Kinston in 1740 was the homestead of William Heritage, a New Bern planter and jurist who had moved to Atkins Banks on the Neuse. In 1762 Governor Dobbs authorized the establishment of a town at Atkins Banks. The main street of the new King's Town (Kingston) was designated King Street in honor of George III. During the Revolution zealous patriots adopted the form Kinston.
Population: 21,677; Growth (since 2000): -8.5%; Density: 1,180.7 persons per square mile; Race: 28.7% White, 68.0% Black/African American, 0.7% Asian, 0.2% American Indian/Alaska Native, 0.1% Native Hawaiian/Other Pacific Islander, 1.3% Two or more races, 2.4% Hispanic of any race; Average household size: 2.23; Median age: 43.7; Age under 18: 23.6%; Age 65 and over: 18.5%; Males per 100 females: 83.0; Marriage status: 37.9% never married, 39.0% now married, 6.2% separated, 10.7% widowed, 12.4% divorced; Foreign born: 2.0%; Speak English only: 95.8%; With disability: 23.2%; Veterans: 9.4%; Ancestry: 10.7% African, 8.2% English, 4.4% American, 3.9% Irish, 2.7% German
Employment: 8.5% management, business, and financial, 2.3% computer, engineering, and science, 9.6% education, legal, community service, arts, and media, 5.2% healthcare practitioners, 25.5% service, 19.4% sales and office, 7.2% natural resources, construction, and maintenance, 22.3% production, transportation, and material moving
Income: Per capita: $18,930; Median household: $29,451; Average household: $43,130; Households with income of $100,000 or more: 7.7%; Poverty rate: 31.8%
Educational Attainment: High school diploma or higher: 78.7%; Bachelor's degree or higher: 15.1%; Graduate/professional degree or higher: 4.1%

School District(s)
Children's Village Academy (KG-08)
   2012-13 Enrollment: 203. . . . . (252) 939-1958
Kinston Charter Acad (KG-08)
   2012-13 Enrollment: 297. . . . . (252) 522-0210
Lenoir County Public Schools (PK-12)
   2012-13 Enrollment: 9,343 . . . . (252) 527-1109
Nc Dept of Juvenile Justice (KG-12)
   2012-13 Enrollment: n/a . . . . (919) 733-3388
Nc Health and Human Resources (KG-12)
   2012-13 Enrollment: n/a . . . . (919) 855-4430
Two-year College(s)
Lenoir Community College (Public)
   Fall 2013 Enrollment: 2,813 . . . . (252) 527-6223
   2013-14 Tuition: In-state $2,407; Out-of-state $8,551
Housing: Homeownership rate: 47.3%; Median home value: $105,600; Median year structure built: 1965; Homeowner vacancy rate: 3.9%; Median gross rent: $616 per month; Rental vacancy rate: 8.9%
Health Insurance: 80.3% have insurance; 44.4% have private insurance; 51.1% have public insurance; 19.7% do not have insurance; 8.5% of children under 18 do not have insurance
Hospitals: Lenoir Memorial Hospital (261 beds)
Safety: Violent crime rate: 126.3 per 10,000 population; Property crime rate: 695.7 per 10,000 population
Newspapers: Free Press (daily circulation 11100); Jones Post (weekly circulation 2800)
Transportation: Commute: 88.4% car, 2.3% public transportation, 4.4% walk, 4.3% work from home; Median travel time to work: 18.7 minutes; Amtrak: Bus service available.
Airports: Kinston Regional Jetport at Stallings Field (general aviation)
Additional Information Contacts
City of Kinston . . . . (252) 939-3110
   http://www.ci.kinston.nc.us

LA GRANGE (town). Covers a land area of 2.305 square miles and a water area of 0.008 square miles. Located at 35.31° N. Lat; 77.79° W. Long. Elevation is 108 feet.

History: La Grange was first known as Rantersville and later Moseley Hall.
Population: 2,873; Growth (since 2000): 1.0%; Density: 1,246.7 persons per square mile; Race: 40.5% White, 55.4% Black/African American, 0.7% Asian, 0.2% American Indian/Alaska Native, 0.1% Native Hawaiian/Other Pacific Islander, 1.1% Two or more races, 3.4% Hispanic of any race; Average household size: 2.33; Median age: 43.2; Age under 18: 23.2%; Age 65 and over: 17.6%; Males per 100 females: 86.3; Marriage status: 22.4% never married, 56.2% now married, 16.1% separated, 6.7% widowed, 14.7% divorced; Foreign born: 0.5%; Speak English only: 99.5%; With disability: 28.9%; Veterans: 12.9%; Ancestry: 9.8% Portuguese, 9.0% English, 8.3% American, 5.8% Irish, 4.6% German
Employment: 4.4% management, business, and financial, 0.0% computer, engineering, and science, 16.1% education, legal, community service, arts, and media, 1.5% healthcare practitioners, 17.6% service, 32.5% sales and office, 10.4% natural resources, construction, and maintenance, 17.6% production, transportation, and material moving
Income: Per capita: $19,937; Median household: $28,160; Average household: $38,165; Households with income of $100,000 or more: 8.9%; Poverty rate: 21.5%
Educational Attainment: High school diploma or higher: 87.2%; Bachelor's degree or higher: 13.5%; Graduate/professional degree or higher: 5.4%
School District(s)
Lenoir County Public Schools (PK-12)
   2012-13 Enrollment: 9,343 . . . . (252) 527-1109
Housing: Homeownership rate: 61.4%; Median home value: $69,000; Median year structure built: 1975; Homeowner vacancy rate: 2.9%; Median gross rent: $685 per month; Rental vacancy rate: 12.3%
Health Insurance: 86.2% have insurance; 58.2% have private insurance; 47.6% have public insurance; 13.8% do not have insurance; 0.0% of children under 18 do not have insurance
Newspapers: Weekly Gazette (weekly circulation 1500)
Transportation: Commute: 92.3% car, 1.5% public transportation, 3.5% walk, 2.7% work from home; Median travel time to work: 24.8 minutes

PINK HILL (town). Covers a land area of 0.469 square miles and a water area of 0 square miles. Located at 35.06° N. Lat; 77.74° W. Long. Elevation is 135 feet.

Population: 552; Growth (since 2000): 6.0%; Density: 1,176.2 persons per square mile; Race: 55.4% White, 28.8% Black/African American, 0.0% Asian, 0.0% American Indian/Alaska Native, 0.0% Native Hawaiian/Other Pacific Islander, 0.7% Two or more races, 20.3% Hispanic of any race; Average household size: 2.60; Median age: 37.3; Age under 18: 25.9%; Age 65 and over: 17.4%; Males per 100 females: 93.7
School District(s)
Lenoir County Public Schools (PK-12)
   2012-13 Enrollment: 9,343 . . . . (252) 527-1109
Housing: Homeownership rate: 50.5%; Homeowner vacancy rate: 2.7%; Rental vacancy rate: 11.0%

Lincoln County

Located in west central North Carolina; in piedmont area, bounded on the east by the Catawba River. Covers a land area of 297.938 square miles, a water area of 9.103 square miles, and is located in the Eastern Time Zone at 35.49° N. Lat., 81.23° W. Long. The county was founded in 1778. County seat is Lincolnton.

Lincoln County is part of the Charlotte-Concord-Gastonia, NC-SC Metropolitan Statistical Area. The entire metro area includes: Cabarrus County, NC; Gaston County, NC; Iredell County, NC; Lincoln County, NC; Mecklenburg County, NC; Rowan County, NC; Union County, NC; Chester County, SC; Lancaster County, SC; York County, SC

Weather Station: Lincolnton 4 W									Elevation: 899 feet		
	Jan	Feb	Mar	Apr	May	Jun	Jul	Aug	Sep	Oct	Nov	Dec
High	51	55	63	72	79	86	89	87	81	72	62	53
Low	29	32	38	46	54	63	67	66	59	47	38	31
Precip	3.8	3.6	4.6	3.5	4.0	4.2	4.1	4.4	3.6	4.2	3.6	3.8
Snow	3.1	1.7	1.0	tr	0.0	0.0	0.0	0.0	0.0	0.0	0.1	0.4

High and Low temperatures in degrees Fahrenheit; Precipitation and Snow in inches

Population: 78,265; Growth (since 2000): 22.7%; Density: 262.7 persons per square mile; Race: 89.4% White, 5.5% Black/African American, 0.5% Asian, 0.3% American Indian/Alaska Native, 0.0% Native Hawaiian/Other Pacific Islander, 1.6% two or more races, 6.7% Hispanic of any race; Average household size: 2.56; Median age: 40.4; Age under 18: 23.6%; Age 65 and over: 13.2%; Males per 100 females: 98.4; Marriage status: 23.0% never married, 60.2% now married, 2.7% separated, 6.5% widowed, 10.3% divorced; Foreign born: 5.0%; Speak English only: 92.4%; With disability: 14.3%; Veterans: 9.9%; Ancestry: 20.3% German, 16.6% American, 13.6% Irish, 11.2% English, 3.2% Italian
Religion: Six largest groups: 26.1% Baptist, 13.1% Methodist/Pietist, 3.7% Lutheran, 2.8% Catholicism, 2.3% Non-denominational Protestant, 1.8% Pentecostal
Economy: Unemployment rate: 5.3%; Leading industries: 15.3% retail trade; 13.6% other services (except public administration); 12.5% construction; Farms: 651 totaling 55,570 acres; Company size: 0 employ 1,000 or more persons, 3 employ 500 to 999 persons, 17 employ 100 to 499 persons, 1,526 employ less than 100 persons; Business ownership: 1,762 women-owned, n/a Black-owned, 335 Hispanic-owned, n/a Asian-owned
Employment: 13.4% management, business, and financial, 4.0% computer, engineering, and science, 7.9% education, legal, community service, arts, and media, 5.0% healthcare practitioners, 13.5% service, 26.6% sales and office, 10.9% natural resources, construction, and maintenance, 18.7% production, transportation, and material moving
Income: Per capita: $25,550; Median household: $48,940; Average household: $65,018; Households with income of $100,000 or more: 19.0%; Poverty rate: 15.6%
Educational Attainment: High school diploma or higher: 83.6%; Bachelor's degree or higher: 19.4%; Graduate/professional degree or higher: 5.0%
Housing: Homeownership rate: 76.1%; Median home value: $154,600; Median year structure built: 1987; Homeowner vacancy rate: 2.2%; Median gross rent: $665 per month; Rental vacancy rate: 10.9%
Vital Statistics: Birth rate: 96.6 per 10,000 population; Death rate: 87.9 per 10,000 population; Age-adjusted cancer mortality rate: 178.5 deaths per 100,000 population
Health Insurance: 83.4% have insurance; 65.4% have private insurance; 29.7% have public insurance; 16.6% do not have insurance; 9.3% of children under 18 do not have insurance
Health Care: Physicians: 7.9 per 10,000 population; Hospital beds: 11.4 per 10,000 population; Hospital admissions: 472.7 per 10,000 population
Air Quality Index: 95.8% good, 4.2% moderate, 0.0% unhealthy for sensitive individuals, 0.0% unhealthy (percent of days)
Transportation: Commute: 94.2% car, 0.3% public transportation, 0.6% walk, 4.2% work from home; Median travel time to work: 29.4 minutes
Presidential Election: 30.0% Obama, 68.7% Romney (2012)
Additional Information Contacts
Lincoln Government . . . . (704) 735-0602
  http://www.lincolncounty.org

Lincoln County Communities

CROUSE (unincorporated postal area)
ZCTA: 28033
  Covers a land area of 15.537 square miles and a water area of 0.086 square miles. Located at 35.42° N. Lat; 81.33° W. Long. Elevation is 856 feet.
  Population: 2,749; Growth (since 2000): 39.8%; Density: 176.9 persons per square mile; Race: 93.5% White, 2.4% Black/African American, 0.0% Asian, 0.3% American Indian/Alaska Native, 0.0% Native Hawaiian/Other Pacific Islander, 1.6% Two or more races, 6.6% Hispanic of any race; Average household size: 2.70; Median age: 39.0; Age under 18: 25.0%; Age 65 and over: 12.6%; Males per 100 females: 97.6; Marriage status: 16.0% never married, 65.9% now married, 2.2% separated, 6.1% widowed, 11.9% divorced; Foreign born: 3.4%; Speak English only: 95.8%; With disability: 14.5%; Veterans: 11.6%; Ancestry: 29.2% American, 26.7% German, 9.4% English, 5.2% Dutch, 4.3% Irish
  Employment: 14.4% management, business, and financial, 4.5% computer, engineering, and science, 3.5% education, legal, community service, arts, and media, 4.4% healthcare practitioners, 8.7% service, 29.9% sales and office, 14.7% natural resources, construction, and maintenance, 19.9% production, transportation, and material moving

Income: Per capita: $19,231; Median household: $44,962; Average household: $49,028; Households with income of $100,000 or more: 8.9%; Poverty rate: 16.8%
Educational Attainment: High school diploma or higher: 79.0%; Bachelor's degree or higher: 6.2%; Graduate/professional degree or higher: 3.3%
Housing: Homeownership rate: 81.6%; Median home value: $107,900; Median year structure built: 1983; Homeowner vacancy rate: 2.5%; Median gross rent: $682 per month; Rental vacancy rate: 12.5%
Health Insurance: 83.6% have insurance; 64.2% have private insurance; 34.8% have public insurance; 16.4% do not have insurance; 11.3% of children under 18 do not have insurance
Transportation: Commute: 98.1% car, 0.0% public transportation, 0.0% walk, 1.4% work from home; Median travel time to work: 33.0 minutes

DENVER (CDP). Covers a land area of 6.216 square miles and a water area of 0.008 square miles. Located at 35.54° N. Lat; 81.04° W. Long. Elevation is 899 feet.
Population: 2,309; Growth (since 2000): n/a; Density: 371.4 persons per square mile; Race: 93.2% White, 2.4% Black/African American, 0.6% Asian, 0.9% American Indian/Alaska Native, 0.0% Native Hawaiian/Other Pacific Islander, 1.2% Two or more races, 3.8% Hispanic of any race; Average household size: 2.38; Median age: 39.5; Age under 18: 24.0%; Age 65 and over: 15.0%; Males per 100 females: 91.6
School District(s)
Lincoln County Schools (PK-12)
  2012-13 Enrollment: 11,860 . . . . (704) 732-2261
Housing: Homeownership rate: 69.9%; Homeowner vacancy rate: 3.3%; Rental vacancy rate: 10.9%

IRON STATION (CDP). Covers a land area of 2.357 square miles and a water area of 0.005 square miles. Located at 35.45° N. Lat; 81.15° W. Long. Elevation is 879 feet.
Population: 755; Growth (since 2000): n/a; Density: 320.3 persons per square mile; Race: 88.7% White, 6.5% Black/African American, 0.5% Asian, 0.7% American Indian/Alaska Native, 0.4% Native Hawaiian/Other Pacific Islander, 1.9% Two or more races, 3.3% Hispanic of any race; Average household size: 2.44; Median age: 43.8; Age under 18: 21.6%; Age 65 and over: 14.8%; Males per 100 females: 92.6
School District(s)
Lincoln County Schools (PK-12)
  2012-13 Enrollment: 11,860 . . . . (704) 732-2261
Housing: Homeownership rate: 80.3%; Homeowner vacancy rate: 2.4%; Rental vacancy rate: 11.6%

LINCOLNTON (city). County seat. Covers a land area of 8.593 square miles and a water area of 0.082 square miles. Located at 35.47° N. Lat; 81.24° W. Long. Elevation is 833 feet.
History: Lincolnton is the oldest town west of the Catawba River. The city and county were named for Colonel Benjamin Lincoln of the Revolutionary Army.
Population: 10,486; Growth (since 2000): 5.2%; Density: 1,220.3 persons per square mile; Race: 76.6% White, 13.7% Black/African American, 0.6% Asian, 0.3% American Indian/Alaska Native, 0.0% Native Hawaiian/Other Pacific Islander, 2.8% Two or more races, 16.0% Hispanic of any race; Average household size: 2.37; Median age: 38.4; Age under 18: 23.5%; Age 65 and over: 16.9%; Males per 100 females: 89.4; Marriage status: 28.2% never married, 47.1% now married, 3.9% separated, 10.8% widowed, 13.8% divorced; Foreign born: 7.1%; Speak English only: 84.8%; With disability: 15.9%; Veterans: 10.1%; Ancestry: 16.8% German, 11.1% Irish, 10.9% American, 10.8% English, 3.6% Dutch
Employment: 13.2% management, business, and financial, 5.3% computer, engineering, and science, 10.6% education, legal, community service, arts, and media, 4.1% healthcare practitioners, 13.8% service, 21.6% sales and office, 10.2% natural resources, construction, and maintenance, 21.1% production, transportation, and material moving
Income: Per capita: $19,514; Median household: $31,162; Average household: $46,500; Households with income of $100,000 or more: 8.6%; Poverty rate: 26.0%
Educational Attainment: High school diploma or higher: 80.8%; Bachelor's degree or higher: 16.9%; Graduate/professional degree or higher: 3.7%
School District(s)
Lincoln Charter (KG-12)
  2012-13 Enrollment: 1,546 . . . . (704) 483-6611

Lincoln County Schools (PK-12)
　2012-13 Enrollment: 11,860 . . . . (704) 732-2261
Housing: Homeownership rate: 48.6%; Median home value: $129,800; Median year structure built: 1971; Homeowner vacancy rate: 3.3%; Median gross rent: $663 per month; Rental vacancy rate: 12.7%
Health Insurance: 82.6% have insurance; 55.4% have private insurance; 39.5% have public insurance; 17.4% do not have insurance; 5.7% of children under 18 do not have insurance
Hospitals: Carolinas Medical Center - Lincoln (87 beds)
Safety: Violent crime rate: 48.7 per 10,000 population; Property crime rate: 497.8 per 10,000 population
Newspapers: Lincoln Times-News (weekly circulation 8000)
Transportation: Commute: 95.8% car, 1.3% public transportation, 1.8% walk, 0.7% work from home; Median travel time to work: 22.5 minutes
Airports: Lincolnton-Lincoln County Regional (general aviation)
Additional Information Contacts
City of Lincolnton. . . . . (704) 735-3096
　http://www.co.lincoln.nc.us/City/cityof1.htm

LOWESVILLE (CDP). Covers a land area of 6.796 square miles and a water area of 0.009 square miles. Located at 35.42° N. Lat; 81.00° W. Long. Elevation is 784 feet.
Population: 2,945; Growth (since 2000): 104.5%; Density: 433.3 persons per square mile; Race: 92.1% White, 4.6% Black/African American, 0.7% Asian, 0.6% American Indian/Alaska Native, 0.0% Native Hawaiian/Other Pacific Islander, 1.0% Two or more races, 2.5% Hispanic of any race; Average household size: 2.62; Median age: 41.1; Age under 18: 24.4%; Age 65 and over: 12.7%; Males per 100 females: 92.5; Marriage status: 25.1% never married, 64.6% now married, 0.7% separated, 2.5% widowed, 7.8% divorced; Foreign born: 1.6%; Speak English only: 96.5%; With disability: 12.1%; Veterans: 7.6%; Ancestry: 22.0% Irish, 17.9% German, 16.4% American, 15.1% Italian, 14.6% English
Employment: 32.8% management, business, and financial, 6.2% computer, engineering, and science, 9.6% education, legal, community service, arts, and media, 4.1% healthcare practitioners, 6.2% service, 21.9% sales and office, 7.4% natural resources, construction, and maintenance, 11.7% production, transportation, and material moving
Income: Per capita: $27,929; Median household: $61,161; Average household: $77,680; Households with income of $100,000 or more: 30.1%; Poverty rate: 9.0%
Educational Attainment: High school diploma or higher: 88.7%; Bachelor's degree or higher: 28.5%; Graduate/professional degree or higher: 9.6%
Housing: Homeownership rate: 86.4%; Median home value: $235,200; Median year structure built: 1997; Homeowner vacancy rate: 2.5%; Median gross rent: $731 per month; Rental vacancy rate: 3.8%
Health Insurance: 86.1% have insurance; 78.7% have private insurance; 19.7% have public insurance; 13.9% do not have insurance; 5.7% of children under 18 do not have insurance
Transportation: Commute: 89.9% car, 1.2% public transportation, 0.6% walk, 8.3% work from home; Median travel time to work: 27.6 minutes

VALE (unincorporated postal area)
ZCTA: 28168
　Covers a land area of 86.744 square miles and a water area of 0.348 square miles. Located at 35.55° N. Lat; 81.43° W. Long. Elevation is 938 feet.
Population: 10,230; Growth (since 2000): 9.2%; Density: 117.9 persons per square mile; Race: 93.8% White, 2.4% Black/African American, 0.8% Asian, 0.3% American Indian/Alaska Native, 0.0% Native Hawaiian/Other Pacific Islander, 1.0% Two or more races, 3.5% Hispanic of any race; Average household size: 2.60; Median age: 40.8; Age under 18: 23.5%; Age 65 and over: 13.4%; Males per 100 females: 99.2; Marriage status: 26.2% never married, 60.6% now married, 5.3% separated, 6.7% widowed, 6.5% divorced; Foreign born: 3.8%; Speak English only: 93.4%; With disability: 15.1%; Veterans: 9.5%; Ancestry: 23.5% American, 20.4% German, 12.8% Irish, 10.1% English, 2.0% Scotch-Irish
Employment: 10.4% management, business, and financial, 3.5% computer, engineering, and science, 6.3% education, legal, community service, arts, and media, 5.0% healthcare practitioners, 14.2% service, 24.8% sales and office, 13.9% natural resources, construction, and maintenance, 21.9% production, transportation, and material moving

Income: Per capita: $20,163; Median household: $44,570; Average household: $54,605; Households with income of $100,000 or more: 11.6%; Poverty rate: 16.2%
Educational Attainment: High school diploma or higher: 79.5%; Bachelor's degree or higher: 16.6%; Graduate/professional degree or higher: 4.4%
School District(s)
Catawba County Schools (PK-12)
　2012-13 Enrollment: 17,256 . . . . (828) 464-8333
Lincoln County Schools (PK-12)
　2012-13 Enrollment: 11,860 . . . . (704) 732-2261
Housing: Homeownership rate: 79.5%; Median home value: $126,800; Median year structure built: 1985; Homeowner vacancy rate: 1.5%; Median gross rent: $595 per month; Rental vacancy rate: 7.4%
Health Insurance: 86.5% have insurance; 66.0% have private insurance; 30.4% have public insurance; 13.5% do not have insurance; 8.5% of children under 18 do not have insurance
Transportation: Commute: 94.1% car, 0.0% public transportation, 2.9% walk, 2.6% work from home; Median travel time to work: 30.0 minutes

WESTPORT (CDP). Covers a land area of 3.670 square miles and a water area of 1.957 square miles. Located at 35.50° N. Lat; 80.98° W. Long. Elevation is 784 feet.
Population: 4,026; Growth (since 2000): 100.7%; Density: 1,096.9 persons per square mile; Race: 95.1% White, 2.7% Black/African American, 0.8% Asian, 0.1% American Indian/Alaska Native, 0.0% Native Hawaiian/Other Pacific Islander, 0.8% Two or more races, 1.7% Hispanic of any race; Average household size: 2.67; Median age: 42.9; Age under 18: 25.4%; Age 65 and over: 12.3%; Males per 100 females: 100.8; Marriage status: 11.8% never married, 72.2% now married, 0.7% separated, 5.7% widowed, 10.3% divorced; Foreign born: 3.0%; Speak English only: 96.8%; With disability: 9.2%; Veterans: 8.5%; Ancestry: 30.4% German, 23.4% English, 9.2% Irish, 7.9% American, 6.1% Dutch
Employment: 29.2% management, business, and financial, 6.7% computer, engineering, and science, 10.5% education, legal, community service, arts, and media, 8.0% healthcare practitioners, 4.1% service, 30.6% sales and office, 5.2% natural resources, construction, and maintenance, 5.7% production, transportation, and material moving
Income: Per capita: $50,820; Median household: $99,425; Average household: $127,566; Households with income of $100,000 or more: 49.3%; Poverty rate: 3.5%
Educational Attainment: High school diploma or higher: 98.4%; Bachelor's degree or higher: 42.9%; Graduate/professional degree or higher: 14.9%
Housing: Homeownership rate: 91.5%; Median home value: $412,800; Median year structure built: 2000; Homeowner vacancy rate: 3.2%; Median gross rent: $646 per month; Rental vacancy rate: 9.2%
Health Insurance: 91.6% have insurance; 83.5% have private insurance; 19.9% have public insurance; 8.4% do not have insurance; 10.5% of children under 18 do not have insurance
Transportation: Commute: 89.4% car, 0.0% public transportation, 0.4% walk, 9.9% work from home; Median travel time to work: 35.9 minutes

Macon County

Located in western North Carolina, partly in the Blue Ridge; bounded on the south by Georgia; crossed by the Nantahala Mountains; drained by the Nantahala and Little Tennessee Rivers; included in Nantahala National Forest. Covers a land area of 515.558 square miles, a water area of 4.129 square miles, and is located in the Eastern Time Zone at 35.15° N. Lat., 83.42° W. Long. The county was founded in 1828. County seat is Franklin.

Weather Station: Coweeta Exp Station									Elevation: 2,249 feet		
	Jan	Feb	Mar	Apr	May	Jun	Jul	Aug	Sep	Oct	Nov	Dec
High	50	54	61	69	76	82	84	83	78	70	61	52
Low	25	28	34	42	49	57	60	60	53	42	34	27
Precip	6.6	6.6	6.8	5.3	5.2	5.8	4.8	4.8	5.9	4.5	6.4	6.2
Snow	1.7	1.2	1.0	0.3	0.0	0.0	0.0	0.0	0.0	0.0	tr	0.2

High and Low temperatures in degrees Fahrenheit; Precipitation and Snow in inches

Weather Station: Franklin 3 W — Elevation: 2,169 feet

	Jan	Feb	Mar	Apr	May	Jun	Jul	Aug	Sep	Oct	Nov	Dec
High	49	53	61	69	76	82	85	84	78	70	61	51
Low	25	28	34	41	49	58	62	62	55	43	34	27
Precip	4.8	4.6	5.1	3.9	4.6	4.6	4.7	4.4	4.3	3.3	4.6	4.5
Snow	2.1	1.4	0.3	0.5	0.0	0.0	0.0	0.0	0.0	0.0	0.1	0.4

High and Low temperatures in degrees Fahrenheit; Precipitation and Snow in inches

Weather Station: Highlands — Elevation: 3,839 feet

	Jan	Feb	Mar	Apr	May	Jun	Jul	Aug	Sep	Oct	Nov	Dec
High	42	46	54	62	70	76	78	77	71	63	53	44
Low	24	26	31	38	47	54	58	57	51	41	33	26
Precip	7.2	6.8	8.0	6.5	6.2	7.0	6.3	6.4	7.7	6.2	8.1	7.9
Snow	4.9	3.0	2.0	0.9	0.2	0.0	0.0	0.0	0.0	tr	0.2	1.8

High and Low temperatures in degrees Fahrenheit; Precipitation and Snow in inches

Population: 33,922; Growth (since 2000): 13.8%; Density: 65.8 persons per square mile; Race: 93.8% White, 1.3% Black/African American, 0.6% Asian, 0.5% American Indian/Alaska Native, 0.0% Native Hawaiian/Other Pacific Islander, 1.1% two or more races, 6.6% Hispanic of any race; Average household size: 2.29; Median age: 47.8; Age under 18: 19.3%; Age 65 and over: 23.8%; Males per 100 females: 94.7; Marriage status: 20.3% never married, 60.1% now married, 2.3% separated, 7.8% widowed, 11.8% divorced; Foreign born: 5.1%; Speak English only: 93.0%; With disability: 18.5%; Veterans: 14.8%; Ancestry: 31.1% American, 12.2% German, 12.1% English, 9.1% Irish, 4.5% Scotch-Irish
Religion: Six largest groups: 37.9% Baptist, 10.0% Methodist/Pietist, 4.9% Pentecostal, 3.6% Catholicism, 2.7% Non-denominational Protestant, 2.2% Presbyterian-Reformed
Economy: Unemployment rate: 5.2%; Leading industries: 20.3% retail trade; 17.5% construction, 13.0% other services (except public administration); Farms: 326 totaling 22,684 acres; Company size: 0 employ 1,000 or more persons, 0 employ 500 to 999 persons, 10 employ 100 to 499 persons, 1,082 employ less than 100 persons; Business ownership: 1,161 women-owned, n/a Black-owned, 25 Hispanic-owned, n/a Asian-owned
Employment: 13.6% management, business, and financial, 2.0% computer, engineering, and science, 6.8% education, legal, community service, arts, and media, 5.8% healthcare practitioners, 24.4% service, 24.8% sales and office, 12.9% natural resources, construction, and maintenance, 9.8% production, transportation, and material moving
Income: Per capita: $23,213; Median household: $37,892; Average household: $51,805; Households with income of $100,000 or more: 9.8%; Poverty rate: 21.3%
Educational Attainment: High school diploma or higher: 85.7%; Bachelor's degree or higher: 20.5%; Graduate/professional degree or higher: 7.8%
Housing: Homeownership rate: 77.3%; Median home value: $165,400; Median year structure built: 1984; Homeowner vacancy rate: 5.1%; Median gross rent: $739 per month; Rental vacancy rate: 14.4%
Vital Statistics: Birth rate: 95.7 per 10,000 population; Death rate: 115.2 per 10,000 population; Age-adjusted cancer mortality rate: 188.3 deaths per 100,000 population
Health Insurance: 79.0% have insurance; 54.3% have private insurance; 43.6% have public insurance; 21.0% do not have insurance; 14.1% of children under 18 do not have insurance
Health Care: Physicians: 17.7 per 10,000 population; Hospital beds: 39.3 per 10,000 population; Hospital admissions: 597.2 per 10,000 population
Air Quality Index: 98.6% good, 1.4% moderate, 0.0% unhealthy for sensitive individuals, 0.0% unhealthy (percent of days)
Transportation: Commute: 92.6% car, 0.4% public transportation, 1.9% walk, 3.8% work from home; Median travel time to work: 21.8 minutes
Presidential Election: 33.9% Obama, 64.3% Romney (2012)
National and State Parks: Nantahala National Forest
Additional Information Contacts
Macon Government. . . . . (828) 349-2000
   http://www.maconnc.org

Macon County Communities

FRANKLIN (town). County seat. Covers a land area of 4.184 square miles and a water area of 0.082 square miles. Located at 35.18° N. Lat; 83.38° W. Long. Elevation is 2,119 feet.
History: Franklin was built on the site of an old Cherokee settlement, Nikwasi, known as Sacred Town. Although twice destroyed and rebuilt, it was occupied by the Cherokee until the land was sold in 1819. Franklin,

named for Jesse Franklin, governor of North Carolina (1820-1821), was known for the beauty of its setting and its mountain climate.
Population: 3,845; Growth (since 2000): 10.2%; Density: 918.9 persons per square mile; Race: 90.1% White, 2.1% Black/African American, 0.8% Asian, 0.5% American Indian/Alaska Native, 0.0% Native Hawaiian/Other Pacific Islander, 1.7% Two or more races, 13.0% Hispanic of any race; Average household size: 2.20; Median age: 40.5; Age under 18: 21.2%; Age 65 and over: 21.9%; Males per 100 females: 86.1; Marriage status: 34.2% never married, 39.3% now married, 1.0% separated, 10.6% widowed, 15.9% divorced; Foreign born: 14.9%; Speak English only: 81.2%; With disability: 21.1%; Veterans: 9.5%; Ancestry: 25.1% American, 12.1% German, 11.9% English, 8.1% Irish, 7.3% Scotch-Irish
Employment: 8.9% management, business, and financial, 2.9% computer, engineering, and science, 8.2% education, legal, community service, arts, and media, 5.7% healthcare practitioners, 31.4% service, 23.5% sales and office, 9.6% natural resources, construction, and maintenance, 9.9% production, transportation, and material moving
Income: Per capita: $18,000; Median household: $29,170; Average household: $38,023; Households with income of $100,000 or more: 4.8%; Poverty rate: 28.2%
Educational Attainment: High school diploma or higher: 77.1%; Bachelor's degree or higher: 22.4%; Graduate/professional degree or higher: 7.8%
School District(s)
Macon County Schools (PK-12)
   2012-13 Enrollment: 4,515 . . . . (828) 524-3314
Housing: Homeownership rate: 55.0%; Median home value: $145,000; Median year structure built: 1977; Homeowner vacancy rate: 6.0%; Median gross rent: $703 per month; Rental vacancy rate: 12.3%
Health Insurance: 72.1% have insurance; 47.6% have private insurance; 39.9% have public insurance; 27.9% do not have insurance; 14.3% of children under 18 do not have insurance
Hospitals: Angel Medical Center (52 beds)
Safety: Violent crime rate: 41.1 per 10,000 population; Property crime rate: 765.3 per 10,000 population
Newspapers: Franklin Press (weekly circulation 9200); Macon County News (weekly circulation 13000)
Transportation: Commute: 91.5% car, 0.0% public transportation, 1.2% walk, 6.6% work from home; Median travel time to work: 28.0 minutes
Airports: Macon County (general aviation)
Additional Information Contacts
Town of Franklin . . . . (828) 524-2516
   http://www.franklinnc.com

HIGHLANDS (town). Covers a land area of 6.010 square miles and a water area of 0.144 square miles. Located at 35.05° N. Lat; 83.20° W. Long. Elevation is 3,832 feet.
History: Since the discovery of a rare plant in 1788 by the French botanist Andre Michaux, Higlands began to attract naturalists who wanted to study the diverse flora.
Population: 924; Growth (since 2000): 1.7%; Density: 153.8 persons per square mile; Race: 94.3% White, 0.0% Black/African American, 0.6% Asian, 0.2% American Indian/Alaska Native, 0.0% Native Hawaiian/Other Pacific Islander, 1.8% Two or more races, 5.7% Hispanic of any race; Average household size: 2.00; Median age: 56.6; Age under 18: 12.1%; Age 65 and over: 33.2%; Males per 100 females: 90.9
School District(s)
Macon County Schools (PK-12)
   2012-13 Enrollment: 4,515 . . . . (828) 524-3314
Housing: Homeownership rate: 76.2%; Homeowner vacancy rate: 16.6%; Rental vacancy rate: 26.5%
Hospitals: Highlands Cashiers Hospital (104 beds)
Safety: Violent crime rate: 21.7 per 10,000 population; Property crime rate: 682.6 per 10,000 population
Newspapers: The Highlander (weekly circulation 4000)
Additional Information Contacts
Town of Highlands. . . . . (828) 526-3645
   http://www.highlandsnc.org

OTTO (unincorporated postal area)
ZCTA: 28763
   Covers a land area of 55.466 square miles and a water area of 0.079 square miles. Located at 35.03° N. Lat; 83.47° W. Long. Elevation is 2,070 feet.

Population: 2,725; Growth (since 2000): 10.5%; Density: 49.1 persons per square mile; Race: 94.0% White, 0.9% Black/African American, 0.3% Asian, 0.3% American Indian/Alaska Native, 0.0% Native Hawaiian/Other Pacific Islander, 1.3% Two or more races, 5.5% Hispanic of any race; Average household size: 2.39; Median age: 47.2; Age under 18: 20.8%; Age 65 and over: 20.8%; Males per 100 females: 97.8; Marriage status: 13.0% never married, 71.0% now married, 2.3% separated, 4.6% widowed, 11.3% divorced; Foreign born: 0.6%; Speak English only: 97.8%; With disability: 15.3%; Veterans: 14.6%; Ancestry: 36.6% American, 16.0% German, 15.3% Irish, 10.9% English, 7.2% Scotch-Irish

Employment: 9.4% management, business, and financial, 1.9% computer, engineering, and science, 4.1% education, legal, community service, arts, and media, 6.2% healthcare practitioners, 17.3% service, 27.0% sales and office, 22.8% natural resources, construction, and maintenance, 11.3% production, transportation, and material moving

Income: Per capita: $22,696; Median household: $43,992; Average household: $49,518; Households with income of $100,000 or more: 10.2%; Poverty rate: 19.0%

Educational Attainment: High school diploma or higher: 89.7%; Bachelor's degree or higher: 14.8%; Graduate/professional degree or higher: 6.9%

Housing: Homeownership rate: 82.5%; Median home value: $169,700; Median year structure built: 1986; Homeowner vacancy rate: 5.6%; Median gross rent: $548 per month; Rental vacancy rate: 15.5%

Health Insurance: 81.8% have insurance; 54.0% have private insurance; 39.4% have public insurance; 18.2% do not have insurance; 0.0% of children under 18 do not have insurance

Transportation: Commute: 94.5% car, 0.0% public transportation, 0.9% walk, 0.0% work from home; Median travel time to work: 23.4 minutes

SCALY MOUNTAIN (unincorporated postal area)
ZCTA: 28775

Covers a land area of 9.839 square miles and a water area of 0.008 square miles. Located at 35.02° N. Lat; 83.32° W. Long. Elevation is 3,481 feet.

Population: 296; Growth (since 2000): n/a; Density: 30.1 persons per square mile; Race: 93.9% White, 2.0% Black/African American, 0.0% Asian, 0.3% American Indian/Alaska Native, 0.0% Native Hawaiian/Other Pacific Islander, 1.0% Two or more races, 6.1% Hispanic of any race; Average household size: 2.23; Median age: 50.9; Age under 18: 15.2%; Age 65 and over: 22.3%; Males per 100 females: 98.7

Housing: Homeownership rate: 78.9%; Homeowner vacancy rate: 4.5%; Rental vacancy rate: 17.1%

TOPTON (unincorporated postal area)
ZCTA: 28781

Covers a land area of 78.254 square miles and a water area of 2.379 square miles. Located at 35.22° N. Lat; 83.64° W. Long..

Population: 939; Growth (since 2000): 6.5%; Density: 12.0 persons per square mile; Race: 97.9% White, 0.2% Black/African American, 0.0% Asian, 1.0% American Indian/Alaska Native, 0.0% Native Hawaiian/Other Pacific Islander, 1.0% Two or more races, 2.7% Hispanic of any race; Average household size: 2.21; Median age: 51.9; Age under 18: 17.1%; Age 65 and over: 28.8%; Males per 100 females: 103.2

School District(s)
Macon County Schools (PK-12)
    2012-13 Enrollment: 4,515 . . . . (828) 524-3314

Housing: Homeownership rate: 82.2%; Homeowner vacancy rate: 3.6%; Rental vacancy rate: 16.1%

Madison County

Located in western North Carolina; mountainous area, bounded on the north by Tennessee; drained by the French Broad River; includes part of Pisgah National Forest, and the Bald Mountains. Covers a land area of 449.570 square miles, a water area of 1.867 square miles, and is located in the Eastern Time Zone at 35.86° N. Lat., 82.71° W. Long. The county was founded in 1851. County seat is Marshall.

Madison County is part of the Asheville, NC Metropolitan Statistical Area. The entire metro area includes: Buncombe County, NC; Haywood County, NC; Henderson County, NC; Madison County, NC

Weather Station: Hot Springs										Elevation: 1,395 feet		
	Jan	Feb	Mar	Apr	May	Jun	Jul	Aug	Sep	Oct	Nov	Dec
High	49	52	61	70	77	84	86	86	81	71	61	51
Low	28	30	36	43	52	60	64	64	57	46	37	31
Precip	3.5	3.3	3.7	3.5	4.3	4.2	4.8	4.4	3.2	1.9	2.9	3.0
Snow	na	na	1.7	1.0	0.0	0.0	0.0	0.0	0.0	0.0	0.1	0.9

High and Low temperatures in degrees Fahrenheit; Precipitation and Snow in inches

Weather Station: Marshall										Elevation: 2,000 feet		
	Jan	Feb	Mar	Apr	May	Jun	Jul	Aug	Sep	Oct	Nov	Dec
High	46	51	59	68	76	82	85	84	79	69	59	50
Low	24	26	32	39	48	57	61	61	54	42	33	27
Precip	3.1	3.1	3.7	3.4	3.8	3.9	4.1	3.8	3.1	2.1	2.8	2.8
Snow	6.2	4.8	4.0	1.6	0.0	0.0	0.0	0.0	0.0	0.1	0.4	3.5

High and Low temperatures in degrees Fahrenheit; Precipitation and Snow in inches

Population: 20,764; Growth (since 2000): 5.7%; Density: 46.2 persons per square mile; Race: 96.5% White, 1.2% Black/African American, 0.3% Asian, 0.2% American Indian/Alaska Native, 0.0% Native Hawaiian/Other Pacific Islander, 1.3% two or more races, 2.0% Hispanic of any race; Average household size: 2.32; Median age: 43.3; Age under 18: 19.7%; Age 65 and over: 17.7%; Males per 100 females: 97.9; Marriage status: 23.2% never married, 56.6% now married, 2.8% separated, 8.3% widowed, 11.9% divorced; Foreign born: 2.5%; Speak English only: 96.9%; With disability: 17.8%; Veterans: 9.0%; Ancestry: 18.3% American, 12.7% German, 11.8% English, 11.4% Irish, 8.1% Scotch-Irish

Religion: Six largest groups: 53.7% Baptist, 2.7% Methodist/Pietist, 1.5% Pentecostal, 1.3% Catholicism, 1.2% Holiness, 0.9% Presbyterian-Reformed

Economy: Unemployment rate: 4.3%; Leading industries: 17.8% construction; 12.7% retail trade; 11.8% other services (except public administration); Farms: 719 totaling 56,282 acres; Company size: 0 employ 1,000 or more persons, 1 employs 500 to 999 persons, 4 employ 100 to 499 persons, 309 employ less than 100 persons; Business ownership: n/a women-owned, n/a Black-owned, n/a Hispanic-owned, n/a Asian-owned

Employment: 11.1% management, business, and financial, 2.3% computer, engineering, and science, 8.8% education, legal, community service, arts, and media, 7.8% healthcare practitioners, 21.0% service, 23.8% sales and office, 10.8% natural resources, construction, and maintenance, 14.4% production, transportation, and material moving

Income: Per capita: $19,902; Median household: $38,598; Average household: $48,740; Households with income of $100,000 or more: 8.8%; Poverty rate: 17.3%

Educational Attainment: High school diploma or higher: 80.8%; Bachelor's degree or higher: 18.6%; Graduate/professional degree or higher: 6.9%

Housing: Homeownership rate: 76.6%; Median home value: $161,700; Median year structure built: 1979; Homeowner vacancy rate: 2.1%; Median gross rent: $619 per month; Rental vacancy rate: 10.2%

Vital Statistics: Birth rate: 87.1 per 10,000 population; Death rate: 100.8 per 10,000 population; Age-adjusted cancer mortality rate: 117.0 deaths per 100,000 population

Health Insurance: 86.2% have insurance; 59.6% have private insurance; 39.6% have public insurance; 13.8% do not have insurance; 5.8% of children under 18 do not have insurance

Health Care: Physicians: 6.2 per 10,000 population; Hospital beds: 0.0 per 10,000 population; Hospital admissions: 0.0 per 10,000 population

Transportation: Commute: 89.7% car, 0.0% public transportation, 2.5% walk, 7.3% work from home; Median travel time to work: 28.5 minutes

Presidential Election: 44.3% Obama, 53.4% Romney (2012)

Additional Information Contacts
Madison Government . . . . (828) 649-2854
    http://www.madisoncountync.org

Madison County Communities

HOT SPRINGS (town). Covers a land area of 3.131 square miles and a water area of 0.265 square miles. Located at 35.89° N. Lat; 82.83° W. Long. Elevation is 1,332 feet.

History: Hot Springs was formerly known as Warm Springs. It was a famous resort until the 1920's. The curative properties of its waters attracted invalids in spite of being on a dangerous road.

Population: 560; Growth (since 2000): -13.2%; Density: 178.9 persons per square mile; Race: 97.9% White, 0.2% Black/African American, 0.0% Asian, 0.0% American Indian/Alaska Native, 0.0% Native Hawaiian/Other

Pacific Islander, 1.6% Two or more races, 2.3% Hispanic of any race; Average household size: 2.11; Median age: 44.0; Age under 18: 23.6%; Age 65 and over: 20.9%; Males per 100 females: 102.2

School District(s)

Madison County Schools (KG-12)
    2012-13 Enrollment: 2,601 . . . . (828) 649-9276
Housing: Homeownership rate: 61.3%; Homeowner vacancy rate: 0.6%; Rental vacancy rate: 14.5%

MARS HILL (town). Covers a land area of 1.975 square miles and a water area of 0 square miles. Located at 35.83° N. Lat; 82.55° W. Long. Elevation is 2,310 feet.

History: Mars Hill College was built in Mars Hill in 1856.
Population: 1,869; Growth (since 2000): 6.0%; Density: 946.2 persons per square mile; Race: 87.1% White, 9.0% Black/African American, 1.0% Asian, 0.2% American Indian/Alaska Native, 0.2% Native Hawaiian/Other Pacific Islander, 1.9% Two or more races, 3.4% Hispanic of any race; Average household size: 2.14; Median age: 22.9; Age under 18: 11.5%; Age 65 and over: 13.4%; Males per 100 females: 96.5

School District(s)

Madison County Schools (KG-12)
    2012-13 Enrollment: 2,601 . . . . (828) 649-9276

Four-year College(s)

Mars Hill University (Private, Not-for-profit)
    Fall 2013 Enrollment: 1,440 . . . . (828) 689-4968
    2013-14 Tuition: In-state $25,636; Out-of-state $25,636
Housing: Homeownership rate: 61.7%; Homeowner vacancy rate: 3.2%; Rental vacancy rate: 11.8%
Safety: Violent crime rate: 14.6 per 10,000 population; Property crime rate: 291.1 per 10,000 population

---

MARSHALL (town). County seat. Covers a land area of 3.763 square miles and a water area of 0.214 square miles. Located at 35.80° N. Lat; 82.68° W. Long. Elevation is 1,644 feet.

History: Marshall was named for Chief Justice John Marshall and became the seat of Madison County in 1855.
Population: 872; Growth (since 2000): 3.8%; Density: 231.8 persons per square mile; Race: 97.5% White, 0.0% Black/African American, 0.1% Asian, 0.8% American Indian/Alaska Native, 0.1% Native Hawaiian/Other Pacific Islander, 1.5% Two or more races, 1.4% Hispanic of any race; Average household size: 2.16; Median age: 41.0; Age under 18: 19.7%; Age 65 and over: 17.8%; Males per 100 females: 106.1

School District(s)

Madison County Schools (KG-12)
    2012-13 Enrollment: 2,601 . . . . (828) 649-9276
Housing: Homeownership rate: 57.4%; Homeowner vacancy rate: 4.6%; Rental vacancy rate: 15.1%
Newspapers: News-Record & Sentinel (weekly circulation 6600)

Martin County

Located in eastern North Carolina; coastal plain area, bounded on the north by the Roanoke River. Covers a land area of 461.217 square miles, a water area of 0.291 square miles, and is located in the Eastern Time Zone at 35.84° N. Lat., 77.11° W. Long. The county was founded in 1774. County seat is Williamston.

Weather Station: Williamston 1 E										Elevation: 20 feet	
	Jan	Feb	Mar	Apr	May	Jun	Jul	Aug	Sep	Oct	Nov	Dec
High	52	55	62	72	79	86	89	87	82	73	64	55
Low	32	34	40	48	57	66	70	68	62	50	42	34
Precip	3.8	2.9	4.1	3.2	3.5	4.9	5.5	5.7	5.6	3.9	3.2	3.2
Snow	0.2	0.4	0.9	0.0	0.0	0.0	0.0	0.0	0.0	0.0	0.0	0.3

High and Low temperatures in degrees Fahrenheit; Precipitation and Snow in inches

Population: 24,505; Growth (since 2000): -4.3%; Density: 53.1 persons per square mile; Race: 53.1% White, 43.5% Black/African American, 0.3% Asian, 0.3% American Indian/Alaska Native, 0.0% Native Hawaiian/Other Pacific Islander, 1.0% two or more races, 3.1% Hispanic of any race; Average household size: 2.36; Median age: 44.0; Age under 18: 22.2%; Age 65 and over: 17.5%; Males per 100 females: 87.5; Marriage status: 27.8% never married, 49.6% now married, 3.0% separated, 11.0% widowed, 11.7% divorced; Foreign born: 2.2%; Speak English only: 96.3%; With disability: 20.2%; Veterans: 8.9%; Ancestry: 11.1% American, 8.9% English, 3.8% Irish, 3.8% German, 1.1% Scottish

Religion: Six largest groups: 32.2% Baptist, 6.7% Pentecostal, 4.4% Non-denominational Protestant, 3.6% Methodist/Pietist, 1.6% Catholicism, 0.8% Presbyterian-Reformed
Economy: Unemployment rate: 6.5%; Leading industries: 17.0% retail trade; 16.3% health care and social assistance; 11.6% other services (except public administration); Farms: 357 totaling 127,187 acres; Company size: 0 employ 1,000 or more persons, 0 employ 500 to 999 persons, 8 employ 100 to 499 persons, 439 employ less than 100 persons; Business ownership: 573 women-owned, 423 Black-owned, n/a Hispanic-owned, n/a Asian-owned
Employment: 10.8% management, business, and financial, 2.9% computer, engineering, and science, 11.0% education, legal, community service, arts, and media, 7.8% healthcare practitioners, 15.2% service, 21.0% sales and office, 13.9% natural resources, construction, and maintenance, 17.4% production, transportation, and material moving
Income: Per capita: $18,783; Median household: $35,111; Average household: $45,746; Households with income of $100,000 or more: 6.8%; Poverty rate: 23.2%
Educational Attainment: High school diploma or higher: 81.5%; Bachelor's degree or higher: 11.9%; Graduate/professional degree or higher: 3.1%
Housing: Homeownership rate: 68.0%; Median home value: $84,600; Median year structure built: 1975; Homeowner vacancy rate: 1.5%; Median gross rent: $591 per month; Rental vacancy rate: 9.3%
Vital Statistics: Birth rate: 95.8 per 10,000 population; Death rate: 124.9 per 10,000 population; Age-adjusted cancer mortality rate: 162.2 deaths per 100,000 population
Health Insurance: 80.6% have insurance; 53.4% have private insurance; 41.1% have public insurance; 19.4% do not have insurance; 9.1% of children under 18 do not have insurance
Health Care: Physicians: 6.7 per 10,000 population; Hospital beds: 20.2 per 10,000 population; Hospital admissions: 915.7 per 10,000 population
Air Quality Index: 78.9% good, 21.1% moderate, 0.0% unhealthy for sensitive individuals, 0.0% unhealthy (percent of days)
Transportation: Commute: 95.2% car, 0.1% public transportation, 2.2% walk, 1.9% work from home; Median travel time to work: 23.8 minutes
Presidential Election: 51.9% Obama, 47.5% Romney (2012)
Additional Information Contacts
Martin Government . . . . (252) 792-1901
    http://www.martincountyncgov.com

Martin County Communities

BEAR GRASS (town). Covers a land area of 0.266 square miles and a water area of 0 square miles. Located at 35.77° N. Lat; 77.13° W. Long. Elevation is 56 feet.

Population: 73; Growth (since 2000): 37.7%; Density: 274.9 persons per square mile; Race: 87.7% White, 8.2% Black/African American, 0.0% Asian, 0.0% American Indian/Alaska Native, 0.0% Native Hawaiian/Other Pacific Islander, 4.1% Two or more races, 0.0% Hispanic of any race; Average household size: 1.97; Median age: 51.3; Age under 18: 13.7%; Age 65 and over: 27.4%; Males per 100 females: 58.7
Housing: Homeownership rate: 73.0%; Homeowner vacancy rate: 3.6%; Rental vacancy rate: 0.0%

EVERETTS (town). Covers a land area of 0.452 square miles and a water area of 0 square miles. Located at 35.83° N. Lat; 77.17° W. Long. Elevation is 56 feet.

Population: 164; Growth (since 2000): -8.4%; Density: 362.8 persons per square mile; Race: 67.7% White, 26.8% Black/African American, 1.2% Asian, 0.0% American Indian/Alaska Native, 0.0% Native Hawaiian/Other Pacific Islander, 3.0% Two or more races, 2.4% Hispanic of any race; Average household size: 2.22; Median age: 49.0; Age under 18: 20.1%; Age 65 and over: 23.2%; Males per 100 females: 72.6
Housing: Homeownership rate: 60.8%; Homeowner vacancy rate: 0.0%; Rental vacancy rate: 3.0%

HAMILTON (town). Covers a land area of 0.486 square miles and a water area of 0 square miles. Located at 35.94° N. Lat; 77.21° W. Long. Elevation is 72 feet.

History: Historic Hamilton Visitor Center; Fort Branch Battlefield State Historic Site. Incorporated 1804.
Population: 408; Growth (since 2000): -20.9%; Density: 838.7 persons per square mile; Race: 37.7% White, 59.6% Black/African American, 0.2% Asian, 0.2% American Indian/Alaska Native, 0.5% Native Hawaiian/Other

Pacific Islander, 1.5% Two or more races, 1.0% Hispanic of any race; Average household size: 2.25; Median age: 47.3; Age under 18: 21.3%; Age 65 and over: 21.6%; Males per 100 females: 75.9

School District(s)

Martin County Schools (PK-12)
    2012-13 Enrollment: 3,623 . . . . (252) 792-1575
Housing: Homeownership rate: 61.3%; Homeowner vacancy rate: 2.6%; Rental vacancy rate: 17.6%

HASSELL (town). Covers a land area of 0.274 square miles and a water area of 0 square miles. Located at 35.91° N. Lat; 77.28° W. Long. Elevation is 79 feet.
Population: 84; Growth (since 2000): 16.7%; Density: 306.2 persons per square mile; Race: 41.7% White, 58.3% Black/African American, 0.0% Asian, 0.0% American Indian/Alaska Native, 0.0% Native Hawaiian/Other Pacific Islander, 0.0% Two or more races, 0.0% Hispanic of any race; Average household size: 2.21; Median age: 46.0; Age under 18: 17.9%; Age 65 and over: 15.5%; Males per 100 females: 82.6
Housing: Homeownership rate: 76.3%; Homeowner vacancy rate: 0.0%; Rental vacancy rate: 10.0%

JAMESVILLE (town). Covers a land area of 1.394 square miles and a water area of 0 square miles. Located at 35.81° N. Lat; 76.90° W. Long. Elevation is 36 feet.
Population: 491; Growth (since 2000): -2.2%; Density: 352.3 persons per square mile; Race: 61.3% White, 34.8% Black/African American, 0.4% Asian, 0.0% American Indian/Alaska Native, 0.0% Native Hawaiian/Other Pacific Islander, 2.9% Two or more races, 2.4% Hispanic of any race; Average household size: 2.40; Median age: 39.7; Age under 18: 25.3%; Age 65 and over: 16.7%; Males per 100 females: 74.7

School District(s)

Martin County Schools (PK-12)
    2012-13 Enrollment: 3,623 . . . . (252) 792-1575
Housing: Homeownership rate: 58.1%; Homeowner vacancy rate: 6.2%; Rental vacancy rate: 7.4%

OAK CITY (town). Covers a land area of 0.459 square miles and a water area of 0 square miles. Located at 35.96° N. Lat; 77.30° W. Long. Elevation is 82 feet.
Population: 317; Growth (since 2000): -6.5%; Density: 690.6 persons per square mile; Race: 37.5% White, 60.3% Black/African American, 0.0% Asian, 0.3% American Indian/Alaska Native, 0.0% Native Hawaiian/Other Pacific Islander, 0.3% Two or more races, 1.9% Hispanic of any race; Average household size: 2.17; Median age: 52.9; Age under 18: 17.7%; Age 65 and over: 27.4%; Males per 100 females: 92.1
Housing: Homeownership rate: 77.4%; Homeowner vacancy rate: 4.2%; Rental vacancy rate: 2.7%

PARMELE (town). Covers a land area of 1.187 square miles and a water area of 0 square miles. Located at 35.82° N. Lat; 77.31° W. Long. Elevation is 72 feet.
Population: 278; Growth (since 2000): -4.1%; Density: 234.3 persons per square mile; Race: 8.6% White, 91.4% Black/African American, 0.0% Asian, 0.0% American Indian/Alaska Native, 0.0% Native Hawaiian/Other Pacific Islander, 0.0% Two or more races, 0.0% Hispanic of any race; Average household size: 2.40; Median age: 43.6; Age under 18: 19.8%; Age 65 and over: 22.7%; Males per 100 females: 82.9
Housing: Homeownership rate: 73.3%; Homeowner vacancy rate: 2.3%; Rental vacancy rate: 16.2%

ROBERSONVILLE (town). Covers a land area of 1.224 square miles and a water area of 0 square miles. Located at 35.82° N. Lat; 77.25° W. Long. Elevation is 72 feet.
History: Settled 1700s; incorporated 1872.
Population: 1,488; Growth (since 2000): -14.0%; Density: 1,215.9 persons per square mile; Race: 30.2% White, 66.6% Black/African American, 0.6% Asian, 0.6% American Indian/Alaska Native, 0.0% Native Hawaiian/Other Pacific Islander, 0.7% Two or more races, 2.8% Hispanic of any race; Average household size: 2.20; Median age: 49.9; Age under 18: 19.0%; Age 65 and over: 23.7%; Males per 100 females: 80.4

School District(s)

Martin County Schools (PK-12)
    2012-13 Enrollment: 3,623 . . . . (252) 792-1575
Housing: Homeownership rate: 58.4%; Homeowner vacancy rate: 3.9%; Rental vacancy rate: 13.7%

WILLIAMSTON (town). County seat. Covers a land area of 3.844 square miles and a water area of 0 square miles. Located at 35.85° N. Lat; 77.07° W. Long. Elevation is 69 feet.
History: Williamston was first called Skewarky. It was later named in honor of Colonel William Williams of the Martin County militia. A port of entry before the Revolutionary War, the town had an old courthouse built in 1774 on stilts over the river. To enter the courthouse people climbed ladders from their boats. When court was declared in session the ladders were removed and no one was permitted to leave.
Population: 5,511; Growth (since 2000): -5.7%; Density: 1,433.7 persons per square mile; Race: 34.6% White, 62.4% Black/African American, 0.5% Asian, 0.2% American Indian/Alaska Native, 0.1% Native Hawaiian/Other Pacific Islander, 1.3% Two or more races, 2.1% Hispanic of any race; Average household size: 2.24; Median age: 41.9; Age under 18: 24.8%; Age 65 and over: 19.0%; Males per 100 females: 73.6; Marriage status: 28.7% never married, 43.0% now married, 4.3% separated, 18.7% widowed, 9.6% divorced; Foreign born: 0.5%; Speak English only: 99.5%; With disability: 20.5%; Veterans: 7.4%; Ancestry: 5.6% English, 4.7% American, 3.5% German, 3.0% Irish, 1.1% Welsh
Employment: 11.8% management, business, and financial, 0.5% computer, engineering, and science, 15.4% education, legal, community service, arts, and media, 6.9% healthcare practitioners, 16.2% service, 19.3% sales and office, 8.1% natural resources, construction, and maintenance, 21.9% production, transportation, and material moving
Income: Per capita: $16,471; Median household: $30,115; Average household: $36,452; Households with income of $100,000 or more: 3.1%; Poverty rate: 25.9%
Educational Attainment: High school diploma or higher: 78.4%; Bachelor's degree or higher: 12.3%; Graduate/professional degree or higher: 3.5%

School District(s)

Bear Grass Charter School (06-12)
    2012-13 Enrollment: 255. . . . . (252) 789-1010
Martin County Schools (PK-12)
    2012-13 Enrollment: 3,623 . . . . (252) 792-1575

Two-year College(s)

Martin Community College (Public)
    Fall 2013 Enrollment: 799 . . . . (252) 792-1521
    2013-14 Tuition: In-state $2,183; Out-of-state $7,943
Housing: Homeownership rate: 45.4%; Median home value: $84,700; Median year structure built: 1967; Homeowner vacancy rate: 3.4%; Median gross rent: $537 per month; Rental vacancy rate: 7.6%
Health Insurance: 85.2% have insurance; 48.6% have private insurance; 49.7% have public insurance; 14.8% do not have insurance; 7.5% of children under 18 do not have insurance
Hospitals: Martin General Hospital (49 beds)
Safety: Violent crime rate: 118.7 per 10,000 population; Property crime rate: 1,007.4 per 10,000 population
Newspapers: The Enterprise (weekly circulation 5100); The Weekly Herald (weekly circulation 1000)
Transportation: Commute: 98.6% car, 0.0% public transportation, 1.4% walk, 0.0% work from home; Median travel time to work: 19.4 minutes
Additional Information Contacts
Town of Williamston . . . . (252) 792-5142
    http://www.townofwilliamston.com

McDowell County

Located in west central North Carolina, in the Blue Ridge; drained by the Catawba River and Lake James; includes part of Pisgah National Forest. Covers a land area of 440.608 square miles, a water area of 5.389 square miles, and is located in the Eastern Time Zone at 35.68° N. Lat., 82.05° W. Long. The county was founded in 1842. County seat is Marion.

McDowell County is part of the Marion, NC Micropolitan Statistical Area. The entire metro area includes: McDowell County, NC

Weather Station: Marion 2 NW										Elevation: 1,465 feet	
	Jan	Feb	Mar	Apr	May	Jun	Jul	Aug	Sep	Oct	Nov	Dec
High	50	55	63	71	78	85	88	87	80	71	62	53
Low	26	29	34	43	51	60	63	62	56	44	35	28
Precip	3.6	3.9	4.4	4.4	4.5	4.7	4.6	4.2	4.6	3.2	4.1	4.0
Snow	2.7	1.9	1.7	0.3	0.0	0.0	0.0	0.0	0.0	0.0	tr	1.3

High and Low temperatures in degrees Fahrenheit; Precipitation and Snow in inches

Population: 44,996; Growth (since 2000): 6.7%; Density: 102.1 persons per square mile; Race: 90.6% White, 3.8% Black/African American, 0.8% Asian, 0.4% American Indian/Alaska Native, 0.0% Native Hawaiian/Other Pacific Islander, 1.2% two or more races, 5.3% Hispanic of any race; Average household size: 2.43; Median age: 41.6; Age under 18: 21.7%; Age 65 and over: 16.4%; Males per 100 females: 100.2; Marriage status: 26.0% never married, 52.5% now married, 3.1% separated, 8.4% widowed, 13.1% divorced; Foreign born: 3.4%; Speak English only: 93.8%; With disability: 22.3%; Veterans: 10.3%; Ancestry: 26.0% American, 13.6% Irish, 11.5% German, 9.7% English, 4.2% Scotch-Irish
Religion: Six largest groups: 27.3% Baptist, 5.5% Methodist/Pietist, 3.3% Non-denominational Protestant, 2.4% Pentecostal, 1.1% Presbyterian-Reformed, 0.9% Latter-day Saints
Economy: Unemployment rate: 5.7%; Leading industries: 17.5% retail trade; 13.3% other services (except public administration); 12.4% health care and social assistance; Farms: 334 totaling 24,903 acres; Company size: 1 employs 1,000 or more persons, 0 employ 500 to 999 persons, 18 employ 100 to 499 persons, 705 employ less than 100 persons; Business ownership: 625 women-owned, n/a Black-owned, n/a Hispanic-owned, 50 Asian-owned
Employment: 9.5% management, business, and financial, 1.7% computer, engineering, and science, 9.6% education, legal, community service, arts, and media, 5.8% healthcare practitioners, 20.2% service, 21.7% sales and office, 9.5% natural resources, construction, and maintenance, 21.9% production, transportation, and material moving
Income: Per capita: $18,932; Median household: $35,297; Average household: $46,025; Households with income of $100,000 or more: 7.7%; Poverty rate: 21.9%
Educational Attainment: High school diploma or higher: 80.8%; Bachelor's degree or higher: 13.9%; Graduate/professional degree or higher: 4.4%
Housing: Homeownership rate: 73.6%; Median home value: $101,200; Median year structure built: 1978; Homeowner vacancy rate: 1.9%; Median gross rent: $569 per month; Rental vacancy rate: 8.8%
Vital Statistics: Birth rate: 99.6 per 10,000 population; Death rate: 101.9 per 10,000 population; Age-adjusted cancer mortality rate: 192.5 deaths per 100,000 population
Health Insurance: 84.8% have insurance; 57.7% have private insurance; 41.4% have public insurance; 15.2% do not have insurance; 4.5% of children under 18 do not have insurance
Health Care: Physicians: 7.3 per 10,000 population; Hospital beds: 10.9 per 10,000 population; Hospital admissions: 407.4 per 10,000 population
Air Quality Index: 88.2% good, 11.8% moderate, 0.0% unhealthy for sensitive individuals, 0.0% unhealthy (percent of days)
Transportation: Commute: 94.6% car, 0.0% public transportation, 0.8% walk, 3.8% work from home; Median travel time to work: 23.6 minutes
Presidential Election: 33.3% Obama, 65.1% Romney (2012)
Additional Information Contacts
McDowell Government . . . . (828) 652-7121
    http://www.mcdowellgov.com

McDowell County Communities

MARION (city). County seat. Covers a land area of 5.388 square miles and a water area of 0.031 square miles. Located at 35.68° N. Lat; 82.00° W. Long. Elevation is 1,430 feet.
History: Marion was named for General Francis Marion, a Revolutionary leader known as the "Swamp Fox." The town was established soon after 1842.
Population: 7,838; Growth (since 2000): 58.6%; Density: 1,454.7 persons per square mile; Race: 76.5% White, 11.1% Black/African American, 0.8% Asian, 0.5% American Indian/Alaska Native, 0.0% Native Hawaiian/Other Pacific Islander, 2.0% Two or more races, 13.1% Hispanic of any race; Average household size: 2.36; Median age: 37.9; Age under 18: 21.3%; Age 65 and over: 16.6%; Males per 100 females: 109.8; Marriage status: 30.9% never married, 41.9% now married, 5.1% separated, 12.2% widowed, 15.0% divorced; Foreign born: 7.5%; Speak English only: 84.5%; With disability: 22.8%; Veterans: 9.3%; Ancestry: 19.8% American, 10.4% German, 9.8% English, 9.6% Irish, 3.9% Scotch-Irish
Employment: 5.9% management, business, and financial, 3.6% computer, engineering, and science, 14.7% education, legal, community service, arts, and media, 9.6% healthcare practitioners, 20.9% service, 14.4% sales and office, 10.0% natural resources, construction, and maintenance, 21.0% production, transportation, and material moving

Income: Per capita: $15,544; Median household: $24,509; Average household: $40,258; Households with income of $100,000 or more: 8.5%; Poverty rate: 41.3%
Educational Attainment: High school diploma or higher: 75.6%; Bachelor's degree or higher: 13.6%; Graduate/professional degree or higher: 5.1%

School District(s)
Mcdowell County Schools (PK-12)
    2012-13 Enrollment: 6,620 . . . . (828) 652-4535
Two-year College(s)
McDowell Technical Community College (Public)
    Fall 2013 Enrollment: 1,152 . . . . (828) 652-6021
    2013-14 Tuition: In-state $1,776; Out-of-state $6,384
Housing: Homeownership rate: 54.4%; Median home value: $83,900; Median year structure built: 1961; Homeowner vacancy rate: 3.4%; Median gross rent: $542 per month; Rental vacancy rate: 5.8%
Health Insurance: 84.5% have insurance; 45.3% have private insurance; 50.2% have public insurance; 15.5% do not have insurance; 4.3% of children under 18 do not have insurance
Hospitals: The Mcdowell Hospital (65 beds)
Safety: Violent crime rate: 37.8 per 10,000 population; Property crime rate: 825.7 per 10,000 population
Newspapers: McDowell News (daily circulation 4700)
Transportation: Commute: 94.3% car, 0.0% public transportation, 2.0% walk, 2.8% work from home; Median travel time to work: 20.6 minutes
Additional Information Contacts
City of Marion . . . . (319) 743-6301
    https://www.cityofmarion.org/#/home

NEBO (unincorporated postal area)
ZCTA: 28761
    Covers a land area of 108.204 square miles and a water area of 6.601 square miles. Located at 35.69° N. Lat; 81.91° W. Long. Elevation is 1,306 feet.
    Population: 7,816; Growth (since 2000): 15.8%; Density: 72.2 persons per square mile; Race: 92.6% White, 2.5% Black/African American, 1.9% Asian, 0.4% American Indian/Alaska Native, 0.0% Native Hawaiian/Other Pacific Islander, 0.7% Two or more races, 3.4% Hispanic of any race; Average household size: 2.50; Median age: 42.9; Age under 18: 22.2%; Age 65 and over: 16.3%; Males per 100 females: 100.8; Marriage status: 31.1% never married, 50.6% now married, 3.8% separated, 6.7% widowed, 11.6% divorced; Foreign born: 3.0%; Speak English only: 96.3%; With disability: 21.6%; Veterans: 10.4%; Ancestry: 29.2% American, 13.6% English, 12.8% German, 11.7% Irish, 3.8% Scottish
    Employment: 5.0% management, business, and financial, 4.0% computer, engineering, and science, 8.5% education, legal, community service, arts, and media, 8.0% healthcare practitioners, 21.1% service, 19.8% sales and office, 13.1% natural resources, construction, and maintenance, 20.6% production, transportation, and material moving
    Income: Per capita: $18,629; Median household: $39,847; Average household: $49,744; Households with income of $100,000 or more: 7.5%; Poverty rate: 22.7%
    Educational Attainment: High school diploma or higher: 80.5%; Bachelor's degree or higher: 15.2%; Graduate/professional degree or higher: 5.5%

School District(s)
Mcdowell County Schools (PK-12)
    2012-13 Enrollment: 6,620 . . . . (828) 652-4535
    Housing: Homeownership rate: 81.0%; Median home value: $96,200; Median year structure built: 1984; Homeowner vacancy rate: 2.1%; Median gross rent: $640 per month; Rental vacancy rate: 9.7%
    Health Insurance: 85.3% have insurance; 57.1% have private insurance; 42.1% have public insurance; 14.7% do not have insurance; 2.6% of children under 18 do not have insurance
    Transportation: Commute: 92.9% car, 0.0% public transportation, 0.5% walk, 5.3% work from home; Median travel time to work: 26.9 minutes

OLD FORT (town). Covers a land area of 1.221 square miles and a water area of 0.008 square miles. Located at 35.63° N. Lat; 82.18° W. Long. Elevation is 1,437 feet.
History: Old Fort is on the site of Davidsons Fort, an early shelter built in 1757.
Population: 908; Growth (since 2000): -5.7%; Density: 743.7 persons per square mile; Race: 83.8% White, 13.5% Black/African American, 0.3%

Asian, 0.1% American Indian/Alaska Native, 0.0% Native Hawaiian/Other Pacific Islander, 1.3% Two or more races, 2.9% Hispanic of any race; Average household size: 2.16; Median age: 44.1; Age under 18: 19.4%; Age 65 and over: 21.0%; Males per 100 females: 90.0

School District(s)
Mcdowell County Schools (PK-12)
    2012-13 Enrollment: 6,620 . . . . (828) 652-4535
Housing: Homeownership rate: 61.8%; Homeowner vacancy rate: 1.5%; Rental vacancy rate: 15.1%

WEST MARION (CDP). Covers a land area of 1.715 square miles and a water area of 0 square miles. Located at 35.65° N. Lat; 82.02° W. Long. Elevation is 1,467 feet.
Population: 1,348; Growth (since 2000): -13.4%; Density: 786.0 persons per square mile; Race: 92.5% White, 4.5% Black/African American, 0.5% Asian, 0.4% American Indian/Alaska Native, 0.0% Native Hawaiian/Other Pacific Islander, 1.0% Two or more races, 3.3% Hispanic of any race; Average household size: 2.28; Median age: 42.2; Age under 18: 21.4%; Age 65 and over: 20.2%; Males per 100 females: 91.2
Housing: Homeownership rate: 68.7%; Homeowner vacancy rate: 1.2%; Rental vacancy rate: 6.1%

Mecklenburg County

Located in southern North Carolina; in piedmont area, bounded on the southwest by South Carolina, and on the west by the Catawba River, with Catawba and Mountain Island Lakes. Covers a land area of 523.842 square miles, a water area of 22.067 square miles, and is located in the Eastern Time Zone at 35.25° N. Lat., 80.83° W. Long. The county was founded in 1762. County seat is Charlotte.

Mecklenburg County is part of the Charlotte-Concord-Gastonia, NC-SC Metropolitan Statistical Area. The entire metro area includes: Cabarrus County, NC; Gaston County, NC; Iredell County, NC; Lincoln County, NC; Mecklenburg County, NC; Rowan County, NC; Union County, NC; Chester County, SC; Lancaster County, SC; York County, SC

Weather Station: Charlotte Douglas Intl Arpt										Elevation: 728 feet		
	Jan	Feb	Mar	Apr	May	Jun	Jul	Aug	Sep	Oct	Nov	Dec
High	51	56	63	72	79	86	89	88	82	72	63	54
Low	32	34	41	49	57	66	70	69	62	50	41	34
Precip	3.4	3.2	4.2	3.1	3.2	3.7	3.7	4.1	3.3	3.4	3.2	3.2
Snow	2.0	1.4	0.8	tr	tr	tr	0.0	tr	0.0	tr	0.1	0.2

High and Low temperatures in degrees Fahrenheit; Precipitation and Snow in inches

Population: 919,628; Growth (since 2000): 32.2%; Density: 1,755.5 persons per square mile; Race: 55.3% White, 30.8% Black/African American, 4.6% Asian, 0.5% American Indian/Alaska Native, 0.1% Native Hawaiian/Other Pacific Islander, 2.6% two or more races, 12.2% Hispanic of any race; Average household size: 2.49; Median age: 33.9; Age under 18: 25.4%; Age 65 and over: 8.8%; Males per 100 females: 93.7; Marriage status: 36.7% never married, 48.7% now married, 2.9% separated, 4.5% widowed, 10.1% divorced; Foreign born: 13.9%; Speak English only: 81.8%; With disability: 8.6%; Veterans: 7.4%; Ancestry: 11.2% German, 8.6% Irish, 8.3% English, 5.4% American, 4.1% Italian
Religion: Six largest groups: 13.3% Baptist, 8.5% Catholicism, 8.0% Methodist/Pietist, 7.7% Non-denominational Protestant, 5.2% Presbyterian-Reformed, 2.5% Pentecostal
Economy: Unemployment rate: 5.7%; Leading industries: 13.9% professional, scientific, and technical services; 12.0% retail trade; 9.2% health care and social assistance; Farms: 237 totaling 15,439 acres; Company size: 33 employ 1,000 or more persons, 78 employ 500 to 999 persons, 738 employ 100 to 499 persons, 27,328 employ less than 100 persons; Business ownership: 27,432 women-owned, 13,873 Black-owned, 4,242 Hispanic-owned, 4,054 Asian-owned
Employment: 19.4% management, business, and financial; 6.0% computer, engineering, and science, 10.8% education, legal, community service, arts, and media, 4.9% healthcare practitioners, 16.4% service, 26.0% sales and office, 6.9% natural resources, construction, and maintenance, 9.6% production, transportation, and material moving
Income: Per capita: $32,482; Median household: $55,444; Average household: $81,675; Households with income of $100,000 or more: 24.7%; Poverty rate: 15.4%
Educational Attainment: High school diploma or higher: 88.8%; Bachelor's degree or higher: 40.7%; Graduate/professional degree or higher: 12.9%

Housing: Homeownership rate: 60.7%; Median home value: $181,900; Median year structure built: 1990; Homeowner vacancy rate: 3.3%; Median gross rent: $889 per month; Rental vacancy rate: 11.3%
Vital Statistics: Birth rate: 141.5 per 10,000 population; Death rate: 56.5 per 10,000 population; Age-adjusted cancer mortality rate: 163.8 deaths per 100,000 population
Health Insurance: 83.0% have insurance; 67.1% have private insurance; 23.6% have public insurance; 17.0% do not have insurance; 7.8% of children under 18 do not have insurance
Health Care: Physicians: 28.8 per 10,000 population; Hospital beds: 24.9 per 10,000 population; Hospital admissions: 1,293.2 per 10,000 population
Air Quality Index: 77.3% good, 22.7% moderate, 0.0% unhealthy for sensitive individuals, 0.0% unhealthy (percent of days)
Transportation: Commute: 87.4% car, 3.4% public transportation, 2.0% walk, 6.0% work from home; Median travel time to work: 24.7 minutes
Presidential Election: 60.7% Obama, 38.2% Romney (2012)
National and State Parks: North Carolina State Wildlife Landing
Additional Information Contacts
Mecklenburg Government . . . . (704) 336-5430
    http://www.charmeck.org

Mecklenburg County Communities

CHARLOTTE (city). County seat. Covers a land area of 297.678 square miles and a water area of 1.988 square miles. Located at 35.21° N. Lat; 80.83° W. Long. Elevation is 761 feet.
History: The present Charlotte area was occupied by the Catawba people when settlers began arriving about 1748. They were Scots-Irish and Germans who came south through Pennsylvania and Virginia, and English, Huguenots and Swiss from Charleston, South Carolina. The county seat was chartered in 1768. The town was named for Queen Charlotte of Mecklenburg-Strelitz, wife of George III. Fertile soil brought more settlers, and in 1771 a college was established. Charlotte claims to have been the site of the first declaration of independence signed by legislators in the Thirteen Colonies, although the document was later destroyed by fire. Gold mining, textiles, and culture have been important to Charlotte's history.
Population: 731,424; Growth (since 2000): 35.2%; Density: 2,457.1 persons per square mile; Race: 50.0% White, 35.0% Black/African American, 5.0% Asian, 0.5% American Indian/Alaska Native, 0.1% Native Hawaiian/Other Pacific Islander, 2.7% Two or more races, 13.1% Hispanic of any race; Average household size: 2.48; Median age: 33.2; Age under 18: 25.2%; Age 65 and over: 8.5%; Males per 100 females: 93.5; Marriage status: 38.9% never married, 46.3% now married, 3.1% separated, 4.6% widowed, 10.3% divorced; Foreign born: 15.0%; Speak English only: 80.3%; With disability: 8.7%; Veterans: 7.2%; Ancestry: 9.7% German, 7.6% Irish, 7.5% English, 4.8% American, 3.5% Italian
Employment: 18.7% management, business, and financial; 6.0% computer, engineering, and science, 10.6% education, legal, community service, arts, and media, 4.8% healthcare practitioners, 16.8% service, 25.9% sales and office, 7.1% natural resources, construction, and maintenance, 10.2% production, transportation, and material moving
Income: Per capita: $31,556; Median household: $52,375; Average household: $78,641; Households with income of $100,000 or more: 22.7%; Poverty rate: 17.1%
Educational Attainment: High school diploma or higher: 88.0%; Bachelor's degree or higher: 39.8%; Graduate/professional degree or higher: 12.7%

School District(s)
Charlotte Secondary School (06-08)
    2012-13 Enrollment: 240 . . . . (704) 295-0137
Charlotte-Mecklenburg Schools (PK-12)
    2012-13 Enrollment: 144,478 . . . . (980) 343-6270
Community Charter School (KG-05)
    2012-13 Enrollment: 147 . . . . (704) 377-3180
Crossroads Charter High (09-12)
    2012-13 Enrollment: 250 . . . . (704) 597-5100
Kennedy Charter (KG-12)
    2012-13 Enrollment: 360 . . . . (704) 688-2939
Kipp: Charlotte (05-08)
    2012-13 Enrollment: 343 . . . . (704) 537-2044
Metrolina Reg Scholars Academy (KG-08)
    2012-13 Enrollment: 361 . . . . (704) 503-1112
Socrates Academy (KG-07)
    2012-13 Enrollment: 607 . . . . (704) 321-1711

Sugar Creek Charter (KG-08)
  2012-13 Enrollment: 878.......................... (704) 509-5470
Four-year College(s)
Charlotte School of Law (Private, For-profit)
  Fall 2013 Enrollment: 1,410 .... (704) 971-8546
DeVry University-North Carolina (Private, For-profit)
  Fall 2013 Enrollment: 737......................... (704) 362-2345
  2013-14 Tuition: In-state $16,010; Out-of-state $16,010
ITT Technical Institute-Charlotte North (Private, For-profit)
  Fall 2013 Enrollment: 416......................... (704) 548-2300
  2013-14 Tuition: In-state $18,048; Out-of-state $18,048
ITT Technical Institute-Charlotte South (Private, For-profit)
  Fall 2013 Enrollment: 369......................... (704) 423-3100
  2013-14 Tuition: In-state $18,048; Out-of-state $18,048
Johnson & Wales University-Charlotte (Private, Not-for-profit)
  Fall 2013 Enrollment: 2,325 .... (980) 598-1000
  2013-14 Tuition: In-state $27,456; Out-of-state $27,456
Johnson C Smith University (Private, Not-for-profit, Historically black)
  Fall 2013 Enrollment: 1,387 .... (704) 378-1000
  2013-14 Tuition: In-state $18,236; Out-of-state $18,236
New Life Theological Seminary (Private, Not-for-profit)
  Fall 2013 Enrollment: 163......................... (704) 334-6882
  2013-14 Tuition: In-state $8,380; Out-of-state $8,380
Queens University of Charlotte (Private, Not-for-profit, Presbyterian Church (USA))
  Fall 2013 Enrollment: 2,285 .... (704) 337-2200
  2013-14 Tuition: In-state $29,800; Out-of-state $29,800
The Art Institute of Charlotte (Private, For-profit)
  Fall 2013 Enrollment: 1,427 .... (704) 357-8020
  2013-14 Tuition: In-state $17,128; Out-of-state $17,128
University of North Carolina at Charlotte (Public)
  Fall 2013 Enrollment: 26,571 .... (704) 687-2000
  2013-14 Tuition: In-state $6,107; Out-of-state $18,636
University of Phoenix-Charlotte Campus (Private, For-profit)
  Fall 2013 Enrollment: 933......................... (866) 766-0766
  2013-14 Tuition: In-state $10,240; Out-of-state $10,240
Two-year College(s)
Carolinas College of Health Sciences (Public)
  Fall 2013 Enrollment: 449......................... (704) 355-5043
Central Piedmont Community College (Public)
  Fall 2013 Enrollment: 20,198 .... (704) 330-2722
  2013-14 Tuition: In-state $2,561; Out-of-state $8,705
Kaplan College-Charlotte (Private, For-profit)
  Fall 2013 Enrollment: 382......................... (704) 567-3700
King's College (Private, For-profit)
  Fall 2013 Enrollment: 381......................... (704) 372-0266
  2013-14 Tuition: In-state $14,280; Out-of-state $14,280
Mercy School of Nursing (Public)
  Fall 2013 Enrollment: 137......................... (704) 512-2010
Vocational/Technical School(s)
Brookstone College-Charlotte (Private, For-profit)
  Fall 2013 Enrollment: 128......................... (704) 547-8600
  2013-14 Tuition: $19,400
Carolina School of Broadcasting (Private, For-profit)
  Fall 2013 Enrollment: 57.......................... (704) 395-9272
  2013-14 Tuition: $15,750
Empire Beauty School-Pineville (Private, For-profit)
  Fall 2013 Enrollment: 105......................... (800) 920-4593
  2013-14 Tuition: $18,360
Regency Beauty Institute-Charlotte (Private, For-profit)
  Fall 2013 Enrollment: 62.......................... (800) 787-6456
  2013-14 Tuition: $16,200
Regina's College of Beauty-Charlotte (Private, For-profit)
  Fall 2013 Enrollment: 102......................... (704) 394-9661
  2013-14 Tuition: $17,495
Southeastern Institute-Charlotte (Private, For-profit)
  Fall 2013 Enrollment: 345......................... (704) 527-4979
  2013-14 Tuition: $15,584
The Hair Design School-Charlotte (Private, For-profit)
  Fall 2013 Enrollment: 134......................... (800) 920-4593
  2013-14 Tuition: $16,260
Housing: Homeownership rate: 57.4%; Median home value: $170,500; Median year structure built: 1988; Homeowner vacancy rate: 3.4%; Median gross rent: $882 per month; Rental vacancy rate: 11.7%

Health Insurance: 81.9% have insurance; 64.6% have private insurance; 24.7% have public insurance; 18.1% do not have insurance; 7.9% of children under 18 do not have insurance
Hospitals: Carolinas Medical Center - Pineville (224 beds); Carolinas Medical Center - University; Carolinas Medical Center/Behaviorial Health (874 beds); Novant Health Charlotte Orthopedic Hospital; Novant Health Presbyterian Medical Center (547 beds)
Safety: Violent crime rate: 60.8 per 10,000 population; Property crime rate: 364.9 per 10,000 population
Newspapers: Charlotte Observer (daily circulation 207000); Mecklenburg Times (weekly circulation 1000); Mint Hill Times (weekly circulation 5000); South Charlotte Weekly (weekly circulation 45000); Union County Weekly (weekly circulation 19000)
Transportation: Commute: 87.1% car, 3.8% public transportation, 2.2% walk, 5.7% work from home; Median travel time to work: 24.3 minutes; Amtrak: Train service available.
Airports: Charlotte/Douglas International (primary service/large hub)
Additional Information Contacts
City of Charlotte............................... (704) 378-1300
  http://www.charmeck.org

CORNELIUS (town). Covers a land area of 12.080 square miles and a water area of 0.304 square miles. Located at 35.47° N. Lat; 80.88° W. Long. Elevation is 784 feet.
History: The town of Cornelius, the second youngest of Mecklenburg County's six incorporated towns, was founded in 1893 but not incorporated until March 4, 1905. The Town's origin has been traced by many historians to a dispute over cotton weighing.
Population: 24,866; Growth (since 2000): 107.8%; Density: 2,058.4 persons per square mile; Race: 88.3% White, 5.8% Black/African American, 2.3% Asian, 0.3% American Indian/Alaska Native, 0.0% Native Hawaiian/Other Pacific Islander, 1.6% Two or more races, 5.3% Hispanic of any race; Average household size: 2.31; Median age: 37.9; Age under 18: 22.9%; Age 65 and over: 10.1%; Males per 100 females: 96.0; Marriage status: 27.2% never married, 55.9% now married, 1.6% separated, 4.6% widowed, 12.3% divorced; Foreign born: 8.9%; Speak English only: 88.9%; With disability: 7.3%; Veterans: 8.7%; Ancestry: 21.8% German, 12.9% English, 12.3% Irish, 7.9% Italian, 6.9% American
Employment: 25.4% management, business, and financial, 7.0% computer, engineering, and science, 9.8% education, legal, community service, arts, and media, 6.3% healthcare practitioners, 16.9% service, 26.0% sales and office, 3.1% natural resources, construction, and maintenance, 5.5% production, transportation, and material moving
Income: Per capita: $47,666; Median household: $80,697; Average household: $113,316; Households with income of $100,000 or more: 39.5%; Poverty rate: 8.5%
Educational Attainment: High school diploma or higher: 93.5%; Bachelor's degree or higher: 50.6%; Graduate/professional degree or higher: 16.5%
School District(s)
Charlotte-Mecklenburg Schools (PK-12)
  2012-13 Enrollment: 144,478 .... (980) 343-6270
Housing: Homeownership rate: 71.3%; Median home value: $247,900; Median year structure built: 1996; Homeowner vacancy rate: 3.3%; Median gross rent: $1,055 per month; Rental vacancy rate: 7.6%
Health Insurance: 87.5% have insurance; 80.4% have private insurance; 16.2% have public insurance; 12.5% do not have insurance; 9.3% of children under 18 do not have insurance
Safety: Violent crime rate: 15.7 per 10,000 population; Property crime rate: 178.8 per 10,000 population
Transportation: Commute: 85.9% car, 3.0% public transportation, 0.8% walk, 9.5% work from home; Median travel time to work: 26.5 minutes
Additional Information Contacts
Town of Cornelius............................... (704) 892-1922
  http://www.cornelius.org

DAVIDSON (town). Covers a land area of 5.751 square miles and a water area of 0.247 square miles. Located at 35.49° N. Lat; 80.83° W. Long. Elevation is 820 feet.
History: Seat of Davidson College (1837).
Population: 10,944; Growth (since 2000): 53.3%; Density: 1,902.9 persons per square mile; Race: 87.8% White, 6.4% Black/African American, 2.8% Asian, 0.2% American Indian/Alaska Native, 0.0% Native Hawaiian/Other Pacific Islander, 1.7% Two or more races, 3.8% Hispanic of any race; Average household size: 2.49; Median age: 35.7; Age under

18: 22.8%; Age 65 and over: 12.5%; Males per 100 females: 90.3; Marriage status: 37.7% never married, 50.8% now married, 3.2% separated, 2.9% widowed, 8.7% divorced; Foreign born: 6.5%; Speak English only: 93.4%; With disability: 7.8%; Veterans: 5.9%; Ancestry: 21.6% German, 16.1% English, 15.6% Irish, 8.2% Scottish, 6.6% Italian
Employment: 25.5% management, business, and financial, 7.6% computer, engineering, and science, 16.1% education, legal, community service, arts, and media, 8.9% healthcare practitioners, 15.8% service, 19.8% sales and office, 3.2% natural resources, construction, and maintenance, 3.2% production, transportation, and material moving
Income: Per capita: $47,565; Median household: $88,750; Average household: $138,044; Households with income of $100,000 or more: 45.4%; Poverty rate: 6.8%
Educational Attainment: High school diploma or higher: 97.3%; Bachelor's degree or higher: 66.0%; Graduate/professional degree or higher: 29.5%

School District(s)
Charlotte-Mecklenburg Schools (PK-12)
  2012-13 Enrollment: 144,478 . . . . (980) 343-6270
Community School Of Davidson (KG-10)
  2012-13 Enrollment: 1,188 . . . . (704) 896-6262
Four-year College(s)
Davidson College (Private, Not-for-profit, Presbyterian Church (USA))
  Fall 2013 Enrollment: 1,788 . . . . (704) 894-2000
  2013-14 Tuition: In-state $42,849; Out-of-state $42,849
Housing: Homeownership rate: 74.8%; Median home value: $391,300; Median year structure built: 1995; Homeowner vacancy rate: 6.2%; Median gross rent: $930 per month; Rental vacancy rate: 9.8%
Health Insurance: 94.1% have insurance; 87.3% have private insurance; 14.7% have public insurance; 5.9% do not have insurance; 1.2% of children under 18 do not have insurance
Safety: Violent crime rate: 9.4 per 10,000 population; Property crime rate: 77.2 per 10,000 population
Newspapers: Herald Weekly (weekly circulation 27000)
Transportation: Commute: 77.1% car, 1.5% public transportation, 6.0% walk, 13.8% work from home; Median travel time to work: 22.5 minutes
Additional Information Contacts
Town of Davidson . . . . (704) 892-7591
  http://www.ci.davidson.nc.us

HUNTERSVILLE (town). Covers a land area of 39.610 square miles and a water area of 0.162 square miles. Located at 35.40° N. Lat; 80.88° W. Long. Elevation is 810 feet.
History: Energy Explorium, hands-on museum at dam.
Population: 46,773; Growth (since 2000): 87.4%; Density: 1,180.8 persons per square mile; Race: 82.8% White, 9.4% Black/African American, 2.7% Asian, 0.3% American Indian/Alaska Native, 0.0% Native Hawaiian/Other Pacific Islander, 2.1% Two or more races, 7.4% Hispanic of any race; Average household size: 2.67; Median age: 35.2; Age under 18: 28.9%; Age 65 and over: 6.8%; Males per 100 females: 96.2; Marriage status: 24.4% never married, 64.0% now married, 1.3% separated, 3.7% widowed, 7.9% divorced; Foreign born: 6.7%; Speak English only: 92.3%; With disability: 6.8%; Veterans: 6.8%; Ancestry: 19.4% German, 15.7% Irish, 13.0% English, 9.4% Italian, 6.8% American
Employment: 25.2% management, business, and financial, 6.7% computer, engineering, and science, 12.2% education, legal, community service, arts, and media, 6.2% healthcare practitioners, 13.6% service, 25.8% sales and office, 5.1% natural resources, construction, and maintenance, 5.2% production, transportation, and material moving
Income: Per capita: $38,409; Median household: $84,486; Average household: $102,816; Households with income of $100,000 or more: 42.9%; Poverty rate: 6.0%
Educational Attainment: High school diploma or higher: 94.2%; Bachelor's degree or higher: 52.5%; Graduate/professional degree or higher: 15.0%

School District(s)
Charlotte-Mecklenburg Schools (PK-12)
  2012-13 Enrollment: 144,478 . . . . (980) 343-6270
Corvian Community School
  2012-13 Enrollment: 88 . . . . (704) 717-7550
Lake Norman Charter (05-12)
  2012-13 Enrollment: 1,594 . . . . (704) 948-8600
Housing: Homeownership rate: 75.5%; Median home value: $245,300; Median year structure built: 1999; Homeowner vacancy rate: 2.2%; Median gross rent: $997 per month; Rental vacancy rate: 7.0%

Health Insurance: 88.9% have insurance; 83.3% have private insurance; 12.0% have public insurance; 11.1% do not have insurance; 6.1% of children under 18 do not have insurance
Hospitals: Novant Health Huntersville Medical Center
Safety: Violent crime rate: 9.8 per 10,000 population; Property crime rate: 187.4 per 10,000 population
Transportation: Commute: 89.0% car, 1.3% public transportation, 0.7% walk, 7.8% work from home; Median travel time to work: 25.9 minutes
Additional Information Contacts
Town of Huntersville . . . . (704) 875-6541
  http://www.huntersville.org

MATTHEWS (town). Covers a land area of 17.110 square miles and a water area of 0.083 square miles. Located at 35.12° N. Lat; 80.71° W. Long. Elevation is 728 feet.
Population: 27,198; Growth (since 2000): 22.9%; Density: 1,589.6 persons per square mile; Race: 81.8% White, 9.6% Black/African American, 4.2% Asian, 0.3% American Indian/Alaska Native, 0.0% Native Hawaiian/Other Pacific Islander, 1.9% Two or more races, 5.8% Hispanic of any race; Average household size: 2.56; Median age: 40.3; Age under 18: 24.9%; Age 65 and over: 13.3%; Males per 100 females: 92.6; Marriage status: 24.2% never married, 61.2% now married, 1.8% separated, 5.4% widowed, 9.2% divorced; Foreign born: 8.7%; Speak English only: 89.0%; With disability: 7.4%; Veterans: 9.7%; Ancestry: 16.6% German, 14.2% Irish, 12.9% English, 9.0% American, 6.8% Italian
Employment: 21.8% management, business, and financial, 6.9% computer, engineering, and science, 15.9% education, legal, community service, arts, and media, 4.9% healthcare practitioners, 11.1% service, 29.3% sales and office, 5.1% natural resources, construction, and maintenance, 5.0% production, transportation, and material moving
Income: Per capita: $33,722; Median household: $68,295; Average household: $87,112; Households with income of $100,000 or more: 31.2%; Poverty rate: 7.9%
Educational Attainment: High school diploma or higher: 94.9%; Bachelor's degree or higher: 48.1%; Graduate/professional degree or higher: 14.8%

School District(s)
Charlotte-Mecklenburg Schools (PK-12)
  2012-13 Enrollment: 144,478 . . . . (980) 343-6270
Union County Public Schools (PK-12)
  2012-13 Enrollment: 40,659 . . . . (704) 296-9898
Vocational/Technical School(s)
Empire Beauty School-Matthews (Private, For-profit)
  Fall 2013 Enrollment: 97 . . . . (800) 920-4593
  2013-14 Tuition: $18,360
Housing: Homeownership rate: 72.5%; Median home value: $217,600; Median year structure built: 1990; Homeowner vacancy rate: 1.8%; Median gross rent: $937 per month; Rental vacancy rate: 5.1%
Health Insurance: 89.1% have insurance; 79.4% have private insurance; 20.8% have public insurance; 10.9% do not have insurance; 7.6% of children under 18 do not have insurance
Hospitals: Presbyterian Hospital Matthews (94 beds)
Safety: Violent crime rate: 19.9 per 10,000 population; Property crime rate: 282.1 per 10,000 population
Newspapers: Matthews Record (weekly circulation 12000)
Transportation: Commute: 88.0% car, 1.6% public transportation, 1.6% walk, 7.5% work from home; Median travel time to work: 25.2 minutes
Additional Information Contacts
Town of Matthews . . . . (704) 847-4411
  http://www.matthewsnc.com

MINT HILL (town). Covers a land area of 23.924 square miles and a water area of 0.227 square miles. Located at 35.18° N. Lat; 80.66° W. Long. Elevation is 787 feet.
Population: 22,722; Growth (since 2000): 52.3%; Density: 949.8 persons per square mile; Race: 78.4% White, 12.3% Black/African American, 2.5% Asian, 0.6% American Indian/Alaska Native, 0.0% Native Hawaiian/Other Pacific Islander, 2.0% Two or more races, 8.3% Hispanic of any race; Average household size: 2.65; Median age: 41.8; Age under 18: 24.2%; Age 65 and over: 14.7%; Males per 100 females: 95.5; Marriage status: 24.9% never married, 62.9% now married, 1.7% separated, 4.1% widowed, 8.1% divorced; Foreign born: 7.8%; Speak English only: 89.8%; With disability: 10.2%; Veterans: 11.3%; Ancestry: 16.9% German, 13.1% Irish, 11.0% English, 10.0% American, 5.4% Scotch-Irish

Employment: 19.5% management, business, and financial, 6.5% computer, engineering, and science, 11.9% education, legal, community service, arts, and media, 3.5% healthcare practitioners, 14.7% service, 26.3% sales and office, 8.4% natural resources, construction, and maintenance, 9.2% production, transportation, and material moving
Income: Per capita: $31,825; Median household: $68,140; Average household: $85,765; Households with income of $100,000 or more: 30.2%; Poverty rate: 8.0%
Educational Attainment: High school diploma or higher: 91.4%; Bachelor's degree or higher: 33.7%; Graduate/professional degree or higher: 9.1%

School District(s)
Queen's Grant Community (KG-12)
    2012-13 Enrollment: 1,284 . . . . (704) 573-6611
Housing: Homeownership rate: 82.1%; Median home value: $207,000; Median year structure built: 1986; Homeowner vacancy rate: 2.8%; Median gross rent: $822 per month; Rental vacancy rate: 11.1%
Health Insurance: 88.8% have insurance; 75.2% have private insurance; 28.3% have public insurance; 11.2% do not have insurance; 7.3% of children under 18 do not have insurance
Safety: Violent crime rate: 18.5 per 10,000 population; Property crime rate: 166.7 per 10,000 population
Transportation: Commute: 93.2% car, 1.0% public transportation, 0.2% walk, 4.9% work from home; Median travel time to work: 28.3 minutes
Additional Information Contacts
Town of Mint Hill . . . . (704) 545-9726
    http://www.minthill.com

PINEVILLE (town). Covers a land area of 6.622 square miles and a water area of 0.037 square miles. Located at 35.09° N. Lat; 80.89° W. Long. Elevation is 571 feet.
History: James K. Polk Memorial State Historical Site, birthplace of President Polk, to East.
Population: 7,479; Growth (since 2000): 116.8%; Density: 1,129.4 persons per square mile; Race: 62.1% White, 22.2% Black/African American, 3.4% Asian, 0.5% American Indian/Alaska Native, 0.1% Native Hawaiian/Other Pacific Islander, 2.7% Two or more races, 20.1% Hispanic of any race; Average household size: 1.97; Median age: 35.0; Age under 18: 20.0%; Age 65 and over: 16.6%; Males per 100 females: 81.0; Marriage status: 37.1% never married, 34.2% now married, 7.6% separated, 12.1% widowed, 16.5% divorced; Foreign born: 17.5%; Speak English only: 74.0%; With disability: 15.4%; Veterans: 5.8%; Ancestry: 13.0% German, 11.9% American, 10.3% Irish, 5.5% English, 4.8% Italian
Employment: 16.5% management, business, and financial, 2.9% computer, engineering, and science, 11.5% education, legal, community service, arts, and media, 2.9% healthcare practitioners, 21.8% service, 30.2% sales and office, 3.7% natural resources, construction, and maintenance, 10.4% production, transportation, and material moving
Income: Per capita: $21,442; Median household: $31,451; Average household: $42,286; Households with income of $100,000 or more: 7.8%; Poverty rate: 21.0%
Educational Attainment: High school diploma or higher: 84.6%; Bachelor's degree or higher: 27.9%; Graduate/professional degree or higher: 6.2%

School District(s)
Charlotte-Mecklenburg Schools (PK-12)
    2012-13 Enrollment: 144,478 . . . . (980) 343-6270
Housing: Homeownership rate: 30.6%; Median home value: $145,200; Median year structure built: 1990; Homeowner vacancy rate: 3.1%; Median gross rent: $805 per month; Rental vacancy rate: 9.4%
Health Insurance: 74.3% have insurance; 52.3% have private insurance; 34.7% have public insurance; 25.7% do not have insurance; 21.1% of children under 18 do not have insurance
Safety: Violent crime rate: 38.6 per 10,000 population; Property crime rate: 1,321.8 per 10,000 population
Transportation: Commute: 87.5% car, 2.9% public transportation, 6.5% walk, 2.6% work from home; Median travel time to work: 26.4 minutes
Additional Information Contacts
Town of Pineville . . . . (704) 889-2291
    http://www.pinevillenc.net

Mitchell County

Located in western North Carolina; bounded on the north by Tennessee, and on the west by the Nolichucky River; includes the Unaka Mountains in the north, and the Blue Ridge in the south; includes part of Pisgah National Forest. Covers a land area of 221.425 square miles, a water area of 0.662 square miles, and is located in the Eastern Time Zone at 36.01° N. Lat., 82.16° W. Long. The county was founded in 1861. County seat is Bakersville.
Population: 15,579; Growth (since 2000): -0.7%; Density: 70.4 persons per square mile; Race: 95.3% White, 0.4% Black/African American, 0.3% Asian, 0.4% American Indian/Alaska Native, 0.0% Native Hawaiian/Other Pacific Islander, 1.1% two or more races, 4.1% Hispanic of any race; Average household size: 2.30; Median age: 45.7; Age under 18: 19.5%; Age 65 and over: 20.9%; Males per 100 females: 95.3; Marriage status: 22.1% never married, 59.6% now married, 8.5% separated, 8.5% widowed, 9.8% divorced; Foreign born: 2.3%; Speak English only: 95.0%; With disability: 21.6%; Veterans: 8.0%; Ancestry: 20.5% American, 12.5% Irish, 12.1% German, 11.1% English, 10.6% Scotch-Irish
Religion: Six largest groups: 56.4% Baptist, 4.4% Methodist/Pietist, 3.8% Non-denominational Protestant, 1.9% Pentecostal, 1.7% Presbyterian-Reformed, 1.5% Catholicism
Economy: Unemployment rate: 6.0%; Leading industries: 16.4% retail trade; 14.6% other services (except public administration); 11.6% construction; Farms: 286 totaling 19,322 acres; Company size: 0 employ 1,000 or more persons, 0 employ 500 to 999 persons, 7 employ 100 to 499 persons, 371 employs less than 100 persons; Business ownership: 349 women-owned, n/a Black-owned, n/a Hispanic-owned, n/a Asian-owned
Employment: 10.1% management, business, and financial, 2.1% computer, engineering, and science, 11.5% education, legal, community service, arts, and media, 5.5% healthcare practitioners, 21.6% service, 16.9% sales and office, 14.5% natural resources, construction, and maintenance, 17.7% production, transportation, and material moving
Income: Per capita: $21,404; Median household: $37,680; Average household: $50,104; Households with income of $100,000 or more: 8.3%; Poverty rate: 18.3%
Educational Attainment: High school diploma or higher: 81.3%; Bachelor's degree or higher: 16.9%; Graduate/professional degree or higher: 4.4%
Housing: Homeownership rate: 76.7%; Median home value: $117,300; Median year structure built: 1975; Homeowner vacancy rate: 2.7%; Median gross rent: $575 per month; Rental vacancy rate: 11.1%
Vital Statistics: Birth rate: 90.0 per 10,000 population; Death rate: 137.7 per 10,000 population; Age-adjusted cancer mortality rate: 160.9 deaths per 100,000 population
Health Insurance: 83.6% have insurance; 61.1% have private insurance; 38.0% have public insurance; 16.4% do not have insurance; 7.2% of children under 18 do not have insurance
Health Care: Physicians: 13.0 per 10,000 population; Hospital beds: 27.3 per 10,000 population; Hospital admissions: 1,338.3 per 10,000 population
Air Quality Index: 84.7% good, 15.3% moderate, 0.0% unhealthy for sensitive individuals, 0.0% unhealthy (percent of days)
Transportation: Commute: 94.8% car, 0.0% public transportation, 1.3% walk, 3.6% work from home; Median travel time to work: 23.0 minutes
Presidential Election: 23.5% Obama, 75.0% Romney (2012)
Additional Information Contacts
Mitchell Government . . . . (828) 688-2139
    http://www.mitchellcounty.org

Mitchell County Communities

BAKERSVILLE (town). County seat. Covers a land area of 0.748 square miles and a water area of 0 square miles. Located at 36.02° N. Lat; 82.16° W. Long. Elevation is 2,470 feet.
Population: 464; Growth (since 2000): 30.0%; Density: 620.3 persons per square mile; Race: 93.3% White, 0.6% Black/African American, 0.0% Asian, 0.4% American Indian/Alaska Native, 0.0% Native Hawaiian/Other Pacific Islander, 3.0% Two or more races, 2.6% Hispanic of any race; Average household size: 2.04; Median age: 45.8; Age under 18: 20.3%; Age 65 and over: 23.3%; Males per 100 females: 73.8

School District(s)
Mitchell County Schools (PK-12)
    2012-13 Enrollment: 2,044 . . . . (828) 766-2220
Housing: Homeownership rate: 46.1%; Homeowner vacancy rate: 2.8%; Rental vacancy rate: 9.6%

SPRUCE PINE (town). Covers a land area of 3.979 square miles and a water area of 0 square miles. Located at 35.91° N. Lat; 82.07° W. Long. Elevation is 2,559 feet.

History: Spruce Pine has been known for the mining and marketing of feldspar and kaolin. The village sprang up when the Carolina, Clinchfield & Ohio Railroad, completed about 1908, built a station on the Toe River.

Population: 2,175; Growth (since 2000): 7.1%; Density: 546.7 persons per square mile; Race: 92.0% White, 0.4% Black/African American, 0.8% Asian, 0.7% American Indian/Alaska Native, 0.0% Native Hawaiian/Other Pacific Islander, 1.1% Two or more races, 7.6% Hispanic of any race; Average household size: 2.37; Median age: 42.5; Age under 18: 22.5%; Age 65 and over: 20.3%; Males per 100 females: 88.1

School District(s)

Mitchell County Schools (PK-12)

    2012-13 Enrollment: 2,044 . . . . (828) 766-2220

Two-year College(s)

Mayland Community College (Public)

    Fall 2013 Enrollment: 1,254 . . . . (828) 766-1273

    2013-14 Tuition: In-state $2,526; Out-of-state $8,461

Housing: Homeownership rate: 60.6%; Homeowner vacancy rate: 4.7%; Rental vacancy rate: 12.2%

Hospitals: Spruce Pine Community Hospital (40 beds)

Newspapers: Mitchell News-Journal (weekly circulation 5600)

Additional Information Contacts

Town of Spruce Pine . . . . (828) 537-0262

    http://www.sprucepine.org

Montgomery County

Located in central North Carolina; bounded on the west by the Yadkin River with Badin and Tillery Lakes. Covers a land area of 491.760 square miles, a water area of 10.034 square miles, and is located in the Eastern Time Zone at 35.34° N. Lat., 79.90° W. Long. The county was founded in 1778. County seat is Troy.

Weather Station: Jackson Springs 5 WNW									Elevation: 729 feet		
	Jan	Feb	Mar	Apr	May	Jun	Jul	Aug	Sep	Oct	Nov	Dec
High	51	55	63	72	79	86	89	88	82	72	63	54
Low	30	33	39	47	56	65	68	67	61	50	41	33
Precip	3.9	3.5	4.3	3.1	3.0	4.1	4.8	5.0	4.3	3.9	3.4	3.3
Snow	2.0	0.7	0.5	0.0	0.0	0.0	0.0	0.0	0.0	0.0	0.0	0.1

High and Low temperatures in degrees Fahrenheit; Precipitation and Snow in inches

Population: 27,798; Growth (since 2000): 3.6%; Density: 56.5 persons per square mile; Race: 68.9% White, 18.8% Black/African American, 1.6% Asian, 0.4% American Indian/Alaska Native, 0.0% Native Hawaiian/Other Pacific Islander, 1.4% two or more races, 14.1% Hispanic of any race; Average household size: 2.53; Median age: 40.2; Age under 18: 24.3%; Age 65 and over: 15.7%; Males per 100 females: 93.8; Marriage status: 29.5% never married, 49.7% now married, 3.2% separated, 9.5% widowed, 11.3% divorced; Foreign born: 8.6%; Speak English only: 84.0%; With disability: 16.3%; Veterans: 8.5%; Ancestry: 10.5% American, 9.1% English, 8.8% Irish, 8.6% German, 5.4% Scotch-Irish

Religion: Six largest groups: 17.3% Baptist, 16.1% Methodist/Pietist, 4.4% Pentecostal, 4.0% Non-denominational Protestant, 2.3% Catholicism, 2.2% Presbyterian-Reformed

Economy: Unemployment rate: 6.1%; Leading industries: 17.0% retail trade; 12.0% other services (except public administration); 11.6% manufacturing; Farms: 250 totaling 35,047 acres; Company size: 0 employ 1,000 or more persons, 0 employ 500 to 999 persons, 13 employ 100 to 499 persons, 480 employ less than 100 persons; Business ownership: 515 women-owned, n/a Black-owned, n/a Hispanic-owned, n/a Asian-owned

Employment: 10.2% management, business, and financial, 2.2% computer, engineering, and science, 10.1% education, legal, community service, arts, and media, 4.6% healthcare practitioners, 18.7% service, 17.7% sales and office, 12.1% natural resources, construction, and maintenance, 24.6% production, transportation, and material moving

Income: Per capita: $18,865; Median household: $31,830; Average household: $47,343; Households with income of $100,000 or more: 11.1%; Poverty rate: 25.6%

Educational Attainment: High school diploma or higher: 71.8%; Bachelor's degree or higher: 15.1%; Graduate/professional degree or higher: 4.1%

Housing: Homeownership rate: 73.1%; Median home value: $88,900; Median year structure built: 1982; Homeowner vacancy rate: 3.0%; Median gross rent: $553 per month; Rental vacancy rate: 10.0%

Vital Statistics: Birth rate: 122.2 per 10,000 population; Death rate: 93.9 per 10,000 population; Age-adjusted cancer mortality rate: 147.5 deaths per 100,000 population

Health Insurance: 80.4% have insurance; 51.3% have private insurance; 40.6% have public insurance; 19.6% do not have insurance; 10.9% of children under 18 do not have insurance

Health Care: Physicians: 3.6 per 10,000 population; Hospital beds: 9.0 per 10,000 population; Hospital admissions: 108.3 per 10,000 population

Air Quality Index: 87.6% good, 12.4% moderate, 0.0% unhealthy for sensitive individuals, 0.0% unhealthy (percent of days)

Transportation: Commute: 94.5% car, 0.2% public transportation, 1.6% walk, 2.5% work from home; Median travel time to work: 25.0 minutes

Presidential Election: 41.9% Obama, 57.0% Romney (2012)

National and State Parks: North Carolina State Reservation; Town Creek Indian Mound State Historic Site; Uwharrie National Forest; Uwharrie National Recreation Trail

Additional Information Contacts

Montgomery Government . . . . (910) 576-4221

    http://www.montgomerycountync.com

Montgomery County Communities

BISCOE (town). Covers a land area of 2.268 square miles and a water area of 0 square miles. Located at 35.36° N. Lat; 79.78° W. Long. Elevation is 617 feet.

Population: 1,700; Growth (since 2000): 0.0%; Density: 749.6 persons per square mile; Race: 50.8% White, 20.5% Black/African American, 0.8% Asian, 0.2% American Indian/Alaska Native, 0.1% Native Hawaiian/Other Pacific Islander, 1.6% Two or more races, 35.5% Hispanic of any race; Average household size: 2.95; Median age: 33.3; Age under 18: 29.5%; Age 65 and over: 15.7%; Males per 100 females: 90.6

School District(s)

Montgomery County Schools (PK-12)

    2012-13 Enrollment: 4,276 . . . . (910) 576-6511

Housing: Homeownership rate: 63.7%; Homeowner vacancy rate: 1.4%; Rental vacancy rate: 9.3%

Safety: Violent crime rate: 17.7 per 10,000 population; Property crime rate: 1,328.2 per 10,000 population

CANDOR (town). Covers a land area of 1.602 square miles and a water area of 0 square miles. Located at 35.29° N. Lat; 79.74° W. Long. Elevation is 735 feet.

Population: 840; Growth (since 2000): 1.8%; Density: 524.3 persons per square mile; Race: 54.8% White, 10.7% Black/African American, 0.4% Asian, 1.9% American Indian/Alaska Native, 0.0% Native Hawaiian/Other Pacific Islander, 3.5% Two or more races, 40.6% Hispanic of any race; Average household size: 2.79; Median age: 35.1; Age under 18: 30.0%; Age 65 and over: 13.1%; Males per 100 females: 96.3

School District(s)

Montgomery County Schools (PK-12)

    2012-13 Enrollment: 4,276 . . . . (910) 576-6511

Housing: Homeownership rate: 67.9%; Homeowner vacancy rate: 2.9%; Rental vacancy rate: 14.4%

MOUNT GILEAD (town). Covers a land area of 3.353 square miles and a water area of 0 square miles. Located at 35.22° N. Lat; 80.00° W. Long. Elevation is 404 feet.

History: Town Creek Indian Mound State Historical Site to Southeast.

Population: 1,181; Growth (since 2000): -15.0%; Density: 352.2 persons per square mile; Race: 41.2% White, 56.0% Black/African American, 0.7% Asian, 0.1% American Indian/Alaska Native, 0.0% Native Hawaiian/Other Pacific Islander, 1.5% Two or more races, 1.2% Hispanic of any race; Average household size: 2.40; Median age: 43.0; Age under 18: 24.5%; Age 65 and over: 19.1%; Males per 100 females: 84.0

School District(s)

Montgomery County Schools (PK-12)

    2012-13 Enrollment: 4,276 . . . . (910) 576-6511

Housing: Homeownership rate: 63.8%; Homeowner vacancy rate: 4.0%; Rental vacancy rate: 14.1%

STAR (town). Covers a land area of 1.237 square miles and a water area of 0 square miles. Located at 35.40° N. Lat; 79.78° W. Long. Elevation is 636 feet.

Population: 876; Growth (since 2000): 8.6%; Density: 707.9 persons per square mile; Race: 78.1% White, 9.7% Black/African American, 0.2% Asian, 0.6% American Indian/Alaska Native, 0.0% Native Hawaiian/Other Pacific Islander, 3.4% Two or more races, 21.6% Hispanic of any race; Average household size: 2.38; Median age: 37.8; Age under 18: 26.9%; Age 65 and over: 14.3%; Males per 100 females: 98.6

School District(s)
Montgomery County Schools (PK-12)
    2012-13 Enrollment: 4,276 . . . . (910) 576-6511
Housing: Homeownership rate: 59.5%; Homeowner vacancy rate: 1.4%; Rental vacancy rate: 8.2%

TROY (town). County seat. Covers a land area of 3.592 square miles and a water area of 0.043 square miles. Located at 35.36° N. Lat; 79.89° W. Long. Elevation is 656 feet.

History: Troy became the seat of Montgomery County in 1779.
Population: 3,189; Growth (since 2000): -7.0%; Density: 887.8 persons per square mile; Race: 58.9% White, 31.8% Black/African American, 1.0% Asian, 0.7% American Indian/Alaska Native, 0.0% Native Hawaiian/Other Pacific Islander, 1.5% Two or more races, 10.3% Hispanic of any race; Average household size: 2.38; Median age: 36.7; Age under 18: 22.8%; Age 65 and over: 13.7%; Males per 100 females: 58.8; Marriage status: 35.7% never married, 43.1% now married, 6.3% separated, 7.8% widowed, 13.4% divorced; Foreign born: 3.7%; Speak English only: 90.8%; With disability: 13.6%; Veterans: 7.6%; Ancestry: 11.1% Irish, 10.4% German, 7.5% American, 7.5% English, 2.7% Scotch-Irish
Employment: 12.9% management, business, and financial, 4.6% computer, engineering, and science, 12.8% education, legal, community service, arts, and media, 4.1% healthcare practitioners, 29.7% service, 17.8% sales and office, 7.6% natural resources, construction, and maintenance, 10.6% production, transportation, and material moving
Income: Per capita: $13,386; Median household: $26,304; Average household: $40,014; Households with income of $100,000 or more: 5.9%; Poverty rate: 39.4%
Educational Attainment: High school diploma or higher: 76.0%; Bachelor's degree or higher: 16.1%; Graduate/professional degree or higher: 5.4%

School District(s)
Montgomery County Schools (PK-12)
    2012-13 Enrollment: 4,276 . . . . (910) 576-6511

Two-year College(s)
Montgomery Community College (Public)
    Fall 2013 Enrollment: 884 . . . . (910) 576-6222
    2013-14 Tuition: In-state $2,363; Out-of-state $8,507
Housing: Homeownership rate: 46.8%; Median home value: $95,500; Median year structure built: 1963; Homeowner vacancy rate: 3.2%; Median gross rent: $518 per month; Rental vacancy rate: 8.9%
Health Insurance: 83.1% have insurance; 48.5% have private insurance; 46.4% have public insurance; 16.9% do not have insurance; 8.8% of children under 18 do not have insurance
Hospitals: Firsthealth Montgomery Memorial Hospital (55 beds)
Safety: Violent crime rate: 40.1 per 10,000 population; Property crime rate: 344.0 per 10,000 population
Newspapers: Montgomery Herald (weekly circulation 6000)
Transportation: Commute: 90.7% car, 1.0% public transportation, 6.0% walk, 1.6% work from home; Median travel time to work: 16.5 minutes
Additional Information Contacts
Town of Troy . . . . (715) 245-2665
    http://townoftroy.org

Moore County

Located in central North Carolina; sand-hill and piedmont area, drained by the Deep River. Covers a land area of 697.843 square miles, a water area of 8.010 square miles, and is located in the Eastern Time Zone at 35.31° N. Lat., 79.48° W. Long. The county was founded in 1784. County seat is Carthage.

Moore County is part of the Pinehurst-Southern Pines, NC Micropolitan Statistical Area. The entire metro area includes: Moore County, NC

Population: 88,247; Growth (since 2000): 18.0%; Density: 126.5 persons per square mile; Race: 80.4% White, 13.4% Black/African American, 0.9% Asian, 0.8% American Indian/Alaska Native, 0.1% Native Hawaiian/Other Pacific Islander, 1.7% two or more races, 6.0% Hispanic of any race; Average household size: 2.33; Median age: 45.0; Age under 18: 21.7%; Age 65 and over: 22.6%; Males per 100 females: 91.5; Marriage status: 20.5% never married, 60.4% now married, 3.0% separated, 9.3% widowed, 9.8% divorced; Foreign born: 5.6%; Speak English only: 92.9%; With disability: 14.5%; Veterans: 14.7%; Ancestry: 17.6% American, 12.5% German, 12.2% English, 11.0% Irish, 5.5% Scottish
Religion: Six largest groups: 15.5% Baptist, 10.4% Methodist/Pietist, 7.4% Non-denominational Protestant, 6.7% Presbyterian-Reformed, 6.4% Catholicism, 1.0% Lutheran
Economy: Unemployment rate: 5.3%; Leading industries: 16.0% retail trade; 12.5% health care and social assistance; 11.0% construction; Farms: 718 totaling 82,462 acres; Company size: 2 employ 1,000 or more persons, 0 employ 500 to 999 persons, 39 employ 100 to 499 persons, 2,137 employ less than 100 persons; Business ownership: 1,971 women-owned, 667 Black-owned, 51 Hispanic-owned, n/a Asian-owned
Employment: 12.5% management, business, and financial, 3.0% computer, engineering, and science, 12.3% education, legal, community service, arts, and media, 9.1% healthcare practitioners, 21.5% service, 21.9% sales and office, 10.3% natural resources, construction, and maintenance, 9.4% production, transportation, and material moving
Income: Per capita: $28,913; Median household: $49,544; Average household: $68,247; Households with income of $100,000 or more: 18.5%; Poverty rate: 15.6%
Educational Attainment: High school diploma or higher: 89.7%; Bachelor's degree or higher: 31.3%; Graduate/professional degree or higher: 11.6%
Housing: Homeownership rate: 74.7%; Median home value: $201,600; Median year structure built: 1988; Homeowner vacancy rate: 2.9%; Median gross rent: $725 per month; Rental vacancy rate: 11.5%
Vital Statistics: Birth rate: 106.9 per 10,000 population; Death rate: 117.2 per 10,000 population; Age-adjusted cancer mortality rate: 162.3 deaths per 100,000 population
Health Insurance: 87.0% have insurance; 65.6% have private insurance; 39.3% have public insurance; 13.0% do not have insurance; 3.9% of children under 18 do not have insurance
Health Care: Physicians: 35.2 per 10,000 population; Hospital beds: 42.4 per 10,000 population; Hospital admissions: 2,311.5 per 10,000 population
Transportation: Commute: 92.9% car, 0.1% public transportation, 1.9% walk, 3.4% work from home; Median travel time to work: 23.9 minutes
Presidential Election: 35.6% Obama, 63.5% Romney (2012)
National and State Parks: Goodwin State Forest
Additional Information Contacts
Moore Government . . . . (910) 947-4636
    http://www.moorecountync.gov

Moore County Communities

ABERDEEN (town). Covers a land area of 8.510 square miles and a water area of 0.116 square miles. Located at 35.13° N. Lat; 79.43° W. Long. Elevation is 331 feet.

History: Aberdeen was originally called Blues Crossing, and became Aberdeen when it was incorporated in 1893. Many of the early settlers were Scottish.
Population: 6,350; Growth (since 2000): 86.8%; Density: 746.2 persons per square mile; Race: 67.9% White, 24.7% Black/African American, 1.8% Asian, 1.3% American Indian/Alaska Native, 0.0% Native Hawaiian/Other Pacific Islander, 2.9% Two or more races, 5.1% Hispanic of any race; Average household size: 2.20; Median age: 35.7; Age under 18: 23.7%; Age 65 and over: 16.2%; Males per 100 females: 86.4; Marriage status: 23.4% never married, 49.2% now married, 2.7% separated, 8.1% widowed, 19.3% divorced; Foreign born: 4.4%; Speak English only: 94.3%; With disability: 14.3%; Veterans: 13.4%; Ancestry: 11.8% Irish, 10.1% German, 8.5% English, 8.3% American, 6.6% Italian
Employment: 12.7% management, business, and financial, 5.8% computer, engineering, and science, 15.9% education, legal, community service, arts, and media, 7.3% healthcare practitioners, 21.9% service, 24.2% sales and office, 5.9% natural resources, construction, and maintenance, 6.3% production, transportation, and material moving
Income: Per capita: $22,392; Median household: $37,470; Average household: $49,883; Households with income of $100,000 or more: 14.2%; Poverty rate: 14.4%

Educational Attainment: High school diploma or higher: 87.0%; Bachelor's degree or higher: 29.4%; Graduate/professional degree or higher: 7.6%

School District(s)

Moore County Schools (PK-12)

    2012-13 Enrollment: 12,912 . . . . (910) 947-2976

Housing: Homeownership rate: 48.0%; Median home value: $180,800; Median year structure built: 1988; Homeowner vacancy rate: 3.6%; Median gross rent: $837 per month; Rental vacancy rate: 4.1%

Health Insurance: 85.5% have insurance; 62.0% have private insurance; 36.0% have public insurance; 14.5% do not have insurance; 2.7% of children under 18 do not have insurance

Safety: Violent crime rate: 34.0 per 10,000 population; Property crime rate: 449.7 per 10,000 population

Transportation: Commute: 94.4% car, 0.8% public transportation, 1.3% walk, 2.6% work from home; Median travel time to work: 18.9 minutes

Additional Information Contacts

Town of Aberdeen . . . . (910) 944-1115

    http://www.townofaberdeen.net

CAMERON (town). Covers a land area of 1.224 square miles and a water area of 0 square miles. Located at 35.33° N. Lat; 79.25° W. Long. Elevation is 358 feet.

Population: 285; Growth (since 2000): 88.7%; Density: 232.8 persons per square mile; Race: 71.2% White, 22.5% Black/African American, 0.4% Asian, 2.1% American Indian/Alaska Native, 0.0% Native Hawaiian/Other Pacific Islander, 3.9% Two or more races, 2.1% Hispanic of any race; Average household size: 2.46; Median age: 43.4; Age under 18: 18.9%; Age 65 and over: 16.8%; Males per 100 females: 75.9

School District(s)

Harnett County Schools (PK-12)

    2012-13 Enrollment: 20,569 . . . . (910) 893-8151

Moore County Schools (PK-12)

    2012-13 Enrollment: 12,912 . . . . (910) 947-2976

Housing: Homeownership rate: 82.7%; Homeowner vacancy rate: 1.0%; Rental vacancy rate: 9.1%

CARTHAGE (town). County seat. Covers a land area of 6.310 square miles and a water area of 0.039 square miles. Located at 35.33° N. Lat; 79.42° W. Long. Elevation is 584 feet.

History: Scottish families from the Cape Fear region settled in Carthage in the middle of the 18th century.

Population: 2,205; Growth (since 2000): 17.9%; Density: 349.4 persons per square mile; Race: 70.7% White, 23.9% Black/African American, 0.7% Asian, 0.7% American Indian/Alaska Native, 0.0% Native Hawaiian/Other Pacific Islander, 2.7% Two or more races, 3.3% Hispanic of any race; Average household size: 2.24; Median age: 42.6; Age under 18: 23.1%; Age 65 and over: 22.0%; Males per 100 females: 80.7

School District(s)

Moore County Schools (PK-12)

    2012-13 Enrollment: 12,912 . . . . (910) 947-2976

Housing: Homeownership rate: 62.6%; Homeowner vacancy rate: 2.7%; Rental vacancy rate: 7.8%

Safety: Violent crime rate: 17.2 per 10,000 population; Property crime rate: 461.0 per 10,000 population

EAGLE SPRINGS (unincorporated postal area)

ZCTA: 27242

    Covers a land area of 53.940 square miles and a water area of 0.246 square miles. Located at 35.33° N. Lat; 79.65° W. Long. Elevation is 669 feet.

    Population: 2,100; Growth (since 2000): -8.1%; Density: 38.9 persons per square mile; Race: 62.7% White, 25.8% Black/African American, 0.1% Asian, 0.5% American Indian/Alaska Native, 0.0% Native Hawaiian/Other Pacific Islander, 1.2% Two or more races, 13.0% Hispanic of any race; Average household size: 2.55; Median age: 38.6; Age under 18: 25.7%; Age 65 and over: 14.4%; Males per 100 females: 97.6

School District(s)

Nc Dept of Juvenile Justice (KG-12)

    2012-13 Enrollment: n/a . . . . (919) 733-3388

    Housing: Homeownership rate: 75.4%; Homeowner vacancy rate: 0.8%; Rental vacancy rate: 20.7%

FOXFIRE (village). Covers a land area of 6.624 square miles and a water area of 0.060 square miles. Located at 35.18° N. Lat; 79.56° W. Long. Elevation is 545 feet.

Population: 902; Growth (since 2000): 90.3%; Density: 136.2 persons per square mile; Race: 89.8% White, 8.5% Black/African American, 0.4% Asian, 0.3% American Indian/Alaska Native, 0.0% Native Hawaiian/Other Pacific Islander, 0.6% Two or more races, 0.7% Hispanic of any race; Average household size: 2.06; Median age: 54.1; Age under 18: 12.6%; Age 65 and over: 29.7%; Males per 100 females: 88.7

Housing: Homeownership rate: 73.2%; Homeowner vacancy rate: 3.3%; Rental vacancy rate: 10.4%

Additional Information Contacts

Village of Foxfire . . . . (910) 215-5107

    http://www.foxfirenc.com

JACKSON SPRINGS (unincorporated postal area)

ZCTA: 27281

    Covers a land area of 52.071 square miles and a water area of 0.112 square miles. Located at 35.19° N. Lat; 79.63° W. Long. Elevation is 443 feet.

    Population: 3,100; Growth (since 2000): 16.9%; Density: 59.5 persons per square mile; Race: 60.7% White, 24.8% Black/African American, 0.4% Asian, 0.4% American Indian/Alaska Native, 0.0% Native Hawaiian/Other Pacific Islander, 1.5% Two or more races, 19.3% Hispanic of any race; Average household size: 2.70; Median age: 38.8; Age under 18: 26.7%; Age 65 and over: 15.4%; Males per 100 females: 95.1; Marriage status: 24.1% never married, 60.7% now married, 1.3% separated, 5.8% widowed, 9.5% divorced; Foreign born: 11.4%; Speak English only: 80.7%; With disability: 14.6%; Veterans: 11.8%; Ancestry: 9.3% American, 8.3% English, 8.1% German, 6.2% Irish, 5.6% Scotch-Irish

    Employment: 9.2% management, business, and financial, 1.4% computer, engineering, and science, 9.7% education, legal, community service, arts, and media, 4.1% healthcare practitioners, 15.8% service, 25.8% sales and office, 12.2% natural resources, construction, and maintenance, 21.8% production, transportation, and material moving

    Income: Per capita: $20,453; Median household: $42,169; Average household: $50,115; Households with income of $100,000 or more: 8.9%; Poverty rate: 15.4%

    Educational Attainment: High school diploma or higher: 79.0%; Bachelor's degree or higher: 22.6%; Graduate/professional degree or higher: 8.0%

    Housing: Homeownership rate: 77.5%; Median home value: $180,400; Median year structure built: 1986; Homeowner vacancy rate: 2.2%; Median gross rent: $647 per month; Rental vacancy rate: 12.4%

    Health Insurance: 80.2% have insurance; 57.8% have private insurance; 40.2% have public insurance; 19.8% do not have insurance; 0.8% of children under 18 do not have insurance

    Transportation: Commute: 94.4% car, 0.0% public transportation, 2.0% walk, 3.1% work from home; Median travel time to work: 23.7 minutes

LAKEVIEW (unincorporated postal area)

ZCTA: 28350

    Covers a land area of 0.647 square miles and a water area of 0.084 square miles. Located at 35.24° N. Lat; 79.31° W. Long. Elevation is 308 feet.

    Population: 305; Growth (since 2000): -17.1%; Density: 471.4 persons per square mile; Race: 69.8% White, 16.1% Black/African American, 1.6% Asian, 3.9% American Indian/Alaska Native, 0.0% Native Hawaiian/Other Pacific Islander, 1.6% Two or more races, 7.5% Hispanic of any race; Average household size: 2.52; Median age: 35.6; Age under 18: 29.2%; Age 65 and over: 13.4%; Males per 100 females: 102.0

    Housing: Homeownership rate: 68.4%; Homeowner vacancy rate: 2.5%; Rental vacancy rate: 14.3%

PINEBLUFF (town). Covers a land area of 2.651 square miles and a water area of 0.033 square miles. Located at 35.11° N. Lat; 79.47° W. Long. Elevation is 417 feet.

Population: 1,337; Growth (since 2000): 20.6%; Density: 504.4 persons per square mile; Race: 81.2% White, 11.8% Black/African American, 0.5% Asian, 1.6% American Indian/Alaska Native, 0.0% Native Hawaiian/Other Pacific Islander, 2.6% Two or more races, 5.9% Hispanic of any race; Average household size: 2.52; Median age: 39.3; Age under 18: 26.3%; Age 65 and over: 13.1%; Males per 100 females: 93.5

Housing: Homeownership rate: 75.7%; Homeowner vacancy rate: 3.8%; Rental vacancy rate: 8.5%
Safety: Violent crime rate: 0.0 per 10,000 population; Property crime rate: 115.8 per 10,000 population

PINEHURST (village). Covers a land area of 13.966 square miles and a water area of 0.592 square miles. Located at 35.19° N. Lat; 79.46° W. Long. Elevation is 525 feet.
History: Developed after 1895; chartered 1911.
Population: 13,124; Growth (since 2000): 35.2%; Density: 939.7 persons per square mile; Race: 92.8% White, 3.8% Black/African American, 1.3% Asian, 0.4% American Indian/Alaska Native, 0.0% Native Hawaiian/Other Pacific Islander, 1.2% Two or more races, 2.1% Hispanic of any race; Average household size: 2.13; Median age: 57.6; Age under 18: 16.1%; Age 65 and over: 37.7%; Males per 100 females: 87.2; Marriage status: 11.7% never married, 72.3% now married, 1.2% separated, 10.2% widowed, 5.8% divorced; Foreign born: 5.2%; Speak English only: 94.8%; With disability: 16.1%; Veterans: 22.6%; Ancestry: 18.8% German, 17.9% English, 17.3% Irish, 9.9% American, 7.8% Italian
Employment: 24.3% management, business, and financial, 3.6% computer, engineering, and science, 16.2% education, legal, community service, arts, and media, 9.6% healthcare practitioners, 15.1% service, 24.2% sales and office, 2.6% natural resources, construction, and maintenance, 4.4% production, transportation, and material moving
Income: Per capita: $45,606; Median household: $70,275; Average household: $98,816; Households with income of $100,000 or more: 28.9%; Poverty rate: 3.3%
Educational Attainment: High school diploma or higher: 97.2%; Bachelor's degree or higher: 52.1%; Graduate/professional degree or higher: 19.3%

School District(s)
Moore County Schools (PK-12)
    2012-13 Enrollment: 12,912 . . . . (910) 947-2976
Two-year College(s)
Sandhills Community College (Public)
    Fall 2013 Enrollment: 4,158 . . . . (910) 692-6185
    2013-14 Tuition: In-state $2,385; Out-of-state $8,529
Housing: Homeownership rate: 84.6%; Median home value: $284,500; Median year structure built: 1994; Homeowner vacancy rate: 3.6%; Median gross rent: $1,388 per month; Rental vacancy rate: 30.0%
Health Insurance: 96.3% have insurance; 84.0% have private insurance; 44.4% have public insurance; 3.7% do not have insurance; 3.3% of children under 18 do not have insurance
Hospitals: Firsthealth Moore Regional Hospital (395 beds)
Safety: Violent crime rate: 5.3 per 10,000 population; Property crime rate: 82.8 per 10,000 population
Transportation: Commute: 90.7% car, 0.0% public transportation, 1.1% walk, 6.7% work from home; Median travel time to work: 21.6 minutes
Airports: Moore County (general aviation)
Additional Information Contacts
Village of Pinehurst . . . . (910) 295-1900
    http://www.villageofpinehurst.org

ROBBINS (town). Covers a land area of 1.408 square miles and a water area of 0 square miles. Located at 35.43° N. Lat; 79.58° W. Long. Elevation is 433 feet.
History: Formerly Hemp. Incorporated 1935.
Population: 1,097; Growth (since 2000): -8.2%; Density: 779.0 persons per square mile; Race: 72.1% White, 2.6% Black/African American, 0.0% Asian, 0.6% American Indian/Alaska Native, 1.5% Native Hawaiian/Other Pacific Islander, 1.7% Two or more races, 50.3% Hispanic of any race; Average household size: 2.87; Median age: 31.4; Age under 18: 31.4%; Age 65 and over: 13.1%; Males per 100 females: 91.1

School District(s)
Moore County Schools (PK-12)
    2012-13 Enrollment: 12,912 . . . . (910) 947-2976
Housing: Homeownership rate: 63.7%; Homeowner vacancy rate: 4.3%; Rental vacancy rate: 14.2%

SEVEN LAKES (CDP). Covers a land area of 8.384 square miles and a water area of 1.665 square miles. Located at 35.26° N. Lat; 79.59° W. Long. Elevation is 571 feet.
History: Ironically, Seven Lakes does not have seven lakes. It has more in the range of 9 or 10, but the official number not exact. Seven Lakes West has added a new addition to its community. Morgan Wood features lots

with more than 3 acres (12,000 m2). These lots are zoned to accommodate home owners who want to own horses or those who would just like a large lot.
Population: 4,888; Growth (since 2000): 52.1%; Density: 583.0 persons per square mile; Race: 94.4% White, 3.0% Black/African American, 0.7% Asian, 0.2% American Indian/Alaska Native, 0.0% Native Hawaiian/Other Pacific Islander, 1.0% Two or more races, 2.0% Hispanic of any race; Average household size: 2.34; Median age: 54.4; Age under 18: 18.4%; Age 65 and over: 32.4%; Males per 100 females: 92.2; Marriage status: 11.5% never married, 75.8% now married, 1.3% separated, 8.9% widowed, 3.8% divorced; Foreign born: 5.1%; Speak English only: 97.3%; With disability: 10.1%; Veterans: 16.0%; Ancestry: 22.4% English, 19.6% German, 17.2% Irish, 12.6% American, 12.5% Scottish
Employment: 20.3% management, business, and financial, 2.5% computer, engineering, and science, 22.4% education, legal, community service, arts, and media, 13.1% healthcare practitioners, 9.1% service, 24.5% sales and office, 3.1% natural resources, construction, and maintenance, 5.0% production, transportation, and material moving
Income: Per capita: $38,232; Median household: $74,854; Average household: $89,639; Households with income of $100,000 or more: 32.1%; Poverty rate: 2.8%
Educational Attainment: High school diploma or higher: 98.1%; Bachelor's degree or higher: 48.1%; Graduate/professional degree or higher: 17.0%
Housing: Homeownership rate: 93.4%; Median home value: $272,200; Median year structure built: 1995; Homeowner vacancy rate: 3.2%; Median gross rent: n/a per month; Rental vacancy rate: 11.4%
Health Insurance: 96.7% have insurance; 87.4% have private insurance; 32.3% have public insurance; 3.3% do not have insurance; 0.0% of children under 18 do not have insurance
Transportation: Commute: 98.0% car, 0.0% public transportation, 0.0% walk, 1.5% work from home; Median travel time to work: 23.9 minutes

SOUTHERN PINES (town). Covers a land area of 16.646 square miles and a water area of 0.177 square miles. Located at 35.19° N. Lat; 79.40° W. Long. Elevation is 499 feet.
History: Area famous for its golf courses. Settled 1885, incorporated 1887.
Population: 12,334; Growth (since 2000): 13.0%; Density: 741.0 persons per square mile; Race: 71.7% White, 24.0% Black/African American, 0.8% Asian, 0.6% American Indian/Alaska Native, 0.1% Native Hawaiian/Other Pacific Islander, 1.4% Two or more races, 3.9% Hispanic of any race; Average household size: 2.07; Median age: 47.0; Age under 18: 20.0%; Age 65 and over: 27.5%; Males per 100 females: 82.0; Marriage status: 25.5% never married, 51.3% now married, 4.9% separated, 13.4% widowed, 9.8% divorced; Foreign born: 8.0%; Speak English only: 92.5%; With disability: 17.8%; Veterans: 14.6%; Ancestry: 15.9% German, 14.6% American, 11.0% English, 9.6% Irish, 6.8% Scottish
Employment: 13.6% management, business, and financial, 2.7% computer, engineering, and science, 16.5% education, legal, community service, arts, and media, 14.6% healthcare practitioners, 23.4% service, 17.5% sales and office, 4.7% natural resources, construction, and maintenance, 7.0% production, transportation, and material moving
Income: Per capita: $36,270; Median household: $49,038; Average household: $78,104; Households with income of $100,000 or more: 25.5%; Poverty rate: 12.0%
Educational Attainment: High school diploma or higher: 89.6%; Bachelor's degree or higher: 40.0%; Graduate/professional degree or higher: 17.9%

School District(s)
Moore County Schools (PK-12)
    2012-13 Enrollment: 12,912 . . . . (910) 947-2976
The Academy of Moore County (KG-05)
    2012-13 Enrollment: 195. . . . . (910) 757-0401
Housing: Homeownership rate: 57.0%; Median home value: $248,000; Median year structure built: 1982; Homeowner vacancy rate: 3.9%; Median gross rent: $724 per month; Rental vacancy rate: 8.0%
Health Insurance: 89.1% have insurance; 67.6% have private insurance; 41.4% have public insurance; 10.9% do not have insurance; 4.8% of children under 18 do not have insurance
Safety: Violent crime rate: 68.5 per 10,000 population; Property crime rate: 435.9 per 10,000 population
Newspapers: Southern Pines Pilot (weekly circulation 16500)
Transportation: Commute: 91.4% car, 0.2% public transportation, 1.9% walk, 2.5% work from home; Median travel time to work: 22.1 minutes; Amtrak: Train service available.

Airports: Moore County (general aviation)
Additional Information Contacts
Town of Southern Pines . . . . (910) 692-7376
  http://www.southernpines.net

TAYLORTOWN (town). Covers a land area of 1.327 square miles and a water area of 0 square miles. Located at 35.21° N. Lat; 79.49° W. Long. Elevation is 479 feet.
Population: 722; Growth (since 2000): -14.6%; Density: 544.2 persons per square mile; Race: 32.0% White, 65.0% Black/African American, 0.8% Asian, 0.4% American Indian/Alaska Native, 0.0% Native Hawaiian/Other Pacific Islander, 1.4% Two or more races, 1.0% Hispanic of any race; Average household size: 2.38; Median age: 43.8; Age under 18: 22.0%; Age 65 and over: 15.7%; Males per 100 females: 83.7
Housing: Homeownership rate: 75.9%; Homeowner vacancy rate: 0.9%; Rental vacancy rate: 3.9%

VASS (town). Covers a land area of 3.278 square miles and a water area of 0.022 square miles. Located at 35.25° N. Lat; 79.28° W. Long. Elevation is 305 feet.
Population: 720; Growth (since 2000): -4.0%; Density: 219.6 persons per square mile; Race: 79.6% White, 13.1% Black/African American, 0.0% Asian, 2.6% American Indian/Alaska Native, 0.1% Native Hawaiian/Other Pacific Islander, 1.5% Two or more races, 9.6% Hispanic of any race; Average household size: 2.38; Median age: 41.1; Age under 18: 23.2%; Age 65 and over: 16.9%; Males per 100 females: 91.5
School District(s)
Moore County Schools (PK-12)
  2012-13 Enrollment: 12,912 . . . . (910) 947-2976
Sandhills Theatre Arts Renaiss (KG-08)
  2012-13 Enrollment: 306. . . . . (910) 695-1004
Housing: Homeownership rate: 66.0%; Homeowner vacancy rate: 4.8%; Rental vacancy rate: 8.6%

WEST END (unincorporated postal area)
ZCTA: 27376
  Covers a land area of 69.758 square miles and a water area of 1.867 square miles. Located at 35.24° N. Lat; 79.52° W. Long. Elevation is 607 feet.
  Population: 9,386; Growth (since 2000): 23.1%; Density: 134.6 persons per square mile; Race: 82.3% White, 13.1% Black/African American, 0.6% Asian, 0.7% American Indian/Alaska Native, 0.0% Native Hawaiian/Other Pacific Islander, 1.7% Two or more races, 3.9% Hispanic of any race; Average household size: 2.40; Median age: 48.1; Age under 18: 21.1%; Age 65 and over: 23.9%; Males per 100 females: 94.0; Marriage status: 18.5% never married, 66.2% now married, 1.7% separated, 8.8% widowed, 6.5% divorced; Foreign born: 3.4%; Speak English only: 97.5%; With disability: 11.6%; Veterans: 13.0%; Ancestry: 18.0% American, 17.8% English, 14.6% German, 12.3% Irish, 9.4% Scottish
  Employment: 14.8% management, business, and financial, 2.5% computer, engineering, and science, 15.0% education, legal, community service, arts, and media, 11.2% healthcare practitioners, 19.8% service, 21.9% sales and office, 9.2% natural resources, construction, and maintenance, 5.6% production, transportation, and material moving
  Income: Per capita: $29,590; Median household: $53,877; Average household: $70,978; Households with income of $100,000 or more: 22.2%; Poverty rate: 15.3%
  Educational Attainment: High school diploma or higher: 95.2%; Bachelor's degree or higher: 36.2%; Graduate/professional degree or higher: 12.9%
School District(s)
Moore County Schools (PK-12)
  2012-13 Enrollment: 12,912 . . . . (910) 947-2976
  Housing: Homeownership rate: 86.2%; Median home value: $224,700; Median year structure built: 1992; Homeowner vacancy rate: 2.9%; Median gross rent: $766 per month; Rental vacancy rate: 6.3%
  Health Insurance: 89.8% have insurance; 75.9% have private insurance; 32.1% have public insurance; 10.2% do not have insurance; 1.5% of children under 18 do not have insurance
  Transportation: Commute: 97.2% car, 0.0% public transportation, 0.6% walk, 1.4% work from home; Median travel time to work: 23.2 minutes

WHISPERING PINES (village). Covers a land area of 3.395 square miles and a water area of 0.626 square miles. Located at 35.25° N. Lat; 79.37° W. Long. Elevation is 371 feet.
Population: 2,928; Growth (since 2000): 40.1%; Density: 862.4 persons per square mile; Race: 95.5% White, 1.3% Black/African American, 1.0% Asian, 0.2% American Indian/Alaska Native, 0.1% Native Hawaiian/Other Pacific Islander, 1.3% Two or more races, 2.9% Hispanic of any race; Average household size: 2.33; Median age: 52.3; Age under 18: 20.2%; Age 65 and over: 33.4%; Males per 100 females: 94.7; Marriage status: 8.1% never married, 80.0% now married, 0.7% separated, 8.7% widowed, 3.2% divorced; Foreign born: 7.2%; Speak English only: 95.5%; With disability: 9.8%; Veterans: 28.6%; Ancestry: 17.8% English, 16.4% American, 13.5% Irish, 13.1% German, 4.7% Scotch-Irish
Employment: 10.7% management, business, and financial, 4.0% computer, engineering, and science, 21.2% education, legal, community service, arts, and media, 11.0% healthcare practitioners, 13.4% service, 26.6% sales and office, 4.0% natural resources, construction, and maintenance, 9.1% production, transportation, and material moving
Income: Per capita: $36,980; Median household: $75,293; Average household: $88,162; Households with income of $100,000 or more: 25.6%; Poverty rate: 1.1%
Educational Attainment: High school diploma or higher: 95.7%; Bachelor's degree or higher: 38.3%; Graduate/professional degree or higher: 14.3%
Housing: Homeownership rate: 92.3%; Median home value: $266,900; Median year structure built: 1982; Homeowner vacancy rate: 2.3%; Median gross rent: $1,155 per month; Rental vacancy rate: 7.5%
Health Insurance: 97.8% have insurance; 85.9% have private insurance; 39.7% have public insurance; 2.2% do not have insurance; 1.1% of children under 18 do not have insurance
Safety: Violent crime rate: 0.0 per 10,000 population; Property crime rate: 141.2 per 10,000 population
Transportation: Commute: 92.8% car, 0.0% public transportation, 0.0% walk, 4.3% work from home; Median travel time to work: 25.9 minutes

Nash County

Located in east central North Carolina; coastal plains area, bounded on the northeast by Fishing Creek; crossed by the Tar River. Covers a land area of 540.406 square miles, a water area of 2.362 square miles, and is located in the Eastern Time Zone at 35.97° N. Lat., 77.99° W. Long. The county was founded in 1777. County seat is Nashville.

Nash County is part of the Rocky Mount, NC Metropolitan Statistical Area. The entire metro area includes: Edgecombe County, NC; Nash County, NC

Population: 95,840; Growth (since 2000): 9.6%; Density: 177.3 persons per square mile; Race: 55.9% White, 37.2% Black/African American, 0.8% Asian, 0.7% American Indian/Alaska Native, 0.0% Native Hawaiian/Other Pacific Islander, 1.6% two or more races, 6.3% Hispanic of any race; Average household size: 2.48; Median age: 39.9; Age under 18: 23.9%; Age 65 and over: 14.0%; Males per 100 females: 93.4; Marriage status: 30.4% never married, 50.4% now married, 4.0% separated, 7.7% widowed, 11.5% divorced; Foreign born: 4.5%; Speak English only: 93.1%; With disability: 14.9%; Veterans: 9.5%; Ancestry: 13.7% American, 11.6% English, 6.7% Irish, 6.6% German, 1.6% Scotch-Irish
Religion: Six largest groups: 24.4% Baptist, 6.7% Methodist/Pietist, 5.2% Pentecostal, 1.5% Catholicism, 1.2% Presbyterian-Reformed, 1.0% Episcopalianism/Anglicanism
Economy: Unemployment rate: 7.1%; Leading industries: 19.5% retail trade; 11.2% health care and social assistance; 11.0% other services (except public administration); Farms: 430 totaling 140,620 acres; Company size: 4 employ 1,000 or more persons, 0 employ 500 to 999 persons, 39 employ 100 to 499 persons, 2,076 employ less than 100 persons; Business ownership: 1,852 women-owned, 1,198 Black-owned, 136 Hispanic-owned, 94 Asian-owned
Employment: 12.2% management, business, and financial, 3.7% computer, engineering, and science, 8.6% education, legal, community service, arts, and media, 5.1% healthcare practitioners, 15.5% service, 26.8% sales and office, 10.0% natural resources, construction, and maintenance, 18.2% production, transportation, and material moving
Income: Per capita: $22,880; Median household: $43,084; Average household: $56,302; Households with income of $100,000 or more: 13.2%; Poverty rate: 17.0%

Educational Attainment: High school diploma or higher: 83.1%; Bachelor's degree or higher: 19.2%; Graduate/professional degree or higher: 4.5%
Housing: Homeownership rate: 64.8%; Median home value: $117,300; Median year structure built: 1983; Homeowner vacancy rate: 2.6%; Median gross rent: $751 per month; Rental vacancy rate: 11.6%
Vital Statistics: Birth rate: 112.9 per 10,000 population; Death rate: 100.8 per 10,000 population; Age-adjusted cancer mortality rate: 198.3 deaths per 100,000 population
Health Insurance: 83.8% have insurance; 61.4% have private insurance; 34.5% have public insurance; 16.2% do not have insurance; 8.3% of children under 18 do not have insurance
Health Care: Physicians: 15.3 per 10,000 population; Hospital beds: 34.4 per 10,000 population; Hospital admissions: 1,350.5 per 10,000 population
Transportation: Commute: 94.6% car, 0.4% public transportation, 1.5% walk, 2.5% work from home; Median travel time to work: 21.0 minutes
Presidential Election: 50.1% Obama, 49.2% Romney (2012)
Additional Information Contacts
Nash Government . . . . (252) 459-9800
  http://www.co.nash.nc.us

Nash County Communities

BAILEY (town). Covers a land area of 0.702 square miles and a water area of 0 square miles. Located at 35.78° N. Lat; 78.11° W. Long. Elevation is 220 feet.
Population: 569; Growth (since 2000): -15.1%; Density: 810.6 persons per square mile; Race: 65.9% White, 20.4% Black/African American, 0.0% Asian, 0.0% American Indian/Alaska Native, 0.0% Native Hawaiian/Other Pacific Islander, 1.4% Two or more races, 13.4% Hispanic of any race; Average household size: 2.51; Median age: 39.6; Age under 18: 23.2%; Age 65 and over: 15.6%; Males per 100 females: 105.4
School District(s)
Nash-Rocky Mount Schools (PK-12)
  2012-13 Enrollment: 16,770 . . . . (252) 459-5220
Housing: Homeownership rate: 71.4%; Homeowner vacancy rate: 2.4%; Rental vacancy rate: 13.2%

BATTLEBORO (unincorporated postal area)
ZCTA: 27809
  Covers a land area of 74.833 square miles and a water area of 0.138 square miles. Located at 36.02° N. Lat; 77.74° W. Long..
  Population: 5,091; Growth (since 2000): -1.4%; Density: 68.0 persons per square mile; Race: 45.8% White, 49.8% Black/African American, 0.2% Asian, 0.8% American Indian/Alaska Native, 0.0% Native Hawaiian/Other Pacific Islander, 1.1% Two or more races, 3.6% Hispanic of any race; Average household size: 2.68; Median age: 41.2; Age under 18: 24.4%; Age 65 and over: 13.1%; Males per 100 females: 93.0; Marriage status: 32.4% never married, 54.7% now married, 2.9% separated, 5.0% widowed, 7.9% divorced; Foreign born: 1.0%; Speak English only: 98.1%; With disability: 16.3%; Veterans: 7.6%; Ancestry: 15.3% American, 13.2% English, 7.0% Irish, 2.7% German, 2.3% French
  Employment: 14.3% management, business, and financial, 5.3% computer, engineering, and science, 6.1% education, legal, community service, arts, and media, 6.7% healthcare practitioners, 15.8% service, 18.7% sales and office, 10.7% natural resources, construction, and maintenance, 22.4% production, transportation, and material moving
  Income: Per capita: $25,372; Median household: $40,400; Average household: $61,887; Households with income of $100,000 or more: 17.9%; Poverty rate: 12.1%
  Educational Attainment: High school diploma or higher: 84.2%; Bachelor's degree or higher: 20.3%; Graduate/professional degree or higher: 2.9%
School District(s)
Edgecombe County Schools (PK-12)
  2012-13 Enrollment: 6,866 . . . . (252) 641-2600
Nash-Rocky Mount Schools (PK-12)
  2012-13 Enrollment: 16,770 . . . . (252) 459-5220
Rocky Mount Preparatory (KG-12)
  2012-13 Enrollment: 1,171 . . . . (252) 443-9923
  Housing: Homeownership rate: 77.7%; Median home value: $94,400; Median year structure built: 1987; Homeowner vacancy rate: 2.1%; Median gross rent: $588 per month; Rental vacancy rate: 7.0%

Health Insurance: 86.1% have insurance; 64.7% have private insurance; 35.8% have public insurance; 13.9% do not have insurance; 4.1% of children under 18 do not have insurance
Transportation: Commute: 96.9% car, 0.0% public transportation, 1.4% walk, 1.3% work from home; Median travel time to work: 19.6 minutes

CASTALIA (town). Covers a land area of 0.753 square miles and a water area of 0 square miles. Located at 36.08° N. Lat; 78.06° W. Long. Elevation is 308 feet.
Population: 268; Growth (since 2000): -21.2%; Density: 356.1 persons per square mile; Race: 51.9% White, 37.7% Black/African American, 1.9% Asian, 2.2% American Indian/Alaska Native, 0.0% Native Hawaiian/Other Pacific Islander, 2.6% Two or more races, 9.0% Hispanic of any race; Average household size: 2.55; Median age: 40.6; Age under 18: 23.5%; Age 65 and over: 15.7%; Males per 100 females: 109.4
Housing: Homeownership rate: 82.9%; Homeowner vacancy rate: 6.5%; Rental vacancy rate: 5.3%

DORTCHES (town). Covers a land area of 7.844 square miles and a water area of 0 square miles. Located at 36.01° N. Lat; 77.86° W. Long. Elevation is 197 feet.
Population: 935; Growth (since 2000): 15.6%; Density: 119.2 persons per square mile; Race: 71.2% White, 24.2% Black/African American, 0.5% Asian, 0.2% American Indian/Alaska Native, 0.0% Native Hawaiian/Other Pacific Islander, 1.7% Two or more races, 3.7% Hispanic of any race; Average household size: 2.44; Median age: 45.9; Age under 18: 20.3%; Age 65 and over: 15.3%; Males per 100 females: 94.4
Housing: Homeownership rate: 81.0%; Homeowner vacancy rate: 3.1%; Rental vacancy rate: 8.8%

MIDDLESEX (town). Covers a land area of 1.045 square miles and a water area of 0 square miles. Located at 35.79° N. Lat; 78.20° W. Long. Elevation is 262 feet.
Population: 822; Growth (since 2000): -1.9%; Density: 786.5 persons per square mile; Race: 52.7% White, 29.6% Black/African American, 0.0% Asian, 0.7% American Indian/Alaska Native, 0.1% Native Hawaiian/Other Pacific Islander, 2.4% Two or more races, 16.2% Hispanic of any race; Average household size: 2.40; Median age: 40.4; Age under 18: 24.7%; Age 65 and over: 19.7%; Males per 100 females: 86.4
School District(s)
Nash-Rocky Mount Schools (PK-12)
  2012-13 Enrollment: 16,770 . . . . (252) 459-5220
Housing: Homeownership rate: 61.2%; Homeowner vacancy rate: 2.3%; Rental vacancy rate: 20.2%

MOMEYER (town). Covers a land area of 1.104 square miles and a water area of 0.003 square miles. Located at 35.96° N. Lat; 78.05° W. Long. Elevation is 272 feet.
Population: 224; Growth (since 2000): -23.0%; Density: 202.8 persons per square mile; Race: 88.8% White, 8.5% Black/African American, 0.0% Asian, 0.0% American Indian/Alaska Native, 0.9% Native Hawaiian/Other Pacific Islander, 1.3% Two or more races, 0.4% Hispanic of any race; Average household size: 2.22; Median age: 44.0; Age under 18: 19.2%; Age 65 and over: 21.0%; Males per 100 females: 94.8
Housing: Homeownership rate: 81.2%; Homeowner vacancy rate: 1.2%; Rental vacancy rate: 5.0%

NASHVILLE (town). County seat. Covers a land area of 4.137 square miles and a water area of 0.004 square miles. Located at 35.97° N. Lat; 77.95° W. Long. Elevation is 187 feet.
History: Nashville and Nash County were named for the Revolutionary patriot, Brigadier General Francis Nash.
Population: 5,352; Growth (since 2000): 24.2%; Density: 1,293.6 persons per square mile; Race: 51.2% White, 45.5% Black/African American, 0.4% Asian, 0.6% American Indian/Alaska Native, 0.0% Native Hawaiian/Other Pacific Islander, 1.3% Two or more races, 1.6% Hispanic of any race; Average household size: 2.37; Median age: 40.1; Age under 18: 23.4%; Age 65 and over: 16.2%; Males per 100 females: 85.7; Marriage status: 34.6% never married, 41.1% now married, 3.5% separated, 8.0% widowed, 16.4% divorced; Foreign born: 0.0%; Speak English only: 99.0%; With disability: 16.3%; Veterans: 10.3%; Ancestry: 12.0% English, 9.3% German, 8.8% American, 5.0% Irish, 4.8% Italian
Employment: 12.1% management, business, and financial, 4.9% computer, engineering, and science, 9.3% education, legal, community service, arts, and media, 6.5% healthcare practitioners, 17.0% service,

25.8% sales and office, 3.1% natural resources, construction, and maintenance, 21.4% production, transportation, and material moving
Income: Per capita: $23,809; Median household: $45,018; Average household: $55,387; Households with income of $100,000 or more: 10.9%; Poverty rate: 16.4%
Educational Attainment: High school diploma or higher: 87.5%; Bachelor's degree or higher: 18.2%; Graduate/professional degree or higher: 5.0%

School District(s)
Nash-Rocky Mount Schools (PK-12)
    2012-13 Enrollment: 16,770 . . . . (252) 459-5220
Housing: Homeownership rate: 59.3%; Median home value: $135,800; Median year structure built: 1977; Homeowner vacancy rate: 1.8%; Median gross rent: $649 per month; Rental vacancy rate: 6.1%
Health Insurance: 86.9% have insurance; 69.1% have private insurance; 31.3% have public insurance; 13.1% do not have insurance; 4.8% of children under 18 do not have insurance
Newspapers: Nashville Graphic (weekly circulation 4500)
Transportation: Commute: 94.5% car, 0.7% public transportation, 1.0% walk, 1.2% work from home; Median travel time to work: 20.7 minutes
Additional Information Contacts
Town of Nashville . . . . (252) 459-4511
    http://www.townofnashville.com

RED OAK (town).
Covers a land area of 19.523 square miles and a water area of 0.009 square miles. Located at 36.06° N. Lat; 77.91° W. Long. Elevation is 203 feet.
Population: 3,430; Growth (since 2000): 26.0%; Density: 175.7 persons per square mile; Race: 87.2% White, 9.7% Black/African American, 0.5% Asian, 0.9% American Indian/Alaska Native, 0.0% Native Hawaiian/Other Pacific Islander, 0.9% Two or more races, 1.7% Hispanic of any race; Average household size: 2.70; Median age: 42.4; Age under 18: 26.1%; Age 65 and over: 11.8%; Males per 100 females: 100.6; Marriage status: 17.4% never married, 71.3% now married, 3.4% separated, 6.7% widowed, 4.6% divorced; Foreign born: 1.9%; Speak English only: 96.8%; With disability: 11.2%; Veterans: 6.5%; Ancestry: 23.9% English, 15.9% American, 10.1% German, 9.6% Irish, 5.2% European
Employment: 17.3% management, business, and financial, 2.3% computer, engineering, and science, 9.9% education, legal, community service, arts, and media, 6.8% healthcare practitioners, 14.3% service, 26.8% sales and office, 14.1% natural resources, construction, and maintenance, 8.5% production, transportation, and material moving
Income: Per capita: $32,165; Median household: $70,288; Average household: $84,202; Households with income of $100,000 or more: 31.2%; Poverty rate: 3.1%
Educational Attainment: High school diploma or higher: 88.4%; Bachelor's degree or higher: 28.5%; Graduate/professional degree or higher: 4.6%

School District(s)
Nash-Rocky Mount Schools (PK-12)
    2012-13 Enrollment: 16,770 . . . . (252) 459-5220
Housing: Homeownership rate: 88.6%; Median home value: $203,000; Median year structure built: 1989; Homeowner vacancy rate: 2.1%; Median gross rent: $1,032 per month; Rental vacancy rate: 9.2%
Health Insurance: 93.3% have insurance; 85.2% have private insurance; 22.1% have public insurance; 6.7% do not have insurance; 0.0% of children under 18 do not have insurance
Transportation: Commute: 99.3% car, 0.0% public transportation, 0.0% walk, 0.7% work from home; Median travel time to work: 19.1 minutes

ROCKY MOUNT (city).
Covers a land area of 43.788 square miles and a water area of 0.216 square miles. Located at 35.97° N. Lat; 77.81° W. Long. Elevation is 98 feet.
History: Rocky Mount was named for the mounds near the site at the Falls of the Tar. The town was incorporated in 1867 with 50 inhabitants.
Population: 57,477; Growth (since 2000): 2.8%; Density: 1,312.6 persons per square mile; Race: 33.5% White, 61.3% Black/African American, 1.0% Asian, 0.6% American Indian/Alaska Native, 0.0% Native Hawaiian/Other Pacific Islander, 1.6% Two or more races, 3.7% Hispanic of any race; Average household size: 2.42; Median age: 38.7; Age under 18: 24.6%; Age 65 and over: 14.2%; Males per 100 females: 84.3; Marriage status: 36.9% never married, 43.2% now married, 5.2% separated, 8.2% widowed, 11.6% divorced; Foreign born: 3.3%; Speak English only: 95.3%; With disability: 16.1%; Veterans: 9.8%; Ancestry: 7.8% English, 7.6% American, 4.1% German, 3.9% Irish, 1.6% Scotch-Irish

Employment: 11.9% management, business, and financial, 3.3% computer, engineering, and science, 8.9% education, legal, community service, arts, and media, 4.3% healthcare practitioners, 18.7% service, 26.4% sales and office, 6.0% natural resources, construction, and maintenance, 20.4% production, transportation, and material moving
Income: Per capita: $20,185; Median household: $36,582; Average household: $48,379; Households with income of $100,000 or more: 9.6%; Poverty rate: 24.5%
Educational Attainment: High school diploma or higher: 82.2%; Bachelor's degree or higher: 19.2%; Graduate/professional degree or higher: 5.0%

School District(s)
Edgecombe County Schools (PK-12)
    2012-13 Enrollment: 6,866 . . . . (252) 641-2600
Nash-Rocky Mount Schools (PK-12)
    2012-13 Enrollment: 16,770 . . . . (252) 459-5220
Four-year College(s)
North Carolina Wesleyan College (Private, Not-for-profit, United Methodist)
    Fall 2013 Enrollment: 1,602 . . . . (252) 985-5100
    2013-14 Tuition: In-state $26,632; Out-of-state $26,632
Two-year College(s)
Nash Community College (Public)
    Fall 2013 Enrollment: 3,279 . . . . (252) 443-4011
    2013-14 Tuition: In-state $2,408; Out-of-state $8,552
Housing: Homeownership rate: 52.5%; Median home value: $105,500; Median year structure built: 1977; Homeowner vacancy rate: 3.5%; Median gross rent: $753 per month; Rental vacancy rate: 14.5%
Health Insurance: 83.3% have insurance; 53.6% have private insurance; 42.4% have public insurance; 16.7% do not have insurance; 7.6% of children under 18 do not have insurance
Hospitals: Nash General Hospital (280 beds)
Safety: Violent crime rate: 105.0 per 10,000 population; Property crime rate: 575.6 per 10,000 population
Newspapers: Rocky Mount Telegram (daily circulation 14200)
Transportation: Commute: 94.2% car, 1.0% public transportation, 1.3% walk, 2.3% work from home; Median travel time to work: 18.7 minutes; Amtrak: Train service available.
Airports: Rocky Mount-Wilson Regional (general aviation)
Additional Information Contacts
City of Rocky Mount . . . . (252) 872-1111
    http://www.ci.rocky-mount.nc.us

SHARPSBURG (town).
Covers a land area of 1.014 square miles and a water area of 0 square miles. Located at 35.87° N. Lat; 77.83° W. Long. Elevation is 138 feet.
Population: 2,024; Growth (since 2000): -16.4%; Density: 1,996.6 persons per square mile; Race: 36.8% White, 58.9% Black/African American, 0.6% Asian, 0.1% American Indian/Alaska Native, 0.0% Native Hawaiian/Other Pacific Islander, 2.2% Two or more races, 2.5% Hispanic of any race; Average household size: 2.45; Median age: 34.9; Age under 18: 26.4%; Age 65 and over: 9.3%; Males per 100 females: 82.8
Housing: Homeownership rate: 50.0%; Homeowner vacancy rate: 2.3%; Rental vacancy rate: 13.3%

SPRING HOPE (town).
Covers a land area of 1.513 square miles and a water area of 0 square miles. Located at 35.94° N. Lat; 78.11° W. Long. Elevation is 262 feet.
History: Spring Hope was built on property acquired in 1887 from the Hendricks family at a price so low that grateful citizens offered the couple a trip anywhere on the Atlantic Coast Line Railroad.
Population: 1,320; Growth (since 2000): 4.7%; Density: 872.5 persons per square mile; Race: 46.9% White, 47.0% Black/African American, 0.5% Asian, 0.7% American Indian/Alaska Native, 0.0% Native Hawaiian/Other Pacific Islander, 1.7% Two or more races, 4.2% Hispanic of any race; Average household size: 2.06; Median age: 47.1; Age under 18: 20.2%; Age 65 and over: 24.2%; Males per 100 females: 76.7
School District(s)
Nash-Rocky Mount Schools (PK-12)
    2012-13 Enrollment: 16,770 . . . . (252) 459-5220
Housing: Homeownership rate: 44.7%; Homeowner vacancy rate: 4.3%; Rental vacancy rate: 6.8%
Safety: Violent crime rate: 52.8 per 10,000 population; Property crime rate: 332.1 per 10,000 population
Newspapers: Spring Hope Enterprise (weekly circulation 3500)

New Hanover County

Located in southeastern North Carolina, on the Atlantic Ocean; bounded on the east by Onslow Bay, on the west by the Cape Fear River, and on the north by Northeast Cape Fear River. Covers a land area of 191.534 square miles, a water area of 136.669 square miles, and is located in the Eastern Time Zone at 34.18° N. Lat., 77.87° W. Long. The county was founded in 1729. County seat is Wilmington.

New Hanover County is part of the Wilmington, NC Metropolitan Statistical Area. The entire metro area includes: New Hanover County, NC; Pender County, NC

Weather Station: Wilmington 7 N										Elevation: 40 feet		
	Jan	Feb	Mar	Apr	May	Jun	Jul	Aug	Sep	Oct	Nov	Dec
High	57	60	66	74	81	88	90	89	84	75	68	60
Low	33	35	42	49	58	67	70	69	63	51	43	35
Precip	4.1	3.6	4.4	3.0	4.7	5.0	7.7	7.0	7.4	3.4	3.3	3.9
Snow	0.3	0.1	0.6	0.0	0.0	0.0	0.0	0.0	0.0	0.0	0.0	0.6

High and Low temperatures in degrees Fahrenheit; Precipitation and Snow in inches

Weather Station: Wilmington New Hanover County										Elevation: 29 feet		
	Jan	Feb	Mar	Apr	May	Jun	Jul	Aug	Sep	Oct	Nov	Dec
High	56	60	66	74	81	87	90	88	84	75	68	59
Low	36	38	44	51	60	68	72	71	66	54	45	38
Precip	3.8	3.5	4.3	2.7	4.4	5.0	7.6	7.8	7.0	3.9	3.2	3.7
Snow	0.7	0.1	0.4	tr	tr	tr	tr	0.0	0.0	0.0	0.0	0.6

High and Low temperatures in degrees Fahrenheit; Precipitation and Snow in inches

Population: 202,667; Growth (since 2000): 26.4%; Density: 1,058.1 persons per square mile; Race: 79.1% White, 14.8% Black/African American, 1.2% Asian, 0.5% American Indian/Alaska Native, 0.1% Native Hawaiian/Other Pacific Islander, 2.0% two or more races, 5.3% Hispanic of any race; Average household size: 2.28; Median age: 37.3; Age under 18: 19.9%; Age 65 and over: 13.9%; Males per 100 females: 94.1; Marriage status: 34.5% never married, 48.5% now married, 2.6% separated, 5.8% widowed, 11.3% divorced; Foreign born: 5.6%; Speak English only: 92.4%; With disability: 12.5%; Veterans: 10.5%; Ancestry: 19.5% American, 12.0% German, 12.0% English, 11.4% Irish, 4.6% Italian

Religion: Six largest groups: 14.7% Baptist, 8.3% Methodist/Pietist, 7.2% Catholicism, 6.0% Non-denominational Protestant, 3.2% Presbyterian-Reformed, 2.3% Episcopalianism/Anglicanism

Economy: Unemployment rate: 5.2%; Leading industries: 15.1% retail trade; 12.7% professional, scientific, and technical services; 11.1% health care and social assistance; Farms: 50 totaling 2,881 acres; Company size: 3 employ 1,000 or more persons, 7 employ 500 to 999 persons, 92 employ 100 to 499 persons, 6,647 employ less than 100 persons; Business ownership: 5,935 women-owned, 1,312 Black-owned, n/a Hispanic-owned, 315 Asian-owned

Employment: 14.6% management, business, and financial, 4.2% computer, engineering, and science, 12.5% education, legal, community service, arts, and media, 7.3% healthcare practitioners, 19.8% service, 25.6% sales and office, 8.2% natural resources, construction, and maintenance, 7.9% production, transportation, and material moving

Income: Per capita: $29,679; Median household: $49,835; Average household: $69,443; Households with income of $100,000 or more: 20.2%; Poverty rate: 16.9%

Educational Attainment: High school diploma or higher: 90.6%; Bachelor's degree or higher: 36.6%; Graduate/professional degree or higher: 12.4%

Housing: Homeownership rate: 59.8%; Median home value: $215,200; Median year structure built: 1988; Homeowner vacancy rate: 3.6%; Median gross rent: $900 per month; Rental vacancy rate: 11.8%

Vital Statistics: Birth rate: 105.8 per 10,000 population; Death rate: 79.3 per 10,000 population; Age-adjusted cancer mortality rate: 179.2 deaths per 100,000 population

Health Insurance: 83.8% have insurance; 68.6% have private insurance; 28.0% have public insurance; 16.2% do not have insurance; 6.4% of children under 18 do not have insurance

Health Care: Physicians: 35.2 per 10,000 population; Hospital beds: 39.0 per 10,000 population; Hospital admissions: 1,870.9 per 10,000 population

Air Quality Index: 80.2% good, 19.8% moderate, 0.0% unhealthy for sensitive individuals, 0.0% unhealthy (percent of days)

Transportation: Commute: 88.9% car, 0.9% public transportation, 2.3% walk, 5.5% work from home; Median travel time to work: 20.2 minutes

Presidential Election: 47.0% Obama, 51.5% Romney (2012)

National and State Parks: Carolina Beach State Park; Fort Fisher State Historic Site; Fort Fisher State Recreation Area

Additional Information Contacts

New Hanover Government . . . . (910) 798-7149
http://www.nhcgov.com

New Hanover County Communities

BAYSHORE (CDP). Covers a land area of 2.425 square miles and a water area of 0.058 square miles. Located at 34.29° N. Lat; 77.80° W. Long. Elevation is 10 feet.

History: Bayshore is part of New Hanover County, formed in 1729 as New Hanover Precinct of Bath County, from Craven Precinct. It was named for the House of Hanover, which was then ruling Great Britain.

Population: 3,393; Growth (since 2000): 35.1%; Density: 1,399.0 persons per square mile; Race: 93.3% White, 2.5% Black/African American, 1.1% Asian, 0.1% American Indian/Alaska Native, 0.0% Native Hawaiian/Other Pacific Islander, 1.3% Two or more races, 3.6% Hispanic of any race; Average household size: 2.54; Median age: 39.5; Age under 18: 26.3%; Age 65 and over: 11.0%; Males per 100 females: 92.2; Marriage status: 22.5% never married, 62.4% now married, 1.0% separated, 2.8% widowed, 12.3% divorced; Foreign born: 3.2%; Speak English only: 93.7%; With disability: 16.2%; Veterans: 8.2%; Ancestry: 28.8% American, 13.6% German, 12.8% Irish, 10.1% English, 3.9% Italian

Employment: 12.3% management, business, and financial, 7.7% computer, engineering, and science, 17.4% education, legal, community service, arts, and media, 4.1% healthcare practitioners, 10.1% service, 28.7% sales and office, 13.1% natural resources, construction, and maintenance, 6.6% production, transportation, and material moving

Income: Per capita: $30,624; Median household: $61,430; Average household: $71,120; Households with income of $100,000 or more: 21.3%; Poverty rate: 3.9%

Educational Attainment: High school diploma or higher: 92.4%; Bachelor's degree or higher: 36.5%; Graduate/professional degree or higher: 11.2%

Housing: Homeownership rate: 80.1%; Median home value: $257,300; Median year structure built: 1993; Homeowner vacancy rate: 1.5%; Median gross rent: $1,240 per month; Rental vacancy rate: 6.3%

Health Insurance: 84.1% have insurance; 77.2% have private insurance; 27.2% have public insurance; 15.9% do not have insurance; 24.5% of children under 18 do not have insurance

Transportation: Commute: 91.9% car, 0.0% public transportation, 0.0% walk, 6.6% work from home; Median travel time to work: 23.9 minutes

BLUE CLAY FARMS (CDP). Covers a land area of 2.439 square miles and a water area of 0.016 square miles. Located at 34.30° N. Lat; 77.89° W. Long.

Population: 33; Growth (since 2000): n/a; Density: 13.5 persons per square mile; Race: 51.5% White, 39.4% Black/African American, 3.0% Asian, 0.0% American Indian/Alaska Native, 0.0% Native Hawaiian/Other Pacific Islander, 3.0% Two or more races, 0.0% Hispanic of any race; Average household size: 2.20; Median age: 49.5; Age under 18: 9.1%; Age 65 and over: 18.2%; Males per 100 females: 120.0

Housing: Homeownership rate: 73.3%; Homeowner vacancy rate: 0.0%; Rental vacancy rate: 0.0%

CAROLINA BEACH (town). Covers a land area of 2.464 square miles and a water area of 0.287 square miles. Located at 34.04° N. Lat; 77.90° W. Long. Elevation is 7 feet.

Population: 5,706; Growth (since 2000): 21.4%; Density: 2,315.9 persons per square mile; Race: 96.1% White, 0.7% Black/African American, 0.4% Asian, 0.7% American Indian/Alaska Native, 0.1% Native Hawaiian/Other Pacific Islander, 1.4% Two or more races, 1.6% Hispanic of any race; Average household size: 2.12; Median age: 43.9; Age under 18: 16.3%; Age 65 and over: 13.2%; Males per 100 females: 102.5; Marriage status: 26.3% never married, 48.4% now married, 5.1% separated, 8.1% widowed, 17.3% divorced; Foreign born: 0.7%; Speak English only: 97.4%; With disability: 9.0%; Veterans: 10.5%; Ancestry: 16.7% Irish, 16.6% German, 13.2% American, 12.8% English, 7.5% Scottish

Employment: 22.6% management, business, and financial, 5.2% computer, engineering, and science, 8.8% education, legal, community service, arts, and media, 6.4% healthcare practitioners, 17.8% service, 25.4% sales and office, 7.4% natural resources, construction, and maintenance, 6.4% production, transportation, and material moving

Income: Per capita: $34,110; Median household: $60,684; Average household: $79,600; Households with income of $100,000 or more: 30.1%; Poverty rate: 10.9%
Educational Attainment: High school diploma or higher: 95.1%; Bachelor's degree or higher: 36.4%; Graduate/professional degree or higher: 15.7%

School District(s)
New Hanover County Schools (PK-12)
    2012-13 Enrollment: 25,836 . . . . (910) 763-5431
Housing: Homeownership rate: 53.9%; Median home value: $258,700; Median year structure built: 1986; Homeowner vacancy rate: 11.5%; Median gross rent: $1,137 per month; Rental vacancy rate: 28.4%
Health Insurance: 81.2% have insurance; 70.2% have private insurance; 23.1% have public insurance; 18.8% do not have insurance; 8.5% of children under 18 do not have insurance
Safety: Violent crime rate: 18.5 per 10,000 population; Property crime rate: 431.2 per 10,000 population
Newspapers: Island Gazette (weekly circulation 8000)
Transportation: Commute: 83.5% car, 2.3% public transportation, 2.4% walk, 9.8% work from home; Median travel time to work: 26.2 minutes
Additional Information Contacts
Town of Carolina Beach . . . . (910) 458-2999
    http://www.carolinabeach.org

CASTLE HAYNE (CDP). Covers a land area of 4.764 square miles and a water area of 0.388 square miles. Located at 34.36° N. Lat; 77.91° W. Long. Elevation is 16 feet.
History: Castle Hayne is one of a number of agricultural colonies developed by Hugh MacRae, Wilmington real estate operator and financier. Its families, mostly from the Netherlands, have been known for their horticultural achievements.
Population: 1,202; Growth (since 2000): 7.7%; Density: 252.3 persons per square mile; Race: 80.4% White, 13.1% Black/African American, 0.4% Asian, 0.6% American Indian/Alaska Native, 0.0% Native Hawaiian/Other Pacific Islander, 1.5% Two or more races, 4.7% Hispanic of any race; Average household size: 2.39; Median age: 39.2; Age under 18: 22.9%; Age 65 and over: 13.1%; Males per 100 females: 99.3

School District(s)
Nc Dept of Juvenile Justice (KG-12)
    2012-13 Enrollment: n/a . . . . (919) 733-3388
New Hanover County Schools (PK-12)
    2012-13 Enrollment: 25,836 . . . . (910) 763-5431
Housing: Homeownership rate: 68.4%; Homeowner vacancy rate: 1.1%; Rental vacancy rate: 13.0%

HIGHTSVILLE (CDP). Covers a land area of 1.475 square miles and a water area of 0.147 square miles. Located at 34.27° N. Lat; 77.94° W. Long. Elevation is 20 feet.
Population: 739; Growth (since 2000): -2.6%; Density: 501.0 persons per square mile; Race: 62.4% White, 33.2% Black/African American, 0.3% Asian, 1.5% American Indian/Alaska Native, 0.0% Native Hawaiian/Other Pacific Islander, 2.0% Two or more races, 2.6% Hispanic of any race; Average household size: 2.28; Median age: 42.0; Age under 18: 8.3%; Age 65 and over: 5.5%; Males per 100 females: 293.1
Housing: Homeownership rate: 69.1%; Homeowner vacancy rate: 6.3%; Rental vacancy rate: 7.8%

KINGS GRANT (CDP). Covers a land area of 4.538 square miles and a water area of 0.018 square miles. Located at 34.27° N. Lat; 77.87° W. Long. Elevation is 30 feet.
Population: 8,113; Growth (since 2000): 4.8%; Density: 1,787.7 persons per square mile; Race: 77.8% White, 14.3% Black/African American, 1.1% Asian, 0.7% American Indian/Alaska Native, 0.1% Native Hawaiian/Other Pacific Islander, 1.9% Two or more races, 6.8% Hispanic of any race; Average household size: 2.47; Median age: 37.4; Age under 18: 20.3%; Age 65 and over: 11.6%; Males per 100 females: 99.5; Marriage status: 28.3% never married, 56.2% now married, 3.4% separated, 6.5% widowed, 9.0% divorced; Foreign born: 9.8%; Speak English only: 86.4%; With disability: 11.4%; Veterans: 11.5%; Ancestry: 19.0% American, 9.9% Irish, 9.7% German, 9.4% English, 3.1% Italian
Employment: 11.5% management, business, and financial, 3.7% computer, engineering, and science, 9.7% education, legal, community service, arts, and media, 3.5% healthcare practitioners, 18.8% service, 27.1% sales and office, 12.8% natural resources, construction, and maintenance, 12.8% production, transportation, and material moving

Income: Per capita: $27,232; Median household: $52,056; Average household: $68,120; Households with income of $100,000 or more: 21.0%; Poverty rate: 8.1%
Educational Attainment: High school diploma or higher: 89.3%; Bachelor's degree or higher: 25.5%; Graduate/professional degree or higher: 6.7%
Housing: Homeownership rate: 70.5%; Median home value: $161,400; Median year structure built: 1980; Homeowner vacancy rate: 2.7%; Median gross rent: $974 per month; Rental vacancy rate: 7.7%
Health Insurance: 76.8% have insurance; 68.2% have private insurance; 20.4% have public insurance; 23.2% do not have insurance; 14.4% of children under 18 do not have insurance
Transportation: Commute: 92.9% car, 0.0% public transportation, 0.3% walk, 5.3% work from home; Median travel time to work: 18.7 minutes

KURE BEACH (town). Covers a land area of 0.841 square miles and a water area of 0.004 square miles. Located at 34.00° N. Lat; 77.91° W. Long. Elevation is 13 feet.
History: State Historical Site to South.
Population: 2,012; Growth (since 2000): 33.5%; Density: 2,391.5 persons per square mile; Race: 97.0% White, 0.8% Black/African American, 0.6% Asian, 0.3% American Indian/Alaska Native, 0.0% Native Hawaiian/Other Pacific Islander, 0.8% Two or more races, 1.8% Hispanic of any race; Average household size: 2.15; Median age: 53.6; Age under 18: 14.5%; Age 65 and over: 25.3%; Males per 100 females: 95.5
Housing: Homeownership rate: 70.1%; Homeowner vacancy rate: 8.2%; Rental vacancy rate: 31.6%

MURRAYSVILLE (CDP). Covers a land area of 8.604 square miles and a water area of 0.072 square miles. Located at 34.29° N. Lat; 77.84° W. Long. Elevation is 36 feet.
Population: 14,215; Growth (since 2000): 95.3%; Density: 1,652.2 persons per square mile; Race: 79.6% White, 13.7% Black/African American, 1.9% Asian, 0.3% American Indian/Alaska Native, 0.1% Native Hawaiian/Other Pacific Islander, 2.1% Two or more races, 5.3% Hispanic of any race; Average household size: 2.45; Median age: 33.1; Age under 18: 23.9%; Age 65 and over: 8.0%; Males per 100 females: 94.5; Marriage status: 31.5% never married, 54.0% now married, 1.4% separated, 5.0% widowed, 9.6% divorced; Foreign born: 6.7%; Speak English only: 92.0%; With disability: 10.5%; Veterans: 11.7%; Ancestry: 21.4% American, 12.2% German, 10.6% Irish, 10.5% English, 5.4% Italian
Employment: 14.2% management, business, and financial, 2.7% computer, engineering, and science, 14.0% education, legal, community service, arts, and media, 6.3% healthcare practitioners, 17.0% service, 27.4% sales and office, 6.6% natural resources, construction, and maintenance, 11.7% production, transportation, and material moving
Income: Per capita: $27,975; Median household: $61,309; Average household: $64,827; Households with income of $100,000 or more: 15.6%; Poverty rate: 6.6%
Educational Attainment: High school diploma or higher: 92.6%; Bachelor's degree or higher: 29.8%; Graduate/professional degree or higher: 8.2%
Housing: Homeownership rate: 73.5%; Median home value: $180,900; Median year structure built: 1999; Homeowner vacancy rate: 2.3%; Median gross rent: $1,052 per month; Rental vacancy rate: 4.9%
Health Insurance: 86.7% have insurance; 78.5% have private insurance; 21.0% have public insurance; 13.3% do not have insurance; 6.6% of children under 18 do not have insurance
Transportation: Commute: 95.8% car, 0.3% public transportation, 0.0% walk, 2.2% work from home; Median travel time to work: 22.0 minutes

MYRTLE GROVE (CDP). Covers a land area of 6.705 square miles and a water area of 0.511 square miles. Located at 34.13° N. Lat; 77.89° W. Long. Elevation is 26 feet.
History: On the night of July 24, 1943, a German U-boat fired at least three shells to attack the "Ethyl-Dow Chemical Company" plant at nearby "Kure's Beach" (post-war: Kure Beach), but instead hit the Cape Fear River. The plant was the only one on the East Coast producing bromine from seawater for use in aviation gasoline.
Population: 8,875; Growth (since 2000): 24.6%; Density: 1,323.7 persons per square mile; Race: 93.0% White, 3.2% Black/African American, 1.2% Asian, 0.3% American Indian/Alaska Native, 0.1% Native Hawaiian/Other Pacific Islander, 1.4% Two or more races, 2.1% Hispanic of any race; Average household size: 2.48; Median age: 43.6; Age under 18: 21.5%; Age 65 and over: 15.9%; Males per 100 females: 95.1; Marriage status:

23.6% never married, 61.1% now married, 2.1% separated, 6.4% widowed, 9.0% divorced; Foreign born: 3.4%; Speak English only: 93.5%; With disability: 11.9%; Veterans: 11.8%; Ancestry: 16.5% English, 16.0% German, 15.3% American, 10.7% Irish, 8.5% Italian
Employment: 17.5% management, business, and financial, 4.5% computer, engineering, and science, 12.6% education, legal, community service, arts, and media, 8.0% healthcare practitioners, 13.7% service, 31.1% sales and office, 7.0% natural resources, construction, and maintenance, 5.6% production, transportation, and material moving
Income: Per capita: $35,475; Median household: $68,807; Average household: $85,505; Households with income of $100,000 or more: 29.8%; Poverty rate: 7.5%
Educational Attainment: High school diploma or higher: 92.8%; Bachelor's degree or higher: 41.0%; Graduate/professional degree or higher: 14.1%
Housing: Homeownership rate: 81.9%; Median home value: $251,100; Median year structure built: 1990; Homeowner vacancy rate: 2.4%; Median gross rent: $990 per month; Rental vacancy rate: 8.9%
Health Insurance: 90.5% have insurance; 77.4% have private insurance; 28.3% have public insurance; 9.5% do not have insurance; 1.4% of children under 18 do not have insurance
Transportation: Commute: 91.0% car, 0.7% public transportation, 0.5% walk, 7.4% work from home; Median travel time to work: 20.0 minutes

NORTHCHASE (CDP). Covers a land area of 1.728 square miles and a water area of 0.029 square miles. Located at 34.31° N. Lat; 77.88° W. Long.

Population: 3,747; Growth (since 2000): n/a; Density: 2,168.1 persons per square mile; Race: 78.6% White, 15.3% Black/African American, 1.7% Asian, 0.7% American Indian/Alaska Native, 0.0% Native Hawaiian/Other Pacific Islander, 2.4% Two or more races, 4.2% Hispanic of any race; Average household size: 2.33; Median age: 36.0; Age under 18: 22.1%; Age 65 and over: 12.8%; Males per 100 females: 89.8; Marriage status: 24.5% never married, 54.1% now married, 1.6% separated, 3.1% widowed, 18.3% divorced; Foreign born: 5.6%; Speak English only: 92.5%; With disability: 14.5%; Veterans: 9.6%; Ancestry: 22.7% German, 15.9% Irish, 15.2% English, 13.0% American, 6.2% Italian
Employment: 12.8% management, business, and financial, 3.3% computer, engineering, and science, 11.1% education, legal, community service, arts, and media, 8.1% healthcare practitioners, 14.3% service, 40.7% sales and office, 2.3% natural resources, construction, and maintenance, 7.4% production, transportation, and material moving
Income: Per capita: $25,447; Median household: $48,281; Average household: $54,572; Households with income of $100,000 or more: 10.1%; Poverty rate: 7.7%
Educational Attainment: High school diploma or higher: 91.7%; Bachelor's degree or higher: 29.6%; Graduate/professional degree or higher: 8.5%
Housing: Homeownership rate: 56.9%; Median home value: $172,800; Median year structure built: 1996; Homeowner vacancy rate: 2.0%; Median gross rent: $865 per month; Rental vacancy rate: 5.5%
Health Insurance: 87.1% have insurance; 66.3% have private insurance; 29.3% have public insurance; 12.9% do not have insurance; 2.5% of children under 18 do not have insurance
Transportation: Commute: 92.9% car, 0.0% public transportation, 2.3% walk, 1.2% work from home; Median travel time to work: 19.2 minutes

OGDEN (CDP). Covers a land area of 4.555 square miles and a water area of 0.257 square miles. Located at 34.26° N. Lat; 77.79° W. Long. Elevation is 46 feet.

History: Originally considered an unimportant fringe suburb of Wilmington, Ogden has become increasingly developed and populated since the late 1990s. This development was furthered by Ogden's location between the luxurious residential communities of Porter's Neck to the north, Middle Sound Loop in the middle, and Landfall to the south.
Population: 6,766; Growth (since 2000): 23.4%; Density: 1,485.5 persons per square mile; Race: 94.4% White, 1.8% Black/African American, 1.1% Asian, 0.4% American Indian/Alaska Native, 0.0% Native Hawaiian/Other Pacific Islander, 1.6% Two or more races, 2.6% Hispanic of any race; Average household size: 2.56; Median age: 40.8; Age under 18: 25.0%; Age 65 and over: 12.3%; Males per 100 females: 97.1; Marriage status: 19.7% never married, 61.1% now married, 3.8% separated, 6.4% widowed, 12.8% divorced; Foreign born: 1.4%; Speak English only: 97.5%; With disability: 9.5%; Veterans: 7.8%; Ancestry: 24.6% American, 18.1% English, 18.1% German, 15.3% Irish, 8.5% Scotch-Irish

Employment: 21.9% management, business, and financial, 6.4% computer, engineering, and science, 12.5% education, legal, community service, arts, and media, 9.8% healthcare practitioners, 18.4% service, 21.4% sales and office, 3.9% natural resources, construction, and maintenance, 5.7% production, transportation, and material moving
Income: Per capita: $34,387; Median household: $68,893; Average household: $89,074; Households with income of $100,000 or more: 26.7%; Poverty rate: 9.6%
Educational Attainment: High school diploma or higher: 95.5%; Bachelor's degree or higher: 47.0%; Graduate/professional degree or higher: 15.3%
Housing: Homeownership rate: 84.2%; Median home value: $236,600; Median year structure built: 1993; Homeowner vacancy rate: 2.1%; Median gross rent: $1,273 per month; Rental vacancy rate: 6.2%
Health Insurance: 87.3% have insurance; 77.7% have private insurance; 19.3% have public insurance; 12.7% do not have insurance; 8.8% of children under 18 do not have insurance
Transportation: Commute: 89.2% car, 0.0% public transportation, 0.5% walk, 9.1% work from home; Median travel time to work: 27.7 minutes

PORTERS NECK (CDP). Covers a land area of 5.365 square miles and a water area of 0.343 square miles. Located at 34.29° N. Lat; 77.77° W. Long.

Population: 6,204; Growth (since 2000): n/a; Density: 1,156.3 persons per square mile; Race: 92.1% White, 3.9% Black/African American, 2.0% Asian, 0.2% American Indian/Alaska Native, 0.0% Native Hawaiian/Other Pacific Islander, 1.3% Two or more races, 2.2% Hispanic of any race; Average household size: 2.34; Median age: 49.1; Age under 18: 19.9%; Age 65 and over: 28.1%; Males per 100 females: 90.0; Marriage status: 15.2% never married, 71.4% now married, 0.5% separated, 7.1% widowed, 6.3% divorced; Foreign born: 4.4%; Speak English only: 94.6%; With disability: 10.5%; Veterans: 16.5%; Ancestry: 19.6% American, 16.7% English, 16.7% German, 12.1% Irish, 5.7% Italian
Employment: 19.4% management, business, and financial, 13.4% computer, engineering, and science, 5.7% education, legal, community service, arts, and media, 13.0% healthcare practitioners, 9.7% service, 25.8% sales and office, 8.3% natural resources, construction, and maintenance, 4.6% production, transportation, and material moving
Income: Per capita: $43,801; Median household: $93,587; Average household: $102,388; Households with income of $100,000 or more: 46.5%; Poverty rate: 3.8%
Educational Attainment: High school diploma or higher: 97.3%; Bachelor's degree or higher: 58.0%; Graduate/professional degree or higher: 25.2%
Housing: Homeownership rate: 74.9%; Median home value: $431,000; Median year structure built: 2001; Homeowner vacancy rate: 3.6%; Median gross rent: $1,195 per month; Rental vacancy rate: 7.8%
Health Insurance: 95.7% have insurance; 88.4% have private insurance; 28.3% have public insurance; 4.3% do not have insurance; 2.7% of children under 18 do not have insurance
Transportation: Commute: 86.0% car, 0.0% public transportation, 1.0% walk, 12.6% work from home; Median travel time to work: 26.7 minutes

SEA BREEZE (CDP). Covers a land area of 1.795 square miles and a water area of 0.227 square miles. Located at 34.07° N. Lat; 77.89° W. Long. Elevation is 7 feet.

Population: 1,969; Growth (since 2000): 50.1%; Density: 1,096.7 persons per square mile; Race: 88.2% White, 8.2% Black/African American, 1.1% Asian, 0.6% American Indian/Alaska Native, 0.1% Native Hawaiian/Other Pacific Islander, 1.5% Two or more races, 1.6% Hispanic of any race; Average household size: 2.35; Median age: 53.0; Age under 18: 14.5%; Age 65 and over: 25.1%; Males per 100 females: 93.8
Housing: Homeownership rate: 83.7%; Homeowner vacancy rate: 4.4%; Rental vacancy rate: 8.7%

SILVER LAKE (CDP). Covers a land area of 2.453 square miles and a water area of 0.049 square miles. Located at 34.14° N. Lat; 77.91° W. Long. Elevation is 33 feet.

Population: 5,598; Growth (since 2000): -3.3%; Density: 2,281.7 persons per square mile; Race: 77.8% White, 8.8% Black/African American, 0.8% Asian, 0.6% American Indian/Alaska Native, 0.1% Native Hawaiian/Other Pacific Islander, 2.3% Two or more races, 12.9% Hispanic of any race; Average household size: 2.65; Median age: 34.4; Age under 18: 26.3%; Age 65 and over: 9.1%; Males per 100 females: 96.1; Marriage status: 33.0% never married, 52.3% now married, 3.5% separated, 7.2%

widowed, 7.4% divorced; Foreign born: 9.5%; Speak English only: 89.3%; With disability: 11.7%; Veterans: 14.6%; Ancestry: 20.3% Irish, 14.5% German, 13.4% American, 12.8% English, 7.3% Italian
Employment: 9.9% management, business, and financial, 2.5% computer, engineering, and science, 8.9% education, legal, community service, arts, and media, 9.1% healthcare practitioners, 23.7% service, 20.3% sales and office, 17.4% natural resources, construction, and maintenance, 8.1% production, transportation, and material moving
Income: Per capita: $20,714; Median household: $49,867; Average household: $53,817; Households with income of $100,000 or more: 9.5%; Poverty rate: 17.4%
Educational Attainment: High school diploma or higher: 85.9%; Bachelor's degree or higher: 14.9%; Graduate/professional degree or higher: 4.0%
Housing: Homeownership rate: 72.5%; Median home value: $156,300; Median year structure built: 1986; Homeowner vacancy rate: 3.3%; Median gross rent: $978 per month; Rental vacancy rate: 9.5%
Health Insurance: 72.1% have insurance; 53.9% have private insurance; 28.6% have public insurance; 27.9% do not have insurance; 17.5% of children under 18 do not have insurance
Transportation: Commute: 91.0% car, 4.1% public transportation, 0.0% walk, 2.7% work from home; Median travel time to work: 21.7 minutes

SKIPPERS CORNER (CDP). Covers a land area of 6.982 square miles and a water area of 0.068 square miles. Located at 34.33° N. Lat; 77.91° W. Long. Elevation is 10 feet.

Population: 2,785; Growth (since 2000): 123.5%; Density: 398.9 persons per square mile; Race: 71.5% White, 20.5% Black/African American, 0.4% Asian, 1.5% American Indian/Alaska Native, 0.0% Native Hawaiian/Other Pacific Islander, 2.1% Two or more races, 10.4% Hispanic of any race; Average household size: 2.57; Median age: 37.0; Age under 18: 18.5%; Age 65 and over: 9.7%; Males per 100 females: 133.4; Marriage status: 39.9% never married, 45.5% now married, 1.1% separated, 7.9% widowed, 6.7% divorced; Foreign born: 15.1%; Speak English only: 82.6%; With disability: 9.5%; Veterans: 12.7%; Ancestry: 17.2% American, 14.7% Irish, 9.9% German, 6.9% English, 2.4% Scotch-Irish
Employment: 11.4% management, business, and financial, 2.1% computer, engineering, and science, 11.0% education, legal, community service, arts, and media, 1.0% healthcare practitioners, 19.1% service, 18.1% sales and office, 22.3% natural resources, construction, and maintenance, 15.1% production, transportation, and material moving
Income: Per capita: $23,583; Median household: $67,602; Average household: $69,430; Households with income of $100,000 or more: 16.9%; Poverty rate: 14.2%
Educational Attainment: High school diploma or higher: 84.8%; Bachelor's degree or higher: 24.7%; Graduate/professional degree or higher: 7.9%
Housing: Homeownership rate: 78.7%; Median home value: $180,700; Median year structure built: 1986; Homeowner vacancy rate: 1.9%; Median gross rent: $793 per month; Rental vacancy rate: 8.4%
Health Insurance: 71.6% have insurance; 57.2% have private insurance; 23.1% have public insurance; 28.4% do not have insurance; 2.4% of children under 18 do not have insurance
Transportation: Commute: 98.0% car, 0.0% public transportation, 0.0% walk, 2.0% work from home; Median travel time to work: 33.6 minutes

WILMINGTON (city). County seat. Covers a land area of 51.493 square miles and a water area of 1.508 square miles. Located at 34.21° N. Lat; 77.89° W. Long. Elevation is 36 feet.

History: Wilmington dates from 1730 when English yeomen built log shacks on a bluff east of the junction of the Northeast and Northwest Branches of the Cape Fear River. The settlement, called New Liverpool, shortly admitted colonists from the lower peninsula, who sought protection from pirates and better harbor facilities. In 1733 John Watson obtained a grant of 640 acres adjoining New Liverpool and called the place New Town (or Newton). Governor Gabriel Johnston, in 1734, changed the name to honor his patron, Spencer Compton, Earl of Wilmington, and the town became a commercial center. In 1745 the assembly authorized the building of Fort Johnston at the mouth of the river as a protection against pirates; it was completed in 1764.
Population: 106,476; Growth (since 2000): 40.4%; Density: 2,067.8 persons per square mile; Race: 73.5% White, 19.9% Black/African American, 1.2% Asian, 0.5% American Indian/Alaska Native, 0.1% Native Hawaiian/Other Pacific Islander, 2.2% Two or more races, 6.1% Hispanic of any race; Average household size: 2.16; Median age: 34.7; Age under

18: 18.4%; Age 65 and over: 14.0%; Males per 100 females: 91.4; Marriage status: 41.2% never married, 41.4% now married, 2.9% separated, 5.6% widowed, 11.9% divorced; Foreign born: 6.2%; Speak English only: 91.6%; With disability: 13.3%; Veterans: 9.5%; Ancestry: 20.0% American, 10.9% English, 10.4% German, 10.1% Irish, 4.2% Italian
Employment: 14.3% management, business, and financial, 3.8% computer, engineering, and science, 13.4% education, legal, community service, arts, and media, 7.1% healthcare practitioners, 22.3% service, 24.4% sales and office, 7.2% natural resources, construction, and maintenance, 7.4% production, transportation, and material moving
Income: Per capita: $29,017; Median household: $41,573; Average household: $65,118; Households with income of $100,000 or more: 17.8%; Poverty rate: 23.2%
Educational Attainment: High school diploma or higher: 89.0%; Bachelor's degree or higher: 39.1%; Graduate/professional degree or higher: 13.7%

School District(s)
Cape Fear Center for Inquiry (KG-08)
    2012-13 Enrollment: 375. . . . . (910) 362-0000
New Hanover County Schools (PK-12)
    2012-13 Enrollment: 25,836 . . . . (910) 763-5431
Wilmington Preparatory Academy (KG-07)
    2012-13 Enrollment: 140. . . . . (910) 799-6776
Four-year College(s)
Miller-Motte College-Wilmington (Private, For-profit)
    Fall 2013 Enrollment: 2,856 . . . . (910) 392-4660
    2013-14 Tuition: In-state $10,485; Out-of-state $10,485
University of North Carolina Wilmington (Public)
    Fall 2013 Enrollment: 13,937 . . . . (910) 962-3000
    2013-14 Tuition: In-state $6,343; Out-of-state $18,480
Two-year College(s)
Cape Fear Community College (Public)
    Fall 2013 Enrollment: 9,246 . . . . (910) 362-7000
    2013-14 Tuition: In-state $2,425; Out-of-state $8,569
Vocational/Technical School(s)
College of Wilmington (Private, For-profit)
    Fall 2013 Enrollment: 182. . . . . (910) 763-4418
    2013-14 Tuition: $14,196
Housing: Homeownership rate: 48.9%; Median home value: $226,200; Median year structure built: 1983; Homeowner vacancy rate: 3.9%; Median gross rent: $855 per month; Rental vacancy rate: 11.3%
Health Insurance: 83.3% have insurance; 65.0% have private insurance; 30.6% have public insurance; 16.7% do not have insurance; 5.2% of children under 18 do not have insurance
Hospitals: New Hanover Regional Medical Center (628 beds)
Safety: Violent crime rate: 61.9 per 10,000 population; Property crime rate: 500.0 per 10,000 population
Newspapers: Star-News (daily circulation 51500)
Transportation: Commute: 86.9% car, 1.2% public transportation, 3.6% walk, 5.3% work from home; Median travel time to work: 17.3 minutes; Amtrak: Bus service available.
Airports: Wilmington International (primary service/small hub)
Additional Information Contacts
City of Wilmington . . . . (910) 341-7816
    http://www.ci.wilmington.nc.us

WRIGHTSBORO (CDP). Covers a land area of 11.148 square miles and a water area of 0.452 square miles. Located at 34.29° N. Lat; 77.93° W. Long. Elevation is 33 feet.

Population: 4,896; Growth (since 2000): 8.9%; Density: 439.2 persons per square mile; Race: 59.9% White, 33.6% Black/African American, 0.4% Asian, 0.8% American Indian/Alaska Native, 0.2% Native Hawaiian/Other Pacific Islander, 2.4% Two or more races, 5.6% Hispanic of any race; Average household size: 2.50; Median age: 39.7; Age under 18: 22.5%; Age 65 and over: 13.7%; Males per 100 females: 95.0; Marriage status: 33.5% never married, 49.8% now married, 2.5% separated, 6.2% widowed, 10.5% divorced; Foreign born: 2.1%; Speak English only: 96.2%; With disability: 14.6%; Veterans: 11.1%; Ancestry: 21.5% American, 8.8% English, 6.0% Irish, 4.9% Scottish, 3.9% German
Employment: 8.7% management, business, and financial, 3.8% computer, engineering, and science, 10.4% education, legal, community service, arts, and media, 5.6% healthcare practitioners, 19.9% service, 22.7% sales and office, 14.1% natural resources, construction, and maintenance, 14.8% production, transportation, and material moving

Income: Per capita: $20,112; Median household: $40,392; Average household: $51,215; Households with income of $100,000 or more: 14.3%; Poverty rate: 15.2%

Educational Attainment: High school diploma or higher: 89.6%; Bachelor's degree or higher: 13.8%; Graduate/professional degree or higher: 2.2%

Housing: Homeownership rate: 76.7%; Median home value: $151,600; Median year structure built: 1979; Homeowner vacancy rate: 2.1%; Median gross rent: $941 per month; Rental vacancy rate: 5.8%

Health Insurance: 80.1% have insurance; 57.9% have private insurance; 35.9% have public insurance; 19.9% do not have insurance; 6.5% of children under 18 do not have insurance

Transportation: Commute: 95.0% car, 0.0% public transportation, 0.0% walk, 4.0% work from home; Median travel time to work: 20.9 minutes

WRIGHTSVILLE BEACH (town). Covers a land area of 1.397 square miles and a water area of 0.880 square miles. Located at 34.21° N. Lat; 77.80° W. Long. Elevation is 3 feet.

Population: 2,477; Growth (since 2000): -4.5%; Density: 1,773.4 persons per square mile; Race: 97.9% White, 0.3% Black/African American, 0.6% Asian, 0.2% American Indian/Alaska Native, 0.0% Native Hawaiian/Other Pacific Islander, 0.6% Two or more races, 1.1% Hispanic of any race; Average household size: 2.13; Median age: 35.6; Age under 18: 12.6%; Age 65 and over: 14.2%; Males per 100 females: 113.0

School District(s)
New Hanover County Schools (PK-12)
    2012-13 Enrollment: 25,836 . . . . (910) 763-5431

Housing: Homeownership rate: 51.3%; Homeowner vacancy rate: 8.5%; Rental vacancy rate: 32.7%

Safety: Violent crime rate: 43.1 per 10,000 population; Property crime rate: 803.6 per 10,000 population

Newspapers: Lumina News (weekly circulation 5000)

Additional Information Contacts
Town of Wrightsville Beach . . . . (910) 256-7900
    http://www.townofwrightsvillebeach.com

Northampton County

Located in northeastern North Carolina; piedmont area, bounded on the north by Virginia, and on the southwest by the Roanoke River; drained by the Meherrin River. Covers a land area of 536.589 square miles, a water area of 14.016 square miles, and is located in the Eastern Time Zone at 36.42° N. Lat., 77.40° W. Long. The county was founded in 1741. County seat is Jackson.

Northampton County is part of the Roanoke Rapids, NC Micropolitan Statistical Area. The entire metro area includes: Halifax County, NC; Northampton County, NC

Weather Station: Jackson | | | | | | | | | Elevation: 129 feet
	Jan	Feb	Mar	Apr	May	Jun	Jul	Aug	Sep	Oct	Nov	Dec
High	50	54	62	72	79	87	90	89	83	73	63	53
Low	29	31	37	45	54	64	68	66	60	47	39	31
Precip	3.6	3.0	4.1	3.5	3.4	4.1	5.2	4.9	4.3	3.6	3.3	3.2
Snow	2.8	1.4	1.1	0.2	0.0	0.0	0.0	0.0	0.0	0.0	tr	0.9

High and Low temperatures in degrees Fahrenheit; Precipitation and Snow in inches

Weather Station: Murfreesboro | | | | | | | | | Elevation: 100 feet
	Jan	Feb	Mar	Apr	May	Jun	Jul	Aug	Sep	Oct	Nov	Dec
High	50	53	61	71	78	85	88	87	81	72	63	53
Low	29	30	36	45	54	63	67	65	59	47	38	31
Precip	3.7	3.5	4.1	3.5	4.0	4.7	4.9	4.4	4.4	3.6	3.2	3.4
Snow	1.6	0.4	0.5	tr	0.0	0.0	0.0	0.0	0.0	0.0	tr	0.7

High and Low temperatures in degrees Fahrenheit; Precipitation and Snow in inches

Population: 22,099; Growth (since 2000): 0.1%; Density: 41.2 persons per square mile; Race: 39.2% White, 58.4% Black/African American, 0.2% Asian, 0.5% American Indian/Alaska Native, 0.0% Native Hawaiian/Other Pacific Islander, 1.0% two or more races, 1.4% Hispanic of any race; Average household size: 2.32; Median age: 45.5; Age under 18: 20.8%; Age 65 and over: 19.6%; Males per 100 females: 94.1; Marriage status: 33.4% never married, 43.5% now married, 5.1% separated, 11.3% widowed, 11.8% divorced; Foreign born: 1.4%; Speak English only: 97.5%; With disability: 25.8%; Veterans: 8.3%; Ancestry: 9.7% American, 7.4% English, 7.0% German, 6.0% Irish, 1.1% African

Religion: Six largest groups: 16.5% Baptist, 12.0% Methodist/Pietist, 0.3% European Free-Church, 0.3% Non-denominational Protestant, 0.2% Episcopalianism/Anglicanism, 0.2% Pentecostal

Economy: Unemployment rate: 7.6%; Leading industries: 17.8% retail trade; 17.8% other services (except public administration); 12.5% health care and social assistance; Farms: 319 totaling 162,758 acres; Company size: 0 employ 1,000 or more persons, 1 employs 500 to 999 persons, 3 employ 100 to 499 persons, 260 employ less than 100 persons; Business ownership: 490 women-owned, 372 Black-owned, n/a Hispanic-owned, n/a Asian-owned

Employment: 10.0% management, business, and financial, 1.2% computer, engineering, and science, 6.7% education, legal, community service, arts, and media, 4.9% healthcare practitioners, 24.0% service, 21.6% sales and office, 11.4% natural resources, construction, and maintenance, 20.3% production, transportation, and material moving

Income: Per capita: $17,919; Median household: $31,433; Average household: $42,499; Households with income of $100,000 or more: 7.0%; Poverty rate: 26.3%

Educational Attainment: High school diploma or higher: 72.9%; Bachelor's degree or higher: 9.4%; Graduate/professional degree or higher: 2.8%

Housing: Homeownership rate: 72.7%; Median home value: $80,000; Median year structure built: 1977; Homeowner vacancy rate: 2.1%; Median gross rent: $622 per month; Rental vacancy rate: 7.7%

Vital Statistics: Birth rate: 87.8 per 10,000 population; Death rate: 133.4 per 10,000 population; Age-adjusted cancer mortality rate: 219.4 deaths per 100,000 population

Health Insurance: 83.1% have insurance; 48.4% have private insurance; 48.6% have public insurance; 16.9% do not have insurance; 7.9% of children under 18 do not have insurance

Health Care: Physicians: 1.9 per 10,000 population; Hospital beds: 0.0 per 10,000 population; Hospital admissions: 0.0 per 10,000 population

Transportation: Commute: 94.3% car, 0.2% public transportation, 2.7% walk, 1.5% work from home; Median travel time to work: 24.9 minutes

Presidential Election: 67.2% Obama, 32.4% Romney (2012)

Additional Information Contacts
Northampton Government . . . . (610) 559-3000
    http://www.northamptonnc.com

Northampton County Communities

CONWAY (town). Covers a land area of 1.824 square miles and a water area of <.001 square miles. Located at 36.44° N. Lat; 77.23° W. Long. Elevation is 102 feet.

Population: 836; Growth (since 2000): 13.9%; Density: 458.4 persons per square mile; Race: 49.3% White, 47.7% Black/African American, 0.0% Asian, 0.0% American Indian/Alaska Native, 0.0% Native Hawaiian/Other Pacific Islander, 1.4% Two or more races, 2.4% Hispanic of any race; Average household size: 2.34; Median age: 38.2; Age under 18: 29.5%; Age 65 and over: 16.6%; Males per 100 females: 70.6

School District(s)
Northampton County Schools (PK-12)
    2012-13 Enrollment: 2,266 . . . . (252) 534-1371

Housing: Homeownership rate: 56.7%; Homeowner vacancy rate: 4.2%; Rental vacancy rate: 7.2%

GARYSBURG (town). Covers a land area of 0.943 square miles and a water area of 0 square miles. Located at 36.45° N. Lat; 77.56° W. Long. Elevation is 135 feet.

Population: 1,057; Growth (since 2000): -15.7%; Density: 1,120.3 persons per square mile; Race: 2.4% White, 95.4% Black/African American, 0.0% Asian, 0.9% American Indian/Alaska Native, 0.1% Native Hawaiian/Other Pacific Islander, 1.2% Two or more races, 0.8% Hispanic of any race; Average household size: 2.29; Median age: 44.7; Age under 18: 22.7%; Age 65 and over: 15.5%; Males per 100 females: 79.2

Housing: Homeownership rate: 66.2%; Homeowner vacancy rate: 1.0%; Rental vacancy rate: 10.9%

Safety: Violent crime rate: 79.1 per 10,000 population; Property crime rate: 326.1 per 10,000 population

GASTON (town). Covers a land area of 1.691 square miles and a water area of 0.139 square miles. Located at 36.50° N. Lat; 77.65° W. Long. Elevation is 180 feet.

History: Incorporated 1950.

Population: 1,152; Growth (since 2000): 18.4%; Density: 681.4 persons per square mile; Race: 57.0% White, 39.3% Black/African American, 0.3% Asian, 0.8% American Indian/Alaska Native, 0.0% Native Hawaiian/Other Pacific Islander, 1.0% Two or more races, 2.3% Hispanic of any race; Average household size: 2.33; Median age: 41.9; Age under 18: 21.5%; Age 65 and over: 18.1%; Males per 100 females: 96.9

School District(s)

Gaston College Preparatory (05-12)

    2012-13 Enrollment: 815. . . . . (252) 308-6932

Northampton County Schools (PK-12)

    2012-13 Enrollment: 2,266 . . . . (252) 534-1371

Housing: Homeownership rate: 58.9%; Homeowner vacancy rate: 1.1%; Rental vacancy rate: 7.2%

HENRICO (unincorporated postal area)

ZCTA: 27842

Covers a land area of 10.793 square miles and a water area of 5.493 square miles. Located at 36.52° N. Lat; 77.85° W. Long. Elevation is 272 feet.

Population: 1,493; Growth (since 2000): 9.3%; Density: 138.3 persons per square mile; Race: 71.9% White, 25.3% Black/African American, 0.5% Asian, 0.4% American Indian/Alaska Native, 0.0% Native Hawaiian/Other Pacific Islander, 1.5% Two or more races, 0.9% Hispanic of any race; Average household size: 2.01; Median age: 59.4; Age under 18: 11.0%; Age 65 and over: 34.8%; Males per 100 females: 96.7

Housing: Homeownership rate: 86.0%; Homeowner vacancy rate: 6.7%; Rental vacancy rate: 14.8%

JACKSON (town). County seat. Covers a land area of 1.010 square miles and a water area of 0 square miles. Located at 36.39° N. Lat; 77.42° W. Long. Elevation is 102 feet.

History: When the first courthouse was built in this town in 1742, it was known as Northampton Courthouse. It was incorporated in 1823 as Jackson, for Andrew Jackson.

Population: 513; Growth (since 2000): -26.2%; Density: 507.9 persons per square mile; Race: 56.3% White, 42.7% Black/African American, 0.0% Asian, 0.2% American Indian/Alaska Native, 0.0% Native Hawaiian/Other Pacific Islander, 0.2% Two or more races, 1.0% Hispanic of any race; Average household size: 2.10; Median age: 49.6; Age under 18: 12.9%; Age 65 and over: 24.4%; Males per 100 females: 118.3

School District(s)

Northampton County Schools (PK-12)

    2012-13 Enrollment: 2,266 . . . . (252) 534-1371

Housing: Homeownership rate: 80.1%; Homeowner vacancy rate: 3.3%; Rental vacancy rate: 2.3%

LASKER (town). Covers a land area of 1.118 square miles and a water area of 0 square miles. Located at 36.35° N. Lat; 77.31° W. Long. Elevation is 85 feet.

Population: 122; Growth (since 2000): 18.4%; Density: 109.1 persons per square mile; Race: 76.2% White, 14.8% Black/African American, 3.3% Asian, 0.0% American Indian/Alaska Native, 0.0% Native Hawaiian/Other Pacific Islander, 2.5% Two or more races, 3.3% Hispanic of any race; Average household size: 2.22; Median age: 47.7; Age under 18: 18.0%; Age 65 and over: 18.9%; Males per 100 females: 100.0

Housing: Homeownership rate: 76.4%; Homeowner vacancy rate: 2.3%; Rental vacancy rate: 7.1%

MARGARETTSVILLE (unincorporated postal area)

ZCTA: 27853

Covers a land area of 42.549 square miles and a water area of 0.103 square miles. Located at 36.51° N. Lat; 77.30° W. Long. Elevation is 52 feet.

Population: 673; Growth (since 2000): -11.8%; Density: 15.8 persons per square mile; Race: 41.9% White, 53.2% Black/African American, 0.0% Asian, 0.4% American Indian/Alaska Native, 0.0% Native Hawaiian/Other Pacific Islander, 1.2% Two or more races, 3.4% Hispanic of any race; Average household size: 2.52; Median age: 44.4; Age under 18: 24.2%; Age 65 and over: 15.8%; Males per 100 females: 99.1

Housing: Homeownership rate: 78.3%; Homeowner vacancy rate: 1.4%; Rental vacancy rate: 4.9%

PENDLETON (unincorporated postal area)

ZCTA: 27862

Covers a land area of 40.090 square miles and a water area of 0.235 square miles. Located at 36.49° N. Lat; 77.19° W. Long. Elevation is 79 feet.

Population: 877; Growth (since 2000): 4.2%; Density: 21.9 persons per square mile; Race: 58.5% White, 40.8% Black/African American, 0.0% Asian, 0.0% American Indian/Alaska Native, 0.0% Native Hawaiian/Other Pacific Islander, 0.7% Two or more races, 0.8% Hispanic of any race; Average household size: 2.34; Median age: 48.2; Age under 18: 19.2%; Age 65 and over: 22.5%; Males per 100 females: 90.2

School District(s)

Northampton County Schools (PK-12)

    2012-13 Enrollment: 2,266 . . . . (252) 534-1371

Housing: Homeownership rate: 81.3%; Homeowner vacancy rate: 1.3%; Rental vacancy rate: 4.1%

RICH SQUARE (town). Covers a land area of 3.086 square miles and a water area of 0 square miles. Located at 36.27° N. Lat; 77.28° W. Long. Elevation is 72 feet.

Population: 958; Growth (since 2000): 2.9%; Density: 310.5 persons per square mile; Race: 35.9% White, 62.6% Black/African American, 0.0% Asian, 0.4% American Indian/Alaska Native, 0.0% Native Hawaiian/Other Pacific Islander, 1.0% Two or more races, 1.5% Hispanic of any race; Average household size: 2.25; Median age: 50.8; Age under 18: 17.7%; Age 65 and over: 29.9%; Males per 100 females: 81.1

Housing: Homeownership rate: 73.6%; Homeowner vacancy rate: 2.6%; Rental vacancy rate: 7.9%

Safety: Violent crime rate: 75.6 per 10,000 population; Property crime rate: 518.4 per 10,000 population

---

SEABOARD (town). Covers a land area of 0.963 square miles and a water area of 0 square miles. Located at 36.49° N. Lat; 77.44° W. Long. Elevation is 131 feet.

Population: 632; Growth (since 2000): -9.1%; Density: 656.3 persons per square mile; Race: 23.6% White, 74.5% Black/African American, 0.2% Asian, 0.2% American Indian/Alaska Native, 0.0% Native Hawaiian/Other Pacific Islander, 1.4% Two or more races, 0.2% Hispanic of any race; Average household size: 2.11; Median age: 47.3; Age under 18: 20.1%; Age 65 and over: 21.0%; Males per 100 females: 74.1

School District(s)

Northampton County Schools (PK-12)

    2012-13 Enrollment: 2,266 . . . . (252) 534-1371

Housing: Homeownership rate: 60.0%; Homeowner vacancy rate: 2.7%; Rental vacancy rate: 6.3%

SEVERN (town). Covers a land area of 1.011 square miles and a water area of 0 square miles. Located at 36.51° N. Lat; 77.19° W. Long. Elevation is 59 feet.

Population: 276; Growth (since 2000): 4.9%; Density: 273.0 persons per square mile; Race: 68.5% White, 31.2% Black/African American, 0.0% Asian, 0.0% American Indian/Alaska Native, 0.0% Native Hawaiian/Other Pacific Islander, 0.4% Two or more races, 1.4% Hispanic of any race; Average household size: 2.19; Median age: 51.5; Age under 18: 12.3%; Age 65 and over: 29.7%; Males per 100 females: 90.3

Housing: Homeownership rate: 79.4%; Homeowner vacancy rate: 2.0%; Rental vacancy rate: 7.1%

WOODLAND (town). Covers a land area of 1.252 square miles and a water area of 0 square miles. Located at 36.33° N. Lat; 77.21° W. Long. Elevation is 66 feet.

Population: 809; Growth (since 2000): -2.9%; Density: 646.4 persons per square mile; Race: 49.2% White, 47.2% Black/African American, 0.5% Asian, 0.7% American Indian/Alaska Native, 0.0% Native Hawaiian/Other Pacific Islander, 1.0% Two or more races, 1.1% Hispanic of any race; Average household size: 2.46; Median age: 40.5; Age under 18: 27.6%; Age 65 and over: 16.4%; Males per 100 females: 84.3

Housing: Homeownership rate: 57.2%; Homeowner vacancy rate: 4.1%; Rental vacancy rate: 4.1%

Onslow County

Located in eastern North Carolina, on the Atlantic Ocean; bounded on the south by Onslow Bay; drained by the New River. Covers a land area of 762.744 square miles, a water area of 143.169 square miles, and is located in the Eastern Time Zone at 34.76° N. Lat., 77.50° W. Long. The county was founded in 1734. County seat is Jacksonville.

Onslow County is part of the Jacksonville, NC Metropolitan Statistical Area. The entire metro area includes: Onslow County, NC

Weather Station: Hofmann Forest									Elevation: 43 feet		
	Jan	Feb	Mar	Apr	May	Jun	Jul	Aug	Sep	Oct	Nov	Dec
High	57	61	68	75	82	88	91	89	84	77	69	60
Low	34	36	41	48	56	65	69	68	63	51	43	35
Precip	4.4	3.8	4.5	3.3	4.1	5.3	6.9	7.3	6.5	4.1	3.8	3.6
Snow	0.5	0.1	0.1	tr	0.0	0.0	0.0	0.0	0.0	0.0	tr	0.7

High and Low temperatures in degrees Fahrenheit; Precipitation and Snow in inches

Population: 177,772; Growth (since 2000): 18.2%; Density: 233.1 persons per square mile; Race: 74.0% White, 15.6% Black/African American, 1.9% Asian, 0.7% American Indian/Alaska Native, 0.3% Native Hawaiian/Other Pacific Islander, 4.4% two or more races, 10.1% Hispanic of any race; Average household size: 2.66; Median age: 25.7; Age under 18: 25.3%; Age 65 and over: 7.5%; Males per 100 females: 115.7; Marriage status: 29.6% never married, 57.2% now married, 3.3% separated, 3.9% widowed, 9.2% divorced; Foreign born: 4.2%; Speak English only: 91.2%; With disability: 14.1%; Veterans: 21.6%; Ancestry: 16.4% German, 15.0% Irish, 8.1% English, 6.9% American, 6.0% Italian

Religion: Six largest groups: 11.7% Baptist, 4.6% Non-denominational Protestant, 4.3% Catholicism, 4.1% Methodist/Pietist, 1.3% Latter-day Saints, 1.0% Pentecostal

Economy: Unemployment rate: 5.9%; Leading industries: 19.8% retail trade; 12.6% accommodation and food services; 11.1% other services (except public administration); Farms: 347 totaling 57,643 acres; Company size: 1 employs 1,000 or more persons, 0 employ 500 to 999 persons, 38 employ 100 to 499 persons, 2,715 employ less than 100 persons; Business ownership: 2,897 women-owned, 913 Black-owned, n/a Hispanic-owned, 265 Asian-owned

Employment: 10.6% management, business, and financial, 2.3% computer, engineering, and science, 10.9% education, legal, community service, arts, and media, 5.2% healthcare practitioners, 22.3% service, 25.4% sales and office, 12.8% natural resources, construction, and maintenance, 10.5% production, transportation, and material moving

Income: Per capita: $21,084; Median household: $45,450; Average household: $55,059; Households with income of $100,000 or more: 11.9%; Poverty rate: 15.2%

Educational Attainment: High school diploma or higher: 90.2%; Bachelor's degree or higher: 18.0%; Graduate/professional degree or higher: 5.3%

Housing: Homeownership rate: 57.1%; Median home value: $151,700; Median year structure built: 1989; Homeowner vacancy rate: 2.1%; Median gross rent: $950 per month; Rental vacancy rate: 5.9%

Vital Statistics: Birth rate: 240.5 per 10,000 population; Death rate: 49.5 per 10,000 population; Age-adjusted cancer mortality rate: 183.2 deaths per 100,000 population

Health Insurance: 85.3% have insurance; 71.3% have private insurance; 25.1% have public insurance; 14.7% do not have insurance; 6.2% of children under 18 do not have insurance

Health Care: Physicians: 10.5 per 10,000 population; Hospital beds: 20.2 per 10,000 population; Hospital admissions: 881.4 per 10,000 population

Transportation: Commute: 85.9% car, 0.2% public transportation, 5.4% walk, 6.8% work from home; Median travel time to work: 24.3 minutes

Presidential Election: 35.9% Obama, 62.8% Romney (2012)

National and State Parks: Hammocks Beach State Park

Additional Information Contacts

Onslow Government . . . . (910) 347-4717
  http://www.onslowcountync.gov

Onslow County Communities

CAMP LEJEUNE (unincorporated postal area)

ZCTA: 28547

Covers a land area of 26.023 square miles and a water area of 11.014 square miles. Located at 34.67° N. Lat; 77.37° W. Long..

Population: 21,884; Growth (since 2000): 1.2%; Density: 840.9 persons per square mile; Race: 77.4% White, 11.6% Black/African American, 2.0% Asian, 1.0% American Indian/Alaska Native, 0.3% Native Hawaiian/Other Pacific Islander, 3.9% Two or more races, 14.2% Hispanic of any race; Average household size: 3.93; Median age: 21.3; Age under 18: 12.1%; Age 65 and over: 0.0%; Males per 100 females: 536.0; Marriage status: 69.2% never married, 28.1% now married, 1.8% separated, 0.1% widowed, 2.6% divorced; Foreign born: 3.6%; Speak English only: 87.2%; With disability: 8.7%; Veterans: 22.0%; Ancestry: 23.4% German, 19.1% Irish, 9.5% Italian, 7.6% English, 3.3% Polish

Employment: 12.4% management, business, and financial, 3.5% computer, engineering, and science, 15.9% education, legal, community service, arts, and media, 8.8% healthcare practitioners, 33.9% service, 19.9% sales and office, 4.6% natural resources, construction, and maintenance, 1.1% production, transportation, and material moving

Income: Per capita: $21,252; Median household: $50,596; Average household: $63,235; Households with income of $100,000 or more: 11.8%; Poverty rate: 5.6%

Educational Attainment: High school diploma or higher: 99.3%; Bachelor's degree or higher: 22.8%; Graduate/professional degree or higher: 8.2%

Housing: Homeownership rate: 0.4%; Median home value: n/a; Median year structure built: 1962; Homeowner vacancy rate: 14.3%; Median gross rent: $1,365 per month; Rental vacancy rate: 4.9%

Health Insurance: 98.0% have insurance; 97.7% have private insurance; 1.5% have public insurance; 2.0% do not have insurance; 0.3% of children under 18 do not have insurance

Transportation: Commute: 47.4% car, 0.3% public transportation, 21.7% walk, 29.6% work from home; Median travel time to work: 9.8 minutes

HALF MOON (CDP). Covers a land area of 7.403 square miles and a water area of 0 square miles. Located at 34.83° N. Lat; 77.46° W. Long. Elevation is 30 feet.

Population: 8,352; Growth (since 2000): 25.7%; Density: 1,128.2 persons per square mile; Race: 68.1% White, 20.8% Black/African American, 2.2% Asian, 0.7% American Indian/Alaska Native, 0.4% Native Hawaiian/Other Pacific Islander, 5.2% Two or more races, 9.8% Hispanic of any race; Average household size: 2.85; Median age: 27.8; Age under 18: 29.8%; Age 65 and over: 6.3%; Males per 100 females: 94.1; Marriage status: 24.4% never married, 63.7% now married, 2.6% separated, 3.3% widowed, 8.6% divorced; Foreign born: 1.6%; Speak English only: 96.6%; With disability: 13.9%; Veterans: 27.5%; Ancestry: 22.0% German, 12.8% Irish, 5.0% English, 4.8% American, 3.1% African

Employment: 11.9% management, business, and financial, 1.3% computer, engineering, and science, 12.9% education, legal, community service, arts, and media, 4.7% healthcare practitioners, 19.5% service, 32.0% sales and office, 9.4% natural resources, construction, and maintenance, 8.2% production, transportation, and material moving

Income: Per capita: $19,191; Median household: $49,380; Average household: $56,454; Households with income of $100,000 or more: 12.5%; Poverty rate: 18.0%

Educational Attainment: High school diploma or higher: 95.8%; Bachelor's degree or higher: 18.6%; Graduate/professional degree or higher: 2.3%

Housing: Homeownership rate: 69.5%; Median home value: $142,500; Median year structure built: 1984; Homeowner vacancy rate: 1.1%; Median gross rent: $803 per month; Rental vacancy rate: 4.4%

Health Insurance: 86.2% have insurance; 76.0% have private insurance; 21.4% have public insurance; 13.8% do not have insurance; 1.2% of children under 18 do not have insurance

Transportation: Commute: 96.0% car, 0.0% public transportation, 0.4% walk, 1.6% work from home; Median travel time to work: 25.8 minutes

HOLLY RIDGE (town). Covers a land area of 3.767 square miles and a water area of 0.003 square miles. Located at 34.49° N. Lat; 77.56° W. Long. Elevation is 62 feet.

History: Incorporated after 1940.

Population: 1,268; Growth (since 2000): 52.6%; Density: 336.6 persons per square mile; Race: 85.4% White, 8.5% Black/African American, 1.0% Asian, 0.2% American Indian/Alaska Native, 0.1% Native Hawaiian/Other Pacific Islander, 3.1% Two or more races, 5.6% Hispanic of any race; Average household size: 2.17; Median age: 30.1; Age under 18: 19.9%; Age 65 and over: 10.6%; Males per 100 females: 102.9

School District(s)

Onslow County Schools (PK-12)

    2012-13 Enrollment: 25,533 . . . . (910) 455-2211

Housing: Homeownership rate: 59.2%; Homeowner vacancy rate: 3.6%; Rental vacancy rate: 5.1%

Safety: Violent crime rate: 24.2 per 10,000 population; Property crime rate: 356.7 per 10,000 population

---

HUBERT (unincorporated postal area)

ZCTA: 28539

    Covers a land area of 48.960 square miles and a water area of 4.663 square miles. Located at 34.70° N. Lat; 77.21° W. Long. Elevation is 39 feet.

    Population: 15,469; Growth (since 2000): 23.7%; Density: 316.0 persons per square mile; Race: 83.5% White, 7.7% Black/African American, 1.5% Asian, 0.7% American Indian/Alaska Native, 0.3% Native Hawaiian/Other Pacific Islander, 4.2% Two or more races, 7.4% Hispanic of any race; Average household size: 2.71; Median age: 28.6; Age under 18: 27.8%; Age 65 and over: 6.9%; Males per 100 females: 100.7; Marriage status: 21.7% never married, 61.3% now married, 4.8% separated, 4.8% widowed, 12.2% divorced; Foreign born: 3.5%; Speak English only: 92.6%; With disability: 17.6%; Veterans: 22.0%; Ancestry: 18.9% German, 16.7% Irish, 9.2% English, 7.4% Italian, 7.2% American

    Employment: 10.8% management, business, and financial, 3.6% computer, engineering, and science, 9.4% education, legal, community service, arts, and media, 6.6% healthcare practitioners, 22.9% service, 20.9% sales and office, 17.7% natural resources, construction, and maintenance, 8.0% production, transportation, and material moving

    Income: Per capita: $21,111; Median household: $47,267; Average household: $55,547; Households with income of $100,000 or more: 9.9%; Poverty rate: 17.7%

    Educational Attainment: High school diploma or higher: 90.6%; Bachelor's degree or higher: 13.2%; Graduate/professional degree or higher: 4.2%

School District(s)

Onslow County Schools (PK-12)

    2012-13 Enrollment: 25,533 . . . . (910) 455-2211

Housing: Homeownership rate: 66.8%; Median home value: $152,500; Median year structure built: 1993; Homeowner vacancy rate: 2.1%; Median gross rent: $923 per month; Rental vacancy rate: 8.0%

Health Insurance: 86.9% have insurance; 72.1% have private insurance; 29.8% have public insurance; 13.1% do not have insurance; 2.7% of children under 18 do not have insurance

Transportation: Commute: 95.0% car, 0.0% public transportation, 1.1% walk, 2.4% work from home; Median travel time to work: 27.4 minutes

---

JACKSONVILLE (city). County seat.

Covers a land area of 46.510 square miles and a water area of 4.198 square miles. Located at 34.74° N. Lat; 77.39° W. Long. Elevation is 13 feet.

History: Settled c.1757.

Population: 70,145; Growth (since 2000): 5.1%; Density: 1,508.2 persons per square mile; Race: 67.7% White, 20.0% Black/African American, 2.5% Asian, 0.7% American Indian/Alaska Native, 0.3% Native Hawaiian/Other Pacific Islander, 4.7% Two or more races, 13.0% Hispanic of any race; Average household size: 2.69; Median age: 22.9; Age under 18: 23.4%; Age 65 and over: 5.4%; Males per 100 females: 142.6; Marriage status: 37.0% never married, 51.7% now married, 3.2% separated, 3.6% widowed, 7.7% divorced; Foreign born: 4.8%; Speak English only: 88.9%; With disability: 13.5%; Veterans: 22.5%; Ancestry: 16.4% German, 15.0% Irish, 6.6% English, 6.6% Italian, 5.3% American

Employment: 10.2% management, business, and financial, 2.3% computer, engineering, and science, 14.5% education, legal, community service, arts, and media, 6.7% healthcare practitioners, 24.8% service, 24.6% sales and office, 7.4% natural resources, construction, and maintenance, 9.6% production, transportation, and material moving

Income: Per capita: $21,210; Median household: $42,459; Average household: $54,194; Households with income of $100,000 or more: 12.1%; Poverty rate: 14.6%

Educational Attainment: High school diploma or higher: 92.2%; Bachelor's degree or higher: 23.1%; Graduate/professional degree or higher: 7.0%

School District(s)

Fort Bragg/camp Lejeune (PK-12)

    2012-13 Enrollment: n/a . . . . (910) 907-0200

Onslow County Schools (PK-12)

    2012-13 Enrollment: 25,533 . . . . (910) 455-2211

Two-year College(s)

Coastal Carolina Community College (Public)

    Fall 2013 Enrollment: 4,433 . . . . (910) 455-1221

    2013-14 Tuition: In-state $2,258; Out-of-state $8,462

Miller-Motte College-Jacksonville (Private, For-profit)

    Fall 2013 Enrollment: 475 . . . . (910) 478-4300

    2013-14 Tuition: In-state $10,080; Out-of-state $10,080

Vocational/Technical School(s)

Cheveux School of Hair Design (Private, For-profit)

    Fall 2013 Enrollment: 34 . . . . (910) 455-5767

    2013-14 Tuition: $9,000

Housing: Homeownership rate: 38.2%; Median home value: $153,600; Median year structure built: 1982; Homeowner vacancy rate: 2.0%; Median gross rent: $1,027 per month; Rental vacancy rate: 4.5%

Health Insurance: 89.8% have insurance; 77.2% have private insurance; 21.9% have public insurance; 10.2% do not have insurance; 3.2% of children under 18 do not have insurance

Hospitals: Onslow Memorial Hospital (162 beds)

Newspapers: Daily News (daily circulation 19900)

Transportation: Commute: 76.3% car, 0.5% public transportation, 9.9% walk, 11.8% work from home; Median travel time to work: 20.3 minutes; Amtrak: Bus service available.

Airports: Albert J Ellis (primary service/non-hub)

Additional Information Contacts

City of Jacksonville . . . . (501) 982-3181

    http://www.cityofjacksonville.net

MIDWAY PARK (unincorporated postal area)

ZCTA: 28544

    Covers a land area of 11.353 square miles and a water area of 0.018 square miles. Located at 34.72° N. Lat; 77.31° W. Long. Elevation is 33 feet.

    Population: 5,368; Growth (since 2000): -15.7%; Density: 472.8 persons per square mile; Race: 62.4% White, 23.2% Black/African American, 1.6% Asian, 0.8% American Indian/Alaska Native, 0.8% Native Hawaiian/Other Pacific Islander, 6.1% Two or more races, 14.7% Hispanic of any race; Average household size: 2.60; Median age: 24.1; Age under 18: 26.2%; Age 65 and over: 5.1%; Males per 100 females: 96.3; Marriage status: 21.7% never married, 63.5% now married, 3.2% separated, 2.5% widowed, 12.3% divorced; Foreign born: 1.1%; Speak English only: 96.9%; With disability: 10.6%; Veterans: 17.2%; Ancestry: 13.5% German, 12.0% Irish, 7.1% English, 6.6% American, 3.7% Italian

    Employment: 8.9% management, business, and financial, 7.5% computer, engineering, and science, 8.1% education, legal, community service, arts, and media, 2.3% healthcare practitioners, 19.6% service, 23.1% sales and office, 15.1% natural resources, construction, and maintenance, 15.3% production, transportation, and material moving

    Income: Per capita: $14,324; Median household: $33,235; Average household: $36,406; Households with income of $100,000 or more: 1.5%; Poverty rate: 23.8%

    Educational Attainment: High school diploma or higher: 88.0%; Bachelor's degree or higher: 10.9%; Graduate/professional degree or higher: 1.2%

    Housing: Homeownership rate: 35.9%; Median home value: $88,000; Median year structure built: 1986; Homeowner vacancy rate: 1.7%; Median gross rent: $937 per month; Rental vacancy rate: 7.6%

    Health Insurance: 80.0% have insurance; 61.1% have private insurance; 25.7% have public insurance; 20.0% do not have insurance; 6.3% of children under 18 do not have insurance

    Transportation: Commute: 92.0% car, 0.0% public transportation, 5.6% walk, 1.3% work from home; Median travel time to work: 21.5 minutes

---

NORTH TOPSAIL BEACH (town).

Covers a land area of 6.350 square miles and a water area of 4.172 square miles. Located at 34.49° N. Lat; 77.44° W. Long. Elevation is 5 feet.

Population: 743; Growth (since 2000): -11.9%; Density: 117.0 persons per square mile; Race: 94.3% White, 1.7% Black/African American, 1.3% Asian, 0.5% American Indian/Alaska Native, 0.4% Native Hawaiian/Other Pacific Islander, 0.5% Two or more races, 3.2% Hispanic of any race; Average household size: 1.86; Median age: 43.5; Age under 18: 8.3%; Age 65 and over: 17.0%; Males per 100 females: 125.2

Housing: Homeownership rate: 51.8%; Homeowner vacancy rate: 12.6%; Rental vacancy rate: 32.4%

Safety: Violent crime rate: 27.2 per 10,000 population; Property crime rate: 1,020.4 per 10,000 population

Additional Information Contacts

Town of North Topsail Beach . . . . (910) 328-1349
http://www.north-topsail-beach.org

PINEY GREEN (CDP). Covers a land area of 13.593 square miles and a water area of 0.090 square miles. Located at 34.77° N. Lat; 77.30° W. Long. Elevation is 39 feet.

Population: 13,293; Growth (since 2000): 14.0%; Density: 977.9 persons per square mile; Race: 63.3% White, 22.4% Black/African American, 2.8% Asian, 0.7% American Indian/Alaska Native, 0.4% Native Hawaiian/Other Pacific Islander, 6.1% Two or more races, 12.2% Hispanic of any race; Average household size: 2.74; Median age: 26.5; Age under 18: 28.3%; Age 65 and over: 6.3%; Males per 100 females: 97.2; Marriage status: 26.3% never married, 58.9% now married, 2.2% separated, 2.9% widowed, 11.9% divorced; Foreign born: 5.6%; Speak English only: 91.6%; With disability: 11.9%; Veterans: 23.4%; Ancestry: 17.1% German, 10.8% Irish, 8.3% English, 7.4% American, 3.9% Italian

Employment: 12.7% management, business, and financial, 4.5% computer, engineering, and science, 7.7% education, legal, community service, arts, and media, 3.4% healthcare practitioners, 22.4% service, 27.9% sales and office, 9.0% natural resources, construction, and maintenance, 12.5% production, transportation, and material moving

Income: Per capita: $20,071; Median household: $47,805; Average household: $54,413; Households with income of $100,000 or more: 9.7%; Poverty rate: 13.9%

Educational Attainment: High school diploma or higher: 89.5%; Bachelor's degree or higher: 14.5%; Graduate/professional degree or higher: 3.8%

Housing: Homeownership rate: 56.5%; Median home value: $146,400; Median year structure built: 1990; Homeowner vacancy rate: 1.9%; Median gross rent: $880 per month; Rental vacancy rate: 5.7%

Health Insurance: 86.5% have insurance; 73.4% have private insurance; 24.7% have public insurance; 13.5% do not have insurance; 4.3% of children under 18 do not have insurance

Transportation: Commute: 92.8% car, 0.0% public transportation, 4.4% walk, 2.0% work from home; Median travel time to work: 25.5 minutes

PUMPKIN CENTER (CDP). Covers a land area of 1.370 square miles and a water area of 0 square miles. Located at 34.79° N. Lat; 77.36° W. Long. Elevation is 43 feet.

Population: 2,222; Growth (since 2000): -0.3%; Density: 1,622.2 persons per square mile; Race: 68.6% White, 17.3% Black/African American, 3.3% Asian, 0.7% American Indian/Alaska Native, 1.0% Native Hawaiian/Other Pacific Islander, 6.1% Two or more races, 10.1% Hispanic of any race; Average household size: 2.80; Median age: 31.7; Age under 18: 24.6%; Age 65 and over: 12.0%; Males per 100 females: 97.2

Housing: Homeownership rate: 75.6%; Homeowner vacancy rate: 1.6%; Rental vacancy rate: 3.9%

RICHLANDS (town). Covers a land area of 1.578 square miles and a water area of 0 square miles. Located at 34.90° N. Lat; 77.54° W. Long. Elevation is 59 feet.

Population: 1,520; Growth (since 2000): 63.8%; Density: 963.3 persons per square mile; Race: 73.9% White, 18.2% Black/African American, 1.0% Asian, 0.3% American Indian/Alaska Native, 0.1% Native Hawaiian/Other Pacific Islander, 4.7% Two or more races, 8.2% Hispanic of any race; Average household size: 2.54; Median age: 30.6; Age under 18: 29.9%; Age 65 and over: 13.0%; Males per 100 females: 87.9

School District(s)

Onslow County Schools (PK-12)
2012-13 Enrollment: 25,533 . . . . (910) 455-2211

Housing: Homeownership rate: 64.9%; Homeowner vacancy rate: 7.0%; Rental vacancy rate: 7.9%

Safety: Violent crime rate: 36.5 per 10,000 population; Property crime rate: 206.9 per 10,000 population

SNEADS FERRY (CDP). Covers a land area of 3.797 square miles and a water area of 2.041 square miles. Located at 34.56° N. Lat; 77.38° W. Long. Elevation is 26 feet.

Population: 2,646; Growth (since 2000): 17.7%; Density: 696.9 persons per square mile; Race: 92.4% White, 3.7% Black/African American, 0.8% Asian, 0.3% American Indian/Alaska Native, 0.0% Native Hawaiian/Other Pacific Islander, 1.8% Two or more races, 3.5% Hispanic of any race;

Average household size: 2.27; Median age: 37.1; Age under 18: 19.4%; Age 65 and over: 15.7%; Males per 100 females: 103.4; Marriage status: 17.7% never married, 68.9% now married, 1.8% separated, 3.7% widowed, 9.7% divorced; Foreign born: 1.0%; Speak English only: 89.0%; With disability: 11.1%; Veterans: 11.9%; Ancestry: 30.5% German, 19.7% Irish, 11.9% English, 11.0% Italian, 10.7% Polish

Employment: 16.9% management, business, and financial, 0.0% computer, engineering, and science, 12.9% education, legal, community service, arts, and media, 0.9% healthcare practitioners, 19.2% service, 22.3% sales and office, 24.3% natural resources, construction, and maintenance, 3.5% production, transportation, and material moving

Income: Per capita: $18,713; Median household: $37,412; Average household: $48,752; Households with income of $100,000 or more: 11.4%; Poverty rate: 26.9%

Educational Attainment: High school diploma or higher: 87.2%; Bachelor's degree or higher: 14.1%; Graduate/professional degree or higher: 2.9%

Housing: Homeownership rate: 65.5%; Median home value: $148,000; Median year structure built: 1992; Homeowner vacancy rate: 2.3%; Median gross rent: $1,288 per month; Rental vacancy rate: 4.7%

Health Insurance: 79.5% have insurance; 53.4% have private insurance; 36.6% have public insurance; 20.5% do not have insurance; 12.9% of children under 18 do not have insurance

Transportation: Commute: 93.0% car, 0.0% public transportation, 1.0% walk, 1.5% work from home; Median travel time to work: 29.5 minutes

STELLA (unincorporated postal area)

ZCTA: 28582

Covers a land area of 16.241 square miles and a water area of 2.496 square miles. Located at 34.75° N. Lat; 77.15° W. Long..

Population: 1,588; Growth (since 2000): 34.8%; Density: 97.8 persons per square mile; Race: 92.3% White, 4.3% Black/African American, 0.3% Asian, 0.5% American Indian/Alaska Native, 0.1% Native Hawaiian/Other Pacific Islander, 1.8% Two or more races, 3.3% Hispanic of any race; Average household size: 2.49; Median age: 42.6; Age under 18: 21.2%; Age 65 and over: 14.7%; Males per 100 females: 101.0

Housing: Homeownership rate: 82.1%; Homeowner vacancy rate: 2.8%; Rental vacancy rate: 4.2%

SWANSBORO (town). Covers a land area of 2.091 square miles and a water area of 0.146 square miles. Located at 34.69° N. Lat; 77.13° W. Long. Elevation is 16 feet.

Population: 2,663; Growth (since 2000): 86.7%; Density: 1,273.5 persons per square mile; Race: 89.9% White, 3.5% Black/African American, 1.8% Asian, 0.4% American Indian/Alaska Native, 0.0% Native Hawaiian/Other Pacific Islander, 3.5% Two or more races, 4.5% Hispanic of any race; Average household size: 2.30; Median age: 38.0; Age under 18: 23.6%; Age 65 and over: 15.4%; Males per 100 females: 85.6; Marriage status: 21.9% never married, 60.6% now married, 2.5% separated, 8.3% widowed, 9.2% divorced; Foreign born: 3.1%; Speak English only: 96.7%; With disability: 13.8%; Veterans: 22.0%; Ancestry: 21.1% Irish, 18.3% English, 16.3% German, 6.8% American, 6.2% French

Employment: 12.4% management, business, and financial, 1.7% computer, engineering, and science, 18.7% education, legal, community service, arts, and media, 4.9% healthcare practitioners, 23.6% service, 26.2% sales and office, 7.3% natural resources, construction, and maintenance, 5.2% production, transportation, and material moving

Income: Per capita: $28,422; Median household: $48,099; Average household: $61,862; Households with income of $100,000 or more: 17.9%; Poverty rate: 12.1%

Educational Attainment: High school diploma or higher: 93.5%; Bachelor's degree or higher: 29.5%; Graduate/professional degree or higher: 13.2%

School District(s)

Onslow County Schools (PK-12)
2012-13 Enrollment: 25,533 . . . . (910) 455-2211

Housing: Homeownership rate: 61.5%; Median home value: $214,800; Median year structure built: 1990; Homeowner vacancy rate: 6.6%; Median gross rent: $909 per month; Rental vacancy rate: 4.9%

Health Insurance: 91.3% have insurance; 80.1% have private insurance; 32.7% have public insurance; 8.7% do not have insurance; 0.0% of children under 18 do not have insurance

Newspapers: Tideland News (weekly circulation 3200)

Transportation: Commute: 88.2% car, 0.0% public transportation, 5.5% walk, 3.6% work from home; Median travel time to work: 25.7 minutes

TARAWA TERRACE (unincorporated postal area)
ZCTA: 28543

Covers a land area of 2.061 square miles and a water area of 0.504 square miles. Located at 34.73° N. Lat; 77.38° W. Long..
Population: 4,699; Growth (since 2000): -26.6%; Density: 2,279.5 persons per square mile; Race: 74.6% White, 13.7% Black/African American, 1.2% Asian, 0.9% American Indian/Alaska Native, 0.3% Native Hawaiian/Other Pacific Islander, 5.8% Two or more races, 15.0% Hispanic of any race; Average household size: 3.38; Median age: 21.4; Age under 18: 44.1%; Age 65 and over: 0.1%; Males per 100 females: 93.5; Marriage status: 6.7% never married, 93.3% now married, 0.4% separated, 0.0% widowed, 0.0% divorced; Foreign born: 6.8%; Speak English only: 81.7%; With disability: 3.7%; Veterans: 11.2%; Ancestry: 14.3% Irish, 12.0% German, 8.6% American, 7.8% Italian, 6.6% English
Employment: 0.0% management, business, and financial, 9.1% computer, engineering, and science, 16.4% education, legal, community service, arts, and media, 4.2% healthcare practitioners, 25.4% service, 23.1% sales and office, 4.6% natural resources, construction, and maintenance, 17.1% production, transportation, and material moving
Income: Per capita: $11,647; Median household: $33,440; Average household: $37,893; Households with income of $100,000 or more: 1.4%; Poverty rate: 17.0%
Educational Attainment: High school diploma or higher: 96.3%; Bachelor's degree or higher: 8.2%; Graduate/professional degree or higher: n/a
School District(s)
Fort Bragg/camp Lejeune (PK-12)
    2012-13 Enrollment: n/a . . . . (910) 907-0200
Housing: Homeownership rate: 1.3%; Median home value: n/a; Median year structure built: 2005; Homeowner vacancy rate: 0.0%; Median gross rent: $1,125 per month; Rental vacancy rate: 2.2%
Health Insurance: 95.2% have insurance; 93.1% have private insurance; 2.6% have public insurance; 4.8% do not have insurance; 1.1% of children under 18 do not have insurance
Transportation: Commute: 93.9% car, 0.0% public transportation, 2.8% walk, 0.9% work from home; Median travel time to work: 23.9 minutes

Orange County

Located in north central North Carolina; piedmont area. Covers a land area of 397.958 square miles, a water area of 3.470 square miles, and is located in the Eastern Time Zone at 36.06° N. Lat., 79.12° W. Long. The county was founded in 1753. County seat is Hillsborough.

Orange County is part of the Durham-Chapel Hill, NC Metropolitan Statistical Area. The entire metro area includes: Chatham County, NC; Durham County, NC; Orange County, NC; Person County, NC

Weather Station: Chapel Hill 2 W										Elevation: 500 feet	
	Jan	Feb	Mar	Apr	May	Jun	Jul	Aug	Sep	Oct	Nov	Dec
High	50	54	62	71	79	86	89	88	82	72	63	53
Low	28	30	37	45	54	63	67	66	59	46	38	31
Precip	3.9	3.4	4.6	3.3	3.8	4.2	4.3	4.6	4.2	3.8	3.8	3.4
Snow	1.9	1.6	0.6	tr	0.0	0.0	0.0	0.0	0.0	0.0	0.1	0.4

High and Low temperatures in degrees Fahrenheit; Precipitation and Snow in inches

Population: 133,801; Growth (since 2000): 13.2%; Density: 336.2 persons per square mile; Race: 74.4% White, 11.9% Black/African American, 6.7% Asian, 0.4% American Indian/Alaska Native, 0.0% Native Hawaiian/Other Pacific Islander, 2.5% two or more races, 8.2% Hispanic of any race; Average household size: 2.41; Median age: 33.1; Age under 18: 20.9%; Age 65 and over: 9.6%; Males per 100 females: 91.6; Marriage status: 40.8% never married, 46.7% now married, 1.9% separated, 3.9% widowed, 8.6% divorced; Foreign born: 12.8%; Speak English only: 84.1%; With disability: 8.5%; Veterans: 5.5%; Ancestry: 14.1% English, 13.7% German, 12.1% Irish, 5.9% American, 4.1% Scottish
Religion: Six largest groups: 10.6% Methodist/Pietist, 10.0% Catholicism, 7.5% Baptist, 3.8% Non-denominational Protestant, 3.4% Presbyterian-Reformed, 2.3% Episcopalianism/Anglicanism
Economy: Unemployment rate: 4.0%; Leading industries: 17.8% professional, scientific, and technical services; 12.7% health care and social assistance; 12.4% retail trade; Farms: 645 totaling 56,666 acres; Company size: 1 employs 1,000 or more persons, 2 employ 500 to 999

persons, 34 employ 100 to 499 persons, 3,040 employ less than 100 persons; Business ownership: 4,575 women-owned, 823 Black-owned, n/a Hispanic-owned, 364 Asian-owned
Employment: 16.0% management, business, and financial, 10.2% computer, engineering, and science, 19.0% education, legal, community service, arts, and media, 10.0% healthcare practitioners, 16.3% service, 17.7% sales and office, 5.7% natural resources, construction, and maintenance, 5.0% production, transportation, and material moving
Income: Per capita: $34,465; Median household: $55,569; Average household: $89,459; Households with income of $100,000 or more: 30.2%; Poverty rate: 17.8%
Educational Attainment: High school diploma or higher: 91.0%; Bachelor's degree or higher: 55.8%; Graduate/professional degree or higher: 30.2%
Housing: Homeownership rate: 60.1%; Median home value: $272,600; Median year structure built: 1984; Homeowner vacancy rate: 2.0%; Median gross rent: $872 per month; Rental vacancy rate: 7.7%
Vital Statistics: Birth rate: 94.0 per 10,000 population; Death rate: 50.3 per 10,000 population; Age-adjusted cancer mortality rate: 169.5 deaths per 100,000 population
Health Insurance: 88.2% have insurance; 77.7% have private insurance; 19.4% have public insurance; 11.8% do not have insurance; 6.8% of children under 18 do not have insurance
Health Care: Physicians: 100.8 per 10,000 population; Hospital beds: 59.1 per 10,000 population; Hospital admissions: 2,797.9 per 10,000 population
Transportation: Commute: 77.6% car, 7.5% public transportation, 5.0% walk, 6.9% work from home; Median travel time to work: 22.0 minutes
Presidential Election: 70.2% Obama, 28.1% Romney (2012)
National and State Parks: Eno River State Park
Additional Information Contacts
Orange Government . . . . (919) 732-8181
    http://www.co.orange.nc.us

Orange County Communities

CARRBORO (town). Covers a land area of 6.462 square miles and a water area of 0.030 square miles. Located at 35.93° N. Lat; 79.09° W. Long. Elevation is 463 feet.
History: The town, which is part of the Durham-Chapel Hill metropolitan statistical area, was named after North Carolina industrialist Julian Shakespeare Carr.
Population: 19,582; Growth (since 2000): 16.7%; Density: 3,030.3 persons per square mile; Race: 70.9% White, 10.1% Black/African American, 8.2% Asian, 0.4% American Indian/Alaska Native, 0.0% Native Hawaiian/Other Pacific Islander, 2.9% Two or more races, 13.8% Hispanic of any race; Average household size: 2.27; Median age: 30.1; Age under 18: 21.5%; Age 65 and over: 5.3%; Males per 100 females: 93.7; Marriage status: 44.3% never married, 44.0% now married, 2.0% separated, 3.2% widowed, 8.4% divorced; Foreign born: 20.2%; Speak English only: 75.5%; With disability: 6.9%; Veterans: 3.5%; Ancestry: 14.3% German, 13.2% English, 11.8% Irish, 4.8% Italian, 4.7% Scottish
Employment: 15.5% management, business, and financial, 11.8% computer, engineering, and science, 24.3% education, legal, community service, arts, and media, 9.3% healthcare practitioners, 18.8% service, 13.4% sales and office, 3.7% natural resources, construction, and maintenance, 3.2% production, transportation, and material moving
Income: Per capita: $33,523; Median household: $46,803; Average household: $78,273; Households with income of $100,000 or more: 25.5%; Poverty rate: 17.0%
Educational Attainment: High school diploma or higher: 90.7%; Bachelor's degree or higher: 65.1%; Graduate/professional degree or higher: 35.6%
School District(s)
Chapel Hill-Carrboro Schools (PK-12)
    2012-13 Enrollment: 12,329 . . . . (919) 967-8211
Housing: Homeownership rate: 38.4%; Median home value: $337,000; Median year structure built: 1984; Homeowner vacancy rate: 2.8%; Median gross rent: $843 per month; Rental vacancy rate: 7.3%
Health Insurance: 83.7% have insurance; 74.2% have private insurance; 14.8% have public insurance; 16.3% do not have insurance; 9.5% of children under 18 do not have insurance
Safety: Violent crime rate: 25.6 per 10,000 population; Property crime rate: 277.2 per 10,000 population
Transportation: Commute: 70.5% car, 15.3% public transportation, 2.5% walk, 5.7% work from home; Median travel time to work: 21.3 minutes

Additional Information Contacts
Town of Carrboro . . . . (919) 942-8541
http://www.ci.carrboro.nc.us

CEDAR GROVE (unincorporated postal area)
ZCTA: 27231
Covers a land area of 36.426 square miles and a water area of 0.647 square miles. Located at 36.21° N. Lat; 79.17° W. Long. Elevation is 709 feet.
Population: 2,148; Growth (since 2000): 9.0%; Density: 59.0 persons per square mile; Race: 66.0% White, 27.7% Black/African American, 0.2% Asian, 0.8% American Indian/Alaska Native, 0.0% Native Hawaiian/Other Pacific Islander, 2.1% Two or more races, 6.5% Hispanic of any race; Average household size: 2.52; Median age: 45.2; Age under 18: 20.1%; Age 65 and over: 15.2%; Males per 100 females: 97.8
Housing: Homeownership rate: 79.2%; Homeowner vacancy rate: 1.4%; Rental vacancy rate: 8.3%

CHAPEL HILL (town). Covers a land area of 21.119 square miles and a water area of 0.152 square miles. Located at 35.93° N. Lat; 79.04° W. Long. Elevation is 486 feet.
History: The University of North Carolina, the first of the nation's state universities, opened in Chapel Hill in 1795. The village takes its name from the little New Hope Chapel that stood in the late 18th century at the crossing of the roads from Petersburg, Virginia, and New Bern, North Carolina.
Population: 57,233; Growth (since 2000): 17.5%; Density: 2,710.0 persons per square mile; Race: 72.8% White, 9.7% Black/African American, 11.9% Asian, 0.3% American Indian/Alaska Native, 0.0% Native Hawaiian/Other Pacific Islander, 2.7% Two or more races, 6.4% Hispanic of any race; Average household size: 2.35; Median age: 25.6; Age under 18: 17.4%; Age 65 and over: 9.2%; Males per 100 females: 87.2; Marriage status: 54.7% never married, 37.5% now married, 1.4% separated, 2.7% widowed, 5.0% divorced; Foreign born: 16.4%; Speak English only: 81.5%; With disability: 6.0%; Veterans: 4.1%; Ancestry: 15.0% English, 14.4% German, 10.6% Irish, 4.2% Scottish, 4.1% Italian
Employment: 14.7% management, business, and financial, 13.3% computer, engineering, and science, 22.9% education, legal, community service, arts, and media, 11.2% healthcare practitioners, 14.7% service, 17.7% sales and office, 2.8% natural resources, construction, and maintenance, 2.7% production, transportation, and material moving
Income: Per capita: $35,714; Median household: $60,802; Average household: $99,212; Households with income of $100,000 or more: 34.0%; Poverty rate: 23.1%
Educational Attainment: High school diploma or higher: 94.7%; Bachelor's degree or higher: 73.9%; Graduate/professional degree or higher: 45.1%

School District(s)
Chapel Hill-Carrboro Schools (PK-12)
  2012-13 Enrollment: 12,329 . . . . (919) 967-8211
Chatham County Schools (PK-12)
  2012-13 Enrollment: 8,454 . . . . (919) 542-3626
Orange County Schools (PK-12)
  2012-13 Enrollment: 7,566 . . . . (919) 732-8126
Pace Academy (09-12)
  2012-13 Enrollment: 128 . . . . (919) 933-7699
Woods Charter (KG-12)
  2012-13 Enrollment: 504 . . . . (919) 960-8353

Four-year College(s)
University of North Carolina at Chapel Hill (Public)
  Fall 2013 Enrollment: 29,127 . . . . (919) 962-2211
  2013-14 Tuition: In-state $8,340; Out-of-state $30,122

Vocational/Technical School(s)
Aveda Institute-Chapel Hill (Private, For-profit)
  Fall 2013 Enrollment: 156 . . . . (919) 960-4769
  2013-14 Tuition: $19,750
Housing: Homeownership rate: 47.6%; Median home value: $367,800; Median year structure built: 1984; Homeowner vacancy rate: 2.6%; Median gross rent: $915 per month; Rental vacancy rate: 7.1%
Health Insurance: 91.5% have insurance; 85.8% have private insurance; 14.3% have public insurance; 8.5% do not have insurance; 6.6% of children under 18 do not have insurance
Hospitals: University of North Carolina Hospital (803 beds)

Safety: Violent crime rate: 12.1 per 10,000 population; Property crime rate: 217.7 per 10,000 population
Newspapers: Chapel Hill News (weekly circulation 25000)
Transportation: Commute: 69.0% car, 11.3% public transportation, 10.1% walk, 6.7% work from home; Median travel time to work: 19.3 minutes
Airports: Horace Williams (general aviation)
Additional Information Contacts
Town of Chapel Hill . . . . (919) 967-8406
http://www.ci.chapel-hill.nc.us

EFLAND (CDP). Covers a land area of 1.802 square miles and a water area of 0.013 square miles. Located at 36.08° N. Lat; 79.17° W. Long. Elevation is 653 feet.
Population: 734; Growth (since 2000): n/a; Density: 407.3 persons per square mile; Race: 62.4% White, 31.9% Black/African American, 0.8% Asian, 0.0% American Indian/Alaska Native, 1.0% Native Hawaiian/Other Pacific Islander, 0.5% Two or more races, 7.4% Hispanic of any race; Average household size: 2.38; Median age: 40.3; Age under 18: 23.7%; Age 65 and over: 14.0%; Males per 100 females: 95.2

School District(s)
Orange County Schools (PK-12)
  2012-13 Enrollment: 7,566 . . . . (919) 732-8126
Housing: Homeownership rate: 74.7%; Homeowner vacancy rate: 1.7%; Rental vacancy rate: 8.0%

HILLSBOROUGH (town). County seat. Covers a land area of 5.331 square miles and a water area of 0.071 square miles. Located at 36.08° N. Lat; 79.10° W. Long. Elevation is 545 feet.
History: An early provincial capital of North Carolina; in 1768, scene of disturbances by the Regulators. Thomas Hart Benton born here. Settled before 1700; plotted 1754.
Population: 6,087; Growth (since 2000): 11.8%; Density: 1,141.8 persons per square mile; Race: 62.9% White, 29.5% Black/African American, 1.7% Asian, 0.6% American Indian/Alaska Native, 0.0% Native Hawaiian/Other Pacific Islander, 2.1% Two or more races, 6.6% Hispanic of any race; Average household size: 2.42; Median age: 38.2; Age under 18: 24.0%; Age 65 and over: 12.2%; Males per 100 females: 97.5; Marriage status: 34.2% never married, 46.2% now married, 3.5% separated, 6.5% widowed, 13.2% divorced; Foreign born: 6.4%; Speak English only: 88.4%; With disability: 11.3%; Veterans: 9.7%; Ancestry: 14.7% Irish, 12.4% German, 10.9% English, 5.6% American, 3.4% Scotch-Irish
Employment: 12.3% management, business, and financial, 5.7% computer, engineering, and science, 15.0% education, legal, community service, arts, and media, 10.3% healthcare practitioners, 21.4% service, 23.1% sales and office, 6.6% natural resources, construction, and maintenance, 5.5% production, transportation, and material moving
Income: Per capita: $23,566; Median household: $47,193; Average household: $60,845; Households with income of $100,000 or more: 19.0%; Poverty rate: 22.2%
Educational Attainment: High school diploma or higher: 84.9%; Bachelor's degree or higher: 36.5%; Graduate/professional degree or higher: 14.8%

School District(s)
Orange Charter (KG-08)
  2012-13 Enrollment: 226 . . . . (919) 644-6272
Orange County Schools (PK-12)
  2012-13 Enrollment: 7,566 . . . . (919) 732-8126
Housing: Homeownership rate: 64.1%; Median home value: $193,600; Median year structure built: 1982; Homeowner vacancy rate: 3.0%; Median gross rent: $834 per month; Rental vacancy rate: 11.6%
Health Insurance: 90.6% have insurance; 64.7% have private insurance; 36.0% have public insurance; 9.4% do not have insurance; 1.3% of children under 18 do not have insurance
Newspapers: News of Orange County (weekly circulation 3300)
Transportation: Commute: 87.0% car, 4.2% public transportation, 1.2% walk, 5.1% work from home; Median travel time to work: 21.9 minutes
Additional Information Contacts
Town of Hillsborough . . . . (919) 732-8156
http://www.hillsborough.net

Pamlico County

Located in eastern North Carolina; swampy, tidewater area, bounded on the north and east by Pamlico Sound of the Atlantic Ocean, and on the

south by the Neuse River. Covers a land area of 336.537 square miles, a water area of 230.213 square miles, and is located in the Eastern Time Zone at 35.15° N. Lat., 76.67° W. Long. The county was founded in 1872. County seat is Bayboro.

Pamlico County is part of the New Bern, NC Metropolitan Statistical Area. The entire metro area includes: Craven County, NC; Jones County, NC; Pamlico County, NC

Weather Station: Bayboro 3 E   Elevation: 9 feet

	Jan	Feb	Mar	Apr	May	Jun	Jul	Aug	Sep	Oct	Nov	Dec
High	56	59	66	74	80	86	89	88	83	75	67	59
Low	34	36	41	49	58	66	70	69	64	52	44	36
Precip	3.9	3.2	4.1	3.4	4.5	5.3	6.6	7.2	5.8	3.8	3.8	3.7
Snow	0.4	0.2	0.7	0.0	0.0	0.0	0.0	0.0	0.0	0.0	0.0	0.5

High and Low temperatures in degrees Fahrenheit; Precipitation and Snow in inches

Population: 13,144; Growth (since 2000): 1.6%; Density: 39.1 persons per square mile; Race: 76.3% White, 20.0% Black/African American, 0.4% Asian, 0.6% American Indian/Alaska Native, 0.1% Native Hawaiian/Other Pacific Islander, 1.4% two or more races, 3.1% Hispanic of any race; Average household size: 2.27; Median age: 48.3; Age under 18: 17.9%; Age 65 and over: 21.7%; Males per 100 females: 104.3; Marriage status: 22.8% never married, 59.0% now married, 4.2% separated, 8.3% widowed, 9.9% divorced; Foreign born: 4.1%; Speak English only: 93.9%; With disability: 20.0%; Veterans: 13.5%; Ancestry: 14.4% English, 12.9% Irish, 10.9% American, 8.8% German, 4.8% Scottish
Religion: Six largest groups: 17.0% Baptist, 16.7% Methodist/Pietist, 4.8% Non-denominational Protestant, 3.2% Presbyterian-Reformed, 1.5% Pentecostal, 1.4% Catholicism
Economy: Unemployment rate: 6.0%; Leading industries: 14.3% retail trade; 13.2% health care and social assistance; 11.8% accommodation and food services; Farms: 80 totaling 46,785 acres; Company size: 0 employ 1,000 or more persons, 0 employ 500 to 999 persons, 0 employ 100 to 499 persons, 280 employ less than 100 persons; Business ownership: 195 women-owned, n/a Black-owned, n/a Hispanic-owned, n/a Asian-owned
Employment: 10.5% management, business, and financial, 3.5% computer, engineering, and science, 9.9% education, legal, community service, arts, and media, 5.6% healthcare practitioners, 20.3% service, 22.6% sales and office, 16.3% natural resources, construction, and maintenance, 11.4% production, transportation, and material moving
Income: Per capita: $23,724; Median household: $43,853; Average household: $57,640; Households with income of $100,000 or more: 14.7%; Poverty rate: 13.8%
Educational Attainment: High school diploma or higher: 85.7%; Bachelor's degree or higher: 18.7%; Graduate/professional degree or higher: 7.0%
Housing: Homeownership rate: 79.0%; Median home value: $157,500; Median year structure built: 1984; Homeowner vacancy rate: 3.5%; Median gross rent: $757 per month; Rental vacancy rate: 13.2%
Vital Statistics: Birth rate: 67.9 per 10,000 population; Death rate: 108.9 per 10,000 population; Age-adjusted cancer mortality rate: 157.4 deaths per 100,000 population
Health Insurance: 83.5% have insurance; 60.6% have private insurance; 45.4% have public insurance; 16.5% do not have insurance; 11.5% of children under 18 do not have insurance
Health Care: Physicians: 5.4 per 10,000 population; Hospital beds: 0.0 per 10,000 population; Hospital admissions: 0.0 per 10,000 population
Transportation: Commute: 92.9% car, 0.0% public transportation, 2.0% walk, 2.7% work from home; Median travel time to work: 24.5 minutes
Presidential Election: 39.1% Obama, 59.9% Romney (2012)
National and State Parks: Goose Creek State Game Refuge
Additional Information Contacts
Pamlico Government. . . . . (252) 745-3133
   http://www.pamlicocounty.org

Pamlico County Communities

ALLIANCE (town). Covers a land area of 2.086 square miles and a water area of 0 square miles. Located at 35.14° N. Lat; 76.81° W. Long. Elevation is 10 feet.
Population: 776; Growth (since 2000): -0.6%; Density: 372.0 persons per square mile; Race: 80.7% White, 15.9% Black/African American, 0.4% Asian, 0.3% American Indian/Alaska Native, 0.0% Native Hawaiian/Other Pacific Islander, 0.8% Two or more races, 3.1% Hispanic of any race;

Average household size: 2.42; Median age: 47.0; Age under 18: 20.0%; Age 65 and over: 26.3%; Males per 100 females: 82.2
Housing: Homeownership rate: 69.0%; Homeowner vacancy rate: 2.0%; Rental vacancy rate: 4.3%

ARAPAHOE (town). Covers a land area of 2.171 square miles and a water area of 0 square miles. Located at 35.02° N. Lat; 76.83° W. Long. Elevation is 39 feet.
Population: 556; Growth (since 2000): 27.5%; Density: 256.1 persons per square mile; Race: 88.3% White, 5.4% Black/African American, 0.0% Asian, 0.2% American Indian/Alaska Native, 1.4% Native Hawaiian/Other Pacific Islander, 1.4% Two or more races, 8.8% Hispanic of any race; Average household size: 2.56; Median age: 40.5; Age under 18: 22.8%; Age 65 and over: 16.5%; Males per 100 females: 101.4
School District(s)
Arapahoe Charter School (KG-08)
   2012-13 Enrollment: 434. . . . . (252) 249-2599
Housing: Homeownership rate: 75.1%; Homeowner vacancy rate: 3.6%; Rental vacancy rate: 3.6%

BAYBORO (town). County seat. Covers a land area of 1.853 square miles and a water area of 0.005 square miles. Located at 35.15° N. Lat; 76.77° W. Long. Elevation is 7 feet.
Population: 1,263; Growth (since 2000): 70.4%; Density: 681.7 persons per square mile; Race: 42.2% White, 54.6% Black/African American, 0.5% Asian, 1.3% American Indian/Alaska Native, 0.0% Native Hawaiian/Other Pacific Islander, 1.2% Two or more races, 3.2% Hispanic of any race; Average household size: 2.13; Median age: 38.9; Age under 18: 10.2%; Age 65 and over: 11.2%; Males per 100 females: 275.9
School District(s)
Pamlico County Schools (PK-12)
   2012-13 Enrollment: 1,330 . . . . (252) 745-4171
Housing: Homeownership rate: 67.7%; Homeowner vacancy rate: 1.9%; Rental vacancy rate: 13.2%

GRANTSBORO (town). Covers a land area of 3.854 square miles and a water area of 0 square miles. Located at 35.14° N. Lat; 76.84° W. Long. Elevation is 39 feet.
Population: 688; Growth (since 2000): n/a; Density: 178.5 persons per square mile; Race: 82.4% White, 10.2% Black/African American, 0.6% Asian, 0.7% American Indian/Alaska Native, 0.0% Native Hawaiian/Other Pacific Islander, 1.7% Two or more races, 5.7% Hispanic of any race; Average household size: 2.45; Median age: 42.4; Age under 18: 22.8%; Age 65 and over: 14.8%; Males per 100 females: 109.8
Two-year College(s)
Pamlico Community College (Public)
   Fall 2013 Enrollment: 597 . . . . (252) 249-1851
   2013-14 Tuition: In-state $2,326; Out-of-state $8,470
Housing: Homeownership rate: 78.8%; Homeowner vacancy rate: 0.0%; Rental vacancy rate: 21.3%

HOBUCKEN (CDP). Covers a land area of 5.079 square miles and a water area of 0.032 square miles. Located at 35.25° N. Lat; 76.57° W. Long. Elevation is 3 feet.
Population: 129; Growth (since 2000): n/a; Density: 25.4 persons per square mile; Race: 98.4% White, 0.0% Black/African American, 0.0% Asian, 0.0% American Indian/Alaska Native, 0.0% Native Hawaiian/Other Pacific Islander, 0.8% Two or more races, 0.8% Hispanic of any race; Average household size: 1.95; Median age: 53.3; Age under 18: 19.4%; Age 65 and over: 32.6%; Males per 100 females: 89.7
Housing: Homeownership rate: 78.8%; Homeowner vacancy rate: 5.5%; Rental vacancy rate: 30.0%

LOWLAND (unincorporated postal area)
ZCTA: 28552
   Covers a land area of 16.374 square miles and a water area of 19.413 square miles. Located at 35.30° N. Lat; 76.55° W. Long. Elevation is 3 feet.
Population: 254; Growth (since 2000): -20.1%; Density: 15.5 persons per square mile; Race: 98.4% White, 0.0% Black/African American, 0.4% Asian, 0.0% American Indian/Alaska Native, 0.0% Native Hawaiian/Other Pacific Islander, 1.2% Two or more races, 0.8% Hispanic of any race; Average household size: 2.48; Median age: 42.3; Age under 18: 26.8%; Age 65 and over: 18.5%; Males per 100 females: 92.4

Housing: Homeownership rate: 76.4%; Homeowner vacancy rate: 7.1%; Rental vacancy rate: 17.2%

MERRITT (unincorporated postal area)
ZCTA: 28556

Covers a land area of 45.250 square miles and a water area of 28.739 square miles. Located at 35.11° N. Lat; 76.63° W. Long. Elevation is 3 feet.

Population: 963; Growth (since 2000): -10.7%; Density: 21.3 persons per square mile; Race: 89.6% White, 7.6% Black/African American, 0.6% Asian, 0.4% American Indian/Alaska Native, 0.0% Native Hawaiian/Other Pacific Islander, 1.0% Two or more races, 1.8% Hispanic of any race; Average household size: 2.17; Median age: 52.8; Age under 18: 14.6%; Age 65 and over: 24.1%; Males per 100 females: 93.0

Housing: Homeownership rate: 86.0%; Homeowner vacancy rate: 5.2%; Rental vacancy rate: 8.6%

MESIC (town).
Covers a land area of 1.032 square miles and a water area of 0.122 square miles. Located at 35.20° N. Lat; 76.65° W. Long. Elevation is 7 feet.

Population: 220; Growth (since 2000): -14.4%; Density: 213.1 persons per square mile; Race: 39.1% White, 60.5% Black/African American, 0.0% Asian, 0.0% American Indian/Alaska Native, 0.0% Native Hawaiian/Other Pacific Islander, 0.0% Two or more races, 0.0% Hispanic of any race; Average household size: 2.39; Median age: 50.0; Age under 18: 16.8%; Age 65 and over: 25.5%; Males per 100 females: 103.7

Housing: Homeownership rate: 75.0%; Homeowner vacancy rate: 0.0%; Rental vacancy rate: 11.1%

MINNESOTT BEACH (town).
Covers a land area of 3.472 square miles and a water area of 0.074 square miles. Located at 34.99° N. Lat; 76.82° W. Long. Elevation is 7 feet.

Population: 440; Growth (since 2000): 41.5%; Density: 126.7 persons per square mile; Race: 94.3% White, 1.8% Black/African American, 1.1% Asian, 0.2% American Indian/Alaska Native, 0.0% Native Hawaiian/Other Pacific Islander, 1.4% Two or more races, 7.0% Hispanic of any race; Average household size: 2.09; Median age: 58.1; Age under 18: 11.8%; Age 65 and over: 30.7%; Males per 100 females: 88.0

Housing: Homeownership rate: 84.3%; Homeowner vacancy rate: 13.1%; Rental vacancy rate: 19.5%

ORIENTAL (town).
Covers a land area of 1.406 square miles and a water area of 0.231 square miles. Located at 35.03° N. Lat; 76.68° W. Long. Elevation is 10 feet.

Population: 900; Growth (since 2000): 2.9%; Density: 640.0 persons per square mile; Race: 92.4% White, 5.7% Black/African American, 0.3% Asian, 0.1% American Indian/Alaska Native, 0.0% Native Hawaiian/Other Pacific Islander, 1.2% Two or more races, 1.1% Hispanic of any race; Average household size: 1.89; Median age: 60.3; Age under 18: 8.9%; Age 65 and over: 38.0%; Males per 100 females: 98.2

Housing: Homeownership rate: 77.6%; Homeowner vacancy rate: 6.9%; Rental vacancy rate: 12.9%

Newspapers: Pamlico News (weekly circulation 3700)

STONEWALL (town).
Covers a land area of 1.707 square miles and a water area of 0.307 square miles. Located at 35.14° N. Lat; 76.74° W. Long. Elevation is 10 feet.

Population: 281; Growth (since 2000): -1.4%; Density: 164.7 persons per square mile; Race: 76.5% White, 20.3% Black/African American, 0.4% Asian, 0.0% American Indian/Alaska Native, 0.0% Native Hawaiian/Other Pacific Islander, 2.8% Two or more races, 1.8% Hispanic of any race; Average household size: 2.40; Median age: 41.6; Age under 18: 24.2%; Age 65 and over: 20.3%; Males per 100 females: 95.1

Housing: Homeownership rate: 76.9%; Homeowner vacancy rate: 3.2%; Rental vacancy rate: 10.0%

VANDEMERE (town).
Covers a land area of 1.522 square miles and a water area of 0.110 square miles. Located at 35.19° N. Lat; 76.66° W. Long. Elevation is 3 feet.

Population: 254; Growth (since 2000): -12.1%; Density: 166.9 persons per square mile; Race: 46.9% White, 45.7% Black/African American, 0.4% Asian, 0.4% American Indian/Alaska Native, 0.8% Native Hawaiian/Other Pacific Islander, 2.8% Two or more races, 4.7% Hispanic of any race;

Average household size: 2.35; Median age: 48.3; Age under 18: 21.7%; Age 65 and over: 24.8%; Males per 100 females: 78.9

Housing: Homeownership rate: 84.3%; Homeowner vacancy rate: 0.0%; Rental vacancy rate: 19.0%

Pasquotank County

Located in northeastern North Carolina; tidewater area, bounded on the south by Albemarle Sound, and on the east by the Pasquotank River. Covers a land area of 226.880 square miles, a water area of 62.557 square miles, and is located in the Eastern Time Zone at 36.27° N. Lat., 76.26° W. Long. The county was founded in 1672. County seat is Elizabeth City.

Pasquotank County is part of the Elizabeth City, NC Micropolitan Statistical Area. The entire metro area includes: Camden County, NC; Pasquotank County, NC; Perquimans County, NC

Weather Station: Elizabeth City										Elevation: 7 feet		
	Jan	Feb	Mar	Apr	May	Jun	Jul	Aug	Sep	Oct	Nov	Dec
High	53	55	63	72	79	86	89	88	83	74	65	56
Low	32	34	40	48	57	66	71	69	64	52	43	35
Precip	3.8	3.3	3.8	3.2	3.7	4.6	5.6	5.6	4.3	3.2	3.3	3.5
Snow	0.1	0.0	0.0	0.0	0.0	0.0	0.0	0.0	0.0	0.0	0.0	0.0

High and Low temperatures in degrees Fahrenheit; Precipitation and Snow in inches

Population: 40,661; Growth (since 2000): 16.5%; Density: 179.2 persons per square mile; Race: 56.7% White, 37.8% Black/African American, 1.1% Asian, 0.3% American Indian/Alaska Native, 0.0% Native Hawaiian/Other Pacific Islander, 2.2% two or more races, 4.0% Hispanic of any race; Average household size: 2.51; Median age: 36.6; Age under 18: 22.6%; Age 65 and over: 13.6%; Males per 100 females: 96.5; Marriage status: 33.8% never married, 49.3% now married, 4.1% separated, 6.2% widowed, 10.7% divorced; Foreign born: 2.9%; Speak English only: 94.7%; With disability: 15.1%; Veterans: 12.9%; Ancestry: 9.7% English, 8.7% American, 6.6% Irish, 6.3% German, 2.7% Italian

Religion: Six largest groups: 14.4% Baptist, 10.2% Methodist/Pietist, 7.7% Non-denominational Protestant, 3.8% Catholicism, 2.9% Pentecostal, 2.3% Latter-day Saints

Economy: Unemployment rate: 7.5%; Leading industries: 20.6% retail trade; 14.6% health care and social assistance; 11.4% other services (except public administration); Farms: 136 totaling 72,270 acres; Company size: 0 employ 1,000 or more persons, 1 employs 500 to 999 persons, 8 employ 100 to 499 persons, 924 employ less than 100 persons; Business ownership: 736 women-owned, 391 Black-owned, n/a Hispanic-owned, 143 Asian-owned

Employment: 10.1% management, business, and financial, 2.1% computer, engineering, and science, 12.5% education, legal, community service, arts, and media, 5.9% healthcare practitioners, 23.2% service, 22.9% sales and office, 11.5% natural resources, construction, and maintenance, 11.8% production, transportation, and material moving

Income: Per capita: $22,745; Median household: $46,053; Average household: $61,081; Households with income of $100,000 or more: 14.6%; Poverty rate: 18.4%

Educational Attainment: High school diploma or higher: 83.7%; Bachelor's degree or higher: 20.1%; Graduate/professional degree or higher: 7.1%

Housing: Homeownership rate: 65.2%; Median home value: $171,600; Median year structure built: 1981; Homeowner vacancy rate: 3.3%; Median gross rent: $885 per month; Rental vacancy rate: 10.3%

Vital Statistics: Birth rate: 121.1 per 10,000 population; Death rate: 94.8 per 10,000 population; Age-adjusted cancer mortality rate: 231.3 deaths per 100,000 population

Health Insurance: 82.4% have insurance; 63.3% have private insurance; 33.6% have public insurance; 17.6% do not have insurance; 7.9% of children under 18 do not have insurance

Health Care: Physicians: 19.3 per 10,000 population; Hospital beds: 34.7 per 10,000 population; Hospital admissions: 1,244.3 per 10,000 population

Transportation: Commute: 91.7% car, 0.4% public transportation, 2.9% walk, 2.0% work from home; Median travel time to work: 24.1 minutes

Presidential Election: 56.7% Obama, 42.2% Romney (2012)

Additional Information Contacts
Pasquotank Government . . . . (252) 335-0865
    http://www.co.pasquotank.nc.us

Pasquotank County Communities

ELIZABETH CITY (city). County seat. Covers a land area of 11.626 square miles and a water area of 0.624 square miles. Located at 36.29° N. Lat; 76.24° W. Long. Elevation is 3 feet.

History: Elizabeth City was first incorporated as Reading in 1793. It was changed to Elizabeth Town, either in honor of Elizabeth Tooley, an early plantation owner, or of Queen Elizabeth. In 1799 it replaced Nixonton (Old Town) as county seat and in 1801 was named Elizabeth City. In the early 1800's ocean-going vessels crowded the docks. Three shipyards were kept busy building, overhauling, and repairing sailing vessels.

Population: 18,683; Growth (since 2000): 8.7%; Density: 1,606.9 persons per square mile; Race: 39.5% White, 54.0% Black/African American, 1.2% Asian, 0.4% American Indian/Alaska Native, 0.1% Native Hawaiian/Other Pacific Islander, 2.3% Two or more races, 5.0% Hispanic of any race; Average household size: 2.38; Median age: 31.3; Age under 18: 22.4%; Age 65 and over: 13.9%; Males per 100 females: 84.5; Marriage status: 44.4% never married, 36.5% now married, 4.7% separated, 7.2% widowed, 12.0% divorced; Foreign born: 3.1%; Speak English only: 92.5%; With disability: 17.8%; Veterans: 11.3%; Ancestry: 6.2% English, 5.4% American, 5.1% German, 4.9% Irish, 2.7% Italian

Employment: 10.4% management, business, and financial, 1.9% computer, engineering, and science, 12.9% education, legal, community service, arts, and media, 5.8% healthcare practitioners, 28.3% service, 22.0% sales and office, 7.4% natural resources, construction, and maintenance, 11.2% production, transportation, and material moving

Income: Per capita: $17,958; Median household: $33,797; Average household: $47,154; Households with income of $100,000 or more: 9.8%; Poverty rate: 29.0%

Educational Attainment: High school diploma or higher: 79.7%; Bachelor's degree or higher: 20.8%; Graduate/professional degree or higher: 7.1%

School District(s)
Elizabeth City-pasquotank Public Schools (PK-12)
    2012-13 Enrollment: 5,997 . . . . (252) 335-2981
Four-year College(s)
Elizabeth City State University (Public, Historically black)
    Fall 2013 Enrollment: 2,421 . . . . (252) 335-3400
    2013-14 Tuition: In-state $4,429; Out-of-state $15,286
Mid-Atlantic Christian University (Private, Not-for-profit, Christian Churches and Churches of Christ)
    Fall 2013 Enrollment: 162 . . . . (252) 334-2000
    2013-14 Tuition: In-state $12,160; Out-of-state $12,160
Two-year College(s)
College of the Albemarle (Public)
    Fall 2013 Enrollment: 2,607 . . . . (252) 335-0821
    2013-14 Tuition: In-state $2,037; Out-of-state $7,489

Housing: Homeownership rate: 46.5%; Median home value: $149,400; Median year structure built: 1967; Homeowner vacancy rate: 5.2%; Median gross rent: $844 per month; Rental vacancy rate: 11.0%

Health Insurance: 76.0% have insurance; 50.8% have private insurance; 37.7% have public insurance; 24.0% do not have insurance; 11.4% of children under 18 do not have insurance

Hospitals: Albemarle Hospital Authority (182 beds)

Safety: Violent crime rate: 59.3 per 10,000 population; Property crime rate: 393.0 per 10,000 population

Newspapers: Daily Advance (daily circulation 10400)

Transportation: Commute: 85.5% car, 0.9% public transportation, 5.9% walk, 2.7% work from home; Median travel time to work: 19.8 minutes

Airports: Elizabeth City CG Air Station/Regional (general aviation)

Additional Information Contacts
City of Elizabeth City . . . . (252) 335-4365
    http://www.elizabethcitychamber.org

Pender County

Located in southeastern North Carolina; tidewater area, bounded on the southeast by Onslow Bay of the Atlantic Ocean; drained by the Northeast Cape Fear River. Covers a land area of 869.795 square miles, a water area of 62.991 square miles, and is located in the Eastern Time Zone at 34.51° N. Lat., 77.89° W. Long. The county was founded in 1875. County seat is Burgaw.

Pender County is part of the Wilmington, NC Metropolitan Statistical Area. The entire metro area includes: New Hanover County, NC; Pender County, NC

Weather Station: Willard 4 SW   Elevation: 55 feet

	Jan	Feb	Mar	Apr	May	Jun	Jul	Aug	Sep	Oct	Nov	Dec
High	57	61	68	76	83	88	91	89	84	75	68	59
Low	34	36	42	49	58	66	70	69	63	52	44	36
Precip	3.8	3.4	4.3	3.4	4.1	5.0	6.7	6.5	5.8	3.3	2.9	3.4
Snow	0.4	0.5	0.6	tr	0.0	0.0	0.0	0.0	0.0	0.0	0.0	0.7

High and Low temperatures in degrees Fahrenheit; Precipitation and Snow in inches

Population: 52,217; Growth (since 2000): 27.1%; Density: 60.0 persons per square mile; Race: 76.1% White, 17.8% Black/African American, 0.4% Asian, 0.6% American Indian/Alaska Native, 0.0% Native Hawaiian/Other Pacific Islander, 1.8% two or more races, 6.1% Hispanic of any race; Average household size: 2.51; Median age: 41.1; Age under 18: 22.8%; Age 65 and over: 15.1%; Males per 100 females: 100.2; Marriage status: 25.3% never married, 56.5% now married, 2.7% separated, 7.1% widowed, 11.2% divorced; Foreign born: 3.9%; Speak English only: 94.3%; With disability: 16.8%; Veterans: 11.9%; Ancestry: 12.5% German, 12.0% Irish, 11.1% American, 9.9% English, 5.0% Italian

Religion: Six largest groups: 15.2% Baptist, 10.1% Methodist/Pietist, 3.8% Catholicism, 2.8% Non-denominational Protestant, 2.2% Presbyterian-Reformed, 1.4% Latter-day Saints

Economy: Unemployment rate: 5.8%; Leading industries: 15.7% retail trade; 15.4% construction; 11.1% other services (except public administration); Farms: 335 totaling 55,775 acres; Company size: 0 employ 1,000 or more persons, 0 employ 500 to 999 persons, 10 employ 100 to 499 persons, 920 employ less than 100 persons; Business ownership: 1,581 women-owned, 511 Black-owned, n/a Hispanic-owned, n/a Asian-owned

Employment: 10.4% management, business, and financial, 4.4% computer, engineering, and science, 8.5% education, legal, community service, arts, and media, 6.3% healthcare practitioners, 18.3% service, 23.5% sales and office, 15.6% natural resources, construction, and maintenance, 12.9% production, transportation, and material moving

Income: Per capita: $23,526; Median household: $44,524; Average household: $60,435; Households with income of $100,000 or more: 15.6%; Poverty rate: 19.3%

Educational Attainment: High school diploma or higher: 86.7%; Bachelor's degree or higher: 21.7%; Graduate/professional degree or higher: 6.7%

Housing: Homeownership rate: 77.3%; Median home value: $155,600; Median year structure built: 1991; Homeowner vacancy rate: 3.0%; Median gross rent: $757 per month; Rental vacancy rate: 16.1%

Vital Statistics: Birth rate: 109.5 per 10,000 population; Death rate: 87.3 per 10,000 population; Age-adjusted cancer mortality rate: 175.3 deaths per 100,000 population

Health Insurance: 81.8% have insurance; 60.9% have private insurance; 35.2% have public insurance; 18.2% do not have insurance; 9.0% of children under 18 do not have insurance

Health Care: Physicians: 5.0 per 10,000 population; Hospital beds: 12.7 per 10,000 population; Hospital admissions: 166.6 per 10,000 population

Transportation: Commute: 94.2% car, 0.2% public transportation, 0.9% walk, 3.5% work from home; Median travel time to work: 29.2 minutes

Presidential Election: 39.2% Obama, 59.6% Romney (2012)

National and State Parks: Moores Creek National Battlefield

Additional Information Contacts
Pender Government . . . . (910) 259-1200
    http://www.pendercountync.gov

Pender County Communities

ATKINSON (town). Covers a land area of 0.990 square miles and a water area of 0 square miles. Located at 34.53° N. Lat; 78.17° W. Long. Elevation is 62 feet.

History: Moore's Creek National Battlefield to Southeast.

Population: 299; Growth (since 2000): 26.7%; Density: 302.1 persons per square mile; Race: 84.6% White, 7.7% Black/African American, 0.0% Asian, 0.0% American Indian/Alaska Native, 0.0% Native Hawaiian/Other Pacific Islander, 0.7% Two or more races, 9.4% Hispanic of any race; Average household size: 2.51; Median age: 41.9; Age under 18: 26.8%; Age 65 and over: 19.4%; Males per 100 females: 92.9

Housing: Homeownership rate: 89.1%; Homeowner vacancy rate: 1.8%; Rental vacancy rate: 21.1%

BURGAW (town). County seat. Covers a land area of 5.460 square miles and a water area of 0.011 square miles. Located at 34.55° N. Lat; 77.92° W. Long. Elevation is 49 feet.

History: Moores Creek National Battlefield to Southwest.

Population: 3,872; Growth (since 2000): 16.0%; Density: 709.1 persons per square mile; Race: 53.8% White, 39.6% Black/African American, 0.4% Asian, 0.8% American Indian/Alaska Native, 0.1% Native Hawaiian/Other Pacific Islander, 1.7% Two or more races, 7.2% Hispanic of any race; Average household size: 2.28; Median age: 39.5; Age under 18: 18.9%; Age 65 and over: 16.0%; Males per 100 females: 127.0; Marriage status: 31.9% never married, 43.1% now married, 5.9% separated, 10.1% widowed, 14.9% divorced; Foreign born: 7.1%; Speak English only: 93.9%; With disability: 24.6%; Veterans: 10.4%; Ancestry: 12.9% English, 7.6% German, 7.5% Irish, 7.2% American, 4.7% Scottish

Employment: 7.8% management, business, and financial, 0.0% computer, engineering, and science, 11.0% education, legal, community service, arts, and media, 4.2% healthcare practitioners, 9.2% service, 33.1% sales and office, 18.0% natural resources, construction, and maintenance, 16.6% production, transportation, and material moving

Income: Per capita: $15,471; Median household: $31,875; Average household: $45,613; Households with income of $100,000 or more: 7.6%; Poverty rate: 33.1%

Educational Attainment: High school diploma or higher: 78.1%; Bachelor's degree or higher: 20.2%; Graduate/professional degree or higher: 5.6%

School District(s)

Pender County Schools (PK-12)

    2012-13 Enrollment: 8,760 . . . . (910) 259-2187

Housing: Homeownership rate: 49.0%; Median home value: $159,900; Median year structure built: 1977; Homeowner vacancy rate: 5.5%; Median gross rent: $641 per month; Rental vacancy rate: 9.3%

Health Insurance: 81.0% have insurance; 43.2% have private insurance; 58.4% have public insurance; 19.0% do not have insurance; 5.0% of children under 18 do not have insurance

Hospitals: Pender Memorial Hospital (68 beds)

Safety: Violent crime rate: 22.5 per 10,000 population; Property crime rate: 289.6 per 10,000 population

Newspapers: Post & Voice (weekly circulation 5000)

Transportation: Commute: 93.0% car, 0.0% public transportation, 3.2% walk, 3.8% work from home; Median travel time to work: 26.4 minutes

Additional Information Contacts

Town of Burgaw . . . . (910) 259-2151

    http://www.townofburgaw.com

CURRIE (unincorporated postal area)

ZCTA: 28435

Covers a land area of 95.617 square miles and a water area of 2.480 square miles. Located at 34.41° N. Lat; 78.11° W. Long. Elevation is 30 feet.

Population: 2,490; Growth (since 2000): 4.7%; Density: 26.0 persons per square mile; Race: 59.4% White, 34.7% Black/African American, 0.1% Asian, 0.9% American Indian/Alaska Native, 0.0% Native Hawaiian/Other Pacific Islander, 2.4% Two or more races, 4.7% Hispanic of any race; Average household size: 2.45; Median age: 44.0; Age under 18: 22.0%; Age 65 and over: 14.7%; Males per 100 females: 100.2

Housing: Homeownership rate: 81.5%; Homeowner vacancy rate: 2.2%; Rental vacancy rate: 23.2%

HAMPSTEAD (CDP). Covers a land area of 20.257 square miles and a water area of 0.138 square miles. Located at 34.36° N. Lat; 77.76° W. Long. Elevation is 36 feet.

Population: 4,083; Growth (since 2000): n/a; Density: 201.6 persons per square mile; Race: 91.9% White, 4.9% Black/African American, 0.5% Asian, 0.2% American Indian/Alaska Native, 0.0% Native Hawaiian/Other Pacific Islander, 1.3% Two or more races, 3.3% Hispanic of any race; Average household size: 2.54; Median age: 42.6; Age under 18: 23.1%; Age 65 and over: 17.3%; Males per 100 females: 98.3; Marriage status: 16.3% never married, 70.4% now married, 0.8% separated, 4.9% widowed, 8.4% divorced; Foreign born: 1.1%; Speak English only: 99.0%; With disability: 9.2%; Veterans: 10.6%; Ancestry: 16.3% German, 16.0% American, 15.3% Irish, 10.2% English, 9.7% Italian

Employment: 11.8% management, business, and financial, 4.7% computer, engineering, and science, 14.4% education, legal, community service, arts, and media, 9.6% healthcare practitioners, 11.8% service,

21.0% sales and office, 21.0% natural resources, construction, and maintenance, 5.6% production, transportation, and material moving

Income: Per capita: $27,137; Median household: $58,077; Average household: $72,141; Households with income of $100,000 or more: 18.7%; Poverty rate: 12.4%

Educational Attainment: High school diploma or higher: 99.5%; Bachelor's degree or higher: 31.1%; Graduate/professional degree or higher: 6.7%

School District(s)

Pender County Schools (PK-12)

    2012-13 Enrollment: 8,760 . . . . (910) 259-2187

Housing: Homeownership rate: 83.4%; Median home value: $217,700; Median year structure built: 1996; Homeowner vacancy rate: 2.8%; Median gross rent: $1,219 per month; Rental vacancy rate: 12.4%

Health Insurance: 92.1% have insurance; 83.2% have private insurance; 22.2% have public insurance; 7.9% do not have insurance; 0.0% of children under 18 do not have insurance

Transportation: Commute: 98.7% car, 0.0% public transportation, 1.3% walk, 0.0% work from home; Median travel time to work: 25.2 minutes

MAPLE HILL (unincorporated postal area)

ZCTA: 28454

Covers a land area of 65.439 square miles and a water area of 0 square miles. Located at 34.68° N. Lat; 77.65° W. Long. Elevation is 33 feet.

Population: 2,545; Growth (since 2000): 0.0%; Density: 38.9 persons per square mile; Race: 55.6% White, 39.1% Black/African American, 0.1% Asian, 0.6% American Indian/Alaska Native, 0.0% Native Hawaiian/Other Pacific Islander, 3.0% Two or more races, 4.8% Hispanic of any race; Average household size: 2.58; Median age: 37.8; Age under 18: 24.8%; Age 65 and over: 13.4%; Males per 100 females: 99.9; Marriage status: 29.6% never married, 45.5% now married, 6.1% separated, 9.3% widowed, 15.6% divorced; Foreign born: 0.3%; Speak English only: 99.8%; With disability: 27.5%; Veterans: 9.6%; Ancestry: 17.1% American, 9.3% German, 8.0% Irish, 2.7% English, 1.8% Scotch-Irish

Employment: 13.2% management, business, and financial, 0.0% computer, engineering, and science, 0.0% education, legal, community service, arts, and media, 5.9% healthcare practitioners, 30.4% service, 19.8% sales and office, 19.0% natural resources, construction, and maintenance, 11.7% production, transportation, and material moving

Income: Per capita: $13,553; Median household: $20,711; Average household: $30,550; Households with income of $100,000 or more: 4.3%; Poverty rate: 27.9%

Educational Attainment: High school diploma or higher: 74.5%; Bachelor's degree or higher: 5.1%; Graduate/professional degree or higher: 1.5%

Housing: Homeownership rate: 82.3%; Median home value: $87,200; Median year structure built: 1982; Homeowner vacancy rate: 1.8%; Median gross rent: $700 per month; Rental vacancy rate: 7.9%

Health Insurance: 75.7% have insurance; 55.9% have private insurance; 36.1% have public insurance; 24.3% do not have insurance; 23.4% of children under 18 do not have insurance

Transportation: Commute: 93.7% car, 0.0% public transportation, 0.0% walk, 6.3% work from home; Median travel time to work: 39.6 minutes

ROCKY POINT (CDP). Covers a land area of 6.924 square miles and a water area of 0 square miles. Located at 34.44° N. Lat; 77.89° W. Long. Elevation is 36 feet.

Population: 1,602; Growth (since 2000): n/a; Density: 231.4 persons per square mile; Race: 61.7% White, 11.6% Black/African American, 0.5% Asian, 0.8% American Indian/Alaska Native, 0.1% Native Hawaiian/Other Pacific Islander, 3.1% Two or more races, 31.8% Hispanic of any race; Average household size: 2.97; Median age: 32.4; Age under 18: 27.8%; Age 65 and over: 9.8%; Males per 100 females: 99.8

School District(s)

Pender County Schools (PK-12)

    2012-13 Enrollment: 8,760 . . . . (910) 259-2187

Housing: Homeownership rate: 65.5%; Homeowner vacancy rate: 1.7%; Rental vacancy rate: 9.7%

SAINT HELENA (village). Covers a land area of 5.638 square miles and a water area of 0 square miles. Located at 34.52° N. Lat; 77.92° W. Long. Elevation is 52 feet.

History: St. Helena was the first of several agricultural colonies developed for immigrants by Hugh MacRae, Wilmington real estate operator. Land

acquired by the development company was cut into small farms and sold to colonists. The first group at St. Helena was composed of seven families from northern Italy, experienced grape growers.

Population: 389; Growth (since 2000): -1.5%; Density: 69.0 persons per square mile; Race: 74.8% White, 21.3% Black/African American, 0.0% Asian, 0.8% American Indian/Alaska Native, 0.0% Native Hawaiian/Other Pacific Islander, 0.3% Two or more races, 4.1% Hispanic of any race; Average household size: 2.48; Median age: 41.2; Age under 18: 24.9%; Age 65 and over: 12.9%; Males per 100 females: 88.8
Housing: Homeownership rate: 88.6%; Homeowner vacancy rate: 0.0%; Rental vacancy rate: 13.6%

SURF CITY (town). Covers a land area of 7.263 square miles and a water area of 2.273 square miles. Located at 34.43° N. Lat; 77.57° W. Long. Elevation is 3 feet.
Population: 1,853; Growth (since 2000): 33.0%; Density: 255.1 persons per square mile; Race: 95.8% White, 0.9% Black/African American, 1.2% Asian, 0.2% American Indian/Alaska Native, 0.2% Native Hawaiian/Other Pacific Islander, 1.0% Two or more races, 3.1% Hispanic of any race; Average household size: 2.18; Median age: 43.1; Age under 18: 13.2%; Age 65 and over: 16.9%; Males per 100 females: 110.1
Housing: Homeownership rate: 58.1%; Homeowner vacancy rate: 14.3%; Rental vacancy rate: 33.5%
Safety: Violent crime rate: 59.9 per 10,000 population; Property crime rate: 743.1 per 10,000 population
Additional Information Contacts
Town of Surf City . . . . (910) 328-4131
  http://surfcity.govoffice.com

TOPSAIL BEACH (town). Covers a land area of 4.394 square miles and a water area of 1.485 square miles. Located at 34.37° N. Lat; 77.65° W. Long. Elevation is 7 feet.
Population: 368; Growth (since 2000): -21.9%; Density: 83.7 persons per square mile; Race: 96.5% White, 1.6% Black/African American, 0.3% Asian, 0.5% American Indian/Alaska Native, 0.0% Native Hawaiian/Other Pacific Islander, 0.8% Two or more races, 0.5% Hispanic of any race; Average household size: 1.97; Median age: 57.4; Age under 18: 8.7%; Age 65 and over: 27.4%; Males per 100 females: 100.0
Housing: Homeownership rate: 74.4%; Homeowner vacancy rate: 7.9%; Rental vacancy rate: 77.9%
Additional Information Contacts
Town of Topsail Beach . . . . (910) 328-5841
  http://topsailbeach.org

WATHA (town). Covers a land area of 1.274 square miles and a water area of 0 square miles. Located at 34.65° N. Lat; 77.96° W. Long. Elevation is 59 feet.
Population: 190; Growth (since 2000): 25.8%; Density: 149.2 persons per square mile; Race: 84.7% White, 7.9% Black/African American, 0.0% Asian, 0.5% American Indian/Alaska Native, 0.0% Native Hawaiian/Other Pacific Islander, 1.6% Two or more races, 7.4% Hispanic of any race; Average household size: 2.50; Median age: 43.3; Age under 18: 24.2%; Age 65 and over: 14.7%; Males per 100 females: 77.6
Housing: Homeownership rate: 85.5%; Homeowner vacancy rate: 0.0%; Rental vacancy rate: 8.3%

WILLARD (unincorporated postal area)
ZCTA: 28478
  Covers a land area of 121.088 square miles and a water area of 0.168 square miles. Located at 34.64° N. Lat; 78.04° W. Long. Elevation is 46 feet.
  Population: 4,588; Growth (since 2000): 103.3%; Density: 37.9 persons per square mile; Race: 64.3% White, 29.8% Black/African American, 0.2% Asian, 0.3% American Indian/Alaska Native, 0.1% Native Hawaiian/Other Pacific Islander, 1.9% Two or more races, 6.5% Hispanic of any race; Average household size: 2.46; Median age: 42.7; Age under 18: 22.5%; Age 65 and over: 16.5%; Males per 100 females: 96.0; Marriage status: 29.9% never married, 46.1% now married, 4.0% separated, 10.8% widowed, 13.3% divorced; Foreign born: 1.4%; Speak English only: 96.9%; With disability: 24.3%; Veterans: 10.1%; Ancestry: 9.3% American, 8.2% Scotch-Irish, 8.2% Irish, 7.0% German, 4.9% English
  Employment: 9.5% management, business, and financial, 0.7% computer, engineering, and science, 6.3% education, legal, community service, arts, and media, 6.6% healthcare practitioners, 18.7% service,

30.6% sales and office, 9.9% natural resources, construction, and maintenance, 17.7% production, transportation, and material moving
  Income: Per capita: $21,332; Median household: $32,293; Average household: $46,758; Households with income of $100,000 or more: 9.4%; Poverty rate: 21.3%
  Educational Attainment: High school diploma or higher: 79.9%; Bachelor's degree or higher: 11.9%; Graduate/professional degree or higher: 2.7%
  School District(s)
  Pender County Schools (PK-12)
    2012-13 Enrollment: 8,760 . . . . (910) 259-2187
  Housing: Homeownership rate: 79.6%; Median home value: $102,300; Median year structure built: 1977; Homeowner vacancy rate: 1.4%; Median gross rent: $634 per month; Rental vacancy rate: 12.0%
  Health Insurance: 83.1% have insurance; 59.4% have private insurance; 39.8% have public insurance; 16.9% do not have insurance; 11.5% of children under 18 do not have insurance
  Transportation: Commute: 96.0% car, 0.0% public transportation, 2.3% walk, 1.7% work from home; Median travel time to work: 29.1 minutes

Perquimans County

Located in northeastern North Carolina; bounded on the south by Albemarle Sound; drained by the Perquimans River; includes Dismal Swamp in the northeast. Covers a land area of 247.089 square miles, a water area of 81.877 square miles, and is located in the Eastern Time Zone at 36.18° N. Lat., 76.40° W. Long. The county was founded in 1672. County seat is Hertford.

Perquimans County is part of the Elizabeth City, NC Micropolitan Statistical Area. The entire metro area includes: Camden County, NC; Pasquotank County, NC; Perquimans County, NC

Population: 13,453; Growth (since 2000): 18.3%; Density: 54.4 persons per square mile; Race: 72.1% White, 24.9% Black/African American, 0.3% Asian, 0.3% American Indian/Alaska Native, 0.0% Native Hawaiian/Other Pacific Islander, 1.3% two or more races, 2.1% Hispanic of any race; Average household size: 2.39; Median age: 46.4; Age under 18: 20.6%; Age 65 and over: 21.5%; Males per 100 females: 92.0; Marriage status: 21.3% never married, 60.6% now married, 2.4% separated, 7.5% widowed, 10.5% divorced; Foreign born: 2.1%; Speak English only: 96.7%; With disability: 19.6%; Veterans: 14.9%; Ancestry: 14.2% American, 13.6% English, 7.7% Irish, 7.1% German, 3.3% Italian
Religion: Six largest groups: 17.9% Methodist/Pietist, 14.3% Baptist, 4.5% Non-denominational Protestant, 1.9% Pentecostal, 1.5% European Free-Church, 1.3% Holiness
Economy: Unemployment rate: 7.4%; Leading industries: 15.9% retail trade; 14.4% construction; 12.4% other services (except public administration); Farms: 185 totaling 80,116 acres; Company size: 0 employ 1,000 or more persons, 0 employ 500 to 999 persons, 0 employ 100 to 499 persons, 201 employs less than 100 persons; Business ownership: 208 women-owned, n/a Black-owned, n/a Hispanic-owned, n/a Asian-owned
Employment: 17.2% management, business, and financial, 2.3% computer, engineering, and science, 8.9% education, legal, community service, arts, and media, 8.4% healthcare practitioners, 17.8% service, 20.2% sales and office, 12.9% natural resources, construction, and maintenance, 12.2% production, transportation, and material moving
Income: Per capita: $23,809; Median household: $43,709; Average household: $58,255; Households with income of $100,000 or more: 14.2%; Poverty rate: 20.2%
Educational Attainment: High school diploma or higher: 83.7%; Bachelor's degree or higher: 18.4%; Graduate/professional degree or higher: 5.2%
Housing: Homeownership rate: 75.7%; Median home value: $170,700; Median year structure built: 1980; Homeowner vacancy rate: 2.6%; Median gross rent: $738 per month; Rental vacancy rate: 11.7%
Vital Statistics: Birth rate: 93.4 per 10,000 population; Death rate: 94.1 per 10,000 population; Age-adjusted cancer mortality rate: 152.2 deaths per 100,000 population
Health Insurance: 83.7% have insurance; 61.8% have private insurance; 42.5% have public insurance; 16.3% do not have insurance; 8.6% of children under 18 do not have insurance
Health Care: Physicians: 3.7 per 10,000 population; Hospital beds: 0.0 per 10,000 population; Hospital admissions: 0.0 per 10,000 population

Transportation: Commute: 92.0% car, 0.9% public transportation, 1.2% walk, 4.1% work from home; Median travel time to work: 29.5 minutes
Presidential Election: 41.5% Obama, 57.5% Romney (2012)
Additional Information Contacts
Perquimans Government . . . . (252) 426-8484
   http://www.perquimanscountync.gov

Perquimans County Communities

BELVIDERE (unincorporated postal area)
ZCTA: 27919
   Covers a land area of 58.224 square miles and a water area of 0.003 square miles. Located at 36.31° N. Lat; 76.50° W. Long. Elevation is 13 feet.
   Population: 1,130; Growth (since 2000): 28.4%; Density: 19.4 persons per square mile; Race: 75.2% White, 23.1% Black/African American, 0.1% Asian, 0.0% American Indian/Alaska Native, 0.1% Native Hawaiian/Other Pacific Islander, 1.2% Two or more races, 1.2% Hispanic of any race; Average household size: 2.35; Median age: 45.4; Age under 18: 20.2%; Age 65 and over: 17.9%; Males per 100 females: 96.5
   Housing: Homeownership rate: 81.7%; Homeowner vacancy rate: 0.5%; Rental vacancy rate: 12.9%

HERTFORD (town). County seat. Covers a land area of 2.856 square miles and a water area of 0.022 square miles. Located at 36.18° N. Lat; 76.47° W. Long. Elevation is 10 feet.
History: Hertford was first called Phelps Point for the owner of the site, and was a port of entry as early as 1701. When incorporated in 1758 it was renamed for the Marquis of Hertford.
Population: 2,143; Growth (since 2000): 3.5%; Density: 750.4 persons per square mile; Race: 46.5% White, 48.1% Black/African American, 0.4% Asian, 0.1% American Indian/Alaska Native, 0.0% Native Hawaiian/Other Pacific Islander, 1.4% Two or more races, 4.8% Hispanic of any race; Average household size: 2.38; Median age: 38.6; Age under 18: 25.2%; Age 65 and over: 18.5%; Males per 100 females: 79.0
                     School District(s)
Perquimans County Schools (PK-12)
   2012-13 Enrollment: 1,848 . . . . (252) 426-5741
Housing: Homeownership rate: 49.4%; Homeowner vacancy rate: 4.6%; Rental vacancy rate: 7.1%
Safety: Violent crime rate: 82.8 per 10,000 population; Property crime rate: 367.8 per 10,000 population
Newspapers: Perquimans Weekly (weekly circulation 2200)

WINFALL (town). Covers a land area of 2.283 square miles and a water area of 0.009 square miles. Located at 36.21° N. Lat; 76.46° W. Long. Elevation is 13 feet.
Population: 594; Growth (since 2000): 7.2%; Density: 260.2 persons per square mile; Race: 57.2% White, 40.1% Black/African American, 0.8% Asian, 0.3% American Indian/Alaska Native, 0.0% Native Hawaiian/Other Pacific Islander, 1.0% Two or more races, 2.0% Hispanic of any race; Average household size: 2.37; Median age: 44.0; Age under 18: 22.9%; Age 65 and over: 21.7%; Males per 100 females: 87.4
                     School District(s)
Perquimans County Schools (PK-12)
   2012-13 Enrollment: 1,848 . . . . (252) 426-5741
Housing: Homeownership rate: 70.4%; Homeowner vacancy rate: 3.9%; Rental vacancy rate: 15.1%

Person County

Located in northern North Carolina; piedmont area, bounded on the north by Virginia. Covers a land area of 392.322 square miles, a water area of 11.757 square miles, and is located in the Eastern Time Zone at 36.39° N. Lat., 78.97° W. Long. The county was founded in 1791. County seat is Roxboro.

Person County is part of the Durham-Chapel Hill, NC Metropolitan Statistical Area. The entire metro area includes: Chatham County, NC; Durham County, NC; Orange County, NC; Person County, NC

Weather Station: Roxboro 7 ESE									Elevation: 709 feet		
	Jan	Feb	Mar	Apr	May	Jun	Jul	Aug	Sep	Oct	Nov	Dec
High	48	53	60	70	77	85	88	87	81	71	62	52
Low	26	28	34	43	52	61	65	64	56	44	35	28
Precip	3.6	3.1	4.5	3.4	3.3	3.8	4.7	4.0	3.7	3.9	3.6	3.6
Snow	2.3	2.6	1.1	tr	0.0	0.0	0.0	0.0	0.0	tr	0.1	0.8

High and Low temperatures in degrees Fahrenheit; Precipitation and Snow in inches

Population: 39,464; Growth (since 2000): 10.8%; Density: 100.6 persons per square mile; Race: 68.3% White, 27.0% Black/African American, 0.3% Asian, 0.7% American Indian/Alaska Native, 0.0% Native Hawaiian/Other Pacific Islander, 1.5% two or more races, 4.0% Hispanic of any race; Average household size: 2.47; Median age: 41.4; Age under 18: 23.1%; Age 65 and over: 15.2%; Males per 100 females: 94.1; Marriage status: 29.5% never married, 50.0% now married, 2.8% separated, 7.8% widowed, 12.8% divorced; Foreign born: 2.6%; Speak English only: 95.6%; With disability: 17.5%; Veterans: 9.3%; Ancestry: 13.8% American, 12.4% English, 9.1% Irish, 6.3% German, 2.9% Scotch-Irish
Religion: Six largest groups: 22.6% Baptist, 10.7% Methodist/Pietist, 2.2% Non-denominational Protestant, 1.9% Pentecostal, 1.6% Catholicism, 0.7% Latter-day Saints
Economy: Unemployment rate: 5.1%; Leading industries: 18.9% retail trade; 13.8% other services (except public administration); 12.5% construction; Farms: 395 totaling 95,299 acres; Company size: 0 employ 1,000 or more persons, 0 employ 500 to 999 persons, 12 employ 100 to 499 persons, 653 employ less than 100 persons; Business ownership: n/a women-owned, n/a Black-owned, 41 Hispanic-owned, n/a Asian-owned
Employment: 10.6% management, business, and financial, 3.4% computer, engineering, and science, 9.2% education, legal, community service, arts, and media, 5.4% healthcare practitioners, 17.2% service, 24.5% sales and office, 13.7% natural resources, construction, and maintenance, 16.1% production, transportation, and material moving
Income: Per capita: $21,292; Median household: $42,317; Average household: $52,555; Households with income of $100,000 or more: 12.3%; Poverty rate: 18.0%
Educational Attainment: High school diploma or higher: 83.0%; Bachelor's degree or higher: 14.7%; Graduate/professional degree or higher: 3.5%
Housing: Homeownership rate: 72.1%; Median home value: $118,800; Median year structure built: 1983; Homeowner vacancy rate: 2.3%; Median gross rent: $622 per month; Rental vacancy rate: 10.0%
Vital Statistics: Birth rate: 98.8 per 10,000 population; Death rate: 105.4 per 10,000 population; Age-adjusted cancer mortality rate: 163.1 deaths per 100,000 population
Health Insurance: 84.5% have insurance; 61.6% have private insurance; 35.2% have public insurance; 15.5% do not have insurance; 6.8% of children under 18 do not have insurance
Health Care: Physicians: 6.9 per 10,000 population; Hospital beds: 27.8 per 10,000 population; Hospital admissions: 510.6 per 10,000 population
Air Quality Index: 99.1% good, 0.9% moderate, 0.0% unhealthy for sensitive individuals, 0.0% unhealthy (percent of days)
Transportation: Commute: 93.5% car, 0.0% public transportation, 0.9% walk, 3.4% work from home; Median travel time to work: 30.1 minutes
Presidential Election: 44.1% Obama, 54.9% Romney (2012)
Additional Information Contacts
Person Government . . . . (336) 597-1741
   http://www.personcounty.net

Person County Communities

HURDLE MILLS (unincorporated postal area)
ZCTA: 27541
   Covers a land area of 69.450 square miles and a water area of 0.254 square miles. Located at 36.26° N. Lat; 79.08° W. Long. Elevation is 610 feet.
   Population: 3,770; Growth (since 2000): 12.7%; Density: 54.3 persons per square mile; Race: 81.4% White, 13.8% Black/African American, 0.3% Asian, 0.2% American Indian/Alaska Native, 0.0% Native Hawaiian/Other Pacific Islander, 1.7% Two or more races, 4.6% Hispanic of any race; Average household size: 2.51; Median age: 43.9; Age under 18: 22.3%; Age 65 and over: 14.6%; Males per 100 females: 100.5; Marriage status: 18.5% never married, 64.7% now married, 1.3% separated, 4.2% widowed, 12.6% divorced; Foreign born: 1.3%; Speak English only: 99.2%; With disability: 11.8%; Veterans: 11.5%; Ancestry:

17.0% American, 12.1% English, 9.8% German, 7.2% Irish, 3.6% Scotch-Irish
Employment: 17.5% management, business, and financial, 2.6% computer, engineering, and science, 8.8% education, legal, community service, arts, and media, 9.6% healthcare practitioners, 12.4% service, 26.6% sales and office, 13.8% natural resources, construction, and maintenance, 8.7% production, transportation, and material moving
Income: Per capita: $27,996; Median household: $56,346; Average household: $67,453; Households with income of $100,000 or more: 14.8%; Poverty rate: 5.8%
Educational Attainment: High school diploma or higher: 88.4%; Bachelor's degree or higher: 20.6%; Graduate/professional degree or higher: 5.4%

School District(s)
Person County Schools (PK-12)
    2012-13 Enrollment: 4,943 . . . . (336) 599-2191
Housing: Homeownership rate: 81.0%; Median home value: $148,000; Median year structure built: 1985; Homeowner vacancy rate: 1.4%; Median gross rent: $902 per month; Rental vacancy rate: 6.9%
Health Insurance: 85.2% have insurance; 71.7% have private insurance; 26.9% have public insurance; 14.8% do not have insurance; 15.6% of children under 18 do not have insurance
Transportation: Commute: 95.2% car, 0.0% public transportation, 0.1% walk, 4.7% work from home; Median travel time to work: 30.0 minutes

ROXBORO (city). County seat. Covers a land area of 6.451 square miles and a water area of 0.007 square miles. Located at 36.39° N. Lat; 78.98° W. Long. Elevation is 715 feet.
History: Roxboro was named for Roxburgh in Scotland. The town was founded when the temporary seat of Person County was moved here and a courthouse was erected.
Population: 8,362; Growth (since 2000): -3.8%; Density: 1,296.3 persons per square mile; Race: 44.9% White, 46.8% Black/African American, 0.4% Asian, 0.6% American Indian/Alaska Native, 0.0% Native Hawaiian/Other Pacific Islander, 2.1% Two or more races, 8.7% Hispanic of any race; Average household size: 2.29; Median age: 40.2; Age under 18: 22.9%; Age 65 and over: 18.6%; Males per 100 females: 82.9; Marriage status: 45.3% never married, 31.1% now married, 3.8% separated, 12.5% widowed, 11.0% divorced; Foreign born: 5.7%; Speak English only: 92.0%; With disability: 20.7%; Veterans: 7.2%; Ancestry: 9.8% American, 7.7% English, 6.3% Irish, 2.3% Scotch-Irish, 2.2% German
Employment: 5.9% management, business, and financial, 2.1% computer, engineering, and science, 4.6% education, legal, community service, arts, and media, 4.7% healthcare practitioners, 21.5% service, 20.3% sales and office, 17.4% natural resources, construction, and maintenance, 23.6% production, transportation, and material moving
Income: Per capita: $12,779; Median household: $20,736; Average household: $29,564; Households with income of $100,000 or more: 2.7%; Poverty rate: 42.8%
Educational Attainment: High school diploma or higher: 70.5%; Bachelor's degree or higher: 10.1%; Graduate/professional degree or higher: 1.5%

School District(s)
Bethel Hill Charter (KG-06)
    2012-13 Enrollment: 377. . . . . (336) 599-2823
Person County Schools (PK-12)
    2012-13 Enrollment: 4,943 . . . . (336) 599-2191
Roxboro Community (06-12)
    2012-13 Enrollment: 646. . . . . (336) 597-0020
Two-year College(s)
Piedmont Community College (Public)
    Fall 2013 Enrollment: 1,591 . . . . (336) 599-1181
    2013-14 Tuition: In-state $2,411; Out-of-state $8,555
Housing: Homeownership rate: 43.3%; Median home value: $88,800; Median year structure built: 1966; Homeowner vacancy rate: 4.3%; Median gross rent: $615 per month; Rental vacancy rate: 12.9%
Health Insurance: 74.6% have insurance; 41.0% have private insurance; 43.3% have public insurance; 25.4% do not have insurance; 9.8% of children under 18 do not have insurance
Hospitals: Person Memorial Hospital (110 beds)
Safety: Violent crime rate: 91.5 per 10,000 population; Property crime rate: 583.6 per 10,000 population
Newspapers: The Courier Times (weekly circulation 9100)
Transportation: Commute: 86.6% car, 0.0% public transportation, 2.3% walk, 3.4% work from home; Median travel time to work: 21.1 minutes

Airports: Person County (general aviation)
Additional Information Contacts
City of Roxboro . . . . (336) 599-3116
    http://www.roxboronc.org

SEMORA (unincorporated postal area)
ZCTA: 27343
    Covers a land area of 46.162 square miles and a water area of 5.294 square miles. Located at 36.50° N. Lat; 79.09° W. Long..
Population: 1,716; Growth (since 2000): 8.9%; Density: 37.2 persons per square mile; Race: 61.5% White, 36.0% Black/African American, 0.2% Asian, 0.3% American Indian/Alaska Native, 0.0% Native Hawaiian/Other Pacific Islander, 1.2% Two or more races, 2.2% Hispanic of any race; Average household size: 2.39; Median age: 47.2; Age under 18: 19.0%; Age 65 and over: 14.4%; Males per 100 females: 93.5
School District(s)
Person County Schools (PK-12)
    2012-13 Enrollment: 4,943 . . . . (336) 599-2191
Housing: Homeownership rate: 77.8%; Homeowner vacancy rate: 5.1%; Rental vacancy rate: 11.2%

TIMBERLAKE (unincorporated postal area)
ZCTA: 27583
    Covers a land area of 46.279 square miles and a water area of 0.139 square miles. Located at 36.29° N. Lat; 78.94° W. Long. Elevation is 591 feet.
Population: 6,921; Growth (since 2000): 48.1%; Density: 149.5 persons per square mile; Race: 82.9% White, 13.7% Black/African American, 0.3% Asian, 0.5% American Indian/Alaska Native, 0.0% Native Hawaiian/Other Pacific Islander, 1.5% Two or more races, 2.2% Hispanic of any race; Average household size: 2.58; Median age: 39.8; Age under 18: 24.8%; Age 65 and over: 11.0%; Males per 100 females: 101.7; Marriage status: 21.2% never married, 59.9% now married, 3.5% separated, 3.5% widowed, 15.5% divorced; Foreign born: 1.6%; Speak English only: 95.8%; With disability: 19.2%; Veterans: 11.2%; Ancestry: 18.3% Irish, 17.1% English, 15.7% American, 5.2% German, 3.1% Scotch-Irish
Employment: 10.2% management, business, and financial, 7.3% computer, engineering, and science, 9.3% education, legal, community service, arts, and media, 6.7% healthcare practitioners, 15.2% service, 28.0% sales and office, 12.1% natural resources, construction, and maintenance, 11.2% production, transportation, and material moving
Income: Per capita: $25,842; Median household: $53,231; Average household: $62,162; Households with income of $100,000 or more: 16.9%; Poverty rate: 8.1%
Educational Attainment: High school diploma or higher: 86.9%; Bachelor's degree or higher: 17.6%; Graduate/professional degree or higher: 3.6%
School District(s)
Person County Schools (PK-12)
    2012-13 Enrollment: 4,943 . . . . (336) 599-2191
Housing: Homeownership rate: 84.6%; Median home value: $137,500; Median year structure built: 1995; Homeowner vacancy rate: 2.1%; Median gross rent: $596 per month; Rental vacancy rate: 7.8%
Health Insurance: 88.9% have insurance; 71.1% have private insurance; 30.0% have public insurance; 11.1% do not have insurance; 7.4% of children under 18 do not have insurance
Transportation: Commute: 97.6% car, 0.0% public transportation, 0.0% walk, 1.3% work from home; Median travel time to work: 36.1 minutes

Pitt County

Located in east central North Carolina; drained by the Tar River. Covers a land area of 651.974 square miles, a water area of 2.850 square miles, and is located in the Eastern Time Zone at 35.59° N. Lat., 77.37° W. Long. The county was founded in 1760. County seat is Greenville.

Pitt County is part of the Greenville, NC Metropolitan Statistical Area. The entire metro area includes: Pitt County, NC

Weather Station: Greenville   Elevation: 32 feet

	Jan	Feb	Mar	Apr	May	Jun	Jul	Aug	Sep	Oct	Nov	Dec
High	52	56	64	73	80	87	90	88	83	74	65	56
Low	32	34	40	49	57	66	70	69	63	50	41	34
Precip	3.9	3.3	4.1	3.2	3.8	4.4	5.3	6.2	5.5	3.4	3.2	3.3
Snow	1.6	1.0	0.8	tr	0.0	0.0	0.0	0.0	0.0	0.0	0.0	0.5

High and Low temperatures in degrees Fahrenheit; Precipitation and Snow in inches

Population: 168,148; Growth (since 2000): 25.7%; Density: 257.9 persons per square mile; Race: 58.9% White, 34.1% Black/African American, 1.6% Asian, 0.3% American Indian/Alaska Native, 0.1% Native Hawaiian/Other Pacific Islander, 2.0% two or more races, 5.5% Hispanic of any race; Average household size: 2.39; Median age: 31.0; Age under 18: 22.5%; Age 65 and over: 9.9%; Males per 100 females: 89.4; Marriage status: 42.8% never married, 42.8% now married, 2.9% separated, 5.3% widowed, 9.2% divorced; Foreign born: 4.8%; Speak English only: 92.8%; With disability: 12.0%; Veterans: 7.3%; Ancestry: 9.4% English, 8.0% Irish, 7.8% American, 7.1% German, 2.6% Italian

Religion: Six largest groups: 10.6% Methodist/Pietist, 10.5% Baptist, 10.1% Non-denominational Protestant, 3.3% Catholicism, 3.0% Pentecostal, 1.3% Presbyterian-Reformed

Economy: Unemployment rate: 5.7%; Leading industries: 17.9% retail trade; 14.3% health care and social assistance; 10.2% accommodation and food services; Farms: 391 totaling 171,821 acres; Company size: 1 employs 1,000 or more persons, 6 employ 500 to 999 persons, 58 employ 100 to 499 persons, 3,512 employ less than 100 persons; Business ownership: 3,685 women-owned, 2,278 Black-owned, 204 Hispanic-owned, n/a Asian-owned

Employment: 12.2% management, business, and financial, 4.3% computer, engineering, and science, 12.4% education, legal, community service, arts, and media, 9.1% healthcare practitioners, 20.0% service, 22.7% sales and office, 8.3% natural resources, construction, and maintenance, 10.9% production, transportation, and material moving

Income: Per capita: $23,029; Median household: $40,718; Average household: $57,292; Households with income of $100,000 or more: 14.9%; Poverty rate: 24.3%

Educational Attainment: High school diploma or higher: 85.8%; Bachelor's degree or higher: 28.1%; Graduate/professional degree or higher: 10.5%

Housing: Homeownership rate: 54.7%; Median home value: $134,900; Median year structure built: 1991; Homeowner vacancy rate: 2.9%; Median gross rent: $716 per month; Rental vacancy rate: 11.6%

Vital Statistics: Birth rate: 123.0 per 10,000 population; Death rate: 69.1 per 10,000 population; Age-adjusted cancer mortality rate: 194.5 deaths per 100,000 population

Health Insurance: 84.3% have insurance; 65.6% have private insurance; 27.0% have public insurance; 15.7% do not have insurance; 7.7% of children under 18 do not have insurance

Health Care: Physicians: 56.3 per 10,000 population; Hospital beds: 54.3 per 10,000 population; Hospital admissions: 2,692.5 per 10,000 population

Air Quality Index: 92.7% good, 7.3% moderate, 0.0% unhealthy for sensitive individuals, 0.0% unhealthy (percent of days)

Transportation: Commute: 93.6% car, 0.9% public transportation, 2.2% walk, 2.4% work from home; Median travel time to work: 19.5 minutes

Presidential Election: 53.1% Obama, 45.9% Romney (2012)

Additional Information Contacts

Pitt Government . . . . (252) 902-1000
  http://www.pittcountync.gov

Pitt County Communities

AYDEN (town). Covers a land area of 3.488 square miles and a water area of 0 square miles. Located at 35.47° N. Lat; 77.42° W. Long. Elevation is 66 feet.

Population: 4,932; Growth (since 2000): 6.7%; Density: 1,413.8 persons per square mile; Race: 48.1% White, 48.3% Black/African American, 0.2% Asian, 0.6% American Indian/Alaska Native, 0.0% Native Hawaiian/Other Pacific Islander, 1.6% Two or more races, 2.5% Hispanic of any race; Average household size: 2.27; Median age: 40.6; Age under 18: 23.8%; Age 65 and over: 19.0%; Males per 100 females: 78.3; Marriage status: 33.3% never married, 43.7% now married, 4.5% separated, 13.4% widowed, 9.6% divorced; Foreign born: 3.5%; Speak English only: 91.5%; With disability: 18.3%; Veterans: 8.1%; Ancestry: 9.1% American, 6.4% English, 5.1% Irish, 4.6% German, 2.5% Italian

Employment: 11.4% management, business, and financial, 1.0% computer, engineering, and science, 11.0% education, legal, community service, arts, and media, 10.2% healthcare practitioners, 19.4% service, 21.6% sales and office, 8.6% natural resources, construction, and maintenance, 16.7% production, transportation, and material moving

Income: Per capita: $17,329; Median household: $30,938; Average household: $42,377; Households with income of $100,000 or more: 6.6%; Poverty rate: 27.1%

Educational Attainment: High school diploma or higher: 75.1%; Bachelor's degree or higher: 13.4%; Graduate/professional degree or higher: 3.1%

School District(s)

Pitt County Schools (PK-12)
  2012-13 Enrollment: 23,791 . . . . (252) 830-4200

Housing: Homeownership rate: 53.1%; Median home value: $105,200; Median year structure built: 1974; Homeowner vacancy rate: 4.1%; Median gross rent: $621 per month; Rental vacancy rate: 7.1%

Health Insurance: 75.1% have insurance; 38.8% have private insurance; 43.9% have public insurance; 24.9% do not have insurance; 15.7% of children under 18 do not have insurance

Safety: Violent crime rate: 53.3 per 10,000 population; Property crime rate: 408.7 per 10,000 population

Transportation: Commute: 94.9% car, 0.0% public transportation, 2.1% walk, 2.5% work from home; Median travel time to work: 23.4 minutes

Additional Information Contacts

Town of Ayden . . . . (252) 746-7030
  http://www.ayden.com

BELL ARTHUR (CDP). Covers a land area of 1.862 square miles and a water area of 0 square miles. Located at 35.59° N. Lat; 77.51° W. Long. Elevation is 79 feet.

Population: 466; Growth (since 2000): n/a; Density: 250.3 persons per square mile; Race: 61.8% White, 33.5% Black/African American, 1.1% Asian, 0.0% American Indian/Alaska Native, 0.0% Native Hawaiian/Other Pacific Islander, 2.1% Two or more races, 4.1% Hispanic of any race; Average household size: 2.56; Median age: 39.8; Age under 18: 23.2%; Age 65 and over: 8.6%; Males per 100 females: 98.3

Housing: Homeownership rate: 79.1%; Homeowner vacancy rate: 2.0%; Rental vacancy rate: 19.1%

BELVOIR (CDP). Covers a land area of 1.976 square miles and a water area of 0 square miles. Located at 35.71° N. Lat; 77.47° W. Long. Elevation is 36 feet.

Population: 307; Growth (since 2000): n/a; Density: 155.3 persons per square mile; Race: 59.9% White, 35.5% Black/African American, 0.0% Asian, 1.0% American Indian/Alaska Native, 0.0% Native Hawaiian/Other Pacific Islander, 2.0% Two or more races, 3.9% Hispanic of any race; Average household size: 2.67; Median age: 37.1; Age under 18: 23.1%; Age 65 and over: 11.4%; Males per 100 females: 83.8

Housing: Homeownership rate: 75.6%; Homeowner vacancy rate: 0.0%; Rental vacancy rate: 3.1%

BETHEL (town). Covers a land area of 1.057 square miles and a water area of 0 square miles. Located at 35.81° N. Lat; 77.38° W. Long. Elevation is 69 feet.

Population: 1,577; Growth (since 2000): -6.2%; Density: 1,491.4 persons per square mile; Race: 38.9% White, 59.5% Black/African American, 0.3% Asian, 0.3% American Indian/Alaska Native, 0.1% Native Hawaiian/Other Pacific Islander, 0.3% Two or more races, 1.0% Hispanic of any race; Average household size: 2.43; Median age: 43.9; Age under 18: 23.3%; Age 65 and over: 17.4%; Males per 100 females: 82.9

School District(s)

Pitt County Schools (PK-12)
  2012-13 Enrollment: 23,791 . . . . (252) 830-4200

Housing: Homeownership rate: 60.6%; Homeowner vacancy rate: 2.2%; Rental vacancy rate: 13.2%

Safety: Violent crime rate: 30.8 per 10,000 population; Property crime rate: 289.2 per 10,000 population

FALKLAND (town). Covers a land area of 0.245 square miles and a water area of 0 square miles. Located at 35.70° N. Lat; 77.51° W. Long. Elevation is 75 feet.

Population: 96; Growth (since 2000): -14.3%; Density: 391.1 persons per square mile; Race: 69.8% White, 18.8% Black/African American, 2.1% Asian, 0.0% American Indian/Alaska Native, 0.0% Native Hawaiian/Other

Pacific Islander, 4.2% Two or more races, 10.4% Hispanic of any race; Average household size: 2.74; Median age: 40.5; Age under 18: 26.0%; Age 65 and over: 18.8%; Males per 100 females: 108.7
Housing: Homeownership rate: 71.5%; Homeowner vacancy rate: 0.0%; Rental vacancy rate: 16.7%

FARMVILLE (town). Covers a land area of 3.364 square miles and a water area of 0 square miles. Located at 35.60° N. Lat; 77.59° W. Long. Elevation is 82 feet.

History: Settled 1860; incorporated 1872.
Population: 4,654; Growth (since 2000): 8.2%; Density: 1,383.6 persons per square mile; Race: 48.1% White, 49.7% Black/African American, 0.4% Asian, 0.2% American Indian/Alaska Native, 0.0% Native Hawaiian/Other Pacific Islander, 0.8% Two or more races, 2.5% Hispanic of any race; Average household size: 2.32; Median age: 42.5; Age under 18: 24.7%; Age 65 and over: 17.4%; Males per 100 females: 81.1; Marriage status: 34.9% never married, 44.1% now married, 6.2% separated, 12.1% widowed, 8.9% divorced; Foreign born: 1.0%; Speak English only: 98.2%; With disability: 23.4%; Veterans: 10.5%; Ancestry: 9.9% American, 8.4% English, 4.0% Irish, 3.8% Scotch-Irish, 2.8% German
Employment: 6.9% management, business, and financial, 3.2% computer, engineering, and science, 6.7% education, legal, community service, arts, and media, 2.4% healthcare practitioners, 25.5% service, 26.6% sales and office, 12.2% natural resources, construction, and maintenance, 16.6% production, transportation, and material moving
Income: Per capita: $18,364; Median household: $29,297; Average household: $41,075; Households with income of $100,000 or more: 8.1%; Poverty rate: 29.9%
Educational Attainment: High school diploma or higher: 80.7%; Bachelor's degree or higher: 15.7%; Graduate/professional degree or higher: 3.7%
School District(s)
Pitt County Schools (PK-12)
    2012-13 Enrollment: 23,791 . . . . (252) 830-4200
Housing: Homeownership rate: 54.9%; Median home value: $123,400; Median year structure built: 1973; Homeowner vacancy rate: 3.4%; Median gross rent: $634 per month; Rental vacancy rate: 11.4%
Health Insurance: 80.0% have insurance; 48.5% have private insurance; 45.4% have public insurance; 20.0% do not have insurance; 12.5% of children under 18 do not have insurance
Safety: Violent crime rate: 73.4 per 10,000 population; Property crime rate: 310.5 per 10,000 population
Newspapers: Farmville Enterprise (weekly circulation 2600)
Transportation: Commute: 86.6% car, 0.0% public transportation, 6.9% walk, 4.9% work from home; Median travel time to work: 18.2 minutes
Additional Information Contacts
Town of Farmville . . . . (252) 753-5116
    http://www.farmville-nc.com

FOUNTAIN (town). Covers a land area of 0.930 square miles and a water area of 0 square miles. Located at 35.67° N. Lat; 77.63° W. Long. Elevation is 112 feet.

Population: 427; Growth (since 2000): -19.9%; Density: 459.2 persons per square mile; Race: 46.6% White, 49.9% Black/African American, 0.0% Asian, 0.0% American Indian/Alaska Native, 0.0% Native Hawaiian/Other Pacific Islander, 2.8% Two or more races, 1.4% Hispanic of any race; Average household size: 2.36; Median age: 44.1; Age under 18: 24.1%; Age 65 and over: 20.6%; Males per 100 females: 88.9
Housing: Homeownership rate: 53.1%; Homeowner vacancy rate: 0.0%; Rental vacancy rate: 9.5%

GREENVILLE (city). County seat. Covers a land area of 34.607 square miles and a water area of 0.755 square miles. Located at 35.60° N. Lat; 77.38° W. Long. Elevation is 56 feet.

History: Greenville was founded in 1786 and named for General Nathanael Greene.
Population: 84,554; Growth (since 2000): 39.8%; Density: 2,443.3 persons per square mile; Race: 56.3% White, 37.0% Black/African American, 2.4% Asian, 0.4% American Indian/Alaska Native, 0.0% Native Hawaiian/Other Pacific Islander, 2.2% Two or more races, 3.8% Hispanic of any race; Average household size: 2.18; Median age: 26.0; Age under 18: 18.7%; Age 65 and over: 8.3%; Males per 100 females: 84.6; Marriage status: 55.2% never married, 32.2% now married, 2.2% separated, 4.2% widowed, 8.4% divorced; Foreign born: 5.1%; Speak English only: 92.9%;

With disability: 10.1%; Veterans: 6.2%; Ancestry: 9.1% Irish, 8.6% English, 7.8% German, 4.6% American, 3.7% Italian
Employment: 12.1% management, business, and financial, 4.3% computer, engineering, and science, 15.2% education, legal, community service, arts, and media, 9.5% healthcare practitioners, 22.9% service, 23.6% sales and office, 3.8% natural resources, construction, and maintenance, 8.6% production, transportation, and material moving
Income: Per capita: $22,836; Median household: $35,137; Average household: $54,786; Households with income of $100,000 or more: 13.8%; Poverty rate: 30.0%
Educational Attainment: High school diploma or higher: 89.7%; Bachelor's degree or higher: 37.1%; Graduate/professional degree or higher: 14.6%
School District(s)
Nc Dept of Juvenile Justice (KG-12)
    2012-13 Enrollment: n/a . . . . (919) 733-3388
Pitt County Schools (PK-12)
    2012-13 Enrollment: 23,791 . . . . (252) 830-4200
Four-year College(s)
East Carolina University (Public)
    Fall 2013 Enrollment: 26,887 . . . . (252) 328-6131
    2013-14 Tuition: In-state $6,143; Out-of-state $20,256
Two-year College(s)
Miller-Motte College-Greenville (Private, For-profit)
    Fall 2013 Enrollment: 446 . . . . (252) 215-2000
    2013-14 Tuition: In-state $10,748; Out-of-state $10,748
Vocational/Technical School(s)
Grace College of Barbering (Private, Not-for-profit)
    Fall 2013 Enrollment: 25 . . . . (252) 917-3223
    2013-14 Tuition: $20,125
Mitchells Hairstyling Academy-Greenville (Private, For-profit)
    Fall 2013 Enrollment: 42 . . . . (252) 756-3050
    2013-14 Tuition: $9,950
Housing: Homeownership rate: 37.1%; Median home value: $149,600; Median year structure built: 1993; Homeowner vacancy rate: 4.5%; Median gross rent: $724 per month; Rental vacancy rate: 11.9%
Health Insurance: 86.0% have insurance; 69.1% have private insurance; 23.8% have public insurance; 14.0% do not have insurance; 5.5% of children under 18 do not have insurance
Hospitals: Vidant Medical Center (745 beds)
Safety: Violent crime rate: 63.1 per 10,000 population; Property crime rate: 438.8 per 10,000 population
Newspapers: Daily Reflector (daily circulation 21000)
Transportation: Commute: 92.0% car, 1.5% public transportation, 3.3% walk, 2.2% work from home; Median travel time to work: 16.8 minutes; Amtrak: Bus service available.
Airports: Pitt-Greenville (primary service/non-hub)
Additional Information Contacts
City of Greenville . . . . (864) 232-2273
    http://www.greenvillenc.gov

GRIFTON (town). Covers a land area of 2.046 square miles and a water area of 0 square miles. Located at 35.38° N. Lat; 77.44° W. Long. Elevation is 26 feet.

Population: 2,617; Growth (since 2000): 26.2%; Density: 1,279.0 persons per square mile; Race: 51.8% White, 40.8% Black/African American, 0.0% Asian, 0.1% American Indian/Alaska Native, 0.0% Native Hawaiian/Other Pacific Islander, 2.4% Two or more races, 9.7% Hispanic of any race; Average household size: 2.51; Median age: 38.8; Age under 18: 26.4%; Age 65 and over: 15.8%; Males per 100 females: 85.9; Marriage status: 29.7% never married, 45.4% now married, 4.7% separated, 10.1% widowed, 14.8% divorced; Foreign born: 4.2%; Speak English only: 96.5%; With disability: 20.8%; Veterans: 8.3%; Ancestry: 10.9% English, 10.2% German, 8.6% American, 6.9% Irish, 3.5% European
Employment: 11.4% management, business, and financial, 3.0% computer, engineering, and science, 8.5% education, legal, community service, arts, and media, 12.0% healthcare practitioners, 26.6% service, 11.3% sales and office, 5.3% natural resources, construction, and maintenance, 22.0% production, transportation, and material moving
Income: Per capita: $20,177; Median household: $34,063; Average household: $45,816; Households with income of $100,000 or more: 10.1%; Poverty rate: 29.0%
Educational Attainment: High school diploma or higher: 88.4%; Bachelor's degree or higher: 18.0%; Graduate/professional degree or higher: 7.2%

School District(s)
Pitt County Schools (PK-12)
   2012-13 Enrollment: 23,791 . . . . (252) 830-4200
Housing: Homeownership rate: 62.3%; Median home value: $110,900; Median year structure built: 1967; Homeowner vacancy rate: 2.2%; Median gross rent: $516 per month; Rental vacancy rate: 4.6%
Health Insurance: 82.9% have insurance; 60.0% have private insurance; 39.0% have public insurance; 17.1% do not have insurance; 21.9% of children under 18 do not have insurance
Newspapers: The Times-Leader (weekly circulation 2600)
Transportation: Commute: 97.2% car, 0.0% public transportation, 0.5% walk, 1.6% work from home; Median travel time to work: 23.1 minutes
Additional Information Contacts
Town of Grifton . . . . (262) 524-5168
  http://www.grifton.com

GRIMESLAND (town). Covers a land area of 0.676 square miles and a water area of 0 square miles. Located at 35.57° N. Lat; 77.20° W. Long. Elevation is 39 feet.
History: Grimesland was built on part of the Grimes plantation.
Population: 441; Growth (since 2000): 0.2%; Density: 652.2 persons per square mile; Race: 60.1% White, 33.3% Black/African American, 0.0% Asian, 0.0% American Indian/Alaska Native, 0.0% Native Hawaiian/Other Pacific Islander, 1.8% Two or more races, 7.7% Hispanic of any race; Average household size: 2.71; Median age: 38.5; Age under 18: 26.5%; Age 65 and over: 15.2%; Males per 100 females: 97.8
School District(s)
Pitt County Schools (PK-12)
   2012-13 Enrollment: 23,791 . . . . (252) 830-4200
Housing: Homeownership rate: 65.1%; Homeowner vacancy rate: 0.9%; Rental vacancy rate: 10.9%

SIMPSON (village). Covers a land area of 0.372 square miles and a water area of 0 square miles. Located at 35.58° N. Lat; 77.28° W. Long. Elevation is 62 feet.
Population: 416; Growth (since 2000): -10.3%; Density: 1,117.0 persons per square mile; Race: 60.6% White, 37.0% Black/African American, 0.0% Asian, 0.0% American Indian/Alaska Native, 0.0% Native Hawaiian/Other Pacific Islander, 0.7% Two or more races, 2.6% Hispanic of any race; Average household size: 2.27; Median age: 39.0; Age under 18: 22.1%; Age 65 and over: 14.9%; Males per 100 females: 88.2
Housing: Homeownership rate: 74.3%; Homeowner vacancy rate: 0.7%; Rental vacancy rate: 9.6%

STOKES (CDP). Covers a land area of 4.429 square miles and a water area of 0 square miles. Located at 35.71° N. Lat; 77.27° W. Long. Elevation is 52 feet.
Population: 376; Growth (since 2000): n/a; Density: 84.9 persons per square mile; Race: 79.5% White, 18.6% Black/African American, 0.3% Asian, 0.3% American Indian/Alaska Native, 0.0% Native Hawaiian/Other Pacific Islander, 1.3% Two or more races, 0.3% Hispanic of any race; Average household size: 2.34; Median age: 43.5; Age under 18: 20.5%; Age 65 and over: 15.7%; Males per 100 females: 98.9
School District(s)
Pitt County Schools (PK-12)
   2012-13 Enrollment: 23,791 . . . . (252) 830-4200
Housing: Homeownership rate: 79.5%; Homeowner vacancy rate: 0.0%; Rental vacancy rate: 17.5%

WINTERVILLE (town). Covers a land area of 4.598 square miles and a water area of <.001 square miles. Located at 35.53° N. Lat; 77.40° W. Long. Elevation is 69 feet.
Population: 9,269; Growth (since 2000): 93.5%; Density: 2,015.7 persons per square mile; Race: 62.8% White, 31.6% Black/African American, 2.1% Asian, 0.3% American Indian/Alaska Native, 0.0% Native Hawaiian/Other Pacific Islander, 1.9% Two or more races, 3.3% Hispanic of any race; Average household size: 2.71; Median age: 34.3; Age under 18: 29.2%; Age 65 and over: 8.7%; Males per 100 females: 87.3; Marriage status: 25.3% never married, 59.3% now married, 2.1% separated, 5.1% widowed, 10.3% divorced; Foreign born: 3.9%; Speak English only: 93.1%; With disability: 11.1%; Veterans: 8.2%; Ancestry: 10.5% German, 9.4% Irish, 9.1% American, 8.4% English, 3.6% Scotch-Irish
Employment: 20.5% management, business, and financial; 8.3% computer, engineering, and science, 11.5% education, legal, community service, arts, and media, 12.9% healthcare practitioners, 12.8% service,

20.8% sales and office, 8.5% natural resources, construction, and maintenance, 4.7% production, transportation, and material moving
Income: Per capita: $26,865; Median household: $57,220; Average household: $74,466; Households with income of $100,000 or more: 26.0%; Poverty rate: 11.2%
Educational Attainment: High school diploma or higher: 91.0%; Bachelor's degree or higher: 37.6%; Graduate/professional degree or higher: 12.2%
School District(s)
Pitt County Schools (PK-12)
   2012-13 Enrollment: 23,791 . . . . (252) 830-4200
Two-year College(s)
Pitt Community College (Public)
   Fall 2013 Enrollment: 8,902 . . . . (252) 493-7200
   2013-14 Tuition: In-state $1,979; Out-of-state $8,122
Housing: Homeownership rate: 81.9%; Median home value: $162,700; Median year structure built: 2001; Homeowner vacancy rate: 1.8%; Median gross rent: $1,097 per month; Rental vacancy rate: 7.5%
Health Insurance: 87.1% have insurance; 76.9% have private insurance; 20.6% have public insurance; 12.9% do not have insurance; 7.8% of children under 18 do not have insurance
Safety: Violent crime rate: 8.4 per 10,000 population; Property crime rate: 88.1 per 10,000 population
Transportation: Commute: 94.4% car, 0.2% public transportation, 0.0% walk, 5.4% work from home; Median travel time to work: 19.9 minutes
Additional Information Contacts
Town of Winterville . . . . (252) 756-2221
  http://www.wintervillenc.com

Polk County

Located in southwestern North Carolina; bounded on the south by South Carolina. Covers a land area of 237.789 square miles, a water area of 0.746 square miles, and is located in the Eastern Time Zone at 35.28° N. Lat., 82.17° W. Long. The county was founded in 1855. County seat is Columbus.

Weather Station: Tryon									Elevation: 1,080 feet			
	Jan	Feb	Mar	Apr	May	Jun	Jul	Aug	Sep	Oct	Nov	Dec
High	52	56	64	73	79	86	89	87	81	72	63	54
Low	32	34	40	47	55	64	67	67	60	49	41	34
Precip	5.0	4.8	6.0	4.7	4.7	5.5	5.5	6.0	5.5	4.6	4.8	5.1
Snow	3.0	1.5	1.0	tr	tr	0.0	0.0	0.0	0.0	0.0	tr	0.4

High and Low temperatures in degrees Fahrenheit; Precipitation and Snow in inches

Population: 20,510; Growth (since 2000): 11.9%; Density: 86.3 persons per square mile; Race: 90.8% White, 4.5% Black/African American, 0.3% Asian, 0.4% American Indian/Alaska Native, 0.0% Native Hawaiian/Other Pacific Islander, 1.4% two or more races, 5.5% Hispanic of any race; Average household size: 2.24; Median age: 49.1; Age under 18: 19.2%; Age 65 and over: 24.3%; Males per 100 females: 92.0; Marriage status: 22.4% never married, 57.0% now married, 2.2% separated, 9.8% widowed, 10.9% divorced; Foreign born: 4.1%; Speak English only: 94.8%; With disability: 15.1%; Veterans: 12.1%; Ancestry: 15.8% German, 15.8% American, 13.6% English, 12.4% Irish, 5.2% Scotch-Irish
Religion: Six largest groups: 27.1% Baptist, 6.0% Methodist/Pietist, 5.7% Presbyterian-Reformed, 5.1% Catholicism, 2.4% Episcopalianism/Anglicanism, 2.0% European Free-Church
Economy: Unemployment rate: 4.2%; Leading industries: 14.3% other services (except public administration); 13.9% retail trade; 13.7% construction; Farms: 290 totaling 24,101 acres; Company size: 0 employ 1,000 or more persons, 0 employ 500 to 999 persons, 4 employ 100 to 499 persons, 478 employ less than 100 persons; Business ownership: 873 women-owned, n/a Black-owned, n/a Hispanic-owned, n/a Asian-owned
Employment: 11.3% management, business, and financial; 2.1% computer, engineering, and science, 9.8% education, legal, community service, arts, and media, 4.1% healthcare practitioners, 17.6% service, 23.7% sales and office, 14.4% natural resources, construction, and maintenance, 17.1% production, transportation, and material moving
Income: Per capita: $24,611; Median household: $44,745; Average household: $55,992; Households with income of $100,000 or more: 14.7%; Poverty rate: 16.7%
Educational Attainment: High school diploma or higher: 87.0%; Bachelor's degree or higher: 26.9%; Graduate/professional degree or higher: 11.6%

Housing: Homeownership rate: 75.6%; Median home value: $170,200; Median year structure built: 1982; Homeowner vacancy rate: 3.7%; Median gross rent: $707 per month; Rental vacancy rate: 12.7%

Vital Statistics: Birth rate: 61.2 per 10,000 population; Death rate: 126.4 per 10,000 population; Age-adjusted cancer mortality rate: 136.5 deaths per 100,000 population

Health Insurance: 84.0% have insurance; 65.5% have private insurance; 39.5% have public insurance; 16.0% do not have insurance; 11.3% of children under 18 do not have insurance

Health Care: Physicians: 12.4 per 10,000 population; Hospital beds: 17.3 per 10,000 population; Hospital admissions: 773.3 per 10,000 population

Transportation: Commute: 90.9% car, 0.4% public transportation, 1.9% walk, 6.7% work from home; Median travel time to work: 24.9 minutes

Presidential Election: 38.6% Obama, 60.0% Romney (2012)

Additional Information Contacts
Polk Government. . . . . (863) 534-6000
http://www.polknc.org

Polk County Communities

COLUMBUS (town). County seat. Covers a land area of 3.557 square miles and a water area of 0.002 square miles. Located at 35.25° N. Lat; 82.21° W. Long. Elevation is 1,106 feet.

History: Columbus was named for Dr. Columbus Mills, who was a member of the General Assembly that created Polk County in 1855.

Population: 999; Growth (since 2000): 0.7%; Density: 280.8 persons per square mile; Race: 81.3% White, 3.6% Black/African American, 0.7% Asian, 2.9% American Indian/Alaska Native, 0.0% Native Hawaiian/Other Pacific Islander, 2.4% Two or more races, 15.4% Hispanic of any race; Average household size: 2.20; Median age: 44.5; Age under 18: 22.0%; Age 65 and over: 25.1%; Males per 100 females: 81.0

School District(s)
Polk County Schools (PK-12)
    2012-13 Enrollment: 2,440 . . . . (828) 894-3051

Housing: Homeownership rate: 57.4%; Homeowner vacancy rate: 1.9%; Rental vacancy rate: 14.4%

Hospitals: Saint Luke's Hospital (73 beds)

Safety: Violent crime rate: 20.3 per 10,000 population; Property crime rate: 274.7 per 10,000 population

Newspapers: Polk Co. News-Journal (weekly circulation 1500)

MILL SPRING (unincorporated postal area)
ZCTA: 28756

Covers a land area of 89.856 square miles and a water area of 0.591 square miles. Located at 35.35° N. Lat; 82.19° W. Long. Elevation is 1,001 feet.

Population: 4,504; Growth (since 2000): 7.4%; Density: 50.1 persons per square mile; Race: 91.5% White, 3.0% Black/African American, 0.3% Asian, 0.5% American Indian/Alaska Native, 0.0% Native Hawaiian/Other Pacific Islander, 1.5% Two or more races, 6.6% Hispanic of any race; Average household size: 2.41; Median age: 42.0; Age under 18: 22.0%; Age 65 and over: 14.5%; Males per 100 females: 98.9; Marriage status: 23.1% never married, 64.0% now married, 2.0% separated, 5.3% widowed, 7.7% divorced; Foreign born: 1.3%; Speak English only: 97.6%; With disability: 13.8%; Veterans: 8.9%; Ancestry: 18.2% Irish, 16.6% German, 16.4% American, 14.8% English, 6.4% Scotch-Irish

Employment: 17.9% management, business, and financial, 2.7% computer, engineering, and science, 7.4% education, legal, community service, arts, and media, 6.4% healthcare practitioners, 13.0% service, 14.6% sales and office, 16.2% natural resources, construction, and maintenance, 21.9% production, transportation, and material moving

Income: Per capita: $21,397; Median household: $33,740; Average household: $51,046; Households with income of $100,000 or more: 16.4%; Poverty rate: 32.7%

Educational Attainment: High school diploma or higher: 85.8%; Bachelor's degree or higher: 11.9%; Graduate/professional degree or higher: 2.6%

School District(s)
Polk County Schools (PK-12)
    2012-13 Enrollment: 2,440 . . . . (828) 894-3051

Housing: Homeownership rate: 76.6%; Median home value: $105,300; Median year structure built: 1989; Homeowner vacancy rate: 3.1%; Median gross rent: $639 per month; Rental vacancy rate: 13.8%

Health Insurance: 82.1% have insurance; 62.3% have private insurance; 36.8% have public insurance; 17.9% do not have insurance; 15.3% of children under 18 do not have insurance

Transportation: Commute: 91.7% car, 0.0% public transportation, 0.1% walk, 8.1% work from home; Median travel time to work: 27.8 minutes

SALUDA (city). Covers a land area of 1.560 square miles and a water area of 0 square miles. Located at 35.24° N. Lat; 82.35° W. Long. Elevation is 2,096 feet.

Population: 713; Growth (since 2000): 24.0%; Density: 457.0 persons per square mile; Race: 95.7% White, 2.7% Black/African American, 0.3% Asian, 0.3% American Indian/Alaska Native, 0.0% Native Hawaiian/Other Pacific Islander, 1.0% Two or more races, 2.0% Hispanic of any race; Average household size: 2.01; Median age: 57.5; Age under 18: 14.6%; Age 65 and over: 34.9%; Males per 100 females: 77.8

School District(s)
Polk County Schools (PK-12)
    2012-13 Enrollment: 2,440 . . . . (828) 894-3051

Housing: Homeownership rate: 75.2%; Homeowner vacancy rate: 5.7%; Rental vacancy rate: 15.4%

TRYON (town). Covers a land area of 1.999 square miles and a water area of 0 square miles. Located at 35.21° N. Lat; 82.24° W. Long. Elevation is 1,102 feet.

History: Tryon lies on the southern slope of the Blue Ridge close to Tryon Peak, for which the town was named. The peak was named for North Carolina's royal governor, William Tryon.

Population: 1,646; Growth (since 2000): -6.5%; Density: 823.3 persons per square mile; Race: 80.0% White, 16.5% Black/African American, 0.4% Asian, 0.1% American Indian/Alaska Native, 0.0% Native Hawaiian/Other Pacific Islander, 1.6% Two or more races, 4.4% Hispanic of any race; Average household size: 1.91; Median age: 56.8; Age under 18: 16.0%; Age 65 and over: 38.0%; Males per 100 females: 78.1

School District(s)
Polk County Schools (PK-12)
    2012-13 Enrollment: 2,440 . . . . (828) 894-3051

Housing: Homeownership rate: 60.2%; Homeowner vacancy rate: 7.3%; Rental vacancy rate: 16.7%

Safety: Violent crime rate: 12.4 per 10,000 population; Property crime rate: 291.0 per 10,000 population

Newspapers: Tryon Daily Bulletin (daily circulation 5000)

Additional Information Contacts
Town of Tryon . . . . (770) 487-4038
http://tyrone.org

Randolph County

Located in central North Carolina; piedmont area, drained by the Deep River. Covers a land area of 782.517 square miles, a water area of 6.833 square miles, and is located in the Eastern Time Zone at 35.71° N. Lat., 79.81° W. Long. The county was founded in 1779. County seat is Asheboro.

Randolph County is part of the Greensboro-High Point, NC Metropolitan Statistical Area. The entire metro area includes: Guilford County, NC; Randolph County, NC; Rockingham County, NC

Weather Station: Asheboro 2 W									Elevation: 870 feet		
	Jan	Feb	Mar	Apr	May	Jun	Jul	Aug	Sep	Oct	Nov	Dec
High	50	55	63	72	78	85	88	87	81	71	62	53
Low	31	34	40	48	56	65	69	67	61	50	41	33
Precip	3.9	3.5	4.1	3.7	3.5	3.9	4.1	4.2	3.9	3.7	3.4	3.2
Snow	3.0	1.7	0.6	tr	0.0	0.0	0.0	0.0	0.0	0.0	0.2	0.3

High and Low temperatures in degrees Fahrenheit; Precipitation and Snow in inches

Population: 141,752; Growth (since 2000): 8.7%; Density: 181.1 persons per square mile; Race: 85.5% White, 5.8% Black/African American, 1.0% Asian, 0.7% American Indian/Alaska Native, 0.0% Native Hawaiian/Other Pacific Islander, 1.7% two or more races, 10.4% Hispanic of any race; Average household size: 2.54; Median age: 39.5; Age under 18: 24.5%; Age 65 and over: 14.1%; Males per 100 females: 97.1; Marriage status: 23.8% never married, 58.0% now married, 3.6% separated, 7.0% widowed, 11.2% divorced; Foreign born: 6.8%; Speak English only: 89.4%; With disability: 13.5%; Veterans: 9.6%; Ancestry: 14.0% American, 11.2% German, 11.2% English, 7.2% Irish, 2.0% Scotch-Irish

Religion: Six largest groups: 12.2% Baptist, 9.7% Methodist/Pietist, 3.9% Non-denominational Protestant, 2.3% Holiness, 2.1% European Free-Church, 2.0% Pentecostal
Economy: Unemployment rate: 5.1%; Leading industries: 15.4% retail trade; 11.7% other services (except public administration); 11.3% manufacturing; Farms: 1,486 totaling 156,813 acres; Company size: 2 employ 1,000 or more persons, 4 employ 500 to 999 persons, 49 employ 100 to 499 persons, 2,531 employs less than 100 persons; Business ownership: 3,235 women-owned, n/a Black-owned, 169 Hispanic-owned, 137 Asian-owned
Employment: 10.8% management, business, and financial, 3.0% computer, engineering, and science, 7.8% education, legal, community service, arts, and media, 4.8% healthcare practitioners, 15.0% service, 24.1% sales and office, 10.8% natural resources, construction, and maintenance, 23.7% production, transportation, and material moving
Income: Per capita: $20,523; Median household: $41,208; Average household: $52,359; Households with income of $100,000 or more: 11.1%; Poverty rate: 17.8%
Educational Attainment: High school diploma or higher: 78.0%; Bachelor's degree or higher: 13.8%; Graduate/professional degree or higher: 3.6%
Housing: Homeownership rate: 73.0%; Median home value: $121,900; Median year structure built: 1982; Homeowner vacancy rate: 2.0%; Median gross rent: $650 per month; Rental vacancy rate: 11.2%
Vital Statistics: Birth rate: 110.0 per 10,000 population; Death rate: 98.2 per 10,000 population; Age-adjusted cancer mortality rate: 165.9 deaths per 100,000 population
Health Insurance: 82.3% have insurance; 58.7% have private insurance; 33.3% have public insurance; 17.7% do not have insurance; 8.9% of children under 18 do not have insurance
Health Care: Physicians: 8.5 per 10,000 population; Hospital beds: 8.6 per 10,000 population; Hospital admissions: 444.0 per 10,000 population
Transportation: Commute: 95.6% car, 0.1% public transportation, 1.4% walk, 2.3% work from home; Median travel time to work: 23.2 minutes
Presidential Election: 24.3% Obama, 74.4% Romney (2012)
Additional Information Contacts
Randolph Government . . . . (336) 318-6301
    http://www.co.randolph.nc.us

Randolph County Communities

ARCHDALE (city). Covers a land area of 8.213 square miles and a water area of 0.022 square miles. Located at 35.90° N. Lat; 79.97° W. Long. Elevation is 866 feet.
History: Archdale was established as Bush Hill in 1773 by Quakers. In 1887 it was renamed for the Quaker John Archdale, governor of the Province (1694-1696).
Population: 11,415; Growth (since 2000): 26.6%; Density: 1,389.8 persons per square mile; Race: 87.8% White, 4.0% Black/African American, 4.8% Asian, 0.6% American Indian/Alaska Native, 0.0% Native Hawaiian/Other Pacific Islander, 1.4% Two or more races, 4.0% Hispanic of any race; Average household size: 2.46; Median age: 40.0; Age under 18: 23.8%; Age 65 and over: 15.6%; Males per 100 females: 90.7; Marriage status: 20.8% never married, 58.8% now married, 3.3% separated, 5.1% widowed, 15.2% divorced; Foreign born: 7.3%; Speak English only: 90.1%; With disability: 13.1%; Veterans: 10.3%; Ancestry: 13.9% German, 13.5% English, 12.1% American, 10.0% Irish, 2.7% Scottish
Employment: 13.1% management, business, and financial, 2.0% computer, engineering, and science, 7.5% education, legal, community service, arts, and media, 4.7% healthcare practitioners, 13.5% service, 30.6% sales and office, 9.1% natural resources, construction, and maintenance, 19.5% production, transportation, and material moving
Income: Per capita: $22,837; Median household: $52,042; Average household: $59,809; Households with income of $100,000 or more: 12.9%; Poverty rate: 11.2%
Educational Attainment: High school diploma or higher: 83.1%; Bachelor's degree or higher: 15.4%; Graduate/professional degree or higher: 4.7%
School District(s)
Randolph County Schools (PK-12)
    2012-13 Enrollment: 18,628 . . . . (336) 318-6100
Housing: Homeownership rate: 72.4%; Median home value: $135,500; Median year structure built: 1985; Homeowner vacancy rate: 2.1%; Median gross rent: $669 per month; Rental vacancy rate: 12.5%

Health Insurance: 86.9% have insurance; 70.1% have private insurance; 25.8% have public insurance; 13.1% do not have insurance; 6.0% of children under 18 do not have insurance
Safety: Violent crime rate: 6.9 per 10,000 population; Property crime rate: 257.7 per 10,000 population
Newspapers: Archdale Trinity News (weekly circulation 3600)
Transportation: Commute: 97.9% car, 0.0% public transportation, 0.1% walk, 1.4% work from home; Median travel time to work: 22.1 minutes
Additional Information Contacts
City of Archdale . . . . (336) 431-9141
    http://www.archdale-nc.gov

ASHEBORO (city). County seat. Covers a land area of 18.532 square miles and a water area of 0.093 square miles. Located at 35.72° N. Lat; 79.81° W. Long. Elevation is 840 feet.
History: Asheboro was named for Samuel Ashe, governor of North Carolina (1795-1798).
Population: 25,012; Growth (since 2000): 15.4%; Density: 1,349.6 persons per square mile; Race: 67.8% White, 12.0% Black/African American, 1.4% Asian, 0.9% American Indian/Alaska Native, 0.1% Native Hawaiian/Other Pacific Islander, 2.8% Two or more races, 26.9% Hispanic of any race; Average household size: 2.46; Median age: 34.0; Age under 18: 27.1%; Age 65 and over: 13.9%; Males per 100 females: 90.8; Marriage status: 29.5% never married, 49.7% now married, 5.6% separated, 8.3% widowed, 12.5% divorced; Foreign born: 16.5%; Speak English only: 75.2%; With disability: 14.0%; Veterans: 9.1%; Ancestry: 10.1% German, 9.5% American, 7.5% English, 5.9% Irish, 1.8% Scotch-Irish
Employment: 9.5% management, business, and financial, 2.8% computer, engineering, and science, 10.8% education, legal, community service, arts, and media, 4.1% healthcare practitioners, 16.4% service, 20.5% sales and office, 7.0% natural resources, construction, and maintenance, 28.9% production, transportation, and material moving
Income: Per capita: $17,448; Median household: $31,846; Average household: $43,024; Households with income of $100,000 or more: 7.0%; Poverty rate: 25.5%
Educational Attainment: High school diploma or higher: 73.1%; Bachelor's degree or higher: 16.8%; Graduate/professional degree or higher: 4.9%
School District(s)
Asheboro City Schools (PK-12)
    2012-13 Enrollment: 4,874 . . . . (336) 625-5104
Randolph County Schools (PK-12)
    2012-13 Enrollment: 18,628 . . . . (336) 318-6100
Two-year College(s)
Randolph Community College (Public)
    Fall 2013 Enrollment: 3,024 . . . . (336) 633-0200
    2013-14 Tuition: In-state $1,790; Out-of-state $6,398
Housing: Homeownership rate: 48.4%; Median home value: $115,900; Median year structure built: 1976; Homeowner vacancy rate: 3.9%; Median gross rent: $625 per month; Rental vacancy rate: 11.8%
Health Insurance: 75.2% have insurance; 46.9% have private insurance; 36.6% have public insurance; 24.8% do not have insurance; 12.4% of children under 18 do not have insurance
Hospitals: Randolph Hospital (145 beds)
Safety: Violent crime rate: 32.0 per 10,000 population; Property crime rate: 639.8 per 10,000 population
Newspapers: Courier-Tribune (daily circulation 13900); The Randolph Guide (weekly circulation 3200)
Transportation: Commute: 95.5% car, 0.4% public transportation, 1.6% walk, 2.1% work from home; Median travel time to work: 20.4 minutes
Airports: Asheboro Regional (general aviation)
Additional Information Contacts
City of Asheboro . . . . (336) 626-1201
    http://www.ci.asheboro.nc.us

CLIMAX (unincorporated postal area)
ZCTA: 27233
    Covers a land area of 24.473 square miles and a water area of 0.128 square miles. Located at 35.89° N. Lat; 79.71° W. Long..
    Population: 3,390; Growth (since 2000): -1.0%; Density: 138.5 persons per square mile; Race: 93.7% White, 2.6% Black/African American, 0.1% Asian, 0.9% American Indian/Alaska Native, 0.0% Native Hawaiian/Other Pacific Islander, 1.5% Two or more races, 3.0% Hispanic of any race; Average household size: 2.52; Median age: 43.4;

Age under 18: 21.2%; Age 65 and over: 15.6%; Males per 100 females: 101.2; Marriage status: 22.4% never married, 64.4% now married, 1.7% separated, 6.9% widowed, 6.3% divorced; Foreign born: 7.1%; Speak English only: 89.2%; With disability: 9.7%; Veterans: 9.1%; Ancestry: 15.8% German, 13.4% American, 12.1% English, 9.1% Irish, 2.4% Dutch
Employment: 12.7% management, business, and financial, 4.6% computer, engineering, and science, 5.4% education, legal, community service, arts, and media, 1.0% healthcare practitioners, 14.9% service, 21.7% sales and office, 10.0% natural resources, construction, and maintenance, 29.7% production, transportation, and material moving
Income: Per capita: $23,199; Median household: $48,250; Average household: $56,088; Households with income of $100,000 or more: 9.4%; Poverty rate: 6.4%
Educational Attainment: High school diploma or higher: 80.8%; Bachelor's degree or higher: 12.9%; Graduate/professional degree or higher: 3.0%

School District(s)
Randolph County Schools (PK-12)
    2012-13 Enrollment: 18,628 . . . . (336) 318-6100
Housing: Homeownership rate: 84.8%; Median home value: $152,800; Median year structure built: 1984; Homeowner vacancy rate: 1.6%; Median gross rent: $728 per month; Rental vacancy rate: 6.8%
Health Insurance: 83.6% have insurance; 69.2% have private insurance; 24.1% have public insurance; 16.4% do not have insurance; 12.1% of children under 18 do not have insurance
Transportation: Commute: 94.6% car, 0.0% public transportation, 0.1% walk, 3.8% work from home; Median travel time to work: 24.2 minutes

FRANKLINVILLE (town). Covers a land area of 1.627 square miles and a water area of 0.021 square miles. Located at 35.74° N. Lat; 79.69° W. Long. Elevation is 469 feet.
History: Franklinville began in 1801 with the founding of a gristmill.
Population: 1,164; Growth (since 2000): -7.5%; Density: 715.2 persons per square mile; Race: 76.2% White, 10.6% Black/African American, 0.0% Asian, 0.0% American Indian/Alaska Native, 0.0% Native Hawaiian/Other Pacific Islander, 1.8% Two or more races, 24.6% Hispanic of any race; Average household size: 3.00; Median age: 32.9; Age under 18: 32.0%; Age 65 and over: 9.3%; Males per 100 females: 96.3
School District(s)
Randolph County Schools (PK-12)
    2012-13 Enrollment: 18,628 . . . . (336) 318-6100
Housing: Homeownership rate: 60.0%; Homeowner vacancy rate: 1.3%; Rental vacancy rate: 11.4%

LIBERTY (town). Covers a land area of 3.110 square miles and a water area of 0.013 square miles. Located at 35.86° N. Lat; 79.57° W. Long. Elevation is 784 feet.
History: Liberty was named for the Liberty Oak under which Union officers are said to have celebrated General Joseph E. Johnston's surrender in 1865.
Population: 2,656; Growth (since 2000): -0.2%; Density: 853.9 persons per square mile; Race: 67.4% White, 20.4% Black/African American, 0.2% Asian, 1.1% American Indian/Alaska Native, 0.0% Native Hawaiian/Other Pacific Islander, 3.7% Two or more races, 14.4% Hispanic of any race; Average household size: 2.42; Median age: 39.5; Age under 18: 25.5%; Age 65 and over: 17.6%; Males per 100 females: 91.8; Marriage status: 24.5% never married, 51.8% now married, 2.9% separated, 9.6% widowed, 14.1% divorced; Foreign born: 4.6%; Speak English only: 87.1%; With disability: 10.2%; Veterans: 7.3%; Ancestry: 15.5% German, 13.6% Irish, 9.5% English, 6.5% American, 2.4% Scotch-Irish
Employment: 16.7% management, business, and financial, 3.3% computer, engineering, and science, 5.3% education, legal, community service, arts, and media, 5.6% healthcare practitioners, 18.4% service, 28.3% sales and office, 10.2% natural resources, construction, and maintenance, 12.3% production, transportation, and material moving
Income: Per capita: $20,645; Median household: $43,167; Average household: $49,252; Households with income of $100,000 or more: 11.3%; Poverty rate: 20.3%
Educational Attainment: High school diploma or higher: 84.7%; Bachelor's degree or higher: 12.7%; Graduate/professional degree or higher: 2.8%
School District(s)
Guilford County Schools (PK-12)
    2012-13 Enrollment: 74,161 . . . . (336) 370-8100

Randolph County Schools (PK-12)
    2012-13 Enrollment: 18,628 . . . . (336) 318-6100
Housing: Homeownership rate: 65.1%; Median home value: $119,100; Median year structure built: 1973; Homeowner vacancy rate: 2.7%; Median gross rent: $600 per month; Rental vacancy rate: 11.5%
Health Insurance: 86.7% have insurance; 67.9% have private insurance; 29.6% have public insurance; 13.3% do not have insurance; 0.4% of children under 18 do not have insurance
Safety: Violent crime rate: 15.0 per 10,000 population; Property crime rate: 63.6 per 10,000 population
Transportation: Commute: 96.3% car, 0.3% public transportation, 0.0% walk, 2.8% work from home; Median travel time to work: 26.7 minutes

RAMSEUR (town). Covers a land area of 1.957 square miles and a water area of 0.268 square miles. Located at 35.74° N. Lat; 79.65° W. Long. Elevation is 486 feet.
History: Settled c.1850; incorporated 1895.
Population: 1,692; Growth (since 2000): 6.5%; Density: 864.7 persons per square mile; Race: 75.6% White, 12.6% Black/African American, 1.4% Asian, 1.0% American Indian/Alaska Native, 0.0% Native Hawaiian/Other Pacific Islander, 3.0% Two or more races, 15.2% Hispanic of any race; Average household size: 2.49; Median age: 39.5; Age under 18: 25.4%; Age 65 and over: 20.3%; Males per 100 females: 91.4
School District(s)
Randolph County Schools (PK-12)
    2012-13 Enrollment: 18,628 . . . . (336) 318-6100
Housing: Homeownership rate: 60.8%; Homeowner vacancy rate: 5.6%; Rental vacancy rate: 14.3%
Safety: Violent crime rate: 64.6 per 10,000 population; Property crime rate: 493.2 per 10,000 population

RANDLEMAN (city). Covers a land area of 4.067 square miles and a water area of 0.041 square miles. Located at 35.82° N. Lat; 79.81° W. Long. Elevation is 689 feet.
History: Richard Petty Museum to North, race memorabilia.
Population: 4,113; Growth (since 2000): 15.6%; Density: 1,011.3 persons per square mile; Race: 86.3% White, 5.9% Black/African American, 0.4% Asian, 0.6% American Indian/Alaska Native, 0.0% Native Hawaiian/Other Pacific Islander, 1.9% Two or more races, 7.6% Hispanic of any race; Average household size: 2.37; Median age: 36.4; Age under 18: 26.4%; Age 65 and over: 12.2%; Males per 100 females: 93.2; Marriage status: 25.7% never married, 50.4% now married, 6.4% separated, 9.5% widowed, 14.4% divorced; Foreign born: 0.5%; Speak English only: 96.1%; With disability: 18.6%; Veterans: 12.1%; Ancestry: 15.7% American, 10.1% Irish, 9.8% German, 9.3% English, 2.8% Italian
Employment: 8.5% management, business, and financial, 6.0% computer, engineering, and science, 5.8% education, legal, community service, arts, and media, 11.4% healthcare practitioners, 16.8% service, 21.3% sales and office, 13.8% natural resources, construction, and maintenance, 16.4% production, transportation, and material moving
Income: Per capita: $18,764; Median household: $33,844; Average household: $41,231; Households with income of $100,000 or more: 6.0%; Poverty rate: 29.4%
Educational Attainment: High school diploma or higher: 74.3%; Bachelor's degree or higher: 9.4%; Graduate/professional degree or higher: 2.1%
School District(s)
Randolph County Schools (PK-12)
    2012-13 Enrollment: 18,628 . . . . (336) 318-6100
Housing: Homeownership rate: 59.6%; Median home value: $120,900; Median year structure built: 1976; Homeowner vacancy rate: 2.3%; Median gross rent: $610 per month; Rental vacancy rate: 8.2%
Health Insurance: 86.3% have insurance; 53.7% have private insurance; 37.6% have public insurance; 13.7% do not have insurance; 0.0% of children under 18 do not have insurance
Safety: Violent crime rate: 24.1 per 10,000 population; Property crime rate: 1,057.0 per 10,000 population
Transportation: Commute: 94.0% car, 0.0% public transportation, 4.0% walk, 0.7% work from home; Median travel time to work: 19.6 minutes
Additional Information Contacts
City of Randleman. . . . . (336) 495-7500
    http://www.randleman.org

SEAGROVE (town). Covers a land area of 1.036 square miles and a water area of 0.005 square miles. Located at 35.54° N. Lat; 79.78° W. Long. Elevation is 748 feet.

History: Pisgah Covered Bridge to West. Potters Museum. Area known for its pottery (over 70 potteries).

Population: 228; Growth (since 2000): -7.3%; Density: 220.1 persons per square mile; Race: 93.9% White, 2.6% Black/African American, 0.0% Asian, 0.0% American Indian/Alaska Native, 0.0% Native Hawaiian/Other Pacific Islander, 3.5% Two or more races, 1.3% Hispanic of any race; Average household size: 2.35; Median age: 45.3; Age under 18: 19.3%; Age 65 and over: 20.2%; Males per 100 females: 88.4

School District(s)
Moore County Schools (PK-12)
    2012-13 Enrollment: 12,912 . . . . (910) 947-2976
Randolph County Schools (PK-12)
    2012-13 Enrollment: 18,628 . . . . (336) 318-6100

Housing: Homeownership rate: 66.0%; Homeowner vacancy rate: 5.2%; Rental vacancy rate: 8.3%

SOPHIA (unincorporated postal area)

ZCTA: 27350

Covers a land area of 37.217 square miles and a water area of 0.637 square miles. Located at 35.81° N. Lat; 79.89° W. Long. Elevation is 778 feet.

Population: 6,530; Growth (since 2000): 10.5%; Density: 175.5 persons per square mile; Race: 95.4% White, 1.1% Black/African American, 0.5% Asian, 0.6% American Indian/Alaska Native, 0.0% Native Hawaiian/Other Pacific Islander, 1.3% Two or more races, 3.5% Hispanic of any race; Average household size: 2.55; Median age: 40.7; Age under 18: 23.4%; Age 65 and over: 13.2%; Males per 100 females: 98.5; Marriage status: 21.0% never married, 61.2% now married, 2.7% separated, 9.2% widowed, 8.6% divorced; Foreign born: 2.8%; Speak English only: 96.5%; With disability: 15.9%; Veterans: 10.5%; Ancestry: 16.3% American, 14.1% English, 12.3% German, 6.5% Irish, 1.5% Dutch

Employment: 5.6% management, business, and financial, 1.9% computer, engineering, and science, 7.1% education, legal, community service, arts, and media, 7.1% healthcare practitioners, 16.2% service, 22.6% sales and office, 15.4% natural resources, construction, and maintenance, 24.2% production, transportation, and material moving

Income: Per capita: $20,731; Median household: $43,957; Average household: $52,146; Households with income of $100,000 or more: 9.3%; Poverty rate: 16.2%

Educational Attainment: High school diploma or higher: 75.9%; Bachelor's degree or higher: 11.0%; Graduate/professional degree or higher: 2.0%

School District(s)
Randolph County Schools (PK-12)
    2012-13 Enrollment: 18,628 . . . . (336) 318-6100

Housing: Homeownership rate: 83.0%; Median home value: $112,900; Median year structure built: 1987; Homeowner vacancy rate: 1.0%; Median gross rent: $739 per month; Rental vacancy rate: 9.8%

Health Insurance: 85.3% have insurance; 59.3% have private insurance; 35.2% have public insurance; 14.7% do not have insurance; 0.9% of children under 18 do not have insurance

Transportation: Commute: 94.7% car, 0.0% public transportation, 3.9% walk, 0.9% work from home; Median travel time to work: 22.3 minutes

STALEY (town). Covers a land area of 1.156 square miles and a water area of 0 square miles. Located at 35.80° N. Lat; 79.55° W. Long. Elevation is 725 feet.

Population: 393; Growth (since 2000): 13.3%; Density: 340.0 persons per square mile; Race: 80.2% White, 8.1% Black/African American, 0.8% Asian, 1.0% American Indian/Alaska Native, 0.0% Native Hawaiian/Other Pacific Islander, 7.4% Two or more races, 9.4% Hispanic of any race; Average household size: 2.62; Median age: 39.1; Age under 18: 27.0%; Age 65 and over: 16.0%; Males per 100 females: 88.0

Housing: Homeownership rate: 78.0%; Homeowner vacancy rate: 0.0%; Rental vacancy rate: 2.9%

TRINITY (city). Covers a land area of 16.866 square miles and a water area of 0.189 square miles. Located at 35.88° N. Lat; 80.01° W. Long. Elevation is 804 feet.

Population: 6,614; Growth (since 2000): -1.1%; Density: 392.1 persons per square mile; Race: 91.7% White, 4.9% Black/African American, 1.2%

Asian, 0.4% American Indian/Alaska Native, 0.0% Native Hawaiian/Other Pacific Islander, 0.8% Two or more races, 2.3% Hispanic of any race; Average household size: 2.50; Median age: 44.0; Age under 18: 21.4%; Age 65 and over: 16.1%; Males per 100 females: 98.7; Marriage status: 17.3% never married, 63.5% now married, 2.0% separated, 5.2% widowed, 14.0% divorced; Foreign born: 1.6%; Speak English only: 96.5%; With disability: 16.1%; Veterans: 11.8%; Ancestry: 14.4% American, 13.9% English, 11.4% German, 10.9% Irish, 3.2% European

Employment: 12.7% management, business, and financial, 3.7% computer, engineering, and science, 8.4% education, legal, community service, arts, and media, 2.9% healthcare practitioners, 15.7% service, 30.3% sales and office, 6.8% natural resources, construction, and maintenance, 19.6% production, transportation, and material moving

Income: Per capita: $24,569; Median household: $46,318; Average household: $59,271; Households with income of $100,000 or more: 9.7%; Poverty rate: 15.1%

Educational Attainment: High school diploma or higher: 81.7%; Bachelor's degree or higher: 10.9%; Graduate/professional degree or higher: 3.0%

School District(s)
Randolph County Schools (PK-12)
    2012-13 Enrollment: 18,628 . . . . (336) 318-6100

Housing: Homeownership rate: 81.1%; Median home value: $125,500; Median year structure built: 1978; Homeowner vacancy rate: 2.3%; Median gross rent: $737 per month; Rental vacancy rate: 9.6%

Health Insurance: 87.6% have insurance; 62.2% have private insurance; 36.6% have public insurance; 12.4% do not have insurance; 5.8% of children under 18 do not have insurance

Transportation: Commute: 97.8% car, 0.0% public transportation, 1.3% walk, 0.6% work from home; Median travel time to work: 18.9 minutes

Additional Information Contacts
City of Trinity . . . . (336) 431-2841
  http://www.trinitynorthcarolina.com

Richmond County

Located in southern North Carolina; bounded on the south by South Carolina, and on the west by the Pee Dee River and Blewett Falls Lake. Covers a land area of 473.821 square miles, a water area of 6.097 square miles, and is located in the Eastern Time Zone at 35.00° N. Lat., 79.75° W. Long. The county was founded in 1779. County seat is Rockingham.

Richmond County is part of the Rockingham, NC Micropolitan Statistical Area. The entire metro area includes: Richmond County, NC

Weather Station: Hamlet   Elevation: 350 feet

	Jan	Feb	Mar	Apr	May	Jun	Jul	Aug	Sep	Oct	Nov	Dec
High	53	58	66	75	82	89	92	90	84	74	65	56
Low	29	32	38	47	56	64	68	67	60	48	39	31
Precip	3.8	3.4	4.0	2.9	3.2	4.6	6.0	4.7	4.6	4.1	3.4	3.1
Snow	0.3	0.3	0.5	0.0	0.0	0.0	0.0	0.0	0.0	0.0	0.0	tr

High and Low temperatures in degrees Fahrenheit; Precipitation and Snow in inches

Population: 46,639; Growth (since 2000): 0.2%; Density: 98.4 persons per square mile; Race: 60.2% White, 30.6% Black/African American, 0.9% Asian, 2.5% American Indian/Alaska Native, 0.1% Native Hawaiian/Other Pacific Islander, 2.1% two or more races, 5.9% Hispanic of any race; Average household size: 2.47; Median age: 38.7; Age under 18: 24.4%; Age 65 and over: 14.3%; Males per 100 females: 96.9; Marriage status: 32.5% never married, 47.6% now married, 4.4% separated, 8.4% widowed, 11.5% divorced; Foreign born: 4.2%; Speak English only: 93.2%; With disability: 20.4%; Veterans: 11.5%; Ancestry: 11.5% American, 7.3% Irish, 6.8% English, 6.5% German, 4.2% Scottish

Religion: Six largest groups: 25.2% Baptist, 14.2% Methodist/Pietist, 5.2% Pentecostal, 5.0% Non-denominational Protestant, 4.1% Presbyterian-Reformed, 0.7% Catholicism

Economy: Unemployment rate: 7.2%; Leading industries: 22.6% retail trade; 14.5% other services (except public administration); 11.7% health care and social assistance; Farms: 277 totaling 47,573 acres; Company size: 1 employs 1,000 or more persons, 0 employ 500 to 999 persons, 15 employ 100 to 499 persons, 830 employ less than 100 persons; Business ownership: 661 women-owned, n/a Black-owned, n/a Hispanic-owned, n/a Asian-owned

Employment: 9.0% management, business, and financial, 1.2% computer, engineering, and science, 10.6% education, legal, community service, arts, and media, 4.8% healthcare practitioners, 19.3% service, 22.3% sales and

office, 12.9% natural resources, construction, and maintenance, 19.8% production, transportation, and material moving
Income: Per capita: $17,236; Median household: $32,384; Average household: $42,891; Households with income of $100,000 or more: 7.6%; Poverty rate: 25.9%
Educational Attainment: High school diploma or higher: 80.1%; Bachelor's degree or higher: 12.4%; Graduate/professional degree or higher: 4.1%
Housing: Homeownership rate: 65.6%; Median home value: $77,500; Median year structure built: 1974; Homeowner vacancy rate: 1.9%; Median gross rent: $583 per month; Rental vacancy rate: 9.5%
Vital Statistics: Birth rate: 125.2 per 10,000 population; Death rate: 114.0 per 10,000 population; Age-adjusted cancer mortality rate: 221.2 deaths per 100,000 population
Health Insurance: 80.1% have insurance; 48.3% have private insurance; 42.6% have public insurance; 19.9% do not have insurance; 10.1% of children under 18 do not have insurance
Health Care: Physicians: 8.0 per 10,000 population; Hospital beds: 33.2 per 10,000 population; Hospital admissions: 1,330.8 per 10,000 population
Transportation: Commute: 95.5% car, 0.3% public transportation, 1.7% walk, 2.1% work from home; Median travel time to work: 19.8 minutes
Presidential Election: 51.0% Obama, 48.1% Romney (2012)
Additional Information Contacts
Richmond Government . . . . (910) 997-8200
  http://www.richmondnc.com

Richmond County Communities

CORDOVA (CDP). Covers a land area of 2.129 square miles and a water area of 0.021 square miles. Located at 34.91° N. Lat; 79.81° W. Long. Elevation is 285 feet.
Population: 1,775; Growth (since 2000): n/a; Density: 833.6 persons per square mile; Race: 82.6% White, 12.2% Black/African American, 1.2% Asian, 2.1% American Indian/Alaska Native, 0.1% Native Hawaiian/Other Pacific Islander, 1.2% Two or more races, 0.7% Hispanic of any race; Average household size: 2.52; Median age: 38.7; Age under 18: 23.6%; Age 65 and over: 12.8%; Males per 100 females: 92.1
Housing: Homeownership rate: 75.3%; Homeowner vacancy rate: 1.7%; Rental vacancy rate: 7.0%

DOBBINS HEIGHTS (town). Covers a land area of 0.882 square miles and a water area of 0 square miles. Located at 34.91° N. Lat; 79.69° W. Long. Elevation is 390 feet.
Population: 866; Growth (since 2000): -7.5%; Density: 982.0 persons per square mile; Race: 10.6% White, 84.6% Black/African American, 0.3% Asian, 1.2% American Indian/Alaska Native, 0.7% Native Hawaiian/Other Pacific Islander, 2.0% Two or more races, 1.6% Hispanic of any race; Average household size: 2.22; Median age: 41.4; Age under 18: 23.6%; Age 65 and over: 16.6%; Males per 100 females: 95.5
Housing: Homeownership rate: 57.2%; Homeowner vacancy rate: 2.2%; Rental vacancy rate: 6.2%

EAST ROCKINGHAM (CDP). Covers a land area of 3.407 square miles and a water area of 0.023 square miles. Located at 34.91° N. Lat; 79.77° W. Long. Elevation is 253 feet.
Population: 3,736; Growth (since 2000): -3.8%; Density: 1,096.5 persons per square mile; Race: 70.1% White, 16.8% Black/African American, 0.6% Asian, 3.5% American Indian/Alaska Native, 0.2% Native Hawaiian/Other Pacific Islander, 2.6% Two or more races, 10.6% Hispanic of any race; Average household size: 2.51; Median age: 37.6; Age under 18: 25.1%; Age 65 and over: 13.0%; Males per 100 females: 100.0; Marriage status: 33.5% never married, 44.2% now married, 4.7% separated, 6.9% widowed, 15.3% divorced; Foreign born: 8.9%; Speak English only: 83.9%; With disability: 19.5%; Veterans: 8.5%; Ancestry: 12.8% American, 9.5% Irish, 6.2% German, 3.4% English, 2.6% Scottish
Employment: 6.6% management, business, and financial, 2.9% computer, engineering, and science, 7.5% education, legal, community service, arts, and media, 1.6% healthcare practitioners, 22.2% service, 21.1% sales and office, 11.4% natural resources, construction, and maintenance, 27.0% production, transportation, and material moving
Income: Per capita: $16,009; Median household: $27,996; Average household: $38,424; Households with income of $100,000 or more: 3.4%; Poverty rate: 39.2%

Educational Attainment: High school diploma or higher: 73.8%; Bachelor's degree or higher: 13.7%; Graduate/professional degree or higher: 1.2%
Housing: Homeownership rate: 61.1%; Median home value: $47,500; Median year structure built: 1967; Homeowner vacancy rate: 2.5%; Median gross rent: $618 per month; Rental vacancy rate: 9.6%
Health Insurance: 72.9% have insurance; 40.7% have private insurance; 39.0% have public insurance; 27.1% do not have insurance; 25.0% of children under 18 do not have insurance
Transportation: Commute: 93.9% car, 0.0% public transportation, 2.2% walk, 3.2% work from home; Median travel time to work: 19.1 minutes

ELLERBE (town). Covers a land area of 1.475 square miles and a water area of 0.006 square miles. Located at 35.07° N. Lat; 79.76° W. Long. Elevation is 538 feet.
Population: 1,054; Growth (since 2000): 3.2%; Density: 714.4 persons per square mile; Race: 48.5% White, 39.1% Black/African American, 0.5% Asian, 0.7% American Indian/Alaska Native, 0.0% Native Hawaiian/Other Pacific Islander, 2.8% Two or more races, 11.1% Hispanic of any race; Average household size: 2.47; Median age: 36.6; Age under 18: 27.9%; Age 65 and over: 14.5%; Males per 100 females: 86.2
School District(s)
Richmond County Schools (PK-12)
  2012-13 Enrollment: 7,870 . . . . (910) 582-5860
Housing: Homeownership rate: 57.9%; Homeowner vacancy rate: 3.1%; Rental vacancy rate: 12.7%

HAMLET (city). Covers a land area of 5.264 square miles and a water area of 0.089 square miles. Located at 34.89° N. Lat; 79.71° W. Long. Elevation is 299 feet.
History: Once had 42 passenger trains per day. National Railroad Museum.
Population: 6,495; Growth (since 2000): 7.9%; Density: 1,233.9 persons per square mile; Race: 55.2% White, 36.6% Black/African American, 0.7% Asian, 1.7% American Indian/Alaska Native, 0.0% Native Hawaiian/Other Pacific Islander, 2.0% Two or more races, 6.2% Hispanic of any race; Average household size: 2.49; Median age: 37.0; Age under 18: 26.9%; Age 65 and over: 15.8%; Males per 100 females: 85.7; Marriage status: 31.6% never married, 45.9% now married, 3.0% separated, 10.4% widowed, 12.1% divorced; Foreign born: 3.6%; Speak English only: 96.2%; With disability: 24.6%; Veterans: 12.5%; Ancestry: 11.3% American, 11.0% English, 7.4% Irish, 5.8% German, 5.8% Scotch-Irish
Employment: 5.8% management, business, and financial, 0.8% computer, engineering, and science, 10.3% education, legal, community service, arts, and media, 6.8% healthcare practitioners, 16.1% service, 27.8% sales and office, 7.7% natural resources, construction, and maintenance, 24.7% production, transportation, and material moving
Income: Per capita: $17,413; Median household: $35,252; Average household: $46,729; Households with income of $100,000 or more: 10.7%; Poverty rate: 24.9%
Educational Attainment: High school diploma or higher: 79.4%; Bachelor's degree or higher: 11.9%; Graduate/professional degree or higher: 3.4%
School District(s)
Richmond County Schools (PK-12)
  2012-13 Enrollment: 7,870 . . . . (910) 582-5860
Scotland County Schools (PK-12)
  2012-13 Enrollment: 6,276 . . . . (910) 276-1138
Two-year College(s)
Richmond Community College (Public)
  Fall 2013 Enrollment: 2,664 . . . . (910) 410-1700
  2013-14 Tuition: In-state $2,366; Out-of-state $8,510
Housing: Homeownership rate: 57.8%; Median home value: $92,100; Median year structure built: 1966; Homeowner vacancy rate: 2.7%; Median gross rent: $594 per month; Rental vacancy rate: 7.6%
Health Insurance: 79.7% have insurance; 44.5% have private insurance; 46.4% have public insurance; 20.3% do not have insurance; 9.1% of children under 18 do not have insurance
Hospitals: Sandhills Regional Medical Center (64 beds)
Safety: Violent crime rate: 74.0 per 10,000 population; Property crime rate: 484.5 per 10,000 population
Transportation: Commute: 97.1% car, 1.5% public transportation, 0.4% walk, 0.6% work from home; Median travel time to work: 18.7 minutes; Amtrak: Train service available.

Additional Information Contacts
City of Hamlet . . . . (910) 895-9058
   http://www.hamletnc.us

HOFFMAN (town). Covers a land area of 3.402 square miles and a
water area of 0 square miles. Located at 35.03° N. Lat; 79.55° W. Long.
Elevation is 427 feet.
Population: 588; Growth (since 2000): -5.8%; Density: 172.9 persons per
square mile; Race: 37.2% White, 56.3% Black/African American, 0.7%
Asian, 4.1% American Indian/Alaska Native, 0.0% Native Hawaiian/Other
Pacific Islander, 1.2% Two or more races, 2.7% Hispanic of any race;
Average household size: 2.75; Median age: 36.4; Age under 18: 26.5%;
Age 65 and over: 11.2%; Males per 100 females: 91.5
Housing: Homeownership rate: 75.0%; Homeowner vacancy rate: 2.4%;
Rental vacancy rate: 3.6%

NORMAN (town). Covers a land area of 0.568 square miles and a
water area of 0 square miles. Located at 35.17° N. Lat; 79.72° W. Long.
Elevation is 623 feet.
Population: 138; Growth (since 2000): 91.7%; Density: 243.1 persons per
square mile; Race: 59.4% White, 19.6% Black/African American, 0.0%
Asian, 5.8% American Indian/Alaska Native, 0.0% Native Hawaiian/Other
Pacific Islander, 0.7% Two or more races, 23.9% Hispanic of any race;
Average household size: 2.56; Median age: 40.5; Age under 18: 24.6%;
Age 65 and over: 11.6%; Males per 100 females: 89.0
Housing: Homeownership rate: 59.3%; Homeowner vacancy rate: 3.0%;
Rental vacancy rate: 18.5%

ROCKINGHAM (city). County seat. Covers a land area of 7.663
square miles and a water area of 0.029 square miles. Located at 34.94° N.
Lat; 79.76° W. Long. Elevation is 282 feet.
History: Rockingham was established in 1785 and named for the Marquis
of Rockingham, who befriended the Colony before the Revolutionary War.
Population: 9,558; Growth (since 2000): -1.2%; Density: 1,247.2 persons
per square mile; Race: 57.4% White, 34.1% Black/African American, 2.1%
Asian, 1.7% American Indian/Alaska Native, 0.0% Native Hawaiian/Other
Pacific Islander, 1.9% Two or more races, 5.1% Hispanic of any race;
Average household size: 2.30; Median age: 38.2; Age under 18: 25.4%;
Age 65 and over: 16.2%; Males per 100 females: 87.0; Marriage status:
33.7% never married, 49.8% now married, 6.2% separated, 8.3%
widowed, 8.3% divorced; Foreign born: 3.9%; Speak English only: 93.7%;
With disability: 18.0%; Veterans: 9.6%; Ancestry: 10.5% American, 6.5%
English, 6.0% German, 5.5% Irish, 4.9% Scotch-Irish
Employment: 12.0% management, business, and financial, 0.8%
computer, engineering, and science, 17.6% education, legal, community
service, arts, and media, 3.3% healthcare practitioners, 19.3% service,
20.0% sales and office, 10.3% natural resources, construction, and
maintenance, 16.7% production, transportation, and material moving
Income: Per capita: $17,767; Median household: $30,638; Average
household: $41,766; Households with income of $100,000 or more: 8.8%;
Poverty rate: 28.1%
Educational Attainment: High school diploma or higher: 81.6%;
Bachelor's degree or higher: 16.8%; Graduate/professional degree or
higher: 7.4%

School District(s)
Nc Dept of Juvenile Justice (KG-12)
   2012-13 Enrollment: n/a . . . . (919) 733-3388
Richmond County Schools (PK-12)
   2012-13 Enrollment: 7,870 . . . . (910) 582-5860
Housing: Homeownership rate: 51.3%; Median home value: $91,200;
Median year structure built: 1967; Homeowner vacancy rate: 3.3%; Median
gross rent: $517 per month; Rental vacancy rate: 11.2%
Health Insurance: 83.7% have insurance; 52.1% have private insurance;
42.3% have public insurance; 16.3% do not have insurance; 8.1% of
children under 18 do not have insurance
Safety: Violent crime rate: 39.0 per 10,000 population; Property crime rate:
1,006.3 per 10,000 population
Newspapers: Richmond County Daily Journal (daily circulation 8000)
Transportation: Commute: 96.1% car, 0.0% public transportation, 0.7%
walk, 2.5% work from home; Median travel time to work: 16.2 minutes
Airports: Richmond County (general aviation)
Additional Information Contacts
City of Rockingham . . . . (609) 683-7132
   http://rockingham.net

Robeson County

Located in southern North Carolina; bounded on the south by South
Carolina; coastal plains area, drained by the Lumber River. Covers a land
area of 949.221 square miles, a water area of 1.766 square miles, and is
located in the Eastern Time Zone at 34.64° N. Lat., 79.10° W. Long. The
county was founded in 1786. County seat is Lumberton.

Robeson County is part of the Lumberton, NC Micropolitan Statistical Area.
The entire metro area includes: Robeson County, NC

Weather Station: Lumberton   Elevation: 111 feet

	Jan	Feb	Mar	Apr	May	Jun	Jul	Aug	Sep	Oct	Nov	Dec
High	53	57	65	74	81	88	90	89	83	74	66	57
Low	31	33	39	47	56	65	69	68	61	49	41	34
Precip	3.8	3.5	3.8	3.2	3.7	4.8	5.6	5.7	4.6	3.4	3.1	3.2
Snow	0.1	0.3	0.8	0.0	0.0	0.0	0.0	0.0	0.0	0.0	0.0	tr

High and Low temperatures in degrees Fahrenheit; Precipitation and Snow in inches

Population: 134,168; Growth (since 2000): 8.8%; Density: 141.3 persons
per square mile; Race: 29.0% White, 24.3% Black/African American, 0.7%
Asian, 38.4% American Indian/Alaska Native, 0.1% Native Hawaiian/Other
Pacific Islander, 2.5% two or more races, 8.1% Hispanic of any race;
Average household size: 2.71; Median age: 34.4; Age under 18: 26.8%;
Age 65 and over: 11.2%; Males per 100 females: 94.7; Marriage status:
38.8% never married, 44.0% now married, 4.9% separated, 7.4%
widowed, 9.8% divorced; Foreign born: 5.6%; Speak English only: 91.2%;
With disability: 17.4%; Veterans: 7.6%; Ancestry: 11.5% American, 3.7%
English, 2.8% Irish, 2.2% German, 1.4% Scotch-Irish
Religion: Six largest groups: 24.0% Baptist, 8.2% Methodist/Pietist, 4.9%
Pentecostal, 3.0% Non-denominational Protestant, 1.8%
Presbyterian-Reformed, 1.1% Catholicism
Economy: Unemployment rate: 8.0%; Leading industries: 21.4% retail
trade; 15.7% health care and social assistance; 11.4% other services
(except public administration); Farms: 941 totaling 265,546 acres;
Company size: 2 employ 1,000 or more persons, 3 employ 500 to 999
persons, 41 employs 100 to 499 persons, 1,793 employ less than 100
persons; Business ownership: 2,671 women-owned, 1,236 Black-owned,
n/a Hispanic-owned, 168 Asian-owned
Employment: 8.7% management, business, and financial, 1.1% computer,
engineering, and science, 11.1% education, legal, community service, arts,
and media, 4.8% healthcare practitioners, 20.2% service, 19.5% sales and
office, 14.5% natural resources, construction, and maintenance, 20.0%
production, transportation, and material moving
Income: Per capita: $15,343; Median household: $29,806; Average
household: $42,420; Households with income of $100,000 or more: 7.2%;
Poverty rate: 31.7%
Educational Attainment: High school diploma or higher: 71.5%;
Bachelor's degree or higher: 12.5%; Graduate/professional degree or
higher: 3.7%
Housing: Homeownership rate: 65.3%; Median home value: $66,800;
Median year structure built: 1983; Homeowner vacancy rate: 1.3%; Median
gross rent: $592 per month; Rental vacancy rate: 9.5%
Vital Statistics: Birth rate: 136.5 per 10,000 population; Death rate: 92.9
per 10,000 population; Age-adjusted cancer mortality rate: 197.4 deaths
per 100,000 population
Health Insurance: 77.1% have insurance; 40.9% have private insurance;
44.5% have public insurance; 22.9% do not have insurance; 7.7% of
children under 18 do not have insurance
Health Care: Physicians: 9.5 per 10,000 population; Hospital beds: 27.6
per 10,000 population; Hospital admissions: 1,067.7 per 10,000 population
Air Quality Index: 86.3% good, 13.7% moderate, 0.0% unhealthy for
sensitive individuals, 0.0% unhealthy (percent of days)
Transportation: Commute: 95.4% car, 0.1% public transportation, 1.9%
walk, 1.5% work from home; Median travel time to work: 23.0 minutes
Presidential Election: 58.2% Obama, 40.8% Romney (2012)
Additional Information Contacts
Robeson Government . . . . (910) 671-3000
   http://www.co.robeson.nc.us

Robeson County Communities

BARKER TEN MILE (CDP). Covers a land area of 2.278 square miles and a water area of 0 square miles. Located at 34.68° N. Lat; 78.99° W. Long. Elevation is 138 feet.
Population: 952; Growth (since 2000): -2.5%; Density: 417.9 persons per square mile; Race: 68.7% White, 12.2% Black/African American, 2.1% Asian, 14.6% American Indian/Alaska Native, 0.0% Native Hawaiian/Other Pacific Islander, 1.6% Two or more races, 2.0% Hispanic of any race; Average household size: 2.53; Median age: 47.3; Age under 18: 20.6%; Age 65 and over: 17.0%; Males per 100 females: 93.9
Housing: Homeownership rate: 90.7%; Homeowner vacancy rate: 1.4%; Rental vacancy rate: 5.4%

ELROD (CDP). Covers a land area of 5.338 square miles and a water area of 0 square miles. Located at 34.61° N. Lat; 79.23° W. Long. Elevation is 161 feet.
Population: 417; Growth (since 2000): -5.4%; Density: 78.1 persons per square mile; Race: 12.2% White, 14.1% Black/African American, 0.0% Asian, 68.3% American Indian/Alaska Native, 0.0% Native Hawaiian/Other Pacific Islander, 4.3% Two or more races, 2.6% Hispanic of any race; Average household size: 2.61; Median age: 41.6; Age under 18: 23.5%; Age 65 and over: 11.0%; Males per 100 females: 91.3
Housing: Homeownership rate: 69.4%; Homeowner vacancy rate: 0.0%; Rental vacancy rate: 23.4%

FAIRMONT (town). Covers a land area of 2.762 square miles and a water area of 0.005 square miles. Located at 34.49° N. Lat; 79.11° W. Long. Elevation is 125 feet.
Population: 2,663; Growth (since 2000): 2.3%; Density: 964.3 persons per square mile; Race: 26.2% White, 56.1% Black/African American, 0.2% Asian, 13.4% American Indian/Alaska Native, 0.0% Native Hawaiian/Other Pacific Islander, 2.7% Two or more races, 1.9% Hispanic of any race; Average household size: 2.34; Median age: 42.5; Age under 18: 25.9%; Age 65 and over: 20.4%; Males per 100 females: 79.3; Marriage status: 40.0% never married, 41.4% now married, 4.8% separated, 8.4% widowed, 10.3% divorced; Foreign born: 4.5%; Speak English only: 95.7%; With disability: 15.4%; Veterans: 9.6%; Ancestry: 4.6% English, 4.2% Scotch-Irish, 3.9% German, 3.9% African, 2.5% American
Employment: 3.8% management, business, and financial, 2.3% computer, engineering, and science, 21.1% education, legal, community service, arts, and media, 6.8% healthcare practitioners, 26.2% service, 17.9% sales and office, 5.8% natural resources, construction, and maintenance, 16.1% production, transportation, and material moving
Income: Per capita: $14,159; Median household: $21,484; Average household: $34,971; Households with income of $100,000 or more: 5.9%; Poverty rate: 49.6%
Educational Attainment: High school diploma or higher: 78.9%; Bachelor's degree or higher: 19.3%; Graduate/professional degree or higher: 5.1%
School District(s)
Robeson County Schools (PK-12)
    2012-13 Enrollment: 24,651 . . . . (910) 671-6000
Housing: Homeownership rate: 49.7%; Median home value: $69,900; Median year structure built: 1968; Homeowner vacancy rate: 3.2%; Median gross rent: $286 per month; Rental vacancy rate: 6.1%
Health Insurance: 82.8% have insurance; 38.5% have private insurance; 54.9% have public insurance; 17.2% do not have insurance; 6.8% of children under 18 do not have insurance
Safety: Violent crime rate: 81.1 per 10,000 population; Property crime rate: 755.3 per 10,000 population
Transportation: Commute: 95.9% car, 0.0% public transportation, 2.7% walk, 1.4% work from home; Median travel time to work: 20.8 minutes

LUMBER BRIDGE (town). Covers a land area of 0.670 square miles and a water area of 0.005 square miles. Located at 34.89° N. Lat; 79.07° W. Long. Elevation is 194 feet.
Population: 94; Growth (since 2000): -20.3%; Density: 140.3 persons per square mile; Race: 75.5% White, 16.0% Black/African American, 1.1% Asian, 4.3% American Indian/Alaska Native, 0.0% Native Hawaiian/Other Pacific Islander, 0.0% Two or more races, 3.2% Hispanic of any race; Average household size: 2.09; Median age: 51.0; Age under 18: 11.7%; Age 65 and over: 20.2%; Males per 100 females: 108.9

School District(s)
Hoke County Schools (PK-12)
    2012-13 Enrollment: 8,404 . . . . (910) 875-4106
Housing: Homeownership rate: 84.5%; Homeowner vacancy rate: 0.0%; Rental vacancy rate: 0.0%

LUMBERTON (city). County seat. Covers a land area of 17.893 square miles and a water area of 0.079 square miles. Located at 34.63° N. Lat; 79.02° W. Long. Elevation is 128 feet.
History: Seat of Pembroke State University to west at Pembroke. Founded 1787, Incorporated 1852.
Population: 21,542; Growth (since 2000): 3.6%; Density: 1,203.9 persons per square mile; Race: 40.8% White, 37.2% Black/African American, 2.4% Asian, 13.1% American Indian/Alaska Native, 0.2% Native Hawaiian/Other Pacific Islander, 2.7% Two or more races, 6.7% Hispanic of any race; Average household size: 2.44; Median age: 36.5; Age under 18: 24.8%; Age 65 and over: 14.6%; Males per 100 females: 93.3; Marriage status: 38.6% never married, 41.4% now married, 4.9% separated, 8.4% widowed, 11.6% divorced; Foreign born: 8.5%; Speak English only: 87.9%; With disability: 16.0%; Veterans: 8.0%; Ancestry: 21.0% American, 6.6% English, 3.6% German, 3.1% Irish, 2.2% Scotch-Irish
Employment: 10.7% management, business, and financial, 1.9% computer, engineering, and science, 13.3% education, legal, community service, arts, and media, 6.7% healthcare practitioners, 18.4% service, 21.5% sales and office, 10.2% natural resources, construction, and maintenance, 17.2% production, transportation, and material moving
Income: Per capita: $18,918; Median household: $30,990; Average household: $50,721; Households with income of $100,000 or more: 11.4%; Poverty rate: 31.3%
Educational Attainment: High school diploma or higher: 72.2%; Bachelor's degree or higher: 18.4%; Graduate/professional degree or higher: 6.7%
School District(s)
Cis Academy (06-08)
    2012-13 Enrollment: 107 . . . . (910) 521-1669
Robeson County Schools (PK-12)
    2012-13 Enrollment: 24,651 . . . . (910) 671-6000
Two-year College(s)
Robeson Community College (Public)
    Fall 2013 Enrollment: 2,260 . . . . (910) 272-3700
    2013-14 Tuition: In-state $2,368; Out-of-state $8,512
Housing: Homeownership rate: 48.3%; Median home value: $100,500; Median year structure built: 1973; Homeowner vacancy rate: 2.4%; Median gross rent: $640 per month; Rental vacancy rate: 7.8%
Health Insurance: 80.3% have insurance; 43.8% have private insurance; 46.3% have public insurance; 19.7% do not have insurance; 5.1% of children under 18 do not have insurance
Hospitals: Southeastern Regional Medical Center (403 beds)
Safety: Violent crime rate: 175.5 per 10,000 population; Property crime rate: 1,398.7 per 10,000 population
Newspapers: The Robesonian (daily circulation 12600)
Transportation: Commute: 95.3% car, 0.3% public transportation, 1.3% walk, 0.8% work from home; Median travel time to work: 19.3 minutes
Additional Information Contacts
City of Lumberton . . . . (910) 671-3800
    http://www.ci.lumberton.nc.us

MARIETTA (town). Covers a land area of 1.117 square miles and a water area of 0 square miles. Located at 34.37° N. Lat; 79.12° W. Long. Elevation is 92 feet.
Population: 175; Growth (since 2000): 6.7%; Density: 156.6 persons per square mile; Race: 42.3% White, 56.6% Black/African American, 0.0% Asian, 0.0% American Indian/Alaska Native, 0.0% Native Hawaiian/Other Pacific Islander, 1.1% Two or more races, 0.0% Hispanic of any race; Average household size: 2.69; Median age: 48.1; Age under 18: 22.3%; Age 65 and over: 16.0%; Males per 100 females: 92.3
Housing: Homeownership rate: 81.5%; Homeowner vacancy rate: 0.0%; Rental vacancy rate: 14.3%

MAXTON (town). Covers a land area of 2.700 square miles and a water area of 0 square miles. Located at 34.74° N. Lat; 79.35° W. Long. Elevation is 194 feet.
History: Maxton was settled by Highland Scots.
Population: 2,426; Growth (since 2000): -4.9%; Density: 898.6 persons per square mile; Race: 19.2% White, 65.0% Black/African American, 0.1%

Asian, 13.8% American Indian/Alaska Native, 0.0% Native Hawaiian/Other Pacific Islander, 1.2% Two or more races, 1.8% Hispanic of any race; Average household size: 2.47; Median age: 37.3; Age under 18: 27.7%; Age 65 and over: 13.6%; Males per 100 females: 78.8

School District(s)
Robeson County Schools (PK-12)
   2012-13 Enrollment: 24,651 . . . . (910) 671-6000
Housing: Homeownership rate: 50.6%; Homeowner vacancy rate: 3.8%; Rental vacancy rate: 9.0%
Airports: Laurinburg-Maxton (general aviation)

MCDONALD (town). Covers a land area of 0.255 square miles and a water area of 0 square miles. Located at 34.55° N. Lat; 79.18° W. Long. Elevation is 148 feet.
Population: 113; Growth (since 2000): -5.0%; Density: 443.0 persons per square mile; Race: 40.7% White, 16.8% Black/African American, 0.0% Asian, 39.8% American Indian/Alaska Native, 0.0% Native Hawaiian/Other Pacific Islander, 1.8% Two or more races, 0.0% Hispanic of any race; Average household size: 2.63; Median age: 40.9; Age under 18: 25.7%; Age 65 and over: 15.9%; Males per 100 females: 82.3
Housing: Homeownership rate: 90.7%; Homeowner vacancy rate: 0.0%; Rental vacancy rate: 0.0%

ORRUM (town). Covers a land area of 0.478 square miles and a water area of 0 square miles. Located at 34.47° N. Lat; 79.01° W. Long. Elevation is 102 feet.
Population: 91; Growth (since 2000): 15.2%; Density: 190.3 persons per square mile; Race: 58.2% White, 26.4% Black/African American, 0.0% Asian, 5.5% American Indian/Alaska Native, 0.0% Native Hawaiian/Other Pacific Islander, 0.0% Two or more races, 14.3% Hispanic of any race; Average household size: 2.33; Median age: 45.8; Age under 18: 19.8%; Age 65 and over: 18.7%; Males per 100 females: 111.6

School District(s)
Robeson County Schools (PK-12)
   2012-13 Enrollment: 24,651 . . . . (910) 671-6000
Housing: Homeownership rate: 71.8%; Homeowner vacancy rate: 3.4%; Rental vacancy rate: 8.3%

PARKTON (town). Covers a land area of 0.679 square miles and a water area of 0 square miles. Located at 34.90° N. Lat; 79.01° W. Long. Elevation is 187 feet.
Population: 436; Growth (since 2000): 1.9%; Density: 642.2 persons per square mile; Race: 72.2% White, 15.1% Black/African American, 0.7% Asian, 5.5% American Indian/Alaska Native, 0.0% Native Hawaiian/Other Pacific Islander, 0.9% Two or more races, 7.1% Hispanic of any race; Average household size: 2.56; Median age: 41.3; Age under 18: 24.1%; Age 65 and over: 17.2%; Males per 100 females: 81.7

School District(s)
Robeson County Schools (PK-12)
   2012-13 Enrollment: 24,651 . . . . (910) 671-6000
Housing: Homeownership rate: 83.6%; Homeowner vacancy rate: 5.3%; Rental vacancy rate: 17.6%

PEMBROKE (town). Covers a land area of 2.866 square miles and a water area of 0 square miles. Located at 34.68° N. Lat; 79.19° W. Long. Elevation is 171 feet.
History: Pembroke was named for the Earl of Pembroke, though it was once known as Scuffletown.
Population: 2,973; Growth (since 2000): 23.9%; Density: 1,037.2 persons per square mile; Race: 16.4% White, 12.3% Black/African American, 0.6% Asian, 66.4% American Indian/Alaska Native, 0.2% Native Hawaiian/Other Pacific Islander, 3.4% Two or more races, 2.2% Hispanic of any race; Average household size: 2.52; Median age: 24.8; Age under 18: 25.7%; Age 65 and over: 11.5%; Males per 100 females: 82.6; Marriage status: 57.9% never married, 24.5% now married, 6.8% separated, 8.5% widowed, 9.2% divorced; Foreign born: 0.2%; Speak English only: 99.3%; With disability: 16.3%; Veterans: 7.8%; Ancestry: 5.3% Irish, 2.9% American, 2.4% German, 2.4% Scotch-Irish, 0.9% Czech
Employment: 6.4% management, business, and financial, 1.0% computer, engineering, and science, 19.3% education, legal, community service, arts, and media, 1.9% healthcare practitioners, 40.4% service, 12.6% sales and office, 9.5% natural resources, construction, and maintenance, 8.8% production, transportation, and material moving

Income: Per capita: $12,227; Median household: $17,489; Average household: $30,034; Households with income of $100,000 or more: 5.0%; Poverty rate: 56.6%
Educational Attainment: High school diploma or higher: 77.9%; Bachelor's degree or higher: 15.7%; Graduate/professional degree or higher: 2.0%

School District(s)
Robeson County Schools (PK-12)
   2012-13 Enrollment: 24,651 . . . . (910) 671-6000
Four-year College(s)
University of North Carolina at Pembroke (Public)
   Fall 2013 Enrollment: 6,222 . . . . (910) 521-6000
   2013-14 Tuition: In-state $5,144; Out-of-state $14,351
Housing: Homeownership rate: 28.4%; Median home value: $68,900; Median year structure built: 1975; Homeowner vacancy rate: 2.1%; Median gross rent: $517 per month; Rental vacancy rate: 9.5%
Health Insurance: 80.7% have insurance; 37.7% have private insurance; 49.5% have public insurance; 19.3% do not have insurance; 12.1% of children under 18 do not have insurance
Transportation: Commute: 94.4% car, 0.0% public transportation, 5.0% walk, 0.0% work from home; Median travel time to work: 19.1 minutes
Additional Information Contacts
Town of Pembroke . . . . (910) 521-9758
   http://www.pembrokenc.com

PROCTORVILLE (town). Covers a land area of 0.454 square miles and a water area of 0 square miles. Located at 34.48° N. Lat; 79.04° W. Long. Elevation is 115 feet.
Population: 117; Growth (since 2000): -12.0%; Density: 257.8 persons per square mile; Race: 73.5% White, 18.8% Black/African American, 0.0% Asian, 5.1% American Indian/Alaska Native, 0.0% Native Hawaiian/Other Pacific Islander, 2.6% Two or more races, 0.0% Hispanic of any race; Average household size: 2.39; Median age: 51.5; Age under 18: 16.2%; Age 65 and over: 20.5%; Males per 100 females: 91.8
Housing: Homeownership rate: 79.6%; Homeowner vacancy rate: 0.0%; Rental vacancy rate: 16.7%

PROSPECT (CDP). Covers a land area of 3.928 square miles and a water area of 0 square miles. Located at 34.74° N. Lat; 79.23° W. Long. Elevation is 190 feet.
Population: 981; Growth (since 2000): 42.2%; Density: 249.7 persons per square mile; Race: 3.9% White, 0.9% Black/African American, 0.0% Asian, 93.1% American Indian/Alaska Native, 0.0% Native Hawaiian/Other Pacific Islander, 1.3% Two or more races, 1.4% Hispanic of any race; Average household size: 2.84; Median age: 36.4; Age under 18: 26.8%; Age 65 and over: 10.5%; Males per 100 females: 98.6
Housing: Homeownership rate: 85.5%; Homeowner vacancy rate: 0.0%; Rental vacancy rate: 16.7%

RAEMON (CDP). Covers a land area of 4.311 square miles and a water area of 0.028 square miles. Located at 34.62° N. Lat; 79.34° W. Long. Elevation is 167 feet.
Population: 282; Growth (since 2000): 33.0%; Density: 65.4 persons per square mile; Race: 15.6% White, 5.3% Black/African American, 0.0% Asian, 78.7% American Indian/Alaska Native, 0.0% Native Hawaiian/Other Pacific Islander, 0.4% Two or more races, 0.0% Hispanic of any race; Average household size: 2.74; Median age: 34.0; Age under 18: 27.7%; Age 65 and over: 9.6%; Males per 100 females: 86.8
Housing: Homeownership rate: 74.8%; Homeowner vacancy rate: 0.0%; Rental vacancy rate: 12.9%

RAYNHAM (town). Covers a land area of 0.122 square miles and a water area of 0 square miles. Located at 34.58° N. Lat; 79.19° W. Long. Elevation is 148 feet.
Population: 72; Growth (since 2000): 7.5%; Density: 591.6 persons per square mile; Race: 52.8% White, 18.1% Black/African American, 6.9% Asian, 18.1% American Indian/Alaska Native, 0.0% Native Hawaiian/Other Pacific Islander, 0.0% Two or more races, 4.2% Hispanic of any race; Average household size: 2.57; Median age: 38.3; Age under 18: 29.2%; Age 65 and over: 11.1%; Males per 100 females: 71.4
Housing: Homeownership rate: 78.5%; Homeowner vacancy rate: 0.0%; Rental vacancy rate: 0.0%

RED SPRINGS (town). Covers a land area of 3.500 square miles and a water area of 0.169 square miles. Located at 34.81° N. Lat; 79.18° W. Long. Elevation is 203 feet.

History: Red Springs grew up at the site of a medicinal spring whose sulphur water was colored by a red pigment. The town was built on land granted to "Sailor" Hector McNeill in 1775. By 1850 it was a recognizable community known as Dora. The General Assembly authorized the change of name to Red Springs in 1885.

Population: 3,428; Growth (since 2000): -1.9%; Density: 979.3 persons per square mile; Race: 32.2% White, 48.8% Black/African American, 0.4% Asian, 12.5% American Indian/Alaska Native, 0.0% Native Hawaiian/Other Pacific Islander, 2.5% Two or more races, 6.4% Hispanic of any race; Average household size: 2.42; Median age: 38.5; Age under 18: 26.3%; Age 65 and over: 17.1%; Males per 100 females: 82.4; Marriage status: 35.5% never married, 40.5% now married, 4.7% separated, 11.2% widowed, 12.9% divorced; Foreign born: 12.2%; Speak English only: 79.7%; With disability: 19.1%; Veterans: 4.6%; Ancestry: 3.3% Scotch-Irish, 3.3% Scottish, 2.9% Other Subsaharan African, 2.8% American, 2.7% German

Employment: 14.7% management, business, and financial, 0.0% computer, engineering, and science, 15.8% education, legal, community service, arts, and media, 1.7% healthcare practitioners, 18.2% service, 9.0% sales and office, 6.2% natural resources, construction, and maintenance, 34.4% production, transportation, and material moving

Income: Per capita: $13,639; Median household: $22,202; Average household: $35,051; Households with income of $100,000 or more: 5.5%; Poverty rate: 58.3%

Educational Attainment: High school diploma or higher: 70.7%; Bachelor's degree or higher: 16.7%; Graduate/professional degree or higher: 6.0%

School District(s)
Hoke County Schools (PK-12)
    2012-13 Enrollment: 8,404 . . . . (910) 875-4106
Robeson County Schools (PK-12)
    2012-13 Enrollment: 24,651 . . . . (910) 671-6000

Housing: Homeownership rate: 57.0%; Median home value: $74,800; Median year structure built: 1962; Homeowner vacancy rate: 3.4%; Median gross rent: $400 per month; Rental vacancy rate: 14.4%

Health Insurance: 82.0% have insurance; 34.9% have private insurance; 55.7% have public insurance; 18.0% do not have insurance; 7.8% of children under 18 do not have insurance

Safety: Violent crime rate: 77.8 per 10,000 population; Property crime rate: 945.5 per 10,000 population

Newspapers: Red Springs Citizen (weekly circulation 2600)

Transportation: Commute: 96.3% car, 0.0% public transportation, 3.7% walk, 0.0% work from home; Median travel time to work: 20.9 minutes

Additional Information Contacts
Town of Red Springs. . . . . (910) 843-5241
    http://www.redsprings.org

RENNERT (town). Covers a land area of 1.103 square miles and a water area of 0 square miles. Located at 34.81° N. Lat; 79.08° W. Long. Elevation is 184 feet.

Population: 383; Growth (since 2000): 35.3%; Density: 347.3 persons per square mile; Race: 15.1% White, 27.7% Black/African American, 0.3% Asian, 43.3% American Indian/Alaska Native, 0.0% Native Hawaiian/Other Pacific Islander, 4.2% Two or more races, 24.3% Hispanic of any race; Average household size: 3.14; Median age: 31.2; Age under 18: 28.2%; Age 65 and over: 10.2%; Males per 100 females: 112.8

Housing: Homeownership rate: 59.9%; Homeowner vacancy rate: 0.0%; Rental vacancy rate: 21.0%

REX (CDP). Covers a land area of 0.742 square miles and a water area of 0 square miles. Located at 34.85° N. Lat; 79.05° W. Long. Elevation is 190 feet.

Population: 55; Growth (since 2000): 0.0%; Density: 74.1 persons per square mile; Race: 58.2% White, 7.3% Black/African American, 0.0% Asian, 27.3% American Indian/Alaska Native, 0.0% Native Hawaiian/Other Pacific Islander, 1.8% Two or more races, 5.5% Hispanic of any race; Average household size: 1.83; Median age: 49.5; Age under 18: 12.7%; Age 65 and over: 14.5%; Males per 100 females: 129.2

Housing: Homeownership rate: 70.0%; Homeowner vacancy rate: 0.0%; Rental vacancy rate: 18.2%

ROWLAND (town). Covers a land area of 1.052 square miles and a water area of 0 square miles. Located at 34.54° N. Lat; 79.29° W. Long. Elevation is 148 feet.

History: Rowland was named for a pioneer family.

Population: 1,037; Growth (since 2000): -9.5%; Density: 985.5 persons per square mile; Race: 21.0% White, 70.3% Black/African American, 0.0% Asian, 6.4% American Indian/Alaska Native, 0.0% Native Hawaiian/Other Pacific Islander, 1.7% Two or more races, 1.6% Hispanic of any race; Average household size: 2.24; Median age: 44.8; Age under 18: 21.1%; Age 65 and over: 21.4%; Males per 100 females: 85.5

School District(s)
Robeson County Schools (PK-12)
    2012-13 Enrollment: 24,651 . . . . (910) 671-6000

Housing: Homeownership rate: 56.8%; Homeowner vacancy rate: 3.2%; Rental vacancy rate: 12.4%

Safety: Violent crime rate: 38.0 per 10,000 population; Property crime rate: 437.3 per 10,000 population

SAINT PAULS (town). Covers a land area of 1.083 square miles and a water area of 0 square miles. Located at 34.81° N. Lat; 78.97° W. Long. Elevation is 167 feet.

Population: 2,035; Growth (since 2000): -4.8%; Density: 1,878.2 persons per square mile; Race: 53.7% White, 19.1% Black/African American, 0.2% Asian, 5.8% American Indian/Alaska Native, 0.1% Native Hawaiian/Other Pacific Islander, 3.4% Two or more races, 25.1% Hispanic of any race; Average household size: 2.55; Median age: 36.7; Age under 18: 25.4%; Age 65 and over: 14.7%; Males per 100 females: 101.7

School District(s)
Robeson County Schools (PK-12)
    2012-13 Enrollment: 24,651 . . . . (910) 671-6000

Housing: Homeownership rate: 55.2%; Homeowner vacancy rate: 0.9%; Rental vacancy rate: 6.9%

Safety: Violent crime rate: 32.8 per 10,000 population; Property crime rate: 323.8 per 10,000 population

Newspapers: St. Pauls Review (weekly circulation 3200)

SHANNON (CDP). Covers a land area of 1.022 square miles and a water area of 0 square miles. Located at 34.85° N. Lat; 79.14° W. Long. Elevation is 200 feet.

Population: 263; Growth (since 2000): 33.5%; Density: 257.5 persons per square mile; Race: 20.9% White, 25.5% Black/African American, 0.0% Asian, 40.7% American Indian/Alaska Native, 0.0% Native Hawaiian/Other Pacific Islander, 0.0% Two or more races, 26.2% Hispanic of any race; Average household size: 3.06; Median age: 30.1; Age under 18: 33.1%; Age 65 and over: 8.7%; Males per 100 females: 94.8

School District(s)
Robeson County Schools (PK-12)
    2012-13 Enrollment: 24,651 . . . . (910) 671-6000

Housing: Homeownership rate: 63.9%; Homeowner vacancy rate: 0.0%; Rental vacancy rate: 6.1%

WAKULLA (CDP). Covers a land area of 0.860 square miles and a water area of 0 square miles. Located at 34.80° N. Lat; 79.26° W. Long. Elevation is 210 feet.

Population: 105; Growth (since 2000): n/a; Density: 122.1 persons per square mile; Race: 12.4% White, 1.0% Black/African American, 0.0% Asian, 86.7% American Indian/Alaska Native, 0.0% Native Hawaiian/Other Pacific Islander, 0.0% Two or more races, 3.8% Hispanic of any race; Average household size: 2.63; Median age: 38.8; Age under 18: 26.7%; Age 65 and over: 6.7%; Males per 100 females: 75.0

Housing: Homeownership rate: 82.5%; Homeowner vacancy rate: 2.9%; Rental vacancy rate: 0.0%

Rockingham County

Located in northern North Carolina; bounded on the north by Virginia; piedmont area, drained by the Dan and Haw Rivers. Covers a land area of 565.551 square miles, a water area of 7.154 square miles, and is located in the Eastern Time Zone at 36.38° N. Lat., 79.78° W. Long. The county was founded in 1785. County seat is Wentworth.

Rockingham County is part of the Greensboro-High Point, NC Metropolitan Statistical Area. The entire metro area includes: Guilford County, NC; Randolph County, NC; Rockingham County, NC

Weather Station: Reidsville 2 NW   Elevation: 890 feet

	Jan	Feb	Mar	Apr	May	Jun	Jul	Aug	Sep	Oct	Nov	Dec
High	48	51	59	69	77	84	88	86	80	70	60	51
Low	28	30	37	46	54	63	67	65	58	47	39	31
Precip	3.8	3.3	4.3	3.9	3.7	4.0	4.7	3.9	4.0	3.4	3.5	3.3
Snow	3.2	3.2	0.9	tr	0.0	0.0	0.0	0.0	0.0	0.0	tr	0.7

High and Low temperatures in degrees Fahrenheit; Precipitation and Snow in inches

Population: 93,643; Growth (since 2000): 1.9%; Density: 165.6 persons per square mile; Race: 75.7% White, 18.9% Black/African American, 0.5% Asian, 0.4% American Indian/Alaska Native, 0.1% Native Hawaiian/Other Pacific Islander, 1.8% two or more races, 5.5% Hispanic of any race; Average household size: 2.39; Median age: 42.2; Age under 18: 22.2%; Age 65 and over: 16.2%; Males per 100 females: 93.2; Marriage status: 25.6% never married, 54.8% now married, 4.5% separated, 7.9% widowed, 11.7% divorced; Foreign born: 3.7%; Speak English only: 94.3%; With disability: 17.9%; Veterans: 9.4%; Ancestry: 15.4% American, 10.7% English, 8.6% Irish, 7.3% German, 2.4% European
Religion: Six largest groups: 18.7% Baptist, 8.1% Methodist/Pietist, 5.8% Non-denominational Protestant, 2.3% Pentecostal, 1.7% Holiness, 1.6% Presbyterian-Reformed
Economy: Unemployment rate: 6.1%; Leading industries: 18.9% retail trade; 13.5% other services (except public administration); 10.9% construction; Farms: 902 totaling 112,166 acres; Company size: 0 employ 1,000 or more persons, 3 employ 500 to 999 persons, 34 employ 100 to 499 persons, 1,663 employ less than 100 persons; Business ownership: 1,503 women-owned, 565 Black-owned, 76 Hispanic-owned, n/a Asian-owned
Employment: 9.3% management, business, and financial, 3.2% computer, engineering, and science, 6.7% education, legal, community service, arts, and media, 5.8% healthcare practitioners, 17.7% service, 23.3% sales and office, 12.7% natural resources, construction, and maintenance, 21.4% production, transportation, and material moving
Income: Per capita: $21,102; Median household: $38,567; Average household: $50,623; Households with income of $100,000 or more: 10.2%; Poverty rate: 17.9%
Educational Attainment: High school diploma or higher: 79.0%; Bachelor's degree or higher: 12.9%; Graduate/professional degree or higher: 3.4%
Housing: Homeownership rate: 69.8%; Median home value: $102,900; Median year structure built: 1974; Homeowner vacancy rate: 2.4%; Median gross rent: $596 per month; Rental vacancy rate: 12.1%
Vital Statistics: Birth rate: 96.3 per 10,000 population; Death rate: 118.9 per 10,000 population; Age-adjusted cancer mortality rate: 189.4 deaths per 100,000 population
Health Insurance: 85.7% have insurance; 61.3% have private insurance; 38.4% have public insurance; 14.3% do not have insurance; 5.4% of children under 18 do not have insurance
Health Care: Physicians: 9.2 per 10,000 population; Hospital beds: 23.0 per 10,000 population; Hospital admissions: 655.1 per 10,000 population
Air Quality Index: 96.3% good, 3.7% moderate, 0.0% unhealthy for sensitive individuals, 0.0% unhealthy (percent of days)
Transportation: Commute: 96.2% car, 0.1% public transportation, 0.6% walk, 2.5% work from home; Median travel time to work: 26.4 minutes
Presidential Election: 38.9% Obama, 60.0% Romney (2012)
National and State Parks: Haw River State Park
Additional Information Contacts
Rockingham Government . . . . (336) 342-8100
  http://www.co.rockingham.nc.us

Rockingham County Communities

EDEN (city). Covers a land area of 13.470 square miles and a water area of 0.161 square miles. Located at 36.50° N. Lat; 79.74° W. Long. Elevation is 594 feet.
Population: 15,527; Growth (since 2000): -2.4%; Density: 1,152.7 persons per square mile; Race: 71.2% White, 23.8% Black/African American, 0.7% Asian, 0.4% American Indian/Alaska Native, 0.2% Native Hawaiian/Other Pacific Islander, 1.9% Two or more races, 4.8% Hispanic of any race; Average household size: 2.29; Median age: 41.2; Age under 18: 22.9%; Age 65 and over: 18.1%; Males per 100 females: 84.2; Marriage status: 30.6% never married, 43.8% now married, 5.9% separated, 9.0% widowed, 16.6% divorced; Foreign born: 3.8%; Speak English only: 94.6%; With disability: 19.9%; Veterans: 10.7%; Ancestry: 12.9% American, 9.6% English, 8.2% Irish, 4.4% German, 2.9% European

Employment: 5.5% management, business, and financial, 3.2% computer, engineering, and science, 6.1% education, legal, community service, arts, and media, 6.3% healthcare practitioners, 24.6% service, 20.6% sales and office, 9.6% natural resources, construction, and maintenance, 24.1% production, transportation, and material moving
Income: Per capita: $17,517; Median household: $31,575; Average household: $39,926; Households with income of $100,000 or more: 5.6%; Poverty rate: 26.0%
Educational Attainment: High school diploma or higher: 78.5%; Bachelor's degree or higher: 12.7%; Graduate/professional degree or higher: 5.2%
School District(s)
Rockingham County Schools (PK-12)
  2012-13 Enrollment: 13,604 . . . . (336) 627-2600
Housing: Homeownership rate: 56.9%; Median home value: $82,500; Median year structure built: 1961; Homeowner vacancy rate: 3.9%; Median gross rent: $611 per month; Rental vacancy rate: 14.0%
Health Insurance: 81.0% have insurance; 52.7% have private insurance; 41.7% have public insurance; 19.0% do not have insurance; 10.0% of children under 18 do not have insurance
Hospitals: Morehead Memorial Hospital (108 beds)
Safety: Violent crime rate: 37.3 per 10,000 population; Property crime rate: 412.3 per 10,000 population
Transportation: Commute: 96.1% car, 0.0% public transportation, 1.1% walk, 1.2% work from home; Median travel time to work: 23.2 minutes
Additional Information Contacts
City of Eden . . . . (336) 623-3336
  http://www.ci.eden.nc.us

MADISON (town). Covers a land area of 3.540 square miles and a water area of 0.017 square miles. Located at 36.39° N. Lat; 79.98° W. Long. Elevation is 614 feet.
History: Madison was laid out in 1818 by Randolph Duke Scales and named for President James Madison, who had relatives living nearby on Mayo River.
Population: 2,246; Growth (since 2000): -0.7%; Density: 634.5 persons per square mile; Race: 65.1% White, 29.2% Black/African American, 0.1% Asian, 0.6% American Indian/Alaska Native, 0.0% Native Hawaiian/Other Pacific Islander, 2.6% Two or more races, 5.1% Hispanic of any race; Average household size: 2.24; Median age: 44.4; Age under 18: 20.4%; Age 65 and over: 17.7%; Males per 100 females: 90.7
School District(s)
Rockingham County Schools (PK-12)
  2012-13 Enrollment: 13,604 . . . . (336) 627-2600
Housing: Homeownership rate: 58.0%; Homeowner vacancy rate: 4.1%; Rental vacancy rate: 11.3%
Safety: Violent crime rate: 13.6 per 10,000 population; Property crime rate: 451.7 per 10,000 population

MAYODAN (town). Covers a land area of 2.876 square miles and a water area of 0.021 square miles. Located at 36.42° N. Lat; 79.97° W. Long. Elevation is 630 feet.
History: Mayodan is named for the Mayo and Dan Rivers.
Population: 2,478; Growth (since 2000): 2.5%; Density: 861.6 persons per square mile; Race: 85.8% White, 10.3% Black/African American, 0.2% Asian, 0.4% American Indian/Alaska Native, 0.1% Native Hawaiian/Other Pacific Islander, 1.5% Two or more races, 4.0% Hispanic of any race; Average household size: 2.11; Median age: 43.8; Age under 18: 20.5%; Age 65 and over: 21.4%; Males per 100 females: 87.2
School District(s)
Rockingham County Schools (PK-12)
  2012-13 Enrollment: 13,604 . . . . (336) 627-2600
Housing: Homeownership rate: 53.6%; Homeowner vacancy rate: 3.1%; Rental vacancy rate: 13.2%
Safety: Violent crime rate: 44.5 per 10,000 population; Property crime rate: 1,048.2 per 10,000 population
Additional Information Contacts
Town of Mayodan . . . . (336) 427-0241
  http://www.townofmayodan.com

REIDSVILLE (city). Covers a land area of 15.047 square miles and a water area of 1.482 square miles. Located at 36.34° N. Lat; 79.68° W. Long. Elevation is 804 feet.
History: Reidsville grew out of a settlement which began in 1815 when Reuben Reid and his family purchased a farm and built their home on the

Danville-Salisbury road. The village was named for Reuben's son, David S. Reid, governor of North Carolina and United States senator.

Population: 14,520; Growth (since 2000): 0.2%; Density: 965.0 persons per square mile; Race: 52.4% White, 41.9% Black/African American, 0.6% Asian, 0.3% American Indian/Alaska Native, 0.0% Native Hawaiian/Other Pacific Islander, 2.1% Two or more races, 4.7% Hispanic of any race; Average household size: 2.27; Median age: 41.7; Age under 18: 22.1%; Age 65 and over: 17.8%; Males per 100 females: 82.5; Marriage status: 27.1% never married, 51.3% now married, 7.1% separated, 9.5% widowed, 12.1% divorced; Foreign born: 2.8%; Speak English only: 97.0%; With disability: 20.1%; Veterans: 9.8%; Ancestry: 9.8% English, 8.6% American, 7.0% Irish, 6.3% German, 2.8% European

Employment: 8.6% management, business, and financial, 2.7% computer, engineering, and science, 6.7% education, legal, community service, arts, and media, 3.5% healthcare practitioners, 17.0% service, 26.8% sales and office, 10.4% natural resources, construction, and maintenance, 24.3% production, transportation, and material moving

Income: Per capita: $21,177; Median household: $37,120; Average household: $46,840; Households with income of $100,000 or more: 6.9%; Poverty rate: 19.3%

Educational Attainment: High school diploma or higher: 84.8%; Bachelor's degree or higher: 16.3%; Graduate/professional degree or higher: 5.0%

School District(s)
Bethany Community Middle (06-08)
    2012-13 Enrollment: 221. . . . . (336) 951-2500
Caswell County Schools (PK-12)
    2012-13 Enrollment: 2,874 . . . . (336) 694-4116
Rockingham County Schools (PK-12)
    2012-13 Enrollment: 13,604 . . . . (336) 627-2600

Housing: Homeownership rate: 51.7%; Median home value: $112,100; Median year structure built: 1964; Homeowner vacancy rate: 4.0%; Median gross rent: $623 per month; Rental vacancy rate: 12.2%

Health Insurance: 90.6% have insurance; 65.3% have private insurance; 43.3% have public insurance; 9.4% do not have insurance; 0.6% of children under 18 do not have insurance

Safety: Violent crime rate: 37.1 per 10,000 population; Property crime rate: 642.6 per 10,000 population

Newspapers: Madison Messenger (weekly circulation 7300); Reidsville Review (weekly circulation 3300)

Transportation: Commute: 95.7% car, 0.2% public transportation, 0.7% walk, 3.3% work from home; Median travel time to work: 21.7 minutes

Airports: Rockingham County Nc Shiloh (general aviation)

Additional Information Contacts
City of Reidsville . . . . (336) 349-1030
    http://www.ci.reidsville.nc.us

RUFFIN (CDP). Covers a land area of 4.524 square miles and a water area of 0.017 square miles. Located at 36.44° N. Lat; 79.53° W. Long. Elevation is 712 feet.

Population: 368; Growth (since 2000): n/a; Density: 81.3 persons per square mile; Race: 82.9% White, 13.9% Black/African American, 0.3% Asian, 1.1% American Indian/Alaska Native, 0.0% Native Hawaiian/Other Pacific Islander, 0.3% Two or more races, 1.6% Hispanic of any race; Average household size: 2.27; Median age: 40.9; Age under 18: 22.6%; Age 65 and over: 12.5%; Males per 100 females: 92.7

School District(s)
Rockingham County Schools (PK-12)
    2012-13 Enrollment: 13,604 . . . . (336) 627-2600

Housing: Homeownership rate: 73.5%; Homeowner vacancy rate: 1.6%; Rental vacancy rate: 14.0%

STONEVILLE (town). Covers a land area of 1.292 square miles and a water area of 0 square miles. Located at 36.47° N. Lat; 79.91° W. Long. Elevation is 823 feet.

Population: 1,056; Growth (since 2000): 5.4%; Density: 817.1 persons per square mile; Race: 78.6% White, 16.2% Black/African American, 0.3% Asian, 0.2% American Indian/Alaska Native, 0.1% Native Hawaiian/Other Pacific Islander, 2.7% Two or more races, 3.8% Hispanic of any race; Average household size: 2.28; Median age: 42.6; Age under 18: 22.1%; Age 65 and over: 20.2%; Males per 100 females: 86.2

School District(s)
Rockingham County Schools (PK-12)
    2012-13 Enrollment: 13,604 . . . . (336) 627-2600

Housing: Homeownership rate: 69.4%; Homeowner vacancy rate: 3.3%; Rental vacancy rate: 10.1%

Additional Information Contacts
Town of Stoneville . . . . (336) 573-9393
    http://www.town.stoneville.nc.us

WENTWORTH (town). County seat. Covers a land area of 14.186 square miles and a water area of 0.065 square miles. Located at 36.40° N. Lat; 79.75° W. Long. Elevation is 735 feet.

Population: 2,807; Growth (since 2000): 1.0%; Density: 197.9 persons per square mile; Race: 82.5% White, 14.4% Black/African American, 0.3% Asian, 0.1% American Indian/Alaska Native, 0.0% Native Hawaiian/Other Pacific Islander, 1.3% Two or more races, 3.6% Hispanic of any race; Average household size: 2.55; Median age: 41.6; Age under 18: 22.0%; Age 65 and over: 13.9%; Males per 100 females: 106.5; Marriage status: 28.0% never married, 57.8% now married, 3.8% separated, 3.6% widowed, 10.7% divorced; Foreign born: 2.1%; Speak English only: 97.5%; With disability: 17.7%; Veterans: 10.0%; Ancestry: 16.1% English, 15.5% American, 14.9% Irish, 9.7% German, 4.6% Scottish

Employment: 7.6% management, business, and financial, 2.3% computer, engineering, and science, 9.8% education, legal, community service, arts, and media, 11.7% healthcare practitioners, 12.7% service, 23.5% sales and office, 11.5% natural resources, construction, and maintenance, 20.8% production, transportation, and material moving

Income: Per capita: $22,741; Median household: $54,412; Average household: $62,704; Households with income of $100,000 or more: 13.7%; Poverty rate: 11.2%

Educational Attainment: High school diploma or higher: 74.8%; Bachelor's degree or higher: 14.1%; Graduate/professional degree or higher: 3.9%

School District(s)
Rockingham County Schools (PK-12)
    2012-13 Enrollment: 13,604 . . . . (336) 627-2600

Two-year College(s)
Rockingham Community College (Public)
    Fall 2013 Enrollment: 1,854 . . . . (336) 342-4261
    2013-14 Tuition: In-state $1,832; Out-of-state $6,428

Housing: Homeownership rate: 82.2%; Median home value: $122,300; Median year structure built: 1977; Homeowner vacancy rate: 1.8%; Median gross rent: $592 per month; Rental vacancy rate: 8.8%

Health Insurance: 86.9% have insurance; 70.7% have private insurance; 29.3% have public insurance; 13.1% do not have insurance; 5.5% of children under 18 do not have insurance

Transportation: Commute: 97.1% car, 0.0% public transportation, 0.0% walk, 2.7% work from home; Median travel time to work: 26.7 minutes

Rowan County

Located in west central North Carolina; piedmont area, bounded on the east by the Yadkin River, and on the north by the South Yadkin River. Covers a land area of 511.374 square miles, a water area of 12.351 square miles, and is located in the Eastern Time Zone at 35.64° N. Lat., 80.53° W. Long. The county was founded in 1753. County seat is Salisbury.

Rowan County is part of the Charlotte-Concord-Gastonia, NC-SC Metropolitan Statistical Area. The entire metro area includes: Cabarrus County, NC; Gaston County, NC; Iredell County, NC; Lincoln County, NC; Mecklenburg County, NC; Rowan County, NC; Union County, NC; Chester County, SC; Lancaster County, SC; York County, SC

Weather Station: Salisbury										Elevation: 700 feet		
	Jan	Feb	Mar	Apr	May	Jun	Jul	Aug	Sep	Oct	Nov	Dec
High	51	56	64	73	80	87	89	88	82	72	63	53
Low	29	32	39	47	55	64	68	67	60	48	39	31
Precip	3.0	3.5	4.2	3.6	3.1	4.0	3.8	3.1	3.5	3.3	3.0	3.1
Snow	2.1	0.9	0.2	0.0	0.0	0.0	0.0	0.0	0.0	0.0	tr	0.3

High and Low temperatures in degrees Fahrenheit; Precipitation and Snow in inches

Weather Station: Salisbury 9 WNW										Elevation: 825 feet		
	Jan	Feb	Mar	Apr	May	Jun	Jul	Aug	Sep	Oct	Nov	Dec
High	49	53	61	70	77	85	88	87	80	71	62	52
Low	27	29	36	45	54	63	67	66	58	45	36	28
Precip	3.4	3.4	4.2	3.7	3.1	4.0	3.3	4.0	3.8	3.3	3.3	3.3
Snow	1.9	1.5	0.4	tr	0.0	0.0	0.0	0.0	0.0	0.0	0.1	0.4

High and Low temperatures in degrees Fahrenheit; Precipitation and Snow in inches

Population: 138,428; Growth (since 2000): 6.2%; Density: 270.7 persons per square mile; Race: 76.5% White, 16.2% Black/African American, 1.0% Asian, 0.3% American Indian/Alaska Native, 0.0% Native Hawaiian/Other Pacific Islander, 1.6% two or more races, 7.7% Hispanic of any race; Average household size: 2.52; Median age: 39.1; Age under 18: 23.8%; Age 65 and over: 14.4%; Males per 100 females: 97.6; Marriage status: 27.5% never married, 53.5% now married, 3.1% separated, 7.4% widowed, 11.6% divorced; Foreign born: 5.3%; Speak English only: 91.2%; With disability: 15.7%; Veterans: 9.8%; Ancestry: 18.5% American, 15.2% German, 7.7% Irish, 7.3% English, 3.7% Scotch-Irish
Religion: Six largest groups: 15.9% Baptist, 8.4% Methodist/Pietist, 7.8% Lutheran, 5.3% Non-denominational Protestant, 3.9% Presbyterian-Reformed, 1.7% Catholicism
Economy: Unemployment rate: 5.6%; Leading industries: 15.9% retail trade; 12.5% other services (except public administration); 10.3% health care and social assistance; Farms: 1,011 totaling 121,145 acres; Company size: 4 employ 1,000 or more persons, 2 employ 500 to 999 persons, 45 employ 100 to 499 persons, 2,496 employ less than 100 persons; Business ownership: 3,229 women-owned, 699 Black-owned, 334 Hispanic-owned, 205 Asian-owned
Employment: 10.0% management, business, and financial, 3.0% computer, engineering, and science, 10.0% education, legal, community service, arts, and media, 5.2% healthcare practitioners, 18.2% service, 22.9% sales and office, 12.6% natural resources, construction, and maintenance, 18.2% production, transportation, and material moving
Income: Per capita: $20,912; Median household: $41,495; Average household: $53,720; Households with income of $100,000 or more: 12.1%; Poverty rate: 18.8%
Educational Attainment: High school diploma or higher: 81.0%; Bachelor's degree or higher: 17.0%; Graduate/professional degree or higher: 5.4%
Housing: Homeownership rate: 69.6%; Median home value: $130,200; Median year structure built: 1978; Homeowner vacancy rate: 2.4%; Median gross rent: $698 per month; Rental vacancy rate: 12.1%
Vital Statistics: Birth rate: 109.7 per 10,000 population; Death rate: 105.9 per 10,000 population; Age-adjusted cancer mortality rate: 194.8 deaths per 100,000 population
Health Insurance: 82.4% have insurance; 58.5% have private insurance; 35.8% have public insurance; 17.6% do not have insurance; 8.5% of children under 18 do not have insurance
Health Care: Physicians: 11.7 per 10,000 population; Hospital beds: 26.6 per 10,000 population; Hospital admissions: 765.5 per 10,000 population
Air Quality Index: 80.0% good, 20.0% moderate, 0.0% unhealthy for sensitive individuals, 0.0% unhealthy (percent of days)
Transportation: Commute: 94.2% car, 0.5% public transportation, 1.0% walk, 3.3% work from home; Median travel time to work: 23.4 minutes
Presidential Election: 36.3% Obama, 62.2% Romney (2012)
Additional Information Contacts
Rowan Government . . . . (704) 636-0361
    http://www.rowancountync.gov

Rowan County Communities

CHINA GROVE (town). Covers a land area of 2.124 square miles and a water area of 0 square miles. Located at 35.57° N. Lat; 80.58° W. Long. Elevation is 827 feet.
Population: 3,563; Growth (since 2000): -1.5%; Density: 1,677.6 persons per square mile; Race: 81.4% White, 7.4% Black/African American, 2.2% Asian, 0.6% American Indian/Alaska Native, 0.0% Native Hawaiian/Other Pacific Islander, 1.5% Two or more races, 9.9% Hispanic of any race; Average household size: 2.54; Median age: 37.9; Age under 18: 23.6%; Age 65 and over: 12.4%; Males per 100 females: 96.6; Marriage status: 27.7% never married, 54.3% now married, 4.5% separated, 7.2% widowed, 10.8% divorced; Foreign born: 10.4%; Speak English only: 82.0%; With disability: 16.4%; Veterans: 12.5%; Ancestry: 10.4% German, 8.8% Irish, 6.7% English, 5.9% Italian, 4.2% American
Employment: 11.6% management, business, and financial, 1.2% computer, engineering, and science, 2.3% education, legal, community service, arts, and media, 7.3% healthcare practitioners, 22.7% service, 17.8% sales and office, 17.1% natural resources, construction, and maintenance, 19.9% production, transportation, and material moving
Income: Per capita: $17,316; Median household: $32,708; Average household: $46,267; Households with income of $100,000 or more: 11.2%; Poverty rate: 27.2%

Educational Attainment: High school diploma or higher: 75.4%; Bachelor's degree or higher: 6.0%; Graduate/professional degree or higher: 4.0%
School District(s)
Rowan-Salisbury Schools (PK-12)
    2012-13 Enrollment: 20,165 . . . . (704) 636-7500
Housing: Homeownership rate: 66.0%; Median home value: $110,200; Median year structure built: 1963; Homeowner vacancy rate: 2.9%; Median gross rent: $691 per month; Rental vacancy rate: 9.8%
Health Insurance: 77.1% have insurance; 43.3% have private insurance; 39.0% have public insurance; 22.9% do not have insurance; 2.7% of children under 18 do not have insurance
Transportation: Commute: 97.0% car, 0.0% public transportation, 0.9% walk, 0.1% work from home; Median travel time to work: 23.6 minutes
Additional Information Contacts
Town of China Grove . . . . (704) 857-2466
    http://www.chinagrovenc.gov

CLEVELAND (town). Covers a land area of 1.550 square miles and a water area of 0 square miles. Located at 35.73° N. Lat; 80.68° W. Long. Elevation is 810 feet.
Population: 871; Growth (since 2000): 7.8%; Density: 561.9 persons per square mile; Race: 66.9% White, 24.1% Black/African American, 2.1% Asian, 0.2% American Indian/Alaska Native, 0.0% Native Hawaiian/Other Pacific Islander, 3.6% Two or more races, 6.5% Hispanic of any race; Average household size: 2.66; Median age: 34.8; Age under 18: 28.4%; Age 65 and over: 11.7%; Males per 100 females: 95.3
School District(s)
Iredell-Statesville Schools (PK-12)
    2012-13 Enrollment: 21,400 . . . . (704) 872-8931
Rowan-Salisbury Schools (PK-12)
    2012-13 Enrollment: 20,165 . . . . (704) 636-7500
Housing: Homeownership rate: 77.1%; Homeowner vacancy rate: 0.8%; Rental vacancy rate: 31.2%
Safety: Violent crime rate: 23.0 per 10,000 population; Property crime rate: 275.9 per 10,000 population

EAST SPENCER (town). Covers a land area of 1.600 square miles and a water area of 0 square miles. Located at 35.68° N. Lat; 80.43° W. Long. Elevation is 715 feet.
Population: 1,534; Growth (since 2000): -12.6%; Density: 958.8 persons per square mile; Race: 11.7% White, 83.5% Black/African American, 0.0% Asian, 0.6% American Indian/Alaska Native, 0.0% Native Hawaiian/Other Pacific Islander, 2.8% Two or more races, 2.4% Hispanic of any race; Average household size: 2.42; Median age: 36.0; Age under 18: 28.7%; Age 65 and over: 13.8%; Males per 100 females: 83.1
Housing: Homeownership rate: 39.0%; Homeowner vacancy rate: 7.3%; Rental vacancy rate: 15.4%

ENOCHVILLE (CDP). Covers a land area of 4.406 square miles and a water area of 0.234 square miles. Located at 35.52° N. Lat; 80.67° W. Long. Elevation is 860 feet.
Population: 2,925; Growth (since 2000): 2.6%; Density: 663.8 persons per square mile; Race: 93.6% White, 1.3% Black/African American, 0.8% Asian, 0.1% American Indian/Alaska Native, 0.0% Native Hawaiian/Other Pacific Islander, 0.8% Two or more races, 5.9% Hispanic of any race; Average household size: 2.52; Median age: 42.2; Age under 18: 21.4%; Age 65 and over: 18.4%; Males per 100 females: 92.8; Marriage status: 16.3% never married, 61.5% now married, 0.9% separated, 12.1% widowed, 10.1% divorced; Foreign born: 2.6%; Speak English only: 96.0%; With disability: 16.5%; Veterans: 12.4%; Ancestry: 16.6% German, 16.1% American, 9.0% Irish, 9.0% English, 3.5% Scotch-Irish
Employment: 13.7% management, business, and financial, 4.5% computer, engineering, and science, 9.7% education, legal, community service, arts, and media, 8.3% healthcare practitioners, 15.3% service, 19.6% sales and office, 19.5% natural resources, construction, and maintenance, 9.3% production, transportation, and material moving
Income: Per capita: $24,626; Median household: $44,444; Average household: $52,699; Households with income of $100,000 or more: 15.5%; Poverty rate: 11.0%
Educational Attainment: High school diploma or higher: 78.6%; Bachelor's degree or higher: 12.0%; Graduate/professional degree or higher: 3.3%

Housing: Homeownership rate: 78.6%; Median home value: $116,000; Median year structure built: 1967; Homeowner vacancy rate: 2.2%; Median gross rent: $759 per month; Rental vacancy rate: 6.4%
Health Insurance: 76.1% have insurance; 62.5% have private insurance; 30.3% have public insurance; 23.9% do not have insurance; 18.5% of children under 18 do not have insurance
Transportation: Commute: 93.0% car, 0.0% public transportation, 1.5% walk, 5.1% work from home; Median travel time to work: 23.0 minutes

FAITH (town).
Covers a land area of 1.074 square miles and a water area of 0 square miles. Located at 35.59° N. Lat; 80.46° W. Long. Elevation is 863 feet.
Population: 807; Growth (since 2000): 16.1%; Density: 751.6 persons per square mile; Race: 96.2% White, 1.6% Black/African American, 0.0% Asian, 0.0% American Indian/Alaska Native, 0.0% Native Hawaiian/Other Pacific Islander, 0.5% Two or more races, 2.7% Hispanic of any race; Average household size: 2.45; Median age: 41.4; Age under 18: 23.5%; Age 65 and over: 15.5%; Males per 100 females: 105.3
School District(s)
Rowan-Salisbury Schools (PK-12)
    2012-13 Enrollment: 20,165 . . . . (704) 636-7500
Housing: Homeownership rate: 77.8%; Homeowner vacancy rate: 1.5%; Rental vacancy rate: 5.2%

GOLD HILL (unincorporated postal area)
ZCTA: 28071
    Covers a land area of 45.588 square miles and a water area of 0.049 square miles. Located at 35.52° N. Lat; 80.32° W. Long. Elevation is 771 feet.
    Population: 2,802; Growth (since 2000): -4.7%; Density: 61.5 persons per square mile; Race: 96.7% White, 0.9% Black/African American, 0.1% Asian, 0.6% American Indian/Alaska Native, 0.0% Native Hawaiian/Other Pacific Islander, 1.1% Two or more races, 1.4% Hispanic of any race; Average household size: 2.58; Median age: 42.1; Age under 18: 23.9%; Age 65 and over: 13.8%; Males per 100 females: 102.3; Marriage status: 22.9% never married, 63.6% now married, 1.1% separated, 6.7% widowed, 6.8% divorced; Foreign born: 0.8%; Speak English only: 97.2%; With disability: 23.5%; Veterans: 11.7%; Ancestry: 17.5% German, 16.8% English, 14.0% American, 8.0% Irish, 6.1% Scotch-Irish
    Employment: 15.4% management, business, and financial, 1.2% computer, engineering, and science, 10.5% education, legal, community service, arts, and media, 2.3% healthcare practitioners, 9.9% service, 19.2% sales and office, 12.2% natural resources, construction, and maintenance, 29.3% production, transportation, and material moving
    Income: Per capita: $31,479; Median household: $46,823; Average household: $85,833; Households with income of $100,000 or more: 16.2%; Poverty rate: 17.6%
    Educational Attainment: High school diploma or higher: 78.6%; Bachelor's degree or higher: 12.6%; Graduate/professional degree or higher: 5.1%
School District(s)
Rowan-Salisbury Schools (PK-12)
    2012-13 Enrollment: 20,165 . . . . (704) 636-7500
    Housing: Homeownership rate: 81.9%; Median home value: $116,000; Median year structure built: 1980; Homeowner vacancy rate: 1.1%; Median gross rent: $861 per month; Rental vacancy rate: 13.6%
    Health Insurance: 86.4% have insurance; 65.8% have private insurance; 33.7% have public insurance; 13.6% do not have insurance; 0.0% of children under 18 do not have insurance
    Transportation: Commute: 94.0% car, 0.0% public transportation, 0.0% walk, 4.5% work from home; Median travel time to work: 28.6 minutes

GRANITE QUARRY (town).
Covers a land area of 2.867 square miles and a water area of 0 square miles. Located at 35.61° N. Lat; 80.45° W. Long. Elevation is 801 feet.
Population: 2,930; Growth (since 2000): 34.7%; Density: 1,022.1 persons per square mile; Race: 87.5% White, 8.3% Black/African American, 1.1% Asian, 0.2% American Indian/Alaska Native, 0.0% Native Hawaiian/Other Pacific Islander, 1.1% Two or more races, 4.0% Hispanic of any race; Average household size: 2.55; Median age: 38.1; Age under 18: 25.5%; Age 65 and over: 13.4%; Males per 100 females: 94.4; Marriage status: 23.2% never married, 59.8% now married, 0.8% separated, 4.9% widowed, 12.1% divorced; Foreign born: 2.4%; Speak English only: 97.6%;

With disability: 13.1%; Veterans: 11.4%; Ancestry: 33.2% German, 16.0% American, 12.7% Irish, 8.5% English, 5.1% Italian
Employment: 13.5% management, business, and financial, 4.8% computer, engineering, and science, 9.8% education, legal, community service, arts, and media, 7.0% healthcare practitioners, 15.5% service, 27.7% sales and office, 7.3% natural resources, construction, and maintenance, 14.4% production, transportation, and material moving
Income: Per capita: $21,157; Median household: $47,557; Average household: $55,657; Households with income of $100,000 or more: 12.2%; Poverty rate: 16.3%
Educational Attainment: High school diploma or higher: 91.1%; Bachelor's degree or higher: 26.4%; Graduate/professional degree or higher: 5.0%
School District(s)
Rowan-Salisbury Schools (PK-12)
    2012-13 Enrollment: 20,165 . . . . (704) 636-7500
Housing: Homeownership rate: 71.1%; Median home value: $145,400; Median year structure built: 1981; Homeowner vacancy rate: 1.9%; Median gross rent: $767 per month; Rental vacancy rate: 7.7%
Health Insurance: 85.7% have insurance; 63.0% have private insurance; 32.6% have public insurance; 14.3% do not have insurance; 3.5% of children under 18 do not have insurance
Transportation: Commute: 88.7% car, 3.0% public transportation, 0.0% walk, 6.7% work from home; Median travel time to work: 25.5 minutes

LANDIS (town).
Covers a land area of 3.489 square miles and a water area of 0.092 square miles. Located at 35.55° N. Lat; 80.61° W. Long. Elevation is 869 feet.
Population: 3,109; Growth (since 2000): 3.8%; Density: 891.2 persons per square mile; Race: 91.9% White, 3.2% Black/African American, 0.5% Asian, 0.5% American Indian/Alaska Native, 0.0% Native Hawaiian/Other Pacific Islander, 0.8% Two or more races, 7.8% Hispanic of any race; Average household size: 2.45; Median age: 39.6; Age under 18: 22.4%; Age 65 and over: 17.6%; Males per 100 females: 94.3; Marriage status: 21.7% never married, 47.9% now married, 3.1% separated, 14.9% widowed, 15.5% divorced; Foreign born: 13.0%; Speak English only: 81.4%; With disability: 13.8%; Veterans: 6.9%; Ancestry: 18.6% German, 11.7% American, 9.5% Scotch-Irish, 8.2% English, 5.7% Irish
Employment: 11.8% management, business, and financial, 2.9% computer, engineering, and science, 2.2% education, legal, community service, arts, and media, 4.9% healthcare practitioners, 13.6% service, 28.8% sales and office, 19.1% natural resources, construction, and maintenance, 16.7% production, transportation, and material moving
Income: Per capita: $22,317; Median household: $38,937; Average household: $47,315; Households with income of $100,000 or more: 13.3%; Poverty rate: 19.9%
Educational Attainment: High school diploma or higher: 88.9%; Bachelor's degree or higher: 15.4%; Graduate/professional degree or higher: 0.7%
School District(s)
Rowan-Salisbury Schools (PK-12)
    2012-13 Enrollment: 20,165 . . . . (704) 636-7500
Housing: Homeownership rate: 74.4%; Median home value: $121,800; Median year structure built: 1971; Homeowner vacancy rate: 3.4%; Median gross rent: $841 per month; Rental vacancy rate: 9.4%
Health Insurance: 76.3% have insurance; 58.2% have private insurance; 33.2% have public insurance; 23.7% do not have insurance; 7.8% of children under 18 do not have insurance
Transportation: Commute: 95.4% car, 0.0% public transportation, 0.0% walk, 4.6% work from home; Median travel time to work: 28.1 minutes

MOUNT ULLA (unincorporated postal area)
ZCTA: 28125
    Covers a land area of 38.465 square miles and a water area of 0.041 square miles. Located at 35.66° N. Lat; 80.70° W. Long. Elevation is 823 feet.
    Population: 2,525; Growth (since 2000): 30.2%; Density: 65.6 persons per square mile; Race: 95.8% White, 2.1% Black/African American, 0.1% Asian, 0.1% American Indian/Alaska Native, 0.0% Native Hawaiian/Other Pacific Islander, 0.9% Two or more races, 1.9% Hispanic of any race; Average household size: 2.56; Median age: 41.9; Age under 18: 22.9%; Age 65 and over: 14.9%; Males per 100 females: 104.0; Marriage status: 22.4% never married, 57.3% now married, 2.5% separated, 8.3% widowed, 12.0% divorced; Foreign born: 1.2%; Speak English only: 98.9%; With disability: 6.3%; Veterans: 8.7%; Ancestry:

28.9% American, 14.0% German, 12.0% English, 5.0% Irish, 3.7% Scottish

Employment: 15.9% management, business, and financial, 2.8% computer, engineering, and science, 14.3% education, legal, community service, arts, and media, 6.6% healthcare practitioners, 15.1% service, 21.2% sales and office, 15.7% natural resources, construction, and maintenance, 8.3% production, transportation, and material moving

Income: Per capita: $28,210; Median household: $48,750; Average household: $69,065; Households with income of $100,000 or more: 21.8%; Poverty rate: 3.5%

Educational Attainment: High school diploma or higher: 90.3%; Bachelor's degree or higher: 29.2%; Graduate/professional degree or higher: 7.2%

School District(s)
Rowan-Salisbury Schools (PK-12)
   2012-13 Enrollment: 20,165 . . . . (704) 636-7500
  Housing: Homeownership rate: 81.7%; Median home value: $181,400; Median year structure built: 1991; Homeowner vacancy rate: 0.7%; Median gross rent: $704 per month; Rental vacancy rate: 5.7%
  Health Insurance: 94.4% have insurance; 88.0% have private insurance; 17.3% have public insurance; 5.6% do not have insurance; 1.8% of children under 18 do not have insurance
  Transportation: Commute: 93.5% car, 0.0% public transportation, 1.2% walk, 5.3% work from home; Median travel time to work: 22.6 minutes

ROCKWELL (town).
Covers a land area of 1.679 square miles and a water area of 0.002 square miles. Located at 35.55° N. Lat; 80.41° W. Long. Elevation is 784 feet.

Population: 2,108; Growth (since 2000): 7.0%; Density: 1,255.8 persons per square mile; Race: 94.8% White, 1.1% Black/African American, 0.7% Asian, 0.0% American Indian/Alaska Native, 0.3% Native Hawaiian/Other Pacific Islander, 1.3% Two or more races, 3.1% Hispanic of any race; Average household size: 2.49; Median age: 39.3; Age under 18: 24.9%; Age 65 and over: 15.1%; Males per 100 females: 89.4

School District(s)
Rowan-Salisbury Schools (PK-12)
   2012-13 Enrollment: 20,165 . . . . (704) 636-7500
  Housing: Homeownership rate: 66.6%; Homeowner vacancy rate: 2.4%; Rental vacancy rate: 6.6%
  Safety: Violent crime rate: 9.5 per 10,000 population; Property crime rate: 279.4 per 10,000 population

SALISBURY (city).
County seat. Covers a land area of 22.141 square miles and a water area of 0 square miles. Located at 35.67° N. Lat; 80.49° W. Long. Elevation is 768 feet.

History: Salisbury is one of the oldest towns of the Piedmont. It was founded in 1753, incorporated in 1755, and named for the Marquis of Salisbury and the English cathedral town.

Population: 33,662; Growth (since 2000): 27.2%; Density: 1,520.3 persons per square mile; Race: 52.4% White, 37.7% Black/African American, 1.6% Asian, 0.4% American Indian/Alaska Native, 0.0% Native Hawaiian/Other Pacific Islander, 2.0% Two or more races, 10.6% Hispanic of any race; Average household size: 2.38; Median age: 36.2; Age under 18: 22.7%; Age 65 and over: 15.9%; Males per 100 females: 98.1; Marriage status: 37.4% never married, 40.7% now married, 4.8% separated, 9.2% widowed, 12.6% divorced; Foreign born: 5.8%; Speak English only: 88.6%; With disability: 16.1%; Veterans: 10.3%; Ancestry: 11.2% German, 11.0% American, 6.5% Irish, 6.5% English, 3.0% Scotch-Irish

Employment: 8.7% management, business, and financial, 2.0% computer, engineering, and science, 14.2% education, legal, community service, arts, and media, 5.7% healthcare practitioners, 24.6% service, 18.7% sales and office, 10.2% natural resources, construction, and maintenance, 15.9% production, transportation, and material moving

Income: Per capita: $18,557; Median household: $34,959; Average household: $48,986; Households with income of $100,000 or more: 9.8%; Poverty rate: 24.8%

Educational Attainment: High school diploma or higher: 80.4%; Bachelor's degree or higher: 22.7%; Graduate/professional degree or higher: 7.3%

School District(s)
Rowan-Salisbury Schools (PK-12)
   2012-13 Enrollment: 20,165 . . . . (704) 636-7500

Four-year College(s)
Catawba College (Private, Not-for-profit)
   Fall 2013 Enrollment: 1,310 . . . . (704) 637-4111
   2013-14 Tuition: In-state $26,820; Out-of-state $26,820
Hood Theological Seminary (Private, Not-for-profit, African Methodist Episcopal Zion Church)
   Fall 2013 Enrollment: 181 . . . . (704) 636-7611
Livingstone College (Private, Not-for-profit, Historically black, African Methodist Episcopal Zion Church)
   Fall 2013 Enrollment: 1,175 . . . . (704) 216-6000
   2013-14 Tuition: In-state $16,024; Out-of-state $16,024

Two-year College(s)
Rowan-Cabarrus Community College (Public)
   Fall 2013 Enrollment: 6,731 . . . . (704) 216-3602
   2013-14 Tuition: In-state $2,420; Out-of-state $8,564

Housing: Homeownership rate: 51.7%; Median home value: $121,600; Median year structure built: 1972; Homeowner vacancy rate: 4.7%; Median gross rent: $717 per month; Rental vacancy rate: 13.7%

Health Insurance: 81.7% have insurance; 55.1% have private insurance; 38.6% have public insurance; 18.3% do not have insurance; 6.5% of children under 18 do not have insurance

Hospitals: Novant Health Rowan Medical Center (188 beds); W G (Bill) Hefner Salisbury VA Medical Center (429 beds)

Safety: Violent crime rate: 77.9 per 10,000 population; Property crime rate: 546.3 per 10,000 population

Newspapers: Salisbury Post (daily circulation 21400)

Transportation: Commute: 91.3% car, 1.5% public transportation, 1.6% walk, 3.3% work from home; Median travel time to work: 19.8 minutes; Amtrak: Train service available.

Additional Information Contacts
City of Salisbury . . . . (704) 638-5270
  http://www.salisburync.gov

SPENCER (town).
Covers a land area of 3.065 square miles and a water area of 0 square miles. Located at 35.70° N. Lat; 80.42° W. Long. Elevation is 709 feet.

Population: 3,267; Growth (since 2000): -2.6%; Density: 1,066.0 persons per square mile; Race: 58.2% White, 32.8% Black/African American, 0.9% Asian, 0.4% American Indian/Alaska Native, 0.2% Native Hawaiian/Other Pacific Islander, 2.3% Two or more races, 9.2% Hispanic of any race; Average household size: 2.56; Median age: 39.1; Age under 18: 24.7%; Age 65 and over: 14.8%; Males per 100 females: 88.6; Marriage status: 38.5% never married, 38.9% now married, 4.7% separated, 6.9% widowed, 15.7% divorced; Foreign born: 2.3%; Speak English only: 96.3%; With disability: 15.7%; Veterans: 12.7%; Ancestry: 15.0% American, 10.6% Irish, 9.9% German, 9.1% English, 3.6% Scottish

Employment: 4.3% management, business, and financial, 7.0% computer, engineering, and science, 4.1% education, legal, community service, arts, and media, 2.8% healthcare practitioners, 24.1% service, 30.2% sales and office, 4.6% natural resources, construction, and maintenance, 22.9% production, transportation, and material moving

Income: Per capita: $15,977; Median household: $37,113; Average household: $41,339; Households with income of $100,000 or more: 5.5%; Poverty rate: 33.0%

Educational Attainment: High school diploma or higher: 82.0%; Bachelor's degree or higher: 11.8%; Graduate/professional degree or higher: 3.1%

School District(s)
Rowan-Salisbury Schools (PK-12)
   2012-13 Enrollment: 20,165 . . . . (704) 636-7500
  Housing: Homeownership rate: 60.9%; Median home value: $98,100; Median year structure built: 1951; Homeowner vacancy rate: 5.4%; Median gross rent: $669 per month; Rental vacancy rate: 11.5%
  Health Insurance: 79.0% have insurance; 45.8% have private insurance; 42.8% have public insurance; 21.0% do not have insurance; 10.3% of children under 18 do not have insurance
  Safety: Violent crime rate: 119.6 per 10,000 population; Property crime rate: 459.8 per 10,000 population
  Transportation: Commute: 94.4% car, 0.0% public transportation, 4.0% walk, 0.0% work from home; Median travel time to work: 21.1 minutes

Additional Information Contacts
Town of Spencer . . . . (704) 633-2231
  http://ci.spencer.nc.us

WOODLEAF (unincorporated postal area)

ZCTA: 27054

Covers a land area of 29.265 square miles and a water area of 0.041 square miles. Located at 35.79° N. Lat; 80.60° W. Long. Elevation is 804 feet.

Population: 2,567; Growth (since 2000): 9.6%; Density: 87.7 persons per square mile; Race: 76.6% White, 14.1% Black/African American, 0.7% Asian, 0.4% American Indian/Alaska Native, 0.0% Native Hawaiian/Other Pacific Islander, 1.2% Two or more races, 8.9% Hispanic of any race; Average household size: 2.73; Median age: 39.1; Age under 18: 25.8%; Age 65 and over: 14.0%; Males per 100 females: 96.4; Marriage status: 27.2% never married, 53.7% now married, 1.3% separated, 8.0% widowed, 11.1% divorced; Foreign born: 3.4%; Speak English only: 95.8%; With disability: 27.8%; Veterans: 11.1%; Ancestry: 29.0% American, 22.9% German, 15.3% English, 8.4% Irish, 2.6% Scotch-Irish

Employment: 0.0% management, business, and financial, 1.9% computer, engineering, and science, 2.4% education, legal, community service, arts, and media, 2.1% healthcare practitioners, 14.9% service, 25.3% sales and office, 15.7% natural resources, construction, and maintenance, 37.8% production, transportation, and material moving

Income: Per capita: $18,364; Median household: $45,114; Average household: $42,786; Households with income of $100,000 or more: n/a; Poverty rate: 25.2%

Educational Attainment: High school diploma or higher: 82.2%; Bachelor's degree or higher: 4.6%; Graduate/professional degree or higher: 1.1%

School District(s)

Rowan-Salisbury Schools (PK-12)

    2012-13 Enrollment: 20,165 . . . . (704) 636-7500

Housing: Homeownership rate: 77.1%; Median home value: $100,900; Median year structure built: 1976; Homeowner vacancy rate: 2.7%; Median gross rent: $657 per month; Rental vacancy rate: 11.5%

Health Insurance: 79.4% have insurance; 44.1% have private insurance; 51.3% have public insurance; 20.6% do not have insurance; 10.3% of children under 18 do not have insurance

Transportation: Commute: 96.4% car, 0.0% public transportation, 0.0% walk, 0.0% work from home; Median travel time to work: 21.0 minutes

Rutherford County

Located in southern North Carolina; bounded on the south by South Carolina; piedmont area, drained by the Broad River. Covers a land area of 564.151 square miles, a water area of 1.699 square miles, and is located in the Eastern Time Zone at 35.40° N. Lat., 81.92° W. Long. The county was founded in 1779. County seat is Rutherfordton.

Rutherford County is part of the Forest City, NC Micropolitan Statistical Area. The entire metro area includes: Rutherford County, NC

Weather Station: Forest City 6 SW   Elevation: 990 feet

	Jan	Feb	Mar	Apr	May	Jun	Jul	Aug	Sep	Oct	Nov	Dec
High	50	55	62	71	79	86	90	88	81	72	63	53
Low	27	30	36	44	52	61	65	64	57	46	37	29
Precip	4.5	4.2	5.1	3.9	4.4	4.0	4.4	4.3	4.0	4.0	4.0	4.0
Snow	3.1	1.3	0.9	tr	0.0	0.0	0.0	0.0	0.0	0.0	tr	0.3

High and Low temperatures in degrees Fahrenheit; Precipitation and Snow in inches

Population: 67,810; Growth (since 2000): 7.8%; Density: 120.2 persons per square mile; Race: 85.9% White, 10.1% Black/African American, 0.4% Asian, 0.3% American Indian/Alaska Native, 0.0% Native Hawaiian/Other Pacific Islander, 1.8% two or more races, 3.5% Hispanic of any race; Average household size: 2.42; Median age: 42.5; Age under 18: 22.5%; Age 65 and over: 17.3%; Males per 100 females: 93.6; Marriage status: 22.4% never married, 56.8% now married, 2.9% separated, 8.0% widowed, 12.8% divorced; Foreign born: 2.8%; Speak English only: 95.9%; With disability: 20.4%; Veterans: 10.6%; Ancestry: 21.3% American, 11.9% Irish, 10.1% German, 9.4% English, 3.6% Scotch-Irish

Religion: Six largest groups: 54.7% Baptist, 11.7% Methodist/Pietist, 2.6% Non-denominational Protestant, 1.2% Pentecostal, 1.0% Presbyterian-Reformed, 1.0% Catholicism

Economy: Unemployment rate: 7.2%; Leading industries: 18.2% retail trade; 15.3% other services (except public administration); 10.5% health care and social assistance; Farms: 638 totaling 59,540 acres; Company size: 1 employs 1,000 or more persons, 1 employs 500 to 999 persons, 23

employ 100 to 499 persons, 1,253 employ less than 100 persons; Business ownership: 1,118 women-owned, 233 Black-owned, n/a Hispanic-owned, n/a Asian-owned

Employment: 9.4% management, business, and financial, 2.1% computer, engineering, and science, 9.9% education, legal, community service, arts, and media, 6.9% healthcare practitioners, 17.6% service, 21.3% sales and office, 11.3% natural resources, construction, and maintenance, 21.4% production, transportation, and material moving

Income: Per capita: $19,551; Median household: $36,334; Average household: $47,542; Households with income of $100,000 or more: 9.2%; Poverty rate: 21.5%

Educational Attainment: High school diploma or higher: 81.6%; Bachelor's degree or higher: 17.0%; Graduate/professional degree or higher: 6.3%

Housing: Homeownership rate: 72.0%; Median home value: $108,600; Median year structure built: 1977; Homeowner vacancy rate: 2.7%; Median gross rent: $587 per month; Rental vacancy rate: 12.5%

Vital Statistics: Birth rate: 103.7 per 10,000 population; Death rate: 118.4 per 10,000 population; Age-adjusted cancer mortality rate: 179.4 deaths per 10,000 population

Health Insurance: 82.0% have insurance; 53.1% have private insurance; 42.6% have public insurance; 18.0% do not have insurance; 6.5% of children under 18 do not have insurance

Health Care: Physicians: 11.3 per 10,000 population; Hospital beds: 17.2 per 10,000 population; Hospital admissions: 817.1 per 10,000 population

Transportation: Commute: 94.2% car, 0.1% public transportation, 1.2% walk, 3.2% work from home; Median travel time to work: 23.1 minutes

Presidential Election: 32.7% Obama, 66.0% Romney (2012)

Additional Information Contacts

Rutherford Government. . . . . (828) 287-6060
  http://www.rutherfordcountync.gov

Rutherford County Communities

BOSTIC (town). Covers a land area of 0.933 square miles and a water area of 0 square miles. Located at 35.36° N. Lat; 81.84° W. Long. Elevation is 925 feet.

Population: 386; Growth (since 2000): 17.7%; Density: 413.9 persons per square mile; Race: 92.7% White, 5.2% Black/African American, 1.0% Asian, 0.0% American Indian/Alaska Native, 0.0% Native Hawaiian/Other Pacific Islander, 1.0% Two or more races, 1.0% Hispanic of any race; Average household size: 2.30; Median age: 42.0; Age under 18: 21.8%; Age 65 and over: 13.0%; Males per 100 females: 82.9

School District(s)

Rutherford County Schools (PK-12)

    2012-13 Enrollment: 8,963 . . . . (828) 288-2200

Housing: Homeownership rate: 83.4%; Homeowner vacancy rate: 1.4%; Rental vacancy rate: 9.7%

CAROLEEN (CDP). Covers a land area of 1.108 square miles and a water area of 0 square miles. Located at 35.28° N. Lat; 81.79° W. Long. Elevation is 843 feet.

Population: 652; Growth (since 2000): n/a; Density: 588.5 persons per square mile; Race: 82.4% White, 10.0% Black/African American, 0.0% Asian, 0.3% American Indian/Alaska Native, 0.0% Native Hawaiian/Other Pacific Islander, 3.2% Two or more races, 6.1% Hispanic of any race; Average household size: 2.55; Median age: 41.4; Age under 18: 23.2%; Age 65 and over: 14.6%; Males per 100 females: 100.6

Housing: Homeownership rate: 71.5%; Homeowner vacancy rate: 1.6%; Rental vacancy rate: 8.6%

CHIMNEY ROCK VILLAGE (village). Covers a land area of 3.147 square miles and a water area of 0.004 square miles. Located at 35.45° N. Lat; 82.26° W. Long. Elevation is 1,096 feet.

Population: 113; Growth (since 2000): -35.4%; Density: 35.9 persons per square mile; Race: 98.2% White, 0.9% Black/African American, 0.0% Asian, 0.0% American Indian/Alaska Native, 0.0% Native Hawaiian/Other Pacific Islander, 0.9% Two or more races, 0.0% Hispanic of any race; Average household size: 1.95; Median age: 53.3; Age under 18: 17.7%; Age 65 and over: 29.2%; Males per 100 females: 105.5

Housing: Homeownership rate: 74.1%; Homeowner vacancy rate: 6.5%; Rental vacancy rate: 31.8%

CLIFFSIDE (CDP). Covers a land area of 2.328 square miles and a water area of 0 square miles. Located at 35.25° N. Lat; 81.77° W. Long. Elevation is 738 feet.
Population: 611; Growth (since 2000): n/a; Density: 262.4 persons per square mile; Race: 90.5% White, 4.9% Black/African American, 0.0% Asian, 0.7% American Indian/Alaska Native, 0.0% Native Hawaiian/Other Pacific Islander, 0.8% Two or more races, 4.1% Hispanic of any race; Average household size: 2.62; Median age: 41.8; Age under 18: 23.6%; Age 65 and over: 14.2%; Males per 100 females: 93.4
School District(s)
Rutherford County Schools (PK-12)
    2012-13 Enrollment: 8,963 . . . . (828) 288-2200
Housing: Homeownership rate: 78.1%; Homeowner vacancy rate: 1.6%; Rental vacancy rate: 17.7%

ELLENBORO (town). Covers a land area of 1.265 square miles and a water area of 0 square miles. Located at 35.33° N. Lat; 81.76° W. Long. Elevation is 1,050 feet.
Population: 873; Growth (since 2000): 82.3%; Density: 690.0 persons per square mile; Race: 79.3% White, 17.1% Black/African American, 0.0% Asian, 0.3% American Indian/Alaska Native, 0.0% Native Hawaiian/Other Pacific Islander, 1.8% Two or more races, 2.1% Hispanic of any race; Average household size: 2.56; Median age: 34.9; Age under 18: 29.8%; Age 65 and over: 14.0%; Males per 100 females: 98.9
School District(s)
Rutherford County Schools (PK-12)
    2012-13 Enrollment: 8,963 . . . . (828) 288-2200
Housing: Homeownership rate: 65.5%; Homeowner vacancy rate: 0.9%; Rental vacancy rate: 18.2%

FOREST CITY (town). Covers a land area of 8.341 square miles and a water area of <.001 square miles. Located at 35.33° N. Lat; 81.87° W. Long. Elevation is 1,014 feet.
History: Forest City was once known as Burnt Chimney and was the muster ground of the Burnt Chimney Volunteers of the Confederate Army.
Population: 7,476; Growth (since 2000): -1.0%; Density: 896.3 persons per square mile; Race: 67.1% White, 24.0% Black/African American, 0.9% Asian, 0.2% American Indian/Alaska Native, 0.0% Native Hawaiian/Other Pacific Islander, 2.9% Two or more races, 9.0% Hispanic of any race; Average household size: 2.32; Median age: 40.0; Age under 18: 24.7%; Age 65 and over: 18.1%; Males per 100 females: 81.3; Marriage status: 29.6% never married, 45.5% now married, 3.3% separated, 11.3% widowed, 13.6% divorced; Foreign born: 4.3%; Speak English only: 92.9%; With disability: 25.7%; Veterans: 6.2%; Ancestry: 20.2% American, 9.1% Irish, 6.0% German, 5.8% English, 2.7% French
Employment: 10.3% management, business, and financial, 3.1% computer, engineering, and science, 14.8% education, legal, community service, arts, and media, 4.0% healthcare practitioners, 16.3% service, 24.3% sales and office, 9.6% natural resources, construction, and maintenance, 17.7% production, transportation, and material moving
Income: Per capita: $14,690; Median household: $22,124; Average household: $32,448; Households with income of $100,000 or more: 2.7%; Poverty rate: 37.5%
Educational Attainment: High school diploma or higher: 70.5%; Bachelor's degree or higher: 12.2%; Graduate/professional degree or higher: 4.3%
School District(s)
Rutherford County Schools (PK-12)
    2012-13 Enrollment: 8,963 . . . . (828) 288-2200
Housing: Homeownership rate: 48.4%; Median home value: $96,500; Median year structure built: 1966; Homeowner vacancy rate: 4.2%; Median gross rent: $576 per month; Rental vacancy rate: 9.7%
Health Insurance: 82.2% have insurance; 38.1% have private insurance; 54.3% have public insurance; 17.8% do not have insurance; 2.3% of children under 18 do not have insurance
Safety: Violent crime rate: 27.0 per 10,000 population; Property crime rate: 791.2 per 10,000 population
Newspapers: Daily Courier (daily circulation 9300)
Transportation: Commute: 89.6% car, 0.3% public transportation, 0.4% walk, 3.9% work from home; Median travel time to work: 17.0 minutes
Additional Information Contacts
Town of Forest City . . . . (828) 245-4747
    http://www.townofforestcity.com

HENRIETTA (CDP). Covers a land area of 0.584 square miles and a water area of 0.004 square miles. Located at 35.26° N. Lat; 81.80° W. Long. Elevation is 784 feet.
Population: 461; Growth (since 2000): n/a; Density: 789.8 persons per square mile; Race: 76.6% White, 14.3% Black/African American, 0.4% Asian, 0.0% American Indian/Alaska Native, 0.0% Native Hawaiian/Other Pacific Islander, 2.4% Two or more races, 10.8% Hispanic of any race; Average household size: 2.39; Median age: 40.7; Age under 18: 23.4%; Age 65 and over: 20.0%; Males per 100 females: 88.2
Housing: Homeownership rate: 67.3%; Homeowner vacancy rate: 0.0%; Rental vacancy rate: 13.3%

LAKE LURE (town). Covers a land area of 13.379 square miles and a water area of 1.209 square miles. Located at 35.45° N. Lat; 82.20° W. Long. Elevation is 1,106 feet.
Population: 1,192; Growth (since 2000): 16.1%; Density: 89.1 persons per square mile; Race: 96.3% White, 1.6% Black/African American, 0.6% Asian, 0.2% American Indian/Alaska Native, 0.1% Native Hawaiian/Other Pacific Islander, 1.0% Two or more races, 1.6% Hispanic of any race; Average household size: 1.97; Median age: 62.4; Age under 18: 8.6%; Age 65 and over: 42.4%; Males per 100 females: 96.1
School District(s)
Lake Lure Classical Academy (KG-08)
    2012-13 Enrollment: 311 . . . . (828) 625-9292
Housing: Homeownership rate: 83.6%; Homeowner vacancy rate: 10.8%; Rental vacancy rate: 42.4%
Safety: Violent crime rate: 0.0 per 10,000 population; Property crime rate: 226.9 per 10,000 population
Additional Information Contacts
Town of Lake Lure . . . . (828) 625-9983
    http://www.townoflakelure.com

RUTH (town). Covers a land area of 0.424 square miles and a water area of 0 square miles. Located at 35.38° N. Lat; 81.94° W. Long. Elevation is 1,037 feet.
History: Called Hampton until 1939.
Population: 440; Growth (since 2000): 33.7%; Density: 1,036.8 persons per square mile; Race: 87.5% White, 6.6% Black/African American, 0.0% Asian, 0.7% American Indian/Alaska Native, 0.0% Native Hawaiian/Other Pacific Islander, 3.4% Two or more races, 2.5% Hispanic of any race; Average household size: 2.49; Median age: 46.1; Age under 18: 17.0%; Age 65 and over: 15.2%; Males per 100 females: 97.3
Housing: Homeownership rate: 80.8%; Homeowner vacancy rate: 0.7%; Rental vacancy rate: 18.6%

RUTHERFORDTON (town). County seat. Covers a land area of 4.131 square miles and a water area of 0 square miles. Located at 35.36° N. Lat; 81.96° W. Long. Elevation is 968 feet.
History: Rutherfordton was established in 1779 and named for Revolutionary General Griffith Rutherford. It was the site of some early gold mines and a muster place for the Kings Mountain Boys. Textiles have also been an important industry.
Population: 4,213; Growth (since 2000): 2.0%; Density: 1,019.8 persons per square mile; Race: 84.9% White, 10.4% Black/African American, 1.6% Asian, 0.3% American Indian/Alaska Native, 0.0% Native Hawaiian/Other Pacific Islander, 1.8% Two or more races, 3.0% Hispanic of any race; Average household size: 2.26; Median age: 44.4; Age under 18: 20.1%; Age 65 and over: 20.5%; Males per 100 females: 84.9; Marriage status: 25.0% never married, 50.9% now married, 1.0% separated, 9.7% widowed, 14.3% divorced; Foreign born: 3.1%; Speak English only: 94.3%; With disability: 17.4%; Veterans: 11.4%; Ancestry: 12.6% American, 12.6% German, 10.9% English, 9.2% Irish, 4.3% Scotch-Irish
Employment: 18.9% management, business, and financial, 5.5% computer, engineering, and science, 9.9% education, legal, community service, arts, and media, 11.4% healthcare practitioners, 20.9% service, 27.0% sales and office, 4.5% natural resources, construction, and maintenance, 2.0% production, transportation, and material moving
Income: Per capita: $26,988; Median household: $43,606; Average household: $63,390; Households with income of $100,000 or more: 16.6%; Poverty rate: 15.1%
Educational Attainment: High school diploma or higher: 85.8%; Bachelor's degree or higher: 26.5%; Graduate/professional degree or higher: 10.5%

School District(s)
Rutherford County Schools (PK-12)
2012-13 Enrollment: 8,963 . . . . (828) 288-2200
Housing: Homeownership rate: 61.2%; Median home value: $172,100; Median year structure built: 1968; Homeowner vacancy rate: 5.0%; Median gross rent: $575 per month; Rental vacancy rate: 11.1%
Health Insurance: 82.0% have insurance; 60.3% have private insurance; 37.0% have public insurance; 18.0% do not have insurance; 17.0% of children under 18 do not have insurance
Hospitals: Rutherford Hospital (143 beds)
Safety: Violent crime rate: 0.0 per 10,000 population; Property crime rate: 332.9 per 10,000 population
Transportation: Commute: 98.0% car, 0.0% public transportation, 0.9% walk, 1.0% work from home; Median travel time to work: 18.4 minutes
Airports: Rutherford County-Marchman Field (general aviation)
Additional Information Contacts
Town of Rutherfordton. . . . . (828) 287-3520
http://www.rutherfordcoc.org

SPINDALE (town). Covers a land area of 5.345 square miles and a water area of 0 square miles. Located at 35.36° N. Lat; 81.92° W. Long. Elevation is 1,086 feet.
Population: 4,321; Growth (since 2000): 7.4%; Density: 808.4 persons per square mile; Race: 68.8% White, 26.7% Black/African American, 0.7% Asian, 0.3% American Indian/Alaska Native, 0.0% Native Hawaiian/Other Pacific Islander, 2.5% Two or more races, 3.3% Hispanic of any race; Average household size: 2.32; Median age: 39.7; Age under 18: 22.0%; Age 65 and over: 15.5%; Males per 100 females: 99.5; Marriage status: 26.7% never married, 46.3% now married, 4.6% separated, 11.6% widowed, 15.5% divorced; Foreign born: 2.1%; Speak English only: 98.3%; With disability: 26.4%; Veterans: 9.2%; Ancestry: 18.4% American, 15.1% Irish, 10.5% English, 8.5% German, 5.4% Dutch
Employment: 6.6% management, business, and financial, 0.0% computer, engineering, and science, 7.9% education, legal, community service, arts, and media, 4.9% healthcare practitioners, 30.6% service, 22.5% sales and office, 7.7% natural resources, construction, and maintenance, 19.8% production, transportation, and material moving
Income: Per capita: $16,829; Median household: $25,670; Average household: $37,240; Households with income of $100,000 or more: 5.0%; Poverty rate: 21.4%
Educational Attainment: High school diploma or higher: 80.6%; Bachelor's degree or higher: 18.0%; Graduate/professional degree or higher: 4.7%
School District(s)
Rutherford County Schools (PK-12)
2012-13 Enrollment: 8,963 . . . . (828) 288-2200
Two-year College(s)
Isothermal Community College (Public)
Fall 2013 Enrollment: 2,390 . . . . (828) 286-3636
2013-14 Tuition: In-state $2,342; Out-of-state $8,486
Housing: Homeownership rate: 54.3%; Median home value: $90,100; Median year structure built: 1960; Homeowner vacancy rate: 6.2%; Median gross rent: $593 per month; Rental vacancy rate: 11.7%
Health Insurance: 87.4% have insurance; 51.0% have private insurance; 52.3% have public insurance; 12.6% do not have insurance; 2.1% of children under 18 do not have insurance
Transportation: Commute: 97.1% car, 0.0% public transportation, 1.2% walk, 1.7% work from home; Median travel time to work: 18.5 minutes
Additional Information Contacts
Town of Spindale. . . . . (828) 286-2541
http://www.spindalenc.net

UNION MILLS (unincorporated postal area)
ZCTA: 28167
Covers a land area of 71.169 square miles and a water area of 0.032 square miles. Located at 35.51° N. Lat; 81.97° W. Long. Elevation is 1,076 feet.
Population: 2,362; Growth (since 2000): -0.1%; Density: 33.2 persons per square mile; Race: 88.4% White, 8.5% Black/African American, 0.7% Asian, 0.7% American Indian/Alaska Native, 0.0% Native Hawaiian/Other Pacific Islander, 1.0% Two or more races, 1.7% Hispanic of any race; Average household size: 2.36; Median age: 47.5; Age under 18: 19.0%; Age 65 and over: 18.1%; Males per 100 females: 104.5

Housing: Homeownership rate: 84.7%; Homeowner vacancy rate: 2.0%; Rental vacancy rate: 13.6%

Sampson County

Located in south central North Carolina; coastal plains area, bounded on the west by the South River; drained by the Black River. Covers a land area of 944.740 square miles, a water area of 1.855 square miles, and is located in the Eastern Time Zone at 34.99° N. Lat., 78.37° W. Long. The county was founded in 1784. County seat is Clinton.

Weather Station: Clinton 2 NE									Elevation: 158 feet			
	Jan	Feb	Mar	Apr	May	Jun	Jul	Aug	Sep	Oct	Nov	Dec
High	52	56	63	73	80	87	90	88	83	74	65	56
Low	31	34	40	49	57	66	70	69	62	50	42	34
Precip	3.7	3.2	4.2	3.0	3.6	4.7	6.2	5.7	5.0	3.3	3.2	3.2
Snow	0.8	0.6	0.6	tr	0.0	0.0	0.0	0.0	0.0	0.0	tr	0.7

High and Low temperatures in degrees Fahrenheit; Precipitation and Snow in inches

Population: 63,431; Growth (since 2000): 5.4%; Density: 67.1 persons per square mile; Race: 56.7% White, 27.0% Black/African American, 0.4% Asian, 2.0% American Indian/Alaska Native, 0.1% Native Hawaiian/Other Pacific Islander, 2.0% two or more races, 16.5% Hispanic of any race; Average household size: 2.60; Median age: 38.2; Age under 18: 25.7%; Age 65 and over: 14.3%; Males per 100 females: 96.2; Marriage status: 29.7% never married, 51.8% now married, 5.1% separated, 8.2% widowed, 10.2% divorced; Foreign born: 9.2%; Speak English only: 84.3%; With disability: 17.7%; Veterans: 9.2%; Ancestry: 11.3% American, 8.1% English, 4.8% Irish, 4.3% German, 2.1% Scottish
Religion: Six largest groups: 33.4% Baptist, 8.3% Methodist/Pietist, 5.5% Catholicism, 4.7% Pentecostal, 2.4% Non-denominational Protestant, 1.0% Presbyterian-Reformed
Economy: Unemployment rate: 5.2%; Leading industries: 19.2% retail trade; 14.2% other services (except public administration); 12.8% health care and social assistance; Farms: 1,067 totaling 291,635 acres; Company size: 1 employs 1,000 or more persons, 1 employs 500 to 999 persons, 16 employ 100 to 499 persons, 995 employ less than 100 persons; Business ownership: 1,242 women-owned, 745 Black-owned, n/a Hispanic-owned, n/a Asian-owned
Employment: 10.8% management, business, and financial, 1.9% computer, engineering, and science, 8.7% education, legal, community service, arts, and media, 5.3% healthcare practitioners, 16.9% service, 19.7% sales and office, 16.2% natural resources, construction, and maintenance, 20.7% production, transportation, and material moving
Income: Per capita: $19,479; Median household: $36,496; Average household: $50,029; Households with income of $100,000 or more: 10.8%; Poverty rate: 22.8%
Educational Attainment: High school diploma or higher: 75.0%; Bachelor's degree or higher: 12.6%; Graduate/professional degree or higher: 3.7%
Housing: Homeownership rate: 69.5%; Median home value: $89,200; Median year structure built: 1981; Homeowner vacancy rate: 1.4%; Median gross rent: $572 per month; Rental vacancy rate: 8.7%
Vital Statistics: Birth rate: 131.3 per 10,000 population; Death rate: 94.9 per 10,000 population; Age-adjusted cancer mortality rate: 158.4 deaths per 100,000 population
Health Insurance: 80.4% have insurance; 51.3% have private insurance; 41.4% have public insurance; 19.6% do not have insurance; 8.0% of children under 18 do not have insurance
Health Care: Physicians: 7.8 per 10,000 population; Hospital beds: 16.5 per 10,000 population; Hospital admissions: 580.4 per 10,000 population
Transportation: Commute: 93.6% car, 0.6% public transportation, 1.6% walk, 3.3% work from home; Median travel time to work: 25.1 minutes
Presidential Election: 44.2% Obama, 55.1% Romney (2012)
Additional Information Contacts
Sampson Government . . . . (910) 592-6308
http://www.sampsonnc.com

Sampson County Communities

AUTRYVILLE (town). Covers a land area of 0.518 square miles and a water area of 0 square miles. Located at 35.00° N. Lat; 78.64° W. Long. Elevation is 105 feet.
Population: 196; Growth (since 2000): 0.0%; Density: 378.2 persons per square mile; Race: 88.3% White, 4.1% Black/African American, 0.0%

Asian, 2.0% American Indian/Alaska Native, 0.0% Native Hawaiian/Other Pacific Islander, 5.6% Two or more races, 1.0% Hispanic of any race; Average household size: 2.15; Median age: 42.7; Age under 18: 25.5%; Age 65 and over: 23.0%; Males per 100 females: 84.9

School District(s)

Sampson County Schools (PK-12)

 2012-13 Enrollment: 8,835 . . . . (910) 592-1401

Housing: Homeownership rate: 60.5%; Homeowner vacancy rate: 0.0%; Rental vacancy rate: 7.7%

BONNETSVILLE (CDP). Covers a land area of 3.306 square miles and a water area of 0.006 square miles. Located at 35.01° N. Lat; 78.40° W. Long. Elevation is 167 feet.

Population: 443; Growth (since 2000): 13.6%; Density: 134.0 persons per square mile; Race: 47.2% White, 30.2% Black/African American, 0.0% Asian, 1.6% American Indian/Alaska Native, 0.0% Native Hawaiian/Other Pacific Islander, 2.0% Two or more races, 23.5% Hispanic of any race; Average household size: 2.59; Median age: 37.3; Age under 18: 20.8%; Age 65 and over: 12.9%; Males per 100 females: 99.5

Housing: Homeownership rate: 54.9%; Homeowner vacancy rate: 0.0%; Rental vacancy rate: 11.5%

CLINTON (city). County seat. Covers a land area of 7.675 square miles and a water area of 0.020 square miles. Located at 35.00° N. Lat; 78.33° W. Long. Elevation is 154 feet.

History: Clinton was founded and laid out in 1818. It was named for Richard Clinton, who gave five acres of land for the county seat.

Population: 8,639; Growth (since 2000): 0.5%; Density: 1,125.6 persons per square mile; Race: 48.9% White, 40.5% Black/African American, 1.1% Asian, 1.2% American Indian/Alaska Native, 0.0% Native Hawaiian/Other Pacific Islander, 2.2% Two or more races, 9.2% Hispanic of any race; Average household size: 2.27; Median age: 42.1; Age under 18: 21.9%; Age 65 and over: 20.6%; Males per 100 females: 90.5; Marriage status: 32.7% never married, 43.4% now married, 5.0% separated, 11.1% widowed, 12.8% divorced; Foreign born: 4.2%; Speak English only: 92.2%; With disability: 18.5%; Veterans: 8.3%; Ancestry: 8.4% American, 7.6% English, 5.0% Irish, 4.1% German, 3.0% Scottish

Employment: 15.8% management, business, and financial, 1.5% computer, engineering, and science, 11.3% education, legal, community service, arts, and media, 7.1% healthcare practitioners, 16.8% service, 23.5% sales and office, 5.9% natural resources, construction, and maintenance, 18.1% production, transportation, and material moving

Income: Per capita: $24,119; Median household: $32,927; Average household: $56,492; Households with income of $100,000 or more: 13.8%; Poverty rate: 27.8%

Educational Attainment: High school diploma or higher: 81.5%; Bachelor's degree or higher: 20.2%; Graduate/professional degree or higher: 6.7%

School District(s)

Clinton City Schools (PK-12)

 2012-13 Enrollment: 3,144 . . . . (910) 592-3132

Sampson County Schools (PK-12)

 2012-13 Enrollment: 8,835 . . . . (910) 592-1401

Two-year College(s)

Sampson Community College (Public)

 Fall 2013 Enrollment: 1,538 . . . . (910) 592-8081

 2013-14 Tuition: In-state $2,365; Out-of-state $8,509

Housing: Homeownership rate: 50.6%; Median home value: $123,700; Median year structure built: 1970; Homeowner vacancy rate: 2.4%; Median gross rent: $559 per month; Rental vacancy rate: 5.2%

Health Insurance: 84.7% have insurance; 54.8% have private insurance; 44.4% have public insurance; 15.3% do not have insurance; 5.6% of children under 18 do not have insurance

Hospitals: Sampson Regional Medical Center (146 beds)

Safety: Violent crime rate: 70.7 per 10,000 population; Property crime rate: 569.9 per 10,000 population

Newspapers: Sampson Independent (daily circulation 8000)

Transportation: Commute: 95.0% car, 0.2% public transportation, 1.3% walk, 2.6% work from home; Median travel time to work: 17.8 minutes

Airports: Clinton-Sampson County (general aviation)

Additional Information Contacts

City of Clinton . . . . (910) 299-4100

 http://www.cityofclintonnc.com

DELWAY (CDP). Covers a land area of 9.632 square miles and a water area of 0.012 square miles. Located at 34.82° N. Lat; 78.21° W. Long. Elevation is 128 feet.

Population: 203; Growth (since 2000): -24.8%; Density: 21.1 persons per square mile; Race: 60.1% White, 26.1% Black/African American, 0.0% Asian, 0.0% American Indian/Alaska Native, 0.0% Native Hawaiian/Other Pacific Islander, 1.5% Two or more races, 24.6% Hispanic of any race; Average household size: 2.48; Median age: 37.8; Age under 18: 24.6%; Age 65 and over: 13.3%; Males per 100 females: 95.2

Housing: Homeownership rate: 70.7%; Homeowner vacancy rate: 0.0%; Rental vacancy rate: 14.3%

GARLAND (town). Covers a land area of 1.076 square miles and a water area of 0.006 square miles. Located at 34.79° N. Lat; 78.39° W. Long. Elevation is 135 feet.

History: Garland was formerly an important lumber-market center.

Population: 625; Growth (since 2000): -22.6%; Density: 580.8 persons per square mile; Race: 47.2% White, 41.1% Black/African American, 0.2% Asian, 0.3% American Indian/Alaska Native, 0.0% Native Hawaiian/Other Pacific Islander, 1.9% Two or more races, 12.8% Hispanic of any race; Average household size: 2.50; Median age: 40.9; Age under 18: 25.6%; Age 65 and over: 21.3%; Males per 100 females: 100.3

Housing: Homeownership rate: 60.8%; Homeowner vacancy rate: 2.6%; Rental vacancy rate: 12.5%

HARRELLS (town). Covers a land area of 3.153 square miles and a water area of 0 square miles. Located at 34.73° N. Lat; 78.20° W. Long. Elevation is 85 feet.

Population: 202; Growth (since 2000): 8.0%; Density: 64.1 persons per square mile; Race: 53.0% White, 32.7% Black/African American, 0.0% Asian, 1.0% American Indian/Alaska Native, 0.0% Native Hawaiian/Other Pacific Islander, 0.0% Two or more races, 17.3% Hispanic of any race; Average household size: 2.46; Median age: 44.5; Age under 18: 21.3%; Age 65 and over: 21.3%; Males per 100 females: 85.3

Housing: Homeownership rate: 79.3%; Homeowner vacancy rate: 4.4%; Rental vacancy rate: 10.5%

INGOLD (CDP). Covers a land area of 5.178 square miles and a water area of 0.011 square miles. Located at 34.83° N. Lat; 78.35° W. Long. Elevation is 98 feet.

Population: 471; Growth (since 2000): -2.7%; Density: 91.0 persons per square mile; Race: 35.5% White, 25.1% Black/African American, 1.1% Asian, 0.0% American Indian/Alaska Native, 0.0% Native Hawaiian/Other Pacific Islander, 0.8% Two or more races, 41.4% Hispanic of any race; Average household size: 2.91; Median age: 30.4; Age under 18: 32.7%; Age 65 and over: 12.3%; Males per 100 females: 97.9

Housing: Homeownership rate: 71.6%; Homeowner vacancy rate: 0.8%; Rental vacancy rate: 17.5%

IVANHOE (CDP). Covers a land area of 5.033 square miles and a water area of 0.008 square miles. Located at 34.58° N. Lat; 78.25° W. Long. Elevation is 30 feet.

Population: 264; Growth (since 2000): -15.1%; Density: 52.5 persons per square mile; Race: 26.1% White, 70.8% Black/African American, 0.0% Asian, 0.0% American Indian/Alaska Native, 0.0% Native Hawaiian/Other Pacific Islander, 0.4% Two or more races, 4.5% Hispanic of any race; Average household size: 2.38; Median age: 44.7; Age under 18: 19.7%; Age 65 and over: 16.7%; Males per 100 females: 98.5

Housing: Homeownership rate: 76.5%; Homeowner vacancy rate: 0.0%; Rental vacancy rate: 7.1%

KEENER (CDP). Covers a land area of 11.172 square miles and a water area of 0.010 square miles. Located at 35.12° N. Lat; 78.30° W. Long. Elevation is 177 feet.

Population: 567; Growth (since 2000): 11.6%; Density: 50.8 persons per square mile; Race: 66.1% White, 14.6% Black/African American, 0.2% Asian, 1.6% American Indian/Alaska Native, 1.1% Native Hawaiian/Other Pacific Islander, 1.4% Two or more races, 18.5% Hispanic of any race; Average household size: 2.50; Median age: 37.7; Age under 18: 24.7%; Age 65 and over: 15.7%; Males per 100 females: 105.4

Housing: Homeownership rate: 69.6%; Homeowner vacancy rate: 2.5%; Rental vacancy rate: 9.2%

NEWTON GROVE (town). Covers a land area of 3.082 square miles and a water area of 0.015 square miles. Located at 35.25° N. Lat; 78.35° W. Long. Elevation is 180 feet.

History: Bentonville Battleground State Historical Site to North.
Population: 569; Growth (since 2000): -6.1%; Density: 184.6 persons per square mile; Race: 71.7% White, 10.7% Black/African American, 0.9% Asian, 1.1% American Indian/Alaska Native, 0.0% Native Hawaiian/Other Pacific Islander, 0.5% Two or more races, 15.1% Hispanic of any race; Average household size: 2.34; Median age: 45.5; Age under 18: 19.2%; Age 65 and over: 24.6%; Males per 100 females: 81.2

School District(s)
Sampson County Schools (PK-12)
   2012-13 Enrollment: 8,835 . . . . (910) 592-1401
Housing: Homeownership rate: 62.6%; Homeowner vacancy rate: 0.7%; Rental vacancy rate: 14.1%

PLAIN VIEW (CDP). Covers a land area of 16.619 square miles and a water area of 0.057 square miles. Located at 35.24° N. Lat; 78.56° W. Long. Elevation is 210 feet.

Population: 1,961; Growth (since 2000): 7.7%; Density: 118.0 persons per square mile; Race: 77.5% White, 16.4% Black/African American, 1.4% Asian, 1.1% American Indian/Alaska Native, 0.0% Native Hawaiian/Other Pacific Islander, 1.4% Two or more races, 5.0% Hispanic of any race; Average household size: 2.57; Median age: 39.1; Age under 18: 24.6%; Age 65 and over: 13.7%; Males per 100 females: 98.9
Housing: Homeownership rate: 78.5%; Homeowner vacancy rate: 1.6%; Rental vacancy rate: 9.4%

ROSEBORO (town). Covers a land area of 1.175 square miles and a water area of <.001 square miles. Located at 34.95° N. Lat; 78.51° W. Long. Elevation is 128 feet.

Population: 1,191; Growth (since 2000): -6.0%; Density: 1,013.4 persons per square mile; Race: 49.0% White, 43.2% Black/African American, 1.3% Asian, 0.7% American Indian/Alaska Native, 0.0% Native Hawaiian/Other Pacific Islander, 2.1% Two or more races, 4.9% Hispanic of any race; Average household size: 2.26; Median age: 43.6; Age under 18: 23.3%; Age 65 and over: 23.1%; Males per 100 females: 81.0

School District(s)
Cumberland County Schools (PK-12)
   2012-13 Enrollment: 52,925 . . . . (910) 678-2300
Sampson County Schools (PK-12)
   2012-13 Enrollment: 8,835 . . . . (910) 592-1401
Housing: Homeownership rate: 55.1%; Homeowner vacancy rate: 1.7%; Rental vacancy rate: 9.8%

SALEMBURG (town). Covers a land area of 0.975 square miles and a water area of 0 square miles. Located at 35.02° N. Lat; 78.50° W. Long. Elevation is 167 feet.

History: Seat of North Carolina Justice Academy.
Population: 435; Growth (since 2000): -7.2%; Density: 446.0 persons per square mile; Race: 88.3% White, 7.1% Black/African American, 0.2% Asian, 1.4% American Indian/Alaska Native, 0.0% Native Hawaiian/Other Pacific Islander, 2.1% Two or more races, 2.1% Hispanic of any race; Average household size: 2.05; Median age: 48.3; Age under 18: 17.9%; Age 65 and over: 24.4%; Males per 100 females: 79.0

School District(s)
Sampson County Schools (PK-12)
   2012-13 Enrollment: 8,835 . . . . (910) 592-1401
Housing: Homeownership rate: 69.2%; Homeowner vacancy rate: 0.7%; Rental vacancy rate: 14.7%

SPIVEY'S CORNER (CDP). Covers a land area of 7.771 square miles and a water area of 0 square miles. Located at 35.20° N. Lat; 78.48° W. Long. Elevation is 190 feet.

Population: 506; Growth (since 2000): 12.9%; Density: 65.1 persons per square mile; Race: 65.0% White, 22.1% Black/African American, 0.0% Asian, 0.8% American Indian/Alaska Native, 0.0% Native Hawaiian/Other Pacific Islander, 1.0% Two or more races, 12.8% Hispanic of any race; Average household size: 2.84; Median age: 37.1; Age under 18: 27.9%; Age 65 and over: 13.4%; Males per 100 females: 101.6
Housing: Homeownership rate: 77.0%; Homeowner vacancy rate: 0.0%; Rental vacancy rate: 16.3%

TURKEY (town). Covers a land area of 0.396 square miles and a water area of 0 square miles. Located at 35.00° N. Lat; 78.18° W. Long. Elevation is 144 feet.

Population: 292; Growth (since 2000): 11.5%; Density: 736.5 persons per square mile; Race: 55.1% White, 26.7% Black/African American, 1.0% Asian, 0.0% American Indian/Alaska Native, 0.0% Native Hawaiian/Other Pacific Islander, 1.0% Two or more races, 19.9% Hispanic of any race; Average household size: 2.63; Median age: 43.9; Age under 18: 24.0%; Age 65 and over: 17.1%; Males per 100 females: 100.0
Housing: Homeownership rate: 79.2%; Homeowner vacancy rate: 0.0%; Rental vacancy rate: 0.0%

VANN CROSSROADS (CDP). Covers a land area of 4.561 square miles and a water area of 0.006 square miles. Located at 35.17° N. Lat; 78.40° W. Long. Elevation is 187 feet.

Population: 336; Growth (since 2000): 3.7%; Density: 73.7 persons per square mile; Race: 82.7% White, 6.0% Black/African American, 0.3% Asian, 1.8% American Indian/Alaska Native, 0.0% Native Hawaiian/Other Pacific Islander, 0.9% Two or more races, 8.3% Hispanic of any race; Average household size: 2.37; Median age: 43.8; Age under 18: 23.2%; Age 65 and over: 22.0%; Males per 100 females: 88.8
Housing: Homeownership rate: 83.8%; Homeowner vacancy rate: 0.8%; Rental vacancy rate: 0.0%

Scotland County

Located in southern North Carolina; bounded on the south by South Carolina; coastal plain and sandhills area, drained by the Lumber River. Covers a land area of 318.845 square miles, a water area of 1.479 square miles, and is located in the Eastern Time Zone at 34.84° N. Lat., 79.48° W. Long. The county was founded in 1899. County seat is Laurinburg.

Scotland County is part of the Laurinburg, NC Micropolitan Statistical Area. The entire metro area includes: Scotland County, NC

Weather Station: Laurinburg											Elevation: 209 feet	
	Jan	Feb	Mar	Apr	May	Jun	Jul	Aug	Sep	Oct	Nov	Dec
High	54	59	66	76	83	89	92	90	84	75	66	57
Low	32	35	41	49	58	66	70	69	63	51	42	34
Precip	3.6	3.4	4.1	2.7	3.1	4.7	4.9	5.1	4.7	3.6	3.1	3.1
Snow	0.9	0.4	0.5	tr	0.0	0.0	0.0	0.0	0.0	0.0	0.0	tr

High and Low temperatures in degrees Fahrenheit; Precipitation and Snow in inches

Population: 36,157; Growth (since 2000): 0.4%; Density: 113.4 persons per square mile; Race: 46.5% White, 38.6% Black/African American, 0.8% Asian, 10.9% American Indian/Alaska Native, 0.0% Native Hawaiian/Other Pacific Islander, 2.2% two or more races, 2.1% Hispanic of any race; Average household size: 2.53; Median age: 38.4; Age under 18: 25.1%; Age 65 and over: 13.6%; Males per 100 females: 93.4; Marriage status: 36.2% never married, 43.8% now married, 5.7% separated, 8.1% widowed, 11.8% divorced; Foreign born: 2.0%; Speak English only: 96.8%; With disability: 21.8%; Veterans: 9.7%; Ancestry: 6.6% American, 5.8% English, 3.9% German, 3.5% Irish, 2.8% Scottish
Religion: Six largest groups: 13.7% Methodist/Pietist, 10.8% Baptist, 5.8% Pentecostal, 4.7% Presbyterian-Reformed, 2.5% Non-denominational Protestant, 1.2% Catholicism
Economy: Unemployment rate: 10.3%; Leading industries: 22.3% retail trade; 17.7% health care and social assistance; 11.9% other services (except public administration); Farms: 150 totaling 68,934 acres; Company size: 0 employ 1,000 or more persons, 1 employs 500 to 999 persons, 16 employ 100 to 499 persons, 614 employ less than 100 persons; Business ownership: 616 women-owned, n/a Black-owned, n/a Hispanic-owned, n/a Asian-owned
Employment: 12.2% management, business, and financial, 2.1% computer, engineering, and science, 12.2% education, legal, community service, arts, and media, 5.0% healthcare practitioners, 18.3% service, 24.2% sales and office, 8.7% natural resources, construction, and maintenance, 17.5% production, transportation, and material moving
Income: Per capita: $15,679; Median household: $29,592; Average household: $40,473; Households with income of $100,000 or more: 8.3%; Poverty rate: 32.3%
Educational Attainment: High school diploma or higher: 77.6%; Bachelor's degree or higher: 14.3%; Graduate/professional degree or higher: 5.2%

Housing: Homeownership rate: 63.8%; Median home value: $77,100; Median year structure built: 1979; Homeowner vacancy rate: 1.7%; Median gross rent: $628 per month; Rental vacancy rate: 9.5%

Vital Statistics: Birth rate: 125.5 per 10,000 population; Death rate: 109.9 per 10,000 population; Age-adjusted cancer mortality rate: 170.1 deaths per 100,000 population

Health Insurance: 83.5% have insurance; 46.9% have private insurance; 48.4% have public insurance; 16.5% do not have insurance; 5.6% of children under 18 do not have insurance

Health Care: Physicians: 16.6 per 10,000 population; Hospital beds: 41.8 per 10,000 population; Hospital admissions: 1,713.7 per 10,000 population

Transportation: Commute: 93.8% car, 0.1% public transportation, 1.3% walk, 3.5% work from home; Median travel time to work: 21.5 minutes

Presidential Election: 58.0% Obama, 41.2% Romney (2012)

Additional Information Contacts

Scotland Government . . . . (910) 277-2406
    http://www.scotlandcounty.org

Scotland County Communities

DEERCROFT (CDP). Covers a land area of 1.292 square miles and a water area of 0.062 square miles. Located at 34.96° N. Lat; 79.43° W. Long.

Population: 411; Growth (since 2000): n/a; Density: 318.2 persons per square mile; Race: 92.5% White, 0.2% Black/African American, 2.7% Asian, 2.7% American Indian/Alaska Native, 0.0% Native Hawaiian/Other Pacific Islander, 1.9% Two or more races, 4.6% Hispanic of any race; Average household size: 2.27; Median age: 54.3; Age under 18: 13.4%; Age 65 and over: 26.0%; Males per 100 females: 102.5

Housing: Homeownership rate: 93.9%; Homeowner vacancy rate: 4.0%; Rental vacancy rate: 0.0%

EAST LAURINBURG (town). Covers a land area of 0.189 square miles and a water area of 0 square miles. Located at 34.77° N. Lat; 79.45° W. Long. Elevation is 213 feet.

Population: 300; Growth (since 2000): 1.7%; Density: 1,584.0 persons per square mile; Race: 60.0% White, 20.3% Black/African American, 0.0% Asian, 15.0% American Indian/Alaska Native, 0.0% Native Hawaiian/Other Pacific Islander, 4.7% Two or more races, 1.3% Hispanic of any race; Average household size: 2.63; Median age: 41.7; Age under 18: 22.7%; Age 65 and over: 16.0%; Males per 100 females: 85.2

Housing: Homeownership rate: 64.9%; Homeowner vacancy rate: 1.3%; Rental vacancy rate: 14.9%

GIBSON (town). Covers a land area of 0.978 square miles and a water area of 0 square miles. Located at 34.76° N. Lat; 79.61° W. Long. Elevation is 249 feet.

Population: 540; Growth (since 2000): -7.5%; Density: 552.0 persons per square mile; Race: 38.0% White, 46.7% Black/African American, 1.1% Asian, 12.0% American Indian/Alaska Native, 0.0% Native Hawaiian/Other Pacific Islander, 1.5% Two or more races, 1.3% Hispanic of any race; Average household size: 2.47; Median age: 37.3; Age under 18: 30.2%; Age 65 and over: 11.3%; Males per 100 females: 82.4

School District(s)

Scotland County Schools (PK-12)
    2012-13 Enrollment: 6,276 . . . . (910) 276-1138

Housing: Homeownership rate: 41.6%; Homeowner vacancy rate: 0.0%; Rental vacancy rate: 7.2%

LAUREL HILL (CDP). Covers a land area of 2.397 square miles and a water area of 0.013 square miles. Located at 34.81° N. Lat; 79.55° W. Long. Elevation is 253 feet.

Population: 1,254; Growth (since 2000): n/a; Density: 523.1 persons per square mile; Race: 65.2% White, 21.3% Black/African American, 0.5% Asian, 10.8% American Indian/Alaska Native, 0.0% Native Hawaiian/Other Pacific Islander, 1.8% Two or more races, 1.1% Hispanic of any race; Average household size: 2.43; Median age: 40.6; Age under 18: 22.4%; Age 65 and over: 14.7%; Males per 100 females: 88.6

School District(s)

Scotland County Schools (PK-12)
    2012-13 Enrollment: 6,276 . . . . (910) 276-1138

Housing: Homeownership rate: 70.5%; Homeowner vacancy rate: 1.9%; Rental vacancy rate: 15.6%

LAURINBURG (city). County seat. Covers a land area of 12.520 square miles and a water area of 0.159 square miles. Located at 34.76° N. Lat; 79.48° W. Long. Elevation is 223 feet.

History: Laurinburg was founded in the 1870's.

Population: 15,962; Growth (since 2000): 0.6%; Density: 1,274.9 persons per square mile; Race: 43.0% White, 46.8% Black/African American, 1.0% Asian, 6.1% American Indian/Alaska Native, 0.0% Native Hawaiian/Other Pacific Islander, 2.0% Two or more races, 2.0% Hispanic of any race; Average household size: 2.40; Median age: 37.7; Age under 18: 25.6%; Age 65 and over: 15.9%; Males per 100 females: 82.0; Marriage status: 35.3% never married, 40.1% now married, 5.8% separated, 10.3% widowed, 14.2% divorced; Foreign born: 2.3%; Speak English only: 96.5%; With disability: 20.4%; Veterans: 9.4%; Ancestry: 6.5% English, 6.0% American, 4.5% German, 3.2% Irish, 3.0% Scottish

Employment: 10.7% management, business, and financial, 1.5% computer, engineering, and science, 16.8% education, legal, community service, arts, and media, 5.5% healthcare practitioners, 16.8% service, 23.9% sales and office, 6.5% natural resources, construction, and maintenance, 18.4% production, transportation, and material moving

Income: Per capita: $15,760; Median household: $26,235; Average household: $38,211; Households with income of $100,000 or more: 8.0%; Poverty rate: 35.9%

Educational Attainment: High school diploma or higher: 78.9%; Bachelor's degree or higher: 18.6%; Graduate/professional degree or higher: 7.6%

School District(s)

Scotland County Schools (PK-12)
    2012-13 Enrollment: 6,276 . . . . (910) 276-1138

Four-year College(s)

St Andrews University (Private, Not-for-profit, Presbyterian Church (USA))
    Fall 2013 Enrollment: 635 . . . . (910) 277-5000
    2013-14 Tuition: In-state $23,332; Out-of-state $23,332

Housing: Homeownership rate: 53.3%; Median home value: $92,900; Median year structure built: 1973; Homeowner vacancy rate: 2.5%; Median gross rent: $613 per month; Rental vacancy rate: 8.0%

Health Insurance: 86.5% have insurance; 49.2% have private insurance; 50.9% have public insurance; 13.5% do not have insurance; 2.9% of children under 18 do not have insurance

Hospitals: Scotland Memorial Hospital (154 beds)

Safety: Violent crime rate: 134.7 per 10,000 population; Property crime rate: 603.6 per 10,000 population

Newspapers: Laurinburg Exchange (daily circulation 8200)

Transportation: Commute: 92.7% car, 0.3% public transportation, 1.9% walk, 3.1% work from home; Median travel time to work: 20.3 minutes

Additional Information Contacts

City of Laurinburg . . . . (910) 276-8324
    http://www.laurinburg.org

MARSTON (unincorporated postal area)
ZCTA: 28363

Covers a land area of 57.301 square miles and a water area of 0.374 square miles. Located at 34.96° N. Lat; 79.55° W. Long..

Population: 1,202; Growth (since 2000): 13.2%; Density: 21.0 persons per square mile; Race: 51.8% White, 36.9% Black/African American, 0.5% Asian, 7.2% American Indian/Alaska Native, 0.0% Native Hawaiian/Other Pacific Islander, 2.7% Two or more races, 2.2% Hispanic of any race; Average household size: 2.51; Median age: 40.6; Age under 18: 24.0%; Age 65 and over: 14.1%; Males per 100 females: 92.3

Housing: Homeownership rate: 75.2%; Homeowner vacancy rate: 1.4%; Rental vacancy rate: 9.1%

OLD HUNDRED (CDP). Covers a land area of 0.971 square miles and a water area of 0 square miles. Located at 34.82° N. Lat; 79.59° W. Long. Elevation is 312 feet.

Population: 287; Growth (since 2000): n/a; Density: 295.6 persons per square mile; Race: 52.3% White, 17.4% Black/African American, 0.0% Asian, 17.4% American Indian/Alaska Native, 0.0% Native Hawaiian/Other Pacific Islander, 9.4% Two or more races, 5.6% Hispanic of any race; Average household size: 2.90; Median age: 29.5; Age under 18: 33.1%; Age 65 and over: 7.7%; Males per 100 females: 97.9

Housing: Homeownership rate: 39.4%; Homeowner vacancy rate: 0.0%; Rental vacancy rate: 3.2%

SCOTCH MEADOWS (CDP). Covers a land area of 0.341 square miles and a water area of 0 square miles. Located at 34.69° N. Lat; 79.52° W. Long.
Population: 580; Growth (since 2000): n/a; Density: 1,702.3 persons per square mile; Race: 88.4% White, 6.0% Black/African American, 2.2% Asian, 2.1% American Indian/Alaska Native, 0.2% Native Hawaiian/Other Pacific Islander, 0.9% Two or more races, 1.0% Hispanic of any race; Average household size: 2.97; Median age: 44.3; Age under 18: 24.8%; Age 65 and over: 15.0%; Males per 100 females: 96.6
Housing: Homeownership rate: 95.8%; Homeowner vacancy rate: 2.1%; Rental vacancy rate: 0.0%

WAGRAM (town). Covers a land area of 1.457 square miles and a water area of 0 square miles. Located at 34.89° N. Lat; 79.37° W. Long. Elevation is 239 feet.
Population: 840; Growth (since 2000): 4.9%; Density: 576.5 persons per square mile; Race: 41.0% White, 49.2% Black/African American, 0.8% Asian, 6.8% American Indian/Alaska Native, 0.1% Native Hawaiian/Other Pacific Islander, 1.8% Two or more races, 1.0% Hispanic of any race; Average household size: 2.53; Median age: 42.6; Age under 18: 22.9%; Age 65 and over: 17.9%; Males per 100 females: 87.1
School District(s)
Scotland County Schools (PK-12)
    2012-13 Enrollment: 6,276 . . . . (910) 276-1138
Housing: Homeownership rate: 70.4%; Homeowner vacancy rate: 0.8%; Rental vacancy rate: 5.8%

Stanly County

Located in south central North Carolina; piedmont area, bounded on the east by the Yadkin River. Covers a land area of 395.086 square miles, a water area of 9.754 square miles, and is located in the Eastern Time Zone at 35.31° N. Lat., 80.25° W. Long. The county was founded in 1841. County seat is Albemarle.

Stanly County is part of the Albemarle, NC Micropolitan Statistical Area. The entire metro area includes: Stanly County, NC

Weather Station: Albemarle   Elevation: 609 feet

	Jan	Feb	Mar	Apr	May	Jun	Jul	Aug	Sep	Oct	Nov	Dec
High	51	56	64	73	80	86	90	88	82	73	64	54
Low	30	33	39	46	55	64	68	67	60	48	40	32
Precip	3.7	3.5	4.9	3.3	3.7	4.6	5.6	4.5	4.1	3.7	3.3	3.4
Snow	1.0	0.9	0.8	tr	0.0	0.0	0.0	0.0	0.0	0.0	tr	0.1

High and Low temperatures in degrees Fahrenheit; Precipitation and Snow in inches

Population: 60,585; Growth (since 2000): 4.3%; Density: 153.3 persons per square mile; Race: 83.6% White, 10.9% Black/African American, 1.8% Asian, 0.3% American Indian/Alaska Native, 0.1% Native Hawaiian/Other Pacific Islander, 1.2% two or more races, 3.6% Hispanic of any race; Average household size: 2.48; Median age: 40.5; Age under 18: 22.7%; Age 65 and over: 15.7%; Males per 100 females: 98.8; Marriage status: 26.3% never married, 53.7% now married, 2.3% separated, 7.9% widowed, 12.1% divorced; Foreign born: 2.9%; Speak English only: 94.1%; With disability: 16.4%; Veterans: 9.2%; Ancestry: 14.7% German, 13.1% American, 10.9% English, 9.8% Irish, 3.4% Scotch-Irish
Religion: Six largest groups: 34.4% Baptist, 17.4% Methodist/Pietist, 4.1% Non-denominational Protestant, 3.2% Pentecostal, 3.1% Presbyterian-Reformed, 2.0% Lutheran
Economy: Unemployment rate: 5.0%; Leading industries: 17.6% retail trade; 13.3% health care and social assistance; 13.0% other services (except public administration); Farms: 664 totaling 93,071 acres; Company size: 0 employ 1,000 or more persons, 2 employ 500 to 999 persons, 18 employ 100 to 499 persons, 1,307 employ less than 100 persons; Business ownership: 1,194 women-owned, n/a Black-owned, n/a Hispanic-owned, n/a Asian-owned
Employment: 10.9% management, business, and financial, 2.8% computer, engineering, and science, 9.7% education, legal, community service, arts, and media, 5.5% healthcare practitioners, 21.1% service, 21.8% sales and office, 13.8% natural resources, construction, and maintenance, 14.3% production, transportation, and material moving
Income: Per capita: $20,504; Median household: $42,518; Average household: $52,171; Households with income of $100,000 or more: 11.5%; Poverty rate: 16.1%

Educational Attainment: High school diploma or higher: 80.6%; Bachelor's degree or higher: 16.0%; Graduate/professional degree or higher: 4.8%
Housing: Homeownership rate: 72.6%; Median home value: $125,100; Median year structure built: 1973; Homeowner vacancy rate: 2.2%; Median gross rent: $638 per month; Rental vacancy rate: 12.1%
Vital Statistics: Birth rate: 104.6 per 10,000 population; Death rate: 107.7 per 10,000 population; Age-adjusted cancer mortality rate: 203.2 deaths per 100,000 population
Health Insurance: 84.8% have insurance; 64.7% have private insurance; 33.5% have public insurance; 15.2% do not have insurance; 6.7% of children under 18 do not have insurance
Health Care: Physicians: 10.9 per 10,000 population; Hospital beds: 16.9 per 10,000 population; Hospital admissions: 825.7 per 10,000 population
Transportation: Commute: 94.8% car, 0.1% public transportation, 1.4% walk, 2.6% work from home; Median travel time to work: 25.7 minutes
Presidential Election: 29.4% Obama, 69.3% Romney (2012)
National and State Parks: Morrow Mountain State Park
Additional Information Contacts
Stanly Government . . . . (704) 986-3600
   http://www.co.stanly.nc.us

Stanly County Communities

ALBEMARLE (city). County seat. Covers a land area of 16.741 square miles and a water area of 0.134 square miles. Located at 35.36° N. Lat; 80.19° W. Long. Elevation is 476 feet.
History: Albemarle was incorporated in 1842.
Population: 15,903; Growth (since 2000): 1.4%; Density: 949.9 persons per square mile; Race: 70.1% White, 22.4% Black/African American, 2.9% Asian, 0.3% American Indian/Alaska Native, 0.0% Native Hawaiian/Other Pacific Islander, 1.8% Two or more races, 4.5% Hispanic of any race; Average household size: 2.34; Median age: 39.6; Age under 18: 23.7%; Age 65 and over: 17.7%; Males per 100 females: 87.2; Marriage status: 29.1% never married, 44.6% now married, 2.3% separated, 10.7% widowed, 15.6% divorced; Foreign born: 3.7%; Speak English only: 91.9%; With disability: 18.2%; Veterans: 7.1%; Ancestry: 13.4% German, 10.2% English, 10.0% American, 7.6% Irish, 3.2% Scotch-Irish
Employment: 8.3% management, business, and financial, 2.7% computer, engineering, and science, 12.4% education, legal, community service, arts, and media, 2.7% healthcare practitioners, 24.9% service, 26.0% sales and office, 11.0% natural resources, construction, and maintenance, 12.1% production, transportation, and material moving
Income: Per capita: $19,592; Median household: $32,859; Average household: $46,213; Households with income of $100,000 or more: 9.3%; Poverty rate: 23.5%
Educational Attainment: High school diploma or higher: 76.5%; Bachelor's degree or higher: 19.5%; Graduate/professional degree or higher: 5.8%
School District(s)
Stanly County Schools (PK-12)
    2012-13 Enrollment: 8,827 . . . . (704) 961-3000
Two-year College(s)
Stanly Community College (Public)
    Fall 2013 Enrollment: 2,885 . . . . (704) 982-0121
    2013-14 Tuition: In-state $2,412; Out-of-state $8,556
Housing: Homeownership rate: 56.2%; Median home value: $119,800; Median year structure built: 1963; Homeowner vacancy rate: 3.2%; Median gross rent: $594 per month; Rental vacancy rate: 14.2%
Health Insurance: 80.9% have insurance; 55.2% have private insurance; 40.0% have public insurance; 19.1% do not have insurance; 9.1% of children under 18 do not have insurance
Hospitals: Stanly Regional Medical Center (119 beds)
Safety: Violent crime rate: 43.9 per 10,000 population; Property crime rate: 549.4 per 10,000 population
Newspapers: Stanly News & Press (weekly circulation 10000)
Transportation: Commute: 96.7% car, 0.0% public transportation, 0.3% walk, 2.2% work from home; Median travel time to work: 22.1 minutes
Airports: Stanly County (general aviation)
Additional Information Contacts
City of Albemarle . . . . (704) 984-9405
   http://www.ci.albemarle.nc.us

AQUADALE (CDP). Covers a land area of 3.255 square miles and a water area of 0 square miles. Located at 35.22° N. Lat; 80.22° W. Long. Elevation is 489 feet.

Population: 397; Growth (since 2000): n/a; Density: 122.0 persons per square mile; Race: 100.0% White, 0.0% Black/African American, 0.0% Asian, 0.0% American Indian/Alaska Native, 0.0% Native Hawaiian/Other Pacific Islander, 0.0% Two or more races, 2.0% Hispanic of any race; Average household size: 2.39; Median age: 41.5; Age under 18: 22.2%; Age 65 and over: 15.4%; Males per 100 females: 111.2

Housing: Homeownership rate: 78.9%; Homeowner vacancy rate: 1.5%; Rental vacancy rate: 7.9%

BADIN (town). Covers a land area of 1.813 square miles and a water area of 0 square miles. Located at 35.41° N. Lat; 80.12° W. Long. Elevation is 515 feet.

History: Badin was established in 1913 and named for Adrien Badin, the French industrialist who first started the construction of an aluminum-reduction plant in the village.

Population: 1,974; Growth (since 2000): 71.1%; Density: 1,088.9 persons per square mile; Race: 55.4% White, 39.0% Black/African American, 0.4% Asian, 0.9% American Indian/Alaska Native, 0.0% Native Hawaiian/Other Pacific Islander, 0.8% Two or more races, 6.4% Hispanic of any race; Average household size: 2.33; Median age: 39.6; Age under 18: 13.2%; Age 65 and over: 11.6%; Males per 100 females: 223.1

School District(s)

Stanly County Schools (PK-12)
    2012-13 Enrollment: 8,827 . . . . (704) 961-3000

Housing: Homeownership rate: 64.4%; Homeowner vacancy rate: 4.6%; Rental vacancy rate: 19.9%

Additional Information Contacts

Town of Badin . . . . (704) 422-3470
    http://www.badin.org

LOCUST (city). Covers a land area of 8.138 square miles and a water area of 0 square miles. Located at 35.27° N. Lat; 80.44° W. Long. Elevation is 725 feet.

History: Read Gold Mine State Historical Site to North first gold mine in U.S. (1799).

Population: 2,930; Growth (since 2000): 21.3%; Density: 360.0 persons per square mile; Race: 93.5% White, 2.3% Black/African American, 0.7% Asian, 0.1% American Indian/Alaska Native, 0.0% Native Hawaiian/Other Pacific Islander, 0.8% Two or more races, 6.0% Hispanic of any race; Average household size: 2.58; Median age: 40.5; Age under 18: 24.3%; Age 65 and over: 15.2%; Males per 100 females: 94.9; Marriage status: 20.4% never married, 61.7% now married, 4.1% separated, 8.3% widowed, 9.5% divorced; Foreign born: 1.6%; Speak English only: 97.4%; With disability: 20.0%; Veterans: 7.1%; Ancestry: 15.1% Irish, 13.1% English, 12.9% American, 12.1% German, 5.7% Scotch-Irish

Employment: 13.9% management, business, and financial, 4.8% computer, engineering, and science, 6.9% education, legal, community service, arts, and media, 7.3% healthcare practitioners, 16.7% service, 30.1% sales and office, 12.8% natural resources, construction, and maintenance, 7.5% production, transportation, and material moving

Income: Per capita: $25,027; Median household: $53,824; Average household: $60,566; Households with income of $100,000 or more: 15.5%; Poverty rate: 8.5%

Educational Attainment: High school diploma or higher: 90.1%; Bachelor's degree or higher: 14.8%; Graduate/professional degree or higher: 6.7%

School District(s)

Stanly County Schools (PK-12)
    2012-13 Enrollment: 8,827 . . . . (704) 961-3000

Housing: Homeownership rate: 81.7%; Median home value: $159,700; Median year structure built: 1983; Homeowner vacancy rate: 5.1%; Median gross rent: $721 per month; Rental vacancy rate: 5.9%

Health Insurance: 87.5% have insurance; 73.4% have private insurance; 27.3% have public insurance; 12.5% do not have insurance; 0.0% of children under 18 do not have insurance

Transportation: Commute: 95.2% car, 0.0% public transportation, 0.0% walk, 4.8% work from home; Median travel time to work: 29.0 minutes

MILLINGPORT (CDP). Covers a land area of 5.682 square miles and a water area of 0 square miles. Located at 35.38° N. Lat; 80.31° W. Long. Elevation is 653 feet.

Population: 599; Growth (since 2000): n/a; Density: 105.4 persons per square mile; Race: 97.0% White, 0.7% Black/African American, 1.7% Asian, 0.2% American Indian/Alaska Native, 0.0% Native Hawaiian/Other Pacific Islander, 0.3% Two or more races, 2.0% Hispanic of any race; Average household size: 2.53; Median age: 41.1; Age under 18: 23.5%; Age 65 and over: 11.5%; Males per 100 females: 97.0

Housing: Homeownership rate: 84.3%; Homeowner vacancy rate: 0.0%; Rental vacancy rate: 5.1%

MISENHEIMER (village). Covers a land area of 1.622 square miles and a water area of 0.003 square miles. Located at 35.48° N. Lat; 80.29° W. Long. Elevation is 669 feet.

Population: 728; Growth (since 2000): n/a; Density: 448.8 persons per square mile; Race: 87.5% White, 7.1% Black/African American, 1.4% Asian, 0.3% American Indian/Alaska Native, 0.0% Native Hawaiian/Other Pacific Islander, 2.2% Two or more races, 4.3% Hispanic of any race; Average household size: 2.09; Median age: 20.9; Age under 18: 4.5%; Age 65 and over: 4.5%; Males per 100 females: 131.1

School District(s)

Gray Stone Day (09-12)
    2012-13 Enrollment: 388 . . . . (704) 463-0567

Four-year College(s)

Pfeiffer University (Private, Not-for-profit, United Methodist)
    Fall 2013 Enrollment: 1,860 . . . . (704) 463-1360
    2013-14 Tuition: In-state $24,150; Out-of-state $24,150

Housing: Homeownership rate: 56.7%; Homeowner vacancy rate: 3.1%; Rental vacancy rate: 12.7%

NEW LONDON (town). Covers a land area of 1.939 square miles and a water area of 0 square miles. Located at 35.43° N. Lat; 80.22° W. Long. Elevation is 728 feet.

Population: 600; Growth (since 2000): 84.0%; Density: 309.5 persons per square mile; Race: 90.0% White, 4.8% Black/African American, 3.8% Asian, 0.3% American Indian/Alaska Native, 0.0% Native Hawaiian/Other Pacific Islander, 0.2% Two or more races, 0.8% Hispanic of any race; Average household size: 2.58; Median age: 40.2; Age under 18: 24.5%; Age 65 and over: 14.7%; Males per 100 females: 91.1

School District(s)

Stanly County Schools (PK-12)
    2012-13 Enrollment: 8,827 . . . . (704) 961-3000

Housing: Homeownership rate: 82.4%; Homeowner vacancy rate: 1.9%; Rental vacancy rate: 19.6%

NORWOOD (town). Covers a land area of 4.479 square miles and a water area of 0.139 square miles. Located at 35.24° N. Lat; 80.11° W. Long. Elevation is 390 feet.

History: Settled c.1800; incorporated 1882.

Population: 2,379; Growth (since 2000): 7.4%; Density: 531.2 persons per square mile; Race: 71.6% White, 21.9% Black/African American, 0.7% Asian, 0.8% American Indian/Alaska Native, 0.0% Native Hawaiian/Other Pacific Islander, 1.1% Two or more races, 5.1% Hispanic of any race; Average household size: 2.47; Median age: 42.2; Age under 18: 23.7%; Age 65 and over: 16.8%; Males per 100 females: 98.3

School District(s)

Stanly County Schools (PK-12)
    2012-13 Enrollment: 8,827 . . . . (704) 961-3000

Housing: Homeownership rate: 68.0%; Homeowner vacancy rate: 3.4%; Rental vacancy rate: 9.9%

OAKBORO (town). Covers a land area of 2.455 square miles and a water area of 0 square miles. Located at 35.23° N. Lat; 80.33° W. Long. Elevation is 518 feet.

Population: 1,859; Growth (since 2000): 55.2%; Density: 757.3 persons per square mile; Race: 78.9% White, 12.9% Black/African American, 0.4% Asian, 0.8% American Indian/Alaska Native, 0.0% Native Hawaiian/Other Pacific Islander, 1.1% Two or more races, 7.9% Hispanic of any race; Average household size: 2.61; Median age: 36.0; Age under 18: 25.2%; Age 65 and over: 14.2%; Males per 100 females: 96.9

School District(s)

Stanly County Schools (PK-12)
    2012-13 Enrollment: 8,827 . . . . (704) 961-3000

Housing: Homeownership rate: 81.0%; Homeowner vacancy rate: 4.3%; Rental vacancy rate: 15.5%

RED CROSS (town). Covers a land area of 3.577 square miles and a water area of 0 square miles. Located at 35.27° N. Lat; 80.36° W. Long. Elevation is 636 feet.
Population: 742; Growth (since 2000): n/a; Density: 207.4 persons per square mile; Race: 96.2% White, 1.3% Black/African American, 0.7% Asian, 0.0% American Indian/Alaska Native, 0.0% Native Hawaiian/Other Pacific Islander, 0.4% Two or more races, 3.2% Hispanic of any race; Average household size: 2.33; Median age: 46.8; Age under 18: 20.1%; Age 65 and over: 18.2%; Males per 100 females: 101.6
Housing: Homeownership rate: 84.3%; Homeowner vacancy rate: 0.4%; Rental vacancy rate: 9.1%

RICHFIELD (town). Covers a land area of 2.246 square miles and a water area of 0.019 square miles. Located at 35.47° N. Lat; 80.26° W. Long. Elevation is 646 feet.
Population: 613; Growth (since 2000): 19.0%; Density: 273.0 persons per square mile; Race: 82.5% White, 8.8% Black/African American, 5.4% Asian, 1.3% American Indian/Alaska Native, 0.0% Native Hawaiian/Other Pacific Islander, 1.3% Two or more races, 0.7% Hispanic of any race; Average household size: 2.70; Median age: 37.4; Age under 18: 24.0%; Age 65 and over: 11.3%; Males per 100 females: 103.7
School District(s)
Stanly County Schools (PK-12)
    2012-13 Enrollment: 8,827 . . . . (704) 961-3000
Housing: Homeownership rate: 74.4%; Homeowner vacancy rate: 2.3%; Rental vacancy rate: 4.9%

STANFIELD (town). Covers a land area of 4.448 square miles and a water area of 0 square miles. Located at 35.23° N. Lat; 80.43° W. Long. Elevation is 607 feet.
Population: 1,486; Growth (since 2000): 33.5%; Density: 334.1 persons per square mile; Race: 94.0% White, 0.9% Black/African American, 0.2% Asian, 0.7% American Indian/Alaska Native, 0.3% Native Hawaiian/Other Pacific Islander, 1.3% Two or more races, 4.8% Hispanic of any race; Average household size: 2.76; Median age: 36.9; Age under 18: 27.6%; Age 65 and over: 11.6%; Males per 100 females: 100.0
School District(s)
Stanly County Schools (PK-12)
    2012-13 Enrollment: 8,827 . . . . (704) 961-3000
Housing: Homeownership rate: 80.3%; Homeowner vacancy rate: 2.0%; Rental vacancy rate: 7.0%

Stokes County

Located in northern North Carolina; bounded on the north by Virginia; piedmont area, drained by the Dan River. Covers a land area of 448.857 square miles, a water area of 6.772 square miles, and is located in the Eastern Time Zone at 36.40° N. Lat., 80.24° W. Long. The county was founded in 1798. County seat is Danbury.

Stokes County is part of the Winston-Salem, NC Metropolitan Statistical Area. The entire metro area includes: Davidson County, NC; Davie County, NC; Forsyth County, NC; Stokes County, NC; Yadkin County, NC

Weather Station: Danbury 1 NW									Elevation: 839 feet		
	Jan	Feb	Mar	Apr	May	Jun	Jul	Aug	Sep	Oct	Nov	Dec
High	48	52	60	70	77	84	87	86	80	70	61	51
Low	25	28	33	42	51	60	65	63	56	43	34	28
Precip	3.3	3.1	4.4	3.7	4.1	4.1	5.0	4.1	4.4	3.4	3.2	3.5
Snow	2.1	3.1	1.3	0.1	0.0	0.0	0.0	0.0	0.0	0.0	tr	1.3

High and Low temperatures in degrees Fahrenheit; Precipitation and Snow in inches

Population: 47,401; Growth (since 2000): 6.0%; Density: 105.6 persons per square mile; Race: 92.9% White, 4.0% Black/African American, 0.3% Asian, 0.3% American Indian/Alaska Native, 0.0% Native Hawaiian/Other Pacific Islander, 1.2% two or more races, 2.6% Hispanic of any race; Average household size: 2.42; Median age: 42.8; Age under 18: 22.2%; Age 65 and over: 16.0%; Males per 100 females: 95.3; Marriage status: 20.6% never married, 62.0% now married, 2.9% separated, 7.0% widowed, 10.3% divorced; Foreign born: 1.5%; Speak English only: 96.8%; With disability: 14.7%; Veterans: 8.6%; Ancestry: 16.7% American, 10.6% German, 10.1% English, 8.0% Irish, 2.3% Scottish

Religion: Six largest groups: 19.5% Baptist, 6.7% Methodist/Pietist, 4.8% Non-denominational Protestant, 1.5% Pentecostal, 1.4% Catholicism, 0.8% Presbyterian-Reformed
Economy: Unemployment rate: 4.9%; Leading industries: 17.0% retail trade; 16.1% construction; 13.1% other services (except public administration); Farms: 926 totaling 91,547 acres; Company size: 0 employ 1,000 or more persons, 0 employ 500 to 999 persons, 4 employ 100 to 499 persons, 606 employ less than 100 persons; Business ownership: 661 women-owned, n/a Black-owned, n/a Hispanic-owned, n/a Asian-owned
Employment: 9.0% management, business, and financial, 2.7% computer, engineering, and science, 8.3% education, legal, community service, arts, and media, 5.4% healthcare practitioners, 16.5% service, 23.8% sales and office, 12.7% natural resources, construction, and maintenance, 21.7% production, transportation, and material moving
Income: Per capita: $21,311; Median household: $42,703; Average household: $52,212; Households with income of $100,000 or more: 10.9%; Poverty rate: 15.8%
Educational Attainment: High school diploma or higher: 81.1%; Bachelor's degree or higher: 13.4%; Graduate/professional degree or higher: 3.8%
Housing: Homeownership rate: 78.0%; Median home value: $118,100; Median year structure built: 1982; Homeowner vacancy rate: 2.2%; Median gross rent: $620 per month; Rental vacancy rate: 9.0%
Vital Statistics: Birth rate: 84.1 per 10,000 population; Death rate: 102.6 per 10,000 population; Age-adjusted cancer mortality rate: 200.6 deaths per 100,000 population
Health Insurance: 87.9% have insurance; 68.6% have private insurance; 33.0% have public insurance; 12.1% do not have insurance; 4.3% of children under 18 do not have insurance
Health Care: Physicians: 3.6 per 10,000 population; Hospital beds: 13.8 per 10,000 population; Hospital admissions: 63.8 per 10,000 population
Transportation: Commute: 94.3% car, 0.2% public transportation, 1.2% walk, 3.5% work from home; Median travel time to work: 28.0 minutes
Presidential Election: 27.8% Obama, 70.5% Romney (2012)
National and State Parks: Hanging Rock State Park
Additional Information Contacts
Stokes Government. . . . . (336) 593-2811
    http://www.co.stokes.nc.us

Stokes County Communities

DANBURY (town). County seat. Covers a land area of 0.800 square miles and a water area of 0.004 square miles. Located at 36.41° N. Lat; 80.21° W. Long. Elevation is 814 feet.
Population: 189; Growth (since 2000): 75.0%; Density: 236.4 persons per square mile; Race: 91.0% White, 5.8% Black/African American, 0.5% Asian, 0.0% American Indian/Alaska Native, 0.0% Native Hawaiian/Other Pacific Islander, 1.1% Two or more races, 4.8% Hispanic of any race; Average household size: 2.62; Median age: 31.7; Age under 18: 18.0%; Age 65 and over: 7.4%; Males per 100 females: 186.4
School District(s)
Stokes County Schools (PK-12)
    2012-13 Enrollment: 6,904 . . . . (336) 593-8146
Housing: Homeownership rate: 80.9%; Homeowner vacancy rate: 2.9%; Rental vacancy rate: 9.1%
Hospitals: Pioneer Community Hospital of Stokes (93 beds)

KING (city). Covers a land area of 5.837 square miles and a water area of 0.055 square miles. Located at 36.27° N. Lat; 80.36° W. Long. Elevation is 1,119 feet.
History: King was one of the earliest settlements in what is now Stokes County.
Population: 6,904; Growth (since 2000): 16.0%; Density: 1,182.7 persons per square mile; Race: 95.1% White, 1.9% Black/African American, 0.8% Asian, 0.3% American Indian/Alaska Native, 0.0% Native Hawaiian/Other Pacific Islander, 1.0% Two or more races, 2.9% Hispanic of any race; Average household size: 2.34; Median age: 43.4; Age under 18: 22.4%; Age 65 and over: 20.0%; Males per 100 females: 84.3; Marriage status: 17.1% never married, 60.9% now married, 1.8% separated, 8.6% widowed, 13.4% divorced; Foreign born: 0.6%; Speak English only: 97.5%; With disability: 12.6%; Veterans: 8.4%; Ancestry: 20.3% American, 15.0% German, 7.9% English, 5.5% Irish, 2.5% European
Employment: 10.0% management, business, and financial, 1.9% computer, engineering, and science, 20.6% education, legal, community

service, arts, and media, 9.1% healthcare practitioners, 11.8% service, 22.3% sales and office, 8.5% natural resources, construction, and maintenance, 15.7% production, transportation, and material moving
Income: Per capita: $24,312; Median household: $53,107; Average household: $60,060; Households with income of $100,000 or more: 13.9%; Poverty rate: 11.2%
Educational Attainment: High school diploma or higher: 89.7%; Bachelor's degree or higher: 24.7%; Graduate/professional degree or higher: 6.4%

School District(s)
Stokes County Schools (PK-12)
    2012-13 Enrollment: 6,904 . . . . (336) 593-8146
Housing: Homeownership rate: 71.4%; Median home value: $142,100; Median year structure built: 1984; Homeowner vacancy rate: 3.5%; Median gross rent: $647 per month; Rental vacancy rate: 7.0%
Health Insurance: 92.2% have insurance; 79.7% have private insurance; 25.5% have public insurance; 7.8% do not have insurance; 1.5% of children under 18 do not have insurance
Safety: Violent crime rate: 19.0 per 10,000 population; Property crime rate: 411.1 per 10,000 population
Newspapers: Weekly Independent (weekly circulation 1800)
Transportation: Commute: 94.7% car, 0.0% public transportation, 0.6% walk, 4.3% work from home; Median travel time to work: 21.8 minutes
Additional Information Contacts
City of King . . . . (336) 983-8265
    http://www.ci.king.nc.us

LAWSONVILLE (unincorporated postal area)
ZCTA: 27022
    Covers a land area of 33.263 square miles and a water area of 0.118 square miles. Located at 36.51° N. Lat; 80.22° W. Long. Elevation is 1,171 feet.
    Population: 1,560; Growth (since 2000): -1.3%; Density: 46.9 persons per square mile; Race: 95.8% White, 1.1% Black/African American, 0.0% Asian, 0.4% American Indian/Alaska Native, 0.0% Native Hawaiian/Other Pacific Islander, 0.6% Two or more races, 3.7% Hispanic of any race; Average household size: 2.41; Median age: 45.1; Age under 18: 18.6%; Age 65 and over: 16.4%; Males per 100 females: 98.5

School District(s)
Stokes County Schools (PK-12)
    2012-13 Enrollment: 6,904 . . . . (336) 593-8146
    Housing: Homeownership rate: 82.5%; Homeowner vacancy rate: 2.4%; Rental vacancy rate: 6.6%

PINE HALL (unincorporated postal area)
ZCTA: 27042
    Covers a land area of 8.613 square miles and a water area of 0.090 square miles. Located at 36.35° N. Lat; 80.06° W. Long. Elevation is 643 feet.
    Population: 834; Growth (since 2000): 28.5%; Density: 96.8 persons per square mile; Race: 86.6% White, 8.4% Black/African American, 0.5% Asian, 0.4% American Indian/Alaska Native, 0.0% Native Hawaiian/Other Pacific Islander, 1.4% Two or more races, 3.6% Hispanic of any race; Average household size: 2.45; Median age: 42.3; Age under 18: 21.9%; Age 65 and over: 17.4%; Males per 100 females: 103.4

School District(s)
Stokes County Schools (PK-12)
    2012-13 Enrollment: 6,904 . . . . (336) 593-8146
    Housing: Homeownership rate: 79.5%; Homeowner vacancy rate: 1.1%; Rental vacancy rate: 15.7%

PINNACLE (CDP).
Covers a land area of 3.611 square miles and a water area of 0.018 square miles. Located at 36.32° N. Lat; 80.42° W. Long. Elevation is 1,079 feet.
Population: 894; Growth (since 2000): n/a; Density: 247.6 persons per square mile; Race: 91.1% White, 6.6% Black/African American, 0.9% Asian, 0.1% American Indian/Alaska Native, 0.0% Native Hawaiian/Other Pacific Islander, 0.8% Two or more races, 1.3% Hispanic of any race; Average household size: 2.55; Median age: 43.5; Age under 18: 23.4%; Age 65 and over: 13.4%; Males per 100 females: 101.4

School District(s)
Stokes County Schools (PK-12)
    2012-13 Enrollment: 6,904 . . . . (336) 593-8146

Surry County Schools (PK-12)
    2012-13 Enrollment: 8,589 . . . . (336) 386-8211
Housing: Homeownership rate: 81.4%; Homeowner vacancy rate: 1.4%; Rental vacancy rate: 14.7%

SANDY RIDGE (unincorporated postal area)
ZCTA: 27046
    Covers a land area of 40.646 square miles and a water area of 0.130 square miles. Located at 36.50° N. Lat; 80.08° W. Long. Elevation is 1,122 feet.
    Population: 2,024; Growth (since 2000): -0.4%; Density: 49.8 persons per square mile; Race: 95.6% White, 1.4% Black/African American, 0.0% Asian, 0.2% American Indian/Alaska Native, 0.0% Native Hawaiian/Other Pacific Islander, 0.8% Two or more races, 4.0% Hispanic of any race; Average household size: 2.42; Median age: 42.0; Age under 18: 20.7%; Age 65 and over: 15.3%; Males per 100 females: 102.2

School District(s)
Stokes County Schools (PK-12)
    2012-13 Enrollment: 6,904 . . . . (336) 593-8146
    Housing: Homeownership rate: 80.3%; Homeowner vacancy rate: 3.8%; Rental vacancy rate: 15.2%

WALNUT COVE (town).
Covers a land area of 2.409 square miles and a water area of 0.029 square miles. Located at 36.29° N. Lat; 80.14° W. Long. Elevation is 656 feet.
History: Walnut Cove was first called Lash for Dr. William A. Lash, upon whose land the town was platted.
Population: 1,425; Growth (since 2000): -2.7%; Density: 591.5 persons per square mile; Race: 79.6% White, 18.2% Black/African American, 0.2% Asian, 0.1% American Indian/Alaska Native, 0.0% Native Hawaiian/Other Pacific Islander, 1.3% Two or more races, 1.5% Hispanic of any race; Average household size: 1.96; Median age: 49.2; Age under 18: 18.2%; Age 65 and over: 29.6%; Males per 100 females: 79.5

School District(s)
Stokes County Schools (PK-12)
    2012-13 Enrollment: 6,904 . . . . (336) 593-8146
Housing: Homeownership rate: 50.7%; Homeowner vacancy rate: 4.2%; Rental vacancy rate: 6.7%
Newspapers: The Stokes News (weekly circulation 8000)

Surry County

Located in northwestern North Carolina; piedmont area, bounded on the north by Virginia, and on the south by the Yadkin River. Covers a land area of 532.166 square miles, a water area of 4.137 square miles, and is located in the Eastern Time Zone at 36.42° N. Lat., 80.69° W. Long. The county was founded in 1770. County seat is Dobson.

Surry County is part of the Mount Airy, NC Micropolitan Statistical Area. The entire metro area includes: Surry County, NC

Weather Station: Mount Airy 2 W   Elevation: 1,040 feet

	Jan	Feb	Mar	Apr	May	Jun	Jul	Aug	Sep	Oct	Nov	Dec
High	48	52	60	70	77	84	87	86	80	70	61	50
Low	26	28	33	41	50	60	64	63	56	43	34	28
Precip	3.6	3.1	4.2	3.9	4.2	4.4	5.1	4.0	4.0	3.3	3.5	3.4
Snow	3.6	2.8	0.8	tr	0.0	0.0	0.0	0.0	0.0	0.0	tr	1.6

High and Low temperatures in degrees Fahrenheit; Precipitation and Snow in inches

Population: 73,673; Growth (since 2000): 3.4%; Density: 138.4 persons per square mile; Race: 88.1% White, 3.7% Black/African American, 0.5% Asian, 0.3% American Indian/Alaska Native, 0.0% Native Hawaiian/Other Pacific Islander, 1.4% two or more races, 9.7% Hispanic of any race; Average household size: 2.43; Median age: 41.2; Age under 18: 23.4%; Age 65 and over: 16.6%; Males per 100 females: 95.4; Marriage status: 22.7% never married, 58.5% now married, 3.5% separated, 7.6% widowed, 11.3% divorced; Foreign born: 5.7%; Speak English only: 90.5%; With disability: 16.9%; Veterans: 8.4%; Ancestry: 26.5% American, 11.1% English, 7.1% German, 6.8% Irish, 2.1% Scotch-Irish
Religion: Six largest groups: 32.3% Baptist, 7.3% Methodist/Pietist, 5.4% Non-denominational Protestant, 1.9% Pentecostal, 1.9% Latter-day Saints, 1.3% Presbyterian-Reformed
Economy: Unemployment rate: 5.6%; Leading industries: 20.1% retail trade; 10.9% construction; 10.9% other services (except public administration); Farms: 1,256 totaling 126,897 acres; Company size: 1

employs 1,000 or more persons, 3 employ 500 to 999 persons, 28 employ 100 to 499 persons, 1,641 employs less than 100 persons; Business ownership: 1,555 women-owned, n/a Black-owned, 195 Hispanic-owned, n/a Asian-owned

Employment: 10.1% management, business, and financial, 2.9% computer, engineering, and science, 9.6% education, legal, community service, arts, and media, 5.5% healthcare practitioners, 17.8% service, 22.5% sales and office, 13.8% natural resources, construction, and maintenance, 17.7% production, transportation, and material moving

Income: Per capita: $20,219; Median household: $35,641; Average household: $48,859; Households with income of $100,000 or more: 10.3%; Poverty rate: 19.9%

Educational Attainment: High school diploma or higher: 75.3%; Bachelor's degree or higher: 15.0%; Graduate/professional degree or higher: 4.9%

Housing: Homeownership rate: 72.7%; Median home value: $109,900; Median year structure built: 1977; Homeowner vacancy rate: 2.1%; Median gross rent: $591 per month; Rental vacancy rate: 9.8%

Vital Statistics: Birth rate: 106.6 per 10,000 population; Death rate: 112.8 per 10,000 population; Age-adjusted cancer mortality rate: 214.1 deaths per 100,000 population

Health Insurance: 82.1% have insurance; 58.7% have private insurance; 37.7% have public insurance; 17.9% do not have insurance; 7.7% of children under 18 do not have insurance

Health Care: Physicians: 12.8 per 10,000 population; Hospital beds: 42.9 per 10,000 population; Hospital admissions: 1,325.1 per 10,000 population

Transportation: Commute: 95.6% car, 0.6% public transportation, 0.7% walk, 2.3% work from home; Median travel time to work: 25.3 minutes

Presidential Election: 30.9% Obama, 67.6% Romney (2012)

National and State Parks: Pilot Mountain State Park

Additional Information Contacts
Surry Government . . . . (336) 401-8201
    http://www.co.surry.nc.us

Surry County Communities

ARARAT (unincorporated postal area)
ZCTA: 27007
    Covers a land area of 21.225 square miles and a water area of 0.118 square miles. Located at 36.39° N. Lat; 80.59° W. Long. Elevation is 902 feet.
    Population: 2,162; Growth (since 2000): 61.5%; Density: 101.9 persons per square mile; Race: 93.8% White, 0.6% Black/African American, 0.1% Asian, 0.1% American Indian/Alaska Native, 0.0% Native Hawaiian/Other Pacific Islander, 1.2% Two or more races, 6.0% Hispanic of any race; Average household size: 2.60; Median age: 39.6; Age under 18: 25.1%; Age 65 and over: 13.1%; Males per 100 females: 100.0
    Housing: Homeownership rate: 81.2%; Homeowner vacancy rate: 1.0%; Rental vacancy rate: 5.4%

DOBSON (town). County seat. Covers a land area of 1.961 square miles and a water area of 0.009 square miles. Located at 36.39° N. Lat; 80.73° W. Long. Elevation is 1,257 feet.
Population: 1,586; Growth (since 2000): 8.9%; Density: 809.0 persons per square mile; Race: 78.3% White, 4.2% Black/African American, 0.3% Asian, 0.9% American Indian/Alaska Native, 0.0% Native Hawaiian/Other Pacific Islander, 1.4% Two or more races, 24.5% Hispanic of any race; Average household size: 2.38; Median age: 36.1; Age under 18: 22.3%; Age 65 and over: 13.6%; Males per 100 females: 113.7
School District(s)
Surry County Schools (PK-12)
    2012-13 Enrollment: 8,589 . . . . (336) 386-8211
Two-year College(s)
Surry Community College (Public)
    Fall 2013 Enrollment: 3,454 . . . . (336) 386-8121
    2013-14 Tuition: In-state $2,401; Out-of-state $8,545
Housing: Homeownership rate: 44.4%; Homeowner vacancy rate: 3.7%; Rental vacancy rate: 6.0%
Safety: Violent crime rate: 37.8 per 10,000 population; Property crime rate: 290.0 per 10,000 population

ELKIN (town). Covers a land area of 6.633 square miles and a water area of 0.079 square miles. Located at 36.26° N. Lat; 80.85° W. Long. Elevation is 896 feet.
History: Elkin is said to have been so named because a man shouted "Elk in" when the elk he pursued fell into the creek here.
Population: 4,001; Growth (since 2000): -2.6%; Density: 603.2 persons per square mile; Race: 78.0% White, 6.4% Black/African American, 0.8% Asian, 0.2% American Indian/Alaska Native, 0.0% Native Hawaiian/Other Pacific Islander, 1.5% Two or more races, 17.8% Hispanic of any race; Average household size: 2.32; Median age: 42.4; Age under 18: 23.3%; Age 65 and over: 21.6%; Males per 100 females: 89.0; Marriage status: 18.0% never married, 57.2% now married, 2.4% separated, 12.4% widowed, 12.3% divorced; Foreign born: 12.6%; Speak English only: 79.2%; With disability: 16.2%; Veterans: 10.0%; Ancestry: 16.9% German, 12.9% American, 9.8% English, 9.1% Irish, 3.6% Scottish
Employment: 12.5% management, business, and financial, 3.0% computer, engineering, and science, 7.5% education, legal, community service, arts, and media, 6.7% healthcare practitioners, 17.5% service, 22.2% sales and office, 9.9% natural resources, construction, and maintenance, 20.8% production, transportation, and material moving
Income: Per capita: $20,934; Median household: $37,429; Average household: $52,667; Households with income of $100,000 or more: 12.4%; Poverty rate: 15.3%
Educational Attainment: High school diploma or higher: 76.4%; Bachelor's degree or higher: 19.2%; Graduate/professional degree or higher: 5.6%
School District(s)
Elkin City Schools (PK-12)
    2012-13 Enrollment: 1,228 . . . . (336) 835-3135
Wilkes County Schools (PK-12)
    2012-13 Enrollment: 10,384 . . . . (336) 667-1121
Housing: Homeownership rate: 60.0%; Median home value: $133,000; Median year structure built: 1965; Homeowner vacancy rate: 3.0%; Median gross rent: $651 per month; Rental vacancy rate: 21.3%
Health Insurance: 74.6% have insurance; 49.3% have private insurance; 39.5% have public insurance; 25.4% do not have insurance; 10.3% of children under 18 do not have insurance
Hospitals: Hugh Chatham Memorial Hospital (222 beds)
Newspapers: The Tribune (weekly circulation 5800)
Transportation: Commute: 93.1% car, 0.0% public transportation, 1.9% walk, 3.8% work from home; Median travel time to work: 20.5 minutes
Airports: Elkin Municipal (general aviation)
Additional Information Contacts
Town of Elkin . . . . (336) 835-9800
    http://www.elkinnc.org

FLAT ROCK (CDP). Covers a land area of 2.613 square miles and a water area of 0.019 square miles. Located at 36.51° N. Lat; 80.58° W. Long. Elevation is 1,145 feet.
Population: 1,556; Growth (since 2000): -7.9%; Density: 595.4 persons per square mile; Race: 85.8% White, 6.5% Black/African American, 0.5% Asian, 0.3% American Indian/Alaska Native, 0.0% Native Hawaiian/Other Pacific Islander, 1.3% Two or more races, 8.2% Hispanic of any race; Average household size: 2.37; Median age: 42.3; Age under 18: 21.2%; Age 65 and over: 18.8%; Males per 100 females: 86.3
Housing: Homeownership rate: 68.9%; Homeowner vacancy rate: 2.4%; Rental vacancy rate: 9.7%

LOWGAP (CDP). Covers a land area of 1.137 square miles and a water area of <.001 square miles. Located at 36.52° N. Lat; 80.87° W. Long. Elevation is 1,457 feet.
Population: 324; Growth (since 2000): n/a; Density: 285.0 persons per square mile; Race: 95.4% White, 0.9% Black/African American, 0.0% Asian, 0.0% American Indian/Alaska Native, 0.0% Native Hawaiian/Other Pacific Islander, 0.9% Two or more races, 4.0% Hispanic of any race; Average household size: 2.45; Median age: 40.8; Age under 18: 26.2%; Age 65 and over: 14.5%; Males per 100 females: 100.0
School District(s)
Surry County Schools (PK-12)
    2012-13 Enrollment: 8,589 . . . . (336) 386-8211
Housing: Homeownership rate: 67.4%; Homeowner vacancy rate: 3.2%; Rental vacancy rate: 6.5%

MOUNT AIRY (city). Covers a land area of 11.653 square miles and a water area of 0.137 square miles. Located at 36.51° N. Lat; 80.61° W. Long. Elevation is 1,099 feet.

History: Incorporated 1885.

Population: 10,388; Growth (since 2000): 22.4%; Density: 891.4 persons per square mile; Race: 84.1% White, 8.2% Black/African American, 1.4% Asian, 0.3% American Indian/Alaska Native, 0.1% Native Hawaiian/Other Pacific Islander, 2.2% Two or more races, 6.7% Hispanic of any race; Average household size: 2.13; Median age: 45.8; Age under 18: 20.2%; Age 65 and over: 22.7%; Males per 100 females: 84.5; Marriage status: 19.3% never married, 56.9% now married, 6.7% separated, 12.1% widowed, 11.6% divorced; Foreign born: 7.4%; Speak English only: 90.5%; With disability: 20.0%; Veterans: 10.6%; Ancestry: 16.4% American, 11.2% English, 8.5% German, 5.7% Irish, 3.9% Scotch-Irish

Employment: 7.8% management, business, and financial, 3.4% computer, engineering, and science, 14.8% education, legal, community service, arts, and media, 7.7% healthcare practitioners, 17.1% service, 23.9% sales and office, 13.4% natural resources, construction, and maintenance, 12.0% production, transportation, and material moving

Income: Per capita: $22,487; Median household: $32,258; Average household: $48,498; Households with income of $100,000 or more: 9.6%; Poverty rate: 21.5%

Educational Attainment: High school diploma or higher: 75.5%; Bachelor's degree or higher: 24.8%; Graduate/professional degree or higher: 8.5%

School District(s)
Millennium Charter Academy (KG-08)
    2012-13 Enrollment: 487 . . . . (336) 789-7570
Mount Airy City Schools (PK-12)
    2012-13 Enrollment: 1,743 . . . . (336) 786-8355
Surry County Schools (PK-12)
    2012-13 Enrollment: 8,589 . . . . (336) 386-8211

Housing: Homeownership rate: 57.1%; Median home value: $129,600; Median year structure built: 1964; Homeowner vacancy rate: 3.6%; Median gross rent: $598 per month; Rental vacancy rate: 8.9%

Health Insurance: 85.6% have insurance; 56.2% have private insurance; 45.9% have public insurance; 14.4% do not have insurance; 3.5% of children under 18 do not have insurance

Hospitals: Northern Hospital of Surry County (113 beds)

Safety: Violent crime rate: 38.3 per 10,000 population; Property crime rate: 500.5 per 10,000 population

Newspapers: Mount Airy News (daily circulation 9300); Surrey Scene (weekly circulation 17000)

Transportation: Commute: 93.7% car, 0.8% public transportation, 1.2% walk, 2.6% work from home; Median travel time to work: 19.6 minutes

Airports: Mount Airy/Surry County (general aviation)

Additional Information Contacts
City of Mount Airy . . . . (336) 786-3501
    http://www.mountairy.org

PILOT MOUNTAIN (town). Covers a land area of 2.000 square miles and a water area of 0.018 square miles. Located at 36.38° N. Lat; 80.47° W. Long. Elevation is 1,155 feet.

Population: 1,477; Growth (since 2000): 15.3%; Density: 738.5 persons per square mile; Race: 89.1% White, 6.5% Black/African American, 0.9% Asian, 0.4% American Indian/Alaska Native, 0.1% Native Hawaiian/Other Pacific Islander, 1.6% Two or more races, 3.3% Hispanic of any race; Average household size: 2.21; Median age: 39.8; Age under 18: 23.6%; Age 65 and over: 17.1%; Males per 100 females: 85.8

School District(s)
Surry County Schools (PK-12)
    2012-13 Enrollment: 8,589 . . . . (336) 386-8211

Housing: Homeownership rate: 56.5%; Homeowner vacancy rate: 2.8%; Rental vacancy rate: 5.2%

Safety: Violent crime rate: 27.1 per 10,000 population; Property crime rate: 819.2 per 10,000 population

Newspapers: The Pilot (weekly circulation 4500)

SILOAM (unincorporated postal area)
ZCTA: 27047
    Covers a land area of 20.312 square miles and a water area of 0.250 square miles. Located at 36.32° N. Lat; 80.57° W. Long. Elevation is 833 feet.

Population: 1,191; Growth (since 2000): -3.4%; Density: 58.6 persons per square mile; Race: 96.7% White, 0.3% Black/African American,

0.2% Asian, 0.4% American Indian/Alaska Native, 0.0% Native Hawaiian/Other Pacific Islander, 1.3% Two or more races, 2.6% Hispanic of any race; Average household size: 2.54; Median age: 40.4; Age under 18: 24.9%; Age 65 and over: 15.8%; Males per 100 females: 99.8

Housing: Homeownership rate: 83.1%; Homeowner vacancy rate: 2.0%; Rental vacancy rate: 6.0%

TOAST (CDP). Covers a land area of 1.513 square miles and a water area of 0.011 square miles. Located at 36.50° N. Lat; 80.64° W. Long. Elevation is 1,066 feet.

Population: 1,450; Growth (since 2000): -24.6%; Density: 958.1 persons per square mile; Race: 89.9% White, 3.2% Black/African American, 0.3% Asian, 0.0% American Indian/Alaska Native, 0.0% Native Hawaiian/Other Pacific Islander, 1.9% Two or more races, 11.1% Hispanic of any race; Average household size: 2.29; Median age: 44.9; Age under 18: 20.8%; Age 65 and over: 18.8%; Males per 100 females: 89.5

Housing: Homeownership rate: 68.7%; Homeowner vacancy rate: 2.2%; Rental vacancy rate: 7.9%

WESTFIELD (unincorporated postal area)
ZCTA: 27053
    Covers a land area of 67.585 square miles and a water area of 0.389 square miles. Located at 36.47° N. Lat; 80.35° W. Long. Elevation is 1,253 feet.

Population: 3,007; Growth (since 2000): 7.0%; Density: 44.5 persons per square mile; Race: 92.6% White, 5.2% Black/African American, 0.1% Asian, 0.3% American Indian/Alaska Native, 0.0% Native Hawaiian/Other Pacific Islander, 0.9% Two or more races, 1.5% Hispanic of any race; Average household size: 2.40; Median age: 44.7; Age under 18: 21.9%; Age 65 and over: 17.3%; Males per 100 females: 101.5; Marriage status: 21.0% never married, 65.6% now married, 3.2% separated, 6.4% widowed, 7.0% divorced; Foreign born: 0.9%; Speak English only: 96.0%; With disability: 17.0%; Veterans: 9.9%; Ancestry: 21.8% American, 18.8% English, 9.4% Irish, 7.0% German, 2.4% Scottish

Employment: 7.5% management, business, and financial, 2.3% computer, engineering, and science, 8.9% education, legal, community service, arts, and media, 2.7% healthcare practitioners, 19.2% service, 29.8% sales and office, 11.2% natural resources, construction, and maintenance, 18.4% production, transportation, and material moving

Income: Per capita: $18,172; Median household: $33,475; Average household: $46,641; Households with income of $100,000 or more: 5.7%; Poverty rate: 18.0%

Educational Attainment: High school diploma or higher: 81.7%; Bachelor's degree or higher: 19.5%; Graduate/professional degree or higher: 6.1%

School District(s)
Stokes County Schools (PK-12)
    2012-13 Enrollment: 6,904 . . . . (336) 593-8146

Housing: Homeownership rate: 82.1%; Median home value: $132,000; Median year structure built: 1976; Homeowner vacancy rate: 1.7%; Median gross rent: $659 per month; Rental vacancy rate: 8.8%

Health Insurance: 86.9% have insurance; 67.4% have private insurance; 31.3% have public insurance; 13.1% do not have insurance; 5.2% of children under 18 do not have insurance

Transportation: Commute: 88.3% car, 2.1% public transportation, 0.3% walk, 6.4% work from home; Median travel time to work: 38.8 minutes

WHITE PLAINS (CDP). Covers a land area of 4.011 square miles and a water area of 0.020 square miles. Located at 36.44° N. Lat; 80.65° W. Long. Elevation is 1,125 feet.

Population: 1,074; Growth (since 2000): 2.4%; Density: 267.8 persons per square mile; Race: 94.0% White, 1.0% Black/African American, 0.5% Asian, 0.8% American Indian/Alaska Native, 0.0% Native Hawaiian/Other Pacific Islander, 0.8% Two or more races, 4.2% Hispanic of any race; Average household size: 2.40; Median age: 41.1; Age under 18: 22.8%; Age 65 and over: 15.1%; Males per 100 females: 95.3

Housing: Homeownership rate: 69.6%; Homeowner vacancy rate: 0.9%; Rental vacancy rate: 8.7%

Swain County

Located in western North Carolina; mountainous area, bounded on the north by Tennessee, and on the west by the Little Tennessee River.

Covers a land area of 527.996 square miles, a water area of 12.648 square miles, and is located in the Eastern Time Zone at 35.57° N. Lat., 83.47° W. Long. The county was founded in 1871. County seat is Bryson City.

Weather Station: Oconaluftee   Elevation: 2,040 feet

	Jan	Feb	Mar	Apr	May	Jun	Jul	Aug	Sep	Oct	Nov	Dec
High	49	53	61	69	77	83	86	85	80	71	61	51
Low	22	24	30	38	46	55	59	58	51	39	30	24
Precip	4.9	4.5	4.9	4.2	5.1	4.3	4.6	4.0	3.7	2.8	4.4	4.6
Snow	3.2	1.1	0.5	0.9	0.0	0.0	0.0	0.0	0.0	0.0	0.1	0.5

High and Low temperatures in degrees Fahrenheit; Precipitation and Snow in inches

Population: 13,981; Growth (since 2000): 7.8%; Density: 26.5 persons per square mile; Race: 66.6% White, 0.5% Black/African American, 0.5% Asian, 27.0% American Indian/Alaska Native, 0.0% Native Hawaiian/Other Pacific Islander, 4.2% two or more races, 3.9% Hispanic of any race; Average household size: 2.42; Median age: 40.8; Age under 18: 23.4%; Age 65 and over: 16.6%; Males per 100 females: 95.0; Marriage status: 25.1% never married, 50.6% now married, 2.2% separated, 8.6% widowed, 15.7% divorced; Foreign born: 2.0%; Speak English only: 97.7%; With disability: 14.3%; Veterans: 10.1%; Ancestry: 13.0% American, 9.2% English, 7.3% German, 6.6% Irish, 4.3% Scotch-Irish
Religion: Six largest groups: 24.3% Baptist, 4.0% Pentecostal, 2.4% Catholicism, 2.4% Non-denominational Protestant, 2.0% Methodist/Pietist, 1.3% Holiness
Economy: Unemployment rate: 6.6%; Leading industries: 26.8% retail trade; 22.9% accommodation and food services; 9.9% construction; Farms: 94 totaling n/a acres; Company size: 0 employ 1,000 or more persons, 0 employ 500 to 999 persons, 5 employ 100 to 499 persons, 357 employ less than 100 persons; Business ownership: 561 women-owned, n/a Black-owned, n/a Hispanic-owned, n/a Asian-owned
Employment: 10.5% management, business, and financial, 3.5% computer, engineering, and science, 9.9% education, legal, community service, arts, and media, 5.5% healthcare practitioners, 27.6% service, 21.7% sales and office, 10.7% natural resources, construction, and maintenance, 10.6% production, transportation, and material moving
Income: Per capita: $19,626; Median household: $36,094; Average household: $47,954; Households with income of $100,000 or more: 8.3%; Poverty rate: 27.2%
Educational Attainment: High school diploma or higher: 82.1%; Bachelor's degree or higher: 16.3%; Graduate/professional degree or higher: 6.0%
Housing: Homeownership rate: 74.1%; Median home value: $132,500; Median year structure built: 1983; Homeowner vacancy rate: 2.8%; Median gross rent: $584 per month; Rental vacancy rate: 22.8%
Vital Statistics: Birth rate: 144.4 per 10,000 population; Death rate: 143.0 per 10,000 population; Age-adjusted cancer mortality rate: 239.7 deaths per 100,000 population
Health Insurance: 73.1% have insurance; 49.1% have private insurance; 37.0% have public insurance; 26.9% do not have insurance; 22.8% of children under 18 do not have insurance
Health Care: Physicians: 12.8 per 10,000 population; Hospital beds: 20.0 per 10,000 population; Hospital admissions: 710.1 per 10,000 population
Air Quality Index: 83.7% good, 16.3% moderate, 0.0% unhealthy for sensitive individuals, 0.0% unhealthy (percent of days)
Transportation: Commute: 95.5% car, 0.2% public transportation, 1.4% walk, 2.6% work from home; Median travel time to work: 19.2 minutes
Presidential Election: 45.7% Obama, 52.0% Romney (2012)
Additional Information Contacts
Swain Government . . . . (828) 488-9273
    http://www.swaincountync.gov

Swain County Communities

ALMOND (unincorporated postal area)
ZCTA: 28702
    Covers a land area of 19.831 square miles and a water area of 1.923 square miles. Located at 35.41° N. Lat; 83.61° W. Long. Elevation is 1,722 feet.
    Population: 366; Growth (since 2000): 1,207.1%; Density: 18.5 persons per square mile; Race: 97.3% White, 0.0% Black/African American, 0.0% Asian, 2.7% American Indian/Alaska Native, 0.0% Native Hawaiian/Other Pacific Islander, 0.0% Two or more races, 0.5% Hispanic of any race; Average household size: 2.07; Median age: 52.5;

Age under 18: 16.1%; Age 65 and over: 27.0%; Males per 100 females: 91.6
Housing: Homeownership rate: 79.1%; Homeowner vacancy rate: 9.0%; Rental vacancy rate: 43.3%

BRYSON CITY (town). County seat. Covers a land area of 2.184 square miles and a water area of 0.109 square miles. Located at 35.43° N. Lat; 83.45° W. Long. Elevation is 1,732 feet.
History: Oconoluftee Indian Village and Museum of the Cherokee Indian at Cherokee Reservation.
Population: 1,424; Growth (since 2000): 0.9%; Density: 652.1 persons per square mile; Race: 89.5% White, 0.5% Black/African American, 0.6% Asian, 4.8% American Indian/Alaska Native, 0.0% Native Hawaiian/Other Pacific Islander, 2.2% Two or more races, 5.4% Hispanic of any race; Average household size: 2.17; Median age: 42.2; Age under 18: 21.0%; Age 65 and over: 21.1%; Males per 100 females: 84.5
School District(s)
Mountain Discovery Charter (KG-08)
    2012-13 Enrollment: 171 . . . . (828) 488-1222
Swain County Schools (PK-12)
    2012-13 Enrollment: 2,081 . . . . (828) 488-3129
Housing: Homeownership rate: 52.1%; Homeowner vacancy rate: 6.4%; Rental vacancy rate: 17.5%
Hospitals: Medwest Swain
Newspapers: Smoky Mountain Times (weekly circulation 4000)

Transylvania County

Located in western North Carolina, in the Blue Ridge; bounded on the south by South Carolina; drained by the French Broad River; includes part of Pisgah National Forest. Covers a land area of 378.528 square miles, a water area of 1.985 square miles, and is located in the Eastern Time Zone at 35.21° N. Lat., 82.82° W. Long. The county was founded in 1861. County seat is Brevard.

Transylvania County is part of the Brevard, NC Micropolitan Statistical Area. The entire metro area includes: Transylvania County, NC

Weather Station: Brevard   Elevation: 2,211 feet

	Jan	Feb	Mar	Apr	May	Jun	Jul	Aug	Sep	Oct	Nov	Dec
High	49	53	61	69	76	81	83	82	77	69	61	51
Low	25	28	33	41	49	58	62	61	54	43	34	27
Precip	5.2	4.9	5.5	4.4	5.0	6.4	5.6	5.5	5.7	4.5	5.3	5.9
Snow	2.6	1.6	0.6	0.5	0.0	0.0	0.0	0.0	0.0	0.0	0.2	0.8

High and Low temperatures in degrees Fahrenheit; Precipitation and Snow in inches

Weather Station: Pisgah Forest 1 N   Elevation: 2,109 feet

	Jan	Feb	Mar	Apr	May	Jun	Jul	Aug	Sep	Oct	Nov	Dec
High	49	53	60	68	75	81	85	83	78	69	61	52
Low	24	26	32	39	47	56	60	59	53	41	32	26
Precip	5.3	5.1	5.7	4.5	4.8	5.2	5.5	5.6	5.4	4.2	5.2	5.0
Snow	3.2	1.7	1.3	0.4	0.0	0.0	0.0	0.0	0.0	0.0	tr	1.2

High and Low temperatures in degrees Fahrenheit; Precipitation and Snow in inches

Population: 33,090; Growth (since 2000): 12.8%; Density: 87.4 persons per square mile; Race: 92.4% White, 3.9% Black/African American, 0.4% Asian, 0.3% American Indian/Alaska Native, 0.0% Native Hawaiian/Other Pacific Islander, 1.7% two or more races, 2.9% Hispanic of any race; Average household size: 2.22; Median age: 48.8; Age under 18: 17.6%; Age 65 and over: 25.8%; Males per 100 females: 93.3; Marriage status: 22.4% never married, 58.3% now married, 1.7% separated, 8.7% widowed, 10.6% divorced; Foreign born: 3.1%; Speak English only: 95.8%; With disability: 18.0%; Veterans: 13.7%; Ancestry: 25.6% American, 12.8% English, 11.4% Irish, 10.3% German, 5.6% Scotch-Irish
Religion: Six largest groups: 32.4% Baptist, 7.3% Catholicism, 5.1% Methodist/Pietist, 1.7% Episcopalianism/Anglicanism, 1.6% Non-denominational Protestant, 1.2% Pentecostal
Economy: Unemployment rate: 5.4%; Leading industries: 16.0% retail trade; 14.7% construction; 12.7% other services (except public administration); Farms: 221 totaling 17,929 acres; Company size: 0 employ 1,000 or more persons, 1 employs 500 to 999 persons, 8 employ 100 to 499 persons, 772 employ less than 100 persons; Business ownership: 638 women-owned, n/a Black-owned, n/a Hispanic-owned, n/a Asian-owned
Employment: 11.5% management, business, and financial, 2.7% computer, engineering, and science, 12.5% education, legal, community

service, arts, and media, 5.0% healthcare practitioners, 24.3% service, 21.0% sales and office, 13.0% natural resources, construction, and maintenance, 9.9% production, transportation, and material moving
Income: Per capita: $23,757; Median household: $41,781; Average household: $54,006; Households with income of $100,000 or more: 10.8%; Poverty rate: 14.3%
Educational Attainment: High school diploma or higher: 88.4%; Bachelor's degree or higher: 27.6%; Graduate/professional degree or higher: 11.1%
Housing: Homeownership rate: 75.6%; Median home value: $171,600; Median year structure built: 1982; Homeowner vacancy rate: 3.7%; Median gross rent: $659 per month; Rental vacancy rate: 10.7%
Vital Statistics: Birth rate: 79.0 per 10,000 population; Death rate: 110.3 per 10,000 population; Age-adjusted cancer mortality rate: 150.3 deaths per 100,000 population
Health Insurance: 81.9% have insurance; 61.2% have private insurance; 43.0% have public insurance; 18.1% do not have insurance; 8.8% of children under 18 do not have insurance
Health Care: Physicians: 14.3 per 10,000 population; Hospital beds: 15.8 per 10,000 population; Hospital admissions: 598.9 per 10,000 population
Transportation: Commute: 91.5% car, 0.0% public transportation, 2.3% walk, 4.5% work from home; Median travel time to work: 23.7 minutes
Presidential Election: 40.7% Obama, 57.5% Romney (2012)
National and State Parks: Gorges State Park
Additional Information Contacts
Transylvania Government . . . . (828) 884-3100
    http://www.transylvaniacounty.org

Transylvania County Communities

BALSAM GROVE (unincorporated postal area)
ZCTA: 28708
    Covers a land area of 48.716 square miles and a water area of 0 square miles. Located at 35.27° N. Lat; 82.86° W. Long. Elevation is 2,828 feet.
    Population: 754; Growth (since 2000): 31.8%; Density: 15.5 persons per square mile; Race: 97.9% White, 0.3% Black/African American, 0.0% Asian, 0.1% American Indian/Alaska Native, 0.0% Native Hawaiian/Other Pacific Islander, 1.7% Two or more races, 0.5% Hispanic of any race; Average household size: 2.44; Median age: 41.6; Age under 18: 23.2%; Age 65 and over: 16.3%; Males per 100 females: 104.3
    Housing: Homeownership rate: 79.6%; Homeowner vacancy rate: 1.2%; Rental vacancy rate: 0.0%

BREVARD (city). County seat. Covers a land area of 5.120 square miles and a water area of 0.003 square miles. Located at 35.24° N. Lat; 82.73° W. Long. Elevation is 2,224 feet.
History: Brevard is named for Ephraim Brevard, Revolutionary soldier and a member of the Mecklenburg Committee. The town was incorporated in 1867 with seven voters, every one of whom held office. The high hat industry once flourished in Brevard.
Population: 7,609; Growth (since 2000): 12.1%; Density: 1,486.0 persons per square mile; Race: 83.3% White, 11.0% Black/African American, 1.0% Asian, 0.3% American Indian/Alaska Native, 0.0% Native Hawaiian/Other Pacific Islander, 2.7% Two or more races, 3.7% Hispanic of any race; Average household size: 2.02; Median age: 46.9; Age under 18: 17.2%; Age 65 and over: 29.5%; Males per 100 females: 78.2; Marriage status: 32.7% never married, 39.1% now married, 1.7% separated, 14.5% widowed, 13.7% divorced; Foreign born: 5.0%; Speak English only: 92.6%; With disability: 15.7%; Veterans: 10.0%; Ancestry: 20.9% American, 11.4% English, 8.7% Irish, 8.5% German, 4.8% Scotch-Irish
Employment: 17.5% management, business, and financial, 5.4% computer, engineering, and science, 13.6% education, legal, community service, arts, and media, 8.4% healthcare practitioners, 21.8% service, 19.8% sales and office, 5.2% natural resources, construction, and maintenance, 8.4% production, transportation, and material moving
Income: Per capita: $22,048; Median household: $35,920; Average household: $49,371; Households with income of $100,000 or more: 10.9%; Poverty rate: 18.2%
Educational Attainment: High school diploma or higher: 87.7%; Bachelor's degree or higher: 35.5%; Graduate/professional degree or higher: 13.3%

School District(s)
Brevard Academy (KG-08)
    2012-13 Enrollment: 201 . . . . (828) 885-2665

Transylvania County Schools (PK-12)
    2012-13 Enrollment: 3,592 . . . . (828) 884-6173
Four-year College(s)
Brevard College (Private, Not-for-profit, United Methodist)
    Fall 2013 Enrollment: 701 . . . . (828) 883-8292
    2013-14 Tuition: In-state $25,200; Out-of-state $25,200
Housing: Homeownership rate: 56.2%; Median home value: $178,500; Median year structure built: 1971; Homeowner vacancy rate: 4.9%; Median gross rent: $641 per month; Rental vacancy rate: 8.2%
Health Insurance: 84.6% have insurance; 61.7% have private insurance; 43.9% have public insurance; 15.4% do not have insurance; 8.6% of children under 18 do not have insurance
Hospitals: Transylvania Regional Hospital (88 beds)
Safety: Violent crime rate: 13.3 per 10,000 population; Property crime rate: 375.5 per 10,000 population
Newspapers: The Transylvania Times (weekly circulation 8500)
Transportation: Commute: 88.5% car, 0.0% public transportation, 6.5% walk, 4.7% work from home; Median travel time to work: 20.4 minutes

CEDAR MOUNTAIN (unincorporated postal area)
ZCTA: 28718
    Covers a land area of 16.533 square miles and a water area of 0.062 square miles. Located at 35.16° N. Lat; 82.63° W. Long. Elevation is 2,703 feet.
    Population: 553; Growth (since 2000): 64.1%; Density: 33.4 persons per square mile; Race: 98.2% White, 0.0% Black/African American, 0.7% Asian, 0.0% American Indian/Alaska Native, 0.0% Native Hawaiian/Other Pacific Islander, 0.5% Two or more races, 3.8% Hispanic of any race; Average household size: 2.32; Median age: 49.2; Age under 18: 17.2%; Age 65 and over: 21.3%; Males per 100 females: 94.7
    Housing: Homeownership rate: 82.8%; Homeowner vacancy rate: 2.5%; Rental vacancy rate: 4.7%

LAKE TOXAWAY (unincorporated postal area)
ZCTA: 28747
    Covers a land area of 52.658 square miles and a water area of 0.844 square miles. Located at 35.16° N. Lat; 82.92° W. Long. Elevation is 3,015 feet.
    Population: 2,198; Growth (since 2000): 14.6%; Density: 41.7 persons per square mile; Race: 94.5% White, 0.0% Black/African American, 0.3% Asian, 0.2% American Indian/Alaska Native, 0.0% Native Hawaiian/Other Pacific Islander, 2.1% Two or more races, 3.6% Hispanic of any race; Average household size: 2.36; Median age: 46.3; Age under 18: 18.5%; Age 65 and over: 20.6%; Males per 100 females: 106.2
School District(s)
Transylvania County Schools (PK-12)
    2012-13 Enrollment: 3,592 . . . . (828) 884-6173
    Housing: Homeownership rate: 82.0%; Homeowner vacancy rate: 6.7%; Rental vacancy rate: 15.2%

PENROSE (unincorporated postal area)
ZCTA: 28766
    Covers a land area of 5.833 square miles and a water area of 0 square miles. Located at 35.25° N. Lat; 82.62° W. Long. Elevation is 2,106 feet.
    Population: 1,262; Growth (since 2000): 49.9%; Density: 216.3 persons per square mile; Race: 96.2% White, 1.1% Black/African American, 0.2% Asian, 0.0% American Indian/Alaska Native, 0.0% Native Hawaiian/Other Pacific Islander, 2.3% Two or more races, 1.3% Hispanic of any race; Average household size: 2.46; Median age: 42.1; Age under 18: 22.0%; Age 65 and over: 14.7%; Males per 100 females: 97.5
    Housing: Homeownership rate: 82.8%; Homeowner vacancy rate: 3.8%; Rental vacancy rate: 16.0%

PISGAH FOREST (unincorporated postal area)
ZCTA: 28768
    Covers a land area of 82.948 square miles and a water area of 0.203 square miles. Located at 35.33° N. Lat; 82.71° W. Long. Elevation is 2,106 feet.
    Population: 6,813; Growth (since 2000): 0.6%; Density: 82.1 persons per square mile; Race: 94.2% White, 3.0% Black/African American, 0.2% Asian, 0.2% American Indian/Alaska Native, 0.0% Native Hawaiian/Other Pacific Islander, 1.3% Two or more races, 3.1%

Hispanic of any race; Average household size: 2.31; Median age: 50.0; Age under 18: 17.6%; Age 65 and over: 24.1%; Males per 100 females: 96.2; Marriage status: 20.5% never married, 63.3% now married, 1.3% separated, 7.9% widowed, 8.4% divorced; Foreign born: 1.7%; Speak English only: 97.9%; With disability: 17.8%; Veterans: 15.0%; Ancestry: 20.2% American, 14.2% Irish, 13.6% English, 11.0% German, 7.1% European

Employment: 10.5% management, business, and financial, 2.6% computer, engineering, and science, 16.1% education, legal, community service, arts, and media, 4.3% healthcare practitioners, 24.4% service, 24.3% sales and office, 8.8% natural resources, construction, and maintenance, 9.0% production, transportation, and material moving

Income: Per capita: $23,489; Median household: $41,315; Average household: $54,104; Households with income of $100,000 or more: 11.7%; Poverty rate: 9.9%

Educational Attainment: High school diploma or higher: 92.7%; Bachelor's degree or higher: 31.0%; Graduate/professional degree or higher: 13.4%

Housing: Homeownership rate: 83.3%; Median home value: $184,200; Median year structure built: 1985; Homeowner vacancy rate: 2.1%; Median gross rent: $696 per month; Rental vacancy rate: 9.8%

Health Insurance: 81.9% have insurance; 68.1% have private insurance; 39.6% have public insurance; 18.1% do not have insurance; 5.7% of children under 18 do not have insurance

Transportation: Commute: 91.6% car, 0.0% public transportation, 1.6% walk, 6.8% work from home; Median travel time to work: 23.8 minutes

ROSMAN (town). Covers a land area of 0.508 square miles and a water area of 0 square miles. Located at 35.15° N. Lat; 82.82° W. Long. Elevation is 2,201 feet.

Population: 576; Growth (since 2000): 17.6%; Density: 1,134.5 persons per square mile; Race: 93.2% White, 0.2% Black/African American, 0.2% Asian, 1.9% American Indian/Alaska Native, 0.0% Native Hawaiian/Other Pacific Islander, 1.9% Two or more races, 10.4% Hispanic of any race; Average household size: 2.50; Median age: 38.0; Age under 18: 26.2%; Age 65 and over: 19.4%; Males per 100 females: 105.7

School District(s)

Transylvania County Schools (PK-12)

    2012-13 Enrollment: 3,592 . . . . (828) 884-6173

Housing: Homeownership rate: 59.6%; Homeowner vacancy rate: 2.8%; Rental vacancy rate: 13.0%

Tyrrell County

Located in northeastern North Carolina; tidewater area, bounded on the north by Albemarle Sound, and on the east by the Alligator River. Covers a land area of 389.035 square miles, a water area of 205.183 square miles, and is located in the Eastern Time Zone at 35.87° N. Lat., 76.17° W. Long. The county was founded in 1729. County seat is Columbia.

Tyrrell County is part of the Kill Devil Hills, NC Micropolitan Statistical Area. The entire metro area includes: Dare County, NC; Tyrrell County, NC

Population: 4,407; Growth (since 2000): 6.2%; Density: 11.3 persons per square mile; Race: 54.5% White, 38.2% Black/African American, 1.8% Asian, 0.4% American Indian/Alaska Native, 0.0% Native Hawaiian/Other Pacific Islander, 1.4% two or more races, 5.4% Hispanic of any race; Average household size: 2.37; Median age: 41.4; Age under 18: 18.0%; Age 65 and over: 16.8%; Males per 100 females: 123.4; Marriage status: 33.7% never married, 47.9% now married, 4.5% separated, 7.8% widowed, 10.6% divorced; Foreign born: 7.5%; Speak English only: 88.0%; With disability: 16.5%; Veterans: 9.6%; Ancestry: 13.0% English, 8.6% American, 7.9% Irish, 6.4% German, 2.1% Scottish

Religion: Six largest groups: 25.7% Baptist, 9.1% Methodist/Pietist, 1.8% Pentecostal, 1.0% Episcopalianism/Anglicanism, 0.5% Catholicism, 0.0% Other Groups

Economy: Unemployment rate: 5.5%; Leading industries: 27.0% retail trade; 14.9% other services (except public administration); 10.8% health care and social assistance; Farms: 78 totaling 64,590 acres; Company size: 0 employ 1,000 or more persons, 0 employ 500 to 999 persons, 0 employ 100 to 499 persons, 74 employ less than 100 persons; Business ownership: n/a women-owned, n/a Black-owned, n/a Hispanic-owned, n/a Asian-owned

Employment: 5.6% management, business, and financial, 0.5% computer, engineering, and science, 7.0% education, legal, community service, arts,

and media, 2.1% healthcare practitioners, 22.3% service, 21.7% sales and office, 22.9% natural resources, construction, and maintenance, 18.0% production, transportation, and material moving

Income: Per capita: $16,658; Median household: $34,216; Average household: $45,278; Households with income of $100,000 or more: 5.7%; Poverty rate: 20.8%

Educational Attainment: High school diploma or higher: 71.5%; Bachelor's degree or higher: 8.4%; Graduate/professional degree or higher: 3.7%

Housing: Homeownership rate: 72.4%; Median home value: $107,100; Median year structure built: 1976; Homeowner vacancy rate: 2.7%; Median gross rent: $643 per month; Rental vacancy rate: 6.9%

Vital Statistics: Birth rate: 109.5 per 10,000 population; Death rate: 73.0 per 10,000 population; Age-adjusted cancer mortality rate: Suppressed deaths per 100,000 population

Health Insurance: 76.6% have insurance; 48.4% have private insurance; 42.3% have public insurance; 23.4% do not have insurance; 11.6% of children under 18 do not have insurance

Health Care: Physicians: 0.0 per 10,000 population; Hospital beds: 0.0 per 10,000 population; Hospital admissions: 0.0 per 10,000 population

Transportation: Commute: 89.6% car, 0.0% public transportation, 8.4% walk, 1.9% work from home; Median travel time to work: 25.6 minutes

Presidential Election: 46.9% Obama, 52.2% Romney (2012)

Additional Information Contacts

Tyrrell Government . . . . (252) 796-1581
    http://albemarle-nc.com/columbia

Tyrrell County Communities

COLUMBIA (town). County seat. Covers a land area of 1.203 square miles and a water area of 0.015 square miles. Located at 35.92° N. Lat; 76.24° W. Long. Elevation is 3 feet.

History: The area around Columbia was explored as early as 1680. In 1800 the town was known as Elizabeth, but ten years later the name was changed to Columbia to honor Christopher Columbus.

Population: 891; Growth (since 2000): 8.8%; Density: 740.3 persons per square mile; Race: 39.3% White, 43.1% Black/African American, 3.3% Asian, 0.3% American Indian/Alaska Native, 0.0% Native Hawaiian/Other Pacific Islander, 0.6% Two or more races, 16.3% Hispanic of any race; Average household size: 2.40; Median age: 42.9; Age under 18: 23.9%; Age 65 and over: 18.6%; Males per 100 females: 86.8

School District(s)

Tyrrell County Schools (PK-12)

    2012-13 Enrollment: 601. . . . . (252) 796-1121

Housing: Homeownership rate: 57.0%; Homeowner vacancy rate: 1.9%; Rental vacancy rate: 4.6%

Union County

Located in southern North Carolina; piedmont area, bounded on the south and southwest by South Carolina, and on the northeast by the Rocky River. Covers a land area of 631.520 square miles, a water area of 8.006 square miles, and is located in the Eastern Time Zone at 34.99° N. Lat., 80.53° W. Long. The county was founded in 1842. County seat is Monroe.

Union County is part of the Charlotte-Concord-Gastonia, NC-SC Metropolitan Statistical Area. The entire metro area includes: Cabarrus County, NC; Gaston County, NC; Iredell County, NC; Lincoln County, NC; Mecklenburg County, NC; Rowan County, NC; Union County, NC; Chester County, SC; Lancaster County, SC; York County, SC

Weather Station: Monroe 4 SE									Elevation: 580 feet		
	Jan	Feb	Mar	Apr	May	Jun	Jul	Aug	Sep	Oct	Nov	Dec
High	52	57	65	73	80	87	90	88	82	73	64	55
Low	31	34	40	48	56	65	68	67	61	49	40	33
Precip	4.0	3.7	4.5	3.1	2.9	4.3	4.3	5.0	4.2	4.1	3.4	3.7
Snow	1.9	0.6	0.6	tr	0.0	0.0	0.0	0.0	0.0	0.0	tr	0.2

High and Low temperatures in degrees Fahrenheit; Precipitation and Snow in inches

Population: 201,292; Growth (since 2000): 62.8%; Density: 318.7 persons per square mile; Race: 79.0% White, 11.7% Black/African American, 1.6% Asian, 0.4% American Indian/Alaska Native, 0.0% Native Hawaiian/Other Pacific Islander, 1.9% two or more races, 10.4% Hispanic of any race; Average household size: 2.94; Median age: 36.2; Age under 18: 30.2%; Age 65 and over: 9.7%; Males per 100 females: 97.5; Marriage status:

24.4% never married, 63.1% now married, 2.3% separated, 4.9% widowed, 7.7% divorced; Foreign born: 9.1%; Speak English only: 87.0%; With disability: 9.1%; Veterans: 8.4%; Ancestry: 13.9% German, 11.8% American, 11.1% Irish, 10.0% English, 5.0% Italian
Religion: Six largest groups: 20.6% Baptist, 11.2% Methodist/Pietist, 7.4% Non-denominational Protestant, 2.0% Presbyterian-Reformed, 1.5% Catholicism, 1.3% Holiness
Economy: Unemployment rate: 4.6%; Leading industries: 15.9% construction; 12.0% retail trade; 10.3% other services (except public administration); Farms: 1,059 totaling 201,655 acres; Company size: 4 employ 1,000 or more persons, 2 employ 500 to 999 persons, 50 employ 100 to 499 persons, 4,005 employ less than 100 persons; Business ownership: 4,446 women-owned, 888 Black-owned, 532 Hispanic-owned, 324 Asian-owned
Employment: 17.7% management, business, and financial, 4.9% computer, engineering, and science, 10.1% education, legal, community service, arts, and media, 5.5% healthcare practitioners, 14.2% service, 26.2% sales and office, 10.7% natural resources, construction, and maintenance, 10.6% production, transportation, and material moving
Income: Per capita: $28,894; Median household: $65,892; Average household: $85,939; Households with income of $100,000 or more: 28.6%; Poverty rate: 9.4%
Educational Attainment: High school diploma or higher: 87.8%; Bachelor's degree or higher: 31.8%; Graduate/professional degree or higher: 8.6%
Housing: Homeownership rate: 81.2%; Median home value: $194,300; Median year structure built: 1994; Homeowner vacancy rate: 2.5%; Median gross rent: $851 per month; Rental vacancy rate: 8.5%
Vital Statistics: Birth rate: 112.9 per 10,000 population; Death rate: 56.1 per 10,000 population; Age-adjusted cancer mortality rate: 156.4 deaths per 100,000 population
Health Insurance: 85.9% have insurance; 72.9% have private insurance; 21.9% have public insurance; 14.1% do not have insurance; 7.8% of children under 18 do not have insurance
Health Care: Physicians: 13.2 per 10,000 population; Hospital beds: 11.6 per 10,000 population; Hospital admissions: 458.4 per 10,000 population
Air Quality Index: 96.6% good, 3.4% moderate, 0.0% unhealthy for sensitive individuals, 0.0% unhealthy (percent of days)
Transportation: Commute: 91.3% car, 0.6% public transportation, 0.7% walk, 6.5% work from home; Median travel time to work: 29.2 minutes
Presidential Election: 34.3% Obama, 64.5% Romney (2012)
Additional Information Contacts
Union Government . . . . (704) 283-3810
  http://www.co.union.nc.us

Union County Communities

FAIRVIEW (town). Covers a land area of 29.922 square miles and a water area of 0.361 square miles. Located at 35.16° N. Lat; 80.53° W. Long. Elevation is 528 feet.
Population: 3,324; Growth (since 2000): n/a; Density: 111.1 persons per square mile; Race: 97.4% White, 0.9% Black/African American, 0.3% Asian, 0.2% American Indian/Alaska Native, 0.0% Native Hawaiian/Other Pacific Islander, 0.4% Two or more races, 1.4% Hispanic of any race; Average household size: 2.71; Median age: 42.6; Age under 18: 25.2%; Age 65 and over: 13.5%; Males per 100 females: 101.2; Marriage status: 22.8% never married, 69.9% now married, 5.0% separated, 3.6% widowed, 3.7% divorced; Foreign born: 0.3%; Speak English only: 98.3%; With disability: 8.4%; Veterans: 7.9%; Ancestry: 19.7% American, 11.6% English, 9.1% German, 6.3% Irish, 6.1% Scottish
Employment: 21.0% management, business, and financial, 3.9% computer, engineering, and science, 3.9% education, legal, community service, arts, and media, 3.9% healthcare practitioners, 18.9% service, 21.4% sales and office, 19.5% natural resources, construction, and maintenance, 7.5% production, transportation, and material moving
Income: Per capita: $29,397; Median household: $73,600; Average household: $85,467; Households with income of $100,000 or more: 29.5%; Poverty rate: 6.2%
Educational Attainment: High school diploma or higher: 92.3%; Bachelor's degree or higher: 20.8%; Graduate/professional degree or higher: 3.1%
Housing: Homeownership rate: 86.0%; Median home value: $252,500; Median year structure built: 1990; Homeowner vacancy rate: 1.0%; Median gross rent: $779 per month; Rental vacancy rate: 3.9%

Health Insurance: 93.3% have insurance; 76.1% have private insurance; 26.6% have public insurance; 6.7% do not have insurance; 0.0% of children under 18 do not have insurance
Transportation: Commute: 92.4% car, 2.2% public transportation, 1.0% walk, 3.5% work from home; Median travel time to work: 32.3 minutes

HEMBY BRIDGE (town). Covers a land area of 2.349 square miles and a water area of 0.038 square miles. Located at 35.10° N. Lat; 80.63° W. Long. Elevation is 636 feet.
Population: 1,520; Growth (since 2000): 69.5%; Density: 647.2 persons per square mile; Race: 88.3% White, 7.2% Black/African American, 1.2% Asian, 0.9% American Indian/Alaska Native, 0.0% Native Hawaiian/Other Pacific Islander, 1.3% Two or more races, 4.4% Hispanic of any race; Average household size: 2.70; Median age: 39.6; Age under 18: 24.3%; Age 65 and over: 14.7%; Males per 100 females: 98.7
Housing: Homeownership rate: 79.7%; Homeowner vacancy rate: 0.9%; Rental vacancy rate: 8.1%

INDIAN TRAIL (town). Covers a land area of 21.689 square miles and a water area of 0.172 square miles. Located at 35.07° N. Lat; 80.65° W. Long. Elevation is 699 feet.
Population: 33,518; Growth (since 2000): 181.5%; Density: 1,545.4 persons per square mile; Race: 81.0% White, 10.0% Black/African American, 1.8% Asian, 0.5% American Indian/Alaska Native, 0.0% Native Hawaiian/Other Pacific Islander, 2.3% Two or more races, 10.9% Hispanic of any race; Average household size: 3.01; Median age: 33.7; Age under 18: 32.7%; Age 65 and over: 6.9%; Males per 100 females: 96,4; Marriage status: 23.4% never married, 66.3% now married, 2.4% separated, 3.1% widowed, 7.2% divorced; Foreign born: 8.8%; Speak English only: 87.0%; With disability: 7.2%; Veterans: 8.6%; Ancestry: 14.2% German, 12.3% Irish, 10.0% American, 9.5% English, 7.0% Italian
Employment: 16.8% management, business, and financial, 5.3% computer, engineering, and science, 11.4% education, legal, community service, arts, and media, 5.0% healthcare practitioners, 14.4% service, 28.0% sales and office, 11.2% natural resources, construction, and maintenance, 8.0% production, transportation, and material moving
Income: Per capita: $26,096; Median household: $66,333; Average household: $80,566; Households with income of $100,000 or more: 25.2%; Poverty rate: 6.3%
Educational Attainment: High school diploma or higher: 93.0%; Bachelor's degree or higher: 35.2%; Graduate/professional degree or higher: 9.3%
School District(s)
Union County Public Schools (PK-12)
  2012-13 Enrollment: 40,659 . . . . (704) 296-9898
Housing: Homeownership rate: 86.0%; Median home value: $172,600; Median year structure built: 2000; Homeowner vacancy rate: 2.2%; Median gross rent: $1,079 per month; Rental vacancy rate: 5.4%
Health Insurance: 83.3% have insurance; 72.1% have private insurance; 18.6% have public insurance; 16.7% do not have insurance; 10.9% of children under 18 do not have insurance
Transportation: Commute: 92.3% car, 0.6% public transportation, 0.2% walk, 5.2% work from home; Median travel time to work: 30.5 minutes
Additional Information Contacts
Town of Indian Trail. . . . . (704) 821-8114
  http://www.indiantrail.org

JAARS (CDP). Covers a land area of 0.859 square miles and a water area of 0.004 square miles. Located at 34.86° N. Lat; 80.75° W. Long. Elevation is 568 feet.
Population: 597; Growth (since 2000): 65.8%; Density: 694.7 persons per square mile; Race: 97.2% White, 1.5% Black/African American, 0.2% Asian, 0.0% American Indian/Alaska Native, 0.3% Native Hawaiian/Other Pacific Islander, 0.3% Two or more races, 1.2% Hispanic of any race; Average household size: 2.70; Median age: 43.5; Age under 18: 27.8%; Age 65 and over: 18.9%; Males per 100 females: 90.1
Housing: Homeownership rate: 63.4%; Homeowner vacancy rate: 2.0%; Rental vacancy rate: 17.4%

LAKE PARK (village). Covers a land area of 0.783 square miles and a water area of 0.025 square miles. Located at 35.08° N. Lat; 80.63° W. Long. Elevation is 656 feet.
History: N.A. Mathisen first requested permission to build his new village in June, 1990. The village charter was approved on July 1, 1994.

Population: 3,422; Growth (since 2000): 63.5%; Density: 4,371.2 persons per square mile; Race: 86.8% White, 7.0% Black/African American, 1.9% Asian, 0.5% American Indian/Alaska Native, 0.0% Native Hawaiian/Other Pacific Islander, 2.2% Two or more races, 5.2% Hispanic of any race; Average household size: 2.77; Median age: 38.6; Age under 18: 28.3%; Age 65 and over: 14.5%; Males per 100 females: 84.9; Marriage status: 22.4% never married, 60.1% now married, 1.3% separated, 5.5% widowed, 11.9% divorced; Foreign born: 9.3%; Speak English only: 86.2%; With disability: 8.8%; Veterans: 9.1%; Ancestry: 15.0% American, 14.6% Irish, 13.2% German, 10.5% English, 4.4% Italian

Employment: 16.8% management, business, and financial, 5.6% computer, engineering, and science, 11.4% education, legal, community service, arts, and media, 10.3% healthcare practitioners, 16.0% service, 24.7% sales and office, 8.6% natural resources, construction, and maintenance, 6.6% production, transportation, and material moving

Income: Per capita: $29,437; Median household: $68,079; Average household: $81,987; Households with income of $100,000 or more: 27.4%; Poverty rate: 5.1%

Educational Attainment: High school diploma or higher: 95.2%; Bachelor's degree or higher: 32.8%; Graduate/professional degree or higher: 7.8%

Housing: Homeownership rate: 88.7%; Median home value: $175,000; Median year structure built: 1997; Homeowner vacancy rate: 2.5%; Median gross rent: $1,339 per month; Rental vacancy rate: 4.9%

Health Insurance: 92.1% have insurance; 80.5% have private insurance; 23.0% have public insurance; 7.9% do not have insurance; 2.2% of children under 18 do not have insurance

Transportation: Commute: 87.9% car, 0.0% public transportation, 0.0% walk, 11.0% work from home; Median travel time to work: 28.3 minutes

Additional Information Contacts
Village of Lake Park . . . . (770) 436-1223
    http://lakeparknc.com

MARSHVILLE (town). Covers a land area of 2.213 square miles and a water area of 0.003 square miles. Located at 34.99° N. Lat; 80.37° W. Long. Elevation is 554 feet.

Population: 2,402; Growth (since 2000): 1.8%; Density: 1,085.3 persons per square mile; Race: 48.0% White, 45.3% Black/African American, 0.2% Asian, 0.6% American Indian/Alaska Native, 0.0% Native Hawaiian/Other Pacific Islander, 1.9% Two or more races, 11.6% Hispanic of any race; Average household size: 2.83; Median age: 35.2; Age under 18: 28.8%; Age 65 and over: 12.9%; Males per 100 females: 85.1

School District(s)
Union County Public Schools (PK-12)
    2012-13 Enrollment: 40,659 . . . . (704) 296-9898
Housing: Homeownership rate: 59.3%; Homeowner vacancy rate: 3.8%; Rental vacancy rate: 11.3%
Newspapers: The Home News (weekly circulation 3000)
Additional Information Contacts
Town of Marshville . . . . (704) 624-2515
    http://marshvillenc.govoffice2.com

MARVIN (village). Covers a land area of 5.892 square miles and a water area of 0.050 square miles. Located at 35.00° N. Lat; 80.82° W. Long. Elevation is 682 feet.

Population: 5,579; Growth (since 2000): 437.0%; Density: 947.0 persons per square mile; Race: 86.2% White, 5.7% Black/African American, 5.4% Asian, 0.2% American Indian/Alaska Native, 0.0% Native Hawaiian/Other Pacific Islander, 1.6% Two or more races, 3.3% Hispanic of any race; Average household size: 3.59; Median age: 36.8; Age under 18: 40.9%; Age 65 and over: 5.0%; Males per 100 females: 100.9; Marriage status: 14.6% never married, 82.1% now married, 0.9% separated, 2.2% widowed, 1.1% divorced; Foreign born: 8.9%; Speak English only: 91.4%; With disability: 2.6%; Veterans: 4.8%; Ancestry: 22.7% German, 14.8% Irish, 10.7% English, 8.1% Italian, 8.0% American

Employment: 37.0% management, business, and financial, 4.7% computer, engineering, and science, 7.2% education, legal, community service, arts, and media, 8.4% healthcare practitioners, 4.3% service, 33.8% sales and office, 1.3% natural resources, construction, and maintenance, 3.3% production, transportation, and material moving

Income: Per capita: $56,629; Median household: $162,917; Average household: $203,208; Households with income of $100,000 or more: 77.4%; Poverty rate: 2.6%

Educational Attainment: High school diploma or higher: 98.8%; Bachelor's degree or higher: 66.3%; Graduate/professional degree or higher: 25.7%

School District(s)
Union County Public Schools (PK-12)
    2012-13 Enrollment: 40,659 . . . . (704) 296-9898
Housing: Homeownership rate: 96.9%; Median home value: $569,100; Median year structure built: 2002; Homeowner vacancy rate: 2.7%; Median gross rent: $1,883 per month; Rental vacancy rate: 2.0%
Health Insurance: 97.3% have insurance; 96.0% have private insurance; 6.8% have public insurance; 2.7% do not have insurance; 2.1% of children under 18 do not have insurance
Transportation: Commute: 85.1% car, 2.6% public transportation, 0.3% walk, 11.5% work from home; Median travel time to work: 31.1 minutes

MINERAL SPRINGS (town). Covers a land area of 8.137 square miles and a water area of 0.072 square miles. Located at 34.94° N. Lat; 80.69° W. Long. Elevation is 633 feet.

Population: 2,639; Growth (since 2000): 92.6%; Density: 324.3 persons per square mile; Race: 81.9% White, 13.9% Black/African American, 0.5% Asian, 0.5% American Indian/Alaska Native, 0.0% Native Hawaiian/Other Pacific Islander, 1.6% Two or more races, 4.6% Hispanic of any race; Average household size: 2.78; Median age: 41.7; Age under 18: 24.9%; Age 65 and over: 11.3%; Males per 100 females: 98.0; Marriage status: 28.1% never married, 59.7% now married, 1.9% separated, 4.4% widowed, 7.8% divorced; Foreign born: 3.1%; Speak English only: 92.2%; With disability: 15.2%; Veterans: 9.7%; Ancestry: 16.7% American, 12.6% German, 11.7% English, 8.8% Irish, 4.7% Scotch-Irish

Employment: 16.0% management, business, and financial, 4.0% computer, engineering, and science, 14.0% education, legal, community service, arts, and media, 4.6% healthcare practitioners, 9.9% service, 29.2% sales and office, 14.2% natural resources, construction, and maintenance, 8.1% production, transportation, and material moving

Income: Per capita: $22,730; Median household: $53,692; Average household: $65,408; Households with income of $100,000 or more: 18.3%; Poverty rate: 11.7%

Educational Attainment: High school diploma or higher: 89.1%; Bachelor's degree or higher: 18.8%; Graduate/professional degree or higher: 7.4%

Housing: Homeownership rate: 86.7%; Median home value: $166,500; Median year structure built: 1988; Homeowner vacancy rate: 2.1%; Median gross rent: $903 per month; Rental vacancy rate: 5.1%

Health Insurance: 87.0% have insurance; 71.5% have private insurance; 25.3% have public insurance; 13.0% do not have insurance; 2.6% of children under 18 do not have insurance

Transportation: Commute: 94.0% car, 0.0% public transportation, 0.5% walk, 5.5% work from home; Median travel time to work: 31.7 minutes

Additional Information Contacts
Town of Mineral Springs . . . . (704) 843-5870
    http://www.mineralspringsnc.com/index.htm

MONROE (city). County seat. Covers a land area of 29.756 square miles and a water area of 0.628 square miles. Located at 35.00° N. Lat; 80.56° W. Long. Elevation is 600 feet.

History: Monroe was named for President James Monroe.

Population: 32,797; Growth (since 2000): 25.0%; Density: 1,102.2 persons per square mile; Race: 52.0% White, 25.2% Black/African American, 0.9% Asian, 0.6% American Indian/Alaska Native, 0.0% Native Hawaiian/Other Pacific Islander, 2.6% Two or more races, 29.4% Hispanic of any race; Average household size: 2.92; Median age: 32.5; Age under 18: 29.6%; Age 65 and over: 11.1%; Males per 100 females: 96.8; Marriage status: 31.5% never married, 50.9% now married, 2.5% separated, 7.3% widowed, 10.3% divorced; Foreign born: 18.8%; Speak English only: 72.2%; With disability: 11.5%; Veterans: 8.7%; Ancestry: 9.7% German, 7.4% American, 6.9% English, 6.0% Irish, 2.2% Scotch-Irish

Employment: 9.5% management, business, and financial, 2.9% computer, engineering, and science, 7.1% education, legal, community service, arts, and media, 4.0% healthcare practitioners, 21.9% service, 23.3% sales and office, 14.8% natural resources, construction, and maintenance, 16.5% production, transportation, and material moving

Income: Per capita: $19,172; Median household: $43,819; Average household: $56,250; Households with income of $100,000 or more: 14.2%; Poverty rate: 20.7%

Educational Attainment: High school diploma or higher: 74.2%; Bachelor's degree or higher: 16.7%; Graduate/professional degree or higher: 4.0%

School District(s)

Union Academy (KG-12)
    2012-13 Enrollment: 1,214 . . . . (704) 238-8883
Union County Public Schools (PK-12)
    2012-13 Enrollment: 40,659 . . . . (704) 296-9898

Vocational/Technical School(s)

Regina's College of Beauty-Monroe (Private, For-profit)
    Fall 2013 Enrollment: 43 . . . . (704) 226-8830
    2013-14 Tuition: $17,595

Housing: Homeownership rate: 56.5%; Median home value: $148,800; Median year structure built: 1983; Homeowner vacancy rate: 4.3%; Median gross rent: $777 per month; Rental vacancy rate: 11.2%

Health Insurance: 74.4% have insurance; 50.7% have private insurance; 32.1% have public insurance; 25.6% do not have insurance; 13.4% of children under 18 do not have insurance

Hospitals: Carolinas Medical Center - Union (157 beds)

Safety: Violent crime rate: 60.2 per 10,000 population; Property crime rate: 522.5 per 10,000 population

Newspapers: Enquirer-Journal (daily circulation 7800)

Transportation: Commute: 94.3% car, 1.1% public transportation, 0.9% walk, 2.5% work from home; Median travel time to work: 26.8 minutes

Airports: Charlotte-Monroe Executive (general aviation)

Additional Information Contacts

City of Monroe. . . . . (704) 282-4500
    http://www.monroenc.org

STALLINGS (town). Covers a land area of 7.909 square miles and a water area of 0.059 square miles. Located at 35.11° N. Lat; 80.66° W. Long. Elevation is 748 feet.

Population: 13,831; Growth (since 2000): 333.7%; Density: 1,748.8 persons per square mile; Race: 88.3% White, 5.6% Black/African American, 2.3% Asian, 0.5% American Indian/Alaska Native, 0.0% Native Hawaiian/Other Pacific Islander, 1.6% Two or more races, 5.8% Hispanic of any race; Average household size: 2.71; Median age: 38.4; Age under 18: 27.7%; Age 65 and over: 10.4%; Males per 100 females: 93.8; Marriage status: 22.2% never married, 64.2% now married, 1.5% separated, 4.7% widowed, 8.8% divorced; Foreign born: 8.0%; Speak English only: 87.5%; With disability: 11.6%; Veterans: 8.5%; Ancestry: 18.2% German, 13.3% English, 11.7% Irish, 10.7% American, 5.4% Scotch-Irish

Employment: 20.6% management, business, and financial, 6.4% computer, engineering, and science, 14.6% education, legal, community service, arts, and media, 10.1% healthcare practitioners, 8.4% service, 26.1% sales and office, 8.1% natural resources, construction, and maintenance, 5.8% production, transportation, and material moving

Income: Per capita: $34,396; Median household: $79,663; Average household: $92,916; Households with income of $100,000 or more: 33.7%; Poverty rate: 6.9%

Educational Attainment: High school diploma or higher: 93.0%; Bachelor's degree or higher: 43.5%; Graduate/professional degree or higher: 11.9%

School District(s)

Union County Public Schools (PK-12)
    2012-13 Enrollment: 40,659 . . . . (704) 296-9898

Housing: Homeownership rate: 89.9%; Median home value: $210,400; Median year structure built: 1998; Homeowner vacancy rate: 1.9%; Median gross rent: $1,006 per month; Rental vacancy rate: 2.4%

Health Insurance: 90.6% have insurance; 79.9% have private insurance; 21.7% have public insurance; 9.4% do not have insurance; 6.4% of children under 18 do not have insurance

Safety: Violent crime rate: 10.3 per 10,000 population; Property crime rate: 163.0 per 10,000 population

Transportation: Commute: 89.5% car, 0.6% public transportation, 0.2% walk, 9.6% work from home; Median travel time to work: 29.7 minutes

Additional Information Contacts

Town of Stallings. . . . . (704) 882-1083
    http://www.stallingsnc.org

UNIONVILLE (town). Covers a land area of 26.958 square miles and a water area of 0.243 square miles. Located at 35.07° N. Lat; 80.52° W. Long. Elevation is 594 feet.

Population: 5,929; Growth (since 2000): 23.6%; Density: 219.9 persons per square mile; Race: 94.9% White, 1.7% Black/African American, 0.6% Asian, 0.2% American Indian/Alaska Native, 0.0% Native Hawaiian/Other Pacific Islander, 1.1% Two or more races, 3.0% Hispanic of any race; Average household size: 2.82; Median age: 39.4; Age under 18: 26.9%; Age 65 and over: 11.4%; Males per 100 females: 99.9; Marriage status: 17.7% never married, 71.7% now married, 3.9% separated, 4.8% widowed, 5.7% divorced; Foreign born: 2.1%; Speak English only: 96.5%; With disability: 9.4%; Veterans: 10.0%; Ancestry: 17.6% American, 11.4% English, 10.6% German, 9.8% Irish, 4.2% Scotch-Irish

Employment: 11.5% management, business, and financial, 3.5% computer, engineering, and science, 9.2% education, legal, community service, arts, and media, 6.5% healthcare practitioners, 19.0% service, 33.2% sales and office, 8.0% natural resources, construction, and maintenance, 9.1% production, transportation, and material moving

Income: Per capita: $28,336; Median household: $63,423; Average household: $76,911; Households with income of $100,000 or more: 19.3%; Poverty rate: 3.4%

Educational Attainment: High school diploma or higher: 93.7%; Bachelor's degree or higher: 20.8%; Graduate/professional degree or higher: 3.7%

Housing: Homeownership rate: 84.7%; Median home value: $200,300; Median year structure built: 1987; Homeowner vacancy rate: 1.5%; Median gross rent: $777 per month; Rental vacancy rate: 5.6%

Health Insurance: 93.6% have insurance; 85.0% have private insurance; 19.2% have public insurance; 6.4% do not have insurance; 3.3% of children under 18 do not have insurance

Transportation: Commute: 94.1% car, 0.0% public transportation, 0.9% walk, 5.0% work from home; Median travel time to work: 28.7 minutes

Additional Information Contacts

Town of Unionville. . . . . (704) 226-1989
    http://www.unionvillenc.com

WAXHAW (town). Covers a land area of 11.544 square miles and a water area of 0.120 square miles. Located at 34.94° N. Lat; 80.74° W. Long. Elevation is 663 feet.

History: Waxhaw was named for the Native Americans who claimed the land between the Rocky and Catawba Rivers.

Population: 9,859; Growth (since 2000): 275.6%; Density: 854.0 persons per square mile; Race: 82.1% White, 11.2% Black/African American, 2.0% Asian, 0.1% American Indian/Alaska Native, 0.0% Native Hawaiian/Other Pacific Islander, 2.9% Two or more races, 6.4% Hispanic of any race; Average household size: 3.04; Median age: 34.5; Age under 18: 34.6%; Age 65 and over: 7.0%; Males per 100 females: 93.7; Marriage status: 20.8% never married, 70.2% now married, 2.1% separated, 4.4% widowed, 4.6% divorced; Foreign born: 8.3%; Speak English only: 91.2%; With disability: 6.2%; Veterans: 10.0%; Ancestry: 15.2% Irish, 14.3% German, 10.7% English, 10.0% American, 6.9% Italian

Employment: 19.9% management, business, and financial, 8.9% computer, engineering, and science, 15.9% education, legal, community service, arts, and media, 4.9% healthcare practitioners, 9.7% service, 28.9% sales and office, 5.3% natural resources, construction, and maintenance, 6.5% production, transportation, and material moving

Income: Per capita: $27,982; Median household: $77,467; Average household: $84,392; Households with income of $100,000 or more: 35.1%; Poverty rate: 5.1%

Educational Attainment: High school diploma or higher: 95.5%; Bachelor's degree or higher: 55.0%; Graduate/professional degree or higher: 15.4%

School District(s)

Union County Public Schools (PK-12)
    2012-13 Enrollment: 40,659 . . . . (704) 296-9898

Housing: Homeownership rate: 86.8%; Median home value: $231,800; Median year structure built: 2003; Homeowner vacancy rate: 3.5%; Median gross rent: $1,124 per month; Rental vacancy rate: 6.5%

Health Insurance: 91.4% have insurance; 84.7% have private insurance; 15.0% have public insurance; 8.6% do not have insurance; 1.8% of children under 18 do not have insurance

Safety: Violent crime rate: 14.3 per 10,000 population; Property crime rate: 153.6 per 10,000 population

Transportation: Commute: 89.8% car, 0.8% public transportation, 0.0% walk, 9.0% work from home; Median travel time to work: 30.2 minutes

Airports: Hawk's Knoll (general aviation)
Additional Information Contacts
Town of Waxhaw................................. (704) 843-2195
   http://www.waxhaw.com

WEDDINGTON (town). Covers a land area of 17.443 square miles and a water area of 0.367 square miles. Located at 35.02° N. Lat; 80.74° W. Long. Elevation is 728 feet.

History: The town's name comes from Reuben B. Weddington's grandfather, who donated the land on which a new church building was constructed. The town charter established the original boundaries of the Town and appointed Mark Teal, our first Mayor, along with four other council members. The act became effective upon ratification on May 2, 1983.

Population: 9,459; Growth (since 2000): 41.3%; Density: 542.3 persons per square mile; Race: 91.2% White, 3.9% Black/African American, 2.6% Asian, 0.2% American Indian/Alaska Native, 0.0% Native Hawaiian/Other Pacific Islander, 1.3% Two or more races, 3.0% Hispanic of any race; Average household size: 3.02; Median age: 43.3; Age under 18: 29.5%; Age 65 and over: 9.4%; Males per 100 females: 101.1; Marriage status: 24.0% never married, 68.5% now married, 2.3% separated, 3.4% widowed, 4.1% divorced; Foreign born: 8.9%; Speak English only: 87.5%; With disability: 4.6%; Veterans: 9.7%; Ancestry: 15.2% German, 13.3% Irish, 12.6% English, 11.4% American, 7.5% Scotch-Irish

Employment: 32.4% management, business, and financial, 10.1% computer, engineering, and science, 5.3% education, legal, community service, arts, and media, 5.1% healthcare practitioners, 11.4% service, 27.7% sales and office, 3.9% natural resources, construction, and maintenance, 4.1% production, transportation, and material moving

Income: Per capita: $53,021; Median household: $141,682; Average household: $162,565; Households with income of $100,000 or more: 70.6%; Poverty rate: 1.8%

Educational Attainment: High school diploma or higher: 97.5%; Bachelor's degree or higher: 53.1%; Graduate/professional degree or higher: 10.9%

Housing: Homeownership rate: 93.6%; Median home value: $391,500; Median year structure built: 1991; Homeowner vacancy rate: 2.9%; Median gross rent: $775 per month; Rental vacancy rate: 2.5%

Health Insurance: 91.7% have insurance; 87.8% have private insurance; 13.3% have public insurance; 8.3% do not have insurance; 2.1% of children under 18 do not have insurance

Transportation: Commute: 88.6% car, 0.0% public transportation, 0.7% walk, 9.9% work from home; Median travel time to work: 30.4 minutes

Additional Information Contacts
Town of Weddington .... (704) 846-2709
   http://www.townofweddington.com

WESLEY CHAPEL (village). Covers a land area of 9.478 square miles and a water area of 0.088 square miles. Located at 35.01° N. Lat; 80.69° W. Long. Elevation is 610 feet.

History: In the early 1800s, a rural meeting place, known as The McWhorter Campground, was established and soon abandoned. This provided the site for the first church in Wesley Chapel, and gave the community its name. Now called the Wesley Chapel United Methodist Church, this venerable religious organization dates to 1832. The church itself was named for John Wesley (1703-1791), the founder of Methodism.

Population: 7,463; Growth (since 2000): 192.8%; Density: 787.4 persons per square mile; Race: 90.7% White, 4.6% Black/African American, 1.5% Asian, 0.2% American Indian/Alaska Native, 0.1% Native Hawaiian/Other Pacific Islander, 1.5% Two or more races, 5.0% Hispanic of any race; Average household size: 3.27; Median age: 38.1; Age under 18: 34.7%; Age 65 and over: 6.4%; Males per 100 females: 102.1; Marriage status: 19.1% never married, 71.6% now married, 1.8% separated, 2.8% widowed, 6.5% divorced; Foreign born: 3.0%; Speak English only: 95.0%; With disability: 4.9%; Veterans: 6.5%; Ancestry: 25.2% German, 18.1% English, 13.4% Irish, 12.9% Italian, 12.7% American

Employment: 25.6% management, business, and financial, 3.3% computer, engineering, and science, 16.8% education, legal, community service, arts, and media, 7.3% healthcare practitioners, 10.0% service, 22.1% sales and office, 8.2% natural resources, construction, and maintenance, 6.7% production, transportation, and material moving

Income: Per capita: $34,189; Median household: $89,701; Average household: $108,428; Households with income of $100,000 or more: 46.2%; Poverty rate: 4.0%

Educational Attainment: High school diploma or higher: 93.9%; Bachelor's degree or higher: 43.7%; Graduate/professional degree or higher: 13.0%

Housing: Homeownership rate: 94.0%; Median home value: $300,700; Median year structure built: 2001; Homeowner vacancy rate: 1.5%; Median gross rent: $1,219 per month; Rental vacancy rate: 4.2%

Health Insurance: 94.6% have insurance; 89.0% have private insurance; 10.9% have public insurance; 5.4% do not have insurance; 2.0% of children under 18 do not have insurance

Transportation: Commute: 89.4% car, 0.2% public transportation, 0.0% walk, 9.4% work from home; Median travel time to work: 28.1 minutes

Additional Information Contacts
Village of Wesley Chapel .... (704) 243-2485
   http://ci.wesley-chapel.nc.us

WINGATE (town). Covers a land area of 1.989 square miles and a water area of 0.005 square miles. Located at 34.98° N. Lat; 80.45° W. Long. Elevation is 568 feet.

History: Seat of Wingate College.

Population: 3,491; Growth (since 2000): 45.1%; Density: 1,754.9 persons per square mile; Race: 60.6% White, 28.8% Black/African American, 0.9% Asian, 0.4% American Indian/Alaska Native, 0.1% Native Hawaiian/Other Pacific Islander, 1.4% Two or more races, 12.4% Hispanic of any race; Average household size: 2.66; Median age: 22.5; Age under 18: 20.0%; Age 65 and over: 8.5%; Males per 100 females: 90.6; Marriage status: 54.9% never married, 32.5% now married, 1.4% separated, 4.1% widowed, 8.5% divorced; Foreign born: 7.0%; Speak English only: 89.3%; With disability: 15.2%; Veterans: 3.6%; Ancestry: 9.0% German, 7.6% English, 6.6% Irish, 4.7% Italian, 4.0% American

Employment: 8.3% management, business, and financial, 2.0% computer, engineering, and science, 19.4% education, legal, community service, arts, and media, 4.6% healthcare practitioners, 16.4% service, 26.9% sales and office, 8.1% natural resources, construction, and maintenance, 14.3% production, transportation, and material moving

Income: Per capita: $17,296; Median household: $38,750; Average household: $53,760; Households with income of $100,000 or more: 8.9%; Poverty rate: 18.1%

Educational Attainment: High school diploma or higher: 84.8%; Bachelor's degree or higher: 21.1%; Graduate/professional degree or higher: 8.5%

School District(s)
Union County Public Schools (PK-12)
   2012-13 Enrollment: 40,659 .... (704) 296-9898
Four-year College(s)
Wingate University (Private, Not-for-profit)
   Fall 2013 Enrollment: 3,002 .... (704) 233-8000
   2013-14 Tuition: In-state $25,040; Out-of-state $25,040

Housing: Homeownership rate: 62.1%; Median home value: $133,500; Median year structure built: 1984; Homeowner vacancy rate: 2.6%; Median gross rent: $530 per month; Rental vacancy rate: 11.3%

Health Insurance: 91.0% have insurance; 76.1% have private insurance; 22.7% have public insurance; 9.0% do not have insurance; 5.1% of children under 18 do not have insurance

Safety: Violent crime rate: 54.0 per 10,000 population; Property crime rate: 310.6 per 10,000 population

Transportation: Commute: 86.8% car, 0.5% public transportation, 11.4% walk, 0.9% work from home; Median travel time to work: 24.4 minutes

Additional Information Contacts
Town of Wingate .... (704) 233-4411
   http://wingate.govoffice.com

Vance County

Located in northern North Carolina; piedmont area, bounded on the north by Virginia, and on the southwest by the Tar River. Covers a land area of 253.517 square miles, a water area of 16.303 square miles, and is located in the Eastern Time Zone at 36.37° N. Lat., 78.41° W. Long. The county was founded in 1881. County seat is Henderson.

Vance County is part of the Henderson, NC Micropolitan Statistical Area. The entire metro area includes: Vance County, NC

Weather Station: Henderson 2 NNW — Elevation: 479 feet

	Jan	Feb	Mar	Apr	May	Jun	Jul	Aug	Sep	Oct	Nov	Dec
High	49	52	61	71	78	86	89	88	81	71	62	52
Low	25	27	34	42	52	62	66	64	57	44	36	28
Precip	3.4	2.8	4.2	3.4	3.3	4.0	4.4	4.5	3.8	3.4	3.6	3.4
Snow	1.3	1.2	0.1	0.0	0.0	0.0	0.0	0.0	0.0	0.0	tr	0.1

High and Low temperatures in degrees Fahrenheit; Precipitation and Snow in inches

Population: 45,422; Growth (since 2000): 5.7%; Density: 179.2 persons per square mile; Race: 44.2% White, 49.9% Black/African American, 0.4% Asian, 0.3% American Indian/Alaska Native, 0.0% Native Hawaiian/Other Pacific Islander, 1.3% two or more races, 6.7% Hispanic of any race; Average household size: 2.56; Median age: 38.6; Age under 18: 25.4%; Age 65 and over: 14.1%; Males per 100 females: 88.4; Marriage status: 35.0% never married, 44.7% now married, 4.5% separated, 8.4% widowed, 11.9% divorced; Foreign born: 3.9%; Speak English only: 94.5%; With disability: 26.2%; Veterans: 9.5%; Ancestry: 18.3% American, 6.9% English, 3.6% Irish, 2.7% German, 1.5% Scotch-Irish
Religion: Six largest groups: 20.0% Baptist, 8.8% Methodist/Pietist, 8.1% Pentecostal, 3.7% Presbyterian-Reformed, 3.5% Non-denominational Protestant, 1.9% Catholicism
Economy: Unemployment rate: 8.3%; Leading industries: 20.8% retail trade; 11.8% other services (except public administration); 11.3% health care and social assistance; Farms: 242 totaling 54,880 acres; Company size: 0 employ 1,000 or more persons, 1 employs 500 to 999 persons, 18 employ 100 to 499 persons, 852 employ less than 100 persons; Business ownership: 881 women-owned, 801 Black-owned, n/a Hispanic-owned, n/a Asian-owned
Employment: 10.1% management, business, and financial, 1.7% computer, engineering, and science, 7.9% education, legal, community service, arts, and media, 4.1% healthcare practitioners, 23.1% service, 24.6% sales and office, 9.4% natural resources, construction, and maintenance, 19.1% production, transportation, and material moving
Income: Per capita: $17,905; Median household: $34,987; Average household: $45,831; Households with income of $100,000 or more: 8.0%; Poverty rate: 28.0%
Educational Attainment: High school diploma or higher: 75.6%; Bachelor's degree or higher: 11.4%; Graduate/professional degree or higher: 3.6%
Housing: Homeownership rate: 61.9%; Median home value: $99,600; Median year structure built: 1980; Homeowner vacancy rate: 2.4%; Median gross rent: $666 per month; Rental vacancy rate: 8.8%
Vital Statistics: Birth rate: 127.2 per 10,000 population; Death rate: 107.3 per 10,000 population; Age-adjusted cancer mortality rate: 184.1 deaths per 100,000 population
Health Insurance: 83.3% have insurance; 50.7% have private insurance; 46.6% have public insurance; 16.7% do not have insurance; 5.8% of children under 18 do not have insurance
Health Care: Physicians: 10.7 per 10,000 population; Hospital beds: 22.6 per 10,000 population; Hospital admissions: 1,078.9 per 10,000 population
Transportation: Commute: 95.3% car, 0.2% public transportation, 2.1% walk, 1.6% work from home; Median travel time to work: 23.0 minutes
Presidential Election: 63.9% Obama, 35.6% Romney (2012)
National and State Parks: Kerr Lake State Recreation Area
Additional Information Contacts
Vance Government . . . . (252) 738-2120
http://www.vancecounty.org

Vance County Communities

HENDERSON (city). County seat. Covers a land area of 8.505 square miles and a water area of 0.006 square miles. Located at 36.33° N. Lat; 78.42° W. Long. Elevation is 505 feet.
History: Henderson was named for Leonard Henderson (1772-1833), Chief Justice of the State Supreme Court, when the town was laid out in 1840.
Population: 15,368; Growth (since 2000): -4.5%; Density: 1,807.0 persons per square mile; Race: 30.0% White, 64.0% Black/African American, 0.8% Asian, 0.3% American Indian/Alaska Native, 0.0% Native Hawaiian/Other Pacific Islander, 1.4% Two or more races, 6.4% Hispanic of any race; Average household size: 2.41; Median age: 38.6; Age under 18: 25.5%; Age 65 and over: 17.3%; Males per 100 females: 79.9; Marriage status: 40.5% never married, 36.9% now married, 5.2% separated, 9.7% widowed, 12.9% divorced; Foreign born: 6.5%; Speak English only: 91.8%;

With disability: 24.2%; Veterans: 8.8%; Ancestry: 11.2% American, 7.4% English, 2.6% German, 2.2% Irish, 0.8% Scotch-Irish
Employment: 10.0% management, business, and financial, 0.8% computer, engineering, and science, 10.0% education, legal, community service, arts, and media, 4.4% healthcare practitioners, 21.6% service, 24.8% sales and office, 8.5% natural resources, construction, and maintenance, 19.8% production, transportation, and material moving
Income: Per capita: $16,188; Median household: $26,149; Average household: $40,599; Households with income of $100,000 or more: 6.2%; Poverty rate: 35.5%
Educational Attainment: High school diploma or higher: 73.7%; Bachelor's degree or higher: 14.1%; Graduate/professional degree or higher: 4.5%
School District(s)
Henderson Collegiate (04-05)
    2012-13 Enrollment: 296 . . . . (252) 598-1038
Vance Charter School (KG-08)
    2012-13 Enrollment: 545 . . . . (252) 431-0440
Vance County Schools (PK-12)
    2012-13 Enrollment: 7,138 . . . . (252) 492-2127
Two-year College(s)
Vance-Granville Community College (Public)
    Fall 2013 Enrollment: 4,008 . . . . (252) 492-2061
    2013-14 Tuition: In-state $1,826; Out-of-state $6,434
Housing: Homeownership rate: 42.3%; Median home value: $116,800; Median year structure built: 1966; Homeowner vacancy rate: 3.6%; Median gross rent: $645 per month; Rental vacancy rate: 9.5%
Health Insurance: 81.5% have insurance; 42.0% have private insurance; 53.7% have public insurance; 18.5% do not have insurance; 4.3% of children under 18 do not have insurance
Hospitals: Maria Parham Medical Center (102 beds)
Safety: Violent crime rate: 139.8 per 10,000 population; Property crime rate: 941.3 per 10,000 population
Newspapers: The Daily Dispatch (daily circulation 7500)
Transportation: Commute: 93.8% car, 0.0% public transportation, 3.4% walk, 1.7% work from home; Median travel time to work: 18.1 minutes
Additional Information Contacts
City of Henderson . . . . (252) 438-8414
http://www.ci.henderson.nc.us

KITTRELL (town). Covers a land area of 0.209 square miles and a water area of 0 square miles. Located at 36.22° N. Lat; 78.44° W. Long. Elevation is 440 feet.
Population: 467; Growth (since 2000): 215.5%; Density: 2,230.7 persons per square mile; Race: 30.2% White, 66.8% Black/African American, 0.2% Asian, 0.0% American Indian/Alaska Native, 0.2% Native Hawaiian/Other Pacific Islander, 1.5% Two or more races, 1.9% Hispanic of any race; Average household size: 2.38; Median age: 20.5; Age under 18: 19.1%; Age 65 and over: 6.0%; Males per 100 females: 93.0
School District(s)
Vance County Schools (PK-12)
    2012-13 Enrollment: 7,138 . . . . (252) 492-2127
Housing: Homeownership rate: 76.1%; Homeowner vacancy rate: 3.6%; Rental vacancy rate: 15.0%

MANSON (unincorporated postal area)
ZCTA: 27553
    Covers a land area of 36.996 square miles and a water area of 6.279 square miles. Located at 36.49° N. Lat; 78.31° W. Long..
Population: 2,937; Growth (since 2000): 49.3%; Density: 79.4 persons per square mile; Race: 27.1% White, 70.4% Black/African American, 0.2% Asian, 0.7% American Indian/Alaska Native, 0.0% Native Hawaiian/Other Pacific Islander, 0.9% Two or more races, 1.9% Hispanic of any race; Average household size: 2.41; Median age: 41.1; Age under 18: 14.2%; Age 65 and over: 12.4%; Males per 100 females: 179.4; Marriage status: 38.2% never married, 39.8% now married, 6.7% separated, 11.3% widowed, 10.6% divorced; Foreign born: 1.0%; Speak English only: 95.2%; With disability: 29.7%; Veterans: 13.5%; Ancestry: 9.9% American, 6.7% English, 6.0% German, 4.8% Scotch-Irish, 4.1% Irish
Employment: 23.2% management, business, and financial, 5.6% computer, engineering, and science, 12.8% education, legal, community service, arts, and media, 1.8% healthcare practitioners, 8.5% service, 25.8% sales and office, 8.3% natural resources, construction, and maintenance, 13.9% production, transportation, and material moving

Income: Per capita: $18,671; Median household: $42,500; Average household: $55,407; Households with income of $100,000 or more: 16.2%; Poverty rate: 32.9%

Educational Attainment: High school diploma or higher: 67.4%; Bachelor's degree or higher: 16.5%; Graduate/professional degree or higher: 5.7%

Housing: Homeownership rate: 77.7%; Median home value: $159,900; Median year structure built: 1987; Homeowner vacancy rate: 1.8%; Median gross rent: $707 per month; Rental vacancy rate: 8.3%

Health Insurance: 87.3% have insurance; 53.0% have private insurance; 49.2% have public insurance; 12.7% do not have insurance; 0.0% of children under 18 do not have insurance

Transportation: Commute: 97.9% car, 0.0% public transportation, 0.0% walk, 2.1% work from home; Median travel time to work: 28.3 minutes

MIDDLEBURG (town).
Covers a land area of 0.566 square miles and a water area of 0 square miles. Located at 36.40° N. Lat; 78.32° W. Long. Elevation is 463 feet.

History: Middleburg, a farming community founded in 1781, was midway between terminals of the Raleigh & Gaston Railroad. Dr. Joseph Hawkins established one of the state's earliest medical schools at his home here in 1808.

Population: 133; Growth (since 2000): -17.9%; Density: 235.0 persons per square mile; Race: 29.3% White, 63.9% Black/African American, 0.0% Asian, 0.0% American Indian/Alaska Native, 0.0% Native Hawaiian/Other Pacific Islander, 3.8% Two or more races, 3.0% Hispanic of any race; Average household size: 2.51; Median age: 43.8; Age under 18: 21.1%; Age 65 and over: 16.5%; Males per 100 females: 84.7

School District(s)

Vance County Schools (PK-12)

   2012-13 Enrollment: 7,138 . . . . (252) 492-2127

Housing: Homeownership rate: 66.0%; Homeowner vacancy rate: 2.8%; Rental vacancy rate: 5.3%

SOUTH HENDERSON (CDP).
Covers a land area of 1.873 square miles and a water area of 0 square miles. Located at 36.30° N. Lat; 78.41° W. Long. Elevation is 505 feet.

Population: 1,213; Growth (since 2000): -0.6%; Density: 647.6 persons per square mile; Race: 33.9% White, 49.9% Black/African American, 0.3% Asian, 0.2% American Indian/Alaska Native, 0.0% Native Hawaiian/Other Pacific Islander, 2.0% Two or more races, 18.2% Hispanic of any race; Average household size: 2.62; Median age: 35.8; Age under 18: 26.3%; Age 65 and over: 12.8%; Males per 100 females: 88.9

Housing: Homeownership rate: 53.2%; Homeowner vacancy rate: 3.6%; Rental vacancy rate: 7.4%

Wake County

Located in central North Carolina; piedmont area, drained by the Neuse River. Covers a land area of 835.219 square miles, a water area of 22.103 square miles, and is located in the Eastern Time Zone at 35.79° N. Lat., 78.65° W. Long. The county was founded in 1770. County seat is Raleigh.

Wake County is part of the Raleigh, NC Metropolitan Statistical Area. The entire metro area includes: Franklin County, NC; Johnston County, NC; Wake County, NC

Weather Station: Raleigh 4 SW   Elevation: 419 feet

	Jan	Feb	Mar	Apr	May	Jun	Jul	Aug	Sep	Oct	Nov	Dec
High	52	56	64	73	80	86	89	88	82	73	64	55
Low	32	34	40	48	57	65	69	68	62	50	42	34
Precip	3.9	3.4	4.4	3.0	3.5	4.9	4.6	4.5	4.2	3.6	3.3	3.1
Snow	1.8	0.8	0.6	tr	0.0	0.0	0.0	0.0	0.0	0.0	0.0	0.2

High and Low temperatures in degrees Fahrenheit; Precipitation and Snow in inches

Weather Station: Raleigh State Univ   Elevation: 399 feet

	Jan	Feb	Mar	Apr	May	Jun	Jul	Aug	Sep	Oct	Nov	Dec
High	50	54	61	71	78	86	89	87	81	71	62	52
Low	31	33	40	48	57	66	70	69	62	50	42	34
Precip	3.8	3.3	4.4	2.9	3.5	4.5	4.4	4.5	4.2	3.7	3.4	3.4
Snow	2.2	0.9	0.7	tr	0.0	0.0	0.0	0.0	0.0	0.0	0.1	0.3

High and Low temperatures in degrees Fahrenheit; Precipitation and Snow in inches

Weather Station: Raleigh-Durham Intl Arpt   Elevation: 416 feet

	Jan	Feb	Mar	Apr	May	Jun	Jul	Aug	Sep	Oct	Nov	Dec
High	51	55	63	72	79	87	90	88	81	72	63	54
Low	31	33	39	47	56	65	69	68	61	49	40	33
Precip	3.5	3.2	4.2	2.9	3.2	3.6	4.7	4.2	4.3	3.2	3.2	3.0
Snow	2.8	1.9	0.8	0.1	tr	tr	tr	0.0	0.0	0.0	0.1	0.4

High and Low temperatures in degrees Fahrenheit; Precipitation and Snow in inches

Population: 900,993; Growth (since 2000): 43.5%; Density: 1,078.8 persons per square mile; Race: 66.3% White, 20.7% Black/African American, 5.4% Asian, 0.5% American Indian/Alaska Native, 0.0% Native Hawaiian/Other Pacific Islander, 2.5% two or more races, 9.8% Hispanic of any race; Average household size: 2.55; Median age: 34.4; Age under 18: 26.0%; Age 65 and over: 8.5%; Males per 100 females: 94.9; Marriage status: 32.5% never married, 54.4% now married, 2.5% separated, 4.0% widowed, 9.1% divorced; Foreign born: 12.8%; Speak English only: 83.4%; With disability: 7.5%; Veterans: 7.9%; Ancestry: 11.8% German, 11.2% English, 10.0% Irish, 9.6% American, 5.1% Italian

Religion: Six largest groups: 11.0% Catholicism, 10.8% Baptist, 7.1% Methodist/Pietist, 5.8% Non-denominational Protestant, 2.5% Presbyterian-Reformed, 2.0% Pentecostal

Economy: Unemployment rate: 4.4%; Leading industries: 17.1% professional, scientific, and technical services; 12.4% retail trade; 10.5% health care and social assistance; Farms: 783 totaling 84,229 acres; Company size: 18 employ 1,000 or more persons, 37 employ 500 to 999 persons, 547 employ 100 to 499 persons, 24,970 employ less than 100 persons; Business ownership: 23,750 women-owned, 9,933 Black-owned, 3,115 Hispanic-owned, 3,992 Asian-owned

Employment: 19.8% management, business, and financial, 11.6% computer, engineering, and science, 12.2% education, legal, community service, arts, and media, 5.8% healthcare practitioners, 14.2% service, 23.6% sales and office, 6.2% natural resources, construction, and maintenance, 6.5% production, transportation, and material moving

Income: Per capita: $33,166; Median household: $66,006; Average household: $86,702; Households with income of $100,000 or more: 30.8%; Poverty rate: 11.0%

Educational Attainment: High school diploma or higher: 91.6%; Bachelor's degree or higher: 48.0%; Graduate/professional degree or higher: 16.6%

Housing: Homeownership rate: 65.1%; Median home value: $229,000; Median year structure built: 1993; Homeowner vacancy rate: 2.5%; Median gross rent: $913 per month; Rental vacancy rate: 8.4%

Vital Statistics: Birth rate: 128.3 per 10,000 population; Death rate: 48.8 per 10,000 population; Age-adjusted cancer mortality rate: 162.4 deaths per 100,000 population

Health Insurance: 86.7% have insurance; 75.1% have private insurance; 19.5% have public insurance; 13.3% do not have insurance; 7.3% of children under 18 do not have insurance

Health Care: Physicians: 24.9 per 10,000 population; Hospital beds: 26.8 per 10,000 population; Hospital admissions: 1,046.9 per 10,000 population

Air Quality Index: 69.3% good, 30.7% moderate, 0.0% unhealthy for sensitive individuals, 0.0% unhealthy (percent of days)

Transportation: Commute: 89.3% car, 1.1% public transportation, 1.5% walk, 6.7% work from home; Median travel time to work: 23.7 minutes

Presidential Election: 54.9% Obama, 43.5% Romney (2012)

National and State Parks: Falls Lake State Recreation Area; Hemlock Bluffs State Natural Area; William B Umstead State Park

Additional Information Contacts

Wake Government . . . . (919) 856-6160
  http://www.wakegov.com

Wake County Communities

APEX (town).
Covers a land area of 15.372 square miles and a water area of 0.061 square miles. Located at 35.73° N. Lat; 78.86° W. Long. Elevation is 499 feet.

History: Apex received its name in the early 1870's when a survey for the Raleigh & Augusta Railroad showed it to be the highest point on the right-of-way between Norfold and Sanford.

Population: 37,476; Growth (since 2000): 85.4%; Density: 2,437.9 persons per square mile; Race: 79.5% White, 7.6% Black/African American, 7.1% Asian, 0.3% American Indian/Alaska Native, 0.1% Native Hawaiian/Other Pacific Islander, 2.5% Two or more races, 7.1% Hispanic of any race; Average household size: 2.82; Median age: 34.3; Age under 18: 33.0%; Age 65 and over: 5.7%; Males per 100 females: 94.7; Marriage

status: 25.0% never married, 63.6% now married, 1.5% separated, 2.6% widowed, 8.8% divorced; Foreign born: 10.0%; Speak English only: 87.7%; With disability: 5.1%; Veterans: 7.3%; Ancestry: 18.1% German, 16.5% Irish, 14.0% English, 9.4% Italian, 8.3% American
Employment: 25.3% management, business, and financial, 16.9% computer, engineering, and science, 12.9% education, legal, community service, arts, and media, 5.9% healthcare practitioners, 12.0% service, 20.6% sales and office, 3.2% natural resources, construction, and maintenance, 3.2% production, transportation, and material moving
Income: Per capita: $34,979; Median household: $89,475; Average household: $100,768; Households with income of $100,000 or more: 45.2%; Poverty rate: 2.5%
Educational Attainment: High school diploma or higher: 96.9%; Bachelor's degree or higher: 61.8%; Graduate/professional degree or higher: 20.9%

School District(s)
Wake County Schools (PK-12)
    2012-13 Enrollment: 150,956 . . . . (919) 431-7400
Housing: Homeownership rate: 74.7%; Median home value: $258,500; Median year structure built: 1998; Homeowner vacancy rate: 1.9%; Median gross rent: $1,055 per month; Rental vacancy rate: 8.0%
Health Insurance: 92.6% have insurance; 87.4% have private insurance; 10.3% have public insurance; 7.4% do not have insurance; 2.9% of children under 18 do not have insurance
Safety: Violent crime rate: 8.7 per 10,000 population; Property crime rate: 129.4 per 10,000 population
Transportation: Commute: 89.8% car, 0.6% public transportation, 1.0% walk, 7.2% work from home; Median travel time to work: 24.2 minutes
Additional Information Contacts
Town of Apex . . . . (919) 249-3418
    http://apexnc.org

CARY (town). Covers a land area of 54.345 square miles and a water area of 1.092 square miles. Located at 35.78° N. Lat; 78.81° W. Long. Elevation is 495 feet.
History: Walter Hines Page born here. Founded 1852; incorporated 1870.
Population: 135,234; Growth (since 2000): 43.1%; Density: 2,488.4 persons per square mile; Race: 73.1% White, 8.0% Black/African American, 13.1% Asian, 0.4% American Indian/Alaska Native, 0.0% Native Hawaiian/Other Pacific Islander, 2.6% Two or more races, 7.7% Hispanic of any race; Average household size: 2.61; Median age: 36.6; Age under 18: 27.7%; Age 65 and over: 8.6%; Males per 100 females: 94.8; Marriage status: 26.5% never married, 62.4% now married, 1.4% separated, 3.7% widowed, 7.3% divorced; Foreign born: 19.3%; Speak English only: 76.9%; With disability: 5.7%; Veterans: 6.7%; Ancestry: 14.0% German, 11.6% English, 11.5% Irish, 7.4% American, 7.1% Italian
Employment: 23.8% management, business, and financial, 17.5% computer, engineering, and science, 11.7% education, legal, community service, arts, and media, 6.4% healthcare practitioners, 12.2% service, 20.6% sales and office, 3.4% natural resources, construction, and maintenance, 4.5% production, transportation, and material moving
Income: Per capita: $41,554; Median household: $90,250; Average household: $110,841; Households with income of $100,000 or more: 45.9%; Poverty rate: 6.2%
Educational Attainment: High school diploma or higher: 95.2%; Bachelor's degree or higher: 62.2%; Graduate/professional degree or higher: 25.1%

School District(s)
Triangle Math and Science
    2012-13 Enrollment: 274 . . . . (919) 297-8709
Wake County Schools (PK-12)
    2012-13 Enrollment: 150,956 . . . . (919) 431-7400
Four-year College(s)
ITT Technical Institute-Cary (Private, For-profit)
    Fall 2013 Enrollment: 282 . . . . (919) 233-2520
    2013-14 Tuition: In-state $18,048; Out-of-state $18,048
Shepherds Theological Seminary (Private, Not-for-profit, Baptist)
    Fall 2013 Enrollment: 76 . . . . (919) 573-5350
    2013-14 Tuition: In-state $7,170; Out-of-state $7,170
Two-year College(s)
Miller-Motte College-Cary (Private, For-profit)
    Fall 2013 Enrollment: 320 . . . . (919) 532-7171
    2013-14 Tuition: In-state $10,659; Out-of-state $10,659

Housing: Homeownership rate: 68.9%; Median home value: $303,700; Median year structure built: 1995; Homeowner vacancy rate: 2.1%; Median gross rent: $965 per month; Rental vacancy rate: 8.9%
Health Insurance: 90.0% have insurance; 84.2% have private insurance; 13.6% have public insurance; 10.0% do not have insurance; 5.5% of children under 18 do not have insurance
Hospitals: Wakemed - Cary Hospital (156 beds)
Safety: Violent crime rate: 6.9 per 10,000 population; Property crime rate: 139.4 per 10,000 population
Transportation: Commute: 88.6% car, 0.6% public transportation, 1.4% walk, 8.2% work from home; Median travel time to work: 22.3 minutes; Amtrak: Train service available.
Additional Information Contacts
Town of Cary . . . . (919) 469-4000
    http://www.townofcary.org

FUQUAY-VARINA (town). Covers a land area of 12.090 square miles and a water area of 0.062 square miles. Located at 35.59° N. Lat; 78.78° W. Long. Elevation is 390 feet.
Population: 17,937; Growth (since 2000): 127.1%; Density: 1,483.6 persons per square mile; Race: 72.3% White, 19.7% Black/African American, 2.0% Asian, 0.6% American Indian/Alaska Native, 0.0% Native Hawaiian/Other Pacific Islander, 2.7% Two or more races, 9.7% Hispanic of any race; Average household size: 2.67; Median age: 34.2; Age under 18: 30.0%; Age 65 and over: 11.2%; Males per 100 females: 89.8; Marriage status: 24.0% never married, 61.6% now married, 4.0% separated, 5.3% widowed, 9.0% divorced; Foreign born: 8.9%; Speak English only: 88.8%; With disability: 9.2%; Veterans: 11.6%; Ancestry: 15.3% German, 14.5% Irish, 12.2% English, 10.1% American, 6.2% Italian
Employment: 16.1% management, business, and financial, 9.4% computer, engineering, and science, 13.4% education, legal, community service, arts, and media, 5.7% healthcare practitioners, 14.8% service, 23.2% sales and office, 7.3% natural resources, construction, and maintenance, 10.2% production, transportation, and material moving
Income: Per capita: $26,372; Median household: $58,588; Average household: $69,735; Households with income of $100,000 or more: 22.5%; Poverty rate: 10.3%
Educational Attainment: High school diploma or higher: 90.7%; Bachelor's degree or higher: 34.5%; Graduate/professional degree or higher: 9.9%

School District(s)
Wake County Schools (PK-12)
    2012-13 Enrollment: 150,956 . . . . (919) 431-7400
Housing: Homeownership rate: 73.2%; Median home value: $191,500; Median year structure built: 2001; Homeowner vacancy rate: 4.7%; Median gross rent: $905 per month; Rental vacancy rate: 8.1%
Health Insurance: 84.5% have insurance; 70.4% have private insurance; 22.2% have public insurance; 15.5% do not have insurance; 7.4% of children under 18 do not have insurance
Newspapers: Cleveland Post (weekly circulation 6500)
Transportation: Commute: 90.4% car, 0.0% public transportation, 2.1% walk, 6.2% work from home; Median travel time to work: 30.2 minutes
Additional Information Contacts
Town of Fuquay-Varina . . . . (919) 552-1029
    http://www.fuquay-varina.org

GARNER (town). Covers a land area of 14.747 square miles and a water area of 0.051 square miles. Located at 35.69° N. Lat; 78.62° W. Long. Elevation is 361 feet.
History: N.C. State University.
Population: 25,745; Growth (since 2000): 45.0%; Density: 1,745.8 persons per square mile; Race: 57.8% White, 32.9% Black/African American, 1.8% Asian, 0.5% American Indian/Alaska Native, 0.0% Native Hawaiian/Other Pacific Islander, 2.3% Two or more races, 9.9% Hispanic of any race; Average household size: 2.49; Median age: 37.1; Age under 18: 24.4%; Age 65 and over: 11.8%; Males per 100 females: 90.5; Marriage status: 26.4% never married, 55.4% now married, 4.9% separated, 7.3% widowed, 10.9% divorced; Foreign born: 4.5%; Speak English only: 92.9%; With disability: 10.8%; Veterans: 11.3%; Ancestry: 11.1% German, 11.1% English, 9.2% Irish, 9.2% American, 3.6% Italian
Employment: 16.5% management, business, and financial, 7.1% computer, engineering, and science, 9.7% education, legal, community service, arts, and media, 6.6% healthcare practitioners, 16.9% service, 25.4% sales and office, 7.2% natural resources, construction, and maintenance, 10.5% production, transportation, and material moving

Income: Per capita: $28,829; Median household: $60,842; Average household: $69,639; Households with income of $100,000 or more: 22.6%; Poverty rate: 8.6%

Educational Attainment: High school diploma or higher: 92.0%; Bachelor's degree or higher: 34.8%; Graduate/professional degree or higher: 9.2%

School District(s)
Johnston County Schools (PK-12)
    2012-13 Enrollment: 33,711 . . . . (919) 934-6031
Wake County Schools (PK-12)
    2012-13 Enrollment: 150,956 . . . . (919) 431-7400

Housing: Homeownership rate: 65.9%; Median home value: $165,600; Median year structure built: 1987; Homeowner vacancy rate: 3.0%; Median gross rent: $920 per month; Rental vacancy rate: 9.1%

Health Insurance: 85.5% have insurance; 73.6% have private insurance; 21.3% have public insurance; 14.5% do not have insurance; 10.9% of children under 18 do not have insurance

Safety: Violent crime rate: 19.2 per 10,000 population; Property crime rate: 436.0 per 10,000 population

Transportation: Commute: 90.7% car, 0.3% public transportation, 1.2% walk, 6.5% work from home; Median travel time to work: 25.8 minutes

Additional Information Contacts
Town of Garner . . . . (919) 733-4407
    http://www.garnernc.gov

HOLLY SPRINGS (town). Covers a land area of 15.013 square miles and a water area of 0.118 square miles. Located at 35.65° N. Lat; 78.84° W. Long. Elevation is 440 feet.

History: The Town of Holly Springs grew around fresh water springs, believed to be the original "holly springs" near the intersection of what is now Avent Ferry Road and Cass Holt Road. These roads linked Raleigh to the Cape Fear River and ultimately to Fayetteville as well as linking Hillsborough to Smithfield.

Population: 24,661; Growth (since 2000): 168.3%; Density: 1,642.7 persons per square mile; Race: 79.8% White, 12.6% Black/African American, 2.9% Asian, 0.4% American Indian/Alaska Native, 0.1% Native Hawaiian/Other Pacific Islander, 2.5% Two or more races, 6.3% Hispanic of any race; Average household size: 3.03; Median age: 33.1; Age under 18: 35.3%; Age 65 and over: 4.9%; Males per 100 females: 94.7; Marriage status: 17.9% never married, 70.5% now married, 1.5% separated, 2.5% widowed, 9.1% divorced; Foreign born: 7.7%; Speak English only: 92.3%; With disability: 6.5%; Veterans: 10.2%; Ancestry: 17.6% German, 14.8% Irish, 12.3% English, 11.8% Italian, 7.1% American

Employment: 21.2% management, business, and financial, 14.1% computer, engineering, and science, 15.4% education, legal, community service, arts, and media, 7.5% healthcare practitioners, 9.8% service, 20.8% sales and office, 5.7% natural resources, construction, and maintenance, 5.5% production, transportation, and material moving

Income: Per capita: $33,517; Median household: $89,644; Average household: $100,703; Households with income of $100,000 or more: 42.7%; Poverty rate: 3.1%

Educational Attainment: High school diploma or higher: 97.0%; Bachelor's degree or higher: 55.4%; Graduate/professional degree or higher: 17.5%

School District(s)
Southern Wake Academy (09-12)
    2012-13 Enrollment: 176 . . . . (919) 567-9955
Wake County Schools (PK-12)
    2012-13 Enrollment: 150,956 . . . . (919) 431-7400

Housing: Homeownership rate: 87.4%; Median home value: $236,300; Median year structure built: 2002; Homeowner vacancy rate: 2.5%; Median gross rent: $1,131 per month; Rental vacancy rate: 15.6%

Health Insurance: 93.5% have insurance; 88.0% have private insurance; 13.1% have public insurance; 6.5% do not have insurance; 5.1% of children under 18 do not have insurance

Safety: Violent crime rate: 8.3 per 10,000 population; Property crime rate: 115.4 per 10,000 population

Transportation: Commute: 88.4% car, 0.2% public transportation, 0.5% walk, 9.3% work from home; Median travel time to work: 27.7 minutes

Additional Information Contacts
Town of Holly Springs . . . . (919) 552-6221
    http://www.hollyspringsnc.us

KNIGHTDALE (town). Covers a land area of 6.206 square miles and a water area of 0.011 square miles. Located at 35.79° N. Lat; 78.50° W. Long. Elevation is 315 feet.

Population: 11,401; Growth (since 2000): 91.4%; Density: 1,837.2 persons per square mile; Race: 50.0% White, 38.3% Black/African American, 1.7% Asian, 0.6% American Indian/Alaska Native, 0.1% Native Hawaiian/Other Pacific Islander, 3.5% Two or more races, 11.4% Hispanic of any race; Average household size: 2.67; Median age: 32.6; Age under 18: 29.4%; Age 65 and over: 6.4%; Males per 100 females: 87.3; Marriage status: 25.6% never married, 60.2% now married, 3.2% separated, 4.8% widowed, 9.4% divorced; Foreign born: 12.3%; Speak English only: 83.7%; With disability: 6.5%; Veterans: 8.5%; Ancestry: 9.7% German, 7.8% African, 7.0% Irish, 6.2% English, 4.5% American

Employment: 16.3% management, business, and financial, 7.9% computer, engineering, and science, 12.7% education, legal, community service, arts, and media, 8.3% healthcare practitioners, 17.8% service, 22.1% sales and office, 7.5% natural resources, construction, and maintenance, 7.3% production, transportation, and material moving

Income: Per capita: $29,263; Median household: $71,066; Average household: $78,147; Households with income of $100,000 or more: 25.6%; Poverty rate: 7.5%

Educational Attainment: High school diploma or higher: 89.6%; Bachelor's degree or higher: 41.6%; Graduate/professional degree or higher: 11.6%

School District(s)
Wake County Schools (PK-12)
    2012-13 Enrollment: 150,956 . . . . (919) 431-7400

Housing: Homeownership rate: 67.9%; Median home value: $168,800; Median year structure built: 2000; Homeowner vacancy rate: 5.1%; Median gross rent: $921 per month; Rental vacancy rate: 14.3%

Health Insurance: 82.6% have insurance; 68.4% have private insurance; 19.8% have public insurance; 17.4% do not have insurance; 10.2% of children under 18 do not have insurance

Safety: Violent crime rate: 14.4 per 10,000 population; Property crime rate: 354.3 per 10,000 population

Transportation: Commute: 93.1% car, 0.0% public transportation, 2.4% walk, 3.5% work from home; Median travel time to work: 25.4 minutes

Additional Information Contacts
Town of Knightdale . . . . (919) 217-2220
    http://www.knightdalenc.gov

MORRISVILLE (town). Covers a land area of 8.258 square miles and a water area of 0.052 square miles. Located at 35.83° N. Lat; 78.84° W. Long. Elevation is 302 feet.

History: The area was originally named in 1852 after Jeremiah Morris. Morris donated land to the North Carolina Railroad for a depot, water tower, and other buildings. The town was officially chartered in 1875 but was disincorporated in 1933. Eventually the town charter was restored in 1947.

Population: 18,576; Growth (since 2000): 256.7%; Density: 2,249.4 persons per square mile; Race: 54.0% White, 12.9% Black/African American, 27.2% Asian, 0.4% American Indian/Alaska Native, 0.1% Native Hawaiian/Other Pacific Islander, 3.4% Two or more races, 5.9% Hispanic of any race; Average household size: 2.43; Median age: 32.5; Age under 18: 27.0%; Age 65 and over: 4.3%; Males per 100 females: 96.7; Marriage status: 23.3% never married, 64.3% now married, 2.5% separated, 2.7% widowed, 9.8% divorced; Foreign born: 27.4%; Speak English only: 64.9%; With disability: 5.5%; Veterans: 7.1%; Ancestry: 10.1% German, 7.7% English, 7.6% Irish, 4.8% Italian, 3.0% American

Employment: 23.9% management, business, and financial, 25.2% computer, engineering, and science, 10.3% education, legal, community service, arts, and media, 5.1% healthcare practitioners, 8.5% service, 20.8% sales and office, 2.1% natural resources, construction, and maintenance, 4.1% production, transportation, and material moving

Income: Per capita: $39,734; Median household: $80,892; Average household: $98,856; Households with income of $100,000 or more: 37.5%; Poverty rate: 3.1%

Educational Attainment: High school diploma or higher: 96.8%; Bachelor's degree or higher: 63.8%; Graduate/professional degree or higher: 23.9%

School District(s)
Sterling Montessori Academy (PK-08)
    2012-13 Enrollment: 584 . . . . (919) 462-8889
Wake County Schools (PK-12)
    2012-13 Enrollment: 150,956 . . . . (919) 431-7400

Four-year College(s)

Strayer University-North Carolina (Private, For-profit)
   Fall 2013 Enrollment: 3,802 . . . . (919) 466-4400
   2013-14 Tuition: In-state $15,495; Out-of-state $15,495

Two-year College(s)

Harrison College-Morrisville (Private, For-profit)
   Fall 2013 Enrollment: 203 . . . . (888) 544-4422
   2013-14 Tuition: In-state $16,740; Out-of-state $16,740

Housing: Homeownership rate: 48.4%; Median home value: $261,600; Median year structure built: 2001; Homeowner vacancy rate: 3.4%; Median gross rent: $980 per month; Rental vacancy rate: 7.6%

Health Insurance: 93.8% have insurance; 88.0% have private insurance; 10.1% have public insurance; 6.2% do not have insurance; 4.4% of children under 18 do not have insurance

Safety: Violent crime rate: 5.7 per 10,000 population; Property crime rate: 197.8 per 10,000 population

Transportation: Commute: 89.5% car, 0.1% public transportation, 0.7% walk, 8.6% work from home; Median travel time to work: 19.9 minutes

Additional Information Contacts

Town of Morrisville . . . . (919) 463-6200
   http://www.ci.morrisville.nc.us

NEW HILL (unincorporated postal area)

ZCTA: 27562

   Covers a land area of 53.772 square miles and a water area of 4.501 square miles. Located at 35.64° N. Lat; 78.99° W. Long. Elevation is 341 feet.

   Population: 1,938; Growth (since 2000): 12.2%; Density: 36.0 persons per square mile; Race: 83.3% White, 10.4% Black/African American, 0.6% Asian, 0.8% American Indian/Alaska Native, 0.0% Native Hawaiian/Other Pacific Islander, 1.9% Two or more races, 4.8% Hispanic of any race; Average household size: 2.51; Median age: 45.8; Age under 18: 22.2%; Age 65 and over: 16.3%; Males per 100 females: 102.5

   Housing: Homeownership rate: 82.9%; Homeowner vacancy rate: 1.4%; Rental vacancy rate: 6.9%

RALEIGH (city). State capital. County seat. Covers a land area of 142.903 square miles and a water area of 1.099 square miles. Located at 35.83° N. Lat; 78.64° W. Long. Elevation is 315 feet.

History: The town of Raleigh was laid out by William Christmas in 1792 with Union Square reserved for the statehouse. The location was chosen by the state convention of 1788 for an "unalterable seat of government." The settlement had formerly been known as Wake Courthouse or Bloomsbury. Cotton and knitting mills, a tobacco warehouse, and an electric power plant were established before 1900. Government employees played a key role in Raleigh's economy.

Population: 403,892; Growth (since 2000): 46.3%; Density: 2,826.3 persons per square mile; Race: 57.5% White, 29.3% Black/African American, 4.3% Asian, 0.5% American Indian/Alaska Native, 0.0% Native Hawaiian/Other Pacific Islander, 2.6% Two or more races, 11.4% Hispanic of any race; Average household size: 2.36; Median age: 31.9; Age under 18: 23.1%; Age 65 and over: 8.2%; Males per 100 females: 93.5; Marriage status: 42.0% never married, 43.8% now married, 2.9% separated, 3.9% widowed, 10.3% divorced; Foreign born: 13.7%; Speak English only: 82.2%; With disability: 7.6%; Veterans: 6.9%; Ancestry: 9.9% English, 9.8% German, 9.7% American, 8.2% Irish, 3.9% Italian

Employment: 18.4% management, business, and financial, 9.7% computer, engineering, and science, 13.4% education, legal, community service, arts, and media, 5.5% healthcare practitioners, 15.9% service, 24.5% sales and office, 6.0% natural resources, construction, and maintenance, 6.6% production, transportation, and material moving

Income: Per capita: $30,470; Median household: $54,448; Average household: $75,640; Households with income of $100,000 or more: 23.0%; Poverty rate: 16.2%

Educational Attainment: High school diploma or higher: 90.0%; Bachelor's degree or higher: 47.5%; Graduate/professional degree or higher: 15.9%

School District(s)

Casa Esperanza Montessori (PK-06)
   2012-13 Enrollment: 385 . . . . (919) 855-9811
Deaf and Blind Schools (PK-12)
   2012-13 Enrollment: 177 . . . . (919) 733-6382
Endeavor Charter School (KG-08)
   2012-13 Enrollment: 475 . . . . (919) 848-0333

Exploris (06-08)
   2012-13 Enrollment: 205 . . . . (919) 715-3690
Hope Elementary (KG-05)
   2012-13 Enrollment: 117 . . . . (919) 834-0941
Magellan Charter (03-08)
   2012-13 Enrollment: 400 . . . . (919) 844-0277
Nc Dept of Juvenile Justice (KG-12)
   2012-13 Enrollment: n/a . . . . (919) 733-3388
Nc Health and Human Resources (KG-12)
   2012-13 Enrollment: n/a . . . . (919) 855-4430
Preeminent Charter (KG-08)
   2012-13 Enrollment: 601 . . . . (919) 235-0511
Quest Academy (KG-08)
   2012-13 Enrollment: 142 . . . . (919) 841-0441
Raleigh Charter High (09-12)
   2012-13 Enrollment: 540 . . . . (919) 715-1155
Torchlight Academy (KG-05)
   2012-13 Enrollment: 416 . . . . (919) 850-9960
Wake County Schools (PK-12)
   2012-13 Enrollment: 150,956 . . . . (919) 431-7400

Four-year College(s)

Living Arts College (Private, For-profit)
   Fall 2013 Enrollment: 513 . . . . (919) 488-8500
   2013-14 Tuition: In-state $16,780; Out-of-state $16,780
Meredith College (Private, Not-for-profit)
   Fall 2013 Enrollment: 1,872 . . . . (919) 760-8600
   2013-14 Tuition: In-state $30,562; Out-of-state $30,562
North Carolina State University at Raleigh (Public)
   Fall 2013 Enrollment: 34,009 . . . . (919) 515-2011
   2013-14 Tuition: In-state $8,206; Out-of-state $21,661
Saint Augustine's University (Private, Not-for-profit, Historically black, Protestant Episcopal)
   Fall 2013 Enrollment: 1,299 . . . . (919) 516-4000
   2013-14 Tuition: In-state $17,890; Out-of-state $17,890
Shaw University (Private, Not-for-profit, Historically black, Baptist)
   Fall 2013 Enrollment: 2,062 . . . . (919) 546-8200
   2013-14 Tuition: In-state $16,480; Out-of-state $16,480
University of Phoenix-Raleigh Campus (Private, For-profit)
   Fall 2013 Enrollment: 166 . . . . (866) 766-0766
   2013-14 Tuition: In-state $10,205; Out-of-state $10,205
William Peace University (Private, Not-for-profit, Presbyterian Church (USA))
   Fall 2013 Enrollment: 1,007 . . . . (919) 508-2000
   2013-14 Tuition: In-state $23,900; Out-of-state $23,900

Two-year College(s)

Miller-Motte College-Raleigh (Private, For-profit)
   Fall 2013 Enrollment: 459 . . . . (919) 723-2820
   2013-14 Tuition: In-state $10,695; Out-of-state $10,695
Wake Technical Community College (Public)
   Fall 2013 Enrollment: 19,160 . . . . (919) 866-5000
   2013-14 Tuition: In-state $2,485; Out-of-state $8,629

Vocational/Technical School(s)

Mitchell's Hair Styling Academy-Raleigh (Private, For-profit)
   Fall 2013 Enrollment: 76 . . . . (919) 851-0962
   2013-14 Tuition: $13,750
MyComputerCareer.com-Raleigh (Private, For-profit)
   Fall 2013 Enrollment: 496 . . . . (919) 371-4820
   2013-14 Tuition: $16,036
Paul Mitchell The School-Raleigh (Private, For-profit)
   Fall 2013 Enrollment: 147 . . . . (919) 789-4500
   2013-14 Tuition: $15,300
The Medical Arts School (Private, For-profit)
   Fall 2013 Enrollment: 163 . . . . (919) 872-6386
   2013-14 Tuition: $12,854

Housing: Homeownership rate: 53.6%; Median home value: $207,000; Median year structure built: 1990; Homeowner vacancy rate: 2.6%; Median gross rent: $897 per month; Rental vacancy rate: 8.0%

Health Insurance: 83.9% have insurance; 69.7% have private insurance; 21.8% have public insurance; 16.1% do not have insurance; 8.9% of children under 18 do not have insurance

Hospitals: Duke Health Raleigh Hospital (222 beds); Rex Hospital (660 beds); Wakemed - Raleigh Campus (515 beds)

Safety: Violent crime rate: 39.2 per 10,000 population; Property crime rate: 306.3 per 10,000 population

Newspapers: Cary News (weekly circulation 50000); News & Observer (daily circulation 165000)
Transportation: Commute: 88.8% car, 2.1% public transportation, 2.1% walk, 5.4% work from home; Median travel time to work: 21.6 minutes; Amtrak: Train service available.
Airports: Raleigh-Durham International (primary service/medium hub)
Additional Information Contacts
City of Raleigh . . . . (919) 890-3100
　http://www.raleigh-nc.org

ROLESVILLE (town). Covers a land area of 3.934 square miles and a water area of 0.013 square miles. Located at 35.92° N. Lat; 78.46° W. Long. Elevation is 443 feet.

Population: 3,786; Growth (since 2000): 317.4%; Density: 962.5 persons per square mile; Race: 74.1% White, 17.8% Black/African American, 3.1% Asian, 0.4% American Indian/Alaska Native, 0.0% Native Hawaiian/Other Pacific Islander, 2.1% Two or more races, 6.2% Hispanic of any race; Average household size: 3.06; Median age: 35.2; Age under 18: 33.3%; Age 65 and over: 7.2%; Males per 100 females: 101.9; Marriage status: 20.6% never married, 72.0% now married, 4.4% separated, 2.7% widowed, 4.6% divorced; Foreign born: 7.3%; Speak English only: 88.8%; With disability: 6.6%; Veterans: 9.1%; Ancestry: 14.5% English, 12.4% Irish, 10.7% German, 8.7% Italian, 5.6% American
Employment: 17.5% management, business, and financial, 7.4% computer, engineering, and science, 11.0% education, legal, community service, arts, and media, 14.1% healthcare practitioners, 11.8% service, 23.4% sales and office, 7.8% natural resources, construction, and maintenance, 7.0% production, transportation, and material moving
Income: Per capita: $28,334; Median household: $79,917; Average household: $87,488; Households with income of $100,000 or more: 33.3%; Poverty rate: 7.5%
Educational Attainment: High school diploma or higher: 86.2%; Bachelor's degree or higher: 33.1%; Graduate/professional degree or higher: 11.5%
School District(s)
Wake County Schools (PK-12)
　2012-13 Enrollment: 150,956 . . . . (919) 431-7400
Housing: Homeownership rate: 87.6%; Median home value: $239,600; Median year structure built: 2002; Homeowner vacancy rate: 4.5%; Median gross rent: $556 per month; Rental vacancy rate: 9.9%
Health Insurance: 88.4% have insurance; 71.8% have private insurance; 24.9% have public insurance; 11.6% do not have insurance; 3.2% of children under 18 do not have insurance
Safety: Violent crime rate: 9.0 per 10,000 population; Property crime rate: 212.5 per 10,000 population
Transportation: Commute: 90.9% car, 0.0% public transportation, 2.1% walk, 7.0% work from home; Median travel time to work: 29.3 minutes

WAKE FOREST (town). Covers a land area of 15.095 square miles and a water area of 0.122 square miles. Located at 35.99° N. Lat; 78.54° W. Long. Elevation is 390 feet.

History: Wake Forest grew up around Wake Forest Institute, which opened in 1834 and was reorganized as a college in 1838.
Population: 30,117; Growth (since 2000): 139.3%; Density: 1,995.2 persons per square mile; Race: 77.3% White, 15.3% Black/African American, 2.9% Asian, 0.4% American Indian/Alaska Native, 0.0% Native Hawaiian/Other Pacific Islander, 2.4% Two or more races, 5.6% Hispanic of any race; Average household size: 2.83; Median age: 34.2; Age under 18: 32.4%; Age 65 and over: 8.1%; Males per 100 females: 92.7; Marriage status: 22.0% never married, 65.9% now married, 1.3% separated, 4.2% widowed, 7.8% divorced; Foreign born: 7.6%; Speak English only: 88.1%; With disability: 6.2%; Veterans: 10.0%; Ancestry: 16.2% Irish, 14.0% German, 13.0% English, 7.5% Italian, 7.1% American
Employment: 21.9% management, business, and financial, 10.5% computer, engineering, and science, 12.8% education, legal, community service, arts, and media, 6.4% healthcare practitioners, 13.6% service, 24.7% sales and office, 4.7% natural resources, construction, and maintenance, 5.4% production, transportation, and material moving
Income: Per capita: $32,474; Median household: $75,050; Average household: $91,608; Households with income of $100,000 or more: 37.4%; Poverty rate: 6.9%
Educational Attainment: High school diploma or higher: 95.2%; Bachelor's degree or higher: 50.4%; Graduate/professional degree or higher: 16.3%

School District(s)
Franklin Academy (KG-12)
　2012-13 Enrollment: 1,624 . . . . (919) 570-8262
Wake County Schools (PK-12)
　2012-13 Enrollment: 150,956 . . . . (919) 431-7400
Four-year College(s)
Southeastern Baptist Theological Seminary (Private, Not-for-profit, Southern Baptist)
　Fall 2013 Enrollment: 2,604 . . . . (919) 761-2100
　2013-14 Tuition: In-state $7,016; Out-of-state $7,016
Housing: Homeownership rate: 72.8%; Median home value: $259,200; Median year structure built: 2001; Homeowner vacancy rate: 3.0%; Median gross rent: $940 per month; Rental vacancy rate: 9.8%
Health Insurance: 92.1% have insurance; 82.3% have private insurance; 18.9% have public insurance; 7.9% do not have insurance; 5.4% of children under 18 do not have insurance
Safety: Violent crime rate: 12.7 per 10,000 population; Property crime rate: 215.9 per 10,000 population
Newspapers: The Wake Weekly (weekly circulation 10000)
Transportation: Commute: 88.5% car, 0.5% public transportation, 0.6% walk, 10.1% work from home; Median travel time to work: 28.8 minutes
Additional Information Contacts
Town of Wake Forest . . . . (919) 554-6100
　http://www.ci.wake-forest.nc.us

WENDELL (town). Covers a land area of 5.204 square miles and a water area of 0.017 square miles. Located at 35.77° N. Lat; 78.42° W. Long. Elevation is 318 feet.

History: Settled c.1890; incorporated 1903.
Population: 5,845; Growth (since 2000): 37.6%; Density: 1,123.1 persons per square mile; Race: 58.1% White, 30.2% Black/African American, 0.9% Asian, 0.8% American Indian/Alaska Native, 0.0% Native Hawaiian/Other Pacific Islander, 3.2% Two or more races, 11.5% Hispanic of any race; Average household size: 2.57; Median age: 33.4; Age under 18: 29.5%; Age 65 and over: 11.6%; Males per 100 females: 85.3; Marriage status: 24.3% never married, 53.9% now married, 2.3% separated, 10.0% widowed, 11.8% divorced; Foreign born: 5.6%; Speak English only: 86.5%; With disability: 14.9%; Veterans: 10.6%; Ancestry: 16.8% American, 12.3% German, 10.6% English, 6.2% Irish, 3.0% Italian
Employment: 15.0% management, business, and financial, 3.1% computer, engineering, and science, 8.4% education, legal, community service, arts, and media, 2.5% healthcare practitioners, 16.7% service, 31.4% sales and office, 10.0% natural resources, construction, and maintenance, 13.0% production, transportation, and material moving
Income: Per capita: $26,525; Median household: $40,968; Average household: $57,376; Households with income of $100,000 or more: 9.6%; Poverty rate: 15.9%
Educational Attainment: High school diploma or higher: 89.8%; Bachelor's degree or higher: 29.0%; Graduate/professional degree or higher: 6.6%
School District(s)
Johnston County Schools (PK-12)
　2012-13 Enrollment: 33,711 . . . . (919) 934-6031
Wake County Schools (PK-12)
　2012-13 Enrollment: 150,956 . . . . (919) 431-7400
Housing: Homeownership rate: 66.5%; Median home value: $127,200; Median year structure built: 1981; Homeowner vacancy rate: 3.3%; Median gross rent: $858 per month; Rental vacancy rate: 4.6%
Health Insurance: 86.5% have insurance; 60.4% have private insurance; 38.0% have public insurance; 13.5% do not have insurance; 4.7% of children under 18 do not have insurance
Safety: Violent crime rate: 20.8 per 10,000 population; Property crime rate: 272.1 per 10,000 population
Transportation: Commute: 92.7% car, 0.9% public transportation, 2.2% walk, 4.2% work from home; Median travel time to work: 31.7 minutes
Additional Information Contacts
Town of Wendell . . . . (919) 365-4450
　http://www.townofwendell.com

WILLOW SPRING (unincorporated postal area)
ZCTA: 27592
　Covers a land area of 41.638 square miles and a water area of 0.216 square miles. Located at 35.56° N. Lat; 78.67° W. Long..
　Population: 15,244; Growth (since 2000): 70.8%; Density: 366.1 persons per square mile; Race: 82.0% White, 9.1% Black/African

American, 0.4% Asian, 0.6% American Indian/Alaska Native, 0.0% Native Hawaiian/Other Pacific Islander, 2.2% Two or more races, 12.3% Hispanic of any race; Average household size: 2.82; Median age: 35.2; Age under 18: 29.2%; Age 65 and over: 7.1%; Males per 100 females: 100.7; Marriage status: 27.2% never married, 57.4% now married, 1.7% separated, 4.6% widowed, 10.9% divorced; Foreign born: 9.3%; Speak English only: 85.6%; With disability: 8.6%; Veterans: 7.7%; Ancestry: 18.8% American, 12.4% German, 10.1% Irish, 7.7% English, 6.7% Italian

Employment: 18.1% management, business, and financial, 8.7% computer, engineering, and science, 8.7% education, legal, community service, arts, and media, 4.5% healthcare practitioners, 16.5% service, 21.3% sales and office, 12.7% natural resources, construction, and maintenance, 9.5% production, transportation, and material moving
Income: Per capita: $22,530; Median household: $56,967; Average household: $63,238; Households with income of $100,000 or more: 19.5%; Poverty rate: 10.4%
Educational Attainment: High school diploma or higher: 87.1%; Bachelor's degree or higher: 28.2%; Graduate/professional degree or higher: 5.8%

School District(s)
Johnston County Schools (PK-12)
    2012-13 Enrollment: 33,711 . . . . (919) 934-6031
Wake County Schools (PK-12)
    2012-13 Enrollment: 150,956 . . . . (919) 431-7400
Housing: Homeownership rate: 83.7%; Median home value: $151,900; Median year structure built: 1997; Homeowner vacancy rate: 2.2%; Median gross rent: $768 per month; Rental vacancy rate: 8.2%
Health Insurance: 79.6% have insurance; 66.0% have private insurance; 19.4% have public insurance; 20.4% do not have insurance; 14.6% of children under 18 do not have insurance
Transportation: Commute: 89.8% car, 0.1% public transportation, 0.6% walk, 7.8% work from home; Median travel time to work: 33.2 minutes

---

ZEBULON (town). Covers a land area of 4.138 square miles and a water area of 0.024 square miles. Located at 35.83° N. Lat; 78.32° W. Long. Elevation is 322 feet.
Population: 4,433; Growth (since 2000): 9.6%; Density: 1,071.4 persons per square mile; Race: 47.3% White, 38.6% Black/African American, 1.0% Asian, 0.5% American Indian/Alaska Native, 0.0% Native Hawaiian/Other Pacific Islander, 3.6% Two or more races, 15.9% Hispanic of any race; Average household size: 2.62; Median age: 35.3; Age under 18: 28.2%; Age 65 and over: 13.1%; Males per 100 females: 84.6; Marriage status: 36.9% never married, 39.7% now married, 4.6% separated, 9.1% widowed, 14.2% divorced; Foreign born: 12.7%; Speak English only: 80.2%; With disability: 15.9%; Veterans: 8.9%; Ancestry: 14.1% American, 10.0% African, 5.9% Irish, 5.8% English, 3.4% Italian
Employment: 5.6% management, business, and financial, 5.9% computer, engineering, and science, 5.1% education, legal, community service, arts, and media, 5.8% healthcare practitioners, 18.7% service, 26.9% sales and office, 10.0% natural resources, construction, and maintenance, 21.9% production, transportation, and material moving
Income: Per capita: $19,529; Median household: $52,599; Average household: $55,765; Households with income of $100,000 or more: 17.8%; Poverty rate: 19.0%
Educational Attainment: High school diploma or higher: 80.9%; Bachelor's degree or higher: 15.7%; Graduate/professional degree or higher: 7.7%

School District(s)
East Wake Academy (KG-12)
    2012-13 Enrollment: 1,122 . . . . (919) 404-0444
Johnston County Schools (PK-12)
    2012-13 Enrollment: 33,711 . . . . (919) 934-6031
Wake County Schools (PK-12)
    2012-13 Enrollment: 150,956 . . . . (919) 431-7400
Housing: Homeownership rate: 56.2%; Median home value: $111,100; Median year structure built: 1984; Homeowner vacancy rate: 4.4%; Median gross rent: $972 per month; Rental vacancy rate: 9.7%
Health Insurance: 78.5% have insurance; 52.5% have private insurance; 37.5% have public insurance; 21.5% do not have insurance; 1.5% of children under 18 do not have insurance
Safety: Violent crime rate: 66.5 per 10,000 population; Property crime rate: 664.7 per 10,000 population
Newspapers: Eastern Wake News (weekly circulation 6900)

Transportation: Commute: 91.1% car, 1.1% public transportation, 1.1% walk, 3.9% work from home; Median travel time to work: 25.7 minutes
Additional Information Contacts
Town of Zebulon . . . . (919) 269-7455
    http://www.townofzebulon.org

Warren County

Located in northern North Carolina; piedmont area, bounded on the north by Virginia; drained by the Roanoke River. Covers a land area of 428.456 square miles, a water area of 15.306 square miles, and is located in the Eastern Time Zone at 36.40° N. Lat., 78.10° W. Long. The county was founded in 1779. County seat is Warrenton.

Weather Station: Arcola										Elevation: 330 feet	
	Jan	Feb	Mar	Apr	May	Jun	Jul	Aug	Sep	Oct	Nov	Dec
High	51	55	63	72	79	87	90	88	83	73	65	55
Low	27	30	36	43	53	61	66	64	57	45	37	31
Precip	3.4	3.3	4.5	3.4	3.5	4.5	5.0	5.1	4.0	3.4	3.4	3.3
Snow	2.6	2.0	0.6	tr	0.0	0.0	0.0	0.0	0.0	0.0	0.1	0.7

High and Low temperatures in degrees Fahrenheit; Precipitation and Snow in inches

Population: 20,972; Growth (since 2000): 5.0%; Density: 48.9 persons per square mile; Race: 38.8% White, 52.3% Black/African American, 0.2% Asian, 5.0% American Indian/Alaska Native, 0.0% Native Hawaiian/Other Pacific Islander, 1.6% two or more races, 3.3% Hispanic of any race; Average household size: 2.38; Median age: 44.9; Age under 18: 20.3%; Age 65 and over: 18.9%; Males per 100 females: 102.1; Marriage status: 32.2% never married, 46.6% now married, 3.6% separated, 9.9% widowed, 11.2% divorced; Foreign born: 2.4%; Speak English only: 96.4%; With disability: 30.0%; Veterans: 11.5%; Ancestry: 15.4% American, 7.9% English, 4.8% German, 3.9% Irish, 1.3% Scotch-Irish
Religion: Six largest groups: 14.5% Baptist, 6.0% Methodist/Pietist, 5.1% Presbyterian-Reformed, 4.1% Non-denominational Protestant, 2.4% Lutheran, 1.0% Pentecostal
Economy: Unemployment rate: 8.1%; Leading industries: 17.3% retail trade; 15.0% other services (except public administration); 14.2% construction; Farms: 256 totaling 65,699 acres; Company size: 0 employ 1,000 or more persons, 0 employ 500 to 999 persons, 4 employ 100 to 499 persons, 250 employ less than 100 persons; Business ownership: 294 women-owned, 458 Black-owned, n/a Hispanic-owned, n/a Asian-owned
Employment: 10.5% management, business, and financial, 1.8% computer, engineering, and science, 8.0% education, legal, community service, arts, and media, 3.9% healthcare practitioners, 21.8% service, 24.4% sales and office, 12.8% natural resources, construction, and maintenance, 16.9% production, transportation, and material moving
Income: Per capita: $19,052; Median household: $34,285; Average household: $48,143; Households with income of $100,000 or more: 11.2%; Poverty rate: 26.2%
Educational Attainment: High school diploma or higher: 76.5%; Bachelor's degree or higher: 13.5%; Graduate/professional degree or higher: 4.7%
Housing: Homeownership rate: 72.6%; Median home value: $98,300; Median year structure built: 1982; Homeowner vacancy rate: 2.3%; Median gross rent: $681 per month; Rental vacancy rate: 8.9%
Vital Statistics: Birth rate: 80.2 per 10,000 population; Death rate: 111.3 per 10,000 population; Age-adjusted cancer mortality rate: 173.2 deaths per 100,000 population
Health Insurance: 82.1% have insurance; 46.5% have private insurance; 49.8% have public insurance; 17.9% do not have insurance; 5.0% of children under 18 do not have insurance
Health Care: Physicians: 2.4 per 10,000 population; Hospital beds: 0.0 per 10,000 population; Hospital admissions: 0.0 per 10,000 population
Transportation: Commute: 94.2% car, 0.0% public transportation, 1.4% walk, 4.2% work from home; Median travel time to work: 29.4 minutes
Presidential Election: 68.7% Obama, 30.9% Romney (2012)
Additional Information Contacts
Warren Government . . . . (252) 257-3115
    http://www.warrencountync.com

Warren County Communities

MACON (town). Covers a land area of 0.471 square miles and a water area of 0 square miles. Located at 36.44° N. Lat; 78.08° W. Long. Elevation is 381 feet.
Population: 119; Growth (since 2000): 3.5%; Density: 252.7 persons per square mile; Race: 84.9% White, 13.4% Black/African American, 0.0% Asian, 0.8% American Indian/Alaska Native, 0.0% Native Hawaiian/Other Pacific Islander, 0.8% Two or more races, 0.0% Hispanic of any race; Average household size: 2.29; Median age: 50.8; Age under 18: 16.8%; Age 65 and over: 17.6%; Males per 100 females: 116.4
Housing: Homeownership rate: 86.5%; Homeowner vacancy rate: 0.0%; Rental vacancy rate: 20.0%

NORLINA (town). Covers a land area of 1.113 square miles and a water area of 0.007 square miles. Located at 36.44° N. Lat; 78.20° W. Long. Elevation is 423 feet.
Population: 1,118; Growth (since 2000): 1.0%; Density: 1,004.8 persons per square mile; Race: 48.5% White, 45.2% Black/African American, 0.4% Asian, 0.2% American Indian/Alaska Native, 0.0% Native Hawaiian/Other Pacific Islander, 2.1% Two or more races, 6.3% Hispanic of any race; Average household size: 2.36; Median age: 38.6; Age under 18: 26.7%; Age 65 and over: 18.3%; Males per 100 females: 85.1
School District(s)
Warren County Schools (PK-12)
    2012-13 Enrollment: 2,469 . . . . (252) 257-3184
Housing: Homeownership rate: 52.9%; Homeowner vacancy rate: 2.3%; Rental vacancy rate: 5.9%

WARRENTON (town). County seat. Covers a land area of 0.974 square miles and a water area of <.001 square miles. Located at 36.40° N. Lat; 78.16° W. Long. Elevation is 387 feet.
History: Warrenton and Warren County were founded in 1779 and named for General Joseph Warren of Massachusetts, who fell at Bunker Hill. The town was laid out in that year by William Christmas. Before the Civil War, it was known as a center of culture and wealth.
Population: 862; Growth (since 2000): 6.3%; Density: 884.8 persons per square mile; Race: 54.6% White, 40.8% Black/African American, 0.2% Asian, 0.8% American Indian/Alaska Native, 0.0% Native Hawaiian/Other Pacific Islander, 1.4% Two or more races, 3.4% Hispanic of any race; Average household size: 1.95; Median age: 54.2; Age under 18: 13.0%; Age 65 and over: 30.6%; Males per 100 females: 90.7
School District(s)
Warren County Schools (PK-12)
    2012-13 Enrollment: 2,469 . . . . (252) 257-3184
Housing: Homeownership rate: 60.5%; Homeowner vacancy rate: 5.2%; Rental vacancy rate: 8.9%
Newspapers: Warren Record (weekly circulation 5800)

Washington County

Located in eastern North Carolina; tidewater area, bounded on the north by Albemarle Sound. Covers a land area of 348.135 square miles, a water area of 75.712 square miles, and is located in the Eastern Time Zone at 35.84° N. Lat., 76.57° W. Long. The county was founded in 1799. County seat is Plymouth.

Weather Station: Plymouth 5 E   Elevation: 20 feet

	Jan	Feb	Mar	Apr	May	Jun	Jul	Aug	Sep	Oct	Nov	Dec
High	54	58	65	74	81	87	90	88	83	75	66	57
Low	33	35	40	48	57	65	70	68	63	51	43	36
Precip	4.0	3.2	4.4	3.5	4.1	5.0	5.5	6.2	5.2	3.6	3.6	3.3
Snow	0.8	0.9	0.7	tr	0.0	0.0	0.0	0.0	0.0	0.0	tr	0.3

High and Low temperatures in degrees Fahrenheit; Precipitation and Snow in inches

Population: 13,228; Growth (since 2000): -3.6%; Density: 38.0 persons per square mile; Race: 46.0% White, 49.8% Black/African American, 0.3% Asian, 0.2% American Indian/Alaska Native, 0.0% Native Hawaiian/Other Pacific Islander, 1.2% two or more races, 3.5% Hispanic of any race; Average household size: 2.37; Median age: 44.0; Age under 18: 23.0%; Age 65 and over: 18.2%; Males per 100 females: 88.8; Marriage status: 34.2% never married, 46.2% now married, 3.3% separated, 11.5% widowed, 8.1% divorced; Foreign born: 2.0%; Speak English only: 97.6%; With disability: 21.9%; Veterans: 10.1%; Ancestry: 11.0% American, 6.4% English, 4.8% Irish, 4.1% German, 2.1% Scottish

Religion: Six largest groups: 30.0% Baptist, 8.3% Methodist/Pietist, 4.7% Non-denominational Protestant, 3.6% Pentecostal, 1.6% Other Groups, 1.5% Catholicism
Economy: Unemployment rate: 6.4%; Leading industries: 19.0% retail trade; 14.3% other services (except public administration); 13.5% health care and social assistance; Farms: 156 totaling 91,398 acres; Company size: 0 employ 1,000 or more persons, 0 employ 500 to 999 persons, 4 employ 100 to 499 persons, 248 employ less than 100 persons; Business ownership: 290 women-owned, 208 Black-owned, n/a Hispanic-owned, n/a Asian-owned
Employment: 12.1% management, business, and financial, 1.3% computer, engineering, and science, 9.2% education, legal, community service, arts, and media, 4.0% healthcare practitioners, 20.1% service, 17.7% sales and office, 12.4% natural resources, construction, and maintenance, 23.2% production, transportation, and material moving
Income: Per capita: $18,779; Median household: $34,936; Average household: $45,728; Households with income of $100,000 or more: 10.0%; Poverty rate: 23.7%
Educational Attainment: High school diploma or higher: 79.0%; Bachelor's degree or higher: 11.7%; Graduate/professional degree or higher: 4.6%
Housing: Homeownership rate: 69.7%; Median home value: $89,000; Median year structure built: 1972; Homeowner vacancy rate: 2.1%; Median gross rent: $585 per month; Rental vacancy rate: 11.6%
Vital Statistics: Birth rate: 101.4 per 10,000 population; Death rate: 112.4 per 10,000 population; Age-adjusted cancer mortality rate: 110.6 deaths per 100,000 population
Health Insurance: 82.0% have insurance; 51.0% have private insurance; 43.5% have public insurance; 18.0% do not have insurance; 6.1% of children under 18 do not have insurance
Health Care: Physicians: 4.7 per 10,000 population; Hospital beds: 19.3 per 10,000 population; Hospital admissions: 524.3 per 10,000 population
Transportation: Commute: 95.6% car, 0.0% public transportation, 2.3% walk, 1.9% work from home; Median travel time to work: 25.3 minutes
Presidential Election: 59.0% Obama, 40.3% Romney (2012)
National and State Parks: Pettigrew State Park
Additional Information Contacts
Washington Government . . . . (252) 793-5823
   http://www.washconc.org

Washington County Communities

CRESWELL (town). Covers a land area of 0.566 square miles and a water area of 0 square miles. Located at 35.87° N. Lat; 76.40° W. Long. Elevation is 7 feet.
History: Creswell was founded in 1874 by William Atkinson and named for John A.J. Creswell, Postmaster General at that time.
Population: 276; Growth (since 2000): -0.7%; Density: 487.7 persons per square mile; Race: 42.0% White, 43.5% Black/African American, 0.0% Asian, 0.0% American Indian/Alaska Native, 0.0% Native Hawaiian/Other Pacific Islander, 2.5% Two or more races, 11.6% Hispanic of any race; Average household size: 2.36; Median age: 42.5; Age under 18: 23.6%; Age 65 and over: 22.1%; Males per 100 females: 86.5
School District(s)
Washington County Schools (PK-12)
    2012-13 Enrollment: 1,816 . . . . (252) 793-5171
Housing: Homeownership rate: 54.7%; Homeowner vacancy rate: 0.0%; Rental vacancy rate: 3.6%

PLYMOUTH (town). County seat. Covers a land area of 4.032 square miles and a water area of 0.005 square miles. Located at 35.86° N. Lat; 76.75° W. Long. Elevation is 16 feet.
History: Plymouth is an old port on the south bank of the Roanoke. It was founded in 1780 with the gift of a site by Arthur Rhodes, a former resident of Plymouth, Massachusetts. It became a thriving shipping point, but was partially destroyed during the Civil War.
Population: 3,878; Growth (since 2000): -5.6%; Density: 961.7 persons per square mile; Race: 29.2% White, 68.4% Black/African American, 0.4% Asian, 0.4% American Indian/Alaska Native, 0.0% Native Hawaiian/Other Pacific Islander, 1.0% Two or more races, 1.2% Hispanic of any race; Average household size: 2.35; Median age: 41.0; Age under 18: 26.3%; Age 65 and over: 19.4%; Males per 100 females: 76.0; Marriage status: 35.1% never married, 44.6% now married, 3.7% separated, 12.7% widowed, 7.6% divorced; Foreign born: 0.4%; Speak English only: 100.0%;

With disability: 24.1%; Veterans: 6.5%; Ancestry: 6.0% Irish, 5.6% English, 5.1% American, 5.1% German, 1.5% Scottish
Employment: 14.7% management, business, and financial, 1.6% computer, engineering, and science, 11.3% education, legal, community service, arts, and media, 5.3% healthcare practitioners, 18.9% service, 17.2% sales and office, 5.6% natural resources, construction, and maintenance, 25.4% production, transportation, and material moving
Income: Per capita: $17,199; Median household: $26,955; Average household: $41,988; Households with income of $100,000 or more: 14.8%; Poverty rate: 34.2%
Educational Attainment: High school diploma or higher: 78.6%; Bachelor's degree or higher: 18.4%; Graduate/professional degree or higher: 7.6%

School District(s)
Northeast Regional School of Biotechnology and Agr (09-09)
 2012-13 Enrollment: 59. . . . . (252) 791-0056
Washington County Schools (PK-12)
 2012-13 Enrollment: 1,816 . . . . (252) 793-5171
Housing: Homeownership rate: 50.5%; Median home value: $91,400; Median year structure built: 1964; Homeowner vacancy rate: 4.6%; Median gross rent: $333 per month; Rental vacancy rate: 10.3%
Health Insurance: 88.7% have insurance; 45.0% have private insurance; 54.8% have public insurance; 11.3% do not have insurance; 1.4% of children under 18 do not have insurance
Hospitals: Washington County Hospital (49 beds)
Newspapers: Roanoke Beacon (weekly circulation 4000)
Transportation: Commute: 96.4% car, 0.0% public transportation, 1.1% walk, 2.5% work from home; Median travel time to work: 18.8 minutes
Additional Information Contacts
Town of Plymouth . . . . (252) 793-4804

ROPER (town). Covers a land area of 0.856 square miles and a water area of 0 square miles. Located at 35.88° N. Lat; 76.62° W. Long. Elevation is 13 feet.
History: Roper was formerly a busy settlement called Lees Mill, which served the needs of the wealthy planters of Tyrrell County in Colonial days.
Population: 611; Growth (since 2000): -0.3%; Density: 713.4 persons per square mile; Race: 18.2% White, 78.6% Black/African American, 0.0% Asian, 0.0% American Indian/Alaska Native, 0.0% Native Hawaiian/Other Pacific Islander, 1.1% Two or more races, 2.9% Hispanic of any race; Average household size: 2.31; Median age: 40.1; Age under 18: 25.2%; Age 65 and over: 16.7%; Males per 100 females: 85.7

School District(s)
Washington County Schools (PK-12)
 2012-13 Enrollment: 1,816 . . . . (252) 793-5171
Housing: Homeownership rate: 48.3%; Homeowner vacancy rate: 5.1%; Rental vacancy rate: 10.5%

Watauga County

Located in northwestern North Carolina, in the Blue Ridge; bounded on the west by Tennessee; drained by the Watauga and South Fork of the New River; includes parts of Yadkin and Pisgah National Forests. Covers a land area of 312.556 square miles, a water area of 0.897 square miles, and is located in the Eastern Time Zone at 36.24° N. Lat., 81.71° W. Long. The county was founded in 1849. County seat is Boone.

Watauga County is part of the Boone, NC Micropolitan Statistical Area. The entire metro area includes: Watauga County, NC

Weather Station: Blowing Rock 1 NW   Elevation: 3,850 feet

	Jan	Feb	Mar	Apr	May	Jun	Jul	Aug	Sep	Oct	Nov	Dec
High	39	42	49	59	66	73	77	75	69	60	51	42
Low	22	24	30	39	47	55	60	58	52	42	33	25
Precip	5.3	4.6	5.7	5.8	5.6	6.2	6.3	5.7	5.3	4.7	5.9	4.6
Snow	7.6	7.1	5.1	1.3	0.0	0.0	0.0	0.0	0.0	tr	0.9	4.6

High and Low temperatures in degrees Fahrenheit; Precipitation and Snow in inches

Weather Station: Boone 1 SE   Elevation: 3,359 feet

	Jan	Feb	Mar	Apr	May	Jun	Jul	Aug	Sep	Oct	Nov	Dec
High	41	44	52	61	68	75	78	77	71	62	53	44
Low	23	25	31	39	47	55	59	58	52	41	33	26
Precip	3.7	3.9	4.7	4.5	4.4	5.1	5.1	5.0	4.4	3.6	4.5	3.5
Snow	9.9	8.8	4.9	3.0	0.1	0.0	0.0	0.0	0.0	0.1	1.4	5.9

High and Low temperatures in degrees Fahrenheit; Precipitation and Snow in inches

Population: 51,079; Growth (since 2000): 19.6%; Density: 163.4 persons per square mile; Race: 94.5% White, 1.7% Black/African American, 0.9% Asian, 0.3% American Indian/Alaska Native, 0.0% Native Hawaiian/Other Pacific Islander, 1.4% two or more races, 3.4% Hispanic of any race; Average household size: 2.24; Median age: 28.4; Age under 18: 13.8%; Age 65 and over: 12.4%; Males per 100 females: 100.8; Marriage status: 47.2% never married, 42.1% now married, 1.3% separated, 4.2% widowed, 6.5% divorced; Foreign born: 3.5%; Speak English only: 94.7%; With disability: 9.5%; Veterans: 7.2%; Ancestry: 21.8% German, 16.3% English, 14.6% Irish, 10.1% American, 5.5% Scottish
Religion: Six largest groups: 21.1% Baptist, 6.3% Methodist/Pietist, 2.9% Lutheran, 2.2% Holiness, 2.1% Presbyterian-Reformed, 2.1% Episcopalianism/Anglicanism
Economy: Unemployment rate: 5.0%; Leading industries: 20.0% retail trade; 13.1% construction; 11.3% accommodation and food services; Farms: 609 totaling 55,765 acres; Company size: 0 employ 1,000 or more persons, 2 employ 500 to 999 persons, 11 employs 100 to 499 persons, 1,559 employ less than 100 persons; Business ownership: 1,276 women-owned, n/a Black-owned, n/a Hispanic-owned, n/a Asian-owned
Employment: 11.3% management, business, and financial, 2.7% computer, engineering, and science, 15.3% education, legal, community service, arts, and media, 3.5% healthcare practitioners, 25.6% service, 26.0% sales and office, 8.6% natural resources, construction, and maintenance, 7.0% production, transportation, and material moving
Income: Per capita: $21,854; Median household: $34,293; Average household: $53,048; Households with income of $100,000 or more: 12.6%; Poverty rate: 31.3%
Educational Attainment: High school diploma or higher: 89.0%; Bachelor's degree or higher: 37.9%; Graduate/professional degree or higher: 15.7%
Housing: Homeownership rate: 56.8%; Median home value: $228,700; Median year structure built: 1984; Homeowner vacancy rate: 5.0%; Median gross rent: $819 per month; Rental vacancy rate: 10.4%
Vital Statistics: Birth rate: 68.7 per 10,000 population; Death rate: 61.3 per 10,000 population; Age-adjusted cancer mortality rate: 174.9 deaths per 100,000 population
Health Insurance: 86.7% have insurance; 75.5% have private insurance; 21.8% have public insurance; 13.3% do not have insurance; 7.5% of children under 18 do not have insurance
Health Care: Physicians: 20.5 per 10,000 population; Hospital beds: 38.0 per 10,000 population; Hospital admissions: 958.5 per 10,000 population
Air Quality Index: 89.3% good, 9.8% moderate, 0.0% unhealthy for sensitive individuals, 0.8% unhealthy (percent of days)
Transportation: Commute: 85.1% car, 1.2% public transportation, 7.0% walk, 5.8% work from home; Median travel time to work: 18.5 minutes
Presidential Election: 47.0% Obama, 50.1% Romney (2012)
National and State Parks: Elk Knob State Natural Area
Additional Information Contacts
Watauga Government . . . . (828) 265-8000
 http://www.wataugacounty.org

Watauga County Communities

BEECH MOUNTAIN (town). Covers a land area of 6.664 square miles and a water area of 0.003 square miles. Located at 36.21° N. Lat; 81.89° W. Long. Elevation is 4,245 feet.
Population: 320; Growth (since 2000): 3.2%; Density: 48.0 persons per square mile; Race: 97.8% White, 0.9% Black/African American, 0.0% Asian, 0.9% American Indian/Alaska Native, 0.0% Native Hawaiian/Other Pacific Islander, 0.0% Two or more races, 3.1% Hispanic of any race; Average household size: 2.08; Median age: 52.0; Age under 18: 10.3%; Age 65 and over: 23.1%; Males per 100 females: 102.5
Housing: Homeownership rate: 82.4%; Homeowner vacancy rate: 23.8%; Rental vacancy rate: 42.0%
Additional Information Contacts
Town of Beech Mountain. . . . . (828) 387-4236
 http://www.townofbeechmountain.com

BLOWING ROCK (town). Covers a land area of 3.000 square miles and a water area of 0.045 square miles. Located at 36.13° N. Lat; 81.67° W. Long. Elevation is 3,573 feet.
History: Blowing Rock was developed in the late 1880's when stages over rough mountain roads were the only means of access. Situated on the Blue Ridge Parkway, Blowing Rock was one of the first resorts in the southern Appalachians. The Blowing Rock itself is an immense cliff

overhanging the Johns River Gorge. It is so called because the rocky walls of the gorge form a flume through which the northwest wind at times sweeps with such force that it blows back up light objects cast over the side.
Population: 1,241; Growth (since 2000): -12.5%; Density: 413.7 persons per square mile; Race: 96.6% White, 0.3% Black/African American, 0.2% Asian, 0.0% American Indian/Alaska Native, 0.0% Native Hawaiian/Other Pacific Islander, 2.5% Two or more races, 1.6% Hispanic of any race; Average household size: 1.89; Median age: 58.9; Age under 18: 10.4%; Age 65 and over: 35.3%; Males per 100 females: 82.5

School District(s)
Watauga County Schools (PK-12)
    2012-13 Enrollment: 4,550 . . . . (828) 264-7190
Housing: Homeownership rate: 71.2%; Homeowner vacancy rate: 11.8%; Rental vacancy rate: 29.7%
Hospitals: Blowing Rock Hospital (100 beds)
Safety: Violent crime rate: 0.0 per 10,000 population; Property crime rate: 324.1 per 10,000 population
Additional Information Contacts
Town of Blowing Rock. . . . . (828) 295-4636
    http://www.blowingrock.com

BOONE (town). County seat. Covers a land area of 6.131 square miles and a water area of 0.016 square miles. Located at 36.21° N. Lat; 81.67° W. Long. Elevation is 3,218 feet.
History: Boone was named for Daniel Boone, whose home was in the section.
Population: 17,122; Growth (since 2000): 27.1%; Density: 2,792.8 persons per square mile; Race: 92.0% White, 3.5% Black/African American, 1.6% Asian, 0.2% American Indian/Alaska Native, 0.0% Native Hawaiian/Other Pacific Islander, 1.7% Two or more races, 3.3% Hispanic of any race; Average household size: 2.08; Median age: 21.5; Age under 18: 5.1%; Age 65 and over: 6.8%; Males per 100 females: 92.4; Marriage status: 81.7% never married, 11.8% now married, 0.2% separated, 2.3% widowed, 4.2% divorced; Foreign born: 3.5%; Speak English only: 93.7%; With disability: 5.4%; Veterans: 2.3%; Ancestry: 26.2% German, 17.0% Irish, 15.5% English, 6.8% Scottish, 5.9% American
Employment: 5.8% management, business, and financial, 2.5% computer, engineering, and science, 13.9% education, legal, community service, arts, and media, 2.2% healthcare practitioners, 39.7% service, 29.8% sales and office, 3.3% natural resources, construction, and maintenance, 2.8% production, transportation, and material moving
Income: Per capita: $12,373; Median household: $14,453; Average household: $32,523; Households with income of $100,000 or more: 6.2%; Poverty rate: 60.6%
Educational Attainment: High school diploma or higher: 92.6%; Bachelor's degree or higher: 48.9%; Graduate/professional degree or higher: 18.9%

School District(s)
Watauga County Schools (PK-12)
    2012-13 Enrollment: 4,550 . . . . (828) 264-7190
Four-year College(s)
Appalachian State University (Public)
    Fall 2013 Enrollment: 17,838 . . . . (828) 262-2000
    2013-14 Tuition: In-state $6,462; Out-of-state $18,670
Housing: Homeownership rate: 23.2%; Median home value: $280,800; Median year structure built: 1981; Homeowner vacancy rate: 7.1%; Median gross rent: $820 per month; Rental vacancy rate: 3.9%
Health Insurance: 91.6% have insurance; 87.3% have private insurance; 9.1% have public insurance; 8.4% do not have insurance; 0.0% of children under 18 do not have insurance
Hospitals: Watauga Medical Center (127 beds)
Safety: Violent crime rate: 22.2 per 10,000 population; Property crime rate: 167.8 per 10,000 population
Newspapers: Avery Journal-Times (weekly circulation 4000); The Blowing Rocket (weekly circulation 3500); The Mountain Times (weekly circulation 14000); Watauga Democrat (weekly circulation 9000)
Transportation: Commute: 71.4% car, 3.1% public transportation, 19.4% walk, 4.5% work from home; Median travel time to work: 12.9 minutes
Additional Information Contacts
Town of Boone . . . . (828) 268-6200
    http://www.townofboone.net

COVE CREEK (CDP). Covers a land area of 8.509 square miles and a water area of 0.004 square miles. Located at 36.29° N. Lat; 81.79° W. Long.
Population: 1,171; Growth (since 2000): n/a; Density: 137.6 persons per square mile; Race: 96.4% White, 0.4% Black/African American, 0.4% Asian, 0.2% American Indian/Alaska Native, 0.0% Native Hawaiian/Other Pacific Islander, 1.4% Two or more races, 3.5% Hispanic of any race; Average household size: 2.41; Median age: 41.0; Age under 18: 20.6%; Age 65 and over: 16.1%; Males per 100 females: 91.0
Housing: Homeownership rate: 75.9%; Homeowner vacancy rate: 2.4%; Rental vacancy rate: 7.7%

DEEP GAP (unincorporated postal area)
ZCTA: 28618
    Covers a land area of 39.550 square miles and a water area of 0.011 square miles. Located at 36.21° N. Lat; 81.52° W. Long. Elevation is 3,002 feet.
    Population: 2,352; Growth (since 2000): 28.9%; Density: 59.5 persons per square mile; Race: 95.6% White, 1.1% Black/African American, 0.3% Asian, 0.2% American Indian/Alaska Native, 0.0% Native Hawaiian/Other Pacific Islander, 1.1% Two or more races, 2.8% Hispanic of any race; Average household size: 2.37; Median age: 41.3; Age under 18: 21.6%; Age 65 and over: 12.9%; Males per 100 females: 106.9
    Housing: Homeownership rate: 77.5%; Homeowner vacancy rate: 4.1%; Rental vacancy rate: 13.6%

FOSCOE (CDP). Covers a land area of 5.778 square miles and a water area of 0.006 square miles. Located at 36.15° N. Lat; 81.77° W. Long. Elevation is 3,041 feet.
Population: 1,370; Growth (since 2000): n/a; Density: 237.1 persons per square mile; Race: 96.9% White, 0.3% Black/African American, 0.3% Asian, 0.2% American Indian/Alaska Native, 0.0% Native Hawaiian/Other Pacific Islander, 1.3% Two or more races, 5.9% Hispanic of any race; Average household size: 2.17; Median age: 41.8; Age under 18: 16.9%; Age 65 and over: 14.5%; Males per 100 females: 102.4
Housing: Homeownership rate: 63.1%; Homeowner vacancy rate: 4.5%; Rental vacancy rate: 17.2%

SEVEN DEVILS (town). Covers a land area of 2.097 square miles and a water area of 0.014 square miles. Located at 36.15° N. Lat; 81.81° W. Long.
Population: 192; Growth (since 2000): 48.8%; Density: 91.5 persons per square mile; Race: 95.3% White, 2.6% Black/African American, 0.5% Asian, 1.0% American Indian/Alaska Native, 0.0% Native Hawaiian/Other Pacific Islander, 0.0% Two or more races, 0.5% Hispanic of any race; Average household size: 2.06; Median age: 49.2; Age under 18: 15.6%; Age 65 and over: 16.7%; Males per 100 females: 108.7
Housing: Homeownership rate: 67.7%; Homeowner vacancy rate: 26.1%; Rental vacancy rate: 31.9%

SUGAR GROVE (unincorporated postal area)
ZCTA: 28679
    Covers a land area of 26.038 square miles and a water area of 0.190 square miles. Located at 36.26° N. Lat; 81.83° W. Long. Elevation is 2,677 feet.
    Population: 2,064; Growth (since 2000): 34.6%; Density: 79.3 persons per square mile; Race: 96.6% White, 0.1% Black/African American, 0.3% Asian, 0.2% American Indian/Alaska Native, 0.0% Native Hawaiian/Other Pacific Islander, 1.7% Two or more races, 2.9% Hispanic of any race; Average household size: 2.42; Median age: 43.0; Age under 18: 19.9%; Age 65 and over: 17.1%; Males per 100 females: 95.6

School District(s)
Watauga County Schools (PK-12)
    2012-13 Enrollment: 4,550 . . . . (828) 264-7190
Four-year College(s)
Jung Tao School of Classical Chinese Medicine (Private, Not-for-profit)
    Fall 2013 Enrollment: 72 . . . . (828) 297-4181
Two-year College(s)
Jung Tao School of Classical Chinese Medicine (Private, Not-for-profit)
    Fall 2013 Enrollment: 72 . . . . (828) 297-4181
Vocational/Technical School(s)
Jung Tao School of Classical Chinese Medicine (Private, Not-for-profit)
    Fall 2013 Enrollment: 72 . . . . (828) 297-4181

Housing: Homeownership rate: 76.3%; Homeowner vacancy rate: 2.8%; Rental vacancy rate: 11.0%

VALLE CRUCIS (CDP). Covers a land area of 4.436 square miles and a water area of <.001 square miles. Located at 36.22° N. Lat; 81.80° W. Long. Elevation is 2,677 feet.
Population: 412; Growth (since 2000): n/a; Density: 92.9 persons per square mile; Race: 98.1% White, 0.0% Black/African American, 0.2% Asian, 0.0% American Indian/Alaska Native, 0.0% Native Hawaiian/Other Pacific Islander, 1.7% Two or more races, 2.4% Hispanic of any race; Average household size: 2.25; Median age: 45.3; Age under 18: 20.4%; Age 65 and over: 18.7%; Males per 100 females: 109.1
Housing: Homeownership rate: 74.8%; Homeowner vacancy rate: 8.6%; Rental vacancy rate: 25.8%

VILAS (unincorporated postal area)
ZCTA: 28692
Covers a land area of 38.479 square miles and a water area of 0.031 square miles. Located at 36.27° N. Lat; 81.81° W. Long. Elevation is 2,746 feet.
Population: 4,067; Growth (since 2000): 16.8%; Density: 105.7 persons per square mile; Race: 96.8% White, 0.6% Black/African American, 0.5% Asian, 0.1% American Indian/Alaska Native, 0.0% Native Hawaiian/Other Pacific Islander, 1.0% Two or more races, 2.2% Hispanic of any race; Average household size: 2.37; Median age: 41.6; Age under 18: 18.9%; Age 65 and over: 17.1%; Males per 100 females: 104.7; Marriage status: 25.4% never married, 62.6% now married, 2.0% separated, 4.2% widowed, 7.7% divorced; Foreign born: 3.5%; Speak English only: 95.1%; With disability: 10.2%; Veterans: 13.1%; Ancestry: 26.4% German, 18.9% English, 15.1% Irish, 12.9% American, 4.8% Scotch-Irish
Employment: 9.7% management, business, and financial, 1.8% computer, engineering, and science, 12.8% education, legal, community service, arts, and media, 3.4% healthcare practitioners, 22.1% service, 26.3% sales and office, 12.6% natural resources, construction, and maintenance, 11.3% production, transportation, and material moving
Income: Per capita: $28,230; Median household: $46,667; Average household: $61,926; Households with income of $100,000 or more: 16.2%; Poverty rate: 12.4%
Educational Attainment: High school diploma or higher: 86.7%; Bachelor's degree or higher: 30.2%; Graduate/professional degree or higher: 14.7%
School District(s)
Watauga County Schools (PK-12)
   2012-13 Enrollment: 4,550 . . . . (828) 264-7190
Housing: Homeownership rate: 73.4%; Median home value: $194,800; Median year structure built: 1986; Homeowner vacancy rate: 4.0%; Median gross rent: $869 per month; Rental vacancy rate: 17.4%
Health Insurance: 86.2% have insurance; 74.4% have private insurance; 26.2% have public insurance; 13.8% do not have insurance; 8.2% of children under 18 do not have insurance
Transportation: Commute: 95.2% car, 0.0% public transportation, 0.0% walk, 4.2% work from home; Median travel time to work: 26.5 minutes

ZIONVILLE (unincorporated postal area)
ZCTA: 28698
Covers a land area of 25.077 square miles and a water area of 0.008 square miles. Located at 36.34° N. Lat; 81.74° W. Long. Elevation is 3,209 feet.
Population: 2,256; Growth (since 2000): -0.1%; Density: 90.0 persons per square mile; Race: 98.1% White, 0.3% Black/African American, 0.3% Asian, 0.1% American Indian/Alaska Native, 0.0% Native Hawaiian/Other Pacific Islander, 0.9% Two or more races, 1.3% Hispanic of any race; Average household size: 2.26; Median age: 42.4; Age under 18: 19.7%; Age 65 and over: 16.8%; Males per 100 females: 101.8
School District(s)
Watauga County Schools (PK-12)
   2012-13 Enrollment: 4,550 . . . . (828) 264-7190
Housing: Homeownership rate: 77.8%; Homeowner vacancy rate: 3.5%; Rental vacancy rate: 12.6%

Wayne County
Located in east central North Carolina; crossed by the Neuse River. Covers a land area of 553.087 square miles, a water area of 3.765 square miles, and is located in the Eastern Time Zone at 35.36° N. Lat., 78.00° W. Long. The county was founded in 1779. County seat is Goldsboro.

Wayne County is part of the Goldsboro, NC Metropolitan Statistical Area. The entire metro area includes: Wayne County, NC

Population: 122,623; Growth (since 2000): 8.2%; Density: 221.7 persons per square mile; Race: 58.8% White, 31.4% Black/African American, 1.2% Asian, 0.4% American Indian/Alaska Native, 0.1% Native Hawaiian/Other Pacific Islander, 2.3% two or more races, 9.9% Hispanic of any race; Average household size: 2.50; Median age: 36.6; Age under 18: 24.9%; Age 65 and over: 13.1%; Males per 100 females: 95.7; Marriage status: 29.8% never married, 52.2% now married, 4.7% separated, 6.6% widowed, 11.4% divorced; Foreign born: 6.9%; Speak English only: 89.1%; With disability: 15.2%; Veterans: 13.4%; Ancestry: 11.5% American, 11.3% English, 8.7% Irish, 8.2% German, 2.3% Italian
Religion: Six largest groups: 11.3% Baptist, 9.9% Non-denominational Protestant, 7.9% Methodist/Pietist, 3.5% Pentecostal, 2.3% Catholicism, 1.9% Latter-day Saints
Economy: Unemployment rate: 6.0%; Leading industries: 21.8% retail trade; 12.7% other services (except public administration); 11.9% health care and social assistance; Farms: 563 totaling 191,195 acres; Company size: 1 employs 1,000 or more persons, 6 employ 500 to 999 persons, 44 employ 100 to 499 persons, 2,084 employ less than 100 persons; Business ownership: 2,206 women-owned, 1,221 Black-owned, 85 Hispanic-owned, 269 Asian-owned
Employment: 12.0% management, business, and financial, 2.2% computer, engineering, and science, 8.9% education, legal, community service, arts, and media, 6.3% healthcare practitioners, 18.4% service, 21.2% sales and office, 13.4% natural resources, construction, and maintenance, 17.5% production, transportation, and material moving
Income: Per capita: $21,557; Median household: $41,731; Average household: $53,695; Households with income of $100,000 or more: 11.5%; Poverty rate: 22.1%
Educational Attainment: High school diploma or higher: 81.7%; Bachelor's degree or higher: 16.4%; Graduate/professional degree or higher: 5.1%
Housing: Homeownership rate: 62.3%; Median home value: $108,600; Median year structure built: 1982; Homeowner vacancy rate: 2.2%; Median gross rent: $694 per month; Rental vacancy rate: 9.4%
Vital Statistics: Birth rate: 139.3 per 10,000 population; Death rate: 98.0 per 10,000 population; Age-adjusted cancer mortality rate: 221.7 deaths per 100,000 population
Health Insurance: 83.6% have insurance; 58.5% have private insurance; 38.5% have public insurance; 16.4% do not have insurance; 5.7% of children under 18 do not have insurance
Health Care: Physicians: 14.0 per 10,000 population; Hospital beds: 42.4 per 10,000 population; Hospital admissions: 1,048.2 per 10,000 population
Air Quality Index: 65.8% good, 34.2% moderate, 0.0% unhealthy for sensitive individuals, 0.0% unhealthy (percent of days)
Transportation: Commute: 94.6% car, 0.5% public transportation, 1.5% walk, 2.6% work from home; Median travel time to work: 21.9 minutes
Presidential Election: 45.4% Obama, 53.8% Romney (2012)
National and State Parks: Cliffs of the Neuse State Park
Additional Information Contacts
Wayne Government . . . . (919) 731-1435
   http://www.waynegov.com

Wayne County Communities

BROGDEN (CDP). Covers a land area of 2.214 square miles and a water area of 0.041 square miles. Located at 35.30° N. Lat; 78.03° W. Long. Elevation is 174 feet.
Population: 2,633; Growth (since 2000): -9.4%; Density: 1,189.3 persons per square mile; Race: 33.9% White, 53.9% Black/African American, 0.7% Asian, 0.3% American Indian/Alaska Native, 0.0% Native Hawaiian/Other Pacific Islander, 1.6% Two or more races, 13.8% Hispanic of any race; Average household size: 2.61; Median age: 37.4; Age under 18: 25.4%; Age 65 and over: 13.2%; Males per 100 females: 94.3; Marriage status: 36.8% never married, 45.7% now married, 2.0% separated, 6.5% widowed, 11.0% divorced; Foreign born: 17.8%; Speak English only:

79.3%; With disability: 9.9%; Veterans: 14.4%; Ancestry: 6.6% American, 5.4% German, 4.7% Irish, 4.3% English, 3.3% Arab

Employment: 8.3% management, business, and financial, 0.0% computer, engineering, and science, 15.4% education, legal, community service, arts, and media, 5.1% healthcare practitioners, 23.7% service, 13.0% sales and office, 12.0% natural resources, construction, and maintenance, 22.5% production, transportation, and material moving

Income: Per capita: $16,830; Median household: $39,261; Average household: $41,834; Households with income of $100,000 or more: 2.9%; Poverty rate: 24.1%

Educational Attainment: High school diploma or higher: 85.6%; Bachelor's degree or higher: 14.6%; Graduate/professional degree or higher: 4.2%

Housing: Homeownership rate: 70.6%; Median home value: $83,800; Median year structure built: 1977; Homeowner vacancy rate: 2.3%; Median gross rent: $704 per month; Rental vacancy rate: 17.8%

Health Insurance: 75.0% have insurance; 44.5% have private insurance; 42.8% have public insurance; 25.0% do not have insurance; 15.9% of children under 18 do not have insurance

Transportation: Commute: 98.8% car, 0.2% public transportation, 1.0% walk, 0.0% work from home; Median travel time to work: 18.3 minutes

---

DUDLEY (unincorporated postal area)

ZCTA: 28333

Covers a land area of 47.245 square miles and a water area of 0.409 square miles. Located at 35.28° N. Lat; 78.01° W. Long. Elevation is 184 feet.

Population: 11,830; Growth (since 2000): 2.5%; Density: 250.4 persons per square mile; Race: 41.3% White, 41.4% Black/African American, 0.7% Asian, 0.4% American Indian/Alaska Native, 0.1% Native Hawaiian/Other Pacific Islander, 2.4% Two or more races, 21.6% Hispanic of any race; Average household size: 2.70; Median age: 34.0; Age under 18: 27.6%; Age 65 and over: 11.0%; Males per 100 females: 95.5; Marriage status: 32.3% never married, 49.4% now married, 4.0% separated, 4.3% widowed, 13.9% divorced; Foreign born: 14.2%; Speak English only: 79.8%; With disability: 14.2%; Veterans: 13.1%; Ancestry: 8.6% American, 5.9% Irish, 5.7% German, 4.2% English, 1.9% Polish

Employment: 8.5% management, business, and financial, 1.1% computer, engineering, and science, 11.9% education, legal, community service, arts, and media, 2.9% healthcare practitioners, 18.9% service, 19.1% sales and office, 17.6% natural resources, construction, and maintenance, 20.0% production, transportation, and material moving

Income: Per capita: $18,667; Median household: $39,632; Average household: $47,174; Households with income of $100,000 or more: 6.7%; Poverty rate: 22.5%

Educational Attainment: High school diploma or higher: 76.7%; Bachelor's degree or higher: 13.5%; Graduate/professional degree or higher: 1.9%

School District(s)

Wayne County Public Schools (PK-12)

2012-13 Enrollment: 19,761 . . . . (919) 731-5900

Housing: Homeownership rate: 65.4%; Median home value: $75,400; Median year structure built: 1984; Homeowner vacancy rate: 2.2%; Median gross rent: $719 per month; Rental vacancy rate: 11.5%

Health Insurance: 74.4% have insurance; 46.1% have private insurance; 38.4% have public insurance; 25.6% do not have insurance; 11.0% of children under 18 do not have insurance

Transportation: Commute: 92.1% car, 0.1% public transportation, 1.8% walk, 5.5% work from home; Median travel time to work: 22.0 minutes

---

ELROY (CDP). Covers a land area of 6.586 square miles and a water area of 0 square miles. Located at 35.33° N. Lat; 77.92° W. Long. Elevation is 112 feet.

Population: 3,869; Growth (since 2000): -0.7%; Density: 587.5 persons per square mile; Race: 64.1% White, 21.9% Black/African American, 1.7% Asian, 0.5% American Indian/Alaska Native, 0.1% Native Hawaiian/Other Pacific Islander, 2.6% Two or more races, 15.1% Hispanic of any race; Average household size: 2.42; Median age: 38.0; Age under 18: 22.1%; Age 65 and over: 13.5%; Males per 100 females: 99.1; Marriage status: 28.4% never married, 51.2% now married, 8.5% separated, 6.0% widowed, 14.4% divorced; Foreign born: 5.1%; Speak English only: 87.8%; With disability: 17.3%; Veterans: 16.8%; Ancestry: 11.3% English, 11.2% German, 11.1% American, 8.3% Irish, 2.6% Scottish

Employment: 7.3% management, business, and financial, 0.9% computer, engineering, and science, 7.2% education, legal, community service, arts,

and media, 6.5% healthcare practitioners, 30.5% service, 18.5% sales and office, 14.8% natural resources, construction, and maintenance, 14.5% production, transportation, and material moving

Income: Per capita: $17,856; Median household: $36,340; Average household: $39,194; Households with income of $100,000 or more: 1.2%; Poverty rate: 32.3%

Educational Attainment: High school diploma or higher: 81.2%; Bachelor's degree or higher: 7.0%; Graduate/professional degree or higher: 2.8%

Housing: Homeownership rate: 64.1%; Median home value: $91,000; Median year structure built: 1987; Homeowner vacancy rate: 1.6%; Median gross rent: $772 per month; Rental vacancy rate: 15.1%

Health Insurance: 86.9% have insurance; 53.1% have private insurance; 49.9% have public insurance; 13.1% do not have insurance; 2.9% of children under 18 do not have insurance

Transportation: Commute: 96.7% car, 2.7% public transportation, 0.0% walk, 0.0% work from home; Median travel time to work: 19.4 minutes

---

EUREKA (town). Covers a land area of 0.361 square miles and a water area of 0 square miles. Located at 35.54° N. Lat; 77.88° W. Long. Elevation is 125 feet.

Population: 197; Growth (since 2000): -19.3%; Density: 545.5 persons per square mile; Race: 73.1% White, 25.4% Black/African American, 0.0% Asian, 0.5% American Indian/Alaska Native, 0.0% Native Hawaiian/Other Pacific Islander, 1.0% Two or more races, 3.6% Hispanic of any race; Average household size: 2.05; Median age: 53.2; Age under 18: 12.2%; Age 65 and over: 27.9%; Males per 100 females: 97.0

Housing: Homeownership rate: 83.9%; Homeowner vacancy rate: 1.3%; Rental vacancy rate: 19.0%

FREMONT (town). Covers a land area of 1.360 square miles and a water area of 0 square miles. Located at 35.54° N. Lat; 77.98° W. Long. Elevation is 148 feet.

History: Charles B. Acock Birthplace State Historical Site to South, former government building built 1859.

Population: 1,255; Growth (since 2000): -14.2%; Density: 922.5 persons per square mile; Race: 47.7% White, 46.9% Black/African American, 0.2% Asian, 0.6% American Indian/Alaska Native, 0.0% Native Hawaiian/Other Pacific Islander, 2.5% Two or more races, 3.5% Hispanic of any race; Average household size: 2.26; Median age: 47.2; Age under 18: 20.0%; Age 65 and over: 19.3%; Males per 100 females: 84.8

School District(s)

Wayne County Public Schools (PK-12)

2012-13 Enrollment: 19,761 . . . . (919) 731-5900

Housing: Homeownership rate: 51.7%; Homeowner vacancy rate: 4.3%; Rental vacancy rate: 7.4%

Newspapers: News-Leader (weekly circulation 2000)

GOLDSBORO (city). County seat. Covers a land area of 28.142 square miles and a water area of 0.020 square miles. Located at 35.38° N. Lat; 77.97° W. Long. Elevation is 108 feet.

History: Goldsboro, formerly Goldsborough, was founded soon after completion in 1840 of the Wilmington & Raleigh Railroad. It was named for a civil engineer who assisted in the rail line survey. Goldsboro was settled by English immigrants. It became the county seat in 1847.

Population: 36,437; Growth (since 2000): -6.7%; Density: 1,294.8 persons per square mile; Race: 39.2% White, 54.3% Black/African American, 1.8% Asian, 0.4% American Indian/Alaska Native, 0.1% Native Hawaiian/Other Pacific Islander, 2.6% Two or more races, 4.3% Hispanic of any race; Average household size: 2.27; Median age: 36.1; Age under 18: 23.1%; Age 65 and over: 14.9%; Males per 100 females: 94.0; Marriage status: 35.3% never married, 43.4% now married, 6.2% separated, 8.3% widowed, 13.0% divorced; Foreign born: 4.9%; Speak English only: 92.5%; With disability: 16.8%; Veterans: 15.4%; Ancestry: 9.0% American, 7.5% German, 7.1% Irish, 6.8% English, 2.5% Italian

Employment: 10.0% management, business, and financial, 3.0% computer, engineering, and science, 11.4% education, legal, community service, arts, and media, 7.5% healthcare practitioners, 19.7% service, 22.3% sales and office, 8.2% natural resources, construction, and maintenance, 18.0% production, transportation, and material moving

Income: Per capita: $20,380; Median household: $34,161; Average household: $46,653; Households with income of $100,000 or more: 8.9%; Poverty rate: 25.7%

Educational Attainment: High school diploma or higher: 83.9%; Bachelor's degree or higher: 18.5%; Graduate/professional degree or higher: 6.5%

School District(s)
Dillard Academy (KG-04)
    2012-13 Enrollment: 199 . . . . (919) 581-0166
Nc Health and Human Resources (KG-12)
    2012-13 Enrollment: n/a . . . . (919) 855-4430
Wayne County Public Schools (PK-12)
    2012-13 Enrollment: 19,761 . . . . (919) 731-5900

Two-year College(s)
Wayne Community College (Public)
    Fall 2013 Enrollment: 3,837 . . . . (919) 735-5151
    2013-14 Tuition: In-state $2,380; Out-of-state $8,524

Vocational/Technical School(s)
Mitchells Hairstyling Academy-Goldsboro (Private, For-profit)
    Fall 2013 Enrollment: 46 . . . . (919) 778-8200
    2013-14 Tuition: $9,950

Housing: Homeownership rate: 41.7%; Median home value: $111,600; Median year structure built: 1972; Homeowner vacancy rate: 3.5%; Median gross rent: $710 per month; Rental vacancy rate: 9.3%

Health Insurance: 86.9% have insurance; 57.4% have private insurance; 46.1% have public insurance; 13.1% do not have insurance; 4.9% of children under 18 do not have insurance

Hospitals: Wayne Memorial Hospital (316 beds)

Safety: Violent crime rate: 76.0 per 10,000 population; Property crime rate: 629.6 per 10,000 population

Newspapers: Goldsboro News-Argus (daily circulation 19200)

Transportation: Commute: 93.8% car, 1.4% public transportation, 2.4% walk, 1.6% work from home; Median travel time to work: 18.0 minutes; Amtrak: Bus service available.

Airports: Seymour Johnson AFB (general aviation); Wayne Executive Jetport (general aviation)

Additional Information Contacts
City of Goldsboro . . . . (919) 580-4362
    http://www.ci.goldsboro.nc.us

MAR-MAC (CDP).
Covers a land area of 4.549 square miles and a water area of 0.027 square miles. Located at 35.33° N. Lat; 78.06° W. Long. Elevation is 112 feet.

Population: 3,615; Growth (since 2000): 20.3%; Density: 794.7 persons per square mile; Race: 56.9% White, 29.7% Black/African American, 1.2% Asian, 0.3% American Indian/Alaska Native, 0.0% Native Hawaiian/Other Pacific Islander, 2.3% Two or more races, 13.7% Hispanic of any race; Average household size: 2.48; Median age: 37.5; Age under 18: 24.0%; Age 65 and over: 13.6%; Males per 100 females: 93.2; Marriage status: 18.3% never married, 64.8% now married, 6.1% separated, 4.8% widowed, 12.2% divorced; Foreign born: 13.7%; Speak English only: 77.5%; With disability: 13.1%; Veterans: 14.7%; Ancestry: 15.1% English, 14.9% Irish, 8.5% German, 8.4% American, 3.0% Italian

Employment: 3.6% management, business, and financial, 0.0% computer, engineering, and science, 5.0% education, legal, community service, arts, and media, 1.1% healthcare practitioners, 23.7% service, 19.0% sales and office, 17.8% natural resources, construction, and maintenance, 29.8% production, transportation, and material moving

Income: Per capita: $18,214; Median household: $36,028; Average household: $44,157; Households with income of $100,000 or more: 5.1%; Poverty rate: 26.4%

Educational Attainment: High school diploma or higher: 75.3%; Bachelor's degree or higher: 10.6%; Graduate/professional degree or higher: 3.9%

Housing: Homeownership rate: 64.1%; Median home value: $88,600; Median year structure built: 1983; Homeowner vacancy rate: 2.3%; Median gross rent: $681 per month; Rental vacancy rate: 5.4%

Health Insurance: 80.2% have insurance; 49.6% have private insurance; 40.0% have public insurance; 19.8% do not have insurance; 14.4% of children under 18 do not have insurance

Transportation: Commute: 93.7% car, 0.0% public transportation, 2.2% walk, 3.4% work from home; Median travel time to work: 21.4 minutes

MOUNT OLIVE (town).
Covers a land area of 2.675 square miles and a water area of 0 square miles. Located at 35.20° N. Lat; 78.07° W. Long. Elevation is 157 feet.

History: Mount Olive was founded upon the advent of the railroad in 1840. Its first industrial plant was a turpentine still.

Population: 4,589; Growth (since 2000): 0.5%; Density: 1,715.8 persons per square mile; Race: 40.4% White, 50.5% Black/African American, 0.4% Asian, 0.8% American Indian/Alaska Native, 0.0% Native Hawaiian/Other Pacific Islander, 1.7% Two or more races, 9.2% Hispanic of any race; Average household size: 2.25; Median age: 36.5; Age under 18: 20.7%; Age 65 and over: 19.1%; Males per 100 females: 81.2; Marriage status: 45.7% never married, 31.9% now married, 3.4% separated, 13.2% widowed, 9.2% divorced; Foreign born: 10.7%; Speak English only: 83.9%; With disability: 18.4%; Veterans: 4.3%; Ancestry: 9.7% English, 9.1% American, 3.6% Haitian, 3.4% German, 3.2% Irish

Employment: 4.9% management, business, and financial, 1.0% computer, engineering, and science, 13.8% education, legal, community service, arts, and media, 4.4% healthcare practitioners, 19.3% service, 14.5% sales and office, 13.2% natural resources, construction, and maintenance, 28.8% production, transportation, and material moving

Income: Per capita: $16,515; Median household: $25,439; Average household: $42,511; Households with income of $100,000 or more: 5.7%; Poverty rate: 33.6%

Educational Attainment: High school diploma or higher: 69.0%; Bachelor's degree or higher: 14.2%; Graduate/professional degree or higher: 6.1%

School District(s)
Wayne County Public Schools (PK-12)
    2012-13 Enrollment: 19,761 . . . . (919) 731-5900

Four-year College(s)
Mount Olive College (Private, Not-for-profit, Original Free Will Baptist)
    Fall 2013 Enrollment: 3,414 . . . . (919) 658-2502
    2013-14 Tuition: In-state $17,300; Out-of-state $17,300

Housing: Homeownership rate: 50.3%; Median home value: $84,200; Median year structure built: 1969; Homeowner vacancy rate: 2.0%; Median gross rent: $621 per month; Rental vacancy rate: 12.4%

Health Insurance: 79.4% have insurance; 45.8% have private insurance; 47.2% have public insurance; 20.6% do not have insurance; 8.5% of children under 18 do not have insurance

Safety: Violent crime rate: 94.2 per 10,000 population; Property crime rate: 665.7 per 10,000 population

Newspapers: Mt. Olive Tribune (weekly circulation 5000)

Transportation: Commute: 86.8% car, 0.0% public transportation, 3.8% walk, 3.5% work from home; Median travel time to work: 23.3 minutes

Additional Information Contacts
Town of Mount Olive . . . . (919) 658-5561
    http://www.townofmountolivenc.com

PIKEVILLE (town).
Covers a land area of 0.703 square miles and a water area of 0 square miles. Located at 35.50° N. Lat; 77.99° W. Long. Elevation is 138 feet.

History: Charles B. Aycock Birthplace State Historical Site to North.

Population: 678; Growth (since 2000): -5.7%; Density: 963.9 persons per square mile; Race: 86.9% White, 8.1% Black/African American, 0.3% Asian, 0.9% American Indian/Alaska Native, 0.0% Native Hawaiian/Other Pacific Islander, 1.3% Two or more races, 4.7% Hispanic of any race; Average household size: 2.27; Median age: 41.8; Age under 18: 24.0%; Age 65 and over: 16.8%; Males per 100 females: 88.3

School District(s)
Wayne County Public Schools (PK-12)
    2012-13 Enrollment: 19,761 . . . . (919) 731-5900

Housing: Homeownership rate: 66.6%; Homeowner vacancy rate: 3.8%; Rental vacancy rate: 9.1%

SEVEN SPRINGS (town).
Covers a land area of 0.334 square miles and a water area of 0 square miles. Located at 35.22° N. Lat; 77.85° W. Long. Elevation is 52 feet.

Population: 110; Growth (since 2000): 27.9%; Density: 328.9 persons per square mile; Race: 81.8% White, 8.2% Black/African American, 0.0% Asian, 0.0% American Indian/Alaska Native, 0.0% Native Hawaiian/Other Pacific Islander, 4.5% Two or more races, 21.8% Hispanic of any race; Average household size: 1.95; Median age: 41.5; Age under 18: 10.9%; Age 65 and over: 20.0%; Males per 100 females: 100.0

School District(s)
Wayne County Public Schools (PK-12)
    2012-13 Enrollment: 19,761 . . . . (919) 731-5900

Housing: Homeownership rate: 67.3%; Homeowner vacancy rate: 2.6%; Rental vacancy rate: 5.3%

WALNUT CREEK (village). Covers a land area of 1.571 square miles and a water area of 0.309 square miles. Located at 35.31° N. Lat; 77.87° W. Long. Elevation is 98 feet.
Population: 835; Growth (since 2000): -2.8%; Density: 531.4 persons per square mile; Race: 91.7% White, 4.1% Black/African American, 1.9% Asian, 0.1% American Indian/Alaska Native, 0.0% Native Hawaiian/Other Pacific Islander, 0.7% Two or more races, 1.7% Hispanic of any race; Average household size: 2.44; Median age: 53.5; Age under 18: 19.2%; Age 65 and over: 22.0%; Males per 100 females: 92.0
Housing: Homeownership rate: 98.2%; Homeowner vacancy rate: 2.9%; Rental vacancy rate: 33.3%

Wilkes County

Located in northwestern North Carolina, mostly in the Blue Ridge; drained by the Yadkin River. Covers a land area of 754.278 square miles, a water area of 2.642 square miles, and is located in the Eastern Time Zone at 36.21° N. Lat., 81.17° W. Long. The county was founded in 1777. County seat is Wilkesboro.

Wilkes County is part of the North Wilkesboro, NC Micropolitan Statistical Area. The entire metro area includes: Wilkes County, NC

Weather Station: North Wilkesboro   Elevation: 1,120 feet

	Jan	Feb	Mar	Apr	May	Jun	Jul	Aug	Sep	Oct	Nov	Dec
High	49	52	60	70	78	85	88	86	80	71	61	51
Low	25	27	33	42	51	60	64	63	55	43	34	27
Precip	4.0	3.6	4.7	4.3	4.2	4.6	4.7	4.2	4.1	3.6	3.5	3.9
Snow	3.2	2.2	1.5	tr	0.0	0.0	0.0	0.0	0.0	0.0	tr	1.9

High and Low temperatures in degrees Fahrenheit; Precipitation and Snow in inches

Weather Station: W Kerr Scott Reservoir   Elevation: 1,069 feet

	Jan	Feb	Mar	Apr	May	Jun	Jul	Aug	Sep	Oct	Nov	Dec
High	49	53	60	70	78	85	88	87	80	71	62	51
Low	25	27	34	42	51	61	64	63	56	44	35	27
Precip	4.0	3.6	4.8	4.4	4.4	4.4	4.5	4.7	4.4	3.6	3.6	4.0
Snow	3.9	2.8	1.4	tr	0.0	0.0	0.0	0.0	0.0	0.0	tr	1.2

High and Low temperatures in degrees Fahrenheit; Precipitation and Snow in inches

Population: 69,340; Growth (since 2000): 5.6%; Density: 91.9 persons per square mile; Race: 90.6% White, 4.1% Black/African American, 0.4% Asian, 0.2% American Indian/Alaska Native, 0.0% Native Hawaiian/Other Pacific Islander, 1.3% two or more races, 5.4% Hispanic of any race; Average household size: 2.41; Median age: 42.4; Age under 18: 22.4%; Age 65 and over: 17.0%; Males per 100 females: 97.7; Marriage status: 22.9% never married, 59.0% now married, 2.8% separated, 7.7% widowed, 10.4% divorced; Foreign born: 3.4%; Speak English only: 95.0%; With disability: 18.4%; Veterans: 8.9%; Ancestry: 39.8% American, 9.4% English, 7.5% German, 6.4% Irish, 2.8% Scotch-Irish
Religion: Six largest groups: 45.2% Baptist, 5.1% Methodist/Pietist, 2.7% Non-denominational Protestant, 1.1% Presbyterian-Reformed, 0.9% Pentecostal, 0.8% Episcopalianism/Anglicanism
Economy: Unemployment rate: 6.0%; Leading industries: 17.9% retail trade; 12.9% other services (except public administration); 11.9% health care and social assistance; Farms: 972 totaling 111,118 acres; Company size: 2 employ 1,000 or more persons, 1 employs 500 to 999 persons, 19 employ 100 to 499 persons, 1,221 employs less than 100 persons; Business ownership: 1,277 women-owned, n/a Black-owned, n/a Hispanic-owned, n/a Asian-owned
Employment: 10.4% management, business, and financial, 1.6% computer, engineering, and science, 9.2% education, legal, community service, arts, and media, 4.4% healthcare practitioners, 16.5% service, 27.3% sales and office, 10.4% natural resources, construction, and maintenance, 20.2% production, transportation, and material moving
Income: Per capita: $19,029; Median household: $33,159; Average household: $46,995; Households with income of $100,000 or more: 8.0%; Poverty rate: 22.7%
Educational Attainment: High school diploma or higher: 74.2%; Bachelor's degree or higher: 12.5%; Graduate/professional degree or higher: 3.5%
Housing: Homeownership rate: 74.4%; Median home value: $111,700; Median year structure built: 1977; Homeowner vacancy rate: 1.7%; Median gross rent: $573 per month; Rental vacancy rate: 12.4%
Vital Statistics: Birth rate: 98.1 per 10,000 population; Death rate: 108.8 per 10,000 population; Age-adjusted cancer mortality rate: 195.3 deaths per 100,000 population

Health Insurance: 83.5% have insurance; 58.0% have private insurance; 39.9% have public insurance; 16.5% do not have insurance; 5.7% of children under 18 do not have insurance
Health Care: Physicians: 8.4 per 10,000 population; Hospital beds: 14.2 per 10,000 population; Hospital admissions: 606.3 per 10,000 population
Transportation: Commute: 95.3% car, 0.3% public transportation, 1.4% walk, 2.5% work from home; Median travel time to work: 24.3 minutes
Presidential Election: 28.0% Obama, 70.4% Romney (2012)
National and State Parks: Rendezvous Mountain State Park; Stone Mountain State Park
Additional Information Contacts
Wilkes Government . . . . (336) 651-7300
  http://www.wilkescounty.net

Wilkes County Communities

BOOMER (unincorporated postal area)
ZCTA: 28606
  Covers a land area of 43.372 square miles and a water area of 0.397 square miles. Located at 36.05° N. Lat; 81.32° W. Long. Elevation is 1,230 feet.
  Population: 2,158; Growth (since 2000): 11.9%; Density: 49.8 persons per square mile; Race: 88.6% White, 8.0% Black/African American, 0.2% Asian, 0.1% American Indian/Alaska Native, 0.0% Native Hawaiian/Other Pacific Islander, 1.3% Two or more races, 2.5% Hispanic of any race; Average household size: 2.41; Median age: 42.1; Age under 18: 23.8%; Age 65 and over: 17.1%; Males per 100 females: 98.0
School District(s)
Wilkes County Schools (PK-12)
  2012-13 Enrollment: 10,384 . . . . (336) 667-1121
  Housing: Homeownership rate: 80.9%; Homeowner vacancy rate: 1.8%; Rental vacancy rate: 11.8%

CRICKET (CDP). Covers a land area of 3.581 square miles and a water area of 0 square miles. Located at 36.17° N. Lat; 81.19° W. Long. Elevation is 1,260 feet.
Population: 1,855; Growth (since 2000): -9.6%; Density: 518.0 persons per square mile; Race: 88.6% White, 1.4% Black/African American, 0.2% Asian, 0.1% American Indian/Alaska Native, 0.1% Native Hawaiian/Other Pacific Islander, 1.6% Two or more races, 12.5% Hispanic of any race; Average household size: 2.38; Median age: 39.3; Age under 18: 22.3%; Age 65 and over: 16.4%; Males per 100 females: 91.6
Housing: Homeownership rate: 66.9%; Homeowner vacancy rate: 1.1%; Rental vacancy rate: 12.2%

FAIRPLAINS (CDP). Covers a land area of 4.214 square miles and a water area of 0 square miles. Located at 36.19° N. Lat; 81.15° W. Long. Elevation is 1,283 feet.
Population: 2,120; Growth (since 2000): 3.4%; Density: 503.1 persons per square mile; Race: 76.1% White, 13.0% Black/African American, 0.2% Asian, 0.2% American Indian/Alaska Native, 0.0% Native Hawaiian/Other Pacific Islander, 2.8% Two or more races, 13.6% Hispanic of any race; Average household size: 2.40; Median age: 39.8; Age under 18: 25.1%; Age 65 and over: 17.4%; Males per 100 females: 94.9
Housing: Homeownership rate: 66.2%; Homeowner vacancy rate: 1.9%; Rental vacancy rate: 13.6%

FERGUSON (unincorporated postal area)
ZCTA: 28624
  Covers a land area of 62.375 square miles and a water area of 0.013 square miles. Located at 36.13° N. Lat; 81.41° W. Long. Elevation is 1,086 feet.
  Population: 1,639; Growth (since 2000): 19.5%; Density: 26.3 persons per square mile; Race: 94.3% White, 3.6% Black/African American, 0.1% Asian, 0.2% American Indian/Alaska Native, 0.0% Native Hawaiian/Other Pacific Islander, 1.4% Two or more races, 0.7% Hispanic of any race; Average household size: 2.31; Median age: 47.6; Age under 18: 19.2%; Age 65 and over: 20.6%; Males per 100 females: 94.2
School District(s)
Wilkes County Schools (PK-12)
  2012-13 Enrollment: 10,384 . . . . (336) 667-1121
  Housing: Homeownership rate: 84.8%; Homeowner vacancy rate: 1.0%; Rental vacancy rate: 11.4%

HAYS (CDP). Covers a land area of 6.158 square miles and a water area of 0 square miles. Located at 36.25° N. Lat; 81.11° W. Long. Elevation is 1,358 feet.
Population: 1,851; Growth (since 2000): 6.9%; Density: 300.6 persons per square mile; Race: 96.2% White, 0.5% Black/African American, 0.2% Asian, 0.0% American Indian/Alaska Native, 0.2% Native Hawaiian/Other Pacific Islander, 1.1% Two or more races, 3.0% Hispanic of any race; Average household size: 2.57; Median age: 39.5; Age under 18: 24.5%; Age 65 and over: 13.3%; Males per 100 females: 94.4
School District(s)
Wilkes County Schools (PK-12)
    2012-13 Enrollment: 10,384 . . . . (336) 667-1121
Housing: Homeownership rate: 75.5%; Homeowner vacancy rate: 1.4%; Rental vacancy rate: 8.8%

MCGRADY (unincorporated postal area)
ZCTA: 28649
    Covers a land area of 34.971 square miles and a water area of <.001 square miles. Located at 36.33° N. Lat; 81.21° W. Long..
    Population: 993; Growth (since 2000): 13.5%; Density: 28.4 persons per square mile; Race: 98.9% White, 0.2% Black/African American, 0.0% Asian, 0.4% American Indian/Alaska Native, 0.0% Native Hawaiian/Other Pacific Islander, 0.5% Two or more races, 0.7% Hispanic of any race; Average household size: 2.45; Median age: 44.5; Age under 18: 20.0%; Age 65 and over: 15.4%; Males per 100 females: 96.2
    Housing: Homeownership rate: 81.5%; Homeowner vacancy rate: 0.3%; Rental vacancy rate: 9.4%

MILLERS CREEK (CDP). Covers a land area of 4.476 square miles and a water area of 0 square miles. Located at 36.19° N. Lat; 81.24° W. Long. Elevation is 1,417 feet.
Population: 2,112; Growth (since 2000): 2.0%; Density: 471.9 persons per square mile; Race: 94.3% White, 0.9% Black/African American, 0.1% Asian, 0.1% American Indian/Alaska Native, 0.0% Native Hawaiian/Other Pacific Islander, 1.5% Two or more races, 4.5% Hispanic of any race; Average household size: 2.37; Median age: 43.7; Age under 18: 22.3%; Age 65 and over: 17.5%; Males per 100 females: 97.4
School District(s)
Wilkes County Schools (PK-12)
    2012-13 Enrollment: 10,384 . . . . (336) 667-1121
Housing: Homeownership rate: 72.8%; Homeowner vacancy rate: 1.4%; Rental vacancy rate: 15.0%

MORAVIAN FALLS (CDP). Covers a land area of 5.030 square miles and a water area of 0.008 square miles. Located at 36.11° N. Lat; 81.19° W. Long. Elevation is 1,194 feet.
History: Moravian Falls received its name from the waterfalls on Moravian Creek.
Population: 1,901; Growth (since 2000): 32.0%; Density: 377.9 persons per square mile; Race: 77.2% White, 4.9% Black/African American, 0.7% Asian, 0.5% American Indian/Alaska Native, 0.0% Native Hawaiian/Other Pacific Islander, 2.3% Two or more races, 25.9% Hispanic of any race; Average household size: 2.52; Median age: 36.8; Age under 18: 26.8%; Age 65 and over: 14.5%; Males per 100 females: 96.2
School District(s)
Wilkes County Schools (PK-12)
    2012-13 Enrollment: 10,384 . . . . (336) 667-1121
Housing: Homeownership rate: 65.5%; Homeowner vacancy rate: 1.6%; Rental vacancy rate: 17.1%

MULBERRY (CDP). Covers a land area of 5.094 square miles and a water area of 0 square miles. Located at 36.23° N. Lat; 81.17° W. Long. Elevation is 1,325 feet.
Population: 2,332; Growth (since 2000): 2.8%; Density: 457.8 persons per square mile; Race: 95.6% White, 1.0% Black/African American, 0.3% Asian, 0.0% American Indian/Alaska Native, 0.0% Native Hawaiian/Other Pacific Islander, 0.6% Two or more races, 3.9% Hispanic of any race; Average household size: 2.40; Median age: 44.0; Age under 18: 21.1%; Age 65 and over: 19.1%; Males per 100 females: 95.5
Housing: Homeownership rate: 79.6%; Homeowner vacancy rate: 1.6%; Rental vacancy rate: 11.6%

NORTH WILKESBORO (town). Covers a land area of 6.587 square miles and a water area of 0 square miles. Located at 36.17° N. Lat; 81.14° W. Long. Elevation is 988 feet.
History: North Wilkesboro was chartered in 1891 when citizens voted to separate from Wilkesboro.
Population: 4,245; Growth (since 2000): 3.1%; Density: 644.4 persons per square mile; Race: 73.0% White, 13.6% Black/African American, 0.6% Asian, 0.4% American Indian/Alaska Native, 0.0% Native Hawaiian/Other Pacific Islander, 2.2% Two or more races, 13.1% Hispanic of any race; Average household size: 2.25; Median age: 40.3; Age under 18: 22.4%; Age 65 and over: 18.8%; Males per 100 females: 97.4; Marriage status: 37.7% never married, 35.1% now married, 3.0% separated, 13.9% widowed, 13.3% divorced; Foreign born: 6.5%; Speak English only: 92.8%; With disability: 19.1%; Veterans: 8.2%; Ancestry: 33.5% American, 8.4% English, 5.9% German, 5.6% Irish, 2.9% Danish
Employment: 12.8% management, business, and financial, 0.0% computer, engineering, and science, 5.7% education, legal, community service, arts, and media, 5.8% healthcare practitioners, 25.9% service, 28.0% sales and office, 5.3% natural resources, construction, and maintenance, 16.4% production, transportation, and material moving
Income: Per capita: $12,935; Median household: $18,182; Average household: $33,006; Households with income of $100,000 or more: 5.3%; Poverty rate: 46.7%
Educational Attainment: High school diploma or higher: 66.6%; Bachelor's degree or higher: 15.7%; Graduate/professional degree or higher: 2.5%
School District(s)
Nc Dept of Juvenile Justice (KG-12)
    2012-13 Enrollment: n/a . . . . (919) 733-3388
Wilkes County Schools (PK-12)
    2012-13 Enrollment: 10,384 . . . . (336) 667-1121
Housing: Homeownership rate: 44.6%; Median home value: $137,300; Median year structure built: 1967; Homeowner vacancy rate: 5.1%; Median gross rent: $444 per month; Rental vacancy rate: 13.7%
Health Insurance: 79.7% have insurance; 44.3% have private insurance; 49.3% have public insurance; 20.3% do not have insurance; 16.2% of children under 18 do not have insurance
Hospitals: Wilkes Regional Medical Center (120 beds)
Safety: Violent crime rate: 47.0 per 10,000 population; Property crime rate: 559.2 per 10,000 population
Newspapers: Wilkes Journal Patriot (weekly circulation 15200)
Transportation: Commute: 96.7% car, 0.0% public transportation, 0.0% walk, 1.7% work from home; Median travel time to work: 19.3 minutes
Airports: Wilkes County (general aviation)
Additional Information Contacts
Town of North Wilkesboro . . . . (336) 667-7129
    http://www.north-wilkesboro.com

PLEASANT HILL (CDP). Covers a land area of 2.584 square miles and a water area of <.001 square miles. Located at 36.25° N. Lat; 80.89° W. Long. Elevation is 1,135 feet.
Population: 878; Growth (since 2000): -20.8%; Density: 339.8 persons per square mile; Race: 96.5% White, 0.9% Black/African American, 0.1% Asian, 0.0% American Indian/Alaska Native, 0.0% Native Hawaiian/Other Pacific Islander, 0.8% Two or more races, 3.4% Hispanic of any race; Average household size: 2.34; Median age: 42.9; Age under 18: 20.5%; Age 65 and over: 19.4%; Males per 100 females: 96.9
Housing: Homeownership rate: 75.5%; Homeowner vacancy rate: 2.6%; Rental vacancy rate: 3.2%

PURLEAR (unincorporated postal area)
ZCTA: 28665
    Covers a land area of 63.158 square miles and a water area of 0 square miles. Located at 36.21° N. Lat; 81.38° W. Long. Elevation is 1,342 feet.
    Population: 2,571; Growth (since 2000): 3.3%; Density: 40.7 persons per square mile; Race: 98.1% White, 0.2% Black/African American, 0.2% Asian, 0.0% American Indian/Alaska Native, 0.0% Native Hawaiian/Other Pacific Islander, 0.9% Two or more races, 1.4% Hispanic of any race; Average household size: 2.42; Median age: 43.1; Age under 18: 21.6%; Age 65 and over: 16.2%; Males per 100 females: 94.9; Marriage status: 20.1% never married, 65.8% now married, 1.0% separated, 5.8% widowed, 8.3% divorced; Foreign born: 1.0%; Speak English only: 99.7%; With disability: 16.5%; Veterans: 8.8%; Ancestry: 47.4% American, 11.2% German, 11.1% Irish, 9.0% English, 3.2% Scotch-Irish

Employment: 8.1% management, business, and financial, 1.3% computer, engineering, and science, 10.9% education, legal, community service, arts, and media, 6.5% healthcare practitioners, 10.0% service, 40.1% sales and office, 5.0% natural resources, construction, and maintenance, 18.0% production, transportation, and material moving
Income: Per capita: $23,422; Median household: $42,661; Average household: $57,007; Households with income of $100,000 or more: 13.4%; Poverty rate: 11.5%
Educational Attainment: High school diploma or higher: 80.7%; Bachelor's degree or higher: 19.2%; Graduate/professional degree or higher: 5.8%
Housing: Homeownership rate: 79.8%; Median home value: $168,100; Median year structure built: 1989; Homeowner vacancy rate: 3.1%; Median gross rent: $688 per month; Rental vacancy rate: 11.4%
Health Insurance: 90.7% have insurance; 67.6% have private insurance; 40.6% have public insurance; 9.3% do not have insurance; 0.0% of children under 18 do not have insurance
Transportation: Commute: 90.1% car, 0.0% public transportation, 3.7% walk, 6.1% work from home; Median travel time to work: 31.1 minutes

ROARING RIVER (unincorporated postal area)
ZCTA: 28669
Covers a land area of 46.298 square miles and a water area of 0.097 square miles. Located at 36.22° N. Lat; 80.99° W. Long. Elevation is 974 feet.
Population: 3,146; Growth (since 2000): 6.2%; Density: 68.0 persons per square mile; Race: 90.1% White, 6.8% Black/African American, 0.2% Asian, 0.1% American Indian/Alaska Native, 0.0% Native Hawaiian/Other Pacific Islander, 1.1% Two or more races, 2.8% Hispanic of any race; Average household size: 2.53; Median age: 41.5; Age under 18: 23.2%; Age 65 and over: 14.7%; Males per 100 females: 102.2; Marriage status: 22.7% never married, 64.6% now married, 0.6% separated, 3.0% widowed, 9.6% divorced; Foreign born: 0.3%; Speak English only: 97.8%; With disability: 15.3%; Veterans: 12.6%; Ancestry: 44.6% American, 7.6% Irish, 6.0% German, 3.9% English, 1.4% Scotch-Irish
Employment: 10.8% management, business, and financial, 1.7% computer, engineering, and science, 4.8% education, legal, community service, arts, and media, 0.0% healthcare practitioners, 20.0% service, 26.3% sales and office, 10.7% natural resources, construction, and maintenance, 25.9% production, transportation, and material moving
Income: Per capita: $16,928; Median household: $29,467; Average household: $42,699; Households with income of $100,000 or more: 6.8%; Poverty rate: 20.7%
Educational Attainment: High school diploma or higher: 73.3%; Bachelor's degree or higher: 4.2%; Graduate/professional degree or higher: 0.6%
School District(s)
Wilkes County Schools (PK-12)
2012-13 Enrollment: 10,384 . . . . (336) 667-1121
Housing: Homeownership rate: 81.2%; Median home value: $100,600; Median year structure built: 1980; Homeowner vacancy rate: 0.7%; Median gross rent: $627 per month; Rental vacancy rate: 11.0%
Health Insurance: 90.8% have insurance; 70.9% have private insurance; 30.8% have public insurance; 9.2% do not have insurance; 0.0% of children under 18 do not have insurance
Transportation: Commute: 95.6% car, 0.0% public transportation, 1.8% walk, 2.6% work from home; Median travel time to work: 25.1 minutes

RONDA (town).
Covers a land area of 1.084 square miles and a water area of 0 square miles. Located at 36.22° N. Lat; 80.94° W. Long. Elevation is 961 feet.
Population: 417; Growth (since 2000): -9.3%; Density: 384.7 persons per square mile; Race: 91.1% White, 2.2% Black/African American, 0.0% Asian, 0.2% American Indian/Alaska Native, 0.0% Native Hawaiian/Other Pacific Islander, 2.2% Two or more races, 9.1% Hispanic of any race; Average household size: 2.41; Median age: 43.1; Age under 18: 20.9%; Age 65 and over: 19.7%; Males per 100 females: 106.4
School District(s)
Wilkes County Schools (PK-12)
2012-13 Enrollment: 10,384 . . . . (336) 667-1121
Housing: Homeownership rate: 71.7%; Homeowner vacancy rate: 2.3%; Rental vacancy rate: 16.9%

STATE ROAD (unincorporated postal area)
ZCTA: 28676
Covers a land area of 28.590 square miles and a water area of 0.139 square miles. Located at 36.33° N. Lat; 80.85° W. Long..
Population: 3,483; Growth (since 2000): 14.3%; Density: 121.8 persons per square mile; Race: 97.4% White, 0.5% Black/African American, 0.2% Asian, 0.2% American Indian/Alaska Native, 0.0% Native Hawaiian/Other Pacific Islander, 0.8% Two or more races, 2.6% Hispanic of any race; Average household size: 2.36; Median age: 45.2; Age under 18: 21.8%; Age 65 and over: 19.4%; Males per 100 females: 94.6; Marriage status: 13.2% never married, 69.7% now married, 2.5% separated, 5.9% widowed, 11.2% divorced; Foreign born: 2.0%; Speak English only: 97.5%; With disability: 19.1%; Veterans: 11.4%; Ancestry: 46.4% American, 11.3% English, 8.1% German, 5.9% Irish, 2.8% Scotch-Irish
Employment: 16.0% management, business, and financial, 0.0% computer, engineering, and science, 11.0% education, legal, community service, arts, and media, 10.7% healthcare practitioners, 19.3% service, 21.0% sales and office, 10.7% natural resources, construction, and maintenance, 11.3% production, transportation, and material moving
Income: Per capita: $24,612; Median household: $35,226; Average household: $54,121; Households with income of $100,000 or more: 10.9%; Poverty rate: 11.0%
Educational Attainment: High school diploma or higher: 79.1%; Bachelor's degree or higher: 21.7%; Graduate/professional degree or higher: 5.5%
School District(s)
Bridges Charter School (KG-08)
2012-13 Enrollment: 139 . . . . (336) 874-2721
Surry County Schools (PK-12)
2012-13 Enrollment: 8,589 . . . . (336) 386-8211
Housing: Homeownership rate: 79.5%; Median home value: $117,100; Median year structure built: 1972; Homeowner vacancy rate: 2.2%; Median gross rent: $693 per month; Rental vacancy rate: 8.5%
Health Insurance: 82.9% have insurance; 68.2% have private insurance; 34.4% have public insurance; 17.1% do not have insurance; 0.0% of children under 18 do not have insurance
Transportation: Commute: 99.0% car, 0.4% public transportation, 0.0% walk, 0.6% work from home; Median travel time to work: 23.1 minutes

THURMOND (unincorporated postal area)
ZCTA: 28683
Covers a land area of 33.364 square miles and a water area of 0.116 square miles. Located at 36.39° N. Lat; 80.91° W. Long..
Population: 1,697; Growth (since 2000): 5.3%; Density: 50.9 persons per square mile; Race: 97.2% White, 0.5% Black/African American, 0.3% Asian, 0.6% American Indian/Alaska Native, 0.0% Native Hawaiian/Other Pacific Islander, 1.2% Two or more races, 1.5% Hispanic of any race; Average household size: 2.36; Median age: 45.5; Age under 18: 20.5%; Age 65 and over: 17.7%; Males per 100 females: 93.3
Housing: Homeownership rate: 82.7%; Homeowner vacancy rate: 2.3%; Rental vacancy rate: 10.1%

TRAPHILL (unincorporated postal area)
ZCTA: 28685
Covers a land area of 60.971 square miles and a water area of 0 square miles. Located at 36.36° N. Lat; 81.06° W. Long. Elevation is 1,299 feet.
Population: 2,076; Growth (since 2000): 3.3%; Density: 34.0 persons per square mile; Race: 96.8% White, 1.4% Black/African American, 0.4% Asian, 0.1% American Indian/Alaska Native, 0.0% Native Hawaiian/Other Pacific Islander, 0.8% Two or more races, 2.5% Hispanic of any race; Average household size: 2.43; Median age: 42.6; Age under 18: 22.6%; Age 65 and over: 16.5%; Males per 100 females: 101.4
School District(s)
Wilkes County Schools (PK-12)
2012-13 Enrollment: 10,384 . . . . (336) 667-1121
Housing: Homeownership rate: 83.9%; Homeowner vacancy rate: 2.0%; Rental vacancy rate: 16.9%

WILKESBORO

WILKESBORO (town). County seat. Covers a land area of 5.896 square miles and a water area of 0 square miles. Located at 36.14° N. Lat; 81.17° W. Long. Elevation is 1,024 feet.

History: Wilkesboro was settled before the Revolution and called Mulberry Fields. The town and Wilkes County were both named for John Wilkes (1727-1797), English statesman and defender of popular rights. John Wilkes Booth, Lincoln's assassin, was related to John Wilkes through his paternal grandmother.

Population: 3,413; Growth (since 2000): 8.0%; Density: 578.9 persons per square mile; Race: 81.5% White, 8.9% Black/African American, 3.0% Asian, 0.2% American Indian/Alaska Native, 0.1% Native Hawaiian/Other Pacific Islander, 2.3% Two or more races, 7.3% Hispanic of any race; Average household size: 2.13; Median age: 45.4; Age under 18: 19.5%; Age 65 and over: 24.6%; Males per 100 females: 86.3; Marriage status: 27.3% never married, 47.9% now married, 7.1% separated, 12.2% widowed, 12.6% divorced; Foreign born: 5.1%; Speak English only: 93.4%; With disability: 20.3%; Veterans: 11.1%; Ancestry: 40.4% American, 9.2% English, 8.0% Irish, 6.6% German, 2.4% Scotch-Irish

Employment: 15.6% management, business, and financial, 2.0% computer, engineering, and science, 16.3% education, legal, community service, arts, and media, 4.3% healthcare practitioners, 13.8% service, 24.7% sales and office, 8.8% natural resources, construction, and maintenance, 14.4% production, transportation, and material moving

Income: Per capita: $24,975; Median household: $33,889; Average household: $54,774; Households with income of $100,000 or more: 13.5%; Poverty rate: 33.2%

Educational Attainment: High school diploma or higher: 75.3%; Bachelor's degree or higher: 23.9%; Graduate/professional degree or higher: 8.9%

School District(s)

Wilkes County Schools (PK-12)
    2012-13 Enrollment: 10,384 . . . . (336) 667-1121

Two-year College(s)

Wilkes Community College (Public)
    Fall 2013 Enrollment: 2,753 . . . . (336) 838-6100
    2013-14 Tuition: In-state $2,418; Out-of-state $8,562

Housing: Homeownership rate: 52.7%; Median home value: $185,000; Median year structure built: 1981; Homeowner vacancy rate: 4.7%; Median gross rent: $562 per month; Rental vacancy rate: 14.6%

Health Insurance: 89.8% have insurance; 60.7% have private insurance; 43.7% have public insurance; 10.2% do not have insurance; 3.0% of children under 18 do not have insurance

Safety: Violent crime rate: 55.4 per 10,000 population; Property crime rate: 944.3 per 10,000 population

Transportation: Commute: 95.6% car, 0.0% public transportation, 0.7% walk, 3.6% work from home; Median travel time to work: 15.7 minutes

Additional Information Contacts
Town of Wilkesboro. . . . . (336) 838-3951
    http://www.wilkesboronorthcarolina.com

Wilson County

Located in east central North Carolina; drained by Contentnea Creek. Covers a land area of 368.174 square miles, a water area of 5.558 square miles, and is located in the Eastern Time Zone at 35.70° N. Lat., 77.92° W. Long. The county was founded in 1855. County seat is Wilson.

Wilson County is part of the Wilson, NC Micropolitan Statistical Area. The entire metro area includes: Wilson County, NC

Weather Station: Wilson 3 SW										Elevation: 109 feet	
	Jan	Feb	Mar	Apr	May	Jun	Jul	Aug	Sep	Oct	Nov	Dec
High	51	55	63	72	80	87	90	89	83	73	65	55
Low	30	32	39	47	56	65	69	67	61	49	40	33
Precip	3.8	3.1	4.3	3.1	3.8	4.1	5.3	4.9	4.8	3.2	3.0	3.3
Snow	1.0	0.9	0.8	tr	0.0	0.0	0.0	0.0	0.0	0.0	tr	0.3

High and Low temperatures in degrees Fahrenheit; Precipitation and Snow in inches

Population: 81,234; Growth (since 2000): 10.1%; Density: 220.6 persons per square mile; Race: 52.0% White, 39.0% Black/African American, 0.8% Asian, 0.3% American Indian/Alaska Native, 0.0% Native Hawaiian/Other Pacific Islander, 1.6% two or more races, 9.5% Hispanic of any race; Average household size: 2.49; Median age: 38.7; Age under 18: 24.7%; Age 65 and over: 14.2%; Males per 100 females: 91.4; Marriage status: 30.6% never married, 50.5% now married, 3.9% separated, 7.7%

widowed, 11.2% divorced; Foreign born: 7.0%; Speak English only: 89.3%; With disability: 15.3%; Veterans: 9.9%; Ancestry: 18.8% American, 9.2% English, 4.9% Irish, 4.4% German, 1.4% Italian

Religion: Six largest groups: 17.3% Baptist, 7.8% Methodist/Pietist, 6.1% Non-denominational Protestant, 3.4% Pentecostal, 2.0% Presbyterian-Reformed, 1.9% Episcopalianism/Anglicanism

Economy: Unemployment rate: 7.9%; Leading industries: 18.5% retail trade; 11.6% health care and social assistance; 11.0% other services (except public administration); Farms: 297 totaling 111,395 acres; Company size: 2 employ 1,000 or more persons, 6 employ 500 to 999 persons, 38 employ 100 to 499 persons, 1,690 employ less than 100 persons; Business ownership: 1,694 women-owned, 1,016 Black-owned, n/a Hispanic-owned, n/a Asian-owned

Employment: 11.0% management, business, and financial, 2.7% computer, engineering, and science, 10.2% education, legal, community service, arts, and media, 5.4% healthcare practitioners, 18.7% service, 23.8% sales and office, 11.8% natural resources, construction, and maintenance, 16.3% production, transportation, and material moving

Income: Per capita: $20,972; Median household: $39,204; Average household: $52,193; Households with income of $100,000 or more: 11.1%; Poverty rate: 23.2%

Educational Attainment: High school diploma or higher: 78.5%; Bachelor's degree or higher: 17.9%; Graduate/professional degree or higher: 4.7%

Housing: Homeownership rate: 60.1%; Median home value: $111,500; Median year structure built: 1980; Homeowner vacancy rate: 2.7%; Median gross rent: $738 per month; Rental vacancy rate: 10.4%

Vital Statistics: Birth rate: 118.8 per 10,000 population; Death rate: 102.9 per 10,000 population; Age-adjusted cancer mortality rate: 195.6 deaths per 100,000 population

Health Insurance: 80.9% have insurance; 56.0% have private insurance; 37.3% have public insurance; 19.1% do not have insurance; 9.2% of children under 18 do not have insurance

Health Care: Physicians: 12.4 per 10,000 population; Hospital beds: 27.0 per 10,000 population; Hospital admissions: 1,001.0 per 10,000 population

Transportation: Commute: 92.6% car, 0.1% public transportation, 1.8% walk, 2.2% work from home; Median travel time to work: 19.7 minutes

Presidential Election: 53.4% Obama, 45.9% Romney (2012)

Additional Information Contacts
Wilson Government. . . . . (252) 399-2803
    http://www.wilson-co.com

Wilson County Communities

BLACK CREEK

BLACK CREEK (town). Covers a land area of 0.717 square miles and a water area of 0.004 square miles. Located at 35.64° N. Lat; 77.93° W. Long. Elevation is 125 feet.

Population: 769; Growth (since 2000): 7.7%; Density: 1,073.2 persons per square mile; Race: 73.0% White, 18.7% Black/African American, 0.7% Asian, 0.1% American Indian/Alaska Native, 0.0% Native Hawaiian/Other Pacific Islander, 1.6% Two or more races, 8.5% Hispanic of any race; Average household size: 2.55; Median age: 36.7; Age under 18: 27.0%; Age 65 and over: 11.2%; Males per 100 females: 91.8

School District(s)

Wilson County Schools (PK-12)
    2012-13 Enrollment: 12,548 . . . . (252) 399-7700

Housing: Homeownership rate: 71.2%; Homeowner vacancy rate: 3.6%; Rental vacancy rate: 10.3%

ELM CITY

ELM CITY (town). Covers a land area of 0.774 square miles and a water area of 0 square miles. Located at 35.81° N. Lat; 77.86° W. Long. Elevation is 135 feet.

Population: 1,298; Growth (since 2000): 11.4%; Density: 1,677.0 persons per square mile; Race: 40.2% White, 56.1% Black/African American, 0.1% Asian, 0.8% American Indian/Alaska Native, 0.0% Native Hawaiian/Other Pacific Islander, 1.2% Two or more races, 4.0% Hispanic of any race; Average household size: 2.34; Median age: 47.1; Age under 18: 19.4%; Age 65 and over: 15.6%; Males per 100 females: 83.1

School District(s)

Nash-Rocky Mount Schools (PK-12)
    2012-13 Enrollment: 16,770 . . . . (252) 459-5220
Wilson County Schools (PK-12)
    2012-13 Enrollment: 12,548 . . . . (252) 399-7700

Housing: Homeownership rate: 64.2%; Homeowner vacancy rate: 2.7%; Rental vacancy rate: 11.9%

Additional Information Contacts
Town of Elm City . . . . (262) 236-4917
    http://elmcity.govoffice.com

LUCAMA (town). Covers a land area of 0.620 square miles and a water area of 0 square miles. Located at 35.64° N. Lat; 78.01° W. Long. Elevation is 131 feet.

Population: 1,108; Growth (since 2000): 30.8%; Density: 1,785.7 persons per square mile; Race: 48.7% White, 24.9% Black/African American, 0.0% Asian, 0.6% American Indian/Alaska Native, 0.2% Native Hawaiian/Other Pacific Islander, 1.8% Two or more races, 27.7% Hispanic of any race; Average household size: 2.77; Median age: 34.8; Age under 18: 25.3%; Age 65 and over: 12.3%; Males per 100 females: 99.6

School District(s)
Wilson County Schools (PK-12)
    2012-13 Enrollment: 12,548 . . . . (252) 399-7700
Housing: Homeownership rate: 61.8%; Homeowner vacancy rate: 3.5%; Rental vacancy rate: 21.6%

SARATOGA (town). Covers a land area of 0.642 square miles and a water area of 0 square miles. Located at 35.65° N. Lat; 77.78° W. Long. Elevation is 118 feet.

History: Incorporated 1939.
Population: 408; Growth (since 2000): 7.7%; Density: 635.8 persons per square mile; Race: 51.7% White, 40.9% Black/African American, 0.0% Asian, 0.5% American Indian/Alaska Native, 0.0% Native Hawaiian/Other Pacific Islander, 0.2% Two or more races, 6.6% Hispanic of any race; Average household size: 2.46; Median age: 45.2; Age under 18: 21.1%; Age 65 and over: 17.6%; Males per 100 females: 91.5
Housing: Homeownership rate: 71.7%; Homeowner vacancy rate: 1.7%; Rental vacancy rate: 11.3%

SIMS (town). Covers a land area of 0.175 square miles and a water area of 0 square miles. Located at 35.76° N. Lat; 78.06° W. Long. Elevation is 197 feet.

History: Sometimes spelled Simms.
Population: 282; Growth (since 2000): 120.3%; Density: 1,614.5 persons per square mile; Race: 71.3% White, 16.3% Black/African American, 0.4% Asian, 0.0% American Indian/Alaska Native, 0.4% Native Hawaiian/Other Pacific Islander, 2.8% Two or more races, 8.9% Hispanic of any race; Average household size: 2.50; Median age: 31.0; Age under 18: 30.1%; Age 65 and over: 11.3%; Males per 100 females: 100.0
Housing: Homeownership rate: 72.5%; Homeowner vacancy rate: 0.0%; Rental vacancy rate: 8.8%

STANTONSBURG (town). Covers a land area of 0.585 square miles and a water area of 0 square miles. Located at 35.61° N. Lat; 77.82° W. Long. Elevation is 85 feet.

History: Stantonsburg was incorporated in 1817 and supposedly named for the founder. It was a thriving village before the Revolution.
Population: 784; Growth (since 2000): 8.0%; Density: 1,340.4 persons per square mile; Race: 51.8% White, 45.4% Black/African American, 0.1% Asian, 0.3% American Indian/Alaska Native, 0.0% Native Hawaiian/Other Pacific Islander, 0.5% Two or more races, 5.6% Hispanic of any race; Average household size: 2.30; Median age: 44.9; Age under 18: 21.6%; Age 65 and over: 20.5%; Males per 100 females: 88.0

School District(s)
Wilson County Schools (PK-12)
    2012-13 Enrollment: 12,548 . . . . (252) 399-7700
Housing: Homeownership rate: 68.4%; Homeowner vacancy rate: 3.8%; Rental vacancy rate: 13.1%

WILSON (city). County seat. Covers a land area of 28.747 square miles and a water area of 0.847 square miles. Located at 35.73° N. Lat; 77.93° W. Long. Elevation is 112 feet.

History: Wilson was named for Colonel Louis D. Wilson.
Population: 49,167; Growth (since 2000): 10.7%; Density: 1,710.3 persons per square mile; Race: 42.9% White, 47.9% Black/African American, 1.2% Asian, 0.3% American Indian/Alaska Native, 0.0% Native Hawaiian/Other Pacific Islander, 1.7% Two or more races, 9.4% Hispanic of any race; Average household size: 2.43; Median age: 37.2; Age under 18: 25.3%; Age 65 and over: 14.1%; Males per 100 females: 87.1; Marriage status: 35.1% never married, 45.9% now married, 3.6% separated, 8.3% widowed, 10.8% divorced; Foreign born: 7.2%; Speak

English only: 89.6%; With disability: 14.9%; Veterans: 10.3%; Ancestry: 16.1% American, 8.5% English, 4.7% Irish, 4.5% German, 1.7% Scottish
Employment: 12.8% management, business, and financial, 3.2% computer, engineering, and science, 11.9% education, legal, community service, arts, and media, 5.7% healthcare practitioners, 19.5% service, 24.4% sales and office, 9.2% natural resources, construction, and maintenance, 13.3% production, transportation, and material moving
Income: Per capita: $21,396; Median household: $37,676; Average household: $53,157; Households with income of $100,000 or more: 12.0%; Poverty rate: 26.5%
Educational Attainment: High school diploma or higher: 78.5%; Bachelor's degree or higher: 23.1%; Graduate/professional degree or higher: 6.3%

School District(s)
Deaf and Blind Schools (PK-12)
    2012-13 Enrollment: 177 . . . . (919) 733-6382
Nc Health and Human Resources (KG-12)
    2012-13 Enrollment: n/a . . . . (919) 855-4430
Sallie B Howard School (KG-08)
    2012-13 Enrollment: 846 . . . . (252) 293-4150
Wilson County Schools (PK-12)
    2012-13 Enrollment: 12,548 . . . . (252) 399-7700
Four-year College(s)
Barton College (Private, Not-for-profit, Christian Church (Disciples of Christ))
    Fall 2013 Enrollment: 1,065 . . . . (252) 399-6300
    2013-14 Tuition: In-state $25,396; Out-of-state $25,396
Two-year College(s)
Wilson Community College (Public)
    Fall 2013 Enrollment: 2,117 . . . . (252) 291-1195
    2013-14 Tuition: In-state $2,393; Out-of-state $8,537
Vocational/Technical School(s)
Mitchells Hairstyling Academy-Wilson (Private, For-profit)
    Fall 2013 Enrollment: 39 . . . . (252) 243-3158
    2013-14 Tuition: $9,950
Housing: Homeownership rate: 50.3%; Median home value: $131,000; Median year structure built: 1979; Homeowner vacancy rate: 3.4%; Median gross rent: $747 per month; Rental vacancy rate: 10.3%
Health Insurance: 81.9% have insurance; 56.1% have private insurance; 37.9% have public insurance; 18.1% do not have insurance; 7.7% of children under 18 do not have insurance
Hospitals: Wilson Medical Center (317 beds)
Newspapers: The Wilson Times (daily circulation 13000)
Transportation: Commute: 92.6% car, 0.1% public transportation, 1.1% walk, 2.0% work from home; Median travel time to work: 18.1 minutes; Amtrak: Train service available.
Additional Information Contacts
City of Wilson . . . . (252) 399-2200
    http://www.wilsonnc.org

Yadkin County

Located in northwestern North Carolina; piedmont area, bounded on the north and east by the Yadkin River. Covers a land area of 334.829 square miles, a water area of 2.677 square miles, and is located in the Eastern Time Zone at 36.16° N. Lat., 80.67° W. Long. The county was founded in 1850. County seat is Yadkinville.

Yadkin County is part of the Winston-Salem, NC Metropolitan Statistical Area. The entire metro area includes: Davidson County, NC; Davie County, NC; Forsyth County, NC; Stokes County, NC; Yadkin County, NC

Weather Station: Yadkinville 6 E									Elevation: 875 feet		
	Jan	Feb	Mar	Apr	May	Jun	Jul	Aug	Sep	Oct	Nov	Dec
High	49	53	62	71	78	85	88	87	80	71	61	51
Low	26	29	35	43	52	61	65	64	57	45	35	28
Precip	3.5	3.2	4.3	3.7	3.8	4.1	4.7	3.5	3.7	3.3	3.2	3.6
Snow	4.0	2.7	0.8	tr	0.0	0.0	0.0	0.0	0.0	0.0	tr	1.2

High and Low temperatures in degrees Fahrenheit; Precipitation and Snow in inches

Population: 38,406; Growth (since 2000): 5.7%; Density: 114.7 persons per square mile; Race: 88.5% White, 3.1% Black/African American, 0.2% Asian, 0.2% American Indian/Alaska Native, 0.0% Native Hawaiian/Other Pacific Islander, 1.2% two or more races, 9.8% Hispanic of any race; Average household size: 2.46; Median age: 41.4; Age under 18: 23.3%; Age 65 and over: 16.3%; Males per 100 females: 96.7; Marriage status:

22.4% never married, 59.1% now married, 3.3% separated, 8.1% widowed, 10.3% divorced; Foreign born: 5.7%; Speak English only: 90.8%; With disability: 15.0%; Veterans: 8.5%; Ancestry: 29.3% American, 11.7% English, 11.4% German, 6.2% Irish, 2.0% Scotch-Irish

Religion: Six largest groups: 33.0% Baptist, 9.0% Methodist/Pietist, 9.0% Non-denominational Protestant, 3.1% Catholicism, 2.7% European Free-Church, 1.8% Pentecostal

Economy: Unemployment rate: 4.4%; Leading industries: 18.3% retail trade; 13.7% other services (except public administration); 11.6% construction; Farms: 952 totaling 100,483 acres; Company size: 0 employ 1,000 or more persons, 4 employ 500 to 999 persons, 7 employ 100 to 499 persons, 594 employ less than 100 persons; Business ownership: n/a women-owned, n/a Black-owned, n/a Hispanic-owned, n/a Asian-owned

Employment: 11.8% management, business, and financial, 2.7% computer, engineering, and science, 8.1% education, legal, community service, arts, and media, 5.8% healthcare practitioners, 15.6% service, 22.5% sales and office, 13.4% natural resources, construction, and maintenance, 20.1% production, transportation, and material moving

Income: Per capita: $22,726; Median household: $40,371; Average household: $56,415; Households with income of $100,000 or more: 12.6%; Poverty rate: 18.5%

Educational Attainment: High school diploma or higher: 78.8%; Bachelor's degree or higher: 13.1%; Graduate/professional degree or higher: 3.1%

Housing: Homeownership rate: 76.2%; Median home value: $121,100; Median year structure built: 1978; Homeowner vacancy rate: 1.5%; Median gross rent: $593 per month; Rental vacancy rate: 11.1%

Vital Statistics: Birth rate: 104.4 per 10,000 population; Death rate: 99.1 per 10,000 population; Age-adjusted cancer mortality rate: 168.1 deaths per 100,000 population

Health Insurance: 84.8% have insurance; 64.9% have private insurance; 35.6% have public insurance; 15.2% do not have insurance; 8.9% of children under 18 do not have insurance

Health Care: Physicians: 4.7 per 10,000 population; Hospital beds: 5.8 per 10,000 population; Hospital admissions: 68.0 per 10,000 population

Transportation: Commute: 94.0% car, 0.1% public transportation, 1.1% walk, 2.7% work from home; Median travel time to work: 28.0 minutes

Presidential Election: 23.5% Obama, 74.8% Romney (2012)

National and State Parks: Pilot Mountain State Park

Additional Information Contacts

Yadkin Government. . . . . (336) 679-4200
  http://www.yadkincounty.gov

Yadkin County Communities

BOONVILLE (town). Covers a land area of 1.238 square miles and a water area of 0 square miles. Located at 36.23° N. Lat; 80.71° W. Long. Elevation is 1,066 feet.

Population: 1,222; Growth (since 2000): 7.4%; Density: 987.3 persons per square mile; Race: 91.6% White, 3.5% Black/African American, 0.1% Asian, 0.3% American Indian/Alaska Native, 0.0% Native Hawaiian/Other Pacific Islander, 1.4% Two or more races, 5.2% Hispanic of any race; Average household size: 2.33; Median age: 42.1; Age under 18: 23.8%; Age 65 and over: 19.9%; Males per 100 females: 83.5

School District(s)

Yadkin County Schools (PK-12)
  2012-13 Enrollment: 5,871 . . . . (336) 679-2051

Housing: Homeownership rate: 69.9%; Homeowner vacancy rate: 2.7%; Rental vacancy rate: 7.6%

EAST BEND (town). Covers a land area of 1.290 square miles and a water area of 0.006 square miles. Located at 36.22° N. Lat; 80.51° W. Long. Elevation is 1,063 feet.

Population: 612; Growth (since 2000): -7.1%; Density: 474.4 persons per square mile; Race: 93.3% White, 1.3% Black/African American, 0.0% Asian, 0.0% American Indian/Alaska Native, 0.2% Native Hawaiian/Other Pacific Islander, 1.3% Two or more races, 4.9% Hispanic of any race; Average household size: 2.42; Median age: 39.4; Age under 18: 25.2%; Age 65 and over: 15.2%; Males per 100 females: 93.7

School District(s)

Yadkin County Schools (PK-12)
  2012-13 Enrollment: 5,871 . . . . (336) 679-2051

Housing: Homeownership rate: 75.8%; Homeowner vacancy rate: 3.5%; Rental vacancy rate: 16.4%

HAMPTONVILLE (unincorporated postal area)

ZCTA: 27020

Covers a land area of 73.446 square miles and a water area of 0.369 square miles. Located at 36.10° N. Lat; 80.80° W. Long. Elevation is 1,020 feet.

Population: 6,421; Growth (since 2000): 8.8%; Density: 87.4 persons per square mile; Race: 88.5% White, 1.5% Black/African American, 0.1% Asian, 0.1% American Indian/Alaska Native, 0.0% Native Hawaiian/Other Pacific Islander, 1.0% Two or more races, 12.0% Hispanic of any race; Average household size: 2.53; Median age: 39.4; Age under 18: 25.4%; Age 65 and over: 15.5%; Males per 100 females: 100.7; Marriage status: 23.1% never married, 60.0% now married, 2.0% separated, 8.9% widowed, 8.1% divorced; Foreign born: 7.7%; Speak English only: 89.1%; With disability: 19.7%; Veterans: 5.9%; Ancestry: 36.5% American, 9.1% English, 8.6% German, 8.0% Irish, 2.7% French

Employment: 10.4% management, business, and financial, 4.2% computer, engineering, and science, 11.3% education, legal, community service, arts, and media, 1.6% healthcare practitioners, 18.8% service, 24.0% sales and office, 7.2% natural resources, construction, and maintenance, 22.4% production, transportation, and material moving

Income: Per capita: $24,777; Median household: $36,770; Average household: $61,234; Households with income of $100,000 or more: 10.9%; Poverty rate: 18.7%

Educational Attainment: High school diploma or higher: 70.8%; Bachelor's degree or higher: 10.9%; Graduate/professional degree or higher: 3.8%

School District(s)

Yadkin County Schools (PK-12)
  2012-13 Enrollment: 5,871 . . . . (336) 679-2051

Housing: Homeownership rate: 77.0%; Median home value: $119,600; Median year structure built: 1977; Homeowner vacancy rate: 0.9%; Median gross rent: $638 per month; Rental vacancy rate: 13.4%

Health Insurance: 81.9% have insurance; 62.6% have private insurance; 42.1% have public insurance; 18.1% do not have insurance; 8.3% of children under 18 do not have insurance

Transportation: Commute: 91.5% car, 0.9% public transportation, 3.3% walk, 3.6% work from home; Median travel time to work: 28.8 minutes

JONESVILLE (town). Covers a land area of 2.835 square miles and a water area of 0.018 square miles. Located at 36.24° N. Lat; 80.84° W. Long. Elevation is 928 feet.

Population: 2,285; Growth (since 2000): 56.1%; Density: 806.0 persons per square mile; Race: 81.6% White, 11.5% Black/African American, 0.1% Asian, 0.2% American Indian/Alaska Native, 0.0% Native Hawaiian/Other Pacific Islander, 2.9% Two or more races, 7.3% Hispanic of any race; Average household size: 2.22; Median age: 41.1; Age under 18: 23.5%; Age 65 and over: 17.6%; Males per 100 females: 85.6

School District(s)

Yadkin County Schools (PK-12)
  2012-13 Enrollment: 5,871 . . . . (336) 679-2051

Housing: Homeownership rate: 56.2%; Homeowner vacancy rate: 3.0%; Rental vacancy rate: 9.0%

YADKINVILLE (town). County seat. Covers a land area of 2.780 square miles and a water area of 0.011 square miles. Located at 36.13° N. Lat; 80.66° W. Long. Elevation is 961 feet.

History: Yadkinville was formed in 1805 and named for the river that forms its northern and eastern boundaries.

Population: 2,959; Growth (since 2000): 5.0%; Density: 1,064.3 persons per square mile; Race: 74.1% White, 7.0% Black/African American, 0.3% Asian, 0.1% American Indian/Alaska Native, 0.0% Native Hawaiian/Other Pacific Islander, 1.3% Two or more races, 23.7% Hispanic of any race; Average household size: 2.47; Median age: 39.1; Age under 18: 23.7%; Age 65 and over: 20.8%; Males per 100 females: 86.2; Marriage status: 23.1% never married, 47.9% now married, 3.5% separated, 15.7% widowed, 13.3% divorced; Foreign born: 9.3%; Speak English only: 83.8%; With disability: 12.6%; Veterans: 5.8%; Ancestry: 17.2% English, 11.7% American, 8.6% German, 8.2% Irish, 1.9% Scotch-Irish

Employment: 10.5% management, business, and financial, 1.7% computer, engineering, and science, 3.9% education, legal, community service, arts, and media, 3.2% healthcare practitioners, 12.2% service, 31.5% sales and office, 14.8% natural resources, construction, and maintenance, 22.1% production, transportation, and material moving

Income: Per capita: $17,638; Median household: $31,494; Average household: $43,966; Households with income of $100,000 or more: 10.7%; Poverty rate: 28.9%

Educational Attainment: High school diploma or higher: 76.1%; Bachelor's degree or higher: 13.8%; Graduate/professional degree or higher: 1.6%

School District(s)
Yadkin County Schools (PK-12)
 2012-13 Enrollment: 5,871 . . . . (336) 679-2051

Housing: Homeownership rate: 59.9%; Median home value: $114,400; Median year structure built: 1973; Homeowner vacancy rate: 2.8%; Median gross rent: $641 per month; Rental vacancy rate: 16.2%

Health Insurance: 77.1% have insurance; 56.0% have private insurance; 33.4% have public insurance; 22.9% do not have insurance; 13.0% of children under 18 do not have insurance

Hospitals: Yadkin Valley Community Hospital (22 beds)

Safety: Violent crime rate: 74.6 per 10,000 population; Property crime rate: 440.8 per 10,000 population

Newspapers: Yadkin Ripple (weekly circulation 5300)

Transportation: Commute: 94.9% car, 0.5% public transportation, 0.6% walk, 2.4% work from home; Median travel time to work: 24.4 minutes

Additional Information Contacts
Town of Yadkinville . . . . (336) 679-8732
 http://www.yadkinville.org

Yancey County

Located in western North Carolina; bounded on the northwest by Tennessee, and on the east by the Nolichucky River; crossed by ranges of the Blue Ridge and Black Mountains, including Mt. Mitchell, the highest point in the state (6,684 ft); includes th e Bald Mountains and parts of Pisgah National Forest. Covers a land area of 312.597 square miles, a water area of 0.563 square miles, and is located in the Eastern Time Zone at 35.89° N. Lat., 82.30° W. Long. The county was founded in 1833. County seat is Burnsville.

Weather Station: Celo 2 S   Elevation: 2,680 feet

	Jan	Feb	Mar	Apr	May	Jun	Jul	Aug	Sep	Oct	Nov	Dec
High	47	50	57	65	73	78	81	80	74	66	58	49
Low	22	25	31	39	47	55	59	58	51	40	32	25
Precip	4.9	4.7	5.6	4.7	4.7	4.6	4.5	5.4	5.0	3.9	4.8	4.1
Snow	5.0	4.2	3.0	1.1	tr	0.0	0.0	0.0	0.0	tr	0.2	1.9

High and Low temperatures in degrees Fahrenheit; Precipitation and Snow in inches

Population: 17,818; Growth (since 2000): 0.2%; Density: 57.0 persons per square mile; Race: 95.2% White, 0.8% Black/African American, 0.2% Asian, 0.4% American Indian/Alaska Native, 0.0% Native Hawaiian/Other Pacific Islander, 0.9% two or more races, 4.6% Hispanic of any race; Average household size: 2.31; Median age: 45.5; Age under 18: 20.0%; Age 65 and over: 20.6%; Males per 100 females: 96.4; Marriage status: 19.2% never married, 63.7% now married, 2.7% separated, 7.2% widowed, 9.9% divorced; Foreign born: 2.7%; Speak English only: 95.4%; With disability: 20.1%; Veterans: 9.1%; Ancestry: 17.3% American, 16.3% German, 12.2% English, 9.7% Irish, 6.3% Scottish

Religion: Six largest groups: 24.6% Baptist, 6.1% Methodist/Pietist, 2.1% Presbyterian-Reformed, 1.1% Non-denominational Protestant, 1.0% Catholicism, 1.0% Pentecostal

Economy: Unemployment rate: 5.6%; Leading industries: 18.3% retail trade; 16.5% construction; 11.7% other services (except public administration); Farms: 450 totaling 31,002 acres; Company size: 0 employ 1,000 or more persons, 0 employ 500 to 999 persons, 7 employ 100 to 499 persons, 327 employ less than 100 persons; Business ownership: 441 women-owned, n/a Black-owned, n/a Hispanic-owned, n/a Asian-owned

Employment: 9.1% management, business, and financial, 1.6% computer, engineering, and science, 11.1% education, legal, community service, arts, and media, 5.9% healthcare practitioners, 22.1% service, 17.4% sales and office, 14.4% natural resources, construction, and maintenance, 18.4% production, transportation, and material moving

Income: Per capita: $20,257; Median household: $38,579; Average household: $48,096; Households with income of $100,000 or more: 6.2%; Poverty rate: 20.1%

Educational Attainment: High school diploma or higher: 83.2%; Bachelor's degree or higher: 17.9%; Graduate/professional degree or higher: 6.0%

Housing: Homeownership rate: 76.4%; Median home value: $135,100; Median year structure built: 1982; Homeowner vacancy rate: 3.8%; Median gross rent: $615 per month; Rental vacancy rate: 15.9%

Vital Statistics: Birth rate: 96.8 per 10,000 population; Death rate: 115.6 per 10,000 population; Age-adjusted cancer mortality rate: 205.0 deaths per 100,000 population

Health Insurance: 82.0% have insurance; 56.9% have private insurance; 39.5% have public insurance; 18.0% do not have insurance; 10.4% of children under 18 do not have insurance

Health Care: Physicians: 7.9 per 10,000 population; Hospital beds: 3.4 per 10,000 population; Hospital admissions: 96.1 per 10,000 population

Air Quality Index: 93.0% good, 7.0% moderate, 0.0% unhealthy for sensitive individuals, 0.0% unhealthy (percent of days)

Transportation: Commute: 90.0% car, 0.0% public transportation, 3.5% walk, 5.6% work from home; Median travel time to work: 27.1 minutes

Presidential Election: 42.1% Obama, 55.8% Romney (2012)

National and State Parks: Mount Mitchell State Park

Additional Information Contacts
Yancey Government . . . . (828) 682-3971
 http://www.yanceycountync.gov

Yancey County Communities

BURNSVILLE (town). County seat. Covers a land area of 1.576 square miles and a water area of 0 square miles. Located at 35.92° N. Lat; 82.30° W. Long. Elevation is 2,825 feet.

History: Burnsville is named for Captain Otway Burns, privateer in the War of 1812.

Population: 1,693; Growth (since 2000): 4.3%; Density: 1,074.1 persons per square mile; Race: 91.6% White, 2.3% Black/African American, 0.1% Asian, 0.6% American Indian/Alaska Native, 0.0% Native Hawaiian/Other Pacific Islander, 1.1% Two or more races, 10.4% Hispanic of any race; Average household size: 2.09; Median age: 45.6; Age under 18: 19.6%; Age 65 and over: 25.1%; Males per 100 females: 89.6

School District(s)
Yancey County Schools (KG-12)
 2012-13 Enrollment: 2,332 . . . . (828) 682-6101

Housing: Homeownership rate: 48.6%; Homeowner vacancy rate: 2.7%; Rental vacancy rate: 12.4%

Newspapers: Times-Journal (weekly circulation 6400)

Additional Information Contacts
Town of Burnsville . . . . (828) 682-2420
 http://www.townofburnsville.org

GREEN MOUNTAIN (unincorporated postal area)
ZCTA: 28740

 Covers a land area of 55.254 square miles and a water area of 0.477 square miles. Located at 36.09° N. Lat; 82.27° W. Long. Elevation is 2,146 feet.

 Population: 1,364; Growth (since 2000): -42.8%; Density: 24.7 persons per square mile; Race: 98.2% White, 0.1% Black/African American, 0.0% Asian, 0.1% American Indian/Alaska Native, 0.0% Native Hawaiian/Other Pacific Islander, 0.7% Two or more races, 1.9% Hispanic of any race; Average household size: 2.33; Median age: 46.2; Age under 18: 18.8%; Age 65 and over: 20.2%; Males per 100 females: 102.7

School District(s)
Mitchell County Schools (PK-12)
 2012-13 Enrollment: 2,044 . . . . (828) 766-2220

 Housing: Homeownership rate: 83.5%; Homeowner vacancy rate: 5.7%; Rental vacancy rate: 13.3%

Place Name Index

Aberdeen (town) Moore County, 172
Advance (CDP) Davie County, 112
Ahoskie (town) Hertford County, 146
Alamance (village) Alamance County, 49
Alamance County, 49
Albemarle (city) Stanly County, 219
Albertson (unincorporated) Duplin County, 113
Alexander (unincorporated) Buncombe County, 69
Alexander County, 52
Alexis (unincorporated) Gaston County, 123
Alleghany County, 53
Alliance (town) Pamlico County, 189
Almond (unincorporated) Swain County, 225
Altamahaw (CDP) Alamance County, 49
Andrews (town) Cherokee County, 91
Angier (town) Harnett County, 139
Anson County, 54
Ansonville (town) Anson County, 54
Apex (town) Wake County, 233
Aquadale (CDP) Stanly County, 220
Arapahoe (town) Pamlico County, 189
Ararat (unincorporated) Surry County, 223
Archdale (city) Randolph County, 200
Archer Lodge (town) Johnston County, 154
Arden (unincorporated) Buncombe County, 69
Ash (unincorporated) Brunswick County, 64
Ashe County, 55
Asheboro (city) Randolph County, 200
Asheville (city) Buncombe County, 70
Ashley Heights (CDP) Hoke County, 148
Askewville (town) Bertie County, 61
Atkinson (town) Pender County, 191
Atlantic (CDP) Carteret County, 81
Atlantic Beach (town) Carteret County, 81
Aulander (town) Bertie County, 61
Aurora (town) Beaufort County, 59
Autryville (town) Sampson County, 215
Avery County, 57
Avery Creek (CDP) Buncombe County, 70
Avon (CDP) Dare County, 107
Ayden (town) Pitt County, 196
Aydlett (unincorporated) Currituck County, 105
Badin (town) Stanly County, 220
Bahama (unincorporated) Durham County, 115
Bailey (town) Nash County, 176
Bakersville (town) Mitchell County, 170
Bald Head Island (village) Brunswick County, 65
Balfour (CDP) Henderson County, 143
Balsam (unincorporated) Jackson County, 152
Balsam Grove (unincorporated) Transylvania County, 226
Banner Elk (town) Avery County, 57
Barco (unincorporated) Currituck County, 105
Barker Heights (CDP) Henderson County, 143
Barker Ten Mile (CDP) Robeson County, 205
Barnardsville (unincorporated) Buncombe County, 70
Bath (town) Beaufort County, 59
Battleboro (unincorporated) Nash County, 176
Bayboro (town) Pamlico County, 189
Bayshore (CDP) New Hanover County, 178
Bayview (CDP) Beaufort County, 59
Bear Creek (unincorporated) Chatham County, 89
Bear Grass (town) Martin County, 164
Beaufort (town) Carteret County, 81
Beaufort County, 58
Beech Mountain (town) Watauga County, 240
Belews Creek (unincorporated) Forsyth County, 119
Belhaven (town) Beaufort County, 59
Bell Arthur (CDP) Pitt County, 196
Belmont (city) Gaston County, 124

Belvidere (unincorporated) Perquimans County, 194
Belville (town) Brunswick County, 65
Belvoir (CDP) Pitt County, 196
Belwood (town) Cleveland County, 93
Bennett (CDP) Chatham County, 89
Benson (town) Johnston County, 154
Bent Creek (CDP) Buncombe County, 70
Bermuda Run (town) Davie County, 112
Bertie County, 61
Bessemer City (city) Gaston County, 124
Bethania (town) Forsyth County, 119
Bethel (town) Pitt County, 196
Bethlehem (CDP) Alexander County, 52
Beulaville (town) Duplin County, 113
Biltmore Forest (town) Buncombe County, 70
Biscoe (town) Montgomery County, 171
Black Creek (town) Wilson County, 248
Black Mountain (town) Buncombe County, 71
Bladen County, 62
Bladenboro (town) Bladen County, 63
Blanch (unincorporated) Caswell County, 84
Blounts Creek (unincorporated) Beaufort County, 59
Blowing Rock (town) Watauga County, 240
Blue Clay Farms (CDP) New Hanover County, 178
Boardman (town) Columbus County, 96
Bogue (town) Carteret County, 81
Boiling Spring Lakes (city) Brunswick County, 65
Boiling Springs (town) Cleveland County, 94
Bolivia (town) Brunswick County, 65
Bolton (town) Columbus County, 96
Bonnetsville (CDP) Sampson County, 216
Boomer (unincorporated) Wilkes County, 245
Boone (town) Watauga County, 241
Boonville (town) Yadkin County, 250
Bostic (town) Rutherford County, 213
Bowmore (CDP) Hoke County, 148
Brasstown (unincorporated) Clay County, 93
Brevard (city) Transylvania County, 226
Brices Creek (CDP) Craven County, 98
Bridgeton (town) Craven County, 99
Broad Creek (CDP) Carteret County, 81
Broadway (town) Lee County, 157
Brogden (CDP) Wayne County, 242
Brookford (town) Catawba County, 86
Browns Summit (unincorporated) Guilford County, 132
Brunswick (town) Columbus County, 96
Brunswick County, 64
Bryson City (town) Swain County, 225
Buies Creek (CDP) Harnett County, 139
Bullock (unincorporated) Granville County, 129
Buncombe County, 68
Bunn (town) Franklin County, 122
Bunnlevel (CDP) Harnett County, 139
Burgaw (town) Pender County, 192
Burke County, 73
Burlington (city) Alamance County, 49
Burnsville (town) Yancey County, 251
Butner (town) Granville County, 129
Butters (CDP) Bladen County, 63
Buxton (CDP) Dare County, 107
Cabarrus County, 75
Cajah's Mountain (town) Caldwell County, 77
Calabash (town) Brunswick County, 65
Caldwell County, 77
Calypso (town) Duplin County, 113
Camden (CDP) Camden County, 80
Camden County, 79
Cameron (town) Moore County, 173

Camp Lejeune (unincorporated) Onslow County, 184
Candler (unincorporated) Buncombe County, 71
Candor (town) Montgomery County, 171
Canton (town) Haywood County, 141
Cape Carteret (town) Carteret County, 81
Caroleen (CDP) Rutherford County, 213
Carolina Beach (town) New Hanover County, 178
Carolina Shores (town) Brunswick County, 65
Carrboro (town) Orange County, 187
Carteret County, 80
Carthage (town) Moore County, 173
Cary (town) Wake County, 234
Casar (town) Cleveland County, 94
Cashiers (CDP) Jackson County, 152
Castalia (town) Nash County, 176
Castle Hayne (CDP) New Hanover County, 179
Caswell Beach (town) Brunswick County, 65
Caswell County, 84
Catawba (town) Catawba County, 86
Catawba County, 85
Cedar Grove (unincorporated) Orange County, 188
Cedar Island (unincorporated) Carteret County, 81
Cedar Mountain (unincorporated) Transylvania County, 226
Cedar Point (town) Carteret County, 82
Cedar Rock (village) Caldwell County, 78
Centerville (town) Franklin County, 122
Cerro Gordo (town) Columbus County, 96
Chadbourn (town) Columbus County, 96
Chapel Hill (town) Orange County, 188
Charlotte (city) Mecklenburg County, 167
Chatham County, 89
Cherokee (CDP) Jackson County, 152
Cherokee County, 90
Cherry Point (unincorporated) Craven County, 99
Cherryville (city) Gaston County, 124
Chimney Rock Village (village) Rutherford County, 213
China Grove (town) Rowan County, 210
Chinquapin (unincorporated) Duplin County, 114
Chocowinity (town) Beaufort County, 60
Chowan County, 91
Claremont (city) Catawba County, 86
Clarendon (unincorporated) Columbus County, 96
Clarkton (town) Bladen County, 63
Clay County, 92
Clayton (town) Johnston County, 154
Clemmons (village) Forsyth County, 119
Cleveland (town) Rowan County, 210
Cleveland County, 93
Cliffside (CDP) Rutherford County, 214
Climax (unincorporated) Randolph County, 200
Clinton (city) Sampson County, 216
Clyde (town) Haywood County, 141
Coats (town) Harnett County, 139
Cofield (village) Hertford County, 146
Coinjock (CDP) Currituck County, 105
Colerain (town) Bertie County, 61
Colfax (unincorporated) Guilford County, 132
Collettsville (unincorporated) Caldwell County, 78
Columbia (town) Tyrrell County, 227
Columbus (town) Polk County, 199
Columbus County, 96
Como (town) Hertford County, 147
Concord (city) Cabarrus County, 76
Conetoe (town) Edgecombe County, 117
Connelly Springs (town) Burke County, 73

CDP = Census Designated Place

CDP = Census Designated Place

Hillsborough (town) Orange County, 188
Hobbsville (unincorporated) Gates County, 128
Hobgood (town) Halifax County, 137
Hobucken (CDP) Pamlico County, 189
Hoffman (town) Richmond County, 204
Hoke County, 147
Holden Beach (town) Brunswick County, 66
Hollister (CDP) Halifax County, 137
Holly Ridge (town) Onslow County, 184
Holly Springs (town) Wake County, 235
Hookerton (town) Greene County, 131
Hoopers Creek (CDP) Henderson County, 145
Hope Mills (town) Cumberland County, 103
Horse Shoe (CDP) Henderson County, 145
Hot Springs (town) Madison County, 163
Hubert (unincorporated) Onslow County, 185
Hudson (town) Caldwell County, 78
Huntersville (town) Mecklenburg County, 169
Hurdle Mills (unincorporated) Person County, 194
Hyde County, 148
Icard (CDP) Burke County, 74
Indian Beach (town) Carteret County, 82
Indian Trail (town) Union County, 228
Ingold (CDP) Sampson County, 216
Iredell County, 149
Iron Station (CDP) Lincoln County, 160
Ivanhoe (CDP) Sampson County, 216
JAARS (CDP) Union County, 228
Jackson (town) Northampton County, 183
Jackson County, 151
Jackson Heights (CDP) Lenoir County, 159
Jackson Springs (unincorporated) Moore County, 173
Jacksonville (city) Onslow County, 185
James City (CDP) Craven County, 100
Jamestown (town) Guilford County, 134
Jamesville (town) Martin County, 165
Jarvisburg (unincorporated) Currituck County, 105
Jefferson (town) Ashe County, 56
Johnston County, 153
Jones County, 156
Jonesville (town) Yadkin County, 250
Julian (unincorporated) Guilford County, 134
Kannapolis (city) Cabarrus County, 76
Keener (CDP) Sampson County, 216
Kelford (town) Bertie County, 61
Kelly (CDP) Bladen County, 63
Kenansville (town) Duplin County, 114
Kenly (town) Johnston County, 155
Kernersville (town) Forsyth County, 119
Kill Devil Hills (town) Dare County, 107
King (city) Stokes County, 221
Kings Grant (CDP) New Hanover County, 179
Kings Mountain (city) Cleveland County, 94
Kingstown (town) Cleveland County, 94
Kinston (city) Lenoir County, 159
Kittrell (town) Vance County, 232
Kitty Hawk (town) Dare County, 108
Knightdale (town) Wake County, 235
Knotts Island (unincorporated) Currituck County, 105
Kure Beach (town) New Hanover County, 179
La Grange (town) Lenoir County, 159
Lake Junaluska (CDP) Haywood County, 141
Lake Lure (town) Rutherford County, 214
Lake Norman of Catawba (CDP) Catawba County, 87
Lake Park (village) Union County, 228
Lake Royale (CDP) Franklin County, 122
Lake Santeetlah (town) Graham County, 129
Lake Toxaway (unincorporated) Transylvania County, 226

Lake Waccamaw (town) Columbus County, 97
Lakeview (unincorporated) Moore County, 173
Landis (town) Rowan County, 211
Lansing (town) Ashe County, 57
Lasker (town) Northampton County, 183
Lattimore (town) Cleveland County, 95
Laurel Hill (CDP) Scotland County, 218
Laurel Park (town) Henderson County, 145
Laurel Springs (unincorporated) Alleghany County, 53
Laurinburg (city) Scotland County, 218
Lawndale (town) Cleveland County, 95
Lawsonville (unincorporated) Stokes County, 222
Leasburg (unincorporated) Caswell County, 84
Lee County, 157
Leggett (town) Edgecombe County, 117
Leicester (unincorporated) Buncombe County, 71
Leland (town) Brunswick County, 66
Lenoir (city) Caldwell County, 79
Lenoir County, 158
Lewiston Woodville (town) Bertie County, 61
Lewisville (town) Forsyth County, 120
Lexington (city) Davidson County, 110
Liberty (town) Randolph County, 201
Light Oak (CDP) Cleveland County, 95
Lilesville (town) Anson County, 54
Lillington (town) Harnett County, 140
Lincoln County, 159
Lincolnton (city) Lincoln County, 160
Linden (town) Cumberland County, 103
Linville (unincorporated) Avery County, 58
Linville Falls (unincorporated) Burke County, 74
Linwood (unincorporated) Davidson County, 110
Littleton (town) Halifax County, 137
Locust (city) Stanly County, 220
Long View (town) Catawba County, 87
Longwood (unincorporated) Brunswick County, 66
Louisburg (town) Franklin County, 123
Love Valley (town) Iredell County, 150
Lowell (city) Gaston County, 126
Lowesville (CDP) Lincoln County, 161
Lowgap (CDP) Surry County, 223
Lowland (unincorporated) Pamlico County, 189
Lucama (town) Wilson County, 249
Lumber Bridge (town) Robeson County, 205
Lumberton (city) Robeson County, 205
Macclesfield (town) Edgecombe County, 117
Macon (town) Warren County, 239
Macon County, 161
Madison (town) Rockingham County, 208
Madison County, 163
Maggie Valley (town) Haywood County, 142
Magnolia (town) Duplin County, 114
Maiden (town) Catawba County, 87
Mamers (CDP) Harnett County, 140
Manns Harbor (CDP) Dare County, 108
Manson (unincorporated) Vance County, 232
Manteo (town) Dare County, 108
Maple (unincorporated) Currituck County, 106
Maple Hill (unincorporated) Pender County, 192
Mar-Mac (CDP) Wayne County, 244
Marble (CDP) Cherokee County, 91
Margarettsville (unincorporated) Northampton County, 183
Marietta (town) Robeson County, 205
Marion (city) McDowell County, 166
Mars Hill (town) Madison County, 164
Marshall (town) Madison County, 164
Marshallberg (CDP) Carteret County, 82
Marshville (town) Union County, 229
Marston (unincorporated) Scotland County, 218

Martin County, 164
Marvin (village) Union County, 229
Matthews (town) Mecklenburg County, 169
Maury (CDP) Greene County, 131
Maxton (town) Robeson County, 205
Mayodan (town) Rockingham County, 208
Maysville (town) Jones County, 156
McAdenville (town) Gaston County, 126
McDonald (town) Robeson County, 206
McDowell County, 165
McFarlan (town) Anson County, 54
McGrady (unincorporated) Wilkes County, 246
McLeansville (CDP) Guilford County, 135
Mebane (city) Alamance County, 51
Mecklenburg County, 167
Merritt (unincorporated) Pamlico County, 190
Merry Hill (unincorporated) Bertie County, 62
Mesic (town) Pamlico County, 190
Micro (town) Johnston County, 155
Middleburg (town) Vance County, 233
Middlesex (town) Nash County, 176
Midland (town) Cabarrus County, 77
Midway (town) Davidson County, 110
Midway Park (unincorporated) Onslow County, 185
Mill Spring (unincorporated) Polk County, 199
Millers Creek (CDP) Wilkes County, 246
Millingport (CDP) Stanly County, 220
Mills River (town) Henderson County, 145
Milton (town) Caswell County, 84
Mineral Springs (town) Union County, 229
Minneapolis (unincorporated) Avery County, 58
Minnesott Beach (town) Pamlico County, 190
Mint Hill (town) Mecklenburg County, 169
Misenheimer (village) Stanly County, 220
Mitchell County, 170
Mocksville (town) Davie County, 112
Momeyer (town) Nash County, 176
Moncure (CDP) Chatham County, 90
Monroe (city) Union County, 229
Montgomery County, 171
Montreat (town) Buncombe County, 72
Moore County, 172
Mooresboro (town) Cleveland County, 95
Mooresville (town) Iredell County, 150
Moravian Falls (CDP) Wilkes County, 246
Morehead City (town) Carteret County, 82
Morganton (city) Burke County, 74
Morrisville (town) Wake County, 235
Morven (town) Anson County, 54
Mount Airy (city) Surry County, 224
Mount Gilead (town) Montgomery County, 171
Mount Holly (city) Gaston County, 126
Mount Olive (town) Wayne County, 244
Mount Pleasant (town) Cabarrus County, 77
Mount Ulla (unincorporated) Rowan County, 211
Mountain Home (CDP) Henderson County, 145
Mountain View (CDP) Catawba County, 87
Moyock (CDP) Currituck County, 106
Mulberry (CDP) Wilkes County, 246
Murfreesboro (town) Hertford County, 147
Murphy (town) Cherokee County, 91
Murraysville (CDP) New Hanover County, 179
Myrtle Grove (CDP) New Hanover County, 179
Nags Head (town) Dare County, 108
Nakina (unincorporated) Columbus County, 97
Nash County, 175
Nashville (town) Nash County, 176
Navassa (town) Brunswick County, 66
Nebo (unincorporated) McDowell County, 166
Neuse Forest (CDP) Craven County, 100
New Bern (city) Craven County, 100
New Hanover County, 178
New Hill (unincorporated) Wake County, 236

CDP = Census Designated Place

Sparta (town) Alleghany County, 54
Speed (town) Edgecombe County, 118
Spencer (town) Rowan County, 212
Spencer Mountain (town) Gaston County, 126
Spindale (town) Rutherford County, 215
Spivey's Corner (CDP) Sampson County, 217
Spring Hope (town) Nash County, 177
Spring Lake (town) Cumberland County, 104
Spruce Pine (town) Mitchell County, 171
Stacy (unincorporated) Carteret County, 84
Staley (town) Randolph County, 202
Stallings (town) Union County, 230
Stanfield (town) Stanly County, 221
Stanley (town) Gaston County, 127
Stanly County, 219
Stantonsburg (town) Wilson County, 249
Star (town) Montgomery County, 172
State Road (unincorporated) Wilkes County, 247
Statesville (city) Iredell County, 151
Stedman (town) Cumberland County, 104
Stella (unincorporated) Onslow County, 186
Stem (town) Granville County, 130
Stokes (CDP) Pitt County, 198
Stokes County, 221
Stokesdale (town) Guilford County, 135
Stoneville (town) Rockingham County, 209
Stonewall (town) Pamlico County, 190
Stony Point (CDP) Alexander County, 52
Stovall (town) Granville County, 130
Stumpy Point (unincorporated) Dare County, 109
Sugar Grove (unincorporated) Watauga County, 241
Sugar Mountain (village) Avery County, 58
Summerfield (town) Guilford County, 136
Sunbury (CDP) Gates County, 128
Sunset Beach (town) Brunswick County, 67
Supply (unincorporated) Brunswick County, 68
Surf City (town) Pender County, 193
Surry County, 222
Swain County, 224
Swan Quarter (CDP) Hyde County, 149
Swannanoa (CDP) Buncombe County, 72
Swanquarter (unincorporated) Hyde County, 149
Swansboro (town) Onslow County, 186
Swepsonville (town) Alamance County, 51
Sylva (town) Jackson County, 153
Tabor City (town) Columbus County, 97
Tar Heel (town) Bladen County, 64
Tarawa Terrace (unincorporated) Onslow County, 187
Tarboro (town) Edgecombe County, 118
Taylorsville (town) Alexander County, 52
Taylortown (town) Moore County, 175
Teachey (town) Duplin County, 114
Terrell (unincorporated) Catawba County, 88
Thomasville (city) Davidson County, 111
Thurmond (unincorporated) Wilkes County, 247
Timberlake (unincorporated) Person County, 195
Toast (CDP) Surry County, 224
Tobaccoville (village) Forsyth County, 120

Todd (unincorporated) Ashe County, 57
Topsail Beach (town) Pender County, 193
Topton (unincorporated) Macon County, 163
Transylvania County, 225
Traphill (unincorporated) Wilkes County, 247
Trent Woods (town) Craven County, 101
Trenton (town) Jones County, 157
Trinity (city) Randolph County, 202
Troutman (town) Iredell County, 151
Troy (town) Montgomery County, 172
Tryon (town) Polk County, 199
Tuckasegee (unincorporated) Jackson County, 153
Turkey (town) Sampson County, 217
Tyner (unincorporated) Chowan County, 92
Tyro (CDP) Davidson County, 111
Tyrrell County, 227
Union County, 227
Union Grove (unincorporated) Iredell County, 151
Union Mills (unincorporated) Rutherford County, 215
Unionville (town) Union County, 230
Valdese (town) Burke County, 75
Vale (unincorporated) Lincoln County, 161
Valle Crucis (CDP) Watauga County, 242
Valley Hill (CDP) Henderson County, 145
Vance County, 231
Vanceboro (town) Craven County, 101
Vandemere (town) Pamlico County, 190
Vander (CDP) Cumberland County, 104
Vann Crossroads (CDP) Sampson County, 217
Varnamtown (town) Brunswick County, 68
Vass (town) Moore County, 175
Vilas (unincorporated) Watauga County, 242
Waco (town) Cleveland County, 95
Wade (town) Cumberland County, 104
Wadesboro (town) Anson County, 55
Wagram (town) Scotland County, 219
Wake County, 233
Wake Forest (town) Wake County, 237
Wakulla (CDP) Robeson County, 207
Walkertown (town) Forsyth County, 121
Wallace (town) Duplin County, 114
Wallburg (town) Davidson County, 111
Walnut Cove (town) Stokes County, 222
Walnut Creek (village) Wayne County, 245
Walstonburg (town) Greene County, 131
Wanchese (CDP) Dare County, 109
Warne (unincorporated) Clay County, 93
Warren County, 238
Warrensville (unincorporated) Ashe County, 57
Warrenton (town) Warren County, 239
Warsaw (town) Duplin County, 115
Washington (city) Beaufort County, 60
Washington County, 239
Washington Park (town) Beaufort County, 60
Watauga County, 240
Watha (town) Pender County, 193
Waves (CDP) Dare County, 109
Waxhaw (town) Union County, 230

Wayne County, 242
Waynesville (town) Haywood County, 142
Weaverville (town) Buncombe County, 72
Webster (town) Jackson County, 153
Weddington (town) Union County, 231
Welcome (CDP) Davidson County, 111
Weldon (town) Halifax County, 138
Wendell (town) Wake County, 237
Wentworth (town) Rockingham County, 209
Wesley Chapel (village) Union County, 231
West Canton (CDP) Haywood County, 142
West End (unincorporated) Moore County, 175
West Jefferson (town) Ashe County, 57
West Marion (CDP) McDowell County, 167
Westfield (unincorporated) Surry County, 224
Westport (CDP) Lincoln County, 161
Whispering Pines (village) Moore County, 175
Whitakers (town) Edgecombe County, 118
White Lake (town) Bladen County, 64
White Oak (CDP) Bladen County, 64
White Plains (CDP) Surry County, 224
Whiteville (city) Columbus County, 98
Whitsett (town) Guilford County, 136
Whittier (unincorporated) Jackson County, 153
Wilkes County, 245
Wilkesboro (town) Wilkes County, 248
Willard (unincorporated) Pender County, 193
Williamston (town) Martin County, 165
Williston (unincorporated) Carteret County, 84
Willow Spring (unincorporated) Wake County, 237
Wilmington (city) New Hanover County, 181
Wilson (city) Wilson County, 249
Wilson County, 248
Wilson's Mills (town) Johnston County, 156
Windsor (town) Bertie County, 62
Winfall (town) Perquimans County, 194
Wingate (town) Union County, 231
Winnabow (unincorporated) Brunswick County, 68
Winston-Salem (city) Forsyth County, 121
Winterville (town) Pitt County, 198
Winton (town) Hertford County, 147
Woodfin (town) Buncombe County, 73
Woodland (town) Northampton County, 183
Woodlawn (CDP) Alamance County, 52
Woodleaf (unincorporated) Rowan County, 213
Wrightsboro (CDP) New Hanover County, 181
Wrightsville Beach (town) New Hanover County, 182
Yadkin County, 249
Yadkinville (town) Yadkin County, 250
Yancey County, 251
Yanceyville (town) Caswell County, 85
Youngsville (town) Franklin County, 123
Zebulon (town) Wake County, 238
Zionville (unincorporated) Watauga County, 242
Zirconia (unincorporated) Henderson County, 146

CDP = Census Designated Place

Sparta (town) Alleghany County, 54
Speed (town) Edgecombe County, 118
Spencer (town) Rowan County, 212
Spencer Mountain (town) Gaston County, 126
Spindale (town) Rutherford County, 215
Spivey's Corner (CDP) Sampson County, 217
Spring Hope (town) Nash County, 177
Spring Lake (town) Cumberland County, 104
Spruce Pine (town) Mitchell County, 171
Stacy (unincorporated) Carteret County, 84
Staley (town) Randolph County, 202
Stallings (town) Union County, 230
Stanfield (town) Stanly County, 221
Stanley (town) Gaston County, 127
Stanly County, 219
Stantonsburg (town) Wilson County, 249
Star (town) Montgomery County, 172
State Road (unincorporated) Wilkes County, 247
Statesville (city) Iredell County, 151
Stedman (town) Cumberland County, 104
Stella (unincorporated) Onslow County, 186
Stem (town) Granville County, 130
Stokes (CDP) Pitt County, 198
Stokes County, 221
Stokesdale (town) Guilford County, 135
Stoneville (town) Rockingham County, 209
Stonewall (town) Pamlico County, 190
Stony Point (CDP) Alexander County, 52
Stovall (town) Granville County, 130
Stumpy Point (unincorporated) Dare County, 109
Sugar Grove (unincorporated) Watauga County, 241
Sugar Mountain (village) Avery County, 58
Summerfield (town) Guilford County, 136
Sunbury (CDP) Gates County, 128
Sunset Beach (town) Brunswick County, 67
Supply (unincorporated) Brunswick County, 68
Surf City (town) Pender County, 193
Surry County, 222
Swain County, 224
Swan Quarter (CDP) Hyde County, 149
Swannanoa (CDP) Buncombe County, 72
Swanquarter (unincorporated) Hyde County, 149
Swansboro (town) Onslow County, 186
Swepsonville (town) Alamance County, 51
Sylva (town) Jackson County, 153
Tabor City (town) Columbus County, 97
Tar Heel (town) Bladen County, 64
Tarawa Terrace (unincorporated) Onslow County, 187
Tarboro (town) Edgecombe County, 118
Taylorsville (town) Alexander County, 52
Taylortown (town) Moore County, 175
Teachey (town) Duplin County, 114
Terrell (unincorporated) Catawba County, 88
Thomasville (city) Davidson County, 111
Thurmond (unincorporated) Wilkes County, 247
Timberlake (unincorporated) Person County, 195
Toast (CDP) Surry County, 224
Tobaccoville (village) Forsyth County, 120

Todd (unincorporated) Ashe County, 57
Topsail Beach (town) Pender County, 193
Topton (unincorporated) Macon County, 163
Transylvania County, 225
Traphill (unincorporated) Wilkes County, 247
Trent Woods (town) Craven County, 101
Trenton (town) Jones County, 157
Trinity (city) Randolph County, 202
Troutman (town) Iredell County, 151
Troy (town) Montgomery County, 172
Tryon (town) Polk County, 199
Tuckasegee (unincorporated) Jackson County, 153
Turkey (town) Sampson County, 217
Tyner (unincorporated) Chowan County, 92
Tyro (CDP) Davidson County, 111
Tyrrell County, 227
Union County, 227
Union Grove (unincorporated) Iredell County, 151
Union Mills (unincorporated) Rutherford County, 215
Unionville (town) Union County, 230
Valdese (town) Burke County, 75
Vale (unincorporated) Lincoln County, 161
Valle Crucis (CDP) Watauga County, 242
Valley Hill (CDP) Henderson County, 145
Vance County, 231
Vanceboro (town) Craven County, 101
Vandemere (town) Pamlico County, 190
Vander (CDP) Cumberland County, 104
Vann Crossroads (CDP) Sampson County, 217
Varnamtown (town) Brunswick County, 68
Vass (town) Moore County, 175
Vilas (unincorporated) Watauga County, 242
Waco (town) Cleveland County, 95
Wade (town) Cumberland County, 104
Wadesboro (town) Anson County, 55
Wagram (town) Scotland County, 219
Wake County, 233
Wake Forest (town) Wake County, 237
Wakulla (CDP) Robeson County, 207
Walkertown (town) Forsyth County, 121
Wallace (town) Duplin County, 114
Wallburg (town) Davidson County, 111
Walnut Cove (town) Stokes County, 222
Walnut Creek (village) Wayne County, 245
Walstonburg (town) Greene County, 131
Wanchese (CDP) Dare County, 109
Warne (unincorporated) Clay County, 93
Warren County, 238
Warrensville (unincorporated) Ashe County, 57
Warrenton (town) Warren County, 239
Warsaw (town) Duplin County, 115
Washington (city) Beaufort County, 60
Washington County, 239
Washington Park (town) Beaufort County, 60
Watauga County, 240
Watha (town) Pender County, 193
Waves (CDP) Dare County, 109
Waxhaw (town) Union County, 230

Wayne County, 242
Waynesville (town) Haywood County, 142
Weaverville (town) Buncombe County, 72
Webster (town) Jackson County, 153
Weddington (town) Union County, 231
Welcome (CDP) Davidson County, 111
Weldon (town) Halifax County, 138
Wendell (town) Wake County, 237
Wentworth (town) Rockingham County, 209
Wesley Chapel (village) Union County, 231
West Canton (CDP) Haywood County, 142
West End (unincorporated) Moore County, 175
West Jefferson (town) Ashe County, 57
West Marion (CDP) McDowell County, 167
Westfield (unincorporated) Surry County, 224
Westport (CDP) Lincoln County, 161
Whispering Pines (village) Moore County, 175
Whitakers (town) Edgecombe County, 118
White Lake (town) Bladen County, 64
White Oak (CDP) Bladen County, 64
White Plains (CDP) Surry County, 224
Whiteville (city) Columbus County, 98
Whitsett (town) Guilford County, 136
Whittier (unincorporated) Jackson County, 153
Wilkes County, 245
Wilkesboro (town) Wilkes County, 248
Willard (unincorporated) Pender County, 193
Williamston (town) Martin County, 165
Williston (unincorporated) Carteret County, 84
Willow Spring (unincorporated) Wake County, 237
Wilmington (city) New Hanover County, 181
Wilson (city) Wilson County, 249
Wilson County, 248
Wilson's Mills (town) Johnston County, 156
Windsor (town) Bertie County, 62
Winfall (town) Perquimans County, 194
Wingate (town) Union County, 231
Winnabow (unincorporated) Brunswick County, 68
Winston-Salem (city) Forsyth County, 121
Winterville (town) Pitt County, 198
Winton (town) Hertford County, 147
Woodfin (town) Buncombe County, 73
Woodland (town) Northampton County, 183
Woodlawn (CDP) Alamance County, 52
Woodleaf (unincorporated) Rowan County, 213
Wrightsboro (CDP) New Hanover County, 181
Wrightsville Beach (town) New Hanover County, 182
Yadkin County, 249
Yadkinville (town) Yadkin County, 250
Yancey County, 251
Yanceyville (town) Caswell County, 85
Youngsville (town) Franklin County, 123
Zebulon (town) Wake County, 238
Zionville (unincorporated) Watauga County, 242
Zirconia (unincorporated) Henderson County, 146

CDP = Census Designated Place

Comparative Statistics

This section compares the 100 largest cities by population in the state, by the following data points:

Population

Place	2000 Census	2010 Census	Growth 2000–2010 (%)
Albemarle city *Stanly Co.*	15,680	15,903	1.4
Apex town *Wake Co.*	20,212	37,476	85.4
Archdale city *Randolph Co.*	9,014	11,415	26.6
Asheboro city *Randolph Co.*	21,672	25,012	15.4
Asheville city *Buncombe Co.*	68,889	83,393	21.0
Belmont city *Gaston Co.*	8,705	10,076	15.7
Boone town *Watauga Co.*	13,472	17,122	27.0
Burlington city *Alamance Co.*	44,917	49,963	11.2
Carrboro town *Orange Co.*	16,782	19,582	16.6
Cary town *Wake Co.*	94,536	135,234	43.0
Chapel Hill town *Orange Co.*	48,715	57,233	17.4
Charlotte city *Mecklenburg Co.*	540,828	731,424	35.2
Clayton town *Johnston Co.*	6,973	16,116	131.1
Clemmons village *Forsyth Co.*	13,827	18,627	34.7
Clinton city *Sampson Co.*	8,600	8,639	0.4
Concord city *Cabarrus Co.*	55,977	79,066	41.2
Conover city *Catawba Co.*	6,604	8,165	23.6
Cornelius town *Mecklenburg Co.*	11,969	24,866	107.7
Davidson town *Mecklenburg Co.*	7,139	10,944	53.3
Dunn city *Harnett Co.*	9,196	9,263	0.7
Durham city *Durham Co.*	187,035	228,330	22.0
Eden city *Rockingham Co.*	15,908	15,527	-2.4
Elizabeth City city *Pasquotank Co.*	17,188	18,683	8.7
Elon town *Alamance Co.*	n/a	9,419	n/a
Fayetteville city *Cumberland Co.*	121,015	200,564	65.7
Fuquay-Varina town *Wake Co.*	7,898	17,937	127.1
Garner town *Wake Co.*	17,757	25,745	44.9
Gastonia city *Gaston Co.*	66,277	71,741	8.2
Goldsboro city *Wayne Co.*	39,043	36,437	-6.6
Graham city *Alamance Co.*	12,833	14,153	10.2
Greensboro city *Guilford Co.*	223,891	269,666	20.4
Greenville city *Pitt Co.*	60,476	84,554	39.8
Half Moon cdp *Onslow Co.*	6,645	8,352	25.6
Harrisburg town *Cabarrus Co.*	4,493	11,526	156.5
Havelock city *Craven Co.*	22,442	20,735	-7.6
Henderson city *Vance Co.*	16,095	15,368	-4.5
Hendersonville city *Henderson Co.*	10,420	13,137	26.0
Hickory city *Catawba Co.*	37,222	40,010	7.4
High Point city *Guilford Co.*	85,839	104,371	21.5
Holly Springs town *Wake Co.*	9,192	24,661	168.2
Hope Mills town *Cumberland Co.*	11,237	15,176	35.0
Huntersville town *Mecklenburg Co.*	24,960	46,773	87.3
Indian Trail town *Union Co.*	11,905	33,518	181.5
Jacksonville city *Onslow Co.*	66,715	70,145	5.1
Kannapolis city *Cabarrus Co.*	36,910	42,625	15.4
Kernersville town *Forsyth Co.*	17,126	23,123	35.0
Kings Mountain city *Cleveland Co.*	9,693	10,296	6.2
Kinston city *Lenoir Co.*	23,688	21,677	-8.4
Knightdale town *Wake Co.*	5,958	11,401	91.3
Laurinburg city *Scotland Co.*	15,874	15,962	0.5

Place	2000 Census	2010 Census	Growth 2000–2010 (%)
Leland town *Brunswick Co.*	1,938	13,527	597.9
Lenoir city *Caldwell Co.*	16,793	18,228	8.5
Lewisville town *Forsyth Co.*	8,826	12,639	43.2
Lexington city *Davidson Co.*	19,953	18,931	-5.1
Lincolnton city *Lincoln Co.*	9,965	10,486	5.2
Lumberton city *Robeson Co.*	20,795	21,542	3.5
Matthews town *Mecklenburg Co.*	22,127	27,198	22.9
Mebane city *Alamance Co.*	7,284	11,393	56.4
Mint Hill town *Mecklenburg Co.*	14,922	22,722	52.2
Monroe city *Union Co.*	26,228	32,797	25.0
Mooresville town *Iredell Co.*	18,823	32,711	73.7
Morehead City town *Carteret Co.*	7,691	8,661	12.6
Morganton city *Burke Co.*	17,310	16,918	-2.2
Morrisville town *Wake Co.*	5,208	18,576	256.6
Mount Airy city *Surry Co.*	8,484	10,388	22.4
Mount Holly city *Gaston Co.*	9,618	13,656	41.9
Murraysville cdp *New Hanover Co.*	7,279	14,215	95.2
Myrtle Grove cdp *New Hanover Co.*	7,125	8,875	24.5
New Bern city *Craven Co.*	23,128	29,524	27.6
Newton city *Catawba Co.*	12,560	12,968	3.2
Oxford city *Granville Co.*	8,338	8,461	1.4
Pinehurst village *Moore Co.*	9,706	13,124	35.2
Piney Green cdp *Onslow Co.*	11,658	13,293	14.0
Raleigh city *Wake Co.*	276,093	403,892	46.2
Reidsville city *Rockingham Co.*	14,485	14,520	0.2
Roanoke Rapids city *Halifax Co.*	16,957	15,754	-7.0
Rockingham city *Richmond Co.*	9,672	9,558	-1.1
Rocky Mount city *Nash Co.*	55,893	57,477	2.8
Roxboro city *Person Co.*	8,696	8,362	-3.8
Saint Stephens cdp *Catawba Co.*	9,439	8,759	-7.2
Salisbury city *Rowan Co.*	26,462	33,662	27.2
Sanford city *Lee Co.*	23,220	28,094	20.9
Shelby city *Cleveland Co.*	19,477	20,323	4.3
Smithfield town *Johnston Co.*	11,510	10,966	-4.7
Southern Pines town *Moore Co.*	10,918	12,334	12.9
Spring Lake town *Cumberland Co.*	8,098	11,964	47.7
Stallings town *Union Co.*	3,189	13,831	333.7
Statesville city *Iredell Co.*	23,320	24,532	5.2
Summerfield town *Guilford Co.*	7,018	10,232	45.8
Tarboro town *Edgecombe Co.*	11,138	11,415	2.4
Thomasville city *Davidson Co.*	19,788	26,757	35.2
Wake Forest town *Wake Co.*	12,588	30,117	139.2
Washington city *Beaufort Co.*	9,583	9,744	1.6
Waxhaw town *Union Co.*	2,625	9,859	275.5
Waynesville town *Haywood Co.*	9,232	9,869	6.9
Weddington town *Union Co.*	6,696	9,459	41.2
Wilmington city *New Hanover Co.*	75,838	106,476	40.4
Wilson city *Wilson Co.*	44,405	49,167	10.7
Winston-Salem city *Forsyth Co.*	185,776	229,617	23.6
Winterville town *Pitt Co.*	4,791	9,269	93.4

SOURCE: U.S. Census Bureau, Census 2010, Census 2000

Physical Characteristics

Place	Density (persons per square mile)	Land Area (square miles)	Water Area (square miles)	Elevation (feet)
Albemarle city *Stanly Co.*	949.9	16.74	0.13	476
Apex town *Wake Co.*	2,437.9	15.37	0.06	499
Archdale city *Randolph Co.*	1,389.8	8.21	0.02	866
Asheboro city *Randolph Co.*	1,349.6	18.53	0.09	840
Asheville city *Buncombe Co.*	1,855.9	44.93	0.30	2,129
Belmont city *Gaston Co.*	1,014.3	9.93	0.18	682
Boone town *Watauga Co.*	2,792.8	6.13	0.02	3,218
Burlington city *Alamance Co.*	1,985.1	25.17	0.21	650
Carrboro town *Orange Co.*	3,030.3	6.46	0.03	463
Cary town *Wake Co.*	2,488.4	54.35	1.09	495
Chapel Hill town *Orange Co.*	2,710.0	21.12	0.15	486
Charlotte city *Mecklenburg Co.*	2,457.1	297.68	1.99	761
Clayton town *Johnston Co.*	1,192.8	13.51	0.02	341
Clemmons village *Forsyth Co.*	1,577.3	11.81	0.21	840
Clinton city *Sampson Co.*	1,125.6	7.68	0.02	154
Concord city *Cabarrus Co.*	1,311.9	60.27	0.04	705
Conover city *Catawba Co.*	749.4	10.90	0.03	1,056
Cornelius town *Mecklenburg Co.*	2,058.4	12.08	0.30	784
Davidson town *Mecklenburg Co.*	1,902.9	5.75	0.25	820
Dunn city *Harnett Co.*	1,431.0	6.47	0.00	207
Durham city *Durham Co.*	2,126.6	107.37	0.91	400
Eden city *Rockingham Co.*	1,152.7	13.47	0.16	594
Elizabeth City city *Pasquotank Co.*	1,606.9	11.63	0.62	3
Elon town *Alamance Co.*	2,424.4	3.89	0.05	705
Fayetteville city *Cumberland Co.*	1,375.2	145.84	1.86	102
Fuquay-Varina town *Wake Co.*	1,483.6	12.09	0.06	390
Garner town *Wake Co.*	1,745.8	14.75	0.05	361
Gastonia city *Gaston Co.*	1,420.5	50.50	0.23	804
Goldsboro city *Wayne Co.*	1,294.8	28.14	0.02	108
Graham city *Alamance Co.*	1,471.6	9.62	0.07	636
Greensboro city *Guilford Co.*	2,131.5	126.52	5.29	827
Greenville city *Pitt Co.*	2,443.3	34.61	0.75	56
Half Moon cdp *Onslow Co.*	1,128.2	7.40	0.00	30
Harrisburg town *Cabarrus Co.*	1,273.4	9.05	0.00	630
Havelock city *Craven Co.*	1,230.7	16.85	0.80	23
Henderson city *Vance Co.*	1,807.0	8.50	0.01	505
Hendersonville city *Henderson Co.*	1,892.9	6.94	0.03	2,159
Hickory city *Catawba Co.*	1,346.8	29.71	0.09	1,148
High Point city *Guilford Co.*	1,939.9	53.80	1.64	922
Holly Springs town *Wake Co.*	1,642.7	15.01	0.12	440
Hope Mills town *Cumberland Co.*	2,186.0	6.94	0.10	112
Huntersville town *Mecklenburg Co.*	1,180.8	39.61	0.16	810
Indian Trail town *Union Co.*	1,545.4	21.69	0.17	699
Jacksonville city *Onslow Co.*	1,508.2	46.51	4.20	13
Kannapolis city *Cabarrus Co.*	1,334.6	31.94	0.56	801
Kernersville town *Forsyth Co.*	1,334.9	17.32	0.11	1,010
Kings Mountain city *Cleveland Co.*	835.6	12.32	0.25	1,007
Kinston city *Lenoir Co.*	1,180.7	18.36	0.16	43
Knightdale town *Wake Co.*	1,837.2	6.21	0.01	315
Laurinburg city *Scotland Co.*	1,274.9	12.52	0.16	223

Place	Density (persons per square mile)	Land Area (square miles)	Water Area (square miles)	Elevation (feet)
Leland town *Brunswick Co.*	683.8	19.78	0.09	23
Lenoir city *Caldwell Co.*	928.1	19.64	0.00	1,171
Lewisville town *Forsyth Co.*	904.8	13.97	0.23	974
Lexington city *Davidson Co.*	1,053.0	17.98	0.00	807
Lincolnton city *Lincoln Co.*	1,220.3	8.59	0.08	833
Lumberton city *Robeson Co.*	1,203.9	17.89	0.08	128
Matthews town *Mecklenburg Co.*	1,589.6	17.11	0.08	728
Mebane city *Alamance Co.*	1,363.3	8.36	0.12	676
Mint Hill town *Mecklenburg Co.*	949.8	23.92	0.23	787
Monroe city *Union Co.*	1,102.2	29.76	0.63	600
Mooresville town *Iredell Co.*	1,562.7	20.93	0.05	909
Morehead City town *Carteret Co.*	1,264.2	6.85	1.67	16
Morganton city *Burke Co.*	883.3	19.15	0.00	1,155
Morrisville town *Wake Co.*	2,249.4	8.26	0.05	302
Mount Airy city *Surry Co.*	891.4	11.65	0.14	1,099
Mount Holly city *Gaston Co.*	1,395.2	9.79	0.20	614
Murraysville cdp *New Hanover Co.*	1,652.2	8.60	0.07	36
Myrtle Grove cdp *New Hanover Co.*	1,323.7	6.70	0.51	26
New Bern city *Craven Co.*	1,045.9	28.23	1.45	10
Newton city *Catawba Co.*	941.8	13.77	0.05	1,007
Oxford city *Granville Co.*	1,398.9	6.05	0.00	482
Pinehurst village *Moore Co.*	939.7	13.97	0.59	525
Piney Green cdp *Onslow Co.*	977.9	13.59	0.09	39
Raleigh city *Wake Co.*	2,826.3	142.90	1.10	315
Reidsville city *Rockingham Co.*	965.0	15.05	1.48	804
Roanoke Rapids city *Halifax Co.*	1,584.0	9.95	0.04	157
Rockingham city *Richmond Co.*	1,247.2	7.66	0.03	282
Rocky Mount city *Nash Co.*	1,312.6	43.79	0.22	98
Roxboro city *Person Co.*	1,296.3	6.45	0.01	715
Saint Stephens cdp *Catawba Co.*	921.7	9.50	0.41	1,119
Salisbury city *Rowan Co.*	1,520.3	22.14	0.00	768
Sanford city *Lee Co.*	1,048.8	26.79	0.25	358
Shelby city *Cleveland Co.*	964.3	21.08	0.04	860
Smithfield town *Johnston Co.*	904.7	12.12	0.01	148
Southern Pines town *Moore Co.*	741.0	16.65	0.18	499
Spring Lake town *Cumberland Co.*	518.8	23.06	0.20	276
Stallings town *Union Co.*	1,748.8	7.91	0.06	748
Statesville city *Iredell Co.*	1,011.5	24.25	0.12	912
Summerfield town *Guilford Co.*	385.3	26.56	0.29	906
Tarboro town *Edgecombe Co.*	1,025.3	11.13	0.04	43
Thomasville city *Davidson Co.*	1,595.8	16.77	0.01	850
Wake Forest town *Wake Co.*	1,995.2	15.10	0.12	390
Washington city *Beaufort Co.*	1,190.0	8.19	0.84	7
Waxhaw town *Union Co.*	854.0	11.54	0.12	663
Waynesville town *Haywood Co.*	1,105.9	8.92	0.00	2,746
Weddington town *Union Co.*	542.3	17.44	0.37	728
Wilmington city *New Hanover Co.*	2,067.8	51.49	1.51	36
Wilson city *Wilson Co.*	1,710.3	28.75	0.85	112
Winston-Salem city *Forsyth Co.*	1,733.6	132.45	1.25	912
Winterville town *Pitt Co.*	2,015.7	4.60	0.00	69

SOURCE: U.S. Census Bureau, Census 2010

Population by Race/Hispanic Origin

Place	White[1] (%)	Black[1] (%)	Asian[1] (%)	AIAN[1,2] (%)	NHOPI[1,3] (%)	Two or More Races (%)	Hispanic[4] (%)
Albemarle city *Stanly Co.*	70.1	22.4	2.9	0.3	0.0	1.8	4.5
Apex town *Wake Co.*	79.5	7.6	7.1	0.3	0.1	2.5	7.1
Archdale city *Randolph Co.*	87.8	4.0	4.8	0.6	0.0	1.4	4.0
Asheboro city *Randolph Co.*	67.8	12.0	1.4	0.9	0.1	2.8	26.9
Asheville city *Buncombe Co.*	79.3	13.4	1.4	0.3	0.2	2.6	6.5
Belmont city *Gaston Co.*	83.6	8.9	4.1	0.3	0.2	1.6	3.5
Boone town *Watauga Co.*	92.0	3.5	1.6	0.2	0.0	1.7	3.3
Burlington city *Alamance Co.*	57.6	28.0	2.1	0.7	0.1	2.4	16.0
Carrboro town *Orange Co.*	70.9	10.1	8.2	0.4	0.0	2.9	13.8
Cary town *Wake Co.*	73.1	8.0	13.1	0.4	0.0	2.6	7.7
Chapel Hill town *Orange Co.*	72.8	9.7	11.9	0.3	0.0	2.7	6.4
Charlotte city *Mecklenburg Co.*	50.0	35.0	5.0	0.5	0.1	2.7	13.1
Clayton town *Johnston Co.*	69.5	21.8	1.4	0.4	0.0	2.1	10.7
Clemmons village *Forsyth Co.*	83.2	6.7	3.7	0.3	0.0	1.5	8.4
Clinton city *Sampson Co.*	48.9	40.5	1.1	1.2	0.0	2.2	9.2
Concord city *Cabarrus Co.*	70.4	17.8	2.6	0.3	0.1	2.3	12.3
Conover city *Catawba Co.*	78.1	9.2	4.2	0.2	0.0	2.5	12.2
Cornelius town *Mecklenburg Co.*	88.3	5.8	2.3	0.3	0.0	1.6	5.3
Davidson town *Mecklenburg Co.*	87.8	6.4	2.8	0.2	0.0	1.7	3.8
Dunn city *Harnett Co.*	50.2	42.5	0.8	1.0	0.1	2.2	5.3
Durham city *Durham Co.*	42.5	41.0	5.1	0.5	0.1	2.7	14.2
Eden city *Rockingham Co.*	71.2	23.8	0.7	0.4	0.2	1.9	4.8
Elizabeth City city *Pasquotank Co.*	39.5	54.0	1.2	0.4	0.1	2.3	5.0
Elon town *Alamance Co.*	86.7	8.5	2.0	0.1	0.0	1.6	2.6
Fayetteville city *Cumberland Co.*	45.7	41.9	2.6	1.1	0.4	4.9	10.1
Fuquay-Varina town *Wake Co.*	72.3	19.7	2.0	0.6	0.0	2.7	9.7
Garner town *Wake Co.*	57.8	32.9	1.8	0.5	0.0	2.3	9.9
Gastonia city *Gaston Co.*	63.0	27.8	1.3	0.4	0.0	2.2	9.6
Goldsboro city *Wayne Co.*	39.2	54.3	1.8	0.4	0.1	2.6	4.3
Graham city *Alamance Co.*	62.9	22.8	1.3	1.2	0.0	2.4	15.7
Greensboro city *Guilford Co.*	48.4	40.6	4.0	0.5	0.1	2.6	7.5
Greenville city *Pitt Co.*	56.3	37.0	2.4	0.4	0.0	2.2	3.8
Half Moon cdp *Onslow Co.*	68.1	20.8	2.2	0.7	0.4	5.2	9.8
Harrisburg town *Cabarrus Co.*	75.8	16.4	4.5	0.5	0.0	2.0	3.7
Havelock city *Craven Co.*	70.0	17.4	2.9	0.7	0.3	4.7	11.6
Henderson city *Vance Co.*	30.0	64.0	0.8	0.3	0.0	1.4	6.4
Hendersonville city *Henderson Co.*	79.7	9.2	1.2	0.4	0.3	2.2	13.5
Hickory city *Catawba Co.*	74.9	14.3	3.2	0.3	0.0	2.2	11.4
High Point city *Guilford Co.*	53.6	33.0	6.1	0.6	0.0	2.3	8.5
Holly Springs town *Wake Co.*	79.8	12.6	2.9	0.4	0.1	2.5	6.3
Hope Mills town *Cumberland Co.*	61.9	26.5	1.8	1.9	0.3	4.6	10.0
Huntersville town *Mecklenburg Co.*	82.8	9.4	2.7	0.3	0.0	2.1	7.4
Indian Trail town *Union Co.*	81.0	10.0	1.8	0.5	0.0	2.3	10.9
Jacksonville city *Onslow Co.*	67.7	20.0	2.5	0.7	0.3	4.7	13.0
Kannapolis city *Cabarrus Co.*	68.5	20.3	1.1	0.3	0.0	2.4	12.1
Kernersville town *Forsyth Co.*	77.8	12.6	1.9	0.5	0.0	2.3	9.7
Kings Mountain city *Cleveland Co.*	73.0	22.5	1.6	0.2	0.0	1.7	2.6
Kinston city *Lenoir Co.*	28.7	68.0	0.7	0.2	0.1	1.3	2.4
Knightdale town *Wake Co.*	50.0	38.3	1.7	0.6	0.1	3.5	11.4
Laurinburg city *Scotland Co.*	43.0	46.8	1.0	6.1	0.0	2.0	2.0

Place	White[1] (%)	Black[1] (%)	Asian[1] (%)	AIAN[1,2] (%)	NHOPI[1,3] (%)	Two or More Races (%)	Hispanic[4] (%)
Leland town Brunswick Co.	83.9	10.0	1.5	0.6	0.0	2.0	4.9
Lenoir city Caldwell Co.	78.4	12.7	0.9	0.4	0.1	2.4	9.0
Lewisville town Forsyth Co.	90.3	5.0	1.7	0.3	0.0	1.6	3.4
Lexington city Davidson Co.	54.7	28.4	2.9	0.7	0.0	2.6	16.3
Lincolnton city Lincoln Co.	76.6	13.7	0.6	0.3	0.0	2.8	16.0
Lumberton city Robeson Co.	40.8	37.2	2.4	13.1	0.2	2.7	6.7
Matthews town Mecklenburg Co.	81.8	9.6	4.2	0.3	0.0	1.9	5.8
Mebane city Alamance Co.	73.5	20.4	1.2	0.5	0.1	2.6	6.0
Mint Hill town Mecklenburg Co.	78.4	12.3	2.5	0.6	0.0	2.0	8.3
Monroe city Union Co.	52.0	25.2	0.9	0.6	0.0	2.6	29.4
Mooresville town Iredell Co.	80.2	10.9	3.3	0.5	0.0	2.4	6.9
Morehead City town Carteret Co.	82.0	10.7	1.6	0.5	0.2	2.5	6.9
Morganton city Burke Co.	70.1	12.2	2.4	0.9	1.5	2.9	16.4
Morrisville town Wake Co.	54.0	12.9	27.2	0.4	0.1	3.4	5.9
Mount Airy city Surry Co.	84.1	8.2	1.4	0.3	0.1	2.2	6.7
Mount Holly city Gaston Co.	80.4	12.7	2.4	0.4	0.1	1.6	5.5
Murraysville cdp New Hanover Co.	79.6	13.7	1.9	0.3	0.1	2.1	5.3
Myrtle Grove cdp New Hanover Co.	93.0	3.2	1.2	0.3	0.1	1.4	2.1
New Bern city Craven Co.	57.9	33.2	3.6	0.4	0.1	2.4	5.8
Newton city Catawba Co.	73.7	13.9	3.3	0.4	0.0	2.6	12.9
Oxford city Granville Co.	38.6	55.6	1.1	0.4	0.0	1.8	4.8
Pinehurst village Moore Co.	92.8	3.8	1.3	0.4	0.0	1.2	2.1
Piney Green cdp Onslow Co.	63.3	22.4	2.8	0.7	0.4	6.1	12.2
Raleigh city Wake Co.	57.5	29.3	4.3	0.5	0.0	2.6	11.4
Reidsville city Rockingham Co.	52.4	41.9	0.6	0.3	0.0	2.1	4.7
Roanoke Rapids city Halifax Co.	63.6	31.2	1.7	0.6	0.0	1.3	3.2
Rockingham city Richmond Co.	57.4	34.1	2.1	1.7	0.0	1.9	5.1
Rocky Mount city Nash Co.	33.5	61.3	1.0	0.6	0.0	1.6	3.7
Roxboro city Person Co.	44.9	46.8	0.4	0.6	0.0	2.1	8.7
Saint Stephens cdp Catawba Co.	82.8	4.2	4.4	0.3	0.1	2.2	10.3
Salisbury city Rowan Co.	52.4	37.7	1.6	0.4	0.0	2.0	10.6
Sanford city Lee Co.	55.2	27.6	1.1	0.8	0.0	2.8	25.6
Shelby city Cleveland Co.	54.7	41.3	0.8	0.4	0.0	1.7	3.1
Smithfield town Johnston Co.	56.9	27.2	0.8	0.5	0.1	1.9	19.3
Southern Pines town Moore Co.	71.7	24.0	0.8	0.6	0.1	1.4	3.9
Spring Lake town Cumberland Co.	47.2	36.3	3.0	1.1	0.5	6.9	15.4
Stallings town Union Co.	88.3	5.6	2.3	0.5	0.0	1.6	5.8
Statesville city Iredell Co.	54.8	34.5	1.9	0.3	0.0	2.4	10.9
Summerfield town Guilford Co.	89.9	4.4	2.2	0.4	0.0	1.5	4.3
Tarboro town Edgecombe Co.	47.2	48.4	0.5	0.1	0.1	0.8	4.9
Thomasville city Davidson Co.	68.3	19.6	1.1	0.7	0.0	2.1	14.4
Wake Forest town Wake Co.	77.3	15.3	2.9	0.4	0.0	2.4	5.6
Washington city Beaufort Co.	49.0	45.5	0.5	0.2	0.1	1.5	5.5
Waxhaw town Union Co.	82.1	11.2	2.0	0.1	0.0	2.9	6.4
Waynesville town Haywood Co.	92.4	2.4	0.4	0.6	0.1	1.3	5.7
Weddington town Union Co.	91.2	3.9	2.6	0.2	0.0	1.3	3.0
Wilmington city New Hanover Co.	73.5	19.9	1.2	0.5	0.1	2.2	6.1
Wilson city Wilson Co.	42.9	47.9	1.2	0.3	0.0	1.7	9.4
Winston-Salem city Forsyth Co.	51.2	34.7	2.0	0.4	0.1	2.4	14.7
Winterville town Pitt Co.	62.8	31.6	2.1	0.3	0.0	1.9	3.3

NOTE: (1) Exclude multiple race combinations; (2) American Indian/Alaska Native; (3) Native Hawaiian/Other Pacific Islander; (4) May be of any race
SOURCE: U.S. Census Bureau, Census 2010

Average Household Size, Age, and Male/Female Ratio

Place	Average Household Size (persons)	Median Age (years)	Age Under 18 (%)	Age 65 and Over (%)	Males per 100 Females
Albemarle city *Stanly Co.*	2.34	39.6	23.7	17.7	87.2
Apex town *Wake Co.*	2.82	34.3	33.0	5.7	94.7
Archdale city *Randolph Co.*	2.46	40.0	23.8	15.6	90.7
Asheboro city *Randolph Co.*	2.46	34.0	27.1	13.9	90.8
Asheville city *Buncombe Co.*	2.12	38.2	18.5	16.3	89.2
Belmont city *Gaston Co.*	2.47	37.0	23.1	10.9	94.1
Boone town *Watauga Co.*	2.08	21.5	5.1	6.8	92.4
Burlington city *Alamance Co.*	2.38	38.3	24.2	15.7	88.0
Carrboro town *Orange Co.*	2.27	30.1	21.5	5.3	93.7
Cary town *Wake Co.*	2.61	36.6	27.7	8.6	94.8
Chapel Hill town *Orange Co.*	2.35	25.6	17.4	9.2	87.2
Charlotte city *Mecklenburg Co.*	2.48	33.2	25.2	8.5	93.5
Clayton town *Johnston Co.*	2.65	33.4	30.9	8.5	90.6
Clemmons village *Forsyth Co.*	2.52	40.6	26.5	14.6	91.1
Clinton city *Sampson Co.*	2.27	42.1	21.9	20.6	90.5
Concord city *Cabarrus Co.*	2.68	34.9	28.4	10.6	93.1
Conover city *Catawba Co.*	2.39	39.8	23.2	17.0	89.7
Cornelius town *Mecklenburg Co.*	2.31	37.9	22.9	10.1	96.0
Davidson town *Mecklenburg Co.*	2.49	35.7	22.8	12.5	90.3
Dunn city *Harnett Co.*	2.29	41.0	23.7	18.8	82.8
Durham city *Durham Co.*	2.34	32.1	22.7	8.8	90.6
Eden city *Rockingham Co.*	2.29	41.2	22.9	18.1	84.2
Elizabeth City city *Pasquotank Co.*	2.38	31.3	22.4	13.9	84.5
Elon town *Alamance Co.*	2.35	21.8	10.5	16.4	77.1
Fayetteville city *Cumberland Co.*	2.45	29.9	25.8	9.7	93.6
Fuquay-Varina town *Wake Co.*	2.67	34.2	30.0	11.2	89.8
Garner town *Wake Co.*	2.49	37.1	24.4	11.8	90.5
Gastonia city *Gaston Co.*	2.52	38.0	24.7	13.6	89.6
Goldsboro city *Wayne Co.*	2.27	36.1	23.1	14.9	94.0
Graham city *Alamance Co.*	2.40	37.5	25.2	14.6	88.0
Greensboro city *Guilford Co.*	2.31	33.4	22.7	11.5	88.7
Greenville city *Pitt Co.*	2.18	26.0	18.7	8.3	84.6
Half Moon cdp *Onslow Co.*	2.85	27.8	29.8	6.3	94.1
Harrisburg town *Cabarrus Co.*	2.87	37.3	30.4	9.2	95.9
Havelock city *Craven Co.*	2.76	23.5	27.0	4.2	121.4
Henderson city *Vance Co.*	2.41	38.6	25.5	17.3	79.9
Hendersonville city *Henderson Co.*	1.96	48.7	17.8	30.2	80.9
Hickory city *Catawba Co.*	2.33	37.7	23.6	14.3	91.1
High Point city *Guilford Co.*	2.46	35.8	25.2	12.0	88.5
Holly Springs town *Wake Co.*	3.03	33.1	35.3	4.9	94.7
Hope Mills town *Cumberland Co.*	2.68	31.9	30.5	7.5	85.1
Huntersville town *Mecklenburg Co.*	2.67	35.2	28.9	6.8	96.2
Indian Trail town *Union Co.*	3.01	33.7	32.7	6.9	96.4
Jacksonville city *Onslow Co.*	2.69	22.9	23.4	5.4	142.6
Kannapolis city *Cabarrus Co.*	2.58	35.6	26.8	13.1	92.0
Kernersville town *Forsyth Co.*	2.29	38.5	23.7	13.1	88.4
Kings Mountain city *Cleveland Co.*	2.44	40.6	24.7	17.3	85.5
Kinston city *Lenoir Co.*	2.23	43.7	23.6	18.5	83.0
Knightdale town *Wake Co.*	2.67	32.6	29.4	6.4	87.3
Laurinburg city *Scotland Co.*	2.40	37.7	25.6	15.9	82.0

Place	Average Household Size (persons)	Median Age (years)	Age Under 18 (%)	Age 65 and Over (%)	Males per 100 Females
Leland town *Brunswick Co.*	2.32	38.9	20.4	15.0	93.2
Lenoir city *Caldwell Co.*	2.32	41.5	22.8	18.5	90.8
Lewisville town *Forsyth Co.*	2.56	43.4	25.0	12.7	94.3
Lexington city *Davidson Co.*	2.44	37.4	24.6	15.1	92.8
Lincolnton city *Lincoln Co.*	2.37	38.4	23.5	16.9	89.4
Lumberton city *Robeson Co.*	2.44	36.5	24.8	14.6	93.3
Matthews town *Mecklenburg Co.*	2.56	40.3	24.9	13.3	92.6
Mebane city *Alamance Co.*	2.41	35.8	26.6	10.8	85.9
Mint Hill town *Mecklenburg Co.*	2.65	41.8	24.2	14.7	95.5
Monroe city *Union Co.*	2.92	32.5	29.6	11.1	96.8
Mooresville town *Iredell Co.*	2.61	34.2	28.4	9.8	94.3
Morehead City town *Carteret Co.*	2.06	42.4	19.4	19.3	87.0
Morganton city *Burke Co.*	2.36	39.7	22.6	18.2	95.4
Morrisville town *Wake Co.*	2.43	32.5	27.0	4.3	96.7
Mount Airy city *Surry Co.*	2.13	45.8	20.2	22.7	84.5
Mount Holly city *Gaston Co.*	2.49	36.2	25.0	10.0	95.4
Murraysville cdp *New Hanover Co.*	2.45	33.1	23.9	8.0	94.5
Myrtle Grove cdp *New Hanover Co.*	2.48	43.6	21.5	15.9	95.1
New Bern city *Craven Co.*	2.25	38.8	22.8	17.9	87.5
Newton city *Catawba Co.*	2.45	38.1	24.2	15.9	91.4
Oxford city *Granville Co.*	2.36	41.4	23.4	19.4	79.4
Pinehurst village *Moore Co.*	2.13	57.6	16.1	37.7	87.2
Piney Green cdp *Onslow Co.*	2.74	26.5	28.3	6.3	97.2
Raleigh city *Wake Co.*	2.36	31.9	23.1	8.2	93.5
Reidsville city *Rockingham Co.*	2.27	41.7	22.1	17.8	82.5
Roanoke Rapids city *Halifax Co.*	2.42	37.9	26.3	14.8	84.8
Rockingham city *Richmond Co.*	2.30	38.2	25.4	16.2	87.0
Rocky Mount city *Nash Co.*	2.42	38.7	24.6	14.2	84.3
Roxboro city *Person Co.*	2.29	40.2	22.9	18.6	82.9
Saint Stephens cdp *Catawba Co.*	2.61	40.5	24.4	15.9	97.1
Salisbury city *Rowan Co.*	2.38	36.2	22.7	15.9	98.1
Sanford city *Lee Co.*	2.60	33.3	28.0	11.7	94.2
Shelby city *Cleveland Co.*	2.32	41.4	23.5	17.7	86.3
Smithfield town *Johnston Co.*	2.35	41.6	22.5	20.8	86.3
Southern Pines town *Moore Co.*	2.07	47.0	20.0	27.5	82.0
Spring Lake town *Cumberland Co.*	2.65	24.9	31.2	4.8	104.0
Stallings town *Union Co.*	2.71	38.4	27.7	10.4	93.8
Statesville city *Iredell Co.*	2.38	37.8	24.6	15.9	88.9
Summerfield town *Guilford Co.*	2.89	42.1	28.9	9.5	101.0
Tarboro town *Edgecombe Co.*	2.35	42.3	22.8	19.1	84.1
Thomasville city *Davidson Co.*	2.50	36.2	26.5	13.9	91.2
Wake Forest town *Wake Co.*	2.83	34.2	32.4	8.1	92.7
Washington city *Beaufort Co.*	2.23	41.6	22.5	18.7	79.9
Waxhaw town *Union Co.*	3.04	34.5	34.6	7.0	93.7
Waynesville town *Haywood Co.*	2.11	46.7	17.8	24.6	87.4
Weddington town *Union Co.*	3.02	43.3	29.5	9.4	101.1
Wilmington city *New Hanover Co.*	2.16	34.7	18.4	14.0	91.4
Wilson city *Wilson Co.*	2.43	37.2	25.3	14.1	87.1
Winston-Salem city *Forsyth Co.*	2.38	34.6	24.6	12.5	88.6
Winterville town *Pitt Co.*	2.71	34.3	29.2	8.7	87.3

SOURCE: U.S. Census Bureau, Census 2010

Foreign Born, Language Spoken, Disabled Persons, and Veterans

Place	Foreign Born (%)	Speak English Only at Home (%)	Individuals with a Disability (%)	Veterans (%)
Albemarle city *Stanly Co.*	3.70	91.9	18.2	7.1
Apex town *Wake Co.*	10.00	87.7	5.1	7.3
Archdale city *Randolph Co.*	7.30	90.1	13.1	10.3
Asheboro city *Randolph Co.*	16.50	75.2	14.0	9.1
Asheville city *Buncombe Co.*	6.90	91.0	13.1	9.7
Belmont city *Gaston Co.*	5.60	93.0	13.5	9.5
Boone town *Watauga Co.*	3.50	93.7	5.4	2.3
Burlington city *Alamance Co.*	8.90	86.0	15.8	9.4
Carrboro town *Orange Co.*	20.20	75.5	6.9	3.5
Cary town *Wake Co.*	19.30	76.9	5.7	6.7
Chapel Hill town *Orange Co.*	16.40	81.5	6.0	4.1
Charlotte city *Mecklenburg Co.*	15.00	80.3	8.7	7.2
Clayton town *Johnston Co.*	5.50	90.9	8.7	10.0
Clemmons village *Forsyth Co.*	10.00	85.2	7.2	11.2
Clinton city *Sampson Co.*	4.20	92.2	18.5	8.3
Concord city *Cabarrus Co.*	10.10	86.8	9.2	9.0
Conover city *Catawba Co.*	10.90	83.0	14.1	12.6
Cornelius town *Mecklenburg Co.*	8.90	88.9	7.3	8.7
Davidson town *Mecklenburg Co.*	6.50	93.4	7.8	5.9
Dunn city *Harnett Co.*	5.10	91.9	19.9	9.3
Durham city *Durham Co.*	14.60	79.8	10.4	6.4
Eden city *Rockingham Co.*	3.80	94.6	19.9	10.7
Elizabeth City city *Pasquotank Co.*	3.10	92.5	17.8	11.3
Elon town *Alamance Co.*	3.70	93.2	10.7	6.1
Fayetteville city *Cumberland Co.*	6.00	88.0	13.6	22.0
Fuquay-Varina town *Wake Co.*	8.90	88.8	9.2	11.6
Garner town *Wake Co.*	4.50	92.9	10.8	11.3
Gastonia city *Gaston Co.*	7.90	88.8	14.7	8.6
Goldsboro city *Wayne Co.*	4.90	92.5	16.8	15.4
Graham city *Alamance Co.*	11.20	80.9	13.3	10.9
Greensboro city *Guilford Co.*	10.70	86.3	9.9	7.6
Greenville city *Pitt Co.*	5.10	92.9	10.1	6.2
Half Moon cdp *Onslow Co.*	1.60	96.6	13.9	27.5
Harrisburg town *Cabarrus Co.*	6.40	91.3	5.5	8.7
Havelock city *Craven Co.*	6.10	88.6	12.1	29.0
Henderson city *Vance Co.*	6.50	91.8	24.2	8.8
Hendersonville city *Henderson Co.*	9.60	87.3	20.8	13.4
Hickory city *Catawba Co.*	9.70	86.7	11.6	7.5
High Point city *Guilford Co.*	12.10	85.0	12.4	7.9
Holly Springs town *Wake Co.*	7.70	92.3	6.5	10.2
Hope Mills town *Cumberland Co.*	5.90	87.4	13.2	18.0
Huntersville town *Mecklenburg Co.*	6.70	92.3	6.8	6.8
Indian Trail town *Union Co.*	8.80	87.0	7.2	8.6
Jacksonville city *Onslow Co.*	4.80	88.9	13.5	22.5
Kannapolis city *Cabarrus Co.*	7.10	88.2	12.4	9.6
Kernersville town *Forsyth Co.*	7.10	89.6	11.0	10.9
Kings Mountain city *Cleveland Co.*	1.00	97.9	21.4	10.1
Kinston city *Lenoir Co.*	2.00	95.8	23.2	9.4
Knightdale town *Wake Co.*	12.30	83.7	6.5	8.5
Laurinburg city *Scotland Co.*	2.30	96.5	20.4	9.4

Place	Foreign Born (%)	Speak English Only at Home (%)	Individuals with a Disability (%)	Veterans (%)
Leland town *Brunswick Co.*	5.70	90.9	11.6	12.9
Lenoir city *Caldwell Co.*	6.10	89.4	19.5	9.0
Lewisville town *Forsyth Co.*	4.10	94.6	8.9	12.1
Lexington city *Davidson Co.*	9.90	81.5	20.3	8.8
Lincolnton city *Lincoln Co.*	7.10	84.8	15.9	10.1
Lumberton city *Robeson Co.*	8.50	87.9	16.0	8.0
Matthews town *Mecklenburg Co.*	8.70	89.0	7.4	9.7
Mebane city *Alamance Co.*	5.70	93.1	9.7	8.9
Mint Hill town *Mecklenburg Co.*	7.80	89.8	10.2	11.3
Monroe city *Union Co.*	18.80	72.2	11.5	8.7
Mooresville town *Iredell Co.*	7.40	90.0	7.8	8.0
Morehead City town *Carteret Co.*	5.40	94.1	19.5	15.1
Morganton city *Burke Co.*	11.30	82.3	21.8	10.2
Morrisville town *Wake Co.*	27.40	64.9	5.5	7.1
Mount Airy city *Surry Co.*	7.40	90.5	20.0	10.6
Mount Holly city *Gaston Co.*	7.00	90.7	13.3	9.9
Murraysville cdp *New Hanover Co.*	6.70	92.0	10.5	11.7
Myrtle Grove cdp *New Hanover Co.*	3.40	93.5	11.9	11.8
New Bern city *Craven Co.*	6.40	89.8	18.7	13.9
Newton city *Catawba Co.*	10.10	83.8	19.1	8.6
Oxford city *Granville Co.*	2.90	95.1	23.4	8.4
Pinehurst village *Moore Co.*	5.20	94.8	16.1	22.6
Piney Green cdp *Onslow Co.*	5.60	91.6	11.9	23.4
Raleigh city *Wake Co.*	13.70	82.2	7.6	6.9
Reidsville city *Rockingham Co.*	2.80	97.0	20.1	9.8
Roanoke Rapids city *Halifax Co.*	1.50	96.4	19.0	8.4
Rockingham city *Richmond Co.*	3.90	93.7	18.0	9.6
Rocky Mount city *Nash Co.*	3.30	95.3	16.1	9.8
Roxboro city *Person Co.*	5.70	92.0	20.7	7.2
Saint Stephens cdp *Catawba Co.*	9.50	84.4	11.6	11.9
Salisbury city *Rowan Co.*	5.80	88.6	16.1	10.3
Sanford city *Lee Co.*	14.50	76.7	14.0	9.5
Shelby city *Cleveland Co.*	3.80	94.6	16.4	10.4
Smithfield town *Johnston Co.*	7.30	88.2	19.9	8.1
Southern Pines town *Moore Co.*	8.00	92.5	17.8	14.6
Spring Lake town *Cumberland Co.*	5.60	86.6	9.5	18.6
Stallings town *Union Co.*	8.00	87.5	11.6	8.5
Statesville city *Iredell Co.*	8.40	87.5	13.9	9.6
Summerfield town *Guilford Co.*	5.30	93.0	8.1	8.7
Tarboro town *Edgecombe Co.*	4.70	94.1	17.8	9.9
Thomasville city *Davidson Co.*	8.40	85.6	14.7	8.7
Wake Forest town *Wake Co.*	7.60	88.1	6.2	10.0
Washington city *Beaufort Co.*	2.60	96.5	21.1	8.9
Waxhaw town *Union Co.*	8.30	91.2	6.2	10.0
Waynesville town *Haywood Co.*	4.80	94.9	19.2	13.6
Weddington town *Union Co.*	8.90	87.5	4.6	9.7
Wilmington city *New Hanover Co.*	6.20	91.6	13.3	9.5
Wilson city *Wilson Co.*	7.20	89.6	14.9	10.3
Winston-Salem city *Forsyth Co.*	11.20	82.9	10.6	8.5
Winterville town *Pitt Co.*	3.90	93.1	11.1	8.2

SOURCE: U.S. Census Bureau, American Community Survey, 2009-2013 Five-Year Estimates

Five Largest Ancestry Groups

Place	Group 1	Group 2	Group 3	Group 4	Group 5
Albemarle city *Stanly Co.*	German (13.4%)	English (10.2%)	American (10.0%)	Irish (7.6%)	Scotch-Irish (3.2%)
Apex town *Wake Co.*	German (18.1%)	Irish (16.5%)	English (14.0%)	Italian (9.4%)	American (8.3%)
Archdale city *Randolph Co.*	German (13.9%)	English (13.5%)	American (12.1%)	Irish (10.0%)	Scottish (2.7%)
Asheboro city *Randolph Co.*	German (10.1%)	American (9.5%)	English (7.5%)	Irish (5.9%)	Scotch-Irish (1.8%)
Asheville city *Buncombe Co.*	German (14.4%)	English (14.3%)	Irish (12.5%)	American (11.7%)	Scotch-Irish (4.2%)
Belmont city *Gaston Co.*	German (16.8%)	Irish (14.2%)	American (13.4%)	English (11.6%)	Scotch-Irish (5.8%)
Boone town *Watauga Co.*	German (26.2%)	Irish (17.0%)	English (15.5%)	Scottish (6.8%)	American (5.9%)
Burlington city *Alamance Co.*	English (9.8%)	German (9.5%)	American (8.5%)	Irish (5.2%)	Scotch-Irish (3.1%)
Carrboro town *Orange Co.*	German (14.3%)	English (13.2%)	Irish (11.8%)	Italian (4.8%)	Scottish (4.7%)
Cary town *Wake Co.*	German (14.0%)	English (11.6%)	Irish (11.5%)	American (7.4%)	Italian (7.1%)
Chapel Hill town *Orange Co.*	English (15.0%)	German (14.4%)	Irish (10.6%)	Scottish (4.2%)	Italian (4.1%)
Charlotte city *Mecklenburg Co.*	German (9.7%)	Irish (7.6%)	English (7.5%)	American (4.8%)	Italian (3.5%)
Clayton town *Johnston Co.*	German (13.5%)	English (12.6%)	Irish (10.2%)	American (10.1%)	Italian (4.5%)
Clemmons village *Forsyth Co.*	German (17.4%)	English (14.7%)	Irish (12.6%)	American (10.4%)	Scottish (5.0%)
Clinton city *Sampson Co.*	American (8.4%)	English (7.6%)	Irish (5.0%)	German (4.1%)	Scottish (3.0%)
Concord city *Cabarrus Co.*	German (13.6%)	Irish (10.2%)	American (8.8%)	English (8.0%)	Italian (4.7%)
Conover city *Catawba Co.*	German (15.6%)	American (11.5%)	Irish (7.1%)	English (5.3%)	Italian (3.8%)
Cornelius town *Mecklenburg Co.*	German (21.8%)	English (12.9%)	Irish (12.3%)	Italian (7.9%)	American (6.9%)
Davidson town *Mecklenburg Co.*	German (21.6%)	English (16.1%)	Irish (15.6%)	Scottish (8.2%)	Italian (6.6%)
Dunn city *Harnett Co.*	American (9.9%)	English (7.7%)	African (5.4%)	Irish (5.2%)	Scottish (2.4%)
Durham city *Durham Co.*	English (7.7%)	German (7.6%)	Irish (5.6%)	American (4.6%)	Italian (2.8%)
Eden city *Rockingham Co.*	American (12.9%)	English (9.6%)	Irish (8.2%)	German (4.4%)	European (2.9%)
Elizabeth City city *Pasquotank Co.*	English (6.2%)	American (5.4%)	German (5.1%)	Irish (4.9%)	Italian (2.7%)
Elon town *Alamance Co.*	German (15.1%)	English (8.8%)	American (7.9%)	Irish (7.6%)	Italian (6.4%)
Fayetteville city *Cumberland Co.*	German (10.4%)	Irish (7.9%)	English (5.4%)	American (4.7%)	Italian (2.8%)
Fuquay-Varina town *Wake Co.*	German (15.3%)	Irish (14.5%)	English (12.2%)	American (10.1%)	Italian (6.2%)
Garner town *Wake Co.*	German (11.1%)	English (11.1%)	Irish (9.2%)	American (9.2%)	Italian (3.6%)
Gastonia city *Gaston Co.*	German (9.0%)	American (8.2%)	English (8.0%)	Irish (7.9%)	Scotch-Irish (3.6%)
Goldsboro city *Wayne Co.*	American (9.0%)	German (7.5%)	Irish (7.1%)	English (6.8%)	Italian (2.5%)
Graham city *Alamance Co.*	American (10.7%)	German (8.9%)	English (8.5%)	Irish (5.3%)	Scotch-Irish (4.4%)
Greensboro city *Guilford Co.*	English (8.1%)	German (7.6%)	Irish (5.8%)	American (5.4%)	Scotch-Irish (2.5%)
Greenville city *Pitt Co.*	Irish (9.1%)	English (8.6%)	German (7.8%)	American (4.6%)	Italian (3.7%)
Half Moon cdp *Onslow Co.*	German (22.0%)	Irish (12.8%)	English (5.0%)	American (4.8%)	African (3.1%)
Harrisburg town *Cabarrus Co.*	Irish (12.2%)	German (11.6%)	American (10.7%)	English (9.0%)	Italian (3.7%)
Havelock city *Craven Co.*	German (19.6%)	Irish (16.6%)	English (9.5%)	Italian (5.9%)	American (4.3%)
Henderson city *Vance Co.*	American (11.2%)	English (7.4%)	German (2.6%)	Irish (2.2%)	Scotch-Irish (0.8%)
Hendersonville city *Henderson Co.*	German (12.2%)	Irish (12.2%)	English (11.3%)	American (10.7%)	Scotch-Irish (5.3%)
Hickory city *Catawba Co.*	German (15.9%)	English (11.6%)	Irish (10.0%)	American (8.3%)	Scotch-Irish (3.1%)
High Point city *Guilford Co.*	German (9.1%)	English (7.8%)	Irish (7.0%)	American (6.2%)	Italian (3.2%)
Holly Springs town *Wake Co.*	German (17.6%)	Irish (14.8%)	English (12.3%)	Italian (11.8%)	American (7.1%)
Hope Mills town *Cumberland Co.*	Irish (9.7%)	American (8.6%)	German (7.4%)	English (5.9%)	Italian (4.1%)
Huntersville town *Mecklenburg Co.*	German (19.4%)	Irish (15.7%)	English (13.0%)	Italian (9.4%)	American (6.8%)
Indian Trail town *Union Co.*	German (14.2%)	Irish (12.3%)	American (10.0%)	English (9.5%)	Italian (7.0%)
Jacksonville city *Onslow Co.*	German (16.4%)	Irish (15.0%)	English (6.6%)	Italian (6.6%)	American (5.3%)
Kannapolis city *Cabarrus Co.*	German (10.9%)	American (9.4%)	Irish (6.8%)	English (5.8%)	Scotch-Irish (2.3%)
Kernersville town *Forsyth Co.*	English (12.6%)	German (11.2%)	American (9.4%)	Irish (8.7%)	Scotch-Irish (2.4%)
Kings Mountain city *Cleveland Co.*	American (29.3%)	German (12.3%)	Irish (8.1%)	English (6.1%)	Scotch-Irish (3.6%)
Kinston city *Lenoir Co.*	African (10.7%)	English (8.2%)	American (4.4%)	Irish (3.9%)	German (2.7%)
Knightdale town *Wake Co.*	German (9.7%)	African (7.8%)	Irish (7.0%)	English (6.2%)	American (4.5%)
Laurinburg city *Scotland Co.*	English (6.5%)	American (6.0%)	German (4.5%)	Irish (3.2%)	Scottish (3.0%)

Place	Group 1	Group 2	Group 3	Group 4	Group 5
Leland town *Brunswick Co.*	German (14.8%)	American (14.1%)	Irish (13.4%)	English (10.7%)	Italian (7.3%)
Lenoir city *Caldwell Co.*	American (14.3%)	German (11.1%)	English (9.6%)	Irish (8.6%)	Scotch-Irish (2.6%)
Lewisville town *Forsyth Co.*	English (15.6%)	Irish (14.7%)	German (13.3%)	American (12.7%)	Italian (5.1%)
Lexington city *Davidson Co.*	German (11.3%)	Irish (8.5%)	English (7.9%)	American (6.6%)	Scotch-Irish (1.6%)
Lincolnton city *Lincoln Co.*	German (16.8%)	Irish (11.1%)	American (10.9%)	English (10.8%)	Dutch (3.6%)
Lumberton city *Robeson Co.*	American (21.0%)	English (6.6%)	German (3.6%)	Irish (3.1%)	Scotch-Irish (2.2%)
Matthews town *Mecklenburg Co.*	German (16.6%)	Irish (14.2%)	English (12.9%)	American (9.0%)	Italian (6.8%)
Mebane city *Alamance Co.*	German (14.5%)	English (13.7%)	Irish (10.1%)	American (9.0%)	French (4.5%)
Mint Hill town *Mecklenburg Co.*	German (16.9%)	Irish (13.1%)	English (11.0%)	American (10.0%)	Scotch-Irish (5.4%)
Monroe city *Union Co.*	German (9.7%)	American (7.4%)	English (6.9%)	Irish (6.0%)	Scotch-Irish (2.2%)
Mooresville town *Iredell Co.*	German (16.2%)	Irish (12.5%)	English (9.4%)	American (8.3%)	Italian (5.7%)
Morehead City town *Carteret Co.*	English (15.6%)	American (13.8%)	Irish (11.7%)	German (9.8%)	Scotch-Irish (4.3%)
Morganton city *Burke Co.*	American (13.9%)	German (12.9%)	Irish (8.1%)	English (7.9%)	Scottish (5.4%)
Morrisville town *Wake Co.*	German (10.1%)	English (7.7%)	Irish (7.6%)	Italian (4.8%)	American (3.0%)
Mount Airy city *Surry Co.*	American (16.4%)	English (11.2%)	German (8.5%)	Irish (5.7%)	Scotch-Irish (3.9%)
Mount Holly city *Gaston Co.*	American (15.6%)	German (14.6%)	Irish (7.2%)	English (6.1%)	Scottish (4.0%)
Murraysville cdp *New Hanover Co.*	American (21.4%)	German (12.2%)	Irish (10.6%)	English (10.5%)	Italian (5.4%)
Myrtle Grove cdp *New Hanover Co.*	English (16.5%)	German (16.0%)	American (15.3%)	Irish (10.7%)	Italian (8.5%)
New Bern city *Craven Co.*	English (12.2%)	Irish (10.9%)	German (9.7%)	American (6.5%)	Scotch-Irish (3.7%)
Newton city *Catawba Co.*	German (13.3%)	American (12.1%)	Irish (9.8%)	English (7.4%)	Italian (2.6%)
Oxford city *Granville Co.*	American (14.9%)	English (8.4%)	Irish (4.5%)	German (4.1%)	Italian (1.6%)
Pinehurst village *Moore Co.*	German (18.8%)	English (17.9%)	Irish (17.3%)	American (9.9%)	Italian (7.8%)
Piney Green cdp *Onslow Co.*	German (17.1%)	Irish (10.8%)	English (8.3%)	American (7.4%)	Italian (3.9%)
Raleigh city *Wake Co.*	English (9.9%)	German (9.8%)	American (9.7%)	Irish (8.2%)	Italian (3.9%)
Reidsville city *Rockingham Co.*	English (9.8%)	American (8.6%)	Irish (7.0%)	German (6.3%)	European (2.8%)
Roanoke Rapids city *Halifax Co.*	English (15.7%)	American (10.3%)	Irish (7.9%)	German (5.0%)	Italian (2.3%)
Rockingham city *Richmond Co.*	American (10.5%)	English (6.5%)	German (6.0%)	Irish (5.5%)	Scotch-Irish (4.9%)
Rocky Mount city *Nash Co.*	English (7.8%)	American (7.6%)	German (4.1%)	Irish (3.9%)	Scotch-Irish (1.6%)
Roxboro city *Person Co.*	American (9.8%)	English (7.7%)	Irish (6.3%)	Scotch-Irish (2.3%)	German (2.2%)
Saint Stephens cdp *Catawba Co.*	German (15.2%)	American (13.4%)	English (9.7%)	Irish (7.6%)	Scottish (3.4%)
Salisbury city *Rowan Co.*	German (11.2%)	American (11.0%)	Irish (6.5%)	English (6.5%)	Scotch-Irish (3.0%)
Sanford city *Lee Co.*	American (8.9%)	English (8.7%)	German (6.9%)	Irish (6.0%)	Scotch-Irish (2.9%)
Shelby city *Cleveland Co.*	American (18.2%)	German (7.7%)	English (7.4%)	Irish (4.6%)	Scotch-Irish (3.0%)
Smithfield town *Johnston Co.*	American (21.0%)	English (12.4%)	Irish (4.9%)	German (2.4%)	Scotch-Irish (2.2%)
Southern Pines town *Moore Co.*	German (15.9%)	American (14.6%)	English (11.0%)	Irish (9.6%)	Scottish (6.8%)
Spring Lake town *Cumberland Co.*	Irish (9.8%)	German (9.5%)	Italian (6.4%)	American (4.8%)	English (4.0%)
Stallings town *Union Co.*	German (18.2%)	English (13.3%)	Irish (11.7%)	American (10.7%)	Scotch-Irish (5.4%)
Statesville city *Iredell Co.*	German (10.3%)	Irish (8.5%)	American (8.1%)	English (7.8%)	Scotch-Irish (3.7%)
Summerfield town *Guilford Co.*	German (18.7%)	English (15.7%)	American (14.9%)	Irish (9.4%)	Italian (4.2%)
Tarboro town *Edgecombe Co.*	American (12.3%)	English (7.3%)	Irish (4.3%)	German (2.4%)	European (2.3%)
Thomasville city *Davidson Co.*	German (9.2%)	American (8.7%)	English (7.6%)	Irish (7.5%)	Scottish (1.7%)
Wake Forest town *Wake Co.*	Irish (16.2%)	German (14.0%)	English (13.0%)	Italian (7.5%)	American (7.1%)
Washington city *Beaufort Co.*	English (12.1%)	American (6.0%)	Irish (5.7%)	German (5.1%)	Italian (1.7%)
Waxhaw town *Union Co.*	Irish (15.2%)	German (14.3%)	English (10.7%)	American (10.0%)	Italian (6.9%)
Waynesville town *Haywood Co.*	American (30.0%)	German (14.3%)	Irish (11.1%)	English (8.5%)	Scotch-Irish (5.8%)
Weddington town *Union Co.*	German (15.2%)	Irish (13.3%)	English (12.6%)	American (11.4%)	Scotch-Irish (7.5%)
Wilmington city *New Hanover Co.*	American (20.0%)	English (10.9%)	German (10.4%)	Irish (10.1%)	Italian (4.2%)
Wilson city *Wilson Co.*	American (16.1%)	English (8.5%)	Irish (4.7%)	German (4.5%)	Scottish (1.7%)
Winston-Salem city *Forsyth Co.*	English (9.6%)	German (8.8%)	Irish (6.5%)	American (5.1%)	Italian (2.4%)
Winterville town *Pitt Co.*	German (10.5%)	Irish (9.4%)	American (9.1%)	English (8.4%)	Scotch-Irish (3.6%)

NOTE: "French" excludes Basque; Please refer to the User Guide for more information.
SOURCE: U.S. Census Bureau, American Community Survey, 2009-2013 Five-Year Estimates

Marriage Status

Place	Never Married (%)	Now Married[1] (%)	Separated (%)	Widowed (%)	Divorced (%)
Albemarle city *Stanly Co.*	29.1	44.6	2.3	10.7	15.6
Apex town *Wake Co.*	25.0	63.6	1.5	2.6	8.8
Archdale city *Randolph Co.*	20.8	58.8	3.3	5.1	15.2
Asheboro city *Randolph Co.*	29.5	49.7	5.6	8.3	12.5
Asheville city *Buncombe Co.*	35.9	41.6	3.4	7.6	14.9
Belmont city *Gaston Co.*	29.4	52.0	3.2	5.9	12.7
Boone town *Watauga Co.*	81.7	11.8	0.2	2.3	4.2
Burlington city *Alamance Co.*	30.7	48.3	3.9	7.3	13.7
Carrboro town *Orange Co.*	44.3	44.0	2.0	3.2	8.4
Cary town *Wake Co.*	26.5	62.4	1.4	3.7	7.3
Chapel Hill town *Orange Co.*	54.7	37.5	1.4	2.7	5.0
Charlotte city *Mecklenburg Co.*	38.9	46.3	3.1	4.6	10.3
Clayton town *Johnston Co.*	24.6	56.3	4.0	6.4	12.7
Clemmons village *Forsyth Co.*	22.2	62.5	2.5	5.4	10.0
Clinton city *Sampson Co.*	32.7	43.4	5.0	11.1	12.8
Concord city *Cabarrus Co.*	28.1	55.9	2.4	5.0	11.1
Conover city *Catawba Co.*	24.6	54.8	2.6	6.6	14.0
Cornelius town *Mecklenburg Co.*	27.2	55.9	1.6	4.6	12.3
Davidson town *Mecklenburg Co.*	37.7	50.8	3.2	2.9	8.7
Dunn city *Harnett Co.*	34.7	41.5	3.8	11.2	12.6
Durham city *Durham Co.*	41.5	43.6	2.9	4.7	10.2
Eden city *Rockingham Co.*	30.6	43.8	5.9	9.0	16.6
Elizabeth City city *Pasquotank Co.*	44.4	36.5	4.7	7.2	12.0
Elon town *Alamance Co.*	56.4	33.2	1.5	7.5	2.9
Fayetteville city *Cumberland Co.*	32.6	49.5	3.8	5.3	12.6
Fuquay-Varina town *Wake Co.*	24.0	61.6	4.0	5.3	9.0
Garner town *Wake Co.*	26.4	55.4	4.9	7.3	10.9
Gastonia city *Gaston Co.*	34.3	47.6	3.8	7.1	11.0
Goldsboro city *Wayne Co.*	35.3	43.4	6.2	8.3	13.0
Graham city *Alamance Co.*	28.7	49.6	4.7	8.7	12.9
Greensboro city *Guilford Co.*	41.2	42.1	3.0	5.8	10.8
Greenville city *Pitt Co.*	55.2	32.2	2.2	4.2	8.4
Half Moon cdp *Onslow Co.*	24.4	63.7	2.6	3.3	8.6
Harrisburg town *Cabarrus Co.*	23.3	66.9	1.3	2.6	7.2
Havelock city *Craven Co.*	32.0	57.3	3.3	2.1	8.6
Henderson city *Vance Co.*	40.5	36.9	5.2	9.7	12.9
Hendersonville city *Henderson Co.*	23.7	48.1	2.6	14.0	14.3
Hickory city *Catawba Co.*	34.9	44.4	3.0	8.0	12.7
High Point city *Guilford Co.*	35.5	46.6	3.8	6.3	11.5
Holly Springs town *Wake Co.*	17.9	70.5	1.5	2.5	9.1
Hope Mills town *Cumberland Co.*	26.8	53.5	3.2	6.5	13.2
Huntersville town *Mecklenburg Co.*	24.4	64.0	1.3	3.7	7.9
Indian Trail town *Union Co.*	23.4	66.3	2.4	3.1	7.2
Jacksonville city *Onslow Co.*	37.0	51.7	3.2	3.6	7.7
Kannapolis city *Cabarrus Co.*	29.8	51.6	4.0	6.8	11.8
Kernersville town *Forsyth Co.*	23.6	56.8	3.4	6.8	12.8
Kings Mountain city *Cleveland Co.*	28.2	51.1	6.8	8.5	12.2
Kinston city *Lenoir Co.*	37.9	39.0	6.2	10.7	12.4
Knightdale town *Wake Co.*	25.6	60.2	3.2	4.8	9.4
Laurinburg city *Scotland Co.*	35.3	40.1	5.8	10.3	14.2

Place	Never Married (%)	Now Married[1] (%)	Separated (%)	Widowed (%)	Divorced (%)
Leland town *Brunswick Co.*	18.8	65.3	2.6	3.8	12.1
Lenoir city *Caldwell Co.*	26.0	46.6	4.8	9.8	17.5
Lewisville town *Forsyth Co.*	21.4	63.3	1.4	5.4	9.9
Lexington city *Davidson Co.*	32.0	46.8	5.6	7.7	13.6
Lincolnton city *Lincoln Co.*	28.2	47.1	3.9	10.8	13.8
Lumberton city *Robeson Co.*	38.6	41.4	4.9	8.4	11.6
Matthews town *Mecklenburg Co.*	24.2	61.2	1.8	5.4	9.2
Mebane city *Alamance Co.*	27.9	56.5	3.7	5.3	10.3
Mint Hill town *Mecklenburg Co.*	24.9	62.9	1.7	4.1	8.1
Monroe city *Union Co.*	31.5	50.9	2.5	7.3	10.3
Mooresville town *Iredell Co.*	28.7	56.0	2.3	4.9	10.4
Morehead City town *Carteret Co.*	24.8	47.7	3.7	9.8	17.6
Morganton city *Burke Co.*	34.1	42.3	3.3	9.4	14.1
Morrisville town *Wake Co.*	23.3	64.3	2.5	2.7	9.8
Mount Airy city *Surry Co.*	19.3	56.9	6.7	12.1	11.6
Mount Holly city *Gaston Co.*	26.0	55.5	3.9	5.7	12.8
Murraysville cdp *New Hanover Co.*	31.5	54.0	1.4	5.0	9.6
Myrtle Grove cdp *New Hanover Co.*	23.6	61.1	2.1	6.4	9.0
New Bern city *Craven Co.*	28.9	50.3	5.0	8.9	12.0
Newton city *Catawba Co.*	33.0	44.7	3.7	10.0	12.3
Oxford city *Granville Co.*	35.4	43.0	6.9	9.3	12.4
Pinehurst village *Moore Co.*	11.7	72.3	1.2	10.2	5.8
Piney Green cdp *Onslow Co.*	26.3	58.9	2.2	2.9	11.9
Raleigh city *Wake Co.*	42.0	43.8	2.9	3.9	10.3
Reidsville city *Rockingham Co.*	27.1	51.3	7.1	9.5	12.1
Roanoke Rapids city *Halifax Co.*	29.4	49.5	4.2	10.0	11.2
Rockingham city *Richmond Co.*	33.7	49.8	6.2	8.3	8.3
Rocky Mount city *Nash Co.*	36.9	43.2	5.2	8.2	11.6
Roxboro city *Person Co.*	45.3	31.1	3.8	12.5	11.0
Saint Stephens cdp *Catawba Co.*	22.6	55.9	1.8	9.1	12.4
Salisbury city *Rowan Co.*	37.4	40.7	4.8	9.2	12.6
Sanford city *Lee Co.*	35.3	46.8	3.4	8.0	9.9
Shelby city *Cleveland Co.*	35.7	44.9	3.3	9.1	10.2
Smithfield town *Johnston Co.*	27.3	45.7	5.3	13.5	13.5
Southern Pines town *Moore Co.*	25.5	51.3	4.9	13.4	9.8
Spring Lake town *Cumberland Co.*	28.1	59.0	4.4	1.6	11.2
Stallings town *Union Co.*	22.2	64.2	1.5	4.7	8.8
Statesville city *Iredell Co.*	34.4	45.1	4.2	7.4	13.0
Summerfield town *Guilford Co.*	18.5	68.7	1.1	4.9	7.9
Tarboro town *Edgecombe Co.*	34.9	44.6	6.1	10.7	9.7
Thomasville city *Davidson Co.*	30.2	44.6	2.9	9.6	15.5
Wake Forest town *Wake Co.*	22.0	65.9	1.3	4.2	7.8
Washington city *Beaufort Co.*	30.2	41.3	3.5	12.7	15.8
Waxhaw town *Union Co.*	20.8	70.2	2.1	4.4	4.6
Waynesville town *Haywood Co.*	22.9	50.3	3.3	10.8	16.0
Weddington town *Union Co.*	24.0	68.5	2.3	3.4	4.1
Wilmington city *New Hanover Co.*	41.2	41.4	2.9	5.6	11.9
Wilson city *Wilson Co.*	35.1	45.9	3.6	8.3	10.8
Winston-Salem city *Forsyth Co.*	38.4	44.1	3.0	6.7	10.8
Winterville town *Pitt Co.*	25.3	59.3	2.1	5.1	10.3

NOTE: (1) Includes separated.
SOURCE: U.S. Census Bureau, American Community Survey, 2009-2013 Five-Year Estimates

Employment by Occupation

Place	MBF[1] (%)	CES[2] (%)	ELCAM[3] (%)	HPT[4] (%)	S[5] (%)	SO[6] (%)	NRCM[7] (%)	PTMM[8] (%)
Albemarle city *Stanly Co.*	8.3	2.7	12.4	2.7	24.9	26.0	11.0	12.1
Apex town *Wake Co.*	25.3	16.9	12.9	5.9	12.0	20.6	3.2	3.2
Archdale city *Randolph Co.*	13.1	2.0	7.5	4.7	13.5	30.6	9.1	19.5
Asheboro city *Randolph Co.*	9.5	2.8	10.8	4.1	16.4	20.5	7.0	28.9
Asheville city *Buncombe Co.*	13.8	4.9	14.9	8.1	21.2	22.8	5.9	8.5
Belmont city *Gaston Co.*	17.9	3.8	14.8	7.1	15.7	25.7	4.8	10.2
Boone town *Watauga Co.*	5.8	2.5	13.9	2.2	39.7	29.8	3.3	2.8
Burlington city *Alamance Co.*	12.3	4.5	9.2	5.4	18.8	24.7	7.3	17.7
Carrboro town *Orange Co.*	15.5	11.8	24.3	9.3	18.8	13.4	3.7	3.2
Cary town *Wake Co.*	23.8	17.5	11.7	6.4	12.2	20.6	3.4	4.5
Chapel Hill town *Orange Co.*	14.7	13.3	22.9	11.2	14.7	17.7	2.8	2.7
Charlotte city *Mecklenburg Co.*	18.7	6.0	10.6	4.8	16.8	25.9	7.1	10.2
Clayton town *Johnston Co.*	14.1	7.3	14.2	6.8	11.1	25.8	12.3	8.5
Clemmons village *Forsyth Co.*	19.0	7.7	13.7	9.6	15.1	21.3	5.0	8.6
Clinton city *Sampson Co.*	15.8	1.5	11.3	7.1	16.8	23.5	5.9	18.1
Concord city *Cabarrus Co.*	17.5	5.7	9.9	6.0	16.0	25.3	8.7	10.8
Conover city *Catawba Co.*	15.4	3.5	7.3	6.6	13.8	23.2	5.2	25.0
Cornelius town *Mecklenburg Co.*	25.4	7.0	9.8	6.3	16.9	26.0	3.1	5.5
Davidson town *Mecklenburg Co.*	25.5	7.6	16.1	8.9	15.8	19.8	3.2	3.2
Dunn city *Harnett Co.*	10.7	1.0	11.7	4.7	24.2	25.9	9.1	12.7
Durham city *Durham Co.*	14.4	10.0	15.6	9.6	17.5	19.2	6.9	6.7
Eden city *Rockingham Co.*	5.5	3.2	6.1	6.3	24.6	20.6	9.6	24.1
Elizabeth City city *Pasquotank Co.*	10.4	1.9	12.9	5.8	28.3	22.0	7.4	11.2
Elon town *Alamance Co.*	20.3	4.8	13.6	6.7	16.0	29.7	3.2	5.8
Fayetteville city *Cumberland Co.*	11.0	2.7	13.2	7.0	21.3	26.5	7.5	10.8
Fuquay-Varina town *Wake Co.*	16.1	9.4	13.4	5.7	14.8	23.2	7.3	10.2
Garner town *Wake Co.*	16.5	7.1	9.7	6.6	16.9	25.4	7.2	10.5
Gastonia city *Gaston Co.*	11.5	3.1	9.9	4.7	18.1	24.4	7.7	20.7
Goldsboro city *Wayne Co.*	10.0	3.0	11.4	7.5	19.7	22.3	8.2	18.0
Graham city *Alamance Co.*	9.9	2.3	9.1	4.4	16.3	27.8	10.5	19.5
Greensboro city *Guilford Co.*	14.1	4.1	12.0	5.7	18.0	27.3	6.4	12.5
Greenville city *Pitt Co.*	12.1	4.3	15.2	9.5	22.9	23.6	3.8	8.6
Half Moon cdp *Onslow Co.*	11.9	1.3	12.9	4.7	19.5	32.0	9.4	8.2
Harrisburg town *Cabarrus Co.*	23.3	7.2	13.0	3.3	12.9	26.8	6.6	6.9
Havelock city *Craven Co.*	6.7	4.0	6.1	6.3	21.4	27.1	18.0	10.3
Henderson city *Vance Co.*	10.0	0.8	10.0	4.4	21.6	24.8	8.5	19.8
Hendersonville city *Henderson Co.*	13.7	2.3	12.2	6.1	18.5	25.4	10.2	12.0
Hickory city *Catawba Co.*	15.8	3.9	10.5	6.7	19.1	22.4	5.6	16.0
High Point city *Guilford Co.*	13.9	4.1	10.2	4.7	18.2	27.6	5.4	15.9
Holly Springs town *Wake Co.*	21.2	14.1	15.4	7.5	9.8	20.8	5.7	5.5
Hope Mills town *Cumberland Co.*	12.0	2.2	14.8	5.6	17.9	26.9	7.2	13.4
Huntersville town *Mecklenburg Co.*	25.2	6.7	12.2	6.2	13.6	25.8	5.1	5.2
Indian Trail town *Union Co.*	16.8	5.3	11.4	5.0	14.4	28.0	11.2	8.0
Jacksonville city *Onslow Co.*	10.2	2.3	14.5	6.7	24.8	24.6	7.4	9.6
Kannapolis city *Cabarrus Co.*	10.4	3.9	10.2	4.4	20.9	25.5	10.6	14.1
Kernersville town *Forsyth Co.*	17.7	6.5	9.2	6.9	16.9	26.2	5.7	11.0
Kings Mountain city *Cleveland Co.*	8.8	1.5	7.5	5.2	17.6	30.0	9.3	20.1
Kinston city *Lenoir Co.*	8.5	2.3	9.6	5.2	25.5	19.4	7.2	22.3
Knightdale town *Wake Co.*	16.3	7.9	12.7	8.3	17.8	22.1	7.5	7.3
Laurinburg city *Scotland Co.*	10.7	1.5	16.8	5.5	16.8	23.9	6.5	18.4

Place	MBF[1] (%)	CES[2] (%)	ELCAM[3] (%)	HPT[4] (%)	S[5] (%)	SO[6] (%)	NRCM[7] (%)	PTMM[8] (%)
Leland town *Brunswick Co.*	17.0	6.0	10.9	8.6	12.7	23.1	9.7	12.1
Lenoir city *Caldwell Co.*	9.4	2.5	9.0	5.3	16.6	24.3	7.6	25.4
Lewisville town *Forsyth Co.*	20.5	8.3	15.3	9.5	12.7	22.1	4.5	7.0
Lexington city *Davidson Co.*	5.2	2.0	8.5	2.6	23.4	19.8	8.8	29.6
Lincolnton city *Lincoln Co.*	13.2	5.3	10.6	4.1	13.8	21.6	10.2	21.1
Lumberton city *Robeson Co.*	10.7	1.9	13.3	6.7	18.4	21.5	10.2	17.2
Matthews town *Mecklenburg Co.*	21.8	6.9	15.9	4.9	11.1	29.3	5.1	5.0
Mebane city *Alamance Co.*	14.3	7.1	14.0	8.3	15.5	23.1	10.2	7.5
Mint Hill town *Mecklenburg Co.*	19.5	6.5	11.9	3.5	14.7	26.3	8.4	9.2
Monroe city *Union Co.*	9.5	2.9	7.1	4.0	21.9	23.3	14.8	16.5
Mooresville town *Iredell Co.*	16.2	6.7	8.3	6.4	20.0	24.4	8.2	9.9
Morehead City town *Carteret Co.*	17.0	2.8	9.9	5.9	21.1	23.1	8.8	11.5
Morganton city *Burke Co.*	11.1	1.7	12.2	7.3	24.6	19.4	7.5	16.1
Morrisville town *Wake Co.*	23.9	25.2	10.3	5.1	8.5	20.8	2.1	4.1
Mount Airy city *Surry Co.*	7.8	3.4	14.8	7.7	17.1	23.9	13.4	12.0
Mount Holly city *Gaston Co.*	14.7	4.7	9.6	5.1	14.8	25.3	8.8	17.0
Murraysville cdp *New Hanover Co.*	14.2	2.7	14.0	6.3	17.0	27.4	6.6	11.7
Myrtle Grove cdp *New Hanover Co.*	17.5	4.5	12.6	8.0	13.7	31.1	7.0	5.6
New Bern city *Craven Co.*	10.2	3.4	12.6	6.4	23.9	20.4	10.6	12.6
Newton city *Catawba Co.*	13.0	2.0	7.7	3.5	20.7	22.0	6.7	24.4
Oxford city *Granville Co.*	11.1	3.3	12.1	10.7	16.8	25.5	4.1	16.4
Pinehurst village *Moore Co.*	24.3	3.6	16.2	9.6	15.1	24.2	2.6	4.4
Piney Green cdp *Onslow Co.*	12.7	4.5	7.7	3.4	22.4	27.9	9.0	12.5
Raleigh city *Wake Co.*	18.4	9.7	13.4	5.5	15.9	24.5	6.0	6.6
Reidsville city *Rockingham Co.*	8.6	2.7	6.7	3.5	17.0	26.8	10.4	24.3
Roanoke Rapids city *Halifax Co.*	12.8	3.4	10.3	7.9	15.7	26.9	9.4	13.6
Rockingham city *Richmond Co.*	12.0	0.8	17.6	3.3	19.3	20.0	10.3	16.7
Rocky Mount city *Nash Co.*	11.9	3.3	8.9	4.3	18.7	26.4	6.0	20.4
Roxboro city *Person Co.*	5.9	2.1	4.6	4.7	21.5	20.3	17.4	23.6
Saint Stephens cdp *Catawba Co.*	8.9	3.3	10.3	6.1	18.8	20.0	8.5	24.1
Salisbury city *Rowan Co.*	8.7	2.0	14.2	5.7	24.6	18.7	10.2	15.9
Sanford city *Lee Co.*	11.4	3.8	9.6	4.8	19.9	22.8	9.1	18.5
Shelby city *Cleveland Co.*	12.8	2.2	13.3	6.3	21.3	23.8	3.1	17.1
Smithfield town *Johnston Co.*	12.6	2.0	9.7	4.7	19.9	20.8	11.7	18.6
Southern Pines town *Moore Co.*	13.6	2.7	16.5	14.6	23.4	17.5	4.7	7.0
Spring Lake town *Cumberland Co.*	8.2	0.4	8.8	6.6	33.3	27.9	4.0	10.7
Stallings town *Union Co.*	20.6	6.4	14.6	10.1	8.4	26.1	8.1	5.8
Statesville city *Iredell Co.*	8.5	2.9	10.4	7.2	13.6	25.5	8.1	23.9
Summerfield town *Guilford Co.*	30.2	4.3	12.8	6.8	9.1	24.8	6.4	5.6
Tarboro town *Edgecombe Co.*	14.0	1.0	11.6	7.6	20.0	22.4	7.5	15.9
Thomasville city *Davidson Co.*	5.0	3.1	7.4	4.4	18.0	28.9	5.9	27.3
Wake Forest town *Wake Co.*	21.9	10.5	12.8	6.4	13.6	24.7	4.7	5.4
Washington city *Beaufort Co.*	9.3	2.2	14.3	9.9	24.8	18.2	9.8	11.5
Waxhaw town *Union Co.*	19.9	8.9	15.9	4.9	9.7	28.9	5.3	6.5
Waynesville town *Haywood Co.*	10.1	1.8	11.7	10.9	23.2	25.7	8.6	8.1
Weddington town *Union Co.*	32.4	10.1	5.3	5.1	11.4	27.7	3.9	4.1
Wilmington city *New Hanover Co.*	14.3	3.8	13.4	7.1	22.3	24.4	7.2	7.4
Wilson city *Wilson Co.*	12.8	3.2	11.9	5.7	19.5	24.4	9.2	13.3
Winston-Salem city *Forsyth Co.*	13.2	4.3	12.6	8.3	19.5	22.6	7.2	12.2
Winterville town *Pitt Co.*	20.5	8.3	11.5	12.9	12.8	20.8	8.5	4.7

NOTES: (1) Management, business, and financial occupations; (2) Computer, engineering, and science occupations; (3) Education, legal, community service, arts, and media occupations; (4) Healthcare practitioners and technical occupations; (5) Service occupations; (6) Sales and office occupations; (7) Natural resources, construction, and maintenance occupations; (8) Production, transportation, and material moving occupations
SOURCE: U.S. Census Bureau, American Community Survey, 2009-2013 Five-Year Estimates

Educational Attainment

Place	Percent of Population 25 Years and Over with:		
	High School Diploma or Higher[1]	Bachelor's Degree or Higher	Graduate/Professional Degree or Higher
Albemarle city *Stanly Co.*	76.5	19.5	5.8
Apex town *Wake Co.*	96.9	61.8	20.9
Archdale city *Randolph Co.*	83.1	15.4	4.7
Asheboro city *Randolph Co.*	73.1	16.8	4.9
Asheville city *Buncombe Co.*	90.2	43.3	15.9
Belmont city *Gaston Co.*	86.9	33.9	13.4
Boone town *Watauga Co.*	92.6	48.9	18.9
Burlington city *Alamance Co.*	82.7	24.0	7.1
Carrboro town *Orange Co.*	90.7	65.1	35.6
Cary town *Wake Co.*	95.2	62.2	25.1
Chapel Hill town *Orange Co.*	94.7	73.9	45.1
Charlotte city *Mecklenburg Co.*	88.0	39.8	12.7
Clayton town *Johnston Co.*	92.1	31.3	8.1
Clemmons village *Forsyth Co.*	93.7	43.8	13.6
Clinton city *Sampson Co.*	81.5	20.2	6.7
Concord city *Cabarrus Co.*	86.3	27.8	8.3
Conover city *Catawba Co.*	87.1	21.6	6.6
Cornelius town *Mecklenburg Co.*	93.5	50.6	16.5
Davidson town *Mecklenburg Co.*	97.3	66.0	29.5
Dunn city *Harnett Co.*	78.5	17.2	5.5
Durham city *Durham Co.*	86.6	46.8	21.8
Eden city *Rockingham Co.*	78.5	12.7	5.2
Elizabeth City city *Pasquotank Co.*	79.7	20.8	7.1
Elon town *Alamance Co.*	90.9	35.8	10.0
Fayetteville city *Cumberland Co.*	90.8	24.7	8.3
Fuquay-Varina town *Wake Co.*	90.7	34.5	9.9
Garner town *Wake Co.*	92.0	34.8	9.2
Gastonia city *Gaston Co.*	80.6	21.6	6.5
Goldsboro city *Wayne Co.*	83.9	18.5	6.5
Graham city *Alamance Co.*	80.0	18.5	5.6
Greensboro city *Guilford Co.*	87.7	35.7	12.3
Greenville city *Pitt Co.*	89.7	37.1	14.6
Half Moon cdp *Onslow Co.*	95.8	18.6	2.3
Harrisburg town *Cabarrus Co.*	96.2	39.9	14.9
Havelock city *Craven Co.*	94.4	12.5	2.8
Henderson city *Vance Co.*	73.7	14.1	4.5
Hendersonville city *Henderson Co.*	83.3	29.8	11.2
Hickory city *Catawba Co.*	84.1	31.0	10.2
High Point city *Guilford Co.*	85.7	28.9	8.6
Holly Springs town *Wake Co.*	97.0	55.4	17.5
Hope Mills town *Cumberland Co.*	89.0	19.6	6.0
Huntersville town *Mecklenburg Co.*	94.2	52.5	15.0
Indian Trail town *Union Co.*	93.0	35.2	9.3
Jacksonville city *Onslow Co.*	92.2	23.1	7.0
Kannapolis city *Cabarrus Co.*	79.0	17.5	5.5
Kernersville town *Forsyth Co.*	90.6	29.9	9.3
Kings Mountain city *Cleveland Co.*	82.4	13.2	4.0
Kinston city *Lenoir Co.*	78.7	15.1	4.1
Knightdale town *Wake Co.*	89.6	41.6	11.6
Laurinburg city *Scotland Co.*	78.9	18.6	7.6

Place	Percent of Population 25 Years and Over with:		
	High School Diploma or Higher[1]	Bachelor's Degree or Higher	Graduate/Professional Degree or Higher
Leland town Brunswick Co.	92.8	41.0	14.8
Lenoir city Caldwell Co.	74.9	14.8	4.9
Lewisville town Forsyth Co.	92.7	38.1	12.8
Lexington city Davidson Co.	70.7	12.2	4.0
Lincolnton city Lincoln Co.	80.8	16.9	3.7
Lumberton city Robeson Co.	72.2	18.4	6.7
Matthews town Mecklenburg Co.	94.9	48.1	14.8
Mebane city Alamance Co.	91.0	32.4	12.9
Mint Hill town Mecklenburg Co.	91.4	33.7	9.1
Monroe city Union Co.	74.2	16.7	4.0
Mooresville town Iredell Co.	90.6	29.0	7.7
Morehead City town Carteret Co.	89.5	27.5	7.4
Morganton city Burke Co.	74.6	22.7	9.0
Morrisville town Wake Co.	96.8	63.8	23.9
Mount Airy city Surry Co.	75.5	24.8	8.5
Mount Holly city Gaston Co.	85.1	24.7	5.6
Murraysville cdp New Hanover Co.	92.6	29.8	8.2
Myrtle Grove cdp New Hanover Co.	92.8	41.0	14.1
New Bern city Craven Co.	83.6	25.0	8.7
Newton city Catawba Co.	76.9	16.0	4.0
Oxford city Granville Co.	81.7	18.3	7.7
Pinehurst village Moore Co.	97.2	52.1	19.3
Piney Green cdp Onslow Co.	89.5	14.5	3.8
Raleigh city Wake Co.	90.0	47.5	15.9
Reidsville city Rockingham Co.	84.8	16.3	5.0
Roanoke Rapids city Halifax Co.	79.8	18.7	7.0
Rockingham city Richmond Co.	81.6	16.8	7.4
Rocky Mount city Nash Co.	82.2	19.2	5.0
Roxboro city Person Co.	70.5	10.1	1.5
Saint Stephens cdp Catawba Co.	80.2	13.1	3.6
Salisbury city Rowan Co.	80.4	22.7	7.3
Sanford city Lee Co.	75.5	22.2	6.4
Shelby city Cleveland Co.	86.0	21.0	7.6
Smithfield town Johnston Co.	77.0	19.4	6.4
Southern Pines town Moore Co.	89.6	40.0	17.9
Spring Lake town Cumberland Co.	90.2	16.1	5.2
Stallings town Union Co.	93.0	43.5	11.9
Statesville city Iredell Co.	80.6	20.5	7.9
Summerfield town Guilford Co.	94.0	51.8	19.0
Tarboro town Edgecombe Co.	78.3	16.9	5.0
Thomasville city Davidson Co.	78.3	13.2	2.7
Wake Forest town Wake Co.	95.2	50.4	16.3
Washington city Beaufort Co.	80.3	23.5	10.3
Waxhaw town Union Co.	95.5	55.0	15.4
Waynesville town Haywood Co.	80.9	23.4	8.2
Weddington town Union Co.	97.5	53.1	10.9
Wilmington city New Hanover Co.	89.0	39.1	13.7
Wilson city Wilson Co.	78.5	23.1	6.3
Winston-Salem city Forsyth Co.	85.0	32.6	12.2
Winterville town Pitt Co.	91.0	37.6	12.2

NOTE: (1) Includes General Equivalency Diploma (GED)
SOURCE: U.S. Census Bureau, American Community Survey, 2009-2013 Five-Year Estimates

Health Insurance

Place	Percent of Total Population with:				Percent of Population[1] Under Age 18 without Health Insurance
	Any Insurance	Private Insurance	Public Insurance	No Insurance	
Albemarle city *Stanly Co.*	80.9	55.2	40.0	19.1	9.1
Apex town *Wake Co.*	92.6	87.4	10.3	7.4	2.9
Archdale city *Randolph Co.*	86.9	70.1	25.8	13.1	6.0
Asheboro city *Randolph Co.*	75.2	46.9	36.6	24.8	12.4
Asheville city *Buncombe Co.*	82.3	61.0	33.4	17.7	6.5
Belmont city *Gaston Co.*	86.9	74.5	24.2	13.1	6.6
Boone town *Watauga Co.*	91.6	87.3	9.1	8.4	0.0
Burlington city *Alamance Co.*	82.8	57.4	38.1	17.2	6.2
Carrboro town *Orange Co.*	83.7	74.2	14.8	16.3	9.5
Cary town *Wake Co.*	90.0	84.2	13.6	10.0	5.5
Chapel Hill town *Orange Co.*	91.5	85.8	14.3	8.5	6.6
Charlotte city *Mecklenburg Co.*	81.9	64.6	24.7	18.1	7.9
Clayton town *Johnston Co.*	85.8	74.6	18.6	14.2	8.2
Clemmons village *Forsyth Co.*	89.3	79.5	22.7	10.7	5.4
Clinton city *Sampson Co.*	84.7	54.8	44.4	15.3	5.6
Concord city *Cabarrus Co.*	83.6	67.4	25.5	16.4	6.5
Conover city *Catawba Co.*	84.3	60.4	36.6	15.7	4.5
Cornelius town *Mecklenburg Co.*	87.5	80.4	16.2	12.5	9.3
Davidson town *Mecklenburg Co.*	94.1	87.3	14.7	5.9	1.2
Dunn city *Harnett Co.*	78.6	47.1	44.2	21.4	10.6
Durham city *Durham Co.*	82.9	65.1	25.9	17.1	7.6
Eden city *Rockingham Co.*	81.0	52.7	41.7	19.0	10.0
Elizabeth City city *Pasquotank Co.*	76.0	50.8	37.7	24.0	11.4
Elon town *Alamance Co.*	92.3	83.2	21.5	7.7	0.0
Fayetteville city *Cumberland Co.*	85.9	66.2	33.9	14.1	5.5
Fuquay-Varina town *Wake Co.*	84.5	70.4	22.2	15.5	7.4
Garner town *Wake Co.*	85.5	73.6	21.3	14.5	10.9
Gastonia city *Gaston Co.*	81.4	55.9	35.7	18.6	9.8
Goldsboro city *Wayne Co.*	86.9	57.4	46.1	13.1	4.9
Graham city *Alamance Co.*	77.1	54.6	33.9	22.9	12.9
Greensboro city *Guilford Co.*	82.6	63.1	28.6	17.4	7.5
Greenville city *Pitt Co.*	86.0	69.1	23.8	14.0	5.5
Half Moon cdp *Onslow Co.*	86.2	76.0	21.4	13.8	1.2
Harrisburg town *Cabarrus Co.*	89.7	80.2	15.5	10.3	7.8
Havelock city *Craven Co.*	85.7	71.7	24.1	14.3	4.9
Henderson city *Vance Co.*	81.5	42.0	53.7	18.5	4.3
Hendersonville city *Henderson Co.*	81.7	52.5	51.9	18.3	12.1
Hickory city *Catawba Co.*	80.7	61.3	29.2	19.3	7.6
High Point city *Guilford Co.*	81.0	58.3	31.5	19.0	11.4
Holly Springs town *Wake Co.*	93.5	88.0	13.1	6.5	5.1
Hope Mills town *Cumberland Co.*	88.8	64.2	34.9	11.2	5.2
Huntersville town *Mecklenburg Co.*	88.9	83.3	12.0	11.1	6.1
Indian Trail town *Union Co.*	83.3	72.1	18.6	16.7	10.9
Jacksonville city *Onslow Co.*	89.8	77.2	21.9	10.2	3.2
Kannapolis city *Cabarrus Co.*	79.7	54.6	34.4	20.3	7.1
Kernersville town *Forsyth Co.*	87.4	73.3	25.6	12.6	6.5
Kings Mountain city *Cleveland Co.*	82.7	53.8	40.5	17.3	2.2
Kinston city *Lenoir Co.*	80.3	44.4	51.1	19.7	8.5
Knightdale town *Wake Co.*	82.6	68.4	19.8	17.4	10.2
Laurinburg city *Scotland Co.*	86.5	49.2	50.9	13.5	2.9

Place	Percent of Total Population with:				Percent of Population[1] Under Age 18 without Health Insurance
	Any Insurance	Private Insurance	Public Insurance	No Insurance	
Leland town *Brunswick Co.*	87.3	74.5	25.9	12.7	4.6
Lenoir city *Caldwell Co.*	82.7	54.9	40.6	17.3	4.0
Lewisville town *Forsyth Co.*	93.5	82.9	22.4	6.5	0.0
Lexington city *Davidson Co.*	77.6	39.7	48.4	22.4	5.8
Lincolnton city *Lincoln Co.*	82.6	55.4	39.5	17.4	5.7
Lumberton city *Robeson Co.*	80.3	43.8	46.3	19.7	5.1
Matthews town *Mecklenburg Co.*	89.1	79.4	20.8	10.9	7.6
Mebane city *Alamance Co.*	89.1	75.8	24.0	10.9	4.8
Mint Hill town *Mecklenburg Co.*	88.8	75.2	28.3	11.2	7.3
Monroe city *Union Co.*	74.4	50.7	32.1	25.6	13.4
Mooresville town *Iredell Co.*	85.7	74.7	18.5	14.3	4.5
Morehead City town *Carteret Co.*	78.3	57.0	39.3	21.7	8.6
Morganton city *Burke Co.*	81.2	50.6	43.9	18.8	3.4
Morrisville town *Wake Co.*	93.8	88.0	10.1	6.2	4.4
Mount Airy city *Surry Co.*	85.6	56.2	45.9	14.4	3.5
Mount Holly city *Gaston Co.*	84.6	67.9	27.6	15.4	7.5
Murraysville cdp *New Hanover Co.*	86.7	78.5	21.0	13.3	6.6
Myrtle Grove cdp *New Hanover Co.*	90.5	77.4	28.3	9.5	1.4
New Bern city *Craven Co.*	83.8	56.5	43.6	16.2	5.0
Newton city *Catawba Co.*	79.9	53.3	40.2	20.1	7.5
Oxford city *Granville Co.*	86.8	58.4	41.0	13.2	3.8
Pinehurst village *Moore Co.*	96.3	84.0	44.4	3.7	3.3
Piney Green cdp *Onslow Co.*	86.5	73.4	24.7	13.5	4.3
Raleigh city *Wake Co.*	83.9	69.7	21.8	16.1	8.9
Reidsville city *Rockingham Co.*	90.6	65.3	43.3	9.4	0.6
Roanoke Rapids city *Halifax Co.*	86.4	56.5	42.1	13.6	6.2
Rockingham city *Richmond Co.*	83.7	52.1	42.3	16.3	8.1
Rocky Mount city *Nash Co.*	83.3	53.6	42.4	16.7	7.6
Roxboro city *Person Co.*	74.6	41.0	43.3	25.4	9.8
Saint Stephens cdp *Catawba Co.*	87.7	69.6	30.1	12.3	3.1
Salisbury city *Rowan Co.*	81.7	55.1	38.6	18.3	6.5
Sanford city *Lee Co.*	78.3	55.4	33.3	21.7	6.9
Shelby city *Cleveland Co.*	83.1	51.9	44.6	16.9	8.0
Smithfield town *Johnston Co.*	81.2	47.3	48.3	18.8	4.1
Southern Pines town *Moore Co.*	89.1	67.6	41.4	10.9	4.8
Spring Lake town *Cumberland Co.*	85.5	66.8	26.8	14.5	5.0
Stallings town *Union Co.*	90.6	79.9	21.7	9.4	6.4
Statesville city *Iredell Co.*	81.1	52.9	39.7	18.9	6.7
Summerfield town *Guilford Co.*	94.9	87.1	16.5	5.1	5.9
Tarboro town *Edgecombe Co.*	80.3	51.1	45.2	19.7	4.8
Thomasville city *Davidson Co.*	81.2	53.3	39.5	18.8	4.6
Wake Forest town *Wake Co.*	92.1	82.3	18.9	7.9	5.4
Washington city *Beaufort Co.*	85.1	49.0	49.6	14.9	4.2
Waxhaw town *Union Co.*	91.4	84.7	15.0	8.6	1.8
Waynesville town *Haywood Co.*	79.4	51.7	43.1	20.6	14.7
Weddington town *Union Co.*	91.7	87.8	13.3	8.3	2.1
Wilmington city *New Hanover Co.*	83.3	65.0	30.6	16.7	5.2
Wilson city *Wilson Co.*	81.9	56.1	37.9	18.1	7.7
Winston-Salem city *Forsyth Co.*	82.0	60.6	31.8	18.0	7.9
Winterville town *Pitt Co.*	87.1	76.9	20.6	12.9	7.8

NOTE: (1) Civilian noninstitutionalized population.
SOURCE: U.S. Census Bureau, American Community Survey, 2009-2013 Five-Year Estimates

Income and Poverty

Place	Average Household Income ($)	Median Household Income ($)	Per Capita Income ($)	Households w/$100,000+ Income (%)	Poverty Rate (%)
Albemarle city *Stanly Co.*	46,213	32,859	19,592	9.3	23.5
Apex town *Wake Co.*	100,768	89,475	34,979	45.2	2.5
Archdale city *Randolph Co.*	59,809	52,042	22,837	12.9	11.2
Asheboro city *Randolph Co.*	43,024	31,846	17,448	7.0	25.5
Asheville city *Buncombe Co.*	58,863	42,016	26,912	15.4	20.0
Belmont city *Gaston Co.*	82,435	54,091	33,624	25.0	9.2
Boone town *Watauga Co.*	32,523	14,453	12,373	6.2	60.6
Burlington city *Alamance Co.*	52,983	36,858	23,127	11.8	21.9
Carrboro town *Orange Co.*	78,273	46,803	33,523	25.5	17.0
Cary town *Wake Co.*	110,841	90,250	41,554	45.9	6.2
Chapel Hill town *Orange Co.*	99,212	60,802	35,714	34.0	23.1
Charlotte city *Mecklenburg Co.*	78,641	52,375	31,556	22.7	17.1
Clayton town *Johnston Co.*	69,552	57,456	26,985	19.7	12.4
Clemmons village *Forsyth Co.*	83,678	64,118	32,955	30.3	7.9
Clinton city *Sampson Co.*	56,492	32,927	24,119	13.8	27.8
Concord city *Cabarrus Co.*	70,842	53,337	25,897	22.6	12.6
Conover city *Catawba Co.*	54,753	42,038	22,327	12.6	17.2
Cornelius town *Mecklenburg Co.*	113,316	80,697	47,666	39.5	8.5
Davidson town *Mecklenburg Co.*	138,044	88,750	47,565	45.4	6.8
Dunn city *Harnett Co.*	44,635	29,399	18,830	8.7	27.6
Durham city *Durham Co.*	68,732	49,160	28,565	20.8	20.0
Eden city *Rockingham Co.*	39,926	31,575	17,517	5.6	26.0
Elizabeth City city *Pasquotank Co.*	47,154	33,797	17,958	9.8	29.0
Elon town *Alamance Co.*	70,374	45,538	22,138	23.8	19.4
Fayetteville city *Cumberland Co.*	57,392	44,900	23,409	13.4	17.6
Fuquay-Varina town *Wake Co.*	69,735	58,588	26,372	22.5	10.3
Garner town *Wake Co.*	69,639	60,842	28,829	22.6	8.6
Gastonia city *Gaston Co.*	56,109	40,053	21,531	13.1	22.3
Goldsboro city *Wayne Co.*	46,653	34,161	20,380	8.9	25.7
Graham city *Alamance Co.*	47,057	38,975	19,243	10.3	24.3
Greensboro city *Guilford Co.*	61,440	41,120	25,861	15.2	20.3
Greenville city *Pitt Co.*	54,786	35,137	22,836	13.8	30.0
Half Moon cdp *Onslow Co.*	56,454	49,380	19,191	12.5	18.0
Harrisburg town *Cabarrus Co.*	88,458	81,808	28,537	32.5	6.2
Havelock city *Craven Co.*	51,527	43,461	20,596	10.4	18.2
Henderson city *Vance Co.*	40,599	26,149	16,188	6.2	35.5
Hendersonville city *Henderson Co.*	47,415	37,060	21,210	7.3	26.0
Hickory city *Catawba Co.*	61,807	39,176	25,310	17.6	19.3
High Point city *Guilford Co.*	57,190	43,083	22,940	15.4	21.4
Holly Springs town *Wake Co.*	100,703	89,644	33,517	42.7	3.1
Hope Mills town *Cumberland Co.*	62,030	51,442	22,913	15.6	15.6
Huntersville town *Mecklenburg Co.*	102,816	84,486	38,409	42.9	6.0
Indian Trail town *Union Co.*	80,566	66,333	26,096	25.2	6.3
Jacksonville city *Onslow Co.*	54,194	42,459	21,210	12.1	14.6
Kannapolis city *Cabarrus Co.*	52,272	39,275	20,482	10.2	20.8
Kernersville town *Forsyth Co.*	64,919	50,032	27,714	19.8	13.5
Kings Mountain city *Cleveland Co.*	47,021	33,701	19,448	8.5	23.6
Kinston city *Lenoir Co.*	43,130	29,451	18,930	7.7	31.8
Knightdale town *Wake Co.*	78,147	71,066	29,263	25.6	7.5
Laurinburg city *Scotland Co.*	38,211	26,235	15,760	8.0	35.9

Place	Average Household Income ($)	Median Household Income ($)	Per Capita Income ($)	Households w/$100,000+ Income (%)	Poverty Rate (%)
Leland town *Brunswick Co.*	74,818	64,471	32,228	26.3	9.0
Lenoir city *Caldwell Co.*	42,281	28,715	17,655	6.7	24.6
Lewisville town *Forsyth Co.*	89,424	72,825	34,550	29.9	8.9
Lexington city *Davidson Co.*	40,105	28,793	16,330	5.1	26.5
Lincolnton city *Lincoln Co.*	46,500	31,162	19,514	8.6	26.0
Lumberton city *Robeson Co.*	50,721	30,990	18,918	11.4	31.3
Matthews town *Mecklenburg Co.*	87,112	68,295	33,722	31.2	7.9
Mebane city *Alamance Co.*	65,594	55,246	27,795	19.7	13.4
Mint Hill town *Mecklenburg Co.*	85,765	68,140	31,825	30.2	8.0
Monroe city *Union Co.*	56,250	43,819	19,172	14.2	20.7
Mooresville town *Iredell Co.*	71,324	61,003	26,392	25.3	9.9
Morehead City town *Carteret Co.*	54,974	35,982	26,548	12.7	22.0
Morganton city *Burke Co.*	47,327	31,083	20,070	11.3	27.9
Morrisville town *Wake Co.*	98,856	80,892	39,734	37.5	3.1
Mount Airy city *Surry Co.*	48,498	32,258	22,487	9.6	21.5
Mount Holly city *Gaston Co.*	66,586	49,351	27,459	20.0	13.9
Murraysville cdp *New Hanover Co.*	64,827	61,309	27,975	15.6	6.6
Myrtle Grove cdp *New Hanover Co.*	85,505	68,807	35,475	29.8	7.5
New Bern city *Craven Co.*	51,503	37,493	22,555	12.7	24.5
Newton city *Catawba Co.*	41,579	32,062	16,720	6.8	23.6
Oxford city *Granville Co.*	51,375	34,018	21,306	10.8	23.5
Pinehurst village *Moore Co.*	98,816	70,275	45,606	28.9	3.3
Piney Green cdp *Onslow Co.*	54,413	47,805	20,071	9.7	13.9
Raleigh city *Wake Co.*	75,640	54,448	30,470	23.0	16.2
Reidsville city *Rockingham Co.*	46,840	37,120	21,177	6.9	19.3
Roanoke Rapids city *Halifax Co.*	47,452	34,975	19,178	11.8	25.6
Rockingham city *Richmond Co.*	41,766	30,638	17,767	8.8	28.1
Rocky Mount city *Nash Co.*	48,379	36,582	20,185	9.6	24.5
Roxboro city *Person Co.*	29,564	20,736	12,779	2.7	42.8
Saint Stephens cdp *Catawba Co.*	63,751	45,945	24,243	14.8	12.5
Salisbury city *Rowan Co.*	48,986	34,959	18,557	9.8	24.8
Sanford city *Lee Co.*	55,844	43,234	20,497	14.9	22.9
Shelby city *Cleveland Co.*	47,374	32,070	19,793	10.5	29.1
Smithfield town *Johnston Co.*	46,313	31,947	18,647	10.3	28.4
Southern Pines town *Moore Co.*	78,104	49,038	36,270	25.5	12.0
Spring Lake town *Cumberland Co.*	42,142	36,538	15,852	2.8	23.4
Stallings town *Union Co.*	92,916	79,663	34,396	33.7	6.9
Statesville city *Iredell Co.*	51,842	32,331	20,803	9.7	29.4
Summerfield town *Guilford Co.*	124,136	98,438	45,508	49.8	4.5
Tarboro town *Edgecombe Co.*	47,229	34,366	19,180	9.9	17.6
Thomasville city *Davidson Co.*	43,132	33,560	17,382	5.7	27.8
Wake Forest town *Wake Co.*	91,608	75,050	32,474	37.4	6.9
Washington city *Beaufort Co.*	40,260	30,479	17,982	6.9	30.5
Waxhaw town *Union Co.*	84,392	77,467	27,982	35.1	5.1
Waynesville town *Haywood Co.*	50,692	36,485	24,725	9.2	20.3
Weddington town *Union Co.*	162,565	141,682	53,021	70.6	1.8
Wilmington city *New Hanover Co.*	65,118	41,573	29,017	17.8	23.2
Wilson city *Wilson Co.*	53,157	37,676	21,396	12.0	26.5
Winston-Salem city *Forsyth Co.*	61,113	40,148	24,858	15.4	23.2
Winterville town *Pitt Co.*	74,466	57,220	26,865	26.0	11.2

SOURCE: U.S. Census Bureau, American Community Survey, 2009-2013 Five-Year Estimates

Housing

Place	Homeownership Rate (%)	Median Home Value ($)	Median Year Structure Built	Homeowner Vacancy Rate (%)	Median Gross Rent ($/month)	Rental Vacancy Rate (%)
Albemarle city *Stanly Co.*	56.2	$119,800	1963	3.2	$594	14.2
Apex town *Wake Co.*	74.7	$258,500	1998	1.9	$1,055	8.0
Archdale city *Randolph Co.*	72.4	$135,500	1985	2.1	$669	12.5
Asheboro city *Randolph Co.*	48.4	$115,900	1976	3.9	$625	11.8
Asheville city *Buncombe Co.*	50.4	$196,300	1972	3.7	$839	7.2
Belmont city *Gaston Co.*	70.6	$152,800	1980	3.9	$741	10.5
Boone town *Watauga Co.*	23.2	$280,800	1981	7.1	$820	3.9
Burlington city *Alamance Co.*	55.3	$126,100	1973	4.1	$728	12.6
Carrboro town *Orange Co.*	38.4	$337,000	1984	2.8	$843	7.3
Cary town *Wake Co.*	68.9	$303,700	1995	2.1	$965	8.9
Chapel Hill town *Orange Co.*	47.6	$367,800	1984	2.6	$915	7.1
Charlotte city *Mecklenburg Co.*	57.4	$170,500	1988	3.4	$882	11.7
Clayton town *Johnston Co.*	65.5	$152,600	2000	4.6	$971	9.8
Clemmons village *Forsyth Co.*	77.9	$206,300	1991	2.9	$820	20.0
Clinton city *Sampson Co.*	50.6	$123,700	1970	2.4	$559	5.2
Concord city *Cabarrus Co.*	67.8	$168,300	1992	2.8	$806	11.8
Conover city *Catawba Co.*	67.6	$134,000	1978	2.6	$627	8.4
Cornelius town *Mecklenburg Co.*	71.3	$247,900	1996	3.3	$1,055	7.6
Davidson town *Mecklenburg Co.*	74.8	$391,300	1995	6.2	$930	9.8
Dunn city *Harnett Co.*	51.6	$107,500	1973	2.6	$619	8.2
Durham city *Durham Co.*	49.8	$180,500	1986	3.2	$852	10.4
Eden city *Rockingham Co.*	56.9	$82,500	1961	3.9	$611	14.0
Elizabeth City city *Pasquotank Co.*	46.5	$149,400	1967	5.2	$844	11.0
Elon town *Alamance Co.*	51.4	$198,300	1988	2.3	$1,209	8.3
Fayetteville city *Cumberland Co.*	50.3	$125,800	1982	3.3	$869	10.5
Fuquay-Varina town *Wake Co.*	73.2	$191,500	2001	4.7	$905	8.1
Garner town *Wake Co.*	65.9	$165,600	1987	3.0	$920	9.1
Gastonia city *Gaston Co.*	56.3	$135,900	1975	3.6	$754	11.7
Goldsboro city *Wayne Co.*	41.7	$111,600	1972	3.5	$710	9.3
Graham city *Alamance Co.*	58.1	$125,700	1976	3.8	$698	13.7
Greensboro city *Guilford Co.*	52.5	$147,400	1981	3.4	$742	11.9
Greenville city *Pitt Co.*	37.1	$149,600	1993	4.5	$724	11.9
Half Moon cdp *Onslow Co.*	69.5	$142,500	1984	1.1	$803	4.4
Harrisburg town *Cabarrus Co.*	90.9	$222,100	2001	2.2	$1,086	6.4
Havelock city *Craven Co.*	42.9	$137,600	1984	2.2	$1,041	5.9
Henderson city *Vance Co.*	42.3	$116,800	1966	3.6	$645	9.5
Hendersonville city *Henderson Co.*	47.8	$164,300	1981	6.4	$712	11.0
Hickory city *Catawba Co.*	54.1	$158,100	1980	3.8	$661	13.1
High Point city *Guilford Co.*	57.1	$146,200	1983	4.0	$762	12.1
Holly Springs town *Wake Co.*	87.4	$236,300	2002	2.5	$1,131	15.6
Hope Mills town *Cumberland Co.*	63.4	$130,500	1992	2.2	$791	8.6
Huntersville town *Mecklenburg Co.*	75.5	$245,300	1999	2.2	$997	7.0
Indian Trail town *Union Co.*	86.0	$172,600	2000	2.2	$1,079	5.4
Jacksonville city *Onslow Co.*	38.2	$153,600	1982	2.0	$1,027	4.5
Kannapolis city *Cabarrus Co.*	62.8	$127,700	1972	3.6	$754	14.2
Kernersville town *Forsyth Co.*	57.2	$174,500	1989	2.7	$720	11.6
Kings Mountain city *Cleveland Co.*	59.3	$105,700	1971	2.6	$606	9.4
Kinston city *Lenoir Co.*	47.3	$105,600	1965	3.9	$616	8.9
Knightdale town *Wake Co.*	67.9	$168,800	2000	5.1	$921	14.3
Laurinburg city *Scotland Co.*	53.3	$92,900	1973	2.5	$613	8.0

Place	Homeownership Rate (%)	Median Home Value ($)	Median Year Structure Built	Homeowner Vacancy Rate (%)	Median Gross Rent ($/month)	Rental Vacancy Rate (%)
Leland town *Brunswick Co.*	76.4	$197,600	2004	4.0	$957	10.2
Lenoir city *Caldwell Co.*	59.3	$105,300	1972	2.8	$577	10.1
Lewisville town *Forsyth Co.*	86.4	$186,100	1984	1.8	$815	15.1
Lexington city *Davidson Co.*	47.6	$100,300	1964	4.7	$635	18.8
Lincolnton city *Lincoln Co.*	48.6	$129,800	1971	3.3	$663	12.7
Lumberton city *Robeson Co.*	48.3	$100,500	1973	2.4	$640	7.8
Matthews town *Mecklenburg Co.*	72.5	$217,600	1990	1.8	$937	5.1
Mebane city *Alamance Co.*	61.5	$163,500	1993	3.2	$800	5.4
Mint Hill town *Mecklenburg Co.*	82.1	$207,000	1986	2.8	$822	11.1
Monroe city *Union Co.*	56.5	$148,800	1983	4.3	$777	11.2
Mooresville town *Iredell Co.*	64.0	$186,500	1997	3.5	$862	12.8
Morehead City town *Carteret Co.*	50.3	$191,300	1981	4.3	$649	7.2
Morganton city *Burke Co.*	54.5	$130,000	1966	3.8	$640	12.6
Morrisville town *Wake Co.*	48.4	$261,600	2001	3.4	$980	7.6
Mount Airy city *Surry Co.*	57.1	$129,600	1964	3.6	$598	8.9
Mount Holly city *Gaston Co.*	66.5	$155,800	1988	3.2	$708	6.7
Murraysville cdp *New Hanover Co.*	73.5	$180,900	1999	2.3	$1,052	4.9
Myrtle Grove cdp *New Hanover Co.*	81.9	$251,100	1990	2.4	$990	8.9
New Bern city *Craven Co.*	54.1	$149,000	1982	5.3	$830	10.4
Newton city *Catawba Co.*	58.4	$109,600	1971	3.5	$674	9.5
Oxford city *Granville Co.*	49.4	$126,000	1969	3.6	$754	7.8
Pinehurst village *Moore Co.*	84.6	$284,500	1994	3.6	$1,388	30.0
Piney Green cdp *Onslow Co.*	56.5	$146,400	1990	1.9	$880	5.7
Raleigh city *Wake Co.*	53.6	$207,000	1990	2.6	$897	8.0
Reidsville city *Rockingham Co.*	51.7	$112,100	1964	4.0	$623	12.2
Roanoke Rapids city *Halifax Co.*	53.3	$112,100	1966	2.4	$660	8.2
Rockingham city *Richmond Co.*	51.3	$91,200	1967	3.3	$517	11.2
Rocky Mount city *Nash Co.*	52.5	$105,500	1977	3.5	$753	14.5
Roxboro city *Person Co.*	43.3	$88,800	1966	4.3	$615	12.9
Saint Stephens cdp *Catawba Co.*	79.0	$124,100	1977	1.8	$647	19.6
Salisbury city *Rowan Co.*	51.7	$121,600	1972	4.7	$717	13.7
Sanford city *Lee Co.*	52.6	$138,100	1978	3.3	$673	7.8
Shelby city *Cleveland Co.*	52.9	$118,100	1969	5.0	$669	15.1
Smithfield town *Johnston Co.*	51.2	$133,100	1972	2.7	$694	8.5
Southern Pines town *Moore Co.*	57.0	$248,000	1982	3.9	$724	8.0
Spring Lake town *Cumberland Co.*	24.7	$92,900	1988	3.1	$995	12.8
Stallings town *Union Co.*	89.9	$210,400	1998	1.9	$1,006	2.4
Statesville city *Iredell Co.*	52.3	$133,500	1971	5.3	$716	14.6
Summerfield town *Guilford Co.*	91.2	$331,000	1996	2.0	$1,571	8.3
Tarboro town *Edgecombe Co.*	54.5	$94,700	1972	2.8	$647	7.3
Thomasville city *Davidson Co.*	57.8	$105,100	1976	3.3	$593	13.0
Wake Forest town *Wake Co.*	72.8	$259,200	2001	3.0	$940	9.8
Washington city *Beaufort Co.*	47.9	$159,900	1973	7.4	$624	5.5
Waxhaw town *Union Co.*	86.8	$231,800	2003	3.5	$1,124	6.5
Waynesville town *Haywood Co.*	57.7	$148,300	1970	4.6	$756	13.1
Weddington town *Union Co.*	93.6	$391,500	1991	2.9	$775	2.5
Wilmington city *New Hanover Co.*	48.9	$226,200	1983	3.9	$855	11.3
Wilson city *Wilson Co.*	50.3	$131,000	1979	3.4	$747	10.3
Winston-Salem city *Forsyth Co.*	56.3	$140,400	1974	3.7	$706	12.5
Winterville town *Pitt Co.*	81.9	$162,700	2001	1.8	$1,097	7.5

SOURCE: *U.S. Census Bureau, Census 2010; U.S. Census Bureau, American Community Survey, 2009-2013 Five-Year Estimates*

Commute to Work

Place	Automobile (%)	Public Transportation (%)	Walk (%)	Work from Home (%)	Median Travel Time to Work (minutes)
Albemarle city *Stanly Co.*	96.7	0.0	0.3	2.2	22.1
Apex town *Wake Co.*	89.8	0.6	1.0	7.2	24.2
Archdale city *Randolph Co.*	97.9	0.0	0.1	1.4	22.1
Asheboro city *Randolph Co.*	95.5	0.4	1.6	2.1	20.4
Asheville city *Buncombe Co.*	84.4	1.6	4.1	8.2	17.8
Belmont city *Gaston Co.*	91.7	0.2	2.2	5.3	22.0
Boone town *Watauga Co.*	71.4	3.1	19.4	4.5	12.9
Burlington city *Alamance Co.*	94.2	0.6	0.9	3.3	21.1
Carrboro town *Orange Co.*	70.5	15.3	2.5	5.7	21.3
Cary town *Wake Co.*	88.6	0.6	1.4	8.2	22.3
Chapel Hill town *Orange Co.*	69.0	11.3	10.1	6.7	19.3
Charlotte city *Mecklenburg Co.*	87.1	3.8	2.2	5.7	24.3
Clayton town *Johnston Co.*	97.8	0.0	0.2	1.9	28.4
Clemmons village *Forsyth Co.*	94.0	0.1	0.9	4.6	20.9
Clinton city *Sampson Co.*	95.0	0.2	1.3	2.6	17.8
Concord city *Cabarrus Co.*	93.6	0.6	0.5	4.4	25.7
Conover city *Catawba Co.*	95.1	0.0	0.0	3.5	16.4
Cornelius town *Mecklenburg Co.*	85.9	3.0	0.8	9.5	26.5
Davidson town *Mecklenburg Co.*	77.1	1.5	6.0	13.8	22.5
Dunn city *Harnett Co.*	92.2	0.8	1.9	3.7	20.4
Durham city *Durham Co.*	86.5	3.9	3.2	4.3	21.1
Eden city *Rockingham Co.*	96.1	0.0	1.1	1.2	23.2
Elizabeth City city *Pasquotank Co.*	85.5	0.9	5.9	2.7	19.8
Elon town *Alamance Co.*	84.2	0.7	7.1	5.1	20.4
Fayetteville city *Cumberland Co.*	90.0	0.8	5.0	3.1	19.7
Fuquay-Varina town *Wake Co.*	90.4	0.0	2.1	6.2	30.2
Garner town *Wake Co.*	90.7	0.3	1.2	6.5	25.8
Gastonia city *Gaston Co.*	95.3	0.9	0.9	2.4	23.7
Goldsboro city *Wayne Co.*	93.8	1.4	2.4	1.6	18.0
Graham city *Alamance Co.*	96.2	0.0	0.4	2.4	20.5
Greensboro city *Guilford Co.*	90.7	1.9	2.0	3.8	20.1
Greenville city *Pitt Co.*	92.0	1.5	3.3	2.2	16.8
Half Moon cdp *Onslow Co.*	96.0	0.0	0.4	1.6	25.8
Harrisburg town *Cabarrus Co.*	93.3	0.5	0.0	6.2	24.5
Havelock city *Craven Co.*	85.6	0.6	6.3	2.7	16.6
Henderson city *Vance Co.*	93.8	0.0	3.4	1.7	18.1
Hendersonville city *Henderson Co.*	89.7	0.2	6.1	3.4	16.6
Hickory city *Catawba Co.*	94.2	0.1	1.3	3.0	18.3
High Point city *Guilford Co.*	91.7	1.8	1.6	3.9	20.1
Holly Springs town *Wake Co.*	88.4	0.2	0.5	9.3	27.7
Hope Mills town *Cumberland Co.*	95.9	0.0	1.1	0.8	24.7
Huntersville town *Mecklenburg Co.*	89.0	1.3	0.7	7.8	25.9
Indian Trail town *Union Co.*	92.3	0.6	0.2	5.2	30.5
Jacksonville city *Onslow Co.*	76.3	0.5	9.9	11.8	20.3
Kannapolis city *Cabarrus Co.*	94.8	0.4	1.6	2.4	24.5
Kernersville town *Forsyth Co.*	93.9	0.0	1.2	4.0	21.8
Kings Mountain city *Cleveland Co.*	95.4	0.0	1.5	2.9	22.6
Kinston city *Lenoir Co.*	88.4	2.3	4.4	4.3	18.7
Knightdale town *Wake Co.*	93.1	0.0	2.4	3.5	25.4
Laurinburg city *Scotland Co.*	92.7	0.3	1.9	3.1	20.3

Place	Automobile (%)	Public Transportation (%)	Walk (%)	Work from Home (%)	Median Travel Time to Work (minutes)
Leland town *Brunswick Co.*	92.2	0.0	0.0	5.0	23.7
Lenoir city *Caldwell Co.*	95.4	0.0	0.9	3.0	20.4
Lewisville town *Forsyth Co.*	91.8	0.0	0.2	7.8	22.7
Lexington city *Davidson Co.*	93.5	0.9	3.2	1.2	22.7
Lincolnton city *Lincoln Co.*	95.8	1.3	1.8	0.7	22.5
Lumberton city *Robeson Co.*	95.3	0.3	1.3	0.8	19.3
Matthews town *Mecklenburg Co.*	88.0	1.6	1.6	7.5	25.2
Mebane city *Alamance Co.*	94.9	0.0	0.9	3.6	24.0
Mint Hill town *Mecklenburg Co.*	93.2	1.0	0.2	4.9	28.3
Monroe city *Union Co.*	94.3	1.1	0.9	2.5	26.8
Mooresville town *Iredell Co.*	90.6	0.7	1.1	4.7	25.3
Morehead City town *Carteret Co.*	90.4	0.6	4.3	2.7	16.5
Morganton city *Burke Co.*	91.4	0.1	3.6	2.2	16.7
Morrisville town *Wake Co.*	89.5	0.1	0.7	8.6	19.9
Mount Airy city *Surry Co.*	93.7	0.8	1.2	2.6	19.6
Mount Holly city *Gaston Co.*	97.1	0.6	0.2	1.8	24.7
Murraysville cdp *New Hanover Co.*	95.8	0.3	0.0	2.2	22.0
Myrtle Grove cdp *New Hanover Co.*	91.0	0.7	0.5	7.4	20.0
New Bern city *Craven Co.*	92.8	0.0	3.1	2.7	19.3
Newton city *Catawba Co.*	97.0	0.2	0.0	2.1	19.7
Oxford city *Granville Co.*	90.9	0.0	5.7	3.0	20.7
Pinehurst village *Moore Co.*	90.7	0.0	1.1	6.7	21.6
Piney Green cdp *Onslow Co.*	92.8	0.0	4.4	2.0	25.5
Raleigh city *Wake Co.*	88.8	2.1	2.1	5.4	21.6
Reidsville city *Rockingham Co.*	95.7	0.2	0.7	3.3	21.7
Roanoke Rapids city *Halifax Co.*	93.9	0.2	2.0	3.1	16.9
Rockingham city *Richmond Co.*	96.1	0.0	0.7	2.5	16.2
Rocky Mount city *Nash Co.*	94.2	1.0	1.3	2.3	18.7
Roxboro city *Person Co.*	86.6	0.0	2.3	3.4	21.1
Saint Stephens cdp *Catawba Co.*	92.6	0.0	0.9	4.9	18.6
Salisbury city *Rowan Co.*	91.3	1.5	1.6	3.3	19.8
Sanford city *Lee Co.*	94.5	0.3	1.5	1.4	22.5
Shelby city *Cleveland Co.*	94.1	0.6	3.0	1.6	19.0
Smithfield town *Johnston Co.*	94.0	0.1	0.7	2.9	22.5
Southern Pines town *Moore Co.*	91.4	0.2	1.9	2.5	22.1
Spring Lake town *Cumberland Co.*	90.7	0.4	4.9	2.8	17.8
Stallings town *Union Co.*	89.5	0.6	0.2	9.6	29.7
Statesville city *Iredell Co.*	94.5	0.0	1.3	1.5	19.5
Summerfield town *Guilford Co.*	91.1	0.0	0.4	7.4	27.5
Tarboro town *Edgecombe Co.*	94.8	0.0	1.4	2.6	19.4
Thomasville city *Davidson Co.*	94.6	0.1	2.2	2.0	20.1
Wake Forest town *Wake Co.*	88.5	0.5	0.6	10.1	28.8
Washington city *Beaufort Co.*	93.5	0.0	2.6	1.6	21.8
Waxhaw town *Union Co.*	89.8	0.8	0.0	9.0	30.2
Waynesville town *Haywood Co.*	93.5	0.3	0.7	4.2	18.0
Weddington town *Union Co.*	88.6	0.0	0.7	9.9	30.4
Wilmington city *New Hanover Co.*	86.9	1.2	3.6	5.3	17.3
Wilson city *Wilson Co.*	92.6	0.1	1.1	2.0	18.1
Winston-Salem city *Forsyth Co.*	90.7	1.7	1.9	3.7	19.2
Winterville town *Pitt Co.*	94.4	0.2	0.0	5.4	19.9

SOURCE: U.S. Census Bureau, American Community Survey, 2009-2013 Five-Year Estimates

Crime

Place	Violent Crime Rate (crimes per 10,000 population)	Property Crime Rate (crimes per 10,000 population)
Albemarle city *Stanly Co.*	43.9	549.4
Apex town *Wake Co.*	8.7	129.4
Archdale city *Randolph Co.*	6.9	257.7
Asheboro city *Randolph Co.*	32.0	639.8
Asheville city *Buncombe Co.*	n/a	n/a
Belmont city *Gaston Co.*	n/a	n/a
Boone town *Watauga Co.*	22.2	167.8
Burlington city *Alamance Co.*	70.4	512.6
Carrboro town *Orange Co.*	25.6	277.2
Cary town *Wake Co.*	6.9	139.4
Chapel Hill town *Orange Co.*	12.1	217.7
Charlotte city *Mecklenburg Co.*	60.8	364.9
Clayton town *Johnston Co.*	16.2	238.5
Clemmons village *Forsyth Co.*	n/a	n/a
Clinton city *Sampson Co.*	70.7	569.9
Concord city *Cabarrus Co.*	14.7	307.5
Conover city *Catawba Co.*	n/a	n/a
Cornelius town *Mecklenburg Co.*	15.7	178.8
Davidson town *Mecklenburg Co.*	9.4	77.2
Dunn city *Harnett Co.*	n/a	n/a
Durham city *Durham Co.*	n/a	n/a
Eden city *Rockingham Co.*	37.3	412.3
Elizabeth City city *Pasquotank Co.*	59.3	393.0
Elon town *Alamance Co.*	2.1	88.3
Fayetteville city *Cumberland Co.*	57.8	605.4
Fuquay-Varina town *Wake Co.*	n/a	n/a
Garner town *Wake Co.*	19.2	436.0
Gastonia city *Gaston Co.*	69.8	529.2
Goldsboro city *Wayne Co.*	76.0	629.6
Graham city *Alamance Co.*	52.6	406.4
Greensboro city *Guilford Co.*	51.9	413.0
Greenville city *Pitt Co.*	63.1	438.8
Half Moon cdp *Onslow Co.*	n/a	n/a
Harrisburg town *Cabarrus Co.*	n/a	n/a
Havelock city *Craven Co.*	21.2	243.2
Henderson city *Vance Co.*	139.8	941.3
Hendersonville city *Henderson Co.*	39.7	637.1
Hickory city *Catawba Co.*	41.6	550.5
High Point city *Guilford Co.*	51.8	418.5
Holly Springs town *Wake Co.*	8.3	115.4
Hope Mills town *Cumberland Co.*	47.1	663.7
Huntersville town *Mecklenburg Co.*	9.8	187.4
Indian Trail town *Union Co.*	n/a	n/a
Jacksonville city *Onslow Co.*	n/a	n/a
Kannapolis city *Cabarrus Co.*	19.7	207.7
Kernersville town *Forsyth Co.*	36.5	430.5
Kings Mountain city *Cleveland Co.*	n/a	n/a
Kinston city *Lenoir Co.*	126.3	695.7
Knightdale town *Wake Co.*	14.4	354.3
Laurinburg city *Scotland Co.*	134.7	603.6

Place	Violent Crime Rate (crimes per 10,000 population)	Property Crime Rate (crimes per 10,000 population)
Leland town *Brunswick Co.*	15.4	252.3
Lenoir city *Caldwell Co.*	n/a	n/a
Lewisville town *Forsyth Co.*	n/a	n/a
Lexington city *Davidson Co.*	44.9	335.8
Lincolnton city *Lincoln Co.*	48.7	497.8
Lumberton city *Robeson Co.*	175.5	1,398.7
Matthews town *Mecklenburg Co.*	19.9	282.1
Mebane city *Alamance Co.*	34.3	543.1
Mint Hill town *Mecklenburg Co.*	18.5	166.7
Monroe city *Union Co.*	60.2	522.5
Mooresville town *Iredell Co.*	22.9	415.4
Morehead City town *Carteret Co.*	62.2	576.5
Morganton city *Burke Co.*	27.9	291.4
Morrisville town *Wake Co.*	5.7	197.8
Mount Airy city *Surry Co.*	38.3	500.5
Mount Holly city *Gaston Co.*	26.1	186.8
Murraysville cdp *New Hanover Co.*	n/a	n/a
Myrtle Grove cdp *New Hanover Co.*	n/a	n/a
New Bern city *Craven Co.*	39.3	513.5
Newton city *Catawba Co.*	40.8	339.8
Oxford city *Granville Co.*	99.9	666.9
Pinehurst village *Moore Co.*	5.3	82.8
Piney Green cdp *Onslow Co.*	n/a	n/a
Raleigh city *Wake Co.*	39.2	306.3
Reidsville city *Rockingham Co.*	37.1	642.6
Roanoke Rapids city *Halifax Co.*	58.7	630.5
Rockingham city *Richmond Co.*	39.0	1,006.3
Rocky Mount city *Nash Co.*	105.0	575.6
Roxboro city *Person Co.*	91.5	583.6
Saint Stephens cdp *Catawba Co.*	n/a	n/a
Salisbury city *Rowan Co.*	77.9	546.3
Sanford city *Lee Co.*	n/a	n/a
Shelby city *Cleveland Co.*	61.7	334.6
Smithfield town *Johnston Co.*	62.0	586.0
Southern Pines town *Moore Co.*	68.5	435.9
Spring Lake town *Cumberland Co.*	n/a	n/a
Stallings town *Union Co.*	10.3	163.0
Statesville city *Iredell Co.*	74.2	662.7
Summerfield town *Guilford Co.*	n/a	n/a
Tarboro town *Edgecombe Co.*	46.9	411.6
Thomasville city *Davidson Co.*	43.5	408.0
Wake Forest town *Wake Co.*	12.7	215.9
Washington city *Beaufort Co.*	n/a	n/a
Waxhaw town *Union Co.*	14.3	153.6
Waynesville town *Haywood Co.*	n/a	n/a
Weddington town *Union Co.*	n/a	n/a
Wilmington city *New Hanover Co.*	61.9	500.0
Wilson city *Wilson Co.*	n/a	n/a
Winston-Salem city *Forsyth Co.*	60.5	545.1
Winterville town *Pitt Co.*	8.4	88.1

NOTE: n/a not available.
SOURCE: Federal Bureau of Investigation, Uniform Crime Reports, 2013

Community Rankings

This section ranks incorporated places and CDPs (Census Designated Places) with populations of 2,500 or more. Unincorporated postal areas were not considered. For each topic below, you will find two tables, one in Descending Order—highest to lowest, and one in Ascending Order—lowest to highest. Four topics are exceptions to this rule, and only include Descending Order—Water Area, Ancestry (five tables), Native Hawaiian/Other Pacific Islander, and Commute to Work: Public Transportation. This is because there are an extraordinarily large number of places that place at the bottom of these topics with zero numbers.

Land Area

Top 150 Places Ranked in *Descending* Order

State Rank	Nat'l Rank	Sq. Miles	Place	State Rank	Nat'l Rank	Sq. Miles	Place
1	25	297.678	**Charlotte** (city) Mecklenburg County	76	2416	12.322	**Kings Mountain** (city) Cleveland County
2	55	145.845	**Fayetteville** (city) Cumberland County	77	2445	12.121	**Smithfield** (town) Johnston County
3	58	142.903	**Raleigh** (city) Wake County	78	2449	12.090	**Fuquay-Varina** (town) Wake County
4	69	132.449	**Winston-Salem** (city) Forsyth County	79	2451	12.080	**Cornelius** (town) Mecklenburg County
5	74	126.515	**Greensboro** (city) Guilford County	80	2488	11.810	**Clemmons** (village) Forsyth County
6	96	107.370	**Durham** (city) Durham County	81	2514	11.653	**Mount Airy** (city) Surry County
7	251	60.267	**Concord** (city) Cabarrus County	82	2520	11.626	**Elizabeth City** (city) Pasquotank County
8	315	54.345	**Cary** (town) Wake County	83	n/a	11.544	**Waxhaw** (town) Union County
9	321	53.803	**High Point** (city) Guilford County	84	n/a	11.328	**Eastover** (town) Cumberland County
10	347	51.493	**Wilmington** (city) New Hanover County	85	n/a	11.148	**Wrightsboro** (CDP) New Hanover County
11	359	50.504	**Gastonia** (city) Gaston County	86	2597	11.133	**Tarboro** (town) Edgecombe County
12	418	46.510	**Jacksonville** (city) Onslow County	87	n/a	10.895	**Conover** (city) Catawba County
13	445	44.933	**Asheville** (city) Buncombe County	88	n/a	10.494	**Moyock** (CDP) Currituck County
14	469	43.788	**Rocky Mount** (city) Nash County	89	n/a	9.984	**Midland** (town) Cabarrus County
15	570	39.610	**Huntersville** (town) Mecklenburg County	90	2797	9.946	**Roanoke Rapids** (city) Halifax County
16	750	34.607	**Greenville** (city) Pitt County	91	2800	9.934	**Belmont** (city) Gaston County
17	893	31.939	**Kannapolis** (city) Cabarrus County	92	2849	9.788	**Mount Holly** (city) Gaston County
18	n/a	29.922	**Fairview** (town) Union County	93	2877	9.618	**Graham** (city) Alamance County
19	986	29.756	**Monroe** (city) Union County	94	n/a	9.504	**Saint Stephens** (CDP) Catawba County
20	987	29.708	**Hickory** (city) Catawba County	95	n/a	9.478	**Wesley Chapel** (village) Union County
21	1039	28.747	**Wilson** (city) Wilson County	96	n/a	9.313	**Welcome** (CDP) Davidson County
22	1070	28.230	**New Bern** (city) Craven County	97	n/a	9.289	**Shallotte** (town) Brunswick County
23	1074	28.142	**Goldsboro** (city) Wayne County	98	n/a	9.278	**Archer Lodge** (town) Johnston County
24	n/a	26.958	**Unionville** (town) Union County	99	2970	9.051	**Harrisburg** (town) Cabarrus County
25	1158	26.786	**Sanford** (city) Lee County	100	n/a	8.924	**Waynesville** (town) Haywood County
26	1171	26.557	**Summerfield** (town) Guilford County	101	n/a	8.905	**Dana** (CDP) Henderson County
27	1240	25.169	**Burlington** (city) Alamance County	102	n/a	8.788	**Woodfin** (town) Buncombe County
28	1291	24.253	**Statesville** (city) Iredell County	103	3062	8.604	**Murraysville** (CDP) New Hanover County
29	1315	23.924	**Mint Hill** (town) Mecklenburg County	104	3066	8.593	**Lincolnton** (city) Lincoln County
30	n/a	23.838	**Lake Norman of Catawba** (CDP) Catawba County	105	n/a	8.510	**Aberdeen** (town) Moore County
31	n/a	23.292	**Boiling Spring Lakes** (city) Brunswick County	106	3083	8.505	**Henderson** (city) Vance County
32	1376	23.059	**Spring Lake** (town) Cumberland County	107	n/a	8.384	**Seven Lakes** (CDP) Moore County
33	n/a	22.386	**Mills River** (town) Henderson County	108	3102	8.357	**Mebane** (city) Alamance County
34	1448	22.141	**Salisbury** (city) Rowan County	109	n/a	8.341	**Forest City** (town) Rutherford County
35	1483	21.689	**Indian Trail** (town) Union County	110	n/a	8.259	**Saint James** (town) Brunswick County
36	1517	21.119	**Chapel Hill** (town) Orange County	111	3126	8.258	**Morrisville** (town) Wake County
37	1518	21.076	**Shelby** (city) Cleveland County	112	3135	8.213	**Archdale** (city) Randolph County
38	1522	20.932	**Mooresville** (town) Iredell County	113	n/a	8.188	**Washington** (city) Beaufort County
39	n/a	20.257	**Hampstead** (CDP) Pender County	114	n/a	8.138	**Locust** (city) Stanly County
40	1626	19.781	**Leland** (town) Brunswick County	115	n/a	8.137	**Mineral Springs** (town) Union County
41	1636	19.640	**Lenoir** (city) Caldwell County	116	n/a	8.117	**Gamewell** (town) Caldwell County
42	n/a	19.523	**Red Oak** (town) Nash County	117	n/a	8.114	**Kitty Hawk** (town) Dare County
43	n/a	19.245	**Stokesdale** (town) Guilford County	118	n/a	8.111	**Flat Rock** (village) Henderson County
44	1671	19.153	**Morganton** (city) Burke County	119	3193	7.909	**Stallings** (town) Union County
45	1724	18.532	**Asheboro** (city) Randolph County	120	n/a	7.844	**Brices Creek** (CDP) Craven County
46	n/a	18.516	**Oak Island** (town) Brunswick County	121	n/a	7.715	**Valdese** (town) Burke County
47	1744	18.360	**Kinston** (city) Lenoir County	122	n/a	7.675	**Clinton** (city) Sampson County
48	1773	17.978	**Lexington** (city) Davidson County	123	n/a	7.672	**Newport** (town) Carteret County
49	1779	17.893	**Lumberton** (city) Robeson County	124	n/a	7.668	**Midway** (town) Davidson County
50	n/a	17.534	**Etowah** (CDP) Henderson County	125	n/a	7.663	**Rockingham** (city) Richmond County
51	n/a	17.443	**Weddington** (town) Union County	126	n/a	7.625	**Bethlehem** (CDP) Alexander County
52	1826	17.322	**Kernersville** (town) Forsyth County	127	n/a	7.587	**James City** (CDP) Craven County
53	1847	17.110	**Matthews** (town) Mecklenburg County	128	n/a	7.536	**Mocksville** (town) Davie County
54	n/a	16.866	**Trinity** (city) Randolph County	129	n/a	7.403	**Half Moon** (CDP) Onslow County
55	1871	16.848	**Havelock** (city) Craven County	130	n/a	7.110	**River Road** (CDP) Beaufort County
56	1879	16.767	**Thomasville** (city) Davidson County	131	n/a	6.982	**Skippers Corner** (CDP) New Hanover County
57	1887	16.741	**Albemarle** (city) Stanly County	132	3410	6.942	**Hope Mills** (town) Cumberland County
58	1891	16.646	**Southern Pines** (town) Moore County	133	3411	6.940	**Hendersonville** (city) Henderson County
59	n/a	15.377	**Oak Ridge** (town) Guilford County	134	n/a	6.851	**Morehead City** (town) Carteret County
60	2040	15.372	**Apex** (town) Wake County	135	n/a	6.796	**Lowesville** (CDP) Lincoln County
61	n/a	15.269	**Pleasant Garden** (town) Guilford County	136	n/a	6.705	**Myrtle Grove** (CDP) New Hanover County
62	2066	15.095	**Wake Forest** (town) Wake County	137	n/a	6.702	**Black Mountain** (town) Buncombe County
63	2073	15.047	**Reidsville** (city) Rockingham County	138	n/a	6.633	**Elkin** (town) Surry County
64	2082	15.013	**Holly Springs** (town) Wake County	139	n/a	6.622	**Pineville** (town) Mecklenburg County
65	2117	14.747	**Garner** (town) Wake County	140	n/a	6.618	**Sawmills** (town) Caldwell County
66	n/a	14.186	**Wentworth** (town) Rockingham County	141	n/a	6.587	**Walkertown** (town) Forsyth County
67	2206	13.969	**Lewisville** (town) Forsyth County	142	n/a	6.587	**North Wilkesboro** (town) Wilkes County
68	2207	13.966	**Pinehurst** (village) Moore County	143	n/a	6.586	**Elroy** (CDP) Wayne County
69	n/a	13.930	**Butner** (town) Granville County	144	n/a	6.582	**Nags Head** (town) Dare County
70	2233	13.770	**Newton** (city) Catawba County	145	n/a	6.473	**Dunn** (city) Harnett County
71	2253	13.593	**Piney Green** (CDP) Onslow County	146	n/a	6.466	**Lake Royale** (CDP) Franklin County
72	2263	13.511	**Clayton** (town) Johnston County	147	3527	6.462	**Carrboro** (town) Orange County
73	2270	13.470	**Eden** (city) Rockingham County	148	n/a	6.451	**Roxboro** (city) Person County
74	n/a	12.850	**Tyro** (CDP) Davidson County	149	n/a	6.447	**Sunset Beach** (town) Brunswick County
75	2392	12.520	**Laurinburg** (city) Scotland County	150	n/a	6.411	**Fletcher** (town) Henderson County

Note: *The state column ranks the top/bottom 150 places in the state with population of 2,500 or more. The national column ranks the top/bottom places in the country with population of 10,000 or more. Places that are unincorporated were not considered in the rankings. n/a indicates data not available. Please refer to the User Guide for additional information.*

Land Area

Top 150 Places Ranked in *Ascending* Order

State Rank	Nat'l Rank	Sq. Miles	Place	State Rank	Nat'l Rank	Sq. Miles	Place
1	n/a	0.783	Lake Park (village) Union County	76	n/a	4.291	East Flat Rock (CDP) Henderson County
2	n/a	1.218	Enfield (town) Halifax County	77	n/a	4.306	Ahoskie (town) Hertford County
3	n/a	1.713	Ranlo (town) Gaston County	78	n/a	4.406	Enochville (CDP) Rowan County
4	n/a	1.728	Northchase (CDP) New Hanover County	79	n/a	4.453	Boiling Springs (town) Cleveland County
5	n/a	1.989	Wingate (town) Union County	80	n/a	4.538	Kings Grant (CDP) New Hanover County
6	n/a	2.046	Grifton (town) Pitt County	81	n/a	4.549	Mar-Mac (CDP) Wayne County
7	n/a	2.091	Swansboro (town) Onslow County	82	n/a	4.555	Ogden (CDP) New Hanover County
8	n/a	2.124	China Grove (town) Rowan County	83	n/a	4.560	Lillington (town) Harnett County
9	n/a	2.214	Brogden (CDP) Wayne County	84	n/a	4.581	Creedmoor (city) Granville County
10	n/a	2.239	Murfreesboro (town) Hertford County	85	n/a	4.598	Winterville (town) Pitt County
11	n/a	2.291	Buies Creek (CDP) Harnett County	86	n/a	4.620	Beaufort (town) Carteret County
12	n/a	2.305	La Grange (town) Lenoir County	87	n/a	4.625	Mountain View (CDP) Catawba County
13	n/a	2.425	Bayshore (CDP) New Hanover County	88	n/a	4.648	Elizabethtown (town) Bladen County
14	n/a	2.453	Silver Lake (CDP) New Hanover County	89	n/a	4.790	Bessemer City (city) Gaston County
15	n/a	2.464	Carolina Beach (town) New Hanover County	90	n/a	4.847	Forest Oaks (CDP) Guilford County
16	n/a	2.509	River Bend (town) Craven County	91	n/a	4.848	Selma (town) Johnston County
17	n/a	2.556	Carolina Shores (town) Brunswick County	92	n/a	4.952	Rockfish (CDP) Hoke County
18	n/a	2.661	Lowell (city) Gaston County	93	n/a	4.990	Emerald Isle (town) Carteret County
19	n/a	2.675	Mount Olive (town) Wayne County	94	n/a	5.120	Brevard (city) Transylvania County
20	n/a	2.683	Stanley (town) Gaston County	95	n/a	5.196	Granite Falls (town) Caldwell County
21	n/a	2.708	Louisburg (town) Franklin County	96	n/a	5.204	Wendell (town) Wake County
22	n/a	2.714	Royal Pines (CDP) Buncombe County	97	n/a	5.264	Hamlet (city) Richmond County
23	n/a	2.762	Fairmont (town) Robeson County	98	n/a	5.331	Hillsborough (town) Orange County
24	n/a	2.780	Yadkinville (town) Yadkin County	99	n/a	5.335	Lake Junaluska (CDP) Haywood County
25	n/a	2.785	Benson (town) Johnston County	100	n/a	5.345	Spindale (town) Rutherford County
26	n/a	2.833	Windsor (town) Bertie County	101	n/a	5.365	Porters Neck (CDP) New Hanover County
27	n/a	2.852	Rural Hall (town) Forsyth County	102	n/a	5.370	Edenton (town) Chowan County
28	n/a	2.866	Pembroke (town) Robeson County	103	n/a	5.388	Marion (city) McDowell County
29	n/a	2.867	Granite Quarry (town) Rowan County	104	n/a	5.460	Burgaw (town) Pender County
30	n/a	2.878	Fairfield Harbour (CDP) Craven County	105	n/a	5.463	Whiteville (city) Columbus County
31	n/a	2.897	Jamestown (town) Guilford County	106	n/a	5.492	Cherryville (city) Gaston County
32	n/a	2.908	Angier (town) Harnett County	107	n/a	5.524	Maiden (town) Catawba County
33	n/a	2.908	Dallas (town) Gaston County	108	n/a	5.576	Wallburg (town) Davidson County
34	n/a	2.951	Trent Woods (town) Craven County	109	n/a	5.618	Kill Devil Hills (town) Dare County
35	n/a	3.053	Warsaw (town) Duplin County	110	963	5.751	Davidson (town) Mecklenburg County
36	n/a	3.065	Spencer (town) Rowan County	111	n/a	5.837	King (city) Stokes County
37	n/a	3.066	Wallace (town) Duplin County	112	n/a	5.892	Marvin (village) Union County
38	n/a	3.110	Liberty (town) Randolph County	113	n/a	5.896	Wilkesboro (town) Wilkes County
39	n/a	3.175	Tabor City (town) Columbus County	114	n/a	6.001	Siler City (town) Chatham County
40	n/a	3.182	Polkton (town) Anson County	115	n/a	6.048	Oxford (city) Granville County
41	n/a	3.191	Sylva (town) Jackson County	116	n/a	6.119	South Rosemary (CDP) Halifax County
42	n/a	3.364	Farmville (town) Pitt County	117	1065	6.131	Boone (town) Watauga County
43	n/a	3.386	Cajah's Mountain (town) Caldwell County	118	1079	6.206	Knightdale (town) Wake County
44	n/a	3.395	Whispering Pines (village) Moore County	119	n/a	6.221	Fairview (CDP) Buncombe County
45	n/a	3.407	East Rockingham (CDP) Richmond County	120	n/a	6.309	Wadesboro (town) Anson County
46	n/a	3.435	Weaverville (town) Buncombe County	121	n/a	6.399	Swannanoa (CDP) Buncombe County
47	n/a	3.488	Ayden (town) Pitt County	122	n/a	6.411	Fletcher (town) Henderson County
48	n/a	3.489	Landis (town) Rowan County	123	n/a	6.447	Sunset Beach (town) Brunswick County
49	n/a	3.495	Gibsonville (town) Guilford County	124	n/a	6.451	Roxboro (city) Person County
50	n/a	3.500	Red Springs (town) Robeson County	125	1129	6.462	Carrboro (town) Orange County
51	n/a	3.505	Cullowhee (CDP) Jackson County	126	n/a	6.466	Lake Royale (CDP) Franklin County
52	n/a	3.518	Glen Raven (CDP) Alamance County	127	n/a	6.473	Dunn (city) Harnett County
53	n/a	3.592	Troy (town) Montgomery County	128	n/a	6.582	Nags Head (town) Dare County
54	n/a	3.670	Westport (CDP) Lincoln County	129	n/a	6.586	Elroy (CDP) Wayne County
55	n/a	3.684	Cramerton (town) Gaston County	130	n/a	6.587	North Wilkesboro (town) Wilkes County
56	n/a	3.728	Hudson (town) Caldwell County	131	n/a	6.587	Walkertown (town) Forsyth County
57	n/a	3.751	Southport (city) Brunswick County	132	n/a	6.618	Sawmills (town) Caldwell County
58	n/a	3.769	Mountain Home (CDP) Henderson County	133	n/a	6.622	Pineville (town) Mecklenburg County
59	n/a	3.775	Canton (town) Haywood County	134	n/a	6.633	Elkin (town) Surry County
60	n/a	3.797	Sneads Ferry (CDP) Onslow County	135	n/a	6.702	Black Mountain (town) Buncombe County
61	n/a	3.826	Icard (CDP) Burke County	136	n/a	6.705	Myrtle Grove (CDP) New Hanover County
62	n/a	3.844	Williamston (town) Martin County	137	n/a	6.796	Lowesville (CDP) Lincoln County
63	n/a	3.885	Elon (town) Alamance County	138	n/a	6.851	Morehead City (town) Carteret County
64	n/a	3.934	Rolesville (town) Wake County	139	1245	6.940	Hendersonville (city) Henderson County
65	n/a	3.937	Long View (town) Catawba County	140	1246	6.942	Hope Mills (town) Cumberland County
66	n/a	3.947	Southern Shores (town) Dare County	141	n/a	6.982	Skippers Corner (CDP) New Hanover County
67	n/a	4.032	Plymouth (town) Washington County	142	n/a	7.110	River Road (CDP) Beaufort County
68	n/a	4.067	Randleman (city) Randolph County	143	n/a	7.403	Half Moon (CDP) Onslow County
69	n/a	4.131	Rutherfordton (town) Rutherford County	144	n/a	7.536	Mocksville (town) Davie County
70	n/a	4.137	Nashville (town) Nash County	145	n/a	7.587	James City (CDP) Craven County
71	n/a	4.138	Zebulon (town) Wake County	146	n/a	7.625	Bethlehem (CDP) Alexander County
72	n/a	4.138	Pittsboro (town) Chatham County	147	n/a	7.663	Rockingham (city) Richmond County
73	n/a	4.184	Franklin (town) Macon County	148	n/a	7.668	Midway (town) Davidson County
74	n/a	4.190	Erwin (town) Harnett County	149	n/a	7.672	Newport (town) Carteret County
75	n/a	4.249	Raeford (city) Hoke County	150	n/a	7.675	Clinton (city) Sampson County

Note: The state column ranks the top/bottom 150 places in the state with population of 2,500 or more. The national column ranks the top/bottom places in the country with population of 10,000 or more. Places that are unincorporated were not considered in the rankings. n/a indicates data not available. Please refer to the User Guide for additional information.

Water Area

Top 150 Places Ranked in *Descending* Order

State Rank	Nat'l Rank	Sq. Miles	Place
1	n/a	8.530	Lake Norman of Catawba (CDP) Catawba County
2	n/a	6.292	James City (CDP) Craven County
3	262	5.286	Greensboro (city) Guilford County
4	303	4.198	Jacksonville (city) Onslow County
5	n/a	2.041	Sneads Ferry (CDP) Onslow County
6	582	1.988	Charlotte (city) Mecklenburg County
7	n/a	1.957	Westport (CDP) Lincoln County
8	608	1.864	Fayetteville (city) Cumberland County
9	n/a	1.665	Morehead City (town) Carteret County
10	n/a	1.665	Seven Lakes (CDP) Moore County
11	671	1.643	High Point (city) Guilford County
12	709	1.508	Wilmington (city) New Hanover County
13	719	1.482	Reidsville (city) Rockingham County
14	738	1.445	New Bern (city) Craven County
15	n/a	1.397	Oak Island (town) Brunswick County
16	n/a	1.256	Bethlehem (CDP) Alexander County
17	n/a	1.247	Fairfield Harbour (CDP) Craven County
18	844	1.247	Winston-Salem (city) Forsyth County
19	904	1.099	Raleigh (city) Wake County
20	909	1.092	Cary (town) Wake County
21	n/a	0.997	Beaufort (town) Carteret County
22	1021	0.910	Durham (city) Durham County
23	n/a	0.897	Sunset Beach (town) Brunswick County
24	1074	0.847	Wilson (city) Wilson County
25	n/a	0.835	Washington (city) Beaufort County
26	1107	0.804	Havelock (city) Craven County
27	1152	0.755	Greenville (city) Pitt County
28	n/a	0.697	Boiling Spring Lakes (city) Brunswick County
29	1269	0.628	Monroe (city) Union County
30	n/a	0.626	Whispering Pines (village) Moore County
31	1272	0.624	Elizabeth City (city) Pasquotank County
32	1302	0.592	Pinehurst (village) Moore County
33	1340	0.563	Kannapolis (city) Cabarrus County
34	n/a	0.539	Lake Royale (CDP) Franklin County
35	n/a	0.511	Myrtle Grove (CDP) New Hanover County
36	n/a	0.491	Brices Creek (CDP) Craven County
37	n/a	0.481	Trent Woods (town) Craven County
38	n/a	0.452	Wrightsboro (CDP) New Hanover County
39	n/a	0.411	Woodfin (town) Buncombe County
40	n/a	0.406	Saint Stephens (CDP) Catawba County
41	n/a	0.367	Weddington (town) Union County
42	n/a	0.361	Fairview (town) Union County
43	n/a	0.343	Porters Neck (CDP) New Hanover County
44	n/a	0.312	Lake Junaluska (CDP) Haywood County
45	1789	0.304	Cornelius (town) Mecklenburg County
46	n/a	0.299	Cramerton (town) Gaston County
47	1806	0.299	Asheville (city) Buncombe County
48	1816	0.294	Summerfield (town) Guilford County
49	n/a	0.287	Carolina Beach (town) New Hanover County
50	n/a	0.257	Ogden (CDP) New Hanover County
51	1932	0.254	Sanford (city) Lee County
52	1952	0.249	Kings Mountain (city) Cleveland County
53	1962	0.247	Davidson (town) Mecklenburg County
54	n/a	0.243	Unionville (town) Union County
55	n/a	0.243	River Bend (town) Craven County
56	n/a	0.234	Enochville (CDP) Rowan County
57	2030	0.227	Mint Hill (town) Mecklenburg County
58	2035	0.226	Gastonia (city) Gaston County
59	2038	0.225	Lewisville (town) Forsyth County
60	n/a	0.224	Creedmoor (city) Granville County
61	2073	0.216	Rocky Mount (city) Nash County
62	n/a	0.212	Etowah (CDP) Henderson County
63	2096	0.209	Clemmons (village) Forsyth County
64	2111	0.207	Burlington (city) Alamance County
65	n/a	0.204	Southern Shores (town) Dare County
66	2122	0.204	Spring Lake (town) Cumberland County
67	n/a	0.198	Edenton (town) Chowan County
68	2150	0.197	Mount Holly (city) Gaston County
69	n/a	0.189	Trinity (city) Randolph County
70	2221	0.177	Southern Pines (town) Moore County
71	2225	0.175	Belmont (city) Gaston County
72	2248	0.172	Indian Trail (town) Union County
73	n/a	0.169	Red Springs (town) Robeson County
74	n/a	0.166	Mills River (town) Henderson County
75	n/a	0.166	Kitty Hawk (town) Dare County
76	2293	0.164	Kinston (city) Lenoir County
77	2303	0.162	Huntersville (town) Mecklenburg County
78	2310	0.161	Eden (city) Rockingham County
79	2322	0.159	Laurinburg (city) Scotland County
80	n/a	0.158	Stokesdale (town) Guilford County
81	2351	0.152	Chapel Hill (town) Orange County
82	n/a	0.146	Swansboro (town) Onslow County
83	n/a	0.142	Oak Ridge (town) Guilford County
84	n/a	0.138	Hampstead (CDP) Pender County
85	2428	0.137	Mount Airy (city) Surry County
86	2456	0.134	Albemarle (city) Stanly County
87	n/a	0.129	Flat Rock (village) Henderson County
88	n/a	0.124	Pleasant Garden (town) Guilford County
89	2534	0.122	Wake Forest (town) Wake County
90	n/a	0.120	Waxhaw (town) Union County
91	2564	0.118	Holly Springs (town) Wake County
92	2579	0.116	Statesville (city) Iredell County
93	n/a	0.116	Aberdeen (town) Moore County
94	2581	0.115	Mebane (city) Alamance County
95	2626	0.110	Kernersville (town) Forsyth County
96	n/a	0.106	Forest Oaks (CDP) Guilford County
97	2698	0.099	Hope Mills (town) Cumberland County
98	n/a	0.095	Rockfish (CDP) Hoke County
99	2744	0.093	Hickory (city) Catawba County
100	2749	0.093	Asheboro (city) Randolph County
101	n/a	0.092	Landis (town) Rowan County
102	2761	0.091	Leland (town) Brunswick County
103	2767	0.090	Piney Green (CDP) Onslow County
104	n/a	0.089	Hamlet (city) Richmond County
105	n/a	0.088	Wesley Chapel (village) Union County
106	n/a	0.085	Emerald Isle (town) Carteret County
107	2828	0.083	Matthews (town) Mecklenburg County
108	2840	0.082	Lincolnton (city) Lincoln County
109	n/a	0.082	Franklin (town) Macon County
110	n/a	0.081	Glen Raven (CDP) Alamance County
111	n/a	0.079	Elkin (town) Surry County
112	2866	0.079	Lumberton (city) Robeson County
113	n/a	0.077	Fletcher (town) Henderson County
114	n/a	0.077	Nags Head (town) Dare County
115	2925	0.072	Murraysville (CDP) New Hanover County
116	n/a	0.072	Mineral Springs (town) Union County
117	n/a	0.071	Hillsborough (town) Orange County
118	n/a	0.068	Skippers Corner (CDP) New Hanover County
119	n/a	0.068	Maiden (town) Catawba County
120	n/a	0.068	Shallotte (town) Brunswick County
121	n/a	0.066	Newport (town) Carteret County
122	n/a	0.065	Wentworth (town) Rockingham County
123	2989	0.065	Graham (city) Alamance County
124	3020	0.062	Fuquay-Varina (town) Wake County
125	3028	0.061	Apex (town) Wake County
126	3056	0.059	Stallings (town) Union County
127	n/a	0.058	Bayshore (CDP) New Hanover County
128	n/a	0.056	Kill Devil Hills (town) Dare County
129	n/a	0.055	King (city) Stokes County
130	n/a	0.052	Murfreesboro (town) Hertford County
131	3125	0.052	Newton (city) Catawba County
132	3126	0.052	Morrisville (town) Wake County
133	3141	0.051	Mooresville (town) Iredell County
134	3143	0.051	Garner (town) Wake County
135	n/a	0.050	Marvin (village) Union County
136	n/a	0.049	Silver Lake (CDP) New Hanover County
137	n/a	0.048	Elon (town) Alamance County
138	n/a	0.044	Granite Falls (town) Caldwell County
139	n/a	0.043	Troy (town) Montgomery County
140	n/a	0.041	Randleman (city) Randolph County
141	n/a	0.041	Brogden (CDP) Wayne County
142	n/a	0.039	Erwin (town) Harnett County
143	n/a	0.038	Saint James (town) Brunswick County
144	n/a	0.038	Bessemer City (city) Gaston County
145	n/a	0.037	Pineville (town) Mecklenburg County
146	n/a	0.037	Moyock (CDP) Currituck County
147	3327	0.037	Tarboro (town) Edgecombe County
148	n/a	0.036	Pittsboro (town) Chatham County
149	3342	0.036	Concord (city) Cabarrus County
150	3348	0.036	Roanoke Rapids (city) Halifax County

Note: *The state column ranks the top/bottom 150 places in the state with population of 2,500 or more. The national column ranks the top/bottom places in the country with population of 10,000 or more. Places that are unincorporated were not considered in the rankings. n/a indicates data not available. Please refer to the User Guide for additional information.*

Elevation

Top 150 Places Ranked in *Descending* Order

State Rank	Nat'l Rank	Feet	Place
1	201	3,218	**Boone** (town) Watauga County
2	n/a	2,746	**Waynesville** (town) Haywood County
3	n/a	2,615	**Canton** (town) Haywood County
4	n/a	2,552	**Lake Junaluska** (CDP) Haywood County
5	n/a	2,398	**Black Mountain** (town) Buncombe County
6	n/a	2,274	**Royal Pines** (CDP) Buncombe County
7	n/a	2,251	**Dana** (CDP) Henderson County
8	n/a	2,224	**Brevard** (city) Transylvania County
8	n/a	2,224	**Fairview** (CDP) Buncombe County
10	n/a	2,208	**East Flat Rock** (CDP) Henderson County
11	n/a	2,205	**Flat Rock** (village) Henderson County
12	n/a	2,198	**Swannanoa** (CDP) Buncombe County
13	n/a	2,178	**Weaverville** (town) Buncombe County
14	276	2,159	**Hendersonville** (city) Henderson County
15	279	2,129	**Asheville** (city) Buncombe County
15	n/a	2,129	**Mountain Home** (CDP) Henderson County
17	n/a	2,119	**Franklin** (town) Macon County
18	n/a	2,116	**Cullowhee** (CDP) Jackson County
18	n/a	2,116	**Fletcher** (town) Henderson County
18	n/a	2,116	**Woodfin** (town) Buncombe County
21	n/a	2,106	**Etowah** (CDP) Henderson County
22	n/a	2,096	**Mills River** (town) Henderson County
23	n/a	2,044	**Sylva** (town) Jackson County
24	n/a	1,430	**Marion** (city) McDowell County
25	n/a	1,312	**Cajah's Mountain** (town) Caldwell County
26	n/a	1,260	**Hudson** (town) Caldwell County
27	n/a	1,234	**Sawmills** (town) Caldwell County
28	n/a	1,207	**Valdese** (town) Burke County
29	n/a	1,194	**Granite Falls** (town) Caldwell County
30	n/a	1,188	**Icard** (CDP) Burke County
31	481	1,171	**Lenoir** (city) Caldwell County
32	n/a	1,155	**Long View** (town) Catawba County
32	495	1,155	**Morganton** (city) Burke County
34	501	1,148	**Hickory** (city) Catawba County
35	n/a	1,129	**Bethlehem** (CDP) Alexander County
36	n/a	1,119	**King** (city) Stokes County
36	n/a	1,119	**Saint Stephens** (CDP) Catawba County
38	n/a	1,102	**Mountain View** (CDP) Catawba County
39	545	1,099	**Mount Airy** (city) Surry County
40	n/a	1,086	**Spindale** (town) Rutherford County
41	n/a	1,070	**Gamewell** (town) Caldwell County
42	n/a	1,056	**Conover** (city) Catawba County
43	n/a	1,024	**Wilkesboro** (town) Wilkes County
44	n/a	1,014	**Forest City** (town) Rutherford County
45	673	1,010	**Kernersville** (town) Forsyth County
45	n/a	1,010	**Rural Hall** (town) Forsyth County
47	677	1,007	**Kings Mountain** (city) Cleveland County
47	677	1,007	**Newton** (city) Catawba County
49	n/a	991	**Walkertown** (town) Forsyth County
50	n/a	988	**North Wilkesboro** (town) Wilkes County
51	n/a	978	**Cherryville** (city) Gaston County
52	732	974	**Lewisville** (town) Forsyth County
53	n/a	968	**Rutherfordton** (town) Rutherford County
54	n/a	961	**Yadkinville** (town) Yadkin County
55	n/a	955	**Stokesdale** (town) Guilford County
56	n/a	938	**Oak Ridge** (town) Guilford County
57	838	922	**High Point** (city) Guilford County
58	n/a	919	**Wallburg** (town) Davidson County
59	852	912	**Statesville** (city) Iredell County
59	852	912	**Winston-Salem** (city) Forsyth County
61	862	909	**Mooresville** (town) Iredell County
62	869	906	**Summerfield** (town) Guilford County
63	n/a	902	**Bessemer City** (city) Gaston County
63	n/a	902	**Midway** (town) Davidson County
65	n/a	899	**Maiden** (town) Catawba County
66	n/a	896	**Elkin** (town) Surry County
67	n/a	883	**Boiling Springs** (town) Cleveland County
68	n/a	869	**Landis** (town) Rowan County
69	981	866	**Archdale** (city) Randolph County
69	n/a	866	**Welcome** (CDP) Davidson County
71	n/a	860	**Enochville** (CDP) Rowan County
71	n/a	860	**Mocksville** (town) Davie County
71	999	860	**Shelby** (city) Cleveland County
74	n/a	856	**Pleasant Garden** (town) Guilford County
75	1021	850	**Thomasville** (city) Davidson County
76	1037	840	**Asheboro** (city) Randolph County
76	1037	840	**Clemmons** (village) Forsyth County
76	n/a	840	**Stanley** (town) Gaston County
79	1055	833	**Lincolnton** (city) Lincoln County
80	n/a	827	**China Grove** (town) Rowan County
80	1073	827	**Greensboro** (city) Guilford County
82	n/a	823	**Tyro** (CDP) Davidson County
83	1088	820	**Davidson** (town) Mecklenburg County
84	n/a	814	**Lake Norman of Catawba** (CDP) Catawba County
85	1109	810	**Huntersville** (town) Mecklenburg County
86	1114	807	**Lexington** (city) Davidson County
87	1122	804	**Gastonia** (city) Gaston County
87	1122	804	**Reidsville** (city) Rockingham County
87	n/a	804	**Trinity** (city) Randolph County
90	n/a	801	**Granite Quarry** (town) Rowan County
90	1131	801	**Kannapolis** (city) Cabarrus County
92	n/a	797	**Ranlo** (town) Gaston County
93	n/a	794	**Dallas** (town) Gaston County
93	n/a	794	**Jamestown** (town) Guilford County
95	1163	787	**Mint Hill** (town) Mecklenburg County
96	1174	784	**Cornelius** (town) Mecklenburg County
96	n/a	784	**Liberty** (town) Randolph County
96	n/a	784	**Lowell** (city) Gaston County
96	n/a	784	**Lowesville** (CDP) Lincoln County
96	n/a	784	**Westport** (CDP) Lincoln County
101	1211	768	**Salisbury** (city) Rowan County
102	1234	761	**Charlotte** (city) Mecklenburg County
102	n/a	761	**Forest Oaks** (CDP) Guilford County
104	1273	748	**Stallings** (town) Union County
105	n/a	735	**Wentworth** (town) Rockingham County
106	1330	728	**Matthews** (town) Mecklenburg County
106	n/a	728	**Weddington** (town) Union County
108	n/a	725	**Locust** (city) Stanly County
109	n/a	718	**Gibsonville** (town) Guilford County
110	n/a	715	**Roxboro** (CDP) Person County
111	n/a	709	**Spencer** (town) Rowan County
112	1403	705	**Concord** (city) Cabarrus County
112	n/a	705	**Elon** (town) Alamance County
114	n/a	699	**Glen Raven** (CDP) Alamance County
114	1424	699	**Indian Trail** (town) Union County
116	n/a	689	**Randleman** (city) Randolph County
117	1466	682	**Belmont** (city) Gaston County
117	n/a	682	**Marvin** (village) Union County
119	1491	676	**Mebane** (city) Alamance County
120	n/a	663	**Waxhaw** (town) Union County
121	n/a	656	**Lake Park** (village) Union County
121	n/a	656	**Troy** (town) Montgomery County
123	1580	650	**Burlington** (city) Alamance County
124	1633	636	**Graham** (city) Alamance County
125	n/a	633	**Mineral Springs** (town) Union County
126	1654	630	**Harrisburg** (town) Cabarrus County
127	1729	614	**Mount Holly** (city) Gaston County
128	n/a	610	**Cramerton** (town) Gaston County
128	n/a	610	**Wesley Chapel** (village) Union County
130	n/a	607	**Siler City** (town) Chatham County
131	1812	600	**Monroe** (city) Union County
132	1851	594	**Eden** (city) Rockingham County
132	n/a	594	**Unionville** (town) Union County
134	n/a	571	**Pineville** (town) Mecklenburg County
134	n/a	571	**Seven Lakes** (CDP) Moore County
136	n/a	568	**Wingate** (town) Union County
137	n/a	545	**Hillsborough** (town) Orange County
138	n/a	528	**Fairview** (town) Union County
139	2011	525	**Pinehurst** (village) Moore County
140	n/a	512	**Wadesboro** (town) Anson County
141	2046	505	**Henderson** (city) Vance County
142	n/a	502	**Midland** (town) Cabarrus County
143	2070	499	**Apex** (town) Wake County
143	2070	499	**Southern Pines** (town) Moore County
145	2079	495	**Cary** (town) Wake County
146	2098	486	**Chapel Hill** (town) Orange County
147	n/a	482	**Oxford** (city) Granville County
148	2120	476	**Albemarle** (city) Stanly County
149	2146	463	**Carrboro** (town) Orange County
150	n/a	443	**Rolesville** (town) Wake County

Note: *The state column ranks the top/bottom 150 places in the state with population of 2,500 or more. The national column ranks the top/bottom places in the country with population of 10,000 or more. Places that are unincorporated were not considered in the rankings. n/a indicates data not available. Please refer to the User Guide for additional information.*

Elevation

Top 150 Places Ranked in *Ascending* Order

State Rank	Nat'l Rank	Feet	Place
1	8	3	**Elizabeth City** (city) Pasquotank County
2	n/a	7	**Carolina Beach** (town) New Hanover County
2	n/a	7	**Fairfield Harbour** (CDP) Craven County
2	n/a	7	**Kill Devil Hills** (town) Dare County
2	n/a	7	**Kitty Hawk** (town) Dare County
2	n/a	7	**Moyock** (CDP) Currituck County
2	n/a	7	**Nags Head** (town) Dare County
2	n/a	7	**Oak Island** (town) Brunswick County
2	n/a	7	**Washington** (city) Beaufort County
2	n/a	7	**Windsor** (town) Bertie County
11	n/a	10	**Bayshore** (CDP) New Hanover County
11	n/a	10	**Beaufort** (town) Carteret County
11	n/a	10	**Edenton** (town) Chowan County
11	n/a	10	**Emerald Isle** (town) Carteret County
11	139	10	**New Bern** (city) Craven County
11	n/a	10	**Saint James** (town) Brunswick County
11	n/a	10	**Skippers Corner** (CDP) New Hanover County
18	n/a	12	**Sunset Beach** (town) Brunswick County
19	217	13	**Jacksonville** (city) Onslow County
19	n/a	13	**James City** (CDP) Craven County
19	n/a	13	**River Bend** (town) Craven County
19	n/a	13	**River Road** (CDP) Beaufort County
19	n/a	13	**Trent Woods** (town) Craven County
24	n/a	16	**Morehead City** (town) Carteret County
24	n/a	16	**Plymouth** (town) Washington County
24	n/a	16	**Shallotte** (town) Brunswick County
24	n/a	16	**Southern Shores** (town) Dare County
24	n/a	16	**Southport** (city) Brunswick County
24	n/a	16	**Swansboro** (town) Onslow County
30	n/a	20	**Newport** (town) Carteret County
31	390	23	**Havelock** (city) Craven County
31	390	23	**Leland** (town) Brunswick County
33	n/a	26	**Brices Creek** (CDP) Craven County
33	n/a	26	**Grifton** (town) Pitt County
33	n/a	26	**Myrtle Grove** (CDP) New Hanover County
33	n/a	26	**Sneads Ferry** (CDP) Onslow County
37	n/a	30	**Half Moon** (CDP) Onslow County
37	n/a	30	**Kings Grant** (CDP) New Hanover County
39	n/a	33	**Silver Lake** (CDP) New Hanover County
39	n/a	33	**Wrightsboro** (CDP) New Hanover County
41	n/a	36	**Hampstead** (CDP) Pender County
41	553	36	**Murraysville** (CDP) New Hanover County
41	553	36	**Wilmington** (city) New Hanover County
44	584	39	**Piney Green** (CDP) Onslow County
45	619	43	**Kinston** (city) Lenoir County
45	619	43	**Tarboro** (town) Edgecombe County
47	n/a	46	**Ahoskie** (town) Hertford County
47	n/a	46	**Carolina Shores** (town) Brunswick County
47	n/a	46	**Ogden** (CDP) New Hanover County
50	n/a	49	**Burgaw** (town) Pender County
50	n/a	49	**Wallace** (town) Duplin County
52	n/a	52	**Boiling Spring Lakes** (city) Brunswick County
53	745	56	**Greenville** (city) Pitt County
54	n/a	66	**Ayden** (town) Pitt County
55	n/a	69	**Williamston** (town) Martin County
55	n/a	69	**Winterville** (town) Pitt County
57	n/a	82	**Farmville** (town) Pitt County
57	n/a	82	**Murfreesboro** (town) Hertford County
59	n/a	95	**Eastover** (town) Cumberland County
60	1071	98	**Rocky Mount** (city) Nash County
60	n/a	98	**Whiteville** (city) Columbus County
62	1097	102	**Fayetteville** (city) Cumberland County
62	n/a	102	**Tabor City** (town) Columbus County
64	n/a	105	**Enfield** (town) Halifax County
65	n/a	108	**Elizabethtown** (town) Bladen County
65	1142	108	**Goldsboro** (city) Wayne County
65	n/a	108	**La Grange** (town) Lenoir County
68	n/a	112	**Elroy** (CDP) Wayne County
68	1159	112	**Hope Mills** (town) Cumberland County
68	n/a	112	**Mar-Mac** (CDP) Wayne County
68	1159	112	**Wilson** (city) Wilson County
72	n/a	125	**Fairmont** (town) Robeson County
73	1239	128	**Lumberton** (city) Robeson County
74	1313	148	**Smithfield** (town) Johnston County
75	n/a	154	**Clinton** (city) Sampson County
75	n/a	154	**Warsaw** (town) Duplin County
77	n/a	157	**Mount Olive** (town) Wayne County
77	1353	157	**Roanoke Rapids** (city) Halifax County
79	n/a	171	**Pembroke** (town) Robeson County
80	n/a	174	**Brogden** (CDP) Wayne County
80	n/a	174	**Selma** (town) Johnston County
82	n/a	187	**Nashville** (town) Nash County
83	n/a	190	**Erwin** (town) Harnett County
84	n/a	194	**Lillington** (town) Harnett County
85	n/a	203	**Red Oak** (town) Nash County
85	n/a	203	**Red Springs** (town) Robeson County
87	n/a	207	**Buies Creek** (CDP) Harnett County
87	n/a	207	**Dunn** (city) Harnett County
89	n/a	217	**Rockfish** (CDP) Hoke County
90	n/a	220	**Louisburg** (town) Franklin County
91	1589	223	**Laurinburg** (city) Scotland County
91	n/a	223	**South Rosemary** (CDP) Halifax County
93	n/a	243	**Benson** (town) Johnston County
94	n/a	253	**East Rockingham** (CDP) Richmond County
95	n/a	262	**Raeford** (city) Hoke County
96	1738	276	**Spring Lake** (town) Cumberland County
97	n/a	282	**Rockingham** (city) Richmond County
98	n/a	292	**Angier** (town) Harnett County
99	n/a	299	**Hamlet** (city) Richmond County
100	1808	302	**Morrisville** (town) Wake County
101	1847	315	**Knightdale** (town) Wake County
101	1847	315	**Raleigh** (city) Wake County
103	n/a	318	**Wendell** (town) Wake County
104	n/a	322	**Zebulon** (town) Wake County
105	n/a	325	**Polkton** (town) Anson County
106	n/a	331	**Aberdeen** (town) Moore County
107	n/a	338	**Archer Lodge** (town) Johnston County
108	1921	341	**Clayton** (town) Johnston County
109	1970	358	**Sanford** (city) Lee County
110	1986	361	**Garner** (town) Wake County
111	n/a	371	**Butner** (town) Granville County
111	n/a	371	**Creedmoor** (city) Granville County
111	n/a	371	**Whispering Pines** (village) Moore County
114	2056	390	**Fuquay-Varina** (town) Wake County
114	2056	390	**Wake Forest** (town) Wake County
116	2079	400	**Durham** (city) Durham County
117	n/a	407	**Pittsboro** (town) Chatham County
118	2162	440	**Holly Springs** (town) Wake County
119	n/a	443	**Rolesville** (town) Wake County
120	2214	463	**Carrboro** (town) Orange County
121	2243	476	**Albemarle** (city) Stanly County
122	n/a	482	**Oxford** (city) Granville County
123	2264	486	**Chapel Hill** (town) Orange County
124	2283	495	**Cary** (town) Wake County
125	2289	499	**Apex** (town) Wake County
125	2289	499	**Southern Pines** (town) Moore County
127	n/a	502	**Midland** (town) Cabarrus County
128	2311	505	**Henderson** (city) Vance County
129	n/a	512	**Wadesboro** (town) Anson County
130	2354	525	**Pinehurst** (village) Moore County
131	n/a	528	**Fairview** (town) Union County
132	n/a	545	**Hillsborough** (town) Orange County
133	n/a	568	**Wingate** (town) Union County
134	n/a	571	**Pineville** (town) Mecklenburg County
134	n/a	571	**Seven Lakes** (CDP) Moore County
136	2503	594	**Eden** (city) Rockingham County
136	n/a	594	**Unionville** (town) Union County
138	2535	600	**Monroe** (city) Union County
139	n/a	607	**Siler City** (town) Chatham County
140	n/a	610	**Cramerton** (town) Gaston County
140	n/a	610	**Wesley Chapel** (village) Union County
142	2619	614	**Mount Holly** (city) Gaston County
143	2697	630	**Harrisburg** (town) Cabarrus County
144	n/a	633	**Mineral Springs** (town) Union County
145	2726	636	**Graham** (city) Alamance County
146	2775	650	**Burlington** (city) Alamance County
147	n/a	656	**Lake Park** (village) Union County
147	n/a	656	**Troy** (town) Montgomery County
149	n/a	663	**Waxhaw** (town) Union County
150	2865	676	**Mebane** (city) Alamance County

Note: The state column ranks the top/bottom 150 places in the state with population of 2,500 or more. The national column ranks the top/bottom places in the country with population of 10,000 or more. Places that are unincorporated were not considered in the rankings. n/a indicates data not available. Please refer to the User Guide for additional information.

Population

Top 150 Places Ranked in *Descending* Order

State Rank	Nat'l Rank	Number	Place
1	22	731,424	**Charlotte** (city) Mecklenburg County
2	50	403,892	**Raleigh** (city) Wake County
3	78	269,666	**Greensboro** (city) Guilford County
4	92	229,617	**Winston-Salem** (city) Forsyth County
5	95	228,330	**Durham** (city) Durham County
6	121	200,564	**Fayetteville** (city) Cumberland County
7	199	135,234	**Cary** (town) Wake County
8	269	106,476	**Wilmington** (city) New Hanover County
9	281	104,371	**High Point** (city) Guilford County
10	397	84,554	**Greenville** (city) Pitt County
11	408	83,393	**Asheville** (city) Buncombe County
12	439	79,066	**Concord** (city) Cabarrus County
13	505	71,741	**Gastonia** (city) Gaston County
14	520	70,145	**Jacksonville** (city) Onslow County
15	689	57,477	**Rocky Mount** (city) Nash County
16	694	57,233	**Chapel Hill** (town) Orange County
17	834	49,963	**Burlington** (city) Alamance County
18	847	49,167	**Wilson** (city) Wilson County
19	917	46,773	**Huntersville** (town) Mecklenburg County
20	1010	42,625	**Kannapolis** (city) Cabarrus County
21	1085	40,010	**Hickory** (city) Catawba County
22	1171	37,476	**Apex** (town) Wake County
23	1210	36,437	**Goldsboro** (city) Wayne County
24	1337	33,662	**Salisbury** (city) Rowan County
25	1343	33,518	**Indian Trail** (town) Union County
26	1387	32,797	**Monroe** (city) Union County
27	1392	32,711	**Mooresville** (town) Iredell County
28	1519	30,117	**Wake Forest** (town) Wake County
29	1560	29,524	**New Bern** (city) Craven County
30	1665	28,094	**Sanford** (city) Lee County
31	1727	27,198	**Matthews** (town) Mecklenburg County
32	1762	26,757	**Thomasville** (city) Davidson County
33	1839	25,745	**Garner** (town) Wake County
34	1906	25,012	**Asheboro** (city) Randolph County
35	1917	24,866	**Cornelius** (town) Mecklenburg County
36	1936	24,661	**Holly Springs** (town) Wake County
37	1942	24,532	**Statesville** (city) Iredell County
38	2079	23,123	**Kernersville** (town) Forsyth County
39	2126	22,722	**Mint Hill** (town) Mecklenburg County
40	2231	21,677	**Kinston** (city) Lenoir County
41	2240	21,542	**Lumberton** (city) Robeson County
42	2326	20,735	**Havelock** (city) Craven County
43	2377	20,323	**Shelby** (city) Cleveland County
44	2469	19,582	**Carrboro** (town) Orange County
45	2569	18,931	**Lexington** (city) Davidson County
46	2607	18,683	**Elizabeth City** (city) Pasquotank County
47	2615	18,627	**Clemmons** (village) Forsyth County
48	2624	18,576	**Morrisville** (town) Wake County
49	2685	18,228	**Lenoir** (city) Caldwell County
50	2732	17,937	**Fuquay-Varina** (town) Wake County
51	2862	17,122	**Boone** (town) Watauga County
52	2883	16,918	**Morganton** (city) Burke County
53	3018	16,116	**Clayton** (town) Johnston County
54	3044	15,962	**Laurinburg** (city) Scotland County
55	3060	15,903	**Albemarle** (city) Stanly County
56	3090	15,754	**Roanoke Rapids** (city) Halifax County
57	3139	15,527	**Eden** (city) Rockingham County
58	3170	15,368	**Henderson** (city) Vance County
59	3213	15,176	**Hope Mills** (town) Cumberland County
60	3360	14,520	**Reidsville** (city) Rockingham County
61	3428	14,215	**Murraysville** (CDP) New Hanover County
62	3445	14,153	**Graham** (city) Alamance County
63	3516	13,831	**Stallings** (town) Union County
64	3562	13,656	**Mount Holly** (city) Gaston County
65	3602	13,527	**Leland** (town) Brunswick County
66	3663	13,293	**Piney Green** (CDP) Onslow County
67	3704	13,137	**Hendersonville** (city) Henderson County
68	3707	13,124	**Pinehurst** (village) Moore County
69	3741	12,968	**Newton** (city) Catawba County
70	3821	12,639	**Lewisville** (town) Forsyth County
71	3893	12,334	**Southern Pines** (town) Moore County
72	3996	11,964	**Spring Lake** (town) Cumberland County
73	4116	11,526	**Harrisburg** (town) Cabarrus County
74	4153	11,415	**Archdale** (city) Randolph County
74	4153	11,415	**Tarboro** (town) Edgecombe County
76	4162	11,401	**Knightdale** (town) Wake County
77	4164	11,393	**Mebane** (city) Alamance County
78	4308	10,966	**Smithfield** (town) Johnston County
79	4315	10,944	**Davidson** (town) Mecklenburg County
80	4484	10,486	**Lincolnton** (city) Lincoln County
81	4516	10,388	**Mount Airy** (city) Surry County
82	4550	10,296	**Kings Mountain** (city) Cleveland County
83	4572	10,232	**Summerfield** (town) Guilford County
84	4636	10,076	**Belmont** (city) Gaston County
85	n/a	9,869	**Waynesville** (town) Haywood County
86	n/a	9,859	**Waxhaw** (town) Union County
87	n/a	9,744	**Washington** (city) Beaufort County
88	n/a	9,558	**Rockingham** (city) Richmond County
89	n/a	9,459	**Weddington** (town) Union County
90	n/a	9,419	**Elon** (town) Alamance County
91	n/a	9,269	**Winterville** (town) Pitt County
92	n/a	9,263	**Dunn** (city) Harnett County
93	n/a	8,875	**Myrtle Grove** (CDP) New Hanover County
94	n/a	8,759	**Saint Stephens** (CDP) Catawba County
95	n/a	8,661	**Morehead City** (town) Carteret County
96	n/a	8,639	**Clinton** (city) Sampson County
97	n/a	8,461	**Oxford** (city) Granville County
98	n/a	8,362	**Roxboro** (city) Person County
99	n/a	8,352	**Half Moon** (CDP) Onslow County
100	n/a	8,165	**Conover** (city) Catawba County
101	n/a	8,113	**Kings Grant** (CDP) New Hanover County
102	n/a	7,887	**Siler City** (town) Chatham County
103	n/a	7,848	**Black Mountain** (town) Buncombe County
104	n/a	7,838	**Marion** (city) McDowell County
105	n/a	7,609	**Brevard** (city) Transylvania County
106	n/a	7,591	**Butner** (town) Granville County
107	n/a	7,479	**Pineville** (town) Mecklenburg County
108	n/a	7,476	**Forest City** (town) Rutherford County
109	n/a	7,463	**Wesley Chapel** (village) Union County
110	n/a	7,411	**Lake Norman of Catawba** (CDP) Catawba County
111	n/a	7,187	**Fletcher** (town) Henderson County
112	n/a	6,944	**Etowah** (CDP) Henderson County
113	n/a	6,904	**King** (city) Stokes County
114	n/a	6,802	**Mills River** (town) Henderson County
115	n/a	6,783	**Oak Island** (town) Brunswick County
116	n/a	6,766	**Ogden** (CDP) New Hanover County
117	n/a	6,683	**Kill Devil Hills** (town) Dare County
118	n/a	6,614	**Trinity** (city) Randolph County
119	n/a	6,495	**Hamlet** (city) Richmond County
120	n/a	6,410	**Gibsonville** (town) Guilford County
121	n/a	6,350	**Aberdeen** (town) Moore County
122	n/a	6,228	**Cullowhee** (CDP) Jackson County
123	n/a	6,204	**Porters Neck** (CDP) New Hanover County
124	n/a	6,185	**Oak Ridge** (town) Guilford County
125	n/a	6,123	**Woodfin** (town) Buncombe County
126	n/a	6,087	**Hillsborough** (town) Orange County
127	n/a	6,073	**Selma** (town) Johnston County
128	n/a	5,929	**Unionville** (town) Union County
129	n/a	5,899	**James City** (CDP) Craven County
130	n/a	5,845	**Wendell** (town) Wake County
131	n/a	5,813	**Wadesboro** (town) Anson County
132	n/a	5,760	**Cherryville** (city) Gaston County
133	n/a	5,706	**Carolina Beach** (town) New Hanover County
134	n/a	5,598	**Silver Lake** (CDP) New Hanover County
135	n/a	5,579	**Marvin** (village) Union County
136	n/a	5,511	**Williamston** (town) Martin County
137	n/a	5,394	**Whiteville** (city) Columbus County
138	n/a	5,372	**Boiling Spring Lakes** (city) Brunswick County
139	n/a	5,352	**Nashville** (town) Nash County
140	n/a	5,340	**Bessemer City** (city) Gaston County
141	n/a	5,240	**Sawmills** (town) Caldwell County
142	n/a	5,051	**Mocksville** (town) Davie County
143	n/a	5,047	**Stokesdale** (town) Guilford County
144	n/a	5,039	**Ahoskie** (town) Hertford County
145	n/a	5,004	**Edenton** (town) Chowan County
146	n/a	4,995	**East Flat Rock** (CDP) Henderson County
147	n/a	4,932	**Ayden** (town) Pitt County
148	n/a	4,896	**Wrightsboro** (CDP) New Hanover County
149	n/a	4,888	**Seven Lakes** (CDP) Moore County
150	n/a	4,871	**Long View** (town) Catawba County

Note: The state column ranks the top/bottom 150 places in the state with population of 2,500 or more. The national column ranks the top/bottom places in the country with population of 10,000 or more. Places that are unincorporated were not considered in the rankings. n/a indicates data not available. Please refer to the User Guide for additional information.

Population

Top 150 Places Ranked in *Ascending* Order

State Rank	Nat'l Rank	Number	Place
1	n/a	2,506	**Lake Royale** (CDP) Franklin County
2	n/a	2,511	**Tabor City** (town) Columbus County
3	n/a	2,532	**Enfield** (town) Halifax County
4	n/a	2,588	**Sylva** (town) Jackson County
5	n/a	2,617	**Grifton** (town) Pitt County
6	n/a	2,633	**Brogden** (CDP) Wayne County
7	n/a	2,639	**Mineral Springs** (town) Union County
8	n/a	2,646	**Sneads Ferry** (CDP) Onslow County
9	n/a	2,656	**Liberty** (town) Randolph County
10	n/a	2,663	**Fairmont** (town) Robeson County
10	n/a	2,663	**Swansboro** (town) Onslow County
12	n/a	2,664	**Icard** (CDP) Burke County
13	n/a	2,678	**Fairview** (CDP) Buncombe County
14	n/a	2,714	**Southern Shores** (town) Dare County
15	n/a	2,734	**Lake Junaluska** (CDP) Haywood County
16	n/a	2,750	**Glen Raven** (CDP) Alamance County
17	n/a	2,757	**Nags Head** (town) Dare County
18	n/a	2,785	**Skippers Corner** (CDP) New Hanover County
19	n/a	2,807	**Wentworth** (town) Rockingham County
20	n/a	2,823	**Cajah's Mountain** (town) Caldwell County
21	n/a	2,833	**Southport** (city) Brunswick County
22	n/a	2,835	**Murfreesboro** (town) Hertford County
23	n/a	2,836	**South Rosemary** (CDP) Halifax County
24	n/a	2,873	**La Grange** (town) Lenoir County
25	n/a	2,925	**Enochville** (CDP) Rowan County
26	n/a	2,928	**Whispering Pines** (village) Moore County
27	n/a	2,930	**Granite Quarry** (town) Rowan County
27	n/a	2,930	**Locust** (city) Stanly County
29	n/a	2,937	**Rural Hall** (town) Forsyth County
30	n/a	2,942	**Buies Creek** (CDP) Harnett County
31	n/a	2,945	**Lowesville** (CDP) Lincoln County
32	n/a	2,952	**Fairfield Harbour** (CDP) Craven County
33	n/a	2,959	**Yadkinville** (town) Yadkin County
34	n/a	2,973	**Pembroke** (town) Robeson County
35	n/a	3,047	**Wallburg** (town) Davidson County
36	n/a	3,048	**Carolina Shores** (town) Brunswick County
37	n/a	3,054	**Warsaw** (town) Duplin County
38	n/a	3,073	**Brices Creek** (CDP) Craven County
38	n/a	3,073	**Midland** (town) Cabarrus County
40	n/a	3,109	**Landis** (town) Rowan County
41	n/a	3,114	**Flat Rock** (village) Henderson County
42	n/a	3,119	**River Bend** (town) Craven County
43	n/a	3,120	**Weaverville** (town) Buncombe County
44	n/a	3,165	**Saint James** (town) Brunswick County
45	n/a	3,189	**Troy** (town) Montgomery County
46	n/a	3,194	**Lillington** (town) Harnett County
47	n/a	3,267	**Spencer** (town) Rowan County
48	n/a	3,272	**Kitty Hawk** (town) Dare County
49	n/a	3,298	**Rockfish** (CDP) Hoke County
50	n/a	3,310	**Maiden** (town) Catawba County
51	n/a	3,311	**Benson** (town) Johnston County
52	n/a	3,324	**Fairview** (town) Union County
53	n/a	3,329	**Dana** (CDP) Henderson County
54	n/a	3,359	**Louisburg** (town) Franklin County
55	n/a	3,375	**Polkton** (town) Anson County
56	n/a	3,382	**Jamestown** (town) Guilford County
57	n/a	3,393	**Bayshore** (CDP) New Hanover County
58	n/a	3,413	**Wilkesboro** (town) Wilkes County
59	n/a	3,422	**Lake Park** (village) Union County
60	n/a	3,428	**Red Springs** (town) Robeson County
61	n/a	3,430	**Red Oak** (town) Nash County
62	n/a	3,434	**Ranlo** (town) Gaston County
63	n/a	3,491	**Wingate** (town) Union County
64	n/a	3,526	**Lowell** (city) Gaston County
65	n/a	3,552	**Mountain View** (CDP) Catawba County
66	n/a	3,556	**Stanley** (town) Gaston County
67	n/a	3,563	**China Grove** (town) Rowan County
68	n/a	3,572	**Sunset Beach** (town) Brunswick County
69	n/a	3,583	**Elizabethtown** (town) Bladen County
70	n/a	3,615	**Mar-Mac** (CDP) Wayne County
71	n/a	3,622	**Mountain Home** (CDP) Henderson County
72	n/a	3,628	**Eastover** (town) Cumberland County
73	n/a	3,630	**Windsor** (town) Bertie County
74	n/a	3,655	**Emerald Isle** (town) Carteret County
75	n/a	3,675	**Shallotte** (town) Brunswick County
76	n/a	3,736	**East Rockingham** (CDP) Richmond County
77	n/a	3,743	**Pittsboro** (town) Chatham County
78	n/a	3,747	**Northchase** (CDP) New Hanover County
79	n/a	3,759	**Moyock** (CDP) Currituck County
80	n/a	3,776	**Hudson** (town) Caldwell County
81	n/a	3,786	**Rolesville** (town) Wake County
82	n/a	3,845	**Franklin** (town) Macon County
83	n/a	3,869	**Elroy** (CDP) Wayne County
84	n/a	3,872	**Burgaw** (town) Pender County
85	n/a	3,878	**Plymouth** (town) Washington County
86	n/a	3,879	**Tyro** (CDP) Davidson County
87	n/a	3,880	**Wallace** (town) Duplin County
88	n/a	3,890	**Forest Oaks** (CDP) Guilford County
89	n/a	4,001	**Elkin** (town) Surry County
90	n/a	4,026	**Westport** (CDP) Lincoln County
91	n/a	4,039	**Beaufort** (town) Carteret County
92	n/a	4,051	**Gamewell** (town) Caldwell County
93	n/a	4,083	**Hampstead** (CDP) Pender County
94	n/a	4,113	**Randleman** (city) Randolph County
95	n/a	4,124	**Creedmoor** (city) Granville County
96	n/a	4,150	**Newport** (town) Carteret County
97	n/a	4,155	**Trent Woods** (town) Craven County
98	n/a	4,162	**Welcome** (CDP) Davidson County
99	n/a	4,165	**Cramerton** (town) Gaston County
100	n/a	4,213	**Rutherfordton** (town) Rutherford County
101	n/a	4,214	**Bethlehem** (CDP) Alexander County
102	n/a	4,227	**Canton** (town) Haywood County
103	n/a	4,245	**North Wilkesboro** (town) Wilkes County
104	n/a	4,272	**Royal Pines** (CDP) Buncombe County
105	n/a	4,292	**Archer Lodge** (town) Johnston County
106	n/a	4,321	**Spindale** (town) Rutherford County
107	n/a	4,350	**Angier** (town) Harnett County
108	n/a	4,394	**River Road** (CDP) Beaufort County
109	n/a	4,405	**Erwin** (town) Harnett County
110	n/a	4,433	**Zebulon** (town) Wake County
111	n/a	4,488	**Dallas** (town) Gaston County
112	n/a	4,489	**Pleasant Garden** (town) Guilford County
113	n/a	4,490	**Valdese** (town) Burke County
114	n/a	4,576	**Swannanoa** (CDP) Buncombe County
115	n/a	4,589	**Mount Olive** (town) Wayne County
116	n/a	4,611	**Raeford** (city) Hoke County
117	n/a	4,647	**Boiling Springs** (town) Cleveland County
118	n/a	4,654	**Farmville** (town) Pitt County
119	n/a	4,675	**Walkertown** (town) Forsyth County
120	n/a	4,679	**Midway** (town) Davidson County
121	n/a	4,722	**Granite Falls** (town) Caldwell County
122	n/a	4,871	**Long View** (town) Catawba County
123	n/a	4,888	**Seven Lakes** (CDP) Moore County
124	n/a	4,896	**Wrightsboro** (CDP) New Hanover County
125	n/a	4,932	**Ayden** (town) Pitt County
126	n/a	4,995	**East Flat Rock** (CDP) Henderson County
127	n/a	5,004	**Edenton** (town) Chowan County
128	n/a	5,039	**Ahoskie** (town) Hertford County
129	n/a	5,047	**Stokesdale** (town) Guilford County
130	n/a	5,051	**Mocksville** (town) Davie County
131	n/a	5,240	**Sawmills** (town) Caldwell County
132	n/a	5,340	**Bessemer City** (city) Gaston County
133	n/a	5,352	**Nashville** (town) Nash County
134	n/a	5,372	**Boiling Spring Lakes** (city) Brunswick County
135	n/a	5,394	**Whiteville** (city) Columbus County
136	n/a	5,511	**Williamston** (town) Martin County
137	n/a	5,579	**Marvin** (village) Union County
138	n/a	5,598	**Silver Lake** (CDP) New Hanover County
139	n/a	5,706	**Carolina Beach** (town) New Hanover County
140	n/a	5,760	**Cherryville** (city) Gaston County
141	n/a	5,813	**Wadesboro** (town) Anson County
142	n/a	5,845	**Wendell** (town) Wake County
143	n/a	5,899	**James City** (CDP) Craven County
144	n/a	5,929	**Unionville** (town) Union County
145	n/a	6,073	**Selma** (town) Johnston County
146	n/a	6,087	**Hillsborough** (town) Orange County
147	n/a	6,123	**Woodfin** (town) Buncombe County
148	n/a	6,185	**Oak Ridge** (town) Guilford County
149	n/a	6,204	**Porters Neck** (CDP) New Hanover County
150	n/a	6,228	**Cullowhee** (CDP) Jackson County

Note: The state column ranks the top/bottom 150 places in the state with population of 2,500 or more. The national column ranks the top/bottom places in the country with population of 10,000 or more. Places that are unincorporated were not considered in the rankings. n/a indicates data not available. Please refer to the User Guide for additional information.

Population Growth

Top 150 Places Ranked in *Descending* Order

State Rank	Nat'l Rank	Percent	Place
1	n/a	3,640.3	**Lake Royale** (CDP) Franklin County
2	17	598.0	**Leland** (town) Brunswick County
3	n/a	437.0	**Marvin** (village) Union County
4	34	333.7	**Stallings** (town) Union County
5	n/a	317.4	**Rolesville** (town) Wake County
6	n/a	293.7	**Saint James** (town) Brunswick County
7	n/a	275.6	**Waxhaw** (town) Union County
8	47	256.7	**Morrisville** (town) Wake County
9	n/a	192.8	**Wesley Chapel** (village) Union County
10	n/a	182.4	**Polkton** (town) Anson County
11	72	181.5	**Indian Trail** (town) Union County
12	83	168.3	**Holly Springs** (town) Wake County
13	n/a	166.1	**Shallotte** (town) Brunswick County
14	n/a	163.7	**Eastover** (town) Cumberland County
15	93	156.5	**Harrisburg** (town) Cabarrus County
16	n/a	151.0	**Etowah** (CDP) Henderson County
17	106	139.3	**Wake Forest** (town) Wake County
18	118	131.1	**Clayton** (town) Johnston County
19	127	127.1	**Fuquay-Varina** (town) Wake County
20	n/a	123.5	**Skippers Corner** (CDP) New Hanover County
21	n/a	116.8	**Pineville** (town) Mecklenburg County
22	152	107.8	**Cornelius** (town) Mecklenburg County
23	n/a	105.7	**Carolina Shores** (town) Brunswick County
24	n/a	104.5	**Lowesville** (CDP) Lincoln County
25	n/a	100.7	**Westport** (CDP) Lincoln County
26	n/a	95.8	**Sunset Beach** (town) Brunswick County
27	168	95.3	**Murraysville** (CDP) New Hanover County
28	n/a	93.6	**Woodfin** (town) Buncombe County
29	n/a	93.5	**Winterville** (town) Pitt County
30	n/a	92.6	**Mineral Springs** (town) Union County
31	180	91.4	**Knightdale** (town) Wake County
32	194	87.4	**Huntersville** (town) Mecklenburg County
33	n/a	86.8	**Aberdeen** (town) Moore County
34	n/a	86.7	**Swansboro** (town) Onslow County
35	200	85.4	**Apex** (town) Wake County
36	n/a	84.8	**Creedmoor** (city) Granville County
37	n/a	80.8	**Boiling Spring Lakes** (city) Brunswick County
38	n/a	74.0	**Cullowhee** (CDP) Jackson County
39	245	73.8	**Mooresville** (town) Iredell County
40	n/a	71.7	**Fletcher** (town) Henderson County
41	n/a	68.1	**Pittsboro** (town) Chatham County
42	n/a	67.0	**Mountain Home** (CDP) Henderson County
43	293	65.7	**Fayetteville** (city) Cumberland County
44	n/a	63.7	**Wadesboro** (town) Anson County
45	n/a	63.5	**Lake Park** (village) Union County
46	n/a	59.0	**Windsor** (town) Bertie County
47	n/a	58.6	**Marion** (city) McDowell County
48	353	56.4	**Mebane** (city) Alamance County
49	n/a	56.2	**Lake Norman of Catawba** (CDP) Catawba County
49	n/a	56.2	**Ranlo** (town) Gaston County
51	n/a	55.1	**Oak Ridge** (town) Guilford County
52	n/a	54.5	**Stokesdale** (town) Guilford County
53	381	53.3	**Davidson** (town) Mecklenburg County
54	391	52.3	**Mint Hill** (town) Mecklenburg County
55	n/a	52.1	**Seven Lakes** (CDP) Moore County
56	n/a	49.2	**Brices Creek** (CDP) Craven County
57	n/a	48.9	**Fairfield Harbour** (CDP) Craven County
58	435	47.7	**Spring Lake** (town) Cumberland County
59	n/a	46.6	**Gibsonville** (town) Guilford County
60	448	46.3	**Raleigh** (city) Wake County
61	454	45.8	**Summerfield** (town) Guilford County
62	n/a	45.1	**Wingate** (town) Union County
63	460	45.0	**Garner** (town) Wake County
64	486	43.2	**Lewisville** (town) Forsyth County
65	488	43.1	**Cary** (town) Wake County
66	505	42.0	**Mount Holly** (city) Gaston County
67	n/a	41.3	**Weddington** (town) Union County
68	512	41.2	**Concord** (city) Cabarrus County
69	528	40.4	**Wilmington** (city) New Hanover County
70	n/a	40.2	**Rockfish** (CDP) Hoke County
71	n/a	40.1	**Whispering Pines** (village) Moore County
72	n/a	40.0	**Cramerton** (town) Gaston County
73	538	39.8	**Greenville** (city) Pitt County
74	n/a	38.6	**Murfreesboro** (town) Hertford County
75	n/a	37.6	**Wendell** (town) Wake County
76	n/a	36.2	**Raeford** (city) Hoke County
77	635	35.2	**Charlotte** (city) Mecklenburg County
77	635	35.2	**Pinehurst** (village) Moore County
77	635	35.2	**Thomasville** (city) Davidson County
80	n/a	35.1	**Bayshore** (CDP) New Hanover County
80	640	35.1	**Hope Mills** (town) Cumberland County
82	642	35.0	**Kernersville** (town) Forsyth County
83	644	34.7	**Clemmons** (village) Forsyth County
83	n/a	34.7	**Granite Quarry** (town) Rowan County
85	n/a	32.8	**Buies Creek** (CDP) Harnett County
86	n/a	32.5	**Lowell** (city) Gaston County
87	n/a	31.9	**Dallas** (town) Gaston County
88	n/a	31.1	**Butner** (town) Granville County
89	n/a	29.1	**Weaverville** (town) Buncombe County
90	798	27.7	**New Bern** (city) Craven County
91	n/a	27.2	**Angier** (town) Harnett County
91	821	27.2	**Salisbury** (city) Rowan County
93	827	27.1	**Boone** (town) Watauga County
94	838	26.6	**Archdale** (city) Randolph County
95	n/a	26.2	**Grifton** (town) Pitt County
96	850	26.1	**Hendersonville** (city) Henderson County
97	n/a	26.0	**Red Oak** (town) Nash County
98	n/a	25.7	**Half Moon** (CDP) Onslow County
99	882	25.0	**Monroe** (city) Union County
100	n/a	24.6	**Myrtle Grove** (CDP) New Hanover County
101	n/a	24.2	**Nashville** (town) Nash County
102	n/a	23.9	**Newport** (town) Carteret County
102	n/a	23.9	**Pembroke** (town) Robeson County
104	n/a	23.6	**Conover** (city) Catawba County
104	n/a	23.6	**Unionville** (town) Union County
104	940	23.6	**Winston-Salem** (city) Forsyth County
107	n/a	23.4	**Ogden** (CDP) New Hanover County
108	n/a	23.3	**Southern Shores** (town) Dare County
109	965	22.9	**Matthews** (town) Mecklenburg County
110	n/a	22.7	**Hudson** (town) Caldwell County
111	987	22.4	**Mount Airy** (city) Surry County
112	1001	22.1	**Durham** (city) Durham County
113	1019	21.6	**High Point** (city) Guilford County
114	n/a	21.4	**Carolina Beach** (town) New Hanover County
114	n/a	21.4	**Flat Rock** (village) Henderson County
116	n/a	21.3	**Locust** (city) Stanly County
117	1047	21.1	**Asheville** (city) Buncombe County
118	1049	21.0	**Sanford** (city) Lee County
119	n/a	20.9	**Mocksville** (town) Davie County
120	n/a	20.5	**Southport** (city) Brunswick County
121	1066	20.4	**Greensboro** (city) Guilford County
122	n/a	20.3	**East Flat Rock** (CDP) Henderson County
122	n/a	20.3	**Mar-Mac** (CDP) Wayne County
124	n/a	20.2	**Boiling Springs** (town) Cleveland County
125	n/a	20.0	**Forest Oaks** (CDP) Guilford County
126	n/a	19.2	**Rural Hall** (town) Forsyth County
127	n/a	17.7	**Sneads Ferry** (CDP) Onslow County
128	n/a	17.6	**Welcome** (CDP) Davidson County
129	1197	17.5	**Chapel Hill** (town) Orange County
130	1234	16.7	**Carrboro** (town) Orange County
131	n/a	16.6	**Walkertown** (town) Forsyth County
132	n/a	16.5	**Stanley** (town) Gaston County
133	n/a	16.0	**Burgaw** (town) Pender County
133	n/a	16.0	**King** (city) Stokes County
133	n/a	16.0	**Wallace** (town) Duplin County
136	1308	15.7	**Belmont** (city) Gaston County
137	n/a	15.6	**Randleman** (city) Randolph County
138	1323	15.5	**Kannapolis** (city) Cabarrus County
139	1331	15.4	**Asheboro** (city) Randolph County
140	1415	14.0	**Piney Green** (CDP) Onslow County
141	n/a	13.5	**Bethlehem** (CDP) Alexander County
142	n/a	13.3	**Benson** (town) Johnston County
142	n/a	13.3	**Kill Devil Hills** (town) Dare County
144	n/a	13.2	**Siler City** (town) Chatham County
145	1493	13.0	**Southern Pines** (town) Moore County
146	n/a	12.6	**Morehead City** (town) Carteret County
147	n/a	12.1	**Brevard** (city) Transylvania County
148	n/a	11.8	**Hillsborough** (town) Orange County
149	n/a	11.4	**Ahoskie** (town) Hertford County
150	1634	11.2	**Burlington** (city) Alamance County

Note: The state column ranks the top/bottom 150 places in the state with population of 2,500 or more. The national column ranks the top/bottom places in the country with population of 10,000 or more. Places that are unincorporated were not considered in the rankings. n/a indicates data not available. Please refer to the User Guide for additional information.

Population Growth

Top 150 Places Ranked in *Ascending* Order

State Rank	Nat'l Rank	Percent	Place
1	n/a	-19.9	**Royal Pines** (CDP) Buncombe County
2	n/a	-9.4	**Brogden** (CDP) Wayne County
3	154	-8.5	**Kinston** (city) Lenoir County
4	195	-7.6	**Havelock** (city) Craven County
5	n/a	-7.2	**Edenton** (town) Chowan County
5	n/a	-7.2	**Saint Stephens** (CDP) Catawba County
7	215	-7.1	**Roanoke Rapids** (city) Halifax County
8	n/a	-7.0	**Troy** (town) Montgomery County
9	238	-6.7	**Goldsboro** (city) Wayne County
10	n/a	-5.7	**Mountain View** (CDP) Catawba County
10	n/a	-5.7	**Williamston** (town) Martin County
12	n/a	-5.6	**Plymouth** (town) Washington County
13	342	-5.1	**Lexington** (city) Davidson County
14	n/a	-4.8	**Pleasant Garden** (town) Guilford County
15	382	-4.7	**Smithfield** (town) Johnston County
16	407	-4.5	**Henderson** (city) Vance County
17	n/a	-3.8	**East Rockingham** (CDP) Richmond County
17	n/a	-3.8	**Roxboro** (city) Person County
19	n/a	-3.3	**Silver Lake** (CDP) New Hanover County
20	n/a	-3.1	**Elizabethtown** (town) Bladen County
21	n/a	-2.9	**Erwin** (town) Harnett County
22	n/a	-2.6	**Elkin** (town) Surry County
22	n/a	-2.6	**Icard** (CDP) Burke County
22	n/a	-2.6	**Spencer** (town) Rowan County
25	653	-2.4	**Eden** (city) Rockingham County
26	665	-2.3	**Morganton** (city) Burke County
27	n/a	-1.9	**Red Springs** (town) Robeson County
28	n/a	-1.5	**China Grove** (town) Rowan County
29	n/a	-1.2	**Rockingham** (city) Richmond County
30	n/a	-1.1	**Trinity** (city) Randolph County
31	n/a	-1.0	**Forest City** (town) Rutherford County
32	n/a	-0.9	**Trent Woods** (town) Craven County
33	n/a	-0.7	**Elroy** (CDP) Wayne County
34	n/a	-0.2	**Liberty** (town) Randolph County
34	n/a	-0.2	**South Rosemary** (CDP) Halifax County
36	n/a	0.0	**Glen Raven** (CDP) Alamance County
37	n/a	0.1	**Tabor City** (town) Columbus County
37	n/a	0.1	**Valdese** (town) Burke County
37	n/a	0.1	**Warsaw** (town) Duplin County
40	1104	0.2	**Reidsville** (city) Rockingham County
41	n/a	0.5	**Clinton** (city) Sampson County
41	n/a	0.5	**Mount Olive** (town) Wayne County
43	1197	0.6	**Laurinburg** (city) Scotland County
44	n/a	0.7	**Dunn** (city) Harnett County
45	n/a	0.9	**Maiden** (town) Catawba County
46	n/a	1.0	**La Grange** (town) Lenoir County
46	n/a	1.0	**Wentworth** (town) Rockingham County
48	1360	1.4	**Albemarle** (city) Stanly County
49	n/a	1.5	**Oxford** (city) Granville County
50	n/a	1.7	**Washington** (city) Beaufort County
51	n/a	2.0	**Rutherfordton** (town) Rutherford County
52	n/a	2.1	**Nags Head** (town) Dare County
53	n/a	2.2	**Lake Junaluska** (CDP) Haywood County
54	n/a	2.3	**Fairmont** (town) Robeson County
55	n/a	2.4	**Granite Falls** (town) Caldwell County
56	1596	2.5	**Tarboro** (town) Edgecombe County
57	n/a	2.6	**Enochville** (CDP) Rowan County
58	n/a	2.7	**Selma** (town) Johnston County
59	1663	2.8	**Rocky Mount** (city) Nash County
60	n/a	3.1	**North Wilkesboro** (town) Wilkes County
61	n/a	3.2	**Long View** (town) Catawba County
61	1746	3.2	**Newton** (city) Catawba County
61	n/a	3.2	**Oak Island** (town) Brunswick County
64	1824	3.6	**Lumberton** (city) Robeson County
65	n/a	3.8	**Landis** (town) Rowan County
66	n/a	4.3	**Bessemer City** (city) Gaston County
66	1978	4.3	**Shelby** (city) Cleveland County
68	n/a	4.5	**Black Mountain** (town) Buncombe County
69	n/a	4.8	**Emerald Isle** (town) Carteret County
69	n/a	4.8	**Kings Grant** (CDP) New Hanover County
69	n/a	4.8	**Whiteville** (city) Columbus County
72	n/a	4.9	**Canton** (town) Haywood County
73	n/a	5.0	**Yadkinville** (town) Yadkin County
74	2101	5.1	**Jacksonville** (city) Onslow County
75	n/a	5.2	**Cajah's Mountain** (town) Caldwell County
75	2129	5.2	**Lincolnton** (city) Lincoln County
75	2129	5.2	**Statesville** (city) Iredell County
78	2275	6.2	**Kings Mountain** (city) Cleveland County
79	n/a	6.3	**Sylva** (town) Jackson County
80	n/a	6.5	**Sawmills** (town) Caldwell County
81	n/a	6.7	**Ayden** (town) Pitt County
81	n/a	6.7	**River Bend** (town) Craven County
83	n/a	6.9	**Waynesville** (town) Haywood County
84	n/a	7.1	**Beaufort** (town) Carteret County
85	n/a	7.3	**Fairview** (CDP) Buncombe County
85	n/a	7.3	**River Road** (CDP) Beaufort County
87	n/a	7.4	**Cherryville** (city) Gaston County
87	n/a	7.4	**Spindale** (town) Rutherford County
89	2456	7.5	**Hickory** (city) Catawba County
90	n/a	7.9	**Enfield** (town) Halifax County
90	n/a	7.9	**Hamlet** (city) Richmond County
92	n/a	8.0	**Louisburg** (town) Franklin County
92	n/a	8.0	**Wilkesboro** (town) Wilkes County
94	n/a	8.2	**Farmville** (town) Pitt County
94	2540	8.2	**Gastonia** (city) Gaston County
96	2571	8.5	**Lenoir** (city) Caldwell County
97	2595	8.7	**Elizabeth City** (city) Pasquotank County
98	n/a	8.8	**James City** (CDP) Craven County
99	n/a	8.9	**Wrightsboro** (CDP) New Hanover County
100	n/a	9.4	**Kitty Hawk** (town) Dare County
101	n/a	9.5	**Jamestown** (town) Guilford County
102	n/a	9.6	**Lillington** (town) Harnett County
102	n/a	9.6	**Zebulon** (town) Wake County
104	n/a	10.2	**Franklin** (town) Macon County
105	2771	10.3	**Graham** (city) Alamance County
106	n/a	10.7	**Swannanoa** (CDP) Buncombe County
106	2812	10.7	**Wilson** (city) Wilson County
108	2851	11.2	**Burlington** (city) Alamance County
108	n/a	11.2	**Gamewell** (town) Caldwell County
110	n/a	11.4	**Ahoskie** (town) Hertford County
111	n/a	11.8	**Hillsborough** (town) Orange County
112	n/a	12.1	**Brevard** (city) Transylvania County
113	n/a	12.6	**Morehead City** (town) Carteret County
114	2990	13.0	**Southern Pines** (town) Moore County
115	n/a	13.2	**Siler City** (town) Chatham County
116	n/a	13.3	**Benson** (town) Johnston County
116	n/a	13.3	**Kill Devil Hills** (town) Dare County
118	n/a	13.5	**Bethlehem** (CDP) Alexander County
119	3070	14.0	**Piney Green** (CDP) Onslow County
120	3156	15.4	**Asheboro** (city) Randolph County
121	3162	15.5	**Kannapolis** (city) Cabarrus County
122	n/a	15.6	**Randleman** (city) Randolph County
123	3175	15.7	**Belmont** (city) Gaston County
124	n/a	16.0	**Burgaw** (town) Pender County
124	n/a	16.0	**King** (city) Stokes County
124	n/a	16.0	**Wallace** (town) Duplin County
127	n/a	16.5	**Stanley** (town) Gaston County
128	n/a	16.6	**Walkertown** (town) Forsyth County
129	3251	16.7	**Carrboro** (town) Orange County
130	3291	17.5	**Chapel Hill** (town) Orange County
131	n/a	17.6	**Welcome** (CDP) Davidson County
132	n/a	17.7	**Sneads Ferry** (CDP) Onslow County
133	n/a	19.2	**Rural Hall** (town) Forsyth County
134	n/a	20.0	**Forest Oaks** (CDP) Guilford County
135	n/a	20.2	**Boiling Springs** (town) Cleveland County
136	n/a	20.3	**East Flat Rock** (CDP) Henderson County
136	n/a	20.3	**Mar-Mac** (CDP) Wayne County
138	3419	20.4	**Greensboro** (city) Guilford County
139	n/a	20.5	**Southport** (city) Brunswick County
140	n/a	20.9	**Mocksville** (town) Davie County
141	3441	21.0	**Sanford** (city) Lee County
142	3444	21.1	**Asheville** (city) Buncombe County
143	n/a	21.3	**Locust** (city) Stanly County
144	n/a	21.4	**Carolina Beach** (town) New Hanover County
144	n/a	21.4	**Flat Rock** (village) Henderson County
146	3470	21.6	**High Point** (city) Guilford County
147	3489	22.1	**Durham** (city) Durham County
148	3502	22.4	**Mount Airy** (city) Surry County
149	n/a	22.7	**Hudson** (town) Caldwell County
150	3523	22.9	**Matthews** (town) Mecklenburg County

Note: *The state column ranks the top/bottom 150 places in the state with population of 2,500 or more. The national column ranks the top/bottom places in the country with population of 10,000 or more. Places that are unincorporated were not considered in the rankings. n/a indicates data not available. Please refer to the User Guide for additional information.*

Population Density

Top 150 Places Ranked in *Descending* Order

State Rank	Nat'l Rank	Pop./ Sq. Mi.	Place
1	n/a	4,371.2	Lake Park (village) Union County
2	1455	3,030.3	Carrboro (town) Orange County
3	1600	2,826.3	Raleigh (city) Wake County
4	1625	2,792.8	Boone (town) Watauga County
5	1681	2,710.0	Chapel Hill (town) Orange County
6	1864	2,488.4	Cary (town) Wake County
7	1885	2,457.1	Charlotte (city) Mecklenburg County
8	1900	2,443.3	Greenville (city) Pitt County
9	1908	2,437.9	Apex (town) Wake County
10	n/a	2,424.4	Elon (town) Alamance County
11	n/a	2,315.9	Carolina Beach (town) New Hanover County
12	n/a	2,281.7	Silver Lake (CDP) New Hanover County
13	2109	2,249.4	Morrisville (town) Wake County
14	2161	2,186.0	Hope Mills (town) Cumberland County
15	n/a	2,168.1	Northchase (CDP) New Hanover County
16	2217	2,131.5	Greensboro (city) Guilford County
17	2225	2,126.6	Durham (city) Durham County
18	n/a	2,078.8	Enfield (town) Halifax County
19	2294	2,067.8	Wilmington (city) New Hanover County
20	2298	2,058.4	Cornelius (town) Mecklenburg County
21	n/a	2,015.7	Winterville (town) Pitt County
22	n/a	2,004.3	Ranlo (town) Gaston County
23	2363	1,995.2	Wake Forest (town) Wake County
24	2374	1,985.1	Burlington (city) Alamance County
25	2420	1,939.9	High Point (city) Guilford County
26	2462	1,902.9	Davidson (town) Mecklenburg County
27	2475	1,892.9	Hendersonville (city) Henderson County
28	2516	1,855.9	Asheville (city) Buncombe County
29	2537	1,837.2	Knightdale (town) Wake County
30	n/a	1,834.9	Gibsonville (town) Guilford County
31	2576	1,807.0	Henderson (city) Vance County
32	n/a	1,787.7	Kings Grant (CDP) New Hanover County
33	n/a	1,777.1	Cullowhee (CDP) Jackson County
34	n/a	1,754.9	Wingate (town) Union County
35	2654	1,748.8	Stallings (town) Union County
36	2656	1,745.8	Garner (town) Wake County
37	2678	1,733.6	Winston-Salem (city) Forsyth County
38	n/a	1,715.8	Mount Olive (town) Wayne County
39	2708	1,710.3	Wilson (city) Wilson County
40	n/a	1,677.6	China Grove (town) Rowan County
41	2789	1,652.2	Murraysville (CDP) New Hanover County
42	2801	1,642.7	Holly Springs (town) Wake County
43	2842	1,606.9	Elizabeth City (city) Pasquotank County
44	2856	1,595.8	Thomasville (city) Davidson County
45	2862	1,589.6	Matthews (town) Mecklenburg County
46	2868	1,584.0	Roanoke Rapids (city) Halifax County
47	2875	1,577.3	Clemmons (village) Forsyth County
48	n/a	1,574.1	Royal Pines (CDP) Buncombe County
49	2889	1,562.7	Mooresville (town) Iredell County
50	2915	1,545.4	Indian Trail (town) Union County
51	n/a	1,543.1	Dallas (town) Gaston County
52	2945	1,520.3	Salisbury (city) Rowan County
53	2968	1,508.2	Jacksonville (city) Onslow County
54	n/a	1,496.0	Angier (town) Harnett County
55	n/a	1,486.0	Brevard (city) Transylvania County
56	n/a	1,485.5	Ogden (CDP) New Hanover County
57	2997	1,483.6	Fuquay-Varina (town) Wake County
58	3008	1,471.6	Graham (city) Alamance County
59	n/a	1,454.7	Marion (city) McDowell County
60	n/a	1,433.7	Williamston (town) Martin County
61	n/a	1,431.0	Dunn (city) Harnett County
62	3091	1,420.5	Gastonia (city) Gaston County
63	n/a	1,413.8	Ayden (town) Pitt County
64	n/a	1,408.0	Trent Woods (town) Craven County
65	n/a	1,399.0	Bayshore (CDP) New Hanover County
66	n/a	1,398.9	Oxford (city) Granville County
67	3127	1,395.2	Mount Holly (city) Gaston County
68	3134	1,389.8	Archdale (city) Randolph County
69	n/a	1,383.6	Farmville (town) Pitt County
70	3154	1,375.2	Fayetteville (city) Cumberland County
71	3171	1,363.3	Mebane (city) Alamance County
72	3193	1,349.6	Asheboro (city) Randolph County
73	3195	1,346.8	Hickory (city) Catawba County
74	3205	1,334.9	Kernersville (town) Forsyth County
75	3206	1,334.6	Kannapolis (city) Cabarrus County
76	n/a	1,325.4	Stanley (town) Gaston County
77	n/a	1,325.0	Lowell (city) Gaston County
78	n/a	1,323.7	Myrtle Grove (CDP) New Hanover County
79	n/a	1,314.2	Siler City (town) Chatham County
80	3240	1,312.6	Rocky Mount (city) Nash County
81	3242	1,311.9	Concord (city) Cabarrus County
82	n/a	1,296.3	Roxboro (city) Person County
83	3258	1,294.8	Goldsboro (city) Wayne County
84	n/a	1,293.6	Nashville (town) Nash County
85	n/a	1,284.3	Buies Creek (CDP) Harnett County
86	n/a	1,281.3	Windsor (town) Bertie County
87	n/a	1,279.0	Grifton (town) Pitt County
88	3284	1,274.9	Laurinburg (city) Scotland County
89	n/a	1,273.5	Swansboro (town) Onslow County
90	3289	1,273.4	Harrisburg (town) Cabarrus County
91	n/a	1,266.0	Murfreesboro (town) Hertford County
92	n/a	1,265.5	Wallace (town) Duplin County
93	n/a	1,264.2	Morehead City (town) Carteret County
94	n/a	1,252.8	Selma (town) Johnston County
95	n/a	1,247.2	Rockingham (city) Richmond County
96	n/a	1,246.7	La Grange (town) Lenoir County
97	n/a	1,243.3	River Bend (town) Craven County
98	n/a	1,240.5	Louisburg (town) Franklin County
99	n/a	1,237.3	Long View (town) Catawba County
100	n/a	1,233.9	Hamlet (city) Richmond County
101	3348	1,230.7	Havelock (city) Craven County
102	3362	1,220.3	Lincolnton (city) Lincoln County
103	3387	1,203.9	Lumberton (city) Robeson County
104	3406	1,192.8	Clayton (town) Johnston County
105	n/a	1,192.3	Carolina Shores (town) Brunswick County
106	n/a	1,190.0	Washington (city) Beaufort County
107	n/a	1,189.6	Kill Devil Hills (town) Dare County
108	n/a	1,189.3	Brogden (CDP) Wayne County
109	n/a	1,189.0	Benson (town) Johnston County
110	n/a	1,182.7	King (city) Stokes County
111	3427	1,180.8	Huntersville (town) Mecklenburg County
112	3428	1,180.7	Kinston (city) Lenoir County
113	n/a	1,171.0	Black Mountain (town) Buncombe County
114	n/a	1,170.2	Ahoskie (town) Hertford County
115	n/a	1,167.2	Jamestown (town) Guilford County
116	n/a	1,164.1	East Flat Rock (CDP) Henderson County
117	n/a	1,156.3	Porters Neck (CDP) New Hanover County
118	3467	1,152.7	Eden (city) Rockingham County
119	n/a	1,141.8	Hillsborough (town) Orange County
120	n/a	1,130.5	Cramerton (town) Gaston County
121	n/a	1,129.4	Pineville (town) Mecklenburg County
122	n/a	1,128.2	Half Moon (CDP) Onslow County
123	n/a	1,125.6	Clinton (city) Sampson County
124	n/a	1,123.1	Wendell (town) Wake County
125	n/a	1,121.0	Fletcher (town) Henderson County
126	n/a	1,119.7	Canton (town) Haywood County
127	n/a	1,114.9	Bessemer City (city) Gaston County
128	n/a	1,105.9	Waynesville (town) Haywood County
129	3538	1,102.2	Monroe (city) Union County
130	n/a	1,096.9	Westport (CDP) Lincoln County
131	n/a	1,096.5	East Rockingham (CDP) Richmond County
132	n/a	1,085.1	Raeford (city) Hoke County
133	n/a	1,071.4	Zebulon (town) Wake County
134	n/a	1,066.0	Spencer (town) Rowan County
135	n/a	1,064.3	Yadkinville (town) Yadkin County
136	n/a	1,060.8	Polkton (town) Anson County
137	3602	1,053.0	Lexington (city) Davidson County
138	n/a	1,051.2	Erwin (town) Harnett County
139	n/a	1,048.9	Cherryville (city) Gaston County
140	3607	1,048.8	Sanford (city) Lee County
141	3613	1,045.9	New Bern (city) Craven County
142	n/a	1,043.6	Boiling Springs (town) Cleveland County
143	n/a	1,037.2	Pembroke (town) Robeson County
144	n/a	1,029.8	Rural Hall (town) Forsyth County
145	n/a	1,025.5	Fairfield Harbour (CDP) Craven County
146	3640	1,025.3	Tarboro (town) Edgecombe County
147	n/a	1,022.1	Granite Quarry (town) Rowan County
148	n/a	1,019.8	Rutherfordton (town) Rutherford County
149	3657	1,014.3	Belmont (city) Gaston County
150	n/a	1,013.0	Hudson (town) Caldwell County

Note: *The state column ranks the top/bottom 150 places in the state with population of 2,500 or more. The national column ranks the top/bottom places in the country with population of 10,000 or more. Places that are unincorporated were not considered in the rankings. n/a indicates data not available. Please refer to the User Guide for additional information.*

Population Density

Top 150 Places Ranked in *Ascending* Order

State Rank	Nat'l Rank	Pop./ Sq. Mi.	Place
1	n/a	111.1	Fairview (town) Union County
2	n/a	175.7	Red Oak (town) Nash County
3	n/a	197.9	Wentworth (town) Rockingham County
4	n/a	201.6	Hampstead (CDP) Pender County
5	n/a	219.9	Unionville (town) Union County
6	n/a	230.6	Boiling Spring Lakes (city) Brunswick County
7	n/a	262.3	Stokesdale (town) Guilford County
8	n/a	294.0	Pleasant Garden (town) Guilford County
9	n/a	301.9	Tyro (CDP) Davidson County
10	n/a	303.8	Mills River (town) Henderson County
11	n/a	307.8	Midland (town) Cabarrus County
12	n/a	310.9	Lake Norman of Catawba (CDP) Catawba County
13	n/a	320.3	Eastover (town) Cumberland County
14	n/a	324.3	Mineral Springs (town) Union County
15	n/a	358.2	Moyock (CDP) Currituck County
16	n/a	360.0	Locust (city) Stanly County
17	n/a	366.3	Oak Island (town) Brunswick County
18	n/a	373.8	Dana (CDP) Henderson County
19	n/a	383.2	Saint James (town) Brunswick County
20	n/a	383.9	Flat Rock (village) Henderson County
21	216	385.3	Summerfield (town) Guilford County
22	n/a	387.5	Lake Royale (CDP) Franklin County
23	n/a	391.8	Brices Creek (CDP) Craven County
24	n/a	392.1	Trinity (city) Randolph County
25	n/a	395.6	Shallotte (town) Brunswick County
26	n/a	396.0	Etowah (CDP) Henderson County
27	n/a	398.9	Skippers Corner (CDP) New Hanover County
28	n/a	402.2	Oak Ridge (town) Guilford County
29	n/a	403.3	Kitty Hawk (town) Dare County
30	n/a	418.9	Nags Head (town) Dare County
31	n/a	430.5	Fairview (CDP) Buncombe County
32	n/a	433.3	Lowesville (CDP) Lincoln County
33	n/a	439.2	Wrightsboro (CDP) New Hanover County
34	n/a	446.9	Welcome (CDP) Davidson County
35	n/a	462.6	Archer Lodge (town) Johnston County
36	n/a	463.4	South Rosemary (CDP) Halifax County
37	n/a	499.1	Gamewell (town) Caldwell County
38	n/a	512.5	Lake Junaluska (CDP) Haywood County
39	371	518.8	Spring Lake (town) Cumberland County
40	n/a	541.0	Newport (town) Carteret County
41	n/a	542.3	Weddington (town) Union County
42	n/a	544.9	Butner (town) Granville County
43	n/a	546.5	Wallburg (town) Davidson County
44	n/a	552.7	Bethlehem (CDP) Alexander County
45	n/a	554.0	Sunset Beach (town) Brunswick County
46	n/a	578.9	Wilkesboro (town) Wilkes County
47	n/a	582.0	Valdese (town) Burke County
48	n/a	583.0	Seven Lakes (CDP) Moore County
49	n/a	587.5	Elroy (CDP) Wayne County
50	n/a	599.2	Maiden (town) Catawba County
51	n/a	603.2	Elkin (town) Surry County
52	n/a	610.2	Midway (town) Davidson County
53	n/a	618.0	River Road (CDP) Beaufort County
54	n/a	644.4	North Wilkesboro (town) Wilkes County
55	n/a	663.8	Enochville (CDP) Rowan County
56	n/a	666.0	Rockfish (CDP) Hoke County
57	n/a	670.2	Mocksville (town) Davie County
58	574	683.8	Leland (town) Brunswick County
59	n/a	687.5	Southern Shores (town) Dare County
60	n/a	696.3	Icard (CDP) Burke County
61	n/a	696.7	Woodfin (town) Buncombe County
62	n/a	696.9	Sneads Ferry (CDP) Onslow County
63	n/a	700.5	Lillington (town) Harnett County
64	n/a	709.1	Burgaw (town) Pender County
65	n/a	709.7	Walkertown (town) Forsyth County
66	n/a	715.1	Swannanoa (CDP) Buncombe County
67	n/a	732.4	Emerald Isle (town) Carteret County
68	641	741.0	Southern Pines (town) Moore County
69	n/a	746.2	Aberdeen (town) Moore County
70	n/a	749.4	Conover (city) Catawba County
71	n/a	755.3	Southport (city) Brunswick County
72	n/a	767.9	Mountain View (CDP) Catawba County
73	n/a	770.9	Elizabethtown (town) Bladen County
74	n/a	777.5	James City (CDP) Craven County
75	n/a	781.7	Glen Raven (CDP) Alamance County
76	n/a	787.4	Wesley Chapel (village) Union County
77	n/a	790.9	Tabor City (town) Columbus County
78	n/a	791.8	Sawmills (town) Caldwell County
79	n/a	794.7	Mar-Mac (CDP) Wayne County
80	n/a	802.5	Forest Oaks (CDP) Guilford County
81	n/a	808.4	Spindale (town) Rutherford County
82	n/a	811.0	Sylva (town) Jackson County
83	n/a	833.8	Cajah's Mountain (town) Caldwell County
84	769	835.6	Kings Mountain (city) Cleveland County
85	n/a	853.9	Liberty (town) Randolph County
86	n/a	854.0	Waxhaw (town) Union County
87	n/a	862.4	Whispering Pines (village) Moore County
88	n/a	874.2	Beaufort (town) Carteret County
89	823	883.3	Morganton (city) Burke County
90	n/a	887.8	Troy (town) Montgomery County
91	n/a	891.2	Landis (town) Rowan County
92	835	891.4	Mount Airy (city) Surry County
93	n/a	896.3	Forest City (town) Rutherford County
94	n/a	900.2	Creedmoor (city) Granville County
95	n/a	904.6	Pittsboro (town) Chatham County
96	854	904.7	Smithfield (town) Johnston County
97	855	904.8	Lewisville (town) Forsyth County
98	n/a	908.4	Weaverville (town) Buncombe County
99	n/a	908.8	Granite Falls (town) Caldwell County
100	n/a	918.9	Franklin (town) Macon County
101	n/a	921.5	Wadesboro (town) Anson County
102	n/a	921.7	Saint Stephens (CDP) Catawba County
103	878	928.1	Lenoir (city) Caldwell County
104	n/a	931.8	Edenton (town) Chowan County
105	895	939.7	Pinehurst (village) Moore County
106	898	941.8	Newton (city) Catawba County
107	n/a	947.0	Marvin (village) Union County
108	910	949.8	Mint Hill (town) Mecklenburg County
109	911	949.9	Albemarle (city) Stanly County
110	n/a	960.9	Mountain Home (CDP) Henderson County
111	n/a	961.7	Plymouth (town) Washington County
112	n/a	962.5	Rolesville (town) Wake County
113	n/a	964.3	Fairmont (town) Robeson County
113	930	964.3	Shelby (city) Cleveland County
115	933	965.0	Reidsville (city) Rockingham County
116	945	977.9	Piney Green (CDP) Onslow County
117	n/a	979.3	Red Springs (town) Robeson County
118	n/a	987.4	Whiteville (city) Columbus County
119	n/a	1,000.3	Warsaw (town) Duplin County
120	n/a	1,011.3	Randleman (city) Randolph County
121	996	1,011.5	Statesville (city) Iredell County
122	n/a	1,013.0	Hudson (town) Caldwell County
123	999	1,014.3	Belmont (city) Gaston County
124	n/a	1,019.8	Rutherfordton (town) Rutherford County
125	n/a	1,022.1	Granite Quarry (town) Rowan County
126	1016	1,025.3	Tarboro (town) Edgecombe County
127	n/a	1,025.5	Fairfield Harbour (CDP) Craven County
128	n/a	1,029.8	Rural Hall (town) Forsyth County
129	n/a	1,037.2	Pembroke (town) Robeson County
130	n/a	1,043.6	Boiling Springs (town) Cleveland County
131	1043	1,045.9	New Bern (city) Craven County
132	1049	1,048.8	Sanford (city) Lee County
133	n/a	1,048.9	Cherryville (city) Gaston County
134	n/a	1,051.2	Erwin (town) Harnett County
135	1054	1,053.0	Lexington (city) Davidson County
136	n/a	1,060.8	Polkton (town) Anson County
137	n/a	1,064.3	Yadkinville (town) Yadkin County
138	n/a	1,066.0	Spencer (town) Rowan County
139	n/a	1,071.4	Zebulon (town) Wake County
140	n/a	1,085.1	Raeford (city) Hoke County
141	n/a	1,096.5	East Rockingham (CDP) Richmond County
142	n/a	1,096.9	Westport (CDP) Lincoln County
143	1118	1,102.2	Monroe (city) Union County
144	n/a	1,105.9	Waynesville (town) Haywood County
145	n/a	1,114.9	Bessemer City (city) Gaston County
146	n/a	1,119.7	Canton (town) Haywood County
147	n/a	1,121.0	Fletcher (town) Henderson County
148	n/a	1,123.1	Wendell (town) Wake County
149	n/a	1,125.6	Clinton (city) Sampson County
150	n/a	1,128.2	Half Moon (CDP) Onslow County

Note: *The state column ranks the top/bottom 150 places in the state with population of 2,500 or more. The national column ranks the top/bottom places in the country with population of 10,000 or more. Places that are unincorporated were not considered in the rankings. n/a indicates data not available. Please refer to the User Guide for additional information.*

White Population

Top 150 Places Ranked in *Descending* Order

State Rank	Nat'l Rank	Percent	Place
1	n/a	98.2	**Flat Rock** (village) Henderson County
2	n/a	97.8	**Lake Junaluska** (CDP) Haywood County
2	n/a	97.8	**Saint James** (town) Brunswick County
2	n/a	97.8	**Southern Shores** (town) Dare County
5	n/a	97.4	**Fairview** (town) Union County
6	n/a	96.8	**Sunset Beach** (town) Brunswick County
7	n/a	96.7	**Emerald Isle** (town) Carteret County
7	n/a	96.7	**Oak Island** (town) Brunswick County
9	n/a	96.6	**Bethlehem** (CDP) Alexander County
10	n/a	96.3	**Kitty Hawk** (town) Dare County
11	n/a	96.1	**Carolina Beach** (town) New Hanover County
11	n/a	96.1	**Trent Woods** (town) Craven County
13	n/a	95.9	**Carolina Shores** (town) Brunswick County
14	n/a	95.5	**Cajah's Mountain** (town) Caldwell County
14	n/a	95.5	**Whispering Pines** (village) Moore County
16	n/a	95.2	**Weaverville** (town) Buncombe County
17	n/a	95.1	**King** (city) Stokes County
17	n/a	95.1	**Westport** (CDP) Lincoln County
19	n/a	95.0	**Lake Norman of Catawba** (CDP) Catawba County
20	n/a	94.9	**Unionville** (town) Union County
20	n/a	94.9	**Wallburg** (town) Davidson County
22	n/a	94.7	**Mills River** (town) Henderson County
23	n/a	94.6	**Nags Head** (town) Dare County
24	n/a	94.5	**Fairfield Harbour** (CDP) Craven County
24	n/a	94.5	**Fairview** (CDP) Buncombe County
26	n/a	94.4	**Ogden** (CDP) New Hanover County
26	n/a	94.4	**Seven Lakes** (CDP) Moore County
28	n/a	94.1	**Sawmills** (town) Caldwell County
29	n/a	93.6	**Canton** (town) Haywood County
29	n/a	93.6	**Enochville** (CDP) Rowan County
31	n/a	93.5	**Granite Falls** (town) Caldwell County
31	n/a	93.5	**Hudson** (town) Caldwell County
31	n/a	93.5	**Locust** (city) Stanly County
31	n/a	93.5	**Tyro** (CDP) Davidson County
35	n/a	93.4	**Etowah** (CDP) Henderson County
36	n/a	93.3	**Bayshore** (CDP) New Hanover County
37	n/a	93.0	**Icard** (CDP) Burke County
37	n/a	93.0	**Myrtle Grove** (CDP) New Hanover County
39	749	92.8	**Pinehurst** (village) Moore County
40	n/a	92.7	**Valdese** (town) Burke County
41	n/a	92.4	**Sneads Ferry** (CDP) Onslow County
41	n/a	92.4	**Waynesville** (town) Haywood County
43	n/a	92.2	**Welcome** (CDP) Davidson County
44	n/a	92.1	**Lowesville** (CDP) Lincoln County
44	n/a	92.1	**Porters Neck** (CDP) New Hanover County
46	n/a	92.0	**Boiling Spring Lakes** (city) Brunswick County
46	896	92.0	**Boone** (town) Watauga County
48	n/a	91.9	**Hampstead** (CDP) Pender County
48	n/a	91.9	**Landis** (town) Rowan County
48	n/a	91.9	**Royal Pines** (CDP) Buncombe County
51	n/a	91.7	**Trinity** (city) Randolph County
52	n/a	91.2	**Weddington** (town) Union County
53	n/a	91.1	**Cramerton** (town) Gaston County
54	n/a	90.9	**Stokesdale** (town) Guilford County
55	n/a	90.7	**Wesley Chapel** (village) Union County
56	1188	90.3	**Lewisville** (town) Forsyth County
57	n/a	90.1	**Franklin** (town) Macon County
58	n/a	90.0	**Black Mountain** (town) Buncombe County
59	n/a	89.9	**Midland** (town) Cabarrus County
59	1250	89.9	**Summerfield** (town) Guilford County
59	n/a	89.9	**Swansboro** (town) Onslow County
62	n/a	89.8	**Kill Devil Hills** (town) Dare County
63	n/a	89.6	**Mountain Home** (CDP) Henderson County
64	n/a	89.5	**Gamewell** (town) Caldwell County
65	n/a	88.9	**Oak Ridge** (town) Guilford County
66	n/a	88.7	**Brices Creek** (CDP) Craven County
67	n/a	88.5	**Moyock** (CDP) Currituck County
68	1494	88.3	**Cornelius** (town) Mecklenburg County
68	n/a	88.3	**Fletcher** (town) Henderson County
68	1494	88.3	**Stallings** (town) Union County
71	n/a	88.2	**Midway** (town) Davidson County
71	n/a	88.2	**River Bend** (town) Craven County
73	1569	87.8	**Archdale** (city) Randolph County
73	1569	87.8	**Davidson** (town) Mecklenburg County
73	n/a	87.8	**Swannanoa** (CDP) Buncombe County
76	n/a	87.6	**Stanley** (town) Gaston County
77	n/a	87.5	**Granite Quarry** (town) Rowan County
78	n/a	87.3	**Woodfin** (town) Buncombe County
79	n/a	87.2	**Red Oak** (town) Nash County
80	n/a	86.8	**Lake Park** (village) Union County
81	n/a	86.7	**Elon** (town) Alamance County
82	n/a	86.3	**Randleman** (city) Randolph County
83	n/a	86.2	**Marvin** (village) Union County
84	n/a	86.1	**Boiling Springs** (town) Cleveland County
85	n/a	85.9	**Lowell** (city) Gaston County
86	n/a	85.8	**Cullowhee** (CDP) Jackson County
86	n/a	85.8	**Mountain View** (CDP) Catawba County
86	n/a	85.8	**Sylva** (town) Jackson County
89	n/a	85.5	**Dana** (CDP) Henderson County
90	n/a	85.2	**Shallotte** (town) Brunswick County
91	n/a	85.1	**Cherryville** (city) Gaston County
92	n/a	84.9	**Rutherfordton** (town) Rutherford County
93	2053	84.1	**Mount Airy** (city) Surry County
94	2077	83.9	**Leland** (town) Brunswick County
95	2107	83.6	**Belmont** (city) Gaston County
95	n/a	83.6	**Maiden** (town) Catawba County
97	n/a	83.3	**Brevard** (city) Transylvania County
98	2152	83.2	**Clemmons** (village) Forsyth County
99	n/a	83.0	**Pleasant Garden** (town) Guilford County
100	2198	82.8	**Huntersville** (town) Mecklenburg County
100	n/a	82.8	**Saint Stephens** (CDP) Catawba County
102	n/a	82.5	**Wentworth** (town) Rockingham County
103	n/a	82.2	**Southport** (city) Brunswick County
104	n/a	82.1	**Lake Royale** (CDP) Franklin County
104	n/a	82.1	**Waxhaw** (town) Union County
106	n/a	82.0	**Morehead City** (town) Carteret County
107	n/a	81.9	**Mineral Springs** (town) Union County
108	2304	81.8	**Matthews** (town) Mecklenburg County
109	n/a	81.7	**Newport** (town) Carteret County
110	n/a	81.5	**Forest Oaks** (CDP) Guilford County
110	n/a	81.5	**Wilkesboro** (town) Wilkes County
112	n/a	81.4	**China Grove** (town) Rowan County
113	n/a	81.0	**Archer Lodge** (town) Johnston County
113	2375	81.0	**Indian Trail** (town) Union County
115	n/a	80.6	**East Flat Rock** (CDP) Henderson County
115	n/a	80.6	**Jamestown** (town) Guilford County
117	2436	80.4	**Mount Holly** (city) Gaston County
118	2459	80.2	**Mooresville** (town) Iredell County
119	n/a	79.9	**James City** (CDP) Craven County
120	2497	79.8	**Holly Springs** (town) Wake County
121	2506	79.7	**Hendersonville** (city) Henderson County
122	n/a	79.6	**Bessemer City** (city) Gaston County
122	2517	79.6	**Murraysville** (CDP) New Hanover County
124	2523	79.5	**Apex** (town) Wake County
125	n/a	79.4	**Gibsonville** (town) Guilford County
126	2539	79.3	**Asheville** (city) Buncombe County
127	n/a	79.0	**Beaufort** (town) Carteret County
128	n/a	78.7	**Glen Raven** (CDP) Alamance County
129	n/a	78.6	**Northchase** (CDP) New Hanover County
130	2622	78.4	**Lenoir** (city) Caldwell County
130	2622	78.4	**Mint Hill** (town) Mecklenburg County
132	n/a	78.3	**Buies Creek** (CDP) Harnett County
133	n/a	78.1	**Conover** (city) Catawba County
134	n/a	78.0	**Elkin** (town) Surry County
135	2669	77.8	**Kernersville** (town) Forsyth County
135	n/a	77.8	**Kings Grant** (CDP) New Hanover County
135	n/a	77.8	**Silver Lake** (CDP) New Hanover County
138	2716	77.3	**Wake Forest** (town) Wake County
139	n/a	76.9	**Walkertown** (town) Forsyth County
140	2769	76.6	**Lincolnton** (city) Lincoln County
141	n/a	76.5	**Marion** (city) McDowell County
142	n/a	76.4	**Dallas** (town) Gaston County
143	2825	75.8	**Harrisburg** (town) Cabarrus County
144	n/a	75.1	**Ranlo** (town) Gaston County
145	n/a	74.9	**Eastover** (town) Cumberland County
145	2912	74.9	**Hickory** (city) Catawba County
147	n/a	74.5	**Long View** (town) Catawba County
148	n/a	74.1	**Rolesville** (town) Wake County
148	n/a	74.1	**Yadkinville** (town) Yadkin County
150	n/a	74.0	**Erwin** (town) Harnett County

Note: The state column ranks the top/bottom 150 places in the state with population of 2,500 or more. The national column ranks the top/bottom places in the country with population of 10,000 or more. Places that are unincorporated were not considered in the rankings. n/a indicates data not available. Please refer to the User Guide for additional information.

White Population

Top 150 Places Ranked in *Ascending* Order

State Rank	Nat'l Rank	Percent	Place
1	n/a	11.8	**Enfield** (town) Halifax County
2	n/a	16.4	**Pembroke** (town) Robeson County
3	n/a	26.2	**Fairmont** (town) Robeson County
4	n/a	28.5	**Ahoskie** (town) Hertford County
5	176	28.7	**Kinston** (city) Lenoir County
6	n/a	29.2	**Plymouth** (town) Washington County
7	192	30.0	**Henderson** (city) Vance County
8	n/a	32.2	**Red Springs** (town) Robeson County
9	n/a	32.8	**Windsor** (town) Bertie County
10	232	33.5	**Rocky Mount** (city) Nash County
10	n/a	33.5	**Warsaw** (town) Duplin County
12	n/a	33.7	**Polkton** (town) Anson County
13	n/a	33.9	**Brogden** (CDP) Wayne County
14	n/a	34.6	**Williamston** (town) Martin County
15	n/a	35.6	**Wadesboro** (town) Anson County
16	n/a	38.6	**Oxford** (city) Granville County
17	n/a	38.8	**Selma** (town) Johnston County
18	308	39.2	**Goldsboro** (city) Wayne County
19	313	39.5	**Elizabeth City** (city) Pasquotank County
20	n/a	40.4	**Mount Olive** (town) Wayne County
21	n/a	40.5	**La Grange** (town) Lenoir County
22	n/a	40.8	**Edenton** (town) Chowan County
22	329	40.8	**Lumberton** (city) Robeson County
24	n/a	41.8	**South Rosemary** (CDP) Halifax County
25	363	42.5	**Durham** (city) Durham County
26	375	42.9	**Wilson** (city) Wilson County
27	377	43.0	**Laurinburg** (city) Scotland County
28	n/a	43.6	**Raeford** (city) Hoke County
29	n/a	43.7	**Elizabethtown** (town) Bladen County
30	n/a	44.0	**Siler City** (town) Chatham County
31	n/a	44.9	**Murfreesboro** (town) Hertford County
31	n/a	44.9	**Roxboro** (city) Person County
33	442	45.7	**Fayetteville** (city) Cumberland County
34	474	47.2	**Spring Lake** (town) Cumberland County
34	474	47.2	**Tarboro** (town) Edgecombe County
36	n/a	47.3	**Louisburg** (town) Franklin County
36	n/a	47.3	**Zebulon** (town) Wake County
38	n/a	48.1	**Ayden** (town) Pitt County
38	n/a	48.1	**Farmville** (town) Pitt County
40	504	48.4	**Greensboro** (city) Guilford County
41	n/a	48.9	**Clinton** (city) Sampson County
42	n/a	49.0	**Washington** (city) Beaufort County
43	549	50.0	**Charlotte** (city) Mecklenburg County
43	549	50.0	**Knightdale** (town) Wake County
45	n/a	50.2	**Dunn** (city) Harnett County
46	n/a	51.2	**Nashville** (town) Nash County
46	589	51.2	**Winston-Salem** (city) Forsyth County
48	n/a	51.8	**Grifton** (town) Pitt County
49	607	52.0	**Monroe** (city) Union County
49	n/a	52.0	**Wallace** (town) Duplin County
51	620	52.4	**Reidsville** (city) Rockingham County
51	620	52.4	**Salisbury** (city) Rowan County
53	n/a	53.2	**Whiteville** (city) Columbus County
54	n/a	53.5	**Lillington** (town) Harnett County
55	654	53.6	**High Point** (city) Guilford County
56	n/a	53.8	**Burgaw** (town) Pender County
57	672	54.0	**Morrisville** (town) Wake County
58	696	54.7	**Lexington** (city) Davidson County
58	696	54.7	**Shelby** (city) Cleveland County
60	699	54.8	**Statesville** (city) Iredell County
61	n/a	55.2	**Hamlet** (city) Richmond County
61	710	55.2	**Sanford** (city) Lee County
63	739	56.3	**Greenville** (city) Pitt County
64	n/a	56.9	**Mar-Mac** (CDP) Wayne County
64	760	56.9	**Smithfield** (town) Johnston County
66	n/a	57.4	**Rockingham** (city) Richmond County
67	780	57.5	**Raleigh** (city) Wake County
68	783	57.6	**Burlington** (city) Alamance County
69	792	57.8	**Garner** (town) Wake County
70	799	57.9	**New Bern** (city) Craven County
71	n/a	58.1	**Wendell** (town) Wake County
72	n/a	58.2	**Spencer** (town) Rowan County
73	n/a	58.9	**Troy** (town) Montgomery County
74	n/a	59.2	**Tabor City** (town) Columbus County
75	n/a	59.5	**Butner** (town) Granville County
76	n/a	59.6	**Creedmoor** (city) Granville County
77	n/a	59.9	**Wrightsboro** (CDP) New Hanover County
78	n/a	60.2	**Benson** (town) Johnston County
79	n/a	60.5	**River Road** (CDP) Beaufort County
80	n/a	60.6	**Wingate** (town) Union County
81	n/a	61.7	**Angier** (town) Harnett County
82	964	61.9	**Hope Mills** (town) Cumberland County
83	n/a	62.1	**Pineville** (town) Mecklenburg County
84	n/a	62.8	**Winterville** (town) Pitt County
85	1019	62.9	**Graham** (city) Alamance County
85	n/a	62.9	**Hillsborough** (town) Orange County
87	1025	63.0	**Gastonia** (city) Gaston County
88	1039	63.3	**Piney Green** (CDP) Onslow County
89	1050	63.6	**Roanoke Rapids** (city) Halifax County
90	n/a	64.1	**Elroy** (CDP) Wayne County
91	n/a	67.1	**Forest City** (town) Rutherford County
92	n/a	67.4	**Liberty** (town) Randolph County
93	1263	67.7	**Jacksonville** (city) Onslow County
94	1273	67.8	**Asheboro** (city) Randolph County
95	n/a	67.9	**Aberdeen** (town) Moore County
95	n/a	67.9	**Rockfish** (CDP) Hoke County
97	n/a	68.1	**Half Moon** (CDP) Onslow County
98	1307	68.3	**Thomasville** (city) Davidson County
99	1319	68.5	**Kannapolis** (city) Cabarrus County
100	n/a	68.8	**Spindale** (town) Rutherford County
101	1373	69.5	**Clayton** (town) Johnston County
102	1411	70.0	**Havelock** (city) Craven County
103	1419	70.1	**Albemarle** (city) Stanly County
103	n/a	70.1	**East Rockingham** (CDP) Richmond County
103	1419	70.1	**Morganton** (city) Burke County
106	1437	70.4	**Concord** (city) Cabarrus County
107	1468	70.9	**Carrboro** (town) Orange County
108	1496	71.2	**Eden** (city) Rockingham County
109	n/a	71.5	**Skippers Corner** (CDP) New Hanover County
110	1528	71.7	**Southern Pines** (town) Moore County
111	n/a	72.2	**Pittsboro** (town) Chatham County
112	1570	72.3	**Fuquay-Varina** (town) Wake County
113	1600	72.8	**Chapel Hill** (town) Orange County
113	n/a	72.8	**Rural Hall** (town) Forsyth County
115	1613	73.0	**Kings Mountain** (city) Cleveland County
115	n/a	73.0	**North Wilkesboro** (town) Wilkes County
117	1622	73.1	**Cary** (town) Wake County
118	1642	73.5	**Mebane** (city) Alamance County
118	1642	73.5	**Wilmington** (city) New Hanover County
120	1657	73.7	**Newton** (city) Catawba County
121	n/a	73.9	**Mocksville** (town) Davie County
122	n/a	74.0	**Erwin** (town) Harnett County
123	n/a	74.1	**Rolesville** (town) Wake County
123	n/a	74.1	**Yadkinville** (town) Yadkin County
125	n/a	74.5	**Long View** (town) Catawba County
126	n/a	74.9	**Eastover** (town) Cumberland County
126	1737	74.9	**Hickory** (city) Catawba County
128	n/a	75.1	**Ranlo** (town) Gaston County
129	1815	75.8	**Harrisburg** (town) Cabarrus County
130	n/a	76.4	**Dallas** (town) Gaston County
131	n/a	76.5	**Marion** (city) McDowell County
132	1880	76.6	**Lincolnton** (city) Lincoln County
133	n/a	76.9	**Walkertown** (town) Forsyth County
134	1932	77.3	**Wake Forest** (town) Wake County
135	1985	77.8	**Kernersville** (town) Forsyth County
135	n/a	77.8	**Kings Grant** (CDP) New Hanover County
135	n/a	77.8	**Silver Lake** (CDP) New Hanover County
138	n/a	78.0	**Elkin** (town) Surry County
139	n/a	78.1	**Conover** (city) Catawba County
140	n/a	78.3	**Buies Creek** (CDP) Harnett County
141	2023	78.4	**Lenoir** (city) Caldwell County
141	2023	78.4	**Mint Hill** (town) Mecklenburg County
143	n/a	78.6	**Northchase** (CDP) New Hanover County
144	n/a	78.7	**Glen Raven** (CDP) Alamance County
145	n/a	79.0	**Beaufort** (town) Carteret County
146	2103	79.3	**Asheville** (city) Buncombe County
147	n/a	79.4	**Gibsonville** (town) Guilford County
148	2127	79.5	**Apex** (town) Wake County
149	n/a	79.6	**Bessemer City** (city) Gaston County
149	2134	79.6	**Murraysville** (CDP) New Hanover County

Note: The state column ranks the top/bottom 150 places in the state with population of 2,500 or more. The national column ranks the top/bottom places in the country with population of 10,000 or more. Places that are unincorporated were not considered in the rankings. n/a indicates data not available. Please refer to the User Guide for additional information.

Black/African American Population

Top 150 Places Ranked in *Descending* Order

State Rank	Nat'l Rank	Percent	Place
1	n/a	87.5	**Enfield** (town) Halifax County
2	n/a	68.4	**Plymouth** (town) Washington County
3	97	68.0	**Kinston** (city) Lenoir County
4	n/a	66.6	**Ahoskie** (town) Hertford County
5	117	64.0	**Henderson** (city) Vance County
6	n/a	62.6	**Windsor** (town) Bertie County
7	n/a	62.4	**Williamston** (town) Martin County
8	133	61.3	**Rocky Mount** (city) Nash County
9	n/a	61.0	**Polkton** (town) Anson County
10	n/a	60.7	**Wadesboro** (town) Anson County
11	n/a	56.1	**Fairmont** (town) Robeson County
12	n/a	55.6	**Oxford** (city) Granville County
13	n/a	55.4	**La Grange** (town) Lenoir County
14	n/a	55.3	**South Rosemary** (CDP) Halifax County
15	n/a	54.8	**Edenton** (town) Chowan County
16	172	54.3	**Goldsboro** (city) Wayne County
17	174	54.0	**Elizabeth City** (city) Pasquotank County
18	n/a	53.9	**Brogden** (CDP) Wayne County
19	n/a	53.0	**Warsaw** (town) Duplin County
20	n/a	51.0	**Elizabethtown** (town) Bladen County
21	n/a	50.9	**Murfreesboro** (town) Hertford County
22	n/a	50.5	**Mount Olive** (town) Wayne County
23	n/a	49.7	**Farmville** (town) Pitt County
24	n/a	48.8	**Red Springs** (town) Robeson County
25	229	48.4	**Tarboro** (town) Edgecombe County
26	n/a	48.3	**Ayden** (town) Pitt County
27	236	47.9	**Wilson** (city) Wilson County
28	n/a	46.9	**Louisburg** (town) Franklin County
29	246	46.8	**Laurinburg** (city) Scotland County
29	n/a	46.8	**Roxboro** (city) Person County
31	n/a	45.5	**Nashville** (town) Nash County
31	n/a	45.5	**Washington** (city) Beaufort County
33	n/a	42.5	**Dunn** (city) Harnett County
34	289	41.9	**Fayetteville** (city) Cumberland County
34	289	41.9	**Reidsville** (city) Rockingham County
36	300	41.3	**Shelby** (city) Cleveland County
37	n/a	41.1	**Raeford** (city) Hoke County
38	303	41.0	**Durham** (city) Durham County
38	n/a	41.0	**Whiteville** (city) Columbus County
40	n/a	40.8	**Grifton** (town) Pitt County
41	313	40.6	**Greensboro** (city) Guilford County
42	n/a	40.5	**Clinton** (city) Sampson County
43	n/a	39.8	**Lillington** (town) Harnett County
44	n/a	39.6	**Burgaw** (town) Pender County
45	n/a	38.6	**Zebulon** (town) Wake County
46	327	38.3	**Knightdale** (town) Wake County
47	335	37.7	**Salisbury** (city) Rowan County
48	339	37.2	**Lumberton** (city) Robeson County
48	n/a	37.2	**Selma** (town) Johnston County
50	343	37.0	**Greenville** (city) Pitt County
51	n/a	36.6	**Hamlet** (city) Richmond County
52	352	36.3	**Spring Lake** (town) Cumberland County
53	n/a	36.2	**Tabor City** (town) Columbus County
54	n/a	35.2	**Creedmoor** (city) Granville County
55	369	35.0	**Charlotte** (city) Mecklenburg County
56	374	34.7	**Winston-Salem** (city) Forsyth County
57	380	34.5	**Statesville** (city) Iredell County
58	n/a	34.1	**Rockingham** (city) Richmond County
59	n/a	33.6	**Wrightsboro** (CDP) New Hanover County
60	401	33.2	**New Bern** (city) Craven County
61	404	33.0	**High Point** (city) Guilford County
62	406	32.9	**Garner** (town) Wake County
63	n/a	32.8	**Spencer** (town) Rowan County
64	n/a	31.8	**Troy** (town) Montgomery County
65	n/a	31.6	**Winterville** (town) Pitt County
66	441	31.2	**Roanoke Rapids** (city) Halifax County
67	n/a	30.2	**Wendell** (town) Wake County
68	n/a	30.1	**Butner** (town) Granville County
69	n/a	29.7	**Mar-Mac** (CDP) Wayne County
70	n/a	29.5	**Hillsborough** (town) Orange County
71	487	29.3	**Raleigh** (city) Wake County
72	n/a	28.8	**Wingate** (town) Union County
73	505	28.4	**Lexington** (city) Davidson County
74	513	28.0	**Burlington** (city) Alamance County
75	522	27.8	**Gastonia** (city) Gaston County
76	530	27.6	**Sanford** (city) Lee County
77	541	27.2	**Smithfield** (town) Johnston County
78	n/a	26.7	**Spindale** (town) Rutherford County
79	n/a	26.6	**Benson** (town) Johnston County
80	558	26.5	**Hope Mills** (town) Cumberland County
81	n/a	26.0	**Wallace** (town) Duplin County
82	593	25.2	**Monroe** (city) Union County
83	n/a	24.7	**Aberdeen** (town) Moore County
84	n/a	24.0	**Forest City** (town) Rutherford County
84	615	24.0	**Southern Pines** (town) Moore County
86	619	23.8	**Eden** (city) Rockingham County
87	654	22.8	**Graham** (city) Alamance County
88	n/a	22.7	**River Road** (CDP) Beaufort County
89	663	22.5	**Kings Mountain** (city) Cleveland County
90	667	22.4	**Albemarle** (city) Stanly County
90	667	22.4	**Piney Green** (CDP) Onslow County
92	n/a	22.2	**Pineville** (town) Mecklenburg County
93	n/a	21.9	**Elroy** (CDP) Wayne County
94	687	21.8	**Clayton** (town) Johnston County
95	n/a	21.7	**Angier** (town) Harnett County
96	n/a	20.8	**Half Moon** (CDP) Onslow County
97	n/a	20.5	**Skippers Corner** (CDP) New Hanover County
98	n/a	20.4	**Liberty** (town) Randolph County
98	728	20.4	**Mebane** (city) Alamance County
100	733	20.3	**Kannapolis** (city) Cabarrus County
101	n/a	20.2	**Rockfish** (CDP) Hoke County
102	744	20.0	**Jacksonville** (city) Onslow County
103	748	19.9	**Wilmington** (city) New Hanover County
104	755	19.7	**Fuquay-Varina** (town) Wake County
105	756	19.6	**Thomasville** (city) Davidson County
106	n/a	19.5	**Pittsboro** (town) Chatham County
107	n/a	19.2	**Eastover** (town) Cumberland County
108	n/a	19.1	**Siler City** (town) Chatham County
109	844	17.8	**Concord** (city) Cabarrus County
109	n/a	17.8	**Rolesville** (town) Wake County
111	n/a	17.5	**Walkertown** (town) Forsyth County
112	856	17.4	**Havelock** (city) Craven County
113	n/a	17.3	**Erwin** (town) Harnett County
114	n/a	17.0	**Beaufort** (town) Carteret County
115	n/a	16.8	**East Rockingham** (CDP) Richmond County
116	907	16.4	**Harrisburg** (town) Cabarrus County
117	n/a	15.9	**Dallas** (town) Gaston County
117	n/a	15.9	**Ranlo** (town) Gaston County
117	n/a	15.9	**Rural Hall** (town) Forsyth County
120	n/a	15.4	**Southport** (city) Brunswick County
121	n/a	15.3	**Northchase** (CDP) New Hanover County
121	977	15.3	**Wake Forest** (town) Wake County
123	n/a	15.2	**Forest Oaks** (CDP) Guilford County
124	n/a	14.8	**Buies Creek** (CDP) Harnett County
125	n/a	14.6	**Gibsonville** (town) Guilford County
125	n/a	14.6	**Mocksville** (town) Davie County
127	n/a	14.5	**Lake Royale** (CDP) Franklin County
128	n/a	14.4	**Bessemer City** (city) Gaston County
128	n/a	14.4	**Wentworth** (town) Rockingham County
130	1036	14.3	**Hickory** (city) Catawba County
130	n/a	14.3	**Kings Grant** (CDP) New Hanover County
132	n/a	13.9	**Mineral Springs** (town) Union County
132	1063	13.9	**Newton** (city) Catawba County
134	1078	13.7	**Lincolnton** (city) Lincoln County
134	1078	13.7	**Murraysville** (CDP) New Hanover County
136	n/a	13.6	**Jamestown** (town) Guilford County
136	n/a	13.6	**North Wilkesboro** (town) Wilkes County
138	n/a	13.5	**James City** (CDP) Craven County
139	1097	13.4	**Asheville** (city) Buncombe County
140	1128	12.9	**Morrisville** (town) Wake County
141	1143	12.7	**Lenoir** (city) Caldwell County
141	1143	12.7	**Mount Holly** (city) Gaston County
143	1154	12.6	**Holly Springs** (town) Wake County
143	1154	12.6	**Kernersville** (town) Forsyth County
145	n/a	12.5	**Glen Raven** (CDP) Alamance County
146	1174	12.3	**Mint Hill** (town) Mecklenburg County
146	n/a	12.3	**Pembroke** (town) Robeson County
148	1180	12.2	**Morganton** (city) Burke County
149	1201	12.0	**Asheboro** (city) Randolph County
150	n/a	11.4	**Long View** (town) Catawba County

Note: The state column ranks the top/bottom 150 places in the state with population of 2,500 or more. The national column ranks the top/bottom places in the country with population of 10,000 or more. Places that are unincorporated were not considered in the rankings. n/a indicates data not available. Please refer to the User Guide for additional information.

Black/African American Population

Top 150 Places Ranked in *Ascending* Order

State Rank	Nat'l Rank	Percent	Place
1	n/a	0.3	**Lake Junaluska** (CDP) Haywood County
1	n/a	0.3	**Southern Shores** (town) Dare County
3	n/a	0.4	**Flat Rock** (village) Henderson County
4	n/a	0.5	**Icard** (CDP) Burke County
5	n/a	0.6	**Emerald Isle** (town) Carteret County
5	n/a	0.6	**Oak Island** (town) Brunswick County
7	n/a	0.7	**Bethlehem** (CDP) Alexander County
7	n/a	0.7	**Carolina Beach** (town) New Hanover County
9	n/a	0.8	**Sunset Beach** (town) Brunswick County
10	n/a	0.9	**Fairview** (town) Union County
10	n/a	0.9	**Sawmills** (town) Caldwell County
10	n/a	0.9	**Wallburg** (town) Davidson County
10	n/a	0.9	**Weaverville** (town) Buncombe County
14	n/a	1.0	**Saint James** (town) Brunswick County
15	n/a	1.1	**Dana** (CDP) Henderson County
15	n/a	1.1	**Etowah** (CDP) Henderson County
15	n/a	1.1	**Kitty Hawk** (town) Dare County
18	n/a	1.2	**Fairview** (CDP) Buncombe County
18	n/a	1.2	**Kill Devil Hills** (town) Dare County
20	n/a	1.3	**Enochville** (CDP) Rowan County
20	n/a	1.3	**Valdese** (town) Burke County
20	n/a	1.3	**Whispering Pines** (village) Moore County
23	n/a	1.5	**Tyro** (CDP) Davidson County
24	n/a	1.6	**Cajah's Mountain** (town) Caldwell County
24	n/a	1.6	**Carolina Shores** (town) Brunswick County
24	n/a	1.6	**Nags Head** (town) Dare County
27	n/a	1.7	**Granite Falls** (town) Caldwell County
27	n/a	1.7	**Mills River** (town) Henderson County
27	n/a	1.7	**Unionville** (town) Union County
30	n/a	1.8	**Canton** (town) Haywood County
30	n/a	1.8	**Ogden** (CDP) New Hanover County
32	n/a	1.9	**Hudson** (town) Caldwell County
32	n/a	1.9	**King** (city) Stokes County
32	n/a	1.9	**Trent Woods** (town) Craven County
35	n/a	2.1	**Franklin** (town) Macon County
36	n/a	2.3	**Locust** (city) Stanly County
37	n/a	2.4	**Waynesville** (town) Haywood County
38	n/a	2.5	**Bayshore** (CDP) New Hanover County
38	n/a	2.5	**Lake Norman of Catawba** (CDP) Catawba County
40	n/a	2.7	**Sylva** (town) Jackson County
40	n/a	2.7	**Westport** (CDP) Lincoln County
42	n/a	3.0	**Seven Lakes** (CDP) Moore County
43	n/a	3.1	**Mountain Home** (CDP) Henderson County
44	n/a	3.2	**Landis** (town) Rowan County
44	n/a	3.2	**Myrtle Grove** (CDP) New Hanover County
46	2089	3.5	**Boone** (town) Watauga County
46	n/a	3.5	**Fairfield Harbour** (CDP) Craven County
46	n/a	3.5	**Swansboro** (town) Onslow County
49	n/a	3.7	**Sneads Ferry** (CDP) Onslow County
49	n/a	3.7	**Welcome** (CDP) Davidson County
51	2177	3.8	**Pinehurst** (village) Moore County
52	n/a	3.9	**Porters Neck** (CDP) New Hanover County
52	n/a	3.9	**Weddington** (town) Union County
54	2242	4.0	**Archdale** (city) Randolph County
55	n/a	4.1	**East Flat Rock** (CDP) Henderson County
55	n/a	4.1	**Fletcher** (town) Henderson County
57	n/a	4.2	**Boiling Spring Lakes** (city) Brunswick County
57	n/a	4.2	**Cramerton** (town) Gaston County
57	n/a	4.2	**Saint Stephens** (CDP) Catawba County
60	n/a	4.4	**Royal Pines** (CDP) Buncombe County
60	2355	4.4	**Summerfield** (town) Guilford County
62	n/a	4.6	**Lowesville** (CDP) Lincoln County
62	n/a	4.6	**Wesley Chapel** (village) Union County
64	n/a	4.7	**Stokesdale** (town) Guilford County
64	n/a	4.7	**Swannanoa** (CDP) Buncombe County
66	n/a	4.9	**Hampstead** (CDP) Pender County
66	n/a	4.9	**Trinity** (city) Randolph County
66	n/a	4.9	**Woodfin** (town) Buncombe County
69	2501	5.0	**Lewisville** (town) Forsyth County
70	n/a	5.2	**Oak Ridge** (town) Guilford County
71	n/a	5.3	**Gamewell** (town) Caldwell County
72	2631	5.6	**Stallings** (town) Union County
73	n/a	5.7	**Marvin** (village) Union County
74	2674	5.8	**Cornelius** (town) Mecklenburg County
75	n/a	5.9	**Randleman** (city) Randolph County
76	n/a	6.0	**Black Mountain** (town) Buncombe County
77	n/a	6.2	**Midland** (town) Cabarrus County
78	2784	6.4	**Davidson** (town) Mecklenburg County
78	n/a	6.4	**Elkin** (town) Surry County
80	2849	6.7	**Clemmons** (village) Forsyth County
81	n/a	6.9	**Moyock** (CDP) Currituck County
82	n/a	7.0	**Lake Park** (village) Union County
82	n/a	7.0	**Yadkinville** (town) Yadkin County
84	n/a	7.1	**Cullowhee** (CDP) Jackson County
85	n/a	7.4	**China Grove** (town) Rowan County
86	2988	7.6	**Apex** (town) Wake County
87	3044	8.0	**Cary** (town) Wake County
88	n/a	8.1	**Mountain View** (CDP) Catawba County
89	n/a	8.2	**Midway** (town) Davidson County
89	3071	8.2	**Mount Airy** (city) Surry County
91	n/a	8.3	**Granite Quarry** (town) Rowan County
92	n/a	8.5	**Elon** (town) Alamance County
93	n/a	8.6	**Brices Creek** (CDP) Craven County
93	n/a	8.6	**River Bend** (town) Craven County
95	n/a	8.7	**Lowell** (city) Gaston County
96	n/a	8.8	**Archer Lodge** (town) Johnston County
96	n/a	8.8	**Silver Lake** (CDP) New Hanover County
98	3147	8.9	**Belmont** (city) Gaston County
98	n/a	8.9	**Wilkesboro** (town) Wilkes County
100	n/a	9.2	**Conover** (city) Catawba County
100	3175	9.2	**Hendersonville** (city) Henderson County
102	n/a	9.3	**Shallotte** (town) Brunswick County
103	3193	9.4	**Huntersville** (town) Mecklenburg County
104	3208	9.6	**Matthews** (town) Mecklenburg County
105	3221	9.7	**Chapel Hill** (town) Orange County
105	n/a	9.7	**Red Oak** (town) Nash County
105	n/a	9.7	**Stanley** (town) Gaston County
108	3249	10.0	**Indian Trail** (town) Union County
108	3249	10.0	**Leland** (town) Brunswick County
110	3265	10.1	**Carrboro** (town) Orange County
111	n/a	10.3	**Cherryville** (city) Gaston County
112	n/a	10.4	**Rutherfordton** (town) Rutherford County
113	n/a	10.7	**Morehead City** (town) Carteret County
113	n/a	10.7	**Pleasant Garden** (town) Guilford County
115	3352	10.9	**Mooresville** (town) Iredell County
116	n/a	11.0	**Brevard** (city) Transylvania County
117	n/a	11.1	**Marion** (city) McDowell County
118	n/a	11.2	**Waxhaw** (town) Union County
119	n/a	11.3	**Boiling Springs** (town) Cleveland County
119	n/a	11.3	**Maiden** (town) Catawba County
119	n/a	11.3	**Newport** (town) Carteret County
122	n/a	11.4	**Long View** (town) Catawba County
123	3447	12.0	**Asheboro** (city) Randolph County
124	3463	12.2	**Morganton** (city) Burke County
125	3477	12.3	**Mint Hill** (town) Mecklenburg County
125	n/a	12.3	**Pembroke** (town) Robeson County
127	n/a	12.5	**Glen Raven** (CDP) Alamance County
128	3494	12.6	**Holly Springs** (town) Wake County
128	3494	12.6	**Kernersville** (town) Forsyth County
130	3503	12.7	**Lenoir** (city) Caldwell County
130	3503	12.7	**Mount Holly** (city) Gaston County
132	3524	12.9	**Morrisville** (town) Wake County
133	3550	13.4	**Asheville** (city) Buncombe County
134	n/a	13.5	**James City** (CDP) Craven County
135	n/a	13.6	**Jamestown** (town) Guilford County
135	n/a	13.6	**North Wilkesboro** (town) Wilkes County
137	3572	13.7	**Lincolnton** (city) Lincoln County
137	3572	13.7	**Murraysville** (CDP) New Hanover County
139	n/a	13.9	**Mineral Springs** (town) Union County
139	3587	13.9	**Newton** (city) Catawba County
141	3611	14.3	**Hickory** (city) Catawba County
141	n/a	14.3	**Kings Grant** (CDP) New Hanover County
143	n/a	14.4	**Bessemer City** (city) Gaston County
143	n/a	14.4	**Wentworth** (town) Rockingham County
145	n/a	14.5	**Lake Royale** (CDP) Franklin County
146	n/a	14.6	**Gibsonville** (town) Guilford County
146	n/a	14.6	**Mocksville** (town) Davie County
148	n/a	14.8	**Buies Creek** (CDP) Harnett County
149	n/a	15.2	**Forest Oaks** (CDP) Guilford County
150	n/a	15.3	**Northchase** (CDP) New Hanover County

Note: *The state column ranks the top/bottom 150 places in the state with population of 2,500 or more. The national column ranks the top/bottom places in the country with population of 10,000 or more. Places that are unincorporated were not considered in the rankings. n/a indicates data not available. Please refer to the User Guide for additional information.*

Asian Population

Top 150 Places Ranked in *Descending* Order

State Rank	Nat'l Rank	Percent	Place
1	101	27.2	**Morrisville** (town) Wake County
2	364	13.1	**Cary** (town) Wake County
3	418	11.9	**Chapel Hill** (town) Orange County
4	689	8.2	**Carrboro** (town) Orange County
5	831	7.1	**Apex** (town) Wake County
6	958	6.1	**High Point** (city) Guilford County
7	n/a	5.4	**Marvin** (village) Union County
8	1163	5.1	**Durham** (city) Durham County
9	1182	5.0	**Charlotte** (city) Mecklenburg County
9	n/a	5.0	**Long View** (town) Catawba County
11	1230	4.8	**Archdale** (city) Randolph County
12	1300	4.5	**Harrisburg** (town) Cabarrus County
13	n/a	4.4	**Saint Stephens** (CDP) Catawba County
14	1361	4.3	**Raleigh** (city) Wake County
15	n/a	4.2	**Conover** (city) Catawba County
15	1388	4.2	**Matthews** (town) Mecklenburg County
17	1423	4.1	**Belmont** (city) Gaston County
18	1457	4.0	**Greensboro** (city) Guilford County
19	1569	3.7	**Clemmons** (village) Forsyth County
20	1618	3.6	**New Bern** (city) Craven County
21	n/a	3.4	**Oak Ridge** (town) Guilford County
21	n/a	3.4	**Pineville** (town) Mecklenburg County
23	1745	3.3	**Mooresville** (town) Iredell County
23	1745	3.3	**Newton** (city) Catawba County
25	1787	3.2	**Hickory** (city) Catawba County
26	n/a	3.1	**Fletcher** (town) Henderson County
26	n/a	3.1	**Rolesville** (town) Wake County
26	n/a	3.1	**Valdese** (town) Burke County
29	1902	3.0	**Spring Lake** (town) Cumberland County
29	n/a	3.0	**Wilkesboro** (town) Wilkes County
31	1953	2.9	**Albemarle** (city) Stanly County
31	1953	2.9	**Havelock** (city) Craven County
31	1953	2.9	**Holly Springs** (town) Wake County
31	1953	2.9	**Lexington** (city) Davidson County
31	1953	2.9	**Wake Forest** (town) Wake County
36	2010	2.8	**Davidson** (town) Mecklenburg County
36	2010	2.8	**Piney Green** (CDP) Onslow County
38	2064	2.7	**Huntersville** (town) Mecklenburg County
38	n/a	2.7	**Icard** (CDP) Burke County
38	n/a	2.7	**Mountain View** (CDP) Catawba County
41	2114	2.6	**Concord** (city) Cabarrus County
41	2114	2.6	**Fayetteville** (city) Cumberland County
41	n/a	2.6	**Weddington** (town) Union County
44	2173	2.5	**Jacksonville** (city) Onslow County
44	n/a	2.5	**Jamestown** (town) Guilford County
44	2173	2.5	**Mint Hill** (town) Mecklenburg County
47	2237	2.4	**Greenville** (city) Pitt County
47	2237	2.4	**Lumberton** (city) Robeson County
47	2237	2.4	**Morganton** (city) Burke County
47	2237	2.4	**Mount Holly** (city) Gaston County
51	2314	2.3	**Cornelius** (town) Mecklenburg County
51	2314	2.3	**Stallings** (town) Union County
53	n/a	2.2	**Buies Creek** (CDP) Harnett County
53	n/a	2.2	**China Grove** (town) Rowan County
53	n/a	2.2	**Cramerton** (town) Gaston County
53	n/a	2.2	**Half Moon** (CDP) Onslow County
53	2384	2.2	**Summerfield** (town) Guilford County
58	2465	2.1	**Burlington** (city) Alamance County
58	n/a	2.1	**Rockingham** (city) Richmond County
58	n/a	2.1	**Winterville** (town) Pitt County
61	n/a	2.0	**Elon** (town) Alamance County
61	2527	2.0	**Fuquay-Varina** (town) Wake County
61	n/a	2.0	**Porters Neck** (CDP) New Hanover County
61	n/a	2.0	**Waxhaw** (town) Union County
61	n/a	2.0	**Windsor** (town) Bertie County
61	2527	2.0	**Winston-Salem** (city) Forsyth County
67	2598	1.9	**Kernersville** (town) Forsyth County
67	n/a	1.9	**Lake Park** (village) Union County
67	2598	1.9	**Murraysville** (CDP) New Hanover County
67	2598	1.9	**Statesville** (city) Iredell County
71	n/a	1.8	**Aberdeen** (town) Moore County
71	2688	1.8	**Garner** (town) Wake County
71	2688	1.8	**Goldsboro** (city) Wayne County
71	2688	1.8	**Hope Mills** (town) Cumberland County
71	2688	1.8	**Indian Trail** (town) Union County
71	n/a	1.8	**Pittsboro** (town) Chatham County
71	n/a	1.8	**Ranlo** (town) Gaston County
71	n/a	1.8	**Swansboro** (town) Onslow County
71	n/a	1.8	**Sylva** (town) Jackson County
80	n/a	1.7	**Elroy** (CDP) Wayne County
80	n/a	1.7	**Hillsborough** (town) Orange County
80	2801	1.7	**Knightdale** (town) Wake County
80	2801	1.7	**Lewisville** (town) Forsyth County
80	n/a	1.7	**Newport** (town) Carteret County
80	n/a	1.7	**Northchase** (CDP) New Hanover County
80	2801	1.7	**Roanoke Rapids** (city) Halifax County
87	2898	1.6	**Boone** (town) Watauga County
87	2898	1.6	**Kings Mountain** (city) Cleveland County
87	n/a	1.6	**Morehead City** (town) Carteret County
87	n/a	1.6	**Rutherfordton** (town) Rutherford County
87	2898	1.6	**Salisbury** (city) Rowan County
92	3009	1.5	**Leland** (town) Brunswick County
92	n/a	1.5	**Wesley Chapel** (village) Union County
94	3111	1.4	**Asheboro** (city) Randolph County
94	3111	1.4	**Asheville** (city) Buncombe County
94	3111	1.4	**Clayton** (town) Johnston County
94	n/a	1.4	**Kill Devil Hills** (town) Dare County
94	3111	1.4	**Mount Airy** (city) Surry County
94	n/a	1.4	**Mountain Home** (CDP) Henderson County
94	n/a	1.4	**Stokesdale** (town) Guilford County
94	n/a	1.4	**Wadesboro** (town) Anson County
94	n/a	1.4	**Welcome** (CDP) Davidson County
103	n/a	1.3	**Ahoskie** (town) Hertford County
103	3229	1.3	**Gastonia** (city) Gaston County
103	3229	1.3	**Graham** (city) Alamance County
103	n/a	1.3	**Maiden** (town) Catawba County
103	3229	1.3	**Pinehurst** (village) Moore County
103	n/a	1.3	**Shallotte** (town) Brunswick County
103	n/a	1.3	**Swannanoa** (CDP) Buncombe County
110	n/a	1.2	**Cullowhee** (CDP) Jackson County
110	3327	1.2	**Elizabeth City** (city) Pasquotank County
110	3327	1.2	**Hendersonville** (city) Henderson County
110	n/a	1.2	**Mar-Mac** (CDP) Wayne County
110	3327	1.2	**Mebane** (city) Alamance County
110	n/a	1.2	**Moyock** (CDP) Currituck County
110	n/a	1.2	**Myrtle Grove** (CDP) New Hanover County
110	n/a	1.2	**Rockfish** (CDP) Hoke County
110	n/a	1.2	**Royal Pines** (CDP) Buncombe County
110	n/a	1.2	**Trinity** (city) Randolph County
110	3327	1.2	**Wilmington** (city) New Hanover County
110	3327	1.2	**Wilson** (city) Wilson County
122	n/a	1.1	**Bayshore** (CDP) New Hanover County
122	n/a	1.1	**Clinton** (city) Sampson County
122	n/a	1.1	**Gibsonville** (town) Guilford County
122	n/a	1.1	**Granite Quarry** (town) Rowan County
122	n/a	1.1	**James City** (CDP) Craven County
122	3443	1.1	**Kannapolis** (city) Cabarrus County
122	n/a	1.1	**Kings Grant** (CDP) New Hanover County
122	n/a	1.1	**Ogden** (CDP) New Hanover County
122	n/a	1.1	**Oxford** (city) Granville County
122	3443	1.1	**Sanford** (city) Lee County
122	3443	1.1	**Thomasville** (city) Davidson County
133	n/a	1.0	**Brevard** (city) Transylvania County
133	3560	1.0	**Laurinburg** (city) Scotland County
133	n/a	1.0	**Lowell** (city) Gaston County
133	n/a	1.0	**Murfreesboro** (town) Hertford County
133	n/a	1.0	**Raeford** (city) Hoke County
133	n/a	1.0	**River Bend** (town) Craven County
133	3560	1.0	**Rocky Mount** (city) Nash County
133	n/a	1.0	**Troy** (town) Montgomery County
133	n/a	1.0	**Whispering Pines** (village) Moore County
133	n/a	1.0	**Zebulon** (town) Wake County
143	n/a	0.9	**Bethlehem** (CDP) Alexander County
143	n/a	0.9	**Butner** (town) Granville County
143	n/a	0.9	**Eastover** (town) Cumberland County
143	n/a	0.9	**Etowah** (CDP) Henderson County
143	n/a	0.9	**Forest City** (town) Rutherford County
143	3694	0.9	**Lenoir** (city) Caldwell County
143	n/a	0.9	**Lillington** (town) Harnett County
143	n/a	0.9	**Louisburg** (town) Franklin County

Note: The state column ranks the top/bottom 150 places in the state with population of 2,500 or more. The national column ranks the top/bottom places in the country with population of 10,000 or more. Places that are unincorporated were not considered in the rankings. n/a indicates data not available. Please refer to the User Guide for additional information.

Asian Population

Top 150 Places Ranked in *Ascending* Order

State Rank	Nat'l Rank	Percent	Place
1	n/a	0.0	**Grifton** (town) Pitt County
2	n/a	0.1	**Canton** (town) Haywood County
2	n/a	0.1	**River Road** (CDP) Beaufort County
2	n/a	0.1	**Southport** (city) Brunswick County
5	n/a	0.2	**Ayden** (town) Pitt County
5	n/a	0.2	**Enfield** (town) Halifax County
5	n/a	0.2	**Fairmont** (town) Robeson County
5	n/a	0.2	**Gamewell** (town) Caldwell County
5	n/a	0.2	**Hudson** (town) Caldwell County
5	n/a	0.2	**Liberty** (town) Randolph County
5	n/a	0.2	**Sawmills** (town) Caldwell County
5	n/a	0.2	**Selma** (town) Johnston County
5	n/a	0.2	**Tabor City** (town) Columbus County
5	n/a	0.2	**Wallace** (town) Duplin County
15	n/a	0.3	**Archer Lodge** (town) Johnston County
15	n/a	0.3	**Erwin** (town) Harnett County
15	n/a	0.3	**Fairview** (town) Union County
15	n/a	0.3	**Lake Junaluska** (CDP) Haywood County
15	n/a	0.3	**Nags Head** (town) Dare County
15	n/a	0.3	**Oak Island** (town) Brunswick County
15	n/a	0.3	**Warsaw** (town) Duplin County
15	n/a	0.3	**Wentworth** (town) Rockingham County
15	n/a	0.3	**Yadkinville** (town) Yadkin County
24	n/a	0.4	**Boiling Springs** (town) Cleveland County
24	n/a	0.4	**Burgaw** (town) Pender County
24	n/a	0.4	**Carolina Beach** (town) New Hanover County
24	n/a	0.4	**Fairview** (CDP) Buncombe County
24	n/a	0.4	**Farmville** (town) Pitt County
24	n/a	0.4	**Flat Rock** (village) Henderson County
24	n/a	0.4	**Mount Olive** (town) Wayne County
24	n/a	0.4	**Nashville** (town) Nash County
24	n/a	0.4	**Plymouth** (town) Washington County
24	n/a	0.4	**Randleman** (city) Randolph County
24	n/a	0.4	**Red Springs** (town) Robeson County
24	n/a	0.4	**Roxboro** (city) Person County
24	n/a	0.4	**Siler City** (town) Chatham County
24	n/a	0.4	**Skippers Corner** (CDP) New Hanover County
24	n/a	0.4	**South Rosemary** (CDP) Halifax County
24	n/a	0.4	**Stanley** (town) Gaston County
24	n/a	0.4	**Waynesville** (town) Haywood County
24	n/a	0.4	**Weaverville** (town) Buncombe County
24	n/a	0.4	**Wrightsboro** (CDP) New Hanover County
43	n/a	0.5	**Benson** (town) Johnston County
43	n/a	0.5	**Boiling Spring Lakes** (city) Brunswick County
43	n/a	0.5	**Carolina Shores** (town) Brunswick County
43	n/a	0.5	**Edenton** (town) Chowan County
43	n/a	0.5	**Fairfield Harbour** (CDP) Craven County
43	n/a	0.5	**Hampstead** (CDP) Pender County
43	n/a	0.5	**Lake Royale** (CDP) Franklin County
43	n/a	0.5	**Landis** (town) Rowan County
43	n/a	0.5	**Midway** (town) Davidson County
43	n/a	0.5	**Mineral Springs** (town) Union County
43	n/a	0.5	**Red Oak** (town) Nash County
43	n/a	0.5	**Rural Hall** (town) Forsyth County
43	198	0.5	**Tarboro** (town) Edgecombe County
43	n/a	0.5	**Tyro** (CDP) Davidson County
43	n/a	0.5	**Washington** (city) Beaufort County
43	n/a	0.5	**Williamston** (town) Martin County
59	n/a	0.6	**Angier** (town) Harnett County
59	n/a	0.6	**Black Mountain** (town) Buncombe County
59	n/a	0.6	**Dallas** (town) Gaston County
59	n/a	0.6	**East Rockingham** (CDP) Richmond County
59	n/a	0.6	**Glen Raven** (CDP) Alamance County
59	321	0.6	**Lincolnton** (city) Lincoln County
59	n/a	0.6	**North Wilkesboro** (town) Wilkes County
59	n/a	0.6	**Pembroke** (town) Robeson County
59	n/a	0.6	**Polkton** (town) Anson County
59	321	0.6	**Reidsville** (city) Rockingham County
59	n/a	0.6	**Saint James** (town) Brunswick County
59	n/a	0.6	**Southern Shores** (town) Dare County
59	n/a	0.6	**Sunset Beach** (town) Brunswick County
59	n/a	0.6	**Trent Woods** (town) Craven County
59	n/a	0.6	**Unionville** (town) Union County
59	n/a	0.6	**Walkertown** (town) Forsyth County
75	n/a	0.7	**Beaufort** (town) Carteret County
75	n/a	0.7	**Bessemer City** (city) Gaston County
75	n/a	0.7	**Brices Creek** (CDP) Craven County
75	n/a	0.7	**Brogden** (CDP) Wayne County
75	n/a	0.7	**Cajah's Mountain** (town) Caldwell County
75	n/a	0.7	**Cherryville** (city) Gaston County
75	n/a	0.7	**Dana** (CDP) Henderson County
75	n/a	0.7	**East Flat Rock** (CDP) Henderson County
75	452	0.7	**Eden** (city) Rockingham County
75	n/a	0.7	**Elizabethtown** (town) Bladen County
75	n/a	0.7	**Forest Oaks** (CDP) Guilford County
75	n/a	0.7	**Granite Falls** (town) Caldwell County
75	n/a	0.7	**Hamlet** (city) Richmond County
75	452	0.7	**Kinston** (city) Lenoir County
75	n/a	0.7	**La Grange** (town) Lenoir County
75	n/a	0.7	**Lake Norman of Catawba** (CDP) Catawba County
75	n/a	0.7	**Locust** (city) Stanly County
75	n/a	0.7	**Lowesville** (CDP) Lincoln County
75	n/a	0.7	**Mills River** (town) Henderson County
75	n/a	0.7	**Pleasant Garden** (town) Guilford County
75	n/a	0.7	**Seven Lakes** (CDP) Moore County
75	n/a	0.7	**Spindale** (town) Rutherford County
97	n/a	0.8	**Creedmoor** (city) Granville County
97	n/a	0.8	**Dunn** (city) Harnett County
97	n/a	0.8	**Elkin** (town) Surry County
97	n/a	0.8	**Emerald Isle** (town) Carteret County
97	n/a	0.8	**Enochville** (CDP) Rowan County
97	n/a	0.8	**Franklin** (town) Macon County
97	629	0.8	**Henderson** (city) Vance County
97	n/a	0.8	**King** (city) Stokes County
97	n/a	0.8	**Kitty Hawk** (town) Dare County
97	n/a	0.8	**Marion** (city) McDowell County
97	n/a	0.8	**Mocksville** (town) Davie County
97	629	0.8	**Shelby** (city) Cleveland County
97	n/a	0.8	**Silver Lake** (CDP) New Hanover County
97	629	0.8	**Smithfield** (town) Johnston County
97	n/a	0.8	**Sneads Ferry** (CDP) Onslow County
97	629	0.8	**Southern Pines** (town) Moore County
97	n/a	0.8	**Wallburg** (town) Davidson County
97	n/a	0.8	**Westport** (CDP) Lincoln County
97	n/a	0.8	**Whiteville** (city) Columbus County
116	n/a	0.9	**Bethlehem** (CDP) Alexander County
116	n/a	0.9	**Butner** (town) Granville County
116	n/a	0.9	**Eastover** (town) Cumberland County
116	n/a	0.9	**Etowah** (CDP) Henderson County
116	n/a	0.9	**Forest City** (town) Rutherford County
116	801	0.9	**Lenoir** (city) Caldwell County
116	n/a	0.9	**Lillington** (town) Harnett County
116	n/a	0.9	**Louisburg** (town) Franklin County
116	n/a	0.9	**Midland** (town) Cabarrus County
116	801	0.9	**Monroe** (city) Union County
116	n/a	0.9	**Spencer** (town) Rowan County
116	n/a	0.9	**Wendell** (town) Wake County
116	n/a	0.9	**Wingate** (town) Union County
116	n/a	0.9	**Woodfin** (town) Buncombe County
130	n/a	1.0	**Brevard** (city) Transylvania County
130	963	1.0	**Laurinburg** (city) Scotland County
130	n/a	1.0	**Lowell** (city) Gaston County
130	n/a	1.0	**Murfreesboro** (town) Hertford County
130	n/a	1.0	**Raeford** (city) Hoke County
130	n/a	1.0	**River Bend** (town) Craven County
130	963	1.0	**Rocky Mount** (city) Nash County
130	n/a	1.0	**Troy** (town) Montgomery County
130	n/a	1.0	**Whispering Pines** (village) Moore County
130	n/a	1.0	**Zebulon** (town) Wake County
140	n/a	1.1	**Bayshore** (CDP) New Hanover County
140	n/a	1.1	**Clinton** (city) Sampson County
140	n/a	1.1	**Gibsonville** (town) Guilford County
140	n/a	1.1	**Granite Quarry** (town) Rowan County
140	n/a	1.1	**James City** (CDP) Craven County
140	1097	1.1	**Kannapolis** (city) Cabarrus County
140	n/a	1.1	**Kings Grant** (CDP) New Hanover County
140	n/a	1.1	**Ogden** (CDP) New Hanover County
140	n/a	1.1	**Oxford** (city) Granville County
140	1097	1.1	**Sanford** (city) Lee County
140	1097	1.1	**Thomasville** (city) Davidson County

Note: The state column ranks the top/bottom 150 places in the state with population of 2,500 or more. The national column ranks the top/bottom places in the country with population of 10,000 or more. Places that are unincorporated were not considered in the rankings. n/a indicates data not available. Please refer to the User Guide for additional information.

American Indian/Alaska Native Population

Top 150 Places Ranked in *Descending* Order

State Rank	Nat'l Rank	Percent	Place
1	n/a	66.4	**Pembroke** (town) Robeson County
2	n/a	13.4	**Fairmont** (town) Robeson County
3	14	13.1	**Lumberton** (city) Robeson County
4	n/a	12.5	**Red Springs** (town) Robeson County
5	35	6.1	**Laurinburg** (city) Scotland County
6	n/a	4.3	**Raeford** (city) Hoke County
7	n/a	3.5	**East Rockingham** (CDP) Richmond County
8	n/a	2.8	**Sylva** (town) Jackson County
9	n/a	1.9	**Eastover** (town) Cumberland County
9	178	1.9	**Hope Mills** (town) Cumberland County
11	n/a	1.7	**Hamlet** (city) Richmond County
11	n/a	1.7	**Rockfish** (CDP) Hoke County
11	n/a	1.7	**Rockingham** (city) Richmond County
11	n/a	1.7	**Siler City** (town) Chatham County
15	n/a	1.6	**Polkton** (town) Anson County
16	n/a	1.5	**Ahoskie** (town) Hertford County
16	n/a	1.5	**Skippers Corner** (CDP) New Hanover County
18	n/a	1.3	**Aberdeen** (town) Moore County
18	n/a	1.3	**Whiteville** (city) Columbus County
20	n/a	1.2	**Clinton** (city) Sampson County
20	390	1.2	**Graham** (city) Alamance County
22	474	1.1	**Fayetteville** (city) Cumberland County
22	n/a	1.1	**Liberty** (town) Randolph County
22	474	1.1	**Spring Lake** (town) Cumberland County
22	n/a	1.1	**Tabor City** (town) Columbus County
26	n/a	1.0	**Dunn** (city) Harnett County
26	n/a	1.0	**River Road** (CDP) Beaufort County
28	667	0.9	**Asheboro** (city) Randolph County
28	n/a	0.9	**Erwin** (town) Harnett County
28	n/a	0.9	**Lillington** (town) Harnett County
28	667	0.9	**Morganton** (city) Burke County
28	n/a	0.9	**Red Oak** (town) Nash County
33	n/a	0.8	**Angier** (town) Harnett County
33	n/a	0.8	**Burgaw** (town) Pender County
33	n/a	0.8	**Mount Olive** (town) Wayne County
33	n/a	0.8	**Ranlo** (town) Gaston County
33	795	0.8	**Sanford** (city) Lee County
33	n/a	0.8	**South Rosemary** (CDP) Halifax County
33	n/a	0.8	**Wendell** (town) Wake County
33	n/a	0.8	**Wrightsboro** (CDP) New Hanover County
41	n/a	0.7	**Buies Creek** (CDP) Harnett County
41	954	0.7	**Burlington** (city) Alamance County
41	n/a	0.7	**Butner** (town) Granville County
41	n/a	0.7	**Canton** (town) Haywood County
41	n/a	0.7	**Carolina Beach** (town) New Hanover County
41	n/a	0.7	**Cullowhee** (CDP) Jackson County
41	n/a	0.7	**Half Moon** (CDP) Onslow County
41	954	0.7	**Havelock** (city) Craven County
41	954	0.7	**Jacksonville** (city) Onslow County
41	n/a	0.7	**Kings Grant** (CDP) New Hanover County
41	n/a	0.7	**Lake Royale** (CDP) Franklin County
41	954	0.7	**Lexington** (city) Davidson County
41	n/a	0.7	**Mountain Home** (CDP) Henderson County
41	n/a	0.7	**Northchase** (CDP) New Hanover County
41	954	0.7	**Piney Green** (CDP) Onslow County
41	n/a	0.7	**Swannanoa** (CDP) Buncombe County
41	954	0.7	**Thomasville** (city) Davidson County
41	n/a	0.7	**Troy** (town) Montgomery County
41	n/a	0.7	**Windsor** (town) Bertie County
60	1134	0.6	**Archdale** (city) Randolph County
60	n/a	0.6	**Archer Lodge** (town) Johnston County
60	n/a	0.6	**Ayden** (town) Pitt County
60	n/a	0.6	**China Grove** (town) Rowan County
60	n/a	0.6	**Cramerton** (town) Gaston County
60	n/a	0.6	**Creedmoor** (city) Granville County
60	1134	0.6	**Fuquay-Varina** (town) Wake County
60	n/a	0.6	**Glen Raven** (CDP) Alamance County
60	1134	0.6	**High Point** (city) Guilford County
60	n/a	0.6	**Hillsborough** (town) Orange County
60	1134	0.6	**Knightdale** (town) Wake County
60	1134	0.6	**Leland** (town) Brunswick County
60	n/a	0.6	**Lowesville** (CDP) Lincoln County
60	1134	0.6	**Mint Hill** (town) Mecklenburg County
60	n/a	0.6	**Mocksville** (town) Davie County
60	1134	0.6	**Monroe** (city) Union County
60	n/a	0.6	**Nashville** (town) Nash County
60	n/a	0.6	**Oak Island** (town) Brunswick County
60	n/a	0.6	**Pleasant Garden** (town) Guilford County
60	n/a	0.6	**Randleman** (city) Randolph County
60	1134	0.6	**Roanoke Rapids** (city) Halifax County
60	1134	0.6	**Rocky Mount** (city) Nash County
60	n/a	0.6	**Roxboro** (city) Person County
60	n/a	0.6	**Shallotte** (town) Brunswick County
60	n/a	0.6	**Silver Lake** (CDP) New Hanover County
60	1134	0.6	**Southern Pines** (town) Moore County
60	n/a	0.6	**Waynesville** (town) Haywood County
60	n/a	0.6	**Woodfin** (town) Buncombe County
88	1413	0.5	**Charlotte** (city) Mecklenburg County
88	1413	0.5	**Durham** (city) Durham County
88	n/a	0.5	**Elizabethtown** (town) Bladen County
88	n/a	0.5	**Elroy** (CDP) Wayne County
88	n/a	0.5	**Fletcher** (town) Henderson County
88	n/a	0.5	**Franklin** (town) Macon County
88	1413	0.5	**Garner** (town) Wake County
88	1413	0.5	**Greensboro** (city) Guilford County
88	1413	0.5	**Harrisburg** (town) Cabarrus County
88	1413	0.5	**Indian Trail** (town) Union County
88	1413	0.5	**Kernersville** (town) Forsyth County
88	n/a	0.5	**Kill Devil Hills** (town) Dare County
88	n/a	0.5	**Lake Junaluska** (CDP) Haywood County
88	n/a	0.5	**Lake Park** (village) Union County
88	n/a	0.5	**Landis** (town) Rowan County
88	n/a	0.5	**Lowell** (city) Gaston County
88	n/a	0.5	**Maiden** (town) Catawba County
88	n/a	0.5	**Marion** (city) McDowell County
88	1413	0.5	**Mebane** (city) Alamance County
88	n/a	0.5	**Mineral Springs** (town) Union County
88	1413	0.5	**Mooresville** (town) Iredell County
88	n/a	0.5	**Morehead City** (town) Carteret County
88	n/a	0.5	**Nags Head** (town) Dare County
88	n/a	0.5	**Newport** (town) Carteret County
88	n/a	0.5	**Pineville** (town) Mecklenburg County
88	1413	0.5	**Raleigh** (city) Wake County
88	n/a	0.5	**Selma** (town) Johnston County
88	1413	0.5	**Smithfield** (town) Johnston County
88	1413	0.5	**Stallings** (town) Union County
88	n/a	0.5	**Tyro** (CDP) Davidson County
88	n/a	0.5	**Wallburg** (town) Davidson County
88	1413	0.5	**Wilmington** (city) New Hanover County
88	n/a	0.5	**Zebulon** (town) Wake County
121	n/a	0.4	**Benson** (town) Johnston County
121	n/a	0.4	**Bessemer City** (city) Gaston County
121	n/a	0.4	**Boiling Spring Lakes** (city) Brunswick County
121	1783	0.4	**Carrboro** (town) Orange County
121	1783	0.4	**Cary** (town) Wake County
121	1783	0.4	**Clayton** (town) Johnston County
121	n/a	0.4	**Dallas** (town) Gaston County
121	n/a	0.4	**Dana** (CDP) Henderson County
121	n/a	0.4	**East Flat Rock** (CDP) Henderson County
121	1783	0.4	**Eden** (city) Rockingham County
121	1783	0.4	**Elizabeth City** (city) Pasquotank County
121	1783	0.4	**Gastonia** (city) Gaston County
121	1783	0.4	**Goldsboro** (city) Wayne County
121	1783	0.4	**Greenville** (city) Pitt County
121	1783	0.4	**Hendersonville** (city) Henderson County
121	1783	0.4	**Holly Springs** (town) Wake County
121	n/a	0.4	**James City** (CDP) Craven County
121	n/a	0.4	**Jamestown** (town) Guilford County
121	1783	0.4	**Lenoir** (city) Caldwell County
121	n/a	0.4	**Long View** (town) Catawba County
121	n/a	0.4	**Midway** (town) Davidson County
121	1783	0.4	**Morrisville** (town) Wake County
121	1783	0.4	**Mount Holly** (city) Gaston County
121	n/a	0.4	**Moyock** (CDP) Currituck County
121	1783	0.4	**New Bern** (city) Craven County
121	1783	0.4	**Newton** (city) Catawba County
121	n/a	0.4	**North Wilkesboro** (town) Wilkes County
121	n/a	0.4	**Oak Ridge** (town) Guilford County
121	n/a	0.4	**Ogden** (CDP) New Hanover County
121	n/a	0.4	**Oxford** (city) Granville County

Note: The state column ranks the top/bottom 150 places in the state with population of 2,500 or more. The national column ranks the top/bottom places in the country with population of 10,000 or more. Places that are unincorporated were not considered in the rankings. n/a indicates data not available. Please refer to the User Guide for additional information.

American Indian/Alaska Native Population

Top 150 Places Ranked in *Ascending* Order

State Rank	Nat'l Rank	Percent	Place
1	n/a	0.0	**Brices Creek** (CDP) Craven County
1	n/a	0.0	**Gamewell** (town) Caldwell County
1	n/a	0.0	**Icard** (CDP) Burke County
1	n/a	0.0	**Weaverville** (town) Buncombe County
5	n/a	0.1	**Bayshore** (CDP) New Hanover County
5	n/a	0.1	**Edenton** (town) Chowan County
5	n/a	0.1	**Elon** (town) Alamance County
5	n/a	0.1	**Enochville** (CDP) Rowan County
5	n/a	0.1	**Fairfield Harbour** (CDP) Craven County
5	n/a	0.1	**Grifton** (town) Pitt County
5	n/a	0.1	**Locust** (city) Stanly County
5	n/a	0.1	**Saint James** (town) Brunswick County
5	n/a	0.1	**Southern Shores** (town) Dare County
5	n/a	0.1	**Southport** (city) Brunswick County
5	61	0.1	**Tarboro** (town) Edgecombe County
5	n/a	0.1	**Valdese** (town) Burke County
5	n/a	0.1	**Waxhaw** (town) Union County
5	n/a	0.1	**Wentworth** (town) Rockingham County
5	n/a	0.1	**Westport** (CDP) Lincoln County
5	n/a	0.1	**Yadkinville** (town) Yadkin County
21	n/a	0.2	**Beaufort** (town) Carteret County
21	n/a	0.2	**Bethlehem** (CDP) Alexander County
21	n/a	0.2	**Boiling Springs** (town) Cleveland County
21	722	0.2	**Boone** (town) Watauga County
21	n/a	0.2	**Cherryville** (city) Gaston County
21	n/a	0.2	**Conover** (city) Catawba County
21	722	0.2	**Davidson** (town) Mecklenburg County
21	n/a	0.2	**Elkin** (town) Surry County
21	n/a	0.2	**Emerald Isle** (town) Carteret County
21	n/a	0.2	**Enfield** (town) Halifax County
21	n/a	0.2	**Etowah** (CDP) Henderson County
21	n/a	0.2	**Fairview** (town) Union County
21	n/a	0.2	**Farmville** (town) Pitt County
21	n/a	0.2	**Flat Rock** (village) Henderson County
21	n/a	0.2	**Forest City** (town) Rutherford County
21	n/a	0.2	**Gibsonville** (town) Guilford County
21	n/a	0.2	**Granite Falls** (town) Caldwell County
21	n/a	0.2	**Granite Quarry** (town) Rowan County
21	n/a	0.2	**Hampstead** (CDP) Pender County
21	722	0.2	**Kings Mountain** (city) Cleveland County
21	722	0.2	**Kinston** (city) Lenoir County
21	n/a	0.2	**Kitty Hawk** (town) Dare County
21	n/a	0.2	**La Grange** (town) Lenoir County
21	n/a	0.2	**Lake Norman of Catawba** (CDP) Catawba County
21	n/a	0.2	**Marvin** (village) Union County
21	n/a	0.2	**Mountain View** (CDP) Catawba County
21	n/a	0.2	**Murfreesboro** (town) Hertford County
21	n/a	0.2	**Porters Neck** (CDP) New Hanover County
21	n/a	0.2	**Royal Pines** (CDP) Buncombe County
21	n/a	0.2	**Rural Hall** (town) Forsyth County
21	n/a	0.2	**Seven Lakes** (CDP) Moore County
21	n/a	0.2	**Trent Woods** (town) Craven County
21	n/a	0.2	**Unionville** (town) Union County
21	n/a	0.2	**Wadesboro** (town) Anson County
21	n/a	0.2	**Washington** (city) Beaufort County
21	n/a	0.2	**Weddington** (town) Union County
21	n/a	0.2	**Welcome** (CDP) Davidson County
21	n/a	0.2	**Wesley Chapel** (village) Union County
21	n/a	0.2	**Whispering Pines** (village) Moore County
21	n/a	0.2	**Wilkesboro** (town) Wilkes County
21	n/a	0.2	**Williamston** (town) Martin County
62	1626	0.3	**Albemarle** (city) Stanly County
62	1626	0.3	**Apex** (town) Wake County
62	1626	0.3	**Asheville** (city) Buncombe County
62	1626	0.3	**Belmont** (city) Gaston County
62	n/a	0.3	**Black Mountain** (town) Buncombe County
62	n/a	0.3	**Brevard** (city) Transylvania County
62	n/a	0.3	**Brogden** (CDP) Wayne County
62	n/a	0.3	**Cajah's Mountain** (town) Caldwell County
62	n/a	0.3	**Carolina Shores** (town) Brunswick County
62	1626	0.3	**Chapel Hill** (town) Orange County
62	1626	0.3	**Clemmons** (village) Forsyth County
62	1626	0.3	**Concord** (city) Cabarrus County
62	1626	0.3	**Cornelius** (town) Mecklenburg County
62	n/a	0.3	**Fairview** (CDP) Buncombe County
62	n/a	0.3	**Forest Oaks** (CDP) Guilford County
62	1626	0.3	**Henderson** (city) Vance County
62	1626	0.3	**Hickory** (city) Catawba County
62	n/a	0.3	**Hudson** (town) Caldwell County
62	1626	0.3	**Huntersville** (town) Mecklenburg County
62	1626	0.3	**Kannapolis** (city) Cabarrus County
62	n/a	0.3	**King** (city) Stokes County
62	1626	0.3	**Lewisville** (town) Forsyth County
62	1626	0.3	**Lincolnton** (city) Lincoln County
62	n/a	0.3	**Louisburg** (town) Franklin County
62	n/a	0.3	**Mar-Mac** (CDP) Wayne County
62	1626	0.3	**Matthews** (town) Mecklenburg County
62	n/a	0.3	**Midland** (town) Cabarrus County
62	n/a	0.3	**Mills River** (town) Henderson County
62	1626	0.3	**Mount Airy** (city) Surry County
62	1626	0.3	**Murraysville** (CDP) New Hanover County
62	n/a	0.3	**Myrtle Grove** (CDP) New Hanover County
62	n/a	0.3	**Pittsboro** (town) Chatham County
62	1626	0.3	**Reidsville** (city) Rockingham County
62	n/a	0.3	**Rutherfordton** (town) Rutherford County
62	n/a	0.3	**Saint Stephens** (CDP) Catawba County
62	n/a	0.3	**Sawmills** (town) Caldwell County
62	n/a	0.3	**Sneads Ferry** (CDP) Onslow County
62	n/a	0.3	**Spindale** (town) Rutherford County
62	1626	0.3	**Statesville** (city) Iredell County
62	n/a	0.3	**Walkertown** (town) Forsyth County
62	1626	0.3	**Wilson** (city) Wilson County
62	n/a	0.3	**Winterville** (town) Pitt County
104	n/a	0.4	**Benson** (town) Johnston County
104	n/a	0.4	**Bessemer City** (city) Gaston County
104	n/a	0.4	**Boiling Spring Lakes** (city) Brunswick County
104	2369	0.4	**Carrboro** (town) Orange County
104	2369	0.4	**Cary** (town) Wake County
104	2369	0.4	**Clayton** (town) Johnston County
104	n/a	0.4	**Dallas** (town) Gaston County
104	n/a	0.4	**Dana** (CDP) Henderson County
104	n/a	0.4	**East Flat Rock** (CDP) Henderson County
104	2369	0.4	**Eden** (city) Rockingham County
104	2369	0.4	**Elizabeth City** (city) Pasquotank County
104	2369	0.4	**Gastonia** (city) Gaston County
104	2369	0.4	**Goldsboro** (city) Wayne County
104	2369	0.4	**Greenville** (city) Pitt County
104	2369	0.4	**Hendersonville** (city) Henderson County
104	2369	0.4	**Holly Springs** (town) Wake County
104	n/a	0.4	**James City** (CDP) Craven County
104	n/a	0.4	**Jamestown** (town) Guilford County
104	2369	0.4	**Lenoir** (city) Caldwell County
104	n/a	0.4	**Long View** (town) Catawba County
104	n/a	0.4	**Midway** (town) Davidson County
104	2369	0.4	**Morrisville** (town) Wake County
104	2369	0.4	**Mount Holly** (city) Gaston County
104	n/a	0.4	**Moyock** (CDP) Currituck County
104	2369	0.4	**New Bern** (city) Craven County
104	2369	0.4	**Newton** (city) Catawba County
104	n/a	0.4	**North Wilkesboro** (town) Wilkes County
104	n/a	0.4	**Oak Ridge** (town) Guilford County
104	n/a	0.4	**Ogden** (CDP) New Hanover County
104	n/a	0.4	**Oxford** (city) Granville County
104	2369	0.4	**Pinehurst** (village) Moore County
104	n/a	0.4	**Plymouth** (town) Washington County
104	n/a	0.4	**River Bend** (town) Craven County
104	n/a	0.4	**Rolesville** (town) Wake County
104	2369	0.4	**Salisbury** (city) Rowan County
104	2369	0.4	**Shelby** (city) Cleveland County
104	n/a	0.4	**Spencer** (town) Rowan County
104	n/a	0.4	**Stanley** (town) Gaston County
104	n/a	0.4	**Stokesdale** (town) Guilford County
104	2369	0.4	**Summerfield** (town) Guilford County
104	n/a	0.4	**Sunset Beach** (town) Brunswick County
104	n/a	0.4	**Swansboro** (town) Onslow County
104	n/a	0.4	**Trinity** (city) Randolph County
104	2369	0.4	**Wake Forest** (town) Wake County
104	n/a	0.4	**Wallace** (town) Duplin County
104	n/a	0.4	**Warsaw** (town) Duplin County
104	n/a	0.4	**Wingate** (town) Union County

Note: The state column ranks the top/bottom 150 places in the state with population of 2,500 or more. The national column ranks the top/bottom places in the country with population of 10,000 or more. Places that are unincorporated were not considered in the rankings. n/a indicates data not available. Please refer to the User Guide for additional information.

Native Hawaiian/Other Pacific Islander Population

Top 150 Places Ranked in *Descending* Order

State Rank	Nat'l Rank	Percent	Place
1	71	1.5	**Morganton** (city) Burke County
2	n/a	0.7	**Mountain Home** (CDP) Henderson County
3	n/a	0.5	**Rockfish** (CDP) Hoke County
3	251	0.5	**Spring Lake** (town) Cumberland County
5	n/a	0.4	**East Flat Rock** (CDP) Henderson County
5	288	0.4	**Fayetteville** (city) Cumberland County
5	n/a	0.4	**Half Moon** (CDP) Onslow County
5	288	0.4	**Piney Green** (CDP) Onslow County
9	374	0.3	**Havelock** (city) Craven County
9	374	0.3	**Hendersonville** (city) Henderson County
9	374	0.3	**Hope Mills** (town) Cumberland County
9	374	0.3	**Jacksonville** (city) Onslow County
9	n/a	0.3	**Lillington** (town) Harnett County
9	n/a	0.3	**Weaverville** (town) Buncombe County
15	510	0.2	**Asheville** (city) Buncombe County
15	510	0.2	**Belmont** (city) Gaston County
15	n/a	0.2	**East Rockingham** (CDP) Richmond County
15	510	0.2	**Eden** (city) Rockingham County
15	n/a	0.2	**Emerald Isle** (town) Carteret County
15	510	0.2	**Lumberton** (city) Robeson County
15	n/a	0.2	**Morehead City** (town) Carteret County
15	n/a	0.2	**Moyock** (CDP) Currituck County
15	n/a	0.2	**Pembroke** (town) Robeson County
15	n/a	0.2	**River Road** (CDP) Beaufort County
15	n/a	0.2	**Siler City** (town) Chatham County
15	n/a	0.2	**Spencer** (town) Rowan County
15	n/a	0.2	**Valdese** (town) Burke County
15	n/a	0.2	**Warsaw** (town) Duplin County
15	n/a	0.2	**Wrightsboro** (CDP) New Hanover County
30	820	0.1	**Apex** (town) Wake County
30	820	0.1	**Asheboro** (city) Randolph County
30	n/a	0.1	**Boiling Spring Lakes** (city) Brunswick County
30	n/a	0.1	**Burgaw** (town) Pender County
30	820	0.1	**Burlington** (city) Alamance County
30	n/a	0.1	**Carolina Beach** (town) New Hanover County
30	n/a	0.1	**Carolina Shores** (town) Brunswick County
30	820	0.1	**Charlotte** (city) Mecklenburg County
30	820	0.1	**Concord** (city) Cabarrus County
30	n/a	0.1	**Creedmoor** (city) Granville County
30	n/a	0.1	**Dana** (CDP) Henderson County
30	n/a	0.1	**Dunn** (city) Harnett County
30	820	0.1	**Durham** (city) Durham County
30	n/a	0.1	**Eastover** (town) Cumberland County
30	820	0.1	**Elizabeth City** (city) Pasquotank County
30	n/a	0.1	**Elroy** (CDP) Wayne County
30	n/a	0.1	**Fletcher** (town) Henderson County
30	n/a	0.1	**Gibsonville** (town) Guilford County
30	820	0.1	**Goldsboro** (city) Wayne County
30	820	0.1	**Greensboro** (city) Guilford County
30	820	0.1	**Holly Springs** (town) Wake County
30	n/a	0.1	**Hudson** (town) Caldwell County
30	n/a	0.1	**James City** (CDP) Craven County
30	n/a	0.1	**Jamestown** (town) Guilford County
30	n/a	0.1	**Kill Devil Hills** (town) Dare County
30	n/a	0.1	**Kings Grant** (CDP) New Hanover County
30	820	0.1	**Kinston** (city) Lenoir County
30	n/a	0.1	**Kitty Hawk** (town) Dare County
30	820	0.1	**Knightdale** (town) Wake County
30	n/a	0.1	**La Grange** (town) Lenoir County
30	820	0.1	**Lenoir** (city) Caldwell County
30	n/a	0.1	**Lowell** (city) Gaston County
30	820	0.1	**Mebane** (city) Alamance County
30	n/a	0.1	**Midway** (town) Davidson County
30	820	0.1	**Morrisville** (town) Wake County
30	820	0.1	**Mount Airy** (city) Surry County
30	820	0.1	**Mount Holly** (city) Gaston County
30	n/a	0.1	**Mountain View** (CDP) Catawba County
30	820	0.1	**Murraysville** (CDP) New Hanover County
30	n/a	0.1	**Myrtle Grove** (CDP) New Hanover County
30	820	0.1	**New Bern** (city) Craven County
30	n/a	0.1	**Newport** (town) Carteret County
30	n/a	0.1	**Pineville** (town) Mecklenburg County
30	n/a	0.1	**Raeford** (city) Hoke County
30	n/a	0.1	**River Bend** (town) Craven County
30	n/a	0.1	**Rural Hall** (town) Forsyth County
30	n/a	0.1	**Saint Stephens** (CDP) Catawba County
30	n/a	0.1	**Selma** (town) Johnston County
30	n/a	0.1	**Shallotte** (town) Brunswick County
30	n/a	0.1	**Silver Lake** (CDP) New Hanover County
30	820	0.1	**Smithfield** (town) Johnston County
30	820	0.1	**Southern Pines** (town) Moore County
30	820	0.1	**Tarboro** (town) Edgecombe County
30	n/a	0.1	**Walkertown** (town) Forsyth County
30	n/a	0.1	**Wallace** (town) Duplin County
30	n/a	0.1	**Washington** (city) Beaufort County
30	n/a	0.1	**Waynesville** (town) Haywood County
30	n/a	0.1	**Wesley Chapel** (village) Union County
30	n/a	0.1	**Whispering Pines** (village) Moore County
30	n/a	0.1	**Whiteville** (city) Columbus County
30	n/a	0.1	**Wilkesboro** (town) Wilkes County
30	n/a	0.1	**Williamston** (town) Martin County
30	820	0.1	**Wilmington** (city) New Hanover County
30	n/a	0.1	**Wingate** (town) Union County
30	820	0.1	**Winston-Salem** (city) Forsyth County
95	n/a	0.0	**Aberdeen** (town) Moore County
95	n/a	0.0	**Ahoskie** (town) Hertford County
95	2061	0.0	**Albemarle** (city) Stanly County
95	n/a	0.0	**Angier** (town) Harnett County
95	2061	0.0	**Archdale** (city) Randolph County
95	n/a	0.0	**Archer Lodge** (town) Johnston County
95	n/a	0.0	**Ayden** (town) Pitt County
95	n/a	0.0	**Bayshore** (CDP) New Hanover County
95	n/a	0.0	**Beaufort** (town) Carteret County
95	n/a	0.0	**Benson** (town) Johnston County
95	n/a	0.0	**Bessemer City** (city) Gaston County
95	n/a	0.0	**Bethlehem** (CDP) Alexander County
95	n/a	0.0	**Black Mountain** (town) Buncombe County
95	n/a	0.0	**Boiling Springs** (town) Cleveland County
95	2061	0.0	**Boone** (town) Watauga County
95	n/a	0.0	**Brevard** (city) Transylvania County
95	n/a	0.0	**Brices Creek** (CDP) Craven County
95	n/a	0.0	**Brogden** (CDP) Wayne County
95	n/a	0.0	**Buies Creek** (CDP) Harnett County
95	n/a	0.0	**Butner** (town) Granville County
95	n/a	0.0	**Cajah's Mountain** (town) Caldwell County
95	n/a	0.0	**Canton** (town) Haywood County
95	2061	0.0	**Carrboro** (town) Orange County
95	2061	0.0	**Cary** (town) Wake County
95	2061	0.0	**Chapel Hill** (town) Orange County
95	n/a	0.0	**Cherryville** (city) Gaston County
95	n/a	0.0	**China Grove** (town) Rowan County
95	2061	0.0	**Clayton** (town) Johnston County
95	2061	0.0	**Clemmons** (village) Forsyth County
95	n/a	0.0	**Clinton** (city) Sampson County
95	n/a	0.0	**Conover** (city) Catawba County
95	2061	0.0	**Cornelius** (town) Mecklenburg County
95	n/a	0.0	**Cramerton** (town) Gaston County
95	n/a	0.0	**Cullowhee** (CDP) Jackson County
95	n/a	0.0	**Dallas** (town) Gaston County
95	2061	0.0	**Davidson** (town) Mecklenburg County
95	n/a	0.0	**Edenton** (town) Chowan County
95	n/a	0.0	**Elizabethtown** (town) Bladen County
95	n/a	0.0	**Elkin** (town) Surry County
95	n/a	0.0	**Elon** (town) Alamance County
95	n/a	0.0	**Enfield** (town) Halifax County
95	n/a	0.0	**Enochville** (CDP) Rowan County
95	n/a	0.0	**Erwin** (town) Harnett County
95	n/a	0.0	**Etowah** (CDP) Henderson County
95	n/a	0.0	**Fairfield Harbour** (CDP) Craven County
95	n/a	0.0	**Fairmont** (town) Robeson County
95	n/a	0.0	**Fairview** (CDP) Buncombe County
95	n/a	0.0	**Fairview** (town) Union County
95	n/a	0.0	**Farmville** (town) Pitt County
95	n/a	0.0	**Flat Rock** (village) Henderson County
95	n/a	0.0	**Forest City** (town) Rutherford County
95	n/a	0.0	**Forest Oaks** (CDP) Guilford County
95	n/a	0.0	**Franklin** (town) Macon County
95	2061	0.0	**Fuquay-Varina** (town) Wake County
95	n/a	0.0	**Gamewell** (town) Caldwell County
95	2061	0.0	**Garner** (town) Wake County

Note: The state column ranks the top/bottom 150 places in the state with population of 2,500 or more. The national column ranks the top/bottom places in the country with population of 10,000 or more. Places that are unincorporated were not considered in the rankings. n/a indicates data not available. Please refer to the User Guide for additional information.

Two or More Races

Top 150 Places Ranked in *Descending* Order

State Rank	Nat'l Rank	Percent	Place
1	95	6.9	**Spring Lake** (town) Cumberland County
2	168	6.1	**Piney Green** (CDP) Onslow County
3	n/a	5.2	**Half Moon** (CDP) Onslow County
4	n/a	5.1	**Rockfish** (CDP) Hoke County
5	426	4.9	**Fayetteville** (city) Cumberland County
6	496	4.7	**Havelock** (city) Craven County
6	496	4.7	**Jacksonville** (city) Onslow County
8	537	4.6	**Hope Mills** (town) Cumberland County
9	n/a	3.7	**Liberty** (town) Randolph County
9	n/a	3.7	**Raeford** (city) Hoke County
11	n/a	3.6	**Zebulon** (town) Wake County
12	1191	3.5	**Knightdale** (town) Wake County
12	n/a	3.5	**Swansboro** (town) Onslow County
14	n/a	3.4	**Mocksville** (town) Davie County
14	1272	3.4	**Morrisville** (town) Wake County
14	n/a	3.4	**Pembroke** (town) Robeson County
14	n/a	3.4	**Siler City** (town) Chatham County
18	n/a	3.2	**East Flat Rock** (CDP) Henderson County
18	n/a	3.2	**Newport** (town) Carteret County
18	n/a	3.2	**Wendell** (town) Wake County
21	n/a	3.0	**Long View** (town) Catawba County
22	n/a	2.9	**Aberdeen** (town) Moore County
22	1717	2.9	**Carrboro** (town) Orange County
22	n/a	2.9	**Forest City** (town) Rutherford County
22	1717	2.9	**Morganton** (city) Burke County
22	n/a	2.9	**Selma** (town) Johnston County
22	n/a	2.9	**Swannanoa** (CDP) Buncombe County
22	n/a	2.9	**Waxhaw** (town) Union County
29	1828	2.8	**Asheboro** (city) Randolph County
29	1828	2.8	**Lincolnton** (city) Lincoln County
29	1828	2.8	**Sanford** (city) Lee County
32	n/a	2.7	**Brevard** (city) Transylvania County
32	1935	2.7	**Chapel Hill** (town) Orange County
32	1935	2.7	**Charlotte** (city) Mecklenburg County
32	1935	2.7	**Durham** (city) Durham County
32	n/a	2.7	**Fairmont** (town) Robeson County
32	1935	2.7	**Fuquay-Varina** (town) Wake County
32	1935	2.7	**Lumberton** (city) Robeson County
32	n/a	2.7	**Pineville** (town) Mecklenburg County
32	n/a	2.7	**Weaverville** (town) Buncombe County
41	2062	2.6	**Asheville** (city) Buncombe County
41	2062	2.6	**Cary** (town) Wake County
41	n/a	2.6	**Dana** (CDP) Henderson County
41	n/a	2.6	**East Rockingham** (CDP) Richmond County
41	n/a	2.6	**Elroy** (CDP) Wayne County
41	n/a	2.6	**Erwin** (town) Harnett County
41	2062	2.6	**Goldsboro** (city) Wayne County
41	2062	2.6	**Greensboro** (city) Guilford County
41	2062	2.6	**Lexington** (city) Davidson County
41	2062	2.6	**Mebane** (city) Alamance County
41	2062	2.6	**Monroe** (city) Union County
41	2062	2.6	**Newton** (city) Catawba County
41	2062	2.6	**Raleigh** (city) Wake County
54	2209	2.5	**Apex** (town) Wake County
54	n/a	2.5	**Conover** (city) Catawba County
54	2209	2.5	**Holly Springs** (town) Wake County
54	n/a	2.5	**Morehead City** (town) Carteret County
54	n/a	2.5	**Red Springs** (town) Robeson County
54	n/a	2.5	**Spindale** (town) Rutherford County
54	n/a	2.5	**Woodfin** (town) Buncombe County
61	n/a	2.4	**Beaufort** (town) Carteret County
61	2357	2.4	**Burlington** (city) Alamance County
61	2357	2.4	**Graham** (city) Alamance County
61	n/a	2.4	**Grifton** (town) Pitt County
61	n/a	2.4	**James City** (CDP) Craven County
61	2357	2.4	**Kannapolis** (city) Cabarrus County
61	2357	2.4	**Lenoir** (city) Caldwell County
61	2357	2.4	**Mooresville** (town) Iredell County
61	2357	2.4	**New Bern** (city) Craven County
61	n/a	2.4	**Northchase** (CDP) New Hanover County
61	n/a	2.4	**Pittsboro** (town) Chatham County
61	n/a	2.4	**Rural Hall** (town) Forsyth County
61	2357	2.4	**Statesville** (city) Iredell County
61	2357	2.4	**Wake Forest** (town) Wake County
61	2357	2.4	**Winston-Salem** (city) Forsyth County
61	n/a	2.4	**Wrightsboro** (CDP) New Hanover County
77	n/a	2.3	**Benson** (town) Johnston County
77	n/a	2.3	**Black Mountain** (town) Buncombe County
77	n/a	2.3	**Butner** (town) Granville County
77	2489	2.3	**Concord** (city) Cabarrus County
77	2489	2.3	**Elizabeth City** (city) Pasquotank County
77	n/a	2.3	**Fairview** (CDP) Buncombe County
77	2489	2.3	**Garner** (town) Wake County
77	2489	2.3	**High Point** (city) Guilford County
77	2489	2.3	**Indian Trail** (town) Union County
77	2489	2.3	**Kernersville** (town) Forsyth County
77	n/a	2.3	**Mar-Mac** (CDP) Wayne County
77	n/a	2.3	**Ranlo** (town) Gaston County
77	n/a	2.3	**Silver Lake** (CDP) New Hanover County
77	n/a	2.3	**Spencer** (town) Rowan County
77	n/a	2.3	**Wilkesboro** (town) Wilkes County
92	n/a	2.2	**Buies Creek** (CDP) Harnett County
92	n/a	2.2	**Clinton** (city) Sampson County
92	n/a	2.2	**Dunn** (city) Harnett County
92	2642	2.2	**Gastonia** (city) Gaston County
92	2642	2.2	**Greenville** (city) Pitt County
92	2642	2.2	**Hendersonville** (city) Henderson County
92	2642	2.2	**Hickory** (city) Catawba County
92	n/a	2.2	**Lake Park** (village) Union County
92	2642	2.2	**Mount Airy** (city) Surry County
92	n/a	2.2	**North Wilkesboro** (town) Wilkes County
92	n/a	2.2	**Saint Stephens** (CDP) Catawba County
92	2642	2.2	**Wilmington** (city) New Hanover County
104	n/a	2.1	**Angier** (town) Harnett County
104	n/a	2.1	**Archer Lodge** (town) Johnston County
104	2791	2.1	**Clayton** (town) Johnston County
104	n/a	2.1	**Creedmoor** (city) Granville County
104	n/a	2.1	**Glen Raven** (CDP) Alamance County
104	n/a	2.1	**Hillsborough** (town) Orange County
104	2791	2.1	**Huntersville** (town) Mecklenburg County
104	n/a	2.1	**Kill Devil Hills** (town) Dare County
104	2791	2.1	**Murraysville** (CDP) New Hanover County
104	2791	2.1	**Reidsville** (city) Rockingham County
104	n/a	2.1	**Rolesville** (town) Wake County
104	n/a	2.1	**Roxboro** (city) Person County
104	n/a	2.1	**Skippers Corner** (CDP) New Hanover County
104	2791	2.1	**Thomasville** (city) Davidson County
118	n/a	2.0	**Fletcher** (town) Henderson County
118	n/a	2.0	**Hamlet** (city) Richmond County
118	2950	2.0	**Harrisburg** (town) Cabarrus County
118	2950	2.0	**Laurinburg** (city) Scotland County
118	2950	2.0	**Leland** (town) Brunswick County
118	n/a	2.0	**Marion** (city) McDowell County
118	2950	2.0	**Mint Hill** (town) Mecklenburg County
118	n/a	2.0	**Moyock** (CDP) Currituck County
118	2950	2.0	**Salisbury** (city) Rowan County
127	n/a	1.9	**Bessemer City** (city) Gaston County
127	n/a	1.9	**Boiling Spring Lakes** (city) Brunswick County
127	n/a	1.9	**Brices Creek** (CDP) Craven County
127	3098	1.9	**Eden** (city) Rockingham County
127	n/a	1.9	**Kings Grant** (CDP) New Hanover County
127	3098	1.9	**Matthews** (town) Mecklenburg County
127	n/a	1.9	**Randleman** (city) Randolph County
127	n/a	1.9	**Rockingham** (city) Richmond County
127	3098	1.9	**Smithfield** (town) Johnston County
127	n/a	1.9	**Winterville** (town) Pitt County
137	3250	1.8	**Albemarle** (city) Stanly County
137	n/a	1.8	**Dallas** (town) Gaston County
137	n/a	1.8	**Eastover** (town) Cumberland County
137	n/a	1.8	**Etowah** (CDP) Henderson County
137	n/a	1.8	**Gamewell** (town) Caldwell County
137	n/a	1.8	**Midland** (town) Cabarrus County
137	n/a	1.8	**Mountain Home** (CDP) Henderson County
137	n/a	1.8	**Oxford** (city) Granville County
137	n/a	1.8	**Rutherfordton** (town) Rutherford County
137	n/a	1.8	**Sneads Ferry** (CDP) Onslow County
137	n/a	1.8	**Tabor City** (town) Columbus County
137	n/a	1.8	**Windsor** (town) Bertie County
149	3438	1.7	**Boone** (town) Watauga County
149	n/a	1.7	**Burgaw** (town) Pender County

Note: The state column ranks the top/bottom 150 places in the state with population of 2,500 or more. The national column ranks the top/bottom places in the country with population of 10,000 or more. Places that are unincorporated were not considered in the rankings. n/a indicates data not available. Please refer to the User Guide for additional information.

Two or More Races

Top 150 Places Ranked in *Ascending* Order

State Rank	Nat'l Rank	Percent	Place
1	n/a	0.3	**Enfield** (town) Halifax County
1	n/a	0.3	**Saint James** (town) Brunswick County
3	n/a	0.4	**Fairview** (town) Union County
4	n/a	0.5	**Lake Junaluska** (CDP) Haywood County
5	n/a	0.6	**Icard** (CDP) Burke County
6	n/a	0.8	**Enochville** (CDP) Rowan County
6	n/a	0.8	**Fairfield Harbour** (CDP) Craven County
6	n/a	0.8	**Farmville** (town) Pitt County
6	n/a	0.8	**Flat Rock** (village) Henderson County
6	n/a	0.8	**Landis** (town) Rowan County
6	n/a	0.8	**Locust** (city) Stanly County
6	n/a	0.8	**Sunset Beach** (town) Brunswick County
6	49	0.8	**Tarboro** (town) Edgecombe County
6	n/a	0.8	**Trinity** (city) Randolph County
6	n/a	0.8	**Westport** (CDP) Lincoln County
16	n/a	0.9	**Cajah's Mountain** (town) Caldwell County
16	n/a	0.9	**Carolina Shores** (town) Brunswick County
16	n/a	0.9	**Midway** (town) Davidson County
16	n/a	0.9	**Polkton** (town) Anson County
16	n/a	0.9	**Red Oak** (town) Nash County
21	n/a	1.0	**Emerald Isle** (town) Carteret County
21	n/a	1.0	**King** (city) Stokes County
21	n/a	1.0	**Lowesville** (CDP) Lincoln County
21	n/a	1.0	**Oak Ridge** (town) Guilford County
21	n/a	1.0	**Plymouth** (town) Washington County
21	n/a	1.0	**River Road** (CDP) Beaufort County
21	n/a	1.0	**Seven Lakes** (CDP) Moore County
21	n/a	1.0	**Trent Woods** (town) Craven County
29	n/a	1.1	**Ahoskie** (town) Hertford County
29	n/a	1.1	**Granite Quarry** (town) Rowan County
29	n/a	1.1	**Hudson** (town) Caldwell County
29	n/a	1.1	**Kitty Hawk** (town) Dare County
29	n/a	1.1	**La Grange** (town) Lenoir County
29	n/a	1.1	**South Rosemary** (CDP) Halifax County
29	n/a	1.1	**Southern Shores** (town) Dare County
29	n/a	1.1	**Unionville** (town) Union County
29	n/a	1.1	**Wallburg** (town) Davidson County
29	n/a	1.1	**Welcome** (CDP) Davidson County
39	n/a	1.2	**Bethlehem** (CDP) Alexander County
39	n/a	1.2	**Lake Norman of Catawba** (CDP) Catawba County
39	n/a	1.2	**Lowell** (city) Gaston County
39	n/a	1.2	**Oak Island** (town) Brunswick County
39	295	1.2	**Pinehurst** (village) Moore County
39	n/a	1.2	**Warsaw** (town) Duplin County
45	n/a	1.3	**Bayshore** (CDP) New Hanover County
45	n/a	1.3	**Edenton** (town) Chowan County
45	n/a	1.3	**Hampstead** (CDP) Pender County
45	415	1.3	**Kinston** (city) Lenoir County
45	n/a	1.3	**Nashville** (town) Nash County
45	n/a	1.3	**Porters Neck** (CDP) New Hanover County
45	n/a	1.3	**River Bend** (town) Craven County
45	415	1.3	**Roanoke Rapids** (city) Halifax County
45	n/a	1.3	**Southport** (city) Brunswick County
45	n/a	1.3	**Stanley** (town) Gaston County
45	n/a	1.3	**Stokesdale** (town) Guilford County
45	n/a	1.3	**Wadesboro** (town) Anson County
45	n/a	1.3	**Waynesville** (town) Haywood County
45	n/a	1.3	**Weddington** (town) Union County
45	n/a	1.3	**Wentworth** (town) Rockingham County
45	n/a	1.3	**Whispering Pines** (village) Moore County
45	n/a	1.3	**Williamston** (town) Martin County
45	n/a	1.3	**Yadkinville** (town) Yadkin County
63	549	1.4	**Archdale** (city) Randolph County
63	n/a	1.4	**Carolina Beach** (town) New Hanover County
63	n/a	1.4	**Forest Oaks** (CDP) Guilford County
63	549	1.4	**Henderson** (city) Vance County
63	n/a	1.4	**Mills River** (town) Henderson County
63	n/a	1.4	**Murfreesboro** (town) Hertford County
63	n/a	1.4	**Myrtle Grove** (CDP) New Hanover County
63	549	1.4	**Southern Pines** (town) Moore County
63	n/a	1.4	**Tyro** (CDP) Davidson County
63	n/a	1.4	**Walkertown** (town) Forsyth County
63	n/a	1.4	**Wallace** (town) Duplin County
63	n/a	1.4	**Wingate** (town) Union County
75	n/a	1.5	**Boiling Springs** (town) Cleveland County
75	n/a	1.5	**China Grove** (town) Rowan County
75	724	1.5	**Clemmons** (village) Forsyth County
75	n/a	1.5	**Cramerton** (town) Gaston County
75	n/a	1.5	**Elkin** (town) Surry County
75	n/a	1.5	**Gibsonville** (town) Guilford County
75	n/a	1.5	**Granite Falls** (town) Caldwell County
75	n/a	1.5	**Maiden** (town) Catawba County
75	n/a	1.5	**Mountain View** (CDP) Catawba County
75	n/a	1.5	**Nags Head** (town) Dare County
75	724	1.5	**Summerfield** (town) Guilford County
75	n/a	1.5	**Troy** (town) Montgomery County
75	n/a	1.5	**Valdese** (town) Burke County
75	n/a	1.5	**Washington** (city) Beaufort County
75	n/a	1.5	**Wesley Chapel** (village) Union County
90	n/a	1.6	**Ayden** (town) Pitt County
90	861	1.6	**Belmont** (city) Gaston County
90	n/a	1.6	**Brogden** (CDP) Wayne County
90	n/a	1.6	**Cherryville** (city) Gaston County
90	861	1.6	**Cornelius** (town) Mecklenburg County
90	n/a	1.6	**Elizabethtown** (town) Bladen County
90	n/a	1.6	**Elon** (town) Alamance County
90	n/a	1.6	**Jamestown** (town) Guilford County
90	n/a	1.6	**Lake Royale** (CDP) Franklin County
90	861	1.6	**Lewisville** (town) Forsyth County
90	n/a	1.6	**Lillington** (town) Harnett County
90	n/a	1.6	**Marvin** (village) Union County
90	n/a	1.6	**Mineral Springs** (town) Union County
90	861	1.6	**Mount Holly** (city) Gaston County
90	n/a	1.6	**Ogden** (CDP) New Hanover County
90	861	1.6	**Rocky Mount** (city) Nash County
90	n/a	1.6	**Sawmills** (town) Caldwell County
90	n/a	1.6	**Shallotte** (town) Brunswick County
90	861	1.6	**Stallings** (town) Union County
109	1050	1.7	**Boone** (town) Watauga County
109	n/a	1.7	**Burgaw** (town) Pender County
109	n/a	1.7	**Canton** (town) Haywood County
109	n/a	1.7	**Cullowhee** (CDP) Jackson County
109	1050	1.7	**Davidson** (town) Mecklenburg County
109	n/a	1.7	**Franklin** (town) Macon County
109	1050	1.7	**Kings Mountain** (city) Cleveland County
109	n/a	1.7	**Louisburg** (town) Franklin County
109	n/a	1.7	**Mount Olive** (town) Wayne County
109	n/a	1.7	**Pleasant Garden** (town) Guilford County
109	n/a	1.7	**Royal Pines** (CDP) Buncombe County
109	1050	1.7	**Shelby** (city) Cleveland County
109	n/a	1.7	**Sylva** (town) Jackson County
109	n/a	1.7	**Whiteville** (city) Columbus County
109	1050	1.7	**Wilson** (city) Wilson County
124	1219	1.8	**Albemarle** (city) Stanly County
124	n/a	1.8	**Dallas** (town) Gaston County
124	n/a	1.8	**Eastover** (town) Cumberland County
124	n/a	1.8	**Etowah** (CDP) Henderson County
124	n/a	1.8	**Gamewell** (town) Caldwell County
124	n/a	1.8	**Midland** (town) Cabarrus County
124	n/a	1.8	**Mountain Home** (CDP) Henderson County
124	n/a	1.8	**Oxford** (city) Granville County
124	n/a	1.8	**Rutherfordton** (town) Rutherford County
124	n/a	1.8	**Sneads Ferry** (CDP) Onslow County
124	n/a	1.8	**Tabor City** (town) Columbus County
124	n/a	1.8	**Windsor** (town) Bertie County
136	n/a	1.9	**Bessemer City** (city) Gaston County
136	n/a	1.9	**Boiling Spring Lakes** (city) Brunswick County
136	n/a	1.9	**Brices Creek** (CDP) Craven County
136	1407	1.9	**Eden** (city) Rockingham County
136	n/a	1.9	**Kings Grant** (CDP) New Hanover County
136	1407	1.9	**Matthews** (town) Mecklenburg County
136	n/a	1.9	**Randleman** (city) Randolph County
136	n/a	1.9	**Rockingham** (city) Richmond County
136	1407	1.9	**Smithfield** (town) Johnston County
136	n/a	1.9	**Winterville** (town) Pitt County
146	n/a	2.0	**Fletcher** (town) Henderson County
146	n/a	2.0	**Hamlet** (city) Richmond County
146	1559	2.0	**Harrisburg** (town) Cabarrus County
146	1559	2.0	**Laurinburg** (city) Scotland County
146	1559	2.0	**Leland** (town) Brunswick County

Note: The state column ranks the top/bottom 150 places in the state with population of 2,500 or more. The national column ranks the top/bottom places in the country with population of 10,000 or more. Places that are unincorporated were not considered in the rankings. n/a indicates data not available. Please refer to the User Guide for additional information.

Hispanic Population

Top 150 Places Ranked in *Descending* Order

State Rank	Nat'l Rank	Percent	Place
1	n/a	49.8	**Siler City** (town) Chatham County
2	n/a	34.8	**Selma** (town) Johnston County
3	644	29.4	**Monroe** (city) Union County
4	732	26.9	**Asheboro** (city) Randolph County
5	772	25.6	**Sanford** (city) Lee County
6	n/a	25.5	**Wallace** (town) Duplin County
7	n/a	23.7	**Yadkinville** (town) Yadkin County
8	n/a	22.4	**East Flat Rock** (CDP) Henderson County
9	n/a	20.3	**Angier** (town) Harnett County
10	n/a	20.1	**Pineville** (town) Mecklenburg County
11	n/a	19.9	**River Road** (CDP) Beaufort County
12	n/a	19.8	**Dana** (CDP) Henderson County
13	1038	19.3	**Smithfield** (town) Johnston County
14	n/a	17.8	**Elkin** (town) Surry County
15	n/a	16.9	**Warsaw** (town) Duplin County
16	1198	16.4	**Morganton** (city) Burke County
17	1207	16.3	**Lexington** (city) Davidson County
18	1234	16.0	**Burlington** (city) Alamance County
18	1234	16.0	**Lincolnton** (city) Lincoln County
20	n/a	15.9	**Zebulon** (town) Wake County
21	1249	15.7	**Graham** (city) Alamance County
22	1277	15.4	**Spring Lake** (town) Cumberland County
23	n/a	15.1	**Elroy** (CDP) Wayne County
24	n/a	14.7	**Butner** (town) Granville County
24	1328	14.7	**Winston-Salem** (city) Forsyth County
26	n/a	14.4	**Liberty** (town) Randolph County
26	1361	14.4	**Thomasville** (city) Davidson County
28	1380	14.2	**Durham** (city) Durham County
29	n/a	14.0	**Benson** (town) Johnston County
30	n/a	13.8	**Brogden** (CDP) Wayne County
30	1418	13.8	**Carrboro** (town) Orange County
32	n/a	13.7	**Mar-Mac** (CDP) Wayne County
33	1443	13.5	**Hendersonville** (city) Henderson County
33	n/a	13.5	**Rural Hall** (town) Forsyth County
35	1481	13.1	**Charlotte** (city) Mecklenburg County
35	n/a	13.1	**Marion** (city) McDowell County
35	n/a	13.1	**North Wilkesboro** (town) Wilkes County
38	n/a	13.0	**Franklin** (town) Macon County
38	1491	13.0	**Jacksonville** (city) Onslow County
40	1504	12.9	**Newton** (city) Catawba County
40	n/a	12.9	**Silver Lake** (CDP) New Hanover County
42	n/a	12.4	**Glen Raven** (CDP) Alamance County
42	n/a	12.4	**Wingate** (town) Union County
44	1569	12.3	**Concord** (city) Cabarrus County
45	n/a	12.2	**Archer Lodge** (town) Johnston County
45	n/a	12.2	**Conover** (city) Catawba County
45	1579	12.2	**Piney Green** (CDP) Onslow County
48	1587	12.1	**Kannapolis** (city) Cabarrus County
49	n/a	12.0	**Mocksville** (town) Davie County
50	1643	11.6	**Havelock** (city) Craven County
50	n/a	11.6	**Rockfish** (CDP) Hoke County
52	n/a	11.5	**Wendell** (town) Wake County
53	1665	11.4	**Hickory** (city) Catawba County
53	1665	11.4	**Knightdale** (town) Wake County
53	1665	11.4	**Raleigh** (city) Wake County
56	1725	10.9	**Indian Trail** (town) Union County
56	1725	10.9	**Statesville** (city) Iredell County
58	1746	10.7	**Clayton** (town) Johnston County
59	n/a	10.6	**East Rockingham** (CDP) Richmond County
59	n/a	10.6	**Long View** (town) Catawba County
59	1762	10.6	**Salisbury** (city) Rowan County
62	n/a	10.4	**Skippers Corner** (CDP) New Hanover County
63	n/a	10.3	**Saint Stephens** (CDP) Catawba County
63	n/a	10.3	**Troy** (town) Montgomery County
65	1822	10.1	**Fayetteville** (city) Cumberland County
66	1829	10.0	**Hope Mills** (town) Cumberland County
67	n/a	9.9	**China Grove** (town) Rowan County
67	1846	9.9	**Garner** (town) Wake County
69	n/a	9.8	**Half Moon** (CDP) Onslow County
70	1866	9.7	**Fuquay-Varina** (town) Wake County
70	n/a	9.7	**Grifton** (town) Pitt County
70	1866	9.7	**Kernersville** (town) Forsyth County
73	1883	9.6	**Gastonia** (city) Gaston County
73	n/a	9.6	**Raeford** (city) Hoke County
75	1913	9.4	**Wilson** (city) Wilson County
76	n/a	9.2	**Clinton** (city) Sampson County
76	n/a	9.2	**Mount Olive** (town) Wayne County
76	n/a	9.2	**Spencer** (town) Rowan County
79	n/a	9.1	**Kill Devil Hills** (town) Dare County
80	n/a	9.0	**Forest City** (town) Rutherford County
80	1951	9.0	**Lenoir** (city) Caldwell County
80	n/a	9.0	**Sylva** (town) Jackson County
83	n/a	8.9	**Pittsboro** (town) Chatham County
83	n/a	8.9	**Swannanoa** (CDP) Buncombe County
85	n/a	8.8	**Lillington** (town) Harnett County
86	n/a	8.7	**Roxboro** (city) Person County
86	n/a	8.7	**Woodfin** (town) Buncombe County
88	n/a	8.6	**Mountain Home** (CDP) Henderson County
89	2034	8.5	**High Point** (city) Guilford County
90	2052	8.4	**Clemmons** (village) Forsyth County
91	2067	8.3	**Mint Hill** (town) Mecklenburg County
92	n/a	8.2	**Polkton** (town) Anson County
93	n/a	8.0	**Dallas** (town) Gaston County
94	n/a	7.8	**Landis** (town) Rowan County
95	2166	7.7	**Cary** (town) Wake County
96	n/a	7.6	**Randleman** (city) Randolph County
97	2200	7.5	**Greensboro** (city) Guilford County
98	n/a	7.4	**Erwin** (town) Harnett County
98	2225	7.4	**Huntersville** (town) Mecklenburg County
100	n/a	7.3	**Ranlo** (town) Gaston County
100	n/a	7.3	**Wilkesboro** (town) Wilkes County
102	n/a	7.2	**Burgaw** (town) Pender County
103	2288	7.1	**Apex** (town) Wake County
104	2334	6.9	**Mooresville** (town) Iredell County
104	n/a	6.9	**Morehead City** (town) Carteret County
106	n/a	6.8	**Kings Grant** (CDP) New Hanover County
107	2382	6.7	**Lumberton** (city) Robeson County
107	2382	6.7	**Mount Airy** (city) Surry County
109	n/a	6.6	**Hillsborough** (town) Orange County
110	2428	6.5	**Asheville** (city) Buncombe County
111	2462	6.4	**Chapel Hill** (town) Orange County
111	2462	6.4	**Henderson** (city) Vance County
111	n/a	6.4	**Red Springs** (town) Robeson County
111	n/a	6.4	**Waxhaw** (town) Union County
115	2495	6.3	**Holly Springs** (town) Wake County
116	n/a	6.2	**Hamlet** (city) Richmond County
116	n/a	6.2	**Maiden** (town) Catawba County
116	n/a	6.2	**Rolesville** (town) Wake County
119	2544	6.1	**Wilmington** (city) New Hanover County
120	n/a	6.0	**Locust** (city) Stanly County
120	2564	6.0	**Mebane** (city) Alamance County
122	n/a	5.9	**Enochville** (CDP) Rowan County
122	n/a	5.9	**Gibsonville** (town) Guilford County
122	n/a	5.9	**James City** (CDP) Craven County
122	2586	5.9	**Morrisville** (town) Wake County
126	n/a	5.8	**Hudson** (town) Caldwell County
126	2613	5.8	**Matthews** (town) Mecklenburg County
126	2613	5.8	**New Bern** (city) Craven County
126	2613	5.8	**Stallings** (town) Union County
130	n/a	5.7	**Lowell** (city) Gaston County
130	n/a	5.7	**Waynesville** (town) Haywood County
132	2661	5.6	**Wake Forest** (town) Wake County
132	n/a	5.6	**Walkertown** (town) Forsyth County
132	n/a	5.6	**Wrightsboro** (CDP) New Hanover County
135	n/a	5.5	**Louisburg** (town) Franklin County
135	2687	5.5	**Mount Holly** (city) Gaston County
135	n/a	5.5	**Washington** (city) Beaufort County
138	n/a	5.4	**Etowah** (CDP) Henderson County
139	2736	5.3	**Cornelius** (town) Mecklenburg County
139	n/a	5.3	**Dunn** (city) Harnett County
139	2736	5.3	**Murraysville** (CDP) New Hanover County
142	n/a	5.2	**Granite Falls** (town) Caldwell County
142	n/a	5.2	**Lake Park** (village) Union County
142	n/a	5.2	**Sawmills** (town) Caldwell County
145	n/a	5.1	**Aberdeen** (town) Moore County
145	n/a	5.1	**Bessemer City** (city) Gaston County
145	n/a	5.1	**Cullowhee** (CDP) Jackson County
145	n/a	5.1	**Rockingham** (city) Richmond County
149	n/a	5.0	**Canton** (town) Haywood County
149	n/a	5.0	**Creedmoor** (city) Granville County

Note: *The state column ranks the top/bottom 150 places in the state with population of 2,500 or more. The national column ranks the top/bottom places in the country with population of 10,000 or more. Places that are unincorporated were not considered in the rankings. n/a indicates data not available. Please refer to the User Guide for additional information.*

Hispanic Population

Top 150 Places Ranked in *Ascending* Order

State Rank	Nat'l Rank	Percent	Place
1	n/a	0.6	**Enfield** (town) Halifax County
2	n/a	0.9	**Saint James** (town) Brunswick County
3	n/a	1.1	**Windsor** (town) Bertie County
4	n/a	1.2	**Flat Rock** (village) Henderson County
4	n/a	1.2	**Plymouth** (town) Washington County
6	n/a	1.3	**Cramerton** (town) Gaston County
7	n/a	1.4	**Fairview** (town) Union County
7	n/a	1.4	**Oak Island** (town) Brunswick County
7	n/a	1.4	**South Rosemary** (CDP) Halifax County
7	n/a	1.4	**Trent Woods** (town) Craven County
11	n/a	1.5	**Brices Creek** (CDP) Craven County
11	n/a	1.5	**Southern Shores** (town) Dare County
13	n/a	1.6	**Ahoskie** (town) Hertford County
13	n/a	1.6	**Carolina Beach** (town) New Hanover County
13	n/a	1.6	**Nashville** (town) Nash County
13	n/a	1.6	**Stanley** (town) Gaston County
17	n/a	1.7	**Lake Junaluska** (CDP) Haywood County
17	n/a	1.7	**Red Oak** (town) Nash County
17	n/a	1.7	**Westport** (CDP) Lincoln County
20	n/a	1.8	**Fairfield Harbour** (CDP) Craven County
20	n/a	1.8	**Royal Pines** (CDP) Buncombe County
20	n/a	1.8	**Wadesboro** (town) Anson County
23	n/a	1.9	**Fairmont** (town) Robeson County
23	n/a	1.9	**Sunset Beach** (town) Brunswick County
25	n/a	2.0	**Bethlehem** (CDP) Alexander County
25	n/a	2.0	**Boiling Springs** (town) Cleveland County
25	n/a	2.0	**Emerald Isle** (town) Carteret County
25	n/a	2.0	**Forest Oaks** (CDP) Guilford County
25	n/a	2.0	**Lake Norman of Catawba** (CDP) Catawba County
25	501	2.0	**Laurinburg** (city) Scotland County
25	n/a	2.0	**Seven Lakes** (CDP) Moore County
32	n/a	2.1	**Carolina Shores** (town) Brunswick County
32	n/a	2.1	**Myrtle Grove** (CDP) New Hanover County
32	563	2.1	**Pinehurst** (village) Moore County
32	n/a	2.1	**Weaverville** (town) Buncombe County
32	n/a	2.1	**Williamston** (town) Martin County
37	n/a	2.2	**Pembroke** (town) Robeson County
37	n/a	2.2	**Porters Neck** (CDP) New Hanover County
39	n/a	2.3	**Lake Royale** (CDP) Franklin County
39	n/a	2.3	**Tabor City** (town) Columbus County
39	n/a	2.3	**Trinity** (city) Randolph County
42	726	2.4	**Kinston** (city) Lenoir County
43	n/a	2.5	**Ayden** (town) Pitt County
43	n/a	2.5	**Black Mountain** (town) Buncombe County
43	n/a	2.5	**Farmville** (town) Pitt County
43	n/a	2.5	**Lowesville** (CDP) Lincoln County
47	n/a	2.6	**Beaufort** (town) Carteret County
47	n/a	2.6	**Elon** (town) Alamance County
47	845	2.6	**Kings Mountain** (city) Cleveland County
47	n/a	2.6	**Ogden** (CDP) New Hanover County
47	n/a	2.6	**River Bend** (town) Craven County
47	n/a	2.6	**Valdese** (town) Burke County
53	n/a	2.7	**Boiling Spring Lakes** (city) Brunswick County
53	n/a	2.7	**Fairview** (CDP) Buncombe County
55	n/a	2.9	**King** (city) Stokes County
55	n/a	2.9	**Kitty Hawk** (town) Dare County
55	n/a	2.9	**Murfreesboro** (town) Hertford County
55	n/a	2.9	**Southport** (city) Brunswick County
55	n/a	2.9	**Whispering Pines** (village) Moore County
60	n/a	3.0	**Eastover** (town) Cumberland County
60	n/a	3.0	**Oak Ridge** (town) Guilford County
60	n/a	3.0	**Rutherfordton** (town) Rutherford County
60	n/a	3.0	**Unionville** (town) Union County
60	n/a	3.0	**Weddington** (town) Union County
65	n/a	3.1	**Cajah's Mountain** (town) Caldwell County
65	1097	3.1	**Shelby** (city) Cleveland County
65	n/a	3.1	**Wallburg** (town) Davidson County
68	n/a	3.2	**Jamestown** (town) Guilford County
68	n/a	3.2	**Nags Head** (town) Dare County
68	1152	3.2	**Roanoke Rapids** (city) Halifax County
71	1195	3.3	**Boone** (town) Watauga County
71	n/a	3.3	**Hampstead** (CDP) Pender County
71	n/a	3.3	**Marvin** (village) Union County
71	n/a	3.3	**Spindale** (town) Rutherford County
71	n/a	3.3	**Whiteville** (city) Columbus County
71	n/a	3.3	**Winterville** (town) Pitt County
77	n/a	3.4	**Edenton** (town) Chowan County
77	n/a	3.4	**La Grange** (town) Lenoir County
77	1236	3.4	**Lewisville** (town) Forsyth County
80	1280	3.5	**Belmont** (city) Gaston County
80	n/a	3.5	**Midland** (town) Cabarrus County
80	n/a	3.5	**Midway** (town) Davidson County
80	n/a	3.5	**Sneads Ferry** (CDP) Onslow County
80	n/a	3.5	**Stokesdale** (town) Guilford County
85	n/a	3.6	**Bayshore** (CDP) New Hanover County
85	n/a	3.6	**Buies Creek** (CDP) Harnett County
85	n/a	3.6	**Moyock** (CDP) Currituck County
85	n/a	3.6	**Welcome** (CDP) Davidson County
85	n/a	3.6	**Wentworth** (town) Rockingham County
90	n/a	3.7	**Brevard** (city) Transylvania County
90	n/a	3.7	**Cherryville** (city) Gaston County
90	1360	3.7	**Harrisburg** (town) Cabarrus County
90	1360	3.7	**Rocky Mount** (city) Nash County
94	1396	3.8	**Davidson** (town) Mecklenburg County
94	1396	3.8	**Greenville** (city) Pitt County
96	n/a	3.9	**Mills River** (town) Henderson County
96	1428	3.9	**Southern Pines** (town) Moore County
98	1459	4.0	**Archdale** (city) Randolph County
98	n/a	4.0	**Granite Quarry** (town) Rowan County
98	n/a	4.0	**Icard** (CDP) Burke County
101	n/a	4.1	**Elizabethtown** (town) Bladen County
102	n/a	4.2	**Mountain View** (CDP) Catawba County
102	n/a	4.2	**Northchase** (CDP) New Hanover County
104	1559	4.3	**Goldsboro** (city) Wayne County
104	1559	4.3	**Summerfield** (town) Guilford County
106	1626	4.5	**Albemarle** (city) Stanly County
106	n/a	4.5	**Gamewell** (town) Caldwell County
106	n/a	4.5	**Swansboro** (town) Onslow County
109	n/a	4.6	**Mineral Springs** (town) Union County
109	n/a	4.6	**Tyro** (CDP) Davidson County
111	n/a	4.7	**Newport** (town) Carteret County
111	n/a	4.7	**Pleasant Garden** (town) Guilford County
111	1696	4.7	**Reidsville** (city) Rockingham County
114	1726	4.8	**Eden** (city) Rockingham County
114	n/a	4.8	**Fletcher** (town) Henderson County
114	n/a	4.8	**Oxford** (city) Granville County
114	n/a	4.8	**Shallotte** (town) Brunswick County
118	1753	4.9	**Leland** (town) Brunswick County
118	1753	4.9	**Tarboro** (town) Edgecombe County
120	n/a	5.0	**Canton** (town) Haywood County
120	n/a	5.0	**Creedmoor** (city) Granville County
120	1787	5.0	**Elizabeth City** (city) Pasquotank County
120	n/a	5.0	**Wesley Chapel** (village) Union County
124	n/a	5.1	**Aberdeen** (town) Moore County
124	n/a	5.1	**Bessemer City** (city) Gaston County
124	n/a	5.1	**Cullowhee** (CDP) Jackson County
124	n/a	5.1	**Rockingham** (city) Richmond County
128	n/a	5.2	**Granite Falls** (town) Caldwell County
128	n/a	5.2	**Lake Park** (village) Union County
128	n/a	5.2	**Sawmills** (town) Caldwell County
131	1887	5.3	**Cornelius** (town) Mecklenburg County
131	n/a	5.3	**Dunn** (city) Harnett County
131	1887	5.3	**Murraysville** (CDP) New Hanover County
134	n/a	5.4	**Etowah** (CDP) Henderson County
135	n/a	5.5	**Louisburg** (town) Franklin County
135	1945	5.5	**Mount Holly** (city) Gaston County
135	n/a	5.5	**Washington** (city) Beaufort County
138	1970	5.6	**Wake Forest** (town) Wake County
138	n/a	5.6	**Walkertown** (town) Forsyth County
138	n/a	5.6	**Wrightsboro** (CDP) New Hanover County
141	n/a	5.7	**Lowell** (city) Gaston County
141	n/a	5.7	**Waynesville** (town) Haywood County
143	n/a	5.8	**Hudson** (town) Caldwell County
143	2017	5.8	**Matthews** (town) Mecklenburg County
143	2017	5.8	**New Bern** (city) Craven County
143	2017	5.8	**Stallings** (town) Union County
147	n/a	5.9	**Enochville** (CDP) Rowan County
147	n/a	5.9	**Gibsonville** (town) Guilford County
147	n/a	5.9	**James City** (CDP) Craven County
147	2044	5.9	**Morrisville** (town) Wake County

Note: *The state column ranks the top/bottom 150 places in the state with population of 2,500 or more. The national column ranks the top/bottom places in the country with population of 10,000 or more. Places that are unincorporated were not considered in the rankings. n/a indicates data not available. Please refer to the User Guide for additional information.*

Average Household Size

Top 150 Places Ranked in *Descending* Order

State Rank	Nat'l Rank	Persons	Place
1	n/a	3.5	**Marvin** (village) Union County
2	n/a	3.2	**Wesley Chapel** (village) Union County
3	n/a	3.1	**Moyock** (CDP) Currituck County
4	n/a	3.0	**Rolesville** (town) Wake County
5	n/a	3.0	**Waxhaw** (town) Union County
6	532	3.0	**Holly Springs** (town) Wake County
7	n/a	3.0	**Weddington** (town) Union County
8	579	3.0	**Indian Trail** (town) Union County
9	n/a	2.9	**Oak Ridge** (town) Guilford County
9	n/a	2.9	**Siler City** (town) Chatham County
11	796	2.9	**Monroe** (city) Union County
12	n/a	2.8	**Archer Lodge** (town) Johnston County
12	863	2.8	**Summerfield** (town) Guilford County
14	931	2.8	**Harrisburg** (town) Cabarrus County
15	n/a	2.8	**Half Moon** (CDP) Onslow County
16	1049	2.8	**Wake Forest** (town) Wake County
17	1077	2.8	**Apex** (town) Wake County
17	n/a	2.8	**Unionville** (town) Union County
19	n/a	2.7	**Mineral Springs** (town) Union County
20	n/a	2.7	**Brices Creek** (CDP) Craven County
20	n/a	2.7	**Lake Park** (village) Union County
22	1283	2.7	**Havelock** (city) Craven County
22	n/a	2.7	**Rockfish** (CDP) Hoke County
24	1353	2.7	**Piney Green** (CDP) Onslow County
24	n/a	2.7	**Selma** (town) Johnston County
26	n/a	2.7	**Stokesdale** (town) Guilford County
27	n/a	2.7	**Fairview** (town) Union County
27	n/a	2.7	**Ranlo** (town) Gaston County
27	1483	2.7	**Stallings** (town) Union County
27	n/a	2.7	**Winterville** (town) Pitt County
31	n/a	2.7	**Red Oak** (town) Nash County
32	1563	2.6	**Jacksonville** (city) Onslow County
32	n/a	2.6	**Polkton** (town) Anson County
34	1617	2.6	**Concord** (city) Cabarrus County
34	1617	2.6	**Hope Mills** (town) Cumberland County
34	n/a	2.6	**Tyro** (CDP) Davidson County
37	1682	2.6	**Fuquay-Varina** (town) Wake County
37	1682	2.6	**Huntersville** (town) Mecklenburg County
37	1682	2.6	**Knightdale** (town) Wake County
37	n/a	2.6	**Westport** (CDP) Lincoln County
41	n/a	2.6	**Wallburg** (town) Davidson County
41	n/a	2.6	**Wingate** (town) Union County
43	1788	2.6	**Clayton** (town) Johnston County
43	1788	2.6	**Mint Hill** (town) Mecklenburg County
43	n/a	2.6	**Silver Lake** (CDP) New Hanover County
43	1788	2.6	**Spring Lake** (town) Cumberland County
47	n/a	2.6	**Creedmoor** (city) Granville County
47	n/a	2.6	**Glen Raven** (CDP) Alamance County
49	n/a	2.6	**Dana** (CDP) Henderson County
50	n/a	2.6	**Lowesville** (CDP) Lincoln County
50	n/a	2.6	**Zebulon** (town) Wake County
52	n/a	2.6	**Brogden** (CDP) Wayne County
52	2001	2.6	**Cary** (town) Wake County
52	n/a	2.6	**Enfield** (town) Halifax County
52	2001	2.6	**Mooresville** (town) Iredell County
52	n/a	2.6	**Saint Stephens** (CDP) Catawba County
57	n/a	2.6	**Mountain View** (CDP) Catawba County
57	2049	2.6	**Sanford** (city) Lee County
59	n/a	2.5	**Angier** (town) Harnett County
59	n/a	2.5	**Bessemer City** (city) Gaston County
59	n/a	2.5	**Boiling Springs** (town) Cleveland County
59	n/a	2.5	**Forest Oaks** (CDP) Guilford County
59	2136	2.5	**Kannapolis** (city) Cabarrus County
59	n/a	2.5	**Locust** (city) Stanly County
59	n/a	2.5	**Midland** (town) Cabarrus County
59	n/a	2.5	**Pleasant Garden** (town) Guilford County
67	n/a	2.5	**Skippers Corner** (CDP) New Hanover County
67	n/a	2.5	**Wendell** (town) Wake County
69	n/a	2.5	**Butner** (town) Granville County
69	2234	2.5	**Lewisville** (town) Forsyth County
69	2234	2.5	**Matthews** (town) Mecklenburg County
69	n/a	2.5	**Ogden** (CDP) New Hanover County
69	n/a	2.5	**Spencer** (town) Rowan County
74	n/a	2.5	**Granite Quarry** (town) Rowan County
74	n/a	2.5	**Wentworth** (town) Rockingham County
76	n/a	2.5	**Bayshore** (CDP) New Hanover County
76	n/a	2.5	**China Grove** (town) Rowan County
76	n/a	2.5	**Hampstead** (CDP) Pender County
79	n/a	2.5	**Boiling Spring Lakes** (city) Brunswick County
79	n/a	2.5	**Sawmills** (town) Caldwell County
81	2464	2.5	**Clemmons** (village) Forsyth County
81	n/a	2.5	**Enochville** (CDP) Rowan County
81	2464	2.5	**Gastonia** (city) Gaston County
81	n/a	2.5	**Pembroke** (town) Robeson County
81	n/a	2.5	**Stanley** (town) Gaston County
86	n/a	2.5	**East Rockingham** (CDP) Richmond County
86	n/a	2.5	**Gamewell** (town) Caldwell County
86	n/a	2.5	**Grifton** (town) Pitt County
86	n/a	2.5	**Midway** (town) Davidson County
90	n/a	2.5	**Dallas** (town) Gaston County
90	n/a	2.5	**Fairview** (CDP) Buncombe County
90	n/a	2.5	**Lowell** (city) Gaston County
90	n/a	2.5	**Maiden** (town) Catawba County
90	2568	2.5	**Thomasville** (city) Davidson County
90	n/a	2.5	**Trinity** (city) Randolph County
90	n/a	2.5	**Wrightsboro** (CDP) New Hanover County
97	2630	2.4	**Davidson** (town) Mecklenburg County
97	n/a	2.4	**East Flat Rock** (CDP) Henderson County
97	2630	2.4	**Garner** (town) Wake County
97	n/a	2.4	**Hamlet** (city) Richmond County
97	2630	2.4	**Mount Holly** (city) Gaston County
102	2698	2.4	**Charlotte** (city) Mecklenburg County
102	n/a	2.4	**Granite Falls** (town) Caldwell County
102	n/a	2.4	**Mar-Mac** (CDP) Wayne County
102	n/a	2.4	**Mocksville** (town) Davie County
102	n/a	2.4	**Myrtle Grove** (CDP) New Hanover County
107	2768	2.4	**Belmont** (city) Gaston County
107	n/a	2.4	**Cajah's Mountain** (town) Caldwell County
107	n/a	2.4	**Gibsonville** (town) Guilford County
107	n/a	2.4	**Kings Grant** (CDP) New Hanover County
107	n/a	2.4	**Yadkinville** (town) Yadkin County
112	2829	2.4	**Archdale** (city) Randolph County
112	2829	2.4	**Asheboro** (city) Randolph County
112	2829	2.4	**High Point** (city) Guilford County
115	2893	2.4	**Fayetteville** (city) Cumberland County
115	n/a	2.4	**Jamestown** (town) Guilford County
115	n/a	2.4	**Landis** (town) Rowan County
115	2893	2.4	**Murraysville** (CDP) New Hanover County
115	2893	2.4	**Newton** (city) Catawba County
115	n/a	2.4	**River Road** (CDP) Beaufort County
121	n/a	2.4	**Cramerton** (town) Gaston County
121	n/a	2.4	**Icard** (CDP) Burke County
121	2968	2.4	**Kings Mountain** (city) Cleveland County
121	2968	2.4	**Lexington** (city) Davidson County
121	2968	2.4	**Lumberton** (city) Robeson County
121	n/a	2.4	**Mountain Home** (CDP) Henderson County
121	n/a	2.4	**Swannanoa** (CDP) Buncombe County
121	n/a	2.4	**Walkertown** (town) Forsyth County
129	n/a	2.4	**Bethlehem** (CDP) Alexander County
129	n/a	2.4	**Erwin** (town) Harnett County
129	n/a	2.4	**Lake Norman of Catawba** (CDP) Catawba County
129	3032	2.4	**Morrisville** (town) Wake County
129	n/a	2.4	**Royal Pines** (CDP) Buncombe County
129	n/a	2.4	**Welcome** (CDP) Davidson County
129	3032	2.4	**Wilson** (city) Wilson County
136	n/a	2.4	**Benson** (town) Johnston County
136	n/a	2.4	**Elroy** (CDP) Wayne County
136	n/a	2.4	**Hillsborough** (town) Orange County
136	n/a	2.4	**James City** (CDP) Craven County
136	n/a	2.4	**Liberty** (town) Randolph County
136	n/a	2.4	**Mills River** (town) Henderson County
136	n/a	2.4	**Red Springs** (town) Robeson County
136	3107	2.4	**Roanoke Rapids** (city) Halifax County
136	3107	2.4	**Rocky Mount** (city) Nash County
145	3179	2.4	**Henderson** (city) Vance County
145	3179	2.4	**Mebane** (city) Alamance County
145	n/a	2.4	**Trent Woods** (town) Craven County
148	n/a	2.4	**Cherryville** (city) Gaston County
148	n/a	2.4	**Eastover** (town) Cumberland County
148	3241	2.4	**Graham** (city) Alamance County

Note: *The state column ranks the top/bottom 150 places in the state with population of 2,500 or more. The national column ranks the top/bottom places in the country with population of 10,000 or more. Places that are unincorporated were not considered in the rankings. n/a indicates data not available. Please refer to the User Guide for additional information.*

Average Household Size

Top 150 Places Ranked in *Ascending* Order

State Rank	Nat'l Rank	Persons	Place
1	n/a	1.7	**Cullowhee** (CDP) Jackson County
2	n/a	1.9	**Sunset Beach** (town) Brunswick County
3	n/a	1.9	**Beaufort** (town) Carteret County
4	n/a	1.9	**Carolina Shores** (town) Brunswick County
4	38	1.9	**Hendersonville** (city) Henderson County
6	n/a	1.9	**Pineville** (town) Mecklenburg County
7	n/a	2.0	**Saint James** (town) Brunswick County
8	n/a	2.0	**Brevard** (city) Transylvania County
8	n/a	2.0	**Fairfield Harbour** (CDP) Craven County
10	n/a	2.0	**Southport** (city) Brunswick County
11	n/a	2.0	**Flat Rock** (village) Henderson County
11	n/a	2.0	**Morehead City** (town) Carteret County
13	n/a	2.0	**Buies Creek** (CDP) Harnett County
13	93	2.0	**Southern Pines** (town) Moore County
15	102	2.0	**Boone** (town) Watauga County
15	n/a	2.0	**River Bend** (town) Craven County
17	n/a	2.0	**Elizabethtown** (town) Bladen County
18	n/a	2.1	**Oak Island** (town) Brunswick County
19	n/a	2.1	**Emerald Isle** (town) Carteret County
19	n/a	2.1	**Waynesville** (town) Haywood County
21	159	2.1	**Asheville** (city) Buncombe County
21	n/a	2.1	**Carolina Beach** (town) New Hanover County
21	n/a	2.1	**Lillington** (town) Harnett County
24	n/a	2.1	**Black Mountain** (town) Buncombe County
24	n/a	2.1	**Lake Junaluska** (CDP) Haywood County
24	170	2.1	**Mount Airy** (city) Surry County
24	170	2.1	**Pinehurst** (village) Moore County
24	n/a	2.1	**Weaverville** (town) Buncombe County
24	n/a	2.1	**Wilkesboro** (town) Wilkes County
30	n/a	2.1	**Whiteville** (city) Columbus County
31	223	2.1	**Wilmington** (city) New Hanover County
32	n/a	2.1	**Louisburg** (town) Franklin County
32	n/a	2.1	**Murfreesboro** (town) Hertford County
32	n/a	2.1	**Sylva** (town) Jackson County
35	278	2.1	**Greenville** (city) Pitt County
36	n/a	2.1	**Nags Head** (town) Dare County
37	n/a	2.2	**Aberdeen** (town) Moore County
37	n/a	2.2	**Franklin** (town) Macon County
39	453	2.2	**Kinston** (city) Lenoir County
39	n/a	2.2	**Washington** (city) Beaufort County
41	n/a	2.2	**Shallotte** (town) Brunswick County
41	n/a	2.2	**Tabor City** (town) Columbus County
41	n/a	2.2	**Williamston** (town) Martin County
44	n/a	2.2	**Mount Olive** (town) Wayne County
44	531	2.2	**New Bern** (city) Craven County
44	n/a	2.2	**North Wilkesboro** (town) Wilkes County
47	n/a	2.2	**Rutherfordton** (town) Rutherford County
48	n/a	2.2	**Ayden** (town) Pitt County
48	623	2.2	**Carrboro** (town) Orange County
48	n/a	2.2	**Clinton** (city) Sampson County
48	623	2.2	**Goldsboro** (city) Wayne County
48	623	2.2	**Reidsville** (city) Rockingham County
48	n/a	2.2	**Sneads Ferry** (CDP) Onslow County
54	n/a	2.2	**Burgaw** (town) Pender County
54	n/a	2.2	**Pittsboro** (town) Chatham County
54	n/a	2.2	**Valdese** (town) Burke County
57	n/a	2.2	**Dunn** (city) Harnett County
57	720	2.2	**Eden** (city) Rockingham County
57	n/a	2.2	**Edenton** (town) Chowan County
57	720	2.2	**Kernersville** (town) Forsyth County
57	n/a	2.2	**Roxboro** (city) Person County
57	n/a	2.2	**Windsor** (town) Bertie County
63	n/a	2.3	**Etowah** (CDP) Henderson County
63	n/a	2.3	**Rockingham** (city) Richmond County
63	n/a	2.3	**Swansboro** (town) Onslow County
66	837	2.3	**Cornelius** (town) Mecklenburg County
66	837	2.3	**Greensboro** (city) Guilford County
66	n/a	2.3	**Kitty Hawk** (town) Dare County
66	n/a	2.3	**Woodfin** (town) Buncombe County
70	n/a	2.3	**Canton** (town) Haywood County
70	n/a	2.3	**Elkin** (town) Surry County
70	n/a	2.3	**Farmville** (town) Pitt County
70	n/a	2.3	**Forest City** (town) Rutherford County
70	892	2.3	**Leland** (town) Brunswick County
70	892	2.3	**Lenoir** (city) Caldwell County
70	892	2.3	**Shelby** (city) Cleveland County
70	n/a	2.3	**Spindale** (town) Rutherford County
78	944	2.3	**Hickory** (city) Catawba County
78	n/a	2.3	**La Grange** (town) Lenoir County
78	n/a	2.3	**Northchase** (CDP) New Hanover County
78	n/a	2.3	**Whispering Pines** (village) Moore County
82	997	2.3	**Albemarle** (city) Stanly County
82	997	2.3	**Durham** (city) Durham County
82	n/a	2.3	**Fairmont** (town) Robeson County
82	n/a	2.3	**King** (city) Stokes County
82	n/a	2.3	**Porters Neck** (CDP) New Hanover County
82	n/a	2.3	**Seven Lakes** (CDP) Moore County
82	n/a	2.3	**Southern Shores** (town) Dare County
89	n/a	2.3	**Ahoskie** (town) Hertford County
89	1049	2.3	**Chapel Hill** (town) Orange County
89	n/a	2.3	**Elon** (town) Alamance County
89	n/a	2.3	**Lake Royale** (CDP) Franklin County
89	n/a	2.3	**Plymouth** (town) Washington County
89	n/a	2.3	**Rural Hall** (town) Forsyth County
89	1049	2.3	**Smithfield** (town) Johnston County
89	1049	2.3	**Tarboro** (town) Edgecombe County
89	n/a	2.3	**Wallace** (town) Duplin County
98	n/a	2.3	**Fletcher** (town) Henderson County
98	n/a	2.3	**Long View** (town) Catawba County
98	n/a	2.3	**Marion** (city) McDowell County
98	1107	2.3	**Morganton** (city) Burke County
98	n/a	2.3	**Oxford** (city) Granville County
98	1107	2.3	**Raleigh** (city) Wake County
104	n/a	2.3	**Kill Devil Hills** (town) Dare County
104	1172	2.3	**Lincolnton** (city) Lincoln County
104	n/a	2.3	**Nashville** (town) Nash County
104	n/a	2.3	**Randleman** (city) Randolph County
104	n/a	2.3	**South Rosemary** (CDP) Halifax County
109	1234	2.3	**Burlington** (city) Alamance County
109	1234	2.3	**Elizabeth City** (city) Pasquotank County
109	n/a	2.3	**Newport** (town) Carteret County
109	n/a	2.3	**Raeford** (city) Hoke County
109	1234	2.3	**Salisbury** (city) Rowan County
109	1234	2.3	**Statesville** (city) Iredell County
109	n/a	2.3	**Troy** (town) Montgomery County
109	1234	2.3	**Winston-Salem** (city) Forsyth County
117	n/a	2.3	**Conover** (city) Catawba County
117	n/a	2.3	**Warsaw** (town) Duplin County
119	n/a	2.4	**Cherryville** (city) Gaston County
119	n/a	2.4	**Eastover** (town) Cumberland County
119	1361	2.4	**Graham** (city) Alamance County
119	n/a	2.4	**Hudson** (town) Caldwell County
119	1361	2.4	**Laurinburg** (city) Scotland County
119	n/a	2.4	**Wadesboro** (town) Anson County
125	1416	2.4	**Henderson** (city) Vance County
125	1416	2.4	**Mebane** (city) Alamance County
125	n/a	2.4	**Trent Woods** (town) Craven County
128	n/a	2.4	**Benson** (town) Johnston County
128	n/a	2.4	**Elroy** (CDP) Wayne County
128	n/a	2.4	**Hillsborough** (town) Orange County
128	n/a	2.4	**James City** (CDP) Craven County
128	n/a	2.4	**Liberty** (town) Randolph County
128	n/a	2.4	**Mills River** (town) Henderson County
128	n/a	2.4	**Red Springs** (town) Robeson County
128	1478	2.4	**Roanoke Rapids** (city) Halifax County
128	1478	2.4	**Rocky Mount** (city) Nash County
137	n/a	2.4	**Bethlehem** (CDP) Alexander County
137	n/a	2.4	**Erwin** (town) Harnett County
137	n/a	2.4	**Lake Norman of Catawba** (CDP) Catawba County
137	1550	2.4	**Morrisville** (town) Wake County
137	n/a	2.4	**Royal Pines** (CDP) Buncombe County
137	n/a	2.4	**Welcome** (CDP) Davidson County
137	1550	2.4	**Wilson** (city) Wilson County
144	n/a	2.4	**Cramerton** (town) Gaston County
144	n/a	2.4	**Icard** (CDP) Burke County
144	1625	2.4	**Kings Mountain** (city) Cleveland County
144	1625	2.4	**Lexington** (city) Davidson County
144	1625	2.4	**Lumberton** (city) Robeson County
144	n/a	2.4	**Mountain Home** (CDP) Henderson County
144	n/a	2.4	**Swannanoa** (CDP) Buncombe County

Note: The state column ranks the top/bottom 150 places in the state with population of 2,500 or more. The national column ranks the top/bottom places in the country with population of 10,000 or more. Places that are unincorporated were not considered in the rankings. n/a indicates data not available. Please refer to the User Guide for additional information.

Median Age

Top 150 Places Ranked in *Descending* Order

State Rank	Nat'l Rank	Years	Place
1	n/a	65.0	**Saint James** (town) Brunswick County
2	n/a	64.9	**Carolina Shores** (town) Brunswick County
3	n/a	64.0	**Flat Rock** (village) Henderson County
3	n/a	64.0	**Sunset Beach** (town) Brunswick County
5	n/a	63.5	**Fairfield Harbour** (CDP) Craven County
6	23	57.6	**Pinehurst** (village) Moore County
7	n/a	56.8	**River Bend** (town) Craven County
8	n/a	55.9	**Southport** (city) Brunswick County
9	n/a	54.4	**Seven Lakes** (CDP) Moore County
10	n/a	54.2	**Southern Shores** (town) Dare County
11	n/a	52.9	**Lake Junaluska** (CDP) Haywood County
12	n/a	52.6	**Oak Island** (town) Brunswick County
13	n/a	52.3	**Whispering Pines** (village) Moore County
14	n/a	52.2	**Emerald Isle** (town) Carteret County
15	n/a	51.4	**Weaverville** (town) Buncombe County
16	n/a	50.7	**Etowah** (CDP) Henderson County
17	n/a	50.2	**Trent Woods** (town) Craven County
18	n/a	49.1	**Porters Neck** (CDP) New Hanover County
19	104	48.7	**Hendersonville** (city) Henderson County
20	n/a	47.7	**Black Mountain** (town) Buncombe County
21	167	47.0	**Southern Pines** (town) Moore County
22	n/a	46.9	**Brevard** (city) Transylvania County
23	n/a	46.8	**Beaufort** (town) Carteret County
23	n/a	46.8	**Forest Oaks** (CDP) Guilford County
23	n/a	46.8	**Nags Head** (town) Dare County
26	n/a	46.7	**Waynesville** (town) Haywood County
27	n/a	46.5	**Lake Norman of Catawba** (CDP) Catawba County
28	n/a	46.3	**Mountain Home** (CDP) Henderson County
29	247	45.8	**Mount Airy** (city) Surry County
30	n/a	45.7	**Mills River** (town) Henderson County
31	n/a	45.6	**Pleasant Garden** (town) Guilford County
32	n/a	45.5	**Bethlehem** (CDP) Alexander County
33	n/a	45.4	**Kitty Hawk** (town) Dare County
33	n/a	45.4	**Wilkesboro** (town) Wilkes County
35	n/a	45.3	**Jamestown** (town) Guilford County
35	n/a	45.3	**Royal Pines** (CDP) Buncombe County
37	n/a	45.0	**Lake Royale** (CDP) Franklin County
38	n/a	44.9	**Eastover** (town) Cumberland County
39	n/a	44.8	**Elizabethtown** (town) Bladen County
40	n/a	44.4	**Rutherfordton** (town) Rutherford County
41	n/a	44.0	**Tabor City** (town) Columbus County
41	n/a	44.0	**Trinity** (city) Randolph County
43	n/a	43.9	**Carolina Beach** (town) New Hanover County
43	n/a	43.9	**Shallotte** (town) Brunswick County
45	552	43.7	**Kinston** (city) Lenoir County
46	n/a	43.6	**Myrtle Grove** (CDP) New Hanover County
47	n/a	43.5	**Valdese** (town) Burke County
48	n/a	43.4	**King** (city) Stokes County
48	613	43.4	**Lewisville** (town) Forsyth County
50	n/a	43.3	**Weddington** (town) Union County
51	n/a	43.2	**Fairview** (CDP) Buncombe County
51	n/a	43.2	**La Grange** (town) Lenoir County
53	n/a	43.1	**Edenton** (town) Chowan County
54	n/a	42.9	**Westport** (CDP) Lincoln County
55	n/a	42.7	**Cajah's Mountain** (town) Caldwell County
56	n/a	42.6	**Fairview** (town) Union County
56	n/a	42.6	**Hampstead** (CDP) Pender County
56	n/a	42.6	**Walkertown** (town) Forsyth County
59	n/a	42.5	**Fairmont** (town) Robeson County
59	n/a	42.5	**Farmville** (town) Pitt County
59	n/a	42.5	**Midway** (town) Davidson County
62	n/a	42.4	**Elkin** (town) Surry County
62	n/a	42.4	**Morehead City** (town) Carteret County
62	n/a	42.4	**Red Oak** (town) Nash County
65	905	42.3	**Tarboro** (town) Edgecombe County
66	n/a	42.2	**Enochville** (CDP) Rowan County
67	n/a	42.1	**Clinton** (city) Sampson County
67	n/a	42.1	**Icard** (CDP) Burke County
67	955	42.1	**Summerfield** (town) Guilford County
70	n/a	41.9	**Brices Creek** (CDP) Craven County
70	n/a	41.9	**Williamston** (town) Martin County
72	1043	41.8	**Mint Hill** (town) Mecklenburg County
72	n/a	41.8	**Oak Ridge** (town) Guilford County
74	n/a	41.7	**Cherryville** (city) Gaston County
74	n/a	41.7	**Mineral Springs** (town) Union County
74	1073	41.7	**Reidsville** (city) Rockingham County
74	n/a	41.7	**South Rosemary** (CDP) Halifax County
74	n/a	41.7	**Welcome** (CDP) Davidson County
79	1100	41.6	**Smithfield** (town) Johnston County
79	n/a	41.6	**Washington** (city) Beaufort County
79	n/a	41.6	**Wentworth** (town) Rockingham County
82	n/a	41.5	**Gamewell** (town) Caldwell County
82	1132	41.5	**Lenoir** (city) Caldwell County
82	n/a	41.5	**Wallburg** (town) Davidson County
85	n/a	41.4	**Oxford** (city) Granville County
85	n/a	41.4	**Pittsboro** (town) Chatham County
85	1167	41.4	**Shelby** (city) Cleveland County
85	n/a	41.4	**Whiteville** (city) Columbus County
89	n/a	41.2	**Boiling Spring Lakes** (city) Brunswick County
89	1244	41.2	**Eden** (city) Rockingham County
91	n/a	41.1	**Lowesville** (CDP) Lincoln County
91	n/a	41.1	**Mountain View** (CDP) Catawba County
93	n/a	41.0	**Dunn** (city) Harnett County
93	n/a	41.0	**Plymouth** (town) Washington County
95	n/a	40.9	**Canton** (town) Haywood County
95	n/a	40.9	**Wallace** (town) Duplin County
97	n/a	40.8	**Ogden** (CDP) New Hanover County
98	n/a	40.6	**Ayden** (town) Pitt County
98	1404	40.6	**Clemmons** (village) Forsyth County
98	n/a	40.6	**James City** (CDP) Craven County
98	1404	40.6	**Kings Mountain** (city) Cleveland County
102	n/a	40.5	**Franklin** (town) Macon County
102	n/a	40.5	**Locust** (city) Stanly County
102	n/a	40.5	**River Road** (CDP) Beaufort County
102	n/a	40.5	**Saint Stephens** (CDP) Catawba County
106	1505	40.3	**Matthews** (town) Mecklenburg County
106	n/a	40.3	**Midland** (town) Cabarrus County
106	n/a	40.3	**North Wilkesboro** (town) Wilkes County
109	n/a	40.2	**Roxboro** (city) Person County
110	n/a	40.1	**Cramerton** (town) Gaston County
110	n/a	40.1	**Erwin** (town) Harnett County
110	n/a	40.1	**Hudson** (town) Caldwell County
110	n/a	40.1	**Nashville** (town) Nash County
114	1610	40.0	**Archdale** (city) Randolph County
114	n/a	40.0	**Enfield** (town) Halifax County
114	n/a	40.0	**Forest City** (town) Rutherford County
117	n/a	39.9	**Stokesdale** (town) Guilford County
118	n/a	39.8	**Conover** (city) Catawba County
118	n/a	39.8	**Wadesboro** (town) Anson County
120	1710	39.7	**Morganton** (city) Burke County
120	n/a	39.7	**Spindale** (town) Rutherford County
120	n/a	39.7	**Wrightsboro** (CDP) New Hanover County
123	1736	39.6	**Albemarle** (city) Stanly County
123	n/a	39.6	**Landis** (town) Rowan County
123	n/a	39.6	**Lillington** (town) Harnett County
126	n/a	39.5	**Ahoskie** (town) Hertford County
126	n/a	39.5	**Bayshore** (CDP) New Hanover County
126	n/a	39.5	**Burgaw** (town) Pender County
126	n/a	39.5	**Liberty** (town) Randolph County
126	n/a	39.5	**Sawmills** (town) Caldwell County
131	n/a	39.4	**Mocksville** (town) Davie County
131	n/a	39.4	**Raeford** (city) Hoke County
131	n/a	39.4	**Unionville** (town) Union County
134	n/a	39.2	**Fletcher** (town) Henderson County
135	n/a	39.1	**Spencer** (town) Rowan County
135	n/a	39.1	**Yadkinville** (town) Yadkin County
137	n/a	38.9	**Granite Falls** (town) Caldwell County
137	1961	38.9	**Leland** (town) Brunswick County
137	n/a	38.9	**Newport** (town) Carteret County
140	n/a	38.8	**Grifton** (town) Pitt County
140	n/a	38.8	**Long View** (town) Catawba County
140	1994	38.8	**New Bern** (city) Craven County
143	2018	38.7	**Rocky Mount** (city) Nash County
143	n/a	38.7	**Stanley** (town) Gaston County
145	2042	38.6	**Henderson** (city) Vance County
145	n/a	38.6	**Lake Park** (village) Union County
145	n/a	38.6	**Windsor** (town) Bertie County
148	2066	38.5	**Kernersville** (town) Forsyth County
148	n/a	38.5	**Red Springs** (town) Robeson County
150	n/a	38.4	**Gibsonville** (town) Guilford County

Note: The state column ranks the top/bottom 150 places in the state with population of 2,500 or more. The national column ranks the top/bottom places in the country with population of 10,000 or more. Places that are unincorporated were not considered in the rankings. n/a indicates data not available. Please refer to the User Guide for additional information.

Median Age

Top 150 Places Ranked in *Ascending* Order

State Rank	Nat'l Rank	Years	Place
1	n/a	20.9	**Buies Creek** (CDP) Harnett County
2	n/a	21.0	**Cullowhee** (CDP) Jackson County
3	19	21.5	**Boone** (town) Watauga County
4	n/a	21.8	**Elon** (town) Alamance County
5	n/a	22.5	**Wingate** (town) Union County
6	62	22.9	**Jacksonville** (city) Onslow County
7	77	23.5	**Havelock** (city) Craven County
8	n/a	24.4	**Boiling Springs** (town) Cleveland County
9	n/a	24.8	**Pembroke** (town) Robeson County
10	112	24.9	**Spring Lake** (town) Cumberland County
11	142	25.6	**Chapel Hill** (town) Orange County
12	153	26.0	**Greenville** (city) Pitt County
13	172	26.5	**Piney Green** (CDP) Onslow County
14	n/a	27.5	**Murfreesboro** (town) Hertford County
15	n/a	27.8	**Half Moon** (CDP) Onslow County
16	n/a	29.6	**Rockfish** (CDP) Hoke County
17	394	29.9	**Fayetteville** (city) Cumberland County
18	421	30.1	**Carrboro** (town) Orange County
19	n/a	31.1	**Siler City** (town) Chatham County
20	590	31.3	**Elizabeth City** (city) Pasquotank County
21	n/a	31.8	**Selma** (town) Johnston County
22	687	31.9	**Hope Mills** (town) Cumberland County
22	687	31.9	**Raleigh** (city) Wake County
24	733	32.1	**Durham** (city) Durham County
25	818	32.5	**Monroe** (city) Union County
25	818	32.5	**Morrisville** (town) Wake County
27	851	32.6	**Knightdale** (town) Wake County
28	959	33.1	**Holly Springs** (town) Wake County
28	959	33.1	**Murraysville** (CDP) New Hanover County
30	982	33.2	**Charlotte** (city) Mecklenburg County
31	1006	33.3	**Sanford** (city) Lee County
32	1027	33.4	**Clayton** (town) Johnston County
32	1027	33.4	**Greensboro** (city) Guilford County
32	n/a	33.4	**Wendell** (town) Wake County
35	1103	33.7	**Indian Trail** (town) Union County
36	1195	34.0	**Asheboro** (city) Randolph County
37	n/a	34.1	**Archer Lodge** (town) Johnston County
38	1249	34.2	**Fuquay-Varina** (town) Wake County
38	1249	34.2	**Mooresville** (town) Iredell County
38	1249	34.2	**Wake Forest** (town) Wake County
41	n/a	34.3	**Angier** (town) Harnett County
41	1279	34.3	**Apex** (town) Wake County
41	n/a	34.3	**Winterville** (town) Pitt County
44	n/a	34.4	**Silver Lake** (CDP) New Hanover County
45	n/a	34.5	**Polkton** (town) Anson County
45	n/a	34.5	**Waxhaw** (town) Union County
47	1339	34.6	**Winston-Salem** (city) Forsyth County
48	1377	34.7	**Wilmington** (city) New Hanover County
49	1439	34.9	**Concord** (city) Cabarrus County
49	n/a	34.9	**Dallas** (town) Gaston County
49	n/a	34.9	**Ranlo** (town) Gaston County
52	n/a	35.0	**Pineville** (town) Mecklenburg County
53	1512	35.2	**Huntersville** (town) Mecklenburg County
53	n/a	35.2	**Rolesville** (town) Wake County
55	n/a	35.3	**Zebulon** (town) Wake County
56	1618	35.6	**Kannapolis** (city) Cabarrus County
57	n/a	35.7	**Aberdeen** (town) Moore County
57	1652	35.7	**Davidson** (town) Mecklenburg County
59	1679	35.8	**High Point** (city) Guilford County
59	1679	35.8	**Mebane** (city) Alamance County
61	n/a	36.0	**Northchase** (CDP) New Hanover County
62	1764	36.1	**Goldsboro** (city) Wayne County
63	1796	36.2	**Mount Holly** (city) Gaston County
63	1796	36.2	**Salisbury** (city) Rowan County
63	1796	36.2	**Thomasville** (city) Davidson County
66	n/a	36.4	**Randleman** (city) Randolph County
66	n/a	36.4	**Sylva** (town) Jackson County
68	1889	36.5	**Lumberton** (city) Robeson County
68	n/a	36.5	**Mount Olive** (town) Wayne County
70	1915	36.6	**Cary** (town) Wake County
70	n/a	36.6	**Creedmoor** (city) Granville County
70	n/a	36.6	**Dana** (CDP) Henderson County
70	n/a	36.6	**Woodfin** (town) Buncombe County
74	n/a	36.7	**Troy** (town) Montgomery County
75	n/a	36.8	**Marvin** (village) Union County
76	n/a	36.9	**Butner** (town) Granville County
77	2042	37.0	**Belmont** (city) Gaston County
77	n/a	37.0	**Bessemer City** (city) Gaston County
77	n/a	37.0	**Hamlet** (city) Richmond County
77	n/a	37.0	**Moyock** (CDP) Currituck County
77	n/a	37.0	**Skippers Corner** (CDP) New Hanover County
82	2082	37.1	**Garner** (town) Wake County
82	n/a	37.1	**Sneads Ferry** (CDP) Onslow County
84	2123	37.2	**Wilson** (city) Wilson County
85	n/a	37.3	**Glen Raven** (CDP) Alamance County
85	2161	37.3	**Harrisburg** (town) Cabarrus County
87	n/a	37.4	**Brogden** (CDP) Wayne County
87	n/a	37.4	**Kings Grant** (CDP) New Hanover County
87	2191	37.4	**Lexington** (city) Davidson County
87	n/a	37.4	**Lowell** (city) Gaston County
91	2225	37.5	**Graham** (city) Alamance County
91	n/a	37.5	**Mar-Mac** (CDP) Wayne County
93	n/a	37.6	**East Flat Rock** (CDP) Henderson County
93	n/a	37.6	**East Rockingham** (CDP) Richmond County
93	n/a	37.6	**Tyro** (CDP) Davidson County
96	2290	37.7	**Hickory** (city) Catawba County
96	2290	37.7	**Laurinburg** (city) Scotland County
98	n/a	37.8	**Kill Devil Hills** (town) Dare County
98	2315	37.8	**Statesville** (city) Iredell County
100	n/a	37.9	**Benson** (town) Johnston County
100	n/a	37.9	**China Grove** (town) Rowan County
100	2348	37.9	**Cornelius** (town) Mecklenburg County
100	n/a	37.9	**Maiden** (town) Catawba County
100	n/a	37.9	**Marion** (city) McDowell County
100	2348	37.9	**Roanoke Rapids** (city) Halifax County
106	n/a	38.0	**Elroy** (CDP) Wayne County
106	2385	38.0	**Gastonia** (city) Gaston County
106	n/a	38.0	**Swansboro** (town) Onslow County
109	n/a	38.1	**Granite Quarry** (town) Rowan County
109	2423	38.1	**Newton** (city) Catawba County
109	n/a	38.1	**Wesley Chapel** (village) Union County
112	2452	38.2	**Asheville** (city) Buncombe County
112	n/a	38.2	**Hillsborough** (town) Orange County
112	n/a	38.2	**Louisburg** (town) Franklin County
112	n/a	38.2	**Rockingham** (city) Richmond County
112	n/a	38.2	**Rural Hall** (town) Forsyth County
112	n/a	38.2	**Swannanoa** (CDP) Buncombe County
118	2482	38.3	**Burlington** (city) Alamance County
119	n/a	38.4	**Gibsonville** (town) Guilford County
119	2520	38.4	**Lincolnton** (city) Lincoln County
119	2520	38.4	**Stallings** (town) Union County
119	n/a	38.4	**Warsaw** (town) Duplin County
123	2550	38.5	**Kernersville** (town) Forsyth County
123	n/a	38.5	**Red Springs** (town) Robeson County
125	2591	38.6	**Henderson** (city) Vance County
125	n/a	38.6	**Lake Park** (village) Union County
125	n/a	38.6	**Windsor** (town) Bertie County
128	2615	38.7	**Rocky Mount** (city) Nash County
128	n/a	38.7	**Stanley** (town) Gaston County
130	n/a	38.8	**Grifton** (town) Pitt County
130	n/a	38.8	**Long View** (town) Catawba County
130	2639	38.8	**New Bern** (city) Craven County
133	n/a	38.9	**Granite Falls** (town) Caldwell County
133	2663	38.9	**Leland** (town) Brunswick County
133	n/a	38.9	**Newport** (town) Carteret County
136	n/a	39.1	**Spencer** (town) Rowan County
136	n/a	39.1	**Yadkinville** (town) Yadkin County
138	n/a	39.2	**Fletcher** (town) Henderson County
139	n/a	39.4	**Mocksville** (town) Davie County
139	n/a	39.4	**Raeford** (city) Hoke County
139	n/a	39.4	**Unionville** (town) Union County
142	n/a	39.5	**Ahoskie** (town) Hertford County
142	n/a	39.5	**Bayshore** (CDP) New Hanover County
142	n/a	39.5	**Burgaw** (town) Pender County
142	n/a	39.5	**Liberty** (town) Randolph County
142	n/a	39.5	**Sawmills** (town) Caldwell County
147	2887	39.6	**Albemarle** (city) Stanly County
147	n/a	39.6	**Landis** (town) Rowan County
147	n/a	39.6	**Lillington** (town) Harnett County
150	2921	39.7	**Morganton** (city) Burke County

Note: The state column ranks the top/bottom 150 places in the state with population of 2,500 or more. The national column ranks the top/bottom places in the country with population of 10,000 or more. Places that are unincorporated were not considered in the rankings. n/a indicates data not available. Please refer to the User Guide for additional information.

Population Under Age 18

Top 150 Places Ranked in *Descending* Order

State Rank	Nat'l Rank	Percent	Place		State Rank	Nat'l Rank	Percent	Place
1	n/a	40.9	**Marvin** (village) Union County		74	n/a	25.4	**Warsaw** (town) Duplin County
2	70	35.3	**Holly Springs** (town) Wake County		74	n/a	25.4	**Westport** (CDP) Lincoln County
3	n/a	34.7	**Wesley Chapel** (village) Union County		78	1718	25.3	**Wilson** (city) Wilson County
4	n/a	34.6	**Waxhaw** (town) Union County		79	1762	25.2	**Charlotte** (city) Mecklenburg County
5	n/a	33.3	**Rolesville** (town) Wake County		79	n/a	25.2	**Fairview** (town) Union County
6	169	33.0	**Apex** (town) Wake County		79	n/a	25.2	**Gibsonville** (town) Guilford County
7	192	32.7	**Indian Trail** (town) Union County		79	1762	25.2	**Graham** (city) Alamance County
8	216	32.4	**Wake Forest** (town) Wake County		79	1762	25.2	**High Point** (city) Guilford County
9	327	31.2	**Spring Lake** (town) Cumberland County		84	n/a	25.1	**East Rockingham** (CDP) Richmond County
10	n/a	31.1	**Rockfish** (CDP) Hoke County		85	1841	25.0	**Lewisville** (town) Forsyth County
11	n/a	30.9	**Archer Lodge** (town) Johnston County		85	1841	25.0	**Mount Holly** (city) Gaston County
11	357	30.9	**Clayton** (town) Johnston County		85	n/a	25.0	**Ogden** (CDP) New Hanover County
13	408	30.5	**Hope Mills** (town) Cumberland County		88	1891	24.9	**Matthews** (town) Mecklenburg County
14	424	30.4	**Harrisburg** (town) Cabarrus County		88	n/a	24.9	**Mineral Springs** (town) Union County
15	n/a	30.1	**Moyock** (CDP) Currituck County		88	n/a	24.9	**Mocksville** (town) Davie County
16	485	30.0	**Fuquay-Varina** (town) Wake County		91	1934	24.8	**Lumberton** (city) Robeson County
17	n/a	29.9	**Oak Ridge** (town) Guilford County		91	n/a	24.8	**Stanley** (town) Gaston County
18	n/a	29.8	**Half Moon** (CDP) Onslow County		91	n/a	24.8	**Williamston** (town) Martin County
18	n/a	29.8	**Selma** (town) Johnston County		94	n/a	24.7	**Farmville** (town) Pitt County
18	n/a	29.8	**Siler City** (town) Chatham County		94	n/a	24.7	**Forest City** (town) Rutherford County
21	554	29.6	**Monroe** (city) Union County		94	1977	24.7	**Gastonia** (city) Gaston County
22	n/a	29.5	**Weddington** (town) Union County		94	n/a	24.7	**Granite Falls** (town) Caldwell County
22	n/a	29.5	**Wendell** (town) Wake County		94	1977	24.7	**Kings Mountain** (city) Cleveland County
24	583	29.4	**Knightdale** (town) Wake County		94	n/a	24.7	**Spencer** (town) Rowan County
25	n/a	29.2	**Winterville** (town) Pitt County		100	2025	24.6	**Lexington** (city) Davidson County
26	663	28.9	**Huntersville** (town) Mecklenburg County		100	2025	24.6	**Rocky Mount** (city) Nash County
26	663	28.9	**Summerfield** (town) Guilford County		100	2025	24.6	**Statesville** (city) Iredell County
28	760	28.4	**Concord** (city) Cabarrus County		100	n/a	24.6	**Wadesboro** (town) Anson County
28	760	28.4	**Mooresville** (town) Iredell County		100	n/a	24.6	**Wallburg** (town) Davidson County
30	n/a	28.3	**Lake Park** (village) Union County		100	2025	24.6	**Winston-Salem** (city) Forsyth County
30	784	28.3	**Piney Green** (CDP) Onslow County		106	2122	24.4	**Garner** (town) Wake County
32	n/a	28.2	**Zebulon** (town) Wake County		106	n/a	24.4	**Lowesville** (CDP) Lincoln County
33	867	28.0	**Sanford** (city) Lee County		106	n/a	24.4	**Saint Stephens** (CDP) Catawba County
34	n/a	27.7	**Angier** (town) Harnett County		109	n/a	24.3	**Edenton** (town) Chowan County
34	946	27.7	**Cary** (town) Wake County		109	n/a	24.3	**Locust** (city) Stanly County
34	946	27.7	**Stallings** (town) Union County		109	n/a	24.3	**Rural Hall** (town) Forsyth County
37	n/a	27.6	**Brices Creek** (CDP) Craven County		112	2205	24.2	**Burlington** (city) Alamance County
38	n/a	27.3	**Creedmoor** (city) Granville County		112	n/a	24.2	**East Flat Rock** (CDP) Henderson County
38	n/a	27.3	**Stokesdale** (town) Guilford County		112	2205	24.2	**Mint Hill** (town) Mecklenburg County
40	1097	27.1	**Asheboro** (city) Randolph County		112	2205	24.2	**Newton** (city) Catawba County
41	1125	27.0	**Havelock** (city) Craven County		116	n/a	24.0	**Hillsborough** (town) Orange County
41	1125	27.0	**Morrisville** (town) Wake County		116	n/a	24.0	**Mar-Mac** (CDP) Wayne County
43	n/a	26.9	**Hamlet** (city) Richmond County		116	n/a	24.0	**River Road** (CDP) Beaufort County
43	n/a	26.9	**Unionville** (town) Union County		119	2343	23.9	**Murraysville** (CDP) New Hanover County
45	1194	26.8	**Kannapolis** (city) Cabarrus County		120	2389	23.8	**Archdale** (city) Randolph County
46	n/a	26.6	**Dana** (CDP) Henderson County		120	n/a	23.8	**Ayden** (town) Pitt County
46	1251	26.6	**Mebane** (city) Alamance County		120	n/a	23.8	**Raeford** (city) Hoke County
48	1290	26.5	**Clemmons** (village) Forsyth County		123	n/a	23.7	**Aberdeen** (town) Moore County
48	1290	26.5	**Thomasville** (city) Davidson County		123	2423	23.7	**Albemarle** (city) Stanly County
48	n/a	26.5	**Tyro** (CDP) Davidson County		123	n/a	23.7	**Cramerton** (town) Gaston County
51	n/a	26.4	**Grifton** (town) Pitt County		123	n/a	23.7	**Dunn** (city) Harnett County
51	n/a	26.4	**Randleman** (city) Randolph County		123	n/a	23.7	**Fletcher** (town) Henderson County
53	n/a	26.3	**Bayshore** (CDP) New Hanover County		123	2423	23.7	**Kernersville** (town) Forsyth County
53	n/a	26.3	**Plymouth** (town) Washington County		123	n/a	23.7	**Lowell** (city) Gaston County
53	n/a	26.3	**Red Springs** (town) Robeson County		123	n/a	23.7	**Yadkinville** (town) Yadkin County
53	1371	26.3	**Roanoke Rapids** (city) Halifax County		131	n/a	23.6	**China Grove** (town) Rowan County
53	n/a	26.3	**Silver Lake** (CDP) New Hanover County		131	2483	23.6	**Hickory** (city) Catawba County
58	n/a	26.2	**Ranlo** (town) Gaston County		131	2483	23.6	**Kinston** (city) Lenoir County
59	n/a	26.1	**Red Oak** (town) Nash County		131	n/a	23.6	**Swansboro** (town) Onslow County
60	n/a	26.0	**Butner** (town) Granville County		131	n/a	23.6	**Wallace** (town) Duplin County
60	n/a	26.0	**Dallas** (town) Gaston County		136	n/a	23.5	**Erwin** (town) Harnett County
60	n/a	26.0	**Glen Raven** (CDP) Alamance County		136	2525	23.5	**Lincolnton** (city) Lincoln County
63	n/a	25.9	**Fairmont** (town) Robeson County		136	n/a	23.5	**Sawmills** (town) Caldwell County
64	1530	25.8	**Fayetteville** (city) Cumberland County		136	2525	23.5	**Shelby** (city) Cleveland County
65	n/a	25.7	**Ahoskie** (town) Hertford County		140	2577	23.4	**Jacksonville** (city) Onslow County
65	n/a	25.7	**Benson** (town) Johnston County		140	n/a	23.4	**Nashville** (town) Nash County
65	n/a	25.7	**Bessemer City** (city) Gaston County		140	n/a	23.4	**Oxford** (city) Granville County
65	n/a	25.7	**Enfield** (town) Halifax County		143	n/a	23.3	**Elkin** (town) Surry County
65	n/a	25.7	**Pembroke** (town) Robeson County		144	n/a	23.2	**Boiling Spring Lakes** (city) Brunswick County
70	1602	25.6	**Laurinburg** (city) Scotland County		144	n/a	23.2	**Conover** (city) Catawba County
71	n/a	25.5	**Granite Quarry** (town) Rowan County		144	n/a	23.2	**La Grange** (town) Lenoir County
71	1643	25.5	**Henderson** (city) Vance County		144	n/a	23.2	**Mountain View** (CDP) Catawba County
71	n/a	25.5	**Liberty** (town) Randolph County		148	2724	23.1	**Belmont** (city) Gaston County
74	n/a	25.4	**Brogden** (CDP) Wayne County		148	2724	23.1	**Goldsboro** (city) Wayne County
74	n/a	25.4	**Rockingham** (city) Richmond County		148	n/a	23.1	**Hampstead** (CDP) Pender County

Note: *The state column ranks the top/bottom 150 places in the state with population of 2,500 or more. The national column ranks the top/bottom places in the country with population of 10,000 or more. Places that are unincorporated were not considered in the rankings. n/a indicates data not available. Please refer to the User Guide for additional information.*

Population Under Age 18

Top 150 Places Ranked in *Ascending* Order

State Rank	Nat'l Rank	Percent	Place
1	n/a	2.5	**Saint James** (town) Brunswick County
2	n/a	4.1	**Cullowhee** (CDP) Jackson County
3	14	5.1	**Boone** (town) Watauga County
4	n/a	5.5	**Buies Creek** (CDP) Harnett County
5	n/a	6.3	**Sunset Beach** (town) Brunswick County
6	n/a	7.2	**Carolina Shores** (town) Brunswick County
7	n/a	9.6	**Fairfield Harbour** (CDP) Craven County
8	n/a	10.1	**Flat Rock** (village) Henderson County
9	n/a	10.3	**Polkton** (town) Anson County
10	n/a	10.5	**Elon** (town) Alamance County
11	n/a	13.5	**River Bend** (town) Craven County
12	n/a	13.8	**Oak Island** (town) Brunswick County
13	n/a	14.0	**Southport** (city) Brunswick County
14	n/a	14.6	**Emerald Isle** (town) Carteret County
15	n/a	15.1	**Lillington** (town) Harnett County
16	n/a	15.3	**Windsor** (town) Bertie County
17	n/a	15.9	**Lake Junaluska** (CDP) Haywood County
18	n/a	16.1	**Beaufort** (town) Carteret County
18	185	16.1	**Pinehurst** (village) Moore County
20	n/a	16.3	**Carolina Beach** (town) New Hanover County
21	n/a	16.6	**Murfreesboro** (town) Hertford County
22	n/a	16.7	**Southern Shores** (town) Dare County
23	n/a	16.9	**Nags Head** (town) Dare County
24	n/a	17.2	**Brevard** (city) Transylvania County
25	276	17.4	**Chapel Hill** (town) Orange County
25	n/a	17.4	**Weaverville** (town) Buncombe County
27	309	17.8	**Hendersonville** (city) Henderson County
27	n/a	17.8	**Waynesville** (town) Haywood County
29	n/a	18.0	**Louisburg** (town) Franklin County
30	n/a	18.3	**Black Mountain** (town) Buncombe County
31	n/a	18.4	**Seven Lakes** (CDP) Moore County
31	368	18.4	**Wilmington** (city) New Hanover County
33	383	18.5	**Asheville** (city) Buncombe County
33	n/a	18.5	**Skippers Corner** (CDP) New Hanover County
35	n/a	18.6	**Etowah** (CDP) Henderson County
36	419	18.7	**Greenville** (city) Pitt County
36	n/a	18.7	**Kitty Hawk** (town) Dare County
36	n/a	18.7	**Woodfin** (town) Buncombe County
39	n/a	18.9	**Burgaw** (town) Pender County
40	n/a	19.4	**Morehead City** (town) Carteret County
40	n/a	19.4	**Sneads Ferry** (CDP) Onslow County
42	n/a	19.5	**Wilkesboro** (town) Wilkes County
43	n/a	19.8	**Lake Norman of Catawba** (CDP) Catawba County
44	n/a	19.9	**Porters Neck** (CDP) New Hanover County
45	n/a	20.0	**Pineville** (town) Mecklenburg County
45	696	20.0	**Southern Pines** (town) Moore County
45	n/a	20.0	**Wingate** (town) Union County
48	n/a	20.1	**Rutherfordton** (town) Rutherford County
48	n/a	20.1	**Sylva** (town) Jackson County
50	749	20.2	**Mount Airy** (city) Surry County
50	n/a	20.2	**Whispering Pines** (village) Moore County
52	n/a	20.3	**Boiling Springs** (town) Cleveland County
52	n/a	20.3	**Kings Grant** (CDP) New Hanover County
54	n/a	20.4	**Bethlehem** (CDP) Alexander County
54	n/a	20.4	**Kill Devil Hills** (town) Dare County
54	807	20.4	**Leland** (town) Brunswick County
57	n/a	20.6	**Mountain Home** (CDP) Henderson County
57	n/a	20.6	**Shallotte** (town) Brunswick County
57	n/a	20.6	**Trent Woods** (town) Craven County
60	n/a	20.7	**Elizabethtown** (town) Bladen County
60	n/a	20.7	**Mount Olive** (town) Wayne County
60	n/a	20.7	**Pittsboro** (town) Chatham County
63	n/a	20.8	**Mills River** (town) Henderson County
64	n/a	20.9	**Lake Royale** (CDP) Franklin County
64	n/a	20.9	**Royal Pines** (CDP) Buncombe County
66	n/a	21.1	**Eastover** (town) Cumberland County
67	n/a	21.2	**Franklin** (town) Macon County
67	n/a	21.2	**Pleasant Garden** (town) Guilford County
69	n/a	21.3	**Marion** (city) McDowell County
70	n/a	21.4	**Enochville** (CDP) Rowan County
70	n/a	21.4	**Trinity** (city) Randolph County
72	1195	21.5	**Carrboro** (town) Orange County
72	n/a	21.5	**Icard** (CDP) Burke County
72	n/a	21.5	**Myrtle Grove** (CDP) New Hanover County
75	n/a	21.6	**Cajah's Mountain** (town) Caldwell County
75	n/a	21.6	**Newport** (town) Carteret County
75	n/a	21.6	**Tabor City** (town) Columbus County
78	n/a	21.8	**Canton** (town) Haywood County
79	n/a	21.9	**Clinton** (city) Sampson County
79	n/a	21.9	**Midway** (town) Davidson County
81	n/a	22.0	**Spindale** (town) Rutherford County
81	n/a	22.0	**Valdese** (town) Burke County
81	n/a	22.0	**Wentworth** (town) Rockingham County
81	n/a	22.0	**Whiteville** (city) Columbus County
85	n/a	22.1	**Elroy** (CDP) Wayne County
85	n/a	22.1	**Forest Oaks** (CDP) Guilford County
85	n/a	22.1	**Northchase** (CDP) New Hanover County
85	1435	22.1	**Reidsville** (city) Rockingham County
89	n/a	22.3	**James City** (CDP) Craven County
89	n/a	22.3	**Long View** (town) Catawba County
91	1565	22.4	**Elizabeth City** (city) Pasquotank County
91	n/a	22.4	**Gamewell** (town) Caldwell County
91	n/a	22.4	**King** (city) Stokes County
91	n/a	22.4	**Landis** (town) Rowan County
91	n/a	22.4	**North Wilkesboro** (town) Wilkes County
91	n/a	22.4	**Walkertown** (town) Forsyth County
97	n/a	22.5	**Fairview** (CDP) Buncombe County
97	1610	22.5	**Smithfield** (town) Johnston County
97	n/a	22.5	**South Rosemary** (CDP) Halifax County
97	n/a	22.5	**Washington** (city) Beaufort County
97	n/a	22.5	**Wrightsboro** (CDP) New Hanover County
102	1650	22.6	**Morganton** (city) Burke County
103	1700	22.7	**Durham** (city) Durham County
103	1700	22.7	**Greensboro** (city) Guilford County
103	1700	22.7	**Jamestown** (town) Guilford County
103	1700	22.7	**Salisbury** (city) Rowan County
103	n/a	22.7	**Swannanoa** (CDP) Buncombe County
103	n/a	22.7	**Welcome** (CDP) Davidson County
109	n/a	22.8	**Cherryville** (city) Gaston County
109	1744	22.8	**Davidson** (town) Mecklenburg County
109	1744	22.8	**Lenoir** (city) Caldwell County
109	1744	22.8	**New Bern** (city) Craven County
109	1744	22.8	**Tarboro** (town) Edgecombe County
109	n/a	22.8	**Troy** (town) Montgomery County
115	1787	22.9	**Cornelius** (town) Mecklenburg County
115	1787	22.9	**Eden** (city) Rockingham County
115	n/a	22.9	**Maiden** (town) Catawba County
115	n/a	22.9	**Roxboro** (city) Person County
119	1881	23.1	**Belmont** (city) Gaston County
119	1881	23.1	**Goldsboro** (city) Wayne County
119	n/a	23.1	**Hampstead** (CDP) Pender County
119	n/a	23.1	**Hudson** (town) Caldwell County
119	n/a	23.1	**Midland** (town) Cabarrus County
119	1881	23.1	**Raleigh** (city) Wake County
125	n/a	23.2	**Boiling Spring Lakes** (city) Brunswick County
125	n/a	23.2	**Conover** (city) Catawba County
125	n/a	23.2	**La Grange** (town) Lenoir County
125	n/a	23.2	**Mountain View** (CDP) Catawba County
129	n/a	23.3	**Elkin** (town) Surry County
130	2033	23.4	**Jacksonville** (city) Onslow County
130	n/a	23.4	**Nashville** (town) Nash County
130	n/a	23.4	**Oxford** (city) Granville County
133	n/a	23.5	**Erwin** (town) Harnett County
133	2080	23.5	**Lincolnton** (city) Lincoln County
133	n/a	23.5	**Sawmills** (town) Caldwell County
133	2080	23.5	**Shelby** (city) Cleveland County
137	n/a	23.6	**China Grove** (town) Rowan County
137	2132	23.6	**Hickory** (city) Catawba County
137	2132	23.6	**Kinston** (city) Lenoir County
137	n/a	23.6	**Swansboro** (town) Onslow County
137	n/a	23.6	**Wallace** (town) Duplin County
142	n/a	23.7	**Aberdeen** (town) Moore County
142	2174	23.7	**Albemarle** (city) Stanly County
142	n/a	23.7	**Cramerton** (town) Gaston County
142	n/a	23.7	**Dunn** (city) Harnett County
142	n/a	23.7	**Fletcher** (town) Henderson County
142	2174	23.7	**Kernersville** (town) Forsyth County
142	n/a	23.7	**Lowell** (city) Gaston County
142	n/a	23.7	**Yadkinville** (town) Yadkin County
150	2234	23.8	**Archdale** (city) Randolph County

Note: The state column ranks the top/bottom 150 places in the state with population of 2,500 or more. The national column ranks the top/bottom places in the country with population of 10,000 or more. Places that are unincorporated were not considered in the rankings. n/a indicates data not available. Please refer to the User Guide for additional information.

Population Age 65 and Over

Top 150 Places Ranked in *Descending* Order

State Rank	Nat'l Rank	Percent	Place
1	n/a	49.8	**Saint James** (town) Brunswick County
2	n/a	49.6	**Carolina Shores** (town) Brunswick County
3	n/a	47.7	**Flat Rock** (village) Henderson County
4	n/a	46.4	**Sunset Beach** (town) Brunswick County
5	n/a	45.9	**Fairfield Harbour** (CDP) Craven County
6	25	37.7	**Pinehurst** (village) Moore County
7	n/a	37.3	**River Bend** (town) Craven County
8	n/a	33.4	**Whispering Pines** (village) Moore County
9	n/a	32.4	**Seven Lakes** (CDP) Moore County
10	n/a	31.3	**Lake Junaluska** (CDP) Haywood County
11	n/a	31.2	**Southport** (city) Brunswick County
12	45	30.2	**Hendersonville** (city) Henderson County
13	n/a	29.5	**Brevard** (city) Transylvania County
14	n/a	28.4	**Etowah** (CDP) Henderson County
15	n/a	28.1	**Porters Neck** (CDP) New Hanover County
16	n/a	27.7	**Weaverville** (town) Buncombe County
17	70	27.5	**Southern Pines** (town) Moore County
17	n/a	27.5	**Southern Shores** (town) Dare County
19	n/a	25.8	**Emerald Isle** (town) Carteret County
20	n/a	24.6	**Waynesville** (town) Haywood County
20	n/a	24.6	**Wilkesboro** (town) Wilkes County
22	n/a	24.5	**Oak Island** (town) Brunswick County
23	n/a	24.1	**Trent Woods** (town) Craven County
24	n/a	23.8	**Mountain Home** (CDP) Henderson County
25	n/a	22.7	**Black Mountain** (town) Buncombe County
25	157	22.7	**Mount Airy** (city) Surry County
27	n/a	22.4	**Shallotte** (town) Brunswick County
28	n/a	21.9	**Franklin** (town) Macon County
29	n/a	21.6	**Elkin** (town) Surry County
30	n/a	21.5	**Elizabethtown** (town) Bladen County
31	n/a	21.4	**Louisburg** (town) Franklin County
32	n/a	21.3	**Edenton** (town) Chowan County
33	237	20.8	**Smithfield** (town) Johnston County
33	n/a	20.8	**Wallace** (town) Duplin County
33	n/a	20.8	**Yadkinville** (town) Yadkin County
36	n/a	20.7	**Beaufort** (town) Carteret County
37	n/a	20.6	**Clinton** (city) Sampson County
38	n/a	20.5	**Rutherfordton** (town) Rutherford County
39	n/a	20.4	**Fairmont** (town) Robeson County
40	n/a	20.0	**King** (city) Stokes County
40	n/a	20.0	**Valdese** (town) Burke County
42	n/a	19.8	**Ahoskie** (town) Hertford County
42	n/a	19.8	**Canton** (town) Haywood County
44	n/a	19.7	**Pittsboro** (town) Chatham County
44	n/a	19.7	**Whiteville** (city) Columbus County
46	n/a	19.4	**Oxford** (city) Granville County
46	n/a	19.4	**Plymouth** (town) Washington County
46	n/a	19.4	**Tabor City** (town) Columbus County
49	n/a	19.3	**Morehead City** (town) Carteret County
50	n/a	19.2	**Cherryville** (city) Gaston County
51	n/a	19.1	**Forest Oaks** (CDP) Guilford County
51	n/a	19.1	**Mount Olive** (town) Wayne County
51	404	19.1	**Tarboro** (town) Edgecombe County
54	n/a	19.0	**Ayden** (town) Pitt County
54	n/a	19.0	**Wadesboro** (town) Anson County
54	n/a	19.0	**Williamston** (town) Martin County
57	n/a	18.8	**Dunn** (city) Harnett County
57	n/a	18.8	**North Wilkesboro** (town) Wilkes County
57	n/a	18.8	**Pleasant Garden** (town) Guilford County
60	n/a	18.7	**Washington** (city) Beaufort County
61	n/a	18.6	**Roxboro** (city) Person County
62	508	18.5	**Kinston** (city) Lenoir County
62	508	18.5	**Lenoir** (city) Caldwell County
64	n/a	18.4	**Cajah's Mountain** (town) Caldwell County
64	n/a	18.4	**Eastover** (town) Cumberland County
64	n/a	18.4	**Enochville** (CDP) Rowan County
67	n/a	18.3	**Mocksville** (town) Davie County
68	556	18.2	**Morganton** (city) Burke County
69	574	18.1	**Eden** (city) Rockingham County
69	n/a	18.1	**Forest City** (town) Rutherford County
71	616	17.9	**New Bern** (city) Craven County
72	635	17.8	**Reidsville** (city) Rockingham County
73	659	17.7	**Albemarle** (city) Stanly County
73	659	17.7	**Shelby** (city) Cleveland County
75	n/a	17.6	**La Grange** (town) Lenoir County
75	n/a	17.6	**Landis** (town) Rowan County
75	n/a	17.6	**Liberty** (town) Randolph County
75	n/a	17.6	**Sylva** (town) Jackson County
79	n/a	17.5	**Benson** (town) Johnston County
79	n/a	17.5	**Bethlehem** (CDP) Alexander County
79	n/a	17.5	**Erwin** (town) Harnett County
82	n/a	17.4	**Farmville** (town) Pitt County
82	n/a	17.4	**Mills River** (town) Henderson County
84	n/a	17.3	**Hampstead** (CDP) Pender County
84	762	17.3	**Henderson** (city) Vance County
84	n/a	17.3	**Hudson** (town) Caldwell County
84	762	17.3	**Kings Mountain** (city) Cleveland County
84	n/a	17.3	**Warsaw** (town) Duplin County
89	n/a	17.2	**Icard** (CDP) Burke County
90	n/a	17.1	**Raeford** (city) Hoke County
90	n/a	17.1	**Red Springs** (town) Robeson County
92	n/a	17.0	**Conover** (city) Catawba County
93	n/a	16.9	**Jamestown** (town) Guilford County
93	874	16.9	**Lincolnton** (city) Lincoln County
95	n/a	16.8	**Nags Head** (town) Dare County
96	n/a	16.6	**Marion** (city) McDowell County
96	n/a	16.6	**Pineville** (town) Mecklenburg County
98	n/a	16.5	**James City** (CDP) Craven County
98	n/a	16.5	**Windsor** (town) Bertie County
100	n/a	16.4	**Elon** (town) Alamance County
101	1033	16.3	**Asheville** (city) Buncombe County
101	n/a	16.3	**Walkertown** (town) Forsyth County
103	n/a	16.2	**Aberdeen** (town) Moore County
103	n/a	16.2	**Nashville** (town) Nash County
103	n/a	16.2	**Rockingham** (city) Richmond County
106	n/a	16.1	**Midway** (town) Davidson County
106	n/a	16.1	**Trinity** (city) Randolph County
108	n/a	16.0	**Burgaw** (town) Pender County
108	n/a	16.0	**Lake Royale** (CDP) Franklin County
110	1150	15.9	**Laurinburg** (city) Scotland County
110	n/a	15.9	**Myrtle Grove** (CDP) New Hanover County
110	1150	15.9	**Newton** (city) Catawba County
110	n/a	15.9	**Saint Stephens** (CDP) Catawba County
110	1150	15.9	**Salisbury** (city) Rowan County
110	1150	15.9	**Statesville** (city) Iredell County
116	n/a	15.8	**Grifton** (town) Pitt County
116	n/a	15.8	**Hamlet** (city) Richmond County
116	n/a	15.8	**Long View** (town) Catawba County
116	n/a	15.8	**River Road** (CDP) Beaufort County
116	n/a	15.8	**Stanley** (town) Gaston County
121	1222	15.7	**Burlington** (city) Alamance County
121	n/a	15.7	**Lake Norman of Catawba** (CDP) Catawba County
121	n/a	15.7	**Sneads Ferry** (CDP) Onslow County
124	1258	15.6	**Archdale** (city) Randolph County
124	n/a	15.6	**South Rosemary** (CDP) Halifax County
126	n/a	15.5	**Enfield** (town) Halifax County
126	n/a	15.5	**Spindale** (town) Rutherford County
128	n/a	15.4	**East Flat Rock** (CDP) Henderson County
128	n/a	15.4	**Gamewell** (town) Caldwell County
128	n/a	15.4	**Royal Pines** (CDP) Buncombe County
128	n/a	15.4	**Swansboro** (town) Onslow County
132	n/a	15.3	**Murfreesboro** (town) Hertford County
133	n/a	15.2	**Locust** (city) Stanly County
134	1433	15.1	**Lexington** (city) Davidson County
135	1466	15.0	**Leland** (town) Brunswick County
135	n/a	15.0	**Welcome** (CDP) Davidson County
137	1502	14.9	**Goldsboro** (city) Wayne County
137	n/a	14.9	**Kitty Hawk** (town) Dare County
137	n/a	14.9	**Rural Hall** (town) Forsyth County
140	1532	14.8	**Roanoke Rapids** (city) Halifax County
140	n/a	14.8	**Spencer** (town) Rowan County
142	1574	14.7	**Mint Hill** (town) Mecklenburg County
143	1615	14.6	**Clemmons** (village) Forsyth County
143	n/a	14.6	**Fairview** (CDP) Buncombe County
143	1615	14.6	**Graham** (city) Alamance County
143	1615	14.6	**Lumberton** (city) Robeson County
143	n/a	14.6	**Newport** (town) Carteret County
148	n/a	14.5	**Lake Park** (village) Union County
149	1740	14.3	**Hickory** (city) Catawba County
150	1781	14.2	**Rocky Mount** (city) Nash County

Note: The state column ranks the top/bottom 150 places in the state with population of 2,500 or more. The national column ranks the top/bottom places in the country with population of 10,000 or more. Places that are unincorporated were not considered in the rankings. n/a indicates data not available. Please refer to the User Guide for additional information.

Population Age 65 and Over

Top 150 Places Ranked in *Ascending* Order

State Rank	Nat'l Rank	Percent	Place	State Rank	Nat'l Rank	Percent	Place
1	n/a	3.8	**Cullowhee** (CDP) Jackson County	76	n/a	12.3	**Ogden** (CDP) New Hanover County
2	41	4.2	**Havelock** (city) Craven County	76	n/a	12.3	**Westport** (CDP) Lincoln County
3	46	4.3	**Morrisville** (town) Wake County	78	n/a	12.4	**China Grove** (town) Rowan County
3	n/a	4.3	**Polkton** (town) Anson County	78	n/a	12.4	**Glen Raven** (CDP) Alamance County
5	n/a	4.5	**Buies Creek** (CDP) Harnett County	80	2075	12.5	**Davidson** (town) Mecklenburg County
6	71	4.8	**Spring Lake** (town) Cumberland County	80	n/a	12.5	**Mountain View** (CDP) Catawba County
7	77	4.9	**Holly Springs** (town) Wake County	80	2075	12.5	**Winston-Salem** (city) Forsyth County
7	n/a	4.9	**Rockfish** (CDP) Hoke County	83	n/a	12.6	**Swannanoa** (CDP) Buncombe County
9	n/a	5.0	**Marvin** (village) Union County	84	2171	12.7	**Lewisville** (town) Forsyth County
10	112	5.3	**Carrboro** (town) Orange County	84	n/a	12.7	**Lowesville** (CDP) Lincoln County
11	n/a	5.4	**Archer Lodge** (town) Johnston County	86	n/a	12.8	**Angier** (town) Harnett County
11	128	5.4	**Jacksonville** (city) Onslow County	86	n/a	12.8	**Northchase** (CDP) New Hanover County
13	164	5.7	**Apex** (town) Wake County	88	n/a	13.0	**Bessemer City** (city) Gaston County
14	n/a	6.3	**Half Moon** (CDP) Onslow County	88	n/a	13.0	**Dana** (CDP) Henderson County
14	222	6.3	**Piney Green** (CDP) Onslow County	88	n/a	13.0	**East Rockingham** (CDP) Richmond County
16	242	6.4	**Knightdale** (town) Wake County	91	n/a	13.1	**Brices Creek** (CDP) Craven County
16	n/a	6.4	**Wesley Chapel** (village) Union County	91	2353	13.1	**Kannapolis** (city) Cabarrus County
18	312	6.8	**Boone** (town) Watauga County	91	2353	13.1	**Kernersville** (town) Forsyth County
18	312	6.8	**Huntersville** (town) Mecklenburg County	91	n/a	13.1	**Zebulon** (town) Wake County
20	331	6.9	**Indian Trail** (town) Union County	95	n/a	13.2	**Brogden** (CDP) Wayne County
21	n/a	7.0	**Waxhaw** (town) Union County	95	n/a	13.2	**Carolina Beach** (town) New Hanover County
22	n/a	7.2	**Rolesville** (town) Wake County	95	n/a	13.2	**Cramerton** (town) Gaston County
23	447	7.5	**Hope Mills** (town) Cumberland County	98	2437	13.3	**Matthews** (town) Mecklenburg County
24	n/a	8.0	**Moyock** (CDP) Currituck County	98	n/a	13.3	**Sawmills** (town) Caldwell County
24	546	8.0	**Murraysville** (CDP) New Hanover County	100	n/a	13.4	**Granite Quarry** (town) Rowan County
26	570	8.1	**Wake Forest** (town) Wake County	100	n/a	13.4	**Wallburg** (town) Davidson County
27	592	8.2	**Raleigh** (city) Wake County	102	n/a	13.5	**Elroy** (CDP) Wayne County
28	614	8.3	**Greenville** (city) Pitt County	102	n/a	13.5	**Fairview** (town) Union County
29	671	8.5	**Charlotte** (city) Mecklenburg County	102	n/a	13.5	**Woodfin** (town) Buncombe County
29	671	8.5	**Clayton** (town) Johnston County	105	2562	13.6	**Gastonia** (city) Gaston County
29	n/a	8.5	**Wingate** (town) Union County	105	n/a	13.6	**Lillington** (town) Harnett County
32	n/a	8.6	**Boiling Springs** (town) Cleveland County	105	n/a	13.6	**Lowell** (city) Gaston County
32	699	8.6	**Cary** (town) Wake County	105	n/a	13.6	**Mar-Mac** (CDP) Wayne County
32	n/a	8.6	**Oak Ridge** (town) Guilford County	109	n/a	13.7	**Midland** (town) Cabarrus County
35	n/a	8.7	**Winterville** (town) Pitt County	109	n/a	13.7	**Troy** (town) Montgomery County
36	767	8.8	**Durham** (city) Durham County	109	n/a	13.7	**Wrightsboro** (CDP) New Hanover County
37	n/a	9.1	**Silver Lake** (CDP) New Hanover County	112	n/a	13.8	**Maiden** (town) Catawba County
38	884	9.2	**Chapel Hill** (town) Orange County	113	2693	13.9	**Asheboro** (city) Randolph County
38	884	9.2	**Harrisburg** (town) Cabarrus County	113	n/a	13.9	**Boiling Spring Lakes** (city) Brunswick County
40	n/a	9.4	**Kill Devil Hills** (town) Dare County	113	2693	13.9	**Elizabeth City** (city) Pasquotank County
40	n/a	9.4	**Weddington** (town) Union County	113	n/a	13.9	**Fletcher** (town) Henderson County
42	976	9.5	**Summerfield** (town) Guilford County	113	2693	13.9	**Thomasville** (city) Davidson County
43	1026	9.7	**Fayetteville** (city) Cumberland County	113	n/a	13.9	**Wentworth** (town) Rockingham County
43	n/a	9.7	**Skippers Corner** (CDP) New Hanover County	119	2746	14.0	**Wilmington** (city) New Hanover County
45	1046	9.8	**Mooresville** (town) Iredell County	120	n/a	14.1	**Granite Falls** (town) Caldwell County
46	1094	10.0	**Mount Holly** (city) Gaston County	120	2792	14.1	**Wilson** (city) Wilson County
47	1137	10.1	**Cornelius** (town) Mecklenburg County	122	2825	14.2	**Rocky Mount** (city) Nash County
48	n/a	10.4	**Butner** (town) Granville County	123	2876	14.3	**Hickory** (city) Catawba County
48	n/a	10.4	**Ranlo** (town) Gaston County	124	n/a	14.5	**Lake Park** (village) Union County
48	1230	10.4	**Stallings** (town) Union County	125	3004	14.6	**Clemmons** (village) Forsyth County
51	n/a	10.5	**Creedmoor** (city) Granville County	125	n/a	14.6	**Fairview** (CDP) Buncombe County
52	1306	10.6	**Concord** (city) Cabarrus County	125	3004	14.6	**Graham** (city) Alamance County
52	n/a	10.6	**Selma** (town) Johnston County	125	3004	14.6	**Lumberton** (city) Robeson County
52	n/a	10.6	**Tyro** (CDP) Davidson County	125	n/a	14.6	**Newport** (town) Carteret County
55	1391	10.8	**Mebane** (city) Alamance County	130	3042	14.7	**Mint Hill** (town) Mecklenburg County
56	1427	10.9	**Belmont** (city) Gaston County	131	3083	14.8	**Roanoke Rapids** (city) Halifax County
57	n/a	11.0	**Bayshore** (CDP) New Hanover County	131	n/a	14.8	**Spencer** (town) Rowan County
58	1498	11.1	**Monroe** (city) Union County	133	3125	14.9	**Goldsboro** (city) Wayne County
59	1532	11.2	**Fuquay-Varina** (town) Wake County	133	n/a	14.9	**Kitty Hawk** (town) Dare County
60	n/a	11.3	**Mineral Springs** (town) Union County	133	n/a	14.9	**Rural Hall** (town) Forsyth County
60	n/a	11.3	**Stokesdale** (town) Guilford County	136	3155	15.0	**Leland** (town) Brunswick County
62	n/a	11.4	**Unionville** (town) Union County	136	n/a	15.0	**Welcome** (CDP) Davidson County
63	n/a	11.5	**Gibsonville** (town) Guilford County	138	3191	15.1	**Lexington** (city) Davidson County
63	1666	11.5	**Greensboro** (city) Guilford County	139	n/a	15.2	**Locust** (city) Stanly County
63	n/a	11.5	**Pembroke** (town) Robeson County	140	n/a	15.3	**Murfreesboro** (town) Hertford County
66	n/a	11.6	**Kings Grant** (CDP) New Hanover County	141	n/a	15.4	**East Flat Rock** (CDP) Henderson County
66	n/a	11.6	**Wendell** (town) Wake County	141	n/a	15.4	**Gamewell** (town) Caldwell County
68	1733	11.7	**Sanford** (city) Lee County	141	n/a	15.4	**Royal Pines** (CDP) Buncombe County
69	1789	11.8	**Garner** (town) Wake County	141	n/a	15.4	**Swansboro** (town) Onslow County
69	n/a	11.8	**Red Oak** (town) Nash County	145	n/a	15.5	**Enfield** (town) Halifax County
71	1877	12.0	**High Point** (city) Guilford County	145	n/a	15.5	**Spindale** (town) Rutherford County
72	n/a	12.1	**Dallas** (town) Gaston County	147	3362	15.6	**Archdale** (city) Randolph County
72	n/a	12.1	**Siler City** (town) Chatham County	147	n/a	15.6	**South Rosemary** (CDP) Halifax County
74	n/a	12.2	**Hillsborough** (town) Orange County	149	3399	15.7	**Burlington** (city) Alamance County
74	n/a	12.2	**Randleman** (city) Randolph County	149	n/a	15.7	**Lake Norman of Catawba** (CDP) Catawba County

Note: *The state column ranks the top/bottom 150 places in the state with population of 2,500 or more. The national column ranks the top/bottom places in the country with population of 10,000 or more. Places that are unincorporated were not considered in the rankings. n/a indicates data not available. Please refer to the User Guide for additional information.*

Males per 100 Females

Top 150 Places Ranked in *Descending* Order

State Rank	Nat'l Rank	Ratio	Place
1	n/a	420.8	**Polkton** (town) Anson County
2	n/a	145.8	**Windsor** (town) Bertie County
3	n/a	145.5	**Lillington** (town) Harnett County
4	38	142.6	**Jacksonville** (city) Onslow County
5	n/a	133.4	**Skippers Corner** (CDP) New Hanover County
6	n/a	127.0	**Burgaw** (town) Pender County
7	78	121.4	**Havelock** (city) Craven County
8	n/a	115.5	**Woodfin** (town) Buncombe County
9	n/a	109.8	**Marion** (city) McDowell County
10	n/a	106.6	**Kill Devil Hills** (town) Dare County
11	n/a	106.5	**Wentworth** (town) Rockingham County
12	n/a	105.6	**Maiden** (town) Catawba County
13	n/a	105.0	**Cullowhee** (CDP) Jackson County
14	n/a	104.8	**Tyro** (CDP) Davidson County
15	290	104.0	**Spring Lake** (town) Cumberland County
16	n/a	103.5	**Emerald Isle** (town) Carteret County
17	n/a	103.4	**Sneads Ferry** (CDP) Onslow County
18	n/a	102.5	**Carolina Beach** (town) New Hanover County
19	n/a	102.2	**Newport** (town) Carteret County
20	n/a	102.1	**Wesley Chapel** (village) Union County
21	n/a	101.9	**Lake Royale** (CDP) Franklin County
21	n/a	101.9	**Rolesville** (town) Wake County
23	n/a	101.2	**Fairview** (town) Union County
24	n/a	101.1	**Oak Ridge** (town) Guilford County
24	n/a	101.1	**Weddington** (town) Union County
26	516	101.0	**Summerfield** (town) Guilford County
27	n/a	100.9	**Marvin** (village) Union County
28	n/a	100.8	**Dana** (CDP) Henderson County
28	n/a	100.8	**Westport** (CDP) Lincoln County
30	n/a	100.6	**Red Oak** (town) Nash County
31	n/a	100.5	**Wallburg** (town) Davidson County
32	n/a	100.0	**East Rockingham** (CDP) Richmond County
33	n/a	99.9	**Unionville** (town) Union County
34	n/a	99.7	**Stokesdale** (town) Guilford County
35	n/a	99.5	**Gamewell** (town) Caldwell County
35	n/a	99.5	**Kings Grant** (CDP) New Hanover County
35	n/a	99.5	**Sawmills** (town) Caldwell County
35	n/a	99.5	**Spindale** (town) Rutherford County
39	n/a	99.3	**River Road** (CDP) Beaufort County
40	n/a	99.1	**Elroy** (CDP) Wayne County
40	n/a	99.1	**Lake Norman of Catawba** (CDP) Catawba County
42	n/a	98.9	**Nags Head** (town) Dare County
43	n/a	98.7	**Trinity** (city) Randolph County
44	n/a	98.4	**Midland** (town) Cabarrus County
45	n/a	98.3	**Hampstead** (CDP) Pender County
46	1043	98.1	**Salisbury** (city) Rowan County
47	n/a	98.0	**Mineral Springs** (town) Union County
48	n/a	97.6	**Kitty Hawk** (town) Dare County
49	n/a	97.5	**Hillsborough** (town) Orange County
49	n/a	97.5	**Midway** (town) Davidson County
51	n/a	97.4	**North Wilkesboro** (town) Wilkes County
52	n/a	97.3	**Boiling Spring Lakes** (city) Brunswick County
52	n/a	97.3	**Butner** (town) Granville County
52	n/a	97.3	**East Flat Rock** (CDP) Henderson County
55	1281	97.2	**Piney Green** (CDP) Onslow County
56	n/a	97.1	**Ogden** (CDP) New Hanover County
56	n/a	97.1	**Saint Stephens** (CDP) Catawba County
58	n/a	97.0	**Archer Lodge** (town) Johnston County
58	n/a	97.0	**James City** (CDP) Craven County
60	n/a	96.8	**Etowah** (CDP) Henderson County
60	1413	96.8	**Monroe** (city) Union County
62	1441	96.7	**Morrisville** (town) Wake County
62	n/a	96.7	**Saint James** (town) Brunswick County
64	n/a	96.6	**China Grove** (town) Rowan County
64	n/a	96.6	**Long View** (town) Catawba County
66	n/a	96.5	**Forest Oaks** (CDP) Guilford County
66	n/a	96.5	**Siler City** (town) Chatham County
68	1532	96.4	**Indian Trail** (town) Union County
69	n/a	96.3	**Oak Island** (town) Brunswick County
69	n/a	96.3	**Rockfish** (CDP) Hoke County
71	1598	96.2	**Huntersville** (town) Mecklenburg County
72	n/a	96.1	**Brices Creek** (CDP) Craven County
72	n/a	96.1	**Silver Lake** (CDP) New Hanover County
74	1685	96.0	**Cornelius** (town) Mecklenburg County
75	1730	95.9	**Harrisburg** (town) Cabarrus County
76	n/a	95.7	**Mountain View** (CDP) Catawba County
77	1882	95.5	**Mint Hill** (town) Mecklenburg County
78	1923	95.4	**Morganton** (city) Burke County
78	1923	95.4	**Mount Holly** (city) Gaston County
80	n/a	95.3	**Icard** (CDP) Burke County
80	n/a	95.3	**Ranlo** (town) Gaston County
82	n/a	95.2	**Mills River** (town) Henderson County
83	n/a	95.1	**Myrtle Grove** (CDP) New Hanover County
84	n/a	95.0	**Bessemer City** (city) Gaston County
84	n/a	95.0	**Wrightsboro** (CDP) New Hanover County
86	n/a	94.9	**Locust** (city) Stanly County
87	2171	94.8	**Cary** (town) Wake County
87	n/a	94.8	**Royal Pines** (CDP) Buncombe County
89	2207	94.7	**Apex** (town) Wake County
89	n/a	94.7	**Fairfield Harbour** (CDP) Craven County
89	2207	94.7	**Holly Springs** (town) Wake County
89	n/a	94.7	**Whispering Pines** (village) Moore County
93	2299	94.5	**Murraysville** (CDP) New Hanover County
94	n/a	94.4	**Granite Quarry** (town) Rowan County
94	n/a	94.4	**Swannanoa** (CDP) Buncombe County
96	n/a	94.3	**Brogden** (CDP) Wayne County
96	n/a	94.3	**Landis** (town) Rowan County
96	2363	94.3	**Lewisville** (town) Forsyth County
96	2363	94.3	**Mooresville** (town) Iredell County
100	n/a	94.2	**Mountain Home** (CDP) Henderson County
100	n/a	94.2	**Pleasant Garden** (town) Guilford County
100	2399	94.2	**Sanford** (city) Lee County
103	2431	94.1	**Belmont** (city) Gaston County
103	n/a	94.1	**Bethlehem** (CDP) Alexander County
103	n/a	94.1	**Half Moon** (CDP) Onslow County
106	2475	94.0	**Goldsboro** (city) Wayne County
106	n/a	94.0	**Southern Shores** (town) Dare County
108	2575	93.8	**Stallings** (town) Union County
109	2620	93.7	**Carrboro** (town) Orange County
109	n/a	93.7	**Waxhaw** (town) Union County
111	2672	93.6	**Fayetteville** (city) Cumberland County
112	2717	93.5	**Charlotte** (city) Mecklenburg County
112	2717	93.5	**Raleigh** (city) Wake County
112	n/a	93.5	**Welcome** (CDP) Davidson County
115	n/a	93.3	**Jamestown** (town) Guilford County
115	2806	93.3	**Lumberton** (city) Robeson County
115	n/a	93.3	**Sylva** (town) Jackson County
118	2846	93.2	**Leland** (town) Brunswick County
118	n/a	93.2	**Mar-Mac** (CDP) Wayne County
118	n/a	93.2	**Randleman** (city) Randolph County
121	2894	93.1	**Concord** (city) Cabarrus County
121	n/a	93.1	**Fairview** (CDP) Buncombe County
121	n/a	93.1	**Hudson** (town) Caldwell County
124	n/a	92.9	**Selma** (town) Johnston County
125	n/a	92.8	**Enochville** (CDP) Rowan County
125	2989	92.8	**Lexington** (city) Davidson County
127	3028	92.7	**Wake Forest** (town) Wake County
128	3076	92.6	**Matthews** (town) Mecklenburg County
129	n/a	92.5	**Flat Rock** (village) Henderson County
129	n/a	92.5	**Lowesville** (CDP) Lincoln County
129	n/a	92.5	**Moyock** (CDP) Currituck County
132	3144	92.4	**Boone** (town) Watauga County
133	n/a	92.3	**Cajah's Mountain** (town) Caldwell County
134	n/a	92.2	**Bayshore** (CDP) New Hanover County
134	n/a	92.2	**Seven Lakes** (CDP) Moore County
136	n/a	92.1	**South Rosemary** (CDP) Halifax County
137	3276	92.0	**Kannapolis** (city) Cabarrus County
138	n/a	91.9	**Eastover** (town) Cumberland County
139	n/a	91.8	**Canton** (town) Haywood County
139	n/a	91.8	**Creedmoor** (city) Granville County
139	n/a	91.8	**Liberty** (town) Randolph County
142	n/a	91.7	**Sunset Beach** (town) Brunswick County
143	n/a	91.6	**Granite Falls** (town) Caldwell County
143	n/a	91.6	**Walkertown** (town) Forsyth County
145	3481	91.4	**Newton** (city) Catawba County
145	3481	91.4	**Wilmington** (city) New Hanover County
147	3540	91.2	**Thomasville** (city) Davidson County
148	3566	91.1	**Clemmons** (village) Forsyth County
148	n/a	91.1	**Dallas** (town) Gaston County
148	3566	91.1	**Hickory** (city) Catawba County

Note: The state column ranks the top/bottom 150 places in the state with population of 2,500 or more. The national column ranks the top/bottom places in the country with population of 10,000 or more. Places that are unincorporated were not considered in the rankings. n/a indicates data not available. Please refer to the User Guide for additional information.

Males per 100 Females

Top 150 Places Ranked in *Ascending* Order

State Rank	Nat'l Rank	Ratio	Place	State Rank	Nat'l Rank	Ratio	Place
1	n/a	58.8	**Troy** (town) Montgomery County	74	353	87.2	**Pinehurst** (village) Moore County
2	n/a	73.6	**Williamston** (town) Martin County	77	364	87.3	**Knightdale** (town) Wake County
3	n/a	76.0	**Plymouth** (town) Washington County	77	n/a	87.3	**Winterville** (town) Pitt County
4	n/a	77.1	**Ahoskie** (town) Hertford County	79	n/a	87.4	**Waynesville** (town) Haywood County
4	n/a	77.1	**Elon** (town) Alamance County	80	387	87.5	**New Bern** (city) Craven County
6	n/a	77.4	**Enfield** (town) Halifax County	81	n/a	87.8	**Carolina Shores** (town) Brunswick County
7	n/a	78.2	**Brevard** (city) Transylvania County	81	n/a	87.8	**Lake Junaluska** (CDP) Haywood County
8	n/a	78.3	**Ayden** (town) Pitt County	83	435	88.0	**Burlington** (city) Alamance County
9	n/a	79.3	**Fairmont** (town) Robeson County	83	435	88.0	**Graham** (city) Alamance County
10	n/a	79.4	**Oxford** (city) Granville County	85	n/a	88.3	**Lowell** (city) Gaston County
11	27	79.9	**Henderson** (city) Vance County	85	n/a	88.3	**Raeford** (city) Hoke County
11	n/a	79.9	**Washington** (city) Beaufort County	87	494	88.4	**Kernersville** (town) Forsyth County
13	n/a	80.2	**Elizabethtown** (town) Bladen County	88	n/a	88.5	**Fletcher** (town) Henderson County
14	n/a	80.8	**Edenton** (town) Chowan County	88	504	88.5	**High Point** (city) Guilford County
14	n/a	80.8	**Valdese** (town) Burke County	90	n/a	88.6	**Spencer** (town) Rowan County
14	n/a	80.8	**Whiteville** (city) Columbus County	90	521	88.6	**Winston-Salem** (city) Forsyth County
17	45	80.9	**Hendersonville** (city) Henderson County	92	532	88.7	**Greensboro** (city) Guilford County
18	n/a	81.0	**Pineville** (town) Mecklenburg County	93	568	88.9	**Statesville** (city) Iredell County
19	n/a	81.1	**Farmville** (town) Pitt County	93	n/a	88.9	**Trent Woods** (town) Craven County
20	n/a	81.2	**Mount Olive** (town) Wayne County	95	n/a	89.0	**Elkin** (town) Surry County
21	n/a	81.3	**Forest City** (town) Rutherford County	95	n/a	89.0	**Murfreesboro** (town) Hertford County
22	n/a	81.4	**Buies Creek** (CDP) Harnett County	97	631	89.2	**Asheville** (city) Buncombe County
23	n/a	81.9	**Wadesboro** (town) Anson County	98	655	89.4	**Lincolnton** (city) Lincoln County
24	65	82.0	**Laurinburg** (city) Scotland County	99	n/a	89.5	**Boiling Springs** (town) Cleveland County
24	65	82.0	**Southern Pines** (town) Moore County	100	689	89.6	**Gastonia** (city) Gaston County
24	n/a	82.0	**Weaverville** (town) Buncombe County	101	n/a	89.7	**Conover** (city) Catawba County
27	n/a	82.3	**Mocksville** (town) Davie County	102	n/a	89.8	**Angier** (town) Harnett County
28	n/a	82.4	**Red Springs** (town) Robeson County	102	n/a	89.8	**Cherryville** (city) Gaston County
28	n/a	82.4	**Warsaw** (town) Duplin County	102	734	89.8	**Fuquay-Varina** (town) Wake County
30	77	82.5	**Reidsville** (city) Rockingham County	102	n/a	89.8	**Louisburg** (town) Franklin County
31	n/a	82.6	**Pembroke** (town) Robeson County	102	n/a	89.8	**Northchase** (CDP) New Hanover County
32	n/a	82.7	**Benson** (town) Johnston County	107	n/a	89.9	**Erwin** (town) Harnett County
33	n/a	82.8	**Dunn** (city) Harnett County	107	n/a	89.9	**Glen Raven** (CDP) Alamance County
34	n/a	82.9	**Roxboro** (city) Person County	109	n/a	90.0	**Porters Neck** (CDP) New Hanover County
35	87	83.0	**Kinston** (city) Lenoir County	110	n/a	90.2	**Beaufort** (town) Carteret County
36	n/a	83.7	**Black Mountain** (town) Buncombe County	111	838	90.3	**Davidson** (town) Mecklenburg County
36	n/a	83.7	**Pittsboro** (town) Chatham County	112	n/a	90.5	**Clinton** (city) Sampson County
38	125	84.1	**Tarboro** (town) Edgecombe County	112	893	90.5	**Garner** (town) Wake County
39	127	84.2	**Eden** (city) Rockingham County	114	921	90.6	**Clayton** (town) Johnston County
40	n/a	84.3	**King** (city) Stokes County	114	921	90.6	**Durham** (city) Durham County
40	131	84.3	**Rocky Mount** (city) Nash County	114	n/a	90.6	**Wingate** (town) Union County
42	n/a	84.4	**Wallace** (town) Duplin County	117	951	90.7	**Archdale** (city) Randolph County
43	143	84.5	**Elizabeth City** (city) Pasquotank County	118	975	90.8	**Asheboro** (city) Randolph County
43	143	84.5	**Mount Airy** (city) Surry County	118	975	90.8	**Lenoir** (city) Caldwell County
45	149	84.6	**Greenville** (city) Pitt County	120	n/a	90.9	**River Bend** (town) Craven County
45	n/a	84.6	**Tabor City** (town) Columbus County	121	1059	91.1	**Clemmons** (village) Forsyth County
45	n/a	84.6	**Zebulon** (town) Wake County	121	n/a	91.1	**Dallas** (town) Gaston County
48	165	84.8	**Roanoke Rapids** (city) Halifax County	121	1059	91.1	**Hickory** (city) Catawba County
49	n/a	84.9	**Lake Park** (village) Union County	121	n/a	91.1	**Rural Hall** (town) Forsyth County
49	n/a	84.9	**Rutherfordton** (town) Rutherford County	125	1091	91.2	**Thomasville** (city) Davidson County
51	180	85.1	**Hope Mills** (town) Cumberland County	126	1142	91.4	**Newton** (city) Catawba County
52	n/a	85.3	**Wendell** (town) Wake County	126	1142	91.4	**Wilmington** (city) New Hanover County
53	n/a	85.5	**Cramerton** (town) Gaston County	128	n/a	91.6	**Granite Falls** (town) Caldwell County
53	210	85.5	**Kings Mountain** (city) Cleveland County	128	n/a	91.6	**Walkertown** (town) Forsyth County
55	n/a	85.6	**Swansboro** (town) Onslow County	130	n/a	91.7	**Sunset Beach** (town) Brunswick County
56	n/a	85.7	**Hamlet** (city) Richmond County	131	n/a	91.8	**Canton** (town) Haywood County
56	n/a	85.7	**Nashville** (town) Nash County	131	n/a	91.8	**Creedmoor** (city) Granville County
58	n/a	85.9	**Grifton** (town) Pitt County	131	n/a	91.8	**Liberty** (town) Randolph County
58	237	85.9	**Mebane** (city) Alamance County	134	n/a	91.9	**Eastover** (town) Cumberland County
58	n/a	85.9	**Shallotte** (town) Brunswick County	135	1343	92.0	**Kannapolis** (city) Cabarrus County
61	n/a	86.0	**Gibsonville** (town) Guilford County	136	n/a	92.1	**South Rosemary** (CDP) Halifax County
62	n/a	86.1	**Franklin** (town) Macon County	137	n/a	92.2	**Bayshore** (CDP) New Hanover County
62	n/a	86.1	**Stanley** (town) Gaston County	137	n/a	92.2	**Seven Lakes** (CDP) Moore County
64	n/a	86.2	**Yadkinville** (town) Yadkin County	139	n/a	92.3	**Cajah's Mountain** (town) Caldwell County
65	n/a	86.3	**La Grange** (town) Lenoir County	140	1487	92.4	**Boone** (town) Watauga County
65	269	86.3	**Shelby** (city) Cleveland County	141	n/a	92.5	**Flat Rock** (village) Henderson County
65	269	86.3	**Smithfield** (town) Johnston County	141	n/a	92.5	**Lowesville** (CDP) Lincoln County
65	n/a	86.3	**Southport** (city) Brunswick County	141	n/a	92.5	**Moyock** (CDP) Currituck County
65	n/a	86.3	**Wilkesboro** (town) Wilkes County	144	1546	92.6	**Matthews** (town) Mecklenburg County
70	n/a	86.4	**Aberdeen** (town) Moore County	145	1581	92.7	**Wake Forest** (town) Wake County
71	n/a	87.0	**Morehead City** (town) Carteret County	146	n/a	92.8	**Enochville** (CDP) Rowan County
71	n/a	87.0	**Rockingham** (city) Richmond County	146	1629	92.8	**Lexington** (city) Davidson County
73	344	87.1	**Wilson** (city) Wilson County	148	n/a	92.9	**Selma** (town) Johnston County
74	353	87.2	**Albemarle** (city) Stanly County	149	1728	93.1	**Concord** (city) Cabarrus County
74	353	87.2	**Chapel Hill** (town) Orange County	149	n/a	93.1	**Fairview** (CDP) Buncombe County

Note: The state column ranks the top/bottom 150 places in the state with population of 2,500 or more. The national column ranks the top/bottom places in the country with population of 10,000 or more. Places that are unincorporated were not considered in the rankings. n/a indicates data not available. Please refer to the User Guide for additional information.

Marriage Status: Never Married

Top 150 Places Ranked in *Descending* Order

State Rank	Nat'l Rank	Percent	Place	State Rank	Nat'l Rank	Percent	Place
1	n/a	87.1	**Buies Creek** (CDP) Harnett County	75	n/a	33.3	**Dallas** (town) Gaston County
2	n/a	84.7	**Cullowhee** (CDP) Jackson County	77	1578	33.0	**Newton** (city) Catawba County
3	7	81.7	**Boone** (town) Watauga County	77	n/a	33.0	**Silver Lake** (CDP) New Hanover County
4	n/a	57.9	**Pembroke** (town) Robeson County	77	n/a	33.0	**Whiteville** (city) Columbus County
5	n/a	56.4	**Elon** (town) Alamance County	80	n/a	32.7	**Brevard** (city) Transylvania County
6	98	55.2	**Greenville** (city) Pitt County	80	n/a	32.7	**Clinton** (city) Sampson County
7	n/a	54.9	**Wingate** (town) Union County	82	1661	32.6	**Fayetteville** (city) Cumberland County
8	106	54.7	**Chapel Hill** (town) Orange County	82	n/a	32.6	**Wallace** (town) Duplin County
9	n/a	54.4	**Polkton** (town) Anson County	84	n/a	32.3	**Warsaw** (town) Duplin County
10	n/a	51.8	**Murfreesboro** (town) Hertford County	85	n/a	32.2	**South Rosemary** (CDP) Halifax County
11	n/a	47.2	**Enfield** (town) Halifax County	86	n/a	32.1	**Raeford** (city) Hoke County
12	n/a	46.4	**Boiling Springs** (town) Cleveland County	87	1793	32.0	**Havelock** (city) Craven County
13	n/a	45.7	**Mount Olive** (town) Wayne County	87	1793	32.0	**Lexington** (city) Davidson County
14	n/a	45.3	**Roxboro** (city) Person County	89	n/a	31.9	**Burgaw** (town) Pender County
15	354	44.4	**Elizabeth City** (city) Pasquotank County	90	n/a	31.8	**Edenton** (town) Chowan County
16	359	44.3	**Carrboro** (town) Orange County	91	n/a	31.7	**Kill Devil Hills** (town) Dare County
17	495	42.0	**Raleigh** (city) Wake County	91	n/a	31.7	**Swannanoa** (CDP) Buncombe County
18	520	41.5	**Durham** (city) Durham County	93	n/a	31.6	**Hamlet** (city) Richmond County
19	540	41.2	**Greensboro** (city) Guilford County	94	1929	31.5	**Monroe** (city) Union County
19	540	41.2	**Wilmington** (city) New Hanover County	94	1929	31.5	**Murraysville** (CDP) New Hanover County
21	n/a	41.0	**Selma** (town) Johnston County	96	n/a	30.9	**Marion** (city) McDowell County
22	597	40.5	**Henderson** (city) Vance County	97	n/a	30.8	**Pittsboro** (town) Chatham County
23	n/a	40.0	**Fairmont** (town) Robeson County	98	2130	30.7	**Burlington** (city) Alamance County
24	n/a	39.9	**Skippers Corner** (CDP) New Hanover County	98	n/a	30.7	**Newport** (town) Carteret County
25	n/a	39.2	**Elizabethtown** (town) Bladen County	100	2158	30.6	**Eden** (city) Rockingham County
26	730	38.9	**Charlotte** (city) Mecklenburg County	101	2241	30.2	**Thomasville** (city) Davidson County
27	n/a	38.8	**Woodfin** (town) Buncombe County	101	2241	30.2	**Washington** (city) Beaufort County
28	767	38.6	**Lumberton** (city) Robeson County	103	2357	29.8	**Kannapolis** (city) Cabarrus County
29	n/a	38.5	**Spencer** (town) Rowan County	104	n/a	29.7	**Grifton** (town) Pitt County
29	n/a	38.5	**Windsor** (town) Bertie County	105	n/a	29.6	**Forest City** (town) Rutherford County
31	783	38.4	**Winston-Salem** (city) Forsyth County	106	2423	29.5	**Asheboro** (city) Randolph County
32	829	37.9	**Kinston** (city) Lenoir County	106	n/a	29.5	**Sylva** (town) Jackson County
33	n/a	37.8	**Siler City** (town) Chatham County	108	2459	29.4	**Belmont** (city) Gaston County
34	847	37.7	**Davidson** (town) Mecklenburg County	108	2459	29.4	**Roanoke Rapids** (city) Halifax County
34	n/a	37.7	**North Wilkesboro** (town) Wilkes County	110	2541	29.1	**Albemarle** (city) Stanly County
36	894	37.4	**Salisbury** (city) Rowan County	111	2587	28.9	**New Bern** (city) Craven County
37	n/a	37.1	**Beaufort** (town) Carteret County	112	2646	28.7	**Graham** (city) Alamance County
37	n/a	37.1	**Pineville** (town) Mecklenburg County	112	2646	28.7	**Mooresville** (town) Iredell County
39	n/a	37.0	**Ahoskie** (town) Hertford County	112	n/a	28.7	**Williamston** (town) Martin County
39	936	37.0	**Jacksonville** (city) Onslow County	115	n/a	28.6	**Bessemer City** (city) Gaston County
39	n/a	37.0	**Louisburg** (town) Franklin County	116	n/a	28.4	**Elroy** (CDP) Wayne County
42	n/a	36.9	**Lillington** (town) Harnett County	116	n/a	28.4	**Walkertown** (town) Forsyth County
42	947	36.9	**Rocky Mount** (city) Nash County	118	n/a	28.3	**Kings Grant** (CDP) New Hanover County
42	n/a	36.9	**Zebulon** (town) Wake County	119	2802	28.2	**Kings Mountain** (city) Cleveland County
45	n/a	36.8	**Brogden** (CDP) Wayne County	119	2802	28.2	**Lincolnton** (city) Lincoln County
46	n/a	36.1	**Benson** (town) Johnston County	119	n/a	28.2	**Maiden** (town) Catawba County
47	n/a	36.0	**Creedmoor** (city) Granville County	119	n/a	28.2	**Tabor City** (town) Columbus County
48	1082	35.9	**Asheville** (city) Buncombe County	123	2834	28.1	**Concord** (city) Cabarrus County
49	1106	35.7	**Shelby** (city) Cleveland County	123	n/a	28.1	**Mineral Springs** (town) Union County
49	n/a	35.7	**Troy** (town) Montgomery County	123	2834	28.1	**Spring Lake** (town) Cumberland County
51	1124	35.5	**High Point** (city) Guilford County	126	n/a	28.0	**Wentworth** (town) Rockingham County
51	n/a	35.5	**Red Springs** (town) Robeson County	127	n/a	27.9	**East Flat Rock** (CDP) Henderson County
53	n/a	35.4	**Oxford** (city) Granville County	127	2901	27.9	**Mebane** (city) Alamance County
54	n/a	35.3	**Butner** (town) Granville County	129	n/a	27.7	**China Grove** (town) Rowan County
54	1158	35.3	**Goldsboro** (city) Wayne County	130	n/a	27.5	**Long View** (town) Catawba County
54	1158	35.3	**Laurinburg** (city) Scotland County	131	3068	27.3	**Smithfield** (town) Johnston County
54	1158	35.3	**Sanford** (city) Lee County	131	n/a	27.3	**Wilkesboro** (town) Wilkes County
58	n/a	35.1	**Plymouth** (town) Washington County	133	n/a	27.2	**Canton** (town) Haywood County
58	1192	35.1	**Wilson** (city) Wilson County	133	3100	27.2	**Cornelius** (town) Mecklenburg County
60	n/a	34.9	**Farmville** (town) Pitt County	133	n/a	27.2	**Hudson** (town) Caldwell County
60	1228	34.9	**Hickory** (city) Catawba County	133	n/a	27.2	**Midland** (town) Cabarrus County
60	1228	34.9	**Tarboro** (town) Edgecombe County	137	3134	27.1	**Reidsville** (city) Rockingham County
63	n/a	34.8	**Wadesboro** (town) Anson County	138	n/a	27.0	**Angier** (town) Harnett County
64	n/a	34.7	**Dunn** (city) Harnett County	138	n/a	27.0	**Fairview** (CDP) Buncombe County
65	n/a	34.6	**Nashville** (town) Nash County	140	3201	26.8	**Hope Mills** (town) Cumberland County
66	1312	34.4	**Statesville** (city) Iredell County	141	n/a	26.7	**Spindale** (town) Rutherford County
67	1342	34.3	**Gastonia** (city) Gaston County	142	n/a	26.6	**Glen Raven** (CDP) Alamance County
68	n/a	34.2	**Franklin** (town) Macon County	143	3302	26.5	**Cary** (town) Wake County
68	n/a	34.2	**Hillsborough** (town) Orange County	143	n/a	26.5	**Ranlo** (town) Gaston County
70	n/a	34.1	**Mocksville** (town) Davie County	145	3330	26.4	**Garner** (town) Wake County
70	1388	34.1	**Morganton** (city) Burke County	146	n/a	26.3	**Carolina Beach** (town) New Hanover County
72	n/a	33.7	**Rockingham** (city) Richmond County	146	3359	26.3	**Piney Green** (CDP) Onslow County
73	n/a	33.5	**East Rockingham** (CDP) Richmond County	146	n/a	26.3	**Tyro** (CDP) Davidson County
73	n/a	33.5	**Wrightsboro** (CDP) New Hanover County	149	3430	26.0	**Lenoir** (city) Caldwell County
75	n/a	33.3	**Ayden** (town) Pitt County	149	3430	26.0	**Mount Holly** (city) Gaston County

Note: *The state column ranks the top/bottom 150 places in the state with population of 2,500 or more. The national column ranks the top/bottom places in the country with population of 10,000 or more. Places that are unincorporated were not considered in the rankings. n/a indicates data not available. Please refer to the User Guide for additional information.*

Marriage Status: Never Married

Top 150 Places Ranked in *Ascending* Order

State Rank	Nat'l Rank	Percent	Place
1	n/a	2.5	**Saint James** (town) Brunswick County
2	n/a	7.7	**Sunset Beach** (town) Brunswick County
3	n/a	8.1	**Whispering Pines** (village) Moore County
4	n/a	8.3	**Carolina Shores** (town) Brunswick County
5	n/a	8.9	**Fairfield Harbour** (CDP) Craven County
6	n/a	11.5	**Seven Lakes** (CDP) Moore County
7	11	11.7	**Pinehurst** (village) Moore County
8	n/a	11.8	**Flat Rock** (village) Henderson County
8	n/a	11.8	**Westport** (CDP) Lincoln County
10	n/a	14.6	**Marvin** (village) Union County
11	n/a	15.0	**Brices Creek** (CDP) Craven County
12	n/a	15.2	**Porters Neck** (CDP) New Hanover County
13	n/a	15.3	**Trent Woods** (town) Craven County
14	n/a	15.6	**Lake Norman of Catawba** (CDP) Catawba County
15	n/a	16.3	**Cajah's Mountain** (town) Caldwell County
15	n/a	16.3	**Enochville** (CDP) Rowan County
15	n/a	16.3	**Hampstead** (CDP) Pender County
18	n/a	17.0	**River Bend** (town) Craven County
19	n/a	17.1	**King** (city) Stokes County
20	n/a	17.3	**Trinity** (city) Randolph County
21	n/a	17.4	**Red Oak** (town) Nash County
21	n/a	17.4	**Southport** (city) Brunswick County
23	n/a	17.5	**Etowah** (CDP) Henderson County
24	n/a	17.7	**Sneads Ferry** (CDP) Onslow County
24	n/a	17.7	**Unionville** (town) Union County
26	n/a	17.9	**Emerald Isle** (town) Carteret County
26	49	17.9	**Holly Springs** (town) Wake County
26	n/a	17.9	**Oak Island** (town) Brunswick County
29	n/a	18.0	**Elkin** (town) Surry County
30	n/a	18.3	**Mar-Mac** (CDP) Wayne County
31	74	18.5	**Summerfield** (town) Guilford County
32	80	18.8	**Leland** (town) Brunswick County
32	n/a	18.8	**Wallburg** (town) Davidson County
34	n/a	18.9	**Oak Ridge** (town) Guilford County
35	n/a	19.1	**Wesley Chapel** (village) Union County
36	100	19.3	**Mount Airy** (city) Surry County
36	n/a	19.3	**Moyock** (CDP) Currituck County
38	n/a	19.4	**Lake Royale** (CDP) Franklin County
38	n/a	19.4	**Midway** (town) Davidson County
38	n/a	19.4	**Southern Shores** (town) Dare County
41	n/a	19.7	**Dana** (CDP) Henderson County
41	n/a	19.7	**Lake Junaluska** (CDP) Haywood County
41	n/a	19.7	**Ogden** (CDP) New Hanover County
44	n/a	20.1	**Weaverville** (town) Buncombe County
45	n/a	20.4	**Locust** (city) Stanly County
46	n/a	20.6	**Rolesville** (town) Wake County
47	203	20.8	**Archdale** (city) Randolph County
47	n/a	20.8	**Waxhaw** (town) Union County
49	n/a	20.9	**Rural Hall** (town) Forsyth County
49	n/a	20.9	**Shallotte** (town) Brunswick County
51	n/a	21.3	**Mills River** (town) Henderson County
52	n/a	21.4	**Gibsonville** (town) Guilford County
52	262	21.4	**Lewisville** (town) Forsyth County
54	n/a	21.5	**Kitty Hawk** (town) Dare County
55	n/a	21.7	**Landis** (town) Rowan County
56	n/a	21.8	**Rockfish** (CDP) Hoke County
57	n/a	21.9	**Forest Oaks** (CDP) Guilford County
57	n/a	21.9	**James City** (CDP) Craven County
57	n/a	21.9	**Swansboro** (town) Onslow County
60	n/a	22.0	**River Road** (CDP) Beaufort County
60	334	22.0	**Wake Forest** (town) Wake County
62	n/a	22.1	**Valdese** (town) Burke County
63	365	22.2	**Clemmons** (village) Forsyth County
63	365	22.2	**Stallings** (town) Union County
65	n/a	22.4	**La Grange** (town) Lenoir County
65	n/a	22.4	**Lake Park** (village) Union County
65	n/a	22.4	**Welcome** (CDP) Davidson County
68	n/a	22.5	**Bayshore** (CDP) New Hanover County
69	n/a	22.6	**Cramerton** (town) Gaston County
69	n/a	22.6	**Saint Stephens** (CDP) Catawba County
71	n/a	22.7	**Bethlehem** (CDP) Alexander County
72	n/a	22.8	**Fairview** (town) Union County
73	n/a	22.9	**Nags Head** (town) Dare County
73	n/a	22.9	**Waynesville** (town) Haywood County
75	n/a	23.0	**Lowell** (city) Gaston County
76	n/a	23.1	**Yadkinville** (town) Yadkin County
77	n/a	23.2	**Granite Quarry** (town) Rowan County
78	593	23.3	**Harrisburg** (town) Cabarrus County
78	593	23.3	**Morrisville** (town) Wake County
80	n/a	23.4	**Aberdeen** (town) Moore County
80	n/a	23.4	**Black Mountain** (town) Buncombe County
80	613	23.4	**Indian Trail** (town) Union County
83	n/a	23.5	**Boiling Spring Lakes** (city) Brunswick County
83	n/a	23.5	**Eastover** (town) Cumberland County
85	671	23.6	**Kernersville** (town) Forsyth County
85	n/a	23.6	**Myrtle Grove** (CDP) New Hanover County
87	691	23.7	**Hendersonville** (city) Henderson County
88	748	24.0	**Fuquay-Varina** (town) Wake County
88	n/a	24.0	**Pleasant Garden** (town) Guilford County
88	n/a	24.0	**Stanley** (town) Gaston County
88	n/a	24.0	**Weddington** (town) Union County
92	794	24.2	**Matthews** (CDP) Mecklenburg County
93	n/a	24.3	**Wendell** (town) Wake County
94	n/a	24.4	**Half Moon** (CDP) Onslow County
94	831	24.4	**Huntersville** (town) Mecklenburg County
94	n/a	24.4	**Mountain Home** (CDP) Henderson County
94	n/a	24.4	**Royal Pines** (CDP) Buncombe County
94	n/a	24.4	**Stokesdale** (town) Guilford County
99	n/a	24.5	**Gamewell** (town) Caldwell County
99	n/a	24.5	**Icard** (CDP) Burke County
99	n/a	24.5	**Liberty** (town) Randolph County
99	n/a	24.5	**Northchase** (CDP) New Hanover County
103	884	24.6	**Clayton** (town) Johnston County
103	n/a	24.6	**Conover** (city) Catawba County
105	n/a	24.7	**Cherryville** (city) Gaston County
106	n/a	24.8	**Archer Lodge** (town) Johnston County
106	n/a	24.8	**Fletcher** (town) Henderson County
106	n/a	24.8	**Jamestown** (town) Guilford County
106	n/a	24.8	**Morehead City** (town) Carteret County
110	947	24.9	**Mint Hill** (town) Mecklenburg County
110	n/a	24.9	**Sawmills** (town) Caldwell County
112	965	25.0	**Apex** (town) Wake County
112	n/a	25.0	**Erwin** (town) Harnett County
112	n/a	25.0	**Rutherfordton** (town) Rutherford County
115	n/a	25.1	**Lowesville** (CDP) Lincoln County
116	n/a	25.3	**Winterville** (town) Pitt County
117	1083	25.5	**Southern Pines** (town) Moore County
118	n/a	25.6	**Granite Falls** (town) Caldwell County
118	1106	25.6	**Knightdale** (town) Wake County
120	n/a	25.7	**Mountain View** (CDP) Catawba County
120	n/a	25.7	**Randleman** (city) Randolph County
122	1203	26.0	**Lenoir** (city) Caldwell County
122	1203	26.0	**Mount Holly** (city) Gaston County
124	n/a	26.3	**Carolina Beach** (town) New Hanover County
124	1281	26.3	**Piney Green** (CDP) Onslow County
124	n/a	26.3	**Tyro** (CDP) Davidson County
127	1298	26.4	**Garner** (town) Wake County
128	1327	26.5	**Cary** (town) Wake County
128	n/a	26.5	**Ranlo** (town) Gaston County
130	n/a	26.6	**Glen Raven** (CDP) Alamance County
131	n/a	26.7	**Spindale** (town) Rutherford County
132	1419	26.8	**Hope Mills** (town) Cumberland County
133	n/a	27.0	**Angier** (town) Harnett County
133	n/a	27.0	**Fairview** (CDP) Buncombe County
135	1502	27.1	**Reidsville** (city) Rockingham County
136	n/a	27.2	**Canton** (town) Haywood County
136	1523	27.2	**Cornelius** (town) Mecklenburg County
136	n/a	27.2	**Hudson** (town) Caldwell County
136	n/a	27.2	**Midland** (town) Cabarrus County
140	1557	27.3	**Smithfield** (town) Johnston County
140	n/a	27.3	**Wilkesboro** (town) Wilkes County
142	n/a	27.5	**Long View** (town) Catawba County
143	n/a	27.7	**China Grove** (town) Rowan County
144	n/a	27.9	**East Flat Rock** (CDP) Henderson County
144	1728	27.9	**Mebane** (city) Alamance County
146	n/a	28.0	**Wentworth** (town) Rockingham County
147	1791	28.1	**Concord** (city) Cabarrus County
147	n/a	28.1	**Mineral Springs** (town) Union County
147	1791	28.1	**Spring Lake** (town) Cumberland County
150	1823	28.2	**Kings Mountain** (city) Cleveland County

Note: The state column ranks the top/bottom 150 places in the state with population of 2,500 or more. The national column ranks the top/bottom places in the country with population of 10,000 or more. Places that are unincorporated were not considered in the rankings. n/a indicates data not available. Please refer to the User Guide for additional information.

Marriage Status: Now Married

Top 150 Places Ranked in *Descending* Order

State Rank	Nat'l Rank	Percent	Place
1	n/a	89.7	**Saint James** (town) Brunswick County
2	n/a	82.1	**Marvin** (village) Union County
3	n/a	80.3	**Fairfield Harbour** (CDP) Craven County
4	n/a	80.1	**Sunset Beach** (town) Brunswick County
5	n/a	80.0	**Whispering Pines** (village) Moore County
6	n/a	78.3	**Brices Creek** (CDP) Craven County
7	n/a	75.8	**Flat Rock** (village) Henderson County
7	n/a	75.8	**Seven Lakes** (CDP) Moore County
9	24	72.3	**Pinehurst** (village) Moore County
10	n/a	72.2	**Westport** (CDP) Lincoln County
11	n/a	72.0	**Rolesville** (town) Wake County
12	n/a	71.7	**Unionville** (town) Union County
13	n/a	71.6	**Wesley Chapel** (village) Union County
14	n/a	71.5	**Lake Norman of Catawba** (CDP) Catawba County
15	n/a	71.4	**Porters Neck** (CDP) New Hanover County
16	n/a	71.3	**Red Oak** (town) Nash County
17	46	70.5	**Holly Springs** (town) Wake County
18	n/a	70.4	**Hampstead** (CDP) Pender County
19	n/a	70.3	**Dana** (CDP) Henderson County
19	n/a	70.3	**Wallburg** (town) Davidson County
21	n/a	70.2	**Oak Ridge** (town) Guilford County
21	n/a	70.2	**Waxhaw** (town) Union County
23	n/a	70.0	**Lake Royale** (CDP) Franklin County
24	n/a	69.9	**Fairview** (town) Union County
25	n/a	69.2	**Emerald Isle** (town) Carteret County
26	n/a	68.9	**Sneads Ferry** (CDP) Onslow County
27	86	68.7	**Summerfield** (town) Guilford County
28	n/a	68.5	**Weddington** (town) Union County
29	n/a	68.3	**Forest Oaks** (CDP) Guilford County
30	n/a	67.5	**Trent Woods** (town) Craven County
31	n/a	67.2	**Archer Lodge** (town) Johnston County
31	n/a	67.2	**Lake Junaluska** (CDP) Haywood County
33	n/a	67.1	**River Bend** (town) Craven County
34	171	66.9	**Harrisburg** (town) Cabarrus County
35	n/a	66.7	**Etowah** (CDP) Henderson County
36	199	66.3	**Indian Trail** (town) Union County
37	227	65.9	**Wake Forest** (town) Wake County
38	n/a	65.5	**Rockfish** (CDP) Hoke County
39	n/a	65.3	**Carolina Shores** (town) Brunswick County
39	262	65.3	**Leland** (town) Brunswick County
41	n/a	65.0	**Southern Shores** (town) Dare County
42	n/a	64.8	**Mar-Mac** (CDP) Wayne County
43	n/a	64.6	**Lowesville** (CDP) Lincoln County
44	n/a	64.4	**Stokesdale** (town) Guilford County
45	347	64.3	**Morrisville** (town) Wake County
46	360	64.2	**Stallings** (town) Union County
47	378	64.0	**Huntersville** (town) Mecklenburg County
48	n/a	63.7	**Half Moon** (CDP) Onslow County
49	416	63.6	**Apex** (town) Wake County
50	n/a	63.5	**Trinity** (city) Randolph County
51	n/a	63.4	**Midway** (town) Davidson County
51	n/a	63.4	**Moyock** (CDP) Currituck County
53	438	63.3	**Lewisville** (town) Forsyth County
54	n/a	63.1	**Mills River** (town) Henderson County
55	n/a	62.9	**Cajah's Mountain** (town) Caldwell County
55	466	62.9	**Mint Hill** (town) Mecklenburg County
57	512	62.5	**Clemmons** (village) Forsyth County
58	n/a	62.4	**Bayshore** (CDP) New Hanover County
58	525	62.4	**Cary** (town) Wake County
60	n/a	62.3	**Bethlehem** (CDP) Alexander County
61	n/a	62.0	**Pleasant Garden** (town) Guilford County
61	n/a	62.0	**Weaverville** (town) Buncombe County
63	n/a	61.9	**Mountain Home** (CDP) Henderson County
64	n/a	61.7	**Locust** (city) Stanly County
65	621	61.6	**Fuquay-Varina** (town) Wake County
66	n/a	61.5	**Enochville** (CDP) Rowan County
67	n/a	61.3	**James City** (CDP) Craven County
68	664	61.2	**Matthews** (town) Mecklenburg County
68	n/a	61.2	**River Road** (CDP) Beaufort County
68	n/a	61.2	**Welcome** (CDP) Davidson County
71	n/a	61.1	**Myrtle Grove** (CDP) New Hanover County
71	n/a	61.1	**Ogden** (CDP) New Hanover County
73	n/a	60.9	**King** (city) Stokes County
74	n/a	60.6	**Swansboro** (town) Onslow County
75	n/a	60.5	**Fairview** (CDP) Buncombe County
76	813	60.2	**Knightdale** (town) Wake County
77	n/a	60.1	**Lake Park** (village) Union County
78	n/a	59.9	**Royal Pines** (CDP) Buncombe County
79	n/a	59.8	**Eastover** (town) Cumberland County
79	n/a	59.8	**Granite Quarry** (town) Rowan County
81	n/a	59.7	**Gibsonville** (town) Guilford County
81	n/a	59.7	**Mineral Springs** (town) Union County
83	n/a	59.5	**Glen Raven** (CDP) Alamance County
84	n/a	59.3	**Winterville** (town) Pitt County
85	991	59.0	**Spring Lake** (town) Cumberland County
86	1006	58.9	**Piney Green** (CDP) Onslow County
87	1025	58.8	**Archdale** (city) Randolph County
88	n/a	58.7	**Rural Hall** (town) Forsyth County
89	n/a	58.1	**Shallotte** (town) Brunswick County
90	n/a	57.8	**Cramerton** (town) Gaston County
90	n/a	57.8	**Wentworth** (town) Rockingham County
92	n/a	57.6	**Tyro** (CDP) Davidson County
93	1260	57.3	**Havelock** (city) Craven County
94	n/a	57.2	**Elkin** (town) Surry County
94	n/a	57.2	**Midland** (town) Cabarrus County
96	1323	56.9	**Mount Airy** (city) Surry County
97	1339	56.8	**Kernersville** (town) Forsyth County
98	n/a	56.7	**Jamestown** (town) Guilford County
98	n/a	56.7	**Oak Island** (town) Brunswick County
100	n/a	56.6	**Boiling Spring Lakes** (city) Brunswick County
101	1399	56.5	**Mebane** (city) Alamance County
102	n/a	56.4	**Hudson** (town) Caldwell County
103	1443	56.3	**Clayton** (town) Johnston County
104	n/a	56.2	**Kings Grant** (CDP) New Hanover County
104	n/a	56.2	**La Grange** (town) Lenoir County
106	1495	56.0	**Mooresville** (town) Iredell County
107	1512	55.9	**Concord** (city) Cabarrus County
107	1512	55.9	**Cornelius** (town) Mecklenburg County
107	n/a	55.9	**Saint Stephens** (CDP) Catawba County
110	n/a	55.7	**Mountain View** (CDP) Catawba County
111	n/a	55.6	**Sawmills** (town) Caldwell County
112	n/a	55.5	**Kitty Hawk** (town) Dare County
112	1595	55.5	**Mount Holly** (city) Gaston County
114	1618	55.4	**Garner** (town) Wake County
115	n/a	55.1	**Stanley** (town) Gaston County
116	n/a	54.8	**Conover** (city) Catawba County
117	n/a	54.5	**Nags Head** (town) Dare County
118	n/a	54.3	**China Grove** (town) Rowan County
119	n/a	54.1	**Northchase** (CDP) New Hanover County
120	1895	54.0	**Murraysville** (CDP) New Hanover County
121	n/a	53.9	**Wendell** (town) Wake County
122	n/a	53.7	**Black Mountain** (town) Buncombe County
123	2003	53.5	**Hope Mills** (town) Cumberland County
124	n/a	53.4	**Fletcher** (town) Henderson County
125	n/a	53.1	**Cherryville** (city) Gaston County
126	n/a	52.4	**Canton** (town) Haywood County
127	n/a	52.3	**Silver Lake** (CDP) New Hanover County
128	2306	52.0	**Belmont** (city) Gaston County
129	n/a	51.8	**Liberty** (town) Randolph County
130	2375	51.7	**Jacksonville** (city) Onslow County
130	n/a	51.7	**Lowell** (city) Gaston County
132	2385	51.6	**Kannapolis** (city) Cabarrus County
133	n/a	51.5	**Ranlo** (town) Gaston County
134	n/a	51.3	**Granite Falls** (town) Caldwell County
134	2435	51.3	**Reidsville** (city) Rockingham County
134	2435	51.3	**Southern Pines** (town) Moore County
137	n/a	51.2	**Elroy** (CDP) Wayne County
138	2482	51.1	**Kings Mountain** (city) Cleveland County
139	n/a	51.0	**Icard** (CDP) Burke County
140	n/a	50.9	**Gamewell** (town) Caldwell County
140	n/a	50.9	**Long View** (town) Catawba County
140	2518	50.9	**Monroe** (city) Union County
140	n/a	50.9	**Rutherfordton** (town) Rutherford County
144	2535	50.8	**Davidson** (town) Mecklenburg County
145	n/a	50.5	**Angier** (town) Harnett County
146	n/a	50.4	**Randleman** (city) Randolph County
147	2651	50.3	**New Bern** (city) Craven County
147	n/a	50.3	**Waynesville** (town) Haywood County
149	n/a	50.1	**Valdese** (town) Burke County
149	n/a	50.1	**Walkertown** (town) Forsyth County

Note: *The state column ranks the top/bottom 150 places in the state with population of 2,500 or more. The national column ranks the top/bottom places in the country with population of 10,000 or more. Places that are unincorporated were not considered in the rankings. n/a indicates data not available. Please refer to the User Guide for additional information.*

Marriage Status: Now Married

Top 150 Places Ranked in *Ascending* Order

State Rank	Nat'l Rank	Percent	Place	State Rank	Nat'l Rank	Percent	Place
1	n/a	9.1	**Buies Creek** (CDP) Harnett County	75	1006	44.9	**Shelby** (city) Cleveland County
2	n/a	10.3	**Cullowhee** (CDP) Jackson County	77	1031	45.1	**Statesville** (city) Iredell County
3	5	11.8	**Boone** (town) Watauga County	78	n/a	45.4	**Grifton** (town) Pitt County
4	n/a	24.5	**Pembroke** (town) Robeson County	79	n/a	45.5	**Forest City** (town) Rutherford County
5	n/a	26.1	**Polkton** (town) Anson County	79	n/a	45.5	**Skippers Corner** (CDP) New Hanover County
6	n/a	31.1	**Roxboro** (city) Person County	81	n/a	45.7	**Brogden** (CDP) Wayne County
7	n/a	31.3	**Lillington** (town) Harnett County	81	1119	45.7	**Smithfield** (town) Johnston County
8	n/a	31.6	**Enfield** (town) Halifax County	83	n/a	45.9	**Hamlet** (city) Richmond County
9	n/a	31.9	**Mount Olive** (town) Wayne County	83	n/a	45.9	**Raeford** (city) Hoke County
10	136	32.2	**Greenville** (city) Pitt County	83	1149	45.9	**Wilson** (city) Wilson County
11	n/a	32.5	**Wingate** (town) Union County	86	n/a	46.2	**Hillsborough** (town) Orange County
12	n/a	32.7	**Elizabethtown** (town) Bladen County	87	1213	46.3	**Charlotte** (city) Mecklenburg County
13	n/a	33.2	**Elon** (town) Alamance County	87	n/a	46.3	**Spindale** (town) Rutherford County
14	n/a	34.2	**Pineville** (town) Mecklenburg County	89	n/a	46.5	**East Flat Rock** (CDP) Henderson County
15	n/a	35.1	**North Wilkesboro** (town) Wilkes County	89	n/a	46.5	**Siler City** (town) Chatham County
16	n/a	35.6	**Murfreesboro** (town) Hertford County	91	1264	46.6	**High Point** (city) Guilford County
17	n/a	36.1	**Whiteville** (city) Columbus County	91	1264	46.6	**Lenoir** (city) Caldwell County
18	285	36.5	**Elizabeth City** (city) Pasquotank County	93	n/a	46.7	**Mocksville** (town) Davie County
19	304	36.9	**Henderson** (city) Vance County	94	1307	46.8	**Lexington** (city) Davidson County
20	n/a	37.1	**Louisburg** (town) Franklin County	94	1307	46.8	**Sanford** (city) Lee County
21	n/a	37.2	**Selma** (town) Johnston County	94	n/a	46.8	**Sylva** (town) Jackson County
22	n/a	37.3	**Beaufort** (town) Carteret County	97	1361	47.1	**Lincolnton** (city) Lincoln County
23	331	37.5	**Chapel Hill** (town) Orange County	98	n/a	47.5	**Newport** (town) Carteret County
24	n/a	38.8	**Windsor** (town) Bertie County	99	n/a	47.6	**Dallas** (town) Gaston County
25	n/a	38.9	**Spencer** (town) Rowan County	99	1437	47.6	**Gastonia** (city) Gaston County
26	427	39.0	**Kinston** (city) Lenoir County	101	n/a	47.7	**Morehead City** (town) Carteret County
27	n/a	39.1	**Brevard** (city) Transylvania County	102	n/a	47.9	**Landis** (town) Rowan County
27	n/a	39.1	**Warsaw** (town) Duplin County	102	n/a	47.9	**Wilkesboro** (town) Wilkes County
29	n/a	39.3	**Franklin** (town) Macon County	102	n/a	47.9	**Yadkinville** (town) Yadkin County
30	n/a	39.7	**Zebulon** (town) Wake County	105	1535	48.1	**Hendersonville** (city) Henderson County
31	n/a	39.8	**Ahoskie** (town) Hertford County	106	1570	48.3	**Burlington** (city) Alamance County
32	n/a	39.9	**Woodfin** (town) Buncombe County	107	n/a	48.4	**Carolina Beach** (town) New Hanover County
33	498	40.1	**Laurinburg** (city) Scotland County	108	n/a	48.6	**Swannanoa** (CDP) Buncombe County
34	n/a	40.5	**Red Springs** (town) Robeson County	109	n/a	48.8	**Butner** (town) Granville County
35	546	40.7	**Salisbury** (city) Rowan County	110	n/a	49.1	**Creedmoor** (city) Granville County
36	n/a	41.0	**South Rosemary** (CDP) Halifax County	111	n/a	49.2	**Aberdeen** (town) Moore County
37	n/a	41.1	**Nashville** (town) Nash County	112	n/a	49.3	**Southport** (city) Brunswick County
38	n/a	41.3	**Boiling Springs** (town) Cleveland County	113	n/a	49.4	**Maiden** (town) Catawba County
38	n/a	41.3	**Washington** (town) Beaufort County	114	1808	49.5	**Fayetteville** (city) Cumberland County
40	n/a	41.4	**Fairmont** (town) Robeson County	114	1808	49.5	**Roanoke Rapids** (city) Halifax County
40	599	41.4	**Lumberton** (city) Robeson County	114	n/a	49.5	**Wallace** (town) Duplin County
40	599	41.4	**Wilmington** (city) New Hanover County	117	1837	49.6	**Graham** (city) Alamance County
43	n/a	41.5	**Dunn** (city) Harnett County	118	1854	49.7	**Asheboro** (city) Randolph County
43	n/a	41.5	**Wadesboro** (town) Anson County	119	n/a	49.8	**Erwin** (town) Harnett County
45	618	41.6	**Asheville** (city) Buncombe County	119	n/a	49.8	**Rockingham** (city) Richmond County
46	n/a	41.7	**Benson** (town) Johnston County	119	n/a	49.8	**Wrightsboro** (CDP) New Hanover County
46	n/a	41.7	**Tabor City** (town) Columbus County	122	n/a	50.1	**Valdese** (town) Burke County
48	n/a	41.9	**Marion** (city) McDowell County	122	n/a	50.1	**Walkertown** (town) Forsyth County
49	658	42.1	**Greensboro** (city) Guilford County	124	1986	50.3	**New Bern** (city) Craven County
50	676	42.3	**Morganton** (city) Burke County	124	n/a	50.3	**Waynesville** (town) Haywood County
51	n/a	42.6	**Edenton** (town) Chowan County	126	n/a	50.4	**Randleman** (city) Randolph County
52	n/a	43.0	**Kill Devil Hills** (town) Dare County	127	n/a	50.5	**Angier** (town) Harnett County
52	n/a	43.0	**Oxford** (city) Granville County	128	2100	50.8	**Davidson** (town) Mecklenburg County
52	n/a	43.0	**Pittsboro** (town) Chatham County	129	n/a	50.9	**Gamewell** (town) Caldwell County
52	n/a	43.0	**Williamston** (town) Martin County	129	n/a	50.9	**Long View** (town) Catawba County
56	n/a	43.1	**Burgaw** (town) Pender County	129	2122	50.9	**Monroe** (city) Union County
56	n/a	43.1	**Troy** (town) Montgomery County	129	n/a	50.9	**Rutherfordton** (town) Rutherford County
58	777	43.2	**Rocky Mount** (city) Nash County	133	n/a	51.0	**Icard** (CDP) Burke County
59	n/a	43.4	**Clinton** (city) Sampson County	134	2157	51.1	**Kings Mountain** (city) Cleveland County
59	804	43.4	**Goldsboro** (city) Wayne County	135	n/a	51.2	**Elroy** (CDP) Wayne County
61	830	43.6	**Durham** (city) Durham County	136	n/a	51.3	**Granite Falls** (town) Caldwell County
62	n/a	43.7	**Ayden** (town) Pitt County	136	2190	51.3	**Reidsville** (city) Rockingham County
63	858	43.8	**Eden** (city) Rockingham County	136	2190	51.3	**Southern Pines** (town) Moore County
63	858	43.8	**Raleigh** (city) Wake County	139	n/a	51.5	**Ranlo** (town) Gaston County
65	883	44.0	**Carrboro** (town) Orange County	140	2250	51.6	**Kannapolis** (city) Cabarrus County
66	n/a	44.1	**Farmville** (town) Pitt County	141	2272	51.7	**Jacksonville** (city) Onslow County
66	896	44.1	**Winston-Salem** (city) Forsyth County	141	n/a	51.7	**Lowell** (city) Gaston County
68	n/a	44.2	**East Rockingham** (CDP) Richmond County	143	n/a	51.8	**Liberty** (town) Randolph County
69	931	44.4	**Hickory** (city) Catawba County	144	2332	52.0	**Belmont** (city) Gaston County
70	956	44.6	**Albemarle** (city) Stanly County	145	n/a	52.3	**Silver Lake** (CDP) New Hanover County
70	n/a	44.6	**Plymouth** (town) Washington County	146	n/a	52.4	**Canton** (town) Haywood County
70	956	44.6	**Tarboro** (town) Edgecombe County	147	n/a	53.1	**Cherryville** (city) Gaston County
70	956	44.6	**Thomasville** (city) Davidson County	148	n/a	53.4	**Fletcher** (town) Henderson County
74	975	44.7	**Newton** (city) Catawba County	149	2625	53.5	**Hope Mills** (town) Cumberland County
75	n/a	44.9	**Bessemer City** (city) Gaston County	150	n/a	53.7	**Black Mountain** (town) Buncombe County

Note: *The state column ranks the top/bottom 150 places in the state with population of 2,500 or more. The national column ranks the top/bottom places in the country with population of 10,000 or more. Places that are unincorporated were not considered in the rankings. n/a indicates data not available. Please refer to the User Guide for additional information.*

Marriage Status: Separated

Top 150 Places Ranked in *Descending* Order

State Rank	Nat'l Rank	Percent	Place
1	n/a	16.1	**La Grange** (town) Lenoir County
2	n/a	8.5	**Elroy** (CDP) Wayne County
3	n/a	8.1	**Warsaw** (town) Duplin County
4	n/a	7.8	**Kitty Hawk** (town) Dare County
4	n/a	7.8	**South Rosemary** (CDP) Halifax County
6	n/a	7.7	**Southport** (city) Brunswick County
7	n/a	7.6	**Pineville** (town) Mecklenburg County
8	n/a	7.3	**Sylva** (town) Jackson County
9	5	7.1	**Reidsville** (city) Rockingham County
9	n/a	7.1	**Wilkesboro** (town) Wilkes County
11	n/a	7.0	**Tabor City** (town) Columbus County
12	n/a	6.9	**Oxford** (city) Granville County
13	n/a	6.8	**Enfield** (town) Halifax County
13	7	6.8	**Kings Mountain** (city) Cleveland County
13	n/a	6.8	**Pembroke** (town) Robeson County
13	n/a	6.8	**Raeford** (city) Hoke County
17	9	6.7	**Mount Airy** (city) Surry County
18	n/a	6.4	**Randleman** (city) Randolph County
19	n/a	6.3	**Troy** (town) Montgomery County
20	n/a	6.2	**Benson** (town) Johnston County
20	n/a	6.2	**Edenton** (town) Chowan County
20	n/a	6.2	**Farmville** (town) Pitt County
20	12	6.2	**Goldsboro** (city) Wayne County
20	12	6.2	**Kinston** (city) Lenoir County
20	n/a	6.2	**Rockingham** (city) Richmond County
26	n/a	6.1	**Creedmoor** (city) Granville County
26	n/a	6.1	**Mar-Mac** (CDP) Wayne County
26	n/a	6.1	**Selma** (town) Johnston County
26	15	6.1	**Tarboro** (town) Edgecombe County
30	n/a	6.0	**Black Mountain** (town) Buncombe County
30	n/a	6.0	**Long View** (town) Catawba County
32	n/a	5.9	**Angier** (town) Harnett County
32	n/a	5.9	**Burgaw** (town) Pender County
32	n/a	5.9	**Dana** (CDP) Henderson County
32	19	5.9	**Eden** (city) Rockingham County
36	21	5.8	**Laurinburg** (city) Scotland County
37	n/a	5.7	**Ahoskie** (town) Hertford County
38	30	5.6	**Asheboro** (city) Randolph County
38	30	5.6	**Lexington** (city) Davidson County
38	n/a	5.6	**Whiteville** (city) Columbus County
41	47	5.3	**Smithfield** (town) Johnston County
42	59	5.2	**Henderson** (city) Vance County
42	59	5.2	**Rocky Mount** (city) Nash County
44	n/a	5.1	**Carolina Beach** (town) New Hanover County
44	n/a	5.1	**Marion** (city) McDowell County
44	n/a	5.1	**Wallace** (town) Duplin County
47	n/a	5.0	**Clinton** (city) Sampson County
47	n/a	5.0	**Fairview** (town) Union County
47	75	5.0	**New Bern** (city) Craven County
50	87	4.9	**Garner** (town) Wake County
50	87	4.9	**Lumberton** (city) Robeson County
50	n/a	4.9	**Newport** (town) Carteret County
50	87	4.9	**Southern Pines** (town) Moore County
54	n/a	4.8	**Cramerton** (town) Gaston County
54	n/a	4.8	**Fairmont** (town) Robeson County
54	98	4.8	**Lenoir** (city) Caldwell County
54	n/a	4.8	**Polkton** (town) Anson County
54	98	4.8	**Salisbury** (city) Rowan County
59	n/a	4.7	**East Rockingham** (CDP) Richmond County
59	112	4.7	**Elizabeth City** (city) Pasquotank County
59	112	4.7	**Graham** (city) Alamance County
59	n/a	4.7	**Grifton** (town) Pitt County
59	n/a	4.7	**Red Springs** (town) Robeson County
59	n/a	4.7	**Spencer** (town) Rowan County
65	n/a	4.6	**River Bend** (town) Craven County
65	n/a	4.6	**Spindale** (town) Rutherford County
65	n/a	4.6	**Windsor** (town) Bertie County
65	n/a	4.6	**Zebulon** (town) Wake County
69	n/a	4.5	**Ayden** (town) Pitt County
69	n/a	4.5	**China Grove** (town) Rowan County
69	n/a	4.5	**Lillington** (town) Harnett County
72	n/a	4.4	**Rolesville** (town) Wake County
72	165	4.4	**Spring Lake** (town) Cumberland County
74	n/a	4.3	**Wallburg** (town) Davidson County
74	n/a	4.3	**Williamston** (town) Martin County
76	n/a	4.2	**Butner** (town) Granville County
76	n/a	4.2	**Lowell** (city) Gaston County
76	212	4.2	**Roanoke Rapids** (city) Halifax County
76	212	4.2	**Statesville** (city) Iredell County
76	n/a	4.2	**Stokesdale** (town) Guilford County
76	n/a	4.2	**Wadesboro** (town) Anson County
82	n/a	4.1	**Locust** (city) Stanly County
83	267	4.0	**Clayton** (town) Johnston County
83	267	4.0	**Fuquay-Varina** (town) Wake County
83	267	4.0	**Kannapolis** (city) Cabarrus County
86	n/a	3.9	**Bessemer City** (city) Gaston County
86	305	3.9	**Burlington** (city) Alamance County
86	n/a	3.9	**Gamewell** (town) Caldwell County
86	305	3.9	**Lincolnton** (city) Lincoln County
86	305	3.9	**Mount Holly** (city) Gaston County
86	n/a	3.9	**Unionville** (town) Union County
92	n/a	3.8	**Dunn** (city) Harnett County
92	n/a	3.8	**Elizabethtown** (town) Bladen County
92	n/a	3.8	**Erwin** (town) Harnett County
92	342	3.8	**Fayetteville** (city) Cumberland County
92	342	3.8	**Gastonia** (city) Gaston County
92	342	3.8	**High Point** (city) Guilford County
92	n/a	3.8	**Maiden** (town) Catawba County
92	n/a	3.8	**Ogden** (CDP) New Hanover County
92	n/a	3.8	**Pittsboro** (town) Chatham County
92	n/a	3.8	**Roxboro** (city) Person County
92	n/a	3.8	**Wentworth** (town) Rockingham County
103	387	3.7	**Mebane** (city) Alamance County
103	n/a	3.7	**Midland** (town) Cabarrus County
103	n/a	3.7	**Mocksville** (town) Davie County
103	n/a	3.7	**Morehead City** (town) Carteret County
103	387	3.7	**Newton** (city) Catawba County
103	n/a	3.7	**Plymouth** (town) Washington County
109	n/a	3.6	**Sawmills** (town) Caldwell County
109	438	3.6	**Wilson** (city) Wilson County
111	n/a	3.5	**Hillsborough** (town) Orange County
111	n/a	3.5	**Kill Devil Hills** (town) Dare County
111	n/a	3.5	**Nashville** (town) Nash County
111	n/a	3.5	**Oak Island** (town) Brunswick County
111	n/a	3.5	**Rural Hall** (town) Forsyth County
111	n/a	3.5	**Silver Lake** (CDP) New Hanover County
111	n/a	3.5	**Washington** (city) Beaufort County
111	n/a	3.5	**Yadkinville** (town) Yadkin County
119	554	3.4	**Asheville** (city) Buncombe County
119	n/a	3.4	**Dallas** (town) Gaston County
119	554	3.4	**Kernersville** (town) Forsyth County
119	n/a	3.4	**Kings Grant** (CDP) New Hanover County
119	n/a	3.4	**Mount Olive** (town) Wayne County
119	n/a	3.4	**Red Oak** (town) Nash County
119	554	3.4	**Sanford** (city) Lee County
119	n/a	3.4	**Walkertown** (town) Forsyth County
127	615	3.3	**Archdale** (city) Randolph County
127	n/a	3.3	**East Flat Rock** (CDP) Henderson County
127	n/a	3.3	**Forest City** (town) Rutherford County
127	615	3.3	**Havelock** (city) Craven County
127	615	3.3	**Morganton** (city) Burke County
127	615	3.3	**Shelby** (city) Cleveland County
127	n/a	3.3	**Waynesville** (town) Haywood County
134	686	3.2	**Belmont** (city) Gaston County
134	686	3.2	**Davidson** (town) Mecklenburg County
134	n/a	3.2	**Fletcher** (town) Henderson County
134	686	3.2	**Hope Mills** (town) Cumberland County
134	686	3.2	**Jacksonville** (city) Onslow County
134	686	3.2	**Knightdale** (town) Wake County
134	n/a	3.2	**Midway** (town) Davidson County
141	747	3.1	**Charlotte** (city) Mecklenburg County
141	n/a	3.1	**Landis** (town) Rowan County
143	n/a	3.0	**Beaufort** (town) Carteret County
143	815	3.0	**Greensboro** (city) Guilford County
143	n/a	3.0	**Hamlet** (city) Richmond County
143	815	3.0	**Hickory** (city) Catawba County
143	n/a	3.0	**North Wilkesboro** (town) Wilkes County
143	815	3.0	**Winston-Salem** (city) Forsyth County
149	906	2.9	**Durham** (city) Durham County
149	n/a	2.9	**Liberty** (town) Randolph County

Note: The state column ranks the top/bottom 150 places in the state with population of 2,500 or more. The national column ranks the top/bottom places in the country with population of 10,000 or more. Places that are unincorporated were not considered in the rankings. n/a indicates data not available. Please refer to the User Guide for additional information.

Marriage Status: Separated

Top 150 Places Ranked in *Ascending* Order

State Rank	Nat'l Rank	Percent	Place
1	n/a	0.0	**Buies Creek** (CDP) Harnett County
1	n/a	0.0	**Flat Rock** (village) Henderson County
1	n/a	0.0	**Saint James** (town) Brunswick County
4	24	0.2	**Boone** (town) Watauga County
5	n/a	0.4	**Glen Raven** (CDP) Alamance County
6	n/a	0.5	**Porters Neck** (CDP) New Hanover County
7	n/a	0.7	**Boiling Springs** (town) Cleveland County
7	n/a	0.7	**Lake Royale** (CDP) Franklin County
7	n/a	0.7	**Lowesville** (CDP) Lincoln County
7	n/a	0.7	**Royal Pines** (CDP) Buncombe County
7	n/a	0.7	**Westport** (CDP) Lincoln County
7	n/a	0.7	**Whispering Pines** (village) Moore County
13	n/a	0.8	**Granite Quarry** (town) Rowan County
13	n/a	0.8	**Hampstead** (CDP) Pender County
13	n/a	0.8	**Louisburg** (town) Franklin County
16	n/a	0.9	**Enochville** (CDP) Rowan County
16	n/a	0.9	**Fairview** (CDP) Buncombe County
16	n/a	0.9	**Marvin** (village) Union County
19	n/a	1.0	**Bayshore** (CDP) New Hanover County
19	n/a	1.0	**Fairfield Harbour** (CDP) Craven County
19	n/a	1.0	**Forest Oaks** (CDP) Guilford County
19	n/a	1.0	**Franklin** (town) Macon County
19	n/a	1.0	**Mountain Home** (CDP) Henderson County
19	n/a	1.0	**Rutherfordton** (town) Rutherford County
25	n/a	1.1	**Canton** (town) Haywood County
25	n/a	1.1	**Skippers Corner** (CDP) New Hanover County
25	923	1.1	**Summerfield** (town) Guilford County
25	n/a	1.1	**Trent Woods** (town) Craven County
29	1096	1.2	**Pinehurst** (village) Moore County
30	1281	1.3	**Harrisburg** (town) Cabarrus County
30	1281	1.3	**Huntersville** (town) Mecklenburg County
30	n/a	1.3	**Lake Park** (village) Union County
30	n/a	1.3	**Seven Lakes** (CDP) Moore County
30	n/a	1.3	**Southern Shores** (town) Dare County
30	n/a	1.3	**Sunset Beach** (town) Brunswick County
30	1281	1.3	**Wake Forest** (town) Wake County
37	1490	1.4	**Cary** (town) Wake County
37	1490	1.4	**Chapel Hill** (town) Orange County
37	1490	1.4	**Lewisville** (town) Forsyth County
37	n/a	1.4	**Mountain View** (CDP) Catawba County
37	1490	1.4	**Murraysville** (CDP) New Hanover County
37	n/a	1.4	**Wingate** (town) Union County
43	1674	1.5	**Apex** (town) Wake County
43	n/a	1.5	**Elon** (town) Alamance County
43	1674	1.5	**Holly Springs** (town) Wake County
43	n/a	1.5	**Jamestown** (town) Guilford County
43	n/a	1.5	**Nags Head** (town) Dare County
43	n/a	1.5	**Oak Ridge** (town) Guilford County
43	1674	1.5	**Stallings** (town) Union County
50	1866	1.6	**Cornelius** (town) Mecklenburg County
50	n/a	1.6	**Northchase** (CDP) New Hanover County
52	n/a	1.7	**Brevard** (city) Transylvania County
52	2054	1.7	**Mint Hill** (town) Mecklenburg County
52	n/a	1.7	**Shallotte** (town) Brunswick County
55	n/a	1.8	**King** (city) Stokes County
55	2235	1.8	**Matthews** (town) Mecklenburg County
55	n/a	1.8	**Saint Stephens** (CDP) Catawba County
55	n/a	1.8	**Sneads Ferry** (CDP) Onslow County
55	n/a	1.8	**Wesley Chapel** (village) Union County
60	n/a	1.9	**Cherryville** (city) Gaston County
60	n/a	1.9	**Gibsonville** (town) Guilford County
60	n/a	1.9	**Hudson** (town) Caldwell County
60	n/a	1.9	**Mineral Springs** (town) Union County
60	n/a	1.9	**Moyock** (CDP) Currituck County
60	n/a	1.9	**Pleasant Garden** (town) Guilford County
60	n/a	1.9	**Tyro** (CDP) Davidson County
60	n/a	1.9	**Welcome** (CDP) Davidson County
68	n/a	2.0	**Boiling Spring Lakes** (city) Brunswick County
68	n/a	2.0	**Brogden** (CDP) Wayne County
68	2539	2.0	**Carrboro** (town) Orange County
68	n/a	2.0	**Granite Falls** (town) Caldwell County
68	n/a	2.0	**River Road** (CDP) Beaufort County
68	n/a	2.0	**Rockfish** (CDP) Hoke County
68	n/a	2.0	**Trinity** (city) Randolph County
75	n/a	2.1	**Carolina Shores** (town) Brunswick County
75	n/a	2.1	**Icard** (CDP) Burke County
75	n/a	2.1	**Lake Junaluska** (CDP) Haywood County
75	n/a	2.1	**Myrtle Grove** (CDP) New Hanover County
75	n/a	2.1	**Waxhaw** (town) Union County
75	n/a	2.1	**Winterville** (town) Pitt County
81	2841	2.2	**Greenville** (city) Pitt County
81	2841	2.2	**Piney Green** (CDP) Onslow County
83	2981	2.3	**Albemarle** (city) Stanly County
83	n/a	2.3	**Cullowhee** (CDP) Jackson County
83	n/a	2.3	**Emerald Isle** (town) Carteret County
83	2981	2.3	**Mooresville** (town) Iredell County
83	n/a	2.3	**Weaverville** (town) Buncombe County
83	n/a	2.3	**Weddington** (town) Union County
83	n/a	2.3	**Wendell** (town) Wake County
90	3107	2.4	**Concord** (city) Cabarrus County
90	n/a	2.4	**Elkin** (town) Surry County
90	n/a	2.4	**Etowah** (CDP) Henderson County
90	3107	2.4	**Indian Trail** (town) Union County
90	n/a	2.4	**Valdese** (town) Burke County
95	n/a	2.5	**Bethlehem** (CDP) Alexander County
95	3238	2.5	**Clemmons** (village) Forsyth County
95	n/a	2.5	**James City** (CDP) Craven County
95	3238	2.5	**Monroe** (city) Union County
95	3238	2.5	**Morrisville** (town) Wake County
95	n/a	2.5	**Swansboro** (town) Onslow County
95	n/a	2.5	**Wrightsboro** (CDP) New Hanover County
102	n/a	2.6	**Brices Creek** (CDP) Craven County
102	n/a	2.6	**Conover** (city) Catawba County
102	n/a	2.6	**Eastover** (town) Cumberland County
102	n/a	2.6	**Half Moon** (CDP) Onslow County
102	3357	2.6	**Hendersonville** (city) Henderson County
102	3357	2.6	**Leland** (town) Brunswick County
102	n/a	2.6	**Mills River** (town) Henderson County
109	n/a	2.7	**Aberdeen** (town) Moore County
109	n/a	2.7	**Lake Norman of Catawba** (CDP) Catawba County
109	n/a	2.7	**Murfreesboro** (town) Hertford County
109	n/a	2.7	**Ranlo** (town) Gaston County
113	n/a	2.8	**Archer Lodge** (town) Johnston County
113	n/a	2.8	**Cajah's Mountain** (town) Caldwell County
113	n/a	2.8	**Siler City** (town) Chatham County
116	3652	2.9	**Durham** (city) Durham County
116	n/a	2.9	**Liberty** (town) Randolph County
116	3652	2.9	**Raleigh** (city) Wake County
116	n/a	2.9	**Stanley** (town) Gaston County
116	n/a	2.9	**Swannanoa** (CDP) Buncombe County
116	3652	2.9	**Thomasville** (city) Davidson County
116	3652	2.9	**Wilmington** (city) New Hanover County
116	n/a	2.9	**Woodfin** (town) Buncombe County
124	n/a	3.0	**Beaufort** (town) Carteret County
124	3751	3.0	**Greensboro** (city) Guilford County
124	n/a	3.0	**Hamlet** (city) Richmond County
124	3751	3.0	**Hickory** (city) Catawba County
124	n/a	3.0	**North Wilkesboro** (town) Wilkes County
124	3751	3.0	**Winston-Salem** (city) Forsyth County
130	3842	3.1	**Charlotte** (city) Mecklenburg County
130	n/a	3.1	**Landis** (town) Rowan County
132	3910	3.2	**Belmont** (city) Gaston County
132	3910	3.2	**Davidson** (town) Mecklenburg County
132	n/a	3.2	**Fletcher** (town) Henderson County
132	3910	3.2	**Hope Mills** (town) Cumberland County
132	3910	3.2	**Jacksonville** (city) Onslow County
132	3910	3.2	**Knightdale** (town) Wake County
132	n/a	3.2	**Midway** (town) Davidson County
139	3971	3.3	**Archdale** (city) Randolph County
139	n/a	3.3	**East Flat Rock** (CDP) Henderson County
139	n/a	3.3	**Forest City** (town) Rutherford County
139	3971	3.3	**Havelock** (city) Craven County
139	3971	3.3	**Morganton** (city) Burke County
139	3971	3.3	**Shelby** (city) Cleveland County
139	n/a	3.3	**Waynesville** (town) Haywood County
146	4042	3.4	**Asheville** (city) Buncombe County
146	n/a	3.4	**Dallas** (town) Gaston County
146	4042	3.4	**Kernersville** (town) Forsyth County
146	n/a	3.4	**Kings Grant** (CDP) New Hanover County
146	n/a	3.4	**Mount Olive** (town) Wayne County

Note: The state column ranks the top/bottom 150 places in the state with population of 2,500 or more. The national column ranks the top/bottom places in the country with population of 10,000 or more. Places that are unincorporated were not considered in the rankings. n/a indicates data not available. Please refer to the User Guide for additional information.

Marriage Status: Widowed

Top 150 Places Ranked in *Descending* Order

State Rank	Nat'l Rank	Percent	Place	State Rank	Nat'l Rank	Percent	Place
1	n/a	19.1	**Louisburg** (town) Franklin County	75	n/a	9.3	**Pittsboro** (town) Chatham County
2	n/a	18.7	**Williamston** (town) Martin County	77	n/a	9.2	**Benson** (town) Johnston County
3	n/a	18.1	**Valdese** (town) Burke County	77	n/a	9.2	**Raeford** (city) Hoke County
4	n/a	17.9	**Warsaw** (town) Duplin County	77	373	9.2	**Salisbury** (city) Rowan County
5	n/a	17.0	**Elizabethtown** (town) Bladen County	80	n/a	9.1	**Saint Stephens** (CDP) Catawba County
6	n/a	15.7	**Yadkinville** (town) Yadkin County	80	403	9.1	**Shelby** (city) Cleveland County
7	n/a	14.9	**Landis** (town) Rowan County	80	n/a	9.1	**Zebulon** (town) Wake County
8	n/a	14.5	**Brevard** (city) Transylvania County	83	433	9.0	**Eden** (city) Rockingham County
9	n/a	14.4	**South Rosemary** (CDP) Halifax County	83	n/a	9.0	**Windsor** (town) Bertie County
10	n/a	14.0	**Edenton** (town) Chowan County	85	452	8.9	**New Bern** (city) Craven County
10	23	14.0	**Hendersonville** (city) Henderson County	85	n/a	8.9	**Seven Lakes** (CDP) Moore County
12	n/a	13.9	**North Wilkesboro** (town) Wilkes County	87	n/a	8.8	**Boiling Spring Lakes** (city) Brunswick County
13	n/a	13.7	**Southport** (city) Brunswick County	88	514	8.7	**Graham** (city) Alamance County
14	27	13.5	**Smithfield** (town) Johnston County	88	n/a	8.7	**Oak Island** (town) Brunswick County
15	n/a	13.4	**Ayden** (town) Pitt County	88	n/a	8.7	**Whispering Pines** (village) Moore County
15	28	13.4	**Southern Pines** (town) Moore County	91	n/a	8.6	**East Flat Rock** (CDP) Henderson County
17	n/a	13.2	**Mount Olive** (town) Wayne County	91	n/a	8.6	**Gamewell** (town) Caldwell County
17	n/a	13.2	**Tabor City** (town) Columbus County	91	n/a	8.6	**King** (city) Stokes County
19	n/a	12.9	**Ahoskie** (town) Hertford County	91	n/a	8.6	**Woodfin** (town) Buncombe County
19	n/a	12.9	**Carolina Shores** (town) Brunswick County	95	n/a	8.5	**Granite Falls** (town) Caldwell County
21	n/a	12.7	**Plymouth** (town) Washington County	95	602	8.5	**Kings Mountain** (city) Cleveland County
21	n/a	12.7	**Washington** (city) Beaufort County	95	n/a	8.5	**Pembroke** (town) Robeson County
23	n/a	12.6	**Erwin** (town) Harnett County	98	n/a	8.4	**Fairmont** (town) Robeson County
24	n/a	12.5	**Roxboro** (city) Person County	98	648	8.4	**Lumberton** (city) Robeson County
25	n/a	12.4	**Elkin** (town) Surry County	100	696	8.3	**Asheboro** (city) Randolph County
26	n/a	12.2	**Marion** (city) McDowell County	100	696	8.3	**Goldsboro** (city) Wayne County
26	n/a	12.2	**Stanley** (town) Gaston County	100	n/a	8.3	**Locust** (city) Stanly County
26	n/a	12.2	**Wilkesboro** (town) Wilkes County	100	n/a	8.3	**Midway** (town) Davidson County
29	n/a	12.1	**Enochville** (CDP) Rowan County	100	n/a	8.3	**Rockingham** (city) Richmond County
29	n/a	12.1	**Farmville** (town) Pitt County	100	n/a	8.3	**Swansboro** (town) Onslow County
29	48	12.1	**Mount Airy** (city) Surry County	100	696	8.3	**Wilson** (city) Wilson County
29	n/a	12.1	**Pineville** (town) Mecklenburg County	107	n/a	8.2	**Fletcher** (town) Henderson County
33	n/a	11.8	**Wadesboro** (town) Anson County	107	743	8.2	**Rocky Mount** (city) Nash County
34	n/a	11.6	**Spindale** (town) Rutherford County	109	n/a	8.1	**Aberdeen** (town) Moore County
34	n/a	11.6	**Whiteville** (city) Columbus County	109	n/a	8.1	**Carolina Beach** (town) New Hanover County
36	n/a	11.4	**Cherryville** (city) Gaston County	109	n/a	8.1	**Weaverville** (town) Buncombe County
36	n/a	11.4	**Enfield** (town) Halifax County	112	833	8.0	**Hickory** (city) Catawba County
38	n/a	11.3	**Forest City** (town) Rutherford County	112	n/a	8.0	**Nashville** (town) Nash County
39	n/a	11.2	**Dunn** (city) Harnett County	112	833	8.0	**Sanford** (city) Lee County
39	n/a	11.2	**Red Springs** (town) Robeson County	115	n/a	7.9	**Mocksville** (town) Davie County
41	n/a	11.1	**Clinton** (city) Sampson County	115	n/a	7.9	**Skippers Corner** (CDP) New Hanover County
42	90	10.8	**Lincolnton** (city) Lincoln County	117	n/a	7.8	**Rural Hall** (town) Forsyth County
42	n/a	10.8	**Waynesville** (town) Haywood County	117	n/a	7.8	**Troy** (town) Montgomery County
44	99	10.7	**Albemarle** (city) Stanly County	119	986	7.7	**Lexington** (city) Davidson County
44	99	10.7	**Kinston** (city) Lenoir County	119	n/a	7.7	**Trent Woods** (town) Craven County
44	99	10.7	**Tarboro** (town) Edgecombe County	121	1048	7.6	**Asheville** (city) Buncombe County
47	n/a	10.6	**Bessemer City** (city) Gaston County	121	n/a	7.6	**Moyock** (CDP) Currituck County
47	n/a	10.6	**Franklin** (town) Macon County	123	n/a	7.5	**Cajah's Mountain** (town) Caldwell County
49	n/a	10.5	**Shallotte** (town) Brunswick County	123	n/a	7.5	**Elon** (town) Alamance County
50	n/a	10.4	**Hamlet** (city) Richmond County	123	n/a	7.5	**Maiden** (town) Catawba County
51	144	10.3	**Laurinburg** (city) Scotland County	123	n/a	7.5	**Mountain Home** (CDP) Henderson County
52	160	10.2	**Pinehurst** (village) Moore County	127	n/a	7.4	**Angier** (town) Harnett County
52	n/a	10.2	**Sylva** (town) Jackson County	127	n/a	7.4	**Newport** (town) Carteret County
54	n/a	10.1	**Burgaw** (town) Pender County	127	n/a	7.4	**River Bend** (town) Craven County
54	n/a	10.1	**Canton** (town) Haywood County	127	1177	7.4	**Statesville** (city) Iredell County
54	n/a	10.1	**Grifton** (town) Pitt County	131	n/a	7.3	**Beaufort** (town) Carteret County
54	n/a	10.1	**Long View** (town) Catawba County	131	1250	7.3	**Burlington** (city) Alamance County
58	197	10.0	**Newton** (city) Catawba County	131	n/a	7.3	**Dallas** (town) Gaston County
58	197	10.0	**Roanoke Rapids** (city) Halifax County	131	1250	7.3	**Garner** (town) Wake County
58	n/a	10.0	**Wendell** (town) Wake County	131	1250	7.3	**Monroe** (city) Union County
61	n/a	9.9	**Lillington** (town) Harnett County	131	n/a	7.3	**Selma** (town) Johnston County
62	234	9.8	**Lenoir** (city) Caldwell County	137	n/a	7.2	**China Grove** (town) Rowan County
62	n/a	9.8	**Lowell** (city) Gaston County	137	1323	7.2	**Elizabeth City** (city) Pasquotank County
62	n/a	9.8	**Morehead City** (town) Carteret County	137	n/a	7.2	**Fairfield Harbour** (CDP) Craven County
65	250	9.7	**Henderson** (city) Vance County	137	n/a	7.2	**Glen Raven** (CDP) Alamance County
65	n/a	9.7	**Rutherfordton** (town) Rutherford County	137	n/a	7.2	**Jamestown** (town) Guilford County
67	n/a	9.6	**Icard** (CDP) Burke County	137	n/a	7.2	**Nags Head** (town) Dare County
67	n/a	9.6	**Liberty** (town) Randolph County	137	n/a	7.2	**Ranlo** (town) Gaston County
67	282	9.6	**Thomasville** (city) Davidson County	137	n/a	7.2	**Silver Lake** (CDP) New Hanover County
70	n/a	9.5	**Randleman** (city) Randolph County	137	n/a	7.2	**Wallace** (town) Duplin County
70	304	9.5	**Reidsville** (city) Rockingham County	146	n/a	7.1	**Dana** (CDP) Henderson County
72	n/a	9.4	**Black Mountain** (town) Buncombe County	146	n/a	7.1	**Eastover** (town) Cumberland County
72	323	9.4	**Morganton** (city) Burke County	146	1398	7.1	**Gastonia** (city) Gaston County
72	n/a	9.4	**Walkertown** (town) Forsyth County	146	n/a	7.1	**James City** (CDP) Craven County
75	n/a	9.3	**Oxford** (city) Granville County	146	n/a	7.1	**Mills River** (town) Henderson County

Note: The state column ranks the top/bottom 150 places in the state with population of 2,500 or more. The national column ranks the top/bottom places in the country with population of 10,000 or more. Places that are unincorporated were not considered in the rankings. n/a indicates data not available. Please refer to the User Guide for additional information.

Marriage Status: Widowed

Top 150 Places Ranked in *Ascending* Order

State Rank	Nat'l Rank	Percent	Place		State Rank	Nat'l Rank	Percent	Place
1	n/a	0.7	**Rockfish** (CDP) Hoke County		76	n/a	5.5	**Bethlehem** (CDP) Alexander County
2	n/a	1.0	**Archer Lodge** (town) Johnston County		76	n/a	5.5	**Boiling Springs** (town) Cleveland County
3	n/a	1.6	**Cullowhee** (CDP) Jackson County		76	n/a	5.5	**Lake Park** (village) Union County
3	28	1.6	**Spring Lake** (town) Cumberland County		76	n/a	5.5	**Siler City** (town) Chatham County
5	n/a	1.8	**Buies Creek** (CDP) Harnett County		80	1891	5.6	**Wilmington** (city) New Hanover County
6	67	2.1	**Havelock** (city) Craven County		81	1974	5.7	**Mount Holly** (city) Gaston County
7	n/a	2.2	**Fairview** (CDP) Buncombe County		81	n/a	5.7	**Westport** (CDP) Lincoln County
7	n/a	2.2	**Marvin** (village) Union County		83	2083	5.8	**Greensboro** (city) Guilford County
9	82	2.3	**Boone** (town) Watauga County		84	2178	5.9	**Belmont** (city) Gaston County
10	117	2.5	**Holly Springs** (town) Wake County		84	n/a	5.9	**Cramerton** (town) Gaston County
10	n/a	2.5	**Lowesville** (CDP) Lincoln County		84	n/a	5.9	**Emerald Isle** (town) Carteret County
12	138	2.6	**Apex** (town) Wake County		84	n/a	5.9	**Sunset Beach** (town) Brunswick County
12	138	2.6	**Harrisburg** (town) Cabarrus County		88	n/a	6.0	**Elroy** (CDP) Wayne County
12	n/a	2.6	**Lake Royale** (CDP) Franklin County		88	n/a	6.0	**Lake Junaluska** (CDP) Haywood County
12	n/a	2.6	**Tyro** (CDP) Davidson County		88	n/a	6.0	**River Road** (CDP) Beaufort County
16	156	2.7	**Chapel Hill** (town) Orange County		91	n/a	6.1	**Sawmills** (town) Caldwell County
16	156	2.7	**Morrisville** (town) Wake County		92	n/a	6.2	**Butner** (town) Granville County
16	n/a	2.7	**Rolesville** (town) Wake County		92	n/a	6.2	**Wrightsboro** (CDP) New Hanover County
19	n/a	2.8	**Bayshore** (CDP) New Hanover County		94	2538	6.3	**High Point** (city) Guilford County
19	n/a	2.8	**Wesley Chapel** (village) Union County		94	n/a	6.3	**Kill Devil Hills** (town) Dare County
21	220	2.9	**Davidson** (town) Mecklenburg County		94	n/a	6.3	**Mountain View** (CDP) Catawba County
21	220	2.9	**Piney Green** (CDP) Onslow County		97	2619	6.4	**Clayton** (town) Johnston County
23	281	3.1	**Indian Trail** (town) Union County		97	n/a	6.4	**Hudson** (town) Caldwell County
23	n/a	3.1	**Northchase** (CDP) New Hanover County		97	n/a	6.4	**Midland** (town) Cabarrus County
25	307	3.2	**Carrboro** (town) Orange County		97	n/a	6.4	**Myrtle Grove** (CDP) New Hanover County
26	n/a	3.3	**Half Moon** (CDP) Onslow County		97	n/a	6.4	**Ogden** (CDP) New Hanover County
27	n/a	3.4	**Weddington** (town) Union County		102	n/a	6.5	**Brogden** (CDP) Wayne County
28	n/a	3.6	**Fairview** (town) Union County		102	n/a	6.5	**Hillsborough** (town) Orange County
28	478	3.6	**Jacksonville** (city) Onslow County		102	2721	6.5	**Hope Mills** (town) Cumberland County
28	n/a	3.6	**Wentworth** (town) Rockingham County		102	n/a	6.5	**Kings Grant** (CDP) New Hanover County
31	519	3.7	**Cary** (town) Wake County		106	n/a	6.6	**Conover** (city) Catawba County
31	519	3.7	**Huntersville** (town) Mecklenburg County		106	n/a	6.6	**Flat Rock** (village) Henderson County
31	n/a	3.7	**Sneads Ferry** (CDP) Onslow County		106	n/a	6.6	**Kitty Hawk** (town) Dare County
34	571	3.8	**Leland** (town) Brunswick County		106	n/a	6.6	**Pleasant Garden** (town) Guilford County
35	n/a	3.9	**Oak Ridge** (town) Guilford County		106	n/a	6.6	**Southern Shores** (town) Dare County
35	629	3.9	**Raleigh** (city) Wake County		111	n/a	6.7	**Etowah** (CDP) Henderson County
37	n/a	4.0	**Forest Oaks** (CDP) Guilford County		111	n/a	6.7	**La Grange** (town) Lenoir County
38	718	4.1	**Mint Hill** (town) Mecklenburg County		111	n/a	6.7	**Red Oak** (town) Nash County
38	n/a	4.1	**Royal Pines** (CDP) Buncombe County		111	2878	6.7	**Winston-Salem** (city) Forsyth County
38	n/a	4.1	**Wingate** (town) Union County		115	2951	6.8	**Kannapolis** (city) Cabarrus County
41	768	4.2	**Greenville** (city) Pitt County		115	2951	6.8	**Kernersville** (town) Forsyth County
41	768	4.2	**Wake Forest** (town) Wake County		117	n/a	6.9	**East Rockingham** (CDP) Richmond County
43	n/a	4.3	**Brices Creek** (CDP) Craven County		117	n/a	6.9	**Spencer** (town) Rowan County
44	n/a	4.4	**Mineral Springs** (town) Union County		119	n/a	7.0	**Murfreesboro** (town) Hertford County
44	n/a	4.4	**Polkton** (town) Anson County		120	n/a	7.1	**Dana** (CDP) Henderson County
44	n/a	4.4	**Stokesdale** (town) Guilford County		120	n/a	7.1	**Eastover** (town) Cumberland County
44	n/a	4.4	**Waxhaw** (town) Union County		120	3179	7.1	**Gastonia** (city) Gaston County
48	1039	4.6	**Charlotte** (city) Mecklenburg County		120	n/a	7.1	**James City** (CDP) Craven County
48	1039	4.6	**Cornelius** (town) Mecklenburg County		120	n/a	7.1	**Mills River** (town) Henderson County
48	n/a	4.6	**Creedmoor** (city) Granville County		120	n/a	7.1	**Porters Neck** (CDP) New Hanover County
51	1132	4.7	**Durham** (city) Durham County		120	n/a	7.1	**Welcome** (CDP) Davidson County
51	1132	4.7	**Stallings** (town) Union County		127	N/a	7.2	**China Grove** (town) Rowan County
51	n/a	4.7	**Swannanoa** (CDP) Buncombe County		127	3259	7.2	**Elizabeth City** (city) Pasquotank County
54	1218	4.8	**Knightdale** (town) Wake County		127	n/a	7.2	**Fairfield Harbour** (CDP) Craven County
54	n/a	4.8	**Mar-Mac** (CDP) Wayne County		127	n/a	7.2	**Glen Raven** (CDP) Alamance County
54	n/a	4.8	**Unionville** (town) Union County		127	n/a	7.2	**Jamestown** (town) Guilford County
57	n/a	4.9	**Granite Quarry** (town) Rowan County		127	n/a	7.2	**Nags Head** (town) Dare County
57	n/a	4.9	**Hampstead** (CDP) Pender County		127	n/a	7.2	**Ranlo** (town) Gaston County
57	1295	4.9	**Mooresville** (town) Iredell County		127	n/a	7.2	**Silver Lake** (CDP) New Hanover County
57	n/a	4.9	**Saint James** (town) Brunswick County		127	n/a	7.2	**Wallace** (town) Duplin County
57	1295	4.9	**Summerfield** (town) Guilford County		136	n/a	7.3	**Beaufort** (town) Carteret County
57	n/a	4.9	**Wallburg** (town) Davidson County		136	3334	7.3	**Burlington** (city) Alamance County
63	1384	5.0	**Concord** (city) Cabarrus County		136	n/a	7.3	**Dallas** (town) Gaston County
63	n/a	5.0	**Lake Norman of Catawba** (CDP) Catawba County		136	3334	7.3	**Garner** (town) Wake County
63	1384	5.0	**Murraysville** (CDP) New Hanover County		136	3334	7.3	**Monroe** (city) Union County
66	1457	5.1	**Archdale** (city) Randolph County		136	n/a	7.3	**Selma** (town) Johnston County
66	n/a	5.1	**Winterville** (town) Pitt County		142	n/a	7.4	**Angier** (town) Harnett County
68	n/a	5.2	**Gibsonville** (town) Guilford County		142	n/a	7.4	**Newport** (town) Carteret County
68	n/a	5.2	**Trinity** (city) Randolph County		142	n/a	7.4	**River Bend** (town) Craven County
70	1606	5.3	**Fayetteville** (city) Cumberland County		142	3407	7.4	**Statesville** (city) Iredell County
70	1606	5.3	**Fuquay-Varina** (town) Wake County		146	n/a	7.5	**Cajah's Mountain** (town) Caldwell County
70	1606	5.3	**Mebane** (city) Alamance County		146	n/a	7.5	**Elon** (town) Alamance County
73	1704	5.4	**Clemmons** (village) Forsyth County		146	n/a	7.5	**Maiden** (town) Catawba County
73	1704	5.4	**Lewisville** (town) Forsyth County		146	n/a	7.5	**Mountain Home** (CDP) Henderson County
73	1704	5.4	**Matthews** (town) Mecklenburg County		150	3547	7.6	**Asheville** (city) Buncombe County

Note: The state column ranks the top/bottom 150 places in the state with population of 2,500 or more. The national column ranks the top/bottom places in the country with population of 10,000 or more. Places that are unincorporated were not considered in the rankings. n/a indicates data not available. Please refer to the User Guide for additional information.

Marriage Status: Divorced

Top 150 Places Ranked in *Descending* Order

State Rank	Nat'l Rank	Percent	Place
1	n/a	21.8	**Lillington** (town) Harnett County
2	n/a	19.6	**Southport** (city) Brunswick County
3	n/a	19.3	**Aberdeen** (town) Moore County
3	n/a	19.3	**Whiteville** (city) Columbus County
5	n/a	19.0	**Kill Devil Hills** (town) Dare County
6	n/a	18.3	**Beaufort** (town) Carteret County
6	n/a	18.3	**Northchase** (CDP) New Hanover County
8	n/a	17.6	**Morehead City** (town) Carteret County
9	80	17.5	**Lenoir** (city) Caldwell County
10	n/a	17.3	**Carolina Beach** (town) New Hanover County
11	n/a	17.1	**East Flat Rock** (CDP) Henderson County
12	n/a	16.9	**Pittsboro** (town) Chatham County
12	n/a	16.9	**Tabor City** (town) Columbus County
14	n/a	16.8	**Oak Island** (town) Brunswick County
15	159	16.6	**Eden** (city) Rockingham County
16	n/a	16.5	**Pineville** (town) Mecklenburg County
17	n/a	16.4	**Kitty Hawk** (town) Dare County
17	n/a	16.4	**Nashville** (town) Nash County
19	n/a	16.0	**Gamewell** (town) Caldwell County
19	n/a	16.0	**Waynesville** (town) Haywood County
21	n/a	15.9	**Bessemer City** (city) Gaston County
21	n/a	15.9	**Franklin** (town) Macon County
23	n/a	15.8	**Washington** (city) Beaufort County
24	n/a	15.7	**Spencer** (town) Rowan County
25	306	15.6	**Albemarle** (city) Stanly County
26	n/a	15.5	**Landis** (town) Rowan County
26	n/a	15.5	**Spindale** (town) Rutherford County
26	321	15.5	**Thomasville** (city) Davidson County
29	n/a	15.4	**Lowell** (city) Gaston County
29	n/a	15.4	**Nags Head** (town) Dare County
31	n/a	15.3	**East Rockingham** (CDP) Richmond County
32	386	15.2	**Archdale** (city) Randolph County
33	n/a	15.1	**Angier** (town) Harnett County
34	n/a	15.0	**Icard** (CDP) Burke County
34	n/a	15.0	**Maiden** (town) Catawba County
34	n/a	15.0	**Marion** (city) McDowell County
34	n/a	15.0	**Polkton** (town) Anson County
34	n/a	15.0	**Swannanoa** (CDP) Buncombe County
39	464	14.9	**Asheville** (city) Buncombe County
39	n/a	14.9	**Burgaw** (town) Pender County
41	n/a	14.8	**Grifton** (town) Pitt County
41	n/a	14.8	**Ranlo** (town) Gaston County
43	n/a	14.7	**La Grange** (town) Lenoir County
44	n/a	14.6	**Granite Falls** (town) Caldwell County
45	n/a	14.5	**Selma** (town) Johnston County
46	n/a	14.4	**Elroy** (CDP) Wayne County
46	n/a	14.4	**Newport** (town) Carteret County
46	n/a	14.4	**Randleman** (city) Randolph County
49	637	14.3	**Hendersonville** (city) Henderson County
49	n/a	14.3	**Rutherfordton** (town) Rutherford County
51	667	14.2	**Laurinburg** (city) Scotland County
51	n/a	14.2	**Zebulon** (town) Wake County
53	n/a	14.1	**Liberty** (town) Randolph County
53	698	14.1	**Morganton** (city) Burke County
55	n/a	14.0	**Conover** (city) Catawba County
55	n/a	14.0	**Trinity** (city) Randolph County
57	n/a	13.8	**Gibsonville** (town) Guilford County
57	809	13.8	**Lincolnton** (city) Lincoln County
57	n/a	13.8	**Windsor** (town) Bertie County
60	n/a	13.7	**Brevard** (city) Transylvania County
60	850	13.7	**Burlington** (city) Alamance County
60	n/a	13.7	**Cramerton** (town) Gaston County
63	n/a	13.6	**Forest City** (town) Rutherford County
63	889	13.6	**Lexington** (city) Davidson County
65	n/a	13.5	**Carolina Shores** (town) Brunswick County
65	n/a	13.5	**Fletcher** (town) Henderson County
65	920	13.5	**Smithfield** (town) Johnston County
65	n/a	13.5	**Tyro** (CDP) Davidson County
69	n/a	13.4	**Black Mountain** (town) Buncombe County
69	n/a	13.4	**King** (city) Stokes County
69	n/a	13.4	**Sawmills** (town) Caldwell County
69	n/a	13.4	**Sylva** (town) Jackson County
69	n/a	13.4	**Troy** (town) Montgomery County
74	n/a	13.3	**Cajah's Mountain** (town) Caldwell County
74	n/a	13.3	**North Wilkesboro** (town) Wilkes County
74	n/a	13.3	**Yadkinville** (town) Yadkin County
77	n/a	13.2	**Hillsborough** (town) Orange County
77	1051	13.2	**Hope Mills** (town) Cumberland County
79	1134	13.0	**Goldsboro** (city) Wayne County
79	1134	13.0	**Statesville** (city) Iredell County
81	n/a	12.9	**Benson** (town) Johnston County
81	1186	12.9	**Graham** (city) Alamance County
81	1186	12.9	**Henderson** (city) Vance County
81	n/a	12.9	**Red Springs** (town) Robeson County
85	n/a	12.8	**Clinton** (city) Sampson County
85	1223	12.8	**Kernersville** (town) Forsyth County
85	1223	12.8	**Mount Holly** (city) Gaston County
85	n/a	12.8	**Ogden** (CDP) New Hanover County
85	n/a	12.8	**Raeford** (city) Hoke County
90	1270	12.7	**Belmont** (city) Gaston County
90	1270	12.7	**Clayton** (town) Johnston County
90	n/a	12.7	**Erwin** (town) Harnett County
90	1270	12.7	**Hickory** (city) Catawba County
90	n/a	12.7	**Woodfin** (town) Buncombe County
95	n/a	12.6	**Dunn** (city) Harnett County
95	1312	12.6	**Fayetteville** (city) Cumberland County
95	n/a	12.6	**Rural Hall** (town) Forsyth County
95	1312	12.6	**Salisbury** (city) Rowan County
95	n/a	12.6	**Wilkesboro** (town) Wilkes County
100	1361	12.5	**Asheboro** (city) Randolph County
100	n/a	12.5	**South Rosemary** (CDP) Halifax County
102	1398	12.4	**Kinston** (city) Lenoir County
102	n/a	12.4	**Oxford** (city) Granville County
102	n/a	12.4	**Saint Stephens** (CDP) Catawba County
105	n/a	12.3	**Bayshore** (CDP) New Hanover County
105	1444	12.3	**Cornelius** (town) Mecklenburg County
105	n/a	12.3	**Elkin** (town) Surry County
105	n/a	12.3	**Mountain View** (CDP) Catawba County
105	1444	12.3	**Newton** (city) Catawba County
110	1497	12.2	**Kings Mountain** (city) Cleveland County
110	n/a	12.2	**Mar-Mac** (CDP) Wayne County
112	n/a	12.1	**Granite Quarry** (town) Rowan County
112	n/a	12.1	**Hamlet** (city) Richmond County
112	1545	12.1	**Leland** (town) Brunswick County
112	1545	12.1	**Reidsville** (city) Rockingham County
112	n/a	12.1	**Walkertown** (town) Forsyth County
117	1604	12.0	**Elizabeth City** (city) Pasquotank County
117	1604	12.0	**New Bern** (city) Craven County
117	n/a	12.0	**Rockfish** (CDP) Hoke County
120	n/a	11.9	**Lake Park** (village) Union County
120	1646	11.9	**Piney Green** (CDP) Onslow County
120	1646	11.9	**Wilmington** (city) New Hanover County
123	n/a	11.8	**Dallas** (town) Gaston County
123	1695	11.8	**Kannapolis** (city) Cabarrus County
123	n/a	11.8	**Wadesboro** (town) Anson County
123	n/a	11.8	**Wendell** (town) Wake County
127	n/a	11.7	**Royal Pines** (CDP) Buncombe County
128	1804	11.6	**Lumberton** (city) Robeson County
128	1804	11.6	**Mount Airy** (city) Surry County
128	1804	11.6	**Rocky Mount** (city) Nash County
131	n/a	11.5	**Edenton** (town) Chowan County
131	1859	11.5	**High Point** (city) Guilford County
131	n/a	11.5	**Long View** (town) Catawba County
134	n/a	11.3	**Jamestown** (town) Guilford County
134	n/a	11.3	**Mocksville** (town) Davie County
136	n/a	11.2	**Boiling Spring Lakes** (city) Brunswick County
136	2009	11.2	**Roanoke Rapids** (city) Halifax County
136	2009	11.2	**Spring Lake** (town) Cumberland County
139	2066	11.1	**Concord** (city) Cabarrus County
139	n/a	11.1	**Elizabethtown** (town) Bladen County
141	n/a	11.0	**Brogden** (CDP) Wayne County
141	2111	11.0	**Gastonia** (city) Gaston County
141	n/a	11.0	**Roxboro** (city) Person County
144	2168	10.9	**Garner** (town) Wake County
145	n/a	10.8	**Cherryville** (city) Gaston County
145	n/a	10.8	**China Grove** (town) Rowan County
145	2216	10.8	**Greensboro** (city) Guilford County
145	2216	10.8	**Wilson** (city) Wilson County
145	2216	10.8	**Winston-Salem** (city) Forsyth County
150	n/a	10.7	**River Road** (CDP) Beaufort County

Note: *The state column ranks the top/bottom 150 places in the state with population of 2,500 or more. The national column ranks the top/bottom places in the country with population of 10,000 or more. Places that are unincorporated were not considered in the rankings. n/a indicates data not available. Please refer to the User Guide for additional information.*

Marriage Status: Divorced

Top 150 Places Ranked in *Ascending* Order

State Rank	Nat'l Rank	Percent	Place
1	n/a	1.1	**Marvin** (village) Union County
2	n/a	2.0	**Buies Creek** (CDP) Harnett County
3	n/a	2.4	**Brices Creek** (CDP) Craven County
4	n/a	2.8	**Dana** (CDP) Henderson County
5	n/a	2.9	**Elon** (town) Alamance County
5	n/a	2.9	**Saint James** (town) Brunswick County
7	n/a	3.2	**Whispering Pines** (village) Moore County
8	n/a	3.4	**Cullowhee** (CDP) Jackson County
9	n/a	3.5	**Fairfield Harbour** (CDP) Craven County
10	n/a	3.7	**Fairview** (town) Union County
11	n/a	3.8	**Seven Lakes** (CDP) Moore County
12	n/a	4.1	**Weddington** (town) Union County
13	61	4.2	**Boone** (town) Watauga County
14	n/a	4.6	**Red Oak** (town) Nash County
14	n/a	4.6	**Rolesville** (town) Wake County
14	n/a	4.6	**Waxhaw** (town) Union County
17	125	5.0	**Chapel Hill** (town) Orange County
18	n/a	5.6	**Murfreesboro** (town) Hertford County
19	n/a	5.7	**Flat Rock** (village) Henderson County
19	n/a	5.7	**Unionville** (town) Union County
21	n/a	5.8	**Forest Oaks** (CDP) Guilford County
21	251	5.8	**Pinehurst** (village) Moore County
23	n/a	5.9	**Wallburg** (town) Davidson County
24	n/a	6.2	**Mountain Home** (CDP) Henderson County
25	n/a	6.3	**Porters Neck** (CDP) New Hanover County
26	n/a	6.4	**Sunset Beach** (town) Brunswick County
27	n/a	6.5	**Wesley Chapel** (village) Union County
28	n/a	6.6	**Glen Raven** (CDP) Alamance County
29	n/a	6.7	**Boiling Springs** (town) Cleveland County
29	n/a	6.7	**Skippers Corner** (CDP) New Hanover County
31	n/a	6.8	**Louisburg** (town) Franklin County
32	n/a	6.9	**Stokesdale** (town) Guilford County
33	n/a	7.0	**Archer Lodge** (town) Johnston County
33	n/a	7.0	**Emerald Isle** (town) Carteret County
33	n/a	7.0	**Lake Junaluska** (CDP) Haywood County
33	n/a	7.0	**Oak Ridge** (town) Guilford County
37	620	7.2	**Harrisburg** (town) Cabarrus County
37	620	7.2	**Indian Trail** (town) Union County
39	655	7.3	**Cary** (town) Wake County
40	n/a	7.4	**Silver Lake** (CDP) New Hanover County
41	n/a	7.5	**Pleasant Garden** (town) Guilford County
42	n/a	7.6	**Plymouth** (town) Washington County
43	808	7.7	**Jacksonville** (city) Onslow County
44	n/a	7.8	**Lake Norman of Catawba** (CDP) Catawba County
44	n/a	7.8	**Lowesville** (CDP) Lincoln County
44	n/a	7.8	**Mineral Springs** (town) Union County
44	849	7.8	**Wake Forest** (town) Wake County
48	902	7.9	**Huntersville** (town) Mecklenburg County
48	902	7.9	**Summerfield** (town) Guilford County
50	n/a	8.0	**Lake Royale** (CDP) Franklin County
51	1000	8.1	**Mint Hill** (town) Mecklenburg County
52	n/a	8.3	**Rockingham** (city) Richmond County
53	1135	8.4	**Carrboro** (town) Orange County
53	1135	8.4	**Greenville** (city) Pitt County
53	n/a	8.4	**Hampstead** (CDP) Pender County
56	n/a	8.5	**River Bend** (town) Craven County
56	n/a	8.5	**Wingate** (town) Union County
58	n/a	8.6	**Half Moon** (CDP) Onslow County
58	1228	8.6	**Havelock** (city) Craven County
58	n/a	8.6	**Mills River** (town) Henderson County
61	1273	8.7	**Davidson** (town) Mecklenburg County
61	n/a	8.7	**Stanley** (town) Gaston County
63	1324	8.8	**Apex** (town) Wake County
63	n/a	8.8	**Midway** (town) Davidson County
63	1324	8.8	**Stallings** (town) Union County
66	n/a	8.9	**Farmville** (town) Pitt County
66	n/a	8.9	**Southern Shores** (town) Dare County
68	1426	9.0	**Fuquay-Varina** (town) Wake County
68	n/a	9.0	**Kings Grant** (CDP) New Hanover County
68	n/a	9.0	**Myrtle Grove** (CDP) New Hanover County
71	n/a	9.1	**Etowah** (CDP) Henderson County
71	1471	9.1	**Holly Springs** (town) Wake County
73	1512	9.2	**Matthews** (town) Mecklenburg County
73	n/a	9.2	**Midland** (town) Cabarrus County
73	n/a	9.2	**Mount Olive** (town) Wayne County
73	n/a	9.2	**Pembroke** (town) Robeson County
73	n/a	9.2	**Swansboro** (town) Onslow County
78	n/a	9.4	**Bethlehem** (CDP) Alexander County
78	1625	9.4	**Knightdale** (town) Wake County
78	n/a	9.4	**Welcome** (CDP) Davidson County
81	n/a	9.5	**Locust** (city) Stanly County
81	n/a	9.5	**Trent Woods** (town) Craven County
83	n/a	9.6	**Ayden** (town) Pitt County
83	n/a	9.6	**Butner** (town) Granville County
83	n/a	9.6	**Moyock** (CDP) Currituck County
83	1730	9.6	**Murraysville** (CDP) New Hanover County
83	n/a	9.6	**Williamston** (town) Martin County
88	n/a	9.7	**Eastover** (town) Cumberland County
88	n/a	9.7	**James City** (CDP) Craven County
88	n/a	9.7	**Sneads Ferry** (CDP) Onslow County
88	1775	9.7	**Tarboro** (town) Edgecombe County
88	n/a	9.7	**Valdese** (town) Burke County
93	n/a	9.8	**Enfield** (town) Halifax County
93	1823	9.8	**Morrisville** (town) Wake County
93	1823	9.8	**Southern Pines** (town) Moore County
93	n/a	9.8	**Weaverville** (town) Buncombe County
97	1878	9.9	**Lewisville** (town) Forsyth County
97	1878	9.9	**Sanford** (city) Lee County
99	1931	10.0	**Clemmons** (village) Forsyth County
100	n/a	10.1	**Enochville** (CDP) Rowan County
100	n/a	10.1	**Hudson** (town) Caldwell County
102	2055	10.2	**Durham** (city) Durham County
102	2055	10.2	**Shelby** (city) Cleveland County
102	n/a	10.2	**Siler City** (town) Chatham County
105	n/a	10.3	**Ahoskie** (town) Hertford County
105	n/a	10.3	**Canton** (town) Haywood County
105	2121	10.3	**Charlotte** (city) Mecklenburg County
105	n/a	10.3	**Creedmoor** (city) Granville County
105	n/a	10.3	**Fairmont** (town) Robeson County
105	n/a	10.3	**Fairview** (CDP) Buncombe County
105	2121	10.3	**Mebane** (city) Alamance County
105	2121	10.3	**Monroe** (city) Union County
105	2121	10.3	**Raleigh** (city) Wake County
105	n/a	10.3	**Westport** (CDP) Lincoln County
105	n/a	10.3	**Winterville** (town) Pitt County
116	2170	10.4	**Mooresville** (town) Iredell County
117	n/a	10.5	**Shallotte** (town) Brunswick County
117	n/a	10.5	**Wrightsboro** (CDP) New Hanover County
119	n/a	10.6	**Warsaw** (town) Duplin County
120	n/a	10.7	**River Road** (CDP) Beaufort County
120	n/a	10.7	**Wallace** (town) Duplin County
120	n/a	10.7	**Wentworth** (town) Rockingham County
123	n/a	10.8	**Cherryville** (city) Gaston County
123	n/a	10.8	**China Grove** (town) Rowan County
123	2380	10.8	**Greensboro** (city) Guilford County
123	2380	10.8	**Wilson** (city) Wilson County
123	2380	10.8	**Winston-Salem** (city) Forsyth County
128	2441	10.9	**Garner** (town) Wake County
129	n/a	11.0	**Brogden** (CDP) Wayne County
129	2489	11.0	**Gastonia** (city) Gaston County
129	n/a	11.0	**Roxboro** (city) Person County
132	2546	11.1	**Concord** (city) Cabarrus County
132	n/a	11.1	**Elizabethtown** (town) Bladen County
134	n/a	11.2	**Boiling Spring Lakes** (city) Brunswick County
134	2591	11.2	**Roanoke Rapids** (city) Halifax County
134	2591	11.2	**Spring Lake** (town) Cumberland County
137	n/a	11.3	**Jamestown** (town) Guilford County
137	n/a	11.3	**Mocksville** (town) Davie County
139	n/a	11.5	**Edenton** (town) Chowan County
139	2747	11.5	**High Point** (city) Guilford County
139	n/a	11.5	**Long View** (town) Catawba County
142	2798	11.6	**Lumberton** (city) Robeson County
142	2798	11.6	**Mount Airy** (city) Surry County
142	2798	11.6	**Rocky Mount** (city) Nash County
145	n/a	11.7	**Royal Pines** (CDP) Buncombe County
146	n/a	11.8	**Dallas** (town) Gaston County
146	2907	11.8	**Kannapolis** (city) Cabarrus County
146	n/a	11.8	**Wadesboro** (town) Anson County
146	n/a	11.8	**Wendell** (town) Wake County
150	n/a	11.9	**Lake Park** (village) Union County

Note: *The state column ranks the top/bottom 150 places in the state with population of 2,500 or more. The national column ranks the top/bottom places in the country with population of 10,000 or more. Places that are unincorporated were not considered in the rankings. n/a indicates data not available. Please refer to the User Guide for additional information.*

Foreign Born

Top 150 Places Ranked in *Descending* Order

State Rank	Nat'l Rank	Percent	Place	State Rank	Nat'l Rank	Percent	Place
1	n/a	32.2	**Siler City** (town) Chatham County	76	2497	7.7	**Holly Springs** (town) Wake County
2	n/a	30.5	**Selma** (town) Johnston County	77	n/a	7.6	**Buies Creek** (CDP) Harnett County
3	506	27.4	**Morrisville** (town) Wake County	77	2528	7.6	**Wake Forest** (town) Wake County
4	n/a	20.4	**River Road** (CDP) Beaufort County	79	n/a	7.5	**Marion** (city) McDowell County
5	887	20.2	**Carrboro** (town) Orange County	80	2588	7.4	**Mooresville** (town) Iredell County
6	945	19.3	**Cary** (town) Wake County	80	2588	7.4	**Mount Airy** (city) Surry County
7	980	18.8	**Monroe** (city) Union County	82	2615	7.3	**Archdale** (city) Randolph County
7	n/a	18.8	**Wallace** (town) Duplin County	82	n/a	7.3	**Rolesville** (town) Wake County
9	n/a	17.8	**Brogden** (CDP) Wayne County	82	2615	7.3	**Smithfield** (town) Johnston County
10	n/a	17.5	**Pineville** (town) Mecklenburg County	85	n/a	7.2	**Whispering Pines** (village) Moore County
11	n/a	16.9	**East Flat Rock** (CDP) Henderson County	85	2648	7.2	**Wilson** (city) Wilson County
12	1171	16.5	**Asheboro** (city) Randolph County	87	n/a	7.1	**Burgaw** (town) Pender County
13	1177	16.4	**Chapel Hill** (town) Orange County	87	2669	7.1	**Kannapolis** (city) Cabarrus County
14	n/a	15.1	**Skippers Corner** (CDP) New Hanover County	87	2669	7.1	**Kernersville** (town) Forsyth County
15	1309	15.0	**Charlotte** (city) Mecklenburg County	87	2669	7.1	**Lincolnton** (city) Lincoln County
16	n/a	14.9	**Franklin** (town) Macon County	87	n/a	7.1	**Mocksville** (town) Davie County
17	1363	14.6	**Durham** (city) Durham County	87	n/a	7.1	**Saint James** (town) Brunswick County
18	1374	14.5	**Sanford** (city) Lee County	93	n/a	7.0	**Cramerton** (town) Gaston County
19	n/a	13.7	**Mar-Mac** (CDP) Wayne County	93	n/a	7.0	**Long View** (town) Catawba County
19	1455	13.7	**Raleigh** (city) Wake County	93	2696	7.0	**Mount Holly** (city) Gaston County
21	n/a	13.0	**Landis** (town) Rowan County	93	n/a	7.0	**River Bend** (town) Craven County
22	n/a	12.7	**Zebulon** (town) Wake County	93	n/a	7.0	**Wingate** (town) Union County
23	n/a	12.6	**Elkin** (town) Surry County	98	2729	6.9	**Asheville** (city) Buncombe County
24	1611	12.3	**Knightdale** (town) Wake County	98	n/a	6.9	**Rural Hall** (town) Forsyth County
25	n/a	12.2	**Red Springs** (town) Robeson County	100	2782	6.7	**Huntersville** (town) Mecklenburg County
26	1645	12.1	**High Point** (city) Guilford County	100	2782	6.7	**Murraysville** (CDP) New Hanover County
27	1764	11.3	**Morganton** (city) Burke County	100	n/a	6.7	**Tyro** (CDP) Davidson County
28	1776	11.2	**Graham** (city) Alamance County	103	2839	6.5	**Davidson** (town) Mecklenburg County
28	1776	11.2	**Winston-Salem** (city) Forsyth County	103	2839	6.5	**Henderson** (city) Vance County
30	n/a	10.9	**Conover** (city) Catawba County	103	n/a	6.5	**North Wilkesboro** (town) Wilkes County
31	1871	10.7	**Greensboro** (city) Guilford County	106	2869	6.4	**Harrisburg** (town) Cabarrus County
31	n/a	10.7	**Mount Olive** (town) Wayne County	106	n/a	6.4	**Hillsborough** (town) Orange County
33	n/a	10.4	**China Grove** (town) Rowan County	106	n/a	6.4	**Kill Devil Hills** (town) Dare County
34	n/a	10.1	**Archer Lodge** (town) Johnston County	106	2869	6.4	**New Bern** (city) Craven County
34	1987	10.1	**Concord** (city) Cabarrus County	106	n/a	6.4	**Sylva** (town) Jackson County
34	1987	10.1	**Newton** (city) Catawba County	111	n/a	6.2	**Lillington** (town) Harnett County
37	2009	10.0	**Apex** (town) Wake County	111	2929	6.2	**Wilmington** (city) New Hanover County
37	2009	10.0	**Clemmons** (village) Forsyth County	113	2955	6.1	**Havelock** (city) Craven County
39	n/a	9.9	**Jamestown** (town) Guilford County	113	2955	6.1	**Lenoir** (city) Caldwell County
39	2031	9.9	**Lexington** (city) Davidson County	115	2990	6.0	**Fayetteville** (city) Cumberland County
41	n/a	9.8	**Angier** (town) Harnett County	116	3011	5.9	**Hope Mills** (town) Cumberland County
41	n/a	9.8	**Kings Grant** (CDP) New Hanover County	116	n/a	5.9	**Welcome** (CDP) Davidson County
43	2083	9.7	**Hickory** (city) Catawba County	118	3039	5.8	**Salisbury** (city) Rowan County
44	n/a	9.6	**Fairview** (CDP) Buncombe County	119	3070	5.7	**Leland** (town) Brunswick County
44	2099	9.6	**Hendersonville** (city) Henderson County	119	3070	5.7	**Mebane** (city) Alamance County
46	n/a	9.5	**Glen Raven** (CDP) Alamance County	119	n/a	5.7	**Roxboro** (city) Person County
46	n/a	9.5	**Saint Stephens** (CDP) Catawba County	122	3093	5.6	**Belmont** (city) Gaston County
46	n/a	9.5	**Silver Lake** (CDP) New Hanover County	122	n/a	5.6	**Northchase** (CDP) New Hanover County
49	n/a	9.3	**Lake Park** (village) Union County	122	3093	5.6	**Piney Green** (CDP) Onslow County
49	n/a	9.3	**Lowell** (city) Gaston County	122	3093	5.6	**Spring Lake** (town) Cumberland County
49	n/a	9.3	**Warsaw** (town) Duplin County	122	n/a	5.6	**Wendell** (town) Wake County
49	n/a	9.3	**Yadkinville** (town) Yadkin County	127	3128	5.5	**Clayton** (town) Johnston County
53	n/a	9.2	**Benson** (town) Johnston County	128	n/a	5.4	**Dana** (CDP) Henderson County
54	2240	8.9	**Burlington** (city) Alamance County	128	n/a	5.4	**Morehead City** (town) Carteret County
54	2240	8.9	**Cornelius** (town) Mecklenburg County	130	n/a	5.3	**Ranlo** (town) Gaston County
54	n/a	8.9	**East Rockingham** (CDP) Richmond County	130	3191	5.3	**Summerfield** (town) Guilford County
54	2240	8.9	**Fuquay-Varina** (town) Wake County	132	n/a	5.2	**Mills River** (town) Henderson County
54	n/a	8.9	**Marvin** (village) Union County	132	3225	5.2	**Pinehurst** (village) Moore County
54	n/a	8.9	**Pittsboro** (town) Chatham County	134	n/a	5.1	**Dunn** (city) Harnett County
54	n/a	8.9	**Weddington** (town) Union County	134	n/a	5.1	**Elroy** (CDP) Wayne County
61	2264	8.8	**Indian Trail** (town) Union County	134	3257	5.1	**Greenville** (city) Pitt County
61	n/a	8.8	**Mountain Home** (CDP) Henderson County	134	n/a	5.1	**Seven Lakes** (CDP) Moore County
63	2283	8.7	**Matthews** (town) Mecklenburg County	134	n/a	5.1	**Wilkesboro** (town) Wilkes County
64	2324	8.5	**Lumberton** (city) Robeson County	139	n/a	5.0	**Brevard** (city) Transylvania County
65	2346	8.4	**Statesville** (city) Iredell County	140	3329	4.9	**Goldsboro** (city) Wayne County
65	2346	8.4	**Thomasville** (city) Davidson County	140	n/a	4.9	**Whiteville** (city) Columbus County
67	n/a	8.3	**Waxhaw** (town) Union County	142	3363	4.8	**Jacksonville** (city) Onslow County
68	n/a	8.2	**Oak Ridge** (town) Guilford County	142	n/a	4.8	**Waynesville** (town) Haywood County
69	n/a	8.0	**Elizabethtown** (town) Bladen County	144	n/a	4.7	**Eastover** (town) Cumberland County
69	2429	8.0	**Southern Pines** (town) Moore County	144	n/a	4.7	**Nags Head** (town) Dare County
69	2429	8.0	**Stallings** (town) Union County	144	3401	4.7	**Tarboro** (town) Edgecombe County
72	2455	7.9	**Gastonia** (city) Gaston County	147	n/a	4.6	**Beaufort** (town) Carteret County
72	n/a	7.9	**Rockfish** (CDP) Hoke County	147	n/a	4.6	**Liberty** (town) Randolph County
72	n/a	7.9	**Woodfin** (town) Buncombe County	147	n/a	4.6	**Swannanoa** (CDP) Buncombe County
75	2475	7.8	**Mint Hill** (town) Mecklenburg County	150	n/a	4.5	**Butner** (town) Granville County

Note: The state column ranks the top/bottom 150 places in the state with population of 2,500 or more. The national column ranks the top/bottom places in the country with population of 10,000 or more. Places that are unincorporated were not considered in the rankings. n/a indicates data not available. Please refer to the User Guide for additional information.

Foreign Born

Top 150 Places Ranked in *Ascending* Order

State Rank	Nat'l Rank	Percent	Place
1	n/a	0.0	**Enfield** (town) Halifax County
1	n/a	0.0	**Midland** (town) Cabarrus County
1	n/a	0.0	**Nashville** (town) Nash County
1	n/a	0.0	**South Rosemary** (CDP) Halifax County
5	n/a	0.2	**Pembroke** (town) Robeson County
6	n/a	0.3	**Fairview** (town) Union County
6	n/a	0.3	**Stanley** (town) Gaston County
8	n/a	0.4	**Cajah's Mountain** (town) Caldwell County
8	n/a	0.4	**Plymouth** (town) Washington County
10	n/a	0.5	**La Grange** (town) Lenoir County
10	n/a	0.5	**Randleman** (city) Randolph County
10	n/a	0.5	**Walkertown** (town) Forsyth County
10	n/a	0.5	**Williamston** (town) Martin County
14	n/a	0.6	**King** (city) Stokes County
14	n/a	0.6	**Midway** (town) Davidson County
16	n/a	0.7	**Carolina Beach** (town) New Hanover County
16	n/a	0.7	**Tabor City** (town) Columbus County
18	n/a	1.0	**Farmville** (town) Pitt County
18	75	1.0	**Kings Mountain** (city) Cleveland County
18	n/a	1.0	**Sneads Ferry** (CDP) Onslow County
21	n/a	1.1	**Hampstead** (CDP) Pender County
22	n/a	1.3	**Lake Junaluska** (CDP) Haywood County
22	n/a	1.3	**Trent Woods** (town) Craven County
24	n/a	1.4	**Bessemer City** (city) Gaston County
24	n/a	1.4	**Gamewell** (town) Caldwell County
24	n/a	1.4	**Ogden** (CDP) New Hanover County
24	n/a	1.4	**Southport** (city) Brunswick County
28	n/a	1.5	**Hudson** (town) Caldwell County
28	182	1.5	**Roanoke Rapids** (city) Halifax County
28	n/a	1.5	**Wallburg** (town) Davidson County
28	n/a	1.5	**Windsor** (town) Bertie County
32	n/a	1.6	**Edenton** (town) Chowan County
32	n/a	1.6	**Half Moon** (CDP) Onslow County
32	n/a	1.6	**Locust** (city) Stanly County
32	n/a	1.6	**Lowesville** (CDP) Lincoln County
32	n/a	1.6	**Trinity** (city) Randolph County
37	n/a	1.7	**Black Mountain** (town) Buncombe County
37	n/a	1.7	**Forest Oaks** (CDP) Guilford County
37	n/a	1.7	**Pleasant Garden** (town) Guilford County
40	n/a	1.8	**Emerald Isle** (town) Carteret County
40	n/a	1.8	**Lake Norman of Catawba** (CDP) Catawba County
40	n/a	1.8	**Murfreesboro** (town) Hertford County
43	n/a	1.9	**Cullowhee** (CDP) Jackson County
43	n/a	1.9	**James City** (CDP) Craven County
43	n/a	1.9	**Red Oak** (town) Nash County
43	n/a	1.9	**Shallotte** (town) Brunswick County
47	n/a	2.0	**Brices Creek** (CDP) Craven County
47	319	2.0	**Kinston** (city) Lenoir County
49	n/a	2.1	**Cherryville** (city) Gaston County
49	n/a	2.1	**Spindale** (town) Rutherford County
49	n/a	2.1	**Unionville** (town) Union County
49	n/a	2.1	**Wentworth** (town) Rockingham County
49	n/a	2.1	**Wrightsboro** (CDP) New Hanover County
54	418	2.3	**Laurinburg** (city) Scotland County
54	n/a	2.3	**Spencer** (town) Rowan County
56	n/a	2.4	**Granite Quarry** (town) Rowan County
57	n/a	2.5	**Bethlehem** (CDP) Alexander County
57	n/a	2.5	**Boiling Spring Lakes** (city) Brunswick County
59	n/a	2.6	**Carolina Shores** (town) Brunswick County
59	n/a	2.6	**Enochville** (CDP) Rowan County
59	n/a	2.6	**Washington** (city) Beaufort County
62	n/a	2.7	**Ahoskie** (town) Hertford County
63	n/a	2.8	**Oak Island** (town) Brunswick County
63	572	2.8	**Reidsville** (city) Rockingham County
65	n/a	2.9	**Oxford** (city) Granville County
66	n/a	3.0	**Erwin** (town) Harnett County
66	n/a	3.0	**Wesley Chapel** (village) Union County
66	n/a	3.0	**Westport** (CDP) Lincoln County
69	n/a	3.1	**Creedmoor** (city) Granville County
69	688	3.1	**Elizabeth City** (city) Pasquotank County
69	n/a	3.1	**Mineral Springs** (town) Union County
69	n/a	3.1	**Mountain View** (CDP) Catawba County
69	n/a	3.1	**Rutherfordton** (town) Rutherford County
69	n/a	3.1	**Swansboro** (town) Onslow County
75	n/a	3.2	**Bayshore** (CDP) New Hanover County
75	n/a	3.2	**Boiling Springs** (town) Cleveland County
75	n/a	3.2	**Southern Shores** (town) Dare County
78	761	3.3	**Rocky Mount** (city) Nash County
78	n/a	3.3	**Sawmills** (town) Caldwell County
78	n/a	3.3	**Sunset Beach** (town) Brunswick County
81	n/a	3.4	**Myrtle Grove** (CDP) New Hanover County
82	n/a	3.5	**Ayden** (town) Pitt County
82	826	3.5	**Boone** (town) Watauga County
82	n/a	3.5	**Dallas** (town) Gaston County
82	n/a	3.5	**Maiden** (town) Catawba County
82	n/a	3.5	**Royal Pines** (CDP) Buncombe County
87	n/a	3.6	**Hamlet** (city) Richmond County
87	n/a	3.6	**Stokesdale** (town) Guilford County
89	902	3.7	**Albemarle** (city) Stanly County
89	n/a	3.7	**Elon** (town) Alamance County
89	n/a	3.7	**Kitty Hawk** (town) Dare County
89	n/a	3.7	**Lake Royale** (CDP) Franklin County
89	n/a	3.7	**Troy** (town) Montgomery County
94	934	3.8	**Eden** (city) Rockingham County
94	n/a	3.8	**Gibsonville** (town) Guilford County
94	934	3.8	**Shelby** (city) Cleveland County
97	n/a	3.9	**Icard** (CDP) Burke County
97	n/a	3.9	**Rockingham** (city) Richmond County
97	n/a	3.9	**Valdese** (town) Burke County
97	n/a	3.9	**Winterville** (town) Pitt County
101	n/a	4.0	**Flat Rock** (village) Henderson County
101	n/a	4.0	**Granite Falls** (town) Caldwell County
101	n/a	4.0	**Weaverville** (town) Buncombe County
104	n/a	4.1	**Etowah** (CDP) Henderson County
104	1032	4.1	**Lewisville** (town) Forsyth County
104	n/a	4.1	**Moyock** (CDP) Currituck County
104	n/a	4.1	**Wadesboro** (town) Anson County
108	n/a	4.2	**Clinton** (city) Sampson County
108	n/a	4.2	**Fairfield Harbour** (CDP) Craven County
108	n/a	4.2	**Grifton** (town) Pitt County
111	n/a	4.3	**Fletcher** (town) Henderson County
111	n/a	4.3	**Forest City** (town) Rutherford County
113	n/a	4.4	**Aberdeen** (town) Moore County
113	n/a	4.4	**Canton** (town) Haywood County
113	n/a	4.4	**Louisburg** (town) Franklin County
113	n/a	4.4	**Newport** (town) Carteret County
113	n/a	4.4	**Porters Neck** (CDP) New Hanover County
113	n/a	4.4	**Raeford** (city) Hoke County
119	n/a	4.5	**Butner** (town) Granville County
119	n/a	4.5	**Fairmont** (town) Robeson County
119	1168	4.5	**Garner** (town) Wake County
119	n/a	4.5	**Polkton** (town) Anson County
123	n/a	4.6	**Beaufort** (town) Carteret County
123	n/a	4.6	**Liberty** (town) Randolph County
123	n/a	4.6	**Swannanoa** (CDP) Buncombe County
126	n/a	4.7	**Eastover** (town) Cumberland County
126	n/a	4.7	**Nags Head** (town) Dare County
126	1224	4.7	**Tarboro** (town) Edgecombe County
129	1256	4.8	**Jacksonville** (city) Onslow County
129	n/a	4.8	**Waynesville** (town) Haywood County
131	1294	4.9	**Goldsboro** (city) Wayne County
131	n/a	4.9	**Whiteville** (city) Columbus County
133	n/a	5.0	**Brevard** (city) Transylvania County
134	n/a	5.1	**Dunn** (city) Harnett County
134	n/a	5.1	**Elroy** (CDP) Wayne County
134	1362	5.1	**Greenville** (city) Pitt County
134	n/a	5.1	**Seven Lakes** (CDP) Moore County
134	n/a	5.1	**Wilkesboro** (town) Wilkes County
139	n/a	5.2	**Mills River** (town) Henderson County
139	1400	5.2	**Pinehurst** (village) Moore County
141	n/a	5.3	**Ranlo** (town) Gaston County
141	1432	5.3	**Summerfield** (town) Guilford County
143	n/a	5.4	**Dana** (CDP) Henderson County
143	n/a	5.4	**Morehead City** (town) Carteret County
145	1492	5.5	**Clayton** (town) Johnston County
146	1529	5.6	**Belmont** (city) Gaston County
146	n/a	5.6	**Northchase** (CDP) New Hanover County
146	1529	5.6	**Piney Green** (CDP) Onslow County
146	1529	5.6	**Spring Lake** (town) Cumberland County
146	n/a	5.6	**Wendell** (town) Wake County

Note: The state column ranks the top/bottom 150 places in the state with population of 2,500 or more. The national column ranks the top/bottom places in the country with population of 10,000 or more. Places that are unincorporated were not considered in the rankings. n/a indicates data not available. Please refer to the User Guide for additional information.

Speak English Only at Home

Top 150 Places Ranked in *Descending* Order

State Rank	Nat'l Rank	Percent	Place
1	n/a	100.0	**Plymouth** (town) Washington County
2	n/a	99.8	**Enfield** (town) Halifax County
3	n/a	99.5	**Cajah's Mountain** (town) Caldwell County
3	n/a	99.5	**La Grange** (town) Lenoir County
3	n/a	99.5	**Williamston** (town) Martin County
6	n/a	99.3	**Midway** (town) Davidson County
6	n/a	99.3	**Pembroke** (town) Robeson County
8	n/a	99.2	**Hudson** (town) Caldwell County
9	n/a	99.0	**Hampstead** (CDP) Pender County
9	n/a	99.0	**Nashville** (town) Nash County
11	n/a	98.9	**Sawmills** (town) Caldwell County
11	n/a	98.9	**Tabor City** (town) Columbus County
13	n/a	98.8	**South Rosemary** (CDP) Halifax County
14	n/a	98.6	**Wallburg** (town) Davidson County
15	n/a	98.5	**Edenton** (town) Chowan County
16	n/a	98.3	**Fairview** (town) Union County
16	n/a	98.3	**Shallotte** (town) Brunswick County
16	n/a	98.3	**Spindale** (town) Rutherford County
19	n/a	98.2	**Boiling Spring Lakes** (city) Brunswick County
19	n/a	98.2	**Farmville** (town) Pitt County
19	n/a	98.2	**Midland** (town) Cabarrus County
22	n/a	98.1	**Stanley** (town) Gaston County
22	n/a	98.1	**Trent Woods** (town) Craven County
24	n/a	97.9	**Forest Oaks** (CDP) Guilford County
24	65	97.9	**Kings Mountain** (city) Cleveland County
26	n/a	97.8	**Kitty Hawk** (town) Dare County
26	n/a	97.8	**Moyock** (CDP) Currituck County
28	n/a	97.7	**Lake Norman of Catawba** (CDP) Catawba County
29	n/a	97.6	**Granite Quarry** (town) Rowan County
30	n/a	97.5	**Creedmoor** (city) Granville County
30	n/a	97.5	**King** (city) Stokes County
30	n/a	97.5	**Murfreesboro** (town) Hertford County
30	n/a	97.5	**Ogden** (CDP) New Hanover County
30	n/a	97.5	**Wentworth** (town) Rockingham County
35	n/a	97.4	**Carolina Beach** (town) New Hanover County
35	n/a	97.4	**Locust** (city) Stanly County
35	n/a	97.4	**Southport** (city) Brunswick County
38	n/a	97.3	**Etowah** (CDP) Henderson County
38	n/a	97.3	**Seven Lakes** (CDP) Moore County
40	n/a	97.2	**Oak Island** (town) Brunswick County
41	191	97.0	**Reidsville** (city) Rockingham County
42	n/a	96.9	**Sunset Beach** (town) Brunswick County
42	n/a	96.9	**Weaverville** (town) Buncombe County
44	n/a	96.8	**Eastover** (town) Cumberland County
44	n/a	96.8	**James City** (CDP) Craven County
44	n/a	96.8	**Red Oak** (town) Nash County
44	n/a	96.8	**Westport** (CDP) Lincoln County
48	n/a	96.7	**Swansboro** (town) Onslow County
49	n/a	96.6	**Black Mountain** (town) Buncombe County
49	n/a	96.6	**Half Moon** (CDP) Onslow County
49	n/a	96.6	**Windsor** (town) Bertie County
52	n/a	96.5	**Ahoskie** (town) Hertford County
52	n/a	96.5	**Grifton** (town) Pitt County
52	301	96.5	**Laurinburg** (city) Scotland County
52	n/a	96.5	**Lowesville** (CDP) Lincoln County
52	n/a	96.5	**Trinity** (city) Randolph County
52	n/a	96.5	**Unionville** (town) Union County
52	n/a	96.5	**Washington** (city) Beaufort County
59	n/a	96.4	**Boiling Springs** (town) Cleveland County
59	318	96.4	**Roanoke Rapids** (city) Halifax County
61	n/a	96.3	**Flat Rock** (village) Henderson County
61	n/a	96.3	**Spencer** (town) Rowan County
63	n/a	96.2	**Hamlet** (city) Richmond County
63	n/a	96.2	**Lake Junaluska** (CDP) Haywood County
63	n/a	96.2	**Royal Pines** (CDP) Buncombe County
63	n/a	96.2	**Wrightsboro** (CDP) New Hanover County
67	n/a	96.1	**Randleman** (city) Randolph County
68	n/a	96.0	**Enochville** (CDP) Rowan County
69	n/a	95.9	**Beaufort** (town) Carteret County
69	n/a	95.9	**Cherryville** (city) Gaston County
69	n/a	95.9	**Emerald Isle** (town) Carteret County
72	456	95.8	**Kinston** (city) Lenoir County
73	n/a	95.7	**Fairmont** (town) Robeson County
74	n/a	95.5	**Bethlehem** (CDP) Alexander County
74	n/a	95.5	**Southern Shores** (town) Dare County
74	n/a	95.5	**Walkertown** (town) Forsyth County
74	n/a	95.5	**Whispering Pines** (village) Moore County
78	n/a	95.4	**Swannanoa** (CDP) Buncombe County
79	n/a	95.3	**Fletcher** (town) Henderson County
79	594	95.3	**Rocky Mount** (city) Nash County
81	n/a	95.2	**Bessemer City** (city) Gaston County
82	n/a	95.1	**Canton** (town) Haywood County
82	n/a	95.1	**Oxford** (city) Granville County
84	n/a	95.0	**Wesley Chapel** (village) Union County
85	n/a	94.9	**Waynesville** (town) Haywood County
86	742	94.8	**Pinehurst** (village) Moore County
87	794	94.6	**Eden** (city) Rockingham County
87	794	94.6	**Lewisville** (town) Forsyth County
87	n/a	94.6	**Porters Neck** (CDP) New Hanover County
87	n/a	94.6	**Saint James** (town) Brunswick County
87	794	94.6	**Shelby** (city) Cleveland County
92	n/a	94.5	**Lake Royale** (CDP) Franklin County
93	n/a	94.3	**Aberdeen** (town) Moore County
93	n/a	94.3	**Pleasant Garden** (town) Guilford County
93	n/a	94.3	**Rutherfordton** (town) Rutherford County
96	n/a	94.2	**Dallas** (town) Gaston County
96	n/a	94.2	**Newport** (town) Carteret County
98	n/a	94.1	**Carolina Shores** (town) Brunswick County
98	n/a	94.1	**Cullowhee** (CDP) Jackson County
98	n/a	94.1	**Maiden** (town) Catawba County
98	n/a	94.1	**Mills River** (town) Henderson County
98	n/a	94.1	**Morehead City** (town) Carteret County
98	n/a	94.1	**Polkton** (town) Anson County
98	904	94.1	**Tarboro** (town) Edgecombe County
105	n/a	94.0	**Brices Creek** (CDP) Craven County
105	n/a	94.0	**Mountain View** (CDP) Catawba County
107	n/a	93.9	**Burgaw** (town) Pender County
107	n/a	93.9	**Fairfield Harbour** (CDP) Craven County
109	n/a	93.7	**Bayshore** (CDP) New Hanover County
109	998	93.7	**Boone** (town) Watauga County
109	n/a	93.7	**Rockingham** (city) Richmond County
112	n/a	93.5	**Myrtle Grove** (CDP) New Hanover County
113	1071	93.4	**Davidson** (town) Mecklenburg County
113	n/a	93.4	**Wilkesboro** (town) Wilkes County
115	n/a	93.3	**Granite Falls** (town) Caldwell County
115	n/a	93.3	**Stokesdale** (town) Guilford County
115	n/a	93.3	**Wadesboro** (town) Anson County
118	n/a	93.2	**Elon** (town) Alamance County
119	n/a	93.1	**Gamewell** (town) Caldwell County
119	n/a	93.1	**Icard** (CDP) Burke County
119	n/a	93.1	**Louisburg** (town) Franklin County
119	1144	93.1	**Mebane** (city) Alamance County
119	n/a	93.1	**Valdese** (town) Burke County
119	n/a	93.1	**Winterville** (town) Pitt County
125	1168	93.0	**Belmont** (city) Gaston County
125	n/a	93.0	**River Bend** (town) Craven County
125	1168	93.0	**Summerfield** (town) Guilford County
128	n/a	92.9	**Forest City** (town) Rutherford County
128	1194	92.9	**Garner** (town) Wake County
128	n/a	92.9	**Gibsonville** (town) Guilford County
128	1194	92.9	**Greenville** (city) Pitt County
132	n/a	92.8	**North Wilkesboro** (town) Wilkes County
133	n/a	92.7	**Raeford** (city) Hoke County
134	n/a	92.6	**Brevard** (city) Transylvania County
134	n/a	92.6	**Erwin** (town) Harnett County
136	1296	92.5	**Elizabeth City** (city) Pasquotank County
136	1296	92.5	**Goldsboro** (city) Wayne County
136	n/a	92.5	**Northchase** (CDP) New Hanover County
136	1296	92.5	**Southern Pines** (town) Moore County
140	1346	92.3	**Holly Springs** (town) Wake County
140	1346	92.3	**Huntersville** (town) Mecklenburg County
140	n/a	92.3	**Kill Devil Hills** (town) Dare County
143	n/a	92.2	**Clinton** (city) Sampson County
143	n/a	92.2	**Elizabethtown** (town) Bladen County
143	n/a	92.2	**Mineral Springs** (town) Union County
146	1416	92.0	**Murraysville** (CDP) New Hanover County
146	n/a	92.0	**Roxboro** (city) Person County
148	1441	91.9	**Albemarle** (city) Stanly County
148	n/a	91.9	**Dunn** (city) Harnett County
148	n/a	91.9	**Fairview** (CDP) Buncombe County

Note: The state column ranks the top/bottom 150 places in the state with population of 2,500 or more. The national column ranks the top/bottom places in the country with population of 10,000 or more. Places that are unincorporated were not considered in the rankings. n/a indicates data not available. Please refer to the User Guide for additional information.

Speak English Only at Home

Top 150 Places Ranked in *Ascending* Order

State Rank	Nat'l Rank	Percent	Place
1	n/a	54.0	Siler City (town) Chatham County
2	n/a	61.3	Selma (town) Johnston County
3	731	64.9	Morrisville (town) Wake County
4	1003	72.2	Monroe (city) Union County
5	n/a	72.4	East Flat Rock (CDP) Henderson County
6	n/a	74.0	Pineville (town) Mecklenburg County
7	1185	75.2	Asheboro (city) Randolph County
8	1201	75.5	Carrboro (town) Orange County
9	n/a	76.1	Wallace (town) Duplin County
10	1272	76.7	Sanford (city) Lee County
11	1284	76.9	Cary (town) Wake County
12	n/a	77.0	River Road (CDP) Beaufort County
13	n/a	77.5	Benson (town) Johnston County
13	n/a	77.5	Mar-Mac (CDP) Wayne County
15	n/a	79.2	Elkin (town) Surry County
16	n/a	79.3	Brogden (CDP) Wayne County
17	n/a	79.7	Red Springs (town) Robeson County
18	1498	79.8	Durham (city) Durham County
19	n/a	80.1	Glen Raven (CDP) Alamance County
20	n/a	80.2	Zebulon (town) Wake County
21	1530	80.3	Charlotte (city) Mecklenburg County
22	1599	80.9	Graham (city) Alamance County
23	n/a	81.2	Franklin (town) Macon County
24	n/a	81.4	Landis (town) Rowan County
25	1648	81.5	Chapel Hill (town) Orange County
25	1648	81.5	Lexington (city) Davidson County
27	n/a	82.0	China Grove (town) Rowan County
28	1713	82.2	Raleigh (city) Wake County
29	1724	82.3	Morganton (city) Burke County
30	n/a	82.4	Archer Lodge (town) Johnston County
31	n/a	82.6	Skippers Corner (CDP) New Hanover County
32	1799	82.9	Winston-Salem (city) Forsyth County
33	n/a	83.0	Conover (city) Catawba County
34	n/a	83.6	Rockfish (CDP) Hoke County
35	1883	83.7	Knightdale (town) Wake County
36	1897	83.8	Newton (city) Catawba County
36	n/a	83.8	Yadkinville (town) Yadkin County
38	n/a	83.9	East Rockingham (CDP) Richmond County
38	n/a	83.9	Mount Olive (town) Wayne County
38	n/a	83.9	Warsaw (town) Duplin County
41	n/a	84.4	Saint Stephens (CDP) Catawba County
42	n/a	84.5	Marion (city) McDowell County
43	n/a	84.7	Pittsboro (town) Chatham County
44	2005	84.8	Lincolnton (city) Lincoln County
45	2032	85.0	High Point (city) Guilford County
46	2069	85.2	Clemmons (village) Forsyth County
46	n/a	85.2	Dana (CDP) Henderson County
48	2117	85.6	Thomasville (city) Davidson County
49	2172	86.0	Burlington (city) Alamance County
50	n/a	86.2	Lake Park (village) Union County
51	2225	86.3	Greensboro (city) Guilford County
52	n/a	86.4	Kings Grant (CDP) New Hanover County
53	n/a	86.5	Wendell (town) Wake County
54	2266	86.6	Spring Lake (town) Cumberland County
55	2282	86.7	Hickory (city) Catawba County
56	2296	86.8	Concord (city) Cabarrus County
57	2320	87.0	Indian Trail (town) Union County
58	n/a	87.1	Liberty (town) Randolph County
59	2360	87.3	Hendersonville (city) Henderson County
59	n/a	87.3	Lowell (city) Gaston County
61	2372	87.4	Hope Mills (town) Cumberland County
61	n/a	87.4	Sylva (town) Jackson County
61	n/a	87.4	Tyro (CDP) Davidson County
64	2386	87.5	Stallings (town) Union County
64	2386	87.5	Statesville (city) Iredell County
64	n/a	87.5	Weddington (town) Union County
67	2410	87.7	Apex (town) Wake County
67	n/a	87.7	Jamestown (town) Guilford County
69	n/a	87.8	Elroy (CDP) Wayne County
70	n/a	87.9	Long View (town) Catawba County
70	2440	87.9	Lumberton (city) Robeson County
72	2459	88.0	Fayetteville (city) Cumberland County
73	2473	88.1	Wake Forest (town) Wake County
74	2492	88.2	Kannapolis (city) Cabarrus County
74	2492	88.2	Smithfield (town) Johnston County
76	n/a	88.3	Angier (town) Harnett County
77	n/a	88.4	Buies Creek (CDP) Harnett County
77	n/a	88.4	Hillsborough (town) Orange County
79	2563	88.6	Havelock (city) Craven County
79	2563	88.6	Salisbury (city) Rowan County
81	2598	88.8	Fuquay-Varina (town) Wake County
81	2598	88.8	Gastonia (city) Gaston County
81	n/a	88.8	Rolesville (town) Wake County
84	n/a	88.9	Butner (town) Granville County
84	2617	88.9	Cornelius (town) Mecklenburg County
84	n/a	88.9	Cramerton (town) Gaston County
84	2617	88.9	Jacksonville (city) Onslow County
88	2633	89.0	Matthews (town) Mecklenburg County
88	n/a	89.0	Ranlo (town) Gaston County
88	n/a	89.0	Sneads Ferry (CDP) Onslow County
91	n/a	89.3	Silver Lake (CDP) New Hanover County
91	n/a	89.3	Wingate (town) Union County
93	2708	89.4	Lenoir (city) Caldwell County
93	n/a	89.4	Woodfin (town) Buncombe County
95	2735	89.6	Kernersville (town) Forsyth County
95	n/a	89.6	Welcome (CDP) Davidson County
95	2735	89.6	Wilson (city) Wilson County
98	2779	89.8	Mint Hill (town) Mecklenburg County
98	2779	89.8	New Bern (city) Craven County
100	2809	90.0	Mooresville (town) Iredell County
101	2829	90.1	Archdale (city) Randolph County
102	n/a	90.2	Nags Head (town) Dare County
103	n/a	90.3	Lillington (town) Harnett County
104	n/a	90.4	Mocksville (town) Davie County
105	2921	90.5	Mount Airy (city) Surry County
105	n/a	90.5	Rural Hall (town) Forsyth County
107	n/a	90.6	Mountain Home (CDP) Henderson County
108	2963	90.7	Mount Holly (city) Gaston County
109	n/a	90.8	Troy (town) Montgomery County
110	2998	90.9	Clayton (town) Johnston County
110	2998	90.9	Leland (town) Brunswick County
112	3018	91.0	Asheville (city) Buncombe County
113	n/a	91.2	Waxhaw (town) Union County
114	3074	91.3	Harrisburg (town) Cabarrus County
114	n/a	91.3	Oak Ridge (town) Guilford County
114	n/a	91.3	Whiteville (city) Columbus County
117	n/a	91.4	Marvin (village) Union County
118	n/a	91.5	Ayden (town) Pitt County
119	3128	91.6	Piney Green (CDP) Onslow County
119	3128	91.6	Wilmington (city) New Hanover County
121	3176	91.8	Henderson (city) Vance County
122	3200	91.9	Albemarle (city) Stanly County
122	n/a	91.9	Dunn (city) Harnett County
122	n/a	91.9	Fairview (CDP) Buncombe County
125	3216	92.0	Murraysville (CDP) New Hanover County
125	n/a	92.0	Roxboro (city) Person County
127	n/a	92.2	Clinton (city) Sampson County
127	n/a	92.2	Elizabethtown (town) Bladen County
127	n/a	92.2	Mineral Springs (town) Union County
130	3287	92.3	Holly Springs (town) Wake County
130	3287	92.3	Huntersville (town) Mecklenburg County
130	n/a	92.3	Kill Devil Hills (town) Dare County
133	3332	92.5	Elizabeth City (city) Pasquotank County
133	3332	92.5	Goldsboro (city) Wayne County
133	n/a	92.5	Northchase (CDP) New Hanover County
133	3332	92.5	Southern Pines (town) Moore County
137	n/a	92.6	Brevard (city) Transylvania County
137	n/a	92.6	Erwin (town) Harnett County
139	n/a	92.7	Raeford (city) Hoke County
140	n/a	92.8	North Wilkesboro (town) Wilkes County
141	n/a	92.9	Forest City (town) Rutherford County
141	3447	92.9	Garner (town) Wake County
141	n/a	92.9	Gibsonville (town) Guilford County
141	3447	92.9	Greenville (city) Pitt County
145	3463	93.0	Belmont (city) Gaston County
145	n/a	93.0	River Bend (town) Craven County
145	3463	93.0	Summerfield (town) Guilford County
148	n/a	93.1	Gamewell (town) Caldwell County
148	n/a	93.1	Icard (CDP) Burke County
148	n/a	93.1	Louisburg (town) Franklin County

Note: The state column ranks the top/bottom 150 places in the state with population of 2,500 or more. The national column ranks the top/bottom places in the country with population of 10,000 or more. Places that are unincorporated were not considered in the rankings. n/a indicates data not available. Please refer to the User Guide for additional information.

Individuals with a Disability

Top 150 Places Ranked in *Descending* Order

State Rank	Nat'l Rank	Percent	Place
1	n/a	30.4	**Tabor City** (town) Columbus County
2	n/a	28.9	**La Grange** (town) Lenoir County
3	n/a	27.3	**Enfield** (town) Halifax County
4	n/a	26.8	**South Rosemary** (CDP) Halifax County
5	n/a	26.6	**East Flat Rock** (CDP) Henderson County
6	n/a	26.4	**Spindale** (town) Rutherford County
7	n/a	26.0	**Stanley** (town) Gaston County
8	n/a	25.7	**Forest City** (town) Rutherford County
9	n/a	24.6	**Burgaw** (town) Pender County
9	n/a	24.6	**Hamlet** (city) Richmond County
11	20	24.2	**Henderson** (city) Vance County
12	n/a	24.1	**Plymouth** (town) Washington County
13	n/a	23.7	**Windsor** (town) Bertie County
14	n/a	23.4	**Farmville** (town) Pitt County
14	n/a	23.4	**Oxford** (city) Granville County
16	34	23.2	**Kinston** (city) Lenoir County
17	n/a	22.8	**Ahoskie** (town) Hertford County
17	n/a	22.8	**Marion** (city) McDowell County
19	n/a	22.7	**Valdese** (town) Burke County
20	n/a	22.5	**Elizabethtown** (town) Bladen County
21	n/a	22.1	**Southport** (city) Brunswick County
22	61	21.8	**Morganton** (city) Burke County
23	n/a	21.5	**Wadesboro** (town) Anson County
24	79	21.4	**Kings Mountain** (city) Cleveland County
25	n/a	21.1	**Franklin** (town) Macon County
25	n/a	21.1	**Washington** (city) Beaufort County
27	n/a	21.0	**Warsaw** (town) Duplin County
28	n/a	20.9	**Butner** (town) Granville County
29	n/a	20.8	**Grifton** (town) Pitt County
29	101	20.8	**Hendersonville** (city) Henderson County
29	n/a	20.8	**Murfreesboro** (town) Hertford County
32	n/a	20.7	**Roxboro** (city) Person County
33	n/a	20.6	**Whiteville** (city) Columbus County
34	n/a	20.5	**Louisburg** (town) Franklin County
34	n/a	20.5	**Williamston** (town) Martin County
36	n/a	20.4	**Carolina Shores** (town) Brunswick County
36	118	20.4	**Laurinburg** (city) Scotland County
38	128	20.3	**Lexington** (city) Davidson County
38	n/a	20.3	**Newport** (town) Carteret County
38	n/a	20.3	**Wilkesboro** (town) Wilkes County
41	141	20.1	**Reidsville** (city) Rockingham County
41	n/a	20.1	**Swannanoa** (CDP) Buncombe County
43	n/a	20.0	**Locust** (city) Stanly County
43	148	20.0	**Mount Airy** (city) Surry County
45	n/a	19.9	**Dunn** (city) Harnett County
45	157	19.9	**Eden** (city) Rockingham County
45	n/a	19.9	**River Bend** (town) Craven County
45	157	19.9	**Smithfield** (town) Johnston County
49	n/a	19.6	**Erwin** (town) Harnett County
50	n/a	19.5	**East Rockingham** (CDP) Richmond County
50	195	19.5	**Lenoir** (city) Caldwell County
50	n/a	19.5	**Morehead City** (town) Carteret County
53	n/a	19.3	**Lillington** (town) Harnett County
54	n/a	19.2	**Waynesville** (town) Haywood County
55	228	19.1	**Newton** (city) Catawba County
55	n/a	19.1	**North Wilkesboro** (town) Wilkes County
55	n/a	19.1	**Red Springs** (town) Robeson County
58	n/a	19.0	**Icard** (CDP) Burke County
58	239	19.0	**Roanoke Rapids** (city) Halifax County
60	n/a	18.9	**Mountain Home** (CDP) Henderson County
61	n/a	18.8	**Black Mountain** (town) Buncombe County
61	n/a	18.8	**Lowell** (city) Gaston County
63	n/a	18.7	**Cajah's Mountain** (town) Caldwell County
63	n/a	18.7	**Creedmoor** (city) Granville County
63	271	18.7	**New Bern** (city) Craven County
63	n/a	18.7	**Ranlo** (town) Gaston County
67	n/a	18.6	**Randleman** (city) Randolph County
68	n/a	18.5	**Clinton** (city) Sampson County
68	n/a	18.5	**Sawmills** (town) Caldwell County
70	n/a	18.4	**Eastover** (town) Cumberland County
70	n/a	18.4	**Mount Olive** (town) Wayne County
72	n/a	18.3	**Ayden** (town) Pitt County
72	n/a	18.3	**Shallotte** (town) Brunswick County
74	318	18.2	**Albemarle** (city) Stanly County
75	n/a	18.1	**Mocksville** (town) Davie County
76	n/a	18.0	**Bessemer City** (city) Gaston County
76	n/a	18.0	**Rockingham** (city) Richmond County
78	357	17.8	**Elizabeth City** (city) Pasquotank County
78	357	17.8	**Southern Pines** (town) Moore County
78	357	17.8	**Tarboro** (town) Edgecombe County
81	n/a	17.7	**Wentworth** (town) Rockingham County
82	n/a	17.5	**Beaufort** (town) Carteret County
83	n/a	17.4	**Rutherfordton** (town) Rutherford County
84	n/a	17.3	**Elroy** (CDP) Wayne County
85	n/a	17.0	**Fairfield Harbour** (CDP) Craven County
86	n/a	16.9	**Benson** (town) Johnston County
86	n/a	16.9	**Gamewell** (town) Caldwell County
88	499	16.8	**Goldsboro** (city) Wayne County
88	n/a	16.8	**Selma** (town) Johnston County
90	n/a	16.6	**Woodfin** (town) Buncombe County
91	n/a	16.5	**Enochville** (CDP) Rowan County
91	n/a	16.5	**Sylva** (town) Jackson County
93	n/a	16.4	**China Grove** (town) Rowan County
93	576	16.4	**Shelby** (city) Cleveland County
95	n/a	16.3	**James City** (CDP) Craven County
95	n/a	16.3	**Nashville** (town) Nash County
95	n/a	16.3	**Pembroke** (town) Robeson County
98	n/a	16.2	**Bayshore** (CDP) New Hanover County
98	n/a	16.2	**Elkin** (town) Surry County
98	n/a	16.2	**Polkton** (town) Anson County
101	n/a	16.1	**Brices Creek** (CDP) Craven County
101	n/a	16.1	**Edenton** (town) Chowan County
101	632	16.1	**Pinehurst** (village) Moore County
101	632	16.1	**Rocky Mount** (city) Nash County
101	632	16.1	**Salisbury** (city) Rowan County
101	n/a	16.1	**Trinity** (city) Randolph County
107	658	16.0	**Lumberton** (city) Robeson County
108	681	15.9	**Lincolnton** (city) Lincoln County
108	n/a	15.9	**Zebulon** (town) Wake County
110	699	15.8	**Burlington** (city) Alamance County
111	n/a	15.7	**Brevard** (city) Transylvania County
111	n/a	15.7	**Spencer** (town) Rowan County
113	n/a	15.5	**Pittsboro** (town) Chatham County
114	n/a	15.4	**Fairmont** (town) Robeson County
114	n/a	15.4	**Pineville** (town) Mecklenburg County
116	n/a	15.3	**Hudson** (town) Caldwell County
117	n/a	15.2	**Cherryville** (city) Gaston County
117	n/a	15.2	**Mineral Springs** (town) Union County
117	n/a	15.2	**Wingate** (town) Union County
120	n/a	15.0	**Long View** (town) Catawba County
121	n/a	14.9	**Wendell** (town) Wake County
121	920	14.9	**Wilson** (city) Wilson County
123	n/a	14.8	**Angier** (town) Harnett County
123	n/a	14.8	**Boiling Spring Lakes** (city) Brunswick County
123	n/a	14.8	**Maiden** (town) Catawba County
123	n/a	14.8	**Midway** (town) Davidson County
123	n/a	14.8	**Saint James** (town) Brunswick County
128	957	14.7	**Gastonia** (city) Gaston County
128	957	14.7	**Thomasville** (city) Davidson County
130	n/a	14.6	**Glen Raven** (CDP) Alamance County
130	n/a	14.6	**Wrightsboro** (CDP) New Hanover County
132	n/a	14.5	**Emerald Isle** (town) Carteret County
132	n/a	14.5	**Northchase** (CDP) New Hanover County
134	n/a	14.4	**Oak Island** (town) Brunswick County
135	n/a	14.3	**Aberdeen** (town) Moore County
136	n/a	14.2	**Nags Head** (town) Dare County
137	n/a	14.1	**Bethlehem** (CDP) Alexander County
137	n/a	14.1	**Conover** (city) Catawba County
139	1145	14.0	**Asheboro** (city) Randolph County
139	1145	14.0	**Sanford** (city) Lee County
139	n/a	14.0	**Wallburg** (town) Davidson County
142	n/a	13.9	**Half Moon** (CDP) Onslow County
142	1177	13.9	**Statesville** (city) Iredell County
144	n/a	13.8	**Landis** (town) Rowan County
144	n/a	13.8	**Swansboro** (town) Onslow County
146	n/a	13.7	**Etowah** (CDP) Henderson County
147	1258	13.6	**Fayetteville** (city) Cumberland County
147	n/a	13.6	**Troy** (town) Montgomery County
149	1298	13.5	**Belmont** (city) Gaston County
149	n/a	13.5	**Dallas** (town) Gaston County

Note: The state column ranks the top/bottom 150 places in the state with population of 2,500 or more. The national column ranks the top/bottom places in the country with population of 10,000 or more. Places that are unincorporated were not considered in the rankings. n/a indicates data not available. Please refer to the User Guide for additional information.

Individuals with a Disability

Top 150 Places Ranked in *Ascending* Order

State Rank	Nat'l Rank	Percent	Place
1	n/a	2.6	**Marvin** (village) Union County
2	n/a	4.6	**Weddington** (town) Union County
3	n/a	4.9	**Wesley Chapel** (village) Union County
4	104	5.1	**Apex** (town) Wake County
5	n/a	5.2	**Buies Creek** (CDP) Harnett County
6	138	5.4	**Boone** (town) Watauga County
7	159	5.5	**Harrisburg** (town) Cabarrus County
7	159	5.5	**Morrisville** (town) Wake County
9	199	5.7	**Cary** (town) Wake County
10	n/a	5.8	**Midland** (town) Cabarrus County
11	258	6.0	**Chapel Hill** (town) Orange County
12	285	6.2	**Wake Forest** (town) Wake County
12	n/a	6.2	**Waxhaw** (town) Union County
14	358	6.5	**Holly Springs** (town) Wake County
14	358	6.5	**Knightdale** (town) Wake County
16	n/a	6.6	**Rolesville** (town) Wake County
17	435	6.8	**Huntersville** (town) Mecklenburg County
18	n/a	6.9	**Archer Lodge** (town) Johnston County
18	465	6.9	**Carrboro** (town) Orange County
18	n/a	6.9	**Fairview** (CDP) Buncombe County
21	550	7.2	**Clemmons** (village) Forsyth County
21	550	7.2	**Indian Trail** (town) Union County
23	589	7.3	**Cornelius** (town) Mecklenburg County
24	624	7.4	**Matthews** (town) Mecklenburg County
25	n/a	7.6	**Oak Ridge** (town) Guilford County
25	703	7.6	**Raleigh** (city) Wake County
25	n/a	7.6	**Stokesdale** (town) Guilford County
28	797	7.8	**Davidson** (town) Mecklenburg County
28	797	7.8	**Mooresville** (town) Iredell County
30	n/a	8.0	**Cullowhee** (CDP) Jackson County
31	953	8.1	**Summerfield** (town) Guilford County
32	n/a	8.4	**Fairview** (town) Union County
33	1228	8.7	**Charlotte** (city) Mecklenburg County
33	1228	8.7	**Clayton** (town) Johnston County
33	n/a	8.7	**Lake Junaluska** (CDP) Haywood County
36	n/a	8.8	**Gibsonville** (town) Guilford County
36	n/a	8.8	**Lake Park** (village) Union County
36	n/a	8.8	**Weaverville** (town) Buncombe County
39	n/a	8.9	**Lake Royale** (CDP) Franklin County
39	1327	8.9	**Lewisville** (town) Forsyth County
39	n/a	8.9	**Royal Pines** (CDP) Buncombe County
42	n/a	9.0	**Carolina Beach** (town) New Hanover County
43	1468	9.2	**Concord** (city) Cabarrus County
43	n/a	9.2	**Forest Oaks** (CDP) Guilford County
43	1468	9.2	**Fuquay-Varina** (town) Wake County
43	n/a	9.2	**Hampstead** (CDP) Pender County
43	n/a	9.2	**Westport** (CDP) Lincoln County
48	n/a	9.4	**Unionville** (town) Union County
49	n/a	9.5	**Ogden** (CDP) New Hanover County
49	n/a	9.5	**Skippers Corner** (CDP) New Hanover County
49	1625	9.5	**Spring Lake** (town) Cumberland County
52	1740	9.7	**Mebane** (city) Alamance County
52	n/a	9.7	**Moyock** (CDP) Currituck County
52	n/a	9.7	**Siler City** (town) Chatham County
55	n/a	9.8	**Whispering Pines** (village) Moore County
56	n/a	9.9	**Brogden** (CDP) Wayne County
56	n/a	9.9	**Canton** (town) Haywood County
56	n/a	9.9	**Fletcher** (town) Henderson County
56	1826	9.9	**Greensboro** (city) Guilford County
56	n/a	9.9	**Lake Norman of Catawba** (CDP) Catawba County
61	1926	10.1	**Greenville** (city) Pitt County
61	n/a	10.1	**Seven Lakes** (CDP) Moore County
63	n/a	10.2	**Liberty** (town) Randolph County
63	1973	10.2	**Mint Hill** (town) Mecklenburg County
65	n/a	10.3	**Jamestown** (town) Guilford County
65	n/a	10.3	**Rockfish** (CDP) Hoke County
67	2058	10.4	**Durham** (city) Durham County
68	2113	10.5	**Murraysville** (CDP) New Hanover County
68	n/a	10.5	**Porters Neck** (CDP) New Hanover County
68	n/a	10.5	**Southern Shores** (town) Dare County
71	n/a	10.6	**Cramerton** (town) Gaston County
71	2162	10.6	**Winston-Salem** (city) Forsyth County
73	n/a	10.7	**Elon** (town) Alamance County
74	2262	10.8	**Garner** (town) Wake County
74	n/a	10.8	**Raeford** (city) Hoke County
76	2350	11.0	**Kernersville** (town) Forsyth County
77	n/a	11.1	**Boiling Springs** (town) Cleveland County
77	n/a	11.1	**Sneads Ferry** (CDP) Onslow County
77	n/a	11.1	**Winterville** (town) Pitt County
80	n/a	11.2	**Red Oak** (town) Nash County
80	n/a	11.2	**Welcome** (CDP) Davidson County
82	n/a	11.3	**Hillsborough** (town) Orange County
82	n/a	11.3	**Walkertown** (town) Forsyth County
84	n/a	11.4	**Kings Grant** (CDP) New Hanover County
85	2575	11.5	**Monroe** (city) Union County
86	2608	11.6	**Hickory** (city) Catawba County
86	2608	11.6	**Leland** (town) Brunswick County
86	n/a	11.6	**River Road** (CDP) Beaufort County
86	n/a	11.6	**Saint Stephens** (CDP) Catawba County
86	2608	11.6	**Stallings** (town) Union County
91	n/a	11.7	**Silver Lake** (CDP) New Hanover County
92	n/a	11.8	**Kitty Hawk** (town) Dare County
93	n/a	11.9	**Dana** (CDP) Henderson County
93	n/a	11.9	**Kill Devil Hills** (town) Dare County
93	n/a	11.9	**Myrtle Grove** (CDP) New Hanover County
93	2745	11.9	**Piney Green** (CDP) Onslow County
93	n/a	11.9	**Pleasant Garden** (town) Guilford County
98	2833	12.1	**Havelock** (city) Craven County
98	n/a	12.1	**Lowesville** (CDP) Lincoln County
98	n/a	12.1	**Mountain View** (CDP) Catawba County
101	n/a	12.3	**Rural Hall** (town) Forsyth County
102	2952	12.4	**High Point** (city) Guilford County
102	2952	12.4	**Kannapolis** (city) Cabarrus County
102	n/a	12.4	**Sunset Beach** (town) Brunswick County
105	n/a	12.6	**Granite Falls** (town) Caldwell County
105	n/a	12.6	**King** (city) Stokes County
105	n/a	12.6	**Yadkinville** (town) Yadkin County
108	n/a	12.7	**Wallace** (town) Duplin County
109	n/a	12.8	**Mills River** (town) Henderson County
109	n/a	12.8	**Trent Woods** (town) Craven County
111	n/a	12.9	**Tyro** (CDP) Davidson County
112	n/a	13.0	**Flat Rock** (village) Henderson County
113	3199	13.1	**Archdale** (city) Randolph County
113	3199	13.1	**Asheville** (city) Buncombe County
113	n/a	13.1	**Granite Quarry** (town) Rowan County
113	n/a	13.1	**Mar-Mac** (CDP) Wayne County
117	3231	13.2	**Hope Mills** (town) Cumberland County
118	3264	13.3	**Graham** (city) Alamance County
118	3264	13.3	**Mount Holly** (city) Gaston County
118	3264	13.3	**Wilmington** (city) New Hanover County
121	3333	13.5	**Belmont** (city) Gaston County
121	n/a	13.5	**Dallas** (town) Gaston County
121	3333	13.5	**Jacksonville** (city) Onslow County
124	3359	13.6	**Fayetteville** (city) Cumberland County
124	n/a	13.6	**Troy** (town) Montgomery County
126	n/a	13.7	**Etowah** (CDP) Henderson County
127	n/a	13.8	**Landis** (town) Rowan County
127	n/a	13.8	**Swansboro** (town) Onslow County
129	n/a	13.9	**Half Moon** (CDP) Onslow County
129	3456	13.9	**Statesville** (city) Iredell County
131	3480	14.0	**Asheboro** (city) Randolph County
131	3480	14.0	**Sanford** (city) Lee County
131	n/a	14.0	**Wallburg** (town) Davidson County
134	n/a	14.1	**Bethlehem** (CDP) Alexander County
134	n/a	14.1	**Conover** (city) Catawba County
136	n/a	14.2	**Nags Head** (town) Dare County
137	n/a	14.3	**Aberdeen** (town) Moore County
138	n/a	14.4	**Oak Island** (town) Brunswick County
139	n/a	14.5	**Emerald Isle** (town) Carteret County
139	n/a	14.5	**Northchase** (CDP) New Hanover County
141	n/a	14.6	**Glen Raven** (CDP) Alamance County
141	n/a	14.6	**Wrightsboro** (CDP) New Hanover County
143	3678	14.7	**Gastonia** (city) Gaston County
143	3678	14.7	**Thomasville** (city) Davidson County
145	n/a	14.8	**Angier** (town) Harnett County
145	n/a	14.8	**Boiling Spring Lakes** (city) Brunswick County
145	n/a	14.8	**Maiden** (town) Catawba County
145	n/a	14.8	**Midway** (town) Davidson County
145	n/a	14.8	**Saint James** (town) Brunswick County
150	n/a	14.9	**Wendell** (town) Wake County

Note: *The state column ranks the top/bottom 150 places in the state with population of 2,500 or more. The national column ranks the top/bottom places in the country with population of 10,000 or more. Places that are unincorporated were not considered in the rankings. n/a indicates data not available. Please refer to the User Guide for additional information.*

Veterans

Top 150 Places Ranked in *Descending* Order

State Rank	Nat'l Rank	Percent	Place		State Rank	Nat'l Rank	Percent	Place
1	4	29.0	**Havelock** (city) Craven County		76	n/a	11.8	**Lillington** (town) Harnett County
2	n/a	28.6	**Whispering Pines** (village) Moore County		76	n/a	11.8	**Myrtle Grove** (CDP) New Hanover County
3	n/a	27.9	**Carolina Shores** (town) Brunswick County		76	n/a	11.8	**Pittsboro** (town) Chatham County
4	n/a	27.5	**Half Moon** (CDP) Onslow County		76	n/a	11.8	**Trinity** (city) Randolph County
5	n/a	26.5	**Fairfield Harbour** (CDP) Craven County		80	n/a	11.7	**Dallas** (town) Gaston County
6	n/a	24.9	**Sunset Beach** (town) Brunswick County		80	720	11.7	**Murraysville** (CDP) New Hanover County
7	n/a	24.3	**River Bend** (town) Craven County		80	n/a	11.7	**Raeford** (city) Hoke County
8	n/a	23.9	**Newport** (town) Carteret County		83	n/a	11.6	**Bethlehem** (CDP) Alexander County
9	n/a	23.8	**Rockfish** (CDP) Hoke County		83	n/a	11.6	**Canton** (town) Haywood County
10	29	23.4	**Piney Green** (CDP) Onslow County		83	756	11.6	**Fuquay-Varina** (town) Wake County
11	36	22.6	**Pinehurst** (village) Moore County		83	n/a	11.6	**Pleasant Garden** (town) Guilford County
12	40	22.5	**Jacksonville** (city) Onslow County		87	n/a	11.5	**Kings Grant** (CDP) New Hanover County
13	46	22.0	**Fayetteville** (city) Cumberland County		87	n/a	11.5	**Lake Norman of Catawba** (CDP) Catawba County
13	n/a	22.0	**Swansboro** (town) Onslow County		89	n/a	11.4	**Granite Quarry** (town) Rowan County
15	n/a	21.0	**Brices Creek** (CDP) Craven County		89	n/a	11.4	**Rutherfordton** (town) Rutherford County
16	n/a	20.0	**James City** (CDP) Craven County		91	858	11.3	**Elizabeth City** (city) Pasquotank County
16	n/a	20.0	**Saint James** (town) Brunswick County		91	858	11.3	**Garner** (town) Wake County
18	n/a	19.4	**Boiling Spring Lakes** (city) Brunswick County		91	858	11.3	**Mint Hill** (town) Mecklenburg County
18	n/a	19.4	**Moyock** (CDP) Currituck County		94	900	11.2	**Clemmons** (village) Forsyth County
20	n/a	19.3	**Trent Woods** (town) Craven County		95	n/a	11.1	**Wilkesboro** (town) Wilkes County
21	n/a	19.2	**Flat Rock** (village) Henderson County		95	n/a	11.1	**Wrightsboro** (CDP) New Hanover County
22	n/a	19.1	**Emerald Isle** (town) Carteret County		97	n/a	11.0	**Midway** (town) Davidson County
23	94	18.6	**Spring Lake** (town) Cumberland County		97	n/a	11.0	**Stanley** (town) Gaston County
24	110	18.0	**Hope Mills** (town) Cumberland County		99	n/a	10.9	**Beaufort** (town) Carteret County
25	n/a	16.9	**Etowah** (CDP) Henderson County		99	1016	10.9	**Graham** (city) Alamance County
25	n/a	16.9	**Southport** (city) Brunswick County		99	1016	10.9	**Kernersville** (town) Forsyth County
27	n/a	16.8	**Elroy** (CDP) Wayne County		99	n/a	10.9	**Swannanoa** (CDP) Buncombe County
28	n/a	16.5	**Porters Neck** (CDP) New Hanover County		103	n/a	10.8	**Jamestown** (town) Guilford County
29	n/a	16.0	**Seven Lakes** (CDP) Moore County		103	n/a	10.8	**Midland** (town) Cabarrus County
30	n/a	15.8	**Eastover** (town) Cumberland County		105	1118	10.7	**Eden** (city) Rockingham County
31	n/a	15.7	**Creedmoor** (city) Granville County		105	n/a	10.7	**Valdese** (town) Burke County
32	219	15.4	**Goldsboro** (city) Wayne County		107	n/a	10.6	**Archer Lodge** (town) Johnston County
33	n/a	15.1	**Morehead City** (town) Carteret County		107	n/a	10.6	**Erwin** (town) Harnett County
34	n/a	14.9	**Lake Royale** (CDP) Franklin County		107	n/a	10.6	**Hampstead** (CDP) Pender County
34	n/a	14.9	**Mountain View** (CDP) Catawba County		107	1169	10.6	**Mount Airy** (city) Surry County
36	n/a	14.7	**Mar-Mac** (CDP) Wayne County		107	n/a	10.6	**Tyro** (CDP) Davidson County
37	n/a	14.6	**Silver Lake** (CDP) New Hanover County		107	n/a	10.6	**Wendell** (town) Wake County
37	276	14.6	**Southern Pines** (town) Moore County		113	n/a	10.5	**Carolina Beach** (town) New Hanover County
39	n/a	14.4	**Brogden** (CDP) Wayne County		113	n/a	10.5	**Farmville** (town) Pitt County
40	n/a	14.1	**Shallotte** (town) Brunswick County		115	n/a	10.4	**Burgaw** (town) Pender County
41	n/a	14.0	**Oak Island** (town) Brunswick County		115	1272	10.4	**Shelby** (city) Cleveland County
42	n/a	13.9	**Mountain Home** (CDP) Henderson County		117	1328	10.3	**Archdale** (city) Randolph County
42	339	13.9	**New Bern** (city) Craven County		117	n/a	10.3	**Nashville** (town) Nash County
44	n/a	13.8	**Cramerton** (town) Gaston County		117	1328	10.3	**Salisbury** (city) Rowan County
45	n/a	13.7	**Mills River** (town) Henderson County		117	1328	10.3	**Wilson** (city) Wilson County
46	n/a	13.6	**Waynesville** (town) Haywood County		121	n/a	10.2	**Cajah's Mountain** (town) Caldwell County
47	n/a	13.4	**Aberdeen** (town) Moore County		121	1386	10.2	**Holly Springs** (town) Wake County
47	388	13.4	**Hendersonville** (city) Henderson County		121	1386	10.2	**Morganton** (city) Burke County
49	n/a	13.2	**Forest Oaks** (CDP) Guilford County		124	1445	10.1	**Kings Mountain** (city) Cleveland County
50	n/a	13.1	**Dana** (CDP) Henderson County		124	1445	10.1	**Lincolnton** (city) Lincoln County
51	n/a	13.0	**Black Mountain** (town) Buncombe County		124	n/a	10.1	**Murfreesboro** (town) Hertford County
51	n/a	13.0	**Nags Head** (town) Dare County		124	n/a	10.1	**Oak Ridge** (town) Guilford County
51	n/a	13.0	**Wadesboro** (town) Anson County		128	n/a	10.0	**Brevard** (city) Transylvania County
54	n/a	12.9	**La Grange** (town) Lenoir County		128	1492	10.0	**Clayton** (town) Johnston County
54	461	12.9	**Leland** (town) Brunswick County		128	n/a	10.0	**Elkin** (town) Surry County
54	n/a	12.9	**Southern Shores** (town) Dare County		128	n/a	10.0	**Long View** (town) Catawba County
57	n/a	12.8	**Butner** (town) Granville County		128	n/a	10.0	**Unionville** (town) Union County
58	n/a	12.7	**Skippers Corner** (CDP) New Hanover County		128	1492	10.0	**Wake Forest** (town) Wake County
58	n/a	12.7	**Spencer** (town) Rowan County		128	n/a	10.0	**Waxhaw** (town) Union County
60	n/a	12.6	**Conover** (city) Catawba County		128	n/a	10.0	**Wentworth** (town) Rockingham County
61	n/a	12.5	**Bessemer City** (city) Gaston County		136	1565	9.9	**Mount Holly** (city) Gaston County
61	n/a	12.5	**China Grove** (town) Rowan County		136	n/a	9.9	**River Road** (CDP) Beaufort County
61	n/a	12.5	**Hamlet** (city) Richmond County		136	1565	9.9	**Tarboro** (town) Edgecombe County
61	n/a	12.5	**Hudson** (town) Caldwell County		139	n/a	9.8	**Fletcher** (town) Henderson County
61	n/a	12.5	**Walkertown** (town) Forsyth County		139	n/a	9.8	**Ranlo** (town) Gaston County
66	n/a	12.4	**Enochville** (CDP) Rowan County		139	1640	9.8	**Reidsville** (city) Rockingham County
66	n/a	12.4	**Fairview** (CDP) Buncombe County		139	1640	9.8	**Rocky Mount** (city) Nash County
66	n/a	12.4	**Wallace** (town) Duplin County		143	1706	9.7	**Asheville** (city) Buncombe County
69	n/a	12.3	**Weaverville** (town) Buncombe County		143	n/a	9.7	**Hillsborough** (town) Orange County
70	n/a	12.2	**Rural Hall** (town) Forsyth County		143	1706	9.7	**Matthews** (town) Mecklenburg County
71	629	12.1	**Lewisville** (town) Forsyth County		143	n/a	9.7	**Mineral Springs** (town) Union County
71	n/a	12.1	**Randleman** (city) Randolph County		143	n/a	9.7	**Weddington** (town) Union County
73	n/a	12.0	**Royal Pines** (CDP) Buncombe County		148	n/a	9.6	**Fairmont** (town) Robeson County
74	n/a	11.9	**Saint Stephens** (CDP) Catawba County		148	1770	9.6	**Kannapolis** (city) Cabarrus County
74	n/a	11.9	**Sneads Ferry** (CDP) Onslow County		148	n/a	9.6	**Northchase** (CDP) New Hanover County

Note: The state column ranks the top/bottom 150 places in the state with population of 2,500 or more. The national column ranks the top/bottom places in the country with population of 10,000 or more. Places that are unincorporated were not considered in the rankings. n/a indicates data not available. Please refer to the User Guide for additional information.

Veterans

Top 150 Places Ranked in *Ascending* Order

State Rank	Nat'l Rank	Percent	Place
1	n/a	2.2	**Cullowhee** (CDP) Jackson County
2	60	2.3	**Boone** (town) Watauga County
3	162	3.5	**Carrboro** (town) Orange County
4	n/a	3.6	**Enfield** (town) Halifax County
4	n/a	3.6	**Wingate** (town) Union County
6	243	4.1	**Chapel Hill** (town) Orange County
7	n/a	4.2	**Buies Creek** (CDP) Harnett County
8	n/a	4.3	**Mount Olive** (town) Wayne County
9	n/a	4.6	**Polkton** (town) Anson County
9	n/a	4.6	**Red Springs** (town) Robeson County
11	n/a	4.8	**Marvin** (village) Union County
11	n/a	4.8	**Siler City** (town) Chatham County
13	n/a	5.3	**Elizabethtown** (town) Bladen County
14	n/a	5.4	**Boiling Springs** (town) Cleveland County
15	n/a	5.8	**Pineville** (town) Mecklenburg County
15	n/a	5.8	**Woodfin** (town) Buncombe County
15	n/a	5.8	**Yadkinville** (town) Yadkin County
18	743	5.9	**Davidson** (town) Mecklenburg County
18	n/a	5.9	**East Flat Rock** (CDP) Henderson County
20	n/a	6.1	**Elon** (town) Alamance County
21	n/a	6.2	**Forest City** (town) Rutherford County
21	868	6.2	**Greenville** (city) Pitt County
23	n/a	6.3	**Lowell** (city) Gaston County
24	952	6.4	**Durham** (city) Durham County
25	n/a	6.5	**Plymouth** (town) Washington County
25	n/a	6.5	**Red Oak** (town) Nash County
25	n/a	6.5	**Wesley Chapel** (village) Union County
28	1064	6.7	**Cary** (town) Wake County
29	n/a	6.8	**Gamewell** (town) Caldwell County
29	1119	6.8	**Huntersville** (town) Mecklenburg County
31	n/a	6.9	**Landis** (town) Rowan County
31	1179	6.9	**Raleigh** (city) Wake County
33	n/a	7.0	**Stokesdale** (town) Guilford County
33	n/a	7.0	**Windsor** (town) Bertie County
35	1286	7.1	**Albemarle** (city) Stanly County
35	n/a	7.1	**Locust** (city) Stanly County
35	1286	7.1	**Morrisville** (town) Wake County
35	n/a	7.1	**Sylva** (town) Jackson County
39	1344	7.2	**Charlotte** (city) Mecklenburg County
39	n/a	7.2	**Lake Junaluska** (CDP) Haywood County
39	n/a	7.2	**Roxboro** (city) Person County
42	1398	7.3	**Apex** (town) Wake County
42	n/a	7.3	**Liberty** (town) Randolph County
44	n/a	7.4	**Icard** (CDP) Burke County
44	n/a	7.4	**South Rosemary** (CDP) Halifax County
44	n/a	7.4	**Williamston** (town) Martin County
47	1507	7.5	**Hickory** (city) Catawba County
47	n/a	7.5	**Welcome** (CDP) Davidson County
49	1552	7.6	**Greensboro** (city) Guilford County
49	n/a	7.6	**Lowesville** (CDP) Lincoln County
49	n/a	7.6	**Troy** (town) Montgomery County
52	n/a	7.7	**Mocksville** (town) Davie County
53	n/a	7.8	**Ogden** (CDP) New Hanover County
53	n/a	7.8	**Pembroke** (town) Robeson County
55	n/a	7.9	**Fairview** (town) Union County
55	n/a	7.9	**Granite Falls** (town) Caldwell County
55	1710	7.9	**High Point** (city) Guilford County
58	1763	8.0	**Lumberton** (city) Robeson County
58	1763	8.0	**Mooresville** (town) Iredell County
58	n/a	8.0	**Selma** (town) Johnston County
61	n/a	8.1	**Ayden** (town) Pitt County
61	n/a	8.1	**Sawmills** (town) Caldwell County
61	1822	8.1	**Smithfield** (town) Johnston County
64	n/a	8.2	**Bayshore** (CDP) New Hanover County
64	n/a	8.2	**North Wilkesboro** (town) Wilkes County
64	n/a	8.2	**Warsaw** (town) Duplin County
64	n/a	8.2	**Winterville** (town) Pitt County
68	n/a	8.3	**Ahoskie** (town) Hertford County
68	n/a	8.3	**Clinton** (city) Sampson County
68	n/a	8.3	**Gibsonville** (town) Guilford County
68	n/a	8.3	**Glen Raven** (CDP) Alamance County
68	n/a	8.3	**Grifton** (town) Pitt County
73	n/a	8.4	**King** (city) Stokes County
73	n/a	8.4	**Oxford** (city) Granville County
73	1991	8.4	**Roanoke Rapids** (city) Halifax County
76	n/a	8.5	**East Rockingham** (CDP) Richmond County
76	2058	8.5	**Knightdale** (town) Wake County
76	2058	8.5	**Stallings** (town) Union County
76	n/a	8.5	**Westport** (CDP) Lincoln County
76	2058	8.5	**Winston-Salem** (city) Forsyth County
81	2122	8.6	**Gastonia** (city) Gaston County
81	2122	8.6	**Indian Trail** (town) Union County
81	2122	8.6	**Newton** (city) Catawba County
84	2189	8.7	**Cornelius** (town) Mecklenburg County
84	n/a	8.7	**Edenton** (town) Chowan County
84	2189	8.7	**Harrisburg** (town) Cabarrus County
84	2189	8.7	**Monroe** (city) Union County
84	2189	8.7	**Summerfield** (town) Guilford County
84	2189	8.7	**Thomasville** (city) Davidson County
90	2274	8.8	**Henderson** (city) Vance County
90	2274	8.8	**Lexington** (city) Davidson County
92	n/a	8.9	**Angier** (town) Harnett County
92	n/a	8.9	**Cherryville** (city) Gaston County
92	2345	8.9	**Mebane** (city) Alamance County
92	n/a	8.9	**Washington** (city) Beaufort County
92	n/a	8.9	**Zebulon** (town) Wake County
97	2404	9.0	**Concord** (city) Cabarrus County
97	2404	9.0	**Lenoir** (city) Caldwell County
99	2479	9.1	**Asheboro** (city) Randolph County
99	n/a	9.1	**Lake Park** (village) Union County
99	n/a	9.1	**Louisburg** (town) Franklin County
99	n/a	9.1	**Rolesville** (town) Wake County
103	n/a	9.2	**Spindale** (town) Rutherford County
103	n/a	9.2	**Whiteville** (city) Columbus County
105	n/a	9.3	**Dunn** (city) Harnett County
105	n/a	9.3	**Kitty Hawk** (town) Dare County
105	n/a	9.3	**Maiden** (town) Catawba County
105	n/a	9.3	**Marion** (city) McDowell County
109	2680	9.4	**Burlington** (city) Alamance County
109	n/a	9.4	**Kill Devil Hills** (town) Dare County
109	2680	9.4	**Kinston** (city) Lenoir County
109	2680	9.4	**Laurinburg** (city) Scotland County
113	2760	9.5	**Belmont** (city) Gaston County
113	n/a	9.5	**Benson** (town) Johnston County
113	n/a	9.5	**Franklin** (town) Macon County
113	2760	9.5	**Sanford** (city) Lee County
113	n/a	9.5	**Wallburg** (town) Davidson County
113	2760	9.5	**Wilmington** (city) New Hanover County
119	n/a	9.6	**Fairmont** (town) Robeson County
119	2825	9.6	**Kannapolis** (city) Cabarrus County
119	n/a	9.6	**Northchase** (CDP) New Hanover County
119	n/a	9.6	**Rockingham** (city) Richmond County
119	2825	9.6	**Statesville** (city) Iredell County
119	n/a	9.6	**Tabor City** (town) Columbus County
125	2887	9.7	**Asheville** (city) Buncombe County
125	n/a	9.7	**Hillsborough** (town) Orange County
125	2887	9.7	**Matthews** (town) Mecklenburg County
125	n/a	9.7	**Mineral Springs** (town) Union County
125	n/a	9.7	**Weddington** (town) Union County
130	n/a	9.8	**Fletcher** (town) Henderson County
130	n/a	9.8	**Ranlo** (town) Gaston County
130	2951	9.8	**Reidsville** (city) Rockingham County
130	2951	9.8	**Rocky Mount** (city) Nash County
134	3017	9.9	**Mount Holly** (city) Gaston County
134	n/a	9.9	**River Road** (CDP) Beaufort County
134	3017	9.9	**Tarboro** (town) Edgecombe County
137	n/a	10.0	**Brevard** (city) Transylvania County
137	3092	10.0	**Clayton** (town) Johnston County
137	n/a	10.0	**Elkin** (town) Surry County
137	n/a	10.0	**Long View** (town) Catawba County
137	n/a	10.0	**Unionville** (town) Union County
137	3092	10.0	**Wake Forest** (town) Wake County
137	n/a	10.0	**Waxhaw** (town) Union County
137	n/a	10.0	**Wentworth** (town) Rockingham County
145	3165	10.1	**Kings Mountain** (city) Cleveland County
145	3165	10.1	**Lincolnton** (city) Lincoln County
145	n/a	10.1	**Murfreesboro** (town) Hertford County
145	n/a	10.1	**Oak Ridge** (town) Guilford County
149	n/a	10.2	**Cajah's Mountain** (town) Caldwell County
149	3212	10.2	**Holly Springs** (town) Wake County

Note: The state column ranks the top/bottom 150 places in the state with population of 2,500 or more. The national column ranks the top/bottom places in the country with population of 10,000 or more. Places that are unincorporated were not considered in the rankings. n/a indicates data not available. Please refer to the User Guide for additional information.

Ancestry: German

Top 150 Places Ranked in *Descending* Order

State Rank	Nat'l Rank	Percent	Place
1	1	76.8	**Chilton** (city) Calumet County
2	2	73.3	**Barton** (town) Washington County
3	3	73.0	**Addison** (town) Washington County
4	4	72.6	**Dyersville** (city) Dubuque County
5	5	70.9	**Jackson** (town) Washington County
6	6	70.5	**Howards Grove** (village) Sheboygan County
7	7	70.3	**Mayville** (city) Dodge County
8	8	69.9	**Minster** (village) Auglaize County
9	9	69.1	**Hartford** (town) Washington County
9	9	69.1	**Polk** (town) Washington County
11	11	68.4	**Medford** (town) Taylor County
12	12	68.1	**Brillion** (city) Calumet County
13	13	67.8	**Kiel** (city) Manitowoc County
14	14	67.7	**Hortonville** (village) Outagamie County
15	15	66.9	**Wakefield** (township) Stearns County
16	16	66.1	**Center** (town) Outagamie County
17	17	66.0	**Plymouth** (town) Sheboygan County
17	17	66.0	**Sheboygan** (town) Sheboygan County
17	17	66.0	**Trenton** (town) Washington County
20	20	65.8	**Fayette** (township) Juniata County
20	20	65.8	**Wheatland** (town) Kenosha County
22	22	65.5	**Kewaskum** (village) Washington County
23	23	65.4	**Springfield** (town) Dane County
24	24	65.2	**Empire** (town) Fond du Lac County
25	25	64.8	**Mukwa** (town) Waupaca County
26	26	64.2	**Albany** (town) Stearns County
27	27	64.0	**Jackson** (village) Washington County
28	28	63.9	**New Bremen** (village) Auglaize County
29	29	63.8	**New Ulm** (city) Brown County
30	30	63.0	**Coldwater** (village) Mercer County
30	30	63.0	**West Bend** (town) Washington County
32	32	62.3	**Breese** (city) Clinton County
33	33	61.9	**Taycheedah** (town) Fond du Lac County
34	34	61.4	**Merrill** (town) Lincoln County
34	34	61.4	**New Holstein** (city) Calumet County
36	36	60.9	**Beaver Dam** (town) Dodge County
36	36	60.9	**Friendship** (town) Fond du Lac County
36	36	60.9	**Mandan** (city) Morton County
39	39	60.8	**Miami Heights** (CDP) Hamilton County
40	40	60.6	**Plymouth** (city) Sheboygan County
40	40	60.6	**Sheboygan Falls** (city) Sheboygan County
42	42	60.4	**Medford** (city) Taylor County
43	43	60.3	**Merrill** (city) Lincoln County
43	43	60.3	**Saint Marys** (city) Elk County
45	45	60.2	**Elizabeth** (township) Lancaster County
46	46	59.7	**Stettin** (town) Marathon County
47	47	59.6	**Merton** (village) Waukesha County
48	48	59.5	**Wales** (village) Waukesha County
49	49	59.4	**Dale** (town) Outagamie County
49	49	59.4	**Germantown** (village) Washington County
49	49	59.4	**Grundy Center** (city) Grundy County
49	49	59.4	**Saint Augusta** (city) Stearns County
53	53	59.3	**Columbus** (city) Columbia County
53	53	59.3	**Farmington** (town) Washington County
55	55	59.2	**Fond du Lac** (town) Fond du Lac County
55	55	59.2	**Wayne** (city) Wayne County
57	57	59.1	**Caledonia** (city) Houston County
58	58	58.9	**Ixonia** (town) Jefferson County
58	58	58.9	**Lodi** (town) Columbia County
60	60	58.3	**Horicon** (city) Dodge County
61	61	58.2	**Johnson Creek** (village) Jefferson County
62	62	58.0	**Oakland** (town) Jefferson County
62	62	58.0	**Sauk Centre** (city) Stearns County
64	64	57.8	**Richfield** (village) Washington County
65	65	57.7	**Harrison** (town) Calumet County
65	65	57.7	**Sebewaing** (township) Huron County
67	67	57.6	**Fox** (township) Elk County
67	67	57.6	**West Bend** (city) Washington County
69	69	57.4	**Grafton** (town) Ozaukee County
69	69	57.4	**Ripon** (city) Fond du Lac County
71	71	57.3	**Harrison** (city) Hamilton County
72	72	57.2	**Carroll** (city) Carroll County
72	72	57.2	**Washington** (township) Schuylkill County
74	74	57.1	**Kronenwetter** (village) Marathon County
75	75	56.9	**Ellington** (town) Outagamie County
76	76	56.8	**Norwood Young America** (city) Carver County
76	76	56.8	**Saukville** (village) Ozaukee County
78	78	56.5	**Sherwood** (village) Calumet County
78	78	56.5	**Slinger** (village) Washington County
80	80	56.4	**Delphos** (city) Allen County
80	80	56.4	**Oregon** (town) Dane County
80	80	56.4	**Shelby** (town) La Crosse County
83	83	56.3	**Lisbon** (town) Waukesha County
83	83	56.3	**Sussex** (village) Waukesha County
85	85	56.2	**Bismarck** (city) Burleigh County
85	85	56.2	**Poynette** (village) Columbia County
87	87	56.0	**Alsace** (township) Berks County
87	87	56.0	**Jordan** (city) Scott County
89	89	55.9	**Eagle** (town) Waukesha County
90	90	55.8	**Waukesha** (town) Waukesha County
91	91	55.7	**Clayton** (town) Winnebago County
91	91	55.7	**Pine Grove** (township) Schuylkill County
93	93	55.6	**Ashippun** (town) Dodge County
93	93	55.6	**Rockland** (township) Berks County
95	95	55.5	**Clintonville** (city) Waupaca County
95	95	55.5	**Pewaukee** (city) Waukesha County
95	95	55.5	**Sevastopol** (town) Door County
98	98	55.3	**Lake Crystal** (city) Blue Earth County
98	98	55.3	**Plainview** (city) Wabasha County
98	98	55.3	**Rock Rapids** (city) Lyon County
101	101	55.2	**De Witt** (city) Clinton County
101	101	55.2	**Merton** (town) Waukesha County
101	101	55.2	**Watertown** (city) Jefferson County
104	104	55.1	**Hartford** (city) Washington County
105	105	55.0	**Upper Augusta** (township) Northumberland County
106	106	54.9	**Delhi Hills** (CDP) Hamilton County
107	107	54.8	**Aberdeen** (city) Brown County
107	107	54.8	**Delafield** (town) Waukesha County
109	109	54.7	**Jamestown** (city) Stutsman County
110	110	54.6	**Cottage Grove** (town) Dane County
110	110	54.6	**Hallam** (borough) York County
110	110	54.6	**Vernon** (town) Waukesha County
113	113	54.5	**Monticello** (city) Jones County
113	113	54.5	**Mukwonago** (town) Waukesha County
115	115	54.4	**Milbank** (city) Grant County
116	116	54.3	**Beulah** (city) Mercer County
116	116	54.3	**Cross Plains** (village) Dane County
116	116	54.3	**Lima** (town) Sheboygan County
119	119	54.2	**Algoma** (city) Kewaunee County
119	119	54.2	**Cold Spring** (city) Stearns County
119	119	54.2	**Lodi** (city) Columbia County
119	119	54.2	**Monfort Heights** (CDP) Hamilton County
123	123	54.1	**Mack** (CDP) Hamilton County
123	123	54.1	**North Mankato** (city) Nicollet County
125	125	54.0	**Menasha** (town) Winnebago County
125	125	54.0	**Rome** (town) Adams County
127	127	53.9	**Hays** (city) Ellis County
128	128	53.8	**Brockway** (township) Stearns County
128	128	53.8	**Dent** (CDP) Hamilton County
128	128	53.8	**Lake Wazeecha** (CDP) Wood County
128	128	53.8	**Sleepy Eye** (city) Brown County
132	132	53.7	**Zumbrota** (city) Goodhue County
133	133	53.6	**Dickinson** (city) Stark County
134	134	53.5	**Beaver Dam** (city) Dodge County
134	134	53.5	**Fond du Lac** (city) Fond du Lac County
134	134	53.5	**Wescott** (town) Shawano County
137	137	53.4	**Eagle Point** (town) Chippewa County
137	137	53.4	**Grafton** (village) Ozaukee County
139	139	53.3	**Freeburg** (village) Saint Clair County
140	140	53.2	**Lake Wisconsin** (CDP) Columbia County
140	140	53.2	**Marshfield** (city) Wood County
142	142	53.1	**Dell Rapids** (city) Minnehaha County
142	142	53.1	**Lake Mills** (city) Jefferson County
142	142	53.1	**Muskego** (city) Waukesha County
142	142	53.1	**Oregon** (village) Dane County
142	142	53.1	**Portage** (city) Columbia County
147	147	53.0	**Hereford** (township) Berks County
147	147	53.0	**Marysville** (city) Marshall County
147	147	53.0	**North Fond du Lac** (village) Fond du Lac County
150	150	52.9	**Blackhawk** (CDP) Meade County

Note: The state column ranks the top/bottom 150 places in the state with population of 2,500 or more. The national column ranks the top/bottom places in the country with population of 10,000 or more. Places that are unincorporated were not considered in the rankings. n/a indicates data not available. Please refer to the User Guide for additional information.

Ancestry: English

Top 150 Places Ranked in *Descending* Order

State Rank	Nat'l Rank	Percent	Place
1	1	84.4	**Hildale** (city) Washington County
2	2	66.2	**Colorado City** (town) Mohave County
3	3	42.2	**Alpine** (city) Utah County
4	4	41.5	**Fruit Heights** (city) Davis County
4	4	41.5	**Manti** (city) Sanpete County
6	6	40.8	**Highland** (city) Utah County
7	7	40.5	**Mapleton** (city) Utah County
8	8	39.1	**Beaver** (city) Beaver County
9	9	38.4	**Centerville** (city) Davis County
10	10	38.2	**Hooper** (city) Weber County
10	10	38.2	**Hopkinton** (town) Merrimack County
12	12	37.8	**Sheridan** (city) Grant County
13	13	36.9	**Santa Clara** (city) Washington County
14	14	36.0	**Saint George** (town) Knox County
15	15	35.9	**Farmingdale** (town) Kennebec County
16	16	35.7	**Bountiful** (city) Davis County
17	17	35.6	**Rockport** (town) Knox County
18	18	35.4	**Kanab** (city) Kane County
18	18	35.4	**McCall** (city) Valley County
20	20	35.0	**Wolfeboro** (CDP) Carroll County
21	21	34.8	**Farr West** (city) Weber County
21	21	34.8	**Providence** (city) Cache County
23	23	34.6	**Bristol** (town) Lincoln County
23	23	34.6	**Rexburg** (city) Madison County
25	25	34.5	**North Logan** (city) Cache County
26	26	34.3	**Boothbay** (town) Lincoln County
26	26	34.3	**Parowan** (city) Iron County
28	28	34.2	**Pleasant View** (city) Weber County
29	29	33.8	**Wellsville** (city) Cache County
30	30	33.6	**Monmouth** (city) Kennebec County
31	31	33.5	**Holladay** (city) Salt Lake County
32	32	33.4	**Hyde Park** (city) Cache County
32	32	33.4	**Trent Woods** (town) Craven County
34	34	33.0	**Salem** (city) Utah County
35	35	32.9	**Delta** (city) Millard County
36	36	32.8	**Freeport** (town) Cumberland County
36	36	32.8	**Midway** (city) Wasatch County
36	36	32.8	**West Bountiful** (city) Davis County
39	39	32.6	**Farmington** (city) Davis County
39	39	32.6	**Kaysville** (city) Davis County
41	41	32.5	**Kennebunkport** (town) York County
42	42	32.4	**Wolfeboro** (town) Carroll County
43	43	32.2	**Woodstock** (town) Windsor County
44	44	32.0	**Santaquin** (city) Utah County
45	45	31.9	**Chichester** (town) Merrimack County
46	46	31.8	**American Fork** (city) Utah County
46	46	31.8	**Anson** (town) Somerset County
46	46	31.8	**Camden** (town) Knox County
46	46	31.8	**Hyrum** (city) Cache County
50	50	31.6	**Spring Arbor** (township) Jackson County
51	51	31.5	**Poland** (town) Androscoggin County
52	52	31.4	**Herriman** (city) Salt Lake County
53	53	31.3	**Morgan** (city) Morgan County
54	54	31.1	**Alamo** (town) Wheeler County
54	54	31.1	**Charlestown** (town) Sullivan County
56	56	31.0	**Spanish Fork** (city) Utah County
56	56	31.0	**Waldoboro** (town) Lincoln County
58	58	30.9	**Ivins** (city) Washington County
59	59	30.8	**Yarmouth** (town) Cumberland County
60	60	30.7	**Cedar Hills** (city) Utah County
61	61	30.6	**Bethel** (town) Oxford County
61	61	30.6	**Bridgton** (town) Cumberland County
61	61	30.6	**Lake San Marcos** (CDP) San Diego County
61	61	30.6	**Rockland** (city) Knox County
61	61	30.6	**Saint George** (city) Washington County
61	61	30.6	**Woods Cross** (city) Davis County
67	67	30.5	**Cedar City** (city) Iron County
68	68	30.3	**North Salt Lake** (city) Davis County
68	68	30.3	**South Jordan** (city) Salt Lake County
70	70	30.2	**Eagle Mountain** (city) Utah County
71	71	30.1	**Preston** (city) Franklin County
72	72	29.9	**Camden** (CDP) Knox County
73	73	29.8	**South Beach** (CDP) Indian River County
74	74	29.7	**Harpswell** (town) Cumberland County
74	74	29.7	**Indian River Shores** (town) Indian River County
76	76	29.5	**Helena** (city) Telfair County
76	76	29.5	**Manchester** (town) Kennebec County
76	76	29.5	**Nephi** (city) Juab County
76	76	29.5	**Washington Terrace** (city) Weber County
80	80	29.4	**Yarmouth** (CDP) Cumberland County
81	81	29.3	**Springville** (city) Utah County
82	82	29.2	**Clinton** (town) Kennebec County
82	82	29.2	**Grantsville** (city) Tooele County
84	84	29.1	**Little Compton** (town) Newport County
84	84	29.1	**Plain City** (city) Weber County
86	86	29.0	**Cottonwood Heights** (city) Salt Lake County
86	86	29.0	**Warren** (town) Knox County
88	88	28.9	**Madison** (town) Carroll County
88	88	28.9	**Washington** (city) Washington County
90	90	28.8	**Lindon** (city) Utah County
90	90	28.8	**Livermore Falls** (town) Androscoggin County
90	90	28.8	**Nibley** (city) Cache County
93	93	28.7	**Orem** (city) Utah County
93	93	28.7	**Woolwich** (town) Sagadahoc County
95	95	28.6	**Pleasant Grove** (city) Utah County
96	96	28.5	**Arundel** (town) York County
96	96	28.5	**China** (town) Kennebec County
98	98	28.4	**Lehi** (city) Utah County
98	98	28.4	**Tamworth** (town) Carroll County
100	100	28.3	**Bradford** (town) Orange County
100	100	28.3	**Enoch** (city) Iron County
102	102	28.2	**Oneida** (town) Scott County
102	102	28.2	**Oxford** (town) Oxford County
102	102	28.2	**South Weber** (city) Davis County
105	105	28.1	**Maeser** (CDP) Uintah County
105	105	28.1	**Walpole** (town) Cheshire County
107	107	28.0	**Hampden** (CDP) Penobscot County
107	107	28.0	**Sandy** (city) Salt Lake County
109	109	27.9	**Northfield** (town) Franklin County
109	109	27.9	**Perry** (city) Box Elder County
111	111	27.8	**Limerick** (town) York County
111	111	27.8	**Orleans** (town) Barnstable County
111	111	27.8	**Riverton** (city) Salt Lake County
114	114	27.7	**Draper** (city) Salt Lake County
114	114	27.7	**Hartland** (town) Windsor County
114	114	27.7	**Otisco** (town) Onondaga County
114	114	27.7	**Saratoga Springs** (city) Utah County
114	114	27.7	**Smithfield** (city) Cache County
119	119	27.6	**Bluffdale** (city) Salt Lake County
119	119	27.6	**Bowdoin** (town) Sagadahoc County
119	119	27.6	**East Bloomfield** (town) Ontario County
119	119	27.6	**North Yarmouth** (town) Cumberland County
119	119	27.6	**Syracuse** (city) Davis County
124	124	27.5	**Harrison** (town) Cumberland County
124	124	27.5	**Highland Park** (town) Dallas County
124	124	27.5	**South Eliot** (CDP) York County
127	127	27.4	**Hampden** (town) Penobscot County
127	127	27.4	**Montpelier** (city) Bear Lake County
127	127	27.4	**Winston** (city) Douglas County
130	130	27.3	**Buxton** (town) York County
130	130	27.3	**North Ogden** (city) Weber County
130	130	27.3	**White Hall** (city) Jefferson County
133	133	27.2	**Thetford** (town) Orange County
134	134	27.1	**Greene** (town) Chenango County
134	134	27.1	**Wakefield** (town) Carroll County
136	136	26.9	**New Durham** (town) Strafford County
136	136	26.9	**Stansbury Park** (CDP) Tooele County
136	136	26.9	**Surfside Beach** (town) Horry County
139	139	26.8	**Stratham** (town) Rockingham County
140	140	26.6	**Concord** (township) Jackson County
140	140	26.6	**Millcreek** (CDP) Salt Lake County
140	140	26.6	**Peterborough** (CDP) Hillsborough County
140	140	26.6	**Turner** (town) Androscoggin County
144	144	26.5	**Foster** (town) Providence County
144	144	26.5	**Hope** (township) Barry County
144	144	26.5	**Norwich** (town) Windsor County
147	147	26.4	**Belle Meade** (city) Davidson County
148	148	26.3	**Belfast** (city) Waldo County
149	149	26.2	**Richfield** (city) Sevier County
149	149	26.2	**South Duxbury** (CDP) Plymouth County

Note: The state column ranks the top/bottom 150 places in the state with population of 2,500 or more. The national column ranks the top/bottom places in the country with population of 10,000 or more. Places that are unincorporated were not considered in the rankings. n/a indicates data not available. Please refer to the User Guide for additional information.

Ancestry: American

Top 150 Places Ranked in *Descending* Order

State Rank	Nat'l Rank	Percent	Place
1	1	66.4	La Follette (city) Campbell County
2	2	60.0	Gloverville (CDP) Aiken County
3	3	54.6	Clearwater (CDP) Aiken County
4	4	54.4	Treasure Lake (CDP) Clearfield County
5	5	51.7	Healdton (city) Carter County
6	6	45.9	Bonifay (city) Holmes County
7	7	45.8	Harlem (CDP) Hendry County
8	8	45.5	Bean Station (city) Grainger County
8	8	45.5	Stanford (city) Lincoln County
10	10	44.5	Pell City (city) Saint Clair County
11	11	44.3	New Tazewell (town) Claiborne County
12	12	43.9	Dresden (town) Weakley County
13	13	43.6	Hartford (city) Ohio County
14	14	43.2	Blue Hill (town) Hancock County
15	15	43.1	Eaton (town) Madison County
16	16	43.0	Church Hill (city) Hawkins County
17	17	42.6	Middlesborough (city) Bell County
18	18	42.1	Temple (city) Carroll County
19	19	41.1	Georgetown (city) Vermilion County
20	20	40.9	Grantville (city) Coweta County
20	20	40.9	Summerville (city) Chattooga County
22	22	40.6	Morehead (city) Rowan County
23	23	40.5	Bayou Vista (CDP) Saint Mary Parish
24	24	40.4	Lone Grove (city) Carter County
24	24	40.4	Wilkesboro (town) Wilkes County
26	26	39.9	Chincoteague (town) Accomack County
27	27	39.8	Bremen (city) Haralson County
28	28	39.7	Cullowhee (CDP) Jackson County
29	29	39.4	Nassau Village-Ratliff (CDP) Nassau County
30	30	38.8	Crab Orchard (CDP) Raleigh County
31	31	38.7	Stanton (city) Powell County
32	32	38.4	Rogersville (town) Hawkins County
33	33	38.2	Cookeville (city) Putnam County
34	34	38.0	Livingston (town) Overton County
35	35	37.6	Gray Summit (CDP) Franklin County
35	35	37.6	Harrogate (city) Claiborne County
37	37	37.4	North Terre Haute (CDP) Vigo County
38	38	37.3	Mount Carmel (CDP) Clermont County
39	39	36.9	Atkins (city) Pope County
39	39	36.9	Burnettown (town) Aiken County
39	39	36.9	De Funiak Springs (city) Walton County
42	42	36.8	Lake of the Woods (CDP) Champaign County
42	42	36.8	Suncoast Estates (CDP) Lee County
44	44	36.7	Lancaster (city) Garrard County
44	44	36.7	Sandy (township) Clearfield County
46	46	36.6	Donalsonville (city) Seminole County
47	47	36.3	Bradford (township) Clearfield County
47	47	36.3	Broadway (town) Rockingham County
47	47	36.3	Jena (town) La Salle Parish
50	50	36.2	Algood (city) Putnam County
50	50	36.2	Sylva (town) Jackson County
52	52	36.0	Unicoi (town) Unicoi County
53	53	35.6	Bloomingdale (CDP) Sullivan County
53	53	35.6	Somerset (city) Pulaski County
53	53	35.6	Timberville (town) Rockingham County
56	56	35.5	Beaver Dam (city) Ohio County
56	56	35.5	Oliver Springs (town) Anderson County
58	58	35.4	Bucksport (CDP) Hancock County
59	59	35.1	England (city) Lonoke County
59	59	35.1	Fairview (CDP) Walker County
59	59	35.1	LaFayette (city) Walker County
62	62	34.9	Bucksport (town) Hancock County
62	62	34.9	Mountain City (town) Johnson County
62	62	34.9	Shepherdsville (city) Bullitt County
65	65	34.8	Blennerhassett (CDP) Wood County
66	66	34.7	South Lebanon (village) Warren County
67	67	34.5	Mount Carmel (town) Hawkins County
68	68	34.3	Hannahs Mill (CDP) Upson County
69	69	34.2	Mills (town) Natrona County
69	69	34.2	Rockwood (city) Roane County
71	71	33.5	North Wilkesboro (town) Wilkes County
71	71	33.5	Odenville (town) Saint Clair County
73	73	33.3	Ward (city) Lonoke County
74	74	33.2	Bawcomville (CDP) Ouachita Parish
75	75	33.1	Bethel (village) Clermont County
75	75	33.1	Grottoes (town) Rockingham County
77	77	33.0	Shelbyville (city) Bedford County
78	78	32.7	Dawson Springs (city) Hopkins County
78	78	32.7	Galena (city) Cherokee County
78	78	32.7	Pike Road (town) Montgomery County
81	81	32.6	Erwin (town) Unicoi County
81	81	32.6	Honea Path (town) Anderson County
83	83	32.5	West Tisbury (town) Dukes County
84	84	32.3	Pearisburg (town) Giles County
85	85	32.2	Evansville (town) Natrona County
86	86	32.0	Moody (city) Saint Clair County
86	86	32.0	Pittsburg (city) Crawford County
88	88	31.9	Woodbury (town) Cannon County
89	89	31.8	Dandridge (town) Jefferson County
90	90	31.7	Withamsville (CDP) Clermont County
91	91	31.5	Margaret (town) Saint Clair County
92	92	31.4	Pigeon Forge (city) Sevier County
93	93	31.3	Alva (CDP) Lee County
94	94	31.1	Hilliard (town) Nassau County
95	95	30.8	Monterey (town) Putnam County
96	96	30.7	Icard (CDP) Burke County
97	97	30.5	Flemingsburg (city) Fleming County
97	97	30.5	Shady Spring (CDP) Raleigh County
99	99	30.4	Irvine (city) Estill County
100	100	30.3	Cloverdale (CDP) Botetourt County
100	100	30.3	Hamilton (town) Madison County
100	100	30.3	Sylacauga (city) Talladega County
100	100	30.3	Underwood-Petersville (CDP) Lauderdale County
104	104	30.2	Central City (city) Muhlenberg County
104	104	30.2	Harriman (city) Roane County
104	104	30.2	Prestonsburg (city) Floyd County
107	107	30.1	Stuarts Draft (CDP) Augusta County
108	108	30.0	Madison (town) Madison County
108	108	30.0	Verona (CDP) Augusta County
108	108	30.0	Waynesville (town) Haywood County
111	111	29.8	Granville (town) Washington County
111	111	29.8	Paris (city) Bourbon County
111	111	29.8	Winchester (city) Clark County
114	114	29.7	Byron (city) Peach County
114	114	29.7	Emmett (city) Gem County
114	114	29.7	Hillview (city) Bullitt County
114	114	29.7	Oak Grove (CDP) Washington County
114	114	29.7	Sunnyvale (town) Dallas County
114	114	29.7	Wickenburg (town) Maricopa County
120	120	29.6	Jefferson City (city) Jefferson County
121	121	29.5	Ball (town) Rapides Parish
121	121	29.5	Corinth (town) Penobscot County
121	121	29.5	Lincoln (city) Talladega County
124	124	29.4	Manchester (city) Coffee County
124	124	29.4	Owensboro (city) Daviess County
126	126	29.3	Kings Mountain (city) Cleveland County
127	127	29.2	Buckner (CDP) Oldham County
127	127	29.2	Malabar (town) Brevard County
129	129	29.1	Baxter Springs (city) Cherokee County
130	130	28.9	Kingston (city) Roane County
130	130	28.9	Morristown (city) Hamblen County
132	132	28.8	Bayshore (CDP) New Hanover County
132	132	28.8	Buena Vista (independent city)
134	134	28.7	Grissom AFB (CDP) Miami County
134	134	28.7	Hodgenville (city) Larue County
136	136	28.5	Claiborne (CDP) Ouachita Parish
136	136	28.5	Inwood (CDP) Polk County
136	136	28.5	Moyock (CDP) Currituck County
136	136	28.5	Richlands (town) Tazewell County
136	136	28.5	Tabor City (town) Columbus County
141	141	28.4	Dundee (town) Polk County
141	141	28.4	Jan Phyl Village (CDP) Polk County
141	141	28.4	Morgan (city) Morgan County
144	144	28.3	West Liberty (city) Morgan County
145	145	28.2	Bicknell (city) Knox County
145	145	28.2	Fort Scott (city) Bourbon County
145	145	28.2	Putney (CDP) Dougherty County
148	148	28.1	Berwick (town) Saint Mary Parish
148	148	28.1	Corinth (town) Saratoga County
148	148	28.1	Middleton (city) Canyon County

Note: *The state column ranks the top/bottom 150 places in the state with population of 2,500 or more. The national column ranks the top/bottom places in the country with population of 10,000 or more. Places that are unincorporated were not considered in the rankings. n/a indicates data not available. Please refer to the User Guide for additional information.*

Ancestry: Irish

Top 150 Places Ranked in *Descending* Order

State Rank	Nat'l Rank	Percent	Place
1	1	52.0	**Pearl River** (CDP) Rockland County
2	2	51.7	**Ocean Bluff-Brant Rock** (CDP) Plymouth County
3	3	50.6	**Green Harbor-Cedar Crest** (CDP) Plymouth County
4	4	49.4	**Rockledge** (borough) Montgomery County
5	5	48.3	**Walpole** (CDP) Norfolk County
6	6	47.4	**North Scituate** (CDP) Plymouth County
7	7	47.0	**Scituate** (CDP) Plymouth County
8	8	46.9	**Marshfield** (town) Plymouth County
9	9	46.2	**Scituate** (town) Plymouth County
10	10	45.8	**Ridley Park** (borough) Delaware County
11	11	45.5	**Spring Lake Heights** (borough) Monmouth County
12	12	45.3	**Oak Valley** (CDP) Gloucester County
13	13	45.2	**Hanover** (town) Plymouth County
14	14	44.7	**Norwell** (town) Plymouth County
15	15	44.2	**Glenside** (CDP) Montgomery County
15	15	44.2	**Manasquan** (borough) Monmouth County
17	17	43.8	**Norwood** (borough) Delaware County
18	18	42.9	**Walpole** (town) Norfolk County
18	18	42.9	**Wynantskill** (CDP) Rensselaer County
20	20	42.8	**Springfield** (township) Delaware County
21	21	42.6	**Folsom** (CDP) Delaware County
21	21	42.6	**Glenolden** (borough) Delaware County
21	21	42.6	**Highlands** (borough) Monmouth County
24	24	42.2	**Marshfield** (CDP) Plymouth County
25	25	41.7	**North Middletown** (CDP) Monmouth County
26	26	41.6	**Braintree Town** (city) Norfolk County
27	27	41.4	**Weymouth Town** (city) Norfolk County
28	28	41.1	**Littleton Common** (CDP) Middlesex County
28	28	41.1	**North Wildwood** (city) Cape May County
30	30	41.0	**Bridgewater** (CDP) Plymouth County
31	31	40.9	**Abington** (cdp/town) Plymouth County
31	31	40.9	**Nahant** (cdp/town) Essex County
31	31	40.9	**Spring Lake** (borough) Monmouth County
34	34	40.6	**Whitman** (town) Plymouth County
35	35	40.5	**Cohasset** (town) Norfolk County
35	35	40.5	**Hopedale** (CDP) Worcester County
35	35	40.5	**Sayville** (CDP) Suffolk County
38	38	40.4	**Brielle** (borough) Monmouth County
39	39	40.3	**Hull** (cdp/town) Plymouth County
40	40	40.2	**Gloucester City** (city) Camden County
41	41	39.9	**Churchville** (CDP) Bucks County
42	42	39.7	**Haddon Heights** (borough) Camden County
43	43	39.6	**Notre Dame** (CDP) Saint Joseph County
44	44	39.5	**Ashland** (borough) Schuylkill County
44	44	39.5	**Hingham** (town) Plymouth County
46	46	39.4	**Avon** (town) Norfolk County
47	47	39.3	**Garden City** (village) Nassau County
47	47	39.3	**Tinicum** (township) Delaware County
49	49	39.2	**Milton** (cdp/town) Norfolk County
49	49	39.2	**Ramtown** (CDP) Monmouth County
51	51	39.1	**Ridley** (township) Delaware County
52	52	38.8	**Bridgewater** (town) Plymouth County
53	53	38.5	**Hanson** (town) Plymouth County
53	53	38.5	**North Reading** (town) Middlesex County
53	53	38.5	**Prospect Park** (borough) Delaware County
53	53	38.5	**Rockland** (town) Plymouth County
57	57	38.4	**Hingham** (CDP) Plymouth County
58	58	38.3	**Foxborough** (town) Norfolk County
59	59	38.1	**Foxborough** (CDP) Norfolk County
60	60	38.0	**Barrington** (borough) Camden County
61	61	37.9	**Aldan** (borough) Delaware County
61	61	37.9	**Mansfield Center** (CDP) Bristol County
61	61	37.9	**National Park** (borough) Gloucester County
64	64	37.8	**East Sandwich** (CDP) Barnstable County
65	65	37.6	**Haverford** (township) Delaware County
65	65	37.6	**West Brandywine** (township) Chester County
67	67	37.5	**East Bridgewater** (town) Plymouth County
68	68	37.4	**Buzzards Bay** (CDP) Barnstable County
69	69	37.3	**Blauvelt** (CDP) Rockland County
69	69	37.3	**East Quogue** (CDP) Suffolk County
71	71	37.2	**Canton** (town) Norfolk County
71	71	37.2	**North Falmouth** (CDP) Barnstable County
73	73	37.1	**Pembroke** (town) Plymouth County
73	73	37.1	**Upton** (CDP) Worcester County
73	73	37.1	**Woodbury Heights** (borough) Gloucester County
76	76	36.9	**Fair Haven** (borough) Monmouth County
77	77	36.8	**Clementon** (borough) Camden County
77	77	36.8	**Duxbury** (town) Plymouth County
79	79	36.7	**Fairview** (CDP) Monmouth County
79	79	36.7	**Folcroft** (borough) Delaware County
79	79	36.7	**Newtown** (township) Delaware County
82	82	36.6	**Rockville Centre** (village) Nassau County
83	83	36.5	**Oceanport** (borough) Monmouth County
83	83	36.5	**West Bridgewater** (town) Plymouth County
85	85	36.2	**Audubon** (borough) Camden County
85	85	36.2	**Campo** (CDP) San Diego County
87	87	36.0	**Orleans** (town) Jefferson County
87	87	36.0	**Shark River Hills** (CDP) Monmouth County
89	89	35.8	**Drexel Hill** (CDP) Delaware County
89	89	35.8	**Trappe** (borough) Montgomery County
89	89	35.8	**West Sayville** (CDP) Suffolk County
92	92	35.5	**Leonardo** (CDP) Monmouth County
92	92	35.5	**Little Silver** (borough) Monmouth County
94	94	35.3	**Bethlehem** (township) Hunterdon County
95	95	35.2	**East Islip** (CDP) Suffolk County
95	95	35.2	**Kingston** (town) Plymouth County
97	97	35.1	**Dedham** (cdp/town) Norfolk County
97	97	35.1	**Hopedale** (town) Worcester County
97	97	35.1	**Wilmington** (cdp/town) Middlesex County
100	100	35.0	**Green Island** (town/village) Albany County
100	100	35.0	**Medford Lakes** (borough) Burlington County
102	102	34.9	**Holbrook** (cdp/town) Norfolk County
102	102	34.9	**Mansfield** (town) Bristol County
104	104	34.8	**LaFayette** (town) Onondaga County
104	104	34.8	**North Plymouth** (CDP) Plymouth County
104	104	34.8	**Norton** (town) Bristol County
104	104	34.8	**Tuckerton** (borough) Ocean County
104	104	34.8	**Wakefield** (cdp/town) Middlesex County
109	109	34.7	**Cape Neddick** (CDP) York County
109	109	34.7	**Tewksbury** (town) Middlesex County
109	109	34.7	**Woodlyn** (CDP) Delaware County
109	109	34.7	**Woolwich** (township) Gloucester County
113	113	34.6	**Wanamassa** (CDP) Monmouth County
114	114	34.5	**East Shoreham** (CDP) Suffolk County
114	114	34.5	**Horsham** (CDP) Montgomery County
114	114	34.5	**Skippack** (CDP) Montgomery County
117	117	34.4	**Plymouth** (town) Plymouth County
117	117	34.4	**Western Springs** (village) Cook County
119	119	34.3	**Bethel** (township) Delaware County
119	119	34.3	**Melrose** (city) Middlesex County
119	119	34.3	**Point Pleasant** (borough) Ocean County
122	122	34.2	**Aston** (township) Delaware County
122	122	34.2	**North Seekonk** (CDP) Bristol County
122	122	34.2	**Wanakah** (CDP) Erie County
122	122	34.2	**Westvale** (CDP) Onondaga County
126	126	34.1	**Reading** (cdp/town) Middlesex County
126	126	34.1	**Winthrop Town** (city) Suffolk County
128	128	34.0	**Atkinson** (town) Rockingham County
128	128	34.0	**Bella Vista** (CDP) Shasta County
128	128	34.0	**Hopkinton** (CDP) Middlesex County
128	128	34.0	**Plymouth** (CDP) Plymouth County
128	128	34.0	**Washington** (town) Dutchess County
128	128	34.0	**Williston Park** (village) Nassau County
134	134	33.9	**Norwood** (cdp/town) Norfolk County
135	135	33.8	**Clinton** (town) Worcester County
135	135	33.8	**Halifax** (town) Plymouth County
135	135	33.8	**Mystic Island** (CDP) Ocean County
135	135	33.8	**Wall** (township) Monmouth County
139	139	33.7	**Massapequa Park** (village) Nassau County
140	140	33.6	**Cold Spring Harbor** (CDP) Suffolk County
140	140	33.6	**Dalton** (town) Berkshire County
142	142	33.5	**Colonie** (village) Albany County
142	142	33.5	**Middletown** (township) Monmouth County
142	142	33.5	**Seabrook** (town) Rockingham County
142	142	33.5	**Waterford** (township) Camden County
146	146	33.4	**Medfield** (CDP) Norfolk County
146	146	33.4	**Montgomery** (village) Orange County
146	146	33.4	**Mount Ephraim** (borough) Camden County
149	149	33.3	**Dover** (town) Dutchess County
149	149	33.3	**Fort Salonga** (CDP) Suffolk County

Note: *The state column ranks the top/bottom 150 places in the state with population of 2,500 or more. The national column ranks the top/bottom places in the country with population of 10,000 or more. Places that are unincorporated were not considered in the rankings. n/a indicates data not available. Please refer to the User Guide for additional information.*

Ancestry: Italian

Top 150 Places Ranked in *Descending* Order

State Rank	Nat'l Rank	Percent	Place
1	1	51.2	**Johnston** (town) Providence County
2	2	50.9	**Fairfield** (township) Essex County
3	3	49.0	**North Massapequa** (CDP) Nassau County
4	4	47.7	**East Haven** (cdp/town) New Haven County
5	5	47.3	**Watertown** (CDP) Litchfield County
6	6	46.3	**Massapequa** (CDP) Nassau County
7	7	45.4	**Eastchester** (CDP) Westchester County
8	8	45.3	**Thornwood** (CDP) Westchester County
9	9	44.4	**Glendora** (CDP) Camden County
10	10	44.0	**Frankfort** (village) Herkimer County
11	11	43.5	**Hawthorne** (CDP) Westchester County
12	12	43.4	**Hammonton** (town) Atlantic County
13	13	43.3	**North Branford** (town) New Haven County
13	13	43.3	**Turnersville** (CDP) Gloucester County
15	15	42.8	**West Islip** (CDP) Suffolk County
16	16	42.6	**Massapequa Park** (village) Nassau County
17	17	42.1	**Franklin Square** (CDP) Nassau County
18	18	41.9	**Islip Terrace** (CDP) Suffolk County
19	19	41.6	**Watertown** (town) Litchfield County
20	20	41.4	**Nesconset** (CDP) Suffolk County
21	21	41.1	**Lake Grove** (village) Suffolk County
22	22	40.4	**North Haven** (cdp/town) New Haven County
23	23	40.3	**Gibbstown** (CDP) Gloucester County
24	24	40.2	**Saint James** (CDP) Suffolk County
24	24	40.2	**Seaford** (CDP) Nassau County
26	26	40.1	**East Hanover** (township) Morris County
26	26	40.1	**Saugus** (cdp/town) Essex County
28	28	39.9	**Marlboro** (CDP) Ulster County
29	29	39.7	**Beach Haven West** (CDP) Ocean County
30	30	39.5	**East Islip** (CDP) Suffolk County
30	30	39.5	**Smithtown** (CDP) Suffolk County
32	32	39.3	**Jefferson Valley-Yorktown** (CDP) Westchester County
33	33	39.2	**Jessup** (borough) Lackawanna County
33	33	39.2	**Monmouth Beach** (borough) Monmouth County
35	35	39.0	**Brightwaters** (village) Suffolk County
36	36	38.7	**South Farmingdale** (CDP) Nassau County
37	37	38.1	**Frankfort** (town) Herkimer County
37	37	38.1	**Richwood** (CDP) Gloucester County
39	39	38.0	**Bayville** (village) Nassau County
39	39	38.0	**Malverne** (village) Nassau County
39	39	38.0	**North Providence** (town) Providence County
42	42	37.9	**Cedar Grove** (township) Essex County
43	43	37.8	**Plainedge** (CDP) Nassau County
44	44	37.7	**Holtsville** (CDP) Suffolk County
44	44	37.7	**Oakville** (CDP) Litchfield County
46	46	37.6	**Blackwood** (CDP) Camden County
46	46	37.6	**Holbrook** (CDP) Suffolk County
48	48	37.4	**Center Moriches** (CDP) Suffolk County
48	48	37.4	**Dunmore** (borough) Lackawanna County
48	48	37.4	**Smithtown** (town) Suffolk County
51	51	37.2	**North Great River** (CDP) Suffolk County
52	52	37.1	**Blue Point** (CDP) Suffolk County
52	52	37.1	**East Norwich** (CDP) Nassau County
52	52	37.1	**Ronkonkoma** (CDP) Suffolk County
52	52	37.1	**West Pittston** (borough) Luzerne County
56	56	36.9	**Hauppauge** (CDP) Suffolk County
57	57	36.8	**Bohemia** (CDP) Suffolk County
57	57	36.8	**Farmingville** (CDP) Suffolk County
57	57	36.8	**Old Forge** (borough) Lackawanna County
57	57	36.8	**Pemberwick** (CDP) Fairfield County
61	61	36.7	**Mechanicville** (city) Saratoga County
61	61	36.7	**Miller Place** (CDP) Suffolk County
61	61	36.7	**Nutley** (township) Essex County
61	61	36.7	**Selden** (CDP) Suffolk County
61	61	36.7	**Wood-Ridge** (borough) Bergen County
66	66	36.6	**Glen Head** (CDP) Nassau County
67	67	36.5	**Pittston** (city) Luzerne County
68	68	36.4	**Centerport** (CDP) Suffolk County
69	69	36.2	**Barnegat** (CDP) Ocean County
70	70	36.1	**Mahopac** (CDP) Putnam County
70	70	36.1	**Ocean Acres** (CDP) Ocean County
72	72	36.0	**Lindenhurst** (village) Suffolk County
72	72	36.0	**Lyncourt** (CDP) Onondaga County
72	72	36.0	**Union Vale** (town) Dutchess County
72	72	36.0	**Washington** (township) Gloucester County
76	76	35.9	**Eastchester** (town) Westchester County
77	77	35.8	**Garden City South** (CDP) Nassau County
77	77	35.8	**Greenwich** (township) Gloucester County
77	77	35.8	**Manorville** (CDP) Suffolk County
80	80	35.7	**Lake Pocotopaug** (CDP) Middlesex County
80	80	35.7	**Moonachie** (borough) Bergen County
80	80	35.7	**Oyster Bay** (CDP) Nassau County
83	83	35.6	**East Freehold** (CDP) Monmouth County
83	83	35.6	**Oakdale** (CDP) Suffolk County
83	83	35.6	**Ramtown** (CDP) Monmouth County
86	86	35.5	**Kensington** (CDP) Hartford County
86	86	35.5	**Pelham Manor** (village) Westchester County
88	88	35.4	**Holiday City-Berkeley** (CDP) Ocean County
88	88	35.4	**Yaphank** (CDP) Suffolk County
90	90	35.2	**Carmel** (town) Putnam County
91	91	35.1	**Commack** (CDP) Suffolk County
92	92	34.9	**Hazlet** (township) Monmouth County
92	92	34.9	**Somers** (town) Westchester County
94	94	34.5	**Bethpage** (CDP) Nassau County
94	94	34.5	**Middle Island** (CDP) Suffolk County
94	94	34.5	**Port Jefferson Station** (CDP) Suffolk County
97	97	34.4	**Lynnfield** (cdp/town) Essex County
98	98	34.3	**Kings Park** (CDP) Suffolk County
98	98	34.3	**North Babylon** (CDP) Suffolk County
98	98	34.3	**West Babylon** (CDP) Suffolk County
101	101	34.2	**Totowa** (borough) Passaic County
102	102	34.1	**Ellwood City** (borough) Lawrence County
102	102	34.1	**Stoneham** (cdp/town) Middlesex County
104	104	34.0	**Cranston** (city) Providence County
104	104	34.0	**Shirley** (CDP) Suffolk County
106	106	33.9	**Pequannock** (township) Morris County
106	106	33.9	**Pine Lake Park** (CDP) Ocean County
108	108	33.8	**East Fishkill** (town) Dutchess County
108	108	33.8	**Montrose** (CDP) Westchester County
110	110	33.7	**Locust Valley** (CDP) Nassau County
110	110	33.7	**Neshannock** (township) Lawrence County
110	110	33.7	**West Bay Shore** (CDP) Suffolk County
110	110	33.7	**Yorktown** (town) Westchester County
114	114	33.6	**Holiday City South** (CDP) Ocean County
114	114	33.6	**Kenmore** (village) Erie County
114	114	33.6	**Lacey** (township) Ocean County
114	114	33.6	**Prospect** (town) New Haven County
114	114	33.6	**Roseland** (borough) Essex County
114	114	33.6	**Wantagh** (CDP) Nassau County
120	120	33.5	**Waldwick** (borough) Bergen County
120	120	33.5	**Wolcott** (town) New Haven County
122	122	33.4	**East Shoreham** (CDP) Suffolk County
122	122	33.4	**South Huntington** (CDP) Suffolk County
122	122	33.4	**West Sayville** (CDP) Suffolk County
125	125	33.3	**Exeter** (borough) Luzerne County
125	125	33.3	**Toms River** (township) Ocean County
127	127	33.2	**East Williston** (village) Nassau County
127	127	33.2	**Lyndhurst** (township) Bergen County
129	129	33.1	**Lake Ronkonkoma** (CDP) Suffolk County
129	129	33.1	**Toms River** (CDP) Ocean County
129	129	33.1	**Westerly** (CDP) Washington County
132	132	33.0	**Cold Spring Harbor** (CDP) Suffolk County
132	132	33.0	**Mount Sinai** (CDP) Suffolk County
134	134	32.9	**Hasbrouck Heights** (borough) Bergen County
134	134	32.9	**Stafford** (township) Ocean County
136	136	32.8	**Berlin** (town) Hartford County
136	136	32.8	**Galeville** (CDP) Onondaga County
136	136	32.8	**West Caldwell** (township) Essex County
139	139	32.7	**Putnam Valley** (town) Putnam County
139	139	32.7	**Sound Beach** (CDP) Suffolk County
141	141	32.6	**Babylon** (village) Suffolk County
141	141	32.6	**Centereach** (CDP) Suffolk County
141	141	32.6	**Elwood** (CDP) Suffolk County
141	141	32.6	**Middletown** (township) Monmouth County
141	141	32.6	**North Patchogue** (CDP) Suffolk County
146	146	32.5	**Lincroft** (CDP) Monmouth County
147	147	32.4	**Barnegat** (township) Ocean County
147	147	32.4	**Caldwell** (borough) Essex County
147	147	32.4	**Levittown** (CDP) Nassau County
147	147	32.4	**Oceanport** (borough) Monmouth County

Note: The state column ranks the top/bottom 150 places in the state with population of 2,500 or more. The national column ranks the top/bottom places in the country with population of 10,000 or more. Places that are unincorporated were not considered in the rankings. n/a indicates data not available. Please refer to the User Guide for additional information.

Employment: Management, Business, and Financial Occupations

Top 150 Places Ranked in *Descending* Order

State Rank	Nat'l Rank	Percent	Place
1	n/a	37.0	**Marvin** (village) Union County
2	n/a	32.8	**Lowesville** (CDP) Lincoln County
3	n/a	32.4	**Weddington** (town) Union County
4	90	30.2	**Summerfield** (town) Guilford County
5	n/a	29.4	**Oak Ridge** (town) Guilford County
6	n/a	29.2	**Westport** (CDP) Lincoln County
7	n/a	27.0	**Nags Head** (town) Dare County
8	n/a	26.6	**Emerald Isle** (town) Carteret County
9	n/a	25.6	**Wesley Chapel** (village) Union County
10	295	25.5	**Davidson** (town) Mecklenburg County
11	307	25.4	**Cornelius** (town) Mecklenburg County
12	316	25.3	**Apex** (town) Wake County
13	329	25.2	**Huntersville** (town) Mecklenburg County
14	388	24.3	**Pinehurst** (village) Moore County
14	n/a	24.3	**Southern Shores** (town) Dare County
16	422	23.9	**Morrisville** (town) Wake County
17	435	23.8	**Cary** (town) Wake County
17	n/a	23.8	**Lake Royale** (CDP) Franklin County
19	477	23.3	**Harrisburg** (town) Cabarrus County
20	n/a	22.6	**Carolina Beach** (town) New Hanover County
21	n/a	21.9	**Jamestown** (town) Guilford County
21	n/a	21.9	**Lake Norman of Catawba** (CDP) Catawba County
21	n/a	21.9	**Ogden** (CDP) New Hanover County
21	619	21.9	**Wake Forest** (town) Wake County
25	634	21.8	**Matthews** (town) Mecklenburg County
26	n/a	21.3	**Saint James** (town) Brunswick County
27	701	21.2	**Holly Springs** (town) Wake County
28	n/a	21.0	**Fairview** (town) Union County
29	781	20.6	**Stallings** (town) Union County
30	800	20.5	**Lewisville** (town) Forsyth County
30	n/a	20.5	**Winterville** (town) Pitt County
32	n/a	20.4	**Stokesdale** (town) Guilford County
33	n/a	20.3	**Elon** (town) Alamance County
33	n/a	20.3	**Seven Lakes** (CDP) Moore County
35	n/a	20.2	**Mills River** (town) Henderson County
36	n/a	19.9	**Waxhaw** (town) Union County
37	n/a	19.8	**Sunset Beach** (town) Brunswick County
38	940	19.5	**Mint Hill** (town) Mecklenburg County
39	n/a	19.4	**Porters Neck** (CDP) New Hanover County
40	1020	19.0	**Clemmons** (village) Forsyth County
41	n/a	18.9	**Rutherfordton** (town) Rutherford County
42	1072	18.7	**Charlotte** (city) Mecklenburg County
42	n/a	18.7	**Forest Oaks** (CDP) Guilford County
42	n/a	18.7	**Weaverville** (town) Buncombe County
45	1141	18.4	**Raleigh** (city) Wake County
46	n/a	18.2	**Kill Devil Hills** (town) Dare County
47	1231	17.9	**Belmont** (city) Gaston County
48	1271	17.7	**Kernersville** (town) Forsyth County
49	n/a	17.6	**Kitty Hawk** (town) Dare County
50	n/a	17.5	**Brevard** (city) Transylvania County
50	1311	17.5	**Concord** (city) Cabarrus County
50	n/a	17.5	**Myrtle Grove** (CDP) New Hanover County
50	n/a	17.5	**Rolesville** (town) Wake County
54	n/a	17.4	**Cramerton** (town) Gaston County
55	n/a	17.3	**Red Oak** (town) Nash County
56	n/a	17.2	**Trent Woods** (town) Craven County
57	n/a	17.1	**Bethlehem** (CDP) Alexander County
58	1419	17.0	**Leland** (town) Brunswick County
58	n/a	17.0	**Morehead City** (town) Carteret County
60	n/a	16.9	**Edenton** (town) Chowan County
60	n/a	16.9	**Fletcher** (town) Henderson County
60	n/a	16.9	**Sneads Ferry** (CDP) Onslow County
63	1457	16.8	**Indian Trail** (town) Union County
63	n/a	16.8	**Lake Park** (village) Union County
65	n/a	16.7	**Liberty** (town) Randolph County
66	n/a	16.6	**Beaufort** (town) Carteret County
66	n/a	16.6	**Fairfield Harbour** (CDP) Craven County
68	1535	16.5	**Garner** (town) Wake County
68	n/a	16.5	**Pineville** (town) Mecklenburg County
70	1577	16.3	**Knightdale** (town) Wake County
70	n/a	16.3	**Oak Island** (town) Brunswick County
72	1600	16.2	**Mooresville** (town) Iredell County
73	1618	16.1	**Fuquay-Varina** (town) Wake County
74	n/a	16.0	**Mineral Springs** (town) Union County
75	n/a	15.8	**Boiling Spring Lakes** (city) Brunswick County
75	n/a	15.8	**Clinton** (city) Sampson County
75	n/a	15.8	**Gibsonville** (town) Guilford County
75	1695	15.8	**Hickory** (city) Catawba County
79	n/a	15.6	**Warsaw** (town) Duplin County
79	n/a	15.6	**Wilkesboro** (town) Wilkes County
81	1772	15.5	**Carrboro** (town) Orange County
82	n/a	15.4	**Archer Lodge** (town) Johnston County
82	n/a	15.4	**Conover** (city) Catawba County
84	n/a	15.2	**Pleasant Garden** (town) Guilford County
85	n/a	15.0	**Wendell** (town) Wake County
86	n/a	14.8	**Moyock** (CDP) Currituck County
87	1983	14.7	**Chapel Hill** (town) Orange County
87	1983	14.7	**Mount Holly** (city) Gaston County
87	n/a	14.7	**Plymouth** (town) Washington County
87	n/a	14.7	**Red Springs** (town) Robeson County
91	n/a	14.6	**Royal Pines** (CDP) Buncombe County
92	n/a	14.5	**Pittsboro** (town) Chatham County
92	n/a	14.5	**Stanley** (town) Gaston County
94	2061	14.4	**Durham** (city) Durham County
95	2085	14.3	**Mebane** (city) Alamance County
95	2085	14.3	**Wilmington** (city) New Hanover County
97	2126	14.2	**Murraysville** (CDP) New Hanover County
98	2155	14.1	**Clayton** (town) Johnston County
98	2155	14.1	**Greensboro** (city) Guilford County
100	n/a	14.0	**Midway** (town) Davidson County
100	2195	14.0	**Tarboro** (town) Edgecombe County
102	n/a	13.9	**Granite Falls** (town) Caldwell County
102	2224	13.9	**High Point** (city) Guilford County
102	n/a	13.9	**Locust** (city) Stanly County
105	2245	13.8	**Asheville** (city) Buncombe County
105	n/a	13.8	**Lake Junaluska** (CDP) Haywood County
107	n/a	13.7	**Enochville** (CDP) Rowan County
107	2274	13.7	**Hendersonville** (city) Henderson County
109	2311	13.6	**Southern Pines** (town) Moore County
110	n/a	13.5	**Carolina Shores** (town) Brunswick County
110	n/a	13.5	**Granite Quarry** (town) Rowan County
112	n/a	13.4	**Lillington** (town) Harnett County
113	n/a	13.3	**Flat Rock** (village) Henderson County
114	2436	13.2	**Lincolnton** (city) Lincoln County
114	2436	13.2	**Winston-Salem** (city) Forsyth County
116	2476	13.1	**Archdale** (city) Randolph County
117	n/a	13.0	**Glen Raven** (CDP) Alamance County
117	2520	13.0	**Newton** (city) Catawba County
119	n/a	12.9	**Maiden** (town) Catawba County
119	n/a	12.9	**Southport** (city) Brunswick County
119	n/a	12.9	**Troy** (town) Montgomery County
122	n/a	12.8	**North Wilkesboro** (town) Wilkes County
122	n/a	12.8	**Northchase** (CDP) New Hanover County
122	2579	12.8	**Roanoke Rapids** (city) Halifax County
122	2579	12.8	**Shelby** (city) Cleveland County
122	2579	12.8	**Wilson** (city) Wilson County
127	n/a	12.7	**Aberdeen** (town) Moore County
127	2613	12.7	**Piney Green** (CDP) Onslow County
127	n/a	12.7	**Trinity** (city) Randolph County
130	2645	12.6	**Smithfield** (town) Johnston County
131	n/a	12.5	**Black Mountain** (town) Buncombe County
131	n/a	12.5	**Eastover** (town) Cumberland County
131	n/a	12.5	**Elkin** (town) Surry County
134	n/a	12.4	**Swansboro** (town) Onslow County
135	n/a	12.3	**Bayshore** (CDP) New Hanover County
135	2733	12.3	**Burlington** (city) Alamance County
135	n/a	12.3	**Canton** (town) Haywood County
135	n/a	12.3	**Hillsborough** (town) Orange County
139	2808	12.1	**Greenville** (city) Pitt County
139	n/a	12.1	**Nashville** (town) Nash County
141	2842	12.0	**Hope Mills** (town) Cumberland County
141	n/a	12.0	**Rockingham** (city) Richmond County
143	n/a	11.9	**Half Moon** (CDP) Onslow County
143	2882	11.9	**Rocky Mount** (city) Nash County
145	n/a	11.8	**Hampstead** (CDP) Pender County
145	n/a	11.8	**Landis** (town) Rowan County
145	n/a	11.8	**Lowell** (city) Gaston County
145	n/a	11.8	**Williamston** (town) Martin County
149	n/a	11.6	**Brices Creek** (CDP) Craven County
149	n/a	11.6	**China Grove** (town) Rowan County

Note: The state column ranks the top/bottom 150 places in the state with population of 2,500 or more. The national column ranks the top/bottom places in the country with population of 10,000 or more. Places that are unincorporated were not considered in the rankings. n/a indicates data not available. Please refer to the User Guide for additional information.

Employment: Management, Business, and Financial Occupations

Top 150 Places Ranked in *Ascending* Order

State Rank	Nat'l Rank	Percent	Place		State Rank	Nat'l Rank	Percent	Place
1	n/a	2.8	**Selma** (town) Johnston County		76	n/a	9.1	**Cherryville** (city) Gaston County
2	n/a	3.4	**Tyro** (CDP) Davidson County		76	n/a	9.1	**Valdese** (town) Burke County
3	n/a	3.5	**Sawmills** (town) Caldwell County		76	n/a	9.1	**Windsor** (town) Bertie County
4	n/a	3.6	**Mar-Mac** (CDP) Wayne County		79	n/a	9.3	**Washington** (city) Beaufort County
5	n/a	3.8	**Fairmont** (town) Robeson County		80	863	9.4	**Lenoir** (city) Caldwell County
6	n/a	4.1	**Gamewell** (town) Caldwell County		80	n/a	9.4	**Midland** (town) Cabarrus County
7	n/a	4.2	**Bessemer City** (city) Gaston County		80	n/a	9.4	**Rockfish** (CDP) Hoke County
8	n/a	4.3	**Spencer** (town) Rowan County		83	904	9.5	**Asheboro** (city) Randolph County
9	n/a	4.4	**La Grange** (town) Lenoir County		83	904	9.5	**Monroe** (city) Union County
10	n/a	4.5	**Wadesboro** (town) Anson County		85	n/a	9.7	**Mountain View** (CDP) Catawba County
11	n/a	4.8	**Siler City** (town) Chatham County		85	n/a	9.7	**Walkertown** (town) Forsyth County
12	n/a	4.9	**Mount Olive** (town) Wayne County		87	1041	9.9	**Graham** (city) Alamance County
13	70	5.0	**Thomasville** (city) Davidson County		87	n/a	9.9	**Silver Lake** (CDP) New Hanover County
14	85	5.2	**Lexington** (city) Davidson County		89	n/a	10.0	**Angier** (town) Harnett County
14	n/a	5.2	**Whiteville** (city) Columbus County		89	n/a	10.0	**Creedmoor** (city) Granville County
16	n/a	5.3	**Butner** (town) Granville County		89	1067	10.0	**Goldsboro** (city) Wayne County
16	n/a	5.3	**Polkton** (town) Anson County		89	1067	10.0	**Henderson** (city) Vance County
18	103	5.5	**Eden** (city) Rockingham County		89	n/a	10.0	**King** (city) Stokes County
18	n/a	5.5	**Wallace** (town) Duplin County		94	n/a	10.1	**Waynesville** (town) Haywood County
20	n/a	5.6	**Zebulon** (town) Wake County		95	1145	10.2	**Jacksonville** (city) Onslow County
21	131	5.8	**Boone** (town) Watauga County		95	1145	10.2	**New Bern** (city) Craven County
21	n/a	5.8	**Hamlet** (city) Richmond County		95	n/a	10.2	**Woodfin** (town) Buncombe County
21	n/a	5.8	**Newport** (town) Carteret County		98	n/a	10.3	**Dana** (CDP) Henderson County
21	n/a	5.8	**Shallotte** (town) Brunswick County		98	n/a	10.3	**Forest City** (town) Rutherford County
25	n/a	5.9	**Marion** (city) McDowell County		100	1224	10.4	**Elizabeth City** (city) Pasquotank County
25	n/a	5.9	**Roxboro** (city) Person County		100	1224	10.4	**Kannapolis** (city) Cabarrus County
25	n/a	5.9	**Rural Hall** (town) Forsyth County		102	n/a	10.5	**Yadkinville** (town) Yadkin County
28	n/a	6.2	**Ranlo** (town) Gaston County		103	n/a	10.6	**Benson** (town) Johnston County
28	n/a	6.2	**South Rosemary** (CDP) Halifax County		104	n/a	10.7	**Dunn** (city) Harnett County
30	n/a	6.3	**Buies Creek** (CDP) Harnett County		104	1321	10.7	**Laurinburg** (city) Scotland County
31	n/a	6.4	**Enfield** (town) Halifax County		104	1321	10.7	**Lumberton** (city) Robeson County
31	n/a	6.4	**Pembroke** (town) Robeson County		104	n/a	10.7	**Swannanoa** (CDP) Buncombe County
31	n/a	6.4	**Raeford** (city) Hoke County		104	n/a	10.7	**Whispering Pines** (village) Moore County
34	n/a	6.6	**East Rockingham** (CDP) Richmond County		109	n/a	11.0	**Erwin** (town) Harnett County
34	n/a	6.6	**Spindale** (town) Rutherford County		109	1422	11.0	**Fayetteville** (city) Cumberland County
36	224	6.7	**Havelock** (city) Craven County		111	1455	11.1	**Morganton** (city) Burke County
37	n/a	6.8	**East Flat Rock** (CDP) Henderson County		111	n/a	11.1	**Oxford** (city) Granville County
37	n/a	6.8	**Murfreesboro** (town) Hertford County		113	n/a	11.4	**Ayden** (town) Pitt County
39	n/a	6.9	**Farmville** (town) Pitt County		113	n/a	11.4	**Grifton** (town) Pitt County
39	n/a	6.9	**Tabor City** (town) Columbus County		113	1556	11.4	**Sanford** (city) Lee County
41	n/a	7.1	**Welcome** (CDP) Davidson County		113	n/a	11.4	**Skippers Corner** (CDP) New Hanover County
42	n/a	7.2	**Cullowhee** (CDP) Jackson County		117	1596	11.5	**Gastonia** (city) Gaston County
42	n/a	7.2	**Fairview** (CDP) Buncombe County		117	n/a	11.5	**Kings Grant** (CDP) New Hanover County
42	n/a	7.2	**Louisburg** (town) Franklin County		117	n/a	11.5	**Mountain Home** (CDP) Henderson County
45	n/a	7.3	**Elroy** (CDP) Wayne County		117	n/a	11.5	**Unionville** (town) Union County
45	n/a	7.3	**Hudson** (town) Caldwell County		121	n/a	11.6	**Brices Creek** (CDP) Craven County
47	n/a	7.4	**Cajah's Mountain** (town) Caldwell County		121	n/a	11.6	**China Grove** (town) Rowan County
48	n/a	7.6	**Wentworth** (town) Rockingham County		121	n/a	11.6	**Dallas** (town) Gaston County
49	n/a	7.7	**Icard** (CDP) Burke County		124	n/a	11.8	**Hampstead** (CDP) Pender County
49	n/a	7.7	**Sylva** (town) Jackson County		124	n/a	11.8	**Landis** (town) Rowan County
51	n/a	7.8	**Burgaw** (town) Pender County		124	n/a	11.8	**Lowell** (city) Gaston County
51	419	7.8	**Mount Airy** (city) Surry County		124	n/a	11.8	**Williamston** (town) Martin County
53	n/a	7.9	**Ahoskie** (town) Hertford County		128	n/a	11.9	**Half Moon** (CDP) Onslow County
54	n/a	8.0	**Boiling Springs** (town) Cleveland County		128	1730	11.9	**Rocky Mount** (city) Nash County
54	n/a	8.0	**River Bend** (town) Craven County		130	1775	12.0	**Hope Mills** (town) Cumberland County
54	n/a	8.0	**River Road** (CDP) Beaufort County		130	n/a	12.0	**Rockingham** (city) Richmond County
57	n/a	8.1	**Elizabethtown** (town) Bladen County		132	1815	12.1	**Greenville** (city) Pitt County
58	497	8.2	**Spring Lake** (town) Cumberland County		132	n/a	12.1	**Nashville** (town) Nash County
59	519	8.3	**Albemarle** (city) Stanly County		134	n/a	12.3	**Bayshore** (CDP) New Hanover County
59	n/a	8.3	**Brogden** (CDP) Wayne County		134	1886	12.3	**Burlington** (city) Alamance County
59	n/a	8.3	**Mocksville** (town) Davie County		134	n/a	12.3	**Canton** (town) Haywood County
59	n/a	8.3	**Wingate** (town) Union County		134	n/a	12.3	**Hillsborough** (town) Orange County
63	n/a	8.5	**Etowah** (CDP) Henderson County		138	n/a	12.4	**Swansboro** (town) Onslow County
63	569	8.5	**Kinston** (city) Lenoir County		139	n/a	12.5	**Black Mountain** (town) Buncombe County
63	n/a	8.5	**Randleman** (city) Randolph County		139	n/a	12.5	**Eastover** (town) Cumberland County
63	569	8.5	**Statesville** (city) Iredell County		139	n/a	12.5	**Elkin** (town) Surry County
67	602	8.6	**Reidsville** (city) Rockingham County		142	1984	12.6	**Smithfield** (town) Johnston County
68	627	8.7	**Salisbury** (city) Rowan County		143	n/a	12.7	**Aberdeen** (town) Moore County
68	n/a	8.7	**Wallburg** (town) Davidson County		143	2012	12.7	**Piney Green** (CDP) Onslow County
68	n/a	8.7	**Wrightsboro** (CDP) New Hanover County		143	n/a	12.7	**Trinity** (city) Randolph County
71	653	8.8	**Kings Mountain** (city) Cleveland County		146	n/a	12.8	**North Wilkesboro** (town) Wilkes County
72	n/a	8.9	**Franklin** (town) Macon County		146	n/a	12.8	**Northchase** (CDP) New Hanover County
72	n/a	8.9	**James City** (CDP) Craven County		146	2044	12.8	**Roanoke Rapids** (city) Halifax County
72	n/a	8.9	**Saint Stephens** (CDP) Catawba County		146	2044	12.8	**Shelby** (city) Cleveland County
75	n/a	9.0	**Long View** (town) Catawba County		146	2044	12.8	**Wilson** (city) Wilson County

Note: *The state column ranks the top/bottom 150 places in the state with population of 2,500 or more. The national column ranks the top/bottom places in the country with population of 10,000 or more. Places that are unincorporated were not considered in the rankings. n/a indicates data not available. Please refer to the User Guide for additional information.*

Employment: Computer, Engineering, and Science Occupations

Top 150 Places Ranked in *Descending* Order

State Rank	Nat'l Rank	Percent	Place	State Rank	Nat'l Rank	Percent	Place
1	9	25.2	**Morrisville** (town) Wake County	76	2244	4.9	**Asheville** (city) Buncombe County
2	56	17.5	**Cary** (town) Wake County	76	n/a	4.9	**Kitty Hawk** (town) Dare County
3	63	16.9	**Apex** (town) Wake County	76	n/a	4.9	**Nashville** (town) Nash County
4	126	14.1	**Holly Springs** (town) Wake County	79	n/a	4.8	**Elon** (town) Alamance County
5	n/a	13.4	**Porters Neck** (CDP) New Hanover County	79	n/a	4.8	**Granite Quarry** (town) Rowan County
6	157	13.3	**Chapel Hill** (town) Orange County	79	n/a	4.8	**Locust** (city) Stanly County
7	262	11.8	**Carrboro** (town) Orange County	79	n/a	4.8	**Pleasant Garden** (town) Guilford County
8	374	10.5	**Wake Forest** (town) Wake County	79	n/a	4.8	**Wallburg** (town) Davidson County
9	n/a	10.3	**Pittsboro** (town) Chatham County	84	n/a	4.7	**Hampstead** (CDP) Pender County
10	n/a	10.1	**Weddington** (town) Union County	84	n/a	4.7	**Marvin** (village) Union County
11	453	10.0	**Durham** (city) Durham County	84	n/a	4.7	**Mocksville** (town) Davie County
11	n/a	10.0	**Oak Ridge** (town) Guilford County	84	2376	4.7	**Mount Holly** (city) Gaston County
13	490	9.7	**Raleigh** (city) Wake County	88	n/a	4.6	**Midway** (town) Davidson County
14	537	9.4	**Fuquay-Varina** (town) Wake County	88	n/a	4.6	**River Bend** (town) Craven County
14	n/a	9.4	**Trent Woods** (town) Craven County	88	n/a	4.6	**Swannanoa** (CDP) Buncombe County
16	n/a	8.9	**Waxhaw** (town) Union County	88	n/a	4.6	**Troy** (town) Montgomery County
17	767	8.3	**Lewisville** (town) Forsyth County	92	2496	4.5	**Burlington** (city) Alamance County
17	n/a	8.3	**Winterville** (town) Pitt County	92	n/a	4.5	**Enochville** (CDP) Rowan County
19	n/a	8.2	**Fairfield Harbour** (CDP) Craven County	92	n/a	4.5	**Myrtle Grove** (CDP) New Hanover County
20	n/a	8.0	**Royal Pines** (CDP) Buncombe County	92	2496	4.5	**Piney Green** (CDP) Onslow County
21	874	7.9	**Knightdale** (town) Wake County	96	n/a	4.4	**Flat Rock** (village) Henderson County
22	n/a	7.7	**Bayshore** (CDP) New Hanover County	97	2627	4.3	**Greenville** (city) Pitt County
22	924	7.7	**Clemmons** (village) Forsyth County	97	n/a	4.3	**Lowell** (city) Gaston County
24	957	7.6	**Davidson** (town) Mecklenburg County	97	2627	4.3	**Summerfield** (town) Guilford County
25	n/a	7.4	**Eastover** (town) Cumberland County	97	2627	4.3	**Winston-Salem** (city) Forsyth County
25	n/a	7.4	**Rolesville** (town) Wake County	101	n/a	4.1	**Etowah** (CDP) Henderson County
27	n/a	7.3	**Butner** (town) Granville County	101	2777	4.1	**Greensboro** (city) Guilford County
27	1061	7.3	**Clayton** (town) Johnston County	101	2777	4.1	**High Point** (city) Guilford County
29	1097	7.2	**Harrisburg** (town) Cabarrus County	104	n/a	4.0	**Boiling Springs** (town) Cleveland County
30	1137	7.1	**Garner** (town) Wake County	104	2835	4.0	**Havelock** (city) Craven County
30	1137	7.1	**Mebane** (city) Alamance County	104	n/a	4.0	**Jamestown** (town) Guilford County
30	n/a	7.1	**Mountain View** (CDP) Catawba County	104	n/a	4.0	**Mineral Springs** (town) Union County
33	1190	7.0	**Cornelius** (town) Mecklenburg County	104	n/a	4.0	**Whispering Pines** (village) Moore County
33	n/a	7.0	**Spencer** (town) Rowan County	109	n/a	3.9	**Fairview** (town) Union County
35	1224	6.9	**Matthews** (town) Mecklenburg County	109	2899	3.9	**Hickory** (city) Catawba County
36	n/a	6.8	**Beaufort** (town) Carteret County	109	2899	3.9	**Kannapolis** (city) Cabarrus County
36	n/a	6.8	**Forest Oaks** (CDP) Guilford County	109	n/a	3.9	**Raeford** (city) Hoke County
38	n/a	6.7	**Emerald Isle** (town) Carteret County	113	2972	3.8	**Belmont** (city) Gaston County
38	1303	6.7	**Huntersville** (town) Mecklenburg County	113	n/a	3.8	**Fletcher** (town) Henderson County
38	1303	6.7	**Mooresville** (town) Iredell County	113	2972	3.8	**Sanford** (city) Lee County
38	n/a	6.7	**Westport** (CDP) Lincoln County	113	2972	3.8	**Wilmington** (city) New Hanover County
42	n/a	6.6	**Newport** (town) Carteret County	113	n/a	3.8	**Wrightsboro** (CDP) New Hanover County
43	1402	6.5	**Kernersville** (town) Forsyth County	118	n/a	3.7	**Bessemer City** (city) Gaston County
43	n/a	6.5	**Lake Royale** (CDP) Franklin County	118	n/a	3.7	**Icard** (CDP) Burke County
43	1402	6.5	**Mint Hill** (town) Mecklenburg County	118	n/a	3.7	**Kings Grant** (CDP) New Hanover County
43	n/a	6.5	**Weaverville** (town) Buncombe County	118	n/a	3.7	**Trinity** (city) Randolph County
47	n/a	6.4	**Ogden** (CDP) New Hanover County	122	n/a	3.6	**Glen Raven** (CDP) Alamance County
47	1445	6.4	**Stallings** (town) Union County	122	n/a	3.6	**Marion** (city) McDowell County
49	n/a	6.3	**Buies Creek** (CDP) Harnett County	122	3093	3.6	**Pinehurst** (village) Moore County
50	n/a	6.2	**Lowesville** (CDP) Lincoln County	125	n/a	3.5	**Conover** (city) Catawba County
51	1624	6.0	**Charlotte** (city) Mecklenburg County	125	n/a	3.5	**Unionville** (town) Union County
51	1624	6.0	**Leland** (town) Brunswick County	127	3220	3.4	**Mount Airy** (city) Surry County
51	n/a	6.0	**Randleman** (city) Randolph County	127	3220	3.4	**New Bern** (city) Craven County
54	n/a	5.9	**Zebulon** (town) Wake County	127	n/a	3.4	**Oak Island** (town) Brunswick County
55	n/a	5.8	**Aberdeen** (town) Moore County	127	3220	3.4	**Roanoke Rapids** (city) Halifax County
55	n/a	5.8	**Angier** (town) Harnett County	131	n/a	3.3	**Cherryville** (city) Gaston County
57	n/a	5.7	**Brices Creek** (CDP) Craven County	131	n/a	3.3	**Fairview** (CDP) Buncombe County
57	1790	5.7	**Concord** (city) Cabarrus County	131	n/a	3.3	**Liberty** (town) Randolph County
57	n/a	5.7	**Hillsborough** (town) Orange County	131	n/a	3.3	**Mills River** (town) Henderson County
60	n/a	5.6	**Gamewell** (town) Caldwell County	131	n/a	3.3	**Northchase** (CDP) New Hanover County
60	n/a	5.6	**Lake Park** (village) Union County	131	n/a	3.3	**Oxford** (city) Granville County
60	n/a	5.6	**Sylva** (town) Jackson County	131	3297	3.3	**Rocky Mount** (city) Nash County
60	n/a	5.6	**Welcome** (CDP) Davidson County	131	n/a	3.3	**Saint Stephens** (CDP) Catawba County
64	n/a	5.5	**Dana** (CDP) Henderson County	131	n/a	3.3	**Wesley Chapel** (village) Union County
64	n/a	5.5	**Rutherfordton** (town) Rutherford County	140	3358	3.2	**Eden** (city) Rockingham County
66	n/a	5.4	**Brevard** (city) Transylvania County	140	n/a	3.2	**Farmville** (town) Pitt County
66	n/a	5.4	**Creedmoor** (city) Granville County	140	n/a	3.2	**Lake Norman of Catawba** (CDP) Catawba County
66	n/a	5.4	**Gibsonville** (town) Guilford County	140	3358	3.2	**Wilson** (city) Wilson County
66	n/a	5.4	**Ranlo** (town) Gaston County	144	n/a	3.1	**Forest City** (town) Rutherford County
70	n/a	5.3	**Archer Lodge** (town) Johnston County	144	3435	3.1	**Gastonia** (city) Gaston County
70	2011	5.3	**Indian Trail** (town) Union County	144	n/a	3.1	**Rural Hall** (town) Forsyth County
70	2011	5.3	**Lincolnton** (city) Lincoln County	144	n/a	3.1	**Southern Shores** (town) Dare County
70	n/a	5.3	**Moyock** (CDP) Currituck County	144	n/a	3.1	**Stanley** (town) Gaston County
74	n/a	5.2	**Carolina Beach** (town) New Hanover County	144	3435	3.1	**Thomasville** (city) Davidson County
75	n/a	5.1	**Stokesdale** (town) Guilford County	144	n/a	3.1	**Wendell** (town) Wake County

Note: The state column ranks the top/bottom 150 places in the state with population of 2,500 or more. The national column ranks the top/bottom places in the country with population of 10,000 or more. Places that are unincorporated were not considered in the rankings. n/a indicates data not available. Please refer to the User Guide for additional information.

Employment: Computer, Engineering, and Science Occupations

Top 150 Places Ranked in *Ascending* Order

State Rank	Nat'l Rank	Percent	Place		State Rank	Nat'l Rank	Percent	Place
1	n/a	0.0	**Benson** (town) Johnston County		73	n/a	2.1	**Roxboro** (city) Person County
1	n/a	0.0	**Brogden** (CDP) Wayne County		73	n/a	2.1	**Saint James** (town) Brunswick County
1	n/a	0.0	**Burgaw** (town) Pender County		73	n/a	2.1	**Siler City** (town) Chatham County
1	n/a	0.0	**Carolina Shores** (town) Brunswick County		73	n/a	2.1	**Skippers Corner** (CDP) New Hanover County
1	n/a	0.0	**La Grange** (town) Lenoir County		80	n/a	2.2	**Cramerton** (town) Gaston County
1	n/a	0.0	**Mar-Mac** (CDP) Wayne County		80	586	2.2	**Hope Mills** (town) Cumberland County
1	n/a	0.0	**North Wilkesboro** (town) Wilkes County		80	n/a	2.2	**Kill Devil Hills** (town) Dare County
1	n/a	0.0	**Red Springs** (town) Robeson County		80	n/a	2.2	**Midland** (town) Cabarrus County
1	n/a	0.0	**Selma** (town) Johnston County		80	586	2.2	**Shelby** (city) Cleveland County
1	n/a	0.0	**Sneads Ferry** (CDP) Onslow County		80	n/a	2.2	**Washington** (city) Beaufort County
1	n/a	0.0	**Spindale** (town) Rutherford County		86	n/a	2.3	**Boiling Spring Lakes** (city) Brunswick County
1	n/a	0.0	**Tyro** (CDP) Davidson County		86	n/a	2.3	**Fairmont** (town) Robeson County
13	n/a	0.3	**Warsaw** (town) Duplin County		86	649	2.3	**Graham** (city) Alamance County
14	21	0.4	**Spring Lake** (town) Cumberland County		86	649	2.3	**Hendersonville** (city) Henderson County
15	n/a	0.5	**Enfield** (town) Halifax County		86	649	2.3	**Jacksonville** (city) Onslow County
15	n/a	0.5	**Long View** (town) Catawba County		86	649	2.3	**Kinston** (city) Lenoir County
15	n/a	0.5	**Louisburg** (town) Franklin County		86	n/a	2.3	**Mountain Home** (CDP) Henderson County
15	n/a	0.5	**Williamston** (town) Martin County		86	n/a	2.3	**Red Oak** (town) Nash County
19	n/a	0.6	**Tabor City** (town) Columbus County		86	n/a	2.3	**Shallotte** (town) Brunswick County
20	n/a	0.7	**Nags Head** (town) Dare County		86	n/a	2.3	**Wentworth** (town) Rockingham County
20	n/a	0.7	**Sunset Beach** (town) Brunswick County		96	754	2.5	**Boone** (town) Watauga County
22	n/a	0.8	**Hamlet** (city) Richmond County		96	754	2.5	**Lenoir** (city) Caldwell County
22	65	0.8	**Henderson** (city) Vance County		96	n/a	2.5	**Seven Lakes** (CDP) Moore County
22	n/a	0.8	**Rockingham** (city) Richmond County		96	n/a	2.5	**Silver Lake** (CDP) New Hanover County
22	n/a	0.8	**Whiteville** (city) Columbus County		100	893	2.7	**Albemarle** (city) Stanly County
26	n/a	0.9	**East Flat Rock** (CDP) Henderson County		100	893	2.7	**Fayetteville** (city) Cumberland County
26	n/a	0.9	**Elroy** (CDP) Wayne County		100	893	2.7	**Murraysville** (CDP) New Hanover County
26	n/a	0.9	**Granite Falls** (town) Caldwell County		100	893	2.7	**Reidsville** (city) Rockingham County
26	n/a	0.9	**Wallace** (town) Duplin County		100	893	2.7	**Southern Pines** (town) Moore County
30	n/a	1.0	**Ayden** (town) Pitt County		100	n/a	2.7	**Valdese** (town) Burke County
30	n/a	1.0	**Dunn** (city) Harnett County		106	952	2.8	**Asheboro** (city) Randolph County
30	n/a	1.0	**Mount Olive** (town) Wayne County		106	n/a	2.8	**Erwin** (town) Harnett County
30	n/a	1.0	**Pembroke** (town) Robeson County		106	n/a	2.8	**Morehead City** (town) Carteret County
30	101	1.0	**Tarboro** (town) Edgecombe County		106	n/a	2.8	**South Rosemary** (CDP) Halifax County
35	n/a	1.2	**China Grove** (town) Rowan County		106	n/a	2.8	**Walkertown** (town) Forsyth County
35	n/a	1.2	**Rockfish** (CDP) Hoke County		111	n/a	2.9	**East Rockingham** (CDP) Richmond County
35	n/a	1.2	**Southport** (city) Brunswick County		111	n/a	2.9	**Franklin** (town) Macon County
38	n/a	1.3	**Ahoskie** (town) Hertford County		111	n/a	2.9	**Landis** (town) Rowan County
38	n/a	1.3	**Elizabethtown** (town) Bladen County		111	1025	2.9	**Monroe** (city) Union County
38	n/a	1.3	**Half Moon** (CDP) Onslow County		111	n/a	2.9	**Pineville** (town) Mecklenburg County
38	n/a	1.3	**River Road** (CDP) Beaufort County		111	1025	2.9	**Statesville** (city) Iredell County
38	n/a	1.3	**Windsor** (town) Bertie County		117	n/a	3.0	**Elkin** (town) Surry County
43	n/a	1.4	**Bethlehem** (CDP) Alexander County		117	1089	3.0	**Goldsboro** (city) Wayne County
43	n/a	1.4	**Polkton** (town) Anson County		117	n/a	3.0	**Grifton** (town) Pitt County
45	n/a	1.5	**Clinton** (city) Sampson County		117	n/a	3.0	**James City** (CDP) Craven County
45	239	1.5	**Kings Mountain** (city) Cleveland County		117	n/a	3.0	**Woodfin** (town) Buncombe County
45	239	1.5	**Laurinburg** (city) Scotland County		122	n/a	3.1	**Forest City** (town) Rutherford County
45	n/a	1.5	**Lillington** (town) Harnett County		122	1168	3.1	**Gastonia** (city) Gaston County
45	n/a	1.5	**Maiden** (town) Catawba County		122	n/a	3.1	**Rural Hall** (town) Forsyth County
45	n/a	1.5	**Wadesboro** (town) Anson County		122	n/a	3.1	**Southern Shores** (town) Dare County
51	n/a	1.6	**Edenton** (town) Chowan County		122	n/a	3.1	**Stanley** (town) Gaston County
51	n/a	1.6	**Plymouth** (town) Washington County		122	1168	3.1	**Thomasville** (city) Davidson County
53	n/a	1.7	**Dallas** (town) Gaston County		122	n/a	3.1	**Wendell** (town) Wake County
53	325	1.7	**Morganton** (city) Burke County		129	1222	3.2	**Eden** (city) Rockingham County
53	n/a	1.7	**Swansboro** (town) Onslow County		129	n/a	3.2	**Farmville** (town) Pitt County
53	n/a	1.7	**Yadkinville** (town) Yadkin County		129	n/a	3.2	**Lake Norman of Catawba** (CDP) Catawba County
57	n/a	1.8	**Cajah's Mountain** (town) Caldwell County		129	1222	3.2	**Wilson** (city) Wilson County
57	n/a	1.8	**Lake Junaluska** (CDP) Haywood County		133	n/a	3.3	**Cherryville** (city) Gaston County
57	n/a	1.8	**Murfreesboro** (town) Hertford County		133	n/a	3.3	**Fairview** (CDP) Buncombe County
57	n/a	1.8	**Waynesville** (town) Haywood County		133	n/a	3.3	**Liberty** (town) Randolph County
61	425	1.9	**Elizabeth City** (city) Pasquotank County		133	n/a	3.3	**Mills River** (town) Henderson County
61	n/a	1.9	**Hudson** (town) Caldwell County		133	n/a	3.3	**Northchase** (CDP) New Hanover County
61	n/a	1.9	**King** (city) Stokes County		133	n/a	3.3	**Oxford** (city) Granville County
61	425	1.9	**Lumberton** (city) Robeson County		133	1299	3.3	**Rocky Mount** (city) Nash County
61	n/a	1.9	**Sawmills** (town) Caldwell County		133	n/a	3.3	**Saint Stephens** (CDP) Catawba County
66	479	2.0	**Archdale** (city) Randolph County		133	n/a	3.3	**Wesley Chapel** (village) Union County
66	479	2.0	**Lexington** (city) Davidson County		142	1360	3.4	**Mount Airy** (city) Surry County
66	479	2.0	**Newton** (city) Catawba County		142	1360	3.4	**New Bern** (city) Craven County
66	479	2.0	**Salisbury** (city) Rowan County		142	n/a	3.4	**Oak Island** (town) Brunswick County
66	479	2.0	**Smithfield** (town) Johnston County		142	1360	3.4	**Roanoke Rapids** (city) Halifax County
66	n/a	2.0	**Wilkesboro** (town) Wilkes County		146	n/a	3.5	**Conover** (city) Catawba County
66	n/a	2.0	**Wingate** (town) Union County		146	n/a	3.5	**Unionville** (town) Union County
73	n/a	2.1	**Black Mountain** (town) Buncombe County		148	n/a	3.6	**Glen Raven** (CDP) Alamance County
73	n/a	2.1	**Canton** (town) Haywood County		148	n/a	3.6	**Marion** (city) McDowell County
73	n/a	2.1	**Cullowhee** (CDP) Jackson County		148	1500	3.6	**Pinehurst** (village) Moore County

Note: *The state column ranks the top/bottom 150 places in the state with population of 2,500 or more. The national column ranks the top/bottom places in the country with population of 10,000 or more. Places that are unincorporated were not considered in the rankings. n/a indicates data not available. Please refer to the User Guide for additional information.*

Employment: Education, Legal, Community Service, Arts, and Media Occupations

Top 150 Places Ranked in *Descending* Order

State Rank	Nat'l Rank	Percent	Place	State Rank	Nat'l Rank	Percent	Place
1	n/a	29.7	**Boiling Springs** (town) Cleveland County	76	n/a	13.3	**Icard** (CDP) Burke County
2	n/a	26.9	**Murfreesboro** (town) Hertford County	76	1045	13.3	**Lumberton** (city) Robeson County
3	50	24.3	**Carrboro** (town) Orange County	76	1045	13.3	**Shelby** (city) Cleveland County
4	75	22.9	**Chapel Hill** (town) Orange County	79	1079	13.2	**Fayetteville** (city) Cumberland County
5	n/a	22.8	**Raeford** (city) Hoke County	79	n/a	13.2	**Fletcher** (town) Henderson County
6	n/a	22.4	**Seven Lakes** (CDP) Moore County	79	n/a	13.2	**Rural Hall** (town) Forsyth County
7	n/a	21.9	**Pittsboro** (town) Chatham County	82	1147	13.0	**Harrisburg** (town) Cabarrus County
8	n/a	21.6	**Benson** (town) Johnston County	82	n/a	13.0	**Stokesdale** (town) Guilford County
9	n/a	21.2	**Whispering Pines** (village) Moore County	82	n/a	13.0	**Woodfin** (town) Buncombe County
10	n/a	21.1	**Fairmont** (town) Robeson County	85	1188	12.9	**Apex** (town) Wake County
11	n/a	20.9	**Lake Junaluska** (CDP) Haywood County	85	1188	12.9	**Elizabeth City** (city) Pasquotank County
12	n/a	20.6	**King** (city) Stokes County	85	n/a	12.9	**Half Moon** (CDP) Onslow County
13	n/a	20.1	**Buies Creek** (CDP) Harnett County	85	n/a	12.9	**Sneads Ferry** (CDP) Onslow County
14	n/a	19.5	**Southport** (city) Brunswick County	89	1228	12.8	**Summerfield** (town) Guilford County
15	n/a	19.4	**Wingate** (town) Union County	89	n/a	12.8	**Troy** (town) Montgomery County
16	n/a	19.3	**Pembroke** (town) Robeson County	89	1228	12.8	**Wake Forest** (town) Wake County
17	n/a	19.2	**Brices Creek** (CDP) Craven County	92	1263	12.7	**Knightdale** (town) Wake County
18	n/a	18.7	**Swansboro** (town) Onslow County	93	n/a	12.6	**Myrtle Grove** (CDP) New Hanover County
19	n/a	18.3	**Louisburg** (town) Franklin County	93	1307	12.6	**New Bern** (city) Craven County
20	n/a	17.6	**Rockingham** (city) Richmond County	93	1307	12.6	**Winston-Salem** (city) Forsyth County
21	n/a	17.4	**Bayshore** (CDP) New Hanover County	96	n/a	12.5	**Cherryville** (city) Gaston County
22	n/a	17.2	**Flat Rock** (village) Henderson County	96	n/a	12.5	**Erwin** (town) Harnett County
23	n/a	17.0	**Fairfield Harbour** (CDP) Craven County	96	n/a	12.5	**Ogden** (CDP) New Hanover County
23	n/a	17.0	**Trent Woods** (town) Craven County	99	1380	12.4	**Albemarle** (city) Stanly County
23	n/a	17.0	**Weaverville** (town) Buncombe County	100	1460	12.2	**Hendersonville** (city) Henderson County
26	366	16.8	**Laurinburg** (city) Scotland County	100	1460	12.2	**Huntersville** (town) Mecklenburg County
26	n/a	16.8	**Wesley Chapel** (village) Union County	100	1460	12.2	**Morganton** (city) Burke County
28	397	16.5	**Southern Pines** (town) Moore County	103	n/a	12.1	**Oxford** (city) Granville County
29	n/a	16.3	**Wilkesboro** (town) Wilkes County	103	n/a	12.1	**River Bend** (town) Craven County
30	435	16.2	**Pinehurst** (village) Moore County	103	n/a	12.1	**Whiteville** (city) Columbus County
31	447	16.1	**Davidson** (town) Mecklenburg County	106	n/a	12.0	**Dana** (CDP) Henderson County
31	n/a	16.1	**La Grange** (town) Lenoir County	106	1552	12.0	**Greensboro** (city) Guilford County
33	n/a	15.9	**Aberdeen** (town) Moore County	106	n/a	12.0	**Mocksville** (town) Davie County
33	471	15.9	**Matthews** (town) Mecklenburg County	109	1586	11.9	**Mint Hill** (town) Mecklenburg County
33	n/a	15.9	**Waxhaw** (town) Union County	109	1586	11.9	**Wilson** (city) Wilson County
36	n/a	15.8	**Red Springs** (town) Robeson County	111	1698	11.7	**Cary** (town) Wake County
37	521	15.6	**Durham** (city) Durham County	111	n/a	11.7	**Dunn** (city) Harnett County
37	n/a	15.6	**Lillington** (town) Harnett County	111	n/a	11.7	**Sunset Beach** (town) Brunswick County
37	n/a	15.6	**Tabor City** (town) Columbus County	111	n/a	11.7	**Waynesville** (town) Haywood County
40	n/a	15.4	**Brogden** (CDP) Wayne County	115	n/a	11.6	**Royal Pines** (CDP) Buncombe County
40	550	15.4	**Holly Springs** (town) Wake County	115	1745	11.6	**Tarboro** (town) Edgecombe County
40	n/a	15.4	**Williamston** (town) Martin County	117	n/a	11.5	**Elizabethtown** (town) Bladen County
43	566	15.3	**Lewisville** (town) Forsyth County	117	n/a	11.5	**Forest Oaks** (CDP) Guilford County
44	583	15.2	**Greenville** (city) Pitt County	117	n/a	11.5	**Kill Devil Hills** (town) Dare County
45	n/a	15.0	**Hillsborough** (town) Orange County	117	n/a	11.5	**Pineville** (town) Mecklenburg County
46	641	14.9	**Asheville** (city) Buncombe County	117	n/a	11.5	**Winterville** (town) Pitt County
46	n/a	14.9	**Cullowhee** (CDP) Jackson County	122	1841	11.4	**Goldsboro** (city) Wayne County
48	656	14.8	**Belmont** (city) Gaston County	122	1841	11.4	**Indian Trail** (town) Union County
48	n/a	14.8	**Forest City** (town) Rutherford County	122	n/a	11.4	**Lake Park** (village) Union County
48	656	14.8	**Hope Mills** (town) Cumberland County	125	n/a	11.3	**Clinton** (city) Sampson County
48	656	14.8	**Mount Airy** (city) Surry County	125	n/a	11.3	**Plymouth** (town) Washington County
48	n/a	14.8	**Walkertown** (town) Forsyth County	127	Nat'l	11.2	**Archer Lodge** (town) Johnston County
53	n/a	14.7	**Enfield** (town) Halifax County	127	Rank	11.2	**Eastover** (town) Cumberland County
53	n/a	14.7	**Marion** (city) McDowell County	129	n/a	11.1	**Northchase** (CDP) New Hanover County
55	701	14.6	**Stallings** (town) Union County	129	n/a	11.1	**Oak Island** (town) Brunswick County
56	718	14.5	**Jacksonville** (city) Onslow County	131	n/a	11.0	**Ayden** (town) Pitt County
57	n/a	14.4	**Hampstead** (CDP) Pender County	131	n/a	11.0	**Burgaw** (town) Pender County
58	n/a	14.3	**Washington** (city) Beaufort County	131	n/a	11.0	**Edenton** (town) Chowan County
59	795	14.2	**Clayton** (town) Johnston County	131	n/a	11.0	**Jamestown** (town) Guilford County
59	795	14.2	**Salisbury** (city) Rowan County	131	n/a	11.0	**Mountain View** (CDP) Catawba County
61	n/a	14.1	**Black Mountain** (town) Buncombe County	131	n/a	11.0	**Rolesville** (town) Wake County
61	n/a	14.1	**Sawmills** (town) Caldwell County	131	n/a	11.0	**Skippers Corner** (CDP) New Hanover County
63	851	14.0	**Mebane** (city) Alamance County	138	n/a	10.9	**Fairview** (CDP) Buncombe County
63	n/a	14.0	**Mineral Springs** (town) Union County	138	2104	10.9	**Leland** (town) Brunswick County
63	851	14.0	**Murraysville** (CDP) New Hanover County	138	n/a	10.9	**Valdese** (town) Burke County
66	878	13.9	**Boone** (town) Watauga County	141	2158	10.8	**Asheboro** (city) Randolph County
67	n/a	13.8	**Mount Olive** (town) Wayne County	142	n/a	10.7	**Oak Ridge** (town) Guilford County
68	931	13.7	**Clemmons** (village) Forsyth County	142	n/a	10.7	**Polkton** (town) Anson County
69	n/a	13.6	**Brevard** (city) Transylvania County	144	2283	10.6	**Charlotte** (city) Mecklenburg County
69	n/a	13.6	**Elon** (town) Alamance County	144	2283	10.6	**Lincolnton** (city) Lincoln County
69	n/a	13.6	**Moyock** (CDP) Currituck County	146	2350	10.5	**Hickory** (city) Catawba County
72	n/a	13.5	**Ahoskie** (town) Hertford County	146	n/a	10.5	**River Road** (CDP) Beaufort County
73	1021	13.4	**Fuquay-Varina** (town) Wake County	146	n/a	10.5	**Westport** (CDP) Lincoln County
73	1021	13.4	**Raleigh** (city) Wake County	149	n/a	10.4	**Angier** (town) Harnett County
73	1021	13.4	**Wilmington** (city) New Hanover County	149	n/a	10.4	**Beaufort** (town) Carteret County

Note: The state column ranks the top/bottom 150 places in the state with population of 2,500 or more. The national column ranks the top/bottom places in the country with population of 10,000 or more. Places that are unincorporated were not considered in the rankings. n/a indicates data not available. Please refer to the User Guide for additional information.

Employment: Education, Legal, Community Service, Arts, and Media Occupations

Top 150 Places Ranked in *Ascending* Order

State Rank	Nat'l Rank	Percent	Place	State Rank	Nat'l Rank	Percent	Place
1	n/a	1.9	Long View (town) Catawba County	76	1440	9.1	Graham (city) Alamance County
2	n/a	2.2	Landis (town) Rowan County	77	1489	9.2	Burlington (city) Alamance County
3	n/a	2.3	China Grove (town) Rowan County	77	1489	9.2	Kernersville (town) Forsyth County
4	n/a	2.6	Midland (town) Cabarrus County	77	n/a	9.2	Lowell (city) Gaston County
5	n/a	2.9	Shallotte (town) Brunswick County	77	n/a	9.2	Ranlo (town) Gaston County
6	n/a	3.8	Warsaw (town) Duplin County	77	n/a	9.2	Unionville (town) Union County
7	n/a	3.9	Fairview (town) Union County	82	n/a	9.3	Etowah (CDP) Henderson County
7	n/a	3.9	Yadkinville (town) Yadkin County	82	n/a	9.3	Nashville (town) Nash County
9	n/a	4.1	Spencer (town) Rowan County	84	n/a	9.4	Glen Raven (CDP) Alamance County
10	n/a	4.6	Maiden (town) Catawba County	85	n/a	9.5	Granite Falls (town) Caldwell County
10	n/a	4.6	Roxboro (city) Person County	85	n/a	9.5	Welcome (CDP) Davidson County
12	n/a	4.7	Dallas (town) Gaston County	87	1715	9.6	Kinston (city) Lenoir County
13	n/a	4.8	Butner (town) Granville County	87	n/a	9.6	Lowesville (CDP) Lincoln County
14	n/a	5.0	Mar-Mac (CDP) Wayne County	87	1715	9.6	Mount Holly (city) Gaston County
15	n/a	5.1	Gamewell (town) Caldwell County	87	1715	9.6	Sanford (city) Lee County
15	n/a	5.1	Zebulon (town) Wake County	87	n/a	9.6	Sylva (town) Jackson County
17	n/a	5.2	Carolina Shores (town) Brunswick County	92	n/a	9.7	Enochville (CDP) Rowan County
18	n/a	5.3	Liberty (town) Randolph County	92	1769	9.7	Garner (town) Wake County
18	n/a	5.3	Weddington (town) Union County	92	n/a	9.7	Gibsonville (town) Guilford County
20	n/a	5.4	Tyro (CDP) Davidson County	92	n/a	9.7	Kings Grant (CDP) New Hanover County
20	n/a	5.4	Wallace (town) Duplin County	92	1769	9.7	Smithfield (town) Johnston County
22	n/a	5.7	North Wilkesboro (town) Wilkes County	92	n/a	9.7	Wallburg (town) Davidson County
22	n/a	5.7	Porters Neck (CDP) New Hanover County	98	1834	9.8	Cornelius (town) Mecklenburg County
24	n/a	5.8	Randleman (city) Randolph County	98	n/a	9.8	Granite Quarry (town) Rowan County
25	257	6.1	Eden (city) Rockingham County	98	n/a	9.8	Newport (town) Carteret County
25	257	6.1	Havelock (city) Craven County	98	n/a	9.8	Wentworth (town) Rockingham County
27	n/a	6.4	Pleasant Garden (town) Guilford County	102	1882	9.9	Concord (city) Cabarrus County
28	n/a	6.5	Southern Shores (town) Dare County	102	n/a	9.9	Cramerton (town) Gaston County
29	n/a	6.7	Bessemer City (city) Gaston County	102	n/a	9.9	Emerald Isle (town) Carteret County
29	n/a	6.7	Farmville (town) Pitt County	102	1882	9.9	Gastonia (city) Gaston County
29	409	6.7	Reidsville (city) Rockingham County	102	n/a	9.9	Morehead City (town) Carteret County
32	n/a	6.8	Mills River (town) Henderson County	102	n/a	9.9	Red Oak (town) Nash County
33	n/a	6.9	Creedmoor (city) Granville County	102	n/a	9.9	Rutherfordton (town) Rutherford County
33	n/a	6.9	Locust (city) Stanly County	109	1938	10.0	Henderson (city) Vance County
35	n/a	7.0	Wadesboro (town) Anson County	109	n/a	10.0	Lake Norman of Catawba (CDP) Catawba County
36	547	7.1	Monroe (city) Union County	111	n/a	10.1	Canton (town) Haywood County
36	n/a	7.1	Swannanoa (CDP) Buncombe County	111	n/a	10.1	Selma (town) Johnston County
38	n/a	7.2	Elroy (CDP) Wayne County	113	2069	10.2	High Point (city) Guilford County
38	n/a	7.2	Marvin (village) Union County	113	2069	10.2	Kannapolis (city) Cabarrus County
38	n/a	7.2	Mountain Home (CDP) Henderson County	115	n/a	10.3	Hamlet (city) Richmond County
38	n/a	7.2	Rockfish (CDP) Hoke County	115	2128	10.3	Morrisville (town) Wake County
42	n/a	7.3	Conover (city) Catawba County	115	2128	10.3	Roanoke Rapids (city) Halifax County
43	646	7.4	Thomasville (city) Davidson County	115	n/a	10.3	Saint Stephens (CDP) Catawba County
44	682	7.5	Archdale (city) Randolph County	119	n/a	10.4	Angier (town) Harnett County
44	n/a	7.5	East Rockingham (CDP) Richmond County	119	n/a	10.4	Beaufort (town) Carteret County
44	n/a	7.5	Elkin (town) Surry County	119	n/a	10.4	Bethlehem (CDP) Alexander County
44	682	7.5	Kings Mountain (city) Cleveland County	119	2191	10.4	Statesville (city) Iredell County
44	n/a	7.5	Lake Royale (CDP) Franklin County	119	n/a	10.4	Wrightsboro (CDP) New Hanover County
44	n/a	7.5	South Rosemary (CDP) Halifax County	124	2243	10.5	Hickory (city) Catawba County
50	n/a	7.6	Midway (town) Davidson County	124	n/a	10.5	River Road (CDP) Beaufort County
50	n/a	7.6	Nags Head (town) Dare County	124	n/a	10.5	Westport (CDP) Lincoln County
52	759	7.7	Newton (city) Catawba County	127	2307	10.6	Charlotte (city) Mecklenburg County
52	759	7.7	Piney Green (CDP) Onslow County	127	2307	10.6	Lincolnton (city) Lincoln County
52	n/a	7.7	Windsor (town) Bertie County	129	n/a	10.7	Oak Ridge (town) Guilford County
55	n/a	7.9	Spindale (town) Rutherford County	129	n/a	10.7	Polkton (town) Anson County
56	n/a	8.0	Siler City (town) Chatham County	131	2446	10.8	Asheboro (city) Randolph County
57	n/a	8.1	Boiling Spring Lakes (city) Brunswick County	132	n/a	10.9	Fairview (CDP) Buncombe County
57	n/a	8.1	Stanley (town) Gaston County	132	2499	10.9	Leland (town) Brunswick County
59	n/a	8.2	Franklin (town) Macon County	132	n/a	10.9	Valdese (town) Burke County
59	n/a	8.2	James City (CDP) Craven County	135	n/a	11.0	Ayden (town) Pitt County
61	1023	8.3	Mooresville (town) Iredell County	135	n/a	11.0	Burgaw (town) Pender County
62	n/a	8.4	Trinity (city) Randolph County	135	n/a	11.0	Edenton (town) Chowan County
62	n/a	8.4	Wendell (town) Wake County	135	n/a	11.0	Jamestown (town) Guilford County
64	n/a	8.5	Grifton (town) Pitt County	135	n/a	11.0	Mountain View (CDP) Catawba County
64	1118	8.5	Lexington (city) Davidson County	135	n/a	11.0	Rolesville (town) Wake County
64	n/a	8.5	Saint James (town) Brunswick County	135	n/a	11.0	Skippers Corner (CDP) New Hanover County
67	n/a	8.8	Carolina Beach (town) New Hanover County	142	n/a	11.1	Northchase (CDP) New Hanover County
67	n/a	8.8	East Flat Rock (CDP) Henderson County	142	n/a	11.1	Oak Island (town) Brunswick County
67	1260	8.8	Spring Lake (town) Cumberland County	144	n/a	11.2	Archer Lodge (town) Johnston County
70	1329	8.9	Rocky Mount (city) Nash County	144	n/a	11.2	Eastover (town) Cumberland County
70	n/a	8.9	Silver Lake (CDP) New Hanover County	146	n/a	11.3	Clinton (city) Sampson County
72	n/a	9.0	Cajah's Mountain (town) Caldwell County	146	n/a	11.3	Plymouth (town) Washington County
72	n/a	9.0	Hudson (town) Caldwell County	148	2760	11.4	Goldsboro (city) Wayne County
72	n/a	9.0	Kitty Hawk (town) Dare County	148	2760	11.4	Indian Trail (town) Union County
72	1388	9.0	Lenoir (city) Caldwell County	148	n/a	11.4	Lake Park (village) Union County

Note: The state column ranks the top/bottom 150 places in the state with population of 2,500 or more. The national column ranks the top/bottom places in the country with population of 10,000 or more. Places that are unincorporated were not considered in the rankings. n/a indicates data not available. Please refer to the User Guide for additional information.

Employment: Healthcare Practitioners

Top 150 Places Ranked in *Descending* Order

State Rank	Nat'l Rank	Percent	Place
1	n/a	16.2	**Fairfield Harbour** (CDP) Craven County
2	n/a	15.0	**Shallotte** (town) Brunswick County
3	n/a	14.9	**Pittsboro** (town) Chatham County
4	12	14.6	**Southern Pines** (town) Moore County
5	n/a	14.1	**Rolesville** (town) Wake County
6	n/a	13.4	**Mountain Home** (CDP) Henderson County
7	n/a	13.1	**Carolina Shores** (town) Brunswick County
7	n/a	13.1	**Seven Lakes** (CDP) Moore County
9	n/a	13.0	**Porters Neck** (CDP) New Hanover County
10	n/a	12.9	**Winterville** (town) Pitt County
11	n/a	12.0	**Grifton** (town) Pitt County
12	n/a	11.7	**Wentworth** (town) Rockingham County
13	n/a	11.4	**Randleman** (town) Randolph County
13	n/a	11.4	**Rutherfordton** (town) Rutherford County
15	92	11.2	**Chapel Hill** (town) Orange County
15	n/a	11.2	**Flat Rock** (village) Henderson County
17	n/a	11.1	**Louisburg** (town) Franklin County
18	n/a	11.0	**Whispering Pines** (village) Moore County
19	n/a	10.9	**Cramerton** (town) Gaston County
19	n/a	10.9	**Waynesville** (town) Haywood County
21	n/a	10.7	**Oxford** (city) Granville County
22	n/a	10.5	**Boiling Springs** (town) Cleveland County
23	n/a	10.3	**Hillsborough** (town) Orange County
23	n/a	10.3	**Lake Park** (village) Union County
25	n/a	10.2	**Ayden** (town) Pitt County
25	n/a	10.2	**Brices Creek** (CDP) Craven County
25	n/a	10.2	**Butner** (town) Granville County
28	173	10.1	**Stallings** (town) Union County
29	n/a	9.9	**Gibsonville** (town) Guilford County
29	n/a	9.9	**Washington** (city) Beaufort County
31	n/a	9.8	**Ogden** (CDP) New Hanover County
32	231	9.6	**Clemmons** (village) Forsyth County
32	231	9.6	**Durham** (city) Durham County
32	n/a	9.6	**Fletcher** (town) Henderson County
32	n/a	9.6	**Hampstead** (CDP) Pender County
32	n/a	9.6	**Marion** (city) McDowell County
32	n/a	9.6	**Mills River** (town) Henderson County
32	231	9.6	**Pinehurst** (village) Moore County
32	n/a	9.6	**Whiteville** (city) Columbus County
40	253	9.5	**Greenville** (city) Pitt County
40	253	9.5	**Lewisville** (town) Forsyth County
42	294	9.3	**Carrboro** (town) Orange County
43	n/a	9.2	**Royal Pines** (CDP) Buncombe County
44	n/a	9.1	**Hudson** (town) Caldwell County
44	n/a	9.1	**King** (city) Stokes County
44	n/a	9.1	**Silver Lake** (CDP) New Hanover County
44	n/a	9.1	**Trent Woods** (town) Craven County
48	n/a	9.0	**Dana** (CDP) Henderson County
48	n/a	9.0	**Lake Royale** (CDP) Franklin County
48	n/a	9.0	**Windsor** (town) Bertie County
51	377	8.9	**Davidson** (town) Mecklenburg County
52	n/a	8.8	**Eastover** (town) Cumberland County
52	n/a	8.8	**River Road** (CDP) Beaufort County
54	n/a	8.7	**Wallburg** (town) Davidson County
55	441	8.6	**Leland** (town) Brunswick County
56	n/a	8.5	**Buies Creek** (CDP) Harnett County
56	n/a	8.5	**Cherryville** (city) Gaston County
56	n/a	8.5	**Creedmoor** (city) Granville County
59	n/a	8.4	**Brevard** (city) Transylvania County
59	n/a	8.4	**Marvin** (village) Union County
59	n/a	8.4	**Oak Island** (town) Brunswick County
62	n/a	8.3	**Enochville** (CDP) Rowan County
62	519	8.3	**Knightdale** (town) Wake County
62	519	8.3	**Mebane** (city) Alamance County
62	519	8.3	**Winston-Salem** (city) Forsyth County
66	n/a	8.2	**Midway** (town) Davidson County
67	597	8.1	**Asheville** (city) Buncombe County
67	n/a	8.1	**Northchase** (CDP) New Hanover County
69	n/a	8.0	**Emerald Isle** (town) Carteret County
69	n/a	8.0	**Myrtle Grove** (CDP) New Hanover County
69	n/a	8.0	**Westport** (CDP) Lincoln County
72	668	7.9	**Roanoke Rapids** (city) Halifax County
73	n/a	7.7	**James City** (CDP) Craven County
73	755	7.7	**Mount Airy** (city) Surry County
73	n/a	7.7	**Nags Head** (town) Dare County
76	804	7.6	**Tarboro** (town) Edgecombe County
77	n/a	7.5	**Ahoskie** (town) Hertford County
77	848	7.5	**Goldsboro** (city) Wayne County
77	848	7.5	**Holly Springs** (town) Wake County
77	n/a	7.5	**River Bend** (town) Craven County
81	n/a	7.4	**Granite Falls** (town) Caldwell County
81	n/a	7.4	**Polkton** (town) Anson County
83	n/a	7.3	**Aberdeen** (town) Moore County
83	n/a	7.3	**China Grove** (town) Rowan County
83	n/a	7.3	**Locust** (city) Stanly County
83	954	7.3	**Morganton** (city) Burke County
83	n/a	7.3	**Wesley Chapel** (village) Union County
88	1026	7.2	**Statesville** (city) Iredell County
88	n/a	7.2	**Stokesdale** (town) Guilford County
90	1083	7.1	**Belmont** (city) Gaston County
90	n/a	7.1	**Clinton** (city) Sampson County
90	1083	7.1	**Wilmington** (city) New Hanover County
93	1138	7.0	**Fayetteville** (city) Cumberland County
93	n/a	7.0	**Granite Quarry** (town) Rowan County
93	n/a	7.0	**Pleasant Garden** (town) Guilford County
93	n/a	7.0	**Wadesboro** (town) Anson County
97	n/a	6.9	**Angier** (town) Harnett County
97	n/a	6.9	**East Flat Rock** (CDP) Henderson County
97	1192	6.9	**Kernersville** (town) Forsyth County
97	n/a	6.9	**Williamston** (town) Martin County
101	1253	6.8	**Clayton** (town) Johnston County
101	n/a	6.8	**Fairmont** (town) Robeson County
101	n/a	6.8	**Hamlet** (city) Richmond County
101	n/a	6.8	**Red Oak** (town) Nash County
101	1253	6.8	**Summerfield** (town) Guilford County
101	n/a	6.8	**Tabor City** (town) Columbus County
107	n/a	6.7	**Elizabethtown** (town) Bladen County
107	n/a	6.7	**Elkin** (town) Surry County
107	n/a	6.7	**Elon** (town) Alamance County
107	1339	6.7	**Hickory** (city) Catawba County
107	1339	6.7	**Jacksonville** (city) Onslow County
107	1339	6.7	**Lumberton** (city) Robeson County
113	n/a	6.6	**Bethlehem** (CDP) Alexander County
113	n/a	6.6	**Conover** (city) Catawba County
113	1404	6.6	**Garner** (town) Wake County
113	1404	6.6	**Spring Lake** (town) Cumberland County
117	n/a	6.5	**Elroy** (CDP) Wayne County
117	n/a	6.5	**Nashville** (town) Nash County
117	n/a	6.5	**Unionville** (town) Union County
120	n/a	6.4	**Carolina Beach** (town) New Hanover County
120	1560	6.4	**Cary** (town) Wake County
120	n/a	6.4	**Glen Raven** (CDP) Alamance County
120	1560	6.4	**Mooresville** (town) Iredell County
120	1560	6.4	**New Bern** (city) Craven County
120	n/a	6.4	**Saint James** (town) Brunswick County
120	n/a	6.4	**Stanley** (town) Gaston County
120	1560	6.4	**Wake Forest** (town) Wake County
120	n/a	6.4	**Weaverville** (town) Buncombe County
129	1625	6.3	**Cornelius** (town) Mecklenburg County
129	1625	6.3	**Eden** (city) Rockingham County
129	1625	6.3	**Havelock** (city) Craven County
129	n/a	6.3	**Mountain View** (CDP) Catawba County
129	1625	6.3	**Murraysville** (CDP) New Hanover County
129	1625	6.3	**Shelby** (city) Cleveland County
135	1723	6.2	**Huntersville** (town) Mecklenburg County
135	n/a	6.2	**Rockfish** (CDP) Hoke County
137	1812	6.1	**Hendersonville** (city) Henderson County
137	n/a	6.1	**Saint Stephens** (CDP) Catawba County
139	1919	6.0	**Concord** (city) Cabarrus County
139	n/a	6.0	**Erwin** (town) Harnett County
139	n/a	6.0	**Fairview** (CDP) Buncombe County
139	n/a	6.0	**Oak Ridge** (town) Guilford County
143	2017	5.9	**Apex** (town) Wake County
143	n/a	5.9	**Morehead City** (town) Carteret County
145	2114	5.8	**Elizabeth City** (city) Pasquotank County
145	n/a	5.8	**North Wilkesboro** (town) Wilkes County
145	n/a	5.8	**Zebulon** (town) Wake County
148	n/a	5.7	**Franklin** (CDP) Macon County
148	2211	5.7	**Fuquay-Varina** (town) Wake County
148	2211	5.7	**Greensboro** (city) Guilford County

Note: *The state column ranks the top/bottom 150 places in the state with population of 2,500 or more. The national column ranks the top/bottom places in the country with population of 10,000 or more. Places that are unincorporated were not considered in the rankings. n/a indicates data not available. Please refer to the User Guide for additional information.*

Employment: Healthcare Practitioners

Top 150 Places Ranked in *Ascending* Order

State Rank	Nat'l Rank	Percent	Place	State Rank	Nat'l Rank	Percent	Place
1	n/a	0.0	**Wallace** (town) Duplin County	72	n/a	4.4	**Rural Hall** (town) Forsyth County
2	n/a	0.7	**Icard** (CDP) Burke County	72	1151	4.4	**Thomasville** (city) Davidson County
3	n/a	0.9	**Gamewell** (town) Caldwell County	78	n/a	4.6	**Mineral Springs** (town) Union County
3	n/a	0.9	**Kitty Hawk** (town) Dare County	78	n/a	4.6	**Sylva** (town) Jackson County
3	n/a	0.9	**Sneads Ferry** (CDP) Onslow County	78	n/a	4.6	**Wingate** (town) Union County
6	n/a	1.0	**Skippers Corner** (CDP) New Hanover County	81	1418	4.7	**Archdale** (city) Randolph County
7	n/a	1.1	**Mar-Mac** (CDP) Wayne County	81	n/a	4.7	**Dunn** (city) Harnett County
8	n/a	1.3	**Siler City** (town) Chatham County	81	1418	4.7	**Gastonia** (city) Gaston County
8	n/a	1.3	**Warsaw** (town) Duplin County	81	n/a	4.7	**Half Moon** (CDP) Onslow County
10	n/a	1.5	**La Grange** (town) Lenoir County	81	1418	4.7	**High Point** (city) Guilford County
11	n/a	1.6	**East Rockingham** (CDP) Richmond County	81	n/a	4.7	**Roxboro** (city) Person County
12	n/a	1.7	**Red Springs** (town) Robeson County	81	1418	4.7	**Smithfield** (town) Johnston County
13	n/a	1.8	**Edenton** (town) Chowan County	88	1502	4.8	**Charlotte** (city) Mecklenburg County
14	n/a	1.9	**Pembroke** (town) Robeson County	88	1502	4.8	**Sanford** (city) Lee County
15	n/a	2.0	**Selma** (town) Johnston County	88	n/a	4.8	**Sunset Beach** (town) Brunswick County
16	140	2.2	**Boone** (town) Watauga County	91	n/a	4.9	**Benson** (town) Johnston County
16	n/a	2.2	**Cullowhee** (CDP) Jackson County	91	n/a	4.9	**Landis** (town) Rowan County
18	n/a	2.4	**Farmville** (town) Pitt County	91	1586	4.9	**Matthews** (town) Mecklenburg County
19	n/a	2.5	**Boiling Spring Lakes** (city) Brunswick County	91	n/a	4.9	**Spindale** (town) Rutherford County
19	n/a	2.5	**Wendell** (town) Wake County	91	n/a	4.9	**Swansboro** (town) Onslow County
21	n/a	2.6	**Lake Norman of Catawba** (CDP) Catawba County	91	n/a	4.9	**Waxhaw** (town) Union County
21	217	2.6	**Lexington** (city) Davidson County	97	n/a	5.0	**Canton** (town) Haywood County
23	253	2.7	**Albemarle** (city) Stanly County	97	1680	5.0	**Indian Trail** (town) Union County
23	n/a	2.7	**Beaufort** (town) Carteret County	97	n/a	5.0	**Ranlo** (town) Gaston County
23	n/a	2.7	**Bessemer City** (city) Gaston County	97	n/a	5.0	**Sawmills** (town) Caldwell County
26	n/a	2.8	**Spencer** (town) Rowan County	101	n/a	5.1	**Black Mountain** (town) Buncombe County
27	n/a	2.9	**Pineville** (town) Mecklenburg County	101	n/a	5.1	**Brogden** (CDP) Wayne County
27	n/a	2.9	**Trinity** (city) Randolph County	101	1762	5.1	**Morrisville** (town) Wake County
29	n/a	3.0	**Murfreesboro** (town) Hertford County	101	1762	5.1	**Mount Holly** (city) Gaston County
30	n/a	3.2	**Kill Devil Hills** (town) Dare County	101	n/a	5.1	**Weddington** (town) Union County
30	n/a	3.2	**Yadkinville** (town) Yadkin County	101	n/a	5.1	**Welcome** (CDP) Davidson County
32	480	3.3	**Harrisburg** (town) Cabarrus County	107	n/a	5.2	**Dallas** (town) Gaston County
32	n/a	3.3	**Lake Junaluska** (CDP) Haywood County	107	n/a	5.2	**Forest Oaks** (CDP) Guilford County
32	n/a	3.3	**Lowell** (city) Gaston County	107	1868	5.2	**Kings Mountain** (city) Cleveland County
32	n/a	3.3	**Rockingham** (city) Richmond County	107	1868	5.2	**Kinston** (city) Lenoir County
36	n/a	3.4	**Enfield** (town) Halifax County	111	1961	5.3	**Lenoir** (city) Caldwell County
36	529	3.4	**Piney Green** (CDP) Onslow County	111	n/a	5.3	**Plymouth** (town) Washington County
38	n/a	3.5	**Kings Grant** (CDP) New Hanover County	113	n/a	5.4	**Archer Lodge** (town) Johnston County
38	n/a	3.5	**Long View** (town) Catawba County	113	2043	5.4	**Burlington** (city) Alamance County
38	n/a	3.5	**Midland** (town) Cabarrus County	115	2138	5.5	**Laurinburg** (city) Scotland County
38	595	3.5	**Mint Hill** (town) Mecklenburg County	115	2138	5.5	**Raleigh** (city) Wake County
38	n/a	3.5	**Moyock** (CDP) Currituck County	117	2234	5.6	**Hope Mills** (town) Cumberland County
38	595	3.5	**Newton** (city) Catawba County	117	n/a	5.6	**Liberty** (town) Randolph County
38	n/a	3.5	**Raeford** (city) Hoke County	117	n/a	5.6	**Wrightsboro** (CDP) New Hanover County
38	595	3.5	**Reidsville** (city) Rockingham County	120	n/a	5.7	**Franklin** (town) Macon County
38	n/a	3.5	**Southern Shores** (town) Dare County	120	2329	5.7	**Fuquay-Varina** (town) Wake County
38	n/a	3.5	**Valdese** (town) Burke County	120	2329	5.7	**Greensboro** (city) Guilford County
48	n/a	3.6	**Lillington** (town) Harnett County	120	2329	5.7	**Salisbury** (city) Rowan County
49	n/a	3.7	**South Rosemary** (CDP) Halifax County	120	2329	5.7	**Wilson** (city) Wilson County
49	n/a	3.7	**Tyro** (CDP) Davidson County	125	2446	5.8	**Elizabeth City** (city) Pasquotank County
49	n/a	3.7	**Woodfin** (town) Buncombe County	125	n/a	5.8	**North Wilkesboro** (town) Wilkes County
52	n/a	3.8	**Southport** (city) Brunswick County	125	n/a	5.8	**Zebulon** (town) Wake County
53	n/a	3.9	**Fairview** (town) Union County	128	2543	5.9	**Apex** (town) Wake County
53	n/a	3.9	**Newport** (town) Carteret County	128	n/a	5.9	**Morehead City** (town) Carteret County
53	n/a	3.9	**Walkertown** (town) Forsyth County	130	2640	6.0	**Concord** (city) Cabarrus County
56	n/a	4.0	**Forest City** (town) Rutherford County	130	n/a	6.0	**Erwin** (town) Harnett County
56	876	4.0	**Monroe** (city) Union County	130	n/a	6.0	**Fairview** (CDP) Buncombe County
58	935	4.1	**Asheboro** (city) Randolph County	130	n/a	6.0	**Oak Ridge** (town) Guilford County
58	n/a	4.1	**Bayshore** (CDP) New Hanover County	134	2738	6.1	**Hendersonville** (city) Henderson County
58	n/a	4.1	**Cajah's Mountain** (town) Caldwell County	134	n/a	6.1	**Saint Stephens** (CDP) Catawba County
58	n/a	4.1	**Jamestown** (town) Guilford County	136	2845	6.2	**Huntersville** (town) Mecklenburg County
58	935	4.1	**Lincolnton** (city) Lincoln County	136	n/a	6.2	**Rockfish** (CDP) Hoke County
58	n/a	4.1	**Lowesville** (CDP) Lincoln County	138	2934	6.3	**Cornelius** (town) Mecklenburg County
58	n/a	4.1	**Maiden** (town) Catawba County	138	2934	6.3	**Eden** (city) Rockingham County
58	n/a	4.1	**Troy** (town) Montgomery County	138	2934	6.3	**Havelock** (city) Craven County
66	n/a	4.2	**Burgaw** (town) Pender County	138	n/a	6.3	**Mountain View** (CDP) Catawba County
66	n/a	4.2	**Swannanoa** (CDP) Buncombe County	138	2934	6.3	**Murraysville** (CDP) New Hanover County
68	n/a	4.3	**Etowah** (CDP) Henderson County	138	2934	6.3	**Shelby** (city) Cleveland County
68	n/a	4.3	**Mocksville** (town) Davie County	144	n/a	6.4	**Carolina Beach** (town) New Hanover County
68	1076	4.3	**Rocky Mount** (city) Nash County	144	3032	6.4	**Cary** (town) Wake County
68	n/a	4.3	**Wilkesboro** (town) Wilkes County	144	n/a	6.4	**Glen Raven** (CDP) Alamance County
72	1151	4.4	**Graham** (city) Alamance County	144	3032	6.4	**Mooresville** (town) Iredell County
72	1151	4.4	**Henderson** (city) Vance County	144	3032	6.4	**New Bern** (city) Craven County
72	1151	4.4	**Kannapolis** (city) Cabarrus County	144	n/a	6.4	**Saint James** (town) Brunswick County
72	n/a	4.4	**Mount Olive** (town) Wayne County	144	n/a	6.4	**Stanley** (town) Gaston County

Note: The state column ranks the top/bottom 150 places in the state with population of 2,500 or more. The national column ranks the top/bottom places in the country with population of 10,000 or more. Places that are unincorporated were not considered in the rankings. n/a indicates data not available. Please refer to the User Guide for additional information.

Employment: Service Occupations

Top 150 Places Ranked in *Descending* Order

State Rank	Nat'l Rank	Percent	Place
1	n/a	40.4	**Pembroke** (town) Robeson County
2	10	39.7	**Boone** (town) Watauga County
3	n/a	37.8	**Sylva** (town) Jackson County
4	n/a	34.8	**Polkton** (town) Anson County
5	n/a	34.3	**Cullowhee** (CDP) Jackson County
6	n/a	33.8	**South Rosemary** (CDP) Halifax County
7	53	33.3	**Spring Lake** (town) Cumberland County
8	n/a	31.4	**Franklin** (town) Macon County
9	n/a	31.1	**Shallotte** (town) Brunswick County
10	n/a	30.6	**Spindale** (town) Rutherford County
11	n/a	30.5	**Elroy** (CDP) Wayne County
12	n/a	30.0	**Buies Creek** (CDP) Harnett County
13	n/a	29.7	**Troy** (town) Montgomery County
14	n/a	29.1	**Icard** (CDP) Burke County
15	n/a	28.4	**Tabor City** (town) Columbus County
16	192	28.3	**Elizabeth City** (city) Pasquotank County
17	n/a	27.4	**Beaufort** (town) Carteret County
18	n/a	27.2	**Swannanoa** (CDP) Buncombe County
19	n/a	26.6	**Grifton** (town) Pitt County
20	n/a	26.3	**Rockfish** (CDP) Hoke County
21	n/a	26.2	**Fairmont** (town) Robeson County
22	n/a	25.9	**North Wilkesboro** (town) Wilkes County
22	n/a	25.9	**Selma** (town) Johnston County
22	n/a	25.9	**Valdese** (town) Burke County
25	n/a	25.8	**Fairview** (CDP) Buncombe County
26	n/a	25.6	**Glen Raven** (CDP) Alamance County
26	n/a	25.6	**Wadesboro** (town) Anson County
28	n/a	25.5	**Canton** (town) Haywood County
28	n/a	25.5	**Farmville** (town) Pitt County
28	384	25.5	**Kinston** (city) Lenoir County
31	n/a	25.2	**Boiling Spring Lakes** (city) Brunswick County
31	n/a	25.2	**Mocksville** (town) Davie County
33	460	24.9	**Albemarle** (city) Stanly County
34	476	24.8	**Jacksonville** (city) Onslow County
34	n/a	24.8	**Washington** (city) Beaufort County
36	n/a	24.7	**Woodfin** (town) Buncombe County
37	505	24.6	**Eden** (city) Rockingham County
37	505	24.6	**Morganton** (city) Burke County
37	505	24.6	**Salisbury** (city) Rowan County
40	n/a	24.5	**Benson** (town) Johnston County
41	n/a	24.2	**Dunn** (city) Harnett County
41	n/a	24.2	**Southern Shores** (town) Dare County
43	n/a	24.1	**Midland** (town) Cabarrus County
43	n/a	24.1	**Spencer** (town) Rowan County
43	n/a	24.1	**Warsaw** (town) Duplin County
46	617	23.9	**New Bern** (city) Craven County
47	n/a	23.7	**Brogden** (CDP) Wayne County
47	n/a	23.7	**Mar-Mac** (CDP) Wayne County
47	n/a	23.7	**Silver Lake** (CDP) New Hanover County
50	n/a	23.6	**Swansboro** (town) Onslow County
51	693	23.4	**Lexington** (city) Davidson County
51	693	23.4	**Southern Pines** (town) Moore County
53	n/a	23.2	**Waynesville** (town) Haywood County
54	n/a	23.0	**Newport** (town) Carteret County
55	794	22.9	**Greenville** (city) Pitt County
56	n/a	22.8	**James City** (CDP) Craven County
56	n/a	22.8	**Ranlo** (town) Gaston County
58	n/a	22.7	**China Grove** (town) Rowan County
59	n/a	22.5	**Stanley** (town) Gaston County
60	n/a	22.4	**Black Mountain** (town) Buncombe County
60	n/a	22.4	**East Flat Rock** (CDP) Henderson County
60	892	22.4	**Piney Green** (CDP) Onslow County
63	n/a	22.3	**River Road** (CDP) Beaufort County
63	915	22.3	**Wilmington** (city) New Hanover County
65	n/a	22.2	**East Rockingham** (CDP) Richmond County
65	n/a	22.2	**Mills River** (town) Henderson County
67	n/a	22.0	**Nags Head** (town) Dare County
67	n/a	22.0	**Sunset Beach** (town) Brunswick County
69	n/a	21.9	**Aberdeen** (town) Moore County
69	n/a	21.9	**Bessemer City** (city) Gaston County
69	1007	21.9	**Monroe** (city) Union County
69	n/a	21.9	**Tyro** (CDP) Davidson County
73	n/a	21.8	**Brevard** (city) Transylvania County
73	n/a	21.8	**Pineville** (town) Mecklenburg County
73	n/a	21.8	**Royal Pines** (CDP) Buncombe County
76	n/a	21.7	**Dallas** (town) Gaston County
76	n/a	21.7	**Kill Devil Hills** (town) Dare County
78	1083	21.6	**Henderson** (city) Vance County
79	n/a	21.5	**Ahoskie** (town) Hertford County
79	n/a	21.5	**Roxboro** (city) Person County
81	1138	21.4	**Havelock** (city) Craven County
81	n/a	21.4	**Hillsborough** (town) Orange County
83	1162	21.3	**Fayetteville** (city) Cumberland County
83	n/a	21.3	**Rural Hall** (town) Forsyth County
83	1162	21.3	**Shelby** (city) Cleveland County
86	1192	21.2	**Asheville** (city) Buncombe County
86	n/a	21.2	**Windsor** (town) Bertie County
88	n/a	21.1	**Lillington** (town) Harnett County
88	n/a	21.1	**Morehead City** (town) Carteret County
90	n/a	21.0	**Etowah** (CDP) Henderson County
91	1272	20.9	**Kannapolis** (city) Cabarrus County
91	n/a	20.9	**Marion** (city) McDowell County
91	n/a	20.9	**Rutherfordton** (town) Rutherford County
94	1332	20.7	**Newton** (city) Catawba County
95	n/a	20.4	**Siler City** (town) Chatham County
95	n/a	20.4	**Whiteville** (city) Columbus County
97	n/a	20.1	**Elizabethtown** (town) Bladen County
98	n/a	20.0	**Butner** (town) Granville County
98	1530	20.0	**Mooresville** (town) Iredell County
98	1530	20.0	**Tarboro** (town) Edgecombe County
101	1565	19.9	**Sanford** (city) Lee County
101	1565	19.9	**Smithfield** (town) Johnston County
101	n/a	19.9	**Wrightsboro** (CDP) New Hanover County
104	n/a	19.8	**Oak Island** (town) Brunswick County
104	n/a	19.8	**Raeford** (city) Hoke County
106	1626	19.7	**Goldsboro** (city) Wayne County
106	n/a	19.7	**Murfreesboro** (town) Hertford County
108	n/a	19.5	**Half Moon** (CDP) Onslow County
108	n/a	19.5	**Trent Woods** (town) Craven County
108	1696	19.5	**Wilson** (city) Wilson County
108	1696	19.5	**Winston-Salem** (city) Forsyth County
112	n/a	19.4	**Ayden** (town) Pitt County
112	n/a	19.4	**Flat Rock** (village) Henderson County
114	n/a	19.3	**Granite Falls** (town) Caldwell County
114	n/a	19.3	**Mount Olive** (town) Wayne County
114	n/a	19.3	**Rockingham** (city) Richmond County
117	n/a	19.2	**Edenton** (town) Chowan County
117	n/a	19.2	**Sneads Ferry** (CDP) Onslow County
119	n/a	19.1	**Creedmoor** (city) Granville County
119	1833	19.1	**Hickory** (city) Catawba County
119	n/a	19.1	**Skippers Corner** (CDP) New Hanover County
122	n/a	19.0	**Erwin** (town) Harnett County
122	n/a	19.0	**Unionville** (town) Union County
124	n/a	18.9	**Fairview** (town) Union County
124	n/a	18.9	**Gamewell** (town) Caldwell County
124	n/a	18.9	**Plymouth** (town) Washington County
124	n/a	18.9	**River Bend** (town) Craven County
124	n/a	18.9	**Wallace** (town) Duplin County
129	1940	18.8	**Burlington** (city) Alamance County
129	1940	18.8	**Carrboro** (town) Orange County
129	n/a	18.8	**Kings Grant** (CDP) New Hanover County
129	n/a	18.8	**Saint Stephens** (CDP) Catawba County
133	1971	18.7	**Rocky Mount** (city) Nash County
133	n/a	18.7	**Zebulon** (town) Wake County
135	n/a	18.6	**Hudson** (town) Caldwell County
136	n/a	18.4	**Liberty** (town) Randolph County
136	2067	18.4	**Lumberton** (city) Robeson County
136	n/a	18.4	**Mountain Home** (CDP) Henderson County
136	n/a	18.4	**Ogden** (CDP) New Hanover County
140	2134	18.2	**Hendersonville** (city) Henderson County
140	2134	18.2	**High Point** (city) Guilford County
140	n/a	18.2	**Red Springs** (town) Robeson County
143	2158	18.1	**Gastonia** (city) Gaston County
144	2185	18.0	**Greensboro** (city) Guilford County
144	2185	18.0	**Thomasville** (city) Davidson County
146	2221	17.9	**Hope Mills** (town) Cumberland County
147	n/a	17.8	**Archer Lodge** (town) Johnston County
147	n/a	17.8	**Carolina Beach** (town) New Hanover County
147	n/a	17.8	**Dana** (CDP) Henderson County
147	2260	17.8	**Knightdale** (town) Wake County

Note: The state column ranks the top/bottom 150 places in the state with population of 2,500 or more. The national column ranks the top/bottom places in the country with population of 10,000 or more. Places that are unincorporated were not considered in the rankings. n/a indicates data not available. Please refer to the User Guide for additional information.

Employment: Service Occupations

Top 150 Places Ranked in *Ascending* Order

State Rank	Nat'l Rank	Percent	Place
1	n/a	4.1	Westport (CDP) Lincoln County
2	n/a	4.3	Marvin (village) Union County
3	n/a	4.6	Lake Royale (CDP) Franklin County
4	n/a	6.2	Lowesville (CDP) Lincoln County
5	n/a	6.8	Fairfield Harbour (CDP) Craven County
6	n/a	7.2	Boiling Springs (town) Cleveland County
7	n/a	7.5	Brices Creek (CDP) Craven County
8	n/a	7.8	Pleasant Garden (town) Guilford County
9	149	8.4	Stallings (town) Union County
10	158	8.5	Morrisville (town) Wake County
11	n/a	9.1	Lake Norman of Catawba (CDP) Catawba County
11	n/a	9.1	Seven Lakes (CDP) Moore County
11	223	9.1	Summerfield (town) Guilford County
14	n/a	9.2	Burgaw (town) Pender County
14	n/a	9.2	Long View (town) Catawba County
16	n/a	9.3	Angier (town) Harnett County
17	n/a	9.7	Porters Neck (CDP) New Hanover County
17	n/a	9.7	Waxhaw (town) Union County
19	295	9.8	Holly Springs (town) Wake County
19	n/a	9.8	Saint James (town) Brunswick County
21	n/a	9.9	Mineral Springs (town) Union County
22	n/a	10.0	Wesley Chapel (village) Union County
23	n/a	10.1	Bayshore (CDP) New Hanover County
24	n/a	10.3	Jamestown (town) Guilford County
25	n/a	10.9	Gibsonville (town) Guilford County
26	485	11.1	Clayton (town) Johnston County
26	485	11.1	Matthews (town) Mecklenburg County
28	n/a	11.2	Wallburg (town) Davidson County
29	n/a	11.3	Sawmills (town) Caldwell County
30	n/a	11.4	Weddington (town) Union County
31	n/a	11.8	Hampstead (CDP) Pender County
31	n/a	11.8	King (city) Stokes County
31	n/a	11.8	Rolesville (town) Wake County
34	n/a	11.9	Oak Ridge (town) Guilford County
35	680	12.0	Apex (town) Wake County
36	n/a	12.1	Forest Oaks (CDP) Guilford County
36	n/a	12.1	Mountain View (CDP) Catawba County
38	722	12.2	Cary (town) Wake County
38	n/a	12.2	Yadkinville (town) Yadkin County
40	n/a	12.3	Cajah's Mountain (town) Caldwell County
40	n/a	12.3	Kitty Hawk (town) Dare County
42	n/a	12.5	Walkertown (town) Forsyth County
43	822	12.7	Leland (town) Brunswick County
43	822	12.7	Lewisville (town) Forsyth County
43	n/a	12.7	Wentworth (town) Rockingham County
46	n/a	12.8	Cramerton (town) Gaston County
46	n/a	12.8	Moyock (CDP) Currituck County
46	n/a	12.8	Winterville (town) Pitt County
49	864	12.9	Harrisburg (town) Cabarrus County
50	n/a	13.1	Pittsboro (town) Chatham County
50	n/a	13.1	Southport (city) Brunswick County
52	n/a	13.2	Cherryville (city) Gaston County
53	n/a	13.3	Eastover (town) Cumberland County
53	n/a	13.3	Lake Junaluska (CDP) Haywood County
55	n/a	13.4	Whispering Pines (village) Moore County
56	1010	13.5	Archdale (city) Randolph County
56	n/a	13.5	Louisburg (town) Franklin County
58	1040	13.6	Huntersville (town) Mecklenburg County
58	n/a	13.6	Landis (town) Rowan County
58	1040	13.6	Statesville (city) Iredell County
58	1040	13.6	Wake Forest (town) Wake County
62	n/a	13.7	Myrtle Grove (CDP) New Hanover County
63	n/a	13.8	Conover (city) Catawba County
63	1085	13.8	Lincolnton (city) Lincoln County
63	n/a	13.8	Weaverville (town) Buncombe County
63	n/a	13.8	Wilkesboro (town) Wilkes County
67	n/a	14.2	Lowell (city) Gaston County
67	n/a	14.2	Stokesdale (town) Guilford County
69	n/a	14.3	Northchase (CDP) New Hanover County
69	n/a	14.3	Red Oak (town) Nash County
71	1246	14.4	Indian Trail (town) Union County
72	1345	14.7	Chapel Hill (town) Orange County
72	n/a	14.7	Emerald Isle (town) Carteret County
72	1345	14.7	Mint Hill (town) Mecklenburg County
75	1375	14.8	Fuquay-Varina (town) Wake County
75	n/a	14.8	Maiden (town) Catawba County
75	1375	14.8	Mount Holly (city) Gaston County
78	1475	15.1	Clemmons (village) Forsyth County
78	1475	15.1	Pinehurst (village) Moore County
80	n/a	15.3	Enochville (CDP) Rowan County
81	n/a	15.5	Granite Quarry (town) Rowan County
81	1592	15.5	Mebane (city) Alamance County
83	1657	15.7	Belmont (city) Gaston County
83	n/a	15.7	Bethlehem (CDP) Alexander County
83	1657	15.7	Roanoke Rapids (city) Halifax County
83	n/a	15.7	Trinity (city) Randolph County
87	1695	15.8	Davidson (town) Mecklenburg County
87	n/a	15.8	Welcome (CDP) Davidson County
89	1728	15.9	Raleigh (city) Wake County
90	1764	16.0	Concord (city) Cabarrus County
90	n/a	16.0	Elon (town) Alamance County
90	n/a	16.0	Lake Park (village) Union County
90	n/a	16.0	Midway (town) Davidson County
94	n/a	16.1	Hamlet (city) Richmond County
95	n/a	16.2	Fletcher (town) Henderson County
95	n/a	16.2	Williamston (town) Martin County
97	n/a	16.3	Forest City (town) Rutherford County
97	1860	16.3	Graham (city) Alamance County
99	1894	16.4	Asheboro (city) Randolph County
99	n/a	16.4	Wingate (town) Union County
101	1965	16.6	Lenoir (city) Caldwell County
102	n/a	16.7	Locust (city) Stanly County
102	n/a	16.7	Wendell (town) Wake County
104	2050	16.8	Charlotte (city) Mecklenburg County
104	n/a	16.8	Clinton (city) Sampson County
104	2050	16.8	Laurinburg (city) Scotland County
104	n/a	16.8	Oxford (city) Granville County
104	n/a	16.8	Randleman (city) Randolph County
109	2072	16.9	Cornelius (town) Mecklenburg County
109	2072	16.9	Garner (town) Wake County
109	2072	16.9	Kernersville (town) Forsyth County
112	2103	17.0	Murraysville (CDP) New Hanover County
112	n/a	17.0	Nashville (town) Nash County
112	2103	17.0	Reidsville (city) Rockingham County
115	2138	17.1	Mount Airy (city) Surry County
116	n/a	17.3	Enfield (town) Halifax County
117	2261	17.5	Durham (city) Durham County
117	n/a	17.5	Elkin (town) Surry County
119	n/a	17.6	Carolina Shores (town) Brunswick County
119	2296	17.6	Kings Mountain (city) Cleveland County
119	n/a	17.6	La Grange (town) Lenoir County
122	n/a	17.8	Archer Lodge (town) Johnston County
122	n/a	17.8	Carolina Beach (town) New Hanover County
122	n/a	17.8	Dana (CDP) Henderson County
122	2366	17.8	Knightdale (town) Wake County
126	2397	17.9	Hope Mills (town) Cumberland County
127	2436	18.0	Greensboro (city) Guilford County
127	2436	18.0	Thomasville (city) Davidson County
129	2472	18.1	Gastonia (city) Gaston County
130	2499	18.2	Hendersonville (city) Henderson County
130	2499	18.2	High Point (city) Guilford County
130	n/a	18.2	Red Springs (town) Robeson County
133	n/a	18.4	Liberty (town) Randolph County
133	2562	18.4	Lumberton (city) Robeson County
133	n/a	18.4	Mountain Home (CDP) Henderson County
133	n/a	18.4	Ogden (CDP) New Hanover County
137	n/a	18.6	Hudson (town) Caldwell County
138	2652	18.7	Rocky Mount (city) Nash County
138	n/a	18.7	Zebulon (town) Wake County
140	2686	18.8	Burlington (city) Alamance County
140	2686	18.8	Carrboro (town) Orange County
140	n/a	18.8	Kings Grant (CDP) New Hanover County
140	n/a	18.8	Saint Stephens (CDP) Catawba County
144	n/a	18.9	Fairview (town) Union County
144	n/a	18.9	Gamewell (town) Caldwell County
144	n/a	18.9	Plymouth (town) Washington County
144	n/a	18.9	River Bend (town) Craven County
144	n/a	18.9	Wallace (town) Duplin County
149	n/a	19.0	Erwin (town) Harnett County
149	n/a	19.0	Unionville (town) Union County

Note: The state column ranks the top/bottom 150 places in the state with population of 2,500 or more. The national column ranks the top/bottom places in the country with population of 10,000 or more. Places that are unincorporated were not considered in the rankings. n/a indicates data not available. Please refer to the User Guide for additional information.

Employment: Sales and Office Occupations

Top 150 Places Ranked in *Descending* Order

State Rank	Nat'l Rank	Percent	Place
1	n/a	44.2	**Saint James** (town) Brunswick County
2	n/a	40.7	**Northchase** (CDP) New Hanover County
3	n/a	37.4	**Whiteville** (city) Columbus County
4	n/a	36.7	**Carolina Shores** (town) Brunswick County
5	n/a	33.8	**Marvin** (village) Union County
6	n/a	33.7	**Hudson** (town) Caldwell County
7	n/a	33.3	**Kitty Hawk** (town) Dare County
8	n/a	33.2	**Unionville** (town) Union County
9	n/a	33.1	**Burgaw** (town) Pender County
10	n/a	32.9	**Angier** (town) Harnett County
11	n/a	32.7	**Jamestown** (town) Guilford County
12	n/a	32.5	**La Grange** (town) Lenoir County
12	n/a	32.5	**Rockfish** (CDP) Hoke County
14	n/a	32.0	**Half Moon** (CDP) Onslow County
15	n/a	31.6	**Midway** (town) Davidson County
16	n/a	31.5	**Yadkinville** (town) Yadkin County
17	n/a	31.4	**Wendell** (town) Wake County
18	n/a	31.3	**Pleasant Garden** (town) Guilford County
19	n/a	31.1	**Lake Norman of Catawba** (CDP) Catawba County
19	n/a	31.1	**Myrtle Grove** (CDP) New Hanover County
21	n/a	30.8	**Tyro** (CDP) Davidson County
22	n/a	30.7	**Wallburg** (town) Davidson County
23	277	30.6	**Archdale** (city) Randolph County
23	n/a	30.6	**Westport** (CDP) Lincoln County
25	n/a	30.3	**Trinity** (city) Randolph County
26	n/a	30.2	**Pineville** (town) Mecklenburg County
26	n/a	30.2	**Spencer** (town) Rowan County
28	n/a	30.1	**Locust** (city) Stanly County
29	363	30.0	**Kings Mountain** (city) Cleveland County
29	n/a	30.0	**Mountain View** (CDP) Catawba County
31	n/a	29.9	**Lake Junaluska** (CDP) Haywood County
32	395	29.8	**Boone** (town) Watauga County
33	n/a	29.7	**Elon** (town) Alamance County
33	n/a	29.7	**Murfreesboro** (town) Hertford County
33	n/a	29.7	**Sunset Beach** (town) Brunswick County
36	n/a	29.4	**Boiling Springs** (town) Cleveland County
37	524	29.3	**Matthews** (town) Mecklenburg County
38	n/a	29.2	**Mineral Springs** (town) Union County
39	624	28.9	**Thomasville** (city) Davidson County
39	n/a	28.9	**Waxhaw** (town) Union County
41	n/a	28.8	**Landis** (town) Rowan County
41	n/a	28.8	**Royal Pines** (CDP) Buncombe County
41	n/a	28.8	**Weaverville** (town) Buncombe County
44	n/a	28.7	**Bayshore** (CDP) New Hanover County
45	n/a	28.6	**Woodfin** (town) Buncombe County
46	n/a	28.3	**Liberty** (town) Randolph County
47	n/a	28.1	**Cajah's Mountain** (town) Caldwell County
48	n/a	28.0	**Granite Falls** (town) Caldwell County
48	904	28.0	**Indian Trail** (town) Union County
48	n/a	28.0	**Louisburg** (town) Franklin County
48	n/a	28.0	**North Wilkesboro** (town) Wilkes County
52	939	27.9	**Piney Green** (CDP) Onslow County
52	939	27.9	**Spring Lake** (town) Cumberland County
54	972	27.8	**Graham** (city) Alamance County
54	n/a	27.8	**Hamlet** (city) Richmond County
56	n/a	27.7	**Cherryville** (city) Gaston County
56	n/a	27.7	**Granite Quarry** (town) Rowan County
56	n/a	27.7	**Weddington** (town) Union County
59	n/a	27.6	**Cullowhee** (CDP) Jackson County
59	1062	27.6	**High Point** (city) Guilford County
61	n/a	27.5	**Dallas** (town) Gaston County
62	n/a	27.4	**Kill Devil Hills** (town) Dare County
62	1156	27.4	**Murraysville** (CDP) New Hanover County
62	n/a	27.4	**Southern Shores** (town) Dare County
65	1198	27.3	**Greensboro** (city) Guilford County
66	n/a	27.2	**Forest Oaks** (CDP) Guilford County
67	1286	27.1	**Havelock** (city) Craven County
67	n/a	27.1	**Kings Grant** (CDP) New Hanover County
69	n/a	27.0	**Rutherfordton** (town) Rutherford County
70	1394	26.9	**Hope Mills** (town) Cumberland County
70	1394	26.9	**Roanoke Rapids** (city) Halifax County
70	n/a	26.9	**Wingate** (town) Union County
70	n/a	26.9	**Zebulon** (town) Wake County
74	1464	26.8	**Harrisburg** (town) Cabarrus County
74	n/a	26.8	**Red Oak** (town) Nash County
74	1464	26.8	**Reidsville** (city) Rockingham County
77	n/a	26.7	**Butner** (town) Granville County
78	n/a	26.6	**Farmville** (town) Pitt County
78	n/a	26.6	**Whispering Pines** (village) Moore County
80	1625	26.5	**Fayetteville** (city) Cumberland County
80	n/a	26.5	**Stanley** (town) Gaston County
82	1681	26.4	**Rocky Mount** (city) Nash County
83	n/a	26.3	**Erwin** (town) Harnett County
83	1738	26.3	**Mint Hill** (town) Mecklenburg County
85	1799	26.2	**Kernersville** (town) Forsyth County
85	n/a	26.2	**Shallotte** (town) Brunswick County
85	n/a	26.2	**Southport** (city) Brunswick County
85	n/a	26.2	**Swansboro** (town) Onslow County
89	1873	26.1	**Stallings** (town) Union County
90	1930	26.0	**Albemarle** (city) Stanly County
90	1930	26.0	**Cornelius** (town) Mecklenburg County
90	n/a	26.0	**Cramerton** (town) Gaston County
93	1997	25.9	**Charlotte** (city) Mecklenburg County
93	n/a	25.9	**Dunn** (city) Harnett County
95	2060	25.8	**Clayton** (town) Johnston County
95	2060	25.8	**Huntersville** (town) Mecklenburg County
95	n/a	25.8	**Nashville** (town) Nash County
95	n/a	25.8	**Porters Neck** (CDP) New Hanover County
99	2116	25.7	**Belmont** (city) Gaston County
99	n/a	25.7	**Waynesville** (town) Haywood County
101	n/a	25.6	**Gibsonville** (town) Guilford County
102	n/a	25.5	**Creedmoor** (city) Granville County
102	2226	25.5	**Kannapolis** (city) Cabarrus County
102	n/a	25.5	**Long View** (town) Catawba County
102	n/a	25.5	**Oxford** (city) Granville County
102	2226	25.5	**Statesville** (city) Iredell County
107	n/a	25.4	**Carolina Beach** (town) New Hanover County
107	n/a	25.4	**Emerald Isle** (town) Carteret County
107	2276	25.4	**Garner** (town) Wake County
107	2276	25.4	**Hendersonville** (city) Henderson County
111	2327	25.3	**Concord** (city) Cabarrus County
111	2327	25.3	**Mount Holly** (city) Gaston County
113	n/a	25.2	**Midland** (town) Cabarrus County
114	n/a	25.1	**Oak Ridge** (town) Guilford County
115	2612	24.8	**Henderson** (city) Vance County
115	n/a	24.8	**Rural Hall** (town) Forsyth County
115	2612	24.8	**Summerfield** (town) Guilford County
118	2671	24.7	**Burlington** (city) Alamance County
118	n/a	24.7	**Lake Park** (village) Union County
118	2671	24.7	**Wake Forest** (town) Wake County
118	n/a	24.7	**Wilkesboro** (town) Wilkes County
122	2724	24.6	**Jacksonville** (city) Onslow County
123	n/a	24.5	**Mountain Home** (CDP) Henderson County
123	2790	24.5	**Raleigh** (city) Wake County
123	n/a	24.5	**Seven Lakes** (CDP) Moore County
123	n/a	24.5	**Tabor City** (town) Columbus County
127	n/a	24.4	**Edenton** (town) Chowan County
127	2857	24.4	**Gastonia** (city) Gaston County
127	2857	24.4	**Mooresville** (town) Iredell County
127	2857	24.4	**Wilmington** (city) New Hanover County
127	2857	24.4	**Wilson** (city) Wilson County
132	n/a	24.3	**Forest City** (town) Rutherford County
132	2911	24.3	**Lenoir** (city) Caldwell County
134	n/a	24.2	**Aberdeen** (town) Moore County
134	n/a	24.2	**Fairview** (CDP) Buncombe County
134	2964	24.2	**Pinehurst** (village) Moore County
134	n/a	24.2	**Walkertown** (town) Forsyth County
138	n/a	24.1	**Fletcher** (town) Henderson County
138	n/a	24.1	**Maiden** (town) Catawba County
140	n/a	24.0	**Ranlo** (town) Gaston County
141	n/a	23.9	**Buies Creek** (CDP) Harnett County
141	n/a	23.9	**Lake Royale** (CDP) Franklin County
141	3102	23.9	**Laurinburg** (city) Scotland County
141	3102	23.9	**Mount Airy** (city) Surry County
145	n/a	23.8	**Brices Creek** (CDP) Craven County
145	3142	23.8	**Shelby** (city) Cleveland County
147	n/a	23.7	**Mocksville** (town) Davie County
148	3236	23.6	**Greenville** (city) Pitt County
149	n/a	23.5	**Clinton** (city) Sampson County
149	n/a	23.5	**Franklin** (town) Macon County

Note: *The state column ranks the top/bottom 150 places in the state with population of 2,500 or more. The national column ranks the top/bottom places in the country with population of 10,000 or more. Places that are unincorporated were not considered in the rankings. n/a indicates data not available. Please refer to the User Guide for additional information.*

Employment: Sales and Office Occupations

Top 150 Places Ranked in *Ascending* Order

State Rank	Nat'l Rank	Percent	Place	State Rank	Nat'l Rank	Percent	Place
1	n/a	9.0	Red Springs (town) Robeson County	76	594	21.3	Clemmons (village) Forsyth County
2	n/a	9.6	Pittsboro (town) Chatham County	76	n/a	21.3	Randleman (city) Randolph County
3	n/a	10.4	Warsaw (town) Duplin County	78	n/a	21.4	Fairview (town) Union County
4	n/a	11.3	Grifton (town) Pitt County	78	n/a	21.4	Ogden (CDP) New Hanover County
5	n/a	12.6	Pembroke (town) Robeson County	80	n/a	21.5	Etowah (CDP) Henderson County
6	n/a	13.0	Bethlehem (CDP) Alexander County	80	643	21.5	Lumberton (city) Robeson County
6	n/a	13.0	Brogden (CDP) Wayne County	80	n/a	21.5	Wadesboro (town) Anson County
8	n/a	13.1	Polkton (town) Anson County	80	n/a	21.5	Wallace (town) Duplin County
9	16	13.4	Carrboro (town) Orange County	84	n/a	21.6	Ayden (town) Pitt County
10	n/a	14.4	Marion (city) McDowell County	84	n/a	21.6	Eastover (town) Cumberland County
11	n/a	14.5	Mount Olive (town) Wayne County	84	675	21.6	Lincolnton (city) Lincoln County
12	n/a	14.6	Gamewell (town) Caldwell County	84	n/a	21.6	Stokesdale (town) Guilford County
12	n/a	14.6	Glen Raven (CDP) Alamance County	88	n/a	21.9	Lowesville (CDP) Lincoln County
14	n/a	14.7	Benson (town) Johnston County	89	787	22.0	Elizabeth City (city) Pasquotank County
14	n/a	14.7	Windsor (town) Bertie County	89	787	22.0	Newton (city) Catawba County
16	n/a	14.9	Siler City (town) Chatham County	91	n/a	22.1	Canton (town) Haywood County
17	n/a	15.5	Fairfield Harbour (CDP) Craven County	91	n/a	22.1	Knightdale (town) Wake County
18	n/a	15.7	Enfield (town) Halifax County	91	812	22.1	Lewisville (town) Forsyth County
19	n/a	15.8	Selma (town) Johnston County	91	812	22.1	Swannanoa (CDP) Buncombe County
20	n/a	16.9	East Flat Rock (CDP) Henderson County	91	n/a	22.1	Wesley Chapel (village) Union County
21	n/a	17.2	Plymouth (town) Washington County	96	n/a	22.2	Elkin (town) Surry County
22	n/a	17.4	Archer Lodge (town) Johnston County	97	881	22.3	Goldsboro (city) Wayne County
23	n/a	17.5	River Road (CDP) Beaufort County	97	n/a	22.3	King (city) Stokes County
23	105	17.5	Southern Pines (town) Moore County	97	n/a	22.3	Sneads Ferry (CDP) Onslow County
25	n/a	17.6	Nags Head (town) Dare County	100	906	22.4	Hickory (city) Catawba County
26	115	17.7	Chapel Hill (town) Orange County	100	n/a	22.4	Oak Island (town) Brunswick County
27	n/a	17.8	China Grove (town) Rowan County	100	906	22.4	Tarboro (town) Edgecombe County
27	n/a	17.8	Troy (town) Montgomery County	103	n/a	22.5	Spindale (town) Rutherford County
29	n/a	17.9	Boiling Spring Lakes (city) Brunswick County	103	n/a	22.5	Trent Woods (town) Craven County
29	n/a	17.9	Fairmont (town) Robeson County	105	974	22.6	Winston-Salem (city) Forsyth County
31	n/a	18.1	Skippers Corner (CDP) New Hanover County	106	n/a	22.7	Wrightsboro (CDP) New Hanover County
31	n/a	18.1	South Rosemary (CDP) Halifax County	107	1041	22.8	Asheville (city) Buncombe County
33	n/a	18.2	Washington (city) Beaufort County	107	n/a	22.8	River Bend (town) Craven County
34	n/a	18.5	Elroy (CDP) Wayne County	107	1041	22.8	Sanford (city) Lee County
35	n/a	18.6	Bessemer City (city) Gaston County	110	n/a	22.9	Flat Rock (village) Henderson County
36	186	18.7	Salisbury (city) Rowan County	111	n/a	23.1	Hillsborough (town) Orange County
37	n/a	18.9	Valdese (town) Burke County	111	1162	23.1	Leland (town) Brunswick County
38	n/a	19.0	Mar-Mac (CDP) Wayne County	111	1162	23.1	Mebane (city) Alamance County
39	231	19.2	Durham (city) Durham County	111	n/a	23.1	Morehead City (town) Carteret County
39	n/a	19.2	Icard (CDP) Burke County	111	n/a	23.1	Moyock (CDP) Currituck County
39	n/a	19.2	Newport (town) Carteret County	116	n/a	23.2	Conover (city) Catawba County
39	n/a	19.2	Sawmills (town) Caldwell County	116	1198	23.2	Fuquay-Varina (town) Wake County
43	n/a	19.3	Lillington (town) Harnett County	118	1239	23.3	Monroe (city) Union County
43	n/a	19.3	Williamston (town) Martin County	119	n/a	23.4	James City (CDP) Craven County
45	257	19.4	Kinston (city) Lenoir County	119	n/a	23.4	Rolesville (town) Wake County
45	257	19.4	Morganton (city) Burke County	121	n/a	23.5	Clinton (city) Sampson County
47	n/a	19.6	Enochville (CDP) Rowan County	121	n/a	23.5	Franklin (town) Macon County
48	n/a	19.8	Brevard (city) Transylvania County	121	n/a	23.5	Wentworth (town) Rockingham County
48	309	19.8	Davidson (town) Mecklenburg County	124	1375	23.6	Greenville (city) Pitt County
48	309	19.8	Lexington (city) Davidson County	125	n/a	23.7	Mocksville (town) Davie County
51	n/a	19.9	Welcome (CDP) Davidson County	126	n/a	23.8	Brices Creek (CDP) Craven County
52	n/a	20.0	Raeford (city) Hoke County	126	1467	23.8	Shelby (city) Cleveland County
52	n/a	20.0	Rockingham (city) Richmond County	128	n/a	23.9	Buies Creek (CDP) Harnett County
52	n/a	20.0	Saint Stephens (CDP) Catawba County	128	n/a	23.9	Lake Royale (CDP) Franklin County
55	n/a	20.2	Mills River (town) Henderson County	128	1515	23.9	Laurinburg (city) Scotland County
56	n/a	20.3	Dana (CDP) Henderson County	128	1515	23.9	Mount Airy (city) Surry County
56	n/a	20.3	Roxboro (city) Person County	132	n/a	24.0	Ranlo (town) Gaston County
56	n/a	20.3	Silver Lake (CDP) New Hanover County	133	n/a	24.1	Fletcher (town) Henderson County
56	n/a	20.3	Sylva (town) Jackson County	133	n/a	24.1	Maiden (town) Catawba County
60	n/a	20.4	Lowell (city) Gaston County	135	n/a	24.2	Aberdeen (town) Moore County
60	401	20.4	New Bern (city) Craven County	135	n/a	24.2	Fairview (CDP) Buncombe County
62	418	20.5	Asheboro (city) Randolph County	135	1648	24.2	Pinehurst (village) Moore County
62	n/a	20.5	Black Mountain (town) Buncombe County	135	n/a	24.2	Walkertown (town) Forsyth County
64	438	20.6	Apex (town) Wake County	139	n/a	24.3	Forest City (town) Rutherford County
64	438	20.6	Cary (town) Wake County	139	1693	24.3	Lenoir (city) Caldwell County
64	438	20.6	Eden (city) Rockingham County	141	n/a	24.4	Edenton (town) Chowan County
67	n/a	20.8	Beaufort (town) Carteret County	141	1746	24.4	Gastonia (city) Gaston County
67	482	20.8	Holly Springs (town) Wake County	141	1746	24.4	Mooresville (town) Iredell County
67	482	20.8	Morrisville (town) Wake County	141	1746	24.4	Wilmington (city) New Hanover County
67	482	20.8	Smithfield (town) Johnston County	141	1746	24.4	Wilson (city) Wilson County
67	n/a	20.8	Winterville (town) Pitt County	146	n/a	24.5	Mountain Home (CDP) Henderson County
72	n/a	21.0	Elizabethtown (town) Bladen County	146	1800	24.5	Raleigh (city) Wake County
72	n/a	21.0	Hampstead (CDP) Pender County	146	n/a	24.5	Seven Lakes (CDP) Moore County
74	n/a	21.1	Ahoskie (town) Hertford County	146	n/a	24.5	Tabor City (town) Columbus County
74	n/a	21.1	East Rockingham (CDP) Richmond County	150	1867	24.6	Jacksonville (city) Onslow County

Note: The state column ranks the top/bottom 150 places in the state with population of 2,500 or more. The national column ranks the top/bottom places in the country with population of 10,000 or more. Places that are unincorporated were not considered in the rankings. n/a indicates data not available. Please refer to the User Guide for additional information.

Employment: Natural Resources, Construction, and Maintenance Occupations

Top 150 Places Ranked in *Descending* Order

State Rank	Nat'l Rank	Percent	Place	State Rank	Nat'l Rank	Percent	Place
1	n/a	31.6	**Wallace** (town) Duplin County	76	938	10.5	**Graham** (city) Alamance County
2	n/a	26.9	**Selma** (town) Johnston County	77	n/a	10.4	**La Grange** (town) Lenoir County
3	n/a	24.3	**Sneads Ferry** (CDP) Onslow County	77	977	10.4	**Reidsville** (city) Rockingham County
4	n/a	23.8	**Newport** (town) Carteret County	79	n/a	10.3	**Rockingham** (city) Richmond County
5	n/a	22.9	**Elizabethtown** (town) Bladen County	80	1044	10.2	**Hendersonville** (city) Henderson County
6	n/a	22.7	**East Flat Rock** (CDP) Henderson County	80	1044	10.2	**Liberty** (town) Randolph County
7	n/a	22.3	**Skippers Corner** (CDP) New Hanover County	80	1044	10.2	**Lincolnton** (city) Lincoln County
8	n/a	21.0	**Hampstead** (CDP) Pender County	80	1044	10.2	**Lumberton** (city) Robeson County
8	n/a	21.0	**River Road** (CDP) Beaufort County	80	1044	10.2	**Mebane** (city) Alamance County
10	n/a	20.2	**Gamewell** (town) Caldwell County	80	1044	10.2	**Salisbury** (city) Rowan County
11	n/a	19.5	**Enochville** (CDP) Rowan County	86	n/a	10.1	**Siler City** (town) Chatham County
11	n/a	19.5	**Fairview** (town) Union County	87	n/a	10.0	**Marion** (city) McDowell County
13	n/a	19.1	**Landis** (town) Rowan County	87	n/a	10.0	**Wendell** (town) Wake County
14	n/a'	18.0	**Burgaw** (town) Pender County	87	n/a	10.0	**Zebulon** (town) Wake County
14	113	18.0	**Havelock** (city) Craven County	90	n/a	9.9	**Elkin** (town) Surry County
16	n/a	17.8	**Mar-Mac** (CDP) Wayne County	90	n/a	9.9	**Enfield** (town) Halifax County
17	n/a	17.7	**Tyro** (CDP) Davidson County	90	n/a	9.9	**Lake Norman of Catawba** (CDP) Catawba County
18	n/a	17.4	**Roxboro** (city) Person County	93	n/a	9.8	**Washington** (city) Beaufort County
18	n/a	17.4	**Silver Lake** (CDP) New Hanover County	94	n/a	9.7	**Beaufort** (town) Carteret County
20	n/a	17.2	**Etowah** (CDP) Henderson County	94	1245	9.7	**Leland** (town) Brunswick County
21	n/a	17.1	**China Grove** (town) Rowan County	96	1289	9.6	**Eden** (city) Rockingham County
22	n/a	16.5	**Moyock** (CDP) Currituck County	96	n/a	9.6	**Forest City** (town) Rutherford County
23	n/a	16.3	**Kitty Hawk** (town) Dare County	96	n/a	9.6	**Franklin** (town) Macon County
23	n/a	16.3	**Nags Head** (town) Dare County	96	n/a	9.6	**Gibsonville** (town) Guilford County
25	n/a	16.2	**Walkertown** (town) Forsyth County	100	n/a	9.5	**Pembroke** (town) Robeson County
26	n/a	15.9	**Bethlehem** (CDP) Alexander County	100	n/a	9.5	**Warsaw** (town) Duplin County
26	n/a	15.9	**River Bend** (town) Craven County	102	n/a	9.4	**Half Moon** (CDP) Onslow County
28	n/a	15.7	**Sawmills** (town) Caldwell County	102	n/a	9.4	**Lake Junaluska** (CDP) Haywood County
29	n/a	14.8	**Elroy** (CDP) Wayne County	102	n/a	9.4	**Midway** (town) Davidson County
29	n/a	14.8	**Maiden** (town) Catawba County	102	1370	9.4	**Roanoke Rapids** (city) Halifax County
29	238	14.8	**Monroe** (city) Union County	106	1418	9.3	**Kings Mountain** (city) Cleveland County
29	n/a	14.8	**Yadkinville** (town) Yadkin County	106	n/a	9.3	**Raeford** (city) Hoke County
33	n/a	14.6	**Welcome** (CDP) Davidson County	106	n/a	9.3	**Rural Hall** (town) Forsyth County
34	n/a	14.3	**Angier** (town) Harnett County	109	1465	9.2	**Wilson** (city) Wilson County
35	n/a	14.2	**Boiling Spring Lakes** (city) Brunswick County	110	1514	9.1	**Archdale** (city) Randolph County
35	n/a	14.2	**Mineral Springs** (town) Union County	110	n/a	9.1	**Dunn** (city) Harnett County
37	n/a	14.1	**Red Oak** (town) Nash County	110	1514	9.1	**Sanford** (city) Lee County
37	n/a	14.1	**Wrightsboro** (CDP) New Hanover County	113	1566	9.0	**Piney Green** (CDP) Onslow County
39	n/a	13.8	**Randleman** (city) Randolph County	114	n/a	8.9	**Dallas** (town) Gaston County
40	n/a	13.5	**Swannanoa** (CDP) Buncombe County	114	n/a	8.9	**Rockfish** (CDP) Hoke County
41	355	13.4	**Mount Airy** (city) Surry County	114	n/a	8.9	**Stokesdale** (town) Guilford County
42	n/a	13.3	**Glen Raven** (CDP) Alamance County	117	n/a	8.8	**Cherryville** (city) Gaston County
43	n/a	13.2	**Mount Olive** (town) Wayne County	117	n/a	8.8	**Eastover** (town) Cumberland County
44	n/a	13.1	**Archer Lodge** (town) Johnston County	117	1683	8.8	**Lexington** (city) Davidson County
44	n/a	13.1	**Bayshore** (CDP) New Hanover County	117	n/a	8.8	**Morehead City** (town) Carteret County
44	n/a	13.1	**Kill Devil Hills** (town) Dare County	117	1683	8.8	**Mount Holly** (city) Gaston County
44	n/a	13.1	**Midland** (town) Cabarrus County	117	n/a	8.8	**Wilkesboro** (town) Wilkes County
48	n/a	13.0	**Butner** (town) Granville County	123	1748	8.7	**Concord** (city) Cabarrus County
49	n/a	12.8	**Kings Grant** (CDP) New Hanover County	124	n/a	8.6	**Ayden** (town) Pitt County
49	n/a	12.8	**Locust** (city) Stanly County	124	n/a	8.6	**Lake Park** (village) Union County
51	n/a	12.6	**Fairfield Harbour** (CDP) Craven County	124	n/a	8.6	**Waynesville** (town) Haywood County
52	n/a	12.5	**Benson** (town) Johnston County	127	1835	8.5	**Henderson** (city) Vance County
52	n/a	12.5	**Cramerton** (town) Gaston County	127	n/a	8.5	**King** (city) Stokes County
54	n/a	12.3	**Carolina Shores** (town) Brunswick County	127	n/a	8.5	**Saint Stephens** (CDP) Catawba County
54	513	12.3	**Clayton** (town) Johnston County	127	n/a	8.5	**Winterville** (town) Pitt County
54	n/a	12.3	**Fairview** (CDP) Buncombe County	131	1887	8.4	**Mint Hill** (town) Mecklenburg County
57	n/a	12.2	**Bessemer City** (city) Gaston County	132	n/a	8.3	**Porters Neck** (CDP) New Hanover County
57	n/a	12.2	**Farmville** (town) Pitt County	133	1984	8.2	**Goldsboro** (city) Wayne County
59	n/a	12.0	**Brogden** (CDP) Wayne County	133	n/a	8.2	**Long View** (town) Catawba County
59	n/a	12.0	**Dana** (CDP) Henderson County	133	1984	8.2	**Mooresville** (town) Iredell County
61	n/a	11.7	**Oak Island** (town) Brunswick County	133	n/a	8.2	**Wesley Chapel** (village) Union County
61	630	11.7	**Smithfield** (town) Johnston County	137	2041	8.1	**Stallings** (town) Union County
63	n/a	11.5	**Cullowhee** (CDP) Jackson County	137	2041	8.1	**Statesville** (city) Iredell County
63	n/a	11.5	**Wentworth** (town) Rockingham County	137	n/a	8.1	**Williamston** (town) Martin County
65	n/a	11.4	**East Rockingham** (CDP) Richmond County	137	n/a	8.1	**Wingate** (town) Union County
66	n/a	11.3	**Cajah's Mountain** (town) Caldwell County	137	n/a	8.1	**Woodfin** (town) Buncombe County
67	736	11.2	**Indian Trail** (town) Union County	142	n/a	8.0	**Ranlo** (town) Gaston County
67	n/a	11.2	**South Rosemary** (CDP) Halifax County	142	n/a	8.0	**Unionville** (town) Union County
69	n/a	11.1	**James City** (CDP) Craven County	142	n/a	8.0	**Windsor** (town) Bertie County
69	n/a	11.1	**Pleasant Garden** (town) Guilford County	145	n/a	7.8	**Edenton** (town) Chowan County
71	789	11.0	**Albemarle** (city) Stanly County	145	n/a	7.8	**Rolesville** (town) Wake County
71	n/a	11.0	**Erwin** (town) Harnett County	147	n/a	7.7	**Black Mountain** (town) Buncombe County
73	n/a	10.9	**Wallburg** (town) Davidson County	147	2240	7.7	**Gastonia** (city) Gaston County
74	904	10.6	**Kannapolis** (city) Cabarrus County	147	n/a	7.7	**Hamlet** (city) Richmond County
74	904	10.6	**New Bern** (city) Craven County	147	n/a	7.7	**Spindale** (town) Rutherford County

Note: The state column ranks the top/bottom 150 places in the state with population of 2,500 or more. The national column ranks the top/bottom places in the country with population of 10,000 or more. Places that are unincorporated were not considered in the rankings. n/a indicates data not available. Please refer to the User Guide for additional information.

Employment: Natural Resources, Construction, and Maintenance Occupations

Top 150 Places Ranked in *Ascending* Order

State Rank	Nat'l Rank	Percent	Place	State Rank	Nat'l Rank	Percent	Place
1	n/a	0.0	**Buies Creek** (CDP) Harnett County	74	1316	6.0	**Rocky Mount** (city) Nash County
2	n/a	0.3	**Icard** (CDP) Burke County	77	n/a	6.2	**Red Springs** (town) Robeson County
3	n/a	0.7	**Shallotte** (town) Brunswick County	78	n/a	6.3	**Southport** (city) Brunswick County
4	n/a	1.3	**Marvin** (village) Union County	78	n/a	6.3	**Whiteville** (city) Columbus County
5	n/a	1.6	**Lake Royale** (CDP) Franklin County	80	1545	6.4	**Greensboro** (city) Guilford County
6	n/a	2.0	**Murfreesboro** (town) Hertford County	80	1545	6.4	**Summerfield** (town) Guilford County
6	n/a	2.0	**Royal Pines** (CDP) Buncombe County	82	n/a	6.5	**Ahoskie** (town) Hertford County
8	99	2.1	**Morrisville** (town) Wake County	82	1622	6.5	**Laurinburg** (city) Scotland County
9	n/a	2.3	**Northchase** (CDP) New Hanover County	84	n/a	6.6	**Brices Creek** (CDP) Craven County
10	n/a	2.5	**Mountain View** (CDP) Catawba County	84	1683	6.6	**Harrisburg** (town) Cabarrus County
11	169	2.6	**Pinehurst** (village) Moore County	84	n/a	6.6	**Hillsborough** (town) Orange County
12	203	2.8	**Chapel Hill** (town) Orange County	84	n/a	6.6	**Hudson** (town) Caldwell County
13	n/a	2.9	**Polkton** (town) Anson County	84	1683	6.6	**Murraysville** (CDP) New Hanover County
14	257	3.1	**Cornelius** (town) Mecklenburg County	84	n/a	6.6	**Southern Shores** (town) Dare County
14	n/a	3.1	**Nashville** (town) Nash County	90	1753	6.7	**Newton** (city) Catawba County
14	n/a	3.1	**Seven Lakes** (CDP) Moore County	91	n/a	6.8	**Trinity** (city) Randolph County
14	257	3.1	**Shelby** (city) Cleveland County	91	n/a	6.8	**Valdese** (town) Burke County
18	281	3.2	**Apex** (town) Wake County	93	1850	6.9	**Durham** (city) Durham County
18	281	3.2	**Davidson** (town) Mecklenburg County	93	n/a	6.9	**Lowell** (city) Gaston County
18	n/a	3.2	**Elon** (town) Alamance County	95	1907	7.0	**Asheboro** (city) Randolph County
21	308	3.3	**Boone** (town) Watauga County	95	n/a	7.0	**Lillington** (town) Harnett County
21	n/a	3.3	**Oak Ridge** (town) Guilford County	95	n/a	7.0	**Louisburg** (town) Franklin County
23	324	3.4	**Cary** (town) Wake County	95	n/a	7.0	**Myrtle Grove** (CDP) New Hanover County
24	n/a	3.6	**Flat Rock** (village) Henderson County	95	n/a	7.0	**Sylva** (town) Jackson County
24	n/a	3.6	**Weaverville** (town) Buncombe County	100	1965	7.1	**Charlotte** (city) Mecklenburg County
26	407	3.7	**Carrboro** (town) Orange County	101	2018	7.2	**Garner** (town) Wake County
26	n/a	3.7	**Pineville** (town) Mecklenburg County	101	2018	7.2	**Hope Mills** (town) Cumberland County
26	n/a	3.7	**Saint James** (town) Brunswick County	101	2018	7.2	**Kinston** (city) Lenoir County
29	n/a	3.8	**Fletcher** (town) Henderson County	101	2018	7.2	**Wilmington** (city) New Hanover County
29	442	3.8	**Greenville** (city) Pitt County	101	2018	7.2	**Winston-Salem** (city) Forsyth County
29	n/a	3.8	**Mountain Home** (CDP) Henderson County	106	2087	7.3	**Burlington** (city) Alamance County
32	n/a	3.9	**Mills River** (town) Henderson County	106	n/a	7.3	**Forest Oaks** (CDP) Guilford County
32	n/a	3.9	**Ogden** (CDP) New Hanover County	106	2087	7.3	**Fuquay-Varina** (town) Wake County
32	n/a	3.9	**Weddington** (town) Union County	106	n/a	7.3	**Granite Quarry** (town) Rowan County
35	500	4.0	**Spring Lake** (town) Cumberland County	106	n/a	7.3	**Sunset Beach** (town) Brunswick County
35	n/a	4.0	**Trent Woods** (town) Craven County	106	n/a	7.3	**Swansboro** (town) Onslow County
35	n/a	4.0	**Whispering Pines** (village) Moore County	112	n/a	7.4	**Carolina Beach** (town) New Hanover County
38	n/a	4.1	**Jamestown** (town) Guilford County	112	2145	7.4	**Elizabeth City** (city) Pasquotank County
38	n/a	4.1	**Oxford** (city) Granville County	112	2145	7.4	**Jacksonville** (city) Onslow County
40	n/a	4.3	**Stanley** (town) Gaston County	112	n/a	7.4	**Lowesville** (CDP) Lincoln County
41	641	4.5	**Lewisville** (town) Forsyth County	116	2218	7.5	**Fayetteville** (city) Cumberland County
41	n/a	4.5	**Rutherfordton** (town) Rutherford County	116	2218	7.5	**Knightdale** (town) Wake County
43	n/a	4.6	**Granite Falls** (town) Caldwell County	116	2218	7.5	**Morganton** (city) Burke County
43	n/a	4.6	**Spencer** (town) Rowan County	116	2218	7.5	**Tarboro** (town) Edgecombe County
45	n/a	4.7	**Boiling Springs** (town) Cleveland County	120	2285	7.6	**Lenoir** (city) Caldwell County
45	729	4.7	**Southern Pines** (town) Moore County	120	n/a	7.6	**Troy** (town) Montgomery County
45	729	4.7	**Wake Forest** (town) Wake County	122	n/a	7.7	**Black Mountain** (town) Buncombe County
48	765	4.8	**Belmont** (city) Gaston County	122	2351	7.7	**Gastonia** (city) Gaston County
49	n/a	4.9	**Emerald Isle** (town) Carteret County	122	n/a	7.7	**Hamlet** (city) Richmond County
49	n/a	4.9	**Mocksville** (town) Davie County	122	n/a	7.7	**Spindale** (town) Rutherford County
49	n/a	4.9	**Wadesboro** (town) Anson County	126	n/a	7.8	**Edenton** (town) Chowan County
52	846	5.0	**Clemmons** (village) Forsyth County	126	n/a	7.8	**Rolesville** (town) Wake County
53	891	5.1	**Huntersville** (town) Mecklenburg County	128	n/a	8.0	**Ranlo** (town) Gaston County
53	891	5.1	**Matthews** (town) Mecklenburg County	128	n/a	8.0	**Unionville** (town) Union County
55	n/a	5.2	**Brevard** (city) Transylvania County	128	n/a	8.0	**Windsor** (town) Bertie County
55	n/a	5.2	**Conover** (city) Catawba County	131	2564	8.1	**Stallings** (town) Union County
55	n/a	5.2	**Westport** (CDP) Lincoln County	131	2564	8.1	**Statesville** (city) Iredell County
58	n/a	5.3	**Grifton** (town) Pitt County	131	n/a	8.1	**Williamston** (town) Martin County
58	n/a	5.3	**North Wilkesboro** (town) Wilkes County	131	n/a	8.1	**Wingate** (town) Union County
58	n/a	5.3	**Tabor City** (town) Columbus County	131	n/a	8.1	**Woodfin** (town) Buncombe County
58	n/a	5.3	**Waxhaw** (town) Union County	136	2616	8.2	**Goldsboro** (city) Wayne County
62	1023	5.4	**High Point** (city) Guilford County	136	n/a	8.2	**Long View** (town) Catawba County
63	n/a	5.5	**Creedmoor** (city) Granville County	136	2616	8.2	**Mooresville** (town) Iredell County
64	n/a	5.6	**Canton** (town) Haywood County	136	n/a	8.2	**Wesley Chapel** (village) Union County
64	1109	5.6	**Hickory** (city) Catawba County	140	n/a	8.3	**Porters Neck** (CDP) New Hanover County
64	n/a	5.6	**Plymouth** (town) Washington County	141	2726	8.4	**Mint Hill** (town) Mecklenburg County
67	1149	5.7	**Holly Springs** (town) Wake County	142	2770	8.5	**Henderson** (city) Vance County
67	1149	5.7	**Kernersville** (town) Forsyth County	142	n/a	8.5	**King** (city) Stokes County
69	n/a	5.8	**Fairmont** (town) Robeson County	142	n/a	8.5	**Saint Stephens** (CDP) Catawba County
70	n/a	5.9	**Aberdeen** (town) Moore County	142	n/a	8.5	**Winterville** (town) Pitt County
70	1246	5.9	**Asheville** (city) Buncombe County	146	n/a	8.6	**Ayden** (town) Pitt County
70	n/a	5.9	**Clinton** (city) Sampson County	146	n/a	8.6	**Lake Park** (village) Union County
70	1246	5.9	**Thomasville** (city) Davidson County	146	n/a	8.6	**Waynesville** (town) Haywood County
74	n/a	6.0	**Pittsboro** (town) Chatham County	149	2866	8.7	**Concord** (city) Cabarrus County
74	1316	6.0	**Raleigh** (city) Wake County	150	n/a	8.8	**Cherryville** (city) Gaston County

Note: The state column ranks the top/bottom 150 places in the state with population of 2,500 or more. The national column ranks the top/bottom places in the country with population of 10,000 or more. Places that are unincorporated were not considered in the rankings. n/a indicates data not available. Please refer to the User Guide for additional information.

Employment: Production, Transportation, and Material Moving Occupations

Top 150 Places Ranked in *Descending* Order

State Rank	Nat'l Rank	Percent	Place	State Rank	Nat'l Rank	Percent	Place
1	n/a	42.3	**Long View** (town) Catawba County	76	718	17.2	**Lumberton** (city) Robeson County
2	n/a	38.4	**Siler City** (town) Chatham County	77	739	17.1	**Shelby** (city) Cleveland County
3	n/a	34.9	**Warsaw** (town) Duplin County	77	n/a	17.1	**Tyro** (CDP) Davidson County
4	n/a	34.4	**Red Springs** (town) Robeson County	79	754	17.0	**Mount Holly** (city) Gaston County
5	n/a	32.2	**Enfield** (town) Halifax County	79	n/a	17.0	**Southport** (city) Brunswick County
6	n/a	30.5	**Gamewell** (town) Caldwell County	81	n/a	16.9	**Cherryville** (city) Gaston County
7	n/a	30.0	**Lowell** (city) Gaston County	81	n/a	16.9	**Mocksville** (town) Davie County
8	n/a	29.9	**Bessemer City** (city) Gaston County	83	n/a	16.7	**Ayden** (town) Pitt County
9	n/a	29.8	**Mar-Mac** (CDP) Wayne County	83	n/a	16.7	**Landis** (town) Rowan County
10	46	29.6	**Lexington** (city) Davidson County	83	n/a	16.7	**Rockingham** (city) Richmond County
11	n/a	29.2	**Sawmills** (town) Caldwell County	83	n/a	16.7	**South Rosemary** (CDP) Halifax County
12	54	28.9	**Asheboro** (city) Randolph County	87	n/a	16.6	**Burgaw** (town) Pender County
13	n/a	28.8	**Mount Olive** (town) Wayne County	87	n/a	16.6	**Farmville** (town) Pitt County
13	n/a	28.8	**Windsor** (town) Bertie County	87	n/a	16.6	**Selma** (town) Johnston County
15	n/a	28.0	**Wadesboro** (town) Anson County	90	n/a	16.5	**Granite Falls** (town) Caldwell County
16	79	27.3	**Thomasville** (city) Davidson County	90	825	16.5	**Monroe** (city) Union County
17	n/a	27.0	**East Rockingham** (CDP) Richmond County	92	n/a	16.4	**North Wilkesboro** (town) Wilkes County
18	n/a	25.9	**Cajah's Mountain** (town) Caldwell County	92	n/a	16.4	**Oxford** (city) Granville County
18	n/a	25.9	**Icard** (CDP) Burke County	92	n/a	16.4	**Pleasant Garden** (town) Guilford County
20	122	25.4	**Lenoir** (city) Caldwell County	92	n/a	16.4	**Randleman** (city) Randolph County
20	n/a	25.4	**Plymouth** (town) Washington County	96	n/a	16.3	**Eastover** (town) Cumberland County
22	n/a	25.0	**Conover** (city) Catawba County	97	n/a	16.2	**Wallace** (town) Duplin County
23	n/a	24.7	**Hamlet** (city) Richmond County	98	n/a	16.1	**Fairmont** (town) Robeson County
24	152	24.4	**Newton** (city) Catawba County	98	890	16.1	**Morganton** (city) Burke County
24	n/a	24.4	**Polkton** (town) Anson County	100	909	16.0	**Hickory** (city) Catawba County
26	158	24.3	**Reidsville** (city) Rockingham County	100	n/a	16.0	**Shallotte** (town) Brunswick County
27	163	24.1	**Eden** (city) Rockingham County	100	n/a	16.0	**Walkertown** (town) Forsyth County
27	n/a	24.1	**Saint Stephens** (CDP) Catawba County	103	929	15.9	**High Point** (city) Guilford County
29	173	23.9	**Statesville** (city) Iredell County	103	929	15.9	**Salisbury** (city) Rowan County
30	n/a	23.6	**Roxboro** (city) Person County	103	929	15.9	**Tarboro** (town) Edgecombe County
31	n/a	23.1	**Lake Royale** (CDP) Franklin County	106	n/a	15.7	**King** (city) Stokes County
31	n/a	23.1	**Maiden** (town) Catawba County	107	n/a	15.6	**Black Mountain** (town) Buncombe County
33	n/a	22.9	**Spencer** (town) Rowan County	108	n/a	15.4	**Brices Creek** (CDP) Craven County
34	n/a	22.5	**Brogden** (CDP) Wayne County	109	n/a	15.3	**Wallburg** (town) Davidson County
35	230	22.3	**Kinston** (city) Lenoir County	110	n/a	15.1	**Skippers Corner** (CDP) New Hanover County
35	n/a	22.3	**Welcome** (CDP) Davidson County	111	n/a	14.8	**James City** (CDP) Craven County
37	n/a	22.1	**Valdese** (town) Burke County	111	n/a	14.8	**Wrightsboro** (CDP) New Hanover County
37	n/a	22.1	**Yadkinville** (town) Yadkin County	113	n/a	14.7	**Stanley** (town) Gaston County
39	n/a	22.0	**Grifton** (town) Pitt County	114	n/a	14.6	**East Flat Rock** (CDP) Henderson County
40	n/a	21.9	**Williamston** (town) Martin County	115	n/a	14.5	**Archer Lodge** (town) Johnston County
40	n/a	21.9	**Zebulon** (town) Wake County	115	n/a	14.5	**Elroy** (CDP) Wayne County
42	n/a	21.4	**Nashville** (town) Nash County	117	n/a	14.4	**Granite Quarry** (town) Rowan County
43	n/a	21.3	**Mountain View** (CDP) Catawba County	117	n/a	14.4	**Louisburg** (town) Franklin County
44	301	21.1	**Lincolnton** (city) Lincoln County	117	n/a	14.4	**Wilkesboro** (town) Wilkes County
45	n/a	21.0	**Marion** (city) McDowell County	120	n/a	14.3	**Raeford** (city) Hoke County
46	n/a	20.8	**Elkin** (town) Surry County	120	n/a	14.3	**Wingate** (town) Union County
46	n/a	20.8	**Wentworth** (town) Rockingham County	122	n/a	14.2	**Boiling Spring Lakes** (city) Brunswick County
48	n/a	20.7	**Ahoskie** (town) Hertford County	123	1288	14.1	**Kannapolis** (city) Cabarrus County
48	332	20.7	**Gastonia** (city) Gaston County	124	n/a	14.0	**Etowah** (CDP) Henderson County
50	368	20.4	**Rocky Mount** (city) Nash County	124	n/a	14.0	**Glen Raven** (CDP) Alamance County
51	391	20.1	**Kings Mountain** (city) Cleveland County	126	n/a	13.8	**Mills River** (town) Henderson County
52	n/a	20.0	**Midland** (town) Cabarrus County	127	n/a	13.7	**Hudson** (town) Caldwell County
53	n/a	19.9	**Bethlehem** (CDP) Alexander County	128	1416	13.6	**Roanoke Rapids** (city) Halifax County
53	n/a	19.9	**China Grove** (town) Rowan County	129	1457	13.4	**Hope Mills** (town) Cumberland County
55	415	19.8	**Henderson** (city) Vance County	130	1483	13.3	**Wilson** (city) Wilson County
55	n/a	19.8	**Spindale** (town) Rutherford County	131	n/a	13.1	**Dana** (CDP) Henderson County
57	n/a	19.6	**Trinity** (city) Randolph County	131	n/a	13.1	**Gibsonville** (town) Guilford County
58	438	19.5	**Archdale** (city) Randolph County	133	n/a	13.0	**Wendell** (town) Wake County
58	438	19.5	**Graham** (city) Alamance County	134	n/a	12.8	**Kings Grant** (CDP) New Hanover County
58	n/a	19.5	**Ranlo** (town) Gaston County	135	n/a	12.7	**Butner** (town) Granville County
61	n/a	18.9	**Creedmoor** (city) Granville County	135	n/a	12.7	**Dunn** (city) Harnett County
61	n/a	18.9	**Mountain Home** (CDP) Henderson County	137	1665	12.6	**New Bern** (city) Craven County
63	n/a	18.7	**Dallas** (town) Gaston County	138	1693	12.5	**Greensboro** (city) Guilford County
64	n/a	18.6	**Lillington** (town) Harnett County	138	1693	12.5	**Piney Green** (CDP) Onslow County
64	522	18.6	**Smithfield** (town) Johnston County	140	n/a	12.3	**Fletcher** (town) Henderson County
66	541	18.5	**Sanford** (city) Lee County	140	n/a	12.3	**Liberty** (town) Randolph County
67	552	18.4	**Laurinburg** (city) Scotland County	142	1778	12.2	**Winston-Salem** (city) Forsyth County
68	n/a	18.1	**Clinton** (city) Sampson County	143	1815	12.1	**Albemarle** (city) Stanly County
69	610	18.0	**Goldsboro** (city) Wayne County	143	n/a	12.1	**Lake Norman of Catawba** (CDP) Catawba County
69	n/a	18.0	**Rural Hall** (town) Forsyth County	143	1815	12.1	**Leland** (town) Brunswick County
71	651	17.7	**Burlington** (city) Alamance County	146	1841	12.0	**Hendersonville** (city) Henderson County
71	n/a	17.7	**Forest City** (town) Rutherford County	146	1841	12.0	**Mount Airy** (city) Surry County
73	n/a	17.6	**La Grange** (town) Lenoir County	146	n/a	12.0	**Tabor City** (town) Columbus County
74	n/a	17.4	**Canton** (town) Haywood County	149	n/a	11.8	**Jamestown** (town) Guilford County
74	n/a	17.4	**Edenton** (town) Chowan County	150	n/a	11.7	**Lowesville** (CDP) Lincoln County

Note: The state column ranks the top/bottom 150 places in the state with population of 2,500 or more. The national column ranks the top/bottom places in the country with population of 10,000 or more. Places that are unincorporated were not considered in the rankings. n/a indicates data not available. Please refer to the User Guide for additional information.

Employment: Production, Transportation, and Material Moving Occupations

Top 150 Places Ranked in *Ascending* Order

State Rank	Nat'l Rank	Percent	Place
1	n/a	0.2	**Cullowhee** (CDP) Jackson County
2	n/a	1.3	**Nags Head** (town) Dare County
2	n/a	1.3	**Trent Woods** (town) Craven County
4	n/a	1.5	**Carolina Shores** (town) Brunswick County
5	n/a	2.0	**Rutherfordton** (town) Rutherford County
6	101	2.7	**Chapel Hill** (town) Orange County
6	n/a	2.7	**Kill Devil Hills** (town) Dare County
8	115	2.8	**Boone** (town) Watauga County
9	168	3.2	**Apex** (town) Wake County
9	168	3.2	**Carrboro** (town) Orange County
9	168	3.2	**Davidson** (town) Mecklenburg County
12	n/a	3.3	**Marvin** (village) Union County
13	n/a	3.5	**Sneads Ferry** (CDP) Onslow County
14	n/a	3.6	**Oak Ridge** (town) Guilford County
15	n/a	3.8	**Emerald Isle** (town) Carteret County
16	n/a	3.9	**Royal Pines** (CDP) Buncombe County
17	331	4.1	**Morrisville** (town) Wake County
17	n/a	4.1	**Sunset Beach** (town) Brunswick County
17	n/a	4.1	**Weddington** (town) Union County
20	n/a	4.2	**Saint James** (town) Brunswick County
21	398	4.4	**Pinehurst** (village) Moore County
21	n/a	4.4	**Southern Shores** (town) Dare County
23	424	4.5	**Cary** (town) Wake County
24	n/a	4.6	**Porters Neck** (CDP) New Hanover County
25	n/a	4.7	**Winterville** (town) Pitt County
26	n/a	5.0	**Buies Creek** (CDP) Harnett County
26	548	5.0	**Matthews** (town) Mecklenburg County
26	n/a	5.0	**Seven Lakes** (CDP) Moore County
29	602	5.2	**Huntersville** (town) Mecklenburg County
29	n/a	5.2	**Swansboro** (town) Onslow County
29	n/a	5.2	**Weaverville** (town) Buncombe County
32	664	5.4	**Wake Forest** (town) Wake County
33	691	5.5	**Cornelius** (town) Mecklenburg County
33	n/a	5.5	**Hillsborough** (town) Orange County
33	691	5.5	**Holly Springs** (town) Wake County
36	n/a	5.6	**Hampstead** (CDP) Pender County
36	n/a	5.6	**Myrtle Grove** (CDP) New Hanover County
36	712	5.6	**Summerfield** (town) Guilford County
39	n/a	5.7	**Beaufort** (town) Carteret County
39	n/a	5.7	**Kitty Hawk** (town) Dare County
39	n/a	5.7	**Ogden** (CDP) New Hanover County
39	n/a	5.7	**Westport** (CDP) Lincoln County
43	n/a	5.8	**Elon** (town) Alamance County
43	764	5.8	**Stallings** (town) Union County
45	n/a	6.3	**Aberdeen** (town) Moore County
46	n/a	6.4	**Boiling Springs** (town) Cleveland County
46	n/a	6.4	**Carolina Beach** (town) New Hanover County
48	n/a	6.5	**Waxhaw** (town) Union County
49	n/a	6.6	**Bayshore** (CDP) New Hanover County
49	n/a	6.6	**Lake Park** (village) Union County
49	993	6.6	**Raleigh** (city) Wake County
52	1020	6.7	**Durham** (city) Durham County
52	n/a	6.7	**Wesley Chapel** (village) Union County
54	1081	6.9	**Harrisburg** (town) Cabarrus County
55	1123	7.0	**Lewisville** (town) Forsyth County
55	n/a	7.0	**Oak Island** (town) Brunswick County
55	n/a	7.0	**Rolesville** (town) Wake County
55	1123	7.0	**Southern Pines** (town) Moore County
59	n/a	7.1	**Fairfield Harbour** (CDP) Craven County
60	1193	7.3	**Knightdale** (town) Wake County
61	n/a	7.4	**Northchase** (CDP) New Hanover County
61	1233	7.4	**Wilmington** (city) New Hanover County
63	n/a	7.5	**Fairview** (town) Union County
63	n/a	7.5	**Locust** (city) Stanly County
63	1265	7.5	**Mebane** (city) Alamance County
63	n/a	7.5	**Sylva** (town) Jackson County
67	n/a	7.6	**Lake Junaluska** (CDP) Haywood County
68	1444	8.0	**Indian Trail** (town) Union County
68	n/a	8.0	**Newport** (town) Carteret County
70	n/a	8.1	**Flat Rock** (village) Henderson County
70	n/a	8.1	**Mineral Springs** (town) Union County
70	n/a	8.1	**Silver Lake** (CDP) New Hanover County
70	n/a	8.1	**Waynesville** (town) Haywood County
74	n/a	8.2	**Half Moon** (CDP) Onslow County
75	n/a	8.3	**Rockfish** (CDP) Hoke County
75	n/a	8.3	**Whiteville** (city) Columbus County
77	n/a	8.4	**Brevard** (city) Transylvania County
77	n/a	8.4	**Cramerton** (town) Gaston County
77	n/a	8.4	**Elizabethtown** (town) Bladen County
80	1617	8.5	**Asheville** (city) Buncombe County
80	1617	8.5	**Clayton** (town) Johnston County
80	n/a	8.5	**Red Oak** (town) Nash County
83	1648	8.6	**Clemmons** (village) Forsyth County
83	1648	8.6	**Greenville** (city) Pitt County
83	n/a	8.6	**Midway** (town) Davidson County
86	n/a	8.7	**Woodfin** (town) Buncombe County
87	n/a	8.8	**Pembroke** (town) Robeson County
88	n/a	9.1	**Unionville** (town) Union County
88	n/a	9.1	**Whispering Pines** (village) Moore County
90	1862	9.2	**Mint Hill** (town) Mecklenburg County
91	n/a	9.3	**Enochville** (CDP) Rowan County
92	1997	9.6	**Jacksonville** (city) Onslow County
92	n/a	9.6	**Pittsboro** (town) Chatham County
94	n/a	9.7	**Stokesdale** (town) Guilford County
95	n/a	9.9	**Franklin** (town) Macon County
95	2106	9.9	**Mooresville** (town) Iredell County
97	n/a	10.1	**Murfreesboro** (town) Hertford County
97	n/a	10.1	**River Bend** (town) Craven County
99	2207	10.2	**Belmont** (city) Gaston County
99	2207	10.2	**Charlotte** (city) Mecklenburg County
99	2207	10.2	**Fuquay-Varina** (town) Wake County
102	n/a	10.3	**Angier** (town) Harnett County
102	n/a	10.3	**Fairview** (CDP) Buncombe County
102	2242	10.3	**Havelock** (city) Craven County
102	n/a	10.3	**Moyock** (CDP) Currituck County
106	n/a	10.4	**Pineville** (town) Mecklenburg County
107	2292	10.5	**Garner** (town) Wake County
107	n/a	10.5	**River Road** (CDP) Beaufort County
107	n/a	10.5	**Swannanoa** (CDP) Buncombe County
110	n/a	10.6	**Troy** (town) Montgomery County
111	2369	10.7	**Spring Lake** (town) Cumberland County
112	2404	10.8	**Concord** (city) Cabarrus County
112	2404	10.8	**Fayetteville** (city) Cumberland County
114	2477	11.0	**Kernersville** (town) Forsyth County
115	n/a	11.2	**Benson** (town) Johnston County
115	2542	11.2	**Elizabeth City** (city) Pasquotank County
117	n/a	11.3	**Erwin** (town) Harnett County
117	n/a	11.3	**Forest Oaks** (CDP) Guilford County
119	n/a	11.5	**Morehead City** (town) Carteret County
119	n/a	11.5	**Washington** (city) Beaufort County
121	n/a	11.7	**Lowesville** (CDP) Lincoln County
121	2699	11.7	**Murraysville** (CDP) New Hanover County
123	n/a	11.8	**Jamestown** (town) Guilford County
124	2789	12.0	**Hendersonville** (city) Henderson County
124	2789	12.0	**Mount Airy** (city) Surry County
124	n/a	12.0	**Tabor City** (town) Columbus County
127	2816	12.1	**Albemarle** (city) Stanly County
127	n/a	12.1	**Lake Norman of Catawba** (CDP) Catawba County
127	2816	12.1	**Leland** (town) Brunswick County
130	2842	12.2	**Winston-Salem** (city) Forsyth County
131	n/a	12.3	**Fletcher** (town) Henderson County
131	n/a	12.3	**Liberty** (town) Randolph County
133	2934	12.5	**Greensboro** (city) Guilford County
133	2934	12.5	**Piney Green** (CDP) Onslow County
135	2964	12.6	**New Bern** (city) Craven County
136	n/a	12.7	**Butner** (town) Granville County
136	n/a	12.7	**Dunn** (city) Harnett County
138	n/a	12.8	**Kings Grant** (CDP) New Hanover County
139	n/a	13.0	**Wendell** (town) Wake County
140	n/a	13.1	**Dana** (CDP) Henderson County
140	n/a	13.1	**Gibsonville** (town) Guilford County
142	3149	13.3	**Wilson** (city) Wilson County
143	3174	13.4	**Hope Mills** (town) Cumberland County
144	3215	13.6	**Roanoke Rapids** (city) Halifax County
145	n/a	13.7	**Hudson** (town) Caldwell County
146	n/a	13.8	**Mills River** (town) Henderson County
147	n/a	14.0	**Etowah** (CDP) Henderson County
147	n/a	14.0	**Glen Raven** (CDP) Alamance County
149	3341	14.1	**Kannapolis** (city) Cabarrus County
150	n/a	14.2	**Boiling Spring Lakes** (city) Brunswick County

Note: The state column ranks the top/bottom 150 places in the state with population of 2,500 or more. The national column ranks the top/bottom places in the country with population of 10,000 or more. Places that are unincorporated were not considered in the rankings. n/a indicates data not available. Please refer to the User Guide for additional information.

Per Capita Income

Top 150 Places Ranked in *Descending* Order

State Rank	Nat'l Rank	Dollars	Place
1	n/a	67,955	**Saint James** (town) Brunswick County
2	n/a	56,629	**Marvin** (village) Union County
3	n/a	53,021	**Weddington** (town) Union County
4	n/a	50,820	**Westport** (CDP) Lincoln County
5	376	47,666	**Cornelius** (town) Mecklenburg County
6	378	47,565	**Davidson** (town) Mecklenburg County
7	451	45,606	**Pinehurst** (village) Moore County
8	457	45,508	**Summerfield** (town) Guilford County
9	n/a	43,982	**Trent Woods** (town) Craven County
10	n/a	43,801	**Porters Neck** (CDP) New Hanover County
11	n/a	43,782	**Flat Rock** (village) Henderson County
12	n/a	42,655	**Sunset Beach** (town) Brunswick County
13	678	41,554	**Cary** (town) Wake County
14	n/a	40,794	**Oak Ridge** (town) Guilford County
15	810	39,734	**Morrisville** (town) Wake County
16	n/a	38,813	**Emerald Isle** (town) Carteret County
17	n/a	38,760	**Southern Shores** (town) Dare County
18	908	38,409	**Huntersville** (town) Mecklenburg County
19	n/a	38,344	**Jamestown** (town) Guilford County
20	n/a	38,232	**Seven Lakes** (CDP) Moore County
21	n/a	37,953	**Lake Junaluska** (CDP) Haywood County
22	n/a	36,980	**Whispering Pines** (village) Moore County
23	n/a	36,959	**Nags Head** (town) Dare County
24	n/a	36,348	**Lake Norman of Catawba** (CDP) Catawba County
25	1091	36,270	**Southern Pines** (town) Moore County
26	1155	35,714	**Chapel Hill** (town) Orange County
27	n/a	35,475	**Myrtle Grove** (CDP) New Hanover County
28	1239	34,979	**Apex** (town) Wake County
29	n/a	34,939	**Fairfield Harbour** (CDP) Craven County
30	1297	34,550	**Lewisville** (town) Forsyth County
31	n/a	34,416	**Royal Pines** (CDP) Buncombe County
32	1315	34,396	**Stallings** (town) Union County
33	n/a	34,387	**Ogden** (CDP) New Hanover County
34	n/a	34,189	**Wesley Chapel** (village) Union County
35	n/a	34,110	**Carolina Beach** (town) New Hanover County
36	1398	33,722	**Matthews** (town) Mecklenburg County
37	1413	33,624	**Belmont** (city) Gaston County
38	n/a	33,613	**Brices Creek** (CDP) Craven County
39	1421	33,523	**Carrboro** (town) Orange County
40	1423	33,517	**Holly Springs** (town) Wake County
41	n/a	33,265	**Kitty Hawk** (town) Dare County
42	1495	32,955	**Clemmons** (village) Forsyth County
43	n/a	32,942	**Forest Oaks** (CDP) Guilford County
44	1560	32,474	**Wake Forest** (town) Wake County
45	n/a	32,434	**Cramerton** (town) Gaston County
46	1592	32,228	**Leland** (town) Brunswick County
47	n/a	32,165	**Red Oak** (town) Nash County
48	1655	31,825	**Mint Hill** (town) Mecklenburg County
49	n/a	31,734	**James City** (CDP) Craven County
50	1689	31,556	**Charlotte** (city) Mecklenburg County
51	n/a	30,624	**Bayshore** (CDP) New Hanover County
52	n/a	30,591	**Stokesdale** (town) Guilford County
53	1868	30,470	**Raleigh** (city) Wake County
54	n/a	30,231	**Weaverville** (town) Buncombe County
55	n/a	30,208	**Oak Island** (town) Brunswick County
56	n/a	29,721	**Kill Devil Hills** (town) Dare County
57	n/a	29,437	**Lake Park** (village) Union County
58	n/a	29,397	**Fairview** (town) Union County
59	n/a	29,391	**Mills River** (town) Henderson County
60	2041	29,263	**Knightdale** (town) Wake County
61	2083	29,017	**Wilmington** (city) New Hanover County
62	2119	28,829	**Garner** (town) Wake County
63	n/a	28,787	**Rural Hall** (town) Forsyth County
64	n/a	28,716	**Carolina Shores** (town) Brunswick County
65	n/a	28,656	**River Bend** (town) Craven County
66	n/a	28,602	**Pleasant Garden** (town) Guilford County
67	2169	28,565	**Durham** (city) Durham County
68	2176	28,537	**Harrisburg** (town) Cabarrus County
69	n/a	28,422	**Swansboro** (town) Onslow County
70	n/a	28,336	**Unionville** (town) Union County
71	n/a	28,334	**Rolesville** (town) Wake County
72	n/a	28,108	**Eastover** (town) Cumberland County
73	n/a	27,982	**Waxhaw** (town) Union County
74	2278	27,975	**Murraysville** (CDP) New Hanover County
75	n/a	27,929	**Lowesville** (CDP) Lincoln County
76	2303	27,795	**Mebane** (city) Alamance County
77	2326	27,714	**Kernersville** (town) Forsyth County
78	n/a	27,626	**Pittsboro** (town) Chatham County
79	n/a	27,513	**Hudson** (town) Caldwell County
80	2364	27,459	**Mount Holly** (city) Gaston County
81	n/a	27,398	**Stanley** (town) Gaston County
82	n/a	27,375	**Archer Lodge** (town) Johnston County
83	n/a	27,232	**Kings Grant** (CDP) New Hanover County
84	n/a	27,137	**Hampstead** (CDP) Pender County
85	n/a	27,028	**Welcome** (CDP) Davidson County
86	n/a	26,988	**Rutherfordton** (town) Rutherford County
87	2439	26,985	**Clayton** (town) Johnston County
88	n/a	26,972	**Wallburg** (town) Davidson County
89	2459	26,912	**Asheville** (city) Buncombe County
90	n/a	26,865	**Winterville** (town) Pitt County
91	n/a	26,815	**Fairview** (CDP) Buncombe County
92	n/a	26,629	**Walkertown** (town) Forsyth County
93	n/a	26,583	**Southport** (city) Brunswick County
94	n/a	26,548	**Morehead City** (town) Carteret County
95	n/a	26,537	**Midway** (town) Davidson County
96	n/a	26,525	**Wendell** (town) Wake County
97	n/a	26,421	**Gibsonville** (town) Guilford County
98	2557	26,392	**Mooresville** (town) Iredell County
99	2561	26,372	**Fuquay-Varina** (town) Wake County
100	n/a	26,362	**Moyock** (CDP) Currituck County
101	2611	26,096	**Indian Trail** (town) Union County
102	n/a	25,974	**Etowah** (CDP) Henderson County
103	2648	25,897	**Concord** (city) Cabarrus County
104	2652	25,861	**Greensboro** (city) Guilford County
105	n/a	25,752	**Lake Royale** (CDP) Franklin County
106	n/a	25,447	**Northchase** (CDP) New Hanover County
107	n/a	25,374	**Fletcher** (town) Henderson County
108	n/a	25,357	**River Road** (CDP) Beaufort County
109	n/a	25,337	**Bethlehem** (CDP) Alexander County
110	2757	25,310	**Hickory** (city) Catawba County
111	n/a	25,027	**Locust** (city) Stanly County
112	n/a	24,975	**Wilkesboro** (town) Wilkes County
113	2839	24,858	**Winston-Salem** (city) Forsyth County
114	n/a	24,725	**Waynesville** (town) Haywood County
115	n/a	24,626	**Enochville** (CDP) Rowan County
116	n/a	24,569	**Trinity** (city) Randolph County
117	n/a	24,410	**Lowell** (city) Gaston County
118	n/a	24,312	**King** (city) Stokes County
119	n/a	24,243	**Saint Stephens** (CDP) Catawba County
120	n/a	24,119	**Clinton** (city) Sampson County
121	n/a	23,899	**Shallotte** (town) Brunswick County
122	n/a	23,809	**Nashville** (town) Nash County
123	n/a	23,583	**Skippers Corner** (CDP) New Hanover County
124	n/a	23,566	**Hillsborough** (town) Orange County
125	n/a	23,445	**Cherryville** (city) Gaston County
126	3115	23,409	**Fayetteville** (city) Cumberland County
127	n/a	23,253	**Midland** (town) Cabarrus County
128	3183	23,127	**Burlington** (city) Alamance County
129	3225	22,940	**High Point** (city) Guilford County
130	3230	22,913	**Hope Mills** (town) Cumberland County
131	3244	22,837	**Archdale** (city) Randolph County
132	3245	22,836	**Greenville** (city) Pitt County
133	n/a	22,822	**Black Mountain** (town) Buncombe County
134	n/a	22,741	**Wentworth** (town) Rockingham County
135	n/a	22,730	**Mineral Springs** (town) Union County
136	n/a	22,627	**Boiling Springs** (town) Cleveland County
137	n/a	22,560	**Mountain View** (CDP) Catawba County
138	3300	22,555	**New Bern** (city) Craven County
139	3319	22,487	**Mount Airy** (city) Surry County
140	n/a	22,392	**Aberdeen** (town) Moore County
141	n/a	22,327	**Conover** (city) Catawba County
142	n/a	22,320	**Mountain Home** (CDP) Henderson County
143	n/a	22,317	**Landis** (town) Rowan County
144	n/a	22,138	**Elon** (town) Alamance County
145	n/a	22,058	**Boiling Spring Lakes** (city) Brunswick County
146	n/a	22,048	**Brevard** (city) Transylvania County
147	n/a	22,044	**Rockfish** (CDP) Hoke County
148	n/a	21,841	**Valdese** (town) Burke County
149	n/a	21,807	**Mocksville** (town) Davie County
150	n/a	21,542	**Creedmoor** (city) Granville County

Note: *The state column ranks the top/bottom 150 places in the state with population of 2,500 or more. The national column ranks the top/bottom places in the country with population of 10,000 or more. Places that are unincorporated were not considered in the rankings. n/a indicates data not available. Please refer to the User Guide for additional information.*

Per Capita Income

Top 150 Places Ranked in *Ascending* Order

State Rank	Nat'l Rank	Dollars	Place
1	n/a	5,854	**Polkton** (town) Anson County
2	n/a	6,828	**Buies Creek** (CDP) Harnett County
3	n/a	7,436	**Cullowhee** (CDP) Jackson County
4	n/a	11,706	**Enfield** (town) Halifax County
5	n/a	11,836	**Selma** (town) Johnston County
6	n/a	12,227	**Pembroke** (town) Robeson County
7	65	12,373	**Boone** (town) Watauga County
8	n/a	12,779	**Roxboro** (city) Person County
9	n/a	12,935	**North Wilkesboro** (town) Wilkes County
10	n/a	13,065	**Lillington** (town) Harnett County
11	n/a	13,386	**Troy** (town) Montgomery County
12	n/a	13,639	**Red Springs** (town) Robeson County
13	n/a	14,159	**Fairmont** (town) Robeson County
14	n/a	14,234	**Siler City** (town) Chatham County
15	n/a	14,690	**Forest City** (town) Rutherford County
16	n/a	14,713	**Warsaw** (town) Duplin County
17	n/a	14,911	**Edenton** (town) Chowan County
18	n/a	14,963	**South Rosemary** (CDP) Halifax County
19	n/a	15,471	**Burgaw** (town) Pender County
20	n/a	15,544	**Marion** (city) McDowell County
21	n/a	15,565	**Long View** (town) Catawba County
22	204	15,760	**Laurinburg** (city) Scotland County
23	210	15,852	**Spring Lake** (town) Cumberland County
24	n/a	15,977	**Spencer** (town) Rowan County
25	n/a	16,009	**East Rockingham** (CDP) Richmond County
26	n/a	16,027	**Benson** (town) Johnston County
27	n/a	16,054	**Windsor** (town) Bertie County
28	n/a	16,118	**Bessemer City** (city) Gaston County
29	n/a	16,138	**Gamewell** (town) Caldwell County
30	242	16,188	**Henderson** (city) Vance County
31	n/a	16,214	**Icard** (CDP) Burke County
32	255	16,330	**Lexington** (city) Davidson County
33	n/a	16,471	**Williamston** (town) Martin County
34	n/a	16,515	**Mount Olive** (town) Wayne County
35	n/a	16,621	**East Flat Rock** (CDP) Henderson County
36	294	16,720	**Newton** (city) Catawba County
37	n/a	16,829	**Spindale** (town) Rutherford County
38	n/a	16,830	**Brogden** (CDP) Wayne County
39	n/a	17,199	**Plymouth** (town) Washington County
40	n/a	17,295	**Wadesboro** (town) Anson County
41	n/a	17,296	**Wingate** (town) Union County
42	n/a	17,316	**China Grove** (town) Rowan County
43	n/a	17,329	**Ayden** (town) Pitt County
44	369	17,382	**Thomasville** (city) Davidson County
45	n/a	17,413	**Hamlet** (city) Richmond County
46	371	17,448	**Asheboro** (city) Randolph County
47	n/a	17,493	**Ahoskie** (town) Hertford County
48	382	17,517	**Eden** (city) Rockingham County
49	n/a	17,638	**Yadkinville** (town) Yadkin County
50	407	17,655	**Lenoir** (city) Caldwell County
51	n/a	17,767	**Rockingham** (city) Richmond County
52	n/a	17,787	**Wallace** (town) Duplin County
53	n/a	17,856	**Elroy** (CDP) Wayne County
54	466	17,958	**Elizabeth City** (city) Pasquotank County
55	n/a	17,982	**Washington** (city) Beaufort County
56	n/a	18,000	**Franklin** (town) Macon County
57	n/a	18,002	**Sawmills** (town) Caldwell County
58	n/a	18,199	**Maiden** (town) Catawba County
59	n/a	18,214	**Mar-Mac** (CDP) Wayne County
60	n/a	18,265	**Elizabethtown** (town) Bladen County
61	n/a	18,364	**Farmville** (town) Pitt County
62	n/a	18,529	**Louisburg** (town) Franklin County
63	n/a	18,545	**Tyro** (CDP) Davidson County
64	556	18,557	**Salisbury** (city) Rowan County
65	576	18,647	**Smithfield** (town) Johnston County
66	n/a	18,663	**Tabor City** (town) Columbus County
67	n/a	18,713	**Sneads Ferry** (CDP) Onslow County
68	n/a	18,764	**Randleman** (city) Randolph County
69	n/a	18,830	**Dunn** (city) Harnett County
70	626	18,918	**Lumberton** (city) Robeson County
71	628	18,930	**Kinston** (city) Lenoir County
72	n/a	18,963	**Dana** (CDP) Henderson County
73	n/a	19,051	**Ranlo** (town) Gaston County
74	n/a	19,098	**Raeford** (city) Hoke County
75	661	19,172	**Monroe** (city) Union County
76	662	19,178	**Roanoke Rapids** (city) Halifax County
77	663	19,180	**Tarboro** (town) Edgecombe County
78	n/a	19,191	**Half Moon** (CDP) Onslow County
79	679	19,243	**Graham** (city) Alamance County
80	710	19,448	**Kings Mountain** (city) Cleveland County
81	n/a	19,460	**Sylva** (town) Jackson County
82	n/a	19,508	**Granite Falls** (town) Caldwell County
83	723	19,514	**Lincolnton** (city) Lincoln County
84	n/a	19,529	**Zebulon** (town) Wake County
85	n/a	19,562	**Woodfin** (town) Buncombe County
86	741	19,592	**Albemarle** (city) Stanly County
87	n/a	19,623	**Cajah's Mountain** (town) Caldwell County
88	779	19,793	**Shelby** (city) Cleveland County
89	n/a	19,937	**La Grange** (town) Lenoir County
90	n/a	19,969	**Erwin** (town) Harnett County
91	n/a	19,996	**Swannanoa** (CDP) Buncombe County
92	833	20,070	**Morganton** (city) Burke County
93	835	20,071	**Piney Green** (CDP) Onslow County
94	n/a	20,112	**Wrightsboro** (CDP) New Hanover County
95	n/a	20,117	**Dallas** (town) Gaston County
96	n/a	20,177	**Grifton** (town) Pitt County
97	862	20,185	**Rocky Mount** (city) Nash County
98	896	20,380	**Goldsboro** (city) Wayne County
99	919	20,482	**Kannapolis** (city) Cabarrus County
100	922	20,497	**Sanford** (city) Lee County
101	n/a	20,530	**Butner** (town) Granville County
102	n/a	20,571	**Canton** (town) Haywood County
103	944	20,596	**Havelock** (city) Craven County
104	n/a	20,645	**Liberty** (town) Randolph County
105	n/a	20,714	**Silver Lake** (CDP) New Hanover County
106	984	20,803	**Statesville** (city) Iredell County
107	n/a	20,904	**Glen Raven** (CDP) Alamance County
108	n/a	20,934	**Elkin** (town) Surry County
109	n/a	20,974	**Angier** (town) Harnett County
110	n/a	21,020	**Newport** (town) Carteret County
111	n/a	21,157	**Granite Quarry** (town) Rowan County
112	1065	21,177	**Reidsville** (city) Rockingham County
113	n/a	21,194	**Murfreesboro** (town) Hertford County
114	n/a	21,202	**Beaufort** (town) Carteret County
115	n/a	21,209	**Whiteville** (city) Columbus County
116	1071	21,210	**Hendersonville** (city) Henderson County
116	1071	21,210	**Jacksonville** (city) Onslow County
118	n/a	21,306	**Oxford** (city) Granville County
119	1116	21,396	**Wilson** (city) Wilson County
120	n/a	21,442	**Pineville** (town) Mecklenburg County
121	1139	21,531	**Gastonia** (city) Gaston County
122	n/a	21,542	**Creedmoor** (city) Granville County
123	n/a	21,807	**Mocksville** (town) Davie County
124	n/a	21,841	**Valdese** (town) Burke County
125	n/a	22,044	**Rockfish** (CDP) Hoke County
126	n/a	22,048	**Brevard** (city) Transylvania County
127	n/a	22,058	**Boiling Spring Lakes** (city) Brunswick County
128	n/a	22,138	**Elon** (town) Alamance County
129	n/a	22,317	**Landis** (town) Rowan County
130	n/a	22,320	**Mountain Home** (CDP) Henderson County
131	n/a	22,327	**Conover** (city) Catawba County
132	n/a	22,392	**Aberdeen** (town) Moore County
133	1337	22,487	**Mount Airy** (city) Surry County
134	1356	22,555	**New Bern** (city) Craven County
135	n/a	22,560	**Mountain View** (CDP) Catawba County
136	n/a	22,627	**Boiling Springs** (town) Cleveland County
137	n/a	22,730	**Mineral Springs** (town) Union County
138	n/a	22,741	**Wentworth** (town) Rockingham County
139	n/a	22,822	**Black Mountain** (town) Buncombe County
140	1411	22,836	**Greenville** (city) Pitt County
141	1412	22,837	**Archdale** (city) Randolph County
142	1426	22,913	**Hope Mills** (town) Cumberland County
143	1431	22,940	**High Point** (city) Guilford County
144	1472	23,127	**Burlington** (city) Alamance County
145	n/a	23,253	**Midland** (town) Cabarrus County
146	1541	23,409	**Fayetteville** (city) Cumberland County
147	n/a	23,445	**Cherryville** (city) Gaston County
148	n/a	23,566	**Hillsborough** (town) Orange County
149	n/a	23,583	**Skippers Corner** (CDP) New Hanover County
150	n/a	23,809	**Nashville** (town) Nash County

Note: The state column ranks the top/bottom 150 places in the state with population of 2,500 or more. The national column ranks the top/bottom places in the country with population of 10,000 or more. Places that are unincorporated were not considered in the rankings. n/a indicates data not available. Please refer to the User Guide for additional information.

Median Household Income

Top 150 Places Ranked in *Descending* Order

State Rank	Nat'l Rank	Dollars	Place
1	n/a	162,917	**Marvin** (village) Union County
2	n/a	141,682	**Weddington** (town) Union County
3	n/a	100,208	**Oak Ridge** (town) Guilford County
4	n/a	99,425	**Westport** (CDP) Lincoln County
5	480	98,438	**Summerfield** (town) Guilford County
6	n/a	93,587	**Porters Neck** (CDP) New Hanover County
7	680	90,250	**Cary** (town) Wake County
8	n/a	89,701	**Wesley Chapel** (village) Union County
9	697	89,644	**Holly Springs** (town) Wake County
10	704	89,475	**Apex** (town) Wake County
11	727	88,750	**Davidson** (town) Mecklenburg County
12	n/a	85,857	**Saint James** (town) Brunswick County
13	n/a	85,554	**Trent Woods** (town) Craven County
14	876	84,486	**Huntersville** (town) Mecklenburg County
15	956	81,808	**Harrisburg** (town) Cabarrus County
16	n/a	81,528	**Moyock** (CDP) Currituck County
17	n/a	81,184	**Southern Shores** (town) Dare County
18	996	80,892	**Morrisville** (town) Wake County
19	1007	80,697	**Cornelius** (town) Mecklenburg County
20	n/a	79,917	**Rolesville** (town) Wake County
21	n/a	79,821	**Brices Creek** (CDP) Craven County
22	1061	79,663	**Stallings** (town) Union County
23	n/a	79,069	**Forest Oaks** (CDP) Guilford County
24	n/a	77,467	**Waxhaw** (town) Union County
25	n/a	77,261	**Jamestown** (town) Guilford County
26	n/a	76,976	**Stokesdale** (town) Guilford County
27	n/a	75,293	**Whispering Pines** (village) Moore County
28	1261	75,050	**Wake Forest** (town) Wake County
29	n/a	74,854	**Seven Lakes** (CDP) Moore County
30	n/a	73,804	**Lake Junaluska** (CDP) Haywood County
31	n/a	73,600	**Fairview** (town) Union County
32	1354	72,825	**Lewisville** (town) Forsyth County
33	n/a	72,276	**Flat Rock** (village) Henderson County
34	1459	71,066	**Knightdale** (town) Wake County
35	n/a	70,288	**Red Oak** (town) Nash County
36	1513	70,275	**Pinehurst** (village) Moore County
37	n/a	69,088	**Royal Pines** (CDP) Buncombe County
38	n/a	68,893	**Ogden** (CDP) New Hanover County
39	n/a	68,807	**Myrtle Grove** (CDP) New Hanover County
40	n/a	68,500	**Cramerton** (town) Gaston County
41	1601	68,295	**Matthews** (town) Mecklenburg County
42	n/a	68,154	**Archer Lodge** (town) Johnston County
43	1609	68,140	**Mint Hill** (town) Mecklenburg County
44	n/a	68,079	**Lake Park** (village) Union County
45	n/a	67,602	**Skippers Corner** (CDP) New Hanover County
46	1712	66,333	**Indian Trail** (town) Union County
47	n/a	65,015	**Lake Norman of Catawba** (CDP) Catawba County
48	n/a	64,563	**Fairfield Harbour** (CDP) Craven County
49	1837	64,471	**Leland** (town) Brunswick County
50	1857	64,118	**Clemmons** (village) Forsyth County
51	n/a	63,423	**Unionville** (town) Union County
52	n/a	63,276	**Pleasant Garden** (town) Guilford County
53	n/a	62,083	**Rockfish** (CDP) Hoke County
54	n/a	61,875	**Boiling Springs** (town) Cleveland County
55	n/a	61,447	**Wallburg** (town) Davidson County
56	n/a	61,430	**Bayshore** (CDP) New Hanover County
57	2047	61,309	**Murraysville** (CDP) New Hanover County
58	n/a	61,161	**Lowesville** (CDP) Lincoln County
59	2064	61,003	**Mooresville** (town) Iredell County
60	2079	60,842	**Garner** (town) Wake County
61	2081	60,802	**Chapel Hill** (town) Orange County
62	n/a	60,684	**Carolina Beach** (town) New Hanover County
63	2224	58,588	**Fuquay-Varina** (town) Wake County
64	n/a	58,566	**Mills River** (town) Henderson County
65	n/a	58,077	**Hampstead** (CDP) Pender County
66	2305	57,456	**Clayton** (town) Johnston County
67	n/a	57,391	**Gibsonville** (town) Guilford County
68	n/a	57,220	**Winterville** (town) Pitt County
69	n/a	56,638	**Bethlehem** (CDP) Alexander County
70	2445	55,246	**Mebane** (city) Alamance County
71	n/a	55,170	**Kill Devil Hills** (town) Dare County
72	n/a	54,900	**Sunset Beach** (town) Brunswick County
73	n/a	54,700	**Weaverville** (town) Buncombe County
74	2510	54,448	**Raleigh** (city) Wake County
75	n/a	54,412	**Wentworth** (town) Rockingham County
76	n/a	54,201	**Emerald Isle** (town) Carteret County
77	2540	54,091	**Belmont** (city) Gaston County
78	n/a	53,824	**Locust** (city) Stanly County
79	n/a	53,692	**Mineral Springs** (town) Union County
80	n/a	53,556	**Fairview** (CDP) Buncombe County
81	2608	53,337	**Concord** (city) Cabarrus County
82	n/a	53,107	**King** (city) Stokes County
83	n/a	53,105	**Pittsboro** (town) Chatham County
84	n/a	52,888	**Midland** (town) Cabarrus County
85	n/a	52,599	**Zebulon** (town) Wake County
86	2692	52,375	**Charlotte** (city) Mecklenburg County
87	n/a	52,355	**Nags Head** (town) Dare County
88	n/a	52,109	**Kitty Hawk** (town) Dare County
89	n/a	52,056	**Kings Grant** (CDP) New Hanover County
90	2719	52,042	**Archdale** (city) Randolph County
91	n/a	51,964	**River Bend** (town) Craven County
92	2761	51,442	**Hope Mills** (town) Cumberland County
93	n/a	51,406	**Creedmoor** (city) Granville County
94	n/a	50,500	**Welcome** (CDP) Davidson County
95	2872	50,032	**Kernersville** (town) Forsyth County
96	n/a	49,867	**Silver Lake** (CDP) New Hanover County
97	n/a	49,735	**James City** (CDP) Craven County
98	n/a	49,497	**Carolina Shores** (town) Brunswick County
99	n/a	49,380	**Half Moon** (CDP) Onslow County
100	2923	49,351	**Mount Holly** (city) Gaston County
101	2938	49,160	**Durham** (city) Durham County
102	2946	49,038	**Southern Pines** (town) Moore County
103	n/a	48,796	**Mountain View** (CDP) Catawba County
104	n/a	48,281	**Northchase** (CDP) New Hanover County
105	n/a	48,099	**Swansboro** (town) Onslow County
106	n/a	48,036	**Hudson** (town) Caldwell County
107	3068	47,805	**Piney Green** (CDP) Onslow County
108	n/a	47,557	**Granite Quarry** (town) Rowan County
109	n/a	47,369	**Oak Island** (town) Brunswick County
110	n/a	47,193	**Hillsborough** (town) Orange County
111	n/a	46,830	**Glen Raven** (CDP) Alamance County
112	3156	46,803	**Carrboro** (town) Orange County
113	n/a	46,681	**Butner** (town) Granville County
114	n/a	46,522	**Rural Hall** (town) Forsyth County
115	n/a	46,318	**Trinity** (city) Randolph County
116	n/a	46,034	**Tyro** (CDP) Davidson County
117	n/a	45,945	**Saint Stephens** (CDP) Catawba County
118	n/a	45,660	**Etowah** (CDP) Henderson County
119	n/a	45,538	**Elon** (town) Alamance County
120	n/a	45,388	**Walkertown** (town) Forsyth County
121	n/a	45,313	**Midway** (town) Davidson County
122	n/a	45,018	**Nashville** (town) Nash County
123	3293	44,900	**Fayetteville** (city) Cumberland County
124	n/a	44,815	**Shallotte** (town) Brunswick County
125	n/a	44,684	**Fletcher** (town) Henderson County
126	n/a	44,444	**Enochville** (CDP) Rowan County
127	n/a	44,019	**Lake Royale** (CDP) Franklin County
128	3395	43,819	**Monroe** (city) Union County
129	n/a	43,625	**Cajah's Mountain** (town) Caldwell County
130	n/a	43,606	**Rutherfordton** (town) Rutherford County
131	n/a	43,504	**Boiling Spring Lakes** (city) Brunswick County
132	3421	43,461	**Havelock** (city) Craven County
133	3458	43,234	**Sanford** (city) Lee County
134	n/a	43,167	**Liberty** (town) Randolph County
135	3472	43,083	**High Point** (city) Guilford County
136	n/a	42,917	**Granite Falls** (town) Caldwell County
137	n/a	42,656	**Cherryville** (city) Gaston County
138	n/a	42,639	**Eastover** (town) Cumberland County
139	3529	42,459	**Jacksonville** (city) Onslow County
140	n/a	42,061	**River Road** (CDP) Beaufort County
141	n/a	42,038	**Conover** (city) Catawba County
142	3574	42,016	**Asheville** (city) Buncombe County
143	n/a	41,842	**Newport** (town) Carteret County
144	n/a	41,607	**Lowell** (city) Gaston County
145	n/a	41,600	**Dana** (CDP) Henderson County
146	3618	41,573	**Wilmington** (city) New Hanover County
147	n/a	41,154	**Murfreesboro** (town) Hertford County
148	3661	41,120	**Greensboro** (city) Guilford County
149	n/a	41,042	**Ranlo** (town) Gaston County
150	n/a	40,968	**Wendell** (town) Wake County

Note: The state column ranks the top/bottom 150 places in the state with population of 2,500 or more. The national column ranks the top/bottom places in the country with population of 10,000 or more. Places that are unincorporated were not considered in the rankings. n/a indicates data not available. Please refer to the User Guide for additional information.

Median Household Income

Top 150 Places Ranked in *Ascending* Order

State Rank	Nat'l Rank	Dollars	Place	State Rank	Nat'l Rank	Dollars	Place
1	1	14,453	**Boone** (town) Watauga County	76	n/a	34,063	**Grifton** (town) Pitt County
2	n/a	17,489	**Pembroke** (town) Robeson County	77	421	34,161	**Goldsboro** (city) Wayne County
3	n/a	17,778	**Cullowhee** (CDP) Jackson County	78	431	34,366	**Tarboro** (town) Edgecombe County
4	n/a	18,182	**North Wilkesboro** (town) Wilkes County	79	n/a	34,434	**Stanley** (town) Gaston County
5	n/a	19,793	**Selma** (town) Johnston County	80	n/a	34,482	**Bessemer City** (city) Gaston County
6	n/a	20,048	**Tabor City** (town) Columbus County	81	478	34,959	**Salisbury** (city) Rowan County
7	n/a	20,698	**Elizabethtown** (town) Bladen County	82	481	34,975	**Roanoke Rapids** (city) Halifax County
8	n/a	20,736	**Roxboro** (city) Person County	83	490	35,137	**Greenville** (city) Pitt County
9	n/a	21,484	**Fairmont** (town) Robeson County	84	n/a	35,252	**Hamlet** (city) Richmond County
10	n/a	22,124	**Forest City** (town) Rutherford County	85	n/a	35,265	**Angier** (town) Harnett County
11	n/a	22,157	**Enfield** (town) Halifax County	86	n/a	35,386	**Icard** (CDP) Burke County
12	n/a	22,202	**Red Springs** (town) Robeson County	87	n/a	35,542	**Erwin** (town) Harnett County
13	n/a	22,861	**Warsaw** (town) Duplin County	88	n/a	35,920	**Brevard** (city) Transylvania County
14	n/a	23,750	**Benson** (town) Johnston County	89	n/a	35,982	**Morehead City** (town) Carteret County
15	n/a	23,955	**Buies Creek** (CDP) Harnett County	90	n/a	36,028	**Mar-Mac** (CDP) Wayne County
16	n/a	24,396	**Edenton** (town) Chowan County	91	n/a	36,102	**Woodfin** (town) Buncombe County
17	n/a	24,509	**Marion** (city) McDowell County	92	n/a	36,150	**Canton** (town) Haywood County
18	n/a	25,439	**Mount Olive** (town) Wayne County	93	n/a	36,340	**Elroy** (CDP) Wayne County
19	n/a	25,670	**Spindale** (town) Rutherford County	94	n/a	36,485	**Waynesville** (town) Haywood County
20	n/a	25,722	**Whiteville** (city) Columbus County	95	592	36,538	**Spring Lake** (town) Cumberland County
21	n/a	25,906	**East Flat Rock** (CDP) Henderson County	96	594	36,582	**Rocky Mount** (city) Nash County
22	61	26,149	**Henderson** (city) Vance County	97	613	36,858	**Burlington** (city) Alamance County
23	65	26,235	**Laurinburg** (city) Scotland County	98	632	37,060	**Hendersonville** (city) Henderson County
24	n/a	26,304	**Troy** (town) Montgomery County	99	n/a	37,113	**Spencer** (town) Rowan County
25	n/a	26,596	**Raeford** (city) Hoke County	100	637	37,120	**Reidsville** (city) Rockingham County
26	n/a	26,955	**Plymouth** (town) Washington County	101	n/a	37,412	**Sneads Ferry** (CDP) Onslow County
27	n/a	27,000	**Ahoskie** (town) Hertford County	102	n/a	37,429	**Elkin** (town) Surry County
28	n/a	27,284	**Windsor** (town) Bertie County	103	n/a	37,470	**Aberdeen** (town) Moore County
29	n/a	27,325	**Louisburg** (town) Franklin County	104	665	37,493	**New Bern** (city) Craven County
30	n/a	27,813	**South Rosemary** (CDP) Halifax County	105	n/a	37,676	**Swannanoa** (CDP) Buncombe County
31	n/a	27,996	**East Rockingham** (CDP) Richmond County	105	679	37,676	**Wilson** (city) Wilson County
32	n/a	28,160	**La Grange** (town) Lenoir County	107	n/a	38,608	**Sawmills** (town) Caldwell County
33	n/a	28,644	**Beaufort** (town) Carteret County	108	n/a	38,750	**Wingate** (town) Union County
34	146	28,715	**Lenoir** (city) Caldwell County	109	n/a	38,937	**Landis** (town) Rowan County
35	149	28,793	**Lexington** (city) Davidson County	110	793	38,975	**Graham** (city) Alamance County
36	n/a	29,170	**Franklin** (town) Macon County	111	n/a	39,136	**Wallace** (town) Duplin County
37	n/a	29,297	**Farmville** (town) Pitt County	112	812	39,176	**Hickory** (city) Catawba County
38	n/a	29,399	**Dunn** (city) Harnett County	113	n/a	39,261	**Brogden** (CDP) Wayne County
39	169	29,451	**Kinston** (city) Lenoir County	114	823	39,275	**Kannapolis** (city) Cabarrus County
40	400	29,554	**Lillington** (town) Harnett County	115	n/a	39,442	**Maiden** (town) Catawba County
41	n/a	29,705	**Long View** (town) Catawba County	116	888	40,053	**Gastonia** (city) Gaston County
42	n/a	29,976	**Gamewell** (town) Caldwell County	117	899	40,148	**Winston-Salem** (city) Forsyth County
43	n/a	30,115	**Williamston** (town) Martin County	118	n/a	40,185	**Black Mountain** (town) Buncombe County
44	n/a	30,479	**Washington** (city) Beaufort County	119	n/a	40,392	**Wrightsboro** (CDP) New Hanover County
45	n/a	30,638	**Rockingham** (city) Richmond County	120	n/a	40,553	**Mocksville** (town) Davie County
46	n/a	30,676	**Siler City** (town) Chatham County	121	n/a	40,647	**Southport** (city) Brunswick County
47	n/a	30,938	**Ayden** (town) Pitt County	122	n/a	40,968	**Wendell** (town) Wake County
48	n/a	30,967	**Wadesboro** (town) Anson County	123	n/a	41,042	**Ranlo** (town) Gaston County
49	233	30,990	**Lumberton** (city) Robeson County	124	995	41,120	**Greensboro** (city) Guilford County
50	238	31,083	**Morganton** (city) Burke County	125	n/a	41,154	**Murfreesboro** (town) Hertford County
51	243	31,162	**Lincolnton** (city) Lincoln County	126	1037	41,573	**Wilmington** (city) New Hanover County
52	n/a	31,451	**Pineville** (town) Mecklenburg County	127	n/a	41,600	**Dana** (CDP) Henderson County
53	n/a	31,494	**Yadkinville** (town) Yadkin County	128	n/a	41,607	**Lowell** (city) Gaston County
54	265	31,575	**Eden** (city) Rockingham County	129	n/a	41,842	**Newport** (town) Carteret County
55	n/a	31,745	**Sylva** (town) Jackson County	130	1082	42,016	**Asheville** (city) Buncombe County
56	282	31,846	**Asheboro** (city) Randolph County	131	n/a	42,038	**Conover** (city) Catawba County
57	n/a	31,875	**Burgaw** (town) Pender County	132	n/a	42,061	**River Road** (CDP) Beaufort County
58	287	31,947	**Smithfield** (town) Johnston County	133	1126	42,459	**Jacksonville** (city) Onslow County
59	290	32,062	**Newton** (city) Catawba County	134	n/a	42,639	**Eastover** (town) Cumberland County
60	292	32,070	**Shelby** (city) Cleveland County	135	n/a	42,656	**Cherryville** (city) Gaston County
61	305	32,258	**Mount Airy** (city) Surry County	136	n/a	42,917	**Granite Falls** (town) Caldwell County
62	309	32,331	**Statesville** (city) Iredell County	137	1184	43,083	**High Point** (city) Guilford County
63	n/a	32,396	**Polkton** (town) Anson County	138	n/a	43,167	**Liberty** (town) Randolph County
64	n/a	32,708	**China Grove** (town) Rowan County	139	1198	43,234	**Sanford** (city) Lee County
65	342	32,859	**Albemarle** (city) Stanly County	140	1235	43,461	**Havelock** (city) Craven County
66	n/a	32,927	**Clinton** (city) Sampson County	141	n/a	43,504	**Boiling Spring Lakes** (city) Brunswick County
67	n/a	33,269	**Mountain Home** (CDP) Henderson County	142	n/a	43,606	**Rutherfordton** (town) Rutherford County
68	n/a	33,424	**Dallas** (town) Gaston County	143	n/a	43,625	**Cajah's Mountain** (town) Caldwell County
69	388	33,560	**Thomasville** (city) Davidson County	144	1261	43,819	**Monroe** (city) Union County
70	400	33,701	**Kings Mountain** (city) Cleveland County	145	n/a	44,019	**Lake Royale** (CDP) Franklin County
71	406	33,797	**Elizabeth City** (city) Pasquotank County	146	n/a	44,444	**Enochville** (CDP) Rowan County
72	n/a	33,844	**Randleman** (city) Randolph County	147	n/a	44,684	**Fletcher** (town) Henderson County
73	n/a	33,889	**Wilkesboro** (town) Wilkes County	148	n/a	44,815	**Shallotte** (town) Brunswick County
74	n/a	34,018	**Oxford** (city) Granville County	149	1363	44,900	**Fayetteville** (city) Cumberland County
75	n/a	34,025	**Valdese** (town) Burke County	150	n/a	45,018	**Nashville** (town) Nash County

Note: The state column ranks the top/bottom 150 places in the state with population of 2,500 or more. The national column ranks the top/bottom places in the country with population of 10,000 or more. Places that are unincorporated were not considered in the rankings. n/a indicates data not available. Please refer to the User Guide for additional information.

Average Household Income

Top 150 Places Ranked in *Descending* Order

State Rank	Nat'l Rank	Dollars	Place		State Rank	Nat'l Rank	Dollars	Place
1	n/a	203,208	**Marvin** (village) Union County		76	n/a	69,695	**Mills River** (town) Henderson County
2	n/a	162,565	**Weddington** (town) Union County		77	2424	69,639	**Garner** (town) Wake County
3	285	138,044	**Davidson** (town) Mecklenburg County		78	2427	69,552	**Clayton** (town) Johnston County
4	n/a	132,391	**Saint James** (town) Brunswick County		79	n/a	69,430	**Skippers Corner** (CDP) New Hanover County
5	n/a	127,566	**Westport** (CDP) Lincoln County		80	2484	68,732	**Durham** (city) Durham County
6	442	124,136	**Summerfield** (town) Guilford County		81	n/a	68,120	**Kings Grant** (CDP) New Hanover County
7	n/a	115,981	**Oak Ridge** (town) Guilford County		82	n/a	67,010	**Rockfish** (CDP) Hoke County
8	616	113,316	**Cornelius** (town) Mecklenburg County		83	n/a	66,998	**Eastover** (town) Cumberland County
9	677	110,841	**Cary** (town) Wake County		84	2646	66,586	**Mount Holly** (city) Gaston County
10	n/a	108,428	**Wesley Chapel** (village) Union County		85	n/a	65,624	**Gibsonville** (town) Guilford County
11	875	102,816	**Huntersville** (town) Mecklenburg County		86	2730	65,594	**Mebane** (city) Alamance County
12	n/a	102,388	**Porters Neck** (CDP) New Hanover County		87	n/a	65,408	**Mineral Springs** (town) Union County
13	n/a	101,664	**Jamestown** (town) Guilford County		88	n/a	65,281	**Pittsboro** (town) Chatham County
14	943	100,768	**Apex** (town) Wake County		89	n/a	65,277	**Wallburg** (town) Davidson County
15	947	100,703	**Holly Springs** (town) Wake County		90	n/a	65,166	**River Bend** (town) Craven County
16	n/a	99,482	**Trent Woods** (town) Craven County		91	2762	65,118	**Wilmington** (city) New Hanover County
17	1001	99,212	**Chapel Hill** (town) Orange County		92	2768	64,919	**Kernersville** (town) Forsyth County
18	1011	98,856	**Morrisville** (town) Wake County		93	n/a	64,832	**Fairview** (CDP) Buncombe County
19	1014	98,816	**Pinehurst** (village) Moore County		94	2776	64,827	**Murraysville** (CDP) New Hanover County
20	n/a	97,663	**Flat Rock** (village) Henderson County		95	n/a	64,262	**Lake Royale** (CDP) Franklin County
21	1235	92,916	**Stallings** (town) Union County		96	n/a	63,867	**Kill Devil Hills** (town) Dare County
22	n/a	92,907	**Southern Shores** (town) Dare County		97	n/a	63,751	**Saint Stephens** (CDP) Catawba County
23	1284	91,608	**Wake Forest** (town) Wake County		98	n/a	63,390	**Rutherfordton** (town) Rutherford County
24	n/a	89,639	**Seven Lakes** (CDP) Moore County		99	n/a	63,229	**Stanley** (town) Gaston County
25	1378	89,424	**Lewisville** (town) Forsyth County		100	n/a	62,860	**Bethlehem** (CDP) Alexander County
26	n/a	89,158	**Royal Pines** (CDP) Buncombe County		101	n/a	62,704	**Wentworth** (town) Rockingham County
27	n/a	89,074	**Ogden** (CDP) New Hanover County		102	2987	62,030	**Hope Mills** (town) Cumberland County
28	n/a	88,768	**Brices Creek** (CDP) Craven County		103	n/a	61,862	**Swansboro** (town) Onslow County
29	n/a	88,651	**Stokesdale** (town) Guilford County		104	3004	61,807	**Hickory** (city) Catawba County
30	1413	88,458	**Harrisburg** (town) Cabarrus County		105	3029	61,440	**Greensboro** (city) Guilford County
31	n/a	88,369	**Lake Norman of Catawba** (CDP) Catawba County		106	n/a	61,369	**Creedmoor** (city) Granville County
32	n/a	88,162	**Whispering Pines** (village) Moore County		107	3057	61,113	**Winston-Salem** (city) Forsyth County
33	n/a	87,488	**Rolesville** (town) Wake County		108	n/a	61,036	**Oak Island** (town) Brunswick County
34	1470	87,112	**Matthews** (town) Mecklenburg County		109	n/a	60,900	**Walkertown** (town) Forsyth County
35	1510	85,765	**Mint Hill** (town) Mecklenburg County		110	n/a	60,845	**Hillsborough** (town) Orange County
36	n/a	85,505	**Myrtle Grove** (CDP) New Hanover County		111	n/a	60,566	**Locust** (city) Stanly County
37	n/a	85,467	**Fairview** (town) Union County		112	n/a	60,060	**King** (city) Stokes County
38	n/a	85,005	**Forest Oaks** (CDP) Guilford County		113	3149	59,809	**Archdale** (city) Randolph County
39	n/a	84,392	**Waxhaw** (town) Union County		114	n/a	59,774	**Midway** (town) Davidson County
40	n/a	84,202	**Red Oak** (town) Nash County		115	n/a	59,747	**Rural Hall** (town) Forsyth County
41	1603	83,678	**Clemmons** (village) Forsyth County		116	n/a	59,271	**Trinity** (city) Randolph County
42	n/a	83,587	**Sunset Beach** (town) Brunswick County		117	3221	58,863	**Asheville** (city) Buncombe County
43	1662	82,435	**Belmont** (city) Gaston County		118	n/a	58,754	**Etowah** (CDP) Henderson County
44	n/a	81,987	**Lake Park** (village) Union County		119	n/a	58,319	**Fletcher** (town) Henderson County
45	n/a	80,629	**Boiling Springs** (town) Cleveland County		120	n/a	58,256	**River Road** (CDP) Beaufort County
46	1759	80,566	**Indian Trail** (town) Union County		121	n/a	57,846	**Midland** (town) Cabarrus County
47	n/a	79,600	**Carolina Beach** (town) New Hanover County		122	n/a	57,699	**Lowell** (city) Gaston County
48	n/a	79,549	**James City** (CDP) Craven County		123	n/a	57,670	**Shallotte** (town) Brunswick County
49	n/a	79,089	**Nags Head** (town) Dare County		124	3349	57,392	**Fayetteville** (city) Cumberland County
50	1874	78,641	**Charlotte** (city) Mecklenburg County		125	n/a	57,376	**Wendell** (town) Wake County
51	n/a	78,633	**Lake Junaluska** (CDP) Haywood County		126	3368	57,190	**High Point** (city) Guilford County
52	n/a	78,486	**Moyock** (CDP) Currituck County		127	n/a	57,044	**Glen Raven** (CDP) Alamance County
53	n/a	78,312	**Emerald Isle** (town) Carteret County		128	n/a	56,492	**Clinton** (city) Sampson County
54	1897	78,273	**Carrboro** (town) Orange County		129	n/a	56,454	**Half Moon** (CDP) Onslow County
55	1903	78,147	**Knightdale** (town) Wake County		130	3446	56,250	**Monroe** (city) Union County
56	1906	78,104	**Southern Pines** (town) Moore County		131	3457	56,109	**Gastonia** (city) Gaston County
57	n/a	77,680	**Lowesville** (CDP) Lincoln County		132	3485	55,844	**Sanford** (city) Lee County
58	n/a	77,610	**Pleasant Garden** (town) Guilford County		133	n/a	55,784	**Murfreesboro** (town) Hertford County
59	n/a	77,599	**Archer Lodge** (town) Johnston County		134	n/a	55,765	**Zebulon** (town) Wake County
60	n/a	77,042	**Cramerton** (town) Gaston County		135	n/a	55,657	**Granite Quarry** (town) Rowan County
61	n/a	76,911	**Unionville** (town) Union County		136	n/a	55,618	**Cherryville** (city) Gaston County
62	2051	75,640	**Raleigh** (city) Wake County		137	n/a	55,387	**Nashville** (town) Nash County
63	2097	74,818	**Leland** (town) Brunswick County		138	n/a	55,066	**Mountain View** (CDP) Catawba County
64	n/a	74,466	**Winterville** (town) Pitt County		139	n/a	54,974	**Morehead City** (town) Carteret County
65	n/a	72,313	**Weaverville** (town) Buncombe County		140	3570	54,786	**Greenville** (city) Pitt County
66	n/a	72,141	**Hampstead** (CDP) Pender County		141	n/a	54,774	**Wilkesboro** (town) Wilkes County
67	n/a	72,139	**Hudson** (town) Caldwell County		142	n/a	54,753	**Conover** (city) Catawba County
68	n/a	71,980	**Kitty Hawk** (town) Dare County		143	n/a	54,572	**Northchase** (CDP) New Hanover County
69	n/a	71,758	**Fairfield Harbour** (CDP) Craven County		144	3615	54,413	**Piney Green** (CDP) Onslow County
70	n/a	71,670	**Welcome** (CDP) Davidson County		145	n/a	54,361	**Butner** (town) Granville County
71	2304	71,324	**Mooresville** (town) Iredell County		146	3640	54,194	**Jacksonville** (city) Onslow County
72	n/a	71,120	**Bayshore** (CDP) New Hanover County		147	n/a	53,817	**Silver Lake** (CDP) New Hanover County
73	2336	70,842	**Concord** (city) Cabarrus County		148	n/a	53,760	**Wingate** (town) Union County
74	n/a	70,374	**Elon** (town) Alamance County		149	n/a	53,485	**Southport** (city) Brunswick County
75	2414	69,735	**Fuquay-Varina** (town) Wake County		150	n/a	53,314	**Carolina Shores** (town) Brunswick County

Note: The state column ranks the top/bottom 150 places in the state with population of 2,500 or more. The national column ranks the top/bottom places in the country with population of 10,000 or more. Places that are unincorporated were not considered in the rankings. n/a indicates data not available. Please refer to the User Guide for additional information.

Average Household Income

Top 150 Places Ranked in *Ascending* Order

State Rank	Nat'l Rank	Dollars	Place
1	n/a	26,249	Cullowhee (CDP) Jackson County
2	n/a	27,873	Selma (town) Johnston County
3	n/a	29,564	Roxboro (city) Person County
4	n/a	29,960	Enfield (town) Halifax County
5	n/a	30,034	Pembroke (town) Robeson County
6	n/a	30,194	Buies Creek (CDP) Harnett County
7	n/a	30,275	Warsaw (town) Duplin County
8	n/a	32,448	Forest City (town) Rutherford County
9	14	32,523	Boone (town) Watauga County
10	n/a	33,006	North Wilkesboro (town) Wilkes County
11	n/a	33,987	South Rosemary (CDP) Halifax County
12	n/a	34,971	Fairmont (town) Robeson County
13	n/a	35,051	Red Springs (town) Robeson County
14	n/a	36,452	Williamston (town) Martin County
15	n/a	36,542	Long View (town) Catawba County
16	n/a	36,748	Edenton (town) Chowan County
17	n/a	36,821	Gamewell (town) Caldwell County
18	n/a	37,240	Spindale (town) Rutherford County
19	n/a	37,470	East Flat Rock (CDP) Henderson County
20	n/a	38,023	Franklin (town) Macon County
21	n/a	38,165	La Grange (town) Lenoir County
22	70	38,211	Laurinburg (city) Scotland County
23	n/a	38,424	East Rockingham (CDP) Richmond County
24	n/a	39,092	Sylva (town) Jackson County
25	n/a	39,194	Elroy (CDP) Wayne County
26	n/a	39,631	Elizabethtown (town) Bladen County
27	n/a	39,910	Siler City (town) Chatham County
28	108	39,926	Eden (city) Rockingham County
29	n/a	40,014	Troy (town) Montgomery County
30	114	40,105	Lexington (city) Davidson County
31	n/a	40,258	Marion (city) McDowell County
32	n/a	40,260	Washington (city) Beaufort County
33	130	40,599	Henderson (city) Vance County
34	n/a	40,852	Lillington (town) Harnett County
35	n/a	40,893	Tabor City (town) Columbus County
36	n/a	41,075	Farmville (town) Pitt County
37	n/a	41,231	Randleman (city) Randolph County
38	n/a	41,302	Ahoskie (town) Hertford County
39	n/a	41,339	Spencer (town) Rowan County
40	n/a	41,409	Wadesboro (town) Anson County
41	162	41,579	Newton (city) Catawba County
42	n/a	41,664	Bessemer City (city) Gaston County
43	n/a	41,666	Polkton (town) Anson County
44	n/a	41,766	Rockingham (city) Richmond County
45	n/a	41,834	Brogden (CDP) Wayne County
46	n/a	41,988	Plymouth (town) Washington County
47	n/a	42,067	Beaufort (town) Carteret County
48	176	42,142	Spring Lake (town) Cumberland County
49	183	42,281	Lenoir (city) Caldwell County
50	n/a	42,286	Pineville (town) Mecklenburg County
51	n/a	42,341	Benson (town) Johnston County
52	n/a	42,377	Ayden (town) Pitt County
53	n/a	42,511	Mount Olive (town) Wayne County
54	215	43,024	Asheboro (city) Randolph County
55	216	43,130	Kinston (city) Lenoir County
56	217	43,132	Thomasville (city) Davidson County
57	n/a	43,162	Icard (CDP) Burke County
58	n/a	43,480	Whiteville (city) Columbus County
59	n/a	43,966	Yadkinville (town) Yadkin County
60	n/a	44,157	Mar-Mac (CDP) Wayne County
61	n/a	44,422	Wallace (town) Duplin County
62	n/a	44,546	Maiden (town) Catawba County
63	n/a	44,635	Dunn (city) Harnett County
64	n/a	45,066	Windsor (town) Bertie County
65	n/a	45,613	Burgaw (town) Pender County
66	n/a	45,816	Grifton (town) Pitt County
67	n/a	46,081	Ranlo (town) Gaston County
68	n/a	46,165	Canton (town) Haywood County
69	390	46,213	Albemarle (city) Stanly County
70	n/a	46,267	China Grove (town) Rowan County
71	398	46,313	Smithfield (town) Johnston County
72	415	46,500	Lincolnton (city) Lincoln County
73	430	46,653	Goldsboro (city) Wayne County
74	n/a	46,729	Hamlet (city) Richmond County
75	n/a	46,798	Louisburg (town) Franklin County
76	n/a	46,828	Tyro (CDP) Davidson County
77	443	46,840	Reidsville (city) Rockingham County
78	n/a	46,903	Swannanoa (CDP) Buncombe County
79	459	47,021	Kings Mountain (city) Cleveland County
80	464	47,036	Dallas (town) Gaston County
81	464	47,057	Graham (city) Alamance County
82	471	47,154	Elizabeth City (city) Pasquotank County
83	475	47,229	Tarboro (town) Edgecombe County
84	n/a	47,315	Landis (town) Rowan County
85	483	47,327	Morganton (city) Burke County
86	487	47,374	Shelby (city) Cleveland County
87	490	47,415	Hendersonville (city) Henderson County
88	494	47,452	Roanoke Rapids (city) Halifax County
89	n/a	47,587	Dana (CDP) Henderson County
90	n/a	48,092	Angier (town) Harnett County
91	n/a	48,145	Valdese (town) Burke County
92	553	48,379	Rocky Mount (city) Nash County
93	n/a	48,405	Sawmills (town) Caldwell County
94	565	48,498	Mount Airy (city) Surry County
95	n/a	48,752	Sneads Ferry (CDP) Onslow County
96	n/a	48,909	Raeford (city) Hoke County
97	618	48,986	Salisbury (city) Rowan County
98	n/a	49,217	Woodfin (town) Buncombe County
99	n/a	49,252	Liberty (town) Randolph County
100	n/a	49,279	Cajah's Mountain (town) Caldwell County
101	n/a	49,371	Brevard (city) Transylvania County
102	n/a	49,883	Aberdeen (town) Moore County
103	n/a	49,942	Boiling Spring Lakes (city) Brunswick County
104	n/a	49,945	Erwin (town) Harnett County
105	n/a	50,314	Granite Falls (town) Caldwell County
106	n/a	50,692	Waynesville (town) Haywood County
107	746	50,721	Lumberton (city) Robeson County
108	n/a	50,955	Black Mountain (town) Buncombe County
109	n/a	51,138	Newport (town) Carteret County
110	n/a	51,215	Wrightsboro (CDP) New Hanover County
111	n/a	51,375	Oxford (city) Granville County
112	803	51,503	New Bern (city) Craven County
113	807	51,527	Havelock (city) Craven County
114	823	51,842	Statesville (city) Iredell County
115	864	52,272	Kannapolis (city) Cabarrus County
116	n/a	52,428	Mocksville (town) Davie County
117	n/a	52,667	Elkin (town) Surry County
118	n/a	52,699	Enochville (CDP) Rowan County
119	n/a	52,963	Mountain Home (CDP) Henderson County
120	919	52,983	Burlington (city) Alamance County
121	938	53,157	Wilson (city) Wilson County
122	n/a	53,314	Carolina Shores (town) Brunswick County
123	n/a	53,485	Southport (city) Brunswick County
124	n/a	53,760	Wingate (town) Union County
125	n/a	53,817	Silver Lake (CDP) New Hanover County
126	1016	54,194	Jacksonville (city) Onslow County
127	n/a	54,361	Butner (town) Granville County
128	1041	54,413	Piney Green (CDP) Onslow County
129	n/a	54,572	Northchase (CDP) New Hanover County
130	n/a	54,753	Conover (city) Catawba County
131	n/a	54,774	Wilkesboro (town) Wilkes County
132	1086	54,786	Greenville (city) Pitt County
133	n/a	54,974	Morehead City (town) Carteret County
134	n/a	55,066	Mountain View (CDP) Catawba County
135	n/a	55,387	Nashville (town) Nash County
136	n/a	55,618	Cherryville (city) Gaston County
137	n/a	55,657	Granite Quarry (town) Rowan County
138	n/a	55,765	Zebulon (town) Wake County
139	n/a	55,784	Murfreesboro (town) Hertford County
140	1171	55,844	Sanford (city) Lee County
141	1199	56,109	Gastonia (city) Gaston County
142	1210	56,250	Monroe (city) Union County
143	n/a	56,454	Half Moon (CDP) Onslow County
144	n/a	56,492	Clinton (city) Sampson County
145	n/a	57,044	Glen Raven (CDP) Alamance County
146	1288	57,190	High Point (city) Guilford County
147	n/a	57,376	Wendell (town) Wake County
148	1306	57,392	Fayetteville (city) Cumberland County
149	n/a	57,670	Shallotte (town) Brunswick County
150	n/a	57,699	Lowell (city) Gaston County

Note: *The state column ranks the top/bottom 150 places in the state with population of 2,500 or more. The national column ranks the top/bottom places in the country with population of 10,000 or more. Places that are unincorporated were not considered in the rankings. n/a indicates data not available. Please refer to the User Guide for additional information.*

Households with Income of $100,000 or More

Top 150 Places Ranked in *Descending* Order

State Rank	Nat'l Rank	Percent	Place
1	n/a	77.4	**Marvin** (village) Union County
2	n/a	70.6	**Weddington** (town) Union County
3	n/a	50.2	**Oak Ridge** (town) Guilford County
4	449	49.8	**Summerfield** (town) Guilford County
5	n/a	49.3	**Westport** (CDP) Lincoln County
6	n/a	46.5	**Porters Neck** (CDP) New Hanover County
7	n/a	46.2	**Wesley Chapel** (village) Union County
8	622	45.9	**Cary** (town) Wake County
9	641	45.4	**Davidson** (town) Mecklenburg County
10	646	45.2	**Apex** (town) Wake County
11	n/a	43.0	**Saint James** (town) Brunswick County
12	753	42.9	**Huntersville** (town) Mecklenburg County
13	767	42.7	**Holly Springs** (town) Wake County
14	950	39.5	**Cornelius** (town) Mecklenburg County
15	1084	37.5	**Morrisville** (town) Wake County
16	1092	37.4	**Wake Forest** (town) Wake County
17	n/a	36.9	**Flat Rock** (village) Henderson County
18	n/a	35.9	**Brices Creek** (CDP) Craven County
19	n/a	35.6	**Southern Shores** (town) Dare County
20	n/a	35.1	**Waxhaw** (town) Union County
21	1342	34.0	**Chapel Hill** (town) Orange County
22	n/a	33.9	**Jamestown** (town) Guilford County
23	1358	33.7	**Stallings** (town) Union County
24	n/a	33.6	**Stokesdale** (town) Guilford County
24	n/a	33.6	**Trent Woods** (town) Craven County
26	n/a	33.3	**Rolesville** (town) Wake County
27	1442	32.5	**Harrisburg** (town) Cabarrus County
28	n/a	32.1	**Seven Lakes** (CDP) Moore County
29	n/a	31.7	**Archer Lodge** (town) Johnston County
30	n/a	31.2	**Forest Oaks** (CDP) Guilford County
30	1523	31.2	**Matthews** (town) Mecklenburg County
30	n/a	31.2	**Red Oak** (town) Nash County
33	1586	30.3	**Clemmons** (village) Forsyth County
34	1591	30.2	**Mint Hill** (town) Mecklenburg County
35	n/a	30.1	**Carolina Beach** (town) New Hanover County
35	n/a	30.1	**Lowesville** (CDP) Lincoln County
37	n/a	29.9	**Lake Junaluska** (CDP) Haywood County
37	1610	29.9	**Lewisville** (town) Forsyth County
39	n/a	29.8	**Myrtle Grove** (CDP) New Hanover County
40	n/a	29.5	**Fairview** (town) Union County
41	1688	28.9	**Pinehurst** (village) Moore County
42	n/a	28.8	**Moyock** (CDP) Currituck County
43	n/a	28.4	**Lake Norman of Catawba** (CDP) Catawba County
44	n/a	28.2	**Royal Pines** (CDP) Buncombe County
45	n/a	27.7	**Emerald Isle** (town) Carteret County
46	n/a	27.5	**Boiling Springs** (town) Cleveland County
47	n/a	27.4	**Lake Park** (village) Union County
48	n/a	27.1	**Pleasant Garden** (town) Guilford County
49	n/a	26.7	**Ogden** (CDP) New Hanover County
50	1907	26.3	**Leland** (town) Brunswick County
51	n/a	26.0	**Winterville** (town) Pitt County
52	n/a	25.8	**Sunset Beach** (town) Brunswick County
53	1986	25.6	**Knightdale** (town) Wake County
53	n/a	25.6	**Whispering Pines** (village) Moore County
55	2003	25.5	**Carrboro** (town) Orange County
55	2003	25.5	**Southern Pines** (town) Moore County
57	2022	25.3	**Mooresville** (town) Iredell County
58	2034	25.2	**Indian Trail** (town) Union County
59	2051	25.0	**Belmont** (city) Gaston County
60	n/a	24.0	**Mills River** (town) Henderson County
61	n/a	23.8	**Elon** (town) Alamance County
62	n/a	23.5	**Cramerton** (town) Gaston County
63	2233	23.0	**Raleigh** (city) Wake County
64	2259	22.7	**Charlotte** (city) Mecklenburg County
64	n/a	22.7	**Weaverville** (town) Buncombe County
66	2266	22.6	**Concord** (city) Cabarrus County
66	2266	22.6	**Garner** (town) Wake County
68	2274	22.5	**Fuquay-Varina** (town) Wake County
69	n/a	21.3	**Bayshore** (CDP) New Hanover County
70	n/a	21.0	**Kings Grant** (CDP) New Hanover County
70	n/a	21.0	**Shallotte** (town) Brunswick County
72	2459	20.8	**Durham** (city) Durham County
73	n/a	20.7	**Welcome** (CDP) Davidson County
74	n/a	20.5	**Lake Royale** (CDP) Franklin County
75	n/a	20.3	**Nags Head** (town) Dare County
76	2562	20.0	**Mount Holly** (city) Gaston County
77	2595	19.8	**Kernersville** (town) Forsyth County
78	2609	19.7	**Clayton** (town) Johnston County
78	n/a	19.7	**Gibsonville** (town) Guilford County
78	2609	19.7	**Mebane** (city) Alamance County
81	n/a	19.4	**Kitty Hawk** (town) Dare County
82	n/a	19.3	**Unionville** (town) Union County
83	n/a	19.0	**Fairfield Harbour** (CDP) Craven County
83	n/a	19.0	**Hillsborough** (town) Orange County
85	n/a	18.7	**Hampstead** (CDP) Pender County
86	n/a	18.6	**Rural Hall** (town) Forsyth County
87	n/a	18.4	**Fairview** (CDP) Buncombe County
88	n/a	18.3	**Mineral Springs** (town) Union County
89	n/a	18.0	**Eastover** (town) Cumberland County
90	n/a	17.9	**Swansboro** (town) Onslow County
91	2842	17.8	**Wilmington** (city) New Hanover County
91	n/a	17.8	**Zebulon** (town) Wake County
93	2865	17.6	**Hickory** (city) Catawba County
94	n/a	17.4	**Cherryville** (city) Gaston County
94	n/a	17.4	**Hudson** (town) Caldwell County
96	n/a	17.3	**Kill Devil Hills** (town) Dare County
97	n/a	16.9	**Skippers Corner** (CDP) New Hanover County
98	n/a	16.6	**Creedmoor** (city) Granville County
98	n/a	16.6	**Rutherfordton** (town) Rutherford County
100	n/a	16.0	**Rockfish** (CDP) Hoke County
101	n/a	15.7	**Bethlehem** (CDP) Alexander County
101	n/a	15.7	**James City** (CDP) Craven County
103	3112	15.6	**Hope Mills** (town) Cumberland County
103	3112	15.6	**Murraysville** (CDP) New Hanover County
103	n/a	15.6	**Oak Island** (town) Brunswick County
106	n/a	15.5	**Enochville** (CDP) Rowan County
106	n/a	15.5	**Locust** (city) Stanly County
108	3136	15.4	**Asheville** (city) Buncombe County
108	3136	15.4	**High Point** (city) Guilford County
108	3136	15.4	**Winston-Salem** (city) Forsyth County
111	3167	15.2	**Greensboro** (city) Guilford County
112	n/a	14.9	**Fletcher** (town) Henderson County
112	3205	14.9	**Sanford** (city) Lee County
112	n/a	14.9	**Wallburg** (town) Davidson County
115	n/a	14.8	**Plymouth** (town) Washington County
115	n/a	14.8	**Saint Stephens** (CDP) Catawba County
115	n/a	14.8	**Southport** (city) Brunswick County
118	n/a	14.7	**Glen Raven** (CDP) Alamance County
119	n/a	14.5	**Mountain Home** (CDP) Henderson County
120	n/a	14.3	**Wrightsboro** (CDP) New Hanover County
121	n/a	14.2	**Aberdeen** (town) Moore County
121	3303	14.2	**Monroe** (city) Union County
123	n/a	14.0	**Midland** (town) Cabarrus County
123	n/a	14.0	**Murfreesboro** (town) Hertford County
125	n/a	13.9	**King** (city) Stokes County
125	n/a	13.9	**Midway** (town) Davidson County
125	n/a	13.9	**Pittsboro** (town) Chatham County
128	n/a	13.8	**Clinton** (city) Sampson County
128	3357	13.8	**Greenville** (city) Pitt County
130	n/a	13.7	**Wentworth** (town) Rockingham County
131	n/a	13.5	**Wilkesboro** (town) Wilkes County
132	3414	13.4	**Fayetteville** (city) Cumberland County
133	n/a	13.3	**Landis** (town) Rowan County
134	n/a	13.2	**Lowell** (city) Gaston County
135	n/a	13.1	**Black Mountain** (town) Buncombe County
135	3463	13.1	**Gastonia** (city) Gaston County
137	n/a	13.0	**Raeford** (city) Hoke County
138	3494	12.9	**Archdale** (city) Randolph County
139	n/a	12.7	**Butner** (town) Granville County
139	n/a	12.7	**Morehead City** (town) Carteret County
139	3512	12.7	**New Bern** (city) Craven County
142	n/a	12.6	**Conover** (city) Catawba County
142	n/a	12.6	**Mocksville** (town) Davie County
142	n/a	12.6	**Tabor City** (town) Columbus County
145	n/a	12.5	**Etowah** (CDP) Henderson County
145	n/a	12.5	**Half Moon** (CDP) Onslow County
147	n/a	12.4	**Elkin** (town) Surry County
148	n/a	12.2	**Granite Quarry** (town) Rowan County
149	3632	12.1	**Jacksonville** (city) Onslow County
149	n/a	12.1	**Walkertown** (town) Forsyth County

Note: The state column ranks the top/bottom 150 places in the state with population of 2,500 or more. The national column ranks the top/bottom places in the country with population of 10,000 or more. Places that are unincorporated were not considered in the rankings. n/a indicates data not available. Please refer to the User Guide for additional information.

Households with Income of $100,000 or More

Top 150 Places Ranked in *Ascending* Order

State Rank	Nat'l Rank	Percent	Place
1	n/a	0.0	**Buies Creek** (CDP) Harnett County
2	n/a	1.1	**Selma** (town) Johnston County
3	n/a	1.2	**Elroy** (CDP) Wayne County
4	n/a	1.8	**South Rosemary** (CDP) Halifax County
5	n/a	2.0	**Maiden** (town) Catawba County
6	n/a	2.3	**Enfield** (town) Halifax County
7	n/a	2.7	**Forest City** (town) Rutherford County
7	n/a	2.7	**Roxboro** (city) Person County
9	n/a	2.8	**Gamewell** (town) Caldwell County
9	16	2.8	**Spring Lake** (town) Cumberland County
11	n/a	2.9	**Brogden** (CDP) Wayne County
11	n/a	2.9	**East Flat Rock** (CDP) Henderson County
13	n/a	3.1	**Williamston** (town) Martin County
14	n/a	3.4	**East Rockingham** (CDP) Richmond County
15	n/a	3.5	**Siler City** (town) Chatham County
15	n/a	3.5	**Warsaw** (town) Duplin County
17	n/a	3.7	**Icard** (CDP) Burke County
18	n/a	3.9	**Cullowhee** (CDP) Jackson County
18	n/a	3.9	**Long View** (town) Catawba County
20	n/a	4.4	**Polkton** (town) Anson County
21	n/a	4.8	**Franklin** (town) Macon County
21	n/a	4.8	**Ranlo** (town) Gaston County
23	n/a	5.0	**Pembroke** (town) Robeson County
23	n/a	5.0	**Spindale** (town) Rutherford County
25	74	5.1	**Lexington** (city) Davidson County
25	n/a	5.1	**Mar-Mac** (CDP) Wayne County
27	n/a	5.3	**North Wilkesboro** (town) Wilkes County
28	n/a	5.4	**Whiteville** (city) Columbus County
29	n/a	5.5	**Benson** (town) Johnston County
29	n/a	5.5	**Red Springs** (town) Robeson County
29	n/a	5.5	**Spencer** (town) Rowan County
29	n/a	5.5	**Sylva** (town) Jackson County
33	105	5.6	**Eden** (city) Rockingham County
34	n/a	5.7	**Mount Olive** (town) Wayne County
34	n/a	5.7	**Newport** (town) Carteret County
34	117	5.7	**Thomasville** (city) Davidson County
37	n/a	5.9	**Fairmont** (town) Robeson County
37	n/a	5.9	**Troy** (town) Montgomery County
37	n/a	5.9	**Wadesboro** (town) Anson County
40	n/a	6.0	**Randleman** (city) Randolph County
41	146	6.2	**Boone** (town) Watauga County
41	n/a	6.2	**Edenton** (town) Chowan County
41	146	6.2	**Henderson** (city) Vance County
44	n/a	6.4	**Lillington** (town) Harnett County
45	n/a	6.5	**Bessemer City** (city) Gaston County
45	n/a	6.5	**Elizabethtown** (town) Bladen County
47	n/a	6.6	**Ayden** (town) Pitt County
48	188	6.7	**Lenoir** (city) Caldwell County
49	199	6.8	**Newton** (city) Catawba County
49	n/a	6.8	**Swannanoa** (CDP) Buncombe County
51	206	6.9	**Reidsville** (city) Rockingham County
51	n/a	6.9	**Washington** (city) Beaufort County
53	213	7.0	**Asheboro** (city) Randolph County
54	n/a	7.1	**Dana** (CDP) Henderson County
55	245	7.3	**Hendersonville** (city) Henderson County
56	n/a	7.4	**Granite Falls** (town) Caldwell County
56	n/a	7.4	**Tyro** (CDP) Davidson County
58	n/a	7.6	**Burgaw** (town) Pender County
59	294	7.7	**Kinston** (city) Lenoir County
60	n/a	7.8	**Cajah's Mountain** (town) Caldwell County
60	n/a	7.8	**Louisburg** (town) Franklin County
60	n/a	7.8	**Pineville** (town) Mecklenburg County
63	334	8.0	**Laurinburg** (city) Scotland County
64	n/a	8.1	**Ahoskie** (town) Hertford County
64	n/a	8.1	**Farmville** (town) Pitt County
66	n/a	8.2	**Dallas** (town) Gaston County
67	n/a	8.4	**Beaufort** (town) Carteret County
67	n/a	8.4	**Boiling Spring Lakes** (city) Brunswick County
69	401	8.5	**Kings Mountain** (city) Cleveland County
69	n/a	8.5	**Marion** (city) McDowell County
71	414	8.6	**Lincolnton** (city) Lincoln County
72	n/a	8.7	**Dunn** (city) Harnett County
73	n/a	8.8	**Rockingham** (city) Richmond County
73	n/a	8.8	**Woodfin** (town) Buncombe County
75	462	8.9	**Goldsboro** (city) Wayne County
75	n/a	8.9	**La Grange** (town) Lenoir County
75	n/a	8.9	**Wingate** (town) Union County
78	n/a	9.2	**Waynesville** (town) Haywood County
79	519	9.3	**Albemarle** (city) Stanly County
80	n/a	9.4	**Stanley** (town) Gaston County
81	n/a	9.5	**Silver Lake** (CDP) New Hanover County
82	567	9.6	**Mount Airy** (city) Surry County
82	567	9.6	**Rocky Mount** (city) Nash County
82	n/a	9.6	**Wallace** (town) Duplin County
82	n/a	9.6	**Wendell** (town) Wake County
86	586	9.7	**Piney Green** (CDP) Onslow County
86	586	9.7	**Statesville** (city) Iredell County
86	n/a	9.7	**Trinity** (city) Randolph County
89	599	9.8	**Elizabeth City** (city) Pasquotank County
89	n/a	9.8	**Erwin** (town) Harnett County
89	599	9.8	**Salisbury** (city) Rowan County
89	n/a	9.8	**Sawmills** (town) Caldwell County
93	621	9.9	**Tarboro** (town) Edgecombe County
94	n/a	10.1	**Grifton** (town) Pitt County
94	n/a	10.1	**Northchase** (CDP) New Hanover County
96	666	10.2	**Kannapolis** (city) Cabarrus County
97	689	10.3	**Graham** (city) Alamance County
97	689	10.3	**Smithfield** (town) Johnston County
99	704	10.4	**Havelock** (city) Craven County
100	719	10.5	**Shelby** (city) Cleveland County
100	n/a	10.5	**Valdese** (town) Burke County
102	n/a	10.7	**Hamlet** (city) Richmond County
102	n/a	10.7	**Yadkinville** (town) Yadkin County
104	n/a	10.8	**Oxford** (city) Granville County
105	n/a	10.9	**Brevard** (city) Transylvania County
105	n/a	10.9	**Nashville** (town) Nash County
107	n/a	11.0	**River Bend** (town) Craven County
107	n/a	11.0	**Windsor** (town) Bertie County
109	n/a	11.2	**China Grove** (town) Rowan County
110	n/a	11.3	**Angier** (town) Harnett County
110	n/a	11.3	**Canton** (town) Haywood County
110	n/a	11.3	**Liberty** (town) Randolph County
110	862	11.3	**Morganton** (city) Burke County
114	878	11.4	**Lumberton** (city) Robeson County
114	n/a	11.4	**Sneads Ferry** (CDP) Onslow County
116	951	11.8	**Burlington** (city) Alamance County
116	n/a	11.8	**Carolina Shores** (town) Brunswick County
116	n/a	11.8	**River Road** (CDP) Beaufort County
116	951	11.8	**Roanoke Rapids** (city) Halifax County
120	n/a	11.9	**Mountain View** (CDP) Catawba County
121	986	12.0	**Wilson** (city) Wilson County
122	1004	12.1	**Jacksonville** (city) Onslow County
122	n/a	12.1	**Walkertown** (town) Forsyth County
124	n/a	12.2	**Granite Quarry** (town) Rowan County
125	n/a	12.4	**Elkin** (town) Surry County
126	n/a	12.5	**Etowah** (CDP) Henderson County
126	n/a	12.5	**Half Moon** (CDP) Onslow County
128	n/a	12.6	**Conover** (city) Catawba County
128	n/a	12.6	**Mocksville** (town) Davie County
128	n/a	12.6	**Tabor City** (town) Columbus County
131	n/a	12.7	**Butner** (town) Granville County
131	n/a	12.7	**Morehead City** (town) Carteret County
131	1126	12.7	**New Bern** (city) Craven County
134	1149	12.9	**Archdale** (city) Randolph County
135	n/a	13.0	**Raeford** (city) Hoke County
136	n/a	13.1	**Black Mountain** (town) Buncombe County
136	1179	13.1	**Gastonia** (city) Gaston County
138	n/a	13.2	**Lowell** (city) Gaston County
139	n/a	13.3	**Landis** (town) Rowan County
140	1223	13.4	**Fayetteville** (city) Cumberland County
141	n/a	13.5	**Wilkesboro** (town) Wilkes County
142	n/a	13.7	**Wentworth** (town) Rockingham County
143	n/a	13.8	**Clinton** (city) Sampson County
143	1288	13.8	**Greenville** (city) Pitt County
145	n/a	13.9	**King** (city) Stokes County
145	n/a	13.9	**Midway** (town) Davidson County
145	n/a	13.9	**Pittsboro** (town) Chatham County
148	n/a	14.0	**Midland** (town) Cabarrus County
148	n/a	14.0	**Murfreesboro** (town) Hertford County
150	n/a	14.2	**Aberdeen** (town) Moore County

Note: The state column ranks the top/bottom 150 places in the state with population of 2,500 or more. The national column ranks the top/bottom places in the country with population of 10,000 or more. Places that are unincorporated were not considered in the rankings. n/a indicates data not available. Please refer to the User Guide for additional information.

Poverty Rate

Top 150 Places Ranked in *Descending* Order

State Rank	Nat'l Rank	Percent	Place
1	2	60.6	**Boone** (town) Watauga County
2	n/a	58.3	**Red Springs** (town) Robeson County
3	n/a	56.6	**Pembroke** (town) Robeson County
4	n/a	53.7	**Cullowhee** (CDP) Jackson County
5	n/a	49.6	**Fairmont** (town) Robeson County
6	n/a	46.7	**North Wilkesboro** (town) Wilkes County
7	n/a	46.3	**Benson** (town) Johnston County
8	n/a	45.4	**Enfield** (town) Halifax County
9	n/a	44.9	**Edenton** (town) Chowan County
10	n/a	43.8	**Selma** (town) Johnston County
11	n/a	42.8	**Roxboro** (city) Person County
12	n/a	41.3	**Marion** (city) McDowell County
13	n/a	39.4	**Troy** (town) Montgomery County
14	n/a	39.3	**Elizabethtown** (town) Bladen County
15	n/a	39.2	**East Rockingham** (CDP) Richmond County
16	n/a	37.7	**Whiteville** (city) Columbus County
17	n/a	37.6	**Warsaw** (town) Duplin County
18	n/a	37.5	**Forest City** (town) Rutherford County
19	100	35.9	**Laurinburg** (city) Scotland County
20	n/a	35.8	**Tabor City** (town) Columbus County
21	111	35.5	**Henderson** (city) Vance County
22	n/a	34.3	**Raeford** (city) Hoke County
23	n/a	34.2	**Plymouth** (town) Washington County
24	n/a	34.0	**Buies Creek** (CDP) Harnett County
25	n/a	33.6	**Mount Olive** (town) Wayne County
26	n/a	33.2	**Wilkesboro** (town) Wilkes County
27	n/a	33.1	**Burgaw** (town) Pender County
28	n/a	33.0	**Spencer** (town) Rowan County
29	n/a	32.9	**East Flat Rock** (CDP) Henderson County
30	n/a	32.4	**Beaufort** (town) Carteret County
31	n/a	32.3	**Elroy** (CDP) Wayne County
32	214	31.8	**Kinston** (city) Lenoir County
33	n/a	31.5	**South Rosemary** (CDP) Halifax County
34	n/a	31.4	**Ahoskie** (town) Hertford County
35	228	31.3	**Lumberton** (city) Robeson County
36	n/a	30.5	**Washington** (city) Beaufort County
37	276	30.0	**Greenville** (city) Pitt County
38	n/a	29.9	**Farmville** (town) Pitt County
39	n/a	29.4	**Randleman** (city) Randolph County
39	303	29.4	**Statesville** (city) Iredell County
41	312	29.1	**Shelby** (city) Cleveland County
42	320	29.0	**Elizabeth City** (city) Pasquotank County
42	n/a	29.0	**Grifton** (town) Pitt County
44	n/a	28.9	**Yadkinville** (town) Yadkin County
45	351	28.4	**Smithfield** (town) Johnston County
46	n/a	28.2	**Franklin** (town) Macon County
47	n/a	28.1	**Rockingham** (city) Richmond County
48	366	27.9	**Morganton** (city) Burke County
49	n/a	27.8	**Clinton** (city) Sampson County
49	371	27.8	**Thomasville** (city) Davidson County
51	n/a	27.6	**Dunn** (city) Harnett County
52	n/a	27.2	**China Grove** (town) Rowan County
53	n/a	27.1	**Ayden** (town) Pitt County
54	n/a	26.9	**Sneads Ferry** (CDP) Onslow County
55	450	26.5	**Lexington** (city) Davidson County
55	450	26.5	**Wilson** (city) Wilson County
57	n/a	26.4	**Mar-Mac** (CDP) Wayne County
58	n/a	26.2	**Dana** (CDP) Henderson County
59	n/a	26.1	**Wadesboro** (town) Anson County
60	488	26.0	**Eden** (city) Rockingham County
60	488	26.0	**Hendersonville** (city) Henderson County
60	488	26.0	**Lincolnton** (city) Lincoln County
63	n/a	25.9	**Williamston** (town) Martin County
64	511	25.7	**Goldsboro** (city) Wayne County
65	514	25.6	**Roanoke Rapids** (city) Halifax County
66	523	25.5	**Asheboro** (city) Randolph County
67	n/a	25.4	**Windsor** (town) Bertie County
68	n/a	25.3	**Lillington** (town) Harnett County
69	n/a	24.9	**Hamlet** (city) Richmond County
70	n/a	24.8	**River Road** (CDP) Beaufort County
70	574	24.8	**Salisbury** (city) Rowan County
72	583	24.6	**Lenoir** (city) Caldwell County
73	589	24.5	**New Bern** (city) Craven County
73	589	24.5	**Rocky Mount** (city) Nash County
75	n/a	24.4	**Long View** (town) Catawba County
76	614	24.3	**Graham** (city) Alamance County
77	n/a	24.1	**Brogden** (CDP) Wayne County
78	n/a	23.7	**Louisburg** (town) Franklin County
78	n/a	23.7	**Polkton** (town) Anson County
80	681	23.6	**Kings Mountain** (city) Cleveland County
80	681	23.6	**Newton** (city) Catawba County
82	690	23.5	**Albemarle** (city) Stanly County
82	n/a	23.5	**Oxford** (city) Granville County
84	700	23.4	**Spring Lake** (town) Cumberland County
85	721	23.2	**Wilmington** (city) New Hanover County
85	721	23.2	**Winston-Salem** (city) Forsyth County
87	732	23.1	**Chapel Hill** (town) Orange County
87	n/a	23.1	**Pittsboro** (town) Chatham County
87	n/a	23.1	**Woodfin** (town) Buncombe County
90	n/a	23.0	**Southport** (city) Brunswick County
91	752	22.9	**Sanford** (city) Lee County
91	n/a	22.9	**Swannanoa** (CDP) Buncombe County
93	814	22.3	**Gastonia** (city) Gaston County
94	n/a	22.2	**Bessemer City** (city) Gaston County
94	n/a	22.2	**Hillsborough** (town) Orange County
94	n/a	22.2	**Siler City** (town) Chatham County
97	n/a	22.0	**Morehead City** (town) Carteret County
98	853	21.9	**Burlington** (city) Alamance County
99	n/a	21.5	**Icard** (CDP) Burke County
99	n/a	21.5	**La Grange** (town) Lenoir County
99	892	21.5	**Mount Airy** (city) Surry County
102	905	21.4	**High Point** (city) Guilford County
102	n/a	21.4	**Spindale** (town) Rutherford County
104	n/a	21.0	**Pineville** (town) Mecklenburg County
105	964	20.8	**Kannapolis** (city) Cabarrus County
105	n/a	20.8	**Sawmills** (town) Caldwell County
107	975	20.7	**Monroe** (city) Union County
108	1021	20.3	**Greensboro** (city) Guilford County
108	n/a	20.3	**Liberty** (town) Randolph County
108	n/a	20.3	**Waynesville** (town) Haywood County
111	n/a	20.1	**Murfreesboro** (town) Hertford County
112	1052	20.0	**Asheville** (city) Buncombe County
112	1052	20.0	**Durham** (city) Durham County
112	n/a	20.0	**Sylva** (town) Jackson County
115	n/a	19.9	**Landis** (town) Rowan County
116	n/a	19.6	**Maiden** (town) Catawba County
117	n/a	19.4	**Elon** (town) Alamance County
118	1145	19.3	**Hickory** (city) Catawba County
118	1145	19.3	**Reidsville** (city) Rockingham County
120	n/a	19.0	**Zebulon** (town) Wake County
121	n/a	18.7	**Mocksville** (town) Davie County
122	n/a	18.6	**Wallace** (town) Duplin County
123	n/a	18.2	**Black Mountain** (town) Buncombe County
123	n/a	18.2	**Brevard** (city) Transylvania County
123	1282	18.2	**Havelock** (city) Craven County
126	n/a	18.1	**Wingate** (town) Union County
127	n/a	18.0	**Half Moon** (CDP) Onslow County
128	n/a	17.7	**Granite Falls** (town) Caldwell County
129	n/a	17.6	**Erwin** (town) Harnett County
129	1368	17.6	**Fayetteville** (city) Cumberland County
129	1368	17.6	**Tarboro** (town) Edgecombe County
132	n/a	17.4	**Silver Lake** (CDP) New Hanover County
133	n/a	17.2	**Conover** (city) Catawba County
134	1437	17.1	**Charlotte** (city) Mecklenburg County
135	1451	17.0	**Carrboro** (town) Orange County
135	n/a	17.0	**Mountain Home** (CDP) Henderson County
137	n/a	16.5	**Pleasant Garden** (town) Guilford County
138	n/a	16.4	**Nashville** (town) Nash County
139	n/a	16.3	**Granite Quarry** (town) Rowan County
140	1561	16.2	**Raleigh** (city) Wake County
141	n/a	15.9	**Canton** (town) Haywood County
141	n/a	15.9	**Wendell** (town) Wake County
143	1638	15.6	**Hope Mills** (town) Cumberland County
144	n/a	15.3	**Elkin** (town) Surry County
145	n/a	15.2	**Stanley** (town) Gaston County
145	n/a	15.2	**Wrightsboro** (CDP) New Hanover County
147	n/a	15.1	**Butner** (town) Granville County
147	n/a	15.1	**Rutherfordton** (town) Rutherford County
147	n/a	15.1	**Trinity** (city) Randolph County
147	n/a	15.1	**Valdese** (town) Burke County

Note: The state column ranks the top/bottom 150 places in the state with population of 2,500 or more. The national column ranks the top/bottom places in the country with population of 10,000 or more. Places that are unincorporated were not considered in the rankings. n/a indicates data not available. Please refer to the User Guide for additional information.

Poverty Rate

Top 150 Places Ranked in *Ascending* Order

State Rank	Nat'l Rank	Percent	Place
1	n/a	0.6	**Brices Creek** (CDP) Craven County
2	n/a	1.0	**Saint James** (town) Brunswick County
3	n/a	1.1	**Whispering Pines** (village) Moore County
4	n/a	1.8	**Weddington** (town) Union County
5	n/a	2.1	**Fairfield Harbour** (CDP) Craven County
6	105	2.5	**Apex** (town) Wake County
7	n/a	2.6	**Marvin** (village) Union County
8	n/a	2.8	**Seven Lakes** (CDP) Moore County
9	n/a	3.0	**Moyock** (CDP) Currituck County
9	n/a	3.0	**Oak Ridge** (town) Guilford County
9	n/a	3.0	**Southern Shores** (town) Dare County
12	220	3.1	**Holly Springs** (town) Wake County
12	n/a	3.1	**Lake Norman of Catawba** (CDP) Catawba County
12	220	3.1	**Morrisville** (town) Wake County
12	n/a	3.1	**Red Oak** (town) Nash County
16	n/a	3.3	**Fairview** (CDP) Buncombe County
16	278	3.3	**Pinehurst** (village) Moore County
16	n/a	3.3	**Trent Woods** (town) Craven County
19	n/a	3.4	**Unionville** (town) Union County
20	n/a	3.5	**Westport** (CDP) Lincoln County
21	n/a	3.8	**Porters Neck** (CDP) New Hanover County
22	n/a	3.9	**Bayshore** (CDP) New Hanover County
23	n/a	4.0	**Wesley Chapel** (village) Union County
24	656	4.5	**Summerfield** (town) Guilford County
25	n/a	4.6	**Weaverville** (town) Buncombe County
26	n/a	4.8	**Lake Junaluska** (CDP) Haywood County
27	n/a	4.9	**Royal Pines** (CDP) Buncombe County
28	n/a	5.1	**Lake Park** (village) Union County
28	n/a	5.1	**Waxhaw** (town) Union County
30	n/a	5.4	**Mountain View** (CDP) Catawba County
31	n/a	5.6	**Rockfish** (CDP) Hoke County
32	n/a	5.8	**Archer Lodge** (town) Johnston County
33	1071	6.0	**Huntersville** (town) Mecklenburg County
34	n/a	6.1	**Midland** (town) Cabarrus County
34	n/a	6.1	**Nags Head** (town) Dare County
36	1134	6.2	**Cary** (town) Wake County
36	n/a	6.2	**Fairview** (town) Union County
36	1134	6.2	**Harrisburg** (town) Cabarrus County
36	n/a	6.2	**Kill Devil Hills** (town) Dare County
40	n/a	6.3	**Emerald Isle** (town) Carteret County
40	1157	6.3	**Indian Trail** (town) Union County
40	n/a	6.3	**Lake Royale** (CDP) Franklin County
43	n/a	6.4	**Flat Rock** (village) Henderson County
44	n/a	6.5	**Etowah** (CDP) Henderson County
45	n/a	6.6	**Cramerton** (town) Gaston County
45	1235	6.6	**Murraysville** (CDP) New Hanover County
47	1303	6.8	**Davidson** (town) Mecklenburg County
48	1329	6.9	**Stallings** (town) Union County
48	1329	6.9	**Wake Forest** (town) Wake County
50	n/a	7.0	**Mills River** (town) Henderson County
51	n/a	7.2	**Kitty Hawk** (town) Dare County
51	n/a	7.2	**River Bend** (town) Craven County
53	n/a	7.3	**Wallburg** (town) Davidson County
54	1482	7.5	**Knightdale** (town) Wake County
54	n/a	7.5	**Myrtle Grove** (CDP) New Hanover County
54	n/a	7.5	**Rolesville** (town) Wake County
57	n/a	7.6	**Fletcher** (town) Henderson County
58	n/a	7.7	**Northchase** (CDP) New Hanover County
59	1601	7.9	**Clemmons** (village) Forsyth County
59	1601	7.9	**Matthews** (town) Mecklenburg County
61	1629	8.0	**Mint Hill** (town) Mecklenburg County
62	n/a	8.1	**Gibsonville** (town) Guilford County
62	n/a	8.1	**Jamestown** (town) Guilford County
62	n/a	8.1	**Kings Grant** (CDP) New Hanover County
65	1754	8.5	**Cornelius** (town) Mecklenburg County
65	n/a	8.5	**Locust** (city) Stanly County
65	n/a	8.5	**Rural Hall** (town) Forsyth County
68	n/a	8.6	**Boiling Springs** (town) Cleveland County
68	1782	8.6	**Garner** (town) Wake County
70	n/a	8.8	**Eastover** (town) Cumberland County
71	1841	8.9	**Lewisville** (town) Forsyth County
71	n/a	8.9	**Oak Island** (town) Brunswick County
73	1865	9.0	**Leland** (town) Brunswick County
73	n/a	9.0	**Lowesville** (CDP) Lincoln County
75	1910	9.2	**Belmont** (city) Gaston County
75	n/a	9.2	**Carolina Shores** (town) Brunswick County
77	n/a	9.6	**Ogden** (CDP) New Hanover County
78	2058	9.9	**Mooresville** (town) Iredell County
79	n/a	10.0	**Cajah's Mountain** (town) Caldwell County
80	2136	10.3	**Fuquay-Varina** (town) Wake County
80	n/a	10.3	**Midway** (town) Davidson County
82	n/a	10.7	**Glen Raven** (CDP) Alamance County
83	n/a	10.8	**Ranlo** (town) Gaston County
84	n/a	10.9	**Bethlehem** (CDP) Alexander County
84	n/a	10.9	**Carolina Beach** (town) New Hanover County
84	n/a	10.9	**Newport** (town) Carteret County
87	n/a	11.0	**Enochville** (CDP) Rowan County
87	n/a	11.0	**Stokesdale** (town) Guilford County
89	n/a	11.1	**Cherryville** (city) Gaston County
90	2308	11.2	**Archdale** (city) Randolph County
90	n/a	11.2	**Forest Oaks** (CDP) Guilford County
90	n/a	11.2	**King** (city) Stokes County
90	n/a	11.2	**Welcome** (CDP) Davidson County
90	n/a	11.2	**Wentworth** (town) Rockingham County
90	n/a	11.2	**Winterville** (town) Pitt County
96	n/a	11.7	**James City** (CDP) Craven County
96	n/a	11.7	**Mineral Springs** (town) Union County
98	n/a	11.8	**Hudson** (town) Caldwell County
99	2455	12.0	**Southern Pines** (town) Moore County
100	n/a	12.1	**Swansboro** (town) Onslow County
101	n/a	12.2	**Walkertown** (town) Forsyth County
102	2530	12.4	**Clayton** (town) Johnston County
102	n/a	12.4	**Hampstead** (CDP) Pender County
104	n/a	12.5	**Saint Stephens** (CDP) Catawba County
105	2565	12.6	**Concord** (city) Cabarrus County
105	n/a	12.6	**Shallotte** (town) Brunswick County
105	n/a	12.6	**Tyro** (CDP) Davidson County
108	n/a	12.7	**Creedmoor** (city) Granville County
109	n/a	12.8	**Lowell** (city) Gaston County
110	n/a	13.2	**Sunset Beach** (town) Brunswick County
111	n/a	13.4	**Gamewell** (town) Caldwell County
111	2662	13.4	**Mebane** (city) Alamance County
113	2678	13.5	**Kernersville** (town) Forsyth County
114	n/a	13.6	**Boiling Spring Lakes** (city) Brunswick County
115	n/a	13.7	**Dallas** (town) Gaston County
116	2743	13.9	**Mount Holly** (city) Gaston County
116	2743	13.9	**Piney Green** (CDP) Onslow County
118	n/a	14.2	**Skippers Corner** (CDP) New Hanover County
119	n/a	14.4	**Aberdeen** (town) Moore County
119	n/a	14.4	**Angier** (town) Harnett County
121	2849	14.6	**Jacksonville** (city) Onslow County
122	n/a	15.1	**Butner** (town) Granville County
122	n/a	15.1	**Rutherfordton** (town) Rutherford County
122	n/a	15.1	**Trinity** (city) Randolph County
122	n/a	15.1	**Valdese** (town) Burke County
126	n/a	15.2	**Stanley** (town) Gaston County
126	n/a	15.2	**Wrightsboro** (CDP) New Hanover County
128	n/a	15.3	**Elkin** (town) Surry County
129	3005	15.6	**Hope Mills** (town) Cumberland County
130	n/a	15.9	**Canton** (town) Haywood County
130	n/a	15.9	**Wendell** (town) Wake County
132	3084	16.2	**Raleigh** (city) Wake County
133	n/a	16.3	**Granite Quarry** (town) Rowan County
134	n/a	16.4	**Nashville** (town) Nash County
135	n/a	16.5	**Pleasant Garden** (town) Guilford County
136	3194	17.0	**Carrboro** (town) Orange County
136	n/a	17.0	**Mountain Home** (CDP) Henderson County
138	3206	17.1	**Charlotte** (city) Mecklenburg County
139	n/a	17.2	**Conover** (city) Catawba County
140	n/a	17.4	**Silver Lake** (CDP) New Hanover County
141	n/a	17.6	**Erwin** (town) Harnett County
141	3270	17.6	**Fayetteville** (city) Cumberland County
141	3270	17.6	**Tarboro** (town) Edgecombe County
144	n/a	17.7	**Granite Falls** (town) Caldwell County
145	n/a	18.0	**Half Moon** (CDP) Onslow County
146	n/a	18.1	**Wingate** (town) Union County
147	n/a	18.2	**Black Mountain** (town) Buncombe County
147	n/a	18.2	**Brevard** (city) Transylvania County
147	3362	18.2	**Havelock** (city) Craven County
150	n/a	18.6	**Wallace** (town) Duplin County

Note: The state column ranks the top/bottom 150 places in the state with population of 2,500 or more. The national column ranks the top/bottom places in the country with population of 10,000 or more. Places that are unincorporated were not considered in the rankings. n/a indicates data not available. Please refer to the User Guide for additional information.

Educational Attainment: High School Diploma or Higher

Top 150 Places Ranked in *Descending* Order

State Rank	Nat'l Rank	Percent	Place
1	n/a	99.5	Hampstead (CDP) Pender County
2	n/a	99.0	Fairfield Harbour (CDP) Craven County
3	n/a	98.8	Marvin (village) Union County
4	n/a	98.6	Trent Woods (town) Craven County
5	n/a	98.4	Flat Rock (village) Henderson County
5	n/a	98.4	Westport (CDP) Lincoln County
7	n/a	98.1	Seven Lakes (CDP) Moore County
8	n/a	97.9	Buies Creek (CDP) Harnett County
9	n/a	97.7	Royal Pines (CDP) Buncombe County
10	n/a	97.5	Weddington (town) Union County
11	202	97.3	Davidson (town) Mecklenburg County
11	n/a	97.3	Porters Neck (CDP) New Hanover County
13	229	97.2	Pinehurst (village) Moore County
14	n/a	97.1	Brices Creek (CDP) Craven County
14	n/a	97.1	Oak Ridge (town) Guilford County
14	n/a	97.1	Saint James (town) Brunswick County
17	270	97.0	Holly Springs (town) Wake County
17	n/a	97.0	Southern Shores (town) Dare County
19	287	96.9	Apex (town) Wake County
20	306	96.8	Morrisville (town) Wake County
20	n/a	96.8	Nags Head (town) Dare County
22	453	96.2	Harrisburg (town) Cabarrus County
23	n/a	96.1	Kill Devil Hills (town) Dare County
23	n/a	96.1	Weaverville (town) Buncombe County
25	n/a	95.8	Emerald Isle (town) Carteret County
25	n/a	95.8	Half Moon (CDP) Onslow County
27	n/a	95.7	Whispering Pines (village) Moore County
28	n/a	95.5	Etowah (CDP) Henderson County
28	n/a	95.5	Ogden (CDP) New Hanover County
28	n/a	95.5	Waxhaw (town) Union County
31	732	95.2	Cary (town) Wake County
31	n/a	95.2	Kitty Hawk (town) Dare County
31	n/a	95.2	Lake Park (village) Union County
31	n/a	95.2	Lake Royale (CDP) Franklin County
31	732	95.2	Wake Forest (town) Wake County
36	n/a	95.1	Carolina Beach (town) New Hanover County
37	n/a	95.0	River Bend (town) Craven County
38	823	94.9	Matthews (town) Mecklenburg County
39	881	94.7	Chapel Hill (town) Orange County
40	n/a	94.5	Lake Junaluska (CDP) Haywood County
41	n/a	94.4	Fairview (CDP) Buncombe County
41	970	94.4	Havelock (city) Craven County
43	1043	94.2	Huntersville (town) Mecklenburg County
44	n/a	94.0	Carolina Shores (town) Brunswick County
44	n/a	94.0	Rockfish (CDP) Hoke County
44	1118	94.0	Summerfield (town) Guilford County
47	n/a	93.9	Wesley Chapel (village) Union County
48	n/a	93.8	Forest Oaks (CDP) Guilford County
49	1224	93.7	Clemmons (village) Forsyth County
49	n/a	93.7	Unionville (town) Union County
51	1301	93.5	Cornelius (town) Mecklenburg County
51	n/a	93.5	Swansboro (town) Onslow County
53	1468	93.0	Indian Trail (town) Union County
53	n/a	93.0	Jamestown (town) Guilford County
53	1468	93.0	Stallings (town) Union County
53	n/a	93.0	Stokesdale (town) Guilford County
57	1532	92.8	Leland (town) Brunswick County
57	n/a	92.8	Myrtle Grove (CDP) New Hanover County
59	1569	92.7	Lewisville (town) Forsyth County
60	1595	92.6	Boone (town) Watauga County
60	1595	92.6	Murraysville (CDP) New Hanover County
62	n/a	92.4	Bayshore (CDP) New Hanover County
62	n/a	92.4	Oak Island (town) Brunswick County
64	n/a	92.3	Fairview (town) Union County
64	n/a	92.3	Mills River (town) Henderson County
66	1734	92.2	Jacksonville (city) Onslow County
67	1768	92.1	Clayton (town) Johnston County
67	n/a	92.1	Sunset Beach (town) Brunswick County
69	1799	92.0	Garner (town) Wake County
70	n/a	91.7	Northchase (CDP) New Hanover County
71	n/a	91.5	Lake Norman of Catawba (CDP) Catawba County
72	n/a	91.4	Creedmoor (city) Granville County
72	1965	91.4	Mint Hill (town) Mecklenburg County
74	n/a	91.2	Boiling Spring Lakes (city) Brunswick County
74	n/a	91.2	Gibsonville (town) Guilford County
76	n/a	91.1	Granite Quarry (town) Rowan County
77	2071	91.0	Mebane (city) Alamance County
77	n/a	91.0	Winterville (town) Pitt County
79	n/a	90.9	Elon (town) Alamance County
80	2137	90.8	Fayetteville (city) Cumberland County
81	2160	90.7	Carrboro (town) Orange County
81	2160	90.7	Fuquay-Varina (town) Wake County
83	2184	90.6	Kernersville (town) Forsyth County
83	2184	90.6	Mooresville (town) Iredell County
85	2293	90.2	Asheville (city) Buncombe County
85	2293	90.2	Spring Lake (town) Cumberland County
87	n/a	90.1	Locust (city) Stanly County
88	2342	90.0	Raleigh (city) Wake County
89	n/a	89.9	Bethlehem (CDP) Alexander County
89	n/a	89.9	Fletcher (town) Henderson County
89	n/a	89.9	Pleasant Garden (town) Guilford County
92	n/a	89.8	Boiling Springs (town) Cleveland County
92	n/a	89.8	Cramerton (town) Gaston County
92	n/a	89.8	Wendell (town) Wake County
95	2407	89.7	Greenville (city) Pitt County
95	n/a	89.7	King (city) Stokes County
97	2430	89.6	Knightdale (town) Wake County
97	n/a	89.6	Murfreesboro (town) Hertford County
97	2430	89.6	Southern Pines (town) Moore County
97	n/a	89.6	Wrightsboro (CDP) New Hanover County
101	n/a	89.5	Morehead City (town) Carteret County
101	2454	89.5	Piney Green (CDP) Onslow County
103	n/a	89.3	Kings Grant (CDP) New Hanover County
104	n/a	89.2	Mountain Home (CDP) Henderson County
105	n/a	89.1	Mineral Springs (town) Union County
106	n/a	89.0	Archer Lodge (town) Johnston County
106	2571	89.0	Hope Mills (town) Cumberland County
106	2571	89.0	Wilmington (city) New Hanover County
109	n/a	88.9	Landis (town) Rowan County
110	n/a	88.7	Lowesville (CDP) Lincoln County
111	n/a	88.4	Grifton (town) Pitt County
111	n/a	88.4	Red Oak (town) Nash County
113	n/a	88.2	Shallotte (town) Brunswick County
114	2805	88.0	Charlotte (city) Mecklenburg County
114	n/a	88.0	James City (CDP) Craven County
116	n/a	87.9	Dana (CDP) Henderson County
117	n/a	87.8	Wallburg (town) Davidson County
118	n/a	87.7	Brevard (city) Transylvania County
118	2873	87.7	Greensboro (city) Guilford County
120	n/a	87.5	Nashville (town) Nash County
121	n/a	87.4	Black Mountain (town) Buncombe County
122	n/a	87.2	La Grange (town) Lenoir County
122	n/a	87.2	Sneads Ferry (CDP) Onslow County
124	n/a	87.1	Conover (city) Catawba County
124	n/a	87.1	Rural Hall (town) Forsyth County
126	n/a	87.0	Aberdeen (town) Moore County
126	n/a	87.0	Hudson (town) Caldwell County
126	n/a	87.0	Moyock (CDP) Currituck County
126	n/a	87.0	Southport (city) Brunswick County
130	3031	86.9	Belmont (city) Gaston County
131	n/a	86.7	Mountain View (CDP) Catawba County
132	n/a	86.6	Cullowhee (CDP) Jackson County
132	3077	86.6	Durham (city) Durham County
134	n/a	86.4	Eastover (town) Cumberland County
135	3120	86.3	Concord (city) Cabarrus County
136	n/a	86.2	Rolesville (town) Wake County
137	n/a	86.1	Woodfin (town) Buncombe County
138	n/a	86.0	Dallas (town) Gaston County
138	3171	86.0	Shelby (city) Cleveland County
140	n/a	85.9	Silver Lake (CDP) New Hanover County
141	n/a	85.8	Rutherfordton (town) Rutherford County
142	3233	85.7	High Point (city) Guilford County
143	n/a	85.6	Brogden (CDP) Wayne County
144	n/a	85.4	Midland (town) Cabarrus County
145	n/a	85.3	Angier (town) Harnett County
146	n/a	85.2	Welcome (CDP) Davidson County
147	3350	85.1	Mount Holly (city) Gaston County
148	3363	85.0	Winston-Salem (city) Forsyth County
149	n/a	84.9	Hillsborough (town) Orange County
150	3385	84.8	Reidsville (city) Rockingham County

Note: The state column ranks the top/bottom 150 places in the state with population of 2,500 or more. The national column ranks the top/bottom places in the country with population of 10,000 or more. Places that are unincorporated were not considered in the rankings. n/a indicates data not available. Please refer to the User Guide for additional information.

Educational Attainment: High School Diploma or Higher

Top 150 Places Ranked in *Ascending* Order

State Rank	Nat'l Rank	Percent	Place
1	n/a	62.8	**Siler City** (town) Chatham County
2	n/a	63.0	**Enfield** (town) Halifax County
3	n/a	64.0	**Selma** (town) Johnston County
4	n/a	66.6	**North Wilkesboro** (town) Wilkes County
5	n/a	66.7	**Polkton** (town) Anson County
6	n/a	67.7	**Windsor** (town) Bertie County
7	n/a	67.8	**Wallace** (town) Duplin County
8	n/a	69.0	**Mount Olive** (town) Wayne County
9	n/a	69.4	**Icard** (CDP) Burke County
10	n/a	70.5	**Forest City** (town) Rutherford County
10	n/a	70.5	**Roxboro** (city) Person County
12	n/a	70.6	**Warsaw** (town) Duplin County
13	222	70.7	**Lexington** (city) Davidson County
13	n/a	70.7	**Red Springs** (town) Robeson County
15	n/a	71.2	**Benson** (town) Johnston County
16	n/a	71.7	**Ahoskie** (town) Hertford County
16	n/a	71.7	**Long View** (town) Catawba County
18	256	72.2	**Lumberton** (city) Robeson County
19	287	73.1	**Asheboro** (city) Randolph County
19	n/a	73.1	**Sawmills** (town) Caldwell County
21	n/a	73.2	**Stanley** (town) Gaston County
22	n/a	73.6	**Maiden** (town) Catawba County
23	306	73.7	**Henderson** (city) Vance County
24	n/a	73.8	**East Rockingham** (CDP) Richmond County
25	329	74.2	**Monroe** (city) Union County
26	n/a	74.3	**Randleman** (city) Randolph County
27	n/a	74.5	**Edenton** (town) Chowan County
28	348	74.6	**Morganton** (city) Burke County
29	n/a	74.8	**Wentworth** (town) Rockingham County
30	361	74.9	**Lenoir** (city) Caldwell County
31	n/a	75.1	**Ayden** (town) Pitt County
32	n/a	75.3	**Mar-Mac** (CDP) Wayne County
32	n/a	75.3	**Wilkesboro** (town) Wilkes County
34	n/a	75.4	**Cajah's Mountain** (town) Caldwell County
34	n/a	75.4	**China Grove** (town) Rowan County
34	n/a	75.4	**Gamewell** (town) Caldwell County
37	386	75.5	**Mount Airy** (city) Surry County
37	386	75.5	**Sanford** (city) Lee County
39	n/a	75.6	**Marion** (city) McDowell County
40	n/a	76.0	**Lillington** (town) Harnett County
40	n/a	76.0	**Troy** (town) Montgomery County
42	n/a	76.1	**Yadkinville** (town) Yadkin County
43	n/a	76.3	**Tabor City** (town) Columbus County
44	n/a	76.4	**Elkin** (town) Surry County
45	431	76.5	**Albemarle** (city) Stanly County
45	n/a	76.5	**Whiteville** (city) Columbus County
47	n/a	76.7	**South Rosemary** (CDP) Halifax County
48	456	76.9	**Newton** (city) Catawba County
49	460	77.0	**Smithfield** (town) Johnston County
50	n/a	77.1	**Franklin** (town) Macon County
51	n/a	77.5	**Elizabethtown** (town) Bladen County
52	n/a	77.9	**Pembroke** (town) Robeson County
53	n/a	78.1	**Burgaw** (town) Pender County
54	n/a	78.2	**River Road** (CDP) Beaufort County
55	n/a	78.3	**Ranlo** (town) Gaston County
55	538	78.3	**Tarboro** (town) Edgecombe County
55	538	78.3	**Thomasville** (city) Davidson County
58	n/a	78.4	**Williamston** (town) Martin County
59	n/a	78.5	**Dunn** (city) Harnett County
59	558	78.5	**Eden** (city) Rockingham County
59	558	78.5	**Wilson** (city) Wilson County
62	n/a	78.6	**Enochville** (CDP) Rowan County
62	n/a	78.6	**Plymouth** (town) Washington County
64	571	78.7	**Kinston** (city) Lenoir County
65	n/a	78.9	**Fairmont** (town) Robeson County
65	585	78.9	**Laurinburg** (city) Scotland County
65	n/a	78.9	**Mocksville** (town) Davie County
68	595	79.0	**Kannapolis** (city) Cabarrus County
69	n/a	79.4	**Hamlet** (city) Richmond County
69	n/a	79.4	**Raeford** (city) Hoke County
71	n/a	79.6	**Butner** (town) Granville County
72	n/a	79.7	**Bessemer City** (city) Gaston County
72	651	79.7	**Elizabeth City** (city) Pasquotank County
74	661	79.8	**Roanoke Rapids** (city) Halifax County
75	n/a	80.0	**East Flat Rock** (CDP) Henderson County
75	678	80.0	**Graham** (city) Alamance County
77	n/a	80.2	**Saint Stephens** (CDP) Catawba County
78	n/a	80.3	**Washington** (city) Beaufort County
79	n/a	80.4	**Cherryville** (city) Gaston County
79	710	80.4	**Salisbury** (city) Rowan County
81	725	80.6	**Gastonia** (city) Gaston County
81	n/a	80.6	**Spindale** (town) Rutherford County
81	725	80.6	**Statesville** (city) Iredell County
81	n/a	80.6	**Tyro** (CDP) Davidson County
85	n/a	80.7	**Farmville** (town) Pitt County
85	n/a	80.7	**Wadesboro** (town) Anson County
87	749	80.8	**Lincolnton** (city) Lincoln County
88	n/a	80.9	**Waynesville** (town) Haywood County
88	n/a	80.9	**Zebulon** (town) Wake County
90	n/a	81.2	**Elroy** (CDP) Wayne County
90	n/a	81.2	**Louisburg** (town) Franklin County
92	n/a	81.4	**Erwin** (town) Harnett County
93	n/a	81.5	**Clinton** (city) Sampson County
93	n/a	81.5	**Sylva** (town) Jackson County
95	n/a	81.6	**Granite Falls** (town) Caldwell County
95	n/a	81.6	**Rockingham** (city) Richmond County
95	n/a	81.6	**Valdese** (town) Burke County
98	n/a	81.7	**Oxford** (city) Granville County
98	n/a	81.7	**Trinity** (city) Randolph County
100	n/a	82.0	**Spencer** (town) Rowan County
101	892	82.2	**Rocky Mount** (city) Nash County
102	911	82.4	**Kings Mountain** (city) Cleveland County
103	951	82.7	**Burlington** (city) Alamance County
104	n/a	83.0	**Beaufort** (town) Carteret County
104	n/a	83.0	**Lowell** (city) Gaston County
106	993	83.1	**Archdale** (city) Randolph County
106	n/a	83.1	**Canton** (town) Haywood County
108	1020	83.3	**Hendersonville** (city) Henderson County
109	n/a	83.5	**Midway** (town) Davidson County
110	1065	83.6	**New Bern** (city) Craven County
111	n/a	83.7	**Walkertown** (town) Forsyth County
112	1121	83.9	**Goldsboro** (city) Wayne County
113	n/a	84.1	**Glen Raven** (CDP) Alamance County
113	1157	84.1	**Hickory** (city) Catawba County
115	n/a	84.3	**Swannanoa** (CDP) Buncombe County
116	n/a	84.5	**Pittsboro** (town) Chatham County
117	n/a	84.6	**Pineville** (town) Mecklenburg County
118	n/a	84.7	**Liberty** (town) Randolph County
118	n/a	84.7	**Newport** (town) Carteret County
120	1250	84.8	**Reidsville** (city) Rockingham County
120	n/a	84.8	**Skippers Corner** (CDP) New Hanover County
120	n/a	84.8	**Wingate** (town) Union County
123	n/a	84.9	**Hillsborough** (town) Orange County
124	1283	85.0	**Winston-Salem** (city) Forsyth County
125	1294	85.1	**Mount Holly** (city) Gaston County
126	n/a	85.2	**Welcome** (CDP) Davidson County
127	n/a	85.3	**Angier** (town) Harnett County
128	n/a	85.4	**Midland** (town) Cabarrus County
129	n/a	85.6	**Brogden** (CDP) Wayne County
130	1403	85.7	**High Point** (city) Guilford County
131	n/a	85.8	**Rutherfordton** (town) Rutherford County
132	n/a	85.9	**Silver Lake** (CDP) New Hanover County
133	n/a	86.0	**Dallas** (town) Gaston County
133	1463	86.0	**Shelby** (city) Cleveland County
135	n/a	86.1	**Woodfin** (town) Buncombe County
136	n/a	86.2	**Rolesville** (town) Wake County
137	1522	86.3	**Concord** (city) Cabarrus County
138	n/a	86.4	**Eastover** (town) Cumberland County
139	n/a	86.6	**Cullowhee** (CDP) Jackson County
139	1569	86.6	**Durham** (city) Durham County
141	n/a	86.7	**Mountain View** (CDP) Catawba County
142	1615	86.9	**Belmont** (city) Gaston County
143	n/a	87.0	**Aberdeen** (town) Moore County
143	n/a	87.0	**Hudson** (town) Caldwell County
143	n/a	87.0	**Moyock** (CDP) Currituck County
143	n/a	87.0	**Southport** (city) Brunswick County
147	n/a	87.1	**Conover** (city) Catawba County
147	n/a	87.1	**Rural Hall** (town) Forsyth County
149	n/a	87.2	**La Grange** (town) Lenoir County
149	n/a	87.2	**Sneads Ferry** (CDP) Onslow County

Note: The state column ranks the top/bottom 150 places in the state with population of 2,500 or more. The national column ranks the top/bottom places in the country with population of 10,000 or more. Places that are unincorporated were not considered in the rankings. n/a indicates data not available. Please refer to the User Guide for additional information.

Educational Attainment: Bachelor's Degree or Higher

Top 150 Places Ranked in *Descending* Order

State Rank	Nat'l Rank	Percent	Place	State Rank	Nat'l Rank	Percent	Place
1	74	73.9	**Chapel Hill** (town) Orange County	76	n/a	32.8	**Lake Park** (village) Union County
2	n/a	66.3	**Marvin** (village) Union County	77	1889	32.6	**Winston-Salem** (city) Forsyth County
3	188	66.0	**Davidson** (town) Mecklenburg County	78	n/a	32.5	**Gibsonville** (town) Guilford County
4	207	65.1	**Carrboro** (town) Orange County	79	1903	32.4	**Mebane** (city) Alamance County
5	238	63.8	**Morrisville** (town) Wake County	80	n/a	32.2	**Bethlehem** (CDP) Alexander County
6	275	62.2	**Cary** (town) Wake County	81	n/a	31.9	**Murfreesboro** (town) Hertford County
7	292	61.8	**Apex** (town) Wake County	82	n/a	31.7	**Oak Island** (town) Brunswick County
8	n/a	59.4	**Flat Rock** (village) Henderson County	83	n/a	31.6	**Glen Raven** (CDP) Alamance County
9	n/a	58.0	**Porters Neck** (CDP) New Hanover County	84	2002	31.3	**Clayton** (town) Johnston County
10	n/a	55.9	**Saint James** (town) Brunswick County	85	n/a	31.2	**Louisburg** (town) Franklin County
11	n/a	55.6	**Buies Creek** (CDP) Harnett County	86	n/a	31.1	**Hampstead** (CDP) Pender County
12	477	55.4	**Holly Springs** (town) Wake County	87	2032	31.0	**Hickory** (city) Catawba County
13	n/a	55.0	**Waxhaw** (town) Union County	88	n/a	30.9	**Lake Royale** (CDP) Franklin County
14	n/a	53.1	**Weddington** (town) Union County	89	n/a	30.3	**Black Mountain** (town) Buncombe County
15	583	52.5	**Huntersville** (town) Mecklenburg County	90	2158	29.9	**Kernersville** (town) Forsyth County
16	600	52.1	**Pinehurst** (village) Moore County	91	2174	29.8	**Hendersonville** (city) Henderson County
17	611	51.8	**Summerfield** (town) Guilford County	91	2174	29.8	**Murraysville** (CDP) New Hanover County
18	n/a	50.9	**Oak Ridge** (town) Guilford County	93	n/a	29.6	**Northchase** (CDP) New Hanover County
19	661	50.6	**Cornelius** (town) Mecklenburg County	94	n/a	29.5	**Swansboro** (town) Onslow County
20	n/a	50.4	**Fairfield Harbour** (CDP) Craven County	95	n/a	29.4	**Aberdeen** (town) Moore County
20	665	50.4	**Wake Forest** (town) Wake County	96	n/a	29.3	**Fletcher** (town) Henderson County
22	n/a	49.3	**Southern Shores** (town) Dare County	96	n/a	29.3	**Mills River** (town) Henderson County
23	n/a	49.0	**Boiling Springs** (town) Cleveland County	98	2265	29.0	**Mooresville** (town) Iredell County
24	735	48.9	**Boone** (town) Watauga County	98	n/a	29.0	**Wendell** (town) Wake County
24	n/a	48.9	**Trent Woods** (town) Craven County	100	2275	28.9	**High Point** (city) Guilford County
26	784	48.1	**Matthews** (town) Mecklenburg County	100	n/a	28.9	**Sylva** (town) Jackson County
26	n/a	48.1	**Seven Lakes** (CDP) Moore County	102	n/a	28.5	**Lowesville** (CDP) Lincoln County
28	n/a	47.5	**Lake Junaluska** (CDP) Haywood County	102	n/a	28.5	**Red Oak** (town) Nash County
28	807	47.5	**Raleigh** (city) Wake County	104	n/a	28.2	**Etowah** (CDP) Henderson County
30	n/a	47.0	**Ogden** (CDP) New Hanover County	104	n/a	28.2	**Kitty Hawk** (town) Dare County
31	841	46.8	**Durham** (city) Durham County	104	n/a	28.2	**River Bend** (town) Craven County
32	n/a	46.5	**Emerald Isle** (town) Carteret County	107	n/a	27.9	**Pineville** (town) Mecklenburg County
33	n/a	46.4	**Royal Pines** (CDP) Buncombe County	108	2387	27.8	**Concord** (city) Cabarrus County
34	n/a	45.2	**Sunset Beach** (town) Brunswick County	109	n/a	27.5	**Morehead City** (town) Carteret County
35	n/a	44.7	**Weaverville** (town) Buncombe County	110	n/a	27.2	**Mountain Home** (CDP) Henderson County
36	n/a	44.0	**Jamestown** (town) Guilford County	111	n/a	26.5	**Rutherfordton** (town) Rutherford County
37	1010	43.8	**Clemmons** (village) Forsyth County	112	n/a	26.4	**Granite Quarry** (town) Rowan County
38	n/a	43.7	**Wesley Chapel** (village) Union County	113	n/a	25.5	**Kings Grant** (CDP) New Hanover County
39	1026	43.5	**Stallings** (town) Union County	114	2722	25.0	**New Bern** (city) Craven County
40	1035	43.3	**Asheville** (city) Buncombe County	115	n/a	24.9	**Shallotte** (town) Brunswick County
41	n/a	42.9	**Westport** (CDP) Lincoln County	116	2747	24.8	**Mount Airy** (city) Surry County
42	n/a	42.1	**Forest Oaks** (CDP) Guilford County	116	n/a	24.8	**Valdese** (town) Burke County
43	1136	41.6	**Knightdale** (town) Wake County	118	2759	24.7	**Fayetteville** (city) Cumberland County
44	1163	41.0	**Leland** (town) Brunswick County	118	n/a	24.7	**King** (city) Stokes County
44	n/a	41.0	**Myrtle Grove** (CDP) New Hanover County	118	2759	24.7	**Mount Holly** (city) Gaston County
46	1245	40.0	**Southern Pines** (town) Moore County	118	n/a	24.7	**Skippers Corner** (CDP) New Hanover County
47	1252	39.9	**Harrisburg** (town) Cabarrus County	122	n/a	24.5	**Woodfin** (town) Buncombe County
48	1258	39.8	**Charlotte** (city) Mecklenburg County	123	n/a	24.2	**River Road** (CDP) Beaufort County
49	n/a	39.7	**Pittsboro** (town) Chatham County	124	n/a	24.0	**Beaufort** (town) Carteret County
50	1306	39.1	**Wilmington** (city) New Hanover County	124	2840	24.0	**Burlington** (city) Alamance County
51	n/a	38.7	**Cullowhee** (CDP) Jackson County	126	n/a	23.9	**Wilkesboro** (town) Wilkes County
52	n/a	38.6	**Nags Head** (town) Dare County	127	n/a	23.5	**Washington** (city) Beaufort County
53	n/a	38.3	**Whispering Pines** (village) Moore County	128	n/a	23.4	**Mocksville** (town) Davie County
54	1383	38.1	**Lewisville** (town) Forsyth County	128	n/a	23.4	**Raeford** (city) Hoke County
55	n/a	37.6	**Brices Creek** (CDP) Craven County	128	n/a	23.4	**Waynesville** (town) Haywood County
55	n/a	37.6	**Winterville** (town) Pitt County	131	n/a	23.1	**Benson** (town) Johnston County
57	1457	37.1	**Greenville** (city) Pitt County	131	2953	23.1	**Jacksonville** (city) Onslow County
58	n/a	36.7	**Southport** (city) Brunswick County	131	2953	23.1	**Wilson** (city) Wilson County
59	n/a	36.5	**Bayshore** (CDP) New Hanover County	134	2998	22.7	**Morganton** (city) Burke County
59	n/a	36.5	**Hillsborough** (town) Orange County	134	2998	22.7	**Salisbury** (city) Rowan County
61	n/a	36.4	**Carolina Beach** (town) New Hanover County	136	n/a	22.4	**Franklin** (town) Macon County
62	n/a	36.1	**Lake Norman of Catawba** (CDP) Catawba County	137	3060	22.2	**Sanford** (city) Lee County
63	n/a	35.8	**Elon** (town) Alamance County	138	n/a	22.1	**Archer Lodge** (town) Johnston County
64	1573	35.7	**Greensboro** (city) Guilford County	139	n/a	22.0	**Eastover** (town) Cumberland County
65	n/a	35.5	**Brevard** (city) Transylvania County	140	n/a	21.6	**Conover** (city) Catawba County
66	1617	35.2	**Indian Trail** (town) Union County	140	3135	21.6	**Gastonia** (city) Gaston County
67	1666	34.8	**Garner** (town) Wake County	142	n/a	21.1	**Wingate** (town) Union County
68	n/a	34.7	**Cramerton** (town) Gaston County	143	n/a	21.0	**Carolina Shores** (town) Brunswick County
69	1696	34.5	**Fuquay-Varina** (town) Wake County	143	3218	21.0	**Shelby** (city) Cleveland County
70	n/a	34.3	**Kill Devil Hills** (town) Dare County	145	n/a	20.9	**Midway** (town) Davidson County
71	n/a	34.2	**Stokesdale** (town) Guilford County	146	3253	20.8	**Elizabeth City** (city) Pasquotank County
72	1752	33.9	**Belmont** (city) Gaston County	146	n/a	20.8	**Fairview** (town) Union County
72	n/a	33.9	**Fairview** (CDP) Buncombe County	146	n/a	20.8	**Unionville** (town) Union County
74	1775	33.7	**Mint Hill** (town) Mecklenburg County	149	n/a	20.7	**Edenton** (town) Chowan County
75	n/a	33.1	**Rolesville** (town) Wake County	150	n/a	20.6	**Mountain View** (CDP) Catawba County

Note: *The state column ranks the top/bottom 150 places in the state with population of 2,500 or more. The national column ranks the top/bottom places in the country with population of 10,000 or more. Places that are unincorporated were not considered in the rankings. n/a indicates data not available. Please refer to the User Guide for additional information.*

Educational Attainment: Bachelor's Degree or Higher

Top 150 Places Ranked in *Ascending* Order

State Rank	Nat'l Rank	Percent	Place
1	n/a	3.0	**Polkton** (town) Anson County
2	n/a	4.4	**South Rosemary** (CDP) Halifax County
3	n/a	6.0	**China Grove** (town) Rowan County
4	n/a	6.1	**Long View** (town) Catawba County
5	n/a	6.3	**Bessemer City** (city) Gaston County
6	n/a	6.5	**Maiden** (town) Catawba County
7	n/a	7.0	**Elroy** (CDP) Wayne County
8	n/a	7.7	**Selma** (town) Johnston County
9	n/a	8.9	**Enfield** (town) Halifax County
10	n/a	9.2	**Newport** (town) Carteret County
11	n/a	9.3	**Gamewell** (town) Caldwell County
11	n/a	9.3	**Sawmills** (town) Caldwell County
13	n/a	9.4	**Randleman** (city) Randolph County
14	n/a	9.6	**Butner** (town) Granville County
15	n/a	10.1	**Roxboro** (city) Person County
16	n/a	10.2	**Icard** (CDP) Burke County
17	n/a	10.6	**Mar-Mac** (CDP) Wayne County
18	n/a	10.8	**Warsaw** (town) Duplin County
19	n/a	10.9	**Trinity** (city) Randolph County
20	n/a	11.2	**Midland** (town) Cabarrus County
20	n/a	11.2	**Tyro** (CDP) Davidson County
22	n/a	11.8	**Spencer** (town) Rowan County
23	n/a	11.9	**Hamlet** (city) Richmond County
24	n/a	12.0	**Enochville** (CDP) Rowan County
25	n/a	12.2	**Forest City** (town) Rutherford County
25	322	12.2	**Lexington** (city) Davidson County
25	n/a	12.2	**Wadesboro** (town) Anson County
28	n/a	12.3	**Williamston** (town) Martin County
29	348	12.5	**Havelock** (city) Craven County
30	366	12.7	**Eden** (city) Rockingham County
30	n/a	12.7	**Liberty** (town) Randolph County
32	n/a	12.9	**Cajah's Mountain** (town) Caldwell County
32	n/a	12.9	**Lillington** (town) Harnett County
34	n/a	13.1	**Saint Stephens** (CDP) Catawba County
35	414	13.2	**Kings Mountain** (city) Cleveland County
35	414	13.2	**Thomasville** (city) Davidson County
35	n/a	13.2	**Wallace** (town) Duplin County
38	n/a	13.4	**Ayden** (town) Pitt County
39	n/a	13.5	**La Grange** (town) Lenoir County
39	n/a	13.5	**Lowell** (city) Gaston County
41	n/a	13.6	**Marion** (city) McDowell County
42	n/a	13.7	**East Rockingham** (CDP) Richmond County
43	n/a	13.8	**Angier** (town) Harnett County
43	n/a	13.8	**Wrightsboro** (CDP) New Hanover County
43	n/a	13.8	**Yadkinville** (town) Yadkin County
46	492	14.1	**Henderson** (city) Vance County
46	n/a	14.1	**Sneads Ferry** (CDP) Onslow County
46	n/a	14.1	**Wentworth** (town) Rockingham County
49	n/a	14.2	**Mount Olive** (town) Wayne County
49	n/a	14.2	**Swannanoa** (CDP) Buncombe County
51	n/a	14.4	**Granite Falls** (town) Caldwell County
51	n/a	14.4	**Siler City** (town) Chatham County
53	525	14.5	**Piney Green** (CDP) Onslow County
54	n/a	14.6	**Brogden** (CDP) Wayne County
55	564	14.8	**Lenoir** (city) Caldwell County
55	n/a	14.8	**Locust** (city) Stanly County
57	n/a	14.9	**Silver Lake** (CDP) New Hanover County
58	n/a	15.0	**East Flat Rock** (CDP) Henderson County
59	619	15.1	**Kinston** (city) Lenoir County
60	649	15.4	**Archdale** (city) Randolph County
60	n/a	15.4	**Landis** (town) Rowan County
62	n/a	15.5	**Stanley** (town) Gaston County
63	n/a	15.7	**Farmville** (town) Pitt County
63	n/a	15.7	**North Wilkesboro** (town) Wilkes County
63	n/a	15.7	**Pembroke** (town) Robeson County
63	n/a	15.7	**Zebulon** (town) Wake County
67	n/a	15.8	**Ranlo** (town) Gaston County
67	n/a	15.8	**Windsor** (town) Bertie County
69	n/a	16.0	**Dallas** (town) Gaston County
69	733	16.0	**Newton** (city) Catawba County
71	n/a	16.1	**Erwin** (town) Harnett County
71	750	16.1	**Spring Lake** (town) Cumberland County
71	n/a	16.1	**Troy** (town) Montgomery County
74	n/a	16.2	**Wallburg** (town) Davidson County
75	774	16.3	**Reidsville** (city) Rockingham County
76	n/a	16.4	**Rockfish** (CDP) Hoke County
76	n/a	16.4	**Welcome** (CDP) Davidson County
78	820	16.7	**Monroe** (city) Union County
78	n/a	16.7	**Red Springs** (town) Robeson County
78	n/a	16.7	**Whiteville** (city) Columbus County
81	829	16.8	**Asheboro** (city) Randolph County
81	n/a	16.8	**Rockingham** (city) Richmond County
83	n/a	16.9	**Hudson** (town) Caldwell County
83	842	16.9	**Lincolnton** (city) Lincoln County
83	842	16.9	**Tarboro** (town) Edgecombe County
86	n/a	17.0	**Ahoskie** (town) Hertford County
86	n/a	17.0	**Elizabethtown** (town) Bladen County
86	n/a	17.0	**Walkertown** (town) Forsyth County
89	n/a	17.2	**Dana** (CDP) Henderson County
89	n/a	17.2	**Dunn** (city) Harnett County
91	n/a	17.4	**Moyock** (CDP) Currituck County
92	922	17.5	**Kannapolis** (city) Cabarrus County
93	n/a	17.7	**Canton** (town) Haywood County
94	n/a	17.8	**Boiling Spring Lakes** (city) Brunswick County
94	n/a	17.8	**James City** (CDP) Craven County
96	n/a	18.0	**Grifton** (town) Pitt County
96	n/a	18.0	**Spindale** (town) Rutherford County
98	n/a	18.2	**Nashville** (town) Nash County
99	n/a	18.3	**Oxford** (city) Granville County
100	1051	18.4	**Lumberton** (city) Robeson County
100	n/a	18.4	**Plymouth** (town) Washington County
102	1067	18.5	**Goldsboro** (city) Wayne County
102	1067	18.5	**Graham** (city) Alamance County
104	n/a	18.6	**Half Moon** (CDP) Onslow County
104	1080	18.6	**Laurinburg** (city) Scotland County
106	1100	18.7	**Roanoke Rapids** (city) Halifax County
107	n/a	18.8	**Mineral Springs** (town) Union County
108	n/a	19.1	**Tabor City** (town) Columbus County
109	n/a	19.2	**Creedmoor** (city) Granville County
109	n/a	19.2	**Elkin** (town) Surry County
109	1169	19.2	**Rocky Mount** (city) Nash County
112	n/a	19.3	**Fairmont** (town) Robeson County
113	n/a	19.4	**Cherryville** (city) Gaston County
113	1197	19.4	**Smithfield** (town) Johnston County
115	1212	19.5	**Albemarle** (city) Stanly County
115	n/a	19.5	**Rural Hall** (town) Forsyth County
117	1228	19.6	**Hope Mills** (town) Cumberland County
118	n/a	19.7	**Pleasant Garden** (town) Guilford County
119	n/a	20.2	**Burgaw** (town) Pender County
119	n/a	20.2	**Clinton** (city) Sampson County
121	1343	20.5	**Statesville** (city) Iredell County
122	n/a	20.6	**Mountain View** (CDP) Catawba County
123	n/a	20.7	**Edenton** (town) Chowan County
124	1385	20.8	**Elizabeth City** (city) Pasquotank County
124	n/a	20.8	**Fairview** (town) Union County
124	n/a	20.8	**Unionville** (town) Union County
127	n/a	20.9	**Midway** (town) Davidson County
128	n/a	21.0	**Carolina Shores** (town) Brunswick County
128	1428	21.0	**Shelby** (city) Cleveland County
130	n/a	21.1	**Wingate** (town) Union County
131	n/a	21.6	**Conover** (city) Catawba County
131	1507	21.6	**Gastonia** (city) Gaston County
133	n/a	22.0	**Eastover** (town) Cumberland County
134	n/a	22.1	**Archer Lodge** (town) Johnston County
135	1588	22.2	**Sanford** (city) Lee County
136	n/a	22.4	**Franklin** (town) Macon County
137	1643	22.7	**Morganton** (city) Burke County
137	1643	22.7	**Salisbury** (city) Rowan County
139	n/a	23.1	**Benson** (town) Johnston County
139	1689	23.1	**Jacksonville** (city) Onslow County
139	1689	23.1	**Wilson** (city) Wilson County
142	n/a	23.4	**Mocksville** (town) Davie County
142	n/a	23.4	**Raeford** (city) Hoke County
142	n/a	23.4	**Waynesville** (town) Haywood County
145	n/a	23.5	**Washington** (city) Beaufort County
146	n/a	23.9	**Wilkesboro** (town) Wilkes County
147	n/a	24.0	**Beaufort** (town) Carteret County
147	1805	24.0	**Burlington** (city) Alamance County
149	n/a	24.2	**River Road** (CDP) Beaufort County
150	n/a	24.5	**Woodfin** (town) Buncombe County

Note: The state column ranks the top/bottom 150 places in the state with population of 2,500 or more. The national column ranks the top/bottom places in the country with population of 10,000 or more. Places that are unincorporated were not considered in the rankings. n/a indicates data not available. Please refer to the User Guide for additional information.

Educational Attainment: Graduate/Professional Degree

Top 150 Places Ranked in *Descending* Order

State Rank	Nat'l Rank	Percent	Place
1	27	45.1	**Chapel Hill** (town) Orange County
2	114	35.6	**Carrboro** (town) Orange County
3	252	29.5	**Davidson** (town) Mecklenburg County
4	n/a	25.7	**Marvin** (village) Union County
5	n/a	25.2	**Porters Neck** (CDP) New Hanover County
6	415	25.1	**Cary** (town) Wake County
7	n/a	24.8	**Boiling Springs** (town) Cleveland County
8	n/a	24.1	**Buies Creek** (CDP) Harnett County
9	468	23.9	**Morrisville** (town) Wake County
10	n/a	22.5	**Saint James** (town) Brunswick County
11	566	21.8	**Durham** (city) Durham County
12	n/a	21.5	**Oak Ridge** (town) Guilford County
13	634	20.9	**Apex** (town) Wake County
13	n/a	20.9	**Flat Rock** (village) Henderson County
15	n/a	20.7	**Cullowhee** (CDP) Jackson County
16	n/a	20.2	**Lake Junaluska** (CDP) Haywood County
17	n/a	19.4	**Fairfield Harbour** (CDP) Craven County
18	778	19.3	**Pinehurst** (village) Moore County
19	804	19.0	**Summerfield** (town) Guilford County
20	811	18.9	**Boone** (town) Watauga County
21	n/a	18.6	**Royal Pines** (CDP) Buncombe County
21	n/a	18.6	**Weaverville** (town) Buncombe County
23	912	17.9	**Southern Pines** (town) Moore County
24	953	17.5	**Holly Springs** (town) Wake County
25	n/a	17.3	**Southern Shores** (town) Dare County
26	n/a	17.0	**Seven Lakes** (CDP) Moore County
27	1071	16.5	**Cornelius** (town) Mecklenburg County
28	1101	16.3	**Wake Forest** (town) Wake County
29	n/a	16.2	**Pittsboro** (town) Chatham County
30	1145	15.9	**Asheville** (city) Buncombe County
30	n/a	15.9	**Emerald Isle** (town) Carteret County
30	1145	15.9	**Raleigh** (city) Wake County
33	n/a	15.8	**Murfreesboro** (town) Hertford County
34	n/a	15.7	**Carolina Beach** (town) New Hanover County
34	n/a	15.7	**Southport** (city) Brunswick County
36	n/a	15.4	**Brices Creek** (CDP) Craven County
36	n/a	15.4	**Waxhaw** (town) Union County
38	n/a	15.3	**Ogden** (CDP) New Hanover County
39	n/a	15.1	**Trent Woods** (town) Craven County
40	1256	15.0	**Huntersville** (town) Mecklenburg County
41	1267	14.9	**Harrisburg** (town) Cabarrus County
41	n/a	14.9	**Westport** (CDP) Lincoln County
43	n/a	14.8	**Hillsborough** (town) Orange County
43	1280	14.8	**Leland** (town) Brunswick County
43	1280	14.8	**Matthews** (town) Mecklenburg County
46	n/a	14.7	**Gibsonville** (town) Guilford County
47	1302	14.6	**Greenville** (city) Pitt County
48	n/a	14.3	**Whispering Pines** (village) Moore County
49	n/a	14.1	**Louisburg** (town) Franklin County
49	n/a	14.1	**Myrtle Grove** (CDP) New Hanover County
51	1443	13.7	**Wilmington** (city) New Hanover County
52	1460	13.6	**Clemmons** (village) Forsyth County
53	n/a	13.5	**Nags Head** (town) Dare County
54	1497	13.4	**Belmont** (city) Gaston County
54	n/a	13.4	**Mills River** (town) Henderson County
54	n/a	13.4	**Sunset Beach** (town) Brunswick County
57	n/a	13.3	**Brevard** (city) Transylvania County
57	n/a	13.3	**Fairview** (CDP) Buncombe County
59	n/a	13.2	**Swansboro** (town) Onslow County
60	n/a	13.1	**Etowah** (CDP) Henderson County
61	n/a	13.0	**Forest Oaks** (CDP) Guilford County
61	n/a	13.0	**Wesley Chapel** (village) Union County
63	1579	12.9	**Mebane** (city) Alamance County
64	1598	12.8	**Lewisville** (town) Forsyth County
64	n/a	12.8	**Stokesdale** (town) Guilford County
66	1617	12.7	**Charlotte** (city) Mecklenburg County
67	n/a	12.5	**Sylva** (town) Jackson County
68	1692	12.3	**Greensboro** (city) Guilford County
69	1719	12.2	**Winston-Salem** (city) Forsyth County
69	n/a	12.2	**Winterville** (town) Pitt County
71	n/a	11.9	**Beaufort** (town) Carteret County
71	n/a	11.9	**Oak Island** (town) Brunswick County
71	1791	11.9	**Stallings** (town) Union County
74	n/a	11.8	**Valdese** (town) Burke County
75	n/a	11.6	**Jamestown** (town) Guilford County
75	1853	11.6	**Knightdale** (town) Wake County
75	n/a	11.6	**Lake Royale** (CDP) Franklin County
78	n/a	11.5	**Rolesville** (town) Wake County
79	n/a	11.3	**Glen Raven** (CDP) Alamance County
80	n/a	11.2	**Bayshore** (CDP) New Hanover County
80	1938	11.2	**Hendersonville** (city) Henderson County
82	n/a	11.0	**Lake Norman of Catawba** (CDP) Catawba County
83	n/a	10.9	**Weddington** (town) Union County
84	n/a	10.5	**Rutherfordton** (town) Rutherford County
85	n/a	10.4	**Hudson** (town) Caldwell County
86	n/a	10.3	**Washington** (city) Beaufort County
87	n/a	10.2	**Bethlehem** (CDP) Alexander County
87	2183	10.2	**Hickory** (city) Catawba County
89	n/a	10.0	**Cramerton** (town) Gaston County
89	n/a	10.0	**Elon** (town) Alamance County
91	2271	9.9	**Fuquay-Varina** (town) Wake County
92	n/a	9.8	**Black Mountain** (town) Buncombe County
93	n/a	9.7	**Dana** (CDP) Henderson County
93	n/a	9.7	**Edenton** (town) Chowan County
95	n/a	9.6	**Lowesville** (CDP) Lincoln County
96	n/a	9.3	**Carolina Shores** (town) Brunswick County
96	2445	9.3	**Indian Trail** (town) Union County
96	2445	9.3	**Kernersville** (town) Forsyth County
99	2471	9.2	**Garner** (town) Wake County
100	2501	9.1	**Mint Hill** (town) Mecklenburg County
100	n/a	9.1	**Mountain Home** (CDP) Henderson County
102	2534	9.0	**Morganton** (city) Burke County
103	n/a	8.9	**Fletcher** (town) Henderson County
103	n/a	8.9	**Wilkesboro** (town) Wilkes County
105	2615	8.7	**New Bern** (city) Craven County
106	2646	8.6	**High Point** (city) Guilford County
107	2683	8.5	**Mount Airy** (city) Surry County
107	n/a	8.5	**Northchase** (CDP) New Hanover County
107	n/a	8.5	**Wingate** (town) Union County
110	n/a	8.4	**Cherryville** (city) Gaston County
111	2749	8.3	**Concord** (city) Cabarrus County
111	2749	8.3	**Fayetteville** (city) Cumberland County
111	n/a	8.3	**Midway** (town) Davidson County
114	n/a	8.2	**Eastover** (town) Cumberland County
114	2785	8.2	**Murraysville** (CDP) New Hanover County
114	n/a	8.2	**River Road** (CDP) Beaufort County
114	n/a	8.2	**Waynesville** (town) Haywood County
114	n/a	8.2	**Woodfin** (town) Buncombe County
119	2814	8.1	**Clayton** (town) Johnston County
119	n/a	8.1	**Tabor City** (town) Columbus County
121	n/a	7.9	**Skippers Corner** (CDP) New Hanover County
121	2882	7.9	**Statesville** (city) Iredell County
123	n/a	7.8	**Franklin** (town) Macon County
123	n/a	7.8	**Lake Park** (village) Union County
125	2960	7.7	**Mooresville** (town) Iredell County
125	n/a	7.7	**Oxford** (city) Granville County
125	n/a	7.7	**Zebulon** (town) Wake County
128	n/a	7.6	**Aberdeen** (town) Moore County
128	2997	7.6	**Laurinburg** (city) Scotland County
128	n/a	7.6	**Plymouth** (town) Washington County
128	2997	7.6	**Shelby** (city) Cleveland County
132	n/a	7.5	**Kill Devil Hills** (town) Dare County
133	n/a	7.4	**Mineral Springs** (town) Union County
133	n/a	7.4	**Mocksville** (town) Davie County
133	n/a	7.4	**Morehead City** (town) Carteret County
133	n/a	7.4	**Rockingham** (city) Richmond County
133	n/a	7.4	**Siler City** (town) Chatham County
138	3086	7.3	**Salisbury** (city) Rowan County
139	n/a	7.2	**Canton** (town) Haywood County
139	n/a	7.2	**Grifton** (town) Pitt County
141	3171	7.1	**Burlington** (city) Alamance County
141	3171	7.1	**Elizabeth City** (city) Pasquotank County
143	3197	7.0	**Jacksonville** (city) Onslow County
143	n/a	7.0	**Kitty Hawk** (town) Dare County
143	3197	7.0	**Roanoke Rapids** (city) Halifax County
143	n/a	7.0	**Shallotte** (town) Brunswick County
147	n/a	6.9	**Rural Hall** (town) Forsyth County
148	n/a	6.7	**Clinton** (city) Sampson County
148	n/a	6.7	**Hampstead** (CDP) Pender County
148	n/a	6.7	**Kings Grant** (CDP) New Hanover County

Note: The state column ranks the top/bottom 150 places in the state with population of 2,500 or more. The national column ranks the top/bottom places in the country with population of 10,000 or more. Places that are unincorporated were not considered in the rankings. n/a indicates data not available. Please refer to the User Guide for additional information.

Educational Attainment: Graduate/Professional Degree

Top 150 Places Ranked in *Ascending* Order

State Rank	Nat'l Rank	Percent	Place	State Rank	Nat'l Rank	Percent	Place
1	n/a	0.7	Landis (town) Rowan County	74	n/a	4.7	Spindale (town) Rutherford County
2	n/a	1.2	East Rockingham (CDP) Richmond County	77	679	4.9	Asheboro (city) Randolph County
3	n/a	1.5	Bessemer City (city) Gaston County	77	679	4.9	Lenoir (city) Caldwell County
3	n/a	1.5	Polkton (town) Anson County	77	n/a	4.9	Raeford (city) Hoke County
3	n/a	1.5	Roxboro (city) Person County	80	n/a	5.0	Granite Quarry (town) Rowan County
3	n/a	1.5	Tyro (CDP) Davidson County	80	n/a	5.0	Nashville (town) Nash County
7	n/a	1.6	Yadkinville (town) Yadkin County	80	726	5.0	Reidsville (city) Rockingham County
8	n/a	1.7	Enfield (town) Halifax County	80	726	5.0	Rocky Mount (city) Nash County
9	n/a	1.8	Gamewell (town) Caldwell County	80	726	5.0	Tarboro (town) Edgecombe County
10	n/a	2.0	Long View (town) Catawba County	85	n/a	5.1	Boiling Spring Lakes (city) Brunswick County
10	n/a	2.0	Midland (town) Cabarrus County	85	n/a	5.1	Fairmont (town) Robeson County
10	n/a	2.0	Pembroke (town) Robeson County	85	n/a	5.1	Marion (city) McDowell County
13	n/a	2.1	Randleman (city) Randolph County	85	n/a	5.1	Stanley (town) Gaston County
13	n/a	2.1	South Rosemary (CDP) Halifax County	89	791	5.2	Eden (city) Rockingham County
13	n/a	2.1	Warsaw (town) Duplin County	89	n/a	5.2	Lowell (city) Gaston County
16	n/a	2.2	Wrightsboro (CDP) New Hanover County	89	791	5.2	Spring Lake (town) Cumberland County
17	n/a	2.3	Half Moon (CDP) Onslow County	92	n/a	5.3	Windsor (town) Bertie County
17	n/a	2.3	James City (CDP) Craven County	93	n/a	5.4	Benson (town) Johnston County
17	n/a	2.3	Welcome (CDP) Davidson County	93	n/a	5.4	Creedmoor (city) Granville County
20	n/a	2.5	Maiden (town) Catawba County	93	n/a	5.4	La Grange (town) Lenoir County
20	n/a	2.5	North Wilkesboro (town) Wilkes County	93	n/a	5.4	Troy (town) Montgomery County
22	n/a	2.7	Newport (town) Carteret County	97	n/a	5.5	Dunn (city) Harnett County
22	163	2.7	Thomasville (city) Davidson County	97	892	5.5	Kannapolis (city) Cabarrus County
22	n/a	2.7	Wallace (town) Duplin County	99	n/a	5.6	Burgaw (town) Pender County
25	n/a	2.8	Elroy (CDP) Wayne County	99	n/a	5.6	Elkin (town) Surry County
25	180	2.8	Havelock (city) Craven County	99	922	5.6	Graham (city) Alamance County
25	n/a	2.8	Liberty (town) Randolph County	99	922	5.6	Mount Holly (city) Gaston County
25	n/a	2.8	Selma (town) Johnston County	103	991	5.8	Albemarle (city) Stanly County
29	n/a	2.9	Sneads Ferry (CDP) Onslow County	104	n/a	5.9	Pleasant Garden (town) Guilford County
30	n/a	3.0	Trinity (city) Randolph County	105	1064	6.0	Hope Mills (town) Cumberland County
30	n/a	3.0	Wallburg (town) Davidson County	105	n/a	6.0	Red Springs (town) Robeson County
32	n/a	3.1	Ayden (town) Pitt County	107	n/a	6.1	Mount Olive (town) Wayne County
32	n/a	3.1	Dallas (town) Gaston County	107	n/a	6.1	Whiteville (city) Columbus County
32	n/a	3.1	Fairview (town) Union County	109	n/a	6.2	Ahoskie (town) Hertford County
32	n/a	3.1	Spencer (town) Rowan County	109	n/a	6.2	Pineville (town) Mecklenburg County
32	n/a	3.1	Walkertown (town) Forsyth County	111	n/a	6.3	River Bend (town) Craven County
37	n/a	3.2	Elizabethtown (town) Bladen County	111	1171	6.3	Wilson (city) Wilson County
38	n/a	3.3	Enochville (CDP) Rowan County	113	n/a	6.4	King (city) Stokes County
39	n/a	3.4	Hamlet (city) Richmond County	113	1208	6.4	Sanford (city) Lee County
40	n/a	3.5	Rockfish (CDP) Hoke County	113	1208	6.4	Smithfield (town) Johnston County
40	n/a	3.5	Williamston (town) Martin County	116	1246	6.5	Gastonia (city) Gaston County
42	n/a	3.6	Archer Lodge (town) Johnston County	116	1246	6.5	Goldsboro (city) Wayne County
42	n/a	3.6	Saint Stephens (CDP) Catawba County	118	n/a	6.6	Conover (city) Catawba County
44	n/a	3.7	Angier (town) Harnett County	118	n/a	6.6	Wendell (town) Wake County
44	n/a	3.7	Farmville (town) Pitt County	120	n/a	6.7	Clinton (city) Sampson County
44	351	3.7	Lincolnton (city) Lincoln County	120	n/a	6.7	Hampstead (CDP) Pender County
44	n/a	3.7	Sawmills (town) Caldwell County	120	n/a	6.7	Kings Grant (CDP) New Hanover County
44	n/a	3.7	Unionville (town) Union County	120	n/a	6.7	Locust (city) Stanly County
49	n/a	3.8	Granite Falls (town) Caldwell County	120	1327	6.7	Lumberton (city) Robeson County
49	378	3.8	Piney Green (CDP) Onslow County	125	n/a	6.9	Rural Hall (town) Forsyth County
51	n/a	3.9	Butner (town) Granville County	126	1426	7.0	Jacksonville (city) Onslow County
51	n/a	3.9	Mar-Mac (CDP) Wayne County	126	n/a	7.0	Kitty Hawk (town) Dare County
51	n/a	3.9	Wentworth (town) Rockingham County	126	1426	7.0	Roanoke Rapids (city) Halifax County
54	n/a	4.0	China Grove (town) Rowan County	126	n/a	7.0	Shallotte (town) Brunswick County
54	415	4.0	Kings Mountain (city) Cleveland County	130	1460	7.1	Burlington (city) Alamance County
54	415	4.0	Lexington (city) Davidson County	130	1460	7.1	Elizabeth City (city) Pasquotank County
54	415	4.0	Monroe (city) Union County	132	n/a	7.2	Canton (town) Haywood County
54	415	4.0	Newton (city) Catawba County	132	n/a	7.2	Grifton (town) Pitt County
54	n/a	4.0	Silver Lake (CDP) New Hanover County	134	1529	7.3	Salisbury (city) Rowan County
54	n/a	4.0	Wadesboro (town) Anson County	135	n/a	7.4	Mineral Springs (town) Union County
61	n/a	4.1	East Flat Rock (CDP) Henderson County	135	n/a	7.4	Mocksville (town) Davie County
61	n/a	4.1	Icard (CDP) Burke County	135	n/a	7.4	Morehead City (town) Carteret County
61	456	4.1	Kinston (city) Lenoir County	135	n/a	7.4	Rockingham (city) Richmond County
61	n/a	4.1	Lillington (town) Harnett County	135	n/a	7.4	Siler City (town) Chatham County
65	n/a	4.2	Brogden (CDP) Wayne County	140	n/a	7.5	Kill Devil Hills (town) Dare County
66	n/a	4.3	Forest City (town) Rutherford County	141	n/a	7.6	Aberdeen (town) Moore County
67	n/a	4.5	Cajah's Mountain (town) Caldwell County	141	1635	7.6	Laurinburg (city) Scotland County
67	551	4.5	Henderson (city) Vance County	141	n/a	7.6	Plymouth (town) Washington County
69	n/a	4.6	Erwin (town) Harnett County	141	1635	7.6	Shelby (city) Cleveland County
69	n/a	4.6	Moyock (CDP) Currituck County	145	1660	7.7	Mooresville (town) Iredell County
69	n/a	4.6	Ranlo (town) Gaston County	145	n/a	7.7	Oxford (city) Granville County
69	n/a	4.6	Red Oak (town) Nash County	145	n/a	7.7	Zebulon (town) Wake County
69	n/a	4.6	Swannanoa (CDP) Buncombe County	148	n/a	7.8	Franklin (town) Macon County
74	620	4.7	Archdale (city) Randolph County	148	n/a	7.8	Lake Park (village) Union County
74	n/a	4.7	Mountain View (CDP) Catawba County	150	n/a	7.9	Skippers Corner (CDP) New Hanover County

Note: *The state column ranks the top/bottom 150 places in the state with population of 2,500 or more. The national column ranks the top/bottom places in the country with population of 10,000 or more. Places that are unincorporated were not considered in the rankings. n/a indicates data not available. Please refer to the User Guide for additional information.*

Homeownership Rate

Top 150 Places Ranked in *Descending* Order

State Rank	Nat'l Rank	Percent	Place
1	n/a	96.9	**Marvin** (village) Union County
2	n/a	95.7	**Saint James** (town) Brunswick County
3	n/a	94.7	**Forest Oaks** (CDP) Guilford County
4	n/a	94.0	**Wesley Chapel** (village) Union County
5	n/a	93.6	**Weddington** (town) Union County
6	n/a	93.4	**Seven Lakes** (CDP) Moore County
7	n/a	92.3	**Whispering Pines** (village) Moore County
8	n/a	92.1	**Oak Ridge** (town) Guilford County
9	n/a	91.5	**Westport** (CDP) Lincoln County
10	n/a	91.2	**Carolina Shores** (town) Brunswick County
10	n/a	91.2	**Flat Rock** (village) Henderson County
10	143	91.2	**Summerfield** (town) Guilford County
13	n/a	91.0	**Moyock** (CDP) Currituck County
14	163	90.9	**Harrisburg** (town) Cabarrus County
15	n/a	90.6	**Brices Creek** (CDP) Craven County
16	210	89.9	**Stallings** (town) Union County
17	n/a	89.3	**Southern Shores** (town) Dare County
18	n/a	89.2	**Trent Woods** (town) Craven County
19	n/a	88.7	**Lake Park** (village) Union County
20	n/a	88.6	**Red Oak** (town) Nash County
21	n/a	88.3	**Sunset Beach** (town) Brunswick County
22	n/a	87.6	**Rolesville** (town) Wake County
23	n/a	87.5	**Wallburg** (town) Davidson County
24	n/a	87.4	**Etowah** (CDP) Henderson County
24	373	87.4	**Holly Springs** (town) Wake County
26	n/a	87.2	**Archer Lodge** (town) Johnston County
26	n/a	87.2	**Fairfield Harbour** (CDP) Craven County
28	n/a	86.8	**Bethlehem** (CDP) Alexander County
28	n/a	86.8	**Waxhaw** (town) Union County
30	n/a	86.7	**Mineral Springs** (town) Union County
31	440	86.4	**Lewisville** (town) Forsyth County
31	n/a	86.4	**Lowesville** (CDP) Lincoln County
33	n/a	86.0	**Fairview** (town) Union County
33	462	86.0	**Indian Trail** (town) Union County
35	n/a	85.7	**Lake Norman of Catawba** (CDP) Catawba County
36	n/a	84.9	**Stokesdale** (town) Guilford County
37	n/a	84.7	**Unionville** (town) Union County
38	563	84.6	**Pinehurst** (village) Moore County
39	n/a	84.2	**Ogden** (CDP) New Hanover County
39	n/a	84.2	**Pleasant Garden** (town) Guilford County
41	n/a	84.1	**Lake Royale** (CDP) Franklin County
42	n/a	84.0	**Mountain View** (CDP) Catawba County
43	n/a	83.5	**Mills River** (town) Henderson County
44	n/a	83.4	**Hampstead** (CDP) Pender County
45	n/a	82.7	**Midway** (town) Davidson County
46	n/a	82.5	**Royal Pines** (CDP) Buncombe County
47	n/a	82.3	**Boiling Spring Lakes** (city) Brunswick County
48	n/a	82.2	**Wentworth** (town) Rockingham County
49	774	82.1	**Mint Hill** (town) Mecklenburg County
50	n/a	81.9	**Myrtle Grove** (CDP) New Hanover County
50	n/a	81.9	**Winterville** (town) Pitt County
52	n/a	81.7	**Locust** (city) Stanly County
53	n/a	81.3	**Fletcher** (town) Henderson County
54	n/a	81.1	**Midland** (town) Cabarrus County
54	n/a	81.1	**Trinity** (city) Randolph County
56	n/a	80.3	**Fairview** (CDP) Buncombe County
57	n/a	80.1	**Bayshore** (CDP) New Hanover County
58	n/a	79.7	**River Bend** (town) Craven County
59	n/a	79.0	**Saint Stephens** (CDP) Catawba County
60	n/a	78.9	**Jamestown** (town) Guilford County
60	n/a	78.9	**Lake Junaluska** (CDP) Haywood County
62	n/a	78.7	**Skippers Corner** (CDP) New Hanover County
63	n/a	78.6	**Enochville** (CDP) Rowan County
63	n/a	78.6	**Walkertown** (town) Forsyth County
65	1169	77.9	**Clemmons** (village) Forsyth County
66	n/a	77.3	**Rockfish** (CDP) Hoke County
66	n/a	77.3	**Tyro** (CDP) Davidson County
68	n/a	76.7	**Wrightsboro** (CDP) New Hanover County
69	n/a	76.6	**Cramerton** (town) Gaston County
70	n/a	76.5	**Gibsonville** (town) Guilford County
71	1309	76.4	**Leland** (town) Brunswick County
72	n/a	76.1	**Ranlo** (town) Gaston County
73	n/a	75.8	**Dana** (CDP) Henderson County
74	1401	75.5	**Huntersville** (town) Mecklenburg County
75	n/a	75.3	**Glen Raven** (CDP) Alamance County
76	n/a	74.9	**Porters Neck** (CDP) New Hanover County
77	1460	74.8	**Davidson** (town) Mecklenburg County
78	1469	74.7	**Apex** (town) Wake County
78	n/a	74.7	**River Road** (CDP) Beaufort County
80	n/a	74.5	**Kitty Hawk** (town) Dare County
81	n/a	74.4	**Eastover** (town) Cumberland County
81	n/a	74.4	**Landis** (town) Rowan County
83	n/a	74.3	**Weaverville** (town) Buncombe County
83	n/a	74.3	**Welcome** (CDP) Davidson County
85	n/a	73.9	**Creedmoor** (city) Granville County
86	n/a	73.6	**Boiling Springs** (town) Cleveland County
86	n/a	73.6	**Gamewell** (town) Caldwell County
88	1586	73.5	**Murraysville** (CDP) New Hanover County
89	n/a	73.4	**Cajah's Mountain** (town) Caldwell County
89	n/a	73.4	**Maiden** (town) Catawba County
91	1619	73.2	**Fuquay-Varina** (town) Wake County
91	n/a	73.2	**James City** (CDP) Craven County
93	1655	72.8	**Wake Forest** (town) Wake County
94	1690	72.5	**Matthews** (town) Mecklenburg County
94	n/a	72.5	**Silver Lake** (CDP) New Hanover County
96	1700	72.4	**Archdale** (city) Randolph County
97	n/a	72.3	**Mountain Home** (CDP) Henderson County
98	n/a	72.2	**Emerald Isle** (town) Carteret County
99	n/a	72.1	**Icard** (CDP) Burke County
100	n/a	71.4	**King** (city) Stokes County
101	1843	71.3	**Cornelius** (town) Mecklenburg County
102	n/a	71.1	**Granite Quarry** (town) Rowan County
103	n/a	70.7	**Oak Island** (town) Brunswick County
104	1916	70.6	**Belmont** (city) Gaston County
104	n/a	70.6	**Brogden** (CDP) Wayne County
106	n/a	70.5	**Kings Grant** (CDP) New Hanover County
107	n/a	70.4	**Cherryville** (city) Gaston County
107	n/a	70.4	**Swannanoa** (CDP) Buncombe County
109	n/a	70.3	**Hudson** (town) Caldwell County
110	n/a	69.6	**Pittsboro** (town) Chatham County
111	n/a	69.5	**Half Moon** (CDP) Onslow County
111	n/a	69.5	**Lowell** (city) Gaston County
113	2088	68.9	**Cary** (town) Wake County
114	n/a	68.2	**Canton** (town) Haywood County
115	2190	67.9	**Knightdale** (town) Wake County
116	2206	67.8	**Concord** (city) Cabarrus County
117	n/a	67.7	**Southport** (city) Brunswick County
118	n/a	67.6	**Conover** (city) Catawba County
118	n/a	67.6	**Nags Head** (town) Dare County
120	n/a	67.5	**Butner** (town) Granville County
121	n/a	67.4	**East Flat Rock** (CDP) Henderson County
122	n/a	67.2	**Erwin** (town) Harnett County
123	n/a	67.0	**Stanley** (town) Gaston County
124	2350	66.5	**Mount Holly** (city) Gaston County
124	n/a	66.5	**Wendell** (town) Wake County
126	n/a	66.3	**Mocksville** (town) Davie County
127	n/a	66.2	**Valdese** (town) Burke County
128	n/a	66.0	**China Grove** (town) Rowan County
129	2416	65.9	**Garner** (town) Wake County
130	n/a	65.7	**South Rosemary** (CDP) Halifax County
131	2461	65.5	**Clayton** (town) Johnston County
131	n/a	65.5	**Sneads Ferry** (CDP) Onslow County
133	n/a	65.2	**Granite Falls** (town) Caldwell County
133	n/a	65.2	**Sawmills** (town) Caldwell County
135	n/a	65.1	**Liberty** (town) Randolph County
136	n/a	64.1	**Elroy** (CDP) Wayne County
136	n/a	64.1	**Hillsborough** (town) Orange County
136	n/a	64.1	**Mar-Mac** (CDP) Wayne County
139	n/a	64.0	**Black Mountain** (town) Buncombe County
139	2602	64.0	**Mooresville** (town) Iredell County
141	2661	63.4	**Hope Mills** (town) Cumberland County
142	2726	62.8	**Kannapolis** (city) Cabarrus County
143	n/a	62.3	**Grifton** (town) Pitt County
144	n/a	62.1	**Rural Hall** (town) Forsyth County
144	n/a	62.1	**Wingate** (town) Union County
146	n/a	61.7	**Bessemer City** (city) Gaston County
146	n/a	61.7	**Newport** (town) Carteret County
148	2865	61.5	**Mebane** (city) Alamance County
148	n/a	61.5	**Swansboro** (town) Onslow County
150	n/a	61.4	**Kill Devil Hills** (town) Dare County

Note: The state column ranks the top/bottom 150 places in the state with population of 2,500 or more. The national column ranks the top/bottom places in the country with population of 10,000 or more. Places that are unincorporated were not considered in the rankings. n/a indicates data not available. Please refer to the User Guide for additional information.

Homeownership Rate

Top 150 Places Ranked in *Ascending* Order

State Rank	Nat'l Rank	Percent	Place
1	n/a	12.0	**Cullowhee** (CDP) Jackson County
2	26	23.2	**Boone** (town) Watauga County
3	31	24.7	**Spring Lake** (town) Cumberland County
4	n/a	28.4	**Pembroke** (town) Robeson County
5	n/a	30.6	**Pineville** (town) Mecklenburg County
6	n/a	35.0	**Buies Creek** (CDP) Harnett County
7	134	37.1	**Greenville** (city) Pitt County
8	157	38.2	**Jacksonville** (city) Onslow County
9	165	38.4	**Carrboro** (town) Orange County
10	n/a	38.8	**Selma** (town) Johnston County
11	242	41.7	**Goldsboro** (city) Wayne County
12	263	42.3	**Henderson** (city) Vance County
13	n/a	42.6	**Lillington** (town) Harnett County
14	n/a	42.7	**Louisburg** (town) Franklin County
15	287	42.9	**Havelock** (city) Craven County
16	n/a	43.3	**Roxboro** (city) Person County
17	n/a	44.1	**Ahoskie** (town) Hertford County
18	n/a	44.6	**North Wilkesboro** (town) Wilkes County
19	n/a	45.4	**Williamston** (town) Martin County
20	n/a	46.4	**Polkton** (town) Anson County
21	426	46.5	**Elizabeth City** (city) Pasquotank County
21	n/a	46.5	**Whiteville** (city) Columbus County
23	n/a	46.6	**Enfield** (town) Halifax County
24	n/a	46.8	**Troy** (town) Montgomery County
24	n/a	46.8	**Warsaw** (town) Duplin County
26	n/a	47.3	**Benson** (town) Johnston County
26	451	47.3	**Kinston** (city) Lenoir County
28	465	47.6	**Chapel Hill** (town) Orange County
28	465	47.6	**Lexington** (city) Davidson County
30	n/a	47.8	**Beaufort** (town) Carteret County
30	480	47.8	**Hendersonville** (city) Henderson County
32	n/a	47.9	**Washington** (city) Beaufort County
33	n/a	48.0	**Aberdeen** (town) Moore County
34	510	48.3	**Lumberton** (city) Robeson County
35	516	48.4	**Asheboro** (city) Randolph County
35	n/a	48.4	**Forest City** (town) Rutherford County
35	516	48.4	**Morrisville** (town) Wake County
38	n/a	48.5	**Edenton** (town) Chowan County
39	529	48.6	**Lincolnton** (city) Lincoln County
40	545	48.9	**Wilmington** (city) New Hanover County
41	n/a	49.0	**Burgaw** (town) Pender County
41	n/a	49.0	**Sylva** (town) Jackson County
43	n/a	49.4	**Oxford** (city) Granville County
44	n/a	49.7	**Fairmont** (town) Robeson County
45	600	49.8	**Durham** (city) Durham County
46	n/a	50.0	**Elizabethtown** (town) Bladen County
47	629	50.3	**Fayetteville** (city) Cumberland County
47	n/a	50.3	**Morehead City** (town) Carteret County
47	n/a	50.3	**Mount Olive** (town) Wayne County
47	629	50.3	**Wilson** (city) Wilson County
51	633	50.4	**Asheville** (city) Buncombe County
52	n/a	50.5	**Plymouth** (town) Washington County
53	n/a	50.6	**Clinton** (city) Sampson County
54	683	51.2	**Smithfield** (town) Johnston County
55	n/a	51.3	**Rockingham** (city) Richmond County
56	n/a	51.4	**Elon** (town) Alamance County
57	n/a	51.6	**Dunn** (city) Harnett County
58	717	51.7	**Reidsville** (city) Rockingham County
58	717	51.7	**Salisbury** (city) Rowan County
60	n/a	52.2	**Wadesboro** (town) Anson County
61	767	52.3	**Statesville** (city) Iredell County
62	795	52.5	**Greensboro** (city) Guilford County
62	795	52.5	**Rocky Mount** (city) Nash County
62	n/a	52.5	**Wallace** (town) Duplin County
65	805	52.6	**Sanford** (city) Lee County
66	n/a	52.7	**Wilkesboro** (town) Wilkes County
67	828	52.9	**Shelby** (city) Cleveland County
67	n/a	52.9	**Woodfin** (town) Buncombe County
69	n/a	53.1	**Ayden** (town) Pitt County
70	853	53.3	**Laurinburg** (city) Scotland County
70	853	53.3	**Roanoke Rapids** (city) Halifax County
72	885	53.6	**Raleigh** (city) Wake County
73	n/a	53.9	**Carolina Beach** (town) New Hanover County
74	932	54.1	**Hickory** (city) Catawba County
74	932	54.1	**New Bern** (city) Craven County
74	n/a	54.1	**Siler City** (town) Chatham County
77	n/a	54.3	**Spindale** (town) Rutherford County
78	n/a	54.4	**Marion** (city) McDowell County
79	964	54.5	**Morganton** (city) Burke County
79	964	54.5	**Tarboro** (town) Edgecombe County
81	n/a	54.9	**Farmville** (town) Pitt County
81	n/a	54.9	**Murfreesboro** (town) Hertford County
83	n/a	55.0	**Franklin** (town) Macon County
84	n/a	55.1	**Tabor City** (town) Columbus County
85	1032	55.3	**Burlington** (city) Alamance County
86	n/a	55.7	**Angier** (town) Harnett County
86	n/a	55.7	**Raeford** (city) Hoke County
88	1135	56.2	**Albemarle** (city) Stanly County
88	n/a	56.2	**Brevard** (city) Transylvania County
88	n/a	56.2	**Zebulon** (town) Wake County
91	1151	56.3	**Gastonia** (city) Gaston County
91	1151	56.3	**Winston-Salem** (city) Forsyth County
93	1178	56.5	**Monroe** (city) Union County
93	1178	56.5	**Piney Green** (CDP) Onslow County
95	1225	56.9	**Eden** (city) Rockingham County
95	n/a	56.9	**Northchase** (CDP) New Hanover County
97	n/a	57.0	**Red Springs** (town) Robeson County
97	1229	57.0	**Southern Pines** (town) Moore County
99	1236	57.1	**High Point** (city) Guilford County
99	1236	57.1	**Mount Airy** (city) Surry County
101	1251	57.2	**Kernersville** (town) Forsyth County
102	1274	57.4	**Charlotte** (city) Mecklenburg County
103	n/a	57.6	**Dallas** (town) Gaston County
104	n/a	57.7	**Waynesville** (town) Haywood County
105	n/a	57.8	**Hamlet** (city) Richmond County
105	1322	57.8	**Thomasville** (city) Davidson County
107	1356	58.1	**Graham** (city) Alamance County
108	1388	58.4	**Newton** (city) Catawba County
109	n/a	58.6	**Long View** (town) Catawba County
110	1504	59.3	**Kings Mountain** (city) Cleveland County
110	1504	59.3	**Lenoir** (city) Caldwell County
110	n/a	59.3	**Nashville** (town) Nash County
113	n/a	59.6	**Randleman** (city) Randolph County
114	n/a	59.9	**Shallotte** (town) Brunswick County
114	n/a	59.9	**Yadkinville** (town) Yadkin County
116	n/a	60.0	**Elkin** (town) Surry County
117	n/a	60.9	**Spencer** (town) Rowan County
118	n/a	61.1	**East Rockingham** (CDP) Richmond County
119	n/a	61.2	**Rutherfordton** (town) Rutherford County
119	n/a	61.2	**Windsor** (town) Bertie County
121	n/a	61.4	**Kill Devil Hills** (town) Dare County
121	n/a	61.4	**La Grange** (town) Lenoir County
123	1782	61.5	**Mebane** (city) Alamance County
123	n/a	61.5	**Swansboro** (town) Onslow County
125	n/a	61.7	**Bessemer City** (city) Gaston County
125	n/a	61.7	**Newport** (town) Carteret County
127	n/a	62.1	**Rural Hall** (town) Forsyth County
127	n/a	62.1	**Wingate** (town) Union County
129	n/a	62.3	**Grifton** (town) Pitt County
130	1916	62.8	**Kannapolis** (city) Cabarrus County
131	1987	63.4	**Hope Mills** (town) Cumberland County
132	n/a	64.0	**Black Mountain** (town) Buncombe County
132	2046	64.0	**Mooresville** (town) Iredell County
134	n/a	64.1	**Elroy** (CDP) Wayne County
134	n/a	64.1	**Hillsborough** (town) Orange County
134	n/a	64.1	**Mar-Mac** (CDP) Wayne County
137	n/a	65.1	**Liberty** (town) Randolph County
138	n/a	65.2	**Granite Falls** (town) Caldwell County
138	n/a	65.2	**Sawmills** (town) Caldwell County
140	2185	65.5	**Clayton** (town) Johnston County
140	n/a	65.5	**Sneads Ferry** (CDP) Onslow County
142	n/a	65.7	**South Rosemary** (CDP) Halifax County
143	2230	65.9	**Garner** (town) Wake County
144	n/a	66.0	**China Grove** (town) Rowan County
145	n/a	66.2	**Valdese** (town) Burke County
146	n/a	66.3	**Mocksville** (town) Davie County
147	2297	66.5	**Mount Holly** (city) Gaston County
147	n/a	66.5	**Wendell** (town) Wake County
149	n/a	67.0	**Stanley** (town) Gaston County
150	n/a	67.2	**Erwin** (town) Harnett County

Note: The state column ranks the top/bottom 150 places in the state with population of 2,500 or more. The national column ranks the top/bottom places in the country with population of 10,000 or more. Places that are unincorporated were not considered in the rankings. n/a indicates data not available. Please refer to the User Guide for additional information.

Median Home Value

Top 150 Places Ranked in *Descending* Order

State Rank	Nat'l Rank	Dollars	Place	State Rank	Nat'l Rank	Dollars	Place
1	n/a	569,100	**Marvin** (village) Union County	76	n/a	188,200	**Mountain Home** (CDP) Henderson County
2	n/a	455,200	**Southern Shores** (town) Dare County	77	2388	186,500	**Mooresville** (town) Iredell County
3	n/a	450,000	**Saint James** (town) Brunswick County	78	2396	186,100	**Lewisville** (town) Forsyth County
4	n/a	431,000	**Porters Neck** (CDP) New Hanover County	79	n/a	185,000	**Wilkesboro** (town) Wilkes County
5	n/a	412,800	**Westport** (CDP) Lincoln County	80	2449	180,900	**Murraysville** (CDP) New Hanover County
6	n/a	391,500	**Weddington** (town) Union County	81	n/a	180,800	**Aberdeen** (town) Moore County
7	615	391,300	**Davidson** (town) Mecklenburg County	82	n/a	180,700	**Skippers Corner** (CDP) New Hanover County
8	n/a	390,600	**Emerald Isle** (town) Carteret County	83	2462	180,500	**Durham** (city) Durham County
9	n/a	389,600	**Flat Rock** (village) Henderson County	84	n/a	180,200	**Etowah** (CDP) Henderson County
10	725	367,800	**Chapel Hill** (town) Orange County	85	n/a	178,500	**Brevard** (city) Transylvania County
11	n/a	352,800	**Lake Norman of Catawba** (CDP) Catawba County	86	n/a	178,100	**Fletcher** (town) Henderson County
12	912	337,000	**Carrboro** (town) Orange County	87	n/a	175,000	**Lake Park** (village) Union County
13	n/a	333,700	**Oak Ridge** (town) Guilford County	88	2560	174,500	**Kernersville** (town) Forsyth County
14	941	331,000	**Summerfield** (town) Guilford County	89	n/a	172,800	**Northchase** (CDP) New Hanover County
15	n/a	326,200	**Nags Head** (town) Dare County	90	2595	172,600	**Indian Trail** (town) Union County
16	n/a	321,100	**Kitty Hawk** (town) Dare County	91	n/a	172,100	**Rutherfordton** (town) Rutherford County
17	1141	303,700	**Cary** (town) Wake County	92	n/a	171,600	**Black Mountain** (town) Buncombe County
18	n/a	300,700	**Wesley Chapel** (village) Union County	93	n/a	170,900	**Boiling Spring Lakes** (city) Brunswick County
19	1276	284,500	**Pinehurst** (village) Moore County	94	2638	170,500	**Charlotte** (city) Mecklenburg County
20	1305	280,800	**Boone** (town) Watauga County	95	n/a	169,400	**Midland** (town) Cabarrus County
21	n/a	273,100	**Sunset Beach** (town) Brunswick County	96	2669	168,800	**Knightdale** (town) Wake County
22	n/a	272,200	**Seven Lakes** (CDP) Moore County	97	2684	168,300	**Concord** (city) Cabarrus County
23	n/a	268,300	**Fairview** (CDP) Buncombe County	98	n/a	166,500	**Mineral Springs** (town) Union County
24	n/a	266,900	**Whispering Pines** (village) Moore County	99	2739	165,600	**Garner** (town) Wake County
25	n/a	261,700	**Moyock** (CDP) Currituck County	100	n/a	165,500	**Cramerton** (town) Gaston County
26	1496	261,600	**Morrisville** (town) Wake County	101	n/a	165,100	**Lake Royale** (CDP) Franklin County
27	n/a	260,900	**Kill Devil Hills** (town) Dare County	102	n/a	164,600	**Cullowhee** (CDP) Jackson County
28	1522	259,200	**Wake Forest** (town) Wake County	103	2770	164,300	**Hendersonville** (city) Henderson County
29	n/a	258,700	**Carolina Beach** (town) New Hanover County	104	n/a	163,600	**Bethlehem** (CDP) Alexander County
30	1534	258,500	**Apex** (town) Wake County	105	2783	163,500	**Mebane** (city) Alamance County
31	n/a	257,300	**Bayshore** (CDP) New Hanover County	106	n/a	162,700	**Rockfish** (CDP) Hoke County
32	n/a	252,500	**Fairview** (town) Union County	106	n/a	162,700	**Winterville** (town) Pitt County
33	n/a	251,400	**Lake Junaluska** (CDP) Haywood County	108	n/a	161,500	**Wallburg** (town) Davidson County
34	n/a	251,100	**Myrtle Grove** (CDP) New Hanover County	109	n/a	161,400	**Kings Grant** (CDP) New Hanover County
35	1611	248,000	**Southern Pines** (town) Moore County	110	n/a	160,800	**Midway** (town) Davidson County
36	1613	247,900	**Cornelius** (town) Mecklenburg County	111	n/a	159,900	**Burgaw** (town) Pender County
37	n/a	246,700	**Brices Creek** (CDP) Craven County	111	n/a	159,900	**Washington** (city) Beaufort County
38	n/a	245,800	**Southport** (city) Brunswick County	113	n/a	159,700	**Locust** (city) Stanly County
39	1645	245,300	**Huntersville** (town) Mecklenburg County	114	n/a	159,500	**Gibsonville** (town) Guilford County
40	n/a	243,200	**Oak Island** (town) Brunswick County	115	n/a	158,700	**Newport** (town) Carteret County
41	n/a	239,600	**Rolesville** (town) Wake County	116	2898	158,100	**Hickory** (city) Catawba County
42	n/a	238,600	**Weaverville** (town) Buncombe County	117	n/a	156,900	**Eastover** (town) Cumberland County
43	n/a	236,600	**Ogden** (CDP) New Hanover County	118	n/a	156,300	**Silver Lake** (CDP) New Hanover County
44	1763	236,300	**Holly Springs** (town) Wake County	119	2951	155,800	**Mount Holly** (city) Gaston County
45	n/a	235,200	**Lowesville** (CDP) Lincoln County	120	n/a	153,600	**Creedmoor** (city) Granville County
46	n/a	231,800	**Waxhaw** (town) Union County	120	2993	153,600	**Jacksonville** (city) Onslow County
47	n/a	228,300	**Trent Woods** (town) Craven County	122	3006	152,800	**Belmont** (city) Gaston County
48	1866	226,200	**Wilmington** (city) New Hanover County	123	3013	152,600	**Clayton** (town) Johnston County
49	n/a	224,900	**Fairfield Harbour** (CDP) Craven County	124	n/a	152,300	**James City** (CDP) Craven County
50	n/a	224,700	**Mills River** (town) Henderson County	125	n/a	151,700	**Boiling Springs** (town) Cleveland County
51	1905	222,100	**Harrisburg** (town) Cabarrus County	126	n/a	151,600	**Wrightsboro** (CDP) New Hanover County
52	n/a	217,700	**Hampstead** (CDP) Pender County	127	n/a	149,700	**Pleasant Garden** (town) Guilford County
53	1963	217,600	**Matthews** (town) Mecklenburg County	128	3089	149,600	**Greenville** (city) Pitt County
54	n/a	214,800	**Swansboro** (town) Onslow County	129	n/a	149,400	**Archer Lodge** (town) Johnston County
55	n/a	212,100	**Jamestown** (town) Guilford County	129	n/a	149,400	**Dana** (CDP) Henderson County
56	2053	210,400	**Stallings** (town) Union County	129	3095	149,400	**Elizabeth City** (city) Pasquotank County
57	2107	207,000	**Mint Hill** (town) Mecklenburg County	132	3106	149,000	**New Bern** (city) Craven County
57	2107	207,000	**Raleigh** (city) Wake County	133	3107	148,800	**Monroe** (city) Union County
59	2119	206,300	**Clemmons** (village) Forsyth County	134	n/a	148,300	**Waynesville** (town) Haywood County
60	n/a	204,200	**Forest Oaks** (CDP) Guilford County	135	n/a	148,000	**Sneads Ferry** (CDP) Onslow County
61	n/a	203,700	**Pittsboro** (town) Chatham County	136	3143	147,400	**Greensboro** (city) Guilford County
62	n/a	203,000	**Red Oak** (town) Nash County	137	n/a	147,000	**Woodfin** (town) Buncombe County
63	n/a	201,600	**Royal Pines** (CDP) Buncombe County	138	3158	146,400	**Piney Green** (CDP) Onslow County
64	n/a	201,300	**Carolina Shores** (town) Brunswick County	139	3160	146,200	**High Point** (city) Guilford County
65	n/a	200,300	**Unionville** (town) Union County	139	n/a	146,200	**Welcome** (CDP) Davidson County
66	n/a	198,300	**Elon** (town) Alamance County	141	n/a	145,800	**River Road** (CDP) Beaufort County
67	2221	197,600	**Leland** (town) Brunswick County	142	n/a	145,400	**Granite Quarry** (town) Rowan County
68	n/a	196,500	**Beaufort** (town) Carteret County	143	n/a	145,200	**Pineville** (town) Mecklenburg County
68	n/a	196,500	**Stokesdale** (town) Guilford County	144	n/a	145,000	**Franklin** (town) Macon County
70	2235	196,300	**Asheville** (city) Buncombe County	145	n/a	144,500	**Mocksville** (town) Davie County
71	n/a	193,700	**Shallotte** (town) Brunswick County	146	n/a	142,500	**Half Moon** (CDP) Onslow County
72	n/a	193,600	**Hillsborough** (town) Orange County	147	n/a	142,100	**King** (city) Stokes County
73	n/a	193,400	**River Bend** (town) Craven County	147	n/a	142,100	**Tyro** (CDP) Davidson County
74	2306	191,500	**Fuquay-Varina** (town) Wake County	149	3272	140,400	**Winston-Salem** (city) Forsyth County
75	n/a	191,300	**Morehead City** (town) Carteret County	150	3309	138,100	**Sanford** (city) Lee County

Note: The state column ranks the top/bottom 150 places in the state with population of 2,500 or more. The national column ranks the top/bottom places in the country with population of 10,000 or more. Places that are unincorporated were not considered in the rankings. n/a indicates data not available. Please refer to the User Guide for additional information.

Median Home Value

Top 150 Places Ranked in *Ascending* Order

State Rank	Nat'l Rank	Dollars	Place
1	n/a	47,500	**East Rockingham** (CDP) Richmond County
2	n/a	64,400	**South Rosemary** (CDP) Halifax County
3	n/a	68,900	**Pembroke** (town) Robeson County
4	n/a	69,000	**La Grange** (town) Lenoir County
5	n/a	69,900	**Fairmont** (town) Robeson County
6	n/a	73,600	**Enfield** (town) Halifax County
7	n/a	74,800	**Red Springs** (town) Robeson County
8	n/a	75,100	**Warsaw** (town) Duplin County
9	n/a	76,200	**Polkton** (town) Anson County
10	n/a	79,500	**Selma** (town) Johnston County
11	n/a	82,100	**Tabor City** (town) Columbus County
12	246	82,500	**Eden** (city) Rockingham County
13	n/a	83,800	**Brogden** (CDP) Wayne County
14	n/a	83,900	**Marion** (city) McDowell County
15	n/a	84,200	**Mount Olive** (town) Wayne County
16	n/a	84,700	**Williamston** (town) Martin County
17	n/a	86,200	**Icard** (CDP) Burke County
18	n/a	87,100	**Long View** (town) Catawba County
19	n/a	87,400	**Windsor** (town) Bertie County
20	n/a	87,600	**Erwin** (town) Harnett County
21	n/a	88,600	**Mar-Mac** (CDP) Wayne County
22	n/a	88,800	**Roxboro** (city) Person County
23	n/a	90,100	**Spindale** (town) Rutherford County
24	n/a	90,200	**Wadesboro** (town) Anson County
25	n/a	90,900	**Ahoskie** (town) Hertford County
26	n/a	91,000	**Elroy** (CDP) Wayne County
27	n/a	91,200	**Rockingham** (city) Richmond County
28	n/a	91,400	**Plymouth** (town) Washington County
29	n/a	92,100	**Hamlet** (city) Richmond County
30	443	92,900	**Laurinburg** (city) Scotland County
30	443	92,900	**Spring Lake** (town) Cumberland County
32	n/a	93,900	**Elizabethtown** (town) Bladen County
33	n/a	94,200	**Buies Creek** (CDP) Harnett County
33	n/a	94,200	**Whiteville** (city) Columbus County
35	481	94,700	**Tarboro** (town) Edgecombe County
36	n/a	95,000	**Bessemer City** (city) Gaston County
37	n/a	95,500	**Troy** (town) Montgomery County
38	n/a	95,700	**Siler City** (town) Chatham County
39	n/a	96,500	**Forest City** (town) Rutherford County
40	n/a	96,800	**Sawmills** (town) Caldwell County
41	n/a	98,100	**Spencer** (town) Rowan County
42	575	100,300	**Lexington** (city) Davidson County
43	579	100,500	**Lumberton** (city) Robeson County
44	n/a	100,600	**Maiden** (town) Catawba County
45	n/a	103,400	**Ranlo** (town) Gaston County
46	n/a	104,300	**Cherryville** (city) Gaston County
47	656	105,100	**Thomasville** (city) Davidson County
48	n/a	105,200	**Ayden** (town) Pitt County
49	662	105,300	**Lenoir** (city) Caldwell County
50	668	105,500	**Rocky Mount** (city) Nash County
51	n/a	105,600	**Benson** (town) Johnston County
51	669	105,600	**Kinston** (city) Lenoir County
53	672	105,700	**Kings Mountain** (city) Cleveland County
54	n/a	107,500	**Dunn** (city) Harnett County
55	737	109,600	**Newton** (city) Catawba County
56	n/a	110,100	**Gamewell** (town) Caldwell County
57	n/a	110,200	**China Grove** (town) Rowan County
58	n/a	110,900	**Grifton** (town) Pitt County
59	n/a	111,100	**Edenton** (town) Chowan County
59	n/a	111,100	**Zebulon** (town) Wake County
61	776	111,600	**Goldsboro** (city) Wayne County
62	n/a	111,900	**Lowell** (city) Gaston County
63	785	112,100	**Reidsville** (city) Rockingham County
63	785	112,100	**Roanoke Rapids** (city) Halifax County
65	n/a	112,200	**Lillington** (town) Harnett County
66	n/a	112,300	**East Flat Rock** (CDP) Henderson County
67	n/a	113,000	**Stanley** (town) Gaston County
68	n/a	114,400	**Yadkinville** (town) Yadkin County
69	n/a	115,100	**Cajah's Mountain** (town) Caldwell County
70	n/a	115,500	**Louisburg** (town) Franklin County
71	n/a	115,800	**Wallace** (town) Duplin County
72	874	115,900	**Asheboro** (city) Randolph County
73	n/a	116,000	**Enochville** (CDP) Rowan County
74	n/a	116,100	**Murfreesboro** (town) Hertford County
75	889	116,800	**Henderson** (city) Vance County
76	n/a	117,900	**Walkertown** (town) Forsyth County
77	922	118,100	**Shelby** (city) Cleveland County
78	n/a	119,100	**Liberty** (town) Randolph County
79	969	119,800	**Albemarle** (city) Stanly County
80	n/a	120,600	**Valdese** (town) Burke County
81	n/a	120,900	**Randleman** (city) Randolph County
82	1008	121,600	**Salisbury** (city) Rowan County
83	n/a	121,700	**Granite Falls** (town) Caldwell County
84	n/a	121,800	**Landis** (town) Rowan County
85	n/a	122,300	**Wentworth** (town) Rockingham County
86	n/a	123,400	**Farmville** (town) Pitt County
87	n/a	123,500	**Dallas** (town) Gaston County
87	n/a	123,500	**Glen Raven** (CDP) Alamance County
89	n/a	123,700	**Clinton** (city) Sampson County
90	n/a	124,100	**Saint Stephens** (CDP) Catawba County
91	n/a	124,400	**Raeford** (city) Hoke County
92	n/a	125,000	**Hudson** (town) Caldwell County
93	n/a	125,500	**Trinity** (city) Randolph County
94	1083	125,700	**Graham** (city) Alamance County
95	1085	125,800	**Fayetteville** (city) Cumberland County
96	n/a	126,000	**Oxford** (city) Granville County
97	1088	126,100	**Burlington** (city) Alamance County
98	n/a	126,900	**Mountain View** (CDP) Catawba County
99	n/a	127,200	**Wendell** (town) Wake County
100	1113	127,700	**Kannapolis** (city) Cabarrus County
101	n/a	128,800	**Butner** (town) Granville County
102	n/a	129,300	**Sylva** (town) Jackson County
103	1157	129,600	**Mount Airy** (city) Surry County
104	1166	129,800	**Lincolnton** (city) Lincoln County
105	n/a	129,900	**Swannanoa** (CDP) Buncombe County
106	1170	130,000	**Morganton** (city) Burke County
107	1182	130,500	**Hope Mills** (town) Cumberland County
108	n/a	130,700	**Canton** (town) Haywood County
109	1191	131,000	**Wilson** (city) Wilson County
110	n/a	133,000	**Elkin** (town) Surry County
111	1237	133,100	**Smithfield** (town) Johnston County
112	1244	133,500	**Statesville** (city) Iredell County
112	n/a	133,500	**Wingate** (town) Union County
114	n/a	134,000	**Conover** (city) Catawba County
115	n/a	134,200	**Angier** (town) Harnett County
116	n/a	134,900	**Rural Hall** (town) Forsyth County
117	1282	135,500	**Archdale** (city) Randolph County
118	n/a	135,800	**Nashville** (town) Nash County
119	1292	135,900	**Gastonia** (city) Gaston County
120	n/a	137,300	**North Wilkesboro** (town) Wilkes County
121	1321	137,600	**Havelock** (city) Craven County
122	1337	138,100	**Sanford** (city) Lee County
123	1376	140,400	**Winston-Salem** (city) Forsyth County
124	n/a	142,100	**King** (city) Stokes County
124	n/a	142,100	**Tyro** (CDP) Davidson County
126	n/a	142,500	**Half Moon** (CDP) Onslow County
127	n/a	144,500	**Mocksville** (town) Davie County
128	n/a	145,000	**Franklin** (town) Macon County
129	n/a	145,200	**Pineville** (town) Mecklenburg County
130	n/a	145,400	**Granite Quarry** (town) Rowan County
131	n/a	145,800	**River Road** (CDP) Beaufort County
132	1485	146,200	**High Point** (city) Guilford County
132	n/a	146,200	**Welcome** (CDP) Davidson County
134	1489	146,400	**Piney Green** (CDP) Onslow County
135	n/a	147,000	**Woodfin** (town) Buncombe County
136	1502	147,400	**Greensboro** (city) Guilford County
137	n/a	148,000	**Sneads Ferry** (CDP) Onslow County
138	n/a	148,300	**Waynesville** (town) Haywood County
139	1540	148,800	**Monroe** (city) Union County
140	1542	149,000	**New Bern** (city) Craven County
141	n/a	149,400	**Archer Lodge** (town) Johnston County
141	n/a	149,400	**Dana** (CDP) Henderson County
141	1550	149,400	**Elizabeth City** (city) Pasquotank County
144	1557	149,600	**Greenville** (city) Pitt County
145	n/a	149,700	**Pleasant Garden** (town) Guilford County
146	n/a	151,600	**Wrightsboro** (CDP) New Hanover County
147	n/a	151,700	**Boiling Springs** (town) Cleveland County
148	n/a	152,300	**James City** (CDP) Craven County
149	1633	152,600	**Clayton** (town) Johnston County
150	1638	152,800	**Belmont** (city) Gaston County

Note: The state column ranks the top/bottom 150 places in the state with population of 2,500 or more. The national column ranks the top/bottom places in the country with population of 10,000 or more. Places that are unincorporated were not considered in the rankings. n/a indicates data not available. Please refer to the User Guide for additional information.

Median Year Structure Built

Top 150 Places Ranked in *Descending* Order

State Rank	Nat'l Rank	Year	Place	State Rank	Nat'l Rank	Year	Place
1	8	2004	**Leland** (town) Brunswick County	72	n/a	1989	**Red Oak** (town) Nash County
2	n/a	2003	**Waxhaw** (town) Union County	77	n/a	1988	**Aberdeen** (town) Moore County
3	56	2002	**Holly Springs** (town) Wake County	77	778	1988	**Charlotte** (city) Mecklenburg County
3	n/a	2002	**Marvin** (village) Union County	77	n/a	1988	**Cullowhee** (CDP) Jackson County
3	n/a	2002	**Rolesville** (town) Wake County	77	n/a	1988	**Elon** (town) Alamance County
3	n/a	2002	**Saint James** (town) Brunswick County	77	n/a	1988	**Emerald Isle** (town) Carteret County
7	84	2001	**Fuquay-Varina** (town) Wake County	77	n/a	1988	**James City** (CDP) Craven County
7	84	2001	**Harrisburg** (town) Cabarrus County	77	n/a	1988	**Mineral Springs** (town) Union County
7	84	2001	**Morrisville** (town) Wake County	77	778	1988	**Mount Holly** (city) Gaston County
7	n/a	2001	**Porters Neck** (CDP) New Hanover County	77	n/a	1988	**Oak Island** (town) Brunswick County
7	n/a	2001	**Shallotte** (town) Brunswick County	77	778	1988	**Spring Lake** (town) Cumberland County
7	84	2001	**Wake Forest** (town) Wake County	87	n/a	1987	**Elroy** (CDP) Wayne County
7	n/a	2001	**Wesley Chapel** (village) Union County	87	851	1987	**Garner** (town) Wake County
7	n/a	2001	**Winterville** (town) Pitt County	87	n/a	1987	**Kitty Hawk** (town) Dare County
15	121	2000	**Clayton** (town) Johnston County	87	n/a	1987	**Mocksville** (town) Davie County
15	121	2000	**Indian Trail** (town) Union County	87	n/a	1987	**Nags Head** (town) Dare County
15	121	2000	**Knightdale** (town) Wake County	87	n/a	1987	**Pittsboro** (town) Chatham County
15	n/a	2000	**Westport** (CDP) Lincoln County	87	n/a	1987	**Southern Shores** (town) Dare County
19	153	1999	**Huntersville** (town) Mecklenburg County	87	n/a	1987	**Southport** (city) Brunswick County
19	153	1999	**Murraysville** (CDP) New Hanover County	87	n/a	1987	**Unionville** (town) Union County
21	181	1998	**Apex** (town) Wake County	96	n/a	1986	**Carolina Beach** (town) New Hanover County
21	n/a	1998	**Boiling Spring Lakes** (city) Brunswick County	96	933	1986	**Durham** (city) Durham County
21	n/a	1998	**Creedmoor** (city) Granville County	96	n/a	1986	**Eastover** (town) Cumberland County
21	n/a	1998	**Lake Royale** (CDP) Franklin County	96	933	1986	**Mint Hill** (town) Mecklenburg County
21	n/a	1998	**Rockfish** (CDP) Hoke County	96	n/a	1986	**Silver Lake** (CDP) New Hanover County
21	181	1998	**Stallings** (town) Union County	96	n/a	1986	**Skippers Corner** (CDP) New Hanover County
27	n/a	1997	**Carolina Shores** (town) Brunswick County	102	1031	1985	**Archdale** (city) Randolph County
27	n/a	1997	**Lake Park** (village) Union County	102	n/a	1985	**Bethlehem** (CDP) Alexander County
27	n/a	1997	**Lowesville** (CDP) Lincoln County	102	n/a	1985	**Midland** (town) Cabarrus County
27	220	1997	**Mooresville** (town) Iredell County	102	n/a	1985	**Newport** (town) Carteret County
27	n/a	1997	**Oak Ridge** (town) Guilford County	102	n/a	1985	**Weaverville** (town) Buncombe County
32	n/a	1996	**Archer Lodge** (town) Johnston County	107	1133	1984	**Carrboro** (town) Orange County
32	266	1996	**Cornelius** (town) Mecklenburg County	107	1133	1984	**Chapel Hill** (town) Orange County
32	n/a	1996	**Hampstead** (CDP) Pender County	107	n/a	1984	**Half Moon** (CDP) Onslow County
32	n/a	1996	**Northchase** (CDP) New Hanover County	107	1133	1984	**Havelock** (city) Craven County
32	n/a	1996	**Stokesdale** (town) Guilford County	107	n/a	1984	**King** (city) Stokes County
32	266	1996	**Summerfield** (town) Guilford County	107	1133	1984	**Lewisville** (town) Forsyth County
38	n/a	1995	**Brices Creek** (CDP) Craven County	107	n/a	1984	**Tyro** (CDP) Davidson County
38	312	1995	**Cary** (town) Wake County	107	n/a	1984	**Wingate** (town) Union County
38	312	1995	**Davidson** (town) Mecklenburg County	107	n/a	1984	**Zebulon** (town) Wake County
38	n/a	1995	**Fletcher** (town) Henderson County	116	1238	1983	**High Point** (city) Guilford County
38	n/a	1995	**Moyock** (CDP) Currituck County	116	n/a	1983	**Jamestown** (town) Guilford County
38	n/a	1995	**Seven Lakes** (CDP) Moore County	116	n/a	1983	**Kill Devil Hills** (town) Dare County
38	n/a	1995	**Sunset Beach** (town) Brunswick County	116	n/a	1983	**Locust** (city) Stanly County
45	369	1994	**Pinehurst** (village) Moore County	116	n/a	1983	**Mar-Mac** (CDP) Wayne County
46	n/a	1993	**Bayshore** (CDP) New Hanover County	116	n/a	1983	**Midway** (town) Davidson County
46	n/a	1993	**Buies Creek** (CDP) Harnett County	116	1238	1983	**Monroe** (city) Union County
46	435	1993	**Greenville** (city) Pitt County	116	n/a	1983	**Mountain Home** (CDP) Henderson County
46	435	1993	**Mebane** (city) Alamance County	116	n/a	1983	**River Bend** (town) Craven County
46	n/a	1993	**Ogden** (CDP) New Hanover County	116	n/a	1983	**Sawmills** (town) Caldwell County
51	n/a	1992	**Boiling Springs** (town) Cleveland County	116	1238	1983	**Wilmington** (city) New Hanover County
51	501	1992	**Concord** (city) Cabarrus County	127	n/a	1982	**Angier** (town) Harnett County
51	501	1992	**Hope Mills** (town) Cumberland County	127	1344	1982	**Fayetteville** (city) Cumberland County
51	n/a	1992	**Sneads Ferry** (CDP) Onslow County	127	n/a	1982	**Granite Falls** (town) Caldwell County
55	n/a	1991	**Butner** (town) Granville County	127	n/a	1982	**Hillsborough** (town) Orange County
55	566	1991	**Clemmons** (village) Forsyth County	127	1344	1982	**Jacksonville** (city) Onslow County
55	n/a	1991	**Cramerton** (town) Gaston County	127	1344	1982	**New Bern** (city) Craven County
55	n/a	1991	**Fairview** (CDP) Buncombe County	127	1344	1982	**Southern Pines** (town) Moore County
55	n/a	1991	**Glen Raven** (CDP) Alamance County	127	n/a	1982	**Welcome** (CDP) Davidson County
55	n/a	1991	**Lake Norman of Catawba** (CDP) Catawba County	127	n/a	1982	**Whispering Pines** (village) Moore County
55	n/a	1991	**Weddington** (town) Union County	136	1463	1981	**Boone** (town) Watauga County
62	n/a	1990	**Dana** (CDP) Henderson County	136	n/a	1981	**East Flat Rock** (CDP) Henderson County
62	n/a	1990	**Fairfield Harbour** (CDP) Craven County	136	n/a	1981	**Granite Quarry** (town) Rowan County
62	n/a	1990	**Fairview** (town) Union County	136	1463	1981	**Greensboro** (city) Guilford County
62	n/a	1990	**Flat Rock** (village) Henderson County	136	1463	1981	**Hendersonville** (city) Henderson County
62	651	1990	**Matthews** (town) Mecklenburg County	136	n/a	1981	**Morehead City** (town) Carteret County
62	n/a	1990	**Myrtle Grove** (CDP) New Hanover County	136	n/a	1981	**Wallburg** (town) Davidson County
62	n/a	1990	**Pineville** (town) Mecklenburg County	136	n/a	1981	**Wendell** (town) Wake County
62	651	1990	**Piney Green** (CDP) Onslow County	136	n/a	1981	**Wilkesboro** (town) Wilkes County
62	651	1990	**Raleigh** (city) Wake County	145	1563	1980	**Belmont** (city) Gaston County
62	n/a	1990	**Swansboro** (town) Onslow County	145	n/a	1980	**Dallas** (town) Gaston County
72	n/a	1989	**Etowah** (CDP) Henderson County	145	1563	1980	**Hickory** (city) Catawba County
72	n/a	1989	**Gibsonville** (town) Guilford County	145	n/a	1980	**Kings Grant** (CDP) New Hanover County
72	715	1989	**Kernersville** (town) Forsyth County	149	n/a	1979	**Elizabethtown** (town) Bladen County
72	n/a	1989	**Mills River** (town) Henderson County	149	n/a	1979	**Royal Pines** (CDP) Buncombe County

Note: The state column ranks the top/bottom 150 places in the state with population of 2,500 or more. The national column ranks the top/bottom places in the country with population of 10,000 or more. Places that are unincorporated were not considered in the rankings. n/a indicates data not available. Please refer to the User Guide for additional information.

Median Year Structure Built

Top 150 Places Ranked in *Ascending* Order

State Rank	Nat'l Rank	Year	Place
1	n/a	1951	**Spencer** (town) Rowan County
2	n/a	1954	**Canton** (town) Haywood County
3	n/a	1959	**Long View** (town) Catawba County
4	n/a	1960	**Enfield** (town) Halifax County
4	n/a	1960	**Erwin** (town) Harnett County
4	n/a	1960	**Spindale** (town) Rutherford County
7	961	1961	**Eden** (city) Rockingham County
7	n/a	1961	**Edenton** (town) Chowan County
7	n/a	1961	**Marion** (city) McDowell County
10	n/a	1962	**Red Springs** (town) Robeson County
10	n/a	1962	**Wadesboro** (town) Anson County
12	1097	1963	**Albemarle** (city) Stanly County
12	n/a	1963	**Cherryville** (city) Gaston County
12	n/a	1963	**China Grove** (town) Rowan County
12	n/a	1963	**Troy** (town) Montgomery County
16	1172	1964	**Lexington** (city) Davidson County
16	1172	1964	**Mount Airy** (city) Surry County
16	n/a	1964	**Plymouth** (town) Washington County
16	1172	1964	**Reidsville** (city) Rockingham County
20	n/a	1965	**Elkin** (town) Surry County
20	1258	1965	**Kinston** (city) Lenoir County
20	n/a	1965	**Valdese** (town) Burke County
23	n/a	1966	**Forest City** (town) Rutherford County
23	n/a	1966	**Hamlet** (city) Richmond County
23	1334	1966	**Henderson** (city) Vance County
23	1334	1966	**Morganton** (city) Burke County
23	1334	1966	**Roanoke Rapids** (city) Halifax County
23	n/a	1966	**Roxboro** (city) Person County
23	n/a	1966	**Windsor** (town) Bertie County
30	n/a	1967	**East Rockingham** (CDP) Richmond County
30	1444	1967	**Elizabeth City** (city) Pasquotank County
30	n/a	1967	**Enochville** (CDP) Rowan County
30	n/a	1967	**Grifton** (town) Pitt County
30	n/a	1967	**Murfreesboro** (town) Hertford County
30	n/a	1967	**North Wilkesboro** (town) Wilkes County
30	n/a	1967	**Rockingham** (city) Richmond County
30	n/a	1967	**Williamston** (town) Martin County
38	n/a	1968	**Ahoskie** (town) Hertford County
38	n/a	1968	**Fairmont** (town) Robeson County
38	n/a	1968	**Rutherfordton** (town) Rutherford County
41	n/a	1969	**Bessemer City** (city) Gaston County
41	n/a	1969	**Maiden** (town) Catawba County
41	n/a	1969	**Mount Olive** (town) Wayne County
41	n/a	1969	**Oxford** (city) Granville County
41	1642	1969	**Shelby** (city) Cleveland County
41	n/a	1969	**Sylva** (town) Jackson County
47	n/a	1970	**Clinton** (city) Sampson County
47	n/a	1970	**Lowell** (city) Gaston County
47	n/a	1970	**Tabor City** (town) Columbus County
47	n/a	1970	**Waynesville** (town) Haywood County
51	n/a	1971	**Brevard** (city) Transylvania County
51	1847	1971	**Kings Mountain** (city) Cleveland County
51	n/a	1971	**Landis** (town) Rowan County
51	1847	1971	**Lincolnton** (city) Lincoln County
51	n/a	1971	**Louisburg** (town) Franklin County
51	1847	1971	**Newton** (city) Catawba County
51	n/a	1971	**South Rosemary** (CDP) Halifax County
51	1847	1971	**Statesville** (city) Iredell County
59	1989	1972	**Asheville** (city) Buncombe County
59	n/a	1972	**Beaufort** (town) Carteret County
59	n/a	1972	**Benson** (town) Johnston County
59	1989	1972	**Goldsboro** (city) Wayne County
59	1989	1972	**Kannapolis** (city) Cabarrus County
59	1989	1972	**Lenoir** (city) Caldwell County
59	n/a	1972	**Lillington** (town) Harnett County
59	1989	1972	**Salisbury** (city) Rowan County
59	1989	1972	**Smithfield** (town) Johnston County
59	1989	1972	**Tarboro** (town) Edgecombe County
59	n/a	1972	**Whiteville** (city) Columbus County
70	n/a	1973	**Black Mountain** (town) Buncombe County
70	2097	1973	**Burlington** (city) Alamance County
70	n/a	1973	**Dunn** (city) Harnett County
70	n/a	1973	**Farmville** (town) Pitt County
70	2097	1973	**Laurinburg** (city) Scotland County
70	n/a	1973	**Liberty** (town) Randolph County
70	2097	1973	**Lumberton** (city) Robeson County
70	n/a	1973	**Siler City** (town) Chatham County
70	n/a	1973	**Stanley** (town) Gaston County
70	n/a	1973	**Wallace** (town) Duplin County
70	n/a	1973	**Warsaw** (town) Duplin County
70	n/a	1973	**Washington** (city) Beaufort County
70	n/a	1973	**Yadkinville** (town) Yadkin County
83	n/a	1974	**Ayden** (town) Pitt County
83	n/a	1974	**Cajah's Mountain** (town) Caldwell County
83	n/a	1974	**Ranlo** (town) Gaston County
83	n/a	1974	**Selma** (town) Johnston County
83	2208	1974	**Winston-Salem** (city) Forsyth County
88	2327	1975	**Gastonia** (city) Gaston County
88	n/a	1975	**La Grange** (town) Lenoir County
88	n/a	1975	**Pembroke** (town) Robeson County
88	n/a	1975	**Trent Woods** (town) Craven County
92	2466	1976	**Asheboro** (city) Randolph County
92	2466	1976	**Graham** (city) Alamance County
92	n/a	1976	**Hudson** (town) Caldwell County
92	n/a	1976	**Icard** (CDP) Burke County
92	n/a	1976	**Pleasant Garden** (town) Guilford County
92	n/a	1976	**Randleman** (city) Randolph County
92	2466	1976	**Thomasville** (city) Davidson County
92	n/a	1976	**Woodfin** (town) Buncombe County
100	n/a	1977	**Brogden** (CDP) Wayne County
100	n/a	1977	**Burgaw** (town) Pender County
100	n/a	1977	**Franklin** (town) Macon County
100	n/a	1977	**Gamewell** (town) Caldwell County
100	n/a	1977	**Lake Junaluska** (CDP) Haywood County
100	n/a	1977	**Nashville** (town) Nash County
100	n/a	1977	**Raeford** (city) Hoke County
100	n/a	1977	**River Road** (CDP) Beaufort County
100	2606	1977	**Rocky Mount** (city) Nash County
100	n/a	1977	**Saint Stephens** (CDP) Catawba County
100	n/a	1977	**Walkertown** (town) Forsyth County
100	n/a	1977	**Wentworth** (town) Rockingham County
112	n/a	1978	**Conover** (city) Catawba County
112	n/a	1978	**Forest Oaks** (CDP) Guilford County
112	n/a	1978	**Mountain View** (CDP) Catawba County
112	n/a	1978	**Polkton** (town) Anson County
112	n/a	1978	**Rural Hall** (town) Forsyth County
112	2725	1978	**Sanford** (city) Lee County
112	n/a	1978	**Swannanoa** (CDP) Buncombe County
112	n/a	1978	**Trinity** (city) Randolph County
120	n/a	1979	**Elizabethtown** (town) Bladen County
120	n/a	1979	**Royal Pines** (CDP) Buncombe County
120	2862	1979	**Wilson** (city) Wilson County
120	n/a	1979	**Wrightsboro** (CDP) New Hanover County
124	2989	1980	**Belmont** (city) Gaston County
124	n/a	1980	**Dallas** (town) Gaston County
124	2989	1980	**Hickory** (city) Catawba County
124	n/a	1980	**Kings Grant** (CDP) New Hanover County
128	3094	1981	**Boone** (town) Watauga County
128	n/a	1981	**East Flat Rock** (CDP) Henderson County
128	n/a	1981	**Granite Quarry** (town) Rowan County
128	3094	1981	**Greensboro** (city) Guilford County
128	3094	1981	**Hendersonville** (city) Henderson County
128	n/a	1981	**Morehead City** (town) Carteret County
128	n/a	1981	**Wallburg** (town) Davidson County
128	n/a	1981	**Wendell** (town) Wake County
128	n/a	1981	**Wilkesboro** (town) Wilkes County
137	n/a	1982	**Angier** (town) Harnett County
137	3194	1982	**Fayetteville** (city) Cumberland County
137	n/a	1982	**Granite Falls** (town) Caldwell County
137	n/a	1982	**Hillsborough** (town) Orange County
137	3194	1982	**Jacksonville** (city) Onslow County
137	3194	1982	**New Bern** (city) Craven County
137	3194	1982	**Southern Pines** (town) Moore County
137	n/a	1982	**Welcome** (CDP) Davidson County
137	n/a	1982	**Whispering Pines** (village) Moore County
146	3313	1983	**High Point** (city) Guilford County
146	n/a	1983	**Jamestown** (town) Guilford County
146	n/a	1983	**Kill Devil Hills** (town) Dare County
146	n/a	1983	**Locust** (city) Stanly County
146	n/a	1983	**Mar-Mac** (CDP) Wayne County

Note: *The state column ranks the top/bottom 150 places in the state with population of 2,500 or more. The national column ranks the top/bottom places in the country with population of 10,000 or more. Places that are unincorporated were not considered in the rankings. n/a indicates data not available. Please refer to the User Guide for additional information.*

Homeowner Vacancy Rate

Top 150 Places Ranked in *Descending* Order

State Rank	Nat'l Rank	Percent	Place	State Rank	Nat'l Rank	Percent	Place
1	n/a	12.0	**Oak Island** (town) Brunswick County	75	539	3.8	**Graham** (city) Alamance County
2	n/a	11.5	**Carolina Beach** (town) New Hanover County	75	539	3.8	**Hickory** (city) Catawba County
3	n/a	10.2	**Southport** (city) Brunswick County	75	539	3.8	**Morganton** (city) Burke County
4	n/a	9.2	**Nags Head** (town) Dare County	79	589	3.7	**Asheville** (city) Buncombe County
4	n/a	9.2	**Shallotte** (town) Brunswick County	79	n/a	3.7	**Cramerton** (town) Gaston County
6	n/a	7.7	**Sunset Beach** (town) Brunswick County	79	n/a	3.7	**Fairfield Harbour** (CDP) Craven County
7	n/a	7.4	**Washington** (city) Beaufort County	79	589	3.7	**Winston-Salem** (city) Forsyth County
8	n/a	7.2	**Lillington** (town) Harnett County	83	n/a	3.6	**Aberdeen** (town) Moore County
9	n/a	7.1	**Beaufort** (town) Carteret County	83	n/a	3.6	**Dallas** (town) Gaston County
9	41	7.1	**Boone** (town) Watauga County	83	641	3.6	**Gastonia** (city) Gaston County
11	n/a	6.6	**Emerald Isle** (town) Carteret County	83	641	3.6	**Henderson** (city) Vance County
11	n/a	6.6	**Swansboro** (town) Onslow County	83	641	3.6	**Kannapolis** (city) Cabarrus County
13	67	6.4	**Hendersonville** (city) Henderson County	83	641	3.6	**Mount Airy** (city) Surry County
14	n/a	6.3	**Carolina Shores** (town) Brunswick County	83	n/a	3.6	**Oxford** (city) Granville County
14	n/a	6.3	**Lake Royale** (CDP) Franklin County	83	641	3.6	**Pinehurst** (village) Moore County
16	83	6.2	**Davidson** (town) Mecklenburg County	83	n/a	3.6	**Porters Neck** (CDP) New Hanover County
16	n/a	6.2	**Spindale** (town) Rutherford County	92	n/a	3.5	**Bessemer City** (city) Gaston County
18	n/a	6.1	**Angier** (town) Harnett County	92	702	3.5	**Goldsboro** (city) Wayne County
19	n/a	6.0	**Franklin** (town) Macon County	92	n/a	3.5	**King** (city) Stokes County
20	n/a	5.6	**Benson** (town) Johnston County	92	702	3.5	**Mooresville** (town) Iredell County
21	n/a	5.5	**Burgaw** (town) Pender County	92	702	3.5	**Newton** (city) Catawba County
22	n/a	5.4	**Edenton** (town) Chowan County	92	702	3.5	**Rocky Mount** (city) Nash County
22	n/a	5.4	**Spencer** (town) Rowan County	92	n/a	3.5	**Valdese** (town) Burke County
24	147	5.3	**New Bern** (city) Craven County	92	n/a	3.5	**Waxhaw** (town) Union County
24	147	5.3	**Statesville** (city) Iredell County	100	765	3.4	**Charlotte** (city) Mecklenburg County
26	158	5.2	**Elizabeth City** (city) Pasquotank County	100	n/a	3.4	**Farmville** (town) Pitt County
26	n/a	5.2	**Flat Rock** (village) Henderson County	100	n/a	3.4	**Glen Raven** (CDP) Alamance County
28	169	5.1	**Knightdale** (town) Wake County	100	765	3.4	**Greensboro** (city) Guilford County
28	n/a	5.1	**Locust** (city) Stanly County	100	n/a	3.4	**Landis** (town) Rowan County
28	n/a	5.1	**North Wilkesboro** (town) Wilkes County	100	n/a	3.4	**Marion** (city) McDowell County
31	n/a	5.0	**Rutherfordton** (town) Rutherford County	100	765	3.4	**Morrisville** (town) Wake County
31	185	5.0	**Shelby** (city) Cleveland County	100	n/a	3.4	**Red Springs** (town) Robeson County
33	n/a	4.9	**Brevard** (city) Transylvania County	100	n/a	3.4	**Sylva** (town) Jackson County
34	242	4.7	**Fuquay-Varina** (town) Wake County	100	n/a	3.4	**Whiteville** (city) Columbus County
34	n/a	4.7	**Kill Devil Hills** (town) Dare County	100	n/a	3.4	**Williamston** (town) Martin County
34	242	4.7	**Lexington** (city) Davidson County	100	765	3.4	**Wilson** (city) Wilson County
34	n/a	4.7	**Louisburg** (town) Franklin County	112	841	3.3	**Cornelius** (town) Mecklenburg County
34	242	4.7	**Salisbury** (city) Rowan County	112	841	3.3	**Fayetteville** (city) Cumberland County
34	n/a	4.7	**Wallace** (town) Duplin County	112	n/a	3.3	**Fletcher** (town) Henderson County
34	n/a	4.7	**Wilkesboro** (town) Wilkes County	112	841	3.3	**Lincolnton** (city) Lincoln County
41	263	4.6	**Clayton** (town) Johnston County	112	n/a	3.3	**Rockingham** (city) Richmond County
41	n/a	4.6	**Plymouth** (town) Washington County	112	841	3.3	**Sanford** (city) Lee County
41	n/a	4.6	**Waynesville** (town) Haywood County	112	n/a	3.3	**Siler City** (town) Chatham County
44	287	4.5	**Greenville** (city) Pitt County	112	n/a	3.3	**Silver Lake** (CDP) New Hanover County
44	n/a	4.5	**Lake Junaluska** (CDP) Haywood County	112	841	3.3	**Thomasville** (city) Davidson County
44	n/a	4.5	**Rolesville** (town) Wake County	112	n/a	3.3	**Warsaw** (town) Duplin County
47	n/a	4.4	**Ahoskie** (town) Hertford County	112	n/a	3.3	**Wendell** (town) Wake County
47	n/a	4.4	**Selma** (town) Johnston County	123	932	3.2	**Albemarle** (city) Stanly County
47	n/a	4.4	**Tabor City** (town) Columbus County	123	n/a	3.2	**Cherryville** (city) Gaston County
47	n/a	4.4	**Zebulon** (town) Wake County	123	932	3.2	**Durham** (city) Durham County
51	340	4.3	**Monroe** (city) Union County	123	n/a	3.2	**Fairmont** (town) Robeson County
51	n/a	4.3	**Morehead City** (town) Carteret County	123	n/a	3.2	**Lake Norman of Catawba** (CDP) Catawba County
51	n/a	4.3	**Roxboro** (city) Person County	123	932	3.2	**Mebane** (city) Alamance County
51	n/a	4.3	**Wadesboro** (town) Anson County	123	932	3.2	**Mount Holly** (city) Gaston County
51	n/a	4.3	**Woodfin** (town) Buncombe County	123	n/a	3.2	**Newport** (town) Carteret County
56	n/a	4.2	**Forest City** (town) Rutherford County	123	n/a	3.2	**Seven Lakes** (CDP) Moore County
56	n/a	4.2	**Polkton** (town) Anson County	123	n/a	3.2	**Troy** (town) Montgomery County
58	n/a	4.1	**Ayden** (town) Pitt County	123	n/a	3.2	**Westport** (CDP) Lincoln County
58	n/a	4.1	**Boiling Spring Lakes** (city) Brunswick County	134	n/a	3.1	**Canton** (town) Haywood County
58	403	4.1	**Burlington** (city) Alamance County	134	n/a	3.1	**Eastover** (town) Cumberland County
58	n/a	4.1	**Etowah** (CDP) Henderson County	134	n/a	3.1	**Jamestown** (town) Guilford County
58	n/a	4.1	**Long View** (town) Catawba County	134	n/a	3.1	**Kitty Hawk** (town) Dare County
58	n/a	4.1	**River Bend** (town) Craven County	134	n/a	3.1	**Pineville** (town) Mecklenburg County
64	444	4.0	**High Point** (city) Guilford County	134	n/a	3.1	**Rural Hall** (town) Forsyth County
64	444	4.0	**Leland** (town) Brunswick County	134	1014	3.1	**Spring Lake** (town) Cumberland County
64	444	4.0	**Reidsville** (city) Rockingham County	141	n/a	3.0	**Brices Creek** (CDP) Craven County
64	n/a	4.0	**Saint James** (town) Brunswick County	141	n/a	3.0	**Dana** (CDP) Henderson County
68	485	3.9	**Asheboro** (city) Randolph County	141	n/a	3.0	**Elkin** (town) Surry County
68	485	3.9	**Belmont** (city) Gaston County	141	1083	3.0	**Garner** (town) Wake County
68	485	3.9	**Eden** (city) Rockingham County	141	n/a	3.0	**Hillsborough** (town) Orange County
68	485	3.9	**Kinston** (city) Lenoir County	141	n/a	3.0	**Rockfish** (CDP) Hoke County
68	n/a	3.9	**Mocksville** (town) Davie County	141	1083	3.0	**Wake Forest** (town) Wake County
68	485	3.9	**Southern Pines** (town) Moore County	148	n/a	2.9	**Black Mountain** (town) Buncombe County
68	485	3.9	**Wilmington** (city) New Hanover County	148	n/a	2.9	**China Grove** (town) Rowan County
75	n/a	3.8	**Buies Creek** (CDP) Harnett County	148	1191	2.9	**Clemmons** (village) Forsyth County

Note: The state column ranks the top/bottom 150 places in the state with population of 2,500 or more. The national column ranks the top/bottom places in the country with population of 10,000 or more. Places that are unincorporated were not considered in the rankings. n/a indicates data not available. Please refer to the User Guide for additional information.

Homeowner Vacancy Rate

Top 150 Places Ranked in *Ascending* Order

State Rank	Nat'l Rank	Percent	Place	State Rank	Nat'l Rank	Percent	Place
1	n/a	1.0	Fairview (town) Union County	72	n/a	2.4	Myrtle Grove (CDP) New Hanover County
1	n/a	1.0	Sawmills (town) Caldwell County	72	2702	2.4	Roanoke Rapids (city) Halifax County
3	n/a	1.1	Half Moon (CDP) Onslow County	78	n/a	2.5	East Flat Rock (CDP) Henderson County
3	n/a	1.1	Midway (town) Davidson County	78	n/a	2.5	East Rockingham (CDP) Richmond County
3	n/a	1.1	Wallburg (town) Davidson County	78	2858	2.5	Holly Springs (town) Wake County
6	n/a	1.2	Gamewell (town) Caldwell County	78	n/a	2.5	Lake Park (village) Union County
6	n/a	1.2	Swannanoa (CDP) Buncombe County	78	2858	2.5	Laurinburg (city) Scotland County
8	n/a	1.4	Archer Lodge (town) Johnston County	78	n/a	2.5	Lowesville (CDP) Lincoln County
8	n/a	1.4	Cullowhee (CDP) Jackson County	78	n/a	2.5	Maiden (town) Catawba County
10	n/a	1.5	Bayshore (CDP) New Hanover County	78	n/a	2.5	Oak Ridge (town) Guilford County
10	n/a	1.5	Cajah's Mountain (town) Caldwell County	78	n/a	2.5	Trent Woods (town) Craven County
10	n/a	1.5	Midland (town) Cabarrus County	78	n/a	2.5	Walkertown (town) Forsyth County
10	n/a	1.5	South Rosemary (CDP) Halifax County	88	2992	2.6	Chapel Hill (town) Orange County
10	n/a	1.5	Unionville (town) Union County	88	n/a	2.6	Conover (city) Catawba County
10	n/a	1.5	Wesley Chapel (village) Union County	88	n/a	2.6	Dunn (city) Harnett County
16	n/a	1.6	Elroy (CDP) Wayne County	88	2992	2.6	Kings Mountain (city) Cleveland County
16	n/a	1.6	Welcome (CDP) Davidson County	88	n/a	2.6	Moyock (CDP) Currituck County
16	n/a	1.6	Windsor (town) Bertie County	88	2992	2.6	Raleigh (city) Wake County
19	n/a	1.7	Icard (CDP) Burke County	88	n/a	2.6	Southern Shores (town) Dare County
19	n/a	1.7	Mountain View (CDP) Catawba County	88	n/a	2.6	Wingate (town) Union County
21	1694	1.8	Lewisville (town) Forsyth County	96	n/a	2.7	Hamlet (city) Richmond County
21	1694	1.8	Matthews (town) Mecklenburg County	96	3109	2.7	Kernersville (town) Forsyth County
21	n/a	1.8	Nashville (town) Nash County	96	n/a	2.7	Kings Grant (CDP) New Hanover County
21	n/a	1.8	Pleasant Garden (town) Guilford County	96	n/a	2.7	Liberty (town) Randolph County
21	n/a	1.8	Saint Stephens (CDP) Catawba County	96	n/a	2.7	Marvin (village) Union County
21	n/a	1.8	Wentworth (town) Rockingham County	96	n/a	2.7	Murfreesboro (town) Hertford County
21	n/a	1.8	Winterville (town) Pitt County	96	n/a	2.7	Pittsboro (town) Chatham County
28	1847	1.9	Apex (town) Wake County	96	n/a	2.7	Raeford (city) Hoke County
28	n/a	1.9	Forest Oaks (CDP) Guilford County	96	n/a	2.7	River Road (CDP) Beaufort County
28	n/a	1.9	Granite Quarry (town) Rowan County	96	3109	2.7	Smithfield (town) Johnston County
28	1847	1.9	Piney Green (CDP) Onslow County	96	n/a	2.7	Weaverville (town) Buncombe County
28	n/a	1.9	Skippers Corner (CDP) New Hanover County	107	3244	2.8	Carrboro (town) Orange County
28	1847	1.9	Stallings (town) Union County	107	3244	2.8	Concord (city) Cabarrus County
34	n/a	2.0	Boiling Springs (town) Cleveland County	107	n/a	2.8	Enfield (town) Halifax County
34	n/a	2.0	Hudson (town) Caldwell County	107	n/a	2.8	Hampstead (CDP) Pender County
34	2036	2.0	Jacksonville (city) Onslow County	107	3244	2.8	Lenoir (city) Caldwell County
34	n/a	2.0	Mount Olive (town) Wayne County	107	3244	2.8	Mint Hill (town) Mecklenburg County
34	n/a	2.0	Northchase (CDP) New Hanover County	107	n/a	2.8	Stanley (town) Gaston County
34	n/a	2.0	Royal Pines (CDP) Buncombe County	107	3244	2.8	Tarboro (town) Edgecombe County
34	2036	2.0	Summerfield (town) Guilford County	107	n/a	2.8	Yadkinville (town) Yadkin County
41	2214	2.1	Archdale (city) Randolph County	116	n/a	2.9	Black Mountain (town) Buncombe County
41	n/a	2.1	Butner (town) Granville County	116	n/a	2.9	China Grove (town) Rowan County
41	2214	2.1	Cary (town) Wake County	116	3361	2.9	Clemmons (village) Forsyth County
41	n/a	2.1	Mineral Springs (town) Union County	116	n/a	2.9	Creedmoor (city) Granville County
41	n/a	2.1	Ogden (CDP) New Hanover County	116	n/a	2.9	Erwin (town) Harnett County
41	n/a	2.1	Pembroke (town) Robeson County	116	n/a	2.9	La Grange (town) Lenoir County
41	n/a	2.1	Red Oak (town) Nash County	116	n/a	2.9	Mills River (town) Henderson County
41	n/a	2.1	Wrightsboro (CDP) New Hanover County	116	n/a	2.9	Mountain Home (CDP) Henderson County
49	n/a	2.2	Elizabethtown (town) Bladen County	116	n/a	2.9	Weddington (town) Union County
49	n/a	2.2	Enochville (CDP) Rowan County	125	n/a	3.0	Brices Creek (CDP) Craven County
49	n/a	2.2	Gibsonville (town) Guilford County	125	n/a	3.0	Dana (CDP) Henderson County
49	n/a	2.2	Grifton (town) Pitt County	125	n/a	3.0	Elkin (town) Surry County
49	2389	2.2	Harrisburg (town) Cabarrus County	125	3466	3.0	Garner (town) Wake County
49	2389	2.2	Havelock (city) Craven County	125	n/a	3.0	Hillsborough (town) Orange County
49	2389	2.2	Hope Mills (town) Cumberland County	125	n/a	3.0	Rockfish (CDP) Hoke County
49	2389	2.2	Huntersville (town) Mecklenburg County	125	3466	3.0	Wake Forest (town) Wake County
49	2389	2.2	Indian Trail (town) Union County	132	n/a	3.1	Canton (town) Haywood County
49	n/a	2.2	James City (CDP) Craven County	132	n/a	3.1	Eastover (town) Cumberland County
49	n/a	2.2	Tyro (CDP) Davidson County	132	n/a	3.1	Jamestown (town) Guilford County
60	n/a	2.3	Brogden (CDP) Wayne County	132	n/a	3.1	Kitty Hawk (town) Dare County
60	n/a	2.3	Elon (town) Alamance County	132	n/a	3.1	Pineville (town) Mecklenburg County
60	n/a	2.3	Fairview (CDP) Buncombe County	132	n/a	3.1	Rural Hall (town) Forsyth County
60	n/a	2.3	Lowell (city) Gaston County	132	3574	3.1	Spring Lake (town) Cumberland County
60	n/a	2.3	Mar-Mac (CDP) Wayne County	139	3643	3.2	Albemarle (city) Stanly County
60	2531	2.3	Murraysville (CDP) New Hanover County	139	n/a	3.2	Cherryville (city) Gaston County
60	n/a	2.3	Randleman (city) Randolph County	139	3643	3.2	Durham (city) Durham County
60	n/a	2.3	Ranlo (town) Gaston County	139	n/a	3.2	Fairmont (town) Robeson County
60	n/a	2.3	Sneads Ferry (CDP) Onslow County	139	n/a	3.2	Lake Norman of Catawba (CDP) Catawba County
60	n/a	2.3	Stokesdale (town) Guilford County	139	3643	3.2	Mebane (city) Alamance County
60	n/a	2.3	Trinity (city) Randolph County	139	3643	3.2	Mount Holly (city) Gaston County
60	n/a	2.3	Whispering Pines (village) Moore County	139	n/a	3.2	Newport (town) Carteret County
72	n/a	2.4	Bethlehem (CDP) Alexander County	139	n/a	3.2	Seven Lakes (CDP) Moore County
72	n/a	2.4	Clinton (city) Sampson County	139	n/a	3.2	Troy (town) Montgomery County
72	n/a	2.4	Granite Falls (town) Caldwell County	139	n/a	3.2	Westport (CDP) Lincoln County
72	2702	2.4	Lumberton (city) Robeson County	150	3725	3.3	Cornelius (town) Mecklenburg County

Note: The state column ranks the top/bottom 150 places in the state with population of 2,500 or more. The national column ranks the top/bottom places in the country with population of 10,000 or more. Places that are unincorporated were not considered in the rankings. n/a indicates data not available. Please refer to the User Guide for additional information.

Median Gross Rent

Top 150 Places Ranked in *Descending* Order

State Rank	Nat'l Rank	Dollars	Place	State Rank	Nat'l Rank	Dollars	Place
1	n/a	1,883	**Marvin** (village) Union County	76	2913	862	**Mooresville** (town) Iredell County
2	n/a	1,646	**Southern Shores** (town) Dare County	77	n/a	858	**Wendell** (town) Wake County
3	n/a	1,588	**Saint James** (town) Brunswick County	78	2961	855	**Wilmington** (city) New Hanover County
4	389	1,571	**Summerfield** (town) Guilford County	79	2979	852	**Durham** (city) Durham County
5	695	1,388	**Pinehurst** (village) Moore County	80	n/a	851	**Pleasant Garden** (town) Guilford County
6	n/a	1,375	**Moyock** (CDP) Currituck County	81	3036	844	**Elizabeth City** (city) Pasquotank County
7	n/a	1,339	**Lake Park** (village) Union County	82	3042	843	**Carrboro** (town) Orange County
8	n/a	1,317	**Lake Royale** (CDP) Franklin County	83	n/a	842	**Newport** (town) Carteret County
9	n/a	1,288	**Sneads Ferry** (CDP) Onslow County	84	n/a	841	**Landis** (town) Rowan County
10	n/a	1,273	**Ogden** (CDP) New Hanover County	85	3066	839	**Asheville** (city) Buncombe County
11	n/a	1,261	**Emerald Isle** (town) Carteret County	86	n/a	837	**Aberdeen** (town) Moore County
12	n/a	1,240	**Bayshore** (CDP) New Hanover County	87	n/a	834	**Hillsborough** (town) Orange County
13	n/a	1,219	**Hampstead** (CDP) Pender County	88	n/a	831	**River Bend** (town) Craven County
13	n/a	1,219	**Wesley Chapel** (village) Union County	89	n/a	830	**Cramerton** (town) Gaston County
15	n/a	1,209	**Elon** (town) Alamance County	89	3120	830	**New Bern** (city) Craven County
16	n/a	1,195	**Porters Neck** (CDP) New Hanover County	91	3169	822	**Mint Hill** (town) Mecklenburg County
17	n/a	1,170	**Fairfield Harbour** (CDP) Craven County	92	3184	820	**Boone** (town) Watauga County
18	n/a	1,155	**Whispering Pines** (village) Moore County	92	3184	820	**Clemmons** (village) Forsyth County
19	n/a	1,137	**Carolina Beach** (town) New Hanover County	94	3209	815	**Lewisville** (town) Forsyth County
20	n/a	1,133	**Rockfish** (CDP) Hoke County	95	n/a	814	**Buies Creek** (CDP) Harnett County
21	1491	1,131	**Holly Springs** (town) Wake County	96	n/a	813	**Pittsboro** (town) Chatham County
22	n/a	1,124	**Waxhaw** (town) Union County	97	n/a	807	**Butner** (town) Granville County
23	n/a	1,116	**Carolina Shores** (town) Brunswick County	98	3259	806	**Concord** (city) Cabarrus County
24	n/a	1,098	**Kitty Hawk** (town) Dare County	99	n/a	805	**Pineville** (town) Mecklenburg County
25	n/a	1,097	**Winterville** (town) Pitt County	100	n/a	803	**Half Moon** (CDP) Onslow County
26	1676	1,086	**Harrisburg** (town) Cabarrus County	101	n/a	801	**Woodfin** (town) Buncombe County
27	n/a	1,079	**Etowah** (CDP) Henderson County	102	3287	800	**Mebane** (city) Alamance County
27	1717	1,079	**Indian Trail** (town) Union County	103	n/a	793	**Skippers Corner** (CDP) New Hanover County
29	1833	1,055	**Apex** (town) Wake County	104	3339	791	**Hope Mills** (town) Cumberland County
29	1833	1,055	**Cornelius** (town) Mecklenburg County	105	n/a	786	**Black Mountain** (town) Buncombe County
29	n/a	1,055	**Kill Devil Hills** (town) Dare County	106	n/a	779	**Fairview** (town) Union County
32	n/a	1,054	**Brices Creek** (CDP) Craven County	106	n/a	779	**Midland** (town) Cabarrus County
33	1850	1,052	**Murraysville** (CDP) New Hanover County	106	n/a	779	**Sunset Beach** (town) Brunswick County
34	1883	1,041	**Havelock** (city) Craven County	109	3423	777	**Monroe** (city) Union County
35	n/a	1,032	**Red Oak** (town) Nash County	109	n/a	777	**Unionville** (town) Union County
36	1941	1,027	**Jacksonville** (city) Onslow County	111	n/a	775	**Weddington** (town) Union County
37	n/a	1,020	**Southport** (city) Brunswick County	112	n/a	772	**Elroy** (CDP) Wayne County
38	n/a	1,019	**Lake Norman of Catawba** (CDP) Catawba County	113	n/a	767	**Granite Quarry** (town) Rowan County
39	2000	1,006	**Stallings** (town) Union County	114	3511	762	**High Point** (city) Guilford County
40	n/a	1,005	**Nags Head** (town) Dare County	115	n/a	760	**Maiden** (town) Catawba County
41	2044	997	**Huntersville** (town) Mecklenburg County	116	n/a	759	**Enochville** (CDP) Rowan County
42	2065	995	**Spring Lake** (town) Cumberland County	117	n/a	756	**Waynesville** (town) Haywood County
43	n/a	990	**Myrtle Grove** (CDP) New Hanover County	118	3560	754	**Gastonia** (city) Gaston County
44	n/a	983	**Flat Rock** (village) Henderson County	118	3560	754	**Kannapolis** (city) Cabarrus County
45	2161	980	**Morrisville** (town) Wake County	118	n/a	754	**Oxford** (city) Granville County
46	n/a	978	**Silver Lake** (CDP) New Hanover County	121	3571	753	**Rocky Mount** (city) Nash County
47	n/a	974	**Kings Grant** (CDP) New Hanover County	122	3603	747	**Wilson** (city) Wilson County
48	n/a	972	**Zebulon** (town) Wake County	123	n/a	744	**Lake Junaluska** (CDP) Haywood County
49	2231	971	**Clayton** (town) Johnston County	124	n/a	743	**Bessemer City** (city) Gaston County
50	2275	965	**Cary** (town) Wake County	124	n/a	743	**Fletcher** (town) Henderson County
51	2333	957	**Leland** (town) Brunswick County	126	3638	742	**Greensboro** (city) Guilford County
52	n/a	954	**Oak Island** (town) Brunswick County	127	n/a	741	**Angier** (town) Harnett County
53	n/a	951	**Royal Pines** (CDP) Buncombe County	127	3652	741	**Belmont** (city) Gaston County
54	n/a	945	**James City** (CDP) Craven County	129	n/a	740	**Oak Ridge** (town) Guilford County
55	n/a	944	**Boiling Spring Lakes** (city) Brunswick County	130	n/a	737	**Trinity** (city) Randolph County
56	n/a	941	**Wrightsboro** (CDP) New Hanover County	131	n/a	734	**Sylva** (town) Jackson County
57	2428	940	**Wake Forest** (town) Wake County	132	n/a	731	**Lowesville** (CDP) Lincoln County
58	n/a	939	**Jamestown** (town) Guilford County	133	3728	728	**Burlington** (city) Alamance County
59	2444	937	**Matthews** (town) Mecklenburg County	134	n/a	726	**Dana** (CDP) Henderson County
60	2481	930	**Davidson** (town) Mecklenburg County	135	n/a	724	**Archer Lodge** (town) Johnston County
61	2547	921	**Knightdale** (town) Wake County	135	3751	724	**Greenville** (city) Pitt County
62	2552	920	**Garner** (town) Wake County	135	3751	724	**Southern Pines** (town) Moore County
63	2578	915	**Chapel Hill** (town) Orange County	138	n/a	721	**Locust** (city) Stanly County
64	n/a	909	**Swansboro** (town) Onslow County	139	3781	720	**Kernersville** (town) Forsyth County
65	2635	905	**Fuquay-Varina** (town) Wake County	140	n/a	719	**Eastover** (town) Cumberland County
66	n/a	903	**Mineral Springs** (town) Union County	141	n/a	717	**East Flat Rock** (CDP) Henderson County
67	2692	897	**Raleigh** (city) Wake County	141	3793	717	**Salisbury** (city) Rowan County
68	n/a	888	**Creedmoor** (city) Granville County	143	3797	716	**Statesville** (city) Iredell County
69	2785	882	**Charlotte** (city) Mecklenburg County	144	n/a	714	**Stokesdale** (town) Guilford County
70	2800	880	**Piney Green** (CDP) Onslow County	145	3819	712	**Hendersonville** (city) Henderson County
71	n/a	871	**Mountain Home** (CDP) Henderson County	146	3833	710	**Goldsboro** (city) Wayne County
71	n/a	871	**Weaverville** (town) Buncombe County	147	n/a	709	**Swannanoa** (CDP) Buncombe County
73	2876	869	**Fayetteville** (city) Cumberland County	148	3845	708	**Mount Holly** (city) Gaston County
74	n/a	866	**Shallotte** (town) Brunswick County	149	3859	706	**Winston-Salem** (city) Forsyth County
75	n/a	865	**Northchase** (CDP) New Hanover County	150	n/a	704	**Brogden** (CDP) Wayne County

Note: *The state column ranks the top/bottom 150 places in the state with population of 2,500 or more. The national column ranks the top/bottom places in the country with population of 10,000 or more. Places that are unincorporated were not considered in the rankings. n/a indicates data not available. Please refer to the User Guide for additional information.*

Median Gross Rent

Top 150 Places Ranked in *Ascending* Order

State Rank	Nat'l Rank	Dollars	Place	State Rank	Nat'l Rank	Dollars	Place
1	n/a	286	Fairmont (town) Robeson County	76	n/a	644	Glen Raven (CDP) Alamance County
2	n/a	333	Plymouth (town) Washington County	77	461	645	Henderson (city) Vance County
3	n/a	335	Elizabethtown (town) Bladen County	77	n/a	645	Walkertown (town) Forsyth County
4	n/a	356	Valdese (town) Burke County	79	n/a	646	Westport (CDP) Lincoln County
5	n/a	400	Red Springs (town) Robeson County	80	n/a	647	King (city) Stokes County
6	n/a	444	North Wilkesboro (town) Wilkes County	80	n/a	647	Saint Stephens (CDP) Catawba County
7	n/a	458	Warsaw (town) Duplin County	80	468	647	Tarboro (town) Edgecombe County
8	n/a	465	Wallburg (town) Davidson County	83	n/a	649	Edenton (town) Chowan County
9	n/a	489	Windsor (town) Bertie County	83	n/a	649	Morehead City (town) Carteret County
10	n/a	492	Fairview (CDP) Buncombe County	83	n/a	649	Nashville (town) Nash County
11	n/a	513	Benson (town) Johnston County	86	n/a	651	Boiling Springs (town) Cleveland County
12	n/a	516	Grifton (town) Pitt County	86	n/a	651	Elkin (town) Surry County
13	n/a	517	Pembroke (town) Robeson County	88	n/a	658	Ranlo (town) Gaston County
13	n/a	517	Rockingham (city) Richmond County	89	541	660	Roanoke Rapids (city) Halifax County
15	n/a	518	Troy (town) Montgomery County	90	n/a	661	Enfield (town) Halifax County
16	n/a	527	Murfreesboro (town) Hertford County	90	542	661	Hickory (city) Catawba County
17	n/a	530	Wingate (town) Union County	92	551	663	Lincolnton (city) Lincoln County
18	n/a	533	Cajah's Mountain (town) Caldwell County	93	n/a	665	Long View (town) Catawba County
19	n/a	537	Williamston (town) Martin County	94	n/a	667	Mills River (town) Henderson County
20	n/a	542	Marion (city) McDowell County	94	n/a	667	Siler City (town) Chatham County
21	n/a	543	Tabor City (town) Columbus County	96	580	669	Archdale (city) Randolph County
22	n/a	554	Cullowhee (CDP) Jackson County	96	580	669	Shelby (city) Cleveland County
23	n/a	556	Rolesville (town) Wake County	96	n/a	669	Spencer (town) Rowan County
24	n/a	557	Raeford (city) Hoke County	99	601	673	Sanford (city) Lee County
25	n/a	559	Clinton (city) Sampson County	100	608	674	Newton (city) Catawba County
26	n/a	561	Whiteville (city) Columbus County	101	n/a	675	Polkton (town) Anson County
27	n/a	562	Wilkesboro (town) Wilkes County	101	n/a	675	Trent Woods (town) Craven County
28	n/a	565	Wallace (town) Duplin County	103	n/a	676	Louisburg (town) Franklin County
29	n/a	566	Midway (town) Davidson County	104	n/a	681	Mar-Mac (CDP) Wayne County
30	n/a	574	Bethlehem (CDP) Alexander County	104	n/a	681	Welcome (CDP) Davidson County
31	n/a	575	Rutherfordton (town) Rutherford County	106	n/a	683	Selma (town) Johnston County
32	n/a	576	Forest City (town) Rutherford County	107	n/a	685	La Grange (town) Lenoir County
33	133	577	Lenoir (city) Caldwell County	108	n/a	690	Cherryville (city) Gaston County
34	n/a	580	Granite Falls (town) Caldwell County	109	n/a	691	China Grove (town) Rowan County
35	n/a	587	Rural Hall (town) Forsyth County	109	n/a	691	Lowell (city) Gaston County
36	n/a	592	Wentworth (town) Rockingham County	109	n/a	691	Wadesboro (town) Anson County
37	n/a	593	Spindale (town) Rutherford County	112	n/a	692	Mountain View (CDP) Catawba County
37	192	593	Thomasville (city) Davidson County	113	n/a	694	Canton (town) Haywood County
39	195	594	Albemarle (city) Stanly County	113	728	694	Smithfield (town) Johnston County
39	n/a	594	Hamlet (city) Richmond County	115	753	698	Graham (city) Alamance County
41	213	598	Mount Airy (city) Surry County	115	n/a	698	Stanley (town) Gaston County
42	n/a	600	Liberty (town) Randolph County	117	n/a	699	Erwin (town) Harnett County
43	n/a	602	Beaufort (town) Carteret County	118	n/a	701	River Road (CDP) Beaufort County
44	n/a	605	Sawmills (town) Caldwell County	119	n/a	703	Franklin (town) Macon County
45	n/a	606	Gamewell (town) Caldwell County	120	n/a	704	Brogden (CDP) Wayne County
45	251	606	Kings Mountain (city) Cleveland County	121	789	706	Winston-Salem (city) Forsyth County
47	n/a	607	Hudson (town) Caldwell County	122	806	708	Mount Holly (city) Gaston County
47	n/a	607	Icard (CDP) Burke County	123	n/a	709	Swannanoa (CDP) Buncombe County
49	n/a	610	Randleman (city) Randolph County	124	818	710	Goldsboro (city) Wayne County
50	267	611	Eden (city) Rockingham County	125	830	712	Hendersonville (city) Henderson County
50	n/a	611	Lillington (town) Harnett County	126	n/a	714	Stokesdale (town) Guilford County
52	287	613	Laurinburg (city) Scotland County	127	853	716	Statesville (city) Iredell County
53	n/a	615	Roxboro (city) Person County	128	n/a	717	East Flat Rock (CDP) Henderson County
54	299	616	Kinston (city) Lenoir County	128	860	717	Salisbury (city) Rowan County
55	n/a	617	Mocksville (town) Davie County	130	n/a	719	Eastover (town) Cumberland County
56	n/a	618	East Rockingham (CDP) Richmond County	131	871	720	Kernersville (town) Forsyth County
57	n/a	619	Dunn (city) Harnett County	132	n/a	721	Locust (city) Stanly County
58	n/a	621	Ayden (town) Pitt County	133	n/a	724	Archer Lodge (town) Johnston County
58	n/a	621	Mount Olive (town) Wayne County	133	894	724	Greenville (city) Pitt County
60	331	623	Reidsville (city) Rockingham County	133	894	724	Southern Pines (town) Moore County
61	n/a	624	Washington (city) Beaufort County	136	n/a	726	Dana (CDP) Henderson County
62	343	625	Asheboro (city) Randolph County	137	921	728	Burlington (city) Alamance County
63	n/a	627	Conover (city) Catawba County	138	n/a	731	Lowesville (CDP) Lincoln County
64	n/a	629	Gibsonville (town) Guilford County	139	n/a	734	Sylva (town) Jackson County
65	n/a	633	Tyro (CDP) Davidson County	140	n/a	737	Trinity (city) Randolph County
66	n/a	634	Farmville (town) Pitt County	141	n/a	740	Oak Ridge (town) Guilford County
67	n/a	635	Ahoskie (town) Hertford County	142	n/a	741	Angier (town) Harnett County
67	n/a	635	Dallas (town) Gaston County	142	998	741	Belmont (city) Gaston County
67	393	635	Lexington (city) Davidson County	144	1005	742	Greensboro (city) Guilford County
70	425	640	Lumberton (city) Robeson County	145	n/a	743	Bessemer City (city) Gaston County
70	425	640	Morganton (city) Burke County	145	n/a	743	Fletcher (town) Henderson County
70	n/a	640	South Rosemary (CDP) Halifax County	147	n/a	744	Lake Junaluska (CDP) Haywood County
73	n/a	641	Brevard (city) Transylvania County	148	1046	747	Wilson (city) Wilson County
73	n/a	641	Burgaw (town) Pender County	149	1080	753	Rocky Mount (city) Nash County
73	n/a	641	Yadkinville (town) Yadkin County	150	1086	754	Gastonia (city) Gaston County

Note: The state column ranks the top/bottom 150 places in the state with population of 2,500 or more. The national column ranks the top/bottom places in the country with population of 10,000 or more. Places that are unincorporated were not considered in the rankings. n/a indicates data not available. Please refer to the User Guide for additional information.

Rental Vacancy Rate

Top 150 Places Ranked in *Descending* Order

State Rank	Nat'l Rank	Percent	Place	State Rank	Nat'l Rank	Percent	Place
1	n/a	73.9	**Sunset Beach** (town) Brunswick County	74	682	11.7	**Gastonia** (city) Gaston County
2	n/a	71.4	**Nags Head** (town) Dare County	74	n/a	11.7	**Moyock** (CDP) Currituck County
3	n/a	65.5	**Emerald Isle** (town) Carteret County	74	n/a	11.7	**Spindale** (town) Rutherford County
4	n/a	37.4	**Kitty Hawk** (town) Dare County	79	n/a	11.6	**Butner** (town) Granville County
5	n/a	36.1	**Flat Rock** (village) Henderson County	79	n/a	11.6	**Hillsborough** (town) Orange County
6	n/a	35.5	**Saint James** (town) Brunswick County	79	706	11.6	**Kernersville** (town) Forsyth County
7	n/a	31.2	**Lake Junaluska** (CDP) Haywood County	82	n/a	11.5	**Dana** (CDP) Henderson County
8	10	30.0	**Pinehurst** (village) Moore County	82	n/a	11.5	**Liberty** (town) Randolph County
9	n/a	28.4	**Carolina Beach** (town) New Hanover County	82	n/a	11.5	**Spencer** (town) Rowan County
10	n/a	27.1	**Oak Island** (town) Brunswick County	85	n/a	11.4	**Cramerton** (town) Gaston County
11	n/a	21.3	**Elkin** (town) Surry County	85	n/a	11.4	**Farmville** (town) Pitt County
12	n/a	21.0	**Buies Creek** (CDP) Harnett County	85	n/a	11.4	**Jamestown** (town) Guilford County
13	n/a	20.6	**Fairfield Harbour** (CDP) Craven County	85	n/a	11.4	**Seven Lakes** (CDP) Moore County
14	50	20.0	**Clemmons** (village) Forsyth County	85	n/a	11.4	**Woodfin** (town) Buncombe County
15	n/a	19.7	**Rural Hall** (town) Forsyth County	90	n/a	11.3	**Dallas** (town) Gaston County
16	n/a	19.6	**Saint Stephens** (CDP) Catawba County	90	778	11.3	**Wilmington** (city) New Hanover County
17	n/a	19.2	**Icard** (CDP) Burke County	90	n/a	11.3	**Wingate** (town) Union County
18	70	18.8	**Lexington** (city) Davidson County	93	805	11.2	**Monroe** (city) Union County
19	n/a	18.0	**Southport** (city) Brunswick County	93	n/a	11.2	**Rockingham** (city) Richmond County
20	n/a	17.8	**Brogden** (CDP) Wayne County	95	831	11.1	**Mint Hill** (town) Mecklenburg County
21	n/a	16.3	**Selma** (town) Johnston County	95	n/a	11.1	**Rutherfordton** (town) Rutherford County
22	n/a	16.2	**Yadkinville** (town) Yadkin County	97	n/a	11.0	**Canton** (town) Haywood County
23	188	15.6	**Holly Springs** (town) Wake County	97	860	11.0	**Elizabeth City** (city) Pasquotank County
24	n/a	15.1	**Elroy** (CDP) Wayne County	97	860	11.0	**Hendersonville** (city) Henderson County
24	211	15.1	**Lewisville** (town) Forsyth County	97	n/a	11.0	**James City** (CDP) Craven County
24	211	15.1	**Shelby** (city) Cleveland County	97	n/a	11.0	**Kill Devil Hills** (town) Dare County
27	246	14.6	**Statesville** (city) Iredell County	97	n/a	11.0	**Welcome** (CDP) Davidson County
27	n/a	14.6	**Wilkesboro** (town) Wilkes County	103	n/a	10.7	**Fairview** (CDP) Buncombe County
29	n/a	14.5	**East Flat Rock** (CDP) Henderson County	103	n/a	10.7	**River Road** (CDP) Beaufort County
29	259	14.5	**Rocky Mount** (town) Nash County	103	n/a	10.7	**Wadesboro** (town) Anson County
31	n/a	14.4	**Red Springs** (town) Robeson County	106	n/a	10.6	**Etowah** (CDP) Henderson County
32	275	14.3	**Knightdale** (town) Wake County	106	n/a	10.6	**Granite Falls** (town) Caldwell County
33	283	14.2	**Albemarle** (city) Stanly County	106	n/a	10.6	**Southern Shores** (town) Dare County
33	n/a	14.2	**Bessemer City** (city) Gaston County	106	n/a	10.6	**Sylva** (town) Jackson County
33	283	14.2	**Kannapolis** (city) Cabarrus County	106	n/a	10.6	**Whiteville** (city) Columbus County
36	303	14.0	**Eden** (city) Rockingham County	111	1024	10.5	**Belmont** (city) Gaston County
37	335	13.7	**Graham** (city) Alamance County	111	1024	10.5	**Fayetteville** (city) Cumberland County
37	n/a	13.7	**North Wilkesboro** (town) Wilkes County	113	1061	10.4	**Durham** (city) Durham County
37	335	13.7	**Salisbury** (city) Rowan County	113	1061	10.4	**New Bern** (city) Craven County
40	n/a	13.2	**Bethlehem** (CDP) Alexander County	113	n/a	10.4	**Stokesdale** (town) Guilford County
41	409	13.1	**Hickory** (city) Catawba County	116	n/a	10.3	**Plymouth** (town) Washington County
41	n/a	13.1	**Waynesville** (town) Haywood County	116	1107	10.3	**Wilson** (city) Wilson County
43	n/a	13.0	**Benson** (town) Johnston County	118	1151	10.2	**Leland** (town) Brunswick County
43	n/a	13.0	**Elizabethtown** (town) Bladen County	118	n/a	10.2	**Mocksville** (town) Davie County
43	428	13.0	**Thomasville** (city) Davidson County	120	n/a	10.1	**Lake Norman of Catawba** (CDP) Catawba County
46	n/a	12.9	**Gibsonville** (town) Guilford County	120	1185	10.1	**Lenoir** (city) Caldwell County
46	n/a	12.9	**Roxboro** (city) Person County	122	n/a	9.9	**Rolesville** (town) Wake County
48	459	12.8	**Mooresville** (town) Iredell County	123	n/a	9.8	**China Grove** (town) Rowan County
48	459	12.8	**Spring Lake** (town) Cumberland County	123	1291	9.8	**Clayton** (town) Johnston County
50	480	12.7	**Lincolnton** (city) Lincoln County	123	1291	9.8	**Davidson** (town) Mecklenburg County
51	493	12.6	**Burlington** (city) Alamance County	123	n/a	9.8	**Ranlo** (town) Gaston County
51	n/a	12.6	**Maiden** (town) Catawba County	123	1291	9.8	**Wake Forest** (town) Wake County
51	493	12.6	**Morganton** (city) Burke County	128	n/a	9.7	**Forest City** (town) Rutherford County
51	n/a	12.6	**Sawmills** (town) Caldwell County	128	n/a	9.7	**Gamewell** (town) Caldwell County
55	512	12.5	**Archdale** (city) Randolph County	128	n/a	9.7	**Zebulon** (town) Wake County
55	512	12.5	**Winston-Salem** (city) Forsyth County	131	n/a	9.6	**East Rockingham** (CDP) Richmond County
57	n/a	12.4	**Cherryville** (city) Gaston County	131	n/a	9.6	**Trinity** (city) Randolph County
57	n/a	12.4	**Hampstead** (CDP) Pender County	131	n/a	9.6	**Walkertown** (town) Forsyth County
57	n/a	12.4	**Mount Olive** (town) Wayne County	134	n/a	9.5	**Boiling Springs** (town) Cleveland County
60	n/a	12.3	**Franklin** (town) Macon County	134	1415	9.5	**Henderson** (city) Vance County
60	n/a	12.3	**La Grange** (town) Lenoir County	134	1415	9.5	**Newton** (city) Catawba County
60	n/a	12.3	**Valdese** (town) Burke County	134	n/a	9.5	**Pembroke** (town) Robeson County
63	n/a	12.2	**Polkton** (town) Anson County	134	n/a	9.5	**Silver Lake** (CDP) New Hanover County
63	561	12.2	**Reidsville** (city) Rockingham County	139	1455	9.4	**Kings Mountain** (city) Cleveland County
63	n/a	12.2	**Tyro** (CDP) Davidson County	139	n/a	9.4	**Landis** (town) Rowan County
66	582	12.1	**High Point** (city) Guilford County	139	n/a	9.4	**Pineville** (town) Mecklenburg County
67	635	11.9	**Greensboro** (city) Guilford County	142	n/a	9.3	**Burgaw** (town) Pender County
67	635	11.9	**Greenville** (city) Pitt County	142	n/a	9.3	**Erwin** (town) Harnett County
67	n/a	11.9	**Mountain Home** (CDP) Henderson County	142	1496	9.3	**Goldsboro** (city) Wayne County
70	656	11.8	**Asheboro** (city) Randolph County	145	n/a	9.2	**Black Mountain** (town) Buncombe County
70	656	11.8	**Concord** (city) Cabarrus County	145	n/a	9.2	**Carolina Shores** (town) Brunswick County
70	n/a	11.8	**River Bend** (town) Craven County	145	n/a	9.2	**Edenton** (town) Chowan County
70	n/a	11.8	**Stanley** (town) Gaston County	145	n/a	9.2	**Red Oak** (town) Nash County
74	682	11.7	**Charlotte** (city) Mecklenburg County	145	n/a	9.2	**Swannanoa** (CDP) Buncombe County
74	n/a	11.7	**Creedmoor** (city) Granville County	145	n/a	9.2	**Westport** (CDP) Lincoln County

Note: *The state column ranks the top/bottom 150 places in the state with population of 2,500 or more. The national column ranks the top/bottom places in the country with population of 10,000 or more. Places that are unincorporated were not considered in the rankings. n/a indicates data not available. Please refer to the User Guide for additional information.*

Rental Vacancy Rate

Top 150 Places Ranked in *Ascending* Order

State Rank	Nat'l Rank	Percent	Place
1	n/a	2.0	**Marvin** (village) Union County
2	33	2.4	**Stallings** (town) Union County
3	n/a	2.5	**Archer Lodge** (town) Johnston County
3	n/a	2.5	**Weddington** (town) Union County
5	n/a	3.8	**Lowesville** (CDP) Lincoln County
5	n/a	3.8	**Rockfish** (CDP) Hoke County
7	274	3.9	**Boone** (town) Watauga County
7	n/a	3.9	**Fairview** (town) Union County
9	n/a	4.1	**Aberdeen** (town) Moore County
10	n/a	4.2	**Wesley Chapel** (village) Union County
11	n/a	4.4	**Half Moon** (CDP) Onslow County
12	n/a	4.5	**Brices Creek** (CDP) Craven County
12	484	4.5	**Jacksonville** (city) Onslow County
14	n/a	4.6	**Grifton** (town) Pitt County
14	n/a	4.6	**Wendell** (town) Wake County
16	n/a	4.7	**Sneads Ferry** (CDP) Onslow County
17	n/a	4.8	**Forest Oaks** (CDP) Guilford County
18	n/a	4.9	**Lake Park** (village) Union County
18	683	4.9	**Murraysville** (CDP) New Hanover County
18	n/a	4.9	**South Rosemary** (CDP) Halifax County
18	n/a	4.9	**Swansboro** (town) Onslow County
22	n/a	5.0	**Trent Woods** (town) Craven County
23	765	5.1	**Matthews** (town) Mecklenburg County
23	n/a	5.1	**Mineral Springs** (town) Union County
25	n/a	5.2	**Clinton** (city) Sampson County
26	949	5.4	**Indian Trail** (town) Union County
26	n/a	5.4	**Mar-Mac** (CDP) Wayne County
26	949	5.4	**Mebane** (city) Alamance County
29	n/a	5.5	**Louisburg** (town) Franklin County
29	n/a	5.5	**Northchase** (CDP) New Hanover County
29	n/a	5.5	**Washington** (city) Beaufort County
32	n/a	5.6	**Unionville** (town) Union County
33	1142	5.7	**Piney Green** (CDP) Onslow County
34	n/a	5.8	**Marion** (city) McDowell County
34	n/a	5.8	**Wrightsboro** (CDP) New Hanover County
36	1255	5.9	**Havelock** (city) Craven County
36	n/a	5.9	**Locust** (city) Stanly County
38	n/a	6.0	**Eastover** (town) Cumberland County
38	n/a	6.0	**Fletcher** (town) Henderson County
40	n/a	6.1	**Fairmont** (town) Robeson County
40	n/a	6.1	**Nashville** (town) Nash County
42	n/a	6.2	**Cajah's Mountain** (town) Caldwell County
42	n/a	6.2	**Ogden** (CDP) New Hanover County
42	n/a	6.2	**Raeford** (city) Hoke County
42	n/a	6.2	**Windsor** (town) Bertie County
46	n/a	6.3	**Bayshore** (CDP) New Hanover County
47	n/a	6.4	**Enochville** (CDP) Rowan County
47	1540	6.4	**Harrisburg** (town) Cabarrus County
49	n/a	6.5	**Newport** (town) Carteret County
49	n/a	6.5	**Waxhaw** (town) Union County
51	1726	6.7	**Mount Holly** (city) Gaston County
52	n/a	6.8	**Hudson** (town) Caldwell County
53	n/a	6.9	**Weaverville** (town) Buncombe County
54	n/a	7.0	**Angier** (town) Harnett County
54	1894	7.0	**Huntersville** (town) Mecklenburg County
54	n/a	7.0	**King** (city) Stokes County
54	n/a	7.0	**Pittsboro** (town) Chatham County
58	n/a	7.1	**Ayden** (town) Pitt County
58	1960	7.1	**Chapel Hill** (town) Orange County
58	n/a	7.1	**Mountain View** (CDP) Catawba County
61	2026	7.2	**Asheville** (city) Buncombe County
61	n/a	7.2	**Morehead City** (town) Carteret County
63	2099	7.3	**Carrboro** (town) Orange County
63	2099	7.3	**Tarboro** (town) Edgecombe County
65	n/a	7.5	**Enfield** (town) Halifax County
65	n/a	7.5	**Lake Royale** (CDP) Franklin County
65	n/a	7.5	**Wallace** (town) Duplin County
65	n/a	7.5	**Whispering Pines** (village) Moore County
65	n/a	7.5	**Winterville** (town) Pitt County
70	2268	7.6	**Cornelius** (town) Mecklenburg County
70	n/a	7.6	**Cullowhee** (CDP) Jackson County
70	n/a	7.6	**Hamlet** (city) Richmond County
70	2268	7.6	**Morrisville** (town) Wake County
70	n/a	7.6	**Tabor City** (town) Columbus County
70	n/a	7.6	**Williamston** (town) Martin County
76	n/a	7.7	**Granite Quarry** (town) Rowan County
76	n/a	7.7	**Kings Grant** (CDP) New Hanover County
76	n/a	7.7	**Midland** (town) Cabarrus County
76	n/a	7.7	**Wallburg** (town) Davidson County
80	n/a	7.8	**Beaufort** (town) Carteret County
80	2372	7.8	**Lumberton** (city) Robeson County
80	n/a	7.8	**Oxford** (city) Granville County
80	n/a	7.8	**Porters Neck** (CDP) New Hanover County
80	2372	7.8	**Sanford** (city) Lee County
85	n/a	8.0	**Ahoskie** (town) Hertford County
85	2481	8.0	**Apex** (town) Wake County
85	2481	8.0	**Laurinburg** (city) Scotland County
85	n/a	8.0	**Lillington** (town) Harnett County
85	2481	8.0	**Raleigh** (city) Wake County
85	2481	8.0	**Southern Pines** (town) Moore County
91	2542	8.1	**Fuquay-Varina** (town) Wake County
91	n/a	8.1	**Lowell** (city) Gaston County
91	n/a	8.1	**Shallotte** (town) Brunswick County
91	n/a	8.1	**Siler City** (town) Chatham County
95	n/a	8.2	**Brevard** (city) Transylvania County
95	n/a	8.2	**Dunn** (city) Harnett County
95	n/a	8.2	**Glen Raven** (CDP) Alamance County
95	n/a	8.2	**Randleman** (city) Randolph County
95	2599	8.2	**Roanoke Rapids** (city) Halifax County
95	n/a	8.2	**Warsaw** (town) Duplin County
101	n/a	8.3	**Elon** (town) Alamance County
101	n/a	8.3	**Royal Pines** (CDP) Buncombe County
101	2664	8.3	**Summerfield** (town) Guilford County
104	n/a	8.4	**Conover** (city) Catawba County
104	n/a	8.4	**Long View** (town) Catawba County
104	n/a	8.4	**Mills River** (town) Henderson County
104	n/a	8.4	**Skippers Corner** (CDP) New Hanover County
108	2765	8.5	**Smithfield** (town) Johnston County
109	2824	8.6	**Hope Mills** (town) Cumberland County
109	n/a	8.6	**Pleasant Garden** (town) Guilford County
111	n/a	8.7	**Boiling Spring Lakes** (city) Brunswick County
112	n/a	8.8	**Murfreesboro** (town) Hertford County
112	n/a	8.8	**Oak Ridge** (town) Guilford County
112	n/a	8.8	**Wentworth** (town) Rockingham County
115	2947	8.9	**Cary** (town) Wake County
115	2947	8.9	**Kinston** (city) Lenoir County
115	2947	8.9	**Mount Airy** (city) Surry County
115	n/a	8.9	**Myrtle Grove** (CDP) New Hanover County
115	n/a	8.9	**Troy** (town) Montgomery County
120	n/a	9.0	**Midway** (town) Davidson County
121	3032	9.1	**Garner** (town) Wake County
122	n/a	9.2	**Black Mountain** (town) Buncombe County
122	n/a	9.2	**Carolina Shores** (town) Brunswick County
122	n/a	9.2	**Edenton** (town) Chowan County
122	n/a	9.2	**Red Oak** (town) Nash County
122	n/a	9.2	**Swannanoa** (CDP) Buncombe County
122	n/a	9.2	**Westport** (CDP) Lincoln County
128	n/a	9.3	**Burgaw** (town) Pender County
128	n/a	9.3	**Erwin** (town) Harnett County
128	3116	9.3	**Goldsboro** (city) Wayne County
131	3161	9.4	**Kings Mountain** (city) Cleveland County
131	n/a	9.4	**Landis** (town) Rowan County
131	n/a	9.4	**Pineville** (town) Mecklenburg County
134	n/a	9.5	**Boiling Springs** (town) Cleveland County
134	3202	9.5	**Henderson** (city) Vance County
134	3202	9.5	**Newton** (city) Catawba County
134	n/a	9.5	**Pembroke** (town) Robeson County
134	n/a	9.5	**Silver Lake** (CDP) New Hanover County
139	n/a	9.6	**East Rockingham** (CDP) Richmond County
139	n/a	9.6	**Trinity** (city) Randolph County
139	n/a	9.6	**Walkertown** (town) Forsyth County
142	n/a	9.7	**Forest City** (town) Rutherford County
142	n/a	9.7	**Gamewell** (town) Caldwell County
142	n/a	9.7	**Zebulon** (town) Wake County
145	n/a	9.8	**China Grove** (town) Rowan County
145	3317	9.8	**Clayton** (town) Johnston County
145	3317	9.8	**Davidson** (town) Mecklenburg County
145	n/a	9.8	**Ranlo** (town) Gaston County
145	3317	9.8	**Wake Forest** (town) Wake County
150	n/a	9.9	**Rolesville** (town) Wake County

Note: The state column ranks the top/bottom 150 places in the state with population of 2,500 or more. The national column ranks the top/bottom places in the country with population of 10,000 or more. Places that are unincorporated were not considered in the rankings. n/a indicates data not available. Please refer to the User Guide for additional information.

Population with Health Insurance

Top 150 Places Ranked in *Descending* Order

State Rank	Nat'l Rank	Percent	Place
1	n/a	98.7	**Saint James** (town) Brunswick County
2	n/a	98.4	**Forest Oaks** (CDP) Guilford County
3	n/a	97.8	**Whispering Pines** (village) Moore County
4	n/a	97.3	**Marvin** (village) Union County
5	n/a	96.7	**Seven Lakes** (CDP) Moore County
6	n/a	96.6	**Brices Creek** (CDP) Craven County
7	291	96.3	**Pinehurst** (village) Moore County
8	n/a	95.7	**Porters Neck** (CDP) New Hanover County
9	n/a	95.0	**Trent Woods** (town) Craven County
10	622	94.9	**Summerfield** (town) Guilford County
10	n/a	94.9	**Sunset Beach** (town) Brunswick County
12	n/a	94.6	**Oak Ridge** (town) Guilford County
12	n/a	94.6	**Wesley Chapel** (village) Union County
14	n/a	94.5	**Buies Creek** (CDP) Harnett County
15	828	94.1	**Davidson** (town) Mecklenburg County
16	n/a	94.0	**Fairfield Harbour** (CDP) Craven County
17	902	93.8	**Morrisville** (town) Wake County
18	n/a	93.7	**Lake Norman of Catawba** (CDP) Catawba County
19	n/a	93.6	**Unionville** (town) Union County
20	989	93.5	**Holly Springs** (town) Wake County
20	989	93.5	**Lewisville** (town) Forsyth County
22	n/a	93.3	**Fairview** (town) Union County
22	n/a	93.3	**Flat Rock** (village) Henderson County
22	n/a	93.3	**Red Oak** (town) Nash County
25	n/a	93.2	**Royal Pines** (CDP) Buncombe County
26	1236	92.6	**Apex** (town) Wake County
27	n/a	92.4	**Midway** (town) Davidson County
28	n/a	92.3	**Elon** (town) Alamance County
29	n/a	92.2	**King** (city) Stokes County
30	n/a	92.1	**Carolina Shores** (town) Brunswick County
30	n/a	92.1	**Hampstead** (CDP) Pender County
30	n/a	92.1	**Lake Park** (village) Union County
30	1366	92.1	**Wake Forest** (town) Wake County
34	n/a	91.7	**Weddington** (town) Union County
35	1499	91.6	**Boone** (town) Watauga County
35	n/a	91.6	**Mills River** (town) Henderson County
35	n/a	91.6	**Westport** (CDP) Lincoln County
38	1525	91.5	**Chapel Hill** (town) Orange County
38	n/a	91.5	**Wallburg** (town) Davidson County
40	n/a	91.4	**Waxhaw** (town) Union County
41	n/a	91.3	**Swansboro** (town) Onslow County
42	n/a	91.2	**Moyock** (CDP) Currituck County
43	n/a	91.1	**Rockfish** (CDP) Hoke County
44	n/a	91.0	**Wingate** (town) Union County
45	n/a	90.9	**Cramerton** (town) Gaston County
46	n/a	90.7	**Emerald Isle** (town) Carteret County
47	n/a	90.6	**Hillsborough** (town) Orange County
47	1759	90.6	**Reidsville** (city) Rockingham County
47	1759	90.6	**Stallings** (town) Union County
50	n/a	90.5	**Boiling Springs** (town) Cleveland County
50	n/a	90.5	**Myrtle Grove** (CDP) New Hanover County
52	n/a	90.4	**Lake Junaluska** (CDP) Haywood County
53	n/a	90.1	**Hudson** (town) Caldwell County
53	n/a	90.1	**Lake Royale** (CDP) Franklin County
55	1898	90.0	**Cary** (town) Wake County
56	1948	89.8	**Jacksonville** (city) Onslow County
56	n/a	89.8	**Wilkesboro** (town) Wilkes County
58	1978	89.7	**Harrisburg** (town) Cabarrus County
58	n/a	89.7	**Shallotte** (town) Brunswick County
58	n/a	89.7	**Weaverville** (town) Buncombe County
61	n/a	89.4	**River Bend** (town) Craven County
62	2068	89.3	**Clemmons** (village) Forsyth County
62	n/a	89.3	**Eastover** (town) Cumberland County
64	n/a	89.2	**Pleasant Garden** (town) Guilford County
65	2117	89.1	**Matthews** (town) Mecklenburg County
65	2117	89.1	**Mebane** (city) Alamance County
65	n/a	89.1	**Murfreesboro** (town) Hertford County
65	2117	89.1	**Southern Pines** (town) Moore County
69	n/a	88.9	**Gibsonville** (town) Guilford County
69	2171	88.9	**Huntersville** (town) Mecklenburg County
71	2194	88.8	**Hope Mills** (town) Cumberland County
71	2194	88.8	**Mint Hill** (town) Mecklenburg County
73	n/a	88.7	**Plymouth** (town) Washington County
73	n/a	88.7	**Valdese** (town) Burke County
75	n/a	88.6	**Rural Hall** (town) Forsyth County
76	n/a	88.4	**Rolesville** (town) Wake County
77	n/a	88.3	**Cullowhee** (CDP) Jackson County
78	n/a	88.2	**Jamestown** (town) Guilford County
79	n/a	88.1	**Beaufort** (town) Carteret County
79	n/a	88.1	**Fletcher** (town) Henderson County
81	n/a	88.0	**Southport** (city) Brunswick County
82	n/a	87.9	**Mountain Home** (CDP) Henderson County
83	n/a	87.7	**Saint Stephens** (CDP) Catawba County
84	n/a	87.6	**Stanley** (town) Gaston County
84	n/a	87.6	**Trinity** (city) Randolph County
86	2504	87.5	**Cornelius** (town) Mecklenburg County
86	n/a	87.5	**Locust** (city) Stanly County
88	2527	87.4	**Kernersville** (town) Forsyth County
88	n/a	87.4	**Spindale** (town) Rutherford County
90	2546	87.3	**Leland** (town) Brunswick County
90	n/a	87.3	**Ogden** (CDP) New Hanover County
92	n/a	87.1	**Northchase** (CDP) New Hanover County
92	n/a	87.1	**Southern Shores** (town) Dare County
92	n/a	87.1	**Winterville** (town) Pitt County
95	n/a	87.0	**Mineral Springs** (town) Union County
96	2638	86.9	**Archdale** (city) Randolph County
96	2638	86.9	**Belmont** (city) Gaston County
96	n/a	86.9	**Elroy** (CDP) Wayne County
96	2638	86.9	**Goldsboro** (city) Wayne County
96	n/a	86.9	**Nashville** (town) Nash County
96	n/a	86.9	**Wentworth** (town) Rockingham County
102	n/a	86.8	**Oxford** (city) Granville County
103	n/a	86.7	**Bethlehem** (CDP) Alexander County
103	n/a	86.7	**Liberty** (town) Randolph County
103	2685	86.7	**Murraysville** (CDP) New Hanover County
103	n/a	86.7	**Stokesdale** (town) Guilford County
107	n/a	86.6	**Cherryville** (city) Gaston County
108	n/a	86.5	**Butner** (town) Granville County
108	2739	86.5	**Laurinburg** (city) Scotland County
108	n/a	86.5	**Louisburg** (town) Franklin County
108	2739	86.5	**Piney Green** (CDP) Onslow County
108	n/a	86.5	**Pittsboro** (town) Chatham County
108	n/a	86.5	**Wendell** (town) Wake County
114	n/a	86.4	**Cajah's Mountain** (town) Caldwell County
114	n/a	86.4	**Nags Head** (town) Dare County
114	2760	86.4	**Roanoke Rapids** (city) Halifax County
114	n/a	86.4	**Windsor** (town) Bertie County
118	n/a	86.3	**Elizabethtown** (town) Bladen County
118	n/a	86.3	**Randleman** (city) Randolph County
120	n/a	86.2	**Half Moon** (CDP) Onslow County
120	n/a	86.2	**La Grange** (town) Lenoir County
122	n/a	86.1	**Lowesville** (CDP) Lincoln County
122	n/a	86.1	**Raeford** (city) Hoke County
124	2844	86.0	**Greenville** (city) Pitt County
125	n/a	85.9	**Edenton** (town) Chowan County
125	2876	85.9	**Fayetteville** (city) Cumberland County
127	2899	85.8	**Clayton** (town) Johnston County
127	n/a	85.8	**Walkertown** (town) Forsyth County
129	n/a	85.7	**Granite Quarry** (town) Rowan County
129	2921	85.7	**Havelock** (city) Craven County
129	2921	85.7	**Mooresville** (town) Iredell County
132	2944	85.6	**Mount Airy** (city) Surry County
133	n/a	85.5	**Aberdeen** (town) Moore County
133	n/a	85.5	**Garner** (town) Wake County
133	n/a	85.5	**Mocksville** (town) Davie County
133	2974	85.5	**Spring Lake** (town) Cumberland County
137	n/a	85.2	**Creedmoor** (city) Granville County
137	n/a	85.2	**Williamston** (town) Martin County
139	n/a	85.1	**Washington** (city) Beaufort County
140	n/a	85.0	**Etowah** (CDP) Henderson County
141	n/a	84.8	**Angier** (town) Harnett County
142	n/a	84.7	**Boiling Spring Lakes** (city) Brunswick County
142	n/a	84.7	**Clinton** (city) Sampson County
144	n/a	84.6	**Brevard** (city) Transylvania County
144	n/a	84.6	**Lillington** (town) Harnett County
144	3128	84.6	**Mount Holly** (city) Gaston County
147	n/a	84.5	**Erwin** (town) Harnett County
147	3146	84.5	**Fuquay-Varina** (town) Wake County
147	n/a	84.5	**James City** (CDP) Craven County
147	n/a	84.5	**Marion** (city) McDowell County

Note: The state column ranks the top/bottom 150 places in the state with population of 2,500 or more. The national column ranks the top/bottom places in the country with population of 10,000 or more. Places that are unincorporated were not considered in the rankings. n/a indicates data not available. Please refer to the User Guide for additional information.

Population with Health Insurance

Top 150 Places Ranked in *Ascending* Order

State Rank	Nat'l Rank	Percent	Place
1	n/a	63.8	**Selma** (town) Johnston County
2	n/a	65.2	**Dana** (CDP) Henderson County
3	n/a	66.8	**Siler City** (town) Chatham County
4	n/a	68.9	**East Flat Rock** (CDP) Henderson County
5	n/a	71.2	**Wallace** (town) Duplin County
6	n/a	71.6	**Icard** (CDP) Burke County
6	n/a	71.6	**Skippers Corner** (CDP) New Hanover County
8	n/a	72.1	**Franklin** (town) Macon County
8	n/a	72.1	**Silver Lake** (CDP) New Hanover County
10	n/a	72.8	**Lowell** (city) Gaston County
11	n/a	72.9	**East Rockingham** (CDP) Richmond County
12	n/a	73.5	**Tyro** (CDP) Davidson County
13	n/a	74.3	**Pineville** (town) Mecklenburg County
14	277	74.4	**Monroe** (city) Union County
15	n/a	74.6	**Elkin** (town) Surry County
15	n/a	74.6	**Gamewell** (town) Caldwell County
15	n/a	74.6	**Roxboro** (city) Person County
18	n/a	75.0	**Brogden** (CDP) Wayne County
19	n/a	75.1	**Ayden** (town) Pitt County
20	323	75.2	**Asheboro** (city) Randolph County
20	n/a	75.2	**Benson** (town) Johnston County
22	n/a	75.7	**Bessemer City** (city) Gaston County
23	363	76.0	**Elizabeth City** (city) Pasquotank County
24	n/a	76.1	**Enochville** (CDP) Rowan County
25	n/a	76.3	**Landis** (town) Rowan County
26	n/a	76.4	**Kill Devil Hills** (town) Dare County
27	n/a	76.7	**Canton** (town) Haywood County
28	n/a	76.8	**Kings Grant** (CDP) New Hanover County
29	n/a	76.9	**Warsaw** (town) Duplin County
30	n/a	77.1	**China Grove** (town) Rowan County
30	445	77.1	**Graham** (city) Alamance County
30	n/a	77.1	**Yadkinville** (town) Yadkin County
33	n/a	77.3	**Woodfin** (town) Buncombe County
34	477	77.6	**Lexington** (city) Davidson County
34	n/a	77.6	**River Road** (CDP) Beaufort County
36	n/a	78.0	**Wadesboro** (town) Anson County
37	n/a	78.1	**Swannanoa** (CDP) Buncombe County
38	n/a	78.2	**Dallas** (town) Gaston County
39	n/a	78.3	**Morehead City** (town) Carteret County
39	538	78.3	**Sanford** (city) Lee County
41	n/a	78.5	**Zebulon** (town) Wake County
42	n/a	78.6	**Dunn** (city) Harnett County
43	n/a	78.9	**Black Mountain** (town) Buncombe County
43	n/a	78.9	**Fairview** (CDP) Buncombe County
45	n/a	79.0	**Spencer** (town) Rowan County
46	n/a	79.4	**Mount Olive** (town) Wayne County
46	n/a	79.4	**Waynesville** (town) Haywood County
48	n/a	79.5	**Sneads Ferry** (CDP) Onslow County
49	n/a	79.7	**Hamlet** (city) Richmond County
49	679	79.7	**Kannapolis** (city) Cabarrus County
49	n/a	79.7	**North Wilkesboro** (town) Wilkes County
52	707	79.9	**Newton** (city) Catawba County
53	n/a	80.0	**Farmville** (town) Pitt County
53	n/a	80.0	**Tabor City** (town) Columbus County
55	n/a	80.1	**Wrightsboro** (CDP) New Hanover County
56	n/a	80.2	**Mar-Mac** (CDP) Wayne County
57	753	80.3	**Kinston** (city) Lenoir County
57	753	80.3	**Lumberton** (city) Robeson County
57	n/a	80.3	**Oak Island** (town) Brunswick County
57	753	80.3	**Tarboro** (town) Edgecombe County
61	n/a	80.4	**Granite Falls** (town) Caldwell County
62	n/a	80.5	**Whiteville** (city) Columbus County
63	n/a	80.6	**Welcome** (CDP) Davidson County
64	n/a	80.7	**Archer Lodge** (town) Johnston County
64	811	80.7	**Hickory** (city) Catawba County
64	n/a	80.7	**Pembroke** (town) Robeson County
67	836	80.9	**Albemarle** (city) Stanly County
68	n/a	81.0	**Burgaw** (town) Pender County
68	849	81.0	**Eden** (city) Rockingham County
68	849	81.0	**High Point** (city) Guilford County
71	n/a	81.1	**Ranlo** (town) Gaston County
71	869	81.1	**Statesville** (city) Iredell County
73	n/a	81.2	**Carolina Beach** (town) New Hanover County
73	884	81.2	**Morganton** (city) Burke County
73	884	81.2	**Smithfield** (town) Johnston County
73	884	81.2	**Thomasville** (city) Davidson County
77	922	81.4	**Gastonia** (city) Gaston County
77	n/a	81.4	**Polkton** (town) Anson County
79	932	81.5	**Henderson** (city) Vance County
79	n/a	81.5	**Kitty Hawk** (town) Dare County
81	969	81.7	**Hendersonville** (city) Henderson County
81	969	81.7	**Salisbury** (city) Rowan County
83	n/a	81.8	**Sylva** (town) Jackson County
84	1000	81.9	**Charlotte** (city) Mecklenburg County
84	1000	81.9	**Wilson** (city) Wilson County
86	n/a	82.0	**Red Springs** (town) Robeson County
86	n/a	82.0	**Rutherfordton** (town) Rutherford County
86	1020	82.0	**Winston-Salem** (city) Forsyth County
89	n/a	82.2	**Forest City** (town) Rutherford County
89	n/a	82.2	**Sawmills** (town) Caldwell County
91	1057	82.3	**Asheville** (city) Buncombe County
92	1115	82.6	**Greensboro** (city) Guilford County
92	1115	82.6	**Knightdale** (town) Wake County
92	1115	82.6	**Lincolnton** (city) Lincoln County
95	1137	82.7	**Kings Mountain** (city) Cleveland County
95	1137	82.7	**Lenoir** (city) Caldwell County
95	n/a	82.7	**Long View** (town) Catawba County
98	1159	82.8	**Burlington** (city) Alamance County
98	n/a	82.8	**Fairmont** (town) Robeson County
100	1177	82.9	**Durham** (city) Durham County
100	n/a	82.9	**Grifton** (town) Pitt County
102	1209	83.1	**Shelby** (city) Cleveland County
102	n/a	83.1	**Troy** (town) Montgomery County
104	n/a	83.3	**Ahoskie** (town) Hertford County
104	1242	83.3	**Indian Trail** (town) Union County
104	n/a	83.3	**Newport** (town) Carteret County
104	1242	83.3	**Rocky Mount** (city) Nash County
104	1242	83.3	**Wilmington** (city) New Hanover County
109	n/a	83.4	**Mountain View** (CDP) Catawba County
110	1311	83.6	**Concord** (city) Cabarrus County
111	1337	83.7	**Carrboro** (town) Orange County
111	n/a	83.7	**Rockingham** (city) Richmond County
113	n/a	83.8	**Enfield** (town) Halifax County
113	1355	83.8	**New Bern** (city) Craven County
115	1373	83.9	**Raleigh** (city) Wake County
116	n/a	84.0	**South Rosemary** (CDP) Halifax County
117	n/a	84.1	**Bayshore** (CDP) New Hanover County
118	n/a	84.2	**Midland** (town) Cabarrus County
119	n/a	84.3	**Conover** (city) Catawba County
119	n/a	84.3	**Maiden** (town) Catawba County
121	n/a	84.4	**Glen Raven** (CDP) Alamance County
122	n/a	84.5	**Erwin** (town) Harnett County
122	1490	84.5	**Fuquay-Varina** (town) Wake County
122	n/a	84.5	**James City** (CDP) Craven County
122	n/a	84.5	**Marion** (city) McDowell County
126	n/a	84.6	**Brevard** (city) Transylvania County
126	n/a	84.6	**Lillington** (town) Harnett County
126	1511	84.6	**Mount Holly** (city) Gaston County
129	n/a	84.7	**Boiling Spring Lakes** (city) Brunswick County
129	n/a	84.7	**Clinton** (city) Sampson County
131	n/a	84.8	**Angier** (town) Harnett County
132	n/a	85.0	**Etowah** (CDP) Henderson County
133	n/a	85.1	**Washington** (city) Beaufort County
134	n/a	85.2	**Creedmoor** (city) Granville County
134	n/a	85.2	**Williamston** (town) Martin County
136	n/a	85.5	**Aberdeen** (town) Moore County
136	1663	85.5	**Garner** (town) Wake County
136	n/a	85.5	**Mocksville** (town) Davie County
136	1663	85.5	**Spring Lake** (town) Cumberland County
140	1683	85.6	**Mount Airy** (city) Surry County
141	n/a	85.7	**Granite Quarry** (town) Rowan County
141	1713	85.7	**Havelock** (city) Craven County
141	1713	85.7	**Mooresville** (town) Iredell County
144	1736	85.8	**Clayton** (town) Johnston County
144	n/a	85.8	**Walkertown** (town) Forsyth County
146	n/a	85.9	**Edenton** (town) Chowan County
146	1758	85.9	**Fayetteville** (city) Cumberland County
148	1781	86.0	**Greenville** (city) Pitt County
149	n/a	86.1	**Lowesville** (CDP) Lincoln County
149	n/a	86.1	**Raeford** (city) Hoke County

Note: The state column ranks the top/bottom 150 places in the state with population of 2,500 or more. The national column ranks the top/bottom places in the country with population of 10,000 or more. Places that are unincorporated were not considered in the rankings. n/a indicates data not available. Please refer to the User Guide for additional information.

Population with Private Health Insurance

Top 150 Places Ranked in *Descending* Order

State Rank	Nat'l Rank	Percent	Place
1	n/a	96.0	**Marvin** (village) Union County
2	n/a	90.8	**Trent Woods** (town) Craven County
3	n/a	90.6	**Oak Ridge** (town) Guilford County
4	n/a	90.5	**Saint James** (town) Brunswick County
5	n/a	89.5	**Brices Creek** (CDP) Craven County
6	n/a	89.1	**Buies Creek** (CDP) Harnett County
7	n/a	89.0	**Wesley Chapel** (village) Union County
8	n/a	88.4	**Porters Neck** (CDP) New Hanover County
9	437	88.0	**Holly Springs** (town) Wake County
9	437	88.0	**Morrisville** (town) Wake County
11	n/a	87.8	**Weddington** (town) Union County
12	520	87.4	**Apex** (town) Wake County
12	n/a	87.4	**Seven Lakes** (CDP) Moore County
14	529	87.3	**Boone** (town) Watauga County
14	529	87.3	**Davidson** (town) Mecklenburg County
16	551	87.1	**Summerfield** (town) Guilford County
17	n/a	86.5	**Lake Norman of Catawba** (CDP) Catawba County
18	n/a	86.2	**Moyock** (CDP) Currituck County
19	n/a	85.9	**Whispering Pines** (village) Moore County
20	711	85.8	**Chapel Hill** (town) Orange County
21	n/a	85.2	**Red Oak** (town) Nash County
22	n/a	85.0	**Unionville** (town) Union County
23	n/a	84.7	**Waxhaw** (town) Union County
24	918	84.2	**Cary** (town) Wake County
25	938	84.0	**Pinehurst** (village) Moore County
26	n/a	83.8	**Royal Pines** (CDP) Buncombe County
27	n/a	83.7	**Forest Oaks** (CDP) Guilford County
28	n/a	83.5	**Cullowhee** (CDP) Jackson County
28	n/a	83.5	**Emerald Isle** (town) Carteret County
28	n/a	83.5	**Westport** (CDP) Lincoln County
31	1030	83.3	**Huntersville** (town) Mecklenburg County
32	n/a	83.2	**Elon** (town) Alamance County
32	n/a	83.2	**Hampstead** (CDP) Pender County
34	1080	82.9	**Lewisville** (town) Forsyth County
34	n/a	82.9	**Wallburg** (town) Davidson County
36	1155	82.3	**Wake Forest** (town) Wake County
37	n/a	81.8	**Lake Junaluska** (CDP) Haywood County
38	n/a	81.7	**Flat Rock** (village) Henderson County
39	n/a	80.5	**Lake Park** (village) Union County
40	1399	80.4	**Cornelius** (town) Mecklenburg County
41	n/a	80.2	**Carolina Shores** (town) Brunswick County
41	1419	80.2	**Harrisburg** (town) Cabarrus County
43	n/a	80.1	**Swansboro** (town) Onslow County
44	1462	79.9	**Stallings** (town) Union County
45	n/a	79.7	**King** (city) Stokes County
46	1514	79.5	**Clemmons** (village) Forsyth County
47	1533	79.4	**Matthews** (town) Mecklenburg County
47	n/a	79.4	**Southern Shores** (town) Dare County
49	n/a	79.0	**Mills River** (town) Henderson County
50	n/a	78.7	**Lowesville** (CDP) Lincoln County
51	n/a	78.5	**Jamestown** (town) Guilford County
51	1638	78.5	**Murraysville** (CDP) New Hanover County
51	n/a	78.5	**Stokesdale** (town) Guilford County
54	n/a	78.2	**Gibsonville** (town) Guilford County
55	n/a	78.1	**Cramerton** (town) Gaston County
56	n/a	78.0	**Rural Hall** (town) Forsyth County
57	n/a	77.7	**Fairfield Harbour** (CDP) Craven County
57	n/a	77.7	**Ogden** (CDP) New Hanover County
59	n/a	77.5	**Midway** (town) Davidson County
60	n/a	77.4	**Myrtle Grove** (CDP) New Hanover County
61	n/a	77.2	**Bayshore** (CDP) New Hanover County
61	n/a	77.2	**Boiling Springs** (town) Cleveland County
61	1761	77.2	**Jacksonville** (city) Onslow County
64	n/a	76.9	**Winterville** (town) Pitt County
65	n/a	76.4	**Bethlehem** (CDP) Alexander County
66	n/a	76.1	**Fairview** (town) Union County
66	n/a	76.1	**Wingate** (town) Union County
68	n/a	76.0	**Half Moon** (CDP) Onslow County
68	n/a	76.0	**Weaverville** (town) Buncombe County
70	1937	75.8	**Mebane** (city) Alamance County
71	1998	75.2	**Mint Hill** (town) Mecklenburg County
72	n/a	75.0	**River Bend** (town) Craven County
73	2055	74.7	**Mooresville** (town) Iredell County
74	2068	74.6	**Clayton** (town) Johnston County
75	2089	74.5	**Belmont** (city) Gaston County
75	2089	74.5	**Leland** (town) Brunswick County
77	n/a	74.3	**Sunset Beach** (town) Brunswick County
78	2120	74.2	**Carrboro** (town) Orange County
79	n/a	73.9	**Nags Head** (town) Dare County
80	2184	73.6	**Garner** (town) Wake County
81	n/a	73.4	**Eastover** (town) Cumberland County
81	n/a	73.4	**Locust** (city) Stanly County
81	2201	73.4	**Piney Green** (CDP) Onslow County
84	2208	73.3	**Kernersville** (town) Forsyth County
85	n/a	73.0	**Newport** (town) Carteret County
86	n/a	72.9	**Archer Lodge** (town) Johnston County
86	n/a	72.9	**Rockfish** (CDP) Hoke County
88	n/a	72.8	**Etowah** (CDP) Henderson County
89	2319	72.1	**Indian Trail** (town) Union County
90	n/a	71.8	**Rolesville** (town) Wake County
91	2354	71.7	**Havelock** (city) Craven County
92	n/a	71.5	**Creedmoor** (city) Granville County
92	n/a	71.5	**Mineral Springs** (town) Union County
94	n/a	70.7	**Wentworth** (town) Rockingham County
95	n/a	70.6	**Lake Royale** (CDP) Franklin County
96	2494	70.4	**Fuquay-Varina** (town) Wake County
97	n/a	70.2	**Carolina Beach** (town) New Hanover County
98	2529	70.1	**Archdale** (city) Randolph County
99	n/a	69.9	**Shallotte** (town) Brunswick County
100	n/a	69.7	**Fletcher** (town) Henderson County
100	2578	69.7	**Raleigh** (city) Wake County
102	n/a	69.6	**Saint Stephens** (CDP) Catawba County
103	n/a	69.4	**Kitty Hawk** (town) Dare County
104	n/a	69.1	**Cajah's Mountain** (town) Caldwell County
104	2636	69.1	**Greenville** (city) Pitt County
104	n/a	69.1	**Nashville** (town) Nash County
107	n/a	68.9	**Hudson** (town) Caldwell County
108	n/a	68.7	**Boiling Spring Lakes** (city) Brunswick County
108	n/a	68.7	**Walkertown** (town) Forsyth County
110	n/a	68.6	**James City** (CDP) Craven County
110	n/a	68.6	**Pleasant Garden** (town) Guilford County
112	2702	68.4	**Knightdale** (town) Wake County
113	n/a	68.2	**Kings Grant** (CDP) New Hanover County
114	n/a	67.9	**Liberty** (town) Randolph County
114	2751	67.9	**Mount Holly** (city) Gaston County
116	n/a	67.7	**Cherryville** (city) Gaston County
117	2776	67.6	**Southern Pines** (town) Moore County
118	2799	67.4	**Concord** (city) Cabarrus County
119	n/a	67.2	**Louisburg** (town) Franklin County
120	n/a	67.1	**Mountain View** (CDP) Catawba County
121	n/a	66.8	**Midland** (town) Cabarrus County
121	2865	66.8	**Spring Lake** (town) Cumberland County
123	n/a	66.7	**Kill Devil Hills** (town) Dare County
124	n/a	66.3	**Northchase** (CDP) New Hanover County
125	2921	66.2	**Fayetteville** (city) Cumberland County
126	n/a	66.1	**Oak Island** (town) Brunswick County
127	2996	65.3	**Reidsville** (city) Rockingham County
128	3015	65.1	**Durham** (city) Durham County
129	3022	65.0	**Wilmington** (city) New Hanover County
130	n/a	64.7	**Hillsborough** (town) Orange County
131	3064	64.6	**Charlotte** (city) Mecklenburg County
132	n/a	64.4	**Valdese** (town) Burke County
133	3104	64.2	**Hope Mills** (town) Cumberland County
134	n/a	63.9	**Angier** (town) Harnett County
134	n/a	63.9	**Pittsboro** (town) Chatham County
136	n/a	63.6	**Mountain Home** (CDP) Henderson County
137	n/a	63.5	**Welcome** (CDP) Davidson County
138	n/a	63.1	**Fairview** (CDP) Buncombe County
138	3216	63.1	**Greensboro** (city) Guilford County
140	n/a	63.0	**Granite Quarry** (town) Rowan County
141	n/a	62.6	**Stanley** (town) Gaston County
142	n/a	62.5	**Enochville** (CDP) Rowan County
143	n/a	62.4	**Sawmills** (town) Caldwell County
144	n/a	62.2	**Trinity** (city) Randolph County
145	n/a	62.0	**Aberdeen** (town) Moore County
146	n/a	61.7	**Brevard** (city) Transylvania County
147	n/a	61.5	**Murfreesboro** (town) Hertford County
148	3367	61.3	**Hickory** (city) Catawba County
149	3392	61.0	**Asheville** (city) Buncombe County
150	n/a	60.7	**Glen Raven** (CDP) Alamance County

Note: The state column ranks the top/bottom 150 places in the state with population of 2,500 or more. The national column ranks the top/bottom places in the country with population of 10,000 or more. Places that are unincorporated were not considered in the rankings. n/a indicates data not available. Please refer to the User Guide for additional information.

Population with Private Health Insurance

Top 150 Places Ranked in *Ascending* Order

State Rank	Nat'l Rank	Percent	Place		State Rank	Nat'l Rank	Percent	Place
1	n/a	26.8	**Selma** (town) Johnston County		76	683	53.8	**Kings Mountain** (city) Cleveland County
2	n/a	33.5	**Enfield** (town) Halifax County		77	n/a	53.9	**Silver Lake** (CDP) New Hanover County
3	n/a	34.9	**Red Springs** (town) Robeson County		78	n/a	54.1	**Black Mountain** (town) Buncombe County
3	n/a	34.9	**Siler City** (town) Chatham County		79	n/a	54.3	**River Road** (CDP) Beaufort County
5	n/a	37.7	**Pembroke** (town) Robeson County		80	739	54.6	**Graham** (city) Alamance County
6	n/a	38.1	**Forest City** (town) Rutherford County		80	739	54.6	**Kannapolis** (city) Cabarrus County
7	n/a	38.5	**Fairmont** (town) Robeson County		82	n/a	54.8	**Canton** (town) Haywood County
8	n/a	38.8	**Ayden** (town) Pitt County		82	n/a	54.8	**Clinton** (city) Sampson County
9	n/a	39.0	**Benson** (town) Johnston County		84	755	54.9	**Lenoir** (city) Caldwell County
10	157	39.7	**Lexington** (city) Davidson County		85	776	55.1	**Salisbury** (city) Rowan County
11	n/a	40.7	**East Rockingham** (CDP) Richmond County		86	785	55.2	**Albemarle** (city) Stanly County
12	n/a	41.0	**Roxboro** (city) Person County		87	805	55.4	**Lincolnton** (city) Lincoln County
13	n/a	41.8	**East Flat Rock** (CDP) Henderson County		87	805	55.4	**Sanford** (city) Lee County
14	198	42.0	**Henderson** (city) Vance County		89	836	55.9	**Gastonia** (city) Gaston County
15	n/a	42.5	**South Rosemary** (CDP) Halifax County		90	n/a	56.0	**Yadkinville** (town) Yadkin County
16	n/a	42.7	**Tabor City** (town) Columbus County		91	852	56.1	**Wilson** (city) Wilson County
17	n/a	43.2	**Burgaw** (town) Pender County		92	863	56.2	**Mount Airy** (city) Surry County
18	n/a	43.3	**China Grove** (town) Rowan County		93	889	56.5	**New Bern** (city) Craven County
19	241	43.8	**Lumberton** (city) Robeson County		93	889	56.5	**Roanoke Rapids** (city) Halifax County
20	n/a	44.1	**Warsaw** (town) Duplin County		95	n/a	56.8	**Swannanoa** (CDP) Buncombe County
21	n/a	44.3	**North Wilkesboro** (town) Wilkes County		96	n/a	57.0	**Beaufort** (town) Carteret County
22	260	44.4	**Kinston** (city) Lenoir County		96	n/a	57.0	**Morehead City** (town) Carteret County
23	n/a	44.5	**Brogden** (CDP) Wayne County		98	n/a	57.2	**Skippers Corner** (CDP) New Hanover County
23	n/a	44.5	**Hamlet** (city) Richmond County		99	966	57.4	**Burlington** (city) Alamance County
25	n/a	45.0	**Plymouth** (town) Washington County		99	966	57.4	**Goldsboro** (city) Wayne County
26	n/a	45.1	**Edenton** (town) Chowan County		101	n/a	57.6	**Butner** (town) Granville County
27	n/a	45.3	**Marion** (city) McDowell County		102	n/a	57.9	**Wrightsboro** (CDP) New Hanover County
28	n/a	45.8	**Mount Olive** (town) Wayne County		103	n/a	58.0	**Lowell** (city) Gaston County
28	n/a	45.8	**Spencer** (town) Rowan County		104	n/a	58.2	**La Grange** (town) Lenoir County
30	n/a	45.9	**Polkton** (town) Anson County		104	n/a	58.2	**Landis** (town) Rowan County
31	n/a	46.3	**Whiteville** (city) Columbus County		106	1044	58.3	**High Point** (city) Guilford County
32	n/a	46.5	**Tyro** (CDP) Davidson County		107	n/a	58.4	**Oxford** (city) Granville County
33	356	46.9	**Asheboro** (city) Randolph County		108	n/a	58.5	**Erwin** (town) Harnett County
34	n/a	47.1	**Dunn** (city) Harnett County		108	n/a	58.5	**Granite Falls** (town) Caldwell County
35	372	47.3	**Smithfield** (town) Johnston County		110	n/a	58.6	**Dallas** (town) Gaston County
35	n/a	47.3	**Wadesboro** (town) Anson County		111	n/a	59.0	**Ranlo** (town) Gaston County
37	n/a	47.4	**Ahoskie** (town) Hertford County		112	n/a	59.1	**Sylva** (town) Jackson County
38	n/a	47.6	**Franklin** (town) Macon County		113	n/a	59.7	**Maiden** (town) Catawba County
39	n/a	48.5	**Farmville** (town) Pitt County		114	n/a	60.0	**Grifton** (town) Pitt County
39	n/a	48.5	**Troy** (town) Montgomery County		115	n/a	60.1	**Southport** (city) Brunswick County
41	n/a	48.6	**Williamston** (town) Martin County		116	n/a	60.3	**Mocksville** (town) Davie County
42	n/a	49.0	**Washington** (city) Beaufort County		116	n/a	60.3	**Rutherfordton** (town) Rutherford County
43	n/a	49.2	**Icard** (CDP) Burke County		118	n/a	60.4	**Conover** (city) Catawba County
43	454	49.2	**Laurinburg** (city) Scotland County		118	n/a	60.4	**Wendell** (town) Wake County
45	n/a	49.3	**Elkin** (town) Surry County		120	1231	60.6	**Winston-Salem** (city) Forsyth County
45	n/a	49.3	**Raeford** (city) Hoke County		121	n/a	60.7	**Glen Raven** (CDP) Alamance County
47	n/a	49.4	**Wallace** (town) Duplin County		121	n/a	60.7	**Wilkesboro** (town) Wilkes County
48	n/a	49.6	**Mar-Mac** (CDP) Wayne County		123	1257	61.0	**Asheville** (city) Buncombe County
49	n/a	49.9	**Gamewell** (town) Caldwell County		124	1279	61.3	**Hickory** (city) Catawba County
50	n/a	50.4	**Bessemer City** (city) Gaston County		125	n/a	61.5	**Murfreesboro** (town) Hertford County
51	527	50.6	**Morganton** (city) Burke County		126	n/a	61.7	**Brevard** (city) Transylvania County
52	529	50.7	**Monroe** (city) Union County		127	Nat'l	62.0	**Aberdeen** (town) Moore County
53	535	50.8	**Elizabeth City** (city) Pasquotank County		128	n/a	62.2	**Trinity** (city) Randolph County
54	n/a	51.0	**Spindale** (town) Rutherford County		129	n/a	62.4	**Sawmills** (town) Caldwell County
55	547	51.1	**Tarboro** (town) Edgecombe County		130	n/a	62.5	**Enochville** (CDP) Rowan County
55	n/a	51.1	**Windsor** (town) Bertie County		131	n/a	62.6	**Stanley** (town) Gaston County
57	n/a	51.5	**Dana** (CDP) Henderson County		132	n/a	63.0	**Granite Quarry** (town) Rowan County
58	n/a	51.7	**Waynesville** (town) Haywood County		133	n/a	63.1	**Fairview** (CDP) Buncombe County
59	n/a	51.9	**Elizabethtown** (town) Bladen County		133	1429	63.1	**Greensboro** (city) Guilford County
59	590	51.9	**Shelby** (city) Cleveland County		135	n/a	63.5	**Welcome** (CDP) Davidson County
61	n/a	52.1	**Rockingham** (city) Richmond County		136	n/a	63.6	**Mountain Home** (CDP) Henderson County
62	n/a	52.3	**Long View** (town) Catawba County		137	n/a	63.9	**Angier** (town) Harnett County
62	n/a	52.3	**Pineville** (town) Mecklenburg County		137	n/a	63.9	**Pittsboro** (town) Chatham County
62	n/a	52.3	**Woodfin** (town) Buncombe County		139	1544	64.2	**Hope Mills** (town) Cumberland County
65	612	52.5	**Hendersonville** (city) Henderson County		140	n/a	64.4	**Valdese** (town) Burke County
65	n/a	52.5	**Zebulon** (town) Wake County		141	1583	64.6	**Charlotte** (city) Mecklenburg County
67	628	52.7	**Eden** (city) Rockingham County		142	n/a	64.7	**Hillsborough** (town) Orange County
68	636	52.9	**Statesville** (city) Iredell County		143	1623	65.0	**Wilmington** (city) New Hanover County
69	n/a	53.1	**Elroy** (CDP) Wayne County		144	1635	65.1	**Durham** (city) Durham County
70	n/a	53.2	**Lillington** (town) Harnett County		145	1651	65.3	**Reidsville** (city) Rockingham County
71	660	53.3	**Newton** (city) Catawba County		146	n/a	66.1	**Oak Island** (town) Brunswick County
71	660	53.3	**Thomasville** (city) Davidson County		147	1726	66.2	**Fayetteville** (city) Cumberland County
73	n/a	53.4	**Sneads Ferry** (CDP) Onslow County		148	n/a	66.3	**Northchase** (CDP) New Hanover County
74	675	53.6	**Rocky Mount** (city) Nash County		149	n/a	66.7	**Kill Devil Hills** (town) Dare County
75	n/a	53.7	**Randleman** (city) Randolph County		150	n/a	66.8	**Midland** (town) Cabarrus County

Note: The state column ranks the top/bottom 150 places in the state with population of 2,500 or more. The national column ranks the top/bottom places in the country with population of 10,000 or more. Places that are unincorporated were not considered in the rankings. n/a indicates data not available. Please refer to the User Guide for additional information.

Population with Public Health Insurance

Top 150 Places Ranked in *Descending* Order

State Rank	Nat'l Rank	Percent	Place
1	n/a	64.6	**Sunset Beach** (town) Brunswick County
2	n/a	61.1	**Enfield** (town) Halifax County
3	n/a	58.4	**Burgaw** (town) Pender County
4	n/a	56.9	**Fairfield Harbour** (CDP) Craven County
5	n/a	55.7	**Red Springs** (town) Robeson County
6	n/a	55.5	**Saint James** (town) Brunswick County
6	n/a	55.5	**South Rosemary** (CDP) Halifax County
8	n/a	55.3	**Carolina Shores** (town) Brunswick County
9	n/a	55.1	**Edenton** (town) Chowan County
10	n/a	54.9	**Fairmont** (town) Robeson County
11	n/a	54.8	**Plymouth** (town) Washington County
12	n/a	54.3	**Forest City** (town) Rutherford County
13	51	53.7	**Henderson** (city) Vance County
14	n/a	52.3	**Spindale** (town) Rutherford County
15	70	51.9	**Hendersonville** (city) Henderson County
16	87	51.1	**Kinston** (city) Lenoir County
17	88	50.9	**Laurinburg** (city) Scotland County
18	n/a	50.4	**Whiteville** (city) Columbus County
19	n/a	50.2	**Marion** (city) McDowell County
19	n/a	50.2	**Windsor** (town) Bertie County
21	n/a	50.0	**Tabor City** (town) Columbus County
22	n/a	49.9	**Elroy** (CDP) Wayne County
23	n/a	49.7	**Ahoskie** (town) Hertford County
23	n/a	49.7	**Williamston** (town) Martin County
25	n/a	49.6	**Washington** (city) Beaufort County
26	n/a	49.5	**Pembroke** (town) Robeson County
27	n/a	49.3	**Benson** (town) Johnston County
27	n/a	49.3	**North Wilkesboro** (town) Wilkes County
27	n/a	49.3	**River Bend** (town) Craven County
30	n/a	48.9	**Southport** (city) Brunswick County
31	n/a	48.6	**Elizabethtown** (town) Bladen County
32	n/a	48.4	**Beaufort** (town) Carteret County
32	141	48.4	**Lexington** (city) Davidson County
34	144	48.3	**Smithfield** (town) Johnston County
35	n/a	47.8	**Raeford** (city) Hoke County
36	n/a	47.6	**La Grange** (town) Lenoir County
37	n/a	47.2	**Mount Olive** (town) Wayne County
38	n/a	46.7	**Flat Rock** (village) Henderson County
39	n/a	46.4	**Hamlet** (city) Richmond County
39	n/a	46.4	**Troy** (town) Montgomery County
41	217	46.3	**Lumberton** (city) Robeson County
41	n/a	46.3	**Selma** (town) Johnston County
43	227	46.1	**Goldsboro** (city) Wayne County
44	n/a	46.0	**Lillington** (town) Harnett County
44	n/a	46.0	**Warsaw** (town) Duplin County
46	235	45.9	**Mount Airy** (city) Surry County
47	n/a	45.4	**Farmville** (town) Pitt County
48	263	45.2	**Tarboro** (town) Edgecombe County
49	n/a	44.7	**Valdese** (town) Burke County
50	291	44.6	**Shelby** (city) Cleveland County
51	n/a	44.5	**Wadesboro** (town) Anson County
52	n/a	44.4	**Clinton** (city) Sampson County
52	n/a	44.4	**Long View** (town) Catawba County
52	303	44.4	**Pinehurst** (village) Moore County
55	n/a	44.2	**Dunn** (city) Harnett County
56	n/a	43.9	**Ayden** (town) Pitt County
56	n/a	43.9	**Brevard** (city) Transylvania County
56	343	43.9	**Morganton** (city) Burke County
59	n/a	43.7	**Polkton** (town) Anson County
59	n/a	43.7	**Wilkesboro** (town) Wilkes County
61	362	43.6	**New Bern** (city) Craven County
62	n/a	43.3	**Mountain Home** (CDP) Henderson County
62	380	43.3	**Reidsville** (city) Rockingham County
62	n/a	43.3	**Roxboro** (city) Person County
65	n/a	43.1	**Waynesville** (town) Haywood County
66	n/a	42.8	**Brogden** (CDP) Wayne County
66	n/a	42.8	**Spencer** (town) Rowan County
68	433	42.4	**Rocky Mount** (city) Nash County
69	n/a	42.3	**Rockingham** (city) Richmond County
70	457	42.1	**Roanoke Rapids** (city) Halifax County
71	486	41.7	**Eden** (city) Rockingham County
72	n/a	41.5	**Butner** (town) Granville County
73	n/a	41.4	**Siler City** (town) Chatham County
73	512	41.4	**Southern Pines** (town) Moore County
75	n/a	41.0	**Oxford** (city) Granville County
76	n/a	40.7	**Black Mountain** (town) Buncombe County
77	564	40.6	**Lenoir** (city) Caldwell County
78	575	40.5	**Kings Mountain** (city) Cleveland County
79	595	40.2	**Newton** (city) Catawba County
80	615	40.0	**Albemarle** (city) Stanly County
80	n/a	40.0	**Mar-Mac** (CDP) Wayne County
82	n/a	39.9	**Franklin** (town) Macon County
82	n/a	39.9	**Oak Island** (town) Brunswick County
84	n/a	39.8	**Erwin** (town) Harnett County
85	n/a	39.7	**Gamewell** (town) Caldwell County
85	640	39.7	**Statesville** (city) Iredell County
85	n/a	39.7	**Whispering Pines** (village) Moore County
88	n/a	39.6	**Mocksville** (town) Davie County
89	n/a	39.5	**Elkin** (town) Surry County
89	655	39.5	**Lincolnton** (city) Lincoln County
89	655	39.5	**Thomasville** (city) Davidson County
92	n/a	39.3	**Morehead City** (town) Carteret County
93	n/a	39.1	**Lake Royale** (CDP) Franklin County
94	n/a	39.0	**China Grove** (town) Rowan County
94	n/a	39.0	**East Rockingham** (CDP) Richmond County
94	n/a	39.0	**Grifton** (town) Pitt County
97	n/a	38.9	**Stanley** (town) Gaston County
98	n/a	38.7	**Woodfin** (town) Buncombe County
99	736	38.6	**Salisbury** (city) Rowan County
100	n/a	38.5	**Canton** (town) Haywood County
101	779	38.1	**Burlington** (city) Alamance County
102	n/a	38.0	**Wendell** (town) Wake County
103	803	37.9	**Wilson** (city) Wilson County
104	n/a	37.8	**East Flat Rock** (CDP) Henderson County
105	825	37.7	**Elizabeth City** (city) Pasquotank County
106	n/a	37.6	**Randleman** (city) Randolph County
107	n/a	37.5	**Zebulon** (town) Wake County
108	n/a	37.0	**Rutherfordton** (town) Rutherford County
109	n/a	36.7	**Hudson** (town) Caldwell County
110	939	36.6	**Asheboro** (city) Randolph County
110	n/a	36.6	**Conover** (city) Catawba County
110	n/a	36.6	**Sneads Ferry** (CDP) Onslow County
110	n/a	36.6	**Trinity** (city) Randolph County
114	n/a	36.5	**Walkertown** (town) Forsyth County
115	n/a	36.3	**Murfreesboro** (town) Hertford County
116	n/a	36.0	**Aberdeen** (town) Moore County
116	n/a	36.0	**Hillsborough** (town) Orange County
118	n/a	35.9	**River Road** (CDP) Beaufort County
118	n/a	35.9	**Weaverville** (town) Buncombe County
118	n/a	35.9	**Wrightsboro** (CDP) New Hanover County
121	n/a	35.8	**Maiden** (town) Catawba County
122	1057	35.7	**Gastonia** (city) Gaston County
123	n/a	35.6	**Lake Junaluska** (CDP) Haywood County
124	n/a	35.5	**Angier** (town) Harnett County
125	n/a	35.4	**Etowah** (CDP) Henderson County
126	n/a	35.3	**Bessemer City** (city) Gaston County
127	1151	34.9	**Hope Mills** (town) Cumberland County
128	n/a	34.7	**Pineville** (town) Mecklenburg County
129	n/a	34.5	**Pleasant Garden** (town) Guilford County
129	n/a	34.5	**Tyro** (CDP) Davidson County
131	1218	34.4	**Kannapolis** (city) Cabarrus County
131	n/a	34.4	**Shallotte** (town) Brunswick County
133	n/a	34.3	**Louisburg** (town) Franklin County
133	n/a	34.3	**Sylva** (town) Jackson County
135	n/a	34.2	**Wallace** (town) Duplin County
136	1292	33.9	**Fayetteville** (city) Cumberland County
136	1292	33.9	**Graham** (city) Alamance County
136	n/a	33.9	**Ranlo** (town) Gaston County
139	n/a	33.7	**Emerald Isle** (town) Carteret County
140	n/a	33.6	**Mountain View** (CDP) Catawba County
141	1376	33.4	**Asheville** (city) Buncombe County
141	n/a	33.4	**Yadkinville** (town) Yadkin County
143	1395	33.3	**Sanford** (city) Lee County
144	n/a	33.2	**Landis** (town) Rowan County
145	n/a	33.0	**Eastover** (town) Cumberland County
145	n/a	33.0	**Fairview** (CDP) Buncombe County
147	n/a	32.8	**Trent Woods** (town) Craven County
148	n/a	32.7	**Sawmills** (town) Caldwell County
148	n/a	32.7	**Swansboro** (town) Onslow County
150	n/a	32.6	**Granite Quarry** (town) Rowan County

Note: The state column ranks the top/bottom 150 places in the state with population of 2,500 or more. The national column ranks the top/bottom places in the country with population of 10,000 or more. Places that are unincorporated were not considered in the rankings. n/a indicates data not available. Please refer to the User Guide for additional information.

Population with Public Health Insurance

Top 150 Places Ranked in *Ascending* Order

State Rank	Nat'l Rank	Percent	Place
1	n/a	6.8	**Marvin** (village) Union County
2	n/a	9.0	**Cullowhee** (CDP) Jackson County
3	37	9.1	**Boone** (town) Watauga County
4	n/a	9.8	**Buies Creek** (CDP) Harnett County
5	52	10.1	**Morrisville** (town) Wake County
6	61	10.3	**Apex** (town) Wake County
7	n/a	10.9	**Wesley Chapel** (village) Union County
8	n/a	11.1	**Oak Ridge** (town) Guilford County
9	113	12.0	**Huntersville** (town) Mecklenburg County
10	160	13.1	**Holly Springs** (town) Wake County
11	n/a	13.2	**Archer Lodge** (town) Johnston County
12	n/a	13.3	**Weddington** (town) Union County
13	181	13.6	**Cary** (town) Wake County
14	230	14.3	**Chapel Hill** (town) Orange County
15	259	14.7	**Davidson** (town) Mecklenburg County
16	267	14.8	**Carrboro** (town) Orange County
17	n/a	15.0	**Waxhaw** (town) Union County
18	n/a	15.1	**Stokesdale** (town) Guilford County
19	320	15.5	**Harrisburg** (town) Cabarrus County
20	381	16.2	**Cornelius** (town) Mecklenburg County
20	n/a	16.2	**Moyock** (CDP) Currituck County
22	405	16.5	**Summerfield** (town) Guilford County
23	655	18.5	**Mooresville** (town) Iredell County
24	668	18.6	**Clayton** (town) Johnston County
24	668	18.6	**Indian Trail** (town) Union County
24	n/a	18.6	**Kill Devil Hills** (town) Dare County
27	713	18.9	**Wake Forest** (town) Wake County
28	n/a	19.2	**Unionville** (town) Union County
29	n/a	19.3	**Ogden** (CDP) New Hanover County
30	n/a	19.7	**Lowesville** (CDP) Lincoln County
31	865	19.8	**Knightdale** (town) Wake County
32	n/a	19.9	**Westport** (CDP) Lincoln County
33	n/a	20.4	**Kings Grant** (CDP) New Hanover County
34	n/a	20.6	**Cramerton** (town) Gaston County
34	n/a	20.6	**Winterville** (town) Pitt County
36	1040	20.8	**Matthews** (town) Mecklenburg County
37	n/a	20.9	**Nags Head** (town) Dare County
38	n/a	21.0	**Boiling Springs** (town) Cleveland County
38	1072	21.0	**Murraysville** (CDP) New Hanover County
40	n/a	21.1	**Wallburg** (town) Davidson County
41	1133	21.3	**Garner** (town) Wake County
42	n/a	21.4	**Half Moon** (CDP) Onslow County
43	n/a	21.5	**Elon** (town) Alamance County
44	1206	21.7	**Stallings** (town) Union County
45	1219	21.8	**Raleigh** (city) Wake County
46	1242	21.9	**Jacksonville** (city) Onslow County
47	n/a	22.1	**Red Oak** (town) Nash County
48	1297	22.2	**Fuquay-Varina** (town) Wake County
48	n/a	22.2	**Hampstead** (CDP) Pender County
50	1336	22.4	**Lewisville** (town) Forsyth County
51	1380	22.7	**Clemmons** (village) Forsyth County
51	n/a	22.7	**Wingate** (town) Union County
53	n/a	22.8	**Royal Pines** (CDP) Buncombe County
54	n/a	23.0	**Lake Park** (village) Union County
55	n/a	23.1	**Carolina Beach** (town) New Hanover County
55	n/a	23.1	**Skippers Corner** (CDP) New Hanover County
57	n/a	23.3	**Dana** (CDP) Henderson County
58	n/a	23.4	**Gibsonville** (town) Guilford County
59	n/a	23.6	**Brices Creek** (CDP) Craven County
60	n/a	23.8	**Creedmoor** (city) Granville County
60	1600	23.8	**Greenville** (city) Pitt County
62	1638	24.0	**Mebane** (city) Alamance County
63	1653	24.1	**Havelock** (city) Craven County
64	1683	24.2	**Belmont** (city) Gaston County
65	n/a	24.3	**Kitty Hawk** (town) Dare County
66	1768	24.7	**Charlotte** (city) Mecklenburg County
66	1768	24.7	**Piney Green** (CDP) Onslow County
68	n/a	24.9	**Rolesville** (town) Wake County
69	n/a	25.0	**Lake Norman of Catawba** (CDP) Catawba County
70	n/a	25.1	**Lowell** (city) Gaston County
71	n/a	25.3	**Mineral Springs** (town) Union County
72	1927	25.5	**Concord** (city) Cabarrus County
72	n/a	25.5	**King** (city) Stokes County
74	1944	25.6	**Kernersville** (town) Forsyth County
75	1983	25.8	**Archdale** (city) Randolph County
76	n/a	25.9	**Bethlehem** (CDP) Alexander County
76	1997	25.9	**Durham** (city) Durham County
76	1997	25.9	**Leland** (town) Brunswick County
79	n/a	26.6	**Fairview** (town) Union County
80	2174	26.8	**Spring Lake** (town) Cumberland County
81	n/a	27.0	**Rural Hall** (town) Forsyth County
82	n/a	27.2	**Bayshore** (CDP) New Hanover County
83	n/a	27.3	**Jamestown** (town) Guilford County
83	n/a	27.3	**Locust** (city) Stanly County
85	2337	27.6	**Mount Holly** (city) Gaston County
86	n/a	27.8	**Forest Oaks** (CDP) Guilford County
87	n/a	27.9	**Newport** (town) Carteret County
88	2462	28.3	**Mint Hill** (town) Mecklenburg County
88	n/a	28.3	**Myrtle Grove** (CDP) New Hanover County
88	n/a	28.3	**Porters Neck** (CDP) New Hanover County
91	2515	28.6	**Greensboro** (city) Guilford County
91	n/a	28.6	**Silver Lake** (CDP) New Hanover County
93	n/a	29.2	**Granite Falls** (town) Caldwell County
93	2617	29.2	**Hickory** (city) Catawba County
95	n/a	29.3	**Northchase** (CDP) New Hanover County
95	n/a	29.3	**Wentworth** (town) Rockingham County
97	n/a	29.5	**Rockfish** (CDP) Hoke County
98	n/a	29.6	**Liberty** (town) Randolph County
99	n/a	29.8	**Swannanoa** (CDP) Buncombe County
100	n/a	29.9	**Fletcher** (town) Henderson County
100	n/a	29.9	**Pittsboro** (town) Chatham County
102	n/a	30.0	**Welcome** (CDP) Davidson County
103	n/a	30.1	**Saint Stephens** (CDP) Catawba County
104	n/a	30.2	**Dallas** (town) Gaston County
105	n/a	30.3	**Enochville** (CDP) Rowan County
106	2841	30.6	**Wilmington** (city) New Hanover County
107	n/a	30.7	**Glen Raven** (CDP) Alamance County
108	n/a	30.8	**Cajah's Mountain** (town) Caldwell County
108	n/a	30.8	**Midland** (town) Cabarrus County
110	n/a	30.9	**Cherryville** (city) Gaston County
111	n/a	31.3	**Nashville** (town) Nash County
112	2989	31.5	**High Point** (city) Guilford County
112	n/a	31.5	**James City** (CDP) Craven County
114	3030	31.8	**Winston-Salem** (city) Forsyth County
115	n/a	31.9	**Southern Shores** (town) Dare County
116	n/a	32.0	**Boiling Spring Lakes** (city) Brunswick County
116	n/a	32.0	**Mills River** (town) Henderson County
118	3078	32.1	**Monroe** (city) Union County
119	n/a	32.3	**Seven Lakes** (CDP) Moore County
120	n/a	32.5	**Icard** (CDP) Burke County
120	n/a	32.5	**Midway** (town) Davidson County
122	n/a	32.6	**Granite Quarry** (town) Rowan County
123	n/a	32.7	**Sawmills** (town) Caldwell County
123	n/a	32.7	**Swansboro** (town) Onslow County
125	n/a	32.8	**Trent Woods** (town) Craven County
126	n/a	33.0	**Eastover** (town) Cumberland County
126	n/a	33.0	**Fairview** (CDP) Buncombe County
128	n/a	33.2	**Landis** (town) Rowan County
129	3247	33.3	**Sanford** (city) Lee County
130	3262	33.4	**Asheville** (city) Buncombe County
130	n/a	33.4	**Yadkinville** (town) Yadkin County
132	n/a	33.6	**Mountain View** (CDP) Catawba County
133	n/a	33.7	**Emerald Isle** (town) Carteret County
134	3347	33.9	**Fayetteville** (city) Cumberland County
134	3347	33.9	**Graham** (city) Alamance County
134	n/a	33.9	**Ranlo** (town) Gaston County
137	n/a	34.2	**Wallace** (town) Duplin County
138	n/a	34.3	**Louisburg** (town) Franklin County
138	n/a	34.3	**Sylva** (town) Jackson County
140	3422	34.4	**Kannapolis** (city) Cabarrus County
140	n/a	34.4	**Shallotte** (town) Brunswick County
142	n/a	34.5	**Pleasant Garden** (town) Guilford County
142	n/a	34.5	**Tyro** (CDP) Davidson County
144	n/a	34.7	**Pineville** (town) Mecklenburg County
145	3487	34.9	**Hope Mills** (town) Cumberland County
146	n/a	35.3	**Bessemer City** (city) Gaston County
147	n/a	35.4	**Etowah** (CDP) Henderson County
148	n/a	35.5	**Angier** (town) Harnett County
149	n/a	35.6	**Lake Junaluska** (CDP) Haywood County
150	3591	35.7	**Gastonia** (city) Gaston County

Note: The state column ranks the top/bottom 150 places in the state with population of 2,500 or more. The national column ranks the top/bottom places in the country with population of 10,000 or more. Places that are unincorporated were not considered in the rankings. n/a indicates data not available. Please refer to the User Guide for additional information.

Population with No Health Insurance

Top 150 Places Ranked in *Descending* Order

State Rank	Nat'l Rank	Percent	Place
1	n/a	36.2	**Selma** (town) Johnston County
2	n/a	34.8	**Dana** (CDP) Henderson County
3	n/a	33.2	**Siler City** (town) Chatham County
4	n/a	31.1	**East Flat Rock** (CDP) Henderson County
5	n/a	28.8	**Wallace** (town) Duplin County
6	n/a	28.4	**Icard** (CDP) Burke County
6	n/a	28.4	**Skippers Corner** (CDP) New Hanover County
8	n/a	27.9	**Franklin** (town) Macon County
8	n/a	27.9	**Silver Lake** (CDP) New Hanover County
10	n/a	27.2	**Lowell** (city) Gaston County
11	n/a	27.1	**East Rockingham** (CDP) Richmond County
12	n/a	26.5	**Tyro** (CDP) Davidson County
13	n/a	25.7	**Pineville** (town) Mecklenburg County
14	277	25.6	**Monroe** (city) Union County
15	n/a	25.4	**Elkin** (town) Surry County
15	n/a	25.4	**Gamewell** (town) Caldwell County
15	n/a	25.4	**Roxboro** (city) Person County
18	n/a	25.0	**Brogden** (CDP) Wayne County
19	n/a	24.9	**Ayden** (town) Pitt County
20	323	24.8	**Asheboro** (city) Randolph County
20	n/a	24.8	**Benson** (town) Johnston County
22	n/a	24.3	**Bessemer City** (city) Gaston County
23	363	24.0	**Elizabeth City** (city) Pasquotank County
24	n/a	23.9	**Enochville** (CDP) Rowan County
25	n/a	23.7	**Landis** (town) Rowan County
26	n/a	23.6	**Kill Devil Hills** (town) Dare County
27	n/a	23.3	**Canton** (town) Haywood County
28	n/a	23.2	**Kings Grant** (CDP) New Hanover County
29	n/a	23.1	**Warsaw** (town) Duplin County
30	n/a	22.9	**China Grove** (town) Rowan County
30	445	22.9	**Graham** (city) Alamance County
30	n/a	22.9	**Yadkinville** (town) Yadkin County
33	n/a	22.7	**Woodfin** (town) Buncombe County
34	477	22.4	**Lexington** (city) Davidson County
34	n/a	22.4	**River Road** (CDP) Beaufort County
36	n/a	22.0	**Wadesboro** (town) Anson County
37	n/a	21.9	**Swannanoa** (CDP) Buncombe County
38	n/a	21.8	**Dallas** (town) Gaston County
39	n/a	21.7	**Morehead City** (town) Carteret County
39	538	21.7	**Sanford** (city) Lee County
41	n/a	21.5	**Zebulon** (town) Wake County
42	n/a	21.4	**Dunn** (city) Harnett County
43	n/a	21.1	**Black Mountain** (town) Buncombe County
43	n/a	21.1	**Fairview** (CDP) Buncombe County
45	n/a	21.0	**Spencer** (town) Rowan County
46	n/a	20.6	**Mount Olive** (town) Wayne County
46	n/a	20.6	**Waynesville** (town) Haywood County
48	n/a	20.5	**Sneads Ferry** (CDP) Onslow County
49	n/a	20.3	**Hamlet** (city) Richmond County
49	679	20.3	**Kannapolis** (city) Cabarrus County
49	n/a	20.3	**North Wilkesboro** (town) Wilkes County
52	707	20.1	**Newton** (city) Catawba County
53	n/a	20.0	**Farmville** (town) Pitt County
53	n/a	20.0	**Tabor City** (town) Columbus County
55	n/a	19.9	**Wrightsboro** (CDP) New Hanover County
56	n/a	19.8	**Mar-Mac** (CDP) Wayne County
57	753	19.7	**Kinston** (city) Lenoir County
57	753	19.7	**Lumberton** (city) Robeson County
57	n/a	19.7	**Oak Island** (town) Brunswick County
57	753	19.7	**Tarboro** (town) Edgecombe County
61	n/a	19.6	**Granite Falls** (town) Caldwell County
62	n/a	19.5	**Whiteville** (city) Columbus County
63	n/a	19.4	**Welcome** (CDP) Davidson County
64	n/a	19.3	**Archer Lodge** (town) Johnston County
64	811	19.3	**Hickory** (city) Catawba County
64	n/a	19.3	**Pembroke** (town) Robeson County
67	836	19.1	**Albemarle** (city) Stanly County
68	n/a	19.0	**Burgaw** (town) Pender County
68	849	19.0	**Eden** (city) Rockingham County
68	849	19.0	**High Point** (city) Guilford County
71	n/a	18.9	**Ranlo** (town) Gaston County
71	869	18.9	**Statesville** (city) Iredell County
73	n/a	18.8	**Carolina Beach** (town) New Hanover County
73	884	18.8	**Morganton** (city) Burke County
73	884	18.8	**Smithfield** (town) Johnston County
73	884	18.8	**Thomasville** (city) Davidson County
77	922	18.6	**Gastonia** (city) Gaston County
77	n/a	18.6	**Polkton** (town) Anson County
79	932	18.5	**Henderson** (city) Vance County
79	n/a	18.5	**Kitty Hawk** (town) Dare County
81	969	18.3	**Hendersonville** (city) Henderson County
81	969	18.3	**Salisbury** (city) Rowan County
83	n/a	18.2	**Sylva** (town) Jackson County
84	1000	18.1	**Charlotte** (city) Mecklenburg County
84	1000	18.1	**Wilson** (city) Wilson County
86	n/a	18.0	**Red Springs** (town) Robeson County
86	n/a	18.0	**Rutherfordton** (town) Rutherford County
86	1020	18.0	**Winston-Salem** (city) Forsyth County
89	n/a	17.8	**Forest City** (town) Rutherford County
89	n/a	17.8	**Sawmills** (town) Caldwell County
91	1057	17.7	**Asheville** (city) Buncombe County
92	1115	17.4	**Greensboro** (city) Guilford County
92	1115	17.4	**Knightdale** (town) Wake County
92	1115	17.4	**Lincolnton** (city) Lincoln County
95	1137	17.3	**Kings Mountain** (city) Cleveland County
95	1137	17.3	**Lenoir** (city) Caldwell County
95	n/a	17.3	**Long View** (town) Catawba County
98	1159	17.2	**Burlington** (city) Alamance County
98	n/a	17.2	**Fairmont** (town) Robeson County
100	1177	17.1	**Durham** (city) Durham County
100	n/a	17.1	**Grifton** (town) Pitt County
102	1209	16.9	**Shelby** (city) Cleveland County
102	n/a	16.9	**Troy** (town) Montgomery County
104	n/a	16.7	**Ahoskie** (town) Hertford County
104	1242	16.7	**Indian Trail** (town) Union County
104	n/a	16.7	**Newport** (town) Carteret County
104	1242	16.7	**Rocky Mount** (city) Nash County
104	1242	16.7	**Wilmington** (city) New Hanover County
109	n/a	16.6	**Mountain View** (CDP) Catawba County
110	1311	16.4	**Concord** (city) Cabarrus County
111	1337	16.3	**Carrboro** (town) Orange County
111	n/a	16.3	**Rockingham** (city) Richmond County
113	n/a	16.2	**Enfield** (town) Halifax County
113	1355	16.2	**New Bern** (city) Craven County
115	1373	16.1	**Raleigh** (city) Wake County
116	n/a	16.0	**South Rosemary** (CDP) Halifax County
117	n/a	15.9	**Bayshore** (CDP) New Hanover County
118	n/a	15.8	**Midland** (town) Cabarrus County
119	n/a	15.7	**Conover** (city) Catawba County
119	n/a	15.7	**Maiden** (town) Catawba County
121	n/a	15.6	**Glen Raven** (CDP) Alamance County
122	n/a	15.5	**Erwin** (town) Harnett County
122	1490	15.5	**Fuquay-Varina** (town) Wake County
122	n/a	15.5	**James City** (CDP) Craven County
122	n/a	15.5	**Marion** (city) McDowell County
126	n/a	15.4	**Brevard** (city) Transylvania County
126	n/a	15.4	**Lillington** (town) Harnett County
126	1511	15.4	**Mount Holly** (city) Gaston County
129	n/a	15.3	**Boiling Spring Lakes** (city) Brunswick County
129	n/a	15.3	**Clinton** (city) Sampson County
131	n/a	15.2	**Angier** (town) Harnett County
132	n/a	15.0	**Etowah** (CDP) Henderson County
133	n/a	14.9	**Washington** (city) Beaufort County
134	n/a	14.8	**Creedmoor** (city) Granville County
134	n/a	14.8	**Williamston** (town) Martin County
136	n/a	14.5	**Aberdeen** (town) Moore County
136	1663	14.5	**Garner** (town) Wake County
136	n/a	14.5	**Mocksville** (town) Davie County
136	1663	14.5	**Spring Lake** (town) Cumberland County
140	1683	14.4	**Mount Airy** (city) Surry County
141	n/a	14.3	**Granite Quarry** (town) Rowan County
141	1713	14.3	**Havelock** (city) Craven County
141	1713	14.3	**Mooresville** (town) Iredell County
144	1736	14.2	**Clayton** (town) Johnston County
144	n/a	14.2	**Walkertown** (town) Forsyth County
146	n/a	14.1	**Edenton** (town) Chowan County
146	1758	14.1	**Fayetteville** (city) Cumberland County
148	1781	14.0	**Greenville** (city) Pitt County
149	n/a	13.9	**Lowesville** (CDP) Lincoln County
149	n/a	13.9	**Raeford** (city) Hoke County

Note: The state column ranks the top/bottom 150 places in the state with population of 2,500 or more. The national column ranks the top/bottom places in the country with population of 10,000 or more. Places that are unincorporated were not considered in the rankings. n/a indicates data not available. Please refer to the User Guide for additional information.

Population with No Health Insurance

Top 150 Places Ranked in *Ascending* Order

State Rank	Nat'l Rank	Percent	Place
1	n/a	1.3	Saint James (town) Brunswick County
2	n/a	1.6	Forest Oaks (CDP) Guilford County
3	n/a	2.2	Whispering Pines (village) Moore County
4	n/a	2.7	Marvin (village) Union County
5	n/a	3.3	Seven Lakes (CDP) Moore County
6	n/a	3.4	Brices Creek (CDP) Craven County
7	291	3.7	Pinehurst (village) Moore County
8	n/a	4.3	Porters Neck (CDP) New Hanover County
9	n/a	5.0	Trent Woods (town) Craven County
10	622	5.1	Summerfield (town) Guilford County
10	n/a	5.1	Sunset Beach (town) Brunswick County
12	n/a	5.4	Oak Ridge (town) Guilford County
12	n/a	5.4	Wesley Chapel (village) Union County
14	n/a	5.5	Buies Creek (CDP) Harnett County
15	828	5.9	Davidson (town) Mecklenburg County
16	n/a	6.0	Fairfield Harbour (CDP) Craven County
17	902	6.2	Morrisville (town) Wake County
18	n/a	6.3	Lake Norman of Catawba (CDP) Catawba County
19	n/a	6.4	Unionville (town) Union County
20	989	6.5	Holly Springs (town) Wake County
20	989	6.5	Lewisville (town) Forsyth County
22	n/a	6.7	Fairview (town) Union County
22	n/a	6.7	Flat Rock (village) Henderson County
22	n/a	6.7	Red Oak (town) Nash County
25	n/a	6.8	Royal Pines (CDP) Buncombe County
26	1236	7.4	Apex (town) Wake County
27	n/a	7.6	Midway (town) Davidson County
28	n/a	7.7	Elon (town) Alamance County
29	n/a	7.8	King (city) Stokes County
30	n/a	7.9	Carolina Shores (town) Brunswick County
30	n/a	7.9	Hampstead (CDP) Pender County
30	n/a	7.9	Lake Park (village) Union County
30	1366	7.9	Wake Forest (town) Wake County
34	1499	8.3	Weddington (town) Union County
35	1499	8.4	Boone (town) Watauga County
35	n/a	8.4	Mills River (town) Henderson County
35	n/a	8.4	Westport (CDP) Lincoln County
38	1525	8.5	Chapel Hill (town) Orange County
38	n/a	8.5	Wallburg (town) Davidson County
40	n/a	8.6	Waxhaw (town) Union County
41	n/a	8.7	Swansboro (town) Onslow County
42	n/a	8.8	Moyock (CDP) Currituck County
43	n/a	8.9	Rockfish (CDP) Hoke County
44	n/a	9.0	Wingate (town) Union County
45	n/a	9.1	Cramerton (town) Gaston County
46	n/a	9.3	Emerald Isle (town) Carteret County
47	n/a	9.4	Hillsborough (town) Orange County
47	1759	9.4	Reidsville (city) Rockingham County
47	1759	9.4	Stallings (town) Union County
50	n/a	9.5	Boiling Springs (town) Cleveland County
50	n/a	9.5	Myrtle Grove (CDP) New Hanover County
52	n/a	9.6	Lake Junaluska (CDP) Haywood County
53	n/a	9.9	Hudson (town) Caldwell County
53	n/a	9.9	Lake Royale (CDP) Franklin County
55	1898	10.0	Cary (town) Wake County
56	1948	10.2	Jacksonville (city) Onslow County
56	n/a	10.2	Wilkesboro (town) Wilkes County
58	1978	10.3	Harrisburg (town) Cabarrus County
58	n/a	10.3	Shallotte (town) Brunswick County
58	n/a	10.3	Weaverville (town) Buncombe County
61	n/a	10.6	River Bend (town) Craven County
62	2068	10.7	Clemmons (village) Forsyth County
62	n/a	10.7	Eastover (town) Cumberland County
64	n/a	10.8	Pleasant Garden (town) Guilford County
65	2117	10.9	Matthews (town) Mecklenburg County
65	2117	10.9	Mebane (city) Alamance County
65	n/a	10.9	Murfreesboro (town) Hertford County
65	2117	10.9	Southern Pines (town) Moore County
69	n/a	11.1	Gibsonville (town) Guilford County
69	2171	11.1	Huntersville (town) Mecklenburg County
71	2194	11.2	Hope Mills (town) Cumberland County
71	2194	11.2	Mint Hill (town) Mecklenburg County
73	n/a	11.3	Plymouth (town) Washington County
73	n/a	11.3	Valdese (town) Burke County
75	n/a	11.4	Rural Hall (town) Forsyth County
76	n/a	11.6	Rolesville (town) Wake County
77	n/a	11.7	Cullowhee (CDP) Jackson County
78	n/a	11.8	Jamestown (town) Guilford County
79	n/a	11.9	Beaufort (town) Carteret County
79	n/a	11.9	Fletcher (town) Henderson County
81	n/a	12.0	Southport (city) Brunswick County
82	n/a	12.1	Mountain Home (CDP) Henderson County
83	n/a	12.3	Saint Stephens (CDP) Catawba County
84	n/a	12.4	Stanley (town) Gaston County
84	n/a	12.4	Trinity (city) Randolph County
86	2504	12.5	Cornelius (town) Mecklenburg County
86	n/a	12.5	Locust (city) Stanly County
88	2527	12.6	Kernersville (town) Forsyth County
88	n/a	12.6	Spindale (town) Rutherford County
90	2546	12.7	Leland (town) Brunswick County
90	n/a	12.7	Ogden (CDP) New Hanover County
92	n/a	12.9	Northchase (CDP) New Hanover County
92	n/a	12.9	Southern Shores (town) Dare County
92	n/a	12.9	Winterville (town) Pitt County
95	n/a	13.0	Mineral Springs (town) Union County
96	2638	13.1	Archdale (city) Randolph County
96	2638	13.1	Belmont (city) Gaston County
96	n/a	13.1	Elroy (CDP) Wayne County
96	2638	13.1	Goldsboro (city) Wayne County
96	n/a	13.1	Nashville (town) Nash County
96	n/a	13.1	Wentworth (town) Rockingham County
102	n/a	13.2	Oxford (city) Granville County
103	n/a	13.3	Bethlehem (CDP) Alexander County
103	n/a	13.3	Liberty (town) Randolph County
103	2685	13.3	Murraysville (CDP) New Hanover County
103	n/a	13.3	Stokesdale (town) Guilford County
107	n/a	13.4	Cherryville (city) Gaston County
108	n/a	13.5	Butner (town) Granville County
108	2739	13.5	Laurinburg (city) Scotland County
108	n/a	13.5	Louisburg (town) Franklin County
108	2739	13.5	Piney Green (CDP) Onslow County
108	n/a	13.5	Pittsboro (town) Chatham County
108	n/a	13.5	Wendell (town) Wake County
114	n/a	13.6	Cajah's Mountain (town) Caldwell County
114	n/a	13.6	Nags Head (town) Dare County
114	2760	13.6	Roanoke Rapids (city) Halifax County
114	n/a	13.6	Windsor (town) Bertie County
118	n/a	13.7	Elizabethtown (town) Bladen County
118	n/a	13.7	Randleman (city) Randolph County
120	n/a	13.8	Half Moon (CDP) Onslow County
120	n/a	13.8	La Grange (town) Lenoir County
122	n/a	13.9	Lowesville (CDP) Lincoln County
122	n/a	13.9	Raeford (city) Hoke County
124	2844	14.0	Greenville (city) Pitt County
125	n/a	14.1	Edenton (town) Chowan County
125	2876	14.1	Fayetteville (city) Cumberland County
127	2899	14.2	Clayton (town) Johnston County
127	n/a	14.2	Walkertown (town) Forsyth County
129	n/a	14.3	Granite Quarry (town) Rowan County
129	2921	14.3	Havelock (city) Craven County
129	2921	14.3	Mooresville (town) Iredell County
132	2944	14.4	Mount Airy (city) Surry County
133	n/a	14.5	Aberdeen (town) Moore County
133	2974	14.5	Garner (town) Wake County
133	n/a	14.5	Mocksville (town) Davie County
133	2974	14.5	Spring Lake (town) Cumberland County
137	n/a	14.8	Creedmoor (city) Granville County
137	n/a	14.8	Williamston (town) Martin County
139	n/a	14.9	Washington (city) Beaufort County
140	n/a	15.0	Etowah (CDP) Henderson County
141	n/a	15.2	Angier (town) Harnett County
142	n/a	15.3	Boiling Spring Lakes (city) Brunswick County
142	n/a	15.3	Clinton (city) Sampson County
144	n/a	15.4	Brevard (city) Transylvania County
144	n/a	15.4	Lillington (town) Harnett County
144	3128	15.4	Mount Holly (city) Gaston County
147	n/a	15.5	Erwin (town) Harnett County
147	3146	15.5	Fuquay-Varina (town) Wake County
147	n/a	15.5	James City (CDP) Craven County
147	n/a	15.5	Marion (city) McDowell County

Note: The state column ranks the top/bottom 150 places in the state with population of 2,500 or more. The national column ranks the top/bottom places in the country with population of 10,000 or more. Places that are unincorporated were not considered in the rankings. n/a indicates data not available. Please refer to the User Guide for additional information.

Population Under 18 Years Old with No Health Insurance

Top 150 Places Ranked in *Descending* Order

State Rank	Nat'l Rank	Percent	Place
1	n/a	31.5	**Dana** (CDP) Henderson County
2	n/a	27.8	**Bessemer City** (city) Gaston County
3	n/a	25.0	**East Rockingham** (CDP) Richmond County
4	n/a	24.5	**Bayshore** (CDP) New Hanover County
5	n/a	24.0	**Gamewell** (town) Caldwell County
6	n/a	21.9	**Grifton** (town) Pitt County
7	n/a	21.7	**Cullowhee** (CDP) Jackson County
8	n/a	21.1	**Pineville** (town) Mecklenburg County
9	n/a	19.5	**Granite Falls** (town) Caldwell County
9	n/a	19.5	**Southern Shores** (town) Dare County
11	n/a	18.5	**Enochville** (CDP) Rowan County
11	n/a	18.5	**Stokesdale** (town) Guilford County
13	n/a	17.9	**Stanley** (town) Gaston County
14	n/a	17.5	**Silver Lake** (CDP) New Hanover County
15	n/a	17.0	**Rutherfordton** (town) Rutherford County
16	n/a	16.3	**Kitty Hawk** (town) Dare County
17	n/a	16.2	**North Wilkesboro** (town) Wilkes County
18	n/a	15.9	**Brogden** (town) Wayne County
18	n/a	15.9	**Fairfield Harbour** (CDP) Craven County
20	n/a	15.7	**Ayden** (town) Pitt County
20	n/a	15.7	**Selma** (town) Johnston County
22	n/a	15.2	**Welcome** (CDP) Davidson County
23	n/a	14.7	**Waynesville** (town) Haywood County
24	n/a	14.4	**Kings Grant** (CDP) New Hanover County
24	n/a	14.4	**Mar-Mac** (CDP) Wayne County
26	n/a	14.3	**Franklin** (town) Macon County
27	n/a	14.0	**Siler City** (town) Chatham County
28	n/a	13.6	**Tyro** (CDP) Davidson County
28	n/a	13.6	**Woodfin** (town) Buncombe County
30	414	13.4	**Monroe** (city) Union County
31	n/a	13.0	**Yadkinville** (town) Yadkin County
32	457	12.9	**Graham** (city) Alamance County
32	n/a	12.9	**Sneads Ferry** (CDP) Onslow County
34	n/a	12.8	**Lowell** (city) Gaston County
35	n/a	12.5	**Creedmoor** (city) Granville County
35	n/a	12.5	**Farmville** (town) Pitt County
37	497	12.4	**Asheboro** (city) Randolph County
38	532	12.1	**Hendersonville** (city) Henderson County
38	n/a	12.1	**Pembroke** (town) Robeson County
38	n/a	12.1	**Tabor City** (town) Columbus County
41	n/a	11.9	**Ranlo** (town) Gaston County
42	n/a	11.8	**Ahoskie** (town) Hertford County
43	n/a	11.6	**River Road** (CDP) Beaufort County
44	n/a	11.5	**Dallas** (town) Gaston County
45	631	11.4	**Elizabeth City** (city) Pasquotank County
45	n/a	11.4	**Etowah** (CDP) Henderson County
45	631	11.4	**High Point** (city) Guilford County
48	698	10.9	**Garner** (town) Wake County
48	698	10.9	**Indian Trail** (town) Union County
50	n/a	10.6	**Dunn** (city) Harnett County
51	n/a	10.5	**Westport** (CDP) Lincoln County
52	n/a	10.3	**Elkin** (town) Surry County
52	n/a	10.3	**Spencer** (town) Rowan County
54	806	10.2	**Knightdale** (town) Wake County
55	n/a	10.1	**Flat Rock** (village) Henderson County
55	n/a	10.1	**Lake Royale** (CDP) Franklin County
55	n/a	10.1	**River Bend** (town) Craven County
58	845	10.0	**Eden** (city) Rockingham County
59	n/a	9.9	**Swannanoa** (CDP) Buncombe County
60	881	9.8	**Gastonia** (city) Gaston County
60	n/a	9.8	**Roxboro** (city) Person County
62	n/a	9.7	**Carolina Shores** (town) Brunswick County
63	954	9.5	**Carrboro** (town) Orange County
64	1004	9.3	**Cornelius** (town) Mecklenburg County
65	1040	9.1	**Albemarle** (city) Stanly County
65	n/a	9.1	**Hamlet** (city) Richmond County
67	n/a	9.0	**Erwin** (town) Harnett County
67	n/a	9.0	**Oak Island** (town) Brunswick County
69	n/a	8.9	**Mountain View** (CDP) Catawba County
69	1083	8.9	**Raleigh** (city) Wake County
71	n/a	8.8	**Ogden** (CDP) New Hanover County
71	n/a	8.8	**Troy** (town) Montgomery County
73	n/a	8.6	**Brevard** (city) Transylvania County
73	n/a	8.6	**Morehead City** (town) Carteret County
75	n/a	8.5	**Canton** (town) Haywood County
75	n/a	8.5	**Carolina Beach** (town) New Hanover County
75	1164	8.5	**Kinston** (city) Lenoir County
75	n/a	8.5	**Mount Olive** (town) Wayne County
79	1227	8.2	**Clayton** (town) Johnston County
80	n/a	8.1	**Fairview** (CDP) Buncombe County
80	n/a	8.1	**Newport** (town) Carteret County
80	n/a	8.1	**Rockingham** (city) Richmond County
80	n/a	8.1	**South Rosemary** (CDP) Halifax County
84	n/a	8.0	**Raeford** (city) Hoke County
84	1279	8.0	**Shelby** (city) Cleveland County
86	1304	7.9	**Charlotte** (city) Mecklenburg County
86	1304	7.9	**Winston-Salem** (city) Forsyth County
88	1335	7.8	**Harrisburg** (town) Cabarrus County
88	n/a	7.8	**Landis** (town) Rowan County
88	n/a	7.8	**Red Springs** (town) Robeson County
88	n/a	7.8	**Winterville** (town) Pitt County
92	n/a	7.7	**Angier** (town) Harnett County
92	1361	7.7	**Wilson** (city) Wilson County
94	1393	7.6	**Durham** (city) Durham County
94	1393	7.6	**Hickory** (city) Catawba County
94	1393	7.6	**Matthews** (town) Mecklenburg County
94	1393	7.6	**Rocky Mount** (city) Nash County
98	1429	7.5	**Greensboro** (city) Guilford County
98	n/a	7.5	**Kill Devil Hills** (town) Dare County
98	1429	7.5	**Mount Holly** (city) Gaston County
98	1429	7.5	**Newton** (city) Catawba County
98	n/a	7.5	**Williamston** (town) Martin County
103	1456	7.4	**Fuquay-Varina** (town) Wake County
104	n/a	7.3	**Black Mountain** (town) Buncombe County
104	n/a	7.3	**Maiden** (town) Catawba County
104	1484	7.3	**Mint Hill** (town) Mecklenburg County
104	n/a	7.3	**Warsaw** (town) Duplin County
108	1551	7.1	**Kannapolis** (city) Cabarrus County
109	1621	6.9	**Sanford** (city) Lee County
110	n/a	6.8	**Fairmont** (town) Robeson County
111	n/a	6.7	**Hudson** (town) Caldwell County
111	n/a	6.7	**Lillington** (town) Harnett County
111	1687	6.7	**Statesville** (city) Iredell County
114	1719	6.6	**Belmont** (city) Gaston County
114	1719	6.6	**Chapel Hill** (town) Orange County
114	1719	6.6	**Murraysville** (CDP) New Hanover County
117	1752	6.5	**Asheville** (city) Buncombe County
117	1752	6.5	**Concord** (city) Cabarrus County
117	1752	6.5	**Kernersville** (town) Forsyth County
117	n/a	6.5	**Long View** (town) Catawba County
117	1752	6.5	**Salisbury** (city) Rowan County
117	n/a	6.5	**Wrightsboro** (CDP) New Hanover County
123	1785	6.4	**Stallings** (town) Union County
124	n/a	6.2	**Archer Lodge** (town) Johnston County
124	1849	6.2	**Burlington** (city) Alamance County
124	n/a	6.2	**Pleasant Garden** (town) Guilford County
124	1849	6.2	**Roanoke Rapids** (city) Halifax County
128	1882	6.1	**Huntersville** (town) Mecklenburg County
129	1922	6.0	**Archdale** (city) Randolph County
129	n/a	6.0	**Boiling Spring Lakes** (city) Brunswick County
129	n/a	6.0	**Lake Norman of Catawba** (CDP) Catawba County
129	n/a	6.0	**Sawmills** (town) Caldwell County
133	1955	5.9	**Summerfield** (town) Guilford County
134	1989	5.8	**Lexington** (city) Davidson County
134	n/a	5.8	**Trinity** (city) Randolph County
136	2025	5.7	**Lincolnton** (city) Lincoln County
136	n/a	5.7	**Lowesville** (CDP) Lincoln County
138	n/a	5.6	**Clinton** (city) Sampson County
138	n/a	5.6	**Icard** (CDP) Burke County
140	2093	5.5	**Cary** (town) Wake County
140	2093	5.5	**Fayetteville** (city) Cumberland County
140	n/a	5.5	**Fletcher** (town) Henderson County
140	2093	5.5	**Greenville** (city) Pitt County
140	n/a	5.5	**Wentworth** (town) Rockingham County
145	2147	5.4	**Clemmons** (village) Forsyth County
145	n/a	5.4	**Pittsboro** (town) Chatham County
145	2147	5.4	**Wake Forest** (town) Wake County
148	2239	5.2	**Hope Mills** (town) Cumberland County
148	n/a	5.2	**Wallburg** (town) Davidson County
148	2239	5.2	**Wilmington** (city) New Hanover County

Note: The state column ranks the top/bottom 150 places in the state with population of 2,500 or more. The national column ranks the top/bottom places in the country with population of 10,000 or more. Places that are unincorporated were not considered in the rankings. n/a indicates data not available. Please refer to the User Guide for additional information.

Population Under 18 Years Old with No Health Insurance

Top 150 Places Ranked in *Ascending* Order

State Rank	Nat'l Rank	Percent	Place	State Rank	Nat'l Rank	Percent	Place
1	n/a	0.0	**Beaufort** (town) Carteret County	76	1411	3.2	**Jacksonville** (city) Onslow County
1	n/a	0.0	**Boiling Springs** (town) Cleveland County	76	n/a	3.2	**Rolesville** (town) Wake County
1	1	0.0	**Boone** (town) Watauga County	76	n/a	3.2	**Wallace** (town) Duplin County
1	n/a	0.0	**Buies Creek** (CDP) Harnett County	76	n/a	3.2	**Weaverville** (town) Buncombe County
1	n/a	0.0	**Eastover** (town) Cumberland County	80	1461	3.3	**Pinehurst** (village) Moore County
1	n/a	0.0	**Edenton** (town) Chowan County	80	n/a	3.3	**Unionville** (town) Union County
1	n/a	0.0	**Elizabethtown** (town) Bladen County	82	1506	3.4	**Morganton** (city) Burke County
1	n/a	0.0	**Elon** (town) Alamance County	83	n/a	3.5	**Granite Quarry** (town) Rowan County
1	n/a	0.0	**Emerald Isle** (town) Carteret County	83	1573	3.5	**Mount Airy** (city) Surry County
1	n/a	0.0	**Enfield** (town) Halifax County	83	n/a	3.5	**Mountain Home** (CDP) Henderson County
1	n/a	0.0	**Fairview** (town) Union County	86	n/a	3.6	**Jamestown** (town) Guilford County
1	n/a	0.0	**Forest Oaks** (CDP) Guilford County	87	n/a	3.8	**Oxford** (city) Granville County
1	n/a	0.0	**Glen Raven** (CDP) Alamance County	88	n/a	4.0	**Benson** (town) Johnston County
1	n/a	0.0	**Hampstead** (CDP) Pender County	88	1832	4.0	**Lenoir** (city) Caldwell County
1	n/a	0.0	**La Grange** (town) Lenoir County	90	1892	4.1	**Smithfield** (town) Johnston County
1	n/a	0.0	**Lake Junaluska** (CDP) Haywood County	91	n/a	4.2	**Wadesboro** (town) Anson County
1	1	0.0	**Lewisville** (town) Forsyth County	91	n/a	4.2	**Washington** (city) Beaufort County
1	n/a	0.0	**Locust** (city) Stanly County	93	1982	4.3	**Henderson** (city) Vance County
1	n/a	0.0	**Louisburg** (town) Franklin County	93	n/a	4.3	**James City** (CDP) Craven County
1	n/a	0.0	**Mills River** (town) Henderson County	93	n/a	4.3	**Marion** (city) McDowell County
1	n/a	0.0	**Nags Head** (town) Dare County	93	1982	4.3	**Piney Green** (CDP) Onslow County
1	n/a	0.0	**Randleman** (city) Randolph County	97	2041	4.4	**Morrisville** (town) Wake County
1	n/a	0.0	**Red Oak** (town) Nash County	97	n/a	4.4	**Moyock** (CDP) Currituck County
1	n/a	0.0	**Saint James** (town) Brunswick County	97	n/a	4.4	**Rural Hall** (town) Forsyth County
1	n/a	0.0	**Seven Lakes** (CDP) Moore County	100	n/a	4.5	**Conover** (city) Catawba County
1	n/a	0.0	**Southport** (city) Brunswick County	100	2079	4.5	**Mooresville** (town) Iredell County
1	n/a	0.0	**Sunset Beach** (town) Brunswick County	102	2117	4.6	**Leland** (town) Brunswick County
1	n/a	0.0	**Swansboro** (town) Onslow County	102	2117	4.6	**Thomasville** (city) Davidson County
29	n/a	0.4	**Liberty** (town) Randolph County	104	n/a	4.7	**Wendell** (town) Wake County
30	177	0.6	**Reidsville** (city) Rockingham County	105	2192	4.8	**Mebane** (city) Alamance County
31	n/a	1.0	**Cajah's Mountain** (town) Caldwell County	105	n/a	4.8	**Nashville** (town) Nash County
32	n/a	1.1	**Polkton** (town) Anson County	105	n/a	4.8	**Royal Pines** (CDP) Buncombe County
32	n/a	1.1	**Sylva** (town) Jackson County	105	2192	4.8	**Southern Pines** (town) Moore County
32	n/a	1.1	**Whispering Pines** (village) Moore County	105	2192	4.8	**Tarboro** (town) Edgecombe County
35	382	1.2	**Davidson** (town) Mecklenburg County	110	n/a	4.9	**Butner** (town) Granville County
35	n/a	1.2	**Half Moon** (CDP) Onslow County	110	n/a	4.9	**Cherryville** (city) Gaston County
37	n/a	1.3	**Hillsborough** (town) Orange County	110	2238	4.9	**Goldsboro** (city) Wayne County
37	n/a	1.3	**Midland** (town) Cabarrus County	110	2238	4.9	**Havelock** (city) Craven County
37	n/a	1.3	**Midway** (town) Davidson County	110	n/a	4.9	**Rockfish** (CDP) Hoke County
40	n/a	1.4	**Bethlehem** (CDP) Alexander County	115	n/a	5.0	**Burgaw** (town) Pender County
40	n/a	1.4	**Murfreesboro** (town) Hertford County	115	n/a	5.0	**Gibsonville** (town) Guilford County
40	n/a	1.4	**Myrtle Grove** (CDP) New Hanover County	115	2279	5.0	**New Bern** (city) Craven County
40	n/a	1.4	**Plymouth** (town) Washington County	115	2279	5.0	**Spring Lake** (town) Cumberland County
40	n/a	1.4	**Windsor** (town) Bertie County	119	2327	5.1	**Holly Springs** (town) Wake County
45	n/a	1.5	**Brices Creek** (CDP) Craven County	119	2327	5.1	**Lumberton** (city) Robeson County
45	n/a	1.5	**King** (city) Stokes County	119	n/a	5.1	**Wingate** (town) Union County
45	n/a	1.5	**Zebulon** (town) Wake County	122	2368	5.2	**Hope Mills** (town) Cumberland County
48	n/a	1.6	**Valdese** (town) Burke County	122	n/a	5.2	**Wallburg** (town) Davidson County
49	n/a	1.8	**Waxhaw** (town) Union County	122	2368	5.2	**Wilmington** (city) New Hanover County
50	n/a	1.9	**Oak Ridge** (town) Guilford County	125	2464	5.4	**Clemmons** (village) Forsyth County
51	n/a	2.0	**Wesley Chapel** (village) Union County	125	n/a	5.4	**Pittsboro** (town) Chatham County
52	n/a	2.1	**Marvin** (village) Union County	125	2464	5.4	**Wake Forest** (town) Wake County
52	n/a	2.1	**Spindale** (town) Rutherford County	128	2510	5.5	**Cary** (town) Wake County
52	n/a	2.1	**Weddington** (town) Union County	128	2510	5.5	**Fayetteville** (city) Cumberland County
55	n/a	2.2	**Cramerton** (town) Gaston County	128	n/a	5.5	**Fletcher** (town) Henderson County
55	876	2.2	**Kings Mountain** (city) Cleveland County	128	2510	5.5	**Greenville** (city) Pitt County
55	n/a	2.2	**Lake Park** (village) Union County	128	n/a	5.5	**Wentworth** (town) Rockingham County
55	n/a	2.2	**Trent Woods** (town) Craven County	133	n/a	5.6	**Clinton** (city) Sampson County
59	n/a	2.3	**East Flat Rock** (CDP) Henderson County	133	n/a	5.6	**Icard** (CDP) Burke County
59	n/a	2.3	**Forest City** (town) Rutherford County	135	2601	5.7	**Lincolnton** (city) Lincoln County
59	n/a	2.3	**Walkertown** (town) Forsyth County	135	n/a	5.7	**Lowesville** (CDP) Lincoln County
62	n/a	2.4	**Skippers Corner** (CDP) New Hanover County	137	2632	5.8	**Lexington** (city) Davidson County
63	n/a	2.5	**Northchase** (CDP) New Hanover County	137	n/a	5.8	**Trinity** (city) Randolph County
63	n/a	2.5	**Whiteville** (city) Columbus County	139	2668	5.9	**Summerfield** (town) Guilford County
65	n/a	2.6	**Mineral Springs** (town) Union County	140	2702	6.0	**Archdale** (city) Randolph County
66	n/a	2.7	**Aberdeen** (town) Moore County	140	n/a	6.0	**Boiling Spring Lakes** (city) Brunswick County
66	n/a	2.7	**China Grove** (town) Rowan County	140	n/a	6.0	**Lake Norman of Catawba** (CDP) Catawba County
66	n/a	2.7	**Mocksville** (town) Davie County	140	n/a	6.0	**Sawmills** (town) Caldwell County
66	n/a	2.7	**Porters Neck** (CDP) New Hanover County	144	2735	6.1	**Huntersville** (town) Mecklenburg County
70	1228	2.9	**Apex** (town) Wake County	145	n/a	6.2	**Archer Lodge** (town) Johnston County
70	n/a	2.9	**Elroy** (CDP) Wayne County	145	2775	6.2	**Burlington** (city) Alamance County
70	1228	2.9	**Laurinburg** (city) Scotland County	145	n/a	6.2	**Pleasant Garden** (town) Guilford County
73	n/a	3.0	**Shallotte** (town) Brunswick County	145	2775	6.2	**Roanoke Rapids** (city) Halifax County
73	n/a	3.0	**Wilkesboro** (town) Wilkes County	149	2835	6.4	**Stallings** (town) Union County
75	n/a	3.1	**Saint Stephens** (CDP) Catawba County	150	2872	6.5	**Asheville** (city) Buncombe County

Note: *The state column ranks the top/bottom 150 places in the state with population of 2,500 or more. The national column ranks the top/bottom places in the country with population of 10,000 or more. Places that are unincorporated were not considered in the rankings. n/a indicates data not available. Please refer to the User Guide for additional information.*

Commute to Work: Car

Top 150 Places Ranked in *Descending* Order

State Rank	Nat'l Rank	Percent	Place	State Rank	Nat'l Rank	Percent	Place
1	n/a	100.0	**Elizabethtown** (town) Bladen County	76	n/a	95.0	**Clinton** (city) Sampson County
2	n/a	99.3	**Red Oak** (town) Nash County	76	n/a	95.0	**Jamestown** (town) Guilford County
3	n/a	99.2	**Creedmoor** (city) Granville County	76	n/a	95.0	**Wrightsboro** (CDP) New Hanover County
4	n/a	98.9	**Hudson** (town) Caldwell County	79	n/a	94.9	**Ayden** (town) Pitt County
4	n/a	98.9	**Wallburg** (town) Davidson County	79	437	94.9	**Mebane** (city) Alamance County
6	n/a	98.8	**Brogden** (CDP) Wayne County	79	n/a	94.9	**Yadkinville** (town) Yadkin County
7	n/a	98.7	**Cajah's Mountain** (town) Caldwell County	82	469	94.8	**Kannapolis** (city) Cabarrus County
7	n/a	98.7	**Gibsonville** (town) Guilford County	82	n/a	94.8	**Lake Junaluska** (CDP) Haywood County
7	n/a	98.7	**Hampstead** (CDP) Pender County	82	469	94.8	**Tarboro** (town) Edgecombe County
10	n/a	98.6	**Williamston** (town) Martin County	85	n/a	94.7	**King** (city) Stokes County
11	n/a	98.4	**Bessemer City** (city) Gaston County	85	n/a	94.7	**Rural Hall** (town) Forsyth County
12	n/a	98.1	**River Road** (CDP) Beaufort County	87	n/a	94.6	**Fairview** (CDP) Buncombe County
13	n/a	98.0	**Rutherfordton** (town) Rutherford County	87	539	94.6	**Thomasville** (city) Davidson County
13	n/a	98.0	**Seven Lakes** (CDP) Moore County	87	n/a	94.6	**Welcome** (CDP) Davidson County
13	n/a	98.0	**Skippers Corner** (CDP) New Hanover County	90	n/a	94.5	**Etowah** (CDP) Henderson County
16	9	97.9	**Archdale** (city) Randolph County	90	n/a	94.5	**Nashville** (town) Nash County
17	n/a	97.8	**Brices Creek** (CDP) Craven County	90	574	94.5	**Sanford** (city) Lee County
17	10	97.8	**Clayton** (town) Johnston County	90	574	94.5	**Statesville** (city) Iredell County
17	n/a	97.8	**Trinity** (city) Randolph County	94	n/a	94.4	**Aberdeen** (town) Moore County
20	n/a	97.7	**Ranlo** (town) Gaston County	94	n/a	94.4	**Gamewell** (town) Caldwell County
20	n/a	97.7	**Whiteville** (city) Columbus County	94	n/a	94.4	**Mountain Home** (CDP) Henderson County
22	n/a	97.6	**Polkton** (town) Anson County	94	n/a	94.4	**Pembroke** (town) Robeson County
22	n/a	97.6	**South Rosemary** (CDP) Halifax County	94	n/a	94.4	**Spencer** (town) Rowan County
24	n/a	97.2	**Grifton** (town) Pitt County	94	n/a	94.4	**Winterville** (town) Pitt County
25	n/a	97.1	**Boiling Spring Lakes** (city) Brunswick County	100	n/a	94.3	**Long View** (town) Catawba County
25	n/a	97.1	**Hamlet** (city) Richmond County	100	n/a	94.3	**Maiden** (town) Catawba County
25	39	97.1	**Mount Holly** (city) Gaston County	100	n/a	94.3	**Marion** (city) McDowell County
25	n/a	97.1	**Spindale** (town) Rutherford County	100	649	94.3	**Monroe** (city) Union County
25	n/a	97.1	**Stanley** (town) Gaston County	104	n/a	94.2	**Ahoskie** (town) Hertford County
25	n/a	97.1	**Wentworth** (town) Rockingham County	104	678	94.2	**Burlington** (city) Alamance County
31	n/a	97.0	**China Grove** (town) Rowan County	104	678	94.2	**Hickory** (city) Catawba County
31	n/a	97.0	**Dana** (CDP) Henderson County	104	678	94.2	**Rocky Mount** (city) Nash County
31	n/a	97.0	**Midland** (town) Cabarrus County	104	n/a	94.2	**Trent Woods** (town) Craven County
31	46	97.0	**Newton** (city) Catawba County	109	n/a	94.1	**Glen Raven** (CDP) Alamance County
35	73	96.7	**Albemarle** (city) Stanly County	109	n/a	94.1	**Moyock** (CDP) Currituck County
35	n/a	96.7	**Elroy** (CDP) Wayne County	109	722	94.1	**Shelby** (city) Cleveland County
35	n/a	96.7	**North Wilkesboro** (town) Wilkes County	109	n/a	94.1	**Unionville** (town) Union County
38	n/a	96.6	**Bethlehem** (CDP) Alexander County	113	767	94.0	**Clemmons** (village) Forsyth County
38	n/a	96.6	**Mountain View** (CDP) Catawba County	113	n/a	94.0	**Mineral Springs** (town) Union County
40	n/a	96.4	**Cherryville** (city) Gaston County	113	n/a	94.0	**Raeford** (city) Hoke County
40	n/a	96.4	**Plymouth** (town) Washington County	113	n/a	94.0	**Randleman** (city) Randolph County
42	n/a	96.3	**Liberty** (town) Randolph County	113	767	94.0	**Smithfield** (town) Johnston County
42	n/a	96.3	**Red Springs** (town) Robeson County	118	n/a	93.9	**East Rockingham** (CDP) Richmond County
44	138	96.2	**Graham** (city) Alamance County	118	816	93.9	**Kernersville** (town) Forsyth County
44	n/a	96.2	**Windsor** (town) Bertie County	118	816	93.9	**Roanoke Rapids** (city) Halifax County
46	150	96.1	**Eden** (city) Rockingham County	121	865	93.8	**Goldsboro** (city) Wayne County
46	n/a	96.1	**Erwin** (town) Harnett County	121	865	93.8	**Henderson** (city) Vance County
46	n/a	96.1	**Rockingham** (city) Richmond County	121	n/a	93.8	**Rockfish** (CDP) Hoke County
49	n/a	96.0	**Half Moon** (CDP) Onslow County	124	n/a	93.7	**Mar-Mac** (CDP) Wayne County
49	n/a	96.0	**Siler City** (town) Chatham County	124	917	93.7	**Mount Airy** (city) Surry County
51	n/a	95.9	**Benson** (town) Johnston County	124	n/a	93.7	**Royal Pines** (CDP) Buncombe County
51	n/a	95.9	**Eastover** (town) Cumberland County	127	964	93.6	**Concord** (city) Cabarrus County
51	n/a	95.9	**Fairmont** (town) Robeson County	127	n/a	93.6	**Mocksville** (town) Davie County
51	177	95.9	**Hope Mills** (town) Cumberland County	129	n/a	93.5	**Dallas** (town) Gaston County
55	198	95.8	**Lincolnton** (city) Lincoln County	129	1000	93.5	**Lexington** (city) Davidson County
55	198	95.8	**Murraysville** (CDP) New Hanover County	129	n/a	93.5	**Washington** (city) Beaufort County
57	228	95.7	**Reidsville** (city) Rockingham County	129	n/a	93.5	**Waynesville** (town) Haywood County
57	n/a	95.7	**Walkertown** (town) Forsyth County	133	1086	93.3	**Harrisburg** (town) Cabarrus County
59	n/a	95.6	**Wilkesboro** (town) Wilkes County	134	1147	93.2	**Mint Hill** (town) Mecklenburg County
60	278	95.5	**Asheboro** (city) Randolph County	134	n/a	93.2	**Warsaw** (town) Duplin County
60	n/a	95.5	**Lillington** (town) Harnett County	136	n/a	93.1	**Elkin** (town) Surry County
60	n/a	95.5	**Shallotte** (town) Brunswick County	136	1193	93.1	**Knightdale** (town) Wake County
63	n/a	95.4	**Butner** (town) Granville County	136	n/a	93.1	**Swannanoa** (CDP) Buncombe County
63	306	95.4	**Kings Mountain** (city) Cleveland County	139	n/a	93.0	**Burgaw** (town) Pender County
63	n/a	95.4	**Landis** (town) Rowan County	139	n/a	93.0	**Enochville** (CDP) Rowan County
63	306	95.4	**Lenoir** (city) Caldwell County	139	n/a	93.0	**Icard** (CDP) Burke County
67	333	95.3	**Gastonia** (city) Gaston County	139	n/a	93.0	**Sneads Ferry** (CDP) Onslow County
67	333	95.3	**Lumberton** (city) Robeson County	143	n/a	92.9	**Kings Grant** (CDP) New Hanover County
67	n/a	95.3	**Tabor City** (town) Columbus County	143	n/a	92.9	**Northchase** (CDP) New Hanover County
70	n/a	95.2	**Locust** (city) Stanly County	145	1322	92.8	**New Bern** (city) Craven County
70	n/a	95.2	**Newport** (town) Carteret County	145	1322	92.8	**Piney Green** (CDP) Onslow County
70	n/a	95.2	**Tyro** (CDP) Davidson County	145	n/a	92.8	**Whispering Pines** (village) Moore County
73	n/a	95.1	**Conover** (city) Catawba County	148	1371	92.7	**Laurinburg** (city) Scotland County
73	n/a	95.1	**Cramerton** (town) Gaston County	148	n/a	92.7	**Wendell** (town) Wake County
73	n/a	95.1	**Midway** (town) Davidson County	150	n/a	92.6	**Fletcher** (town) Henderson County

Note: The state column ranks the top/bottom 150 places in the state with population of 2,500 or more. The national column ranks the top/bottom places in the country with population of 10,000 or more. Places that are unincorporated were not considered in the rankings. n/a indicates data not available. Please refer to the User Guide for additional information.

Commute to Work: Car

Top 150 Places Ranked in *Ascending* Order

State Rank	Nat'l Rank	Percent	Place
1	172	69.0	**Chapel Hill** (town) Orange County
2	197	70.5	**Carrboro** (town) Orange County
3	211	71.4	**Boone** (town) Watauga County
4	n/a	72.2	**Saint James** (town) Brunswick County
5	n/a	72.5	**Cullowhee** (CDP) Jackson County
6	n/a	73.1	**Sunset Beach** (town) Brunswick County
7	339	76.3	**Jacksonville** (city) Onslow County
8	368	77.1	**Davidson** (town) Mecklenburg County
9	n/a	77.2	**Buies Creek** (CDP) Harnett County
10	n/a	78.6	**Fairfield Harbour** (CDP) Craven County
11	n/a	80.5	**Beaufort** (town) Carteret County
12	n/a	83.5	**Carolina Beach** (town) New Hanover County
13	n/a	83.6	**Nags Head** (town) Dare County
14	n/a	84.2	**Elon** (town) Alamance County
15	n/a	84.3	**East Flat Rock** (CDP) Henderson County
16	884	84.4	**Asheville** (city) Buncombe County
17	n/a	84.7	**Emerald Isle** (town) Carteret County
17	n/a	84.7	**Valdese** (town) Burke County
19	n/a	85.0	**Selma** (town) Johnston County
20	n/a	85.1	**Marvin** (village) Union County
21	n/a	85.4	**Black Mountain** (town) Buncombe County
21	n/a	85.4	**Southport** (city) Brunswick County
23	n/a	85.5	**Boiling Springs** (town) Cleveland County
23	1025	85.5	**Elizabeth City** (city) Pasquotank County
25	1041	85.6	**Havelock** (city) Craven County
26	1095	85.9	**Cornelius** (town) Mecklenburg County
27	n/a	86.0	**Porters Neck** (CDP) New Hanover County
28	n/a	86.1	**Lake Norman of Catawba** (CDP) Catawba County
29	1203	86.5	**Durham** (city) Durham County
30	n/a	86.6	**Farmville** (town) Pitt County
30	n/a	86.6	**Roxboro** (city) Person County
32	n/a	86.7	**Edenton** (town) Chowan County
32	n/a	86.7	**Wallace** (town) Duplin County
34	n/a	86.8	**Mount Olive** (town) Wayne County
34	n/a	86.8	**Wingate** (town) Union County
36	1276	86.9	**Wilmington** (city) New Hanover County
37	n/a	87.0	**Hillsborough** (town) Orange County
38	1313	87.1	**Charlotte** (city) Mecklenburg County
39	n/a	87.5	**Flat Rock** (village) Henderson County
39	n/a	87.5	**Pineville** (town) Mecklenburg County
41	n/a	87.9	**Lake Park** (village) Union County
42	1509	88.0	**Matthews** (town) Mecklenburg County
43	n/a	88.2	**Swansboro** (town) Onslow County
44	1625	88.4	**Holly Springs** (town) Wake County
44	1625	88.4	**Kinston** (city) Lenoir County
46	n/a	88.5	**Brevard** (city) Transylvania County
46	1664	88.5	**Wake Forest** (town) Wake County
48	1685	88.6	**Cary** (town) Wake County
48	n/a	88.6	**Weddington** (town) Union County
50	n/a	88.7	**Granite Quarry** (town) Rowan County
51	1736	88.8	**Raleigh** (city) Wake County
52	n/a	88.9	**Southern Shores** (town) Dare County
52	n/a	88.9	**Sylva** (town) Jackson County
54	1790	89.0	**Huntersville** (town) Mecklenburg County
54	n/a	89.0	**Pittsboro** (town) Chatham County
56	n/a	89.2	**Lake Royale** (CDP) Franklin County
56	n/a	89.2	**Ogden** (CDP) New Hanover County
56	n/a	89.2	**Woodfin** (town) Buncombe County
59	n/a	89.4	**Mills River** (town) Henderson County
59	n/a	89.4	**Wesley Chapel** (village) Union County
59	n/a	89.4	**Westport** (CDP) Lincoln County
62	1953	89.5	**Morrisville** (town) Wake County
62	1953	89.5	**Stallings** (town) Union County
64	n/a	89.6	**Forest City** (town) Rutherford County
64	n/a	89.6	**Weaverville** (town) Buncombe County
66	2028	89.7	**Hendersonville** (city) Henderson County
67	2053	89.8	**Apex** (town) Wake County
67	n/a	89.8	**Sawmills** (town) Caldwell County
67	n/a	89.8	**Waxhaw** (town) Union County
70	n/a	89.9	**Lowesville** (CDP) Lincoln County
71	2127	90.0	**Fayetteville** (city) Cumberland County
72	n/a	90.1	**Pleasant Garden** (town) Guilford County
73	2274	90.4	**Fuquay-Varina** (town) Wake County
73	n/a	90.4	**Granite Falls** (town) Caldwell County
73	n/a	90.4	**Morehead City** (town) Carteret County
73	n/a	90.4	**River Bend** (town) Craven County
77	n/a	90.6	**Kitty Hawk** (town) Dare County
77	2349	90.6	**Mooresville** (town) Iredell County
79	2381	90.7	**Garner** (town) Wake County
79	2381	90.7	**Greensboro** (city) Guilford County
79	n/a	90.7	**James City** (CDP) Craven County
79	2381	90.7	**Pinehurst** (village) Moore County
79	2381	90.7	**Spring Lake** (town) Cumberland County
79	n/a	90.7	**Troy** (town) Montgomery County
79	2381	90.7	**Winston-Salem** (city) Forsyth County
86	n/a	90.9	**Forest Oaks** (CDP) Guilford County
86	n/a	90.9	**Murfreesboro** (town) Hertford County
86	n/a	90.9	**Oxford** (city) Granville County
86	n/a	90.9	**Rolesville** (town) Wake County
90	n/a	91.0	**Myrtle Grove** (CDP) New Hanover County
90	n/a	91.0	**Silver Lake** (CDP) New Hanover County
92	2545	91.1	**Summerfield** (town) Guilford County
92	n/a	91.1	**Zebulon** (town) Wake County
94	n/a	91.2	**Lowell** (city) Gaston County
95	n/a	91.3	**Angier** (town) Harnett County
95	2634	91.3	**Salisbury** (city) Rowan County
95	n/a	91.3	**Wadesboro** (town) Anson County
98	2676	91.4	**Morganton** (city) Burke County
98	2676	91.4	**Southern Pines** (town) Moore County
100	n/a	91.5	**Franklin** (town) Macon County
101	n/a	91.6	**Enfield** (town) Halifax County
102	2800	91.7	**Belmont** (city) Gaston County
102	2800	91.7	**High Point** (city) Guilford County
104	n/a	91.8	**Archer Lodge** (town) Johnston County
104	2838	91.8	**Lewisville** (town) Forsyth County
104	n/a	91.8	**Oak Ridge** (town) Guilford County
107	n/a	91.9	**Bayshore** (CDP) New Hanover County
107	n/a	91.9	**Stokesdale** (town) Guilford County
109	n/a	92.0	**Carolina Shores** (town) Brunswick County
109	2913	92.0	**Greenville** (city) Pitt County
111	n/a	92.1	**Louisburg** (town) Franklin County
112	n/a	92.2	**Canton** (town) Haywood County
112	n/a	92.2	**Dunn** (city) Harnett County
112	n/a	92.2	**Kill Devil Hills** (town) Dare County
112	3013	92.2	**Leland** (town) Brunswick County
116	3049	92.3	**Indian Trail** (town) Union County
116	n/a	92.3	**La Grange** (town) Lenoir County
118	n/a	92.4	**Fairview** (town) Union County
119	n/a	92.6	**Fletcher** (town) Henderson County
119	n/a	92.6	**Oak Island** (town) Brunswick County
119	n/a	92.6	**Saint Stephens** (CDP) Catawba County
119	3191	92.6	**Wilson** (city) Wilson County
123	3241	92.7	**Laurinburg** (city) Scotland County
123	n/a	92.7	**Wendell** (town) Wake County
125	3286	92.8	**New Bern** (city) Craven County
125	3286	92.8	**Piney Green** (CDP) Onslow County
125	n/a	92.8	**Whispering Pines** (village) Moore County
128	n/a	92.9	**Kings Grant** (CDP) New Hanover County
128	n/a	92.9	**Northchase** (CDP) New Hanover County
130	n/a	93.0	**Burgaw** (town) Pender County
130	n/a	93.0	**Enochville** (CDP) Rowan County
130	n/a	93.0	**Icard** (CDP) Burke County
130	n/a	93.0	**Sneads Ferry** (CDP) Onslow County
134	n/a	93.1	**Elkin** (town) Surry County
134	3420	93.1	**Knightdale** (town) Wake County
134	n/a	93.1	**Swannanoa** (CDP) Buncombe County
137	3464	93.2	**Mint Hill** (town) Mecklenburg County
137	n/a	93.2	**Warsaw** (town) Duplin County
139	3510	93.3	**Harrisburg** (town) Cabarrus County
140	n/a	93.5	**Dallas** (town) Gaston County
140	3614	93.5	**Lexington** (city) Davidson County
140	n/a	93.5	**Washington** (city) Beaufort County
140	n/a	93.5	**Waynesville** (town) Haywood County
144	3657	93.6	**Concord** (city) Cabarrus County
144	n/a	93.6	**Mocksville** (town) Davie County
146	n/a	93.7	**Mar-Mac** (CDP) Wayne County
146	3693	93.7	**Mount Airy** (city) Surry County
146	n/a	93.7	**Royal Pines** (CDP) Buncombe County
149	3740	93.8	**Goldsboro** (city) Wayne County
149	3740	93.8	**Henderson** (city) Vance County

Note: *The state column ranks the top/bottom 150 places in the state with population of 2,500 or more. The national column ranks the top/bottom places in the country with population of 10,000 or more. Places that are unincorporated were not considered in the rankings. n/a indicates data not available. Please refer to the User Guide for additional information.*

Commute to Work: Public Transportation

Top 150 Places Ranked in *Descending* Order

State Rank	Nat'l Rank	Percent	Place
1	202	15.3	**Carrboro** (town) Orange County
2	322	11.3	**Chapel Hill** (town) Orange County
3	n/a	4.7	**Southport** (city) Brunswick County
4	n/a	4.2	**Hillsborough** (town) Orange County
5	n/a	4.1	**Silver Lake** (CDP) New Hanover County
6	1186	3.9	**Durham** (city) Durham County
7	1208	3.8	**Charlotte** (city) Mecklenburg County
8	1446	3.1	**Boone** (town) Watauga County
9	1476	3.0	**Cornelius** (town) Mecklenburg County
9	n/a	3.0	**Granite Quarry** (town) Rowan County
11	n/a	2.9	**Pineville** (town) Mecklenburg County
12	n/a	2.7	**Elroy** (CDP) Wayne County
13	n/a	2.6	**Marvin** (village) Union County
14	n/a	2.4	**Canton** (town) Haywood County
15	n/a	2.3	**Carolina Beach** (town) New Hanover County
15	1801	2.3	**Kinston** (city) Lenoir County
17	n/a	2.2	**Fairview** (town) Union County
17	n/a	2.2	**Wadesboro** (town) Anson County
19	1897	2.1	**Raleigh** (city) Wake County
20	2005	1.9	**Greensboro** (city) Guilford County
20	n/a	1.9	**Lowell** (city) Gaston County
22	2054	1.8	**High Point** (city) Guilford County
23	n/a	1.7	**Beaufort** (town) Carteret County
23	n/a	1.7	**Pittsboro** (town) Chatham County
23	2111	1.7	**Winston-Salem** (city) Forsyth County
26	2157	1.6	**Asheville** (city) Buncombe County
26	2157	1.6	**Matthews** (town) Mecklenburg County
26	n/a	1.6	**Sylva** (town) Jackson County
29	n/a	1.5	**Ahoskie** (town) Hertford County
29	2239	1.5	**Davidson** (town) Mecklenburg County
29	2239	1.5	**Greenville** (city) Pitt County
29	n/a	1.5	**Hamlet** (city) Richmond County
29	n/a	1.5	**La Grange** (town) Lenoir County
29	2239	1.5	**Salisbury** (city) Rowan County
35	2324	1.4	**Goldsboro** (city) Wayne County
36	2411	1.3	**Huntersville** (town) Mecklenburg County
36	2411	1.3	**Lincolnton** (city) Lincoln County
36	n/a	1.3	**Oak Island** (town) Brunswick County
36	n/a	1.3	**Walkertown** (town) Forsyth County
40	n/a	1.2	**Lowesville** (CDP) Lincoln County
40	n/a	1.2	**South Rosemary** (CDP) Halifax County
40	2496	1.2	**Wilmington** (city) New Hanover County
43	n/a	1.1	**Lake Norman of Catawba** (CDP) Catawba County
43	2599	1.1	**Monroe** (city) Union County
43	n/a	1.1	**Zebulon** (town) Wake County
46	n/a	1.0	**Archer Lodge** (town) Johnston County
46	n/a	1.0	**Boiling Springs** (town) Cleveland County
46	2684	1.0	**Mint Hill** (town) Mecklenburg County
46	n/a	1.0	**Raeford** (city) Hoke County
46	n/a	1.0	**River Bend** (town) Craven County
46	2684	1.0	**Rocky Mount** (city) Nash County
46	n/a	1.0	**Troy** (town) Montgomery County
53	2793	0.9	**Elizabeth City** (city) Pasquotank County
53	2793	0.9	**Gastonia** (city) Gaston County
53	2793	0.9	**Lexington** (city) Davidson County
53	n/a	0.9	**Siler City** (town) Chatham County
53	n/a	0.9	**Wendell** (town) Wake County
58	n/a	0.8	**Aberdeen** (town) Moore County
58	n/a	0.8	**Dunn** (city) Harnett County
58	2912	0.8	**Fayetteville** (city) Cumberland County
58	n/a	0.8	**Flat Rock** (village) Henderson County
58	2912	0.8	**Mount Airy** (city) Surry County
58	n/a	0.8	**Tabor City** (town) Columbus County
58	n/a	0.8	**Waxhaw** (town) Union County
65	n/a	0.7	**Elon** (town) Alamance County
65	3031	0.7	**Mooresville** (town) Iredell County
65	n/a	0.7	**Myrtle Grove** (CDP) New Hanover County
65	n/a	0.7	**Nashville** (town) Nash County
65	n/a	0.7	**Shallotte** (town) Brunswick County
70	3184	0.6	**Apex** (town) Wake County
70	3184	0.6	**Burlington** (city) Alamance County
70	3184	0.6	**Cary** (town) Wake County
70	3184	0.6	**Concord** (city) Cabarrus County
70	n/a	0.6	**Granite Falls** (town) Caldwell County
70	3184	0.6	**Havelock** (city) Craven County

State Rank	Nat'l Rank	Percent	Place
70	3184	0.6	**Indian Trail** (town) Union County
70	n/a	0.6	**Morehead City** (town) Carteret County
70	3184	0.6	**Mount Holly** (city) Gaston County
70	3184	0.6	**Shelby** (city) Cleveland County
70	3184	0.6	**Stallings** (town) Union County
81	3338	0.5	**Harrisburg** (town) Cabarrus County
81	3338	0.5	**Jacksonville** (city) Onslow County
81	n/a	0.5	**Ranlo** (town) Gaston County
81	3338	0.5	**Wake Forest** (town) Wake County
81	n/a	0.5	**Wingate** (town) Union County
81	n/a	0.5	**Yadkinville** (town) Yadkin County
87	3488	0.4	**Asheboro** (city) Randolph County
87	3488	0.4	**Kannapolis** (city) Cabarrus County
87	n/a	0.4	**Selma** (town) Johnston County
87	3488	0.4	**Spring Lake** (town) Cumberland County
91	n/a	0.3	**Erwin** (town) Harnett County
91	n/a	0.3	**Forest City** (town) Rutherford County
91	3669	0.3	**Garner** (town) Wake County
91	3669	0.3	**Laurinburg** (city) Scotland County
91	n/a	0.3	**Liberty** (town) Randolph County
91	3669	0.3	**Lumberton** (city) Robeson County
91	3669	0.3	**Murraysville** (CDP) New Hanover County
91	3669	0.3	**Sanford** (city) Lee County
91	n/a	0.3	**Waynesville** (town) Haywood County
100	3876	0.2	**Belmont** (city) Gaston County
100	n/a	0.2	**Brogden** (CDP) Wayne County
100	n/a	0.2	**Clinton** (city) Sampson County
100	3876	0.2	**Hendersonville** (city) Henderson County
100	3876	0.2	**Holly Springs** (town) Wake County
100	n/a	0.2	**Lillington** (town) Harnett County
100	3876	0.2	**Newton** (city) Catawba County
100	3876	0.2	**Reidsville** (city) Rockingham County
100	3876	0.2	**Roanoke Rapids** (city) Halifax County
100	3876	0.2	**Southern Pines** (town) Moore County
100	n/a	0.2	**Wesley Chapel** (village) Union County
100	n/a	0.2	**Winterville** (town) Pitt County
112	4109	0.1	**Clemmons** (village) Forsyth County
112	n/a	0.1	**Gibsonville** (town) Guilford County
112	4109	0.1	**Hickory** (city) Catawba County
112	4109	0.1	**Morganton** (city) Burke County
112	4109	0.1	**Morrisville** (town) Wake County
112	n/a	0.1	**Mountain Home** (CDP) Henderson County
112	4109	0.1	**Smithfield** (town) Johnston County
112	4109	0.1	**Thomasville** (city) Davidson County
112	4109	0.1	**Wilson** (city) Wilson County
121	4278	0.0	**Albemarle** (city) Stanly County
121	n/a	0.0	**Angier** (town) Harnett County
121	4278	0.0	**Archdale** (city) Randolph County
121	n/a	0.0	**Ayden** (town) Pitt County
121	n/a	0.0	**Bayshore** (CDP) New Hanover County
121	n/a	0.0	**Benson** (town) Johnston County
121	n/a	0.0	**Bessemer City** (city) Gaston County
121	n/a	0.0	**Bethlehem** (CDP) Alexander County
121	n/a	0.0	**Black Mountain** (town) Buncombe County
121	n/a	0.0	**Boiling Spring Lakes** (city) Brunswick County
121	n/a	0.0	**Brevard** (city) Transylvania County
121	n/a	0.0	**Brices Creek** (CDP) Craven County
121	n/a	0.0	**Buies Creek** (CDP) Harnett County
121	n/a	0.0	**Burgaw** (town) Pender County
121	n/a	0.0	**Butner** (town) Granville County
121	n/a	0.0	**Cajah's Mountain** (town) Caldwell County
121	n/a	0.0	**Carolina Shores** (town) Brunswick County
121	n/a	0.0	**Cherryville** (city) Gaston County
121	n/a	0.0	**China Grove** (town) Rowan County
121	4278	0.0	**Clayton** (town) Johnston County
121	n/a	0.0	**Conover** (city) Catawba County
121	n/a	0.0	**Cramerton** (town) Gaston County
121	n/a	0.0	**Creedmoor** (city) Granville County
121	n/a	0.0	**Cullowhee** (CDP) Jackson County
121	n/a	0.0	**Dallas** (town) Gaston County
121	n/a	0.0	**Dana** (CDP) Henderson County
121	n/a	0.0	**East Flat Rock** (CDP) Henderson County
121	n/a	0.0	**East Rockingham** (CDP) Richmond County
121	n/a	0.0	**Eastover** (town) Cumberland County
121	4278	0.0	**Eden** (city) Rockingham County

Note: The state column ranks the top/bottom 150 places in the state with population of 2,500 or more. The national column ranks the top/bottom places in the country with population of 10,000 or more. Places that are unincorporated were not considered in the rankings. n/a indicates data not available. Please refer to the User Guide for additional information.

Commute to Work: Walk

Top 150 Places Ranked in *Descending* Order

State Rank	Nat'l Rank	Percent	Place
1	n/a	25.4	**Cullowhee** (CDP) Jackson County
2	34	19.4	**Boone** (town) Watauga County
3	n/a	13.1	**Buies Creek** (CDP) Harnett County
4	n/a	11.7	**Saint James** (town) Brunswick County
5	n/a	11.4	**Wingate** (town) Union County
6	n/a	10.5	**Boiling Springs** (town) Cleveland County
7	152	10.1	**Chapel Hill** (town) Orange County
8	157	9.9	**Jacksonville** (city) Onslow County
9	n/a	8.8	**Wallace** (town) Duplin County
10	n/a	7.9	**Louisburg** (town) Franklin County
11	n/a	7.6	**Murfreesboro** (town) Hertford County
12	n/a	7.1	**Elon** (town) Alamance County
13	n/a	7.0	**Icard** (CDP) Burke County
14	n/a	6.9	**Farmville** (town) Pitt County
15	n/a	6.7	**Edenton** (town) Chowan County
16	n/a	6.5	**Brevard** (city) Transylvania County
16	n/a	6.5	**Pineville** (town) Mecklenburg County
18	353	6.3	**Havelock** (city) Craven County
19	n/a	6.1	**East Flat Rock** (CDP) Henderson County
19	373	6.1	**Hendersonville** (city) Henderson County
21	381	6.0	**Davidson** (town) Mecklenburg County
21	n/a	6.0	**Troy** (town) Montgomery County
23	387	5.9	**Elizabeth City** (city) Pasquotank County
24	n/a	5.7	**Enfield** (town) Halifax County
24	n/a	5.7	**Oxford** (city) Granville County
26	n/a	5.5	**Swansboro** (town) Onslow County
27	n/a	5.4	**Dallas** (town) Gaston County
28	493	5.0	**Fayetteville** (city) Cumberland County
28	n/a	5.0	**Pembroke** (town) Robeson County
30	506	4.9	**Spring Lake** (town) Cumberland County
31	n/a	4.5	**Sylva** (town) Jackson County
32	589	4.4	**Kinston** (city) Lenoir County
32	589	4.4	**Piney Green** (CDP) Onslow County
32	n/a	4.4	**Valdese** (town) Burke County
35	n/a	4.3	**Morehead City** (town) Carteret County
36	660	4.1	**Asheville** (city) Buncombe County
37	n/a	4.0	**Randleman** (city) Randolph County
37	n/a	4.0	**Spencer** (town) Rowan County
39	n/a	3.8	**Mount Olive** (town) Wayne County
39	n/a	3.8	**Rockfish** (CDP) Hoke County
41	n/a	3.7	**Lake Royale** (CDP) Franklin County
41	n/a	3.7	**Red Springs** (town) Robeson County
41	n/a	3.7	**Welcome** (CDP) Davidson County
44	n/a	3.6	**Beaufort** (town) Carteret County
44	799	3.6	**Morganton** (city) Burke County
44	799	3.6	**Wilmington** (city) New Hanover County
47	n/a	3.5	**La Grange** (town) Lenoir County
47	n/a	3.5	**Warsaw** (town) Duplin County
49	879	3.4	**Henderson** (city) Vance County
49	n/a	3.4	**Southport** (city) Brunswick County
51	925	3.3	**Greenville** (city) Pitt County
52	n/a	3.2	**Burgaw** (town) Pender County
52	965	3.2	**Durham** (city) Durham County
52	965	3.2	**Lexington** (city) Davidson County
52	n/a	3.2	**Maiden** (town) Catawba County
56	1009	3.1	**New Bern** (city) Craven County
57	n/a	3.0	**Carolina Shores** (town) Brunswick County
57	n/a	3.0	**Dana** (CDP) Henderson County
57	1053	3.0	**Shelby** (city) Cleveland County
60	n/a	2.8	**Black Mountain** (town) Buncombe County
61	n/a	2.7	**Fairmont** (town) Robeson County
62	n/a	2.6	**Lillington** (town) Harnett County
62	n/a	2.6	**Washington** (city) Beaufort County
64	1347	2.5	**Carrboro** (town) Orange County
65	n/a	2.4	**Ahoskie** (town) Hertford County
65	n/a	2.4	**Carolina Beach** (town) New Hanover County
65	1439	2.4	**Goldsboro** (city) Wayne County
65	1439	2.4	**Knightdale** (town) Wake County
65	n/a	2.4	**Weaverville** (town) Buncombe County
70	n/a	2.3	**Mocksville** (town) Davie County
70	n/a	2.3	**Northchase** (CDP) New Hanover County
70	n/a	2.3	**Roxboro** (city) Person County
73	1584	2.2	**Belmont** (city) Gaston County
73	1584	2.2	**Charlotte** (city) Mecklenburg County
73	n/a	2.2	**East Rockingham** (CDP) Richmond County

State Rank	Nat'l Rank	Percent	Place
73	n/a	2.2	**Mar-Mac** (CDP) Wayne County
73	1584	2.2	**Thomasville** (city) Davidson County
73	n/a	2.2	**Wadesboro** (town) Anson County
73	n/a	2.2	**Wendell** (town) Wake County
80	n/a	2.1	**Ayden** (town) Pitt County
80	n/a	2.1	**Cherryville** (city) Gaston County
80	n/a	2.1	**Eastover** (town) Cumberland County
80	n/a	2.1	**Emerald Isle** (town) Carteret County
80	1686	2.1	**Fuquay-Varina** (town) Wake County
80	1686	2.1	**Raleigh** (city) Wake County
80	n/a	2.1	**Rolesville** (town) Wake County
87	1781	2.0	**Greensboro** (city) Guilford County
87	n/a	2.0	**Marion** (city) McDowell County
87	1781	2.0	**Roanoke Rapids** (city) Halifax County
90	n/a	1.9	**Dunn** (city) Harnett County
90	n/a	1.9	**Elkin** (town) Surry County
90	n/a	1.9	**Fairfield Harbour** (CDP) Craven County
90	1886	1.9	**Laurinburg** (city) Scotland County
90	1886	1.9	**Southern Pines** (town) Moore County
90	1886	1.9	**Winston-Salem** (city) Forsyth County
96	n/a	1.8	**Benson** (town) Johnston County
96	1994	1.8	**Lincolnton** (city) Lincoln County
98	n/a	1.7	**Newport** (town) Carteret County
98	n/a	1.7	**Windsor** (town) Bertie County
100	2230	1.6	**Asheboro** (city) Randolph County
100	n/a	1.6	**Canton** (town) Haywood County
100	n/a	1.6	**Etowah** (CDP) Henderson County
100	n/a	1.6	**Flat Rock** (village) Henderson County
100	2230	1.6	**High Point** (city) Guilford County
100	2230	1.6	**Kannapolis** (city) Cabarrus County
100	n/a	1.6	**Lake Junaluska** (CDP) Haywood County
100	2230	1.6	**Matthews** (town) Mecklenburg County
100	2230	1.6	**Salisbury** (city) Rowan County
100	n/a	1.6	**Sawmills** (town) Caldwell County
110	n/a	1.5	**Enochville** (CDP) Rowan County
110	2367	1.5	**Kings Mountain** (city) Cleveland County
110	n/a	1.5	**Pittsboro** (town) Chatham County
110	2367	1.5	**Sanford** (city) Lee County
114	2500	1.4	**Cary** (town) Wake County
114	2500	1.4	**Tarboro** (town) Edgecombe County
114	n/a	1.4	**Williamston** (town) Martin County
117	n/a	1.3	**Aberdeen** (town) Moore County
117	n/a	1.3	**Clinton** (city) Sampson County
117	n/a	1.3	**Hampstead** (CDP) Pender County
117	2661	1.3	**Hickory** (city) Catawba County
117	2661	1.3	**Lumberton** (city) Robeson County
117	2661	1.3	**Rocky Mount** (city) Nash County
117	n/a	1.3	**South Rosemary** (CDP) Halifax County
117	n/a	1.3	**Stanley** (town) Gaston County
117	2661	1.3	**Statesville** (city) Iredell County
117	n/a	1.3	**Trinity** (city) Randolph County
127	n/a	1.2	**Franklin** (town) Macon County
127	2817	1.2	**Garner** (town) Wake County
127	n/a	1.2	**Hillsborough** (town) Orange County
127	2817	1.2	**Kernersville** (town) Forsyth County
127	2817	1.2	**Mount Airy** (city) Surry County
127	n/a	1.2	**Spindale** (town) Rutherford County
133	2976	1.1	**Eden** (city) Rockingham County
133	2976	1.1	**Hope Mills** (town) Cumberland County
133	2976	1.1	**Mooresville** (town) Iredell County
133	n/a	1.1	**Moyock** (CDP) Currituck County
133	n/a	1.1	**Pinehurst** (village) Moore County
133	n/a	1.1	**Plymouth** (town) Washington County
133	2976	1.1	**Wilson** (city) Wilson County
133	n/a	1.1	**Zebulon** (town) Wake County
141	3154	1.0	**Apex** (town) Wake County
141	n/a	1.0	**Brogden** (CDP) Wayne County
141	n/a	1.0	**Fairview** (town) Union County
141	n/a	1.0	**Nashville** (town) Nash County
141	n/a	1.0	**Polkton** (town) Anson County
141	n/a	1.0	**Porters Neck** (CDP) New Hanover County
141	n/a	1.0	**Sneads Ferry** (CDP) Onslow County
148	3333	0.9	**Burlington** (city) Alamance County
148	n/a	0.9	**China Grove** (town) Rowan County
148	3333	0.9	**Clemmons** (village) Forsyth County

Note: The state column ranks the top/bottom 150 places in the state with population of 2,500 or more. The national column ranks the top/bottom places in the country with population of 10,000 or more. Places that are unincorporated were not considered in the rankings. n/a indicates data not available. Please refer to the User Guide for additional information.

Commute to Work: Walk

Top 150 Places Ranked in *Ascending* Order

State Rank	Nat'l Rank	Percent	Place
1	n/a	0.0	Archer Lodge (town) Johnston County
1	n/a	0.0	Bayshore (CDP) New Hanover County
1	n/a	0.0	Bessemer City (city) Gaston County
1	n/a	0.0	Bethlehem (CDP) Alexander County
1	n/a	0.0	Boiling Spring Lakes (city) Brunswick County
1	n/a	0.0	Brices Creek (CDP) Craven County
1	n/a	0.0	Conover (city) Catawba County
1	n/a	0.0	Creedmoor (city) Granville County
1	n/a	0.0	Elizabethtown (town) Bladen County
1	n/a	0.0	Elroy (CDP) Wayne County
1	n/a	0.0	Fairview (CDP) Buncombe County
1	n/a	0.0	Fletcher (town) Henderson County
1	n/a	0.0	Gamewell (town) Caldwell County
1	n/a	0.0	Gibsonville (town) Guilford County
1	n/a	0.0	Glen Raven (CDP) Alamance County
1	n/a	0.0	Granite Quarry (town) Rowan County
1	1	0.0	Harrisburg (town) Cabarrus County
1	n/a	0.0	Hudson (town) Caldwell County
1	n/a	0.0	Kitty Hawk (town) Dare County
1	n/a	0.0	Lake Park (village) Union County
1	n/a	0.0	Landis (town) Rowan County
1	1	0.0	Leland (town) Brunswick County
1	n/a	0.0	Liberty (town) Randolph County
1	n/a	0.0	Locust (city) Stanly County
1	n/a	0.0	Midland (town) Cabarrus County
1	n/a	0.0	Midway (town) Davidson County
1	n/a	0.0	Mountain Home (CDP) Henderson County
1	n/a	0.0	Mountain View (CDP) Catawba County
1	1	0.0	Murraysville (CDP) New Hanover County
1	1	0.0	Newton (city) Catawba County
1	n/a	0.0	North Wilkesboro (town) Wilkes County
1	n/a	0.0	Ranlo (town) Gaston County
1	n/a	0.0	Red Oak (town) Nash County
1	n/a	0.0	River Bend (town) Craven County
1	n/a	0.0	Seven Lakes (CDP) Moore County
1	n/a	0.0	Silver Lake (CDP) New Hanover County
1	n/a	0.0	Skippers Corner (CDP) New Hanover County
1	n/a	0.0	Trent Woods (town) Craven County
1	n/a	0.0	Tyro (CDP) Davidson County
1	n/a	0.0	Wallburg (town) Davidson County
1	n/a	0.0	Waxhaw (town) Union County
1	n/a	0.0	Wentworth (town) Rockingham County
1	n/a	0.0	Wesley Chapel (village) Union County
1	n/a	0.0	Whispering Pines (village) Moore County
1	n/a	0.0	Whiteville (city) Columbus County
1	n/a	0.0	Winterville (town) Pitt County
1	n/a	0.0	Wrightsboro (CDP) New Hanover County
48	93	0.1	Archdale (city) Randolph County
48	n/a	0.1	Walkertown (town) Forsyth County
50	151	0.2	Clayton (town) Johnston County
50	151	0.2	Indian Trail (town) Union County
50	151	0.2	Lewisville (town) Forsyth County
50	151	0.2	Mint Hill (town) Mecklenburg County
50	151	0.2	Mount Holly (city) Gaston County
50	151	0.2	Stallings (town) Union County
56	246	0.3	Albemarle (city) Stanly County
56	n/a	0.3	Angier (town) Harnett County
56	n/a	0.3	Cajah's Mountain (town) Caldwell County
56	n/a	0.3	Kings Grant (CDP) New Hanover County
56	n/a	0.3	Lake Norman of Catawba (CDP) Catawba County
56	n/a	0.3	Marvin (village) Union County
56	n/a	0.3	Mills River (town) Henderson County
56	n/a	0.3	Nags Head (town) Dare County
56	n/a	0.3	Raeford (city) Hoke County
65	n/a	0.4	Butner (town) Granville County
65	n/a	0.4	Cramerton (town) Gaston County
65	n/a	0.4	Forest City (town) Rutherford County
65	358	0.4	Graham (city) Alamance County
65	n/a	0.4	Half Moon (CDP) Onslow County
65	n/a	0.4	Hamlet (city) Richmond County
65	n/a	0.4	James City (CDP) Craven County
65	n/a	0.4	Pleasant Garden (town) Guilford County
65	358	0.4	Summerfield (town) Guilford County
65	n/a	0.4	Westport (CDP) Lincoln County
65	n/a	0.4	Woodfin (town) Buncombe County
76	497	0.5	Concord (city) Cabarrus County
76	n/a	0.5	Erwin (town) Harnett County
76	n/a	0.5	Grifton (town) Pitt County
76	497	0.5	Holly Springs (town) Wake County
76	n/a	0.5	Kill Devil Hills (town) Dare County
76	n/a	0.5	Mineral Springs (town) Union County
76	n/a	0.5	Myrtle Grove (CDP) New Hanover County
76	n/a	0.5	Ogden (CDP) New Hanover County
76	n/a	0.5	River Road (CDP) Beaufort County
76	n/a	0.5	Royal Pines (CDP) Buncombe County
76	n/a	0.5	Southern Shores (town) Dare County
87	n/a	0.6	Jamestown (town) Guilford County
87	n/a	0.6	King (city) Stokes County
87	n/a	0.6	Long View (town) Catawba County
87	n/a	0.6	Lowesville (CDP) Lincoln County
87	n/a	0.6	Oak Island (town) Brunswick County
87	n/a	0.6	Selma (town) Johnston County
87	n/a	0.6	Stokesdale (town) Guilford County
87	n/a	0.6	Tabor City (town) Columbus County
87	651	0.6	Wake Forest (town) Wake County
87	n/a	0.6	Yadkinville (town) Yadkin County
97	n/a	0.7	Forest Oaks (CDP) Guilford County
97	802	0.7	Huntersville (town) Mecklenburg County
97	802	0.7	Morrisville (town) Wake County
97	n/a	0.7	Oak Ridge (town) Guilford County
97	802	0.7	Reidsville (city) Rockingham County
97	n/a	0.7	Rockingham (city) Richmond County
97	n/a	0.7	Shallotte (town) Brunswick County
97	n/a	0.7	Siler City (town) Chatham County
97	802	0.7	Smithfield (town) Johnston County
97	n/a	0.7	Waynesville (town) Haywood County
97	n/a	0.7	Weddington (town) Union County
97	n/a	0.7	Wilkesboro (town) Wilkes County
109	970	0.8	Cornelius (town) Mecklenburg County
109	n/a	0.8	Lowell (city) Gaston County
109	n/a	0.8	Rural Hall (town) Forsyth County
109	n/a	0.8	Sunset Beach (town) Brunswick County
109	n/a	0.8	Swannanoa (CDP) Buncombe County
114	1154	0.9	Burlington (city) Alamance County
114	n/a	0.9	China Grove (town) Rowan County
114	1154	0.9	Clemmons (village) Forsyth County
114	1154	0.9	Gastonia (city) Gaston County
114	n/a	0.9	Granite Falls (town) Caldwell County
114	1154	0.9	Lenoir (city) Caldwell County
114	1154	0.9	Mebane (city) Alamance County
114	1154	0.9	Monroe (city) Union County
114	n/a	0.9	Rutherfordton (town) Rutherford County
114	n/a	0.9	Saint Stephens (CDP) Catawba County
114	n/a	0.9	Unionville (town) Union County
125	1324	1.0	Apex (town) Wake County
125	n/a	1.0	Brogden (CDP) Wayne County
125	n/a	1.0	Fairview (town) Union County
125	n/a	1.0	Nashville (town) Nash County
125	n/a	1.0	Polkton (town) Anson County
125	n/a	1.0	Porters Neck (CDP) New Hanover County
125	n/a	1.0	Sneads Ferry (CDP) Onslow County
132	1503	1.1	Eden (city) Rockingham County
132	1503	1.1	Hope Mills (town) Cumberland County
132	1503	1.1	Mooresville (town) Iredell County
132	n/a	1.1	Moyock (CDP) Currituck County
132	1503	1.1	Pinehurst (village) Moore County
132	n/a	1.1	Plymouth (town) Washington County
132	1503	1.1	Wilson (city) Wilson County
132	n/a	1.1	Zebulon (town) Wake County
140	n/a	1.2	Franklin (town) Macon County
140	1681	1.2	Garner (town) Wake County
140	n/a	1.2	Hillsborough (town) Orange County
140	1681	1.2	Kernersville (town) Forsyth County
140	1681	1.2	Mount Airy (city) Surry County
140	n/a	1.2	Spindale (town) Rutherford County
146	n/a	1.3	Aberdeen (town) Moore County
146	n/a	1.3	Clinton (city) Sampson County
146	n/a	1.3	Hampstead (CDP) Pender County
146	1840	1.3	Hickory (city) Catawba County
146	1840	1.3	Lumberton (city) Robeson County

Note: *The state column ranks the top/bottom 150 places in the state with population of 2,500 or more. The national column ranks the top/bottom places in the country with population of 10,000 or more. Places that are unincorporated were not considered in the rankings. n/a indicates data not available. Please refer to the User Guide for additional information.*

Commute to Work: Work from Home

Top 150 Places Ranked in *Descending* Order

State Rank	Nat'l Rank	Percent	Place	State Rank	Nat'l Rank	Percent	Place
1	n/a	19.5	**Fairfield Harbour** (CDP) Craven County	76	n/a	5.1	**Elon** (town) Alamance County
2	n/a	16.6	**Sunset Beach** (town) Brunswick County	76	n/a	5.1	**Enochville** (CDP) Rowan County
3	n/a	16.2	**Saint James** (town) Brunswick County	76	n/a	5.1	**Fletcher** (town) Henderson County
4	34	13.8	**Davidson** (town) Mecklenburg County	76	n/a	5.1	**Hillsborough** (town) Orange County
5	n/a	13.1	**Nags Head** (town) Dare County	80	n/a	5.0	**Carolina Shores** (town) Brunswick County
6	n/a	12.6	**Porters Neck** (CDP) New Hanover County	80	1209	5.0	**Leland** (town) Brunswick County
7	59	11.8	**Jacksonville** (city) Onslow County	80	n/a	5.0	**Unionville** (town) Union County
8	n/a	11.5	**Marvin** (village) Union County	83	n/a	4.9	**Farmville** (town) Pitt County
9	n/a	11.0	**Lake Park** (village) Union County	83	1254	4.9	**Mint Hill** (town) Mecklenburg County
10	n/a	10.9	**Lake Norman of Catawba** (CDP) Catawba County	83	n/a	4.9	**Moyock** (CDP) Currituck County
11	n/a	10.8	**Valdese** (town) Burke County	83	n/a	4.9	**Saint Stephens** (CDP) Catawba County
12	n/a	10.2	**Emerald Isle** (town) Carteret County	87	n/a	4.8	**Locust** (city) Stanly County
13	130	10.1	**Wake Forest** (town) Wake County	88	n/a	4.7	**Brevard** (city) Transylvania County
14	n/a	10.0	**Mills River** (town) Henderson County	88	1372	4.7	**Mooresville** (town) Iredell County
15	n/a	9.9	**Weddington** (town) Union County	90	1429	4.6	**Clemmons** (village) Forsyth County
15	n/a	9.9	**Westport** (CDP) Lincoln County	90	n/a	4.6	**Landis** (town) Rowan County
17	n/a	9.8	**Carolina Beach** (town) New Hanover County	92	1495	4.5	**Boone** (town) Watauga County
18	152	9.6	**Stallings** (town) Union County	93	1566	4.4	**Concord** (city) Cabarrus County
19	160	9.5	**Cornelius** (town) Mecklenburg County	93	n/a	4.4	**Jamestown** (town) Guilford County
20	n/a	9.4	**Wesley Chapel** (village) Union County	93	n/a	4.4	**Swannanoa** (CDP) Buncombe County
21	177	9.3	**Holly Springs** (town) Wake County	96	1650	4.3	**Durham** (city) Durham County
22	n/a	9.1	**Ogden** (CDP) New Hanover County	96	n/a	4.3	**King** (city) Stokes County
23	n/a	9.0	**Southern Shores** (town) Dare County	96	1650	4.3	**Kinston** (city) Lenoir County
23	n/a	9.0	**Waxhaw** (town) Union County	96	n/a	4.3	**Mountain Home** (CDP) Henderson County
25	n/a	8.8	**Black Mountain** (town) Buncombe County	96	n/a	4.3	**Whispering Pines** (village) Moore County
26	234	8.6	**Morrisville** (town) Wake County	101	n/a	4.2	**Waynesville** (town) Haywood County
27	n/a	8.5	**Pleasant Garden** (town) Guilford County	101	n/a	4.2	**Wendell** (town) Wake County
28	n/a	8.3	**East Flat Rock** (CDP) Henderson County	103	n/a	4.1	**Glen Raven** (CDP) Alamance County
28	n/a	8.3	**Lowesville** (CDP) Lincoln County	104	1884	4.0	**Kernersville** (town) Forsyth County
30	272	8.2	**Asheville** (city) Buncombe County	104	n/a	4.0	**Wrightsboro** (CDP) New Hanover County
30	272	8.2	**Cary** (town) Wake County	106	n/a	3.9	**Butner** (town) Granville County
32	n/a	8.0	**Flat Rock** (village) Henderson County	106	n/a	3.9	**Forest City** (town) Rutherford County
32	n/a	8.0	**Kitty Hawk** (town) Dare County	106	1952	3.9	**High Point** (city) Guilford County
34	328	7.8	**Huntersville** (town) Mecklenburg County	106	n/a	3.9	**Tyro** (CDP) Davidson County
34	328	7.8	**Lewisville** (town) Forsyth County	106	n/a	3.9	**Zebulon** (town) Wake County
36	n/a	7.7	**Forest Oaks** (CDP) Guilford County	111	n/a	3.8	**Burgaw** (town) Pender County
37	387	7.5	**Matthews** (town) Mecklenburg County	111	n/a	3.8	**Elkin** (town) Surry County
38	n/a	7.4	**Buies Creek** (CDP) Harnett County	111	2046	3.8	**Greensboro** (city) Guilford County
38	n/a	7.4	**Myrtle Grove** (CDP) New Hanover County	114	n/a	3.7	**Cramerton** (town) Gaston County
38	404	7.4	**Summerfield** (town) Guilford County	114	n/a	3.7	**Dunn** (city) Harnett County
38	n/a	7.4	**Weaverville** (town) Buncombe County	114	2137	3.7	**Winston-Salem** (city) Forsyth County
42	451	7.2	**Apex** (town) Wake County	117	n/a	3.6	**Lake Junaluska** (CDP) Haywood County
43	n/a	7.1	**Lake Royale** (CDP) Franklin County	117	2227	3.6	**Mebane** (city) Alamance County
44	n/a	7.0	**Rolesville** (town) Wake County	117	n/a	3.6	**Swansboro** (town) Onslow County
45	n/a	6.9	**Oak Ridge** (town) Guilford County	117	n/a	3.6	**Wilkesboro** (town) Wilkes County
46	n/a	6.8	**Woodfin** (town) Buncombe County	121	n/a	3.5	**Conover** (city) Catawba County
47	572	6.7	**Chapel Hill** (town) Orange County	121	n/a	3.5	**Fairview** (town) Union County
47	n/a	6.7	**Granite Quarry** (town) Rowan County	121	2321	3.5	**Knightdale** (town) Wake County
47	572	6.7	**Pinehurst** (village) Moore County	121	n/a	3.5	**Mount Olive** (town) Wayne County
50	n/a	6.6	**Bayshore** (CDP) New Hanover County	125	n/a	3.4	**Bethlehem** (CDP) Alexander County
50	n/a	6.6	**Franklin** (town) Macon County	125	2433	3.4	**Hendersonville** (city) Henderson County
52	623	6.5	**Garner** (town) Wake County	125	n/a	3.4	**Mar-Mac** (CDP) Wayne County
52	n/a	6.5	**Stokesdale** (town) Guilford County	125	n/a	3.4	**Roxboro** (city) Person County
54	n/a	6.3	**Angier** (town) Harnett County	129	2522	3.3	**Burlington** (city) Alamance County
54	n/a	6.3	**Granite Falls** (town) Caldwell County	129	n/a	3.3	**Lowell** (city) Gaston County
54	n/a	6.3	**James City** (CDP) Craven County	129	n/a	3.3	**Midway** (town) Davidson County
57	n/a	6.2	**Archer Lodge** (town) Johnston County	129	n/a	3.3	**Mocksville** (town) Davie County
57	n/a	6.2	**Beaufort** (town) Carteret County	129	2522	3.3	**Reidsville** (city) Rockingham County
57	701	6.2	**Fuquay-Varina** (town) Wake County	129	2522	3.3	**Salisbury** (city) Rowan County
57	701	6.2	**Harrisburg** (town) Cabarrus County	135	n/a	3.2	**Canton** (town) Haywood County
61	n/a	6.0	**Sawmills** (town) Caldwell County	135	n/a	3.2	**East Rockingham** (CDP) Richmond County
62	n/a	5.8	**Royal Pines** (CDP) Buncombe County	135	n/a	3.2	**Wallace** (town) Duplin County
62	n/a	5.8	**Trent Woods** (town) Craven County	138	2729	3.1	**Fayetteville** (city) Cumberland County
64	887	5.7	**Carrboro** (town) Orange County	138	2729	3.1	**Laurinburg** (city) Scotland County
64	887	5.7	**Charlotte** (city) Mecklenburg County	138	2729	3.1	**Roanoke Rapids** (city) Halifax County
66	n/a	5.5	**Kill Devil Hills** (town) Dare County	141	n/a	3.0	**Boiling Springs** (town) Cleveland County
66	n/a	5.5	**Mineral Springs** (town) Union County	141	2821	3.0	**Hickory** (city) Catawba County
68	n/a	5.4	**Fairview** (CDP) Buncombe County	141	2821	3.0	**Lenoir** (city) Caldwell County
68	1010	5.4	**Raleigh** (city) Wake County	141	n/a	3.0	**Midland** (town) Cabarrus County
68	n/a	5.4	**Winterville** (town) Pitt County	141	n/a	3.0	**Oxford** (city) Granville County
71	1060	5.3	**Belmont** (city) Gaston County	146	n/a	2.9	**Edenton** (town) Chowan County
71	n/a	5.3	**Kings Grant** (CDP) New Hanover County	146	2913	2.9	**Kings Mountain** (city) Cleveland County
71	1060	5.3	**Wilmington** (city) New Hanover County	146	2913	2.9	**Smithfield** (town) Johnston County
74	1109	5.2	**Indian Trail** (town) Union County	146	n/a	2.9	**Wadesboro** (town) Anson County
74	n/a	5.2	**Southport** (city) Brunswick County	146	n/a	2.9	**Walkertown** (town) Forsyth County

Note: The state column ranks the top/bottom 150 places in the state with population of 2,500 or more. The national column ranks the top/bottom places in the country with population of 10,000 or more. Places that are unincorporated were not considered in the rankings. n/a indicates data not available. Please refer to the User Guide for additional information.

Commute to Work: Work from Home

Top 150 Places Ranked in *Ascending* Order

State Rank	Nat'l Rank	Percent	Place
1	n/a	0.0	**Brogden** (CDP) Wayne County
1	n/a	0.0	**Dana** (CDP) Henderson County
1	n/a	0.0	**Elizabethtown** (town) Bladen County
1	n/a	0.0	**Elroy** (CDP) Wayne County
1	n/a	0.0	**Gamewell** (town) Caldwell County
1	n/a	0.0	**Hampstead** (CDP) Pender County
1	n/a	0.0	**Icard** (CDP) Burke County
1	n/a	0.0	**Louisburg** (town) Franklin County
1	n/a	0.0	**Pembroke** (town) Robeson County
1	n/a	0.0	**Red Springs** (town) Robeson County
1	n/a	0.0	**South Rosemary** (CDP) Halifax County
1	n/a	0.0	**Spencer** (town) Rowan County
1	n/a	0.0	**Williamston** (town) Martin County
14	n/a	0.1	**China Grove** (town) Rowan County
15	n/a	0.4	**Lillington** (town) Harnett County
15	n/a	0.4	**Murfreesboro** (town) Hertford County
17	n/a	0.5	**Dallas** (town) Gaston County
17	n/a	0.5	**Hudson** (town) Caldwell County
17	n/a	0.5	**Whiteville** (city) Columbus County
20	n/a	0.6	**Hamlet** (city) Richmond County
20	n/a	0.6	**Mountain View** (CDP) Catawba County
20	n/a	0.6	**Trinity** (city) Randolph County
23	n/a	0.7	**Cherryville** (city) Gaston County
23	40	0.7	**Lincolnton** (city) Lincoln County
23	n/a	0.7	**Randleman** (city) Randolph County
23	n/a	0.7	**Red Oak** (town) Nash County
27	n/a	0.8	**Creedmoor** (city) Granville County
27	59	0.8	**Hope Mills** (town) Cumberland County
27	59	0.8	**Lumberton** (city) Robeson County
30	n/a	0.9	**Ahoskie** (town) Hertford County
30	n/a	0.9	**Cajah's Mountain** (town) Caldwell County
30	n/a	0.9	**Raeford** (city) Hoke County
30	n/a	0.9	**Wingate** (town) Union County
34	n/a	1.0	**Rutherfordton** (town) Rutherford County
34	n/a	1.0	**Siler City** (town) Chatham County
34	n/a	1.0	**Windsor** (town) Bertie County
37	n/a	1.1	**Maiden** (town) Catawba County
37	n/a	1.1	**Ranlo** (town) Gaston County
37	n/a	1.1	**Wallburg** (town) Davidson County
40	180	1.2	**Eden** (city) Rockingham County
40	180	1.2	**Lexington** (city) Davidson County
40	n/a	1.2	**Nashville** (town) Nash County
40	n/a	1.2	**Northchase** (CDP) New Hanover County
40	n/a	1.2	**Stanley** (town) Gaston County
45	n/a	1.3	**Enfield** (town) Halifax County
45	n/a	1.3	**Etowah** (CDP) Henderson County
45	n/a	1.3	**Gibsonville** (town) Guilford County
45	n/a	1.3	**Rockfish** (CDP) Hoke County
49	272	1.4	**Archdale** (city) Randolph County
49	n/a	1.4	**Fairmont** (town) Robeson County
49	n/a	1.4	**Polkton** (town) Anson County
49	n/a	1.4	**River Road** (CDP) Beaufort County
49	272	1.4	**Sanford** (city) Lee County
54	n/a	1.5	**Seven Lakes** (CDP) Moore County
54	n/a	1.5	**Sneads Ferry** (CDP) Onslow County
54	327	1.5	**Statesville** (city) Iredell County
57	n/a	1.6	**Bessemer City** (city) Gaston County
57	398	1.6	**Goldsboro** (city) Wayne County
57	n/a	1.6	**Grifton** (town) Pitt County
57	n/a	1.6	**Half Moon** (CDP) Onslow County
57	398	1.6	**Shelby** (city) Cleveland County
57	n/a	1.6	**Troy** (town) Montgomery County
57	n/a	1.6	**Warsaw** (town) Duplin County
57	n/a	1.6	**Washington** (city) Beaufort County
65	467	1.7	**Henderson** (city) Vance County
65	n/a	1.7	**North Wilkesboro** (town) Wilkes County
65	n/a	1.7	**Spindale** (town) Rutherford County
65	n/a	1.7	**Welcome** (CDP) Davidson County
69	539	1.8	**Mount Holly** (city) Gaston County
70	634	1.9	**Clayton** (town) Johnston County
70	n/a	1.9	**Long View** (town) Catawba County
72	n/a	2.0	**Eastover** (town) Cumberland County
72	710	2.0	**Piney Green** (CDP) Onslow County
72	n/a	2.0	**Skippers Corner** (CDP) New Hanover County
72	710	2.0	**Thomasville** (city) Davidson County
72	710	2.0	**Wilson** (city) Wilson County
77	818	2.1	**Asheboro** (city) Randolph County
77	n/a	2.1	**Boiling Spring Lakes** (city) Brunswick County
77	n/a	2.1	**Newport** (town) Carteret County
77	818	2.1	**Newton** (city) Catawba County
81	905	2.2	**Albemarle** (city) Stanly County
81	n/a	2.2	**Brices Creek** (CDP) Craven County
81	n/a	2.2	**Cullowhee** (CDP) Jackson County
81	905	2.2	**Greenville** (city) Pitt County
81	905	2.2	**Morganton** (city) Burke County
81	905	2.2	**Murraysville** (CDP) New Hanover County
81	n/a	2.2	**Oak Island** (town) Brunswick County
88	n/a	2.3	**Benson** (town) Johnston County
88	1012	2.3	**Rocky Mount** (city) Nash County
88	n/a	2.3	**Rural Hall** (town) Forsyth County
88	n/a	2.3	**Tabor City** (town) Columbus County
92	1104	2.4	**Gastonia** (city) Gaston County
92	1104	2.4	**Graham** (city) Alamance County
92	1104	2.4	**Kannapolis** (city) Cabarrus County
92	n/a	2.4	**Yadkinville** (town) Yadkin County
96	n/a	2.5	**Ayden** (town) Pitt County
96	n/a	2.5	**Erwin** (town) Harnett County
96	1206	2.5	**Monroe** (city) Union County
96	n/a	2.5	**Plymouth** (town) Washington County
96	n/a	2.5	**Rockingham** (city) Richmond County
96	1206	2.5	**Southern Pines** (town) Moore County
96	n/a	2.5	**Sylva** (town) Jackson County
103	n/a	2.6	**Aberdeen** (town) Moore County
103	n/a	2.6	**Clinton** (city) Sampson County
103	1321	2.6	**Mount Airy** (city) Surry County
103	n/a	2.6	**Pineville** (town) Mecklenburg County
103	n/a	2.6	**River Bend** (town) Craven County
103	n/a	2.6	**Shallotte** (town) Brunswick County
103	1321	2.6	**Tarboro** (town) Edgecombe County
110	1426	2.7	**Elizabeth City** (city) Pasquotank County
110	1426	2.7	**Havelock** (city) Craven County
110	n/a	2.7	**La Grange** (town) Lenoir County
110	n/a	2.7	**Morehead City** (town) Carteret County
110	1426	2.7	**New Bern** (city) Craven County
110	n/a	2.7	**Pittsboro** (town) Chatham County
110	n/a	2.7	**Selma** (town) Johnston County
110	n/a	2.7	**Silver Lake** (CDP) New Hanover County
110	n/a	2.7	**Wentworth** (town) Rockingham County
119	n/a	2.8	**Liberty** (town) Randolph County
119	n/a	2.8	**Marion** (city) McDowell County
119	1547	2.8	**Spring Lake** (town) Cumberland County
122	n/a	2.9	**Edenton** (town) Chowan County
122	1631	2.9	**Kings Mountain** (city) Cleveland County
122	1631	2.9	**Smithfield** (town) Johnston County
122	n/a	2.9	**Wadesboro** (town) Anson County
122	n/a	2.9	**Walkertown** (town) Forsyth County
127	n/a	3.0	**Boiling Springs** (town) Cleveland County
127	1744	3.0	**Hickory** (city) Catawba County
127	1744	3.0	**Lenoir** (city) Caldwell County
127	n/a	3.0	**Midland** (town) Cabarrus County
127	n/a	3.0	**Oxford** (city) Granville County
132	1836	3.1	**Fayetteville** (city) Cumberland County
132	1836	3.1	**Laurinburg** (city) Scotland County
132	1836	3.1	**Roanoke Rapids** (city) Halifax County
135	n/a	3.2	**Canton** (town) Haywood County
135	n/a	3.2	**East Rockingham** (CDP) Richmond County
135	n/a	3.2	**Wallace** (town) Duplin County
138	2036	3.3	**Burlington** (city) Alamance County
138	n/a	3.3	**Lowell** (city) Gaston County
138	n/a	3.3	**Midway** (town) Davidson County
138	n/a	3.3	**Mocksville** (town) Davie County
138	2036	3.3	**Reidsville** (city) Rockingham County
138	2036	3.3	**Salisbury** (city) Rowan County
144	n/a	3.4	**Bethlehem** (CDP) Alexander County
144	2135	3.4	**Hendersonville** (city) Henderson County
144	n/a	3.4	**Mar-Mac** (CDP) Wayne County
144	n/a	3.4	**Roxboro** (city) Person County
148	n/a	3.5	**Conover** (city) Catawba County
148	n/a	3.5	**Fairview** (town) Union County
148	2224	3.5	**Knightdale** (town) Wake County

Note: The state column ranks the top/bottom 150 places in the state with population of 2,500 or more. The national column ranks the top/bottom places in the country with population of 10,000 or more. Places that are unincorporated were not considered in the rankings. n/a indicates data not available. Please refer to the User Guide for additional information.

Median Travel Time to Work

Top 150 Places Ranked in *Descending* Order

State Rank	Nat'l Rank	Minutes	Place
1	n/a	38.2	**Lake Norman of Catawba** (CDP) Catawba County
2	n/a	36.5	**Selma** (town) Johnston County
3	n/a	36.2	**Lake Royale** (CDP) Franklin County
4	n/a	35.9	**Westport** (CDP) Lincoln County
5	n/a	35.0	**Fairfield Harbour** (CDP) Craven County
6	n/a	33.6	**Skippers Corner** (CDP) New Hanover County
7	n/a	33.3	**Angier** (town) Harnett County
8	n/a	32.3	**Fairview** (town) Union County
9	n/a	31.8	**Moyock** (CDP) Currituck County
10	n/a	31.7	**Mineral Springs** (town) Union County
10	n/a	31.7	**Wendell** (town) Wake County
12	n/a	31.6	**Midland** (town) Cabarrus County
13	n/a	31.1	**Marvin** (village) Union County
14	847	30.5	**Indian Trail** (town) Union County
15	n/a	30.4	**Weddington** (town) Union County
16	921	30.2	**Fuquay-Varina** (town) Wake County
16	n/a	30.2	**Waxhaw** (town) Union County
18	n/a	30.0	**Archer Lodge** (town) Johnston County
19	1018	29.7	**Stallings** (town) Union County
20	n/a	29.5	**Sneads Ferry** (CDP) Onslow County
21	n/a	29.3	**Rolesville** (town) Wake County
22	n/a	29.0	**Locust** (city) Stanly County
23	1211	28.8	**Wake Forest** (town) Wake County
24	n/a	28.7	**Unionville** (town) Union County
25	n/a	28.6	**Brices Creek** (CDP) Craven County
25	n/a	28.6	**Maiden** (town) Catawba County
27	1306	28.4	**Clayton** (town) Johnston County
28	n/a	28.3	**Lake Park** (village) Union County
28	1335	28.3	**Mint Hill** (town) Mecklenburg County
28	n/a	28.3	**Pittsboro** (town) Chatham County
31	n/a	28.1	**Landis** (town) Rowan County
31	n/a	28.1	**Polkton** (town) Anson County
31	n/a	28.1	**Wesley Chapel** (village) Union County
34	n/a	28.0	**Franklin** (town) Macon County
35	1461	27.7	**Holly Springs** (town) Wake County
35	n/a	27.7	**Ogden** (CDP) New Hanover County
35	n/a	27.7	**Pleasant Garden** (town) Guilford County
38	n/a	27.6	**Lowesville** (CDP) Lincoln County
39	1519	27.5	**Summerfield** (town) Guilford County
40	n/a	27.0	**Rockfish** (CDP) Hoke County
41	n/a	26.9	**Oak Island** (town) Brunswick County
42	1674	26.8	**Monroe** (city) Union County
43	n/a	26.7	**Liberty** (town) Randolph County
43	n/a	26.7	**Porters Neck** (CDP) New Hanover County
43	n/a	26.7	**Wentworth** (town) Rockingham County
46	1751	26.5	**Cornelius** (town) Mecklenburg County
47	n/a	26.4	**Burgaw** (town) Pender County
47	n/a	26.4	**Pineville** (town) Mecklenburg County
49	n/a	26.2	**Carolina Beach** (town) New Hanover County
50	1910	25.9	**Huntersville** (town) Mecklenburg County
50	n/a	25.9	**Lowell** (city) Gaston County
50	n/a	25.9	**Whispering Pines** (village) Moore County
53	1939	25.8	**Garner** (town) Wake County
53	n/a	25.8	**Half Moon** (CDP) Onslow County
55	n/a	25.7	**Boiling Spring Lakes** (city) Brunswick County
55	1966	25.7	**Concord** (city) Cabarrus County
55	n/a	25.7	**Swansboro** (town) Onslow County
55	n/a	25.7	**Zebulon** (town) Wake County
59	n/a	25.6	**Stokesdale** (town) Guilford County
60	n/a	25.5	**Granite Quarry** (town) Rowan County
60	2014	25.5	**Piney Green** (CDP) Onslow County
60	n/a	25.5	**Ranlo** (town) Gaston County
63	n/a	25.4	**Erwin** (town) Harnett County
63	2037	25.4	**Knightdale** (town) Wake County
63	n/a	25.4	**Welcome** (CDP) Davidson County
66	2067	25.3	**Mooresville** (town) Iredell County
67	n/a	25.2	**Hampstead** (CDP) Pender County
67	2097	25.2	**Matthews** (town) Mecklenburg County
69	n/a	25.0	**Forest Oaks** (CDP) Guilford County
70	n/a	24.8	**Cajah's Mountain** (town) Caldwell County
70	n/a	24.8	**Elizabethtown** (town) Bladen County
70	n/a	24.8	**La Grange** (town) Lenoir County
73	n/a	24.7	**Creedmoor** (city) Granville County
73	2239	24.7	**Hope Mills** (town) Cumberland County
73	2239	24.7	**Mount Holly** (city) Gaston County
76	n/a	24.6	**East Flat Rock** (CDP) Henderson County
76	n/a	24.6	**Murfreesboro** (town) Hertford County
76	n/a	24.6	**Oak Ridge** (town) Guilford County
76	n/a	24.6	**Siler City** (town) Chatham County
80	2284	24.5	**Harrisburg** (town) Cabarrus County
80	n/a	24.5	**Hudson** (town) Caldwell County
80	2284	24.5	**Kannapolis** (city) Cabarrus County
83	n/a	24.4	**Wingate** (town) Union County
83	n/a	24.4	**Yadkinville** (town) Yadkin County
85	n/a	24.3	**Canton** (town) Haywood County
85	2350	24.3	**Charlotte** (city) Mecklenburg County
87	2386	24.2	**Apex** (town) Wake County
88	n/a	24.1	**Eastover** (town) Cumberland County
89	n/a	24.0	**Bethlehem** (CDP) Alexander County
89	n/a	24.0	**Cherryville** (city) Gaston County
89	2445	24.0	**Mebane** (city) Alamance County
92	n/a	23.9	**Bayshore** (CDP) New Hanover County
92	n/a	23.9	**Cramerton** (town) Gaston County
92	n/a	23.9	**Seven Lakes** (CDP) Moore County
95	n/a	23.8	**Butner** (town) Granville County
95	n/a	23.8	**Lillington** (town) Harnett County
95	n/a	23.8	**Sawmills** (town) Caldwell County
95	n/a	23.8	**Windsor** (town) Bertie County
99	n/a	23.7	**Carolina Shores** (town) Brunswick County
99	2543	23.7	**Gastonia** (city) Gaston County
99	2543	23.7	**Leland** (town) Brunswick County
102	n/a	23.6	**China Grove** (town) Rowan County
102	n/a	23.6	**Walkertown** (town) Forsyth County
104	n/a	23.5	**Buies Creek** (CDP) Harnett County
105	n/a	23.4	**Ayden** (town) Pitt County
105	n/a	23.4	**Edenton** (town) Chowan County
105	n/a	23.4	**Emerald Isle** (town) Carteret County
105	n/a	23.4	**Glen Raven** (CDP) Alamance County
109	n/a	23.3	**Enfield** (town) Halifax County
109	n/a	23.3	**Gibsonville** (town) Guilford County
109	n/a	23.3	**Mount Olive** (town) Wayne County
109	n/a	23.3	**Wallburg** (town) Davidson County
113	2697	23.2	**Eden** (city) Rockingham County
113	n/a	23.2	**Tyro** (CDP) Davidson County
115	n/a	23.1	**Grifton** (town) Pitt County
115	n/a	23.1	**Southern Shores** (town) Dare County
117	n/a	23.0	**Enochville** (CDP) Rowan County
118	n/a	22.9	**Wadesboro** (town) Anson County
119	n/a	22.7	**Dallas** (town) Gaston County
119	2818	22.7	**Lewisville** (town) Forsyth County
119	2818	22.7	**Lexington** (city) Davidson County
122	2845	22.6	**Kings Mountain** (city) Cleveland County
122	n/a	22.6	**Louisburg** (town) Franklin County
122	n/a	22.6	**Warsaw** (town) Duplin County
125	2871	22.5	**Davidson** (town) Mecklenburg County
125	2871	22.5	**Lincolnton** (city) Lincoln County
125	n/a	22.5	**River Road** (CDP) Beaufort County
125	2871	22.5	**Sanford** (city) Lee County
125	2871	22.5	**Smithfield** (town) Johnston County
130	n/a	22.4	**Mocksville** (town) Davie County
131	2943	22.3	**Cary** (town) Wake County
131	n/a	22.3	**Stanley** (town) Gaston County
133	3005	22.1	**Albemarle** (city) Stanly County
133	3005	22.1	**Archdale** (city) Randolph County
133	n/a	22.1	**Beaufort** (town) Carteret County
133	3005	22.1	**Southern Pines** (town) Moore County
137	3038	22.0	**Belmont** (city) Gaston County
137	3038	22.0	**Murraysville** (CDP) New Hanover County
139	n/a	21.9	**Hillsborough** (town) Orange County
139	n/a	21.9	**Newport** (town) Carteret County
141	3095	21.8	**Kernersville** (town) Forsyth County
141	n/a	21.8	**King** (city) Stokes County
141	n/a	21.8	**Mountain Home** (CDP) Henderson County
141	n/a	21.8	**Washington** (city) Beaufort County
145	n/a	21.7	**Boiling Springs** (town) Cleveland County
145	n/a	21.7	**Mountain View** (CDP) Catawba County
145	3114	21.7	**Reidsville** (city) Rockingham County
145	n/a	21.7	**Silver Lake** (CDP) New Hanover County
149	3142	21.6	**Pinehurst** (village) Moore County
149	3142	21.6	**Raleigh** (city) Wake County

Note: The state column ranks the top/bottom 150 places in the state with population of 2,500 or more. The national column ranks the top/bottom places in the country with population of 10,000 or more. Places that are unincorporated were not considered in the rankings. n/a indicates data not available. Please refer to the User Guide for additional information.

Median Travel Time to Work

Top 150 Places Ranked in *Ascending* Order

State Rank	Nat'l Rank	Minutes	Place
1	46	12.9	**Boone** (town) Watauga County
2	n/a	14.3	**Lake Junaluska** (CDP) Haywood County
2	n/a	14.3	**Whiteville** (city) Columbus County
4	n/a	15.7	**Wilkesboro** (town) Wilkes County
5	n/a	15.8	**Kitty Hawk** (town) Dare County
6	n/a	16.2	**Cullowhee** (CDP) Jackson County
6	n/a	16.2	**Rockingham** (city) Richmond County
8	n/a	16.4	**Conover** (city) Catawba County
8	n/a	16.4	**Nags Head** (town) Dare County
10	n/a	16.5	**Morehead City** (town) Carteret County
10	n/a	16.5	**Troy** (town) Montgomery County
12	384	16.6	**Havelock** (city) Craven County
12	384	16.6	**Hendersonville** (city) Henderson County
14	397	16.7	**Morganton** (city) Burke County
15	419	16.8	**Greenville** (city) Pitt County
16	441	16.9	**Roanoke Rapids** (city) Halifax County
17	n/a	17.0	**Forest City** (town) Rutherford County
18	507	17.3	**Wilmington** (city) New Hanover County
19	n/a	17.7	**Woodfin** (town) Buncombe County
20	590	17.8	**Asheville** (city) Buncombe County
20	n/a	17.8	**Clinton** (city) Sampson County
20	590	17.8	**Spring Lake** (town) Cumberland County
23	n/a	17.9	**Royal Pines** (CDP) Buncombe County
24	630	18.0	**Goldsboro** (city) Wayne County
24	n/a	18.0	**Waynesville** (town) Haywood County
26	643	18.1	**Henderson** (city) Vance County
26	643	18.1	**Wilson** (city) Wilson County
28	n/a	18.2	**Farmville** (town) Pitt County
28	n/a	18.2	**Trent Woods** (town) Craven County
30	n/a	18.3	**Brogden** (CDP) Wayne County
30	686	18.3	**Hickory** (city) Catawba County
30	n/a	18.3	**James City** (CDP) Craven County
30	n/a	18.3	**Southport** (city) Brunswick County
34	n/a	18.4	**Rutherfordton** (town) Rutherford County
35	n/a	18.5	**Spindale** (town) Rutherford County
36	n/a	18.6	**Saint Stephens** (CDP) Catawba County
36	n/a	18.6	**Shallotte** (town) Brunswick County
38	n/a	18.7	**Hamlet** (city) Richmond County
38	n/a	18.7	**Kings Grant** (CDP) New Hanover County
38	756	18.7	**Kinston** (city) Lenoir County
38	756	18.7	**Rocky Mount** (city) Nash County
42	n/a	18.8	**Plymouth** (town) Washington County
43	n/a	18.9	**Aberdeen** (town) Moore County
43	n/a	18.9	**Black Mountain** (town) Buncombe County
43	n/a	18.9	**Trinity** (city) Randolph County
46	811	19.0	**Shelby** (city) Cleveland County
46	n/a	19.0	**South Rosemary** (CDP) Halifax County
46	n/a	19.0	**Sunset Beach** (town) Brunswick County
46	n/a	19.0	**Weaverville** (town) Buncombe County
50	n/a	19.1	**East Rockingham** (CDP) Richmond County
50	n/a	19.1	**Pembroke** (town) Robeson County
50	n/a	19.1	**Red Oak** (town) Nash County
53	n/a	19.2	**Fletcher** (town) Henderson County
53	n/a	19.2	**Northchase** (CDP) New Hanover County
53	862	19.2	**Winston-Salem** (city) Forsyth County
56	883	19.3	**Chapel Hill** (town) Orange County
56	883	19.3	**Lumberton** (city) Robeson County
56	883	19.3	**New Bern** (city) Craven County
56	n/a	19.3	**North Wilkesboro** (town) Wilkes County
56	n/a	19.3	**Swannanoa** (CDP) Buncombe County
61	n/a	19.4	**Dana** (CDP) Henderson County
61	n/a	19.4	**Elroy** (CDP) Wayne County
61	n/a	19.4	**Long View** (town) Catawba County
61	909	19.4	**Tarboro** (town) Edgecombe County
61	n/a	19.4	**Williamston** (town) Martin County
66	937	19.5	**Statesville** (city) Iredell County
66	n/a	19.5	**Sylva** (town) Jackson County
68	n/a	19.6	**Granite Falls** (town) Caldwell County
68	973	19.6	**Mount Airy** (city) Surry County
68	n/a	19.6	**Randleman** (city) Randolph County
71	n/a	19.7	**Ahoskie** (town) Hertford County
71	996	19.7	**Fayetteville** (city) Cumberland County
71	n/a	19.7	**Jamestown** (town) Guilford County
71	996	19.7	**Newton** (city) Catawba County
75	1019	19.8	**Elizabeth City** (city) Pasquotank County
75	n/a	19.8	**Saint James** (town) Brunswick County
75	1019	19.8	**Salisbury** (city) Rowan County
78	1045	19.9	**Morrisville** (town) Wake County
78	n/a	19.9	**Winterville** (town) Pitt County
80	2000	20.0	**Icard** (CDP) Burke County
80	n/a	20.0	**Myrtle Grove** (CDP) New Hanover County
82	1085	20.1	**Greensboro** (city) Guilford County
82	1085	20.1	**High Point** (city) Guilford County
82	n/a	20.1	**Rural Hall** (town) Forsyth County
82	1085	20.1	**Thomasville** (city) Davidson County
86	n/a	20.2	**Raeford** (city) Hoke County
87	1151	20.3	**Jacksonville** (city) Onslow County
87	1151	20.3	**Laurinburg** (city) Scotland County
87	n/a	20.3	**Mills River** (town) Henderson County
87	n/a	20.3	**Tabor City** (town) Columbus County
91	1179	20.4	**Asheboro** (city) Randolph County
91	n/a	20.4	**Brevard** (city) Transylvania County
91	n/a	20.4	**Dunn** (city) Harnett County
91	n/a	20.4	**Elon** (town) Alamance County
91	1179	20.4	**Lenoir** (city) Caldwell County
96	n/a	20.5	**Elkin** (town) Surry County
96	1204	20.5	**Graham** (city) Alamance County
98	n/a	20.6	**Marion** (city) McDowell County
98	n/a	20.6	**Wallace** (town) Duplin County
100	n/a	20.7	**Bessemer City** (city) Gaston County
100	n/a	20.7	**Nashville** (town) Nash County
100	n/a	20.7	**Oxford** (city) Granville County
103	n/a	20.8	**Benson** (town) Johnston County
103	n/a	20.8	**Fairmont** (town) Robeson County
103	n/a	20.8	**Flat Rock** (village) Henderson County
106	1298	20.9	**Clemmons** (village) Forsyth County
106	n/a	20.9	**Fairview** (CDP) Buncombe County
106	n/a	20.9	**Gamewell** (town) Caldwell County
106	n/a	20.9	**Red Springs** (town) Robeson County
106	n/a	20.9	**Wrightsboro** (CDP) New Hanover County
111	1348	21.1	**Burlington** (city) Alamance County
111	1348	21.1	**Durham** (city) Durham County
111	n/a	21.1	**Roxboro** (city) Person County
111	n/a	21.1	**Spencer** (town) Rowan County
115	n/a	21.2	**River Bend** (town) Craven County
115	n/a	21.2	**Valdese** (town) Burke County
117	1406	21.3	**Carrboro** (town) Orange County
117	n/a	21.3	**Midway** (town) Davidson County
119	n/a	21.4	**Mar-Mac** (CDP) Wayne County
120	n/a	21.5	**Etowah** (CDP) Henderson County
120	n/a	21.5	**Kill Devil Hills** (town) Dare County
122	1491	21.6	**Pinehurst** (village) Moore County
122	1491	21.6	**Raleigh** (city) Wake County
124	n/a	21.7	**Boiling Springs** (town) Cleveland County
124	n/a	21.7	**Mountain View** (CDP) Catawba County
124	1515	21.7	**Reidsville** (city) Rockingham County
124	n/a	21.7	**Silver Lake** (CDP) New Hanover County
128	1543	21.8	**Kernersville** (town) Forsyth County
128	n/a	21.8	**King** (city) Stokes County
128	n/a	21.8	**Mountain Home** (CDP) Henderson County
128	n/a	21.8	**Washington** (city) Beaufort County
132	n/a	21.9	**Hillsborough** (town) Orange County
132	n/a	21.9	**Newport** (town) Carteret County
134	1593	22.0	**Belmont** (city) Gaston County
134	1593	22.0	**Murraysville** (CDP) New Hanover County
136	1619	22.1	**Albemarle** (city) Stanly County
136	1619	22.1	**Archdale** (city) Randolph County
136	n/a	22.1	**Beaufort** (town) Carteret County
136	1619	22.1	**Southern Pines** (town) Moore County
140	1680	22.3	**Cary** (town) Wake County
140	n/a	22.3	**Stanley** (town) Gaston County
142	n/a	22.4	**Mocksville** (town) Davie County
143	1746	22.5	**Davidson** (town) Mecklenburg County
143	1746	22.5	**Lincolnton** (city) Lincoln County
143	n/a	22.5	**River Road** (CDP) Beaufort County
143	1746	22.5	**Sanford** (city) Lee County
143	1746	22.5	**Smithfield** (town) Johnston County
148	1786	22.6	**Kings Mountain** (city) Cleveland County
148	n/a	22.6	**Louisburg** (town) Franklin County
148	n/a	22.6	**Warsaw** (town) Duplin County

Note: The state column ranks the top/bottom 150 places in the state with population of 2,500 or more. The national column ranks the top/bottom places in the country with population of 10,000 or more. Places that are unincorporated were not considered in the rankings. n/a indicates data not available. Please refer to the User Guide for additional information.

Violent Crime Rate per 10,000 Population

Top 150 Places Ranked in *Descending* Order

State Rank	Nat'l Rank	Rate	Place
1	n/a	177.5	Whiteville (city) Columbus County
2	21	175.5	Lumberton (city) Robeson County
3	n/a	141.0	Wadesboro (town) Anson County
4	51	139.8	Henderson (city) Vance County
5	57	134.7	Laurinburg (city) Scotland County
6	71	126.3	Kinston (city) Lenoir County
7	n/a	119.6	Spencer (town) Rowan County
8	n/a	118.7	Williamston (town) Martin County
9	111	105.0	Rocky Mount (city) Nash County
10	n/a	99.9	Oxford (city) Granville County
11	n/a	94.2	Mount Olive (town) Wayne County
12	n/a	91.5	Roxboro (city) Person County
13	n/a	86.9	Benson (town) Johnston County
14	n/a	81.1	Fairmont (town) Robeson County
15	n/a	78.1	Edenton (town) Chowan County
16	255	77.9	Salisbury (city) Rowan County
17	n/a	77.8	Red Springs (town) Robeson County
18	n/a	76.5	Sylva (town) Jackson County
19	269	76.0	Goldsboro (city) Wayne County
20	n/a	74.6	Yadkinville (town) Yadkin County
21	281	74.2	Statesville (city) Iredell County
22	n/a	74.0	Hamlet (city) Richmond County
23	n/a	73.4	Farmville (town) Pitt County
24	n/a	72.4	Enfield (town) Halifax County
25	n/a	70.7	Clinton (city) Sampson County
26	316	70.4	Burlington (city) Alamance County
27	322	69.8	Gastonia (city) Gaston County
28	337	68.5	Southern Pines (town) Moore County
29	n/a	66.5	Zebulon (town) Wake County
30	396	63.1	Greenville (city) Pitt County
31	n/a	62.2	Morehead City (town) Carteret County
32	411	62.0	Smithfield (town) Johnston County
33	414	61.9	Wilmington (city) New Hanover County
34	417	61.7	Shelby (city) Cleveland County
35	n/a	61.1	Kill Devil Hills (town) Dare County
35	n/a	61.1	Selma (town) Johnston County
37	436	60.8	Charlotte (city) Mecklenburg County
38	441	60.5	Winston-Salem (city) Forsyth County
39	444	60.2	Monroe (city) Union County
40	454	59.3	Elizabeth City (city) Pasquotank County
40	n/a	59.3	Raeford (city) Hoke County
42	464	58.7	Roanoke Rapids (city) Halifax County
43	475	57.8	Fayetteville (city) Cumberland County
44	n/a	55.4	Tabor City (town) Columbus County
44	n/a	55.4	Wilkesboro (town) Wilkes County
46	n/a	55.2	Canton (town) Haywood County
47	n/a	54.0	Wingate (town) Union County
48	n/a	53.3	Ayden (town) Pitt County
49	548	52.6	Graham (city) Alamance County
50	n/a	52.1	Shallotte (town) Brunswick County
51	564	51.9	Greensboro (city) Guilford County
52	569	51.8	High Point (city) Guilford County
53	n/a	51.4	Long View (town) Catawba County
54	621	48.7	Lincolnton (city) Lincoln County
55	655	47.1	Hope Mills (town) Cumberland County
56	n/a	47.0	North Wilkesboro (town) Wilkes County
57	661	46.9	Tarboro (town) Edgecombe County
58	725	44.9	Lexington (city) Davidson County
59	n/a	44.1	Warsaw (town) Duplin County
60	739	43.9	Albemarle (city) Stanly County
61	747	43.5	Thomasville (city) Davidson County
62	790	41.6	Hickory (city) Catawba County
63	n/a	41.1	Franklin (town) Macon County
64	809	40.8	Newton (city) Catawba County
65	n/a	40.7	Pittsboro (town) Chatham County
66	n/a	40.1	Troy (town) Montgomery County
67	841	39.7	Hendersonville (city) Henderson County
68	852	39.3	New Bern (city) Craven County
69	858	39.2	Raleigh (city) Wake County
70	n/a	39.0	Beaufort (town) Carteret County
70	n/a	39.0	Rockingham (city) Richmond County
72	n/a	38.6	Pineville (town) Mecklenburg County
73	883	38.3	Mount Airy (city) Surry County
74	n/a	38.2	Oak Island (town) Brunswick County
75	n/a	37.8	Marion (city) McDowell County
76	914	37.3	Eden (city) Rockingham County
77	922	37.1	Reidsville (city) Rockingham County
78	940	36.5	Kernersville (town) Forsyth County
79	1018	34.3	Mebane (city) Alamance County
80	n/a	34.0	Aberdeen (town) Moore County
81	n/a	32.8	Siler City (town) Chatham County
82	n/a	32.7	Emerald Isle (town) Carteret County
83	n/a	32.4	Wallace (town) Duplin County
84	n/a	32.1	Louisburg (town) Franklin County
85	1099	32.0	Asheboro (city) Randolph County
86	n/a	30.9	Cherryville (city) Gaston County
87	n/a	28.1	Windsor (town) Bertie County
88	1279	27.9	Morganton (city) Burke County
89	n/a	27.5	Woodfin (town) Buncombe County
90	n/a	27.0	Forest City (town) Rutherford County
91	n/a	26.1	Butner (town) Granville County
91	1355	26.1	Mount Holly (city) Gaston County
93	1378	25.6	Carrboro (town) Orange County
94	n/a	24.9	Murfreesboro (town) Hertford County
95	n/a	24.1	Randleman (city) Randolph County
96	n/a	24.0	Maiden (town) Catawba County
97	n/a	23.5	Creedmoor (city) Granville County
98	1503	22.9	Mooresville (town) Iredell County
99	n/a	22.5	Burgaw (town) Pender County
100	1531	22.2	Boone (town) Watauga County
101	n/a	21.6	Mocksville (town) Davie County
102	1595	21.2	Havelock (city) Craven County
103	n/a	20.8	Wendell (town) Wake County
104	1679	19.9	Matthews (town) Mecklenburg County
105	1691	19.7	Kannapolis (city) Cabarrus County
106	n/a	19.5	Erwin (town) Harnett County
107	n/a	19.4	Granite Falls (town) Caldwell County
108	1715	19.2	Garner (town) Wake County
109	n/a	19.0	King (city) Stokes County
110	n/a	18.5	Carolina Beach (town) New Hanover County
110	1769	18.5	Mint Hill (town) Mecklenburg County
112	n/a	18.0	Boiling Spring Lakes (city) Brunswick County
113	n/a	16.7	Newport (town) Carteret County
114	1924	16.2	Clayton (town) Johnston County
115	1966	15.7	Cornelius (town) Mecklenburg County
116	1992	15.4	Leland (town) Brunswick County
117	n/a	15.0	Liberty (town) Randolph County
118	2041	14.7	Concord (city) Cabarrus County
119	2067	14.4	Knightdale (town) Wake County
120	n/a	14.3	Waxhaw (town) Union County
121	n/a	13.9	Stanley (town) Gaston County
122	n/a	13.3	Brevard (city) Transylvania County
123	2208	12.7	Wake Forest (town) Wake County
124	2259	12.1	Chapel Hill (town) Orange County
125	2397	10.3	Stallings (town) Union County
126	2430	9.8	Huntersville (town) Mecklenburg County
127	n/a	9.6	Fletcher (town) Henderson County
128	2467	9.4	Davidson (town) Mecklenburg County
129	n/a	9.0	Kitty Hawk (town) Dare County
129	n/a	9.0	Rolesville (town) Wake County
131	2529	8.7	Apex (town) Wake County
131	n/a	8.7	Black Mountain (town) Buncombe County
133	n/a	8.4	Winterville (town) Pitt County
134	2568	8.3	Holly Springs (town) Wake County
135	n/a	8.1	Hudson (town) Caldwell County
136	n/a	7.9	Weaverville (town) Buncombe County
137	n/a	7.1	Trent Woods (town) Craven County
138	2730	6.9	Archdale (city) Randolph County
138	2730	6.9	Cary (town) Wake County
140	2865	5.7	Morrisville (town) Wake County
141	2910	5.3	Pinehurst (village) Moore County
142	n/a	4.5	Gibsonville (town) Guilford County
142	n/a	4.5	Valdese (town) Burke County
144	n/a	3.6	Southern Shores (town) Dare County
145	n/a	2.7	Sunset Beach (town) Brunswick County
146	n/a	2.1	Elon (town) Alamance County
147	n/a	0.0	River Bend (town) Craven County
147	n/a	0.0	Rutherfordton (town) Rutherford County
147	n/a	0.0	Whispering Pines (village) Moore County
150	n/a	n/a	Ahoskie (town) Hertford County

Note: The state column ranks the top/bottom 150 places in the state with population of 2,500 or more. The national column ranks the top/bottom places in the country with population of 10,000 or more. Places that are unincorporated were not considered in the rankings. n/a indicates data not available. Please refer to the User Guide for additional information.

Violent Crime Rate per 10,000 Population

Top 150 Places Ranked in *Ascending* Order

State Rank	Nat'l Rank	Rate	Place
1	n/a	0.0	**River Bend** (town) Craven County
1	n/a	0.0	**Rutherfordton** (town) Rutherford County
1	n/a	0.0	**Whispering Pines** (village) Moore County
4	n/a	2.1	**Elon** (town) Alamance County
5	n/a	2.7	**Sunset Beach** (town) Brunswick County
6	n/a	3.6	**Southern Shores** (town) Dare County
7	n/a	4.5	**Gibsonville** (town) Guilford County
7	n/a	4.5	**Valdese** (town) Burke County
9	354	5.3	**Pinehurst** (village) Moore County
10	392	5.7	**Morrisville** (town) Wake County
11	531	6.9	**Archdale** (city) Randolph County
11	531	6.9	**Cary** (town) Wake County
13	n/a	7.1	**Trent Woods** (town) Craven County
14	n/a	7.9	**Weaverville** (town) Buncombe County
15	n/a	8.1	**Hudson** (town) Caldwell County
16	689	8.3	**Holly Springs** (town) Wake County
17	n/a	8.4	**Winterville** (town) Pitt County
18	736	8.7	**Apex** (town) Wake County
18	n/a	8.7	**Black Mountain** (town) Buncombe County
20	n/a	9.0	**Kitty Hawk** (town) Dare County
20	n/a	9.0	**Rolesville** (town) Wake County
22	793	9.4	**Davidson** (town) Mecklenburg County
23	n/a	9.6	**Fletcher** (town) Henderson County
24	835	9.8	**Huntersville** (town) Mecklenburg County
25	871	10.3	**Stallings** (town) Union County
26	1003	12.1	**Chapel Hill** (town) Orange County
27	1052	12.7	**Wake Forest** (town) Wake County
28	n/a	13.3	**Brevard** (city) Transylvania County
29	n/a	13.9	**Stanley** (town) Gaston County
30	n/a	14.3	**Waxhaw** (town) Union County
31	1195	14.4	**Knightdale** (town) Wake County
32	1222	14.7	**Concord** (city) Cabarrus County
33	n/a	15.0	**Liberty** (town) Randolph County
34	1270	15.4	**Leland** (town) Brunswick County
35	1299	15.7	**Cornelius** (town) Mecklenburg County
36	1337	16.2	**Clayton** (town) Johnston County
37	n/a	16.7	**Newport** (town) Carteret County
38	n/a	18.0	**Boiling Spring Lakes** (city) Brunswick County
39	n/a	18.5	**Carolina Beach** (town) New Hanover County
39	1492	18.5	**Mint Hill** (town) Mecklenburg County
41	n/a	19.0	**King** (city) Stokes County
42	1548	19.2	**Garner** (town) Wake County
43	n/a	19.4	**Granite Falls** (town) Caldwell County
44	n/a	19.5	**Erwin** (town) Harnett County
45	1573	19.7	**Kannapolis** (city) Cabarrus County
46	1587	19.9	**Matthews** (town) Mecklenburg County
47	n/a	20.8	**Wendell** (town) Wake County
48	1666	21.2	**Havelock** (city) Craven County
49	n/a	21.6	**Mocksville** (town) Davie County
50	1737	22.2	**Boone** (town) Watauga County
51	n/a	22.5	**Burgaw** (town) Pender County
52	1765	22.9	**Mooresville** (town) Iredell County
53	n/a	23.5	**Creedmoor** (city) Granville County
54	n/a	24.0	**Maiden** (town) Catawba County
55	n/a	24.1	**Randleman** (city) Randolph County
56	n/a	24.9	**Murfreesboro** (town) Hertford County
57	1890	25.6	**Carrboro** (town) Orange County
58	n/a	26.1	**Butner** (town) Granville County
58	1913	26.1	**Mount Holly** (city) Gaston County
60	n/a	27.0	**Forest City** (town) Rutherford County
61	n/a	27.5	**Woodfin** (town) Buncombe County
62	1987	27.9	**Morganton** (city) Burke County
63	n/a	28.1	**Windsor** (town) Bertie County
64	n/a	30.9	**Cherryville** (city) Gaston County
65	2161	32.0	**Asheboro** (city) Randolph County
66	n/a	32.1	**Louisburg** (town) Franklin County
67	n/a	32.4	**Wallace** (town) Duplin County
68	n/a	32.7	**Emerald Isle** (town) Carteret County
69	n/a	32.8	**Siler City** (town) Chatham County
70	n/a	34.0	**Aberdeen** (town) Moore County
71	2251	34.3	**Mebane** (city) Alamance County
72	2329	36.5	**Kernersville** (town) Forsyth County
73	2346	37.1	**Reidsville** (city) Rockingham County
74	2352	37.3	**Eden** (city) Rockingham County
75	n/a	37.8	**Marion** (city) McDowell County
76	n/a	38.2	**Oak Island** (town) Brunswick County
77	2385	38.3	**Mount Airy** (city) Surry County
78	n/a	38.6	**Pineville** (town) Mecklenburg County
79	n/a	39.0	**Beaufort** (town) Carteret County
79	n/a	39.0	**Rockingham** (city) Richmond County
81	2408	39.2	**Raleigh** (city) Wake County
82	2414	39.3	**New Bern** (city) Craven County
83	2427	39.7	**Hendersonville** (city) Henderson County
84	n/a	40.1	**Troy** (town) Montgomery County
85	n/a	40.7	**Pittsboro** (town) Chatham County
86	2459	40.8	**Newton** (city) Catawba County
87	n/a	41.1	**Franklin** (town) Macon County
88	2479	41.6	**Hickory** (city) Catawba County
89	2521	43.5	**Thomasville** (city) Davidson County
90	2530	43.9	**Albemarle** (city) Stanly County
91	n/a	44.1	**Warsaw** (town) Duplin County
92	2545	44.9	**Lexington** (city) Davidson County
93	2606	46.9	**Tarboro** (town) Edgecombe County
94	n/a	47.0	**North Wilkesboro** (town) Wilkes County
95	2612	47.1	**Hope Mills** (town) Cumberland County
96	2646	48.7	**Lincolnton** (city) Lincoln County
97	n/a	51.4	**Long View** (town) Catawba County
98	2701	51.8	**High Point** (city) Guilford County
99	2703	51.9	**Greensboro** (city) Guilford County
100	n/a	52.1	**Shallotte** (town) Brunswick County
101	2722	52.6	**Graham** (city) Alamance County
102	n/a	53.3	**Ayden** (town) Pitt County
103	n/a	54.0	**Wingate** (town) Union County
104	n/a	55.2	**Canton** (town) Haywood County
105	n/a	55.4	**Tabor City** (town) Columbus County
105	n/a	55.4	**Wilkesboro** (town) Wilkes County
107	2796	57.8	**Fayetteville** (city) Cumberland County
108	2805	58.7	**Roanoke Rapids** (city) Halifax County
109	2817	59.3	**Elizabeth City** (city) Pasquotank County
109	n/a	59.3	**Raeford** (city) Hoke County
111	2827	60.2	**Monroe** (city) Union County
112	2828	60.5	**Winston-Salem** (city) Forsyth County
113	2834	60.8	**Charlotte** (city) Mecklenburg County
114	n/a	61.1	**Kill Devil Hills** (town) Dare County
114	n/a	61.1	**Selma** (town) Johnston County
116	2853	61.7	**Shelby** (city) Cleveland County
117	2856	61.9	**Wilmington** (city) New Hanover County
118	2858	62.0	**Smithfield** (town) Johnston County
119	n/a	62.2	**Morehead City** (town) Carteret County
120	2873	63.1	**Greenville** (city) Pitt County
121	n/a	66.5	**Zebulon** (town) Wake County
122	2933	68.5	**Southern Pines** (town) Moore County
123	2947	69.8	**Gastonia** (city) Gaston County
124	2955	70.4	**Burlington** (city) Alamance County
125	n/a	70.7	**Clinton** (city) Sampson County
126	n/a	72.4	**Enfield** (town) Halifax County
127	n/a	73.4	**Farmville** (town) Pitt County
128	n/a	74.0	**Hamlet** (city) Richmond County
129	2987	74.2	**Statesville** (city) Iredell County
130	n/a	74.6	**Yadkinville** (town) Yadkin County
131	3002	76.0	**Goldsboro** (city) Wayne County
132	n/a	76.5	**Sylva** (town) Jackson County
133	n/a	77.8	**Red Springs** (town) Robeson County
134	3014	77.9	**Salisbury** (city) Rowan County
135	n/a	78.1	**Edenton** (town) Chowan County
136	n/a	81.1	**Fairmont** (town) Robeson County
137	n/a	86.9	**Benson** (town) Johnston County
138	n/a	91.5	**Roxboro** (city) Person County
139	n/a	94.2	**Mount Olive** (town) Wayne County
140	n/a	99.9	**Oxford** (city) Granville County
141	3160	105.0	**Rocky Mount** (city) Nash County
142	n/a	118.7	**Williamston** (town) Martin County
143	n/a	119.6	**Spencer** (town) Rowan County
144	3200	126.3	**Kinston** (city) Lenoir County
145	3214	134.7	**Laurinburg** (city) Scotland County
146	3220	139.8	**Henderson** (city) Vance County
147	n/a	141.0	**Wadesboro** (town) Anson County
148	3250	175.5	**Lumberton** (city) Robeson County
149	n/a	177.5	**Whiteville** (city) Columbus County

Note: The state column ranks the top/bottom 150 places in the state with population of 2,500 or more. The national column ranks the top/bottom places in the country with population of 10,000 or more. Places that are unincorporated were not considered in the rankings. n/a indicates data not available. Please refer to the User Guide for additional information.

Property Crime Rate per 10,000 Population

Top 150 Places Ranked in *Descending* Order

State Rank	Nat'l Rank	Rate	Place
1	4	1,398.7	**Lumberton** (city) Robeson County
2	n/a	1,321.8	**Pineville** (town) Mecklenburg County
3	n/a	1,143.4	**Whiteville** (city) Columbus County
4	n/a	1,057.0	**Randleman** (city) Randolph County
5	n/a	1,007.4	**Williamston** (town) Martin County
6	n/a	1,006.3	**Rockingham** (city) Richmond County
7	n/a	945.5	**Red Springs** (town) Robeson County
8	n/a	944.3	**Wilkesboro** (town) Wilkes County
9	19	941.3	**Henderson** (city) Vance County
10	n/a	825.7	**Marion** (city) McDowell County
11	n/a	791.2	**Forest City** (town) Rutherford County
12	n/a	765.3	**Franklin** (town) Macon County
13	n/a	755.3	**Fairmont** (town) Robeson County
14	87	695.7	**Kinston** (city) Lenoir County
15	n/a	682.2	**Wadesboro** (town) Anson County
16	n/a	670.6	**Sylva** (town) Jackson County
17	n/a	666.9	**Oxford** (city) Granville County
18	n/a	665.7	**Mount Olive** (town) Wayne County
19	n/a	664.7	**Zebulon** (town) Wake County
20	107	663.7	**Hope Mills** (town) Cumberland County
21	108	662.7	**Statesville** (city) Iredell County
22	n/a	654.1	**Emerald Isle** (town) Carteret County
23	129	642.6	**Reidsville** (city) Rockingham County
24	132	639.8	**Asheboro** (city) Randolph County
25	140	637.1	**Hendersonville** (city) Henderson County
26	144	630.5	**Roanoke Rapids** (city) Halifax County
27	148	629.6	**Goldsboro** (city) Wayne County
28	n/a	629.2	**Canton** (town) Haywood County
29	n/a	624.1	**Granite Falls** (town) Caldwell County
30	176	605.4	**Fayetteville** (city) Cumberland County
31	179	603.6	**Laurinburg** (city) Scotland County
32	196	586.0	**Smithfield** (town) Johnston County
33	n/a	583.6	**Roxboro** (city) Person County
34	n/a	576.5	**Benson** (town) Johnston County
34	n/a	576.5	**Morehead City** (town) Carteret County
36	212	575.6	**Rocky Mount** (city) Nash County
37	n/a	569.9	**Clinton** (city) Sampson County
38	n/a	559.2	**North Wilkesboro** (town) Wilkes County
39	252	550.5	**Hickory** (city) Catawba County
40	255	549.4	**Albemarle** (city) Stanly County
41	n/a	547.3	**Shallotte** (town) Brunswick County
42	259	546.3	**Salisbury** (city) Rowan County
43	261	545.1	**Winston-Salem** (city) Forsyth County
44	264	543.1	**Mebane** (city) Alamance County
45	n/a	532.2	**Long View** (town) Catawba County
46	298	529.2	**Gastonia** (city) Gaston County
47	n/a	525.1	**Raeford** (city) Hoke County
48	310	522.5	**Monroe** (city) Union County
49	328	513.5	**New Bern** (city) Craven County
50	331	512.6	**Burlington** (city) Alamance County
51	n/a	506.0	**Weaverville** (town) Buncombe County
52	367	500.5	**Mount Airy** (city) Surry County
53	371	500.0	**Wilmington** (city) New Hanover County
54	375	497.8	**Lincolnton** (city) Lincoln County
55	n/a	484.5	**Hamlet** (city) Richmond County
56	n/a	482.9	**Enfield** (town) Halifax County
57	n/a	466.5	**Selma** (town) Johnston County
58	n/a	462.9	**Kill Devil Hills** (town) Dare County
59	n/a	462.6	**Edenton** (town) Chowan County
60	n/a	459.8	**Spencer** (town) Rowan County
61	n/a	449.7	**Aberdeen** (town) Moore County
62	n/a	440.8	**Wallace** (town) Duplin County
62	n/a	440.8	**Yadkinville** (town) Yadkin County
64	572	438.8	**Greenville** (city) Pitt County
65	583	436.0	**Garner** (town) Wake County
66	584	435.9	**Southern Pines** (town) Moore County
67	n/a	435.6	**Mocksville** (town) Davie County
68	n/a	431.2	**Carolina Beach** (town) New Hanover County
69	605	430.5	**Kernersville** (town) Forsyth County
70	653	418.5	**High Point** (city) Guilford County
71	664	415.4	**Mooresville** (town) Iredell County
72	675	413.0	**Greensboro** (city) Guilford County
73	677	412.3	**Eden** (city) Rockingham County
74	679	411.6	**Tarboro** (town) Edgecombe County
75	n/a	411.5	**Beaufort** (town) Carteret County
76	n/a	411.1	**King** (city) Stokes County
77	n/a	408.7	**Ayden** (town) Pitt County
78	695	408.0	**Thomasville** (city) Davidson County
79	699	406.4	**Graham** (city) Alamance County
80	n/a	403.2	**Kitty Hawk** (town) Dare County
81	n/a	394.3	**Siler City** (town) Chatham County
82	750	393.0	**Elizabeth City** (city) Pasquotank County
83	n/a	386.2	**Stanley** (town) Gaston County
84	n/a	380.4	**Tabor City** (town) Columbus County
85	n/a	375.5	**Brevard** (city) Transylvania County
86	n/a	375.2	**Warsaw** (town) Duplin County
87	873	364.9	**Charlotte** (city) Mecklenburg County
88	n/a	358.2	**Oak Island** (town) Brunswick County
89	932	354.3	**Knightdale** (town) Wake County
90	n/a	344.1	**Hudson** (town) Caldwell County
91	n/a	344.0	**Troy** (town) Montgomery County
92	1000	339.8	**Newton** (city) Catawba County
93	1023	335.8	**Lexington** (city) Davidson County
94	1029	334.6	**Shelby** (city) Cleveland County
95	n/a	332.9	**Rutherfordton** (town) Rutherford County
96	n/a	321.4	**Cherryville** (city) Gaston County
97	n/a	313.9	**Erwin** (town) Harnett County
98	n/a	310.6	**Wingate** (town) Union County
99	n/a	310.5	**Farmville** (town) Pitt County
100	1199	307.5	**Concord** (city) Cabarrus County
101	1206	306.3	**Raleigh** (city) Wake County
102	n/a	297.7	**Louisburg** (town) Franklin County
103	n/a	297.6	**Butner** (town) Granville County
104	n/a	296.4	**Maiden** (town) Catawba County
105	1304	291.4	**Morganton** (city) Burke County
106	n/a	289.6	**Burgaw** (town) Pender County
107	1366	282.1	**Matthews** (town) Mecklenburg County
108	1407	277.2	**Carrboro** (town) Orange County
109	n/a	272.1	**Wendell** (town) Wake County
110	n/a	264.4	**Sunset Beach** (town) Brunswick County
111	n/a	260.1	**Murfreesboro** (town) Hertford County
112	1577	257.7	**Archdale** (city) Randolph County
113	n/a	253.2	**Newport** (town) Carteret County
114	1622	252.3	**Leland** (town) Brunswick County
115	1692	243.2	**Havelock** (city) Craven County
116	1727	238.5	**Clayton** (town) Johnston County
117	n/a	233.9	**Pittsboro** (town) Chatham County
118	1901	217.7	**Chapel Hill** (town) Orange County
119	1928	215.9	**Wake Forest** (town) Wake County
120	n/a	212.5	**Rolesville** (town) Wake County
121	2011	207.7	**Kannapolis** (city) Cabarrus County
122	n/a	204.9	**Southern Shores** (town) Dare County
123	n/a	200.8	**Fletcher** (town) Henderson County
124	n/a	199.8	**Creedmoor** (city) Granville County
125	2110	197.8	**Morrisville** (town) Wake County
126	2211	187.4	**Huntersville** (town) Mecklenburg County
127	2221	186.8	**Mount Holly** (city) Gaston County
128	2284	178.8	**Cornelius** (town) Mecklenburg County
129	n/a	178.1	**Woodfin** (town) Buncombe County
130	n/a	176.7	**Boiling Spring Lakes** (city) Brunswick County
131	n/a	171.9	**Gibsonville** (town) Guilford County
132	2370	167.8	**Boone** (town) Watauga County
133	2381	166.7	**Mint Hill** (town) Mecklenburg County
134	2416	163.0	**Stallings** (town) Union County
135	n/a	153.6	**Valdese** (town) Burke County
135	n/a	153.6	**Waxhaw** (town) Union County
137	n/a	147.3	**Black Mountain** (town) Buncombe County
138	n/a	145.9	**Windsor** (town) Bertie County
139	n/a	141.2	**Whispering Pines** (village) Moore County
140	2616	139.4	**Cary** (town) Wake County
141	2692	129.4	**Apex** (town) Wake County
142	n/a	125.3	**Trent Woods** (town) Craven County
143	n/a	119.7	**River Bend** (town) Craven County
144	2811	115.4	**Holly Springs** (town) Wake County
145	n/a	88.3	**Elon** (town) Alamance County
146	n/a	88.1	**Winterville** (town) Pitt County
147	3066	82.8	**Pinehurst** (village) Moore County
148	3102	77.2	**Davidson** (town) Mecklenburg County
149	n/a	63.6	**Liberty** (town) Randolph County

Note: The state column ranks the top/bottom 150 places in the state with population of 2,500 or more. The national column ranks the top/bottom places in the country with population of 10,000 or more. Places that are unincorporated were not considered in the rankings. n/a indicates data not available. Please refer to the User Guide for additional information.

Property Crime Rate per 10,000 Population

Top 150 Places Ranked in *Ascending* Order

State Rank	Nat'l Rank	Rate	Place	State Rank	Nat'l Rank	Rate	Place
1	n/a	63.6	**Liberty** (town) Randolph County	76	2591	411.6	**Tarboro** (town) Edgecombe County
2	168	77.2	**Davidson** (town) Mecklenburg County	77	2593	412.3	**Eden** (city) Rockingham County
3	203	82.8	**Pinehurst** (village) Moore County	78	2595	413.0	**Greensboro** (city) Guilford County
4	n/a	88.1	**Winterville** (town) Pitt County	79	2606	415.4	**Mooresville** (town) Iredell County
5	n/a	88.3	**Elon** (town) Alamance County	80	2617	418.5	**High Point** (city) Guilford County
6	459	115.4	**Holly Springs** (town) Wake County	81	2665	430.5	**Kernersville** (town) Forsyth County
7	n/a	119.7	**River Bend** (town) Craven County	82	n/a	431.2	**Carolina Beach** (town) New Hanover County
8	n/a	125.3	**Trent Woods** (town) Craven County	83	n/a	435.6	**Mocksville** (town) Davie County
9	577	129.4	**Apex** (town) Wake County	84	2686	435.9	**Southern Pines** (town) Moore County
10	654	139.4	**Cary** (town) Wake County	85	2687	436.0	**Garner** (town) Wake County
11	n/a	141.2	**Whispering Pines** (village) Moore County	86	2697	438.8	**Greenville** (city) Pitt County
12	n/a	145.9	**Windsor** (town) Bertie County	87	n/a	440.8	**Wallace** (town) Duplin County
13	n/a	147.3	**Black Mountain** (town) Buncombe County	87	n/a	440.8	**Yadkinville** (town) Yadkin County
14	n/a	153.6	**Valdese** (town) Burke County	89	n/a	449.7	**Aberdeen** (town) Moore County
14	n/a	153.6	**Waxhaw** (town) Union County	90	n/a	459.8	**Spencer** (town) Rowan County
16	854	163.0	**Stallings** (town) Union County	91	n/a	462.6	**Edenton** (town) Chowan County
17	888	166.7	**Mint Hill** (town) Mecklenburg County	92	n/a	462.9	**Kill Devil Hills** (town) Dare County
18	899	167.8	**Boone** (town) Watauga County	93	n/a	466.5	**Selma** (town) Johnston County
19	n/a	171.9	**Gibsonville** (town) Guilford County	94	n/a	482.9	**Enfield** (town) Halifax County
20	n/a	176.7	**Boiling Spring Lakes** (city) Brunswick County	95	n/a	484.5	**Hamlet** (city) Richmond County
21	n/a	178.1	**Woodfin** (town) Buncombe County	96	2894	497.8	**Lincolnton** (city) Lincoln County
22	986	178.8	**Cornelius** (town) Mecklenburg County	97	2899	500.0	**Wilmington** (city) New Hanover County
23	1048	186.8	**Mount Holly** (city) Gaston County	98	2902	500.5	**Mount Airy** (city) Surry County
24	1059	187.4	**Huntersville** (town) Mecklenburg County	99	n/a	506.0	**Weaverville** (town) Buncombe County
25	1159	197.8	**Morrisville** (town) Wake County	100	2939	512.6	**Burlington** (city) Alamance County
26	n/a	199.8	**Creedmoor** (city) Granville County	101	2942	513.5	**New Bern** (city) Craven County
27	n/a	200.8	**Fletcher** (town) Henderson County	102	2960	522.5	**Monroe** (city) Union County
28	n/a	204.9	**Southern Shores** (town) Dare County	103	n/a	525.1	**Raeford** (city) Hoke County
29	1259	207.7	**Kannapolis** (city) Cabarrus County	104	2972	529.2	**Gastonia** (city) Gaston County
30	n/a	212.5	**Rolesville** (town) Wake County	105	n/a	532.2	**Long View** (town) Catawba County
31	1340	215.9	**Wake Forest** (town) Wake County	106	3005	543.1	**Mebane** (city) Alamance County
32	1368	217.7	**Chapel Hill** (town) Orange County	107	3009	545.1	**Winston-Salem** (city) Forsyth County
33	n/a	233.9	**Pittsboro** (town) Chatham County	108	3011	546.3	**Salisbury** (city) Rowan County
34	1542	238.5	**Clayton** (town) Johnston County	109	n/a	547.3	**Shallotte** (town) Brunswick County
35	1578	243.2	**Havelock** (city) Craven County	110	3014	549.4	**Albemarle** (city) Stanly County
36	1647	252.2	**Leland** (town) Brunswick County	111	3018	550.5	**Hickory** (city) Catawba County
37	n/a	253.2	**Newport** (town) Carteret County	112	n/a	559.2	**North Wilkesboro** (town) Wilkes County
38	1693	257.7	**Archdale** (city) Randolph County	113	n/a	569.9	**Clinton** (city) Sampson County
39	n/a	260.1	**Murfreesboro** (town) Hertford County	114	3058	575.6	**Rocky Mount** (city) Nash County
40	n/a	264.4	**Sunset Beach** (town) Brunswick County	115	n/a	576.5	**Benson** (town) Johnston County
41	n/a	272.1	**Wendell** (town) Wake County	115	n/a	576.5	**Morehead City** (town) Carteret County
42	1863	277.2	**Carrboro** (town) Orange County	117	n/a	583.6	**Roxboro** (city) Person County
43	1904	282.1	**Matthews** (town) Mecklenburg County	118	3074	586.0	**Smithfield** (town) Johnston County
44	n/a	289.6	**Burgaw** (town) Pender County	119	3091	603.6	**Laurinburg** (city) Scotland County
45	1965	291.4	**Morganton** (city) Burke County	120	3094	605.4	**Fayetteville** (city) Cumberland County
46	n/a	296.4	**Maiden** (town) Catawba County	121	n/a	624.1	**Granite Falls** (town) Caldwell County
47	n/a	297.6	**Butner** (town) Granville County	122	n/a	629.2	**Canton** (town) Haywood County
48	n/a	297.7	**Louisburg** (town) Franklin County	123	3122	629.6	**Goldsboro** (city) Wayne County
49	2064	306.3	**Raleigh** (city) Wake County	124	3126	630.5	**Roanoke Rapids** (city) Halifax County
50	2071	307.5	**Concord** (city) Cabarrus County	125	3130	637.1	**Hendersonville** (city) Henderson County
51	n/a	310.5	**Farmville** (town) Pitt County	126	3137	639.8	**Asheboro** (city) Randolph County
52	n/a	310.6	**Wingate** (town) Union County	127	3141	642.6	**Reidsville** (city) Rockingham County
53	n/a	313.9	**Erwin** (town) Harnett County	128	n/a	654.1	**Emerald Isle** (town) Carteret County
54	n/a	321.4	**Cherryville** (city) Gaston County	129	3162	662.7	**Statesville** (city) Iredell County
55	n/a	332.9	**Rutherfordton** (town) Rutherford County	130	3163	663.7	**Hope Mills** (town) Cumberland County
56	2241	334.6	**Shelby** (city) Cleveland County	131	n/a	664.7	**Zebulon** (town) Wake County
57	2247	335.8	**Lexington** (city) Davidson County	132	n/a	665.7	**Mount Olive** (town) Wayne County
58	2270	339.8	**Newton** (city) Catawba County	133	n/a	666.9	**Oxford** (city) Granville County
59	n/a	344.0	**Troy** (town) Montgomery County	134	n/a	670.6	**Sylva** (town) Jackson County
60	n/a	344.1	**Hudson** (town) Caldwell County	135	n/a	682.2	**Wadesboro** (town) Anson County
61	2338	354.3	**Knightdale** (town) Wake County	136	3183	695.7	**Kinston** (city) Lenoir County
62	n/a	358.2	**Oak Island** (town) Brunswick County	137	n/a	755.3	**Fairmont** (town) Robeson County
63	2396	364.9	**Charlotte** (city) Mecklenburg County	138	n/a	765.3	**Franklin** (town) Macon County
64	n/a	375.2	**Warsaw** (town) Duplin County	139	n/a	791.2	**Forest City** (town) Rutherford County
65	n/a	375.5	**Brevard** (city) Transylvania County	140	n/a	825.7	**Marion** (city) McDowell County
66	n/a	380.4	**Tabor City** (town) Columbus County	141	3251	941.3	**Henderson** (city) Vance County
67	n/a	386.2	**Stanley** (town) Gaston County	142	n/a	944.3	**Wilkesboro** (town) Wilkes County
68	2518	393.0	**Elizabeth City** (city) Pasquotank County	143	n/a	945.5	**Red Springs** (town) Robeson County
69	n/a	394.3	**Siler City** (town) Chatham County	144	n/a	1,006.3	**Rockingham** (city) Richmond County
70	n/a	403.2	**Kitty Hawk** (town) Dare County	145	n/a	1,007.4	**Williamston** (town) Martin County
71	2571	406.4	**Graham** (city) Alamance County	146	n/a	1,057.0	**Randleman** (city) Randolph County
72	2575	408.0	**Thomasville** (city) Davidson County	147	n/a	1,143.4	**Whiteville** (city) Columbus County
73	n/a	408.7	**Ayden** (town) Pitt County	148	n/a	1,321.8	**Pineville** (town) Mecklenburg County
74	n/a	411.1	**King** (city) Stokes County	149	3266	1,398.7	**Lumberton** (city) Robeson County
75	n/a	411.5	**Beaufort** (town) Carteret County				

Note: The state column ranks the top/bottom 150 places in the state with population of 2,500 or more. The national column ranks the top/bottom places in the country with population of 10,000 or more. Places that are unincorporated were not considered in the rankings. n/a indicates data not available. Please refer to the User Guide for additional information.

Education

North Carolina Public School Educational Profile

Category	Value	Category	Value
Schools *(2011-2012)*	2,609	**Diploma Recipients** *(2009-2010)*	88,704
Instructional Level		White, Non-Hispanic	52,339
Primary	1,417	Black, Non-Hispanic	25,181
Middle	497	Asian/Pacific Islander, Non-Hispanic	2,243
High	495	American Indian/Alaskan Native, Non-Hispanic	1,243
Other/Not Reported	200	Hawaiian Native/Pacific Islander, Non-Hispanic	n/a
Curriculum		Two or More Races, Non-Hispanic	n/a
Regular	2,489	Hispanic of Any Race	5,681
Special Education	30	**Staff** *(2011-2012)*	
Vocational	1	Teachers (FTE)	97,309.1
Alternative	89	Salary[1] ($)	45,355
Type		Librarians/Media Specialists (FTE)	2,193.3
Magnet	111	Guidance Counselors (FTE)	3,925.5
Charter	108	**Ratios** *(2011-2012)*	
Title I Eligible	2,077	Number of Students per Teacher	15.5 to 1
School-wide Title I	1,945	Number of Students per Librarian	687.5 to 1
Students *(2011-2012)*	1,507,864	Number of Students per Guidance Counselor	384.1 to 1
Gender (%)		**Finances** *(2010-2011)*	
Male	51.4	Current Expenditures ($ per student)	
Female	48.6	Total	8,267
Race/Ethnicity (%)		Instruction	5,167
White, Non-Hispanic	52.4	Support Services	2,653
Black, Non-Hispanic	26.4	Other	447
Asian, Non-Hispanic	2.5	General Revenue ($ per student)	
American Indian/Alaskan Native, Non-Hisp.	1.5	Total	8,875
Hawaiian Native/Pacific Islander, Non-Hisp.	0.1	From Federal Sources	1,435
Two or More Races, Non-Hispanic	3.7	From State Sources	5,158
Hispanic of Any Race	13.5	From Local Sources	2,282
Special Programs (%)		Long-Term Debt Outstanding ($ per student)	
Individual Education Program (IEP)	12.4	At Beginning of Fiscal Year	6,255
English Language Learner (ELL)	6.6	Issued During Fiscal Year	549
Eligible for Free Lunch Program	44.6	Retired During Fiscal Year	840
Eligible for Reduced-Price Lunch Program	7.6	At End of Fiscal Year	5,965
Average Freshman Grad. Rate (%) *(2009-2010)*	76.9	**College Entrance Exam Scores**	
White, Non-Hispanic	80.6	SAT Reasoning Test™ *(2013)*	
Black, Non-Hispanic	69.5	Participation Rate (%)	62
Asian/Pacific Islander, Non-Hispanic	93.1	Mean Critical Reading Score	495
American Indian/Alaskan Native, Non-Hispanic	75.2	Mean Math Score	506
Hispanic of Any Race	67.4	Mean Writing Score	478
High School Drop-out Rate (%) *(2009-2010)*	4.7	ACT *(2013)*	
White, Non-Hispanic	4.0	Participation Rate (%)	100
Black, Non-Hispanic	5.4	Mean Composite Score	18.7
Asian/Pacific Islander, Non-Hispanic	2.0	Mean English Score	17.1
American Indian/Alaskan Native, Non-Hispanic	6.1	Mean Math Score	19.6
Hawaiian Native/Pacific Islander, Non-Hispanic	n/a	Mean Reading Score	18.8
Two or More Races, Non-Hispanic	n/a	Mean Science Score	18.7
Hispanic of Any Race	6.1		

Note: *For an explanation of data, please refer to the User's Guide in the front of the book; (1) Average salary for classroom teachers in 2013-14*

Number of Schools

Rank	Number	District Name	City
1	174	Charlotte-Mecklenburg Schools	Charlotte
2	170	Wake County Schools	Raleigh
3	123	Guilford County Schools	Greensboro
4	88	Cumberland County Schools	Fayetteville
5	81	Forsyth County Schools	Winston Salem
6	56	Durham Public Schools	Durham
6	56	Gaston County Schools	Gastonia
8	52	Union County Public Schools	Monroe
9	44	Johnston County Schools	Smithfield
10	43	Buncombe County Schools	Asheville
11	42	Robeson County Schools	Lumberton
12	41	New Hanover County Schools	Wilmington
13	38	Cabarrus County Schools	Concord
14	37	Pitt County Schools	Greenville
15	36	Iredell-Statesville Schools	Statesville
16	35	Alamance-Burlington Schools	Burlington
16	35	Davidson County Schools	Lexington
16	35	Onslow County Schools	Jacksonville
16	35	Rowan-Salisbury Schools	Salisbury
20	31	Cleveland County Schools	Shelby
20	31	Randolph County Schools	Asheboro
20	31	Wayne County Public Schools	Goldsboro
23	28	Catawba County Schools	Newton
24	27	Burke County Schools	Morganton
24	27	Harnett County Schools	Lillington
24	27	Nash-Rocky Mount Schools	Nashville
27	26	Caldwell County Schools	Lenoir
27	26	Rockingham County Schools	Eden
29	25	Craven County Schools	New Bern
29	25	Wilson County Schools	Wilson
31	24	Lincoln County Schools	Lincolnton
31	24	Moore County Schools	Carthage
33	23	Henderson County Schools	Hendersonville
34	22	Stanly County Schools	Albemarle
34	22	Wilkes County Schools	North Wilkesb
36	20	Granville County Schools	Oxford
36	20	Scotland County Schools	Laurinburg
36	20	Stokes County Schools	Danbury
39	19	Brunswick County Schools	Bolivia
39	19	Chapel Hill-Carrboro Schools	Chapel Hill
39	19	Columbus County Schools	Whiteville
39	19	Surry County Schools	Dobson
43	18	Rutherford County Schools	Forest City
43	18	Sampson County Schools	Clinton
45	17	Chatham County Schools	Pittsboro
45	17	Lenoir County Public Schools	Kinston
45	17	Richmond County Schools	Hamlet
48	16	Carteret County Public Schools	Beaufort
48	16	Duplin County Schools	Kenansville
48	16	Haywood County Schools	Waynesville
48	16	Lee County Schools	Sanford
48	16	Pender County Schools	Burgaw
48	16	Vance County Schools	Henderson
54	15	Edgecombe County Schools	Tarboro
54	15	Franklin County Schools	Louisburg
56	14	Beaufort County Schools	Washington
56	14	Cherokee County Schools	Murphy
56	14	Hoke County Schools	Raeford
56	14	Yadkin County Schools	Yadkinville
60	13	Bladen County Schools	Elizabethtown
60	13	Orange County Schools	Hillsborough
62	12	Davie County Schools	Mocksville
62	12	Mcdowell County Schools	Marion
62	12	Pasquotank County Schools	Elizabeth City
65	11	Anson County Schools	Wadesboro
65	11	Dare County Schools	Nags Head
65	11	Halifax County Schools	Halifax
65	11	Macon County Schools	Franklin
65	11	Martin County Schools	Williamston
65	11	Montgomery County Schools	Troy
71	10	Alexander County Schools	Taylorsville
71	10	Avery County Schools	Newland
71	10	Currituck County Schools	Currituck
71	10	Hickory City Schools	Hickory
71	10	Person County Schools	Roxboro
76	9	Asheville City Schools	Asheville
76	9	Jackson County Schools	Sylva
76	9	Mitchell County Schools	Bakersville
76	9	Northampton County Schools	Jackson
76	9	Transylvania County Schools	Brevard
76	9	Watauga County Schools	Boone
76	9	Yancey County Schools	Burnsville
83	8	Asheboro City Schools	Asheboro
83	8	Bertie County Schools	Windsor
83	8	Kannapolis City Schools	Kannapolis
83	8	Mooresville City Schools	Mooresville
83	8	Warren County Schools	Warrenton
88	7	Hertford County Schools	Winton
88	7	Lexington City Schools	Lexington
88	7	Madison County Schools	Marshall
88	7	Newton Conover City Schools	Newton
88	7	Polk County Schools	Columbus
93	6	Caswell County Schools	Yanceyville
93	6	Clinton City Schools	Clinton
93	6	Greene County Schools	Snow Hill
96	5	Ashe County Schools	Jefferson
96	5	Camden County Schools	Camden
96	5	Gates County Schools	Gatesville
96	5	Swain County Schools	Bryson City
96	5	Washington County Schools	Plymouth
96	5	Whiteville City Schools	Whiteville
102	4	Alleghany County Schools	Sparta
102	4	Edenton/chowan Schools	Edenton
102	4	Mount Airy City Schools	Mount Airy
102	4	Perquimans County Schools	Hertford
102	4	Roanoke Rapids City Schools	Roanoke Rapids
102	4	Thomasville City Schools	Thomasville
108	1	Franklin Academy	Wake Forest
108	1	Lake Norman Charter	Huntersville
108	1	Pine Lake Preparatory	Mooresville

Number of Teachers

Rank	Number	District Name	City
1	9,439.8	Wake County Schools	Raleigh
2	8,790.5	Charlotte-Mecklenburg Schools	Charlotte
3	4,938.4	Guilford County Schools	Greensboro
4	3,625.9	Forsyth County Schools	Winston Salem
5	3,587.7	Cumberland County Schools	Fayetteville
6	2,383.3	Union County Public Schools	Monroe
7	2,156.7	Johnston County Schools	Smithfield
8	2,138.4	Durham Public Schools	Durham
9	1,856.7	Gaston County Schools	Gastonia
10	1,852.4	Cabarrus County Schools	Concord
11	1,614.5	New Hanover County Schools	Wilmington
12	1,606.7	Buncombe County Schools	Asheville
13	1,599.1	Pitt County Schools	Greenville
14	1,512.2	Robeson County Schools	Lumberton
15	1,486.9	Alamance-Burlington Schools	Burlington
16	1,421.6	Onslow County Schools	Jacksonville
17	1,353.7	Rowan-Salisbury Schools	Salisbury
18	1,318.4	Iredell-Statesville Schools	Statesville
19	1,261.5	Wayne County Public Schools	Goldsboro
20	1,214.5	Harnett County Schools	Lillington
21	1,198.9	Davidson County Schools	Lexington
22	1,166.6	Randolph County Schools	Asheboro
23	1,115.5	Cleveland County Schools	Shelby
24	1,074.7	Nash-Rocky Mount Schools	Nashville
25	1,062.7	Catawba County Schools	Newton
26	941.8	Craven County Schools	New Bern
27	927.2	Chapel Hill-Carrboro Schools	Chapel Hill
28	904.8	Henderson County Schools	Hendersonville
29	903.1	Rockingham County Schools	Eden
30	846.7	Caldwell County Schools	Lenoir
31	803.1	Burke County Schools	Morganton
32	796.3	Moore County Schools	Carthage
33	781.5	Lincoln County Schools	Lincolnton
34	752.6	Brunswick County Schools	Bolivia
35	749.3	Wilson County Schools	Wilson
36	634.2	Stanly County Schools	Albemarle
37	628.7	Wilkes County Schools	North Wilkesb
38	616.5	Lee County Schools	Sanford
39	613.6	Carteret County Public Schools	Beaufort
40	601.8	Duplin County Schools	Kenansville
41	596.9	Lenoir County Public Schools	Kinston
42	582.7	Franklin County Schools	Louisburg
43	570.8	Rutherford County Schools	Forest City
44	561.5	Hoke County Schools	Raeford
45	559.9	Surry County Schools	Dobson
46	557.7	Sampson County Schools	Clinton
47	557.4	Chatham County Schools	Pittsboro
48	531.7	Granville County Schools	Oxford
49	529.2	Orange County Schools	Hillsborough
50	522.0	Haywood County Schools	Waynesville
51	520.3	Pender County Schools	Burgaw
52	517.9	Vance County Schools	Henderson
53	499.6	Beaufort County Schools	Washington
54	487.9	Stokes County Schools	Danbury
55	485.7	Richmond County Schools	Hamlet
56	462.1	Scotland County Schools	Laurinburg
57	451.3	Mcdowell County Schools	Marion
58	447.5	Edgecombe County Schools	Tarboro
59	439.8	Pasquotank County Schools	Elizabeth City
60	433.4	Davie County Schools	Mocksville
61	429.9	Columbus County Schools	Whiteville
62	397.8	Yadkin County Schools	Yadkinville
63	390.3	Dare County Schools	Nags Head
64	382.7	Kannapolis City Schools	Kannapolis
65	354.1	Bladen County Schools	Elizabethtown
66	352.4	Watauga County Schools	Boone
67	342.1	Asheboro City Schools	Asheboro
68	341.2	Alexander County Schools	Taylorsville
69	336.0	Macon County Schools	Franklin
70	335.6	Person County Schools	Roxboro
71	328.6	Asheville City Schools	Asheville
72	324.9	Mooresville City Schools	Mooresville
73	295.9	Hickory City Schools	Hickory
74	282.7	Montgomery County Schools	Troy
75	278.1	Martin County Schools	Williamston
76	261.0	Transylvania County Schools	Brevard
77	257.2	Halifax County Schools	Halifax
78	249.8	Anson County Schools	Wadesboro
79	249.0	Cherokee County Schools	Murphy
80	242.8	Jackson County Schools	Sylva
81	240.8	Currituck County Schools	Currituck
82	235.2	Ashe County Schools	Jefferson
83	225.8	Lexington City Schools	Lexington
84	220.5	Hertford County Schools	Winton
85	217.1	Greene County Schools	Snow Hill
86	209.2	Clinton City Schools	Clinton
87	201.9	Caswell County Schools	Yanceyville
88	199.3	Newton Conover City Schools	Newton
89	190.3	Roanoke Rapids City Schools	Roanoke Rapids
90	185.7	Bertie County Schools	Windsor
91	181.1	Madison County Schools	Marshall
92	178.8	Polk County Schools	Columbus
93	176.8	Warren County Schools	Warrenton
94	174.9	Yancey County Schools	Burnsville
95	174.5	Thomasville City Schools	Thomasville
96	167.8	Northampton County Schools	Jackson
97	165.0	Avery County Schools	Newland
98	161.7	Edenton/chowan Schools	Edenton
99	155.8	Mitchell County Schools	Bakersville
100	146.6	Whiteville City Schools	Whiteville
101	139.0	Gates County Schools	Gatesville
102	136.4	Washington County Schools	Plymouth
103	131.4	Swain County Schools	Bryson City
104	123.5	Camden County Schools	Camden
105	120.8	Alleghany County Schools	Sparta
106	120.0	Perquimans County Schools	Hertford
107	114.9	Mount Airy City Schools	Mount Airy
108	100.3	Franklin Academy	Wake Forest
109	92.3	Pine Lake Preparatory	Mooresville
110	89.4	Lake Norman Charter	Huntersville

Number of Students

Rank	Number	District Name	City
1	148,154	Wake County Schools	Raleigh
2	141,728	Charlotte-Mecklenburg Schools	Charlotte
3	74,086	Guilford County Schools	Greensboro
4	53,340	Forsyth County Schools	Winston Salem
5	53,053	Cumberland County Schools	Fayetteville
6	40,111	Union County Public Schools	Monroe
7	33,256	Durham Public Schools	Durham
8	33,097	Johnston County Schools	Smithfield
9	31,696	Gaston County Schools	Gastonia
10	29,747	Cabarrus County Schools	Concord
11	25,656	Buncombe County Schools	Asheville
12	25,131	New Hanover County Schools	Wilmington
13	24,996	Robeson County Schools	Lumberton
14	24,989	Onslow County Schools	Jacksonville
15	23,919	Pitt County Schools	Greenville
16	22,851	Alamance-Burlington Schools	Burlington
17	21,494	Iredell-Statesville Schools	Statesville
18	20,340	Rowan-Salisbury Schools	Salisbury
19	20,338	Davidson County Schools	Lexington
20	19,912	Wayne County Public Schools	Goldsboro
21	19,681	Harnett County Schools	Lillington
22	18,711	Randolph County Schools	Asheboro

Note: This section only includes districts with 1,500 or more students; All categories are ranked from high to low

23	17,364	Catawba County Schools	Newton
24	16,952	Nash-Rocky Mount Schools	Nashville
25	16,229	Cleveland County Schools	Shelby
26	15,229	Craven County Schools	New Bern
27	13,893	Rockingham County Schools	Eden
28	13,536	Henderson County Schools	Hendersonville
29	13,504	Burke County Schools	Morganton
30	12,652	Moore County Schools	Carthage
31	12,570	Caldwell County Schools	Lenoir
32	12,380	Wilson County Schools	Wilson
33	12,269	Brunswick County Schools	Bolivia
34	12,092	Chapel Hill-Carrboro Schools	Chapel Hill
35	11,982	Lincoln County Schools	Lincolnton
36	10,485	Wilkes County Schools	North Wilkesb
37	9,931	Lee County Schools	Sanford
38	9,404	Duplin County Schools	Kenansville
39	9,375	Lenoir County Public Schools	Kinston
40	9,092	Rutherford County Schools	Forest City
41	9,074	Stanly County Schools	Albemarle
42	8,755	Sampson County Schools	Clinton
43	8,710	Granville County Schools	Oxford
44	8,662	Franklin County Schools	Louisburg
45	8,658	Surry County Schools	Dobson
46	8,605	Carteret County Public Schools	Beaufort
47	8,520	Pender County Schools	Burgaw
48	8,393	Chatham County Schools	Pittsboro
49	8,389	Hoke County Schools	Raeford
50	7,888	Richmond County Schools	Hamlet
51	7,708	Haywood County Schools	Waynesville
52	7,556	Orange County Schools	Hillsborough
53	7,380	Edgecombe County Schools	Tarboro
54	7,247	Vance County Schools	Henderson
55	7,161	Beaufort County Schools	Washington
56	7,003	Stokes County Schools	Danbury
57	6,763	Mcdowell County Schools	Marion
58	6,702	Columbus County Schools	Whiteville
59	6,651	Davie County Schools	Mocksville
60	6,297	Scotland County Schools	Laurinburg
61	6,076	Pasquotank County Schools	Elizabeth City
62	5,959	Yadkin County Schools	Yadkinville
63	5,639	Mooresville City Schools	Mooresville
64	5,480	Kannapolis City Schools	Kannapolis
65	5,475	Alexander County Schools	Taylorsville
66	5,386	Bladen County Schools	Elizabethtown
67	5,079	Person County Schools	Roxboro
68	5,017	Dare County Schools	Nags Head
69	4,927	Asheboro City Schools	Asheboro
70	4,588	Watauga County Schools	Boone
71	4,512	Hickory City Schools	Hickory
72	4,506	Macon County Schools	Franklin
73	4,299	Montgomery County Schools	Troy
74	4,096	Asheville City Schools	Asheville
75	3,997	Currituck County Schools	Currituck
76	3,908	Halifax County Schools	Halifax
77	3,899	Martin County Schools	Williamston
78	3,770	Anson County Schools	Wadesboro
79	3,686	Jackson County Schools	Sylva
80	3,557	Transylvania County Schools	Brevard
81	3,528	Cherokee County Schools	Murphy
82	3,342	Greene County Schools	Snow Hill
83	3,277	Ashe County Schools	Jefferson
84	3,219	Hertford County Schools	Winton
85	3,165	Lexington City Schools	Lexington
86	3,131	Clinton City Schools	Clinton
87	3,090	Roanoke Rapids City Schools	Roanoke Rapids
88	3,025	Newton Conover City Schools	Newton
89	2,879	Caswell County Schools	Yanceyville
90	2,874	Bertie County Schools	Windsor
91	2,574	Warren County Schools	Warrenton
92	2,564	Madison County Schools	Marshall
93	2,528	Thomasville City Schools	Thomasville
94	2,421	Yancey County Schools	Burnsville
95	2,412	Polk County Schools	Columbus
96	2,392	Northampton County Schools	Jackson
97	2,356	Edenton/chowan Schools	Edenton
98	2,324	Whiteville City Schools	Whiteville
99	2,262	Avery County Schools	Newland
100	2,090	Mitchell County Schools	Bakersville
101	2,064	Swain County Schools	Bryson City
102	1,939	Camden County Schools	Camden
103	1,857	Gates County Schools	Gatesville
104	1,846	Washington County Schools	Plymouth
105	1,773	Perquimans County Schools	Hertford
106	1,689	Mount Airy City Schools	Mount Airy
107	1,607	Franklin Academy	Wake Forest
108	1,598	Lake Norman Charter	Huntersville
109	1,593	Pine Lake Preparatory	Mooresville
110	1,555	Alleghany County Schools	Sparta

Male Students

Rank	Percent	District Name	City
1	53.8	Yancey County Schools	Burnsville
2	53.6	Northampton County Schools	Jackson
3	52.9	Kannapolis City Schools	Kannapolis
3	52.9	Yadkin County Schools	Yadkinville
5	52.7	Caswell County Schools	Yanceyville
5	52.7	Cherokee County Schools	Murphy
5	52.7	Mitchell County Schools	Bakersville
8	52.6	Lenoir County Public Schools	Kinston
9	52.4	Granville County Schools	Oxford
9	52.4	Jackson County Schools	Sylva
9	52.4	Washington County Schools	Plymouth
12	52.3	Randolph County Schools	Asheboro
13	52.2	Edenton/chowan Schools	Edenton
13	52.2	Hickory City Schools	Hickory
15	52.1	Haywood County Schools	Waynesville
15	52.1	Lincoln County Schools	Lincolnton
15	52.1	Madison County Schools	Marshall
18	52.0	Cabarrus County Schools	Concord
18	52.0	Newton Conover City Schools	Newton
20	51.9	Beaufort County Schools	Washington
20	51.9	Carteret County Public Schools	Beaufort
20	51.9	Chapel Hill-Carrboro Schools	Chapel Hill
20	51.9	Duplin County Schools	Kenansville
20	51.9	Harnett County Schools	Lillington
20	51.9	Hoke County Schools	Raeford
20	51.9	Macon County Schools	Franklin
20	51.9	Pitt County Schools	Greenville
20	51.9	Stanly County Schools	Albemarle
20	51.9	Wayne County Public Schools	Goldsboro
30	51.8	Cleveland County Schools	Shelby
30	51.8	Mcdowell County Schools	Marion
30	51.8	Mooresville City Schools	Mooresville
30	51.8	New Hanover County Schools	Wilmington
30	51.8	Orange County Schools	Hillsborough
30	51.8	Rutherford County Schools	Forest City
36	51.7	Alamance-Burlington Schools	Burlington
36	51.7	Asheville City Schools	Asheville
36	51.7	Burke County Schools	Morganton
36	51.7	Dare County Schools	Nags Head
36	51.7	Gaston County Schools	Gastonia
36	51.7	Person County Schools	Roxboro
36	51.7	Robeson County Schools	Lumberton
36	51.7	Rockingham County Schools	Eden
36	51.7	Swain County Schools	Bryson City
45	51.6	Franklin County Schools	Louisburg
45	51.6	Johnston County Schools	Smithfield
45	51.6	Wilkes County Schools	North Wilkesb
48	51.5	Buncombe County Schools	Asheville
48	51.5	Cumberland County Schools	Fayetteville
48	51.5	Davie County Schools	Mocksville
48	51.5	Iredell-Statesville Schools	Statesville
48	51.5	Moore County Schools	Carthage
48	51.5	Nash-Rocky Mount Schools	Nashville
48	51.5	Pasquotank County Schools	Elizabeth City
48	51.5	Scotland County Schools	Laurinburg
48	51.5	Surry County Schools	Dobson
48	51.5	Watauga County Schools	Boone
48	51.5	Whiteville City Schools	Whiteville
59	51.4	Alexander County Schools	Taylorsville
59	51.4	Brunswick County Schools	Bolivia
59	51.4	Catawba County Schools	Newton
59	51.4	Guilford County Schools	Greensboro
59	51.4	Onslow County Schools	Jacksonville
64	51.3	Chatham County Schools	Pittsboro
64	51.3	Davidson County Schools	Lexington
64	51.3	Edgecombe County Schools	Tarboro
64	51.3	Greene County Schools	Snow Hill
64	51.3	Halifax County Schools	Halifax
64	51.3	Henderson County Schools	Hendersonville
64	51.3	Mount Airy City Schools	Mount Airy
64	51.3	Rowan-Salisbury Schools	Salisbury
64	51.3	Union County Public Schools	Monroe
64	51.3	Vance County Schools	Henderson
64	51.3	Wilson County Schools	Wilson
75	51.2	Bladen County Schools	Elizabethtown
75	51.2	Forsyth County Schools	Winston Salem
75	51.2	Pender County Schools	Burgaw
75	51.2	Wake County Schools	Raleigh
79	51.1	Gates County Schools	Gatesville
79	51.1	Lee County Schools	Sanford
79	51.1	Montgomery County Schools	Troy
79	51.1	Richmond County Schools	Hamlet
79	51.1	Sampson County Schools	Clinton
84	51.0	Charlotte-Mecklenburg Schools	Charlotte
84	51.0	Hertford County Schools	Winton
84	51.0	Stokes County Schools	Danbury
87	50.9	Ashe County Schools	Jefferson
88	50.8	Caldwell County Schools	Lenoir
88	50.8	Craven County Schools	New Bern
88	50.8	Warren County Schools	Warrenton
91	50.7	Bertie County Schools	Windsor
91	50.7	Polk County Schools	Columbus
91	50.7	Transylvania County Schools	Brevard
94	50.6	Avery County Schools	Newland
94	50.6	Lexington City Schools	Lexington
96	50.5	Clinton City Schools	Clinton
96	50.5	Durham Public Schools	Durham
96	50.5	Roanoke Rapids City Schools	Roanoke Rapids
96	50.5	Thomasville City Schools	Thomasville
100	50.4	Anson County Schools	Wadesboro
101	50.3	Currituck County Schools	Currituck
102	50.2	Lake Norman Charter	Huntersville
102	50.2	Martin County Schools	Williamston
102	50.2	Pine Lake Preparatory	Mooresville
105	50.1	Perquimans County Schools	Hertford
106	50.0	Camden County Schools	Camden
107	49.8	Asheboro City Schools	Asheboro
108	49.3	Alleghany County Schools	Sparta
109	49.2	Columbus County Schools	Whiteville
110	48.1	Franklin Academy	Wake Forest

Female Students

Rank	Percent	District Name	City
1	51.9	Franklin Academy	Wake Forest
2	50.8	Columbus County Schools	Whiteville
3	50.7	Alleghany County Schools	Sparta
4	50.2	Asheboro City Schools	Asheboro
5	50.0	Camden County Schools	Camden
6	49.9	Perquimans County Schools	Hertford
7	49.8	Lake Norman Charter	Huntersville
7	49.8	Martin County Schools	Williamston
7	49.8	Pine Lake Preparatory	Mooresville
10	49.7	Currituck County Schools	Currituck
11	49.6	Anson County Schools	Wadesboro
12	49.5	Clinton City Schools	Clinton
12	49.5	Durham Public Schools	Durham
12	49.5	Roanoke Rapids City Schools	Roanoke Rapids
12	49.5	Thomasville City Schools	Thomasville
16	49.4	Avery County Schools	Newland
16	49.4	Lexington City Schools	Lexington
18	49.3	Bertie County Schools	Windsor
18	49.3	Polk County Schools	Columbus
18	49.3	Transylvania County Schools	Brevard
21	49.2	Caldwell County Schools	Lenoir
21	49.2	Craven County Schools	New Bern
21	49.2	Warren County Schools	Warrenton
24	49.1	Ashe County Schools	Jefferson
25	49.0	Charlotte-Mecklenburg Schools	Charlotte
25	49.0	Hertford County Schools	Winton
25	49.0	Stokes County Schools	Danbury
28	48.9	Gates County Schools	Gatesville
28	48.9	Lee County Schools	Sanford
28	48.9	Montgomery County Schools	Troy
28	48.9	Richmond County Schools	Hamlet
28	48.9	Sampson County Schools	Clinton
33	48.8	Bladen County Schools	Elizabethtown
33	48.8	Forsyth County Schools	Winston Salem
33	48.8	Pender County Schools	Burgaw
33	48.8	Wake County Schools	Raleigh
37	48.7	Chatham County Schools	Pittsboro
37	48.7	Davidson County Schools	Lexington
37	48.7	Edgecombe County Schools	Tarboro
37	48.7	Greene County Schools	Snow Hill
37	48.7	Halifax County Schools	Halifax
37	48.7	Henderson County Schools	Hendersonville
37	48.7	Mount Airy City Schools	Mount Airy
37	48.7	Rowan-Salisbury Schools	Salisbury
37	48.7	Union County Public Schools	Monroe
37	48.7	Vance County Schools	Henderson
37	48.7	Wilson County Schools	Wilson

Note: This section only includes districts with 1,500 or more students; All categories are ranked from high to low

48	48.6	Alexander County Schools	Taylorsville
48	48.6	Brunswick County Schools	Bolivia
48	48.6	Catawba County Schools	Newton
48	48.6	Guilford County Schools	Greensboro
48	48.6	Onslow County Schools	Jacksonville
53	48.5	Buncombe County Schools	Asheville
53	48.5	Cumberland County Schools	Fayetteville
53	48.5	Davie County Schools	Mocksville
53	48.5	Iredell-Statesville Schools	Statesville
53	48.5	Moore County Schools	Carthage
53	48.5	Nash-Rocky Mount Schools	Nashville
53	48.5	Pasquotank County Schools	Elizabeth City
53	48.5	Scotland County Schools	Laurinburg
53	48.5	Surry County Schools	Dobson
53	48.5	Watauga County Schools	Boone
53	48.5	Whiteville City Schools	Whiteville
64	48.4	Franklin County Schools	Louisburg
64	48.4	Johnston County Schools	Smithfield
64	48.4	Wilkes County Schools	North Wilkesb
67	48.3	Alamance-Burlington Schools	Burlington
67	48.3	Asheville City Schools	Asheville
67	48.3	Burke County Schools	Morganton
67	48.3	Dare County Schools	Nags Head
67	48.3	Gaston County Schools	Gastonia
67	48.3	Person County Schools	Roxboro
67	48.3	Robeson County Schools	Lumberton
67	48.3	Rockingham County Schools	Eden
67	48.3	Swain County Schools	Bryson City
76	48.2	Cleveland County Schools	Shelby
76	48.2	Mcdowell County Schools	Marion
76	48.2	Mooresville City Schools	Mooresville
76	48.2	New Hanover County Schools	Wilmington
76	48.2	Orange County Schools	Hillsborough
76	48.2	Rutherford County Schools	Forest City
82	48.1	Beaufort County Schools	Washington
82	48.1	Carteret County Public Schools	Beaufort
82	48.1	Chapel Hill-Carrboro Schools	Chapel Hill
82	48.1	Duplin County Schools	Kenansville
82	48.1	Harnett County Schools	Lillington
82	48.1	Hoke County Schools	Raeford
82	48.1	Macon County Schools	Franklin
82	48.1	Pitt County Schools	Greenville
82	48.1	Stanly County Schools	Albemarle
82	48.1	Wayne County Public Schools	Goldsboro
92	48.0	Cabarrus County Schools	Concord
92	48.0	Newton Conover City Schools	Newton
94	47.9	Haywood County Schools	Waynesville
94	47.9	Lincoln County Schools	Lincolnton
94	47.9	Madison County Schools	Marshall
97	47.8	Edenton/chowan Schools	Edenton
97	47.8	Hickory City Schools	Hickory
99	47.7	Randolph County Schools	Asheboro
100	47.6	Granville County Schools	Oxford
100	47.6	Jackson County Schools	Sylva
100	47.6	Washington County Schools	Plymouth
103	47.4	Lenoir County Public Schools	Kinston
104	47.3	Caswell County Schools	Yanceyville
104	47.3	Cherokee County Schools	Murphy
104	47.3	Mitchell County Schools	Bakersville
107	47.1	Kannapolis City Schools	Kannapolis
107	47.1	Yadkin County Schools	Yadkinville
109	46.4	Northampton County Schools	Jackson
110	46.2	Yancey County Schools	Burnsville

Individual Education Program Students

Rank	Percent	District Name	City
1	18.9	Stokes County Schools	Danbury
2	17.9	Mount Airy City Schools	Mount Airy
3	17.4	Stanly County Schools	Albemarle
4	17.0	Mitchell County Schools	Bakersville
5	16.8	Macon County Schools	Franklin
6	16.4	Gates County Schools	Gatesville
7	16.3	Watauga County Schools	Boone
8	16.2	Anson County Schools	Wadesboro
8	16.2	Robeson County Schools	Lumberton
8	16.2	Swain County Schools	Bryson City
11	15.9	Yancey County Schools	Burnsville
12	15.6	Burke County Schools	Morganton
12	15.6	Caswell County Schools	Yanceyville
12	15.6	Haywood County Schools	Waynesville
15	15.5	Ashe County Schools	Jefferson
15	15.5	Perquimans County Schools	Hertford
17	15.2	Scotland County Schools	Laurinburg

18	15.1	Jackson County Schools	Sylva
19	14.9	Warren County Schools	Warrenton
20	14.7	Alexander County Schools	Taylorsville
21	14.6	Kannapolis City Schools	Kannapolis
21	14.6	Pasquotank County Schools	Elizabeth City
21	14.6	Rutherford County Schools	Forest City
24	14.5	Martin County Schools	Williamston
24	14.5	Rockingham County Schools	Eden
24	14.5	Yadkin County Schools	Yadkinville
27	14.4	Beaufort County Schools	Washington
27	14.4	Lenoir County Public Schools	Kinston
27	14.4	Polk County Schools	Columbus
30	14.2	Johnston County Schools	Smithfield
30	14.2	Vance County Schools	Henderson
32	14.1	Bertie County Schools	Windsor
32	14.1	Mcdowell County Schools	Marion
32	14.1	Orange County Schools	Hillsborough
32	14.1	Person County Schools	Roxboro
36	13.9	Transylvania County Schools	Brevard
37	13.8	Buncombe County Schools	Asheville
37	13.8	Montgomery County Schools	Troy
37	13.8	Wayne County Public Schools	Goldsboro
40	13.7	Alleghany County Schools	Sparta
40	13.7	Guilford County Schools	Greensboro
42	13.6	Edenton/chowan Schools	Edenton
43	13.5	Chatham County Schools	Pittsboro
43	13.5	Cherokee County Schools	Murphy
43	13.5	Cumberland County Schools	Fayetteville
46	13.4	Carteret County Public Schools	Beaufort
46	13.4	Cleveland County Schools	Shelby
46	13.4	Halifax County Schools	Halifax
46	13.4	Madison County Schools	Marshall
50	13.2	Hertford County Schools	Winton
50	13.2	Lincoln County Schools	Lincolnton
50	13.2	Wake County Schools	Raleigh
53	13.1	Asheville City Schools	Asheville
53	13.1	Durham Public Schools	Durham
55	12.9	Cabarrus County Schools	Concord
56	12.8	Henderson County Schools	Hendersonville
56	12.8	Nash-Rocky Mount Schools	Nashville
58	12.6	Davidson County Schools	Lexington
58	12.6	Rowan-Salisbury Schools	Salisbury
60	12.4	Avery County Schools	Newland
60	12.4	Camden County Schools	Camden
60	12.4	Forsyth County Schools	Winston Salem
63	12.3	Hoke County Schools	Raeford
63	12.3	Washington County Schools	Plymouth
65	12.2	Caldwell County Schools	Lenoir
65	12.2	Davie County Schools	Mocksville
65	12.2	Gaston County Schools	Gastonia
65	12.2	Surry County Schools	Dobson
69	12.1	Harnett County Schools	Lillington
70	12.0	Lexington City Schools	Lexington
70	12.0	Roanoke Rapids City Schools	Roanoke Rapids
72	11.9	Alamance-Burlington Schools	Burlington
72	11.9	Newton Conover City Schools	Newton
72	11.9	Northampton County Schools	Jackson
75	11.8	Mooresville City Schools	Mooresville
76	11.7	Greene County Schools	Snow Hill
76	11.7	Wilkes County Schools	North Wilkesb
78	11.6	Catawba County Schools	Newton
78	11.6	Onslow County Schools	Jacksonville
80	11.5	New Hanover County Schools	Wilmington
81	11.4	Bladen County Schools	Elizabethtown
81	11.4	Pitt County Schools	Greenville
81	11.4	Randolph County Schools	Asheboro
84	11.3	Asheboro City Schools	Asheboro
84	11.3	Pender County Schools	Burgaw
86	11.2	Brunswick County Schools	Bolivia
86	11.2	Hickory City Schools	Hickory
88	11.0	Columbus County Schools	Whiteville
89	10.9	Edgecombe County Schools	Tarboro
89	10.9	Franklin County Schools	Louisburg
89	10.9	Granville County Schools	Oxford
92	10.8	Moore County Schools	Carthage
93	10.7	Richmond County Schools	Hamlet
94	10.6	Craven County Schools	New Bern
94	10.6	Iredell-Statesville Schools	Statesville
94	10.6	Lee County Schools	Sanford
94	10.6	Pine Lake Preparatory	Mooresville
94	10.6	Sampson County Schools	Clinton
99	10.5	Whiteville City Schools	Whiteville
100	10.1	Dare County Schools	Nags Head
101	9.6	Charlotte-Mecklenburg Schools	Charlotte
102	9.5	Duplin County Schools	Kenansville

102	9.5	Union County Public Schools	Monroe
104	9.1	Chapel Hill-Carrboro Schools	Chapel Hill
104	9.1	Wilson County Schools	Wilson
106	9.0	Currituck County Schools	Currituck
107	8.9	Thomasville City Schools	Thomasville
108	8.3	Clinton City Schools	Clinton
109	6.3	Franklin Academy	Wake Forest
110	5.9	Lake Norman Charter	Huntersville

English Language Learner Students

Rank	Percent	District Name	City
1	18.4	Duplin County Schools	Kenansville
2	18.3	Lexington City Schools	Lexington
3	18.2	Asheboro City Schools	Asheboro
4	16.1	Sampson County Schools	Clinton
5	15.9	Greene County Schools	Snow Hill
6	14.8	Chatham County Schools	Pittsboro
7	14.5	Thomasville City Schools	Thomasville
8	14.3	Montgomery County Schools	Troy
9	13.5	Durham Public Schools	Durham
9	13.5	Lee County Schools	Sanford
11	12.9	Newton Conover City Schools	Newton
12	12.2	Hickory City Schools	Hickory
13	11.8	Forsyth County Schools	Winston Salem
14	11.2	Chapel Hill-Carrboro Schools	Chapel Hill
15	11.1	Kannapolis City Schools	Kannapolis
16	10.9	Alamance-Burlington Schools	Burlington
17	9.8	Charlotte-Mecklenburg Schools	Charlotte
18	9.5	Henderson County Schools	Hendersonville
19	9.0	Clinton City Schools	Clinton
20	8.9	Surry County Schools	Dobson
21	8.7	Johnston County Schools	Smithfield
22	8.1	Yadkin County Schools	Yadkinville
23	7.9	Guilford County Schools	Greensboro
24	7.7	Wayne County Public Schools	Goldsboro
25	7.5	Wake County Schools	Raleigh
26	7.1	Catawba County Schools	Newton
26	7.1	Macon County Schools	Franklin
26	7.1	Rowan-Salisbury Schools	Salisbury
29	6.9	Burke County Schools	Morganton
29	6.9	Hoke County Schools	Raeford
29	6.9	Vance County Schools	Henderson
32	6.7	Buncombe County Schools	Asheville
32	6.7	Harnett County Schools	Lillington
32	6.7	Randolph County Schools	Asheboro
35	6.6	Cabarrus County Schools	Concord
36	6.4	Alleghany County Schools	Sparta
36	6.4	Yancey County Schools	Burnsville
38	6.3	Robeson County Schools	Lumberton
39	6.2	Orange County Schools	Hillsborough
40	6.1	Beaufort County Schools	Washington
40	6.1	Wilson County Schools	Wilson
42	6.0	Mount Airy City Schools	Mount Airy
43	5.5	Franklin County Schools	Louisburg
44	5.4	Avery County Schools	Newland
44	5.4	Granville County Schools	Oxford
44	5.4	Lenoir County Public Schools	Kinston
44	5.4	Union County Public Schools	Monroe
48	5.1	Bladen County Schools	Elizabethtown
48	5.1	Dare County Schools	Nags Head
50	5.0	Iredell-Statesville Schools	Statesville
50	5.0	Wilkes County Schools	North Wilkesb
52	4.8	Mcdowell County Schools	Marion
52	4.8	Richmond County Schools	Hamlet
52	4.8	Rockingham County Schools	Eden
55	4.7	Gaston County Schools	Gastonia
56	4.6	Nash-Rocky Mount Schools	Nashville
57	4.5	Craven County Schools	New Bern
57	4.5	Edgecombe County Schools	Tarboro
59	4.3	Mitchell County Schools	Bakersville
60	4.0	Pitt County Schools	Greenville
61	3.9	Davie County Schools	Mocksville
61	3.9	Moore County Schools	Carthage
61	3.9	Stanly County Schools	Albemarle
64	3.8	Ashe County Schools	Jefferson
64	3.8	Brunswick County Schools	Bolivia
64	3.8	Pender County Schools	Burgaw
64	3.8	Whiteville City Schools	Whiteville
68	3.7	Polk County Schools	Columbus
69	3.6	Mooresville City Schools	Mooresville
70	3.5	Jackson County Schools	Sylva
70	3.5	New Hanover County Schools	Wilmington
72	3.4	Alexander County Schools	Taylorsville

Note: This section only includes districts with 1,500 or more students; All categories are ranked from high to low

73	3.3	Lincoln County Schools	Lincolnton
74	3.1	Person County Schools	Roxboro
74	3.1	Washington County Schools	Plymouth
76	3.0	Caldwell County Schools	Lenoir
76	3.0	Columbus County Schools	Whiteville
76	3.0	Roanoke Rapids City Schools	Roanoke Rapids
79	2.9	Watauga County Schools	Boone
80	2.6	Anson County Schools	Wadesboro
80	2.6	Warren County Schools	Warrenton
82	2.4	Rutherford County Schools	Forest City
83	2.2	Asheville City Schools	Asheville
83	2.2	Haywood County Schools	Waynesville
85	2.0	Carteret County Public Schools	Beaufort
85	2.0	Cumberland County Schools	Fayetteville
87	1.9	Davidson County Schools	Lexington
87	1.9	Transylvania County Schools	Brevard
89	1.8	Cleveland County Schools	Shelby
89	1.8	Northampton County Schools	Jackson
91	1.7	Edenton/chowan Schools	Edenton
92	1.6	Pasquotank County Schools	Elizabeth City
92	1.6	Swain County Schools	Bryson City
94	1.5	Martin County Schools	Williamston
94	1.5	Stokes County Schools	Danbury
96	1.4	Madison County Schools	Marshall
97	1.3	Caswell County Schools	Yanceyville
97	1.3	Hertford County Schools	Winton
97	1.3	Onslow County Schools	Jacksonville
100	1.2	Halifax County Schools	Halifax
101	0.9	Bertie County Schools	Windsor
102	0.8	Perquimans County Schools	Hertford
103	0.7	Currituck County Schools	Currituck
103	0.7	Scotland County Schools	Laurinburg
105	0.6	Cherokee County Schools	Murphy
106	0.4	Camden County Schools	Camden
107	0.3	Pine Lake Preparatory	Mooresville
108	0.2	Franklin Academy	Wake Forest
108	0.2	Gates County Schools	Gatesville
108	0.2	Lake Norman Charter	Huntersville

Students Eligible for Free Lunch

Rank	Percent	District Name	City
1	79.6	Thomasville City Schools	Thomasville
2	78.8	Lexington City Schools	Lexington
3	77.5	Northampton County Schools	Jackson
4	76.5	Halifax County Schools	Halifax
5	76.0	Vance County Schools	Henderson
6	75.1	Bertie County Schools	Windsor
7	73.5	Hertford County Schools	Winton
8	73.0	Washington County Schools	Plymouth
9	72.3	Robeson County Schools	Lumberton
10	69.3	Anson County Schools	Wadesboro
11	68.9	Warren County Schools	Warrenton
12	68.6	Edgecombe County Schools	Tarboro
13	65.8	Greene County Schools	Snow Hill
14	65.5	Bladen County Schools	Elizabethtown
14	65.5	Montgomery County Schools	Troy
16	64.7	Richmond County Schools	Hamlet
17	63.1	Columbus County Schools	Whiteville
18	62.5	Asheboro City Schools	Asheboro
19	61.8	Whiteville City Schools	Whiteville
20	61.7	Duplin County Schools	Kenansville
21	61.4	Clinton City Schools	Clinton
22	61.1	Sampson County Schools	Clinton
23	59.2	Caswell County Schools	Yanceyville
23	59.2	Lenoir County Public Schools	Kinston
25	59.1	Kannapolis City Schools	Kannapolis
26	58.0	Rutherford County Schools	Forest City
27	57.2	Martin County Schools	Williamston
28	57.0	Nash-Rocky Mount Schools	Nashville
29	56.5	Beaufort County Schools	Washington
30	56.3	Lee County Schools	Sanford
31	55.7	Wilson County Schools	Wilson
32	54.9	Hickory City Schools	Hickory
32	54.9	Mcdowell County Schools	Marion
34	54.7	Alleghany County Schools	Sparta
35	54.0	Cleveland County Schools	Shelby
36	53.9	Durham Public Schools	Durham
37	53.7	Edenton/chowan Schools	Edenton
38	53.6	Newton Conover City Schools	Newton
39	53.2	Wayne County Public Schools	Goldsboro
39	53.2	Wilkes County Schools	North Wilkesb
41	52.7	Hoke County Schools	Raeford
42	52.4	Cherokee County Schools	Murphy
43	52.3	Surry County Schools	Dobson
44	52.1	Macon County Schools	Franklin
44	52.1	Rowan-Salisbury Schools	Salisbury
46	51.6	Madison County Schools	Marshall
47	51.3	Brunswick County Schools	Bolivia
47	51.3	Pasquotank County Schools	Elizabeth City
49	51.0	Franklin County Schools	Louisburg
50	50.9	Perquimans County Schools	Hertford
50	50.9	Pitt County Schools	Greenville
52	50.3	Person County Schools	Roxboro
53	49.9	Roanoke Rapids City Schools	Roanoke Rapids
53	49.9	Rockingham County Schools	Eden
53	49.9	Transylvania County Schools	Brevard
56	49.5	Caldwell County Schools	Lenoir
57	48.9	Polk County Schools	Columbus
58	48.8	Charlotte-Mecklenburg Schools	Charlotte
59	48.6	Guilford County Schools	Greensboro
60	48.4	Swain County Schools	Bryson City
61	48.3	Burke County Schools	Morganton
61	48.3	Forsyth County Schools	Winston Salem
63	48.1	Yancey County Schools	Burnsville
64	48.0	Jackson County Schools	Sylva
65	47.9	Cumberland County Schools	Fayetteville
66	47.7	Harnett County Schools	Lillington
67	47.2	Mount Airy City Schools	Mount Airy
67	47.2	Pender County Schools	Burgaw
69	47.1	Alamance-Burlington Schools	Burlington
70	46.4	Randolph County Schools	Asheboro
71	46.0	Buncombe County Schools	Asheville
72	45.6	Avery County Schools	Newland
72	45.6	Stanly County Schools	Albemarle
72	45.6	Yadkin County Schools	Yadkinville
75	45.5	Granville County Schools	Oxford
75	45.5	Haywood County Schools	Waynesville
75	45.5	Henderson County Schools	Hendersonville
78	44.9	Alexander County Schools	Taylorsville
79	44.3	Mitchell County Schools	Bakersville
80	43.3	Craven County Schools	New Bern
81	43.1	Chatham County Schools	Pittsboro
82	42.2	Asheville City Schools	Asheville
83	41.8	Gates County Schools	Gatesville
84	41.4	Catawba County Schools	Newton
85	40.7	Lincoln County Schools	Lincolnton
86	40.2	Stokes County Schools	Danbury
87	39.2	Moore County Schools	Carthage
88	38.3	Davie County Schools	Mocksville
88	38.3	Johnston County Schools	Smithfield
90	38.2	New Hanover County Schools	Wilmington
91	36.9	Davidson County Schools	Lexington
92	36.4	Ashe County Schools	Jefferson
93	35.5	Iredell-Statesville Schools	Statesville
94	35.0	Carteret County Public Schools	Beaufort
95	34.6	Orange County Schools	Hillsborough
96	33.9	Cabarrus County Schools	Concord
97	32.8	Dare County Schools	Nags Head
98	31.9	Onslow County Schools	Jacksonville
99	31.6	Mooresville City Schools	Mooresville
100	30.8	Watauga County Schools	Boone
101	29.6	Wake County Schools	Raleigh
102	28.9	Union County Public Schools	Monroe
103	28.3	Currituck County Schools	Currituck
104	23.7	Camden County Schools	Camden
105	22.0	Chapel Hill-Carrboro Schools	Chapel Hill
106	6.9	Gaston County Schools	Gastonia
107	2.9	Pine Lake Preparatory	Mooresville
108	2.7	Franklin Academy	Wake Forest
109	0.1	Lake Norman Charter	Huntersville
n/a	n/a	Scotland County Schools	Laurinburg

Students Eligible for Reduced-Price Lunch

Rank	Percent	District Name	City
1	50.9	Gaston County Schools	Gastonia
2	13.0	Mitchell County Schools	Bakersville
3	12.5	Avery County Schools	Newland
4	12.1	Swain County Schools	Bryson City
5	11.9	Cherokee County Schools	Murphy
6	11.4	Alleghany County Schools	Sparta
7	10.2	Yancey County Schools	Burnsville
8	10.0	Macon County Schools	Franklin
9	9.9	Jackson County Schools	Sylva
10	9.8	Burke County Schools	Morganton
11	9.7	Ashe County Schools	Jefferson
12	9.6	Mcdowell County Schools	Marion
13	9.5	Craven County Schools	New Bern
14	9.1	Edenton/chowan Schools	Edenton
14	9.1	Madison County Schools	Marshall
16	9.0	Brunswick County Schools	Bolivia
17	8.9	Bertie County Schools	Windsor
17	8.9	Columbus County Schools	Whiteville
17	8.9	Hoke County Schools	Raeford
17	8.9	Onslow County Schools	Jacksonville
21	8.8	Montgomery County Schools	Troy
21	8.8	Newton Conover City Schools	Newton
23	8.7	Pender County Schools	Burgaw
23	8.7	Polk County Schools	Columbus
23	8.7	Stanly County Schools	Albemarle
23	8.7	Stokes County Schools	Danbury
27	8.6	Pasquotank County Schools	Elizabeth City
27	8.6	Warren County Schools	Warrenton
29	8.5	Haywood County Schools	Waynesville
29	8.5	Surry County Schools	Dobson
31	8.4	Camden County Schools	Camden
31	8.4	Harnett County Schools	Lillington
33	8.3	Sampson County Schools	Clinton
34	8.2	Cumberland County Schools	Fayetteville
34	8.2	Edgecombe County Schools	Tarboro
34	8.2	Franklin County Schools	Louisburg
34	8.2	Henderson County Schools	Hendersonville
38	8.1	Rowan-Salisbury Schools	Salisbury
38	8.1	Transylvania County Schools	Brevard
38	8.1	Yadkin County Schools	Yadkinville
41	8.0	Caswell County Schools	Yanceyville
41	8.0	Perquimans County Schools	Hertford
43	7.9	Buncombe County Schools	Asheville
43	7.9	Caldwell County Schools	Lenoir
43	7.9	Catawba County Schools	Newton
43	7.9	Lenoir County Public Schools	Kinston
43	7.9	Wilkes County Schools	North Wilkesb
48	7.8	Duplin County Schools	Kenansville
48	7.8	Gates County Schools	Gatesville
50	7.7	Richmond County Schools	Hamlet
50	7.7	Watauga County Schools	Boone
52	7.5	Clinton City Schools	Clinton
52	7.5	Nash-Rocky Mount Schools	Nashville
52	7.5	Randolph County Schools	Asheboro
52	7.5	Roanoke Rapids City Schools	Roanoke Rapids
56	7.4	Alexander County Schools	Taylorsville
57	7.3	Wayne County Public Schools	Goldsboro
58	7.2	Anson County Schools	Wadesboro
58	7.2	Rockingham County Schools	Eden
58	7.2	Rutherford County Schools	Forest City
61	7.1	Lincoln County Schools	Lincolnton
62	7.0	Carteret County Public Schools	Beaufort
62	7.0	Granville County Schools	Oxford
62	7.0	Lee County Schools	Sanford
65	6.9	Bladen County Schools	Elizabethtown
66	6.8	Franklin Academy	Wake Forest
66	6.8	Mooresville City Schools	Mooresville
68	6.7	Currituck County Schools	Currituck
68	6.7	Iredell-Statesville Schools	Statesville
68	6.7	Martin County Schools	Williamston
68	6.7	Person County Schools	Roxboro
68	6.7	Washington County Schools	Plymouth
73	6.6	Alamance-Burlington Schools	Burlington
73	6.6	Dare County Schools	Nags Head
73	6.6	Hertford County Schools	Winton
73	6.6	Wilson County Schools	Wilson
77	6.5	Robeson County Schools	Lumberton
78	6.4	Beaufort County Schools	Washington
78	6.4	Kannapolis City Schools	Kannapolis
78	6.4	Vance County Schools	Henderson
81	6.3	Northampton County Schools	Jackson
82	6.2	Asheboro City Schools	Asheboro
82	6.2	Davidson County Schools	Lexington
84	6.1	Guilford County Schools	Greensboro
85	6.0	Greene County Schools	Snow Hill
85	6.0	Thomasville City Schools	Thomasville
87	5.9	Cabarrus County Schools	Concord
87	5.9	Charlotte-Mecklenburg Schools	Charlotte
87	5.9	Cleveland County Schools	Shelby
87	5.9	Hickory City Schools	Hickory
91	5.7	Forsyth County Schools	Winston Salem
92	5.6	Whiteville City Schools	Whiteville
93	5.5	Johnston County Schools	Smithfield
93	5.5	New Hanover County Schools	Wilmington
95	5.4	Chatham County Schools	Pittsboro
96	5.3	Lexington City Schools	Lexington

Note: This section only includes districts with 1,500 or more students; All categories are ranked from high to low

96	5.3	Moore County Schools	Carthage
96	5.3	Union County Public Schools	Monroe
99	5.0	Davie County Schools	Mocksville
100	4.9	Wake County Schools	Raleigh
101	4.7	Durham Public Schools	Durham
102	4.6	Halifax County Schools	Halifax
102	4.6	Orange County Schools	Hillsborough
102	4.6	Pitt County Schools	Greenville
105	4.3	Asheville City Schools	Asheville
105	4.3	Mount Airy City Schools	Mount Airy
107	2.8	Chapel Hill-Carrboro Schools	Chapel Hill
108	1.9	Pine Lake Preparatory	Mooresville
109	0.3	Lake Norman Charter	Huntersville
n/a	n/a	Scotland County Schools	Laurinburg

Student/Teacher Ratio
(number of students per teacher)

Rank	Number	District Name	City
1	12.5	Asheville City Schools	Asheville
2	12.9	Alleghany County Schools	Sparta
2	12.9	Dare County Schools	Nags Head
4	13.0	Chapel Hill-Carrboro Schools	Chapel Hill
4	13.0	Watauga County Schools	Boone
6	13.4	Gates County Schools	Gatesville
6	13.4	Macon County Schools	Franklin
6	13.4	Mitchell County Schools	Bakersville
9	13.5	Polk County Schools	Columbus
9	13.5	Washington County Schools	Plymouth
11	13.6	Scotland County Schools	Laurinburg
11	13.6	Transylvania County Schools	Brevard
13	13.7	Avery County Schools	Newland
14	13.8	Pasquotank County Schools	Elizabeth City
14	13.8	Yancey County Schools	Burnsville
16	13.9	Ashe County Schools	Jefferson
17	14.0	Carteret County Public Schools	Beaufort
17	14.0	Lexington City Schools	Lexington
17	14.0	Martin County Schools	Williamston
17	14.0	Vance County Schools	Henderson
21	14.2	Cherokee County Schools	Murphy
21	14.2	Madison County Schools	Marshall
23	14.3	Beaufort County Schools	Washington
23	14.3	Caswell County Schools	Yanceyville
23	14.3	Kannapolis City Schools	Kannapolis
23	14.3	Northampton County Schools	Jackson
23	14.3	Orange County Schools	Hillsborough
23	14.3	Stanly County Schools	Albemarle
29	14.4	Asheboro City Schools	Asheboro
29	14.4	Stokes County Schools	Danbury
31	14.5	Cleveland County Schools	Shelby
31	14.5	Thomasville City Schools	Thomasville
33	14.6	Edenton/chowan Schools	Edenton
33	14.6	Hertford County Schools	Winton
33	14.6	Warren County Schools	Warrenton
36	14.7	Forsyth County Schools	Winston Salem
36	14.7	Mount Airy City Schools	Mount Airy
38	14.8	Caldwell County Schools	Lenoir
38	14.8	Cumberland County Schools	Fayetteville
38	14.8	Haywood County Schools	Waynesville
38	14.8	Perquimans County Schools	Hertford
42	14.9	Franklin County Schools	Louisburg
42	14.9	Hoke County Schools	Raeford
44	15.0	Clinton City Schools	Clinton
44	15.0	Guilford County Schools	Greensboro
44	15.0	Henderson County Schools	Hendersonville
44	15.0	Mcdowell County Schools	Marion
44	15.0	Pitt County Schools	Greenville
44	15.0	Rowan-Salisbury Schools	Salisbury
44	15.0	Yadkin County Schools	Yadkinville
51	15.1	Anson County Schools	Wadesboro
51	15.1	Chatham County Schools	Pittsboro
51	15.1	Person County Schools	Roxboro
54	15.2	Bladen County Schools	Elizabethtown
54	15.2	Halifax County Schools	Halifax
54	15.2	Hickory City Schools	Hickory
54	15.2	Jackson County Schools	Sylva
54	15.2	Montgomery County Schools	Troy
54	15.2	Newton Conover City Schools	Newton
60	15.3	Davie County Schools	Mocksville
60	15.3	Johnston County Schools	Smithfield
60	15.3	Lincoln County Schools	Lincolnton
63	15.4	Alamance-Burlington Schools	Burlington
63	15.4	Greene County Schools	Snow Hill
63	15.4	Rockingham County Schools	Eden
66	15.5	Bertie County Schools	Windsor
66	15.5	Surry County Schools	Dobson
68	15.6	Columbus County Schools	Whiteville
68	15.6	Duplin County Schools	Kenansville
68	15.6	Durham Public Schools	Durham
68	15.6	New Hanover County Schools	Wilmington
72	15.7	Camden County Schools	Camden
72	15.7	Lenoir County Public Schools	Kinston
72	15.7	Sampson County Schools	Clinton
72	15.7	Swain County Schools	Bryson City
72	15.7	Wake County Schools	Raleigh
77	15.8	Nash-Rocky Mount Schools	Nashville
77	15.8	Wayne County Public Schools	Goldsboro
79	15.9	Moore County Schools	Carthage
79	15.9	Rutherford County Schools	Forest City
79	15.9	Whiteville City Schools	Whiteville
82	16.0	Alexander County Schools	Taylorsville
82	16.0	Buncombe County Schools	Asheville
82	16.0	Franklin Academy	Wake Forest
82	16.0	Randolph County Schools	Asheboro
86	16.1	Cabarrus County Schools	Concord
86	16.1	Charlotte-Mecklenburg Schools	Charlotte
86	16.1	Lee County Schools	Sanford
89	16.2	Craven County Schools	New Bern
89	16.2	Harnett County Schools	Lillington
89	16.2	Richmond County Schools	Hamlet
89	16.2	Roanoke Rapids City Schools	Roanoke Rapids
93	16.3	Brunswick County Schools	Bolivia
93	16.3	Catawba County Schools	Newton
93	16.3	Iredell-Statesville Schools	Statesville
96	16.4	Granville County Schools	Oxford
96	16.4	Pender County Schools	Burgaw
98	16.5	Edgecombe County Schools	Tarboro
98	16.5	Robeson County Schools	Lumberton
98	16.5	Wilson County Schools	Wilson
101	16.6	Currituck County Schools	Currituck
102	16.7	Wilkes County Schools	North Wilkesb
103	16.8	Burke County Schools	Morganton
103	16.8	Union County Public Schools	Monroe
105	17.0	Davidson County Schools	Lexington
106	17.1	Gaston County Schools	Gastonia
107	17.3	Pine Lake Preparatory	Mooresville
108	17.4	Mooresville City Schools	Mooresville
109	17.6	Onslow County Schools	Jacksonville
110	17.9	Lake Norman Charter	Huntersville

Student/Librarian Ratio
(number of students per librarian)

Rank	Number	District Name	City
1	341.7	Northampton County Schools	Jackson
2	347.3	Yancey County Schools	Burnsville
3	348.3	Mitchell County Schools	Bakersville
4	371.4	Gates County Schools	Gatesville
5	393.4	Martin County Schools	Williamston
6	394.2	Columbus County Schools	Whiteville
7	411.9	Stokes County Schools	Danbury
8	414.6	Bladen County Schools	Elizabethtown
9	415.9	Polk County Schools	Columbus
10	427.3	Madison County Schools	Marshall
11	443.3	Perquimans County Schools	Hertford
12	444.1	Currituck County Schools	Currituck
13	444.6	Transylvania County Schools	Brevard
14	468.0	Warren County Schools	Warrenton
15	476.6	Halifax County Schools	Halifax
16	479.8	Caswell County Schools	Yanceyville
17	497.7	Alexander County Schools	Taylorsville
18	500.3	Sampson County Schools	Clinton
19	507.9	Person County Schools	Roxboro
20	509.3	Surry County Schools	Dobson
21	509.7	Macon County Schools	Franklin
22	512.0	Asheville City Schools	Asheville
23	513.7	Yadkin County Schools	Yadkinville
24	513.9	Haywood County Schools	Waynesville
25	514.3	Cherokee County Schools	Murphy
26	516.0	Swain County Schools	Bryson City
27	521.8	Clinton City Schools	Clinton
28	524.6	Chatham County Schools	Pittsboro
29	537.4	Montgomery County Schools	Troy
30	538.3	Wilson County Schools	Wilson
31	545.4	Bertie County Schools	Windsor
32	547.4	Asheboro City Schools	Asheboro
33	563.6	Mcdowell County Schools	Marion
34	564.0	Hickory City Schools	Hickory
35	565.1	Buncombe County Schools	Asheville
36	567.1	Stanly County Schools	Albemarle
37	569.4	Pasquotank County Schools	Elizabeth City
38	573.4	Caldwell County Schools	Lenoir
39	575.1	Moore County Schools	Carthage
40	575.5	Lexington City Schools	Lexington
41	578.9	Rockingham County Schools	Eden
42	581.0	Whiteville City Schools	Whiteville
43	584.7	Randolph County Schools	Asheboro
44	585.9	Lenoir County Public Schools	Kinston
45	589.0	Edenton/chowan Schools	Edenton
46	594.2	Rutherford County Schools	Forest City
47	597.7	Beaufort County Schools	Washington
48	599.6	Cumberland County Schools	Fayetteville
49	604.6	Davie County Schools	Mocksville
50	605.0	Newton Conover City Schools	Newton
51	608.6	Pender County Schools	Burgaw
52	614.3	Jackson County Schools	Sylva
53	614.5	Lincoln County Schools	Lincolnton
54	615.0	Edgecombe County Schools	Tarboro
55	615.3	Washington County Schools	Plymouth
56	615.5	Gaston County Schools	Gastonia
57	616.4	Rowan-Salisbury Schools	Salisbury
58	616.8	Wilkes County Schools	North Wilkesb
59	623.6	Carteret County Public Schools	Beaufort
60	624.9	Robeson County Schools	Lumberton
61	626.9	Duplin County Schools	Kenansville
62	627.9	Nash-Rocky Mount Schools	Nashville
63	631.0	Richmond County Schools	Hamlet
64	632.0	Thomasville City Schools	Thomasville
65	634.5	Craven County Schools	New Bern
66	641.6	Franklin County Schools	Louisburg
67	643.8	Hertford County Schools	Winton
68	646.3	Camden County Schools	Camden
69	649.2	Cleveland County Schools	Shelby
70	655.4	Ashe County Schools	Jefferson
71	659.0	Guilford County Schools	Greensboro
72	667.4	Durham Public Schools	Durham
73	667.8	Catawba County Schools	Newton
74	668.1	Pitt County Schools	Greenville
75	676.3	Alamance-Burlington Schools	Burlington
76	684.6	Onslow County Schools	Jacksonville
77	686.9	Orange County Schools	Hillsborough
78	696.6	Johnston County Schools	Smithfield
79	699.1	Hoke County Schools	Raeford
80	704.9	Mooresville City Schools	Mooresville
81	709.6	Iredell-Statesville Schools	Statesville
82	722.2	New Hanover County Schools	Wilmington
83	726.4	Davidson County Schools	Lexington
84	731.3	Greene County Schools	Snow Hill
85	741.3	Brunswick County Schools	Bolivia
86	745.2	Harnett County Schools	Lillington
87	749.6	Scotland County Schools	Laurinburg
88	754.0	Anson County Schools	Wadesboro
89	755.8	Chapel Hill-Carrboro Schools	Chapel Hill
90	772.5	Roanoke Rapids City Schools	Roanoke Rapids
91	777.5	Alleghany County Schools	Sparta
92	778.2	Wake County Schools	Raleigh
93	792.2	Forsyth County Schools	Winston Salem
94	793.1	Kannapolis City Schools	Kannapolis
95	796.2	Henderson County Schools	Hendersonville
96	796.5	Wayne County Public Schools	Goldsboro
97	805.2	Vance County Schools	Henderson
98	808.4	Union County Public Schools	Monroe
99	841.6	Lee County Schools	Sanford
100	844.5	Mount Airy City Schools	Mount Airy
101	854.7	Burke County Schools	Morganton
102	864.7	Cabarrus County Schools	Concord
103	963.5	Charlotte-Mecklenburg Schools	Charlotte
104	1,088.8	Granville County Schools	Oxford
105	1,158.7	Dare County Schools	Nags Head
106	1,240.0	Watauga County Schools	Boone
107	1,300.0	Avery County Schools	Newland
n/a	n/a	Franklin Academy	Wake Forest
n/a	n/a	Lake Norman Charter	Huntersville
n/a	n/a	Pine Lake Preparatory	Mooresville

Student/Counselor Ratio
(number of students per counselor)

Rank	Number	District Name	City
1	257.4	Warren County Schools	Warrenton
2	261.6	Polk County Schools	Columbus
3	279.9	Hertford County Schools	Winton

Note: This section only includes districts with 1,500 or more students; All categories are ranked from high to low

4	288.5	Nash-Rocky Mount Schools	Nashville
5	289.3	Chapel Hill-Carrboro Schools	Chapel Hill
6	291.0	Caldwell County Schools	Lenoir
7	300.3	Asheville City Schools	Asheville
8	300.4	Rowan-Salisbury Schools	Salisbury
9	309.5	Gates County Schools	Gatesville
10	311.2	Hickory City Schools	Hickory
11	312.3	Buncombe County Schools	Asheville
12	313.6	Dare County Schools	Nags Head
13	314.2	Anson County Schools	Wadesboro
14	316.5	Lexington City Schools	Lexington
15	318.5	Bladen County Schools	Elizabethtown
15	318.5	Stokes County Schools	Danbury
17	318.7	Gaston County Schools	Gastonia
18	319.9	Caswell County Schools	Yanceyville
19	321.5	Mitchell County Schools	Bakersville
20	322.5	Rockingham County Schools	Eden
21	322.8	Edgecombe County Schools	Tarboro
22	326.8	Granville County Schools	Oxford
23	327.3	Halifax County Schools	Halifax
24	329.4	Guilford County Schools	Greensboro
25	332.0	Whiteville City Schools	Whiteville
26	332.8	Lincoln County Schools	Lincolnton
27	333.7	Durham Public Schools	Durham
28	335.3	Mcdowell County Schools	Marion
29	336.0	Cherokee County Schools	Murphy
30	336.7	Rutherford County Schools	Forest City
31	336.8	Cleveland County Schools	Shelby
32	337.5	Orange County Schools	Hillsborough
33	340.4	Jackson County Schools	Sylva
34	343.7	Davie County Schools	Mocksville
35	345.1	Vance County Schools	Henderson
36	346.3	Perquimans County Schools	Hertford
37	347.2	Lenoir County Public Schools	Kinston
38	350.1	Bertie County Schools	Windsor
39	350.2	Alamance-Burlington Schools	Burlington
40	351.2	Pender County Schools	Burgaw
41	356.7	Cabarrus County Schools	Concord
42	361.0	Robeson County Schools	Lumberton
43	361.1	Thomasville City Schools	Thomasville
44	361.3	Davidson County Schools	Lexington
45	363.8	Scotland County Schools	Laurinburg
46	365.0	Alexander County Schools	Taylorsville
47	366.3	Madison County Schools	Marshall
48	368.0	Beaufort County Schools	Washington
49	368.6	Northampton County Schools	Jackson
50	369.6	Macon County Schools	Franklin
51	371.3	Martin County Schools	Williamston
52	371.5	Person County Schools	Roxboro
53	372.4	Yadkin County Schools	Yadkinville
54	372.8	Pasquotank County Schools	Elizabeth City
55	375.9	Wake County Schools	Raleigh
56	376.4	Surry County Schools	Dobson
57	377.7	Yancey County Schools	Burnsville
58	378.1	Stanly County Schools	Albemarle
59	380.0	Newton Conover City Schools	Newton
60	382.2	Washington County Schools	Plymouth
61	382.6	Randolph County Schools	Asheboro
62	385.8	Pitt County Schools	Greenville
63	385.9	Harnett County Schools	Lillington
64	386.9	Wilson County Schools	Wilson
65	387.3	Duplin County Schools	Kenansville
66	387.9	Cumberland County Schools	Fayetteville
67	388.8	Alleghany County Schools	Sparta
68	394.2	Catawba County Schools	Newton
69	395.2	Transylvania County Schools	Brevard
70	396.9	Carteret County Public Schools	Beaufort
71	397.2	Burke County Schools	Morganton
72	397.8	Chatham County Schools	Pittsboro
73	400.8	Craven County Schools	New Bern
74	403.0	Forsyth County Schools	Winston Salem
75	406.2	Edenton/chowan Schools	Edenton
76	409.2	New Hanover County Schools	Wilmington
77	411.2	Wilkes County Schools	North Wilkesb
78	413.7	Johnston County Schools	Smithfield
79	416.4	Henderson County Schools	Hendersonville
80	416.9	Sampson County Schools	Clinton
81	417.8	Greene County Schools	Snow Hill
82	420.8	Wayne County Public Schools	Goldsboro
83	422.3	Mount Airy City Schools	Mount Airy
84	423.5	Brunswick County Schools	Bolivia
85	424.3	Moore County Schools	Carthage
86	425.7	Franklin County Schools	Louisburg
87	425.8	Iredell-Statesville Schools	Statesville
88	427.9	Union County Public Schools	Monroe

89	429.9	Montgomery County Schools	Troy
90	435.0	Haywood County Schools	Waynesville
91	438.2	Richmond County Schools	Hamlet
92	441.4	Roanoke Rapids City Schools	Roanoke Rapids
93	446.1	Mooresville City Schools	Mooresville
94	446.8	Columbus County Schools	Whiteville
95	451.2	Clinton City Schools	Clinton
96	453.3	Asheboro City Schools	Asheboro
97	460.0	Charlotte-Mecklenburg Schools	Charlotte
98	466.1	Hoke County Schools	Raeford
99	468.1	Ashe County Schools	Jefferson
100	485.4	Lee County Schools	Sanford
101	487.9	Swain County Schools	Bryson City
102	489.1	Watauga County Schools	Boone
103	499.6	Currituck County Schools	Currituck
104	510.0	Onslow County Schools	Jacksonville
105	532.7	Lake Norman Charter	Huntersville
106	646.3	Camden County Schools	Camden
107	685.0	Kannapolis City Schools	Kannapolis
108	1,396.3	Avery County Schools	Newland
109	1,593.0	Pine Lake Preparatory	Mooresville
n/a	n/a	Franklin Academy	Wake Forest

Current Expenditures per Student

Rank	Dollars	District Name	City
1	12,131	Asheville City Schools	Asheville
2	10,971	Washington County Schools	Plymouth
3	10,806	Dare County Schools	Nags Head
4	10,728	Northampton County Schools	Jackson
5	10,708	Edenton/chowan Schools	Edenton
6	10,701	Mitchell County Schools	Bakersville
7	10,697	Alleghany County Schools	Sparta
8	10,696	Chapel Hill-Carrboro Schools	Chapel Hill
9	10,427	Warren County Schools	Warrenton
10	10,413	Scotland County Schools	Laurinburg
11	10,280	Avery County Schools	Newland
12	10,208	Gates County Schools	Gatesville
13	10,154	Lexington City Schools	Lexington
14	10,070	Polk County Schools	Columbus
15	9,968	Halifax County Schools	Halifax
16	9,904	Bertie County Schools	Windsor
17	9,891	Hertford County Schools	Winton
18	9,796	Anson County Schools	Wadesboro
19	9,795	Thomasville City Schools	Thomasville
20	9,781	Orange County Schools	Hillsborough
21	9,763	Perquimans County Schools	Hertford
22	9,744	Greene County Schools	Snow Hill
23	9,655	Yancey County Schools	Burnsville
24	9,624	Martin County Schools	Williamston
25	9,484	Transylvania County Schools	Brevard
26	9,364	Macon County Schools	Franklin
27	9,327	Madison County Schools	Marshall
27	9,327	Mount Airy City Schools	Mount Airy
29	9,300	Durham Public Schools	Durham
30	9,288	Bladen County Schools	Elizabethtown
31	9,284	Chatham County Schools	Pittsboro
32	9,279	Caswell County Schools	Yanceyville
33	9,215	Cherokee County Schools	Murphy
34	9,202	Ashe County Schools	Jefferson
35	9,111	Watauga County Schools	Boone
36	9,073	Rutherford County Schools	Forest City
37	9,069	Jackson County Schools	Sylva
38	9,059	Vance County Schools	Henderson
39	9,051	Currituck County Schools	Currituck
40	9,016	Beaufort County Schools	Washington
41	8,974	Asheboro City Schools	Asheboro
42	8,971	Kannapolis City Schools	Kannapolis
43	8,951	Swain County Schools	Bryson City
44	8,921	Whiteville City Schools	Whiteville
45	8,861	Pasquotank County Schools	Elizabeth City
45	8,861	Robeson County Schools	Lumberton
47	8,807	Brunswick County Schools	Bolivia
48	8,779	Montgomery County Schools	Troy
49	8,759	New Hanover County Schools	Wilmington
50	8,705	Cleveland County Schools	Shelby
51	8,684	Guilford County Schools	Greensboro
52	8,671	Columbus County Schools	Whiteville
53	8,632	Carteret County Public Schools	Beaufort
54	8,613	Person County Schools	Roxboro
55	8,604	Forsyth County Schools	Winston Salem
56	8,551	Stokes County Schools	Danbury
57	8,539	Nash-Rocky Mount Schools	Nashville
58	8,529	Duplin County Schools	Kenansville

59	8,502	Haywood County Schools	Waynesville
60	8,477	Roanoke Rapids City Schools	Roanoke Rapids
61	8,427	Lee County Schools	Sanford
62	8,418	Richmond County Schools	Hamlet
63	8,400	Clinton City Schools	Clinton
64	8,351	Rowan-Salisbury Schools	Salisbury
65	8,330	Buncombe County Schools	Asheville
66	8,289	Stanly County Schools	Albemarle
67	8,286	Camden County Schools	Camden
68	8,278	Sampson County Schools	Clinton
69	8,251	Pitt County Schools	Greenville
70	8,248	Rockingham County Schools	Eden
71	8,237	Johnston County Schools	Smithfield
72	8,212	Hickory City Schools	Hickory
73	8,199	Henderson County Schools	Hendersonville
73	8,199	Newton Conover City Schools	Newton
75	8,177	Surry County Schools	Dobson
76	8,173	Lenoir County Public Schools	Kinston
77	8,168	Cumberland County Schools	Fayetteville
78	8,158	Mcdowell County Schools	Marion
79	8,129	Edgecombe County Schools	Tarboro
79	8,129	Hoke County Schools	Raeford
81	8,109	Granville County Schools	Oxford
82	8,057	Yadkin County Schools	Yadkinville
83	8,050	Charlotte-Mecklenburg Schools	Charlotte
84	8,036	Moore County Schools	Carthage
85	8,023	Wilson County Schools	Wilson
86	8,018	Pender County Schools	Burgaw
87	7,955	Wilkes County Schools	North Wilkesb
88	7,917	Caldwell County Schools	Lenoir
89	7,907	Lincoln County Schools	Lincolnton
90	7,893	Alexander County Schools	Taylorsville
91	7,880	Franklin County Schools	Louisburg
92	7,868	Catawba County Schools	Newton
93	7,778	Onslow County Schools	Jacksonville
94	7,758	Davie County Schools	Mocksville
95	7,751	Wayne County Public Schools	Goldsboro
96	7,750	Alamance-Burlington Schools	Burlington
97	7,725	Mooresville City Schools	Mooresville
98	7,719	Craven County Schools	New Bern
99	7,714	Randolph County Schools	Asheboro
99	7,714	Wake County Schools	Raleigh
101	7,669	Burke County Schools	Morganton
102	7,592	Gaston County Schools	Gastonia
103	7,511	Union County Public Schools	Monroe
104	7,509	Iredell-Statesville Schools	Statesville
105	7,463	Cabarrus County Schools	Concord
106	7,182	Harnett County Schools	Lillington
107	6,975	Davidson County Schools	Lexington
108	5,979	Franklin Academy	Wake Forest
109	5,591	Lake Norman Charter	Huntersville
110	5,249	Pine Lake Preparatory	Mooresville

Total General Revenue per Student

Rank	Dollars	District Name	City
1	20,220	Pine Lake Preparatory	Mooresville
2	18,502	Orange County Schools	Hillsborough
3	13,844	Dare County Schools	Nags Head
4	12,957	Asheville City Schools	Asheville
5	12,585	Northampton County Schools	Jackson
6	12,576	Johnston County Schools	Smithfield
7	12,521	Lincoln County Schools	Lincolnton
8	12,245	Union County Public Schools	Monroe
9	12,060	Rutherford County Schools	Forest City
10	12,048	Alleghany County Schools	Sparta
11	11,923	Cabarrus County Schools	Concord
12	11,749	Chatham County Schools	Pittsboro
13	11,611	Avery County Schools	Newland
14	11,591	Warren County Schools	Warrenton
15	11,567	Wilkes County Schools	North Wilkesb
16	11,519	Watauga County Schools	Boone
17	11,503	Gates County Schools	Gatesville
18	11,446	Edenton/chowan Schools	Edenton
19	11,426	Halifax County Schools	Halifax
20	11,423	Washington County Schools	Plymouth
21	11,385	Chapel Hill-Carrboro Schools	Chapel Hill
22	11,360	Rockingham County Schools	Eden
23	11,289	Polk County Schools	Columbus
24	11,181	Mitchell County Schools	Bakersville
25	11,076	Scotland County Schools	Laurinburg
26	11,073	Forsyth County Schools	Winston Salem
27	11,043	Greene County Schools	Snow Hill
28	11,028	Jackson County Schools	Sylva

Note: This section only includes districts with 1,500 or more students; All categories are ranked from high to low

29	10,873	Ashe County Schools	Jefferson
30	10,870	Thomasville City Schools	Thomasville
31	10,863	Guilford County Schools	Greensboro
32	10,759	Transylvania County Schools	Brevard
33	10,744	Bertie County Schools	Windsor
34	10,688	Macon County Schools	Franklin
35	10,642	Lexington City Schools	Lexington
36	10,626	Hertford County Schools	Winton
37	10,565	Cherokee County Schools	Murphy
38	10,548	Mount Airy City Schools	Mount Airy
39	10,454	Pender County Schools	Burgaw
40	10,425	Wilson County Schools	Wilson
41	10,416	Carteret County Public Schools	Beaufort
42	10,402	Brunswick County Schools	Bolivia
43	10,397	Martin County Schools	Williamston
44	10,384	Anson County Schools	Wadesboro
45	10,373	Durham Public Schools	Durham
46	10,333	New Hanover County Schools	Wilmington
47	10,263	Madison County Schools	Marshall
48	10,221	Bladen County Schools	Elizabethtown
49	10,220	Caswell County Schools	Yanceyville
50	10,200	Person County Schools	Roxboro
51	10,180	Yancey County Schools	Burnsville
52	10,166	Nash-Rocky Mount Schools	Nashville
53	10,159	Currituck County Schools	Currituck
54	10,141	Charlotte-Mecklenburg Schools	Charlotte
55	10,138	Perquimans County Schools	Hertford
56	10,037	Swain County Schools	Bryson City
57	9,958	Stokes County Schools	Danbury
58	9,892	Beaufort County Schools	Washington
59	9,867	Newton Conover City Schools	Newton
60	9,865	Buncombe County Schools	Asheville
61	9,824	Vance County Schools	Henderson
62	9,752	Cleveland County Schools	Shelby
63	9,679	Sampson County Schools	Clinton
64	9,638	Whiteville City Schools	Whiteville
65	9,576	Franklin County Schools	Louisburg
66	9,567	Lee County Schools	Sanford
67	9,566	Pasquotank County Schools	Elizabeth City
68	9,563	Surry County Schools	Dobson
69	9,530	Henderson County Schools	Hendersonville
70	9,520	Robeson County Schools	Lumberton
71	9,506	Montgomery County Schools	Troy
72	9,503	Catawba County Schools	Newton
73	9,487	Columbus County Schools	Whiteville
74	9,486	Granville County Schools	Oxford
75	9,479	Asheboro City Schools	Asheboro
76	9,473	Lenoir County Public Schools	Kinston
77	9,461	Camden County Schools	Camden
78	9,458	Duplin County Schools	Kenansville
79	9,411	Cumberland County Schools	Fayetteville
80	9,333	Rowan-Salisbury Schools	Salisbury
81	9,297	Richmond County Schools	Hamlet
82	9,286	Hickory City Schools	Hickory
83	9,285	Iredell-Statesville Schools	Statesville
84	9,250	Haywood County Schools	Waynesville
85	9,181	Moore County Schools	Carthage
86	9,082	Yadkin County Schools	Yadkinville
87	9,080	Kannapolis City Schools	Kannapolis
88	9,066	Onslow County Schools	Jacksonville
89	9,034	Roanoke Rapids City Schools	Roanoke Rapids
90	8,993	Clinton City Schools	Clinton
91	8,976	Stanly County Schools	Albemarle
92	8,965	Caldwell County Schools	Lenoir
93	8,928	Davie County Schools	Mocksville
94	8,910	Hoke County Schools	Raeford
95	8,887	Randolph County Schools	Asheboro
96	8,820	Harnett County Schools	Lillington
97	8,761	Burke County Schools	Morganton
98	8,754	Gaston County Schools	Gastonia
99	8,732	Edgecombe County Schools	Tarboro
100	8,669	Pitt County Schools	Greenville
101	8,659	Alamance-Burlington Schools	Burlington
102	8,629	Mcdowell County Schools	Marion
103	8,553	Craven County Schools	New Bern
104	8,504	Alexander County Schools	Taylorsville
105	8,225	Wayne County Public Schools	Goldsboro
106	8,215	Mooresville City Schools	Mooresville
107	8,208	Wake County Schools	Raleigh
108	7,979	Davidson County Schools	Lexington
109	7,616	Lake Norman Charter	Huntersville
110	7,317	Franklin Academy	Wake Forest

Long-Term Debt per Student (end of FY)

Rank	Dollars	District Name	City
1	19,235	Dare County Schools	Nags Head
2	17,726	Orange County Schools	Hillsborough
3	15,309	Watauga County Schools	Boone
4	12,338	Union County Public Schools	Monroe
5	11,123	Wake County Schools	Raleigh
6	10,882	Iredell-Statesville Schools	Statesville
7	10,472	Cabarrus County Schools	Concord
8	10,205	Franklin County Schools	Louisburg
9	10,009	Johnston County Schools	Smithfield
10	9,856	Lincoln County Schools	Lincolnton
11	9,335	Charlotte-Mecklenburg Schools	Charlotte
12	9,204	Forsyth County Schools	Winston Salem
13	8,775	Macon County Schools	Franklin
14	8,046	Sampson County Schools	Clinton
15	7,729	New Hanover County Schools	Wilmington
16	7,640	Durham Public Schools	Durham
17	7,538	Chatham County Schools	Pittsboro
18	7,283	Carteret County Public Schools	Beaufort
19	7,169	Guilford County Schools	Greensboro
20	7,092	Pender County Schools	Burgaw
21	7,019	Lee County Schools	Sanford
22	6,606	Lenoir County Public Schools	Kinston
23	6,580	Brunswick County Schools	Bolivia
24	6,239	Granville County Schools	Oxford
25	6,133	Catawba County Schools	Newton
26	5,633	Henderson County Schools	Hendersonville
27	5,505	Harnett County Schools	Lillington
28	5,426	Gaston County Schools	Gastonia
29	5,424	Randolph County Schools	Asheboro
30	4,979	Moore County Schools	Carthage
31	4,910	Pitt County Schools	Greenville
32	4,874	Surry County Schools	Dobson
33	4,861	Yadkin County Schools	Yadkinville
34	4,542	Onslow County Schools	Jacksonville
35	4,516	Davidson County Schools	Lexington
36	4,464	Buncombe County Schools	Asheville
37	4,315	Alleghany County Schools	Sparta
38	4,259	Wilkes County Schools	North Wilkesb
39	4,255	Rutherford County Schools	Forest City
40	4,195	Avery County Schools	Newland
41	4,083	Pasquotank County Schools	Elizabeth City
42	3,850	Martin County Schools	Williamston
43	3,714	Beaufort County Schools	Washington
44	3,713	Halifax County Schools	Halifax
45	3,375	Rowan-Salisbury Schools	Salisbury
46	3,371	Transylvania County Schools	Brevard
47	3,367	Montgomery County Schools	Troy
48	3,306	Camden County Schools	Camden
49	3,300	Craven County Schools	New Bern
50	3,259	Gates County Schools	Gatesville
51	3,243	Ashe County Schools	Jefferson
52	3,146	Northampton County Schools	Jackson
53	3,040	Stanly County Schools	Albemarle
54	2,954	Jackson County Schools	Sylva
55	2,915	Polk County Schools	Columbus
56	2,883	Richmond County Schools	Hamlet
57	2,876	Wilson County Schools	Wilson
58	2,874	Burke County Schools	Morganton
59	2,843	Rockingham County Schools	Eden
60	2,814	Swain County Schools	Bryson City
61	2,770	Edenton/chowan Schools	Edenton
62	2,758	Davie County Schools	Mocksville
63	2,744	Bertie County Schools	Windsor
64	2,728	Haywood County Schools	Waynesville
65	2,721	Stokes County Schools	Danbury
66	2,712	Bladen County Schools	Elizabethtown
67	2,661	Vance County Schools	Henderson
68	2,638	Cherokee County Schools	Murphy
69	2,584	Alamance-Burlington Schools	Burlington
70	2,343	Person County Schools	Roxboro
71	2,234	Cumberland County Schools	Fayetteville
72	2,002	Hoke County Schools	Raeford
73	1,831	Currituck County Schools	Currituck
74	1,829	Nash-Rocky Mount Schools	Nashville
75	1,416	Edgecombe County Schools	Tarboro
76	1,357	Alexander County Schools	Taylorsville
77	1,274	Cleveland County Schools	Shelby
78	999	Caldwell County Schools	Lenoir
79	990	Scotland County Schools	Laurinburg
80	821	Mitchell County Schools	Bakersville
81	759	Caswell County Schools	Yanceyville
82	618	Warren County Schools	Warrenton

83	509	Robeson County Schools	Lumberton
84	448	Duplin County Schools	Kenansville
85	425	Mcdowell County Schools	Marion
86	380	Madison County Schools	Marshall
87	250	Columbus County Schools	Whiteville
88	246	Anson County Schools	Wadesboro
89	0	Asheboro City Schools	Asheboro
89	0	Asheville City Schools	Asheville
89	0	Chapel Hill-Carrboro Schools	Chapel Hill
89	0	Clinton City Schools	Clinton
89	0	Franklin Academy	Wake Forest
89	0	Greene County Schools	Snow Hill
89	0	Hertford County Schools	Winton
89	0	Hickory City Schools	Hickory
89	0	Kannapolis City Schools	Kannapolis
89	0	Lake Norman Charter	Huntersville
89	0	Lexington City Schools	Lexington
89	0	Mooresville City Schools	Mooresville
89	0	Mount Airy City Schools	Mount Airy
89	0	Newton Conover City Schools	Newton
89	0	Perquimans County Schools	Hertford
89	0	Pine Lake Preparatory	Mooresville
89	0	Roanoke Rapids City Schools	Roanoke Rapids
89	0	Thomasville City Schools	Thomasville
89	0	Washington County Schools	Plymouth
89	0	Wayne County Public Schools	Goldsboro
89	0	Whiteville City Schools	Whiteville
89	0	Yancey County Schools	Burnsville

Number of Diploma Recipients

Rank	Number	District Name	City
1	8,186	Wake County Schools	Raleigh
2	7,052	Charlotte-Mecklenburg Schools	Charlotte
3	4,616	Guilford County Schools	Greensboro
4	3,327	Cumberland County Schools	Fayetteville
5	3,150	Forsyth County Schools	Winston Salem
6	2,136	Union County Public Schools	Monroe
7	2,035	Gaston County Schools	Gastonia
8	1,813	Durham Public Schools	Durham
9	1,628	Buncombe County Schools	Asheville
10	1,625	Johnston County Schools	Smithfield
11	1,591	Cabarrus County Schools	Concord
12	1,472	Onslow County Schools	Jacksonville
13	1,462	New Hanover County Schools	Wilmington
14	1,407	Iredell-Statesville Schools	Statesville
15	1,389	Robeson County Schools	Lumberton
16	1,352	Rowan-Salisbury Schools	Salisbury
17	1,349	Alamance-Burlington Schools	Burlington
18	1,298	Pitt County Schools	Greenville
19	1,289	Davidson County Schools	Lexington
20	1,170	Wayne County Public Schools	Goldsboro
21	1,166	Catawba County Schools	Newton
22	1,108	Harnett County Schools	Lillington
23	1,049	Nash-Rocky Mount Schools	Nashville
24	1,035	Randolph County Schools	Asheboro
25	1,027	Cleveland County Schools	Shelby
26	990	Burke County Schools	Morganton
27	898	Rockingham County Schools	Eden
28	867	Craven County Schools	New Bern
29	851	Lincoln County Schools	Lincolnton
30	825	Henderson County Schools	Hendersonville
31	811	Chapel Hill-Carrboro Schools	Chapel Hill
32	769	Caldwell County Schools	Lenoir
33	714	Moore County Schools	Carthage
34	684	Brunswick County Schools	Bolivia
35	629	Rutherford County Schools	Forest City
35	629	Wilson County Schools	Wilson
37	614	Stanly County Schools	Albemarle
38	608	Lenoir County Public Schools	Kinston
39	586	Lee County Schools	Sanford
40	566	Wilkes County Schools	North Wilkesb
41	564	Carteret County Public Schools	Beaufort
42	543	Surry County Schools	Dobson
43	541	Pender County Schools	Burgaw
44	500	Franklin County Schools	Louisburg
45	492	Stokes County Schools	Danbury
46	490	Granville County Schools	Oxford
47	485	Orange County Schools	Hillsborough
48	477	Vance County Schools	Henderson
49	476	Haywood County Schools	Waynesville
50	470	Chatham County Schools	Pittsboro
50	470	Richmond County Schools	Hamlet
52	468	Duplin County Schools	Kenansville

Note: This section only includes districts with 1,500 or more students; All categories are ranked from high to low

53	446	Edgecombe County Schools	Tarboro
54	445	Beaufort County Schools	Washington
55	435	Columbus County Schools	Whiteville
56	400	Sampson County Schools	Clinton
57	397	Yadkin County Schools	Yadkinville
58	389	Scotland County Schools	Laurinburg
59	384	Mcdowell County Schools	Marion
60	375	Davie County Schools	Mocksville
61	354	Pasquotank County Schools	Elizabeth City
62	352	Dare County Schools	Nags Head
63	347	Watauga County Schools	Boone
64	342	Alexander County Schools	Taylorsville
64	342	Mooresville City Schools	Mooresville
66	334	Hoke County Schools	Raeford
67	331	Bladen County Schools	Elizabethtown
67	331	Person County Schools	Roxboro
69	286	Halifax County Schools	Halifax
70	282	Currituck County Schools	Currituck
71	277	Hickory City Schools	Hickory
72	273	Macon County Schools	Franklin
73	271	Montgomery County Schools	Troy
74	255	Cherokee County Schools	Murphy
75	253	Asheville City Schools	Asheville
76	251	Transylvania County Schools	Brevard
77	244	Asheboro City Schools	Asheboro
78	242	Martin County Schools	Williamston
79	239	Anson County Schools	Wadesboro
80	236	Hertford County Schools	Winton
81	233	Kannapolis City Schools	Kannapolis
82	218	Ashe County Schools	Jefferson
83	201	Jackson County Schools	Sylva
84	189	Caswell County Schools	Yanceyville
85	185	Yancey County Schools	Burnsville
86	182	Greene County Schools	Snow Hill
87	179	Warren County Schools	Warrenton
88	178	Newton Conover City Schools	Newton
89	175	Clinton City Schools	Clinton
90	174	Roanoke Rapids City Schools	Roanoke Rapids
91	170	Bertie County Schools	Windsor
92	168	Polk County Schools	Columbus
93	166	Edenton/chowan Schools	Edenton
94	161	Whiteville City Schools	Whiteville
95	157	Lexington City Schools	Lexington
96	146	Avery County Schools	Newland
97	144	Northampton County Schools	Jackson
98	140	Madison County Schools	Marshall
99	139	Thomasville City Schools	Thomasville
100	134	Mount Airy City Schools	Mount Airy
101	130	Swain County Schools	Bryson City
102	129	Washington County Schools	Plymouth
103	128	Mitchell County Schools	Bakersville
104	123	Gates County Schools	Gatesville
105	120	Camden County Schools	Camden
106	102	Perquimans County Schools	Hertford
107	87	Alleghany County Schools	Sparta
108	71	Franklin Academy	Wake Forest
n/a	n/a	Lake Norman Charter	Huntersville
n/a	n/a	Pine Lake Preparatory	Mooresville

High School Drop-out Rate

Rank	Percent	District Name	City
1	10.3	Hickory City Schools	Hickory
2	9.0	Jackson County Schools	Sylva
3	8.6	Caswell County Schools	Yanceyville
3	8.6	Rutherford County Schools	Forest City
5	8.4	Swain County Schools	Bryson City
6	8.3	Madison County Schools	Marshall
7	8.1	Cleveland County Schools	Shelby
8	8.0	Alamance-Burlington Schools	Burlington
9	7.8	Roanoke Rapids City Schools	Roanoke Rapids
10	7.6	Beaufort County Schools	Washington
11	7.5	Martin County Schools	Williamston
11	7.5	Yancey County Schools	Burnsville
13	7.4	Granville County Schools	Oxford
13	7.4	Wilkes County Schools	North Wilkesb
15	7.3	Edgecombe County Schools	Tarboro
15	7.3	Vance County Schools	Henderson
17	7.2	Richmond County Schools	Hamlet
17	7.2	Thomasville City Schools	Thomasville
19	7.1	Mitchell County Schools	Bakersville
20	7.0	Halifax County Schools	Halifax
20	7.0	Nash-Rocky Mount Schools	Nashville
22	6.9	Ashe County Schools	Jefferson
22	6.9	Sampson County Schools	Clinton
24	6.8	Clinton City Schools	Clinton
25	6.7	Greene County Schools	Snow Hill
25	6.7	Haywood County Schools	Waynesville
25	6.7	Robeson County Schools	Lumberton
28	6.6	Davie County Schools	Mocksville
28	6.6	Northampton County Schools	Jackson
28	6.6	Pitt County Schools	Greenville
28	6.6	Rockingham County Schools	Eden
32	6.5	Mcdowell County Schools	Marion
33	6.4	Davidson County Schools	Lexington
33	6.4	Gates County Schools	Gatesville
35	6.3	Charlotte-Mecklenburg Schools	Charlotte
35	6.3	Harnett County Schools	Lillington
35	6.3	Montgomery County Schools	Troy
35	6.3	Randolph County Schools	Asheboro
39	6.2	Currituck County Schools	Currituck
39	6.2	Duplin County Schools	Kenansville
39	6.2	Person County Schools	Roxboro
39	6.2	Wilson County Schools	Wilson
43	6.1	Bladen County Schools	Elizabethtown
43	6.1	Gaston County Schools	Gastonia
43	6.1	Kannapolis City Schools	Kannapolis
43	6.1	Lee County Schools	Sanford
43	6.1	Rowan-Salisbury Schools	Salisbury
48	6.0	Forsyth County Schools	Winston Salem
48	6.0	Whiteville City Schools	Whiteville
50	5.9	Caldwell County Schools	Lenoir
50	5.9	Perquimans County Schools	Hertford
52	5.8	Asheville City Schools	Asheville
52	5.8	Lenoir County Public Schools	Kinston
52	5.8	Lexington City Schools	Lexington
52	5.8	New Hanover County Schools	Wilmington
56	5.7	Alexander County Schools	Taylorsville
56	5.7	Asheboro City Schools	Asheboro
56	5.7	Franklin County Schools	Louisburg
59	5.6	Brunswick County Schools	Bolivia
59	5.6	Stokes County Schools	Danbury
59	5.6	Wayne County Public Schools	Goldsboro
62	5.5	Surry County Schools	Dobson
63	5.4	Burke County Schools	Morganton
63	5.4	Transylvania County Schools	Brevard
65	5.3	Hoke County Schools	Raeford
65	5.3	Johnston County Schools	Smithfield
65	5.3	Watauga County Schools	Boone
68	5.2	Henderson County Schools	Hendersonville
68	5.2	Pasquotank County Schools	Elizabeth City
68	5.2	Pender County Schools	Burgaw
71	5.1	Durham Public Schools	Durham
71	5.1	Polk County Schools	Columbus
71	5.1	Warren County Schools	Warrenton
74	5.0	Cabarrus County Schools	Concord
74	5.0	Chatham County Schools	Pittsboro
74	5.0	Craven County Schools	New Bern
74	5.0	Orange County Schools	Hillsborough
78	4.9	Stanly County Schools	Albemarle
79	4.8	Macon County Schools	Franklin
79	4.8	Washington County Schools	Plymouth
81	4.7	Buncombe County Schools	Asheville
81	4.7	Carteret County Public Schools	Beaufort
81	4.7	Lincoln County Schools	Lincolnton
81	4.7	Onslow County Schools	Jacksonville
85	4.5	Camden County Schools	Camden
85	4.5	Columbus County Schools	Whiteville
85	4.5	Moore County Schools	Carthage
85	4.5	Mooresville City Schools	Mooresville
89	4.3	Wake County Schools	Raleigh
90	4.2	Bertie County Schools	Windsor
90	4.2	Catawba County Schools	Newton
92	4.1	Edenton/chowan Schools	Edenton
93	4.0	Cherokee County Schools	Murphy
94	3.9	Scotland County Schools	Laurinburg
95	3.8	Alleghany County Schools	Sparta
95	3.8	Cumberland County Schools	Fayetteville
97	3.7	Avery County Schools	Newland
98	3.6	Hertford County Schools	Winton
98	3.6	Iredell-Statesville Schools	Statesville
100	3.3	Union County Public Schools	Monroe
101	3.1	Anson County Schools	Wadesboro
101	3.1	Guilford County Schools	Greensboro
101	3.1	Yadkin County Schools	Yadkinville
104	2.6	Mount Airy City Schools	Mount Airy
105	2.2	Newton Conover City Schools	Newton
106	1.9	Dare County Schools	Nags Head
107	1.5	Chapel Hill-Carrboro Schools	Chapel Hill
108	0.0	Franklin Academy	Wake Forest
n/a	n/a	Lake Norman Charter	Huntersville
n/a	n/a	Pine Lake Preparatory	Mooresville

Average Freshman Graduation Rate

Rank	Percent	District Name	City
1	100.0	Franklin Academy	Wake Forest
2	87.9	Mooresville City Schools	Mooresville
3	87.6	Union County Public Schools	Monroe
4	85.9	Iredell-Statesville Schools	Statesville
5	85.5	Watauga County Schools	Boone
6	84.7	Wake County Schools	Raleigh
7	84.5	Lincoln County Schools	Lincolnton
8	83.9	Cherokee County Schools	Murphy
9	83.8	Dare County Schools	Nags Head
10	83.4	Avery County Schools	Newland
10	83.4	Chapel Hill-Carrboro Schools	Chapel Hill
12	83.3	Camden County Schools	Camden
13	83.2	Polk County Schools	Columbus
14	82.3	Ashe County Schools	Jefferson
15	81.9	Onslow County Schools	Jacksonville
16	81.8	Catawba County Schools	Newton
17	81.0	Currituck County Schools	Currituck
18	80.8	Yancey County Schools	Burnsville
19	80.5	Whiteville City Schools	Whiteville
20	80.4	Cabarrus County Schools	Concord
20	80.4	Guilford County Schools	Greensboro
20	80.4	Henderson County Schools	Hendersonville
23	80.2	Swain County Schools	Bryson City
24	79.9	Yadkin County Schools	Yadkinville
25	79.4	Macon County Schools	Franklin
25	79.4	Stokes County Schools	Danbury
27	78.8	Burke County Schools	Morganton
28	78.6	Chatham County Schools	Pittsboro
29	78.5	Pender County Schools	Burgaw
30	78.4	Newton Conover City Schools	Newton
31	78.3	Forsyth County Schools	Winston Salem
32	78.0	Surry County Schools	Dobson
33	77.9	Alexander County Schools	Taylorsville
34	77.7	Davidson County Schools	Lexington
35	77.2	Hickory City Schools	Hickory
36	77.0	Carteret County Public Schools	Beaufort
36	77.0	Orange County Schools	Hillsborough
38	76.8	Franklin County Schools	Louisburg
39	76.4	Cumberland County Schools	Fayetteville
40	76.3	Moore County Schools	Carthage
41	76.1	Perquimans County Schools	Hertford
42	75.9	Rowan-Salisbury Schools	Salisbury
43	75.8	Haywood County Schools	Waynesville
44	75.5	Wayne County Public Schools	Goldsboro
45	75.3	Asheville City Schools	Asheville
46	75.2	Buncombe County Schools	Asheville
47	75.0	Alleghany County Schools	Sparta
48	74.9	Lee County Schools	Sanford
48	74.9	Montgomery County Schools	Troy
50	74.6	Brunswick County Schools	Bolivia
51	74.4	Stanly County Schools	Albemarle
52	74.3	Transylvania County Schools	Brevard
53	74.2	Craven County Schools	New Bern
54	74.1	Mcdowell County Schools	Marion
55	74.0	Johnston County Schools	Smithfield
56	73.8	Edenton/chowan Schools	Edenton
57	73.4	Richmond County Schools	Hamlet
58	73.3	Rutherford County Schools	Forest City
59	73.2	Mount Airy City Schools	Mount Airy
59	73.2	Rockingham County Schools	Eden
61	73.1	Harnett County Schools	Lillington
62	73.0	Davie County Schools	Mocksville
63	72.8	Asheboro City Schools	Asheboro
64	72.6	Gaston County Schools	Gastonia
65	72.3	Alamance-Burlington Schools	Burlington
66	72.2	Caldwell County Schools	Lenoir
67	72.1	New Hanover County Schools	Wilmington
68	72.0	Beaufort County Schools	Washington
69	71.7	Washington County Schools	Plymouth
70	70.8	Nash-Rocky Mount Schools	Nashville
71	70.7	Gates County Schools	Gatesville
71	70.7	Hertford County Schools	Winton
73	70.4	Columbus County Schools	Whiteville
74	70.3	Robeson County Schools	Lumberton
75	70.1	Durham Public Schools	Durham
76	69.5	Edgecombe County Schools	Tarboro
77	69.3	Roanoke Rapids City Schools	Roanoke Rapids

Note: This section only includes districts with 1,500 or more students; All categories are ranked from high to low

78	69.2	Charlotte-Mecklenburg Schools	Charlotte	87	67.0	Person County Schools	Roxboro	100	63.6	Sampson County Schools	Clinton
78	69.2	Pitt County Schools	Greenville	87	67.0	Warren County Schools	Warrenton	101	63.5	Kannapolis City Schools	Kannapolis
78	69.2	Randolph County Schools	Asheboro	91	66.2	Scotland County Schools	Laurinburg	102	63.2	Thomasville City Schools	Thomasville
81	69.1	Martin County Schools	Williamston	92	66.1	Bladen County Schools	Elizabethtown	103	62.8	Jackson County Schools	Sylva
82	68.6	Cleveland County Schools	Shelby	92	66.1	Hoke County Schools	Raeford	104	62.7	Anson County Schools	Wadesboro
83	68.4	Wilkes County Schools	North Wilkesb	94	65.2	Granville County Schools	Oxford	105	61.4	Wilson County Schools	Wilson
84	68.3	Pasquotank County Schools	Elizabeth City	94	65.2	Greene County Schools	Snow Hill	106	60.9	Madison County Schools	Marshall
85	67.7	Mitchell County Schools	Bakersville	96	65.1	Bertie County Schools	Windsor	107	59.5	Northampton County Schools	Jackson
86	67.3	Caswell County Schools	Yanceyville	97	64.1	Clinton City Schools	Clinton	108	59.2	Lexington City Schools	Lexington
87	67.0	Duplin County Schools	Kenansville	97	64.1	Vance County Schools	Henderson	n/a	n/a	Lake Norman Charter	Huntersville
87	67.0	Lenoir County Public Schools	Kinston	99	63.8	Halifax County Schools	Halifax	n/a	n/a	Pine Lake Preparatory	Mooresville

Note: This section only includes districts with 1,500 or more students; All categories are ranked from high to low

The Nation's Report Card — **Mathematics**
2013 State Snapshot Report

North Carolina
Grade 4
Public Schools

Overall Results

- In 2013, the average score of fourth-grade students in North Carolina was 245. This was higher than the average score of 241 for public school students in the nation.
- The average score for students in North Carolina in 2013 (245) was not significantly different from their average score in 2011 (245) and was higher than their average score in 1992 (213).
- The score gap between higher performing students in North Carolina (those at the 75th percentile) and lower performing students (those at the 25th percentile) was 37 points in 2013. This performance gap was narrower than that in 1992 (45 points).
- The percentage of students in North Carolina who performed at or above the NAEP *Proficient* level was 45 percent in 2013. This percentage was not significantly different from that in 2011 (44 percent) and was greater than that in 1992 (13 percent).
- The percentage of students in North Carolina who performed at or above the NAEP *Basic* level was 87 percent in 2013. This percentage was not significantly different from that in 2011 (88 percent) and was greater than that in 1992 (50 percent).

Achievement-Level Percentages and Average Score Results

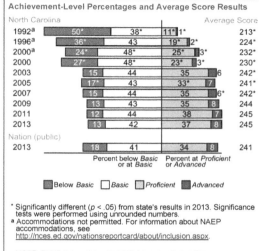

North Carolina / Average Score

Year	Percent below *Basic* or at *Basic*	Percent at *Proficient* or *Advanced*	Average Score
1992a	50* / 38*	11* / 1*	213*
1996a	36* / 43	19* / 2*	224*
2000a	24* / 48*	25* / 3*	232*
2000	27* / 48*	23* / 3*	230*
2003	15 / 44	35 / 6	242*
2005	17* / 43	33* / 7	241*
2007	15 / 44	35 / 6*	242*
2009	13 / 43	35 / 8	244
2011	12 / 44	38 / 7	245
2013	13 / 42	37 / 8	245

Nation (public)

| 2013 | 18 / 41 | 34 / 8 | 241 |

■ Below *Basic*   □ *Basic*   ▨ *Proficient*   ■ *Advanced*

* Significantly different (*p* < .05) from state's results in 2013. Significance tests were performed using unrounded numbers.
a Accommodations not permitted. For information about NAEP accommodations, see http://nces.ed.gov/nationsreportcard/about/inclusion.aspx.

NOTE: Detail may not sum to totals because of rounding.

Compare the Average Score in 2013 to Other States/Jurisdictions

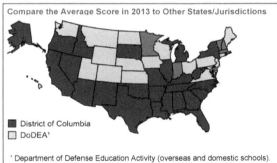

■ District of Columbia
□ DoDEA[1]

[1] Department of Defense Education Activity (overseas and domestic schools).

In 2013, the average score in North Carolina (245) was
- lower than those in 5 states/jurisdictions
- higher than those in 26 states/jurisdictions
- not significantly different from those in 20 states/jurisdictions

Average Scores for State/Jurisdiction and Nation (public)

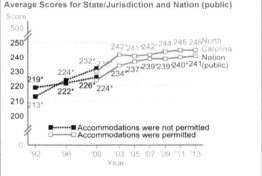

North Carolina: 242 241 242* 244 245 245
Nation (public): 234 237 239 239 240* 241
219* 224* 232* 236
222* 226* 224*
213*

■····■ Accommodations were not permitted
□—□ Accommodations were permitted

* Significantly different (*p* < .05) from 2013. Significance tests were performed using unrounded numbers.

NOTE: For information about NAEP accommodations, see http://nces.ed.gov/nationsreportcard/about/inclusion.aspx.

Results for Student Groups in 2013

Reporting Groups	Percent of students	Avg. score	Percentages at or above — Basic	Proficient	Percent at Advanced
Race/Ethnicity					
White	49	254	94	60	12
Black	26	230	76	22	1
Hispanic	16	239	85	35	3
Asian	3	261	90	67	30
American Indian/Alaska Native	2	225	68	16	#
Native Hawaiian/Pacific Islander	#	‡	‡	‡	‡
Two or more races	4	248	92	49	7
Gender					
Male	51	245	86	46	8
Female	49	245	87	45	8
National School Lunch Program					
Eligible	57	235	80	29	2
Not eligible	41	259	96	67	16

Rounds to zero.   ‡ Reporting standards not met.

NOTE: Detail may not sum to totals because of rounding, and because the "Information not available" category for the National School Lunch Program, which provides free/reduced-price lunches, is not displayed. Black includes African American and Hispanic includes Latino. Race categories exclude Hispanic origin.

Score Gaps for Student Groups

- In 2013, Black students had an average score that was 24 points lower than White students. This performance gap was narrower than that in 1992 (30 points).
- In 2013, Hispanic students had an average score that was 15 points lower than White students. Data are not reported for Hispanic students in 1992, because reporting standards were not met.
- In 2013, male students in North Carolina had an average score that was not significantly different from female students.
- In 2013, students who were eligible for free/reduced-price school lunch, an indicator of low family income, had an average score that was 24 points lower than students who were not eligible for free/reduced-price school lunch. This performance gap was not significantly different from that in 1996 (25 points).

ies NATIONAL CENTER FOR EDUCATION STATISTICS Institute of Education Sciences

NOTE: Statistical comparisons are calculated on the basis of unrounded scale scores or percentages.
SOURCE: U.S. Department of Education, Institute of Education Sciences, National Center for Education Statistics, National Assessment of Educational Progress (NAEP), various years, 1992–2013 Mathematics Assessments.

The Nation's Report Card Mathematics 2013 State Snapshot Report

North Carolina
Grade 8
Public Schools

Overall Results

- In 2013, the average score of eighth-grade students in North Carolina was 286. This was not significantly different from the average score of 284 for public school students in the nation.
- The average score for students in North Carolina in 2013 (286) was not significantly different from their average score in 2011 (286) and was higher than their average score in 1990 (250).
- The score gap between higher performing students in North Carolina (those at the 75th percentile) and lower performing students (those at the 25th percentile) was 49 points in 2013. This performance gap was not significantly different from that in 1990 (50 points).
- The percentage of students in North Carolina who performed at or above the NAEP *Proficient* level was 36 percent in 2013. This percentage was not significantly different from that in 2011 (37 percent) and was greater than that in 1990 (9 percent).
- The percentage of students in North Carolina who performed at or above the NAEP *Basic* level was 75 percent in 2013. This percentage was not significantly different from that in 2011 (75 percent) and was greater than that in 1990 (38 percent).

Achievement-Level Percentages and Average Score Results

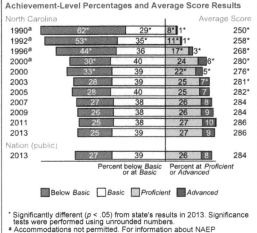

North Carolina   Average Score

Year	Below Basic	Basic	Proficient	Advanced	Average Score
1990ᵃ	62*	29*	8*	1*	250*
1992ᵃ	53*	35*	11*	1*	258*
1996ᵃ	44*	36	17*	3*	268*
2000ᵃ	30*	40	24	6*	280*
2000	33*	39	22*	5*	276*
2003	28	39	25	7*	281*
2005	28	40	25	7	282*
2007	27	38	26	8	284
2009	26	38	26	9	284
2011	25	38	27	10	286
2013	25	39	27	9	286

Nation (public)
| 2013 | 27 | 39 | 26 | 8 | 284 |

Percent below *Basic* or at *Basic*   Percent at *Proficient* or *Advanced*

■ Below *Basic*   □ *Basic*   ■ *Proficient*   ■ *Advanced*

* Significantly different (*p* < .05) from state's results in 2013. Significance tests were performed using unrounded numbers.
ᵃ Accommodations not permitted. For information about NAEP accommodations, see http://nces.ed.gov/nationsreportcard/about/inclusion.aspx.

NOTE: Detail may not sum to totals because of rounding.

Compare the Average Score in 2013 to Other States/Jurisdictions

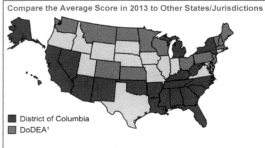

■ District of Columbia
■ DoDEA¹

¹ Department of Defense Education Activity (overseas and domestic schools).

In 2013, the average score in North Carolina (286) was
- lower than those in 15 states/jurisdictions
- higher than those in 21 states/jurisdictions
- not significantly different from those in 15 states/jurisdictions

Average Scores for State/Jurisdiction and Nation (public)

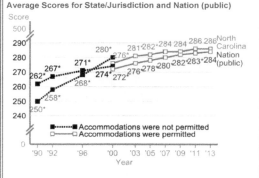

■------■ Accommodations were not permitted
□------□ Accommodations were permitted

* Significantly different (*p* < .05) from 2013. Significance tests were performed using unrounded numbers.

NOTE: For information about NAEP accommodations, see http://nces.ed.gov/nationsreportcard/about/inclusion.aspx.

Results for Student Groups in 2013

Reporting Groups	Percent of students	Avg. score	Percentages at or above Basic	Percentages at or above Proficient	Percent at Advanced
Race/Ethnicity					
White	53	296	85	48	14
Black	28	268	58	17	2
Hispanic	13	279	71	27	5
Asian	2	301	81	55	25
American Indian/Alaska Native	1	‡	‡	‡	‡
Native Hawaiian/Pacific Islander	#	‡	‡	‡	‡
Two or more races	3	283	69	36	11
Gender					
Male	51	285	74	36	10
Female	49	286	76	36	9
National School Lunch Program					
Eligible	54	274	65	23	4
Not eligible	45	300	87	53	16

\# Rounds to zero.   ‡ Reporting standards not met.

NOTE: Detail may not sum to totals because of rounding, and because the "Information not available" category for the National School Lunch Program, which provides free/reduced-price lunches, is not displayed. Black includes African American and Hispanic includes Latino. Race categories exclude Hispanic origin.

Score Gaps for Student Groups

- In 2013, Black students had an average score that was 28 points lower than White students. This performance gap was not significantly different from that in 1990 (30 points).
- In 2013, Hispanic students had an average score that was 17 points lower than White students. Data are not reported for Hispanic students in 1990, because reporting standards were not met.
- In 2013, male students in North Carolina had an average score that was not significantly different from female students.
- In 2013, students who were eligible for free/reduced-price school lunch, an indicator of low family income, had an average score that was 25 points lower than students who were not eligible for free/reduced-price school lunch. This performance gap was not significantly different from that in 1996 (27 points).

NOTE: Statistical comparisons are calculated on the basis of unrounded scale scores or percentages.
SOURCE: U.S. Department of Education, Institute of Education Sciences, National Center for Education Statistics, National Assessment of Educational Progress (NAEP), various years, 1990–2013 Mathematics Assessments.

The Nation's Report Card — Reading
2013 State Snapshot Report

North Carolina
Grade 4
Public Schools

Overall Results

- In 2013, the average score of fourth-grade students in North Carolina was 222. This was not significantly different from the average score of 221 for public school students in the nation.
- The average score for students in North Carolina in 2013 (222) was not significantly different from their average score in 2011 (221) and was higher than their average score in 1992 (212).
- The score gap between higher performing students in North Carolina (those at the 75th percentile) and lower performing students (those at the 25th percentile) was 46 points in 2013. This performance gap was not significantly different from that in 1992 (50 points).
- The percentage of students in North Carolina who performed at or above the NAEP *Proficient* level was 35 percent in 2013. This percentage was not significantly different from that in 2011 (34 percent) and was greater than that in 1992 (25 percent).
- The percentage of students in North Carolina who performed at or above the NAEP *Basic* level was 69 percent in 2013. This percentage was not significantly different from that in 2011 (68 percent) and was greater than that in 1992 (56 percent).

Achievement-Level Percentages and Average Score Results

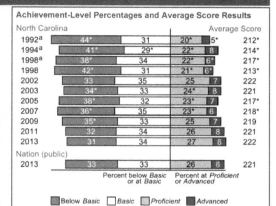

North Carolina / Average Score

Year	Below Basic	Basic	Proficient	Advanced	Average Score
1992[a]	44*	31	20*	5*	212*
1994[a]	41*	29*	22*	8	214*
1998[a]	38*	34	22*	6*	217*
1998	42*	31	21*	6*	213*
2002	33	35	25	7	222
2003	34*	33	24*	8	221
2005	38*	32	23*	7	217*
2007	36*	35	23*	6	218*
2009	35*	33	25	7	219
2011	32	34	26	8	221
2013	31	34	27	8	222

Nation (public)

| 2013 | 33 | 33 | 26 | 8 | 221 |

Percent below *Basic* or at *Basic* — Percent at *Proficient* or *Advanced*

■ Below *Basic*   □ *Basic*   ▨ *Proficient*   ■ *Advanced*

* Significantly different (*p* < .05) from state's results in 2013. Significance tests were performed using unrounded numbers.
[a] Accommodations not permitted. For information about NAEP accommodations, see http://nces.ed.gov/nationsreportcard/about/inclusion.aspx.

NOTE: Detail may not sum to totals because of rounding.

Compare the Average Score in 2013 to Other States/Jurisdictions

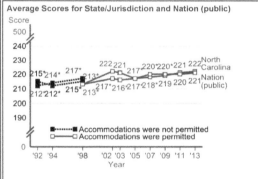

■ District of Columbia
▨ DoDEA[1]

[1] Department of Defense Education Activity (overseas and domestic schools).

In 2013, the average score in North Carolina (222) was
- lower than those in 14 states/jurisdictions
- higher than those in 18 states/jurisdictions
- not significantly different from those in 19 states/jurisdictions

Average Scores for State/Jurisdiction and Nation (public)

(graph) Score vs Year

North Carolina: 215*, 214*, 217*, 213*, 222, 221, 217*, 220*, 220*, 221, 222
Nation (public): 212*, 212*, 215*, 213*, 217*, 216*, 217*, 218*, 219, 220, 221

■┄┄■ Accommodations were not permitted
□—□ Accommodations were permitted

'92 '94 '98 '02 '03 '05 '07 '09 '11 '13   Year

* Significantly different (*p* < .05) from 2013. Significance tests were performed using unrounded numbers.

NOTE: For information about NAEP accommodations, see http://nces.ed.gov/nationsreportcard/about/inclusion.aspx.

Results for Student Groups in 2013

Reporting Groups	Percent of students	Avg. score	Percentages at or above Basic	Percentages at or above Proficient	Percent at Advanced
Race/Ethnicity					
White	49	232	81	47	11
Black	26	210	55	20	2
Hispanic	16	210	56	23	4
Asian	3	238	81	57	20
American Indian/Alaska Native	2	206	55	16	2
Native Hawaiian/Pacific Islander	#	‡	‡	‡	‡
Two or more races	4	225	71	38	10
Gender					
Male	51	219	65	32	6
Female	49	226	73	39	10
National School Lunch Program					
Eligible	58	211	58	22	3
Not eligible	41	237	84	53	15

Rounds to zero.   ‡ Reporting standards not met.

NOTE: Detail may not sum to totals because of rounding, and because the "Information not available" category for the National School Lunch Program, which provides free/reduced-price lunches, is not displayed. Black includes African American and Hispanic includes Latino. Race categories exclude Hispanic origin.

Score Gaps for Student Groups

- In 2013, Black students had an average score that was 23 points lower than White students. This performance gap was not significantly different from that in 1992 (26 points).
- In 2013, Hispanic students had an average score that was 22 points lower than White students. Data are not reported for Hispanic students in 1992, because reporting standards were not met.
- In 2013, female students in North Carolina had an average score that was higher than male students by 8 points.
- In 2013, students who were eligible for free/reduced-price school lunch, an indicator of low family income, had an average score that was 26 points lower than students who were not eligible for free/reduced-price school lunch. This performance gap was not significantly different from that in 1998 (26 points).

NOTE: Statistical comparisons are calculated on the basis of unrounded scale scores or percentages.
SOURCE: U.S. Department of Education, Institute of Education Sciences, National Center for Education Statistics, National Assessment of Educational Progress (NAEP), various years, 1992–2013 Reading Assessments.

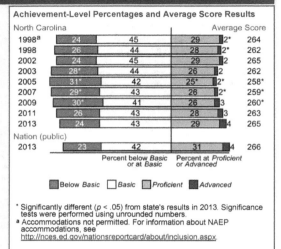

Overall Results

- In 2013, the average score of eighth-grade students in North Carolina was 265. This was not significantly different from the average score of 266 for public school students in the nation.
- The average score for students in North Carolina in 2013 (265) was not significantly different from their average score in 2011 (263) and in 1998 (262).
- The score gap between higher performing students in North Carolina (those at the 75th percentile) and lower performing students (those at the 25th percentile) was 44 points in 2013. This performance gap was not significantly different from that in 1998 (44 points).
- The percentage of students in North Carolina who performed at or above the NAEP *Proficient* level was 33 percent in 2013. This percentage was not significantly different from that in 2011 (31 percent) and in 1998 (30 percent).
- The percentage of students in North Carolina who performed at or above the NAEP *Basic* level was 76 percent in 2013. This percentage was not significantly different from that in 2011 (74 percent) and in 1998 (74 percent).

Achievement-Level Percentages and Average Score Results

* Significantly different (*p* < .05) from state's results in 2013. Significance tests were performed using unrounded numbers.
a Accommodations not permitted. For information about NAEP accommodations, see http://nces.ed.gov/nationsreportcard/about/inclusion.aspx.

NOTE: Detail may not sum to totals because of rounding.

Compare the Average Score in 2013 to Other States/Jurisdictions

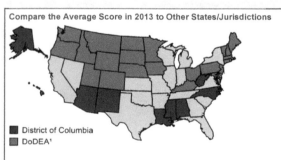

- District of Columbia
- DoDEA[1]

[1] Department of Defense Education Activity (overseas and domestic schools).

In 2013, the average score in North Carolina (265) was
- lower than those in 23 states/jurisdictions
- higher than those in 9 states/jurisdictions
- not significantly different from those in 19 states/jurisdictions

Average Scores for State/Jurisdiction and Nation (public)

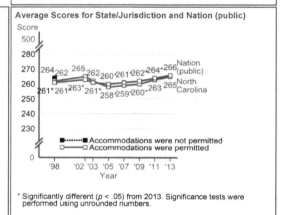

* Significantly different (*p* < .05) from 2013. Significance tests were performed using unrounded numbers.

NOTE: For information about NAEP accommodations, see http://nces.ed.gov/nationsreportcard/about/inclusion.aspx.

Results for Student Groups in 2013

Reporting Groups	Percent of students	Avg. score	Percentages at or above Basic	Proficient	Percent at Advanced
Race/Ethnicity					
White	53	273	83	43	6
Black	28	251	63	16	1
Hispanic	13	258	72	23	1
Asian	2	273	84	45	6
American Indian/Alaska Native	1	‡	‡	‡	‡
Native Hawaiian/Pacific Islander	#	‡	‡	‡	‡
Two or more races	3	266	73	34	5
Gender					
Male	51	258	70	26	2
Female	49	271	81	40	6
National School Lunch Program					
Eligible	54	253	66	19	1
Not eligible	45	278	88	49	7

Rounds to zero.   ‡ Reporting standards not met.

NOTE: Detail may not sum to totals because of rounding, and because the "Information not available" category for the National School Lunch Program, which provides free/reduced-price lunches, is not displayed. Black includes African American and Hispanic includes Latino. Race categories exclude Hispanic origin.

Score Gaps for Student Groups

- In 2013, Black students had an average score that was 23 points lower than White students. This performance gap was not significantly different from that in 1998 (25 points).
- In 2013, Hispanic students had an average score that was 15 points lower than White students. Data are not reported for Hispanic students in 1998, because reporting standards were not met.
- In 2013, female students in North Carolina had an average score that was higher than male students by 13 points.
- In 2013, students who were eligible for free/reduced-price school lunch, an indicator of low family income, had an average score that was 25 points lower than students who were not eligible for free/reduced-price school lunch. This performance gap was not significantly different from that in 1998 (24 points).

North Carolina
Grade 4
Public Schools

Science 2009

State Snapshot Report

2009 Science Assessment Content

Guided by a new framework, the NAEP science assessment was updated in 2009 to keep the content current with key developments in science, curriculum standards, assessments, and research. The 2009 framework organizes science content into three broad content areas.
Physical science includes concepts related to properties and changes of matter, forms of energy, energy transfer and conservation, position and motion of objects, and forces affecting motion.
Life science includes concepts related to organization and development, matter and energy transformations, interdependence, heredity and reproduction, and evolution and diversity.
Earth and space sciences includes concepts related to objects in the universe, the history of the Earth, properties of Earth materials, tectonics, energy in Earth systems, climate and weather, and biogeochemical cycles.
The 2009 science assessment was composed of 143 questions at grade 4, 162 at grade 8, and 179 at grade 12. Students responded to only a portion of the questions, which included both multiple-choice questions and questions that required a written response.

Compare the Average Score in 2009 to Other States/Jurisdictions

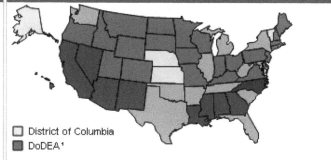

☐ District of Columbia
■ DoDEA[1]

[1] Department of Defense Education Activity (overseas and domestic schools).

In 2009, the average score in **North Carolina** was
- lower than those in 24 states/jurisdictions
- higher than those in 9 states/jurisdictions
- not significantly different from those in 13 states/jurisdictions
- 5 states/jurisdictions did not participate

Overall Results

- In 2009, the average score of fourth-grade students in North Carolina was 148. This was not significantly different from the average score of 149 for public school students in the nation.
- The percentage of students in North Carolina who performed at or above the NAEP *Proficient* level was 30 percent in 2009. This percentage was not significantly different from the nation (32 percent).
- The percentage of students in North Carolina who performed at or above the NAEP *Basic* level was 69 percent in 2009. This percentage was not significantly different from the nation (71 percent).

Achievement-Level Percentages and Average Score Results

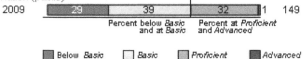

NOTE: Detail may not sum to totals because of rounding.

Results for Student Groups in 2009

Reporting Groups	Percent of students	Avg. score	Percentages at or above Basic	Proficient	Percent at Advanced
Gender					
Male	51	149	70	33	1
Female	49	146	68	27	#
Race/Ethnicity					
White	54	162	86	45	1
Black	28	126	44	9	#
Hispanic	11	132	51	11	#
Asian/Pacific Islander	2	163	83	52	#
American Indian/Alaska Native	1	128	46	10	#
National School Lunch Program					
Eligible	48	133	53	13	#
Not eligible	51	162	84	46	1

Rounds to zero.

NOTE: Detail may not sum to totals because of rounding, and because the "Information not available" category for the National School Lunch Program, which provides free/reduced-price lunches, and the "Unclassified" category for race/ethnicity are not displayed.

Score Gaps for Student Groups

- In 2009, male students in North Carolina had an average score that was higher than female students.
- In 2009, Black students had an average score that was 36 points lower than White students. This performance gap was not significantly different from the nation (35 points).
- In 2009, Hispanic students had an average score that was 30 points lower than White students. This performance gap was not significantly different from the nation (32 points).
- In 2009, students who were eligible for free/reduced-price school lunch, an indicator of low family income, had an average score that was 29 points lower than students who were not eligible for free/reduced-price school lunch. This performance gap was not significantly different from the nation (29 points).

NOTE: Statistical comparisons are calculated on the basis of unrounded scale scores or percentages.
SOURCE: U.S. Department of Education, Institute of Education Sciences, National Center for Education Statistics, National Assessment of Educational Progress (NAEP), 2009 Science Assessment.

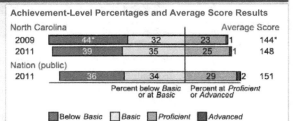

Overall Results

- In 2011, the average score of eighth-grade students in North Carolina was 148. This was lower than the average score of 151 for public school students in the nation.
- The average score for students in North Carolina in 2011 (148) was higher than their average score in 2009 (144).
- In 2011, the score gap between students in North Carolina at the 75th percentile and students at the 25th percentile was 44 points. This performance gap was not significantly different from that of 2009 (48 points).
- The percentage of students in North Carolina who performed at or above the NAEP *Proficient* level was 26 percent in 2011. This percentage was not significantly different from that in 2009 (24 percent).
- The percentage of students in North Carolina who performed at or above the NAEP *Basic* level was 61 percent in 2011. This percentage was greater than that in 2009 (56 percent).

Achievement-Level Percentages and Average Score Results

		Average Score
North Carolina		
2009	44* / 32 / 23 / 1	144*
2011	39 / 35 / 25 / 1	148
Nation (public)		
2011	36 / 34 / 29 / 2	151

■ Below *Basic*　□ *Basic*　▦ *Proficient*　■ *Advanced*

* Significantly different (*p* < .05) from state's results in 2011. Significance tests were performed using unrounded numbers.

NOTE: Detail may not sum to totals because of rounding.

Compare the Average Score in 2011 to Other States/Jurisdictions

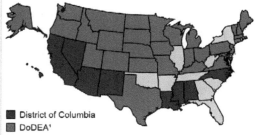

■ District of Columbia
▦ DoDEA[1]

[1] Department of Defense Education Activity (overseas and domestic schools).

In 2011, the average score in North Carolina (148) was
- lower than those in 31 states/jurisdictions
- higher than those in 9 states/jurisdictions
- not significantly different from those in 11 states/jurisdictions

Average Scores for State/Jurisdiction and Nation (public)

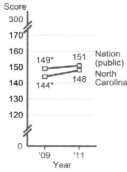

Nation (public): 149* → 151
North Carolina: 144* → 148

* Significantly different (*p* < .05) from 2011. Significance tests were performed using unrounded numbers.

Results for Student Groups in 2011

Reporting Groups	Percent of students	Avg. score	Percentages at or above Basic	Percentages at or above Proficient	Percent at Advanced
Race/Ethnicity					
White	55	160	76	38	2
Black	26	125	33	7	#
Hispanic	11	138	50	15	#
Asian	3	161	79	35	5
American Indian/Alaska Native	1	136	51	13	#
Native Hawaiian/Pacific Islander	#	‡	‡	‡	‡
Two or more races	4	143	59	20	#
Gender					
Male	51	149	62	30	2
Female	49	147	60	23	1
National School Lunch Program					
Eligible	50	136	47	14	#
Not eligible	49	160	76	39	2

Rounds to zero.　　‡ Reporting standards not met.

NOTE: Detail may not sum to totals because of rounding, and because the "Information not available" category for the National School Lunch Program, which provides free/reduced-price lunches, is not displayed. Black includes African American and Hispanic includes Latino. Race categories exclude Hispanic origin.

Score Gaps for Student Groups

- In 2011, Black students had an average score that was 34 points lower than White students. This performance gap was not significantly different from that in 2009 (37 points).
- In 2011, Hispanic students had an average score that was 22 points lower than White students. This performance gap was not significantly different from that in 2009 (26 points).
- In 2011, male students in North Carolina had an average score that was not significantly different from female students.
- In 2011, students who were eligible for free/reduced-price school lunch, an indicator of low family income, had an average score that was 24 points lower than students who were not eligible for free/reduced-price school lunch. This performance gap was not significantly different from that in 2009 (28 points).

NCES
National Center for
Education Statistics

The Nation's Report Card
State **Writing** 2002
Snapshot Report

North Carolina
Grade 4
Public School

NCES 2003-532NC4

The writing assessment of the National Assessment of Educational Progress (NAEP) measures narrative, informative, and persuasive writing–three purposes identified in the NAEP framework. The NAEP writing scale ranges from 0 to 300.

Overall Writing Results for North Carolina

- The average scale score for fourth-grade students in North Carolina was 159.

- North Carolina's average score (159) was higher[1] than that of the nation's public schools (153).

- Students' average scale scores in North Carolina were higher than those in 30 jurisdictions[2], not significantly different from those in 14 jurisdictions, and lower than those in 3 jurisdictions.

- The percentage of students who performed at or above the NAEP *Proficient* level was 32 percent. The percentage of students who performed at or above the *Basic* level was 88 percent.

Student Percentage at Each Achievement Level

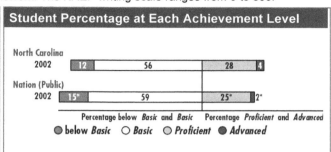

North Carolina
2002 | 12 | 56 | 28 | 4

Nation (Public)
2002 | 15* | 59 | 25* | 2*

Percentage below *Basic* and *Basic*   Percentage *Proficient* and *Advanced*
● below *Basic*   ○ *Basic*   ○ *Proficient*   ● *Advanced*

Performance of NAEP Reporting Groups in North Carolina

Reporting groups	Percentage of students	Average Score	Below *Basic*	*Basic*	*Proficient*	*Advanced*
Male	50	151 ↑	16 ↓	59	23 ↑	2 ↑
Female	50	167 ↑	8	53	34	5 ↑
White	58	167 ↑	8 ↓	52 ↓	34 ↑	6 ↑
Black	31	147 ↑	18 ↓	62	19 ↑	1
Hispanic	6	145	21	59	19	1
Asian/Pacific Islander	2	161	14	46	34	6
American Indian/Alaska Native	2	---	---	---	---	---
Free/reduced-priced school lunch						
Eligible	49	146 ↑	19	61	19 ↑	1
Not eligible	47	172 ↑	5 ↓	49 ↓	38 ↑	7 ↑
Information not available	4	159	10	59	28	3

Average Score Gaps Between Selected Groups

- Female students in North Carolina had an average score that was higher than that of male students (16 points). This performance gap was not significantly different from that of the Nation (18 points).

- White students had an average score that was higher than that of Black students (20 points). This performance gap was not significantly different from that of the Nation (20 points).

- White students had an average score that was higher than that of Hispanic students (22 points). This performance gap was not significantly different from that of the Nation (19 points).

- Students who were not eligible for free/reduced-price school lunch had an average score that was higher than that of students who were eligible (25 points). This performance gap was not significantly different from that of the Nation (22 points).

Writing Scale Scores at Selected Percentiles

Scale Score Distribution

	25th Percentile	50th Percentile	75th Percentile
North Carolina	133	159 ↑	184 ↑
Nation (Public)	128	153	178

An examination of scores at different percentiles on the 0-300 NAEP writing scale at each grade indicates how well students at lower, middle, and higher levels of the distribution performed. For example, the data above shows that 75 percent of students in public schools nationally scored below *178*, while 75 percent of students in North Carolina scored below *184*.

\# Percentage rounds to zero.   --- Reporting standards not met; sample size insufficient to permit a reliable estimate.
* Significantly different from North Carolina.   ↑ Significantly higher than, ↓ lower than appropriate subgroup in the nation (public).
[1] Comparisons (higher/lower/not different) are based on statistical tests. The .05 level was used for testing statistical significance.
[2] "Jurisdictions" includes participating states and other jurisdictions (such as Guam or the District of Columbia).
NOTE: Detail may not sum to totals because of rounding. Score gaps are calculated based on differences between unrounded average scale scores.
Visit http://nces.ed.gov/nationsreportcard/states/ for additional results and detailed information.
SOURCE: U.S. Department of Education, Institute of Education Sciences, National Center for Education Statistics, National Assessment of Educational Progress (NAEP), 2002 Writing Assessment.

NCES 2008-470NC8

The Nation's Report Card Writing 2007 State Snapshot Report

North Carolina
Grade 8
Public Schools

The National Assessment of Educational Progress (NAEP) assesses writing for three purposes identified in the NAEP framework: narrative, informative, and persuasive. The NAEP writing scale ranges from 0 to 300.

Overall Writing Results for North Carolina

- In 2007, the average scale score for eighth-grade students in North Carolina was 153. This was lower than their average score in 2002 (157) and was not significantly different from their average score in 1998 (150).[1]
- North Carolina's average score (153) in 2007 was not significantly different from that of the nation's public schools (154).
- Of the 45 states and one other jurisdiction that participated in the 2007 eighth-grade assessment, students' average scale score in North Carolina was higher than those in 10 jurisdictions, not significantly different from those in 17 jurisdictions, and lower than those in 18 jurisdictions.[2]
- The percentage of students in North Carolina who performed at or above the NAEP *Proficient* level was 29 percent in 2007. This percentage was smaller than that in 2002 (34 percent) and was not significantly different from that in 1998 (27 percent).
- The percentage of students in North Carolina who performed at or above the NAEP *Basic* level was 87 percent in 2007. This percentage was not significantly different from that in 2002 (87 percent) and was not significantly different from that in 1998 (85 percent).

Percentages at NAEP Achievement Levels and Average Score

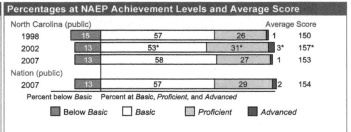

NOTE: The NAEP grade 8 writing achievement levels correspond to the following scale points: Below *Basic*, 113 or lower; *Basic*, 114–172; *Proficient*, 173–223; *Advanced*, 224 or above.

Performance of NAEP Reporting Groups in North Carolina: 2007

Reporting groups	Percent of students	Average score	Percent below *Basic*	Percent of students at or above *Basic*	Percent of students at or above *Proficient*	Percent *Advanced*
Male	51	142	20	80	18↓	#
Female	49	164	6	94	40	2↓
White	57↓	162	8	92	38	2↓
Black	29	138	21	79	12	#
Hispanic	7↑	138	25	75	16	#
Asian/Pacific Islander	2	164	9	91	45	3
American Indian/Alaska Native	1↑	145	22	78	23	4
Eligible for National School Lunch Program	44↑	141	20	80	16	#
Not eligible for National School Lunch Program	55	163	7	93	39	2↓

Average Score Gaps Between Selected Groups

- In 2007, male students in North Carolina had an average score that was lower than that of female students by 22 points. This performance gap was not significantly different from that of 1998 (21 points).
- In 2007, Black students had an average score that was lower than that of White students by 24 points. This performance gap was not significantly different from that of 1998 (25 points).
- In 2007, Hispanic students had an average score that was lower than that of White students by 24 points. Data are not reported for Hispanic students in 1998, because reporting standards were not met.
- In 2007, students who were eligible for free/reduced-price school lunch, an indicator of poverty, had an average score that was lower than that of students who were not eligible for free/reduced-price school lunch by 22 points. This performance gap was narrower than that of 1998 (28 points).
- In 2007, the score gap between students at the 75th percentile and students at the 25th percentile was 46 points. This performance gap was not significantly different from that of 1998 (48 points).

Writing Scores at Selected Percentiles in North Carolina

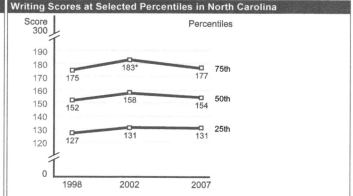

NOTE: Scores at selected percentiles on the NAEP writing scale indicate how well students at lower, middle, and higher levels performed.

Rounds to zero.
‡ Reporting standards not met.
* Significantly different from 2007.
↑ Significantly higher than 2002. ↓ Significantly lower than 2002.
[1] Comparisons (higher/lower/narrower/wider/not different) are based on statistical tests. The .05 level with appropriate adjustments for multiple comparisons was used for testing statistical significance. Statistical comparisons are calculated on the basis of unrounded scale scores or percentages. Comparisons across jurisdictions and comparisons with the nation or within a jurisdiction across years may be affected by differences in exclusion rates for students with disabilities (SD) and English language learners (ELL). The exclusion rates for SD and ELL in North Carolina were 2 percent and "percentage rounds to zero" in 2007, respectively. For more information on NAEP significance testing, see http://nces.ed.gov/nationsreportcard/writing/interpret-results.asp#statistical.
[2] "Jurisdiction" refers to states, the District of Columbia, and the Department of Defense Education Activity schools.
NOTE: Detail may not sum to totals because of rounding and because the "Information not available" category for the National School Lunch Program, which provides free and reduced-price lunches, and the "Unclassified" category for race/ethnicity are not displayed. Visit http://nces.ed.gov/nationsreportcard/states/ for additional results and detailed information.
SOURCE: U.S. Department of Education, Institute of Education Sciences, National Center for Education Statistics, National Assessment of Educational Progress (NAEP), 1998, 2002, and 2007 Writing Assessments.

Table 2. 2013–14 End-of-Grade Statewide Participation and Performance
Grade 3 English Language Arts (ELA)

CATEGORY	# Verified Mbership[1]	% of Verified Mbership	GENERAL TEST		ALTERNATE ASSESSMENTS				# Medical Exclusions	% Medical Exclusions	NOT TESTED						TOTAL FOR ALL TESTS			
			# Tested (General Test)	% Tested (General Test)	# Tested NC EXTEND2	% Tested NC EXTEND2	# Tested NC EXTEND1	% Tested NC EXTEND1			# LEP Exclusions	% LEP Exclusions	# Absent	% Absent	# Other[2]	% Other	# Participating	% Participating	# Proficient	% Proficient
All Students	**116,184**	**100.0**	**111,182**	**95.7**	**3,136**	**2.7**	**1,063**	**0.9**	**475**	**0.4**	**79**	**0.1**	**249**	**0.2**	**0**	**0.0**	**115,381**	**99.4**	**69,471**	**60.2**
Female	56,773	48.9	55,082	97.0	975	1.7	331	0.6	234	0.4	38	0.1	113	0.2	0	0.0	56,388	99.4	35,889	63.6
Male	59,411	51.1	56,100	94.4	2,161	3.6	732	1.2	241	0.4	41	0.1	136	0.2	0	0.0	58,993	99.4	33,582	56.9
American Indian	1,459	1.3	1,396	95.7	36	2.5	18	1.2	6	0.4	1	0.1	2	0.1	0	0.0	1,450	99.5	662	45.7
Asian	3,398	2.9	3,212	94.5	41	1.2	30	0.9	96	2.8	0	0.0	19	0.6	0	0.0	3,283	96.6	2,473	75.3
Black	29,404	25.3	27,897	94.9	991	3.4	385	1.3	42	0.1	19	0.1	70	0.2	0	0.0	29,273	99.6	12,699	43.4
Hispanic	19,382	16.7	18,334	94.6	569	2.9	156	0.8	269	1.4	10	0.1	44	0.2	0	0.0	19,059	98.4	8,572	45.0
Multi-Racial	4,254	3.7	4,077	95.8	114	2.7	42	1.0	3	0.1	1	0.0	17	0.4	0	0.0	4,233	99.5	2,657	62.8
Native Hawaiian/Pacific Islander	133	0.1	127	95.5	3	2.3	0	0.0	3	2.3	0	0.0	0	0.0	0	0.0	130	97.7	70	53.8
White	58,154	50.1	56,139	96.5	1,382	2.4	432	0.7	56	0.1	48	0.1	97	0.2	0	0.0	57,953	99.7	42,338	73.1
Economically Disadvantaged	**66,471**	**57.2**	**62,869**	**94.6**	**2,387**	**3.6**	**777**	**1.2**	**263**	**0.4**	**42**	**0.1**	**133**	**0.2**	**0**	**0.0**	**66,033**	**99.4**	**30,409**	**46.1**
Not Economically Disadvantaged	49,713	42.8	48,313	97.2	749	1.5	286	0.6	212	0.4	37	0.1	116	0.2	0	0.0	49,348	99.3	39,062	79.2
Migrant	161	0.1	159	98.8	1	0.6	0	0.0	1	0.6	0	0.0	0	0.0	0	0.0	160	99.4	54	33.8
Not Migrant	116,023	99.9	111,023	95.7	3,135	2.7	1,063	0.9	474	0.4	79	0.1	249	0.2	0	0.0	115,221	99.4	69,417	60.2
Limited English Proficient (LEP)	**13,094**	**11.3**	**11,982**	**91.5**	**487**	**3.7**	**94**	**0.7**	**475**	**3.6**	**4**	**0.0**	**52**	**0.4**	**0**	**0.0**	**12,563**	**96.0**	**4,090**	**32.6**
Not LEP	103,090	88.7	99,200	96.2	2,649	2.6	969	0.9	0	0.0	75	0.1	197	0.2	0	0.0	102,818	99.8	65,381	63.6
All Students with Disabilities	**17,016**	**14.6**	**12,876**	**75.7**	**2,977**	**17.5**	**1,041**	**6.1**	**8**	**0.0**	**56**	**0.3**	**58**	**0.3**	**0**	**0.0**	**16,894**	**99.6**	**5,221**	**30.9**
Students Without Disabilities	99,168	85.4	98,306	99.1	159	0.2	22	0.0	467	0.5	23	0.0	191	0.2	0	0.0	98,487	99.3	64,250	65.2
Autism	1,318	1.1	620	47.0	322	24.4	364	27.6	0	0.0	3	0.2	9	0.7	0	0.0	1,306	99.3	500	38.3
Deaf-Blindness	1	0.0	0	0.0	0	0.0	0	0.0	0	0.0	1	100.0	0	0.0	0	0.0	0		*	*
Deafness	9	0.0	2	22.2	4	44.4	3	33.3	0	0.0	0	0.0	0	0.0	0	0.0	9	100.0	3	33.3
Serious Emotional Disability	410	0.4	301	73.4	97	23.7	5	1.2	0	0.0	0	0.0	7	1.7	0	0.0	403	98.3	116	28.8
Hearing Impairment	144	0.1	109	75.7	35	24.3	0	0.0	0	0.0	0	0.0	0	0.0	0	0.0	144	100.0	42	29.2
Intellectual Disability - Mild	773	0.7	221	28.6	390	50.5	155	20.1	2	0.3	1	0.1	4	0.5	0	0.0	766	99.2	146	19.1
Intellectual Disability - Moderate	264	0.2	6	2.3	30	11.4	228	86.4	0	0.0	0	0.0	0	0.0	0	0.0	264	100.0	135	51.1
Intellectual Disability - Severe	63	0.1	0	0.0	1	1.6	55	87.3	0	0.0	7	11.1	0	0.0	0	0.0	56	100.0	10	17.9
Specific Learning Disability	5,928	5.1	4,475	75.5	1,426	24.1	7	0.1	3	0.1	3	0.1	14	0.2	0	0.0	5,908	99.7	843	14.3
Multiple Disabilities	197	0.2	6	3.0	18	9.1	142	72.1	0	0.0	26	13.2	5	2.5	0	0.0	166	97.1	52	31.3
Other Health Impairment	2,525	2.2	1,853	73.4	584	23.1	68	2.7	1	0.0	11	0.4	8	0.3	0	0.0	2,505	99.6	556	22.2
Orthopedic Impairment	55	0.0	38	69.1	9	16.4	6	10.9	0	0.0	0	0.0	2	3.6	0	0.0	53	96.4	22	41.5
Speech or Language Impairment	5,269	4.5	5,207	98.8	49	0.9	2	0.0	1	0.0	1	0.0	9	0.2	0	0.0	5,258	99.8	2,778	52.8
Traumatic Brain Injury	23	0.0	9	39.1	7	30.4	5	21.7	0	0.0	0	0.0	0	0.0	0	0.0	21	100.0	4	19.0
Visual Impairment	37	0.0	29	78.4	5	13.5	1	2.7	1	2.7	1	2.7	0	0.0	0	0.0	35	97.2	14	40.0

[1]The "Verified Membership" for the end-of-grade tests is the number of student grade and course enrollment records in PowerSchool on the first day of test administration in the testing cycle.

[2]Data for "Other" includes misadministrations, transfers, and unknown causes.

*Performance data are not reported when membership is fewer than five. Performance data that are less than or equal to 5.0 percent, or greater than or equal to 95.0 percent, are not displayed. Some columns may not add up to the total due to miscoding or rounding. The disability categories were revised in 2007–08.

Notes: The total for "All Students with Disabilities" includes Section 504.

Data received from local education agencies, charter schools, and regional school after December 5, 2014 are not included in this table.

Prepared by the NCDPI Division of Accountability Services/Test Development Section.

Table 2a. 2013–14 End-of-Grade Statewide Participation and Performance
Grade 3 Mathematics

MATHEMATICS

CATEGORY	# Verified Mbership[1]	% of Verified Mbership	GENERAL TEST		ALTERNATE ASSESSMENTS				NOT TESTED								TOTAL FOR ALL TESTS			
			# Tested (General Test)	% Tested (General Test)	# Tested NC EXTEND2	% Tested NC EXTEND2	# Tested NC EXTEND1	% Tested NC EXTEND1	# Medical Exclusions	% Medical Exclusions	# LEP Exclusions	% LEP Exclusions	# Absent	% Absent	# Other[2]	% Other	# Participating	% Participating	# Proficient	% Proficient
(All)	**116,184**	**100.0**	**112,017**	**96.4**	**2,327**	**2.0**	**1,063**	**0.9**	**479**	**0.4**	**78**	**0.1**	**220**	**0.2**	**0**	**0.0**	**115,407**	**99.4**	**70,302**	**60.9**
Female	56,773	48.9	55,329	97.5	743	1.3	331	0.6	236	0.4	37	0.1	97	0.2	0	0.0	56,403	99.4	34,941	61.9
Male	59,411	51.1	56,688	95.4	1,584	2.7	732	1.2	243	0.4	41	0.1	123	0.2	0	0.0	59,004	99.4	35,361	59.9
American Indian	1,459	1.3	1,404	96.2	28	1.9	18	1.2	7	0.5	1	0.1	9	0.1	0	0.0	1,450	99.5	662	45.7
Asian	3,398	2.9	3,233	95.1	26	0.8	30	0.9	100	2.9	0	0.0	9	0.3	0	0.0	3,289	96.8	2,704	82.2
Black	29,404	25.3	28,055	95.4	832	2.8	385	1.3	41	0.1	19	0.1	72	0.2	0	0.0	29,272	99.6	12,274	41.9
Hispanic	19,382	16.7	18,528	95.6	392	2.0	156	0.8	267	1.4	10	0.1	29	0.1	0	0.0	19,076	98.5	10,024	52.5
Multi-Racial	4,254	3.7	4,102	96.4	91	2.1	42	1.0	3	0.1	1	0.0	15	0.4	0	0.0	4,235	99.6	2,591	61.2
Native Hawaiian/Pacific Islander	133	0.1	128	96.2	2	1.5	0	0.0	3	2.3	0	0.0	0	0.0	0	0.0	130	97.7	73	56.2
White	58,154	50.1	56,567	97.3	956	1.6	432	0.7	58	0.1	47	0.1	94	0.2	0	0.0	57,955	99.7	41,974	72.4
Economically Disadvantaged	**66,471**	**57.2**	**63,432**	**95.4**	**1,831**	**2.8**	**777**	**1.2**	**264**	**0.4**	**42**	**0.1**	**125**	**0.2**	**0**	**0.0**	**66,040**	**99.4**	**31,548**	**47.8**
Not Economically Disadvantaged	49,713	42.8	48,585	97.7	496	1.0	286	0.6	215	0.4	36	0.1	95	0.2	0	0.0	49,367	99.4	38,754	78.5
Migrant	161	0.1	159	98.8	1	0.6	0	0.0	1	0.6	0	0.0	0	0.0	0	0.0	160	99.4	71	44.4
Not Migrant	116,023	99.9	111,858	96.4	2,326	2.0	1,063	0.9	478	0.4	78	0.1	220	0.2	0	0.0	115,247	99.4	70,231	60.9
Limited English Proficient (LEP)	**13,094**	**11.3**	**12,157**	**92.8**	**337**	**2.6**	**94**	**0.7**	**479**	**3.7**	**4**	**0.0**	**23**	**0.2**	**0**	**0.0**	**12,588**	**96.2**	**5,648**	**44.9**
Not LEP	103,090	88.7	99,860	96.9	1,990	1.9	969	0.9	0	0.0	74	0.1	197	0.2	0	0.0	102,819	99.8	64,654	62.9
All Students with Disabilities	**17,016**	**14.6**	**13,640**	**80.2**	**2,215**	**13.0**	**1,041**	**6.1**	**9**	**0.1**	**55**	**0.3**	**56**	**0.3**	**0**	**0.0**	**16,896**	**99.6**	**5,833**	**34.5**
Students Without Disabilities	99,168	85.4	98,377	99.2	112	0.1	22	0.0	470	0.5	23	0.0	164	0.2	0	0.0	98,511	99.4	64,469	65.4
Autism	1,318	1.1	663	50.3	280	21.2	364	27.6	1	0.1	3	0.2	7	0.5	0	0.0	1,307	99.4	466	35.7
Deaf-Blindness	1	0.0	0	0.0	0	0.0	0	0.0	0	0.0	1	100.0	0	0.0	0	0.0	0		*	*
Deafness	9	0.0	3	33.3	3	33.3	3	33.3	0	0.0	0	0.0	0	0.0	0	0.0	9	100.0	2	22.2
Serious Emotional Disability	410	0.4	318	77.6	80	19.5	5	1.2	0	0.0	0	0.0	7	1.7	0	0.0	403	98.3	92	22.8
Hearing Impairment	144	0.1	118	81.9	26	18.1	0	0.0	0	0.0	0	0.0	0	0.0	0	0.0	144	100.0	51	35.4
Intellectual Disability - Mild	773	0.7	232	30.0	378	48.9	155	20.1	2	0.3	1	0.1	5	0.6	0	0.0	765	99.1	118	15.4
Intellectual Disability - Moderate	264	0.2	8	3.0	27	10.2	228	86.4	0	0.0	0	0.0	1	0.4	0	0.0	263	99.6	100	38.0
Intellectual Disability - Severe	63	0.1	0	0.0	1	1.6	55	87.3	0	0.0	7	11.1	0	0.0	0	0.0	56	100.0	12	21.4
Specific Learning Disability	5,928	5.1	5,022	84.7	879	14.8	7	0.1	3	0.1	3	0.1	14	0.2	0	0.0	5,908	99.7	1,330	22.5
Multiple Disabilities	197	0.2	8	4.1	17	8.6	142	72.1	0	0.0	26	13.2	4	2.0	0	0.0	167	97.7	35	21.0
Other Health Impairment	2,525	2.2	1,964	77.8	474	18.8	68	2.7	1	0.0	10	0.4	8	0.3	0	0.0	2,506	99.6	538	21.5
Orthopedic Impairment	55	0.0	41	74.5	6	10.9	6	10.9	0	0.0	0	0.0	2	3.6	0	0.0	53	96.4	17	32.1
Speech or Language Impairment	5,269	4.5	5,223	99.1	34	0.6	2	0.0	1	0.0	1	0.0	8	0.2	0	0.0	5,259	99.8	3,053	58.1
Traumatic Brain Injury	23	0.0	9	39.1	7	30.4	5	21.7	0	0.0	2	8.7	0	0.0	0	0.0	21	100.0	4	19.0
Visual Impairment	37	0.0	31	83.8	3	8.1	1	2.7	1	2.7	2	2.7	0	0.0	0	0.0	35	97.2	15	42.9

[1] The "Verified Membership" for the end-of-grade tests is the number of student grade and course enrollment records in PowerSchool on the first day of test administration in the testing cycle.

[2] Data for "Other" includes misadministrations, transfers, and unknown causes.

*Performance data are not reported when membership is fewer than five. Performance data that are less than or equal to 5.0 percent, or greater than or equal to 95.0 percent, are not displayed. Some columns may not add up to the total due to miscoding or rounding. The disability categories were revised in 2007–08.

Notes:　The total for "All Students with Disabilities" includes Section 504.

Data received from local education agencies, charter schools, and regional school after December 5, 2014 are not included in this table.

Prepared by the NCDPI Division of Accountability Services/Test Development Section.

Table 2b. 2013–14 End-of-Grade Statewide Participation and Performance
Grade 4 English Language Arts (ELA)

ELA

CATEGORY	GENERAL TEST				ALTERNATE ASSESSMENTS				NOT TESTED								TOTAL FOR ALL TESTS			
	# Verified Mbership[1]	% of Verified Mbership	# Tested (General Test)	% Tested (General Test)	# Tested NC EXTEND2	% Tested NC EXTEND2	# Tested NC EXTEND1	% Tested NC EXTEND1	# Medical Exclusions	% Medical Exclusions	# LEP Exclusions	% LEP Exclusions	# Absent	% Absent	# Other[2]	% Other	# Participating	% Participating	# Proficient	% Proficient
	108,350	100.0	103,553	95.6	3,004	2.8	1,018	0.9	469	0.4	80	0.1	226	0.2	0	0.0	107,575	99.4	59,854	55.6
Male	52,581	48.5	50,912	96.8	964	1.8	339	0.6	234	0.4	33	0.1	99	0.2	0	0.0	52,215	99.4	30,929	59.2
Female	55,769	51.5	52,641	94.4	2,040	3.7	679	1.2	235	0.4	47	0.1	127	0.2	0	0.0	55,360	99.4	28,925	52.2
American Indian	1,371	1.3	1,301	94.9	46	3.4	11	0.8	10	0.7	2	0.1	1	0.1	0	0.0	1,358	99.2	560	41.2
Asian	3,187	2.9	2,988	93.8	46	1.4	23	0.7	113	3.5	1	0.0	16	0.5	0	0.0	3,057	96.0	2,191	71.7
Black	26,669	24.6	25,115	94.2	1,110	4.2	329	1.2	28	0.1	22	0.1	65	0.2	0	0.0	26,554	99.7	9,858	37.1
Hispanic	17,014	15.7	15,990	94.0	571	3.4	142	0.8	269	1.6	6	0.0	36	0.2	0	0.0	16,703	98.2	6,333	37.9
Multi-Racial	4,426	4.1	4,259	96.2	104	2.3	49	1.1	0	0.0	3	0.1	11	0.2	0	0.0	4,412	99.8	2,627	59.5
Native Hawaiian/Pacific Islander	99	0.1	90	90.9	5	5.1	1	1.0	0	0.0	0	0.0	0	0.0	0	0.0	96	97.0	55	57.3
White	55,584	51.3	53,810	96.8	1,122	2.0	463	0.8	46	0.1	46	0.1	97	0.2	0	0.0	55,395	99.7	38,230	69.0
Economically Disadvantaged	60,488	55.8	57,027	94.3	2,377	3.9	687	1.1	241	0.4	38	0.1	118	0.2	0	0.0	60,091	99.4	24,322	40.5
Not Economically Disadvantaged	47,862	44.2	46,526	97.2	627	1.3	331	0.7	228	0.5	42	0.1	108	0.2	0	0.0	47,484	99.3	35,532	74.8
Migrant	146	0.1	139	95.2	5	3.4	0	0.0	0	0.0	0	0.0	2	1.4	0	0.0	144	98.6	45	31.3
Not Migrant	108,204	99.9	103,414	95.6	2,999	2.8	1,018	0.9	469	0.4	80	0.1	224	0.2	0	0.0	107,431	99.4	59,809	55.7
Limited English Proficient (LEP)	6,910	6.4	5,825	84.3	500	7.2	79	1.1	469	6.8	2	0.0	35	0.5	0	0.0	6,404	92.7	786	12.3
Not LEP	101,440	93.6	97,728	96.3	2,504	2.5	939	0.9	0	0.0	78	0.1	191	0.2	0	0.0	101,171	99.8	59,068	58.4
All Students with Disabilities	17,582	16.2	13,491	76.7	2,962	16.8	1,006	5.7	9	0.1	46	0.3	68	0.4	0	0.0	17,459	99.6	4,413	25.3
Students Without Disabilities	90,768	83.8	90,062	99.2	42	0.0	12	0.0	460	0.5	34	0.0	158	0.2	0	0.0	90,116	99.3	55,441	61.5
Autism	1,327	1.2	660	49.7	281	21.2	373	28.1	1	0.1	3	0.2	9	0.7	0	0.0	1,314	99.2	420	32.0
Deaf-Blindness	2	0.0	0	0.0	1	50.0	1	50.0	0	0.0	0	0.0	0	0.0	0	0.0	2	100.0	*	*
Deafness	4	0.0	2	50.0	2	50.0	0	0.0	0	0.0	0	0.0	0	0.0	0	0.0	4	100.0	*	*
Serious Emotional Disability	431	0.4	332	77.0	89	20.6	2	0.5	1	0.2	1	0.2	6	1.4	0	0.0	423	98.4	93	22.0
Hearing Impairment	145	0.1	117	80.7	27	18.6	1	0.7	0	0.0	0	0.0	0	0.0	0	0.0	145	100.0	34	23.4
Intellectual Disability - Mild	929	0.9	272	29.3	493	53.1	159	17.1	0	0.0	0	0.0	5	0.5	0	0.0	924	99.5	145	15.7
Intellectual Disability - Moderate	270	0.2	8	3.0	22	8.1	235	87.0	1	0.4	0	0.0	4	1.5	0	0.0	265	98.1	139	52.5
Intellectual Disability - Severe	53	0.0	0	0.0	0	0.0	48	90.6	1	0.4	4	7.5	1	1.9	0	0.0	48	98.0	20	41.7
Specific Learning Disability	7,246	6.7	5,804	80.1	1,414	19.5	7	0.1	5	0.1	3	0.0	13	0.2	0	0.0	7,225	99.8	931	12.9
Multiple Disabilities	186	0.2	10	5.4	20	10.8	126	67.7	0	0.0	24	12.9	6	3.2	0	0.0	156	96.3	51	32.7
Other Health Impairment	2,975	2.7	2,342	78.7	568	19.1	42	1.4	1	0.0	11	0.4	11	0.4	0	0.0	2,952	99.6	574	19.4
Orthopedic Impairment	55	0.1	43	78.2	11	20.0	1	1.8	0	0.0	0	0.0	0	0.0	0	0.0	55	100.0	18	32.7
Speech or Language Impairment	3,881	3.6	3,844	99.0	22	0.6	3	0.1	0	0.0	0	0.0	12	0.3	0	0.0	3,869	99.7	1,968	50.9
Traumatic Brain Injury	29	0.0	14	48.3	8	27.6	6	20.7	0	0.0	0	0.0	1	3.4	0	0.0	28	96.6	*	<=5%
Visual Impairment	49	0.0	43	87.8	4	8.2	2	4.1	0	0.0	0	0.0	0	0.0	0	0.0	49	100.0	19	38.8

[1] The "Verified Membership" for the end-of-grade tests is the number of student grade and course enrollment records in PowerSchool on the first day of test administration in the testing cycle.

[2] Data for "Other" includes misadministrations, transfers, and unknown causes.

*Performance data are not reported when membership is fewer than five. Performance data that are less than or equal to 5.0 percent, or greater than or equal to 95.0 percent, are not displayed. Some columns may not add up to the total due to miscoding or rounding. The disability categories were revised in 2007–08.

Notes: The total for "All Students with Disabilities" includes Section 504.

Data received from local education agencies, charter schools, and regional school after December 5, 2014 are not included in this table.

Prepared by the NCDPI Division of Accountability Services/Test Development Section.

Table 2c. 2013–14 End-of-Grade Statewide Participation and Performance
Grade 4 Mathematics

MATHEMATICS

CATEGORY	# Verified Mbership[1]	% of Verified Mbership	GENERAL TEST		ALTERNATE ASSESSMENTS				NOT TESTED								TOTAL FOR ALL TESTS			
			# Tested (General Test)	% Tested (General Test)	# Tested NC EXTEND2	% Tested NC EXTEND2	# Tested NC EXTEND1	% Tested NC EXTEND1	# Medical Exclusions	% Medical Exclusions	# LEP Exclusions	% LEP Exclusions	# Absent	% Absent	# Other[2]	% Other	# Participating	% Participating	# Proficient	% Proficient
All Students	108,350	100.0	103,977	96.0	2,586	2.4	1,018	0.9	468	0.4	82	0.1	219	0.2	0	0.0	107,581	99.4	58,438	54.3
Female	52,581	48.5	50,995	97.0	884	1.7	339	0.6	235	0.4	34	0.1	94	0.2	0	0.0	52,218	99.4	28,252	54.1
Male	55,769	51.5	52,982	95.0	1,702	3.1	679	1.2	233	0.4	48	0.1	125	0.2	0	0.0	55,363	99.4	30,186	54.5
American Indian	1,371	1.3	1,307	95.3	41	3.0	11	0.8	10	0.7	2	0.1	0	0.0	0	0.0	1,359	99.3	532	39.1
Asian	3,187	2.9	3,001	94.2	37	1.2	23	0.7	114	3.6	1	0.0	11	0.3	0	0.0	3,061	96.1	2,395	78.2
Black	26,669	24.6	25,209	94.5	1,015	3.8	329	1.2	28	0.1	22	0.1	66	0.2	0	0.0	26,553	99.6	8,706	32.8
Hispanic	17,014	15.7	16,113	94.7	455	2.7	142	0.8	267	1.6	6	0.0	31	0.2	0	0.0	16,710	98.2	7,216	43.2
Multi-Racial	4,426	4.1	4,272	96.5	91	2.1	49	1.1	0	0.0	3	0.1	11	0.2	0	0.0	4,412	99.8	2,430	55.1
Native Hawaiian/Pacific Islander	99	0.1	90	90.9	5	5.1	1	1.0	3	3.0	0	0.0	0	0.0	0	0.0	96	97.0	56	58.3
White	55,584	51.3	53,985	97.1	942	1.7	463	0.8	46	0.1	48	0.1	100	0.2	0	0.0	55,390	99.7	37,103	67.0
Economically Disadvantaged	60,488	55.8	57,352	94.8	2,059	3.4	687	1.1	243	0.4	38	0.1	109	0.2	0	0.0	60,098	99.4	23,817	39.6
Not Economically Disadvantaged	47,862	44.2	46,625	97.4	527	1.1	331	0.7	225	0.5	44	0.1	110	0.2	0	0.0	47,483	99.3	34,621	72.9
Migrant	146	0.1	139	95.2	5	3.4	0	0.0	0	0.0	0	0.0	2	1.4	0	0.0	144	98.6	45	31.3
Not Migrant	108,204	99.9	103,838	96.0	2,581	2.4	1,018	0.9	468	0.4	82	0.1	217	0.2	0	0.0	107,437	99.4	58,393	54.4
Limited English Proficient (LEP)	6,910	6.4	5,935	85.9	399	5.8	79	1.1	468	6.8	2	0.0	27	0.4	0	0.0	6,413	92.8	1,415	22.1
Not LEP	101,440	93.6	98,042	96.7	2,187	2.2	939	0.9	0	0.0	80	0.1	192	0.2	0	0.0	101,168	99.8	57,023	56.4
All Students with Disabilities	17,582	16.2	13,899	79.1	2,554	14.5	1,006	5.7	9	0.1	46	0.3	68	0.4	0	0.0	17,459	99.6	4,652	26.6
Students Without Disabilities	90,768	83.8	90,078	99.2	32	0.0	12	0.0	459	0.5	36	0.0	151	0.2	0	0.0	90,122	99.3	53,786	59.7
Autism	1,327	1.2	669	50.4	270	20.3	373	28.1	1	0.1	3	0.2	11	0.8	0	0.0	1,312	99.1	435	33.2
Deaf-Blindness	2	0.0	0	0.0	1	50.0	1	50.0	0	0.0	0	0.0	0	0.0	0	0.0	2	100.0	*	*
Deafness	4	0.0	2	50.0	2	50.0	0	0.0	0	0.0	0	0.0	0	0.0	0	0.0	4	100.0	*	*
Serious Emotional Disability	431	0.4	343	79.6	77	17.9	2	0.5	1	0.2	1	0.2	7	1.6	0	0.0	422	98.1	65	15.4
Hearing Impairment	145	0.1	119	82.1	25	17.2	1	0.7	0	0.0	0	0.0	0	0.0	0	0.0	145	100.0	39	26.9
Intellectual Disability - Mild	929	0.9	270	29.1	495	53.3	159	17.1	0	0.0	0	0.0	5	0.5	0	0.0	924	99.5	145	15.7
Intellectual Disability - Moderate	270	0.2	8	3.0	22	8.1	235	87.0	1	0.4	0	0.0	4	1.5	0	0.0	265	98.1	128	48.3
Intellectual Disability - Severe	53	0.0	1	1.9	0	0.0	48	90.6	0	0.0	4	7.5	0	0.0	0	0.0	49	100.0	22	44.9
Specific Learning Disability	7,246	6.7	6,143	84.8	1,076	14.8	7	0.1	5	0.1	3	0.0	12	0.2	0	0.0	7,226	99.8	1,221	16.9
Multiple Disabilities	186	0.2	10	5.4	20	10.8	126	67.7	0	0.0	24	12.9	6	3.2	0	0.0	156	96.3	54	34.6
Other Health Impairment	2,975	2.7	2,386	80.2	525	17.6	42	1.4	1	0.0	11	0.4	10	0.3	0	0.0	2,953	99.6	460	15.6
Orthopedic Impairment	55	0.1	42	76.4	12	21.8	1	1.8	0	0.0	0	0.0	0	0.0	0	0.0	55	100.0	10	18.2
Speech or Language Impairment	3,881	3.6	3,849	99.2	17	0.4	3	0.1	0	0.0	0	0.0	12	0.3	0	0.0	3,869	99.7	2,051	53.0
Traumatic Brain Injury	29	0.0	14	48.3	8	27.6	6	20.7	0	0.0	0	0.0	1	3.4	0	0.0	28	96.6	4	14.3
Visual Impairment	49	0.0	43	87.8	4	8.2	2	4.1	0	0.0	0	0.0	0	0.0	0	0.0	49	100.0	17	34.7

[1] The "Verified Membership" for the end-of-grade tests is the number of student grade and course enrollment records in PowerSchool on the first day of test administration in the testing cycle.

[2] Data for "Other" includes misadministrations, transfers, and unknown causes.

*Performance data are not reported when membership is fewer than five. Performance data that are less than or equal to 5.0 percent, or greater than or equal to 95.0 percent, are not displayed. Some columns may not add up to the total due to miscoding or rounding. The disability categories were revised in 2007–08.

Notes: The total for "All Students with Disabilities" includes Section 504.

Data received from local education agencies, charter schools, and regional school after December 5, 2014 are not included in this table.

Prepared by the NCDPI Division of Accountability Services/Test Development Section.

Table 2d. 2013–14 End-of-Grade Statewide Participation and Performance
Grade 5 English Language Arts (ELA)

CATEGORY	# Verified Mbership[1]	% of Verified Mbership	GENERAL TEST		ALTERNATE ASSESSMENTS				NOT TESTED								TOTAL FOR ALL TESTS			
			# Tested (General Test)	% Tested (General Test)	# Tested NC EXTEND2	% Tested NC EXTEND2	# Tested NC EXTEND1	% Tested NC EXTEND1	# Medical Exclusions	% Medical Exclusions	# LEP Exclusions	% LEP Exclusions	# Absent	% Absent	# Other[2]	% Other	# Participating	% Participating	# Proficient	% Proficient
All Students	116,683	100.0	111,175	95.3	3,664	3.1	1,121	1.0	422	0.4	103	0.1	192	0.2	0	0.0	115,960	99.5	62,341	53.8
Female	56,843	48.7	54,950	96.7	1,207	2.1	368	0.6	200	0.4	44	0.1	72	0.1	0	0.0	56,525	99.5	31,525	55.8
Male	59,840	51.3	56,225	94.0	2,457	4.1	753	1.3	222	0.4	59	0.1	120	0.2	0	0.0	59,435	99.4	30,816	51.8
American Indian	1,555	1.3	1,488	95.7	38	2.4	19	1.2	5	0.3	1	0.1	4	0.3	0	0.0	1,545	99.4	580	37.5
Asian	3,371	2.9	3,191	94.7	49	1.5	27	0.8	89	2.6	0	0.0	15	0.4	0	0.0	3,267	96.9	2,318	71.0
Black	29,231	25.1	27,373	93.6	1,375	4.7	394	1.3	21	0.1	24	0.1	44	0.2	0	0.0	29,142	99.8	10,220	35.1
Hispanic	17,916	15.4	16,872	94.2	630	3.5	136	0.8	235	1.3	13	0.1	27	0.2	0	0.0	17,638	98.5	6,590	37.4
Multi-Racial	4,670	4.0	4,466	95.6	144	3.1	44	0.9	5	0.1	4	0.1	7	0.1	0	0.0	4,654	99.7	2,603	55.9
Native Hawiian/Pacific Islander	115	0.1	107	93.0	3	2.6	0	0.0	5	4.3	0	0.0	0	0.0	0	0.0	110	95.7	62	56.4
White	59,825	51.3	57,678	96.4	1,425	2.4	501	0.8	62	0.1	61	0.1	95	0.2	0	0.0	59,604	99.7	39,968	67.1
Economically Disadvantaged	64,925	55.6	60,889	93.8	2,859	4.4	775	1.2	253	0.4	48	0.1	100	0.2	0	0.0	64,523	99.5	24,767	38.4
Not Economically Disadvantaged	51,758	44.4	50,286	97.2	805	1.6	346	0.7	169	0.3	55	0.1	92	0.2	0	0.0	51,437	99.5	37,574	73.0
Migrant	138	0.1	129	93.5	2	1.4	2	1.4	5	3.6	0	0.0	0	0.0	0	0.0	133	96.4	27	20.3
Not Migrant	116,545	99.9	111,046	95.3	3,662	3.1	1,119	1.0	417	0.4	103	0.1	192	0.2	0	0.0	115,827	99.5	62,314	53.8
Limited English Proficient (LEP)	5,520	4.7	4,460	80.8	513	9.3	81	1.5	422	7.8	4	0.1	34	0.6	0	0.0	5,054	91.6	467	9.2
Not LEP	111,163	95.3	106,715	96.0	3,151	2.8	1,040	0.9	0	0.0	99	0.1	158	0.1	0	0.0	110,906	99.9	61,874	55.8
All Students with Disabilities	18,710	16.0	13,846	74.0	3,627	19.4	1,107	5.9	8	0.0	66	0.4	56	0.3	0	0.0	18,580	99.7	4,355	23.4
Students Without Disabilities	97,973	84.0	97,329	99.3	37	0.0	14	0.0	414	0.4	37	0.0	136	0.1	0	0.0	97,380	99.4	57,986	59.5
Autism	1,427	1.2	663	46.5	359	25.2	394	27.6	0	0.0	5	0.4	6	0.4	0	0.0	1,416	99.6	571	40.3
Deaf-Blindness	2	0.0	0	0.0	1	50.0	1	50.0	0	0.0	0	0.0	0	0.0	0	0.0	2	100.0	*	*
Deafness	11	0.0	4	36.4	6	54.5	0	0.0	0	0.0	0	0.0	1	9.1	0	0.0	10	90.9	*	*
Serious Emotional Disability	506	0.4	383	75.7	115	22.7	2	0.4	0	0.0	2	0.4	4	0.8	0	0.0	500	99.2	117	23.4
Hearing Impairment	149	0.1	110	73.8	33	22.1	6	4.0	0	0.0	0	0.0	0	0.0	0	0.0	149	100.0	25	16.8
Intellectual Disability - Mild	1,023	0.9	318	31.1	532	52.0	168	16.4	0	0.0	0	0.0	5	0.5	0	0.0	1,018	99.5	163	16.0
Intellectual Disability - Moderate	342	0.3	10	2.9	46	13.5	282	82.5	1	0.3	2	0.6	1	0.3	0	0.0	338	99.4	218	64.5
Intellectual Disability - Severe	61	0.1	0	0.0	0	0.0	52	85.2	0	0.0	8	13.1	1	1.6	0	0.0	52	98.1	23	44.2
Specific Learning Disability	8,247	7.1	6,474	78.5	1,750	21.2	3	0.0	5	0.1	4	0.0	11	0.1	0	0.0	8,227	99.8	1,012	12.3
Multiple Disabilities	206	0.2	8	3.9	16	7.8	142	68.9	0	0.0	34	16.5	6	2.9	0	0.0	166	96.5	73	44.0
Other Health Impairment	3,457	3.0	2689	77.8	709	20.5	39	1.1	1	0.0	7	0.2	12	0.3	0	0.0	3,437	99.6	637	18.5
Orthopedic Impairment	69	0.1	36	52.2	20	29.0	11	15.9	0	0.0	2	2.9	0	0.0	0	0.0	67	100.0	23	34.3
Speech or Language Impairment	3,131	2.7	3,098	98.9	22	0.7	1	0.0	0	0.0	1	0.0	9	0.3	0	0.0	3,121	99.7	1,472	47.2
Traumatic Brain Injury	28	0.0	11	39.3	11	39.3	6	21.4	0	0.0	0	0.0	0	0.0	0	0.0	28	100.0	6	21.4
Visual Impairment	50	0.0	42	84.0	6	12.0	0	0.0	1	2.0	1	2.0	0	0.0	0	0.0	48	98.0	14	29.2

[1]The "Verified Membership" for the end-of-grade tests is the number of student grade and course enrollment records in PowerSchool on the first day of test administration in the testing cycle.

[2]Data for "Other" includes misadministrations, transfers, and unknown causes.

*Performance data are not reported when membership is fewer than five. Performance data that are less than or equal to 5.0 percent, or greater than or equal to 95.0 percent, are not displayed. Some columns may not add up to the total due to miscoding or rounding. The disability categories were revised in 2007–08.

Notes: The total for "All Students with Disabilities" includes Section 504.

Data received from local education agencies, charter schools, and regional school after December 5, 2014 are not included in this table.

Prepared by the NCDPI Division of Accountability Services/Test Development Section.

Table 2e. 2013–14 End-of-Grade Statewide Participation and Performance
Grade 5 Mathematics

MATHEMATICS

CATEGORY	# Verified Mbership[1]	% of Verified Mbership	GENERAL TEST # Tested (General Test)	GENERAL TEST % Tested (General Test)	ALTERNATE ASSESSMENTS # Tested NC EXTEND2	ALTERNATE ASSESSMENTS % Tested NC EXTEND2	ALTERNATE ASSESSMENTS # Tested NC EXTEND1	ALTERNATE ASSESSMENTS % Tested NC EXTEND1	NOT TESTED # Medical Exclusions	NOT TESTED % Medical Exclusions	NOT TESTED # LEP Exclusions	NOT TESTED % LEP Exclusions	NOT TESTED # Absent	NOT TESTED % Absent	NOT TESTED # Other[2]	NOT TESTED % Other	TOTAL # Participating	TOTAL % Participating	TOTAL # Proficient	TOTAL % Proficient
All Students	**116,683**	**100.0**	**111,718**	**95.7**	**3,135**	**2.7**	**1,120**	**1.0**	**431**	**0.4**	**108**	**0.1**	**171**	**0.1**	**0**	**0.0**	**115,973**	**99.5**	**65,412**	**56.4**
Female	56,843	48.7	55,065	96.9	1,097	1.9	367	0.6	204	0.4	47	0.1	63	0.1	0	0.0	56,529	99.5	32,640	57.7
Male	59,840	51.3	56,653	94.7	2,038	3.4	753	1.3	227	0.4	61	0.1	108	0.2	0	0.0	59,444	99.4	32,772	55.1
American Indian	1,555	1.3	1,494	96.1	33	2.1	19	1.2	5	0.3	1	0.1	3	0.2	0	0.0	1,546	99.5	577	37.3
Asian	3,371	2.9	3,197	94.8	45	1.3	27	0.8	93	2.8	0	0.0	9	0.3	0	0.0	3,269	97.0	2,638	80.7
Black	29,231	25.1	27,514	94.1	1,228	4.2	394	1.3	21	0.1	26	0.1	48	0.2	0	0.0	29,136	99.8	10,571	36.3
Hispanic	17,916	15.4	17,038	95.1	478	2.7	136	0.8	238	1.3	13	0.1	13	0.1	0	0.0	17,652	98.6	8,608	48.8
Multi-Racial	4,670	4.0	4,492	96.2	118	2.5	44	0.9	6	0.1	4	0.1	6	0.1	0	0.0	4,654	99.7	2,659	57.1
Native Hawaiian/Pacific Islander	115	0.1	107	93.0	3	2.6	0	0.0	5	4.3	0	0.0	0	0.0	0	0.0	110	95.7	61	55.5
White	59,825	51.3	57,876	96.7	1,230	2.1	500	0.8	63	0.1	64	0.1	92	0.2	0	0.0	59,606	99.7	40,298	67.6
Economically Disadvantaged	**64,925**	**55.6**	**61,322**	**94.5**	**2,426**	**3.7**	**775**	**1.2**	**256**	**0.4**	**51**	**0.1**	**95**	**0.1**	**0**	**0.0**	**64,523**	**99.5**	**27,334**	**42.4**
Not Economically Disadvantaged	51,758	44.4	50,396	97.4	709	1.4	345	0.7	175	0.3	57	0.1	76	0.1	0	0.0	51,450	99.5	38,078	74.0
Migrant	138	0.1	129	93.5	2	1.4	2	1.4	5	3.6	0	0.0	0	0.0	0	0.0	133	96.4	46	34.6
Not Migrant	116,545	99.9	111,589	95.7	3,133	2.7	1,118	1.0	426	0.4	108	0.1	171	0.1	0	0.0	115,840	99.5	65,366	56.4
Limited English Proficient (LEP)	**5,520**	**4.7**	**4,605**	**83.4**	**388**	**7.0**	**81**	**1.5**	**431**	**7.8**	**5**	**0.1**	**10**	**0.2**	**0**	**0.0**	**5,074**	**92.0**	**1,111**	**21.9**
Not LEP	111,163	95.3	107,113	96.4	2,747	2.5	1,039	0.9	0	0.0	103	0.1	161	0.1	0	0.0	110,899	99.9	64,301	58.0
All Students with Disabilities	**18,710**	**16.0**	**14,369**	**76.8**	**3,099**	**16.6**	**1,106**	**5.9**	**9**	**0.0**	**70**	**0.4**	**57**	**0.3**	**0**	**0.0**	**18,574**	**99.6**	**4,701**	**25.3**
Students Without Disabilities	97,973	84.0	97,349	99.4	36	0.0	14	0.0	422	0.4	38	0.0	114	0.1	0	0.0	97,399	99.5	60,711	62.3
Autism	1,427	1.2	673	47.2	349	24.5	394	27.6	0	0.0	5	0.4	6	0.4	0	0.0	1,416	99.6	504	35.6
Deaf-Blindness	2	0.0	0	0.0	1	50.0	1	50.0	0	0.0	0	0.0	0	0.0	0	0.0	2	100.0	*	*
Deafness	11	0.0	5	45.5	5	45.5	0	0.0	0	0.0	0	0.0	1	9.1	0	0.0	10	90.9	*	*
Serious Emotional Disability	506	0.4	388	76.7	111	21.9	2	0.4	0	0.0	3	0.6	2	0.4	0	0.0	501	99.6	79	15.8
Hearing Impairment	149	0.1	115	77.2	28	18.8	6	4.0	0	0.0	0	0.0	0	0.0	0	0.0	149	100.0	36	24.2
Intellectual Disability - Mild	1,023	0.9	314	30.7	535	52.3	168	16.4	0	0.0	0	0.0	6	0.6	0	0.0	1,017	99.4	129	12.7
Intellectual Disability - Moderate	342	0.3	11	3.2	45	13.2	281	82.2	1	0.3	2	0.6	2	0.6	0	0.0	337	99.1	135	40.1
Intellectual Disability - Severe	61	0.1	0	0.0	0	0.0	52	85.2	1	1.6	8	13.1	0	0.0	0	0.0	52	98.1	16	30.8
Specific Learning Disability	8,247	7.1	6,915	83.8	1,308	15.9	3	0.0	5	0.1	5	0.1	11	0.1	0	0.0	8,226	99.8	1,517	18.4
Multiple Disabilities	206	0.2	8	3.9	16	7.8	142	68.9	0	0.0	34	16.5	6	2.9	0	0.0	166	96.5	49	29.5
Other Health Impairment	3,457	3.0	2,746	79.4	648	18.7	39	1.1	1	0.0	9	0.3	14	0.4	0	0.0	3,433	99.6	581	16.9
Orthopedic Impairment	69	0.1	36	52.2	19	27.5	11	15.9	0	0.0	2	2.9	1	1.4	0	0.0	66	98.5	24	36.4
Speech or Language Impairment	3,131	2.7	3,105	99.2	16	0.5	1	0.0	0	0.0	1	0.0	8	0.3	0	0.0	3,122	99.7	1,605	51.4
Traumatic Brain Injury	28	0.0	11	39.3	11	39.3	6	21.4	0	0.0	0	0.0	0	0.0	0	0.0	28	100.0	6	21.4
Visual Impairment	50	0.0	42	84.0	6	12.0	0	0.0	1	2.0	0	2.0	0	0.0	0	0.0	48	98.0	19	39.6

[1] The "Verified Membership" for the end-of-grade tests is the number of student grade and course enrollment records in PowerSchool on the first day of test administration in the testing cycle.

[2] Data for "Other" includes misadministrations, transfers, and unknown causes.

*Performance data are not reported when membership is fewer than five. Performance data that are less than or equal to 5.0 percent, or greater than or equal to 95.0 percent, are not displayed. Some columns may not add up to the total due to miscoding or rounding. The disability categories were revised in 2007–08.

Notes: The total for "All Students with Disabilities" includes Section 504.

Data received from local education agencies, charter schools, and regional school after December 5, 2014 are not included in this table.

Prepared by the NCDPI Division of Accountability Services/Test Development Section.

Table 2f. 2013–14 End-of-Grade Statewide Participation and Performance
Grade 6 English Language Arts (ELA)

CATEGORY	GENERAL TEST				ALTERNATE ASSESSMENTS				NOT TESTED								TOTAL FOR ALL TESTS			
	# Verified Mbership[1]	% of Verified Mbership	# Tested (General Test)	% Tested (General Test)	# Tested NC EXTEND2	% Tested NC EXTEND2	# Tested NC EXTEND1	% Tested NC EXTEND1	# Medical Exclusions	% Medical Exclusions	# LEP Exclusions	% LEP Exclusions	# Absent	% Absent	# Other[2]	% Other	# Participating	% Participating	# Proficient	% Proficient
All Students	116,667	100.0	110,955	95.1	3,733	3.2	1,103	0.9	418	0.4	82	0.1	376	0.3	0	0.0	115,791	99.4	65,806	56.8
Female	56,589	48.5	54,630	96.5	1,237	2.2	332	0.6	191	0.3	40	0.1	159	0.3	0	0.0	56,199	99.4	33,570	59.7
Male	60,078	51.5	56,325	93.8	2,496	4.2	771	1.3	227	0.4	42	0.1	217	0.4	0	0.0	59,592	99.3	32,236	54.1
American Indian	1,535	1.3	1,473	96.0	38	2.5	13	0.8	8	0.5	1	0.1	2	0.1	0	0.0	1,524	99.3	638	41.9
Asian	3,210	2.8	3,060	95.3	33	1.0	14	0.4	87	2.7	4	0.1	12	0.4	0	0.0	3,107	96.9	2,281	73.4
Black	30,356	26.0	28,327	93.3	1,463	4.8	374	1.2	37	0.1	20	0.1	135	0.4	0	0.0	30,164	99.4	11,343	37.6
Hispanic	17,443	15.0	16,385	93.9	646	3.7	127	0.7	223	1.3	13	0.1	49	0.3	0	0.0	17,158	98.4	7,156	41.7
Multi-Racial	4,319	3.7	4,135	95.7	123	2.8	43	1.0	2	0.0	1	0.0	15	0.3	0	0.0	4,301	99.6	2,531	58.8
Native Hawaiian/Pacific Islander	130	0.1	121	93.1	3	2.3	0	0	5	3.8	0	0.0	1	0.8	0	0.0	124	95.4	61	49.2
White	59,674	51.1	57,454	96.3	1,427	2.4	532	0.9	56	0.1	43	0.1	162	0.3	0	0.0	59,413	99.6	41,796	70.3
Economically Disadvantaged	64,720	55.5	60,543	93.5	2,929	4.5	726	1.1	234	0.4	48	0.1	240	0.4	0	0.0	64,198	99.3	26,584	41.4
Not Economically Disadvantaged	51,947	44.5	50,412	97.0	804	1.5	377	0.7	184	0.4	34	0.1	136	0.3	0	0.0	51,593	99.4	39,222	76.0
Migrant	146	0.1	136	93.2	4	2.7	0	0.0	5	3.4	0	0.0	1	0.7	0	0.0	140	95.9	37	26.4
Not Migrant	116,521	99.9	110,819	95.1	3,729	3.2	1,103	0.9	413	0.4	82	0.1	375	0.3	0	0.0	115,651	99.3	65,769	56.9
Limited English Proficient (LEP)	5,389	4.6	4,305	79.9	546	10.1	80	1.5	418	7.8	5	0.1	35	0.6	0	0.0	4,931	91.6	492	10.0
Not LEP	111,278	95.4	106,650	95.8	3,187	2.9	1,023	0.9	0	0.0	77	0.1	341	0.3	0	0.0	110,860	99.7	65,314	58.9
All Students with Disabilities	18,168	15.6	13,183	72.6	3,705	20.4	1,095	6.0	10	0.1	50	0.3	125	0.7	0	0.0	17,983	99.3	4,039	22.5
Students Without Disabilities	98,499	84.4	97,772	99.3	28	0.0	8	0.0	408	0.4	32	0.0	251	0.3	0	0.0	97,808	99.3	61,767	63.2
Autism	1,311	1.1	616	47.0	320	24.4	362	27.6	0	0.0	4	0.3	9	0.7	0	0.0	1,298	99.3	487	37.5
Deaf-Blindness	1	0.0	0	0.0	0	0.0	0	0.0	0	0.0	1	100.0	0	0.0	0	0.0	0	0.0	*	*
Deafness	20	0.0	5	25.0	14	70.0	1	5.0	0	0.0	0	0.0	0	0.0	0	0.0	20	100.0	*	<=5%
Serious Emotional Disability	592	0.5	456	77.0	113	19.1	3	0.5	0	0.0	0	0.0	20	3.4	0	0.0	572	96.6	114	19.9
Hearing Impairment	138	0.1	109	79.0	26	18.8	3	2.2	0	0.0	0	0.0	0	0.0	0	0.0	138	100.0	37	26.8
Intellectual Disability - Mild	1,147	1.0	324	28.2	627	54.7	183	16.0	1	0.1	0	0.0	12	1.0	0	0.0	1,134	98.9	161	14.2
Intellectual Disability - Moderate	316	0.3	7	2.2	28	8.9	278	88.0	0	0.0	1	0.3	2	0.6	0	0.0	313	99.4	162	51.8
Intellectual Disability - Severe	65	0.1	0	0.0	0	0.0	57	87.7	0	0.0	7	10.8	1	1.5	0	0.0	57	98.3	10	17.5
Specific Learning Disability	8,540	7.3	6,692	78.4	1,788	20.9	7	0.1	6	0.1	8	0.1	39	0.5	0	0.0	8,487	99.5	1,267	14.9
Multiple Disabilities	198	0.2	11	5.6	18	9.1	142	71.7	2	1.0	20	10.1	5	2.5	0	0.0	171	96.1	50	29.2
Other Health Impairment	3,610	3.1	2,814	78.0	712	19.7	47	1.3	1	0.0	5	0.1	31	0.9	0	0.0	3,573	99.1	668	18.7
Orthopedic Impairment	64	0.1	40	62.5	14	21.9	6	9.4	0	0.0	1	1.6	3	4.7	0	0.0	60	95.2	21	35.0
Speech or Language Impairment	2,075	1.8	2,047	98.7	23	1.1	1	0.0	0	0.0	1	0.0	3	0.1	0	0.0	2,071	99.9	1,036	50.0
Traumatic Brain Injury	33	0.0	18	54.5	10	30.3	4	12.1	0	0.0	1	3.0	0	0.0	0	0.0	32	100.0	4	12.5
Visual Impairment	58	0.0	44	75.9	12	20.7	1	1.7	0	0.0	1	1.7	0	0.0	0	0.0	57	100.0	21	36.8

[1]The "Verified Membership" for the end-of-grade tests is the number of student grade and course enrollment records in PowerSchool on the first day of test administration in the testing cycle.

[2]Data for "Other" includes misadministrations, transfers, and unknown causes.

*Performance data are not reported when membership is fewer than five. Performance data that are less than or equal to 5.0 percent, or greater than or equal to 95.0 percent, are not displayed. Some columns may not add up to the total due to miscoding or rounding. The disability categories were revised in 2007–08.

Notes: The total for "All Students with Disabilities" includes Section 504.

Data received from local education agencies, charter schools, and regional school after December 5, 2014 are not included in this table.

Prepared by the NCDPI Division of Accountability Services/Test Development Section.

Table 2g. 2013–14 End-of-Grade Statewide Participation and Performance
Grade 6 Mathematics

MATHEMATICS

CATEGORY	# Verified Mbership[1]	% of Verified Mbership	GENERAL TEST # Tested (General Test)	GENERAL TEST % Tested (General Test)	ALTERNATE ASSESSMENTS # Tested NC EXTEND2	% Tested NC EXTEND2	# Tested NC EXTEND1	% Tested NC EXTEND1	NOT TESTED # Medical Exclusions	% Medical Exclusions	# LEP Exclusions	% LEP Exclusions	# Absent	% Absent	# Other[2]	% Other	TOTAL FOR ALL TESTS # Participating	% Participating	# Proficient	% Proficient
All Students	116,667	100.0	111,470	95.5	3,218	2.8	1,102	0.9	413	0.4	83	0.1	381	0.3	0	0.0	115,790	99.3	54,223	46.8
Female	56,589	48.5	54,754	96.8	1,116	2.0	330	0.6	188	0.3	40	0.1	161	0.3	0	0.0	56,200	99.3	27,174	48.4
Male	60,078	51.5	56,716	94.4	2,102	3.5	772	1.3	225	0.4	43	0.1	220	0.4	0	0.0	59,590	99.3	27,049	45.4
American Indian	1,535	1.3	1,478	96.3	31	2.0	13	0.8	8	0.5	1	0.1	4	0.3	0	0.0	1,522	99.2	474	31.1
Asian	3,210	2.8	3,068	95.6	28	0.9	15	0.5	87	2.7	4	0.1	8	0.2	0	0.0	3,111	97.0	2,403	77.2
Black	30,356	26.0	28,432	93.7	1,345	4.4	375	1.2	37	0.1	21	0.1	146	0.5	0	0.0	30,152	99.4	7,853	26.0
Hispanic	17,443	15.0	16,539	94.8	495	2.8	125	0.7	218	1.2	13	0.1	53	0.3	0	0.0	17,159	98.4	6,431	37.5
Multi-Racial	4,319	3.7	4,153	96.2	107	2.5	43	1.0	2	0.0	1	0.0	13	0.3	0	0.0	4,303	99.7	1,936	45.0
Native Hawaiian/Pacific Islander	130	0.1	121	93.1	3	2.3	0	0.0	5	3.8	0	0.0	1	0.8	0	0.0	124	95.4	57	46.0
White	59,674	51.1	57,679	96.7	1,209	2.0	531	0.9	56	0.1	43	0.1	156	0.3	0	0.0	59,419	99.6	35,069	59.0
Economically Disadvantaged	64,720	55.5	60,948	94.2	2,509	3.9	726	1.1	232	0.4	49	0.1	256	0.4	0	0.0	64,183	99.2	20,047	31.2
Not Economically Disadvantaged	51,947	44.5	50,522	97.3	709	1.4	376	0.7	181	0.3	34	0.1	125	0.2	0	0.0	51,607	99.4	34,176	66.2
Migrant	146	0.1	138	94.5	2	1.4	0	0.0	5	3.4	0	0.0	1	0.7	0	0.0	140	95.9	39	27.9
Not Migrant	116,521	99.9	111,332	95.5	3,216	2.8	1,102	0.9	408	0.4	83	0.1	380	0.3	0	0.0	115,650	99.3	54,184	46.9
Limited English Proficient (LEP)	5,389	4.6	4,436	82.3	421	7.8	79	1.5	413	7.7	6	0.1	34	0.6	0	0.0	4,936	91.7	662	13.4
Not LEP	111,278	95.4	107,034	96.2	2,797	2.5	1,023	0.9	0	0.0	77	0.1	347	0.3	0	0.0	110,854	99.7	53,561	48.3
All Students with Disabilities	18,168	15.6	13,682	75.3	3,191	17.6	1,093	6.0	10	0.1	50	0.3	142	0.8	0	0.0	17,966	99.2	3,167	17.6
Students Without Disabilities	98,499	84.4	97,788	99.3	27	0.0	9	0.0	403	0.4	33	0.0	239	0.2	0	0.0	97,824	99.3	51,056	52.2
Autism	1,311	1.1	623	47.5	313	23.9	362	27.6	0	0.0	4	0.3	9	0.7	0	0.0	1,298	99.3	399	30.7
Deaf-Blindness	1	0.0	0	0.0	0	0.0	0	0.0	0	0.0	1	100.0	0	0.0	0	0.0	0	*	*	*
Deafness	20	0.0	7	35.0	12	60.0	1	5.0	0	0.0	0	0.0	0	0.0	0	0.0	20	100.0	*	<=5%
Serious Emotional Disability	592	0.5	460	77.7	111	18.8	3	0.5	0	0.0	0	0.0	18	3.0	0	0.0	574	97.0	53	9.2
Hearing Impairment	138	0.1	115	83.3	20	14.5	3	2.2	0	0.0	0	0.0	0	0.0	0	0.0	138	100.0	35	25.4
Intellectual Disability - Mild	1,147	1.0	322	28.1	627	54.7	184	16.0	1	0.1	0	0.0	13	1.1	0	0.0	1,133	98.8	144	12.7
Intellectual Disability - Moderate	316	0.3	8	2.5	28	8.9	277	87.7	0	0.0	1	0.3	2	0.6	0	0.0	313	99.4	132	42.2
Intellectual Disability - Severe	65	0.1	0	0.0	0	0.0	57	87.7	0	0.0	7	10.8	1	1.5	0	0.0	57	98.3	8	14.0
Specific Learning Disability	8,540	7.3	7,126	83.4	1,340	15.7	7	0.1	6	0.1	8	0.1	53	0.6	0	0.0	8,473	99.3	1,036	12.2
Multiple Disabilities	198	0.2	13	6.6	16	8.1	140	70.7	0	0.0	20	10.1	7	3.5	0	0.0	169	94.9	42	24.9
Other Health Impairment	3,610	3.1	2,852	79.0	672	18.6	47	1.3	2	1.0	5	0.1	33	0.9	0	0.0	3,571	99.1	400	11.2
Orthopedic Impairment	64	0.1	40	62.5	14	21.9	6	9.4	0	0.0	1	1.6	3	4.7	0	0.0	60	95.2	12	20.0
Speech or Language Impairment	2,075	1.8	2,050	98.8	20	1.0	1	0.0	0	0.0	0	0.0	3	0.1	0	0.0	2,071	99.9	886	42.8
Traumatic Brain Injury	33	0.0	19	57.6	9	27.3	4	12.1	0	0.0	1	3.0	0	0.0	0	0.0	32	100.0	4	12.5
Visual Impairment	58	0.0	47	81.0	9	15.5	1	1.7	0	0.0	1	1.7	0	0.0	0	0.0	57	100.0	15	26.3

[1]The "Verified Membership" for the end-of-grade tests is the number of student grade and course enrollment records in PowerSchool on the first day of test administration in the testing cycle.

[2]Data for "Other" includes misadministrations, transfers, and unknown causes.

*Performance data are not reported when membership is fewer than five. Performance data that are less than or equal to 5.0 percent, or greater than or equal to 95.0 percent, are not displayed. Some columns may not add up to the total due to miscoding or rounding. The disability categories were revised in 2007–08.

Notes: The total for "All Students with Disabilities" includes Section 504.
Data received from local education agencies, charter schools, and regional school after December 5, 2014 are not included in this table.
Prepared by the NCDPI Division of Accountability Services/Test Development Section.

Table 2h. 2013–14 End-of-Grade Statewide Participation and Performance
Grade 7 English Language Arts (ELA)

CATEGORY	# Verified Mbership[1]	% of Verified Mbership	# Tested (General Test)	% Tested (General Test)	# Tested NC EXTEND2	% Tested NC EXTEND2	# Tested NC EXTEND1	% Tested NC EXTEND1	# Medical Exclusions	% Medical Exclusions	# LEP Exclusions	% LEP Exclusions	# Absent	% Absent	# Other[2]	% Other	# Participating	% Participating	# Proficient	% Proficient
All Students	119,060	100.0	113,012	94.9	3,810	3.2	1,170	1.0	490	0.4	114	0.1	464	0.4	0	0.0	117,992	99.2	67,604	57.3
Female	57,992	48.7	55,820	96.3	1,283	2.2	390	0.7	240	0.4	58	0.1	201	0.3	0	0.0	57,493	99.2	34,612	60.2
Male	61,068	51.3	57,192	93.7	2,527	4.1	780	1.3	250	0.4	56	0.1	263	0.4	0	0.0	60,499	99.2	32,992	54.5
American Indian	1,629	1.4	1,555	95.5	38	2.3	18	1.1	9	0.6	1	0.1	8	0.5	0	0.0	1,611	99.0	672	41.7
Asian	3,149	2.6	2,986	94.8	32	1.0	26	0.8	87	2.8	2	0.1	16	0.5	0	0.0	3,044	96.7	2,237	73.5
Black	31,500	26.5	29,294	93.0	1,568	5.0	411	1.3	30	0.1	24	0.1	173	0.5	0	0.0	31,273	99.4	11,867	37.9
Hispanic	16,935	14.2	15,856	93.6	587	3.5	125	0.7	297	1.8	7	0.0	63	0.4	0	0.0	16,568	97.9	7,373	44.5
Multi-Racial	4,251	3.6	4,062	95.6	132	3.1	31	0.7	0	0.0	5	0.1	21	0.5	0	0.0	4,225	99.5	2,503	59.2
Native Hawaiian/Pacific Islander	114	0.1	107	93.9	3	2.6	2	1.8	2	1.8	0	0.0	0	0.0	0	0.0	112	98.2	54	48.2
White	61,482	51.6	59,152	96.2	1,450	2.4	557	0.9	65	0.1	75	0.1	183	0.3	0	0.0	61,159	99.6	42,898	70.1
Economically Disadvantaged	64,898	54.5	60,460	93.2	3,004	4.6	771	1.2	294	0.5	55	0.1	314	0.5	0	0.0	64,235	99.1	27,407	42.7
Not Economically Disadvantaged	54,162	45.5	52,552	97.0	806	1.5	399	0.7	196	0.4	59	0.1	150	0.3	0	0.0	53,757	99.4	40,197	74.8
Migrant	114	0.1	110	96.5	3	2.6	0	0.0	1	0.9	0	0.0	0	0.0	0	0.0	113	99.1	42	37.2
Not Migrant	118,946	99.9	112,902	94.9	3,807	3.2	1,170	1.0	489	0.4	114	0.1	464	0.4	0	0.0	117,879	99.2	67,562	57.3
Limited English Proficient (LEP)	5,529	4.6	4,409	79.7	501	9.1	84	1.5	490	8.9	2	0.0	43	0.8	0	0.0	4,994	90.4	541	10.8
Not LEP	113,531	95.4	108,603	95.7	3,309	2.9	1,086	1.0	0	0.0	112	0.1	421	0.4	0	0.0	112,998	99.6	67,063	59.3
All Students with Disabilities	17,487	14.7	12,315	70.4	3,797	21.7	1,160	6.6	3	0.0	58	0.3	154	0.9	0	0.0	17,272	99.1	3,705	21.5
Students Without Disabilities	101,573	85.3	100,697	99.1	13	0.0	10	0.0	487	0.5	56	0.1	310	0.3	0	0.0	100,720	99.2	63,899	63.4
Autism	1,219	1.0	576	47.3	302	24.8	326	26.7	1	0.1	5	0.4	9	0.7	0	0.0	1,204	99.2	404	33.6
Deaf-Blindness	2	0.0	1	50.0	0	0.0	1	50.0	0	0.0	0	0.0	0	0.0	0	0.0	2	100.0	*	*
Deafness	9	0.0	0	0.0	7	77.8	2	22.2	0	0.0	0	0.0	0	0.0	0	0.0	9	100.0	1	11.1
Serious Emotional Disability	677	0.6	507	74.9	142	21.0	2	0.3	0	0.0	2	0.3	24	3.5	0	0.0	651	96.4	138	21.2
Hearing Impairment	156	0.1	105	67.3	46	29.5	4	2.6	0	0.0	0	0.0	1	0.6	0	0.0	155	99.4	34	21.9
Intellectual Disability - Mild	1,226	1.0	296	24.1	693	56.5	217	17.7	0	0.0	3	0.2	17	1.4	0	0.0	1,206	98.6	198	16.4
Intellectual Disability - Moderate	378	0.3	10	2.6	33	8.7	326	86.2	1	0.3	4	1.1	4	1.1	0	0.0	369	98.7	165	44.7
Intellectual Disability - Severe	58	0.0	0	0.0	1	1.7	51	87.9	0	0.0	4	6.9	2	3.4	0	0.0	52	96.3	*	<=5%
Specific Learning Disability	8,331	7.0	6,538	78.5	1,737	20.8	2	0.0	1	0.0	3	0.0	50	0.6	0	0.0	8,277	99.4	1,337	16.2
Multiple Disabilities	194	0.2	4	2.1	16	8.2	151	77.8	0	0.0	18	9.3	5	2.6	0	0.0	171	97.2	47	27.5
Other Health Impairment	3,857	3.2	2,991	77.5	761	19.7	56	1.5	0	0.0	12	0.3	37	1.0	0	0.0	3,808	99.0	749	19.7
Orthopedic Impairment	85	0.1	48	56.5	25	29.4	10	11.8	0	0.0	1	1.2	1	1.2	0	0.0	83	98.8	26	31.3
Speech or Language Impairment	1,197	1.0	1,176	98.2	16	1.3	1	0.1	0	0.0	2	0.2	2	0.2	0	0.0	1,193	99.8	571	47.9
Traumatic Brain Injury	33	0.0	18	54.5	7	21.2	6	18.2	0	0.0	2	6.1	2	0.2	0	0.0	31	100.0	8	25.8
Visual Impairment	65	0.1	45	69.2	11	16.9	5	7.7	0	0.0	2	3.1	2	3.1	0	0.0	61	96.8	24	39.3

[1] The "Verified Membership" for the end-of-grade tests is the number of student grade and course enrollment records in PowerSchool on the first day of test administration in the testing cycle.

[2] Data for "Other" includes misadministrations, transfers, and unknown causes.

*Performance data are not reported when membership is fewer than five. Performance data that are less than or equal to 5.0 percent, or greater than or equal to 95.0 percent, are not displayed. Some columns may not add up to the total due to miscoding or rounding. The disability categories were revised in 2007–08.

Notes: The total for "All Students with Disabilities" includes Section 504.

Data received from local education agencies, charter schools, and regional school after December 5, 2014 are not included in this table.

Prepared by the NCDPI Division of Accountability Services/Test Development Section.

Table 2i: 2013–14 End-of-Grade Statewide Participation and Performance
Grade 7 Mathematics

MATHEMATICS

CATEGORY	# Verified Mbership[1]	% of Verified Mbership	GENERAL TEST # Tested (General Test)	% Tested (General Test)	ALTERNATE ASSESSMENTS # Tested NC EXTEND2	% Tested NC EXTEND2	# Tested NC EXTEND1	% Tested NC EXTEND1	NOT TESTED # Medical Exclusions	% Medical Exclusions	# LEP Exclusions	% LEP Exclusions	# Absent	% Absent	# Other[2]	% Other	TOTAL FOR ALL TESTS # Participating	% Participating	# Proficient	% Proficient
All Students	119,060	100.0	113,416	95.3	3,410	2.9	1,168	1.0	484	0.4	114	0.1	468	0.4	0	0.0	117,994	99.2	54,203	45.9
Female	57,992	48.7	55,884	96.4	1,216	2.1	390	0.7	237	0.4	58	0.1	207	0.4	0	0.0	57,490	99.2	27,434	47.7
Male	61,068	51.3	57,532	94.2	2,194	3.6	778	1.3	247	0.4	56	0.1	261	0.4	0	0.0	60,504	99.2	26,769	44.2
American Indian	1,629	1.4	1,558	95.6	34	2.1	18	1.1	9	0.6	1	0.1	9	0.6	0	0.0	1,610	98.9	503	31.2
Asian	3,149	2.6	2,998	95.2	23	0.7	26	0.8	87	2.8	2	0.1	13	0.4	0	0.0	3,047	96.8	2,320	76.1
Black	31,500	26.5	29,405	93.3	1,450	4.6	410	1.3	29	0.1	24	0.1	182	0.6	0	0.0	31,265	99.3	7,982	25.5
Hispanic	16,935	14.2	15,978	94.3	475	2.8	125	0.7	293	1.7	7	0.0	57	0.3	0	0.0	16,578	97.9	6,017	36.3
Multi-Racial	4,251	3.6	4,077	95.9	116	2.7	31	0.7	0	0.0	5	0.1	22	0.5	0	0.0	4,224	99.5	1,891	44.8
Native Hawaiian/Pacific Islander	114	0.1	107	93.9	3	2.6	2	1.8	2	1.8	0	0.0	0	0.0	0	0.0	112	98.2	43	38.4
White	61,482	51.6	59,293	96.4	1,309	2.1	556	0.9	64	0.1	75	0.1	185	0.3	0	0.0	61,158	99.6	35,447	58.0
Economically Disadvantaged	64,898	54.5	60,796	93.7	2,660	4.1	769	1.2	292	0.4	55	0.1	326	0.5	0	0.0	64,225	99.0	19,453	30.3
Not Economically Disadvantaged	54,162	45.5	52,620	97.2	750	1.4	399	0.7	192	0.4	59	0.1	142	0.3	0	0.0	53,769	99.4	34,750	64.6
Migrant	114	0.1	110	96.5	3	2.6	0	0.0	1	0.9	0	0.0	0	0.0	0	0.0	113	99.1	47	41.6
Not Migrant	118,946	99.9	113,306	95.3	3,407	2.9	1,168	1.0	483	0.4	114	0.1	468	0.4	0	0.0	117,881	99.2	54,156	45.9
Limited English Proficient (LEP)	5,529	4.6	4,527	81.9	396	7.2	84	1.5	484	8.8	2	0.0	36	0.7	0	0.0	5,007	90.6	615	12.3
Not LEP	113,531	95.4	108,889	95.9	3,014	2.7	1,084	1.0	0	0.0	112	0.1	432	0.4	0	0.0	112,987	99.6	53,588	47.4
All Students with Disabilities	17,487	14.7	12,707	72.7	3,395	19.4	1,158	6.6	3	0.0	58	0.3	166	0.9	0	0.0	17,260	99.0	2,414	14.0
Students Without Disabilities	101,573	85.3	100,709	99.1	15	0.0	10	0.0	481	0.5	56	0.1	302	0.3	0	0.0	100,734	99.2	51,789	51.4
Autism	1,219	1.0	582	47.7	294	24.1	325	26.7	1	0.1	5	0.4	12	1.0	0	0.0	1,201	98.9	307	25.6
Deaf-Blindness	2	0.0	1	50.0	0	0.0	1	50.0	0	0.0	0	0.0	0	0.0	0	0.0	2	100.0	*	*
Deafness	9	0.0	1	11.1	6	66.7	2	22.2	0	0.0	0	0.0	0	0.0	0	0.0	9	100.0	1	11.1
Serious Emotional Disability	677	0.6	505	74.6	142	21.0	2	0.3	0	0.0	2	0.3	26	3.8	0	0.0	649	96.1	64	9.9
Hearing Impairment	156	0.1	112	71.8	38	24.4	4	2.6	0	0.0	0	0.0	2	1.3	0	0.0	154	98.7	30	19.5
Intellectual Disability - Mild	1,226	1.0	297	24.2	693	56.5	217	17.7	0	0.0	3	0.2	16	1.3	0	0.0	1,207	98.7	112	9.3
Intellectual Disability - Moderate	378	0.3	9	2.4	34	9.0	325	86.0	1	0.3	4	1.1	5	1.3	0	0.0	368	98.4	77	20.9
Intellectual Disability - Severe	58	0.0	0	0.0	1	1.7	51	87.9	0	0.0	4	6.9	2	3.4	0	0.0	52	96.3	5	9.6
Specific Learning Disability	8,331	7.0	6,904	82.9	1,372	16.5	2	0.0	1	0.0	3	0.0	49	0.6	0	0.0	8,278	99.4	890	10.8
Multiple Disabilities	194	0.2	4	2.1	16	8.2	151	77.8	0	0.0	18	9.3	5	2.6	0	0.0	171	97.2	29	17.0
Other Health Impairment	3,857	3.2	3,004	77.9	742	19.2	56	1.5	0	0.0	12	0.3	43	1.1	0	0.0	3,802	98.9	377	9.9
Orthopedic Impairment	85	0.1	46	54.1	27	31.8	10	11.8	0	0.0	1	1.2	1	1.2	0	0.0	83	98.8	15	18.1
Speech or Language Impairment	1,197	1.0	1,179	98.5	13	1.1	1	0.1	0	0.0	2	0.2	2	0.2	0	0.0	1,193	99.8	487	40.8
Traumatic Brain Injury	33	0.0	18	54.5	6	18.2	6	18.2	0	0.0	2	6.1	1	3.0	0	0.0	30	96.8	6	20.0
Visual Impairment	65	0.1	45	69.2	11	16.9	5	7.7	0	0.0	2	3.1	2	3.1	0	0.0	61	96.8	13	21.3

[1]The "Verified Membership" for the end-of-grade tests is the number of student grade and course enrollment records in PowerSchool on the first day of test administration in the testing cycle.

[2]Data for "Other" includes misadministrations, transfers, and unknown causes.

*Performance data are not reported when membership is fewer than five. Performance data that are less than or equal to 5.0 percent, or greater than or equal to 95.0 percent, are not displayed. Some columns may not add up to the total due to miscoding or rounding. The disability categories were revised in 2007–08.

Notes: The total for "All Students with Disabilities" includes Section 504.

Data received from local education agencies, charter schools, and regional school after December 5, 2014 are not included in this table.

Prepared by the NCDPI Division of Accountability Services/Test Development Section.

Table 2j. 2013–14 End-of-Grade Statewide Participation and Performance
Grade 8 English Language Arts (ELA)

CATEGORY	# Verified Mbership[1]	% of Verified Mbership	GENERAL TEST		ALTERNATE ASSESSMENTS				NOT TESTED								TOTAL FOR ALL TESTS			
			# Tested (General Test)	% Tested (General Test)	# Tested NC EXTEND2	% Tested NC EXTEND2	# Tested NC EXTEND1	% Tested NC EXTEND1	# Medical Exclusions	% Medical Exclusions	# LEP Exclusions	% LEP Exclusions	# Absent	% Absent	# Other[2]	% Other	# Participating	% Participating	# Proficient	% Proficient
All Students	117,665	100.0	111,946	95.1	3,445	2.9	1,235	1.0	411	0.4	115	0.1	502	0.4	0	0.0	116,626	99.2	63,174	54.2
Female	57,454	48.8	55,395	96.4	1,123	2.0	453	0.8	213	0.4	63	0.1	203	0.4	0	0.0	56,971	99.3	33,799	59.3
Male	60,211	51.2	56,551	93.9	2,322	3.9	782	1.3	198	0.3	52	0.1	299	0.5	0	0.0	59,655	99.2	29,375	49.2
American Indian	1,743	1.5	1,658	95.1	40	2.3	23	1.3	8	0.5	1	0.1	13	0.7	0	0.0	1,721	98.8	622	36.1
Asian	3,122	2.7	2,979	95.4	27	0.9	28	0.9	72	2.4	1	0.0	12	0.4	0	0.0	3,034	97.2	2,133	70.3
Black	31,377	26.7	29,268	93.3	1,444	4.6	435	1.4	27	0.1	24	0.1	179	0.6	0	0.0	31,147	99.3	11,230	36.1
Hispanic	15,747	13.4	14,746	93.6	502	3.2	135	0.9	252	1.7	11	0.1	93	0.6	0	0.0	15,383	97.8	6,425	41.8
Multi-Racial	4,045	3.4	3,887	96.1	105	2.6	29	0.7	5	0.1	4	0.1	15	0.4	0	0.0	4,021	99.5	2,186	54.4
Native Hawaiian/Pacific Islander	128	0.1	125	97.7	2	1.6	1	0.8	0	0.0	0	0.0	0	0.0	0	0.0	128	100.0	56	43.8
White	61,503	52.3	59,283	96.4	1,325	2.2	584	0.9	47	0.1	74	0.1	190	0.3	0	0.0	61,192	99.6	40,522	66.2
Economically Disadvantaged	62,062	52.7	57,908	93.3	2,676	4.3	827	1.3	232	0.4	57	0.1	358	0.6	0	0.0	61,411	99.0	23,901	38.9
Not Economically Disadvantaged	55,603	47.3	54,038	97.2	769	1.4	408	0.7	179	0.3	58	0.1	144	0.3	0	0.0	55,215	99.4	39,273	71.1
Migrant	94	0.1	91	96.8	1	1.1	0	0.0	0	0.0	0	0.0	2	2.1	0	0.0	92	97.9	21	22.8
Not Migrant	117,571	99.9	111,855	95.1	3,444	2.9	1,235	1.1	411	0.4	115	0.1	500	0.4	0	0.0	116,534	99.2	63,153	54.2
Limited English Proficient (LEP)	5,516	4.7	4,516	81.9	421	7.6	79	1.4	411	7.7	7	0.1	71	1.3	0	0.0	5,016	91.1	471	9.4
Not LEP	112,149	95.3	107,430	95.8	3,024	2.7	1,156	1.0	0	0.0	108	0.1	431	0.4	0	0.0	111,610	99.6	62,703	56.2
All Students with Disabilities	16,279	13.8	11,394	70.0	3,429	21.1	1,227	7.5	6	0.0	55	0.3	168	1.0	0	0.0	16,050	98.9	2,972	18.5
Students Without Disabilities	101,386	86.2	100,552	99.2	16	0.0	8	0.0	405	0.4	60	0.1	334	0.3	0	0.0	100,576	99.3	60,202	59.9
Autism	1,166	1.0	560	48.0	273	23.4	321	27.5	0	0.0	3	0.3	9	0.8	0	0.0	1,154	99.2	412	35.7
Deaf-Blindness	0	0.0	0	0.0	0	0	0	0	0	0.0	0	0	0	0	0	0	0	0	*	*
Deafness	16	0.0	2	12.5	12	75.0	1	6.3	0	0.0	0	0.0	1	6.3	0	0.0	15	93.8	1	6.7
Serious Emotional Disability	649	0.6	502	77.3	113	17.4	5	0.8	1	0.2	5	0.8	23	3.5	0	0.0	620	96.3	81	13.1
Hearing Impairment	166	0.1	128	77.1	36	21.7	2	1.2	0	0.0	0	0.0	0	0.0	0	0.0	166	100.0	26	15.7
Intellectual Disability - Mild	1,184	1.0	298	25.2	678	57.3	190	16.0	1	0.1	3	0.3	14	1.2	0	0.0	1,166	98.7	172	14.8
Intellectual Disability - Moderate	460	0.4	7	1.5	41	8.9	408	88.7	0	0.0	1	0.2	3	0.7	0	0.0	456	99.3	250	54.8
Intellectual Disability - Severe	76	0.1	0	0.0	0	0.0	69	90.8	0	0.0	4	5.3	3	3.9	0	0.0	69	95.8	13	18.8
Specific Learning Disability	8,060	6.8	6,438	79.9	1,545	19.2	8	0.1	4	0.0	3	0.0	62	0.8	0	0.0	7,991	99.2	1,112	13.9
Multiple Disabilities	213	0.2	13	6.1	12	5.6	161	75.6	0	0.0	20	9.4	7	3.3	0	0.0	186	96.4	55	29.6
Other Health Impairment	3,593	3.1	2,812	78.3	689	19.2	38	1.1	0	0.0	9	0.3	45	1.3	0	0.0	3,539	98.7	588	16.6
Orthopedic Impairment	54	0.0	34	63.0	8	14.8	7	13.0	0	0.0	4	7.4	1	1.9	0	0.0	49	98.0	23	46.9
Speech or Language Impairment	551	0.5	545	98.9	6	1.1	0	0.0	0	0.0	0	0.0	0	0.0	0	0.0	551	100.0	212	38.5
Traumatic Brain Injury	42	0.0	18	42.9	9	21.4	15	35.7	0	0.0	0	0.0	0	0.0	0	0.0	42	100.0	10	23.8
Visual Impairment	49	0.0	37	75.5	7	14.3	2	4.1	0	0.0	3	6.1	0	0.0	0	0.0	46	100.0	17	37.0

[1] The "Verified Membership" for the end-of-grade tests is the number of student grade and course enrollment records in PowerSchool on the first day of test administration in the testing cycle.

[2] Data for "Other" includes misadministrations, transfers, and unknown causes.

*Performance data are not reported when membership is fewer than five. Performance data that are less than or equal to 5.0 percent, or greater than or equal to 95.0 percent, are not displayed. Some columns may not add up to the total due to miscoding or rounding. The disability categories were revised in 2007–08.

Notes: The total for "All Students with Disabilities" includes Section 504.

Data received from local education agencies, charter schools, and regional school after December 5, 2014 are not included in this table.

Prepared by the NCDPI Division of Accountability Services/Test Development Section.

Table 2k. 2013–14 End-of-Grade Statewide Participation and Performance
Grade 8 Mathematics

MATHEMATICS

CATEGORY	# Verified Mbership[1]	% of Verified Mbership	GENERAL TEST # Tested (General Test)	GENERAL TEST % Tested (General Test)	ALTERNATE ASSESSMENTS # Tested NC EXTEND2	% Tested NC EXTEND2	# Tested NC EXTEND1	% Tested NC EXTEND1	NOT TESTED # Medical Exclusions	% Medical Exclusions	# LEP Exclusions	% LEP Exclusions	# Absent	% Absent	# Other[2]	% Other	TOTAL FOR ALL TESTS # Participating	% Participating	# Proficient	% Proficient
All Students	117,665	100.0	112,243	95.4	3,171	2.7	1,235	1.0	421	0.4	116	0.1	479	0.4	0	0.0	116,649	99.2	49,184	42.2
Female	57,454	48.8	55,443	96.5	1,074	1.9	453	0.8	216	0.4	63	0.1	205	0.4	0	0.0	56,970	99.3	24,434	42.9
Male	60,211	51.2	56,800	94.3	2,097	3.5	782	1.3	205	0.3	53	0.1	274	0.5	0	0.0	59,679	99.2	24,750	41.5
American Indian	1,743	1.5	1,660	95.2	38	2.2	23	1.3	8	0.5	1	0.1	13	0.7	0	0.0	1,721	98.8	430	25.0
Asian	3,122	2.7	2,991	95.8	21	0.7	28	0.9	77	2.5	1	0.0	4	0.1	0	0.0	3,040	97.4	2,212	72.8
Black	31,377	26.7	29,349	93.5	1,362	4.3	435	1.4	27	0.1	24	0.1	180	0.6	0	0.0	31,146	99.3	6,708	21.5
Hispanic	15,747	13.4	14,848	94.3	422	2.7	135	0.9	257	1.6	11	0.1	74	0.5	0	0.0	15,405	97.9	4,960	32.2
Multi-Racial	4,045	3.4	3,887	96.1	104	2.6	29	0.7	5	0.1	4	0.1	16	0.4	0	0.0	4,020	99.5	1,604	39.9
Native Hawaiian/Pacific Islander	128	0.1	125	97.7	2	1.6	1	0.8	0	0.0	0	0.0	0	0.0	0	0.0	128	100.0	51	39.8
White	61,503	52.3	59,383	96.6	1,222	2.0	584	0.9	47	0.1	75	0.1	192	0.3	0	0.0	61,189	99.6	33,219	54.3
Economically Disadvantaged	62,062	52.7	58,136	93.7	2,456	4.0	827	1.3	237	0.4	58	0.1	348	0.6	0	0.0	61,419	99.1	16,398	26.7
Not Economically Disadvantaged	55,603	47.3	54,107	97.3	715	1.3	408	0.7	184	0.3	58	0.1	131	0.2	0	0.0	55,230	99.4	32,786	59.4
Migrant	94	0.1	92	97.9	1	1.1	0	0.0	0	0.0	0	0.0	1	1.1	0	0.0	93	98.9	20	21.5
Not Migrant	117,571	99.9	112,151	95.4	3,170	2.7	1,235	1.1	421	0.4	116	0.1	478	0.4	0	0.0	116,556	99.2	49,164	42.2
Limited English Proficient (LEP)	5,516	4.7	4,620	83.8	344	6.2	79	1.4	421	7.6	7	0.1	45	0.8	0	0.0	5,043	91.5	553	11.0
Not LEP	112,149	95.3	107,623	96.0	2,827	2.5	1,156	1.0	0	0.0	109	0.1	434	0.4	0	0.0	111,606	99.6	48,631	43.6
All Students with Disabilities	16,279	13.8	11,660	71.6	3,155	19.4	1,227	7.5	6	0.0	56	0.3	175	1.1	0	0.0	16,042	98.9	1,962	12.2
Students Without Disabilities	101,386	86.2	100,583	99.2	16	0.0	8	0.0	415	0.4	60	0.1	304	0.3	0	0.0	100,607	99.3	47,222	46.9
Autism	1,166	1.0	555	47.6	278	23.8	321	27.5	0	0.0	3	0.3	9	0.8	0	0.0	1,154	99.2	314	27.2
Deaf-Blindness	0	0.0	0	0.0	0	0.0	0	0.0	0	0.0	0	0.0	0	0.0	0	0.0	0	0.0	*	*
Deafness	16	0.0	2	12.5	12	75.0	1	6.3	0	0.0	0	0.0	1	6.3	0	0.0	15	93.8	1	6.7
Serious Emotional Disability	649	0.6	499	76.9	116	17.9	5	0.8	1	0.2	5	0.8	23	3.5	0	0.0	620	96.3	44	7.1
Hearing Impairment	166	0.1	134	80.7	28	16.9	2	1.2	0	0.0	0	0.0	2	1.2	0	0.0	164	98.8	31	18.9
Intellectual Disability - Mild	1,184	1.0	302	25.5	670	56.6	190	16.0	1	0.1	3	0.3	18	1.5	0	0.0	1,162	98.4	103	8.9
Intellectual Disability - Moderate	460	0.4	7	1.5	41	8.9	408	88.7	0	0.0	1	0.2	3	0.7	0	0.0	456	99.3	114	25.0
Intellectual Disability - Severe	76	0.1	0	0.0	0	0.0	69	90.8	0	0.0	4	5.3	3	3.9	0	0.0	69	95.8	5	7.2
Specific Learning Disability	8,060	6.8	6,709	83.2	1,266	15.7	8	0.1	4	0.0	4	0.0	69	0.9	0	0.0	7,983	99.1	790	9.9
Multiple Disabilities	213	0.2	11	5.2	14	6.6	161	75.6	0	0.0	20	9.4	7	3.3	0	0.0	186	96.4	30	16.1
Other Health Impairment	3,593	3.1	2,808	78.2	699	19.5	38	1.1	0	0.0	9	0.3	39	1.1	0	0.0	3,545	98.9	312	8.8
Orthopedic Impairment	54	0.0	34	63.0	8	14.8	7	13.0	0	0.0	4	7.4	1	1.9	0	0.0	49	98.0	11	22.4
Speech or Language Impairment	551	0.5	545	98.9	6	1.1	0	0.0	0	0.0	0	0.0	0	0.0	0	0.0	551	100.0	186	33.8
Traumatic Brain Injury	42	0.0	17	40.5	10	23.8	15	35.7	0	0.0	0	0.0	0	0.0	0	0.0	42	100.0	4	9.5
Visual Impairment	49	0.0	37	75.5	7	14.3	2	4.1	0	0.0	3	6.1	0	0.0	0	0.0	46	100.0	17	37.0

[1] The "Verified Membership" for the end-of-grade tests is the number of student grade and course enrollment records in PowerSchool on the first day of test administration in the testing cycle.

[2] Data for "Other" includes misadministrations, transfers, and unknown causes.

*Performance data are not reported when membership is fewer than five. Performance data that are less than or equal to 5.0 percent, or greater than or equal to 95.0 percent, are not displayed. Some columns may not add up to the total due to miscoding or rounding. The disability categories were revised in 2007–08.

Notes: The total for "All Students with Disabilities" includes Section 504.

Data received from local education agencies, charter schools, and regional school after December 5, 2014 are not included in this table.

Prepared by the NCDPI Division of Accountability Services/Test Development Section.

Table 4. 2013–14 End-of-Grade Statewide Participation and Performance
Grade 5 Science

CATEGORY	# Verified Mbership[1]	% of Verified Mbership[1]	GENERAL TEST # Tested	GENERAL TEST % Tested	# Tested NC EXTEND2	% Tested NC EXTEND2	# Tested NC EXTEND1	% Tested NC EXTEND1	NOT TESTED # LEP Exclusions	% LEP Exclusions	# Medical Exclusions	% Medical Exclusions	# Absent	% Absent	# Other[2]	% Other	TOTAL OF ALL TESTS # Participating	% Participating	# Proficient	% Proficient
All Students	116,683	100.0	111,659	95.7	3,151	2.7	1,114	1.0	430	100.0	99	0.1	230	0.2	0	0.0	115,924	99.4	74,438	64.2
Female	56,843	48.7	55,088	96.9	1,059	1.9	365	0.6	204	100.0	44	0.1	83	0.1	0	0.0	56,512	99.5	35,603	63.0
Male	59,840	51.3	56,571	94.5	2,092	3.5	749	1.3	226	100.0	55	0.1	147	0.2	0	0.0	59,412	99.4	38,835	65.4
American Indian	1,555	1.3	1,488	95.7	35	2.3	19	1.2	5	100.0	1	0.1	7	0.5	0	0.0	1,542	99.2	791	51.3
Asian	3,371	2.9	3,197	94.8	45	1.3	27	0.8	93	100.0	0	0.0	9	0.3	0	0.0	3,269	97.0	2,616	80.0
Black	29,231	25.1	27,486	94.0	1,245	4.3	391	1.3	21	100.0	25	0.1	63	0.2	0	0.0	29,122	99.7	12,825	44.0
Hispanic	17,916	15.4	17,007	94.9	498	2.8	136	0.8	237	100.0	9	0.1	29	0.2	0	0.0	17,641	98.5	9,250	52.4
Multi-Racial	4,670	4.0	4,492	96.2	115	2.5	44	0.9	6	100.0	4	0.1	9	0.2	0	0.0	4,651	99.7	3,139	67.5
Native Hawaiian/Pacific Islander	115	0.1	106	92.2	3	2.6	0	0.0	5	100.0	0	0.0	1	0.9	0	0.0	109	94.8	73	67.0
White	59,825	51.3	57,883	96.8	1,210	2.0	497	0.8	63	100.0	60	0.1	112	0.2	0	0.0	59,590	99.7	45,744	76.8
Economically Disadvantaged	64,925	55.6	61,246	94.3	2,469	3.8	770	1.2	256	100.0	45	0.1	139	0.2	0	0.0	64,485	99.4	32,774	50.8
Not Economically Disadvantaged	51,758	44.4	50,413	97.4	682	1.3	344	0.7	174	100.0	54	0.1	91	0.2	0	0.0	51,439	99.5	41,664	81.0
Migrant	138	0.1	129	93.5	2	1.4	2	1.4	5	100.0	0	0.0	0	0.0	0	0.0	133	96.4	48	36.1
Not Migrant	116,545	99.9	111,530	95.7	3,149	2.7	1,112	1.0	425	100.0	99	0.1	230	0.2	0	0.0	115,791	99.4	74,390	64.2
Limited English Proficient (LEP)	5,520	4.7	4,576	82.9	412	7.5	81	1.5	430	100.0	4	0.1	17	0.3	0	0.0	5,069	91.9	1,171	23.1
Not LEP	111,163	95.3	107,083	96.3	2,739	2.5	1,033	0.9	0	0.0	95	0.1	213	0.2	0	0.0	110,855	99.8	73,267	66.1
All Students with Disabilities	18,710	16.0	14,336	76.6	3,118	16.7	1,100	5.9	9	100.0	65	0.3	82	0.4	0	0.0	18,554	99.5	6,333	34.1
Students without Disabilities	97,973	84.0	97,323	99.3	33	0.0	14	0.0	421	100.0	34	0.0	148	0.2	0	0.0	97,370	99.4	68,105	69.9
Autism	1,427	1.2	684	47.9	341	23.9	391	27.4	0	0.0	5	0.4	6	0.4	0	0.0	1,416	99.6	629	44.4
Deaf-Blindness	2	0.0	0	0.0	1	50.0	1	50.0	0	0.0	0	0.0	0	0.0	0	0.0	2	100.0	*	*
Deafness	11	0.0	5	45.5	5	45.5	0	0.0	0	0.0	0	0.0	1	9.1	0	0.0	10	90.9	1	10.0
Serious Emotional Disability	506	0.4	393	77.7	105	20.8	2	0.4	0	0.0	3	0.6	3	0.6	0	0.0	500	99.4	154	30.8
Hearing Impairment	149	0.1	114	76.5	29	19.5	6	4.0	0	0.0	0	0.0	0	0.0	0	0.0	149	100.0	43	28.9
Intellectual Disability-Mild	1,023	0.9	319	31.2	527	51.5	168	16.4	0	0.0	1	0.3	9	0.9	0	0.0	1,014	99.1	167	16.5
Intellectual Disability-Moderate	342	0.3	11	3.2	46	13.5	280	81.9	0	100.0	3	0.9	3	0.9	0	0.0	337	98.8	186	55.2
Intellectual Disability-Severe	61	0.1	0	0.0	0	0.0	52	85.2	1	100.0	6	9.8	2	3.3	0	0.0	52	94.5	13	25.0
Specific Learning Disability	8,247	7.1	6,853	83.1	1,363	16.5	3	0.0	5	100.0	4	0.0	19	0.2	0	0.0	8,219	99.7	2,283	27.8
Multiple Disabilities	206	0.2	8	3.9	15	7.3	141	68.4	0	0.0	34	16.5	8	3.9	0	0.0	164	95.3	57	34.8
Other Health Impairment	3,457	3.0	2,755	79.7	633	18.3	39	1.1	1	100.0	9	0.3	20	0.6	0	0.0	3,427	99.4	941	27.5
Orthopedic Impairment	69	0.1	36	52.2	19	27.5	11	15.9	0	0.0	2	2.9	1	1.4	0	0.0	66	98.5	24	36.4
Speech or Language Impairment	3,131	2.7	3,103	99.1	17	0.5	1	0.0	0	0.0	1	0.0	9	0.3	0	0.0	3,121	99.7	1,812	58.1
Traumatic Brain Injury	28	0.0	12	42.9	11	39.3	5	17.9	0	0.0	0	0.0	0	0.0	0	0.0	28	100.0	4	14.3
Visual Impairment incl. Blindness	50	0.0	43	86.0	5	10.0	0	0.0	1	100.0	0	0.0	0	2.0	0	0.0	48	96.0	19	39.6

[1] The "Verified Membership" for the end-of-grade science tests is the number of student grade and course enrollment records in PowerSchool on the first day of test administration in the testing cycle.

[2] Data for "Other" includes misadministrations, transfers, and unknown causes.

*Performance data are not reported when membership is fewer than five. Performance data that are less than or equal to 5.0 percent, or greater than or equal to 95.0 percent, are not displayed. Some columns may not add up to the total due to miscoding or rounding. The disability categories were revised in 2007–08.

Notes: The total for "All Students with Disabilities" includes Section 504.

Data received from local education agencies, charter schools, and regional school after December 5, 2014 are not included in this table.

Prepared by the NCDPI Division of Accountability Services/Test Development Section.

Table 4a. 2013-14 End-of-Grade Statewide Participation and Performance
Grade 8 Science

CATEGORY	# Verified Mbership[1]	% of Verified Mbership	GENERAL TEST # Tested (General Test)	% Tested (General Test)	# Tested NC EXTEND2	% Tested NC EXTEND2	# Tested NC EXTEND1	% Tested NC EXTEND1	# LEP Exclusions	% LEP Exclusions	# Medical Exclusions	% Medical Exclusions	NOT TESTED # Absent	% Absent	# Other[2]	% Other	TOTAL OF ALL TESTS # Participating	% Participating	# Proficient	% Proficient
All Students	117,665	100.0	112,108	95.3	3,152	2.7	1,234	1.0	417	100.0	111	0.1	643	0.5	0	0.0	116,494	99.1	83,156	71.4
Female	57,454	48.8	55,427	96.5	1,043	1.8	453	0.8	216	100.0	62	0.1	253	0.4	0	0.0	56,923	99.2	40,476	71.1
Male	60,211	51.2	56,681	94.1	2,109	3.5	781	1.3	201	100.0	49	0.1	390	0.6	0	0.0	59,571	99.0	42,680	71.6
American Indian	1,743	1.5	1,648	94.5	39	2.2	23	1.3	8	100.0	1	0.1	24	1.4	0	0.0	1,710	98.2	927	54.2
Asian	3,122	2.7	2,985	95.6	24	0.8	28	0.9	74	100.0	1	0.0	10	0.3	0	0.0	3,037	97.3	2,588	85.2
Black	31,377	26.7	29,311	93.4	1,339	4.3	434	1.4	27	100.0	24	0.1	242	0.8	0	0.0	31,084	99.1	16,656	53.6
Hispanic	15,747	13.4	14,817	94.1	438	2.8	135	0.9	256	100.0	10	0.1	91	0.6	0	0.0	15,390	97.8	9,726	63.2
Multi-Racial	4,045	3.4	3,884	96.0	96	2.4	29	0.7	5	100.0	4	0.1	27	0.7	0	0.0	4,009	99.2	2,915	72.7
Native Hawaiian/Pacific Islander	128	0.1	125	97.7	2	1.6	1	0.8	0	0.0	0	0.0	0	0.0	0	0.0	128	100.0	83	64.8
White	61,503	52.3	59,338	96.5	1,214	2.0	584	0.9	47	100.0	71	0.1	249	0.4	0	0.0	61,136	99.5	50,261	82.2
Economically Disadvantaged	62,062	52.7	58,005	93.5	2,460	4.0	826	1.3	235	100.0	54	0.1	482	0.8	0	0.0	61,291	98.8	36,019	58.8
Not Economically Disadvantaged	55,603	47.3	54,103	97.3	692	1.2	408	0.7	182	100.0	57	0.1	161	0.3	0	0.0	55,203	99.4	47,137	85.4
Migrant	94	0.1	90	95.7	1	1.1	0	0.0	0	0.0	0	0.0	3	3.2	0	0.0	91	96.8	45	49.5
Not Migrant	117,571	99.9	112,018	95.3	3,151	2.7	1,234	1.0	417	100.0	111	0.1	640	0.5	0	0.0	116,403	99.1	83,111	71.4
Limited English Proficient (LEP)	5,516	4.7	4,589	83.2	363	6.6	79	1.4	417	100.0	6	0.1	62	1.1	0	0.0	5,031	91.3	1,597	31.7
Not LEP	112,149	95.3	107,519	95.9	2,789	2.5	1,155	1.0	0	0.0	105	0.1	581	0.5	0	0.0	111,463	99.5	81,559	73.2
All Students with Disabilities	16,279	13.8	11,637	71.5	3,139	19.3	1,226	7.5	6	100.0	54	0.3	217	1.3	0	0.0	16,002	98.6	6,086	38.0
Students without Disabilities	101,386	86.2	100,471	99.1	13	0.0	8	0.0	411	100.0	57	0.1	426	0.4	0	0.0	100,492	99.2	77,070	76.7
Autism	1,166	1.0	566	48.5	262	22.5	321	27.5	0	0.0	3	0.3	14	1.2	0	0.0	1,149	98.8	636	55.4
Deaf-Blindness	0	0.0	0	0.0	0	0.0	0	0.0	0	0.0	0	0.0	0	0.0	0	0.0	0	0.0	*	*
Deafness	16	0.0	2	12.5	12	75.0	1	6.3	0	0.0	0	0.0	1	6.3	0	0.0	15	93.8	3	20.0
Serious Emotional Disability	649	0.6	503	77.5	107	16.5	5	0.8	1	100.0	5	0.8	28	4.3	0	0.0	615	95.5	186	30.2
Hearing Impairment	166	0.1	131	78.9	32	19.3	2	1.2	0	0.0	0	0.0	1	0.6	0	0.0	165	99.4	64	38.8
Intellectual Disability-Mild	1,184	1.0	311	26.3	655	55.3	189	16.0	1	100.0	3	0.3	25	2.1	0	0.0	1,155	97.8	205	17.7
Intellectual Disability-Moderate	460	0.4	8	1.7	39	8.5	408	88.7	0	0.0	1	0.2	4	0.9	0	0.0	455	99.1	269	59.1
Intellectual Disability-Severe	76	0.1	0	0.0	0	0.0	69	90.8	0	0.0	4	5.3	3	3.9	0	0.0	69	95.8	17	24.6
Specific Learning Disability	8,060	6.8	6,636	82.3	1,330	16.5	8	0.1	4	100.0	3	0.0	79	1.0	0	0.0	7,974	99.0	2,922	36.6
Multiple Disabilities	213	0.2	13	6.1	14	6.6	161	75.6	0	0.0	19	8.9	6	2.8	0	0.0	188	96.9	65	34.6
Other Health Impairment	3,593	3.1	2,832	78.8	660	18.4	38	1.1	0	0.0	9	0.3	54	1.5	0	0.0	3,530	98.5	1,313	37.2
Orthopedic Impairment	54	0.0	34	63.0	8	14.8	7	13.0	0	0.0	4	7.4	1	1.9	0	0.0	49	98.0	30	61.2
Speech or Language Impairment	551	0.5	547	99.3	3	0.5	0	0.0	0	0.0	0	0.0	1	0.2	0	0.0	550	99.8	331	60.2
Traumatic Brain Injury	42	0.0	17	40.5	10	23.8	15	35.7	0	0.0	0	0.0	0	0.0	0	0.0	42	100.0	16	38.1
Visual Impairment incl. Blindness	49	0.0	37	75.5	7	14.3	2	4.1	0	0.0	3	6.1	0	0.0	0	0.0	46	100.0	29	63.0

[1]The "Verified Membership" for the end-of-grade science tests is the number of student grade and course enrollment records in PowerSchool on the first day of test administration in the testing cycle.

[2]Data for "Other" includes misadministrations, transfers, and unknown causes.

*Performance data are not reported when membership is fewer than five. Performance data that are less than or equal to 5.0 percent, or greater than or equal to 95.0 percent, are not displayed. Some columns may not add up to the total due to miscoding or rounding. The disability categories were revised in 2007–08.

Notes: The total for "All Students with Disabilities" includes Section 504.
Data received from local education agencies, charter schools, and regional school after December 5, 2014 are not included in this table.
Prepared by the NCDPI Division of Accountability Services/Test Development Section.

Table 5. 2013–14 Statewide Participation and Performance End-of-Course Biology

Biology

Category	# Verified Mbership[1]	% of Verified Mbership	Tested				Not Tested		# Eligible	# Participating	% Participating	# Proficient	% Proficient
			# Tested	% Tested	# Medical Exclusions	% Medical Exclusions	# Absent/Other	% Absent/Other					
All Students	**108,137**	**100.0**	**106,639**	**98.6**	**67**	**0.1**	**1,375**	**1.3**	**108,070**	**106,639**	**98.6**	**59,135**	**55.4**
Female	53,311	49.3	52,698	98.9	41	0.1	547	1.0	53,270	52,698	98.9	29,055	55.1
Male	54,826	50.7	53,941	98.4	26	0.0	828	1.5	54,800	53,941	98.4	30,080	55.7
American Indian	1,543	1.4	1,518	98.4	0	0.0	24	1.6	1,543	1,518	98.4	661	43.5
Asian	3,048	2.8	3,011	98.8	0	0.0	20	0.7	3,048	3,011	98.8	2,189	72.7
Black	28,720	26.6	28,160	98.1	16	0.1	542	1.9	28,704	28,160	98.1	9,592	34.0
Hispanic	12,927	12.0	12,642	97.8	5	0.0	254	2.0	12,922	12,642	97.8	5,655	44.6
Multi-Racial	3,619	3.3	3,568	98.6	4	0.1	47	1.3	3,615	3,568	98.6	1,983	55.5
Native Hawaiian/Pacific Islander	120	0.1	116	96.7	0	0.0	3	2.5	120	116	96.7	49	41.9
White	58,160	53.8	57,624	99.1	42	0.1	485	0.8	58,118	57,624	99.1	39,006	67.6
Economically Disadvantaged	**50,172**	**46.4**	**49,168**	**98.0**	**27**	**0.1**	**946**	**1.9**	**50,145**	**49,168**	**98.0**	**19,465**	**39.5**
Not Economically Disadvantaged	57,965	53.6	57,471	99.1	40	0.1	429	0.7	57,925	57,471	99.1	39,670	69.0
Title I	0	0.0	0	0.0	0	0.0	0	0.0	0	0	0.0	*	*
Not Title I	0	0.0	0	0.0	0	0.0	0	0.0	0	0	0.0	*	*
Schoolwide Title I Program	0	0.0	0	0.0	0	0.0	0	0.0	0	0	0.0	*	*
Targeted Assistance	0	0.0	0	0.0	0	0.0	0	0.0	0	0	0.0	*	*
Migrant	0	0.0	0	0.0	0	0.0	0	0.0	0	0	0.0	*	*
Not Migrant	0	0.0	0	0.0	0	0.0	0	0.0	0	0	0.0	*	*
Limited English Proficient (LEP)	**2,835**	**2.6**	**2,688**	**94.8**	**1**	**0.0**	**90**	**3.2**	**2,834**	**2,688**	**94.8**	**324**	**12.0**
Not LEP	105,302	97.4	103,951	98.7	66	0.1	1,285	1.2	105,236	103,951	98.7	58,811	56.5
Not Exceptional	**78,044**	**72.2**	**76,924**	**98.6**	**38**	**0.0**	**1,029**	**1.3**	**78,006**	**76,924**	**98.6**	**38,370**	**49.8**
Academically/Intellectually Gifted	19,889	18.4	19,827	99.7	10	0.1	50	0.3	19,879	19,827	99.7	18,373	92.7
Students with IEPs	**10,204**	**9.4**	**9,888**	**96.9**	**19**	**0.2**	**296**	**2.9**	**10,185**	**9,888**	**96.9**	**2,392**	**24.1**
Students without IEPs	97,933	90.6	96,751	98.8	48	0.0	1,079	1.1	97,885	96,751	98.8	56,743	58.6
Students with Disabilities	**10,204**	**9.4**	**9,888**	**96.9**	**19**	**0.2**	**296**	**2.9**	**10,185**	**9,888**	**96.9**	**2,392**	**24.1**
Students without Disabilities	97,933	90.6	96,751	98.8	48	0.0	1,079	1.1	97,885	96,751	98.8	56,743	58.6
Autism	501	0.5	495	98.8	2	0.4	4	0.8	499	495	98.8	285	57.6
Deaf-Blindness	2	0.0	2	100.0	0	0.0	0	0.0	2	2	100.0	*	*
Deafness	9	0.0	9	100.0	0	0.0	0	0.0	9	9	100.0	4	44.4
Serious Emotional Disability	496	0.5	453	91.3	1	0.2	42	8.5	495	453	91.3	99	21.7
Hearing Impairment	124	0.1	122	98.4	0	0.0	2	1.6	124	122	98.4	31	25.2
Intellectual Disability-Mild	342	0.3	309	90.4	1	0.3	32	9.4	341	309	90.4	*	<=5%
Intellectual Disability-Moderate	8	0.0	6	75.0	0	0.0	2	25.0	8	6	75.0	1	16.7
Intellectual Disability-Severe	0	0.0	0	0.0	0	0.0	0	0.0	0	0	0.0	*	*
Specific Learning Disability	5,712	5.3	5,573	97.6	5	0.1	133	2.3	5,707	5,573	97.6	1,200	21.5
Multiple Disabilities	4	0.0	4	100.0	0	0.0	0	0.0	4	4	100.0	*	*
Other Health Impairment	2,703	2.5	2,620	96.9	8	0.3	75	2.8	2,695	2,620	96.9	638	24.3
Orthopedic Impairment	48	0.0	48	100.0	0	0.0	0	0.0	48	48	100.0	16	33.3
Speech or Language Impairment	176	0.2	172	97.7	1	0.6	3	1.7	175	172	97.7	85	49.4
Traumatic Brain Injury	36	0.0	32	88.9	1	2.8	3	8.3	35	32	88.9	2	6.3
Visual Impairment incl. Blindness	43	0.0	43	100.0	0	0.0	0	0.0	43	43	100.0	27	62.8

[1] The "Verified Membership" for the end-of-course tests is the number of student grade and course enrollment records in PowerSchool on the first day of test administration in the testing cycle.

[2] Data for "Other" includes misadministrations, transfers, and unknown causes. Some columns may not add up to the total due to miscoding or rounding.

Notes: The disability categories were revised in 2007–08.

The total for "All Students with Disabilities" includes Section 504.

Data received from by local education agencies, charter schools, and regional school after December 5, 2014 are not included in this table.

Prepared by the NCDPI Division of Accountability Services/Test Development Section.

Table 5a. 2013–14 Statewide Participation and Performance
End-of-Course English II

Category	# Verified Mbership[1]	% of Verified Mbership[1]	Tested		Not Tested				# Eligible	# Participating	% Participating	# Proficient	% Proficient
			# Tested	% Tested	# Medical Exclusions	% Medical Exclusions	# Absent/Other	% Absent/Other					
All Students	**111,237**	**100.0**	**109,569**	**98.5**	**71**	**0.1**	**1,409**	**1.3**	**111,166**	**109,569**	**98.5**	**69,019**	**62.7**
Female	54,562	49.1	53,936	98.9	38	0.1	494	0.9	54,524	53,936	98.9	37,148	68.7
Male	56,675	50.9	55,633	98.2	33	0.1	915	1.6	56,642	55,633	98.2	31,871	57.0
American Indian	1,561	1.4	1,532	98.1	1	0.1	25	1.6	1,560	1,532	98.1	688	44.7
Asian	3,049	2.7	2,992	98.1	1	0.0	16	0.5	3,048	2,992	98.1	2,146	71.6
Black	29,521	26.5	28,927	98.0	18	0.1	561	1.9	29,503	28,927	98.0	13,305	45.7
Hispanic	13,516	12.2	13,101	96.9	4	0.0	311	2.3	13,512	13,101	96.9	6,768	51.3
Multi-Racial	3,893	3.5	3,840	98.6	3	0.1	49	1.3	3,890	3,840	98.6	2,534	65.7
Native Hawaiian/Pacific Islander	132	0.1	130	98.5	1	0.8	0	0.0	131	130	98.5	72	55.0
White	59,565	53.5	59,047	99.1	43	0.1	447	0.8	59,522	59,047	99.1	43,506	73.5
Economically Disadvantaged	**52,319**	**47.0**	**51,150**	**97.8**	**27**	**0.1**	**1,035**	**2.0**	**52,292**	**51,150**	**97.8**	**24,339**	**47.3**
Not Economically Disadvantaged	58,918	53.0	58,419	99.2	44	0.1	374	0.6	58,874	58,419	99.2	44,680	76.3
Title I	0	0.0	0	0.0	0	0.0	0	0.0	0	0	0.0	*	*
Not Title I	0	0.0	0	0.0	0	0.0	0	0.0	0	0	0.0	*	*
Schoolwide Title I Program	0	0.0	0	0.0	0	0.0	0	0.0	0	0	0.0	*	*
Targeted Assistance	0	0.0	0	0.0	0	0.0	0	0.0	0	0	0.0	*	*
Migrant	0	0.0	0	0.0	0	0.0	0	0.0	0	0	0.0	*	*
Not Migrant	0	0.0	0	0.0	0	0.0	0	0.0	0	0	0.0	*	*
Limited English Proficient (LEP)	**3,312**	**3.0**	**2,980**	**90.0**	**1**	**0.0**	**143**	**4.3**	**3,311**	**2,980**	**90.0**	**250**	**8.3**
Not LEP	107,925	97.0	106,589	98.8	70	0.1	1,266	1.2	107,855	106,589	98.8	68,769	64.3
Not Exceptional	**80,157**	**72.1**	**78,921**	**98.5**	**41**	**0.1**	**1,007**	**1.3**	**80,116**	**78,921**	**98.5**	**47,123**	**59.4**
Academically/Intellectually Gifted	20,314	18.3	20,271	99.8	11	0.1	32	0.2	20,303	20,271	99.8	*	>=95%
Students with IEPs	**10,766**	**9.7**	**10,377**	**96.4**	**19**	**0.2**	**370**	**3.4**	**10,747**	**10,377**	**96.4**	**2,397**	**22.9**
Students without IEPs	100,471	90.3	99,192	98.7	52	0.1	1,039	1.0	100,419	99,192	98.7	66,622	66.9
Students with Disabilities	**10,766**	**9.7**	**10,377**	**96.4**	**19**	**0.2**	**370**	**3.4**	**10,747**	**10,377**	**96.4**	**2,397**	**22.9**
Students without Disabilities	100,471	90.3	99,192	98.7	52	0.1	1,039	1.0	100,419	99,192	98.7	66,622	66.9
Autism	499	0.4	491	98.4	0	0.0	8	1.6	499	491	98.4	253	51.3
Deaf-Blindness	1	0.0	1	100.0	0	0.0	0	0.0	1	1	100.0	*	*
Deafness	5	0.0	5	100.0	0	0.0	0	0.0	5	5	100.0	*	*
Serious Emotional Disability	532	0.5	478	89.8	1	0.2	53	10.0	531	478	89.8	133	27.2
Hearing Impairment	115	0.1	113	98.3	0	0.0	2	1.7	115	113	98.3	37	32.7
Intellectual Disability-Mild	390	0.4	336	86.2	1	0.3	53	13.6	389	336	86.2	*	<=5%
Intellectual Disability-Moderate	12	0.0	10	83.3	0	0.0	2	16.7	12	10	83.3	*	*
Intellectual Disability-Severe	0	0.0	0	0.0	0	0.0	0	0.0	0	0	0.0	*	*
Specific Learning Disability	6,017	5.4	5,866	97.5	5	0.1	146	2.4	6,012	5,866	97.5	1,162	19.7
Multiple Disabilities	6	0.0	5	83.3	0	0.0	1	16.7	6	5	83.3	3	60.0
Other Health Impairment	2,837	2.6	2,730	96.2	8	0.3	99	3.5	2,829	2,730	96.2	676	24.6
Orthopedic Impairment	52	0.0	51	98.1	1	1.9	0	0.0	51	51	98.1	20	39.2
Speech or Language Impairment	220	0.2	215	97.7	2	0.9	3	1.4	218	215	97.7	80	37.0
Traumatic Brain Injury	37	0.0	34	91.9	1	2.7	2	5.4	36	34	91.9	6	17.6
Visual Impairment incl. Blindness	43	0.0	42	97.7	0	0.0	1	2.3	43	42	97.7	25	59.5

[1] The "Verified Membership" for the end-of-course tests is the number of student grade and course enrollment records in PowerSchool on the first day of test administration in the testing cycle.

[2] Data for "Other" includes misadministrations, transfers, and unknown causes. Some columns may not add up to the total due to miscoding or rounding.

Notes: The disability categories were revised in 2007–08.
The total for "All Students with Disabilities" includes Section 504.
Data received from by local education agencies, charter schools, and regional school after December 5, 2014 are not included in this table.
Prepared by the NCDPI Division of Accountability Services/Test Development Section.

Table 5b. 2013–14 Statewide Participation and Performance End-of-Course Math I

Category	# Verified Mbership[1]	% of Verified Mbership	Tested		Not Tested				Math I				
			# Tested	% Tested	# Medical Exclusions	% Medical Exclusions	# Absent/Other	% Absent/Other	# Eligible	# Participating	% Participating	# Proficient	% Proficient
All Students	118,858	100.0	116,462	98.0	65	0.1	1,854	1.6	118,793	116,462	98.0	63,526	54.5
Female	57,899	48.7	57,020	98.5	36	0.1	641	1.1	57,863	57,020	98.5	31,987	56.1
Male	60,959	51.3	59,442	97.5	29	0.0	1,213	2.0	60,930	59,442	97.5	31,539	53.1
American Indian	1,621	1.4	1,569	96.8	1	0.1	39	2.4	1,620	1,569	96.8	666	42.4
Asian	3,245	2.7	3,140	96.8	0	0.0	7	0.2	3,245	3,140	96.8	2,435	77.5
Black	32,444	27.3	31,629	97.5	15	0.0	751	2.3	32,429	31,629	97.5	10,969	34.7
Hispanic	15,435	13.0	14,820	96.0	4	0.0	350	2.3	15,431	14,820	96.0	6,863	46.3
Multi-Racial	4,032	3.4	3,964	98.3	1	0.0	64	1.6	4,031	3,964	98.3	2,119	53.5
Native Hawaiian/Pacific Islander	146	0.1	138	94.5	0	0.0	2	1.4	146	138	94.5	63	45.7
White	61,935	52.1	61,202	98.8	44	0.1	641	1.0	61,891	61,202	98.8	40,411	66.0
Economically Disadvantaged	60,733	51.1	58,996	97.1	29	0.0	1,386	2.3	60,704	58,996	97.1	23,544	39.9
Not Economically Disadvantaged	58,125	48.9	57,466	98.9	36	0.1	468	0.8	58,089	57,466	98.9	39,982	69.6
Title I	0	0.0	0	0.0	0	0.0	0	0.0	0	0	0.0	*	*
Not Title I	0	0.0	0	0.0	0	0.0	0	0.0	0	0	0.0	*	*
Schoolwide Title I Program	0	0.0	0	0.0	0	0.0	0	0.0	0	0	0.0	*	*
Targeted Assistance	0	0.0	0	0.0	0	0.0	0	0.0	0	0	0.0	*	*
Migrant	0	0.0	0	0.0	0	0.0	0	0.0	0	0	0.0	*	*
Not Migrant	0	0.0	0	0.0	0	0.0	0	0.0	0	0	0.0	*	*
Limited English Proficient (LEP)	5,822	4.9	5,158	88.6	4	0.1	183	3.1	5,818	5,158	88.6	1,065	20.6
Not LEP	113,036	95.1	111,304	98.5	61	0.1	1,671	1.5	112,975	111,304	98.5	62,461	56.1
Not Exceptional	85,557	72.0	83,725	97.9	36	0.0	1,322	1.5	85,521	83,725	97.9	41,789	49.9
Academically/Intellectually Gifted	20,318	17.1	20,274	99.8	10	0.0	34	0.2	20,308	20,274	99.8	*	>=95%
Students with IEPs	12,983	10.9	12,463	96.0	19	0.1	498	3.8	12,964	12,463	96.0	2,388	19.2
Students without IEPs	105,875	89.1	103,999	98.2	46	0.0	1,356	1.3	105,829	103,999	98.2	61,138	58.8
Students with Disabilities	12,983	10.9	12,463	96.0	19	0.1	498	3.8	12,964	12,463	96.0	2,388	19.2
Students without Disabilities	105,875	89.1	103,999	98.2	46	0.0	1,356	1.3	105,829	103,999	98.2	61,138	58.8
Autism	602	0.5	591	98.2	1	0.2	10	1.7	601	591	98.2	274	46.4
Deaf-Blindness	2	0.0	2	100.0	0	0.0	0	0.0	2	2	100.0	*	*
Deafness	6	0.0	6	100.0	0	0.0	0	0.0	6	6	100.0	1	16.7
Serious Emotional Disability	651	0.5	580	89.1	1	0.2	70	10.8	650	580	89.1	98	16.9
Hearing Impairment	130	0.1	126	96.9	0	0.0	4	3.1	130	126	96.9	39	31.0
Intellectual Disability-Mild	440	0.4	399	90.7	1	0.2	39	8.9	439	399	90.7	*	<=5%
Intellectual Disability-Moderate	17	0.0	16	94.1	0	0.0	1	5.9	17	16	94.1	*	*
Intellectual Disability-Severe	0	0.0	0	0.0	0	0.0	0	0.0	0	0	0.0	*	*
Specific Learning Disability	7,261	6.1	7,026	96.8	5	0.1	228	3.1	7,256	7,026	96.8	1,236	17.6
Multiple Disabilities	7	0.0	6	85.7	1	14.3	0	0.0	6	6	85.7	1	16.7
Other Health Impairment	3,335	2.8	3,185	95.5	10	0.3	140	4.2	3,325	3,185	95.5	521	16.4
Orthopedic Impairment	48	0.0	48	100.0	0	0.0	0	0.0	48	48	100.0	15	31.3
Speech or Language Impairment	406	0.3	403	99.3	0	0.0	3	0.7	406	403	99.3	174	43.2
Traumatic Brain Injury	30	0.0	27	90.0	0	0.0	3	10.0	30	27	90.0	5	18.5
Visual Impairment incl. Blindness	48	0.0	48	100.0	0	0.0	0	0.0	48	48	100.0	21	43.8

[1] The "Verified Membership" for the end-of-course tests is the number of student grade and course enrollment records in PowerSchool on the first day of test administration in the testing cycle.

[2] Data for "Other" includes misadministrations, transfers, and unknown causes. Some columns may not add up to the total due to miscoding or rounding.

Notes: The disability categories were revised in 2007–08.

The total for "All Students with Disabilities" includes Section 504.

Data received from by local education agencies, charter schools, and regional school after December 5, 2014 are not included in this table.

Prepared by the NCDPI Division of Accountability Services/Test Development Section.

Table 6. 2013–14 End-of-Course *NCEXTEND2* Alternate Assessment Results

Biology

Category	# Verified Mbership[1]	% of Verified Mbership	Tested		Not Tested				# Eligible	# Participating	% Participating	# Proficient	% Proficient
			# Tested	% Tested	# Medical Exclusions	% Medical Exclusions	# Absent/Other	% Absent/Other					
All Students	**3,550**	**100.0**	**2,052**	**57.8**	**67**	**1.9**	**1,375**	**38.7**	**3,483**	**2,052**	**57.8**	*	<=5%
Female	1,289	36.3	676	52.4	41	3.2	547	42.4	1,248	676	52.4	*	<=5%
Male	2,261	63.7	1,376	60.9	26	1.1	828	36.6	2,235	1,376	60.9	*	<=5%
American Indian	70	2.0	45	64.3	0	0.0	24	34.3	70	45	64.3	*	<=5%
Asian	53	1.5	16	30.2	0	0.0	20	37.7	53	16	30.2	*	*
Black	1,436	40.5	876	61.0	16	1.1	542	37.7	1,420	876	61.0	*	<=5%
Hispanic	479	13.5	194	40.5	5	1.0	254	53.0	474	194	40.5	*	<=5%
Multi-Racial	115	3.2	64	55.7	4	3.5	47	40.9	111	64	55.7	*	<=5%
Native Hawaiian/Pacific Islander	7	0.2	3	42.9	0	0.0	3	42.9	7	3	42.9	*	*
White	1,390	39.2	854	61.4	42	3.0	485	34.9	1,348	854	61.4	*	<=5%
Economically Disadvantaged	**2,482**	**69.9**	**1,478**	**59.5**	**27**	**1.1**	**946**	**38.1**	**2,455**	**1,478**	**59.5**	*	<=5%
Not Economically Disadvantaged	1,068	30.1	574	53.7	40	3.7	429	40.2	1,028	574	53.7	*	<=5%
Limited English Proficient (LEP)	**302**	**8.5**	**155**	**51.3**	**1**	**0.3**	**90**	**29.8**	**301**	**155**	**51.3**	*	<=5%
Not LEP	3,248	91.5	1,897	58.4	66	2.0	1,285	39.6	3,182	1,897	58.4	*	<=5%
Not Exceptional	**1,124**	**31.7**	**4**	**0.4**	**38**	**3.4**	**1,029**	**91.5**	**1,086**	**4**	**0.4**	*	*
Academically/Intellectually Gifted	62	1.7	0	0.0	10	0.0	50	80.6	52	0	0.0	*	*
Students with IEPs	**2,364**	**66.6**	**2,048**	**86.6**	**19**	**0.8**	**296**	**12.5**	**2,345**	**2,048**	**86.6**	*	<=5%
Students without IEPs	1,186	33.4	4	0.3	48	4.0	1,079	91.0	1,138	4	0.3	*	*
Students with Disabilities	**2,364**	**66.6**	**2,048**	**86.6**	**19**	**0.8**	**296**	**12.5**	**2,345**	**2,048**	**86.6**	*	<=5%
Students without Disabilities	1,186	33.4	4	0.3	48	4.0	1,079	91.0	1,138	4	0.3	*	*
Autism	166	4.7	160	96.4	2	1.2	4	2.4	164	160	96.4	11	6.9
Deaf-Blindness	1	0.0	1	100.0	0	0.0	0	0.0	1	1	100.0	*	*
Deafness	6	0.2	6	100.0	0	0.0	0	0.0	6	6	100.0	*	*
Serious Emotional Disability	113	3.2	70	61.9	1	0.9	42	37.2	112	70	61.9	4	5.7
Hearing Impairment	19	0.5	17	89.5	0	0.0	2	10.5	19	17	89.5	*	*
Intellectual Disability-Mild	746	21.0	713	95.6	1	0.1	32	4.3	745	713	95.6	*	<=5%
Intellectual Disability-Moderate	51	1.4	49	96.1	0	0.0	2	3.9	51	49	96.1	*	<=5%
Intellectual Disability-Severe	0	0.0	0	0.0	0	0.0	0	0.0	0	0	0.0	*	*
Specific Learning Disability	716	20.2	577	80.6	5	0.7	133	18.6	711	577	80.6	*	<=5%
Multiple Disabilities	10	0.3	10	100.0	0	0.0	0	0.0	10	10	100.0	*	*
Other Health Impairment	481	13.5	398	82.7	8	1.7	75	15.6	473	398	82.7	*	<=5%
Orthopedic Impairment	21	0.6	21	100.0	0	0.0	0	0.0	21	21	100.0	*	<=5%
Speech or Language Impairment	4	0.1	0	0.0	1	0.0	3	75.0	3	0	0.0	*	*
Traumatic Brain Injury	21	0.6	17	81.0	1	4.8	3	14.3	20	17	81.0	*	*
Visual Impairment incl. Blindness	9	0.3	9	100.0	0	0.0	0	0.0	9	9	100.0	*	*

[1]The "Verified Membership" for the end-of-course tests is the number of student grade and course enrollment records in PowerSchool on the first day of test administration in the testing cycle.

[2]Data for "Other" includes misadministrations, transfers, and unknown causes. Some columns may not add up to the total due to miscoding or rounding.

Notes: The disability categories were revised in 2007–08.
The total for "All Students with Disabilities" includes Section 504.
Data received from by local education agencies, charter schools, and regional school after December 5, 2014 are not included in this table.
Prepared by the NCDPI Division of Accountability Services/Test Development Section.

Table 6a. 2013–14 End-of-Course *NCEXTEND2* Alternate Assessment Results
English II

Category	# Verified Mbership¹	% of Verified Mbership	Tested		Not Tested				# Eligible	# Participating	% Participating	# Proficient	% Proficient
			# Tested	% Tested	# Medical Exclusions	% Medical Exclusions	# Absent/Other	% Absent/Other					
All Students	**3,874**	**100.0**	**2,206**	**56.9**	**71**	**1.8**	**1,409**	**36.4**	**3,803**	**2,206**	**56.9**	**115**	**5.1**
Female	1,339	34.6	713	53.2	38	2.8	494	36.9	1,301	713	53.2	*	<=5%
Male	2,535	65.4	1,493	58.9	33	1.3	915	36.1	2,502	1,493	58.9	80	5.3
American Indian	72	1.9	43	59.7	1	1.4	25	34.7	71	43	59.7	*	<=5%
Asian	75	1.9	18	24.0	1	1.3	16	21.3	74	18	24.0	*	*
Black	1,554	40.1	960	61.8	18	1.2	561	36.1	1,536	960	61.8	*	<=5%
Hispanic	617	15.9	202	32.7	4	0.6	311	50.4	613	202	32.7	12	5.8
Multi-Racial	122	3.1	69	56.6	3	2.5	49	40.2	119	69	56.6	5	7.2
Native Hawaiian/Pacific Islander	5	0.1	3	60.0	1	20.0	0	0.0	4	3	60.0	*	*
White	1,429	36.9	911	63.8	43	3.0	447	31.3	1,386	911	63.8	68	7.4
Economically Disadvantaged	**2,818**	**72.7**	**1,649**	**58.5**	**27**	**1.0**	**1,035**	**36.7**	**2,791**	**1,649**	**58.5**	*	**<=5%**
Not Economically Disadvantaged	1,056	27.3	557	52.7	44	4.2	374	35.4	1,012	557	52.7	44	7.8
Limited English Proficient (LEP)	**489**	**12.6**	**157**	**32.1**	**1**	**0.2**	**143**	**29.2**	**488**	**157**	**32.1**	*	**<=5%**
Not LEP	3,385	87.4	2,049	60.5	70	2.1	1,266	37.4	3,315	2,049	60.5	108	5.2
Not Exceptional	**1,244**	**32.1**	**8**	**0.6**	**41**	**3.3**	**1,007**	**80.9**	**1,203**	**8**	**0.6**	*	*
Academically/Intellectually Gifted	43	1.1	0	0.0	11	0.0	32	74.4	32	0	0.0	*	*
Students with IEPs	**2,587**	**66.8**	**2,198**	**85.0**	**19**	**0.7**	**370**	**14.3**	**2,568**	**2,198**	**85.0**	**115**	**5.1**
Students without IEPs	1,287	33.2	8	0.6	52	4.0	1,039	80.7	1,235	8	0.6	*	*
Students with Disabilities	**2,587**	**66.8**	**2,198**	**85.0**	**19**	**0.7**	**370**	**14.3**	**2,568**	**2,198**	**85.0**	**115**	**5.1**
Students without Disabilities	1,287	33.2	8	0.6	52	4.0	1,039	80.7	1,235	8	0.6	*	*
Autism	206	5.3	198	96.1	0	0.0	8	3.9	206	198	96.1	17	8.5
Deaf-Blindness	1	0.0	1	100.0	0	0.0	0	0.0	1	1	100.0	*	*
Deafness	11	0.3	11	100.0	0	0.0	0	0.0	11	11	100.0	*	*
Serious Emotional Disability	137	3.5	83	60.6	1	0.7	53	38.7	136	83	60.6	*	<=5%
Hearing Impairment	23	0.6	21	91.3	0	0.0	2	8.7	23	21	91.3	*	<=5%
Intellectual Disability-Mild	737	19.0	683	92.7	1	0.1	53	7.2	736	683	92.7	*	<=5%
Intellectual Disability-Moderate	62	1.6	60	96.8	0	0.0	2	3.2	62	60	96.8	*	<=5%
Intellectual Disability-Severe	0	0.0	0	0.0	0	0.0	0	0.0	0	0	0.0	*	*
Specific Learning Disability	792	20.4	641	80.9	5	0.6	146	18.4	787	641	80.9	53	8.2
Multiple Disabilities	12	0.3	11	91.7	0	0.0	1	8.3	12	11	91.7	*	*
Other Health Impairment	559	14.4	452	80.9	8	1.4	99	17.7	551	452	80.9	35	7.6
Orthopedic Impairment	19	0.5	18	94.7	1	5.3	0	0.0	18	18	94.7	*	*
Speech or Language Impairment	5	0.1	0	0.0	2	0.0	3	60.0	3	0	0.0	*	*
Traumatic Brain Injury	13	0.3	10	76.9	1	7.7	2	15.4	12	10	76.9	*	*
Visual Impairment incl. Blindness	10	0.3	9	90.0	0	0.0	1	10.0	10	9	90.0	1	11.1

¹The "Verified Membership" for the end-of-course tests is the number of student grade and course enrollment records in PowerSchool on the first day of test administration in the testing cycle.

²Data for "Other" includes misadministrations, transfers, and unknown causes. Some columns may not add up to the total due to miscoding or rounding.

Notes: The disability categories were revised in 2007–08.

The total for "All Students with Disabilities" includes Section 504.

Data received from by local education agencies, charter schools, and regional school after December 5, 2014 are not included in this table.

Prepared by the NCDPI Division of Accountability Services/Test Development Section.

Table 6b. 2013–14 End-of-Course *NCEXTEND2* Alternate Assessment Results
Math I

Category	# Verified Mbership[1]	% of Verified Mbership	Tested		Not Tested				# Eligible	# Participating	% Participating	# Proficient	% Proficient
			# Tested	% Tested	# Medical Exclusions	% Medical Exclusions	# Absent/Other	% Absent/Other					
All Students	**4,931**	**100.0**	**2,535**	**51.4**	**65**	**1.3**	**1,854**	**37.6**	**4,866**	**2,535**	**51.4**	**276**	**10.9**
Female	1,712	34.7	833	48.7	36	2.1	641	37.4	1,676	833	48.7	79	9.5
Male	3,219	65.3	1,702	52.9	29	0.9	1,213	37.7	3,190	1,702	52.9	197	11.6
American Indian	94	1.9	42	44.7	1	1.1	39	41.5	93	42	44.7	*	<=5%
Asian	123	2.5	18	14.6	0	0.0	7	5.7	123	18	14.6	7	38.9
Black	1,895	38.4	1,080	57.0	15	0.8	751	39.6	1,880	1,080	57.0	85	7.9
Hispanic	878	17.8	263	30.0	4	0.5	350	39.9	874	263	30.0	27	10.3
Multi-Racial	139	2.8	71	51.1	1	0.7	64	46.0	138	71	51.1	6	8.5
Native Hawaiian/Pacific Islander	9	0.2	1	11.1	0	0.0	2	22.2	9	1	11.1	*	*
White	1,793	36.4	1,060	59.1	44	2.5	641	35.8	1,749	1,060	59.1	149	14.1
Economically Disadvantaged	**3,666**	**74.3**	**1,929**	**52.6**	**29**	**0.8**	**1,386**	**37.8**	**3,637**	**1,929**	**52.6**	**207**	**10.7**
Not Economically Disadvantaged	1,265	25.7	606	47.9	36	2.8	468	37.0	1,229	606	47.9	69	11.4
Limited English Proficient (LEP)	**861**	**17.5**	**197**	**22.9**	**4**	**0.5**	**183**	**21.3**	**857**	**197**	**22.9**	**21**	**10.7**
Not LEP	4,070	82.5	2,338	57.4	61	1.5	1,671	41.1	4,009	2,338	57.4	255	10.9
Not Exceptional	**1,840**	**37.3**	**8**	**0.4**	**36**	**2.0**	**1,322**	**71.8**	**1,804**	**8**	**0.4**	*	*
Academically/Intellectually Gifted	44	0.9	0	0.0	10	0.0	34	77.3	34	0	0.0	*	*
Students with IEPs	**3,047**	**61.8**	**2,527**	**82.9**	**19**	**0.6**	**498**	**16.3**	**3,028**	**2,527**	**82.9**	**276**	**10.9**
Students without IEPs	1,884	38.2	8	0.4	46	2.4	1,356	72.0	1,838	8	0.4	*	*
Students with Disabilities	**3,047**	**61.8**	**2,527**	**82.9**	**19**	**0.6**	**498**	**16.3**	**3,028**	**2,527**	**82.9**	**276**	**10.9**
Students without Disabilities	1,884	38.2	8	0.4	46	2.4	1,356	72.0	1,838	8	0.4	*	*
Autism	234	4.7	223	95.3	1	0.4	10	4.3	233	223	95.3	38	17.0
Deaf-Blindness	0	0.0	0	0.0	0	0.0	0	0.0	0	0	0.0	*	*
Deafness	9	0.2	9	100.0	0	0.0	0	0.0	9	9	100.0	*	*
Serious Emotional Disability	156	3.2	85	54.5	1	0.6	70	44.9	155	85	54.5	6	7.1
Hearing Impairment	31	0.6	27	87.1	0	0.0	4	12.9	31	27	87.1	2	7.4
Intellectual Disability-Mild	773	15.7	732	94.7	1	0.1	39	5.0	772	732	94.7	40	5.5
Intellectual Disability-Moderate	52	1.1	51	98.1	0	0.0	1	1.9	52	51	98.1	*	<=5%
Intellectual Disability-Severe	0	0.0	0	0.0	0	0.0	0	0.0	0	0	0.0	*	*
Specific Learning Disability	1,043	21.2	808	77.5	5	0.5	228	21.9	1,038	808	77.5	125	15.5
Multiple Disabilities	12	0.2	11	91.7	1	8.3	0	0.0	11	11	91.7	*	*
Other Health Impairment	695	14.1	545	78.4	10	1.4	140	20.1	685	545	78.4	60	11.0
Orthopedic Impairment	16	0.3	16	100.0	0	0.0	0	0.0	16	16	100.0	1	6.3
Speech or Language Impairment	4	0.1	1	25.0	0	0.0	3	75.0	4	1	25.0	*	*
Traumatic Brain Injury	15	0.3	12	80.0	0	0.0	3	20.0	15	12	80.0	2	16.7
Visual Impairment incl. Blindness	7	0.1	7	100.0	0	0.0	0	0.0	7	7	100.0	1	14.3

[1] The "Verified Membership" for the end-of-course tests is the number of student grade and course enrollment records in PowerSchool on the first day of test administration in the testing cycle.

[2] Data for "Other" includes misadministrations, transfers, and unknown causes. Some columns may not add up to the total due to miscoding or rounding.

Notes: The disability categories were revised in 2007–08.
   The total for "All Students with Disabilities" includes Section 504.
   Data received from by local education agencies, charter schools, and regional school after December 5, 2014 are not included in this table.
   Prepared by the NCDPI Division of Accountability Services/Test Development Section.

Table 7. 2013–14 End-of-Course NCEXTEND1 Alternate Assessment Results

Biology

Category	# Verified Mbership[1]	% of Verified Mbership	Tested		Not Tested				# Eligible	# Participating	% Participating	# Proficient	% Proficient
			# Tested	% Tested	# Medical Exclusions	% Medical Exclusions	# Absent/Other	% Absent/Other					
All Students	**2,409**	**100.0**	**911**	**37.8**	**67**	**2.8**	**1,375**	**57.1**	**2,342**	**911**	**37.8**	**578**	**63.4**
Female	942	39.1	329	34.9	41	4.4	547	58.1	901	329	34.9	205	62.3
Male	1,467	60.9	582	39.7	26	1.8	828	56.4	1,441	582	39.7	373	64.1
American Indian	44	1.8	19	43.2	0	0.0	24	54.5	44	19	43.2	14	73.7
Asian	44	1.8	7	15.9	0	0.0	20	45.5	44	7	15.9	5	71.4
Black	916	38.0	356	38.9	16	1.7	542	59.2	900	356	38.9	224	62.9
Hispanic	365	15.2	80	21.9	5	1.4	254	69.6	360	80	21.9	41	51.3
Multi-Racial	82	3.4	31	37.8	4	4.9	47	57.3	78	31	37.8	20	64.5
Native Hawaiian/Pacific Islander	4	0.2	0	0.0	0	0.0	3	75.0	4	0	0.0	*	*
White	954	39.6	418	43.8	42	4.4	485	50.8	912	418	43.8	274	65.6
Economically Disadvantaged	**1,615**	**67.0**	**611**	**37.8**	**27**	**1.7**	**946**	**58.6**	**1,588**	**611**	**37.8**	**402**	**65.8**
Not Economically Disadvantaged	794	33.0	300	37.8	40	5.0	429	54.0	754	300	37.8	176	58.7
Limited English Proficient (LEP)	**185**	**7.7**	**38**	**20.5**	**1**	**0.5**	**90**	**48.6**	**184**	**38**	**20.5**	**24**	**63.2**
Not LEP	2,224	92.3	873	39.3	66	3.0	1,285	57.8	2,158	873	39.3	554	63.5
Not Exceptional	**1,126**	**46.7**	**6**	**0.5**	**38**	**3.4**	**1,029**	**91.4**	**1,088**	**6**	**0.5**	**4**	**66.7**
Academically/Intellectually Gifted	62	2.6	0	0.0	10	0.0	50	80.6	52	0	0.0	*	*
Students with IEPs	**1,221**	**50.7**	**905**	**74.1**	**19**	**1.6**	**296**	**24.2**	**1,202**	**905**	**74.1**	**574**	**63.4**
Students without IEPs	1,188	49.3	6	0.5	48	4.0	1,079	90.8	1,140	6	0.5	4	66.7
Students with Disabilities	**1,221**	**50.7**	**905**	**74.1**	**19**	**1.6**	**296**	**24.2**	**1,202**	**905**	**74.1**	**574**	**63.4**
Students without Disabilities	1,188	49.3	6	0.5	48	4.0	1,079	90.8	1,140	6	0.5	4	66.7
Autism	245	10.2	239	97.6	2	0.8	4	1.6	243	239	97.6	131	54.8
Deaf-Blindness	1	0.0	1	100.0	0	0.0	0	0.0	1	1	100.0	*	*
Deafness	2	0.1	2	100.0	0	0.0	0	0.0	2	2	100.0	*	*
Serious Emotional Disability	45	1.9	2	4.4	1	2.2	42	93.3	44	2	4.4	*	*
Hearing Impairment	5	0.2	3	60.0	0	0.0	2	40.0	5	3	60.0	*	*
Intellectual Disability-Mild	171	7.1	138	80.7	1	0.6	32	18.7	170	138	80.7	127	92.0
Intellectual Disability-Moderate	307	12.7	305	99.3	0	0.0	2	0.7	307	305	99.3	203	66.6
Intellectual Disability-Severe	45	1.9	45	100.0	0	0.0	0	0.0	45	45	100.0	14	31.1
Specific Learning Disability	139	5.8	0	0.0	5	0.0	133	95.7	134	0	0.0	*	*
Multiple Disabilities	127	5.3	127	100.0	0	0.0	0	0.0	127	127	100.0	60	47.2
Other Health Impairment	112	4.6	29	25.9	8	7.1	75	67.0	104	29	25.9	21	72.4
Orthopedic Impairment	4	0.2	4	100.0	0	0.0	0	0.0	4	4	100.0	*	*
Speech or Language Impairment	4	0.2	0	0.0	1	0.0	3	75.0	3	0	0.0	*	*
Traumatic Brain Injury	12	0.5	8	66.7	1	8.3	3	25.0	11	8	66.7	5	62.5
Visual Impairment incl. Blindness	2	0.1	2	100.0	0	0.0	0	0.0	2	2	100.0	*	*

[1]The "Verified Membership" for the end-of-course tests is the number of student grade and course enrollment records in PowerSchool on the first day of test administration in the testing cycle.

[2]Data for "Other" includes misadministrations, transfers, and unknown causes. Some columns may not add up to the total due to miscoding or rounding.

Notes: The disability categories were revised in 2007–08.
The total for "All Students with Disabilities" includes Section 504.
Data received from by local education agencies, charter schools, and regional school after December 5, 2014 are not included in this table.
Prepared by the NCDPI Division of Accountability Services/Test Development Section.

Table 7a. 2013–14 End-of-Course *NCEXTEND1* Alternate Assessment Results

English II

Category	# Verified Mbership[1]	% of Verified Mbership	Tested		# Medical Exclusions	% Medical Exclusions	Not Tested		# Eligible	# Partici-pating	% Partici-pating	# Proficient	% Proficient
			# Tested	% Tested			# Absent/ Other	% Absent/ Other					
All Students	**2,572**	**100.0**	**904**	**35.1**	**71**	**2.8**	**1,409**	**54.8**	**2,501**	**904**	**35.1**	**593**	**65.6**
Female	952	37.0	326	34.2	38	4.0	494	51.9	914	326	34.2	216	66.3
Male	1,620	63.0	578	35.7	33	2.0	915	56.5	1,587	578	35.7	377	65.2
American Indian	48	1.9	19	39.6	1	2.1	25	52.1	47	19	39.6	14	73.7
Asian	64	2.5	7	10.9	1	1.6	16	25.0	63	7	10.9	4	57.1
Black	948	36.9	354	37.3	18	1.9	561	59.2	930	354	37.3	233	65.8
Hispanic	495	19.2	80	16.2	4	0.8	311	62.8	491	80	16.2	50	62.5
Multi-Racial	83	3.2	30	36.1	3	3.6	49	59.0	80	30	36.1	19	63.3
Native Hawaiian/Pacific Islander	2	0.1	0	0.0	1	0.0	0	0.0	1	0	0.0	*	*
White	932	36.2	414	44.4	43	4.6	447	48.0	889	414	44.4	273	65.9
Economically Disadvantaged	**1,775**	**69.0**	**606**	**34.1**	**27**	**1.5**	**1,035**	**58.3**	**1,748**	**606**	**34.1**	**409**	**67.5**
Not Economically Disadvantaged	797	31.0	298	37.4	44	5.5	374	46.9	753	298	37.4	184	61.7
Limited English Proficient (LEP)	**370**	**14.4**	**38**	**10.3**	**1**	**0.3**	**143**	**38.6**	**369**	**38**	**10.3**	**29**	**76.3**
Not LEP	2,202	85.6	866	39.3	70	3.2	1,266	57.5	2,132	866	39.3	564	65.1
Not Exceptional	**1,242**	**48.3**	**6**	**0.5**	**41**	**3.3**	**1,007**	**81.1**	**1,201**	**6**	**0.5**	**5**	**83.3**
Academically/Intellectually Gifted	43	1.7	0	0.0	11	0.0	32	74.4	32	0	0.0	*	*
Students with IEPs	**1,287**	**50.0**	**898**	**69.8**	**19**	**1.5**	**370**	**28.7**	**1,268**	**898**	**69.8**	**588**	**65.5**
Students without IEPs	1,285	50.0	6	0.5	52	4.0	1,039	80.9	1,233	6	0.5	5	83.3
Students with Disabilities	**1,287**	**50.0**	**898**	**69.8**	**19**	**1.5**	**370**	**28.7**	**1,268**	**898**	**69.8**	**588**	**65.5**
Students without Disabilities	1,285	50.0	6	0.5	52	4.0	1,039	80.9	1,233	6	0.5	5	83.3
Autism	244	9.5	236	96.7	0	0.0	8	3.3	244	236	96.7	145	61.4
Deaf-Blindness	1	0.0	1	100.0	0	0.0	0	0.0	1	1	100.0	*	*
Deafness	2	0.1	2	100.0	0	0.0	0	0.0	2	2	100.0	*	*
Serious Emotional Disability	56	2.2	2	3.6	1	1.8	53	94.6	55	2	3.6	*	*
Hearing Impairment	5	0.2	3	60.0	0	0.0	2	40.0	5	3	60.0	*	*
Intellectual Disability-Mild	192	7.5	138	71.9	1	0.5	53	27.6	191	138	71.9	125	90.6
Intellectual Disability-Moderate	304	11.8	302	99.3	0	0.0	2	0.7	304	302	99.3	196	64.9
Intellectual Disability-Severe	44	1.7	44	100.0	0	0.0	0	0.0	44	44	100.0	19	43.2
Specific Learning Disability	151	5.9	0	0.0	5	0.0	146	96.7	146	0	0.0	*	*
Multiple Disabilities	128	5.0	127	99.2	0	0.0	1	0.8	128	127	99.2	61	48.0
Other Health Impairment	136	5.3	29	21.3	8	5.9	99	72.8	128	29	21.3	26	89.7
Orthopedic Impairment	5	0.2	4	80.0	1	20.0	0	0.0	4	4	80.0	*	*
Speech or Language Impairment	5	0.2	0	0.0	2	0.0	3	60.0	3	0	0.0	*	*
Traumatic Brain Injury	11	0.4	8	72.7	1	9.1	2	18.2	10	8	72.7	6	75.0
Visual Impairment incl. Blindness	3	0.1	2	66.7	0	0.0	1	33.3	3	2	66.7	*	*

[1] The "Verified Membership" for the end-of-course tests is the number of student grade and course enrollment records in PowerSchool on the first day of test administration in the testing cycle.

[2] Data for "Other" includes misadministrations, transfers, and unknown causes. Some columns may not add up to the total due to miscoding or rounding.

Notes: The disability categories were revised in 2007–08.
The total for "All Students with Disabilities" includes Section 504.
Data received from by local education agencies, charter schools, and regional school after December 5, 2014 are not included in this table.
Prepared by the NCDPI Division of Accountability Services/Test Development Section.

Table 7b. 2013–14 End-of-Course *NCEXTEND1* Alternate Assessment Results
Math I

Category	# Verified Mbership[1]	% of Verified Mbership	Tested		Not Tested				# Eligible	# Participating	% Participating	# Proficient	% Proficient
			# Tested	% Tested	# Medical Exclusions	% Medical Exclusions	# Absent/Other	% Absent/Other					
All Students	**3,307**	**100.0**	**911**	**27.5**	**65**	**2.0**	**1,854**	**56.1**	**3,242**	**911**	**27.5**	**569**	**62.5**
Female	1,208	36.5	329	27.2	36	3.0	641	53.1	1,172	329	27.2	196	59.6
Male	2,099	63.5	582	27.7	29	1.4	1,213	57.8	2,070	582	27.7	373	64.1
American Indian	71	2.1	19	26.8	1	1.4	39	54.9	70	19	26.8	13	68.4
Asian	112	3.4	7	6.3	0	0.0	7	6.3	112	7	6.3	4	57.1
Black	1,171	35.4	356	30.4	15	1.3	751	64.1	1,156	356	30.4	227	63.8
Hispanic	695	21.0	80	11.5	4	0.6	350	50.4	691	80	11.5	48	60.0
Multi-Racial	99	3.0	31	31.3	1	1.0	64	64.6	98	31	31.3	18	58.1
Native Hawaiian/Pacific Islander	8	0.2	0	0.0	0	0.0	2	25.0	8	0	0.0	*	*
White	1,151	34.8	418	36.3	44	3.8	641	55.7	1,107	418	36.3	259	62.0
Economically Disadvantaged	**2,348**	**71.0**	**611**	**26.0**	**29**	**1.2**	**1,386**	**59.0**	**2,319**	**611**	**26.0**	**407**	**66.6**
Not Economically Disadvantaged	959	29.0	300	31.3	36	3.8	468	48.8	923	300	31.3	162	54.0
Limited English Proficient (LEP)	**702**	**21.2**	**38**	**5.4**	**4**	**0.6**	**183**	**26.1**	**698**	**38**	**5.4**	**29**	**76.3**
Not LEP	2,605	78.8	873	33.5	61	2.3	1,671	64.1	2,544	873	33.5	540	61.9
Not Exceptional	**1,838**	**55.6**	**6**	**0.3**	**36**	**2.0**	**1,322**	**71.9**	**1,802**	**6**	**0.3**	**3**	**50.0**
Academically/Intellectually Gifted	44	1.3	0	0.0	10	0.0	34	77.3	34	0	0.0	*	*
Students with IEPs	**1,425**	**43.1**	**905**	**63.5**	**19**	**1.3**	**498**	**34.9**	**1,406**	**905**	**63.5**	**566**	**62.5**
Students without IEPs	1,882	56.9	6	0.3	46	2.4	1,356	72.1	1,836	6	0.3	3	50.0
Students with Disabilities	**1,425**	**43.1**	**905**	**63.5**	**19**	**1.3**	**498**	**34.9**	**1,406**	**905**	**63.5**	**566**	**62.5**
Students without Disabilities	1,882	56.9	6	0.3	46	2.4	1,356	72.1	1,836	6	0.3	3	50.0
Autism	250	7.6	239	95.6	1	0.4	10	4.0	249	239	95.6	153	64.0
Deaf-Blindness	1	0.0	1	100.0	0	0.0	0	0.0	1	1	100.0	*	*
Deafness	2	0.1	2	100.0	0	0.0	0	0.0	2	2	100.0	*	*
Serious Emotional Disability	73	2.2	2	2.7	1	1.4	70	95.9	72	2	2.7	*	*
Hearing Impairment	7	0.2	3	42.9	0	0.0	4	57.1	7	3	42.9	*	*
Intellectual Disability-Mild	179	5.4	138	77.1	1	0.6	39	21.8	178	138	77.1	105	76.1
Intellectual Disability-Moderate	306	9.3	305	99.7	0	0.0	1	0.3	306	305	99.7	181	59.3
Intellectual Disability-Severe	45	1.4	45	100.0	0	0.0	0	0.0	45	45	100.0	21	46.7
Specific Learning Disability	235	7.1	0	0.0	5	0.0	228	97.0	230	0	0.0	*	*
Multiple Disabilities	128	3.9	127	99.2	1	0.8	0	0.0	127	127	99.2	67	52.8
Other Health Impairment	179	5.4	29	16.2	10	5.6	140	78.2	169	29	16.2	24	82.8
Orthopedic Impairment	4	0.1	4	100.0	0	0.0	0	0.0	4	4	100.0	*	*
Speech or Language Impairment	3	0.1	0	0.0	0	0.0	3	100.0	3	0	0.0	*	*
Traumatic Brain Injury	11	0.3	8	72.7	0	0.0	3	27.3	11	8	72.7	5	62.5
Visual Impairment incl. Blindness	2	0.1	2	100.0	0	0.0	0	0.0	2	2	100.0	*	*

[1] The "Verified Membership" for the end-of-course tests is the number of student grade and course enrollment records in PowerSchool on the first day of test administration in the testing cycle.

[2] Data for "Other" includes misadministrations, transfers, and unknown causes. Some columns may not add up to the total due to miscoding or rounding.

Notes: The disability categories were revised in 2007–08.
The total for "All Students with Disabilities" includes Section 504.
Data received from by local education agencies, charter schools, and regional school after December 5, 2014 are not included in this table.
Prepared by the NCDPI Division of Accountability Services/Test Development Section.

Ancestry and Ethnicity

State Profile

Population: 9,535,483

Ancestry	Population	%
Afghan (749)	841	0.01
African, Sub-Saharan (68,388)	80,649	0.87
African (45,994)	55,748	0.60
Cape Verdean (269)	568	0.01
Ethiopian (2,732)	2,813	0.03
Ghanaian (1,729)	1,745	0.02
Kenyan (1,416)	1,597	0.02
Liberian (1,765)	1,963	0.02
Nigerian (5,732)	6,162	0.07
Senegalese (156)	156	<0.01
Sierra Leonean (565)	590	0.01
Somalian (1,173)	1,308	0.01
South African (1,159)	1,690	0.02
Sudanese (1,804)	1,880	0.02
Ugandan (38)	38	<0.01
Zimbabwean (68)	79	<0.01
Other Sub-Saharan African (3,788)	4,312	0.05
Albanian (379)	762	0.01
Alsatian (69)	255	<0.01
American (1,066,458)	1,066,458	11.50
Arab (19,860)	29,140	0.31
Arab (4,327)	5,243	0.06
Egyptian (3,017)	3,860	0.04
Iraqi (164)	241	<0.01
Jordanian (1,111)	1,457	0.02
Lebanese (5,468)	10,370	0.11
Moroccan (1,703)	1,893	0.02
Palestinian (1,136)	1,551	0.02
Syrian (779)	1,848	0.02
Other Arab (2,155)	2,677	0.03
Armenian (1,742)	3,644	0.04
Assyrian/Chaldean/Syriac (102)	138	<0.01
Australian (887)	2,088	0.02
Austrian (2,639)	11,896	0.13
Basque (149)	245	<0.01
Belgian (1,756)	5,418	0.06
Brazilian (3,131)	4,247	0.05
British (24,221)	43,114	0.47
Bulgarian (1,188)	1,544	0.02
Cajun (653)	1,416	0.02
Canadian (8,325)	15,051	0.16
Carpatho Rusyn (56)	70	<0.01
Celtic (911)	1,789	0.02
Croatian (1,437)	4,404	0.05
Cypriot (104)	135	<0.01
Czech (5,482)	18,171	0.20
Czechoslovakian (2,026)	5,381	0.06
Danish (4,096)	15,824	0.17
Dutch (24,394)	119,440	1.29
Eastern European (4,541)	5,437	0.06
English (477,665)	981,696	10.59
Estonian (254)	450	<0.01
European (84,064)	95,883	1.03
Finnish (2,297)	6,261	0.07
French, ex. Basque (37,176)	170,948	1.84
French Canadian (13,727)	32,892	0.35
German (372,466)	1,078,399	11.63
German Russian (74)	350	<0.01
Greek (13,391)	25,926	0.28
Guyanese (1,530)	2,234	0.02
Hungarian (7,549)	25,192	0.27
Icelander (539)	946	0.01
Iranian (3,300)	4,273	0.05
Irish (302,526)	879,734	9.49
Israeli (689)	1,071	0.01
Italian (102,391)	284,213	3.07
Latvian (458)	1,364	0.01
Lithuanian (3,043)	9,457	0.10
Luxemburger (64)	220	<0.01
Macedonian (187)	269	<0.01
Maltese (190)	623	0.01
New Zealander (422)	562	0.01
Northern European (3,766)	4,055	0.04

Ancestry (cont.)	Population	%
Norwegian (13,455)	43,446	0.47
Pennsylvania German (1,244)	2,855	0.03
Polish (40,165)	131,740	1.42
Portuguese (4,345)	11,957	0.13
Romanian (3,889)	7,511	0.08
Russian (15,415)	41,674	0.45
Scandinavian (2,968)	8,125	0.09
Scotch-Irish (192,818)	340,482	3.67
Scottish (102,868)	246,993	2.66
Serbian (948)	2,490	0.03
Slavic (685)	2,554	0.03
Slovak (3,362)	10,408	0.11
Slovene (678)	1,847	0.02
Soviet Union (14)	14	<0.01
Swedish (14,472)	52,952	0.57
Swiss (4,057)	15,605	0.17
Turkish (2,540)	3,355	0.04
Ukrainian (7,553)	15,628	0.17
Welsh (13,091)	54,197	0.58
West Indian, ex. Hispanic (18,847)	31,296	0.34
Bahamian (536)	974	0.01
Barbadian (598)	877	0.01
Belizean (283)	459	<0.01
Bermudan (67)	141	<0.01
British West Indian (471)	1,029	0.01
Dutch West Indian (270)	653	0.01
Haitian (3,310)	4,878	0.05
Jamaican (8,187)	12,897	0.14
Trinidadian/Tobagonian (1,662)	2,499	0.03
U.S. Virgin Islander (133)	177	<0.01
West Indian (3,297)	6,660	0.07
Other West Indian (33)	52	<0.01
Yugoslavian (2,603)	4,917	0.05

Hispanic Origin	Population	%
Hispanic or Latino (of any race)	800,120	8.39
Central American, ex. Mexican	105,066	1.10
Costa Rican	4,658	0.05
Guatemalan	20,206	0.21
Honduran	30,900	0.32
Nicaraguan	4,964	0.05
Panamanian	5,708	0.06
Salvadoran	37,778	0.40
Other Central American	852	0.01
Cuban	18,079	0.19
Dominican Republic	15,225	0.16
Mexican	486,960	5.11
Puerto Rican	71,800	0.75
South American	46,307	0.49
Argentinean	3,210	0.03
Bolivian	878	0.01
Chilean	2,525	0.03
Colombian	17,648	0.19
Ecuadorian	8,110	0.09
Paraguayan	245	<0.01
Peruvian	8,247	0.09
Uruguayan	980	0.01
Venezuelan	4,070	0.04
Other South American	394	<0.01
Other Hispanic or Latino	56,683	0.59

Race*	Population	%
African-American/Black (2,048,628)	2,151,456	22.56
Not Hispanic (2,019,854)	2,107,630	22.10
Hispanic (28,774)	43,826	0.46
American Indian/Alaska Native (122,110)	184,082	1.93
Not Hispanic (108,829)	162,311	1.70
Hispanic (13,281)	21,771	0.23
Alaska Athabascan (Ala. Nat.) (58)	78	<0.01
Aleut (Alaska Native) (83)	111	<0.01
Apache (295)	927	0.01
Arapaho (13)	50	<0.01
Blackfeet (348)	2,231	0.02
Canadian/French Am. Ind. (77)	179	<0.01
Central American Ind. (285)	523	0.01
Cherokee (13,942)	32,030	0.34

Race* (cont.)	Population	%
Cheyenne (66)	158	<0.01
Chickasaw (127)	298	<0.01
Chippewa (566)	1,032	0.01
Choctaw (437)	1,130	0.01
Colville (16)	24	<0.01
Comanche (78)	199	<0.01
Cree (32)	104	<0.01
Creek (278)	671	0.01
Crow (25)	145	<0.01
Delaware (85)	249	<0.01
Hopi (25)	68	<0.01
Houma (37)	61	<0.01
Inupiat (Alaska Native) (69)	130	<0.01
Iroquois (1,515)	2,507	0.03
Kiowa (42)	68	<0.01
Lumbee (52,905)	58,306	0.61
Menominee (31)	49	<0.01
Mexican American Ind. (2,871)	3,826	0.04
Navajo (418)	774	0.01
Osage (53)	131	<0.01
Ottawa (48)	87	<0.01
Paiute (27)	39	<0.01
Pima (27)	58	<0.01
Potawatomi (114)	210	<0.01
Pueblo (86)	210	<0.01
Puget Sound Salish (26)	40	<0.01
Seminole (96)	466	<0.01
Shoshone (36)	95	<0.01
Sioux (533)	1,283	0.01
South American Ind. (295)	783	0.01
Spanish American Ind. (337)	543	0.01
Tlingit-Haida (Alaska Native) (52)	73	<0.01
Tohono O'Odham (28)	47	<0.01
Tsimshian (Alaska Native) (4)	5	<0.01
Ute (17)	37	<0.01
Yakama (19)	29	<0.01
Yaqui (30)	76	<0.01
Yuman (14)	26	<0.01
Yup'ik (Alaska Native) (29)	45	<0.01
Asian (208,962)	252,585	2.65
Not Hispanic (206,579)	245,810	2.58
Hispanic (2,383)	6,775	0.07
Bangladeshi (854)	945	0.01
Bhutanese (487)	614	0.01
Burmese (3,478)	3,779	0.04
Cambodian (3,559)	4,345	0.05
Chinese, ex. Taiwanese (32,301)	38,764	0.41
Filipino (18,643)	29,314	0.31
Hmong (10,433)	10,864	0.11
Indian (57,400)	63,852	0.67
Indonesian (767)	1,121	0.01
Japanese (6,411)	12,878	0.14
Korean (19,221)	25,420	0.27
Laotian (5,566)	6,562	0.07
Malaysian (214)	363	<0.01
Nepalese (875)	1,039	0.01
Pakistani (5,757)	6,477	0.07
Sri Lankan (612)	721	0.01
Taiwanese (1,780)	2,151	0.02
Thai (2,947)	4,782	0.05
Vietnamese (27,304)	30,665	0.32
Hawaii Native/Pacific Islander (6,604)	14,774	0.15
Not Hispanic (5,259)	11,417	0.12
Hispanic (1,345)	3,357	0.04
Fijian (34)	76	<0.01
Guamanian/Chamorro (2,505)	3,682	0.04
Marshallese (152)	182	<0.01
Native Hawaiian (1,389)	4,182	0.04
Samoan (716)	1,600	0.02
Tongan (54)	123	<0.01
White (6,528,950)	6,697,465	70.24
Not Hispanic (6,223,995)	6,354,005	66.64
Hispanic (304,955)	343,460	3.60

*Notes: † The Census 2010 population figure is used to calculate the percentages in the Hispanic Origin and Race categories. Ancestry percentages are based on the 2006-2010 American Community Survey population (not shown); ‡ Numbers in parentheses indicate the number of people reporting a single ancestry; * Numbers in parentheses indicate the number of persons reporting this race alone, not in combination with any other race; Please refer to the Explanation of Data for more information.*

County Profiles

Alamance County

Population: 151,131

Ancestry	Population	%
Afghan (0)	18	0.01
African, Sub-Saharan (296)	531	0.36
African (199)	390	0.27
Cape Verdean (0)	0	<0.01
Ethiopian (0)	0	<0.01
Ghanaian (0)	0	<0.01
Kenyan (0)	0	<0.01
Liberian (0)	0	<0.01
Nigerian (0)	0	<0.01
Senegalese (0)	0	<0.01
Sierra Leonean (0)	0	<0.01
Somalian (0)	0	<0.01
South African (49)	93	0.06
Sudanese (48)	48	0.03
Ugandan (0)	0	<0.01
Zimbabwean (0)	0	<0.01
Other Sub-Saharan African (0)	0	<0.01
Albanian (0)	0	<0.01
Alsatian (18)	18	0.01
American (15,467)	15,467	10.52
Arab (153)	278	0.19
Arab (14)	14	0.01
Egyptian (19)	19	0.01
Iraqi (0)	0	<0.01
Jordanian (0)	0	<0.01
Lebanese (108)	151	0.10
Moroccan (0)	0	<0.01
Palestinian (12)	12	0.01
Syrian (0)	64	0.04
Other Arab (0)	18	0.01
Armenian (14)	57	0.04
Assyrian/Chaldean/Syriac (0)	0	<0.01
Australian (0)	12	0.01
Austrian (43)	159	0.11
Basque (0)	0	<0.01
Belgian (0)	44	0.03
Brazilian (32)	50	0.03
British (287)	384	0.26
Bulgarian (9)	9	0.01
Cajun (10)	10	0.01
Canadian (119)	162	0.11
Carpatho Rusyn (0)	0	<0.01
Celtic (103)	114	0.08
Croatian (11)	47	0.03
Cypriot (12)	34	0.02
Czech (15)	93	0.06
Czechoslovakian (22)	22	0.01
Danish (74)	210	0.14
Dutch (207)	1,611	1.10
Eastern European (12)	12	0.01
English (7,691)	16,090	10.94
Estonian (0)	0	<0.01
European (1,196)	1,275	0.87
Finnish (18)	29	0.02
French, ex. Basque (348)	2,671	1.82
French Canadian (156)	339	0.23
German (5,831)	17,379	11.82
German Russian (0)	0	<0.01
Greek (162)	380	0.26
Guyanese (0)	0	<0.01
Hungarian (90)	307	0.21
Icelander (0)	0	<0.01
Iranian (10)	20	0.01
Irish (4,358)	13,342	9.07
Israeli (0)	0	<0.01
Italian (1,469)	3,872	2.63
Latvian (0)	0	<0.01
Lithuanian (35)	50	0.03
Luxemburger (0)	0	<0.01
Macedonian (0)	0	<0.01
Maltese (0)	0	<0.01
New Zealander (0)	0	<0.01
Northern European (0)	0	<0.01
Norwegian (209)	590	0.40
Pennsylvania German (0)	30	0.02
Polish (274)	1,305	0.89
Portuguese (128)	202	0.14
Romanian (0)	7	<0.01
Russian (215)	556	0.38
Scandinavian (10)	62	0.04
Scotch-Irish (3,636)	6,384	4.34
Scottish (1,822)	3,688	2.51
Serbian (16)	32	0.02
Slavic (28)	28	0.02
Slovak (66)	162	0.11
Slovene (0)	0	<0.01
Soviet Union (0)	0	<0.01
Swedish (227)	641	0.44
Swiss (73)	239	0.16
Turkish (53)	66	0.04
Ukrainian (46)	260	0.18
Welsh (139)	457	0.31
West Indian, ex. Hispanic (0)	160	0.11
Bahamian (0)	0	<0.01
Barbadian (0)	0	<0.01
Belizean (0)	0	<0.01
Bermudan (0)	0	<0.01
British West Indian (0)	0	<0.01
Dutch West Indian (0)	0	<0.01
Haitian (0)	0	<0.01
Jamaican (0)	124	0.08
Trinidadian/Tobagonian (0)	0	<0.01
U.S. Virgin Islander (0)	0	<0.01
West Indian (0)	36	0.02
Other West Indian (0)	0	<0.01
Yugoslavian (9)	26	0.02

Hispanic Origin	Population	%
Hispanic or Latino (of any race)	16,639	11.01
Central American, ex. Mexican	2,247	1.49
Costa Rican	41	0.03
Guatemalan	180	0.12
Honduran	441	0.29
Nicaraguan	85	0.06
Panamanian	37	0.02
Salvadoran	1,456	0.96
Other Central American	7	<0.01
Cuban	186	0.12
Dominican Republic	163	0.11
Mexican	11,664	7.72
Puerto Rican	861	0.57
South American	518	0.34
Argentinean	37	0.02
Bolivian	15	0.01
Chilean	64	0.04
Colombian	136	0.09
Ecuadorian	154	0.10
Paraguayan	5	<0.01
Peruvian	56	0.04
Uruguayan	13	0.01
Venezuelan	35	0.02
Other South American	3	<0.01
Other Hispanic or Latino	1,000	0.66

Race*	Population	%
African-American/Black (28,369)	30,027	19.87
Not Hispanic (27,985)	29,405	19.46
Hispanic (384)	622	0.41
American Indian/Alaska Native (1,020)	1,881	1.24
Not Hispanic (542)	1,209	0.80
Hispanic (478)	672	0.44
Alaska Athabascan (Ala. Nat.) (1)	1	<0.01
Aleut (Alaska Native) (0)	0	<0.01
Apache (2)	10	0.01
Arapaho (0)	0	<0.01
Blackfeet (6)	31	0.02
Canadian/French Am. Ind. (2)	2	<0.01
Central American Ind. (10)	12	0.01
Cherokee (79)	302	0.20
Cheyenne (1)	2	<0.01
Chickasaw (3)	8	0.01
Chippewa (11)	17	0.01
Choctaw (6)	7	<0.01
Colville (0)	0	<0.01
Comanche (0)	4	<0.01
Cree (0)	0	<0.01
Creek (3)	11	0.01
Crow (0)	4	<0.01
Delaware (0)	0	<0.01
Hopi (0)	0	<0.01
Houma (1)	1	<0.01
Inupiat (Alaska Native) (0)	0	<0.01
Iroquois (2)	9	0.01
Kiowa (1)	3	<0.01
Lumbee (76)	102	0.07
Menominee (0)	0	<0.01
Mexican American Ind. (106)	129	0.09
Navajo (1)	4	<0.01
Osage (0)	1	<0.01
Ottawa (0)	0	<0.01
Paiute (0)	0	<0.01
Pima (0)	0	<0.01
Potawatomi (3)	3	<0.01
Pueblo (2)	2	<0.01
Puget Sound Salish (0)	0	<0.01
Seminole (3)	6	<0.01
Shoshone (0)	0	<0.01
Sioux (10)	15	0.01
South American Ind. (5)	9	0.01
Spanish American Ind. (41)	60	0.04
Tlingit-Haida (Alaska Native) (3)	3	<0.01
Tohono O'Odham (4)	4	<0.01
Tsimshian (Alaska Native) (0)	0	<0.01
Ute (1)	1	<0.01
Yakama (0)	0	<0.01
Yaqui (0)	2	<0.01
Yuman (0)	0	<0.01
Yup'ik (Alaska Native) (0)	0	<0.01
Asian (1,837)	2,294	1.52
Not Hispanic (1,806)	2,203	1.46
Hispanic (31)	91	0.06
Bangladeshi (10)	10	0.01
Bhutanese (0)	0	<0.01
Burmese (13)	14	0.01
Cambodian (6)	7	<0.01
Chinese, ex. Taiwanese (234)	292	0.19
Filipino (147)	235	0.16
Hmong (46)	46	0.03
Indian (459)	532	0.35
Indonesian (7)	7	<0.01
Japanese (35)	90	0.06
Korean (201)	272	0.18
Laotian (250)	298	0.20
Malaysian (0)	1	<0.01
Nepalese (1)	1	<0.01
Pakistani (74)	86	0.06
Sri Lankan (0)	0	<0.01
Taiwanese (12)	17	0.01
Thai (19)	45	0.03
Vietnamese (240)	259	0.17
Hawaii Native/Pacific Islander (58)	166	0.11
Not Hispanic (55)	133	0.09
Hispanic (3)	33	0.02
Fijian (0)	2	<0.01
Guamanian/Chamorro (14)	29	0.02
Marshallese (1)	1	<0.01
Native Hawaiian (15)	57	0.04
Samoan (8)	22	0.01
Tongan (0)	0	<0.01
White (107,420)	110,017	72.80
Not Hispanic (101,718)	103,571	68.53
Hispanic (5,702)	6,446	4.27

*Notes: † The Census 2010 population figure is used to calculate the percentages in the Hispanic Origin and Race categories. Ancestry percentages are based on the 2006-2010 American Community Survey population (not shown); ‡ Numbers in parentheses indicate the number of people reporting a single ancestry; * Numbers in parentheses indicate the number of persons reporting this race alone, not in combination with any other race; Please refer to the Explanation of Data for more information.*

Brunswick County

Population: 107,431

Ancestry	Population	%
Afghan (0)	0	<0.01
African, Sub-Saharan (108)	114	0.11
African (90)	93	0.09
Cape Verdean (0)	0	<0.01
Ethiopian (17)	17	0.02
Ghanaian (0)	0	<0.01
Kenyan (0)	0	<0.01
Liberian (0)	0	<0.01
Nigerian (0)	0	<0.01
Senegalese (0)	0	<0.01
Sierra Leonean (0)	0	<0.01
Somalian (0)	0	<0.01
South African (1)	4	<0.01
Sudanese (0)	0	<0.01
Ugandan (0)	0	<0.01
Zimbabwean (0)	0	<0.01
Other Sub-Saharan African (0)	0	<0.01
Albanian (0)	0	<0.01
Alsatian (0)	0	<0.01
American (11,907)	11,907	11.67
Arab (109)	132	0.13
Arab (3)	3	<0.01
Egyptian (18)	18	0.02
Iraqi (0)	0	<0.01
Jordanian (0)	0	<0.01
Lebanese (72)	72	0.07
Moroccan (0)	0	<0.01
Palestinian (0)	0	<0.01
Syrian (16)	39	0.04
Other Arab (0)	0	<0.01
Armenian (0)	20	0.02
Assyrian/Chaldean/Syriac (0)	0	<0.01
Australian (46)	46	0.05
Austrian (66)	299	0.29
Basque (0)	0	<0.01
Belgian (35)	35	0.03
Brazilian (38)	38	0.04
British (293)	449	0.44
Bulgarian (17)	27	0.03
Cajun (36)	51	0.05
Canadian (84)	103	0.10
Carpatho Rusyn (0)	14	0.01
Celtic (0)	0	<0.01
Croatian (7)	50	0.05
Cypriot (0)	0	<0.01
Czech (103)	167	0.16
Czechoslovakian (25)	40	0.04
Danish (92)	153	0.15
Dutch (189)	1,356	1.33
Eastern European (5)	5	<0.01
English (7,087)	14,996	14.70
Estonian (6)	6	0.01
European (626)	716	0.70
Finnish (37)	86	0.08
French, ex. Basque (781)	2,968	2.91
French Canadian (244)	591	0.58
German (5,886)	16,308	15.99
German Russian (0)	0	<0.01
Greek (227)	266	0.26
Guyanese (0)	0	<0.01
Hungarian (155)	543	0.53
Icelander (4)	4	<0.01
Iranian (46)	46	0.05
Irish (5,426)	13,978	13.70
Israeli (0)	0	<0.01
Italian (2,645)	5,683	5.57
Latvian (0)	7	0.01
Lithuanian (180)	249	0.24
Luxemburger (12)	12	0.01
Macedonian (0)	16	0.02
Maltese (0)	0	<0.01
New Zealander (0)	0	<0.01
Northern European (84)	129	0.13
Norwegian (204)	487	0.48
Pennsylvania German (42)	76	0.07

Ancestry (cont.)	Population	%
Polish (778)	2,060	2.02
Portuguese (51)	179	0.18
Romanian (15)	71	0.07
Russian (101)	415	0.41
Scandinavian (41)	84	0.08
Scotch-Irish (2,349)	4,506	4.42
Scottish (1,502)	3,730	3.66
Serbian (2)	21	0.02
Slavic (0)	30	0.03
Slovak (150)	267	0.26
Slovene (37)	42	0.04
Soviet Union (0)	0	<0.01
Swedish (387)	1,189	1.17
Swiss (34)	235	0.23
Turkish (0)	43	0.04
Ukrainian (71)	168	0.16
Welsh (245)	1,045	1.02
West Indian, ex. Hispanic (173)	189	0.19
Bahamian (2)	2	<0.01
Barbadian (0)	0	<0.01
Belizean (0)	0	<0.01
Bermudan (0)	0	<0.01
British West Indian (31)	31	0.03
Dutch West Indian (0)	0	<0.01
Haitian (40)	42	0.04
Jamaican (100)	114	0.11
Trinidadian/Tobagonian (0)	0	<0.01
U.S. Virgin Islander (0)	0	<0.01
West Indian (0)	0	<0.01
Other West Indian (0)	0	<0.01
Yugoslavian (24)	47	0.05

Hispanic Origin	Population	%
Hispanic or Latino (of any race)	5,549	5.17
Central American, ex. Mexican	407	0.38
Costa Rican	32	0.03
Guatemalan	97	0.09
Honduran	115	0.11
Nicaraguan	11	0.01
Panamanian	25	0.02
Salvadoran	122	0.11
Other Central American	5	<0.01
Cuban	85	0.08
Dominican Republic	46	0.04
Mexican	3,802	3.54
Puerto Rican	658	0.61
South American	176	0.16
Argentinean	14	0.01
Bolivian	3	<0.01
Chilean	10	0.01
Colombian	60	0.06
Ecuadorian	33	0.03
Paraguayan	2	<0.01
Peruvian	29	0.03
Uruguayan	6	0.01
Venezuelan	14	0.01
Other South American	5	<0.01
Other Hispanic or Latino	375	0.35

Race*	Population	%
African-American/Black (12,291)	13,177	12.27
Not Hispanic (12,120)	12,941	12.05
Hispanic (171)	236	0.22
American Indian/Alaska Native (761)	1,519	1.41
Not Hispanic (652)	1,354	1.26
Hispanic (109)	165	0.15
Alaska Athabascan (Ala. Nat.) (1)	1	<0.01
Aleut (Alaska Native) (2)	4	<0.01
Apache (3)	13	0.01
Arapaho (0)	1	<0.01
Blackfeet (5)	38	0.04
Canadian/French Am. Ind. (0)	1	<0.01
Central American Ind. (3)	4	<0.01
Cherokee (81)	291	0.27
Cheyenne (0)	1	<0.01
Chickasaw (4)	7	0.01
Chippewa (7)	12	0.01
Choctaw (2)	9	0.01
Colville (0)	0	<0.01

Race* (cont.)	Population	%
Comanche (0)	2	<0.01
Cree (0)	1	<0.01
Creek (8)	14	0.01
Crow (1)	2	<0.01
Delaware (2)	3	<0.01
Hopi (0)	1	<0.01
Houma (0)	0	<0.01
Inupiat (Alaska Native) (1)	5	<0.01
Iroquois (26)	43	0.04
Kiowa (3)	3	<0.01
Lumbee (198)	273	0.25
Menominee (0)	0	<0.01
Mexican American Ind. (19)	21	0.02
Navajo (2)	8	0.01
Osage (0)	1	<0.01
Ottawa (0)	0	<0.01
Paiute (0)	0	<0.01
Pima (0)	0	<0.01
Potawatomi (3)	6	0.01
Pueblo (0)	0	<0.01
Puget Sound Salish (0)	0	<0.01
Seminole (5)	17	0.02
Shoshone (0)	0	<0.01
Sioux (11)	20	0.02
South American Ind. (3)	11	0.01
Spanish American Ind. (14)	15	0.01
Tlingit-Haida (Alaska Native) (0)	0	<0.01
Tohono O'Odham (2)	3	<0.01
Tsimshian (Alaska Native) (0)	0	<0.01
Ute (0)	0	<0.01
Yakama (0)	0	<0.01
Yaqui (0)	0	<0.01
Yuman (0)	0	<0.01
Yup'ik (Alaska Native) (0)	0	<0.01
Asian (579)	843	0.78
Not Hispanic (560)	806	0.75
Hispanic (19)	37	0.03
Bangladeshi (0)	0	<0.01
Bhutanese (0)	0	<0.01
Burmese (0)	0	<0.01
Cambodian (5)	5	<0.01
Chinese, ex. Taiwanese (133)	158	0.15
Filipino (107)	184	0.17
Hmong (0)	0	<0.01
Indian (52)	81	0.08
Indonesian (4)	7	0.01
Japanese (22)	63	0.06
Korean (81)	109	0.10
Laotian (8)	11	0.01
Malaysian (2)	2	<0.01
Nepalese (0)	0	<0.01
Pakistani (6)	7	0.01
Sri Lankan (4)	4	<0.01
Taiwanese (1)	3	<0.01
Thai (25)	36	0.03
Vietnamese (108)	128	0.12
Hawaii Native/Pacific Islander (38)	86	0.08
Not Hispanic (33)	63	0.06
Hispanic (5)	23	0.02
Fijian (0)	3	<0.01
Guamanian/Chamorro (16)	19	0.02
Marshallese (3)	3	<0.01
Native Hawaiian (14)	26	0.02
Samoan (0)	6	0.01
Tongan (0)	0	<0.01
White (89,193)	90,901	84.61
Not Hispanic (86,818)	88,223	82.12
Hispanic (2,375)	2,678	2.49

Notes: † The Census 2010 population figure is used to calculate the percentages in the Hispanic Origin and Race categories. Ancestry percentages are based on the 2006-2010 American Community Survey population (not shown); ‡ Numbers in parentheses indicate the number of people reporting a single ancestry; * Numbers in parentheses indicate the number of persons reporting this race alone, not in combination with any other race; Please refer to the Explanation of Data for more information.

Buncombe County

Population: 238,318

Ancestry	Population	%
Afghan (0)	0	<0.01
African, Sub-Saharan (789)	923	0.40
African (647)	721	0.31
Cape Verdean (18)	18	0.01
Ethiopian (12)	12	0.01
Ghanaian (0)	0	<0.01
Kenyan (0)	0	<0.01
Liberian (56)	56	0.02
Nigerian (0)	0	<0.01
Senegalese (0)	0	<0.01
Sierra Leonean (0)	0	<0.01
Somalian (0)	0	<0.01
South African (14)	74	0.03
Sudanese (0)	0	<0.01
Ugandan (0)	0	<0.01
Zimbabwean (15)	15	0.01
Other Sub-Saharan African (27)	27	0.01
Albanian (13)	27	0.01
Alsatian (10)	10	<0.01
American (31,776)	31,776	13.62
Arab (130)	469	0.20
Arab (27)	27	0.01
Egyptian (0)	0	<0.01
Iraqi (9)	9	<0.01
Jordanian (0)	12	0.01
Lebanese (63)	318	0.14
Moroccan (16)	16	0.01
Palestinian (0)	12	0.01
Syrian (15)	35	0.02
Other Arab (0)	40	0.02
Armenian (58)	122	0.05
Assyrian/Chaldean/Syriac (0)	0	<0.01
Australian (4)	22	0.01
Austrian (74)	512	0.22
Basque (0)	0	<0.01
Belgian (12)	228	0.10
Brazilian (109)	109	0.05
British (876)	1,626	0.70
Bulgarian (12)	12	0.01
Cajun (17)	17	0.01
Canadian (165)	488	0.21
Carpatho Rusyn (8)	8	<0.01
Celtic (152)	249	0.11
Croatian (47)	142	0.06
Cypriot (0)	0	<0.01
Czech (202)	836	0.36
Czechoslovakian (14)	229	0.10
Danish (255)	1,035	0.44
Dutch (1,051)	4,701	2.02
Eastern European (309)	313	0.13
English (12,470)	32,204	13.81
Estonian (0)	19	0.01
European (2,867)	3,266	1.40
Finnish (101)	261	0.11
French, ex. Basque (1,205)	6,589	2.82
French Canadian (424)	1,028	0.44
German (9,885)	34,353	14.73
German Russian (0)	53	0.02
Greek (582)	1,036	0.44
Guyanese (0)	0	<0.01
Hungarian (205)	827	0.35
Icelander (8)	19	0.01
Iranian (60)	98	0.04
Irish (9,577)	30,205	12.95
Israeli (27)	41	0.02
Italian (2,191)	7,773	3.33
Latvian (24)	68	0.03
Lithuanian (61)	268	0.11
Luxemburger (0)	15	0.01
Macedonian (0)	0	<0.01
Maltese (0)	0	<0.01
New Zealander (12)	12	0.01
Northern European (195)	208	0.09
Norwegian (483)	1,771	0.76
Pennsylvania German (37)	63	0.03

Ancestry	Population	%
Polish (1,745)	4,848	2.08
Portuguese (188)	640	0.27
Romanian (877)	998	0.43
Russian (758)	1,643	0.70
Scandinavian (149)	466	0.20
Scotch-Irish (8,485)	14,972	6.42
Scottish (3,357)	9,933	4.26
Serbian (8)	129	0.06
Slavic (0)	51	0.02
Slovak (80)	117	0.05
Slovene (41)	118	0.05
Soviet Union (0)	0	<0.01
Swedish (407)	1,960	0.84
Swiss (278)	915	0.39
Turkish (20)	74	0.03
Ukrainian (1,427)	1,816	0.78
Welsh (712)	2,666	1.14
West Indian, ex. Hispanic (221)	365	0.16
Bahamian (0)	0	<0.01
Barbadian (0)	0	<0.01
Belizean (33)	50	0.02
Bermudan (0)	0	<0.01
British West Indian (0)	0	<0.01
Dutch West Indian (0)	14	0.01
Haitian (20)	20	0.01
Jamaican (68)	146	0.06
Trinidadian/Tobagonian (100)	116	0.05
U.S. Virgin Islander (0)	0	<0.01
West Indian (0)	0	<0.01
Other West Indian (0)	19	0.01
Yugoslavian (24)	46	0.02

Hispanic Origin	Population	%
Hispanic or Latino (of any race)	14,254	5.98
Central American, ex. Mexican	1,981	0.83
Costa Rican	54	0.02
Guatemalan	320	0.13
Honduran	402	0.17
Nicaraguan	81	0.03
Panamanian	53	0.02
Salvadoran	1,062	0.45
Other Central American	9	<0.01
Cuban	527	0.22
Dominican Republic	67	0.03
Mexican	8,953	3.76
Puerto Rican	891	0.37
South American	793	0.33
Argentinean	105	0.04
Bolivian	13	0.01
Chilean	82	0.03
Colombian	277	0.12
Ecuadorian	122	0.05
Paraguayan	5	<0.01
Peruvian	70	0.03
Uruguayan	16	0.01
Venezuelan	91	0.04
Other South American	12	0.01
Other Hispanic or Latino	1,042	0.44

Race*	Population	%
African-American/Black (15,211)	17,445	7.32
Not Hispanic (14,979)	17,019	7.14
Hispanic (232)	426	0.18
American Indian/Alaska Native (948)	2,647	1.11
Not Hispanic (778)	2,332	0.98
Hispanic (170)	315	0.13
Alaska Athabascan (Ala. Nat.) (1)	1	<0.01
Aleut (Alaska Native) (4)	5	<0.01
Apache (18)	44	0.02
Arapaho (0)	2	<0.01
Blackfeet (16)	54	0.02
Canadian/French Am. Ind. (0)	6	<0.01
Central American Ind. (7)	19	0.01
Cherokee (325)	1,025	0.43
Cheyenne (2)	3	<0.01
Chickasaw (6)	10	<0.01
Chippewa (13)	32	0.01
Choctaw (9)	31	0.01
Colville (2)	2	<0.01

Race*	Population	%
Comanche (6)	13	0.01
Cree (0)	3	<0.01
Creek (6)	12	0.01
Crow (0)	7	<0.01
Delaware (0)	5	<0.01
Hopi (0)	0	<0.01
Houma (1)	1	<0.01
Inupiat (Alaska Native) (1)	4	<0.01
Iroquois (10)	36	0.02
Kiowa (0)	0	<0.01
Lumbee (63)	98	0.04
Menominee (1)	5	<0.01
Mexican American Ind. (48)	62	0.03
Navajo (11)	17	0.01
Osage (2)	5	<0.01
Ottawa (0)	0	<0.01
Paiute (0)	1	<0.01
Pima (2)	2	<0.01
Potawatomi (3)	3	<0.01
Pueblo (1)	4	<0.01
Puget Sound Salish (0)	0	<0.01
Seminole (3)	12	0.01
Shoshone (5)	7	<0.01
Sioux (11)	31	0.01
South American Ind. (6)	10	<0.01
Spanish American Ind. (9)	11	<0.01
Tlingit-Haida (Alaska Native) (1)	2	<0.01
Tohono O'Odham (0)	0	<0.01
Tsimshian (Alaska Native) (0)	0	<0.01
Ute (1)	1	<0.01
Yakama (1)	1	<0.01
Yaqui (0)	4	<0.01
Yuman (4)	5	<0.01
Yup'ik (Alaska Native) (3)	3	<0.01
Asian (2,417)	3,229	1.35
Not Hispanic (2,388)	3,132	1.31
Hispanic (29)	97	0.04
Bangladeshi (4)	4	<0.01
Bhutanese (1)	1	<0.01
Burmese (12)	14	0.01
Cambodian (57)	58	0.02
Chinese, ex. Taiwanese (485)	609	0.26
Filipino (360)	553	0.23
Hmong (9)	11	<0.01
Indian (456)	576	0.24
Indonesian (44)	52	0.02
Japanese (118)	266	0.11
Korean (407)	487	0.20
Laotian (2)	10	<0.01
Malaysian (3)	9	<0.01
Nepalese (16)	16	0.01
Pakistani (54)	66	0.03
Sri Lankan (9)	10	<0.01
Taiwanese (6)	14	0.01
Thai (69)	99	0.04
Vietnamese (212)	239	0.10
Hawaii Native/Pacific Islander (289)	450	0.19
Not Hispanic (271)	396	0.17
Hispanic (18)	54	0.02
Fijian (0)	1	<0.01
Guamanian/Chamorro (31)	38	0.02
Marshallese (51)	58	0.02
Native Hawaiian (30)	93	0.04
Samoan (21)	37	0.02
Tongan (1)	3	<0.01
White (208,192)	212,749	89.27
Not Hispanic (201,241)	205,018	86.03
Hispanic (6,951)	7,731	3.24

*Notes: † The Census 2010 population figure is used to calculate the percentages in the Hispanic Origin and Race categories. Ancestry percentages are based on the 2006-2010 American Community Survey population (not shown); ‡ Numbers in parentheses indicate the number of people reporting a single ancestry; * Numbers in parentheses indicate the number of persons reporting this race alone, not in combination with any other race; Please refer to the Explanation of Data for more information.*

Burke County

Population: 90,912

Ancestry	Population	%
Afghan (0)	0	<0.01
African, Sub-Saharan (112)	149	0.16
African (112)	149	0.16
Cape Verdean (0)	0	<0.01
Ethiopian (0)	0	<0.01
Ghanaian (0)	0	<0.01
Kenyan (0)	0	<0.01
Liberian (0)	0	<0.01
Nigerian (0)	0	<0.01
Senegalese (0)	0	<0.01
Sierra Leonean (0)	0	<0.01
Somalian (0)	0	<0.01
South African (0)	0	<0.01
Sudanese (0)	0	<0.01
Ugandan (0)	0	<0.01
Zimbabwean (0)	0	<0.01
Other Sub-Saharan African (0)	0	<0.01
Albanian (0)	0	<0.01
Alsatian (0)	0	<0.01
American (19,631)	19,631	21.68
Arab (130)	225	0.25
Arab (0)	0	<0.01
Egyptian (34)	34	0.04
Iraqi (0)	0	<0.01
Jordanian (0)	0	<0.01
Lebanese (20)	46	0.05
Moroccan (0)	0	<0.01
Palestinian (76)	145	0.16
Syrian (0)	0	<0.01
Other Arab (0)	0	<0.01
Armenian (0)	0	<0.01
Assyrian/Chaldean/Syriac (5)	5	0.01
Australian (8)	15	0.02
Austrian (25)	141	0.16
Basque (0)	0	<0.01
Belgian (0)	8	0.01
Brazilian (0)	0	<0.01
British (289)	399	0.44
Bulgarian (0)	0	<0.01
Cajun (0)	0	<0.01
Canadian (14)	77	0.09
Carpatho Rusyn (0)	0	<0.01
Celtic (0)	12	0.01
Croatian (0)	0	<0.01
Cypriot (8)	17	0.02
Czech (34)	65	0.07
Czechoslovakian (0)	17	0.02
Danish (15)	90	0.10
Dutch (392)	1,878	2.07
Eastern European (0)	26	0.03
English (4,154)	8,255	9.12
Estonian (0)	0	<0.01
European (506)	587	0.65
Finnish (10)	57	0.06
French, ex. Basque (438)	1,337	1.48
French Canadian (176)	198	0.22
German (6,919)	15,163	16.74
German Russian (0)	0	<0.01
Greek (0)	137	0.15
Guyanese (0)	0	<0.01
Hungarian (54)	161	0.18
Icelander (0)	0	<0.01
Iranian (0)	0	<0.01
Irish (4,885)	11,312	12.49
Israeli (0)	0	<0.01
Italian (876)	1,792	1.98
Latvian (0)	9	0.01
Lithuanian (36)	36	0.04
Luxemburger (0)	0	<0.01
Macedonian (0)	0	<0.01
Maltese (9)	9	0.01
New Zealander (0)	0	<0.01
Northern European (0)	0	<0.01
Norwegian (175)	333	0.37
Pennsylvania German (5)	5	0.01

Ancestry (cont.)	Population	%
Polish (68)	471	0.52
Portuguese (30)	57	0.06
Romanian (10)	10	0.01
Russian (24)	114	0.13
Scandinavian (6)	19	0.02
Scotch-Irish (2,206)	3,721	4.11
Scottish (1,751)	3,635	4.01
Serbian (0)	0	<0.01
Slavic (0)	0	<0.01
Slovak (3)	16	0.02
Slovene (0)	13	0.01
Soviet Union (0)	0	<0.01
Swedish (123)	342	0.38
Swiss (9)	46	0.05
Turkish (0)	0	<0.01
Ukrainian (0)	13	0.01
Welsh (236)	439	0.48
West Indian, ex. Hispanic (0)	5	0.01
Bahamian (0)	0	<0.01
Barbadian (0)	0	<0.01
Belizean (0)	0	<0.01
Bermudan (0)	0	<0.01
British West Indian (0)	0	<0.01
Dutch West Indian (0)	2	<0.01
Haitian (0)	0	<0.01
Jamaican (0)	0	<0.01
Trinidadian/Tobagonian (0)	0	<0.01
U.S. Virgin Islander (0)	0	<0.01
West Indian (0)	3	<0.01
Other West Indian (0)	0	<0.01
Yugoslavian (0)	0	<0.01

Hispanic Origin	Population	%
Hispanic or Latino (of any race)	4,634	5.10
Central American, ex. Mexican	1,978	2.18
Costa Rican	26	0.03
Guatemalan	1,721	1.89
Honduran	110	0.12
Nicaraguan	6	0.01
Panamanian	10	0.01
Salvadoran	99	0.11
Other Central American	6	0.01
Cuban	71	0.08
Dominican Republic	13	0.01
Mexican	1,659	1.82
Puerto Rican	154	0.17
South American	60	0.07
Argentinean	6	0.01
Bolivian	1	<0.01
Chilean	4	<0.01
Colombian	26	0.03
Ecuadorian	4	<0.01
Paraguayan	0	<0.01
Peruvian	9	0.01
Uruguayan	0	<0.01
Venezuelan	10	0.01
Other South American	0	<0.01
Other Hispanic or Latino	699	0.77

Race*	Population	%
African-American/Black (6,012)	6,729	7.40
Not Hispanic (5,953)	6,637	7.30
Hispanic (59)	92	0.10
American Indian/Alaska Native (325)	829	0.91
Not Hispanic (207)	652	0.72
Hispanic (118)	177	0.19
Alaska Athabascan (Ala. Nat.) (0)	0	<0.01
Aleut (Alaska Native) (0)	0	<0.01
Apache (4)	10	0.01
Arapaho (0)	0	<0.01
Blackfeet (0)	18	0.02
Canadian/French Am. Ind. (0)	0	<0.01
Central American Ind. (20)	31	0.03
Cherokee (65)	253	0.28
Cheyenne (0)	0	<0.01
Chickasaw (0)	1	<0.01
Chippewa (11)	11	0.01
Choctaw (6)	13	0.01
Colville (0)	0	<0.01

Race* (cont.)	Population	%
Comanche (0)	1	<0.01
Cree (0)	0	<0.01
Creek (2)	3	<0.01
Crow (0)	0	<0.01
Delaware (0)	1	<0.01
Hopi (1)	4	<0.01
Houma (0)	1	<0.01
Inupiat (Alaska Native) (0)	0	<0.01
Iroquois (1)	5	0.01
Kiowa (0)	0	<0.01
Lumbee (33)	56	0.06
Menominee (0)	0	<0.01
Mexican American Ind. (77)	90	0.10
Navajo (0)	1	<0.01
Osage (0)	0	<0.01
Ottawa (2)	3	<0.01
Paiute (0)	1	<0.01
Pima (0)	0	<0.01
Potawatomi (0)	0	<0.01
Pueblo (2)	6	0.01
Puget Sound Salish (0)	0	<0.01
Seminole (0)	1	<0.01
Shoshone (0)	0	<0.01
Sioux (5)	14	0.02
South American Ind. (2)	3	<0.01
Spanish American Ind. (1)	4	<0.01
Tlingit-Haida (Alaska Native) (0)	0	<0.01
Tohono O'Odham (0)	0	<0.01
Tsimshian (Alaska Native) (0)	0	<0.01
Ute (0)	0	<0.01
Yakama (0)	0	<0.01
Yaqui (0)	0	<0.01
Yuman (0)	0	<0.01
Yup'ik (Alaska Native) (0)	0	<0.01
Asian (3,185)	3,426	3.77
Not Hispanic (3,163)	3,357	3.69
Hispanic (22)	69	0.08
Bangladeshi (4)	4	<0.01
Bhutanese (0)	0	<0.01
Burmese (0)	0	<0.01
Cambodian (2)	3	<0.01
Chinese, ex. Taiwanese (100)	120	0.13
Filipino (90)	129	0.14
Hmong (2,281)	2,351	2.59
Indian (217)	260	0.29
Indonesian (7)	8	0.01
Japanese (22)	40	0.04
Korean (18)	36	0.04
Laotian (191)	200	0.22
Malaysian (1)	1	<0.01
Nepalese (4)	4	<0.01
Pakistani (8)	10	0.01
Sri Lankan (0)	0	<0.01
Taiwanese (0)	5	0.01
Thai (19)	28	0.03
Vietnamese (19)	29	0.03
Hawaii Native/Pacific Islander (303)	371	0.41
Not Hispanic (162)	199	0.22
Hispanic (141)	172	0.19
Fijian (0)	2	<0.01
Guamanian/Chamorro (281)	291	0.32
Marshallese (0)	0	<0.01
Native Hawaiian (7)	24	0.03
Samoan (1)	5	0.01
Tongan (0)	0	<0.01
White (76,716)	78,135	85.95
Not Hispanic (75,472)	76,619	84.28
Hispanic (1,244)	1,516	1.67

*Notes: † The Census 2010 population figure is used to calculate the percentages in the Hispanic Origin and Race categories. Ancestry percentages are based on the 2006-2010 American Community Survey population (not shown); ‡ Numbers in parentheses indicate the number of people reporting a single ancestry; * Numbers in parentheses indicate the number of persons reporting this race alone, not in combination with any other race; Please refer to the Explanation of Data for more information.*

Cabarrus County

Population: 178,011

Ancestry	Population	%
Afghan (0)	0	<0.01
African, Sub-Saharan (402)	493	0.29
African (319)	410	0.24
Cape Verdean (0)	0	<0.01
Ethiopian (0)	0	<0.01
Ghanaian (0)	0	<0.01
Kenyan (0)	0	<0.01
Liberian (52)	52	0.03
Nigerian (0)	0	<0.01
Senegalese (0)	0	<0.01
Sierra Leonean (0)	0	<0.01
Somalian (0)	0	<0.01
South African (23)	23	0.01
Sudanese (8)	8	<0.01
Ugandan (0)	0	<0.01
Zimbabwean (0)	0	<0.01
Other Sub-Saharan African (0)	0	<0.01
Albanian (0)	38	0.02
Alsatian (0)	3	<0.01
American (18,464)	18,464	10.86
Arab (134)	316	0.19
Arab (8)	42	0.02
Egyptian (31)	31	0.02
Iraqi (0)	0	<0.01
Jordanian (0)	0	<0.01
Lebanese (81)	154	0.09
Moroccan (7)	25	0.01
Palestinian (0)	0	<0.01
Syrian (0)	57	0.03
Other Arab (7)	7	<0.01
Armenian (28)	28	0.02
Assyrian/Chaldean/Syriac (0)	0	<0.01
Australian (0)	0	<0.01
Austrian (0)	151	0.09
Basque (0)	0	<0.01
Belgian (54)	80	0.05
Brazilian (15)	15	0.01
British (451)	764	0.45
Bulgarian (0)	21	0.01
Cajun (0)	0	<0.01
Canadian (99)	172	0.10
Carpatho Rusyn (0)	0	<0.01
Celtic (0)	28	0.02
Croatian (11)	65	0.04
Cypriot (0)	0	<0.01
Czech (94)	299	0.18
Czechoslovakian (150)	178	0.10
Danish (104)	353	0.21
Dutch (457)	3,451	2.03
Eastern European (4)	15	0.01
English (6,910)	15,639	9.20
Estonian (0)	0	<0.01
European (1,690)	1,778	1.05
Finnish (40)	52	0.03
French, ex. Basque (946)	3,377	1.99
French Canadian (348)	583	0.34
German (11,368)	29,262	17.21
German Russian (0)	0	<0.01
Greek (199)	479	0.28
Guyanese (215)	284	0.17
Hungarian (204)	471	0.28
Icelander (31)	63	0.04
Iranian (0)	0	<0.01
Irish (4,328)	15,944	9.38
Israeli (0)	0	<0.01
Italian (2,977)	7,005	4.12
Latvian (0)	0	<0.01
Lithuanian (43)	214	0.13
Luxemburger (0)	0	<0.01
Macedonian (0)	0	<0.01
Maltese (0)	0	<0.01
New Zealander (37)	37	0.02
Northern European (81)	81	0.05
Norwegian (115)	483	0.28
Pennsylvania German (61)	70	0.04
Polish (674)	2,969	1.75
Portuguese (67)	254	0.15
Romanian (29)	129	0.08
Russian (244)	978	0.58
Scandinavian (101)	115	0.07
Scotch-Irish (4,286)	7,935	4.67
Scottish (2,052)	4,890	2.88
Serbian (0)	57	0.03
Slavic (2)	48	0.03
Slovak (102)	201	0.12
Slovene (0)	0	<0.01
Soviet Union (0)	0	<0.01
Swedish (166)	674	0.40
Swiss (141)	287	0.17
Turkish (49)	49	0.03
Ukrainian (12)	206	0.12
Welsh (263)	891	0.52
West Indian, ex. Hispanic (702)	975	0.57
Bahamian (0)	0	<0.01
Barbadian (25)	26	0.02
Belizean (0)	0	<0.01
Bermudan (0)	0	<0.01
British West Indian (0)	7	<0.01
Dutch West Indian (0)	0	<0.01
Haitian (305)	305	0.18
Jamaican (200)	254	0.15
Trinidadian/Tobagonian (111)	193	0.11
U.S. Virgin Islander (0)	0	<0.01
West Indian (61)	190	0.11
Other West Indian (0)	0	<0.01
Yugoslavian (0)	16	0.01

Hispanic Origin	Population	%
Hispanic or Latino (of any race)	16,767	9.42
Central American, ex. Mexican	1,193	0.67
Costa Rican	54	0.03
Guatemalan	227	0.13
Honduran	316	0.18
Nicaraguan	100	0.06
Panamanian	78	0.04
Salvadoran	414	0.23
Other Central American	4	<0.01
Cuban	542	0.30
Dominican Republic	311	0.17
Mexican	11,229	6.31
Puerto Rican	1,555	0.87
South American	1,051	0.59
Argentinean	72	0.04
Bolivian	13	0.01
Chilean	39	0.02
Colombian	373	0.21
Ecuadorian	254	0.14
Paraguayan	2	<0.01
Peruvian	197	0.11
Uruguayan	20	0.01
Venezuelan	70	0.04
Other South American	11	0.01
Other Hispanic or Latino	886	0.50

Race*	Population	%
African-American/Black (27,219)	29,187	16.40
Not Hispanic (26,660)	28,300	15.90
Hispanic (559)	887	0.50
American Indian/Alaska Native (659)	1,549	0.87
Not Hispanic (497)	1,277	0.72
Hispanic (162)	272	0.15
Alaska Athabascan (Ala. Nat.) (0)	0	<0.01
Aleut (Alaska Native) (2)	2	<0.01
Apache (2)	15	0.01
Arapaho (0)	0	<0.01
Blackfeet (2)	34	0.02
Canadian/French Am. Ind. (1)	3	<0.01
Central American Ind. (8)	9	0.01
Cherokee (92)	411	0.23
Cheyenne (0)	1	<0.01
Chickasaw (2)	4	<0.01
Chippewa (5)	19	0.01
Choctaw (13)	26	0.01
Colville (1)	1	<0.01

	Population	%
Comanche (0)	0	<0.01
Cree (0)	0	<0.01
Creek (6)	20	0.01
Crow (2)	2	<0.01
Delaware (0)	0	<0.01
Hopi (0)	0	<0.01
Houma (1)	3	<0.01
Inupiat (Alaska Native) (0)	2	<0.01
Iroquois (17)	26	0.01
Kiowa (1)	1	<0.01
Lumbee (153)	219	0.12
Menominee (0)	0	<0.01
Mexican American Ind. (55)	59	0.03
Navajo (9)	18	0.01
Osage (1)	1	<0.01
Ottawa (2)	2	<0.01
Paiute (0)	0	<0.01
Pima (0)	0	<0.01
Potawatomi (1)	2	<0.01
Pueblo (1)	2	<0.01
Puget Sound Salish (6)	6	<0.01
Seminole (0)	4	<0.01
Shoshone (0)	0	<0.01
Sioux (1)	8	<0.01
South American Ind. (5)	7	<0.01
Spanish American Ind. (4)	6	<0.01
Tlingit-Haida (Alaska Native) (0)	0	<0.01
Tohono O'Odham (1)	6	<0.01
Tsimshian (Alaska Native) (0)	0	<0.01
Ute (0)	0	<0.01
Yakama (0)	0	<0.01
Yaqui (1)	1	<0.01
Yuman (0)	0	<0.01
Yup'ik (Alaska Native) (1)	2	<0.01
Asian (3,513)	4,210	2.37
Not Hispanic (3,460)	4,073	2.29
Hispanic (53)	137	0.08
Bangladeshi (4)	5	<0.01
Bhutanese (0)	0	<0.01
Burmese (8)	8	<0.01
Cambodian (15)	30	0.02
Chinese, ex. Taiwanese (462)	565	0.32
Filipino (327)	492	0.28
Hmong (237)	249	0.14
Indian (1,391)	1,507	0.85
Indonesian (16)	21	0.01
Japanese (70)	138	0.08
Korean (258)	330	0.19
Laotian (167)	196	0.11
Malaysian (1)	3	<0.01
Nepalese (16)	16	0.01
Pakistani (59)	65	0.04
Sri Lankan (12)	16	0.01
Taiwanese (15)	18	0.01
Thai (28)	60	0.03
Vietnamese (279)	340	0.19
Hawaii Native/Pacific Islander (65)	191	0.11
Not Hispanic (60)	144	0.08
Hispanic (5)	47	0.03
Fijian (0)	0	<0.01
Guamanian/Chamorro (12)	28	0.02
Marshallese (0)	0	<0.01
Native Hawaiian (17)	63	0.04
Samoan (8)	27	0.02
Tongan (0)	0	<0.01
White (134,149)	137,293	77.13
Not Hispanic (127,526)	129,954	73.00
Hispanic (6,623)	7,339	4.12

*Notes: † The Census 2010 population figure is used to calculate the percentages in the Hispanic Origin and Race categories. Ancestry percentages are based on the 2006-2010 American Community Survey population (not shown); ‡ Numbers in parentheses indicate the number of people reporting a single ancestry; * Numbers in parentheses indicate the number of persons reporting this race alone, not in combination with any other race; Please refer to the Explanation of Data for more information.*

Caldwell County

Population: 83,029

Ancestry	Population	%
Afghan (0)	0	<0.01
African, Sub-Saharan (37)	47	0.06
African (10)	20	0.02
Cape Verdean (0)	0	<0.01
Ethiopian (27)	27	0.03
Ghanaian (0)	0	<0.01
Kenyan (0)	0	<0.01
Liberian (0)	0	<0.01
Nigerian (0)	0	<0.01
Senegalese (0)	0	<0.01
Sierra Leonean (0)	0	<0.01
Somalian (0)	0	<0.01
South African (0)	0	<0.01
Sudanese (0)	0	<0.01
Ugandan (0)	0	<0.01
Zimbabwean (0)	0	<0.01
Other Sub-Saharan African (0)	0	<0.01
Albanian (0)	0	<0.01
Alsatian (0)	0	<0.01
American (15,175)	15,175	18.47
Arab (0)	0	<0.01
Arab (0)	0	<0.01
Egyptian (0)	0	<0.01
Iraqi (0)	0	<0.01
Jordanian (0)	0	<0.01
Lebanese (0)	0	<0.01
Moroccan (0)	0	<0.01
Palestinian (0)	0	<0.01
Syrian (0)	0	<0.01
Other Arab (0)	0	<0.01
Armenian (11)	11	0.01
Assyrian/Chaldean/Syriac (0)	0	<0.01
Australian (0)	0	<0.01
Austrian (12)	36	0.04
Basque (0)	0	<0.01
Belgian (0)	37	0.05
Brazilian (0)	0	<0.01
British (99)	244	0.30
Bulgarian (0)	0	<0.01
Cajun (0)	0	<0.01
Canadian (0)	0	<0.01
Carpatho Rusyn (0)	0	<0.01
Celtic (26)	61	0.07
Croatian (0)	0	<0.01
Cypriot (0)	0	<0.01
Czech (0)	68	0.08
Czechoslovakian (10)	10	0.01
Danish (152)	209	0.25
Dutch (465)	1,927	2.35
Eastern European (0)	0	<0.01
English (4,541)	8,590	10.45
Estonian (0)	0	<0.01
European (662)	718	0.87
Finnish (26)	50	0.06
French, ex. Basque (225)	943	1.15
French Canadian (85)	96	0.12
German (4,092)	11,709	14.25
German Russian (0)	0	<0.01
Greek (13)	27	0.03
Guyanese (0)	0	<0.01
Hungarian (11)	40	0.05
Icelander (0)	0	<0.01
Iranian (0)	0	<0.01
Irish (2,851)	8,786	10.69
Israeli (0)	64	0.08
Italian (429)	1,470	1.79
Latvian (0)	0	<0.01
Lithuanian (13)	43	0.05
Luxemburger (0)	0	<0.01
Macedonian (0)	0	<0.01
Maltese (0)	0	<0.01
New Zealander (0)	0	<0.01
Northern European (63)	63	0.08
Norwegian (40)	186	0.23
Pennsylvania German (25)	46	0.06

Ancestry	Population	%
Polish (148)	410	0.50
Portuguese (0)	0	<0.01
Romanian (9)	9	0.01
Russian (37)	172	0.21
Scandinavian (35)	55	0.07
Scotch-Irish (1,396)	2,501	3.04
Scottish (644)	1,804	2.20
Serbian (0)	0	<0.01
Slavic (0)	75	0.09
Slovak (0)	29	0.04
Slovene (0)	0	<0.01
Soviet Union (0)	0	<0.01
Swedish (106)	250	0.30
Swiss (19)	106	0.13
Turkish (3)	3	<0.01
Ukrainian (26)	63	0.08
Welsh (88)	292	0.36
West Indian, ex. Hispanic (40)	61	0.07
Bahamian (0)	0	<0.01
Barbadian (0)	0	<0.01
Belizean (0)	0	<0.01
Bermudan (0)	0	<0.01
British West Indian (26)	26	0.03
Dutch West Indian (0)	9	0.01
Haitian (0)	0	<0.01
Jamaican (0)	12	0.01
Trinidadian/Tobagonian (0)	0	<0.01
U.S. Virgin Islander (0)	0	<0.01
West Indian (14)	14	0.02
Other West Indian (0)	0	<0.01
Yugoslavian (34)	39	0.05

Hispanic Origin	Population	%
Hispanic or Latino (of any race)	3,796	4.57
Central American, ex. Mexican	1,192	1.44
Costa Rican	22	0.03
Guatemalan	235	0.28
Honduran	548	0.66
Nicaraguan	12	0.01
Panamanian	7	0.01
Salvadoran	367	0.44
Other Central American	1	<0.01
Cuban	138	0.17
Dominican Republic	11	0.01
Mexican	1,592	1.92
Puerto Rican	237	0.29
South American	138	0.17
Argentinean	4	<0.01
Bolivian	2	<0.01
Chilean	16	0.02
Colombian	65	0.08
Ecuadorian	6	0.01
Paraguayan	0	<0.01
Peruvian	29	0.03
Uruguayan	3	<0.01
Venezuelan	13	0.02
Other South American	0	<0.01
Other Hispanic or Latino	488	0.59

Race*	Population	%
African-American/Black (4,086)	4,723	5.69
Not Hispanic (4,025)	4,613	5.56
Hispanic (61)	110	0.13
American Indian/Alaska Native (257)	631	0.76
Not Hispanic (159)	482	0.58
Hispanic (98)	149	0.18
Alaska Athabascan (Ala. Nat.) (0)	1	<0.01
Aleut (Alaska Native) (6)	6	0.01
Apache (6)	10	0.01
Arapaho (0)	0	<0.01
Blackfeet (2)	18	0.02
Canadian/French Am. Ind. (0)	0	<0.01
Central American Ind. (0)	1	<0.01
Cherokee (64)	207	0.25
Cheyenne (1)	1	<0.01
Chickasaw (0)	1	<0.01
Chippewa (3)	7	0.01
Choctaw (1)	3	<0.01
Colville (0)	0	<0.01

Race* (cont.)	Population	%
Comanche (1)	1	<0.01
Cree (0)	0	<0.01
Creek (0)	1	<0.01
Crow (0)	1	<0.01
Delaware (0)	0	<0.01
Hopi (0)	0	<0.01
Houma (0)	0	<0.01
Inupiat (Alaska Native) (0)	0	<0.01
Iroquois (3)	6	0.01
Kiowa (0)	0	<0.01
Lumbee (15)	32	0.04
Menominee (0)	0	<0.01
Mexican American Ind. (16)	19	0.02
Navajo (3)	4	<0.01
Osage (0)	3	<0.01
Ottawa (0)	0	<0.01
Paiute (2)	2	<0.01
Pima (0)	0	<0.01
Potawatomi (0)	0	<0.01
Pueblo (0)	0	<0.01
Puget Sound Salish (0)	0	<0.01
Seminole (0)	0	<0.01
Shoshone (0)	0	<0.01
Sioux (3)	5	0.01
South American Ind. (1)	1	<0.01
Spanish American Ind. (0)	2	<0.01
Tlingit-Haida (Alaska Native) (0)	0	<0.01
Tohono O'Odham (0)	0	<0.01
Tsimshian (Alaska Native) (0)	0	<0.01
Ute (0)	0	<0.01
Yakama (0)	0	<0.01
Yaqui (0)	1	<0.01
Yuman (0)	0	<0.01
Yup'ik (Alaska Native) (0)	0	<0.01
Asian (428)	551	0.66
Not Hispanic (421)	528	0.64
Hispanic (7)	23	0.03
Bangladeshi (0)	0	<0.01
Bhutanese (0)	0	<0.01
Burmese (0)	0	<0.01
Cambodian (0)	1	<0.01
Chinese, ex. Taiwanese (64)	82	0.10
Filipino (54)	88	0.11
Hmong (103)	108	0.13
Indian (78)	90	0.11
Indonesian (0)	0	<0.01
Japanese (9)	20	0.02
Korean (37)	53	0.06
Laotian (10)	14	0.02
Malaysian (0)	0	<0.01
Nepalese (3)	3	<0.01
Pakistani (0)	0	<0.01
Sri Lankan (0)	0	<0.01
Taiwanese (1)	4	<0.01
Thai (6)	15	0.02
Vietnamese (40)	49	0.06
Hawaii Native/Pacific Islander (27)	68	0.08
Not Hispanic (16)	41	0.05
Hispanic (11)	27	0.03
Fijian (0)	0	<0.01
Guamanian/Chamorro (12)	18	0.02
Marshallese (0)	0	<0.01
Native Hawaiian (6)	17	0.02
Samoan (1)	2	<0.01
Tongan (0)	0	<0.01
White (74,925)	76,097	91.65
Not Hispanic (73,565)	74,502	89.73
Hispanic (1,360)	1,595	1.92

*Notes: † The Census 2010 population figure is used to calculate the percentages in the Hispanic Origin and Race categories. Ancestry percentages are based on the 2006-2010 American Community Survey population (not shown); ‡ Numbers in parentheses indicate the number of people reporting a single ancestry; * Numbers in parentheses indicate the number of persons reporting this race alone, not in combination with any other race; Please refer to the Explanation of Data for more information.*

Carteret County

Population: 66,469

Ancestry	Population	%
Afghan (0)	0	<0.01
African, Sub-Saharan (82)	148	0.23
African (78)	129	0.20
Cape Verdean (0)	0	<0.01
Ethiopian (0)	0	<0.01
Ghanaian (0)	0	<0.01
Kenyan (0)	0	<0.01
Liberian (0)	0	<0.01
Nigerian (4)	4	0.01
Senegalese (0)	0	<0.01
Sierra Leonean (0)	0	<0.01
Somalian (0)	0	<0.01
South African (0)	0	<0.01
Sudanese (0)	0	<0.01
Ugandan (0)	0	<0.01
Zimbabwean (0)	0	<0.01
Other Sub-Saharan African (0)	15	0.02
Albanian (0)	0	<0.01
Alsatian (0)	0	<0.01
American (8,686)	8,686	13.35
Arab (126)	165	0.25
Arab (16)	16	0.02
Egyptian (11)	11	0.02
Iraqi (0)	0	<0.01
Jordanian (0)	0	<0.01
Lebanese (99)	138	0.21
Moroccan (0)	0	<0.01
Palestinian (0)	0	<0.01
Syrian (0)	0	<0.01
Other Arab (0)	0	<0.01
Armenian (10)	52	0.08
Assyrian/Chaldean/Syriac (0)	0	<0.01
Australian (0)	10	0.02
Austrian (12)	95	0.15
Basque (0)	0	<0.01
Belgian (0)	15	0.02
Brazilian (33)	33	0.05
British (314)	447	0.69
Bulgarian (0)	0	<0.01
Cajun (0)	0	<0.01
Canadian (46)	144	0.22
Carpatho Rusyn (0)	0	<0.01
Celtic (6)	6	0.01
Croatian (20)	61	0.09
Cypriot (0)	0	<0.01
Czech (69)	270	0.41
Czechoslovakian (60)	84	0.13
Danish (14)	105	0.16
Dutch (108)	738	1.13
Eastern European (0)	0	<0.01
English (7,089)	12,839	19.73
Estonian (0)	0	<0.01
European (1,036)	1,083	1.66
Finnish (37)	79	0.12
French, ex. Basque (494)	1,805	2.77
French Canadian (141)	193	0.30
German (2,929)	8,977	13.80
German Russian (0)	12	0.02
Greek (106)	139	0.21
Guyanese (34)	34	0.05
Hungarian (74)	192	0.30
Icelander (2)	2	<0.01
Iranian (0)	0	<0.01
Irish (3,454)	8,677	13.34
Israeli (0)	0	<0.01
Italian (945)	2,315	3.56
Latvian (42)	42	0.06
Lithuanian (43)	83	0.13
Luxemburger (0)	0	<0.01
Macedonian (0)	0	<0.01
Maltese (18)	18	0.03
New Zealander (22)	22	0.03
Northern European (122)	122	0.19
Norwegian (178)	437	0.67
Pennsylvania German (60)	143	0.22

Ancestry (cont.)	Population	%
Polish (471)	1,327	2.04
Portuguese (21)	104	0.16
Romanian (50)	50	0.08
Russian (85)	267	0.41
Scandinavian (11)	23	0.04
Scotch-Irish (1,637)	2,663	4.09
Scottish (925)	2,067	3.18
Serbian (20)	24	0.04
Slavic (0)	61	0.09
Slovak (26)	108	0.17
Slovene (9)	9	0.01
Soviet Union (0)	0	<0.01
Swedish (175)	442	0.68
Swiss (27)	33	0.05
Turkish (0)	0	<0.01
Ukrainian (5)	20	0.03
Welsh (159)	596	0.92
West Indian, ex. Hispanic (17)	24	0.04
Bahamian (0)	0	<0.01
Barbadian (0)	0	<0.01
Belizean (17)	17	0.03
Bermudan (0)	0	<0.01
British West Indian (0)	0	<0.01
Dutch West Indian (0)	0	<0.01
Haitian (0)	0	<0.01
Jamaican (0)	0	<0.01
Trinidadian/Tobagonian (0)	0	<0.01
U.S. Virgin Islander (0)	0	<0.01
West Indian (0)	7	0.01
Other West Indian (0)	0	<0.01
Yugoslavian (30)	58	0.09

Hispanic Origin	Population	%
Hispanic or Latino (of any race)	2,241	3.37
Central American, ex. Mexican	142	0.21
Costa Rican	11	0.02
Guatemalan	34	0.05
Honduran	36	0.05
Nicaraguan	14	0.02
Panamanian	21	0.03
Salvadoran	23	0.03
Other Central American	3	<0.01
Cuban	86	0.13
Dominican Republic	10	0.02
Mexican	1,422	2.14
Puerto Rican	304	0.46
South American	90	0.14
Argentinean	11	0.02
Bolivian	2	<0.01
Chilean	6	0.01
Colombian	24	0.04
Ecuadorian	14	0.02
Paraguayan	1	<0.01
Peruvian	12	0.02
Uruguayan	5	0.01
Venezuelan	13	0.02
Other South American	2	<0.01
Other Hispanic or Latino	187	0.28

Race*	Population	%
African-American/Black (4,041)	4,603	6.93
Not Hispanic (3,986)	4,493	6.76
Hispanic (55)	110	0.17
American Indian/Alaska Native (316)	759	1.14
Not Hispanic (283)	684	1.03
Hispanic (33)	75	0.11
Alaska Athabascan (Ala. Nat.) (2)	2	<0.01
Aleut (Alaska Native) (1)	1	<0.01
Apache (2)	3	<0.01
Arapaho (0)	1	<0.01
Blackfeet (2)	17	0.03
Canadian/French Am. Ind. (0)	0	<0.01
Central American Ind. (1)	1	<0.01
Cherokee (61)	210	0.32
Cheyenne (1)	1	<0.01
Chickasaw (0)	3	<0.01
Chippewa (7)	12	0.02
Choctaw (1)	11	0.02
Colville (0)	0	<0.01

Race* (cont.)	Population	%
Comanche (0)	0	<0.01
Cree (1)	2	<0.01
Creek (0)	8	0.01
Crow (0)	0	<0.01
Delaware (3)	3	<0.01
Hopi (0)	0	<0.01
Houma (0)	0	<0.01
Inupiat (Alaska Native) (1)	2	<0.01
Iroquois (3)	12	0.02
Kiowa (0)	0	<0.01
Lumbee (65)	121	0.18
Menominee (0)	0	<0.01
Mexican American Ind. (10)	13	0.02
Navajo (2)	2	<0.01
Osage (2)	4	0.01
Ottawa (0)	0	<0.01
Paiute (0)	0	<0.01
Pima (0)	1	<0.01
Potawatomi (1)	5	0.01
Pueblo (5)	7	0.01
Puget Sound Salish (0)	0	<0.01
Seminole (0)	4	0.01
Shoshone (0)	1	<0.01
Sioux (1)	6	0.01
South American Ind. (1)	2	<0.01
Spanish American Ind. (4)	9	0.01
Tlingit-Haida (Alaska Native) (1)	3	<0.01
Tohono O'Odham (1)	1	<0.01
Tsimshian (Alaska Native) (0)	0	<0.01
Ute (0)	0	<0.01
Yakama (0)	0	<0.01
Yaqui (3)	3	<0.01
Yuman (0)	0	<0.01
Yup'ik (Alaska Native) (3)	3	<0.01
Asian (580)	905	1.36
Not Hispanic (576)	861	1.30
Hispanic (4)	44	0.07
Bangladeshi (0)	0	<0.01
Bhutanese (0)	0	<0.01
Burmese (21)	22	0.03
Cambodian (3)	3	<0.01
Chinese, ex. Taiwanese (93)	129	0.19
Filipino (119)	239	0.36
Hmong (10)	10	0.02
Indian (70)	105	0.16
Indonesian (1)	1	<0.01
Japanese (104)	175	0.26
Korean (43)	73	0.11
Laotian (0)	0	<0.01
Malaysian (4)	4	0.01
Nepalese (0)	0	<0.01
Pakistani (8)	8	0.01
Sri Lankan (0)	1	<0.01
Taiwanese (7)	8	0.01
Thai (21)	28	0.04
Vietnamese (54)	69	0.10
Hawaii Native/Pacific Islander (67)	125	0.19
Not Hispanic (63)	108	0.16
Hispanic (4)	17	0.03
Fijian (2)	3	<0.01
Guamanian/Chamorro (27)	31	0.05
Marshallese (0)	0	<0.01
Native Hawaiian (22)	49	0.07
Samoan (5)	14	0.02
Tongan (0)	0	<0.01
White (59,346)	60,541	91.08
Not Hispanic (58,101)	59,161	89.01
Hispanic (1,245)	1,380	2.08

*Notes: † The Census 2010 population figure is used to calculate the percentages in the Hispanic Origin and Race categories. Ancestry percentages are based on the 2006-2010 American Community Survey population (not shown); ‡ Numbers in parentheses indicate the number of people reporting a single ancestry; * Numbers in parentheses indicate the number of persons reporting this race alone, not in combination with any other race; Please refer to the Explanation of Data for more information.*

Catawba County

Population: 154,358

Ancestry	Population	%
Afghan (0)	0	<0.01
African, Sub-Saharan (96)	126	0.08
African (50)	80	0.05
Cape Verdean (0)	0	<0.01
Ethiopian (10)	10	0.01
Ghanaian (0)	0	<0.01
Kenyan (0)	0	<0.01
Liberian (36)	36	0.02
Nigerian (0)	0	<0.01
Senegalese (0)	0	<0.01
Sierra Leonean (0)	0	<0.01
Somalian (0)	0	<0.01
South African (0)	0	<0.01
Sudanese (0)	0	<0.01
Ugandan (0)	0	<0.01
Zimbabwean (0)	0	<0.01
Other Sub-Saharan African (0)	0	<0.01
Albanian (0)	0	<0.01
Alsatian (0)	0	<0.01
American (20,562)	20,562	13.43
Arab (74)	99	0.06
Arab (4)	8	0.01
Egyptian (0)	10	0.01
Iraqi (0)	0	<0.01
Jordanian (0)	0	<0.01
Lebanese (48)	48	0.03
Moroccan (0)	0	<0.01
Palestinian (22)	22	0.01
Syrian (0)	0	<0.01
Other Arab (0)	11	0.01
Armenian (0)	0	<0.01
Assyrian/Chaldean/Syriac (0)	0	<0.01
Australian (0)	0	<0.01
Austrian (41)	149	0.10
Basque (0)	0	<0.01
Belgian (34)	39	0.03
Brazilian (0)	0	<0.01
British (217)	393	0.26
Bulgarian (0)	0	<0.01
Cajun (24)	24	0.02
Canadian (67)	196	0.13
Carpatho Rusyn (0)	0	<0.01
Celtic (0)	20	0.01
Croatian (0)	12	0.01
Cypriot (0)	0	<0.01
Czech (45)	205	0.13
Czechoslovakian (18)	55	0.04
Danish (16)	231	0.15
Dutch (667)	3,151	2.06
Eastern European (62)	62	0.04
English (6,855)	14,470	9.45
Estonian (0)	0	<0.01
European (1,384)	1,512	0.99
Finnish (13)	68	0.04
French, ex. Basque (498)	2,197	1.43
French Canadian (173)	533	0.35
German (14,099)	30,122	19.67
German Russian (0)	0	<0.01
Greek (116)	228	0.15
Guyanese (80)	80	0.05
Hungarian (228)	542	0.35
Icelander (0)	0	<0.01
Iranian (9)	9	0.01
Irish (5,510)	15,866	10.36
Israeli (0)	0	<0.01
Italian (1,163)	3,181	2.08
Latvian (5)	19	0.01
Lithuanian (53)	117	0.08
Luxemburger (22)	22	0.01
Macedonian (0)	0	<0.01
Maltese (0)	0	<0.01
New Zealander (0)	0	<0.01
Northern European (70)	70	0.05
Norwegian (132)	570	0.37
Pennsylvania German (13)	13	0.01

Ancestry	Population	%
Polish (615)	1,574	1.03
Portuguese (55)	90	0.06
Romanian (196)	196	0.13
Russian (168)	526	0.34
Scandinavian (14)	26	0.02
Scotch-Irish (2,465)	4,979	3.25
Scottish (1,331)	3,815	2.49
Serbian (0)	0	<0.01
Slavic (29)	51	0.03
Slovak (44)	183	0.12
Slovene (9)	22	0.01
Soviet Union (0)	0	<0.01
Swedish (301)	756	0.49
Swiss (81)	293	0.19
Turkish (0)	0	<0.01
Ukrainian (37)	92	0.06
Welsh (357)	622	0.41
West Indian, ex. Hispanic (27)	71	0.05
Bahamian (0)	0	<0.01
Barbadian (0)	0	<0.01
Belizean (0)	0	<0.01
Bermudan (0)	0	<0.01
British West Indian (0)	0	<0.01
Dutch West Indian (7)	7	<0.01
Haitian (20)	37	0.02
Jamaican (0)	11	0.01
Trinidadian/Tobagonian (0)	16	0.01
U.S. Virgin Islander (0)	0	<0.01
West Indian (0)	0	<0.01
Other West Indian (0)	0	<0.01
Yugoslavian (0)	0	<0.01

Hispanic Origin	Population	%
Hispanic or Latino (of any race)	13,032	8.44
Central American, ex. Mexican	1,363	0.88
Costa Rican	375	0.24
Guatemalan	274	0.18
Honduran	216	0.14
Nicaraguan	105	0.07
Panamanian	43	0.03
Salvadoran	344	0.22
Other Central American	6	<0.01
Cuban	174	0.11
Dominican Republic	124	0.08
Mexican	9,446	6.12
Puerto Rican	673	0.44
South American	623	0.40
Argentinean	19	0.01
Bolivian	4	<0.01
Chilean	40	0.03
Colombian	352	0.23
Ecuadorian	46	0.03
Paraguayan	0	<0.01
Peruvian	114	0.07
Uruguayan	3	<0.01
Venezuelan	42	0.03
Other South American	3	<0.01
Other Hispanic or Latino	629	0.41

Race*	Population	%
African-American/Black (13,041)	14,577	9.44
Not Hispanic (12,857)	14,221	9.21
Hispanic (184)	356	0.23
American Indian/Alaska Native (489)	1,097	0.71
Not Hispanic (342)	883	0.57
Hispanic (147)	214	0.14
Alaska Athabascan (Ala. Nat.) (0)	3	<0.01
Aleut (Alaska Native) (0)	0	<0.01
Apache (0)	10	0.01
Arapaho (0)	0	<0.01
Blackfeet (6)	35	0.02
Canadian/French Am. Ind. (2)	2	<0.01
Central American Ind. (1)	1	<0.01
Cherokee (92)	286	0.19
Cheyenne (0)	0	<0.01
Chickasaw (0)	1	<0.01
Chippewa (18)	28	0.02
Choctaw (0)	5	<0.01
Colville (0)	0	<0.01

Race*	Population	%
Comanche (0)	2	<0.01
Cree (0)	2	<0.01
Creek (1)	11	0.01
Crow (0)	2	<0.01
Delaware (0)	2	<0.01
Hopi (1)	1	<0.01
Houma (0)	0	<0.01
Inupiat (Alaska Native) (2)	2	<0.01
Iroquois (5)	9	0.01
Kiowa (0)	0	<0.01
Lumbee (67)	94	0.06
Menominee (2)	2	<0.01
Mexican American Ind. (38)	54	0.03
Navajo (1)	8	0.01
Osage (0)	2	<0.01
Ottawa (1)	1	<0.01
Paiute (0)	0	<0.01
Pima (0)	0	<0.01
Potawatomi (2)	7	<0.01
Pueblo (1)	1	<0.01
Puget Sound Salish (0)	0	<0.01
Seminole (0)	2	<0.01
Shoshone (0)	2	<0.01
Sioux (6)	7	<0.01
South American Ind. (1)	4	<0.01
Spanish American Ind. (0)	4	<0.01
Tlingit-Haida (Alaska Native) (1)	1	<0.01
Tohono O'Odham (0)	0	<0.01
Tsimshian (Alaska Native) (0)	0	<0.01
Ute (0)	0	<0.01
Yakama (0)	0	<0.01
Yaqui (0)	0	<0.01
Yuman (0)	1	<0.01
Yup'ik (Alaska Native) (0)	1	<0.01
Asian (5,352)	5,819	3.77
Not Hispanic (5,311)	5,724	3.71
Hispanic (41)	95	0.06
Bangladeshi (0)	0	<0.01
Bhutanese (0)	0	<0.01
Burmese (2)	2	<0.01
Cambodian (13)	23	0.01
Chinese, ex. Taiwanese (252)	300	0.19
Filipino (158)	231	0.15
Hmong (3,180)	3,262	2.11
Indian (324)	412	0.27
Indonesian (3)	6	<0.01
Japanese (63)	125	0.08
Korean (72)	132	0.09
Laotian (301)	354	0.23
Malaysian (0)	3	<0.01
Nepalese (3)	5	<0.01
Pakistani (52)	65	0.04
Sri Lankan (2)	2	<0.01
Taiwanese (6)	6	<0.01
Thai (121)	152	0.10
Vietnamese (507)	561	0.36
Hawaii Native/Pacific Islander (53)	103	0.07
Not Hispanic (34)	74	0.05
Hispanic (19)	29	0.02
Fijian (0)	0	<0.01
Guamanian/Chamorro (20)	29	0.02
Marshallese (1)	1	<0.01
Native Hawaiian (17)	40	0.03
Samoan (3)	19	0.01
Tongan (0)	0	<0.01
White (126,151)	128,718	83.39
Not Hispanic (120,388)	122,400	79.30
Hispanic (5,763)	6,318	4.09

*Notes: † The Census 2010 population figure is used to calculate the percentages in the Hispanic Origin and Race categories. Ancestry percentages are based on the 2006-2010 American Community Survey population (not shown); ‡ Numbers in parentheses indicate the number of people reporting a single ancestry; * Numbers in parentheses indicate the number of persons reporting this race alone, not in combination with any other race; Please refer to the Explanation of Data for more information.*

Chatham County

Population: 63,505

Ancestry	Population	%
Afghan (0)	0	<0.01
African, Sub-Saharan (371)	407	0.66
African (328)	346	0.56
Cape Verdean (0)	0	<0.01
Ethiopian (0)	0	<0.01
Ghanaian (0)	0	<0.01
Kenyan (0)	0	<0.01
Liberian (0)	0	<0.01
Nigerian (0)	0	<0.01
Senegalese (0)	0	<0.01
Sierra Leonean (0)	0	<0.01
Somalian (0)	0	<0.01
South African (43)	43	0.07
Sudanese (0)	0	<0.01
Ugandan (0)	0	<0.01
Zimbabwean (0)	0	<0.01
Other Sub-Saharan African (0)	18	0.03
Albanian (0)	0	<0.01
Alsatian (0)	0	<0.01
American (5,463)	5,463	8.89
Arab (0)	54	0.09
Arab (0)	0	<0.01
Egyptian (0)	27	0.04
Iraqi (0)	0	<0.01
Jordanian (0)	0	<0.01
Lebanese (0)	0	<0.01
Moroccan (0)	0	<0.01
Palestinian (0)	0	<0.01
Syrian (0)	27	0.04
Other Arab (0)	0	<0.01
Armenian (0)	0	<0.01
Assyrian/Chaldean/Syriac (0)	0	<0.01
Australian (26)	26	0.04
Austrian (48)	106	0.17
Basque (0)	0	<0.01
Belgian (16)	123	0.20
Brazilian (0)	23	0.04
British (183)	365	0.59
Bulgarian (0)	0	<0.01
Cajun (0)	0	<0.01
Canadian (60)	86	0.14
Carpatho Rusyn (0)	0	<0.01
Celtic (0)	9	0.01
Croatian (0)	0	<0.01
Cypriot (0)	0	<0.01
Czech (40)	135	0.22
Czechoslovakian (37)	83	0.14
Danish (33)	131	0.21
Dutch (257)	968	1.58
Eastern European (100)	100	0.16
English (3,687)	9,073	14.77
Estonian (0)	0	<0.01
European (994)	1,132	1.84
Finnish (26)	61	0.10
French, ex. Basque (97)	1,644	2.68
French Canadian (60)	143	0.23
German (2,754)	7,841	12.76
German Russian (0)	0	<0.01
Greek (16)	85	0.14
Guyanese (22)	22	0.04
Hungarian (84)	313	0.51
Icelander (0)	0	<0.01
Iranian (12)	12	0.02
Irish (1,882)	6,476	10.54
Israeli (0)	0	<0.01
Italian (895)	1,796	2.92
Latvian (0)	0	<0.01
Lithuanian (22)	72	0.12
Luxemburger (0)	0	<0.01
Macedonian (0)	0	<0.01
Maltese (0)	0	<0.01
New Zealander (0)	5	0.01
Northern European (72)	72	0.12
Norwegian (142)	545	0.89
Pennsylvania German (13)	25	0.04

Ancestry	Population	%
Polish (400)	1,263	2.06
Portuguese (28)	28	0.05
Romanian (10)	54	0.09
Russian (138)	445	0.72
Scandinavian (0)	49	0.08
Scotch-Irish (1,559)	2,852	4.64
Scottish (665)	2,211	3.60
Serbian (0)	0	<0.01
Slavic (0)	33	0.05
Slovak (28)	119	0.19
Slovene (0)	0	<0.01
Soviet Union (0)	0	<0.01
Swedish (152)	344	0.56
Swiss (40)	238	0.39
Turkish (0)	12	0.02
Ukrainian (209)	329	0.54
Welsh (218)	374	0.61
West Indian, ex. Hispanic (16)	60	0.10
Bahamian (0)	0	<0.01
Barbadian (0)	0	<0.01
Belizean (0)	0	<0.01
Bermudan (0)	0	<0.01
British West Indian (0)	0	<0.01
Dutch West Indian (0)	0	<0.01
Haitian (0)	0	<0.01
Jamaican (0)	0	<0.01
Trinidadian/Tobagonian (0)	44	0.07
U.S. Virgin Islander (0)	0	<0.01
West Indian (16)	16	0.03
Other West Indian (0)	0	<0.01
Yugoslavian (9)	23	0.04

Hispanic Origin	Population	%
Hispanic or Latino (of any race)	8,228	12.96
Central American, ex. Mexican	1,493	2.35
Costa Rican	17	0.03
Guatemalan	649	1.02
Honduran	176	0.28
Nicaraguan	28	0.04
Panamanian	18	0.03
Salvadoran	584	0.92
Other Central American	21	0.03
Cuban	70	0.11
Dominican Republic	30	0.05
Mexican	5,842	9.20
Puerto Rican	210	0.33
South American	149	0.23
Argentinean	18	0.03
Bolivian	7	0.01
Chilean	12	0.02
Colombian	55	0.09
Ecuadorian	5	0.01
Paraguayan	1	<0.01
Peruvian	28	0.04
Uruguayan	3	<0.01
Venezuelan	20	0.03
Other South American	0	<0.01
Other Hispanic or Latino	434	0.68

Race*	Population	%
African-American/Black (8,392)	8,925	14.05
Not Hispanic (8,272)	8,721	13.73
Hispanic (120)	204	0.32
American Indian/Alaska Native (344)	657	1.03
Not Hispanic (163)	406	0.64
Hispanic (181)	251	0.40
Alaska Athabascan (Ala. Nat.) (0)	0	<0.01
Aleut (Alaska Native) (0)	0	<0.01
Apache (0)	4	0.01
Arapaho (0)	0	<0.01
Blackfeet (0)	5	0.01
Canadian/French Am. Ind. (0)	1	<0.01
Central American Ind. (2)	6	0.01
Cherokee (27)	101	0.16
Cheyenne (0)	0	<0.01
Chickasaw (0)	0	<0.01
Chippewa (4)	7	0.01
Choctaw (2)	8	0.01
Colville (0)	0	<0.01

	Population	%
Comanche (0)	2	<0.01
Cree (0)	0	<0.01
Creek (1)	1	<0.01
Crow (0)	0	<0.01
Delaware (0)	0	<0.01
Hopi (0)	1	<0.01
Houma (0)	0	<0.01
Inupiat (Alaska Native) (0)	0	<0.01
Iroquois (2)	11	0.02
Kiowa (0)	0	<0.01
Lumbee (60)	80	0.13
Menominee (0)	0	<0.01
Mexican American Ind. (41)	62	0.10
Navajo (0)	0	<0.01
Osage (0)	1	<0.01
Ottawa (0)	0	<0.01
Paiute (0)	0	<0.01
Pima (0)	0	<0.01
Potawatomi (0)	0	<0.01
Pueblo (0)	0	<0.01
Puget Sound Salish (0)	1	<0.01
Seminole (0)	1	<0.01
Shoshone (0)	0	<0.01
Sioux (5)	17	0.03
South American Ind. (1)	7	0.01
Spanish American Ind. (5)	10	0.02
Tlingit-Haida (Alaska Native) (0)	0	<0.01
Tohono O'Odham (0)	0	<0.01
Tsimshian (Alaska Native) (0)	0	<0.01
Ute (0)	0	<0.01
Yakama (0)	0	<0.01
Yaqui (0)	0	<0.01
Yuman (0)	0	<0.01
Yup'ik (Alaska Native) (0)	0	<0.01
Asian (703)	921	1.45
Not Hispanic (694)	891	1.40
Hispanic (9)	30	0.05
Bangladeshi (0)	0	<0.01
Bhutanese (0)	0	<0.01
Burmese (4)	4	0.01
Cambodian (1)	6	0.01
Chinese, ex. Taiwanese (162)	207	0.33
Filipino (97)	142	0.22
Hmong (8)	8	0.01
Indian (175)	206	0.32
Indonesian (3)	3	<0.01
Japanese (23)	54	0.09
Korean (103)	135	0.21
Laotian (9)	13	0.02
Malaysian (1)	1	<0.01
Nepalese (5)	5	0.01
Pakistani (16)	20	0.03
Sri Lankan (4)	4	0.01
Taiwanese (14)	18	0.03
Thai (18)	30	0.05
Vietnamese (27)	46	0.07
Hawaii Native/Pacific Islander (24)	54	0.09
Not Hispanic (15)	42	0.07
Hispanic (9)	12	0.02
Fijian (3)	5	0.01
Guamanian/Chamorro (17)	18	0.03
Marshallese (0)	0	<0.01
Native Hawaiian (1)	6	0.01
Samoan (1)	6	0.01
Tongan (0)	0	<0.01
White (48,237)	49,243	77.54
Not Hispanic (45,185)	45,921	72.31
Hispanic (3,052)	3,322	5.23

*Notes: † The Census 2010 population figure is used to calculate the percentages in the Hispanic Origin and Race categories. Ancestry percentages are based on the 2006-2010 American Community Survey population (not shown); ‡ Numbers in parentheses indicate the number of people reporting a single ancestry; * Numbers in parentheses indicate the number of persons reporting this race alone, not in combination with any other race; Please refer to the Explanation of Data for more information.*

Cleveland County

Population: 98,078

Ancestry	Population	%
Afghan (0)	0	<0.01
African, Sub-Saharan (407)	473	0.48
African (285)	351	0.36
Cape Verdean (0)	0	<0.01
Ethiopian (0)	0	<0.01
Ghanaian (0)	0	<0.01
Kenyan (0)	0	<0.01
Liberian (0)	0	<0.01
Nigerian (22)	22	0.02
Senegalese (0)	0	<0.01
Sierra Leonean (0)	0	<0.01
Somalian (0)	0	<0.01
South African (0)	0	<0.01
Sudanese (0)	0	<0.01
Ugandan (0)	0	<0.01
Zimbabwean (0)	0	<0.01
Other Sub-Saharan African (100)	100	0.10
Albanian (0)	20	0.02
Alsatian (0)	0	<0.01
American (18,906)	18,906	19.33
Arab (0)	80	0.08
Arab (0)	0	<0.01
Egyptian (0)	0	<0.01
Iraqi (0)	0	<0.01
Jordanian (0)	0	<0.01
Lebanese (0)	80	0.08
Moroccan (0)	0	<0.01
Palestinian (0)	0	<0.01
Syrian (0)	0	<0.01
Other Arab (0)	0	<0.01
Armenian (22)	22	0.02
Assyrian/Chaldean/Syriac (0)	0	<0.01
Australian (27)	27	0.03
Austrian (15)	37	0.04
Basque (0)	0	<0.01
Belgian (0)	0	<0.01
Brazilian (31)	31	0.03
British (98)	139	0.14
Bulgarian (0)	29	0.03
Cajun (18)	18	0.02
Canadian (57)	57	0.06
Carpatho Rusyn (0)	0	<0.01
Celtic (0)	0	<0.01
Croatian (0)	0	<0.01
Cypriot (0)	0	<0.01
Czech (32)	38	0.04
Czechoslovakian (0)	17	0.02
Danish (0)	49	0.05
Dutch (349)	1,205	1.23
Eastern European (12)	12	0.01
English (4,902)	8,754	8.95
Estonian (9)	9	0.01
European (634)	869	0.89
Finnish (17)	34	0.03
French, ex. Basque (184)	959	0.98
French Canadian (122)	221	0.23
German (3,965)	10,191	10.42
German Russian (0)	0	<0.01
Greek (33)	150	0.15
Guyanese (0)	0	<0.01
Hungarian (58)	91	0.09
Icelander (0)	0	<0.01
Iranian (0)	0	<0.01
Irish (3,082)	8,049	8.23
Israeli (0)	0	<0.01
Italian (354)	1,566	1.60
Latvian (0)	0	<0.01
Lithuanian (0)	15	0.02
Luxemburger (0)	0	<0.01
Macedonian (0)	0	<0.01
Maltese (0)	0	<0.01
New Zealander (0)	0	<0.01
Northern European (21)	21	0.02
Norwegian (150)	388	0.40
Pennsylvania German (0)	21	0.02

Ancestry	Population	%
Polish (324)	618	0.63
Portuguese (0)	22	0.02
Romanian (40)	40	0.04
Russian (17)	44	0.04
Scandinavian (10)	26	0.03
Scotch-Irish (2,043)	3,333	3.41
Scottish (929)	1,813	1.85
Serbian (13)	13	0.01
Slavic (0)	0	<0.01
Slovak (14)	46	0.05
Slovene (8)	8	0.01
Soviet Union (0)	0	<0.01
Swedish (41)	373	0.38
Swiss (9)	34	0.03
Turkish (0)	0	<0.01
Ukrainian (25)	44	0.04
Welsh (100)	318	0.33
West Indian, ex. Hispanic (143)	157	0.16
Bahamian (0)	14	0.01
Barbadian (0)	0	<0.01
Belizean (0)	0	<0.01
Bermudan (0)	0	<0.01
British West Indian (0)	0	<0.01
Dutch West Indian (0)	0	<0.01
Haitian (113)	113	0.12
Jamaican (12)	12	0.01
Trinidadian/Tobagonian (18)	18	0.02
U.S. Virgin Islander (0)	0	<0.01
West Indian (0)	0	<0.01
Other West Indian (0)	0	<0.01
Yugoslavian (0)	31	0.03

Hispanic Origin	Population	%
Hispanic or Latino (of any race)	2,756	2.81
Central American, ex. Mexican	182	0.19
Costa Rican	40	0.04
Guatemalan	13	0.01
Honduran	18	0.02
Nicaraguan	35	0.04
Panamanian	29	0.03
Salvadoran	47	0.05
Other Central American	0	<0.01
Cuban	109	0.11
Dominican Republic	36	0.04
Mexican	1,742	1.78
Puerto Rican	313	0.32
South American	116	0.12
Argentinean	9	0.01
Bolivian	0	<0.01
Chilean	4	<0.01
Colombian	52	0.05
Ecuadorian	7	0.01
Paraguayan	0	<0.01
Peruvian	18	0.02
Uruguayan	8	0.01
Venezuelan	12	0.01
Other South American	6	0.01
Other Hispanic or Latino	258	0.26

Race*	Population	%
African-American/Black (20,332)	21,220	21.64
Not Hispanic (20,237)	21,062	21.47
Hispanic (95)	158	0.16
American Indian/Alaska Native (232)	629	0.64
Not Hispanic (193)	549	0.56
Hispanic (39)	80	0.08
Alaska Athabascan (Ala. Nat.) (0)	0	<0.01
Aleut (Alaska Native) (0)	0	<0.01
Apache (0)	3	<0.01
Arapaho (0)	0	<0.01
Blackfeet (2)	18	0.02
Canadian/French Am. Ind. (1)	1	<0.01
Central American Ind. (2)	3	<0.01
Cherokee (42)	170	0.17
Cheyenne (0)	1	<0.01
Chickasaw (2)	8	0.01
Chippewa (1)	1	<0.01
Choctaw (1)	4	<0.01
Colville (0)	0	<0.01

Race*	Population	%
Comanche (0)	0	<0.01
Cree (0)	0	<0.01
Creek (1)	1	<0.01
Crow (1)	2	<0.01
Delaware (0)	0	<0.01
Hopi (0)	0	<0.01
Houma (0)	0	<0.01
Inupiat (Alaska Native) (1)	1	<0.01
Iroquois (7)	9	0.01
Kiowa (0)	0	<0.01
Lumbee (19)	30	0.03
Menominee (0)	0	<0.01
Mexican American Ind. (6)	6	0.01
Navajo (5)	12	0.01
Osage (1)	3	<0.01
Ottawa (0)	0	<0.01
Paiute (0)	0	<0.01
Pima (0)	0	<0.01
Potawatomi (0)	0	<0.01
Pueblo (0)	0	<0.01
Puget Sound Salish (0)	0	<0.01
Seminole (1)	2	<0.01
Shoshone (0)	0	<0.01
Sioux (5)	9	0.01
South American Ind. (0)	0	<0.01
Spanish American Ind. (0)	0	<0.01
Tlingit-Haida (Alaska Native) (0)	0	<0.01
Tohono O'Odham (0)	0	<0.01
Tsimshian (Alaska Native) (0)	0	<0.01
Ute (0)	0	<0.01
Yakama (0)	0	<0.01
Yaqui (0)	0	<0.01
Yuman (0)	0	<0.01
Yup'ik (Alaska Native) (0)	0	<0.01
Asian (756)	951	0.97
Not Hispanic (735)	914	0.93
Hispanic (21)	37	0.04
Bangladeshi (5)	5	<0.01
Bhutanese (0)	0	<0.01
Burmese (0)	0	<0.01
Cambodian (1)	3	<0.01
Chinese, ex. Taiwanese (89)	121	0.12
Filipino (43)	64	0.07
Hmong (32)	36	0.04
Indian (142)	188	0.19
Indonesian (0)	0	<0.01
Japanese (23)	45	0.05
Korean (24)	49	0.05
Laotian (264)	311	0.32
Malaysian (0)	0	<0.01
Nepalese (1)	1	<0.01
Pakistani (16)	20	0.02
Sri Lankan (0)	0	<0.01
Taiwanese (1)	9	0.01
Thai (9)	22	0.02
Vietnamese (48)	62	0.06
Hawaii Native/Pacific Islander (24)	68	0.07
Not Hispanic (22)	63	0.06
Hispanic (2)	5	0.01
Fijian (0)	0	<0.01
Guamanian/Chamorro (3)	7	0.01
Marshallese (0)	0	<0.01
Native Hawaiian (10)	28	0.03
Samoan (4)	9	0.01
Tongan (0)	3	<0.01
White (74,123)	75,412	76.89
Not Hispanic (72,793)	73,923	75.37
Hispanic (1,330)	1,489	1.52

Notes: † The Census 2010 population figure is used to calculate the percentages in the Hispanic Origin and Race categories. Ancestry percentages are based on the 2006-2010 American Community Survey population (not shown); ‡ Numbers in parentheses indicate the number of people reporting a single ancestry; * Numbers in parentheses indicate the number of persons reporting this race alone, not in combination with any other race; Please refer to the Explanation of Data for more information.

Columbus County

Population: 58,098

Ancestry	Population	%
Afghan (0)	0	<0.01
African, Sub-Saharan (172)	180	0.32
African (172)	180	0.32
Cape Verdean (0)	0	<0.01
Ethiopian (0)	0	<0.01
Ghanaian (0)	0	<0.01
Kenyan (0)	0	<0.01
Liberian (0)	0	<0.01
Nigerian (0)	0	<0.01
Senegalese (0)	0	<0.01
Sierra Leonean (0)	0	<0.01
Somalian (0)	0	<0.01
South African (0)	0	<0.01
Sudanese (0)	0	<0.01
Ugandan (0)	0	<0.01
Zimbabwean (0)	0	<0.01
Other Sub-Saharan African (0)	0	<0.01
Albanian (0)	0	<0.01
Alsatian (0)	0	<0.01
American (11,853)	11,853	20.85
Arab (71)	85	0.15
Arab (0)	0	<0.01
Egyptian (0)	0	<0.01
Iraqi (0)	0	<0.01
Jordanian (0)	0	<0.01
Lebanese (25)	39	0.07
Moroccan (43)	43	0.08
Palestinian (0)	0	<0.01
Syrian (0)	0	<0.01
Other Arab (3)	3	0.01
Armenian (0)	0	<0.01
Assyrian/Chaldean/Syriac (0)	0	<0.01
Australian (0)	0	<0.01
Austrian (15)	15	0.03
Basque (0)	0	<0.01
Belgian (0)	10	0.02
Brazilian (0)	0	<0.01
British (16)	70	0.12
Bulgarian (0)	0	<0.01
Cajun (0)	0	<0.01
Canadian (22)	22	0.04
Carpatho Rusyn (0)	0	<0.01
Celtic (0)	0	<0.01
Croatian (9)	9	0.02
Cypriot (0)	0	<0.01
Czech (0)	56	0.10
Czechoslovakian (0)	27	0.05
Danish (19)	30	0.05
Dutch (15)	251	0.44
Eastern European (0)	0	<0.01
English (2,880)	4,412	7.76
Estonian (0)	0	<0.01
European (174)	174	0.31
Finnish (0)	4	0.01
French, ex. Basque (314)	790	1.39
French Canadian (11)	33	0.06
German (890)	2,345	4.12
German Russian (0)	0	<0.01
Greek (26)	83	0.15
Guyanese (0)	0	<0.01
Hungarian (26)	46	0.08
Icelander (0)	0	<0.01
Iranian (0)	0	<0.01
Irish (2,088)	3,970	6.98
Israeli (0)	0	<0.01
Italian (216)	645	1.13
Latvian (0)	0	<0.01
Lithuanian (0)	7	0.01
Luxemburger (0)	0	<0.01
Macedonian (0)	0	<0.01
Maltese (0)	0	<0.01
New Zealander (0)	0	<0.01
Northern European (0)	0	<0.01
Norwegian (28)	77	0.14
Pennsylvania German (8)	8	0.01

Ancestry	Population	%
Polish (28)	133	0.23
Portuguese (0)	16	0.03
Romanian (0)	0	<0.01
Russian (7)	152	0.27
Scandinavian (10)	10	0.02
Scotch-Irish (1,340)	1,841	3.24
Scottish (479)	884	1.55
Serbian (0)	0	<0.01
Slavic (3)	3	0.01
Slovak (0)	12	0.02
Slovene (0)	0	<0.01
Soviet Union (0)	0	<0.01
Swedish (4)	211	0.37
Swiss (0)	0	<0.01
Turkish (0)	0	<0.01
Ukrainian (9)	9	0.02
Welsh (22)	61	0.11
West Indian, ex. Hispanic (83)	101	0.18
Bahamian (0)	0	<0.01
Barbadian (0)	0	<0.01
Belizean (0)	0	<0.01
Bermudan (0)	0	<0.01
British West Indian (0)	0	<0.01
Dutch West Indian (0)	0	<0.01
Haitian (0)	0	<0.01
Jamaican (3)	21	0.04
Trinidadian/Tobagonian (65)	65	0.11
U.S. Virgin Islander (0)	0	<0.01
West Indian (15)	15	0.03
Other West Indian (0)	0	<0.01
Yugoslavian (0)	0	<0.01

Hispanic Origin	Population	%
Hispanic or Latino (of any race)	2,662	4.58
Central American, ex. Mexican	88	0.15
Costa Rican	8	0.01
Guatemalan	23	0.04
Honduran	20	0.03
Nicaraguan	8	0.01
Panamanian	6	0.01
Salvadoran	22	0.04
Other Central American	1	<0.01
Cuban	19	0.03
Dominican Republic	9	0.02
Mexican	2,154	3.71
Puerto Rican	133	0.23
South American	25	0.04
Argentinean	1	<0.01
Bolivian	3	0.01
Chilean	0	<0.01
Colombian	6	0.01
Ecuadorian	1	<0.01
Paraguayan	0	<0.01
Peruvian	2	<0.01
Uruguayan	0	<0.01
Venezuelan	12	0.02
Other South American	0	<0.01
Other Hispanic or Latino	234	0.40

Race*	Population	%
African-American/Black (17,713)	18,162	31.26
Not Hispanic (17,587)	18,007	30.99
Hispanic (126)	155	0.27
American Indian/Alaska Native (1,845)	2,339	4.03
Not Hispanic (1,788)	2,243	3.86
Hispanic (57)	96	0.17
Alaska Athabascan (Ala. Nat.) (2)	2	<0.01
Aleut (Alaska Native) (0)	0	<0.01
Apache (3)	5	0.01
Arapaho (0)	0	<0.01
Blackfeet (0)	10	0.02
Canadian/French Am. Ind. (0)	0	<0.01
Central American Ind. (2)	2	<0.01
Cherokee (63)	163	0.28
Cheyenne (0)	0	<0.01
Chickasaw (0)	0	<0.01
Chippewa (2)	3	0.01
Choctaw (4)	6	0.01
Colville (0)	2	<0.01

Race* (cont.)	Population	%
Comanche (0)	0	<0.01
Cree (0)	0	<0.01
Creek (10)	10	0.02
Crow (1)	1	<0.01
Delaware (0)	0	<0.01
Hopi (0)	0	<0.01
Houma (0)	0	<0.01
Inupiat (Alaska Native) (0)	0	<0.01
Iroquois (21)	32	0.06
Kiowa (0)	0	<0.01
Lumbee (237)	305	0.52
Menominee (0)	0	<0.01
Mexican American Ind. (13)	14	0.02
Navajo (4)	6	0.01
Osage (0)	0	<0.01
Ottawa (0)	0	<0.01
Paiute (0)	0	<0.01
Pima (0)	0	<0.01
Potawatomi (0)	0	<0.01
Pueblo (0)	0	<0.01
Puget Sound Salish (0)	0	<0.01
Seminole (0)	1	<0.01
Shoshone (0)	2	<0.01
Sioux (17)	20	0.03
South American Ind. (0)	3	0.01
Spanish American Ind. (1)	3	0.01
Tlingit-Haida (Alaska Native) (0)	0	<0.01
Tohono O'Odham (0)	0	<0.01
Tsimshian (Alaska Native) (0)	0	<0.01
Ute (0)	0	<0.01
Yakama (0)	0	<0.01
Yaqui (0)	0	<0.01
Yuman (0)	0	<0.01
Yup'ik (Alaska Native) (0)	0	<0.01
Asian (154)	237	0.41
Not Hispanic (143)	219	0.38
Hispanic (11)	18	0.03
Bangladeshi (0)	0	<0.01
Bhutanese (0)	0	<0.01
Burmese (0)	0	<0.01
Cambodian (1)	1	<0.01
Chinese, ex. Taiwanese (30)	38	0.07
Filipino (41)	56	0.10
Hmong (0)	0	<0.01
Indian (23)	37	0.06
Indonesian (0)	0	<0.01
Japanese (3)	9	0.02
Korean (6)	19	0.03
Laotian (0)	6	0.01
Malaysian (1)	1	<0.01
Nepalese (0)	0	<0.01
Pakistani (0)	0	<0.01
Sri Lankan (0)	0	<0.01
Taiwanese (0)	0	<0.01
Thai (2)	3	0.01
Vietnamese (25)	28	0.05
Hawaii Native/Pacific Islander (27)	51	0.09
Not Hispanic (26)	45	0.08
Hispanic (1)	6	0.01
Fijian (0)	0	<0.01
Guamanian/Chamorro (11)	15	0.03
Marshallese (0)	0	<0.01
Native Hawaiian (14)	21	0.04
Samoan (0)	1	<0.01
Tongan (0)	2	<0.01
White (35,735)	36,374	62.61
Not Hispanic (35,068)	35,612	61.30
Hispanic (667)	762	1.31

*Notes: † The Census 2010 population figure is used to calculate the percentages in the Hispanic Origin and Race categories. Ancestry percentages are based on the 2006-2010 American Community Survey population (not shown); ‡ Numbers in parentheses indicate the number of people reporting a single ancestry; * Numbers in parentheses indicate the number of persons reporting this race alone, not in combination with any other race; Please refer to the Explanation of Data for more information.*

Craven County

Population: 103,505

Ancestry	Population	%
Afghan (0)	0	<0.01
African, Sub-Saharan (996)	1,246	1.25
African (905)	1,074	1.07
Cape Verdean (19)	55	0.05
Ethiopian (64)	64	0.06
Ghanaian (0)	0	<0.01
Kenyan (0)	7	0.01
Liberian (0)	0	<0.01
Nigerian (8)	8	0.01
Senegalese (0)	0	<0.01
Sierra Leonean (0)	0	<0.01
Somalian (0)	0	<0.01
South African (0)	38	0.04
Sudanese (0)	0	<0.01
Ugandan (0)	0	<0.01
Zimbabwean (0)	0	<0.01
Other Sub-Saharan African (0)	0	<0.01
Albanian (0)	0	<0.01
Alsatian (0)	0	<0.01
American (8,720)	8,720	8.72
Arab (87)	226	0.23
Arab (0)	0	<0.01
Egyptian (11)	11	0.01
Iraqi (0)	0	<0.01
Jordanian (0)	0	<0.01
Lebanese (76)	203	0.20
Moroccan (0)	0	<0.01
Palestinian (0)	0	<0.01
Syrian (0)	10	0.01
Other Arab (0)	2	<0.01
Armenian (16)	16	0.02
Assyrian/Chaldean/Syriac (0)	0	<0.01
Australian (8)	15	0.01
Austrian (133)	133	0.13
Basque (0)	0	<0.01
Belgian (28)	91	0.09
Brazilian (0)	25	0.02
British (337)	494	0.49
Bulgarian (0)	0	<0.01
Cajun (21)	21	0.02
Canadian (90)	115	0.11
Carpatho Rusyn (0)	0	<0.01
Celtic (0)	0	<0.01
Croatian (10)	95	0.09
Cypriot (0)	0	<0.01
Czech (90)	174	0.17
Czechoslovakian (64)	98	0.10
Danish (104)	343	0.34
Dutch (272)	1,431	1.43
Eastern European (17)	38	0.04
English (5,991)	13,543	13.54
Estonian (0)	0	<0.01
European (1,103)	1,183	1.18
Finnish (11)	46	0.05
French, ex. Basque (787)	3,082	3.08
French Canadian (193)	362	0.36
German (3,944)	13,037	13.04
German Russian (0)	0	<0.01
Greek (72)	221	0.22
Guyanese (13)	13	0.01
Hungarian (198)	553	0.55
Icelander (11)	22	0.02
Iranian (10)	10	0.01
Irish (4,032)	13,419	13.42
Israeli (0)	0	<0.01
Italian (1,474)	4,413	4.41
Latvian (0)	0	<0.01
Lithuanian (75)	131	0.13
Luxemburger (0)	0	<0.01
Macedonian (26)	26	0.03
Maltese (16)	16	0.02
New Zealander (0)	0	<0.01
Northern European (22)	22	0.02
Norwegian (306)	629	0.63
Pennsylvania German (37)	49	0.05

	Population	%
Polish (686)	1,979	1.98
Portuguese (49)	118	0.12
Romanian (0)	7	0.01
Russian (97)	410	0.41
Scandinavian (97)	287	0.29
Scotch-Irish (1,409)	2,935	2.93
Scottish (845)	2,481	2.48
Serbian (0)	0	<0.01
Slavic (0)	0	<0.01
Slovak (0)	107	0.11
Slovene (0)	0	<0.01
Soviet Union (0)	0	<0.01
Swedish (234)	960	0.96
Swiss (73)	244	0.24
Turkish (0)	0	<0.01
Ukrainian (77)	134	0.13
Welsh (120)	709	0.71
West Indian, ex. Hispanic (402)	529	0.53
Bahamian (0)	0	<0.01
Barbadian (0)	0	<0.01
Belizean (70)	102	0.10
Bermudan (0)	0	<0.01
British West Indian (38)	38	0.04
Dutch West Indian (0)	0	<0.01
Haitian (39)	48	0.05
Jamaican (202)	276	0.28
Trinidadian/Tobagonian (0)	0	<0.01
U.S. Virgin Islander (0)	0	<0.01
West Indian (53)	65	0.06
Other West Indian (0)	0	<0.01
Yugoslavian (54)	54	0.05

Hispanic Origin	Population	%
Hispanic or Latino (of any race)	6,272	6.06
Central American, ex. Mexican	407	0.39
Costa Rican	13	0.01
Guatemalan	74	0.07
Honduran	127	0.12
Nicaraguan	31	0.03
Panamanian	44	0.04
Salvadoran	118	0.11
Other Central American	0	<0.01
Cuban	162	0.16
Dominican Republic	156	0.15
Mexican	3,447	3.33
Puerto Rican	1,268	1.23
South American	313	0.30
Argentinean	17	0.02
Bolivian	19	0.02
Chilean	8	0.01
Colombian	155	0.15
Ecuadorian	39	0.04
Paraguayan	15	0.01
Peruvian	31	0.03
Uruguayan	5	<0.01
Venezuelan	23	0.02
Other South American	1	<0.01
Other Hispanic or Latino	519	0.50

Race*	Population	%
African-American/Black (23,193)	24,562	23.73
Not Hispanic (22,868)	24,082	23.27
Hispanic (325)	480	0.46
American Indian/Alaska Native (504)	1,176	1.14
Not Hispanic (420)	1,015	0.98
Hispanic (84)	161	0.16
Alaska Athabascan (Ala. Nat.) (0)	0	<0.01
Aleut (Alaska Native) (3)	3	<0.01
Apache (8)	16	0.02
Arapaho (2)	2	<0.01
Blackfeet (4)	26	0.03
Canadian/French Am. Ind. (2)	5	<0.01
Central American Ind. (0)	0	<0.01
Cherokee (62)	227	0.22
Cheyenne (0)	2	<0.01
Chickasaw (3)	8	0.01
Chippewa (3)	9	0.01
Choctaw (2)	11	0.01
Colville (0)	0	<0.01

	Population	%
Comanche (1)	2	<0.01
Cree (1)	5	<0.01
Creek (6)	9	0.01
Crow (0)	4	<0.01
Delaware (3)	9	0.01
Hopi (0)	0	<0.01
Houma (3)	4	<0.01
Inupiat (Alaska Native) (0)	2	<0.01
Iroquois (24)	37	0.04
Kiowa (2)	3	<0.01
Lumbee (57)	71	0.07
Menominee (1)	1	<0.01
Mexican American Ind. (15)	21	0.02
Navajo (32)	42	0.04
Osage (0)	1	<0.01
Ottawa (1)	1	<0.01
Paiute (0)	0	<0.01
Pima (0)	2	<0.01
Potawatomi (4)	5	<0.01
Pueblo (4)	5	<0.01
Puget Sound Salish (0)	0	<0.01
Seminole (1)	3	<0.01
Shoshone (0)	0	<0.01
Sioux (12)	28	0.03
South American Ind. (0)	1	<0.01
Spanish American Ind. (5)	6	0.01
Tlingit-Haida (Alaska Native) (0)	2	<0.01
Tohono O'Odham (2)	2	<0.01
Tsimshian (Alaska Native) (0)	0	<0.01
Ute (0)	0	<0.01
Yakama (0)	0	<0.01
Yaqui (1)	1	<0.01
Yuman (0)	0	<0.01
Yup'ik (Alaska Native) (0)	0	<0.01
Asian (2,099)	2,892	2.79
Not Hispanic (2,058)	2,781	2.69
Hispanic (41)	111	0.11
Bangladeshi (3)	6	0.01
Bhutanese (0)	0	<0.01
Burmese (592)	630	0.61
Cambodian (15)	27	0.03
Chinese, ex. Taiwanese (143)	208	0.20
Filipino (471)	806	0.78
Hmong (7)	9	0.01
Indian (119)	152	0.15
Indonesian (6)	8	0.01
Japanese (219)	411	0.40
Korean (102)	184	0.18
Laotian (11)	15	0.01
Malaysian (1)	8	0.01
Nepalese (5)	8	0.01
Pakistani (12)	13	0.01
Sri Lankan (0)	1	<0.01
Taiwanese (7)	13	0.01
Thai (39)	80	0.08
Vietnamese (222)	259	0.25
Hawaii Native/Pacific Islander (135)	326	0.31
Not Hispanic (106)	262	0.25
Hispanic (29)	64	0.06
Fijian (0)	0	<0.01
Guamanian/Chamorro (73)	112	0.11
Marshallese (3)	3	<0.01
Native Hawaiian (20)	82	0.08
Samoan (20)	40	0.04
Tongan (0)	0	<0.01
White (72,441)	74,753	72.22
Not Hispanic (69,425)	71,302	68.89
Hispanic (3,016)	3,451	3.33

*Notes: † The Census 2010 population figure is used to calculate the percentages in the Hispanic Origin and Race categories. Ancestry percentages are based on the 2006-2010 American Community Survey population (not shown); ‡ Numbers in parentheses indicate the number of people reporting a single ancestry; * Numbers in parentheses indicate the number of persons reporting this race alone, not in combination with any other race; Please refer to the Explanation of Data for more information.*

Cumberland County

Population: 319,431

Ancestry	Population	%
Afghan (0)	0	<0.01
African, Sub-Saharan (2,190)	3,036	0.97
African (1,295)	1,906	0.61
Cape Verdean (13)	46	0.01
Ethiopian (56)	56	0.02
Ghanaian (121)	121	0.04
Kenyan (0)	0	<0.01
Liberian (11)	11	<0.01
Nigerian (355)	412	0.13
Senegalese (0)	0	<0.01
Sierra Leonean (36)	36	0.01
Somalian (33)	134	0.04
South African (55)	55	0.02
Sudanese (107)	107	0.03
Ugandan (0)	0	<0.01
Zimbabwean (0)	0	<0.01
Other Sub-Saharan African (108)	152	0.05
Albanian (3)	3	<0.01
Alsatian (0)	0	<0.01
American (17,940)	17,940	5.73
Arab (430)	615	0.20
Arab (87)	142	0.05
Egyptian (21)	21	0.01
Iraqi (26)	26	0.01
Jordanian (0)	0	<0.01
Lebanese (121)	236	0.08
Moroccan (41)	56	0.02
Palestinian (0)	0	<0.01
Syrian (0)	0	<0.01
Other Arab (134)	134	0.04
Armenian (58)	100	0.03
Assyrian/Chaldean/Syriac (21)	21	0.01
Australian (38)	51	0.02
Austrian (213)	519	0.17
Basque (29)	29	0.01
Belgian (10)	59	0.02
Brazilian (89)	89	0.03
British (439)	783	0.25
Bulgarian (18)	18	0.01
Cajun (84)	118	0.04
Canadian (197)	352	0.11
Carpatho Rusyn (0)	0	<0.01
Celtic (0)	0	<0.01
Croatian (11)	109	0.03
Cypriot (0)	0	<0.01
Czech (163)	423	0.14
Czechoslovakian (26)	141	0.05
Danish (180)	559	0.18
Dutch (400)	2,888	0.92
Eastern European (29)	32	0.01
English (8,574)	21,283	6.80
Estonian (14)	64	0.02
European (1,772)	2,250	0.72
Finnish (106)	318	0.10
French, ex. Basque (1,269)	6,825	2.18
French Canadian (555)	1,460	0.47
German (10,954)	34,341	10.97
German Russian (17)	38	0.01
Greek (411)	768	0.25
Guyanese (147)	177	0.06
Hungarian (281)	915	0.29
Icelander (37)	64	0.02
Iranian (82)	100	0.03
Irish (8,138)	28,175	9.00
Israeli (0)	0	<0.01
Italian (2,756)	10,458	3.34
Latvian (16)	33	0.01
Lithuanian (83)	289	0.09
Luxemburger (0)	0	<0.01
Macedonian (7)	7	<0.01
Maltese (15)	25	0.01
New Zealander (0)	0	<0.01
Northern European (23)	23	0.01
Norwegian (459)	1,716	0.55
Pennsylvania German (19)	190	0.06

Ancestry	Population	%
Polish (1,129)	4,638	1.48
Portuguese (253)	572	0.18
Romanian (42)	65	0.02
Russian (327)	1,154	0.37
Scandinavian (19)	108	0.03
Scotch-Irish (5,619)	9,783	3.13
Scottish (3,726)	8,462	2.70
Serbian (9)	36	0.01
Slavic (27)	27	0.01
Slovak (115)	283	0.09
Slovene (0)	21	0.01
Soviet Union (0)	0	<0.01
Swedish (469)	1,982	0.63
Swiss (58)	254	0.08
Turkish (119)	183	0.06
Ukrainian (112)	281	0.09
Welsh (88)	1,364	0.44
West Indian, ex. Hispanic (1,936)	3,378	1.08
Bahamian (0)	42	0.01
Barbadian (21)	40	0.01
Belizean (0)	7	<0.01
Bermudan (0)	0	<0.01
British West Indian (86)	333	0.11
Dutch West Indian (28)	28	0.01
Haitian (155)	459	0.15
Jamaican (860)	1,245	0.40
Trinidadian/Tobagonian (130)	175	0.06
U.S. Virgin Islander (44)	61	0.02
West Indian (612)	988	0.32
Other West Indian (0)	0	<0.01
Yugoslavian (7)	100	0.03

Hispanic Origin	Population	%
Hispanic or Latino (of any race)	30,190	9.45
Central American, ex. Mexican	3,201	1.00
Costa Rican	115	0.04
Guatemalan	301	0.09
Honduran	387	0.12
Nicaraguan	239	0.07
Panamanian	1,614	0.51
Salvadoran	524	0.16
Other Central American	21	0.01
Cuban	772	0.24
Dominican Republic	1,007	0.32
Mexican	10,073	3.15
Puerto Rican	11,214	3.51
South American	1,656	0.52
Argentinean	80	0.03
Bolivian	65	0.02
Chilean	80	0.03
Colombian	679	0.21
Ecuadorian	253	0.08
Paraguayan	15	<0.01
Peruvian	335	0.10
Uruguayan	20	0.01
Venezuelan	115	0.04
Other South American	14	<0.01
Other Hispanic or Latino	2,267	0.71

Race*	Population	%
African-American/Black (117,117)	125,620	39.33
Not Hispanic (113,939)	120,645	37.77
Hispanic (3,178)	4,975	1.56
American Indian/Alaska Native (5,140)	9,549	2.99
Not Hispanic (4,655)	8,368	2.62
Hispanic (485)	1,181	0.37
Alaska Athabascan (Ala. Nat.) (6)	10	<0.01
Aleut (Alaska Native) (3)	8	<0.01
Apache (22)	84	0.03
Arapaho (2)	5	<0.01
Blackfeet (29)	208	0.07
Canadian/French Am. Ind. (2)	5	<0.01
Central American Ind. (11)	24	0.01
Cherokee (383)	1,380	0.43
Cheyenne (9)	18	0.01
Chickasaw (11)	27	0.01
Chippewa (39)	95	0.03
Choctaw (46)	98	0.03
Colville (1)	1	<0.01

Race* (cont.)	Population	%
Comanche (10)	19	0.01
Cree (2)	11	<0.01
Creek (22)	43	0.01
Crow (0)	9	<0.01
Delaware (7)	26	0.01
Hopi (4)	10	<0.01
Houma (4)	6	<0.01
Inupiat (Alaska Native) (4)	9	<0.01
Iroquois (83)	144	0.05
Kiowa (4)	9	<0.01
Lumbee (1,890)	2,484	0.78
Menominee (3)	5	<0.01
Mexican American Ind. (43)	79	0.02
Navajo (93)	137	0.04
Osage (3)	7	<0.01
Ottawa (2)	5	<0.01
Paiute (5)	5	<0.01
Pima (4)	8	<0.01
Potawatomi (12)	23	0.01
Pueblo (6)	13	<0.01
Puget Sound Salish (3)	5	<0.01
Seminole (4)	33	0.01
Shoshone (3)	11	<0.01
Sioux (70)	146	0.05
South American Ind. (23)	129	0.04
Spanish American Ind. (24)	26	0.01
Tlingit-Haida (Alaska Native) (6)	8	<0.01
Tohono O'Odham (2)	5	<0.01
Tsimshian (Alaska Native) (0)	0	<0.01
Ute (0)	1	<0.01
Yakama (4)	6	<0.01
Yaqui (2)	4	<0.01
Yuman (0)	0	<0.01
Yup'ik (Alaska Native) (5)	5	<0.01
Asian (7,090)	10,877	3.41
Not Hispanic (6,885)	10,172	3.18
Hispanic (205)	705	0.22
Bangladeshi (52)	56	0.02
Bhutanese (5)	5	<0.01
Burmese (39)	44	0.01
Cambodian (58)	93	0.03
Chinese, ex. Taiwanese (564)	1,003	0.31
Filipino (1,304)	2,432	0.76
Hmong (13)	24	0.01
Indian (954)	1,212	0.38
Indonesian (11)	30	0.01
Japanese (446)	1,119	0.35
Korean (2,162)	3,197	1.00
Laotian (63)	101	0.03
Malaysian (1)	1	<0.01
Nepalese (12)	12	<0.01
Pakistani (80)	101	0.03
Sri Lankan (17)	21	0.01
Taiwanese (35)	44	0.01
Thai (301)	544	0.17
Vietnamese (610)	811	0.25
Hawaii Native/Pacific Islander (1,225)	2,321	0.73
Not Hispanic (1,114)	1,932	0.60
Hispanic (111)	389	0.12
Fijian (3)	7	<0.01
Guamanian/Chamorro (504)	747	0.23
Marshallese (25)	34	0.01
Native Hawaiian (225)	685	0.21
Samoan (194)	329	0.10
Tongan (11)	22	0.01
White (164,064)	175,430	54.92
Not Hispanic (150,749)	159,580	49.96
Hispanic (13,315)	15,850	4.96

*Notes: † The Census 2010 population figure is used to calculate the percentages in the Hispanic Origin and Race categories. Ancestry percentages are based on the 2006-2010 American Community Survey population (not shown); ‡ Numbers in parentheses indicate the number of people reporting a single ancestry; * Numbers in parentheses indicate the number of persons reporting this race alone, not in combination with any other race; Please refer to the Explanation of Data for more information.*

Davidson County

Population: 162,878

Ancestry	Population	%
Afghan (0)	0	<0.01
African, Sub-Saharan (250)	259	0.16
African (250)	250	0.16
Cape Verdean (0)	0	<0.01
Ethiopian (0)	0	<0.01
Ghanaian (0)	0	<0.01
Kenyan (0)	9	0.01
Liberian (0)	0	<0.01
Nigerian (0)	0	<0.01
Senegalese (0)	0	<0.01
Sierra Leonean (0)	0	<0.01
Somalian (0)	0	<0.01
South African (0)	0	<0.01
Sudanese (0)	0	<0.01
Ugandan (0)	0	<0.01
Zimbabwean (0)	0	<0.01
Other Sub-Saharan African (0)	0	<0.01
Albanian (0)	0	<0.01
Alsatian (0)	0	<0.01
American (20,912)	20,912	13.02
Arab (149)	149	0.09
Arab (0)	0	<0.01
Egyptian (0)	0	<0.01
Iraqi (0)	0	<0.01
Jordanian (53)	53	0.03
Lebanese (44)	44	0.03
Moroccan (0)	0	<0.01
Palestinian (24)	24	0.01
Syrian (0)	0	<0.01
Other Arab (28)	28	0.02
Armenian (18)	18	0.01
Assyrian/Chaldean/Syriac (0)	0	<0.01
Australian (0)	0	<0.01
Austrian (9)	97	0.06
Basque (0)	0	<0.01
Belgian (43)	76	0.05
Brazilian (33)	33	0.02
British (216)	427	0.27
Bulgarian (0)	0	<0.01
Cajun (23)	135	0.08
Canadian (56)	163	0.10
Carpatho Rusyn (0)	0	<0.01
Celtic (0)	0	<0.01
Croatian (41)	52	0.03
Cypriot (0)	0	<0.01
Czech (67)	132	0.08
Czechoslovakian (0)	0	<0.01
Danish (14)	102	0.06
Dutch (516)	3,065	1.91
Eastern European (5)	5	<0.01
English (8,798)	15,573	9.69
Estonian (0)	0	<0.01
European (1,090)	1,212	0.75
Finnish (0)	26	0.02
French, ex. Basque (858)	2,899	1.80
French Canadian (164)	428	0.27
German (13,411)	28,914	18.00
German Russian (0)	0	<0.01
Greek (150)	417	0.26
Guyanese (33)	33	0.02
Hungarian (86)	258	0.16
Icelander (0)	0	<0.01
Iranian (0)	0	<0.01
Irish (5,173)	14,788	9.21
Israeli (0)	0	<0.01
Italian (1,174)	2,860	1.78
Latvian (0)	0	<0.01
Lithuanian (33)	59	0.04
Luxemburger (0)	0	<0.01
Macedonian (0)	0	<0.01
Maltese (0)	0	<0.01
New Zealander (0)	0	<0.01
Northern European (0)	0	<0.01
Norwegian (257)	642	0.40
Pennsylvania German (0)	37	0.02

Ancestry	Population	%
Polish (313)	1,110	0.69
Portuguese (26)	74	0.05
Romanian (56)	56	0.03
Russian (246)	421	0.26
Scandinavian (33)	234	0.15
Scotch-Irish (2,731)	4,656	2.90
Scottish (1,756)	3,695	2.30
Serbian (125)	136	0.08
Slavic (0)	10	0.01
Slovak (28)	61	0.04
Slovene (10)	10	0.01
Soviet Union (0)	0	<0.01
Swedish (200)	785	0.49
Swiss (81)	446	0.28
Turkish (0)	0	<0.01
Ukrainian (48)	121	0.08
Welsh (92)	502	0.31
West Indian, ex. Hispanic (7)	30	0.02
Bahamian (0)	0	<0.01
Barbadian (0)	0	<0.01
Belizean (0)	0	<0.01
Bermudan (0)	0	<0.01
British West Indian (0)	0	<0.01
Dutch West Indian (7)	30	0.02
Haitian (0)	0	<0.01
Jamaican (0)	0	<0.01
Trinidadian/Tobagonian (0)	0	<0.01
U.S. Virgin Islander (0)	0	<0.01
West Indian (0)	0	<0.01
Other West Indian (0)	0	<0.01
Yugoslavian (0)	0	<0.01

Hispanic Origin	Population	%
Hispanic or Latino (of any race)	10,408	6.39
Central American, ex. Mexican	1,054	0.65
Costa Rican	29	0.02
Guatemalan	111	0.07
Honduran	283	0.17
Nicaraguan	18	0.01
Panamanian	36	0.02
Salvadoran	574	0.35
Other Central American	3	<0.01
Cuban	115	0.07
Dominican Republic	139	0.09
Mexican	7,599	4.67
Puerto Rican	498	0.31
South American	258	0.16
Argentinean	14	0.01
Bolivian	3	<0.01
Chilean	10	0.01
Colombian	127	0.08
Ecuadorian	30	0.02
Paraguayan	1	<0.01
Peruvian	33	0.02
Uruguayan	8	<0.01
Venezuelan	20	0.01
Other South American	12	0.01
Other Hispanic or Latino	745	0.46

Race*	Population	%
African-American/Black (14,421)	15,456	9.49
Not Hispanic (14,269)	15,181	9.32
Hispanic (152)	275	0.17
American Indian/Alaska Native (794)	1,586	0.97
Not Hispanic (634)	1,341	0.82
Hispanic (160)	245	0.15
Alaska Athabascan (Ala. Nat.) (0)	0	<0.01
Aleut (Alaska Native) (2)	2	<0.01
Apache (8)	25	0.02
Arapaho (0)	1	<0.01
Blackfeet (1)	23	0.01
Canadian/French Am. Ind. (0)	1	<0.01
Central American Ind. (2)	2	<0.01
Cherokee (150)	428	0.26
Cheyenne (3)	5	<0.01
Chickasaw (2)	2	<0.01
Chippewa (7)	12	0.01
Choctaw (7)	18	0.01
Colville (0)	0	<0.01

Race* (cont.)	Population	%
Comanche (2)	4	<0.01
Cree (2)	2	<0.01
Creek (5)	12	0.01
Crow (0)	1	<0.01
Delaware (2)	4	<0.01
Hopi (3)	3	<0.01
Houma (0)	1	<0.01
Inupiat (Alaska Native) (1)	1	<0.01
Iroquois (19)	30	0.02
Kiowa (0)	1	<0.01
Lumbee (195)	275	0.17
Menominee (0)	0	<0.01
Mexican American Ind. (34)	49	0.03
Navajo (2)	6	<0.01
Osage (0)	0	<0.01
Ottawa (0)	0	<0.01
Paiute (0)	0	<0.01
Pima (0)	0	<0.01
Potawatomi (1)	1	<0.01
Pueblo (0)	0	<0.01
Puget Sound Salish (0)	0	<0.01
Seminole (2)	5	<0.01
Shoshone (0)	0	<0.01
Sioux (4)	20	0.01
South American Ind. (7)	10	0.01
Spanish American Ind. (5)	7	<0.01
Tlingit-Haida (Alaska Native) (1)	1	<0.01
Tohono O'Odham (0)	0	<0.01
Tsimshian (Alaska Native) (0)	0	<0.01
Ute (1)	1	<0.01
Yakama (0)	0	<0.01
Yaqui (0)	0	<0.01
Yuman (0)	0	<0.01
Yup'ik (Alaska Native) (0)	0	<0.01
Asian (1,994)	2,425	1.49
Not Hispanic (1,957)	2,339	1.44
Hispanic (37)	86	0.05
Bangladeshi (3)	3	<0.01
Bhutanese (0)	0	<0.01
Burmese (8)	8	<0.01
Cambodian (789)	891	0.55
Chinese, ex. Taiwanese (118)	173	0.11
Filipino (201)	287	0.18
Hmong (3)	3	<0.01
Indian (205)	250	0.15
Indonesian (1)	6	<0.01
Japanese (28)	60	0.04
Korean (86)	133	0.08
Laotian (106)	135	0.08
Malaysian (5)	7	<0.01
Nepalese (0)	0	<0.01
Pakistani (98)	107	0.07
Sri Lankan (1)	2	<0.01
Taiwanese (6)	9	0.01
Thai (27)	44	0.03
Vietnamese (175)	218	0.13
Hawaii Native/Pacific Islander (27)	89	0.05
Not Hispanic (26)	75	0.05
Hispanic (1)	14	0.01
Fijian (0)	0	<0.01
Guamanian/Chamorro (4)	16	0.01
Marshallese (1)	1	<0.01
Native Hawaiian (7)	31	0.02
Samoan (1)	2	<0.01
Tongan (0)	0	<0.01
White (137,359)	139,470	85.63
Not Hispanic (133,486)	135,208	83.01
Hispanic (3,873)	4,262	2.62

*Notes: † The Census 2010 population figure is used to calculate the percentages in the Hispanic Origin and Race categories. Ancestry percentages are based on the 2006-2010 American Community Survey population (not shown); ‡ Numbers in parentheses indicate the number of people reporting a single ancestry; * Numbers in parentheses indicate the number of persons reporting this race alone, not in combination with any other race; Please refer to the Explanation of Data for more information.*

Duplin County

Population: 58,505

Ancestry	Population	%
Afghan (0)	0	<0.01
African, Sub-Saharan (95)	114	0.20
African (95)	114	0.20
Cape Verdean (0)	0	<0.01
Ethiopian (0)	0	<0.01
Ghanaian (0)	0	<0.01
Kenyan (0)	0	<0.01
Liberian (0)	0	<0.01
Nigerian (0)	0	<0.01
Senegalese (0)	0	<0.01
Sierra Leonean (0)	0	<0.01
Somalian (0)	0	<0.01
South African (0)	0	<0.01
Sudanese (0)	0	<0.01
Ugandan (0)	0	<0.01
Zimbabwean (0)	0	<0.01
Other Sub-Saharan African (0)	0	<0.01
Albanian (0)	0	<0.01
Alsatian (0)	0	<0.01
American (6,676)	6,676	11.78
Arab (0)	0	<0.01
Arab (0)	0	<0.01
Egyptian (0)	0	<0.01
Iraqi (0)	0	<0.01
Jordanian (0)	0	<0.01
Lebanese (0)	0	<0.01
Moroccan (0)	0	<0.01
Palestinian (0)	0	<0.01
Syrian (0)	0	<0.01
Other Arab (0)	0	<0.01
Armenian (0)	0	<0.01
Assyrian/Chaldean/Syriac (0)	0	<0.01
Australian (0)	0	<0.01
Austrian (0)	0	<0.01
Basque (0)	0	<0.01
Belgian (5)	5	0.01
Brazilian (0)	0	<0.01
British (22)	101	0.18
Bulgarian (0)	0	<0.01
Cajun (0)	0	<0.01
Canadian (17)	27	0.05
Carpatho Rusyn (4)	4	0.01
Celtic (15)	15	0.03
Croatian (0)	0	<0.01
Cypriot (0)	0	<0.01
Czech (0)	51	0.09
Czechoslovakian (0)	0	<0.01
Danish (4)	13	0.02
Dutch (39)	238	0.42
Eastern European (19)	19	0.03
English (2,171)	3,755	6.63
Estonian (0)	0	<0.01
European (298)	302	0.53
Finnish (0)	0	<0.01
French, ex. Basque (278)	602	1.06
French Canadian (0)	0	<0.01
German (1,173)	2,778	4.90
German Russian (0)	0	<0.01
Greek (27)	38	0.07
Guyanese (0)	0	<0.01
Hungarian (0)	4	0.01
Icelander (0)	0	<0.01
Iranian (0)	0	<0.01
Irish (1,389)	3,058	5.40
Israeli (0)	0	<0.01
Italian (138)	300	0.53
Latvian (4)	12	0.02
Lithuanian (0)	0	<0.01
Luxemburger (0)	0	<0.01
Macedonian (0)	0	<0.01
Maltese (0)	0	<0.01
New Zealander (0)	0	<0.01
Northern European (19)	19	0.03
Norwegian (15)	109	0.19
Pennsylvania German (0)	0	<0.01

Ancestry	Population	%
Polish (83)	249	0.44
Portuguese (43)	56	0.10
Romanian (7)	7	0.01
Russian (15)	46	0.08
Scandinavian (0)	8	0.01
Scotch-Irish (850)	1,250	2.21
Scottish (629)	891	1.57
Serbian (0)	0	<0.01
Slavic (0)	0	<0.01
Slovak (0)	65	0.11
Slovene (0)	0	<0.01
Soviet Union (0)	0	<0.01
Swedish (6)	127	0.22
Swiss (6)	10	0.02
Turkish (0)	0	<0.01
Ukrainian (4)	4	0.01
Welsh (36)	77	0.14
West Indian, ex. Hispanic (117)	117	0.21
Bahamian (0)	0	<0.01
Barbadian (0)	0	<0.01
Belizean (0)	0	<0.01
Bermudan (0)	0	<0.01
British West Indian (0)	0	<0.01
Dutch West Indian (0)	0	<0.01
Haitian (24)	24	0.04
Jamaican (0)	0	<0.01
Trinidadian/Tobagonian (93)	93	0.16
U.S. Virgin Islander (0)	0	<0.01
West Indian (0)	0	<0.01
Other West Indian (0)	0	<0.01
Yugoslavian (0)	0	<0.01

Hispanic Origin	Population	%
Hispanic or Latino (of any race)	12,059	20.61
Central American, ex. Mexican	3,379	5.78
Costa Rican	13	0.02
Guatemalan	858	1.47
Honduran	2,207	3.77
Nicaraguan	20	0.03
Panamanian	11	0.02
Salvadoran	268	0.46
Other Central American	2	<0.01
Cuban	83	0.14
Dominican Republic	36	0.06
Mexican	7,150	12.22
Puerto Rican	261	0.45
South American	63	0.11
Argentinean	1	<0.01
Bolivian	1	<0.01
Chilean	1	<0.01
Colombian	41	0.07
Ecuadorian	2	<0.01
Paraguayan	0	<0.01
Peruvian	6	0.01
Uruguayan	0	<0.01
Venezuelan	11	0.02
Other South American	0	<0.01
Other Hispanic or Latino	1,087	1.86

Race*	Population	%
African-American/Black (14,773)	15,134	25.87
Not Hispanic (14,640)	14,917	25.50
Hispanic (133)	217	0.37
American Indian/Alaska Native (267)	580	0.99
Not Hispanic (173)	388	0.66
Hispanic (94)	192	0.33
Alaska Athabascan (Ala. Nat.) (0)	0	<0.01
Aleut (Alaska Native) (0)	0	<0.01
Apache (2)	3	0.01
Arapaho (0)	0	<0.01
Blackfeet (2)	8	0.01
Canadian/French Am. Ind. (1)	1	<0.01
Central American Ind. (0)	3	0.01
Cherokee (31)	87	0.15
Cheyenne (0)	0	<0.01
Chickasaw (0)	0	<0.01
Chippewa (2)	3	0.01
Choctaw (1)	3	0.01
Colville (0)	0	<0.01

Race*	Population	%
Comanche (0)	0	<0.01
Cree (2)	2	<0.01
Creek (3)	5	0.01
Crow (0)	0	<0.01
Delaware (1)	1	<0.01
Hopi (0)	0	<0.01
Houma (0)	1	<0.01
Inupiat (Alaska Native) (0)	1	<0.01
Iroquois (1)	4	0.01
Kiowa (0)	0	<0.01
Lumbee (21)	46	0.08
Menominee (0)	0	<0.01
Mexican American Ind. (29)	50	0.09
Navajo (2)	2	<0.01
Osage (0)	0	<0.01
Ottawa (0)	4	0.01
Paiute (0)	0	<0.01
Pima (0)	0	<0.01
Potawatomi (0)	0	<0.01
Pueblo (0)	1	<0.01
Puget Sound Salish (0)	0	<0.01
Seminole (1)	3	0.01
Shoshone (0)	0	<0.01
Sioux (1)	8	0.01
South American Ind. (1)	3	0.01
Spanish American Ind. (1)	3	0.01
Tlingit-Haida (Alaska Native) (0)	0	<0.01
Tohono O'Odham (0)	0	<0.01
Tsimshian (Alaska Native) (0)	0	<0.01
Ute (0)	0	<0.01
Yakama (0)	1	<0.01
Yaqui (4)	4	0.01
Yuman (0)	0	<0.01
Yup'ik (Alaska Native) (0)	0	<0.01
Asian (155)	207	0.35
Not Hispanic (135)	179	0.31
Hispanic (20)	28	0.05
Bangladeshi (0)	0	<0.01
Bhutanese (0)	0	<0.01
Burmese (0)	0	<0.01
Cambodian (0)	0	<0.01
Chinese, ex. Taiwanese (37)	45	0.08
Filipino (35)	47	0.08
Hmong (0)	0	<0.01
Indian (27)	31	0.05
Indonesian (0)	0	<0.01
Japanese (17)	28	0.05
Korean (24)	26	0.04
Laotian (2)	4	0.01
Malaysian (0)	0	<0.01
Nepalese (0)	0	<0.01
Pakistani (0)	0	<0.01
Sri Lankan (0)	0	<0.01
Taiwanese (0)	0	<0.01
Thai (2)	2	<0.01
Vietnamese (8)	12	0.02
Hawaii Native/Pacific Islander (65)	115	0.20
Not Hispanic (28)	49	0.08
Hispanic (37)	66	0.11
Fijian (0)	0	<0.01
Guamanian/Chamorro (52)	68	0.12
Marshallese (0)	0	<0.01
Native Hawaiian (9)	28	0.05
Samoan (4)	5	0.01
Tongan (0)	0	<0.01
White (33,449)	34,176	58.42
Not Hispanic (30,959)	31,346	53.58
Hispanic (2,490)	2,830	4.84

Notes: † The Census 2010 population figure is used to calculate the percentages in the Hispanic Origin and Race categories. Ancestry percentages are based on the 2006-2010 American Community Survey population (not shown); ‡ Numbers in parentheses indicate the number of people reporting a single ancestry; * Numbers in parentheses indicate the number of persons reporting this race alone, not in combination with any other race; Please refer to the Explanation of Data for more information.

Durham County

Population: 267,587

Ancestry	Population	%
Afghan (27)	27	0.01
African, Sub-Saharan (4,816)	5,689	2.20
African (3,055)	3,769	1.46
Cape Verdean (0)	0	<0.01
Ethiopian (264)	311	0.12
Ghanaian (144)	144	0.06
Kenyan (120)	127	0.05
Liberian (191)	265	0.10
Nigerian (618)	624	0.24
Senegalese (16)	16	0.01
Sierra Leonean (58)	83	0.03
Somalian (11)	11	<0.01
South African (75)	75	0.03
Sudanese (134)	134	0.05
Ugandan (0)	0	<0.01
Zimbabwean (0)	0	<0.01
Other Sub-Saharan African (130)	130	0.05
Albanian (27)	38	0.01
Alsatian (0)	0	<0.01
American (13,032)	13,032	5.04
Arab (518)	833	0.32
Arab (131)	279	0.11
Egyptian (110)	110	0.04
Iraqi (28)	28	0.01
Jordanian (22)	22	0.01
Lebanese (61)	166	0.06
Moroccan (81)	98	0.04
Palestinian (14)	27	0.01
Syrian (13)	45	0.02
Other Arab (58)	58	0.02
Armenian (103)	356	0.14
Assyrian/Chaldean/Syriac (13)	13	0.01
Australian (9)	127	0.05
Austrian (111)	487	0.19
Basque (0)	11	<0.01
Belgian (10)	43	0.02
Brazilian (31)	56	0.02
British (1,056)	1,957	0.76
Bulgarian (87)	87	0.03
Cajun (0)	0	<0.01
Canadian (514)	898	0.35
Carpatho Rusyn (0)	0	<0.01
Celtic (16)	129	0.05
Croatian (79)	254	0.10
Cypriot (0)	0	<0.01
Czech (123)	438	0.17
Czechoslovakian (23)	145	0.06
Danish (122)	428	0.17
Dutch (483)	1,995	0.77
Eastern European (389)	414	0.16
English (9,195)	23,435	9.06
Estonian (57)	87	0.03
European (2,846)	3,277	1.27
Finnish (88)	326	0.13
French, ex. Basque (754)	3,967	1.53
French Canadian (266)	886	0.34
German (6,717)	23,628	9.14
German Russian (13)	47	0.02
Greek (345)	736	0.28
Guyanese (30)	108	0.04
Hungarian (176)	666	0.26
Icelander (0)	0	<0.01
Iranian (124)	163	0.06
Irish (5,243)	18,631	7.21
Israeli (112)	130	0.05
Italian (2,118)	7,212	2.79
Latvian (51)	51	0.02
Lithuanian (118)	324	0.13
Luxemburger (0)	0	<0.01
Macedonian (0)	11	<0.01
Maltese (0)	0	<0.01
New Zealander (0)	12	<0.01
Northern European (447)	465	0.18
Norwegian (333)	1,509	0.58
Pennsylvania German (28)	72	0.03

Ancestry	Population	%
Polish (1,167)	4,447	1.72
Portuguese (158)	344	0.13
Romanian (213)	449	0.17
Russian (773)	1,933	0.75
Scandinavian (133)	308	0.12
Scotch-Irish (3,864)	7,703	2.98
Scottish (1,805)	5,735	2.22
Serbian (68)	74	0.03
Slavic (28)	82	0.03
Slovak (107)	340	0.13
Slovene (46)	104	0.04
Soviet Union (0)	0	<0.01
Swedish (358)	1,571	0.61
Swiss (58)	427	0.17
Turkish (274)	274	0.11
Ukrainian (254)	737	0.29
Welsh (316)	1,736	0.67
West Indian, ex. Hispanic (1,036)	2,417	0.93
Bahamian (0)	42	0.02
Barbadian (0)	0	<0.01
Belizean (0)	0	<0.01
Bermudan (0)	0	<0.01
British West Indian (11)	60	0.02
Dutch West Indian (16)	46	0.02
Haitian (269)	461	0.18
Jamaican (395)	973	0.38
Trinidadian/Tobagonian (41)	95	0.04
U.S. Virgin Islander (8)	8	<0.01
West Indian (296)	732	0.28
Other West Indian (0)	0	<0.01
Yugoslavian (40)	142	0.05

Hispanic Origin	Population	%
Hispanic or Latino (of any race)	36,077	13.48
Central American, ex. Mexican	8,619	3.22
Costa Rican	68	0.03
Guatemalan	1,399	0.52
Honduran	3,597	1.34
Nicaraguan	82	0.03
Panamanian	176	0.07
Salvadoran	3,230	1.21
Other Central American	67	0.03
Cuban	519	0.19
Dominican Republic	458	0.17
Mexican	19,939	7.45
Puerto Rican	1,824	0.68
South American	1,603	0.60
Argentinean	232	0.09
Bolivian	63	0.02
Chilean	150	0.06
Colombian	542	0.20
Ecuadorian	189	0.07
Paraguayan	6	<0.01
Peruvian	210	0.08
Uruguayan	34	0.01
Venezuelan	158	0.06
Other South American	19	0.01
Other Hispanic or Latino	3,115	1.16

Race*	Population	%
African-American/Black (101,577)	105,142	39.29
Not Hispanic (100,260)	103,287	38.60
Hispanic (1,317)	1,855	0.69
American Indian/Alaska Native (1,339)	3,148	1.18
Not Hispanic (722)	2,154	0.80
Hispanic (617)	994	0.37
Alaska Athabascan (Ala. Nat.) (1)	1	<0.01
Aleut (Alaska Native) (0)	1	<0.01
Apache (4)	12	<0.01
Arapaho (0)	0	<0.01
Blackfeet (9)	71	0.03
Canadian/French Am. Ind. (2)	5	<0.01
Central American Ind. (30)	32	0.01
Cherokee (81)	496	0.19
Cheyenne (0)	1	<0.01
Chickasaw (1)	12	<0.01
Chippewa (9)	15	0.01
Choctaw (9)	30	0.01
Colville (0)	0	<0.01

	Population	%
Comanche (0)	7	<0.01
Cree (2)	3	<0.01
Creek (3)	17	0.01
Crow (1)	1	<0.01
Delaware (4)	11	<0.01
Hopi (1)	3	<0.01
Houma (0)	0	<0.01
Inupiat (Alaska Native) (0)	0	<0.01
Iroquois (8)	38	0.01
Kiowa (1)	1	<0.01
Lumbee (119)	177	0.07
Menominee (0)	0	<0.01
Mexican American Ind. (128)	175	0.07
Navajo (2)	17	<0.01
Osage (0)	4	<0.01
Ottawa (1)	1	<0.01
Paiute (6)	7	<0.01
Pima (0)	0	<0.01
Potawatomi (1)	2	<0.01
Pueblo (0)	4	<0.01
Puget Sound Salish (0)	0	<0.01
Seminole (1)	13	<0.01
Shoshone (0)	1	<0.01
Sioux (17)	40	0.01
South American Ind. (13)	33	0.01
Spanish American Ind. (15)	22	0.01
Tlingit-Haida (Alaska Native) (3)	3	<0.01
Tohono O'Odham (1)	1	<0.01
Tsimshian (Alaska Native) (0)	0	<0.01
Ute (0)	3	<0.01
Yakama (3)	5	<0.01
Yaqui (2)	3	<0.01
Yuman (0)	0	<0.01
Yup'ik (Alaska Native) (0)	0	<0.01
Asian (12,278)	14,077	5.26
Not Hispanic (12,180)	13,799	5.16
Hispanic (98)	278	0.10
Bangladeshi (90)	96	0.04
Bhutanese (13)	29	0.01
Burmese (83)	90	0.03
Cambodian (77)	92	0.03
Chinese, ex. Taiwanese (2,954)	3,373	1.26
Filipino (1,236)	1,572	0.59
Hmong (19)	20	0.01
Indian (3,152)	3,508	1.31
Indonesian (25)	49	0.02
Japanese (407)	639	0.24
Korean (1,012)	1,232	0.46
Laotian (19)	25	0.01
Malaysian (11)	20	0.01
Nepalese (30)	49	0.02
Pakistani (272)	307	0.11
Sri Lankan (28)	35	0.01
Taiwanese (239)	276	0.10
Thai (168)	232	0.09
Vietnamese (790)	897	0.34
Hawaii Native/Pacific Islander (172)	362	0.14
Not Hispanic (135)	277	0.10
Hispanic (37)	85	0.03
Fijian (2)	3	<0.01
Guamanian/Chamorro (38)	55	0.02
Marshallese (0)	0	<0.01
Native Hawaiian (34)	86	0.03
Samoan (15)	36	0.01
Tongan (0)	2	<0.01
White (124,274)	129,383	48.35
Not Hispanic (112,697)	116,260	43.45
Hispanic (11,577)	13,123	4.90

Notes: † The Census 2010 population figure is used to calculate the percentages in the Hispanic Origin and Race categories. Ancestry percentages are based on the 2006-2010 American Community Survey population (not shown); ‡ Numbers in parentheses indicate the number of people reporting a single ancestry; * Numbers in parentheses indicate the number of persons reporting this race alone, not in combination with any other race; Please refer to the Explanation of Data for more information.

Edgecombe County

Population: 56,552

Ancestry	Population	%
Afghan (0)	0	<0.01
African, Sub-Saharan (407)	641	1.14
African (407)	568	1.01
Cape Verdean (0)	0	<0.01
Ethiopian (0)	0	<0.01
Ghanaian (0)	0	<0.01
Kenyan (0)	0	<0.01
Liberian (0)	0	<0.01
Nigerian (0)	0	<0.01
Senegalese (0)	0	<0.01
Sierra Leonean (0)	0	<0.01
Somalian (0)	0	<0.01
South African (0)	0	<0.01
Sudanese (0)	0	<0.01
Ugandan (0)	0	<0.01
Zimbabwean (0)	0	<0.01
Other Sub-Saharan African (0)	73	0.13
Albanian (0)	0	<0.01
Alsatian (0)	0	<0.01
American (5,416)	5,416	9.63
Arab (193)	193	0.34
Arab (160)	160	0.28
Egyptian (33)	33	0.06
Iraqi (0)	0	<0.01
Jordanian (0)	0	<0.01
Lebanese (0)	0	<0.01
Moroccan (0)	0	<0.01
Palestinian (0)	0	<0.01
Syrian (0)	0	<0.01
Other Arab (0)	0	<0.01
Armenian (0)	0	<0.01
Assyrian/Chaldean/Syriac (16)	16	0.03
Australian (0)	0	<0.01
Austrian (0)	0	<0.01
Basque (0)	0	<0.01
Belgian (0)	12	0.02
Brazilian (0)	0	<0.01
British (46)	46	0.08
Bulgarian (0)	0	<0.01
Cajun (0)	0	<0.01
Canadian (9)	38	0.07
Carpatho Rusyn (0)	0	<0.01
Celtic (27)	27	0.05
Croatian (0)	0	<0.01
Cypriot (0)	0	<0.01
Czech (0)	0	<0.01
Czechoslovakian (0)	21	0.04
Danish (0)	0	<0.01
Dutch (59)	228	0.41
Eastern European (0)	0	<0.01
English (2,896)	4,190	7.45
Estonian (0)	0	<0.01
European (424)	529	0.94
Finnish (0)	0	<0.01
French, ex. Basque (191)	341	0.61
French Canadian (25)	25	0.04
German (624)	1,687	3.00
German Russian (0)	0	<0.01
Greek (0)	72	0.13
Guyanese (0)	0	<0.01
Hungarian (0)	0	<0.01
Icelander (0)	0	<0.01
Iranian (26)	26	0.05
Irish (745)	2,133	3.79
Israeli (0)	0	<0.01
Italian (146)	412	0.73
Latvian (0)	0	<0.01
Lithuanian (0)	0	<0.01
Luxemburger (0)	0	<0.01
Macedonian (0)	0	<0.01
Maltese (0)	0	<0.01
New Zealander (0)	0	<0.01
Northern European (19)	19	0.03
Norwegian (0)	82	0.15
Pennsylvania German (11)	11	0.02

	Population	%
Polish (33)	33	0.06
Portuguese (0)	24	0.04
Romanian (0)	0	<0.01
Russian (0)	48	0.09
Scandinavian (0)	0	<0.01
Scotch-Irish (702)	872	1.55
Scottish (257)	481	0.86
Serbian (0)	0	<0.01
Slavic (0)	0	<0.01
Slovak (0)	0	<0.01
Slovene (0)	57	0.10
Soviet Union (0)	0	<0.01
Swedish (16)	51	0.09
Swiss (20)	20	0.04
Turkish (0)	0	<0.01
Ukrainian (0)	48	0.09
Welsh (19)	61	0.11
West Indian, ex. Hispanic (114)	237	0.42
Bahamian (0)	0	<0.01
Barbadian (0)	0	<0.01
Belizean (0)	0	<0.01
Bermudan (0)	0	<0.01
British West Indian (0)	0	<0.01
Dutch West Indian (0)	0	<0.01
Haitian (0)	39	0.07
Jamaican (93)	177	0.31
Trinidadian/Tobagonian (0)	0	<0.01
U.S. Virgin Islander (0)	0	<0.01
West Indian (21)	21	0.04
Other West Indian (0)	0	<0.01
Yugoslavian (0)	0	<0.01

Hispanic Origin	Population	%
Hispanic or Latino (of any race)	2,104	3.72
Central American, ex. Mexican	113	0.20
Costa Rican	5	0.01
Guatemalan	50	0.09
Honduran	19	0.03
Nicaraguan	0	<0.01
Panamanian	12	0.02
Salvadoran	27	0.05
Other Central American	0	<0.01
Cuban	15	0.03
Dominican Republic	30	0.05
Mexican	1,627	2.88
Puerto Rican	114	0.20
South American	50	0.09
Argentinean	0	<0.01
Bolivian	0	<0.01
Chilean	0	<0.01
Colombian	31	0.05
Ecuadorian	1	<0.01
Paraguayan	1	<0.01
Peruvian	8	0.01
Uruguayan	5	0.01
Venezuelan	4	0.01
Other South American	0	<0.01
Other Hispanic or Latino	155	0.27

Race*	Population	%
African-American/Black (32,435)	32,806	58.01
Not Hispanic (32,318)	32,665	57.76
Hispanic (117)	141	0.25
American Indian/Alaska Native (169)	385	0.68
Not Hispanic (128)	334	0.59
Hispanic (41)	51	0.09
Alaska Athabascan (Ala. Nat.) (0)	0	<0.01
Aleut (Alaska Native) (0)	0	<0.01
Apache (1)	6	0.01
Arapaho (0)	0	<0.01
Blackfeet (0)	5	0.01
Canadian/French Am. Ind. (0)	0	<0.01
Central American Ind. (0)	0	<0.01
Cherokee (3)	46	0.08
Cheyenne (0)	0	<0.01
Chickasaw (0)	0	<0.01
Chippewa (0)	1	<0.01
Choctaw (1)	1	<0.01
Colville (0)	0	<0.01

	Population	%
Comanche (2)	2	<0.01
Cree (0)	0	<0.01
Creek (2)	2	<0.01
Crow (0)	1	<0.01
Delaware (0)	0	<0.01
Hopi (0)	0	<0.01
Houma (0)	0	<0.01
Inupiat (Alaska Native) (0)	0	<0.01
Iroquois (1)	3	0.01
Kiowa (0)	0	<0.01
Lumbee (7)	13	0.02
Menominee (0)	0	<0.01
Mexican American Ind. (4)	6	0.01
Navajo (0)	0	<0.01
Osage (0)	0	<0.01
Ottawa (0)	0	<0.01
Paiute (0)	0	<0.01
Pima (0)	0	<0.01
Potawatomi (0)	0	<0.01
Pueblo (0)	0	<0.01
Puget Sound Salish (0)	0	<0.01
Seminole (0)	1	<0.01
Shoshone (0)	0	<0.01
Sioux (0)	2	<0.01
South American Ind. (0)	0	<0.01
Spanish American Ind. (0)	0	<0.01
Tlingit-Haida (Alaska Native) (0)	0	<0.01
Tohono O'Odham (0)	0	<0.01
Tsimshian (Alaska Native) (0)	0	<0.01
Ute (0)	0	<0.01
Yakama (0)	0	<0.01
Yaqui (0)	0	<0.01
Yuman (0)	0	<0.01
Yup'ik (Alaska Native) (0)	0	<0.01
Asian (113)	180	0.32
Not Hispanic (113)	177	0.31
Hispanic (0)	3	0.01
Bangladeshi (0)	0	<0.01
Bhutanese (0)	0	<0.01
Burmese (0)	0	<0.01
Cambodian (1)	1	<0.01
Chinese, ex. Taiwanese (36)	44	0.08
Filipino (14)	28	0.05
Hmong (0)	0	<0.01
Indian (23)	34	0.06
Indonesian (0)	0	<0.01
Japanese (1)	10	0.02
Korean (8)	18	0.03
Laotian (1)	1	<0.01
Malaysian (0)	0	<0.01
Nepalese (0)	0	<0.01
Pakistani (1)	1	<0.01
Sri Lankan (0)	0	<0.01
Taiwanese (2)	2	<0.01
Thai (4)	5	0.01
Vietnamese (16)	19	0.03
Hawaii Native/Pacific Islander (15)	40	0.07
Not Hispanic (7)	25	0.04
Hispanic (8)	15	0.03
Fijian (0)	0	<0.01
Guamanian/Chamorro (9)	9	0.02
Marshallese (0)	0	<0.01
Native Hawaiian (3)	10	0.02
Samoan (1)	2	<0.01
Tongan (0)	0	<0.01
White (21,923)	22,337	39.50
Not Hispanic (21,360)	21,699	38.37
Hispanic (563)	638	1.13

*Notes: † The Census 2010 population figure is used to calculate the percentages in the Hispanic Origin and Race categories. Ancestry percentages are based on the 2006-2010 American Community Survey population (not shown); ‡ Numbers in parentheses indicate the number of people reporting a single ancestry; * Numbers in parentheses indicate the number of persons reporting this race alone, not in combination with any other race; Please refer to the Explanation of Data for more information.*

Forsyth County

Population: 350,670

Ancestry	Population	%
Afghan (0)	0	<0.01
African, Sub-Saharan (1,504)	2,287	0.67
African (1,018)	1,499	0.44
Cape Verdean (0)	0	<0.01
Ethiopian (16)	16	<0.01
Ghanaian (70)	70	0.02
Kenyan (0)	145	0.04
Liberian (51)	117	0.03
Nigerian (254)	254	0.07
Senegalese (0)	0	<0.01
Sierra Leonean (0)	0	<0.01
Somalian (0)	0	<0.01
South African (95)	149	0.04
Sudanese (0)	0	<0.01
Ugandan (0)	0	<0.01
Zimbabwean (0)	0	<0.01
Other Sub-Saharan African (0)	37	0.01
Albanian (0)	0	<0.01
Alsatian (0)	14	<0.01
American (26,383)	26,383	7.69
Arab (731)	970	0.28
Arab (120)	143	0.04
Egyptian (117)	176	0.05
Iraqi (0)	0	<0.01
Jordanian (66)	79	0.02
Lebanese (302)	395	0.12
Moroccan (43)	43	0.01
Palestinian (13)	13	<0.01
Syrian (26)	70	0.02
Other Arab (44)	51	0.01
Armenian (53)	110	0.03
Assyrian/Chaldean/Syriac (0)	15	<0.01
Australian (22)	68	0.02
Austrian (221)	580	0.17
Basque (9)	9	<0.01
Belgian (71)	135	0.04
Brazilian (101)	140	0.04
British (1,222)	1,810	0.53
Bulgarian (25)	63	0.02
Cajun (47)	47	0.01
Canadian (180)	385	0.11
Carpatho Rusyn (0)	0	<0.01
Celtic (31)	64	0.02
Croatian (36)	104	0.03
Cypriot (0)	0	<0.01
Czech (204)	581	0.17
Czechoslovakian (35)	150	0.04
Danish (146)	496	0.14
Dutch (669)	4,345	1.27
Eastern European (133)	217	0.06
English (18,275)	37,365	10.89
Estonian (0)	0	<0.01
European (3,642)	4,021	1.17
Finnish (68)	141	0.04
French, ex. Basque (1,611)	5,910	1.72
French Canadian (437)	877	0.26
German (15,453)	41,468	12.09
German Russian (21)	21	0.01
Greek (1,250)	1,859	0.54
Guyanese (67)	130	0.04
Hungarian (301)	878	0.26
Icelander (37)	37	0.01
Iranian (413)	487	0.14
Irish (9,809)	29,839	8.70
Israeli (0)	0	<0.01
Italian (3,260)	8,774	2.56
Latvian (10)	102	0.03
Lithuanian (91)	397	0.12
Luxemburger (0)	13	<0.01
Macedonian (0)	10	<0.01
Maltese (0)	0	<0.01
New Zealander (12)	12	<0.01
Northern European (184)	257	0.07
Norwegian (643)	1,990	0.58
Pennsylvania German (37)	64	0.02

Ancestry	Population	%
Polish (1,211)	4,314	1.26
Portuguese (187)	456	0.13
Romanian (128)	302	0.09
Russian (642)	1,566	0.46
Scandinavian (89)	404	0.12
Scotch-Irish (5,523)	11,110	3.24
Scottish (3,435)	8,479	2.47
Serbian (21)	99	0.03
Slavic (4)	10	<0.01
Slovak (110)	495	0.14
Slovene (12)	33	0.01
Soviet Union (0)	0	<0.01
Swedish (420)	1,628	0.47
Swiss (122)	512	0.15
Turkish (63)	63	0.02
Ukrainian (131)	325	0.09
Welsh (505)	2,486	0.72
West Indian, ex. Hispanic (784)	1,236	0.36
Bahamian (0)	9	<0.01
Barbadian (222)	222	0.06
Belizean (0)	30	0.01
Bermudan (0)	0	<0.01
British West Indian (0)	0	<0.01
Dutch West Indian (0)	0	<0.01
Haitian (160)	191	0.06
Jamaican (272)	582	0.17
Trinidadian/Tobagonian (87)	98	0.03
U.S. Virgin Islander (18)	18	0.01
West Indian (25)	86	0.03
Other West Indian (0)	0	<0.01
Yugoslavian (141)	337	0.10

Hispanic Origin	Population	%
Hispanic or Latino (of any race)	41,775	11.91
Central American, ex. Mexican	4,696	1.34
Costa Rican	110	0.03
Guatemalan	1,055	0.30
Honduran	579	0.17
Nicaraguan	244	0.07
Panamanian	155	0.04
Salvadoran	2,521	0.72
Other Central American	32	0.01
Cuban	743	0.21
Dominican Republic	593	0.17
Mexican	28,440	8.11
Puerto Rican	2,605	0.74
South American	1,930	0.55
Argentinean	191	0.05
Bolivian	20	0.01
Chilean	104	0.03
Colombian	682	0.19
Ecuadorian	327	0.09
Paraguayan	14	<0.01
Peruvian	309	0.09
Uruguayan	25	0.01
Venezuelan	241	0.07
Other South American	17	<0.01
Other Hispanic or Latino	2,768	0.79

Race*	Population	%
African-American/Black (91,227)	95,429	27.21
Not Hispanic (89,533)	92,878	26.49
Hispanic (1,694)	2,551	0.73
American Indian/Alaska Native (1,457)	3,385	0.97
Not Hispanic (894)	2,496	0.71
Hispanic (563)	889	0.25
Alaska Athabascan (Ala. Nat.) (1)	2	<0.01
Aleut (Alaska Native) (0)	0	<0.01
Apache (10)	28	0.01
Arapaho (0)	0	<0.01
Blackfeet (13)	88	0.03
Canadian/French Am. Ind. (1)	5	<0.01
Central American Ind. (21)	32	0.01
Cherokee (162)	707	0.20
Cheyenne (3)	7	<0.01
Chickasaw (14)	23	0.01
Chippewa (16)	27	0.01
Choctaw (15)	34	0.01
Colville (0)	0	<0.01

Race*	Population	%
Comanche (0)	3	<0.01
Cree (1)	3	<0.01
Creek (4)	16	<0.01
Crow (0)	4	<0.01
Delaware (1)	6	<0.01
Hopi (0)	0	<0.01
Houma (0)	0	<0.01
Inupiat (Alaska Native) (2)	2	<0.01
Iroquois (12)	25	0.01
Kiowa (2)	4	<0.01
Lumbee (218)	322	0.09
Menominee (0)	0	<0.01
Mexican American Ind. (181)	229	0.07
Navajo (11)	17	<0.01
Osage (2)	4	<0.01
Ottawa (1)	1	<0.01
Paiute (0)	0	<0.01
Pima (0)	0	<0.01
Potawatomi (1)	5	<0.01
Pueblo (2)	13	<0.01
Puget Sound Salish (0)	2	<0.01
Seminole (0)	10	<0.01
Shoshone (1)	6	<0.01
Sioux (4)	29	0.01
South American Ind. (13)	32	0.01
Spanish American Ind. (4)	4	<0.01
Tlingit-Haida (Alaska Native) (6)	6	<0.01
Tohono O'Odham (1)	1	<0.01
Tsimshian (Alaska Native) (0)	0	<0.01
Ute (0)	0	<0.01
Yakama (0)	0	<0.01
Yaqui (1)	2	<0.01
Yuman (0)	0	<0.01
Yup'ik (Alaska Native) (0)	0	<0.01
Asian (6,495)	7,978	2.28
Not Hispanic (6,427)	7,756	2.21
Hispanic (68)	222	0.06
Bangladeshi (10)	11	<0.01
Bhutanese (0)	0	<0.01
Burmese (156)	156	0.04
Cambodian (114)	136	0.04
Chinese, ex. Taiwanese (1,358)	1,614	0.46
Filipino (979)	1,279	0.36
Hmong (38)	50	0.01
Indian (1,674)	1,906	0.54
Indonesian (93)	108	0.03
Japanese (184)	427	0.12
Korean (524)	681	0.19
Laotian (87)	95	0.03
Malaysian (6)	7	<0.01
Nepalese (37)	38	0.01
Pakistani (191)	226	0.06
Sri Lankan (31)	39	0.01
Taiwanese (46)	54	0.02
Thai (70)	119	0.03
Vietnamese (623)	728	0.21
Hawaii Native/Pacific Islander (223)	471	0.13
Not Hispanic (156)	321	0.09
Hispanic (67)	150	0.04
Fijian (0)	1	<0.01
Guamanian/Chamorro (90)	137	0.04
Marshallese (42)	44	0.01
Native Hawaiian (37)	118	0.03
Samoan (8)	17	<0.01
Tongan (1)	1	<0.01
White (218,517)	224,561	64.04
Not Hispanic (205,934)	210,263	59.96
Hispanic (12,583)	14,298	4.08

Notes: † The Census 2010 population figure is used to calculate the percentages in the Hispanic Origin and Race categories. Ancestry percentages are based on the 2006-2010 American Community Survey population (not shown); ‡ Numbers in parentheses indicate the number of people reporting a single ancestry; * Numbers in parentheses indicate the number of persons reporting this race alone, not in combination with any other race; Please refer to the Explanation of Data for more information.

Franklin County

Population: 60,619

Ancestry	Population	%
Afghan (0)	0	<0.01
African, Sub-Saharan (293)	433	0.74
African (293)	418	0.71
Cape Verdean (0)	0	<0.01
Ethiopian (0)	0	<0.01
Ghanaian (0)	0	<0.01
Kenyan (0)	0	<0.01
Liberian (0)	0	<0.01
Nigerian (0)	0	<0.01
Senegalese (0)	0	<0.01
Sierra Leonean (0)	0	<0.01
Somalian (0)	0	<0.01
South African (0)	0	<0.01
Sudanese (0)	0	<0.01
Ugandan (0)	0	<0.01
Zimbabwean (0)	0	<0.01
Other Sub-Saharan African (0)	15	0.03
Albanian (0)	0	<0.01
Alsatian (0)	0	<0.01
American (9,525)	9,525	16.29
Arab (43)	43	0.07
Arab (0)	0	<0.01
Egyptian (0)	0	<0.01
Iraqi (0)	0	<0.01
Jordanian (0)	0	<0.01
Lebanese (33)	33	0.06
Moroccan (10)	10	0.02
Palestinian (0)	0	<0.01
Syrian (0)	0	<0.01
Other Arab (0)	0	<0.01
Armenian (58)	58	0.10
Assyrian/Chaldean/Syriac (0)	0	<0.01
Australian (0)	0	<0.01
Austrian (20)	58	0.10
Basque (0)	0	<0.01
Belgian (0)	59	0.10
Brazilian (0)	0	<0.01
British (40)	89	0.15
Bulgarian (19)	19	0.03
Cajun (0)	0	<0.01
Canadian (0)	25	0.04
Carpatho Rusyn (0)	0	<0.01
Celtic (0)	0	<0.01
Croatian (0)	0	<0.01
Cypriot (0)	0	<0.01
Czech (15)	48	0.08
Czechoslovakian (0)	75	0.13
Danish (14)	62	0.11
Dutch (60)	255	0.44
Eastern European (0)	0	<0.01
English (3,757)	7,352	12.57
Estonian (0)	0	<0.01
European (550)	606	1.04
Finnish (14)	26	0.04
French, ex. Basque (221)	983	1.68
French Canadian (55)	301	0.51
German (1,583)	5,269	9.01
German Russian (0)	0	<0.01
Greek (30)	131	0.22
Guyanese (11)	15	0.03
Hungarian (13)	115	0.20
Icelander (0)	0	<0.01
Iranian (0)	0	<0.01
Irish (1,754)	5,314	9.09
Israeli (0)	0	<0.01
Italian (527)	1,710	2.92
Latvian (0)	0	<0.01
Lithuanian (4)	56	0.10
Luxemburger (0)	0	<0.01
Macedonian (0)	0	<0.01
Maltese (0)	0	<0.01
New Zealander (0)	0	<0.01
Northern European (37)	37	0.06
Norwegian (59)	354	0.61
Pennsylvania German (18)	18	0.03

Ancestry	Population	%
Polish (183)	730	1.25
Portuguese (21)	56	0.10
Romanian (0)	0	<0.01
Russian (82)	95	0.16
Scandinavian (55)	84	0.14
Scotch-Irish (556)	1,133	1.94
Scottish (477)	1,001	1.71
Serbian (0)	22	0.04
Slavic (0)	0	<0.01
Slovak (0)	0	<0.01
Slovene (0)	15	0.03
Soviet Union (0)	0	<0.01
Swedish (58)	270	0.46
Swiss (0)	0	<0.01
Turkish (0)	0	<0.01
Ukrainian (10)	10	0.02
Welsh (14)	147	0.25
West Indian, ex. Hispanic (43)	174	0.30
Bahamian (0)	0	<0.01
Barbadian (0)	0	<0.01
Belizean (0)	0	<0.01
Bermudan (0)	0	<0.01
British West Indian (0)	15	0.03
Dutch West Indian (0)	0	<0.01
Haitian (0)	9	0.02
Jamaican (18)	60	0.10
Trinidadian/Tobagonian (13)	78	0.13
U.S. Virgin Islander (0)	0	<0.01
West Indian (12)	12	0.02
Other West Indian (0)	0	<0.01
Yugoslavian (0)	0	<0.01

Hispanic Origin	Population	%
Hispanic or Latino (of any race)	4,776	7.88
Central American, ex. Mexican	312	0.51
Costa Rican	13	0.02
Guatemalan	42	0.07
Honduran	67	0.11
Nicaraguan	30	0.05
Panamanian	14	0.02
Salvadoran	144	0.24
Other Central American	2	<0.01
Cuban	122	0.20
Dominican Republic	63	0.10
Mexican	3,456	5.70
Puerto Rican	367	0.61
South American	165	0.27
Argentinean	13	0.02
Bolivian	2	<0.01
Chilean	9	0.01
Colombian	82	0.14
Ecuadorian	11	0.02
Paraguayan	1	<0.01
Peruvian	18	0.03
Uruguayan	2	<0.01
Venezuelan	25	0.04
Other South American	2	<0.01
Other Hispanic or Latino	291	0.48

Race*	Population	%
African-American/Black (16,212)	16,768	27.66
Not Hispanic (15,995)	16,468	27.17
Hispanic (217)	300	0.49
American Indian/Alaska Native (329)	710	1.17
Not Hispanic (253)	581	0.96
Hispanic (76)	129	0.21
Alaska Athabascan (Ala. Nat.) (1)	1	<0.01
Aleut (Alaska Native) (0)	0	<0.01
Apache (1)	4	0.01
Arapaho (0)	0	<0.01
Blackfeet (1)	4	0.01
Canadian/French Am. Ind. (1)	1	<0.01
Central American Ind. (0)	0	<0.01
Cherokee (39)	159	0.26
Cheyenne (0)	0	<0.01
Chickasaw (0)	0	<0.01
Chippewa (5)	7	0.01
Choctaw (8)	14	0.02
Colville (0)	0	<0.01

	Population	%
Comanche (0)	0	<0.01
Cree (0)	2	<0.01
Creek (4)	13	0.02
Crow (0)	0	<0.01
Delaware (0)	0	<0.01
Hopi (0)	0	<0.01
Houma (0)	0	<0.01
Inupiat (Alaska Native) (0)	0	<0.01
Iroquois (4)	8	0.01
Kiowa (0)	0	<0.01
Lumbee (18)	26	0.04
Menominee (0)	0	<0.01
Mexican American Ind. (16)	21	0.03
Navajo (1)	2	<0.01
Osage (0)	0	<0.01
Ottawa (0)	0	<0.01
Paiute (2)	2	<0.01
Pima (0)	0	<0.01
Potawatomi (0)	0	<0.01
Pueblo (0)	0	<0.01
Puget Sound Salish (0)	0	<0.01
Seminole (2)	6	0.01
Shoshone (0)	0	<0.01
Sioux (4)	14	0.02
South American Ind. (2)	6	0.01
Spanish American Ind. (0)	0	<0.01
Tlingit-Haida (Alaska Native) (0)	0	<0.01
Tohono O'Odham (0)	0	<0.01
Tsimshian (Alaska Native) (0)	0	<0.01
Ute (0)	0	<0.01
Yakama (0)	0	<0.01
Yaqui (0)	0	<0.01
Yuman (0)	0	<0.01
Yup'ik (Alaska Native) (0)	0	<0.01
Asian (288)	456	0.75
Not Hispanic (272)	412	0.68
Hispanic (16)	44	0.07
Bangladeshi (8)	8	0.01
Bhutanese (0)	0	<0.01
Burmese (4)	4	0.01
Cambodian (0)	0	<0.01
Chinese, ex. Taiwanese (38)	56	0.09
Filipino (67)	110	0.18
Hmong (0)	0	<0.01
Indian (35)	56	0.09
Indonesian (2)	2	<0.01
Japanese (19)	43	0.07
Korean (12)	35	0.06
Laotian (0)	0	<0.01
Malaysian (1)	3	<0.01
Nepalese (0)	0	<0.01
Pakistani (18)	22	0.04
Sri Lankan (1)	1	<0.01
Taiwanese (6)	6	0.01
Thai (3)	9	0.01
Vietnamese (53)	63	0.10
Hawaii Native/Pacific Islander (12)	53	0.09
Not Hispanic (5)	29	0.05
Hispanic (7)	24	0.04
Fijian (0)	0	<0.01
Guamanian/Chamorro (6)	6	0.01
Marshallese (0)	0	<0.01
Native Hawaiian (4)	17	0.03
Samoan (2)	6	0.01
Tongan (0)	0	<0.01
White (40,003)	40,881	67.44
Not Hispanic (38,478)	39,100	64.50
Hispanic (1,525)	1,781	2.94

Notes: † The Census 2010 population figure is used to calculate the percentages in the Hispanic Origin and Race categories. Ancestry percentages are based on the 2006-2010 American Community Survey population (not shown); ‡ Numbers in parentheses indicate the number of people reporting a single ancestry; * Numbers in parentheses indicate the number of persons reporting this race alone, not in combination with any other race; Please refer to the Explanation of Data for more information.

Gaston County

Population: 206,086

Ancestry	Population	%
Afghan (0)	0	<0.01
African, Sub-Saharan (729)	860	0.42
African (502)	633	0.31
Cape Verdean (0)	0	<0.01
Ethiopian (96)	96	0.05
Ghanaian (0)	0	<0.01
Kenyan (13)	13	0.01
Liberian (0)	0	<0.01
Nigerian (87)	87	0.04
Senegalese (8)	8	<0.01
Sierra Leonean (0)	0	<0.01
Somalian (23)	23	0.01
South African (0)	0	<0.01
Sudanese (0)	0	<0.01
Ugandan (0)	0	<0.01
Zimbabwean (0)	0	<0.01
Other Sub-Saharan African (0)	0	<0.01
Albanian (9)	9	<0.01
Alsatian (0)	0	<0.01
American (24,321)	24,321	12.00
Arab (441)	650	0.32
Arab (16)	42	0.02
Egyptian (100)	124	0.06
Iraqi (0)	0	<0.01
Jordanian (175)	205	0.10
Lebanese (30)	77	0.04
Moroccan (13)	13	0.01
Palestinian (0)	7	<0.01
Syrian (32)	99	0.05
Other Arab (75)	83	0.04
Armenian (0)	82	0.04
Assyrian/Chaldean/Syriac (0)	0	<0.01
Australian (13)	13	0.01
Austrian (40)	133	0.07
Basque (0)	0	<0.01
Belgian (0)	42	0.02
Brazilian (14)	14	0.01
British (298)	575	0.28
Bulgarian (109)	109	0.05
Cajun (0)	18	0.01
Canadian (67)	122	0.06
Carpatho Rusyn (0)	0	<0.01
Celtic (0)	0	<0.01
Croatian (22)	45	0.02
Cypriot (0)	0	<0.01
Czech (50)	324	0.16
Czechoslovakian (39)	61	0.03
Danish (60)	109	0.05
Dutch (833)	3,850	1.90
Eastern European (48)	52	0.03
English (7,896)	17,178	8.48
Estonian (0)	0	<0.01
European (1,043)	1,335	0.66
Finnish (155)	233	0.11
French, ex. Basque (786)	3,337	1.65
French Canadian (241)	560	0.28
German (10,217)	27,250	13.45
German Russian (0)	0	<0.01
Greek (350)	810	0.40
Guyanese (0)	0	<0.01
Hungarian (60)	222	0.11
Icelander (0)	0	<0.01
Iranian (0)	0	<0.01
Irish (6,642)	19,979	9.86
Israeli (6)	6	<0.01
Italian (1,593)	3,701	1.83
Latvian (0)	0	<0.01
Lithuanian (5)	82	0.04
Luxemburger (0)	0	<0.01
Macedonian (0)	0	<0.01
Maltese (0)	0	<0.01
New Zealander (0)	0	<0.01
Northern European (21)	21	0.01
Norwegian (109)	338	0.17
Pennsylvania German (11)	52	0.03

Ancestry	Population	%
Polish (327)	1,548	0.76
Portuguese (75)	162	0.08
Romanian (11)	47	0.02
Russian (119)	441	0.22
Scandinavian (45)	76	0.04
Scotch-Irish (5,633)	9,583	4.73
Scottish (2,380)	4,871	2.40
Serbian (0)	0	<0.01
Slavic (14)	35	0.02
Slovak (45)	188	0.09
Slovene (0)	47	0.02
Soviet Union (0)	0	<0.01
Swedish (199)	515	0.25
Swiss (63)	303	0.15
Turkish (10)	10	<0.01
Ukrainian (26)	78	0.04
Welsh (214)	723	0.36
West Indian, ex. Hispanic (261)	277	0.14
Bahamian (12)	12	0.01
Barbadian (12)	12	0.01
Belizean (0)	0	<0.01
Bermudan (0)	0	<0.01
British West Indian (0)	0	<0.01
Dutch West Indian (10)	10	<0.01
Haitian (49)	65	0.03
Jamaican (52)	52	0.03
Trinidadian/Tobagonian (36)	36	0.02
U.S. Virgin Islander (0)	0	<0.01
West Indian (90)	90	0.04
Other West Indian (0)	0	<0.01
Yugoslavian (19)	19	0.01

Hispanic Origin	Population	%
Hispanic or Latino (of any race)	12,201	5.92
Central American, ex. Mexican	1,136	0.55
Costa Rican	212	0.10
Guatemalan	159	0.08
Honduran	293	0.14
Nicaraguan	123	0.06
Panamanian	61	0.03
Salvadoran	263	0.13
Other Central American	25	0.01
Cuban	308	0.15
Dominican Republic	226	0.11
Mexican	6,928	3.36
Puerto Rican	1,157	0.56
South American	1,520	0.74
Argentinean	24	0.01
Bolivian	11	0.01
Chilean	83	0.04
Colombian	1,059	0.51
Ecuadorian	164	0.08
Paraguayan	2	<0.01
Peruvian	102	0.05
Uruguayan	31	0.02
Venezuelan	41	0.02
Other South American	3	<0.01
Other Hispanic or Latino	926	0.45

Race*	Population	%
African-American/Black (31,431)	33,352	16.18
Not Hispanic (31,002)	32,762	15.90
Hispanic (429)	590	0.29
American Indian/Alaska Native (850)	1,948	0.95
Not Hispanic (707)	1,742	0.85
Hispanic (143)	206	0.10
Alaska Athabascan (Ala. Nat.) (1)	1	<0.01
Aleut (Alaska Native) (0)	0	<0.01
Apache (5)	12	0.01
Arapaho (0)	0	<0.01
Blackfeet (7)	34	0.02
Canadian/French Am. Ind. (1)	2	<0.01
Central American Ind. (7)	7	<0.01
Cherokee (196)	616	0.30
Cheyenne (1)	1	<0.01
Chickasaw (1)	1	<0.01
Chippewa (9)	15	0.01
Choctaw (14)	31	0.02
Colville (0)	0	<0.01

Race*	Population	%
Comanche (0)	1	<0.01
Cree (0)	0	<0.01
Creek (26)	37	0.02
Crow (1)	2	<0.01
Delaware (3)	4	<0.01
Hopi (0)	0	<0.01
Houma (0)	0	<0.01
Inupiat (Alaska Native) (1)	2	<0.01
Iroquois (4)	12	0.01
Kiowa (1)	1	<0.01
Lumbee (177)	248	0.12
Menominee (0)	0	<0.01
Mexican American Ind. (36)	40	0.02
Navajo (3)	6	<0.01
Osage (0)	1	<0.01
Ottawa (0)	1	<0.01
Paiute (0)	0	<0.01
Pima (0)	0	<0.01
Potawatomi (0)	3	<0.01
Pueblo (0)	0	<0.01
Puget Sound Salish (0)	0	<0.01
Seminole (0)	9	<0.01
Shoshone (3)	3	<0.01
Sioux (4)	13	0.01
South American Ind. (4)	9	<0.01
Spanish American Ind. (2)	5	<0.01
Tlingit-Haida (Alaska Native) (0)	0	<0.01
Tohono O'Odham (0)	0	<0.01
Tsimshian (Alaska Native) (0)	0	<0.01
Ute (0)	0	<0.01
Yakama (0)	0	<0.01
Yaqui (1)	1	<0.01
Yuman (1)	1	<0.01
Yup'ik (Alaska Native) (0)	0	<0.01
Asian (2,478)	3,068	1.49
Not Hispanic (2,462)	3,012	1.46
Hispanic (16)	56	0.03
Bangladeshi (0)	0	<0.01
Bhutanese (0)	0	<0.01
Burmese (1)	2	<0.01
Cambodian (42)	58	0.03
Chinese, ex. Taiwanese (251)	310	0.15
Filipino (175)	292	0.14
Hmong (66)	67	0.03
Indian (659)	772	0.37
Indonesian (14)	19	0.01
Japanese (56)	140	0.07
Korean (120)	189	0.09
Laotian (314)	363	0.18
Malaysian (2)	2	<0.01
Nepalese (4)	4	<0.01
Pakistani (149)	168	0.08
Sri Lankan (7)	8	<0.01
Taiwanese (4)	5	<0.01
Thai (24)	58	0.03
Vietnamese (472)	536	0.26
Hawaii Native/Pacific Islander (63)	177	0.09
Not Hispanic (44)	136	0.07
Hispanic (19)	41	0.02
Fijian (1)	1	<0.01
Guamanian/Chamorro (22)	34	0.02
Marshallese (0)	0	<0.01
Native Hawaiian (18)	48	0.02
Samoan (10)	21	0.01
Tongan (0)	0	<0.01
White (161,166)	164,531	79.84
Not Hispanic (156,310)	159,104	77.20
Hispanic (4,856)	5,427	2.63

*Notes: † The Census 2010 population figure is used to calculate the percentages in the Hispanic Origin and Race categories. Ancestry percentages are based on the 2006-2010 American Community Survey population (not shown); ‡ Numbers in parentheses indicate the number of people reporting a single ancestry; * Numbers in parentheses indicate the number of persons reporting this race alone, not in combination with any other race; Please refer to the Explanation of Data for more information.*

Granville County

Population: 59,916

Ancestry	Population	%
Afghan (0)	0	<0.01
African, Sub-Saharan (323)	397	0.68
African (315)	389	0.67
Cape Verdean (0)	0	<0.01
Ethiopian (0)	0	<0.01
Ghanaian (0)	0	<0.01
Kenyan (0)	0	<0.01
Liberian (0)	0	<0.01
Nigerian (8)	8	0.01
Senegalese (0)	0	<0.01
Sierra Leonean (0)	0	<0.01
Somalian (0)	0	<0.01
South African (0)	0	<0.01
Sudanese (0)	0	<0.01
Ugandan (0)	0	<0.01
Zimbabwean (0)	0	<0.01
Other Sub-Saharan African (0)	0	<0.01
Albanian (0)	0	<0.01
Alsatian (0)	0	<0.01
American (9,130)	9,130	15.72
Arab (54)	143	0.25
Arab (0)	0	<0.01
Egyptian (0)	37	0.06
Iraqi (0)	0	<0.01
Jordanian (0)	0	<0.01
Lebanese (16)	56	0.10
Moroccan (34)	34	0.06
Palestinian (4)	16	0.03
Syrian (0)	0	<0.01
Other Arab (0)	0	<0.01
Armenian (0)	0	<0.01
Assyrian/Chaldean/Syriac (0)	0	<0.01
Australian (0)	0	<0.01
Austrian (8)	62	0.11
Basque (0)	0	<0.01
Belgian (0)	0	<0.01
Brazilian (0)	0	<0.01
British (125)	133	0.23
Bulgarian (0)	0	<0.01
Cajun (0)	0	<0.01
Canadian (53)	53	0.09
Carpatho Rusyn (0)	0	<0.01
Celtic (0)	0	<0.01
Croatian (32)	50	0.09
Cypriot (0)	0	<0.01
Czech (23)	68	0.12
Czechoslovakian (0)	0	<0.01
Danish (43)	88	0.15
Dutch (68)	313	0.54
Eastern European (0)	0	<0.01
English (2,590)	5,047	8.69
Estonian (0)	0	<0.01
European (469)	544	0.94
Finnish (0)	8	0.01
French, ex. Basque (242)	883	1.52
French Canadian (12)	174	0.30
German (1,442)	3,824	6.59
German Russian (0)	0	<0.01
Greek (8)	57	0.10
Guyanese (0)	9	0.02
Hungarian (45)	97	0.17
Icelander (0)	0	<0.01
Iranian (0)	0	<0.01
Irish (1,462)	3,609	6.21
Israeli (0)	0	<0.01
Italian (226)	892	1.54
Latvian (0)	8	0.01
Lithuanian (0)	12	0.02
Luxemburger (0)	0	<0.01
Macedonian (0)	0	<0.01
Maltese (0)	0	<0.01
New Zealander (0)	0	<0.01
Northern European (61)	81	0.14
Norwegian (67)	147	0.25
Pennsylvania German (8)	8	0.01

Ancestry	Population	%
Polish (135)	396	0.68
Portuguese (0)	8	0.01
Romanian (0)	0	<0.01
Russian (24)	197	0.34
Scandinavian (0)	27	0.05
Scotch-Irish (651)	1,029	1.77
Scottish (433)	980	1.69
Serbian (27)	105	0.18
Slavic (3)	36	0.06
Slovak (0)	34	0.06
Slovene (0)	0	<0.01
Soviet Union (0)	0	<0.01
Swedish (105)	365	0.63
Swiss (9)	74	0.13
Turkish (0)	0	<0.01
Ukrainian (21)	46	0.08
Welsh (16)	143	0.25
West Indian, ex. Hispanic (115)	131	0.23
Bahamian (0)	0	<0.01
Barbadian (0)	0	<0.01
Belizean (0)	0	<0.01
Bermudan (0)	0	<0.01
British West Indian (7)	7	0.01
Dutch West Indian (0)	0	<0.01
Haitian (33)	49	0.08
Jamaican (53)	53	0.09
Trinidadian/Tobagonian (0)	0	<0.01
U.S. Virgin Islander (0)	0	<0.01
West Indian (22)	22	0.04
Other West Indian (0)	0	<0.01
Yugoslavian (0)	0	<0.01

Hispanic Origin	Population	%
Hispanic or Latino (of any race)	4,482	7.48
Central American, ex. Mexican	284	0.47
Costa Rican	4	0.01
Guatemalan	43	0.07
Honduran	77	0.13
Nicaraguan	2	<0.01
Panamanian	17	0.03
Salvadoran	135	0.23
Other Central American	6	0.01
Cuban	120	0.20
Dominican Republic	43	0.07
Mexican	3,289	5.49
Puerto Rican	385	0.64
South American	104	0.17
Argentinean	9	0.02
Bolivian	0	<0.01
Chilean	8	0.01
Colombian	38	0.06
Ecuadorian	26	0.04
Paraguayan	0	<0.01
Peruvian	22	0.04
Uruguayan	1	<0.01
Venezuelan	0	<0.01
Other South American	0	<0.01
Other Hispanic or Latino	257	0.43

Race*	Population	%
African-American/Black (19,652)	20,239	33.78
Not Hispanic (19,454)	19,972	33.33
Hispanic (198)	267	0.45
American Indian/Alaska Native (338)	659	1.10
Not Hispanic (250)	526	0.88
Hispanic (88)	133	0.22
Alaska Athabascan (Ala. Nat.) (0)	0	<0.01
Aleut (Alaska Native) (0)	0	<0.01
Apache (4)	4	0.01
Arapaho (0)	0	<0.01
Blackfeet (8)	21	0.04
Canadian/French Am. Ind. (0)	1	<0.01
Central American Ind. (0)	0	<0.01
Cherokee (46)	141	0.24
Cheyenne (0)	0	<0.01
Chickasaw (0)	1	<0.01
Chippewa (4)	5	0.01
Choctaw (1)	4	0.01
Colville (0)	1	<0.01

Race*	Population	%
Comanche (0)	3	0.01
Cree (1)	1	<0.01
Creek (3)	5	0.01
Crow (0)	0	<0.01
Delaware (2)	3	0.01
Hopi (0)	0	<0.01
Houma (0)	0	<0.01
Inupiat (Alaska Native) (0)	0	<0.01
Iroquois (6)	9	0.02
Kiowa (0)	0	<0.01
Lumbee (32)	45	0.08
Menominee (0)	0	<0.01
Mexican American Ind. (26)	35	0.06
Navajo (3)	4	0.01
Osage (0)	3	0.01
Ottawa (0)	0	<0.01
Paiute (0)	0	<0.01
Pima (0)	0	<0.01
Potawatomi (0)	0	<0.01
Pueblo (0)	0	<0.01
Puget Sound Salish (0)	0	<0.01
Seminole (4)	6	0.01
Shoshone (0)	0	<0.01
Sioux (7)	8	0.01
South American Ind. (1)	5	0.01
Spanish American Ind. (1)	1	<0.01
Tlingit-Haida (Alaska Native) (0)	0	<0.01
Tohono O'Odham (0)	0	<0.01
Tsimshian (Alaska Native) (0)	0	<0.01
Ute (0)	0	<0.01
Yakama (0)	0	<0.01
Yaqui (0)	3	0.01
Yuman (0)	0	<0.01
Yup'ik (Alaska Native) (0)	0	<0.01
Asian (326)	490	0.82
Not Hispanic (321)	454	0.76
Hispanic (5)	36	0.06
Bangladeshi (8)	8	0.01
Bhutanese (0)	0	<0.01
Burmese (0)	0	<0.01
Cambodian (0)	0	<0.01
Chinese, ex. Taiwanese (40)	60	0.10
Filipino (42)	87	0.15
Hmong (13)	13	0.02
Indian (93)	120	0.20
Indonesian (0)	2	<0.01
Japanese (12)	35	0.06
Korean (18)	37	0.06
Laotian (11)	17	0.03
Malaysian (0)	1	<0.01
Nepalese (0)	0	<0.01
Pakistani (5)	8	0.01
Sri Lankan (0)	0	<0.01
Taiwanese (2)	2	<0.01
Thai (4)	4	0.01
Vietnamese (54)	60	0.10
Hawaii Native/Pacific Islander (34)	72	0.12
Not Hispanic (22)	44	0.07
Hispanic (12)	28	0.05
Fijian (0)	0	<0.01
Guamanian/Chamorro (14)	22	0.04
Marshallese (0)	0	<0.01
Native Hawaiian (2)	17	0.03
Samoan (0)	0	<0.01
Tongan (0)	0	<0.01
White (36,205)	37,048	61.83
Not Hispanic (34,550)	35,203	58.75
Hispanic (1,655)	1,845	3.08

Notes: † The Census 2010 population figure is used to calculate the percentages in the Hispanic Origin and Race categories. Ancestry percentages are based on the 2006-2010 American Community Survey population (not shown); ‡ Numbers in parentheses indicate the number of people reporting a single ancestry; * Numbers in parentheses indicate the number of persons reporting this race alone, not in combination with any other race; Please refer to the Explanation of Data for more information.

Guilford County

Population: 488,406

Ancestry	Population	%
Afghan (16)	16	<0.01
African, Sub-Saharan (7,408)	8,250	1.73
African (2,827)	3,489	0.73
Cape Verdean (29)	44	0.01
Ethiopian (353)	353	0.07
Ghanaian (402)	402	0.08
Kenyan (15)	15	<0.01
Liberian (551)	580	0.12
Nigerian (656)	711	0.15
Senegalese (13)	13	<0.01
Sierra Leonean (210)	210	0.04
Somalian (118)	118	0.02
South African (24)	61	0.01
Sudanese (1,454)	1,471	0.31
Ugandan (38)	38	0.01
Zimbabwean (0)	0	<0.01
Other Sub-Saharan African (718)	745	0.16
Albanian (0)	0	<0.01
Alsatian (12)	12	<0.01
American (32,345)	32,345	6.80
Arab (1,055)	1,577	0.33
Arab (183)	239	0.05
Egyptian (137)	151	0.03
Iraqi (0)	0	<0.01
Jordanian (126)	159	0.03
Lebanese (287)	535	0.11
Moroccan (49)	58	0.01
Palestinian (65)	131	0.03
Syrian (82)	155	0.03
Other Arab (126)	149	0.03
Armenian (84)	107	0.02
Assyrian/Chaldean/Syriac (0)	0	<0.01
Australian (10)	89	0.02
Austrian (167)	698	0.15
Basque (21)	21	<0.01
Belgian (96)	270	0.06
Brazilian (220)	247	0.05
British (1,249)	2,467	0.52
Bulgarian (87)	112	0.02
Cajun (58)	88	0.02
Canadian (433)	675	0.14
Carpatho Rusyn (0)	0	<0.01
Celtic (46)	59	0.01
Croatian (170)	330	0.07
Cypriot (0)	0	<0.01
Czech (202)	1,104	0.23
Czechoslovakian (83)	242	0.05
Danish (224)	873	0.18
Dutch (1,112)	5,236	1.10
Eastern European (474)	539	0.11
English (21,386)	45,054	9.47
Estonian (0)	0	<0.01
European (5,020)	5,808	1.22
Finnish (35)	379	0.08
French, ex. Basque (1,719)	7,544	1.59
French Canadian (438)	1,450	0.30
German (16,064)	46,903	9.86
German Russian (0)	0	<0.01
Greek (556)	955	0.20
Guyanese (182)	416	0.09
Hungarian (324)	1,456	0.31
Icelander (0)	14	<0.01
Iranian (390)	450	0.09
Irish (11,969)	35,178	7.39
Israeli (0)	0	<0.01
Italian (5,028)	12,548	2.64
Latvian (9)	26	0.01
Lithuanian (87)	439	0.09
Luxemburger (0)	9	<0.01
Macedonian (0)	0	<0.01
Maltese (9)	9	<0.01
New Zealander (0)	8	<0.01
Northern European (145)	165	0.03
Norwegian (552)	2,023	0.43
Pennsylvania German (57)	164	0.03

	Population	%
Polish (1,988)	5,843	1.23
Portuguese (77)	572	0.12
Romanian (183)	354	0.07
Russian (705)	2,076	0.44
Scandinavian (136)	461	0.10
Scotch-Irish (8,756)	16,167	3.40
Scottish (4,697)	11,352	2.39
Serbian (125)	351	0.07
Slavic (74)	147	0.03
Slovak (187)	511	0.11
Slovene (28)	85	0.02
Soviet Union (0)	0	<0.01
Swedish (713)	2,447	0.51
Swiss (218)	644	0.14
Turkish (15)	57	0.01
Ukrainian (191)	676	0.14
Welsh (582)	2,422	0.51
West Indian, ex. Hispanic (1,314)	2,230	0.47
Bahamian (155)	170	0.04
Barbadian (29)	57	0.01
Belizean (0)	0	<0.01
Bermudan (34)	92	0.02
British West Indian (0)	22	<0.01
Dutch West Indian (27)	27	0.01
Haitian (218)	305	0.06
Jamaican (605)	1,040	0.22
Trinidadian/Tobagonian (173)	309	0.06
U.S. Virgin Islander (0)	0	<0.01
West Indian (73)	208	0.04
Other West Indian (0)	0	<0.01
Yugoslavian (290)	521	0.11

Hispanic Origin	Population	%
Hispanic or Latino (of any race)	34,826	7.13
Central American, ex. Mexican	3,653	0.75
Costa Rican	210	0.04
Guatemalan	737	0.15
Honduran	735	0.15
Nicaraguan	199	0.04
Panamanian	301	0.06
Salvadoran	1,457	0.30
Other Central American	14	<0.01
Cuban	960	0.20
Dominican Republic	889	0.18
Mexican	21,425	4.39
Puerto Rican	3,175	0.65
South American	2,393	0.49
Argentinean	153	0.03
Bolivian	50	0.01
Chilean	166	0.03
Colombian	962	0.20
Ecuadorian	232	0.05
Paraguayan	17	<0.01
Peruvian	459	0.09
Uruguayan	38	0.01
Venezuelan	289	0.06
Other South American	27	0.01
Other Hispanic or Latino	2,331	0.48

Race*	Population	%
African-American/Black (158,899)	165,677	33.92
Not Hispanic (156,982)	162,809	33.33
Hispanic (1,917)	2,868	0.59
American Indian/Alaska Native (2,594)	5,887	1.21
Not Hispanic (2,071)	4,968	1.02
Hispanic (523)	919	0.19
Alaska Athabascan (Ala. Nat.) (0)	0	<0.01
Aleut (Alaska Native) (1)	2	<0.01
Apache (11)	49	0.01
Arapaho (0)	1	<0.01
Blackfeet (17)	161	0.03
Canadian/French Am. Ind. (1)	6	<0.01
Central American Ind. (18)	29	0.01
Cherokee (291)	1,259	0.26
Cheyenne (2)	4	<0.01
Chickasaw (2)	6	<0.01
Chippewa (24)	53	0.01
Choctaw (9)	45	0.01
Colville (0)	0	<0.01

	Population	%
Comanche (4)	20	<0.01
Cree (1)	5	<0.01
Creek (5)	33	0.01
Crow (1)	3	<0.01
Delaware (3)	8	<0.01
Hopi (0)	3	<0.01
Houma (0)	0	<0.01
Inupiat (Alaska Native) (2)	4	<0.01
Iroquois (24)	83	0.02
Kiowa (1)	1	<0.01
Lumbee (638)	900	0.18
Menominee (0)	0	<0.01
Mexican American Ind. (119)	169	0.03
Navajo (14)	38	0.01
Osage (3)	3	<0.01
Ottawa (3)	6	<0.01
Paiute (0)	1	<0.01
Pima (0)	1	<0.01
Potawatomi (8)	15	<0.01
Pueblo (2)	12	<0.01
Puget Sound Salish (0)	0	<0.01
Seminole (2)	12	<0.01
Shoshone (0)	0	<0.01
Sioux (12)	41	0.01
South American Ind. (6)	24	<0.01
Spanish American Ind. (10)	13	<0.01
Tlingit-Haida (Alaska Native) (1)	1	<0.01
Tohono O'Odham (1)	1	<0.01
Tsimshian (Alaska Native) (0)	0	<0.01
Ute (0)	0	<0.01
Yakama (2)	2	<0.01
Yaqui (0)	1	<0.01
Yuman (1)	2	<0.01
Yup'ik (Alaska Native) (1)	1	<0.01
Asian (19,176)	21,685	4.44
Not Hispanic (19,059)	21,382	4.38
Hispanic (117)	303	0.06
Bangladeshi (58)	73	0.01
Bhutanese (202)	234	0.05
Burmese (652)	680	0.14
Cambodian (684)	840	0.17
Chinese, ex. Taiwanese (1,684)	2,078	0.43
Filipino (874)	1,329	0.27
Hmong (121)	124	0.03
Indian (3,054)	3,498	0.72
Indonesian (24)	40	0.01
Japanese (330)	610	0.12
Korean (1,659)	2,054	0.42
Laotian (928)	1,068	0.22
Malaysian (19)	28	0.01
Nepalese (204)	228	0.05
Pakistani (1,620)	1,763	0.36
Sri Lankan (44)	52	0.01
Taiwanese (86)	105	0.02
Thai (202)	314	0.06
Vietnamese (5,658)	6,045	1.24
Hawaii Native/Pacific Islander (235)	658	0.13
Not Hispanic (193)	520	0.11
Hispanic (42)	138	0.03
Fijian (1)	5	<0.01
Guamanian/Chamorro (67)	121	0.02
Marshallese (8)	9	<0.01
Native Hawaiian (67)	197	0.04
Samoan (24)	66	0.01
Tongan (0)	2	<0.01
White (278,525)	287,040	58.77
Not Hispanic (265,228)	272,050	55.70
Hispanic (13,297)	14,990	3.07

Notes: † The Census 2010 population figure is used to calculate the percentages in the Hispanic Origin and Race categories. Ancestry percentages are based on the 2006-2010 American Community Survey population (not shown); ‡ Numbers in parentheses indicate the number of people reporting a single ancestry; * Numbers in parentheses indicate the number of persons reporting this race alone, not in combination with any other race; Please refer to the Explanation of Data for more information.

Halifax County

Population: 54,691

Ancestry	Population	%
Afghan (0)	0	<0.01
African, Sub-Saharan (556)	642	1.16
African (537)	623	1.13
Cape Verdean (0)	0	<0.01
Ethiopian (19)	19	0.03
Ghanaian (0)	0	<0.01
Kenyan (0)	0	<0.01
Liberian (0)	0	<0.01
Nigerian (0)	0	<0.01
Senegalese (0)	0	<0.01
Sierra Leonean (0)	0	<0.01
Somalian (0)	0	<0.01
South African (0)	0	<0.01
Sudanese (0)	0	<0.01
Ugandan (0)	0	<0.01
Zimbabwean (0)	0	<0.01
Other Sub-Saharan African (0)	0	<0.01
Albanian (0)	0	<0.01
Alsatian (0)	0	<0.01
American (4,740)	4,740	8.57
Arab (175)	193	0.35
Arab (117)	117	0.21
Egyptian (0)	0	<0.01
Iraqi (0)	0	<0.01
Jordanian (0)	0	<0.01
Lebanese (11)	11	0.02
Moroccan (0)	18	0.03
Palestinian (0)	0	<0.01
Syrian (0)	0	<0.01
Other Arab (47)	47	0.09
Armenian (0)	0	<0.01
Assyrian/Chaldean/Syriac (0)	0	<0.01
Australian (0)	0	<0.01
Austrian (0)	0	<0.01
Basque (0)	0	<0.01
Belgian (17)	30	0.05
Brazilian (0)	0	<0.01
British (67)	80	0.14
Bulgarian (0)	0	<0.01
Cajun (0)	0	<0.01
Canadian (52)	56	0.10
Carpatho Rusyn (0)	0	<0.01
Celtic (0)	0	<0.01
Croatian (0)	0	<0.01
Cypriot (0)	0	<0.01
Czech (0)	19	0.03
Czechoslovakian (13)	39	0.07
Danish (35)	42	0.08
Dutch (96)	158	0.29
Eastern European (0)	0	<0.01
English (2,949)	4,728	8.55
Estonian (0)	0	<0.01
European (170)	230	0.42
Finnish (0)	19	0.03
French, ex. Basque (42)	380	0.69
French Canadian (23)	412	0.75
German (509)	2,115	3.83
German Russian (0)	0	<0.01
Greek (19)	44	0.08
Guyanese (8)	8	0.01
Hungarian (28)	93	0.17
Icelander (0)	0	<0.01
Iranian (14)	14	0.03
Irish (1,627)	3,323	6.01
Israeli (0)	0	<0.01
Italian (527)	949	1.72
Latvian (0)	0	<0.01
Lithuanian (0)	0	<0.01
Luxemburger (0)	0	<0.01
Macedonian (0)	0	<0.01
Maltese (0)	0	<0.01
New Zealander (0)	0	<0.01
Northern European (0)	0	<0.01
Norwegian (5)	39	0.07
Pennsylvania German (0)	0	<0.01

Ancestry	Population	%
Polish (47)	149	0.27
Portuguese (0)	7	0.01
Romanian (16)	16	0.03
Russian (16)	38	0.07
Scandinavian (0)	0	<0.01
Scotch-Irish (502)	991	1.79
Scottish (498)	1,025	1.85
Serbian (0)	0	<0.01
Slavic (0)	13	0.02
Slovak (0)	31	0.06
Slovene (0)	0	<0.01
Soviet Union (0)	0	<0.01
Swedish (40)	105	0.19
Swiss (18)	60	0.11
Turkish (0)	0	<0.01
Ukrainian (0)	0	<0.01
Welsh (12)	37	0.07
West Indian, ex. Hispanic (123)	549	0.99
Bahamian (0)	141	0.26
Barbadian (0)	0	<0.01
Belizean (0)	0	<0.01
Bermudan (0)	0	<0.01
British West Indian (60)	168	0.30
Dutch West Indian (0)	0	<0.01
Haitian (0)	0	<0.01
Jamaican (61)	238	0.43
Trinidadian/Tobagonian (2)	2	<0.01
U.S. Virgin Islander (0)	0	<0.01
West Indian (0)	0	<0.01
Other West Indian (0)	0	<0.01
Yugoslavian (11)	11	0.02

Hispanic Origin	Population	%
Hispanic or Latino (of any race)	1,152	2.11
Central American, ex. Mexican	122	0.22
Costa Rican	3	0.01
Guatemalan	25	0.05
Honduran	12	0.02
Nicaraguan	11	0.02
Panamanian	7	0.01
Salvadoran	64	0.12
Other Central American	0	<0.01
Cuban	12	0.02
Dominican Republic	8	0.01
Mexican	712	1.30
Puerto Rican	133	0.24
South American	35	0.06
Argentinean	0	<0.01
Bolivian	0	<0.01
Chilean	1	<0.01
Colombian	15	0.03
Ecuadorian	2	<0.01
Paraguayan	1	<0.01
Peruvian	15	0.03
Uruguayan	0	<0.01
Venezuelan	1	<0.01
Other South American	0	<0.01
Other Hispanic or Latino	130	0.24

Race*	Population	%
African-American/Black (29,109)	29,531	54.00
Not Hispanic (28,986)	29,380	53.72
Hispanic (123)	151	0.28
American Indian/Alaska Native (2,071)	2,337	4.27
Not Hispanic (2,008)	2,259	4.13
Hispanic (63)	78	0.14
Alaska Athabascan (Ala. Nat.) (0)	0	<0.01
Aleut (Alaska Native) (0)	0	<0.01
Apache (2)	2	<0.01
Arapaho (0)	0	<0.01
Blackfeet (8)	14	0.03
Canadian/French Am. Ind. (1)	1	<0.01
Central American Ind. (0)	0	<0.01
Cherokee (30)	90	0.16
Cheyenne (1)	1	<0.01
Chickasaw (0)	0	<0.01
Chippewa (2)	2	<0.01
Choctaw (1)	3	0.01
Colville (0)	0	<0.01

Race*	Population	%
Comanche (0)	0	<0.01
Cree (0)	0	<0.01
Creek (1)	1	<0.01
Crow (0)	0	<0.01
Delaware (0)	3	0.01
Hopi (0)	0	<0.01
Houma (0)	0	<0.01
Inupiat (Alaska Native) (0)	0	<0.01
Iroquois (4)	8	0.01
Kiowa (0)	0	<0.01
Lumbee (26)	30	0.05
Menominee (0)	0	<0.01
Mexican American Ind. (2)	4	0.01
Navajo (1)	1	<0.01
Osage (0)	0	<0.01
Ottawa (0)	0	<0.01
Paiute (0)	0	<0.01
Pima (0)	0	<0.01
Potawatomi (0)	0	<0.01
Pueblo (0)	0	<0.01
Puget Sound Salish (0)	0	<0.01
Seminole (0)	0	<0.01
Shoshone (0)	0	<0.01
Sioux (3)	3	0.01
South American Ind. (0)	0	<0.01
Spanish American Ind. (8)	8	0.01
Tlingit-Haida (Alaska Native) (0)	0	<0.01
Tohono O'Odham (0)	0	<0.01
Tsimshian (Alaska Native) (0)	0	<0.01
Ute (0)	0	<0.01
Yakama (0)	0	<0.01
Yaqui (0)	0	<0.01
Yuman (0)	1	<0.01
Yup'ik (Alaska Native) (0)	0	<0.01
Asian (362)	448	0.82
Not Hispanic (357)	431	0.79
Hispanic (5)	17	0.03
Bangladeshi (0)	0	<0.01
Bhutanese (0)	0	<0.01
Burmese (0)	0	<0.01
Cambodian (1)	1	<0.01
Chinese, ex. Taiwanese (71)	74	0.14
Filipino (99)	118	0.22
Hmong (0)	0	<0.01
Indian (102)	123	0.22
Indonesian (0)	0	<0.01
Japanese (5)	13	0.02
Korean (8)	15	0.03
Laotian (0)	0	<0.01
Malaysian (0)	0	<0.01
Nepalese (0)	0	<0.01
Pakistani (6)	6	0.01
Sri Lankan (0)	0	<0.01
Taiwanese (0)	0	<0.01
Thai (5)	7	0.01
Vietnamese (60)	64	0.12
Hawaii Native/Pacific Islander (19)	48	0.09
Not Hispanic (8)	32	0.06
Hispanic (11)	16	0.03
Fijian (0)	0	<0.01
Guamanian/Chamorro (11)	15	0.03
Marshallese (0)	0	<0.01
Native Hawaiian (2)	13	0.02
Samoan (1)	6	0.01
Tongan (0)	0	<0.01
White (21,890)	22,348	40.86
Not Hispanic (21,569)	21,961	40.15
Hispanic (321)	387	0.71

*Notes: † The Census 2010 population figure is used to calculate the percentages in the Hispanic Origin and Race categories. Ancestry percentages are based on the 2006-2010 American Community Survey population (not shown); ‡ Numbers in parentheses indicate the number of people reporting a single ancestry; * Numbers in parentheses indicate the number of persons reporting this race alone, not in combination with any other race; Please refer to the Explanation of Data for more information.*

Harnett County

Population: 114,678

Ancestry	Population	%
Afghan (0)	0	<0.01
African, Sub-Saharan (972)	1,093	1.00
African (957)	1,052	0.96
Cape Verdean (0)	0	<0.01
Ethiopian (0)	0	<0.01
Ghanaian (0)	0	<0.01
Kenyan (0)	0	<0.01
Liberian (0)	0	<0.01
Nigerian (0)	0	<0.01
Senegalese (15)	15	0.01
Sierra Leonean (0)	0	<0.01
Somalian (0)	0	<0.01
South African (0)	26	0.02
Sudanese (0)	0	<0.01
Ugandan (0)	0	<0.01
Zimbabwean (0)	0	<0.01
Other Sub-Saharan African (0)	0	<0.01
Albanian (0)	0	<0.01
Alsatian (0)	0	<0.01
American (12,790)	12,790	11.73
Arab (46)	89	0.08
Arab (21)	21	0.02
Egyptian (0)	0	<0.01
Iraqi (0)	0	<0.01
Jordanian (0)	0	<0.01
Lebanese (4)	47	0.04
Moroccan (21)	21	0.02
Palestinian (0)	0	<0.01
Syrian (0)	0	<0.01
Other Arab (0)	0	<0.01
Armenian (0)	0	<0.01
Assyrian/Chaldean/Syriac (0)	0	<0.01
Australian (0)	0	<0.01
Austrian (0)	75	0.07
Basque (8)	41	0.04
Belgian (0)	0	<0.01
Brazilian (40)	46	0.04
British (341)	581	0.53
Bulgarian (0)	0	<0.01
Cajun (25)	187	0.17
Canadian (51)	90	0.08
Carpatho Rusyn (0)	0	<0.01
Celtic (0)	23	0.02
Croatian (0)	8	0.01
Cypriot (0)	0	<0.01
Czech (67)	158	0.14
Czechoslovakian (20)	27	0.02
Danish (33)	148	0.14
Dutch (86)	813	0.75
Eastern European (0)	0	<0.01
English (4,476)	9,420	8.64
Estonian (0)	0	<0.01
European (1,106)	1,138	1.04
Finnish (20)	84	0.08
French, ex. Basque (429)	2,008	1.84
French Canadian (234)	481	0.44
German (3,582)	11,490	10.54
German Russian (0)	0	<0.01
Greek (181)	252	0.23
Guyanese (0)	0	<0.01
Hungarian (260)	323	0.30
Icelander (28)	28	0.03
Iranian (0)	0	<0.01
Irish (4,156)	10,799	9.90
Israeli (0)	0	<0.01
Italian (858)	2,621	2.40
Latvian (11)	11	0.01
Lithuanian (42)	73	0.07
Luxemburger (0)	0	<0.01
Macedonian (0)	0	<0.01
Maltese (0)	0	<0.01
New Zealander (0)	0	<0.01
Northern European (0)	8	0.01
Norwegian (128)	324	0.30
Pennsylvania German (37)	46	0.04

Ancestry	Population	%
Polish (313)	1,019	0.93
Portuguese (105)	133	0.12
Romanian (11)	12	0.01
Russian (28)	186	0.17
Scandinavian (22)	45	0.04
Scotch-Irish (2,805)	4,876	4.47
Scottish (1,544)	3,022	2.77
Serbian (0)	20	0.02
Slavic (0)	0	<0.01
Slovak (0)	18	0.02
Slovene (0)	26	0.02
Soviet Union (0)	0	<0.01
Swedish (283)	620	0.57
Swiss (11)	75	0.07
Turkish (3)	12	0.01
Ukrainian (12)	37	0.03
Welsh (151)	502	0.46
West Indian, ex. Hispanic (278)	547	0.50
Bahamian (0)	0	<0.01
Barbadian (0)	0	<0.01
Belizean (0)	0	<0.01
Bermudan (0)	0	<0.01
British West Indian (9)	34	0.03
Dutch West Indian (0)	0	<0.01
Haitian (180)	337	0.31
Jamaican (89)	169	0.16
Trinidadian/Tobagonian (0)	0	<0.01
U.S. Virgin Islander (0)	0	<0.01
West Indian (0)	7	0.01
Other West Indian (0)	0	<0.01
Yugoslavian (0)	11	0.01

Hispanic Origin	Population	%
Hispanic or Latino (of any race)	12,359	10.78
Central American, ex. Mexican	1,017	0.89
Costa Rican	50	0.04
Guatemalan	247	0.22
Honduran	260	0.23
Nicaraguan	55	0.05
Panamanian	164	0.14
Salvadoran	234	0.20
Other Central American	7	0.01
Cuban	149	0.13
Dominican Republic	102	0.09
Mexican	8,408	7.33
Puerto Rican	1,667	1.45
South American	277	0.24
Argentinean	26	0.02
Bolivian	2	<0.01
Chilean	20	0.02
Colombian	106	0.09
Ecuadorian	35	0.03
Paraguayan	1	<0.01
Peruvian	58	0.05
Uruguayan	3	<0.01
Venezuelan	21	0.02
Other South American	5	<0.01
Other Hispanic or Latino	739	0.64

Race*	Population	%
African-American/Black (23,973)	25,837	22.53
Not Hispanic (23,591)	25,187	21.96
Hispanic (382)	650	0.57
American Indian/Alaska Native (1,392)	2,520	2.20
Not Hispanic (991)	1,940	1.69
Hispanic (401)	580	0.51
Alaska Athabascan (Ala. Nat.) (2)	2	<0.01
Aleut (Alaska Native) (0)	0	<0.01
Apache (8)	17	0.01
Arapaho (0)	0	<0.01
Blackfeet (4)	36	0.03
Canadian/French Am. Ind. (4)	4	<0.01
Central American Ind. (0)	2	<0.01
Cherokee (131)	453	0.40
Cheyenne (0)	1	<0.01
Chickasaw (0)	0	<0.01
Chippewa (15)	17	0.01
Choctaw (23)	36	0.03
Colville (0)	0	<0.01

Race*	Population	%
Comanche (3)	3	<0.01
Cree (0)	2	<0.01
Creek (0)	5	<0.01
Crow (0)	2	<0.01
Delaware (0)	1	<0.01
Hopi (0)	0	<0.01
Houma (0)	0	<0.01
Inupiat (Alaska Native) (3)	3	<0.01
Iroquois (19)	36	0.03
Kiowa (4)	8	0.01
Lumbee (207)	286	0.25
Menominee (0)	0	<0.01
Mexican American Ind. (56)	71	0.06
Navajo (11)	18	0.02
Osage (1)	2	<0.01
Ottawa (0)	0	<0.01
Paiute (0)	0	<0.01
Pima (0)	0	<0.01
Potawatomi (2)	2	<0.01
Pueblo (0)	4	<0.01
Puget Sound Salish (1)	2	<0.01
Seminole (4)	17	0.01
Shoshone (0)	1	<0.01
Sioux (9)	35	0.03
South American Ind. (11)	12	0.01
Spanish American Ind. (0)	0	<0.01
Tlingit-Haida (Alaska Native) (2)	2	<0.01
Tohono O'Odham (0)	0	<0.01
Tsimshian (Alaska Native) (0)	0	<0.01
Ute (1)	1	<0.01
Yakama (3)	3	<0.01
Yaqui (1)	3	<0.01
Yuman (0)	0	<0.01
Yup'ik (Alaska Native) (1)	3	<0.01
Asian (1,029)	1,757	1.53
Not Hispanic (983)	1,636	1.43
Hispanic (46)	121	0.11
Bangladeshi (0)	0	<0.01
Bhutanese (0)	0	<0.01
Burmese (0)	5	<0.01
Cambodian (7)	15	0.01
Chinese, ex. Taiwanese (123)	184	0.16
Filipino (292)	522	0.46
Hmong (17)	21	0.02
Indian (121)	193	0.17
Indonesian (2)	5	<0.01
Japanese (59)	172	0.15
Korean (197)	359	0.31
Laotian (3)	16	0.01
Malaysian (0)	0	<0.01
Nepalese (0)	0	<0.01
Pakistani (5)	6	0.01
Sri Lankan (1)	1	<0.01
Taiwanese (2)	10	0.01
Thai (54)	94	0.08
Vietnamese (74)	113	0.10
Hawaii Native/Pacific Islander (139)	338	0.29
Not Hispanic (126)	286	0.25
Hispanic (13)	52	0.05
Fijian (0)	0	<0.01
Guamanian/Chamorro (55)	96	0.08
Marshallese (0)	0	<0.01
Native Hawaiian (26)	100	0.09
Samoan (31)	80	0.07
Tongan (0)	0	<0.01
White (78,300)	81,202	70.81
Not Hispanic (73,707)	75,953	66.23
Hispanic (4,593)	5,249	4.58

Notes: † The Census 2010 population figure is used to calculate the percentages in the Hispanic Origin and Race categories. Ancestry percentages are based on the 2006-2010 American Community Survey population (not shown); ‡ Numbers in parentheses indicate the number of people reporting a single ancestry; * Numbers in parentheses indicate the number of persons reporting this race alone, not in combination with any other race; Please refer to the Explanation of Data for more information.

Haywood County

Population: 59,036

Ancestry	Population	%
Afghan (0)	0	<0.01
African, Sub-Saharan (24)	40	0.07
African (0)	16	0.03
Cape Verdean (0)	0	<0.01
Ethiopian (0)	0	<0.01
Ghanaian (0)	0	<0.01
Kenyan (0)	0	<0.01
Liberian (0)	0	<0.01
Nigerian (0)	0	<0.01
Senegalese (0)	0	<0.01
Sierra Leonean (0)	0	<0.01
Somalian (0)	0	<0.01
South African (24)	24	0.04
Sudanese (0)	0	<0.01
Ugandan (0)	0	<0.01
Zimbabwean (0)	0	<0.01
Other Sub-Saharan African (0)	0	<0.01
Albanian (0)	0	<0.01
Alsatian (0)	0	<0.01
American (13,920)	13,920	23.76
Arab (0)	0	<0.01
Arab (0)	0	<0.01
Egyptian (0)	0	<0.01
Iraqi (0)	0	<0.01
Jordanian (0)	0	<0.01
Lebanese (0)	0	<0.01
Moroccan (0)	0	<0.01
Palestinian (0)	0	<0.01
Syrian (0)	0	<0.01
Other Arab (0)	0	<0.01
Armenian (15)	15	0.03
Assyrian/Chaldean/Syriac (0)	0	<0.01
Australian (32)	32	0.05
Austrian (8)	8	0.01
Basque (0)	0	<0.01
Belgian (0)	19	0.03
Brazilian (0)	0	<0.01
British (208)	324	0.55
Bulgarian (0)	0	<0.01
Cajun (0)	18	0.03
Canadian (81)	167	0.28
Carpatho Rusyn (0)	0	<0.01
Celtic (0)	0	<0.01
Croatian (0)	0	<0.01
Cypriot (0)	0	<0.01
Czech (86)	176	0.30
Czechoslovakian (0)	0	<0.01
Danish (11)	59	0.10
Dutch (287)	1,295	2.21
Eastern European (17)	17	0.03
English (4,344)	8,058	13.75
Estonian (0)	0	<0.01
European (533)	543	0.93
Finnish (44)	61	0.10
French, ex. Basque (268)	1,369	2.34
French Canadian (73)	468	0.80
German (2,542)	7,415	12.65
German Russian (0)	0	<0.01
Greek (35)	65	0.11
Guyanese (0)	0	<0.01
Hungarian (40)	85	0.15
Icelander (3)	39	0.07
Iranian (0)	0	<0.01
Irish (3,189)	7,732	13.20
Israeli (0)	0	<0.01
Italian (723)	1,662	2.84
Latvian (0)	0	<0.01
Lithuanian (5)	8	0.01
Luxemburger (0)	0	<0.01
Macedonian (0)	0	<0.01
Maltese (0)	0	<0.01
New Zealander (27)	27	0.05
Northern European (36)	36	0.06
Norwegian (121)	321	0.55
Pennsylvania German (17)	62	0.11
Polish (123)	556	0.95
Portuguese (3)	33	0.06
Romanian (9)	17	0.03
Russian (118)	232	0.40
Scandinavian (12)	19	0.03
Scotch-Irish (3,346)	5,092	8.69
Scottish (851)	2,055	3.51
Serbian (0)	4	0.01
Slavic (0)	0	<0.01
Slovak (10)	34	0.06
Slovene (12)	12	0.02
Soviet Union (0)	0	<0.01
Swedish (203)	564	0.96
Swiss (44)	64	0.11
Turkish (0)	20	0.03
Ukrainian (3)	3	0.01
Welsh (119)	625	1.07
West Indian, ex. Hispanic (0)	30	0.05
Bahamian (0)	0	<0.01
Barbadian (0)	0	<0.01
Belizean (0)	0	<0.01
Bermudan (0)	0	<0.01
British West Indian (0)	0	<0.01
Dutch West Indian (0)	0	<0.01
Haitian (0)	0	<0.01
Jamaican (0)	0	<0.01
Trinidadian/Tobagonian (0)	0	<0.01
U.S. Virgin Islander (0)	0	<0.01
West Indian (0)	30	0.05
Other West Indian (0)	0	<0.01
Yugoslavian (11)	11	0.02

Hispanic Origin	Population	%
Hispanic or Latino (of any race)	1,999	3.39
Central American, ex. Mexican	69	0.12
Costa Rican	3	0.01
Guatemalan	22	0.04
Honduran	24	0.04
Nicaraguan	7	0.01
Panamanian	6	0.01
Salvadoran	7	0.01
Other Central American	0	<0.01
Cuban	104	0.18
Dominican Republic	7	0.01
Mexican	1,486	2.52
Puerto Rican	137	0.23
South American	65	0.11
Argentinean	10	0.02
Bolivian	0	<0.01
Chilean	5	0.01
Colombian	9	0.02
Ecuadorian	18	0.03
Paraguayan	0	<0.01
Peruvian	15	0.03
Uruguayan	0	<0.01
Venezuelan	8	0.01
Other South American	0	<0.01
Other Hispanic or Latino	131	0.22

Race*	Population	%
African-American/Black (624)	779	1.32
Not Hispanic (615)	759	1.29
Hispanic (9)	20	0.03
American Indian/Alaska Native (303)	637	1.08
Not Hispanic (270)	578	0.98
Hispanic (33)	59	0.10
Alaska Athabascan (Ala. Nat.) (0)	0	<0.01
Aleut (Alaska Native) (0)	0	<0.01
Apache (1)	8	0.01
Arapaho (0)	0	<0.01
Blackfeet (1)	9	0.02
Canadian/French Am. Ind. (0)	1	<0.01
Central American Ind. (0)	3	0.01
Cherokee (152)	327	0.55
Cheyenne (0)	1	<0.01
Chickasaw (2)	2	<0.01
Chippewa (2)	3	0.01
Choctaw (1)	9	0.02
Colville (0)	0	<0.01
Comanche (0)	4	0.01
Cree (0)	1	<0.01
Creek (0)	2	<0.01
Crow (0)	4	0.01
Delaware (1)	2	<0.01
Hopi (0)	0	<0.01
Houma (0)	0	<0.01
Inupiat (Alaska Native) (0)	0	<0.01
Iroquois (4)	7	0.01
Kiowa (0)	0	<0.01
Lumbee (23)	27	0.05
Menominee (0)	0	<0.01
Mexican American Ind. (16)	19	0.03
Navajo (0)	2	<0.01
Osage (0)	0	<0.01
Ottawa (0)	0	<0.01
Paiute (0)	0	<0.01
Pima (0)	0	<0.01
Potawatomi (0)	0	<0.01
Pueblo (0)	2	<0.01
Puget Sound Salish (0)	0	<0.01
Seminole (0)	3	0.01
Shoshone (0)	1	<0.01
Sioux (1)	4	0.01
South American Ind. (1)	1	<0.01
Spanish American Ind. (0)	0	<0.01
Tlingit-Haida (Alaska Native) (0)	0	<0.01
Tohono O'Odham (0)	0	<0.01
Tsimshian (Alaska Native) (0)	0	<0.01
Ute (0)	0	<0.01
Yakama (0)	0	<0.01
Yaqui (0)	0	<0.01
Yuman (0)	0	<0.01
Yup'ik (Alaska Native) (0)	0	<0.01
Asian (215)	313	0.53
Not Hispanic (212)	309	0.52
Hispanic (3)	4	0.01
Bangladeshi (0)	0	<0.01
Bhutanese (0)	0	<0.01
Burmese (0)	0	<0.01
Cambodian (1)	1	<0.01
Chinese, ex. Taiwanese (37)	67	0.11
Filipino (52)	85	0.14
Hmong (0)	0	<0.01
Indian (35)	43	0.07
Indonesian (0)	1	<0.01
Japanese (13)	26	0.04
Korean (19)	28	0.05
Laotian (1)	2	<0.01
Malaysian (0)	0	<0.01
Nepalese (0)	0	<0.01
Pakistani (0)	0	<0.01
Sri Lankan (2)	2	<0.01
Taiwanese (0)	0	<0.01
Thai (4)	17	0.03
Vietnamese (21)	32	0.05
Hawaii Native/Pacific Islander (15)	40	0.07
Not Hispanic (8)	25	0.04
Hispanic (7)	15	0.03
Fijian (0)	0	<0.01
Guamanian/Chamorro (6)	13	0.02
Marshallese (0)	0	<0.01
Native Hawaiian (2)	7	0.01
Samoan (0)	5	0.01
Tongan (0)	0	<0.01
White (56,405)	57,015	96.58
Not Hispanic (55,368)	55,891	94.67
Hispanic (1,037)	1,124	1.90

*Notes: † The Census 2010 population figure is used to calculate the percentages in the Hispanic Origin and Race categories. Ancestry percentages are based on the 2006-2010 American Community Survey population (not shown); ‡ Numbers in parentheses indicate the number of people reporting a single ancestry; * Numbers in parentheses indicate the number of persons reporting this race alone, not in combination with any other race; Please refer to the Explanation of Data for more information.*

Henderson County

Population: 106,740

Ancestry	Population	%
Afghan (0)	0	<0.01
African, Sub-Saharan (46)	74	0.07
African (31)	50	0.05
Cape Verdean (0)	0	<0.01
Ethiopian (0)	0	<0.01
Ghanaian (0)	0	<0.01
Kenyan (0)	0	<0.01
Liberian (0)	0	<0.01
Nigerian (0)	9	0.01
Senegalese (0)	0	<0.01
Sierra Leonean (0)	0	<0.01
Somalian (0)	0	<0.01
South African (15)	15	0.01
Sudanese (0)	0	<0.01
Ugandan (0)	0	<0.01
Zimbabwean (0)	0	<0.01
Other Sub-Saharan African (0)	0	<0.01
Albanian (0)	14	0.01
Alsatian (0)	0	<0.01
American (11,596)	11,596	11.16
Arab (31)	36	0.03
Arab (0)	0	<0.01
Egyptian (12)	12	0.01
Iraqi (0)	0	<0.01
Jordanian (0)	0	<0.01
Lebanese (19)	24	0.02
Moroccan (0)	0	<0.01
Palestinian (0)	0	<0.01
Syrian (0)	0	<0.01
Other Arab (0)	0	<0.01
Armenian (0)	0	<0.01
Assyrian/Chaldean/Syriac (20)	20	0.02
Australian (0)	0	<0.01
Austrian (62)	307	0.30
Basque (0)	0	<0.01
Belgian (46)	56	0.05
Brazilian (36)	53	0.05
British (377)	624	0.60
Bulgarian (0)	0	<0.01
Cajun (18)	31	0.03
Canadian (57)	274	0.26
Carpatho Rusyn (0)	0	<0.01
Celtic (0)	22	0.02
Croatian (14)	40	0.04
Cypriot (0)	0	<0.01
Czech (97)	221	0.21
Czechoslovakian (115)	142	0.14
Danish (101)	273	0.26
Dutch (490)	2,415	2.32
Eastern European (53)	84	0.08
English (6,958)	16,636	16.01
Estonian (9)	9	0.01
European (1,156)	1,321	1.27
Finnish (38)	107	0.10
French, ex. Basque (687)	2,905	2.80
French Canadian (323)	593	0.57
German (5,836)	17,073	16.44
German Russian (20)	20	0.02
Greek (43)	218	0.21
Guyanese (20)	28	0.03
Hungarian (128)	317	0.31
Icelander (0)	0	<0.01
Iranian (0)	0	<0.01
Irish (4,846)	13,716	13.20
Israeli (0)	0	<0.01
Italian (823)	2,641	2.54
Latvian (0)	11	0.01
Lithuanian (96)	301	0.29
Luxemburger (0)	0	<0.01
Macedonian (54)	54	0.05
Maltese (0)	0	<0.01
New Zealander (0)	0	<0.01
Northern European (54)	54	0.05
Norwegian (353)	1,197	1.15
Pennsylvania German (0)	15	0.01
Polish (905)	2,092	2.01
Portuguese (49)	179	0.17
Romanian (83)	196	0.19
Russian (466)	839	0.81
Scandinavian (87)	177	0.17
Scotch-Irish (3,154)	6,347	6.11
Scottish (2,052)	4,967	4.78
Serbian (0)	0	<0.01
Slavic (16)	34	0.03
Slovak (78)	135	0.13
Slovene (0)	22	0.02
Soviet Union (0)	0	<0.01
Swedish (570)	1,381	1.33
Swiss (76)	184	0.18
Turkish (0)	12	0.01
Ukrainian (267)	395	0.38
Welsh (193)	1,065	1.03
West Indian, ex. Hispanic (74)	111	0.11
Bahamian (0)	0	<0.01
Barbadian (0)	0	<0.01
Belizean (0)	0	<0.01
Bermudan (0)	0	<0.01
British West Indian (0)	0	<0.01
Dutch West Indian (0)	0	<0.01
Haitian (29)	29	0.03
Jamaican (45)	82	0.08
Trinidadian/Tobagonian (0)	0	<0.01
U.S. Virgin Islander (0)	0	<0.01
West Indian (0)	0	<0.01
Other West Indian (0)	0	<0.01
Yugoslavian (19)	19	0.02

Hispanic Origin	Population	%
Hispanic or Latino (of any race)	10,424	9.77
Central American, ex. Mexican	500	0.47
Costa Rican	88	0.08
Guatemalan	107	0.10
Honduran	74	0.07
Nicaraguan	28	0.03
Panamanian	19	0.02
Salvadoran	178	0.17
Other Central American	6	0.01
Cuban	178	0.17
Dominican Republic	28	0.03
Mexican	8,488	7.95
Puerto Rican	347	0.33
South American	337	0.32
Argentinean	33	0.03
Bolivian	5	<0.01
Chilean	57	0.05
Colombian	143	0.13
Ecuadorian	22	0.02
Paraguayan	8	0.01
Peruvian	33	0.03
Uruguayan	9	0.01
Venezuelan	27	0.03
Other South American	0	<0.01
Other Hispanic or Latino	546	0.51

Race*	Population	%
African-American/Black (3,224)	3,963	3.71
Not Hispanic (3,149)	3,826	3.58
Hispanic (75)	137	0.13
American Indian/Alaska Native (449)	1,122	1.05
Not Hispanic (318)	908	0.85
Hispanic (131)	214	0.20
Alaska Athabascan (Ala. Nat.) (0)	0	<0.01
Aleut (Alaska Native) (0)	0	<0.01
Apache (7)	17	0.02
Arapaho (0)	0	<0.01
Blackfeet (2)	22	0.02
Canadian/French Am. Ind. (0)	0	<0.01
Central American Ind. (0)	2	<0.01
Cherokee (122)	397	0.37
Cheyenne (0)	0	<0.01
Chickasaw (1)	3	<0.01
Chippewa (4)	9	0.01
Choctaw (2)	12	0.01
Colville (0)	0	<0.01
Comanche (0)	2	<0.01
Cree (0)	0	<0.01
Creek (2)	3	<0.01
Crow (0)	0	<0.01
Delaware (0)	0	<0.01
Hopi (4)	4	<0.01
Houma (0)	0	<0.01
Inupiat (Alaska Native) (11)	11	0.01
Iroquois (7)	40	0.04
Kiowa (0)	1	<0.01
Lumbee (35)	49	0.05
Menominee (0)	0	<0.01
Mexican American Ind. (64)	92	0.09
Navajo (1)	3	<0.01
Osage (0)	2	<0.01
Ottawa (0)	0	<0.01
Paiute (1)	2	<0.01
Pima (0)	0	<0.01
Potawatomi (2)	3	<0.01
Pueblo (1)	7	0.01
Puget Sound Salish (1)	1	<0.01
Seminole (2)	8	0.01
Shoshone (0)	1	<0.01
Sioux (4)	10	0.01
South American Ind. (3)	6	0.01
Spanish American Ind. (6)	6	0.01
Tlingit-Haida (Alaska Native) (1)	2	<0.01
Tohono O'Odham (0)	0	<0.01
Tsimshian (Alaska Native) (0)	0	<0.01
Ute (0)	1	<0.01
Yakama (0)	0	<0.01
Yaqui (0)	0	<0.01
Yuman (0)	0	<0.01
Yup'ik (Alaska Native) (0)	0	<0.01
Asian (1,022)	1,319	1.24
Not Hispanic (994)	1,277	1.20
Hispanic (28)	42	0.04
Bangladeshi (0)	2	<0.01
Bhutanese (0)	0	<0.01
Burmese (1)	3	<0.01
Cambodian (137)	164	0.15
Chinese, ex. Taiwanese (149)	188	0.18
Filipino (207)	261	0.24
Hmong (12)	12	0.01
Indian (116)	164	0.15
Indonesian (7)	9	0.01
Japanese (46)	108	0.10
Korean (128)	177	0.17
Laotian (1)	4	<0.01
Malaysian (1)	2	<0.01
Nepalese (0)	0	<0.01
Pakistani (28)	31	0.03
Sri Lankan (0)	1	<0.01
Taiwanese (5)	6	0.01
Thai (33)	49	0.05
Vietnamese (91)	104	0.10
Hawaii Native/Pacific Islander (178)	251	0.24
Not Hispanic (165)	224	0.21
Hispanic (13)	27	0.03
Fijian (1)	5	<0.01
Guamanian/Chamorro (15)	19	0.02
Marshallese (0)	0	<0.01
Native Hawaiian (32)	47	0.04
Samoan (0)	6	0.01
Tongan (1)	2	<0.01
White (94,914)	96,803	90.69
Not Hispanic (90,105)	91,504	85.73
Hispanic (4,809)	5,299	4.96

Notes: † The Census 2010 population figure is used to calculate the percentages in the Hispanic Origin and Race categories. Ancestry percentages are based on the 2006-2010 American Community Survey population (not shown); ‡ Numbers in parentheses indicate the number of people reporting a single ancestry; * Numbers in parentheses indicate the number of persons reporting this race alone, not in combination with any other race; Please refer to the Explanation of Data for more information.

Iredell County

Population: 159,437

Ancestry	Population	%
Afghan (0)	0	<0.01
African, Sub-Saharan (223)	278	0.18
African (124)	179	0.12
Cape Verdean (41)	41	0.03
Ethiopian (0)	0	<0.01
Ghanaian (58)	58	0.04
Kenyan (0)	0	<0.01
Liberian (0)	0	<0.01
Nigerian (0)	0	<0.01
Senegalese (0)	0	<0.01
Sierra Leonean (0)	0	<0.01
Somalian (0)	0	<0.01
South African (0)	0	<0.01
Sudanese (0)	0	<0.01
Ugandan (0)	0	<0.01
Zimbabwean (0)	0	<0.01
Other Sub-Saharan African (0)	0	<0.01
Albanian (0)	0	<0.01
Alsatian (0)	0	<0.01
American (18,052)	18,052	11.67
Arab (211)	347	0.22
Arab (137)	137	0.09
Egyptian (0)	0	<0.01
Iraqi (0)	0	<0.01
Jordanian (0)	0	<0.01
Lebanese (65)	153	0.10
Moroccan (0)	0	<0.01
Palestinian (0)	0	<0.01
Syrian (9)	57	0.04
Other Arab (0)	0	<0.01
Armenian (0)	15	0.01
Assyrian/Chaldean/Syriac (0)	0	<0.01
Australian (53)	62	0.04
Austrian (48)	170	0.11
Basque (0)	0	<0.01
Belgian (16)	16	0.01
Brazilian (13)	13	0.01
British (281)	694	0.45
Bulgarian (0)	0	<0.01
Cajun (0)	0	<0.01
Canadian (160)	201	0.13
Carpatho Rusyn (0)	0	<0.01
Celtic (0)	0	<0.01
Croatian (39)	77	0.05
Cypriot (0)	0	<0.01
Czech (76)	246	0.16
Czechoslovakian (51)	67	0.04
Danish (57)	243	0.16
Dutch (755)	2,711	1.75
Eastern European (51)	51	0.03
English (7,967)	15,595	10.09
Estonian (0)	0	<0.01
European (1,264)	1,454	0.94
Finnish (60)	231	0.15
French, ex. Basque (552)	2,933	1.90
French Canadian (191)	367	0.24
German (8,937)	22,644	14.64
German Russian (0)	0	<0.01
Greek (130)	392	0.25
Guyanese (0)	0	<0.01
Hungarian (234)	601	0.39
Icelander (0)	0	<0.01
Iranian (0)	0	<0.01
Irish (6,538)	16,978	10.98
Israeli (16)	16	0.01
Italian (2,530)	6,424	4.15
Latvian (0)	0	<0.01
Lithuanian (55)	135	0.09
Luxemburger (0)	0	<0.01
Macedonian (0)	0	<0.01
Maltese (0)	6	<0.01
New Zealander (44)	44	0.03
Northern European (14)	14	0.01
Norwegian (426)	914	0.59
Pennsylvania German (21)	63	0.04

Ancestry	Population	%
Polish (811)	2,752	1.78
Portuguese (45)	327	0.21
Romanian (80)	105	0.07
Russian (234)	650	0.42
Scandinavian (91)	289	0.19
Scotch-Irish (4,059)	7,509	4.86
Scottish (1,730)	3,773	2.44
Serbian (0)	0	<0.01
Slavic (0)	0	<0.01
Slovak (70)	217	0.14
Slovene (0)	10	0.01
Soviet Union (0)	0	<0.01
Swedish (216)	971	0.63
Swiss (127)	357	0.23
Turkish (0)	0	<0.01
Ukrainian (108)	175	0.11
Welsh (372)	977	0.63
West Indian, ex. Hispanic (364)	535	0.35
Bahamian (0)	14	0.01
Barbadian (0)	0	<0.01
Belizean (0)	0	<0.01
Bermudan (0)	0	<0.01
British West Indian (0)	0	<0.01
Dutch West Indian (0)	0	<0.01
Haitian (228)	228	0.15
Jamaican (0)	0	<0.01
Trinidadian/Tobagonian (32)	32	0.02
U.S. Virgin Islander (9)	9	0.01
West Indian (95)	252	0.16
Other West Indian (0)	0	<0.01
Yugoslavian (45)	45	0.03

Hispanic Origin	Population	%
Hispanic or Latino (of any race)	10,844	6.80
Central American, ex. Mexican	1,454	0.91
Costa Rican	72	0.05
Guatemalan	130	0.08
Honduran	273	0.17
Nicaraguan	111	0.07
Panamanian	32	0.02
Salvadoran	825	0.52
Other Central American	11	0.01
Cuban	280	0.18
Dominican Republic	170	0.11
Mexican	6,029	3.78
Puerto Rican	839	0.53
South American	1,333	0.84
Argentinean	40	0.03
Bolivian	6	<0.01
Chilean	66	0.04
Colombian	888	0.56
Ecuadorian	168	0.11
Paraguayan	0	<0.01
Peruvian	95	0.06
Uruguayan	10	0.01
Venezuelan	59	0.04
Other South American	1	<0.01
Other Hispanic or Latino	739	0.46

Race*	Population	%
African-American/Black (19,047)	20,440	12.82
Not Hispanic (18,748)	19,984	12.53
Hispanic (299)	456	0.29
American Indian/Alaska Native (547)	1,349	0.85
Not Hispanic (416)	1,108	0.69
Hispanic (131)	241	0.15
Alaska Athabascan (Ala. Nat.) (0)	0	<0.01
Aleut (Alaska Native) (0)	0	<0.01
Apache (6)	17	0.01
Arapaho (0)	0	<0.01
Blackfeet (5)	41	0.03
Canadian/French Am. Ind. (0)	0	<0.01
Central American Ind. (5)	5	<0.01
Cherokee (120)	385	0.24
Cheyenne (0)	0	<0.01
Chickasaw (0)	1	<0.01
Chippewa (5)	8	0.01
Choctaw (8)	17	0.01
Colville (0)	0	<0.01

Race*	Population	%
Comanche (2)	3	<0.01
Cree (0)	2	<0.01
Creek (1)	7	<0.01
Crow (4)	4	<0.01
Delaware (1)	2	<0.01
Hopi (0)	1	<0.01
Houma (0)	0	<0.01
Inupiat (Alaska Native) (1)	1	<0.01
Iroquois (17)	32	0.02
Kiowa (0)	0	<0.01
Lumbee (70)	112	0.07
Menominee (0)	0	<0.01
Mexican American Ind. (18)	37	0.02
Navajo (1)	5	<0.01
Osage (0)	1	<0.01
Ottawa (2)	2	<0.01
Paiute (1)	1	<0.01
Pima (0)	0	<0.01
Potawatomi (0)	0	<0.01
Pueblo (1)	1	<0.01
Puget Sound Salish (0)	0	<0.01
Seminole (1)	5	<0.01
Shoshone (0)	9	<0.01
Sioux (7)	21	0.01
South American Ind. (2)	5	<0.01
Spanish American Ind. (5)	6	<0.01
Tlingit-Haida (Alaska Native) (2)	2	<0.01
Tohono O'Odham (0)	0	<0.01
Tsimshian (Alaska Native) (0)	0	<0.01
Ute (1)	1	<0.01
Yakama (0)	0	<0.01
Yaqui (0)	1	<0.01
Yuman (0)	0	<0.01
Yup'ik (Alaska Native) (1)	1	<0.01
Asian (2,922)	3,471	2.18
Not Hispanic (2,899)	3,386	2.12
Hispanic (23)	85	0.05
Bangladeshi (0)	0	<0.01
Bhutanese (0)	0	<0.01
Burmese (0)	0	<0.01
Cambodian (16)	18	0.01
Chinese, ex. Taiwanese (325)	407	0.26
Filipino (229)	348	0.22
Hmong (616)	659	0.41
Indian (948)	1,042	0.65
Indonesian (7)	13	0.01
Japanese (118)	196	0.12
Korean (145)	193	0.12
Laotian (146)	172	0.11
Malaysian (1)	1	<0.01
Nepalese (2)	2	<0.01
Pakistani (38)	41	0.03
Sri Lankan (0)	0	<0.01
Taiwanese (6)	6	<0.01
Thai (23)	36	0.02
Vietnamese (176)	224	0.14
Hawaii Native/Pacific Islander (43)	130	0.08
Not Hispanic (36)	96	0.06
Hispanic (7)	34	0.02
Fijian (0)	0	<0.01
Guamanian/Chamorro (20)	28	0.02
Marshallese (0)	0	<0.01
Native Hawaiian (15)	53	0.03
Samoan (0)	1	<0.01
Tongan (0)	0	<0.01
White (128,646)	131,180	82.28
Not Hispanic (124,107)	126,088	79.08
Hispanic (4,539)	5,092	3.19

Notes: † The Census 2010 population figure is used to calculate the percentages in the Hispanic Origin and Race categories. Ancestry percentages are based on the 2006-2010 American Community Survey population (not shown); ‡ Numbers in parentheses indicate the number of people reporting a single ancestry; * Numbers in parentheses indicate the number of persons reporting this race alone, not in combination with any other race; Please refer to the Explanation of Data for more information.

Johnston County

Population: 168,878

Ancestry	Population	%
Afghan (0)	0	<0.01
African, Sub-Saharan (1,469)	1,597	0.99
African (1,275)	1,403	0.87
Cape Verdean (0)	0	<0.01
Ethiopian (0)	0	<0.01
Ghanaian (0)	0	<0.01
Kenyan (0)	0	<0.01
Liberian (109)	109	0.07
Nigerian (7)	7	<0.01
Senegalese (0)	0	<0.01
Sierra Leonean (0)	0	<0.01
Somalian (0)	0	<0.01
South African (0)	0	<0.01
Sudanese (0)	0	<0.01
Ugandan (0)	0	<0.01
Zimbabwean (0)	0	<0.01
Other Sub-Saharan African (78)	78	0.05
Albanian (0)	87	0.05
Alsatian (0)	35	0.02
American (24,682)	24,682	15.36
Arab (387)	585	0.36
Arab (127)	168	0.10
Egyptian (33)	33	0.02
Iraqi (0)	0	<0.01
Jordanian (0)	0	<0.01
Lebanese (85)	132	0.08
Moroccan (39)	72	0.04
Palestinian (35)	76	0.05
Syrian (0)	0	<0.01
Other Arab (68)	104	0.06
Armenian (22)	83	0.05
Assyrian/Chaldean/Syriac (0)	0	<0.01
Australian (0)	15	0.01
Austrian (13)	181	0.11
Basque (0)	0	<0.01
Belgian (20)	109	0.07
Brazilian (17)	17	0.01
British (287)	617	0.38
Bulgarian (0)	0	<0.01
Cajun (0)	0	<0.01
Canadian (303)	441	0.27
Carpatho Rusyn (0)	0	<0.01
Celtic (3)	27	0.02
Croatian (0)	12	0.01
Cypriot (0)	0	<0.01
Czech (14)	188	0.12
Czechoslovakian (42)	157	0.10
Danish (21)	127	0.08
Dutch (427)	1,660	1.03
Eastern European (34)	65	0.04
English (10,513)	17,903	11.14
Estonian (0)	0	<0.01
European (1,234)	1,406	0.88
Finnish (55)	73	0.05
French, ex. Basque (537)	2,817	1.75
French Canadian (283)	727	0.45
German (4,317)	13,712	8.53
German Russian (0)	0	<0.01
Greek (177)	323	0.20
Guyanese (0)	0	<0.01
Hungarian (166)	500	0.31
Icelander (0)	0	<0.01
Iranian (21)	23	0.01
Irish (5,276)	15,434	9.61
Israeli (0)	0	<0.01
Italian (1,940)	5,774	3.59
Latvian (0)	32	0.02
Lithuanian (57)	247	0.15
Luxemburger (0)	0	<0.01
Macedonian (0)	0	<0.01
Maltese (0)	0	<0.01
New Zealander (0)	0	<0.01
Northern European (51)	60	0.04
Norwegian (109)	461	0.29
Pennsylvania German (26)	67	0.04

Ancestry	Population	%
Polish (792)	2,692	1.68
Portuguese (110)	293	0.18
Romanian (58)	83	0.05
Russian (57)	520	0.32
Scandinavian (16)	135	0.08
Scotch-Irish (2,375)	4,155	2.59
Scottish (1,522)	3,491	2.17
Serbian (36)	50	0.03
Slavic (20)	20	0.01
Slovak (48)	134	0.08
Slovene (0)	0	<0.01
Soviet Union (0)	0	<0.01
Swedish (229)	947	0.59
Swiss (41)	179	0.11
Turkish (17)	41	0.03
Ukrainian (73)	191	0.12
Welsh (168)	721	0.45
West Indian, ex. Hispanic (403)	494	0.31
Bahamian (0)	0	<0.01
Barbadian (67)	67	0.04
Belizean (59)	59	0.04
Bermudan (0)	0	<0.01
British West Indian (9)	28	0.02
Dutch West Indian (0)	0	<0.01
Haitian (3)	43	0.03
Jamaican (161)	171	0.11
Trinidadian/Tobagonian (0)	0	<0.01
U.S. Virgin Islander (0)	0	<0.01
West Indian (104)	126	0.08
Other West Indian (0)	0	<0.01
Yugoslavian (8)	8	<0.01

Hispanic Origin	Population	%
Hispanic or Latino (of any race)	21,814	12.92
Central American, ex. Mexican	2,523	1.49
Costa Rican	63	0.04
Guatemalan	358	0.21
Honduran	1,508	0.89
Nicaraguan	85	0.05
Panamanian	87	0.05
Salvadoran	403	0.24
Other Central American	19	0.01
Cuban	350	0.21
Dominican Republic	371	0.22
Mexican	15,119	8.95
Puerto Rican	1,408	0.83
South American	686	0.41
Argentinean	51	0.03
Bolivian	10	0.01
Chilean	35	0.02
Colombian	208	0.12
Ecuadorian	160	0.09
Paraguayan	0	<0.01
Peruvian	88	0.05
Uruguayan	34	0.02
Venezuelan	99	0.06
Other South American	1	<0.01
Other Hispanic or Latino	1,357	0.80

Race*	Population	%
African-American/Black (25,546)	27,005	15.99
Not Hispanic (25,082)	26,268	15.55
Hispanic (464)	737	0.44
American Indian/Alaska Native (939)	1,876	1.11
Not Hispanic (689)	1,482	0.88
Hispanic (250)	394	0.23
Alaska Athabascan (Ala. Nat.) (0)	1	<0.01
Aleut (Alaska Native) (2)	3	<0.01
Apache (3)	11	0.01
Arapaho (0)	2	<0.01
Blackfeet (3)	40	0.02
Canadian/French Am. Ind. (0)	2	<0.01
Central American Ind. (4)	5	<0.01
Cherokee (117)	374	0.22
Cheyenne (5)	7	<0.01
Chickasaw (1)	4	<0.01
Chippewa (8)	12	0.01
Choctaw (10)	16	0.01
Colville (0)	0	<0.01

Race*	Population	%
Comanche (1)	1	<0.01
Cree (0)	0	<0.01
Creek (4)	7	<0.01
Crow (0)	0	<0.01
Delaware (1)	5	<0.01
Hopi (2)	4	<0.01
Houma (0)	0	<0.01
Inupiat (Alaska Native) (1)	6	<0.01
Iroquois (10)	18	0.01
Kiowa (0)	0	<0.01
Lumbee (236)	316	0.19
Menominee (0)	0	<0.01
Mexican American Ind. (40)	64	0.04
Navajo (9)	17	0.01
Osage (1)	1	<0.01
Ottawa (3)	4	<0.01
Paiute (1)	1	<0.01
Pima (3)	3	<0.01
Potawatomi (0)	3	<0.01
Pueblo (1)	9	0.01
Puget Sound Salish (0)	0	<0.01
Seminole (0)	5	<0.01
Shoshone (0)	6	<0.01
Sioux (10)	15	0.01
South American Ind. (2)	9	0.01
Spanish American Ind. (0)	2	<0.01
Tlingit-Haida (Alaska Native) (0)	0	<0.01
Tohono O'Odham (0)	0	<0.01
Tsimshian (Alaska Native) (0)	0	<0.01
Ute (0)	0	<0.01
Yakama (0)	0	<0.01
Yaqui (0)	1	<0.01
Yuman (0)	0	<0.01
Yup'ik (Alaska Native) (0)	0	<0.01
Asian (1,021)	1,560	0.92
Not Hispanic (976)	1,445	0.86
Hispanic (45)	115	0.07
Bangladeshi (0)	0	<0.01
Bhutanese (0)	0	<0.01
Burmese (2)	3	<0.01
Cambodian (5)	7	<0.01
Chinese, ex. Taiwanese (180)	252	0.15
Filipino (207)	357	0.21
Hmong (12)	13	0.01
Indian (222)	267	0.16
Indonesian (2)	6	<0.01
Japanese (41)	127	0.08
Korean (106)	180	0.11
Laotian (8)	12	0.01
Malaysian (1)	1	<0.01
Nepalese (4)	4	<0.01
Pakistani (13)	14	<0.01
Sri Lankan (0)	0	<0.01
Taiwanese (3)	8	<0.01
Thai (26)	54	0.03
Vietnamese (134)	153	0.09
Hawaii Native/Pacific Islander (51)	183	0.11
Not Hispanic (33)	116	0.07
Hispanic (18)	67	0.04
Fijian (0)	0	<0.01
Guamanian/Chamorro (15)	27	0.02
Marshallese (0)	0	<0.01
Native Hawaiian (9)	44	0.03
Samoan (2)	6	<0.01
Tongan (1)	3	<0.01
White (125,349)	128,227	75.93
Not Hispanic (117,869)	119,814	70.95
Hispanic (7,480)	8,413	4.98

*Notes: † The Census 2010 population figure is used to calculate the percentages in the Hispanic Origin and Race categories. Ancestry percentages are based on the 2006-2010 American Community Survey population (not shown); ‡ Numbers in parentheses indicate the number of people reporting a single ancestry; * Numbers in parentheses indicate the number of persons reporting this race alone, not in combination with any other race; Please refer to the Explanation of Data for more information.*

Lee County

Population: 57,866

Ancestry	Population	%
Afghan (0)	0	<0.01
African, Sub-Saharan (96)	120	0.22
African (96)	120	0.22
Cape Verdean (0)	0	<0.01
Ethiopian (0)	0	<0.01
Ghanaian (0)	0	<0.01
Kenyan (0)	0	<0.01
Liberian (0)	0	<0.01
Nigerian (0)	0	<0.01
Senegalese (0)	0	<0.01
Sierra Leonean (0)	0	<0.01
Somalian (0)	0	<0.01
South African (0)	0	<0.01
Sudanese (0)	0	<0.01
Ugandan (0)	0	<0.01
Zimbabwean (0)	0	<0.01
Other Sub-Saharan African (0)	0	<0.01
Albanian (0)	0	<0.01
Alsatian (0)	0	<0.01
American (5,847)	5,847	10.52
Arab (84)	168	0.30
Arab (40)	40	0.07
Egyptian (0)	0	<0.01
Iraqi (0)	0	<0.01
Jordanian (0)	0	<0.01
Lebanese (12)	86	0.15
Moroccan (0)	0	<0.01
Palestinian (0)	0	<0.01
Syrian (18)	28	0.05
Other Arab (14)	14	0.03
Armenian (13)	17	0.03
Assyrian/Chaldean/Syriac (0)	0	<0.01
Australian (37)	37	0.07
Austrian (0)	13	0.02
Basque (0)	0	<0.01
Belgian (10)	16	0.03
Brazilian (0)	0	<0.01
British (60)	75	0.13
Bulgarian (0)	0	<0.01
Cajun (0)	0	<0.01
Canadian (8)	25	0.04
Carpatho Rusyn (0)	0	<0.01
Celtic (42)	42	0.08
Croatian (44)	58	0.10
Cypriot (0)	0	<0.01
Czech (15)	33	0.06
Czechoslovakian (0)	0	<0.01
Danish (36)	55	0.10
Dutch (198)	593	1.07
Eastern European (0)	16	0.03
English (2,785)	5,428	9.77
Estonian (0)	0	<0.01
European (880)	899	1.62
Finnish (0)	0	<0.01
French, ex. Basque (247)	888	1.60
French Canadian (99)	196	0.35
German (1,731)	4,516	8.13
German Russian (0)	0	<0.01
Greek (0)	95	0.17
Guyanese (0)	0	<0.01
Hungarian (47)	193	0.35
Icelander (0)	0	<0.01
Iranian (0)	0	<0.01
Irish (1,335)	3,339	6.01
Israeli (0)	0	<0.01
Italian (331)	950	1.71
Latvian (0)	0	<0.01
Lithuanian (32)	45	0.08
Luxemburger (0)	0	<0.01
Macedonian (0)	0	<0.01
Maltese (0)	0	<0.01
New Zealander (0)	0	<0.01
Northern European (0)	0	<0.01
Norwegian (52)	70	0.13
Pennsylvania German (0)	12	0.02

	Population	%
Polish (185)	631	1.14
Portuguese (14)	70	0.13
Romanian (0)	13	0.02
Russian (43)	152	0.27
Scandinavian (0)	0	<0.01
Scotch-Irish (1,112)	2,124	3.82
Scottish (1,105)	1,922	3.46
Serbian (0)	0	<0.01
Slavic (0)	13	0.02
Slovak (0)	12	0.02
Slovene (0)	0	<0.01
Soviet Union (0)	0	<0.01
Swedish (94)	242	0.44
Swiss (0)	22	0.04
Turkish (0)	0	<0.01
Ukrainian (13)	13	0.02
Welsh (98)	248	0.45
West Indian, ex. Hispanic (82)	101	0.18
Bahamian (0)	0	<0.01
Barbadian (0)	0	<0.01
Belizean (0)	0	<0.01
Bermudan (0)	0	<0.01
British West Indian (0)	0	<0.01
Dutch West Indian (0)	0	<0.01
Haitian (14)	14	0.03
Jamaican (20)	20	0.04
Trinidadian/Tobagonian (23)	23	0.04
U.S. Virgin Islander (0)	0	<0.01
West Indian (25)	44	0.08
Other West Indian (0)	0	<0.01
Yugoslavian (0)	0	<0.01

Hispanic Origin	Population	%
Hispanic or Latino (of any race)	10,576	18.28
Central American, ex. Mexican	2,189	3.78
Costa Rican	26	0.04
Guatemalan	527	0.91
Honduran	422	0.73
Nicaraguan	46	0.08
Panamanian	55	0.10
Salvadoran	1,105	1.91
Other Central American	8	0.01
Cuban	43	0.07
Dominican Republic	97	0.17
Mexican	6,898	11.92
Puerto Rican	594	1.03
South American	209	0.36
Argentinean	5	0.01
Bolivian	5	0.01
Chilean	2	<0.01
Colombian	83	0.14
Ecuadorian	26	0.04
Paraguayan	4	0.01
Peruvian	68	0.12
Uruguayan	4	0.01
Venezuelan	12	0.02
Other South American	0	<0.01
Other Hispanic or Latino	546	0.94

Race*	Population	%
African-American/Black (11,565)	12,169	21.03
Not Hispanic (11,369)	11,821	20.43
Hispanic (196)	348	0.60
American Indian/Alaska Native (407)	759	1.31
Not Hispanic (253)	527	0.91
Hispanic (154)	232	0.40
Alaska Athabascan (Ala. Nat.) (0)	0	<0.01
Aleut (Alaska Native) (0)	0	<0.01
Apache (1)	3	0.01
Arapaho (1)	1	<0.01
Blackfeet (2)	10	0.02
Canadian/French Am. Ind. (1)	2	<0.01
Central American Ind. (9)	15	0.03
Cherokee (61)	177	0.31
Cheyenne (0)	0	<0.01
Chickasaw (0)	0	<0.01
Chippewa (4)	7	0.01
Choctaw (3)	6	0.01
Colville (0)	0	<0.01

	Population	%
Comanche (0)	2	<0.01
Cree (0)	0	<0.01
Creek (1)	2	<0.01
Crow (0)	0	<0.01
Delaware (2)	7	0.01
Hopi (0)	0	<0.01
Houma (0)	0	<0.01
Inupiat (Alaska Native) (0)	1	<0.01
Iroquois (11)	25	0.04
Kiowa (0)	0	<0.01
Lumbee (54)	93	0.16
Menominee (0)	0	<0.01
Mexican American Ind. (39)	57	0.10
Navajo (2)	3	0.01
Osage (0)	0	<0.01
Ottawa (0)	0	<0.01
Paiute (0)	0	<0.01
Pima (1)	2	<0.01
Potawatomi (3)	3	0.01
Pueblo (0)	0	<0.01
Puget Sound Salish (0)	0	<0.01
Seminole (1)	1	<0.01
Shoshone (1)	1	<0.01
Sioux (4)	11	0.02
South American Ind. (2)	5	0.01
Spanish American Ind. (5)	5	0.01
Tlingit-Haida (Alaska Native) (0)	0	<0.01
Tohono O'Odham (0)	0	<0.01
Tsimshian (Alaska Native) (0)	0	<0.01
Ute (0)	0	<0.01
Yakama (0)	0	<0.01
Yaqui (0)	0	<0.01
Yuman (0)	0	<0.01
Yup'ik (Alaska Native) (0)	0	<0.01
Asian (489)	699	1.21
Not Hispanic (475)	652	1.13
Hispanic (14)	47	0.08
Bangladeshi (0)	0	<0.01
Bhutanese (0)	0	<0.01
Burmese (0)	0	<0.01
Cambodian (4)	4	0.01
Chinese, ex. Taiwanese (56)	64	0.11
Filipino (97)	161	0.28
Hmong (1)	1	<0.01
Indian (111)	146	0.25
Indonesian (0)	0	<0.01
Japanese (23)	41	0.07
Korean (36)	64	0.11
Laotian (2)	2	<0.01
Malaysian (0)	0	<0.01
Nepalese (0)	0	<0.01
Pakistani (13)	14	0.02
Sri Lankan (0)	0	<0.01
Taiwanese (0)	0	<0.01
Thai (19)	30	0.05
Vietnamese (98)	124	0.21
Hawaii Native/Pacific Islander (20)	69	0.12
Not Hispanic (13)	42	0.07
Hispanic (7)	27	0.05
Fijian (0)	1	<0.01
Guamanian/Chamorro (7)	15	0.03
Marshallese (0)	0	<0.01
Native Hawaiian (3)	15	0.03
Samoan (3)	7	0.01
Tongan (1)	3	0.01
White (38,688)	39,835	68.84
Not Hispanic (34,321)	34,972	60.44
Hispanic (4,367)	4,863	8.40

Notes: † The Census 2010 population figure is used to calculate the percentages in the Hispanic Origin and Race categories. Ancestry percentages are based on the 2006-2010 American Community Survey population (not shown); ‡ Numbers in parentheses indicate the number of people reporting a single ancestry; * Numbers in parentheses indicate the number of persons reporting this race alone, not in combination with any other race; Please refer to the Explanation of Data for more information.

Lenoir County

Population: 59,495

Ancestry	Population	%
Afghan (0)	0	<0.01
African, Sub-Saharan (805)	963	1.62
African (739)	885	1.49
Cape Verdean (0)	0	<0.01
Ethiopian (0)	0	<0.01
Ghanaian (0)	0	<0.01
Kenyan (0)	0	<0.01
Liberian (14)	14	0.02
Nigerian (9)	9	0.02
Senegalese (0)	0	<0.01
Sierra Leonean (0)	0	<0.01
Somalian (0)	0	<0.01
South African (0)	0	<0.01
Sudanese (0)	0	<0.01
Ugandan (0)	0	<0.01
Zimbabwean (0)	0	<0.01
Other Sub-Saharan African (43)	55	0.09
Albanian (0)	0	<0.01
Alsatian (0)	0	<0.01
American (8,588)	8,588	14.48
Arab (55)	55	0.09
Arab (33)	33	0.06
Egyptian (0)	0	<0.01
Iraqi (0)	0	<0.01
Jordanian (0)	0	<0.01
Lebanese (22)	22	0.04
Moroccan (0)	0	<0.01
Palestinian (0)	0	<0.01
Syrian (0)	0	<0.01
Other Arab (0)	0	<0.01
Armenian (11)	21	0.04
Assyrian/Chaldean/Syriac (0)	0	<0.01
Australian (0)	0	<0.01
Austrian (0)	11	0.02
Basque (0)	0	<0.01
Belgian (0)	0	<0.01
Brazilian (0)	0	<0.01
British (103)	112	0.19
Bulgarian (0)	0	<0.01
Cajun (0)	0	<0.01
Canadian (10)	10	0.02
Carpatho Rusyn (0)	0	<0.01
Celtic (0)	0	<0.01
Croatian (0)	0	<0.01
Cypriot (0)	0	<0.01
Czech (19)	30	0.05
Czechoslovakian (11)	11	0.02
Danish (14)	42	0.07
Dutch (43)	182	0.31
Eastern European (0)	0	<0.01
English (3,539)	5,962	10.05
Estonian (0)	0	<0.01
European (417)	449	0.76
Finnish (0)	0	<0.01
French, ex. Basque (179)	546	0.92
French Canadian (51)	63	0.11
German (900)	2,362	3.98
German Russian (0)	36	0.06
Greek (9)	64	0.11
Guyanese (0)	0	<0.01
Hungarian (7)	25	0.04
Icelander (0)	0	<0.01
Iranian (0)	0	<0.01
Irish (1,542)	3,684	6.21
Israeli (0)	0	<0.01
Italian (232)	687	1.16
Latvian (0)	0	<0.01
Lithuanian (0)	22	0.04
Luxemburger (0)	0	<0.01
Macedonian (0)	0	<0.01
Maltese (0)	0	<0.01
New Zealander (0)	0	<0.01
Northern European (0)	0	<0.01
Norwegian (84)	318	0.54
Pennsylvania German (0)	0	<0.01

Ancestry (cont.)	Population	%
Polish (70)	121	0.20
Portuguese (0)	19	0.03
Romanian (0)	0	<0.01
Russian (24)	100	0.17
Scandinavian (0)	0	<0.01
Scotch-Irish (557)	1,036	1.75
Scottish (439)	803	1.35
Serbian (0)	0	<0.01
Slavic (0)	0	<0.01
Slovak (0)	0	<0.01
Slovene (0)	0	<0.01
Soviet Union (0)	0	<0.01
Swedish (85)	146	0.25
Swiss (9)	23	0.04
Turkish (0)	0	<0.01
Ukrainian (0)	18	0.03
Welsh (13)	76	0.13
West Indian, ex. Hispanic (107)	187	0.32
Bahamian (0)	0	<0.01
Barbadian (0)	40	0.07
Belizean (0)	0	<0.01
Bermudan (0)	0	<0.01
British West Indian (0)	0	<0.01
Dutch West Indian (0)	0	<0.01
Haitian (0)	0	<0.01
Jamaican (87)	110	0.19
Trinidadian/Tobagonian (20)	37	0.06
U.S. Virgin Islander (0)	0	<0.01
West Indian (0)	0	<0.01
Other West Indian (0)	0	<0.01
Yugoslavian (0)	0	<0.01

Hispanic Origin	Population	%
Hispanic or Latino (of any race)	3,917	6.58
Central American, ex. Mexican	218	0.37
Costa Rican	1	<0.01
Guatemalan	36	0.06
Honduran	125	0.21
Nicaraguan	6	0.01
Panamanian	5	0.01
Salvadoran	44	0.07
Other Central American	1	<0.01
Cuban	24	0.04
Dominican Republic	21	0.04
Mexican	3,204	5.39
Puerto Rican	181	0.30
South American	59	0.10
Argentinean	5	0.01
Bolivian	1	<0.01
Chilean	13	0.02
Colombian	21	0.04
Ecuadorian	5	0.01
Paraguayan	0	<0.01
Peruvian	6	0.01
Uruguayan	0	<0.01
Venezuelan	4	0.01
Other South American	4	0.01
Other Hispanic or Latino	210	0.35

Race*	Population	%
African-American/Black (24,121)	24,565	41.29
Not Hispanic (23,968)	24,366	40.95
Hispanic (153)	199	0.33
American Indian/Alaska Native (222)	434	0.73
Not Hispanic (163)	365	0.61
Hispanic (59)	69	0.12
Alaska Athabascan (Ala. Nat.) (0)	0	<0.01
Aleut (Alaska Native) (0)	0	<0.01
Apache (0)	0	<0.01
Arapaho (0)	1	<0.01
Blackfeet (0)	7	0.01
Canadian/French Am. Ind. (0)	0	<0.01
Central American Ind. (1)	3	0.01
Cherokee (26)	86	0.14
Cheyenne (0)	0	<0.01
Chickasaw (0)	0	<0.01
Chippewa (0)	0	<0.01
Choctaw (2)	6	0.01
Colville (0)	0	<0.01

Race* (cont.)	Population	%
Comanche (0)	0	<0.01
Cree (0)	0	<0.01
Creek (2)	4	0.01
Crow (0)	0	<0.01
Delaware (0)	0	<0.01
Hopi (0)	0	<0.01
Houma (0)	0	<0.01
Inupiat (Alaska Native) (0)	0	<0.01
Iroquois (1)	4	0.01
Kiowa (1)	1	<0.01
Lumbee (25)	36	0.06
Menominee (0)	0	<0.01
Mexican American Ind. (7)	7	0.01
Navajo (0)	1	<0.01
Osage (0)	0	<0.01
Ottawa (0)	0	<0.01
Paiute (0)	0	<0.01
Pima (0)	0	<0.01
Potawatomi (0)	0	<0.01
Pueblo (0)	0	<0.01
Puget Sound Salish (0)	0	<0.01
Seminole (0)	2	<0.01
Shoshone (0)	0	<0.01
Sioux (0)	2	<0.01
South American Ind. (0)	0	<0.01
Spanish American Ind. (0)	0	<0.01
Tlingit-Haida (Alaska Native) (0)	0	<0.01
Tohono O'Odham (0)	0	<0.01
Tsimshian (Alaska Native) (0)	0	<0.01
Ute (0)	0	<0.01
Yakama (0)	0	<0.01
Yaqui (0)	0	<0.01
Yuman (0)	0	<0.01
Yup'ik (Alaska Native) (0)	0	<0.01
Asian (262)	389	0.65
Not Hispanic (256)	372	0.63
Hispanic (6)	17	0.03
Bangladeshi (0)	0	<0.01
Bhutanese (0)	0	<0.01
Burmese (0)	0	<0.01
Cambodian (0)	0	<0.01
Chinese, ex. Taiwanese (50)	61	0.10
Filipino (43)	77	0.13
Hmong (0)	0	<0.01
Indian (60)	74	0.12
Indonesian (1)	1	<0.01
Japanese (7)	14	0.02
Korean (25)	49	0.08
Laotian (10)	12	0.02
Malaysian (0)	0	<0.01
Nepalese (0)	0	<0.01
Pakistani (8)	8	0.01
Sri Lankan (0)	0	<0.01
Taiwanese (1)	1	<0.01
Thai (22)	38	0.06
Vietnamese (28)	40	0.07
Hawaii Native/Pacific Islander (48)	95	0.16
Not Hispanic (26)	64	0.11
Hispanic (22)	31	0.05
Fijian (0)	0	<0.01
Guamanian/Chamorro (31)	37	0.06
Marshallese (0)	0	<0.01
Native Hawaiian (2)	3	0.01
Samoan (9)	26	0.04
Tongan (3)	13	0.02
White (31,758)	32,367	54.40
Not Hispanic (30,492)	30,971	52.06
Hispanic (1,266)	1,396	2.35

Notes: † The Census 2010 population figure is used to calculate the percentages in the Hispanic Origin and Race categories. Ancestry percentages are based on the 2006-2010 American Community Survey population (not shown); ‡ Numbers in parentheses indicate the number of people reporting a single ancestry; * Numbers in parentheses indicate the number of persons reporting this race alone, not in combination with any other race; Please refer to the Explanation of Data for more information.

Lincoln County

Population: 78,265

Ancestry	Population	%
Afghan (0)	0	<0.01
African, Sub-Saharan (19)	46	0.06
African (19)	46	0.06
Cape Verdean (0)	0	<0.01
Ethiopian (0)	0	<0.01
Ghanaian (0)	0	<0.01
Kenyan (0)	0	<0.01
Liberian (0)	0	<0.01
Nigerian (0)	0	<0.01
Senegalese (0)	0	<0.01
Sierra Leonean (0)	0	<0.01
Somalian (0)	0	<0.01
South African (0)	0	<0.01
Sudanese (0)	0	<0.01
Ugandan (0)	0	<0.01
Zimbabwean (0)	0	<0.01
Other Sub-Saharan African (0)	0	<0.01
Albanian (0)	0	<0.01
Alsatian (0)	0	<0.01
American (11,238)	11,238	14.85
Arab (51)	51	0.07
Arab (33)	33	0.04
Egyptian (0)	0	<0.01
Iraqi (0)	0	<0.01
Jordanian (0)	0	<0.01
Lebanese (18)	18	0.02
Moroccan (0)	0	<0.01
Palestinian (0)	0	<0.01
Syrian (0)	0	<0.01
Other Arab (0)	0	<0.01
Armenian (7)	15	0.02
Assyrian/Chaldean/Syriac (0)	0	<0.01
Australian (25)	25	0.03
Austrian (13)	49	0.06
Basque (0)	0	<0.01
Belgian (22)	41	0.05
Brazilian (0)	0	<0.01
British (55)	128	0.17
Bulgarian (0)	10	0.01
Cajun (0)	0	<0.01
Canadian (126)	192	0.25
Carpatho Rusyn (0)	0	<0.01
Celtic (0)	31	0.04
Croatian (19)	27	0.04
Cypriot (0)	0	<0.01
Czech (17)	172	0.23
Czechoslovakian (0)	15	0.02
Danish (0)	47	0.06
Dutch (174)	2,096	2.77
Eastern European (51)	51	0.07
English (4,315)	8,480	11.20
Estonian (0)	0	<0.01
European (548)	568	0.75
Finnish (31)	184	0.24
French, ex. Basque (184)	1,271	1.68
French Canadian (170)	267	0.35
German (6,718)	15,465	20.43
German Russian (0)	0	<0.01
Greek (64)	99	0.13
Guyanese (0)	0	<0.01
Hungarian (56)	86	0.11
Icelander (0)	0	<0.01
Iranian (13)	13	0.02
Irish (2,795)	10,000	13.21
Israeli (0)	0	<0.01
Italian (722)	2,018	2.67
Latvian (0)	0	<0.01
Lithuanian (22)	39	0.05
Luxemburger (0)	0	<0.01
Macedonian (0)	0	<0.01
Maltese (0)	0	<0.01
New Zealander (28)	28	0.04
Northern European (0)	0	<0.01
Norwegian (92)	196	0.26
Pennsylvania German (0)	0	<0.01
Polish (339)	961	1.27
Portuguese (26)	124	0.16
Romanian (21)	21	0.03
Russian (91)	174	0.23
Scandinavian (0)	0	<0.01
Scotch-Irish (1,615)	2,829	3.74
Scottish (680)	1,844	2.44
Serbian (7)	15	0.02
Slavic (0)	0	<0.01
Slovak (18)	24	0.03
Slovene (0)	0	<0.01
Soviet Union (0)	0	<0.01
Swedish (17)	175	0.23
Swiss (20)	166	0.22
Turkish (64)	64	0.08
Ukrainian (13)	25	0.03
Welsh (86)	364	0.48
West Indian, ex. Hispanic (37)	37	0.05
Bahamian (0)	0	<0.01
Barbadian (0)	0	<0.01
Belizean (0)	0	<0.01
Bermudan (0)	0	<0.01
British West Indian (0)	0	<0.01
Dutch West Indian (0)	0	<0.01
Haitian (0)	0	<0.01
Jamaican (0)	0	<0.01
Trinidadian/Tobagonian (0)	0	<0.01
U.S. Virgin Islander (37)	37	0.05
West Indian (0)	0	<0.01
Other West Indian (0)	0	<0.01
Yugoslavian (39)	39	0.05

Hispanic Origin	Population	%
Hispanic or Latino (of any race)	5,238	6.69
Central American, ex. Mexican	1,355	1.73
Costa Rican	1,037	1.32
Guatemalan	67	0.09
Honduran	73	0.09
Nicaraguan	64	0.08
Panamanian	13	0.02
Salvadoran	99	0.13
Other Central American	2	<0.01
Cuban	119	0.15
Dominican Republic	107	0.14
Mexican	2,824	3.61
Puerto Rican	249	0.32
South American	271	0.35
Argentinean	61	0.08
Bolivian	5	0.01
Chilean	18	0.02
Colombian	77	0.10
Ecuadorian	24	0.03
Paraguayan	0	<0.01
Peruvian	50	0.06
Uruguayan	21	0.03
Venezuelan	13	0.02
Other South American	2	<0.01
Other Hispanic or Latino	313	0.40

Race*	Population	%
African-American/Black (4,340)	4,833	6.18
Not Hispanic (4,269)	4,712	6.02
Hispanic (71)	121	0.15
American Indian/Alaska Native (250)	563	0.72
Not Hispanic (222)	514	0.66
Hispanic (28)	49	0.06
Alaska Athabascan (Ala. Nat.) (0)	0	<0.01
Aleut (Alaska Native) (0)	0	<0.01
Apache (6)	12	0.02
Arapaho (0)	0	<0.01
Blackfeet (1)	7	0.01
Canadian/French Am. Ind. (0)	0	<0.01
Central American Ind. (1)	1	<0.01
Cherokee (59)	178	0.23
Cheyenne (0)	6	0.01
Chickasaw (1)	3	<0.01
Chippewa (3)	8	0.01
Choctaw (7)	9	0.01
Colville (1)	1	<0.01

	Population	%
Comanche (0)	0	<0.01
Cree (0)	0	<0.01
Creek (1)	2	<0.01
Crow (0)	0	<0.01
Delaware (0)	0	<0.01
Hopi (0)	0	<0.01
Houma (0)	0	<0.01
Inupiat (Alaska Native) (0)	0	<0.01
Iroquois (9)	13	0.02
Kiowa (0)	0	<0.01
Lumbee (42)	60	0.08
Menominee (0)	1	<0.01
Mexican American Ind. (7)	8	0.01
Navajo (0)	3	<0.01
Osage (0)	0	<0.01
Ottawa (0)	1	<0.01
Paiute (0)	0	<0.01
Pima (0)	0	<0.01
Potawatomi (2)	2	<0.01
Pueblo (0)	0	<0.01
Puget Sound Salish (0)	0	<0.01
Seminole (0)	1	<0.01
Shoshone (0)	0	<0.01
Sioux (3)	4	0.01
South American Ind. (1)	1	<0.01
Spanish American Ind. (0)	0	<0.01
Tlingit-Haida (Alaska Native) (3)	3	<0.01
Tohono O'Odham (0)	0	<0.01
Tsimshian (Alaska Native) (0)	0	<0.01
Ute (0)	1	<0.01
Yakama (0)	0	<0.01
Yaqui (0)	0	<0.01
Yuman (0)	0	<0.01
Yup'ik (Alaska Native) (0)	0	<0.01
Asian (421)	606	0.77
Not Hispanic (415)	578	0.74
Hispanic (6)	28	0.04
Bangladeshi (0)	0	<0.01
Bhutanese (0)	0	<0.01
Burmese (2)	2	<0.01
Cambodian (10)	11	0.01
Chinese, ex. Taiwanese (68)	86	0.11
Filipino (77)	122	0.16
Hmong (40)	47	0.06
Indian (46)	78	0.10
Indonesian (6)	6	0.01
Japanese (11)	38	0.05
Korean (48)	87	0.11
Laotian (5)	11	0.01
Malaysian (0)	0	<0.01
Nepalese (0)	2	<0.01
Pakistani (2)	2	<0.01
Sri Lankan (0)	0	<0.01
Taiwanese (0)	1	<0.01
Thai (4)	11	0.01
Vietnamese (59)	74	0.09
Hawaii Native/Pacific Islander (17)	49	0.06
Not Hispanic (13)	30	0.04
Hispanic (4)	19	0.02
Fijian (0)	0	<0.01
Guamanian/Chamorro (5)	7	0.01
Marshallese (0)	0	<0.01
Native Hawaiian (2)	17	0.02
Samoan (0)	2	<0.01
Tongan (0)	0	<0.01
White (69,940)	71,064	90.80
Not Hispanic (67,139)	67,981	86.86
Hispanic (2,801)	3,083	3.94

Notes: † The Census 2010 population figure is used to calculate the percentages in the Hispanic Origin and Race categories. Ancestry percentages are based on the 2006-2010 American Community Survey population (not shown); ‡ Numbers in parentheses indicate the number of people reporting a single ancestry; * Numbers in parentheses indicate the number of persons reporting this race alone, not in combination with any other race; Please refer to the Explanation of Data for more information.

Mecklenburg County

Population: 919,628

Ancestry	Population	%
Afghan (0)	13	<0.01
African, Sub-Saharan (11,344)	12,696	1.44
African (5,044)	6,136	0.70
Cape Verdean (27)	48	0.01
Ethiopian (1,177)	1,177	0.13
Ghanaian (544)	560	0.06
Kenyan (354)	354	0.04
Liberian (618)	633	0.07
Nigerian (1,244)	1,254	0.14
Senegalese (47)	47	0.01
Sierra Leonean (70)	70	0.01
Somalian (485)	485	0.05
South African (181)	226	0.03
Sudanese (42)	101	0.01
Ugandan (0)	0	<0.01
Zimbabwean (14)	14	<0.01
Other Sub-Saharan African (1,497)	1,591	0.18
Albanian (149)	194	0.02
Alsatian (0)	19	<0.01
American (43,953)	43,953	4.98
Arab (4,057)	5,546	0.63
Arab (806)	902	0.10
Egyptian (642)	743	0.08
Iraqi (0)	0	<0.01
Jordanian (241)	252	0.03
Lebanese (930)	2,016	0.23
Moroccan (368)	390	0.04
Palestinian (175)	186	0.02
Syrian (212)	318	0.04
Other Arab (683)	739	0.08
Armenian (440)	722	0.08
Assyrian/Chaldean/Syriac (7)	7	<0.01
Australian (43)	163	0.02
Austrian (352)	1,596	0.18
Basque (6)	6	<0.01
Belgian (327)	938	0.11
Brazilian (1,163)	1,459	0.17
British (2,692)	4,973	0.56
Bulgarian (91)	123	0.01
Cajun (115)	228	0.03
Canadian (1,088)	1,982	0.22
Carpatho Rusyn (15)	15	<0.01
Celtic (38)	100	0.01
Croatian (272)	968	0.11
Cypriot (0)	0	<0.01
Czech (735)	2,279	0.26
Czechoslovakian (287)	995	0.11
Danish (511)	2,092	0.24
Dutch (1,952)	10,335	1.17
Eastern European (961)	999	0.11
English (31,062)	81,519	9.23
Estonian (30)	41	<0.01
European (8,537)	9,249	1.05
Finnish (202)	575	0.07
French, ex. Basque (3,344)	16,856	1.91
French Canadian (1,430)	3,667	0.42
German (31,247)	102,490	11.61
German Russian (0)	9	<0.01
Greek (3,232)	5,084	0.58
Guyanese (268)	364	0.04
Hungarian (908)	3,236	0.37
Icelander (11)	25	<0.01
Iranian (724)	849	0.10
Irish (22,900)	77,732	8.81
Israeli (44)	59	0.01
Italian (13,986)	40,415	4.58
Latvian (75)	188	0.02
Lithuanian (460)	1,219	0.14
Luxemburger (0)	0	<0.01
Macedonian (19)	30	<0.01
Maltese (0)	156	0.02
New Zealander (34)	72	0.01
Northern European (399)	428	0.05
Norwegian (1,382)	4,573	0.52
Pennsylvania German (55)	281	0.03
Polish (4,841)	16,672	1.89
Portuguese (674)	1,459	0.17
Romanian (681)	1,694	0.19
Russian (3,208)	7,208	0.82
Scandinavian (428)	1,007	0.11
Scotch-Irish (21,055)	35,321	4.00
Scottish (8,460)	23,405	2.65
Serbian (134)	470	0.05
Slavic (149)	507	0.06
Slovak (573)	2,029	0.23
Slovene (176)	334	0.04
Soviet Union (0)	0	<0.01
Swedish (1,615)	5,941	0.67
Swiss (429)	2,217	0.25
Turkish (730)	848	0.10
Ukrainian (1,553)	2,902	0.33
Welsh (1,675)	6,715	0.76
West Indian, ex. Hispanic (3,151)	4,737	0.54
Bahamian (102)	148	0.02
Barbadian (83)	148	0.02
Belizean (13)	20	<0.01
Bermudan (0)	16	<0.01
British West Indian (82)	82	0.01
Dutch West Indian (34)	56	0.01
Haitian (328)	465	0.05
Jamaican (1,751)	2,586	0.29
Trinidadian/Tobagonian (141)	270	0.03
U.S. Virgin Islander (0)	12	<0.01
West Indian (596)	913	0.10
Other West Indian (21)	21	<0.01
Yugoslavian (1,212)	1,509	0.17

Hispanic Origin	Population	%
Hispanic or Latino (of any race)	111,944	12.17
Central American, ex. Mexican	24,822	2.70
Costa Rican	782	0.09
Guatemalan	2,775	0.30
Honduran	8,138	0.88
Nicaraguan	1,521	0.17
Panamanian	709	0.08
Salvadoran	10,625	1.16
Other Central American	272	0.03
Cuban	3,571	0.39
Dominican Republic	3,895	0.42
Mexican	47,403	5.15
Puerto Rican	9,523	1.04
South American	13,184	1.43
Argentinean	652	0.07
Bolivian	172	0.02
Chilean	452	0.05
Colombian	4,221	0.46
Ecuadorian	3,582	0.39
Paraguayan	37	<0.01
Peruvian	2,663	0.29
Uruguayan	296	0.03
Venezuelan	1,013	0.11
Other South American	96	0.01
Other Hispanic or Latino	9,546	1.04

Race*	Population	%
African-American/Black (282,804)	295,316	32.11
Not Hispanic (278,042)	288,390	31.36
Hispanic (4,762)	6,926	0.75
American Indian/Alaska Native (4,261)	10,095	1.10
Not Hispanic (2,843)	7,461	0.81
Hispanic (1,418)	2,634	0.29
Alaska Athabascan (Ala. Nat.) (4)	5	<0.01
Aleut (Alaska Native) (10)	14	<0.01
Apache (10)	56	0.01
Arapaho (4)	4	<0.01
Blackfeet (39)	223	0.02
Canadian/French Am. Ind. (2)	15	<0.01
Central American Ind. (21)	72	0.01
Cherokee (359)	1,629	0.18
Cheyenne (3)	7	<0.01
Chickasaw (13)	40	<0.01
Chippewa (37)	70	0.01
Choctaw (39)	102	0.01
Colville (0)	0	<0.01
Comanche (2)	5	<0.01
Cree (6)	10	<0.01
Creek (19)	55	0.01
Crow (1)	14	<0.01
Delaware (11)	28	<0.01
Hopi (0)	1	<0.01
Houma (1)	2	<0.01
Inupiat (Alaska Native) (6)	12	<0.01
Iroquois (62)	132	0.01
Kiowa (0)	6	<0.01
Lumbee (739)	1,021	0.11
Menominee (5)	10	<0.01
Mexican American Ind. (283)	390	0.04
Navajo (9)	39	<0.01
Osage (3)	6	<0.01
Ottawa (5)	8	<0.01
Paiute (0)	3	<0.01
Pima (1)	1	<0.01
Potawatomi (6)	9	<0.01
Pueblo (2)	20	<0.01
Puget Sound Salish (3)	3	<0.01
Seminole (6)	39	<0.01
Shoshone (2)	9	<0.01
Sioux (29)	79	0.01
South American Ind. (29)	104	0.01
Spanish American Ind. (17)	103	0.01
Tlingit-Haida (Alaska Native) (2)	4	<0.01
Tohono O'Odham (1)	1	<0.01
Tsimshian (Alaska Native) (1)	1	<0.01
Ute (1)	4	<0.01
Yakama (0)	0	<0.01
Yaqui (1)	6	<0.01
Yuman (1)	4	<0.01
Yup'ik (Alaska Native) (1)	2	<0.01
Asian (42,352)	47,979	5.22
Not Hispanic (41,991)	47,051	5.12
Hispanic (361)	928	0.10
Bangladeshi (66)	87	0.01
Bhutanese (224)	277	0.03
Burmese (526)	568	0.06
Cambodian (1,137)	1,331	0.14
Chinese, ex. Taiwanese (5,041)	5,988	0.65
Filipino (1,971)	2,965	0.32
Hmong (1,447)	1,537	0.17
Indian (14,985)	16,069	1.75
Indonesian (155)	207	0.02
Japanese (865)	1,460	0.16
Korean (3,201)	3,941	0.43
Laotian (1,398)	1,605	0.17
Malaysian (55)	96	0.01
Nepalese (120)	173	0.02
Pakistani (665)	758	0.08
Sri Lankan (70)	90	0.01
Taiwanese (220)	256	0.03
Thai (323)	552	0.06
Vietnamese (8,143)	8,878	0.97
Hawaii Native/Pacific Islander (668)	1,539	0.17
Not Hispanic (518)	1,178	0.13
Hispanic (150)	361	0.04
Fijian (6)	13	<0.01
Guamanian/Chamorro (208)	293	0.03
Marshallese (3)	5	<0.01
Native Hawaiian (110)	314	0.03
Samoan (66)	161	0.02
Tongan (19)	34	<0.01
White (508,946)	526,746	57.28
Not Hispanic (465,372)	478,016	51.98
Hispanic (43,574)	48,730	5.30

Notes: † The Census 2010 population figure is used to calculate the percentages in the Hispanic Origin and Race categories. Ancestry percentages are based on the 2006-2010 American Community Survey population (not shown); ‡ Numbers in parentheses indicate the number of people reporting a single ancestry; * Numbers in parentheses indicate the number of persons reporting this race alone, not in combination with any other race; Please refer to the Explanation of Data for more information.

Moore County

Population: 88,247

Ancestry	Population	%
Afghan (0)	0	<0.01
African, Sub-Saharan (178)	198	0.23
African (125)	145	0.17
Cape Verdean (0)	0	<0.01
Ethiopian (0)	0	<0.01
Ghanaian (0)	0	<0.01
Kenyan (0)	0	<0.01
Liberian (0)	0	<0.01
Nigerian (53)	53	0.06
Senegalese (0)	0	<0.01
Sierra Leonean (0)	0	<0.01
Somalian (0)	0	<0.01
South African (0)	0	<0.01
Sudanese (0)	0	<0.01
Ugandan (0)	0	<0.01
Zimbabwean (0)	0	<0.01
Other Sub-Saharan African (0)	0	<0.01
Albanian (0)	0	<0.01
Alsatian (0)	0	<0.01
American (10,485)	10,485	12.20
Arab (114)	410	0.48
Arab (0)	0	<0.01
Egyptian (0)	12	0.01
Iraqi (0)	0	<0.01
Jordanian (0)	0	<0.01
Lebanese (107)	391	0.46
Moroccan (0)	0	<0.01
Palestinian (0)	0	<0.01
Syrian (7)	7	0.01
Other Arab (0)	0	<0.01
Armenian (13)	57	0.07
Assyrian/Chaldean/Syriac (0)	0	<0.01
Australian (28)	34	0.04
Austrian (29)	139	0.16
Basque (0)	0	<0.01
Belgian (68)	113	0.13
Brazilian (65)	65	0.08
British (300)	415	0.48
Bulgarian (0)	0	<0.01
Cajun (0)	0	<0.01
Canadian (169)	273	0.32
Carpatho Rusyn (0)	0	<0.01
Celtic (0)	23	0.03
Croatian (19)	66	0.08
Cypriot (0)	0	<0.01
Czech (72)	210	0.24
Czechoslovakian (3)	117	0.14
Danish (54)	291	0.34
Dutch (579)	1,549	1.80
Eastern European (61)	69	0.08
English (9,215)	15,538	18.09
Estonian (0)	0	<0.01
European (537)	648	0.75
Finnish (24)	31	0.04
French, ex. Basque (343)	2,475	2.88
French Canadian (149)	319	0.37
German (3,842)	10,882	12.67
German Russian (0)	0	<0.01
Greek (117)	258	0.30
Guyanese (0)	0	<0.01
Hungarian (145)	301	0.35
Icelander (28)	28	0.03
Iranian (0)	8	0.01
Irish (3,697)	8,738	10.17
Israeli (0)	0	<0.01
Italian (1,503)	3,111	3.62
Latvian (0)	0	<0.01
Lithuanian (80)	269	0.31
Luxemburger (0)	0	<0.01
Macedonian (0)	12	0.01
Maltese (4)	56	0.07
New Zealander (0)	0	<0.01
Northern European (31)	31	0.04
Norwegian (133)	504	0.59
Pennsylvania German (18)	56	0.07

Ancestry (cont.)	Population	%
Polish (622)	1,781	2.07
Portuguese (54)	114	0.13
Romanian (17)	30	0.03
Russian (90)	382	0.44
Scandinavian (13)	29	0.03
Scotch-Irish (2,314)	3,845	4.48
Scottish (2,721)	4,907	5.71
Serbian (0)	0	<0.01
Slavic (15)	79	0.09
Slovak (22)	160	0.19
Slovene (17)	60	0.07
Soviet Union (0)	0	<0.01
Swedish (149)	828	0.96
Swiss (89)	282	0.33
Turkish (11)	11	0.01
Ukrainian (33)	116	0.14
Welsh (310)	1,024	1.19
West Indian, ex. Hispanic (68)	123	0.14
Bahamian (0)	0	<0.01
Barbadian (0)	0	<0.01
Belizean (0)	0	<0.01
Bermudan (0)	0	<0.01
British West Indian (0)	0	<0.01
Dutch West Indian (0)	0	<0.01
Haitian (0)	0	<0.01
Jamaican (68)	110	0.13
Trinidadian/Tobagonian (0)	0	<0.01
U.S. Virgin Islander (0)	0	<0.01
West Indian (0)	13	0.02
Other West Indian (0)	0	<0.01
Yugoslavian (14)	30	0.03

Hispanic Origin	Population	%
Hispanic or Latino (of any race)	5,261	5.96
Central American, ex. Mexican	223	0.25
Costa Rican	10	0.01
Guatemalan	106	0.12
Honduran	16	0.02
Nicaraguan	8	0.01
Panamanian	36	0.04
Salvadoran	43	0.05
Other Central American	4	<0.01
Cuban	79	0.09
Dominican Republic	36	0.04
Mexican	4,027	4.56
Puerto Rican	384	0.44
South American	146	0.17
Argentinean	25	0.03
Bolivian	4	<0.01
Chilean	11	0.01
Colombian	63	0.07
Ecuadorian	9	0.01
Paraguayan	1	<0.01
Peruvian	27	0.03
Uruguayan	0	<0.01
Venezuelan	6	0.01
Other South American	0	<0.01
Other Hispanic or Latino	366	0.41

Race*	Population	%
African-American/Black (11,839)	12,518	14.19
Not Hispanic (11,727)	12,339	13.98
Hispanic (112)	179	0.20
American Indian/Alaska Native (732)	1,261	1.43
Not Hispanic (689)	1,166	1.32
Hispanic (43)	95	0.11
Alaska Athabascan (Ala. Nat.) (0)	0	<0.01
Aleut (Alaska Native) (0)	0	<0.01
Apache (1)	2	<0.01
Arapaho (0)	5	0.01
Blackfeet (2)	9	0.01
Canadian/French Am. Ind. (0)	0	<0.01
Central American Ind. (0)	0	<0.01
Cherokee (87)	246	0.28
Cheyenne (0)	2	<0.01
Chickasaw (0)	0	<0.01
Chippewa (7)	8	0.01
Choctaw (2)	3	<0.01
Colville (0)	0	<0.01

Race* (cont.)	Population	%
Comanche (0)	1	<0.01
Cree (0)	0	<0.01
Creek (0)	11	0.01
Crow (1)	6	0.01
Delaware (0)	1	<0.01
Hopi (0)	0	<0.01
Houma (11)	11	0.01
Inupiat (Alaska Native) (2)	3	<0.01
Iroquois (11)	22	0.02
Kiowa (0)	0	<0.01
Lumbee (326)	423	0.48
Menominee (0)	0	<0.01
Mexican American Ind. (7)	12	0.01
Navajo (3)	4	<0.01
Osage (3)	3	<0.01
Ottawa (0)	0	<0.01
Paiute (0)	0	<0.01
Pima (0)	0	<0.01
Potawatomi (1)	1	<0.01
Pueblo (3)	5	0.01
Puget Sound Salish (0)	0	<0.01
Seminole (1)	1	<0.01
Shoshone (0)	0	<0.01
Sioux (7)	10	0.01
South American Ind. (1)	5	0.01
Spanish American Ind. (0)	0	<0.01
Tlingit-Haida (Alaska Native) (1)	3	<0.01
Tohono O'Odham (0)	0	<0.01
Tsimshian (Alaska Native) (0)	0	<0.01
Ute (0)	0	<0.01
Yakama (0)	0	<0.01
Yaqui (1)	1	<0.01
Yuman (0)	1	<0.01
Yup'ik (Alaska Native) (0)	0	<0.01
Asian (754)	1,062	1.20
Not Hispanic (736)	1,029	1.17
Hispanic (18)	33	0.04
Bangladeshi (0)	0	<0.01
Bhutanese (0)	0	<0.01
Burmese (9)	9	0.01
Cambodian (10)	13	0.01
Chinese, ex. Taiwanese (118)	144	0.16
Filipino (143)	227	0.26
Hmong (31)	33	0.04
Indian (95)	122	0.14
Indonesian (1)	1	<0.01
Japanese (64)	130	0.15
Korean (106)	162	0.18
Laotian (42)	59	0.07
Malaysian (0)	0	<0.01
Nepalese (0)	0	<0.01
Pakistani (3)	3	<0.01
Sri Lankan (1)	1	<0.01
Taiwanese (2)	2	<0.01
Thai (31)	55	0.06
Vietnamese (70)	84	0.10
Hawaii Native/Pacific Islander (64)	120	0.14
Not Hispanic (25)	70	0.08
Hispanic (39)	50	0.06
Fijian (0)	0	<0.01
Guamanian/Chamorro (44)	66	0.07
Marshallese (0)	0	<0.01
Native Hawaiian (8)	29	0.03
Samoan (3)	6	0.01
Tongan (0)	0	<0.01
White (70,913)	72,223	81.84
Not Hispanic (68,487)	69,546	78.81
Hispanic (2,426)	2,677	3.03

*Notes: † The Census 2010 population figure is used to calculate the percentages in the Hispanic Origin and Race categories. Ancestry percentages are based on the 2006-2010 American Community Survey population (not shown); ‡ Numbers in parentheses indicate the number of people reporting a single ancestry; * Numbers in parentheses indicate the number of persons reporting this race alone, not in combination with any other race; Please refer to the Explanation of Data for more information.*

Nash County

Population: 95,840

Ancestry	Population	%
Afghan (0)	0	<0.01
African, Sub-Saharan (1,092)	1,295	1.37
African (1,072)	1,275	1.35
Cape Verdean (0)	0	<0.01
Ethiopian (13)	13	0.01
Ghanaian (7)	7	0.01
Kenyan (0)	0	<0.01
Liberian (0)	0	<0.01
Nigerian (0)	0	<0.01
Senegalese (0)	0	<0.01
Sierra Leonean (0)	0	<0.01
Somalian (0)	0	<0.01
South African (0)	0	<0.01
Sudanese (0)	0	<0.01
Ugandan (0)	0	<0.01
Zimbabwean (0)	0	<0.01
Other Sub-Saharan African (0)	0	<0.01
Albanian (0)	0	<0.01
Alsatian (0)	0	<0.01
American (10,912)	10,912	11.56
Arab (586)	599	0.63
Arab (74)	74	0.08
Egyptian (0)	0	<0.01
Iraqi (0)	0	<0.01
Jordanian (47)	47	0.05
Lebanese (107)	107	0.11
Moroccan (14)	14	0.01
Palestinian (234)	234	0.25
Syrian (0)	13	0.01
Other Arab (110)	110	0.12
Armenian (0)	0	<0.01
Assyrian/Chaldean/Syriac (0)	0	<0.01
Australian (0)	0	<0.01
Austrian (0)	67	0.07
Basque (0)	0	<0.01
Belgian (25)	88	0.09
Brazilian (0)	0	<0.01
British (233)	309	0.33
Bulgarian (0)	0	<0.01
Cajun (0)	0	<0.01
Canadian (58)	64	0.07
Carpatho Rusyn (0)	0	<0.01
Celtic (0)	0	<0.01
Croatian (15)	25	0.03
Cypriot (0)	0	<0.01
Czech (0)	89	0.09
Czechoslovakian (0)	0	<0.01
Danish (13)	36	0.04
Dutch (96)	675	0.72
Eastern European (13)	30	0.03
English (6,821)	10,566	11.19
Estonian (0)	0	<0.01
European (525)	583	0.62
Finnish (18)	18	0.02
French, ex. Basque (328)	1,276	1.35
French Canadian (258)	434	0.46
German (1,700)	6,352	6.73
German Russian (0)	47	0.05
Greek (20)	20	0.02
Guyanese (0)	0	<0.01
Hungarian (82)	213	0.23
Icelander (0)	0	<0.01
Iranian (0)	0	<0.01
Irish (2,610)	7,813	8.28
Israeli (0)	0	<0.01
Italian (616)	1,226	1.30
Latvian (0)	4	<0.01
Lithuanian (18)	48	0.05
Luxemburger (0)	0	<0.01
Macedonian (0)	0	<0.01
Maltese (0)	0	<0.01
New Zealander (0)	0	<0.01
Northern European (9)	28	0.03
Norwegian (85)	248	0.26
Pennsylvania German (0)	16	0.02

Ancestry	Population	%
Polish (215)	646	0.68
Portuguese (45)	76	0.08
Romanian (0)	69	0.07
Russian (60)	151	0.16
Scandinavian (0)	3	<0.01
Scotch-Irish (1,498)	1,952	2.07
Scottish (614)	1,210	1.28
Serbian (21)	21	0.02
Slavic (0)	16	0.02
Slovak (78)	108	0.11
Slovene (0)	0	<0.01
Soviet Union (0)	0	<0.01
Swedish (90)	315	0.33
Swiss (21)	73	0.08
Turkish (0)	0	<0.01
Ukrainian (21)	45	0.05
Welsh (68)	288	0.31
West Indian, ex. Hispanic (101)	128	0.14
Bahamian (18)	18	0.02
Barbadian (0)	27	0.03
Belizean (0)	0	<0.01
Bermudan (0)	0	<0.01
British West Indian (0)	0	<0.01
Dutch West Indian (0)	0	<0.01
Haitian (13)	13	0.01
Jamaican (70)	70	0.07
Trinidadian/Tobagonian (0)	0	<0.01
U.S. Virgin Islander (0)	0	<0.01
West Indian (0)	0	<0.01
Other West Indian (0)	0	<0.01
Yugoslavian (0)	27	0.03

Hispanic Origin	Population	%
Hispanic or Latino (of any race)	6,015	6.28
Central American, ex. Mexican	328	0.34
Costa Rican	10	0.01
Guatemalan	90	0.09
Honduran	94	0.10
Nicaraguan	17	0.02
Panamanian	23	0.02
Salvadoran	93	0.10
Other Central American	1	<0.01
Cuban	55	0.06
Dominican Republic	46	0.05
Mexican	4,701	4.91
Puerto Rican	408	0.43
South American	144	0.15
Argentinean	18	0.02
Bolivian	4	<0.01
Chilean	6	0.01
Colombian	47	0.05
Ecuadorian	20	0.02
Paraguayan	2	<0.01
Peruvian	36	0.04
Uruguayan	0	<0.01
Venezuelan	11	0.01
Other South American	0	<0.01
Other Hispanic or Latino	333	0.35

Race*	Population	%
African-American/Black (35,650)	36,621	38.21
Not Hispanic (35,449)	36,275	37.85
Hispanic (201)	346	0.36
American Indian/Alaska Native (657)	1,238	1.29
Not Hispanic (567)	1,083	1.13
Hispanic (90)	155	0.16
Alaska Athabascan (Ala. Nat.) (0)	0	<0.01
Aleut (Alaska Native) (3)	3	<0.01
Apache (5)	16	0.02
Arapaho (0)	0	<0.01
Blackfeet (6)	29	0.03
Canadian/French Am. Ind. (0)	0	<0.01
Central American Ind. (0)	6	0.01
Cherokee (34)	136	0.14
Cheyenne (3)	5	0.01
Chickasaw (0)	0	<0.01
Chippewa (3)	4	<0.01
Choctaw (2)	5	0.01
Colville (0)	0	<0.01

	Population	%
Comanche (0)	1	<0.01
Cree (0)	3	<0.01
Creek (0)	0	<0.01
Crow (0)	3	<0.01
Delaware (0)	0	<0.01
Hopi (0)	0	<0.01
Houma (0)	0	<0.01
Inupiat (Alaska Native) (0)	0	<0.01
Iroquois (3)	7	0.01
Kiowa (0)	0	<0.01
Lumbee (56)	71	0.07
Menominee (0)	0	<0.01
Mexican American Ind. (52)	63	0.07
Navajo (1)	3	<0.01
Osage (0)	0	<0.01
Ottawa (0)	0	<0.01
Paiute (0)	0	<0.01
Pima (0)	0	<0.01
Potawatomi (0)	1	<0.01
Pueblo (0)	0	<0.01
Puget Sound Salish (0)	1	<0.01
Seminole (0)	1	<0.01
Shoshone (0)	0	<0.01
Sioux (3)	6	0.01
South American Ind. (0)	1	<0.01
Spanish American Ind. (1)	2	<0.01
Tlingit-Haida (Alaska Native) (0)	0	<0.01
Tohono O'Odham (0)	1	<0.01
Tsimshian (Alaska Native) (0)	0	<0.01
Ute (1)	2	<0.01
Yakama (0)	0	<0.01
Yaqui (0)	0	<0.01
Yuman (0)	0	<0.01
Yup'ik (Alaska Native) (0)	0	<0.01
Asian (747)	954	1.00
Not Hispanic (713)	886	0.92
Hispanic (34)	68	0.07
Bangladeshi (15)	15	0.02
Bhutanese (0)	0	<0.01
Burmese (0)	0	<0.01
Cambodian (0)	0	<0.01
Chinese, ex. Taiwanese (122)	151	0.16
Filipino (119)	173	0.18
Hmong (9)	9	0.01
Indian (218)	242	0.25
Indonesian (1)	2	<0.01
Japanese (16)	46	0.05
Korean (52)	76	0.08
Laotian (2)	2	<0.01
Malaysian (3)	8	0.01
Nepalese (0)	0	<0.01
Pakistani (28)	34	0.04
Sri Lankan (2)	2	<0.01
Taiwanese (0)	0	<0.01
Thai (6)	6	0.01
Vietnamese (111)	119	0.12
Hawaii Native/Pacific Islander (19)	73	0.08
Not Hispanic (17)	53	0.06
Hispanic (2)	20	0.02
Fijian (0)	0	<0.01
Guamanian/Chamorro (4)	16	0.02
Marshallese (0)	0	<0.01
Native Hawaiian (8)	39	0.04
Samoan (5)	13	0.01
Tongan (0)	0	<0.01
White (53,531)	54,685	57.06
Not Hispanic (51,770)	52,668	54.95
Hispanic (1,761)	2,017	2.10

Notes: † The Census 2010 population figure is used to calculate the percentages in the Hispanic Origin and Race categories. Ancestry percentages are based on the 2006-2010 American Community Survey population (not shown); ‡ Numbers in parentheses indicate the number of people reporting a single ancestry; * Numbers in parentheses indicate the number of persons reporting this race alone, not in combination with any other race; Please refer to the Explanation of Data for more information.

New Hanover County
Population: 202,667

Ancestry	Population	%
Afghan (0)	0	<0.01
African, Sub-Saharan (326)	594	0.30
African (158)	426	0.22
Cape Verdean (0)	0	<0.01
Ethiopian (0)	0	<0.01
Ghanaian (0)	0	<0.01
Kenyan (0)	0	<0.01
Liberian (0)	0	<0.01
Nigerian (96)	96	0.05
Senegalese (0)	0	<0.01
Sierra Leonean (0)	0	<0.01
Somalian (0)	0	<0.01
South African (19)	19	0.01
Sudanese (0)	0	<0.01
Ugandan (0)	0	<0.01
Zimbabwean (0)	0	<0.01
Other Sub-Saharan African (53)	53	0.03
Albanian (0)	0	<0.01
Alsatian (0)	0	<0.01
American (29,771)	29,771	15.09
Arab (339)	471	0.24
Arab (94)	94	0.05
Egyptian (80)	120	0.06
Iraqi (0)	0	<0.01
Jordanian (0)	0	<0.01
Lebanese (138)	201	0.10
Moroccan (0)	0	<0.01
Palestinian (0)	0	<0.01
Syrian (0)	14	0.01
Other Arab (27)	42	0.02
Armenian (34)	97	0.05
Assyrian/Chaldean/Syriac (0)	0	<0.01
Australian (141)	181	0.09
Austrian (65)	400	0.20
Basque (0)	0	<0.01
Belgian (23)	75	0.04
Brazilian (113)	124	0.06
British (887)	1,295	0.66
Bulgarian (58)	66	0.03
Cajun (0)	0	<0.01
Canadian (220)	393	0.20
Carpatho Rusyn (0)	0	<0.01
Celtic (38)	51	0.03
Croatian (47)	278	0.14
Cypriot (0)	0	<0.01
Czech (399)	638	0.32
Czechoslovakian (137)	244	0.12
Danish (115)	624	0.32
Dutch (545)	2,439	1.24
Eastern European (93)	133	0.07
English (11,282)	27,634	14.01
Estonian (0)	0	<0.01
European (1,711)	1,895	0.96
Finnish (70)	186	0.09
French, ex. Basque (992)	5,860	2.97
French Canadian (400)	942	0.48
German (7,390)	26,107	13.23
German Russian (0)	18	0.01
Greek (661)	1,213	0.61
Guyanese (0)	0	<0.01
Hungarian (190)	720	0.36
Icelander (0)	11	0.01
Iranian (174)	174	0.09
Irish (8,730)	25,401	12.88
Israeli (25)	25	0.01
Italian (4,380)	11,143	5.65
Latvian (17)	51	0.03
Lithuanian (159)	477	0.24
Luxemburger (0)	0	<0.01
Macedonian (0)	0	<0.01
Maltese (14)	14	0.01
New Zealander (34)	64	0.03
Northern European (81)	81	0.04
Norwegian (399)	1,308	0.66
Pennsylvania German (53)	97	0.05
Polish (1,356)	4,302	2.18
Portuguese (189)	401	0.20
Romanian (134)	283	0.14
Russian (458)	1,185	0.60
Scandinavian (87)	257	0.13
Scotch-Irish (5,057)	9,848	4.99
Scottish (2,589)	6,872	3.48
Serbian (0)	0	<0.01
Slavic (46)	222	0.11
Slovak (106)	480	0.24
Slovene (57)	79	0.04
Soviet Union (0)	0	<0.01
Swedish (431)	1,698	0.86
Swiss (68)	329	0.17
Turkish (130)	224	0.11
Ukrainian (262)	697	0.35
Welsh (355)	1,617	0.82
West Indian, ex. Hispanic (237)	364	0.18
Bahamian (0)	0	<0.01
Barbadian (38)	38	0.02
Belizean (0)	0	<0.01
Bermudan (0)	0	<0.01
British West Indian (0)	0	<0.01
Dutch West Indian (0)	0	<0.01
Haitian (18)	43	0.02
Jamaican (138)	148	0.08
Trinidadian/Tobagonian (14)	14	0.01
U.S. Virgin Islander (0)	0	<0.01
West Indian (29)	121	0.06
Other West Indian (0)	0	<0.01
Yugoslavian (103)	245	0.12

Hispanic Origin	Population	%
Hispanic or Latino (of any race)	10,716	5.29
Central American, ex. Mexican	1,310	0.65
Costa Rican	37	0.02
Guatemalan	294	0.15
Honduran	544	0.27
Nicaraguan	36	0.02
Panamanian	110	0.05
Salvadoran	279	0.14
Other Central American	10	<0.01
Cuban	317	0.16
Dominican Republic	160	0.08
Mexican	5,932	2.93
Puerto Rican	1,312	0.65
South American	698	0.34
Argentinean	84	0.04
Bolivian	26	0.01
Chilean	73	0.04
Colombian	243	0.12
Ecuadorian	86	0.04
Paraguayan	4	<0.01
Peruvian	112	0.06
Uruguayan	16	0.01
Venezuelan	50	0.02
Other South American	4	<0.01
Other Hispanic or Latino	987	0.49

Race*	Population	%
African-American/Black (29,907)	31,747	15.66
Not Hispanic (29,469)	31,067	15.33
Hispanic (438)	680	0.34
American Indian/Alaska Native (1,005)	2,214	1.09
Not Hispanic (798)	1,848	0.91
Hispanic (207)	366	0.18
Alaska Athabascan (Ala. Nat.) (0)	0	<0.01
Aleut (Alaska Native) (0)	1	<0.01
Apache (7)	22	0.01
Arapaho (0)	2	<0.01
Blackfeet (7)	41	0.02
Canadian/French Am. Ind. (3)	5	<0.01
Central American Ind. (15)	30	0.01
Cherokee (122)	490	0.24
Cheyenne (1)	3	<0.01
Chickasaw (6)	10	<0.01
Chippewa (22)	26	0.01
Choctaw (5)	16	0.01
Colville (0)	0	<0.01

	Population	%
Comanche (4)	4	<0.01
Cree (2)	3	<0.01
Creek (7)	14	0.01
Crow (1)	3	<0.01
Delaware (6)	8	<0.01
Hopi (1)	2	<0.01
Houma (0)	0	<0.01
Inupiat (Alaska Native) (1)	1	<0.01
Iroquois (12)	38	0.02
Kiowa (0)	0	<0.01
Lumbee (174)	244	0.12
Menominee (3)	3	<0.01
Mexican American Ind. (54)	77	0.04
Navajo (3)	13	0.01
Osage (4)	6	<0.01
Ottawa (2)	6	<0.01
Paiute (2)	2	<0.01
Pima (1)	1	<0.01
Potawatomi (0)	0	<0.01
Pueblo (2)	3	<0.01
Puget Sound Salish (2)	2	<0.01
Seminole (6)	20	0.01
Shoshone (0)	0	<0.01
Sioux (9)	28	0.01
South American Ind. (6)	11	0.01
Spanish American Ind. (2)	2	<0.01
Tlingit-Haida (Alaska Native) (0)	0	<0.01
Tohono O'Odham (0)	2	<0.01
Tsimshian (Alaska Native) (0)	0	<0.01
Ute (0)	0	<0.01
Yakama (0)	0	<0.01
Yaqui (0)	1	<0.01
Yuman (0)	1	<0.01
Yup'ik (Alaska Native) (0)	0	<0.01
Asian (2,410)	3,443	1.70
Not Hispanic (2,380)	3,319	1.64
Hispanic (30)	124	0.06
Bangladeshi (15)	15	0.01
Bhutanese (0)	0	<0.01
Burmese (14)	16	0.01
Cambodian (5)	12	0.01
Chinese, ex. Taiwanese (565)	707	0.35
Filipino (288)	565	0.28
Hmong (1)	1	<0.01
Indian (410)	499	0.25
Indonesian (18)	33	0.02
Japanese (126)	290	0.14
Korean (335)	473	0.23
Laotian (20)	23	0.01
Malaysian (3)	7	<0.01
Nepalese (4)	5	<0.01
Pakistani (16)	23	0.01
Sri Lankan (5)	5	<0.01
Taiwanese (20)	24	0.01
Thai (56)	95	0.05
Vietnamese (379)	438	0.22
Hawaii Native/Pacific Islander (130)	364	0.18
Not Hispanic (108)	310	0.15
Hispanic (22)	54	0.03
Fijian (0)	0	<0.01
Guamanian/Chamorro (34)	58	0.03
Marshallese (0)	0	<0.01
Native Hawaiian (43)	127	0.06
Samoan (22)	56	0.03
Tongan (1)	1	<0.01
White (160,298)	163,708	80.78
Not Hispanic (155,631)	158,395	78.16
Hispanic (4,667)	5,313	2.62

Onslow County
Population: 177,772

Ancestry	Population	%
Afghan (5)	5	<0.01
African, Sub-Saharan (891)	1,785	1.05
African (879)	1,737	1.03
Cape Verdean (0)	12	0.01
Ethiopian (0)	0	<0.01
Ghanaian (0)	0	<0.01
Kenyan (0)	0	<0.01
Liberian (0)	0	<0.01
Nigerian (0)	14	0.01
Senegalese (12)	12	0.01
Sierra Leonean (0)	0	<0.01
Somalian (0)	0	<0.01
South African (0)	10	0.01
Sudanese (0)	0	<0.01
Ugandan (0)	0	<0.01
Zimbabwean (0)	0	<0.01
Other Sub-Saharan African (0)	0	<0.01
Albanian (0)	0	<0.01
Alsatian (0)	0	<0.01
American (10,314)	10,314	6.10
Arab (225)	550	0.33
Arab (0)	15	0.01
Egyptian (32)	32	0.02
Iraqi (46)	46	0.03
Jordanian (0)	0	<0.01
Lebanese (86)	306	0.18
Moroccan (0)	0	<0.01
Palestinian (19)	19	0.01
Syrian (24)	84	0.05
Other Arab (18)	48	0.03
Armenian (16)	16	0.01
Assyrian/Chaldean/Syriac (0)	0	<0.01
Australian (0)	21	0.01
Austrian (42)	100	0.06
Basque (0)	0	<0.01
Belgian (19)	71	0.04
Brazilian (30)	66	0.04
British (530)	898	0.53
Bulgarian (0)	0	<0.01
Cajun (0)	58	0.03
Canadian (238)	618	0.37
Carpatho Rusyn (11)	11	0.01
Celtic (0)	26	0.02
Croatian (14)	83	0.05
Cypriot (19)	19	0.01
Czech (82)	314	0.19
Czechoslovakian (31)	102	0.06
Danish (154)	413	0.24
Dutch (427)	2,024	1.20
Eastern European (65)	65	0.04
English (5,824)	15,703	9.28
Estonian (0)	0	<0.01
European (1,334)	1,491	0.88
Finnish (24)	108	0.06
French, ex. Basque (1,136)	5,843	3.45
French Canadian (486)	1,226	0.72
German (8,292)	28,515	16.85
German Russian (0)	0	<0.01
Greek (233)	410	0.24
Guyanese (67)	67	0.04
Hungarian (152)	716	0.42
Icelander (8)	17	0.01
Iranian (0)	0	<0.01
Irish (8,677)	27,744	16.40
Israeli (20)	36	0.02
Italian (3,644)	9,899	5.85
Latvian (0)	0	<0.01
Lithuanian (28)	99	0.06
Luxemburger (10)	22	0.01
Macedonian (0)	0	<0.01
Maltese (7)	10	0.01
New Zealander (0)	23	0.01
Northern European (33)	33	0.02
Norwegian (537)	1,723	1.02
Pennsylvania German (76)	132	0.08

	Population	%
Polish (1,435)	4,786	2.83
Portuguese (250)	445	0.26
Romanian (91)	147	0.09
Russian (237)	922	0.54
Scandinavian (30)	259	0.15
Scotch-Irish (2,273)	4,333	2.56
Scottish (1,436)	4,164	2.46
Serbian (52)	95	0.06
Slavic (12)	100	0.06
Slovak (141)	241	0.14
Slovene (14)	14	0.01
Soviet Union (0)	0	<0.01
Swedish (396)	1,406	0.83
Swiss (19)	252	0.15
Turkish (0)	0	<0.01
Ukrainian (64)	218	0.13
Welsh (161)	895	0.53
West Indian, ex. Hispanic (700)	1,321	0.78
Bahamian (9)	9	0.01
Barbadian (13)	13	0.01
Belizean (0)	15	0.01
Bermudan (0)	0	<0.01
British West Indian (0)	0	<0.01
Dutch West Indian (0)	13	0.01
Haitian (115)	142	0.08
Jamaican (306)	635	0.38
Trinidadian/Tobagonian (86)	103	0.06
U.S. Virgin Islander (0)	0	<0.01
West Indian (171)	391	0.23
Other West Indian (0)	0	<0.01
Yugoslavian (0)	99	0.06

Hispanic Origin	Population	%
Hispanic or Latino (of any race)	17,896	10.07
Central American, ex. Mexican	1,293	0.73
Costa Rican	80	0.05
Guatemalan	207	0.12
Honduran	236	0.13
Nicaraguan	140	0.08
Panamanian	286	0.16
Salvadoran	335	0.19
Other Central American	9	0.01
Cuban	698	0.39
Dominican Republic	653	0.37
Mexican	7,924	4.46
Puerto Rican	4,727	2.66
South American	1,121	0.63
Argentinean	40	0.02
Bolivian	55	0.03
Chilean	79	0.04
Colombian	485	0.27
Ecuadorian	161	0.09
Paraguayan	8	<0.01
Peruvian	194	0.11
Uruguayan	12	0.01
Venezuelan	68	0.04
Other South American	19	0.01
Other Hispanic or Latino	1,480	0.83

Race*	Population	%
African-American/Black (27,672)	31,426	17.68
Not Hispanic (26,577)	29,643	16.67
Hispanic (1,095)	1,783	1.00
American Indian/Alaska Native (1,238)	2,897	1.63
Not Hispanic (1,013)	2,396	1.35
Hispanic (225)	501	0.28
Alaska Athabascan (Ala. Nat.) (2)	2	<0.01
Aleut (Alaska Native) (2)	3	<0.01
Apache (15)	42	0.02
Arapaho (2)	3	<0.01
Blackfeet (12)	82	0.05
Canadian/French Am. Ind. (8)	20	0.01
Central American Ind. (4)	10	0.01
Cherokee (184)	649	0.37
Cheyenne (3)	9	0.01
Chickasaw (4)	9	0.01
Chippewa (33)	69	0.04
Choctaw (19)	57	0.03
Colville (1)	2	<0.01

	Population	%
Comanche (3)	4	<0.01
Cree (2)	4	<0.01
Creek (9)	27	0.02
Crow (1)	13	0.01
Delaware (3)	12	0.01
Hopi (2)	4	<0.01
Houma (2)	4	<0.01
Inupiat (Alaska Native) (2)	8	<0.01
Iroquois (24)	55	0.03
Kiowa (6)	7	<0.01
Lumbee (172)	252	0.14
Menominee (1)	1	<0.01
Mexican American Ind. (41)	54	0.03
Navajo (67)	89	0.05
Osage (0)	0	<0.01
Ottawa (1)	8	<0.01
Paiute (2)	2	<0.01
Pima (2)	6	<0.01
Potawatomi (13)	22	0.01
Pueblo (5)	16	0.01
Puget Sound Salish (4)	6	<0.01
Seminole (4)	22	0.01
Shoshone (4)	4	<0.01
Sioux (32)	66	0.04
South American Ind. (2)	8	<0.01
Spanish American Ind. (3)	3	<0.01
Tlingit-Haida (Alaska Native) (4)	4	<0.01
Tohono O'Odham (2)	2	<0.01
Tsimshian (Alaska Native) (0)	0	<0.01
Ute (0)	0	<0.01
Yakama (2)	6	<0.01
Yaqui (2)	4	<0.01
Yuman (2)	2	<0.01
Yup'ik (Alaska Native) (1)	1	<0.01
Asian (3,355)	5,757	3.24
Not Hispanic (3,163)	5,232	2.94
Hispanic (192)	525	0.30
Bangladeshi (1)	2	<0.01
Bhutanese (0)	0	<0.01
Burmese (3)	5	<0.01
Cambodian (38)	54	0.03
Chinese, ex. Taiwanese (286)	554	0.31
Filipino (1,366)	2,460	1.38
Hmong (40)	43	0.02
Indian (182)	334	0.19
Indonesian (13)	22	0.01
Japanese (542)	1,166	0.66
Korean (243)	441	0.25
Laotian (42)	59	0.03
Malaysian (2)	5	<0.01
Nepalese (0)	0	<0.01
Pakistani (16)	20	0.01
Sri Lankan (1)	1	<0.01
Taiwanese (13)	17	0.01
Thai (124)	217	0.12
Vietnamese (246)	343	0.19
Hawaii Native/Pacific Islander (487)	1,031	0.58
Not Hispanic (438)	882	0.50
Hispanic (49)	149	0.08
Fijian (2)	3	<0.01
Guamanian/Chamorro (136)	219	0.12
Marshallese (1)	5	<0.01
Native Hawaiian (139)	386	0.22
Samoan (87)	164	0.09
Tongan (3)	8	<0.01
White (131,590)	138,114	77.69
Not Hispanic (122,558)	127,597	71.78
Hispanic (9,032)	10,517	5.92

Notes: † The Census 2010 population figure is used to calculate the percentages in the Hispanic Origin and Race categories. Ancestry percentages are based on the 2006-2010 American Community Survey population (not shown); ‡ Numbers in parentheses indicate the number of people reporting a single ancestry; * Numbers in parentheses indicate the number of persons reporting this race alone, not in combination with any other race; Please refer to the Explanation of Data for more information.

Orange County

Population: 133,801

Ancestry	Population	%
Afghan (0)	0	<0.01
African, Sub-Saharan (962)	1,145	0.88
African (538)	660	0.51
Cape Verdean (0)	0	<0.01
Ethiopian (20)	20	0.02
Ghanaian (26)	26	0.02
Kenyan (44)	44	0.03
Liberian (5)	5	<0.01
Nigerian (148)	203	0.16
Senegalese (0)	0	<0.01
Sierra Leonean (0)	0	<0.01
Somalian (0)	0	<0.01
South African (35)	41	0.03
Sudanese (0)	0	<0.01
Ugandan (0)	0	<0.01
Zimbabwean (39)	39	0.03
Other Sub-Saharan African (107)	107	0.08
Albanian (7)	26	0.02
Alsatian (0)	14	0.01
American (6,349)	6,349	4.90
Arab (398)	658	0.51
Arab (63)	96	0.07
Egyptian (23)	60	0.05
Iraqi (0)	20	0.02
Jordanian (2)	2	<0.01
Lebanese (275)	334	0.26
Moroccan (26)	26	0.02
Palestinian (0)	14	0.01
Syrian (0)	60	0.05
Other Arab (9)	46	0.04
Armenian (33)	98	0.08
Assyrian/Chaldean/Syriac (0)	0	<0.01
Australian (64)	74	0.06
Austrian (84)	384	0.30
Basque (0)	0	<0.01
Belgian (148)	247	0.19
Brazilian (12)	12	0.01
British (848)	1,725	1.33
Bulgarian (118)	194	0.15
Cajun (17)	17	0.01
Canadian (282)	511	0.39
Carpatho Rusyn (0)	0	<0.01
Celtic (76)	112	0.09
Croatian (31)	113	0.09
Cypriot (10)	10	0.01
Czech (233)	730	0.56
Czechoslovakian (28)	191	0.15
Danish (88)	545	0.42
Dutch (425)	2,171	1.68
Eastern European (281)	326	0.25
English (7,693)	21,730	16.77
Estonian (28)	48	0.04
European (2,775)	3,055	2.36
Finnish (26)	130	0.10
French, ex. Basque (374)	3,396	2.62
French Canadian (311)	832	0.64
German (4,638)	18,929	14.61
German Russian (0)	0	<0.01
Greek (225)	766	0.59
Guyanese (0)	27	0.02
Hungarian (112)	744	0.57
Icelander (14)	27	0.02
Iranian (75)	95	0.07
Irish (4,126)	15,447	11.92
Israeli (98)	123	0.09
Italian (1,404)	5,336	4.12
Latvian (28)	176	0.14
Lithuanian (162)	611	0.47
Luxemburger (0)	73	0.06
Macedonian (0)	9	0.01
Maltese (0)	0	<0.01
New Zealander (49)	49	0.04
Northern European (161)	161	0.12
Norwegian (272)	884	0.68
Pennsylvania German (13)	83	0.06

Ancestry	Population	%
Polish (1,060)	3,649	2.82
Portuguese (30)	273	0.21
Romanian (88)	213	0.16
Russian (746)	2,141	1.65
Scandinavian (66)	186	0.14
Scotch-Irish (3,494)	6,998	5.40
Scottish (1,719)	5,309	4.10
Serbian (24)	33	0.03
Slavic (72)	182	0.14
Slovak (28)	172	0.13
Slovene (11)	43	0.03
Soviet Union (0)	0	<0.01
Swedish (302)	1,642	1.27
Swiss (169)	721	0.56
Turkish (98)	111	0.09
Ukrainian (229)	442	0.34
Welsh (261)	1,299	1.00
West Indian, ex. Hispanic (373)	647	0.50
Bahamian (0)	0	<0.01
Barbadian (0)	14	0.01
Belizean (0)	0	<0.01
Bermudan (0)	0	<0.01
British West Indian (44)	55	0.04
Dutch West Indian (0)	0	<0.01
Haitian (28)	114	0.09
Jamaican (274)	343	0.26
Trinidadian/Tobagonian (0)	64	0.05
U.S. Virgin Islander (0)	0	<0.01
West Indian (27)	57	0.04
Other West Indian (0)	0	<0.01
Yugoslavian (11)	104	0.08

Hispanic Origin	Population	%
Hispanic or Latino (of any race)	11,017	8.23
Central American, ex. Mexican	1,391	1.04
Costa Rican	47	0.04
Guatemalan	465	0.35
Honduran	282	0.21
Nicaraguan	38	0.03
Panamanian	74	0.06
Salvadoran	472	0.35
Other Central American	13	0.01
Cuban	333	0.25
Dominican Republic	84	0.06
Mexican	6,860	5.13
Puerto Rican	669	0.50
South American	971	0.73
Argentinean	128	0.10
Bolivian	24	0.02
Chilean	87	0.07
Colombian	366	0.27
Ecuadorian	67	0.05
Paraguayan	23	0.02
Peruvian	156	0.12
Uruguayan	12	0.01
Venezuelan	100	0.07
Other South American	8	0.01
Other Hispanic or Latino	709	0.53

Race*	Population	%
African-American/Black (15,928)	17,145	12.81
Not Hispanic (15,722)	16,774	12.54
Hispanic (206)	371	0.28
American Indian/Alaska Native (570)	1,537	1.15
Not Hispanic (383)	1,169	0.87
Hispanic (187)	368	0.28
Alaska Athabascan (Ala. Nat.) (0)	0	<0.01
Aleut (Alaska Native) (4)	5	<0.01
Apache (2)	8	0.01
Arapaho (0)	0	<0.01
Blackfeet (0)	26	0.02
Canadian/French Am. Ind. (1)	2	<0.01
Central American Ind. (1)	1	<0.01
Cherokee (62)	344	0.26
Cheyenne (2)	2	<0.01
Chickasaw (2)	2	<0.01
Chippewa (16)	25	0.02
Choctaw (6)	33	0.02
Colville (0)	0	<0.01

Race* (cont.)	Population	%
Comanche (0)	0	<0.01
Cree (1)	3	<0.01
Creek (3)	12	0.01
Crow (0)	1	<0.01
Delaware (1)	8	0.01
Hopi (1)	6	<0.01
Houma (0)	0	<0.01
Inupiat (Alaska Native) (0)	0	<0.01
Iroquois (14)	34	0.03
Kiowa (1)	1	<0.01
Lumbee (101)	142	0.11
Menominee (1)	1	<0.01
Mexican American Ind. (61)	103	0.08
Navajo (5)	14	0.01
Osage (2)	2	<0.01
Ottawa (0)	1	<0.01
Paiute (0)	1	<0.01
Pima (0)	0	<0.01
Potawatomi (1)	8	0.01
Pueblo (1)	4	<0.01
Puget Sound Salish (0)	0	<0.01
Seminole (1)	1	<0.01
Shoshone (0)	0	<0.01
Sioux (4)	14	0.01
South American Ind. (7)	31	0.02
Spanish American Ind. (1)	6	<0.01
Tlingit-Haida (Alaska Native) (1)	1	<0.01
Tohono O'Odham (0)	0	<0.01
Tsimshian (Alaska Native) (0)	0	<0.01
Ute (0)	0	<0.01
Yakama (0)	0	<0.01
Yaqui (0)	0	<0.01
Yuman (2)	2	<0.01
Yup'ik (Alaska Native) (0)	0	<0.01
Asian (9,023)	10,253	7.66
Not Hispanic (8,996)	10,158	7.59
Hispanic (27)	95	0.07
Bangladeshi (45)	46	0.03
Bhutanese (0)	0	<0.01
Burmese (732)	780	0.58
Cambodian (16)	27	0.02
Chinese, ex. Taiwanese (3,331)	3,683	2.75
Filipino (320)	507	0.38
Hmong (13)	13	0.01
Indian (1,694)	1,929	1.44
Indonesian (18)	28	0.02
Japanese (386)	587	0.44
Korean (1,483)	1,644	1.23
Laotian (12)	15	0.01
Malaysian (17)	24	0.02
Nepalese (11)	11	0.01
Pakistani (82)	118	0.09
Sri Lankan (48)	55	0.04
Taiwanese (202)	239	0.18
Thai (102)	138	0.10
Vietnamese (250)	302	0.23
Hawaii Native/Pacific Islander (41)	141	0.11
Not Hispanic (35)	121	0.09
Hispanic (6)	20	0.01
Fijian (1)	4	<0.01
Guamanian/Chamorro (16)	25	0.02
Marshallese (0)	0	<0.01
Native Hawaiian (10)	35	0.03
Samoan (7)	14	0.01
Tongan (0)	2	<0.01
White (99,495)	102,477	76.59
Not Hispanic (94,671)	96,999	72.49
Hispanic (4,824)	5,478	4.09

*Notes: † The Census 2010 population figure is used to calculate the percentages in the Hispanic Origin and Race categories. Ancestry percentages are based on the 2006-2010 American Community Survey population (not shown); ‡ Numbers in parentheses indicate the number of people reporting a single ancestry; * Numbers in parentheses indicate the number of persons reporting this race alone, not in combination with any other race; Please refer to the Explanation of Data for more information.*

Pender County

Population: 52,217

Ancestry	Population	%
Afghan (20)	20	0.04
African, Sub-Saharan (57)	104	0.21
African (57)	104	0.21
Cape Verdean (0)	0	<0.01
Ethiopian (0)	0	<0.01
Ghanaian (0)	0	<0.01
Kenyan (0)	0	<0.01
Liberian (0)	0	<0.01
Nigerian (0)	0	<0.01
Senegalese (0)	0	<0.01
Sierra Leonean (0)	0	<0.01
Somalian (0)	0	<0.01
South African (0)	0	<0.01
Sudanese (0)	0	<0.01
Ugandan (0)	0	<0.01
Zimbabwean (0)	0	<0.01
Other Sub-Saharan African (0)	0	<0.01
Albanian (0)	0	<0.01
Alsatian (0)	14	0.03
American (7,170)	7,170	14.27
Arab (8)	75	0.15
Arab (0)	0	<0.01
Egyptian (0)	0	<0.01
Iraqi (0)	0	<0.01
Jordanian (0)	0	<0.01
Lebanese (0)	33	0.07
Moroccan (8)	8	0.02
Palestinian (0)	0	<0.01
Syrian (0)	34	0.07
Other Arab (0)	0	<0.01
Armenian (0)	0	<0.01
Assyrian/Chaldean/Syriac (0)	0	<0.01
Australian (44)	44	0.09
Austrian (8)	10	0.02
Basque (0)	0	<0.01
Belgian (0)	7	0.01
Brazilian (0)	0	<0.01
British (204)	251	0.50
Bulgarian (0)	0	<0.01
Cajun (0)	0	<0.01
Canadian (30)	30	0.06
Carpatho Rusyn (0)	0	<0.01
Celtic (0)	52	0.10
Croatian (0)	0	<0.01
Cypriot (0)	0	<0.01
Czech (0)	92	0.18
Czechoslovakian (0)	8	0.02
Danish (9)	39	0.08
Dutch (56)	413	0.82
Eastern European (0)	0	<0.01
English (2,651)	5,987	11.91
Estonian (0)	0	<0.01
European (199)	252	0.50
Finnish (0)	14	0.03
French, ex. Basque (286)	1,196	2.38
French Canadian (100)	180	0.36
German (1,976)	6,003	11.94
German Russian (0)	0	<0.01
Greek (30)	82	0.16
Guyanese (0)	0	<0.01
Hungarian (33)	286	0.57
Icelander (0)	0	<0.01
Iranian (9)	9	0.02
Irish (2,251)	5,652	11.25
Israeli (0)	0	<0.01
Italian (882)	2,160	4.30
Latvian (15)	15	0.03
Lithuanian (0)	76	0.15
Luxemburger (0)	0	<0.01
Macedonian (0)	0	<0.01
Maltese (0)	0	<0.01
New Zealander (0)	14	0.03
Northern European (0)	0	<0.01
Norwegian (90)	424	0.84
Pennsylvania German (0)	5	0.01

Ancestry (cont.)	Population	%
Polish (311)	790	1.57
Portuguese (30)	56	0.11
Romanian (0)	0	<0.01
Russian (91)	243	0.48
Scandinavian (44)	77	0.15
Scotch-Irish (1,444)	2,590	5.15
Scottish (654)	1,553	3.09
Serbian (0)	0	<0.01
Slavic (0)	3	0.01
Slovak (28)	69	0.14
Slovene (0)	0	<0.01
Soviet Union (0)	0	<0.01
Swedish (75)	284	0.57
Swiss (66)	100	0.20
Turkish (0)	0	<0.01
Ukrainian (16)	46	0.09
Welsh (81)	347	0.69
West Indian, ex. Hispanic (27)	27	0.05
Bahamian (0)	0	<0.01
Barbadian (0)	0	<0.01
Belizean (0)	0	<0.01
Bermudan (0)	0	<0.01
British West Indian (0)	0	<0.01
Dutch West Indian (0)	0	<0.01
Haitian (0)	0	<0.01
Jamaican (3)	3	0.01
Trinidadian/Tobagonian (24)	24	0.05
U.S. Virgin Islander (0)	0	<0.01
West Indian (0)	0	<0.01
Other West Indian (0)	0	<0.01
Yugoslavian (0)	15	0.03

Hispanic Origin	Population	%
Hispanic or Latino (of any race)	3,194	6.12
Central American, ex. Mexican	240	0.46
Costa Rican	15	0.03
Guatemalan	31	0.06
Honduran	146	0.28
Nicaraguan	7	0.01
Panamanian	18	0.03
Salvadoran	12	0.02
Other Central American	11	0.02
Cuban	47	0.09
Dominican Republic	28	0.05
Mexican	2,334	4.47
Puerto Rican	209	0.40
South American	93	0.18
Argentinean	5	0.01
Bolivian	2	<0.01
Chilean	1	<0.01
Colombian	38	0.07
Ecuadorian	15	0.03
Paraguayan	0	<0.01
Peruvian	19	0.04
Uruguayan	4	0.01
Venezuelan	5	0.01
Other South American	4	0.01
Other Hispanic or Latino	243	0.47

Race*	Population	%
African-American/Black (9,269)	9,673	18.52
Not Hispanic (9,208)	9,569	18.33
Hispanic (61)	104	0.20
American Indian/Alaska Native (291)	663	1.27
Not Hispanic (237)	570	1.09
Hispanic (54)	93	0.18
Alaska Athabascan (Ala. Nat.) (1)	1	<0.01
Aleut (Alaska Native) (0)	0	<0.01
Apache (1)	3	0.01
Arapaho (0)	1	<0.01
Blackfeet (4)	15	0.03
Canadian/French Am. Ind. (1)	6	0.01
Central American Ind. (0)	0	<0.01
Cherokee (46)	151	0.29
Cheyenne (0)	0	<0.01
Chickasaw (0)	0	<0.01
Chippewa (5)	8	0.02
Choctaw (2)	4	0.01
Colville (0)	0	<0.01

Race* (cont.)	Population	%
Comanche (0)	0	<0.01
Cree (1)	1	<0.01
Creek (4)	5	0.01
Crow (0)	0	<0.01
Delaware (0)	3	0.01
Hopi (0)	1	<0.01
Houma (0)	0	<0.01
Inupiat (Alaska Native) (2)	2	<0.01
Iroquois (1)	8	0.02
Kiowa (0)	0	<0.01
Lumbee (41)	57	0.11
Menominee (0)	0	<0.01
Mexican American Ind. (29)	31	0.06
Navajo (3)	7	0.01
Osage (0)	0	<0.01
Ottawa (0)	0	<0.01
Paiute (0)	0	<0.01
Pima (0)	0	<0.01
Potawatomi (0)	3	0.01
Pueblo (1)	2	<0.01
Puget Sound Salish (0)	1	<0.01
Seminole (0)	1	<0.01
Shoshone (0)	3	0.01
Sioux (5)	30	0.06
South American Ind. (0)	3	0.01
Spanish American Ind. (0)	0	<0.01
Tlingit-Haida (Alaska Native) (0)	0	<0.01
Tohono O'Odham (0)	0	<0.01
Tsimshian (Alaska Native) (0)	0	<0.01
Ute (0)	0	<0.01
Yakama (0)	0	<0.01
Yaqui (0)	0	<0.01
Yuman (0)	0	<0.01
Yup'ik (Alaska Native) (0)	0	<0.01
Asian (207)	348	0.67
Not Hispanic (197)	323	0.62
Hispanic (10)	25	0.05
Bangladeshi (0)	0	<0.01
Bhutanese (0)	0	<0.01
Burmese (0)	0	<0.01
Cambodian (0)	1	<0.01
Chinese, ex. Taiwanese (61)	82	0.16
Filipino (33)	70	0.13
Hmong (0)	0	<0.01
Indian (34)	48	0.09
Indonesian (5)	7	0.01
Japanese (19)	57	0.11
Korean (12)	22	0.04
Laotian (1)	2	<0.01
Malaysian (0)	0	<0.01
Nepalese (0)	0	<0.01
Pakistani (0)	0	<0.01
Sri Lankan (0)	0	<0.01
Taiwanese (1)	3	0.01
Thai (22)	32	0.06
Vietnamese (7)	12	0.02
Hawaii Native/Pacific Islander (18)	57	0.11
Not Hispanic (11)	43	0.08
Hispanic (7)	14	0.03
Fijian (1)	1	<0.01
Guamanian/Chamorro (9)	12	0.02
Marshallese (2)	2	<0.01
Native Hawaiian (3)	25	0.05
Samoan (2)	2	<0.01
Tongan (0)	0	<0.01
White (39,756)	40,572	77.70
Not Hispanic (38,568)	39,227	75.12
Hispanic (1,188)	1,345	2.58

Notes: † The Census 2010 population figure is used to calculate the percentages in the Hispanic Origin and Race categories. Ancestry percentages are based on the 2006-2010 American Community Survey population (not shown); ‡ Numbers in parentheses indicate the number of people reporting a single ancestry; * Numbers in parentheses indicate the number of persons reporting this race alone, not in combination with any other race; Please refer to the Explanation of Data for more information.

Pitt County

Population: 168,148

Ancestry	Population	%
Afghan (0)	0	<0.01
African, Sub-Saharan (713)	858	0.53
African (453)	598	0.37
Cape Verdean (0)	0	<0.01
Ethiopian (0)	0	<0.01
Ghanaian (165)	165	0.10
Kenyan (14)	14	0.01
Liberian (12)	12	0.01
Nigerian (69)	69	0.04
Senegalese (0)	0	<0.01
Sierra Leonean (0)	0	<0.01
Somalian (0)	0	<0.01
South African (0)	0	<0.01
Sudanese (0)	0	<0.01
Ugandan (0)	0	<0.01
Zimbabwean (0)	0	<0.01
Other Sub-Saharan African (0)	0	<0.01
Albanian (0)	0	<0.01
Alsatian (0)	0	<0.01
American (12,569)	12,569	7.79
Arab (723)	751	0.47
Arab (98)	98	0.06
Egyptian (368)	368	0.23
Iraqi (0)	0	<0.01
Jordanian (10)	10	0.01
Lebanese (144)	172	0.11
Moroccan (44)	44	0.03
Palestinian (48)	48	0.03
Syrian (0)	0	<0.01
Other Arab (11)	11	0.01
Armenian (14)	14	0.01
Assyrian/Chaldean/Syriac (0)	0	<0.01
Australian (25)	89	0.06
Austrian (41)	152	0.09
Basque (0)	0	<0.01
Belgian (7)	36	0.02
Brazilian (95)	135	0.08
British (403)	625	0.39
Bulgarian (30)	30	0.02
Cajun (51)	67	0.04
Canadian (113)	220	0.14
Carpatho Rusyn (18)	18	0.01
Celtic (0)	0	<0.01
Croatian (6)	30	0.02
Cypriot (0)	0	<0.01
Czech (34)	175	0.11
Czechoslovakian (20)	20	0.01
Danish (43)	239	0.15
Dutch (270)	1,335	0.83
Eastern European (29)	29	0.02
English (9,363)	17,024	10.55
Estonian (0)	0	<0.01
European (1,656)	1,967	1.22
Finnish (29)	91	0.06
French, ex. Basque (864)	2,915	1.81
French Canadian (172)	448	0.28
German (3,873)	12,489	7.74
German Russian (0)	0	<0.01
Greek (192)	544	0.34
Guyanese (0)	0	<0.01
Hungarian (116)	378	0.23
Icelander (0)	33	0.02
Iranian (101)	101	0.06
Irish (4,320)	13,424	8.32
Israeli (27)	27	0.02
Italian (1,515)	4,399	2.73
Latvian (0)	14	0.01
Lithuanian (54)	325	0.20
Luxemburger (0)	0	<0.01
Macedonian (0)	0	<0.01
Maltese (0)	0	<0.01
New Zealander (0)	0	<0.01
Northern European (54)	67	0.04
Norwegian (174)	645	0.40
Pennsylvania German (27)	27	0.02

Ancestry	Population	%
Polish (599)	1,948	1.21
Portuguese (72)	218	0.14
Romanian (37)	61	0.04
Russian (115)	480	0.30
Scandinavian (0)	27	0.02
Scotch-Irish (2,368)	4,247	2.63
Scottish (1,239)	3,487	2.16
Serbian (0)	0	<0.01
Slavic (0)	23	0.01
Slovak (37)	98	0.06
Slovene (24)	54	0.03
Soviet Union (0)	0	<0.01
Swedish (102)	398	0.25
Swiss (97)	193	0.12
Turkish (31)	43	0.03
Ukrainian (28)	190	0.12
Welsh (251)	745	0.46
West Indian, ex. Hispanic (358)	473	0.29
Bahamian (0)	0	<0.01
Barbadian (0)	0	<0.01
Belizean (0)	0	<0.01
Bermudan (0)	0	<0.01
British West Indian (0)	0	<0.01
Dutch West Indian (0)	8	<0.01
Haitian (0)	35	0.02
Jamaican (183)	219	0.14
Trinidadian/Tobagonian (163)	199	0.12
U.S. Virgin Islander (0)	0	<0.01
West Indian (12)	12	0.01
Other West Indian (0)	0	<0.01
Yugoslavian (89)	103	0.06

Hispanic Origin	Population	%
Hispanic or Latino (of any race)	9,202	5.47
Central American, ex. Mexican	572	0.34
Costa Rican	53	0.03
Guatemalan	120	0.07
Honduran	128	0.08
Nicaraguan	46	0.03
Panamanian	45	0.03
Salvadoran	173	0.10
Other Central American	7	<0.01
Cuban	189	0.11
Dominican Republic	94	0.06
Mexican	6,422	3.82
Puerto Rican	870	0.52
South American	401	0.24
Argentinean	26	0.02
Bolivian	7	<0.01
Chilean	27	0.02
Colombian	170	0.10
Ecuadorian	46	0.03
Paraguayan	9	0.01
Peruvian	62	0.04
Uruguayan	4	<0.01
Venezuelan	40	0.02
Other South American	10	0.01
Other Hispanic or Latino	654	0.39

Race*	Population	%
African-American/Black (57,257)	59,217	35.22
Not Hispanic (56,813)	58,527	34.81
Hispanic (444)	690	0.41
American Indian/Alaska Native (582)	1,361	0.81
Not Hispanic (474)	1,166	0.69
Hispanic (108)	195	0.12
Alaska Athabascan (Ala. Nat.) (2)	2	<0.01
Aleut (Alaska Native) (6)	6	<0.01
Apache (1)	10	0.01
Arapaho (0)	0	<0.01
Blackfeet (4)	24	0.01
Canadian/French Am. Ind. (7)	10	0.01
Central American Ind. (1)	8	<0.01
Cherokee (60)	250	0.15
Cheyenne (0)	4	<0.01
Chickasaw (0)	4	<0.01
Chippewa (8)	21	0.01
Choctaw (6)	13	0.01
Colville (0)	0	<0.01

	Population	%
Comanche (1)	7	<0.01
Cree (2)	2	<0.01
Creek (1)	9	0.01
Crow (0)	1	<0.01
Delaware (1)	3	<0.01
Hopi (1)	3	<0.01
Houma (0)	0	<0.01
Inupiat (Alaska Native) (0)	1	<0.01
Iroquois (13)	23	0.01
Kiowa (0)	0	<0.01
Lumbee (93)	121	0.07
Menominee (0)	0	<0.01
Mexican American Ind. (30)	40	0.02
Navajo (7)	9	0.01
Osage (1)	3	<0.01
Ottawa (1)	2	<0.01
Paiute (0)	0	<0.01
Pima (0)	4	<0.01
Potawatomi (1)	1	<0.01
Pueblo (2)	2	<0.01
Puget Sound Salish (0)	0	<0.01
Seminole (3)	7	<0.01
Shoshone (1)	1	<0.01
Sioux (6)	11	0.01
South American Ind. (7)	9	0.01
Spanish American Ind. (0)	0	<0.01
Tlingit-Haida (Alaska Native) (1)	1	<0.01
Tohono O'Odham (1)	1	<0.01
Tsimshian (Alaska Native) (0)	0	<0.01
Ute (0)	0	<0.01
Yakama (0)	0	<0.01
Yaqui (0)	0	<0.01
Yuman (0)	0	<0.01
Yup'ik (Alaska Native) (0)	0	<0.01
Asian (2,613)	3,442	2.05
Not Hispanic (2,561)	3,337	1.98
Hispanic (52)	105	0.06
Bangladeshi (7)	10	0.01
Bhutanese (0)	0	<0.01
Burmese (14)	30	0.02
Cambodian (4)	10	0.01
Chinese, ex. Taiwanese (528)	620	0.37
Filipino (279)	456	0.27
Hmong (57)	61	0.04
Indian (781)	894	0.53
Indonesian (2)	14	0.01
Japanese (173)	300	0.18
Korean (259)	390	0.23
Laotian (13)	16	0.01
Malaysian (3)	6	<0.01
Nepalese (2)	2	<0.01
Pakistani (117)	149	0.09
Sri Lankan (3)	3	<0.01
Taiwanese (24)	28	0.02
Thai (28)	52	0.03
Vietnamese (175)	228	0.14
Hawaii Native/Pacific Islander (97)	240	0.14
Not Hispanic (71)	176	0.10
Hispanic (26)	64	0.04
Fijian (1)	1	<0.01
Guamanian/Chamorro (31)	51	0.03
Marshallese (0)	0	<0.01
Native Hawaiian (26)	63	0.04
Samoan (11)	27	0.02
Tongan (3)	4	<0.01
White (99,075)	101,773	60.53
Not Hispanic (96,038)	98,235	58.42
Hispanic (3,037)	3,538	2.10

Notes: † The Census 2010 population figure is used to calculate the percentages in the Hispanic Origin and Race categories. Ancestry percentages are based on the 2006-2010 American Community Survey population (not shown); ‡ Numbers in parentheses indicate the number of people reporting a single ancestry; * Numbers in parentheses indicate the number of persons reporting this race alone, not in combination with any other race; Please refer to the Explanation of Data for more information.

Randolph County

Population: 141,752

Ancestry	Population	%
Afghan (0)	0	<0.01
African, Sub-Saharan (121)	121	0.09
African (102)	102	0.07
Cape Verdean (0)	0	<0.01
Ethiopian (0)	0	<0.01
Ghanaian (0)	0	<0.01
Kenyan (0)	0	<0.01
Liberian (19)	19	0.01
Nigerian (0)	0	<0.01
Senegalese (0)	0	<0.01
Sierra Leonean (0)	0	<0.01
Somalian (0)	0	<0.01
South African (0)	0	<0.01
Sudanese (0)	0	<0.01
Ugandan (0)	0	<0.01
Zimbabwean (0)	0	<0.01
Other Sub-Saharan African (0)	0	<0.01
Albanian (0)	0	<0.01
Alsatian (0)	0	<0.01
American (19,879)	19,879	14.20
Arab (167)	195	0.14
Arab (24)	35	0.02
Egyptian (55)	68	0.05
Iraqi (0)	0	<0.01
Jordanian (0)	0	<0.01
Lebanese (24)	28	0.02
Moroccan (0)	0	<0.01
Palestinian (17)	17	0.01
Syrian (0)	0	<0.01
Other Arab (47)	47	0.03
Armenian (17)	73	0.05
Assyrian/Chaldean/Syriac (0)	0	<0.01
Australian (8)	8	0.01
Austrian (14)	174	0.12
Basque (0)	0	<0.01
Belgian (33)	135	0.10
Brazilian (41)	41	0.03
British (279)	490	0.35
Bulgarian (0)	0	<0.01
Cajun (0)	54	0.04
Canadian (230)	396	0.28
Carpatho Rusyn (0)	0	<0.01
Celtic (0)	0	<0.01
Croatian (65)	65	0.05
Cypriot (0)	0	<0.01
Czech (159)	354	0.25
Czechoslovakian (11)	11	0.01
Danish (17)	94	0.07
Dutch (294)	1,930	1.38
Eastern European (13)	13	0.01
English (9,070)	16,067	11.47
Estonian (0)	0	<0.01
European (966)	1,138	0.81
Finnish (207)	301	0.21
French, ex. Basque (392)	1,606	1.15
French Canadian (99)	194	0.14
German (6,463)	16,557	11.82
German Russian (0)	0	<0.01
Greek (28)	119	0.08
Guyanese (0)	0	<0.01
Hungarian (40)	83	0.06
Icelander (0)	0	<0.01
Iranian (0)	0	<0.01
Irish (4,626)	11,947	8.53
Israeli (0)	95	0.07
Italian (756)	2,265	1.62
Latvian (13)	23	0.02
Lithuanian (0)	44	0.03
Luxemburger (0)	0	<0.01
Macedonian (0)	0	<0.01
Maltese (22)	22	0.02
New Zealander (112)	112	0.08
Northern European (19)	19	0.01
Norwegian (117)	415	0.30
Pennsylvania German (17)	20	0.01

	Population	%
Polish (376)	893	0.64
Portuguese (61)	116	0.08
Romanian (25)	25	0.02
Russian (38)	146	0.10
Scandinavian (48)	92	0.07
Scotch-Irish (2,594)	4,014	2.87
Scottish (1,632)	3,278	2.34
Serbian (0)	0	<0.01
Slavic (0)	0	<0.01
Slovak (11)	11	0.01
Slovene (0)	18	0.01
Soviet Union (0)	0	<0.01
Swedish (94)	397	0.28
Swiss (115)	203	0.14
Turkish (0)	0	<0.01
Ukrainian (18)	37	0.03
Welsh (179)	674	0.48
West Indian, ex. Hispanic (42)	92	0.07
Bahamian (17)	17	0.01
Barbadian (0)	8	0.01
Belizean (0)	0	<0.01
Bermudan (0)	0	<0.01
British West Indian (0)	0	<0.01
Dutch West Indian (0)	0	<0.01
Haitian (0)	0	<0.01
Jamaican (4)	12	0.01
Trinidadian/Tobagonian (0)	0	<0.01
U.S. Virgin Islander (0)	0	<0.01
West Indian (21)	55	0.04
Other West Indian (0)	0	<0.01
Yugoslavian (0)	9	0.01

Hispanic Origin	Population	%
Hispanic or Latino (of any race)	14,698	10.37
Central American, ex. Mexican	1,045	0.74
Costa Rican	63	0.04
Guatemalan	280	0.20
Honduran	148	0.10
Nicaraguan	166	0.12
Panamanian	28	0.02
Salvadoran	355	0.25
Other Central American	5	<0.01
Cuban	194	0.14
Dominican Republic	147	0.10
Mexican	11,960	8.44
Puerto Rican	383	0.27
South American	223	0.16
Argentinean	13	0.01
Bolivian	1	<0.01
Chilean	21	0.01
Colombian	95	0.07
Ecuadorian	26	0.02
Paraguayan	12	0.01
Peruvian	35	0.02
Uruguayan	4	<0.01
Venezuelan	12	0.01
Other South American	4	<0.01
Other Hispanic or Latino	746	0.53

Race*	Population	%
African-American/Black (8,176)	9,163	6.46
Not Hispanic (7,979)	8,848	6.24
Hispanic (197)	315	0.22
American Indian/Alaska Native (952)	1,671	1.18
Not Hispanic (674)	1,272	0.90
Hispanic (278)	399	0.28
Alaska Athabascan (Ala. Nat.) (1)	1	<0.01
Aleut (Alaska Native) (0)	0	<0.01
Apache (5)	25	0.02
Arapaho (0)	1	<0.01
Blackfeet (5)	27	0.02
Canadian/French Am. Ind. (0)	1	<0.01
Central American Ind. (1)	1	<0.01
Cherokee (108)	367	0.26
Cheyenne (0)	0	<0.01
Chickasaw (3)	3	<0.01
Chippewa (2)	6	<0.01
Choctaw (16)	19	0.01
Colville (0)	0	<0.01

	Population	%
Comanche (1)	4	<0.01
Cree (2)	3	<0.01
Creek (4)	7	<0.01
Crow (0)	0	<0.01
Delaware (4)	8	0.01
Hopi (1)	1	<0.01
Houma (2)	4	<0.01
Inupiat (Alaska Native) (0)	6	<0.01
Iroquois (8)	12	0.01
Kiowa (0)	0	<0.01
Lumbee (274)	361	0.25
Menominee (0)	0	<0.01
Mexican American Ind. (62)	92	0.06
Navajo (0)	1	<0.01
Osage (0)	1	<0.01
Ottawa (0)	0	<0.01
Paiute (0)	0	<0.01
Pima (0)	0	<0.01
Potawatomi (1)	3	<0.01
Pueblo (2)	3	<0.01
Puget Sound Salish (0)	1	<0.01
Seminole (3)	3	<0.01
Shoshone (0)	0	<0.01
Sioux (4)	17	0.01
South American Ind. (3)	5	<0.01
Spanish American Ind. (7)	8	<0.01
Tlingit-Haida (Alaska Native) (0)	0	<0.01
Tohono O'Odham (0)	0	<0.01
Tsimshian (Alaska Native) (0)	0	<0.01
Ute (0)	6	<0.01
Yakama (0)	0	<0.01
Yaqui (1)	7	<0.01
Yuman (1)	1	<0.01
Yup'ik (Alaska Native) (0)	0	<0.01
Asian (1,431)	1,710	1.21
Not Hispanic (1,406)	1,654	1.17
Hispanic (25)	56	0.04
Bangladeshi (2)	2	<0.01
Bhutanese (0)	0	<0.01
Burmese (0)	0	<0.01
Cambodian (64)	81	0.06
Chinese, ex. Taiwanese (106)	132	0.09
Filipino (99)	155	0.11
Hmong (19)	21	0.01
Indian (236)	271	0.19
Indonesian (8)	12	0.01
Japanese (25)	74	0.05
Korean (89)	125	0.09
Laotian (55)	75	0.05
Malaysian (1)	1	<0.01
Nepalese (0)	0	<0.01
Pakistani (350)	373	0.26
Sri Lankan (0)	0	<0.01
Taiwanese (4)	6	<0.01
Thai (22)	39	0.03
Vietnamese (246)	263	0.19
Hawaii Native/Pacific Islander (33)	105	0.07
Not Hispanic (20)	60	0.04
Hispanic (13)	45	0.03
Fijian (0)	0	<0.01
Guamanian/Chamorro (16)	22	0.02
Marshallese (0)	0	<0.01
Native Hawaiian (11)	30	0.02
Samoan (3)	9	0.01
Tongan (0)	0	<0.01
White (121,169)	123,369	87.03
Not Hispanic (115,205)	116,711	82.33
Hispanic (5,964)	6,658	4.70

Notes: † The Census 2010 population figure is used to calculate the percentages in the Hispanic Origin and Race categories. Ancestry percentages are based on the 2006-2010 American Community Survey population (not shown); ‡ Numbers in parentheses indicate the number of people reporting a single ancestry; * Numbers in parentheses indicate the number of persons reporting this race alone, not in combination with any other race; Please refer to the Explanation of Data for more information.

Robeson County

Population: 134,168

Ancestry	Population	%
Afghan (0)	0	<0.01
African, Sub-Saharan (417)	442	0.34
African (417)	442	0.34
Cape Verdean (0)	0	<0.01
Ethiopian (0)	0	<0.01
Ghanaian (0)	0	<0.01
Kenyan (0)	0	<0.01
Liberian (0)	0	<0.01
Nigerian (0)	0	<0.01
Senegalese (0)	0	<0.01
Sierra Leonean (0)	0	<0.01
Somalian (0)	0	<0.01
South African (0)	0	<0.01
Sudanese (0)	0	<0.01
Ugandan (0)	0	<0.01
Zimbabwean (0)	0	<0.01
Other Sub-Saharan African (0)	0	<0.01
Albanian (0)	0	<0.01
Alsatian (0)	0	<0.01
American (5,929)	5,929	4.50
Arab (152)	517	0.39
Arab (58)	94	0.07
Egyptian (0)	0	<0.01
Iraqi (0)	0	<0.01
Jordanian (31)	182	0.14
Lebanese (0)	21	0.02
Moroccan (0)	9	0.01
Palestinian (26)	174	0.13
Syrian (0)	0	<0.01
Other Arab (37)	37	0.03
Armenian (41)	57	0.04
Assyrian/Chaldean/Syriac (0)	0	<0.01
Australian (0)	0	<0.01
Austrian (0)	0	<0.01
Basque (0)	0	<0.01
Belgian (0)	16	0.01
Brazilian (0)	0	<0.01
British (23)	66	0.05
Bulgarian (0)	0	<0.01
Cajun (0)	0	<0.01
Canadian (20)	21	0.02
Carpatho Rusyn (0)	0	<0.01
Celtic (0)	0	<0.01
Croatian (0)	0	<0.01
Cypriot (0)	0	<0.01
Czech (8)	41	0.03
Czechoslovakian (4)	4	<0.01
Danish (34)	61	0.05
Dutch (24)	159	0.12
Eastern European (0)	0	<0.01
English (3,331)	5,291	4.02
Estonian (0)	0	<0.01
European (88)	179	0.14
Finnish (0)	8	0.01
French, ex. Basque (277)	631	0.48
French Canadian (13)	41	0.03
German (879)	3,181	2.42
German Russian (0)	0	<0.01
Greek (13)	59	0.04
Guyanese (2)	2	<0.01
Hungarian (14)	41	0.03
Icelander (0)	0	<0.01
Iranian (0)	0	<0.01
Irish (1,704)	3,788	2.88
Israeli (0)	0	<0.01
Italian (296)	659	0.50
Latvian (0)	0	<0.01
Lithuanian (26)	26	0.02
Luxemburger (0)	0	<0.01
Macedonian (0)	0	<0.01
Maltese (0)	0	<0.01
New Zealander (0)	0	<0.01
Northern European (0)	0	<0.01
Norwegian (28)	162	0.12
Pennsylvania German (0)	0	<0.01

Ancestry	Population	%
Polish (116)	438	0.33
Portuguese (47)	81	0.06
Romanian (15)	15	0.01
Russian (51)	51	0.04
Scandinavian (9)	70	0.05
Scotch-Irish (1,827)	2,420	1.84
Scottish (875)	1,333	1.01
Serbian (0)	0	<0.01
Slavic (2)	11	0.01
Slovak (0)	0	<0.01
Slovene (0)	0	<0.01
Soviet Union (0)	0	<0.01
Swedish (0)	54	0.04
Swiss (0)	45	0.03
Turkish (0)	12	0.01
Ukrainian (0)	14	0.01
Welsh (79)	176	0.13
West Indian, ex. Hispanic (421)	439	0.33
Bahamian (0)	0	<0.01
Barbadian (0)	0	<0.01
Belizean (0)	0	<0.01
Bermudan (0)	0	<0.01
British West Indian (0)	0	<0.01
Dutch West Indian (0)	0	<0.01
Haitian (379)	389	0.30
Jamaican (42)	42	0.03
Trinidadian/Tobagonian (0)	0	<0.01
U.S. Virgin Islander (0)	0	<0.01
West Indian (0)	8	0.01
Other West Indian (0)	0	<0.01
Yugoslavian (0)	0	<0.01

Hispanic Origin	Population	%
Hispanic or Latino (of any race)	10,932	8.15
Central American, ex. Mexican	738	0.55
Costa Rican	8	0.01
Guatemalan	325	0.24
Honduran	246	0.18
Nicaraguan	43	0.03
Panamanian	30	0.02
Salvadoran	79	0.06
Other Central American	7	0.01
Cuban	80	0.06
Dominican Republic	76	0.06
Mexican	8,616	6.42
Puerto Rican	629	0.47
South American	100	0.07
Argentinean	2	<0.01
Bolivian	0	<0.01
Chilean	6	<0.01
Colombian	47	0.04
Ecuadorian	14	0.01
Paraguayan	0	<0.01
Peruvian	23	0.02
Uruguayan	0	<0.01
Venezuelan	8	0.01
Other South American	0	<0.01
Other Hispanic or Latino	693	0.52

Race*	Population	%
African-American/Black (32,637)	34,012	25.35
Not Hispanic (32,347)	33,569	25.02
Hispanic (290)	443	0.33
American Indian/Alaska Native (51,502)	53,756	40.07
Not Hispanic (50,866)	52,915	39.44
Hispanic (636)	841	0.63
Alaska Athabascan (Ala. Nat.) (1)	1	<0.01
Aleut (Alaska Native) (0)	0	<0.01
Apache (14)	16	0.01
Arapaho (0)	2	<0.01
Blackfeet (10)	20	0.01
Canadian/French Am. Ind. (1)	1	<0.01
Central American Ind. (16)	17	0.01
Cherokee (283)	488	0.36
Cheyenne (1)	1	<0.01
Chickasaw (1)	2	<0.01
Chippewa (10)	11	0.01
Choctaw (3)	22	0.02
Colville (0)	0	<0.01

Race*	Population	%
Comanche (5)	7	0.01
Cree (0)	0	<0.01
Creek (5)	10	0.01
Crow (0)	1	<0.01
Delaware (0)	0	<0.01
Hopi (0)	0	<0.01
Houma (0)	0	<0.01
Inupiat (Alaska Native) (0)	0	<0.01
Iroquois (704)	767	0.57
Kiowa (0)	1	<0.01
Lumbee (37,833)	39,067	29.12
Menominee (3)	4	<0.01
Mexican American Ind. (60)	98	0.07
Navajo (18)	25	0.02
Osage (1)	1	<0.01
Ottawa (0)	1	<0.01
Paiute (0)	0	<0.01
Pima (0)	4	<0.01
Potawatomi (8)	8	0.01
Pueblo (1)	1	<0.01
Puget Sound Salish (0)	0	<0.01
Seminole (2)	5	<0.01
Shoshone (1)	1	<0.01
Sioux (50)	61	0.05
South American Ind. (0)	1	<0.01
Spanish American Ind. (12)	15	0.01
Tlingit-Haida (Alaska Native) (0)	0	<0.01
Tohono O'Odham (3)	3	<0.01
Tsimshian (Alaska Native) (0)	0	<0.01
Ute (0)	0	<0.01
Yakama (0)	0	<0.01
Yaqui (1)	1	<0.01
Yuman (0)	1	<0.01
Yup'ik (Alaska Native) (0)	0	<0.01
Asian (993)	1,271	0.95
Not Hispanic (971)	1,231	0.92
Hispanic (22)	40	0.03
Bangladeshi (0)	0	<0.01
Bhutanese (0)	0	<0.01
Burmese (131)	182	0.14
Cambodian (4)	4	<0.01
Chinese, ex. Taiwanese (184)	200	0.15
Filipino (169)	231	0.17
Hmong (17)	17	0.01
Indian (172)	304	0.23
Indonesian (2)	5	<0.01
Japanese (23)	43	0.03
Korean (65)	82	0.06
Laotian (4)	5	<0.01
Malaysian (0)	0	<0.01
Nepalese (0)	0	<0.01
Pakistani (26)	28	0.02
Sri Lankan (0)	0	<0.01
Taiwanese (0)	0	<0.01
Thai (35)	42	0.03
Vietnamese (46)	66	0.05
Hawaii Native/Pacific Islander (86)	186	0.14
Not Hispanic (60)	146	0.11
Hispanic (26)	40	0.03
Fijian (0)	0	<0.01
Guamanian/Chamorro (39)	56	0.04
Marshallese (0)	0	<0.01
Native Hawaiian (20)	50	0.04
Samoan (13)	29	0.02
Tongan (0)	0	<0.01
White (38,877)	41,140	30.66
Not Hispanic (36,160)	37,898	28.25
Hispanic (2,717)	3,242	2.42

Notes: † The Census 2010 population figure is used to calculate the percentages in the Hispanic Origin and Race categories. Ancestry percentages are based on the 2006-2010 American Community Survey population (not shown); ‡ Numbers in parentheses indicate the number of people reporting a single ancestry; * Numbers in parentheses indicate the number of persons reporting this race alone, not in combination with any other race; Please refer to the Explanation of Data for more information.

Rockingham County

Population: 93,643

Ancestry	Population	%
Afghan (0)	0	<0.01
African, Sub-Saharan (157)	190	0.20
African (157)	190	0.20
Cape Verdean (0)	0	<0.01
Ethiopian (0)	0	<0.01
Ghanaian (0)	0	<0.01
Kenyan (0)	0	<0.01
Liberian (0)	0	<0.01
Nigerian (0)	0	<0.01
Senegalese (0)	0	<0.01
Sierra Leonean (0)	0	<0.01
Somalian (0)	0	<0.01
South African (0)	0	<0.01
Sudanese (0)	0	<0.01
Ugandan (0)	0	<0.01
Zimbabwean (0)	0	<0.01
Other Sub-Saharan African (0)	0	<0.01
Albanian (0)	0	<0.01
Alsatian (0)	0	<0.01
American (13,396)	13,396	14.35
Arab (102)	114	0.12
Arab (9)	9	0.01
Egyptian (61)	61	0.07
Iraqi (0)	0	<0.01
Jordanian (0)	0	<0.01
Lebanese (0)	0	<0.01
Moroccan (32)	32	0.03
Palestinian (0)	0	<0.01
Syrian (0)	12	0.01
Other Arab (0)	0	<0.01
Armenian (0)	26	0.03
Assyrian/Chaldean/Syriac (0)	10	0.01
Australian (0)	0	<0.01
Austrian (0)	109	0.12
Basque (0)	0	<0.01
Belgian (0)	10	0.01
Brazilian (0)	72	0.08
British (155)	232	0.25
Bulgarian (0)	0	<0.01
Cajun (0)	0	<0.01
Canadian (10)	10	0.01
Carpatho Rusyn (0)	0	<0.01
Celtic (0)	12	0.01
Croatian (0)	11	0.01
Cypriot (0)	0	<0.01
Czech (14)	33	0.04
Czechoslovakian (25)	25	0.03
Danish (0)	21	0.02
Dutch (192)	1,288	1.38
Eastern European (0)	0	<0.01
English (6,511)	10,347	11.09
Estonian (0)	0	<0.01
European (894)	1,624	1.74
Finnish (0)	0	<0.01
French, ex. Basque (214)	1,111	1.19
French Canadian (35)	65	0.07
German (2,296)	7,683	8.23
German Russian (0)	0	<0.01
Greek (8)	43	0.05
Guyanese (0)	0	<0.01
Hungarian (14)	14	0.02
Icelander (18)	43	0.05
Iranian (0)	49	0.05
Irish (3,929)	9,162	9.82
Israeli (0)	73	0.08
Italian (654)	1,604	1.72
Latvian (0)	0	<0.01
Lithuanian (15)	15	0.02
Luxemburger (0)	0	<0.01
Macedonian (0)	0	<0.01
Maltese (0)	0	<0.01
New Zealander (0)	0	<0.01
Northern European (21)	21	0.02
Norwegian (104)	217	0.23
Pennsylvania German (0)	0	<0.01

	Population	%
Polish (279)	723	0.77
Portuguese (13)	27	0.03
Romanian (0)	37	0.04
Russian (113)	204	0.22
Scandinavian (0)	0	<0.01
Scotch-Irish (1,234)	2,088	2.24
Scottish (874)	1,893	2.03
Serbian (0)	0	<0.01
Slavic (0)	0	<0.01
Slovak (10)	10	0.01
Slovene (0)	0	<0.01
Soviet Union (0)	0	<0.01
Swedish (155)	349	0.37
Swiss (0)	45	0.05
Turkish (0)	0	<0.01
Ukrainian (25)	25	0.03
Welsh (98)	487	0.52
West Indian, ex. Hispanic (67)	77	0.08
Bahamian (0)	0	<0.01
Barbadian (0)	0	<0.01
Belizean (0)	0	<0.01
Bermudan (0)	0	<0.01
British West Indian (0)	0	<0.01
Dutch West Indian (0)	0	<0.01
Haitian (0)	0	<0.01
Jamaican (67)	67	0.07
Trinidadian/Tobagonian (0)	0	<0.01
U.S. Virgin Islander (0)	0	<0.01
West Indian (0)	10	0.01
Other West Indian (0)	0	<0.01
Yugoslavian (8)	34	0.04

Hispanic Origin	Population	%
Hispanic or Latino (of any race)	5,159	5.51
Central American, ex. Mexican	297	0.32
Costa Rican	6	0.01
Guatemalan	129	0.14
Honduran	59	0.06
Nicaraguan	11	0.01
Panamanian	14	0.01
Salvadoran	76	0.08
Other Central American	2	<0.01
Cuban	51	0.05
Dominican Republic	6	0.01
Mexican	4,216	4.50
Puerto Rican	200	0.21
South American	70	0.07
Argentinean	7	0.01
Bolivian	0	<0.01
Chilean	6	0.01
Colombian	27	0.03
Ecuadorian	8	0.01
Paraguayan	1	<0.01
Peruvian	14	0.01
Uruguayan	2	<0.01
Venezuelan	4	<0.01
Other South American	1	<0.01
Other Hispanic or Latino	319	0.34

Race*	Population	%
African-American/Black (17,655)	18,577	19.84
Not Hispanic (17,529)	18,388	19.64
Hispanic (126)	189	0.20
American Indian/Alaska Native (345)	874	0.93
Not Hispanic (307)	798	0.85
Hispanic (38)	76	0.08
Alaska Athabascan (Ala. Nat.) (0)	0	<0.01
Aleut (Alaska Native) (3)	3	<0.01
Apache (2)	12	0.01
Arapaho (0)	0	<0.01
Blackfeet (3)	19	0.02
Canadian/French Am. Ind. (0)	0	<0.01
Central American Ind. (2)	2	<0.01
Cherokee (76)	275	0.29
Cheyenne (0)	0	<0.01
Chickasaw (2)	2	<0.01
Chippewa (6)	8	0.01
Choctaw (3)	4	<0.01
Colville (0)	0	<0.01

	Population	%
Comanche (0)	0	<0.01
Cree (0)	2	<0.01
Creek (0)	2	<0.01
Crow (0)	1	<0.01
Delaware (2)	2	<0.01
Hopi (0)	0	<0.01
Houma (0)	0	<0.01
Inupiat (Alaska Native) (0)	0	<0.01
Iroquois (4)	8	0.01
Kiowa (0)	0	<0.01
Lumbee (100)	120	0.13
Menominee (0)	0	<0.01
Mexican American Ind. (10)	11	0.01
Navajo (0)	0	<0.01
Osage (0)	0	<0.01
Ottawa (0)	0	<0.01
Paiute (0)	1	<0.01
Pima (0)	0	<0.01
Potawatomi (0)	0	<0.01
Pueblo (0)	0	<0.01
Puget Sound Salish (0)	0	<0.01
Seminole (0)	8	0.01
Shoshone (0)	0	<0.01
Sioux (1)	9	0.01
South American Ind. (1)	2	<0.01
Spanish American Ind. (1)	1	<0.01
Tlingit-Haida (Alaska Native) (1)	1	<0.01
Tohono O'Odham (0)	0	<0.01
Tsimshian (Alaska Native) (0)	0	<0.01
Ute (0)	0	<0.01
Yakama (0)	0	<0.01
Yaqui (0)	1	<0.01
Yuman (0)	0	<0.01
Yup'ik (Alaska Native) (0)	0	<0.01
Asian (430)	592	0.63
Not Hispanic (423)	569	0.61
Hispanic (7)	23	0.02
Bangladeshi (0)	0	<0.01
Bhutanese (0)	0	<0.01
Burmese (0)	0	<0.01
Cambodian (5)	8	0.01
Chinese, ex. Taiwanese (80)	99	0.11
Filipino (51)	79	0.08
Hmong (10)	11	0.01
Indian (113)	138	0.15
Indonesian (0)	0	<0.01
Japanese (15)	50	0.05
Korean (39)	59	0.06
Laotian (11)	16	0.02
Malaysian (3)	3	<0.01
Nepalese (1)	1	<0.01
Pakistani (35)	40	0.04
Sri Lankan (0)	0	<0.01
Taiwanese (0)	0	<0.01
Thai (7)	12	0.01
Vietnamese (36)	55	0.06
Hawaii Native/Pacific Islander (60)	103	0.11
Not Hispanic (44)	79	0.08
Hispanic (16)	24	0.03
Fijian (1)	1	<0.01
Guamanian/Chamorro (32)	37	0.04
Marshallese (0)	0	<0.01
Native Hawaiian (16)	34	0.04
Samoan (6)	7	0.01
Tongan (0)	0	<0.01
White (70,875)	72,382	77.30
Not Hispanic (68,744)	69,967	74.72
Hispanic (2,131)	2,415	2.58

Rowan County

Population: 138,428

Ancestry	Population	%
Afghan (0)	0	<0.01
African, Sub-Saharan (3,445)	3,529	2.58
African (3,422)	3,506	2.56
Cape Verdean (0)	0	<0.01
Ethiopian (0)	0	<0.01
Ghanaian (0)	0	<0.01
Kenyan (0)	0	<0.01
Liberian (0)	0	<0.01
Nigerian (23)	23	0.02
Senegalese (0)	0	<0.01
Sierra Leonean (0)	0	<0.01
Somalian (0)	0	<0.01
South African (0)	0	<0.01
Sudanese (0)	0	<0.01
Ugandan (0)	0	<0.01
Zimbabwean (0)	0	<0.01
Other Sub-Saharan African (0)	0	<0.01
Albanian (31)	31	0.02
Alsatian (0)	0	<0.01
American (24,405)	24,405	17.83
Arab (80)	108	0.08
Arab (18)	18	0.01
Egyptian (21)	33	0.02
Iraqi (0)	0	<0.01
Jordanian (0)	0	<0.01
Lebanese (32)	48	0.04
Moroccan (0)	0	<0.01
Palestinian (0)	0	<0.01
Syrian (9)	9	0.01
Other Arab (0)	0	<0.01
Armenian (0)	0	<0.01
Assyrian/Chaldean/Syriac (0)	0	<0.01
Australian (0)	8	0.01
Austrian (13)	52	0.04
Basque (0)	0	<0.01
Belgian (8)	31	0.02
Brazilian (0)	22	0.02
British (270)	432	0.32
Bulgarian (0)	0	<0.01
Cajun (0)	0	<0.01
Canadian (140)	143	0.10
Carpatho Rusyn (0)	0	<0.01
Celtic (0)	0	<0.01
Croatian (0)	28	0.02
Cypriot (0)	0	<0.01
Czech (63)	205	0.15
Czechoslovakian (32)	43	0.03
Danish (16)	49	0.04
Dutch (640)	2,596	1.90
Eastern European (38)	38	0.03
English (5,019)	10,069	7.36
Estonian (0)	0	<0.01
European (603)	669	0.49
Finnish (34)	115	0.08
French, ex. Basque (343)	2,009	1.47
French Canadian (241)	446	0.33
German (11,966)	24,773	18.10
German Russian (0)	0	<0.01
Greek (81)	211	0.15
Guyanese (13)	13	0.01
Hungarian (97)	219	0.16
Icelander (0)	6	<0.01
Iranian (16)	78	0.06
Irish (3,682)	11,426	8.35
Israeli (0)	0	<0.01
Italian (1,009)	2,572	1.88
Latvian (0)	0	<0.01
Lithuanian (18)	37	0.03
Luxemburger (0)	0	<0.01
Macedonian (0)	0	<0.01
Maltese (11)	11	0.01
New Zealander (0)	0	<0.01
Northern European (23)	23	0.02
Norwegian (84)	363	0.27
Pennsylvania German (10)	10	0.01

Ancestry	Population	%
Polish (369)	1,251	0.91
Portuguese (18)	41	0.03
Romanian (0)	28	0.02
Russian (51)	319	0.23
Scandinavian (45)	86	0.06
Scotch-Irish (3,168)	6,025	4.40
Scottish (1,034)	2,581	1.89
Serbian (5)	5	<0.01
Slavic (8)	55	0.04
Slovak (11)	79	0.06
Slovene (0)	11	0.01
Soviet Union (0)	0	<0.01
Swedish (123)	796	0.58
Swiss (69)	169	0.12
Turkish (0)	12	0.01
Ukrainian (0)	22	0.02
Welsh (182)	450	0.33
West Indian, ex. Hispanic (36)	60	0.04
Bahamian (20)	20	0.01
Barbadian (0)	0	<0.01
Belizean (0)	0	<0.01
Bermudan (0)	0	<0.01
British West Indian (0)	0	<0.01
Dutch West Indian (0)	0	<0.01
Haitian (2)	15	0.01
Jamaican (7)	7	0.01
Trinidadian/Tobagonian (0)	0	<0.01
U.S. Virgin Islander (0)	0	<0.01
West Indian (7)	18	0.01
Other West Indian (0)	0	<0.01
Yugoslavian (68)	93	0.07

Hispanic Origin	Population	%
Hispanic or Latino (of any race)	10,644	7.69
Central American, ex. Mexican	1,605	1.16
Costa Rican	9	0.01
Guatemalan	117	0.08
Honduran	772	0.56
Nicaraguan	27	0.02
Panamanian	25	0.02
Salvadoran	633	0.46
Other Central American	22	0.02
Cuban	331	0.24
Dominican Republic	67	0.05
Mexican	7,426	5.36
Puerto Rican	455	0.33
South American	206	0.15
Argentinean	9	0.01
Bolivian	7	0.01
Chilean	10	0.01
Colombian	79	0.06
Ecuadorian	56	0.04
Paraguayan	0	<0.01
Peruvian	28	0.02
Uruguayan	4	<0.01
Venezuelan	12	0.01
Other South American	1	<0.01
Other Hispanic or Latino	554	0.40

Race*	Population	%
African-American/Black (22,392)	23,485	16.97
Not Hispanic (22,153)	23,135	16.71
Hispanic (239)	350	0.25
American Indian/Alaska Native (468)	1,199	0.87
Not Hispanic (376)	1,060	0.77
Hispanic (92)	139	0.10
Alaska Athabascan (Ala. Nat.) (1)	2	<0.01
Aleut (Alaska Native) (0)	0	<0.01
Apache (3)	10	0.01
Arapaho (0)	0	<0.01
Blackfeet (7)	34	0.02
Canadian/French Am. Ind. (1)	5	<0.01
Central American Ind. (0)	1	<0.01
Cherokee (101)	348	0.25
Cheyenne (1)	1	<0.01
Chickasaw (4)	8	0.01
Chippewa (14)	16	0.01
Choctaw (2)	18	0.01
Colville (0)	0	<0.01

Race* (continued)	Population	%
Comanche (1)	3	<0.01
Cree (0)	1	<0.01
Creek (0)	5	<0.01
Crow (0)	2	<0.01
Delaware (1)	1	<0.01
Hopi (1)	1	<0.01
Houma (0)	0	<0.01
Inupiat (Alaska Native) (1)	1	<0.01
Iroquois (3)	11	0.01
Kiowa (0)	0	<0.01
Lumbee (89)	134	0.10
Menominee (0)	0	<0.01
Mexican American Ind. (22)	28	0.02
Navajo (7)	9	0.01
Osage (0)	5	<0.01
Ottawa (1)	2	<0.01
Paiute (0)	0	<0.01
Pima (0)	0	<0.01
Potawatomi (0)	0	<0.01
Pueblo (0)	0	<0.01
Puget Sound Salish (0)	0	<0.01
Seminole (1)	2	<0.01
Shoshone (0)	0	<0.01
Sioux (3)	13	0.01
South American Ind. (3)	4	<0.01
Spanish American Ind. (5)	5	<0.01
Tlingit-Haida (Alaska Native) (0)	1	<0.01
Tohono O'Odham (0)	0	<0.01
Tsimshian (Alaska Native) (0)	0	<0.01
Ute (0)	0	<0.01
Yakama (0)	0	<0.01
Yaqui (0)	0	<0.01
Yuman (0)	0	<0.01
Yup'ik (Alaska Native) (0)	0	<0.01
Asian (1,386)	1,660	1.20
Not Hispanic (1,353)	1,598	1.15
Hispanic (33)	62	0.04
Bangladeshi (0)	0	<0.01
Bhutanese (0)	0	<0.01
Burmese (0)	0	<0.01
Cambodian (3)	8	0.01
Chinese, ex. Taiwanese (143)	194	0.14
Filipino (141)	215	0.16
Hmong (194)	205	0.15
Indian (227)	263	0.19
Indonesian (2)	2	<0.01
Japanese (14)	41	0.03
Korean (68)	107	0.08
Laotian (207)	226	0.16
Malaysian (0)	0	<0.01
Nepalese (0)	0	<0.01
Pakistani (18)	19	0.01
Sri Lankan (1)	1	<0.01
Taiwanese (10)	12	0.01
Thai (38)	66	0.05
Vietnamese (220)	258	0.19
Hawaii Native/Pacific Islander (49)	116	0.08
Not Hispanic (44)	89	0.06
Hispanic (5)	27	0.02
Fijian (0)	0	<0.01
Guamanian/Chamorro (12)	14	0.01
Marshallese (0)	0	<0.01
Native Hawaiian (19)	43	0.03
Samoan (9)	22	0.02
Tongan (0)	0	<0.01
White (105,923)	107,856	77.91
Not Hispanic (101,986)	103,526	74.79
Hispanic (3,937)	4,330	3.13

*Notes: † The Census 2010 population figure is used to calculate the percentages in the Hispanic Origin and Race categories. Ancestry percentages are based on the 2006-2010 American Community Survey population (not shown); ‡ Numbers in parentheses indicate the number of people reporting a single ancestry; * Numbers in parentheses indicate the number of persons reporting this race alone, not in combination with any other race; Please refer to the Explanation of Data for more information.*

Rutherford County

Population: 67,810

Ancestry	Population	%
Afghan (0)	0	<0.01
African, Sub-Saharan (180)	288	0.43
African (78)	186	0.28
Cape Verdean (0)	0	<0.01
Ethiopian (0)	0	<0.01
Ghanaian (0)	0	<0.01
Kenyan (0)	0	<0.01
Liberian (0)	0	<0.01
Nigerian (102)	102	0.15
Senegalese (0)	0	<0.01
Sierra Leonean (0)	0	<0.01
Somalian (0)	0	<0.01
South African (0)	0	<0.01
Sudanese (0)	0	<0.01
Ugandan (0)	0	<0.01
Zimbabwean (0)	0	<0.01
Other Sub-Saharan African (0)	0	<0.01
Albanian (0)	0	<0.01
Alsatian (0)	0	<0.01
American (13,277)	13,277	19.84
Arab (10)	64	0.10
Arab (0)	0	<0.01
Egyptian (0)	0	<0.01
Iraqi (0)	0	<0.01
Jordanian (0)	0	<0.01
Lebanese (10)	64	0.10
Moroccan (0)	0	<0.01
Palestinian (0)	0	<0.01
Syrian (0)	0	<0.01
Other Arab (0)	0	<0.01
Armenian (100)	100	0.15
Assyrian/Chaldean/Syriac (0)	0	<0.01
Australian (0)	0	<0.01
Austrian (12)	103	0.15
Basque (0)	9	0.01
Belgian (0)	31	0.05
Brazilian (87)	104	0.16
British (61)	135	0.20
Bulgarian (0)	0	<0.01
Cajun (0)	0	<0.01
Canadian (130)	194	0.29
Carpatho Rusyn (0)	0	<0.01
Celtic (24)	92	0.14
Croatian (0)	0	<0.01
Cypriot (0)	0	<0.01
Czech (95)	187	0.28
Czechoslovakian (17)	33	0.05
Danish (11)	43	0.06
Dutch (146)	1,064	1.59
Eastern European (0)	0	<0.01
English (3,477)	6,287	9.39
Estonian (0)	0	<0.01
European (283)	320	0.48
Finnish (65)	76	0.11
French, ex. Basque (252)	1,210	1.81
French Canadian (118)	229	0.34
German (2,231)	6,892	10.30
German Russian (0)	0	<0.01
Greek (0)	45	0.07
Guyanese (0)	0	<0.01
Hungarian (55)	67	0.10
Icelander (0)	0	<0.01
Iranian (0)	0	<0.01
Irish (3,822)	8,934	13.35
Israeli (0)	22	0.03
Italian (409)	1,028	1.54
Latvian (0)	0	<0.01
Lithuanian (18)	32	0.05
Luxemburger (0)	0	<0.01
Macedonian (0)	0	<0.01
Maltese (0)	0	<0.01
New Zealander (0)	0	<0.01
Northern European (0)	0	<0.01
Norwegian (65)	203	0.30
Pennsylvania German (0)	0	<0.01

	Population	%
Polish (104)	407	0.61
Portuguese (14)	129	0.19
Romanian (16)	67	0.10
Russian (18)	236	0.35
Scandinavian (22)	47	0.07
Scotch-Irish (2,162)	3,128	4.67
Scottish (557)	1,545	2.31
Serbian (0)	8	0.01
Slavic (0)	25	0.04
Slovak (0)	18	0.03
Slovene (0)	0	<0.01
Soviet Union (14)	14	0.02
Swedish (62)	360	0.54
Swiss (27)	90	0.13
Turkish (0)	9	0.01
Ukrainian (14)	118	0.18
Welsh (34)	201	0.30
West Indian, ex. Hispanic (0)	13	0.02
Bahamian (0)	0	<0.01
Barbadian (0)	13	0.02
Belizean (0)	0	<0.01
Bermudan (0)	0	<0.01
British West Indian (0)	0	<0.01
Dutch West Indian (0)	0	<0.01
Haitian (0)	0	<0.01
Jamaican (0)	0	<0.01
Trinidadian/Tobagonian (0)	0	<0.01
U.S. Virgin Islander (0)	0	<0.01
West Indian (0)	0	<0.01
Other West Indian (0)	0	<0.01
Yugoslavian (5)	5	0.01

Hispanic Origin	Population	%
Hispanic or Latino (of any race)	2,397	3.53
Central American, ex. Mexican	346	0.51
Costa Rican	9	0.01
Guatemalan	35	0.05
Honduran	82	0.12
Nicaraguan	50	0.07
Panamanian	11	0.02
Salvadoran	152	0.22
Other Central American	7	0.01
Cuban	68	0.10
Dominican Republic	38	0.06
Mexican	1,522	2.24
Puerto Rican	151	0.22
South American	97	0.14
Argentinean	5	0.01
Bolivian	0	<0.01
Chilean	7	0.01
Colombian	51	0.08
Ecuadorian	8	0.01
Paraguayan	0	<0.01
Peruvian	21	0.03
Uruguayan	0	<0.01
Venezuelan	4	0.01
Other South American	1	<0.01
Other Hispanic or Latino	175	0.26

Race*	Population	%
African-American/Black (6,854)	7,561	11.15
Not Hispanic (6,804)	7,482	11.03
Hispanic (50)	79	0.12
American Indian/Alaska Native (171)	547	0.81
Not Hispanic (156)	490	0.72
Hispanic (15)	57	0.08
Alaska Athabascan (Ala. Nat.) (0)	0	<0.01
Aleut (Alaska Native) (0)	0	<0.01
Apache (2)	2	<0.01
Arapaho (0)	0	<0.01
Blackfeet (0)	15	0.02
Canadian/French Am. Ind. (0)	1	<0.01
Central American Ind. (0)	5	0.01
Cherokee (43)	207	0.31
Cheyenne (0)	0	<0.01
Chickasaw (0)	0	<0.01
Chippewa (1)	2	<0.01
Choctaw (1)	1	<0.01
Colville (0)	0	<0.01

	Population	%
Comanche (1)	1	<0.01
Cree (0)	0	<0.01
Creek (1)	1	<0.01
Crow (0)	2	<0.01
Delaware (0)	0	<0.01
Hopi (0)	0	<0.01
Houma (0)	0	<0.01
Inupiat (Alaska Native) (0)	0	<0.01
Iroquois (4)	15	0.02
Kiowa (0)	0	<0.01
Lumbee (19)	24	0.04
Menominee (0)	0	<0.01
Mexican American Ind. (2)	4	0.01
Navajo (0)	1	<0.01
Osage (0)	0	<0.01
Ottawa (0)	0	<0.01
Paiute (0)	0	<0.01
Pima (0)	0	<0.01
Potawatomi (0)	0	<0.01
Pueblo (1)	2	<0.01
Puget Sound Salish (0)	0	<0.01
Seminole (0)	2	<0.01
Shoshone (0)	0	<0.01
Sioux (2)	4	0.01
South American Ind. (0)	0	<0.01
Spanish American Ind. (1)	1	<0.01
Tlingit-Haida (Alaska Native) (0)	0	<0.01
Tohono O'Odham (0)	0	<0.01
Tsimshian (Alaska Native) (0)	0	<0.01
Ute (0)	0	<0.01
Yakama (0)	0	<0.01
Yaqui (0)	0	<0.01
Yuman (0)	0	<0.01
Yup'ik (Alaska Native) (0)	0	<0.01
Asian (296)	438	0.65
Not Hispanic (289)	403	0.59
Hispanic (7)	35	0.05
Bangladeshi (0)	0	<0.01
Bhutanese (0)	0	<0.01
Burmese (0)	0	<0.01
Cambodian (6)	6	0.01
Chinese, ex. Taiwanese (33)	48	0.07
Filipino (66)	124	0.18
Hmong (2)	4	0.01
Indian (83)	98	0.14
Indonesian (0)	1	<0.01
Japanese (11)	32	0.05
Korean (5)	14	0.02
Laotian (6)	6	0.01
Malaysian (1)	1	<0.01
Nepalese (0)	1	<0.01
Pakistani (9)	9	0.01
Sri Lankan (0)	0	<0.01
Taiwanese (2)	2	<0.01
Thai (5)	7	0.01
Vietnamese (54)	63	0.09
Hawaii Native/Pacific Islander (5)	52	0.08
Not Hispanic (5)	36	0.05
Hispanic (0)	16	0.02
Fijian (0)	0	<0.01
Guamanian/Chamorro (0)	9	0.01
Marshallese (0)	0	<0.01
Native Hawaiian (5)	20	0.03
Samoan (0)	4	0.01
Tongan (0)	0	<0.01
White (58,221)	59,325	87.49
Not Hispanic (57,054)	58,010	85.55
Hispanic (1,167)	1,315	1.94

*Notes: † The Census 2010 population figure is used to calculate the percentages in the Hispanic Origin and Race categories. Ancestry percentages are based on the 2006-2010 American Community Survey population (not shown); ‡ Numbers in parentheses indicate the number of people reporting a single ancestry; * Numbers in parentheses indicate the number of persons reporting this race alone, not in combination with any other race; Please refer to the Explanation of Data for more information.*

Sampson County

Population: 63,431.

Ancestry	Population	%
Afghan (0)	0	<0.01
African, Sub-Saharan (182)	321	0.51
African (176)	240	0.38
Cape Verdean (0)	0	<0.01
Ethiopian (0)	0	<0.01
Ghanaian (6)	6	0.01
Kenyan (0)	0	<0.01
Liberian (0)	0	<0.01
Nigerian (0)	75	0.12
Senegalese (0)	0	<0.01
Sierra Leonean (0)	0	<0.01
Somalian (0)	0	<0.01
South African (0)	0	<0.01
Sudanese (0)	0	<0.01
Ugandan (0)	0	<0.01
Zimbabwean (0)	0	<0.01
Other Sub-Saharan African (0)	0	<0.01
Albanian (0)	0	<0.01
Alsatian (0)	0	<0.01
American (6,548)	6,548	10.42
Arab (216)	231	0.37
Arab (2)	2	<0.01
Egyptian (0)	0	<0.01
Iraqi (0)	0	<0.01
Jordanian (0)	0	<0.01
Lebanese (213)	228	0.36
Moroccan (1)	1	<0.01
Palestinian (0)	0	<0.01
Syrian (0)	0	<0.01
Other Arab (0)	0	<0.01
Armenian (8)	8	0.01
Assyrian/Chaldean/Syriac (0)	0	<0.01
Australian (0)	0	<0.01
Austrian (4)	39	0.06
Basque (0)	0	<0.01
Belgian (0)	3	<0.01
Brazilian (4)	7	0.01
British (92)	108	0.17
Bulgarian (0)	0	<0.01
Cajun (0)	0	<0.01
Canadian (8)	19	0.03
Carpatho Rusyn (0)	0	<0.01
Celtic (0)	0	<0.01
Croatian (5)	5	0.01
Cypriot (0)	0	<0.01
Czech (0)	9	0.01
Czechoslovakian (7)	17	0.03
Danish (10)	37	0.06
Dutch (98)	387	0.62
Eastern European (4)	4	0.01
English (3,436)	5,020	7.99
Estonian (0)	0	<0.01
European (209)	346	0.55
Finnish (0)	0	<0.01
French, ex. Basque (172)	400	0.64
French Canadian (46)	87	0.14
German (1,296)	3,330	5.30
German Russian (0)	0	<0.01
Greek (18)	21	0.03
Guyanese (44)	44	0.07
Hungarian (16)	31	0.05
Icelander (0)	0	<0.01
Iranian (0)	0	<0.01
Irish (2,110)	3,736	5.95
Israeli (0)	0	<0.01
Italian (171)	561	0.89
Latvian (83)	83	0.13
Lithuanian (0)	0	<0.01
Luxemburger (3)	3	<0.01
Macedonian (0)	0	<0.01
Maltese (0)	0	<0.01
New Zealander (0)	0	<0.01
Northern European (0)	0	<0.01
Norwegian (129)	157	0.25
Pennsylvania German (18)	18	0.03

Ancestry	Population	%
Polish (124)	289	0.46
Portuguese (5)	61	0.10
Romanian (0)	0	<0.01
Russian (5)	29	0.05
Scandinavian (8)	31	0.05
Scotch-Irish (1,090)	1,660	2.64
Scottish (994)	1,642	2.61
Serbian (0)	0	<0.01
Slavic (0)	0	<0.01
Slovak (0)	7	0.01
Slovene (0)	0	<0.01
Soviet Union (0)	0	<0.01
Swedish (58)	290	0.46
Swiss (14)	18	0.03
Turkish (0)	0	<0.01
Ukrainian (0)	0	<0.01
Welsh (110)	314	0.50
West Indian, ex. Hispanic (77)	209	0.33
Bahamian (0)	0	<0.01
Barbadian (0)	0	<0.01
Belizean (0)	0	<0.01
Bermudan (0)	0	<0.01
British West Indian (0)	0	<0.01
Dutch West Indian (13)	13	0.02
Haitian (0)	34	0.05
Jamaican (10)	102	0.16
Trinidadian/Tobagonian (4)	4	0.01
U.S. Virgin Islander (0)	0	<0.01
West Indian (50)	56	0.09
Other West Indian (0)	0	<0.01
Yugoslavian (0)	0	<0.01

Hispanic Origin	Population	%
Hispanic or Latino (of any race)	10,440	16.46
Central American, ex. Mexican	1,667	2.63
Costa Rican	23	0.04
Guatemalan	223	0.35
Honduran	1,028	1.62
Nicaraguan	78	0.12
Panamanian	22	0.03
Salvadoran	286	0.45
Other Central American	7	0.01
Cuban	50	0.08
Dominican Republic	58	0.09
Mexican	7,482	11.80
Puerto Rican	510	0.80
South American	91	0.14
Argentinean	4	0.01
Bolivian	2	<0.01
Chilean	14	0.02
Colombian	29	0.05
Ecuadorian	14	0.02
Paraguayan	0	<0.01
Peruvian	15	0.02
Uruguayan	4	0.01
Venezuelan	9	0.01
Other South American	0	<0.01
Other Hispanic or Latino	582	0.92

Race*	Population	%
African-American/Black (17,128)	17,724	27.94
Not Hispanic (16,948)	17,443	27.50
Hispanic (180)	281	0.44
American Indian/Alaska Native (1,297)	1,794	2.83
Not Hispanic (1,130)	1,549	2.44
Hispanic (167)	245	0.39
Alaska Athabascan (Ala. Nat.) (0)	0	<0.01
Aleut (Alaska Native) (5)	5	0.01
Apache (3)	6	0.01
Arapaho (0)	0	<0.01
Blackfeet (2)	17	0.03
Canadian/French Am. Ind. (0)	0	<0.01
Central American Ind. (0)	0	<0.01
Cherokee (48)	166	0.26
Cheyenne (1)	2	<0.01
Chickasaw (0)	0	<0.01
Chippewa (4)	5	0.01
Choctaw (0)	0	<0.01
Colville (0)	0	<0.01

	Population	%
Comanche (1)	1	<0.01
Cree (0)	0	<0.01
Creek (1)	1	<0.01
Crow (0)	0	<0.01
Delaware (0)	0	<0.01
Hopi (0)	0	<0.01
Houma (0)	0	<0.01
Inupiat (Alaska Native) (0)	1	<0.01
Iroquois (4)	11	0.02
Kiowa (0)	0	<0.01
Lumbee (166)	244	0.38
Menominee (0)	0	<0.01
Mexican American Ind. (44)	49	0.08
Navajo (2)	4	0.01
Osage (0)	0	<0.01
Ottawa (0)	0	<0.01
Paiute (0)	0	<0.01
Pima (0)	0	<0.01
Potawatomi (0)	0	<0.01
Pueblo (0)	0	<0.01
Puget Sound Salish (0)	0	<0.01
Seminole (0)	0	<0.01
Shoshone (0)	0	<0.01
Sioux (7)	13	0.02
South American Ind. (4)	4	0.01
Spanish American Ind. (19)	25	0.04
Tlingit-Haida (Alaska Native) (1)	1	<0.01
Tohono O'Odham (0)	0	<0.01
Tsimshian (Alaska Native) (0)	0	<0.01
Ute (0)	0	<0.01
Yakama (0)	0	<0.01
Yaqui (0)	0	<0.01
Yuman (0)	0	<0.01
Yup'ik (Alaska Native) (0)	0	<0.01
Asian (242)	336	0.53
Not Hispanic (217)	294	0.46
Hispanic (25)	42	0.07
Bangladeshi (0)	0	<0.01
Bhutanese (0)	0	<0.01
Burmese (0)	0	<0.01
Cambodian (0)	0	<0.01
Chinese, ex. Taiwanese (56)	73	0.12
Filipino (31)	48	0.08
Hmong (0)	0	<0.01
Indian (38)	57	0.09
Indonesian (0)	0	<0.01
Japanese (8)	18	0.03
Korean (37)	53	0.08
Laotian (15)	15	0.02
Malaysian (0)	0	<0.01
Nepalese (3)	3	<0.01
Pakistani (0)	0	<0.01
Sri Lankan (0)	0	<0.01
Taiwanese (0)	0	<0.01
Thai (7)	11	0.02
Vietnamese (23)	27	0.04
Hawaii Native/Pacific Islander (72)	113	0.18
Not Hispanic (43)	60	0.09
Hispanic (29)	53	0.08
Fijian (1)	1	<0.01
Guamanian/Chamorro (43)	55	0.09
Marshallese (0)	0	<0.01
Native Hawaiian (7)	18	0.03
Samoan (5)	16	0.03
Tongan (0)	0	<0.01
White (35,985)	36,979	58.30
Not Hispanic (33,754)	34,398	54.23
Hispanic (2,231)	2,581	4.07

*Notes: † The Census 2010 population figure is used to calculate the percentages in the Hispanic Origin and Race categories. Ancestry percentages are based on the 2006-2010 American Community Survey population (not shown); ‡ Numbers in parentheses indicate the number of people reporting a single ancestry; * Numbers in parentheses indicate the number of persons reporting this race alone, not in combination with any other race; Please refer to the Explanation of Data for more information.*

Stanly County

Population: 60,585

Ancestry	Population	%
Afghan (0)	0	<0.01
African, Sub-Saharan (245)	308	0.51
African (245)	306	0.51
Cape Verdean (0)	0	<0.01
Ethiopian (0)	0	<0.01
Ghanaian (0)	0	<0.01
Kenyan (0)	0	<0.01
Liberian (0)	0	<0.01
Nigerian (0)	2	<0.01
Senegalese (0)	0	<0.01
Sierra Leonean (0)	0	<0.01
Somalian (0)	0	<0.01
South African (0)	0	<0.01
Sudanese (0)	0	<0.01
Ugandan (0)	0	<0.01
Zimbabwean (0)	0	<0.01
Other Sub-Saharan African (0)	0	<0.01
Albanian (9)	9	0.01
Alsatian (0)	0	<0.01
American (8,537)	8,537	14.20
Arab (50)	162	0.27
Arab (10)	10	0.02
Egyptian (0)	0	<0.01
Iraqi (0)	0	<0.01
Jordanian (0)	0	<0.01
Lebanese (27)	139	0.23
Moroccan (0)	0	<0.01
Palestinian (13)	13	0.02
Syrian (0)	0	<0.01
Other Arab (0)	0	<0.01
Armenian (0)	41	0.07
Assyrian/Chaldean/Syriac (0)	0	<0.01
Australian (0)	0	<0.01
Austrian (0)	8	0.01
Basque (0)	0	<0.01
Belgian (45)	60	0.10
Brazilian (0)	0	<0.01
British (33)	76	0.13
Bulgarian (0)	0	<0.01
Cajun (0)	36	0.06
Canadian (33)	148	0.25
Carpatho Rusyn (0)	0	<0.01
Celtic (7)	21	0.03
Croatian (0)	0	<0.01
Cypriot (0)	0	<0.01
Czech (24)	24	0.04
Czechoslovakian (0)	12	0.02
Danish (80)	85	0.14
Dutch (158)	1,395	2.32
Eastern European (0)	0	<0.01
English (5,821)	8,575	14.27
Estonian (0)	0	<0.01
European (504)	536	0.89
Finnish (0)	0	<0.01
French, ex. Basque (210)	784	1.30
French Canadian (9)	61	0.10
German (4,339)	8,772	14.59
German Russian (0)	0	<0.01
Greek (0)	61	0.10
Guyanese (0)	0	<0.01
Hungarian (21)	53	0.09
Icelander (0)	0	<0.01
Iranian (0)	0	<0.01
Irish (1,915)	4,882	8.12
Israeli (0)	0	<0.01
Italian (331)	751	1.25
Latvian (0)	0	<0.01
Lithuanian (0)	0	<0.01
Luxemburger (0)	0	<0.01
Macedonian (0)	0	<0.01
Maltese (0)	0	<0.01
New Zealander (0)	0	<0.01
Northern European (0)	0	<0.01
Norwegian (24)	50	0.08
Pennsylvania German (8)	8	0.01

Ancestry	Population	%
Polish (133)	482	0.80
Portuguese (3)	14	0.02
Romanian (14)	14	0.02
Russian (12)	32	0.05
Scandinavian (12)	101	0.17
Scotch-Irish (955)	1,680	2.79
Scottish (519)	1,490	2.48
Serbian (3)	25	0.04
Slavic (0)	15	0.02
Slovak (17)	60	0.10
Slovene (0)	0	<0.01
Soviet Union (0)	0	<0.01
Swedish (60)	272	0.45
Swiss (10)	180	0.30
Turkish (0)	33	0.05
Ukrainian (16)	90	0.15
Welsh (91)	184	0.31
West Indian, ex. Hispanic (82)	93	0.15
Bahamian (0)	0	<0.01
Barbadian (0)	11	0.02
Belizean (0)	0	<0.01
Bermudan (0)	0	<0.01
British West Indian (0)	0	<0.01
Dutch West Indian (0)	0	<0.01
Haitian (0)	0	<0.01
Jamaican (82)	82	0.14
Trinidadian/Tobagonian (0)	0	<0.01
U.S. Virgin Islander (0)	0	<0.01
West Indian (0)	0	<0.01
Other West Indian (0)	0	<0.01
Yugoslavian (0)	0	<0.01

Hispanic Origin	Population	%
Hispanic or Latino (of any race)	2,166	3.58
Central American, ex. Mexican	94	0.16
Costa Rican	3	<0.01
Guatemalan	7	0.01
Honduran	36	0.06
Nicaraguan	2	<0.01
Panamanian	13	0.02
Salvadoran	30	0.05
Other Central American	3	<0.01
Cuban	19	0.03
Dominican Republic	18	0.03
Mexican	1,754	2.90
Puerto Rican	113	0.19
South American	34	0.06
Argentinean	0	<0.01
Bolivian	1	<0.01
Chilean	1	<0.01
Colombian	10	0.02
Ecuadorian	10	0.02
Paraguayan	1	<0.01
Peruvian	2	<0.01
Uruguayan	3	<0.01
Venezuelan	6	0.01
Other South American	0	<0.01
Other Hispanic or Latino	134	0.22

Race*	Population	%
African-American/Black (6,630)	7,013	11.58
Not Hispanic (6,590)	6,954	11.48
Hispanic (40)	59	0.10
American Indian/Alaska Native (197)	380	0.63
Not Hispanic (175)	355	0.59
Hispanic (22)	25	0.04
Alaska Athabascan (Ala. Nat.) (1)	1	<0.01
Aleut (Alaska Native) (0)	0	<0.01
Apache (0)	2	<0.01
Arapaho (0)	0	<0.01
Blackfeet (0)	2	<0.01
Canadian/French Am. Ind. (0)	0	<0.01
Central American Ind. (0)	0	<0.01
Cherokee (41)	97	0.16
Cheyenne (0)	0	<0.01
Chickasaw (1)	1	<0.01
Chippewa (3)	4	0.01
Choctaw (0)	1	<0.01
Colville (0)	0	<0.01

	Population	%
Comanche (0)	0	<0.01
Cree (0)	0	<0.01
Creek (0)	2	<0.01
Crow (0)	1	<0.01
Delaware (0)	0	<0.01
Hopi (0)	1	<0.01
Houma (0)	0	<0.01
Inupiat (Alaska Native) (1)	1	<0.01
Iroquois (1)	2	<0.01
Kiowa (0)	0	<0.01
Lumbee (54)	82	0.14
Menominee (0)	0	<0.01
Mexican American Ind. (5)	5	0.01
Navajo (0)	1	<0.01
Osage (1)	1	<0.01
Ottawa (2)	2	<0.01
Paiute (0)	0	<0.01
Pima (0)	0	<0.01
Potawatomi (0)	0	<0.01
Pueblo (0)	0	<0.01
Puget Sound Salish (0)	0	<0.01
Seminole (0)	2	<0.01
Shoshone (1)	1	<0.01
Sioux (1)	1	<0.01
South American Ind. (0)	0	<0.01
Spanish American Ind. (0)	0	<0.01
Tlingit-Haida (Alaska Native) (0)	0	<0.01
Tohono O'Odham (0)	0	<0.01
Tsimshian (Alaska Native) (0)	0	<0.01
Ute (0)	0	<0.01
Yakama (0)	0	<0.01
Yaqui (0)	0	<0.01
Yuman (0)	0	<0.01
Yup'ik (Alaska Native) (0)	0	<0.01
Asian (1,118)	1,232	2.03
Not Hispanic (1,108)	1,211	2.00
Hispanic (10)	21	0.03
Bangladeshi (0)	0	<0.01
Bhutanese (0)	0	<0.01
Burmese (2)	2	<0.01
Cambodian (0)	3	<0.01
Chinese, ex. Taiwanese (41)	59	0.10
Filipino (44)	68	0.11
Hmong (706)	730	1.20
Indian (96)	128	0.21
Indonesian (0)	0	<0.01
Japanese (18)	34	0.06
Korean (20)	27	0.04
Laotian (43)	48	0.08
Malaysian (0)	0	<0.01
Nepalese (0)	0	<0.01
Pakistani (4)	5	0.01
Sri Lankan (0)	0	<0.01
Taiwanese (6)	6	0.01
Thai (32)	33	0.05
Vietnamese (23)	26	0.04
Hawaii Native/Pacific Islander (42)	61	0.10
Not Hispanic (10)	23	0.04
Hispanic (32)	38	0.06
Fijian (1)	1	<0.01
Guamanian/Chamorro (30)	31	0.05
Marshallese (0)	0	<0.01
Native Hawaiian (6)	10	0.02
Samoan (5)	6	0.01
Tongan (0)	0	<0.01
White (50,623)	51,274	84.63
Not Hispanic (49,877)	50,457	83.28
Hispanic (746)	817	1.35

*Notes: † The Census 2010 population figure is used to calculate the percentages in the Hispanic Origin and Race categories. Ancestry percentages are based on the 2006-2010 American Community Survey population (not shown); ‡ Numbers in parentheses indicate the number of people reporting a single ancestry; * Numbers in parentheses indicate the number of persons reporting this race alone, not in combination with any other race; Please refer to the Explanation of Data for more information.*

Surry County

Population: 73,673

Ancestry	Population	%
Afghan (0)	0	<0.01
African, Sub-Saharan (98)	107	0.15
African (98)	107	0.15
Cape Verdean (0)	0	<0.01
Ethiopian (0)	0	<0.01
Ghanaian (0)	0	<0.01
Kenyan (0)	0	<0.01
Liberian (0)	0	<0.01
Nigerian (0)	0	<0.01
Senegalese (0)	0	<0.01
Sierra Leonean (0)	0	<0.01
Somalian (0)	0	<0.01
South African (0)	0	<0.01
Sudanese (0)	0	<0.01
Ugandan (0)	0	<0.01
Zimbabwean (0)	0	<0.01
Other Sub-Saharan African (0)	0	<0.01
Albanian (0)	0	<0.01
Alsatian (0)	0	<0.01
American (18,639)	18,639	25.43
Arab (30)	57	0.08
Arab (0)	0	<0.01
Egyptian (0)	0	<0.01
Iraqi (0)	0	<0.01
Jordanian (0)	0	<0.01
Lebanese (30)	57	0.08
Moroccan (0)	0	<0.01
Palestinian (0)	0	<0.01
Syrian (0)	0	<0.01
Other Arab (0)	0	<0.01
Armenian (0)	7	0.01
Assyrian/Chaldean/Syriac (0)	0	<0.01
Australian (0)	14	0.02
Austrian (17)	117	0.16
Basque (0)	0	<0.01
Belgian (0)	63	0.09
Brazilian (0)	0	<0.01
British (184)	431	0.59
Bulgarian (64)	64	0.09
Cajun (0)	0	<0.01
Canadian (22)	51	0.07
Carpatho Rusyn (0)	0	<0.01
Celtic (0)	10	0.01
Croatian (0)	0	<0.01
Cypriot (0)	0	<0.01
Czech (12)	85	0.12
Czechoslovakian (24)	43	0.06
Danish (40)	94	0.13
Dutch (182)	1,220	1.66
Eastern European (0)	0	<0.01
English (5,223)	8,342	11.38
Estonian (0)	0	<0.01
European (437)	481	0.66
Finnish (0)	0	<0.01
French, ex. Basque (203)	989	1.35
French Canadian (140)	177	0.24
German (3,070)	7,047	9.62
German Russian (0)	0	<0.01
Greek (31)	31	0.04
Guyanese (0)	0	<0.01
Hungarian (7)	47	0.06
Icelander (0)	0	<0.01
Iranian (0)	0	<0.01
Irish (2,441)	6,546	8.93
Israeli (0)	0	<0.01
Italian (653)	1,059	1.45
Latvian (0)	0	<0.01
Lithuanian (0)	0	<0.01
Luxemburger (0)	0	<0.01
Macedonian (0)	0	<0.01
Maltese (0)	0	<0.01
New Zealander (0)	0	<0.01
Northern European (71)	71	0.10
Norwegian (19)	35	0.05
Pennsylvania German (13)	23	0.03

Ancestry	Population	%
Polish (252)	824	1.12
Portuguese (9)	25	0.03
Romanian (39)	52	0.07
Russian (128)	192	0.26
Scandinavian (41)	41	0.06
Scotch-Irish (1,099)	2,032	2.77
Scottish (702)	1,174	1.60
Serbian (0)	0	<0.01
Slavic (0)	20	0.03
Slovak (14)	17	0.02
Slovene (0)	0	<0.01
Soviet Union (0)	0	<0.01
Swedish (71)	336	0.46
Swiss (9)	24	0.03
Turkish (0)	0	<0.01
Ukrainian (36)	36	0.05
Welsh (49)	460	0.63
West Indian, ex. Hispanic (28)	28	0.04
Bahamian (14)	14	0.02
Barbadian (0)	0	<0.01
Belizean (0)	0	<0.01
Bermudan (0)	0	<0.01
British West Indian (3)	3	<0.01
Dutch West Indian (0)	0	<0.01
Haitian (0)	0	<0.01
Jamaican (0)	0	<0.01
Trinidadian/Tobagonian (0)	0	<0.01
U.S. Virgin Islander (0)	0	<0.01
West Indian (11)	11	0.02
Other West Indian (0)	0	<0.01
Yugoslavian (0)	0	<0.01

Hispanic Origin	Population	%
Hispanic or Latino (of any race)	7,155	9.71
Central American, ex. Mexican	231	0.31
Costa Rican	9	0.01
Guatemalan	110	0.15
Honduran	35	0.05
Nicaraguan	16	0.02
Panamanian	6	0.01
Salvadoran	54	0.07
Other Central American	1	<0.01
Cuban	51	0.07
Dominican Republic	15	0.02
Mexican	6,323	8.58
Puerto Rican	132	0.18
South American	64	0.09
Argentinean	17	0.02
Bolivian	0	<0.01
Chilean	4	0.01
Colombian	15	0.02
Ecuadorian	0	<0.01
Paraguayan	0	<0.01
Peruvian	11	0.01
Uruguayan	0	<0.01
Venezuelan	14	0.02
Other South American	3	<0.01
Other Hispanic or Latino	339	0.46

Race*	Population	%
African-American/Black (2,749)	3,145	4.27
Not Hispanic (2,644)	3,002	4.07
Hispanic (105)	143	0.19
American Indian/Alaska Native (219)	516	0.70
Not Hispanic (173)	439	0.60
Hispanic (46)	77	0.10
Alaska Athabascan (Ala. Nat.) (3)	5	0.01
Aleut (Alaska Native) (3)	3	<0.01
Apache (1)	5	0.01
Arapaho (0)	0	<0.01
Blackfeet (1)	7	0.01
Canadian/French Am. Ind. (1)	2	<0.01
Central American Ind. (1)	1	<0.01
Cherokee (51)	165	0.22
Cheyenne (0)	0	<0.01
Chickasaw (9)	10	0.01
Chippewa (3)	3	<0.01
Choctaw (0)	2	<0.01
Colville (0)	0	<0.01

	Population	%
Comanche (2)	3	<0.01
Cree (0)	0	<0.01
Creek (1)	4	0.01
Crow (0)	0	<0.01
Delaware (0)	3	<0.01
Hopi (0)	0	<0.01
Houma (0)	0	<0.01
Inupiat (Alaska Native) (1)	1	<0.01
Iroquois (0)	3	<0.01
Kiowa (0)	0	<0.01
Lumbee (28)	38	0.05
Menominee (0)	0	<0.01
Mexican American Ind. (17)	19	0.03
Navajo (0)	0	<0.01
Osage (0)	0	<0.01
Ottawa (0)	0	<0.01
Paiute (0)	0	<0.01
Pima (0)	0	<0.01
Potawatomi (1)	1	<0.01
Pueblo (0)	0	<0.01
Puget Sound Salish (0)	0	<0.01
Seminole (0)	0	<0.01
Shoshone (0)	0	<0.01
Sioux (2)	6	0.01
South American Ind. (1)	1	<0.01
Spanish American Ind. (0)	0	<0.01
Tlingit-Haida (Alaska Native) (2)	5	0.01
Tohono O'Odham (0)	0	<0.01
Tsimshian (Alaska Native) (0)	0	<0.01
Ute (0)	0	<0.01
Yakama (0)	0	<0.01
Yaqui (0)	0	<0.01
Yuman (0)	0	<0.01
Yup'ik (Alaska Native) (0)	0	<0.01
Asian (347)	469	0.64
Not Hispanic (339)	430	0.58
Hispanic (8)	39	0.05
Bangladeshi (0)	0	<0.01
Bhutanese (0)	0	<0.01
Burmese (0)	0	<0.01
Cambodian (1)	1	<0.01
Chinese, ex. Taiwanese (44)	59	0.08
Filipino (55)	88	0.12
Hmong (67)	68	0.09
Indian (55)	82	0.11
Indonesian (5)	5	0.01
Japanese (18)	37	0.05
Korean (17)	28	0.04
Laotian (17)	19	0.03
Malaysian (0)	0	<0.01
Nepalese (0)	0	<0.01
Pakistani (7)	7	0.01
Sri Lankan (0)	0	<0.01
Taiwanese (0)	0	<0.01
Thai (3)	5	0.01
Vietnamese (45)	52	0.07
Hawaii Native/Pacific Islander (18)	48	0.07
Not Hispanic (9)	24	0.03
Hispanic (9)	24	0.03
Fijian (0)	0	<0.01
Guamanian/Chamorro (8)	8	0.01
Marshallese (0)	0	<0.01
Native Hawaiian (3)	15	0.02
Samoan (1)	3	<0.01
Tongan (1)	3	<0.01
White (64,926)	65,842	89.37
Not Hispanic (62,611)	63,266	85.87
Hispanic (2,315)	2,576	3.50

Notes: † The Census 2010 population figure is used to calculate the percentages in the Hispanic Origin and Race categories. Ancestry percentages are based on the 2006-2010 American Community Survey population (not shown); ‡ Numbers in parentheses indicate the number of people reporting a single ancestry; * Numbers in parentheses indicate the number of persons reporting this race alone, not in combination with any other race; Please refer to the Explanation of Data for more information.

Union County

Population: 201,292

Ancestry	Population	%
Afghan (0)	15	0.01
African, Sub-Saharan (1,074)	1,146	0.60
African (817)	881	0.46
Cape Verdean (0)	0	<0.01
Ethiopian (89)	89	0.05
Ghanaian (0)	0	<0.01
Kenyan (0)	0	<0.01
Liberian (32)	32	0.02
Nigerian (71)	71	0.04
Senegalese (0)	0	<0.01
Sierra Leonean (0)	0	<0.01
Somalian (0)	0	<0.01
South African (28)	36	0.02
Sudanese (0)	0	<0.01
Ugandan (0)	0	<0.01
Zimbabwean (0)	0	<0.01
Other Sub-Saharan African (37)	37	0.02
Albanian (5)	28	0.01
Alsatian (0)	0	<0.01
American (28,569)	28,569	15.01
Arab (426)	662	0.35
Arab (38)	38	0.02
Egyptian (9)	27	0.01
Iraqi (0)	0	<0.01
Jordanian (81)	81	0.04
Lebanese (38)	174	0.09
Moroccan (95)	106	0.06
Palestinian (0)	0	<0.01
Syrian (165)	218	0.11
Other Arab (0)	18	0.01
Armenian (121)	249	0.13
Assyrian/Chaldean/Syriac (0)	0	<0.01
Australian (0)	0	<0.01
Austrian (107)	445	0.23
Basque (0)	5	<0.01
Belgian (53)	188	0.10
Brazilian (218)	230	0.12
British (525)	1,233	0.65
Bulgarian (15)	26	0.01
Cajun (0)	0	<0.01
Canadian (207)	449	0.24
Carpatho Rusyn (0)	0	<0.01
Celtic (44)	44	0.02
Croatian (87)	156	0.08
Cypriot (12)	12	0.01
Czech (163)	425	0.22
Czechoslovakian (85)	217	0.11
Danish (150)	528	0.28
Dutch (566)	2,357	1.24
Eastern European (59)	62	0.03
English (9,334)	19,503	10.25
Estonian (0)	0	<0.01
European (1,576)	1,750	0.92
Finnish (66)	112	0.06
French, ex. Basque (714)	3,488	1.83
French Canadian (468)	938	0.49
German (9,878)	29,329	15.41
German Russian (0)	25	0.01
Greek (296)	699	0.37
Guyanese (0)	0	<0.01
Hungarian (203)	798	0.42
Icelander (0)	0	<0.01
Iranian (71)	71	0.04
Irish (6,923)	22,365	11.75
Israeli (0)	7	<0.01
Italian (3,759)	10,277	5.40
Latvian (0)	24	0.01
Lithuanian (38)	171	0.09
Luxemburger (17)	34	0.02
Macedonian (65)	65	0.03
Maltese (41)	41	0.02
New Zealander (0)	0	<0.01
Northern European (20)	20	0.01
Norwegian (332)	928	0.49
Pennsylvania German (36)	98	0.05

Ancestry	Population	%
Polish (1,254)	4,811	2.53
Portuguese (90)	301	0.16
Romanian (82)	229	0.12
Russian (933)	1,526	0.80
Scandinavian (133)	244	0.13
Scotch-Irish (4,539)	8,271	4.35
Scottish (1,992)	5,001	2.63
Serbian (9)	57	0.03
Slavic (0)	20	0.01
Slovak (90)	259	0.14
Slovene (56)	105	0.06
Soviet Union (0)	0	<0.01
Swedish (579)	1,470	0.77
Swiss (106)	355	0.19
Turkish (0)	12	0.01
Ukrainian (555)	794	0.42
Welsh (206)	1,223	0.64
West Indian, ex. Hispanic (192)	499	0.26
Bahamian (0)	0	<0.01
Barbadian (0)	0	<0.01
Belizean (0)	0	<0.01
Bermudan (0)	0	<0.01
British West Indian (0)	0	<0.01
Dutch West Indian (21)	227	0.12
Haitian (0)	29	0.02
Jamaican (146)	186	0.10
Trinidadian/Tobagonian (13)	13	0.01
U.S. Virgin Islander (0)	0	<0.01
West Indian (12)	44	0.02
Other West Indian (0)	0	<0.01
Yugoslavian (74)	140	0.07

Hispanic Origin	Population	%
Hispanic or Latino (of any race)	20,967	10.42
Central American, ex. Mexican	1,677	0.83
Costa Rican	109	0.05
Guatemalan	549	0.27
Honduran	264	0.13
Nicaraguan	115	0.06
Panamanian	88	0.04
Salvadoran	539	0.27
Other Central American	13	0.01
Cuban	577	0.29
Dominican Republic	409	0.20
Mexican	13,439	6.68
Puerto Rican	1,811	0.90
South American	1,916	0.95
Argentinean	128	0.06
Bolivian	17	0.01
Chilean	55	0.03
Colombian	801	0.40
Ecuadorian	436	0.22
Paraguayan	4	<0.01
Peruvian	293	0.15
Uruguayan	11	0.01
Venezuelan	155	0.08
Other South American	16	0.01
Other Hispanic or Latino	1,138	0.57

Race*	Population	%
African-American/Black (23,558)	25,238	12.54
Not Hispanic (23,134)	24,546	12.19
Hispanic (424)	692	0.34
American Indian/Alaska Native (815)	1,760	0.87
Not Hispanic (605)	1,436	0.71
Hispanic (210)	324	0.16
Alaska Athabascan (Ala. Nat.) (0)	0	<0.01
Aleut (Alaska Native) (3)	8	<0.01
Apache (2)	10	<0.01
Arapaho (0)	0	<0.01
Blackfeet (4)	33	0.02
Canadian/French Am. Ind. (1)	1	<0.01
Central American Ind. (4)	6	<0.01
Cherokee (97)	380	0.19
Cheyenne (1)	2	<0.01
Chickasaw (0)	1	<0.01
Chippewa (6)	11	0.01
Choctaw (9)	31	0.02
Colville (0)	0	<0.01

Race*	Population	%
Comanche (0)	6	<0.01
Cree (0)	3	<0.01
Creek (6)	17	0.01
Crow (1)	1	<0.01
Delaware (2)	9	<0.01
Hopi (0)	5	<0.01
Houma (1)	1	<0.01
Inupiat (Alaska Native) (4)	5	<0.01
Iroquois (27)	44	0.02
Kiowa (1)	1	<0.01
Lumbee (235)	349	0.17
Menominee (0)	3	<0.01
Mexican American Ind. (45)	54	0.03
Navajo (1)	5	<0.01
Osage (3)	4	<0.01
Ottawa (4)	6	<0.01
Paiute (0)	0	<0.01
Pima (0)	0	<0.01
Potawatomi (0)	2	<0.01
Pueblo (1)	1	<0.01
Puget Sound Salish (0)	2	<0.01
Seminole (0)	9	<0.01
Shoshone (0)	1	<0.01
Sioux (6)	11	0.01
South American Ind. (7)	22	0.01
Spanish American Ind. (7)	12	0.01
Tlingit-Haida (Alaska Native) (0)	0	<0.01
Tohono O'Odham (0)	0	<0.01
Tsimshian (Alaska Native) (0)	0	<0.01
Ute (0)	0	<0.01
Yakama (0)	1	<0.01
Yaqui (1)	5	<0.01
Yuman (0)	0	<0.01
Yup'ik (Alaska Native) (0)	0	<0.01
Asian (3,271)	4,154	2.06
Not Hispanic (3,243)	4,013	1.99
Hispanic (28)	141	0.07
Bangladeshi (0)	2	<0.01
Bhutanese (0)	0	<0.01
Burmese (3)	3	<0.01
Cambodian (29)	34	0.02
Chinese, ex. Taiwanese (518)	674	0.33
Filipino (386)	645	0.32
Hmong (79)	84	0.04
Indian (1,064)	1,182	0.59
Indonesian (21)	29	0.01
Japanese (69)	171	0.08
Korean (492)	633	0.31
Laotian (29)	42	0.02
Malaysian (1)	7	<0.01
Nepalese (1)	1	<0.01
Pakistani (14)	18	0.01
Sri Lankan (7)	9	<0.01
Taiwanese (10)	14	0.01
Thai (21)	44	0.02
Vietnamese (382)	426	0.21
Hawaii Native/Pacific Islander (63)	166	0.08
Not Hispanic (58)	131	0.07
Hispanic (5)	35	0.02
Fijian (0)	0	<0.01
Guamanian/Chamorro (14)	22	0.01
Marshallese (0)	0	<0.01
Native Hawaiian (13)	49	0.02
Samoan (13)	30	0.01
Tongan (4)	6	<0.01
White (158,954)	162,317	80.64
Not Hispanic (150,098)	152,561	75.79
Hispanic (8,856)	9,756	4.85

Wake County

Population: 900,993

Ancestry	Population	%
Afghan (681)	727	0.09
African, Sub-Saharan (14,726)	16,682	1.96
African (9,601)	10,818	1.27
Cape Verdean (120)	302	0.04
Ethiopian (479)	490	0.06
Ghanaian (173)	173	0.02
Kenyan (841)	854	0.10
Liberian (0)	14	<0.01
Nigerian (1,701)	1,806	0.21
Senegalese (45)	45	0.01
Sierra Leonean (191)	191	0.02
Somalian (503)	537	0.06
South African (210)	390	0.05
Sudanese (0)	0	<0.01
Ugandan (0)	0	<0.01
Zimbabwean (0)	11	<0.01
Other Sub-Saharan African (862)	1,051	0.12
Albanian (114)	215	0.03
Alsatian (29)	105	0.01
American (82,720)	82,720	9.73
Arab (4,968)	6,671	0.78
Arab (1,327)	1,429	0.17
Egyptian (981)	1,368	0.16
Iraqi (55)	112	0.01
Jordanian (205)	285	0.03
Lebanese (950)	1,633	0.19
Moroccan (559)	594	0.07
Palestinian (323)	345	0.04
Syrian (70)	216	0.03
Other Arab (498)	689	0.08
Armenian (255)	552	0.06
Assyrian/Chaldean/Syriac (18)	18	<0.01
Australian (91)	499	0.06
Austrian (316)	1,742	0.20
Basque (57)	95	0.01
Belgian (251)	1,025	0.12
Brazilian (380)	723	0.09
British (3,612)	6,690	0.79
Bulgarian (355)	384	0.05
Cajun (70)	131	0.02
Canadian (1,464)	2,510	0.30
Carpatho Rusyn (0)	0	<0.01
Celtic (74)	82	0.01
Croatian (106)	512	0.06
Cypriot (43)	43	0.01
Czech (849)	3,594	0.42
Czechoslovakian (242)	632	0.07
Danish (425)	2,200	0.26
Dutch (2,657)	10,723	1.26
Eastern European (875)	1,251	0.15
English (42,392)	101,808	11.97
Estonian (87)	119	0.01
European (13,469)	15,706	1.85
Finnish (230)	712	0.08
French, ex. Basque (3,451)	18,721	2.20
French Canadian (1,884)	4,696	0.55
German (29,350)	105,592	12.41
German Russian (0)	13	<0.01
Greek (1,533)	3,090	0.36
Guyanese (179)	243	0.03
Hungarian (928)	3,681	0.43
Icelander (35)	120	0.01
Iranian (812)	1,069	0.13
Irish (25,691)	86,855	10.21
Israeli (180)	212	0.02
Italian (14,897)	44,365	5.22
Latvian (39)	169	0.02
Lithuanian (442)	1,585	0.19
Luxemburger (0)	17	<0.01
Macedonian (0)	13	<0.01
Maltese (40)	187	0.02
New Zealander (11)	11	<0.01
Northern European (726)	740	0.09
Norwegian (1,885)	6,009	0.71
Pennsylvania German (91)	187	0.02
Polish (5,838)	21,156	2.49
Portuguese (389)	1,442	0.17
Romanian (438)	1,013	0.12
Russian (2,363)	6,597	0.78
Scandinavian (500)	1,225	0.14
Scotch-Irish (14,657)	28,676	3.37
Scottish (8,927)	25,344	2.98
Serbian (89)	328	0.04
Slavic (54)	261	0.03
Slovak (634)	1,969	0.23
Slovene (42)	276	0.03
Soviet Union (0)	0	<0.01
Swedish (1,814)	6,901	0.81
Swiss (495)	2,258	0.27
Turkish (714)	859	0.10
Ukrainian (1,164)	2,475	0.29
Welsh (1,442)	7,154	0.84
West Indian, ex. Hispanic (2,783)	4,364	0.51
Bahamian (169)	284	0.03
Barbadian (26)	57	0.01
Belizean (63)	120	0.01
Bermudan (24)	24	<0.01
British West Indian (28)	83	0.01
Dutch West Indian (0)	0	<0.01
Haitian (346)	484	0.06
Jamaican (1,199)	1,588	0.19
Trinidadian/Tobagonian (185)	244	0.03
U.S. Virgin Islander (14)	26	<0.01
West Indian (717)	1,442	0.17
Other West Indian (12)	12	<0.01
Yugoslavian (149)	495	0.06

Hispanic Origin	Population	%
Hispanic or Latino (of any race)	87,922	9.76
Central American, ex. Mexican	11,997	1.33
Costa Rican	390	0.04
Guatemalan	1,950	0.22
Honduran	3,401	0.38
Nicaraguan	488	0.05
Panamanian	588	0.07
Salvadoran	5,068	0.56
Other Central American	112	0.01
Cuban	2,616	0.29
Dominican Republic	3,441	0.38
Mexican	47,680	5.29
Puerto Rican	8,869	0.98
South American	7,493	0.83
Argentinean	631	0.07
Bolivian	187	0.02
Chilean	433	0.05
Colombian	2,667	0.30
Ecuadorian	855	0.09
Paraguayan	26	<0.01
Peruvian	1,528	0.17
Uruguayan	235	0.03
Venezuelan	883	0.10
Other South American	48	0.01
Other Hispanic or Latino	5,826	0.65

Race*	Population	%
African-American/Black (186,510)	197,078	21.87
Not Hispanic (182,793)	191,447	21.25
Hispanic (3,717)	5,631	0.62
American Indian/Alaska Native (4,503)	10,150	1.13
Not Hispanic (2,537)	7,076	0.79
Hispanic (1,966)	3,074	0.34
Alaska Athabascan (Ala. Nat.) (15)	19	<0.01
Aleut (Alaska Native) (6)	9	<0.01
Apache (10)	60	0.01
Arapaho (0)	7	<0.01
Blackfeet (32)	221	0.02
Canadian/French Am. Ind. (11)	23	<0.01
Central American Ind. (29)	67	0.01
Cherokee (374)	1,793	0.20
Cheyenne (7)	17	<0.01
Chickasaw (8)	29	<0.01
Chippewa (45)	105	0.01
Choctaw (26)	108	0.01
Colville (0)	1	<0.01

	Population	%
Comanche (10)	17	<0.01
Cree (3)	11	<0.01
Creek (16)	59	0.01
Crow (2)	19	<0.01
Delaware (7)	28	<0.01
Hopi (1)	4	<0.01
Houma (3)	6	<0.01
Inupiat (Alaska Native) (2)	10	<0.01
Iroquois (48)	145	0.02
Kiowa (2)	2	<0.01
Lumbee (635)	923	0.10
Menominee (2)	3	<0.01
Mexican American Ind. (350)	450	0.05
Navajo (19)	50	0.01
Osage (9)	18	<0.01
Ottawa (5)	8	<0.01
Paiute (2)	4	<0.01
Pima (4)	5	<0.01
Potawatomi (9)	19	<0.01
Pueblo (8)	18	<0.01
Puget Sound Salish (4)	4	<0.01
Seminole (5)	57	0.01
Shoshone (3)	3	<0.01
Sioux (35)	98	0.01
South American Ind. (64)	149	0.02
Spanish American Ind. (62)	79	0.01
Tlingit-Haida (Alaska Native) (4)	6	<0.01
Tohono O'Odham (5)	8	<0.01
Tsimshian (Alaska Native) (1)	2	<0.01
Ute (2)	4	<0.01
Yakama (0)	0	<0.01
Yaqui (4)	8	<0.01
Yuman (1)	2	<0.01
Yup'ik (Alaska Native) (1)	6	<0.01
Asian (48,553)	55,721	6.18
Not Hispanic (48,287)	54,905	6.09
Hispanic (266)	816	0.09
Bangladeshi (413)	438	0.05
Bhutanese (42)	68	0.01
Burmese (369)	414	0.05
Cambodian (103)	162	0.02
Chinese, ex. Taiwanese (9,143)	10,436	1.16
Filipino (3,096)	4,598	0.51
Hmong (87)	91	0.01
Indian (19,935)	21,220	2.36
Indonesian (166)	258	0.03
Japanese (1,023)	2,042	0.23
Korean (4,213)	5,169	0.57
Laotian (328)	392	0.04
Malaysian (54)	80	0.01
Nepalese (369)	424	0.05
Pakistani (1,376)	1,530	0.17
Sri Lankan (297)	339	0.04
Taiwanese (708)	824	0.09
Thai (444)	664	0.07
Vietnamese (4,967)	5,542	0.62
Hawaii Native/Pacific Islander (387)	1,195	0.13
Not Hispanic (317)	939	0.10
Hispanic (70)	256	0.03
Fijian (3)	7	<0.01
Guamanian/Chamorro (129)	243	0.03
Marshallese (1)	4	<0.01
Native Hawaiian (105)	346	0.04
Samoan (20)	87	0.01
Tongan (2)	7	<0.01
White (597,546)	615,587	68.32
Not Hispanic (560,536)	574,351	63.75
Hispanic (37,010)	41,236	4.58

*Notes: † The Census 2010 population figure is used to calculate the percentages in the Hispanic Origin and Race categories. Ancestry percentages are based on the 2006-2010 American Community Survey population (not shown); ‡ Numbers in parentheses indicate the number of people reporting a single ancestry; * Numbers in parentheses indicate the number of persons reporting this race alone, not in combination with any other race; Please refer to the Explanation of Data for more information.*

Watauga County

Population: 51,079

Ancestry	Population	%
Afghan (0)	0	<0.01
African, Sub-Saharan (4)	4	0.01
African (4)	4	0.01
Cape Verdean (0)	0	<0.01
Ethiopian (0)	0	<0.01
Ghanaian (0)	0	<0.01
Kenyan (0)	0	<0.01
Liberian (0)	0	<0.01
Nigerian (0)	0	<0.01
Senegalese (0)	0	<0.01
Sierra Leonean (0)	0	<0.01
Somalian (0)	0	<0.01
South African (0)	0	<0.01
Sudanese (0)	0	<0.01
Ugandan (0)	0	<0.01
Zimbabwean (0)	0	<0.01
Other Sub-Saharan African (0)	0	<0.01
Albanian (0)	4	0.01
Alsatian (0)	0	<0.01
American (4,465)	4,465	8.98
Arab (94)	122	0.25
Arab (0)	0	<0.01
Egyptian (10)	10	0.02
Iraqi (0)	0	<0.01
Jordanian (0)	0	<0.01
Lebanese (84)	112	0.23
Moroccan (0)	0	<0.01
Palestinian (0)	0	<0.01
Syrian (0)	0	<0.01
Other Arab (0)	0	<0.01
Armenian (0)	24	0.05
Assyrian/Chaldean/Syriac (0)	0	<0.01
Australian (0)	3	0.01
Austrian (13)	79	0.16
Basque (0)	0	<0.01
Belgian (0)	0	<0.01
Brazilian (0)	0	<0.01
British (253)	396	0.80
Bulgarian (0)	0	<0.01
Cajun (0)	0	<0.01
Canadian (12)	19	0.04
Carpatho Rusyn (0)	0	<0.01
Celtic (0)	0	<0.01
Croatian (0)	3	0.01
Cypriot (0)	0	<0.01
Czech (65)	281	0.57
Czechoslovakian (76)	135	0.27
Danish (48)	229	0.46
Dutch (235)	845	1.70
Eastern European (4)	4	0.01
English (3,798)	8,042	16.18
Estonian (0)	0	<0.01
European (565)	619	1.25
Finnish (0)	38	0.08
French, ex. Basque (424)	1,165	2.34
French Canadian (29)	40	0.08
German (4,482)	11,703	23.54
German Russian (0)	0	<0.01
Greek (188)	262	0.53
Guyanese (0)	0	<0.01
Hungarian (131)	295	0.59
Icelander (0)	69	0.14
Iranian (0)	95	0.19
Irish (2,476)	6,693	13.47
Israeli (0)	0	<0.01
Italian (511)	1,732	3.48
Latvian (0)	0	<0.01
Lithuanian (14)	52	0.10
Luxemburger (0)	0	<0.01
Macedonian (0)	0	<0.01
Maltese (0)	0	<0.01
New Zealander (0)	0	<0.01
Northern European (7)	7	0.01
Norwegian (107)	704	1.42
Pennsylvania German (16)	38	0.08

Ancestry (cont.)	Population	%
Polish (256)	778	1.57
Portuguese (56)	129	0.26
Romanian (25)	48	0.10
Russian (133)	407	0.82
Scandinavian (33)	136	0.27
Scotch-Irish (1,574)	3,266	6.57
Scottish (903)	2,676	5.38
Serbian (29)	29	0.06
Slavic (15)	15	0.03
Slovak (31)	75	0.15
Slovene (0)	0	<0.01
Soviet Union (0)	0	<0.01
Swedish (67)	392	0.79
Swiss (48)	131	0.26
Turkish (54)	79	0.16
Ukrainian (42)	73	0.15
Welsh (80)	551	1.11
West Indian, ex. Hispanic (23)	53	0.11
Bahamian (0)	0	<0.01
Barbadian (0)	0	<0.01
Belizean (0)	0	<0.01
Bermudan (0)	0	<0.01
British West Indian (0)	0	<0.01
Dutch West Indian (10)	10	0.02
Haitian (0)	0	<0.01
Jamaican (0)	18	0.04
Trinidadian/Tobagonian (13)	13	0.03
U.S. Virgin Islander (0)	0	<0.01
West Indian (0)	12	0.02
Other West Indian (0)	0	<0.01
Yugoslavian (0)	34	0.07

Hispanic Origin	Population	%
Hispanic or Latino (of any race)	1,713	3.35
Central American, ex. Mexican	121	0.24
Costa Rican	12	0.02
Guatemalan	40	0.08
Honduran	41	0.08
Nicaraguan	12	0.02
Panamanian	3	0.01
Salvadoran	13	0.03
Other Central American	0	<0.01
Cuban	122	0.24
Dominican Republic	12	0.02
Mexican	1,076	2.11
Puerto Rican	155	0.30
South American	122	0.24
Argentinean	10	0.02
Bolivian	2	<0.01
Chilean	9	0.02
Colombian	63	0.12
Ecuadorian	7	0.01
Paraguayan	1	<0.01
Peruvian	11	0.02
Uruguayan	5	0.01
Venezuelan	14	0.03
Other South American	0	<0.01
Other Hispanic or Latino	105	0.21

Race*	Population	%
African-American/Black (877)	1,072	2.10
Not Hispanic (855)	1,025	2.01
Hispanic (22)	47	0.09
American Indian/Alaska Native (129)	438	0.86
Not Hispanic (117)	390	0.76
Hispanic (12)	48	0.09
Alaska Athabascan (Ala. Nat.) (0)	0	<0.01
Aleut (Alaska Native) (0)	0	<0.01
Apache (1)	10	0.02
Arapaho (0)	0	<0.01
Blackfeet (1)	11	0.02
Canadian/French Am. Ind. (1)	1	<0.01
Central American Ind. (1)	1	<0.01
Cherokee (27)	162	0.32
Cheyenne (1)	3	0.01
Chickasaw (0)	0	<0.01
Chippewa (8)	13	0.03
Choctaw (8)	9	0.02
Colville (0)	0	<0.01

Race* (cont.)	Population	%
Comanche (0)	0	<0.01
Cree (0)	2	<0.01
Creek (0)	2	<0.01
Crow (0)	1	<0.01
Delaware (2)	3	0.01
Hopi (0)	0	<0.01
Houma (0)	0	<0.01
Inupiat (Alaska Native) (0)	0	<0.01
Iroquois (3)	9	0.02
Kiowa (0)	0	<0.01
Lumbee (11)	22	0.04
Menominee (0)	1	<0.01
Mexican American Ind. (0)	3	0.01
Navajo (1)	2	<0.01
Osage (0)	0	<0.01
Ottawa (0)	0	<0.01
Paiute (0)	0	<0.01
Pima (0)	0	<0.01
Potawatomi (3)	3	0.01
Pueblo (0)	0	<0.01
Puget Sound Salish (0)	0	<0.01
Seminole (0)	1	<0.01
Shoshone (0)	0	<0.01
Sioux (4)	8	0.02
South American Ind. (1)	5	0.01
Spanish American Ind. (0)	3	0.01
Tlingit-Haida (Alaska Native) (0)	0	<0.01
Tohono O'Odham (0)	0	<0.01
Tsimshian (Alaska Native) (0)	0	<0.01
Ute (0)	0	<0.01
Yakama (0)	0	<0.01
Yaqui (0)	0	<0.01
Yuman (0)	0	<0.01
Yup'ik (Alaska Native) (0)	0	<0.01
Asian (475)	650	1.27
Not Hispanic (467)	629	1.23
Hispanic (8)	21	0.04
Bangladeshi (0)	0	<0.01
Bhutanese (0)	0	<0.01
Burmese (2)	2	<0.01
Cambodian (1)	1	<0.01
Chinese, ex. Taiwanese (155)	180	0.35
Filipino (39)	85	0.17
Hmong (21)	22	0.04
Indian (70)	94	0.18
Indonesian (2)	3	0.01
Japanese (26)	63	0.12
Korean (56)	81	0.16
Laotian (5)	5	0.01
Malaysian (1)	1	<0.01
Nepalese (3)	3	0.01
Pakistani (5)	5	0.01
Sri Lankan (1)	1	<0.01
Taiwanese (7)	11	0.02
Thai (6)	12	0.02
Vietnamese (52)	66	0.13
Hawaii Native/Pacific Islander (13)	44	0.09
Not Hispanic (13)	38	0.07
Hispanic (0)	6	0.01
Fijian (0)	0	<0.01
Guamanian/Chamorro (1)	7	0.01
Marshallese (1)	1	<0.01
Native Hawaiian (5)	19	0.04
Samoan (3)	4	0.01
Tongan (0)	0	<0.01
White (48,272)	48,945	95.82
Not Hispanic (47,268)	47,831	93.64
Hispanic (1,004)	1,114	2.18

Notes: † The Census 2010 population figure is used to calculate the percentages in the Hispanic Origin and Race categories. Ancestry percentages are based on the 2006-2010 American Community Survey population (not shown); ‡ Numbers in parentheses indicate the number of people reporting a single ancestry; * Numbers in parentheses indicate the number of persons reporting this race alone, not in combination with any other race; Please refer to the Explanation of Data for more information.

Wayne County

Population: 122,623

Ancestry	Population	%
Afghan (0)	0	<0.01
African, Sub-Saharan (375)	499	0.42
African (334)	416	0.35
Cape Verdean (0)	0	<0.01
Ethiopian (0)	0	<0.01
Ghanaian (0)	0	<0.01
Kenyan (0)	0	<0.01
Liberian (0)	0	<0.01
Nigerian (41)	83	0.07
Senegalese (0)	0	<0.01
Sierra Leonean (0)	0	<0.01
Somalian (0)	0	<0.01
South African (0)	0	<0.01
Sudanese (0)	0	<0.01
Ugandan (0)	0	<0.01
Zimbabwean (0)	0	<0.01
Other Sub-Saharan African (0)	0	<0.01
Albanian (0)	0	<0.01
Alsatian (0)	0	<0.01
American (15,495)	15,495	12.90
Arab (213)	273	0.23
Arab (76)	94	0.08
Egyptian (18)	18	0.01
Iraqi (0)	0	<0.01
Jordanian (25)	25	0.02
Lebanese (53)	74	0.06
Moroccan (0)	3	<0.01
Palestinian (16)	16	0.01
Syrian (16)	16	0.01
Other Arab (9)	27	0.02
Armenian (0)	0	<0.01
Assyrian/Chaldean/Syriac (0)	0	<0.01
Australian (20)	30	0.02
Austrian (9)	48	0.04
Basque (0)	0	<0.01
Belgian (39)	43	0.04
Brazilian (14)	17	0.01
British (290)	435	0.36
Bulgarian (0)	0	<0.01
Cajun (12)	12	0.01
Canadian (27)	106	0.09
Carpatho Rusyn (0)	0	<0.01
Celtic (0)	0	<0.01
Croatian (0)	35	0.03
Cypriot (0)	0	<0.01
Czech (30)	188	0.16
Czechoslovakian (9)	9	0.01
Danish (6)	196	0.16
Dutch (168)	991	0.83
Eastern European (8)	22	0.02
English (6,650)	11,415	9.50
Estonian (0)	0	<0.01
European (795)	829	0.69
Finnish (0)	40	0.03
French, ex. Basque (436)	1,530	1.27
French Canadian (136)	275	0.23
German (2,579)	8,314	6.92
German Russian (0)	0	<0.01
Greek (32)	233	0.19
Guyanese (0)	0	<0.01
Hungarian (46)	173	0.14
Icelander (0)	11	0.01
Iranian (22)	26	0.02
Irish (3,738)	9,352	7.79
Israeli (0)	0	<0.01
Italian (709)	2,274	1.89
Latvian (0)	10	0.01
Lithuanian (16)	58	0.05
Luxemburger (0)	0	<0.01
Macedonian (0)	0	<0.01
Maltese (0)	0	<0.01
New Zealander (0)	0	<0.01
Northern European (18)	18	0.01
Norwegian (207)	539	0.45
Pennsylvania German (45)	60	0.05

	Population	%
Polish (300)	1,062	0.88
Portuguese (128)	278	0.23
Romanian (0)	19	0.02
Russian (25)	93	0.08
Scandinavian (24)	27	0.02
Scotch-Irish (1,574)	2,843	2.37
Scottish (836)	2,143	1.78
Serbian (10)	17	0.01
Slavic (0)	3	<0.01
Slovak (18)	22	0.02
Slovene (3)	35	0.03
Soviet Union (0)	0	<0.01
Swedish (228)	616	0.51
Swiss (19)	93	0.08
Turkish (38)	38	0.03
Ukrainian (22)	48	0.04
Welsh (48)	343	0.29
West Indian, ex. Hispanic (233)	416	0.35
Bahamian (0)	0	<0.01
Barbadian (46)	46	0.04
Belizean (0)	0	<0.01
Bermudan (9)	9	0.01
British West Indian (37)	37	0.03
Dutch West Indian (7)	7	0.01
Haitian (21)	30	0.02
Jamaican (77)	141	0.12
Trinidadian/Tobagonian (18)	18	0.01
U.S. Virgin Islander (3)	3	<0.01
West Indian (15)	125	0.10
Other West Indian (0)	0	<0.01
Yugoslavian (3)	3	<0.01

Hispanic Origin	Population	%
Hispanic or Latino (of any race)	12,162	9.92
Central American, ex. Mexican	1,979	1.61
Costa Rican	17	0.01
Guatemalan	1,058	0.86
Honduran	445	0.36
Nicaraguan	29	0.02
Panamanian	75	0.06
Salvadoran	343	0.28
Other Central American	12	0.01
Cuban	129	0.11
Dominican Republic	95	0.08
Mexican	7,921	6.46
Puerto Rican	905	0.74
South American	200	0.16
Argentinean	18	0.01
Bolivian	1	<0.01
Chilean	8	0.01
Colombian	68	0.06
Ecuadorian	38	0.03
Paraguayan	1	<0.01
Peruvian	34	0.03
Uruguayan	1	<0.01
Venezuelan	26	0.02
Other South American	5	<0.01
Other Hispanic or Latino	933	0.76

Race*	Population	%
African-American/Black (38,499)	39,932	32.56
Not Hispanic (38,107)	39,348	32.09
Hispanic (392)	584	0.48
American Indian/Alaska Native (481)	1,118	0.91
Not Hispanic (333)	881	0.72
Hispanic (148)	237	0.19
Alaska Athabascan (Ala. Nat.) (1)	1	<0.01
Aleut (Alaska Native) (1)	2	<0.01
Apache (8)	17	0.01
Arapaho (0)	2	<0.01
Blackfeet (2)	25	0.02
Canadian/French Am. Ind. (3)	5	<0.01
Central American Ind. (6)	12	0.01
Cherokee (47)	224	0.18
Cheyenne (0)	0	<0.01
Chickasaw (1)	3	<0.01
Chippewa (4)	15	0.01
Choctaw (3)	3	<0.01
Colville (0)	0	<0.01

	Population	%
Comanche (0)	0	<0.01
Cree (0)	0	<0.01
Creek (5)	9	0.01
Crow (0)	0	<0.01
Delaware (0)	0	<0.01
Hopi (0)	0	<0.01
Houma (0)	3	<0.01
Inupiat (Alaska Native) (0)	0	<0.01
Iroquois (10)	22	0.02
Kiowa (0)	0	<0.01
Lumbee (50)	79	0.06
Menominee (0)	0	<0.01
Mexican American Ind. (50)	62	0.05
Navajo (0)	6	<0.01
Osage (0)	0	<0.01
Ottawa (0)	0	<0.01
Paiute (0)	0	<0.01
Pima (1)	3	<0.01
Potawatomi (4)	7	0.01
Pueblo (1)	3	<0.01
Puget Sound Salish (0)	0	<0.01
Seminole (7)	9	0.01
Shoshone (0)	0	<0.01
Sioux (2)	11	0.01
South American Ind. (7)	10	0.01
Spanish American Ind. (6)	10	0.01
Tlingit-Haida (Alaska Native) (0)	0	<0.01
Tohono O'Odham (0)	0	<0.01
Tsimshian (Alaska Native) (0)	0	<0.01
Ute (0)	0	<0.01
Yakama (0)	0	<0.01
Yaqui (1)	1	<0.01
Yuman (0)	0	<0.01
Yup'ik (Alaska Native) (0)	0	<0.01
Asian (1,431)	2,186	1.78
Not Hispanic (1,405)	2,092	1.71
Hispanic (26)	94	0.08
Bangladeshi (8)	9	0.01
Bhutanese (0)	0	<0.01
Burmese (1)	1	<0.01
Cambodian (5)	7	0.01
Chinese, ex. Taiwanese (257)	312	0.25
Filipino (378)	609	0.50
Hmong (9)	9	0.01
Indian (132)	190	0.15
Indonesian (0)	0	<0.01
Japanese (103)	221	0.18
Korean (205)	317	0.26
Laotian (10)	15	0.01
Malaysian (1)	1	<0.01
Nepalese (0)	0	<0.01
Pakistani (29)	31	0.03
Sri Lankan (3)	3	<0.01
Taiwanese (12)	15	0.01
Thai (106)	174	0.14
Vietnamese (82)	108	0.09
Hawaii Native/Pacific Islander (64)	200	0.16
Not Hispanic (47)	136	0.11
Hispanic (17)	64	0.05
Fijian (1)	1	<0.01
Guamanian/Chamorro (28)	46	0.04
Marshallese (0)	0	<0.01
Native Hawaiian (20)	76	0.06
Samoan (3)	11	0.01
Tongan (0)	1	<0.01
White (72,135)	74,431	60.70
Not Hispanic (68,216)	69,958	57.05
Hispanic (3,919)	4,473	3.65

Notes: † The Census 2010 population figure is used to calculate the percentages in the Hispanic Origin and Race categories. Ancestry percentages are based on the 2006-2010 American Community Survey population (not shown); ‡ Numbers in parentheses indicate the number of people reporting a single ancestry; * Numbers in parentheses indicate the number of persons reporting this race alone, not in combination with any other race; Please refer to the Explanation of Data for more information.

Wilkes County
Population: 69,340

Ancestry	Population	%
Afghan (0)	0	<0.01
African, Sub-Saharan (48)	110	0.16
African (35)	97	0.14
Cape Verdean (0)	0	<0.01
Ethiopian (0)	0	<0.01
Ghanaian (13)	13	0.02
Kenyan (0)	0	<0.01
Liberian (0)	0	<0.01
Nigerian (0)	0	<0.01
Senegalese (0)	0	<0.01
Sierra Leonean (0)	0	<0.01
Somalian (0)	0	<0.01
South African (0)	0	<0.01
Sudanese (0)	0	<0.01
Ugandan (0)	0	<0.01
Zimbabwean (0)	0	<0.01
Other Sub-Saharan African (0)	0	<0.01
Albanian (0)	0	<0.01
Alsatian (0)	0	<0.01
American (25,895)	25,895	37.49
Arab (0)	40	0.06
Arab (0)	0	<0.01
Egyptian (0)	0	<0.01
Iraqi (0)	0	<0.01
Jordanian (0)	0	<0.01
Lebanese (0)	26	0.04
Moroccan (0)	0	<0.01
Palestinian (0)	0	<0.01
Syrian (0)	14	0.02
Other Arab (0)	0	<0.01
Armenian (0)	0	<0.01
Assyrian/Chaldean/Syriac (0)	0	<0.01
Australian (0)	0	<0.01
Austrian (0)	11	0.02
Basque (0)	0	<0.01
Belgian (0)	10	0.01
Brazilian (0)	0	<0.01
British (140)	356	0.52
Bulgarian (0)	0	<0.01
Cajun (0)	0	<0.01
Canadian (50)	76	0.11
Carpatho Rusyn (0)	0	<0.01
Celtic (20)	20	0.03
Croatian (0)	0	<0.01
Cypriot (0)	0	<0.01
Czech (12)	61	0.09
Czechoslovakian (14)	28	0.04
Danish (0)	0	<0.01
Dutch (215)	915	1.32
Eastern European (0)	14	0.02
English (4,420)	7,194	10.42
Estonian (0)	26	0.04
European (528)	553	0.80
Finnish (0)	0	<0.01
French, ex. Basque (276)	789	1.14
French Canadian (21)	79	0.11
German (2,356)	6,442	9.33
German Russian (0)	0	<0.01
Greek (48)	90	0.13
Guyanese (0)	0	<0.01
Hungarian (21)	72	0.10
Icelander (0)	0	<0.01
Iranian (0)	0	<0.01
Irish (1,927)	4,591	6.65
Israeli (0)	0	<0.01
Italian (293)	722	1.05
Latvian (0)	0	<0.01
Lithuanian (0)	48	0.07
Luxemburger (0)	0	<0.01
Macedonian (0)	0	<0.01
Maltese (0)	0	<0.01
New Zealander (0)	0	<0.01
Northern European (0)	0	<0.01
Norwegian (39)	171	0.25
Pennsylvania German (0)	14	0.02

	Population	%
Polish (139)	459	0.66
Portuguese (10)	12	0.02
Romanian (2)	2	<0.01
Russian (20)	66	0.10
Scandinavian (9)	9	0.01
Scotch-Irish (1,230)	2,215	3.21
Scottish (501)	1,541	2.23
Serbian (0)	0	<0.01
Slavic (0)	0	<0.01
Slovak (9)	9	0.01
Slovene (0)	0	<0.01
Soviet Union (0)	0	<0.01
Swedish (87)	137	0.20
Swiss (15)	68	0.10
Turkish (0)	8	0.01
Ukrainian (0)	5	0.01
Welsh (64)	211	0.31
West Indian, ex. Hispanic (0)	69	0.10
Bahamian (0)	0	<0.01
Barbadian (0)	0	<0.01
Belizean (0)	0	<0.01
Bermudan (0)	0	<0.01
British West Indian (0)	0	<0.01
Dutch West Indian (0)	29	0.04
Haitian (0)	0	<0.01
Jamaican (0)	0	<0.01
Trinidadian/Tobagonian (0)	0	<0.01
U.S. Virgin Islander (0)	0	<0.01
West Indian (0)	40	0.06
Other West Indian (0)	0	<0.01
Yugoslavian (12)	12	0.02

Hispanic Origin	Population	%
Hispanic or Latino (of any race)	3,772	5.44
Central American, ex. Mexican	733	1.06
Costa Rican	6	0.01
Guatemalan	281	0.41
Honduran	192	0.28
Nicaraguan	24	0.03
Panamanian	3	<0.01
Salvadoran	212	0.31
Other Central American	15	0.02
Cuban	86	0.12
Dominican Republic	12	0.02
Mexican	2,498	3.60
Puerto Rican	136	0.20
South American	53	0.08
Argentinean	2	<0.01
Bolivian	2	<0.01
Chilean	2	<0.01
Colombian	18	0.03
Ecuadorian	16	0.02
Paraguayan	0	<0.01
Peruvian	3	<0.01
Uruguayan	2	<0.01
Venezuelan	8	0.01
Other South American	0	<0.01
Other Hispanic or Latino	254	0.37

Race*	Population	%
African-American/Black (2,830)	3,266	4.71
Not Hispanic (2,785)	3,201	4.62
Hispanic (45)	65	0.09
American Indian/Alaska Native (133)	393	0.57
Not Hispanic (110)	344	0.50
Hispanic (23)	49	0.07
Alaska Athabascan (Ala. Nat.) (0)	0	<0.01
Aleut (Alaska Native) (0)	0	<0.01
Apache (0)	3	<0.01
Arapaho (0)	0	<0.01
Blackfeet (0)	8	0.01
Canadian/French Am. Ind. (0)	0	<0.01
Central American Ind. (0)	1	<0.01
Cherokee (39)	128	0.18
Cheyenne (0)	0	<0.01
Chickasaw (0)	1	<0.01
Chippewa (1)	1	<0.01
Choctaw (0)	0	<0.01
Colville (0)	0	<0.01

	Population	%
Comanche (0)	2	<0.01
Cree (0)	0	<0.01
Creek (0)	1	<0.01
Crow (1)	1	<0.01
Delaware (0)	0	<0.01
Hopi (0)	0	<0.01
Houma (0)	0	<0.01
Inupiat (Alaska Native) (0)	0	<0.01
Iroquois (1)	2	<0.01
Kiowa (0)	0	<0.01
Lumbee (16)	26	0.04
Menominee (0)	0	<0.01
Mexican American Ind. (10)	18	0.03
Navajo (2)	2	<0.01
Osage (1)	1	<0.01
Ottawa (1)	1	<0.01
Paiute (0)	0	<0.01
Pima (0)	0	<0.01
Potawatomi (0)	0	<0.01
Pueblo (0)	0	<0.01
Puget Sound Salish (0)	0	<0.01
Seminole (0)	2	<0.01
Shoshone (0)	0	<0.01
Sioux (1)	7	0.01
South American Ind. (0)	0	<0.01
Spanish American Ind. (0)	0	<0.01
Tlingit-Haida (Alaska Native) (0)	0	<0.01
Tohono O'Odham (0)	0	<0.01
Tsimshian (Alaska Native) (0)	0	<0.01
Ute (0)	0	<0.01
Yakama (0)	0	<0.01
Yaqui (0)	0	<0.01
Yuman (0)	0	<0.01
Yup'ik (Alaska Native) (0)	0	<0.01
Asian (296)	384	0.55
Not Hispanic (295)	378	0.55
Hispanic (1)	6	0.01
Bangladeshi (0)	0	<0.01
Bhutanese (0)	0	<0.01
Burmese (0)	0	<0.01
Cambodian (0)	0	<0.01
Chinese, ex. Taiwanese (56)	58	0.08
Filipino (23)	42	0.06
Hmong (1)	1	<0.01
Indian (136)	157	0.23
Indonesian (0)	0	<0.01
Japanese (11)	19	0.03
Korean (16)	31	0.04
Laotian (1)	2	<0.01
Malaysian (0)	0	<0.01
Nepalese (0)	0	<0.01
Pakistani (0)	0	<0.01
Sri Lankan (0)	0	<0.01
Taiwanese (0)	0	<0.01
Thai (4)	5	0.01
Vietnamese (31)	42	0.06
Hawaii Native/Pacific Islander (20)	48	0.07
Not Hispanic (15)	34	0.05
Hispanic (5)	14	0.02
Fijian (0)	0	<0.01
Guamanian/Chamorro (14)	17	0.02
Marshallese (0)	0	<0.01
Native Hawaiian (4)	17	0.02
Samoan (0)	4	0.01
Tongan (0)	0	<0.01
White (62,824)	63,683	91.84
Not Hispanic (61,587)	62,250	89.78
Hispanic (1,237)	1,433	2.07

Notes: † The Census 2010 population figure is used to calculate the percentages in the Hispanic Origin and Race categories. Ancestry percentages are based on the 2006-2010 American Community Survey population (not shown); ‡ Numbers in parentheses indicate the number of people reporting a single ancestry; * Numbers in parentheses indicate the number of persons reporting this race alone, not in combination with any other race; Please refer to the Explanation of Data for more information.

Wilson County

Population: 81,234

Ancestry	Population	%
Afghan (0)	0	<0.01
African, Sub-Saharan (416)	522	0.66
African (401)	507	0.64
Cape Verdean (0)	0	<0.01
Ethiopian (0)	0	<0.01
Ghanaian (0)	0	<0.01
Kenyan (15)	15	0.02
Liberian (0)	0	<0.01
Nigerian (0)	0	<0.01
Senegalese (0)	0	<0.01
Sierra Leonean (0)	0	<0.01
Somalian (0)	0	<0.01
South African (0)	0	<0.01
Sudanese (0)	0	<0.01
Ugandan (0)	0	<0.01
Zimbabwean (0)	0	<0.01
Other Sub-Saharan African (0)	0	<0.01
Albanian (0)	0	<0.01
Alsatian (0)	0	<0.01
American (12,481)	12,481	15.69
Arab (482)	583	0.73
Arab (306)	306	0.38
Egyptian (0)	0	<0.01
Iraqi (0)	0	<0.01
Jordanian (0)	0	<0.01
Lebanese (77)	133	0.17
Moroccan (39)	39	0.05
Palestinian (0)	0	<0.01
Syrian (15)	48	0.06
Other Arab (45)	57	0.07
Armenian (0)	0	<0.01
Assyrian/Chaldean/Syriac (0)	0	<0.01
Australian (0)	0	<0.01
Austrian (0)	0	<0.01
Basque (0)	0	<0.01
Belgian (38)	52	0.07
Brazilian (0)	32	0.04
British (148)	191	0.24
Bulgarian (0)	0	<0.01
Cajun (0)	0	<0.01
Canadian (0)	17	0.02
Carpatho Rusyn (0)	0	<0.01
Celtic (27)	27	0.03
Croatian (0)	0	<0.01
Cypriot (0)	0	<0.01
Czech (13)	39	0.05
Czechoslovakian (0)	0	<0.01
Danish (0)	90	0.11
Dutch (163)	451	0.57
Eastern European (0)	0	<0.01
English (4,654)	7,401	9.31
Estonian (0)	0	<0.01
European (591)	622	0.78
Finnish (0)	0	<0.01
French, ex. Basque (217)	904	1.14
French Canadian (26)	338	0.42
German (1,617)	4,277	5.38
German Russian (0)	0	<0.01
Greek (104)	143	0.18
Guyanese (10)	10	0.01
Hungarian (28)	73	0.09
Icelander (0)	0	<0.01
Iranian (0)	0	<0.01
Irish (1,505)	4,366	5.49
Israeli (0)	0	<0.01
Italian (411)	1,016	1.28
Latvian (0)	0	<0.01
Lithuanian (0)	0	<0.01
Luxemburger (0)	0	<0.01
Macedonian (0)	0	<0.01
Maltese (0)	0	<0.01
New Zealander (0)	0	<0.01
Northern European (18)	18	0.02
Norwegian (107)	170	0.21
Pennsylvania German (0)	0	<0.01

Ancestry	Population	%
Polish (50)	297	0.37
Portuguese (0)	22	0.03
Romanian (0)	3	<0.01
Russian (69)	140	0.18
Scandinavian (0)	35	0.04
Scotch-Irish (1,024)	1,636	2.06
Scottish (465)	1,193	1.50
Serbian (0)	0	<0.01
Slavic (0)	0	<0.01
Slovak (0)	12	0.02
Slovene (0)	0	<0.01
Soviet Union (0)	0	<0.01
Swedish (27)	149	0.19
Swiss (10)	15	0.02
Turkish (0)	0	<0.01
Ukrainian (9)	29	0.04
Welsh (73)	303	0.38
West Indian, ex. Hispanic (62)	210	0.26
Bahamian (18)	18	0.02
Barbadian (0)	0	<0.01
Belizean (13)	13	0.02
Bermudan (0)	0	<0.01
British West Indian (0)	0	<0.01
Dutch West Indian (0)	0	<0.01
Haitian (0)	13	0.02
Jamaican (31)	60	0.08
Trinidadian/Tobagonian (0)	0	<0.01
U.S. Virgin Islander (0)	0	<0.01
West Indian (0)	106	0.13
Other West Indian (0)	0	<0.01
Yugoslavian (0)	0	<0.01

Hispanic Origin	Population	%
Hispanic or Latino (of any race)	7,724	9.51
Central American, ex. Mexican	393	0.48
Costa Rican	7	0.01
Guatemalan	69	0.08
Honduran	95	0.12
Nicaraguan	35	0.04
Panamanian	11	0.01
Salvadoran	173	0.21
Other Central American	3	<0.01
Cuban	47	0.06
Dominican Republic	32	0.04
Mexican	6,123	7.54
Puerto Rican	321	0.40
South American	139	0.17
Argentinean	20	0.02
Bolivian	1	<0.01
Chilean	6	0.01
Colombian	29	0.04
Ecuadorian	26	0.03
Paraguayan	0	<0.01
Peruvian	28	0.03
Uruguayan	16	0.02
Venezuelan	13	0.02
Other South American	0	<0.01
Other Hispanic or Latino	669	0.82

Race*	Population	%
African-American/Black (31,686)	32,387	39.87
Not Hispanic (31,462)	32,082	39.49
Hispanic (224)	305	0.38
American Indian/Alaska Native (238)	545	0.67
Not Hispanic (190)	461	0.57
Hispanic (48)	84	0.10
Alaska Athabascan (Ala. Nat.) (1)	1	<0.01
Aleut (Alaska Native) (0)	0	<0.01
Apache (0)	2	<0.01
Arapaho (0)	0	<0.01
Blackfeet (0)	11	0.01
Canadian/French Am. Ind. (4)	4	<0.01
Central American Ind. (0)	3	<0.01
Cherokee (19)	105	0.13
Cheyenne (0)	0	<0.01
Chickasaw (0)	0	<0.01
Chippewa (7)	11	0.01
Choctaw (0)	3	<0.01
Colville (0)	0	<0.01

Race*	Population	%
Comanche (5)	7	0.01
Cree (0)	0	<0.01
Creek (2)	3	<0.01
Crow (1)	1	<0.01
Delaware (0)	0	<0.01
Hopi (0)	0	<0.01
Houma (0)	0	<0.01
Inupiat (Alaska Native) (0)	0	<0.01
Iroquois (0)	17	0.02
Kiowa (0)	0	<0.01
Lumbee (25)	34	0.04
Menominee (0)	0	<0.01
Mexican American Ind. (15)	16	0.02
Navajo (0)	0	<0.01
Osage (0)	0	<0.01
Ottawa (0)	0	<0.01
Paiute (0)	0	<0.01
Pima (0)	3	<0.01
Potawatomi (1)	1	<0.01
Pueblo (1)	1	<0.01
Puget Sound Salish (0)	0	<0.01
Seminole (0)	1	<0.01
Shoshone (0)	0	<0.01
Sioux (0)	1	<0.01
South American Ind. (1)	4	<0.01
Spanish American Ind. (0)	0	<0.01
Tlingit-Haida (Alaska Native) (0)	0	<0.01
Tohono O'Odham (1)	1	<0.01
Tsimshian (Alaska Native) (0)	0	<0.01
Ute (0)	0	<0.01
Yakama (0)	0	<0.01
Yaqui (0)	0	<0.01
Yuman (0)	0	<0.01
Yup'ik (Alaska Native) (0)	0	<0.01
Asian (668)	864	1.06
Not Hispanic (664)	832	1.02
Hispanic (4)	32	0.04
Bangladeshi (9)	9	<0.01
Bhutanese (0)	0	<0.01
Burmese (0)	0	<0.01
Cambodian (17)	21	0.03
Chinese, ex. Taiwanese (88)	114	0.14
Filipino (98)	149	0.18
Hmong (0)	0	<0.01
Indian (261)	281	0.35
Indonesian (0)	3	<0.01
Japanese (32)	47	0.06
Korean (40)	65	0.08
Laotian (0)	3	<0.01
Malaysian (0)	0	<0.01
Nepalese (0)	0	<0.01
Pakistani (7)	12	0.01
Sri Lankan (1)	1	<0.01
Taiwanese (2)	2	<0.01
Thai (12)	23	0.03
Vietnamese (85)	100	0.12
Hawaii Native/Pacific Islander (25)	85	0.10
Not Hispanic (22)	71	0.09
Hispanic (3)	14	0.02
Fijian (0)	0	<0.01
Guamanian/Chamorro (13)	24	0.03
Marshallese (0)	0	<0.01
Native Hawaiian (6)	29	0.04
Samoan (2)	6	0.01
Tongan (0)	0	<0.01
White (42,222)	43,259	53.25
Not Hispanic (40,157)	40,903	50.35
Hispanic (2,065)	2,356	2.90

*Notes: † The Census 2010 population figure is used to calculate the percentages in the Hispanic Origin and Race categories. Ancestry percentages are based on the 2006-2010 American Community Survey population (not shown); ‡ Numbers in parentheses indicate the number of people reporting a single ancestry; * Numbers in parentheses indicate the number of persons reporting this race alone, not in combination with any other race; Please refer to the Explanation of Data for more information.*

Place Profiles

Asheville

Place Type: City
County: Buncombe
Population: 83,393

Ancestry	Population	%
Afghan (0)	0	<0.01
African, Sub-Saharan (298)	355	0.43
African (286)	302	0.37
Cape Verdean (0)	0	<0.01
Ethiopian (12)	12	0.01
Ghanaian (0)	0	<0.01
Kenyan (0)	0	<0.01
Liberian (0)	0	<0.01
Nigerian (0)	0	<0.01
Senegalese (0)	0	<0.01
Sierra Leonean (0)	0	<0.01
Somalian (0)	0	<0.01
South African (0)	41	0.05
Sudanese (0)	0	<0.01
Ugandan (0)	0	<0.01
Zimbabwean (0)	0	<0.01
Other Sub-Saharan African (0)	0	<0.01
Albanian (13)	13	0.02
Alsatian (10)	10	0.01
American (9,825)	9,825	11.99
Arab (67)	361	0.44
Arab (13)	13	0.02
Egyptian (0)	0	<0.01
Iraqi (0)	0	<0.01
Jordanian (0)	12	0.01
Lebanese (39)	259	0.32
Moroccan (0)	0	<0.01
Palestinian (0)	12	0.01
Syrian (15)	25	0.03
Other Arab (0)	40	0.05
Armenian (13)	50	0.06
Assyrian/Chaldean/Syriac (0)	0	<0.01
Australian (0)	7	0.01
Austrian (34)	207	0.25
Basque (0)	0	<0.01
Belgian (0)	56	0.07
Brazilian (0)	0	<0.01
British (278)	635	0.77
Bulgarian (12)	12	0.01
Cajun (17)	17	0.02
Canadian (109)	192	0.23
Carpatho Rusyn (8)	8	0.01
Celtic (73)	84	0.10
Croatian (47)	98	0.12
Cypriot (0)	0	<0.01
Czech (113)	366	0.45
Czechoslovakian (0)	58	0.07
Danish (145)	465	0.57
Dutch (175)	1,295	1.58
Eastern European (139)	139	0.17
English (4,371)	12,259	14.96
Estonian (0)	0	<0.01
European (1,274)	1,449	1.77
Finnish (26)	78	0.10
French, ex. Basque (389)	2,612	3.19
French Canadian (176)	357	0.44
German (3,116)	12,009	14.65
German Russian (0)	53	0.06
Greek (244)	443	0.54
Guyanese (0)	0	<0.01
Hungarian (66)	174	0.21
Icelander (0)	11	0.01
Iranian (24)	41	0.05
Irish (2,766)	9,641	11.76
Israeli (27)	27	0.03
Italian (825)	2,842	3.47
Latvian (12)	21	0.03
Lithuanian (31)	173	0.21
Luxemburger (0)	12	0.01
Macedonian (0)	0	<0.01

Ancestry	Population	%
Maltese (0)	0	<0.01
New Zealander (0)	0	<0.01
Northern European (132)	132	0.16
Norwegian (230)	841	1.03
Pennsylvania German (7)	21	0.03
Polish (950)	2,531	3.09
Portuguese (35)	63	0.08
Romanian (732)	759	0.93
Russian (348)	655	0.80
Scandinavian (62)	279	0.34
Scotch-Irish (2,496)	4,845	5.91
Scottish (1,092)	3,480	4.25
Serbian (0)	10	0.01
Slavic (0)	32	0.04
Slovak (25)	25	0.03
Slovene (0)	44	0.05
Soviet Union (0)	0	<0.01
Swedish (125)	620	0.76
Swiss (108)	492	0.60
Turkish (20)	20	0.02
Ukrainian (540)	745	0.91
Welsh (313)	1,103	1.35
West Indian, ex. Hispanic (180)	239	0.29
Bahamian (0)	0	<0.01
Barbadian (0)	0	<0.01
Belizean (0)	0	<0.01
Bermudan (0)	0	<0.01
British West Indian (0)	0	<0.01
Dutch West Indian (0)	0	<0.01
Haitian (20)	20	0.02
Jamaican (68)	127	0.15
Trinidadian/Tobagonian (92)	92	0.11
U.S. Virgin Islander (0)	0	<0.01
West Indian (0)	0	<0.01
Other West Indian (0)	0	<0.01
Yugoslavian (8)	8	0.01

Hispanic Origin	Population	%
Hispanic or Latino (of any race)	5,455	6.54
Central American, ex. Mexican	847	1.02
Costa Rican	17	0.02
Guatemalan	87	0.10
Honduran	181	0.22
Nicaraguan	26	0.03
Panamanian	11	0.01
Salvadoran	525	0.63
Other Central American	0	<0.01
Cuban	223	0.27
Dominican Republic	27	0.03
Mexican	3,059	3.67
Puerto Rican	419	0.50
South American	404	0.48
Argentinean	57	0.07
Bolivian	4	<0.01
Chilean	38	0.05
Colombian	135	0.16
Ecuadorian	61	0.07
Paraguayan	2	<0.01
Peruvian	43	0.05
Uruguayan	3	<0.01
Venezuelan	53	0.06
Other South American	8	0.01
Other Hispanic or Latino	476	0.57

Race*	Population	%
African-American/Black (11,134)	12,247	14.69
Not Hispanic (11,024)	12,038	14.44
Hispanic (110)	209	0.25
American Indian/Alaska Native (280)	932	1.12
Not Hispanic (217)	798	0.96
Hispanic (63)	134	0.16
Alaska Athabascan (Ala. Nat.) (1)	1	<0.01
Aleut (Alaska Native) (1)	1	<0.01
Apache (2)	12	0.01
Arapaho (0)	1	<0.01
Blackfeet (4)	20	0.02

Race*	Population	%
Canadian/French Am. Ind. (0)	3	<0.01
Central American Ind. (0)	8	0.01
Cherokee (89)	342	0.41
Cheyenne (1)	2	<0.01
Chickasaw (0)	1	<0.01
Chippewa (2)	8	0.01
Choctaw (3)	12	0.01
Colville (0)	0	<0.01
Comanche (1)	2	<0.01
Cree (0)	2	<0.01
Creek (1)	2	<0.01
Crow (0)	0	<0.01
Delaware (0)	1	<0.01
Hopi (0)	0	<0.01
Houma (1)	1	<0.01
Inupiat (Alaska Native) (0)	0	<0.01
Iroquois (4)	13	0.02
Kiowa (0)	0	<0.01
Lumbee (25)	37	0.04
Menominee (0)	0	<0.01
Mexican American Ind. (11)	16	0.02
Navajo (6)	12	0.01
Osage (0)	0	<0.01
Ottawa (0)	0	<0.01
Paiute (0)	1	<0.01
Pima (0)	0	<0.01
Potawatomi (1)	1	<0.01
Pueblo (0)	0	<0.01
Puget Sound Salish (0)	0	<0.01
Seminole (0)	6	0.01
Shoshone (0)	1	<0.01
Sioux (4)	9	0.01
South American Ind. (4)	7	0.01
Spanish American Ind. (4)	4	<0.01
Tlingit-Haida (Alaska Native) (0)	0	<0.01
Tohono O'Odham (0)	0	<0.01
Tsimshian (Alaska Native) (0)	0	<0.01
Ute (1)	1	<0.01
Yakama (0)	0	<0.01
Yaqui (0)	4	<0.01
Yuman (0)	1	<0.01
Yup'ik (Alaska Native) (0)	0	<0.01
Asian (1,142)	1,518	1.82
Not Hispanic (1,130)	1,491	1.79
Hispanic (12)	27	0.03
Bangladeshi (0)	0	<0.01
Bhutanese (1)	1	<0.01
Burmese (2)	2	<0.01
Cambodian (11)	12	0.01
Chinese, ex. Taiwanese (230)	290	0.35
Filipino (175)	250	0.30
Hmong (4)	4	<0.01
Indian (241)	292	0.35
Indonesian (30)	32	0.04
Japanese (71)	146	0.18
Korean (179)	220	0.26
Laotian (5)	5	0.01
Malaysian (1)	2	<0.01
Nepalese (6)	6	0.01
Pakistani (16)	20	0.02
Sri Lankan (3)	4	<0.01
Taiwanese (4)	8	0.01
Thai (33)	39	0.05
Vietnamese (85)	97	0.12
Hawaii Native/Pacific Islander (126)	203	0.24
Not Hispanic (123)	179	0.21
Hispanic (3)	24	0.03
Fijian (0)	1	<0.01
Guamanian/Chamorro (5)	5	0.01
Marshallese (22)	26	0.03
Native Hawaiian (8)	41	0.05
Samoan (15)	22	0.03
Tongan (0)	1	<0.01
White (66,143)	68,075	81.63
Not Hispanic (63,508)	65,118	78.09
Hispanic (2,635)	2,957	3.55

Notes: † The Census 2010 population figure is used to calculate the percentages in the Hispanic Origin and Race categories. Ancestry percentages are based on the 2006-2010 American Community Survey population (not shown); ‡ Numbers in parentheses indicate the number of people reporting a single ancestry; * Numbers in parentheses indicate the number of persons reporting this race alone, not in combination with any other race; Please refer to the Explanation of Data for more information.

Cary

Place Type: Town
County: Wake
Population: 135,234

Ancestry	Population	%
Afghan (369)	369	0.29
African, Sub-Saharan (627)	900	0.71
African (453)	618	0.48
Cape Verdean (0)	0	<0.01
Ethiopian (0)	0	<0.01
Ghanaian (0)	0	<0.01
Kenyan (60)	60	0.05
Liberian (0)	0	<0.01
Nigerian (101)	101	0.08
Senegalese (0)	0	<0.01
Sierra Leonean (0)	0	<0.01
Somalian (0)	0	<0.01
South African (13)	121	0.09
Sudanese (0)	0	<0.01
Ugandan (0)	0	<0.01
Zimbabwean (0)	0	<0.01
Other Sub-Saharan African (0)	0	<0.01
Albanian (48)	48	0.04
Alsatian (0)	16	0.01
American (9,424)	9,424	7.39
Arab (1,035)	1,244	0.98
Arab (59)	71	0.06
Egyptian (200)	271	0.21
Iraqi (12)	12	0.01
Jordanian (75)	75	0.06
Lebanese (189)	315	0.25
Moroccan (301)	301	0.24
Palestinian (108)	108	0.08
Syrian (14)	14	0.01
Other Arab (77)	77	0.06
Armenian (54)	206	0.16
Assyrian/Chaldean/Syriac (0)	0	<0.01
Australian (0)	0	<0.01
Austrian (71)	407	0.32
Basque (25)	38	0.03
Belgian (56)	343	0.27
Brazilian (19)	69	0.05
British (638)	1,185	0.93
Bulgarian (215)	215	0.17
Cajun (29)	40	0.03
Canadian (399)	525	0.41
Carpatho Rusyn (0)	0	<0.01
Celtic (21)	29	0.02
Croatian (10)	86	0.07
Cypriot (0)	0	<0.01
Czech (155)	642	0.50
Czechoslovakian (32)	139	0.11
Danish (87)	498	0.39
Dutch (379)	1,854	1.45
Eastern European (229)	320	0.25
English (7,252)	17,916	14.04
Estonian (11)	11	0.01
European (2,831)	3,166	2.48
Finnish (38)	148	0.12
French, ex. Basque (539)	3,176	2.49
French Canadian (430)	1,019	0.80
German (5,605)	19,577	15.34
German Russian (0)	13	0.01
Greek (313)	728	0.57
Guyanese (18)	18	0.01
Hungarian (388)	950	0.74
Icelander (11)	11	0.01
Iranian (116)	205	0.16
Irish (4,338)	15,501	12.15
Israeli (102)	102	0.08
Italian (3,188)	9,428	7.39
Latvian (8)	30	0.02
Lithuanian (27)	356	0.28
Luxemburger (0)	0	<0.01
Macedonian (0)	13	0.01
Maltese (0)	29	0.02
New Zealander (0)	0	<0.01
Northern European (236)	236	0.18
Norwegian (379)	1,260	0.99
Pennsylvania German (0)	10	0.01
Polish (988)	4,181	3.28
Portuguese (63)	267	0.21
Romanian (46)	211	0.17
Russian (490)	1,625	1.27
Scandinavian (164)	251	0.20
Scotch-Irish (2,326)	4,549	3.57
Scottish (1,239)	3,944	3.09
Serbian (0)	36	0.03
Slavic (0)	41	0.03
Slovak (141)	448	0.35
Slovene (20)	70	0.05
Soviet Union (0)	0	<0.01
Swedish (455)	1,679	1.32
Swiss (83)	345	0.27
Turkish (130)	147	0.12
Ukrainian (140)	630	0.49
Welsh (212)	1,388	1.09
West Indian, ex. Hispanic (782)	1,010	0.79
Bahamian (0)	0	<0.01
Barbadian (0)	0	<0.01
Belizean (18)	40	0.03
Bermudan (0)	0	<0.01
British West Indian (0)	0	<0.01
Dutch West Indian (0)	0	<0.01
Haitian (126)	151	0.12
Jamaican (280)	325	0.25
Trinidadian/Tobagonian (35)	96	0.08
U.S. Virgin Islander (0)	12	0.01
West Indian (323)	386	0.30
Other West Indian (0)	0	<0.01
Yugoslavian (35)	202	0.16

Hispanic Origin	Population	%
Hispanic or Latino (of any race)	10,364	7.66
Central American, ex. Mexican	1,351	1.00
Costa Rican	82	0.06
Guatemalan	391	0.29
Honduran	244	0.18
Nicaraguan	89	0.07
Panamanian	78	0.06
Salvadoran	450	0.33
Other Central American	17	0.01
Cuban	529	0.39
Dominican Republic	248	0.18
Mexican	5,012	3.71
Puerto Rican	1,169	0.86
South American	1,259	0.93
Argentinean	115	0.09
Bolivian	40	0.03
Chilean	83	0.06
Colombian	423	0.31
Ecuadorian	140	0.10
Paraguayan	9	0.01
Peruvian	258	0.19
Uruguayan	23	0.02
Venezuelan	156	0.12
Other South American	12	0.01
Other Hispanic or Latino	796	0.59

Race*	Population	%
African-American/Black (10,787)	11,966	8.85
Not Hispanic (10,485)	11,504	8.51
Hispanic (302)	462	0.34
American Indian/Alaska Native (559)	1,353	1.00
Not Hispanic (284)	949	0.70
Hispanic (275)	404	0.30
Alaska Athabascan (Ala. Nat.) (9)	10	0.01
Aleut (Alaska Native) (0)	0	<0.01
Apache (2)	11	0.01
Arapaho (0)	0	<0.01
Blackfeet (14)	39	0.03
Canadian/French Am. Ind. (1)	2	<0.01
Central American Ind. (5)	6	<0.01
Cherokee (31)	214	0.16
Cheyenne (0)	1	<0.01
Chickasaw (0)	5	<0.01
Chippewa (11)	21	0.02
Choctaw (4)	20	0.01
Colville (0)	1	<0.01
Comanche (0)	0	<0.01
Cree (1)	3	<0.01
Creek (2)	6	<0.01
Crow (0)	6	<0.01
Delaware (1)	5	<0.01
Hopi (0)	1	<0.01
Houma (0)	0	<0.01
Inupiat (Alaska Native) (0)	0	<0.01
Iroquois (8)	24	0.02
Kiowa (1)	1	<0.01
Lumbee (78)	124	0.09
Menominee (0)	0	<0.01
Mexican American Ind. (50)	59	0.04
Navajo (1)	6	<0.01
Osage (0)	7	0.01
Ottawa (1)	2	<0.01
Paiute (0)	0	<0.01
Pima (1)	1	<0.01
Potawatomi (0)	1	<0.01
Pueblo (2)	2	<0.01
Puget Sound Salish (3)	3	<0.01
Seminole (1)	8	0.01
Shoshone (0)	0	<0.01
Sioux (5)	14	0.01
South American Ind. (20)	39	0.03
Spanish American Ind. (0)	0	<0.01
Tlingit-Haida (Alaska Native) (1)	1	<0.01
Tohono O'Odham (0)	0	<0.01
Tsimshian (Alaska Native) (0)	0	<0.01
Ute (0)	0	<0.01
Yakama (0)	0	<0.01
Yaqui (1)	1	<0.01
Yuman (0)	0	<0.01
Yup'ik (Alaska Native) (0)	0	<0.01
Asian (17,668)	19,370	14.32
Not Hispanic (17,620)	19,231	14.22
Hispanic (48)	139	0.10
Bangladeshi (115)	124	0.09
Bhutanese (0)	0	<0.01
Burmese (1)	5	<0.01
Cambodian (15)	31	0.02
Chinese, ex. Taiwanese (3,979)	4,330	3.20
Filipino (582)	847	0.63
Hmong (0)	10	0.01
Indian (8,769)	9,217	6.82
Indonesian (28)	70	0.05
Japanese (314)	561	0.41
Korean (1,273)	1,455	1.08
Laotian (23)	26	0.02
Malaysian (10)	14	0.01
Nepalese (184)	190	0.14
Pakistani (506)	579	0.43
Sri Lankan (137)	161	0.12
Taiwanese (305)	346	0.26
Thai (74)	114	0.08
Vietnamese (969)	1,081	0.80
Hawaii Native/Pacific Islander (46)	179	0.13
Not Hispanic (39)	160	0.12
Hispanic (7)	19	0.01
Fijian (1)	2	<0.01
Guamanian/Chamorro (15)	28	0.02
Marshallese (0)	0	<0.01
Native Hawaiian (19)	54	0.04
Samoan (1)	7	0.01
Tongan (0)	0	<0.01
White (98,907)	101,785	75.27
Not Hispanic (93,202)	95,613	70.70
Hispanic (5,705)	6,172	4.56

*Notes: † The Census 2010 population figure is used to calculate the percentages in the Hispanic Origin and Race categories. Ancestry percentages are based on the 2006-2010 American Community Survey population (not shown); ‡ Numbers in parentheses indicate the number of people reporting a single ancestry; * Numbers in parentheses indicate the number of persons reporting this race alone, not in combination with any other race; Please refer to the Explanation of Data for more information.*

Chapel Hill

Place Type: Town
County: Orange
Population: 57,233

Ancestry	Population	%
Afghan (0)	0	<0.01
African, Sub-Saharan (353)	429	0.78
African (172)	216	0.39
Cape Verdean (0)	0	<0.01
Ethiopian (20)	20	0.04
Ghanaian (26)	26	0.05
Kenyan (32)	32	0.06
Liberian (0)	0	<0.01
Nigerian (44)	70	0.13
Senegalese (0)	0	<0.01
Sierra Leonean (0)	0	<0.01
Somalian (0)	0	<0.01
South African (5)	11	0.02
Sudanese (0)	0	<0.01
Ugandan (0)	0	<0.01
Zimbabwean (39)	39	0.07
Other Sub-Saharan African (15)	15	0.03
Albanian (7)	19	0.03
Alsatian (0)	14	0.03
American (1,650)	1,650	2.99
Arab (193)	381	0.69
Arab (63)	96	0.17
Egyptian (23)	43	0.08
Iraqi (0)	20	0.04
Jordanian (2)	2	<0.01
Lebanese (98)	148	0.27
Moroccan (7)	7	0.01
Palestinian (0)	14	0.03
Syrian (0)	14	0.03
Other Arab (0)	37	0.07
Armenian (33)	91	0.16
Assyrian/Chaldean/Syriac (0)	0	<0.01
Australian (34)	44	0.08
Austrian (53)	243	0.44
Basque (0)	0	<0.01
Belgian (70)	116	0.21
Brazilian (0)	0	<0.01
British (612)	1,225	2.22
Bulgarian (46)	75	0.14
Cajun (0)	0	<0.01
Canadian (181)	279	0.51
Carpatho Rusyn (0)	0	<0.01
Celtic (0)	36	0.07
Croatian (8)	84	0.15
Cypriot (0)	0	<0.01
Czech (144)	430	0.78
Czechoslovakian (0)	33	0.06
Danish (12)	217	0.39
Dutch (284)	1,052	1.91
Eastern European (171)	196	0.36
English (3,591)	10,042	18.20
Estonian (17)	17	0.03
European (1,345)	1,435	2.60
Finnish (26)	78	0.14
French, ex. Basque (184)	1,546	2.80
French Canadian (123)	477	0.86
German (2,021)	8,076	14.64
German Russian (0)	0	<0.01
Greek (146)	442	0.80
Guyanese (0)	15	0.03
Hungarian (77)	281	0.51
Icelander (14)	27	0.05
Iranian (47)	47	0.09
Irish (1,255)	5,429	9.84
Israeli (84)	109	0.20
Italian (636)	2,665	4.83
Latvian (28)	68	0.12
Lithuanian (85)	224	0.41
Luxemburger (0)	0	<0.01
Macedonian (0)	0	<0.01
Maltese (0)	0	<0.01
New Zealander (49)	49	0.09
Northern European (156)	156	0.28

	Population	%
Norwegian (180)	526	0.95
Pennsylvania German (0)	16	0.03
Polish (474)	1,646	2.98
Portuguese (0)	96	0.17
Romanian (75)	176	0.32
Russian (318)	946	1.71
Scandinavian (25)	102	0.18
Scotch-Irish (1,278)	2,806	5.09
Scottish (827)	2,770	5.02
Serbian (3)	3	0.01
Slavic (33)	122	0.22
Slovak (51)	124	0.22
Slovene (0)	32	0.06
Soviet Union (0)	0	<0.01
Swedish (128)	795	1.44
Swiss (127)	422	0.76
Turkish (55)	68	0.12
Ukrainian (144)	334	0.61
Welsh (180)	805	1.46
West Indian, ex. Hispanic (317)	411	0.74
Bahamian (0)	0	<0.01
Barbadian (0)	14	0.03
Belizean (0)	0	<0.01
Bermudan (0)	0	<0.01
British West Indian (44)	55	0.10
Dutch West Indian (0)	0	<0.01
Haitian (19)	57	0.10
Jamaican (227)	258	0.47
Trinidadian/Tobagonian (0)	0	<0.01
U.S. Virgin Islander (0)	0	<0.01
West Indian (27)	27	0.05
Other West Indian (0)	0	<0.01
Yugoslavian (11)	54	0.10

Hispanic Origin	Population	%
Hispanic or Latino (of any race)	3,638	6.36
Central American, ex. Mexican	667	1.17
Costa Rican	29	0.05
Guatemalan	223	0.39
Honduran	112	0.20
Nicaraguan	29	0.05
Panamanian	43	0.08
Salvadoran	227	0.40
Other Central American	4	0.01
Cuban	197	0.34
Dominican Republic	45	0.08
Mexican	1,566	2.74
Puerto Rican	332	0.58
South American	529	0.92
Argentinean	74	0.13
Bolivian	12	0.02
Chilean	45	0.08
Colombian	204	0.36
Ecuadorian	35	0.06
Paraguayan	12	0.02
Peruvian	78	0.14
Uruguayan	7	0.01
Venezuelan	58	0.10
Other South American	4	0.01
Other Hispanic or Latino	302	0.53

Race*	Population	%
African-American/Black (5,530)	6,061	10.59
Not Hispanic (5,460)	5,915	10.33
Hispanic (70)	146	0.26
American Indian/Alaska Native (176)	471	0.82
Not Hispanic (152)	396	0.69
Hispanic (24)	75	0.13
Alaska Athabascan (Ala. Nat.) (0)	0	<0.01
Aleut (Alaska Native) (0)	1	<0.01
Apache (0)	2	<0.01
Arapaho (0)	0	<0.01
Blackfeet (0)	7	0.01
Canadian/French Am. Ind. (0)	0	<0.01
Central American Ind. (2)	3	0.01
Cherokee (30)	109	0.19
Cheyenne (0)	0	<0.01
Chickasaw (1)	1	<0.01
Chippewa (5)	13	0.02

	Population	%
Choctaw (1)	15	0.03
Colville (0)	0	<0.01
Comanche (0)	4	0.01
Cree (0)	0	<0.01
Creek (1)	2	<0.01
Crow (0)	0	<0.01
Delaware (0)	7	0.01
Hopi (1)	1	<0.01
Houma (0)	0	<0.01
Inupiat (Alaska Native) (0)	0	<0.01
Iroquois (4)	10	0.02
Kiowa (1)	1	<0.01
Lumbee (48)	65	0.11
Menominee (0)	0	<0.01
Mexican American Ind. (15)	24	0.04
Navajo (2)	8	0.01
Osage (0)	0	<0.01
Ottawa (0)	0	<0.01
Paiute (0)	0	<0.01
Pima (0)	0	<0.01
Potawatomi (0)	0	<0.01
Pueblo (0)	3	0.01
Puget Sound Salish (0)	0	<0.01
Seminole (0)	0	<0.01
Shoshone (0)	0	<0.01
Sioux (1)	4	0.01
South American Ind. (1)	12	0.02
Spanish American Ind. (0)	2	<0.01
Tlingit-Haida (Alaska Native) (0)	0	<0.01
Tohono O'Odham (0)	0	<0.01
Tsimshian (Alaska Native) (0)	0	<0.01
Ute (0)	0	<0.01
Yakama (0)	0	<0.01
Yaqui (0)	0	<0.01
Yuman (0)	0	<0.01
Yup'ik (Alaska Native) (0)	0	<0.01
Asian (6,788)	7,548	13.19
Not Hispanic (6,775)	7,495	13.10
Hispanic (13)	53	0.09
Bangladeshi (34)	35	0.06
Bhutanese (0)	0	<0.01
Burmese (380)	393	0.69
Cambodian (7)	13	0.02
Chinese, ex. Taiwanese (2,638)	2,866	5.01
Filipino (155)	269	0.47
Hmong (6)	6	0.01
Indian (1,260)	1,418	2.48
Indonesian (15)	20	0.03
Japanese (293)	387	0.68
Korean (1,285)	1,377	2.41
Laotian (4)	6	0.01
Malaysian (8)	8	0.01
Nepalese (11)	11	0.02
Pakistani (66)	89	0.16
Sri Lankan (38)	42	0.07
Taiwanese (170)	201	0.35
Thai (77)	105	0.18
Vietnamese (186)	216	0.38
Hawaii Native/Pacific Islander (14)	55	0.10
Not Hispanic (11)	47	0.08
Hispanic (3)	8	0.01
Fijian (1)	3	0.01
Guamanian/Chamorro (3)	7	0.01
Marshallese (0)	0	<0.01
Native Hawaiian (3)	9	0.02
Samoan (2)	6	0.01
Tongan (0)	0	<0.01
White (41,641)	43,000	75.13
Not Hispanic (39,777)	40,897	71.46
Hispanic (1,864)	2,103	3.67

*Notes: † The Census 2010 population figure is used to calculate the percentages in the Hispanic Origin and Race categories. Ancestry percentages are based on the 2006-2010 American Community Survey population (not shown); ‡ Numbers in parentheses indicate the number of people reporting a single ancestry; * Numbers in parentheses indicate the number of persons reporting this race alone, not in combination with any other race; Please refer to the Explanation of Data for more information.*

Charlotte

Place Type: City
County: Mecklenburg
Population: 731,424

Ancestry	Population	%
Afghan (0)	13	<0.01
African, Sub-Saharan (10,123)	11,247	1.59
African (4,575)	5,460	0.77
Cape Verdean (27)	48	0.01
Ethiopian (954)	954	0.14
Ghanaian (523)	539	0.08
Kenyan (282)	282	0.04
Liberian (618)	633	0.09
Nigerian (1,182)	1,192	0.17
Senegalese (47)	47	0.01
Sierra Leonean (70)	70	0.01
Somalian (485)	485	0.07
South African (170)	194	0.03
Sudanese (42)	101	0.01
Ugandan (0)	0	<0.01
Zimbabwean (0)	0	<0.01
Other Sub-Saharan African (1,148)	1,242	0.18
Albanian (149)	177	0.03
Alsatian (0)	19	<0.01
American (30,441)	30,441	4.31
Arab (3,391)	4,490	0.64
Arab (754)	840	0.12
Egyptian (522)	604	0.09
Iraqi (0)	0	<0.01
Jordanian (106)	117	0.02
Lebanese (850)	1,598	0.23
Moroccan (368)	382	0.05
Palestinian (111)	122	0.02
Syrian (163)	254	0.04
Other Arab (517)	573	0.08
Armenian (397)	612	0.09
Assyrian/Chaldean/Syriac (7)	7	<0.01
Australian (32)	152	0.02
Austrian (261)	1,273	0.18
Basque (6)	6	<0.01
Belgian (294)	690	0.10
Brazilian (1,163)	1,399	0.20
British (1,891)	3,557	0.50
Bulgarian (91)	123	0.02
Cajun (115)	208	0.03
Canadian (819)	1,520	0.22
Carpatho Rusyn (15)	15	<0.01
Celtic (38)	100	0.01
Croatian (178)	618	0.09
Cypriot (0)	0	<0.01
Czech (505)	1,654	0.23
Czechoslovakian (207)	759	0.11
Danish (414)	1,486	0.21
Dutch (1,395)	7,656	1.08
Eastern European (831)	862	0.12
English (22,165)	58,078	8.23
Estonian (30)	41	0.01
European (5,975)	6,521	0.92
Finnish (166)	402	0.06
French, ex. Basque (2,435)	12,074	1.71
French Canadian (973)	2,489	0.35
German (21,410)	71,671	10.15
German Russian (0)	9	<0.01
Greek (2,642)	4,046	0.57
Guyanese (246)	298	0.04
Hungarian (528)	2,059	0.29
Icelander (11)	11	<0.01
Iranian (661)	786	0.11
Irish (15,980)	54,824	7.77
Israeli (36)	51	0.01
Italian (9,960)	28,643	4.06
Latvian (52)	105	0.01
Lithuanian (401)	856	0.12
Luxemburger (0)	0	<0.01
Macedonian (0)	0	<0.01
Maltese (0)	156	0.02
New Zealander (34)	72	0.01
Northern European (328)	357	0.05

Ancestry	Population	%
Norwegian (1,027)	3,212	0.46
Pennsylvania German (42)	203	0.03
Polish (3,483)	12,055	1.71
Portuguese (509)	1,157	0.16
Romanian (487)	1,248	0.18
Russian (2,439)	5,549	0.79
Scandinavian (316)	609	0.09
Scotch-Irish (15,704)	25,971	3.68
Scottish (6,409)	17,085	2.42
Serbian (79)	362	0.05
Slavic (112)	340	0.05
Slovak (410)	1,441	0.20
Slovene (124)	255	0.04
Soviet Union (0)	0	<0.01
Swedish (1,191)	4,136	0.59
Swiss (284)	1,724	0.24
Turkish (691)	809	0.11
Ukrainian (989)	1,867	0.26
Welsh (1,158)	4,719	0.67
West Indian, ex. Hispanic (2,750)	4,254	0.60
Bahamian (76)	122	0.02
Barbadian (83)	148	0.02
Belizean (13)	20	<0.01
Bermudan (0)	16	<0.01
British West Indian (82)	82	0.01
Dutch West Indian (34)	56	0.01
Haitian (266)	403	0.06
Jamaican (1,489)	2,278	0.32
Trinidadian/Tobagonian (128)	241	0.03
U.S. Virgin Islander (0)	12	<0.01
West Indian (558)	855	0.12
Other West Indian (21)	21	<0.01
Yugoslavian (1,013)	1,220	0.17

Hispanic Origin	Population	%
Hispanic or Latino (of any race)	95,688	13.08
Central American, ex. Mexican	22,359	3.06
Costa Rican	673	0.09
Guatemalan	2,421	0.33
Honduran	7,557	1.03
Nicaraguan	1,320	0.18
Panamanian	608	0.08
Salvadoran	9,516	1.30
Other Central American	264	0.04
Cuban	2,902	0.40
Dominican Republic	3,280	0.45
Mexican	40,601	5.55
Puerto Rican	7,521	1.03
South American	10,729	1.47
Argentinean	514	0.07
Bolivian	138	0.02
Chilean	368	0.05
Colombian	3,338	0.46
Ecuadorian	3,008	0.41
Paraguayan	28	<0.01
Peruvian	2,177	0.30
Uruguayan	262	0.04
Venezuelan	818	0.11
Other South American	78	0.01
Other Hispanic or Latino	8,296	1.13

Race*	Population	%
African-American/Black (256,241)	266,822	36.48
Not Hispanic (252,007)	260,726	35.65
Hispanic (4,234)	6,096	0.83
American Indian/Alaska Native (3,483)	8,397	1.15
Not Hispanic (2,250)	6,096	0.83
Hispanic (1,233)	2,301	0.31
Alaska Athabascan *(Ala. Nat.)* (4)	5	<0.01
Aleut *(Alaska Native)* (5)	8	<0.01
Apache (9)	46	0.01
Arapaho (1)	1	<0.01
Blackfeet (29)	186	0.03
Canadian/French Am. Ind. (2)	15	<0.01
Central American Ind. (20)	67	0.01
Cherokee (270)	1,294	0.18
Cheyenne (3)	5	<0.01
Chickasaw (10)	36	<0.01
Chippewa (31)	60	0.01

Race* (cont.)	Population	%
Choctaw (19)	67	0.01
Colville (0)	0	<0.01
Comanche (2)	5	<0.01
Cree (6)	10	<0.01
Creek (14)	38	0.01
Crow (1)	13	<0.01
Delaware (11)	26	<0.01
Hopi (0)	1	<0.01
Houma (1)	1	<0.01
Inupiat *(Alaska Native)* (6)	12	<0.01
Iroquois (56)	116	0.02
Kiowa (0)	2	<0.01
Lumbee (548)	763	0.10
Menominee (0)	4	<0.01
Mexican American Ind. (236)	331	0.05
Navajo (9)	33	<0.01
Osage (3)	5	<0.01
Ottawa (1)	2	<0.01
Paiute (0)	0	<0.01
Pima (1)	1	<0.01
Potawatomi (1)	4	<0.01
Pueblo (1)	18	<0.01
Puget Sound Salish (2)	2	<0.01
Seminole (5)	34	<0.01
Shoshone (1)	4	<0.01
Sioux (23)	66	0.01
South American Ind. (25)	88	0.01
Spanish American Ind. (15)	101	0.01
Tlingit-Haida *(Alaska Native)* (2)	3	<0.01
Tohono O'Odham (1)	1	<0.01
Tsimshian *(Alaska Native)* (1)	1	<0.01
Ute (4)	4	<0.01
Yakama (0)	0	<0.01
Yaqui (1)	6	<0.01
Yuman (1)	4	<0.01
Yup'ik *(Alaska Native)* (1)	2	<0.01
Asian (36,403)	40,918	5.59
Not Hispanic (36,115)	40,149	5.49
Hispanic (288)	769	0.11
Bangladeshi (62)	82	0.01
Bhutanese (224)	277	0.04
Burmese (503)	542	0.07
Cambodian (1,071)	1,236	0.17
Chinese, ex. Taiwanese (4,139)	4,883	0.67
Filipino (1,508)	2,240	0.31
Hmong (1,230)	1,304	0.18
Indian (13,329)	14,258	1.95
Indonesian (118)	163	0.02
Japanese (710)	1,149	0.16
Korean (2,575)	3,168	0.43
Laotian (1,245)	1,426	0.19
Malaysian (50)	78	0.01
Nepalese (107)	157	0.02
Pakistani (548)	625	0.09
Sri Lankan (51)	66	0.01
Taiwanese (192)	223	0.03
Thai (272)	461	0.06
Vietnamese (6,964)	7,550	1.03
Hawaii Native/Pacific Islander (581)	1,315	0.18
Not Hispanic (436)	986	0.13
Hispanic (145)	329	0.04
Fijian (3)	8	<0.01
Guamanian/Chamorro (196)	268	0.04
Marshallese (3)	5	<0.01
Native Hawaiian (95)	268	0.04
Samoan (58)	139	0.02
Tongan (11)	20	<0.01
White (365,384)	379,739	51.92
Not Hispanic (329,545)	339,512	46.42
Hispanic (35,839)	40,227	5.50

*Notes: † The Census 2010 population figure is used to calculate the percentages in the Hispanic Origin and Race categories. Ancestry percentages are based on the 2006-2010 American Community Survey population (not shown); ‡ Numbers in parentheses indicate the number of people reporting a single ancestry; * Numbers in parentheses indicate the number of persons reporting this race alone, not in combination with any other race; Please refer to the Explanation of Data for more information.*

Concord

Place Type: City
County: Cabarrus
Population: 79,066

Ancestry	Population	%
Afghan (0)	0	<0.01
African, Sub-Saharan (161)	203	0.27
African (95)	137	0.18
Cape Verdean (0)	0	<0.01
Ethiopian (0)	0	<0.01
Ghanaian (0)	0	<0.01
Kenyan (0)	0	<0.01
Liberian (52)	52	0.07
Nigerian (0)	0	<0.01
Senegalese (0)	0	<0.01
Sierra Leonean (0)	0	<0.01
Somalian (0)	0	<0.01
South African (14)	14	0.02
Sudanese (0)	0	<0.01
Ugandan (0)	0	<0.01
Zimbabwean (0)	0	<0.01
Other Sub-Saharan African (0)	0	<0.01
Albanian (0)	0	<0.01
Alsatian (0)	0	<0.01
American (6,736)	6,736	8.96
Arab (61)	168	0.22
Arab (0)	21	0.03
Egyptian (31)	31	0.04
Iraqi (0)	0	<0.01
Jordanian (0)	0	<0.01
Lebanese (30)	54	0.07
Moroccan (0)	18	0.02
Palestinian (0)	0	<0.01
Syrian (0)	44	0.06
Other Arab (0)	0	<0.01
Armenian (14)	14	0.02
Assyrian/Chaldean/Syriac (0)	0	<0.01
Australian (0)	0	<0.01
Austrian (0)	41	0.05
Basque (0)	0	<0.01
Belgian (0)	0	<0.01
Brazilian (0)	0	<0.01
British (272)	391	0.52
Bulgarian (0)	8	0.01
Cajun (0)	0	<0.01
Canadian (27)	45	0.06
Carpatho Rusyn (0)	0	<0.01
Celtic (0)	28	0.04
Croatian (0)	18	0.02
Cypriot (0)	0	<0.01
Czech (38)	151	0.20
Czechoslovakian (129)	157	0.21
Danish (104)	340	0.45
Dutch (283)	1,450	1.93
Eastern European (0)	0	<0.01
English (3,070)	7,361	9.79
Estonian (0)	0	<0.01
European (746)	822	1.09
Finnish (40)	52	0.07
French, ex. Basque (358)	1,485	1.98
French Canadian (134)	261	0.35
German (4,245)	11,684	15.54
German Russian (0)	0	<0.01
Greek (84)	200	0.27
Guyanese (191)	260	0.35
Hungarian (170)	385	0.51
Icelander (31)	63	0.08
Iranian (0)	0	<0.01
Irish (2,196)	7,316	9.73
Israeli (0)	0	<0.01
Italian (1,860)	4,223	5.62
Latvian (0)	0	<0.01
Lithuanian (0)	76	0.10
Luxemburger (0)	0	<0.01
Macedonian (0)	0	<0.01
Maltese (0)	0	<0.01
New Zealander (0)	0	<0.01
Northern European (81)	81	0.11

Ancestry	Population	%
Norwegian (55)	211	0.28
Pennsylvania German (48)	48	0.06
Polish (302)	1,562	2.08
Portuguese (0)	56	0.07
Romanian (29)	104	0.14
Russian (243)	594	0.79
Scandinavian (36)	50	0.07
Scotch-Irish (1,842)	3,224	4.29
Scottish (706)	1,983	2.64
Serbian (0)	9	0.01
Slavic (2)	16	0.02
Slovak (29)	50	0.07
Slovene (0)	0	<0.01
Soviet Union (0)	0	<0.01
Swedish (81)	272	0.36
Swiss (60)	125	0.17
Turkish (0)	0	<0.01
Ukrainian (6)	139	0.18
Welsh (68)	399	0.53
West Indian, ex. Hispanic (620)	794	1.06
Bahamian (0)	0	<0.01
Barbadian (0)	0	<0.01
Belizean (0)	0	<0.01
Bermudan (0)	0	<0.01
British West Indian (0)	0	<0.01
Dutch West Indian (0)	0	<0.01
Haitian (248)	248	0.33
Jamaican (200)	233	0.31
Trinidadian/Tobagonian (111)	193	0.26
U.S. Virgin Islander (0)	0	<0.01
West Indian (61)	120	0.16
Other West Indian (0)	0	<0.01
Yugoslavian (0)	0	<0.01

Hispanic Origin	Population	%
Hispanic or Latino (of any race)	9,754	12.34
Central American, ex. Mexican	708	0.90
Costa Rican	43	0.05
Guatemalan	137	0.17
Honduran	180	0.23
Nicaraguan	72	0.09
Panamanian	47	0.06
Salvadoran	225	0.28
Other Central American	4	0.01
Cuban	314	0.40
Dominican Republic	188	0.24
Mexican	6,528	8.26
Puerto Rican	881	1.11
South American	591	0.75
Argentinean	41	0.05
Bolivian	4	0.01
Chilean	22	0.03
Colombian	226	0.29
Ecuadorian	151	0.19
Paraguayan	0	<0.01
Peruvian	92	0.12
Uruguayan	9	0.01
Venezuelan	35	0.04
Other South American	11	0.01
Other Hispanic or Latino	544	0.69

Race*	Population	%
African-American/Black (14,110)	15,064	19.05
Not Hispanic (13,717)	14,518	18.36
Hispanic (393)	546	0.69
American Indian/Alaska Native (274)	664	0.84
Not Hispanic (189)	535	0.68
Hispanic (85)	129	0.16
Alaska Athabascan (Ala. Nat.) (0)	0	<0.01
Aleut (Alaska Native) (1)	1	<0.01
Apache (1)	4	0.01
Arapaho (0)	0	<0.01
Blackfeet (1)	21	0.03
Canadian/French Am. Ind. (0)	0	<0.01
Central American Ind. (1)	1	<0.01
Cherokee (35)	188	0.24
Cheyenne (0)	1	<0.01
Chickasaw (0)	2	<0.01
Chippewa (3)	5	0.01

Race*	Population	%
Choctaw (4)	7	0.01
Colville (1)	1	<0.01
Comanche (0)	0	<0.01
Cree (0)	0	<0.01
Creek (0)	8	0.01
Crow (2)	2	<0.01
Delaware (0)	0	<0.01
Hopi (0)	0	<0.01
Houma (1)	3	<0.01
Inupiat (Alaska Native) (0)	0	<0.01
Iroquois (8)	10	0.01
Kiowa (1)	1	<0.01
Lumbee (54)	87	0.11
Menominee (0)	0	<0.01
Mexican American Ind. (33)	34	0.04
Navajo (1)	3	<0.01
Osage (0)	0	<0.01
Ottawa (2)	2	<0.01
Paiute (0)	0	<0.01
Pima (0)	0	<0.01
Potawatomi (0)	0	<0.01
Pueblo (1)	1	<0.01
Puget Sound Salish (2)	2	<0.01
Seminole (1)	1	<0.01
Shoshone (0)	0	<0.01
Sioux (5)	5	0.01
South American Ind. (3)	3	<0.01
Spanish American Ind. (3)	3	<0.01
Tlingit-Haida (Alaska Native) (0)	0	<0.01
Tohono O'Odham (0)	5	0.01
Tsimshian (Alaska Native) (0)	0	<0.01
Ute (0)	0	<0.01
Yakama (0)	0	<0.01
Yaqui (0)	0	<0.01
Yuman (0)	0	<0.01
Yup'ik (Alaska Native) (1)	1	<0.01
Asian (2,046)	2,436	3.08
Not Hispanic (2,018)	2,374	3.00
Hispanic (28)	62	0.08
Bangladeshi (0)	0	<0.01
Bhutanese (0)	0	<0.01
Burmese (5)	5	0.01
Cambodian (12)	23	0.03
Chinese, ex. Taiwanese (249)	319	0.40
Filipino (227)	331	0.42
Hmong (62)	70	0.09
Indian (954)	1,017	1.29
Indonesian (12)	12	0.02
Japanese (47)	88	0.11
Korean (136)	169	0.21
Laotian (49)	66	0.08
Malaysian (0)	0	<0.01
Nepalese (3)	3	<0.01
Pakistani (34)	38	0.05
Sri Lankan (9)	11	0.01
Taiwanese (6)	6	0.01
Thai (11)	28	0.04
Vietnamese (160)	197	0.25
Hawaii Native/Pacific Islander (50)	108	0.14
Not Hispanic (47)	90	0.11
Hispanic (3)	18	0.02
Fijian (0)	0	<0.01
Guamanian/Chamorro (8)	16	0.02
Marshallese (0)	0	<0.01
Native Hawaiian (15)	43	0.05
Samoan (2)	18	0.02
Tongan (0)	0	<0.01
White (55,691)	57,201	72.35
Not Hispanic (51,843)	53,001	67.03
Hispanic (3,848)	4,200	5.31

Notes: † The Census 2010 population figure is used to calculate the percentages in the Hispanic Origin and Race categories. Ancestry percentages are based on the 2006-2010 American Community Survey population (not shown); ‡ Numbers in parentheses indicate the number of people reporting a single ancestry; * Numbers in parentheses indicate the number of persons reporting this race alone, not in combination with any other race; Please refer to the Explanation of Data for more information.

Durham

Place Type: City
County: Durham
Population: 228,330

Ancestry	Population	%
Afghan (27)	27	0.01
African, Sub-Saharan (4,325)	5,147	2.34
African (2,755)	3,418	1.55
Cape Verdean (0)	0	<0.01
Ethiopian (156)	203	0.09
Ghanaian (144)	144	0.07
Kenyan (57)	64	0.03
Liberian (191)	265	0.12
Nigerian (598)	604	0.27
Senegalese (16)	16	0.01
Sierra Leonean (58)	83	0.04
Somalian (11)	11	<0.01
South African (75)	75	0.03
Sudanese (134)	134	0.06
Ugandan (0)	0	<0.01
Zimbabwean (0)	0	<0.01
Other Sub-Saharan African (130)	130	0.06
Albanian (27)	38	0.02
Alsatian (0)	0	<0.01
American (8,730)	8,730	3.96
Arab (436)	751	0.34
Arab (131)	279	0.13
Egyptian (94)	94	0.04
Iraqi (28)	28	0.01
Jordanian (22)	22	0.01
Lebanese (15)	120	0.05
Moroccan (61)	78	0.04
Palestinian (14)	27	0.01
Syrian (13)	45	0.02
Other Arab (58)	58	0.03
Armenian (103)	340	0.15
Assyrian/Chaldean/Syriac (13)	13	0.01
Australian (9)	127	0.06
Austrian (70)	423	0.19
Basque (0)	11	<0.01
Belgian (10)	43	0.02
Brazilian (31)	56	0.03
British (768)	1,500	0.68
Bulgarian (52)	52	0.02
Cajun (0)	0	<0.01
Canadian (501)	821	0.37
Carpatho Rusyn (0)	0	<0.01
Celtic (16)	119	0.05
Croatian (62)	165	0.07
Cypriot (0)	0	<0.01
Czech (123)	388	0.18
Czechoslovakian (0)	113	0.05
Danish (106)	348	0.16
Dutch (410)	1,816	0.82
Eastern European (350)	375	0.17
English (6,753)	18,137	8.23
Estonian (22)	43	0.02
European (2,211)	2,559	1.16
Finnish (28)	229	0.10
French, ex. Basque (601)	3,230	1.47
French Canadian (241)	649	0.29
German (5,215)	18,806	8.54
German Russian (13)	47	0.02
Greek (268)	448	0.20
Guyanese (30)	108	0.05
Hungarian (136)	571	0.26
Icelander (0)	0	<0.01
Iranian (124)	163	0.07
Irish (4,097)	14,557	6.61
Israeli (112)	130	0.06
Italian (1,809)	6,105	2.77
Latvian (0)	42	0.02
Lithuanian (106)	270	0.12
Luxemburger (0)	0	<0.01
Macedonian (0)	11	<0.01
Maltese (0)	0	<0.01
New Zealander (0)	12	0.01
Northern European (243)	261	0.12

Ancestry	Population	%
Norwegian (267)	1,246	0.57
Pennsylvania German (17)	53	0.02
Polish (948)	3,725	1.69
Portuguese (123)	279	0.13
Romanian (185)	421	0.19
Russian (676)	1,774	0.81
Scandinavian (124)	287	0.13
Scotch-Irish (2,989)	6,163	2.80
Scottish (1,532)	4,809	2.18
Serbian (68)	74	0.03
Slavic (28)	67	0.03
Slovak (84)	281	0.13
Slovene (46)	104	0.05
Soviet Union (0)	0	<0.01
Swedish (274)	1,342	0.61
Swiss (58)	381	0.17
Turkish (262)	262	0.12
Ukrainian (226)	597	0.27
Welsh (235)	1,397	0.63
West Indian, ex. Hispanic (1,002)	2,283	1.04
Bahamian (0)	42	0.02
Barbadian (0)	0	<0.01
Belizean (0)	0	<0.01
Bermudan (0)	0	<0.01
British West Indian (11)	60	0.03
Dutch West Indian (16)	46	0.02
Haitian (260)	452	0.21
Jamaican (370)	885	0.40
Trinidadian/Tobagonian (41)	58	0.03
U.S. Virgin Islander (8)	8	<0.01
West Indian (296)	732	0.33
Other West Indian (0)	0	<0.01
Yugoslavian (0)	66	0.03

Hispanic Origin	Population	%
Hispanic or Latino (of any race)	32,459	14.22
Central American, ex. Mexican	8,052	3.53
Costa Rican	64	0.03
Guatemalan	1,323	0.58
Honduran	3,451	1.51
Nicaraguan	77	0.03
Panamanian	159	0.07
Salvadoran	2,929	1.28
Other Central American	49	0.02
Cuban	445	0.19
Dominican Republic	428	0.19
Mexican	17,626	7.72
Puerto Rican	1,641	0.72
South American	1,448	0.63
Argentinean	210	0.09
Bolivian	58	0.03
Chilean	140	0.06
Colombian	478	0.21
Ecuadorian	169	0.07
Paraguayan	6	<0.01
Peruvian	193	0.08
Uruguayan	33	0.01
Venezuelan	143	0.06
Other South American	18	0.01
Other Hispanic or Latino	2,819	1.23

Race*	Population	%
African-American/Black (93,517)	96,706	42.35
Not Hispanic (92,285)	94,986	41.60
Hispanic (1,232)	1,720	0.75
American Indian/Alaska Native (1,161)	2,744	1.20
Not Hispanic (611)	1,853	0.81
Hispanic (550)	891	0.39
Alaska Athabascan (Ala. Nat.) (1)	1	<0.01
Aleut (Alaska Native) (0)	1	<0.01
Apache (4)	11	<0.01
Arapaho (0)	0	<0.01
Blackfeet (9)	57	0.02
Canadian/French Am. Ind. (2)	4	<0.01
Central American Ind. (28)	29	0.01
Cherokee (54)	417	0.18
Cheyenne (0)	1	<0.01
Chickasaw (1)	11	<0.01
Chippewa (6)	10	<0.01

Race*	Population	%
Choctaw (9)	25	0.01
Colville (0)	0	<0.01
Comanche (0)	3	<0.01
Cree (2)	3	<0.01
Creek (2)	14	0.01
Crow (0)	0	<0.01
Delaware (4)	7	<0.01
Hopi (2)	2	<0.01
Houma (0)	0	<0.01
Inupiat (Alaska Native) (0)	0	<0.01
Iroquois (8)	34	0.01
Kiowa (1)	1	<0.01
Lumbee (102)	155	0.07
Menominee (0)	0	<0.01
Mexican American Ind. (111)	156	0.07
Navajo (2)	16	0.01
Osage (0)	4	<0.01
Ottawa (1)	1	<0.01
Paiute (0)	1	<0.01
Pima (0)	0	<0.01
Potawatomi (1)	2	<0.01
Pueblo (0)	4	<0.01
Puget Sound Salish (0)	0	<0.01
Seminole (1)	13	0.01
Shoshone (0)	1	<0.01
Sioux (10)	29	0.01
South American Ind. (10)	24	0.01
Spanish American Ind. (15)	22	0.01
Tlingit-Haida (Alaska Native) (3)	3	<0.01
Tohono O'Odham (1)	1	<0.01
Tsimshian (Alaska Native) (0)	0	<0.01
Ute (0)	2	<0.01
Yakama (3)	5	<0.01
Yaqui (2)	3	<0.01
Yuman (0)	0	<0.01
Yup'ik (Alaska Native) (0)	0	<0.01
Asian (11,574)	13,147	5.76
Not Hispanic (11,478)	12,897	5.65
Hispanic (96)	250	0.11
Bangladeshi (90)	96	0.04
Bhutanese (13)	29	0.01
Burmese (83)	90	0.04
Cambodian (65)	80	0.04
Chinese, ex. Taiwanese (2,777)	3,150	1.38
Filipino (1,130)	1,419	0.62
Hmong (19)	20	0.01
Indian (2,982)	3,306	1.45
Indonesian (23)	44	0.02
Japanese (380)	589	0.26
Korean (947)	1,146	0.50
Laotian (18)	23	0.01
Malaysian (10)	19	0.01
Nepalese (29)	48	0.02
Pakistani (261)	294	0.13
Sri Lankan (28)	35	0.02
Taiwanese (233)	269	0.12
Thai (156)	207	0.09
Vietnamese (701)	795	0.35
Hawaii Native/Pacific Islander (166)	331	0.14
Not Hispanic (129)	256	0.11
Hispanic (37)	75	0.03
Fijian (2)	3	<0.01
Guamanian/Chamorro (33)	49	0.02
Marshallese (0)	0	<0.01
Native Hawaiian (34)	79	0.03
Samoan (14)	34	0.01
Tongan (0)	2	<0.01
White (96,932)	101,410	44.41
Not Hispanic (86,519)	89,618	39.25
Hispanic (10,413)	11,792	5.16

Notes: † The Census 2010 population figure is used to calculate the percentages in the Hispanic Origin and Race categories. Ancestry percentages are based on the 2006-2010 American Community Survey population (not shown); ‡ Numbers in parentheses indicate the number of people reporting a single ancestry; * Numbers in parentheses indicate the number of persons reporting this race alone, not in combination with any other race; Please refer to the Explanation of Data for more information.

Fayetteville

Place Type: City
County: Cumberland
Population: 200,564

Ancestry	Population	%
Afghan (0)	0	<0.01
African, Sub-Saharan (1,702)	2,422	1.22
African (844)	1,373	0.69
Cape Verdean (13)	46	0.02
Ethiopian (56)	56	0.03
Ghanaian (106)	106	0.05
Kenyan (0)	0	<0.01
Liberian (11)	11	<0.01
Nigerian (355)	412	0.21
Senegalese (0)	0	<0.01
Sierra Leonean (36)	36	0.02
Somalian (33)	134	0.07
South African (33)	33	0.02
Sudanese (107)	107	0.05
Ugandan (0)	0	<0.01
Zimbabwean (0)	0	<0.01
Other Sub-Saharan African (108)	108	0.05
Albanian (0)	0	<0.01
Alsatian (0)	0	<0.01
American (8,601)	8,601	4.32
Arab (229)	327	0.16
Arab (87)	87	0.04
Egyptian (0)	0	<0.01
Iraqi (26)	26	0.01
Jordanian (0)	0	<0.01
Lebanese (97)	195	0.10
Moroccan (0)	0	<0.01
Palestinian (0)	0	<0.01
Syrian (0)	0	<0.01
Other Arab (19)	19	0.01
Armenian (48)	48	0.02
Assyrian/Chaldean/Syriac (0)	0	<0.01
Australian (27)	40	0.02
Austrian (200)	349	0.18
Basque (29)	29	0.01
Belgian (0)	36	0.02
Brazilian (0)	0	<0.01
British (262)	512	0.26
Bulgarian (18)	18	0.01
Cajun (0)	16	0.01
Canadian (170)	303	0.15
Carpatho Rusyn (0)	0	<0.01
Celtic (0)	0	<0.01
Croatian (11)	67	0.03
Cypriot (0)	0	<0.01
Czech (129)	353	0.18
Czechoslovakian (7)	70	0.04
Danish (75)	345	0.17
Dutch (208)	1,635	0.82
Eastern European (0)	0	<0.01
English (4,711)	12,565	6.32
Estonian (14)	64	0.03
European (1,063)	1,435	0.72
Finnish (82)	255	0.13
French, ex. Basque (787)	3,489	1.75
French Canadian (346)	899	0.45
German (7,097)	21,911	11.02
German Russian (0)	8	<0.01
Greek (363)	542	0.27
Guyanese (131)	139	0.07
Hungarian (170)	488	0.25
Icelander (0)	27	0.01
Iranian (82)	100	0.05
Irish (4,648)	16,748	8.42
Israeli (0)	0	<0.01
Italian (1,731)	6,535	3.29
Latvian (16)	33	0.02
Lithuanian (67)	165	0.08
Luxemburger (0)	0	<0.01
Macedonian (0)	0	<0.01
Maltese (15)	25	0.01
New Zealander (0)	0	<0.01
Northern European (23)	23	0.01

Ancestry	Population	%
Norwegian (311)	1,032	0.52
Pennsylvania German (19)	45	0.02
Polish (604)	2,868	1.44
Portuguese (242)	503	0.25
Romanian (28)	51	0.03
Russian (295)	914	0.46
Scandinavian (19)	98	0.05
Scotch-Irish (3,290)	5,414	2.72
Scottish (2,220)	4,887	2.46
Serbian (2)	29	0.01
Slavic (27)	27	0.01
Slovak (89)	174	0.09
Slovene (0)	21	0.01
Soviet Union (0)	0	<0.01
Swedish (318)	1,416	0.71
Swiss (30)	144	0.07
Turkish (94)	124	0.06
Ukrainian (72)	192	0.10
Welsh (62)	983	0.49
West Indian, ex. Hispanic (1,230)	2,462	1.24
Bahamian (0)	31	0.02
Barbadian (12)	31	0.02
Belizean (0)	7	<0.01
Bermudan (0)	0	<0.01
British West Indian (86)	333	0.17
Dutch West Indian (28)	28	0.01
Haitian (102)	406	0.20
Jamaican (511)	803	0.40
Trinidadian/Tobagonian (121)	147	0.07
U.S. Virgin Islander (44)	61	0.03
West Indian (326)	615	0.31
Other West Indian (0)	0	<0.01
Yugoslavian (0)	33	0.02

Hispanic Origin	Population	%
Hispanic or Latino (of any race)	20,256	10.10
Central American, ex. Mexican	2,238	1.12
Costa Rican	81	0.04
Guatemalan	176	0.09
Honduran	282	0.14
Nicaraguan	157	0.08
Panamanian	1,154	0.58
Salvadoran	379	0.19
Other Central American	9	<0.01
Cuban	534	0.27
Dominican Republic	730	0.36
Mexican	6,448	3.21
Puerto Rican	7,526	3.75
South American	1,227	0.61
Argentinean	74	0.04
Bolivian	53	0.03
Chilean	55	0.03
Colombian	492	0.25
Ecuadorian	195	0.10
Paraguayan	14	0.01
Peruvian	244	0.12
Uruguayan	10	<0.01
Venezuelan	80	0.04
Other South American	10	<0.01
Other Hispanic or Latino	1,553	0.77

Race*	Population	%
African-American/Black (84,040)	89,916	44.83
Not Hispanic (81,768)	86,376	43.07
Hispanic (2,272)	3,540	1.77
American Indian/Alaska Native (2,165)	4,901	2.44
Not Hispanic (1,907)	4,180	2.08
Hispanic (258)	721	0.36
Alaska Athabascan (Ala. Nat.) (5)	8	<0.01
Aleut (Alaska Native) (3)	7	<0.01
Apache (16)	52	0.03
Arapaho (1)	3	<0.01
Blackfeet (17)	143	0.07
Canadian/French Am. Ind. (2)	4	<0.01
Central American Ind. (5)	17	0.01
Cherokee (169)	815	0.41
Cheyenne (5)	12	0.01
Chickasaw (3)	12	0.01
Chippewa (17)	55	0.03

Race*	Population	%
Choctaw (26)	55	0.03
Colville (1)	1	<0.01
Comanche (6)	13	0.01
Cree (2)	11	0.01
Creek (11)	29	0.01
Crow (0)	4	<0.01
Delaware (1)	12	0.01
Hopi (2)	4	<0.01
Houma (1)	3	<0.01
Inupiat (Alaska Native) (0)	2	<0.01
Iroquois (40)	60	0.03
Kiowa (2)	7	<0.01
Lumbee (630)	893	0.45
Menominee (1)	2	<0.01
Mexican American Ind. (14)	27	0.01
Navajo (80)	109	0.05
Osage (3)	7	<0.01
Ottawa (1)	4	<0.01
Paiute (2)	2	<0.01
Pima (4)	8	<0.01
Potawatomi (4)	9	<0.01
Pueblo (4)	11	0.01
Puget Sound Salish (3)	5	<0.01
Seminole (4)	24	0.01
Shoshone (3)	11	0.01
Sioux (41)	87	0.04
South American Ind. (12)	94	0.05
Spanish American Ind. (14)	15	0.01
Tlingit-Haida (Alaska Native) (6)	6	<0.01
Tohono O'Odham (2)	4	<0.01
Tsimshian (Alaska Native) (0)	0	<0.01
Ute (0)	1	<0.01
Yakama (0)	0	<0.01
Yaqui (2)	4	<0.01
Yuman (0)	0	<0.01
Yup'ik (Alaska Native) (3)	3	<0.01
Asian (5,291)	7,899	3.94
Not Hispanic (5,147)	7,423	3.70
Hispanic (144)	476	0.24
Bangladeshi (48)	51	0.03
Bhutanese (0)	0	<0.01
Burmese (34)	37	0.02
Cambodian (44)	73	0.04
Chinese, ex. Taiwanese (418)	741	0.37
Filipino (956)	1,754	0.87
Hmong (9)	16	0.01
Indian (717)	908	0.45
Indonesian (5)	21	0.01
Japanese (327)	775	0.39
Korean (1,590)	2,323	1.16
Laotian (49)	67	0.03
Malaysian (1)	1	<0.01
Nepalese (12)	12	0.01
Pakistani (70)	85	0.04
Sri Lankan (15)	19	0.01
Taiwanese (27)	32	0.02
Thai (220)	364	0.18
Vietnamese (471)	611	0.30
Hawaii Native/Pacific Islander (896)	1,631	0.81
Not Hispanic (823)	1,376	0.69
Hispanic (73)	255	0.13
Fijian (3)	4	<0.01
Guamanian/Chamorro (367)	528	0.26
Marshallese (17)	22	0.01
Native Hawaiian (158)	473	0.24
Samoan (143)	226	0.11
Tongan (4)	10	<0.01
White (91,653)	99,113	49.42
Not Hispanic (82,797)	88,521	44.14
Hispanic (8,856)	10,592	5.28

Notes: † The Census 2010 population figure is used to calculate the percentages in the Hispanic Origin and Race categories. Ancestry percentages are based on the 2006-2010 American Community Survey population (not shown); ‡ Numbers in parentheses indicate the number of people reporting a single ancestry; * Numbers in parentheses indicate the number of persons reporting this race alone, not in combination with any other race; Please refer to the Explanation of Data for more information.

Gastonia

Place Type: City
County: Gaston
Population: 71,741

Ancestry	Population	%
Afghan (0)	0	<0.01
African, Sub-Saharan (622)	682	0.96
African (395)	455	0.64
Cape Verdean (0)	0	<0.01
Ethiopian (96)	96	0.14
Ghanaian (0)	0	<0.01
Kenyan (13)	13	0.02
Liberian (0)	0	<0.01
Nigerian (87)	87	0.12
Senegalese (8)	8	0.01
Sierra Leonean (0)	0	<0.01
Somalian (23)	23	0.03
South African (0)	0	<0.01
Sudanese (0)	0	<0.01
Ugandan (0)	0	<0.01
Zimbabwean (0)	0	<0.01
Other Sub-Saharan African (0)	0	<0.01
Albanian (9)	9	0.01
Alsatian (0)	0	<0.01
American (5,604)	5,604	7.93
Arab (90)	208	0.29
Arab (0)	26	0.04
Egyptian (15)	39	0.06
Iraqi (0)	0	<0.01
Jordanian (0)	0	<0.01
Lebanese (30)	30	0.04
Moroccan (13)	13	0.02
Palestinian (0)	0	<0.01
Syrian (32)	92	0.13
Other Arab (0)	8	0.01
Armenian (0)	69	0.10
Assyrian/Chaldean/Syriac (0)	0	<0.01
Australian (13)	13	0.02
Austrian (28)	67	0.09
Basque (0)	0	<0.01
Belgian (0)	13	0.02
Brazilian (14)	14	0.02
British (129)	289	0.41
Bulgarian (79)	79	0.11
Cajun (0)	0	<0.01
Canadian (19)	67	0.09
Carpatho Rusyn (0)	0	<0.01
Celtic (0)	0	<0.01
Croatian (0)	23	0.03
Cypriot (0)	0	<0.01
Czech (0)	87	0.12
Czechoslovakian (39)	47	0.07
Danish (22)	22	0.03
Dutch (215)	1,116	1.58
Eastern European (26)	30	0.04
English (2,543)	5,568	7.87
Estonian (0)	0	<0.01
European (354)	473	0.67
Finnish (47)	47	0.07
French, ex. Basque (158)	901	1.27
French Canadian (115)	268	0.38
German (2,591)	7,258	10.26
German Russian (0)	0	<0.01
Greek (270)	576	0.81
Guyanese (0)	0	<0.01
Hungarian (0)	15	0.02
Icelander (0)	0	<0.01
Iranian (0)	0	<0.01
Irish (1,788)	5,979	8.46
Israeli (0)	0	<0.01
Italian (327)	1,119	1.58
Latvian (0)	0	<0.01
Lithuanian (0)	0	<0.01
Luxemburger (0)	0	<0.01
Macedonian (0)	0	<0.01
Maltese (0)	0	<0.01
New Zealander (0)	0	<0.01
Northern European (14)	14	0.02

	Population	%
Norwegian (5)	42	0.06
Pennsylvania German (11)	11	0.02
Polish (135)	514	0.73
Portuguese (34)	45	0.06
Romanian (0)	11	0.02
Russian (67)	214	0.30
Scandinavian (0)	0	<0.01
Scotch-Irish (2,096)	3,416	4.83
Scottish (1,049)	1,911	2.70
Serbian (0)	0	<0.01
Slavic (0)	0	<0.01
Slovak (20)	65	0.09
Slovene (0)	0	<0.01
Soviet Union (0)	0	<0.01
Swedish (41)	182	0.26
Swiss (0)	61	0.09
Turkish (10)	10	0.01
Ukrainian (6)	20	0.03
Welsh (122)	327	0.46
West Indian, ex. Hispanic (135)	135	0.19
Bahamian (12)	12	0.02
Barbadian (0)	0	<0.01
Belizean (0)	0	<0.01
Bermudan (0)	0	<0.01
British West Indian (0)	0	<0.01
Dutch West Indian (0)	0	<0.01
Haitian (36)	36	0.05
Jamaican (9)	9	0.01
Trinidadian/Tobagonian (0)	0	<0.01
U.S. Virgin Islander (0)	0	<0.01
West Indian (78)	78	0.11
Other West Indian (0)	0	<0.01
Yugoslavian (19)	19	0.03

Hispanic Origin	Population	%
Hispanic or Latino (of any race)	6,901	9.62
Central American, ex. Mexican	606	0.84
Costa Rican	72	0.10
Guatemalan	79	0.11
Honduran	206	0.29
Nicaraguan	73	0.10
Panamanian	18	0.03
Salvadoran	134	0.19
Other Central American	24	0.03
Cuban	136	0.19
Dominican Republic	171	0.24
Mexican	3,849	5.37
Puerto Rican	561	0.78
South American	1,042	1.45
Argentinean	10	0.01
Bolivian	3	<0.01
Chilean	63	0.09
Colombian	812	1.13
Ecuadorian	72	0.10
Paraguayan	0	<0.01
Peruvian	52	0.07
Uruguayan	15	0.02
Venezuelan	13	0.02
Other South American	2	<0.01
Other Hispanic or Latino	536	0.75

Race*	Population	%
African-American/Black (19,953)	20,917	29.16
Not Hispanic (19,661)	20,521	28.60
Hispanic (292)	396	0.55
American Indian/Alaska Native (289)	691	0.96
Not Hispanic (201)	576	0.80
Hispanic (88)	115	0.16
Alaska Athabascan (Ala. Nat.) (0)	0	<0.01
Aleut (Alaska Native) (0)	0	<0.01
Apache (2)	5	0.01
Arapaho (0)	0	<0.01
Blackfeet (1)	14	0.02
Canadian/French Am. Ind. (0)	0	<0.01
Central American Ind. (1)	1	<0.01
Cherokee (61)	184	0.26
Cheyenne (1)	1	<0.01
Chickasaw (0)	0	<0.01
Chippewa (4)	6	0.01

	Population	%
Choctaw (5)	9	0.01
Colville (0)	0	<0.01
Comanche (0)	0	<0.01
Cree (0)	0	<0.01
Creek (8)	10	0.01
Crow (0)	1	<0.01
Delaware (1)	1	<0.01
Hopi (0)	0	<0.01
Houma (0)	0	<0.01
Inupiat (Alaska Native) (0)	0	<0.01
Iroquois (1)	2	<0.01
Kiowa (1)	1	<0.01
Lumbee (27)	44	0.06
Menominee (0)	0	<0.01
Mexican American Ind. (22)	23	0.03
Navajo (1)	3	<0.01
Osage (0)	1	<0.01
Ottawa (0)	0	<0.01
Paiute (0)	0	<0.01
Pima (0)	0	<0.01
Potawatomi (0)	3	<0.01
Pueblo (0)	0	<0.01
Puget Sound Salish (0)	0	<0.01
Seminole (0)	9	0.01
Shoshone (0)	0	<0.01
Sioux (2)	4	0.01
South American Ind. (4)	7	0.01
Spanish American Ind. (2)	2	<0.01
Tlingit-Haida (Alaska Native) (0)	0	<0.01
Tohono O'Odham (0)	0	<0.01
Tsimshian (Alaska Native) (0)	0	<0.01
Ute (0)	0	<0.01
Yakama (0)	0	<0.01
Yaqui (0)	0	<0.01
Yuman (1)	1	<0.01
Yup'ik (Alaska Native) (0)	0	<0.01
Asian (964)	1,175	1.64
Not Hispanic (956)	1,144	1.59
Hispanic (8)	31	0.04
Bangladeshi (0)	0	<0.01
Bhutanese (0)	0	<0.01
Burmese (0)	0	<0.01
Cambodian (13)	17	0.02
Chinese, ex. Taiwanese (143)	161	0.22
Filipino (69)	96	0.13
Hmong (15)	15	0.02
Indian (339)	389	0.54
Indonesian (11)	13	0.02
Japanese (23)	49	0.07
Korean (52)	75	0.10
Laotian (37)	51	0.07
Malaysian (1)	1	<0.01
Nepalese (0)	0	<0.01
Pakistani (92)	98	0.14
Sri Lankan (7)	8	0.01
Taiwanese (0)	0	<0.01
Thai (12)	28	0.04
Vietnamese (112)	143	0.20
Hawaii Native/Pacific Islander (16)	53	0.07
Not Hispanic (7)	36	0.05
Hispanic (9)	17	0.02
Fijian (1)	1	<0.01
Guamanian/Chamorro (1)	5	0.01
Marshallese (0)	0	<0.01
Native Hawaiian (6)	14	0.02
Samoan (8)	10	0.01
Tongan (0)	0	<0.01
White (45,199)	46,580	64.93
Not Hispanic (42,614)	43,719	60.94
Hispanic (2,585)	2,861	3.99

Notes: † The Census 2010 population figure is used to calculate the percentages in the Hispanic Origin and Race categories. Ancestry percentages are based on the 2006-2010 American Community Survey population (not shown); ‡ Numbers in parentheses indicate the number of people reporting a single ancestry; * Numbers in parentheses indicate the number of persons reporting this race alone, not in combination with any other race; Please refer to the Explanation of Data for more information.

Greensboro

Place Type: City
County: Guilford
Population: 269,666

Ancestry	Population	%
Afghan (16)	16	0.01
African, Sub-Saharan (5,627)	6,270	2.38
African (2,320)	2,798	1.06
Cape Verdean (0)	0	<0.01
Ethiopian (87)	87	0.03
Ghanaian (375)	375	0.14
Kenyan (15)	15	0.01
Liberian (175)	204	0.08
Nigerian (498)	553	0.21
Senegalese (13)	13	<0.01
Sierra Leonean (210)	210	0.08
Somalian (118)	118	0.04
South African (8)	45	0.02
Sudanese (1,127)	1,144	0.43
Ugandan (38)	38	0.01
Zimbabwean (0)	0	<0.01
Other Sub-Saharan African (643)	670	0.25
Albanian (0)	0	<0.01
Alsatian (0)	0	<0.01
American (12,778)	12,778	4.85
Arab (813)	1,120	0.43
Arab (108)	151	0.06
Egyptian (137)	151	0.06
Iraqi (0)	0	<0.01
Jordanian (126)	159	0.06
Lebanese (254)	361	0.14
Moroccan (17)	26	0.01
Palestinian (65)	111	0.04
Syrian (75)	130	0.05
Other Arab (31)	31	0.01
Armenian (0)	0	<0.01
Assyrian/Chaldean/Syriac (0)	0	<0.01
Australian (10)	66	0.03
Austrian (119)	326	0.12
Basque (21)	21	0.01
Belgian (46)	193	0.07
Brazilian (205)	232	0.09
British (839)	1,727	0.66
Bulgarian (37)	52	0.02
Cajun (36)	66	0.03
Canadian (271)	359	0.14
Carpatho Rusyn (0)	0	<0.01
Celtic (38)	51	0.02
Croatian (101)	166	0.06
Cypriot (0)	0	<0.01
Czech (94)	523	0.20
Czechoslovakian (50)	136	0.05
Danish (95)	372	0.14
Dutch (414)	2,321	0.88
Eastern European (422)	476	0.18
English (10,090)	22,926	8.71
Estonian (0)	0	<0.01
European (2,522)	2,845	1.08
Finnish (35)	292	0.11
French, ex. Basque (750)	4,077	1.55
French Canadian (189)	633	0.24
German (7,590)	22,704	8.62
German Russian (0)	0	<0.01
Greek (325)	526	0.20
Guyanese (182)	209	0.08
Hungarian (121)	666	0.25
Icelander (0)	14	0.01
Iranian (365)	397	0.15
Irish (6,207)	18,092	6.87
Israeli (0)	0	<0.01
Italian (2,254)	6,358	2.41
Latvian (9)	9	<0.01
Lithuanian (37)	243	0.09
Luxemburger (0)	9	<0.01
Macedonian (0)	0	<0.01
Maltese (9)	9	<0.01
New Zealander (0)	0	<0.01
Northern European (116)	116	0.04

Ancestry (cont.)	Population	%
Norwegian (207)	1,013	0.38
Pennsylvania German (37)	143	0.05
Polish (1,041)	3,312	1.26
Portuguese (66)	273	0.10
Romanian (125)	160	0.06
Russian (561)	1,444	0.55
Scandinavian (77)	313	0.12
Scotch-Irish (4,966)	8,719	3.31
Scottish (2,606)	6,491	2.46
Serbian (61)	93	0.04
Slavic (38)	38	0.01
Slovak (109)	331	0.13
Slovene (11)	38	0.01
Soviet Union (0)	0	<0.01
Swedish (435)	1,509	0.57
Swiss (130)	367	0.14
Turkish (15)	32	0.01
Ukrainian (137)	323	0.12
Welsh (300)	1,239	0.47
West Indian, ex. Hispanic (725)	1,334	0.51
Bahamian (0)	15	0.01
Barbadian (29)	57	0.02
Belizean (0)	0	<0.01
Bermudan (34)	34	0.01
British West Indian (0)	0	<0.01
Dutch West Indian (0)	0	<0.01
Haitian (34)	45	0.02
Jamaican (470)	860	0.33
Trinidadian/Tobagonian (85)	123	0.05
U.S. Virgin Islander (0)	0	<0.01
West Indian (73)	200	0.08
Other West Indian (0)	0	<0.01
Yugoslavian (202)	252	0.10

Hispanic Origin	Population	%
Hispanic or Latino (of any race)	20,336	7.54
Central American, ex. Mexican	2,246	0.83
Costa Rican	132	0.05
Guatemalan	518	0.19
Honduran	352	0.13
Nicaraguan	159	0.06
Panamanian	191	0.07
Salvadoran	887	0.33
Other Central American	7	<0.01
Cuban	520	0.19
Dominican Republic	568	0.21
Mexican	12,293	4.56
Puerto Rican	1,872	0.69
South American	1,456	0.54
Argentinean	89	0.03
Bolivian	32	0.01
Chilean	102	0.04
Colombian	562	0.21
Ecuadorian	128	0.05
Paraguayan	7	<0.01
Peruvian	285	0.11
Uruguayan	27	0.01
Venezuelan	203	0.08
Other South American	21	0.01
Other Hispanic or Latino	1,381	0.51

Race*	Population	%
African-American/Black (109,586)	114,156	42.33
Not Hispanic (108,233)	112,136	41.58
Hispanic (1,353)	2,020	0.75
American Indian/Alaska Native (1,385)	3,454	1.28
Not Hispanic (1,096)	2,892	1.07
Hispanic (289)	562	0.21
Alaska Athabascan (Ala. Nat.) (0)	0	<0.01
Aleut (Alaska Native) (1)	2	<0.01
Apache (4)	23	0.01
Arapaho (0)	1	<0.01
Blackfeet (12)	123	0.05
Canadian/French Am. Ind. (1)	4	<0.01
Central American Ind. (11)	19	0.01
Cherokee (159)	789	0.29
Cheyenne (2)	4	<0.01
Chickasaw (2)	6	<0.01
Chippewa (15)	33	0.01

Race* (cont.)	Population	%
Choctaw (2)	22	0.01
Colville (0)	0	<0.01
Comanche (1)	7	<0.01
Cree (0)	1	<0.01
Creek (1)	11	<0.01
Crow (1)	2	<0.01
Delaware (2)	5	<0.01
Hopi (0)	2	<0.01
Houma (0)	0	<0.01
Inupiat (Alaska Native) (1)	2	<0.01
Iroquois (13)	56	0.02
Kiowa (1)	1	<0.01
Lumbee (336)	488	0.18
Menominee (0)	0	<0.01
Mexican American Ind. (44)	72	0.03
Navajo (7)	21	0.01
Osage (0)	0	<0.01
Ottawa (1)	3	<0.01
Paiute (0)	0	<0.01
Pima (0)	0	<0.01
Potawatomi (1)	1	<0.01
Pueblo (0)	3	<0.01
Puget Sound Salish (0)	0	<0.01
Seminole (1)	5	<0.01
Shoshone (0)	0	<0.01
Sioux (10)	24	0.01
South American Ind. (5)	18	0.01
Spanish American Ind. (7)	8	<0.01
Tlingit-Haida (Alaska Native) (1)	1	<0.01
Tohono O'Odham (1)	1	<0.01
Tsimshian (Alaska Native) (0)	0	<0.01
Ute (0)	0	<0.01
Yakama (0)	0	<0.01
Yaqui (0)	0	<0.01
Yuman (0)	1	<0.01
Yup'ik (Alaska Native) (1)	1	<0.01
Asian (10,772)	12,291	4.56
Not Hispanic (10,711)	12,120	4.49
Hispanic (61)	171	0.06
Bangladeshi (38)	43	0.02
Bhutanese (158)	173	0.06
Burmese (266)	272	0.10
Cambodian (551)	648	0.24
Chinese, ex. Taiwanese (961)	1,197	0.44
Filipino (384)	672	0.25
Hmong (84)	85	0.03
Indian (1,810)	2,030	0.75
Indonesian (21)	35	0.01
Japanese (183)	369	0.14
Korean (778)	997	0.37
Laotian (328)	389	0.14
Malaysian (7)	14	0.01
Nepalese (74)	81	0.03
Pakistani (205)	230	0.09
Sri Lankan (31)	37	0.01
Taiwanese (46)	59	0.02
Thai (112)	177	0.07
Vietnamese (4,198)	4,474	1.66
Hawaii Native/Pacific Islander (157)	429	0.16
Not Hispanic (128)	342	0.13
Hispanic (29)	87	0.03
Fijian (1)	4	<0.01
Guamanian/Chamorro (35)	72	0.03
Marshallese (7)	7	<0.01
Native Hawaiian (50)	125	0.05
Samoan (16)	47	0.02
Tongan (2)	2	<0.01
White (130,396)	135,483	50.24
Not Hispanic (122,888)	126,944	47.07
Hispanic (7,508)	8,539	3.17

Notes: † The Census 2010 population figure is used to calculate the percentages in the Hispanic Origin and Race categories. Ancestry percentages are based on the 2006-2010 American Community Survey population (not shown); ‡ Numbers in parentheses indicate the number of people reporting a single ancestry; * Numbers in parentheses indicate the number of persons reporting this race alone, not in combination with any other race; Please refer to the Explanation of Data for more information.

Greenville

Place Type: City
County: Pitt
Population: 84,554

Ancestry	Population	%
Afghan (0)	0	<0.01
African, Sub-Saharan (393)	462	0.57
African (169)	238	0.30
Cape Verdean (0)	0	<0.01
Ethiopian (0)	0	<0.01
Ghanaian (129)	129	0.16
Kenyan (14)	14	0.02
Liberian (12)	12	0.01
Nigerian (69)	69	0.09
Senegalese (0)	0	<0.01
Sierra Leonean (0)	0	<0.01
Somalian (0)	0	<0.01
South African (0)	0	<0.01
Sudanese (0)	0	<0.01
Ugandan (0)	0	<0.01
Zimbabwean (0)	0	<0.01
Other Sub-Saharan African (0)	0	<0.01
Albanian (0)	0	<0.01
Alsatian (0)	0	<0.01
American (3,891)	3,891	4.84
Arab (642)	670	0.83
Arab (86)	86	0.11
Egyptian (368)	368	0.46
Iraqi (0)	0	<0.01
Jordanian (10)	10	0.01
Lebanese (123)	151	0.19
Moroccan (44)	44	0.05
Palestinian (0)	0	<0.01
Syrian (0)	0	<0.01
Other Arab (11)	11	0.01
Armenian (14)	14	0.02
Assyrian/Chaldean/Syriac (0)	0	<0.01
Australian (0)	11	0.01
Austrian (41)	110	0.14
Basque (0)	0	<0.01
Belgian (7)	36	0.04
Brazilian (11)	51	0.06
British (220)	359	0.45
Bulgarian (30)	30	0.04
Cajun (16)	32	0.04
Canadian (74)	136	0.17
Carpatho Rusyn (18)	18	0.02
Celtic (0)	0	<0.01
Croatian (0)	0	<0.01
Cypriot (0)	0	<0.01
Czech (27)	129	0.16
Czechoslovakian (20)	20	0.02
Danish (26)	97	0.12
Dutch (164)	705	0.88
Eastern European (22)	22	0.03
English (3,459)	7,419	9.22
Estonian (0)	0	<0.01
European (880)	1,041	1.29
Finnish (13)	40	0.05
French, ex. Basque (320)	1,491	1.85
French Canadian (62)	314	0.39
German (1,999)	6,913	8.59
German Russian (0)	0	<0.01
Greek (50)	170	0.21
Guyanese (0)	0	<0.01
Hungarian (105)	274	0.34
Icelander (0)	33	0.04
Iranian (101)	101	0.13
Irish (2,568)	7,908	9.83
Israeli (27)	27	0.03
Italian (1,157)	3,183	3.96
Latvian (0)	14	0.02
Lithuanian (54)	130	0.16
Luxemburger (0)	0	<0.01
Macedonian (0)	0	<0.01
Maltese (0)	0	<0.01
New Zealander (0)	0	<0.01
Northern European (11)	24	0.03
Norwegian (139)	536	0.67
Pennsylvania German (13)	13	0.02
Polish (362)	1,159	1.44
Portuguese (56)	183	0.23
Romanian (12)	12	0.01
Russian (77)	232	0.29
Scandinavian (0)	9	0.01
Scotch-Irish (1,266)	2,036	2.53
Scottish (819)	2,193	2.73
Serbian (0)	0	<0.01
Slavic (0)	17	0.02
Slovak (26)	65	0.08
Slovene (11)	11	0.01
Soviet Union (0)	0	<0.01
Swedish (61)	287	0.36
Swiss (87)	142	0.18
Turkish (31)	31	0.04
Ukrainian (28)	161	0.20
Welsh (206)	536	0.67
West Indian, ex. Hispanic (247)	339	0.42
Bahamian (0)	0	<0.01
Barbadian (0)	0	<0.01
Belizean (0)	0	<0.01
Bermudan (0)	0	<0.01
British West Indian (0)	0	<0.01
Dutch West Indian (0)	8	0.01
Haitian (0)	35	0.04
Jamaican (84)	101	0.13
Trinidadian/Tobagonian (163)	195	0.24
U.S. Virgin Islander (0)	0	<0.01
West Indian (0)	0	<0.01
Other West Indian (0)	0	<0.01
Yugoslavian (62)	62	0.08

Hispanic Origin	Population	%
Hispanic or Latino (of any race)	3,183	3.76
Central American, ex. Mexican	350	0.41
Costa Rican	38	0.04
Guatemalan	44	0.05
Honduran	65	0.08
Nicaraguan	39	0.05
Panamanian	35	0.04
Salvadoran	125	0.15
Other Central American	4	<0.01
Cuban	111	0.13
Dominican Republic	72	0.09
Mexican	1,558	1.84
Puerto Rican	547	0.65
South American	277	0.33
Argentinean	14	0.02
Bolivian	2	<0.01
Chilean	23	0.03
Colombian	112	0.13
Ecuadorian	29	0.03
Paraguayan	7	0.01
Peruvian	48	0.06
Uruguayan	3	<0.01
Venezuelan	29	0.03
Other South American	10	0.01
Other Hispanic or Latino	268	0.32

Race*	Population	%
African-American/Black (31,272)	32,386	38.30
Not Hispanic (31,010)	31,978	37.82
Hispanic (262)	408	0.48
American Indian/Alaska Native (303)	735	0.87
Not Hispanic (265)	651	0.77
Hispanic (38)	84	0.10
Alaska Athabascan (Ala. Nat.) (0)	0	<0.01
Aleut (Alaska Native) (5)	5	0.01
Apache (0)	0	<0.01
Arapaho (0)	0	<0.01
Blackfeet (1)	11	0.01
Canadian/French Am. Ind. (5)	7	0.01
Central American Ind. (1)	8	0.01
Cherokee (33)	134	0.16
Cheyenne (0)	4	<0.01
Chickasaw (0)	1	<0.01
Chippewa (5)	12	0.01

	Population	%
Choctaw (4)	9	0.01
Colville (0)	0	<0.01
Comanche (1)	7	0.01
Cree (1)	1	<0.01
Creek (1)	6	<0.01
Crow (0)	0	<0.01
Delaware (1)	1	<0.01
Hopi (0)	0	<0.01
Houma (0)	0	<0.01
Inupiat (Alaska Native) (0)	1	<0.01
Iroquois (9)	17	0.02
Kiowa (0)	0	<0.01
Lumbee (53)	72	0.09
Menominee (0)	0	<0.01
Mexican American Ind. (5)	12	0.01
Navajo (2)	2	<0.01
Osage (0)	0	<0.01
Ottawa (1)	1	<0.01
Paiute (0)	0	<0.01
Pima (0)	0	<0.01
Potawatomi (1)	1	<0.01
Pueblo (0)	2	<0.01
Puget Sound Salish (0)	0	<0.01
Seminole (1)	5	0.01
Shoshone (1)	1	<0.01
Sioux (1)	6	0.01
South American Ind. (6)	8	0.01
Spanish American Ind. (0)	0	<0.01
Tlingit-Haida (Alaska Native) (1)	1	<0.01
Tohono O'Odham (0)	0	<0.01
Tsimshian (Alaska Native) (0)	0	<0.01
Ute (0)	0	<0.01
Yakama (0)	0	<0.01
Yaqui (0)	0	<0.01
Yuman (0)	0	<0.01
Yup'ik (Alaska Native) (0)	0	<0.01
Asian (2,025)	2,560	3.03
Not Hispanic (1,996)	2,504	2.96
Hispanic (29)	56	0.07
Bangladeshi (7)	10	0.01
Bhutanese (0)	0	<0.01
Burmese (14)	30	0.04
Cambodian (4)	8	0.01
Chinese, ex. Taiwanese (412)	468	0.55
Filipino (196)	308	0.36
Hmong (39)	41	0.05
Indian (665)	733	0.87
Indonesian (0)	11	0.01
Japanese (96)	173	0.20
Korean (200)	285	0.34
Laotian (8)	11	0.01
Malaysian (1)	3	<0.01
Nepalese (2)	2	<0.01
Pakistani (100)	116	0.14
Sri Lankan (1)	1	<0.01
Taiwanese (24)	28	0.03
Thai (21)	39	0.05
Vietnamese (125)	166	0.20
Hawaii Native/Pacific Islander (34)	100	0.12
Not Hispanic (31)	87	0.10
Hispanic (3)	13	0.02
Fijian (1)	1	<0.01
Guamanian/Chamorro (11)	20	0.02
Marshallese (0)	0	<0.01
Native Hawaiian (4)	19	0.02
Samoan (8)	15	0.02
Tongan (3)	3	<0.01
White (47,579)	49,010	57.96
Not Hispanic (46,368)	47,591	56.28
Hispanic (1,211)	1,419	1.68

*Notes: † The Census 2010 population figure is used to calculate the percentages in the Hispanic Origin and Race categories. Ancestry percentages are based on the 2006-2010 American Community Survey population (not shown); ‡ Numbers in parentheses indicate the number of people reporting a single ancestry; * Numbers in parentheses indicate the number of persons reporting this race alone, not in combination with any other race; Please refer to the Explanation of Data for more information.*

High Point

Place Type: City
County: Guilford
Population: 104,371

Ancestry	Population	%
Afghan (0)	0	<0.01
African, Sub-Saharan (1,677)	1,717	1.70
African (496)	536	0.53
Cape Verdean (0)	0	<0.01
Ethiopian (266)	266	0.26
Ghanaian (27)	27	0.03
Kenyan (0)	0	<0.01
Liberian (376)	376	0.37
Nigerian (110)	110	0.11
Senegalese (0)	0	<0.01
Sierra Leonean (0)	0	<0.01
Somalian (0)	0	<0.01
South African (0)	0	<0.01
Sudanese (327)	327	0.32
Ugandan (0)	0	<0.01
Zimbabwean (0)	0	<0.01
Other Sub-Saharan African (75)	75	0.07
Albanian (0)	0	<0.01
Alsatian (0)	0	<0.01
American (5,633)	5,633	5.58
Arab (18)	134	0.13
Arab (0)	13	0.01
Egyptian (0)	0	<0.01
Iraqi (0)	0	<0.01
Jordanian (0)	0	<0.01
Lebanese (11)	114	0.11
Moroccan (0)	0	<0.01
Palestinian (0)	0	<0.01
Syrian (7)	7	0.01
Other Arab (0)	0	<0.01
Armenian (73)	73	0.07
Assyrian/Chaldean/Syriac (0)	0	<0.01
Australian (0)	8	0.01
Austrian (19)	162	0.16
Basque (0)	0	<0.01
Belgian (0)	15	0.01
Brazilian (0)	0	<0.01
British (91)	155	0.15
Bulgarian (0)	10	0.01
Cajun (0)	0	<0.01
Canadian (12)	69	0.07
Carpatho Rusyn (0)	0	<0.01
Celtic (0)	0	<0.01
Croatian (28)	98	0.10
Cypriot (0)	0	<0.01
Czech (54)	432	0.43
Czechoslovakian (0)	66	0.07
Danish (60)	102	0.10
Dutch (161)	959	0.95
Eastern European (15)	15	0.01
English (4,724)	9,115	9.03
Estonian (0)	0	<0.01
European (771)	974	0.97
Finnish (0)	70	0.07
French, ex. Basque (301)	1,210	1.20
French Canadian (121)	335	0.33
German (3,102)	9,603	9.52
German Russian (0)	0	<0.01
Greek (211)	468	0.46
Guyanese (0)	207	0.21
Hungarian (70)	265	0.26
Icelander (0)	0	<0.01
Iranian (9)	9	0.01
Irish (2,379)	7,037	6.97
Israeli (0)	0	<0.01
Italian (1,172)	2,523	2.50
Latvian (0)	17	0.02
Lithuanian (28)	78	0.08
Luxemburger (0)	0	<0.01
Macedonian (0)	0	<0.01
Maltese (0)	0	<0.01
New Zealander (0)	0	<0.01
Northern European (11)	11	0.01

Ancestry (cont.)	Population	%
Norwegian (208)	629	0.62
Pennsylvania German (12)	12	0.01
Polish (398)	983	0.97
Portuguese (0)	253	0.25
Romanian (19)	31	0.03
Russian (56)	196	0.19
Scandinavian (0)	19	0.02
Scotch-Irish (1,704)	3,160	3.13
Scottish (986)	2,043	2.02
Serbian (64)	250	0.25
Slavic (36)	109	0.11
Slovak (64)	96	0.10
Slovene (17)	34	0.03
Soviet Union (0)	0	<0.01
Swedish (161)	838	0.83
Swiss (18)	73	0.07
Turkish (0)	0	<0.01
Ukrainian (14)	239	0.24
Welsh (170)	402	0.40
West Indian, ex. Hispanic (436)	626	0.62
Bahamian (155)	155	0.15
Barbadian (0)	0	<0.01
Belizean (0)	0	<0.01
Bermudan (0)	0	<0.01
British West Indian (0)	22	0.02
Dutch West Indian (7)	24	0.02
Haitian (115)	115	0.11
Jamaican (71)	116	0.11
Trinidadian/Tobagonian (88)	186	0.18
U.S. Virgin Islander (0)	0	<0.01
West Indian (0)	8	0.01
Other West Indian (0)	0	<0.01
Yugoslavian (88)	269	0.27

Hispanic Origin	Population	%
Hispanic or Latino (of any race)	8,847	8.48
Central American, ex. Mexican	1,086	1.04
Costa Rican	43	0.04
Guatemalan	157	0.15
Honduran	380	0.36
Nicaraguan	21	0.02
Panamanian	72	0.07
Salvadoran	408	0.39
Other Central American	5	<0.01
Cuban	253	0.24
Dominican Republic	258	0.25
Mexican	5,092	4.88
Puerto Rican	883	0.85
South American	700	0.67
Argentinean	37	0.04
Bolivian	18	0.02
Chilean	49	0.05
Colombian	318	0.30
Ecuadorian	93	0.09
Paraguayan	1	<0.01
Peruvian	131	0.13
Uruguayan	6	0.01
Venezuelan	45	0.04
Other South American	2	<0.01
Other Hispanic or Latino	575	0.55

Race*	Population	%
African-American/Black (34,394)	35,767	34.27
Not Hispanic (33,983)	35,168	33.70
Hispanic (411)	599	0.57
American Indian/Alaska Native (579)	1,205	1.15
Not Hispanic (436)	981	0.94
Hispanic (143)	224	0.21
Alaska Athabascan (Ala. Nat.) (0)	0	<0.01
Aleut (Alaska Native) (0)	0	<0.01
Apache (6)	13	0.01
Arapaho (0)	0	<0.01
Blackfeet (3)	22	0.02
Canadian/French Am. Ind. (0)	1	<0.01
Central American Ind. (6)	8	0.01
Cherokee (56)	216	0.21
Cheyenne (0)	2	<0.01
Chickasaw (0)	0	<0.01
Chippewa (5)	13	0.01

Race* (cont.)	Population	%
Choctaw (3)	13	0.01
Colville (0)	0	<0.01
Comanche (3)	7	0.01
Cree (0)	2	<0.01
Creek (2)	7	0.01
Crow (0)	1	<0.01
Delaware (1)	2	<0.01
Hopi (0)	1	<0.01
Houma (0)	0	<0.01
Inupiat (Alaska Native) (0)	1	<0.01
Iroquois (7)	17	0.02
Kiowa (0)	0	<0.01
Lumbee (107)	161	0.15
Menominee (0)	0	<0.01
Mexican American Ind. (38)	52	0.05
Navajo (2)	11	0.01
Osage (0)	0	<0.01
Ottawa (1)	2	<0.01
Paiute (0)	0	<0.01
Pima (0)	0	<0.01
Potawatomi (0)	3	<0.01
Pueblo (2)	3	<0.01
Puget Sound Salish (0)	0	<0.01
Seminole (1)	2	<0.01
Shoshone (0)	0	<0.01
Sioux (1)	9	0.01
South American Ind. (1)	5	<0.01
Spanish American Ind. (1)	1	<0.01
Tlingit-Haida (Alaska Native) (0)	0	<0.01
Tohono O'Odham (0)	0	<0.01
Tsimshian (Alaska Native) (0)	0	<0.01
Ute (0)	0	<0.01
Yakama (0)	0	<0.01
Yaqui (0)	1	<0.01
Yuman (1)	1	<0.01
Yup'ik (Alaska Native) (0)	0	<0.01
Asian (6,345)	6,916	6.63
Not Hispanic (6,302)	6,828	6.54
Hispanic (43)	88	0.08
Bangladeshi (9)	16	0.02
Bhutanese (44)	61	0.06
Burmese (384)	406	0.39
Cambodian (72)	111	0.11
Chinese, ex. Taiwanese (387)	468	0.45
Filipino (352)	459	0.44
Hmong (11)	13	0.01
Indian (978)	1,152	1.10
Indonesian (1)	1	<0.01
Japanese (79)	119	0.11
Korean (560)	630	0.60
Laotian (515)	579	0.55
Malaysian (12)	12	0.01
Nepalese (130)	147	0.14
Pakistani (1,293)	1,399	1.34
Sri Lankan (7)	7	0.01
Taiwanese (16)	21	0.02
Thai (56)	81	0.08
Vietnamese (1,032)	1,085	1.04
Hawaii Native/Pacific Islander (45)	135	0.13
Not Hispanic (38)	104	0.10
Hispanic (7)	31	0.03
Fijian (0)	0	<0.01
Guamanian/Chamorro (13)	27	0.03
Marshallese (0)	0	<0.01
Native Hawaiian (5)	31	0.03
Samoan (6)	15	0.01
Tongan (0)	0	<0.01
White (55,989)	57,866	55.44
Not Hispanic (52,612)	54,075	51.81
Hispanic (3,377)	3,791	3.63

*Notes: † The Census 2010 population figure is used to calculate the percentages in the Hispanic Origin and Race categories. Ancestry percentages are based on the 2006-2010 American Community Survey population (not shown); ‡ Numbers in parentheses indicate the number of people reporting a single ancestry; * Numbers in parentheses indicate the number of persons reporting this race alone, not in combination with any other race; Please refer to the Explanation of Data for more information.*

Jacksonville

Place Type: City
County: Onslow
Population: 70,145

Ancestry	Population	%
Afghan (5)	5	0.01
African, Sub-Saharan (512)	1,157	1.68
African (500)	1,109	1.61
Cape Verdean (0)	12	0.02
Ethiopian (0)	0	<0.01
Ghanaian (0)	0	<0.01
Kenyan (0)	0	<0.01
Liberian (0)	0	<0.01
Nigerian (0)	14	0.02
Senegalese (12)	12	0.02
Sierra Leonean (0)	0	<0.01
Somalian (0)	0	<0.01
South African (0)	10	0.01
Sudanese (0)	0	<0.01
Ugandan (0)	0	<0.01
Zimbabwean (0)	0	<0.01
Other Sub-Saharan African (0)	0	<0.01
Albanian (0)	0	<0.01
Alsatian (0)	0	<0.01
American (2,778)	2,778	4.03
Arab (173)	306	0.44
Arab (0)	15	0.02
Egyptian (7)	7	0.01
Iraqi (46)	46	0.07
Jordanian (0)	0	<0.01
Lebanese (86)	133	0.19
Moroccan (0)	0	<0.01
Palestinian (0)	0	<0.01
Syrian (16)	76	0.11
Other Arab (18)	29	0.04
Armenian (16)	16	0.02
Assyrian/Chaldean/Syriac (0)	0	<0.01
Australian (0)	0	<0.01
Austrian (0)	30	0.04
Basque (0)	0	<0.01
Belgian (19)	31	0.04
Brazilian (14)	32	0.05
British (279)	525	0.76
Bulgarian (0)	0	<0.01
Cajun (0)	48	0.07
Canadian (43)	168	0.24
Carpatho Rusyn (11)	11	0.02
Celtic (0)	12	0.02
Croatian (1)	1	<0.01
Cypriot (19)	19	0.03
Czech (50)	156	0.23
Czechoslovakian (13)	48	0.07
Danish (37)	194	0.28
Dutch (129)	606	0.88
Eastern European (26)	26	0.04
English (1,635)	5,174	7.50
Estonian (0)	0	<0.01
European (818)	889	1.29
Finnish (22)	88	0.13
French, ex. Basque (448)	2,249	3.26
French Canadian (244)	505	0.73
German (3,786)	12,255	17.76
German Russian (0)	0	<0.01
Greek (54)	161	0.23
Guyanese (59)	59	0.09
Hungarian (51)	377	0.55
Icelander (0)	0	<0.01
Iranian (0)	0	<0.01
Irish (3,487)	11,545	16.73
Israeli (9)	25	0.04
Italian (1,684)	4,366	6.33
Latvian (0)	0	<0.01
Lithuanian (9)	33	0.05
Luxemburger (10)	22	0.03
Macedonian (0)	0	<0.01
Maltese (0)	0	<0.01
New Zealander (0)	23	0.03
Northern European (0)	0	<0.01
Norwegian (129)	487	0.71
Pennsylvania German (39)	39	0.06
Polish (540)	1,751	2.54
Portuguese (177)	317	0.46
Romanian (83)	102	0.15
Russian (155)	471	0.68
Scandinavian (30)	120	0.17
Scotch-Irish (939)	1,730	2.51
Scottish (703)	1,917	2.78
Serbian (52)	95	0.14
Slavic (12)	54	0.08
Slovak (22)	74	0.11
Slovene (14)	14	0.02
Soviet Union (0)	0	<0.01
Swedish (161)	661	0.96
Swiss (19)	95	0.14
Turkish (0)	0	<0.01
Ukrainian (38)	120	0.17
Welsh (129)	397	0.58
West Indian, ex. Hispanic (440)	773	1.12
Bahamian (0)	0	<0.01
Barbadian (6)	6	0.01
Belizean (0)	15	0.02
Bermudan (0)	0	<0.01
British West Indian (0)	0	<0.01
Dutch West Indian (0)	13	0.02
Haitian (65)	89	0.13
Jamaican (223)	450	0.65
Trinidadian/Tobagonian (35)	52	0.08
U.S. Virgin Islander (0)	0	<0.01
West Indian (111)	148	0.21
Other West Indian (0)	0	<0.01
Yugoslavian (0)	72	0.10

Hispanic Origin	Population	%
Hispanic or Latino (of any race)	9,106	12.98
Central American, ex. Mexican	641	0.91
Costa Rican	43	0.06
Guatemalan	111	0.16
Honduran	90	0.13
Nicaraguan	80	0.11
Panamanian	115	0.16
Salvadoran	196	0.28
Other Central American	6	0.01
Cuban	367	0.52
Dominican Republic	413	0.59
Mexican	4,045	5.77
Puerto Rican	2,356	3.36
South American	577	0.82
Argentinean	23	0.03
Bolivian	27	0.04
Chilean	36	0.05
Colombian	249	0.35
Ecuadorian	95	0.14
Paraguayan	3	<0.01
Peruvian	85	0.12
Uruguayan	4	0.01
Venezuelan	44	0.06
Other South American	11	0.02
Other Hispanic or Latino	707	1.01

Race*	Population	%
African-American/Black (14,055)	15,798	22.52
Not Hispanic (13,453)	14,855	21.18
Hispanic (602)	943	1.34
American Indian/Alaska Native (502)	1,150	1.64
Not Hispanic (390)	899	1.28
Hispanic (112)	251	0.36
Alaska Athabascan (Ala. Nat.) (1)	1	<0.01
Aleut (Alaska Native) (0)	0	<0.01
Apache (11)	17	0.02
Arapaho (2)	2	<0.01
Blackfeet (9)	45	0.06
Canadian/French Am. Ind. (1)	2	<0.01
Central American Ind. (0)	4	0.01
Cherokee (58)	220	0.31
Cheyenne (1)	1	<0.01
Chickasaw (3)	5	0.01
Chippewa (15)	23	0.03
Choctaw (9)	17	0.02
Colville (0)	0	<0.01
Comanche (0)	2	<0.01
Cree (0)	2	<0.01
Creek (5)	8	0.01
Crow (0)	1	<0.01
Delaware (1)	2	<0.01
Hopi (1)	3	<0.01
Houma (2)	2	<0.01
Inupiat (Alaska Native) (0)	6	0.01
Iroquois (9)	24	0.03
Kiowa (3)	4	0.01
Lumbee (51)	77	0.11
Menominee (1)	1	<0.01
Mexican American Ind. (19)	25	0.04
Navajo (44)	52	0.07
Osage (0)	0	<0.01
Ottawa (1)	2	<0.01
Paiute (2)	2	<0.01
Pima (0)	4	0.01
Potawatomi (1)	7	0.01
Pueblo (2)	7	0.01
Puget Sound Salish (2)	4	0.01
Seminole (2)	7	0.01
Shoshone (1)	1	<0.01
Sioux (15)	31	0.04
South American Ind. (1)	2	<0.01
Spanish American Ind. (1)	1	<0.01
Tlingit-Haida (Alaska Native) (0)	0	<0.01
Tohono O'Odham (2)	2	<0.01
Tsimshian (Alaska Native) (0)	0	<0.01
Ute (0)	0	<0.01
Yakama (1)	5	0.01
Yaqui (1)	3	<0.01
Yuman (0)	0	<0.01
Yup'ik (Alaska Native) (0)	0	<0.01
Asian (1,748)	2,775	3.96
Not Hispanic (1,653)	2,531	3.61
Hispanic (95)	244	0.35
Bangladeshi (1)	2	<0.01
Bhutanese (0)	0	<0.01
Burmese (2)	3	<0.01
Cambodian (19)	24	0.03
Chinese, ex. Taiwanese (168)	271	0.39
Filipino (689)	1,167	1.66
Hmong (33)	33	0.05
Indian (130)	219	0.31
Indonesian (11)	16	0.02
Japanese (201)	449	0.64
Korean (129)	229	0.33
Laotian (35)	45	0.06
Malaysian (2)	3	<0.01
Nepalese (0)	0	<0.01
Pakistani (13)	17	0.02
Sri Lankan (0)	0	<0.01
Taiwanese (4)	5	0.01
Thai (53)	87	0.12
Vietnamese (156)	212	0.30
Hawaii Native/Pacific Islander (208)	432	0.62
Not Hispanic (184)	376	0.54
Hispanic (24)	56	0.08
Fijian (1)	2	<0.01
Guamanian/Chamorro (54)	93	0.13
Marshallese (0)	0	<0.01
Native Hawaiian (48)	144	0.21
Samoan (35)	67	0.10
Tongan (0)	1	<0.01
White (47,460)	50,136	71.47
Not Hispanic (42,797)	44,804	63.87
Hispanic (4,663)	5,332	7.60

Notes: † The Census 2010 population figure is used to calculate the percentages in the Hispanic Origin and Race categories. Ancestry percentages are based on the 2006-2010 American Community Survey population (not shown); ‡ Numbers in parentheses indicate the number of people reporting a single ancestry; * Numbers in parentheses indicate the number of persons reporting this race alone, not in combination with any other race; Please refer to the Explanation of Data for more information.

Raleigh

Place Type: City
County: Wake
Population: 403,892

Ancestry	Population	%
Afghan (272)	318	0.08
African, Sub-Saharan (11,388)	12,222	3.19
African (7,418)	7,836	2.05
Cape Verdean (75)	95	0.02
Ethiopian (312)	323	0.08
Ghanaian (109)	109	0.03
Kenyan (753)	766	0.20
Liberian (0)	14	<0.01
Nigerian (1,281)	1,375	0.36
Senegalese (45)	45	0.01
Sierra Leonean (161)	161	0.04
Somalian (462)	496	0.13
South African (108)	163	0.04
Sudanese (0)	0	<0.01
Ugandan (0)	0	<0.01
Zimbabwean (0)	0	<0.01
Other Sub-Saharan African (664)	839	0.22
Albanian (66)	94	0.02
Alsatian (17)	17	<0.01
American (37,404)	37,404	9.77
Arab (2,923)	3,836	1.00
Arab (1,015)	1,105	0.29
Egyptian (530)	703	0.18
Iraqi (30)	87	0.02
Jordanian (106)	186	0.05
Lebanese (521)	837	0.22
Moroccan (258)	258	0.07
Palestinian (97)	119	0.03
Syrian (25)	85	0.02
Other Arab (341)	456	0.12
Armenian (153)	213	0.06
Assyrian/Chaldean/Syriac (18)	18	<0.01
Australian (44)	356	0.09
Austrian (103)	670	0.18
Basque (0)	25	0.01
Belgian (40)	288	0.08
Brazilian (265)	444	0.12
British (1,389)	2,874	0.75
Bulgarian (71)	85	0.02
Cajun (9)	49	0.01
Canadian (406)	740	0.19
Carpatho Rusyn (0)	0	<0.01
Celtic (53)	53	0.01
Croatian (59)	221	0.06
Cypriot (27)	27	0.01
Czech (387)	959	0.25
Czechoslovakian (68)	198	0.05
Danish (161)	689	0.18
Dutch (955)	4,068	1.06
Eastern European (404)	549	0.14
English (16,908)	39,630	10.35
Estonian (45)	77	0.02
European (4,570)	5,405	1.41
Finnish (76)	310	0.08
French, ex. Basque (1,448)	7,025	1.84
French Canadian (601)	1,561	0.41
German (10,684)	38,247	9.99
German Russian (0)	0	<0.01
Greek (717)	1,389	0.36
Guyanese (138)	202	0.05
Hungarian (210)	972	0.25
Icelander (24)	67	0.02
Iranian (411)	532	0.14
Irish (10,384)	31,339	8.19
Israeli (63)	95	0.02
Italian (4,925)	14,642	3.83
Latvian (22)	119	0.03
Lithuanian (215)	566	0.15
Luxemburger (0)	17	<0.01
Macedonian (0)	0	<0.01
Maltese (33)	94	0.02
New Zealander (0)	0	<0.01
Northern European (261)	261	0.07

Ancestry	Population	%
Norwegian (810)	2,108	0.55
Pennsylvania German (17)	44	0.01
Polish (2,380)	7,411	1.94
Portuguese (156)	370	0.10
Romanian (208)	418	0.11
Russian (795)	2,411	0.63
Scandinavian (132)	318	0.08
Scotch-Irish (6,243)	12,189	3.18
Scottish (3,579)	10,633	2.78
Serbian (60)	72	0.02
Slavic (25)	66	0.02
Slovak (283)	651	0.17
Slovene (0)	39	0.01
Soviet Union (0)	0	<0.01
Swedish (676)	2,719	0.71
Swiss (185)	846	0.22
Turkish (260)	329	0.09
Ukrainian (520)	846	0.22
Welsh (671)	3,130	0.82
West Indian, ex. Hispanic (1,182)	2,282	0.60
Bahamian (69)	184	0.05
Barbadian (0)	31	0.01
Belizean (29)	29	0.01
Bermudan (0)	0	<0.01
British West Indian (28)	83	0.02
Dutch West Indian (0)	0	<0.01
Haitian (198)	300	0.08
Jamaican (618)	914	0.24
Trinidadian/Tobagonian (65)	107	0.03
U.S. Virgin Islander (14)	14	<0.01
West Indian (161)	620	0.16
Other West Indian (0)	0	<0.01
Yugoslavian (79)	196	0.05

Hispanic Origin	Population	%
Hispanic or Latino (of any race)	45,868	11.36
Central American, ex. Mexican	7,519	1.86
Costa Rican	164	0.04
Guatemalan	978	0.24
Honduran	2,345	0.58
Nicaraguan	184	0.05
Panamanian	313	0.08
Salvadoran	3,476	0.86
Other Central American	59	0.01
Cuban	1,082	0.27
Dominican Republic	2,378	0.59
Mexican	23,867	5.91
Puerto Rican	4,340	1.07
South American	3,574	0.88
Argentinean	313	0.08
Bolivian	94	0.02
Chilean	196	0.05
Colombian	1,261	0.31
Ecuadorian	352	0.09
Paraguayan	9	<0.01
Peruvian	729	0.18
Uruguayan	146	0.04
Venezuelan	457	0.11
Other South American	17	<0.01
Other Hispanic or Latino	3,108	0.77

Race*	Population	%
African-American/Black (118,471)	124,035	30.71
Not Hispanic (115,976)	120,403	29.81
Hispanic (2,495)	3,632	0.90
American Indian/Alaska Native (1,963)	4,541	1.12
Not Hispanic (1,019)	3,015	0.75
Hispanic (944)	1,526	0.38
Alaska Athabascan (Ala. Nat.) (2)	3	<0.01
Aleut (Alaska Native) (4)	5	<0.01
Apache (4)	26	0.01
Arapaho (0)	1	<0.01
Blackfeet (12)	101	0.03
Canadian/French Am. Ind. (7)	11	<0.01
Central American Ind. (6)	23	0.01
Cherokee (149)	775	0.19
Cheyenne (3)	9	<0.01
Chickasaw (6)	9	<0.01
Chippewa (9)	36	0.01

Race*	Population	%
Choctaw (11)	36	0.01
Colville (0)	0	<0.01
Comanche (0)	4	<0.01
Cree (1)	6	<0.01
Creek (3)	21	0.01
Crow (2)	4	<0.01
Delaware (4)	10	<0.01
Hopi (0)	2	<0.01
Houma (2)	2	<0.01
Inupiat (Alaska Native) (0)	3	<0.01
Iroquois (13)	52	0.01
Kiowa (0)	0	<0.01
Lumbee (268)	392	0.10
Menominee (1)	2	<0.01
Mexican American Ind. (201)	242	0.06
Navajo (6)	19	<0.01
Osage (9)	9	<0.01
Ottawa (1)	1	<0.01
Paiute (2)	2	<0.01
Pima (3)	3	<0.01
Potawatomi (1)	2	<0.01
Pueblo (6)	13	<0.01
Puget Sound Salish (1)	1	<0.01
Seminole (1)	20	<0.01
Shoshone (0)	0	<0.01
Sioux (11)	42	0.01
South American Ind. (8)	46	0.01
Spanish American Ind. (37)	44	0.01
Tlingit-Haida (Alaska Native) (1)	2	<0.01
Tohono O'Odham (5)	5	<0.01
Tsimshian (Alaska Native) (0)	1	<0.01
Ute (1)	2	<0.01
Yakama (0)	0	<0.01
Yaqui (1)	1	<0.01
Yuman (0)	0	<0.01
Yup'ik (Alaska Native) (0)	3	<0.01
Asian (17,434)	20,389	5.05
Not Hispanic (17,309)	20,006	4.95
Hispanic (125)	383	0.09
Bangladeshi (167)	177	0.04
Bhutanese (42)	68	0.02
Burmese (360)	397	0.10
Cambodian (39)	63	0.02
Chinese, ex. Taiwanese (3,135)	3,607	0.89
Filipino (1,486)	2,141	0.53
Hmong (53)	55	0.01
Indian (4,681)	5,143	1.27
Indonesian (91)	121	0.03
Japanese (443)	821	0.20
Korean (1,957)	2,357	0.58
Laotian (219)	259	0.06
Malaysian (31)	44	0.01
Nepalese (101)	140	0.03
Pakistani (497)	545	0.13
Sri Lankan (71)	75	0.02
Taiwanese (230)	269	0.07
Thai (232)	343	0.08
Vietnamese (2,954)	3,210	0.79
Hawaii Native/Pacific Islander (173)	595	0.15
Not Hispanic (139)	417	0.10
Hispanic (34)	178	0.04
Fijian (2)	3	<0.01
Guamanian/Chamorro (56)	121	0.03
Marshallese (0)	0	<0.01
Native Hawaiian (49)	156	0.04
Samoan (10)	43	0.01
Tongan (1)	1	<0.01
White (232,377)	240,430	59.53
Not Hispanic (215,204)	221,203	54.77
Hispanic (17,173)	19,227	4.76

Notes: † The Census 2010 population figure is used to calculate the percentages in the Hispanic Origin and Race categories. Ancestry percentages are based on the 2006-2010 American Community Survey population (not shown); ‡ Numbers in parentheses indicate the number of people reporting a single ancestry; * Numbers in parentheses indicate the number of persons reporting this race alone, not in combination with any other race; Please refer to the Explanation of Data for more information.

Rocky Mount

Place Type: City
County: Nash
Population: 57,477

Ancestry	Population	%
Afghan (0)	0	<0.01
African, Sub-Saharan (938)	1,253	2.17
African (925)	1,167	2.02
Cape Verdean (0)	0	<0.01
Ethiopian (13)	13	0.02
Ghanaian (0)	0	<0.01
Kenyan (0)	0	<0.01
Liberian (0)	0	<0.01
Nigerian (0)	0	<0.01
Senegalese (0)	0	<0.01
Sierra Leonean (0)	0	<0.01
Somalian (0)	0	<0.01
South African (0)	0	<0.01
Sudanese (0)	0	<0.01
Ugandan (0)	0	<0.01
Zimbabwean (0)	0	<0.01
Other Sub-Saharan African (0)	73	0.13
Albanian (0)	0	<0.01
Alsatian (0)	0	<0.01
American (3,523)	3,523	6.10
Arab (492)	492	0.85
Arab (74)	74	0.13
Egyptian (0)	0	<0.01
Iraqi (0)	0	<0.01
Jordanian (47)	47	0.08
Lebanese (55)	55	0.10
Moroccan (0)	0	<0.01
Palestinian (222)	222	0.38
Syrian (0)	0	<0.01
Other Arab (94)	94	0.16
Armenian (0)	0	<0.01
Assyrian/Chaldean/Syriac (0)	0	<0.01
Australian (0)	0	<0.01
Austrian (0)	27	0.05
Basque (0)	0	<0.01
Belgian (12)	75	0.13
Brazilian (0)	0	<0.01
British (91)	150	0.26
Bulgarian (0)	0	<0.01
Cajun (0)	0	<0.01
Canadian (34)	34	0.06
Carpatho Rusyn (0)	0	<0.01
Celtic (0)	0	<0.01
Croatian (15)	15	0.03
Cypriot (0)	0	<0.01
Czech (0)	29	0.05
Czechoslovakian (0)	0	<0.01
Danish (0)	7	0.01
Dutch (111)	457	0.79
Eastern European (10)	27	0.05
English (2,975)	4,711	8.15
Estonian (0)	0	<0.01
European (140)	140	0.24
Finnish (18)	18	0.03
French, ex. Basque (123)	619	1.07
French Canadian (53)	94	0.16
German (561)	2,438	4.22
German Russian (0)	47	0.08
Greek (10)	69	0.12
Guyanese (0)	0	<0.01
Hungarian (31)	117	0.20
Icelander (0)	0	<0.01
Iranian (0)	0	<0.01
Irish (1,178)	3,313	5.73
Israeli (0)	0	<0.01
Italian (293)	684	1.18
Latvian (0)	4	0.01
Lithuanian (18)	18	0.03
Luxemburger (0)	0	<0.01
Macedonian (0)	0	<0.01
Maltese (0)	0	<0.01
New Zealander (0)	0	<0.01
Northern European (0)	19	0.03
Norwegian (13)	116	0.20
Pennsylvania German (0)	16	0.03
Polish (120)	172	0.30
Portuguese (14)	33	0.06
Romanian (0)	17	0.03
Russian (46)	52	0.09
Scandinavian (0)	0	<0.01
Scotch-Irish (857)	1,076	1.86
Scottish (280)	507	0.88
Serbian (0)	0	<0.01
Slavic (0)	16	0.03
Slovak (53)	53	0.09
Slovene (0)	0	<0.01
Soviet Union (0)	0	<0.01
Swedish (13)	140	0.24
Swiss (5)	25	0.04
Turkish (0)	0	<0.01
Ukrainian (21)	45	0.08
Welsh (50)	123	0.21
West Indian, ex. Hispanic (120)	270	0.47
Bahamian (0)	0	<0.01
Barbadian (0)	27	0.05
Belizean (0)	0	<0.01
Bermudan (0)	0	<0.01
British West Indian (0)	0	<0.01
Dutch West Indian (0)	0	<0.01
Haitian (0)	39	0.07
Jamaican (120)	204	0.35
Trinidadian/Tobagonian (0)	0	<0.01
U.S. Virgin Islander (0)	0	<0.01
West Indian (0)	0	<0.01
Other West Indian (0)	0	<0.01
Yugoslavian (0)	27	0.05

Hispanic Origin	Population	%
Hispanic or Latino (of any race)	2,106	3.66
Central American, ex. Mexican	183	0.32
Costa Rican	10	0.02
Guatemalan	30	0.05
Honduran	60	0.10
Nicaraguan	5	0.01
Panamanian	21	0.04
Salvadoran	57	0.10
Other Central American	0	<0.01
Cuban	29	0.05
Dominican Republic	22	0.04
Mexican	1,376	2.39
Puerto Rican	253	0.44
South American	94	0.16
Argentinean	12	0.02
Bolivian	2	<0.01
Chilean	4	0.01
Colombian	40	0.07
Ecuadorian	12	0.02
Paraguayan	2	<0.01
Peruvian	16	0.03
Uruguayan	0	<0.01
Venezuelan	6	0.01
Other South American	0	<0.01
Other Hispanic or Latino	149	0.26

Race*	Population	%
African-American/Black (35,245)	35,854	62.38
Not Hispanic (35,069)	35,605	61.95
Hispanic (176)	249	0.43
American Indian/Alaska Native (350)	660	1.15
Not Hispanic (329)	615	1.07
Hispanic (21)	45	0.08
Alaska Athabascan (Ala. Nat.) (0)	0	<0.01
Aleut (Alaska Native) (3)	3	0.01
Apache (0)	0	<0.01
Arapaho (0)	0	<0.01
Blackfeet (3)	18	0.03
Canadian/French Am. Ind. (0)	0	<0.01
Central American Ind. (0)	3	0.01
Cherokee (10)	63	0.11
Cheyenne (0)	1	<0.01
Chickasaw (0)	0	<0.01
Chippewa (0)	0	<0.01
Choctaw (1)	4	0.01
Colville (0)	0	<0.01
Comanche (0)	0	<0.01
Cree (0)	3	0.01
Creek (2)	2	<0.01
Crow (0)	2	<0.01
Delaware (0)	0	<0.01
Hopi (0)	0	<0.01
Houma (0)	0	<0.01
Inupiat (Alaska Native) (0)	0	<0.01
Iroquois (0)	4	0.01
Kiowa (0)	0	<0.01
Lumbee (15)	24	0.04
Menominee (0)	0	<0.01
Mexican American Ind. (11)	13	0.02
Navajo (0)	0	<0.01
Osage (0)	0	<0.01
Ottawa (0)	0	<0.01
Paiute (0)	0	<0.01
Pima (0)	0	<0.01
Potawatomi (0)	1	<0.01
Pueblo (0)	0	<0.01
Puget Sound Salish (0)	0	<0.01
Seminole (0)	1	<0.01
Shoshone (0)	0	<0.01
Sioux (0)	1	<0.01
South American Ind. (0)	1	<0.01
Spanish American Ind. (1)	2	<0.01
Tlingit-Haida (Alaska Native) (0)	0	<0.01
Tohono O'Odham (0)	0	<0.01
Tsimshian (Alaska Native) (0)	0	<0.01
Ute (0)	0	<0.01
Yakama (0)	0	<0.01
Yaqui (0)	0	<0.01
Yuman (0)	0	<0.01
Yup'ik (Alaska Native) (0)	0	<0.01
Asian (563)	714	1.24
Not Hispanic (540)	677	1.18
Hispanic (23)	37	0.06
Bangladeshi (15)	15	0.03
Bhutanese (0)	0	<0.01
Burmese (0)	0	<0.01
Cambodian (1)	1	<0.01
Chinese, ex. Taiwanese (73)	91	0.16
Filipino (87)	127	0.22
Hmong (9)	9	0.02
Indian (180)	198	0.34
Indonesian (1)	1	<0.01
Japanese (10)	20	0.03
Korean (43)	59	0.10
Laotian (0)	0	<0.01
Malaysian (3)	8	0.01
Nepalese (0)	0	<0.01
Pakistani (29)	29	0.05
Sri Lankan (2)	2	<0.01
Taiwanese (0)	0	<0.01
Thai (6)	7	0.01
Vietnamese (75)	81	0.14
Hawaii Native/Pacific Islander (12)	52	0.09
Not Hispanic (10)	41	0.07
Hispanic (2)	11	0.02
Fijian (0)	0	<0.01
Guamanian/Chamorro (2)	4	0.01
Marshallese (0)	0	<0.01
Native Hawaiian (4)	23	0.04
Samoan (4)	8	0.01
Tongan (0)	0	<0.01
White (19,228)	19,851	34.54
Not Hispanic (18,610)	19,138	33.30
Hispanic (618)	713	1.24

Notes: † The Census 2010 population figure is used to calculate the percentages in the Hispanic Origin and Race categories. Ancestry percentages are based on the 2006-2010 American Community Survey population (not shown); ‡ Numbers in parentheses indicate the number of people reporting a single ancestry; * Numbers in parentheses indicate the number of persons reporting this race alone, not in combination with any other race; Please refer to the Explanation of Data for more information.

Wilmington

Place Type: City
County: New Hanover
Population: 106,476

Ancestry	Population	%
Afghan (0)	0	<0.01
African, Sub-Saharan (103)	316	0.30
African (83)	296	0.28
Cape Verdean (0)	0	<0.01
Ethiopian (0)	0	<0.01
Ghanaian (0)	0	<0.01
Kenyan (0)	0	<0.01
Liberian (0)	0	<0.01
Nigerian (20)	20	0.02
Senegalese (0)	0	<0.01
Sierra Leonean (0)	0	<0.01
Somalian (0)	0	<0.01
South African (0)	0	<0.01
Sudanese (0)	0	<0.01
Ugandan (0)	0	<0.01
Zimbabwean (0)	0	<0.01
Other Sub-Saharan African (0)	0	<0.01
Albanian (0)	0	<0.01
Alsatian (0)	0	<0.01
American (15,339)	15,339	14.65
Arab (189)	262	0.25
Arab (31)	31	0.03
Egyptian (67)	67	0.06
Iraqi (0)	0	<0.01
Jordanian (0)	0	<0.01
Lebanese (64)	122	0.12
Moroccan (0)	0	<0.01
Palestinian (0)	0	<0.01
Syrian (0)	0	<0.01
Other Arab (27)	42	0.04
Armenian (17)	43	0.04
Assyrian/Chaldean/Syriac (0)	0	<0.01
Australian (66)	106	0.10
Austrian (22)	224	0.21
Basque (0)	0	<0.01
Belgian (9)	54	0.05
Brazilian (61)	61	0.06
British (547)	713	0.68
Bulgarian (58)	66	0.06
Cajun (0)	0	<0.01
Canadian (68)	148	0.14
Carpatho Rusyn (0)	0	<0.01
Celtic (38)	38	0.04
Croatian (15)	102	0.10
Cypriot (0)	0	<0.01
Czech (279)	393	0.38
Czechoslovakian (16)	46	0.04
Danish (75)	270	0.26
Dutch (281)	1,097	1.05
Eastern European (10)	27	0.03
English (5,762)	13,829	13.20
Estonian (0)	0	<0.01
European (745)	808	0.77
Finnish (26)	142	0.14
French, ex. Basque (445)	2,934	2.80
French Canadian (121)	395	0.38
German (3,534)	11,884	11.35
German Russian (0)	0	<0.01
Greek (291)	544	0.52
Guyanese (0)	0	<0.01
Hungarian (99)	476	0.45
Icelander (0)	11	0.01
Iranian (35)	35	0.03
Irish (4,386)	11,876	11.34
Israeli (0)	0	<0.01
Italian (2,262)	5,142	4.91
Latvian (17)	51	0.05
Lithuanian (74)	272	0.26
Luxemburger (0)	0	<0.01
Macedonian (0)	0	<0.01
Maltese (0)	0	<0.01
New Zealander (0)	30	0.03
Northern European (29)	29	0.03

Ancestry	Population	%
Norwegian (176)	634	0.61
Pennsylvania German (17)	30	0.03
Polish (602)	1,997	1.91
Portuguese (111)	242	0.23
Romanian (64)	82	0.08
Russian (300)	603	0.58
Scandinavian (7)	21	0.02
Scotch-Irish (2,648)	5,317	5.08
Scottish (1,472)	3,498	3.34
Serbian (0)	0	<0.01
Slavic (25)	90	0.09
Slovak (39)	195	0.19
Slovene (15)	24	0.02
Soviet Union (0)	0	<0.01
Swedish (206)	598	0.57
Swiss (38)	161	0.15
Turkish (92)	186	0.18
Ukrainian (156)	256	0.24
Welsh (169)	993	0.95
West Indian, ex. Hispanic (189)	306	0.29
Bahamian (0)	0	<0.01
Barbadian (38)	38	0.04
Belizean (0)	0	<0.01
Bermudan (0)	0	<0.01
British West Indian (0)	0	<0.01
Dutch West Indian (0)	0	<0.01
Haitian (0)	25	0.02
Jamaican (122)	122	0.12
Trinidadian/Tobagonian (0)	0	<0.01
U.S. Virgin Islander (0)	0	<0.01
West Indian (29)	121	0.12
Other West Indian (0)	0	<0.01
Yugoslavian (54)	181	0.17

Hispanic Origin	Population	%
Hispanic or Latino (of any race)	6,487	6.09
Central American, ex. Mexican	826	0.78
Costa Rican	21	0.02
Guatemalan	212	0.20
Honduran	389	0.37
Nicaraguan	26	0.02
Panamanian	52	0.05
Salvadoran	122	0.11
Other Central American	4	<0.01
Cuban	170	0.16
Dominican Republic	93	0.09
Mexican	3,654	3.43
Puerto Rican	692	0.65
South American	423	0.40
Argentinean	62	0.06
Bolivian	16	0.02
Chilean	40	0.04
Colombian	160	0.15
Ecuadorian	50	0.05
Paraguayan	3	<0.01
Peruvian	52	0.05
Uruguayan	13	0.01
Venezuelan	26	0.02
Other South American	1	<0.01
Other Hispanic or Latino	629	0.59

Race*	Population	%
African-American/Black (21,158)	22,287	20.93
Not Hispanic (20,850)	21,808	20.48
Hispanic (308)	479	0.45
American Indian/Alaska Native (514)	1,276	1.20
Not Hispanic (379)	1,018	0.96
Hispanic (135)	258	0.24
Alaska Athabascan (Ala. Nat.) (0)	0	<0.01
Aleut (Alaska Native) (0)	0	<0.01
Apache (3)	15	0.01
Arapaho (0)	2	<0.01
Blackfeet (2)	25	0.02
Canadian/French Am. Ind. (1)	2	<0.01
Central American Ind. (12)	25	0.02
Cherokee (72)	297	0.28
Cheyenne (0)	0	<0.01
Chickasaw (3)	6	0.01
Chippewa (6)	8	0.01

Race*	Population	%
Choctaw (3)	9	0.01
Colville (0)	0	<0.01
Comanche (2)	2	<0.01
Cree (2)	3	<0.01
Creek (4)	8	0.01
Crow (1)	3	<0.01
Delaware (1)	2	<0.01
Hopi (0)	1	<0.01
Houma (0)	0	<0.01
Inupiat (Alaska Native) (0)	0	<0.01
Iroquois (8)	25	0.02
Kiowa (0)	0	<0.01
Lumbee (78)	120	0.11
Menominee (3)	3	<0.01
Mexican American Ind. (37)	57	0.05
Navajo (1)	10	0.01
Osage (0)	1	<0.01
Ottawa (0)	2	<0.01
Paiute (1)	1	<0.01
Pima (0)	0	<0.01
Potawatomi (0)	0	<0.01
Pueblo (0)	0	<0.01
Puget Sound Salish (0)	0	<0.01
Seminole (4)	13	0.01
Shoshone (0)	0	<0.01
Sioux (2)	19	0.02
South American Ind. (6)	10	0.01
Spanish American Ind. (2)	2	<0.01
Tlingit-Haida (Alaska Native) (0)	0	<0.01
Tohono O'Odham (0)	0	<0.01
Tsimshian (Alaska Native) (0)	0	<0.01
Ute (0)	0	<0.01
Yakama (0)	0	<0.01
Yaqui (0)	1	<0.01
Yuman (0)	0	<0.01
Yup'ik (Alaska Native) (0)	0	<0.01
Asian (1,263)	1,829	1.72
Not Hispanic (1,246)	1,766	1.66
Hispanic (17)	63	0.06
Bangladeshi (4)	4	<0.01
Bhutanese (0)	0	<0.01
Burmese (6)	6	0.01
Cambodian (2)	2	<0.01
Chinese, ex. Taiwanese (345)	408	0.38
Filipino (135)	282	0.26
Hmong (1)	1	<0.01
Indian (223)	284	0.27
Indonesian (13)	26	0.02
Japanese (78)	162	0.15
Korean (176)	238	0.22
Laotian (11)	11	0.01
Malaysian (3)	5	<0.01
Nepalese (4)	5	<0.01
Pakistani (14)	18	0.02
Sri Lankan (3)	3	<0.01
Taiwanese (10)	11	0.01
Thai (19)	35	0.03
Vietnamese (152)	182	0.17
Hawaii Native/Pacific Islander (78)	189	0.18
Not Hispanic (61)	152	0.14
Hispanic (17)	37	0.03
Fijian (0)	0	<0.01
Guamanian/Chamorro (24)	39	0.04
Marshallese (0)	0	<0.01
Native Hawaiian (27)	61	0.06
Samoan (15)	34	0.03
Tongan (1)	1	<0.01
White (78,286)	80,213	75.33
Not Hispanic (75,432)	76,964	72.28
Hispanic (2,854)	3,249	3.05

*Notes: † The Census 2010 population figure is used to calculate the percentages in the Hispanic Origin and Race categories. Ancestry percentages are based on the 2006-2010 American Community Survey population (not shown); ‡ Numbers in parentheses indicate the number of people reporting a single ancestry; * Numbers in parentheses indicate the number of persons reporting this race alone, not in combination with any other race; Please refer to the Explanation of Data for more information.*

Winston-Salem

Place Type: City
County: Forsyth
Population: 229,617

Ancestry	Population	%
Afghan (0)	0	<0.01
African, Sub-Saharan (1,249)	1,923	0.86
African (857)	1,251	0.56
Cape Verdean (0)	0	<0.01
Ethiopian (16)	16	0.01
Ghanaian (70)	70	0.03
Kenyan (0)	145	0.06
Liberian (40)	106	0.05
Nigerian (254)	254	0.11
Senegalese (0)	0	<0.01
Sierra Leonean (0)	0	<0.01
Somalian (0)	0	<0.01
South African (12)	66	0.03
Sudanese (0)	0	<0.01
Ugandan (0)	0	<0.01
Zimbabwean (0)	0	<0.01
Other Sub-Saharan African (0)	15	0.01
Albanian (0)	0	<0.01
Alsatian (0)	0	<0.01
American (11,710)	11,710	5.21
Arab (602)	806	0.36
Arab (111)	134	0.06
Egyptian (117)	176	0.08
Iraqi (0)	0	<0.01
Jordanian (50)	50	0.02
Lebanese (249)	320	0.14
Moroccan (43)	43	0.02
Palestinian (6)	6	<0.01
Syrian (26)	70	0.03
Other Arab (0)	7	<0.01
Armenian (17)	74	0.03
Assyrian/Chaldean/Syriac (0)	0	<0.01
Australian (11)	34	0.02
Austrian (121)	325	0.14
Basque (9)	9	<0.01
Belgian (71)	120	0.05
Brazilian (64)	103	0.05
British (656)	1,064	0.47
Bulgarian (25)	25	0.01
Cajun (38)	38	0.02
Canadian (97)	168	0.07
Carpatho Rusyn (0)	0	<0.01
Celtic (31)	64	0.03
Croatian (29)	65	0.03
Cypriot (0)	0	<0.01
Czech (113)	321	0.14
Czechoslovakian (24)	90	0.04
Danish (82)	256	0.11
Dutch (363)	2,351	1.05
Eastern European (117)	135	0.06
English (10,465)	22,468	10.00
Estonian (0)	0	<0.01
European (2,088)	2,316	1.03
Finnish (68)	124	0.06
French, ex. Basque (925)	3,360	1.49
French Canadian (194)	520	0.23
German (7,850)	22,499	10.01
German Russian (21)	21	0.01
Greek (706)	1,114	0.50
Guyanese (47)	82	0.04
Hungarian (267)	554	0.25
Icelander (0)	0	<0.01
Iranian (373)	431	0.19
Irish (5,460)	17,469	7.77
Israeli (0)	0	<0.01
Italian (2,074)	5,218	2.32
Latvian (10)	102	0.05
Lithuanian (35)	252	0.11
Luxemburger (0)	0	<0.01
Macedonian (0)	0	<0.01
Maltese (0)	0	<0.01
New Zealander (12)	12	0.01
Northern European (58)	58	0.03
Norwegian (500)	1,252	0.56
Pennsylvania German (21)	34	0.02
Polish (637)	2,333	1.04
Portuguese (91)	268	0.12
Romanian (112)	194	0.09
Russian (435)	1,097	0.49
Scandinavian (57)	344	0.15
Scotch-Irish (3,388)	6,601	2.94
Scottish (2,174)	4,986	2.22
Serbian (21)	99	0.04
Slavic (0)	0	<0.01
Slovak (78)	196	0.09
Slovene (0)	21	0.01
Soviet Union (0)	0	<0.01
Swedish (247)	928	0.41
Swiss (52)	272	0.12
Turkish (25)	25	0.01
Ukrainian (105)	251	0.11
Welsh (360)	1,806	0.80
West Indian, ex. Hispanic (601)	968	0.43
Bahamian (0)	9	<0.01
Barbadian (222)	222	0.10
Belizean (0)	30	0.01
Bermudan (0)	0	<0.01
British West Indian (0)	0	<0.01
Dutch West Indian (0)	0	<0.01
Haitian (160)	191	0.08
Jamaican (112)	398	0.18
Trinidadian/Tobagonian (64)	75	0.03
U.S. Virgin Islander (18)	18	0.01
West Indian (25)	25	0.01
Other West Indian (0)	0	<0.01
Yugoslavian (26)	45	0.02

Hispanic Origin	Population	%
Hispanic or Latino (of any race)	33,753	14.70
Central American, ex. Mexican	3,757	1.64
Costa Rican	78	0.03
Guatemalan	882	0.38
Honduran	497	0.22
Nicaraguan	199	0.09
Panamanian	115	0.05
Salvadoran	1,954	0.85
Other Central American	32	0.01
Cuban	503	0.22
Dominican Republic	472	0.21
Mexican	23,427	10.20
Puerto Rican	1,965	0.86
South American	1,344	0.59
Argentinean	121	0.05
Bolivian	17	0.01
Chilean	79	0.03
Colombian	463	0.20
Ecuadorian	243	0.11
Paraguayan	10	<0.01
Peruvian	236	0.10
Uruguayan	25	0.01
Venezuelan	137	0.06
Other South American	13	0.01
Other Hispanic or Latino	2,285	1.00

Race*	Population	%
African-American/Black (79,598)	82,853	36.08
Not Hispanic (78,065)	80,608	35.11
Hispanic (1,533)	2,245	0.98
American Indian/Alaska Native (991)	2,391	1.04
Not Hispanic (567)	1,726	0.75
Hispanic (424)	665	0.29
Alaska Athabascan (Ala. Nat.) (0)	1	<0.01
Aleut (Alaska Native) (0)	0	<0.01
Apache (6)	17	0.01
Arapaho (0)	0	<0.01
Blackfeet (9)	72	0.03
Canadian/French Am. Ind. (0)	4	<0.01
Central American Ind. (15)	25	0.01
Cherokee (98)	470	0.20
Cheyenne (0)	2	<0.01
Chickasaw (3)	11	<0.01
Chippewa (9)	17	0.01
Choctaw (6)	18	0.01
Colville (0)	0	<0.01
Comanche (0)	1	<0.01
Cree (0)	2	<0.01
Creek (1)	10	<0.01
Crow (0)	4	<0.01
Delaware (1)	3	<0.01
Hopi (0)	0	<0.01
Houma (0)	0	<0.01
Inupiat (Alaska Native) (2)	2	<0.01
Iroquois (8)	18	0.01
Kiowa (1)	1	<0.01
Lumbee (120)	180	0.08
Menominee (0)	0	<0.01
Mexican American Ind. (128)	151	0.07
Navajo (8)	11	<0.01
Osage (0)	2	<0.01
Ottawa (0)	0	<0.01
Paiute (0)	0	<0.01
Pima (0)	0	<0.01
Potawatomi (1)	4	<0.01
Pueblo (1)	12	0.01
Puget Sound Salish (0)	2	<0.01
Seminole (0)	10	<0.01
Shoshone (0)	1	<0.01
Sioux (4)	18	0.01
South American Ind. (11)	22	0.01
Spanish American Ind. (4)	4	<0.01
Tlingit-Haida (Alaska Native) (3)	3	<0.01
Tohono O'Odham (0)	1	<0.01
Tsimshian (Alaska Native) (0)	0	<0.01
Ute (0)	0	<0.01
Yakama (0)	0	<0.01
Yaqui (0)	0	<0.01
Yuman (0)	0	<0.01
Yup'ik (Alaska Native) (0)	0	<0.01
Asian (4,581)	5,669	2.47
Not Hispanic (4,536)	5,513	2.40
Hispanic (45)	156	0.07
Bangladeshi (9)	10	<0.01
Bhutanese (0)	0	<0.01
Burmese (154)	154	0.07
Cambodian (64)	84	0.04
Chinese, ex. Taiwanese (912)	1,116	0.49
Filipino (707)	922	0.40
Hmong (35)	47	0.02
Indian (1,206)	1,391	0.61
Indonesian (90)	97	0.04
Japanese (143)	298	0.13
Korean (344)	451	0.20
Laotian (51)	58	0.03
Malaysian (5)	5	<0.01
Nepalese (37)	38	0.02
Pakistani (124)	155	0.07
Sri Lankan (30)	36	0.02
Taiwanese (31)	38	0.02
Thai (49)	79	0.03
Vietnamese (376)	456	0.20
Hawaii Native/Pacific Islander (182)	374	0.16
Not Hispanic (138)	261	0.11
Hispanic (44)	113	0.05
Fijian (0)	0	<0.01
Guamanian/Chamorro (68)	100	0.04
Marshallese (42)	44	0.02
Native Hawaiian (29)	90	0.04
Samoan (2)	11	<0.01
Tongan (1)	1	<0.01
White (117,600)	121,879	53.08
Not Hispanic (108,222)	111,232	48.44
Hispanic (9,378)	10,647	4.64

*Notes: † The Census 2010 population figure is used to calculate the percentages in the Hispanic Origin and Race categories. Ancestry percentages are based on the 2006-2010 American Community Survey population (not shown); ‡ Numbers in parentheses indicate the number of people reporting a single ancestry; * Numbers in parentheses indicate the number of persons reporting this race alone, not in combination with any other race; Please refer to the Explanation of Data for more information.*

Ancestry Group Rankings

Afghan

Top 10 Places Sorted by Population
Based on all places, regardless of total population

Place	Population	%
Cary (town) Wake County	369	0.29
Raleigh (city) Wake County	318	0.08
Durham (city) Durham County	27	0.01
Greensboro (city) Guilford County	16	0.01
Waxhaw (town) Union County	15	0.17
Charlotte (city) Mecklenburg County	13	<0.01
Jacksonville (city) Onslow County	5	0.01
Aberdeen (town) Moore County	0	0.00
Advance (cdp) Davie County	0	0.00
Ahoskie (town) Hertford County	0	0.00

Top 10 Places Sorted by Percent of Total Population
Based on all places, regardless of total population

Place	Population	%
Cary (town) Wake County	369	0.29
Waxhaw (town) Union County	15	0.17
Raleigh (city) Wake County	318	0.08
Durham (city) Durham County	27	0.01
Greensboro (city) Guilford County	16	0.01
Jacksonville (city) Onslow County	5	0.01
Charlotte (city) Mecklenburg County	13	<0.01
Aberdeen (town) Moore County	0	0.00
Advance (cdp) Davie County	0	0.00
Ahoskie (town) Hertford County	0	0.00

Top 10 Places Sorted by Percent of Total Population
Based on places with total population of 50,000 or more

Place	Population	%
Cary (town) Wake County	369	0.29
Raleigh (city) Wake County	318	0.08
Durham (city) Durham County	27	0.01
Greensboro (city) Guilford County	16	0.01
Jacksonville (city) Onslow County	5	0.01
Charlotte (city) Mecklenburg County	13	<0.01
Asheville (city) Buncombe County	0	0.00
Chapel Hill (town) Orange County	0	0.00
Concord (city) Cabarrus County	0	0.00
Fayetteville (city) Cumberland County	0	0.00

African, Sub-Saharan

Top 10 Places Sorted by Population
Based on all places, regardless of total population

Place	Population	%
Raleigh (city) Wake County	12,222	3.19
Charlotte (city) Mecklenburg County	11,247	1.59
Greensboro (city) Guilford County	6,270	2.38
Durham (city) Durham County	5,147	2.34
Fayetteville (city) Cumberland County	2,422	1.22
Winston-Salem (city) Forsyth County	1,923	0.86
Salisbury (city) Rowan County	1,859	5.63
High Point (city) Guilford County	1,717	1.70
Rocky Mount (city) Nash County	1,253	2.17
Jacksonville (city) Onslow County	1,157	1.68

Top 10 Places Sorted by Percent of Total Population
Based on all places, regardless of total population

Place	Population	%
Winton (town) Hertford County	184	19.96
East Spencer (town) Rowan County	305	17.76
Princeton (town) Johnston County	170	13.04
Spencer (town) Rowan County	400	12.17
Knightdale (town) Wake County	953	9.10
Micro (town) Johnston County	36	9.02
Powellsville (town) Bertie County	16	7.62
Five Points (cdp) Hoke County	61	7.21
Dunn (city) Harnett County	534	5.85
Salisbury (city) Rowan County	1,859	5.63

Top 10 Places Sorted by Percent of Total Population
Based on places with total population of 50,000 or more

Place	Population	%
Raleigh (city) Wake County	12,222	3.19
Greensboro (city) Guilford County	6,270	2.38
Durham (city) Durham County	5,147	2.34
Rocky Mount (city) Nash County	1,253	2.17
High Point (city) Guilford County	1,717	1.70
Jacksonville (city) Onslow County	1,157	1.68
Charlotte (city) Mecklenburg County	11,247	1.59
Fayetteville (city) Cumberland County	2,422	1.22
Gastonia (city) Gaston County	682	0.96
Winston-Salem (city) Forsyth County	1,923	0.86

African, Sub-Saharan: African

Top 10 Places Sorted by Population
Based on all places, regardless of total population

Place	Population	%
Raleigh (city) Wake County	7,836	2.05
Charlotte (city) Mecklenburg County	5,460	0.77
Durham (city) Durham County	3,418	1.55
Greensboro (city) Guilford County	2,798	1.06
Salisbury (city) Rowan County	1,836	5.56
Fayetteville (city) Cumberland County	1,373	0.69
Winston-Salem (city) Forsyth County	1,251	0.56
Rocky Mount (city) Nash County	1,167	2.02
Jacksonville (city) Onslow County	1,109	1.61
Kinston (city) Lenoir County	759	3.45

Top 10 Places Sorted by Percent of Total Population
Based on all places, regardless of total population

Place	Population	%
Winton (town) Hertford County	184	19.96
East Spencer (town) Rowan County	305	17.76
Princeton (town) Johnston County	170	13.04
Spencer (town) Rowan County	400	12.17
Micro (town) Johnston County	36	9.02
Powellsville (town) Bertie County	16	7.62
Five Points (cdp) Hoke County	61	7.21
Dunn (city) Harnett County	534	5.85
Salisbury (city) Rowan County	1,836	5.56
Bayboro (town) Pamlico County	76	5.41

Top 10 Places Sorted by Percent of Total Population
Based on places with total population of 50,000 or more

Place	Population	%
Raleigh (city) Wake County	7,836	2.05
Rocky Mount (city) Nash County	1,167	2.02
Jacksonville (city) Onslow County	1,109	1.61
Durham (city) Durham County	3,418	1.55
Greensboro (city) Guilford County	2,798	1.06
Charlotte (city) Mecklenburg County	5,460	0.77
Fayetteville (city) Cumberland County	1,373	0.69
Gastonia (city) Gaston County	455	0.64
Winston-Salem (city) Forsyth County	1,251	0.56
High Point (city) Guilford County	536	0.53

African, Sub-Saharan: Cape Verdean

Top 10 Places Sorted by Population
Based on all places, regardless of total population

Place	Population	%
Apex (town) Wake County	192	0.56
Raleigh (city) Wake County	95	0.02
Havelock (city) Craven County	55	0.27
Charlotte (city) Mecklenburg County	48	0.01
Fayetteville (city) Cumberland County	46	0.02
Statesville (city) Iredell County	24	0.10
Mooresville (town) Iredell County	17	0.06
Jacksonville (city) Onslow County	12	0.02
Aberdeen (town) Moore County	0	0.00
Advance (cdp) Davie County	0	0.00

Top 10 Places Sorted by Percent of Total Population
Based on all places, regardless of total population

Place	Population	%
Apex (town) Wake County	192	0.56
Havelock (city) Craven County	55	0.27
Statesville (city) Iredell County	24	0.10
Mooresville (town) Iredell County	17	0.06
Raleigh (city) Wake County	95	0.02
Fayetteville (city) Cumberland County	46	0.02
Jacksonville (city) Onslow County	12	0.02
Charlotte (city) Mecklenburg County	48	0.01
Aberdeen (town) Moore County	0	0.00
Advance (cdp) Davie County	0	0.00

Top 10 Places Sorted by Percent of Total Population
Based on places with total population of 50,000 or more

Place	Population	%
Raleigh (city) Wake County	95	0.02
Fayetteville (city) Cumberland County	46	0.02
Jacksonville (city) Onslow County	12	0.02
Charlotte (city) Mecklenburg County	48	0.01
Asheville (city) Buncombe County	0	0.00
Cary (town) Wake County	0	0.00
Chapel Hill (town) Orange County	0	0.00
Concord (city) Cabarrus County	0	0.00
Durham (city) Durham County	0	0.00
Gastonia (city) Gaston County	0	0.00

African, Sub-Saharan: Ethiopian

Top 10 Places Sorted by Population
Based on all places, regardless of total population

Place	Population	%
Charlotte (city) Mecklenburg County	954	0.14
Raleigh (city) Wake County	323	0.08
High Point (city) Guilford County	266	0.26
Durham (city) Durham County	203	0.09
Matthews (town) Mecklenburg County	181	0.68
Gastonia (city) Gaston County	96	0.14
Indian Trail (town) Union County	89	0.29
Greensboro (city) Guilford County	87	0.03
Wake Forest (town) Wake County	72	0.27
Havelock (city) Craven County	64	0.31

Top 10 Places Sorted by Percent of Total Population
Based on all places, regardless of total population

Place	Population	%
Matthews (town) Mecklenburg County	181	0.68
Lilesville (town) Anson County	3	0.49
Havelock (city) Craven County	64	0.31
Indian Trail (town) Union County	89	0.29
Wake Forest (town) Wake County	72	0.27
High Point (city) Guilford County	266	0.26
Holly Springs (town) Wake County	43	0.20
Lenoir (city) Caldwell County	27	0.15
Charlotte (city) Mecklenburg County	954	0.14
Gastonia (city) Gaston County	96	0.14

Top 10 Places Sorted by Percent of Total Population
Based on places with total population of 50,000 or more

Place	Population	%
High Point (city) Guilford County	266	0.26
Charlotte (city) Mecklenburg County	954	0.14
Gastonia (city) Gaston County	96	0.14
Durham (city) Durham County	203	0.09
Raleigh (city) Wake County	323	0.08
Chapel Hill (town) Orange County	20	0.04
Greensboro (city) Guilford County	87	0.03
Fayetteville (city) Cumberland County	56	0.03
Rocky Mount (city) Nash County	13	0.02
Winston-Salem (city) Forsyth County	16	0.01

African, Sub-Saharan: Ghanaian

Top 10 Places Sorted by Population
Based on all places, regardless of total population

Place	Population	%
Charlotte (city) Mecklenburg County	539	0.08
Greensboro (city) Guilford County	375	0.14
Durham (city) Durham County	144	0.07
Greenville (city) Pitt County	129	0.16
Raleigh (city) Wake County	109	0.03
Fayetteville (city) Cumberland County	106	0.05
Winston-Salem (city) Forsyth County	70	0.03
Wake Forest (town) Wake County	64	0.24
Mooresville (town) Iredell County	58	0.19
Winterville (town) Pitt County	36	0.43

Top 10 Places Sorted by Percent of Total Population
Based on all places, regardless of total population

Place	Population	%
Winterville (town) Pitt County	36	0.43
Wake Forest (town) Wake County	64	0.24
Red Oak (town) Nash County	7	0.21
Mooresville (town) Iredell County	58	0.19
Greenville (city) Pitt County	129	0.16
Greensboro (city) Guilford County	375	0.14
Mint Hill (town) Mecklenburg County	21	0.10
Charlotte (city) Mecklenburg County	539	0.08
Durham (city) Durham County	144	0.07
Fayetteville (city) Cumberland County	106	0.05

Top 10 Places Sorted by Percent of Total Population
Based on places with total population of 50,000 or more

Place	Population	%
Greenville (city) Pitt County	129	0.16
Greensboro (city) Guilford County	375	0.14
Charlotte (city) Mecklenburg County	539	0.08
Durham (city) Durham County	144	0.07
Fayetteville (city) Cumberland County	106	0.05
Chapel Hill (town) Orange County	26	0.05
Raleigh (city) Wake County	109	0.03
Winston-Salem (city) Forsyth County	70	0.03
High Point (city) Guilford County	27	0.03
Asheville (city) Buncombe County	0	0.00

African, Sub-Saharan: Kenyan

Top 10 Places Sorted by Population
Based on all places, regardless of total population

Place	Population	%
Raleigh (city) Wake County	766	0.20
Charlotte (city) Mecklenburg County	282	0.04
Winston-Salem (city) Forsyth County	145	0.06
Davidson (town) Mecklenburg County	72	0.70
Durham (city) Durham County	64	0.03
Cary (town) Wake County	60	0.05
Chapel Hill (town) Orange County	32	0.06
Holly Springs (town) Wake County	17	0.08
Wilson (city) Wilson County	15	0.03
Greensboro (city) Guilford County	15	0.01

Top 10 Places Sorted by Percent of Total Population
Based on all places, regardless of total population

Place	Population	%
Davidson (town) Mecklenburg County	72	0.70
Raleigh (city) Wake County	766	0.20
Holly Springs (town) Wake County	17	0.08
Winston-Salem (city) Forsyth County	145	0.06
Chapel Hill (town) Orange County	32	0.06
Cary (town) Wake County	60	0.05
Garner (town) Wake County	11	0.05
Lexington (city) Davidson County	9	0.05
Charlotte (city) Mecklenburg County	282	0.04
Durham (city) Durham County	64	0.03

Top 10 Places Sorted by Percent of Total Population
Based on places with total population of 50,000 or more

Place	Population	%
Raleigh (city) Wake County	766	0.20
Winston-Salem (city) Forsyth County	145	0.06
Chapel Hill (town) Orange County	32	0.06
Cary (town) Wake County	60	0.05

Charlotte (city) Mecklenburg County	282	0.04
Durham (city) Durham County	64	0.03
Greenville (city) Pitt County	14	0.02
Gastonia (city) Gaston County	13	0.02
Greensboro (city) Guilford County	15	0.01
Asheville (city) Buncombe County	0	0.00

African, Sub-Saharan: Liberian

Top 10 Places Sorted by Population
Based on all places, regardless of total population

Place	Population	%
Charlotte (city) Mecklenburg County	633	0.09
High Point (city) Guilford County	376	0.37
Durham (city) Durham County	265	0.12
Greensboro (city) Guilford County	204	0.08
Winston-Salem (city) Forsyth County	106	0.05
Concord (city) Cabarrus County	52	0.07
Archdale (city) Randolph County	19	0.17
Kinston (city) Lenoir County	14	0.06
Raleigh (city) Wake County	14	<0.01
Greenville (city) Pitt County	12	0.01

Top 10 Places Sorted by Percent of Total Population
Based on all places, regardless of total population

Place	Population	%
High Point (city) Guilford County	376	0.37
Archdale (city) Randolph County	19	0.17
Durham (city) Durham County	265	0.12
Charlotte (city) Mecklenburg County	633	0.09
Greensboro (city) Guilford County	204	0.08
Concord (city) Cabarrus County	52	0.07
Kinston (city) Lenoir County	14	0.06
Winston-Salem (city) Forsyth County	106	0.05
Kernersville (town) Forsyth County	11	0.05
Carrboro (town) Orange County	5	0.03

Top 10 Places Sorted by Percent of Total Population
Based on places with total population of 50,000 or more

Place	Population	%
High Point (city) Guilford County	376	0.37
Durham (city) Durham County	265	0.12
Charlotte (city) Mecklenburg County	633	0.09
Greensboro (city) Guilford County	204	0.08
Concord (city) Cabarrus County	52	0.07
Winston-Salem (city) Forsyth County	106	0.05
Greenville (city) Pitt County	12	0.01
Fayetteville (city) Cumberland County	11	0.01
Raleigh (city) Wake County	14	<0.01
Asheville (city) Buncombe County	0	0.00

African, Sub-Saharan: Nigerian

Top 10 Places Sorted by Population
Based on all places, regardless of total population

Place	Population	%
Raleigh (city) Wake County	1,375	0.36
Charlotte (city) Mecklenburg County	1,192	0.17
Durham (city) Durham County	604	0.27
Greensboro (city) Guilford County	553	0.21
Fayetteville (city) Cumberland County	412	0.21
Winston-Salem (city) Forsyth County	254	0.11
Knightdale (town) Wake County	199	1.90
High Point (city) Guilford County	110	0.11
Carrboro (town) Orange County	104	0.55
Cary (town) Wake County	101	0.08

Top 10 Places Sorted by Percent of Total Population
Based on all places, regardless of total population

Place	Population	%
Knightdale (town) Wake County	199	1.90
Silver Lake (cdp) New Hanover County	76	1.40
Seven Lakes (cdp) Moore County	53	1.14
Carrboro (town) Orange County	104	0.55
Raleigh (city) Wake County	1,375	0.36
Stallings (town) Union County	36	0.28
Durham (city) Durham County	604	0.27
Morrisville (town) Wake County	43	0.27
Greensboro (city) Guilford County	553	0.21
Fayetteville (city) Cumberland County	412	0.21

Top 10 Places Sorted by Percent of Total Population
Based on places with total population of 50,000 or more

Place	Population	%
Raleigh (city) Wake County	1,375	0.36
Durham (city) Durham County	604	0.27
Greensboro (city) Guilford County	553	0.21
Fayetteville (city) Cumberland County	412	0.21
Charlotte (city) Mecklenburg County	1,192	0.17
Chapel Hill (town) Orange County	70	0.13
Gastonia (city) Gaston County	87	0.12
Winston-Salem (city) Forsyth County	254	0.11
High Point (city) Guilford County	110	0.11
Greenville (city) Pitt County	69	0.09

African, Sub-Saharan: Senegalese

Top 10 Places Sorted by Population
Based on all places, regardless of total population

Place	Population	%
Charlotte (city) Mecklenburg County	47	0.01
Raleigh (city) Wake County	45	0.01
Durham (city) Durham County	16	0.01
Greensboro (city) Guilford County	13	<0.01
Jacksonville (city) Onslow County	12	0.02
Gastonia (city) Gaston County	8	0.01
Aberdeen (town) Moore County	0	0.00
Advance (cdp) Davie County	0	0.00
Ahoskie (town) Hertford County	0	0.00
Alamance (village) Alamance County	0	0.00

Top 10 Places Sorted by Percent of Total Population
Based on all places, regardless of total population

Place	Population	%
Jacksonville (city) Onslow County	12	0.02
Charlotte (city) Mecklenburg County	47	0.01
Raleigh (city) Wake County	45	0.01
Durham (city) Durham County	16	0.01
Gastonia (city) Gaston County	8	0.01
Greensboro (city) Guilford County	13	<0.01
Aberdeen (town) Moore County	0	0.00
Advance (cdp) Davie County	0	0.00
Ahoskie (town) Hertford County	0	0.00
Alamance (village) Alamance County	0	0.00

Top 10 Places Sorted by Percent of Total Population
Based on places with total population of 50,000 or more

Place	Population	%
Jacksonville (city) Onslow County	12	0.02
Charlotte (city) Mecklenburg County	47	0.01
Raleigh (city) Wake County	45	0.01
Durham (city) Durham County	16	0.01
Gastonia (city) Gaston County	8	0.01
Greensboro (city) Guilford County	13	<0.01
Asheville (city) Buncombe County	0	0.00
Cary (town) Wake County	0	0.00
Chapel Hill (town) Orange County	0	0.00
Concord (city) Cabarrus County	0	0.00

African, Sub-Saharan: Sierra Leonean

Top 10 Places Sorted by Population
Based on all places, regardless of total population

Place	Population	%
Greensboro (city) Guilford County	210	0.08
Raleigh (city) Wake County	161	0.04
Durham (city) Durham County	83	0.04
Charlotte (city) Mecklenburg County	70	0.01
Fayetteville (city) Cumberland County	36	0.02
Holly Springs (town) Wake County	30	0.14
Aberdeen (town) Moore County	0	0.00
Advance (cdp) Davie County	0	0.00
Ahoskie (town) Hertford County	0	0.00
Alamance (village) Alamance County	0	0.00

Top 10 Places Sorted by Percent of Total Population
Based on all places, regardless of total population

Place	Population	%
Holly Springs (town) Wake County	30	0.14
Greensboro (city) Guilford County	210	0.08
Raleigh (city) Wake County	161	0.04

Place	Population	%
Durham (city) Durham County	83	0.04
Fayetteville (city) Cumberland County	36	0.02
Charlotte (city) Mecklenburg County	70	0.01
Aberdeen (town) Moore County	0	0.00
Advance (cdp) Davie County	0	0.00
Ahoskie (town) Hertford County	0	0.00
Alamance (village) Alamance County	0	0.00

Top 10 Places Sorted by Percent of Total Population
Based on places with total population of 50,000 or more

Place	Population	%
Greensboro (city) Guilford County	210	0.08
Raleigh (city) Wake County	161	0.04
Durham (city) Durham County	83	0.04
Fayetteville (city) Cumberland County	36	0.02
Charlotte (city) Mecklenburg County	70	0.01
Asheville (city) Buncombe County	0	0.00
Cary (town) Wake County	0	0.00
Chapel Hill (town) Orange County	0	0.00
Concord (city) Cabarrus County	0	0.00
Gastonia (city) Gaston County	0	0.00

African, Sub-Saharan: Somalian

Top 10 Places Sorted by Population
Based on all places, regardless of total population

Place	Population	%
Raleigh (city) Wake County	496	0.13
Charlotte (city) Mecklenburg County	485	0.07
Fayetteville (city) Cumberland County	134	0.07
Greensboro (city) Guilford County	118	0.04
Apex (town) Wake County	41	0.12
Gastonia (city) Gaston County	23	0.03
Durham (city) Durham County	11	<0.01
Aberdeen (town) Moore County	0	0.00
Advance (cdp) Davie County	0	0.00
Ahoskie (town) Hertford County	0	0.00

Top 10 Places Sorted by Percent of Total Population
Based on all places, regardless of total population

Place	Population	%
Raleigh (city) Wake County	496	0.13
Apex (town) Wake County	41	0.12
Charlotte (city) Mecklenburg County	485	0.07
Fayetteville (city) Cumberland County	134	0.07
Greensboro (city) Guilford County	118	0.04
Gastonia (city) Gaston County	23	0.03
Durham (city) Durham County	11	<0.01
Aberdeen (town) Moore County	0	0.00
Advance (cdp) Davie County	0	0.00
Ahoskie (town) Hertford County	0	0.00

Top 10 Places Sorted by Percent of Total Population
Based on places with total population of 50,000 or more

Place	Population	%
Raleigh (city) Wake County	496	0.13
Charlotte (city) Mecklenburg County	485	0.07
Fayetteville (city) Cumberland County	134	0.07
Greensboro (city) Guilford County	118	0.04
Gastonia (city) Gaston County	23	0.03
Durham (city) Durham County	11	<0.01
Asheville (city) Buncombe County	0	0.00
Cary (town) Wake County	0	0.00
Chapel Hill (town) Orange County	0	0.00
Concord (city) Cabarrus County	0	0.00

African, Sub-Saharan: South African

Top 10 Places Sorted by Population
Based on all places, regardless of total population

Place	Population	%
Charlotte (city) Mecklenburg County	194	0.03
Raleigh (city) Wake County	163	0.04
Cary (town) Wake County	121	0.09
Clemmons (village) Forsyth County	83	0.46
Durham (city) Durham County	75	0.03
Winston-Salem (city) Forsyth County	66	0.03
Greensboro (city) Guilford County	45	0.02
Burlington (city) Alamance County	42	0.09
Asheville (city) Buncombe County	41	0.05
New Bern (city) Craven County	38	0.14

Top 10 Places Sorted by Percent of Total Population
Based on all places, regardless of total population

Place	Population	%
Haw River (town) Alamance County	35	1.89
Biltmore Forest (town) Buncombe County	14	0.90
Weaverville (town) Buncombe County	19	0.61
Clemmons (village) Forsyth County	83	0.46
Ossipee (town) Alamance County	2	0.36
Carolina Beach (town) New Hanover County	19	0.34
Rolesville (town) Wake County	9	0.27
Morrisville (town) Wake County	37	0.23
Carrboro (town) Orange County	30	0.16
New Bern (city) Craven County	38	0.14

Top 10 Places Sorted by Percent of Total Population
Based on places with total population of 50,000 or more

Place	Population	%
Cary (town) Wake County	121	0.09
Asheville (city) Buncombe County	41	0.05
Raleigh (city) Wake County	163	0.04
Charlotte (city) Mecklenburg County	194	0.03
Durham (city) Durham County	75	0.03
Winston-Salem (city) Forsyth County	66	0.03
Greensboro (city) Guilford County	45	0.02
Fayetteville (city) Cumberland County	33	0.02
Concord (city) Cabarrus County	14	0.02
Chapel Hill (town) Orange County	11	0.02

African, Sub-Saharan: Sudanese

Top 10 Places Sorted by Population
Based on all places, regardless of total population

Place	Population	%
Greensboro (city) Guilford County	1,144	0.43
High Point (city) Guilford County	327	0.32
Durham (city) Durham County	134	0.06
Fayetteville (city) Cumberland County	107	0.05
Charlotte (city) Mecklenburg County	101	0.01
Burlington (city) Alamance County	48	0.10
Mars Hill (town) Madison County	11	0.40
Harrisburg (town) Cabarrus County	8	0.08
Aberdeen (town) Moore County	0	0.00
Advance (cdp) Davie County	0	0.00

Top 10 Places Sorted by Percent of Total Population
Based on all places, regardless of total population

Place	Population	%
Greensboro (city) Guilford County	1,144	0.43
Mars Hill (town) Madison County	11	0.40
High Point (city) Guilford County	327	0.32
Burlington (city) Alamance County	48	0.10
Harrisburg (town) Cabarrus County	8	0.08
Durham (city) Durham County	134	0.06
Fayetteville (city) Cumberland County	107	0.05
Charlotte (city) Mecklenburg County	101	0.01
Aberdeen (town) Moore County	0	0.00
Advance (cdp) Davie County	0	0.00

Top 10 Places Sorted by Percent of Total Population
Based on places with total population of 50,000 or more

Place	Population	%
Greensboro (city) Guilford County	1,144	0.43
High Point (city) Guilford County	327	0.32
Durham (city) Durham County	134	0.06
Fayetteville (city) Cumberland County	107	0.05
Charlotte (city) Mecklenburg County	101	0.01
Asheville (city) Buncombe County	0	0.00
Cary (town) Wake County	0	0.00
Chapel Hill (town) Orange County	0	0.00
Concord (city) Cabarrus County	0	0.00
Gastonia (city) Gaston County	0	0.00

African, Sub-Saharan: Ugandan

Top 10 Places Sorted by Population
Based on all places, regardless of total population

Place	Population	%
Greensboro (city) Guilford County	38	0.01
Aberdeen (town) Moore County	0	0.00
Advance (cdp) Davie County	0	0.00

Place	Population	%
Ahoskie (town) Hertford County	0	0.00
Alamance (village) Alamance County	0	0.00
Albemarle (city) Stanly County	0	0.00
Alliance (town) Pamlico County	0	0.00
Altamahaw (cdp) Alamance County	0	0.00
Andrews (town) Cherokee County	0	0.00
Angier (town) Harnett County	0	0.00

Top 10 Places Sorted by Percent of Total Population
Based on all places, regardless of total population

Place	Population	%
Greensboro (city) Guilford County	38	0.01
Aberdeen (town) Moore County	0	0.00
Advance (cdp) Davie County	0	0.00
Ahoskie (town) Hertford County	0	0.00
Alamance (village) Alamance County	0	0.00
Albemarle (city) Stanly County	0	0.00
Alliance (town) Pamlico County	0	0.00
Altamahaw (cdp) Alamance County	0	0.00
Andrews (town) Cherokee County	0	0.00
Angier (town) Harnett County	0	0.00

Top 10 Places Sorted by Percent of Total Population
Based on places with total population of 50,000 or more

Place	Population	%
Greensboro (city) Guilford County	38	0.01
Asheville (city) Buncombe County	0	0.00
Cary (town) Wake County	0	0.00
Chapel Hill (town) Orange County	0	0.00
Charlotte (city) Mecklenburg County	0	0.00
Concord (city) Cabarrus County	0	0.00
Durham (city) Durham County	0	0.00
Fayetteville (city) Cumberland County	0	0.00
Gastonia (city) Gaston County	0	0.00
Greenville (city) Pitt County	0	0.00

African, Sub-Saharan: Zimbabwean

Top 10 Places Sorted by Population
Based on all places, regardless of total population

Place	Population	%
Chapel Hill (town) Orange County	39	0.07
Davidson (town) Mecklenburg County	14	0.14
Morrisville (town) Wake County	11	0.07
Aberdeen (town) Moore County	0	0.00
Advance (cdp) Davie County	0	0.00
Ahoskie (town) Hertford County	0	0.00
Alamance (village) Alamance County	0	0.00
Albemarle (city) Stanly County	0	0.00
Alliance (town) Pamlico County	0	0.00
Altamahaw (cdp) Alamance County	0	0.00

Top 10 Places Sorted by Percent of Total Population
Based on all places, regardless of total population

Place	Population	%
Davidson (town) Mecklenburg County	14	0.14
Chapel Hill (town) Orange County	39	0.07
Morrisville (town) Wake County	11	0.07
Aberdeen (town) Moore County	0	0.00
Advance (cdp) Davie County	0	0.00
Ahoskie (town) Hertford County	0	0.00
Alamance (village) Alamance County	0	0.00
Albemarle (city) Stanly County	0	0.00
Alliance (town) Pamlico County	0	0.00
Altamahaw (cdp) Alamance County	0	0.00

Top 10 Places Sorted by Percent of Total Population
Based on places with total population of 50,000 or more

Place	Population	%
Chapel Hill (town) Orange County	39	0.07
Asheville (city) Buncombe County	0	0.00
Cary (town) Wake County	0	0.00
Charlotte (city) Mecklenburg County	0	0.00
Concord (city) Cabarrus County	0	0.00
Durham (city) Durham County	0	0.00
Fayetteville (city) Cumberland County	0	0.00
Gastonia (city) Gaston County	0	0.00
Greensboro (city) Guilford County	0	0.00
Greenville (city) Pitt County	0	0.00

African, Sub-Saharan: Other

Top 10 Places Sorted by Population
Based on all places, regardless of total population

Place	Population	%
Charlotte (city) Mecklenburg County	1,242	0.18
Raleigh (city) Wake County	839	0.22
Greensboro (city) Guilford County	670	0.25
Knightdale (town) Wake County	198	1.89
Durham (city) Durham County	130	0.06
Fayetteville (city) Cumberland County	108	0.05
Shelby (city) Cleveland County	100	0.49
Hillsborough (town) Orange County	92	1.54
Clayton (town) Johnston County	78	0.53
High Point (city) Guilford County	75	0.07

Top 10 Places Sorted by Percent of Total Population
Based on all places, regardless of total population

Place	Population	%
Knightdale (town) Wake County	198	1.89
Hillsborough (town) Orange County	92	1.54
Porters Neck (cdp) New Hanover County	53	1.06
Franklinton (town) Franklin County	15	0.72
Clayton (town) Johnston County	78	0.53
Shelby (city) Cleveland County	100	0.49
Beaufort (town) Carteret County	15	0.38
Spring Lake (town) Cumberland County	44	0.37
Greensboro (city) Guilford County	670	0.25
Kinston (city) Lenoir County	55	0.25

Top 10 Places Sorted by Percent of Total Population
Based on places with total population of 50,000 or more

Place	Population	%
Greensboro (city) Guilford County	670	0.25
Raleigh (city) Wake County	839	0.22
Charlotte (city) Mecklenburg County	1,242	0.18
Rocky Mount (city) Nash County	73	0.13
High Point (city) Guilford County	75	0.07
Durham (city) Durham County	130	0.06
Fayetteville (city) Cumberland County	108	0.05
Chapel Hill (town) Orange County	15	0.03
Winston-Salem (city) Forsyth County	15	0.01
Asheville (city) Buncombe County	0	0.00

Albanian

Top 10 Places Sorted by Population
Based on all places, regardless of total population

Place	Population	%
Charlotte (city) Mecklenburg County	177	0.03
Raleigh (city) Wake County	94	0.02
Apex (town) Wake County	73	0.21
Cary (town) Wake County	48	0.04
Durham (city) Durham County	38	0.02
Salisbury (city) Rowan County	31	0.09
Lake Park (village) Union County	20	0.62
Shelby (city) Cleveland County	20	0.10
Chapel Hill (town) Orange County	19	0.03
Huntersville (town) Mecklenburg County	17	0.04

Top 10 Places Sorted by Percent of Total Population
Based on all places, regardless of total population

Place	Population	%
Beech Mountain (town) Watauga County	4	0.69
Lake Park (village) Union County	20	0.62
Stedman (town) Cumberland County	3	0.28
Cullowhee (cdp) Jackson County	12	0.25
Apex (town) Wake County	73	0.21
Shelby (city) Cleveland County	20	0.10
Salisbury (city) Rowan County	31	0.09
Harrisburg (town) Cabarrus County	8	0.08
Albemarle (city) Stanly County	9	0.06
Cary (town) Wake County	48	0.04

Top 10 Places Sorted by Percent of Total Population
Based on places with total population of 50,000 or more

Place	Population	%
Cary (town) Wake County	48	0.04
Charlotte (city) Mecklenburg County	177	0.03
Chapel Hill (town) Orange County	19	0.03
Raleigh (city) Wake County	94	0.02

Durham (city) Durham County	38	0.02
Asheville (city) Buncombe County	13	0.02
Gastonia (city) Gaston County	9	0.01
Concord (city) Cabarrus County	0	0.00
Fayetteville (city) Cumberland County	0	0.00
Greensboro (city) Guilford County	0	0.00

Alsatian

Top 10 Places Sorted by Population
Based on all places, regardless of total population

Place	Population	%
Morrisville (town) Wake County	23	0.14
Charlotte (city) Mecklenburg County	19	<0.01
Woodlawn (cdp) Alamance County	18	1.44
Raleigh (city) Wake County	17	<0.01
Cary (town) Wake County	16	0.01
Lewisville (town) Forsyth County	14	0.11
Chapel Hill (town) Orange County	14	0.03
Summerfield (town) Guilford County	12	0.12
Asheville (city) Buncombe County	10	0.01
Banner Elk (town) Avery County	4	0.43

Top 10 Places Sorted by Percent of Total Population
Based on all places, regardless of total population

Place	Population	%
Woodlawn (cdp) Alamance County	18	1.44
Banner Elk (town) Avery County	4	0.43
Mount Pleasant (town) Cabarrus County	3	0.17
Morrisville (town) Wake County	23	0.14
Summerfield (town) Guilford County	12	0.12
Lewisville (town) Forsyth County	14	0.11
Chapel Hill (town) Orange County	14	0.03
Cary (town) Wake County	16	0.01
Asheville (city) Buncombe County	10	0.01
Charlotte (city) Mecklenburg County	19	<0.01

Top 10 Places Sorted by Percent of Total Population
Based on places with total population of 50,000 or more

Place	Population	%
Chapel Hill (town) Orange County	14	0.03
Cary (town) Wake County	16	0.01
Asheville (city) Buncombe County	10	0.01
Charlotte (city) Mecklenburg County	19	<0.01
Raleigh (city) Wake County	17	<0.01
Concord (city) Cabarrus County	0	0.00
Durham (city) Durham County	0	0.00
Fayetteville (city) Cumberland County	0	0.00
Gastonia (city) Gaston County	0	0.00
Greensboro (city) Guilford County	0	0.00

American

Top 10 Places Sorted by Population
Based on all places, regardless of total population

Place	Population	%
Raleigh (city) Wake County	37,404	9.77
Charlotte (city) Mecklenburg County	30,441	4.31
Wilmington (city) New Hanover County	15,339	14.65
Greensboro (city) Guilford County	12,778	4.85
Winston-Salem (city) Forsyth County	11,710	5.21
Asheville (city) Buncombe County	9,825	11.99
Cary (town) Wake County	9,424	7.39
Durham (city) Durham County	8,730	3.96
Fayetteville (city) Cumberland County	8,601	4.32
Concord (city) Cabarrus County	6,736	8.96

Top 10 Places Sorted by Percent of Total Population
Based on all places, regardless of total population

Place	Population	%
Macon (town) Warren County	376	66.67
Spencer Mountain (town) Gaston County	12	57.14
Lowgap (cdp) Surry County	164	56.94
Coinjock (cdp) Currituck County	123	56.16
Jefferson (town) Ashe County	876	54.65
Sunbury (cdp) Gates County	168	50.76
Ronda (town) Wilkes County	167	49.70
Norman (town) Richmond County	42	48.28
West Jefferson (town) Ashe County	689	48.01
Pinnacle (cdp) Stokes County	355	45.51

Top 10 Places Sorted by Percent of Total Population
Based on places with total population of 50,000 or more

Place	Population	%
Wilmington (city) New Hanover County	15,339	14.65
Asheville (city) Buncombe County	9,825	11.99
Raleigh (city) Wake County	37,404	9.77
Concord (city) Cabarrus County	6,736	8.96
Gastonia (city) Gaston County	5,604	7.93
Cary (town) Wake County	9,424	7.39
Rocky Mount (city) Nash County	3,523	6.10
High Point (city) Guilford County	5,633	5.58
Winston-Salem (city) Forsyth County	11,710	5.21
Greensboro (city) Guilford County	12,778	4.85

Arab: Total

Top 10 Places Sorted by Population
Based on all places, regardless of total population

Place	Population	%
Charlotte (city) Mecklenburg County	4,490	0.64
Raleigh (city) Wake County	3,836	1.00
Cary (town) Wake County	1,244	0.98
Greensboro (city) Guilford County	1,120	0.43
Winston-Salem (city) Forsyth County	806	0.36
Durham (city) Durham County	751	0.34
Greenville (city) Pitt County	670	0.83
Wilson (city) Wilson County	574	1.19
Rocky Mount (city) Nash County	492	0.85
Lumberton (city) Robeson County	406	1.89

Top 10 Places Sorted by Percent of Total Population
Based on all places, regardless of total population

Place	Population	%
Falcon (town) Cumberland County	27	10.23
Rougemont (cdp) Durham County	46	5.87
Mooresboro (town) Cleveland County	17	4.80
Gaston (town) Northampton County	58	4.60
Wanchese (cdp) Dare County	79	4.51
Brunswick (town) Columbus County	43	3.86
South Rosemary (cdp) Halifax County	117	3.75
Robbinsville (town) Graham County	31	3.11
Brogden (cdp) Wayne County	76	3.05
Pine Knoll Shores (town) Carteret County	39	2.60

Top 10 Places Sorted by Percent of Total Population
Based on places with total population of 50,000 or more

Place	Population	%
Raleigh (city) Wake County	3,836	1.00
Cary (town) Wake County	1,244	0.98
Rocky Mount (city) Nash County	492	0.85
Greenville (city) Pitt County	670	0.83
Chapel Hill (town) Orange County	381	0.69
Charlotte (city) Mecklenburg County	4,490	0.64
Asheville (city) Buncombe County	361	0.44
Jacksonville (city) Onslow County	306	0.44
Greensboro (city) Guilford County	1,120	0.43
Winston-Salem (city) Forsyth County	806	0.36

Arab: Arab

Top 10 Places Sorted by Population
Based on all places, regardless of total population

Place	Population	%
Raleigh (city) Wake County	1,105	0.29
Charlotte (city) Mecklenburg County	840	0.12
Wilson (city) Wilson County	297	0.62
Durham (city) Durham County	279	0.13
Tarboro (town) Edgecombe County	160	1.40
Greensboro (city) Guilford County	151	0.06
Winston-Salem (city) Forsyth County	134	0.06
South Rosemary (cdp) Halifax County	117	3.75
Smithfield (town) Johnston County	101	0.92
Chapel Hill (town) Orange County	96	0.17

Top 10 Places Sorted by Percent of Total Population
Based on all places, regardless of total population

Place	Population	%
Wanchese (cdp) Dare County	79	4.51
South Rosemary (cdp) Halifax County	117	3.75
Brogden (cdp) Wayne County	76	3.05

Place	Population	%
Tarboro (town) Edgecombe County	160	1.40
Stantonsburg (town) Wilson County	9	1.17
Bayboro (town) Pamlico County	16	1.14
Pine Knoll Shores (town) Carteret County	16	1.07
Gaston (town) Northampton County	12	0.95
Smithfield (town) Johnston County	101	0.92
St. Pauls (town) Robeson County	14	0.68

Top 10 Places Sorted by Percent of Total Population
Based on places with total population of 50,000 or more

Place	Population	%
Raleigh (city) Wake County	1,105	0.29
Chapel Hill (town) Orange County	96	0.17
Durham (city) Durham County	279	0.13
Rocky Mount (city) Nash County	74	0.13
Charlotte (city) Mecklenburg County	840	0.12
Greenville (city) Pitt County	86	0.11
Greensboro (city) Guilford County	151	0.06
Winston-Salem (city) Forsyth County	134	0.06
Cary (town) Wake County	71	0.06
Fayetteville (city) Cumberland County	87	0.04

Arab: Egyptian

Top 10 Places Sorted by Population
Based on all places, regardless of total population

Place	Population	%
Raleigh (city) Wake County	703	0.18
Charlotte (city) Mecklenburg County	604	0.09
Greenville (city) Pitt County	368	0.46
Cary (town) Wake County	271	0.21
Winston-Salem (city) Forsyth County	176	0.08
Greensboro (city) Guilford County	151	0.06
Huntersville (town) Mecklenburg County	99	0.23
Fuquay-Varina (town) Wake County	96	0.59
Durham (city) Durham County	94	0.04
Knightdale (town) Wake County	88	0.84

Top 10 Places Sorted by Percent of Total Population
Based on all places, regardless of total population

Place	Population	%
Warrenton (town) Warren County	14	1.28
Knightdale (town) Wake County	88	0.84
Cherryville (city) Gaston County	44	0.77
Ogden (cdp) New Hanover County	40	0.60
Fuquay-Varina (town) Wake County	96	0.59
Cramerton (town) Gaston County	20	0.51
Greenville (city) Pitt County	368	0.46
Oxford (city) Granville County	37	0.44
Whispering Pines (village) Moore County	12	0.43
Kill Devil Hills (town) Dare County	26	0.39

Top 10 Places Sorted by Percent of Total Population
Based on places with total population of 50,000 or more

Place	Population	%
Greenville (city) Pitt County	368	0.46
Cary (town) Wake County	271	0.21
Raleigh (city) Wake County	703	0.18
Charlotte (city) Mecklenburg County	604	0.09
Winston-Salem (city) Forsyth County	176	0.08
Chapel Hill (town) Orange County	43	0.08
Greensboro (city) Guilford County	151	0.06
Wilmington (city) New Hanover County	67	0.06
Gastonia (city) Gaston County	39	0.06
Durham (city) Durham County	94	0.04

Arab: Iraqi

Top 10 Places Sorted by Population
Based on all places, regardless of total population

Place	Population	%
Raleigh (city) Wake County	87	0.02
Jacksonville (city) Onslow County	46	0.07
Durham (city) Durham County	28	0.01
Fayetteville (city) Cumberland County	26	0.01
Chapel Hill (town) Orange County	20	0.04
Cary (town) Wake County	12	0.01
Biltmore Forest (town) Buncombe County	9	0.58
Aberdeen (town) Moore County	0	0.00
Advance (cdp) Davie County	0	0.00
Ahoskie (town) Hertford County	0	0.00

Top 10 Places Sorted by Percent of Total Population
Based on all places, regardless of total population

Place	Population	%
Biltmore Forest (town) Buncombe County	9	0.58
Jacksonville (city) Onslow County	46	0.07
Chapel Hill (town) Orange County	20	0.04
Raleigh (city) Wake County	87	0.02
Durham (city) Durham County	28	0.01
Fayetteville (city) Cumberland County	26	0.01
Cary (town) Wake County	12	0.01
Aberdeen (town) Moore County	0	0.00
Advance (cdp) Davie County	0	0.00
Ahoskie (town) Hertford County	0	0.00

Top 10 Places Sorted by Percent of Total Population
Based on places with total population of 50,000 or more

Place	Population	%
Jacksonville (city) Onslow County	46	0.07
Chapel Hill (town) Orange County	20	0.04
Raleigh (city) Wake County	87	0.02
Durham (city) Durham County	28	0.01
Fayetteville (city) Cumberland County	26	0.01
Cary (town) Wake County	12	0.01
Asheville (city) Buncombe County	0	0.00
Charlotte (city) Mecklenburg County	0	0.00
Concord (city) Cabarrus County	0	0.00
Gastonia (city) Gaston County	0	0.00

Arab: Jordanian

Top 10 Places Sorted by Population
Based on all places, regardless of total population

Place	Population	%
Mount Holly (city) Gaston County	205	1.59
Raleigh (city) Wake County	186	0.05
Lumberton (city) Robeson County	179	0.83
Greensboro (city) Guilford County	159	0.06
Charlotte (city) Mecklenburg County	117	0.02
Indian Trail (town) Union County	81	0.27
Cary (town) Wake County	75	0.06
Tyro (cdp) Davidson County	53	1.35
Winston-Salem (city) Forsyth County	50	0.02
Rocky Mount (city) Nash County	47	0.08

Top 10 Places Sorted by Percent of Total Population
Based on all places, regardless of total population

Place	Population	%
Mount Holly (city) Gaston County	205	1.59
Tyro (cdp) Davidson County	53	1.35
Lumberton (city) Robeson County	179	0.83
Indian Trail (town) Union County	81	0.27
Huntersville (town) Mecklenburg County	39	0.09
Clemmons (village) Forsyth County	16	0.09
Morrisville (town) Wake County	14	0.09
Rocky Mount (city) Nash County	47	0.08
Greensboro (city) Guilford County	159	0.06
Cary (town) Wake County	75	0.06

Top 10 Places Sorted by Percent of Total Population
Based on places with total population of 50,000 or more

Place	Population	%
Rocky Mount (city) Nash County	47	0.08
Greensboro (city) Guilford County	159	0.06
Cary (town) Wake County	75	0.06
Raleigh (city) Wake County	186	0.05
Charlotte (city) Mecklenburg County	117	0.02
Winston-Salem (city) Forsyth County	50	0.02
Durham (city) Durham County	22	0.01
Asheville (city) Buncombe County	12	0.01
Greenville (city) Pitt County	10	0.01
Chapel Hill (town) Orange County	2	<0.01

Arab: Lebanese

Top 10 Places Sorted by Population
Based on all places, regardless of total population

Place	Population	%
Charlotte (city) Mecklenburg County	1,598	0.23
Raleigh (city) Wake County	837	0.22
Greensboro (city) Guilford County	361	0.14

Place	Population	%
Winston-Salem (city) Forsyth County	320	0.14
Cary (town) Wake County	315	0.25
Asheville (city) Buncombe County	259	0.32
Pinehurst (village) Moore County	206	1.65
Fayetteville (city) Cumberland County	195	0.10
Matthews (town) Mecklenburg County	163	0.61
Greenville (city) Pitt County	151	0.19

Top 10 Places Sorted by Percent of Total Population
Based on all places, regardless of total population

Place	Population	%
Rougemont (cdp) Durham County	46	5.87
Mooresboro (town) Cleveland County	17	4.80
Robbinsville (town) Graham County	31	3.11
Nags Head (town) Dare County	50	1.80
Pinehurst (village) Moore County	206	1.65
Williamston (town) Martin County	90	1.63
Half Moon (cdp) Onslow County	131	1.60
Red Oak (town) Nash County	52	1.58
Vandemere (town) Pamlico County	3	1.54
Pine Knoll Shores (town) Carteret County	23	1.53

Top 10 Places Sorted by Percent of Total Population
Based on places with total population of 50,000 or more

Place	Population	%
Asheville (city) Buncombe County	259	0.32
Chapel Hill (town) Orange County	148	0.27
Cary (town) Wake County	315	0.25
Charlotte (city) Mecklenburg County	1,598	0.23
Raleigh (city) Wake County	837	0.22
Greenville (city) Pitt County	151	0.19
Jacksonville (city) Onslow County	133	0.19
Greensboro (city) Guilford County	361	0.14
Winston-Salem (city) Forsyth County	320	0.14
Wilmington (city) New Hanover County	122	0.12

Arab: Moroccan

Top 10 Places Sorted by Population
Based on all places, regardless of total population

Place	Population	%
Charlotte (city) Mecklenburg County	382	0.05
Cary (town) Wake County	301	0.24
Raleigh (city) Wake County	258	0.07
Durham (city) Durham County	78	0.04
Waxhaw (town) Union County	72	0.82
Greenville (city) Pitt County	44	0.05
Brunswick (town) Columbus County	43	3.86
Winston-Salem (city) Forsyth County	43	0.02
Spring Lake (town) Cumberland County	41	0.35
Wilson (city) Wilson County	39	0.08

Top 10 Places Sorted by Percent of Total Population
Based on all places, regardless of total population

Place	Population	%
Brunswick (town) Columbus County	43	3.86
Wilson's Mills (town) Johnston County	33	1.56
Bayboro (town) Pamlico County	17	1.21
Waxhaw (town) Union County	72	0.82
Sharpsburg (town) Nash County	14	0.65
Selma (town) Johnston County	31	0.51
Polkton (town) Anson County	16	0.49
Lillington (town) Harnett County	15	0.47
Butner (town) Granville County	34	0.46
Wendell (town) Wake County	21	0.38

Top 10 Places Sorted by Percent of Total Population
Based on places with total population of 50,000 or more

Place	Population	%
Cary (town) Wake County	301	0.24
Raleigh (city) Wake County	258	0.07
Charlotte (city) Mecklenburg County	382	0.05
Greenville (city) Pitt County	44	0.05
Durham (city) Durham County	78	0.04
Winston-Salem (city) Forsyth County	43	0.02
Concord (city) Cabarrus County	18	0.02
Gastonia (city) Gaston County	13	0.02
Greensboro (city) Guilford County	26	0.01
Chapel Hill (town) Orange County	7	0.01

Arab: Palestinian

Top 10 Places Sorted by Population
Based on all places, regardless of total population

Place	Population	%
Rocky Mount (city) Nash County	222	0.38
Lumberton (city) Robeson County	174	0.81
Charlotte (city) Mecklenburg County	122	0.02
Raleigh (city) Wake County	119	0.03
Greensboro (city) Guilford County	111	0.04
Cary (town) Wake County	108	0.08
Morrisville (town) Wake County	63	0.39
Winterville (town) Pitt County	39	0.46
Durham (city) Durham County	27	0.01
Thomasville (city) Davidson County	23	0.09

Top 10 Places Sorted by Percent of Total Population
Based on all places, regardless of total population

Place	Population	%
Lumberton (city) Robeson County	174	0.81
Norwood (town) Stanly County	13	0.61
Winterville (town) Pitt County	39	0.46
Morrisville (town) Wake County	63	0.39
Rocky Mount (city) Nash County	222	0.38
Mount Olive (town) Wayne County	16	0.35
Lake Norman of Catawba (cdp) Catawba County	22	0.32
Oxford (city) Granville County	16	0.19
Thomasville (city) Davidson County	23	0.09
Cary (town) Wake County	108	0.08

Top 10 Places Sorted by Percent of Total Population
Based on places with total population of 50,000 or more

Place	Population	%
Rocky Mount (city) Nash County	222	0.38
Cary (town) Wake County	108	0.08
Greensboro (city) Guilford County	111	0.04
Raleigh (city) Wake County	119	0.03
Chapel Hill (town) Orange County	14	0.03
Charlotte (city) Mecklenburg County	122	0.02
Durham (city) Durham County	27	0.01
Asheville (city) Buncombe County	12	0.01
Winston-Salem (city) Forsyth County	6	<0.01
Concord (city) Cabarrus County	0	0.00

Arab: Syrian

Top 10 Places Sorted by Population
Based on all places, regardless of total population

Place	Population	%
Charlotte (city) Mecklenburg County	254	0.04
Greensboro (city) Guilford County	130	0.05
Gastonia (city) Gaston County	92	0.13
Raleigh (city) Wake County	85	0.02
Jacksonville (city) Onslow County	76	0.11
Winston-Salem (city) Forsyth County	70	0.03
Burlington (city) Alamance County	64	0.13
Apex (town) Wake County	62	0.18
Mooresville (town) Iredell County	48	0.16
Wilson (city) Wilson County	48	0.10

Top 10 Places Sorted by Percent of Total Population
Based on all places, regardless of total population

Place	Population	%
Bryson City (town) Swain County	11	0.71
Carolina Shores (town) Brunswick County	16	0.56
Hillsborough (town) Orange County	31	0.52
Red Oak (town) Nash County	13	0.39
Siler City (town) Chatham County	27	0.35
Sunset Beach (town) Brunswick County	11	0.33
Swansboro (town) Onslow County	8	0.33
Hamlet (city) Richmond County	17	0.26
Whispering Pines (village) Moore County	7	0.25
Apex (town) Wake County	62	0.18

Top 10 Places Sorted by Percent of Total Population
Based on places with total population of 50,000 or more

Place	Population	%
Gastonia (city) Gaston County	92	0.13
Jacksonville (city) Onslow County	76	0.11
Concord (city) Cabarrus County	44	0.06
Greensboro (city) Guilford County	130	0.05

Charlotte (city) Mecklenburg County	254	0.04
Winston-Salem (city) Forsyth County	70	0.03
Asheville (city) Buncombe County	25	0.03
Chapel Hill (town) Orange County	14	0.03
Raleigh (city) Wake County	85	0.02
Durham (city) Durham County	45	0.02

Arab: Other

Top 10 Places Sorted by Population
Based on all places, regardless of total population

Place	Population	%
Charlotte (city) Mecklenburg County	573	0.08
Raleigh (city) Wake County	456	0.12
Rocky Mount (city) Nash County	94	0.16
Holly Springs (town) Wake County	79	0.36
Cary (town) Wake County	77	0.06
Durham (city) Durham County	58	0.03
Wilson (city) Wilson County	57	0.12
Smithfield (town) Johnston County	53	0.48
Mount Holly (city) Gaston County	50	0.39
Asheboro (city) Randolph County	47	0.19

Top 10 Places Sorted by Percent of Total Population
Based on all places, regardless of total population

Place	Population	%
Falcon (town) Cumberland County	27	10.23
Gaston (town) Northampton County	46	3.65
St. Pauls (town) Robeson County	37	1.80
Sharpsburg (town) Nash County	16	0.74
Pleasant Garden (town) Guilford County	31	0.68
Smithfield (town) Johnston County	53	0.48
Mount Holly (city) Gaston County	50	0.39
Holly Springs (town) Wake County	79	0.36
Lake Waccamaw (town) Columbus County	3	0.29
Belmont (city) Gaston County	25	0.25

Top 10 Places Sorted by Percent of Total Population
Based on places with total population of 50,000 or more

Place	Population	%
Rocky Mount (city) Nash County	94	0.16
Raleigh (city) Wake County	456	0.12
Charlotte (city) Mecklenburg County	573	0.08
Chapel Hill (town) Orange County	37	0.07
Cary (town) Wake County	77	0.06
Asheville (city) Buncombe County	40	0.05
Wilmington (city) New Hanover County	42	0.04
Jacksonville (city) Onslow County	29	0.04
Durham (city) Durham County	58	0.03
Greensboro (city) Guilford County	31	0.01

Armenian

Top 10 Places Sorted by Population
Based on all places, regardless of total population

Place	Population	%
Charlotte (city) Mecklenburg County	612	0.09
Durham (city) Durham County	340	0.15
Raleigh (city) Wake County	213	0.06
Cary (town) Wake County	206	0.16
Indian Trail (town) Union County	121	0.40
Huntersville (town) Mecklenburg County	110	0.26
Chapel Hill (town) Orange County	91	0.16
Winston-Salem (city) Forsyth County	74	0.03
High Point (city) Guilford County	73	0.07
Gastonia (city) Gaston County	69	0.10

Top 10 Places Sorted by Percent of Total Population
Based on all places, regardless of total population

Place	Population	%
Barker Ten Mile (cdp) Robeson County	41	3.48
Swepsonville (town) Alamance County	22	1.82
Rutherfordton (town) Rutherford County	63	1.50
Foxfire (village) Moore County	10	1.28
Royal Pines (cdp) Buncombe County	52	1.24
Stanfield (town) Stanly County	10	0.64
Sunset Beach (town) Brunswick County	20	0.60
Beech Mountain (town) Watauga County	3	0.51
Morehead City (town) Carteret County	39	0.46
Bethlehem (cdp) Alexander County	19	0.45

Top 10 Places Sorted by Percent of Total Population
Based on places with total population of 50,000 or more

Place	Population	%
Cary (town) Wake County	206	0.16
Chapel Hill (town) Orange County	91	0.16
Durham (city) Durham County	340	0.15
Gastonia (city) Gaston County	69	0.10
Charlotte (city) Mecklenburg County	612	0.09
High Point (city) Guilford County	73	0.07
Raleigh (city) Wake County	213	0.06
Asheville (city) Buncombe County	50	0.06
Wilmington (city) New Hanover County	43	0.04
Winston-Salem (city) Forsyth County	74	0.03

Assyrian/Chaldean/Syriac

Top 10 Places Sorted by Population
Based on all places, regardless of total population

Place	Population	%
Mountain Home (cdp) Henderson County	20	0.62
Raleigh (city) Wake County	18	<0.01
Tarboro (town) Edgecombe County	16	0.14
Kernersville (town) Forsyth County	15	0.07
Durham (city) Durham County	13	0.01
Advance (cdp) Davie County	11	0.96
Charlotte (city) Mecklenburg County	7	<0.01
Aberdeen (town) Moore County	0	0.00
Ahoskie (town) Hertford County	0	0.00
Alamance (village) Alamance County	0	0.00

Top 10 Places Sorted by Percent of Total Population
Based on all places, regardless of total population

Place	Population	%
Advance (cdp) Davie County	11	0.96
Mountain Home (cdp) Henderson County	20	0.62
Tarboro (town) Edgecombe County	16	0.14
Kernersville (town) Forsyth County	15	0.07
Durham (city) Durham County	13	0.01
Raleigh (city) Wake County	18	<0.01
Charlotte (city) Mecklenburg County	7	<0.01
Aberdeen (town) Moore County	0	0.00
Ahoskie (town) Hertford County	0	0.00
Alamance (village) Alamance County	0	0.00

Top 10 Places Sorted by Percent of Total Population
Based on places with total population of 50,000 or more

Place	Population	%
Durham (city) Durham County	13	0.01
Raleigh (city) Wake County	18	<0.01
Charlotte (city) Mecklenburg County	7	<0.01
Asheville (city) Buncombe County	0	0.00
Cary (town) Wake County	0	0.00
Chapel Hill (town) Orange County	0	0.00
Concord (city) Cabarrus County	0	0.00
Fayetteville (city) Cumberland County	0	0.00
Gastonia (city) Gaston County	0	0.00
Greensboro (city) Guilford County	0	0.00

Australian

Top 10 Places Sorted by Population
Based on all places, regardless of total population

Place	Population	%
Raleigh (city) Wake County	356	0.09
Charlotte (city) Mecklenburg County	152	0.02
Durham (city) Durham County	127	0.06
Wilmington (city) New Hanover County	106	0.10
Greensboro (city) Guilford County	66	0.03
Troy (town) Montgomery County	58	1.80
Apex (town) Wake County	45	0.13
Chapel Hill (town) Orange County	44	0.08
Fayetteville (city) Cumberland County	40	0.02
Porters Neck (cdp) New Hanover County	38	0.76

Top 10 Places Sorted by Percent of Total Population
Based on all places, regardless of total population

Place	Population	%
Hamilton (town) Martin County	13	2.92
Troy (town) Montgomery County	58	1.80
Clyde (town) Haywood County	11	1.10

Place	Population	%
Sunset Beach (town) Brunswick County	28	0.84
Toast (cdp) Surry County	14	0.79
Porters Neck (cdp) New Hanover County	38	0.76
Westport (cdp) Lincoln County	25	0.76
Boiling Springs (town) Cleveland County	27	0.60
Taylorsville (town) Alexander County	11	0.58
Kings Grant (cdp) New Hanover County	37	0.44

Top 10 Places Sorted by Percent of Total Population
Based on places with total population of 50,000 or more

Place	Population	%
Wilmington (city) New Hanover County	106	0.10
Raleigh (city) Wake County	356	0.09
Chapel Hill (town) Orange County	44	0.08
Durham (city) Durham County	127	0.06
Greensboro (city) Guilford County	66	0.03
Charlotte (city) Mecklenburg County	152	0.02
Fayetteville (city) Cumberland County	40	0.02
Winston-Salem (city) Forsyth County	34	0.02
Gastonia (city) Gaston County	13	0.02
Greenville (city) Pitt County	11	0.01

Austrian

Top 10 Places Sorted by Population
Based on all places, regardless of total population

Place	Population	%
Charlotte (city) Mecklenburg County	1,273	0.18
Raleigh (city) Wake County	670	0.18
Durham (city) Durham County	423	0.19
Cary (town) Wake County	407	0.32
Fayetteville (city) Cumberland County	349	0.18
Greensboro (city) Guilford County	326	0.12
Winston-Salem (city) Forsyth County	325	0.14
Chapel Hill (town) Orange County	243	0.44
Wilmington (city) New Hanover County	224	0.21
Asheville (city) Buncombe County	207	0.25

Top 10 Places Sorted by Percent of Total Population
Based on all places, regardless of total population

Place	Population	%
Rodanthe (cdp) Dare County	27	6.46
Danbury (town) Stokes County	8	5.56
Buxton (cdp) Dare County	46	4.80
Neuse Forest (cdp) Craven County	51	3.35
Forest Oaks (cdp) Guilford County	100	2.94
Shallotte (town) Brunswick County	90	2.68
JAARS (cdp) Union County	11	2.25
Spring Hope (town) Nash County	28	2.23
Topsail Beach (town) Pender County	8	2.12
Wingate (town) Union County	70	2.06

Top 10 Places Sorted by Percent of Total Population
Based on places with total population of 50,000 or more

Place	Population	%
Chapel Hill (town) Orange County	243	0.44
Cary (town) Wake County	407	0.32
Asheville (city) Buncombe County	207	0.25
Wilmington (city) New Hanover County	224	0.21
Durham (city) Durham County	423	0.19
Charlotte (city) Mecklenburg County	1,273	0.18
Raleigh (city) Wake County	670	0.18
Fayetteville (city) Cumberland County	349	0.18
High Point (city) Guilford County	162	0.16
Winston-Salem (city) Forsyth County	325	0.14

Basque

Top 10 Places Sorted by Population
Based on all places, regardless of total population

Place	Population	%
Coats (town) Harnett County	41	1.94
Cary (town) Wake County	38	0.03
Fayetteville (city) Cumberland County	29	0.01
Raleigh (city) Wake County	25	0.01
Greensboro (city) Guilford County	21	0.01
Durham (city) Durham County	11	<0.01
Winston-Salem (city) Forsyth County	9	<0.01
Charlotte (city) Mecklenburg County	6	<0.01
Lake Park (village) Union County	5	0.15
Aberdeen (town) Moore County	0	0.00

Top 10 Places Sorted by Percent of Total Population
Based on all places, regardless of total population

Place	Population	%
Coats (town) Harnett County	41	1.94
Lake Park (village) Union County	5	0.15
Cary (town) Wake County	38	0.03
Fayetteville (city) Cumberland County	29	0.01
Raleigh (city) Wake County	25	0.01
Greensboro (city) Guilford County	21	0.01
Durham (city) Durham County	11	<0.01
Winston-Salem (city) Forsyth County	9	<0.01
Charlotte (city) Mecklenburg County	6	<0.01
Aberdeen (town) Moore County	0	0.00

Top 10 Places Sorted by Percent of Total Population
Based on places with total population of 50,000 or more

Place	Population	%
Cary (town) Wake County	38	0.03
Fayetteville (city) Cumberland County	29	0.01
Raleigh (city) Wake County	25	0.01
Greensboro (city) Guilford County	21	0.01
Durham (city) Durham County	11	<0.01
Winston-Salem (city) Forsyth County	9	<0.01
Charlotte (city) Mecklenburg County	6	<0.01
Asheville (city) Buncombe County	0	0.00
Chapel Hill (town) Orange County	0	0.00
Concord (city) Cabarrus County	0	0.00

Belgian

Top 10 Places Sorted by Population
Based on all places, regardless of total population

Place	Population	%
Charlotte (city) Mecklenburg County	690	0.10
Cary (town) Wake County	343	0.27
Raleigh (city) Wake County	288	0.08
Greensboro (city) Guilford County	193	0.07
Winston-Salem (city) Forsyth County	120	0.05
Chapel Hill (town) Orange County	116	0.21
Holly Springs (town) Wake County	103	0.47
Huntersville (town) Mecklenburg County	103	0.24
Stallings (town) Union County	98	0.77
Randleman (city) Randolph County	93	2.32

Top 10 Places Sorted by Percent of Total Population
Based on all places, regardless of total population

Place	Population	%
Dillsboro (town) Jackson County	8	6.02
Randleman (city) Randolph County	93	2.32
Spruce Pine (town) Mitchell County	40	1.78
Avery Creek (cdp) Buncombe County	38	1.68
Mount Pleasant (town) Cabarrus County	28	1.62
Stallings (town) Union County	98	0.77
St. James (town) Brunswick County	21	0.75
Robersonville (town) Martin County	9	0.58
Saluda (city) Polk County	4	0.57
Trent Woods (town) Craven County	21	0.51

Top 10 Places Sorted by Percent of Total Population
Based on places with total population of 50,000 or more

Place	Population	%
Cary (town) Wake County	343	0.27
Chapel Hill (town) Orange County	116	0.21
Rocky Mount (city) Nash County	75	0.13
Charlotte (city) Mecklenburg County	690	0.10
Raleigh (city) Wake County	288	0.08
Greensboro (city) Guilford County	193	0.07
Asheville (city) Buncombe County	56	0.07
Winston-Salem (city) Forsyth County	120	0.05
Wilmington (city) New Hanover County	54	0.05
Greenville (city) Pitt County	36	0.04

Brazilian

Top 10 Places Sorted by Population
Based on all places, regardless of total population

Place	Population	%
Charlotte (city) Mecklenburg County	1,399	0.20
Raleigh (city) Wake County	444	0.12
Greensboro (city) Guilford County	232	0.09

Place	Population	%
Indian Trail (town) Union County	150	0.49
Winston-Salem (city) Forsyth County	103	0.05
Cary (town) Wake County	69	0.05
Winterville (town) Pitt County	64	0.76
Wilmington (city) New Hanover County	61	0.06
Durham (city) Durham County	56	0.03
Apex (town) Wake County	54	0.16

Top 10 Places Sorted by Percent of Total Population
Based on all places, regardless of total population

Place	Population	%
Richlands (town) Onslow County	25	1.67
Horse Shoe (cdp) Henderson County	39	1.39
Carolina Shores (town) Brunswick County	38	1.33
Spindale (town) Rutherford County	49	1.15
Bayshore (cdp) New Hanover County	46	1.09
Duck (town) Dare County	4	1.03
Hightsville (cdp) New Hanover County	6	0.87
Newport (town) Carteret County	33	0.83
Winterville (town) Pitt County	64	0.76
Welcome (cdp) Davidson County	33	0.74

Top 10 Places Sorted by Percent of Total Population
Based on places with total population of 50,000 or more

Place	Population	%
Charlotte (city) Mecklenburg County	1,399	0.20
Raleigh (city) Wake County	444	0.12
Greensboro (city) Guilford County	232	0.09
Wilmington (city) New Hanover County	61	0.06
Greenville (city) Pitt County	51	0.06
Winston-Salem (city) Forsyth County	103	0.05
Cary (town) Wake County	69	0.05
Jacksonville (city) Onslow County	32	0.05
Durham (city) Durham County	56	0.03
Gastonia (city) Gaston County	14	0.02

British

Top 10 Places Sorted by Population
Based on all places, regardless of total population

Place	Population	%
Charlotte (city) Mecklenburg County	3,557	0.50
Raleigh (city) Wake County	2,874	0.75
Greensboro (city) Guilford County	1,727	0.66
Durham (city) Durham County	1,500	0.68
Chapel Hill (town) Orange County	1,225	2.22
Cary (town) Wake County	1,185	0.93
Winston-Salem (city) Forsyth County	1,064	0.47
Wilmington (city) New Hanover County	713	0.68
Asheville (city) Buncombe County	635	0.77
Jacksonville (city) Onslow County	525	0.76

Top 10 Places Sorted by Percent of Total Population
Based on all places, regardless of total population

Place	Population	%
Seven Springs (town) Wayne County	25	18.66
Stokes (cdp) Pitt County	32	13.33
Swan Quarter (cdp) Hyde County	34	7.93
Bunnlevel (cdp) Harnett County	26	4.66
Maggie Valley (town) Haywood County	45	4.21
Montreat (town) Buncombe County	30	3.77
Marshallberg (cdp) Carteret County	12	3.70
Kenansville (town) Duplin County	34	3.14
Whispering Pines (village) Moore County	82	2.96
Trent Woods (town) Craven County	121	2.94

Top 10 Places Sorted by Percent of Total Population
Based on places with total population of 50,000 or more

Place	Population	%
Chapel Hill (town) Orange County	1,225	2.22
Cary (town) Wake County	1,185	0.93
Asheville (city) Buncombe County	635	0.77
Jacksonville (city) Onslow County	525	0.76
Raleigh (city) Wake County	2,874	0.75
Durham (city) Durham County	1,500	0.68
Wilmington (city) New Hanover County	713	0.68
Greensboro (city) Guilford County	1,727	0.66
Concord (city) Cabarrus County	391	0.52
Charlotte (city) Mecklenburg County	3,557	0.50

Bulgarian

Top 10 Places Sorted by Population
Based on all places, regardless of total population

Place	Population	%
Cary (town) Wake County	215	0.17
Charlotte (city) Mecklenburg County	123	0.02
Carrboro (town) Orange County	88	0.46
Raleigh (city) Wake County	85	0.02
Gastonia (city) Gaston County	79	0.11
Chapel Hill (town) Orange County	75	0.14
Wilmington (city) New Hanover County	66	0.06
Mount Airy (city) Surry County	64	0.61
Durham (city) Durham County	52	0.02
Greensboro (city) Guilford County	52	0.02

Top 10 Places Sorted by Percent of Total Population
Based on all places, regardless of total population

Place	Population	%
Mount Airy (city) Surry County	64	0.61
Carrboro (town) Orange County	88	0.46
Southport (city) Brunswick County	8	0.29
Kill Devil Hills (town) Dare County	17	0.26
Mount Holly (city) Gaston County	30	0.23
Cary (town) Wake County	215	0.17
Chapel Hill (town) Orange County	75	0.14
Harrisburg (town) Cabarrus County	13	0.13
Gastonia (city) Gaston County	79	0.11
Morrisville (town) Wake County	17	0.11

Top 10 Places Sorted by Percent of Total Population
Based on places with total population of 50,000 or more

Place	Population	%
Cary (town) Wake County	215	0.17
Chapel Hill (town) Orange County	75	0.14
Gastonia (city) Gaston County	79	0.11
Wilmington (city) New Hanover County	66	0.06
Greenville (city) Pitt County	30	0.04
Charlotte (city) Mecklenburg County	123	0.02
Raleigh (city) Wake County	85	0.02
Durham (city) Durham County	52	0.02
Greensboro (city) Guilford County	52	0.02
Winston-Salem (city) Forsyth County	25	0.01

Cajun

Top 10 Places Sorted by Population
Based on all places, regardless of total population

Place	Population	%
Charlotte (city) Mecklenburg County	208	0.03
Thomasville (city) Davidson County	105	0.40
Greensboro (city) Guilford County	66	0.03
Raleigh (city) Wake County	49	0.01
Jacksonville (city) Onslow County	48	0.07
Apex (town) Wake County	42	0.12
Vander (cdp) Cumberland County	41	4.12
Cary (town) Wake County	40	0.03
Erwin (town) Harnett County	38	0.87
Winston-Salem (city) Forsyth County	38	0.02

Top 10 Places Sorted by Percent of Total Population
Based on all places, regardless of total population

Place	Population	%
Vander (cdp) Cumberland County	41	4.12
Erwin (town) Harnett County	38	0.87
Fletcher (town) Henderson County	31	0.46
Oak Island (town) Brunswick County	31	0.45
Thomasville (city) Davidson County	105	0.40
Washington (city) Beaufort County	15	0.15
Apex (town) Wake County	42	0.12
Hope Mills (town) Cumberland County	18	0.12
Havelock (city) Craven County	21	0.10
Jacksonville (city) Onslow County	48	0.07

Top 10 Places Sorted by Percent of Total Population
Based on places with total population of 50,000 or more

Place	Population	%
Jacksonville (city) Onslow County	48	0.07
Greenville (city) Pitt County	32	0.04
Charlotte (city) Mecklenburg County	208	0.03
Greensboro (city) Guilford County	66	0.03

Cary (town) Wake County	40	0.03
Winston-Salem (city) Forsyth County	38	0.02
Asheville (city) Buncombe County	17	0.02
Raleigh (city) Wake County	49	0.01
Fayetteville (city) Cumberland County	16	0.01
Chapel Hill (town) Orange County	0	0.00

Canadian

Top 10 Places Sorted by Population
Based on all places, regardless of total population

Place	Population	%
Charlotte (city) Mecklenburg County	1,520	0.22
Durham (city) Durham County	821	0.37
Raleigh (city) Wake County	740	0.19
Cary (town) Wake County	525	0.41
Greensboro (city) Guilford County	359	0.14
Fayetteville (city) Cumberland County	303	0.15
Chapel Hill (town) Orange County	279	0.51
Wake Forest (town) Wake County	206	0.77
Apex (town) Wake County	205	0.60
Asheville (city) Buncombe County	192	0.23

Top 10 Places Sorted by Percent of Total Population
Based on all places, regardless of total population

Place	Population	%
Rhodhiss (town) Burke County	63	4.95
Seaboard (town) Northampton County	41	4.80
Atlantic (cdp) Carteret County	22	4.14
Aquadale (cdp) Stanly County	14	2.86
Bridgeton (town) Craven County	7	2.46
McLeansville (cdp) Guilford County	18	2.30
China Grove (town) Rowan County	82	2.29
Vass (town) Moore County	12	1.98
West Canton (cdp) Haywood County	22	1.90
Half Moon (cdp) Onslow County	150	1.84

Top 10 Places Sorted by Percent of Total Population
Based on places with total population of 50,000 or more

Place	Population	%
Chapel Hill (town) Orange County	279	0.51
Cary (town) Wake County	525	0.41
Durham (city) Durham County	821	0.37
Jacksonville (city) Onslow County	168	0.24
Asheville (city) Buncombe County	192	0.23
Charlotte (city) Mecklenburg County	1,520	0.22
Raleigh (city) Wake County	740	0.19
Greenville (city) Pitt County	136	0.17
Fayetteville (city) Cumberland County	303	0.15
Greensboro (city) Guilford County	359	0.14

Carpatho Rusyn

Top 10 Places Sorted by Population
Based on all places, regardless of total population

Place	Population	%
Greenville (city) Pitt County	18	0.02
Charlotte (city) Mecklenburg County	15	<0.01
Sunset Beach (town) Brunswick County	14	0.42
Jacksonville (city) Onslow County	11	0.02
Asheville (city) Buncombe County	8	0.01
Faison (town) Duplin County	4	0.34
Aberdeen (town) Moore County	0	0.00
Advance (cdp) Davie County	0	0.00
Ahoskie (town) Hertford County	0	0.00
Alamance (village) Alamance County	0	0.00

Top 10 Places Sorted by Percent of Total Population
Based on all places, regardless of total population

Place	Population	%
Sunset Beach (town) Brunswick County	14	0.42
Faison (town) Duplin County	4	0.34
Greenville (city) Pitt County	18	0.02
Jacksonville (city) Onslow County	11	0.02
Asheville (city) Buncombe County	8	0.01
Charlotte (city) Mecklenburg County	15	<0.01
Aberdeen (town) Moore County	0	0.00
Advance (cdp) Davie County	0	0.00
Ahoskie (town) Hertford County	0	0.00
Alamance (village) Alamance County	0	0.00

Top 10 Places Sorted by Percent of Total Population
Based on places with total population of 50,000 or more

Place	Population	%
Greenville (city) Pitt County	18	0.02
Jacksonville (city) Onslow County	11	0.02
Asheville (city) Buncombe County	8	0.01
Charlotte (city) Mecklenburg County	15	<0.01
Cary (town) Wake County	0	0.00
Chapel Hill (town) Orange County	0	0.00
Concord (city) Cabarrus County	0	0.00
Durham (city) Durham County	0	0.00
Fayetteville (city) Cumberland County	0	0.00
Gastonia (city) Gaston County	0	0.00

Celtic

Top 10 Places Sorted by Population
Based on all places, regardless of total population

Place	Population	%
Durham (city) Durham County	119	0.05
Charlotte (city) Mecklenburg County	100	0.01
Asheville (city) Buncombe County	84	0.10
Forest City (town) Rutherford County	65	0.87
Winston-Salem (city) Forsyth County	64	0.03
Carrboro (town) Orange County	62	0.33
Raleigh (city) Wake County	53	0.01
Rocky Point (cdp) Pender County	52	2.87
Greensboro (city) Guilford County	51	0.02
Wilmington (city) New Hanover County	38	0.04

Top 10 Places Sorted by Percent of Total Population
Based on all places, regardless of total population

Place	Population	%
Rocky Point (cdp) Pender County	52	2.87
Dillsboro (town) Jackson County	3	2.26
Chimney Rock Village (village) Rutherford County	3	1.63
Columbia (town) Tyrrell County	15	1.61
Rose Hill (town) Duplin County	15	1.07
McLeansville (cdp) Guilford County	8	1.02
Jackson (town) Northampton County	5	0.97
Forest City (town) Rutherford County	65	0.87
Kure Beach (town) New Hanover County	13	0.80
Bent Creek (cdp) Buncombe County	10	0.70

Top 10 Places Sorted by Percent of Total Population
Based on places with total population of 50,000 or more

Place	Population	%
Asheville (city) Buncombe County	84	0.10
Chapel Hill (town) Orange County	36	0.07
Durham (city) Durham County	119	0.05
Wilmington (city) New Hanover County	38	0.04
Concord (city) Cabarrus County	28	0.04
Winston-Salem (city) Forsyth County	64	0.03
Greensboro (city) Guilford County	51	0.02
Cary (town) Wake County	29	0.02
Jacksonville (city) Onslow County	12	0.02
Charlotte (city) Mecklenburg County	100	0.01

Croatian

Top 10 Places Sorted by Population
Based on all places, regardless of total population

Place	Population	%
Charlotte (city) Mecklenburg County	618	0.09
Raleigh (city) Wake County	221	0.06
Huntersville (town) Mecklenburg County	180	0.42
Greensboro (city) Guilford County	166	0.06
Durham (city) Durham County	165	0.07
Wilmington (city) New Hanover County	102	0.10
Asheville (city) Buncombe County	98	0.12
High Point (city) Guilford County	98	0.10
Cary (town) Wake County	86	0.07
Chapel Hill (town) Orange County	84	0.15

Top 10 Places Sorted by Percent of Total Population
Based on all places, regardless of total population

Place	Population	%
Avon (cdp) Dare County	22	9.69
Buxton (cdp) Dare County	23	2.40
Moyock (cdp) Currituck County	81	2.03

Place	Population	%
Bayshore (cdp) New Hanover County	68	1.61
Pumpkin Center (cdp) Onslow County	30	1.57
Duck (town) Dare County	6	1.54
Carolina Beach (town) New Hanover County	59	1.04
North Topsail Beach (town) Onslow County	7	0.71
Lowell (city) Gaston County	22	0.65
Horse Shoe (cdp) Henderson County	18	0.64

Top 10 Places Sorted by Percent of Total Population
Based on places with total population of 50,000 or more

Place	Population	%
Chapel Hill (town) Orange County	84	0.15
Asheville (city) Buncombe County	98	0.12
Wilmington (city) New Hanover County	102	0.10
High Point (city) Guilford County	98	0.10
Charlotte (city) Mecklenburg County	618	0.09
Durham (city) Durham County	165	0.07
Cary (town) Wake County	86	0.07
Raleigh (city) Wake County	221	0.06
Greensboro (city) Guilford County	166	0.06
Fayetteville (city) Cumberland County	67	0.03

Cypriot

Top 10 Places Sorted by Population
Based on all places, regardless of total population

Place	Population	%
Elon (town) Alamance County	34	0.38
Raleigh (city) Wake County	27	0.01
Jacksonville (city) Onslow County	19	0.03
Carrboro (town) Orange County	10	0.05
Aberdeen (town) Moore County	0	0.00
Advance (cdp) Davie County	0	0.00
Ahoskie (town) Hertford County	0	0.00
Alamance (village) Alamance County	0	0.00
Albemarle (city) Stanly County	0	0.00
Alliance (town) Pamlico County	0	0.00

Top 10 Places Sorted by Percent of Total Population
Based on all places, regardless of total population

Place	Population	%
Elon (town) Alamance County	34	0.38
Carrboro (town) Orange County	10	0.05
Jacksonville (city) Onslow County	19	0.03
Raleigh (city) Wake County	27	0.01
Aberdeen (town) Moore County	0	0.00
Advance (cdp) Davie County	0	0.00
Ahoskie (town) Hertford County	0	0.00
Alamance (village) Alamance County	0	0.00
Albemarle (city) Stanly County	0	0.00
Alliance (town) Pamlico County	0	0.00

Top 10 Places Sorted by Percent of Total Population
Based on places with total population of 50,000 or more

Place	Population	%
Jacksonville (city) Onslow County	19	0.03
Raleigh (city) Wake County	27	0.01
Asheville (city) Buncombe County	0	0.00
Cary (town) Wake County	0	0.00
Chapel Hill (town) Orange County	0	0.00
Charlotte (city) Mecklenburg County	0	0.00
Concord (city) Cabarrus County	0	0.00
Durham (city) Durham County	0	0.00
Fayetteville (city) Cumberland County	0	0.00
Gastonia (city) Gaston County	0	0.00

Czech

Top 10 Places Sorted by Population
Based on all places, regardless of total population

Place	Population	%
Charlotte (city) Mecklenburg County	1,654	0.23
Raleigh (city) Wake County	959	0.25
Cary (town) Wake County	642	0.50
Greensboro (city) Guilford County	523	0.20
High Point (city) Guilford County	432	0.43
Chapel Hill (town) Orange County	430	0.78
Wilmington (city) New Hanover County	393	0.38
Durham (city) Durham County	388	0.18
Asheville (city) Buncombe County	366	0.45
Fayetteville (city) Cumberland County	353	0.18

Top 10 Places Sorted by Percent of Total Population
Based on all places, regardless of total population

Place	Population	%
Cove Creek (cdp) Watauga County	86	5.80
North Topsail Beach (town) Onslow County	54	5.49
Marshallberg (cdp) Carteret County	12	3.70
Youngsville (town) Franklin County	33	2.98
Deercroft (cdp) Scotland County	11	2.43
Chimney Rock Village (village) Rutherford County	4	2.17
Tabor City (town) Columbus County	49	1.95
Royal Pines (cdp) Buncombe County	76	1.81
Maiden (town) Catawba County	59	1.77
Morrisville (town) Wake County	277	1.72

Top 10 Places Sorted by Percent of Total Population
Based on places with total population of 50,000 or more

Place	Population	%
Chapel Hill (town) Orange County	430	0.78
Cary (town) Wake County	642	0.50
Asheville (city) Buncombe County	366	0.45
High Point (city) Guilford County	432	0.43
Wilmington (city) New Hanover County	393	0.38
Raleigh (city) Wake County	959	0.25
Charlotte (city) Mecklenburg County	1,654	0.23
Jacksonville (city) Onslow County	156	0.23
Greensboro (city) Guilford County	523	0.20
Concord (city) Cabarrus County	151	0.20

Czechoslovakian

Top 10 Places Sorted by Population
Based on all places, regardless of total population

Place	Population	%
Charlotte (city) Mecklenburg County	759	0.11
Raleigh (city) Wake County	198	0.05
Silver Lake (cdp) New Hanover County	184	3.39
Concord (city) Cabarrus County	157	0.21
Cary (town) Wake County	139	0.11
Greensboro (city) Guilford County	136	0.05
Durham (city) Durham County	113	0.05
Holly Springs (town) Wake County	92	0.42
Unionville (town) Union County	90	1.54
Winston-Salem (city) Forsyth County	90	0.04

Top 10 Places Sorted by Percent of Total Population
Based on all places, regardless of total population

Place	Population	%
Valle Crucis (cdp) Watauga County	29	4.59
Foscoe (cdp) Watauga County	29	3.54
Silver Lake (cdp) New Hanover County	184	3.39
Rougemont (cdp) Durham County	23	2.94
Lake Royale (cdp) Franklin County	39	1.57
Unionville (town) Union County	90	1.54
Severn (town) Northampton County	5	1.39
Kenly (town) Johnston County	20	1.18
Richlands (town) Onslow County	17	1.14
Tabor City (town) Columbus County	27	1.07

Top 10 Places Sorted by Percent of Total Population
Based on places with total population of 50,000 or more

Place	Population	%
Concord (city) Cabarrus County	157	0.21
Charlotte (city) Mecklenburg County	759	0.11
Cary (town) Wake County	139	0.11
High Point (city) Guilford County	66	0.07
Asheville (city) Buncombe County	58	0.07
Jacksonville (city) Onslow County	48	0.07
Gastonia (city) Gaston County	47	0.07
Chapel Hill (town) Orange County	33	0.06
Raleigh (city) Wake County	198	0.05
Greensboro (city) Guilford County	136	0.05

Danish

Top 10 Places Sorted by Population
Based on all places, regardless of total population

Place	Population	%
Charlotte (city) Mecklenburg County	1,486	0.21
Raleigh (city) Wake County	689	0.18
Cary (town) Wake County	498	0.39

Place	Population	%
Asheville (city) Buncombe County	465	0.57
Greensboro (city) Guilford County	372	0.14
Durham (city) Durham County	348	0.16
Fayetteville (city) Cumberland County	345	0.17
Concord (city) Cabarrus County	340	0.45
Wilmington (city) New Hanover County	270	0.26
Huntersville (town) Mecklenburg County	266	0.62

Top 10 Places Sorted by Percent of Total Population
Based on all places, regardless of total population

Place	Population	%
Seven Springs (town) Wayne County	25	18.66
Lansing (town) Ashe County	14	7.87
Bald Head Island (village) Brunswick County	4	5.33
Harrells (town) Sampson County	10	5.10
McDonald (town) Robeson County	2	4.55
Whispering Pines (village) Moore County	88	3.17
Mountain View (cdp) Catawba County	96	2.75
Laurel Park (town) Henderson County	52	2.27
Porters Neck (cdp) New Hanover County	109	2.19
Fairfield Harbour (cdp) Craven County	57	2.06

Top 10 Places Sorted by Percent of Total Population
Based on places with total population of 50,000 or more

Place	Population	%
Asheville (city) Buncombe County	465	0.57
Concord (city) Cabarrus County	340	0.45
Cary (town) Wake County	498	0.39
Chapel Hill (town) Orange County	217	0.39
Jacksonville (city) Onslow County	194	0.28
Wilmington (city) New Hanover County	270	0.26
Charlotte (city) Mecklenburg County	1,486	0.21
Raleigh (city) Wake County	689	0.18
Fayetteville (city) Cumberland County	345	0.17
Durham (city) Durham County	348	0.16

Dutch

Top 10 Places Sorted by Population
Based on all places, regardless of total population

Place	Population	%
Charlotte (city) Mecklenburg County	7,656	1.08
Raleigh (city) Wake County	4,068	1.06
Winston-Salem (city) Forsyth County	2,351	1.05
Greensboro (city) Guilford County	2,321	0.88
Cary (town) Wake County	1,854	1.45
Durham (city) Durham County	1,816	0.82
Fayetteville (city) Cumberland County	1,635	0.82
Concord (city) Cabarrus County	1,450	1.93
Asheville (city) Buncombe County	1,295	1.58
Gastonia (city) Gaston County	1,116	1.58

Top 10 Places Sorted by Percent of Total Population
Based on all places, regardless of total population

Place	Population	%
Ocracoke (cdp) Hyde County	72	16.74
Stony Point (cdp) Alexander County	215	14.92
Buxton (cdp) Dare County	142	14.82
Rodanthe (cdp) Dare County	57	13.64
Northlakes (cdp) Caldwell County	201	11.53
Hot Springs (town) Madison County	56	11.43
Godwin (town) Cumberland County	15	11.19
Waco (town) Cleveland County	23	8.95
Westport (cdp) Lincoln County	278	8.41
Red Cross (town) Stanly County	60	8.11

Top 10 Places Sorted by Percent of Total Population
Based on places with total population of 50,000 or more

Place	Population	%
Concord (city) Cabarrus County	1,450	1.93
Chapel Hill (town) Orange County	1,052	1.91
Asheville (city) Buncombe County	1,295	1.58
Gastonia (city) Gaston County	1,116	1.58
Cary (town) Wake County	1,854	1.45
Charlotte (city) Mecklenburg County	7,656	1.08
Raleigh (city) Wake County	4,068	1.06
Winston-Salem (city) Forsyth County	2,351	1.05
Wilmington (city) New Hanover County	1,097	1.05
High Point (city) Guilford County	959	0.95

Eastern European

Top 10 Places Sorted by Population
Based on all places, regardless of total population

Place	Population	%
Charlotte (city) Mecklenburg County	862	0.12
Raleigh (city) Wake County	549	0.14
Greensboro (city) Guilford County	476	0.18
Durham (city) Durham County	375	0.17
Cary (town) Wake County	320	0.25
Apex (town) Wake County	198	0.58
Chapel Hill (town) Orange County	196	0.36
Asheville (city) Buncombe County	139	0.17
Winston-Salem (city) Forsyth County	135	0.06
Carrboro (town) Orange County	103	0.54

Top 10 Places Sorted by Percent of Total Population
Based on all places, regardless of total population

Place	Population	%
Butters (cdp) Bladen County	84	35.29
Royal Pines (cdp) Buncombe County	65	1.55
Millers Creek (cdp) Wilkes County	14	0.88
Archer Lodge (town) Johnston County	34	0.84
Salemburg (town) Sampson County	4	0.81
Fairfield Harbour (cdp) Craven County	21	0.76
Seven Lakes (cdp) Moore County	33	0.71
Oak Ridge (town) Guilford County	37	0.64
Fearrington Village (cdp) Chatham County	15	0.64
Mountain Home (cdp) Henderson County	19	0.59

Top 10 Places Sorted by Percent of Total Population
Based on places with total population of 50,000 or more

Place	Population	%
Chapel Hill (town) Orange County	196	0.36
Cary (town) Wake County	320	0.25
Greensboro (city) Guilford County	476	0.18
Durham (city) Durham County	375	0.17
Asheville (city) Buncombe County	139	0.17
Raleigh (city) Wake County	549	0.14
Charlotte (city) Mecklenburg County	862	0.12
Winston-Salem (city) Forsyth County	135	0.06
Rocky Mount (city) Nash County	27	0.05
Gastonia (city) Gaston County	30	0.04

English

Top 10 Places Sorted by Population
Based on all places, regardless of total population

Place	Population	%
Charlotte (city) Mecklenburg County	58,078	8.23
Raleigh (city) Wake County	39,630	10.35
Greensboro (city) Guilford County	22,926	8.71
Winston-Salem (city) Forsyth County	22,468	10.00
Durham (city) Durham County	18,137	8.23
Cary (town) Wake County	17,916	14.04
Wilmington (city) New Hanover County	13,829	13.20
Fayetteville (city) Cumberland County	12,565	6.32
Asheville (city) Buncombe County	12,259	14.96
Chapel Hill (town) Orange County	10,042	18.20

Top 10 Places Sorted by Percent of Total Population
Based on all places, regardless of total population

Place	Population	%
Waves (cdp) Dare County	74	71.84
Old Hundred (cdp) Scotland County	26	66.67
Rodanthe (cdp) Dare County	266	63.64
Harkers Island (cdp) Carteret County	634	58.01
Love Valley (town) Iredell County	9	47.37
Grandfather (village) Avery County	55	46.61
Gulf (cdp) Chatham County	24	45.28
Lasker (town) Northampton County	56	44.09
Ocracoke (cdp) Hyde County	181	42.09
Bayview (cdp) Beaufort County	154	41.96

Top 10 Places Sorted by Percent of Total Population
Based on places with total population of 50,000 or more

Place	Population	%
Chapel Hill (town) Orange County	10,042	18.20
Asheville (city) Buncombe County	12,259	14.96
Cary (town) Wake County	17,916	14.04
Wilmington (city) New Hanover County	13,829	13.20

Raleigh (city) Wake County	39,630	10.35
Winston-Salem (city) Forsyth County	22,468	10.00
Concord (city) Cabarrus County	7,361	9.79
Greenville (city) Pitt County	7,419	9.22
High Point (city) Guilford County	9,115	9.03
Greensboro (city) Guilford County	22,926	8.71

Estonian

Top 10 Places Sorted by Population
Based on all places, regardless of total population

Place	Population	%
Raleigh (city) Wake County	77	0.02
Garner (town) Wake County	66	0.27
Fayetteville (city) Cumberland County	64	0.03
Durham (city) Durham County	43	0.02
Charlotte (city) Mecklenburg County	41	0.01
Carrboro (town) Orange County	20	0.10
Chapel Hill (town) Orange County	17	0.03
Cary (town) Wake County	11	0.01
Flat Rock (village) Henderson County	9	0.30
Shelby (city) Cleveland County	9	0.04

Top 10 Places Sorted by Percent of Total Population
Based on all places, regardless of total population

Place	Population	%
Varnam (town) Brunswick County	6	1.00
Flat Rock (village) Henderson County	9	0.30
Garner (town) Wake County	66	0.27
Carrboro (town) Orange County	20	0.10
Shelby (city) Cleveland County	9	0.04
Fayetteville (city) Cumberland County	64	0.03
Chapel Hill (town) Orange County	17	0.03
Raleigh (city) Wake County	77	0.02
Durham (city) Durham County	43	0.02
Charlotte (city) Mecklenburg County	41	0.01

Top 10 Places Sorted by Percent of Total Population
Based on places with total population of 50,000 or more

Place	Population	%
Fayetteville (city) Cumberland County	64	0.03
Chapel Hill (town) Orange County	17	0.03
Raleigh (city) Wake County	77	0.02
Durham (city) Durham County	43	0.02
Charlotte (city) Mecklenburg County	41	0.01
Cary (town) Wake County	11	0.01
Asheville (city) Buncombe County	0	0.00
Concord (city) Cabarrus County	0	0.00
Gastonia (city) Gaston County	0	0.00
Greensboro (city) Guilford County	0	0.00

European

Top 10 Places Sorted by Population
Based on all places, regardless of total population

Place	Population	%
Charlotte (city) Mecklenburg County	6,521	0.92
Raleigh (city) Wake County	5,405	1.41
Cary (town) Wake County	3,166	2.48
Greensboro (city) Guilford County	2,845	1.08
Durham (city) Durham County	2,559	1.16
Winston-Salem (city) Forsyth County	2,316	1.03
Asheville (city) Buncombe County	1,449	1.77
Chapel Hill (town) Orange County	1,435	2.60
Fayetteville (city) Cumberland County	1,435	0.72
Greenville (city) Pitt County	1,041	1.29

Top 10 Places Sorted by Percent of Total Population
Based on all places, regardless of total population

Place	Population	%
Earl (town) Cleveland County	48	20.69
Bald Head Island (village) Brunswick County	10	13.33
Orrum (town) Robeson County	12	13.04
Iron Station (cdp) Lincoln County	115	11.59
Harrellsville (town) Hertford County	15	10.42
Cliffside (cdp) Rutherford County	38	9.50
Atlantic (cdp) Carteret County	50	9.40
Lowgap (cdp) Surry County	24	8.33
West Marion (cdp) McDowell County	137	6.81
Mountain Home (cdp) Henderson County	212	6.62

Top 10 Places Sorted by Percent of Total Population
Based on places with total population of 50,000 or more

Place	Population	%
Chapel Hill (town) Orange County	1,435	2.60
Cary (town) Wake County	3,166	2.48
Asheville (city) Buncombe County	1,449	1.77
Raleigh (city) Wake County	5,405	1.41
Greenville (city) Pitt County	1,041	1.29
Jacksonville (city) Onslow County	889	1.29
Durham (city) Durham County	2,559	1.16
Concord (city) Cabarrus County	822	1.09
Greensboro (city) Guilford County	2,845	1.08
Winston-Salem (city) Forsyth County	2,316	1.03

Finnish

Top 10 Places Sorted by Population
Based on all places, regardless of total population

Place	Population	%
Charlotte (city) Mecklenburg County	402	0.06
Raleigh (city) Wake County	310	0.08
Greensboro (city) Guilford County	292	0.11
Fayetteville (city) Cumberland County	255	0.13
Durham (city) Durham County	229	0.10
Cary (town) Wake County	148	0.12
Wilmington (city) New Hanover County	142	0.14
Winston-Salem (city) Forsyth County	124	0.06
Westport (cdp) Lincoln County	118	3.57
Elizabeth City (city) Pasquotank County	90	0.48

Top 10 Places Sorted by Percent of Total Population
Based on all places, regardless of total population

Place	Population	%
Westport (cdp) Lincoln County	118	3.57
Maggie Valley (town) Haywood County	34	3.18
Halifax (town) Halifax County	4	1.90
Bunnlevel (cdp) Harnett County	9	1.61
Lowesville (cdp) Lincoln County	33	1.25
Bent Creek (cdp) Buncombe County	17	1.19
Flat Rock (village) Henderson County	32	1.05
Saluda (city) Polk County	7	1.00
Stanley (town) Gaston County	33	0.95
Alliance (town) Pamlico County	9	0.90

Top 10 Places Sorted by Percent of Total Population
Based on places with total population of 50,000 or more

Place	Population	%
Wilmington (city) New Hanover County	142	0.14
Chapel Hill (town) Orange County	78	0.14
Fayetteville (city) Cumberland County	255	0.13
Jacksonville (city) Onslow County	88	0.13
Cary (town) Wake County	148	0.12
Greensboro (city) Guilford County	292	0.11
Durham (city) Durham County	229	0.10
Asheville (city) Buncombe County	78	0.10
Raleigh (city) Wake County	310	0.08
High Point (city) Guilford County	70	0.07

French, except Basque

Top 10 Places Sorted by Population
Based on all places, regardless of total population

Place	Population	%
Charlotte (city) Mecklenburg County	12,074	1.71
Raleigh (city) Wake County	7,025	1.84
Greensboro (city) Guilford County	4,077	1.55
Fayetteville (city) Cumberland County	3,489	1.75
Winston-Salem (city) Forsyth County	3,360	1.49
Durham (city) Durham County	3,230	1.47
Cary (town) Wake County	3,176	2.49
Wilmington (city) New Hanover County	2,934	2.80
Asheville (city) Buncombe County	2,612	3.19
Jacksonville (city) Onslow County	2,249	3.26

Top 10 Places Sorted by Percent of Total Population
Based on all places, regardless of total population

Place	Population	%
Danbury (town) Stokes County	39	27.08
Bolivia (town) Brunswick County	29	21.17
Avon (cdp) Dare County	40	17.62

Place	Population	%
Ocracoke (cdp) Hyde County	73	16.98
Marble (cdp) Cherokee County	16	14.95
Chimney Rock Village (village) Rutherford County	22	11.96
Saluda (city) Polk County	69	9.84
Grimesland (town) Pitt County	46	8.71
Seven Devils (town) Watauga County	16	8.47
Glen Raven (cdp) Alamance County	224	8.41

Top 10 Places Sorted by Percent of Total Population
Based on places with total population of 50,000 or more

Place	Population	%
Jacksonville (city) Onslow County	2,249	3.26
Asheville (city) Buncombe County	2,612	3.19
Wilmington (city) New Hanover County	2,934	2.80
Chapel Hill (town) Orange County	1,546	2.80
Cary (town) Wake County	3,176	2.49
Concord (city) Cabarrus County	1,485	1.98
Greenville (city) Pitt County	1,491	1.85
Raleigh (city) Wake County	7,025	1.84
Fayetteville (city) Cumberland County	3,489	1.75
Charlotte (city) Mecklenburg County	12,074	1.71

French Canadian

Top 10 Places Sorted by Population
Based on all places, regardless of total population

Place	Population	%
Charlotte (city) Mecklenburg County	2,489	0.35
Raleigh (city) Wake County	1,561	0.41
Cary (town) Wake County	1,019	0.80
Fayetteville (city) Cumberland County	899	0.45
Durham (city) Durham County	649	0.29
Greensboro (city) Guilford County	633	0.24
Winston-Salem (city) Forsyth County	520	0.23
Jacksonville (city) Onslow County	505	0.73
Chapel Hill (town) Orange County	477	0.86
Huntersville (town) Mecklenburg County	463	1.07

Top 10 Places Sorted by Percent of Total Population
Based on all places, regardless of total population

Place	Population	%
Castle Hayne (cdp) New Hanover County	82	6.26
Falcon (town) Cumberland County	16	6.06
Efland (cdp) Orange County	30	5.08
Ellenboro (town) Rutherford County	42	5.05
Saratoga (town) Wilson County	15	3.82
Moyock (cdp) Currituck County	135	3.39
Forest Oaks (cdp) Guilford County	111	3.27
Hillsdale (cdp) Davie County	18	3.27
Sims (town) Wilson County	11	3.01
Broad Creek (cdp) Carteret County	64	2.86

Top 10 Places Sorted by Percent of Total Population
Based on places with total population of 50,000 or more

Place	Population	%
Chapel Hill (town) Orange County	477	0.86
Cary (town) Wake County	1,019	0.80
Jacksonville (city) Onslow County	505	0.73
Fayetteville (city) Cumberland County	899	0.45
Asheville (city) Buncombe County	357	0.44
Raleigh (city) Wake County	1,561	0.41
Greenville (city) Pitt County	314	0.39
Wilmington (city) New Hanover County	395	0.38
Gastonia (city) Gaston County	268	0.38
Charlotte (city) Mecklenburg County	2,489	0.35

German

Top 10 Places Sorted by Population
Based on all places, regardless of total population

Place	Population	%
Charlotte (city) Mecklenburg County	71,671	10.15
Raleigh (city) Wake County	38,247	9.99
Greensboro (city) Guilford County	22,704	8.62
Winston-Salem (city) Forsyth County	22,499	10.01
Fayetteville (city) Cumberland County	21,911	11.02
Cary (town) Wake County	19,577	15.34
Durham (city) Durham County	18,806	8.54
Jacksonville (city) Onslow County	12,255	17.76
Asheville (city) Buncombe County	12,009	14.65
Wilmington (city) New Hanover County	11,884	11.35

Top 10 Places Sorted by Percent of Total Population
Based on all places, regardless of total population

Place	Population	%
Salvo (cdp) Dare County	50	56.82
JAARS (cdp) Union County	245	50.10
Grandfather (village) Avery County	51	43.22
Ruffin (cdp) Rockingham County	234	38.55
Advance (cdp) Davie County	439	38.24
Seven Devils (town) Watauga County	72	38.10
Foscoe (cdp) Watauga County	279	34.07
Old Hundred (cdp) Scotland County	13	33.33
Mount Pleasant (town) Cabarrus County	573	33.18
Saxapahaw (cdp) Alamance County	367	32.54

Top 10 Places Sorted by Percent of Total Population
Based on places with total population of 50,000 or more

Place	Population	%
Jacksonville (city) Onslow County	12,255	17.76
Concord (city) Cabarrus County	11,684	15.54
Cary (town) Wake County	19,577	15.34
Asheville (city) Buncombe County	12,009	14.65
Chapel Hill (town) Orange County	8,076	14.64
Wilmington (city) New Hanover County	11,884	11.35
Fayetteville (city) Cumberland County	21,911	11.02
Gastonia (city) Gaston County	7,258	10.26
Charlotte (city) Mecklenburg County	71,671	10.15
Winston-Salem (city) Forsyth County	22,499	10.01

German Russian

Top 10 Places Sorted by Population
Based on all places, regardless of total population

Place	Population	%
Asheville (city) Buncombe County	53	0.06
Rocky Mount (city) Nash County	47	0.08
Durham (city) Durham County	47	0.02
Kinston (city) Lenoir County	36	0.16
Lake Park (village) Union County	25	0.77
Winston-Salem (city) Forsyth County	21	0.01
Northchase (cdp) New Hanover County	18	0.61
Hope Mills (town) Cumberland County	17	0.12
Cary (town) Wake County	13	0.01
Charlotte (city) Mecklenburg County	9	<0.01

Top 10 Places Sorted by Percent of Total Population
Based on all places, regardless of total population

Place	Population	%
Lake Park (village) Union County	25	0.77
Northchase (cdp) New Hanover County	18	0.61
Robersonville (town) Martin County	3	0.19
Kinston (city) Lenoir County	36	0.16
Hope Mills (town) Cumberland County	17	0.12
Rocky Mount (city) Nash County	47	0.08
Asheville (city) Buncombe County	53	0.06
Durham (city) Durham County	47	0.02
Winston-Salem (city) Forsyth County	21	0.01
Cary (town) Wake County	13	0.01

Top 10 Places Sorted by Percent of Total Population
Based on places with total population of 50,000 or more

Place	Population	%
Rocky Mount (city) Nash County	47	0.08
Asheville (city) Buncombe County	53	0.06
Durham (city) Durham County	47	0.02
Winston-Salem (city) Forsyth County	21	0.01
Cary (town) Wake County	13	0.01
Charlotte (city) Mecklenburg County	9	<0.01
Fayetteville (city) Cumberland County	8	<0.01
Chapel Hill (town) Orange County	0	0.00
Concord (city) Cabarrus County	0	0.00
Gastonia (city) Gaston County	0	0.00

Greek

Top 10 Places Sorted by Population
Based on all places, regardless of total population

Place	Population	%
Charlotte (city) Mecklenburg County	4,046	0.57
Raleigh (city) Wake County	1,389	0.36
Winston-Salem (city) Forsyth County	1,114	0.50

Place	Population	%
Cary (town) Wake County	728	0.57
Gastonia (city) Gaston County	576	0.81
Wilmington (city) New Hanover County	544	0.52
Fayetteville (city) Cumberland County	542	0.27
Greensboro (city) Guilford County	526	0.27
High Point (city) Guilford County	468	0.46
Durham (city) Durham County	448	0.20

Top 10 Places Sorted by Percent of Total Population
Based on all places, regardless of total population

Place	Population	%
Bethania (town) Forsyth County	16	5.61
Rhodhiss (town) Burke County	63	4.95
Holden Beach (town) Brunswick County	33	4.34
Polkville (city) Cleveland County	26	3.87
Wrightsville Beach (town) New Hanover County	91	3.52
Evergreen (cdp) Columbus County	14	3.03
Iron Station (cdp) Lincoln County	30	3.02
Buies Creek (cdp) Harnett County	112	3.01
Vanceboro (town) Craven County	24	2.94
Caswell Beach (town) Brunswick County	18	2.88

Top 10 Places Sorted by Percent of Total Population
Based on places with total population of 50,000 or more

Place	Population	%
Gastonia (city) Gaston County	576	0.81
Chapel Hill (town) Orange County	442	0.80
Charlotte (city) Mecklenburg County	4,046	0.57
Cary (town) Wake County	728	0.57
Asheville (city) Buncombe County	443	0.54
Wilmington (city) New Hanover County	544	0.52
Winston-Salem (city) Forsyth County	1,114	0.50
High Point (city) Guilford County	468	0.46
Raleigh (city) Wake County	1,389	0.36
Fayetteville (city) Cumberland County	542	0.27

Guyanese

Top 10 Places Sorted by Population
Based on all places, regardless of total population

Place	Population	%
Charlotte (city) Mecklenburg County	298	0.04
Concord (city) Cabarrus County	260	0.35
Greensboro (city) Guilford County	209	0.08
High Point (city) Guilford County	207	0.21
Raleigh (city) Wake County	202	0.05
Fayetteville (city) Cumberland County	139	0.07
Durham (city) Durham County	108	0.05
Winston-Salem (city) Forsyth County	82	0.04
Jacksonville (city) Onslow County	59	0.09
Laurinburg (city) Scotland County	47	0.29

Top 10 Places Sorted by Percent of Total Population
Based on all places, regardless of total population

Place	Population	%
Newport (town) Carteret County	34	0.85
East Rockingham (cdp) Richmond County	26	0.65
Pittsboro (town) Chatham County	22	0.62
Concord (city) Cabarrus County	260	0.35
Louisburg (town) Franklin County	11	0.33
Laurinburg (city) Scotland County	47	0.29
Harrisburg (town) Cabarrus County	24	0.23
Rockingham (city) Richmond County	22	0.23
Williamston (town) Martin County	12	0.22
High Point (city) Guilford County	207	0.21

Top 10 Places Sorted by Percent of Total Population
Based on places with total population of 50,000 or more

Place	Population	%
Concord (city) Cabarrus County	260	0.35
High Point (city) Guilford County	207	0.21
Jacksonville (city) Onslow County	59	0.09
Greensboro (city) Guilford County	209	0.08
Fayetteville (city) Cumberland County	139	0.07
Raleigh (city) Wake County	202	0.05
Durham (city) Durham County	108	0.05
Charlotte (city) Mecklenburg County	298	0.04
Winston-Salem (city) Forsyth County	82	0.04
Chapel Hill (town) Orange County	15	0.03

Hungarian

Top 10 Places Sorted by Population
Based on all places, regardless of total population

Place	Population	%
Charlotte (city) Mecklenburg County	2,059	0.29
Raleigh (city) Wake County	972	0.25
Cary (town) Wake County	950	0.74
Greensboro (city) Guilford County	666	0.25
Durham (city) Durham County	571	0.26
Winston-Salem (city) Forsyth County	554	0.25
Fayetteville (city) Cumberland County	488	0.25
Wilmington (city) New Hanover County	476	0.45
Concord (city) Cabarrus County	385	0.51
Jacksonville (city) Onslow County	377	0.55

Top 10 Places Sorted by Percent of Total Population
Based on all places, regardless of total population

Place	Population	%
River Bend (town) Craven County	199	6.54
Buxton (cdp) Dare County	46	4.80
Holly Ridge (town) Onslow County	25	3.75
Ocean Isle Beach (town) Brunswick County	33	3.62
Gloucester (cdp) Carteret County	12	3.01
Lake Norman of Catawba (cdp) Catawba County	203	2.93
Fairfield Harbour (cdp) Craven County	69	2.50
Red Oak (town) Nash County	73	2.22
Bent Creek (cdp) Buncombe County	31	2.17
Oak Ridge (town) Guilford County	125	2.15

Top 10 Places Sorted by Percent of Total Population
Based on places with total population of 50,000 or more

Place	Population	%
Cary (town) Wake County	950	0.74
Jacksonville (city) Onslow County	377	0.55
Concord (city) Cabarrus County	385	0.51
Chapel Hill (town) Orange County	281	0.51
Wilmington (city) New Hanover County	476	0.45
Greenville (city) Pitt County	274	0.34
Charlotte (city) Mecklenburg County	2,059	0.29
Durham (city) Durham County	571	0.26
High Point (city) Guilford County	265	0.26
Raleigh (city) Wake County	972	0.25

Icelander

Top 10 Places Sorted by Population
Based on all places, regardless of total population

Place	Population	%
Boone (town) Watauga County	69	0.42
Raleigh (city) Wake County	67	0.02
Concord (city) Cabarrus County	63	0.08
Apex (town) Wake County	42	0.12
Greenville (city) Pitt County	33	0.04
Seven Lakes (cdp) Moore County	28	0.60
Chapel Hill (town) Orange County	27	0.05
Fayetteville (city) Cumberland County	27	0.01
Kill Devil Hills (town) Dare County	21	0.32
Cullowhee (cdp) Jackson County	15	0.32

Top 10 Places Sorted by Percent of Total Population
Based on all places, regardless of total population

Place	Population	%
Faith (town) Rowan County	6	0.66
Seven Lakes (cdp) Moore County	28	0.60
Boone (town) Watauga County	69	0.42
Bayboro (town) Pamlico County	5	0.36
Kill Devil Hills (town) Dare County	21	0.32
Cullowhee (cdp) Jackson County	15	0.32
Maggie Valley (town) Haywood County	3	0.28
Cedar Point (town) Carteret County	2	0.16
Carolina Shores (town) Brunswick County	4	0.14
Apex (town) Wake County	42	0.12

Top 10 Places Sorted by Percent of Total Population
Based on places with total population of 50,000 or more

Place	Population	%
Concord (city) Cabarrus County	63	0.08
Chapel Hill (town) Orange County	27	0.05
Greenville (city) Pitt County	33	0.04
Raleigh (city) Wake County	67	0.02

Fayetteville (city) Cumberland County	27	0.01
Greensboro (city) Guilford County	14	0.01
Asheville (city) Buncombe County	11	0.01
Cary (town) Wake County	11	0.01
Wilmington (city) New Hanover County	11	0.01
Charlotte (city) Mecklenburg County	11	<0.01

Iranian

Top 10 Places Sorted by Population
Based on all places, regardless of total population

Place	Population	%
Charlotte (city) Mecklenburg County	786	0.11
Raleigh (city) Wake County	532	0.14
Winston-Salem (city) Forsyth County	431	0.19
Greensboro (city) Guilford County	397	0.15
Cary (town) Wake County	205	0.16
Durham (city) Durham County	163	0.07
Carolina Beach (town) New Hanover County	120	2.12
Greenville (city) Pitt County	101	0.13
Fayetteville (city) Cumberland County	100	0.05
Boone (town) Watauga County	95	0.57

Top 10 Places Sorted by Percent of Total Population
Based on all places, regardless of total population

Place	Population	%
Carolina Beach (town) New Hanover County	120	2.12
Bermuda Run (town) Davie County	14	0.84
Boone (town) Watauga County	95	0.57
Surf City (town) Pender County	9	0.52
Oak Ridge (town) Guilford County	28	0.48
Morrisville (town) Wake County	76	0.47
Lewisville (town) Forsyth County	56	0.45
East Rockingham (cdp) Richmond County	15	0.38
Waxhaw (town) Union County	31	0.35
Eden (city) Rockingham County	49	0.31

Top 10 Places Sorted by Percent of Total Population
Based on places with total population of 50,000 or more

Place	Population	%
Winston-Salem (city) Forsyth County	431	0.19
Cary (town) Wake County	205	0.16
Greensboro (city) Guilford County	397	0.15
Raleigh (city) Wake County	532	0.14
Greenville (city) Pitt County	101	0.13
Charlotte (city) Mecklenburg County	786	0.11
Chapel Hill (town) Orange County	47	0.09
Durham (city) Durham County	163	0.07
Fayetteville (city) Cumberland County	100	0.05
Asheville (city) Buncombe County	41	0.05

Irish

Top 10 Places Sorted by Population
Based on all places, regardless of total population

Place	Population	%
Charlotte (city) Mecklenburg County	54,824	7.77
Raleigh (city) Wake County	31,339	8.19
Greensboro (city) Guilford County	18,092	6.87
Winston-Salem (city) Forsyth County	17,469	7.77
Fayetteville (city) Cumberland County	16,748	8.42
Cary (town) Wake County	15,501	12.15
Durham (city) Durham County	14,557	6.61
Wilmington (city) New Hanover County	11,876	11.34
Jacksonville (city) Onslow County	11,545	16.73
Asheville (city) Buncombe County	9,641	11.76

Top 10 Places Sorted by Percent of Total Population
Based on all places, regardless of total population

Place	Population	%
Cashiers (cdp) Jackson County	24	47.06
Rodanthe (cdp) Dare County	186	44.50
Waves (cdp) Dare County	45	43.69
Bakersville (town) Mitchell County	126	33.60
Ruffin (cdp) Rockingham County	196	32.29
Wakulla (cdp) Robeson County	96	31.17
Godwin (town) Cumberland County	38	28.36
Gulf (cdp) Chatham County	15	28.30
Ossipee (town) Alamance County	159	28.29
Hobucken (cdp) Pamlico County	65	27.78

Top 10 Places Sorted by Percent of Total Population
Based on places with total population of 50,000 or more

Place	Population	%
Jacksonville (city) Onslow County	11,545	16.73
Cary (town) Wake County	15,501	12.15
Asheville (city) Buncombe County	9,641	11.76
Wilmington (city) New Hanover County	11,876	11.34
Chapel Hill (town) Orange County	5,429	9.84
Greenville (city) Pitt County	7,908	9.83
Concord (city) Cabarrus County	7,316	9.73
Gastonia (city) Gaston County	5,979	8.46
Fayetteville (city) Cumberland County	16,748	8.42
Raleigh (city) Wake County	31,339	8.19

Israeli

Top 10 Places Sorted by Population
Based on all places, regardless of total population

Place	Population	%
Durham (city) Durham County	130	0.06
Chapel Hill (town) Orange County	109	0.20
Cary (town) Wake County	102	0.08
Raleigh (city) Wake County	95	0.02
Lenoir (city) Caldwell County	64	0.35
Charlotte (city) Mecklenburg County	51	0.01
Scotch Meadows (cdp) Scotland County	46	5.61
Asheville (city) Buncombe County	27	0.03
Greenville (city) Pitt County	27	0.03
Jacksonville (city) Onslow County	25	0.04

Top 10 Places Sorted by Percent of Total Population
Based on all places, regardless of total population

Place	Population	%
Scotch Meadows (cdp) Scotland County	46	5.61
Lenoir (city) Caldwell County	64	0.35
Chapel Hill (town) Orange County	109	0.20
Ogden (cdp) New Hanover County	11	0.17
Myrtle Grove (cdp) New Hanover County	14	0.16
Cramerton (town) Gaston County	6	0.15
Morrisville (town) Wake County	15	0.09
Cary (town) Wake County	102	0.08
Carrboro (town) Orange County	14	0.07
Durham (city) Durham County	130	0.06

Top 10 Places Sorted by Percent of Total Population
Based on places with total population of 50,000 or more

Place	Population	%
Chapel Hill (town) Orange County	109	0.20
Cary (town) Wake County	102	0.08
Durham (city) Durham County	130	0.06
Jacksonville (city) Onslow County	25	0.04
Asheville (city) Buncombe County	27	0.03
Greenville (city) Pitt County	27	0.03
Raleigh (city) Wake County	95	0.02
Charlotte (city) Mecklenburg County	51	0.01
Concord (city) Cabarrus County	0	0.00
Fayetteville (city) Cumberland County	0	0.00

Italian

Top 10 Places Sorted by Population
Based on all places, regardless of total population

Place	Population	%
Charlotte (city) Mecklenburg County	28,643	4.06
Raleigh (city) Wake County	14,642	3.83
Cary (town) Wake County	9,428	7.39
Fayetteville (city) Cumberland County	6,535	3.29
Greensboro (city) Guilford County	6,358	2.41
Durham (city) Durham County	6,105	2.77
Winston-Salem (city) Forsyth County	5,218	2.32
Wilmington (city) New Hanover County	5,142	4.91
Huntersville (town) Mecklenburg County	4,606	10.69
Jacksonville (city) Onslow County	4,366	6.33

Top 10 Places Sorted by Percent of Total Population
Based on all places, regardless of total population

Place	Population	%
Avon (cdp) Dare County	58	25.55
Hatteras (cdp) Dare County	123	23.75
Gatesville (town) Gates County	58	17.68

Place	Population	%
Casar (town) Cleveland County	61	16.76
Love Valley (town) Iredell County	3	15.79
Flat Rock (cdp) Surry County	181	13.44
Sunset Beach (town) Brunswick County	431	12.93
Bowmore (cdp) Hoke County	16	12.70
Wesley Chapel (village) Union County	838	12.50
Porters Neck (cdp) New Hanover County	600	12.03

Top 10 Places Sorted by Percent of Total Population
Based on places with total population of 50,000 or more

Place	Population	%
Cary (town) Wake County	9,428	7.39
Jacksonville (city) Onslow County	4,366	6.33
Concord (city) Cabarrus County	4,223	5.62
Wilmington (city) New Hanover County	5,142	4.91
Chapel Hill (town) Orange County	2,665	4.83
Charlotte (city) Mecklenburg County	28,643	4.06
Greenville (city) Pitt County	3,183	3.96
Raleigh (city) Wake County	14,642	3.83
Asheville (city) Buncombe County	2,842	3.47
Fayetteville (city) Cumberland County	6,535	3.29

Latvian

Top 10 Places Sorted by Population
Based on all places, regardless of total population

Place	Population	%
Raleigh (city) Wake County	119	0.03
Charlotte (city) Mecklenburg County	105	0.01
Winston-Salem (city) Forsyth County	102	0.05
Chapel Hill (town) Orange County	68	0.12
Wilmington (city) New Hanover County	51	0.05
Durham (city) Durham County	42	0.02
Marion (city) McDowell County	38	0.47
Fayetteville (city) Cumberland County	33	0.02
Cary (town) Wake County	30	0.02
Huntersville (town) Mecklenburg County	23	0.05

Top 10 Places Sorted by Percent of Total Population
Based on all places, regardless of total population

Place	Population	%
Walnut Creek (village) Wayne County	10	1.05
Beulaville (town) Duplin County	8	0.48
Marion (city) McDowell County	38	0.47
Valley Hill (cdp) Henderson County	11	0.42
Kitty Hawk (town) Dare County	11	0.34
Woodfin (town) Buncombe County	14	0.24
Carolina Shores (town) Brunswick County	7	0.24
Andrews (town) Cherokee County	5	0.24
Lake Park (village) Union County	6	0.19
Biltmore Forest (town) Buncombe County	3	0.19

Top 10 Places Sorted by Percent of Total Population
Based on places with total population of 50,000 or more

Place	Population	%
Chapel Hill (town) Orange County	68	0.12
Winston-Salem (city) Forsyth County	102	0.05
Wilmington (city) New Hanover County	51	0.05
Raleigh (city) Wake County	119	0.03
Asheville (city) Buncombe County	21	0.03
Durham (city) Durham County	42	0.02
Fayetteville (city) Cumberland County	33	0.02
Cary (town) Wake County	30	0.02
High Point (city) Guilford County	17	0.02
Greenville (city) Pitt County	14	0.02

Lithuanian

Top 10 Places Sorted by Population
Based on all places, regardless of total population

Place	Population	%
Charlotte (city) Mecklenburg County	856	0.12
Raleigh (city) Wake County	566	0.15
Cary (town) Wake County	356	0.28
Wilmington (city) New Hanover County	272	0.26
Durham (city) Durham County	270	0.12
Winston-Salem (city) Forsyth County	252	0.11
Greensboro (city) Guilford County	243	0.09
Chapel Hill (town) Orange County	224	0.41
Pinehurst (village) Moore County	206	1.65
Clayton (town) Johnston County	191	1.30

Top 10 Places Sorted by Percent of Total Population
Based on all places, regardless of total population

Place	Population	%
Bolivia (town) Brunswick County	8	5.84
Duck (town) Dare County	11	2.82
Fruitland (cdp) Henderson County	39	2.48
Atlantic Beach (town) Carteret County	37	1.93
Carolina Shores (town) Brunswick County	54	1.89
Pinehurst (village) Moore County	206	1.65
Hampstead (cdp) Pender County	54	1.46
Porters Neck (cdp) New Hanover County	72	1.44
Clayton (town) Johnston County	191	1.30
Whispering Pines (village) Moore County	32	1.15

Top 10 Places Sorted by Percent of Total Population
Based on places with total population of 50,000 or more

Place	Population	%
Chapel Hill (town) Orange County	224	0.41
Cary (town) Wake County	356	0.28
Wilmington (city) New Hanover County	272	0.26
Asheville (city) Buncombe County	173	0.21
Greenville (city) Pitt County	130	0.16
Raleigh (city) Wake County	566	0.15
Charlotte (city) Mecklenburg County	856	0.12
Durham (city) Durham County	270	0.12
Winston-Salem (city) Forsyth County	252	0.11
Concord (city) Cabarrus County	76	0.10

Luxemburger

Top 10 Places Sorted by Population
Based on all places, regardless of total population

Place	Population	%
Hillsborough (town) Orange County	73	1.22
St. Stephens (cdp) Catawba County	22	0.24
Jacksonville (city) Onslow County	22	0.03
Lake Park (village) Union County	17	0.52
Monroe (city) Union County	17	0.05
Raleigh (city) Wake County	17	<0.01
Clemmons (village) Forsyth County	13	0.07
Asheville (city) Buncombe County	12	0.01
Greensboro (city) Guilford County	9	<0.01
Biltmore Forest (town) Buncombe County	3	0.19

Top 10 Places Sorted by Percent of Total Population
Based on all places, regardless of total population

Place	Population	%
Hillsborough (town) Orange County	73	1.22
Lake Park (village) Union County	17	0.52
St. Stephens (cdp) Catawba County	22	0.24
Biltmore Forest (town) Buncombe County	3	0.19
Clemmons (village) Forsyth County	13	0.07
Monroe (city) Union County	17	0.05
Jacksonville (city) Onslow County	22	0.03
Asheville (city) Buncombe County	12	0.01
Raleigh (city) Wake County	17	<0.01
Greensboro (city) Guilford County	9	<0.01

Top 10 Places Sorted by Percent of Total Population
Based on places with total population of 50,000 or more

Place	Population	%
Jacksonville (city) Onslow County	22	0.03
Asheville (city) Buncombe County	12	0.01
Raleigh (city) Wake County	17	<0.01
Greensboro (city) Guilford County	9	<0.01
Cary (town) Wake County	0	0.00
Chapel Hill (town) Orange County	0	0.00
Charlotte (city) Mecklenburg County	0	0.00
Concord (city) Cabarrus County	0	0.00
Durham (city) Durham County	0	0.00
Fayetteville (city) Cumberland County	0	0.00

Macedonian

Top 10 Places Sorted by Population
Based on all places, regardless of total population

Place	Population	%
Cornelius (town) Mecklenburg County	19	0.08
Southern Shores (town) Dare County	16	0.60
St. James (town) Brunswick County	16	0.57

Place	Population	%
New Bern (city) Craven County	14	0.05
Cary (town) Wake County	13	0.01
Havelock (city) Craven County	12	0.06
Huntersville (town) Mecklenburg County	11	0.03
Durham (city) Durham County	11	<0.01
Mineral Springs (town) Union County	3	0.12
Aberdeen (town) Moore County	0	0.00

Top 10 Places Sorted by Percent of Total Population
Based on all places, regardless of total population

Place	Population	%
Southern Shores (town) Dare County	16	0.60
St. James (town) Brunswick County	16	0.57
Mineral Springs (town) Union County	3	0.12
Cornelius (town) Mecklenburg County	19	0.08
Havelock (city) Craven County	12	0.06
New Bern (city) Craven County	14	0.05
Huntersville (town) Mecklenburg County	11	0.03
Cary (town) Wake County	13	0.01
Durham (city) Durham County	11	<0.01
Aberdeen (town) Moore County	0	0.00

Top 10 Places Sorted by Percent of Total Population
Based on places with total population of 50,000 or more

Place	Population	%
Cary (town) Wake County	13	0.01
Durham (city) Durham County	11	<0.01
Asheville (city) Buncombe County	0	0.00
Chapel Hill (town) Orange County	0	0.00
Charlotte (city) Mecklenburg County	0	0.00
Concord (city) Cabarrus County	0	0.00
Fayetteville (city) Cumberland County	0	0.00
Gastonia (city) Gaston County	0	0.00
Greensboro (city) Guilford County	0	0.00
Greenville (city) Pitt County	0	0.00

Maltese

Top 10 Places Sorted by Population
Based on all places, regardless of total population

Place	Population	%
Charlotte (city) Mecklenburg County	156	0.02
Raleigh (city) Wake County	94	0.02
Pinehurst (village) Moore County	45	0.36
Wake Forest (town) Wake County	45	0.17
Stallings (town) Union County	41	0.32
Cary (town) Wake County	29	0.02
Fayetteville (city) Cumberland County	25	0.01
Edenton (town) Chowan County	19	0.37
Morehead City (town) Carteret County	18	0.21
Trent Woods (town) Craven County	16	0.39

Top 10 Places Sorted by Percent of Total Population
Based on all places, regardless of total population

Place	Population	%
Whispering Pines (village) Moore County	11	0.40
Trent Woods (town) Craven County	16	0.39
Edenton (town) Chowan County	19	0.37
Pinehurst (village) Moore County	45	0.36
Stallings (town) Union County	41	0.32
Morehead City (town) Carteret County	18	0.21
Wake Forest (town) Wake County	45	0.17
Swansboro (town) Onslow County	3	0.12
Murraysville (cdp) New Hanover County	14	0.11
Morrisville (town) Wake County	12	0.07

Top 10 Places Sorted by Percent of Total Population
Based on places with total population of 50,000 or more

Place	Population	%
Charlotte (city) Mecklenburg County	156	0.02
Raleigh (city) Wake County	94	0.02
Cary (town) Wake County	29	0.02
Fayetteville (city) Cumberland County	25	0.01
Greensboro (city) Guilford County	9	<0.01
Asheville (city) Buncombe County	0	0.00
Chapel Hill (town) Orange County	0	0.00
Concord (city) Cabarrus County	0	0.00
Durham (city) Durham County	0	0.00
Gastonia (city) Gaston County	0	0.00

New Zealander

Top 10 Places Sorted by Population
Based on all places, regardless of total population

Place	Population	%
Charlotte (city) Mecklenburg County	72	0.01
Chapel Hill (town) Orange County	49	0.09
Mooresville (town) Iredell County	44	0.14
Kannapolis (city) Cabarrus County	37	0.09
Kings Grant (cdp) New Hanover County	34	0.41
Wilmington (city) New Hanover County	30	0.03
Lake Junaluska (cdp) Haywood County	27	0.99
Jacksonville (city) Onslow County	23	0.03
Morehead City (town) Carteret County	22	0.26
Hampstead (cdp) Pender County	14	0.38

Top 10 Places Sorted by Percent of Total Population
Based on all places, regardless of total population

Place	Population	%
Lake Junaluska (cdp) Haywood County	27	0.99
Kings Grant (cdp) New Hanover County	34	0.41
Westport (cdp) Lincoln County	13	0.39
Hampstead (cdp) Pender County	14	0.38
Swannanoa (cdp) Buncombe County	12	0.29
Morehead City (town) Carteret County	22	0.26
Mooresville (town) Iredell County	44	0.14
Pittsboro (town) Chatham County	5	0.14
Chapel Hill (town) Orange County	49	0.09
Kannapolis (city) Cabarrus County	37	0.09

Top 10 Places Sorted by Percent of Total Population
Based on places with total population of 50,000 or more

Place	Population	%
Chapel Hill (town) Orange County	49	0.09
Wilmington (city) New Hanover County	30	0.03
Jacksonville (city) Onslow County	23	0.03
Charlotte (city) Mecklenburg County	72	0.01
Durham (city) Durham County	12	0.01
Winston-Salem (city) Forsyth County	12	0.01
Asheville (city) Buncombe County	0	0.00
Cary (town) Wake County	0	0.00
Concord (city) Cabarrus County	0	0.00
Fayetteville (city) Cumberland County	0	0.00

Northern European

Top 10 Places Sorted by Population
Based on all places, regardless of total population

Place	Population	%
Charlotte (city) Mecklenburg County	357	0.05
Durham (city) Durham County	261	0.12
Raleigh (city) Wake County	261	0.07
Cary (town) Wake County	236	0.18
Chapel Hill (town) Orange County	156	0.28
Asheville (city) Buncombe County	132	0.16
Clemmons (village) Forsyth County	126	0.69
Greensboro (city) Guilford County	116	0.04
Carrboro (town) Orange County	84	0.44
Concord (city) Cabarrus County	81	0.11

Top 10 Places Sorted by Percent of Total Population
Based on all places, regardless of total population

Place	Population	%
Germanton (cdp) Forsyth County	14	2.08
Flat Rock (village) Henderson County	30	0.98
Duck (town) Dare County	3	0.77
Mountain Home (cdp) Henderson County	24	0.75
Clemmons (village) Forsyth County	126	0.69
Beaufort (town) Carteret County	27	0.68
St. James (town) Brunswick County	18	0.65
Rolesville (town) Wake County	21	0.64
Blowing Rock (town) Watauga County	7	0.54
Whispering Pines (village) Moore County	14	0.51

Top 10 Places Sorted by Percent of Total Population
Based on places with total population of 50,000 or more

Place	Population	%
Chapel Hill (town) Orange County	156	0.28
Cary (town) Wake County	236	0.18
Asheville (city) Buncombe County	132	0.16
Durham (city) Durham County	261	0.12

Concord (city) Cabarrus County	81	0.11
Raleigh (city) Wake County	261	0.07
Charlotte (city) Mecklenburg County	357	0.05
Greensboro (city) Guilford County	116	0.04
Winston-Salem (city) Forsyth County	58	0.03
Wilmington (city) New Hanover County	29	0.03

Norwegian

Top 10 Places Sorted by Population
Based on all places, regardless of total population

Place	Population	%
Charlotte (city) Mecklenburg County	3,212	0.46
Raleigh (city) Wake County	2,108	0.55
Cary (town) Wake County	1,260	0.99
Winston-Salem (city) Forsyth County	1,252	0.56
Durham (city) Durham County	1,246	0.57
Fayetteville (city) Cumberland County	1,032	0.52
Greensboro (city) Guilford County	1,013	0.38
Asheville (city) Buncombe County	841	1.03
Wilmington (city) New Hanover County	634	0.61
High Point (city) Guilford County	629	0.62

Top 10 Places Sorted by Percent of Total Population
Based on all places, regardless of total population

Place	Population	%
Godwin (town) Cumberland County	18	13.43
Rodanthe (cdp) Dare County	35	8.37
Linden (town) Cumberland County	10	8.33
Keener (cdp) Sampson County	16	5.78
Horse Shoe (cdp) Henderson County	123	4.39
Aurora (town) Beaufort County	23	4.22
Bunnlevel (cdp) Harnett County	23	4.12
Bald Head Island (village) Brunswick County	3	4.00
Cameron (town) Moore County	13	3.88
Caswell Beach (town) Brunswick County	22	3.51

Top 10 Places Sorted by Percent of Total Population
Based on places with total population of 50,000 or more

Place	Population	%
Asheville (city) Buncombe County	841	1.03
Cary (town) Wake County	1,260	0.99
Chapel Hill (town) Orange County	526	0.95
Jacksonville (city) Onslow County	487	0.71
Greenville (city) Pitt County	536	0.67
High Point (city) Guilford County	629	0.62
Wilmington (city) New Hanover County	634	0.61
Durham (city) Durham County	1,246	0.57
Winston-Salem (city) Forsyth County	1,252	0.56
Raleigh (city) Wake County	2,108	0.55

Pennsylvania German

Top 10 Places Sorted by Population
Based on all places, regardless of total population

Place	Population	%
Charlotte (city) Mecklenburg County	203	0.03
Greensboro (city) Guilford County	143	0.05
Huntersville (town) Mecklenburg County	78	0.18
Durham (city) Durham County	53	0.02
Concord (city) Cabarrus County	48	0.06
Fayetteville (city) Cumberland County	45	0.02
Raleigh (city) Wake County	44	0.01
Goldsboro (city) Wayne County	39	0.11
Jacksonville (city) Onslow County	39	0.06
New Bern (city) Craven County	37	0.13

Top 10 Places Sorted by Percent of Total Population
Based on all places, regardless of total population

Place	Population	%
Sandy Creek (town) Brunswick County	17	4.51
Gloucester (cdp) Carteret County	13	3.26
Swansboro (town) Onslow County	27	1.12
Caswell Beach (town) Brunswick County	6	0.96
Duck (town) Dare County	3	0.77
Bayshore (cdp) New Hanover County	31	0.73
Royal Pines (cdp) Buncombe County	30	0.71
Zebulon (town) Wake County	28	0.64
Sugar Mountain (village) Avery County	3	0.63
Staley (town) Randolph County	3	0.59

Top 10 Places Sorted by Percent of Total Population
Based on places with total population of 50,000 or more

Place	Population	%
Concord (city) Cabarrus County	48	0.06
Jacksonville (city) Onslow County	39	0.06
Greensboro (city) Guilford County	143	0.05
Charlotte (city) Mecklenburg County	203	0.03
Wilmington (city) New Hanover County	30	0.03
Asheville (city) Buncombe County	21	0.03
Chapel Hill (town) Orange County	16	0.03
Rocky Mount (city) Nash County	16	0.03
Durham (city) Durham County	53	0.02
Fayetteville (city) Cumberland County	45	0.02

Polish

Top 10 Places Sorted by Population
Based on all places, regardless of total population

Place	Population	%
Charlotte (city) Mecklenburg County	12,055	1.71
Raleigh (city) Wake County	7,411	1.94
Cary (town) Wake County	4,181	3.28
Durham (city) Durham County	3,725	1.69
Greensboro (city) Guilford County	3,312	1.26
Fayetteville (city) Cumberland County	2,868	1.44
Asheville (city) Buncombe County	2,531	3.09
Winston-Salem (city) Forsyth County	2,333	1.04
Wilmington (city) New Hanover County	1,997	1.91
Jacksonville (city) Onslow County	1,751	2.54

Top 10 Places Sorted by Percent of Total Population
Based on all places, regardless of total population

Place	Population	%
Salvo (cdp) Dare County	25	28.41
Elk Park (town) Avery County	135	20.21
Waves (cdp) Dare County	15	14.56
Hatteras (cdp) Dare County	73	14.09
Bowmore (cdp) Hoke County	16	12.70
Lake Santeetlah (town) Graham County	9	12.50
St. Helena (village) Pender County	49	10.65
Barker Heights (cdp) Henderson County	135	9.13
Bethania (town) Forsyth County	26	9.12
Marvin (village) Union County	429	8.77

Top 10 Places Sorted by Percent of Total Population
Based on places with total population of 50,000 or more

Place	Population	%
Cary (town) Wake County	4,181	3.28
Asheville (city) Buncombe County	2,531	3.09
Chapel Hill (town) Orange County	1,646	2.98
Jacksonville (city) Onslow County	1,751	2.54
Concord (city) Cabarrus County	1,562	2.08
Raleigh (city) Wake County	7,411	1.94
Wilmington (city) New Hanover County	1,997	1.91
Charlotte (city) Mecklenburg County	12,055	1.71
Durham (city) Durham County	3,725	1.69
Fayetteville (city) Cumberland County	2,868	1.44

Portuguese

Top 10 Places Sorted by Population
Based on all places, regardless of total population

Place	Population	%
Charlotte (city) Mecklenburg County	1,157	0.16
Fayetteville (city) Cumberland County	503	0.25
Raleigh (city) Wake County	370	0.10
Jacksonville (city) Onslow County	317	0.46
Durham (city) Durham County	279	0.13
Greensboro (city) Guilford County	273	0.10
Winston-Salem (city) Forsyth County	268	0.12
Cary (town) Wake County	267	0.21
High Point (city) Guilford County	253	0.25
Black Mountain (town) Buncombe County	247	3.16

Top 10 Places Sorted by Percent of Total Population
Based on all places, regardless of total population

Place	Population	%
Hassell (town) Martin County	5	8.93
Foscoe (cdp) Watauga County	60	7.33
Crossnore (town) Avery County	9	4.84

Place	Population	%
Delco (cdp) Columbus County	16	4.60
Middlesex (town) Nash County	31	4.09
Avery Creek (cdp) Buncombe County	89	3.93
Black Mountain (town) Buncombe County	247	3.16
Neuse Forest (cdp) Craven County	37	2.43
Ossipee (town) Alamance County	10	1.78
Rich Square (town) Northampton County	21	1.77

Top 10 Places Sorted by Percent of Total Population
Based on places with total population of 50,000 or more

Place	Population	%
Jacksonville (city) Onslow County	317	0.46
Fayetteville (city) Cumberland County	503	0.25
High Point (city) Guilford County	253	0.25
Wilmington (city) New Hanover County	242	0.23
Greenville (city) Pitt County	183	0.23
Cary (town) Wake County	267	0.21
Chapel Hill (town) Orange County	96	0.17
Charlotte (city) Mecklenburg County	1,157	0.16
Durham (city) Durham County	279	0.13
Winston-Salem (city) Forsyth County	268	0.12

Romanian

Top 10 Places Sorted by Population
Based on all places, regardless of total population

Place	Population	%
Charlotte (city) Mecklenburg County	1,248	0.18
Asheville (city) Buncombe County	759	0.93
Durham (city) Durham County	421	0.19
Raleigh (city) Wake County	418	0.11
Cary (town) Wake County	211	0.17
Winston-Salem (city) Forsyth County	194	0.09
Huntersville (town) Mecklenburg County	188	0.44
Chapel Hill (town) Orange County	176	0.32
Greensboro (city) Guilford County	160	0.06
Concord (city) Cabarrus County	104	0.14

Top 10 Places Sorted by Percent of Total Population
Based on all places, regardless of total population

Place	Population	%
Fairview (cdp) Buncombe County	74	2.71
Skippers Corner (cdp) New Hanover County	58	2.53
Sharpsburg (town) Nash County	50	2.32
James (town) Guilford County	76	2.30
Royal Pines (cdp) Buncombe County	66	1.57
Sugar Mountain (village) Avery County	7	1.46
East Flat Rock (cdp) Henderson County	72	1.25
Woodfin (town) Buncombe County	71	1.20
Misenheimer (village) Stanly County	10	1.09
St. James (town) Brunswick County	30	1.08

Top 10 Places Sorted by Percent of Total Population
Based on places with total population of 50,000 or more

Place	Population	%
Asheville (city) Buncombe County	759	0.93
Chapel Hill (town) Orange County	176	0.32
Durham (city) Durham County	421	0.19
Charlotte (city) Mecklenburg County	1,248	0.18
Cary (town) Wake County	211	0.17
Jacksonville (city) Onslow County	102	0.15
Concord (city) Cabarrus County	104	0.14
Raleigh (city) Wake County	418	0.11
Winston-Salem (city) Forsyth County	194	0.09
Wilmington (city) New Hanover County	82	0.08

Russian

Top 10 Places Sorted by Population
Based on all places, regardless of total population

Place	Population	%
Charlotte (city) Mecklenburg County	5,549	0.79
Raleigh (city) Wake County	2,411	0.63
Durham (city) Durham County	1,774	0.81
Cary (town) Wake County	1,625	1.27
Greensboro (city) Guilford County	1,444	0.55
Winston-Salem (city) Forsyth County	1,097	0.49
Chapel Hill (town) Orange County	946	1.71
Fayetteville (city) Cumberland County	914	0.46
Asheville (city) Buncombe County	655	0.80
Wilmington (city) New Hanover County	603	0.58

Top 10 Places Sorted by Percent of Total Population
Based on all places, regardless of total population

Place	Population	%
Lake Santeetlah (town) Graham County	6	8.33
Autryville (town) Sampson County	16	7.41
Neuse Forest (cdp) Craven County	93	6.11
Marshallberg (cdp) Carteret County	19	5.86
Balfour (cdp) Henderson County	62	5.73
St. Helena (village) Pender County	23	5.00
Fearrington Village (cdp) Chatham County	113	4.81
Blowing Rock (town) Watauga County	55	4.27
Saxapahaw (cdp) Alamance County	48	4.26
Whispering Pines (village) Moore County	115	4.15

Top 10 Places Sorted by Percent of Total Population
Based on places with total population of 50,000 or more

Place	Population	%
Chapel Hill (town) Orange County	946	1.71
Cary (town) Wake County	1,625	1.27
Durham (city) Durham County	1,774	0.81
Asheville (city) Buncombe County	655	0.80
Charlotte (city) Mecklenburg County	5,549	0.79
Concord (city) Cabarrus County	594	0.79
Jacksonville (city) Onslow County	471	0.68
Raleigh (city) Wake County	2,411	0.63
Wilmington (city) New Hanover County	603	0.58
Greensboro (city) Guilford County	1,444	0.55

Scandinavian

Top 10 Places Sorted by Population
Based on all places, regardless of total population

Place	Population	%
Charlotte (city) Mecklenburg County	609	0.09
Winston-Salem (city) Forsyth County	344	0.15
Raleigh (city) Wake County	318	0.08
Greensboro (city) Guilford County	313	0.12
Durham (city) Durham County	287	0.13
Asheville (city) Buncombe County	279	0.34
Cary (town) Wake County	251	0.20
Statesville (city) Iredell County	180	0.73
Morrisville (town) Wake County	159	0.98
Huntersville (town) Mecklenburg County	144	0.33

Top 10 Places Sorted by Percent of Total Population
Based on all places, regardless of total population

Place	Population	%
Polkville (city) Cleveland County	23	3.42
Severn (town) Northampton County	9	2.50
Varnam (town) Brunswick County	14	2.34
Southport (city) Brunswick County	50	1.80
East Spencer (town) Rowan County	23	1.34
Montreat (town) Buncombe County	10	1.26
Seagrove (town) Randolph County	2	1.12
Louisburg (town) Franklin County	37	1.11
Franklinton (town) Franklin County	23	1.11
Bunn (town) Franklin County	5	1.11

Top 10 Places Sorted by Percent of Total Population
Based on places with total population of 50,000 or more

Place	Population	%
Asheville (city) Buncombe County	279	0.34
Cary (town) Wake County	251	0.20
Chapel Hill (town) Orange County	102	0.18
Jacksonville (city) Onslow County	120	0.17
Winston-Salem (city) Forsyth County	344	0.15
Durham (city) Durham County	287	0.13
Greensboro (city) Guilford County	313	0.12
Charlotte (city) Mecklenburg County	609	0.09
Raleigh (city) Wake County	318	0.08
Concord (city) Cabarrus County	50	0.07

Scotch-Irish

Top 10 Places Sorted by Population
Based on all places, regardless of total population

Place	Population	%
Charlotte (city) Mecklenburg County	25,971	3.68
Raleigh (city) Wake County	12,189	3.18
Greensboro (city) Guilford County	8,719	3.31

Place	Population	%
Winston-Salem (city) Forsyth County	6,601	2.94
Durham (city) Durham County	6,163	2.80
Fayetteville (city) Cumberland County	5,414	2.72
Wilmington (city) New Hanover County	5,317	5.08
Asheville (city) Buncombe County	4,845	5.91
Cary (town) Wake County	4,549	3.57
Gastonia (city) Gaston County	3,416	4.83

Top 10 Places Sorted by Percent of Total Population
Based on all places, regardless of total population

Place	Population	%
Mamers (cdp) Harnett County	265	28.25
Chimney Rock Village (village) Rutherford County	51	27.72
Cliffside (cdp) Rutherford County	109	27.25
White Oak (cdp) Bladen County	37	26.06
Dublin (town) Bladen County	49	23.44
Hillsdale (cdp) Davie County	117	21.27
Webster (town) Jackson County	108	19.60
Lake Junaluska (cdp) Haywood County	527	19.40
Marshallberg (cdp) Carteret County	61	18.83
Horse Shoe (cdp) Henderson County	517	18.46

Top 10 Places Sorted by Percent of Total Population
Based on places with total population of 50,000 or more

Place	Population	%
Asheville (city) Buncombe County	4,845	5.91
Chapel Hill (town) Orange County	2,806	5.09
Wilmington (city) New Hanover County	5,317	5.08
Gastonia (city) Gaston County	3,416	4.83
Concord (city) Cabarrus County	3,224	4.29
Charlotte (city) Mecklenburg County	25,971	3.68
Cary (town) Wake County	4,549	3.57
Greensboro (city) Guilford County	8,719	3.31
Raleigh (city) Wake County	12,189	3.18
High Point (city) Guilford County	3,160	3.13

Scottish

Top 10 Places Sorted by Population
Based on all places, regardless of total population

Place	Population	%
Charlotte (city) Mecklenburg County	17,085	2.42
Raleigh (city) Wake County	10,633	2.78
Greensboro (city) Guilford County	6,491	2.46
Winston-Salem (city) Forsyth County	4,986	2.22
Fayetteville (city) Cumberland County	4,887	2.46
Durham (city) Durham County	4,809	2.18
Cary (town) Wake County	3,944	3.09
Wilmington (city) New Hanover County	3,498	3.34
Asheville (city) Buncombe County	3,480	4.25
Chapel Hill (town) Orange County	2,770	5.02

Top 10 Places Sorted by Percent of Total Population
Based on all places, regardless of total population

Place	Population	%
Salvo (cdp) Dare County	25	28.41
Deercroft (cdp) Scotland County	95	21.02
Gerton (cdp) Henderson County	78	20.00
Ingold (cdp) Sampson County	84	17.65
Buxton (cdp) Dare County	168	17.54
Montreat (town) Buncombe County	120	15.09
Crossnore (town) Avery County	28	15.05
Centerville (town) Franklin County	14	14.74
Indian Beach (town) Carteret County	18	14.63
Pikeville (town) Wayne County	85	14.46

Top 10 Places Sorted by Percent of Total Population
Based on places with total population of 50,000 or more

Place	Population	%
Chapel Hill (town) Orange County	2,770	5.02
Asheville (city) Buncombe County	3,480	4.25
Wilmington (city) New Hanover County	3,498	3.34
Cary (town) Wake County	3,944	3.09
Raleigh (city) Wake County	10,633	2.78
Jacksonville (city) Onslow County	1,917	2.78
Greenville (city) Pitt County	2,193	2.73
Gastonia (city) Gaston County	1,911	2.70
Concord (city) Cabarrus County	1,983	2.64
Greensboro (city) Guilford County	6,491	2.46

Serbian

Top 10 Places Sorted by Population
Based on all places, regardless of total population

Place	Population	%
Charlotte (city) Mecklenburg County	362	0.05
High Point (city) Guilford County	250	0.25
Winston-Salem (city) Forsyth County	99	0.04
Jacksonville (city) Onslow County	95	0.14
Greensboro (city) Guilford County	93	0.04
Thomasville (city) Davidson County	88	0.33
Durham (city) Durham County	74	0.03
Raleigh (city) Wake County	72	0.02
Swannanoa (cdp) Buncombe County	60	1.43
King (city) Stokes County	56	0.84

Top 10 Places Sorted by Percent of Total Population
Based on all places, regardless of total population

Place	Population	%
Swannanoa (cdp) Buncombe County	60	1.43
Banner Elk (town) Avery County	13	1.40
Pine Level (town) Johnston County	14	0.91
King (city) Stokes County	56	0.84
Biscoe (town) Montgomery County	17	0.68
Cherokee (cdp) Jackson County	17	0.53
Creedmoor (city) Granville County	20	0.52
Mars Hill (town) Madison County	14	0.51
Butner (town) Granville County	36	0.49
Maggie Valley (town) Haywood County	4	0.37

Top 10 Places Sorted by Percent of Total Population
Based on places with total population of 50,000 or more

Place	Population	%
High Point (city) Guilford County	250	0.25
Jacksonville (city) Onslow County	95	0.14
Charlotte (city) Mecklenburg County	362	0.05
Winston-Salem (city) Forsyth County	99	0.04
Greensboro (city) Guilford County	93	0.04
Durham (city) Durham County	74	0.03
Cary (town) Wake County	36	0.03
Raleigh (city) Wake County	72	0.02
Fayetteville (city) Cumberland County	29	0.01
Asheville (city) Buncombe County	10	0.01

Slavic

Top 10 Places Sorted by Population
Based on all places, regardless of total population

Place	Population	%
Charlotte (city) Mecklenburg County	340	0.05
Chapel Hill (town) Orange County	122	0.22
High Point (city) Guilford County	109	0.11
Huntersville (town) Mecklenburg County	96	0.22
Wilmington (city) New Hanover County	90	0.09
Lenoir (city) Caldwell County	75	0.41
Durham (city) Durham County	67	0.03
Raleigh (city) Wake County	66	0.02
Aberdeen (town) Moore County	64	1.09
Jacksonville (city) Onslow County	54	0.08

Top 10 Places Sorted by Percent of Total Population
Based on all places, regardless of total population

Place	Population	%
Aquadale (cdp) Stanly County	15	3.06
Parkton (town) Robeson County	11	2.45
Bogue (town) Carteret County	13	1.62
Aberdeen (town) Moore County	64	1.09
Winfall (town) Perquimans County	7	0.93
Pittsboro (town) Chatham County	26	0.73
St. Helena (village) Pender County	3	0.65
Half Moon (cdp) Onslow County	46	0.56
Pine Level (town) Johnston County	8	0.52
Foxfire (village) Moore County	4	0.51

Top 10 Places Sorted by Percent of Total Population
Based on places with total population of 50,000 or more

Place	Population	%
Chapel Hill (town) Orange County	122	0.22
High Point (city) Guilford County	109	0.11
Wilmington (city) New Hanover County	90	0.09
Jacksonville (city) Onslow County	54	0.08

Place	Population	%
Charlotte (city) Mecklenburg County	340	0.05
Asheville (city) Buncombe County	32	0.04
Durham (city) Durham County	67	0.03
Cary (town) Wake County	41	0.03
Rocky Mount (city) Nash County	16	0.03
Raleigh (city) Wake County	66	0.02

Slovak

Top 10 Places Sorted by Population
Based on all places, regardless of total population

Place	Population	%
Charlotte (city) Mecklenburg County	1,441	0.20
Raleigh (city) Wake County	651	0.17
Cary (town) Wake County	448	0.35
Greensboro (city) Guilford County	331	0.13
Durham (city) Durham County	281	0.13
Huntersville (town) Mecklenburg County	277	0.64
Apex (town) Wake County	263	0.76
Winston-Salem (city) Forsyth County	196	0.09
Wilmington (city) New Hanover County	195	0.19
Fayetteville (city) Cumberland County	174	0.09

Top 10 Places Sorted by Percent of Total Population
Based on all places, regardless of total population

Place	Population	%
Richlands (town) Onslow County	42	2.81
Belville (town) Brunswick County	34	1.80
Bogue (town) Carteret County	13	1.62
Minnesott Beach (town) Pamlico County	6	1.56
Locust (city) Stanly County	46	1.55
Laurel Hill (cdp) Scotland County	20	1.38
Walnut Creek (village) Wayne County	11	1.16
Vander (cdp) Cumberland County	11	1.11
Murraysville (cdp) New Hanover County	144	1.08
Sunset Beach (town) Brunswick County	35	1.05

Top 10 Places Sorted by Percent of Total Population
Based on places with total population of 50,000 or more

Place	Population	%
Cary (town) Wake County	448	0.35
Chapel Hill (town) Orange County	124	0.22
Charlotte (city) Mecklenburg County	1,441	0.20
Wilmington (city) New Hanover County	195	0.19
Raleigh (city) Wake County	651	0.17
Greensboro (city) Guilford County	331	0.13
Durham (city) Durham County	281	0.13
Jacksonville (city) Onslow County	74	0.11
High Point (city) Guilford County	96	0.10
Winston-Salem (city) Forsyth County	196	0.09

Slovene

Top 10 Places Sorted by Population
Based on all places, regardless of total population

Place	Population	%
Charlotte (city) Mecklenburg County	255	0.04
Durham (city) Durham County	104	0.05
Cary (town) Wake County	70	0.05
Pinehurst (village) Moore County	60	0.48
Apex (town) Wake County	60	0.17
Tarboro (town) Edgecombe County	57	0.50
Asheville (city) Buncombe County	44	0.05
Wake Forest (town) Wake County	42	0.16
Raleigh (city) Wake County	39	0.01
Greensboro (city) Guilford County	38	0.01

Top 10 Places Sorted by Percent of Total Population
Based on all places, regardless of total population

Place	Population	%
Kure Beach (town) New Hanover County	24	1.48
Cramerton (town) Gaston County	32	0.81
Franklin (town) Macon County	29	0.75
Calabash (town) Brunswick County	12	0.64
Buies Creek (cdp) Harnett County	23	0.62
Tarboro (town) Edgecombe County	57	0.50
Pinehurst (village) Moore County	60	0.48
Pine Knoll Shores (town) Carteret County	6	0.40
Ogden (cdp) New Hanover County	18	0.27
Clyde (town) Haywood County	2	0.20

Top 10 Places Sorted by Percent of Total Population
Based on places with total population of 50,000 or more

Place	Population	%
Chapel Hill (town) Orange County	32	0.06
Durham (city) Durham County	104	0.05
Cary (town) Wake County	70	0.05
Asheville (city) Buncombe County	44	0.05
Charlotte (city) Mecklenburg County	255	0.04
High Point (city) Guilford County	34	0.03
Wilmington (city) New Hanover County	24	0.02
Jacksonville (city) Onslow County	14	0.02
Raleigh (city) Wake County	39	0.01
Greensboro (city) Guilford County	38	0.01

Soviet Union

Top 10 Places Sorted by Population
Based on all places, regardless of total population

Place	Population	%
Aberdeen (town) Moore County	0	0.00
Advance (cdp) Davie County	0	0.00
Ahoskie (town) Hertford County	0	0.00
Alamance (village) Alamance County	0	0.00
Albemarle (city) Stanly County	0	0.00
Alliance (town) Pamlico County	0	0.00
Altamahaw (cdp) Alamance County	0	0.00
Andrews (town) Cherokee County	0	0.00
Angier (town) Harnett County	0	0.00
Ansonville (town) Anson County	0	0.00

Top 10 Places Sorted by Percent of Total Population
Based on all places, regardless of total population

Place	Population	%
Aberdeen (town) Moore County	0	0.00
Advance (cdp) Davie County	0	0.00
Ahoskie (town) Hertford County	0	0.00
Alamance (village) Alamance County	0	0.00
Albemarle (city) Stanly County	0	0.00
Alliance (town) Pamlico County	0	0.00
Altamahaw (cdp) Alamance County	0	0.00
Andrews (town) Cherokee County	0	0.00
Angier (town) Harnett County	0	0.00
Ansonville (town) Anson County	0	0.00

Top 10 Places Sorted by Percent of Total Population
Based on places with total population of 50,000 or more

Place	Population	%
Asheville (city) Buncombe County	0	0.00
Cary (town) Wake County	0	0.00
Chapel Hill (town) Orange County	0	0.00
Charlotte (city) Mecklenburg County	0	0.00
Concord (city) Cabarrus County	0	0.00
Durham (city) Durham County	0	0.00
Fayetteville (city) Cumberland County	0	0.00
Gastonia (city) Gaston County	0	0.00
Greensboro (city) Guilford County	0	0.00
Greenville (city) Pitt County	0	0.00

Swedish

Top 10 Places Sorted by Population
Based on all places, regardless of total population

Place	Population	%
Charlotte (city) Mecklenburg County	4,136	0.59
Raleigh (city) Wake County	2,719	0.71
Cary (town) Wake County	1,679	1.32
Greensboro (city) Guilford County	1,509	0.57
Fayetteville (city) Cumberland County	1,416	0.71
Durham (city) Durham County	1,342	0.61
Winston-Salem (city) Forsyth County	928	0.41
High Point (city) Guilford County	838	0.83
Chapel Hill (town) Orange County	795	1.44
Jacksonville (city) Onslow County	661	0.96

Top 10 Places Sorted by Percent of Total Population
Based on all places, regardless of total population

Place	Population	%
Riegelwood (cdp) Columbus County	91	14.51
Watha (town) Pender County	16	7.96
Flat Rock (village) Henderson County	218	7.15

Place	Population	%
Avery Creek (cdp) Buncombe County	162	7.15
Grandfather (village) Avery County	8	6.78
Wade (town) Cumberland County	30	6.67
Chimney Rock Village (village) Rutherford County	9	4.89
Stoneville (town) Rockingham County	49	4.72
Bolivia (town) Brunswick County	6	4.38
Seven Devils (town) Watauga County	8	4.23

Top 10 Places Sorted by Percent of Total Population
Based on places with total population of 50,000 or more

Place	Population	%
Chapel Hill (town) Orange County	795	1.44
Cary (town) Wake County	1,679	1.32
Jacksonville (city) Onslow County	661	0.96
High Point (city) Guilford County	838	0.83
Asheville (city) Buncombe County	620	0.76
Raleigh (city) Wake County	2,719	0.71
Fayetteville (city) Cumberland County	1,416	0.71
Durham (city) Durham County	1,342	0.61
Charlotte (city) Mecklenburg County	4,136	0.59
Greensboro (city) Guilford County	1,509	0.57

Swiss

Top 10 Places Sorted by Population
Based on all places, regardless of total population

Place	Population	%
Charlotte (city) Mecklenburg County	1,724	0.24
Raleigh (city) Wake County	846	0.22
Asheville (city) Buncombe County	492	0.60
Chapel Hill (town) Orange County	422	0.76
Durham (city) Durham County	381	0.17
Greensboro (city) Guilford County	367	0.14
Cary (town) Wake County	345	0.27
Winston-Salem (city) Forsyth County	272	0.12
Apex (town) Wake County	205	0.60
Huntersville (town) Mecklenburg County	194	0.45

Top 10 Places Sorted by Percent of Total Population
Based on all places, regardless of total population

Place	Population	%
JAARS (cdp) Union County	48	9.82
Avon (cdp) Dare County	17	7.49
Caswell Beach (town) Brunswick County	41	6.55
Oriental (town) Pamlico County	49	5.08
Watha (town) Pender County	5	2.49
Tyro (cdp) Davidson County	90	2.29
Minnesott Beach (town) Pamlico County	7	1.82
Seven Devils (town) Watauga County	3	1.59
Stedman (town) Cumberland County	17	1.58
Pikeville (town) Wayne County	9	1.53

Top 10 Places Sorted by Percent of Total Population
Based on places with total population of 50,000 or more

Place	Population	%
Chapel Hill (town) Orange County	422	0.76
Asheville (city) Buncombe County	492	0.60
Cary (town) Wake County	345	0.27
Charlotte (city) Mecklenburg County	1,724	0.24
Raleigh (city) Wake County	846	0.22
Greenville (city) Pitt County	142	0.18
Durham (city) Durham County	381	0.17
Concord (city) Cabarrus County	125	0.17
Wilmington (city) New Hanover County	161	0.15
Greensboro (city) Guilford County	367	0.14

Turkish

Top 10 Places Sorted by Population
Based on all places, regardless of total population

Place	Population	%
Charlotte (city) Mecklenburg County	809	0.11
Raleigh (city) Wake County	329	0.09
Durham (city) Durham County	262	0.12
Wilmington (city) New Hanover County	186	0.18
Fuquay-Varina (town) Wake County	168	1.04
Cary (town) Wake County	147	0.12
Fayetteville (city) Cumberland County	124	0.06
Holly Springs (town) Wake County	78	0.36
Chapel Hill (town) Orange County	68	0.12
Apex (town) Wake County	64	0.19

Top 10 Places Sorted by Percent of Total Population
Based on all places, regardless of total population

Place	Population	%
Rougemont (cdp) Durham County	12	1.53
Fuquay-Varina (town) Wake County	168	1.04
Mar-Mac (cdp) Wayne County	35	1.03
Mars Hill (town) Madison County	14	0.51
Holly Springs (town) Wake County	78	0.36
Leland (town) Brunswick County	43	0.36
Lewisville (town) Forsyth County	38	0.30
Murraysville (cdp) New Hanover County	38	0.29
Rhodhiss (town) Burke County	3	0.24
Rutherfordton (town) Rutherford County	9	0.21

Top 10 Places Sorted by Percent of Total Population
Based on places with total population of 50,000 or more

Place	Population	%
Wilmington (city) New Hanover County	186	0.18
Durham (city) Durham County	262	0.12
Cary (town) Wake County	147	0.12
Chapel Hill (town) Orange County	68	0.12
Charlotte (city) Mecklenburg County	809	0.11
Raleigh (city) Wake County	329	0.09
Fayetteville (city) Cumberland County	124	0.06
Greenville (city) Pitt County	31	0.04
Asheville (city) Buncombe County	20	0.02
Greensboro (city) Guilford County	32	0.01

Ukrainian

Top 10 Places Sorted by Population
Based on all places, regardless of total population

Place	Population	%
Charlotte (city) Mecklenburg County	1,867	0.26
Raleigh (city) Wake County	846	0.22
Asheville (city) Buncombe County	745	0.91
Cary (town) Wake County	630	0.49
Durham (city) Durham County	597	0.27
Indian Trail (town) Union County	418	1.38
Chapel Hill (town) Orange County	334	0.61
Greensboro (city) Guilford County	323	0.12
Wilmington (city) New Hanover County	256	0.24
Winston-Salem (city) Forsyth County	251	0.11

Top 10 Places Sorted by Percent of Total Population
Based on all places, regardless of total population

Place	Population	%
Balfour (cdp) Henderson County	68	6.28
Camden (cdp) Camden County	28	5.24
Fairview (cdp) Buncombe County	124	4.55
Ocracoke (cdp) Hyde County	17	3.95
St. Helena (village) Pender County	12	2.61
Vander (cdp) Cumberland County	22	2.21
Mills River (town) Henderson County	140	2.11
Foscoe (cdp) Watauga County	15	1.83
Misenheimer (village) Stanly County	16	1.74
Saluda (city) Polk County	11	1.57

Top 10 Places Sorted by Percent of Total Population
Based on places with total population of 50,000 or more

Place	Population	%
Asheville (city) Buncombe County	745	0.91
Chapel Hill (town) Orange County	334	0.61
Cary (town) Wake County	630	0.49
Durham (city) Durham County	597	0.27
Charlotte (city) Mecklenburg County	1,867	0.26
Wilmington (city) New Hanover County	256	0.24
High Point (city) Guilford County	239	0.24
Raleigh (city) Wake County	846	0.22
Greenville (city) Pitt County	161	0.20
Concord (city) Cabarrus County	139	0.18

Welsh

Top 10 Places Sorted by Population
Based on all places, regardless of total population

Place	Population	%
Charlotte (city) Mecklenburg County	4,719	0.67
Raleigh (city) Wake County	3,130	0.82
Winston-Salem (city) Forsyth County	1,806	0.80

Place	Population	%
Durham (city) Durham County	1,397	0.63
Cary (town) Wake County	1,388	1.09
Greensboro (city) Guilford County	1,239	0.47
Asheville (city) Buncombe County	1,103	1.35
Wilmington (city) New Hanover County	993	0.95
Fayetteville (city) Cumberland County	983	0.49
Chapel Hill (town) Orange County	805	1.46

Top 10 Places Sorted by Percent of Total Population
Based on all places, regardless of total population

Place	Population	%
Bayview (cdp) Beaufort County	35	9.54
Banner Elk (town) Avery County	75	8.06
Hoopers Creek (cdp) Henderson County	76	7.04
Hobucken (cdp) Pamlico County	16	6.84
Ocracoke (cdp) Hyde County	29	6.74
Davis (cdp) Carteret County	27	6.00
Lake Santeetlah (town) Graham County	4	5.56
Bald Head Island (village) Brunswick County	4	5.33
Sunset Beach (town) Brunswick County	159	4.77
Grandfather (village) Avery County	5	4.24

Top 10 Places Sorted by Percent of Total Population
Based on places with total population of 50,000 or more

Place	Population	%
Chapel Hill (town) Orange County	805	1.46
Asheville (city) Buncombe County	1,103	1.35
Cary (town) Wake County	1,388	1.09
Wilmington (city) New Hanover County	993	0.95
Raleigh (city) Wake County	3,130	0.82
Winston-Salem (city) Forsyth County	1,806	0.80
Charlotte (city) Mecklenburg County	4,719	0.67
Greenville (city) Pitt County	536	0.67
Durham (city) Durham County	1,397	0.63
Jacksonville (city) Onslow County	397	0.58

West Indian, excluding Hispanic

Top 10 Places Sorted by Population
Based on all places, regardless of total population

Place	Population	%
Charlotte (city) Mecklenburg County	4,254	0.60
Fayetteville (city) Cumberland County	2,462	1.24
Durham (city) Durham County	2,283	1.04
Raleigh (city) Wake County	2,282	0.60
Greensboro (city) Guilford County	1,334	0.51
Cary (town) Wake County	1,010	0.79
Winston-Salem (city) Forsyth County	968	0.43
Concord (city) Cabarrus County	794	1.06
Jacksonville (city) Onslow County	773	1.12
High Point (city) Guilford County	626	0.62

Top 10 Places Sorted by Percent of Total Population
Based on all places, regardless of total population

Place	Population	%
Saxapahaw (cdp) Alamance County	124	10.99
Coats (town) Harnett County	160	7.55
Greenevers (town) Duplin County	68	7.17
Hassell (town) Martin County	4	7.14
East Arcadia (town) Bladen County	31	6.20
Rolesville (town) Wake County	165	5.02
Dover (town) Craven County	16	3.09
Hertford (town) Perquimans County	56	3.03
Kittrell (town) Vance County	27	3.03
Stedman (town) Cumberland County	31	2.88

Top 10 Places Sorted by Percent of Total Population
Based on places with total population of 50,000 or more

Place	Population	%
Fayetteville (city) Cumberland County	2,462	1.24
Jacksonville (city) Onslow County	773	1.12
Concord (city) Cabarrus County	794	1.06
Durham (city) Durham County	2,283	1.04
Cary (town) Wake County	1,010	0.79
Chapel Hill (town) Orange County	411	0.74
High Point (city) Guilford County	626	0.62
Charlotte (city) Mecklenburg County	4,254	0.60
Raleigh (city) Wake County	2,282	0.60
Greensboro (city) Guilford County	1,334	0.51

West Indian: Bahamian, excluding Hispanic

Top 10 Places Sorted by Population
Based on all places, regardless of total population

Place	Population	%
Raleigh (city) Wake County	184	0.05
High Point (city) Guilford County	155	0.15
Roanoke Rapids (city) Halifax County	141	0.89
Charlotte (city) Mecklenburg County	122	0.02
Durham (city) Durham County	42	0.02
Fayetteville (city) Cumberland County	31	0.02
Pineville (town) Mecklenburg County	26	0.36
Salisbury (city) Rowan County	20	0.06
Knightdale (town) Wake County	18	0.17
Wilson (city) Wilson County	18	0.04

Top 10 Places Sorted by Percent of Total Population
Based on all places, regardless of total population

Place	Population	%
Whitakers (town) Edgecombe County	8	1.23
Roanoke Rapids (city) Halifax County	141	0.89
Pineville (town) Mecklenburg County	26	0.36
Knightdale (town) Wake County	18	0.17
High Point (city) Guilford County	155	0.15
Kings Mountain (city) Cleveland County	14	0.13
Mount Airy (city) Surry County	14	0.13
Navassa (town) Brunswick County	2	0.11
Hope Mills (town) Cumberland County	11	0.08
Salisbury (city) Rowan County	20	0.06

Top 10 Places Sorted by Percent of Total Population
Based on places with total population of 50,000 or more

Place	Population	%
High Point (city) Guilford County	155	0.15
Raleigh (city) Wake County	184	0.05
Charlotte (city) Mecklenburg County	122	0.02
Durham (city) Durham County	42	0.02
Fayetteville (city) Cumberland County	31	0.02
Gastonia (city) Gaston County	12	0.02
Greensboro (city) Guilford County	15	0.01
Winston-Salem (city) Forsyth County	9	<0.01
Asheville (city) Buncombe County	0	0.00
Cary (town) Wake County	0	0.00

West Indian: Barbadian, excluding Hispanic

Top 10 Places Sorted by Population
Based on all places, regardless of total population

Place	Population	%
Winston-Salem (city) Forsyth County	222	0.10
Charlotte (city) Mecklenburg County	148	0.02
Greensboro (city) Guilford County	57	0.02
Kinston (city) Lenoir County	40	0.18
Wilmington (city) New Hanover County	38	0.04
Fayetteville (city) Cumberland County	31	0.02
Raleigh (city) Wake County	31	0.01
Rocky Mount (city) Nash County	27	0.05
Rolesville (town) Wake County	26	0.79
East Arcadia (town) Bladen County	22	4.40

Top 10 Places Sorted by Percent of Total Population
Based on all places, regardless of total population

Place	Population	%
East Arcadia (town) Bladen County	22	4.40
Rolesville (town) Wake County	26	0.79
Kinston (city) Lenoir County	40	0.18
Washington (city) Beaufort County	16	0.16
Winston-Salem (city) Forsyth County	222	0.10
Archdale (city) Randolph County	8	0.07
Rocky Mount (city) Nash County	27	0.05
Wilmington (city) New Hanover County	38	0.04
Chapel Hill (town) Orange County	14	0.03
Charlotte (city) Mecklenburg County	148	0.02

Top 10 Places Sorted by Percent of Total Population
Based on places with total population of 50,000 or more

Place	Population	%
Winston-Salem (city) Forsyth County	222	0.10

Place	Population	%
Rocky Mount (city) Nash County	27	0.05
Wilmington (city) New Hanover County	38	0.04
Chapel Hill (town) Orange County	14	0.03
Charlotte (city) Mecklenburg County	148	0.02
Greensboro (city) Guilford County	57	0.02
Fayetteville (city) Cumberland County	31	0.02
Raleigh (city) Wake County	31	0.01
Jacksonville (city) Onslow County	6	0.01
Asheville (city) Buncombe County	0	0.00

West Indian: Belizean, excluding Hispanic

Top 10 Places Sorted by Population
Based on all places, regardless of total population

Place	Population	%
New Bern (city) Craven County	70	0.25
Woodfin (town) Buncombe County	50	0.85
Cary (town) Wake County	40	0.03
Wake Forest (town) Wake County	35	0.13
Havelock (city) Craven County	32	0.16
Winston-Salem (city) Forsyth County	30	0.01
Raleigh (city) Wake County	29	0.01
Charlotte (city) Mecklenburg County	20	<0.01
Newport (town) Carteret County	17	0.43
Garner (town) Wake County	16	0.07

Top 10 Places Sorted by Percent of Total Population
Based on all places, regardless of total population

Place	Population	%
Woodfin (town) Buncombe County	50	0.85
Saluda (city) Polk County	5	0.71
Newport (town) Carteret County	17	0.43
New Bern (city) Craven County	70	0.25
Havelock (city) Craven County	32	0.16
Wake Forest (town) Wake County	35	0.13
Garner (town) Wake County	16	0.07
Rockingham (city) Richmond County	5	0.05
Cary (town) Wake County	40	0.03
Wilson (city) Wilson County	13	0.03

Top 10 Places Sorted by Percent of Total Population
Based on places with total population of 50,000 or more

Place	Population	%
Cary (town) Wake County	40	0.03
Jacksonville (city) Onslow County	15	0.02
Winston-Salem (city) Forsyth County	30	0.01
Raleigh (city) Wake County	29	0.01
Charlotte (city) Mecklenburg County	20	<0.01
Fayetteville (city) Cumberland County	7	<0.01
Asheville (city) Buncombe County	0	0.00
Chapel Hill (town) Orange County	0	0.00
Concord (city) Cabarrus County	0	0.00
Durham (city) Durham County	0	0.00

West Indian: Bermudan, excluding Hispanic

Top 10 Places Sorted by Population
Based on all places, regardless of total population

Place	Population	%
Forest Oaks (cdp) Guilford County	58	1.71
Greensboro (city) Guilford County	34	0.01
Charlotte (city) Mecklenburg County	16	<0.01
Apex (town) Wake County	10	0.03
Aberdeen (town) Moore County	0	0.00
Advance (cdp) Davie County	0	0.00
Ahoskie (town) Hertford County	0	0.00
Alamance (village) Alamance County	0	0.00
Albemarle (city) Stanly County	0	0.00
Alliance (town) Pamlico County	0	0.00

Top 10 Places Sorted by Percent of Total Population
Based on all places, regardless of total population

Place	Population	%
Forest Oaks (cdp) Guilford County	58	1.71
Apex (town) Wake County	10	0.03
Greensboro (city) Guilford County	34	0.01
Charlotte (city) Mecklenburg County	16	<0.01
Aberdeen (town) Moore County	0	0.00
Advance (cdp) Davie County	0	0.00
Ahoskie (town) Hertford County	0	0.00

Place	Population	%
Alamance (village) Alamance County	0	0.00
Albemarle (city) Stanly County	0	0.00
Alliance (town) Pamlico County	0	0.00

Top 10 Places Sorted by Percent of Total Population
Based on places with total population of 50,000 or more

Place	Population	%
Greensboro (city) Guilford County	34	0.01
Charlotte (city) Mecklenburg County	16	<0.01
Asheville (city) Buncombe County	0	0.00
Cary (town) Wake County	0	0.00
Chapel Hill (town) Orange County	0	0.00
Concord (city) Cabarrus County	0	0.00
Durham (city) Durham County	0	0.00
Fayetteville (city) Cumberland County	0	0.00
Gastonia (city) Gaston County	0	0.00
Greenville (city) Pitt County	0	0.00

West Indian: British West Indian, excluding Hispanic

Top 10 Places Sorted by Population
Based on all places, regardless of total population

Place	Population	%
Fayetteville (city) Cumberland County	333	0.17
Roanoke Rapids (city) Halifax County	142	0.90
Raleigh (city) Wake County	83	0.02
Charlotte (city) Mecklenburg County	82	0.01
Durham (city) Durham County	60	0.03
Chapel Hill (town) Orange County	55	0.10
Havelock (city) Craven County	38	0.18
Lenoir (city) Caldwell County	26	0.14
High Point (city) Guilford County	22	0.02
Goldsboro (city) Wayne County	8	0.02

Top 10 Places Sorted by Percent of Total Population
Based on all places, regardless of total population

Place	Population	%
Roanoke Rapids (city) Halifax County	142	0.90
Havelock (city) Craven County	38	0.18
Fayetteville (city) Cumberland County	333	0.17
Dobson (town) Surry County	3	0.16
Lenoir (city) Caldwell County	26	0.14
Chapel Hill (town) Orange County	55	0.10
Oxford (city) Granville County	7	0.08
Durham (city) Durham County	60	0.03
Raleigh (city) Wake County	83	0.02
High Point (city) Guilford County	22	0.02

Top 10 Places Sorted by Percent of Total Population
Based on places with total population of 50,000 or more

Place	Population	%
Fayetteville (city) Cumberland County	333	0.17
Chapel Hill (town) Orange County	55	0.10
Durham (city) Durham County	60	0.03
Raleigh (city) Wake County	83	0.02
High Point (city) Guilford County	22	0.02
Charlotte (city) Mecklenburg County	82	0.01
Asheville (city) Buncombe County	0	0.00
Cary (town) Wake County	0	0.00
Concord (city) Cabarrus County	0	0.00
Gastonia (city) Gaston County	0	0.00

West Indian: Dutch West Indian, excluding Hispanic

Top 10 Places Sorted by Population
Based on all places, regardless of total population

Place	Population	%
Charlotte (city) Mecklenburg County	56	0.01
Durham (city) Durham County	46	0.02
Fayetteville (city) Cumberland County	28	0.01
High Point (city) Guilford County	24	0.02
Hemby Bridge (town) Union County	21	1.34
Roseboro (town) Sampson County	13	0.84
Jacksonville (city) Onslow County	13	0.02
High Shoals (town) Gaston County	10	1.86
Oak Ridge (town) Guilford County	10	0.17
Greenville (city) Pitt County	8	0.01

Please refer to the Explanation of Data in the front of the book for more detailed information.

Top 10 Places Sorted by Percent of Total Population
Based on all places, regardless of total population

Place	Population	%
High Shoals (town) Gaston County	10	1.86
Hemby Bridge (town) Union County	21	1.34
Roseboro (town) Sampson County	13	0.84
Wallburg (town) Davidson County	6	0.20
Oak Ridge (town) Guilford County	10	0.17
Connelly Springs (town) Burke County	2	0.13
Durham (city) Durham County	46	0.02
High Point (city) Guilford County	24	0.02
Jacksonville (city) Onslow County	13	0.02
Goldsboro (city) Wayne County	7	0.02

Top 10 Places Sorted by Percent of Total Population
Based on places with total population of 50,000 or more

Place	Population	%
Durham (city) Durham County	46	0.02
High Point (city) Guilford County	24	0.02
Jacksonville (city) Onslow County	13	0.02
Charlotte (city) Mecklenburg County	56	0.01
Fayetteville (city) Cumberland County	28	0.01
Greenville (city) Pitt County	8	0.01
Asheville (city) Buncombe County	0	0.00
Cary (town) Wake County	0	0.00
Chapel Hill (town) Orange County	0	0.00
Concord (city) Cabarrus County	0	0.00

West Indian: Haitian, excluding Hispanic

Top 10 Places Sorted by Population
Based on all places, regardless of total population

Place	Population	%
Durham (city) Durham County	452	0.21
Fayetteville (city) Cumberland County	406	0.20
Charlotte (city) Mecklenburg County	403	0.06
Raleigh (city) Wake County	300	0.08
Concord (city) Cabarrus County	248	0.33
Mooresville (town) Iredell County	219	0.72
Winston-Salem (city) Forsyth County	191	0.08
Coats (town) Harnett County	160	7.55
Cary (town) Wake County	151	0.12
High Point (city) Guilford County	115	0.11

Top 10 Places Sorted by Percent of Total Population
Based on all places, regardless of total population

Place	Population	%
Coats (town) Harnett County	160	7.55
Hassell (town) Martin County	4	7.14
Wanchese (cdp) Dare County	47	2.68
Bayboro (town) Pamlico County	15	1.07
Four Oaks (town) Johnston County	16	0.86
Murfreesboro (town) Hertford County	23	0.83
Warsaw (town) Duplin County	24	0.78
Mooresville (town) Iredell County	219	0.72
Summerfield (town) Guilford County	65	0.68
Shelby (city) Cleveland County	113	0.55

Top 10 Places Sorted by Percent of Total Population
Based on places with total population of 50,000 or more

Place	Population	%
Concord (city) Cabarrus County	248	0.33
Durham (city) Durham County	452	0.21
Fayetteville (city) Cumberland County	406	0.20
Jacksonville (city) Onslow County	89	0.13
Cary (town) Wake County	151	0.12
High Point (city) Guilford County	115	0.11
Chapel Hill (town) Orange County	57	0.10
Raleigh (city) Wake County	300	0.08
Winston-Salem (city) Forsyth County	191	0.08
Rocky Mount (city) Nash County	39	0.07

West Indian: Jamaican, excluding Hispanic

Top 10 Places Sorted by Population
Based on all places, regardless of total population

Place	Population	%
Charlotte (city) Mecklenburg County	2,278	0.32
Raleigh (city) Wake County	914	0.24

Place	Population	%
Durham (city) Durham County	885	0.40
Greensboro (city) Guilford County	860	0.33
Fayetteville (city) Cumberland County	803	0.40
Jacksonville (city) Onslow County	450	0.65
Winston-Salem (city) Forsyth County	398	0.18
Cary (town) Wake County	325	0.25
Havelock (city) Craven County	260	1.26
Chapel Hill (town) Orange County	258	0.47

Top 10 Places Sorted by Percent of Total Population
Based on all places, regardless of total population

Place	Population	%
Saxapahaw (cdp) Alamance County	124	10.99
Rolesville (town) Wake County	103	3.13
Dover (town) Craven County	16	3.09
Kittrell (town) Vance County	27	3.03
Stedman (town) Cumberland County	31	2.88
Hertford (town) Perquimans County	48	2.60
Barker Heights (cdp) Henderson County	32	2.16
Havelock (city) Craven County	260	1.26
Stanley (town) Gaston County	43	1.24
Garland (town) Sampson County	7	0.97

Top 10 Places Sorted by Percent of Total Population
Based on places with total population of 50,000 or more

Place	Population	%
Jacksonville (city) Onslow County	450	0.65
Chapel Hill (town) Orange County	258	0.47
Durham (city) Durham County	885	0.40
Fayetteville (city) Cumberland County	803	0.40
Rocky Mount (city) Nash County	204	0.35
Greensboro (city) Guilford County	860	0.33
Charlotte (city) Mecklenburg County	2,278	0.32
Concord (city) Cabarrus County	233	0.31
Cary (town) Wake County	325	0.25
Raleigh (city) Wake County	914	0.24

West Indian: Trinidadian and Tobagonian, excluding Hispanic

Top 10 Places Sorted by Population
Based on all places, regardless of total population

Place	Population	%
Charlotte (city) Mecklenburg County	241	0.03
Greenville (city) Pitt County	195	0.24
Concord (city) Cabarrus County	193	0.26
High Point (city) Guilford County	186	0.18
Fayetteville (city) Cumberland County	147	0.07
Greensboro (city) Guilford County	123	0.05
Raleigh (city) Wake County	107	0.03
Cary (town) Wake County	96	0.08
Asheville (city) Buncombe County	92	0.11
Winston-Salem (city) Forsyth County	75	0.03

Top 10 Places Sorted by Percent of Total Population
Based on all places, regardless of total population

Place	Population	%
Greenevers (town) Duplin County	68	7.17
Kenansville (town) Duplin County	25	2.31
Louisburg (town) Franklin County	65	1.95
East Arcadia (town) Bladen County	9	1.80
St. Helena (village) Pender County	3	0.65
Mars Hill (town) Madison County	13	0.48
Rolesville (town) Wake County	14	0.43
Hertford (town) Perquimans County	8	0.43
Windsor (town) Bertie County	13	0.39
Yanceyville (town) Caswell County	9	0.36

Top 10 Places Sorted by Percent of Total Population
Based on places with total population of 50,000 or more

Place	Population	%
Concord (city) Cabarrus County	193	0.26
Greenville (city) Pitt County	195	0.24
High Point (city) Guilford County	186	0.18
Asheville (city) Buncombe County	92	0.11
Cary (town) Wake County	96	0.08
Jacksonville (city) Onslow County	52	0.08
Fayetteville (city) Cumberland County	147	0.07
Greensboro (city) Guilford County	123	0.05
Charlotte (city) Mecklenburg County	241	0.03
Raleigh (city) Wake County	107	0.03

West Indian: U.S. Virgin Islander, excluding Hispanic

Top 10 Places Sorted by Population
Based on all places, regardless of total population

Place	Population	%
Fayetteville (city) Cumberland County	61	0.03
Winston-Salem (city) Forsyth County	18	0.01
Raleigh (city) Wake County	14	<0.01
Cary (town) Wake County	12	0.01
Charlotte (city) Mecklenburg County	12	0.01
Durham (city) Durham County	8	<0.01
Pollocksville (town) Jones County	3	0.83
Goldsboro (city) Wayne County	3	0.01
Aberdeen (town) Moore County	0	0.00
Advance (cdp) Davie County	0	0.00

Top 10 Places Sorted by Percent of Total Population
Based on all places, regardless of total population

Place	Population	%
Pollocksville (town) Jones County	3	0.83
Fayetteville (city) Cumberland County	61	0.03
Winston-Salem (city) Forsyth County	18	0.01
Cary (town) Wake County	12	0.01
Goldsboro (city) Wayne County	3	0.01
Raleigh (city) Wake County	14	<0.01
Charlotte (city) Mecklenburg County	12	<0.01
Durham (city) Durham County	8	<0.01
Aberdeen (town) Moore County	0	0.00
Advance (cdp) Davie County	0	0.00

Top 10 Places Sorted by Percent of Total Population
Based on places with total population of 50,000 or more

Place	Population	%
Fayetteville (city) Cumberland County	61	0.03
Winston-Salem (city) Forsyth County	18	0.01
Cary (town) Wake County	12	0.01
Raleigh (city) Wake County	14	<0.01
Charlotte (city) Mecklenburg County	12	<0.01
Durham (city) Durham County	8	<0.01
Asheville (city) Buncombe County	0	0.00
Chapel Hill (town) Orange County	0	0.00
Concord (city) Cabarrus County	0	0.00
Gastonia (city) Gaston County	0	0.00

West Indian: West Indian, excluding Hispanic

Top 10 Places Sorted by Population
Based on all places, regardless of total population

Place	Population	%
Charlotte (city) Mecklenburg County	855	0.12
Durham (city) Durham County	732	0.33
Raleigh (city) Wake County	620	0.16
Fayetteville (city) Cumberland County	615	0.31
Cary (town) Wake County	386	0.30
Greensboro (city) Guilford County	200	0.08
Piney Green (cdp) Onslow County	182	1.31
Hope Mills (town) Cumberland County	174	1.21
Jacksonville (city) Onslow County	148	0.21
Spring Lake (town) Cumberland County	138	1.17

Top 10 Places Sorted by Percent of Total Population
Based on all places, regardless of total population

Place	Population	%
Richlands (town) Onslow County	36	2.41
Bolton (town) Columbus County	15	2.06
Wendell (town) Wake County	100	1.80
Piney Green (cdp) Onslow County	182	1.31
Cofield (village) Hertford County	4	1.28
Hope Mills (town) Cumberland County	174	1.21
Spring Lake (town) Cumberland County	138	1.17
Rolesville (town) Wake County	22	0.67
Polkton (town) Anson County	18	0.55
Statesville (city) Iredell County	128	0.52

Top 10 Places Sorted by Percent of Total Population
Based on places with total population of 50,000 or more

Place	Population	%
Durham (city) Durham County	732	0.33

Fayetteville (city) Cumberland County	615	0.31
Cary (town) Wake County	386	0.30
Jacksonville (city) Onslow County	148	0.21
Raleigh (city) Wake County	620	0.16
Concord (city) Cabarrus County	120	0.16
Charlotte (city) Mecklenburg County	855	0.12
Wilmington (city) New Hanover County	121	0.12
Gastonia (city) Gaston County	78	0.11
Greensboro (city) Guilford County	200	0.08

West Indian: Other, excluding Hispanic

Top 10 Places Sorted by Population
Based on all places, regardless of total population

Place	Population	%
Charlotte (city) Mecklenburg County	21	<0.01
Aberdeen (town) Moore County	0	0.00
Advance (cdp) Davie County	0	0.00
Ahoskie (town) Hertford County	0	0.00
Alamance (village) Alamance County	0	0.00
Albemarle (city) Stanly County	0	0.00
Alliance (town) Pamlico County	0	0.00
Altamahaw (cdp) Alamance County	0	0.00
Andrews (town) Cherokee County	0	0.00
Angier (town) Harnett County	0	0.00

Top 10 Places Sorted by Percent of Total Population
Based on all places, regardless of total population

Place	Population	%
Charlotte (city) Mecklenburg County	21	<0.01
Aberdeen (town) Moore County	0	0.00
Advance (cdp) Davie County	0	0.00
Ahoskie (town) Hertford County	0	0.00
Alamance (village) Alamance County	0	0.00
Albemarle (city) Stanly County	0	0.00
Alliance (town) Pamlico County	0	0.00
Altamahaw (cdp) Alamance County	0	0.00
Andrews (town) Cherokee County	0	0.00
Angier (town) Harnett County	0	0.00

Top 10 Places Sorted by Percent of Total Population
Based on places with total population of 50,000 or more

Place	Population	%
Charlotte (city) Mecklenburg County	21	<0.01
Asheville (city) Buncombe County	0	0.00
Cary (town) Wake County	0	0.00
Chapel Hill (town) Orange County	0	0.00
Concord (city) Cabarrus County	0	0.00
Durham (city) Durham County	0	0.00
Fayetteville (city) Cumberland County	0	0.00
Gastonia (city) Gaston County	0	0.00
Greensboro (city) Guilford County	0	0.00
Greenville (city) Pitt County	0	0.00

Yugoslavian

Top 10 Places Sorted by Population
Based on all places, regardless of total population

Place	Population	%
Charlotte (city) Mecklenburg County	1,220	0.17
High Point (city) Guilford County	269	0.27
Greensboro (city) Guilford County	252	0.10
Cary (town) Wake County	202	0.16
Raleigh (city) Wake County	196	0.05
Wilmington (city) New Hanover County	181	0.17
Kernersville (town) Forsyth County	98	0.44
Indian Trail (town) Union County	84	0.28
Mint Hill (town) Mecklenburg County	79	0.36
Jacksonville (city) Onslow County	72	0.10

Top 10 Places Sorted by Percent of Total Population
Based on all places, regardless of total population

Place	Population	%
Walstonburg (town) Greene County	9	2.88
Ocean Isle Beach (town) Brunswick County	23	2.52
Granite Quarry (town) Rowan County	29	1.04
Cape Carteret (town) Carteret County	19	0.97
King (city) Stokes County	56	0.84
Creswell (town) Washington County	3	0.84
Fairview (cdp) Buncombe County	22	0.81
Wendell (town) Wake County	33	0.59

Alliance (town) Pamlico County	5	0.50
Kernersville (town) Forsyth County	98	0.44

Top 10 Places Sorted by Percent of Total Population
Based on places with total population of 50,000 or more

Place	Population	%
High Point (city) Guilford County	269	0.27
Charlotte (city) Mecklenburg County	1,220	0.17
Wilmington (city) New Hanover County	181	0.17
Cary (town) Wake County	202	0.16
Greensboro (city) Guilford County	252	0.10
Jacksonville (city) Onslow County	72	0.10
Chapel Hill (town) Orange County	54	0.10
Greenville (city) Pitt County	62	0.08
Raleigh (city) Wake County	196	0.05
Rocky Mount (city) Nash County	27	0.05

Hispanic Origin Rankings

Hispanic or Latino (of any race)

Top 10 Places Sorted by Population
Based on all places, regardless of total population

Place	Population	%
Charlotte (city) Mecklenburg County	95,688	13.08
Raleigh (city) Wake County	45,868	11.36
Winston-Salem (city) Forsyth County	33,753	14.70
Durham (city) Durham County	32,459	14.22
Greensboro (city) Guilford County	20,336	7.54
Fayetteville (city) Cumberland County	20,256	10.10
Cary (town) Wake County	10,364	7.66
Concord (city) Cabarrus County	9,754	12.34
Monroe (city) Union County	9,651	29.43
Jacksonville (city) Onslow County	9,106	12.98

Top 10 Places Sorted by Percent of Total Population
Based on all places, regardless of total population

Place	Population	%
Robbins (town) Moore County	552	50.32
Siler City (town) Chatham County	3,925	49.77
Ingold (cdp) Sampson County	195	41.40
Candor (town) Montgomery County	341	40.60
Magnolia (town) Duplin County	378	40.26
Faison (town) Duplin County	370	38.50
Barker Heights (cdp) Henderson County	456	36.36
Biscoe (town) Montgomery County	604	35.53
Selma (town) Johnston County	2,115	34.83
Rocky Point (cdp) Pender County	510	31.84

Top 10 Places Sorted by Percent of Total Population
Based on places with total population of 50,000 or more

Place	Population	%
Winston-Salem (city) Forsyth County	33,753	14.70
Durham (city) Durham County	32,459	14.22
Charlotte (city) Mecklenburg County	95,688	13.08
Jacksonville (city) Onslow County	9,106	12.98
Concord (city) Cabarrus County	9,754	12.34
Raleigh (city) Wake County	45,868	11.36
Fayetteville (city) Cumberland County	20,256	10.10
Gastonia (city) Gaston County	6,901	9.62
High Point (city) Guilford County	8,847	8.48
Cary (town) Wake County	10,364	7.66

Central American, excluding Mexican

Top 10 Places Sorted by Population
Based on all places, regardless of total population

Place	Population	%
Charlotte (city) Mecklenburg County	22,359	3.06
Durham (city) Durham County	8,052	3.53
Raleigh (city) Wake County	7,519	1.86
Winston-Salem (city) Forsyth County	3,757	1.64
Greensboro (city) Guilford County	2,246	0.83
Fayetteville (city) Cumberland County	2,238	1.12
Sanford (city) Lee County	1,749	6.23
Morganton (city) Burke County	1,633	9.65
Cary (town) Wake County	1,351	1.00
Burlington (city) Alamance County	1,275	2.55

Top 10 Places Sorted by Percent of Total Population
Based on all places, regardless of total population

Place	Population	%
Wallace (town) Duplin County	639	16.47
Magnolia (town) Duplin County	140	14.91
Siler City (town) Chatham County	995	12.62
Teachey (town) Duplin County	44	11.70
Bonnetsville (cdp) Sampson County	47	10.61
Rose Hill (town) Duplin County	168	10.33
Selma (town) Johnston County	591	9.73
Morganton (city) Burke County	1,633	9.65
Faison (town) Duplin County	75	7.80
Seven Springs (town) Wayne County	8	7.27

Top 10 Places Sorted by Percent of Total Population
Based on places with total population of 50,000 or more

Place	Population	%
Durham (city) Durham County	8,052	3.53
Charlotte (city) Mecklenburg County	22,359	3.06
Raleigh (city) Wake County	7,519	1.86
Winston-Salem (city) Forsyth County	3,757	1.64
Chapel Hill (town) Orange County	667	1.17
Fayetteville (city) Cumberland County	2,238	1.12
High Point (city) Guilford County	1,086	1.04
Asheville (city) Buncombe County	847	1.02
Cary (town) Wake County	1,351	1.00
Jacksonville (city) Onslow County	641	0.91

Central American: Costa Rican

Top 10 Places Sorted by Population
Based on all places, regardless of total population

Place	Population	%
Charlotte (city) Mecklenburg County	673	0.09
Lincolnton (city) Lincoln County	431	4.11
Raleigh (city) Wake County	164	0.04
Greensboro (city) Guilford County	132	0.05
Hickory (city) Catawba County	105	0.26
Cary (town) Wake County	82	0.06
Fayetteville (city) Cumberland County	81	0.04
Winston-Salem (city) Forsyth County	78	0.03
Gastonia (city) Gaston County	72	0.10
Durham (city) Durham County	64	0.03

Top 10 Places Sorted by Percent of Total Population
Based on all places, regardless of total population

Place	Population	%
Lincolnton (city) Lincoln County	431	4.11
Love Valley (town) Iredell County	2	2.22
Maiden (town) Catawba County	46	1.39
Falcon (town) Cumberland County	2	0.78
White Oak (cdp) Bladen County	2	0.59
Dallas (town) Gaston County	19	0.42
Moncure (cdp) Chatham County	3	0.42
St. Stephens (cdp) Catawba County	30	0.34
Cherryville (city) Gaston County	17	0.30
Mills River (town) Henderson County	19	0.28

Top 10 Places Sorted by Percent of Total Population
Based on places with total population of 50,000 or more

Place	Population	%
Gastonia (city) Gaston County	72	0.10
Charlotte (city) Mecklenburg County	673	0.09
Cary (town) Wake County	82	0.06
Jacksonville (city) Onslow County	43	0.06
Greensboro (city) Guilford County	132	0.05
Concord (city) Cabarrus County	43	0.05
Chapel Hill (town) Orange County	29	0.05
Raleigh (city) Wake County	164	0.04
Fayetteville (city) Cumberland County	81	0.04
High Point (city) Guilford County	43	0.04

Central American: Guatemalan

Top 10 Places Sorted by Population
Based on all places, regardless of total population

Place	Population	%
Charlotte (city) Mecklenburg County	2,421	0.33
Morganton (city) Burke County	1,507	8.91
Durham (city) Durham County	1,323	0.58
Raleigh (city) Wake County	978	0.24
Winston-Salem (city) Forsyth County	882	0.38
Greensboro (city) Guilford County	518	0.19
Siler City (town) Chatham County	502	6.36
Sanford (city) Lee County	429	1.53
Cary (town) Wake County	391	0.29
Monroe (city) Union County	342	1.04

Central American: Honduran

Top 10 Places Sorted by Percent of Total Population
Based on all places, regardless of total population

Place	Population	%
Morganton (city) Burke County	1,507	8.91
Seven Springs (town) Wayne County	8	7.27
Faison (town) Duplin County	67	6.97
Siler City (town) Chatham County	502	6.36
Dobson (town) Surry County	41	2.59
Robbins (town) Moore County	28	2.55
Mount Olive (town) Wayne County	99	2.16
North Wilkesboro (town) Wilkes County	91	2.14
Drexel (town) Burke County	37	1.99
Moravian Falls (cdp) Wilkes County	33	1.74

Top 10 Places Sorted by Percent of Total Population
Based on places with total population of 50,000 or more

Place	Population	%
Durham (city) Durham County	1,323	0.58
Chapel Hill (town) Orange County	223	0.39
Winston-Salem (city) Forsyth County	882	0.38
Charlotte (city) Mecklenburg County	2,421	0.33
Cary (town) Wake County	391	0.29
Raleigh (city) Wake County	978	0.24
Wilmington (city) New Hanover County	212	0.20
Greensboro (city) Guilford County	518	0.19
Concord (city) Cabarrus County	137	0.17
Jacksonville (city) Onslow County	111	0.16

Central American: Honduran

Top 10 Places Sorted by Population
Based on all places, regardless of total population

Place	Population	%
Charlotte (city) Mecklenburg County	7,557	1.03
Durham (city) Durham County	3,451	1.51
Raleigh (city) Wake County	2,345	0.58
Wallace (town) Duplin County	605	15.59
Winston-Salem (city) Forsyth County	497	0.22
Salisbury (city) Rowan County	488	1.45
Selma (town) Johnston County	416	6.85
Wilmington (city) New Hanover County	389	0.37
High Point (city) Guilford County	380	0.36
Greensboro (city) Guilford County	352	0.13

Top 10 Places Sorted by Percent of Total Population
Based on all places, regardless of total population

Place	Population	%
Wallace (town) Duplin County	605	15.59
Magnolia (town) Duplin County	113	12.03
Teachey (town) Duplin County	43	11.44
Rose Hill (town) Duplin County	160	9.84
Bonnetsville (cdp) Sampson County	35	7.90
Selma (town) Johnston County	416	6.85
Greenevers (town) Duplin County	22	3.47
Spencer (town) Rowan County	87	2.66
Watha (town) Pender County	5	2.63
Smithfield (town) Johnston County	274	2.50

Top 10 Places Sorted by Percent of Total Population
Based on places with total population of 50,000 or more

Place	Population	%
Durham (city) Durham County	3,451	1.51
Charlotte (city) Mecklenburg County	7,557	1.03
Raleigh (city) Wake County	2,345	0.58
Wilmington (city) New Hanover County	389	0.37
High Point (city) Guilford County	380	0.36
Gastonia (city) Gaston County	206	0.29
Concord (city) Cabarrus County	180	0.23
Winston-Salem (city) Forsyth County	497	0.22
Asheville (city) Buncombe County	181	0.22
Chapel Hill (town) Orange County	112	0.20

Central American: Nicaraguan

Top 10 Places Sorted by Population
Based on all places, regardless of total population

Place	Population	%
Charlotte (city) Mecklenburg County	1,320	0.18
Winston-Salem (city) Forsyth County	199	0.09
Raleigh (city) Wake County	184	0.05
Greensboro (city) Guilford County	159	0.06
Fayetteville (city) Cumberland County	157	0.08
Asheboro (city) Randolph County	98	0.39
Cary (town) Wake County	89	0.07
Jacksonville (city) Onslow County	80	0.11
Durham (city) Durham County	77	0.03
Gastonia (city) Gaston County	73	0.10

Top 10 Places Sorted by Percent of Total Population
Based on all places, regardless of total population

Place	Population	%
Harrells (town) Sampson County	6	2.97
Bonnetsville (cdp) Sampson County	5	1.13
Orrum (town) Robeson County	1	1.10
Turkey (town) Sampson County	3	1.03
Youngsville (town) Franklin County	9	0.78
Caroleen (cdp) Rutherford County	5	0.77
Fairplains (cdp) Wilkes County	14	0.66
Barker Heights (cdp) Henderson County	8	0.64
Brookford (town) Catawba County	2	0.52
Asheboro (city) Randolph County	98	0.39

Top 10 Places Sorted by Percent of Total Population
Based on places with total population of 50,000 or more

Place	Population	%
Charlotte (city) Mecklenburg County	1,320	0.18
Jacksonville (city) Onslow County	80	0.11
Gastonia (city) Gaston County	73	0.10
Winston-Salem (city) Forsyth County	199	0.09
Concord (city) Cabarrus County	72	0.09
Fayetteville (city) Cumberland County	157	0.08
Cary (town) Wake County	89	0.07
Greensboro (city) Guilford County	159	0.06
Raleigh (city) Wake County	184	0.05
Greenville (city) Pitt County	39	0.05

Central American: Panamanian

Top 10 Places Sorted by Population
Based on all places, regardless of total population

Place	Population	%
Fayetteville (city) Cumberland County	1,154	0.58
Charlotte (city) Mecklenburg County	608	0.08
Raleigh (city) Wake County	313	0.08
Greensboro (city) Guilford County	191	0.07
Durham (city) Durham County	159	0.07
Jacksonville (city) Onslow County	115	0.16
Winston-Salem (city) Forsyth County	115	0.05
Hope Mills (town) Cumberland County	88	0.58
Spring Lake (town) Cumberland County	80	0.67
Cary (town) Wake County	78	0.06

Top 10 Places Sorted by Percent of Total Population
Based on all places, regardless of total population

Place	Population	%
Falcon (town) Cumberland County	3	1.16
Rockfish (cdp) Hoke County	29	0.88
Aquadale (cdp) Stanly County	3	0.76
Spring Lake (town) Cumberland County	80	0.67
North Topsail Beach (town) Onslow County	5	0.67
Whitakers (town) Edgecombe County	5	0.67
Pumpkin Center (cdp) Onslow County	14	0.63
Fayetteville (city) Cumberland County	1,154	0.58
Hope Mills (town) Cumberland County	88	0.58
Millingport (cdp) Stanly County	3	0.50

Top 10 Places Sorted by Percent of Total Population
Based on places with total population of 50,000 or more

Place	Population	%
Fayetteville (city) Cumberland County	1,154	0.58
Jacksonville (city) Onslow County	115	0.16
Charlotte (city) Mecklenburg County	608	0.08
Raleigh (city) Wake County	313	0.08

Chapel Hill (town) Orange County	43	0.08
Greensboro (city) Guilford County	191	0.07
Durham (city) Durham County	159	0.07
High Point (city) Guilford County	72	0.07
Cary (town) Wake County	78	0.06
Concord (city) Cabarrus County	47	0.06

Central American: Salvadoran

Top 10 Places Sorted by Population
Based on all places, regardless of total population

Place	Population	%
Charlotte (city) Mecklenburg County	9,516	1.30
Raleigh (city) Wake County	3,476	0.86
Durham (city) Durham County	2,929	1.28
Winston-Salem (city) Forsyth County	1,954	0.85
Greensboro (city) Guilford County	887	0.33
Sanford (city) Lee County	880	3.13
Burlington (city) Alamance County	859	1.72
Asheville (city) Buncombe County	525	0.63
Cary (town) Wake County	450	0.33
High Point (city) Guilford County	408	0.39

Top 10 Places Sorted by Percent of Total Population
Based on all places, regardless of total population

Place	Population	%
Harmony (town) Iredell County	26	4.90
Siler City (town) Chatham County	370	4.69
Sanford (city) Lee County	880	3.13
Lucama (town) Wilson County	29	2.62
Staley (town) Randolph County	9	2.29
Delway (cdp) Sampson County	4	1.97
Moravian Falls (cdp) Wilkes County	35	1.84
Burlington (city) Alamance County	859	1.72
Magnolia (town) Duplin County	15	1.60
Cooleemee (town) Davie County	15	1.56

Top 10 Places Sorted by Percent of Total Population
Based on places with total population of 50,000 or more

Place	Population	%
Charlotte (city) Mecklenburg County	9,516	1.30
Durham (city) Durham County	2,929	1.28
Raleigh (city) Wake County	3,476	0.86
Winston-Salem (city) Forsyth County	1,954	0.85
Asheville (city) Buncombe County	525	0.63
Chapel Hill (town) Orange County	227	0.40
High Point (city) Guilford County	408	0.39
Greensboro (city) Guilford County	887	0.33
Cary (town) Wake County	450	0.33
Concord (city) Cabarrus County	225	0.28

Central American: Other Central American

Top 10 Places Sorted by Population
Based on all places, regardless of total population

Place	Population	%
Charlotte (city) Mecklenburg County	264	0.04
Raleigh (city) Wake County	59	0.01
Durham (city) Durham County	49	0.02
Winston-Salem (city) Forsyth County	32	0.01
Gastonia (city) Gaston County	24	0.03
Siler City (town) Chatham County	20	0.25
Cary (town) Wake County	17	0.01
Salisbury (city) Rowan County	14	0.04
Smithfield (town) Johnston County	9	0.08
Fayetteville (city) Cumberland County	9	<0.01

Top 10 Places Sorted by Percent of Total Population
Based on all places, regardless of total population

Place	Population	%
Moravian Falls (cdp) Wilkes County	5	0.26
Siler City (town) Chatham County	20	0.25
Hampstead (cdp) Pender County	6	0.15
Southport (city) Brunswick County	4	0.14
Burgaw (town) Pender County	5	0.13
Selma (town) Johnston County	7	0.12
Red Springs (town) Robeson County	4	0.12
Mountain View (cdp) Catawba County	4	0.11
Glen Raven (cdp) Alamance County	3	0.11
Cherokee (cdp) Jackson County	2	0.09

Top 10 Places Sorted by Percent of Total Population
Based on places with total population of 50,000 or more

Place	Population	%
Charlotte (city) Mecklenburg County	264	0.04
Gastonia (city) Gaston County	24	0.03
Durham (city) Durham County	49	0.02
Raleigh (city) Wake County	59	0.01
Winston-Salem (city) Forsyth County	32	0.01
Cary (town) Wake County	17	0.01
Jacksonville (city) Onslow County	6	0.01
Chapel Hill (town) Orange County	4	0.01
Concord (city) Cabarrus County	4	0.01
Fayetteville (city) Cumberland County	9	<0.01

Cuban

Top 10 Places Sorted by Population
Based on all places, regardless of total population

Place	Population	%
Charlotte (city) Mecklenburg County	2,902	0.40
Raleigh (city) Wake County	1,082	0.27
Fayetteville (city) Cumberland County	534	0.27
Cary (town) Wake County	529	0.39
Greensboro (city) Guilford County	520	0.19
Winston-Salem (city) Forsyth County	503	0.22
Durham (city) Durham County	445	0.19
Jacksonville (city) Onslow County	367	0.52
Concord (city) Cabarrus County	314	0.40
High Point (city) Guilford County	253	0.24

Top 10 Places Sorted by Percent of Total Population
Based on all places, regardless of total population

Place	Population	%
Orrum (town) Robeson County	10	10.99
Deercroft (cdp) Scotland County	15	3.65
Ronda (town) Wilkes County	9	2.16
Hot Springs (town) Madison County	8	1.43
Conetoe (town) Edgecombe County	3	1.02
Oak City (town) Martin County	3	0.95
Beech Mountain (town) Watauga County	3	0.94
Bethania (town) Forsyth County	3	0.91
Hollister (cdp) Halifax County	6	0.89
Bunn (town) Franklin County	3	0.87

Top 10 Places Sorted by Percent of Total Population
Based on places with total population of 50,000 or more

Place	Population	%
Jacksonville (city) Onslow County	367	0.52
Charlotte (city) Mecklenburg County	2,902	0.40
Concord (city) Cabarrus County	314	0.40
Cary (town) Wake County	529	0.39
Chapel Hill (town) Orange County	197	0.34
Raleigh (city) Wake County	1,082	0.27
Fayetteville (city) Cumberland County	534	0.27
Asheville (city) Buncombe County	223	0.27
High Point (city) Guilford County	253	0.24
Winston-Salem (city) Forsyth County	503	0.22

Dominican Republic

Top 10 Places Sorted by Population
Based on all places, regardless of total population

Place	Population	%
Charlotte (city) Mecklenburg County	3,280	0.45
Raleigh (city) Wake County	2,378	0.59
Fayetteville (city) Cumberland County	730	0.36
Greensboro (city) Guilford County	568	0.21
Winston-Salem (city) Forsyth County	472	0.21
Durham (city) Durham County	428	0.19
Jacksonville (city) Onslow County	413	0.59
High Point (city) Guilford County	258	0.25
Cary (town) Wake County	248	0.18
Concord (city) Cabarrus County	188	0.24

Top 10 Places Sorted by Percent of Total Population
Based on all places, regardless of total population

Place	Population	%
Zebulon (town) Wake County	90	2.03
Selma (town) Johnston County	104	1.71
Pineville (town) Mecklenburg County	99	1.32

Place	Population	%
Winfall (town) Perquimans County	5	0.84
Lincolnton (city) Lincoln County	76	0.72
Raleigh (city) Wake County	2,378	0.59
Jacksonville (city) Onslow County	413	0.59
Misenheimer (village) Stanly County	4	0.55
Magnolia (town) Duplin County	5	0.53
Havelock (city) Craven County	102	0.49

Top 10 Places Sorted by Percent of Total Population
Based on places with total population of 50,000 or more

Place	Population	%
Raleigh (city) Wake County	2,378	0.59
Jacksonville (city) Onslow County	413	0.59
Charlotte (city) Mecklenburg County	3,280	0.45
Fayetteville (city) Cumberland County	730	0.36
High Point (city) Guilford County	258	0.25
Concord (city) Cabarrus County	188	0.24
Gastonia (city) Gaston County	171	0.24
Greensboro (city) Guilford County	568	0.21
Winston-Salem (city) Forsyth County	472	0.21
Durham (city) Durham County	428	0.19

Mexican

Top 10 Places Sorted by Population
Based on all places, regardless of total population

Place	Population	%
Charlotte (city) Mecklenburg County	40,601	5.55
Raleigh (city) Wake County	23,867	5.91
Winston-Salem (city) Forsyth County	23,427	10.20
Durham (city) Durham County	17,626	7.72
Greensboro (city) Guilford County	12,293	4.56
Monroe (city) Union County	7,773	23.70
Concord (city) Cabarrus County	6,528	8.26
Fayetteville (city) Cumberland County	6,448	3.21
Asheboro (city) Randolph County	5,469	21.87
Burlington (city) Alamance County	5,402	10.81

Top 10 Places Sorted by Percent of Total Population
Based on all places, regardless of total population

Place	Population	%
Robbins (town) Moore County	493	44.94
Ingold (cdp) Sampson County	179	38.00
Candor (town) Montgomery County	315	37.50
Biscoe (town) Montgomery County	585	34.41
Siler City (town) Chatham County	2,638	33.45
Rocky Point (cdp) Pender County	482	30.09
Barker Heights (cdp) Henderson County	376	29.98
Faison (town) Duplin County	276	28.72
Green Level (town) Alamance County	570	27.14
Shannon (cdp) Robeson County	69	26.24

Top 10 Places Sorted by Percent of Total Population
Based on places with total population of 50,000 or more

Place	Population	%
Winston-Salem (city) Forsyth County	23,427	10.20
Concord (city) Cabarrus County	6,528	8.26
Durham (city) Durham County	17,626	7.72
Raleigh (city) Wake County	23,867	5.91
Jacksonville (city) Onslow County	4,045	5.77
Charlotte (city) Mecklenburg County	40,601	5.55
Gastonia (city) Gaston County	3,849	5.37
High Point (city) Guilford County	5,092	4.88
Greensboro (city) Guilford County	12,293	4.56
Cary (town) Wake County	5,012	3.71

Puerto Rican

Top 10 Places Sorted by Population
Based on all places, regardless of total population

Place	Population	%
Fayetteville (city) Cumberland County	7,526	3.75
Charlotte (city) Mecklenburg County	7,521	1.03
Raleigh (city) Wake County	4,340	1.07
Jacksonville (city) Onslow County	2,356	3.36
Winston-Salem (city) Forsyth County	1,965	0.86
Greensboro (city) Guilford County	1,872	0.69
Durham (city) Durham County	1,641	0.72
Cary (town) Wake County	1,169	0.86
High Point (city) Guilford County	883	0.85
Concord (city) Cabarrus County	881	1.11

Top 10 Places Sorted by Percent of Total Population
Based on all places, regardless of total population

Place	Population	%
Spring Lake (town) Cumberland County	740	6.19
Rockfish (cdp) Hoke County	149	4.52
Hope Mills (town) Cumberland County	649	4.28
Piney Green (cdp) Onslow County	531	3.99
Fayetteville (city) Cumberland County	7,526	3.75
Pumpkin Center (cdp) Onslow County	80	3.60
Jacksonville (city) Onslow County	2,356	3.36
Richlands (town) Onslow County	48	3.16
Falcon (town) Cumberland County	8	3.10
Norman (town) Richmond County	4	2.90

Top 10 Places Sorted by Percent of Total Population
Based on places with total population of 50,000 or more

Place	Population	%
Fayetteville (city) Cumberland County	7,526	3.75
Jacksonville (city) Onslow County	2,356	3.36
Concord (city) Cabarrus County	881	1.11
Raleigh (city) Wake County	4,340	1.07
Charlotte (city) Mecklenburg County	7,521	1.03
Winston-Salem (city) Forsyth County	1,965	0.86
Cary (town) Wake County	1,169	0.86
High Point (city) Guilford County	883	0.85
Gastonia (city) Gaston County	561	0.78
Durham (city) Durham County	1,641	0.72

South American

Top 10 Places Sorted by Population
Based on all places, regardless of total population

Place	Population	%
Charlotte (city) Mecklenburg County	10,729	1.47
Raleigh (city) Wake County	3,574	0.88
Greensboro (city) Guilford County	1,456	0.54
Durham (city) Durham County	1,448	0.63
Winston-Salem (city) Forsyth County	1,344	0.59
Cary (town) Wake County	1,259	0.93
Fayetteville (city) Cumberland County	1,227	0.61
Gastonia (city) Gaston County	1,042	1.45
Indian Trail (town) Union County	706	2.11
High Point (city) Guilford County	700	0.67

Top 10 Places Sorted by Percent of Total Population
Based on all places, regardless of total population

Place	Population	%
Pineville (town) Mecklenburg County	344	4.60
Manteo (town) Dare County	47	3.28
Sunbury (cdp) Gates County	7	2.42
Indian Trail (town) Union County	706	2.11
Statesville (city) Iredell County	483	1.97
Ranlo (town) Gaston County	65	1.89
Selma (town) Johnston County	97	1.60
Morrisville (town) Wake County	286	1.54
Staley (town) Randolph County	6	1.53
Charlotte (city) Mecklenburg County	10,729	1.47

Top 10 Places Sorted by Percent of Total Population
Based on places with total population of 50,000 or more

Place	Population	%
Charlotte (city) Mecklenburg County	10,729	1.47
Gastonia (city) Gaston County	1,042	1.45
Cary (town) Wake County	1,259	0.93
Chapel Hill (town) Orange County	529	0.92
Raleigh (city) Wake County	3,574	0.88
Jacksonville (city) Onslow County	577	0.82
Concord (city) Cabarrus County	591	0.75
High Point (city) Guilford County	700	0.67
Durham (city) Durham County	1,448	0.63
Fayetteville (city) Cumberland County	1,227	0.61

South American: Argentinean

Top 10 Places Sorted by Population
Based on all places, regardless of total population

Place	Population	%
Charlotte (city) Mecklenburg County	514	0.07
Raleigh (city) Wake County	313	0.08
Durham (city) Durham County	210	0.09

Place	Population	%
Winston-Salem (city) Forsyth County	121	0.05
Cary (town) Wake County	115	0.09
Greensboro (city) Guilford County	89	0.03
Chapel Hill (town) Orange County	74	0.13
Fayetteville (city) Cumberland County	74	0.04
Wilmington (city) New Hanover County	62	0.06
Asheville (city) Buncombe County	57	0.07

Top 10 Places Sorted by Percent of Total Population
Based on all places, regardless of total population

Place	Population	%
Wilson's Mills (town) Johnston County	9	0.40
Elm City (town) Wilson County	4	0.31
Avon (cdp) Dare County	2	0.26
King (city) Stokes County	17	0.25
Lincolnton (city) Lincoln County	24	0.23
Pineville (town) Mecklenburg County	17	0.23
Mineral Springs (town) Union County	6	0.23
Carrboro (town) Orange County	40	0.20
Maysville (town) Jones County	2	0.20
Elkin (town) Surry County	7	0.17

Top 10 Places Sorted by Percent of Total Population
Based on places with total population of 50,000 or more

Place	Population	%
Chapel Hill (town) Orange County	74	0.13
Durham (city) Durham County	210	0.09
Cary (town) Wake County	115	0.09
Raleigh (city) Wake County	313	0.08
Charlotte (city) Mecklenburg County	514	0.07
Asheville (city) Buncombe County	57	0.07
Wilmington (city) New Hanover County	62	0.06
Winston-Salem (city) Forsyth County	121	0.05
Concord (city) Cabarrus County	41	0.05
Fayetteville (city) Cumberland County	74	0.04

South American: Bolivian

Top 10 Places Sorted by Population
Based on all places, regardless of total population

Place	Population	%
Charlotte (city) Mecklenburg County	138	0.02
Raleigh (city) Wake County	94	0.02
Durham (city) Durham County	58	0.03
Fayetteville (city) Cumberland County	53	0.03
Cary (town) Wake County	40	0.03
Greensboro (city) Guilford County	32	0.01
Jacksonville (city) Onslow County	27	0.04
High Point (city) Guilford County	18	0.02
Winston-Salem (city) Forsyth County	17	0.01
Wilmington (city) New Hanover County	16	0.02

Top 10 Places Sorted by Percent of Total Population
Based on all places, regardless of total population

Place	Population	%
Bell Arthur (cdp) Pitt County	3	0.64
Sylva (town) Jackson County	4	0.15
Pittsboro (town) Chatham County	4	0.11
Banner Elk (town) Avery County	1	0.10
Maysville (town) Jones County	1	0.10
Denver (cdp) Lincoln County	2	0.09
Swansboro (town) Onslow County	2	0.08
Belmont (city) Gaston County	7	0.07
James City (cdp) Craven County	4	0.07
Garner (town) Wake County	14	0.05

Top 10 Places Sorted by Percent of Total Population
Based on places with total population of 50,000 or more

Place	Population	%
Jacksonville (city) Onslow County	27	0.04
Durham (city) Durham County	58	0.03
Fayetteville (city) Cumberland County	53	0.03
Cary (town) Wake County	40	0.03
Charlotte (city) Mecklenburg County	138	0.02
Raleigh (city) Wake County	94	0.02
High Point (city) Guilford County	18	0.02
Wilmington (city) New Hanover County	16	0.02
Chapel Hill (town) Orange County	12	0.02
Greensboro (city) Guilford County	32	0.01

South American: Chilean

Top 10 Places Sorted by Population
Based on all places, regardless of total population

Place	Population	%
Charlotte (city) Mecklenburg County	368	0.05
Raleigh (city) Wake County	196	0.05
Durham (city) Durham County	140	0.06
Greensboro (city) Guilford County	102	0.04
Cary (town) Wake County	83	0.06
Winston-Salem (city) Forsyth County	79	0.03
Gastonia (city) Gaston County	63	0.09
Fayetteville (city) Cumberland County	55	0.03
High Point (city) Guilford County	49	0.05
Chapel Hill (town) Orange County	45	0.08

Top 10 Places Sorted by Percent of Total Population
Based on all places, regardless of total population

Place	Population	%
Manteo (town) Dare County	6	0.42
Castle Hayne (cdp) New Hanover County	5	0.42
Mars Hill (town) Madison County	7	0.37
Princeton (town) Johnston County	3	0.25
Ramseur (town) Randolph County	4	0.24
Bermuda Run (town) Davie County	4	0.23
Cajah's Mountain (town) Caldwell County	6	0.21
Mountain Home (cdp) Henderson County	6	0.17
Haw River (town) Alamance County	4	0.17
East Flat Rock (cdp) Henderson County	8	0.16

Top 10 Places Sorted by Percent of Total Population
Based on places with total population of 50,000 or more

Place	Population	%
Gastonia (city) Gaston County	63	0.09
Chapel Hill (town) Orange County	45	0.08
Durham (city) Durham County	140	0.06
Cary (town) Wake County	83	0.06
Charlotte (city) Mecklenburg County	368	0.05
Raleigh (city) Wake County	196	0.05
High Point (city) Guilford County	49	0.05
Asheville (city) Buncombe County	38	0.05
Jacksonville (city) Onslow County	36	0.05
Greensboro (city) Guilford County	102	0.04

South American: Colombian

Top 10 Places Sorted by Population
Based on all places, regardless of total population

Place	Population	%
Charlotte (city) Mecklenburg County	3,338	0.46
Raleigh (city) Wake County	1,261	0.31
Gastonia (city) Gaston County	812	1.13
Greensboro (city) Guilford County	562	0.21
Fayetteville (city) Cumberland County	492	0.25
Durham (city) Durham County	478	0.21
Winston-Salem (city) Forsyth County	463	0.20
Cary (town) Wake County	423	0.31
Statesville (city) Iredell County	365	1.49
High Point (city) Guilford County	318	0.30

Top 10 Places Sorted by Percent of Total Population
Based on all places, regardless of total population

Place	Population	%
Staley (town) Randolph County	6	1.53
Statesville (city) Iredell County	365	1.49
Pineville (town) Mecklenburg County	95	1.27
Ranlo (town) Gaston County	42	1.22
Gastonia (city) Gaston County	812	1.13
Jamesville (town) Martin County	5	1.02
Indian Trail (town) Union County	316	0.94
Troutman (town) Iredell County	19	0.80
Falcon (town) Cumberland County	2	0.78
Pumpkin Center (cdp) Onslow County	17	0.77

Top 10 Places Sorted by Percent of Total Population
Based on places with total population of 50,000 or more

Place	Population	%
Gastonia (city) Gaston County	812	1.13
Charlotte (city) Mecklenburg County	3,338	0.46
Chapel Hill (town) Orange County	204	0.36
Jacksonville (city) Onslow County	249	0.35

Raleigh (city) Wake County	1,261	0.31
Cary (town) Wake County	423	0.31
High Point (city) Guilford County	318	0.30
Concord (city) Cabarrus County	226	0.29
Fayetteville (city) Cumberland County	492	0.25
Greensboro (city) Guilford County	562	0.21

South American: Ecuadorian

Top 10 Places Sorted by Population
Based on all places, regardless of total population

Place	Population	%
Charlotte (city) Mecklenburg County	3,008	0.41
Raleigh (city) Wake County	352	0.09
Winston-Salem (city) Forsyth County	243	0.11
Fayetteville (city) Cumberland County	195	0.10
Indian Trail (town) Union County	178	0.53
Durham (city) Durham County	169	0.07
Concord (city) Cabarrus County	151	0.19
Cary (town) Wake County	140	0.10
Greensboro (city) Guilford County	128	0.05
Burlington (city) Alamance County	123	0.25

Top 10 Places Sorted by Percent of Total Population
Based on all places, regardless of total population

Place	Population	%
Pineville (town) Mecklenburg County	108	1.44
Kenly (town) Johnston County	9	0.67
Selma (town) Johnston County	36	0.59
Indian Trail (town) Union County	178	0.53
Ranlo (town) Gaston County	18	0.52
Hillsdale (cdp) Davie County	5	0.51
Waxhaw (town) Union County	47	0.48
Simpson (village) Pitt County	2	0.48
Peletier (town) Carteret County	3	0.47
Lowell (city) Gaston County	16	0.45

Top 10 Places Sorted by Percent of Total Population
Based on places with total population of 50,000 or more

Place	Population	%
Charlotte (city) Mecklenburg County	3,008	0.41
Concord (city) Cabarrus County	151	0.19
Jacksonville (city) Onslow County	95	0.14
Winston-Salem (city) Forsyth County	243	0.11
Fayetteville (city) Cumberland County	195	0.10
Cary (town) Wake County	140	0.10
Gastonia (city) Gaston County	72	0.10
Raleigh (city) Wake County	352	0.09
High Point (city) Guilford County	93	0.09
Durham (city) Durham County	169	0.07

South American: Paraguayan

Top 10 Places Sorted by Population
Based on all places, regardless of total population

Place	Population	%
Charlotte (city) Mecklenburg County	28	<0.01
Fayetteville (city) Cumberland County	14	0.01
New Bern (city) Craven County	13	0.04
Chapel Hill (town) Orange County	12	0.02
Winston-Salem (city) Forsyth County	10	<0.01
Cary (town) Wake County	9	0.01
Raleigh (city) Wake County	9	0.01
Greenville (city) Pitt County	7	0.01
Greensboro (city) Guilford County	7	<0.01
Durham (city) Durham County	6	<0.01

Top 10 Places Sorted by Percent of Total Population
Based on all places, regardless of total population

Place	Population	%
Winton (town) Hertford County	1	0.13
Columbus (town) Polk County	1	0.10
Richlands (town) Onslow County	1	0.07
Jefferson (town) Ashe County	1	0.06
Cherokee (cdp) Jackson County	1	0.05
New Bern (city) Craven County	13	0.04
Fletcher (town) Henderson County	3	0.04
East Flat Rock (cdp) Henderson County	2	0.04
Southport (city) Brunswick County	1	0.04
Carrboro (town) Orange County	5	0.03

Top 10 Places Sorted by Percent of Total Population
Based on places with total population of 50,000 or more

Place	Population	%
Chapel Hill (town) Orange County	12	0.02
Fayetteville (city) Cumberland County	14	0.01
Cary (town) Wake County	9	0.01
Greenville (city) Pitt County	7	0.01
Charlotte (city) Mecklenburg County	28	<0.01
Winston-Salem (city) Forsyth County	10	<0.01
Raleigh (city) Wake County	9	<0.01
Greensboro (city) Guilford County	7	<0.01
Durham (city) Durham County	6	<0.01
Jacksonville (city) Onslow County	3	<0.01

South American: Peruvian

Top 10 Places Sorted by Population
Based on all places, regardless of total population

Place	Population	%
Charlotte (city) Mecklenburg County	2,177	0.30
Raleigh (city) Wake County	729	0.18
Greensboro (city) Guilford County	285	0.11
Cary (town) Wake County	258	0.19
Fayetteville (city) Cumberland County	244	0.12
Winston-Salem (city) Forsyth County	236	0.10
Durham (city) Durham County	193	0.08
High Point (city) Guilford County	131	0.13
Pineville (town) Mecklenburg County	95	1.27
Indian Trail (town) Union County	95	0.28

Top 10 Places Sorted by Percent of Total Population
Based on all places, regardless of total population

Place	Population	%
Manteo (town) Dare County	40	2.79
Sunbury (cdp) Gates County	7	2.42
Pineville (town) Mecklenburg County	95	1.27
Rodanthe (cdp) Dare County	2	0.77
Lake Park (village) Union County	18	0.53
Watha (town) Pender County	1	0.53
JAARS (cdp) Union County	3	0.50
St. Pauls (town) Robeson County	10	0.49
Manns Harbor (cdp) Dare County	4	0.49
Holly Ridge (town) Onslow County	6	0.47

Top 10 Places Sorted by Percent of Total Population
Based on places with total population of 50,000 or more

Place	Population	%
Charlotte (city) Mecklenburg County	2,177	0.30
Cary (town) Wake County	258	0.19
Raleigh (city) Wake County	729	0.18
Chapel Hill (town) Orange County	78	0.14
High Point (city) Guilford County	131	0.13
Fayetteville (city) Cumberland County	244	0.12
Concord (city) Cabarrus County	92	0.12
Jacksonville (city) Onslow County	85	0.12
Greensboro (city) Guilford County	285	0.11
Winston-Salem (city) Forsyth County	236	0.10

South American: Uruguayan

Top 10 Places Sorted by Population
Based on all places, regardless of total population

Place	Population	%
Charlotte (city) Mecklenburg County	262	0.04
Raleigh (city) Wake County	146	0.04
Durham (city) Durham County	33	0.01
Greensboro (city) Guilford County	27	0.01
Winston-Salem (city) Forsyth County	25	0.01
Cary (town) Wake County	23	0.02
Wilson (city) Wilson County	16	0.03
Gastonia (city) Gaston County	15	0.02
Selma (town) Johnston County	14	0.23
Lincolnton (city) Lincoln County	13	0.12

Top 10 Places Sorted by Percent of Total Population
Based on all places, regardless of total population

Place	Population	%
Grover (town) Cleveland County	8	1.13
Selma (town) Johnston County	14	0.23
Valley Hill (cdp) Henderson County	3	0.14

Please refer to the Explanation of Data in the front of the book for more detailed information.

Montreat (town) Buncombe County	1	0.14
Lincolnton (city) Lincoln County	13	0.12
Jefferson (town) Ashe County	2	0.12
Knightdale (town) Wake County	13	0.11
Hays (cdp) Wilkes County	2	0.11
Pineville (town) Mecklenburg County	7	0.09
Mount Gilead (town) Montgomery County	1	0.08

Top 10 Places Sorted by Percent of Total Population
Based on places with total population of 50,000 or more

Place	Population	%
Charlotte (city) Mecklenburg County	262	0.04
Raleigh (city) Wake County	146	0.04
Cary (town) Wake County	23	0.02
Gastonia (city) Gaston County	15	0.02
Durham (city) Durham County	33	0.01
Greensboro (city) Guilford County	27	0.01
Winston-Salem (city) Forsyth County	25	0.01
Wilmington (city) New Hanover County	13	0.01
Concord (city) Cabarrus County	9	0.01
Chapel Hill (town) Orange County	7	0.01

South American: Venezuelan

Top 10 Places Sorted by Population
Based on all places, regardless of total population

Place	Population	%
Charlotte (city) Mecklenburg County	818	0.11
Raleigh (city) Wake County	457	0.11
Greensboro (city) Guilford County	203	0.08
Cary (town) Wake County	156	0.12
Durham (city) Durham County	143	0.06
Winston-Salem (city) Forsyth County	137	0.06
Fayetteville (city) Cumberland County	80	0.04
Chapel Hill (town) Orange County	58	0.10
Asheville (city) Buncombe County	53	0.06
Huntersville (town) Mecklenburg County	52	0.11

Top 10 Places Sorted by Percent of Total Population
Based on all places, regardless of total population

Place	Population	%
Pikeville (town) Wayne County	3	0.44
Lake Park (village) Union County	14	0.41
Mars Hill (town) Madison County	5	0.27
Misenheimer (village) Stanly County	2	0.27
Duck (town) Dare County	1	0.27
Clemmons (village) Forsyth County	49	0.26
Spring Hope (town) Nash County	3	0.23
Engelhard (cdp) Hyde County	1	0.22
Belville (town) Brunswick County	4	0.21
Columbus (town) Polk County	2	0.20

Top 10 Places Sorted by Percent of Total Population
Based on places with total population of 50,000 or more

Place	Population	%
Cary (town) Wake County	156	0.12
Charlotte (city) Mecklenburg County	818	0.11
Raleigh (city) Wake County	457	0.11
Chapel Hill (town) Orange County	58	0.10
Greensboro (city) Guilford County	203	0.08
Durham (city) Durham County	143	0.06
Winston-Salem (city) Forsyth County	137	0.06
Asheville (city) Buncombe County	53	0.06
Jacksonville (city) Onslow County	44	0.06
Fayetteville (city) Cumberland County	80	0.04

South American: Other South American

Top 10 Places Sorted by Population
Based on all places, regardless of total population

Place	Population	%
Charlotte (city) Mecklenburg County	78	0.01
Greensboro (city) Guilford County	21	0.01
Durham (city) Durham County	18	0.01
Raleigh (city) Wake County	17	<0.01
Winston-Salem (city) Forsyth County	13	0.01
Cary (town) Wake County	12	0.01
Jacksonville (city) Onslow County	11	0.02
Concord (city) Cabarrus County	11	0.01
Greenville (city) Pitt County	10	0.01
Fayetteville (city) Cumberland County	10	<0.01

Top 10 Places Sorted by Percent of Total Population
Based on all places, regardless of total population

Place	Population	%
White Lake (town) Bladen County	2	0.25
East Rockingham (cdp) Richmond County	5	0.13
Fairview (cdp) Buncombe County	3	0.11
White Plains (cdp) Surry County	1	0.09
Manteo (town) Dare County	1	0.07
Oak Ridge (town) Guilford County	4	0.06
Stallings (town) Union County	7	0.05
Lexington (city) Davidson County	8	0.04
Silver Lake (cdp) New Hanover County	2	0.04
Gibsonville (town) Guilford County	2	0.03

Top 10 Places Sorted by Percent of Total Population
Based on places with total population of 50,000 or more

Place	Population	%
Jacksonville (city) Onslow County	11	0.02
Charlotte (city) Mecklenburg County	78	0.01
Greensboro (city) Guilford County	21	0.01
Durham (city) Durham County	18	0.01
Winston-Salem (city) Forsyth County	13	0.01
Cary (town) Wake County	12	0.01
Concord (city) Cabarrus County	11	0.01
Greenville (city) Pitt County	10	0.01
Asheville (city) Buncombe County	8	0.01
Chapel Hill (town) Orange County	4	0.01

Other Hispanic or Latino

Top 10 Places Sorted by Population
Based on all places, regardless of total population

Place	Population	%
Charlotte (city) Mecklenburg County	8,296	1.13
Raleigh (city) Wake County	3,108	0.77
Durham (city) Durham County	2,819	1.23
Winston-Salem (city) Forsyth County	2,285	1.00
Fayetteville (city) Cumberland County	1,553	0.77
Greensboro (city) Guilford County	1,381	0.51
Cary (town) Wake County	796	0.59
Jacksonville (city) Onslow County	707	1.01
Wilmington (city) New Hanover County	629	0.59
High Point (city) Guilford County	575	0.55

Top 10 Places Sorted by Percent of Total Population
Based on all places, regardless of total population

Place	Population	%
Lake Santeetlah (town) Graham County	4	8.89
Polkton (town) Anson County	262	7.76
Gorman (cdp) Durham County	67	6.63
McFarlan (town) Anson County	7	5.98
Rex (cdp) Robeson County	3	5.45
Saratoga (town) Wilson County	21	5.15
Magnolia (town) Duplin County	48	5.11
Seven Springs (town) Wayne County	5	4.55
Brunswick (town) Columbus County	49	4.38
Falcon (town) Cumberland County	10	3.88

Top 10 Places Sorted by Percent of Total Population
Based on places with total population of 50,000 or more

Place	Population	%
Durham (city) Durham County	2,819	1.23
Charlotte (city) Mecklenburg County	8,296	1.13
Jacksonville (city) Onslow County	707	1.01
Winston-Salem (city) Forsyth County	2,285	1.00
Raleigh (city) Wake County	3,108	0.77
Fayetteville (city) Cumberland County	1,553	0.77
Gastonia (city) Gaston County	536	0.75
Concord (city) Cabarrus County	544	0.69
Cary (town) Wake County	796	0.59
Wilmington (city) New Hanover County	629	0.59

Racial Group Rankings

African-American/Black

Top 10 Places Sorted by Population
Based on all places, regardless of total population

Place	Population	%
Charlotte (city) Mecklenburg County	266,822	36.48
Raleigh (city) Wake County	124,035	30.71
Greensboro (city) Guilford County	114,156	42.33
Durham (city) Durham County	96,706	42.35
Fayetteville (city) Cumberland County	89,916	44.83
Winston-Salem (city) Forsyth County	82,853	36.08
Rocky Mount (city) Nash County	35,854	62.38
High Point (city) Guilford County	35,767	34.27
Greenville (city) Pitt County	32,386	38.30
Wilson (city) Wilson County	24,034	48.88

Top 10 Places Sorted by Percent of Total Population
Based on all places, regardless of total population

Place	Population	%
Garysburg (town) Northampton County	1,021	96.59
Princeville (town) Edgecombe County	2,010	96.54
East Arcadia (town) Bladen County	453	93.02
Silver City (cdp) Hoke County	818	92.74
Parmele (town) Martin County	254	91.37
Kings (town) Cleveland County	614	90.16
Enfield (town) Halifax County	2,222	87.76
Dobbins Heights (town) Richmond County	747	86.26
East Spencer (town) Rowan County	1,320	86.05
Cofield (village) Hertford County	344	83.29

Top 10 Places Sorted by Percent of Total Population
Based on places with total population of 50,000 or more

Place	Population	%
Rocky Mount (city) Nash County	35,854	62.38
Fayetteville (city) Cumberland County	89,916	44.83
Durham (city) Durham County	96,706	42.35
Greensboro (city) Guilford County	114,156	42.33
Greenville (city) Pitt County	32,386	38.30
Charlotte (city) Mecklenburg County	266,822	36.48
Winston-Salem (city) Forsyth County	82,853	36.08
High Point (city) Guilford County	35,767	34.27
Raleigh (city) Wake County	124,035	30.71
Gastonia (city) Gaston County	20,917	29.16

African-American/Black: Not Hispanic

Top 10 Places Sorted by Population
Based on all places, regardless of total population

Place	Population	%
Charlotte (city) Mecklenburg County	260,726	35.65
Raleigh (city) Wake County	120,403	29.81
Greensboro (city) Guilford County	112,136	41.58
Durham (city) Durham County	94,986	41.60
Fayetteville (city) Cumberland County	86,376	43.07
Winston-Salem (city) Forsyth County	80,608	35.11
Rocky Mount (city) Nash County	35,605	61.95
High Point (city) Guilford County	35,168	33.70
Greenville (city) Pitt County	31,978	37.82
Wilson (city) Wilson County	23,803	48.41

Top 10 Places Sorted by Percent of Total Population
Based on all places, regardless of total population

Place	Population	%
Princeville (town) Edgecombe County	2,010	96.54
Garysburg (town) Northampton County	1,015	96.03
Silver City (cdp) Hoke County	817	92.63
East Arcadia (town) Bladen County	448	91.99
Parmele (town) Martin County	254	91.37
Kings (town) Cleveland County	614	90.16
Enfield (town) Halifax County	2,210	87.28
East Spencer (town) Rowan County	1,316	85.79
Dobbins Heights (town) Richmond County	740	85.45
Greenevers (town) Duplin County	525	82.81

Top 10 Places Sorted by Percent of Total Population
Based on places with total population of 50,000 or more

Place	Population	%
Rocky Mount (city) Nash County	35,605	61.95
Fayetteville (city) Cumberland County	86,376	43.07
Durham (city) Durham County	94,986	41.60
Greensboro (city) Guilford County	112,136	41.58
Greenville (city) Pitt County	31,978	37.82
Charlotte (city) Mecklenburg County	260,726	35.65
Winston-Salem (city) Forsyth County	80,608	35.11
High Point (city) Guilford County	35,168	33.70
Raleigh (city) Wake County	120,403	29.81
Gastonia (city) Gaston County	20,521	28.60

African-American/Black: Hispanic

Top 10 Places Sorted by Population
Based on all places, regardless of total population

Place	Population	%
Charlotte (city) Mecklenburg County	6,096	0.83
Raleigh (city) Wake County	3,632	0.90
Fayetteville (city) Cumberland County	3,540	1.77
Winston-Salem (city) Forsyth County	2,245	0.98
Greensboro (city) Guilford County	2,020	0.75
Durham (city) Durham County	1,720	0.75
Jacksonville (city) Onslow County	943	1.34
High Point (city) Guilford County	599	0.57
Concord (city) Cabarrus County	546	0.69
Wilmington (city) New Hanover County	479	0.45

Top 10 Places Sorted by Percent of Total Population
Based on all places, regardless of total population

Place	Population	%
Norman (town) Richmond County	4	2.90
Spring Lake (town) Cumberland County	335	2.80
Falcon (town) Cumberland County	5	1.94
Bell Arthur (cdp) Pitt County	9	1.93
Fayetteville (city) Cumberland County	3,540	1.77
Pantego (town) Beaufort County	3	1.68
Calypso (town) Duplin County	9	1.67
Hope Mills (town) Cumberland County	238	1.57
Pumpkin Center (cdp) Onslow County	33	1.49
Delway (cdp) Sampson County	3	1.48

Top 10 Places Sorted by Percent of Total Population
Based on places with total population of 50,000 or more

Place	Population	%
Fayetteville (city) Cumberland County	3,540	1.77
Jacksonville (city) Onslow County	943	1.34
Winston-Salem (city) Forsyth County	2,245	0.98
Raleigh (city) Wake County	3,632	0.90
Charlotte (city) Mecklenburg County	6,096	0.83
Greensboro (city) Guilford County	2,020	0.75
Durham (city) Durham County	1,720	0.75
Concord (city) Cabarrus County	546	0.69
High Point (city) Guilford County	599	0.57
Gastonia (city) Gaston County	396	0.55

American Indian/Alaska Native

Top 10 Places Sorted by Population
Based on all places, regardless of total population

Place	Population	%
Charlotte (city) Mecklenburg County	8,397	1.15
Fayetteville (city) Cumberland County	4,901	2.44
Raleigh (city) Wake County	4,541	1.12
Greensboro (city) Guilford County	3,454	1.28
Lumberton (city) Robeson County	3,178	14.75
Durham (city) Durham County	2,744	1.20
Winston-Salem (city) Forsyth County	2,391	1.04
Pembroke (town) Robeson County	2,043	68.72
Cherokee (cdp) Jackson County	1,756	82.13
Cary (town) Wake County	1,353	1.00

Top 10 Places Sorted by Percent of Total Population
Based on all places, regardless of total population

Place	Population	%
Prospect (cdp) Robeson County	925	94.29
Wakulla (cdp) Robeson County	91	86.67
Cherokee (cdp) Jackson County	1,756	82.13
Raemon (cdp) Robeson County	223	79.08
Hollister (cdp) Halifax County	483	71.66
Elrod (cdp) Robeson County	298	71.46
Pembroke (town) Robeson County	2,043	68.72
Rennert (town) Robeson County	177	46.21
McDonald (town) Robeson County	47	41.59
Shannon (cdp) Robeson County	107	40.68

Top 10 Places Sorted by Percent of Total Population
Based on places with total population of 50,000 or more

Place	Population	%
Fayetteville (city) Cumberland County	4,901	2.44
Jacksonville (city) Onslow County	1,150	1.64
Greensboro (city) Guilford County	3,454	1.28
Durham (city) Durham County	2,744	1.20
Wilmington (city) New Hanover County	1,276	1.20
Charlotte (city) Mecklenburg County	8,397	1.15
High Point (city) Guilford County	1,205	1.15
Rocky Mount (city) Nash County	660	1.15
Raleigh (city) Wake County	4,541	1.12
Asheville (city) Buncombe County	932	1.12

American Indian/Alaska Native: Not Hispanic

Top 10 Places Sorted by Population
Based on all places, regardless of total population

Place	Population	%
Charlotte (city) Mecklenburg County	6,096	0.83
Fayetteville (city) Cumberland County	4,180	2.08
Lumberton (city) Robeson County	3,076	14.28
Raleigh (city) Wake County	3,015	0.75
Greensboro (city) Guilford County	2,892	1.07
Pembroke (town) Robeson County	2,015	67.78
Durham (city) Durham County	1,853	0.81
Winston-Salem (city) Forsyth County	1,726	0.75
Cherokee (cdp) Jackson County	1,682	78.67
Laurinburg (city) Scotland County	1,170	7.33

Top 10 Places Sorted by Percent of Total Population
Based on all places, regardless of total population

Place	Population	%
Prospect (cdp) Robeson County	919	93.68
Wakulla (cdp) Robeson County	91	86.67
Raemon (cdp) Robeson County	223	79.08
Cherokee (cdp) Jackson County	1,682	78.67
Elrod (cdp) Robeson County	297	71.22
Hollister (cdp) Halifax County	465	68.99
Pembroke (town) Robeson County	2,015	67.78
McDonald (town) Robeson County	47	41.59
Shannon (cdp) Robeson County	107	40.68
Rennert (town) Robeson County	149	38.90

Top 10 Places Sorted by Percent of Total Population
Based on places with total population of 50,000 or more

Place	Population	%
Fayetteville (city) Cumberland County	4,180	2.08
Jacksonville (city) Onslow County	899	1.28
Greensboro (city) Guilford County	2,892	1.07
Rocky Mount (city) Nash County	615	1.07
Wilmington (city) New Hanover County	1,018	0.96
Asheville (city) Buncombe County	798	0.96
High Point (city) Guilford County	981	0.94
Charlotte (city) Mecklenburg County	6,096	0.83
Durham (city) Durham County	1,853	0.81
Gastonia (city) Gaston County	576	0.80

American Indian/Alaska Native: Hispanic

Top 10 Places Sorted by Population
Based on all places, regardless of total population

Place	Population	%
Charlotte (city) Mecklenburg County	2,301	0.31
Raleigh (city) Wake County	1,526	0.38
Durham (city) Durham County	891	0.39
Fayetteville (city) Cumberland County	721	0.36
Winston-Salem (city) Forsyth County	665	0.29
Greensboro (city) Guilford County	562	0.21
Cary (town) Wake County	404	0.30
Wilmington (city) New Hanover County	258	0.24
Burlington (city) Alamance County	256	0.51
Jacksonville (city) Onslow County	251	0.36

Top 10 Places Sorted by Percent of Total Population
Based on all places, regardless of total population

Place	Population	%
Rennert (town) Robeson County	28	7.31
Cherokee (cdp) Jackson County	74	3.46
Columbus (town) Polk County	30	3.00
Hollister (cdp) Halifax County	18	2.67
Bald Head Island (village) Brunswick County	4	2.53
Castalia (town) Nash County	6	2.24
Lake Santeetlah (town) Graham County	1	2.22
Ashley Heights (cdp) Hoke County	8	2.11
Cameron (town) Moore County	6	2.11
Siler City (town) Chatham County	162	2.05

Top 10 Places Sorted by Percent of Total Population
Based on places with total population of 50,000 or more

Place	Population	%
Durham (city) Durham County	891	0.39
Raleigh (city) Wake County	1,526	0.38
Fayetteville (city) Cumberland County	721	0.36
Jacksonville (city) Onslow County	251	0.36
Charlotte (city) Mecklenburg County	2,301	0.31
Cary (town) Wake County	404	0.30
Winston-Salem (city) Forsyth County	665	0.29
Wilmington (city) New Hanover County	258	0.24
Greensboro (city) Guilford County	562	0.21
High Point (city) Guilford County	224	0.21

Alaska Native: Alaska Athabascan

Top 10 Places Sorted by Population
Based on all places, regardless of total population

Place	Population	%
Cary (town) Wake County	10	0.01
Fayetteville (city) Cumberland County	8	<0.01
Charlotte (city) Mecklenburg County	5	<0.01
Hickory (city) Catawba County	3	0.01
Raleigh (city) Wake County	3	<0.01
Winterville (town) Pitt County	2	0.02
Wake Forest (town) Wake County	2	0.01
Kannapolis (city) Cabarrus County	2	<0.01
Rennert (town) Robeson County	1	0.26
Stanfield (town) Stanly County	1	0.07

Top 10 Places Sorted by Percent of Total Population
Based on all places, regardless of total population

Place	Population	%
Rennert (town) Robeson County	1	0.26
Stanfield (town) Stanly County	1	0.07
Wilson's Mills (town) Johnston County	1	0.04
Winterville (town) Pitt County	2	0.02
Cullowhee (cdp) Jackson County	1	0.02
Erwin (town) Harnett County	1	0.02
Cary (town) Wake County	10	0.01
Hickory (city) Catawba County	3	0.01
Wake Forest (town) Wake County	2	0.01
Clemmons (village) Forsyth County	1	0.01

Top 10 Places Sorted by Percent of Total Population
Based on places with total population of 50,000 or more

Place	Population	%
Cary (town) Wake County	10	0.01
Fayetteville (city) Cumberland County	8	<0.01
Charlotte (city) Mecklenburg County	5	<0.01
Raleigh (city) Wake County	3	<0.01

Place	Population	%
Asheville (city) Buncombe County	1	<0.01
Durham (city) Durham County	1	<0.01
Jacksonville (city) Onslow County	1	<0.01
Winston-Salem (city) Forsyth County	1	<0.01
Chapel Hill (town) Orange County	0	0.00
Concord (city) Cabarrus County	0	0.00

Alaska Native: Aleut

Top 10 Places Sorted by Population
Based on all places, regardless of total population

Place	Population	%
Charlotte (city) Mecklenburg County	8	<0.01
Fayetteville (city) Cumberland County	7	<0.01
Lenoir (city) Caldwell County	6	0.03
Greenville (city) Pitt County	5	0.01
Raleigh (city) Wake County	5	<0.01
Hillsborough (town) Orange County	4	0.07
James City (cdp) Craven County	3	0.05
Apex (town) Wake County	3	0.01
Indian Trail (town) Union County	3	0.01
Mint Hill (town) Mecklenburg County	3	0.01

Top 10 Places Sorted by Percent of Total Population
Based on all places, regardless of total population

Place	Population	%
Harrells (town) Sampson County	1	0.50
Richlands (town) Onslow County	2	0.13
Hillsborough (town) Orange County	4	0.07
James City (cdp) Craven County	3	0.05
Ahoskie (town) Hertford County	2	0.04
Broad Creek (cdp) Carteret County	1	0.04
Lenoir (city) Caldwell County	6	0.03
Mar-Mac (cdp) Wayne County	1	0.03
Mount Airy (city) Surry County	2	0.02
Carolina Beach (town) New Hanover County	1	0.02

Top 10 Places Sorted by Percent of Total Population
Based on places with total population of 50,000 or more

Place	Population	%
Greenville (city) Pitt County	5	0.01
Rocky Mount (city) Nash County	3	0.01
Charlotte (city) Mecklenburg County	8	<0.01
Fayetteville (city) Cumberland County	7	<0.01
Raleigh (city) Wake County	5	<0.01
Greensboro (city) Guilford County	2	<0.01
Asheville (city) Buncombe County	1	<0.01
Chapel Hill (town) Orange County	1	<0.01
Concord (city) Cabarrus County	1	<0.01
Durham (city) Durham County	1	<0.01

American Indian: Apache

Top 10 Places Sorted by Population
Based on all places, regardless of total population

Place	Population	%
Fayetteville (city) Cumberland County	52	0.03
Charlotte (city) Mecklenburg County	46	0.01
Raleigh (city) Wake County	26	0.01
Greensboro (city) Guilford County	23	0.01
Jacksonville (city) Onslow County	17	0.02
Winston-Salem (city) Forsyth County	17	0.01
Wilmington (city) New Hanover County	15	0.01
Asheboro (city) Randolph County	14	0.06
High Point (city) Guilford County	13	0.01
Asheville (city) Buncombe County	12	0.01

Top 10 Places Sorted by Percent of Total Population
Based on all places, regardless of total population

Place	Population	%
Love Valley (town) Iredell County	1	1.11
Macon (town) Warren County	1	0.84
Rosman (town) Transylvania County	4	0.69
Sandyfield (town) Columbus County	2	0.45
Staley (town) Randolph County	1	0.25
Cherokee (cdp) Jackson County	4	0.19
Bailey (town) Nash County	1	0.18
Keener (cdp) Sampson County	1	0.18
Polkville (city) Cleveland County	1	0.18
Plain View (cdp) Sampson County	3	0.15

Top 10 Places Sorted by Percent of Total Population
Based on places with total population of 50,000 or more

Place	Population	%
Fayetteville (city) Cumberland County	52	0.03
Jacksonville (city) Onslow County	17	0.02
Charlotte (city) Mecklenburg County	46	0.01
Raleigh (city) Wake County	26	0.01
Greensboro (city) Guilford County	23	0.01
Winston-Salem (city) Forsyth County	17	0.01
Wilmington (city) New Hanover County	15	0.01
High Point (city) Guilford County	13	0.01
Asheville (city) Buncombe County	12	0.01
Cary (town) Wake County	11	0.01

American Indian: Arapaho

Top 10 Places Sorted by Population
Based on all places, regardless of total population

Place	Population	%
Holly Springs (town) Wake County	5	0.02
Fayetteville (city) Cumberland County	3	<0.01
Pine Level (town) Johnston County	2	0.12
Moyock (cdp) Currituck County	2	0.05
Roxboro (city) Person County	2	0.02
Lumberton (city) Robeson County	2	0.01
New Bern (city) Craven County	2	0.01
Jacksonville (city) Onslow County	2	<0.01
Wilmington (city) New Hanover County	2	<0.01
Fairview (cdp) Buncombe County	1	0.04

Top 10 Places Sorted by Percent of Total Population
Based on all places, regardless of total population

Place	Population	%
Pine Level (town) Johnston County	2	0.12
Moyock (cdp) Currituck County	2	0.05
Fairview (cdp) Buncombe County	1	0.04
Southport (city) Brunswick County	1	0.04
Emerald Isle (town) Carteret County	1	0.03
Holly Springs (town) Wake County	5	0.02
Roxboro (city) Person County	2	0.02
Aberdeen (town) Moore County	1	0.02
Lumberton (city) Robeson County	2	0.01
New Bern (city) Craven County	2	0.01

Top 10 Places Sorted by Percent of Total Population
Based on places with total population of 50,000 or more

Place	Population	%
Fayetteville (city) Cumberland County	3	<0.01
Jacksonville (city) Onslow County	2	<0.01
Wilmington (city) New Hanover County	2	<0.01
Asheville (city) Buncombe County	1	<0.01
Charlotte (city) Mecklenburg County	1	<0.01
Greensboro (city) Guilford County	1	<0.01
Raleigh (city) Wake County	1	<0.01
Cary (town) Wake County	0	0.00
Chapel Hill (town) Orange County	0	0.00
Concord (city) Cabarrus County	0	0.00

American Indian: Blackfeet

Top 10 Places Sorted by Population
Based on all places, regardless of total population

Place	Population	%
Charlotte (city) Mecklenburg County	186	0.03
Fayetteville (city) Cumberland County	143	0.07
Greensboro (city) Guilford County	123	0.05
Raleigh (city) Wake County	101	0.03
Winston-Salem (city) Forsyth County	72	0.03
Durham (city) Durham County	57	0.02
Jacksonville (city) Onslow County	45	0.06
Cary (town) Wake County	39	0.03
Wilmington (city) New Hanover County	25	0.02
High Point (city) Guilford County	22	0.02

Top 10 Places Sorted by Percent of Total Population
Based on all places, regardless of total population

Place	Population	%
Grimesland (town) Pitt County	3	0.68
Peachland (town) Anson County	2	0.46
Rodanthe (cdp) Dare County	1	0.38

Place	Population	%
Ossipee (town) Alamance County	2	0.37
Old Hundred (cdp) Scotland County	1	0.35
Fallston (town) Cleveland County	2	0.33
Pembroke (town) Robeson County	7	0.24
Spring Hope (town) Nash County	3	0.23
West Jefferson (town) Ashe County	3	0.23
Creedmoor (city) Granville County	9	0.22

Top 10 Places Sorted by Percent of Total Population
Based on places with total population of 50,000 or more

Place	Population	%
Fayetteville (city) Cumberland County	143	0.07
Jacksonville (city) Onslow County	45	0.06
Greensboro (city) Guilford County	123	0.05
Charlotte (city) Mecklenburg County	186	0.03
Raleigh (city) Wake County	101	0.03
Winston-Salem (city) Forsyth County	72	0.03
Cary (town) Wake County	39	0.03
Concord (city) Cabarrus County	21	0.03
Rocky Mount (city) Nash County	18	0.03
Durham (city) Durham County	57	0.02

American Indian: Canadian/French American Indian

Top 10 Places Sorted by Population
Based on all places, regardless of total population

Place	Population	%
Charlotte (city) Mecklenburg County	15	<0.01
Raleigh (city) Wake County	11	<0.01
Greenville (city) Pitt County	7	0.01
Wilson (city) Wilson County	4	0.01
Durham (city) Durham County	4	<0.01
Fayetteville (city) Cumberland County	4	<0.01
Greensboro (city) Guilford County	4	<0.01
Winston-Salem (city) Forsyth County	4	<0.01
Asheville (city) Buncombe County	3	<0.01
Cherokee (cdp) Jackson County	2	0.09

Top 10 Places Sorted by Percent of Total Population
Based on all places, regardless of total population

Place	Population	%
Hollister (cdp) Halifax County	1	0.15
Marshall (town) Madison County	1	0.11
Cherokee (cdp) Jackson County	2	0.09
Broadway (town) Lee County	1	0.08
Skippers Corner (cdp) New Hanover County	2	0.07
Mar-Mac (cdp) Wayne County	2	0.06
Belhaven (town) Beaufort County	1	0.06
Burnsville (town) Yancey County	1	0.06
Dobson (town) Surry County	1	0.06
James City (cdp) Craven County	2	0.03

Top 10 Places Sorted by Percent of Total Population
Based on places with total population of 50,000 or more

Place	Population	%
Greenville (city) Pitt County	7	0.01
Charlotte (city) Mecklenburg County	15	<0.01
Raleigh (city) Wake County	11	<0.01
Durham (city) Durham County	4	<0.01
Fayetteville (city) Cumberland County	4	<0.01
Greensboro (city) Guilford County	4	<0.01
Winston-Salem (city) Forsyth County	4	<0.01
Asheville (city) Buncombe County	3	<0.01
Cary (town) Wake County	2	<0.01
Jacksonville (city) Onslow County	2	<0.01

American Indian: Central American Indian

Top 10 Places Sorted by Population
Based on all places, regardless of total population

Place	Population	%
Charlotte (city) Mecklenburg County	67	0.01
Morganton (city) Burke County	31	0.18
Durham (city) Durham County	29	0.01
Wilmington (city) New Hanover County	25	0.02
Winston-Salem (city) Forsyth County	25	0.01
Raleigh (city) Wake County	23	0.01
Greensboro (city) Guilford County	19	0.01
Fayetteville (city) Cumberland County	17	0.01
Lumberton (city) Robeson County	14	0.06

Place	Population	%
Sanford (city) Lee County	14	0.05

Top 10 Places Sorted by Percent of Total Population
Based on all places, regardless of total population

Place	Population	%
Morganton (city) Burke County	31	0.18
Zebulon (town) Wake County	7	0.16
Rolesville (town) Wake County	5	0.13
La Grange (town) Lenoir County	3	0.10
St. James (town) Brunswick County	3	0.09
Pittsboro (town) Chatham County	3	0.08
Edneyville (cdp) Henderson County	2	0.08
Forest City (town) Rutherford County	5	0.07
Navassa (town) Brunswick County	1	0.07
Lumberton (city) Robeson County	14	0.06

Top 10 Places Sorted by Percent of Total Population
Based on places with total population of 50,000 or more

Place	Population	%
Wilmington (city) New Hanover County	25	0.02
Charlotte (city) Mecklenburg County	67	0.01
Durham (city) Durham County	29	0.01
Winston-Salem (city) Forsyth County	25	0.01
Raleigh (city) Wake County	23	0.01
Greensboro (city) Guilford County	19	0.01
Fayetteville (city) Cumberland County	17	0.01
Asheville (city) Buncombe County	8	0.01
Greenville (city) Pitt County	8	0.01
High Point (city) Guilford County	8	0.01

American Indian: Cherokee

Top 10 Places Sorted by Population
Based on all places, regardless of total population

Place	Population	%
Cherokee (cdp) Jackson County	1,593	74.51
Charlotte (city) Mecklenburg County	1,294	0.18
Fayetteville (city) Cumberland County	815	0.41
Greensboro (city) Guilford County	789	0.29
Raleigh (city) Wake County	775	0.19
Winston-Salem (city) Forsyth County	470	0.20
Durham (city) Durham County	417	0.18
Asheville (city) Buncombe County	342	0.41
Wilmington (city) New Hanover County	297	0.28
Jacksonville (city) Onslow County	220	0.31

Top 10 Places Sorted by Percent of Total Population
Based on all places, regardless of total population

Place	Population	%
Cherokee (cdp) Jackson County	1,593	74.51
Bryson City (town) Swain County	77	5.41
East Laurinburg (town) Scotland County	13	4.33
Rex (cdp) Robeson County	2	3.64
Old Hundred (cdp) Scotland County	8	2.79
Robbinsville (town) Graham County	17	2.74
Sylva (town) Jackson County	64	2.47
Shannon (cdp) Robeson County	6	2.28
Marble (cdp) Cherokee County	7	2.18
Webster (town) Jackson County	7	1.93

Top 10 Places Sorted by Percent of Total Population
Based on places with total population of 50,000 or more

Place	Population	%
Fayetteville (city) Cumberland County	815	0.41
Asheville (city) Buncombe County	342	0.41
Jacksonville (city) Onslow County	220	0.31
Greensboro (city) Guilford County	789	0.29
Wilmington (city) New Hanover County	297	0.28
Gastonia (city) Gaston County	184	0.26
Concord (city) Cabarrus County	188	0.24
High Point (city) Guilford County	216	0.21
Winston-Salem (city) Forsyth County	470	0.20
Raleigh (city) Wake County	775	0.19

American Indian: Cheyenne

Top 10 Places Sorted by Population
Based on all places, regardless of total population

Place	Population	%
Fayetteville (city) Cumberland County	12	0.01

Place	Population	%
Raleigh (city) Wake County	9	<0.01
Charlotte (city) Mecklenburg County	5	<0.01
Cherokee (cdp) Jackson County	4	0.19
Spring Lake (town) Cumberland County	4	0.03
Greensboro (city) Guilford County	4	<0.01
Greenville (city) Pitt County	4	<0.01
Westport (cdp) Lincoln County	3	0.07
Silver Lake (cdp) New Hanover County	3	0.05
Piney Green (cdp) Onslow County	3	0.02

Top 10 Places Sorted by Percent of Total Population
Based on all places, regardless of total population

Place	Population	%
Cherokee (cdp) Jackson County	4	0.19
Pinebluff (town) Moore County	2	0.15
Middlesex (town) Nash County	1	0.12
Westport (cdp) Lincoln County	3	0.07
Silver Lake (cdp) New Hanover County	3	0.05
Yanceyville (town) Caswell County	1	0.05
Nashville (town) Nash County	2	0.04
Spring Lake (town) Cumberland County	4	0.03
Hamlet (city) Richmond County	2	0.03
East Rockingham (cdp) Richmond County	1	0.03

Top 10 Places Sorted by Percent of Total Population
Based on places with total population of 50,000 or more

Place	Population	%
Fayetteville (city) Cumberland County	12	0.01
Raleigh (city) Wake County	9	<0.01
Charlotte (city) Mecklenburg County	5	<0.01
Greensboro (city) Guilford County	4	<0.01
Greenville (city) Pitt County	4	<0.01
Asheville (city) Buncombe County	2	<0.01
High Point (city) Guilford County	2	<0.01
Winston-Salem (city) Forsyth County	2	<0.01
Cary (town) Wake County	1	<0.01
Concord (city) Cabarrus County	1	<0.01

American Indian: Chickasaw

Top 10 Places Sorted by Population
Based on all places, regardless of total population

Place	Population	%
Charlotte (city) Mecklenburg County	36	<0.01
Fayetteville (city) Cumberland County	12	0.01
Durham (city) Durham County	11	<0.01
Winston-Salem (city) Forsyth County	11	<0.01
Raleigh (city) Wake County	9	<0.01
Wilmington (city) New Hanover County	6	0.01
Greensboro (city) Guilford County	6	<0.01
Jacksonville (city) Onslow County	5	0.01
Cary (town) Wake County	5	<0.01
Hope Mills (town) Cumberland County	4	0.03

Top 10 Places Sorted by Percent of Total Population
Based on all places, regardless of total population

Place	Population	%
Peletier (town) Carteret County	3	0.47
East Bend (town) Yadkin County	1	0.16
Neuse Forest (cdp) Craven County	3	0.15
Advance (cdp) Davie County	1	0.09
Boiling Springs (town) Cleveland County	3	0.06
Murphy (town) Cherokee County	1	0.06
Belville (town) Brunswick County	1	0.05
Brevard (city) Transylvania County	3	0.04
Edneyville (cdp) Henderson County	1	0.04
Tobaccoville (village) Forsyth County	1	0.04

Top 10 Places Sorted by Percent of Total Population
Based on places with total population of 50,000 or more

Place	Population	%
Fayetteville (city) Cumberland County	12	0.01
Wilmington (city) New Hanover County	6	0.01
Jacksonville (city) Onslow County	5	0.01
Charlotte (city) Mecklenburg County	36	<0.01
Durham (city) Durham County	11	<0.01
Winston-Salem (city) Forsyth County	11	<0.01
Raleigh (city) Wake County	9	<0.01
Greensboro (city) Guilford County	6	<0.01
Cary (town) Wake County	5	<0.01
Concord (city) Cabarrus County	2	<0.01

American Indian: Chippewa

Top 10 Places Sorted by Population
Based on all places, regardless of total population

Place	Population	%
Charlotte (city) Mecklenburg County	60	0.01
Fayetteville (city) Cumberland County	55	0.03
Raleigh (city) Wake County	36	0.01
Greensboro (city) Guilford County	33	0.01
Jacksonville (city) Onslow County	23	0.03
Cary (town) Wake County	21	0.02
Winston-Salem (city) Forsyth County	17	0.01
Chapel Hill (town) Orange County	13	0.02
High Point (city) Guilford County	13	0.01
Greenville (city) Pitt County	12	0.01

Top 10 Places Sorted by Percent of Total Population
Based on all places, regardless of total population

Place	Population	%
Sugar Mountain (village) Avery County	2	1.01
Seven Devils (town) Watauga County	1	0.52
Sandyfield (town) Columbus County	1	0.22
Winfall (town) Perquimans County	1	0.17
Pinebluff (town) Moore County	2	0.15
Pumpkin Center (cdp) Onslow County	3	0.14
Spruce Pine (town) Mitchell County	3	0.14
Madison (town) Rockingham County	3	0.13
Hudson (town) Caldwell County	4	0.11
Calabash (town) Brunswick County	2	0.11

Top 10 Places Sorted by Percent of Total Population
Based on places with total population of 50,000 or more

Place	Population	%
Fayetteville (city) Cumberland County	55	0.03
Jacksonville (city) Onslow County	23	0.03
Cary (town) Wake County	21	0.02
Chapel Hill (town) Orange County	13	0.02
Charlotte (city) Mecklenburg County	60	0.01
Raleigh (city) Wake County	36	0.01
Greensboro (city) Guilford County	33	0.01
Winston-Salem (city) Forsyth County	17	0.01
High Point (city) Guilford County	13	0.01
Greenville (city) Pitt County	12	0.01

American Indian: Choctaw

Top 10 Places Sorted by Population
Based on all places, regardless of total population

Place	Population	%
Charlotte (city) Mecklenburg County	67	0.01
Fayetteville (city) Cumberland County	55	0.03
Raleigh (city) Wake County	36	0.01
Durham (city) Durham County	25	0.01
Greensboro (city) Guilford County	22	0.01
Cary (town) Wake County	20	0.01
Winston-Salem (city) Forsyth County	18	0.01
Jacksonville (city) Onslow County	17	0.02
Piney Green (cdp) Onslow County	15	0.11
Chapel Hill (town) Orange County	15	0.03

Top 10 Places Sorted by Percent of Total Population
Based on all places, regardless of total population

Place	Population	%
Grantsboro (town) Pamlico County	3	0.44
Cherokee (cdp) Jackson County	7	0.33
Bunn (town) Franklin County	1	0.29
Laurel Hill (cdp) Scotland County	3	0.24
Cofield (village) Hertford County	1	0.24
Minnesott Beach (town) Pamlico County	1	0.23
Southmont (cdp) Davidson County	3	0.20
Rolesville (town) Wake County	7	0.18
Troutman (town) Iredell County	4	0.17
Chadbourn (town) Columbus County	3	0.16

Top 10 Places Sorted by Percent of Total Population
Based on places with total population of 50,000 or more

Place	Population	%
Fayetteville (city) Cumberland County	55	0.03
Chapel Hill (town) Orange County	15	0.03
Jacksonville (city) Onslow County	17	0.02
Charlotte (city) Mecklenburg County	67	0.01

Raleigh (city) Wake County	36	0.01
Durham (city) Durham County	25	0.01
Greensboro (city) Guilford County	22	0.01
Cary (town) Wake County	20	0.01
Winston-Salem (city) Forsyth County	18	0.01
High Point (city) Guilford County	13	0.01

American Indian: Colville

Top 10 Places Sorted by Population
Based on all places, regardless of total population

Place	Population	%
Cherokee (cdp) Jackson County	7	0.33
Lake Waccamaw (town) Columbus County	2	0.14
Lowesville (cdp) Lincoln County	1	0.03
Half Moon (cdp) Onslow County	1	0.01
Laurinburg (city) Scotland County	1	0.01
Oxford (city) Granville County	1	0.01
Piney Green (cdp) Onslow County	1	0.01
Cary (town) Wake County	1	<0.01
Concord (city) Cabarrus County	1	<0.01
Fayetteville (city) Cumberland County	1	<0.01

Top 10 Places Sorted by Percent of Total Population
Based on all places, regardless of total population

Place	Population	%
Cherokee (cdp) Jackson County	7	0.33
Lake Waccamaw (town) Columbus County	2	0.14
Lowesville (cdp) Lincoln County	1	0.03
Half Moon (cdp) Onslow County	1	0.01
Laurinburg (city) Scotland County	1	0.01
Oxford (city) Granville County	1	0.01
Piney Green (cdp) Onslow County	1	0.01
Cary (town) Wake County	1	<0.01
Concord (city) Cabarrus County	1	<0.01
Fayetteville (city) Cumberland County	1	<0.01

Top 10 Places Sorted by Percent of Total Population
Based on places with total population of 50,000 or more

Place	Population	%
Cary (town) Wake County	1	<0.01
Concord (city) Cabarrus County	1	<0.01
Fayetteville (city) Cumberland County	1	<0.01
Asheville (city) Buncombe County	0	0.00
Chapel Hill (town) Orange County	0	0.00
Charlotte (city) Mecklenburg County	0	0.00
Durham (city) Durham County	0	0.00
Gastonia (city) Gaston County	0	0.00
Greensboro (city) Guilford County	0	0.00
Greenville (city) Pitt County	0	0.00

American Indian: Comanche

Top 10 Places Sorted by Population
Based on all places, regardless of total population

Place	Population	%
Fayetteville (city) Cumberland County	13	0.01
Greenville (city) Pitt County	7	0.01
High Point (city) Guilford County	7	0.01
Greensboro (city) Guilford County	7	<0.01
Sedalia (town) Guilford County	6	0.96
King (city) Stokes County	6	0.09
Charlotte (city) Mecklenburg County	5	<0.01
Swepsonville (town) Alamance County	4	0.35
Chapel Hill (town) Orange County	4	0.01
Wilson (city) Wilson County	4	0.01

Top 10 Places Sorted by Percent of Total Population
Based on all places, regardless of total population

Place	Population	%
Linden (town) Cumberland County	2	1.54
Sedalia (town) Guilford County	6	0.96
South Mills (cdp) Camden County	2	0.44
Swepsonville (town) Alamance County	4	0.35
Elm City (town) Wilson County	2	0.15
King (city) Stokes County	6	0.09
Holly Ridge (town) Onslow County	1	0.08
Pembroke (town) Robeson County	2	0.07
Mountain Home (cdp) Henderson County	2	0.06
Butner (town) Granville County	3	0.04

American Indian: Colville (percent, 50,000+)
(See above)

Top 10 Places Sorted by Percent of Total Population
Based on places with total population of 50,000 or more

Place	Population	%
Fayetteville (city) Cumberland County	13	0.01
Greenville (city) Pitt County	7	0.01
High Point (city) Guilford County	7	0.01
Chapel Hill (town) Orange County	4	0.01
Greensboro (city) Guilford County	7	<0.01
Charlotte (city) Mecklenburg County	5	<0.01
Raleigh (city) Wake County	4	<0.01
Durham (city) Durham County	3	<0.01
Asheville (city) Buncombe County	2	<0.01
Wilmington (city) New Hanover County	2	<0.01

American Indian: Cree

Top 10 Places Sorted by Population
Based on all places, regardless of total population

Place	Population	%
Fayetteville (city) Cumberland County	11	0.01
Charlotte (city) Mecklenburg County	10	0.01
Raleigh (city) Wake County	6	<0.01
River Road (cdp) Beaufort County	3	0.07
Rocky Mount (city) Nash County	3	0.01
Cary (town) Wake County	3	<0.01
Durham (city) Durham County	3	<0.01
Wilmington (city) New Hanover County	3	<0.01
Kenansville (town) Duplin County	2	0.23
Asheboro (city) Randolph County	2	0.01

Top 10 Places Sorted by Percent of Total Population
Based on all places, regardless of total population

Place	Population	%
Kenansville (town) Duplin County	2	0.23
River Road (cdp) Beaufort County	3	0.07
Franklinton (town) Franklin County	1	0.05
Southport (city) Brunswick County	1	0.04
Mountain View (cdp) Catawba County	1	0.03
Beaufort (town) Carteret County	1	0.02
Cullowhee (cdp) Jackson County	1	0.02
Newport (town) Carteret County	1	0.02
Royal Pines (cdp) Buncombe County	1	0.02
Fayetteville (city) Cumberland County	11	0.01

Top 10 Places Sorted by Percent of Total Population
Based on places with total population of 50,000 or more

Place	Population	%
Fayetteville (city) Cumberland County	11	0.01
Rocky Mount (city) Nash County	3	0.01
Charlotte (city) Mecklenburg County	10	<0.01
Raleigh (city) Wake County	6	<0.01
Cary (town) Wake County	3	<0.01
Durham (city) Durham County	3	<0.01
Wilmington (city) New Hanover County	3	<0.01
Asheville (city) Buncombe County	2	<0.01
High Point (city) Guilford County	2	<0.01
Jacksonville (city) Onslow County	2	<0.01

American Indian: Creek

Top 10 Places Sorted by Population
Based on all places, regardless of total population

Place	Population	%
Charlotte (city) Mecklenburg County	38	0.01
Fayetteville (city) Cumberland County	29	0.01
Raleigh (city) Wake County	21	0.01
Durham (city) Durham County	14	0.01
Greensboro (city) Guilford County	11	<0.01
Gastonia (city) Gaston County	10	0.01
Winston-Salem (city) Forsyth County	10	<0.01
Mount Holly (city) Gaston County	9	0.07
Concord (city) Cabarrus County	8	0.01
Jacksonville (city) Onslow County	8	0.01

Top 10 Places Sorted by Percent of Total Population
Based on all places, regardless of total population

Place	Population	%
Pollocksville (town) Jones County	4	1.29
Bolton (town) Columbus County	3	0.43
Swepsonville (town) Alamance County	4	0.35

Place	Population	%
Cherokee (cdp) Jackson County	6	0.28
Caswell Beach (town) Brunswick County	1	0.25
Deercroft (cdp) Scotland County	1	0.24
Belhaven (town) Beaufort County	3	0.18
Atlantic (cdp) Carteret County	1	0.18
Castle Hayne (cdp) New Hanover County	2	0.17
Cliffside (cdp) Rutherford County	1	0.16

Top 10 Places Sorted by Percent of Total Population
Based on places with total population of 50,000 or more

Place	Population	%
Charlotte (city) Mecklenburg County	38	0.01
Fayetteville (city) Cumberland County	29	0.01
Raleigh (city) Wake County	21	0.01
Durham (city) Durham County	14	0.01
Gastonia (city) Gaston County	10	0.01
Concord (city) Cabarrus County	8	0.01
Jacksonville (city) Onslow County	8	0.01
Wilmington (city) New Hanover County	8	0.01
High Point (city) Guilford County	7	0.01
Greenville (city) Pitt County	6	0.01

American Indian: Crow

Top 10 Places Sorted by Population
Based on all places, regardless of total population

Place	Population	%
Charlotte (city) Mecklenburg County	13	<0.01
Wake Forest (town) Wake County	6	0.02
Cary (town) Wake County	6	<0.01
Carthage (town) Moore County	5	0.23
Piney Green (cdp) Onslow County	4	0.03
Mooresville (town) Iredell County	4	0.01
Fayetteville (city) Cumberland County	4	<0.01
Raleigh (city) Wake County	4	<0.01
Winston-Salem (city) Forsyth County	4	<0.01
Laurinburg (city) Scotland County	3	0.02

Top 10 Places Sorted by Percent of Total Population
Based on all places, regardless of total population

Place	Population	%
Caswell Beach (town) Brunswick County	1	0.25
Carthage (town) Moore County	5	0.23
Spring Hope (town) Nash County	2	0.15
Pumpkin Center (cdp) Onslow County	2	0.09
West Canton (cdp) Haywood County	1	0.08
Long View (town) Catawba County	2	0.04
Southport (city) Brunswick County	1	0.04
Piney Green (cdp) Onslow County	4	0.03
Forest City (town) Rutherford County	2	0.03
Wake Forest (town) Wake County	6	0.02

Top 10 Places Sorted by Percent of Total Population
Based on places with total population of 50,000 or more

Place	Population	%
Charlotte (city) Mecklenburg County	13	<0.01
Cary (town) Wake County	6	<0.01
Fayetteville (city) Cumberland County	4	<0.01
Raleigh (city) Wake County	4	<0.01
Winston-Salem (city) Forsyth County	4	<0.01
Wilmington (city) New Hanover County	3	<0.01
Concord (city) Cabarrus County	2	<0.01
Greensboro (city) Guilford County	2	<0.01
Rocky Mount (city) Nash County	2	<0.01
Gastonia (city) Gaston County	1	<0.01

American Indian: Delaware

Top 10 Places Sorted by Population
Based on all places, regardless of total population

Place	Population	%
Charlotte (city) Mecklenburg County	26	<0.01
Fayetteville (city) Cumberland County	12	0.01
Raleigh (city) Wake County	10	0.01
Chapel Hill (town) Orange County	7	0.01
Durham (city) Durham County	7	<0.01
Havelock (city) Craven County	5	0.02
Cary (town) Wake County	5	<0.01
Greensboro (city) Guilford County	5	<0.01
Archer Lodge (town) Johnston County	4	0.09
Half Moon (cdp) Onslow County	4	0.05

Top 10 Places Sorted by Percent of Total Population
Based on all places, regardless of total population

Place	Population	%
Hobucken (cdp) Pamlico County	1	0.78
Warrenton (town) Warren County	1	0.12
Mineral Springs (town) Union County	3	0.11
Archer Lodge (town) Johnston County	4	0.09
Laurel Hill (cdp) Scotland County	1	0.08
Randleman (city) Randolph County	3	0.07
Half Moon (cdp) Onslow County	4	0.05
Kitty Hawk (town) Dare County	1	0.03
Shallotte (town) Brunswick County	1	0.03
Havelock (city) Craven County	5	0.02

Top 10 Places Sorted by Percent of Total Population
Based on places with total population of 50,000 or more

Place	Population	%
Fayetteville (city) Cumberland County	12	0.01
Chapel Hill (town) Orange County	7	0.01
Charlotte (city) Mecklenburg County	26	<0.01
Raleigh (city) Wake County	10	<0.01
Durham (city) Durham County	7	<0.01
Cary (town) Wake County	5	<0.01
Greensboro (city) Guilford County	5	<0.01
Winston-Salem (city) Forsyth County	3	<0.01
High Point (city) Guilford County	2	<0.01
Jacksonville (city) Onslow County	2	<0.01

American Indian: Hopi

Top 10 Places Sorted by Population
Based on all places, regardless of total population

Place	Population	%
Indian Trail (town) Union County	5	0.01
Horse Shoe (cdp) Henderson County	4	0.17
Hillsborough (town) Orange County	4	0.07
Fayetteville (city) Cumberland County	4	<0.01
Thomasville (city) Davidson County	3	<0.01
Jacksonville (city) Onslow County	3	<0.01
Durham (city) Durham County	2	<0.01
Greensboro (city) Guilford County	2	<0.01
Raleigh (city) Wake County	2	<0.01
Stanfield (town) Stanly County	1	0.07

Top 10 Places Sorted by Percent of Total Population
Based on all places, regardless of total population

Place	Population	%
Horse Shoe (cdp) Henderson County	4	0.17
Hillsborough (town) Orange County	4	0.07
Stanfield (town) Stanly County	1	0.07
Jonesville (town) Yadkin County	1	0.04
Pittsboro (town) Chatham County	1	0.03
Carolina Beach (town) New Hanover County	1	0.02
Indian Trail (town) Union County	5	0.01
Thomasville (city) Davidson County	3	0.01
Kill Devil Hills (town) Dare County	1	0.01
Leland (town) Brunswick County	1	0.01

Top 10 Places Sorted by Percent of Total Population
Based on places with total population of 50,000 or more

Place	Population	%
Fayetteville (city) Cumberland County	4	<0.01
Jacksonville (city) Onslow County	3	<0.01
Durham (city) Durham County	2	<0.01
Greensboro (city) Guilford County	2	<0.01
Raleigh (city) Wake County	2	<0.01
Cary (town) Wake County	1	<0.01
Chapel Hill (town) Orange County	1	<0.01
Charlotte (city) Mecklenburg County	1	<0.01
High Point (city) Guilford County	1	<0.01
Wilmington (city) New Hanover County	1	<0.01

American Indian: Houma

Top 10 Places Sorted by Population
Based on all places, regardless of total population

Place	Population	%
Woodland (town) Northampton County	3	0.37
Franklin (town) Macon County	3	0.08
Goldsboro (city) Wayne County	3	0.01

Place	Population	%
Holly Springs (town) Wake County	3	0.01
Concord (city) Cabarrus County	3	<0.01
Fayetteville (city) Cumberland County	3	<0.01
Spring Lake (town) Cumberland County	2	0.02
Havelock (city) Craven County	2	<0.01
Jacksonville (city) Onslow County	2	<0.01
Raleigh (city) Wake County	2	<0.01

Top 10 Places Sorted by Percent of Total Population
Based on all places, regardless of total population

Place	Population	%
Woodland (town) Northampton County	3	0.37
Franklin (town) Macon County	3	0.08
West Marion (cdp) McDowell County	1	0.07
Spring Lake (town) Cumberland County	2	0.02
Goldsboro (city) Wayne County	3	0.01
Holly Springs (town) Wake County	3	0.01
Havelock (city) Craven County	2	0.01
Knightdale (town) Wake County	1	0.01
Concord (city) Cabarrus County	3	<0.01
Fayetteville (city) Cumberland County	3	<0.01

Top 10 Places Sorted by Percent of Total Population
Based on places with total population of 50,000 or more

Place	Population	%
Concord (city) Cabarrus County	3	<0.01
Fayetteville (city) Cumberland County	3	<0.01
Jacksonville (city) Onslow County	2	<0.01
Raleigh (city) Wake County	2	<0.01
Asheville (city) Buncombe County	1	<0.01
Charlotte (city) Mecklenburg County	1	<0.01
Cary (town) Wake County	0	0.00
Chapel Hill (town) Orange County	0	0.00
Durham (city) Durham County	0	0.00
Gastonia (city) Gaston County	0	0.00

Alaska Native: Inupiat (Eskimo)

Top 10 Places Sorted by Population
Based on all places, regardless of total population

Place	Population	%
Charlotte (city) Mecklenburg County	12	<0.01
Mountain Home (cdp) Henderson County	8	0.22
Jacksonville (city) Onslow County	6	0.01
Weddington (town) Union County	4	0.04
Randleman (city) Randolph County	3	0.07
Cullowhee (cdp) Jackson County	3	0.05
Elizabeth City (city) Pasquotank County	3	0.02
Raleigh (city) Wake County	3	<0.01
Broad Creek (cdp) Carteret County	2	0.09
Lake Norman of Catawba (cdp) Catawba County	2	0.03

Top 10 Places Sorted by Percent of Total Population
Based on all places, regardless of total population

Place	Population	%
Caswell Beach (town) Brunswick County	1	0.25
Mountain Home (cdp) Henderson County	8	0.22
Broad Creek (cdp) Carteret County	2	0.09
Barker Heights (cdp) Henderson County	1	0.08
Randleman (city) Randolph County	3	0.07
Flat Rock (cdp) Surry County	1	0.06
Cullowhee (cdp) Jackson County	3	0.05
Cherokee (cdp) Jackson County	1	0.05
Valley Hill (cdp) Henderson County	1	0.05
Weddington (town) Union County	4	0.04

Top 10 Places Sorted by Percent of Total Population
Based on places with total population of 50,000 or more

Place	Population	%
Jacksonville (city) Onslow County	6	0.01
Charlotte (city) Mecklenburg County	12	<0.01
Raleigh (city) Wake County	3	<0.01
Fayetteville (city) Cumberland County	2	<0.01
Greensboro (city) Guilford County	2	<0.01
Winston-Salem (city) Forsyth County	2	<0.01
Greenville (city) Pitt County	1	<0.01
High Point (city) Guilford County	1	<0.01
Asheville (city) Buncombe County	0	0.00
Cary (town) Wake County	0	0.00

American Indian: Iroquois

Top 10 Places Sorted by Population
Based on all places, regardless of total population

Place	Population	%
Charlotte (city) Mecklenburg County	116	0.02
Fayetteville (city) Cumberland County	60	0.03
Greensboro (city) Guilford County	56	0.02
Raleigh (city) Wake County	52	0.01
Durham (city) Durham County	34	0.01
Wilmington (city) New Hanover County	25	0.02
Jacksonville (city) Onslow County	24	0.03
Cary (town) Wake County	24	0.02
Maxton (town) Robeson County	23	0.95
Winston-Salem (city) Forsyth County	18	0.01

Top 10 Places Sorted by Percent of Total Population
Based on all places, regardless of total population

Place	Population	%
Bowmore (cdp) Hoke County	10	9.71
Shannon (cdp) Robeson County	4	1.52
Parkton (town) Robeson County	5	1.15
Bolton (town) Columbus County	7	1.01
Maxton (town) Robeson County	23	0.95
Wakulla (cdp) Robeson County	1	0.95
Marshall (town) Madison County	8	0.92
Prospect (cdp) Robeson County	6	0.61
Watha (town) Pender County	1	0.53
Pembroke (town) Robeson County	15	0.50

Top 10 Places Sorted by Percent of Total Population
Based on places with total population of 50,000 or more

Place	Population	%
Fayetteville (city) Cumberland County	60	0.03
Jacksonville (city) Onslow County	24	0.03
Charlotte (city) Mecklenburg County	116	0.02
Greensboro (city) Guilford County	56	0.02
Wilmington (city) New Hanover County	25	0.02
Cary (town) Wake County	24	0.02
Greenville (city) Pitt County	17	0.02
High Point (city) Guilford County	17	0.02
Asheville (city) Buncombe County	13	0.02
Chapel Hill (town) Orange County	10	0.02

American Indian: Kiowa

Top 10 Places Sorted by Population
Based on all places, regardless of total population

Place	Population	%
Fayetteville (city) Cumberland County	7	<0.01
Mint Hill (town) Mecklenburg County	4	0.02
Jacksonville (city) Onslow County	4	0.01
Cherokee (cdp) Jackson County	3	0.14
Piney Green (cdp) Onslow County	2	0.02
Havelock (city) Craven County	2	0.01
Charlotte (city) Mecklenburg County	2	<0.01
Mountain Home (cdp) Henderson County	1	0.03
Tyro (cdp) Davidson County	1	0.03
James City (cdp) Craven County	1	0.02

Top 10 Places Sorted by Percent of Total Population
Based on all places, regardless of total population

Place	Population	%
Cherokee (cdp) Jackson County	3	0.14
Mountain Home (cdp) Henderson County	1	0.03
Tyro (cdp) Davidson County	1	0.03
Mint Hill (town) Mecklenburg County	4	0.02
Piney Green (cdp) Onslow County	2	0.02
James City (cdp) Craven County	1	0.02
Jacksonville (city) Onslow County	4	0.01
Havelock (city) Craven County	2	0.01
Hope Mills (town) Cumberland County	1	0.01
Fayetteville (city) Cumberland County	7	<0.01

Top 10 Places Sorted by Percent of Total Population
Based on places with total population of 50,000 or more

Place	Population	%
Jacksonville (city) Onslow County	4	0.01
Fayetteville (city) Cumberland County	7	<0.01
Charlotte (city) Mecklenburg County	2	<0.01
Cary (town) Wake County	1	<0.01

Chapel Hill (town) Orange County	1	<0.01
Concord (city) Cabarrus County	1	<0.01
Durham (city) Durham County	1	<0.01
Gastonia (city) Gaston County	1	<0.01
Greensboro (city) Guilford County	1	<0.01
Winston-Salem (city) Forsyth County	1	<0.01

American Indian: Lumbee

Top 10 Places Sorted by Population
Based on all places, regardless of total population

Place	Population	%
Lumberton (city) Robeson County	1,952	9.06
Pembroke (town) Robeson County	1,599	53.78
Fayetteville (city) Cumberland County	893	0.45
Charlotte (city) Mecklenburg County	763	0.10
Prospect (cdp) Robeson County	754	76.86
Laurinburg (city) Scotland County	662	4.15
Greensboro (city) Guilford County	488	0.18
Raleigh (city) Wake County	392	0.10
Red Springs (town) Robeson County	301	8.78
Fairmont (town) Robeson County	274	10.29

Top 10 Places Sorted by Percent of Total Population
Based on all places, regardless of total population

Place	Population	%
Prospect (cdp) Robeson County	754	76.86
Wakulla (cdp) Robeson County	68	64.76
Raemon (cdp) Robeson County	163	57.80
Pembroke (town) Robeson County	1,599	53.78
Elrod (cdp) Robeson County	217	52.04
Rennert (town) Robeson County	127	33.16
Shannon (cdp) Robeson County	87	33.08
McDonald (town) Robeson County	25	22.12
Rex (cdp) Robeson County	11	20.00
Bowmore (cdp) Hoke County	12	11.65

Top 10 Places Sorted by Percent of Total Population
Based on places with total population of 50,000 or more

Place	Population	%
Fayetteville (city) Cumberland County	893	0.45
Greensboro (city) Guilford County	488	0.18
High Point (city) Guilford County	161	0.15
Wilmington (city) New Hanover County	120	0.11
Concord (city) Cabarrus County	87	0.11
Jacksonville (city) Onslow County	77	0.11
Chapel Hill (town) Orange County	65	0.11
Charlotte (city) Mecklenburg County	763	0.10
Raleigh (city) Wake County	392	0.10
Cary (town) Wake County	124	0.09

American Indian: Menominee

Top 10 Places Sorted by Population
Based on all places, regardless of total population

Place	Population	%
Charlotte (city) Mecklenburg County	4	<0.01
Waxhaw (town) Union County	3	0.03
Hope Mills (town) Cumberland County	3	0.02
Wilmington (city) New Hanover County	3	<0.01
Fayetteville (city) Cumberland County	2	<0.01
Huntersville (town) Mecklenburg County	2	<0.01
Raleigh (city) Wake County	2	<0.01
Cherokee (cdp) Jackson County	1	0.05
Kitty Hawk (town) Dare County	1	0.03
Carrboro (town) Orange County	1	0.01

Top 10 Places Sorted by Percent of Total Population
Based on all places, regardless of total population

Place	Population	%
Cherokee (cdp) Jackson County	1	0.05
Waxhaw (town) Union County	3	0.03
Kitty Hawk (town) Dare County	1	0.03
Hope Mills (town) Cumberland County	3	0.02
Carrboro (town) Orange County	1	0.01
Knightdale (town) Wake County	1	0.01
Charlotte (city) Mecklenburg County	4	<0.01
Wilmington (city) New Hanover County	3	<0.01
Fayetteville (city) Cumberland County	2	<0.01
Huntersville (town) Mecklenburg County	2	<0.01

Top 10 Places Sorted by Percent of Total Population
Based on places with total population of 50,000 or more

Place	Population	%
Charlotte (city) Mecklenburg County	4	<0.01
Wilmington (city) New Hanover County	3	<0.01
Fayetteville (city) Cumberland County	2	<0.01
Raleigh (city) Wake County	2	<0.01
Jacksonville (city) Onslow County	1	<0.01
Asheville (city) Buncombe County	0	0.00
Cary (town) Wake County	0	0.00
Chapel Hill (town) Orange County	0	0.00
Concord (city) Cabarrus County	0	0.00
Durham (city) Durham County	0	0.00

American Indian: Mexican American Indian

Top 10 Places Sorted by Population
Based on all places, regardless of total population

Place	Population	%
Charlotte (city) Mecklenburg County	331	0.05
Raleigh (city) Wake County	242	0.06
Durham (city) Durham County	156	0.07
Winston-Salem (city) Forsyth County	151	0.07
Morganton (city) Burke County	80	0.47
Greensboro (city) Guilford County	72	0.03
Cary (town) Wake County	59	0.04
Wilmington (city) New Hanover County	57	0.05
High Point (city) Guilford County	52	0.05
Siler City (town) Chatham County	50	0.63

Top 10 Places Sorted by Percent of Total Population
Based on all places, regardless of total population

Place	Population	%
Rennert (town) Robeson County	4	1.04
Belvoir (cdp) Pitt County	3	0.98
Rocky Point (cdp) Pender County	12	0.75
Siler City (town) Chatham County	50	0.63
St. Pauls (town) Robeson County	12	0.59
Pikeville (town) Wayne County	4	0.59
Burnsville (town) Yancey County	9	0.53
Wilson's Mills (town) Johnston County	11	0.48
Morganton (city) Burke County	80	0.47
Sparta (town) Alleghany County	8	0.45

Top 10 Places Sorted by Percent of Total Population
Based on places with total population of 50,000 or more

Place	Population	%
Durham (city) Durham County	156	0.07
Winston-Salem (city) Forsyth County	151	0.07
Raleigh (city) Wake County	242	0.06
Charlotte (city) Mecklenburg County	331	0.05
Wilmington (city) New Hanover County	57	0.05
High Point (city) Guilford County	52	0.05
Cary (town) Wake County	59	0.04
Concord (city) Cabarrus County	34	0.04
Jacksonville (city) Onslow County	25	0.04
Chapel Hill (town) Orange County	24	0.04

American Indian: Navajo

Top 10 Places Sorted by Population
Based on all places, regardless of total population

Place	Population	%
Fayetteville (city) Cumberland County	109	0.05
Jacksonville (city) Onslow County	52	0.07
Charlotte (city) Mecklenburg County	33	<0.01
Havelock (city) Craven County	23	0.11
Greensboro (city) Guilford County	21	0.01
Raleigh (city) Wake County	19	<0.01
Durham (city) Durham County	16	0.01
Asheville (city) Buncombe County	12	0.01
High Point (city) Guilford County	11	0.01
Winston-Salem (city) Forsyth County	11	<0.01

Top 10 Places Sorted by Percent of Total Population
Based on all places, regardless of total population

Place	Population	%
Falcon (town) Cumberland County	3	1.16
Macon (town) Warren County	1	0.84

Place	Population	%
Winton (town) Hertford County	3	0.39
Beech Mountain (town) Watauga County	1	0.31
Cherokee (cdp) Jackson County	4	0.19
Spring Hope (town) Nash County	2	0.15
Grover (town) Cleveland County	1	0.14
Boiling Springs (town) Cleveland County	6	0.13
River Bend (town) Craven County	4	0.13
Wagram (town) Scotland County	1	0.12

Top 10 Places Sorted by Percent of Total Population
Based on places with total population of 50,000 or more

Place	Population	%
Jacksonville (city) Onslow County	52	0.07
Fayetteville (city) Cumberland County	109	0.05
Greensboro (city) Guilford County	21	0.01
Durham (city) Durham County	16	0.01
Asheville (city) Buncombe County	12	0.01
High Point (city) Guilford County	11	0.01
Wilmington (city) New Hanover County	10	0.01
Chapel Hill (town) Orange County	8	0.01
Charlotte (city) Mecklenburg County	33	<0.01
Raleigh (city) Wake County	19	<0.01

American Indian: Osage

Top 10 Places Sorted by Population
Based on all places, regardless of total population

Place	Population	%
Raleigh (city) Wake County	9	<0.01
Cary (town) Wake County	7	0.01
Fayetteville (city) Cumberland County	7	<0.01
Salisbury (city) Rowan County	5	0.01
Charlotte (city) Mecklenburg County	5	<0.01
Tryon (town) Polk County	4	0.24
Monroe (city) Union County	4	0.01
Durham (city) Durham County	4	<0.01
Plymouth (town) Washington County	2	0.05
Summerfield (town) Guilford County	2	0.02

Top 10 Places Sorted by Percent of Total Population
Based on all places, regardless of total population

Place	Population	%
Como (town) Hertford County	1	1.10
Tryon (town) Polk County	4	0.24
Parkton (town) Robeson County	1	0.23
Foxfire (village) Moore County	1	0.11
Balfour (cdp) Henderson County	1	0.08
Robersonville (town) Martin County	1	0.07
Plymouth (town) Washington County	2	0.05
Cherokee (cdp) Jackson County	1	0.05
Four Oaks (town) Johnston County	1	0.05
Pittsboro (town) Chatham County	1	0.03

Top 10 Places Sorted by Percent of Total Population
Based on places with total population of 50,000 or more

Place	Population	%
Cary (town) Wake County	7	0.01
Raleigh (city) Wake County	9	<0.01
Fayetteville (city) Cumberland County	7	<0.01
Charlotte (city) Mecklenburg County	5	<0.01
Durham (city) Durham County	4	<0.01
Winston-Salem (city) Forsyth County	2	<0.01
Gastonia (city) Gaston County	1	<0.01
Wilmington (city) New Hanover County	1	<0.01
Asheville (city) Buncombe County	0	0.00
Chapel Hill (town) Orange County	0	0.00

American Indian: Ottawa

Top 10 Places Sorted by Population
Based on all places, regardless of total population

Place	Population	%
Rose Hill (town) Duplin County	4	0.25
Fayetteville (city) Cumberland County	4	<0.01
Indian Trail (town) Union County	3	0.01
Greensboro (city) Guilford County	3	<0.01
Kill Devil Hills (town) Dare County	2	0.03
Davidson (town) Mecklenburg County	2	0.02
Cornelius (town) Mecklenburg County	2	0.01
Elizabeth City (city) Pasquotank County	2	0.01
Wake Forest (town) Wake County	2	0.01

Place	Population	%
Cary (town) Wake County	2	<0.01

Top 10 Places Sorted by Percent of Total Population
Based on all places, regardless of total population

Place	Population	%
Rose Hill (town) Duplin County	4	0.25
Winton (town) Hertford County	1	0.13
Stanfield (town) Stanly County	1	0.07
Kure Beach (town) New Hanover County	1	0.05
Pumpkin Center (cdp) Onslow County	1	0.05
Wilson's Mills (town) Johnston County	1	0.04
Kill Devil Hills (town) Dare County	2	0.03
Davidson (town) Mecklenburg County	2	0.02
Gibsonville (town) Guilford County	1	0.02
Mocksville (town) Davie County	1	0.02

Top 10 Places Sorted by Percent of Total Population
Based on places with total population of 50,000 or more

Place	Population	%
Fayetteville (city) Cumberland County	4	<0.01
Greensboro (city) Guilford County	3	<0.01
Cary (town) Wake County	2	<0.01
Charlotte (city) Mecklenburg County	2	<0.01
Concord (city) Cabarrus County	2	<0.01
High Point (city) Guilford County	2	<0.01
Jacksonville (city) Onslow County	2	<0.01
Wilmington (city) New Hanover County	2	<0.01
Durham (city) Durham County	1	<0.01
Greenville (city) Pitt County	1	<0.01

American Indian: Paiute

Top 10 Places Sorted by Population
Based on all places, regardless of total population

Place	Population	%
Huntersville (town) Mecklenburg County	3	0.01
Fayetteville (city) Cumberland County	2	<0.01
Jacksonville (city) Onslow County	2	<0.01
Raleigh (city) Wake County	2	<0.01
Kure Beach (town) New Hanover County	1	0.05
East Flat Rock (cdp) Henderson County	1	0.02
Sawmills (town) Caldwell County	1	0.02
Eden (city) Rockingham County	1	0.01
Morganton (city) Burke County	1	0.01
Apex (town) Wake County	1	<0.01

Top 10 Places Sorted by Percent of Total Population
Based on all places, regardless of total population

Place	Population	%
Kure Beach (town) New Hanover County	1	0.05
East Flat Rock (cdp) Henderson County	1	0.02
Sawmills (town) Caldwell County	1	0.02
Huntersville (town) Mecklenburg County	3	0.01
Eden (city) Rockingham County	1	0.01
Morganton (city) Burke County	1	0.01
Fayetteville (city) Cumberland County	2	<0.01
Jacksonville (city) Onslow County	2	<0.01
Raleigh (city) Wake County	2	<0.01
Apex (town) Wake County	1	<0.01

Top 10 Places Sorted by Percent of Total Population
Based on places with total population of 50,000 or more

Place	Population	%
Fayetteville (city) Cumberland County	2	<0.01
Jacksonville (city) Onslow County	2	<0.01
Raleigh (city) Wake County	2	<0.01
Asheville (city) Buncombe County	1	<0.01
Durham (city) Durham County	1	<0.01
Wilmington (city) New Hanover County	1	<0.01
Cary (town) Wake County	0	0.00
Chapel Hill (town) Orange County	0	0.00
Charlotte (city) Mecklenburg County	0	0.00
Concord (city) Cabarrus County	0	0.00

American Indian: Pima

Top 10 Places Sorted by Population
Based on all places, regardless of total population

Place	Population	%
Fayetteville (city) Cumberland County	8	<0.01

Place	Population	%
Jacksonville (city) Onslow County	4	0.01
Wilson (city) Wilson County	3	0.01
Raleigh (city) Wake County	3	<0.01
Fremont (town) Wayne County	2	0.16
Havelock (city) Craven County	2	0.01
North Topsail Beach (town) Onslow County	1	0.13
Carolina Beach (town) New Hanover County	1	0.02
Morehead City (town) Carteret County	1	0.01
Cary (town) Wake County	1	<0.01

Top 10 Places Sorted by Percent of Total Population
Based on all places, regardless of total population

Place	Population	%
Fremont (town) Wayne County	2	0.16
North Topsail Beach (town) Onslow County	1	0.13
Carolina Beach (town) New Hanover County	1	0.02
Jacksonville (city) Onslow County	4	0.01
Wilson (city) Wilson County	3	0.01
Havelock (city) Craven County	2	0.01
Morehead City (town) Carteret County	1	0.01
Fayetteville (city) Cumberland County	8	<0.01
Raleigh (city) Wake County	3	<0.01
Cary (town) Wake County	1	<0.01

Top 10 Places Sorted by Percent of Total Population
Based on places with total population of 50,000 or more

Place	Population	%
Jacksonville (city) Onslow County	4	0.01
Fayetteville (city) Cumberland County	8	<0.01
Raleigh (city) Wake County	3	<0.01
Cary (town) Wake County	1	<0.01
Charlotte (city) Mecklenburg County	1	<0.01
Asheville (city) Buncombe County	0	0.00
Chapel Hill (town) Orange County	0	0.00
Concord (city) Cabarrus County	0	0.00
Durham (city) Durham County	0	0.00
Gastonia (city) Gaston County	0	0.00

American Indian: Potawatomi

Top 10 Places Sorted by Population
Based on all places, regardless of total population

Place	Population	%
Fayetteville (city) Cumberland County	9	<0.01
Jacksonville (city) Onslow County	7	0.01
Hickory (city) Catawba County	5	0.01
Forest Oaks (cdp) Guilford County	4	0.10
Garner (town) Wake County	4	0.02
Wake Forest (town) Wake County	4	0.01
Charlotte (city) Mecklenburg County	4	<0.01
Winston-Salem (city) Forsyth County	4	<0.01
Broadway (town) Lee County	3	0.24
Mount Olive (town) Wayne County	3	0.07

Top 10 Places Sorted by Percent of Total Population
Based on all places, regardless of total population

Place	Population	%
Marble (cdp) Cherokee County	1	0.31
Broadway (town) Lee County	3	0.24
Bryson City (town) Swain County	2	0.14
Forest Oaks (cdp) Guilford County	4	0.10
Bent Creek (cdp) Buncombe County	1	0.08
Mount Olive (town) Wayne County	3	0.07
Atlantic Beach (town) Carteret County	1	0.07
Troy (town) Montgomery County	2	0.06
Bermuda Run (town) Davie County	1	0.06
Murfreesboro (town) Hertford County	1	0.04

Top 10 Places Sorted by Percent of Total Population
Based on places with total population of 50,000 or more

Place	Population	%
Jacksonville (city) Onslow County	7	0.01
Fayetteville (city) Cumberland County	9	<0.01
Charlotte (city) Mecklenburg County	4	<0.01
Winston-Salem (city) Forsyth County	4	<0.01
Gastonia (city) Gaston County	3	<0.01
High Point (city) Guilford County	3	<0.01
Durham (city) Durham County	2	<0.01
Raleigh (city) Wake County	2	<0.01
Asheville (city) Buncombe County	1	<0.01
Cary (town) Wake County	1	<0.01

American Indian: Pueblo

Top 10 Places Sorted by Population
Based on all places, regardless of total population

Place	Population	%
Charlotte (city) Mecklenburg County	18	<0.01
Raleigh (city) Wake County	13	<0.01
Winston-Salem (city) Forsyth County	12	0.01
Fayetteville (city) Cumberland County	11	0.01
Jacksonville (city) Onslow County	7	0.01
Forest Oaks (cdp) Guilford County	5	0.13
Fletcher (town) Henderson County	5	0.07
Havelock (city) Craven County	4	0.02
Durham (city) Durham County	4	<0.01
Newport (town) Carteret County	3	0.07

Top 10 Places Sorted by Percent of Total Population
Based on all places, regardless of total population

Place	Population	%
Ellenboro (town) Rutherford County	2	0.23
Forest Oaks (cdp) Guilford County	5	0.13
Kenansville (town) Duplin County	1	0.12
Cherokee (cdp) Jackson County	2	0.09
Balfour (cdp) Henderson County	1	0.08
Fletcher (town) Henderson County	5	0.07
Newport (town) Carteret County	3	0.07
Ramseur (town) Randolph County	1	0.06
Coats (town) Harnett County	1	0.05
Laurel Park (town) Henderson County	1	0.05

Top 10 Places Sorted by Percent of Total Population
Based on places with total population of 50,000 or more

Place	Population	%
Winston-Salem (city) Forsyth County	12	0.01
Fayetteville (city) Cumberland County	11	0.01
Jacksonville (city) Onslow County	7	0.01
Chapel Hill (town) Orange County	3	0.01
Charlotte (city) Mecklenburg County	18	<0.01
Raleigh (city) Wake County	13	<0.01
Durham (city) Durham County	4	<0.01
Greensboro (city) Guilford County	3	<0.01
High Point (city) Guilford County	3	<0.01
Cary (town) Wake County	2	<0.01

American Indian: Puget Sound Salish

Top 10 Places Sorted by Population
Based on all places, regardless of total population

Place	Population	%
Fayetteville (city) Cumberland County	5	<0.01
Jacksonville (city) Onslow County	4	0.01
Cary (town) Wake County	3	<0.01
Marvin (village) Union County	2	0.04
Kings Grant (cdp) New Hanover County	2	0.02
Charlotte (city) Mecklenburg County	2	<0.01
Concord (city) Cabarrus County	2	<0.01
Winston-Salem (city) Forsyth County	2	<0.01
Archdale (city) Randolph County	1	0.01
Davidson (town) Mecklenburg County	1	0.01

Top 10 Places Sorted by Percent of Total Population
Based on all places, regardless of total population

Place	Population	%
Marvin (village) Union County	2	0.04
Kings Grant (cdp) New Hanover County	2	0.02
Jacksonville (city) Onslow County	4	0.01
Archdale (city) Randolph County	1	0.01
Davidson (town) Mecklenburg County	1	0.01
Fayetteville (city) Cumberland County	5	<0.01
Cary (town) Wake County	3	<0.01
Charlotte (city) Mecklenburg County	2	<0.01
Concord (city) Cabarrus County	2	<0.01
Winston-Salem (city) Forsyth County	2	<0.01

Top 10 Places Sorted by Percent of Total Population
Based on places with total population of 50,000 or more

Place	Population	%
Jacksonville (city) Onslow County	4	0.01
Fayetteville (city) Cumberland County	5	<0.01
Cary (town) Wake County	3	<0.01
Charlotte (city) Mecklenburg County	2	<0.01

Concord (city) Cabarrus County	2	<0.01
Winston-Salem (city) Forsyth County	2	<0.01
Raleigh (city) Wake County	1	<0.01
Asheville (city) Buncombe County	0	0.00
Chapel Hill (town) Orange County	0	0.00
Durham (city) Durham County	0	0.00

American Indian: Seminole

Top 10 Places Sorted by Population
Based on all places, regardless of total population

Place	Population	%
Charlotte (city) Mecklenburg County	34	<0.01
Fayetteville (city) Cumberland County	24	0.01
Raleigh (city) Wake County	20	<0.01
Durham (city) Durham County	13	0.01
Wilmington (city) New Hanover County	13	0.01
Wake Forest (town) Wake County	10	0.03
Winston-Salem (city) Forsyth County	10	<0.01
Gastonia (city) Gaston County	9	0.01
Cary (town) Wake County	8	0.01
Jacksonville (city) Onslow County	7	0.01

Top 10 Places Sorted by Percent of Total Population
Based on all places, regardless of total population

Place	Population	%
Trenton (town) Jones County	2	0.70
Camden (cdp) Camden County	4	0.67
East Bend (town) Yadkin County	2	0.33
Aurora (town) Beaufort County	1	0.19
Calabash (town) Brunswick County	3	0.17
East Spencer (town) Rowan County	2	0.13
Manns Harbor (cdp) Dare County	1	0.12
Bladenboro (town) Bladen County	2	0.11
Carolina Beach (town) New Hanover County	5	0.09
Cherokee (cdp) Jackson County	2	0.09

Top 10 Places Sorted by Percent of Total Population
Based on places with total population of 50,000 or more

Place	Population	%
Fayetteville (city) Cumberland County	24	0.01
Durham (city) Durham County	13	0.01
Wilmington (city) New Hanover County	13	0.01
Gastonia (city) Gaston County	9	0.01
Cary (town) Wake County	8	0.01
Jacksonville (city) Onslow County	7	0.01
Asheville (city) Buncombe County	6	0.01
Greenville (city) Pitt County	5	0.01
Charlotte (city) Mecklenburg County	34	<0.01
Raleigh (city) Wake County	20	<0.01

American Indian: Shoshone

Top 10 Places Sorted by Population
Based on all places, regardless of total population

Place	Population	%
Fayetteville (city) Cumberland County	11	0.01
Woodland (town) Northampton County	6	0.74
Statesville (city) Iredell County	6	0.02
Cherokee (cdp) Jackson County	5	0.23
Huntersville (town) Mecklenburg County	5	0.01
Charlotte (city) Mecklenburg County	4	<0.01
Half Moon (cdp) Onslow County	3	0.04
Mooresville (town) Iredell County	3	0.01
Wake Forest (town) Wake County	3	0.01
Long View (town) Catawba County	2	0.04

Top 10 Places Sorted by Percent of Total Population
Based on all places, regardless of total population

Place	Population	%
Woodland (town) Northampton County	6	0.74
Cherokee (cdp) Jackson County	5	0.23
Broadway (town) Lee County	1	0.08
Four Oaks (town) Johnston County	1	0.05
Spruce Pine (town) Mitchell County	1	0.05
Half Moon (cdp) Onslow County	3	0.04
Long View (town) Catawba County	2	0.04
Statesville (city) Iredell County	6	0.02
Beaufort (town) Carteret County	1	0.02
Fayetteville (city) Cumberland County	11	0.01

Top 10 Places Sorted by Percent of Total Population
Based on places with total population of 50,000 or more

Place	Population	%
Fayetteville (city) Cumberland County	11	0.01
Charlotte (city) Mecklenburg County	4	<0.01
Asheville (city) Buncombe County	1	<0.01
Durham (city) Durham County	1	<0.01
Greenville (city) Pitt County	1	<0.01
Jacksonville (city) Onslow County	1	<0.01
Winston-Salem (city) Forsyth County	1	<0.01
Cary (town) Wake County	0	0.00
Chapel Hill (town) Orange County	0	0.00
Concord (city) Cabarrus County	0	0.00

American Indian: Sioux

Top 10 Places Sorted by Population
Based on all places, regardless of total population

Place	Population	%
Fayetteville (city) Cumberland County	87	0.04
Charlotte (city) Mecklenburg County	66	0.01
Raleigh (city) Wake County	42	0.01
Jacksonville (city) Onslow County	31	0.04
Durham (city) Durham County	29	0.01
Greensboro (city) Guilford County	24	0.01
Spring Lake (town) Cumberland County	22	0.18
Wilmington (city) New Hanover County	19	0.02
Winston-Salem (city) Forsyth County	18	0.01
Havelock (city) Craven County	16	0.08

Top 10 Places Sorted by Percent of Total Population
Based on all places, regardless of total population

Place	Population	%
Patterson Springs (town) Cleveland County	4	0.64
Gibson (town) Scotland County	3	0.56
Hollister (cdp) Halifax County	3	0.45
Stoneville (town) Rockingham County	4	0.38
Castalia (town) Nash County	1	0.37
Newton Grove (town) Sampson County	2	0.35
Gorman (cdp) Durham County	3	0.30
Northwest (city) Brunswick County	2	0.27
Pinnacle (cdp) Stokes County	2	0.22
Prospect (cdp) Robeson County	2	0.20

Top 10 Places Sorted by Percent of Total Population
Based on places with total population of 50,000 or more

Place	Population	%
Fayetteville (city) Cumberland County	87	0.04
Jacksonville (city) Onslow County	31	0.04
Wilmington (city) New Hanover County	19	0.02
Charlotte (city) Mecklenburg County	66	0.01
Raleigh (city) Wake County	42	0.01
Durham (city) Durham County	29	0.01
Greensboro (city) Guilford County	24	0.01
Winston-Salem (city) Forsyth County	18	0.01
Cary (town) Wake County	14	0.01
Asheville (city) Buncombe County	9	0.01

American Indian: South American Indian

Top 10 Places Sorted by Population
Based on all places, regardless of total population

Place	Population	%
Fayetteville (city) Cumberland County	94	0.05
Charlotte (city) Mecklenburg County	88	0.01
Raleigh (city) Wake County	46	0.01
Cary (town) Wake County	39	0.03
Durham (city) Durham County	24	0.01
Winston-Salem (city) Forsyth County	22	0.01
Greensboro (city) Guilford County	18	0.01
Fuquay-Varina (town) Wake County	13	0.07
Chapel Hill (town) Orange County	12	0.02
Carrboro (town) Orange County	11	0.06

Top 10 Places Sorted by Percent of Total Population
Based on all places, regardless of total population

Place	Population	%
Sunbury (cdp) Gates County	2	0.69
Hemby Bridge (town) Union County	4	0.26
Rockfish (cdp) Hoke County	6	0.18

Belville (town) Brunswick County	3	0.15
Siler City (town) Chatham County	6	0.08
Mineral Springs (town) Union County	2	0.08
Fuquay-Varina (town) Wake County	13	0.07
Richlands (town) Onslow County	1	0.07
Carrboro (town) Orange County	11	0.06
Murphy (town) Cherokee County	1	0.06

Top 10 Places Sorted by Percent of Total Population
Based on places with total population of 50,000 or more

Place	Population	%
Fayetteville (city) Cumberland County	94	0.05
Cary (town) Wake County	39	0.03
Chapel Hill (town) Orange County	12	0.02
Charlotte (city) Mecklenburg County	88	0.01
Raleigh (city) Wake County	46	0.01
Durham (city) Durham County	24	0.01
Winston-Salem (city) Forsyth County	22	0.01
Greensboro (city) Guilford County	18	0.01
Wilmington (city) New Hanover County	10	0.01
Greenville (city) Pitt County	8	0.01

American Indian: Spanish American Indian

Top 10 Places Sorted by Population
Based on all places, regardless of total population

Place	Population	%
Charlotte (city) Mecklenburg County	101	0.01
Raleigh (city) Wake County	44	0.01
Burlington (city) Alamance County	25	0.05
Durham (city) Durham County	22	0.01
Fayetteville (city) Cumberland County	15	0.01
Graham (city) Alamance County	13	0.09
Fuquay-Varina (town) Wake County	12	0.07
Siler City (town) Chatham County	10	0.13
Apex (town) Wake County	8	0.02
Greensboro (city) Guilford County	8	<0.01

Top 10 Places Sorted by Percent of Total Population
Based on all places, regardless of total population

Place	Population	%
Rennert (town) Robeson County	5	1.31
Hollister (cdp) Halifax County	4	0.59
Liberty (town) Randolph County	6	0.23
Sunset Beach (town) Brunswick County	6	0.17
Whitsett (town) Guilford County	1	0.17
Siler City (town) Chatham County	10	0.13
River Bend (town) Craven County	4	0.13
Graham (city) Alamance County	13	0.09
Brunswick (town) Columbus County	1	0.09
Fuquay-Varina (town) Wake County	12	0.07

Top 10 Places Sorted by Percent of Total Population
Based on places with total population of 50,000 or more

Place	Population	%
Charlotte (city) Mecklenburg County	101	0.01
Raleigh (city) Wake County	44	0.01
Durham (city) Durham County	22	0.01
Fayetteville (city) Cumberland County	15	0.01
Greensboro (city) Guilford County	8	<0.01
Asheville (city) Buncombe County	4	<0.01
Winston-Salem (city) Forsyth County	4	<0.01
Concord (city) Cabarrus County	3	<0.01
Chapel Hill (town) Orange County	2	<0.01
Gastonia (city) Gaston County	2	<0.01

Alaska Native: Tlingit-Haida

Top 10 Places Sorted by Population
Based on all places, regardless of total population

Place	Population	%
Fayetteville (city) Cumberland County	6	<0.01
Broad Creek (cdp) Carteret County	3	0.13
Haw River (town) Alamance County	3	0.13
Half Moon (cdp) Onslow County	3	0.04
Lincolnton (city) Lincoln County	3	0.03
Charlotte (city) Mecklenburg County	3	<0.01
Durham (city) Durham County	3	<0.01
Winston-Salem (city) Forsyth County	3	<0.01
Elizabeth (town) Bladen County	2	0.06

Spring Lake (town) Cumberland County	2	0.02

Top 10 Places Sorted by Percent of Total Population
Based on all places, regardless of total population

Place	Population	%
Broad Creek (cdp) Carteret County	3	0.13
Haw River (town) Alamance County	3	0.13
Laurel Hill (cdp) Scotland County	1	0.08
Elizabeth (town) Bladen County	2	0.06
Half Moon (cdp) Onslow County	3	0.04
Tobaccoville (village) Forsyth County	1	0.04
Lincolnton (city) Lincoln County	3	0.03
Dana (cdp) Henderson County	1	0.03
Spring Lake (town) Cumberland County	2	0.02
Havelock (city) Craven County	2	0.01

Top 10 Places Sorted by Percent of Total Population
Based on places with total population of 50,000 or more

Place	Population	%
Fayetteville (city) Cumberland County	6	<0.01
Charlotte (city) Mecklenburg County	3	<0.01
Durham (city) Durham County	3	<0.01
Winston-Salem (city) Forsyth County	3	<0.01
Raleigh (city) Wake County	2	<0.01
Cary (town) Wake County	1	<0.01
Greensboro (city) Guilford County	1	<0.01
Greenville (city) Pitt County	1	<0.01
Asheville (city) Buncombe County	0	0.00
Chapel Hill (town) Orange County	0	0.00

American Indian: Tohono O'Odham

Top 10 Places Sorted by Population
Based on all places, regardless of total population

Place	Population	%
Concord (city) Cabarrus County	5	0.01
Raleigh (city) Wake County	5	<0.01
Graham (city) Alamance County	4	0.03
Fayetteville (city) Cumberland County	4	<0.01
Bald Head Island (village) Brunswick County	3	1.90
Knightdale (town) Wake County	3	0.03
Elizabeth City (city) Pasquotank County	3	0.02
Porters Neck (cdp) New Hanover County	2	0.03
New Bern (city) Craven County	2	0.01
Jacksonville (city) Onslow County	2	<0.01

Top 10 Places Sorted by Percent of Total Population
Based on all places, regardless of total population

Place	Population	%
Bald Head Island (village) Brunswick County	3	1.90
Maysville (town) Jones County	1	0.10
Graham (city) Alamance County	4	0.03
Knightdale (town) Wake County	3	0.03
Porters Neck (cdp) New Hanover County	2	0.03
Elizabeth City (city) Pasquotank County	3	0.02
Concord (city) Cabarrus County	5	0.01
New Bern (city) Craven County	2	0.01
Spring Lake (town) Cumberland County	1	0.01
Raleigh (city) Wake County	5	<0.01

Top 10 Places Sorted by Percent of Total Population
Based on places with total population of 50,000 or more

Place	Population	%
Concord (city) Cabarrus County	5	0.01
Raleigh (city) Wake County	5	<0.01
Fayetteville (city) Cumberland County	4	<0.01
Jacksonville (city) Onslow County	2	<0.01
Charlotte (city) Mecklenburg County	1	<0.01
Durham (city) Durham County	1	<0.01
Greensboro (city) Guilford County	1	<0.01
Winston-Salem (city) Forsyth County	1	<0.01
Asheville (city) Buncombe County	0	0.00
Cary (town) Wake County	0	0.00

Alaska Native: Tsimshian

Top 10 Places Sorted by Population
Based on all places, regardless of total population

Place	Population	%
Charlotte (city) Mecklenburg County	1	<0.01

Garner (town) Wake County	1	<0.01
Raleigh (city) Wake County	1	<0.01
Aberdeen (town) Moore County	0	0.00
Advance (cdp) Davie County	0	0.00
Ahoskie (town) Hertford County	0	0.00
Alamance (village) Alamance County	0	0.00
Albemarle (city) Stanly County	0	0.00
Alliance (town) Pamlico County	0	0.00
Altamahaw (cdp) Alamance County	0	0.00

Top 10 Places Sorted by Percent of Total Population
Based on all places, regardless of total population

Place	Population	%
Charlotte (city) Mecklenburg County	1	<0.01
Garner (town) Wake County	1	<0.01
Raleigh (city) Wake County	1	<0.01
Aberdeen (town) Moore County	0	0.00
Advance (cdp) Davie County	0	0.00
Ahoskie (town) Hertford County	0	0.00
Alamance (village) Alamance County	0	0.00
Albemarle (city) Stanly County	0	0.00
Alliance (town) Pamlico County	0	0.00
Altamahaw (cdp) Alamance County	0	0.00

Top 10 Places Sorted by Percent of Total Population
Based on places with total population of 50,000 or more

Place	Population	%
Charlotte (city) Mecklenburg County	1	<0.01
Raleigh (city) Wake County	1	<0.01
Asheville (city) Buncombe County	0	0.00
Cary (town) Wake County	0	0.00
Chapel Hill (town) Orange County	0	0.00
Concord (city) Cabarrus County	0	0.00
Durham (city) Durham County	0	0.00
Fayetteville (city) Cumberland County	0	0.00
Gastonia (city) Gaston County	0	0.00
Greensboro (city) Guilford County	0	0.00

American Indian: Ute

Top 10 Places Sorted by Population
Based on all places, regardless of total population

Place	Population	%
Charlotte (city) Mecklenburg County	4	<0.01
Asheboro (city) Randolph County	2	0.01
Durham (city) Durham County	2	<0.01
Raleigh (city) Wake County	2	<0.01
Asheville (city) Buncombe County	1	<0.01
Burlington (city) Alamance County	1	<0.01
Fayetteville (city) Cumberland County	1	<0.01
Statesville (city) Iredell County	1	<0.01
Wake Forest (town) Wake County	1	<0.01
Aberdeen (town) Moore County	0	0.00

Top 10 Places Sorted by Percent of Total Population
Based on all places, regardless of total population

Place	Population	%
Asheboro (city) Randolph County	2	0.01
Charlotte (city) Mecklenburg County	4	<0.01
Durham (city) Durham County	2	<0.01
Raleigh (city) Wake County	2	<0.01
Asheville (city) Buncombe County	1	<0.01
Burlington (city) Alamance County	1	<0.01
Fayetteville (city) Cumberland County	1	<0.01
Statesville (city) Iredell County	1	<0.01
Wake Forest (town) Wake County	1	<0.01
Aberdeen (town) Moore County	0	0.00

Top 10 Places Sorted by Percent of Total Population
Based on places with total population of 50,000 or more

Place	Population	%
Charlotte (city) Mecklenburg County	4	<0.01
Durham (city) Durham County	2	<0.01
Raleigh (city) Wake County	2	<0.01
Asheville (city) Buncombe County	1	<0.01
Fayetteville (city) Cumberland County	1	<0.01
Cary (town) Wake County	0	0.00
Chapel Hill (town) Orange County	0	0.00
Concord (city) Cabarrus County	0	0.00
Gastonia (city) Gaston County	0	0.00
Greensboro (city) Guilford County	0	0.00

American Indian: Yakama

Top 10 Places Sorted by Population
Based on all places, regardless of total population

Place	Population	%
Jacksonville (city) Onslow County	5	0.01
Durham (city) Durham County	5	<0.01
Stokesdale (town) Guilford County	2	0.04
Murphy (town) Cherokee County	1	0.06
Avery Creek (cdp) Buncombe County	1	0.05
Indian Trail (town) Union County	1	<0.01
Aberdeen (town) Moore County	0	0.00
Advance (cdp) Davie County	0	0.00
Ahoskie (town) Hertford County	0	0.00
Alamance (village) Alamance County	0	0.00

Top 10 Places Sorted by Percent of Total Population
Based on all places, regardless of total population

Place	Population	%
Murphy (town) Cherokee County	1	0.06
Avery Creek (cdp) Buncombe County	1	0.05
Stokesdale (town) Guilford County	2	0.04
Jacksonville (city) Onslow County	5	0.01
Durham (city) Durham County	5	<0.01
Indian Trail (town) Union County	1	<0.01
Aberdeen (town) Moore County	0	0.00
Advance (cdp) Davie County	0	0.00
Ahoskie (town) Hertford County	0	0.00
Alamance (village) Alamance County	0	0.00

Top 10 Places Sorted by Percent of Total Population
Based on places with total population of 50,000 or more

Place	Population	%
Jacksonville (city) Onslow County	5	0.01
Durham (city) Durham County	5	<0.01
Asheville (city) Buncombe County	0	0.00
Cary (town) Wake County	0	0.00
Chapel Hill (town) Orange County	0	0.00
Charlotte (city) Mecklenburg County	0	0.00
Concord (city) Cabarrus County	0	0.00
Fayetteville (city) Cumberland County	0	0.00
Gastonia (city) Gaston County	0	0.00
Greensboro (city) Guilford County	0	0.00

American Indian: Yaqui

Top 10 Places Sorted by Population
Based on all places, regardless of total population

Place	Population	%
Asheboro (city) Randolph County	6	0.02
Charlotte (city) Mecklenburg County	6	<0.01
Asheville (city) Buncombe County	4	<0.01
Fayetteville (city) Cumberland County	4	<0.01
Monroe (city) Union County	3	0.01
Durham (city) Durham County	3	<0.01
Jacksonville (city) Onslow County	3	<0.01
West Jefferson (town) Ashe County	1	0.08
Zebulon (town) Wake County	1	0.02
Archdale (city) Randolph County	1	0.01

Top 10 Places Sorted by Percent of Total Population
Based on all places, regardless of total population

Place	Population	%
West Jefferson (town) Ashe County	1	0.08
Asheboro (city) Randolph County	6	0.02
Zebulon (town) Wake County	1	0.02
Monroe (city) Union County	3	0.01
Archdale (city) Randolph County	1	0.01
Elizabeth City (city) Pasquotank County	1	0.01
Lenoir (city) Caldwell County	1	0.01
Mebane (city) Alamance County	1	0.01
Smithfield (town) Johnston County	1	0.01
Southern Pines (town) Moore County	1	0.01

Top 10 Places Sorted by Percent of Total Population
Based on places with total population of 50,000 or more

Place	Population	%
Charlotte (city) Mecklenburg County	6	<0.01
Asheville (city) Buncombe County	4	<0.01
Fayetteville (city) Cumberland County	4	<0.01
Durham (city) Durham County	3	<0.01

Place	Population	%
Jacksonville (city) Onslow County	3	<0.01
Cary (town) Wake County	1	<0.01
High Point (city) Guilford County	1	<0.01
Raleigh (city) Wake County	1	<0.01
Wilmington (city) New Hanover County	1	<0.01
Chapel Hill (town) Orange County	0	0.00

American Indian: Yuman

Top 10 Places Sorted by Population
Based on all places, regardless of total population

Place	Population	%
Charlotte (city) Mecklenburg County	4	<0.01
Hillsborough (town) Orange County	2	0.03
South Rosemary (cdp) Halifax County	1	0.04
Aberdeen (town) Moore County	1	0.02
Carolina Beach (town) New Hanover County	1	0.02
Asheville (city) Buncombe County	1	<0.01
Gastonia (city) Gaston County	1	<0.01
Greensboro (city) Guilford County	1	<0.01
High Point (city) Guilford County	1	<0.01
Wake Forest (town) Wake County	1	<0.01

Top 10 Places Sorted by Percent of Total Population
Based on all places, regardless of total population

Place	Population	%
South Rosemary (cdp) Halifax County	1	0.04
Hillsborough (town) Orange County	2	0.03
Aberdeen (town) Moore County	1	0.02
Carolina Beach (town) New Hanover County	1	0.02
Charlotte (city) Mecklenburg County	4	<0.01
Asheville (city) Buncombe County	1	<0.01
Gastonia (city) Gaston County	1	<0.01
Greensboro (city) Guilford County	1	<0.01
High Point (city) Guilford County	1	<0.01
Wake Forest (town) Wake County	1	<0.01

Top 10 Places Sorted by Percent of Total Population
Based on places with total population of 50,000 or more

Place	Population	%
Charlotte (city) Mecklenburg County	4	<0.01
Asheville (city) Buncombe County	1	<0.01
Gastonia (city) Gaston County	1	<0.01
Greensboro (city) Guilford County	1	<0.01
High Point (city) Guilford County	1	<0.01
Cary (town) Wake County	0	0.00
Chapel Hill (town) Orange County	0	0.00
Concord (city) Cabarrus County	0	0.00
Durham (city) Durham County	0	0.00
Fayetteville (city) Cumberland County	0	0.00

Alaska Native: Yup'ik

Top 10 Places Sorted by Population
Based on all places, regardless of total population

Place	Population	%
Cedar Point (town) Carteret County	3	0.23
Fayetteville (city) Cumberland County	3	<0.01
Raleigh (city) Wake County	3	<0.01
Maysville (town) Jones County	2	0.20
Wake Forest (town) Wake County	2	0.01
Charlotte (city) Mecklenburg County	2	<0.01
Eastover (town) Cumberland County	1	0.03
Ahoskie (town) Hertford County	1	0.02
Fuquay-Varina (town) Wake County	1	0.01
Concord (city) Cabarrus County	1	<0.01

Top 10 Places Sorted by Percent of Total Population
Based on all places, regardless of total population

Place	Population	%
Cedar Point (town) Carteret County	3	0.23
Maysville (town) Jones County	2	0.20
Eastover (town) Cumberland County	1	0.03
Ahoskie (town) Hertford County	1	0.02
Wake Forest (town) Wake County	2	0.01
Fuquay-Varina (town) Wake County	1	0.01
Fayetteville (city) Cumberland County	3	<0.01
Raleigh (city) Wake County	3	<0.01
Charlotte (city) Mecklenburg County	2	<0.01
Concord (city) Cabarrus County	1	<0.01

Top 10 Places Sorted by Percent of Total Population
Based on places with total population of 50,000 or more

Place	Population	%
Fayetteville (city) Cumberland County	3	<0.01
Raleigh (city) Wake County	3	<0.01
Charlotte (city) Mecklenburg County	2	<0.01
Concord (city) Cabarrus County	1	<0.01
Greensboro (city) Guilford County	1	<0.01
Asheville (city) Buncombe County	0	0.00
Cary (town) Wake County	0	0.00
Chapel Hill (town) Orange County	0	0.00
Durham (city) Durham County	0	0.00
Gastonia (city) Gaston County	0	0.00

Asian

Top 10 Places Sorted by Population
Based on all places, regardless of total population

Place	Population	%
Charlotte (city) Mecklenburg County	40,918	5.59
Raleigh (city) Wake County	20,389	5.05
Cary (town) Wake County	19,370	14.32
Durham (city) Durham County	13,147	5.76
Greensboro (city) Guilford County	12,291	4.56
Fayetteville (city) Cumberland County	7,899	3.94
Chapel Hill (town) Orange County	7,548	13.19
High Point (city) Guilford County	6,916	6.63
Winston-Salem (city) Forsyth County	5,669	2.47
Morrisville (town) Wake County	5,378	28.95

Top 10 Places Sorted by Percent of Total Population
Based on all places, regardless of total population

Place	Population	%
Morrisville (town) Wake County	5,378	28.95
Cary (town) Wake County	19,370	14.32
Chapel Hill (town) Orange County	7,548	13.19
Carrboro (town) Orange County	1,822	9.30
Apex (town) Wake County	3,083	8.23
Connelly Springs (town) Burke County	123	7.37
Raynham (town) Robeson County	5	6.94
High Point (city) Guilford County	6,916	6.63
Glen Alpine (town) Burke County	93	6.13
Marvin (village) Union County	340	6.09

Top 10 Places Sorted by Percent of Total Population
Based on places with total population of 50,000 or more

Place	Population	%
Cary (town) Wake County	19,370	14.32
Chapel Hill (town) Orange County	7,548	13.19
High Point (city) Guilford County	6,916	6.63
Durham (city) Durham County	13,147	5.76
Charlotte (city) Mecklenburg County	40,918	5.59
Raleigh (city) Wake County	20,389	5.05
Greensboro (city) Guilford County	12,291	4.56
Jacksonville (city) Onslow County	2,775	3.96
Fayetteville (city) Cumberland County	7,899	3.94
Concord (city) Cabarrus County	2,436	3.08

Asian: Not Hispanic

Top 10 Places Sorted by Population
Based on all places, regardless of total population

Place	Population	%
Charlotte (city) Mecklenburg County	40,149	5.49
Raleigh (city) Wake County	20,006	4.95
Cary (town) Wake County	19,231	14.22
Durham (city) Durham County	12,897	5.65
Greensboro (city) Guilford County	12,120	4.49
Chapel Hill (town) Orange County	7,495	13.10
Fayetteville (city) Cumberland County	7,423	3.70
High Point (city) Guilford County	6,828	6.54
Winston-Salem (city) Forsyth County	5,513	2.40
Morrisville (town) Wake County	5,354	28.82

Top 10 Places Sorted by Percent of Total Population
Based on all places, regardless of total population

Place	Population	%
Morrisville (town) Wake County	5,354	28.82
Cary (town) Wake County	19,231	14.22
Chapel Hill (town) Orange County	7,495	13.10

Place	Population	%
Carrboro (town) Orange County	1,802	9.20
Apex (town) Wake County	3,045	8.13
Connelly Springs (town) Burke County	123	7.37
Raynham (town) Robeson County	5	6.94
High Point (city) Guilford County	6,828	6.54
Marvin (village) Union County	340	6.09
Glen Alpine (town) Burke County	92	6.06

Top 10 Places Sorted by Percent of Total Population
Based on places with total population of 50,000 or more

Place	Population	%
Cary (town) Wake County	19,231	14.22
Chapel Hill (town) Orange County	7,495	13.10
High Point (city) Guilford County	6,828	6.54
Durham (city) Durham County	12,897	5.65
Charlotte (city) Mecklenburg County	40,149	5.49
Raleigh (city) Wake County	20,006	4.95
Greensboro (city) Guilford County	12,120	4.49
Fayetteville (city) Cumberland County	7,423	3.70
Jacksonville (city) Onslow County	2,531	3.61
Concord (city) Cabarrus County	2,374	3.00

Asian: Hispanic

Top 10 Places Sorted by Population
Based on all places, regardless of total population

Place	Population	%
Charlotte (city) Mecklenburg County	769	0.11
Fayetteville (city) Cumberland County	476	0.24
Raleigh (city) Wake County	383	0.09
Durham (city) Durham County	250	0.11
Jacksonville (city) Onslow County	244	0.35
Greensboro (city) Guilford County	171	0.06
Winston-Salem (city) Forsyth County	156	0.07
Cary (town) Wake County	139	0.10
High Point (city) Guilford County	88	0.08
Spring Lake (town) Cumberland County	67	0.56

Top 10 Places Sorted by Percent of Total Population
Based on all places, regardless of total population

Place	Population	%
Falcon (town) Cumberland County	4	1.55
Hatteras (cdp) Dare County	6	1.19
Ingold (cdp) Sampson County	5	1.06
Coinjock (cdp) Currituck County	3	0.90
Bunn (town) Franklin County	3	0.87
Old Hundred (cdp) Scotland County	2	0.70
Sunbury (cdp) Gates County	2	0.69
Butters (cdp) Bladen County	2	0.68
Ellerbe (town) Richmond County	7	0.66
Spring Lake (town) Cumberland County	67	0.56

Top 10 Places Sorted by Percent of Total Population
Based on places with total population of 50,000 or more

Place	Population	%
Jacksonville (city) Onslow County	244	0.35
Fayetteville (city) Cumberland County	476	0.24
Charlotte (city) Mecklenburg County	769	0.11
Durham (city) Durham County	250	0.11
Cary (town) Wake County	139	0.10
Raleigh (city) Wake County	383	0.09
Chapel Hill (town) Orange County	53	0.09
High Point (city) Guilford County	88	0.08
Concord (city) Cabarrus County	62	0.08
Winston-Salem (city) Forsyth County	156	0.07

Asian: Bangladeshi

Top 10 Places Sorted by Population
Based on all places, regardless of total population

Place	Population	%
Raleigh (city) Wake County	177	0.04
Cary (town) Wake County	124	0.09
Durham (city) Durham County	96	0.04
Charlotte (city) Mecklenburg County	82	0.01
Fayetteville (city) Cumberland County	51	0.03
Greensboro (city) Guilford County	43	0.02
Morrisville (town) Wake County	41	0.22
Apex (town) Wake County	35	0.09
Chapel Hill (town) Orange County	35	0.06
High Point (city) Guilford County	16	0.02

Top 10 Places Sorted by Percent of Total Population
Based on all places, regardless of total population

Place	Population	%
Walnut Creek (village) Wayne County	3	0.36
Morrisville (town) Wake County	41	0.22
Porters Neck (cdp) New Hanover County	11	0.18
Butner (town) Granville County	8	0.11
Eastover (town) Cumberland County	4	0.11
Cary (town) Wake County	124	0.09
Apex (town) Wake County	35	0.09
Chapel Hill (town) Orange County	35	0.06
Holly Springs (town) Wake County	12	0.05
Rockingham (city) Richmond County	5	0.05

Top 10 Places Sorted by Percent of Total Population
Based on places with total population of 50,000 or more

Place	Population	%
Cary (town) Wake County	124	0.09
Chapel Hill (town) Orange County	35	0.06
Raleigh (city) Wake County	177	0.04
Durham (city) Durham County	96	0.04
Fayetteville (city) Cumberland County	51	0.03
Rocky Mount (city) Nash County	15	0.03
Greensboro (city) Guilford County	43	0.02
High Point (city) Guilford County	16	0.02
Charlotte (city) Mecklenburg County	82	0.01
Greenville (city) Pitt County	10	0.01

Asian: Bhutanese

Top 10 Places Sorted by Population
Based on all places, regardless of total population

Place	Population	%
Charlotte (city) Mecklenburg County	277	0.04
Greensboro (city) Guilford County	173	0.06
Raleigh (city) Wake County	68	0.02
High Point (city) Guilford County	61	0.06
Durham (city) Durham County	29	0.01
Asheville (city) Buncombe County	1	<0.01
Aberdeen (town) Moore County	0	0.00
Advance (cdp) Davie County	0	0.00
Ahoskie (town) Hertford County	0	0.00
Alamance (village) Alamance County	0	0.00

Top 10 Places Sorted by Percent of Total Population
Based on all places, regardless of total population

Place	Population	%
Greensboro (city) Guilford County	173	0.06
High Point (city) Guilford County	61	0.06
Charlotte (city) Mecklenburg County	277	0.04
Raleigh (city) Wake County	68	0.02
Durham (city) Durham County	29	0.01
Asheville (city) Buncombe County	1	<0.01
Aberdeen (town) Moore County	0	0.00
Advance (cdp) Davie County	0	0.00
Ahoskie (town) Hertford County	0	0.00
Alamance (village) Alamance County	0	0.00

Top 10 Places Sorted by Percent of Total Population
Based on places with total population of 50,000 or more

Place	Population	%
Greensboro (city) Guilford County	173	0.06
High Point (city) Guilford County	61	0.06
Charlotte (city) Mecklenburg County	277	0.04
Raleigh (city) Wake County	68	0.02
Durham (city) Durham County	29	0.01
Asheville (city) Buncombe County	1	<0.01
Cary (town) Wake County	0	0.00
Chapel Hill (town) Orange County	0	0.00
Concord (city) Cabarrus County	0	0.00
Fayetteville (city) Cumberland County	0	0.00

Asian: Burmese

Top 10 Places Sorted by Population
Based on all places, regardless of total population

Place	Population	%
New Bern (city) Craven County	623	2.11
Charlotte (city) Mecklenburg County	542	0.07
High Point (city) Guilford County	406	0.39

Place	Population	%
Raleigh (city) Wake County	397	0.10
Chapel Hill (town) Orange County	393	0.69
Carrboro (town) Orange County	339	1.73
Greensboro (city) Guilford County	272	0.10
Winston-Salem (city) Forsyth County	154	0.07
Lumberton (city) Robeson County	134	0.62
Durham (city) Durham County	90	0.04

Top 10 Places Sorted by Percent of Total Population
Based on all places, regardless of total population

Place	Population	%
New Bern (city) Craven County	623	2.11
Carrboro (town) Orange County	339	1.73
Chapel Hill (town) Orange County	393	0.69
Lumberton (city) Robeson County	134	0.62
Rockingham (city) Richmond County	44	0.46
High Point (city) Guilford County	406	0.39
Woodland (town) Northampton County	3	0.37
Lewiston Woodville (town) Bertie County	2	0.36
Avery Creek (cdp) Buncombe County	5	0.26
Youngsville (town) Franklin County	3	0.26

Top 10 Places Sorted by Percent of Total Population
Based on places with total population of 50,000 or more

Place	Population	%
Chapel Hill (town) Orange County	393	0.69
High Point (city) Guilford County	406	0.39
Raleigh (city) Wake County	397	0.10
Greensboro (city) Guilford County	272	0.10
Charlotte (city) Mecklenburg County	542	0.07
Winston-Salem (city) Forsyth County	154	0.07
Durham (city) Durham County	90	0.04
Greenville (city) Pitt County	30	0.04
Fayetteville (city) Cumberland County	37	0.02
Wilmington (city) New Hanover County	6	0.01

Asian: Cambodian

Top 10 Places Sorted by Population
Based on all places, regardless of total population

Place	Population	%
Charlotte (city) Mecklenburg County	1,236	0.17
Greensboro (city) Guilford County	648	0.24
Lexington (city) Davidson County	365	1.93
High Point (city) Guilford County	111	0.11
Winston-Salem (city) Forsyth County	84	0.04
Durham (city) Durham County	80	0.04
Fayetteville (city) Cumberland County	73	0.04
Raleigh (city) Wake County	63	0.02
Welcome (cdp) Davidson County	42	1.01
Archdale (city) Randolph County	34	0.30

Top 10 Places Sorted by Percent of Total Population
Based on all places, regardless of total population

Place	Population	%
Lexington (city) Davidson County	365	1.93
Welcome (cdp) Davidson County	42	1.01
Valley Hill (cdp) Henderson County	12	0.58
Barker Heights (cdp) Henderson County	6	0.48
East Flat Rock (cdp) Henderson County	22	0.44
Seagrove (town) Randolph County	1	0.44
Etowah (cdp) Henderson County	28	0.40
Swannanoa (cdp) Buncombe County	17	0.37
Archdale (city) Randolph County	34	0.30
Midway (town) Davidson County	14	0.30

Top 10 Places Sorted by Percent of Total Population
Based on places with total population of 50,000 or more

Place	Population	%
Greensboro (city) Guilford County	648	0.24
Charlotte (city) Mecklenburg County	1,236	0.17
High Point (city) Guilford County	111	0.11
Winston-Salem (city) Forsyth County	84	0.04
Durham (city) Durham County	80	0.04
Fayetteville (city) Cumberland County	73	0.04
Jacksonville (city) Onslow County	24	0.03
Concord (city) Cabarrus County	23	0.03
Raleigh (city) Wake County	63	0.02
Cary (town) Wake County	31	0.02

Asian: Chinese, except Taiwanese

Top 10 Places Sorted by Population
Based on all places, regardless of total population

Place	Population	%
Charlotte (city) Mecklenburg County	4,883	0.67
Cary (town) Wake County	4,330	3.20
Raleigh (city) Wake County	3,607	0.89
Durham (city) Durham County	3,150	1.38
Chapel Hill (town) Orange County	2,866	5.01
Greensboro (city) Guilford County	1,197	0.44
Winston-Salem (city) Forsyth County	1,116	0.49
Fayetteville (city) Cumberland County	741	0.37
Apex (town) Wake County	652	1.74
Carrboro (town) Orange County	595	3.04

Top 10 Places Sorted by Percent of Total Population
Based on all places, regardless of total population

Place	Population	%
Chapel Hill (town) Orange County	2,866	5.01
Teachey (town) Duplin County	13	3.46
Cary (town) Wake County	4,330	3.20
Carrboro (town) Orange County	595	3.04
Blue Clay Farms (cdp) New Hanover County	1	3.03
Morrisville (town) Wake County	502	2.70
Falkland (town) Pitt County	2	2.08
Salvo (cdp) Dare County	4	1.75
Apex (town) Wake County	652	1.74
Oak Ridge (town) Guilford County	89	1.44

Top 10 Places Sorted by Percent of Total Population
Based on places with total population of 50,000 or more

Place	Population	%
Chapel Hill (town) Orange County	2,866	5.01
Cary (town) Wake County	4,330	3.20
Durham (city) Durham County	3,150	1.38
Raleigh (city) Wake County	3,607	0.89
Charlotte (city) Mecklenburg County	4,883	0.67
Greenville (city) Pitt County	468	0.55
Winston-Salem (city) Forsyth County	1,116	0.49
High Point (city) Guilford County	468	0.45
Greensboro (city) Guilford County	1,197	0.44
Concord (city) Cabarrus County	319	0.40

Asian: Filipino

Top 10 Places Sorted by Population
Based on all places, regardless of total population

Place	Population	%
Charlotte (city) Mecklenburg County	2,240	0.31
Raleigh (city) Wake County	2,141	0.53
Fayetteville (city) Cumberland County	1,754	0.87
Durham (city) Durham County	1,419	0.62
Jacksonville (city) Onslow County	1,167	1.66
Winston-Salem (city) Forsyth County	922	0.40
Cary (town) Wake County	847	0.63
Greensboro (city) Guilford County	672	0.25
High Point (city) Guilford County	459	0.44
Havelock (city) Craven County	432	2.08

Top 10 Places Sorted by Percent of Total Population
Based on all places, regardless of total population

Place	Population	%
Lasker (town) Northampton County	6	4.92
Pumpkin Center (cdp) Onslow County	79	3.56
Piney Green (cdp) Onslow County	284	2.14
Half Moon (cdp) Onslow County	176	2.11
Havelock (city) Craven County	432	2.08
Neuse Forest (cdp) Craven County	40	2.00
Jacksonville (city) Onslow County	1,167	1.66
Windsor (town) Bertie County	57	1.57
Spring Lake (town) Cumberland County	178	1.49
Moyock (cdp) Currituck County	52	1.38

Top 10 Places Sorted by Percent of Total Population
Based on places with total population of 50,000 or more

Place	Population	%
Jacksonville (city) Onslow County	1,167	1.66
Fayetteville (city) Cumberland County	1,754	0.87
Cary (town) Wake County	847	0.63
Durham (city) Durham County	1,419	0.62

Place	Population	%
Raleigh (city) Wake County	2,141	0.53
Chapel Hill (town) Orange County	269	0.47
High Point (city) Guilford County	459	0.44
Concord (city) Cabarrus County	331	0.42
Winston-Salem (city) Forsyth County	922	0.40
Greenville (city) Pitt County	308	0.36

Asian: Hmong

Top 10 Places Sorted by Population
Based on all places, regardless of total population

Place	Population	%
Charlotte (city) Mecklenburg County	1,304	0.18
Hickory (city) Catawba County	479	1.20
Albemarle (city) Stanly County	291	1.83
Newton (city) Catawba County	262	2.02
St. Stephens (cdp) Catawba County	250	2.85
Morganton (city) Burke County	163	0.96
Conover (city) Catawba County	160	1.96
Long View (town) Catawba County	158	3.24
Statesville (city) Iredell County	140	0.57
Connelly Springs (town) Burke County	100	5.99

Top 10 Places Sorted by Percent of Total Population
Based on all places, regardless of total population

Place	Population	%
Raynham (town) Robeson County	5	6.94
Connelly Springs (town) Burke County	100	5.99
Richfield (town) Stanly County	25	4.08
Long View (town) Catawba County	158	3.24
Glen Alpine (town) Burke County	46	3.03
Hildebran (town) Burke County	60	2.97
St. Stephens (cdp) Catawba County	250	2.85
Drexel (town) Burke County	43	2.31
New London (town) Stanly County	13	2.17
Valdese (town) Burke County	92	2.05

Top 10 Places Sorted by Percent of Total Population
Based on places with total population of 50,000 or more

Place	Population	%
Charlotte (city) Mecklenburg County	1,304	0.18
Concord (city) Cabarrus County	70	0.09
Greenville (city) Pitt County	41	0.05
Jacksonville (city) Onslow County	33	0.05
Greensboro (city) Guilford County	85	0.03
Winston-Salem (city) Forsyth County	47	0.02
Gastonia (city) Gaston County	15	0.02
Rocky Mount (city) Nash County	9	0.02
Raleigh (city) Wake County	55	0.01
Durham (city) Durham County	20	0.01

Asian: Indian

Top 10 Places Sorted by Population
Based on all places, regardless of total population

Place	Population	%
Charlotte (city) Mecklenburg County	14,258	1.95
Cary (town) Wake County	9,217	6.82
Raleigh (city) Wake County	5,143	1.27
Morrisville (town) Wake County	3,809	20.50
Durham (city) Durham County	3,306	1.45
Greensboro (city) Guilford County	2,030	0.75
Chapel Hill (town) Orange County	1,418	2.48
Winston-Salem (city) Forsyth County	1,391	0.61
Apex (town) Wake County	1,339	3.57
High Point (city) Guilford County	1,152	1.10

Top 10 Places Sorted by Percent of Total Population
Based on all places, regardless of total population

Place	Population	%
Morrisville (town) Wake County	3,809	20.50
Cary (town) Wake County	9,217	6.82
Apex (town) Wake County	1,339	3.57
Marvin (village) Union County	164	2.94
Chapel Hill (town) Orange County	1,418	2.48
Wilkesboro (town) Wilkes County	79	2.31
Bennett (cdp) Chatham County	6	2.13
Avery Creek (cdp) Buncombe County	39	2.00
Charlotte (city) Mecklenburg County	14,258	1.95
Harrisburg (town) Cabarrus County	211	1.83

Top 10 Places Sorted by Percent of Total Population
Based on places with total population of 50,000 or more

Place	Population	%
Cary (town) Wake County	9,217	6.82
Chapel Hill (town) Orange County	1,418	2.48
Charlotte (city) Mecklenburg County	14,258	1.95
Durham (city) Durham County	3,306	1.45
Concord (city) Cabarrus County	1,017	1.29
Raleigh (city) Wake County	5,143	1.27
High Point (city) Guilford County	1,152	1.10
Greenville (city) Pitt County	733	0.87
Greensboro (city) Guilford County	2,030	0.75
Winston-Salem (city) Forsyth County	1,391	0.61

Asian: Indonesian

Top 10 Places Sorted by Population
Based on all places, regardless of total population

Place	Population	%
Charlotte (city) Mecklenburg County	163	0.02
Raleigh (city) Wake County	121	0.03
Winston-Salem (city) Forsyth County	97	0.04
Cary (town) Wake County	70	0.05
Durham (city) Durham County	44	0.02
Greensboro (city) Guilford County	35	0.01
Asheville (city) Buncombe County	32	0.04
Wilmington (city) New Hanover County	26	0.02
Fayetteville (city) Cumberland County	21	0.01
Chapel Hill (town) Orange County	20	0.03

Top 10 Places Sorted by Percent of Total Population
Based on all places, regardless of total population

Place	Population	%
Cherokee (cdp) Jackson County	7	0.33
Bryson City (town) Swain County	2	0.14
Pineville (town) Mecklenburg County	10	0.13
Brevard (city) Transylvania County	8	0.11
Swannanoa (cdp) Buncombe County	5	0.11
Cramerton (town) Gaston County	4	0.10
Sea Breeze (cdp) New Hanover County	2	0.10
Royal Pines (cdp) Buncombe County	4	0.09
Hertford (town) Perquimans County	2	0.09
Morrisville (town) Wake County	14	0.08

Top 10 Places Sorted by Percent of Total Population
Based on places with total population of 50,000 or more

Place	Population	%
Cary (town) Wake County	70	0.05
Winston-Salem (city) Forsyth County	97	0.04
Asheville (city) Buncombe County	32	0.04
Raleigh (city) Wake County	121	0.03
Chapel Hill (town) Orange County	20	0.03
Charlotte (city) Mecklenburg County	163	0.02
Durham (city) Durham County	44	0.02
Wilmington (city) New Hanover County	26	0.02
Jacksonville (city) Onslow County	16	0.02
Gastonia (city) Gaston County	13	0.02

Asian: Japanese

Top 10 Places Sorted by Population
Based on all places, regardless of total population

Place	Population	%
Charlotte (city) Mecklenburg County	1,149	0.16
Raleigh (city) Wake County	821	0.20
Fayetteville (city) Cumberland County	775	0.39
Durham (city) Durham County	589	0.26
Cary (town) Wake County	561	0.41
Jacksonville (city) Onslow County	449	0.64
Chapel Hill (town) Orange County	387	0.68
Greensboro (city) Guilford County	369	0.14
Winston-Salem (city) Forsyth County	298	0.13
Havelock (city) Craven County	201	0.97

Top 10 Places Sorted by Percent of Total Population
Based on all places, regardless of total population

Place	Population	%
Godwin (town) Cumberland County	2	1.44
Piney Green (cdp) Onslow County	178	1.34
Newport (town) Carteret County	49	1.18

Place	Population	%
Neuse Forest (cdp) Craven County	23	1.15
Frisco (cdp) Dare County	2	1.00
Havelock (city) Craven County	201	0.97
Half Moon (cdp) Onslow County	77	0.92
Bakersville (town) Mitchell County	4	0.86
Bell Arthur (cdp) Pitt County	4	0.86
Pumpkin Center (cdp) Onslow County	17	0.77

Top 10 Places Sorted by Percent of Total Population
Based on places with total population of 50,000 or more

Place	Population	%
Chapel Hill (town) Orange County	387	0.68
Jacksonville (city) Onslow County	449	0.64
Cary (town) Wake County	561	0.41
Fayetteville (city) Cumberland County	775	0.39
Durham (city) Durham County	589	0.26
Raleigh (city) Wake County	821	0.20
Greenville (city) Pitt County	173	0.20
Asheville (city) Buncombe County	146	0.18
Charlotte (city) Mecklenburg County	1,149	0.16
Wilmington (city) New Hanover County	162	0.15

Asian: Korean

Top 10 Places Sorted by Population
Based on all places, regardless of total population

Place	Population	%
Charlotte (city) Mecklenburg County	3,168	0.43
Raleigh (city) Wake County	2,357	0.58
Fayetteville (city) Cumberland County	2,323	1.16
Cary (town) Wake County	1,455	1.08
Chapel Hill (town) Orange County	1,377	2.41
Durham (city) Durham County	1,146	0.50
Greensboro (city) Guilford County	997	0.37
High Point (city) Guilford County	630	0.60
Winston-Salem (city) Forsyth County	451	0.20
Greenville (city) Pitt County	285	0.34

Top 10 Places Sorted by Percent of Total Population
Based on all places, regardless of total population

Place	Population	%
Chapel Hill (town) Orange County	1,377	2.41
Falcon (town) Cumberland County	5	1.94
Bald Head Island (village) Brunswick County	3	1.90
Spring Lake (town) Cumberland County	200	1.67
Deercroft (cdp) Scotland County	5	1.22
Fayetteville (city) Cumberland County	2,323	1.16
Rockfish (cdp) Hoke County	38	1.15
Cary (town) Wake County	1,455	1.08
Wade (town) Cumberland County	6	1.08
Morrisville (town) Wake County	198	1.07

Top 10 Places Sorted by Percent of Total Population
Based on places with total population of 50,000 or more

Place	Population	%
Chapel Hill (town) Orange County	1,377	2.41
Fayetteville (city) Cumberland County	2,323	1.16
Cary (town) Wake County	1,455	1.08
High Point (city) Guilford County	630	0.60
Raleigh (city) Wake County	2,357	0.58
Durham (city) Durham County	1,146	0.50
Charlotte (city) Mecklenburg County	3,168	0.43
Greensboro (city) Guilford County	997	0.37
Greenville (city) Pitt County	285	0.34
Jacksonville (city) Onslow County	229	0.33

Asian: Laotian

Top 10 Places Sorted by Population
Based on all places, regardless of total population

Place	Population	%
Charlotte (city) Mecklenburg County	1,426	0.19
High Point (city) Guilford County	579	0.55
Greensboro (city) Guilford County	389	0.14
Raleigh (city) Wake County	259	0.06
Burlington (city) Alamance County	178	0.36
Mount Holly (city) Gaston County	170	1.24
Kannapolis (city) Cabarrus County	116	0.27
Kings Mountain (city) Cleveland County	111	1.08
Graham (city) Alamance County	67	0.47
Fayetteville (city) Cumberland County	67	0.03

Top 10 Places Sorted by Percent of Total Population
Based on all places, regardless of total population

Place	Population	%
Glen Alpine (town) Burke County	26	1.71
Grover (town) Cleveland County	10	1.41
Drexel (town) Burke County	25	1.35
Mount Holly (city) Gaston County	170	1.24
Kings Mountain (city) Cleveland County	111	1.08
China Grove (town) Rowan County	34	0.95
Catawba (town) Catawba County	5	0.83
Millingport (cdp) Stanly County	4	0.67
High Point (city) Guilford County	579	0.55
Graham (city) Alamance County	67	0.47

Top 10 Places Sorted by Percent of Total Population
Based on places with total population of 50,000 or more

Place	Population	%
High Point (city) Guilford County	579	0.55
Charlotte (city) Mecklenburg County	1,426	0.19
Greensboro (city) Guilford County	389	0.14
Concord (city) Cabarrus County	66	0.08
Gastonia (city) Gaston County	51	0.07
Raleigh (city) Wake County	259	0.06
Jacksonville (city) Onslow County	45	0.06
Fayetteville (city) Cumberland County	67	0.03
Winston-Salem (city) Forsyth County	58	0.03
Cary (town) Wake County	26	0.02

Asian: Malaysian

Top 10 Places Sorted by Population
Based on all places, regardless of total population

Place	Population	%
Charlotte (city) Mecklenburg County	78	0.01
Raleigh (city) Wake County	44	0.01
Durham (city) Durham County	19	0.01
Cary (town) Wake County	14	0.01
Greensboro (city) Guilford County	14	0.01
High Point (city) Guilford County	12	0.01
Morrisville (town) Wake County	11	0.06
Chapel Hill (town) Orange County	8	0.01
Rocky Mount (city) Nash County	8	0.01
New Bern (city) Craven County	7	0.02

Top 10 Places Sorted by Percent of Total Population
Based on all places, regardless of total population

Place	Population	%
Pine Knoll Shores (town) Carteret County	1	0.07
Morrisville (town) Wake County	11	0.06
Royal Pines (cdp) Buncombe County	2	0.05
Mebane (city) Alamance County	5	0.04
Brevard (city) Transylvania County	3	0.04
Wesley Chapel (village) Union County	3	0.04
Tabor City (town) Columbus County	1	0.04
Carrboro (town) Orange County	5	0.03
Kill Devil Hills (town) Dare County	2	0.03
Emerald Isle (town) Carteret County	1	0.03

Top 10 Places Sorted by Percent of Total Population
Based on places with total population of 50,000 or more

Place	Population	%
Charlotte (city) Mecklenburg County	78	0.01
Raleigh (city) Wake County	44	0.01
Durham (city) Durham County	19	0.01
Cary (town) Wake County	14	0.01
Greensboro (city) Guilford County	14	0.01
High Point (city) Guilford County	12	0.01
Chapel Hill (town) Orange County	8	0.01
Rocky Mount (city) Nash County	8	0.01
Wilmington (city) New Hanover County	5	<0.01
Winston-Salem (city) Forsyth County	5	<0.01

Asian: Nepalese

Top 10 Places Sorted by Population
Based on all places, regardless of total population

Place	Population	%
Cary (town) Wake County	190	0.14
Charlotte (city) Mecklenburg County	157	0.02
High Point (city) Guilford County	147	0.14

Place	Population	%
Raleigh (city) Wake County	140	0.03
Greensboro (city) Guilford County	81	0.03
Morrisville (town) Wake County	70	0.38
Durham (city) Durham County	48	0.02
Winston-Salem (city) Forsyth County	38	0.02
Harrisburg (town) Cabarrus County	13	0.11
Fuquay-Varina (town) Wake County	13	0.07

Top 10 Places Sorted by Percent of Total Population
Based on all places, regardless of total population

Place	Population	%
Turkey (town) Sampson County	3	1.03
Morrisville (town) Wake County	70	0.38
Cary (town) Wake County	190	0.14
High Point (city) Guilford County	147	0.14
Brices Creek (cdp) Craven County	4	0.13
Alliance (town) Pamlico County	1	0.13
Ranlo (town) Gaston County	4	0.12
Harrisburg (town) Cabarrus County	13	0.11
Marion (city) McDowell County	7	0.09
Franklin (town) Macon County	3	0.08

Top 10 Places Sorted by Percent of Total Population
Based on places with total population of 50,000 or more

Place	Population	%
Cary (town) Wake County	190	0.14
High Point (city) Guilford County	147	0.14
Raleigh (city) Wake County	140	0.03
Greensboro (city) Guilford County	81	0.03
Charlotte (city) Mecklenburg County	157	0.02
Durham (city) Durham County	48	0.02
Winston-Salem (city) Forsyth County	38	0.02
Chapel Hill (town) Orange County	11	0.02
Fayetteville (city) Cumberland County	12	0.01
Asheville (city) Buncombe County	6	0.01

Asian: Pakistani

Top 10 Places Sorted by Population
Based on all places, regardless of total population

Place	Population	%
High Point (city) Guilford County	1,399	1.34
Charlotte (city) Mecklenburg County	625	0.09
Cary (town) Wake County	579	0.43
Raleigh (city) Wake County	545	0.13
Durham (city) Durham County	294	0.13
Greensboro (city) Guilford County	230	0.09
Archdale (city) Randolph County	211	1.85
Winston-Salem (city) Forsyth County	155	0.07
Morrisville (town) Wake County	144	0.78
Greenville (city) Pitt County	116	0.14

Top 10 Places Sorted by Percent of Total Population
Based on all places, regardless of total population

Place	Population	%
Archdale (city) Randolph County	211	1.85
High Point (city) Guilford County	1,399	1.34
Scotch Meadows (cdp) Scotland County	6	1.03
Ramseur (town) Randolph County	15	0.89
Morrisville (town) Wake County	144	0.78
Staley (town) Randolph County	3	0.76
Trinity (city) Randolph County	37	0.56
Cary (town) Wake County	579	0.43
Belmont (city) Gaston County	30	0.30
Apex (town) Wake County	104	0.28

Top 10 Places Sorted by Percent of Total Population
Based on places with total population of 50,000 or more

Place	Population	%
High Point (city) Guilford County	1,399	1.34
Cary (town) Wake County	579	0.43
Chapel Hill (town) Orange County	89	0.16
Greenville (city) Pitt County	116	0.14
Gastonia (city) Gaston County	98	0.14
Raleigh (city) Wake County	545	0.13
Durham (city) Durham County	294	0.13
Charlotte (city) Mecklenburg County	625	0.09
Greensboro (city) Guilford County	230	0.09
Winston-Salem (city) Forsyth County	155	0.07

Asian: Sri Lankan

Top 10 Places Sorted by Population
Based on all places, regardless of total population

Place	Population	%
Cary (town) Wake County	161	0.12
Raleigh (city) Wake County	75	0.02
Charlotte (city) Mecklenburg County	66	0.01
Chapel Hill (town) Orange County	42	0.07
Greensboro (city) Guilford County	37	0.01
Winston-Salem (city) Forsyth County	36	0.02
Durham (city) Durham County	35	0.02
Morrisville (town) Wake County	34	0.18
Apex (town) Wake County	27	0.07
Fayetteville (city) Cumberland County	19	0.01

Top 10 Places Sorted by Percent of Total Population
Based on all places, regardless of total population

Place	Population	%
Laurel Hill (cdp) Scotland County	4	0.32
Morrisville (town) Wake County	34	0.18
Cary (town) Wake County	161	0.12
Sea Breeze (cdp) New Hanover County	2	0.10
Banner Elk (town) Avery County	1	0.10
Chapel Hill (town) Orange County	42	0.07
Apex (town) Wake County	27	0.07
Foscoe (cdp) Watauga County	1	0.07
Carrboro (town) Orange County	12	0.06
Davidson (town) Mecklenburg County	4	0.04

Top 10 Places Sorted by Percent of Total Population
Based on places with total population of 50,000 or more

Place	Population	%
Cary (town) Wake County	161	0.12
Chapel Hill (town) Orange County	42	0.07
Raleigh (city) Wake County	75	0.02
Winston-Salem (city) Forsyth County	36	0.02
Durham (city) Durham County	35	0.02
Charlotte (city) Mecklenburg County	66	0.01
Greensboro (city) Guilford County	37	0.01
Fayetteville (city) Cumberland County	19	0.01
Concord (city) Cabarrus County	11	0.01
Gastonia (city) Gaston County	8	0.01

Asian: Taiwanese

Top 10 Places Sorted by Population
Based on all places, regardless of total population

Place	Population	%
Cary (town) Wake County	346	0.26
Durham (city) Durham County	269	0.12
Raleigh (city) Wake County	269	0.07
Charlotte (city) Mecklenburg County	223	0.03
Chapel Hill (town) Orange County	201	0.35
Greensboro (city) Guilford County	59	0.02
Apex (town) Wake County	50	0.13
Carrboro (town) Orange County	40	0.20
Winston-Salem (city) Forsyth County	38	0.02
Fayetteville (city) Cumberland County	32	0.02

Top 10 Places Sorted by Percent of Total Population
Based on all places, regardless of total population

Place	Population	%
Chapel Hill (town) Orange County	201	0.35
Cary (town) Wake County	346	0.26
Neuse Forest (cdp) Craven County	5	0.25
Carrboro (town) Orange County	40	0.20
Rockwell (town) Rowan County	4	0.19
Banner Elk (town) Avery County	2	0.19
Morrisville (town) Wake County	29	0.16
High Shoals (town) Gaston County	1	0.14
Apex (town) Wake County	50	0.13
North Topsail Beach (town) Onslow County	1	0.13

Top 10 Places Sorted by Percent of Total Population
Based on places with total population of 50,000 or more

Place	Population	%
Chapel Hill (town) Orange County	201	0.35
Cary (town) Wake County	346	0.26
Durham (city) Durham County	269	0.12
Raleigh (city) Wake County	269	0.07

Charlotte (city) Mecklenburg County	223	0.03
Greenville (city) Pitt County	28	0.03
Greensboro (city) Guilford County	59	0.02
Winston-Salem (city) Forsyth County	38	0.02
Fayetteville (city) Cumberland County	32	0.02
High Point (city) Guilford County	21	0.02

Asian: Thai

Top 10 Places Sorted by Population
Based on all places, regardless of total population

Place	Population	%
Charlotte (city) Mecklenburg County	461	0.06
Fayetteville (city) Cumberland County	364	0.18
Raleigh (city) Wake County	343	0.08
Durham (city) Durham County	207	0.09
Greensboro (city) Guilford County	177	0.07
Cary (town) Wake County	114	0.08
Chapel Hill (town) Orange County	105	0.18
Jacksonville (city) Onslow County	87	0.12
High Point (city) Guilford County	81	0.08
Winston-Salem (city) Forsyth County	79	0.03

Top 10 Places Sorted by Percent of Total Population
Based on all places, regardless of total population

Place	Population	%
New London (town) Stanly County	10	1.67
Cameron (town) Moore County	2	0.70
Catawba (town) Catawba County	3	0.50
Surf City (town) Pender County	9	0.49
Glen Alpine (town) Burke County	7	0.46
Elroy (cdp) Wayne County	17	0.44
Henrietta (cdp) Rutherford County	2	0.43
Spring Lake (town) Cumberland County	50	0.42
Conover (city) Catawba County	34	0.42
Wade (town) Cumberland County	2	0.36

Top 10 Places Sorted by Percent of Total Population
Based on places with total population of 50,000 or more

Place	Population	%
Fayetteville (city) Cumberland County	364	0.18
Chapel Hill (town) Orange County	105	0.18
Jacksonville (city) Onslow County	87	0.12
Durham (city) Durham County	207	0.09
Raleigh (city) Wake County	343	0.08
Cary (town) Wake County	114	0.08
High Point (city) Guilford County	81	0.08
Greensboro (city) Guilford County	177	0.07
Charlotte (city) Mecklenburg County	461	0.06
Asheville (city) Buncombe County	39	0.05

Asian: Vietnamese

Top 10 Places Sorted by Population
Based on all places, regardless of total population

Place	Population	%
Charlotte (city) Mecklenburg County	7,550	1.03
Greensboro (city) Guilford County	4,474	1.66
Raleigh (city) Wake County	3,210	0.79
High Point (city) Guilford County	1,085	1.04
Cary (town) Wake County	1,081	0.80
Durham (city) Durham County	795	0.35
Fayetteville (city) Cumberland County	611	0.30
Winston-Salem (city) Forsyth County	456	0.20
Matthews (town) Mecklenburg County	335	1.23
Hickory (city) Catawba County	315	0.79

Top 10 Places Sorted by Percent of Total Population
Based on all places, regardless of total population

Place	Population	%
Columbia (town) Tyrrell County	19	2.13
Belmont (city) Gaston County	190	1.89
Greensboro (city) Guilford County	4,474	1.66
Matthews (town) Mecklenburg County	335	1.23
Archdale (city) Randolph County	133	1.17
High Point (city) Guilford County	1,085	1.04
Bostic (town) Rutherford County	4	1.04
Crossnore (town) Avery County	2	1.04
Charlotte (city) Mecklenburg County	7,550	1.03
Morrisville (town) Wake County	181	0.97

Top 10 Places Sorted by Percent of Total Population
Based on places with total population of 50,000 or more

Place	Population	%
Greensboro (city) Guilford County	4,474	1.66
High Point (city) Guilford County	1,085	1.04
Charlotte (city) Mecklenburg County	7,550	1.03
Cary (town) Wake County	1,081	0.80
Raleigh (city) Wake County	3,210	0.79
Chapel Hill (town) Orange County	216	0.38
Durham (city) Durham County	795	0.35
Fayetteville (city) Cumberland County	611	0.30
Jacksonville (city) Onslow County	212	0.30
Concord (city) Cabarrus County	197	0.25

Hawaii Native/Pacific Islander

Top 10 Places Sorted by Population
Based on all places, regardless of total population

Place	Population	%
Fayetteville (city) Cumberland County	1,631	0.81
Charlotte (city) Mecklenburg County	1,315	0.18
Raleigh (city) Wake County	595	0.15
Jacksonville (city) Onslow County	432	0.62
Greensboro (city) Guilford County	429	0.16
Winston-Salem (city) Forsyth County	374	0.16
Durham (city) Durham County	331	0.14
Morganton (city) Burke County	272	1.61
Asheville (city) Buncombe County	203	0.24
Wilmington (city) New Hanover County	189	0.18

Top 10 Places Sorted by Percent of Total Population
Based on all places, regardless of total population

Place	Population	%
Seven Springs (town) Wayne County	4	3.64
Pumpkin Center (cdp) Onslow County	46	2.07
Arapahoe (town) Pamlico County	9	1.62
Morganton (city) Burke County	272	1.61
Robbins (town) Moore County	17	1.55
Coinjock (cdp) Currituck County	5	1.49
Keener (cdp) Sampson County	8	1.41
Lansing (town) Ashe County	2	1.27
Spring Lake (town) Cumberland County	144	1.20
Lewiston Woodville (town) Bertie County	6	1.09

Top 10 Places Sorted by Percent of Total Population
Based on places with total population of 50,000 or more

Place	Population	%
Fayetteville (city) Cumberland County	1,631	0.81
Jacksonville (city) Onslow County	432	0.62
Asheville (city) Buncombe County	203	0.24
Charlotte (city) Mecklenburg County	1,315	0.18
Wilmington (city) New Hanover County	189	0.18
Greensboro (city) Guilford County	429	0.16
Winston-Salem (city) Forsyth County	374	0.16
Raleigh (city) Wake County	595	0.15
Durham (city) Durham County	331	0.14
Concord (city) Cabarrus County	108	0.14

Hawaii Native/Pacific Islander: Not Hispanic

Top 10 Places Sorted by Population
Based on all places, regardless of total population

Place	Population	%
Fayetteville (city) Cumberland County	1,376	0.69
Charlotte (city) Mecklenburg County	986	0.13
Raleigh (city) Wake County	417	0.10
Jacksonville (city) Onslow County	376	0.54
Greensboro (city) Guilford County	342	0.13
Winston-Salem (city) Forsyth County	261	0.11
Durham (city) Durham County	256	0.11
Asheville (city) Buncombe County	179	0.21
Cary (town) Wake County	160	0.12
Wilmington (city) New Hanover County	152	0.14

Top 10 Places Sorted by Percent of Total Population
Based on all places, regardless of total population

Place	Population	%
Pumpkin Center (cdp) Onslow County	45	2.03
Arapahoe (town) Pamlico County	9	1.62

Place	Population	%
Lansing (town) Ashe County	2	1.27
Mamers (cdp) Harnett County	8	0.97
Efland (cdp) Orange County	7	0.95
Momeyer (town) Nash County	2	0.89
Morganton (city) Burke County	139	0.82
East Bend (town) Yadkin County	5	0.82
Spring Lake (town) Cumberland County	94	0.79
Vandemere (town) Pamlico County	2	0.79

Top 10 Places Sorted by Percent of Total Population
Based on places with total population of 50,000 or more

Place	Population	%
Fayetteville (city) Cumberland County	1,376	0.69
Jacksonville (city) Onslow County	376	0.54
Asheville (city) Buncombe County	179	0.21
Wilmington (city) New Hanover County	152	0.14
Charlotte (city) Mecklenburg County	986	0.13
Greensboro (city) Guilford County	342	0.13
Cary (town) Wake County	160	0.12
Winston-Salem (city) Forsyth County	261	0.11
Durham (city) Durham County	256	0.11
Concord (city) Cabarrus County	90	0.11

Hawaii Native/Pacific Islander: Hispanic

Top 10 Places Sorted by Population
Based on all places, regardless of total population

Place	Population	%
Charlotte (city) Mecklenburg County	329	0.04
Fayetteville (city) Cumberland County	255	0.13
Raleigh (city) Wake County	178	0.04
Morganton (city) Burke County	133	0.79
Winston-Salem (city) Forsyth County	113	0.05
Greensboro (city) Guilford County	87	0.03
Durham (city) Durham County	75	0.03
Jacksonville (city) Onslow County	56	0.08
Spring Lake (town) Cumberland County	50	0.42
Piney Green (cdp) Onslow County	44	0.33

Top 10 Places Sorted by Percent of Total Population
Based on all places, regardless of total population

Place	Population	%
Seven Springs (town) Wayne County	4	3.64
Robbins (town) Moore County	17	1.55
Lewiston Woodville (town) Bertie County	6	1.09
Keener (cdp) Sampson County	6	1.06
Coinjock (cdp) Currituck County	3	0.90
Morganton (city) Burke County	133	0.79
Hamilton (town) Martin County	3	0.74
Faison (town) Duplin County	6	0.62
Newland (town) Avery County	4	0.57
Parkton (town) Robeson County	2	0.46

Top 10 Places Sorted by Percent of Total Population
Based on places with total population of 50,000 or more

Place	Population	%
Fayetteville (city) Cumberland County	255	0.13
Jacksonville (city) Onslow County	56	0.08
Winston-Salem (city) Forsyth County	113	0.05
Charlotte (city) Mecklenburg County	329	0.04
Raleigh (city) Wake County	178	0.04
Greensboro (city) Guilford County	87	0.03
Durham (city) Durham County	75	0.03
Wilmington (city) New Hanover County	37	0.03
High Point (city) Guilford County	31	0.03
Asheville (city) Buncombe County	24	0.03

Hawaii Native/Pacific Islander: Fijian

Top 10 Places Sorted by Population
Based on all places, regardless of total population

Place	Population	%
Charlotte (city) Mecklenburg County	8	<0.01
Fayetteville (city) Cumberland County	4	<0.01
Greensboro (city) Guilford County	4	<0.01
Leland (town) Brunswick County	3	0.02
Chapel Hill (town) Orange County	3	0.01
Huntersville (town) Mecklenburg County	3	0.01
Durham (city) Durham County	3	<0.01
Raleigh (city) Wake County	3	<0.01
Atlantic Beach (town) Carteret County	2	0.13

Place	Population	%
Wendell (town) Wake County	2	0.03

Top 10 Places Sorted by Percent of Total Population
Based on all places, regardless of total population

Place	Population	%
Atlantic Beach (town) Carteret County	2	0.13
Wendell (town) Wake County	2	0.03
Leland (town) Brunswick County	3	0.02
Chapel Hill (town) Orange County	3	0.01
Huntersville (town) Mecklenburg County	3	0.01
Cornelius (town) Mecklenburg County	2	0.01
Albemarle (city) Stanly County	1	0.01
Morehead City (town) Carteret County	1	0.01
Charlotte (city) Mecklenburg County	8	<0.01
Fayetteville (city) Cumberland County	4	<0.01

Top 10 Places Sorted by Percent of Total Population
Based on places with total population of 50,000 or more

Place	Population	%
Chapel Hill (town) Orange County	3	0.01
Charlotte (city) Mecklenburg County	8	<0.01
Fayetteville (city) Cumberland County	4	<0.01
Greensboro (city) Guilford County	4	<0.01
Durham (city) Durham County	3	<0.01
Raleigh (city) Wake County	3	<0.01
Cary (town) Wake County	2	<0.01
Jacksonville (city) Onslow County	2	<0.01
Asheville (city) Buncombe County	1	<0.01
Gastonia (city) Gaston County	1	<0.01

Hawaii Native/Pacific Islander: Guamanian or Chamorro

Top 10 Places Sorted by Population
Based on all places, regardless of total population

Place	Population	%
Fayetteville (city) Cumberland County	528	0.26
Charlotte (city) Mecklenburg County	268	0.04
Morganton (city) Burke County	246	1.45
Raleigh (city) Wake County	121	0.03
Winston-Salem (city) Forsyth County	100	0.04
Jacksonville (city) Onslow County	93	0.13
Greensboro (city) Guilford County	72	0.03
Havelock (city) Craven County	67	0.32
Durham (city) Durham County	49	0.02
Wilmington (city) New Hanover County	39	0.04

Top 10 Places Sorted by Percent of Total Population
Based on all places, regardless of total population

Place	Population	%
Robbins (town) Moore County	17	1.55
Morganton (city) Burke County	246	1.45
Keener (cdp) Sampson County	7	1.23
Lewiston Woodville (town) Bertie County	6	1.09
Arapahoe (town) Pamlico County	5	0.90
Momeyer (town) Nash County	2	0.89
Efland (cdp) Orange County	6	0.82
Lansing (town) Ashe County	1	0.63
Pumpkin Center (cdp) Onslow County	13	0.59
Faison (town) Duplin County	5	0.52

Top 10 Places Sorted by Percent of Total Population
Based on places with total population of 50,000 or more

Place	Population	%
Fayetteville (city) Cumberland County	528	0.26
Jacksonville (city) Onslow County	93	0.13
Charlotte (city) Mecklenburg County	268	0.04
Winston-Salem (city) Forsyth County	100	0.04
Wilmington (city) New Hanover County	39	0.04
Raleigh (city) Wake County	121	0.03
Greensboro (city) Guilford County	72	0.03
High Point (city) Guilford County	27	0.03
Durham (city) Durham County	49	0.02
Cary (town) Wake County	28	0.02

Hawaii Native/Pacific Islander: Marshallese

Top 10 Places Sorted by Population
Based on all places, regardless of total population

Place	Population	%
Winston-Salem (city) Forsyth County	44	0.02
Asheville (city) Buncombe County	26	0.03
Fayetteville (city) Cumberland County	22	0.01
Greensboro (city) Guilford County	7	<0.01
Piney Green (cdp) Onslow County	5	0.04
Charlotte (city) Mecklenburg County	5	<0.01
Wake Forest (town) Wake County	4	0.01
Boiling Spring Lakes (city) Brunswick County	3	0.06
Woodfin (town) Buncombe County	3	0.05
New Bern (city) Craven County	3	0.01

Top 10 Places Sorted by Percent of Total Population
Based on all places, regardless of total population

Place	Population	%
Surf City (town) Pender County	2	0.11
Boiling Spring Lakes (city) Brunswick County	3	0.06
Woodfin (town) Buncombe County	3	0.05
Piney Green (cdp) Onslow County	5	0.04
Asheville (city) Buncombe County	26	0.03
Winston-Salem (city) Forsyth County	44	0.02
Fayetteville (city) Cumberland County	22	0.01
Wake Forest (town) Wake County	4	0.01
New Bern (city) Craven County	3	0.01
Boone (town) Watauga County	1	0.01

Top 10 Places Sorted by Percent of Total Population
Based on places with total population of 50,000 or more

Place	Population	%
Asheville (city) Buncombe County	26	0.03
Winston-Salem (city) Forsyth County	44	0.02
Fayetteville (city) Cumberland County	22	0.01
Greensboro (city) Guilford County	7	<0.01
Charlotte (city) Mecklenburg County	5	<0.01
Cary (town) Wake County	0	0.00
Chapel Hill (town) Orange County	0	0.00
Concord (city) Cabarrus County	0	0.00
Durham (city) Durham County	0	0.00
Gastonia (city) Gaston County	0	0.00

Hawaii Native/Pacific Islander: Native Hawaiian

Top 10 Places Sorted by Population
Based on all places, regardless of total population

Place	Population	%
Fayetteville (city) Cumberland County	473	0.24
Charlotte (city) Mecklenburg County	268	0.04
Raleigh (city) Wake County	156	0.04
Jacksonville (city) Onslow County	144	0.21
Greensboro (city) Guilford County	125	0.05
Winston-Salem (city) Forsyth County	90	0.04
Durham (city) Durham County	79	0.03
Wilmington (city) New Hanover County	61	0.06
Cary (town) Wake County	54	0.04
Concord (city) Cabarrus County	43	0.05

Top 10 Places Sorted by Percent of Total Population
Based on all places, regardless of total population

Place	Population	%
Coinjock (cdp) Currituck County	4	1.19
East Bend (town) Yadkin County	5	0.82
Pumpkin Center (cdp) Onslow County	18	0.81
Rodanthe (cdp) Dare County	2	0.77
Calypso (town) Duplin County	4	0.74
Newland (town) Avery County	5	0.72
Dobbins Heights (town) Richmond County	6	0.69
Lansing (town) Ashe County	1	0.63
Ellerbe (town) Richmond County	6	0.57
Polkville (city) Cleveland County	3	0.55

Top 10 Places Sorted by Percent of Total Population
Based on places with total population of 50,000 or more

Place	Population	%
Fayetteville (city) Cumberland County	473	0.24

Place	Population	%
Jacksonville (city) Onslow County	144	0.21
Wilmington (city) New Hanover County	61	0.06
Greensboro (city) Guilford County	125	0.05
Concord (city) Cabarrus County	43	0.05
Asheville (city) Buncombe County	41	0.05
Charlotte (city) Mecklenburg County	268	0.04
Raleigh (city) Wake County	156	0.04
Winston-Salem (city) Forsyth County	90	0.04
Cary (town) Wake County	54	0.04

Hawaii Native/Pacific Islander: Samoan

Top 10 Places Sorted by Population
Based on all places, regardless of total population

Place	Population	%
Fayetteville (city) Cumberland County	226	0.11
Charlotte (city) Mecklenburg County	139	0.02
Jacksonville (city) Onslow County	67	0.10
Greensboro (city) Guilford County	47	0.02
Raleigh (city) Wake County	43	0.01
Wilmington (city) New Hanover County	34	0.03
Durham (city) Durham County	34	0.01
Spring Lake (town) Cumberland County	31	0.26
Asheville (city) Buncombe County	22	0.03
Half Moon (cdp) Onslow County	20	0.24

Top 10 Places Sorted by Percent of Total Population
Based on all places, regardless of total population

Place	Population	%
Mamers (cdp) Harnett County	8	0.97
South Weldon (cdp) Halifax County	4	0.57
Pumpkin Center (cdp) Onslow County	12	0.54
Rockwell (town) Rowan County	6	0.28
Spring Lake (town) Cumberland County	31	0.26
Mountain View (cdp) Catawba County	9	0.25
Half Moon (cdp) Onslow County	20	0.24
Bridgeton (town) Craven County	1	0.22
Richlands (town) Onslow County	3	0.20
Spivey's Corner (cdp) Sampson County	1	0.20

Top 10 Places Sorted by Percent of Total Population
Based on places with total population of 50,000 or more

Place	Population	%
Fayetteville (city) Cumberland County	226	0.11
Jacksonville (city) Onslow County	67	0.10
Wilmington (city) New Hanover County	34	0.03
Asheville (city) Buncombe County	22	0.03
Charlotte (city) Mecklenburg County	139	0.02
Greensboro (city) Guilford County	47	0.02
Concord (city) Cabarrus County	18	0.02
Greenville (city) Pitt County	15	0.02
Raleigh (city) Wake County	43	0.01
Durham (city) Durham County	34	0.01

Hawaii Native/Pacific Islander: Tongan

Top 10 Places Sorted by Population
Based on all places, regardless of total population

Place	Population	%
Charlotte (city) Mecklenburg County	20	<0.01
Fayetteville (city) Cumberland County	10	<0.01
Kinston (city) Lenoir County	8	0.04
Holly Springs (town) Wake County	4	0.02
Spring Lake (town) Cumberland County	3	0.03
Sanford (city) Lee County	3	0.01
Shelby (city) Cleveland County	3	0.01
Greenville (city) Pitt County	3	<0.01
Carrboro (town) Orange County	2	0.01
Clayton (town) Johnston County	2	0.01

Top 10 Places Sorted by Percent of Total Population
Based on all places, regardless of total population

Place	Population	%
Montreat (town) Buncombe County	1	0.14
Laurel Park (town) Henderson County	1	0.05
Kinston (city) Lenoir County	8	0.04
Spring Lake (town) Cumberland County	3	0.03
Holly Springs (town) Wake County	4	0.02
Elkin (town) Surry County	1	0.02
Sanford (city) Lee County	3	0.01
Shelby (city) Cleveland County	3	0.01

Place	Population	%
Carrboro (town) Orange County	2	0.01
Clayton (town) Johnston County	2	0.01

Top 10 Places Sorted by Percent of Total Population
Based on places with total population of 50,000 or more

Place	Population	%
Charlotte (city) Mecklenburg County	20	<0.01
Fayetteville (city) Cumberland County	10	<0.01
Greenville (city) Pitt County	3	<0.01
Durham (city) Durham County	2	<0.01
Greensboro (city) Guilford County	2	<0.01
Asheville (city) Buncombe County	1	<0.01
Jacksonville (city) Onslow County	1	<0.01
Raleigh (city) Wake County	1	<0.01
Wilmington (city) New Hanover County	1	<0.01
Winston-Salem (city) Forsyth County	1	<0.01

White

Top 10 Places Sorted by Population
Based on all places, regardless of total population

Place	Population	%
Charlotte (city) Mecklenburg County	379,739	51.92
Raleigh (city) Wake County	240,430	59.53
Greensboro (city) Guilford County	135,483	50.24
Winston-Salem (city) Forsyth County	121,879	53.08
Cary (town) Wake County	101,785	75.27
Durham (city) Durham County	101,410	44.41
Fayetteville (city) Cumberland County	99,113	49.42
Wilmington (city) New Hanover County	80,213	75.33
Asheville (city) Buncombe County	68,075	81.63
High Point (city) Guilford County	57,866	55.44

Top 10 Places Sorted by Percent of Total Population
Based on all places, regardless of total population

Place	Population	%
Aquadale (cdp) Stanly County	397	100.00
Grandfather (village) Avery County	25	100.00
Valle Crucis (cdp) Watauga County	411	99.76
Cedar Rock (village) Caldwell County	299	99.67
Casar (town) Cleveland County	296	99.66
Hatteras (cdp) Dare County	502	99.60
Harkers Island (cdp) Carteret County	1,201	99.50
Frisco (cdp) Dare County	199	99.50
Hot Springs (town) Madison County	557	99.46
Denton (town) Davidson County	1,625	99.33

Top 10 Places Sorted by Percent of Total Population
Based on places with total population of 50,000 or more

Place	Population	%
Asheville (city) Buncombe County	68,075	81.63
Wilmington (city) New Hanover County	80,213	75.33
Cary (town) Wake County	101,785	75.27
Chapel Hill (town) Orange County	43,000	75.13
Concord (city) Cabarrus County	57,201	72.35
Jacksonville (city) Onslow County	50,136	71.47
Gastonia (city) Gaston County	46,580	64.93
Raleigh (city) Wake County	240,430	59.53
Greenville (city) Pitt County	49,010	57.96
High Point (city) Guilford County	57,866	55.44

White: Not Hispanic

Top 10 Places Sorted by Population
Based on all places, regardless of total population

Place	Population	%
Charlotte (city) Mecklenburg County	339,512	46.42
Raleigh (city) Wake County	221,203	54.77
Greensboro (city) Guilford County	126,944	47.07
Winston-Salem (city) Forsyth County	111,232	48.44
Cary (town) Wake County	95,613	70.70
Durham (city) Durham County	89,618	39.25
Fayetteville (city) Cumberland County	88,521	44.14
Wilmington (city) New Hanover County	76,964	72.28
Asheville (city) Buncombe County	65,118	78.09
High Point (city) Guilford County	54,075	51.81

Top 10 Places Sorted by Percent of Total Population
Based on all places, regardless of total population

Place	Population	%
Grandfather (village) Avery County	25	100.00
Harkers Island (cdp) Carteret County	1,200	99.42
Hobucken (cdp) Pamlico County	128	99.22
Davis (cdp) Carteret County	418	99.05
Gloucester (cdp) Carteret County	530	98.70
Denton (town) Davidson County	1,614	98.66
Frisco (cdp) Dare County	197	98.50
Biltmore Forest (town) Buncombe County	1,320	98.29
Marshallberg (cdp) Carteret County	396	98.26
Chimney Rock Village (village) Rutherford County	111	98.23

Top 10 Places Sorted by Percent of Total Population
Based on places with total population of 50,000 or more

Place	Population	%
Asheville (city) Buncombe County	65,118	78.09
Wilmington (city) New Hanover County	76,964	72.28
Chapel Hill (town) Orange County	40,897	71.46
Cary (town) Wake County	95,613	70.70
Concord (city) Cabarrus County	53,001	67.03
Jacksonville (city) Onslow County	44,804	63.87
Gastonia (city) Gaston County	43,719	60.94
Greenville (city) Pitt County	47,591	56.28
Raleigh (city) Wake County	221,203	54.77
High Point (city) Guilford County	54,075	51.81

White: Hispanic

Top 10 Places Sorted by Population
Based on all places, regardless of total population

Place	Population	%
Charlotte (city) Mecklenburg County	40,227	5.50
Raleigh (city) Wake County	19,227	4.76
Durham (city) Durham County	11,792	5.16
Winston-Salem (city) Forsyth County	10,647	4.64
Fayetteville (city) Cumberland County	10,592	5.28
Greensboro (city) Guilford County	8,539	3.17
Cary (town) Wake County	6,172	4.56
Jacksonville (city) Onslow County	5,332	7.60
Concord (city) Cabarrus County	4,200	5.31
High Point (city) Guilford County	3,791	3.63

Top 10 Places Sorted by Percent of Total Population
Based on all places, regardless of total population

Place	Population	%
Robbins (town) Moore County	296	26.98
Ocracoke (cdp) Hyde County	166	17.51
Siler City (town) Chatham County	1,288	16.33
Barker Heights (cdp) Henderson County	191	15.23
Shannon (cdp) Robeson County	35	13.31
Selma (town) Johnston County	803	13.22
Franklinville (town) Randolph County	152	13.06
Seven Springs (town) Wayne County	14	12.73
Star (town) Montgomery County	110	12.56
Delway (cdp) Sampson County	25	12.32

Top 10 Places Sorted by Percent of Total Population
Based on places with total population of 50,000 or more

Place	Population	%
Jacksonville (city) Onslow County	5,332	7.60
Charlotte (city) Mecklenburg County	40,227	5.50
Concord (city) Cabarrus County	4,200	5.31
Fayetteville (city) Cumberland County	10,592	5.28
Durham (city) Durham County	11,792	5.16
Raleigh (city) Wake County	19,227	4.76
Winston-Salem (city) Forsyth County	10,647	4.64
Cary (town) Wake County	6,172	4.56
Gastonia (city) Gaston County	2,861	3.99
Chapel Hill (town) Orange County	2,103	3.67

Climate

North Carolina Physical Features and Climate Narrative

PHYSICAL FEATURES. North Carolina lies between 33.5° and 37° N. latitude and between 75° and 84.5° W. longitude. The span of longitude is greater than that of any other state east of the Mississippi River. The greatest length from east to west is 503 miles. The greatest breadth from north to south is 187 miles. The total area is 52,712 square miles: 49,142 square miles of land and 3,570 square miles of water.

The range of altitude is also the greatest of any eastern state. North Carolina rises from sea level along the Atlantic coast to 6,684 feet at the summit of Mount Mitchell, the highest peak in the eastern United States. Mount Mitchell is in the heart of the Blue Ridge Range. This Range, along with the Great Smokies, lies partly in North Carolina and partly in Tennessee and forms the highest part of the Appalachian Mountains.

The three principal physiographic divisions of the eastern United States are particularly well developed in North Carolina. Beginning in the east, they are: the Coastal Plain, the Piedmont, and the Mountains. The land and water areas of the Coastal Plain Division comprise nearly half the area of the State. The tidewater portion is generally flat and swampy, while the interior is gently sloping and, for the most part, naturally well drained. The Piedmont Division rises gently from about 200 feet at the fall line to near 1,500 feet at the base of the mountains; its area is about one-third of the State. The land is mostly gently rolling. There are several ranges of steeper hills. The Mountain Division is the smallest of the three, little more than one-fifth of the State's area. In elevation it ranges downward from Mount Mitchell's peak to about 1,000 feet above mean sea level in the lowest valleys. There are more than 40 peaks higher than 6,000 feet and about 80 others over 5,000 feet high.

North Carolina rivers fall into two groups: those that flow into the Atlantic Ocean and those that drain westward into the Mississippi River system. The two are separated by a ridge averaging 2,200 feet above mean sea level. A second chain of mountains ranging up to 6,000 feet marks the western boundary of the State. Most of the State, including the Coastal Plain, the Piedmont, and the eastern and southern slopes, drains into the Atlantic Ocean. The principal rivers involved are the Roanoke, Tar, Neuse, Cape Fear, Yadkin, and Catawba. The main stream draining the extreme western part of North Carolina is the French Broad River. The northern mountains are drained by streams flowing into the Ohio River system. All eventually reach the Mississippi.

GENERAL CLIMATE. North Carolina has the most varied climate of any eastern state. This is due mainly to its wide range in elevation and distance from the ocean. In all seasons of the year the average temperature varies more than 20 from the lower coast to the highest mountain elevations. Altitude also has an important effect on rainfall. The rainiest part of the eastern United States, with an annual average of more than 80 inches, is in southwestern North Carolina where moist southerly winds are forced upward in passing over the mountain barrier.

In winter the greater part of North Carolina is partially protected by the mountain ranges from the frequent outbreaks of cold which move southeastward across the Central States. Such outbreaks often spread southward all the way to the Gulf of Mexico without attaining strength and depth to cross the Appalachian Range. When cold waves do break across they are usually modified by the crossing and the descent on the eastern slopes. The temperature drops to around 10 over central North Carolina once or twice during an average winter. Near the coast a comparable figure is some 10 degrees higher, and in the upper mountains 10 degrees lower. Temperatures as low as 0 are rare outside the mountains, but have occurred at one time or another throughout the western part of the State.

Winter temperatures in the eastern Coastal Plain are modified by the proximity of the Atlantic Ocean. This effect raises the average winter temperature and reduces the average day-to-night range. The Gulf Stream, contrary to popular opinion, has little direct effect on North Carolina temperatures, even on the immediate coast. The Stream lies some 50 miles offshore at its nearest point. The southern reaches of the cold Labrador Current pass between the Gulf Stream and the North Carolina coast. This offsets any warming effect the Stream might otherwise have on coastal temperatures. The meeting of the two opposing currents does provide a breeding ground for rough weather. Not infrequently low pressure storms having their origin there develop major proportions, causing rain on the North Carolina coast and over states to the north.

In spring the storm systems that bring cold weather southward reach North Carolina less forcefully than in winter, and temperatures begin to modify. Day-to-day variations in temperature are less pronounced, and warm weather is more likely to occur in conjunction with fair weather. During the summer, when the drying of the air is sufficient to keep cloudiness at a minimum for several days, temperatures may occasionally reach 100°F. or a little higher in interior sections at elevations below 1,500 feet. Ordinarily, however, summer cloudiness develops to limit the sun's heating while temperatures are still in the 90°F. range. Autumn is the season of most rapidly changing temperature, the daily downward trend being greater than the corresponding rise in spring. The dropoff is most rapid in October and continues almost as fast in November.

PRECIPITATION. There are no distinct wet and dry seasons in North Carolina. There is some seasonal variation in average precipitation. Summer rainfall is normally the greatest, and July the wettest month. Since the rain at this time of year comes mostly with thunderstorms and convective showers, it is also more variable than at other seasons. Daily showers are not uncommon, nor are periods of one or two weeks without rain. Autumn is the driest season, and October the driest month. Precipitation in winter and spring occurs mostly with migratory low pressure storms. It appears with greater regularity and more even distribution than summer showers.

Winter precipitation usually occurs with southerly through easterly winds, and is seldom associated with very cold weather. Snow and sleet occur on an average of once or twice a year near the coast, and not much more often over the southeastern half of the State. Over the Mountains and western Piedmont frozen precipitation sometimes occurs with interior low pressure storms. In the extreme west it can happen with a cold front passage from northwest. Average winter snowfall ranges from about one inch per year on the Outer Banks and the lower coast, to about nine inches in the northern Piedmont and southern Mountains. Some of the higher mountain peaks and upper slopes receive an average of nearly 50 inches a year.

OTHER CLIMATIC ELEMENTS. Relative humidity may vary greatly from day to day and even from hour to hour, especially in winter. The average relative humidity, however, does not vary greatly from season to season, there being a slight tendency for highest averages in winter and lowest in spring. The lowest relative humidities are found over the southern Piedmont; the highest are along the immediate coast.

Sunshine is abundant, the average annual percentage of possible ranging from 60 to 65 percent at most recording points. Measurable rain falls on about 120 days. Prevailing winds blow from southwest 10 months of the year, and from northeast during September and October. The average wind speed for interior locations is about eight m.p.h., for coastal points about 12 m.p.h.

STORMS AND FLOODS. Intense rainstorms occur in the precipitous mountain terrain, especially in the southern portion. Streams here rise quickly to flood, and almost as quickly subside when rain ends. Floods occur frequently, affecting some part of North Carolina each year. Floods may occur at any season, but are most frequent in early spring, summer, and early fall. Rains associated with West Indian hurricanes are the main cause of summer and fall floods. The greatest economic loss entailed in North Carolina because of stormy weather is that due to summer thunderstorms. These usually affect only limited areas. In any given locality, 40 to 50 days with thunderstorms may be expected in a year.

North Carolina is outside the principal tornado area of the United States, experiencing an average of less than 4 per year. Tropical hurricanes come close enough to influence North Carolina weather about twice in an average year. Only about once in 10 years, on the average, does this type storm strike the State with sufficient force to do much damage.

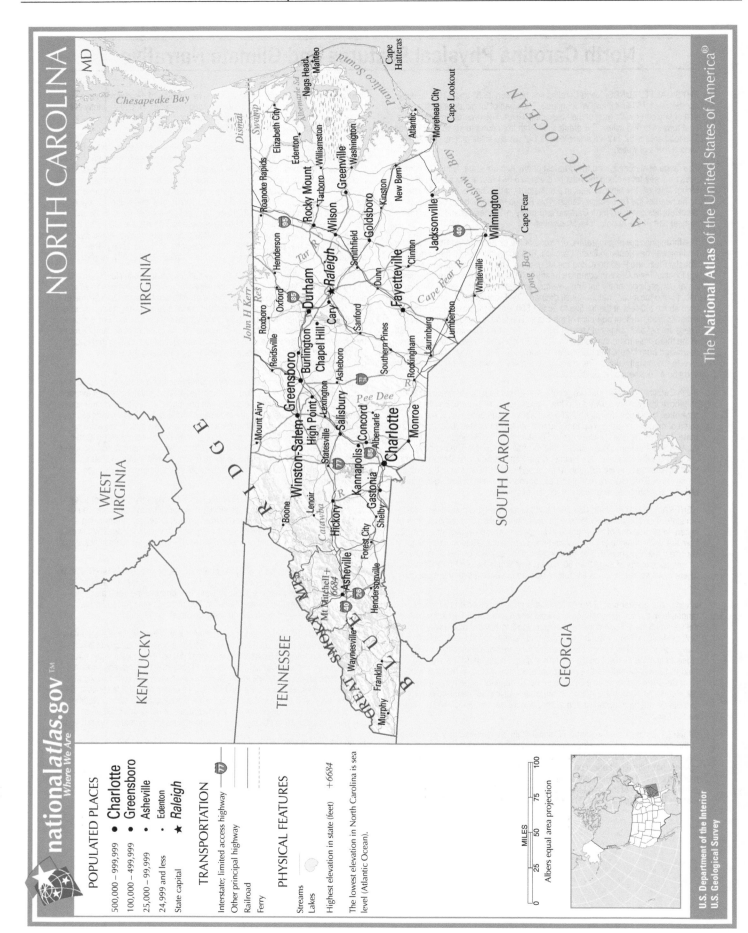

NORTH CAROLINA

nationalatlas.gov™
Where We Are

POPULATED PLACES

500,000 – 999,999   ● **Charlotte**
100,000 – 499,999   ● **Greensboro**
25,000 – 99,999   ● Asheville
24,999 and less   · Edenton
State capital   ★ *Raleigh*

TRANSPORTATION

Interstate; limited access highway   ⑰
Other principal highway
Railroad
Ferry

PHYSICAL FEATURES

Streams
Lakes
Highest elevation in state (feet)   +6684

The lowest elevation in North Carolina is sea
level (Atlantic Ocean).

MILES
0   25   50   75   100
Albers equal area projection

The **National Atlas** of the United States of America®

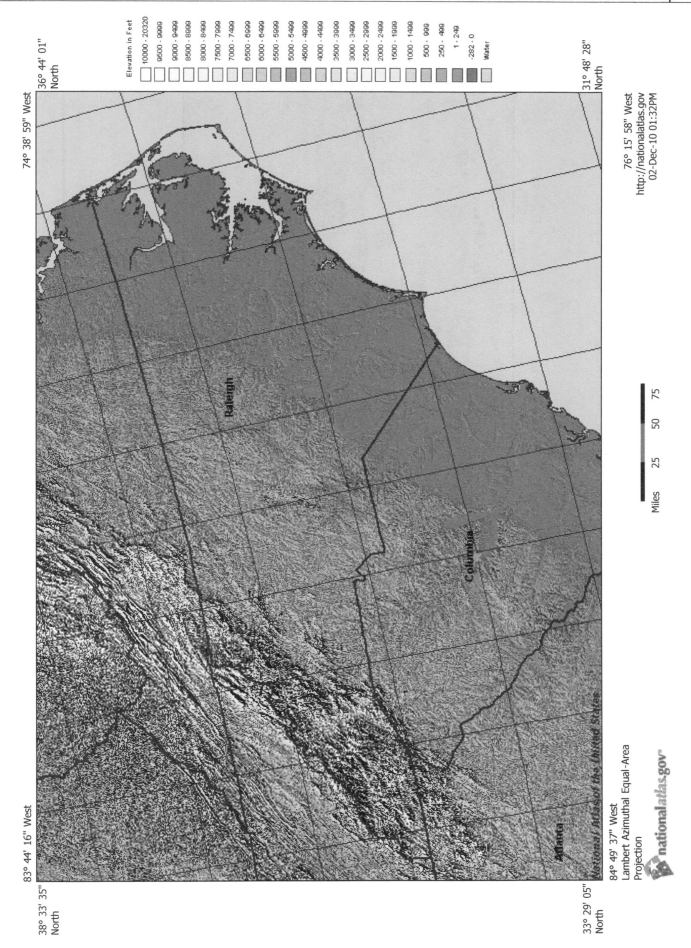

Elevation in Feet

10000 - 20320
9500 - 9999
9000 - 9499
8500 - 8999
8000 - 8499
7500 - 7999
7000 - 7499
6500 - 6999
6000 - 6499
5500 - 5999
5000 - 5499
4500 - 4999
4000 - 4499
3500 - 3999
3000 - 3499
2500 - 2999
2000 - 2499
1500 - 1999
1000 - 1499
500 - 999
250 - 499
1 - 249
-282 - 0
Water

36° 44' 01"
North

74° 38' 59" West

83° 44' 16" West

38° 33' 35"
North

31° 48' 28"
North

33° 29' 05"
North

84° 49' 37" West
Lambert Azimuthal Equal-Area
Projection

76° 15' 58" West
http://nationalatlas.gov
02-Dec-10 01:32PM

Raleigh

Columbia

Atlanta

National Atlas of the United States

nationalatlas.gov

Miles   25   50   75

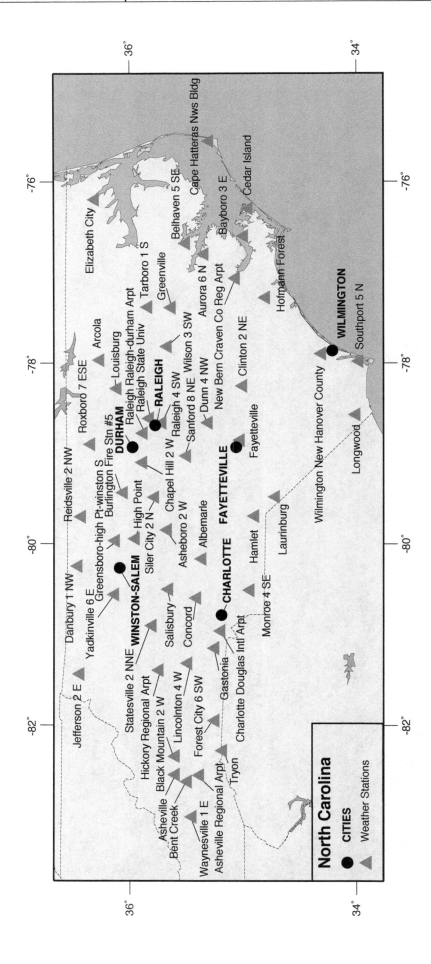

North Carolina Weather Stations by County

County	Station Name
Alamance	Burlington Fire Stn #5
Ashe	Jefferson 2 E
Beaufort	Aurora 6 N Belhaven 5 SE
Brunswick	Longwood Southport 5 N
Buncombe	Asheville Asheville Regional Arpt Bent Creek Black Mountain 2 W
Burke	Hickory Regional Arpt
Cabarrus	Concord
Carteret	Cedar Island
Chatham	Siler City 2 N
Craven	New Bern Craven Co Reg Arpt
Cumberland	Fayetteville
Dare	Cape Hatteras NWS Bldg
Edgecombe	Tarboro 1 S
Franklin	Louisburg
Gaston	Gastonia
Guilford	Greensboro-High Pt-Winston Salem High Point
Harnett	Dunn 4 NW
Haywood	Waynesville 1 E
Iredell	Statesville 2 NNE
Lee	Sanford 8 NE
Lincoln	Lincolnton 4 W
Mecklenburg	Charlotte Douglas Intl Arpt
New Hanover	Wilmington New Hanover County
Onslow	Hofmann Forest
Orange	Chapel Hill 2 W
Pamlico	Bayboro 3 E
Pasquotank	Elizabeth City
Person	Roxboro 7 ESE
Pitt	Greenville

County	Station Name
Polk	Tryon
Randolph	Asheboro 2 W
Richmond	Hamlet
Rockingham	Reidsville 2 NW
Rowan	Salisbury
Rutherford	Forest City 6 SW
Sampson	Clinton 2 NE
Scotland	Laurinburg
Stanly	Albemarle
Stokes	Danbury 1 NW
Union	Monroe 4 SE
Wake	Raleigh 4 SW Raleigh State Univ Raleigh-Durham Intl Arpt
Warren	Arcola
Wilson	Wilson 3 SW
Yadkin	Yadkinville 6 E

See User Guide for station inclusion criteria.

North Carolina Weather Stations by City

City	Station Name	Miles
Apex	Chapel Hill 2 W	17.8
	Raleigh-Durham Intl Arpt	9.9
	Raleigh 4 SW	9.8
	Raleigh State Univ	9.9
	Sanford 8 NE	17.7
Asheville	Asheville Regional Arpt	10.3
	Asheville	1.7
	Bent Creek	6.2
	Black Mountain 2 W	11.7
	Waynesville 1 E	24.2
Burlington	Burlington Fire Stn #5	1.6
	Chapel Hill 2 W	23.4
	Reidsville 2 NW	24.8
	Siler City 2 N	22.4
Cary	Chapel Hill 2 W	18.7
	Raleigh-Durham Intl Arpt	6.5
	Raleigh 4 SW	7.2
	Raleigh State Univ	5.9
	Sanford 8 NE	21.7
Chapel Hill	Burlington Fire Stn #5	24.8
	Chapel Hill 2 W	2.4
	Raleigh-Durham Intl Arpt	15.0
	Raleigh 4 SW	24.1
	Raleigh State Univ	21.0
Charlotte	Charlotte Douglas Intl Arpt	7.8
	Concord	19.3
	Gastonia	18.6
	Monroe 4 SE	23.9
	Winthrop University, SC	22.1
Concord	Albemarle	24.3
	Charlotte Douglas Intl Arpt	22.9
	Concord	1.3
	Salisbury	20.8
Durham	Chapel Hill 2 W	10.6
	Raleigh-Durham Intl Arpt	11.0
	Raleigh 4 SW	21.7
	Raleigh State Univ	17.5
	Roxboro 7 ESE	22.9
Fayetteville	Dunn 4 NW	21.9
	Fayetteville	3.8
Fort Bragg	Dunn 4 NW	21.8
	Fayetteville	9.1
Gastonia	Charlotte Douglas Intl Arpt	12.9
	Gastonia	2.6
	Lincolnton 4 W	17.4
	Winthrop University, SC	23.3
Goldsboro	Wilson 3 SW	22.2
Greensboro	Burlington Fire Stn #5	20.9
	Greensboro-High Pt-Winston Salem	7.2
	High Point	11.2
	Reidsville 2 NW	22.1

City	Station Name	Miles
Greenville	Greenville	3.2
	Tarboro 1 S	22.0
Hickory	Hickory Regional Arpt	3.4
	Lincolnton 4 W	19.5
High Point	Asheboro 2 W	21.4
	Greensboro-High Pt-Winston Salem	8.6
	High Point	1.9
Huntersville	Charlotte Douglas Intl Arpt	14.6
	Concord	15.0
	Gastonia	18.3
Jacksonville	Hofmann Forest	8.6
Kannapolis	Concord	5.0
	Salisbury	15.6
Matthews	Charlotte Douglas Intl Arpt	14.9
	Concord	21.7
	Monroe 4 SE	16.0
	Winthrop University, SC	22.0
Monroe	Monroe 4 SE	3.5
	Pageland, SC	17.9
New Bern	Aurora 6 N	25.0
	Bayboro 3 E	20.5
	Hofmann Forest	23.1
	New Bern Craven Co Reg Arpt	3.5
Raleigh	Raleigh-Durham Intl Arpt	8.4
	Raleigh 4 SW	6.6
	Raleigh State Univ	3.6
Rocky Mount	Arcola	24.7
	Tarboro 1 S	16.2
	Wilson 3 SW	19.3
Salisbury	Concord	18.8
	Salisbury	1.0
	Statesville 2 NNE	24.9
Sanford	Sanford 8 NE	8.2
Statesville	Salisbury	23.3
	Statesville 2 NNE	2.0
Wake Forest	Louisburg	14.9
	Raleigh-Durham Intl Arpt	16.7
	Raleigh 4 SW	19.1
	Raleigh State Univ	15.8
Wilmington	Southport 5 N	16.5
	Wilmington New Hanover County	3.3
Wilson	Tarboro 1 S	24.2
	Wilson 3 SW	2.7
Winston-Salem	Danbury 1 NW	21.8
	Greensboro-High Pt-Winston Salem	17.7
	High Point	19.3
	Yadkinville 6 E	15.9

Note: Miles is the distance between the geographic center of the city and the weather station.

North Carolina Weather Stations by Elevation

Feet	Station Name
2,770	Jefferson 2 E
2,658	Waynesville 1 E
2,290	Black Mountain 2 W
2,240	Asheville
2,140	Asheville Regional Arpt
2,109	Bent Creek
1,143	Hickory Regional Arpt
1,080	Tryon
990	Forest City 6 SW
950	Statesville 2 NNE
899	High Point
899	Lincolnton 4 W
896	Greensboro-High Pt-Winston Salem
890	Reidsville 2 NW
875	Yadkinville 6 E
870	Asheboro 2 W
839	Danbury 1 NW
728	Charlotte Douglas Intl Arpt
709	Roxboro 7 ESE
700	Gastonia
700	Salisbury
689	Concord
660	Burlington Fire Stn #5
609	Albemarle
609	Siler City 2 N
580	Monroe 4 SE
500	Chapel Hill 2 W
419	Raleigh 4 SW
416	Raleigh-Durham Intl Arpt
399	Raleigh State Univ
350	Hamlet
330	Arcola
262	Sanford 8 NE
259	Louisburg
209	Laurinburg
200	Dunn 4 NW
158	Clinton 2 NE
109	Wilson 3 SW
96	Fayetteville
43	Hofmann Forest
40	Longwood
35	Tarboro 1 S
32	Greenville
29	Wilmington New Hanover County
20	Aurora 6 N
20	Southport 5 N
16	New Bern Craven Co Reg Arpt
9	Bayboro 3 E
9	Cape Hatteras NWS Bldg
7	Belhaven 5 SE
7	Cedar Island
7	Elizabeth City

See User Guide for station inclusion criteria.

Asheville Regional Airport

The city of Asheville is located on both banks of the French Broad River, near the center of the French Broad Basin. Upstream from Asheville, the valley runs south for 18 miles and then curves toward the south-southwest. Downstream from the city, the valley is oriented toward the north-northwest. Two miles upstream from the principal section of Asheville, the Swannanoa River joins the French Broad from the east. The entire valley is known as the Asheville Plateau, having an average elevation near 2,200 feet above sea level, and is flanked by mountain ridges to the east and west, whose peaks range from 2,000 to 4,400 feet above the valley floor. At the Carolina-Tennessee border, about 25 miles north-northwest of Asheville, a relatively high ridge of mountains blocks the northern end of the valley. Thirty miles south, the Blue Ridge Mountains form a steep slope, having a general elevation of about 2,700 feet above sea level.

Asheville has a temperate, but invigorating, climate. Considerable variation in temperature often occurs from day to day in summer, as well as during the other seasons.

The growing season in this area is of sufficient length for commercial crops, the average length of freeze-free period being about 195 days. The average last occurrence in spring of a temperature 32 degrees or lower is mid-April and the average first occurrence in fall of 32 degrees is late October.

The orientation of the French Broad Valley appears to have a pronounced influence on the wind direction. Prevailing winds are from the northwest during all months of the year. Also, the shielding effect of the nearby mountain barriers apparently has a direct bearing on the annual amount of precipitation received in this vicinity. In an area northwest of Asheville, the average annual precipitation is the lowest in North Carolina. Precipitation increases sharply in all other directions, especially to the south and southwest.

Destructive events caused directly by meteorological conditions are infrequent. The most frequent, occurring at approximately 12-year intervals, are floods on the French Broad River. These floods are usually associated with heavy rains caused by storms moving out of the Gulf of Mexico. Snowstorms which have seriously disrupted normal life in this community are infrequent. Hailstorms that cause property damage are extremely rare.

Asheville Regional Airport *Buncombe County*   Elevation: 2,140 ft.   Latitude: 35° 26' N   Longitude: 82° 32' W

	JAN	FEB	MAR	APR	MAY	JUN	JUL	AUG	SEP	OCT	NOV	DEC	YEAR
Mean Maximum Temp. (°F)	47.8	51.4	58.8	67.6	74.9	81.3	84.2	83.1	77.0	68.1	58.9	50.1	66.9
Mean Temp. (°F)	37.4	40.5	47.2	55.3	63.1	70.4	73.9	73.0	66.4	56.3	47.4	39.7	55.9
Mean Minimum Temp. (°F)	27.0	29.5	35.5	42.9	51.2	59.5	63.6	62.8	55.8	44.5	35.8	29.3	44.8
Extreme Maximum Temp. (°F)	80	78	83	88	93	95	96	100	92	86	81	75	100
Extreme Minimum Temp. (°F)	-16	-1	2	20	28	37	44	42	35	24	15	-7	-16
Days Maximum Temp. ≥ 90°F	0	0	0	0	0	2	4	3	0	0	0	0	9
Days Maximum Temp. ≤ 32°F	2	1	0	0	0	0	0	0	0	0	0	1	4
Days Minimum Temp. ≤ 32°F	22	18	12	4	0	0	0	0	0	3	13	21	93
Days Minimum Temp. ≤ 0°F	0	0	0	0	0	0	0	0	0	0	0	0	0
Heating Degree Days (base 65°F)	848	687	545	293	105	11	1	2	52	271	523	777	4,115
Cooling Degree Days (base 65°F)	0	0	0	8	52	180	283	256	101	11	0	0	892
Mean Precipitation (in.)	3.55	3.70	3.96	3.42	3.65	4.77	4.31	4.37	3.85	2.89	3.57	3.58	45.62
Maximum Precipitation (in.)*	7.5	7.0	9.9	7.3	8.8	10.7	10.4	11.3	9.1	9.1	9.9	8.5	64.9
Minimum Precipitation (in.)*	0.4	0.2	0.8	0.3	0.5	0.9	0.5	0.5	0.2	0.2	0.8	0.2	26.6
Extreme Maximum Daily Precip. (in.)	4.42	3.36	3.79	2.03	2.93	3.97	2.95	4.32	3.78	3.32	2.41	2.46	4.42
Days With ≥ 0.1" Precipitation	6	6	7	6	7	8	8	7	6	5	6	6	78
Days With ≥ 0.5" Precipitation	2	2	3	3	2	3	3	2	3	2	3	2	30
Days With ≥ 1.0" Precipitation	1	1	1	1	1	1	1	1	1	1	1	1	12
Mean Snowfall (in.)	4.1	2.5	2.1	0.8	trace	trace	trace	trace	0.0	trace	0.1	1.6	11.2
Maximum Snowfall (in.)*	18	26	18	12	trace	0	0	0	0	trace	10	16	50
Maximum 24-hr. Snowfall (in.)*	14	9	14	12	trace	0	0	0	0	trace	5	16	16
Maximum Snow Depth (in.)	14	7	18	12	trace	trace	trace	trace	0	trace	1	10	18
Days With ≥ 1.0" Snow Depth	3	1	1	0	0	0	0	0	0	0	0	1	6
Thunderstorm Days*	< 1	1	2	3	7	9	10	9	3	1	1	< 1	46
Foggy Days*	14	11	12	10	19	23	26	29	26	20	14	14	218
Predominant Sky Cover*	OVR	OVR	OVR	OVR	OVR	OVR	BRK	OVR	OVR	CLR	OVR	OVR	OVR
Mean Relative Humidity 7am (%)*	84	83	83	84	90	92	94	96	96	93	87	85	89
Mean Relative Humidity 4pm (%)*	57	53	50	47	56	60	63	64	62	54	54	56	56
Mean Dewpoint (°F)*	27	28	34	42	53	61	65	64	58	46	36	29	45
Prevailing Wind Direction*	NNW	NNW	NNW	NNW	NNW	NNW	NNW	NNW	NNW	NNW	NNW	NNW	NNW
Prevailing Wind Speed (mph)*	14	14	14	13	10	9	8	8	9	10	13	13	12
Maximum Wind Gust (mph)*	58	54	64	58	49	52	61	43	51	58	55	53	64

Note: (*) Period of record is 1948-1995

Cape Hatteras NWS Bldg

Hatteras Island is the largest and easternmost island in North Carolina. The average elevation of the island is less than 10 feet above mean sea level. It is separated from the mainland by the Pamlico Sound and is part of a chain of islands known as the Outer Banks. The Island is narrow, ranging from a few hundred yards wide to a few miles wide and is about 54 miles long. Much of the island is a National Park and waterfowl reserve.

The Weather Office is located in the village of Buxton about one mile west-northwest of the famous Cape Hatteras Lighthouse. Weather observations have been taken continuously since 1874 from locations all within 10 miles of the present stations location.

With its maritime climate, Cape Hatteras is very humid, with cooler summers and warmer winters than mainland North Carolina. Ninety degree temperatures are rare in summer, as are the teens in winter. The average first occurrence of freezing temperatures is early December, and the average last occurrence is late February.

Average rainfall is greater than any other coastal station in the state. Rainfall is rather evenly distributed throughout the year, with the maximum during July, August, and September. Snowfall is rare and generally light, usually melting as it falls.

Winter storms frequently breed offshore where the warm waters of the Gulf Stream and the southernmost penetration of the Labrador Current meet some 20 to 50 miles off the coast. Late summer and fall tracks of tropical cyclones occasionally threaten the island. These storms produce strong winds, heavy rains and tidal flooding from both the ocean and Pamlico Sound. Many ships have been lost near, or wrecked on, the beaches of the island.

More than a million tourists visit the island each year. The proximity of the gulfstream, natural beaches, excellent surf, and offshore fishing make Cape Hatteras a preferred place for vacationers, sportsmen, and campers. The surfing conditions are said to be the best on the east coast.

Cape Hatteras NWS Bldg *Dare County*   Elevation: 9 ft.   Latitude: 35° 16' N   Longitude: 75° 33' W

	JAN	FEB	MAR	APR	MAY	JUN	JUL	AUG	SEP	OCT	NOV	DEC	YEAR
Mean Maximum Temp. (°F)	53.4	54.5	59.6	67.4	74.8	81.9	85.5	85.0	80.8	72.8	64.8	57.1	69.8
Mean Temp. (°F)	46.2	47.2	52.1	60.1	67.7	75.5	79.6	79.0	74.9	66.2	58.0	50.1	63.0
Mean Minimum Temp. (°F)	39.0	39.8	44.5	52.7	60.6	69.0	73.5	72.9	68.9	59.6	51.1	43.0	56.2
Extreme Maximum Temp. (°F)	75	75	81	89	91	92	96	93	91	89	81	78	96
Extreme Minimum Temp. (°F)	6	15	22	32	40	47	55	59	46	36	27	12	6
Days Maximum Temp. ≥ 90°F	0	0	0	0	0	1	3	2	0	0	0	0	6
Days Maximum Temp. ≤ 32°F	1	0	0	0	0	0	0	0	0	0	0	0	1
Days Minimum Temp. ≤ 32°F	8	6	2	0	0	0	0	0	0	0	1	4	21
Days Minimum Temp. ≤ 0°F	0	0	0	0	0	0	0	0	0	0	0	0	0
Heating Degree Days (base 65°F)	577	499	398	172	40	2	0	0	2	65	228	459	2,442
Cooling Degree Days (base 65°F)	1	1	5	31	130	324	459	441	306	110	24	4	1,836
Mean Precipitation (in.)	5.28	3.94	4.83	3.72	3.49	4.13	4.90	6.65	6.02	5.41	5.08	4.28	57.73
Maximum Precipitation (in.)*	12.4	8.4	11.2	9.6	11.4	10.8	10.0	16.1	20.0	15.0	16.2	9.6	90.8
Minimum Precipitation (in.)*	1.8	1.1	1.0	0.4	0.3	0.4	0.4	1.0	0.1	0.5	1.1	0.6	41.5
Extreme Maximum Daily Precip. (in.)	5.95	3.03	4.57	2.73	4.98	4.00	3.75	8.69	5.50	8.30	7.69	2.96	8.69
Days With ≥ 0.1" Precipitation	8	6	7	6	5	7	8	8	7	6	7	6	81
Days With ≥ 0.5" Precipitation	3	3	3	3	2	3	3	4	3	3	3	3	36
Days With ≥ 1.0" Precipitation	2	1	1	1	1	1	1	2	2	2	1	1	16
Mean Snowfall (in.)	na	na	na	na	na	na	na	na	na	na	na	na	na
Maximum Snowfall (in.)*	4	4	9	trace	0	0	0	0	0	0	trace	14	14
Maximum 24-hr. Snowfall (in.)*	4	4	7	trace	0	0	0	0	0	0	trace	8	8
Maximum Snow Depth (in.)	na	na	na	na	na	na	na	na	na	na	na	na	na
Days With ≥ 1.0" Snow Depth	na	na	na	na	na	na	na	na	na	na	na	na	na
Thunderstorm Days*	1	2	2	3	5	5	8	8	3	2	1	1	41
Foggy Days*	13	11	12	8	10	9	8	9	7	10	10	11	118
Predominant Sky Cover*	OVR	OVR	OVR	OVR	OVR	OVR	OVR	OVR	OVR	OVR	OVR	OVR	OVR
Mean Relative Humidity 7am (%)*	80	80	80	78	81	82	85	86	83	82	81	80	82
Mean Relative Humidity 4pm (%)*	69	66	65	62	67	70	72	72	69	68	69	69	68
Mean Dewpoint (°F)*	37	37	43	50	59	67	72	72	67	57	49	41	54
Prevailing Wind Direction*	N	NNE	NNE	SW	SW	SW	SW	SW	NE	NNE	NNE	N	NNE
Prevailing Wind Speed (mph)*	13	14	14	13	12	12	12	12	12	13	13	12	13
Maximum Wind Gust (mph)*	60	69	69	83	55	64	62	98	94	66	78	64	98

Note: (*) Period of record is 1957-1995

Charlotte Douglas Int'l Airport

Charlotte is located in the Piedmont of the Carolinas, a transitional area of rolling country between the mountains to the west and the Coastal Plain to the east. The mountains are to the northwest about 80 miles from Charlotte. The general elevation of the area around Charlotte is about 730 feet. The Atlantic ocean is about 160 miles southeast.

The mountains have a moderating effect on winter temperatures, causing appreciable warming of cold air from the northwest winds. The ocean is too far away to have any immediate effect on summer temperatures but in winter an occasional general and sustained flow of air from the warm ocean waters results in considerable warming.

Charlotte enjoys a moderate climate, characterized by cool winters and quite warm summers. Temperatures fall as low as the freezing point on a little over one-half of the days in the winter months. Winter weather is changeable, with occasional cold periods, but extreme cold is rare. Snow is infrequent, and the first snowfall of the season usually comes in late November or December. Heavy snowfalls have occurred, but any appreciable accumulation of snow on the ground for more than a day or two is rare.

Summers are long and quite warm, with afternoon temperatures frequently in the low 90s. The growing season is also long, the average length of the freeze-free period being 216 days. On the average, the last occurrence in spring with a temperature of 32 degrees is early April. In the fall the average first occurrence of 32 degrees is early November.

Rainfall is generally rather evenly distributed throughout the year, the driest weather usually coming in the fall. Summer rainfall comes principally from thunderstorms with occasional dry spells of one to three weeks duration.

Hurricanes which strike the Carolina coast may produce heavy rain but seldom cause dangerous winds.

Charlotte Douglas Int'l Airport *Mecklenburg County*   Elevation: 728 ft.   Latitude: 35° 13' N   Longitude: 80° 57' W

	JAN	FEB	MAR	APR	MAY	JUN	JUL	AUG	SEP	OCT	NOV	DEC	YEAR
Mean Maximum Temp. (°F)	51.2	55.6	63.4	72.2	79.3	86.3	89.4	88.0	81.6	72.0	62.7	53.6	71.3
Mean Temp. (°F)	41.4	45.0	52.2	60.4	68.4	76.2	79.5	78.4	71.9	61.2	51.8	43.7	60.8
Mean Minimum Temp. (°F)	31.5	34.4	41.0	48.6	57.4	66.1	69.6	68.7	62.1	50.4	40.9	33.8	50.4
Extreme Maximum Temp. (°F)	79	81	87	91	94	100	103	104	96	93	83	80	104
Extreme Minimum Temp. (°F)	-5	7	4	21	35	45	56	50	39	26	13	4	-5
Days Maximum Temp. ≥ 90°F	0	0	0	0	2	10	16	12	3	0	0	0	43
Days Maximum Temp. ≤ 32°F	1	0	0	0	0	0	0	0	0	0	0	0	1
Days Minimum Temp. ≤ 32°F	17	13	6	1	0	0	0	0	0	1	6	15	59
Days Minimum Temp. ≤ 0°F	0	0	0	0	0	0	0	0	0	0	0	0	0
Heating Degree Days (base 65°F)	725	560	399	173	39	2	0	0	16	160	393	655	3,122
Cooling Degree Days (base 65°F)	0	1	8	43	151	345	458	422	229	50	5	1	1,713
Mean Precipitation (in.)	3.40	3.24	4.15	3.07	3.19	3.72	3.69	4.12	3.28	3.41	3.22	3.21	41.70
Maximum Precipitation (in.)*	7.4	7.6	8.8	7.6	12.5	8.3	8.3	10.0	9.7	14.7	8.7	7.5	62.1
Minimum Precipitation (in.)*	0.4	0.2	0.6	0.3	0.3	0.1	0.5	0.6	trace	trace	0.5	0.4	26.9
Extreme Maximum Daily Precip. (in.)	2.35	2.20	2.34	2.07	3.50	2.76	6.88	5.36	3.38	4.21	3.26	2.37	6.88
Days With ≥ 0.1" Precipitation	7	6	7	6	6	6	6	6	5	5	5	6	71
Days With ≥ 0.5" Precipitation	2	2	3	2	2	3	2	3	2	2	3	2	28
Days With ≥ 1.0" Precipitation	1	1	1	1	1	1	1	1	1	1	1	1	12
Mean Snowfall (in.)	2.0	1.4	0.8	trace	trace	trace	0.0	trace	0.0	trace	0.1	0.2	4.5
Maximum Snowfall (in.)*	12	15	19	trace	0	0	0	0	0	0	3	8	23
Maximum 24-hr. Snowfall (in.)*	12	10	10	trace	0	0	0	0	0	0	2	8	12
Maximum Snow Depth (in.)	12	13	9	trace	trace	trace	0	trace	0	trace	trace	2	13
Days With ≥ 1.0" Snow Depth	2	1	0	0	0	0	0	0	0	0	0	0	3
Thunderstorm Days*	1	1	2	3	6	7	9	7	3	1	1	< 1	41
Foggy Days*	13	11	12	9	13	13	16	18	16	13	13	13	160
Predominant Sky Cover*	OVR	OVR	OVR	OVR	OVR	OVR	OVR	OVR	OVR	CLR	CLR	OVR	OVR
Mean Relative Humidity 7am (%)*	78	77	78	78	82	83	86	88	88	86	83	79	82
Mean Relative Humidity 4pm (%)*	53	48	46	43	49	51	54	55	54	50	50	53	51
Mean Dewpoint (°F)*	29	30	36	44	55	63	67	67	61	50	39	32	48
Prevailing Wind Direction*	SW	SW	SW	SW	SW	SW	SW	NE	NE	NNE	NNE	SW	SW
Prevailing Wind Speed (mph)*	10	12	12	12	9	8	8	8	8	9	9	9	9
Maximum Wind Gust (mph)*	64	53	60	56	48	60	55	77	87	40	51	52	87

Note: (*) Period of record is 1948-1995

Greensboro Airport

The Greensboro-High Point-Winston-Salem Regional Airport is located in the west-central part of Guilford County, in the northern Piedmont section of North Carolina. The location is near the headwaters of the Haw and Deep Rivers, both branches of the Cape Fear River system. A few miles west is a ridge beyond which lies the Yadkin River Basin. To the north, across a similar ridge, the waters of the Dan River flow northeastward into the Roanoke. West, beyond the Yadkin River Basin, the land gradually rises into the Brushy Mountains. To the northwest, other outcroppings southeast of the Blue Ridge rise into peaks occasionally exceeding 2,500 feet. Winter temperatures and rainfall are both modified by the mountain barrier, but to a lesser extent than in areas closer to the Appalachian Range. Shallow cold air masses from the west tend to be stopped by the mountains, while deeper masses are lifted over the range, losing moisture and warming during the passage. For this reason the lowest temperatures recorded in Forsyth and Guilford Counties usually occur when clear, cold air drifts southward, east of the Appalachian Range. The summer temperatures vary, but are generally mild.

Northwesterly winds seldom bring heavy or prolonged winter rain or snow. Flurries of light snow may fall when cold air blows across the mountains, but the heavier winter precipitation comes with winds blowing from northeast through east and south to southwest. When moist winds blowing from an easterly or southerly direction meet cold air moving out of the north or northwest in the vicinity of North Carolina, snow, sleet, or glaze may occur.

Seasonal snowfall has a wide range and there have been a few winters with only a trace of snow. Snow seldom stays on the ground more than a few days.

Summer precipitation is largely from thunderstorms, mostly local in character. The frequency of these showers and the amount of rain received varies greatly from year to year and from place to place. Sizeable areas are sometimes without significant rain in late spring or early summer for two or more weeks, while other areas in the vicinity may be well watered.

Damaging storms are infrequent in the Northern Piedmont area. The highest winds to occur have been associated with thunderstorms, and were of brief duration. Hail is reported within Guilford and Forsyth Counties each year. The occurrence of tornadoes is rare. Hurricanes have produced heavy rainfall here, but no winds of destructive force.

Based on the 1951-1980 period, the average first occurrence of 32 degrees Fahrenheit in the fall is October 27 and the average last occurrence in the spring is April 11.

Greensboro Airport *Guilford County*   Elevation: 896 ft.   Latitude: 36° 06' N   Longitude: 79° 57' W

	JAN	FEB	MAR	APR	MAY	JUN	JUL	AUG	SEP	OCT	NOV	DEC	YEAR
Mean Maximum Temp. (°F)	48.2	52.4	60.5	69.8	77.2	84.4	87.7	86.1	79.4	69.8	60.5	50.8	68.9
Mean Temp. (°F)	38.6	42.0	49.4	58.2	66.3	74.4	78.1	76.7	69.8	59.0	49.7	41.2	58.6
Mean Minimum Temp. (°F)	29.0	31.6	38.4	46.6	55.2	64.3	68.4	67.2	60.0	48.1	38.9	31.5	48.3
Extreme Maximum Temp. (°F)	78	79	86	91	93	98	101	103	97	92	82	78	103
Extreme Minimum Temp. (°F)	-8	1	8	24	32	45	49	45	37	28	17	1	-8
Days Maximum Temp. ≥ 90°F	0	0	0	0	1	6	12	9	2	0	0	0	30
Days Maximum Temp. ≤ 32°F	2	1	0	0	0	0	0	0	0	0	0	1	4
Days Minimum Temp. ≤ 32°F	21	17	9	1	0	0	0	0	0	1	8	18	75
Days Minimum Temp. ≤ 0°F	0	0	0	0	0	0	0	0	0	0	0	0	0
Heating Degree Days (base 65°F)	811	643	480	227	68	5	0	1	30	212	454	732	3,663
Cooling Degree Days (base 65°F)	0	0	5	31	113	294	412	371	179	32	2	1	1,440
Mean Precipitation (in.)	3.04	2.92	3.73	3.62	3.35	3.79	4.32	3.84	4.06	3.09	3.17	2.93	41.86
Maximum Precipitation (in.)*	7.7	5.8	8.8	8.0	8.3	9.5	12.7	11.7	13.1	12.6	8.3	6.4	56.5
Minimum Precipitation (in.)*	0.7	0.4	0.7	0.4	0.4	trace	1.0	0.7	trace	0.3	0.3	0.3	29.7
Extreme Maximum Daily Precip. (in.)	1.77	2.14	3.60	3.97	3.24	2.63	4.16	4.94	3.94	4.08	2.49	1.90	4.94
Days With ≥ 0.1" Precipitation	6	6	7	7	7	7	8	6	5	5	5	6	75
Days With ≥ 0.5" Precipitation	2	2	3	2	2	3	3	2	3	2	2	2	28
Days With ≥ 1.0" Precipitation	1	1	1	1	1	1	1	1	1	1	1	1	12
Mean Snowfall (in.)	3.3	2.5	1.0	trace	trace	trace	trace	trace	0.0	0.0	0.1	0.7	7.6
Maximum Snowfall (in.)*	23	16	21	trace	0	0	0	0	0	0	6	8	32
Maximum 24-hr. Snowfall (in.)*	10	9	11	trace	0	0	0	0	0	0	3	5	11
Maximum Snow Depth (in.)	9	8	8	trace	trace	trace	trace	trace	0	0	1	5	9
Days With ≥ 1.0" Snow Depth	3	2	0	0	0	0	0	0	0	0	0	1	6
Thunderstorm Days*	< 1	1	2	3	6	8	10	8	3	1	1	< 1	43
Foggy Days*	13	12	12	10	14	16	18	21	18	13	12	12	171
Predominant Sky Cover*	OVR	OVR	OVR	OVR	OVR	OVR	OVR	OVR	OVR	CLR	OVR	OVR	OVR
Mean Relative Humidity 7am (%)*	79	77	78	77	82	84	87	90	90	88	83	79	83
Mean Relative Humidity 4pm (%)*	54	49	46	44	52	54	57	58	56	51	51	53	52
Mean Dewpoint (°F)*	27	28	34	43	54	63	67	66	60	48	37	29	46
Prevailing Wind Direction*	SW	SW	SW	SW	SW	SW	SW	SW	NE	NE	SW	SW	SW
Prevailing Wind Speed (mph)*	9	9	9	9	8	8	7	7	9	9	8	8	8
Maximum Wind Gust (mph)*	63	62	53	55	59	51	98	81	54	60	48	47	98

Note: (*) Period of record is 1948-1995

Raleigh-Durham Airport

The Raleigh-Durham Airport is located in the zone of transition between the Coastal Plain and the Piedmont Plateau. The surrounding terrain is rolling, with an average elevation of around 400 feet, the range over a 10-mile radius is roughly between 200 and 550 feet. Being centrally located between the mountains on the west and the coast on the south and east, the Raleigh-Durham area enjoys a favorable climate. The mountains form a partial barrier to cold air masses moving eastward from the interior of the nation. As a result, there are few days in the heart of the winter season when the temperature falls below 20 degrees. Tropical air is present over the eastern and central sections of North Carolina during much of the summer season, bringing warm temperatures and rather high humidities to the Raleigh-Durham area. Afternoon temperatures reach 90 degrees or higher on about one-fourth of the days in the middle of summer, but reach 100 degrees less than once per year. Even in the hottest weather, early morning temperatures almost always drop into the lower 70s.

Rainfall is well distributed throughout the year as a whole. July and August have the greatest amount of rainfall, and October and November the least. There are times in spring and summer when soil moisture is scanty. This usually results from too many days between rains rather than from a shortage of total rainfall, but occasionally the accumulated total during the growing season falls short of plant needs. Most summer rain is produced by thunderstorms, which may occasionally be accompanied by strong winds, intense rains, and hail. The Raleigh-Durham area is far enough from the coast so that the bad weather effects of coastal storms are reduced.

From September 1887 to December 1950, the office was located in the downtown areas of Raleigh. The various buildings occupied were within an area of three blocks. All thermometers were exposed on the roof, and this, plus the smoke over the city, had an effect on the temperature record of that period. Lowest temperatures at the city office were frequently from two to five degrees higher than those recorded in surrounding rural areas. Maximum temperatures in the city were generally a degree or two lower.

From September 1946 to May 1954, simultaneous records were kept at a surface location on the North Carolina State College campus in Raleigh, and at the Raleigh-Durham Airport 10 and a half air miles to the northwest.

Based on the 1951-1980 period, the average first occurrence of 32 degrees Fahrenheit in the fall is October 27 and the average last occurrence in the spring is April 11.

Raleigh-Durham Airport *Wake County*   Elevation: 416 ft.   Latitude: 35° 52' N   Longitude: 78° 47' W

	JAN	FEB	MAR	APR	MAY	JUN	JUL	AUG	SEP	OCT	NOV	DEC	YEAR
Mean Maximum Temp. (°F)	50.5	54.8	62.7	72.0	79.1	86.5	89.6	88.0	81.5	72.1	63.1	53.5	71.1
Mean Temp. (°F)	40.5	43.9	51.0	59.7	67.5	75.8	79.4	78.0	71.3	60.6	51.6	43.2	60.2
Mean Minimum Temp. (°F)	30.5	33.0	39.2	47.3	55.8	64.9	69.2	67.9	61.1	49.1	40.0	32.9	49.2
Extreme Maximum Temp. (°F)	80	83	90	95	95	101	104	105	101	94	86	81	105
Extreme Minimum Temp. (°F)	-9	0	11	23	36	42	51	49	37	28	18	4	-9
Days Maximum Temp. ≥ 90°F	0	0	0	1	2	11	16	13	4	0	0	0	47
Days Maximum Temp. ≤ 32°F	2	1	0	0	0	0	0	0	0	0	0	1	4
Days Minimum Temp. ≤ 32°F	19	15	8	2	0	0	0	0	0	1	8	17	70
Days Minimum Temp. ≤ 0°F	0	0	0	0	0	0	0	0	0	0	0	0	0
Heating Degree Days (base 65°F)	751	590	439	198	55	4	0	1	20	180	401	671	3,310
Cooling Degree Days (base 65°F)	1	1	10	46	139	333	454	410	216	50	6	2	1,668
Mean Precipitation (in.)	3.52	3.21	4.19	2.93	3.18	3.61	4.70	4.21	4.27	3.24	3.17	3.03	43.26
Maximum Precipitation (in.)*	7.5	6.4	7.8	6.1	7.7	9.4	10.3	12.2	6.8	9.1	8.2	6.6	54.1
Minimum Precipitation (in.)*	0.9	0.3	1.0	0.2	0.9	0.3	0.8	0.8	0.2	0.4	0.6	0.3	33.7
Extreme Maximum Daily Precip. (in.)	3.01	1.88	3.17	2.22	2.46	5.63	4.18	4.18	4.96	5.33	2.97	2.30	5.63
Days With ≥ 0.1" Precipitation	7	6	7	6	6	7	8	6	5	5	5	5	73
Days With ≥ 0.5" Precipitation	2	2	3	2	2	2	3	3	3	2	2	2	28
Days With ≥ 1.0" Precipitation	1	1	1	1	0	1	1	1	1	1	1	1	11
Mean Snowfall (in.)	2.8	1.9	0.8	0.1	trace	trace	trace	0.0	0.0	0.0	0.1	0.4	6.1
Maximum Snowfall (in.)*	14	17	14	2	0	0	0	0	0	0	3	11	21
Maximum 24-hr. Snowfall (in.)*	9	10	9	2	0	0	0	0	0	0	3	9	10
Maximum Snow Depth (in.)	20	6	11	trace	trace	trace	trace	0	0	0	2	3	20
Days With ≥ 1.0" Snow Depth	2	2	0	0	0	0	0	0	0	0	0	0	4
Thunderstorm Days*	< 1	1	2	3	6	7	11	8	3	1	1	< 1	43
Foggy Days*	12	12	12	11	16	18	20	22	19	16	13	13	184
Predominant Sky Cover*	OVR	OVR	OVR	OVR	OVR	OVR	OVR	OVR	OVR	CLR	CLR	OVR	OVR
Mean Relative Humidity 7am (%)*	79	78	80	80	84	86	89	91	92	90	84	80	84
Mean Relative Humidity 4pm (%)*	53	48	46	42	51	54	57	58	57	52	51	53	52
Mean Dewpoint (°F)*	28	29	35	44	56	64	68	68	61	50	39	31	48
Prevailing Wind Direction*	SW	SW	SW	SW	SW	SW	SW	SSW	NE	NNE	SW	SW	SW
Prevailing Wind Speed (mph)*	9	10	10	10	9	8	8	7	8	9	9	9	9
Maximum Wind Gust (mph)*	55	62	60	56	55	51	48	61	46	44	41	55	62

Note: (*) Period of record is 1948-1995

Wilmington Airport

Wilmington is located in the tidewater section of southeastern North Carolina, near the Atlantic Ocean. The city proper is built adjacent to the east bank of the Cape Fear River. Because of the curvature of the coastline in this area, the ocean lies about five miles east and about 20 miles south. The surrounding terrain is typical of coastal Carolina. It is low-lying with an average elevation of less than 40 feet, and is characterized by level to gently rolling land with rivers, creeks, and lakes.

The maritime location makes the climate of Wilmington unusually mild for its latitude. All wind directions from the east-northeast through southwest have some moderating effects on temperatures throughout the year, because the ocean is relatively warm in winter and cool in summer. The daily range in temperatures is moderate compared to a continental type of climate. As a rule, summers are quite warm and humid, but excessive heat is rare. Sea breezes, arriving early in the afternoon, tend to alleviate the heat further inland. Long-term averages show afternoon temperatures reach 90 degrees or higher on one-third of the days in midsummer, but several years may pass without 100 degree weather. During the colder part of the year, numerous outbreaks of polar air masses reach the Atlantic Coast, causing sharp drops in temperatures. However, these cold outbreaks are significantly moderated by the long trajectories from the source regions, the effects of passing over the Appalachian Range, and the warming effects of the ocean air. As a result, most winters are short and quite mild.

Rainfall in this area is usually ample and well-distributed throughout the year, the greatest amount occurring in the summer. Summer rainfall comes principally from thunderstorms, and is therefore usually of short duration, but often heavy and unevenly distributed. Thunderstorms occur about one out of three days from June through August. Winter rain is more likely to be of the slow, steady type, lasting one or two days. Generally, the winter rain is evenly distributed and associated with slow-moving, low-pressure systems. Seldom is there a winter without a few flakes of snow, but several years may pass without a measurable amount. Hail occurs less than once a year. Sunshine is abundant, with the area receiving about two-thirds of the sunshine hours possible at its latitude.

Because of these many factors, the growing season is long, averaging 244 days, but records show the range is from 180 days to as long as 302 days.

In common with most Atlantic Coastal localities, the area is subject to the effects of coastal storms and occasional hurricanes which produce high winds, above normal tides, and heavy rains.

Wilmington Airport *New Hanover County*   Elevation: 29 ft.   Latitude: 34° 16' N   Longitude: 77° 54' W

	JAN	FEB	MAR	APR	MAY	JUN	JUL	AUG	SEP	OCT	NOV	DEC	YEAR
Mean Maximum Temp. (°F)	56.4	59.7	66.1	74.0	80.6	86.6	89.7	88.0	83.5	75.4	67.7	59.5	73.9
Mean Temp. (°F)	46.0	48.7	54.8	62.8	70.1	77.5	81.1	79.6	74.6	64.9	56.5	48.7	63.8
Mean Minimum Temp. (°F)	35.6	37.7	43.5	51.5	59.7	68.4	72.4	71.2	65.6	54.4	45.2	37.9	53.6
Extreme Maximum Temp. (°F)	81	82	88	94	96	101	101	103	96	95	86	82	103
Extreme Minimum Temp. (°F)	5	11	9	29	38	48	55	55	44	32	23	0	0
Days Maximum Temp. ≥ 90°F	0	0	0	1	2	9	16	11	4	0	0	0	43
Days Maximum Temp. ≤ 32°F	0	0	0	0	0	0	0	0	0	0	0	0	0
Days Minimum Temp. ≤ 32°F	13	9	4	0	0	0	0	0	0	0	3	10	39
Days Minimum Temp. ≤ 0°F	0	0	0	0	0	0	0	0	0	0	0	0	0
Heating Degree Days (base 65°F)	584	457	325	130	26	1	0	0	4	93	272	503	2,395
Cooling Degree Days (base 65°F)	3	4	16	69	192	384	505	460	298	98	23	5	2,057
Mean Precipitation (in.)	3.81	3.53	4.26	2.74	4.39	4.95	7.64	7.77	6.98	3.85	3.20	3.69	56.81
Maximum Precipitation (in.)*	10.2	8.7	8.3	8.2	9.1	12.9	18.0	14.1	18.9	9.8	7.9	7.1	66.6
Minimum Precipitation (in.)*	0.7	0.6	0.9	0.2	0.9	0.9	1.6	1.7	0.7	0.2	0.5	0.5	36.9
Extreme Maximum Daily Precip. (in.)	3.03	3.37	4.38	2.94	5.02	3.82	6.51	9.55	13.38	6.34	3.83	3.49	13.38
Days With ≥ 0.1" Precipitation	7	6	6	5	6	7	10	9	6	5	5	6	78
Days With ≥ 0.5" Precipitation	3	3	3	2	3	3	5	4	4	2	2	3	37
Days With ≥ 1.0" Precipitation	1	1	1	1	1	2	2	2	2	1	1	1	16
Mean Snowfall (in.)	0.7	0.1	0.4	trace	trace	trace	trace	0.0	0.0	0.0	0.0	0.6	1.8
Maximum Snowfall (in.)*	5	13	7	trace	0	0	0	0	0	0	trace	15	16
Maximum 24-hr. Snowfall (in.)*	5	7	5	trace	0	0	0	0	0	0	trace	10	10
Maximum Snow Depth (in.)	3	trace	7	trace	trace	trace	trace	0	0	0	0	13	13
Days With ≥ 1.0" Snow Depth	0	0	0	0	0	0	0	0	0	0	0	0	0
Thunderstorm Days*	< 1	1	2	3	6	8	12	9	4	1	1	< 1	47
Foggy Days*	15	12	14	12	15	16	14	17	17	16	15	14	177
Predominant Sky Cover*	OVR	OVR	OVR	CLR	OVR	OVR	SCT	OVR	OVR	CLR	CLR	OVR	OVR
Mean Relative Humidity 7am (%)*	82	80	82	81	84	85	87	90	90	89	86	82	85
Mean Relative Humidity 4pm (%)*	58	55	54	51	58	62	66	67	66	60	58	58	59
Mean Dewpoint (°F)*	36	37	43	50	60	68	72	71	66	56	46	38	54
Prevailing Wind Direction*	N	SW	SW	SW	SW	SW	SW	SW	NNE	N	N	N	SW
Prevailing Wind Speed (mph)*	9	12	12	12	10	9	9	8	9	10	10	9	10
Maximum Wind Gust (mph)*	64	63	77	59	55	64	78	64	74	52	54	55	78

Note: (*) Period of record is 1948-1995

Albemarle *Stanly County*   Elevation: 609 ft.   Latitude: 35° 22' N   Longitude: 80° 11' W

	JAN	FEB	MAR	APR	MAY	JUN	JUL	AUG	SEP	OCT	NOV	DEC	YEAR
Mean Maximum Temp. (°F)	51.5	55.8	64.2	72.6	79.6	86.5	89.6	88.1	81.9	72.7	63.7	54.3	71.7
Mean Temp. (°F)	40.9	44.2	51.7	59.5	67.3	75.3	78.9	77.6	71.0	60.4	51.8	43.4	60.2
Mean Minimum Temp. (°F)	30.2	32.6	39.3	46.3	55.1	64.2	68.1	67.0	60.1	48.2	39.8	32.5	48.6
Extreme Maximum Temp. (°F)	79	81	87	92	95	99	103	107	99	94	83	80	107
Extreme Minimum Temp. (°F)	-6	2	5	23	29	42	50	50	35	25	17	2	-6
Days Maximum Temp. ≥ 90°F	0	0	0	0	2	10	16	13	3	0	0	0	44
Days Maximum Temp. ≤ 32°F	1	0	0	0	0	0	0	0	0	0	0	0	1
Days Minimum Temp. ≤ 32°F	19	15	8	2	0	0	0	0	0	1	8	17	70
Days Minimum Temp. ≤ 0°F	0	0	0	0	0	0	0	0	0	0	0	0	0
Heating Degree Days (base 65°F)	742	582	410	196	53	4	0	0	19	177	395	664	3,242
Cooling Degree Days (base 65°F)	0	1	7	37	133	320	438	397	208	43	5	1	1,590
Mean Precipitation (in.)	3.73	3.48	4.85	3.34	3.65	4.57	5.57	4.51	4.12	3.65	3.33	3.35	48.15
Extreme Maximum Daily Precip. (in.)	*2.98*	2.45	*3.02*	4.67	3.22	3.80	*5.25*	4.01	6.25	9.32	2.90	*2.01*	*9.32*
Days With ≥ 0.1" Precipitation	7	6	7	6	7	6	8	6	5	5	5	6	74
Days With ≥ 0.5" Precipitation	2	3	4	2	3	3	4	3	3	2	2	2	33
Days With ≥ 1.0" Precipitation	1	1	2	1	1	1	1	1	1	1	1	1	13
Mean Snowfall (in.)	1.0	0.9	0.8	trace	0.0	0.0	0.0	0.0	0.0	0.0	trace	0.1	2.8
Maximum Snow Depth (in.)	9	6	*7*	trace	0	0	0	0	0	0	trace	1	*9*
Days With ≥ 1.0" Snow Depth	*0*	0	*0*	0	0	0	0	0	0	0	0	0	*0*

Arcola *Warren County*   Elevation: 330 ft.   Latitude: 36° 17' N   Longitude: 77° 59' W

	JAN	FEB	MAR	APR	MAY	JUN	JUL	AUG	SEP	OCT	NOV	DEC	YEAR
Mean Maximum Temp. (°F)	50.7	55.1	*63.1*	72.5	79.4	86.7	90.1	88.3	82.5	73.4	64.5	54.8	*71.8*
Mean Temp. (°F)	*38.4*	42.7	*49.3*	58.0	66.0	74.0	78.0	76.1	69.9	59.4	50.8	42.9	*58.8*
Mean Minimum Temp. (°F)	*26.5*	30.2	*35.5*	43.4	52.6	61.2	65.6	64.0	57.2	45.1	37.1	30.8	*45.8*
Extreme Maximum Temp. (°F)	80	82	*89*	95	96	100	*102*	103	100	94	82	79	*103*
Extreme Minimum Temp. (°F)	-7	-3	*11*	19	30	37	47	43	36	20	17	3	*-7*
Days Maximum Temp. ≥ 90°F	0	0	0	1	2	11	19	14	4	0	0	0	51
Days Maximum Temp. ≤ 32°F	1	0	0	0	0	0	0	0	0	0	0	1	2
Days Minimum Temp. ≤ 32°F	23	18	11	4	0	0	0	0	0	2	11	19	88
Days Minimum Temp. ≤ 0°F	0	0	0	0	0	0	0	0	0	0	0	0	0
Heating Degree Days (base 65°F)	*817*	624	*482*	231	67	5	0	1	25	200	422	680	*3,554*
Cooling Degree Days (base 65°F)	*0*	0	*3*	27	106	281	409	352	178	33	3	1	*1,393*
Mean Precipitation (in.)	3.40	3.26	4.45	3.37	3.47	4.50	5.01	5.09	4.01	3.36	3.36	3.28	46.56
Extreme Maximum Daily Precip. (in.)	2.41	3.72	3.54	5.01	3.98	4.28	5.54	4.02	8.45	4.30	3.40	2.05	8.45
Days With ≥ 0.1" Precipitation	6	6	7	7	6	7	7	7	5	5	5	6	74
Days With ≥ 0.5" Precipitation	2	2	4	2	2	3	3	3	3	2	3	2	31
Days With ≥ 1.0" Precipitation	1	1	1	1	1	1	2	2	1	1	1	1	14
Mean Snowfall (in.)	2.6	2.0	0.6	trace	0.0	0.0	0.0	0.0	0.0	0.0	0.1	0.6	5.9
Maximum Snow Depth (in.)	12	5	11	0	0	0	0	0	0	0	1	3	12
Days With ≥ 1.0" Snow Depth	3	1	0	0	0	0	0	0	0	0	0	0	4

Asheboro 2 W *Randolph County*   Elevation: 870 ft.   Latitude: 35° 42' N   Longitude: 79° 50' W

	JAN	FEB	MAR	APR	MAY	JUN	JUL	AUG	SEP	OCT	NOV	DEC	YEAR
Mean Maximum Temp. (°F)	49.9	54.6	62.9	72.0	78.2	84.9	88.2	86.8	80.6	71.2	62.3	52.9	70.4
Mean Temp. (°F)	40.4	44.1	51.5	59.9	67.1	74.8	78.4	77.1	70.8	60.4	51.5	43.2	59.9
Mean Minimum Temp. (°F)	31.0	33.6	40.1	47.8	55.9	64.6	68.6	67.4	60.9	49.6	40.7	33.4	49.5
Extreme Maximum Temp. (°F)	78	81	90	93	94	97	101	105	100	93	83	79	105
Extreme Minimum Temp. (°F)	-8	2	8	24	33	39	51	49	39	29	16	-1	-8
Days Maximum Temp. ≥ 90°F	0	0	0	0	1	7	13	10	3	0	0	0	34
Days Maximum Temp. ≤ 32°F	2	1	0	0	0	0	0	0	0	0	0	1	4
Days Minimum Temp. ≤ 32°F	18	14	7	1	0	0	0	0	0	1	7	16	64
Days Minimum Temp. ≤ 0°F	0	0	0	0	0	0	0	0	0	0	0	0	0
Heating Degree Days (base 65°F)	756	585	421	189	54	4	0	0	21	180	403	671	3,284
Cooling Degree Days (base 65°F)	0	1	10	43	126	304	424	383	201	44	4	1	1,541
Mean Precipitation (in.)	3.86	3.51	4.11	3.66	3.48	3.90	4.11	4.19	3.93	3.70	3.43	3.24	45.12
Extreme Maximum Daily Precip. (in.)	1.90	2.46	2.66	4.04	2.74	5.17	2.73	3.69	4.69	5.26	2.90	2.23	5.26
Days With ≥ 0.1" Precipitation	7	6	7	6	6	6	7	7	5	5	6	6	74
Days With ≥ 0.5" Precipitation	3	3	3	2	2	3	3	3	3	2	3	2	32
Days With ≥ 1.0" Precipitation	1	1	1	1	1	1	1	1	1	1	1	1	12
Mean Snowfall (in.)	3.0	1.7	0.6	trace	0.0	0.0	0.0	0.0	0.0	0.0	0.2	0.3	5.8
Maximum Snow Depth (in.)	8	3	6	trace	0	0	0	0	0	0	0	2	8
Days With ≥ 1.0" Snow Depth	1	1	0	0	0	0	0	0	0	0	0	0	2

Asheville *Buncombe County*   Elevation: 2,240 ft.   Latitude: 35° 36' N   Longitude: 82° 32' W

	JAN	FEB	MAR	APR	MAY	JUN	JUL	AUG	SEP	OCT	NOV	DEC	YEAR
Mean Maximum Temp. (°F)	46.8	50.4	58.0	67.2	74.9	81.5	84.8	83.7	77.1	67.8	58.3	49.3	66.6
Mean Temp. (°F)	37.4	40.6	47.6	56.1	64.0	71.2	74.7	73.7	67.1	57.0	48.0	40.0	56.4
Mean Minimum Temp. (°F)	28.0	30.8	37.1	45.0	52.9	60.8	64.5	63.7	57.0	46.1	37.6	30.6	46.2
Extreme Maximum Temp. (°F)	78	78	87	89	93	95	98	99	92	86	81	75	99
Extreme Minimum Temp. (°F)	-17	-5	4	19	30	42	51	46	36	26	14	-8	-17
Days Maximum Temp. ≥ 90°F	0	0	0	0	0	2	6	4	0	0	0	0	12
Days Maximum Temp. ≤ 32°F	3	2	1	0	0	0	0	0	0	0	0	2	8
Days Minimum Temp. ≤ 32°F	21	17	11	3	0	0	0	0	0	2	10	19	83
Days Minimum Temp. ≤ 0°F	0	0	0	0	0	0	0	0	0	0	0	0	0
Heating Degree Days (base 65°F)	849	683	534	277	95	10	0	2	48	256	505	769	4,028
Cooling Degree Days (base 65°F)	0	0	2	16	69	203	307	278	116	15	1	0	1,007
Mean Precipitation (in.)	2.83	3.13	3.40	3.11	3.28	3.39	3.32	3.36	3.27	2.18	2.88	2.72	36.87
Extreme Maximum Daily Precip. (in.)	3.34	2.96	2.79	1.83	2.56	3.08	2.08	3.43	3.76	3.07	2.13	2.10	3.76
Days With ≥ 0.1" Precipitation	6	6	7	6	7	7	8	7	6	4	5	6	75
Days With ≥ 0.5" Precipitation	2	2	2	2	2	2	2	2	2	1	2	2	23
Days With ≥ 1.0" Precipitation	0	1	1	1	1	1	1	1	1	0	1	1	10
Mean Snowfall (in.)	4.1	2.7	2.1	1.1	trace	trace	0.0	0.0	0.0	trace	0.4	2.2	12.6
Maximum Snow Depth (in.)	14	4	20	15	trace	trace	0	0	0	trace	2	11	20
Days With ≥ 1.0" Snow Depth	3	1	2	1	0	0	0	0	0	0	1	2	8

The period of record for all cooperative weather station data is 1980 – 2009. See User Guide for detailed explanation of data.

Aurora 6 N *Beaufort County*　Elevation: 20 ft.　Latitude: 35° 23' N　Longitude: 76° 47' W

	JAN	FEB	MAR	APR	MAY	JUN	JUL	AUG	SEP	OCT	NOV	DEC	YEAR
Mean Maximum Temp. (°F)	53.0	55.8	62.4	71.7	79.1	85.9	89.3	87.3	82.5	73.4	64.5	56.1	71.7
Mean Temp. (°F)	43.7	46.2	52.4	61.4	69.3	77.0	80.7	79.0	74.2	64.4	55.4	47.0	62.6
Mean Minimum Temp. (°F)	34.3	36.6	42.3	51.1	59.5	68.1	72.2	70.5	65.8	55.3	46.2	37.8	53.3
Extreme Maximum Temp. (°F)	79	81	90	93	96	101	100	103	100	93	86	82	103
Extreme Minimum Temp. (°F)	-1	8	11	28	44	51	59	55	46	33	21	10	-1
Days Maximum Temp. ≥ 90°F	0	0	0	1	2	9	15	11	3	0	0	0	41
Days Maximum Temp. ≤ 32°F	1	0	0	0	0	0	0	0	0	0	0	0	1
Days Minimum Temp. ≤ 32°F	13	9	3	0	0	0	0	0	0	0	1	8	34
Days Minimum Temp. ≤ 0°F	0	0	0	0	0	0	0	0	0	0	0	0	0
Heating Degree Days (base 65°F)	656	526	393	154	32	2	0	0	3	98	295	555	2,714
Cooling Degree Days (base 65°F)	1	2	10	54	173	368	495	440	285	85	14	3	1,930
Mean Precipitation (in.)	3.90	3.10	4.07	3.31	3.89	4.93	5.63	6.33	4.57	3.41	3.03	3.25	49.42
Extreme Maximum Daily Precip. (in.)	2.94	*2.39*	2.64	3.93	*3.81*	*4.96*	8.82	5.08	*5.87*	*4.02*	6.07	3.45	*8.82*
Days With ≥ 0.1" Precipitation	7	6	6	5	6	7	8	8	6	4	5	6	74
Days With ≥ 0.5" Precipitation	3	2	3	2	2	3	4	4	3	2	2	2	32
Days With ≥ 1.0" Precipitation	1	1	1	1	1	1	2	2	1	1	1	1	14
Mean Snowfall (in.)	0.3	0.0	trace	0.0	0.0	0.0	0.0	0.0	0.0	0.0	0.0	trace	0.3
Maximum Snow Depth (in.)	trace	trace	trace	0	0	0	0	0	0	0	0	0	trace
Days With ≥ 1.0" Snow Depth	0	0	0	0	0	0	0	0	0	0	0	0	0

Bayboro 3 E *Pamlico County*　Elevation: 9 ft.　Latitude: 35° 09' N　Longitude: 76° 43' W

	JAN	FEB	MAR	APR	MAY	JUN	JUL	AUG	SEP	OCT	NOV	DEC	YEAR
Mean Maximum Temp. (°F)	55.9	59.5	65.8	*74.2*	80.4	86.5	89.1	88.0	83.3	75.0	67.3	58.8	*73.6*
Mean Temp. (°F)	44.9	47.8	53.5	*61.7*	69.1	76.5	79.8	78.5	73.5	63.6	55.5	47.7	*62.7*
Mean Minimum Temp. (°F)	33.9	36.0	41.2	*49.2*	57.7	66.4	70.4	68.9	63.6	52.1	43.6	36.4	*51.6*
Extreme Maximum Temp. (°F)	80	83	91	*93*	96	102	100	107	98	96	88	82	*107*
Extreme Minimum Temp. (°F)	-1	5	10	*26*	35	46	52	51	40	27	16	-4	*-4*
Days Maximum Temp. ≥ 90°F	0	0	0	*1*	2	9	15	12	3	0	0	0	*42*
Days Maximum Temp. ≤ 32°F	0	0	0	*0*	0	0	0	0	0	0	0	0	*0*
Days Minimum Temp. ≤ 32°F	14	11	7	*1*	0	0	0	0	0	1	5	12	*51*
Days Minimum Temp. ≤ 0°F	0	0	0	*0*	0	0	0	0	0	0	0	0	*0*
Heating Degree Days (base 65°F)	618	485	363	*150*	34	2	0	0	5	115	296	535	*2,603*
Cooling Degree Days (base 65°F)	2	3	14	*57*	168	353	465	425	266	77	17	4	*1,851*
Mean Precipitation (in.)	3.89	3.18	4.13	*3.41*	4.46	5.29	6.56	7.24	5.82	3.81	3.75	3.66	*55.20*
Extreme Maximum Daily Precip. (in.)	3.15	2.62	3.24	*5.10*	5.05	3.50	4.72	*4.78*	5.48	5.42	5.83	2.77	*5.83*
Days With ≥ 0.1" Precipitation	7	6	6	*5*	6	8	9	8	7	5	5	6	*78*
Days With ≥ 0.5" Precipitation	3	2	3	*2*	3	4	4	4	3	2	2	2	*34*
Days With ≥ 1.0" Precipitation	1	1	1	*1*	1	2	2	2	2	1	1	1	*16*
Mean Snowfall (in.)	0.4	0.2	0.7	*0.0*	0.0	0.0	0.0	0.0	0.0	0.0	0.0	0.5	*1.8*
Maximum Snow Depth (in.)	4	3	0	*0*	0	0	0	0	0	0	0	12	*12*
Days With ≥ 1.0" Snow Depth	0	0	0	*0*	0	0	0	0	0	0	0	0	*0*

Belhaven 5 SE *Beaufort County*　Elevation: 7 ft.　Latitude: 35° 30' N　Longitude: 76° 41' W

	JAN	FEB	MAR	APR	MAY	JUN	JUL	AUG	SEP	OCT	NOV	DEC	YEAR
Mean Maximum Temp. (°F)	52.4	55.7	62.6	71.5	79.0	85.6	*88.3*	86.8	82.1	73.7	64.9	56.0	*71.6*
Mean Temp. (°F)	42.6	45.4	51.8	60.6	68.8	76.4	*79.7*	78.0	72.8	62.9	54.4	46.1	*61.6*
Mean Minimum Temp. (°F)	32.8	35.0	41.0	49.7	58.5	67.1	71.1	69.3	63.5	52.0	43.9	36.1	51.7
Extreme Maximum Temp. (°F)	79	82	89	94	96	101	100	101	97	94	84	81	101
Extreme Minimum Temp. (°F)	-10	4	15	28	40	44	55	51	44	30	23	8	-10
Days Maximum Temp. ≥ 90°F	0	0	0	1	2	8	12	9	2	0	0	0	34
Days Maximum Temp. ≤ 32°F	1	0	0	0	0	0	0	0	0	0	0	0	1
Days Minimum Temp. ≤ 32°F	16	12	6	0	0	0	0	0	0	0	4	12	50
Days Minimum Temp. ≤ 0°F	0	0	0	0	0	0	0	0	0	0	0	0	0
Heating Degree Days (base 65°F)	688	548	411	174	40	2	*0*	0	8	128	322	582	*2,903*
Cooling Degree Days (base 65°F)	1	1	9	49	164	350	*463*	411	249	69	11	2	*1,779*
Mean Precipitation (in.)	3.77	2.93	4.24	3.23	3.78	4.96	6.07	6.31	4.54	2.54	3.20	2.98	48.55
Extreme Maximum Daily Precip. (in.)	2.72	2.05	3.20	3.42	3.37	6.02	4.62	6.00	6.37	3.99	6.90	2.18	6.90
Days With ≥ 0.1" Precipitation	8	6	7	5	7	7	9	8	6	4	5	5	77
Days With ≥ 0.5" Precipitation	3	2	3	2	3	4	4	4	3	2	2	2	34
Days With ≥ 1.0" Precipitation	1	1	1	1	1	2	2	2	1	1	1	1	15
Mean Snowfall (in.)	0.7	0.6	0.9	0.2	0.0	0.0	0.0	0.0	0.0	0.0	0.0	0.6	3.0
Maximum Snow Depth (in.)	4	6	16	4	0	0	0	0	0	0	0	5	16
Days With ≥ 1.0" Snow Depth	0	0	0	0	0	0	0	0	0	0	0	0	0

Bent Creek *Buncombe County*　Elevation: 2,109 ft.　Latitude: 35° 30' N　Longitude: 82° 36' W

	JAN	FEB	MAR	APR	MAY	JUN	JUL	AUG	SEP	OCT	NOV	DEC	YEAR
Mean Maximum Temp. (°F)	48.2	51.9	59.7	68.9	75.8	81.5	84.4	83.4	77.7	68.8	59.4	50.1	67.5
Mean Temp. (°F)	37.1	40.1	46.9	55.1	62.8	69.8	73.2	72.5	66.2	56.3	47.0	39.2	55.5
Mean Minimum Temp. (°F)	26.0	28.2	34.0	41.1	49.7	58.0	62.0	61.4	54.8	43.7	34.6	28.3	43.5
Extreme Maximum Temp. (°F)	81	80	83	90	91	95	97	100	95	88	81	76	100
Extreme Minimum Temp. (°F)	-16	-5	-1	19	26	36	42	41	31	20	11	-5	-16
Days Maximum Temp. ≥ 90°F	0	0	0	0	0	1	5	4	1	0	0	0	11
Days Maximum Temp. ≤ 32°F	2	1	0	0	0	0	0	0	0	0	0	1	4
Days Minimum Temp. ≤ 32°F	23	20	14	5	1	0	0	0	0	5	15	22	105
Days Minimum Temp. ≤ 0°F	0	0	0	0	0	0	0	0	0	0	0	0	0
Heating Degree Days (base 65°F)	858	699	555	299	112	13	1	2	54	274	534	792	4,193
Cooling Degree Days (base 65°F)	0	0	1	8	49	163	262	240	98	10	1	0	832
Mean Precipitation (in.)	3.83	3.79	4.59	3.77	3.75	4.54	4.49	3.98	4.51	2.99	4.09	3.35	47.68
Extreme Maximum Daily Precip. (in.)	3.45	3.44	3.75	2.34	2.68	2.80	3.02	3.95	4.48	3.54	4.34	2.21	4.48
Days With ≥ 0.1" Precipitation	6	6	7	6	6	8	7	7	6	4	5	6	74
Days With ≥ 0.5" Precipitation	2	2	3	2	2	3	3	2	3	2	3	2	29
Days With ≥ 1.0" Precipitation	1	1	1	1	1	1	1	1	1	1	1	1	12
Mean Snowfall (in.)	2.5	1.4	1.1	0.5	0.0	0.0	0.0	0.0	0.0	trace	0.0	*0.4*	*5.9*
Maximum Snow Depth (in.)	12	4	17	13	0	0	0	0	0	trace	2	10	17
Days With ≥ 1.0" Snow Depth	2	1	1	0	0	0	0	0	0	0	0	1	5

Black Mountain 2 W *Buncombe County*   Elevation: 2,290 ft.   Latitude: 35° 37' N   Longitude: 82° 21' W

	JAN	FEB	MAR	APR	MAY	JUN	JUL	AUG	SEP	OCT	NOV	DEC	YEAR
Mean Maximum Temp. (°F)	49.1	52.1	60.0	68.0	75.2	81.2	84.3	83.2	77.2	69.1	59.9	51.1	67.5
Mean Temp. (°F)	37.5	40.5	47.0	54.6	62.2	69.3	72.8	72.0	65.7	56.3	47.3	39.7	55.4
Mean Minimum Temp. (°F)	26.0	28.8	34.0	41.2	49.2	57.4	61.2	60.7	54.1	43.5	34.6	28.2	43.2
Extreme Maximum Temp. (°F)	77	76	86	90	90	93	99	97	92	85	79	76	99
Extreme Minimum Temp. (°F)	-14	-7	7	18	26	32	44	43	28	19	12	-13	-14
Days Maximum Temp. ≥ 90°F	0	0	0	0	0	2	4	3	0	0	0	0	9
Days Maximum Temp. ≤ 32°F	2	1	0	0	0	0	0	0	0	0	0	1	4
Days Minimum Temp. ≤ 32°F	22	19	14	5	1	0	0	0	0	5	13	21	100
Days Minimum Temp. ≤ 0°F	0	0	0	0	0	0	0	0	0	0	0	0	0
Heating Degree Days (base 65°F)	838	685	550	311	119	17	1	3	60	272	525	779	4,160
Cooling Degree Days (base 65°F)	0	0	1	7	42	152	249	226	87	11	1	0	776
Mean Precipitation (in.)	3.50	3.56	4.09	3.75	4.09	4.58	3.83	3.94	4.43	3.07	3.62	3.42	45.88
Extreme Maximum Daily Precip. (in.)	5.20	3.21	3.30	2.05	4.00	4.22	2.05	6.80	10.00	3.90	2.75	2.00	10.00
Days With ≥ 0.1" Precipitation	6	6	6	7	8	8	8	7	6	5	6	6	79
Days With ≥ 0.5" Precipitation	2	2	3	3	3	3	2	2	3	2	3	3	31
Days With ≥ 1.0" Precipitation	1	1	1	1	1	1	1	1	1	1	1	1	12
Mean Snowfall (in.)	2.6	2.0	1.2	0.6	0.0	0.0	0.0	0.0	0.0	0.0	0.1	1.4	7.9
Maximum Snow Depth (in.)	12	5	5	4	0	0	0	0	0	0	0	5	12
Days With ≥ 1.0" Snow Depth	1	1	0	0	0	0	0	0	0	0	0	0	2

Burlington Fire Stn #5 *Alamance County*   Elevation: 660 ft.   Latitude: 36° 04' N   Longitude: 79° 27' W

	JAN	FEB	MAR	APR	MAY	JUN	JUL	AUG	SEP	OCT	NOV	DEC	YEAR
Mean Maximum Temp. (°F)	50.1	54.0	62.2	71.8	79.1	86.8	90.1	88.7	81.8	72.2	63.1	53.3	71.1
Mean Temp. (°F)	39.4	42.5	49.9	58.7	66.8	75.3	79.0	77.4	70.4	59.4	50.7	42.1	59.3
Mean Minimum Temp. (°F)	28.6	30.9	37.5	45.6	54.3	63.9	67.8	66.3	59.0	46.6	38.2	30.9	47.5
Extreme Maximum Temp. (°F)	84	80	89	95	98	101	102	104	100	93	85	79	104
Extreme Minimum Temp. (°F)	-6	4	8	22	29	43	48	41	36	25	15	-4	-6
Days Maximum Temp. ≥ 90°F	0	0	0	1	2	11	19	14	4	0	0	0	51
Days Maximum Temp. ≤ 32°F	2	1	0	0	0	0	0	0	0	0	0	1	4
Days Minimum Temp. ≤ 32°F	22	17	10	2	0	0	0	0	0	1	9	19	80
Days Minimum Temp. ≤ 0°F	0	0	0	0	0	0	0	0	0	0	0	0	0
Heating Degree Days (base 65°F)	787	630	468	217	65	4	0	1	24	201	427	702	3,526
Cooling Degree Days (base 65°F)	0	0	6	35	126	319	441	393	194	35	3	0	1,552
Mean Precipitation (in.)	3.33	3.05	4.15	3.47	3.44	4.00	4.62	3.95	3.76	3.28	3.19	3.14	43.38
Extreme Maximum Daily Precip. (in.)	2.20	2.81	3.10	3.38	2.40	4.60	4.30	4.67	5.15	2.91	3.20	2.20	5.15
Days With ≥ 0.1" Precipitation	6	5	7	6	6	6	7	6	5	5	6	5	70
Days With ≥ 0.5" Precipitation	3	2	3	2	3	2	3	2	2	2	2	2	28
Days With ≥ 1.0" Precipitation	1	1	1	1	1	1	1	1	1	1	1	1	12
Mean Snowfall (in.)	1.5	1.0	0.2	trace	0.0	0.0	0.0	0.0	0.0	0.0	0.0	trace	2.7
Maximum Snow Depth (in.)	10	5	4	trace	0	0	0	0	0	0	0	3	10
Days With ≥ 1.0" Snow Depth	0	0	0	0	0	0	0	0	0	0	0	0	0

Cedar Island *Carteret County*   Elevation: 7 ft.   Latitude: 34° 59' N   Longitude: 76° 18' W

	JAN	FEB	MAR	APR	MAY	JUN	JUL	AUG	SEP	OCT	NOV	DEC	YEAR
Mean Maximum Temp. (°F)	54.5	57.0	63.8	72.7	79.8	86.4	89.6	87.8	82.6	74.2	65.6	57.3	72.6
Mean Temp. (°F)	45.5	47.8	54.2	62.7	70.1	77.3	80.7	79.4	74.8	65.6	56.8	48.5	63.6
Mean Minimum Temp. (°F)	36.6	38.6	44.6	52.6	60.4	68.2	71.8	71.0	67.0	57.0	47.8	39.6	54.6
Extreme Maximum Temp. (°F)	79	78	88	93	98	101	102	102	98	98	85	79	102
Extreme Minimum Temp. (°F)	2	13	10	28	38	48	51	57	44	33	22	8	2
Days Maximum Temp. ≥ 90°F	0	0	0	0	2	9	16	12	3	0	0	0	42
Days Maximum Temp. ≤ 32°F	1	0	0	0	0	0	0	0	0	0	0	0	1
Days Minimum Temp. ≤ 32°F	11	8	3	0	0	0	0	0	0	0	2	8	32
Days Minimum Temp. ≤ 0°F	0	0	0	0	0	0	0	0	0	0	0	0	0
Heating Degree Days (base 65°F)	597	481	339	124	21	0	0	0	1	74	258	508	2,403
Cooling Degree Days (base 65°F)	1	1	12	60	186	377	495	454	303	100	17	3	2,009
Mean Precipitation (in.)	4.63	3.41	4.54	3.46	3.93	4.11	6.23	7.33	6.13	4.69	4.03	4.42	56.91
Extreme Maximum Daily Precip. (in.)	2.75	2.12	3.95	2.81	4.68	4.57	5.08	8.90	4.45	4.50	6.35	4.15	8.90
Days With ≥ 0.1" Precipitation	8	7	7	6	6	7	9	9	7	6	6	7	85
Days With ≥ 0.5" Precipitation	3	2	3	2	2	3	4	4	3	3	3	3	35
Days With ≥ 1.0" Precipitation	1	1	1	1	1	1	2	2	2	2	1	1	16
Mean Snowfall (in.)	1.1	0.2	0.6	trace	0.0	0.0	0.0	0.0	0.0	0.0	trace	0.6	2.5
Maximum Snow Depth (in.)	8	1	12	trace	0	0	0	0	0	0	trace	11	12
Days With ≥ 1.0" Snow Depth	0	0	0	0	0	0	0	0	0	0	0	0	0

Chapel Hill 2 W *Orange County*   Elevation: 500 ft.   Latitude: 35° 55' N   Longitude: 79° 05' W

	JAN	FEB	MAR	APR	MAY	JUN	JUL	AUG	SEP	OCT	NOV	DEC	YEAR
Mean Maximum Temp. (°F)	50.1	54.1	61.9	71.4	78.6	85.9	89.3	88.0	81.5	71.7	63.0	53.3	70.7
Mean Temp. (°F)	39.2	42.3	49.5	58.5	66.5	74.6	78.3	77.2	70.4	59.1	50.5	42.1	59.0
Mean Minimum Temp. (°F)	28.3	30.4	37.0	45.5	54.3	63.3	67.2	66.2	59.1	46.4	37.9	30.8	47.2
Extreme Maximum Temp. (°F)	80	83	89	94	95	100	104	106	100	94	87	80	106
Extreme Minimum Temp. (°F)	-8	3	9	23	29	42	48	40	36	24	17	0	-8
Days Maximum Temp. ≥ 90°F	0	0	0	1	2	10	16	13	3	0	0	0	45
Days Maximum Temp. ≤ 32°F	2	1	0	0	0	0	0	0	0	0	0	1	4
Days Minimum Temp. ≤ 32°F	22	18	11	2	0	0	0	0	0	2	10	19	84
Days Minimum Temp. ≤ 0°F	0	0	0	0	0	0	0	0	0	0	0	0	0
Heating Degree Days (base 65°F)	794	636	481	226	69	5	0	1	26	210	434	704	3,586
Cooling Degree Days (base 65°F)	0	1	7	37	122	301	419	385	194	35	4	1	1,506
Mean Precipitation (in.)	3.85	3.44	4.60	3.32	3.82	4.19	4.32	4.58	4.15	3.84	3.76	3.42	47.29
Extreme Maximum Daily Precip. (in.)	3.20	2.42	3.27	2.10	3.27	4.62	5.12	4.80	7.68	4.11	4.42	1.96	7.68
Days With ≥ 0.1" Precipitation	7	6	7	7	7	7	7	7	5	5	6	6	77
Days With ≥ 0.5" Precipitation	3	3	3	2	3	3	3	3	3	3	2	2	33
Days With ≥ 1.0" Precipitation	1	1	1	1	1	1	1	1	1	1	1	1	12
Mean Snowfall (in.)	1.9	1.6	0.6	trace	0.0	0.0	0.0	0.0	0.0	0.0	0.1	0.4	4.6
Maximum Snow Depth (in.)	6	4	0	0	0	0	0	0	0	0	trace	trace	6
Days With ≥ 1.0" Snow Depth	0	0	0	0	0	0	0	0	0	0	0	0	0

Clinton 2 NE *Sampson County*   Elevation: 158 ft.   Latitude: 35° 01' N   Longitude: 78° 17' W

	JAN	FEB	MAR	APR	MAY	JUN	JUL	AUG	SEP	OCT	NOV	DEC	YEAR
Mean Maximum Temp. (°F)	52.4	56.1	63.4	73.0	80.0	86.9	89.9	88.4	82.9	73.9	65.2	55.7	72.3
Mean Temp. (°F)	41.9	45.1	52.0	60.8	68.6	76.5	80.0	78.5	72.6	61.9	53.5	44.9	61.4
Mean Minimum Temp. (°F)	31.4	34.1	40.5	48.5	57.1	65.9	70.1	68.6	62.3	49.9	41.7	34.0	50.3
Extreme Maximum Temp. (°F)	78	83	89	94	96	101	101	104	100	96	84	81	104
Extreme Minimum Temp. (°F)	-2	3	8	26	35	47	53	52	40	27	20	5	-2
Days Maximum Temp. ≥ 90°F	0	0	0	1	3	11	17	14	5	0	0	0	51
Days Maximum Temp. ≤ 32°F	1	0	0	0	0	0	0	0	0	0	0	0	1
Days Minimum Temp. ≤ 32°F	18	14	7	1	0	0	0	0	0	1	6	15	62
Days Minimum Temp. ≤ 0°F	0	0	0	0	0	0	0	0	0	0	0	0	0
Heating Degree Days (base 65°F)	711	557	408	172	44	3	0	0	12	151	351	620	3,029
Cooling Degree Days (base 65°F)	1	2	10	52	163	353	472	427	247	63	12	2	1,804
Mean Precipitation (in.)	3.68	3.17	4.19	2.98	3.57	4.72	6.15	5.71	4.98	3.25	3.16	3.20	48.76
Extreme Maximum Daily Precip. (in.)	3.01	3.03	3.75	2.08	2.70	4.00	4.45	5.40	10.05	4.45	3.93	2.08	10.05
Days With ≥ 0.1" Precipitation	7	6	7	5	7	7	8	8	6	5	5	6	77
Days With ≥ 0.5" Precipitation	3	2	2	2	2	3	4	3	3	2	2	3	31
Days With ≥ 1.0" Precipitation	1	1	1	1	1	1	2	2	1	1	1	1	14
Mean Snowfall (in.)	0.8	0.6	0.6	trace	0.0	0.0	0.0	0.0	0.0	0.0	trace	0.6	2.6
Maximum Snow Depth (in.)	6	5	10	trace	0	0	0	0	0	0	trace	10	10
Days With ≥ 1.0" Snow Depth	1	0	0	0	0	0	0	0	0	0	0	0	1

Concord *Cabarrus County*   Elevation: 689 ft.   Latitude: 35° 25' N   Longitude: 80° 36' W

	JAN	FEB	MAR	APR	MAY	JUN	JUL	AUG	SEP	OCT	NOV	DEC	YEAR
Mean Maximum Temp. (°F)	51.2	55.5	63.4	72.6	79.9	87.1	90.3	88.9	82.5	72.7	63.5	54.1	71.8
Mean Temp. (°F)	40.0	43.4	50.8	59.5	67.7	76.0	79.7	78.4	71.5	60.3	51.0	42.6	60.1
Mean Minimum Temp. (°F)	28.8	31.2	38.1	46.3	55.5	64.8	68.9	67.8	60.4	47.9	38.5	31.0	48.3
Extreme Maximum Temp. (°F)	79	82	89	95	98	100	105	107	100	96	85	81	107
Extreme Minimum Temp. (°F)	-5	6	1	24	32	43	53	50	40	28	17	4	-5
Days Maximum Temp. ≥ 90°F	0	0	0	1	3	12	19	15	5	0	0	0	55
Days Maximum Temp. ≤ 32°F	1	0	0	0	0	0	0	0	0	0	0	0	1
Days Minimum Temp. ≤ 32°F	21	17	9	1	0	0	0	0	0	1	9	19	77
Days Minimum Temp. ≤ 0°F	0	0	0	0	0	0	0	0	0	0	0	0	0
Heating Degree Days (base 65°F)	768	605	440	201	53	4	0	0	19	182	418	689	3,379
Cooling Degree Days (base 65°F)	0	0	7	42	143	341	461	422	220	45	4	1	1,686
Mean Precipitation (in.)	3.55	3.30	4.34	3.61	3.47	4.27	5.10	3.98	3.88	3.75	3.44	3.15	45.84
Extreme Maximum Daily Precip. (in.)	2.24	2.71	2.77	2.85	3.03	3.87	6.40	8.80	4.62	5.60	3.47	2.10	8.80
Days With ≥ 0.1" Precipitation	7	6	7	6	6	7	7	6	5	5	6	6	74
Days With ≥ 0.5" Precipitation	3	2	3	2	2	3	3	2	2	2	2	2	28
Days With ≥ 1.0" Precipitation	1	1	1	1	1	1	1	1	1	1	1	1	12
Mean Snowfall (in.)	1.7	1.4	0.7	trace	0.0	0.0	0.0	0.0	0.0	0.0	trace	0.1	3.9
Maximum Snow Depth (in.)	9	11	7	trace	0	0	0	0	0	0	1	3	11
Days With ≥ 1.0" Snow Depth	2	1	0	0	0	0	0	0	0	0	0	0	3

Danbury 1 NW *Stokes County*   Elevation: 839 ft.   Latitude: 36° 25' N   Longitude: 80° 13' W

	JAN	FEB	MAR	APR	MAY	JUN	JUL	AUG	SEP	OCT	NOV	DEC	YEAR
Mean Maximum Temp. (°F)	47.7	51.7	59.6	69.7	77.0	84.3	87.4	86.0	79.7	70.3	60.7	50.9	68.8
Mean Temp. (°F)	36.3	39.7	46.5	55.9	63.9	72.3	76.0	74.7	67.8	56.8	47.5	39.4	56.4
Mean Minimum Temp. (°F)	25.0	27.5	33.2	42.0	50.8	60.3	64.7	63.3	55.9	43.1	34.3	27.8	44.0
Extreme Maximum Temp. (°F)	80	79	87	92	99	100	100	103	100	92	86	80	103
Extreme Minimum Temp. (°F)	-10	-8	8	22	28	40	47	42	33	21	12	-1	-10
Days Maximum Temp. ≥ 90°F	0	0	0	0	1	6	12	8	3	0	0	0	30
Days Maximum Temp. ≤ 32°F	2	1	0	0	0	0	0	0	0	0	0	1	4
Days Minimum Temp. ≤ 32°F	25	21	14	4	0	0	0	0	0	4	14	22	104
Days Minimum Temp. ≤ 0°F	0	0	0	0	0	0	0	0	0	0	0	0	0
Heating Degree Days (base 65°F)	881	710	570	287	103	10	1	2	46	265	518	787	4,180
Cooling Degree Days (base 65°F)	0	0	2	19	76	235	350	310	138	17	1	0	1,148
Mean Precipitation (in.)	3.32	3.07	4.41	3.67	4.07	4.07	5.00	4.09	4.43	3.43	3.19	3.52	46.27
Extreme Maximum Daily Precip. (in.)	2.05	2.27	4.00	4.27	4.01	3.62	4.35	5.27	4.60	4.70	2.84	2.20	5.27
Days With ≥ 0.1" Precipitation	6	6	7	6	7	7	8	6	5	5	6	6	75
Days With ≥ 0.5" Precipitation	2	2	3	3	3	3	4	2	3	2	2	3	32
Days With ≥ 1.0" Precipitation	1	1	1	1	1	1	1	1	2	1	1	1	13
Mean Snowfall (in.)	2.1	3.1	1.3	0.1	0.0	0.0	0.0	0.0	0.0	0.0	trace	1.3	7.9
Maximum Snow Depth (in.)	15	9	7	0	0	0	0	0	0	0	trace	8	15
Days With ≥ 1.0" Snow Depth	3	1	0	0	0	0	0	0	0	0	0	1	5

Dunn 4 NW *Harnett County*   Elevation: 200 ft.   Latitude: 35° 19' N   Longitude: 78° 41' W

	JAN	FEB	MAR	APR	MAY	JUN	JUL	AUG	SEP	OCT	NOV	DEC	YEAR
Mean Maximum Temp. (°F)	52.0	56.2	63.9	73.1	79.9	86.8	89.6	87.9	82.4	73.1	64.4	55.0	72.0
Mean Temp. (°F)	41.1	44.4	51.4	60.1	67.8	76.0	79.5	78.0	71.9	61.0	52.0	43.8	60.6
Mean Minimum Temp. (°F)	30.1	32.6	38.9	47.0	55.7	65.1	69.3	68.1	61.3	48.8	39.4	32.4	49.1
Extreme Maximum Temp. (°F)	79	82	89	93	97	101	102	108	100	95	85	80	108
Extreme Minimum Temp. (°F)	-4	4	10	25	35	45	52	53	37	24	20	1	-4
Days Maximum Temp. ≥ 90°F	0	0	0	1	2	10	16	12	4	0	0	0	45
Days Maximum Temp. ≤ 32°F	1	0	0	0	0	0	0	0	0	0	0	0	1
Days Minimum Temp. ≤ 32°F	19	15	9	1	0	0	0	0	0	1	9	18	72
Days Minimum Temp. ≤ 0°F	0	0	0	0	0	0	0	0	0	0	0	0	0
Heating Degree Days (base 65°F)	734	575	423	186	49	2	0	0	15	170	392	651	3,197
Cooling Degree Days (base 65°F)	1	1	9	45	143	339	455	411	228	52	7	2	1,693
Mean Precipitation (in.)	3.52	3.30	3.99	3.34	3.49	4.61	6.25	5.36	4.18	3.23	3.10	3.25	47.62
Extreme Maximum Daily Precip. (in.)	2.10	2.95	4.50	3.03	2.42	5.85	4.06	4.85	7.40	4.20	2.83	2.42	7.40
Days With ≥ 0.1" Precipitation	7	6	6	6	6	6	9	7	5	4	5	6	73
Days With ≥ 0.5" Precipitation	3	2	3	2	2	3	4	4	3	2	2	2	32
Days With ≥ 1.0" Precipitation	1	1	1	1	1	2	2	2	1	1	1	1	15
Mean Snowfall (in.)	1.1	0.5	0.4	0.0	0.0	0.0	0.0	0.0	0.0	0.0	0.0	0.3	2.3
Maximum Snow Depth (in.)	5	7	8	0	0	0	0	0	0	0	0	0	8
Days With ≥ 1.0" Snow Depth	0	0	0	0	0	0	0	0	0	0	0	0	0

The period of record for all cooperative weather station data is 1980 – 2009. See User Guide for detailed explanation of data.

Elizabeth City *Pasquotank County*   Elevation: 7 ft.   Latitude: 36° 19' N   Longitude: 76° 12' W

	JAN	FEB	MAR	APR	MAY	JUN	JUL	AUG	SEP	OCT	NOV	DEC	YEAR
Mean Maximum Temp. (°F)	52.5	55.4	63.0	71.9	79.3	86.0	89.3	87.6	82.6	74.0	65.0	55.8	71.9
Mean Temp. (°F)	42.4	44.7	51.5	59.9	67.9	76.0	80.1	78.3	73.1	63.0	54.2	45.5	61.4
Mean Minimum Temp. (°F)	32.1	34.1	40.0	48.2	56.5	66.0	70.8	69.0	63.6	52.1	43.3	35.2	50.9
Extreme Maximum Temp. (°F)	78	82	90	95	98	100	102	103	98	94	85	81	103
Extreme Minimum Temp. (°F)	-2	5	14	26	22	43	54	50	44	30	22	5	-2
Days Maximum Temp. ≥ 90°F	0	0	0	0	2	9	14	11	3	0	0	0	39
Days Maximum Temp. ≤ 32°F	1	0	0	0	0	0	0	0	0	0	0	0	1
Days Minimum Temp. ≤ 32°F	17	13	7	1	0	0	0	0	0	0	5	14	57
Days Minimum Temp. ≤ 0°F	0	0	0	0	0	0	0	0	0	0	0	0	0
Heating Degree Days (base 65°F)	696	568	418	187	50	3	0	0	6	125	327	599	2,979
Cooling Degree Days (base 65°F)	0	1	8	42	146	340	474	420	257	71	10	1	1,770
Mean Precipitation (in.)	3.80	3.25	3.79	3.23	3.74	4.60	5.59	5.55	4.27	3.21	3.33	3.50	47.86
Extreme Maximum Daily Precip. (in.)	2.23	2.26	3.70	4.65	3.52	3.35	4.50	3.14	5.40	4.29	4.29	2.50	5.40
Days With ≥ 0.1" Precipitation	7	6	7	6	6	6	8	7	6	5	5	6	75
Days With ≥ 0.5" Precipitation	3	2	3	2	2	3	3	4	3	2	2	2	31
Days With ≥ 1.0" Precipitation	1	1	1	1	1	1	2	2	1	1	1	1	14
Mean Snowfall (in.)	0.1	0.0	0.0	0.0	0.0	0.0	0.0	0.0	0.0	0.0	0.0	0.0	0.1
Maximum Snow Depth (in.)	2	0	0	0	0	0	0	0	0	0	0	0	2
Days With ≥ 1.0" Snow Depth	0	0	0	0	0	0	0	0	0	0	0	0	0

Fayetteville *Cumberland County*   Elevation: 96 ft.   Latitude: 35° 04' N   Longitude: 78° 52' W

	JAN	FEB	MAR	APR	MAY	JUN	JUL	AUG	SEP	OCT	NOV	DEC	YEAR
Mean Maximum Temp. (°F)	52.6	56.4	64.1	73.4	80.4	87.2	90.3	88.4	82.7	73.4	65.1	55.9	72.5
Mean Temp. (°F)	41.8	44.5	51.6	60.3	68.4	76.6	80.4	78.7	72.5	61.5	52.8	44.5	61.1
Mean Minimum Temp. (°F)	30.9	32.7	39.0	47.3	56.4	65.8	70.4	69.0	62.3	49.7	40.5	33.3	49.8
Extreme Maximum Temp. (°F)	79	83	88	95	97	102	103	105	98	96	86	81	105
Extreme Minimum Temp. (°F)	-1	5	14	20	34	47	53	53	41	29	21	4	-1
Days Maximum Temp. ≥ 90°F	0	0	0	1	3	12	18	13	4	0	0	0	51
Days Maximum Temp. ≤ 32°F	1	0	0	0	0	0	0	0	0	0	0	0	1
Days Minimum Temp. ≤ 32°F	18	15	8	1	0	0	0	0	0	1	8	16	67
Days Minimum Temp. ≤ 0°F	0	0	0	0	0	0	0	0	0	0	0	0	0
Heating Degree Days (base 65°F)	713	573	419	182	45	3	0	0	14	156	367	629	3,101
Cooling Degree Days (base 65°F)	1	1	9	50	158	356	484	432	245	56	9	2	1,803
Mean Precipitation (in.)	3.52	3.09	3.95	3.15	3.17	4.48	5.37	5.33	4.47	3.29	2.99	3.07	45.88
Extreme Maximum Daily Precip. (in.)	2.25	2.70	3.84	2.45	5.10	4.18	3.20	3.30	8.25	3.83	2.77	2.03	8.25
Days With ≥ 0.1" Precipitation	7	6	7	5	6	7	8	8	6	5	5	6	76
Days With ≥ 0.5" Precipitation	3	2	3	2	2	3	4	4	3	2	2	2	32
Days With ≥ 1.0" Precipitation	1	1	1	1	1	1	2	2	1	1	1	1	14
Mean Snowfall (in.)	0.4	trace	0.2	0.0	0.0	0.0	0.0	0.0	0.0	0.0	trace	0.0	0.6
Maximum Snow Depth (in.)	5	6	11	0	0	0	0	0	0	0	trace	2	11
Days With ≥ 1.0" Snow Depth	0	0	0	0	0	0	0	0	0	0	0	0	0

Forest City 6 SW *Rutherford County*   Elevation: 990 ft.   Latitude: 35° 16' N   Longitude: 81° 56' W

	JAN	FEB	MAR	APR	MAY	JUN	JUL	AUG	SEP	OCT	NOV	DEC	YEAR
Mean Maximum Temp. (°F)	50.4	55.0	62.4	71.2	79.1	86.0	89.7	87.6	81.3	72.0	62.6	53.1	70.9
Mean Temp. (°F)	38.5	42.4	49.1	57.3	65.7	73.4	77.3	75.6	69.1	58.8	49.7	41.0	58.2
Mean Minimum Temp. (°F)	26.5	29.8	35.8	43.5	52.3	60.8	64.8	63.6	56.8	45.5	36.7	28.9	45.4
Extreme Maximum Temp. (°F)	78	82	87	93	97	101	106	107	97	91	82	78	107
Extreme Minimum Temp. (°F)	-8	2	5	23	27	39	50	45	35	25	18	-3	-8
Days Maximum Temp. ≥ 90°F	0	0	0	0	1	10	16	12	4	0	0	0	43
Days Maximum Temp. ≤ 32°F	1	0	0	0	0	0	0	0	0	0	0	1	2
Days Minimum Temp. ≤ 32°F	23	18	11	3	0	0	0	0	0	2	11	21	89
Days Minimum Temp. ≤ 0°F	0	0	0	0	0	0	0	0	0	0	0	0	0
Heating Degree Days (base 65°F)	815	633	489	245	71	4	1	1	31	211	455	736	3,692
Cooling Degree Days (base 65°F)	0	0	3	23	100	265	388	337	160	25	2	0	1,303
Mean Precipitation (in.)	4.45	4.24	5.11	3.89	4.44	3.99	4.41	4.25	4.03	4.04	4.03	3.96	50.84
Extreme Maximum Daily Precip. (in.)	3.12	4.00	3.71	2.32	3.40	3.50	3.30	6.50	6.65	4.35	3.05	2.95	6.65
Days With ≥ 0.1" Precipitation	7	7	7	7	8	7	7	8	6	6	5	6	81
Days With ≥ 0.5" Precipitation	3	3	4	3	3	3	3	3	3	2	3	3	36
Days With ≥ 1.0" Precipitation	2	1	1	1	1	1	1	1	1	1	1	1	13
Mean Snowfall (in.)	3.1	1.3	0.9	trace	0.0	0.0	0.0	0.0	0.0	0.0	trace	0.3	5.6
Maximum Snow Depth (in.)	13	7	9	trace	0	0	0	0	0	0	1	2	13
Days With ≥ 1.0" Snow Depth	2	1	1	0	0	0	0	0	0	0	0	0	3

Gastonia *Gaston County*   Elevation: 700 ft.   Latitude: 35° 16' N   Longitude: 81° 08' W

	JAN	FEB	MAR	APR	MAY	JUN	JUL	AUG	SEP	OCT	NOV	DEC	YEAR
Mean Maximum Temp. (°F)	52.0	56.1	64.1	72.5	79.8	86.7	89.9	88.5	82.3	72.7	63.6	54.0	71.9
Mean Temp. (°F)	41.5	44.7	52.1	60.3	68.4	76.2	79.6	78.6	72.1	61.4	52.2	43.4	60.9
Mean Minimum Temp. (°F)	30.8	33.3	40.1	48.1	56.9	65.6	69.4	68.7	61.9	50.1	40.8	32.8	49.9
Extreme Maximum Temp. (°F)	79	80	87	91	94	100	102	104	98	94	83	80	104
Extreme Minimum Temp. (°F)	-5	11	-1	25	32	44	54	49	39	28	18	3	-5
Days Maximum Temp. ≥ 90°F	0	0	0	0	2	10	17	14	4	0	0	0	47
Days Maximum Temp. ≤ 32°F	1	0	0	0	0	0	0	0	0	0	0	0	1
Days Minimum Temp. ≤ 32°F	17	14	7	1	0	0	0	0	0	1	7	16	63
Days Minimum Temp. ≤ 0°F	0	0	0	0	0	0	0	0	0	0	0	0	0
Heating Degree Days (base 65°F)	722	568	400	177	38	2	0	0	15	153	383	662	3,120
Cooling Degree Days (base 65°F)	0	1	8	43	150	345	461	429	235	50	5	1	1,728
Mean Precipitation (in.)	3.57	3.36	3.79	2.86	3.13	3.83	3.26	4.47	3.66	3.69	3.04	3.24	41.90
Extreme Maximum Daily Precip. (in.)	2.10	2.35	2.20	2.08	2.65	2.91	3.00	6.10	3.94	4.35	2.88	3.11	6.10
Days With ≥ 0.1" Precipitation	6	6	6	6	6	6	6	6	5	5	5	5	68
Days With ≥ 0.5" Precipitation	3	2	3	2	2	2	2	3	2	2	2	2	27
Days With ≥ 1.0" Precipitation	1	1	1	1	1	1	1	1	1	1	1	1	12
Mean Snowfall (in.)	0.5	0.2	0.0	0.0	0.0	0.0	0.0	0.0	0.0	0.0	0.0	trace	0.7
Maximum Snow Depth (in.)	8	11	0	0	0	0	0	0	0	0	0	trace	11
Days With ≥ 1.0" Snow Depth	0	0	0	0	0	0	0	0	0	0	0	0	0

The period of record for all cooperative weather station data is 1980 – 2009. See User Guide for detailed explanation of data.

Greenville *Pitt County*   Elevation: 32 ft.   Latitude: 35° 38' N   Longitude: 77° 24' W

	JAN	FEB	MAR	APR	MAY	JUN	JUL	AUG	SEP	OCT	NOV	DEC	YEAR
Mean Maximum Temp. (°F)	52.2	56.2	63.9	73.0	80.2	86.9	90.0	88.4	82.8	73.7	64.9	55.6	72.3
Mean Temp. (°F)	42.0	45.1	52.1	60.9	68.7	76.6	80.2	78.6	72.7	62.0	53.0	44.8	61.4
Mean Minimum Temp. (°F)	31.8	34.0	40.3	48.7	57.3	66.2	70.3	68.8	62.5	50.2	41.1	33.9	50.4
Extreme Maximum Temp. (°F)	80	84	91	96	97	103	103	104	100	95	86	82	104
Extreme Minimum Temp. (°F)	-4	4	15	27	37	45	53	50	40	27	19	1	-4
Days Maximum Temp. ≥ 90°F	0	0	0	1	3	11	18	13	4	0	0	0	50
Days Maximum Temp. ≤ 32°F	1	0	0	0	0	0	0	0	0	0	0	1	2
Days Minimum Temp. ≤ 32°F	17	14	7	1	0	0	0	0	0	1	7	15	62
Days Minimum Temp. ≤ 0°F	0	0	0	0	0	0	0	0	0	0	0	0	0
Heating Degree Days (base 65°F)	707	559	405	173	42	1	0	0	12	151	363	623	3,036
Cooling Degree Days (base 65°F)	2	2	13	57	164	356	478	428	249	64	11	3	1,827
Mean Precipitation (in.)	3.85	3.26	4.05	3.24	3.81	4.44	5.27	6.24	5.46	3.39	3.17	3.28	49.46
Extreme Maximum Daily Precip. (in.)	3.49	3.29	2.24	2.99	3.17	3.63	4.11	7.60	10.75	5.60	3.46	1.94	10.75
Days With ≥ 0.1" Precipitation	8	6	7	6	7	7	8	7	6	5	5	6	78
Days With ≥ 0.5" Precipitation	3	2	3	2	3	3	4	4	3	2	2	2	33
Days With ≥ 1.0" Precipitation	1	1	1	1	1	1	2	2	2	1	1	1	15
Mean Snowfall (in.)	1.6	1.0	0.8	trace	0.0	0.0	0.0	0.0	0.0	0.0	0.0	0.5	3.9
Maximum Snow Depth (in.)	8	7	16	trace	0	0	0	0	0	0	0	6	16
Days With ≥ 1.0" Snow Depth	0	0	0	0	0	0	0	0	0	0	0	0	0

Hamlet *Richmond County*   Elevation: 350 ft.   Latitude: 34° 53' N   Longitude: 79° 42' W

	JAN	FEB	MAR	APR	MAY	JUN	JUL	AUG	SEP	OCT	NOV	DEC	YEAR
Mean Maximum Temp. (°F)	53.1	57.8	65.9	75.0	82.2	88.7	91.5	89.6	83.6	74.2	65.3	56.2	73.6
Mean Temp. (°F)	41.3	44.9	52.1	60.9	68.9	76.6	80.0	78.4	72.0	61.3	52.0	43.7	61.0
Mean Minimum Temp. (°F)	29.5	31.9	38.2	46.7	55.7	64.4	68.3	67.1	60.3	48.3	38.6	31.1	48.4
Extreme Maximum Temp. (°F)	80	84	94	95	99	103	106	108	100	96	85	81	108
Extreme Minimum Temp. (°F)	-6	5	7	17	27	32	49	41	35	24	15	3	-6
Days Maximum Temp. ≥ 90°F	0	0	0	1	5	15	21	16	5	1	0	0	64
Days Maximum Temp. ≤ 32°F	1	0	0	0	0	0	0	0	0	0	0	0	1
Days Minimum Temp. ≤ 32°F	20	16	10	2	0	0	0	0	0	2	10	19	79
Days Minimum Temp. ≤ 0°F	0	0	0	0	0	0	0	0	0	0	0	0	0
Heating Degree Days (base 65°F)	728	563	404	169	36	3	0	0	16	163	391	654	3,127
Cooling Degree Days (base 65°F)	1	1	10	54	165	356	471	423	233	56	7	1	1,778
Mean Precipitation (in.)	3.81	3.41	4.00	2.89	3.17	4.58	6.01	4.74	4.63	4.07	3.37	3.13	47.81
Extreme Maximum Daily Precip. (in.)	3.06	1.90	2.35	1.93	3.09	4.32	6.10	3.72	4.60	5.41	3.61	1.72	6.10
Days With ≥ 0.1" Precipitation	7	6	7	6	6	7	9	7	6	6	6	6	79
Days With ≥ 0.5" Precipitation	3	3	3	2	2	3	4	3	3	2	2	2	32
Days With ≥ 1.0" Precipitation	1	1	1	1	1	1	2	1	1	1	1	1	13
Mean Snowfall (in.)	0.3	0.3	0.5	0.0	0.0	0.0	0.0	0.0	0.0	0.0	0.0	trace	1.1
Maximum Snow Depth (in.)	12	trace	8	0	0	0	0	0	0	0	0	1	12
Days With ≥ 1.0" Snow Depth	0	0	0	0	0	0	0	0	0	0	0	0	0

Hickory Regional Arpt *Burke County*   Elevation: 1,143 ft.   Latitude: 35° 44' N   Longitude: 81° 23' W

	JAN	FEB	MAR	APR	MAY	JUN	JUL	AUG	SEP	OCT	NOV	DEC	YEAR
Mean Maximum Temp. (°F)	49.3	53.4	61.1	70.1	77.5	84.7	87.8	86.4	79.6	70.3	61.0	51.5	69.4
Mean Temp. (°F)	39.4	42.8	50.1	58.5	66.3	74.4	77.9	76.6	69.8	59.3	50.2	41.6	58.9
Mean Minimum Temp. (°F)	29.6	32.2	38.9	46.9	55.1	64.0	67.8	66.9	59.9	48.4	39.4	31.7	48.4
Extreme Maximum Temp. (°F)	77	83	86	92	96	100	102	104	95	91	82	78	104
Extreme Minimum Temp. (°F)	-8	2	9	25	30	46	52	45	40	27	17	2	-8
Days Maximum Temp. ≥ 90°F	0	0	0	0	1	7	13	9	2	0	0	0	32
Days Maximum Temp. ≤ 32°F	2	1	0	0	0	0	0	0	0	0	0	1	4
Days Minimum Temp. ≤ 32°F	19	16	8	1	0	0	0	0	0	1	8	18	71
Days Minimum Temp. ≤ 0°F	0	0	0	0	0	0	0	0	0	0	0	0	0
Heating Degree Days (base 65°F)	785	621	460	217	59	3	0	1	25	200	439	719	3,529
Cooling Degree Days (base 65°F)	0	0	4	30	108	293	406	368	175	32	2	0	1,418
Mean Precipitation (in.)	3.59	3.55	4.39	3.78	3.69	4.16	4.38	4.16	3.80	3.44	3.50	3.72	46.16
Extreme Maximum Daily Precip. (in.)	2.60	3.55	3.86	2.74	2.26	4.56	3.96	4.04	4.01	6.31	2.79	2.73	6.31
Days With ≥ 0.1" Precipitation	6	6	7	7	7	7	7	6	6	5	6	6	76
Days With ≥ 0.5" Precipitation	3	2	3	3	2	3	3	3	2	2	2	3	31
Days With ≥ 1.0" Precipitation	1	1	1	1	1	1	1	1	1	1	1	1	12
Mean Snowfall (in.)	na	na	na	na	na	na	na	na	na	na	na	na	na
Maximum Snow Depth (in.)	na	na	na	na	na	na	na	na	na	na	na	na	na
Days With ≥ 1.0" Snow Depth	na	na	na	na	na	na	na	na	na	na	na	na	na

High Point *Guilford County*   Elevation: 899 ft.   Latitude: 35° 58' N   Longitude: 79° 58' W

	JAN	FEB	MAR	APR	MAY	JUN	JUL	AUG	SEP	OCT	NOV	DEC	YEAR
Mean Maximum Temp. (°F)	50.8	55.4	63.4	72.8	79.7	86.5	89.3	88.1	81.8	72.4	62.5	53.0	71.3
Mean Temp. (°F)	40.2	43.9	51.1	59.9	67.4	75.1	78.4	77.2	70.6	60.3	51.1	42.5	59.8
Mean Minimum Temp. (°F)	29.6	32.3	38.6	46.8	55.1	63.7	67.3	66.3	59.4	48.0	39.7	32.0	48.2
Extreme Maximum Temp. (°F)	80	80	88	94	95	102	101	104	98	94	89	80	104
Extreme Minimum Temp. (°F)	-7	2	7	22	33	39	49	46	35	19	16	0	-7
Days Maximum Temp. ≥ 90°F	0	0	0	0	2	9	16	13	4	0	0	0	44
Days Maximum Temp. ≤ 32°F	1	0	0	0	0	0	0	0	0	0	0	1	2
Days Minimum Temp. ≤ 32°F	20	16	9	2	0	0	0	0	0	1	8	17	73
Days Minimum Temp. ≤ 0°F	0	0	0	0	0	0	0	0	0	0	0	0	0
Heating Degree Days (base 65°F)	762	591	433	190	51	4	0	0	23	181	413	692	3,340
Cooling Degree Days (base 65°F)	0	0	8	43	134	314	421	386	198	40	4	1	1,549
Mean Precipitation (in.)	3.54	3.42	4.18	3.84	3.47	3.87	4.49	4.30	3.91	3.41	3.47	3.37	45.27
Extreme Maximum Daily Precip. (in.)	2.50	2.03	2.80	5.10	2.90	3.78	2.94	5.14	4.50	5.61	2.71	1.92	5.61
Days With ≥ 0.1" Precipitation	7	6	8	7	7	7	8	6	6	5	6	6	79
Days With ≥ 0.5" Precipitation	3	3	3	2	2	3	3	3	3	2	3	2	32
Days With ≥ 1.0" Precipitation	1	1	1	1	1	1	1	1	1	1	1	1	12
Mean Snowfall (in.)	1.4	1.4	0.4	trace	0.0	0.0	0.0	0.0	0.0	0.0	trace	0.3	3.5
Maximum Snow Depth (in.)	15	7	8	trace	0	0	0	0	0	0	trace	2	15
Days With ≥ 1.0" Snow Depth	1	1	0	0	0	0	0	0	0	0	0	0	2

Hofmann Forest *Onslow County*   Elevation: 43 ft.   Latitude: 34° 50' N   Longitude: 77° 18' W

	JAN	FEB	MAR	APR	MAY	JUN	JUL	AUG	SEP	OCT	NOV	DEC	YEAR
Mean Maximum Temp. (°F)	56.8	60.9	67.6	75.4	81.8	87.7	90.5	89.1	84.4	76.7	68.7	59.7	74.9
Mean Temp. (°F)	*45.2*	48.3	54.1	61.8	69.0	76.4	80.0	78.7	73.5	64.1	55.8	47.6	*62.9*
Mean Minimum Temp. (°F)	*33.6*	35.7	40.5	48.2	56.3	65.1	69.5	68.4	62.6	51.4	42.7	35.5	*50.8*
Extreme Maximum Temp. (°F)	81	85	92	97	98	104	102	104	98	93	90	82	104
Extreme Minimum Temp. (°F)	2	10	11	25	32	37	50	50	38	23	14	-2	-2
Days Maximum Temp. ≥ 90°F	0	0	0	1	4	12	19	15	5	1	0	0	57
Days Maximum Temp. ≤ 32°F	0	0	0	0	0	0	0	0	0	0	0	0	0
Days Minimum Temp. ≤ 32°F	14	12	8	2	0	0	0	0	0	1	7	14	58
Days Minimum Temp. ≤ 0°F	0	0	0	0	0	0	0	0	0	0	0	0	0
Heating Degree Days (base 65°F)	*608*	470	346	148	35	2	0	0	7	111	292	537	2,556
Cooling Degree Days (base 65°F)	2	4	14	61	168	350	471	432	269	89	21	4	1,885
Mean Precipitation (in.)	4.35	3.84	4.54	3.30	4.13	5.32	6.89	7.31	6.52	4.10	3.83	3.55	57.68
Extreme Maximum Daily Precip. (in.)	4.19	5.15	5.10	3.05	3.90	3.35	4.85	6.20	7.40	4.55	6.20	2.94	7.40
Days With ≥ 0.1" Precipitation	7	6	7	6	7	8	10	9	7	5	5	6	83
Days With ≥ 0.5" Precipitation	3	2	3	2	3	3	4	5	3	2	2	2	34
Days With ≥ 1.0" Precipitation	1	1	1	1	1	2	2	2	2	1	1	1	16
Mean Snowfall (in.)	0.5	0.1	0.1	trace	0.0	0.0	0.0	0.0	0.0	0.0	trace	0.7	1.4
Maximum Snow Depth (in.)	trace	trace	0	trace	0	0	0	0	0	0	trace	3	3
Days With ≥ 1.0" Snow Depth	0	0	0	0	0	0	0	0	0	0	0	0	0

Jefferson 2 E *Ashe County*   Elevation: 2,770 ft.   Latitude: 36° 25' N   Longitude: 81° 26' W

	JAN	FEB	MAR	APR	MAY	JUN	JUL	AUG	SEP	OCT	NOV	DEC	YEAR
Mean Maximum Temp. (°F)	43.5	46.3	54.1	63.0	71.0	77.9	81.0	80.4	74.2	65.0	56.0	46.5	63.2
Mean Temp. (°F)	32.9	35.3	42.0	50.1	58.2	66.0	69.7	68.7	62.1	51.7	43.2	35.3	51.3
Mean Minimum Temp. (°F)	22.3	24.3	29.8	37.2	45.3	54.0	58.3	57.1	50.0	38.4	30.3	24.0	39.3
Extreme Maximum Temp. (°F)	74	74	81	83	90	93	94	96	94	85	79	74	96
Extreme Minimum Temp. (°F)	-15	-6	2	13	22	28	36	33	26	16	6	-9	-15
Days Maximum Temp. ≥ 90°F	0	0	0	0	0	0	1	1	0	0	0	0	2
Days Maximum Temp. ≤ 32°F	5	3	1	0	0	0	0	0	0	0	0	3	12
Days Minimum Temp. ≤ 32°F	26	23	19	9	3	0	0	0	1	9	19	25	134
Days Minimum Temp. ≤ 0°F	1	0	0	0	0	0	0	0	0	0	0	0	1
Heating Degree Days (base 65°F)	987	832	707	442	218	44	10	15	121	407	647	914	5,344
Cooling Degree Days (base 65°F)	0	0	0	2	14	80	162	138	41	2	0	0	439
Mean Precipitation (in.)	3.65	3.45	4.12	3.91	4.23	3.94	4.60	3.99	3.77	2.93	3.78	3.40	45.77
Extreme Maximum Daily Precip. (in.)	4.12	2.60	3.45	2.53	2.52	4.52	3.30	5.22	4.53	5.36	3.52	2.72	5.36
Days With ≥ 0.1" Precipitation	6	6	7	7	8	7	9	7	6	4	6	6	79
Days With ≥ 0.5" Precipitation	2	2	3	3	3	2	3	3	2	2	2	2	29
Days With ≥ 1.0" Precipitation	1	1	1	1	1	1	1	1	1	1	1	1	12
Mean Snowfall (in.)	4.2	3.9	3.0	0.4	0.0	0.0	0.0	0.0	0.0	trace	0.1	2.8	14.4
Maximum Snow Depth (in.)	20	14	24	3	0	0	0	0	0	trace	2	14	24
Days With ≥ 1.0" Snow Depth	3	3	1	0	0	0	0	0	0	0	0	2	9

Laurinburg *Scotland County*   Elevation: 209 ft.   Latitude: 34° 45' N   Longitude: 79° 27' W

	JAN	FEB	MAR	APR	MAY	JUN	JUL	AUG	SEP	OCT	NOV	DEC	YEAR
Mean Maximum Temp. (°F)	53.9	58.7	66.5	75.7	82.8	89.1	91.7	89.8	84.2	75.4	66.1	56.7	74.2
Mean Temp. (°F)	43.0	46.7	53.8	62.2	70.3	77.7	80.9	79.4	73.4	63.0	54.1	45.5	62.5
Mean Minimum Temp. (°F)	32.1	34.6	41.1	48.6	57.7	66.3	70.1	69.0	62.6	50.7	42.0	34.3	50.8
Extreme Maximum Temp. (°F)	80	84	91	96	98	104	104	107	100	97	87	81	107
Extreme Minimum Temp. (°F)	-3	6	8	24	34	47	55	53	41	28	19	6	-3
Days Maximum Temp. ≥ 90°F	0	0	0	1	5	16	21	16	6	1	0	0	66
Days Maximum Temp. ≤ 32°F	1	0	0	0	0	0	0	0	0	0	0	0	1
Days Minimum Temp. ≤ 32°F	17	12	6	1	0	0	0	0	0	1	6	15	58
Days Minimum Temp. ≤ 0°F	0	0	0	0	0	0	0	0	0	0	0	0	0
Heating Degree Days (base 65°F)	675	514	352	141	27	1	0	0	9	127	333	600	2,779
Cooling Degree Days (base 65°F)	1	2	13	64	198	391	500	454	268	73	13	2	1,979
Mean Precipitation (in.)	3.64	3.40	4.07	2.73	3.06	4.73	4.94	5.13	4.65	3.62	3.11	3.07	46.15
Extreme Maximum Daily Precip. (in.)	2.79	2.50	2.99	1.95	3.02	4.19	4.70	4.75	5.58	4.11	3.27	2.05	5.58
Days With ≥ 0.1" Precipitation	7	6	7	5	6	7	8	7	6	5	5	6	75
Days With ≥ 0.5" Precipitation	3	3	3	2	2	3	3	3	3	2	2	2	31
Days With ≥ 1.0" Precipitation	1	1	1	1	1	1	1	2	1	1	1	1	13
Mean Snowfall (in.)	0.9	0.4	0.5	trace	0.0	0.0	0.0	0.0	0.0	0.0	0.0	trace	1.8
Maximum Snow Depth (in.)	8	4	9	trace	0	0	0	0	0	0	0	1	9
Days With ≥ 1.0" Snow Depth	1	0	0	0	0	0	0	0	0	0	0	0	1

Lincolnton 4 W *Lincoln County*   Elevation: 899 ft.   Latitude: 35° 28' N   Longitude: 81° 20' W

	JAN	FEB	MAR	APR	MAY	JUN	JUL	AUG	SEP	OCT	NOV	DEC	YEAR
Mean Maximum Temp. (°F)	50.7	55.3	63.3	72.0	78.9	85.5	88.5	87.1	80.8	71.6	62.0	52.7	70.7
Mean Temp. (°F)	40.1	43.7	50.9	59.0	66.6	74.3	77.7	76.5	69.9	59.5	50.2	42.0	59.2
Mean Minimum Temp. (°F)	29.4	31.9	38.4	45.9	54.4	63.0	66.7	65.8	59.0	47.4	38.5	31.2	47.6
Extreme Maximum Temp. (°F)	78	80	86	91	94	100	102	105	96	92	83	78	105
Extreme Minimum Temp. (°F)	-6	2	6	22	28	41	50	47	36	23	13	1	-6
Days Maximum Temp. ≥ 90°F	0	0	0	0	1	7	13	9	3	0	0	0	33
Days Maximum Temp. ≤ 32°F	1	0	0	0	0	0	0	0	0	0	0	0	1
Days Minimum Temp. ≤ 32°F	19	16	9	2	0	0	0	0	0	2	9	18	75
Days Minimum Temp. ≤ 0°F	0	0	0	0	0	0	0	0	0	0	0	0	0
Heating Degree Days (base 65°F)	765	597	436	204	55	4	0	1	25	197	438	707	3,429
Cooling Degree Days (base 65°F)	0	0	4	30	112	289	399	364	180	35	2	1	1,416
Mean Precipitation (in.)	3.75	3.56	4.59	3.49	4.04	4.23	4.11	4.40	3.56	4.19	3.63	3.82	47.37
Extreme Maximum Daily Precip. (in.)	2.42	3.48	3.87	3.00	2.71	3.74	4.25	4.95	3.80	5.46	3.09	2.40	5.46
Days With ≥ 0.1" Precipitation	6	6	7	6	7	8	7	6	6	5	6	6	76
Days With ≥ 0.5" Precipitation	3	3	3	3	3	3	3	2	2	3	3	3	34
Days With ≥ 1.0" Precipitation	1	1	1	1	1	1	1	1	1	2	1	1	13
Mean Snowfall (in.)	3.1	1.7	1.0	trace	0.0	0.0	0.0	0.0	0.0	0.0	0.1	0.4	6.3
Maximum Snow Depth (in.)	14	6	9	trace	0	0	0	0	0	0	2	4	14
Days With ≥ 1.0" Snow Depth	2	1	0	0	0	0	0	0	0	0	0	0	3

The period of record for all cooperative weather station data is 1980 – 2009. See User Guide for detailed explanation of data.

Longwood *Brunswick County* Elevation: 40 ft. Latitude: 34° 01' N Longitude: 78° 33' W

	JAN	FEB	MAR	APR	MAY	JUN	JUL	AUG	SEP	OCT	NOV	DEC	YEAR
Mean Maximum Temp. (°F)	56.1	59.6	66.1	73.7	80.6	86.2	89.3	88.1	83.4	75.6	67.9	59.1	73.8
Mean Temp. (°F)	44.4	47.2	53.3	60.8	68.5	75.9	79.6	78.3	72.9	63.2	55.0	46.9	62.2
Mean Minimum Temp. (°F)	32.8	34.8	40.4	47.8	56.2	65.6	69.9	68.5	62.3	50.7	42.1	34.7	50.5
Extreme Maximum Temp. (°F)	80	83	87	94	97	101	101	103	98	95	87	82	103
Extreme Minimum Temp. (°F)	0	11	5	21	32	44	50	51	35	26	19	-4	-4
Days Maximum Temp. ≥ 90°F	0	0	0	1	2	7	14	11	4	0	0	0	39
Days Maximum Temp. ≤ 32°F	0	0	0	0	0	0	0	0	0	0	0	0	0
Days Minimum Temp. ≤ 32°F	17	12	8	1	0	0	0	0	0	1	7	15	61
Days Minimum Temp. ≤ 0°F	0	0	0	0	0	0	0	0	0	0	0	0	0
Heating Degree Days (base 65°F)	631	499	365	162	39	2	0	0	9	123	310	557	2,697
Cooling Degree Days (base 65°F)	1	2	9	43	152	336	461	420	253	73	18	4	1,772
Mean Precipitation (in.)	4.02	3.52	4.06	3.06	3.41	5.01	5.55	7.02	6.75	3.73	3.25	3.76	53.14
Extreme Maximum Daily Precip. (in.)	3.53	4.85	4.38	3.10	3.45	3.23	3.63	6.42	12.85	4.86	2.90	4.65	12.85
Days With ≥ 0.1" Precipitation	7	6	6	5	6	7	9	9	7	5	5	6	78
Days With ≥ 0.5" Precipitation	3	2	3	2	2	3	4	4	3	2	2	2	32
Days With ≥ 1.0" Precipitation	1	1	1	1	1	1	2	2	2	1	1	1	15
Mean Snowfall (in.)	0.2	0.1	0.7	0.0	0.0	0.0	0.0	0.0	0.0	0.0	0.0	0.7	1.7
Maximum Snow Depth (in.)	3	1	11	0	0	0	0	0	0	0	0	trace	11
Days With ≥ 1.0" Snow Depth	0	0	0	0	0	0	0	0	0	0	0	0	0

Louisburg *Franklin County* Elevation: 259 ft. Latitude: 36° 06' N Longitude: 78° 18' W

	JAN	FEB	MAR	APR	MAY	JUN	JUL	AUG	SEP	OCT	NOV	DEC	YEAR
Mean Maximum Temp. (°F)	50.8	54.6	62.7	72.3	79.1	86.8	89.6	88.4	82.1	72.5	63.5	54.0	71.4
Mean Temp. (°F)	38.3	40.9	48.6	57.5	65.2	73.9	77.5	**75.9**	**69.5**	58.5	49.2	41.0	**58.0**
Mean Minimum Temp. (°F)	25.5	27.4	34.4	42.6	51.4	61.0	65.4	63.5	56.8	44.1	35.2	27.8	44.6
Extreme Maximum Temp. (°F)	81	83	91	95	96	101	102	105	100	94	85	80	105
Extreme Minimum Temp. (°F)	-10	-1	8	20	30	36	44	40	33	22	11	3	-10
Days Maximum Temp. ≥ 90°F	0	0	0	1	2	11	17	13	4	0	0	0	48
Days Maximum Temp. ≤ 32°F	2	1	0	0	0	0	0	0	0	0	0	1	4
Days Minimum Temp. ≤ 32°F	23	20	15	4	0	0	0	0	0	4	14	22	102
Days Minimum Temp. ≤ 0°F	0	0	0	0	0	0	0	0	0	0	0	0	0
Heating Degree Days (base 65°F)	821	675	507	249	84	8	1	**2**	**33**	224	469	737	**3,810**
Cooling Degree Days (base 65°F)	0	0	6	31	98	283	394	**346**	**173**	29	3	1	**1,364**
Mean Precipitation (in.)	3.62	3.12	4.25	3.24	3.80	3.90	4.57	5.31	4.18	3.45	3.21	3.07	45.72
Extreme Maximum Daily Precip. (in.)	2.50	2.00	3.37	3.70	4.00	4.90	7.24	6.38	7.55	6.10	2.95	2.10	7.55
Days With ≥ 0.1" Precipitation	7	5	7	6	6	6	7	6	6	5	5	6	72
Days With ≥ 0.5" Precipitation	2	2	3	2	3	3	3	4	3	2	2	2	31
Days With ≥ 1.0" Precipitation	1	1	1	1	1	1	1	2	1	1	1	1	13
Mean Snowfall (in.)	1.4	0.4	0.2	trace	0.0	0.0	0.0	0.0	0.0	0.0	trace	0.2	2.2
Maximum Snow Depth (in.)	10	5	2	trace	0	0	0	0	0	0	trace	1	10
Days With ≥ 1.0" Snow Depth	1	0	0	0	0	0	0	0	0	0	0	0	1

Monroe 4 SE *Union County* Elevation: 580 ft. Latitude: 34° 58' N Longitude: 80° 30' W

	JAN	FEB	MAR	APR	MAY	JUN	JUL	AUG	SEP	OCT	NOV	DEC	YEAR
Mean Maximum Temp. (°F)	52.3	56.6	64.5	73.3	80.3	87.3	90.1	88.5	82.4	73.1	63.8	54.7	72.2
Mean Temp. (°F)	41.7	45.1	52.2	60.4	68.2	76.1	79.3	78.0	71.6	61.0	51.8	43.8	60.8
Mean Minimum Temp. (°F)	31.1	33.5	39.9	47.5	56.1	64.8	68.5	67.4	60.7	48.9	39.7	32.9	49.2
Extreme Maximum Temp. (°F)	79	81	86	92	95	100	103	107	98	93	83	79	107
Extreme Minimum Temp. (°F)	-5	6	5	24	32	44	53	51	38	22	14	5	-5
Days Maximum Temp. ≥ 90°F	0	0	0	0	2	11	17	13	4	0	0	0	47
Days Maximum Temp. ≤ 32°F	1	0	0	0	0	0	0	0	0	0	0	0	1
Days Minimum Temp. ≤ 32°F	18	14	8	2	0	0	0	0	0	2	9	17	70
Days Minimum Temp. ≤ 0°F	0	0	0	0	0	0	0	0	0	0	0	0	0
Heating Degree Days (base 65°F)	715	558	398	175	42	3	0	0	17	165	396	651	3,120
Cooling Degree Days (base 65°F)	0	1	9	45	148	342	450	409	221	49	6	1	1,681
Mean Precipitation (in.)	3.96	3.69	4.53	3.07	2.91	4.27	4.34	5.03	4.22	4.09	3.41	3.66	47.18
Extreme Maximum Daily Precip. (in.)	3.62	2.65	3.93	2.70	3.11	2.70	4.54	5.01	6.74	7.72	3.20	2.40	7.72
Days With ≥ 0.1" Precipitation	7	6	7	6	6	7	7	7	5	5	5	6	74
Days With ≥ 0.5" Precipitation	3	3	3	2	2	3	3	3	3	3	3	2	33
Days With ≥ 1.0" Precipitation	1	1	1	1	1	1	1	2	1	1	1	1	13
Mean Snowfall (in.)	1.9	0.6	0.6	trace	0.0	0.0	0.0	0.0	0.0	0.0	trace	0.2	3.3
Maximum Snow Depth (in.)	12	8	5	trace	0	0	0	0	0	0	trace	1	12
Days With ≥ 1.0" Snow Depth	1	1	0	0	0	0	0	0	0	0	0	0	2

New Bern Craven Co Reg Arpt *Craven County* Elevation: 16 ft. Latitude: 35° 04' N Longitude: 77° 03' W

	JAN	FEB	MAR	APR	MAY	JUN	JUL	AUG	SEP	OCT	NOV	DEC	YEAR
Mean Maximum Temp. (°F)	*54.3*	*58.0*	64.8	73.4	80.3	86.7	89.5	88.0	83.0	*74.6*	66.8	*57.8*	*73.1*
Mean Temp. (°F)	*44.0*	*46.9*	53.4	61.9	69.5	77.1	80.6	79.3	74.0	*64.0*	55.6	*47.0*	*62.8*
Mean Minimum Temp. (°F)	*33.7*	*35.9*	42.0	50.3	58.7	67.4	71.6	70.6	65.0	*53.5*	44.3	*36.1*	*52.4*
Extreme Maximum Temp. (°F)	80	*83*	90	95	96	101	102	101	98	*95*	86	*81*	*102*
Extreme Minimum Temp. (°F)	*1*	*15*	16	29	38	51	56	56	45	*29*	23	*-4*	*-4*
Days Maximum Temp. ≥ 90°F	*0*	*0*	0	1	2	9	16	13	4	*0*	0	*0*	*45*
Days Maximum Temp. ≤ 32°F	*0*	*0*	0	0	0	0	0	0	0	*0*	0	*0*	*0*
Days Minimum Temp. ≤ 32°F	*14*	*11*	5	0	0	0	0	0	0	0	*3*	*13*	*46*
Days Minimum Temp. ≤ 0°F	*0*	*0*	0	0	0	0	0	0	0	*0*	0	*0*	*0*
Heating Degree Days (base 65°F)	*645*	*508*	365	147	30	0	0	0	5	*109*	293	*556*	*2,658*
Cooling Degree Days (base 65°F)	*2*	*4*	13	60	176	369	490	451	283	*86*	17	*4*	*1,955*
Mean Precipitation (in.)	*3.88*	*3.45*	4.59	3.34	4.21	4.41	6.38	6.74	5.21	*3.29*	3.51	*3.51*	*52.52*
Extreme Maximum Daily Precip. (in.)	*3.84*	*3.20*	3.28	3.52	3.89	3.65	3.49	8.85	6.79	*6.52*	3.99	*2.87*	*8.85*
Days With ≥ 0.1" Precipitation	*7*	*6*	7	6	7	8	10	9	6	*5*	5	*6*	*82*
Days With ≥ 0.5" Precipitation	*3*	*3*	3	2	3	3	5	4	3	*2*	2	*2*	*35*
Days With ≥ 1.0" Precipitation	*1*	*1*	1	1	1	1	2	2	2	*1*	1	*1*	*15*
Mean Snowfall (in.)	na	na	na	na	na	na	na	na	na	na	na	na	na
Maximum Snow Depth (in.)	na	na	na	na	na	na	na	na	na	na	na	na	na
Days With ≥ 1.0" Snow Depth	na	na	na	na	na	na	na	na	na	na	na	na	na

The period of record for all cooperative weather station data is 1980 – 2009. See User Guide for detailed explanation of data.

Raleigh 4 SW *Wake County* Elevation: 419 ft. Latitude: 35° 44' N Longitude: 78° 41' W

	JAN	FEB	MAR	APR	MAY	JUN	JUL	AUG	SEP	OCT	NOV	DEC	YEAR
Mean Maximum Temp. (°F)	52.1	56.4	64.0	72.9	79.8	86.3	89.1	87.9	82.3	72.8	63.7	54.7	71.8
Mean Temp. (°F)	42.1	45.4	52.3	60.6	68.2	75.7	79.0	77.9	71.9	61.5	52.6	44.6	61.0
Mean Minimum Temp. (°F)	31.9	34.3	40.3	48.3	56.5	65.1	68.9	67.8	61.5	50.2	41.5	34.5	50.1
Extreme Maximum Temp. (°F)	78	80	87	92	93	99	103	103	99	92	84	78	103
Extreme Minimum Temp. (°F)	-6	11	12	24	34	46	51	49	37	24	19	5	-6
Days Maximum Temp. ≥ 90°F	0	0	0	0	1	8	15	11	3	0	0	0	38
Days Maximum Temp. ≤ 32°F	1	0	0	0	0	0	0	0	0	0	0	0	1
Days Minimum Temp. ≤ 32°F	17	13	7	1	0	0	0	0	0	1	6	14	59
Days Minimum Temp. ≤ 0°F	0	0	0	0	0	0	0	0	0	0	0	0	0
Heating Degree Days (base 65°F)	705	549	397	174	43	3	0	0	16	156	371	627	3,041
Cooling Degree Days (base 65°F)	1	1	9	50	149	332	442	405	230	55	7	1	1,682
Mean Precipitation (in.)	3.93	3.38	4.39	3.02	3.46	4.88	4.59	4.54	4.18	3.63	3.28	3.14	46.42
Extreme Maximum Daily Precip. (in.)	2.90	2.44	3.76	2.04	3.75	6.72	3.97	3.97	4.85	4.10	3.66	2.65	6.72
Days With ≥ 0.1" Precipitation	6	6	7	6	6	7	7	7	6	5	6	6	75
Days With ≥ 0.5" Precipitation	3	3	3	2	2	3	3	3	3	2	3	2	32
Days With ≥ 1.0" Precipitation	1	1	1	1	1	1	1	1	1	1	1	1	12
Mean Snowfall (in.)	1.8	0.8	0.6	trace	0.0	0.0	0.0	0.0	0.0	0.0	0.0	0.2	3.4
Maximum Snow Depth (in.)	12	5	2	trace	0	0	0	0	0	0	0	3	2	12
Days With ≥ 1.0" Snow Depth	1	1	0	0	0	0	0	0	0	0	0	0	2

Raleigh State Univ *Wake County* Elevation: 399 ft. Latitude: 35° 48' N Longitude: 78° 42' W

	JAN	FEB	MAR	APR	MAY	JUN	JUL	AUG	SEP	OCT	NOV	DEC	YEAR
Mean Maximum Temp. (°F)	49.6	53.8	61.4	70.9	78.5	85.8	89.0	87.4	81.1	71.0	62.1	52.5	70.2
Mean Temp. (°F)	40.3	43.5	50.6	59.7	67.9	75.9	79.5	78.0	71.6	60.6	52.0	43.1	60.2
Mean Minimum Temp. (°F)	30.9	33.3	39.8	48.5	57.2	65.8	69.9	68.6	62.1	50.1	41.8	33.6	50.1
Extreme Maximum Temp. (°F)	80	81	88	93	94	101	103	104	100	92	83	80	104
Extreme Minimum Temp. (°F)	-6	2	12	26	39	47	55	49	42	30	20	4	-6
Days Maximum Temp. ≥ 90°F	0	0	0	1	2	9	15	12	3	0	0	0	42
Days Maximum Temp. ≤ 32°F	2	1	0	0	0	0	0	0	0	0	0	1	4
Days Minimum Temp. ≤ 32°F	18	14	7	1	0	0	0	0	0	0	5	15	60
Days Minimum Temp. ≤ 0°F	0	0	0	0	0	0	0	0	0	0	0	0	0
Heating Degree Days (base 65°F)	760	601	446	196	50	4	0	0	17	175	389	674	3,312
Cooling Degree Days (base 65°F)	1	1	8	44	146	336	455	411	223	45	5	1	1,676
Mean Precipitation (in.)	3.80	3.30	4.35	2.86	3.51	4.51	4.38	4.47	4.22	3.69	3.40	3.35	45.84
Extreme Maximum Daily Precip. (in.)	2.70	2.16	3.21	2.30	3.60	5.37	3.13	3.80	6.04	5.34	4.67	2.58	6.04
Days With ≥ 0.1" Precipitation	7	6	7	6	6	7	7	7	6	5	5	6	74
Days With ≥ 0.5" Precipitation	2	2	3	2	2	3	3	3	3	2	2	3	30
Days With ≥ 1.0" Precipitation	1	1	1	1	1	1	1	2	1	1	1	1	13
Mean Snowfall (in.)	2.2	0.9	0.6	trace	0.0	0.0	0.0	0.0	0.0	0.0	0.1	0.3	4.1
Maximum Snow Depth (in.)	14	6	8	trace	0	0	0	0	0	0	trace	4	14
Days With ≥ 1.0" Snow Depth	2	1	0	0	0	0	0	0	0	0	0	0	3

Reidsville 2 NW *Rockingham County* Elevation: 890 ft. Latitude: 36° 23' N Longitude: 79° 42' W

	JAN	FEB	MAR	APR	MAY	JUN	JUL	AUG	SEP	OCT	NOV	DEC	YEAR
Mean Maximum Temp. (°F)	47.5	51.5	59.2	68.9	76.6	84.3	87.7	86.4	79.8	69.9	60.4	50.7	68.6
Mean Temp. (°F)	37.8	40.9	48.1	57.5	65.5	73.9	77.4	76.0	69.1	58.3	49.5	40.9	57.9
Mean Minimum Temp. (°F)	28.1	30.4	37.0	46.1	54.3	63.4	67.0	65.5	58.4	46.7	38.6	31.0	47.2
Extreme Maximum Temp. (°F)	79	80	87	92	95	99	100	103	98	93	83	80	103
Extreme Minimum Temp. (°F)	-9	0	10	23	34	44	50	45	35	27	16	-1	-9
Days Maximum Temp. ≥ 90°F	0	0	0	0	1	7	12	10	3	0	0	0	33
Days Maximum Temp. ≤ 32°F	3	1	0	0	0	0	0	0	0	0	0	1	5
Days Minimum Temp. ≤ 32°F	21	17	10	2	0	0	0	0	0	1	8	19	78
Days Minimum Temp. ≤ 0°F	0	0	0	0	0	0	0	0	0	0	0	0	0
Heating Degree Days (base 65°F)	835	674	521	247	83	7	1	2	35	230	460	742	3,837
Cooling Degree Days (base 65°F)	0	0	5	30	104	281	390	348	165	30	2	0	1,355
Mean Precipitation (in.)	3.75	3.29	4.28	3.93	3.71	3.99	4.69	3.87	4.04	3.36	3.48	3.25	45.64
Extreme Maximum Daily Precip. (in.)	2.52	2.65	3.15	5.07	3.60	4.27	3.62	4.45	4.70	4.00	3.00	2.50	5.07
Days With ≥ 0.1" Precipitation	7	6	7	7	7	7	7	6	5	5	5	6	75
Days With ≥ 0.5" Precipitation	3	3	3	3	2	3	3	2	2	2	3	2	31
Days With ≥ 1.0" Precipitation	1	1	1	1	1	1	2	1	1	1	1	1	13
Mean Snowfall (in.)	3.2	3.2	0.9	trace	0.0	0.0	0.0	0.0	0.0	0.0	trace	0.7	8.0
Maximum Snow Depth (in.)	13	10	9	trace	0	0	0	0	0	0	trace	6	13
Days With ≥ 1.0" Snow Depth	3	2	1	0	0	0	0	0	0	0	0	1	7

Roxboro 7 ESE *Person County* Elevation: 709 ft. Latitude: 36° 19' N Longitude: 78° 54' W

	JAN	FEB	MAR	APR	MAY	JUN	JUL	AUG	SEP	OCT	NOV	DEC	YEAR
Mean Maximum Temp. (°F)	48.3	52.6	60.5	70.4	77.2	84.7	88.1	87.1	80.6	70.9	62.1	51.5	69.5
Mean Temp. (°F)	37.1	40.3	47.3	56.7	64.8	72.7	76.6	75.4	68.4	57.4	48.5	39.7	57.1
Mean Minimum Temp. (°F)	25.8	27.9	34.1	43.0	52.3	60.7	65.1	63.7	56.2	43.8	35.1	27.8	44.6
Extreme Maximum Temp. (°F)	79	81	87	96	92	98	102	103	99	93	83	80	103
Extreme Minimum Temp. (°F)	-9	-8	7	20	30	38	45	41	37	22	13	-1	-9
Days Maximum Temp. ≥ 90°F	0	0	0	1	1	7	12	11	3	0	0	0	35
Days Maximum Temp. ≤ 32°F	3	1	0	0	0	0	0	0	0	0	0	1	5
Days Minimum Temp. ≤ 32°F	23	21	14	4	0	0	0	0	0	4	13	21	100
Days Minimum Temp. ≤ 0°F	0	0	0	0	0	0	0	0	0	0	0	0	0
Heating Degree Days (base 65°F)	859	693	546	265	92	10	1	2	42	253	490	778	4,031
Cooling Degree Days (base 65°F)	0	0	4	24	92	249	368	332	151	23	2	0	1,245
Mean Precipitation (in.)	3.63	3.08	4.48	3.43	3.33	3.84	4.65	3.95	3.72	3.90	3.55	3.56	45.12
Extreme Maximum Daily Precip. (in.)	**3.47**	**2.25**	3.70	2.41	**2.92**	**3.21**	3.37	5.21	6.78	4.30	4.71	3.40	**6.78**
Days With ≥ 0.1" Precipitation	6	6	7	6	6	6	7	5	5	5	5	5	69
Days With ≥ 0.5" Precipitation	3	2	3	2	2	2	3	2	2	2	3	2	28
Days With ≥ 1.0" Precipitation	1	1	1	1	1	1	2	1	1	2	1	1	14
Mean Snowfall (in.)	2.3	2.6	1.1	trace	0.0	0.0	0.0	0.0	0.0	trace	0.1	0.8	6.9
Maximum Snow Depth (in.)	10	13	12	trace	0	0	0	0	0	trace	1	6	13
Days With ≥ 1.0" Snow Depth	2	2	1	0	0	0	0	0	0	0	0	1	5

The period of record for all cooperative weather station data is 1980 – 2009. See User Guide for detailed explanation of data.

Salisbury Rowan County   Elevation: 700 ft.   Latitude: 35° 41' N   Longitude: 80° 29' W

	JAN	FEB	MAR	APR	MAY	JUN	JUL	AUG	SEP	OCT	NOV	DEC	YEAR
Mean Maximum Temp. (°F)	51.5	56.0	64.0	73.0	79.9	86.5	89.4	88.4	81.7	72.4	63.1	53.3	71.6
Mean Temp. (°F)	40.5	44.2	51.4	60.0	67.7	75.5	78.8	77.9	70.7	60.1	51.2	42.4	60.0
Mean Minimum Temp. (°F)	29.5	32.3	38.7	47.0	55.5	64.4	68.3	67.3	59.7	47.7	39.2	31.4	48.4
Extreme Maximum Temp. (°F)	78	80	89	93	98	98	103	105	99	92	82	79	105
Extreme Minimum Temp. (°F)	-4	4	2	21	32	44	50	48	35	21	18	3	-4
Days Maximum Temp. ≥ 90°F	0	0	0	0	2	10	16	12	4	0	0	0	44
Days Maximum Temp. ≤ 32°F	1	0	0	0	0	0	0	0	0	0	0	0	1
Days Minimum Temp. ≤ 32°F	20	16	8	2	0	0	0	0	0	2	9	18	75
Days Minimum Temp. ≤ 0°F	0	0	0	0	0	0	0	0	0	0	0	0	0
Heating Degree Days (base 65°F)	752	582	422	182	46	3	0	0	22	184	411	696	3,300
Cooling Degree Days (base 65°F)	0	1	6	40	137	324	436	405	201	39	3	1	1,593
Mean Precipitation (in.)	3.03	3.46	4.21	3.56	3.05	3.96	3.84	3.13	3.46	3.31	2.97	3.05	41.03
Extreme Maximum Daily Precip. (in.)	1.80	2.25	2.96	3.32	2.18	3.69	3.30	5.90	4.17	4.48	*2.90*	2.30	*5.90*
Days With ≥ 0.1" Precipitation	6	6	7	6	6	6	6	5	5	5	5	5	68
Days With ≥ 0.5" Precipitation	2	3	3	3	2	2	3	2	2	2	2	2	28
Days With ≥ 1.0" Precipitation	1	1	1	1	1	1	1	1	1	1	1	1	12
Mean Snowfall (in.)	2.1	0.9	0.2	0.0	0.0	0.0	0.0	0.0	0.0	0.0	trace	0.3	3.5
Maximum Snow Depth (in.)	8	10	0	0	0	0	0	0	0	0	*trace*	2	*10*
Days With ≥ 1.0" Snow Depth	*0*	0	0	0	0	0	0	0	0	0	0	0	*0*

Sanford 8 NE Lee County   Elevation: 262 ft.   Latitude: 35° 32' N   Longitude: 79° 03' W

	JAN	FEB	MAR	APR	MAY	JUN	JUL	AUG	SEP	OCT	NOV	DEC	YEAR
Mean Maximum Temp. (°F)	52.8	57.4	65.6	74.9	81.4	87.9	90.8	89.0	83.0	73.8	64.3	55.3	73.0
Mean Temp. (°F)	41.0	44.5	51.7	60.2	67.7	75.4	79.0	77.4	71.0	60.4	51.2	43.2	60.2
Mean Minimum Temp. (°F)	29.2	31.5	37.7	45.4	54.0	62.9	67.2	65.8	59.0	46.9	38.1	31.2	47.4
Extreme Maximum Temp. (°F)	80	83	91	93	96	101	104	107	100	93	86	80	107
Extreme Minimum Temp. (°F)	-3	0	11	19	29	35	41	45	34	19	11	2	-3
Days Maximum Temp. ≥ 90°F	0	0	0	1	3	13	19	14	5	0	0	0	55
Days Maximum Temp. ≤ 32°F	1	0	0	0	0	0	0	0	0	0	0	0	1
Days Minimum Temp. ≤ 32°F	20	16	11	4	0	0	0	0	0	3	11	19	84
Days Minimum Temp. ≤ 0°F	0	0	0	0	0	0	0	0	0	0	0	0	0
Heating Degree Days (base 65°F)	737	575	417	187	53	4	0	1	21	184	412	669	3,260
Cooling Degree Days (base 65°F)	1	1	10	49	144	323	441	393	208	47	6	1	1,624
Mean Precipitation (in.)	3.81	3.44	4.07	2.93	3.48	4.71	5.03	4.64	4.18	3.70	3.34	2.96	46.29
Extreme Maximum Daily Precip. (in.)	2.88	2.50	2.60	2.06	3.34	6.10	3.50	4.35	6.14	3.50	3.76	2.16	6.14
Days With ≥ 0.1" Precipitation	6	6	7	5	6	6	8	7	5	5	6	5	72
Days With ≥ 0.5" Precipitation	3	3	3	2	3	3	3	3	3	2	2	2	32
Days With ≥ 1.0" Precipitation	1	1	1	1	1	2	1	1	1	1	1	1	13
Mean Snowfall (in.)	1.3	0.5	0.4	trace	0.0	0.0	0.0	0.0	0.0	0.0	trace	0.2	2.4
Maximum Snow Depth (in.)	17	5	trace	0	0	0	0	0	0	0	1	2	17
Days With ≥ 1.0" Snow Depth	1	0	0	0	0	0	0	0	0	0	0	0	1

Siler City 2 N Chatham County   Elevation: 609 ft.   Latitude: 35° 46' N   Longitude: 79° 28' W

	JAN	FEB	MAR	APR	MAY	JUN	JUL	AUG	SEP	OCT	NOV	DEC	YEAR
Mean Maximum Temp. (°F)	49.7	53.7	61.7	70.8	77.8	85.0	88.3	87.1	80.5	70.8	62.0	52.6	70.0
Mean Temp. (°F)	39.4	42.5	49.9	58.5	66.4	74.5	78.1	76.7	69.9	59.1	50.5	42.3	59.0
Mean Minimum Temp. (°F)	29.0	31.2	38.1	46.2	54.9	63.8	67.7	66.3	59.2	47.3	39.1	32.0	47.9
Extreme Maximum Temp. (°F)	79	81	88	92	96	99	101	105	99	92	85	79	105
Extreme Minimum Temp. (°F)	-11	2	0	23	33	44	52	47	34	25	16	1	-11
Days Maximum Temp. ≥ 90°F	0	0	0	0	1	7	13	11	3	0	0	0	35
Days Maximum Temp. ≤ 32°F	2	1	0	0	0	0	0	0	0	0	0	1	4
Days Minimum Temp. ≤ 32°F	21	16	9	2	0	0	0	0	0	1	9	18	76
Days Minimum Temp. ≤ 0°F	0	0	0	0	0	0	0	0	0	0	0	0	0
Heating Degree Days (base 65°F)	788	631	466	226	68	6	0	1	28	211	430	697	3,552
Cooling Degree Days (base 65°F)	0	1	7	37	117	296	412	372	182	33	4	1	1,462
Mean Precipitation (in.)	3.87	3.42	4.61	3.47	3.86	3.89	4.60	4.27	4.09	3.85	3.55	3.22	46.70
Extreme Maximum Daily Precip. (in.)	3.08	2.85	4.65	2.83	3.15	2.79	4.27	6.15	6.00	4.93	2.91	2.04	6.15
Days With ≥ 0.1" Precipitation	7	6	7	6	6	7	7	6	5	5	6	6	74
Days With ≥ 0.5" Precipitation	2	2	3	2	3	3	3	3	2	2	3	2	30
Days With ≥ 1.0" Precipitation	1	1	1	1	1	1	1	1	1	1	1	1	12
Mean Snowfall (in.)	1.2	0.7	0.4	trace	0.0	0.0	0.0	0.0	0.0	0.0	0.0	0.1	2.4
Maximum Snow Depth (in.)	22	3	5	trace	0	0	0	0	0	0	0	trace	22
Days With ≥ 1.0" Snow Depth	0	0	0	0	0	0	0	0	0	0	0	0	0

Southport 5 N Brunswick County   Elevation: 20 ft.   Latitude: 34° 00' N   Longitude: 78° 01' W

	JAN	FEB	MAR	APR	MAY	JUN	JUL	AUG	SEP	OCT	NOV	DEC	YEAR
Mean Maximum Temp. (°F)	57.1	59.1	65.6	73.1	79.8	85.9	89.2	*88.3*	83.6	76.0	68.6	59.8	*73.8*
Mean Temp. (°F)	45.3	47.4	54.0	61.3	69.0	76.6	80.4	*79.1*	73.7	64.1	56.1	47.8	*62.9*
Mean Minimum Temp. (°F)	33.3	35.6	42.0	49.6	58.1	67.3	71.6	*69.9*	63.7	52.1	43.6	35.7	*51.9*
Extreme Maximum Temp. (°F)	83	81	88	94	94	101	102	102	96	94	88	83	102
Extreme Minimum Temp. (°F)	0	9	8	25	37	46	52	54	35	25	16	-3	-3
Days Maximum Temp. ≥ 90°F	0	0	0	0	1	7	14	11	3	0	0	0	36
Days Maximum Temp. ≤ 32°F	0	0	0	0	0	0	0	0	0	0	0	0	0
Days Minimum Temp. ≤ 32°F	15	12	6	1	0	0	0	0	0	1	5	13	53
Days Minimum Temp. ≤ 0°F	0	0	0	0	0	0	0	0	0	0	0	0	0
Heating Degree Days (base 65°F)	604	491	344	152	30	2	0	*0*	6	110	280	532	*2,551*
Cooling Degree Days (base 65°F)	1	1	10	48	160	356	483	*444*	273	87	20	5	*1,888*
Mean Precipitation (in.)	4.20	3.73	4.30	2.90	3.58	4.42	5.85	6.94	8.44	4.19	3.63	3.95	56.13
Extreme Maximum Daily Precip. (in.)	2.56	5.00	5.02	*5.10*	5.24	3.86	4.50	10.00	18.30	8.60	3.30	2.74	*18.30*
Days With ≥ 0.1" Precipitation	7	6	6	4	6	6	8	9	7	5	5	6	75
Days With ≥ 0.5" Precipitation	3	3	3	2	3	3	4	4	4	2	2	2	35
Days With ≥ 1.0" Precipitation	1	1	1	1	1	1	2	2	3	1	1	1	16
Mean Snowfall (in.)	trace	0.0	0.3	0.0	0.0	0.0	0.0	0.0	0.0	0.0	0.0	0.5	0.8
Maximum Snow Depth (in.)	0	0	8	0	0	0	0	0	0	*0*	0	0	*8*
Days With ≥ 1.0" Snow Depth	0	0	0	0	0	0	0	0	0	0	0	0	0

The period of record for all cooperative weather station data is 1980 – 2009. See User Guide for detailed explanation of data.

Statesville 2 NNE *Iredell County*   Elevation: 950 ft.   Latitude: 35° 49' N   Longitude: 80° 53' W

	JAN	FEB	MAR	APR	MAY	JUN	JUL	AUG	SEP	OCT	NOV	DEC	YEAR
Mean Maximum Temp. (°F)	50.4	54.6	62.8	72.0	79.1	85.8	88.6	87.2	80.8	71.5	61.9	52.1	70.6
Mean Temp. (°F)	38.7	42.0	49.3	57.9	66.1	73.9	77.3	76.1	69.3	58.6	48.9	40.4	58.2
Mean Minimum Temp. (°F)	27.0	29.2	35.8	43.6	52.9	61.9	66.0	65.0	57.8	45.7	35.9	28.9	45.8
Extreme Maximum Temp. (°F)	78	81	88	94	97	101	102	106	99	92	82	79	106
Extreme Minimum Temp. (°F)	-7	2	10	17	29	41	46	44	33	21	13	1	-7
Days Maximum Temp. ≥ 90°F	0	0	0	1	2	9	14	10	3	0	0	0	39
Days Maximum Temp. ≤ 32°F	1	0	0	0	0	0	0	0	0	0	0	1	2
Days Minimum Temp. ≤ 32°F	22	19	12	4	0	0	0	0	0	3	13	21	94
Days Minimum Temp. ≤ 0°F	0	0	0	0	0	0	0	0	0	0	0	0	0
Heating Degree Days (base 65°F)	808	645	482	235	69	5	0	1	30	220	478	756	3,729
Cooling Degree Days (base 65°F)	0	0	3	27	109	277	389	352	166	29	2	1	1,355
Mean Precipitation (in.)	3.40	3.29	4.24	3.59	3.38	4.29	4.06	3.84	3.66	3.38	3.35	3.58	44.06
Extreme Maximum Daily Precip. (in.)	2.29	2.14	4.20	3.73	3.24	6.02	3.24	4.53	4.20	2.80	2.35	2.30	6.02
Days With ≥ 0.1" Precipitation	6	6	7	7	6	7	7	6	5	5	6	6	74
Days With ≥ 0.5" Precipitation	2	2	3	2	2	3	2	2	2	2	3	3	28
Days With ≥ 1.0" Precipitation	1	1	1	1	1	1	1	1	1	1	1	1	12
Mean Snowfall (in.)	2.2	1.2	0.6	0.0	0.0	0.0	0.0	0.0	0.0	0.0	trace	0.4	4.4
Maximum Snow Depth (in.)	8	6	4	0	0	0	0	0	0	0	trace	4	8
Days With ≥ 1.0" Snow Depth	1	1	0	0	0	0	0	0	0	0	0	0	2

Tarboro 1 S *Edgecombe County*   Elevation: 35 ft.   Latitude: 35° 53' N   Longitude: 77° 32' W

	JAN	FEB	MAR	APR	MAY	JUN	JUL	AUG	SEP	OCT	NOV	DEC	YEAR
Mean Maximum Temp. (°F)	51.9	55.4	63.2	72.5	79.9	87.1	90.0	88.5	82.8	73.4	64.1	54.8	72.0
Mean Temp. (°F)	40.8	43.6	50.6	59.4	67.6	75.8	79.4	77.9	71.9	61.2	51.8	43.4	60.3
Mean Minimum Temp. (°F)	29.5	31.6	38.0	46.3	55.3	64.5	68.8	67.3	61.0	48.8	39.5	32.1	48.6
Extreme Maximum Temp. (°F)	79	84	91	96	98	101	103	105	100	94	85	82	105
Extreme Minimum Temp. (°F)	-5	2	8	26	34	44	49	48	37	25	20	0	-5
Days Maximum Temp. ≥ 90°F	0	0	0	1	3	11	17	14	4	0	0	0	50
Days Maximum Temp. ≤ 32°F	1	0	0	0	0	0	0	0	0	0	0	0	1
Days Minimum Temp. ≤ 32°F	20	16	9	2	0	0	0	0	0	1	9	17	74
Days Minimum Temp. ≤ 0°F	0	0	0	0	0	0	0	0	0	0	0	0	0
Heating Degree Days (base 65°F)	745	600	446	202	54	3	0	0	13	165	395	663	3,286
Cooling Degree Days (base 65°F)	1	1	8	42	142	334	454	408	227	53	7	1	1,678
Mean Precipitation (in.)	3.64	3.25	3.90	3.15	3.26	3.93	4.74	5.00	4.28	2.96	2.89	3.02	44.02
Extreme Maximum Daily Precip. (in.)	3.73	2.33	2.18	2.17	3.44	2.80	4.00	3.27	5.80	2.93	5.60	2.50	5.80
Days With ≥ 0.1" Precipitation	7	6	7	6	6	6	7	7	5	4	5	6	72
Days With ≥ 0.5" Precipitation	3	3	3	2	2	3	3	3	2	2	2	3	30
Days With ≥ 1.0" Precipitation	1	1	1	1	1	1	1	2	1	1	1	1	13
Mean Snowfall (in.)	1.8	1.6	1.1	trace	0.0	0.0	0.0	0.0	0.0	0.0	trace	0.8	5.3
Maximum Snow Depth (in.)	8	3	12	trace	0	0	0	0	0	0	trace	12	12
Days With ≥ 1.0" Snow Depth	1	0	0	0	0	0	0	0	0	0	0	0	1

Tryon *Polk County*   Elevation: 1,080 ft.   Latitude: 35° 12' N   Longitude: 82° 14' W

	JAN	FEB	MAR	APR	MAY	JUN	JUL	AUG	SEP	OCT	NOV	DEC	YEAR
Mean Maximum Temp. (°F)	52.2	56.3	64.3	72.8	79.5	85.6	88.5	87.3	81.0	72.1	62.8	54.0	71.4
Mean Temp. (°F)	41.9	45.1	52.2	60.1	67.5	74.6	78.0	76.9	70.6	60.8	52.0	43.9	60.3
Mean Minimum Temp. (°F)	31.6	33.9	40.0	47.3	55.4	63.5	67.5	66.6	60.2	49.3	41.0	33.7	49.2
Extreme Maximum Temp. (°F)	80	82	89	94	97	98	102	103	96	91	83	81	103
Extreme Minimum Temp. (°F)	-8	8	14	26	33	44	51	49	40	26	20	3	-8
Days Maximum Temp. ≥ 90°F	0	0	0	1	1	9	13	11	3	0	0	0	38
Days Maximum Temp. ≤ 32°F	1	0	0	0	0	0	0	0	0	0	0	0	1
Days Minimum Temp. ≤ 32°F	17	13	6	1	0	0	0	0	0	1	6	15	59
Days Minimum Temp. ≤ 0°F	0	0	0	0	0	0	0	0	0	0	0	0	0
Heating Degree Days (base 65°F)	708	556	397	178	44	3	0	0	17	162	387	648	3,100
Cooling Degree Days (base 65°F)	0	0	6	37	127	297	410	378	191	38	3	1	1,488
Mean Precipitation (in.)	4.98	4.75	6.00	4.67	4.73	5.45	5.46	6.02	5.50	4.56	4.81	5.14	62.07
Extreme Maximum Daily Precip. (in.)	4.00	4.69	4.60	2.58	5.50	6.25	6.55	7.15	8.47	5.06	3.83	4.28	8.47
Days With ≥ 0.1" Precipitation	7	7	7	7	8	8	8	7	7	5	6	7	84
Days With ≥ 0.5" Precipitation	3	3	4	3	3	3	3	3	3	3	3	4	38
Days With ≥ 1.0" Precipitation	2	1	2	2	1	2	1	2	2	2	2	2	21
Mean Snowfall (in.)	3.0	1.5	1.0	trace	trace	0.0	0.0	0.0	0.0	0.0	trace	0.4	5.9
Maximum Snow Depth (in.)	16	7	10	trace	trace	0	0	0	0	0	trace	3	16
Days With ≥ 1.0" Snow Depth	2	1	1	0	0	0	0	0	0	0	0	0	4

Waynesville 1 E *Haywood County*   Elevation: 2,658 ft.   Latitude: 35° 29' N   Longitude: 82° 58' W

	JAN	FEB	MAR	APR	MAY	JUN	JUL	AUG	SEP	OCT	NOV	DEC	YEAR
Mean Maximum Temp. (°F)	49.2	52.5	59.7	67.6	74.8	80.9	83.5	82.7	77.0	68.8	60.0	51.5	67.4
Mean Temp. (°F)	36.5	39.3	45.9	53.3	60.9	68.0	71.3	70.6	64.4	54.7	45.9	38.7	54.1
Mean Minimum Temp. (°F)	23.6	26.1	32.0	38.9	47.1	55.1	59.0	58.4	51.7	40.4	31.7	25.7	40.8
Extreme Maximum Temp. (°F)	75	79	84	87	92	92	95	94	92	85	81	72	95
Extreme Minimum Temp. (°F)	-22	-13	-8	15	24	34	40	41	28	17	7	-6	-22
Days Maximum Temp. ≥ 90°F	0	0	0	0	0	1	2	2	0	0	0	0	5
Days Maximum Temp. ≤ 32°F	2	1	0	0	0	0	0	0	0	0	0	1	4
Days Minimum Temp. ≤ 32°F	24	21	17	8	2	0	0	0	0	8	17	23	120
Days Minimum Temp. ≤ 0°F	1	0	0	0	0	0	0	0	0	0	0	0	1
Heating Degree Days (base 65°F)	878	720	587	349	149	23	2	5	76	319	567	810	4,485
Cooling Degree Days (base 65°F)	0	0	1	4	30	120	205	185	64	5	0	0	614
Mean Precipitation (in.)	4.31	4.41	4.63	3.80	4.35	4.03	3.71	4.19	3.95	2.67	3.72	3.95	47.72
Extreme Maximum Daily Precip. (in.)	3.78	3.90	3.45	2.05	3.80	1.78	2.65	3.90	5.25	3.88	3.10	2.37	5.25
Days With ≥ 0.1" Precipitation	8	7	8	8	8	8	9	8	7	5	6	8	90
Days With ≥ 0.5" Precipitation	3	3	3	3	3	3	3	2	3	2	3	3	33
Days With ≥ 1.0" Precipitation	1	1	1	1	1	1	1	1	1	1	1	1	12
Mean Snowfall (in.)	4.4	3.1	2.4	1.2	0.2	0.0	0.0	0.0	0.0	trace	0.4	1.8	13.5
Maximum Snow Depth (in.)	17	5	18	16	5	0	0	0	0	trace	3	13	18
Days With ≥ 1.0" Snow Depth	3	2	2	1	0	0	0	0	0	0	0	1	7

Wilson 3 SW *Wilson County*   Elevation: 109 ft.   Latitude: 35° 42' N   Longitude: 77° 57' W

	JAN	FEB	MAR	APR	MAY	JUN	JUL	AUG	SEP	OCT	NOV	DEC	YEAR
Mean Maximum Temp. (°F)	51.4	55.2	62.8	72.2	79.8	87.3	90.3	88.8	82.9	73.3	64.5	54.7	71.9
Mean Temp. (°F)	40.9	43.7	50.8	59.6	67.8	76.1	79.6	78.1	71.9	61.1	52.4	43.8	60.5
Mean Minimum Temp. (°F)	30.3	32.3	38.7	47.0	55.8	64.8	68.8	67.4	60.8	48.8	40.2	32.8	49.0
Extreme Maximum Temp. (°F)	81	83	91	96	96	102	104	105	101	94	86	81	105
Extreme Minimum Temp. (°F)	-5	5	7	26	36	43	49	49	38	25	18	3	-5
Days Maximum Temp. ≥ 90°F	0	0	0	1	3	11	18	15	5	0	0	0	53
Days Maximum Temp. ≤ 32°F	1	0	0	0	0	0	0	0	0	0	0	1	2
Days Minimum Temp. ≤ 32°F	19	15	8	1	0	0	0	0	0	1	7	16	67
Days Minimum Temp. ≤ 0°F	0	0	0	0	0	0	0	0	0	0	0	0	0
Heating Degree Days (base 65°F)	741	596	442	197	51	3	0	1	16	167	379	653	3,246
Cooling Degree Days (base 65°F)	1	1	8	43	146	342	459	414	229	51	8	1	1,703
Mean Precipitation (in.)	3.76	3.10	4.29	3.08	3.79	4.08	5.34	4.92	4.79	3.21	2.99	3.26	46.61
Extreme Maximum Daily Precip. (in.)	2.10	2.35	3.66	2.24	4.00	3.77	4.08	5.20	9.53	4.95	2.12	2.28	9.53
Days With ≥ 0.1" Precipitation	7	6	7	6	7	7	8	7	6	5	5	6	77
Days With ≥ 0.5" Precipitation	3	2	3	2	3	3	3	3	3	2	2	2	31
Days With ≥ 1.0" Precipitation	1	1	1	1	1	1	2	2	2	1	1	1	15
Mean Snowfall (in.)	1.0	0.9	0.8	trace	0.0	0.0	0.0	0.0	0.0	0.0	trace	0.3	3.0
Maximum Snow Depth (in.)	8	6	12	trace	0	0	0	0	0	0	trace	4	12
Days With ≥ 1.0" Snow Depth	0	0	0	0	0	0	0	0	0	0	0	0	0

Yadkinville 6 E *Yadkin County*   Elevation: 875 ft.   Latitude: 36° 08' N   Longitude: 80° 33' W

	JAN	FEB	MAR	APR	MAY	JUN	JUL	AUG	SEP	OCT	NOV	DEC	YEAR
Mean Maximum Temp. (°F)	48.9	53.3	61.7	71.2	78.0	85.1	88.0	86.7	80.2	70.7	61.2	51.2	69.7
Mean Temp. (°F)	37.6	40.9	48.3	57.1	64.9	73.0	76.5	75.3	68.6	57.7	48.3	39.8	57.3
Mean Minimum Temp. (°F)	26.3	28.5	34.9	42.9	51.7	60.9	65.0	64.0	57.0	44.7	35.4	28.3	45.0
Extreme Maximum Temp. (°F)	78	82	89	92	96	102	102	104	99	94	83	80	104
Extreme Minimum Temp. (°F)	-8	-1	6	22	30	40	47	44	34	23	12	0	-8
Days Maximum Temp. ≥ 90°F	0	0	0	0	1	8	13	10	3	0	0	0	35
Days Maximum Temp. ≤ 32°F	2	1	0	0	0	0	0	0	0	0	0	1	4
Days Minimum Temp. ≤ 32°F	23	20	13	4	0	0	0	0	0	3	13	22	98
Days Minimum Temp. ≤ 0°F	0	0	0	0	0	0	0	0	0	0	0	0	0
Heating Degree Days (base 65°F)	842	674	514	253	84	7	0	1	36	242	495	776	3,924
Cooling Degree Days (base 65°F)	0	0	3	21	88	255	365	328	151	23	1	0	1,235
Mean Precipitation (in.)	3.45	3.22	4.25	3.67	3.76	4.14	4.65	3.47	3.73	3.29	3.18	3.56	44.37
Extreme Maximum Daily Precip. (in.)	2.42	2.40	4.25	3.25	3.14	3.40	4.00	4.57	3.76	4.50	2.69	2.60	4.57
Days With ≥ 0.1" Precipitation	6	6	7	7	8	8	8	6	5	5	6	6	78
Days With ≥ 0.5" Precipitation	3	2	3	3	2	3	3	2	3	2	2	3	31
Days With ≥ 1.0" Precipitation	1	1	1	1	1	1	1	1	1	1	1	1	12
Mean Snowfall (in.)	4.0	2.7	0.8	trace	0.0	0.0	0.0	0.0	0.0	0.0	trace	1.2	8.7
Maximum Snow Depth (in.)	16	10	6	trace	0	0	0	0	0	0	0	8	16
Days With ≥ 1.0" Snow Depth	3	2	0	0	0	0	0	0	0	0	0	1	6

North Carolina Weather Station Rankings

Annual Extreme Maximum Temperature

	Highest			Lowest	
Rank	Station Name	°F	Rank	Station Name	°F
1	Dunn 4 NW	108	1	Waynesville 1 E	95
1	Hamlet	108	2	Cape Hatteras NWS Bldg	96
3	Albemarle	107	2	Jefferson 2 E	96
3	Bayboro 3 E	*107*	4	Asheville	99
3	Concord	107	4	Black Mountain 2 W	99
3	Forest City 6 SW	*107*	6	Asheville Regional Arpt	100
3	Laurinburg	107	6	Bent Creek	100
3	Monroe 4 SE	107	8	Belhaven 5 SE	101
3	Sanford 8 NE	107	9	Cedar Island	102
10	Chapel Hill 2 W	106	9	New Bern Craven Co Reg Arpt	*102*
10	Statesville 2 NNE	106	9	Southport 5 N	102
12	Asheboro 2 W	105	12	Arcola	*103*
12	Fayetteville	105	12	Aurora 6 N	103
12	Lincolnton 4 W	105	12	Danbury 1 NW	103
12	Louisburg	105	12	Elizabeth City	103
12	Raleigh-Durham Intl Arpt	105	12	Longwood	103
12	Salisbury	105	12	Greensboro-High Pt-Winston Salem	103
12	Siler City 2 N	105	12	Raleigh 4 SW	103
12	Tarboro 1 S	105	12	Reidsville 2 NW	103
12	Wilson 3 SW	105	12	Roxboro 7 ESE	103
21	Burlington Fire Stn #5	104	12	Tryon	103
21	Charlotte Douglas Intl Arpt	104	12	Wilmington New Hanover County	103
21	Clinton 2 NE	104	23	Burlington Fire Stn #5	104
21	Gastonia	104	23	Charlotte Douglas Intl Arpt	104
21	Greenville	104	23	Clinton 2 NE	104

Annual Mean Maximum Temperature

	Highest			Lowest	
Rank	Station Name	°F	Rank	Station Name	°F
1	Hofmann Forest	74.9	1	Jefferson 2 E	63.2
2	Laurinburg	74.2	2	Asheville	66.6
3	Wilmington New Hanover County	73.9	3	Asheville Regional Arpt	66.9
4	Longwood	73.8	4	Waynesville 1 E	67.4
4	Southport 5 N	*73.8*	5	Bent Creek	67.5
6	Bayboro 3 E	*73.7*	5	Black Mountain 2 W	67.5
7	Hamlet	73.6	7	Reidsville 2 NW	68.6
8	New Bern Craven Co Reg Arpt	*73.1*	8	Danbury 1 NW	68.8
9	Sanford 8 NE	73.0	9	Greensboro-High Pt-Winston Salem	68.9
10	Cedar Island	72.6	10	Hickory Regional Arpt	69.4
11	Fayetteville	72.5	11	Roxboro 7 ESE	69.5
12	Clinton 2 NE	72.3	12	Yadkinville 6 E	69.7
12	Greenville	72.3	13	Cape Hatteras NWS Bldg	69.8
14	Monroe 4 SE	72.2	14	Siler City 2 N	70.0
15	Dunn 4 NW	72.0	15	Raleigh State Univ	70.3
15	Tarboro 1 S	72.0	16	Asheboro 2 W	70.4
17	Elizabeth City	71.9	17	Statesville 2 NNE	70.6
17	Gastonia	71.9	18	Chapel Hill 2 W	70.7
17	Raleigh 4 SW	71.9	18	Lincolnton 4 W	70.7
17	Wilson 3 SW	71.9	20	Forest City 6 SW	*70.9*
21	Arcola	*71.8*	21	Burlington Fire Stn #5	71.1
21	Concord	71.8	21	Raleigh-Durham Intl Arpt	71.1
23	Albemarle	71.7	23	Charlotte Douglas Intl Arpt	71.3
23	Aurora 6 N	71.7	23	High Point	71.3
25	Belhaven 5 SE	*71.6*	25	Louisburg	71.4

Rankings include 25 highest/lowest stations. If state has less than 25 stations, all stations are included. The period of record is 1980–2009. See User Guide for detailed explanation of data.

Annual Mean Temperature

Highest			Lowest		
Rank	Station Name	°F	Rank	Station Name	°F
1	Wilmington New Hanover County	63.8	1	Jefferson 2 E	51.3
2	Cedar Island	63.6	2	Waynesville 1 E	54.1
3	Cape Hatteras NWS Bldg	63.0	3	Black Mountain 2 W	55.4
4	Hofmann Forest	62.9	4	Bent Creek	55.5
4	Southport 5 N	62.9	5	Asheville Regional Arpt	55.9
6	New Bern Craven Co Reg Arpt	62.8	6	Asheville	56.4
7	Bayboro 3 E	62.7	6	Danbury 1 NW	56.4
8	Aurora 6 N	62.6	8	Roxboro 7 ESE	57.1
9	Laurinburg	62.5	9	Yadkinville 6 E	57.3
10	Longwood	62.2	10	Reidsville 2 NW	57.9
11	Belhaven 5 SE	61.6	11	Louisburg	58.0
12	Clinton 2 NE	61.4	12	Forest City 6 SW	58.2
12	Elizabeth City	61.4	12	Statesville 2 NNE	58.2
12	Greenville	61.4	14	Greensboro-High Pt-Winston Salem	58.6
15	Fayetteville	61.2	15	Arcola	58.8
16	Hamlet	61.0	16	Hickory Regional Arpt	58.9
16	Raleigh 4 SW	61.0	17	Chapel Hill 2 W	59.0
18	Gastonia	60.9	17	Siler City 2 N	59.0
19	Charlotte Douglas Intl Arpt	60.8	19	Lincolnton 4 W	59.2
19	Monroe 4 SE	60.8	20	Burlington Fire Stn #5	59.3
21	Dunn 4 NW	60.6	21	High Point	59.8
22	Wilson 3 SW	60.5	22	Asheboro 2 W	59.9
23	Tarboro 1 S	60.3	23	Salisbury	60.0
23	Tryon	60.3	24	Concord	60.1
25	Albemarle	60.2	25	Albemarle	60.2

Annual Mean Minimum Temperature

Highest			Lowest		
Rank	Station Name	°F	Rank	Station Name	°F
1	Cape Hatteras NWS Bldg	56.2	1	Jefferson 2 E	39.3
2	Cedar Island	54.6	2	Waynesville 1 E	40.8
3	Wilmington New Hanover County	53.6	3	Black Mountain 2 W	43.2
4	Aurora 6 N	53.3	4	Bent Creek	43.5
5	New Bern Craven Co Reg Arpt	52.4	5	Danbury 1 NW	44.0
6	Southport 5 N	51.9	6	Louisburg	44.6
7	Belhaven 5 SE	51.7	6	Roxboro 7 ESE	44.6
8	Bayboro 3 E	51.6	8	Asheville Regional Arpt	44.8
9	Elizabeth City	50.9	9	Yadkinville 6 E	45.0
10	Hofmann Forest	50.8	10	Forest City 6 SW	45.4
10	Laurinburg	50.8	11	Arcola	45.8
12	Longwood	50.5	11	Statesville 2 NNE	45.8
13	Charlotte Douglas Intl Arpt	50.4	13	Asheville	46.2
13	Greenville	50.4	14	Chapel Hill 2 W	47.2
15	Clinton 2 NE	50.3	14	Reidsville 2 NW	47.2
16	Raleigh 4 SW	50.1	16	Sanford 8 NE	47.4
16	Raleigh State Univ	50.1	17	Burlington Fire Stn #5	47.5
18	Gastonia	49.9	18	Lincolnton 4 W	47.6
19	Fayetteville	49.8	19	Siler City 2 N	47.9
20	Asheboro 2 W	49.5	20	High Point	48.2
21	Monroe 4 SE	49.2	21	Concord	48.3
21	Raleigh-Durham Intl Arpt	49.2	21	Greensboro-High Pt-Winston Salem	48.3
21	Tryon	49.2	23	Hamlet	48.4
24	Dunn 4 NW	49.1	23	Hickory Regional Arpt	48.4
25	Wilson 3 SW	49.0	23	Salisbury	48.4

Rankings include 25 highest/lowest stations. If state has less than 25 stations, all stations are included. The period of record is 1980–2009. See User Guide for detailed explanation of data.

Annual Extreme Minimum Temperature

	Highest				Lowest	
Rank	Station Name	°F		Rank	Station Name	°F
1	Cape Hatteras NWS Bldg	6		1	Waynesville 1 E	-22
2	Cedar Island	2		2	Asheville	-17
3	Wilmington New Hanover County	0		3	Asheville Regional Arpt	-16
4	Aurora 6 N	-1		3	Bent Creek	-16
4	Fayetteville	-1		5	Jefferson 2 E	-15
6	Clinton 2 NE	-2		6	Black Mountain 2 W	-14
6	Elizabeth City	-2		7	Siler City 2 N	-11
6	Hofmann Forest	-2		8	Belhaven 5 SE	-10
9	Laurinburg	-3		8	Danbury 1 NW	-10
9	Sanford 8 NE	-3		8	Louisburg	-10
9	Southport 5 N	-3		11	Raleigh-Durham Intl Arpt	-9
12	Bayboro 3 E	*-4*		11	Reidsville 2 NW	-9
12	Dunn 4 NW	-4		11	Roxboro 7 ESE	-9
12	Greenville	-4		14	Asheboro 2 W	-8
12	Longwood	-4		14	Chapel Hill 2 W	-8
12	New Bern Craven Co Reg Arpt	*-4*		14	Forest City 6 SW	*-8*
12	Salisbury	-4		14	Hickory Regional Arpt	-8
18	Charlotte Douglas Intl Arpt	-5		14	Greensboro-High Pt-Winston Salem	-8
18	Concord	-5		14	Tryon	-8
18	Gastonia	-5		14	Yadkinville 6 E	-8
18	Monroe 4 SE	-5		21	Arcola	*-7*
18	Tarboro 1 S	-5		21	High Point	-7
18	Wilson 3 SW	-5		21	Statesville 2 NNE	-7
24	Albemarle	-6		24	Albemarle	-6
24	Burlington Fire Stn #5	-6		24	Burlington Fire Stn #5	-6

July Mean Maximum Temperature

	Highest				Lowest	
Rank	Station Name	°F		Rank	Station Name	°F
1	Laurinburg	91.7		1	Jefferson 2 E	81.0
2	Hamlet	91.5		2	Waynesville 1 E	83.5
3	Sanford 8 NE	90.8		3	Asheville Regional Arpt	84.2
4	Hofmann Forest	90.5		4	Black Mountain 2 W	84.3
5	Concord	90.4		5	Bent Creek	84.4
6	Fayetteville	90.3		6	Asheville	84.8
6	Wilson 3 SW	90.3		7	Cape Hatteras NWS Bldg	85.5
8	Arcola	90.2		8	Danbury 1 NW	87.4
9	Burlington Fire Stn #5	90.1		9	Greensboro-High Pt-Winston Salem	87.7
9	Monroe 4 SE	90.1		9	Reidsville 2 NW	87.7
11	Greenville	90.0		11	Hickory Regional Arpt	87.8
11	Tarboro 1 S	90.0		12	Yadkinville 6 E	88.0
13	Clinton 2 NE	89.9		13	Roxboro 7 ESE	88.1
13	Gastonia	89.9		14	Asheboro 2 W	88.2
15	Forest City 6 SW	*89.7*		15	Belhaven 5 SE	*88.3*
15	Wilmington New Hanover County	89.7		16	Siler City 2 N	88.4
17	Albemarle	89.6		17	Lincolnton 4 W	88.5
17	Cedar Island	89.6		17	Tryon	88.5
17	Dunn 4 NW	89.6		19	Statesville 2 NNE	88.6
17	Louisburg	89.6		20	Raleigh State Univ	89.0
17	Raleigh-Durham Intl Arpt	89.6		21	Bayboro 3 E	89.1
22	New Bern Craven Co Reg Arpt	89.5		21	Raleigh 4 SW	89.1
23	Charlotte Douglas Intl Arpt	89.4		23	Southport 5 N	89.2
23	Salisbury	89.4		24	Aurora 6 N	89.3
25	Aurora 6 N	89.3		24	Chapel Hill 2 W	89.3

Rankings include 25 highest/lowest stations. If state has less than 25 stations, all stations are included. The period of record is 1980–2009. See User Guide for detailed explanation of data.

January Mean Minimum Temperature

	Highest				Lowest	
Rank	Station Name	°F		Rank	Station Name	°F
1	Cape Hatteras NWS Bldg	39.0		1	Jefferson 2 E	22.3
2	Cedar Island	36.6		2	Waynesville 1 E	23.6
3	Wilmington New Hanover County	35.6		3	Danbury 1 NW	25.0
4	Aurora 6 N	34.3		4	Louisburg	25.5
5	Bayboro 3 E	33.9		5	Roxboro 7 ESE	25.9
6	New Bern Craven Co Reg Arpt	*33.7*		6	Bent Creek	26.0
7	Hofmann Forest	*33.6*		6	Black Mountain 2 W	26.0
8	Southport 5 N	33.3		8	Yadkinville 6 E	26.3
9	Belhaven 5 SE	32.8		9	Arcola	*26.5*
9	Longwood	32.8		9	Forest City 6 SW	*26.5*
11	Elizabeth City	32.1		11	Asheville Regional Arpt	27.0
11	Laurinburg	32.1		11	Statesville 2 NNE	27.0
13	Raleigh 4 SW	31.9		13	Asheville	28.0
14	Greenville	31.8		14	Reidsville 2 NW	28.1
15	Charlotte Douglas Intl Arpt	31.6		15	Chapel Hill 2 W	28.3
15	Tryon	31.6		16	Burlington Fire Stn #5	28.6
17	Clinton 2 NE	31.4		17	Concord	28.8
18	Monroe 4 SE	31.1		18	Greensboro-High Pt-Winston Salem	29.0
19	Asheboro 2 W	31.0		18	Siler City 2 N	29.0
20	Fayetteville	30.9		20	Sanford 8 NE	29.2
20	Raleigh State Univ	30.9		21	Lincolnton 4 W	29.4
22	Gastonia	30.8		22	Hamlet	29.5
23	Raleigh-Durham Intl Arpt	30.5		22	Salisbury	29.5
24	Wilson 3 SW	30.3		22	Tarboro 1 S	29.5
25	Albemarle	30.2		25	Hickory Regional Arpt	29.6

Number of Days Annually Maximum Temperature ≥ 90°F

	Highest				Lowest	
Rank	Station Name	Days		Rank	Station Name	Days
1	Laurinburg	66		1	Jefferson 2 E	2
2	Hamlet	64		2	Waynesville 1 E	5
3	Hofmann Forest	57		3	Cape Hatteras NWS Bldg	6
4	Concord	55		4	Asheville Regional Arpt	9
4	Sanford 8 NE	55		4	Black Mountain 2 W	9
6	Wilson 3 SW	53		6	Bent Creek	11
7	Arcola	51		7	Asheville	12
7	Burlington Fire Stn #5	51		8	Danbury 1 NW	30
7	Clinton 2 NE	51		8	Greensboro-High Pt-Winston Salem	30
7	Fayetteville	51		10	Hickory Regional Arpt	32
11	Greenville	50		11	Lincolnton 4 W	33
11	Tarboro 1 S	50		11	Reidsville 2 NW	33
13	Louisburg	48		13	Asheboro 2 W	34
14	Gastonia	47		13	Belhaven 5 SE	34
14	Monroe 4 SE	47		15	Roxboro 7 ESE	35
14	Raleigh-Durham Intl Arpt	47		15	Siler City 2 N	35
17	Chapel Hill 2 W	45		15	Yadkinville 6 E	35
17	Dunn 4 NW	45		18	Southport 5 N	36
17	New Bern Craven Co Reg Arpt	*45*		19	Raleigh 4 SW	38
20	Albemarle	44		19	Tryon	38
20	High Point	44		21	Elizabeth City	39
20	Salisbury	44		21	Longwood	39
23	Charlotte Douglas Intl Arpt	43		21	Statesville 2 NNE	39
23	Forest City 6 SW	*43*		24	Aurora 6 N	41
23	Wilmington New Hanover County	43		25	Bayboro 3 E	*42*

Rankings include 25 highest/lowest stations. If state has less than 25 stations, all stations are included. The period of record is 1980–2009. See User Guide for detailed explanation of data.

Number of Days Annually Maximum Temperature ≤ 32°F

	Highest			Lowest	
Rank	Station Name	Days	Rank	Station Name	Days
1	Jefferson 2 E	12	1	Bayboro 3 E	*0*
2	Asheville	8	1	Hofmann Forest	0
3	Reidsville 2 NW	5	1	Longwood	0
3	Roxboro 7 ESE	5	1	New Bern Craven Co Reg Arpt	*0*
5	Asheboro 2 W	4	1	Southport 5 N	0
5	Asheville Regional Arpt	4	1	Wilmington New Hanover County	0
5	Bent Creek	4	7	Albemarle	1
5	Black Mountain 2 W	4	7	Aurora 6 N	1
5	Burlington Fire Stn #5	4	7	Belhaven 5 SE	1
5	Chapel Hill 2 W	4	7	Cape Hatteras NWS Bldg	1
5	Danbury 1 NW	4	7	Cedar Island	1
5	Hickory Regional Arpt	4	7	Charlotte Douglas Intl Arpt	1
5	Louisburg	4	7	Clinton 2 NE	1
5	Greensboro-High Pt-Winston Salem	4	7	Concord	1
5	Raleigh-Durham Intl Arpt	4	7	Dunn 4 NW	1
5	Raleigh State Univ	4	7	Elizabeth City	1
5	Siler City 2 N	4	7	Fayetteville	1
5	Waynesville 1 E	4	7	Gastonia	1
5	Yadkinville 6 E	4	7	Hamlet	1
20	Arcola	2	7	Laurinburg	1
20	Forest City 6 SW	*2*	7	Lincolnton 4 W	1
20	Greenville	2	7	Monroe 4 SE	1
20	High Point	2	7	Raleigh 4 SW	1
20	Statesville 2 NNE	2	7	Salisbury	1
20	Wilson 3 SW	2	7	Sanford 8 NE	1

Number of Days Annually Minimum Temperature ≤ 32°F

	Highest			Lowest	
Rank	Station Name	Days	Rank	Station Name	Days
1	Jefferson 2 E	134	1	Cape Hatteras NWS Bldg	21
2	Waynesville 1 E	120	2	Cedar Island	32
3	Bent Creek	105	3	Aurora 6 N	34
4	Danbury 1 NW	104	4	Wilmington New Hanover County	39
5	Louisburg	102	5	New Bern Craven Co Reg Arpt	*46*
6	Black Mountain 2 W	100	6	Belhaven 5 SE	50
6	Roxboro 7 ESE	100	7	Bayboro 3 E	*51*
8	Yadkinville 6 E	98	8	Southport 5 N	53
9	Statesville 2 NNE	94	9	Elizabeth City	57
10	Asheville Regional Arpt	93	10	Hofmann Forest	58
11	Forest City 6 SW	*89*	10	Laurinburg	58
12	Arcola	88	12	Charlotte Douglas Intl Arpt	59
13	Chapel Hill 2 W	84	12	Raleigh 4 SW	59
13	Sanford 8 NE	84	12	Tryon	59
15	Asheville	83	15	Raleigh State Univ	60
16	Burlington Fire Stn #5	80	16	Longwood	61
17	Hamlet	79	17	Clinton 2 NE	62
18	Reidsville 2 NW	78	17	Greenville	62
19	Concord	77	19	Gastonia	63
20	Siler City 2 N	76	20	Asheboro 2 W	64
21	Lincolnton 4 W	75	21	Fayetteville	67
21	Greensboro-High Pt-Winston Salem	75	21	Wilson 3 SW	67
21	Salisbury	75	23	Albemarle	70
24	Tarboro 1 S	74	23	Monroe 4 SE	70
25	High Point	73	23	Raleigh-Durham Intl Arpt	70

Rankings include 25 highest/lowest stations. If state has less than 25 stations, all stations are included. The period of record is 1980–2009. See User Guide for detailed explanation of data.

Number of Days Annually Minimum Temperature ≤ 0°F

	Highest			Lowest	
Rank	Station Name	Days	Rank	Station Name	Days
1	Jefferson 2 E	1	1	Albemarle	0
1	Waynesville 1 E	1	1	Arcola	0
3	Albemarle	0	1	Asheboro 2 W	0
3	Arcola	0	1	Asheville	0
3	Asheboro 2 W	0	1	Asheville Regional Arpt	0
3	Asheville	0	1	Aurora 6 N	0
3	Asheville Regional Arpt	0	1	Bayboro 3 E	*0*
3	Aurora 6 N	0	1	Belhaven 5 SE	0
3	Bayboro 3 E	*0*	1	Bent Creek	0
3	Belhaven 5 SE	0	1	Black Mountain 2 W	0
3	Bent Creek	0	1	Burlington Fire Stn #5	0
3	Black Mountain 2 W	0	1	Cape Hatteras NWS Bldg	0
3	Burlington Fire Stn #5	0	1	Cedar Island	0
3	Cape Hatteras NWS Bldg	0	1	Chapel Hill 2 W	0
3	Cedar Island	0	1	Charlotte Douglas Intl Arpt	0
3	Chapel Hill 2 W	0	1	Clinton 2 NE	0
3	Charlotte Douglas Intl Arpt	0	1	Concord	0
3	Clinton 2 NE	0	1	Danbury 1 NW	0
3	Concord	0	1	Dunn 4 NW	0
3	Danbury 1 NW	0	1	Elizabeth City	0
3	Dunn 4 NW	0	1	Fayetteville	0
3	Elizabeth City	0	1	Forest City 6 SW	*0*
3	Fayetteville	0	1	Gastonia	0
3	Forest City 6 SW	*0*	1	Greenville	0
3	Gastonia	0	1	Hamlet	0

Number of Annual Heating Degree Days

	Highest			Lowest	
Rank	Station Name	Num.	Rank	Station Name	Num.
1	Jefferson 2 E	5,344	1	Wilmington New Hanover County	2,395
2	Waynesville 1 E	4,485	2	Cedar Island	2,403
3	Bent Creek	4,193	3	Cape Hatteras NWS Bldg	2,442
4	Danbury 1 NW	4,180	4	Southport 5 N	*2,551*
5	Black Mountain 2 W	4,160	5	Hofmann Forest	*2,556*
6	Asheville Regional Arpt	4,115	6	Bayboro 3 E	*2,603*
7	Roxboro 7 ESE	4,031	7	New Bern Craven Co Reg Arpt	*2,658*
8	Asheville	4,028	8	Longwood	2,697
9	Yadkinville 6 E	3,924	9	Aurora 6 N	2,714
10	Reidsville 2 NW	3,837	10	Laurinburg	2,779
11	Louisburg	*3,810*	11	Belhaven 5 SE	*2,903*
12	Statesville 2 NNE	3,729	12	Elizabeth City	2,979
13	Forest City 6 SW	*3,692*	13	Clinton 2 NE	3,029
14	Greensboro-High Pt-Winston Salem	3,663	14	Greenville	3,036
15	Chapel Hill 2 W	3,586	15	Raleigh 4 SW	3,041
16	Arcola	*3,554*	16	Tryon	3,100
17	Siler City 2 N	3,552	17	Fayetteville	3,101
18	Hickory Regional Arpt	3,529	18	Gastonia	3,120
19	Burlington Fire Stn #5	3,526	18	Monroe 4 SE	3,120
20	Lincolnton 4 W	3,429	20	Charlotte Douglas Intl Arpt	3,122
21	Concord	3,379	21	Hamlet	3,127
22	High Point	3,340	22	Dunn 4 NW	3,197
23	Raleigh State Univ	3,312	23	Albemarle	3,242
24	Raleigh-Durham Intl Arpt	3,310	24	Wilson 3 SW	3,246
25	Salisbury	3,300	25	Sanford 8 NE	3,260

Rankings include 25 highest/lowest stations. If state has less than 25 stations, all stations are included. The period of record is 1980–2009. See User Guide for detailed explanation of data.

Number of Annual Cooling Degree Days

	Highest			Lowest	
Rank	Station Name	Num.	Rank	Station Name	Num.
1	Wilmington New Hanover County	2,057	1	Jefferson 2 E	439
2	Cedar Island	2,009	2	Waynesville 1 E	614
3	Laurinburg	1,979	3	Black Mountain 2 W	776
4	New Bern Craven Co Reg Arpt	1,955	4	Bent Creek	832
5	Aurora 6 N	1,930	5	Asheville Regional Arpt	892
6	Southport 5 N	1,888	6	Asheville	1,007
7	Hofmann Forest	1,885	7	Danbury 1 NW	1,148
8	Bayboro 3 E	1,851	8	Yadkinville 6 E	1,235
9	Cape Hatteras NWS Bldg	1,836	9	Roxboro 7 ESE	1,245
10	Greenville	1,827	10	Forest City 6 SW	1,303
11	Clinton 2 NE	1,804	11	Reidsville 2 NW	1,355
12	Fayetteville	1,803	11	Statesville 2 NNE	1,355
13	Belhaven 5 SE	1,779	13	Louisburg	1,364
14	Hamlet	1,778	14	Arcola	1,393
15	Longwood	1,772	15	Lincolnton 4 W	1,416
16	Elizabeth City	1,770	16	Hickory Regional Arpt	1,418
17	Gastonia	1,728	17	Greensboro-High Pt-Winston Salem	1,440
18	Charlotte Douglas Intl Arpt	1,713	18	Siler City 2 N	1,462
19	Wilson 3 SW	1,703	19	Tryon	1,488
20	Dunn 4 NW	1,693	20	Chapel Hill 2 W	1,506
21	Concord	1,686	21	Asheboro 2 W	1,541
22	Raleigh 4 SW	1,682	22	High Point	1,549
23	Monroe 4 SE	1,681	23	Burlington Fire Stn #5	1,552
24	Tarboro 1 S	1,678	24	Albemarle	1,590
25	Raleigh State Univ	1,676	25	Salisbury	1,593

Annual Precipitation

	Highest			Lowest	
Rank	Station Name	Inches	Rank	Station Name	Inches
1	Tryon	62.07	1	Asheville	36.87
2	Cape Hatteras NWS Bldg	57.73	2	Salisbury	41.03
3	Hofmann Forest	57.68	3	Charlotte Douglas Intl Arpt	41.70
4	Cedar Island	56.91	4	Greensboro-High Pt-Winston Salem	41.86
5	Wilmington New Hanover County	56.81	5	Gastonia	41.90
6	Southport 5 N	56.13	6	Raleigh-Durham Intl Arpt	43.26
7	Bayboro 3 E	55.20	7	Burlington Fire Stn #5	43.38
8	Longwood	53.14	8	Tarboro 1 S	44.02
9	New Bern Craven Co Reg Arpt	52.52	9	Statesville 2 NNE	44.06
10	Forest City 6 SW	50.84	10	Yadkinville 6 E	44.37
11	Greenville	49.46	11	Asheboro 2 W	45.12
12	Aurora 6 N	49.42	11	Roxboro 7 ESE	45.12
13	Clinton 2 NE	48.76	13	High Point	45.27
14	Belhaven 5 SE	48.55	14	Asheville Regional Arpt	45.62
15	Albemarle	48.15	15	Reidsville 2 NW	45.64
16	Elizabeth City	47.86	16	Louisburg	45.72
17	Hamlet	47.81	17	Jefferson 2 E	45.77
18	Waynesville 1 E	47.72	18	Concord	45.84
19	Bent Creek	47.68	18	Raleigh State Univ	45.84
20	Dunn 4 NW	47.62	20	Black Mountain 2 W	45.88
21	Lincolnton 4 W	47.37	20	Fayetteville	45.88
22	Chapel Hill 2 W	47.29	22	Laurinburg	46.15
23	Monroe 4 SE	47.18	23	Hickory Regional Arpt	46.16
24	Siler City 2 N	46.70	24	Danbury 1 NW	46.27
25	Wilson 3 SW	46.61	25	Sanford 8 NE	46.29

Rankings include 25 highest/lowest stations. If state has less than 25 stations, all stations are included. The period of record is 1980–2009. See User Guide for detailed explanation of data.

Annual Extreme Maximum Daily Precipitation

	Highest			Lowest	
Rank	Station Name	Inches	Rank	Station Name	Inches
1	Southport 5 N	*18.30*	1	Asheville	3.76
2	Wilmington New Hanover County	13.38	2	Asheville Regional Arpt	4.42
3	Longwood	12.85	3	Bent Creek	4.48
4	Greenville	10.75	4	Yadkinville 6 E	4.57
5	Clinton 2 NE	10.05	5	Greensboro-High Pt-Winston Salem	4.94
6	Black Mountain 2 W	10.00	6	Reidsville 2 NW	5.07
7	Wilson 3 SW	9.53	7	Burlington Fire Stn #5	5.15
8	Albemarle	*9.32*	8	Waynesville 1 E	5.25
9	Cedar Island	8.90	9	Asheboro 2 W	5.26
10	New Bern Craven Co Reg Arpt	*8.85*	10	Danbury 1 NW	5.27
11	Aurora 6 N	*8.82*	11	Jefferson 2 E	5.36
12	Concord	8.80	12	Elizabeth City	5.40
13	Cape Hatteras NWS Bldg	8.69	13	Lincolnton 4 W	5.46
14	Tryon	8.47	14	Laurinburg	5.58
15	Arcola	8.45	15	High Point	5.61
16	Fayetteville	8.25	16	Raleigh-Durham Intl Arpt	5.63
17	Monroe 4 SE	7.72	17	Tarboro 1 S	5.80
18	Chapel Hill 2 W	7.68	18	Bayboro 3 E	*5.83*
19	Louisburg	7.55	19	Salisbury	*5.90*
20	Dunn 4 NW	7.40	20	Statesville 2 NNE	6.02
20	Hofmann Forest	7.40	21	Raleigh State Univ	6.04
22	Belhaven 5 SE	6.90	22	Gastonia	6.10
23	Charlotte Douglas Intl Arpt	6.88	22	Hamlet	6.10
24	Roxboro 7 ESE	*6.78*	24	Sanford 8 NE	6.14
25	Raleigh 4 SW	6.72	25	Siler City 2 N	6.15

Number of Days Annually With ≥ 0.1 Inches of Precipitation

	Highest			Lowest	
Rank	Station Name	Days	Rank	Station Name	Days
1	Waynesville 1 E	90	1	Gastonia	68
2	Cedar Island	85	1	Salisbury	68
3	Tryon	84	3	Roxboro 7 ESE	69
4	Hofmann Forest	83	4	Burlington Fire Stn #5	70
5	New Bern Craven Co Reg Arpt	*82*	5	Charlotte Douglas Intl Arpt	71
6	Cape Hatteras NWS Bldg	81	6	Louisburg	72
6	Forest City 6 SW	*81*	6	Sanford 8 NE	72
8	Black Mountain 2 W	79	6	Tarboro 1 S	72
8	Hamlet	79	9	Dunn 4 NW	73
8	High Point	79	9	Raleigh-Durham Intl Arpt	73
8	Jefferson 2 E	79	11	Albemarle	74
12	Asheville Regional Arpt	78	11	Arcola	74
12	Bayboro 3 E	*78*	11	Asheboro 2 W	74
12	Greenville	78	11	Aurora 6 N	74
12	Longwood	78	11	Bent Creek	74
12	Wilmington New Hanover County	78	11	Concord	74
12	Yadkinville 6 E	78	11	Monroe 4 SE	74
18	Belhaven 5 SE	77	11	Raleigh State Univ	74
18	Chapel Hill 2 W	77	11	Siler City 2 N	74
18	Clinton 2 NE	77	11	Statesville 2 NNE	74
18	Wilson 3 SW	77	21	Asheville	75
22	Fayetteville	76	21	Danbury 1 NW	75
22	Hickory Regional Arpt	76	21	Elizabeth City	75
22	Lincolnton 4 W	76	21	Laurinburg	75
25	Asheville	75	21	Greensboro-High Pt-Winston Salem	75

Rankings include 25 highest/lowest stations. If state has less than 25 stations, all stations are included. The period of record is 1980–2009. See User Guide for detailed explanation of data.

Number of Days Annually With ≥ 0.5 Inches of Precipitation

	Highest			Lowest	
Rank	**Station Name**	**Days**	**Rank**	**Station Name**	**Days**
1	Tryon	38	1	Asheville	23
2	Wilmington New Hanover County	37	2	Gastonia	27
3	Cape Hatteras NWS Bldg	36	3	Burlington Fire Stn #5	28
3	Forest City 6 SW	*36*	3	Charlotte Douglas Intl Arpt	28
5	Cedar Island	35	3	Concord	28
5	New Bern Craven Co Reg Arpt	*35*	3	Greensboro-High Pt-Winston Salem	28
5	Southport 5 N	35	3	Raleigh-Durham Intl Arpt	28
8	Bayboro 3 E	*34*	3	Roxboro 7 ESE	28
8	Belhaven 5 SE	34	3	Salisbury	28
8	Hofmann Forest	34	3	Statesville 2 NNE	28
8	Lincolnton 4 W	34	11	Bent Creek	29
12	Albemarle	33	11	Jefferson 2 E	29
12	Chapel Hill 2 W	33	13	Asheville Regional Arpt	30
12	Greenville	33	13	Raleigh State Univ	30
12	Monroe 4 SE	33	13	Siler City 2 N	30
12	Waynesville 1 E	33	13	Tarboro 1 S	30
17	Asheboro 2 W	32	17	Arcola	31
17	Aurora 6 N	32	17	Black Mountain 2 W	31
17	Danbury 1 NW	32	17	Clinton 2 NE	31
17	Dunn 4 NW	32	17	Elizabeth City	31
17	Fayetteville	32	17	Hickory Regional Arpt	31
17	Hamlet	32	17	Laurinburg	31
17	High Point	32	17	Louisburg	31
17	Longwood	32	17	Reidsville 2 NW	31
17	Raleigh 4 SW	32	17	Wilson 3 SW	31

Number of Days Annually With ≥ 1.0 Inches of Precipitation

	Highest			Lowest	
Rank	**Station Name**	**Days**	**Rank**	**Station Name**	**Days**
1	Tryon	21	1	Asheville	10
2	Bayboro 3 E	*16*	2	Raleigh-Durham Intl Arpt	11
2	Cape Hatteras NWS Bldg	16	3	Asheboro 2 W	12
2	Cedar Island	16	3	Asheville Regional Arpt	12
2	Hofmann Forest	16	3	Bent Creek	12
2	Southport 5 N	16	3	Black Mountain 2 W	12
2	Wilmington New Hanover County	16	3	Burlington Fire Stn #5	12
8	Belhaven 5 SE	15	3	Chapel Hill 2 W	12
8	Dunn 4 NW	15	3	Charlotte Douglas Intl Arpt	12
8	Greenville	15	3	Concord	12
8	Longwood	15	3	Gastonia	12
8	New Bern Craven Co Reg Arpt	*15*	3	Hickory Regional Arpt	12
8	Wilson 3 SW	15	3	High Point	12
14	Arcola	14	3	Jefferson 2 E	12
14	Aurora 6 N	14	3	Greensboro-High Pt-Winston Salem	12
14	Clinton 2 NE	14	3	Raleigh 4 SW	12
14	Elizabeth City	14	3	Salisbury	12
14	Fayetteville	14	3	Siler City 2 N	12
14	Roxboro 7 ESE	14	3	Statesville 2 NNE	12
20	Albemarle	13	3	Waynesville 1 E	12
20	Danbury 1 NW	13	3	Yadkinville 6 E	12
20	Forest City 6 SW	*13*	22	Albemarle	13
20	Hamlet	13	22	Danbury 1 NW	13
20	Laurinburg	13	22	Forest City 6 SW	*13*
20	Lincolnton 4 W	13	22	Hamlet	13

Annual Snowfall

	Highest			Lowest	
Rank	Station Name	Inches	Rank	Station Name	Inches
1	Jefferson 2 E	14.4	1	Elizabeth City	0.1
2	Waynesville 1 E	13.5	2	Aurora 6 N	0.3
3	Asheville	12.6	3	Fayetteville	0.6
4	Asheville Regional Arpt	11.2	4	Gastonia	0.7
5	Yadkinville 6 E	8.7	5	Southport 5 N	0.8
6	Reidsville 2 NW	8.0	6	Hamlet	1.1
7	Black Mountain 2 W	7.9	7	Hofmann Forest	1.4
7	Danbury 1 NW	7.9	8	Longwood	1.7
9	Greensboro-High Pt-Winston Salem	7.6	9	Bayboro 3 E	1.8
10	Roxboro 7 ESE	6.9	9	Laurinburg	1.8
11	Lincolnton 4 W	6.3	9	Wilmington New Hanover County	1.8
12	Raleigh-Durham Intl Arpt	6.1	12	Louisburg	2.2
13	Arcola	5.9	13	Dunn 4 NW	2.3
13	Bent Creek	5.9	14	Sanford 8 NE	2.4
13	Tryon	5.9	14	Siler City 2 N	2.4
16	Asheboro 2 W	5.8	16	Cedar Island	2.5
17	Forest City 6 SW	5.6	17	Clinton 2 NE	2.6
18	Tarboro 1 S	5.3	18	Burlington Fire Stn #5	2.7
19	Chapel Hill 2 W	4.6	19	Albemarle	2.8
20	Charlotte Douglas Intl Arpt	4.5	20	Belhaven 5 SE	3.0
21	Statesville 2 NNE	4.4	20	Wilson 3 SW	3.0
22	Raleigh State Univ	4.1	22	Monroe 4 SE	3.3
23	Concord	3.9	23	Raleigh 4 SW	3.4
23	Greenville	3.9	24	High Point	3.5
25	High Point	3.5	24	Salisbury	3.5

Annual Maximum Snow Depth

	Highest			Lowest	
Rank	Station Name	Inches	Rank	Station Name	Inches
1	Jefferson 2 E	24	1	Aurora 6 N	Trace
2	Siler City 2 N	22	2	Elizabeth City	2
3	Asheville	20	3	Hofmann Forest	3
3	Raleigh-Durham Intl Arpt	20	4	Chapel Hill 2 W	6
5	Asheville Regional Arpt	18	5	Asheboro 2 W	8
5	Waynesville 1 E	18	5	Dunn 4 NW	8
7	Bent Creek	17	5	Southport 5 N	8
7	Sanford 8 NE	17	5	Statesville 2 NNE	8
9	Belhaven 5 SE	16	9	Albemarle	9
9	Greenville	16	9	Laurinburg	9
9	Tryon	16	9	Greensboro-High Pt-Winston Salem	9
9	Yadkinville 6 E	16	12	Burlington Fire Stn #5	10
13	Danbury 1 NW	15	12	Clinton 2 NE	10
13	High Point	15	12	Louisburg	10
15	Lincolnton 4 W	14	12	Salisbury	10
15	Raleigh State Univ	14	16	Concord	11
17	Charlotte Douglas Intl Arpt	13	16	Fayetteville	11
17	Forest City 6 SW	13	16	Gastonia	11
17	Reidsville 2 NW	13	16	Longwood	11
17	Roxboro 7 ESE	13	20	Arcola	12
17	Wilmington New Hanover County	13	20	Bayboro 3 E	12
22	Arcola	12	20	Black Mountain 2 W	12
22	Bayboro 3 E	12	20	Cedar Island	12
22	Black Mountain 2 W	12	20	Hamlet	12
22	Cedar Island	12	20	Monroe 4 SE	12

Rankings include 25 highest/lowest stations. If state has less than 25 stations, all stations are included. The period of record is 1980–2009. See User Guide for detailed explanation of data.

Number of Days Annually With ≥ 1.0 Inch Snow Depth

	Highest			Lowest	
Rank	Station Name	Days	Rank	Station Name	Days
1	Jefferson 2 E	9	1	Albemarle	*0*
2	Asheville	8	1	Aurora 6 N	0
3	Reidsville 2 NW	7	1	Bayboro 3 E	*0*
3	Waynesville 1 E	7	1	Belhaven 5 SE	0
5	Asheville Regional Arpt	6	1	Burlington Fire Stn #5	0
5	Greensboro-High Pt-Winston Salem	6	1	Cedar Island	0
5	Yadkinville 6 E	6	1	Chapel Hill 2 W	0
8	Bent Creek	5	1	Dunn 4 NW	0
8	Danbury 1 NW	*5*	1	Elizabeth City	0
8	Roxboro 7 ESE	5	1	Fayetteville	0
11	Arcola	4	1	Gastonia	0
11	Raleigh-Durham Intl Arpt	4	1	Greenville	0
11	Tryon	4	1	Hamlet	0
14	Charlotte Douglas Intl Arpt	3	1	Hofmann Forest	0
14	Concord	3	1	Longwood	0
14	Forest City 6 SW	*3*	1	Salisbury	*0*
14	Lincolnton 4 W	3	1	Siler City 2 N	0
14	Raleigh State Univ	3	1	Southport 5 N	0
19	Asheboro 2 W	2	1	Wilmington New Hanover County	0
19	Black Mountain 2 W	2	1	Wilson 3 SW	0
19	High Point	2	21	Clinton 2 NE	1
19	Monroe 4 SE	2	21	Laurinburg	1
19	Raleigh 4 SW	2	21	Louisburg	1
19	Statesville 2 NNE	2	21	Sanford 8 NE	1
25	Clinton 2 NE	1	21	Tarboro 1 S	1

Rankings include 25 highest/lowest stations. If state has less than 25 stations, all stations are included. The period of record is 1980–2009. See User Guide for detailed explanation of data.

Significant Storm Events in North Carolina: 2000 – 2009

Location or County	Date	Type	Mag.	Deaths	Injuries	Property Damage ($mil.)	Crop Damage ($mil.)
McDowell County	04/13/00	Fog	na	1	14	0.0	0.0
Northwest Piedmont Region	12/04/02	Ice Storm	na	0	0	100.0	0.0
Southwest Piedmont, Charlotte Metro Area	12/04/02	Ice Storm	na	0	0	99.0	0.0
Stanly	06/16/03	Flash Flood	na	5	0	0.0	0.0
Eastern North Carolina	09/17/03	Hurricane Isabel	na	0	0	435.6	14.2
Northeastern North Carolina	09/18/03	Hurricane Isabel	na	1	0	16.9	0.0
Northeast North Carolina	09/18/03	Hurricane Isabel	na	1	0	7.2	0.0
Bladen, Columbus, Pender and Robeson Co.	01/26/04	Ice Storm	na	0	0	13.0	0.0
Coastal Counties, and Outer Banks	08/03/04	Hurricane Alex	na	0	0	7.5	0.0
Pender	08/13/04	Tornado	F2	3	29	1.3	0.0
Bladen, Brunswick, Columbus, New Hanover, and Pender Counties	08/14/04	Hurricane Charley	na	0	3	10.4	2.5
Buncombe Co.	09/07/04	Flood	na	0	0	40.0	1.0
Avery, Burke, Caldwell, McDowell, Mitchell, and Yancey Counties	09/07/04	Flood	na	0	0	25.0	5.5
Haywood, Henderson and Transylvania Co.	09/07/04	Flood	na	0	0	10.5	11.5
Buncombe County	09/08/04	Landslide	na	0	0	10.0	0.0
Buncombe Co.	09/16/04	Flood	na	2	0	40.0	0.0
Haywood Co.	09/16/04	Flood	na	3	0	15.0	0.0
Madison County	09/16/04	Flood	na	0	0	8.0	0.9
Buncombe County	09/17/04	Landslide	na	0	0	10.0	0.0
Avery, Burke, Caldwell, McDowell, and Mitchell Counties	09/17/04	Flood	na	0	0	8.2	4.0
Southeast North Carolina	09/13/05	Hurricane Ophelia	na	0	5	42.1	11.5
Brunswick, New Hanover, and Pender Counties	09/14/05	Hurricane Ophelia	na	0	0	8.3	0.0
Columbus	11/16/06	Tornado	F3	8	20	0.5	0.0
Mecklenburg	08/27/08	Flash Flood	na	0	0	8.5	0.0

Note: Deaths, injuries, and damages are date and location specific.

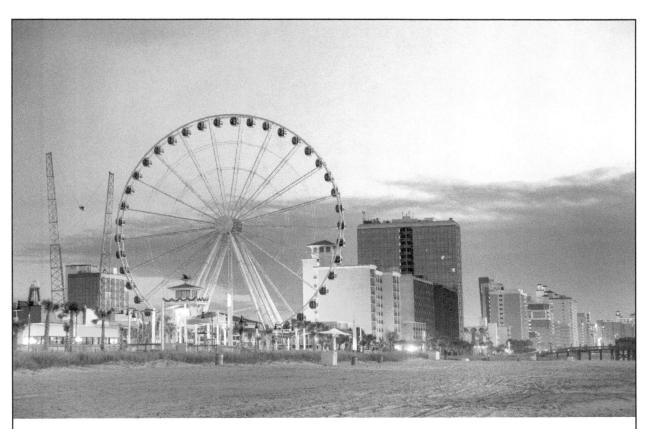

South Carolina

About South Carolina

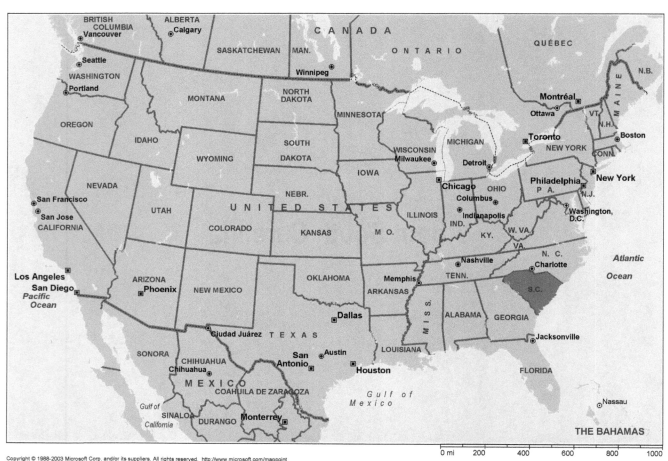

Governor	**Nimrata Nikki Randhawa Haley (R)**
Lt Governor	**Henry Dargan McMaster (R)**
State Capital	Columbia
Date of Statehood	May 23, 1788 (8th state)
Before Statehood	Province of South Carolina
State Nickname	The Palmetto State
Largest City	Columbia
Demonym	South Carolinian
Highest Point	Sassafras Mountain (3,560 feet)
Lowest Point	Atlantic Ocean (sea level)
Time Zone	Eastern
State American Folk Dance	Square Dance
State Amphibian	Spotted Salamander *(Ambystoma maculatum)*
State Animal	White-tailed Deer *(Odocoileus virginianus)*
State Beverage	Milk
State Bird	Carolina Wren *(Thryothorus ludovicianus)*
State Butterfly	Eastern Tiger Swallowtail *(Papilio glaucus)*
State Color	Indigo Blue
State Craft	Sweetgrass Basket Weaving
State Dance	Shag
State Dog	Boykin Spaniel
State Duck	Wood Duck *(Aix sponsa)*
State Fish	Striped Bass or Rockfish *(Morone saxatilis)*
State Flower	Yellow Jessamine *(Gelsemium sempervirens)*
State Fossil	Columbian Mammoth *(Mammuthus columbi)*
State Fruit	Peach *(Prunus persica)*
State Gemstone	Amethyst
State Grass	Indian Grass *(Sorghastrum nutans)*
State Heritage Horse	Carolina Marsh Tacky
State Heritage Work Animal	Mule
State Hospitality Beverage	Tea *(Camellia sinensis)*
State Insect	Carolina Mantid *(Stagmomantis Carolina)*
State Marine Mammal	Bottlenose Dolphin *(Tursiops truncatus)*
State Migratory Marine Mammal . .	Northern Right Whale *(Eubalaena glacialis)*
State Mottos	"While I breathe, I hope" *("Dum spiro spero")*, and
	"Ready in soul and resource" *("Animis opibusque parati")*
State Music	Spiritual
State Popular Music	Beach Music
State Reptile	Loggerhead Sea Turtle *(Caretta caretta)*
State Shell	Lettered Olive *(Oliva sayana)*
State Snack	Boiled Peanuts
State Songs	"Carolina" (1911) and "South Carolina On My Mind" (1984)
State Spider	Carolina Wolf Spider *(Hogna carolinensis)*
State Stone	Blue Granite
State Tapestry	"From the Mountains to the Sea"
State Tartan	The Carolina Tartan
State Tree	Sabal Palmetto *(Sabal palmetto)*
State Waltz	Richardson Waltz
State Wild Game Bird	Wild Turkey *(Meleagris gallopavo)*
State Wildflower	Goldenrod *(solidago altissima)*

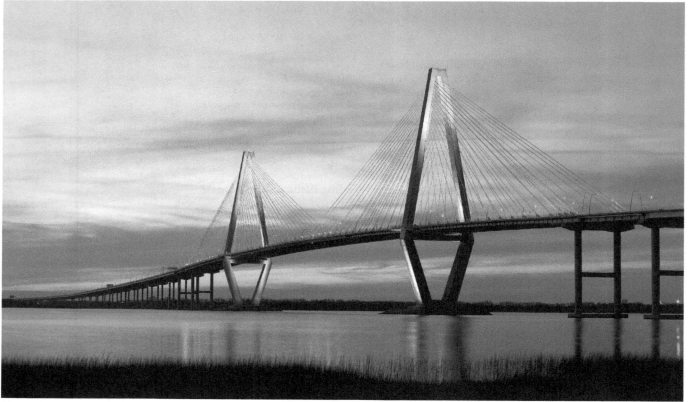

The South Carolina State House, pictured top, is located in the capital city of Columbia. Built in 1855 in the Greek Revival style, the building is both a National Historic Landmark, and on the National Registry of Historic Places. The bottom photo shows the Arthur Ravenel Jr. Bridge, connecting the cities of Charleston and Mount Pleasant. Crossing the Cooper River, this cable-stayed bridge opened in 2005 to replace two obsolete cantilever truss bridges.

The Federal style John A. Cuthbert House, built in 1811 in Beaufort, is typical of the city's gracious waterfront homes and part of the Beaufort Historic District. Originally built for Mary B. Williamson, wife of John Cuthbert, during the Civil War, the house became the property of US Army Brigadier General Rufus Saxon. It became a National Registry property in 1972.

The top photograph is of Fort Sumter, a sea fort located in Charleston. Now a National Monument with a Visitor Education Center, it is noted for two historic battles during the American Civil War. The skyline of Columbia is shown in the bottom photograph. It is the capital and largest city in the state, 13 miles northwest of the state's geographic center, and was named for Christopher Columbus.

History of South Carolina

Early History

Humans arrived in the area of South Carolina around 13,000 BC. These people were hunters with crude tools made from stones and bones. Around 10,000 BC, they used spears and hunted big game. Over the Archaic period of 8000 to 2000 BC, the people gathered nuts, berries, fish and shellfish as part of their diets. Trade between the coastal plain and the piedmont developed. There is evidence of plant domestication and pottery in the late Archaic. The Woodland period brought more serious agriculture, more sophisticated pottery, and the bow and arrow.

By the time of the first European exploration, twenty-nine tribes or nations of Native Americans, divided by major language families, lived within the boundaries of what became South Carolina. Algonquian-speaking tribes lived in the low country, Siouan and Iroquoian-speaking in the Piedmont and uplands, respectively.

Colonial Period

The Carolina Colonies

By the end of the 16th century, the Spanish and French had left the area of South Carolina after several reconnaissance missions, expeditions and failed colonization attempts, notably the French outpost of Charlesfort followed by the Spanish mission of Santa Elena on modern-day Parris Island between 1562 and 1587. In 1629, Charles I, King of England, granted his attorney general a charter to everything between latitudes 36 and 31. He called this land the Province of Carlana, which would later be changed to "Carolina" for pronunciation, after the Latin form of his own name.

In 1663, Charles II granted the land to eight Lords Proprietors in return for their financial and political assistance in restoring him to the throne in 1660. Charles II intended for the newly created Province of Carolina to serve as an English bulwark to contest lands claimed by Spanish Florida and prevent Spanish expansion northward. The eight nobles ruled the Province of Carolina as a proprietary colony. After the Yamasee War of 1715-1717, the Lords Proprietors came under increasing pressure from settlers and were forced to relinquish their charter to the Crown in 1719. The proprietors retained their right to the land until 1719, when the colony was officially split into the provinces of North Carolina and South Carolina as crown colonies.

In April 1670 settlers arrived at Albemarle Point, at the confluence of the Ashley and Cooper rivers. They founded Charles Town, named in honor of King Charles II. Throughout the Colonial Period, the Carolinas participated in many wars against the Spanish and the Native Americans, including the Yamasee and Cherokee tribes. In its first decades, the colony's plantations were relatively small and its wealth came from Indian trade, mainly in Indian slaves and deerskins.

The slave trade adversely affected tribes throughout the Southeast and exacerbated enmity and competition among some of them. Historians estimate that Carolinians exported 24,000-51,000 Indian slaves from 1670–1717, sending them to markets ranging from Boston in North America to the Barbados. Planters financed the purchase of African slaves by their sale of Indians, finding they were somewhat easier to control, as they did not know the territory for escape.

18th Century

In the 1700-1770 era, the colony possessed many advantages—entrepreneurial planters and businessmen, a major harbor, the expansion of cost-efficient African slave labor, and an attractive physical environment, with rich soil and a long growing season, albeit with endemic malaria. Planters established rice and indigo as commodity crops, based in developing large plantations, with long-staple cotton grown on the sea islands. As the demand for labor increased, planters imported increasing numbers of African slaves, and gradually they began to reproduce themselves, so that the majority of slaves in the colony came to be native-born. This became one of the wealthiest of the British colonies. Rich colonials became avid consumers of services from outside the colony, such as mercantile services, medical education, and legal training in England. Almost everyone in

18th-century South Carolina felt the pressures, constraints, and opportunities associated with the growing importance of trade.

Yemasee War

A pan-Indian alliance rose up against the settlers in the Yamasee War (1715–1717), in part due to tribes' opposition to the Indian slave trade. The Native Americans nearly destroyed the colony. But the colonists and Indian allies defeated the Yemasee and their allies, such as the Iroquoian-speaking Tuscarora people. The latter emigrated from the colony north to western New York state, where by 1722 they declared the migration ended. They were accepted as the sixth nation of the Iroquois Confederacy. Combined with exposure to European infectious diseases, the backcountry's Yemasee population was greatly reduced by the fierce warfare.

Slaves

After the Yamasee War, the planters turned exclusively to importing African slaves for labor. With the establishment of rice and indigo as commodity export crops, South Carolina became a slave society, with slavery central to its economy. By 1708 black slaves comprised a majority of the population in the colony; they comprised the majority of population in the state into the 20th century. Beginning about 1910, tens of thousands of blacks left the state in the Great Migration, traveling for work and other opportunities in the northern and midwestern industrial cities. Planters used slave labor to support cultivation and processing of rice and indigo as commodity crops. Building dams, irrigation ditches and related infrastructure, enslaved Africans created the equivalent of huge earthworks to regulate water for the rice culture.

Most of the slaves came from West Africa. In the Low Country, including the Sea Islands, where large populations of Africans lived together, they developed a creolized culture and language known as Gullah /Geechee (the latter a term used in Georgia). They interacted with and adopted some elements of the English language and colonial culture and language. The Gullah adapted to multiple factors in American society during the slavery years. Since the late nineteenth century, they have marketed or otherwise used their distinctive lifeways, products, and language to perpetuate their unique ethnic identity.

Low Country

The Low Country was settled first, dominated by wealthy English men who became owners of large amounts of land on which they created plantations. They first transported white indentured servants as laborers, mostly teenage youth from England who came to work off their passage in hopes of learning to farm and buying their own land. Planters also imported African laborers to the colony.

In the early colonial years, social boundaries were fluid between indentured laborers and slaves, and there was considerable intermarriage. Gradually the terms of enslavement became more rigid, and slavery became a racial caste. South Carolina used Virginia's model of declaring all children born to slave mothers as slaves, regardless of the race or nationality of the father. In the Upper South, there were many mixed-race slaves with white planter fathers. With a decrease in English settlers as the economy improved in England before the beginning of the 18th century, the planters began to rely chiefly on enslaved Africans for labor.

The market for land functioned efficiently and reflected both rapid economic development and widespread optimism regarding future economic growth. The frequency and turnover rate for land sales were tied to the general business cycle; the overall trend was upward, with almost half of the sales occurring in the decade before the American Revolution. Prices also rose over time, parallel with the rise in the price for rice. Prices dropped dramatically, however, in the years just before the war, when fears arose about future prospects outside the system of English mercantilist trade.

Back Country

In contrast to the Tidewater, the back country was settled later in the 18th century, chiefly by Scotch-Irish and North British migrants, who had quickly moved down from Pennsylvania and Virginia. The immigrants from Ulster, the Scottish lowlands and the north of England (the border counties) comprised the largest group from the British Isles before the Revolution. They came mostly in the 18th century, later than other colonial immigrants. Such "North Britons were a large majority in much of the South Carolina upcountry." The character of this environment was "well matched to the culture of the British borderlands."

They settled in the backcountry throughout the South and relied on subsistence farming. Mostly they did not own slaves. Given the differences in background, class, slave holding, economics, and culture, there was long-standing competition between the Low Country and Upcountry that played out in politics.

Rice

In the early period, planters earned wealth from two major crops: rice and indigo (see below), both of which relied on slave labor for their cultivation. Historians no longer believe that the blacks brought the art of rice cultivation from Africa, but they certainly contributed expertise. Exports of these crops led South Carolina to become one of the wealthiest colonies prior to the Revolution. Near the beginning of the 18th century, planters began rice culture along the coast, mainly in the Georgetown and Charleston areas. The rice became known as Carolina Gold, both for its color and its ability to produce great fortunes for plantation owners.

Indigo Production

In the 1740s, Eliza Lucas Pinckney began indigo culture and processing in coastal South Carolina. Indigo was in heavy demand in Europe for making dyes for clothing. An "Indigo Bonanza" followed, with South Carolina production approaching a million pounds (400 plus Tonnes) in the late 1750s. This growth was stimulated by a British bounty of six pence per pound.

South Carolina did not have a monopoly of the British market, but the demand was strong and many planters switched to the new crop when the price of rice fell. Carolina indigo had a mediocre reputation because Carolina planters failed to achieve consistent high quality production standards. Carolina indigo nevertheless succeeded in displacing French and Spanish indigo in the British and in some continental markets, reflecting the demand for cheap dyestuffs from manufacturers of low-cost textiles, the fastest-growing sectors of the European textile industries at the onset of industrialization.

In addition, the colonial economy depended on sales of pelts (primarily deerskins), and naval stores and timber. Coastal towns began shipbuilding to support their trade, using the prime timbers of the live oak.

Jews

South Carolina's liberal constitution and early flourishing trade attracted Sephardic Jewish immigrants as early as the 17th century. They were mostly elite businessmen from London and Barbados, where they had been involved in the rum and sugar trades. Many became slaveholders. In 1800, Charleston had the largest Jewish population of any city in the United States.

Revolutionary War

Prior to the American Revolution, the British began taxing American colonies to raise revenue. Residents of South Carolina were outraged by the Townsend Acts that taxed tea, paper, wine, glass, and oil. To protest the Stamp Act, South Carolina sent the wealthy rice planter Thomas Lynch, twenty-six-year-old lawyer John Rutledge, and Christopher Gadsden to the Stamp Act Congress, held in 1765 in New York. Other taxes were removed, but tea taxes remained. Soon residents of South Carolina, like those of the Boston Tea Party, began to dump tea into the Charleston Harbor, followed by boycotts and protests.

South Carolina set up its state government and constitution on March 26, 1776. Because of the colony's longstanding trade ties with Great Britain, the Low Country cities had numerous Loyalists. Many of the Patriot battles fought in South Carolina during the American Revolution were against loyalist Carolinians and the Cherokee Nation, which was allied with the British. This was to British General Henry Clinton's advantage, as his strategy was to march his troops north from St. Augustine and sandwich George Washington in the North. Clinton alienated Loyalists and enraged Patriots by attacking and nearly annihilating a fleeing army of Patriot soldiers who posed no threat.

White colonists were not the only ones with a desire for freedom. Estimates are that about 25,000 slaves escaped, migrated or died during the disruption of the war, 30 percent of the state's slave population. About 13,000 joined the British, who had promised them freedom if they left rebel masters and fought with them.

From 1770 to 1790, the proportion of the state's population made up of blacks (almost all of whom were enslaved), dropped from 60.5 percent to 43.8 percent.

On October 7, 1780, at Kings Mountain, John Sevier and William Campbell, assaulted the 'high heel' of the wooded mountain, the smallest area but highest point, while the other seven groups, led by Colonels Shelby, Williams, Lacey, Cleveland, Hambright, Winston and McDowell attacked the main Loyalist position by surrounding the 'ball' base beside the 'heel' crest of the mountain. North and South Carolinians attacked the British Major Patrick Ferguson and his body of Loyalists on a hilltop. This was a major victory for the Patriots, especially because it was won by militiamen and not trained Continentals. Thomas Jefferson called it, "The turn of the tide of success." It was the first Patriot victory since the British had taken Charleston.

While tensions mounted between the Crown and the Carolinas, some key southern Pastors became a target of King George: "...this church (Bullock Creek) was noted as one of the "Four Bees" in King George's bonnet due to its pastor, Rev. Joseph Alexander, preaching open rebellion to the British Crown in June 1780. Bullock Creek Presbyterian Church was a place noted for being a Whig party stronghold. Under a ground swell of such Calvin Protestant leadership, South Carolina moved from a back seat to the front in the war against tyranny. Patriots went on to regain control of Charleston and South Carolina with untrained militiamen by trapping Colonel Banastre "No Quarter" Tarleton's troops along a river.

In 1787, John Rutledge, Charles Pinckney, Charles Cotesworth Pinckney, and Pierce Butler went to Philadelphia where the Constitutional Convention was being held and constructed what served as a detailed outline for the U.S. Constitution. The federal Constitution was ratified by the state in 1787. The new state constitution was ratified in 1790 without the support of the Upcountry.

Scotch-Irish
During the American Revolution, the Scotch-Irish in the back country in most states were noted as strong patriots. One exception was the Waxhaw settlement on the lower Catawba River along the North Carolina-South Carolina boundary, where Loyalism was strong. The area had two main settlement periods of Scotch Irish. During the 1750s-1760s, second- and third-generation Scotch Irish Americans moved from Pennsylvania, Virginia, and North Carolina. This particular group had large families, and as a group they produced goods for themselves and for others. They generally were patriots.

In addition to these, The Earl of Donegal arrived in Charleston on December 22, 1767 from Belfast bringing approximately fifty families over who received land grants under the Bounty Act. Most of these families settled in the upstate. A portion of these eventually migrated into Georgia and on into Alabama.

Just prior to the Revolution, a second stream of immigrants came directly from northern Ireland via Charleston. Mostly poor, this group settled in an underdeveloped area because they could not afford expensive land. Most of this group remained loyal to the Crown or neutral when the war began. Prior to Charles Cornwallis's march into the backcountry in 1780, two-thirds of the men among the Waxhaw settlement had declined to serve in the army. British victory at the Battle of the Waxhaws resulted in anti-British sentiment in a bitterly divided region. While many individuals chose to take up arms against the British, the British forced the people to choose sides, as they were trying to recruit Loyalists for a militia.

Antebellum South Carolina

South Carolina led opposition to national law during the Nullification Crisis. It was the first state to declare its secession in 1860 in response to the election of Abraham Lincoln. Dominated by major planters, it was the only state in which slaveholders comprised a majority of the legislature.

Politics and Slavery
After the Revolutionary War, numerous slaves were freed. Most of the northern states abolished slavery, sometimes combined with gradual emancipation. In the Upper South, inspired by the revolutionary ideals and activist preachers , state legislatures passed laws making it easier for slaveholders to manumit their slaves both during their lifetimes or by wills. Quakers, Methodists and Baptists urged slaveholders to free their slaves. In

the period from 1790-1810, the proportion and number of free blacks rose dramatically in the Upper South and overall, from less than 1 percent to more than 10 percent.

Slave owners had more control over the state government of South Carolina than of any other state. Elite planters played the role of English aristocrats more than did the planters of other states. In the late antebellum years the newer Southern states, such as Alabama and Mississippi, allowed more political equality among whites. Although all white male residents were allowed to vote, property requirements for office holders were higher in South Carolina than in any other state. It was the only state legislature in which slave owners held the majority of seats. The legislature elected the governor, all judges and state electors for federal elections, as well as the US senators into the 20th century, so its members had considerable political power. The state's chief executive was a figurehead who had no authority to veto legislative law.

With its society disrupted by slave losses during the Revolution, South Carolina did not embrace manumission as readily as states of the Upper South. Most of its small number of free blacks were of mixed race, often the children of major planters or their sons and slave mothers. Their wealthy fathers sometimes passed on social capital to such mixed-race children, arranging for their manumission even if officially denying them as legal heirs. Fathers sometimes arranged to have their slave children educated, arranged apprenticeships in skilled trades, and other preparation for independent adulthood. Some planters sent their mixed-race slave children to schools and colleges in the North for education.

In the early 19th century, the state legislature passed laws making manumission more difficult. The manumission law of 1820 required slaveholders to gain legislative approval for each act of manumission and generally required other free adults to testify that the person to be freed could support himself. This meant that free people of color were thwarted from freeing their children if born into slavery. So, while some slaves were freed during this period and might earn enough to purchase relatives, they could not readily free them. The first law required that five citizens attest to the ability of the person proposed to be freed to earn a living; this prevented slaveholders from freeing their own children before they became adults. In 1820, the legislature ended personal manumissions, requiring all slaveholders to gain individual permission from the legislature before manumitting even family members.

The majority of the population in South Carolina was black, with concentrations in the plantation areas of the Low Country: by 1860 the population of the state was 703,620, with 57 percent or slightly more than 402,000 classified as enslaved African Americans. Free blacks numbered slightly less than 10,000. A concentration of free people of color lived in Charleston, where they formed an elite racial caste of people who had more skills and education than most blacks. Unlike Virginia, where most of the larger plantations and slaves were concentrated in the eastern part of the state, in South Carolina plantations and slaves became common throughout much of the state. After 1794, Eli Whitney's cotton gin allowed cotton plantations for short-staple cotton to be widely developed in the Piedmont area, which became known as the Black Belt.

By 1830, 85 percent of inhabitants of rice plantations in the Low Country were slaves. When rice planters left the malarial low country for cities such as Charleston during the social season, up to 98 percent of the Low Country residents were slaves. This led to a preservation of West African customs while developing the Creole culture known as Gullah. By 1830, two-thirds of South Carolina's counties had populations with 40 percent or more enslaved; even in the two counties with the lowest rates of slavery, 23 percent of the population were slaves.

In 1822, a black freedman named Denmark Vesey and compatriots around Charleston organized a plan for thousands of slaves to participate in an armed uprising to gain freedom. Vesey's plan, inspired by the 1791 Haitian Revolution, called for thousands of armed black men to kill their slaveholders, seize the city of Charleston, and escape from the United States by sailing to Haiti. The plot was discovered when two slaves opposed to the plan leaked word of it to white authorities. Charleston authorities charged 131 men with participating in the conspiracy. In total, the state convicted 67 men and killed 35 of them by hanging, including Denmark Vesey. White fear of slave insurrections after the Vesey conspiracy led to a 9:15 pm curfew for slaves in Charleston, and the establishment of a municipal guard of 150 white men in Charleston, with half the men stationed in an arsenal called the Citadel.

Plantations in older Southern states such as South Carolina wore out the soil to such an extent that 42 percent of state residents left the state for the lower South, to develop plantations with newer soil. The remaining South Carolina plantations were especially hard hit when worldwide cotton markets turned down in 1826-32 and again in 1837-49. Economic hardships caused many South Carolinians to believe that a "Forty Bale theory" explained their problems.

Nullification
The white minority in South Carolina felt more threatened than in other parts of the South, and reacted more to the economic Panic of 1819, the Missouri Controversy of 1820, and attempts at emancipation in the form of the Ohio Resolutions of 1824 and the American Colonization Petition of 1827. South Carolina's first attempt at nullification occurred in 1822, when South Carolina adopted a policy of jailing foreign black sailors at South Carolina ports. This policy violated a treaty between the United Kingdom and the United States, but South Carolina defied a complaint from Britain through American Secretary of State John Quincy Adams and a United States Supreme Court justice's federal circuit decision condemning the jailings. Foreign blacks from Santo Domingo previously communicated with Vesey's conspirators, and the South Carolina state Senate declared that the need to prevent insurrections was more important than laws, treaties or constitutions.

South Carolinian George McDuffie popularized the "Forty Bale theory" to explain South Carolina's economic woes. He said that tariffs that became progressively higher in 1816, 1824 and 1828 had the same effect as if a thief stole forty bales out of a hundred from every barn. The tariffs applied to imports of goods such as iron, wool and finished cotton products. The Forty Bale theory was based on faulty math, as Britain could sell finished cotton goods made from Southern raw cotton around the world, not just to the United States. Still, the theory was a popular explanation for economic problems that were caused in large part by overproduction of cotton in the Deep South competing with South Carolina's declining crops because of its depleted soil. South Carolinians, rightly or wrongly, blamed the tariff for the fact that cotton prices fell from 18 cents a pound to 9 cents a pound during the 1820s.

While the effects of the tariff were exaggerated, manufactured imports from Europe were cheaper than American-made products without the tariff, and the tariff did reduce British imports of cotton to some extent. These were largely short-term problems that existed before United States factories and textile makers could compete with Europe. Also, the tariff replaced a tax system where slave states previously had to pay more in taxes for the increased representation they got in the U.S. House of Representatives under the three-fifths clause.

The Tariff of 1828, which South Carolina agitators called the Tariff of Abominations, set the tariff rate at 50 percent. Although John C. Calhoun previously supported tariffs, he anonymously wrote the South Carolina Exposition and Protest, which was a states' rights argument for nullifying the tariff. Calhoun's theory was that the threat of secession would lead to a "concurrent majority" that would possess every white minority's consent, as opposed to a "tyrannical majority" of Northerners controlling the South. Both Calhoun and Robert Barnwell Rhett foresaw that the same arguments could be used to defend slavery when necessary.

President Andrew Jackson successfully forced the nullifiers to back down and allowed a gradual reduction of tariff rates. Calhoun and Senator Henry Clay agreed upon the Compromise Tariff of 1833, which would lower rates over 10 years. Calhoun later supported national protection for slavery in the form of the Fugitive Slave Law of 1850 and federal protection of slavery in the territories conquered from Mexico, in contradiction to his previous support for nullification and states' rights.

Censorship and Slavery
On July 29, 1835, Charleston Postmaster Alfred Huger found abolitionist literature in the mail, and refused to deliver it. Slave owners seized the mail and built a bonfire with it, and other Southern states followed South Carolina's lead in censoring abolitionist literature. South Carolina's James Henry Hammond started the gag rule controversy by demanding a ban on petitions for ending slavery from being introduced before Congress in 1835. The 1856 caning of Republican Charles Sumner by the South Carolinian Preston Brooks after Sumner's Crime Against Kansas speech heightened Northern fears that the alleged aggressions of the slave power threatened republican government for Northern whites.

Secession and War

South Carolina was the first state to secede from the Union after the election of Abraham Lincoln in 1860. South Carolina adopted the Declaration of the Immediate Causes Which Induce and Justify the Secession of South Carolina from the Federal Union on December 20, 1860. All of the violations of the alleged rights of Southern states mentioned in the document were about slavery. President Buchanan protested but made no military response aside from a failed attempt to resupply Fort Sumter via the ship Star of the West, which was fired upon by South Carolina forces and turned back before it reached the fort.

American Civil War

Prewar Tensions

Few white South Carolinians considered abolition of slavery as an option. Having lived as a minority among the majority-black slaves, they feared that, if freed, the slaves would try to "Africanize" the whites' cherished society and culture. This was what they believed had happened after slave revolutions in Haiti, in which numerous whites and free people of color were killed during the revolution. South Carolina's white politicians were divided between devoted Unionists who opposed any sort of secession, and those who believed secession was a state's right.

John C. Calhoun noted that the dry and barren West could not support a plantation system and would remain without slaves. Calhoun proposed that Congress should not exclude slavery from territories but let each state choose for itself whether it would allow slaves within its borders. After Calhoun's death in 1850, however, South Carolina was left without a leader great enough in national standing and character to prevent action by those more militant South Carolinian factions who wanted to secede immediately. Andrew Pickens Butler argued against Charleston publisher Robert Barnwell Rhett, who advocated immediate secession and, if necessary, independence. Butler won the battle, but Rhett outlived him.

When people began to believe that Abraham Lincoln would be elected President, states in the Deep South organized conventions to discuss their options. South Carolina was the first state to organize such a convention, meeting in December following the national election. On December 20, 1860, delegates convened in Charleston and voted unanimously to secede from the Union. President James Buchanan declared the secession illegal, but did not act to stop it. The first six states to secede with the largest slaveholding states in the South, demonstrating that the slavery societies were an integral part of the secession question.

Fort Sumter

On February 4, a seven seceded states approved a new constitution for the Confederate States of America. Lincoln argued that the United States were "one nation, indivisible," and denied the Southern states' right to secede. South Carolina entered the Confederacy on February 8, 1861, thus ending fewer than six weeks of being an independent State of South Carolina. Meanwhile Major Robert Anderson, commander of the U.S. troops in Charleston, withdrew his men into the small island fortress of Fort Sumter in Charleston Harbor and raised the U.S. flag. Fort Sumter was vastly outgunned by shore batteries and was too small to be a military threat but it had high symbolic value. In a letter delivered January 31, 1861, South Carolina Governor Pickens demanded of President Buchanan that he surrender Fort Sumter because, "I regard that possession is not consistent with the dignity or safety of the State of South Carolina." Buchanan refused. Lincoln was determined to hold it to assert national power and prestige; he wanted the Confederacy to fire the first shot. If it was to be a dignified independent nation the Confederacy could not tolerate a foreign fort in its second largest harbor.

About 6,000 Confederate men were stationed around the rim of the harbor, ready to take on the 60 men in Fort Sumter. At 4:30 a.m. on April 12, after two days of fruitless negotiations, and with Union ships just outside the harbor, the Confederates opened fire on orders from President Jefferson Davis. Edmund Ruffin had the honor firing the first shot. Thirty-four hours later, Anderson's men raised the white flag and were allowed to leave the fort with colors flying and drums beating, saluting the U.S. flag with a 50-gun salute before taking it down. During this salute, one of the guns exploded, killing a young soldier—the only casualty of the bombardment and the first casualty of the war. In a mass frenzy North and South men rushed to enlist, as Lincoln called up troops to recapture the fort.

Civil War Devastates the State

The South was at a disadvantage in number, weaponry, and maritime skills—few southerners were sailors. Federal ships sailed south and blocked off one port after another. As early as November, Union troops occupied the Sea Islands in the Beaufort area, and established an important base for the men and ships that would obstruct the ports at Charleston and Savannah. Many plantation owners had already fled to distant interior refuges, sometimes taking their slaves with them.

Those African Americans who remained on the Sea Islands became the first "freedmen" of the war. Undder military supervision, the Sea Islands became a laboratory for education, with Northern missionary teachers finding former enslaved adults as well as children eager for learning. The supervisors assigned plots of plantation land to individual freedmen households, who began to do subsistence farming, generally of food crops and cotton or rice.

Despite South Carolina's important role, and the Union's unsuccessful attempt to take Charleston from 1863 onward, few military engagements occurred within the state's borders until 1865. Having completed his March to the Sea at Savannah in 1865, Union General Sherman took his Army to Columbia, then north into North Carolina. There was little resistance to his advance. South Carolina suffered the worst devastation during the March, as many of Sherman's troops were particularly angry at the state and its citizens, who they blamed for starting the war. Sherman's 1865 march through the Carolinas resulted in the burning of the capital of Columbia and numerous other towns.

On February 21, 1865, with the Confederate forces finally evacuated from Charleston, the black 54th Massachusetts Regiment, led by Thomas Baker, Albert Adams, David Adams, Nelson R. Anderson, William H. Alexander, Beverly Harris, Joseph Anderson, Robert Abram, Elijah Brown, Wiley Abbott, marched through the city. At a ceremony at which the U.S. flag was raised over Fort Sumter, former fort commander Robert Anderson was joined on the platform by two African Americans: Union hero Robert Smalls, who had piloted a Confederate ship to Union lines, and the son of Denmark Vesey.

Continuing to rely on agriculture in a declining market, landowners in the state struggled with the change to free labor, as well as the aftermath of the war's destruction. There was an agricultural depression and deep financial recession in 1873, and changes in the labor market disrupted agriculture. South Carolina lost proportionally more of its young men of fighting age than did any other Southern state. Recorded deaths were 18,666 but fatalities may have reached 21,146. This was 31-35% of the total of white men of ages 18–45 recorded in the 1860 census for South Carolina. As with other military forces, most of the men died of disease rather than being wounded in battle.

Reconstruction 1865–1877

African Americans had long comprised the majority of the state's population but in 1860, only 2 percent of the state's black population were free; most were mulattos or free people of color, with ties of kinship to white families. They were well established as more educated and skilled artisans in Charleston and some other cities despite social restrictions, and sometimes as landowners and slaveholders. As a result, free people of color before the war became important leaders in the South Carolina government during Reconstruction; they made up 26 percent of blacks elected to office in the state between 1868 and 1876 and played important roles in the Republican Party, prepared by their education, skills and experiences before the war.

Despite the anti-Northern fury of prewar and wartime politics, most South Carolinians, including the state's leading opinion-maker, Wade Hampton III, believed that white citizens would do well to accept President Johnson's terms for full reentry to the Union. However, the state legislature, in 1865, passed "Black Codes" to control the work and movement of freedmen. This angered Northerners, who accused the state of imposing semi-slavery on the freedmen. The South Carolina Black Codes have been described:

> Persons of color contracting for service were to be known as "servants", and those with whom
> they contracted, as "masters." On farms the hours of labor would be from sunrise to sunset
> daily, except on Sunday. The negroes were to get out of bed at dawn. Time lost would be

deducted from their wages, as would be the cost of food, nursing, etc., during absence from sickness. Absentees on Sunday must return to the plantation by sunset. House servants were to be at call at all hours of the day and night on all days of the week. They must be "especially civil and polite to their masters, their masters' families and guests", and they in return would receive "gentle and kind treatment." Corporal and other punishment was to be administered only upon order of the district judge or other civil magistrate. A vagrant law of some severity was enacted to keep the negroes from roaming the roads and living the lives of beggars and thieves.

The Black Codes outraged northern opinion and apparently were never put into effect in any state.

Republican Rule

After winning the 1866 elections, the Radical Republicans took control of the Reconstruction process. The Army registered all male voters, and elections returned a Republican government composed of a coalition of freedmen, carpetbaggers, and scalawags. By a constitutional convention, new voters created the constitution of 1868; this brought democratic reforms to the state, including its first public school system. Native white Republicans supported it, but white Democrats viewed the Republican government as representative of black interests only and were largely unsupportive.

Adding to the interracial animosity was the sense of many whites that their former slaves had betrayed them. Before the war, slaveholders had convinced themselves that they were treating their slaves well and had earned their slaves' loyalty. When the Union Army rolled in and slaves deserted by the thousands, slaveholders were stunned. The black population scrambled to preserve its new rights while the white population attempted to claw its way back up the social ladder by denying blacks those same rights and reviving white supremacy.

The Ku Klux Klan raids began shortly after the end of the war, as a first stage of insurgency. Secret chapters had members who terrorized and murdered blacks and their sympathizers in an attempt to reestablish white supremacy. These raids were particularly prevalent in the upstate and they reached a climax in 1870-71. Congress passed a series of Enforcement Acts aimed at curbing Klan activity, and the Grant administration eventually declared martial law in the upstate counties of Spartanburg, York, Marion, Chester, Laurens, Newberry, Fairfield, Lancaster, and Chesterfield in October 1870.

The declaration was followed by mass arrests and a series of Congressional hearings to investigate the violence in the region. Though the federal program resulted in over 700 indictments, there were few successful prosecutions, and many of those individuals later received pardons. The ultimate weakness of the response helped to undermine federal authority in the state, though formal Klan activity declined precipitously following federal intervention. The violence in the state did not subside, however. New insurgent groups formed as paramilitary units and rifle clubs who operated openly in the 1870s to disrupt Republican organizing and suppress black voting; such groups included the Red Shirts, as of 1874, and their violence killed more than 100 blacks during the political season of 1876.

Spending and Debt

A major Theme of conservative opposition to Republican state government was the escalating state that, and the rising taxes paid by a white population that was much poorer than before the war. Much of the state money had been squandered or wasted. Simkins and Woody say that, "The state debt increased rapidly, interest was seldom paid, and credit of the state was almost wiped out; yet with one or two exceptions the offenders were not brought to justice."

Reconstruction government established public education for the first time, and new charitable institutions, together with improved prisons. There was corruption, but it was mostly white Southerners who benefited, particularly by investments to develop railroads and other infrastructure. Taxes had been exceedingly low before the war because the planter class refused to support programs such as education welfare. The exigencies of the postwar period caused the state debt to climb rapidly. When Republicans came to power in 1868, the debt stood at $5.4 million. By the time Republicans lost control in 1877, state debt had risen to $18.5 million.

The 1876 Gubernatorial Election

From 1868 on, elections were accompanied by increasing violence from white paramilitary groups such as the Red Shirts. Because of the violence in 1870, Republican Governor Chamberlain requested assistance from Washington to try to keep control. President Ulysses S. Grant sent federal troops to try to preserve order and ensure a fair election.

Using as a model the "Mississippi Plan," which had redeemed that state in 1874, South Carolina whites used intimidation, violence, persuasion, and control of the blacks. In 1876, tensions were high, especially in Piedmont towns where the numbers of blacks were fewer than whites. In these counties, blacks sometimes made up a narrow majority. There were numerous demonstrations by the Red Shirts—white Democrats determined to win the upcoming elections by any means possible. The Red Shirts turned the tide in South Carolina, convincing whites that this could indeed be the year they regain control and terrorizing blacks to stay away from voting, due to incidents such as the Hamburg Massacre in July, the Ellenton riots in October, and other similar events in Aiken County and Edgefield District. Armed with heavy pistols and rifles, they rode on horseback to every Republican meeting, and demanded a chance to speak. The Red Shirts milled among the crowds. Each selected a black man to watch, privately threatening to shoot him if he raised a disturbance. The Redeemers organized hundreds of rifle clubs. Obeying proclamations to disband, they sometimes reorganized as missionary societies or dancing clubs—with rifles.

They set up an ironclad economic boycott against Black activists and scalawags who refused to vote the Democratic ticket. People lost jobs over their political views. They beat down the opposition—but always just within the law. In 1876 Wade Hampton made more than forty speeches across the state. Some Black Republicans joined his cause; donning the Red Shirts, they paraded with the whites.

On election day, there was intimidation and fraud on all sides, employed by both parties. Edgefield and Laurens counties had more votes for Democratic candidate Wade Hampton III than the total number of registered voters in either county. The returns were disputed all the way to Washington, where they played a central role in the Compromise of 1877. Both parties claimed victory. For a while, two separate state assemblies did business side by side on the floor of the State House (their Speakers shared the Speaker's desk, but each had his own gavel), until the Democrats moved to their own building. There the Democrats continued to pass resolutions and conducted the state's business, just as the Republicans were doing. The Republican State Assembly tossed out results of the tainted election and reelected Chamberlain as governor. A week later, General Wade Hampton III took the oath of office for the Democrats.

Finally, in return for the South's support of his own convoluted presidential "victory" over Samuel Tilden, President Rutherford B. Hayes withdrew federal troops from Columbia and the rest of the South in 1877. The Republican government dissolved and Chamberlain headed north, as Wade Hampton and his Redeemers took control.

Memory

Whites and blacks in South Carolina developed different memories of Reconstruction and used them to justify their politics. James Shepherd Pike, a prominent Republican journalist, visited the state in 1873 and wrote accounts that were widely reprinted and published as a book, The Prostrate State (1874). Historian Eric Foner writes:

> The book depicted a state engulfed by political corruption, drained by governmental extravagance, and under the control of "a mass of black barbarism." The South's problems, he insisted, arose from "Negro government." The solution was to restore leading whites to political power.

Similar views were developed in scholarly monographs by academic historians of the Dunning School based at Columbia University in the early 20th century; they served as historians at major colleges in the South, influencing interpretation of Reconstruction into the 1960s. They argued that corrupt Yankee carpetbaggers controlled for financial profit the mass of ignorant black voters and nearly plunged South Carolina into economic ruin and social chaos. The heroes in this version were the Red Shirts: white paramilitary insurgents who, beginning in 1874, rescued the state from misrule and preserved democracy, expelled blacks from the

public square by intimidation during elections, restored law and order, and created a long era of comity between the races.

The black version, beginning with W.E.B. Du Bois' Black Reconstruction (1935), examines the period more objectively and notes its achievements in establishing public school education, and numerous social and welfare institutions to benefit all the citizens. Other historians also evaluated Reconstruction against similar periods. Their work provided intellectual support for the Civil Rights Movement.

In the 1980s, social battles over the display of the Confederate flag following the achievements of the African American Civil Rights Movement were related to these differing interpretations and the blacks' nearly century of struggle to regain the exercise of constitutional rights lost to Conservative Democrats after Reconstruction.

Conservative Rule 1877–1890

The Democrats were led by General Wade Hampton III and other former Confederate veterans who espoused a return to the policies of the antebellum period. Known as the Conservatives, or the Bourbons, they favored a minimalist approach by the government and a conciliatory policy towards blacks while maintaining white supremacy. Also of interest to the Conservatives was the restoration of the University of South Carolina to its prominent prewar status as the leading institution of higher education in the state and the region. They closed the college before passing a law to restrict admission to whites only. The legislature designated Claflin College for higher education for blacks. (The Reconstruction legislature had opened the college to blacks and established supplemental programs to prepare them for study.)

Once in power, the Democrats quickly consolidated their position and sought to unravel the legacy of the Radical Republicans. They pressured Republicans to resign from their positions, which included violence and intimidation by members of the Red Shirts, a paramilitary group described the historian George Rabe as the "military arm of the Democratic Party," who also worked to suppress black voting. Within a year both the legislative and judiciary were firmly in the control of the Democrats. The Democrats launched investigations into the corruption and frauds committed by Republicans during Reconstruction. They dropped the charges when the Federal government dropped its charges against whites accused of violence in the 1876 election campaign.

With their position secure, the Democrats next tackled the state debt. Many Democrats from the upcountry, led by General Martin Gary, who had developed the Edgefield Plan for targeted violence to take back the state, pushed for the entire state debt to be canceled, but Gary was opposed by Charleston holders of the bonds. A compromise moderated by Wade Hampton was achieved and by October 1882, the state debt was reduced to $6.5 million.

Other legislative initiatives by the Conservatives benefited its primary supporters, the planters and business class. Taxes across the board were reduced, and funding was cut for public social and educational programs that assisted poor whites and blacks. Oral contracts were made to be legally binding, breach of contract was enforced as a criminal offense, and those in debt to planters could be forced to work off their debt. In addition, the University of South Carolina along with The Citadel were reopened to elite classes and generously supported by the state government.

By the late 1880s, the agrarian movement swept through the state and encouraged subsistence farmers to assert their political rights. They pressured the legislature to establish an agriculture college. Reluctantly the legislature complied by adding an agriculture college to the University of South Carolina in 1887. Ben Tillman inspired the farmers to demand a separate agriculture college isolated from the politics of Columbia. The Conservatives finally gave them one in 1889.

Tillman Era and Disfranchisement, 1890–1914

n 1890, Ben Tillman set his sights on the gubernatorial contest. The farmers rallied behind his candidacy and Tillman easily defeated the conservative nominee, A.C. Haskell. The conservatives failed to grasp the strength

of the farmers' movement in the state. The planter elite no longer engendered automatic respect for having fought in the Civil War. Not only that, but Tillman's "humorous and coarse speech appealed to a majority no more delicate than he in matters of taste."

The Tillman movement succeeded in enacting a number of Tillman's proposals and pet projects. Among those was the crafting of a new state constitution and a state dispensary system for alcohol. Tillman held a "pathological fear of Negro rule." White elites created a new constitution with provisions to suppress voting by blacks and poor whites following the 1890 model of Mississippi, which had survived an appeal to the US Supreme Court.

They followed what was known as the Mississippi Plan, which had survived a US Supreme Court challenge. Disfranchisement was chiefly accomplished through provisions related to making voter registration more difficult, such as poll taxes and literacy tests, which in practice adversely affected African Americans and poor whites. After promulgation of the new Constitution of 1895, voting was essentially restricted to whites for more than 60 years, establishing a one-party Democratic state. White Democrats benefited by controlling the total Congressional apportionment based on total state population, although the number of voters had been drastically reduced. Blacks were excluded from the political system in every way, including excluded from juries and serving in local offices.

During Reconstruction, black legislators had been a majority in the lower house of the legislature. The new requirements, applied under white authority, led to only about 15,000 of the 140,000 eligible blacks qualifying to register. In practice, many more blacks were prohibited from voting by the subjective voter registration process controlled by white registrars. In addition, the Democratic Party primary was restricted to whites only. By October 1896 there were 50,000 whites registered, but only 5,500 blacks, in a state in which blacks were the majority.

The 1900 census demonstrated the extent of disfranchisement: African Americans comprised more than 58% of the state's population, with a total of 782,509 citizens, who were essentially without any representation. The political loss affected educated and illiterate men alike. It meant that without their interests represented, blacks were unfairly treated within the state. They were unable to serve on juries; segregated schools and services were underfunded; law enforcement was dominated by whites. African Americans did not recover the ability to exercise suffrage and political rights until the Civil Rights Movement won passage of Federal legislation in 1964 and 1965.

The state Dispensary, described as "Ben Tillman's Baby", was never popular in the state, and violence broke out in Darlington over its enforcement. In 1907, the Dispensary Act was repealed. In 1915, the legal sale of alcohol was prohibited by referendum.

Tillman's influence on the politics of South Carolina began to wane after he was elected by the legislature to the U.S. Senate in 1895. The Conservatives recaptured the legislature in 1902. The elite planter, Duncan Clinch Heyward, won the gubernatorial election. He made no substantial changes and Heyward continued to enforce the Dispensary Act at great difficulty. The state continued its rapid pace of industrialization, which gave rise to a new class of white voters, the cotton mill workers.

White sharecroppers and mill workers coalesced behind the candidacy of Tillmanite Cole Blease in the gubernatorial election of 1910. They believed that Blease was including them as an important part of the political force of the state. Once in office, however, Blease did not initiate any policies that were beneficial to the mill workers or poor farmers. Instead, his four years in office were highly erratic in behavior. This helped to pave the way for a progressive, Richard I. Manning, to win the governorship in 1914.

Economic Booms and Busts

In the 1880s Atlanta editor Henry W. Grady won attention in the state for his vision of a "New South," a South based on the modern industrial model. By now, the idea had already struck some enterprising South Carolinians that the cotton they were shipping north could also be processed in South Carolina mills. The idea was not new;

in 1854, De Bow's Commercial Review of the South & West had boasted to investors of South Carolina's potential for manufacturing, citing its three lines of railroads, inexpensive raw materials, non-freezing rivers, and labor pool. Slavery was so profitable before 1860 that it absorbed available capital and repelled Northern investors, but now the time for industrialization was at hand. By 1900 the textile industry was established in upland areas, which had water-power and an available white labor force, comprising men, women and children willing to move from hard-scrabble farms to mill towns.

In 1902, the Charleston Expedition drew visitors from around the world. President Theodore Roosevelt, whose mother had attended school in Columbia, called for reconciliation of still simmering animosities between the North and the South.

The Progressive Movement came to the state with Governor Richard Irvine Manning III in 1914. The expansion of bright-leaf tobacco around 1900 from North Carolina brought an agricultural boom. This was broken by the Great Depression starting in 1929, but the tobacco industry recovered and prospered until near the end of the 20th century. Cotton remained by far the dominant crop, despite low prices. The arrival of boll weevil infestation sharply reduced acreage, and especially yields. Farmers shifted to other crops.

Black sharecroppers and laborers began heading North in large numbers in the era of World War I, a Great Migration that continued for the rest of the century, as they sought higher wages and much more favorable political conditions.

Civil Rights Movement

Compared to hot spots such as Mississippi and Alabama, desegregation went rather smoothly during the 1950s and 1960s in South Carolina. As early as 1948, however, when Strom Thurmond ran for president on the States Rights ticket, South Carolina whites were showing discontent with the Democrats' post-World War II continuation of the New Deal's federalization of power.

In 1944, George Stinney, a 14-year-old black youth, was accused of murdering two girls, aged 11 and 8 near Alcolu at Clarendon County. Alcolu was a small working-class mill town, where residences of whites and blacks were separated by railroad tracks. Stinney was interrogated by police in a locked room with several white officers and no other witnesses, and it was claimed that he had confessed to the killing within an hour. Stinney's father was fired from his job at local lumber mill, and his family had to either leave the city or risk getting lynched. Given the two white female victims, and an all-white male jury, Stinney was rapidly convicted. Stinney's court-appointed attorney Charles Plowden was a tax commissioner with political aspirations, and scholars have considered him ineffective. On June 16, 1944, Stinney was executed at South Carolina State Penitentiary in Columbia. On December 17, 2014, Stinney's conviction was vacated on the grounds that his constitutional rights had been violated, and his confession had most likely been coerced.

South Carolina blacks had problems with the Southern version of states' rights; by 1940 the voter registration provisions written into the 1895 constitution effectively still limited African American voters to 3,000 - only 0.8 percent of those of voting age in the state. African Americans had not been able to elect a representative since the 19th century. Hundreds of thousands left the state for industrial cities in the Great Migration of the 20th century. By 1960, during the Civil Rights Movement, South Carolina had a population of 2,382,594, of whom nearly 35%, or 829,291 were African Americans, who had been without representation for 60 years. In addition, the state enforced legal racial segregation in public facilities.

Non-violent action against segregation began in Rock Hill in 1961, when nine black Friendship Junior College students took seats at the whites-only lunch counter at a downtown McCrory's and refused to leave. When police arrested them, the students were given the choice of paying $200 fines or serving 30 days of hard labor in the York County jail. The Friendship Nine, as they became known, chose the latter, gaining national attention in the American Civil Rights Movement because of their decision to use the "jail, no bail" strategy.

In 1962, federal courts ordered Clemson University to admit its first African-American student, Harvey Gantt, into classes. The state and the college's board of trustees had exhausted legal recourse to prevent his admission;

influential whites ensured that word was widespread that no violence or otherwise unseemly behavior would be tolerated. Gantt's entrance into the school occurred without incident. The March 16, 1963, Saturday Evening Post praised the state's handling of the crisis, with an article titled "Desegregation with Dignity: The Inside Story of How South Carolina Kept the Peace". Gantt graduated in architecture with honors, served on the Charlotte City Council beginning in 1974 and, in 1983, was elected to the first of two terms as Charlotte's first black mayor.

In 1964, Barry Goldwater's platform galvanized South Carolina's conservative Democrats and led to major defections of whites into the Republican Party, led by Senator Strom Thurmond. With the federal Civil Rights Act of 1964 and Voting Rights Act of 1965, the national government under the Democrat Lyndon B. Johnson worked to enforce rights for South Carolina and other blacks to participate in public life and regain the power of suffrage. Since then African Americans have been regularly elected to national, state and local offices in the state.

In 1968, the tragic shooting at Orangeburg shattered the state's peaceful desegregation. When police overreacted to the violence of students' protesting a segregated bowling alley, they killed three students and wounded 27 others.

In 1970, when South Carolina celebrated its Tricentennial, more than 80% of its residents had been born in the state. Since then, people from the North and Midwest have discovered South Carolina's golf courses, beaches and mild climate. The state, particularly the coastal areas but increasingly inland as well, has become more popular as a tourist destination and magnet for new arrivals and retirees. Descendants of black South Carolinians who moved out of the South during the Jim Crow years have moved back in a reverse migration. Despite these new arrivals, about 69% of residents are native born.

Recent Events

Economic Change
The rapid decline of agriculture in the state has been one of the most important developments since the 1960s. As late as 1960, more than half the state's cotton was picked by hand. Over the next twenty years, mechanization eliminated tens of thousands of jobs in rural counties. By 2000 only 24,000 farms were left, with fewer than 2% of the population; many others lived in rural areas on what were once farms, but they commuted to non-farm jobs. Cotton was no longer king, as cotton lands were converted into timberlands. Until the 1970s rural areas had controlled the legislature.

After 1972, both houses of the state legislature were reapportioned into single-member districts, ending another rural advantage. Coupled with the federal Voting Rights Act of 1965, which protected voting for African Americans, the reapportionment transformed South Carolina politics. The South Carolina Democratic party, which dominated the state for nearly a century after Reconstruction, due to suppression of black voting, began to decline at the state and county level with the 1994 elections. The majority white voters had been supporting Republican presidential candidates since the late 1960s and gradually elected the party candidates to local and state offices as well. Republicans won all but one statewide constitutional office, and control of the state house of representatives.

Fritz Hollings, governor 1959–1963, who was a key supporter of development, executed a campaign to promote industrial training programs and implemented a state-wide economic development strategy. The end of the Cold War in 1990 brought the closing of military installations, such as the naval facilities in North Charleston, which Rep. Mendel Rivers had long sponsored. The quest for new jobs became a high state priority. Starting in 1975 the state used its attractive climate, lack of powerful labor unions, and low wage rates to attract foreign investment in factories, including Michelin, which located its U.S. headquarters in the state. The stretch of Interstate 85 from the North Carolina line to Greenville became "UN Alley" as international companies opened operations.

Tourism became a major industry, especially in the Myrtle Beach area. With its semitropical climate, cheap land and low construction costs (because of low wages), the state became a developer's dream. Barrier islands, such

as Kiawah and Hilton Head, were developed as retirement communities for wealthy outsiders. The state's attempts to manage coastal development in an orderly and environmentally sound manner have run afoul of federal court decisions. The U.S. Supreme Court (in Lucas v. South Carolina Coastal Council) ruled that the state, in forbidding construction on threatened beachfront property, had, in effect, seized the plaintiff's property without due process of law. The rush to build upscale housing along the coast paid its price in the billions of dollars of losses as Hurricane Hugo swept through on September 21–22, 1989. Charleston was more used to hurricanes; historical preservation groups immediately stepped in to begin salvage and reconstruction, with the result that one year after Hugo, the city was virtually returned to normal.

By the late 1980s, however, the state's economic growth rate flattened. South Carolina's development plan focused on offering low taxes and attracting low-wage industries, but the state's low levels of education have failed to attract high wage, high tech industries.

In 1991, under the leadership of then Governor Carroll A. Campbell, the state successfully recruited BMW's (Bavarian Motor Works) only U.S. auto factory to the city of Greer, in Spartanburg County. Second-tier and third-tier auto parts suppliers to BMW likewise established assembly and distribution facilities near the factory, creating a significant shift in manufacturing from textiles to automotive.

In 2009, the state outbid the state of Washington for a giant new Boeing plant, to be constructed in North Charleston. Boeing must create at least 3,800 jobs and invest more than $750 million within seven years to take advantage of the various tax inducements, worth $450 million.

Politics
In the 1970s, South Carolina white voters elected the state's first Republican governor since Reconstruction. In 1987 and 1991, the state elected and reelected Governor Carroll Campbell, another Republican. Many politicians switched from the Democratic Party to the GOP, including David Beasley, a former Democrat who claimed to have undergone a spiritual rebirth; he was elected governor as a Republican. In 1996 Beasley surprised citizens by announcing that he could not justify keeping the Confederate flag flying over the capitol. He said that a "spate of racially motivated violence compelled him to reconsider the politics and symbolism of the Confederate flag, and he concluded it should be moved." Traditionalists were further surprised when Bob Jones III, head of Bob Jones University, announced he held the same view.

Beasley was upset for reelection in 1998 by the little-known Jim Hodges, a state assemblyman from Lancaster. Hodges attacked Beasley's opposition to the creation of a state lottery to support education. Hodges called for a fresh tax base to improve public education. Despite Hodges' unwillingness to join Beasley in his opposition to flying the Confederate flag, the NAACP announced its support for Hodges. (At the same time the NAACP demanded a boycott of conferences in the state over the flag issue). Hodges reportedly accepted millions in contributions from the gambling industry, which some estimated spent a total of $10 million to defeat Beasely.

After the election, with public opinions steadfastly against video gambling, Hodges asked for a statewide referendum on the issue. He claimed that he would personally join the expected majority in saying "no" on legalized gambling, but vowed not to campaign against it. Critics in both parties suggested that Hodges' debts to the state's gambling interests were keeping him from campaigning against legalized gambling. The state constitution does not provide for referendums except for ratification of amendments. State legislators shut down the state's video casinos soon after Hodges took office.

Upon his election, Hodges announced that he agreed with Beasley's increasingly popular compromise proposal on the Confederate flag issue. He supported the flag's transfer to a Confederate monument on the State House's grounds. Many South Carolinians agreed with this position as the only solution. Further, they admired Hodges' solution to nuclear waste shipments to the state. Hodges alienated moderate voters sufficiently so that in 2002, most of the state's major newspapers supported the Republican Mark Sanford to replace him. Hodges was held responsible for the state's mishandling of the Hurricane Floyd evacuation in 1999. By 2002, most of the funds from Hodges' "South Carolina Education Lottery" were used to pay for college scholarships, rather than to improve impoverished rural and inner-city schools. Religious leaders denounced the lottery as taxing the poor to pay for higher education for the middle class.

In the lottery's first year, Hodges' administration awarded $40 million for "LIFE Scholarships", granted to any South Carolinian student with a B average, graduation in the top 30% of the student's high school class, and an 1,100 SAT score. Hodges' administration awarded $5.8 million for "HOPE Scholarships", which had lower GPA requirements.

Hodges lost his campaign for reelection in 2002 against the Republican conservative Mark Sanford, a former U.S. congressman from Sullivan's Island.
Source: Wikipedia, "History of South Carolina"

Timeline of South Carolina History

1521
First recorded Spanish expedition reached Carolina coast

1524
First French ship explored Carolina coast

1526
Spanish settlement, San Miguel de Guadalupe near Winvah Bay; failed within one year

1562
French attempted settlement of Charlesfort on Parris Island; failed within one year

1566
Spanish built coastal forts to discourage French settlements

1629
King Charles I granted charter to Sir Robert Heath for all territory between 31° and 36° N (from Albemarle Sound in North Carolina to Jekyll Island off Georgia's coast

1663
King Charles II granted region of Carolina to eight Lords Proprietors

1666
Capt. Robert Sanford explored, named Ashley River; took formal possession of Carolina region for England and Lords Proprietors

1669
Fundamental Constitution of Carolina approved by Lords Proprietors; guaranteed religious freedom

1670
First permanent England settlements and capital city, Charles Town, (Charleston founded; City Assembly established tax-supported free library

1680
First group French Huguenots arrived; Charles Town moved to Oyster Point, current site

1700
Hurricane struck Charleston, 98 killed

1706
French, Spanish attacked Charles Town during Queen Anne's War; colonial forces captured French vessel and crew

1712
Territory of Carolina divided into North and South; each had own governor

1713
Hurricane struck; heavy flooding, 70 killed

1715 – 1717
Yemassee Indian Wars

1718
Pirate Blackbeard sailed into Charles Town Harbor; took hostages for ransom; pirate Stede Bonnet captured, hanged in Charles Town

1719
Citizens of South Carolina rebel against Lords Proprietors; James Moore elected governor

1721
South Carolina became Crown Colony; General Sir Francis Nicholson appointed governor

1728
Passenger, shipping service began between Charles Town and New York

1729
Seven Lord Proprietors surrendered right to King George II

1730
Nine townships laid out; settlers began move into interior

1730 – 1739
About 20,000 enslaved Africans brought to South Carolina

1739
40 blacks, 21 whites died in Stono slave revolt

1740
Fire swept through Charles Town

1742
Spanish prevented from taking Charles Town in Battle of Bloody Marsh

1747
Treaty signed with Choctaw Indians; treaty established trade with Choctaws for not attacking French settlements

1752
Hurricane struck, 103 killed

1760 – 1761
Cherokee Wars

1761
Cherokee War ended; Treaty opened land for settlement; Bounty Act offered public land tax free for 10 year in Up Country, settlers began to move in

1769
Nine judicial district established

1774
Henry Middleton, John and Edward Rutledge, Thomas Lynch, Christopher Gadsden named delegates to First Continental Congress; Middleton chosen President of Continental Congress

1775
Carolina's First Provincial Congress met

1776
First major battle of the Revolution; 15 British warships, 1,500 troops attack Ft. Moultrie, forced away; Declaration of Independence arrived in Charles Town

1777
New state government required each male citizen to denounce King, pledge loyalty to state

1778
Major fire in Charles Town destroyed many building, arson suspected

1779
British prepared sea and land expedition against Charles Town; General Washington ordered 1,400 Continental troops to Charles Town

1780
British troops landed on Seabrook Island, warships anchored within broadside range of Charles Town, Army crossed Ashley river and established line of breastworks; encircled civilian population; siege lasted 40 days; Charles Town surrendered to British

1781
Revolutionary leader, Col. Isaac Hayne, hanged by British outside Charles Town city limits; American forces retake most of South Carolina, advanced to within 15 miles of Charles Town

1782
British Army defeated; left Charles Town

1783
Charles Town renamed Charleston

1785
General Assembly legislation laid out counties, established county courts

1786
Capital moved from Charleston to Columbia

1788
South Carolina became 8th state

1792
Law passed—all free African-Americans between 16 – 50 to pay annual "head tax" of $2.00

1804
Hurricane struck South Carolina

1822
Denmark Vesey conspiracy discovered (Vesey and other slave followers planned to capture Charleston, kill most of the whites, escape to Caribbean or Africa); Vesey and 33 others hanged

1830
First steam locomotive in U.S. began passenger route service between Charleston and Hamburg, South Carolina

1838
Fire destroyed most of Ansonborough

1843
Citadel opened for first class of cadets

1860
South Carolina first state to secede from the Union prior to Civil War

1861
First shots of Civil War fired by Confederate forces upon Ft. Sumter; Union forces sunk "Stone Fleet" in Charleston harbor channel

1862
Confederates repulsed Union attack at Battle of Seccessionville on James Island; Battle of Simmons Bluff occurred, Union victorious

1863
Federal fleet attacked by Confederate ironclads; Union sent fleet of warships to attack Ft. Sumter; Union assault on Battery Wagner at Morris Island led by all black unit; 587 day bombardment of downtown Charleston began

1864
Confederate submarine sank Union's Housatonic

1865
Gen. Sherman's troops reached Middleton Place Plantation, left it in ruins; burned Columbia; Civil War ended

1868
South Carolina readmitted to Union; new Constitution written; Sen. B.F. Randolph murdered by radical whites in Abbeville County

1869
Joseph Rainey first African-American in South Carolina to become U. S. Representative

1886
Low Country struck by estimated 7.5 earthquake, 83 killed, $6 million in damages

1925
New dance craze in Charleston's pubs, dance halls began, spread across nation, named "Charleston"

1934
George Gershwin arrived in Charleston to write Porgy and Bess, first American opera

1954
Hurricane Hazel struck Garden City, left two of 275 homes habitable; severe coastal damage ocurred

1963
Rivers High School in Charleston became first racially integrated high school in South Carolina

1964
Civil Rights Act passed; segregation ends

1968
Orangeburg Massacre at S. C. State campus occurred; three students killed, 28 wounded

1970
Angry whites overturned school bus with young black children on way to integrate local schools in Lamar; state restored order, enforced law

1986
Lake City native, astronaut and physicist Ron McNair, killed in Space Shuttle Challenger explosion

1989
Hurricane Hugo struck; barrier islands lost 80% of homes; Charleston suffered significant damages; total losses $2.8 billion

1990
Hurricane Klaus struck; 80 bridges destroyed, 40 more damaged; secondary roads washed out

1995
Divers discovered wreck of Confederate submarine H. L. Hunley in waters off Sullivan's Island

2000
South Carolina moved the last Confederate flag flying above the U.S. Statehouse to a location on the grounds

2002
Sen. Strom Thurmond retires at age 100

2004
Hurricane Gaston caused major flooding; damaged structures

2007
Nine fire fighters killed in furniture warehouse fire in Charleston

2009

Atlantic Coast Conference moved three future baseball tournaments out of state due to concerns from NAACP over state-sponsored display of Confederate flag

2010

Legislation introduced mandating gold and silver to replace federal currency in the state

2011

State's immigration laws challenged by 16 nations from Latin America and Caribbean

2014

South Carolina became the 35th state to legalize same-sex marriage

2015

In the wake of the Charleston Emanuel AME Church massacre by white supremacist Dylann Roof, Governor Nikki Haley called for the removal of the Confederate flag from the grounds of the Statehouse

Source: http://www.worldatlas.com, June 26, 2015; Original research

An Introduction to South Carolina State Government

Overview

South Carolina's state government consists of the Executive, Legislative, and Judicial branches.

South Carolina has historically had a weak executive branch and a strong legislature. Before 1865, governors in South Carolina were appointed by the General Assembly, and held the title "President of State." The 1865 Constitution changed this process, requiring a popular election for governor. Democratic representation was increased under the constitution of 1867, which established home rule for counties.

This was changed in the 1895 constitution, which reduced counties to a role as agents of state government. They were essentially governed by the General Assembly through their legislative delegation, in which the state senator from each county exercised the most power. This system held until 1973. It meant that rural counties held power disproportionate to their population. After a federal case of 1964 required reapportionment according to the principle of "one man, one vote," the legislature made other changes to county government structure, passing a 1973 constitutional amendment to establish home rule. The Home Rule Act in 1975 implemented this.

In 1926 the governor's term was changed to four years. In 1982 governors were allowed to run for a second term. In 1993 a limited cabinet was created, all of whom must be popularly elected.

The Executive Branch

The South Carolina Constitution since 1993 provides for separate election of nine executive officers, making a limited cabinet. This is a large number of elective offices compared to most states, which generally give the governor the executive power to appoint members of the cabinet. The nine officers are:
- Governor of South Carolina
- Lieutenant Governor of South Carolina
- South Carolina Attorney General
- South Carolina Adjutant General
- South Carolina Commissioner of Agriculture
- South Carolina Comptroller General
- Secretary of State of South Carolina
- South Carolina State Treasurer
- South Carolina Superintendent of Education

The Governor of South Carolina is the chief executive of the state. The governor is elected for a four-year term and may serve up to two consecutive terms. The current governor is Republican Nikki Haley. Haley was elected in 2010 as the state's first female governor, as well the second Indian American governor in the United States.

Each officer is elected at the same time as the governor. The separately elected positions allow for the possibility of multiple parties to be represented in the executive branch. The Governor's Cabinet also contains several appointed positions. In most cases, persons who fill cabinet-level positions are recommended by the governor and appointed by the Senate.

The Legislative Branch

The legislative power of the State of South Carolina is vested in a bicameral General Assembly comprised of the Senate and the House of Representatives. The Senate consists of 46 members who are elected from single member districts of approximately 87,200 citizens. Senators must be citizens of the United States and the State of South Carolina, at least 25 years old at the time of their election, and residents of the district in which they are elected. Senators serve four year terms. The political make up of the current Senate is 28 Republicans and 18 Democrats.

The South Carolina House of Representatives consists of 124 part-time citizen legislators elected every two years to represent our state's 124 separate single-member districts. The current House membership is made up of 77 Republicans and 46 Democrats with 1 vacancy. As outlined by our state's constitution, the General Assembly's annual session begins on the second Tuesday in January and runs through the first Thursday in June.

The two houses meet in the South Carolina State House in Columbia.

The Judicial Branch

The Family Court deals with all matters of domestic and family relationships, as well as generally maintaining exclusive jurisdiction over cases involving minors under the age of seventeen, excepting traffic and game law violations. Some criminal charges may come under Circuit Court jurisdiction.

The South Carolina Circuit Court is the trial court of general jurisdiction court for South Carolina. It consists of a civil division (the Court of Common Pleas) and a criminal division . (the Court of General Sessions). It is also a superior court, having limited appellate jurisdiction over appeals from the lower Probate Court, Magistrate's Court, and Municipal Court, and appeals from the Administrative Law Judge Division, which hears matters relating to state administrative and regulatory agencies. South Carolina's 46 counties are divided into 16 judicial circuits, and there are currently 46 judges. Circuit court judges are elected by the General Assembly to staggered six-year terms.

The South Carolina Court of Appeals is the state intermediate appellate court. It hears all Circuit Court and Family Court appeals, excepting appeals that are within the seven classes of exclusive Supreme Court jurisdiction. The Court of Appeals is selected by the General Assembly to staggered six-year terms. The court comprises a chief judge, and eight associate judges, and may hear cases as the whole court, or as three panels with three judges each. The court may preside in any county.

The South Carolina Supreme Court is the state supreme court. The Chief Justice and four Associate Justices are elected to staggered ten-year terms. There are no limits on the number of terms a justice may serve, but there is a mandatory retirement age of 72. The overwhelming majority of vacancies on the Court occur when Justices reach this age, not through the refusal of the General Assembly to elect a sitting Justice to another term.

Source: South Carolina Legislative Services Agency, http://www.scstatehouse.gov; Wikipedia, "South Carolina Government and Politics," June 24, 2015

SOUTH CAROLINA

NORTH CAROLINA

nationalatlas.gov™
Where We Are

CONGRESSIONAL DISTRICTS
113th Congress (January 2013–January 2015)

The Constitution prescribes Congressional apportionment based on decennial census population data. Each state has at least one Representative, no matter how small its population. Since 1941, distribution of Representatives has been based on total U.S. population, so that the average population per Representative has the least possible variation between one state and any other. Congress fixes the number of voting Representatives at each apportionment. States delineate the district boundaries. The first House of Representatives in 1789 had 65 members; currently there are 435. There are non-voting delegates from American Samoa, the District of Columbia, Guam, Puerto Rico, and the Virgin Islands.

ATLANTIC OCEAN

The **National Atlas** of the United States of America®

GEORGIA

MILES
0   10   20   30   40   50   60
Albers equal area projection

U.S. Department of the Interior
U.S. Geological Survey

Percent of Population Who Voted for Barack Obama in 2012

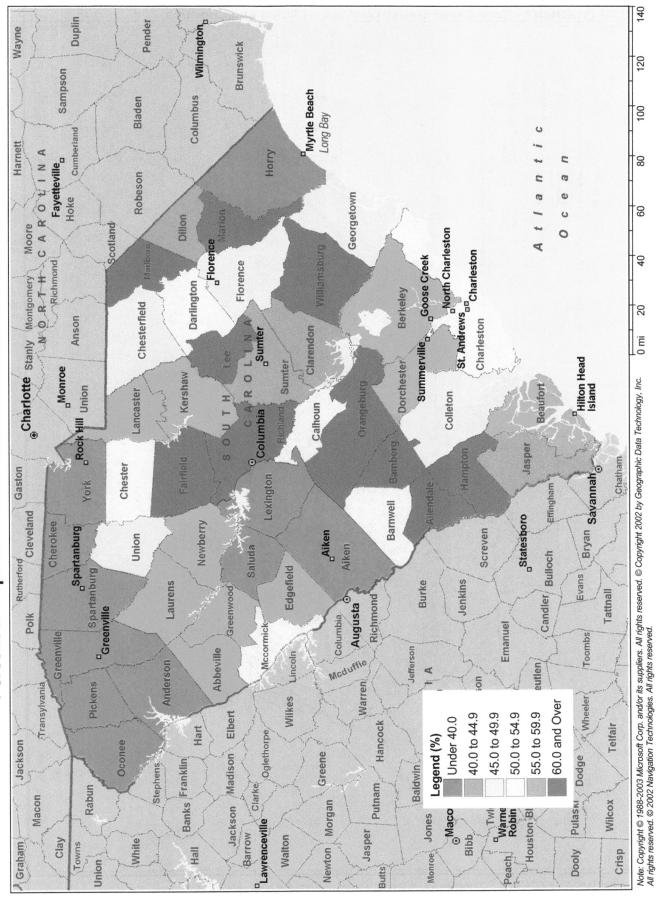

Legend (%)
- Under 40.0
- 40.0 to 44.9
- 45.0 to 49.9
- 50.0 to 54.9
- 55.0 to 59.9
- 60.0 and Over

SOUTH CAROLINA - Core Based Statistical Areas (CBSAs) and Counties

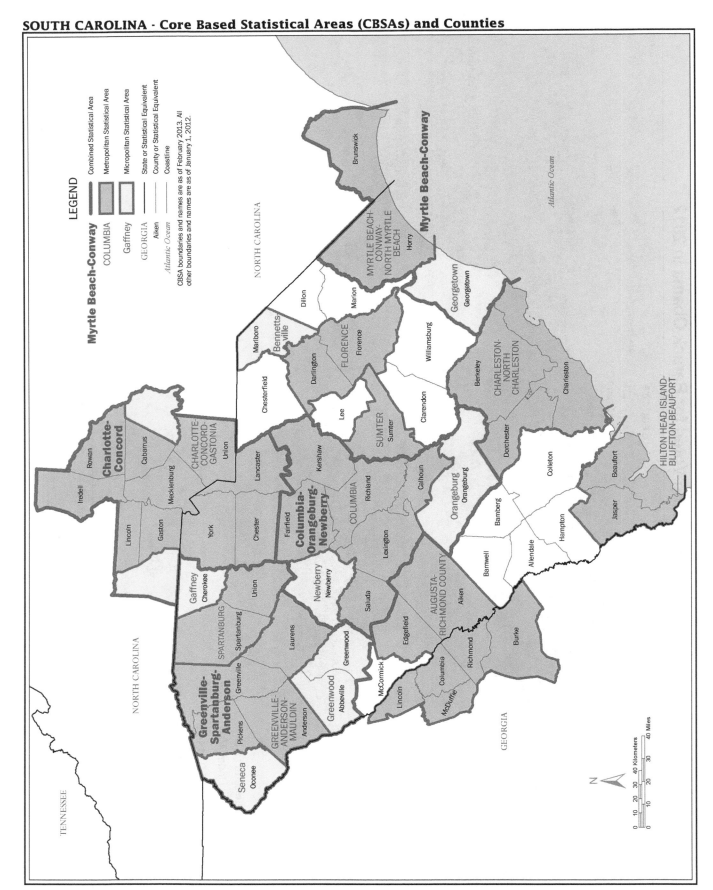

Land and Natural Resources

Topic	Value	Time Period
Total Surface Area (acres)	19,939,300	2010
Land	19,123,300	2010
Federal Land	1,036,200	2010
Non-Federal Land, Developed	2,651,500	2010
Non-Federal Land, Rural	15,435,600	2010
Cropland	2,205,900	2010
CRP Land	129,900	2010
Pastureland	1,108,700	2010
Rangeland	0	2010
Forest Land	11,166,100	2010
Other Rural Land	825,000	2010
Water	816,000	2010
World Heritage Sites	0	FY Ending 9/30/2014
National Heritage Areas	2	FY Ending 9/30/2014
National Natural Landmarks	6	FY Ending 9/30/2014
National Historic Landmarks	76	FY Ending 9/30/2014
National Register of Historic Places Listings	1,511	FY Ending 9/30/2014
National Parks	6	FY Ending 9/30/2014
Visitors to National Parks	1,519,746	FY Ending 9/30/2014
Archeological Sites in National Parks	101	FY Ending 9/30/2014
Threatened and Endangered Species in National Parks	6	FY Ending 9/30/2014
Places Recorded by Heritage Documentation Programs	1,162	FY Ending 9/30/2014
Economic Benefit from National Park Tourism	$81,100,000	FY Ending 9/30/2014
Historic Preservation Grants	$32,070,571	Since 1969
Historic Rehabilitation Projects Stimulated by Tax Incentives	$313,533,907	Since 1995
Land & Water Conservation Fund Grants	$61,416,357	Since 1965
Acres Transferred by Federal Lands to Local Parks	7,850	Since 1948

Sources: *United States Department of Agriculture, Natural Resources Conservation Service, National Resources Inventory; U.S. Department of the Interior, National Park Service, State Profiles*

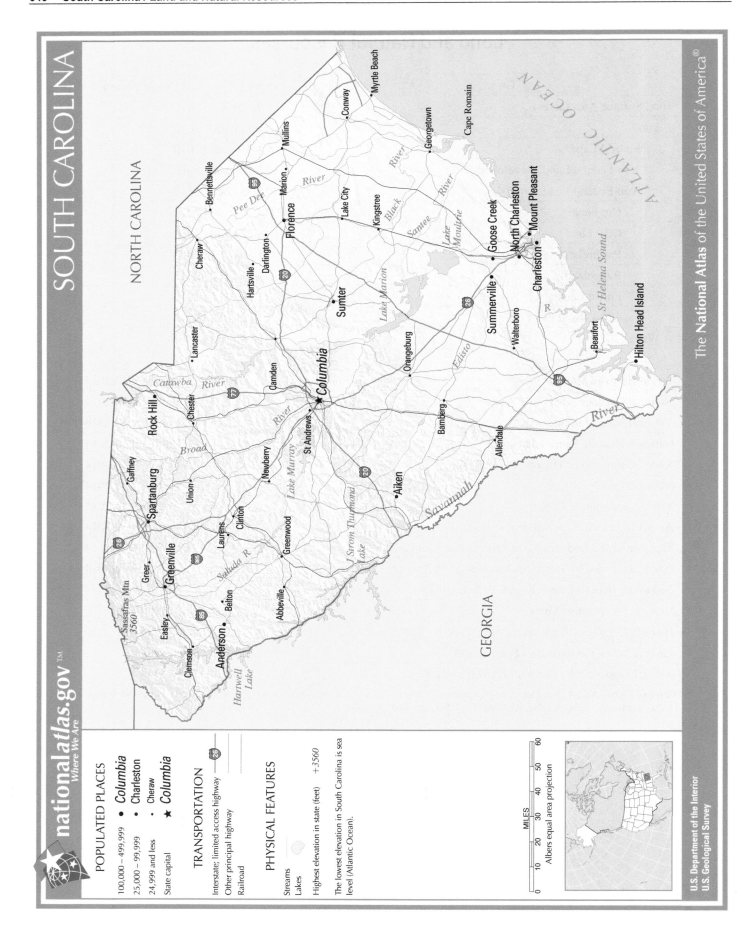

SOUTH CAROLINA

NORTH CAROLINA

ATLANTIC OCEAN

GEORGIA

The National Atlas of the United States of America®

nationalatlas.gov™
Where We Are

POPULATED PLACES

100,000 – 499,999   ● Columbia
25,000 – 99,999   ● Charleston
24,999 and less   · Cheraw
State capital   ★ Columbia

TRANSPORTATION

Interstate; limited access highway
Other principal highway
Railroad

PHYSICAL FEATURES

Streams
Lakes
Highest elevation in state (feet)   +3560

The lowest elevation in South Carolina is sea
level (Atlantic Ocean).

MILES
0   10   20   30   40   50   60
Albers equal area projection

U.S. Department of the Interior
U.S. Geological Survey

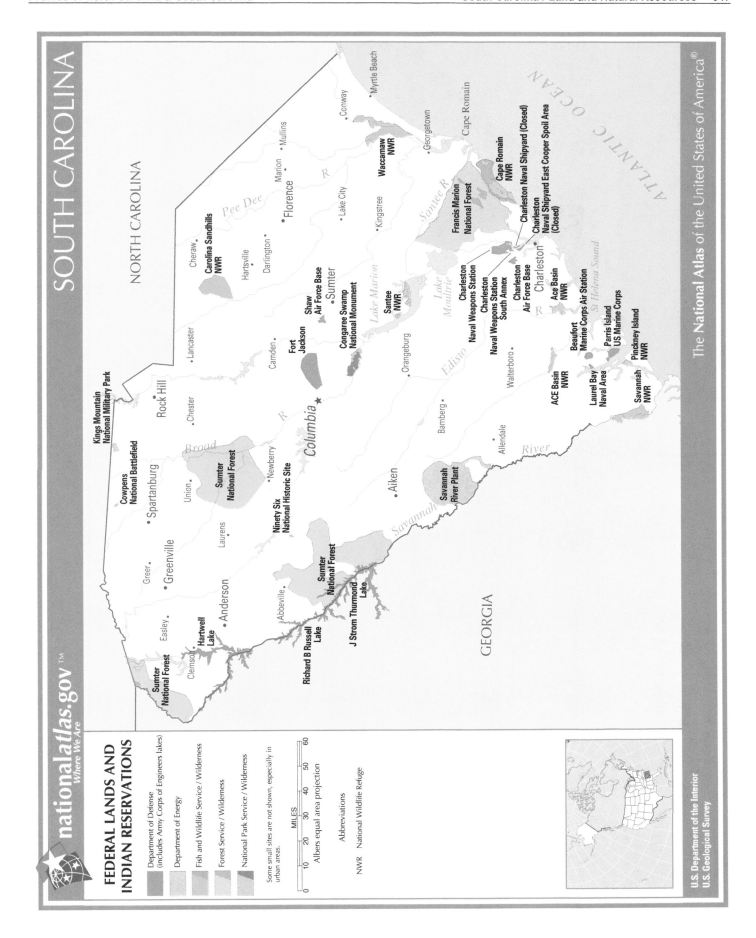

SOUTH CAROLINA

NORTH CAROLINA

ATLANTIC OCEAN

The National Atlas of the United States of America®

nationalatlas.gov™
Where We Are

FEDERAL LANDS AND
INDIAN RESERVATIONS

Department of Defense
(includes Army Corps of Engineers lakes)

Department of Energy

Fish and Wildlife Service / Wilderness

Forest Service / Wilderness

National Park Service / Wilderness

Some small sites are not shown, especially in
urban areas.

MILES

0 10 20 30 40 50 60

Albers equal area projection

Abbreviations

NWR National Wildlife Refuge

U.S. Department of the Interior
U.S. Geological Survey

Myrtle Beach
Conway
Mullins
Marion
Florence
Lake City
Cheraw
Hartsville
Darlington
Kingstree
Georgetown
Cape Romain
Cape Romain NWR
Waccamaw NWR
Pee Dee R
Francis Marion National Forest
Charleston Naval Shipyard (Closed)
Charleston Naval Shipyard East Cooper Spoil Area (Closed)
Charleston Naval Shipyard (Closed)
Carolina Sandhills NWR
Santee R
Lake Marion
Lake Moultrie
Shaw Air Force Base
Sumter
Congaree Swamp National Monument
Santee NWR
Charleston Naval Weapons Station
Charleston Naval Weapons Station South Annex
Charleston Air Force Base
Charleston
Ace Basin NWR
St Helena Sound
Fort Jackson
Camden
Lancaster
Orangeburg
Walterboro
Beaufort Marine Corps Air Station
Parris Island US Marine Corps
Pinckney Island NWR
Laurel Bay Naval Area
Savannah NWR
ACE Basin NWR
Edisto R
Bamberg
Allendale
River
Kings Mountain National Military Park
Rock Hill
Chester
Newberry
Columbia
Broad R
Cowpens National Battlefield
Spartanburg
Union
Sumter National Forest
Ninety Six National Historic Site
Savannah River Plant
Aiken
Savannah R
Greer
Greenville
Laurens
Anderson
Easley
Abbeville
Clemson
Hartwell Lake
Sumter National Forest
Richard B Russell Lake
J Strom Thurmond Lake
GEORGIA

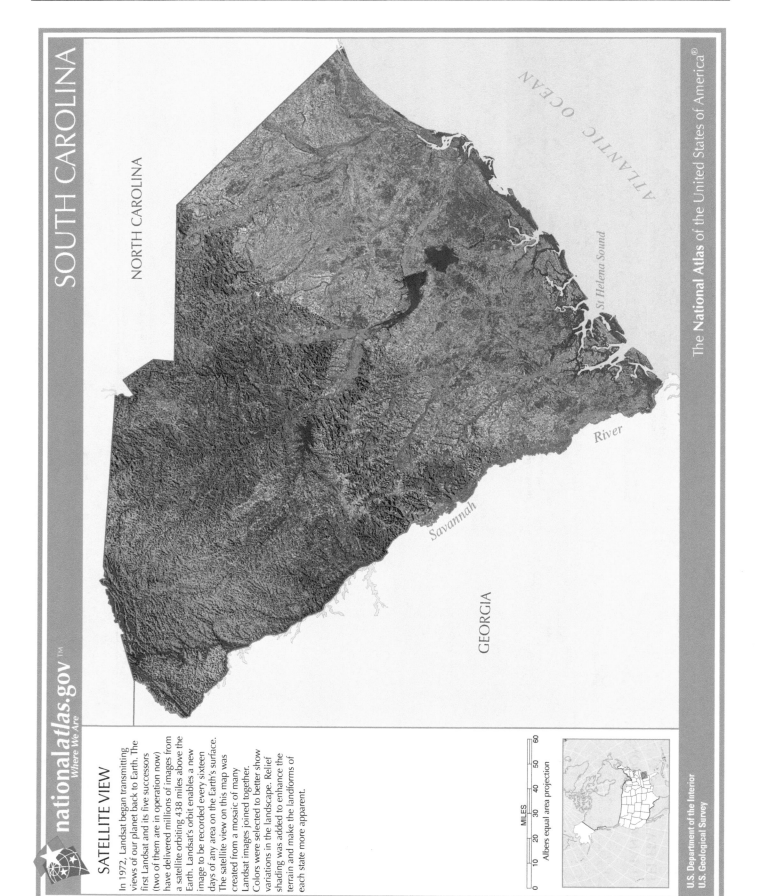

SOUTH CAROLINA

NORTH CAROLINA

ATLANTIC OCEAN

St Helena Sound

River

Savannah

GEORGIA

nationalatlas.gov™
Where We Are

SATELLITE VIEW

In 1972, Landsat began transmitting views of our planet back to Earth. The first Landsat and its five successors (two of them are in operation now) have delivered millions of images from a satellite orbiting 438 miles above the Earth. Landsat's orbit enables a new image to be recorded every sixteen days of any area on the Earth's surface. The satellite view on this map was created from a mosaic of many Landsat images joined together. Colors were selected to better show variations in the landscape. Relief shading was added to enhance the terrain and make the landforms of each state more apparent.

MILES

0   10   20   30   40   50   60

Albers equal area projection

U.S. Department of the Interior
U.S. Geological Survey

The **National Atlas** of the United States of America®

Economic Losses from Hazard Events, 1960-2009

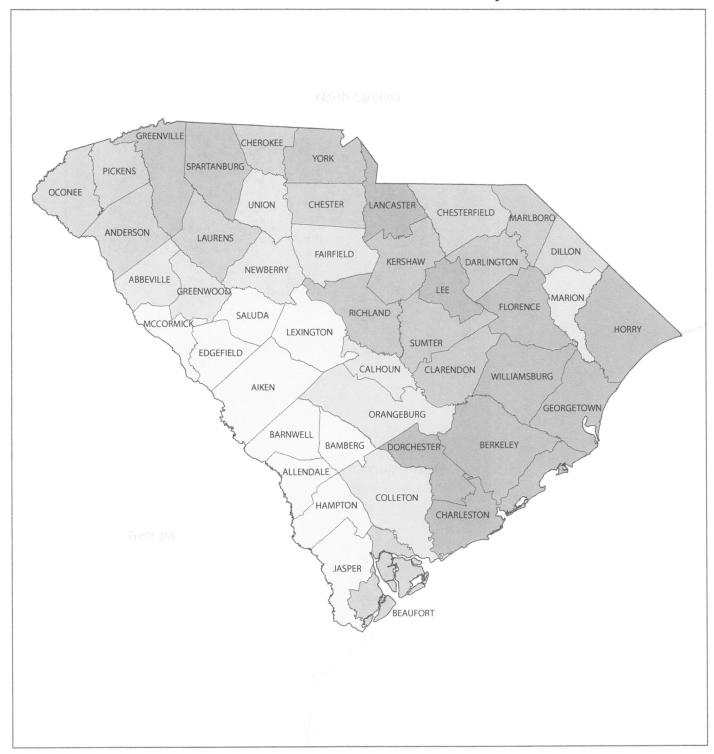

SOUTH CAROLINA

Total Losses (Property and Crop)

- 47,434,300 - 59,898,122
- 59,898,123 - 71,748,810
- 71,748,811 - 93,864,295
- 93,864,296 - 224,239,154
- 224,239,155 - 1,915,976,150

Source: SHELDUS v. 8.0
Classification: Quantiles
Losses adjusted to 2009 Dollars

0   25   50 Miles

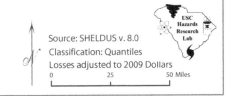

SOUTH CAROLINA

Hazard Losses
1960-2009

Distribution of Losses by Hazard Type
(in 2009 USD million)

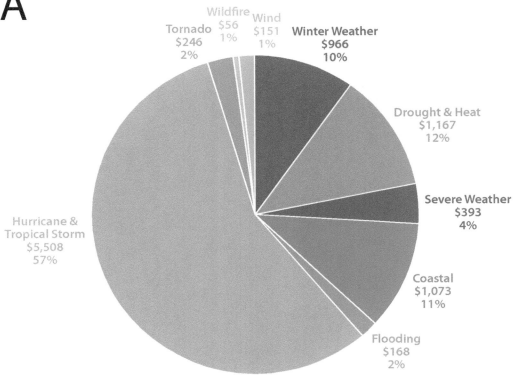

Distribution of Hazard Events
(number of events)

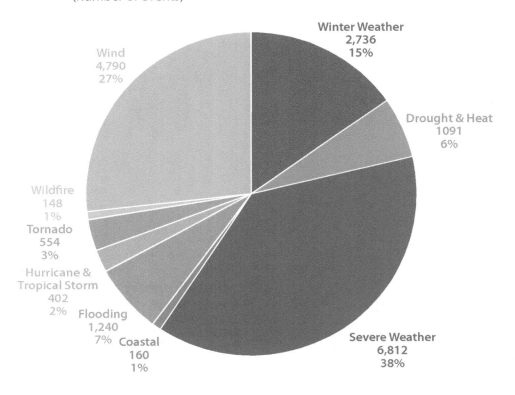

South Carolina Energy Profile

Quick Facts

- In 2014, South Carolina was eighth in the nation in per capita retail electricity sales, in part because of high air conditioning demand during the hot summer months and the widespread use of electricity for home heating in winter.
- South Carolina's electric power sector received 34% of its domestic coal deliveries from Kentucky and 29% from Pennslyvania in 2013.
- South Carolina's four existing nuclear power plants supplied 54% of the state's net electricity generation in 2014. Two new reactors are under construction at the V.C. Summer Nuclear Station site in Fairfield County.
- In 2013, renewable energy resources accounted for 5.0% of South Carolina's net electricity generation; almost 59% of that generation came from conventional hydroelectric power.
- South Carolina enacted a renewable portfolio standard in 2014 authorizing the creation of distributed energy resource programs to encourage the development of in-state renewable energy generation capacity.

Analysis

Overview

South Carolina's primary energy resource is nuclear power. Although the state does not have any fossil fuel reserves or production, it does have renewable resources. South Carolina's system of rivers and lakes provides considerable hydroelectric power potential. Elevations increase gradually in South Carolina from the southeast to the northwest, and the state is crossed by many rivers. The Low Country, or coastal plain, which covers two-thirds of the state, extends from the coast to the west until it reaches the Fall Line, an area of waterfalls and rapids. The remaining one-third of the state, known as the Up Country, has the forested hills of the Piedmont region and the South Carolina Blue Ridge Mountains. Forest occupies two-thirds of South Carolina's land area and is widely distributed in both the Low Country and the Up Country. The wood waste from the state's forests and the associated mills yields significant amounts of biomass, while landfill gas and municipal solid waste from more densely populated areas provide South Carolina with additional biomass resources.

Industry is South Carolina's largest energy-consuming sector, accounting for nearly one-third of the state's total energy consumption. South Carolina's manufacturing activities include chemicals, pharmaceuticals, plastics, forestry products, paper products, metals, machinery, textiles, food products and processing, and aeronautical and automotive assembly. The transportation sector is the state's second-largest energy consumer, using more than one-fourth of the state's total energy supply, primarily in the form of motor gasoline.

Petroleum

No indications of crude oil have been found in South Carolina. There are no petroleum refineries in the state, and all petroleum products arrive from out of state. Petroleum products enter South Carolina at the Port of Charleston and arrive from the Gulf Coast by way of the Colonial Pipeline and the Plantation Pipeline. The Dixie Pipeline, also originating in the Gulf Coast, delivers propane to South Carolina. Petroleum coke is handled at the Port of Georgetown and provides fuel for industrial processes like aluminum smelting.

South Carolina's total petroleum consumption is at the national median. Almost all of the petroleum used in the state is consumed by the transportation sector, primarily by passenger vehicles. Motor gasoline consumption per capita in South Carolina is among the highest in the nation because of extensive motor travel on the state's major interstate corridors. South Carolina allows the statewide use of conventional motor gasoline. Although South Carolina has no ethanol plants and blended gasoline is not required in the state, about 2% of the nation's fuel ethanol consumption occurs in South Carolina.

Natural Gas

Because South Carolina has no natural gas production, all natural gas consumed in the state arrives via interstate pipeline. Several major interstate pipeline systems transport natural gas from the Gulf Coast and deliver it through Georgia to South Carolina. The state consumes substantial amounts of natural gas, but, because of the large volumes in the interstate pipeline system, more than four-fifths of the supply that enters South Carolina continues on to North Carolina on its way to markets in the Northeast.

Natural gas use in South Carolina has increased since 2008, most dramatically in the electric power sector, where consumption more than doubled between 2008 and 2012. Natural gas use by the electric power sector in 2014 decreased slightly from its 2012 peak but still exceeded that of any other sector. Industrial demand has remained fairly constant, and the industrial sector, which had led the state in natural gas use prior to 2009, is the second-largest natural gas consuming-sector after the electric power sector. Winters are generally mild and overall demand for heating in South Carolina is relatively low. Almost one-fourth of South Carolina households use natural gas for home heating, but residential sector natural gas consumption lags behind that of the electric power sector and of the industrial sector.

Coal

Coal in South Carolina is used almost exclusively for electricity generation. Because the state does not produce any coal, fuel for South Carolina's coal-fired power plants arrives by rail, mostly from Kentucky, Pennsylvania, Illinois, and Tennessee. Minor amounts of coal are also delivered to industrial plants in the state. Coal imports arrive by ship at the Port of Charleston. Appalachian coal shipments that transit the state are exported from the Port of Charleston as well.

Electricity

Nuclear energy dominates electricity generation in South Carolina. Ranked third in the nation in nuclear generating capacity, South Carolina produces more than half of its electricity from nuclear power. There are currently seven operating reactors at four nuclear power plants in the state, and two more reactors are under construction. Coal-fired power plants supply another three-tenths of South Carolina's electricity generation. Natural gas fuels another tenth and almost all of the remaining electricity generation is provided by conventional and pumped hydroelectric power plants and by biomass-fueled facilities that use wood waste, landfill gas, and municipal solid waste. South Carolina generates much more electricity than it consumes and sends its surplus to other states.

More than one-third of retail electricity sales in South Carolina are to the residential sector. Per capita retail electricity sales in South Carolina are among the highest in the nation, in part because of the high demand for air conditioning during the hot and humid summer months. Electricity consumption is also high because more than two-thirds of South Carolina households use electricity as their primary energy source for home heating.

Renewable Energy

Hydropower and biomass, South Carolina's primary renewable resources, contribute about 5% of the state's total net generation. There are dozens of hydroelectric generating plants in South Carolina, primarily in the western part of the state, and additional development potential exists at sites throughout South Carolina. Biomass contributes almost as much to South Carolina's net generation as hydropower. The state has about 13 million acres of forest, and forestry is a leading industry in South Carolina. Logging residue is considered to be the state's greatest source of underused biomass. Even though the manufacture and export of wood pellets are growing industries, South Carolina mills produced 9 million tons of wood residues that were either burned as waste or disposed of in landfills in 2011.

The U.S. Department of Energy, using biomass fuel from forest debris collected within 100 miles of its Savannah River Site in Aiken, has replaced coal-fired cogeneration facilities with those fueled by biomass. The Savannah River facilities have operated since 2012 and are the largest publicly operated biomass facilities in the nation. In 2001, Santee Cooper, a state-owned electric utility, became the first utility in South Carolina to produce electricity using methane gas from landfills. Additionally, the state's first anaerobic digester project came online in 2011. The anaerobic digester project generates power from methane gas captured at a hog farm.

South Carolina also has biomass resources in the form of agricultural residues from corn, wheat, cotton, and soybean crops. Although the state has no ethanol production facilities, it does have three biodiesel plants.

South Carolina does not have any appreciable onshore wind energy resource and does not have any installed wind capacity, but manufacturers and assemblers of wind turbine components are located in the state. A small but increasing share of South Carolina's renewable generation comes from solar and geothermal resources. Solar resources are modest, although the state does offer tax incentives to encourage the use of solar technologies. Geothermal resource applications in South Carolina focus on geothermal heat pumps.

In 2014, South Carolina's legislature authorized the creation of distributed energy resource programs by electric utilities and required the Public Service Commission to develop new accompanying net metering rules. Participation in an energy resource program by an electric utility is voluntary. The legislation's goal is to encourage the development of in-state renewable energy generation capacity by allowing a participating utility to recover costs connected with meeting the utility's renewable generation target. Additionally, South Carolina's Energy Efficiency Act requires that public buildings develop energy conservation plans to reduce their energy consumption. The ultimate conservation goal of the act is a 20% reduction in energy use from year 2000 levels by 2020.

Source: U.S. Energy Information Administration, State Profile and Energy Estimates, May 21, 2015

Population

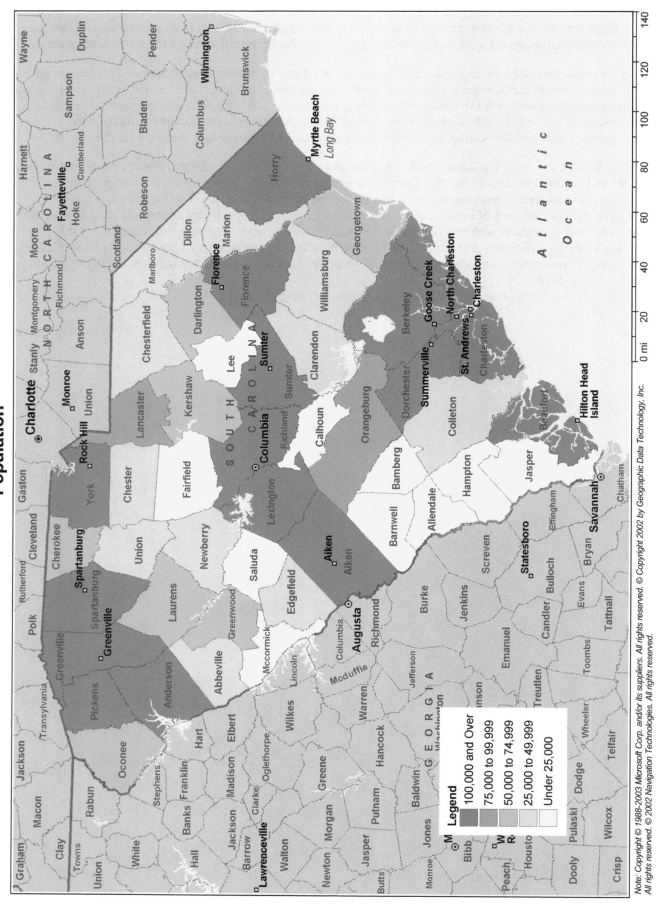

Legend

- 100,000 and Over
- 75,000 to 99,999
- 50,000 to 74,999
- 25,000 to 49,999
- Under 25,000

Percent White

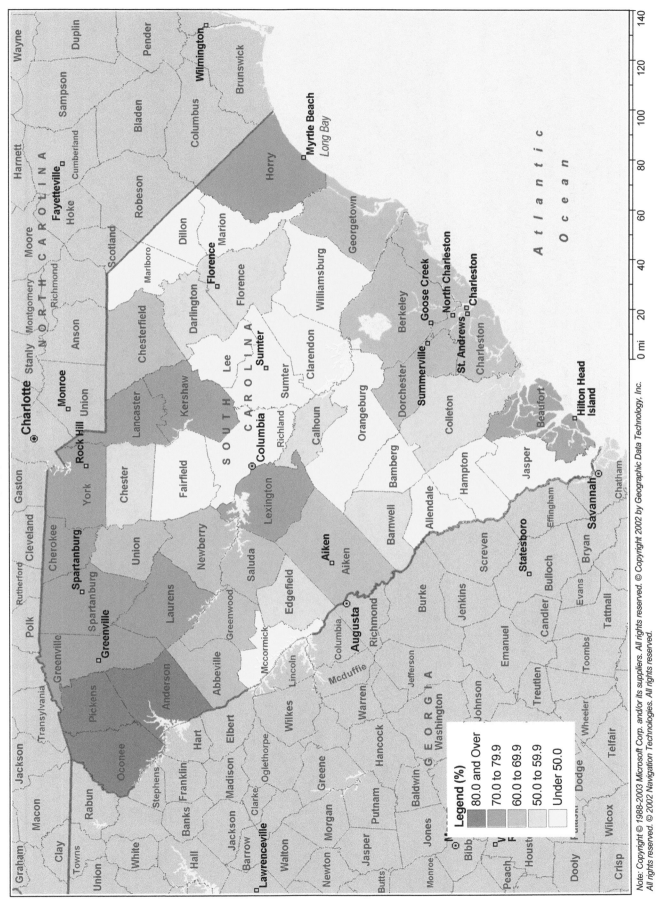

Legend (%)
- 80.0 and Over
- 70.0 to 79.9
- 60.0 to 69.9
- 50.0 to 59.9
- Under 50.0

Percent Black

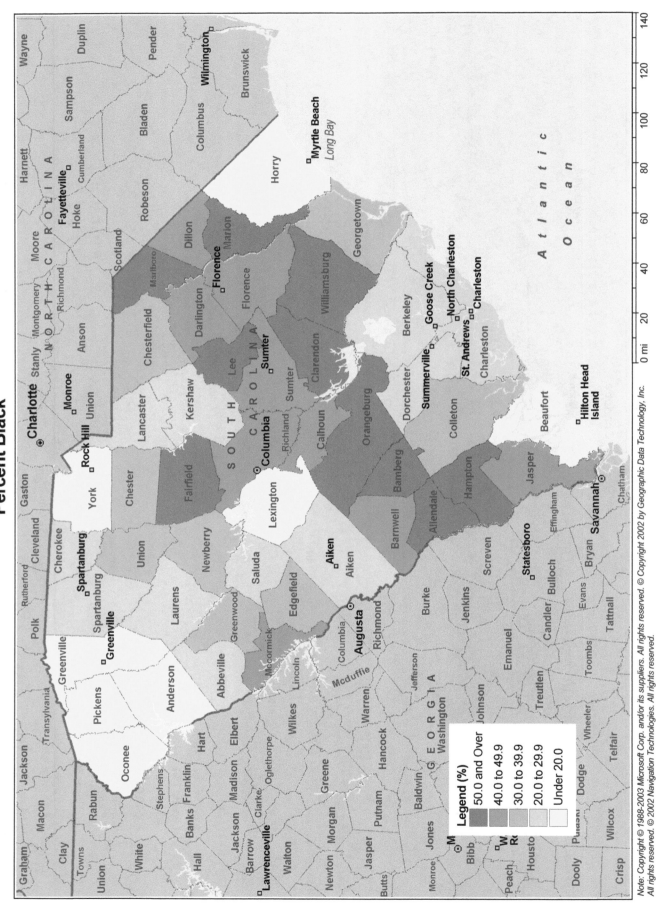

Legend (%)
- 50.0 and Over
- 40.0 to 49.9
- 30.0 to 39.9
- 20.0 to 29.9
- Under 20.0

Percent Asian

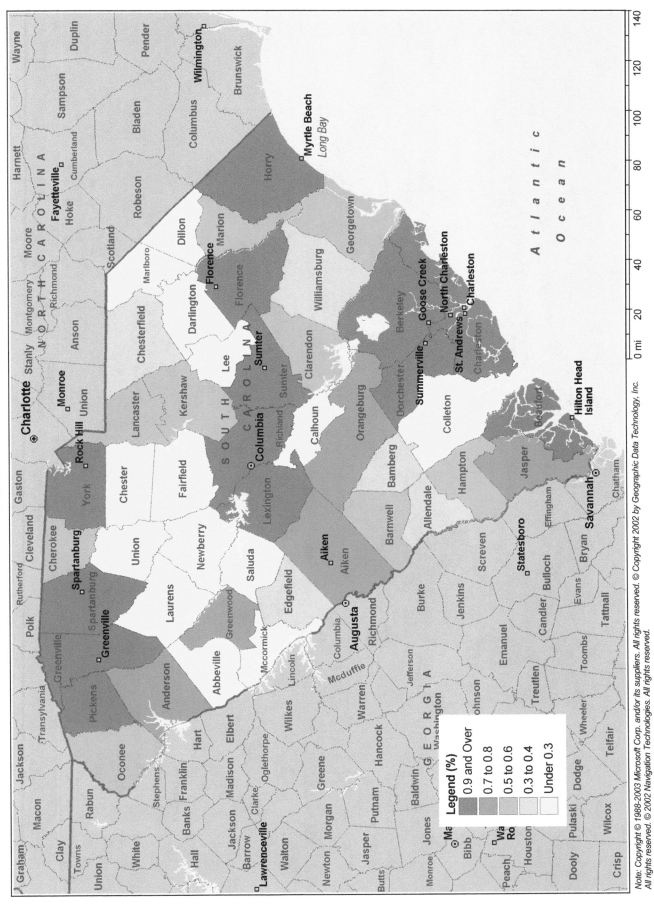

Legend (%)

- 0.9 and Over
- 0.7 to 0.8
- 0.5 to 0.6
- 0.3 to 0.4
- Under 0.3

Percent Hispanic

Legend (%)
- 6.0 and Over
- 4.5 to 5.9
- 3.0 to 4.4
- 1.5 to 2.9
- Under 1.5

Median Age

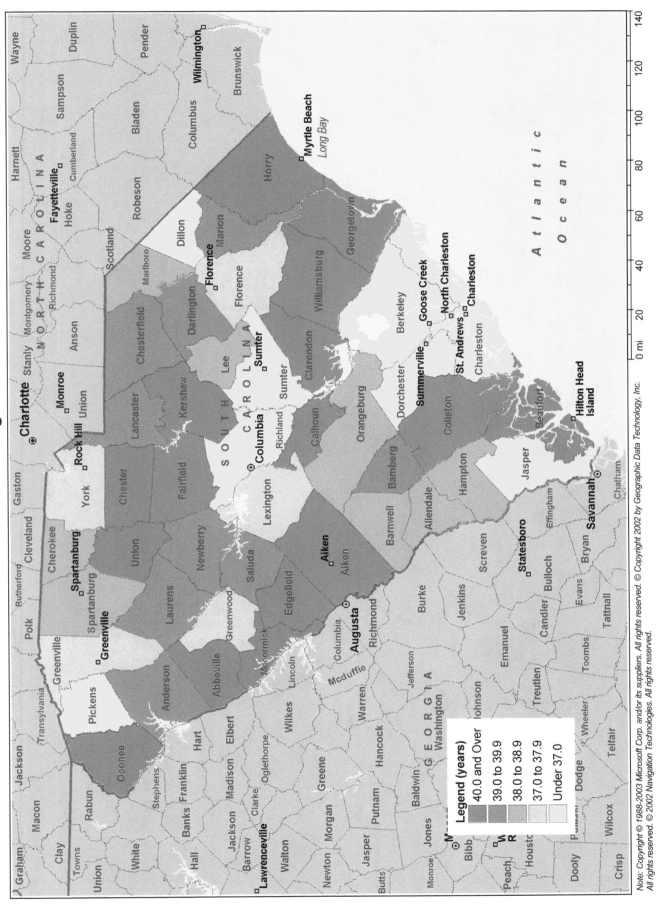

Legend (years)
- 40.0 and Over
- 39.0 to 39.9
- 38.0 to 38.9
- 37.0 to 37.9
- Under 37.0

Median Household Income

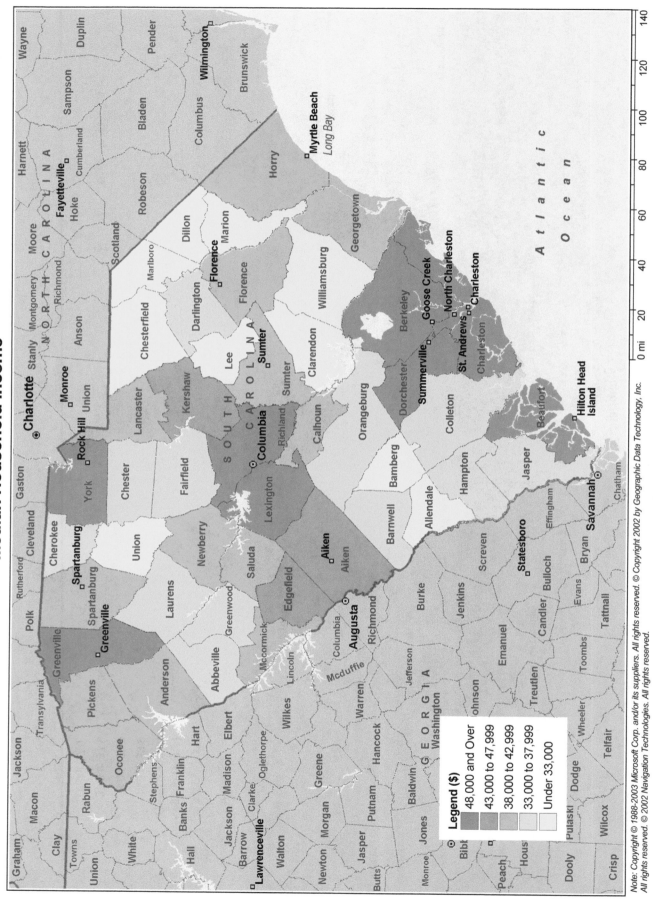

Legend ($)
- 48,000 and Over
- 43,000 to 47,999
- 38,000 to 42,999
- 33,000 to 37,999
- Under 33,000

Median Home Value

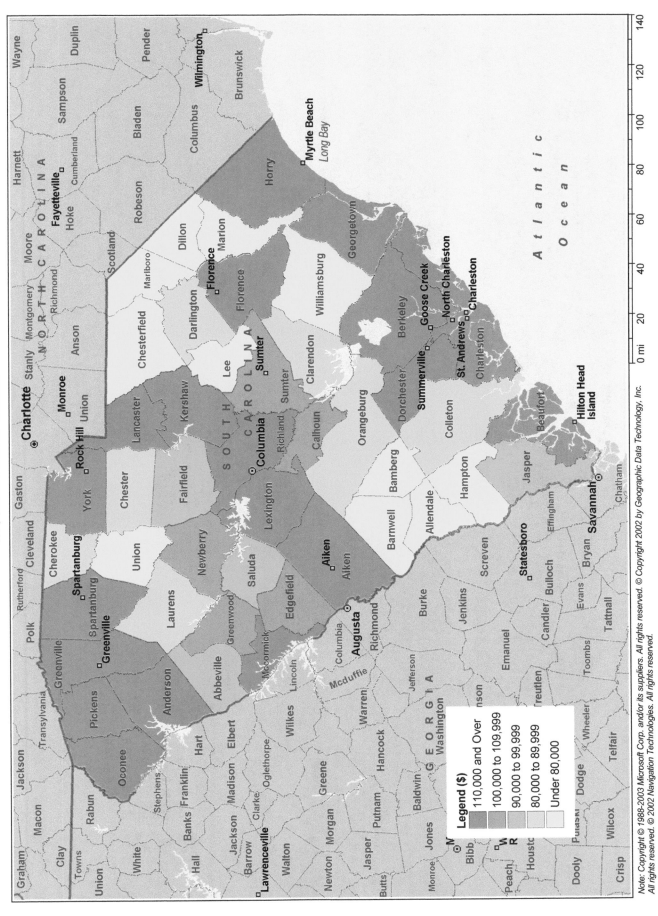

Legend ($)
- 110,000 and Over
- 100,000 to 109,999
- 90,000 to 99,999
- 80,000 to 89,999
- Under 80,000

High School Graduates*

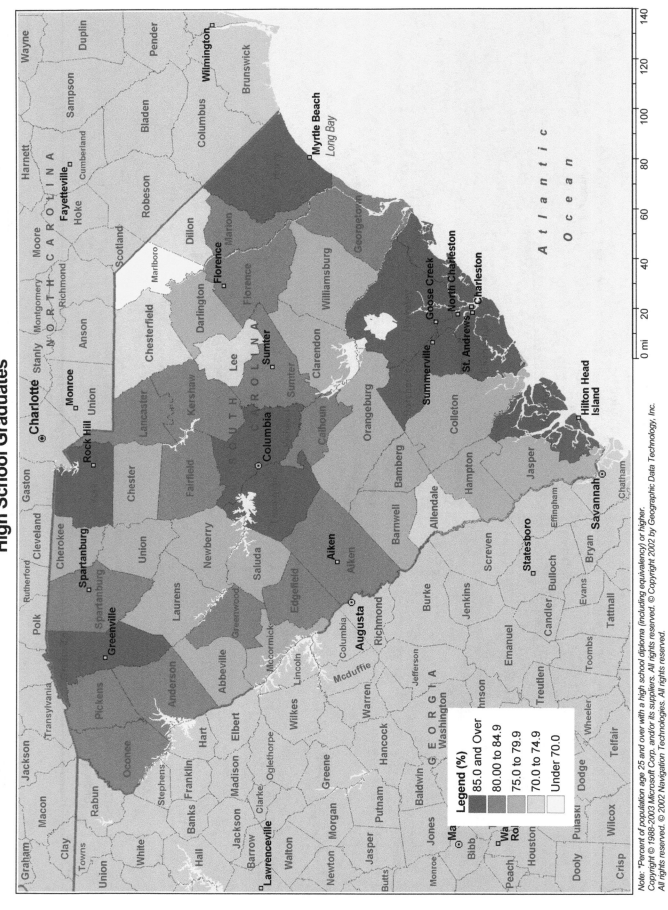

Legend (%)

- 85.0 and Over
- 80.00 to 84.9
- 75.0 to 79.9
- 70.0 to 74.9
- Under 70.0

College Graduates*

Legend (%)

- 20.0 and Over
- 17.0 to 19.9
- 14.0 to 16.9
- 11.0 to 13.9
- Under 11.0

Profiles

Abbeville County

Located in northwestern South Carolina; bounded on the west by the Savannah River and the Georgia border, and on the northeast by the Saluda River; includes part of Sumter National Forest. Covers a land area of 490.484 square miles, a water area of 20.508 square miles, and is located in the Eastern Time Zone at 34.21° N. Lat., 82.46° W. Long. The county was founded in 1785. County seat is Abbeville.

Abbeville County is part of the Greenwood, SC Micropolitan Statistical Area. The entire metro area includes: Abbeville County, SC; Greenwood County, SC

Weather Station: Calhoun Falls   Elevation: 529 feet

	Jan	Feb	Mar	Apr	May	Jun	Jul	Aug	Sep	Oct	Nov	Dec
High	54	58	66	74	81	88	92	90	84	74	65	56
Low	32	34	40	47	57	66	70	69	62	50	40	33
Precip	4.1	4.3	4.9	3.0	3.0	4.1	4.4	3.6	3.2	3.3	3.6	3.8
Snow	0.1	0.1	0.5	0.0	0.0	0.0	0.0	0.0	0.0	0.0	0.0	tr

High and Low temperatures in degrees Fahrenheit; Precipitation and Snow in inches

Population: 25,417; Growth (since 2000): -2.9%; Density: 51.8 persons per square mile; Race: 69.6% White, 28.3% Black/African American, 0.3% Asian, 0.2% American Indian/Alaska Native, 0.0% Native Hawaiian/Other Pacific Islander, 1.1% two or more races, 1.0% Hispanic of any race; Average household size: 2.45; Median age: 41.6; Age under 18: 22.8%; Age 65 and over: 16.5%; Males per 100 females: 94.1; Marriage status: 28.7% never married, 53.5% now married, 3.4% separated, 8.6% widowed, 9.1% divorced; Foreign born: 1.0%; Speak English only: 97.7%; With disability: 19.8%; Veterans: 9.9%; Ancestry: 19.3% American, 9.4% Irish, 8.5% German, 7.8% English, 3.8% Scotch-Irish

Religion: Six largest groups: 31.7% Baptist, 20.3% Methodist/Pietist, 4.5% Pentecostal, 4.1% Presbyterian-Reformed, 2.5% Non-denominational Protestant, 0.9% European Free-Church

Economy: Unemployment rate: 7.1%; Leading industries: 18.3% retail trade; 14.2% other services (except public administration); 12.1% construction; Farms: 574 totaling 92,047 acres; Company size: 0 employ 1,000 or more persons, 0 employ 500 to 999 persons, 7 employ 100 to 499 persons, 331 employs less than 100 persons; Business ownership: 462 women-owned, 265 Black-owned, n/a Hispanic-owned, n/a Asian-owned

Employment: 8.4% management, business, and financial, 1.8% computer, engineering, and science, 10.0% education, legal, community service, arts, and media, 6.3% healthcare practitioners, 17.2% service, 20.4% sales and office, 11.0% natural resources, construction, and maintenance, 24.7% production, transportation, and material moving

Income: Per capita: $18,134; Median household: $35,947; Average household: $45,632; Households with income of $100,000 or more: 7.7%; Poverty rate: 21.6%

Educational Attainment: High school diploma or higher: 76.8%; Bachelor's degree or higher: 12.2%; Graduate/professional degree or higher: 4.4%

Housing: Homeownership rate: 76.6%; Median home value: $91,200; Median year structure built: 1976; Homeowner vacancy rate: 1.9%; Median gross rent: $629 per month; Rental vacancy rate: 11.1%

Vital Statistics: Birth rate: 108.4 per 10,000 population; Death rate: 100.0 per 10,000 population; Age-adjusted cancer mortality rate: 223.0 deaths per 100,000 population

Health Insurance: 83.9% have insurance; 57.3% have private insurance; 39.2% have public insurance; 16.1% do not have insurance; 10.8% of children under 18 do not have insurance

Health Care: Physicians: 5.6 per 10,000 population; Hospital beds: 10.0 per 10,000 population; Hospital admissions: 291.8 per 10,000 population

Air Quality Index: 99.1% good, 0.9% moderate, 0.0% unhealthy for sensitive individuals, 0.0% unhealthy (percent of days)

Transportation: Commute: 95.0% car, 0.0% public transportation, 1.8% walk, 2.6% work from home; Median travel time to work: 27.1 minutes

Presidential Election: 42.6% Obama, 56.0% Romney (2012)

Additional Information Contacts

Abbeville Government . . . . (864) 366-4210
    http://www.abbevillecountysc.com

Abbeville County Communities

ABBEVILLE (city). County seat. Covers a land area of 6.116 square miles and a water area of 0.012 square miles. Located at 34.18° N. Lat; 82.38° W. Long. Elevation is 591 feet.

History: Named for Abbeville, France, by Huguenot settlers, the town of Abbeville was often referred to as "The cradle and the grave of the Confederacy." Here, it is claimed, the meeting that began the secession movement was held on November 22, 1860, and the last confederate cabinet meeting of President Jefferson Davis was held on May 2, 1865.

Population: 5,237; Growth (since 2000): -10.3%; Density: 856.3 persons per square mile; Race: 46.9% White, 50.5% Black/African American, 0.4% Asian, 0.2% American Indian/Alaska Native, 0.0% Native Hawaiian/Other Pacific Islander, 1.5% Two or more races, 0.9% Hispanic of any race; Average household size: 2.30; Median age: 40.4; Age under 18: 24.0%; Age 65 and over: 17.5%; Males per 100 females: 81.3; Marriage status: 34.8% never married, 45.3% now married, 4.1% separated, 10.3% widowed, 9.6% divorced; Foreign born: 0.5%; Speak English only: 98.0%; With disability: 24.5%; Veterans: 9.4%; Ancestry: 14.6% American, 6.2% Irish, 5.1% Scotch-Irish, 3.6% Scottish, 3.3% English

Employment: 9.5% management, business, and financial, 1.1% computer, engineering, and science, 11.7% education, legal, community service, arts, and media, 3.8% healthcare practitioners, 26.4% service, 24.6% sales and office, 4.9% natural resources, construction, and maintenance, 18.0% production, transportation, and material moving

Income: Per capita: $14,771; Median household: $23,027; Average household: $35,608; Households with income of $100,000 or more: 5.1%; Poverty rate: 37.4%

Educational Attainment: High school diploma or higher: 74.6%; Bachelor's degree or higher: 11.6%; Graduate/professional degree or higher: 4.5%

School District(s)

Abbeville 60 (PK-12)
    2012-13 Enrollment: 3,165 . . . . (864) 366-5427

Housing: Homeownership rate: 59.3%; Median home value: $87,200; Median year structure built: 1962; Homeowner vacancy rate: 3.4%; Median gross rent: $678 per month; Rental vacancy rate: 13.2%

Health Insurance: 86.9% have insurance; 52.8% have private insurance; 49.0% have public insurance; 13.1% do not have insurance; 1.0% of children under 18 do not have insurance

Hospitals: Abbeville Area Medical Center (25 beds)

Safety: Violent crime rate: 77.5 per 10,000 population; Property crime rate: 416.4 per 10,000 population

Newspapers: Abbeville Press & Banner (weekly circulation 7500)

Transportation: Commute: 94.8% car, 0.0% public transportation, 2.1% walk, 1.9% work from home; Median travel time to work: 24.9 minutes

Additional Information Contacts

City of Abbeville. . . . . (864) 459-2109
    http://abbevillecitysc.sc.gov

ANTREVILLE (CDP). Covers a land area of 3.879 square miles and a water area of 0.016 square miles. Located at 34.30° N. Lat; 82.56° W. Long. Elevation is 722 feet.

Population: 140; Growth (since 2000): 18.6%; Density: 36.1 persons per square mile; Race: 87.1% White, 12.1% Black/African American, 0.0% Asian, 0.0% American Indian/Alaska Native, 0.0% Native Hawaiian/Other Pacific Islander, 0.7% Two or more races, 0.0% Hispanic of any race; Average household size: 2.39; Median age: 46.5; Age under 18: 20.7%; Age 65 and over: 25.7%; Males per 100 females: 79.5

Housing: Homeownership rate: 80.7%; Homeowner vacancy rate: 0.0%; Rental vacancy rate: 26.7%

CALHOUN FALLS (town). Covers a land area of 3.386 square miles and a water area of 0.074 square miles. Located at 34.09° N. Lat; 82.60° W. Long. Elevation is 528 feet.

History: Calhoun Falls is named for the Calhoun family whose property holdings extended for many miles along the Savannah River.

Population: 2,004; Growth (since 2000): -13.0%; Density: 591.8 persons per square mile; Race: 44.0% White, 53.1% Black/African American, 0.0% Asian, 0.5% American Indian/Alaska Native, 0.0% Native Hawaiian/Other Pacific Islander, 1.9% Two or more races, 1.2% Hispanic of any race; Average household size: 2.43; Median age: 40.8; Age under 18: 24.3%; Age 65 and over: 16.1%; Males per 100 females: 88.3

School District(s)

Abbeville 60 (PK-12)

    2012-13 Enrollment: 3,165 . . . . (864) 366-5427

Sc Public Charter SD (PK-12)

    2012-13 Enrollment: 11,500 . . . . (803) 734-8322

Housing: Homeownership rate: 65.2%; Homeowner vacancy rate: 2.4%; Rental vacancy rate: 7.9%

Additional Information Contacts

Town of Calhoun Falls. . . . . (864) 418-8512

DONALDS (town). Covers a land area of 0.832 square miles and a water area of 0.006 square miles. Located at 34.38° N. Lat; 82.35° W. Long. Elevation is 761 feet.

Population: 348; Growth (since 2000): -1.7%; Density: 418.4 persons per square mile; Race: 82.2% White, 13.8% Black/African American, 0.6% Asian, 0.0% American Indian/Alaska Native, 0.0% Native Hawaiian/Other Pacific Islander, 1.7% Two or more races, 1.4% Hispanic of any race; Average household size: 2.58; Median age: 38.1; Age under 18: 27.3%; Age 65 and over: 15.5%; Males per 100 females: 87.1

School District(s)

Abbeville 60 (PK-12)

    2012-13 Enrollment: 3,165 . . . . (864) 366-5427

Housing: Homeownership rate: 71.8%; Homeowner vacancy rate: 1.0%; Rental vacancy rate: 9.5%

DUE WEST (town). Covers a land area of 1.635 square miles and a water area of 0.005 square miles. Located at 34.33° N. Lat; 82.39° W. Long. Elevation is 699 feet.

History: Once an old trading center called Duett's or DeWitt's Corner, Due West was the location of Erskin College, founded in 1849 by the Associate Reformed Presbyterian Church.

Population: 1,247; Growth (since 2000): 3.1%; Density: 762.5 persons per square mile; Race: 81.6% White, 15.6% Black/African American, 0.6% Asian, 0.1% American Indian/Alaska Native, 0.0% Native Hawaiian/Other Pacific Islander, 1.5% Two or more races, 1.4% Hispanic of any race; Average household size: 2.25; Median age: 22.4; Age under 18: 11.2%; Age 65 and over: 16.1%; Males per 100 females: 87.0

School District(s)

Abbeville 60 (PK-12)

    2012-13 Enrollment: 3,165 . . . . (864) 366-5427

Four-year College(s)

Erskine College (Private, Not-for-profit, Reformed Presbyterian Church)

    Fall 2013 Enrollment: 815 . . . . (864) 379-2131

    2013-14 Tuition: In-state $31,580; Out-of-state $31,580

Housing: Homeownership rate: 64.9%; Homeowner vacancy rate: 3.0%; Rental vacancy rate: 11.8%

Safety: Violent crime rate: 0.0 per 10,000 population; Property crime rate: 80.8 per 10,000 population

Additional Information Contacts

Town of Due West. . . . . (864) 379-2385

    http://www.abbevillescchamber.com

LAKE SECESSION (CDP). Covers a land area of 5.630 square miles and a water area of 1.585 square miles. Located at 34.29° N. Lat; 82.59° W. Long. Elevation is 551 feet.

Population: 1,083; Growth (since 2000): 16.7%; Density: 192.4 persons per square mile; Race: 95.7% White, 2.5% Black/African American, 0.1% Asian, 0.4% American Indian/Alaska Native, 0.0% Native Hawaiian/Other Pacific Islander, 1.4% Two or more races, 0.4% Hispanic of any race; Average household size: 2.27; Median age: 51.3; Age under 18: 17.8%; Age 65 and over: 24.1%; Males per 100 females: 96.9

Housing: Homeownership rate: 85.3%; Homeowner vacancy rate: 5.1%; Rental vacancy rate: 4.1%

LOWNDESVILLE (town). Covers a land area of 0.775 square miles and a water area of 0 square miles. Located at 34.21° N. Lat; 82.65° W. Long. Elevation is 607 feet.

History: Lowndesville was incorporated in 1839 as a depot for shipping cotton to the coast by floating it down the river.

Population: 128; Growth (since 2000): -22.9%; Density: 165.3 persons per square mile; Race: 78.1% White, 19.5% Black/African American, 0.0% Asian, 0.0% American Indian/Alaska Native, 0.0% Native Hawaiian/Other Pacific Islander, 1.6% Two or more races, 3.1% Hispanic of any race; Average household size: 2.17; Median age: 45.0; Age under 18: 25.8%; Age 65 and over: 19.5%; Males per 100 females: 141.5

Housing: Homeownership rate: 52.6%; Homeowner vacancy rate: 5.0%; Rental vacancy rate: 0.0%

Aiken County

Located in western South Carolina, at the edge of the piedmont region in the Sand Hills Belt; bounded on the west by the Savannah River and the Georgia border, and on the northeast by the North Fork of the Edisto River. Covers a land area of 1,071.034 square miles, a water area of 9.562 square miles, and is located in the Eastern Time Zone at 33.55° N. Lat., 81.63° W. Long. The county was founded in 1871. County seat is Aiken.

Aiken County is part of the Augusta-Richmond County, GA-SC Metropolitan Statistical Area. The entire metro area includes: Burke County, GA; Columbia County, GA; Lincoln County, GA; McDuffie County, GA; Richmond County, GA; Aiken County, SC; Edgefield County, SC

Weather Station: Aiken 4 NE										Elevation: 399 feet		
	Jan	Feb	Mar	Apr	May	Jun	Jul	Aug	Sep	Oct	Nov	Dec
High	58	63	70	79	86	91	94	92	87	78	69	60
Low	33	36	42	49	58	66	70	69	62	51	42	34
Precip	4.9	4.3	5.1	3.1	3.3	5.5	4.9	5.2	4.0	3.4	3.3	3.6
Snow	0.4	tr	tr	0.0	0.0	0.0	0.0	0.0	0.0	0.0	tr	0.0

High and Low temperatures in degrees Fahrenheit; Precipitation and Snow in inches

Population: 160,099; Growth (since 2000): 12.3%; Density: 149.5 persons per square mile; Race: 69.6% White, 24.6% Black/African American, 0.8% Asian, 0.4% American Indian/Alaska Native, 0.0% Native Hawaiian/Other Pacific Islander, 1.9% two or more races, 4.9% Hispanic of any race; Average household size: 2.45; Median age: 40.0; Age under 18: 23.0%; Age 65 and over: 15.4%; Males per 100 females: 93.9; Marriage status: 28.9% never married, 52.7% now married, 3.0% separated, 7.2% widowed, 11.2% divorced; Foreign born: 3.4%; Speak English only: 94.8%; With disability: 14.1%; Veterans: 11.3%; Ancestry: 23.8% American, 9.0% German, 8.6% Irish, 8.2% English, 2.2% Italian

Religion: Six largest groups: 32.0% Baptist, 8.7% Non-denominational Protestant, 5.2% Catholicism, 4.5% Methodist/Pietist, 3.8% Pentecostal, 1.8% Presbyterian-Reformed

Economy: Unemployment rate: 6.4%; Leading industries: 19.0% retail trade; 11.5% health care and social assistance; 11.2% other services (except public administration); Farms: 1,102 totaling 154,351 acres; Company size: 5 employ 1,000 or more persons, 4 employ 500 to 999 persons, 56 employ 100 to 499 persons, 2,614 employ less than 100 persons; Business ownership: 3,694 women-owned, 1,337 Black-owned, 285 Hispanic-owned, 219 Asian-owned

Employment: 12.6% management, business, and financial, 5.9% computer, engineering, and science, 9.8% education, legal, community service, arts, and media, 6.6% healthcare practitioners, 16.5% service, 23.0% sales and office, 10.6% natural resources, construction, and maintenance, 15.1% production, transportation, and material moving

Income: Per capita: $24,769; Median household: $44,509; Average household: $60,728; Households with income of $100,000 or more: 17.2%; Poverty rate: 18.9%

Educational Attainment: High school diploma or higher: 84.8%; Bachelor's degree or higher: 24.0%; Graduate/professional degree or higher: 9.1%

Housing: Homeownership rate: 73.1%; Median home value: $124,600; Median year structure built: 1984; Homeowner vacancy rate: 2.4%; Median gross rent: $705 per month; Rental vacancy rate: 9.1%

Vital Statistics: Birth rate: 115.0 per 10,000 population; Death rate: 98.6 per 10,000 population; Age-adjusted cancer mortality rate: 168.0 deaths per 100,000 population

Health Insurance: 84.6% have insurance; 64.2% have private insurance; 34.1% have public insurance; 15.4% do not have insurance; 7.9% of children under 18 do not have insurance

Health Care: Physicians: 11.7 per 10,000 population; Hospital beds: 15.8 per 10,000 population; Hospital admissions: 768.5 per 10,000 population

Air Quality Index: 97.8% good, 2.2% moderate, 0.0% unhealthy for sensitive individuals, 0.0% unhealthy (percent of days)

Transportation: Commute: 94.4% car, 0.1% public transportation, 1.1% walk, 3.1% work from home; Median travel time to work: 25.2 minutes

Presidential Election: 36.0% Obama, 62.6% Romney (2012)

National and State Parks: Aiken State Park; Redcliffe State Park

Additional Information Contacts

Aiken Government. . . . . (803) 642-1715

    http://www.aikencountysc.gov

Aiken County Communities

AIKEN (city). County seat. Covers a land area of 20.697 square miles and a water area of 0.142 square miles. Located at 33.53° N. Lat; 81.73° W. Long. Elevation is 515 feet.

History: Aiken was named in 1834 for William Aiken, father of Governor Aiken, when a townsite was laid out near the western terminus of the Charleston-Hamburg railroad. The nation's first passenger train and the first train carrying U.S. mail passed through Aiken. Though incorporated in 1835, the new settlement made little progress until 1845, when William Gregg built a cotton mill in Horse Creek Valley, six miles away. Aiken witnessed a Civil War battle in 1865 when General H.J. Kilpatrick, ordered by Sherman to destroy the mills at Graniteville, was defeated by General Joe Wheeler in a confrontation on the main street of Aiken.

Population: 29,524; Growth (since 2000): 16.5%; Density: 1,426.5 persons per square mile; Race: 66.8% White, 28.5% Black/African American, 1.9% Asian, 0.4% American Indian/Alaska Native, 0.1% Native Hawaiian/Other Pacific Islander, 1.5% Two or more races, 2.6% Hispanic of any race; Average household size: 2.20; Median age: 44.8; Age under 18: 19.6%; Age 65 and over: 21.9%; Males per 100 females: 85.3; Marriage status: 34.4% never married, 47.3% now married, 1.5% separated, 10.2% widowed, 8.2% divorced; Foreign born: 4.0%; Speak English only: 96.0%; With disability: 12.0%; Veterans: 12.5%; Ancestry: 14.7% American, 11.2% German, 10.5% English, 9.5% Irish, 3.5% Italian

Employment: 17.2% management, business, and financial, 9.7% computer, engineering, and science, 12.1% education, legal, community service, arts, and media, 6.3% healthcare practitioners, 18.5% service, 21.9% sales and office, 5.1% natural resources, construction, and maintenance, 9.2% production, transportation, and material moving

Income: Per capita: $31,853; Median household: $53,127; Average household: $74,298; Households with income of $100,000 or more: 25.7%; Poverty rate: 17.0%

Educational Attainment: High school diploma or higher: 90.8%; Bachelor's degree or higher: 43.1%; Graduate/professional degree or higher: 18.7%

School District(s)
Aiken 01 (PK-12)
    2012-13 Enrollment: 24,686 . . . . (803) 641-2430

Four-year College(s)
University of South Carolina-Aiken (Public)
    Fall 2013 Enrollment: 3,299 . . . . (803) 648-6851
    2013-14 Tuition: In-state $9,308; Out-of-state $18,340

Vocational/Technical School(s)
Aiken School of Cosmetology (Private, For-profit)
    Fall 2013 Enrollment: 33 . . . . (803) 644-7133
    2013-14 Tuition: $14,100
Lacy Cosmetology School-Aiken (Private, For-profit)
    Fall 2013 Enrollment: 17 . . . . (803) 648-6181
    2013-14 Tuition: $17,065

Housing: Homeownership rate: 66.0%; Median home value: $179,100; Median year structure built: 1986; Homeowner vacancy rate: 3.5%; Median gross rent: $839 per month; Rental vacancy rate: 6.8%

Health Insurance: 90.1% have insurance; 71.5% have private insurance; 36.8% have public insurance; 9.9% do not have insurance; 5.8% of children under 18 do not have insurance

Hospitals: Aiken Regional Medical Center (230 beds)

Safety: Violent crime rate: 32.0 per 10,000 population; Property crime rate: 493.6 per 10,000 population

Newspapers: Aiken Standard (daily circulation 15000)

Transportation: Commute: 91.0% car, 0.3% public transportation, 2.1% walk, 4.7% work from home; Median travel time to work: 21.4 minutes

Airports: Aiken Municipal (general aviation)

Additional Information Contacts
City of Aiken . . . . (803) 642-7654
    http://www.aiken.net

BATH (unincorporated postal area)
ZCTA: 29816
    Covers a land area of 0.985 square miles and a water area of 0.020 square miles. Located at 33.50° N. Lat; 81.87° W. Long. Elevation is 164 feet.
    Population: 1,033; Growth (since 2000): 1.7%; Density: 1,049.0 persons per square mile; Race: 78.9% White, 7.0% Black/African American, 1.3% Asian, 0.6% American Indian/Alaska Native, 0.0%

    Native Hawaiian/Other Pacific Islander, 4.5% Two or more races, 12.3% Hispanic of any race; Average household size: 2.58; Median age: 38.4; Age under 18: 24.5%; Age 65 and over: 13.7%; Males per 100 females: 89.5
    Housing: Homeownership rate: 63.3%; Homeowner vacancy rate: 1.1%; Rental vacancy rate: 3.9%

BEECH ISLAND (unincorporated postal area)
ZCTA: 29842
    Covers a land area of 39.113 square miles and a water area of 0.508 square miles. Located at 33.45° N. Lat; 81.86° W. Long. Elevation is 226 feet.
    Population: 7,675; Growth (since 2000): 13.2%; Density: 196.2 persons per square mile; Race: 56.5% White, 35.5% Black/African American, 0.2% Asian, 0.4% American Indian/Alaska Native, 0.0% Native Hawaiian/Other Pacific Islander, 2.7% Two or more races, 7.1% Hispanic of any race; Average household size: 2.58; Median age: 38.4; Age under 18: 24.4%; Age 65 and over: 12.3%; Males per 100 females: 95.3; Marriage status: 28.1% never married, 47.0% now married, 4.3% separated, 7.0% widowed, 17.9% divorced; Foreign born: 2.4%; Speak English only: 94.2%; With disability: 19.3%; Veterans: 8.5%; Ancestry: 38.7% American, 6.4% Irish, 5.3% German, 2.8% English, 2.8% African
    Employment: 3.4% management, business, and financial, 0.7% computer, engineering, and science, 8.7% education, legal, community service, arts, and media, 5.0% healthcare practitioners, 16.5% service, 31.1% sales and office, 9.2% natural resources, construction, and maintenance, 25.5% production, transportation, and material moving
    Income: Per capita: $15,873; Median household: $30,537; Average household: $40,307; Households with income of $100,000 or more: 4.8%; Poverty rate: 32.6%
    Educational Attainment: High school diploma or higher: 79.3%; Bachelor's degree or higher: 9.4%; Graduate/professional degree or higher: 4.5%
    Housing: Homeownership rate: 72.7%; Median home value: $76,100; Median year structure built: 1981; Homeowner vacancy rate: 3.0%; Median gross rent: $649 per month; Rental vacancy rate: 9.7%
    Health Insurance: 73.7% have insurance; 49.0% have private insurance; 34.8% have public insurance; 26.3% do not have insurance; 20.7% of children under 18 do not have insurance
    Transportation: Commute: 91.7% car, 0.0% public transportation, 1.0% walk, 3.9% work from home; Median travel time to work: 23.6 minutes

BELVEDERE (CDP). Covers a land area of 3.504 square miles and a water area of 0.006 square miles. Located at 33.54° N. Lat; 81.94° W. Long. Elevation is 486 feet.
Population: 5,792; Growth (since 2000): 2.9%; Density: 1,653.1 persons per square mile; Race: 66.8% White, 26.2% Black/African American, 0.4% Asian, 0.3% American Indian/Alaska Native, 0.1% Native Hawaiian/Other Pacific Islander, 2.6% Two or more races, 6.0% Hispanic of any race; Average household size: 2.54; Median age: 36.2; Age under 18: 25.0%; Age 65 and over: 15.0%; Males per 100 females: 94.0; Marriage status: 24.2% never married, 49.9% now married, 6.0% separated, 9.9% widowed, 16.0% divorced; Foreign born: 5.6%; Speak English only: 91.3%; With disability: 14.4%; Veterans: 14.8%; Ancestry: 18.4% American, 7.2% Irish, 5.3% German, 5.3% English, 1.3% Scotch-Irish
Employment: 10.6% management, business, and financial, 2.1% computer, engineering, and science, 9.6% education, legal, community service, arts, and media, 6.9% healthcare practitioners, 16.5% service, 22.2% sales and office, 11.4% natural resources, construction, and maintenance, 20.7% production, transportation, and material moving
Income: Per capita: $20,229; Median household: $42,208; Average household: $53,782; Households with income of $100,000 or more: 9.4%; Poverty rate: 24.2%
Educational Attainment: High school diploma or higher: 82.2%; Bachelor's degree or higher: 11.8%; Graduate/professional degree or higher: 5.6%

School District(s)
Aiken 01 (PK-12)
    2012-13 Enrollment: 24,686 . . . . (803) 641-2430
Housing: Homeownership rate: 69.2%; Median home value: $95,100; Median year structure built: 1969; Homeowner vacancy rate: 2.8%; Median gross rent: $704 per month; Rental vacancy rate: 7.5%
Health Insurance: 83.1% have insurance; 56.1% have private insurance; 40.8% have public insurance; 16.9% do not have insurance; 5.3% of children under 18 do not have insurance

Transportation: Commute: 93.5% car, 0.0% public transportation, 2.7% walk, 1.2% work from home; Median travel time to work: 25.2 minutes

BURNETTOWN (town). Covers a land area of 5.477 square miles and a water area of 0.553 square miles. Located at 33.52° N. Lat; 81.86° W. Long. Elevation is 177 feet.

Population: 2,673; Growth (since 2000): -1.7%; Density: 488.1 persons per square mile; Race: 78.3% White, 14.2% Black/African American, 0.7% Asian, 0.6% American Indian/Alaska Native, 0.0% Native Hawaiian/Other Pacific Islander, 2.1% Two or more races, 6.4% Hispanic of any race; Average household size: 2.56; Median age: 41.3; Age under 18: 23.1%; Age 65 and over: 16.2%; Males per 100 females: 100.7; Marriage status: 26.5% never married, 57.5% now married, 2.0% separated, 6.6% widowed, 9.4% divorced; Foreign born: 1.6%; Speak English only: 96.4%; With disability: 17.6%; Veterans: 11.8%; Ancestry: 36.9% American, 8.3% English, 6.0% German, 4.1% Irish, 1.9% Greek

Employment: 8.0% management, business, and financial, 4.0% computer, engineering, and science, 6.2% education, legal, community service, arts, and media, 3.3% healthcare practitioners, 24.4% service, 22.8% sales and office, 19.3% natural resources, construction, and maintenance, 12.0% production, transportation, and material moving

Income: Per capita: $18,470; Median household: $36,739; Average household: $44,795; Households with income of $100,000 or more: 7.2%; Poverty rate: 17.6%

Educational Attainment: High school diploma or higher: 80.0%; Bachelor's degree or higher: 11.5%; Graduate/professional degree or higher: 3.8%

Housing: Homeownership rate: 79.8%; Median home value: $88,200; Median year structure built: 1967; Homeowner vacancy rate: 2.0%; Median gross rent: $706 per month; Rental vacancy rate: 7.9%

Health Insurance: 80.8% have insurance; 54.8% have private insurance; 38.4% have public insurance; 19.2% do not have insurance; 17.3% of children under 18 do not have insurance

Safety: Violent crime rate: 36.6 per 10,000 population; Property crime rate: 124.4 per 10,000 population

Transportation: Commute: 94.0% car, 0.0% public transportation, 0.4% walk, 5.0% work from home; Median travel time to work: 22.8 minutes

Additional Information Contacts

Town of Burnettown . . . . (803) 593-2676
   http://www.burnettown.com

CLEARWATER (CDP). Covers a land area of 4.189 square miles and a water area of 0.122 square miles. Located at 33.50° N. Lat; 81.91° W. Long. Elevation is 148 feet.

Population: 4,370; Growth (since 2000): 4.1%; Density: 1,043.2 persons per square mile; Race: 69.6% White, 16.3% Black/African American, 0.2% Asian, 0.6% American Indian/Alaska Native, 0.0% Native Hawaiian/Other Pacific Islander, 1.9% Two or more races, 13.6% Hispanic of any race; Average household size: 2.52; Median age: 36.0; Age under 18: 24.6%; Age 65 and over: 14.2%; Males per 100 females: 99.4; Marriage status: 28.5% never married, 49.9% now married, 4.6% separated, 4.9% widowed, 16.8% divorced; Foreign born: 3.5%; Speak English only: 89.7%; With disability: 23.4%; Veterans: 8.5%; Ancestry: 54.6% American, 5.5% English, 4.7% Irish, 4.6% German, 1.8% Danish

Employment: 3.2% management, business, and financial, 4.6% computer, engineering, and science, 4.0% education, legal, community service, arts, and media, 6.8% healthcare practitioners, 10.6% service, 28.3% sales and office, 16.6% natural resources, construction, and maintenance, 26.0% production, transportation, and material moving

Income: Per capita: $14,672; Median household: $26,555; Average household: $35,681; Households with income of $100,000 or more: 3.7%; Poverty rate: 40.4%

Educational Attainment: High school diploma or higher: 79.3%; Bachelor's degree or higher: 10.9%; Graduate/professional degree or higher: 4.0%

School District(s)

Aiken 01 (PK-12)
   2012-13 Enrollment: 24,686 . . . . (803) 641-2430

Housing: Homeownership rate: 62.1%; Median home value: $112,500; Median year structure built: 1978; Homeowner vacancy rate: 3.3%; Median gross rent: $549 per month; Rental vacancy rate: 9.7%

Health Insurance: 67.6% have insurance; 40.9% have private insurance; 36.4% have public insurance; 32.4% do not have insurance; 26.4% of children under 18 do not have insurance

Transportation: Commute: 90.6% car, 0.0% public transportation, 2.0% walk, 5.7% work from home; Median travel time to work: 19.2 minutes

GLOVERVILLE (CDP). Covers a land area of 3.628 square miles and a water area of 0.009 square miles. Located at 33.53° N. Lat; 81.81° W. Long. Elevation is 203 feet.

Population: 2,831; Growth (since 2000): 0.9%; Density: 780.2 persons per square mile; Race: 80.9% White, 13.5% Black/African American, 0.2% Asian, 0.7% American Indian/Alaska Native, 0.0% Native Hawaiian/Other Pacific Islander, 3.0% Two or more races, 3.1% Hispanic of any race; Average household size: 2.43; Median age: 38.0; Age under 18: 25.3%; Age 65 and over: 14.1%; Males per 100 females: 97.4; Marriage status: 30.8% never married, 43.7% now married, 3.4% separated, 11.4% widowed, 14.0% divorced; Foreign born: 0.0%; Speak English only: 100.0%; With disability: 21.0%; Veterans: 7.0%; Ancestry: 60.0% American, 3.6% German, 3.2% Irish, 2.5% English, 1.7% Scottish

Employment: 4.7% management, business, and financial, 0.0% computer, engineering, and science, 5.4% education, legal, community service, arts, and media, 7.0% healthcare practitioners, 12.4% service, 20.9% sales and office, 16.3% natural resources, construction, and maintenance, 33.3% production, transportation, and material moving

Income: Per capita: $14,382; Median household: $23,798; Average household: $31,314; Households with income of $100,000 or more: 2.8%; Poverty rate: 33.4%

Educational Attainment: High school diploma or higher: 59.3%; Bachelor's degree or higher: 6.6%; Graduate/professional degree or higher: 2.4%

School District(s)

Aiken 01 (PK-12)
   2012-13 Enrollment: 24,686 . . . . (803) 641-2430

Housing: Homeownership rate: 62.1%; Median home value: $65,000; Median year structure built: 1980; Homeowner vacancy rate: 1.5%; Median gross rent: $615 per month; Rental vacancy rate: 12.2%

Health Insurance: 78.0% have insurance; 36.9% have private insurance; 48.3% have public insurance; 22.0% do not have insurance; 16.1% of children under 18 do not have insurance

Transportation: Commute: 100.0% car, 0.0% public transportation, 0.0% walk, 0.0% work from home; Median travel time to work: 22.8 minutes

GRANITEVILLE (CDP). Covers a land area of 3.307 square miles and a water area of 0.018 square miles. Located at 33.56° N. Lat; 81.81° W. Long. Elevation is 233 feet.

Population: 2,614; Growth (since 2000): n/a; Density: 790.5 persons per square mile; Race: 65.3% White, 28.6% Black/African American, 0.0% Asian, 0.7% American Indian/Alaska Native, 0.1% Native Hawaiian/Other Pacific Islander, 2.5% Two or more races, 5.9% Hispanic of any race; Average household size: 2.49; Median age: 34.5; Age under 18: 27.5%; Age 65 and over: 15.0%; Males per 100 females: 90.8; Marriage status: 41.3% never married, 44.3% now married, 7.6% separated, 5.9% widowed, 8.4% divorced; Foreign born: 0.0%; Speak English only: 98.1%; With disability: 10.7%; Veterans: 7.1%; Ancestry: 14.6% American, 9.3% English, 8.1% Irish, 6.4% African, 4.1% German

Employment: 5.5% management, business, and financial, 0.9% computer, engineering, and science, 8.0% education, legal, community service, arts, and media, 6.1% healthcare practitioners, 22.9% service, 36.2% sales and office, 11.9% natural resources, construction, and maintenance, 8.4% production, transportation, and material moving

Income: Per capita: $16,524; Median household: $23,790; Average household: $35,633; Households with income of $100,000 or more: 8.3%; Poverty rate: 28.8%

Educational Attainment: High school diploma or higher: 83.9%; Bachelor's degree or higher: 9.4%; Graduate/professional degree or higher: 1.8%

School District(s)

Aiken 01 (PK-12)
   2012-13 Enrollment: 24,686 . . . . (803) 641-2430

Two-year College(s)

Aiken Technical College (Public)
   Fall 2013 Enrollment: 2,583 . . . . (803) 508-7263
   2013-14 Tuition: In-state $4,163; Out-of-state $9,630

Housing: Homeownership rate: 63.6%; Median home value: $78,100; Median year structure built: 1970; Homeowner vacancy rate: 3.2%; Median gross rent: $645 per month; Rental vacancy rate: 8.0%

Health Insurance: 79.0% have insurance; 46.0% have private insurance; 42.9% have public insurance; 21.0% do not have insurance; 4.3% of children under 18 do not have insurance
Transportation: Commute: 97.5% car, 0.0% public transportation, 0.0% walk, 1.9% work from home; Median travel time to work: 23.5 minutes

JACKSON (town). Covers a land area of 3.545 square miles and a water area of <.001 square miles. Located at 33.33° N. Lat; 81.79° W. Long. Elevation is 203 feet.

History: Grew with establishment nearby (1951) of Savannah River Nuclear Power Plant of Atomic Energy Commission.
Population: 1,700; Growth (since 2000): 4.6%; Density: 479.6 persons per square mile; Race: 83.8% White, 13.7% Black/African American, 0.8% Asian, 0.4% American Indian/Alaska Native, 0.0% Native Hawaiian/Other Pacific Islander, 1.2% Two or more races, 1.9% Hispanic of any race; Average household size: 2.41; Median age: 44.3; Age under 18: 20.6%; Age 65 and over: 18.7%; Males per 100 females: 88.7

School District(s)
Aiken 01 (PK-12)
    2012-13 Enrollment: 24,686 . . . . (803) 641-2430
Housing: Homeownership rate: 77.8%; Homeowner vacancy rate: 1.9%; Rental vacancy rate: 13.3%
Safety: Violent crime rate: 0.0 per 10,000 population; Property crime rate: 241.7 per 10,000 population

LANGLEY (CDP). Covers a land area of 1.148 square miles and a water area of 0.005 square miles. Located at 33.52° N. Lat; 81.84° W. Long. Elevation is 194 feet.

Population: 1,447; Growth (since 2000): n/a; Density: 1,260.0 persons per square mile; Race: 91.9% White, 4.8% Black/African American, 0.3% Asian, 0.3% American Indian/Alaska Native, 0.1% Native Hawaiian/Other Pacific Islander, 1.8% Two or more races, 2.6% Hispanic of any race; Average household size: 2.44; Median age: 38.7; Age under 18: 23.4%; Age 65 and over: 14.0%; Males per 100 females: 95.3
Housing: Homeownership rate: 66.4%; Homeowner vacancy rate: 1.2%; Rental vacancy rate: 17.2%

MONETTA (town). Covers a land area of 0.737 square miles and a water area of 0 square miles. Located at 33.85° N. Lat; 81.61° W. Long. Elevation is 633 feet.

Population: 236; Growth (since 2000): 7.3%; Density: 320.3 persons per square mile; Race: 73.3% White, 18.6% Black/African American, 0.0% Asian, 0.0% American Indian/Alaska Native, 0.0% Native Hawaiian/Other Pacific Islander, 4.2% Two or more races, 13.6% Hispanic of any race; Average household size: 2.62; Median age: 43.4; Age under 18: 21.6%; Age 65 and over: 16.1%; Males per 100 females: 82.9

School District(s)
Aiken 01 (PK-12)
    2012-13 Enrollment: 24,686 . . . . (803) 641-2430
Housing: Homeownership rate: 76.7%; Homeowner vacancy rate: 0.0%; Rental vacancy rate: 8.7%

NEW ELLENTON (town). Covers a land area of 4.771 square miles and a water area of 0.006 square miles. Located at 33.42° N. Lat; 81.68° W. Long. Elevation is 410 feet.

History: Grew with the establishment of the Department of Energy's Savannah River Nuclear Site.
Population: 2,052; Growth (since 2000): -8.8%; Density: 430.1 persons per square mile; Race: 58.2% White, 36.7% Black/African American, 0.4% Asian, 0.1% American Indian/Alaska Native, 0.0% Native Hawaiian/Other Pacific Islander, 2.9% Two or more races, 3.3% Hispanic of any race; Average household size: 2.34; Median age: 42.1; Age under 18: 20.4%; Age 65 and over: 18.0%; Males per 100 females: 95.4

School District(s)
Aiken 01 (PK-12)
    2012-13 Enrollment: 24,686 . . . . (803) 641-2430
Housing: Homeownership rate: 74.1%; Homeowner vacancy rate: 2.4%; Rental vacancy rate: 14.6%
Safety: Violent crime rate: 38.2 per 10,000 population; Property crime rate: 396.4 per 10,000 population

NORTH AUGUSTA (city). Covers a land area of 20.032 square miles and a water area of 0.461 square miles. Located at 33.52° N. Lat; 81.95° W. Long. Elevation is 387 feet.

History: Settled c.1860, Incorporated 1906.

Population: 21,348; Growth (since 2000): 21.5%; Density: 1,065.7 persons per square mile; Race: 74.2% White, 20.4% Black/African American, 1.1% Asian, 0.3% American Indian/Alaska Native, 0.0% Native Hawaiian/Other Pacific Islander, 2.0% Two or more races, 4.2% Hispanic of any race; Average household size: 2.34; Median age: 37.9; Age under 18: 23.4%; Age 65 and over: 14.7%; Males per 100 females: 88.5; Marriage status: 27.9% never married, 51.0% now married, 4.1% separated, 7.7% widowed, 13.4% divorced; Foreign born: 3.6%; Speak English only: 94.9%; With disability: 12.7%; Veterans: 12.6%; Ancestry: 20.7% American, 12.3% English, 10.5% Irish, 10.2% German, 3.0% French
Employment: 15.8% management, business, and financial, 7.3% computer, engineering, and science, 12.6% education, legal, community service, arts, and media, 11.4% healthcare practitioners, 15.8% service, 22.6% sales and office, 4.7% natural resources, construction, and maintenance, 9.7% production, transportation, and material moving
Income: Per capita: $29,025; Median household: $49,027; Average household: $66,181; Households with income of $100,000 or more: 18.7%; Poverty rate: 11.6%
Educational Attainment: High school diploma or higher: 92.0%; Bachelor's degree or higher: 33.6%; Graduate/professional degree or higher: 13.1%

School District(s)
Aiken 01 (PK-12)
    2012-13 Enrollment: 24,686 . . . . (803) 641-2430
Edgefield 01 (PK-12)
    2012-13 Enrollment: 3,508 . . . . (803) 275-4601
Sc Public Charter SD (PK-12)
    2012-13 Enrollment: 11,500 . . . . (803) 734-8322
Vocational/Technical School(s)
Kenneth Shuler School of Cosmetology-North Augusta (Private, For-profit)
    Fall 2013 Enrollment: 85 . . . . (803) 278-1200
    2013-14 Tuition: $16,750
Housing: Homeownership rate: 66.8%; Median home value: $147,200; Median year structure built: 1979; Homeowner vacancy rate: 2.7%; Median gross rent: $688 per month; Rental vacancy rate: 7.3%
Health Insurance: 88.8% have insurance; 74.6% have private insurance; 27.0% have public insurance; 11.2% do not have insurance; 6.6% of children under 18 do not have insurance
Safety: Violent crime rate: 18.6 per 10,000 population; Property crime rate: 376.3 per 10,000 population
Newspapers: The Star (weekly circulation 3800)
Transportation: Commute: 94.2% car, 0.1% public transportation, 1.7% walk, 3.0% work from home; Median travel time to work: 24.4 minutes
Additional Information Contacts
City of North Augusta . . . . (803) 441-4202
    http://www.northaugusta.net

PERRY (town). Covers a land area of 1.162 square miles and a water area of 0 square miles. Located at 33.63° N. Lat; 81.31° W. Long. Elevation is 440 feet.

Population: 233; Growth (since 2000): -1.7%; Density: 200.4 persons per square mile; Race: 60.1% White, 37.3% Black/African American, 0.0% Asian, 0.9% American Indian/Alaska Native, 0.0% Native Hawaiian/Other Pacific Islander, 1.7% Two or more races, 0.0% Hispanic of any race; Average household size: 2.65; Median age: 35.1; Age under 18: 26.2%; Age 65 and over: 15.0%; Males per 100 females: 102.6
Housing: Homeownership rate: 82.9%; Homeowner vacancy rate: 1.2%; Rental vacancy rate: 0.0%

SALLEY (town). Covers a land area of 0.750 square miles and a water area of 0.011 square miles. Located at 33.57° N. Lat; 81.30° W. Long. Elevation is 374 feet.

History: Known for its Chitlin Festival.
Population: 398; Growth (since 2000): -2.9%; Density: 530.9 persons per square mile; Race: 44.0% White, 52.8% Black/African American, 0.0% Asian, 0.5% American Indian/Alaska Native, 0.0% Native Hawaiian/Other Pacific Islander, 2.8% Two or more races, 1.8% Hispanic of any race; Average household size: 2.46; Median age: 40.5; Age under 18: 25.9%; Age 65 and over: 19.1%; Males per 100 females: 84.3
Housing: Homeownership rate: 68.5%; Homeowner vacancy rate: 3.5%; Rental vacancy rate: 12.1%
Safety: Violent crime rate: 0.0 per 10,000 population; Property crime rate: 121.4 per 10,000 population

VAUCLUSE (unincorporated postal area)
ZCTA: 29850

Covers a land area of 2.035 square miles and a water area of 0.137 square miles. Located at 33.61° N. Lat; 81.82° W. Long. Elevation is 331 feet.

Population: 111; Growth (since 2000): 24.7%; Density: 54.5 persons per square mile; Race: 86.5% White, 1.8% Black/African American, 1.8% Asian, 0.9% American Indian/Alaska Native, 0.0% Native Hawaiian/Other Pacific Islander, 7.2% Two or more races, 6.3% Hispanic of any race; Average household size: 1.88; Median age: 52.5; Age under 18: 9.0%; Age 65 and over: 23.4%; Males per 100 females: 82.0

Housing: Homeownership rate: 72.9%; Homeowner vacancy rate: 0.0%; Rental vacancy rate: 0.0%

WAGENER (town).
Covers a land area of 1.174 square miles and a water area of 0.007 square miles. Located at 33.65° N. Lat; 81.36° W. Long. Elevation is 466 feet.

Population: 797; Growth (since 2000): -7.6%; Density: 678.8 persons per square mile; Race: 32.0% White, 64.7% Black/African American, 0.4% Asian, 0.5% American Indian/Alaska Native, 0.0% Native Hawaiian/Other Pacific Islander, 2.4% Two or more races, 1.5% Hispanic of any race; Average household size: 2.59; Median age: 38.4; Age under 18: 26.6%; Age 65 and over: 16.2%; Males per 100 females: 83.6

School District(s)
Aiken 01 (PK-12)

    2012-13 Enrollment: 24,686 . . . . (803) 641-2430

Housing: Homeownership rate: 67.0%; Homeowner vacancy rate: 3.4%; Rental vacancy rate: 15.4%

Safety: Violent crime rate: 24.6 per 10,000 population; Property crime rate: 566.5 per 10,000 population

WARRENVILLE (CDP).
Covers a land area of 1.084 square miles and a water area of 0.009 square miles. Located at 33.55° N. Lat; 81.80° W. Long. Elevation is 233 feet.

Population: 1,233; Growth (since 2000): n/a; Density: 1,137.0 persons per square mile; Race: 85.8% White, 5.4% Black/African American, 0.2% Asian, 0.9% American Indian/Alaska Native, 0.0% Native Hawaiian/Other Pacific Islander, 3.6% Two or more races, 6.8% Hispanic of any race; Average household size: 2.25; Median age: 41.2; Age under 18: 21.9%; Age 65 and over: 18.7%; Males per 100 females: 88.8

School District(s)
Aiken 01 (PK-12)

    2012-13 Enrollment: 24,686 . . . . (803) 641-2430

Housing: Homeownership rate: 66.8%; Homeowner vacancy rate: 2.4%; Rental vacancy rate: 8.1%

WINDSOR (town).
Covers a land area of 0.658 square miles and a water area of 0 square miles. Located at 33.48° N. Lat; 81.51° W. Long. Elevation is 387 feet.

Population: 121; Growth (since 2000): -4.7%; Density: 183.9 persons per square mile; Race: 82.6% White, 8.3% Black/African American, 0.8% Asian, 0.0% American Indian/Alaska Native, 0.0% Native Hawaiian/Other Pacific Islander, 4.1% Two or more races, 14.0% Hispanic of any race; Average household size: 2.88; Median age: 30.5; Age under 18: 32.2%; Age 65 and over: 15.7%; Males per 100 females: 89.1

Housing: Homeownership rate: 83.3%; Homeowner vacancy rate: 2.8%; Rental vacancy rate: 0.0%

Allendale County

Located in southwestern South Carolina; bounded on the west by the Savannah River and the Georgia border. Covers a land area of 408.090 square miles, a water area of 4.327 square miles, and is located in the Eastern Time Zone at 32.98° N. Lat., 81.36° W. Long. The county was founded in 1919. County seat is Allendale.

Weather Station: Allendale 2 NW   Elevation: 180 feet

	Jan	Feb	Mar	Apr	May	Jun	Jul	Aug	Sep	Oct	Nov	Dec
High	58	63	70	77	85	90	93	91	86	78	70	61
Low	34	37	43	49	58	67	70	69	63	52	43	36
Precip	4.1	3.5	4.0	2.9	3.0	5.6	4.9	5.3	3.6	3.1	3.0	3.6
Snow	tr	0.1	tr	0.0	0.0	0.0	0.0	0.0	0.0	0.0	tr	0.0

High and Low temperatures in degrees Fahrenheit; Precipitation and Snow in inches

Population: 10,419; Growth (since 2000): -7.1%; Density: 25.5 persons per square mile; Race: 23.7% White, 73.6% Black/African American, 0.4% Asian, 0.2% American Indian/Alaska Native, 0.0% Native Hawaiian/Other Pacific Islander, 0.8% two or more races, 2.3% Hispanic of any race; Average household size: 2.45; Median age: 38.8; Age under 18: 22.3%; Age 65 and over: 13.2%; Males per 100 females: 113.5; Marriage status: 42.8% never married, 38.2% now married, 4.2% separated, 9.1% widowed, 9.9% divorced; Foreign born: 1.4%; Speak English only: 97.4%; With disability: 22.9%; Veterans: 7.8%; Ancestry: 7.2% American, 2.9% German, 2.4% English, 2.0% Irish, 0.4% African

Religion: Six largest groups: 22.8% Baptist, 13.7% Methodist/Pietist, 1.8% Non-denominational Protestant, 1.4% Lutheran, 1.1% Catholicism, 0.6% Pentecostal

Economy: Unemployment rate: 10.8%; Leading industries: 20.8% retail trade; 10.8% other services (except public administration); 10.0% health care and social assistance; Farms: 141 totaling 124,350 acres; Company size: 0 employ 1,000 or more persons, 0 employ 500 to 999 persons, 5 employ 100 to 499 persons, 115 employ less than 100 persons; Business ownership: n/a women-owned, n/a Black-owned, n/a Hispanic-owned, n/a Asian-owned

Employment: 8.2% management, business, and financial, 1.2% computer, engineering, and science, 13.1% education, legal, community service, arts, and media, 4.7% healthcare practitioners, 21.8% service, 17.2% sales and office, 10.1% natural resources, construction, and maintenance, 23.8% production, transportation, and material moving

Income: Per capita: $13,334; Median household: $25,252; Average household: $37,189; Households with income of $100,000 or more: 6.7%; Poverty rate: 36.0%

Educational Attainment: High school diploma or higher: 71.9%; Bachelor's degree or higher: 15.0%; Graduate/professional degree or higher: 4.0%

Housing: Homeownership rate: 64.6%; Median home value: $65,400; Median year structure built: 1974; Homeowner vacancy rate: 2.6%; Median gross rent: $564 per month; Rental vacancy rate: 10.5%

Vital Statistics: Birth rate: 99.6 per 10,000 population; Death rate: 97.6 per 10,000 population; Age-adjusted cancer mortality rate: 216.9 deaths per 100,000 population

Health Insurance: 76.1% have insurance; 46.3% have private insurance; 42.7% have public insurance; 23.9% do not have insurance; 7.7% of children under 18 do not have insurance

Health Care: Physicians: 8.0 per 10,000 population; Hospital beds: 67.3 per 10,000 population; Hospital admissions: 342.2 per 10,000 population

Transportation: Commute: 91.2% car, 0.5% public transportation, 4.6% walk, 3.4% work from home; Median travel time to work: 23.4 minutes

Presidential Election: 79.2% Obama, 20.1% Romney (2012)

Additional Information Contacts

Allendale Government . . . . (803) 584-2737

    http://www.allendalecounty.com

Allendale County Communities

ALLENDALE (town).
County seat. Covers a land area of 3.310 square miles and a water area of 0 square miles. Located at 33.01° N. Lat; 81.31° W. Long. Elevation is 187 feet.

History: Allendale grew from a settlement about four miles southwest when pioneers in the mid-1800's established large estates in the area. A post office was secured in 1849, and the town was named for the first postmaster, Paul H. Allen. When, 23 years later, the railroad picked a route several miles away from the town, the citizens purchased several plantations near the railroad line and moved their town there.

Population: 3,482; Growth (since 2000): -14.1%; Density: 1,051.9 persons per square mile; Race: 12.8% White, 83.4% Black/African American, 0.7% Asian, 0.2% American Indian/Alaska Native, 0.1% Native Hawaiian/Other Pacific Islander, 1.4% Two or more races, 2.8% Hispanic of any race; Average household size: 2.51; Median age: 35.4; Age under 18: 28.0%; Age 65 and over: 12.8%; Males per 100 females: 87.7; Marriage status: 49.8% never married, 35.2% now married, 3.0% separated, 8.8% widowed, 6.2% divorced; Foreign born: 0.4%; Speak English only: 99.4%; With disability: 21.7%; Veterans: 7.6%; Ancestry: 4.1% American, 0.9% German, 0.5% European, 0.4% Scottish

Employment: 11.1% management, business, and financial, 0.0% computer, engineering, and science, 19.1% education, legal, community service, arts, and media, 5.3% healthcare practitioners, 23.5% service, 14.6% sales and office, 8.0% natural resources, construction, and maintenance, 18.5% production, transportation, and material moving

Income: Per capita: $11,182; Median household: $22,946; Average household: $30,134; Households with income of $100,000 or more: 4.8%; Poverty rate: 39.3%

Educational Attainment: High school diploma or higher: 69.5%; Bachelor's degree or higher: 20.8%; Graduate/professional degree or higher: 4.5%

School District(s)
Allendale 01 (PK-12)
    2012-13 Enrollment: 1,329 . . . . (803) 584-4603

Two-year College(s)
University of South Carolina-Salkehatchie (Public)
    Fall 2013 Enrollment: 1,021 . . . . (800) 922-5500
    2013-14 Tuition: In-state $6,482; Out-of-state $15,632

Housing: Homeownership rate: 57.0%; Median home value: $75,100; Median year structure built: 1971; Homeowner vacancy rate: 3.1%; Median gross rent: $417 per month; Rental vacancy rate: 8.6%

Health Insurance: 71.9% have insurance; 40.8% have private insurance; 41.9% have public insurance; 28.1% do not have insurance; 5.4% of children under 18 do not have insurance

Safety: Violent crime rate: 149.8 per 10,000 population; Property crime rate: 458.4 per 10,000 population

Transportation: Commute: 92.9% car, 1.1% public transportation, 1.2% walk, 4.8% work from home; Median travel time to work: 25.5 minutes

Airports: Allendale County (general aviation)

Additional Information Contacts
Town of Allendale . . . . (803) 584-4619
    http://www.allendalesc.org

FAIRFAX (town). Covers a land area of 3.312 square miles and a water area of <.001 square miles. Located at 32.96° N. Lat; 81.24° W. Long. Elevation is 135 feet.

History: Settled 1876, incorporated 1898.

Population: 2,025; Growth (since 2000): -36.8%; Density: 611.4 persons per square mile; Race: 19.8% White, 78.6% Black/African American, 0.6% Asian, 0.1% American Indian/Alaska Native, 0.0% Native Hawaiian/Other Pacific Islander, 0.2% Two or more races, 1.5% Hispanic of any race; Average household size: 2.38; Median age: 40.8; Age under 18: 24.5%; Age 65 and over: 15.7%; Males per 100 females: 79.0

School District(s)
Allendale 01 (PK-12)
    2012-13 Enrollment: 1,329 . . . . (803) 584-4603
Dept of Correction N04 (09-12)
    2012-13 Enrollment: 752 . . . . (803) 896-8556

Housing: Homeownership rate: 54.6%; Homeowner vacancy rate: 3.6%; Rental vacancy rate: 11.8%

Hospitals: Allendale County Hospital

Additional Information Contacts
Town of Fairfax . . . . (803) 632-2836
    http://www.allendalecounty.comfairfax.htm

MARTIN (unincorporated postal area)

ZCTA: 29836
    Covers a land area of 170.109 square miles and a water area of 1.589 square miles. Located at 33.12° N. Lat; 81.56° W. Long. Elevation is 92 feet.
    Population: 482; Growth (since 2000): -26.7%; Density: 2.8 persons per square mile; Race: 24.1% White, 71.6% Black/African American, 0.0% Asian, 0.8% American Indian/Alaska Native, 0.0% Native Hawaiian/Other Pacific Islander, 1.7% Two or more races, 2.5% Hispanic of any race; Average household size: 2.25; Median age: 50.1; Age under 18: 20.7%; Age 65 and over: 14.5%; Males per 100 females: 99.2
    Housing: Homeownership rate: 84.1%; Homeowner vacancy rate: 0.6%; Rental vacancy rate: 12.8%

SYCAMORE (town). Covers a land area of 3.171 square miles and a water area of 0.009 square miles. Located at 33.03° N. Lat; 81.22° W. Long. Elevation is 148 feet.

History: Sycamore was named for the sycamore or plane tree that grew abundantly in the woodlands and marshes here.

Population: 180; Growth (since 2000): -2.7%; Density: 56.8 persons per square mile; Race: 67.2% White, 32.2% Black/African American, 0.6% Asian, 0.0% American Indian/Alaska Native, 0.0% Native Hawaiian/Other Pacific Islander, 0.0% Two or more races, 1.1% Hispanic of any race;

Average household size: 2.28; Median age: 47.5; Age under 18: 19.4%; Age 65 and over: 18.9%; Males per 100 females: 106.9

Housing: Homeownership rate: 70.9%; Homeowner vacancy rate: 0.0%; Rental vacancy rate: 17.9%

ULMER (town). Covers a land area of 2.739 square miles and a water area of 0.013 square miles. Located at 33.10° N. Lat; 81.21° W. Long. Elevation is 161 feet.

Population: 88; Growth (since 2000): -13.7%; Density: 32.1 persons per square mile; Race: 69.3% White, 28.4% Black/African American, 0.0% Asian, 2.3% American Indian/Alaska Native, 0.0% Native Hawaiian/Other Pacific Islander, 0.0% Two or more races, 2.3% Hispanic of any race; Average household size: 2.10; Median age: 41.0; Age under 18: 20.5%; Age 65 and over: 14.8%; Males per 100 females: 91.3

Housing: Homeownership rate: 64.3%; Homeowner vacancy rate: 0.0%; Rental vacancy rate: 20.0%

Anderson County

Located in northwestern South Carolina; bounded on the west by the Tugaloo and Savannah Rivers, and on the east by the Saluda River. Covers a land area of 715.426 square miles, a water area of 42.010 square miles, and is located in the Eastern Time Zone at 34.52° N. Lat., 82.64° W. Long. The county was founded in 1826. County seat is Anderson.

Anderson County is part of the Greenville-Anderson-Mauldin, SC Metropolitan Statistical Area. The entire metro area includes: Anderson County, SC; Greenville County, SC; Laurens County, SC; Pickens County, SC

Weather Station: Anderson   Elevation: 799 feet

	Jan	Feb	Mar	Apr	May	Jun	Jul	Aug	Sep	Oct	Nov	Dec
High	54	59	66	75	82	89	92	90	84	74	65	56
Low	31	34	40	47	56	64	68	67	61	50	40	33
Precip	4.4	4.3	4.9	3.3	3.2	3.3	4.1	4.0	4.0	3.6	4.1	4.5
Snow	0.7	0.7	0.4	0.0	0.0	0.0	0.0	0.0	0.0	0.0	0.0	0.1

High and Low temperatures in degrees Fahrenheit; Precipitation and Snow in inches

Weather Station: Anderson County Arpt   Elevation: 759 feet

	Jan	Feb	Mar	Apr	May	Jun	Jul	Aug	Sep	Oct	Nov	Dec
High	53	57	65	73	81	88	91	89	83	73	64	55
Low	32	35	42	48	57	66	69	69	62	51	41	34
Precip	3.9	4.0	4.6	3.2	3.2	3.6	3.6	3.8	4.1	3.2	3.6	4.1
Snow	na	na	na	na	na	na	na	na	na	na	na	na

High and Low temperatures in degrees Fahrenheit; Precipitation and Snow in inches

Weather Station: West Pelzer 2 W   Elevation: 861 feet

	Jan	Feb	Mar	Apr	May	Jun	Jul	Aug	Sep	Oct	Nov	Dec
High	52	57	65	73	80	87	91	89	82	73	64	55
Low	30	33	40	47	56	65	68	68	61	49	40	32
Precip	4.2	4.0	4.5	3.0	3.0	3.2	3.3	3.5	3.6	3.3	3.7	4.0
Snow	1.2	0.8	0.7	0.0	0.0	0.0	0.0	0.0	0.0	0.0	0.1	0.1

High and Low temperatures in degrees Fahrenheit; Precipitation and Snow in inches

Population: 187,126; Growth (since 2000): 12.9%; Density: 261.6 persons per square mile; Race: 80.1% White, 16.0% Black/African American, 0.8% Asian, 0.3% American Indian/Alaska Native, 0.0% Native Hawaiian/Other Pacific Islander, 1.5% two or more races, 2.9% Hispanic of any race; Average household size: 2.50; Median age: 39.7; Age under 18: 24.0%; Age 65 and over: 15.1%; Males per 100 females: 93.2; Marriage status: 25.9% never married, 56.0% now married, 3.4% separated, 7.4% widowed, 10.7% divorced; Foreign born: 2.5%; Speak English only: 96.2%; With disability: 16.3%; Veterans: 10.3%; Ancestry: 15.8% American, 12.5% Irish, 10.6% English, 9.7% German, 3.6% Scotch-Irish

Religion: Six largest groups: 44.1% Baptist, 6.0% Pentecostal, 5.3% Methodist/Pietist, 4.2% Non-denominational Protestant, 2.2% Presbyterian-Reformed, 1.5% Catholicism

Economy: Unemployment rate: 5.6%; Leading industries: 19.1% retail trade; 12.4% other services (except public administration); 10.4% accommodation and food services; Farms: 1,498 totaling 159,106 acres; Company size: 4 employ 1,000 or more persons, 7 employ 500 to 999 persons, 67 employ 100 to 499 persons, 3,594 employ less than 100 persons; Business ownership: 3,411 women-owned, 754 Black-owned, 108 Hispanic-owned, 142 Asian-owned

Employment: 10.9% management, business, and financial, 3.7% computer, engineering, and science, 9.3% education, legal, community

service, arts, and media, 6.0% healthcare practitioners, 16.1% service, 25.4% sales and office, 10.2% natural resources, construction, and maintenance, 18.6% production, transportation, and material moving
Income: Per capita: $22,081; Median household: $41,579; Average household: $55,713; Households with income of $100,000 or more: 13.9%; Poverty rate: 16.8%
Educational Attainment: High school diploma or higher: 81.7%; Bachelor's degree or higher: 19.3%; Graduate/professional degree or higher: 6.6%
Housing: Homeownership rate: 71.8%; Median home value: $123,400; Median year structure built: 1981; Homeowner vacancy rate: 3.1%; Median gross rent: $655 per month; Rental vacancy rate: 12.2%
Vital Statistics: Birth rate: 116.7 per 10,000 population; Death rate: 102.4 per 10,000 population; Age-adjusted cancer mortality rate: 183.8 deaths per 100,000 population
Health Insurance: 83.9% have insurance; 63.2% have private insurance; 33.2% have public insurance; 16.1% do not have insurance; 8.7% of children under 18 do not have insurance
Health Care: Physicians: 18.9 per 10,000 population; Hospital beds: 28.7 per 10,000 population; Hospital admissions: 1,131.2 per 10,000 population
Air Quality Index: 99.2% good, 0.8% moderate, 0.0% unhealthy for sensitive individuals, 0.0% unhealthy (percent of days)
Transportation: Commute: 94.9% car, 0.5% public transportation, 1.3% walk, 2.2% work from home; Median travel time to work: 23.4 minutes
Presidential Election: 31.0% Obama, 67.5% Romney (2012)
National and State Parks: Sadlers Creek State Park
Additional Information Contacts
Anderson Government . . . . (864) 260-4053
   http://www.andersoncountysc.org

Anderson County Communities

ANDERSON (city). County seat. Covers a land area of 14.595 square miles and a water area of 0.044 square miles. Located at 34.52° N. Lat; 82.65° W. Long. Elevation is 787 feet.
History: Anderson was named for General Robert Anderson, a soldier in the Revolutionary War, who in 1801 had founded a river port called Andersonville about 12 miles from the site of Anderson. Settlement began here after the treaty with the Cherokee in 1777. During the Civil War Anderson was an ammunition-manufacturing center and supplier for Confederate soldiers. Only two minor skirmishes were fought in this area. Anderson was incorporated in 1882. A hydroelectric plant built nearby on the Seneca River is believed to be the first such plant in the U.S.
Population: 26,686; Growth (since 2000): 4.6%; Density: 1,828.5 persons per square mile; Race: 61.4% White, 33.6% Black/African American, 1.0% Asian, 0.3% American Indian/Alaska Native, 0.0% Native Hawaiian/Other Pacific Islander, 2.1% Two or more races, 4.1% Hispanic of any race; Average household size: 2.25; Median age: 36.8; Age under 18: 23.4%; Age 65 and over: 17.9%; Males per 100 females: 80.2; Marriage status: 37.1% never married, 41.5% now married, 4.8% separated, 11.6% widowed, 9.8% divorced; Foreign born: 3.7%; Speak English only: 94.5%; With disability: 17.2%; Veterans: 8.9%; Ancestry: 12.7% American, 10.0% English, 9.7% Irish, 6.7% German, 3.8% Scotch-Irish
Employment: 10.7% management, business, and financial, 2.6% computer, engineering, and science, 10.0% education, legal, community service, arts, and media, 6.2% healthcare practitioners, 21.7% service, 23.5% sales and office, 8.1% natural resources, construction, and maintenance, 17.1% production, transportation, and material moving
Income: Per capita: $18,845; Median household: $30,032; Average household: $44,150; Households with income of $100,000 or more: 10.0%; Poverty rate: 27.5%
Educational Attainment: High school diploma or higher: 78.9%; Bachelor's degree or higher: 21.8%; Graduate/professional degree or higher: 7.6%
School District(s)
Anderson 03 (PK-12)
   2012-13 Enrollment: 2,563 . . . . (864) 348-6196
Anderson 05 (PK-12)
   2012-13 Enrollment: 12,716 . . . . (864) 260-5000
Four-year College(s)
Anderson University (Private, Not-for-profit, Baptist)
   Fall 2013 Enrollment: 2,966 . . . . (864) 231-2000
   2013-14 Tuition: In-state $22,790; Out-of-state $22,790

Two-year College(s)
Forrest College (Private, For-profit)
   Fall 2013 Enrollment: 135 . . . . (864) 225-7653
   2013-14 Tuition: In-state $9,420; Out-of-state $9,420
Housing: Homeownership rate: 49.3%; Median home value: $122,100; Median year structure built: 1969; Homeowner vacancy rate: 4.7%; Median gross rent: $629 per month; Rental vacancy rate: 12.4%
Health Insurance: 82.0% have insurance; 53.8% have private insurance; 40.7% have public insurance; 18.0% do not have insurance; 8.7% of children under 18 do not have insurance
Hospitals: Anmed Health (461 beds)
Safety: Violent crime rate: 103.7 per 10,000 population; Property crime rate: 901.5 per 10,000 population
Newspapers: Anderson Independent-Mail (daily circulation 34800)
Transportation: Commute: 91.5% car, 2.6% public transportation, 2.9% walk, 1.6% work from home; Median travel time to work: 18.9 minutes
Airports: Anderson Regional (general aviation)
Additional Information Contacts
City of Anderson . . . . (864) 231-2200
   http://www.cityofandersonsc.com

BELTON (city). Covers a land area of 3.842 square miles and a water area of 0.013 square miles. Located at 34.52° N. Lat; 82.49° W. Long. Elevation is 883 feet.
History: Belton was named for Judge Belton O'Neall, an early railroad magnate, lawyer, and historian.
Population: 4,134; Growth (since 2000): -7.3%; Density: 1,076.0 persons per square mile; Race: 80.7% White, 16.6% Black/African American, 0.3% Asian, 0.2% American Indian/Alaska Native, 0.0% Native Hawaiian/Other Pacific Islander, 1.8% Two or more races, 1.9% Hispanic of any race; Average household size: 2.31; Median age: 40.8; Age under 18: 23.3%; Age 65 and over: 18.1%; Males per 100 females: 84.8; Marriage status: 29.0% never married, 51.7% now married, 6.1% separated, 6.9% widowed, 12.4% divorced; Foreign born: 1.0%; Speak English only: 96.0%; With disability: 23.0%; Veterans: 14.1%; Ancestry: 13.4% English, 12.9% American, 12.3% Irish, 5.6% German, 3.5% French
Employment: 14.3% management, business, and financial, 2.9% computer, engineering, and science, 8.5% education, legal, community service, arts, and media, 5.2% healthcare practitioners, 15.7% service, 19.8% sales and office, 13.5% natural resources, construction, and maintenance, 20.1% production, transportation, and material moving
Income: Per capita: $20,491; Median household: $30,263; Average household: $46,744; Households with income of $100,000 or more: 11.9%; Poverty rate: 21.5%
Educational Attainment: High school diploma or higher: 77.6%; Bachelor's degree or higher: 15.6%; Graduate/professional degree or higher: 6.4%
School District(s)
Anderson 02 (PK-12)
   2012-13 Enrollment: 3,706 . . . . (864) 369-7364
Housing: Homeownership rate: 63.1%; Median home value: $82,100; Median year structure built: 1960; Homeowner vacancy rate: 3.9%; Median gross rent: $563 per month; Rental vacancy rate: 12.5%
Health Insurance: 75.3% have insurance; 50.3% have private insurance; 38.2% have public insurance; 24.7% do not have insurance; 15.5% of children under 18 do not have insurance
Safety: Violent crime rate: 78.2 per 10,000 population; Property crime rate: 518.7 per 10,000 population
Newspapers: Belton News Chronicle (weekly circulation 3900)
Transportation: Commute: 94.1% car, 0.0% public transportation, 4.9% walk, 0.5% work from home; Median travel time to work: 20.7 minutes
Additional Information Contacts
City of Belton . . . . (864) 338-7773
   http://www.cityofbeltonsc.com

CENTERVILLE (CDP). Covers a land area of 5.905 square miles and a water area of 0.031 square miles. Located at 34.53° N. Lat; 82.72° W. Long. Elevation is 833 feet.
Population: 6,586; Growth (since 2000): 27.1%; Density: 1,115.4 persons per square mile; Race: 83.3% White, 13.3% Black/African American, 1.1% Asian, 0.2% American Indian/Alaska Native, 0.0% Native Hawaiian/Other Pacific Islander, 1.3% Two or more races, 2.7% Hispanic of any race; Average household size: 2.46; Median age: 39.3; Age under 18: 23.1%; Age 65 and over: 15.7%; Males per 100 females: 90.6; Marriage status: 24.7% never married, 61.4% now married, 4.5% separated, 4.8%

widowed, 9.1% divorced; Foreign born: 2.9%; Speak English only: 96.5%; With disability: 12.4%; Veterans: 9.1%; Ancestry: 13.6% Irish, 12.9% American, 11.7% German, 11.4% English, 5.1% Scotch-Irish
Employment: 11.2% management, business, and financial, 5.3% computer, engineering, and science, 11.1% education, legal, community service, arts, and media, 8.3% healthcare practitioners, 14.3% service, 21.3% sales and office, 6.0% natural resources, construction, and maintenance, 22.5% production, transportation, and material moving
Income: Per capita: $21,925; Median household: $43,004; Average household: $53,958; Households with income of $100,000 or more: 12.8%; Poverty rate: 7.1%
Educational Attainment: High school diploma or higher: 85.8%; Bachelor's degree or higher: 19.4%; Graduate/professional degree or higher: 6.4%
Housing: Homeownership rate: 76.1%; Median home value: $132,500; Median year structure built: 1988; Homeowner vacancy rate: 5.6%; Median gross rent: $561 per month; Rental vacancy rate: 8.0%
Health Insurance: 85.7% have insurance; 70.4% have private insurance; 28.9% have public insurance; 14.3% do not have insurance; 12.4% of children under 18 do not have insurance
Transportation: Commute: 96.8% car, 0.0% public transportation, 0.4% walk, 2.0% work from home; Median travel time to work: 19.1 minutes

HOMELAND PARK (CDP).
Covers a land area of 4.714 square miles and a water area of 0.011 square miles. Located at 34.46° N. Lat; 82.66° W. Long. Elevation is 784 feet.
Population: 6,296; Growth (since 2000): -0.6%; Density: 1,335.7 persons per square mile; Race: 62.5% White, 31.8% Black/African American, 0.3% Asian, 0.2% American Indian/Alaska Native, 0.0% Native Hawaiian/Other Pacific Islander, 2.3% Two or more races, 5.6% Hispanic of any race; Average household size: 2.45; Median age: 36.1; Age under 18: 25.8%; Age 65 and over: 14.9%; Males per 100 females: 91.4; Marriage status: 32.6% never married, 41.8% now married, 4.7% separated, 9.0% widowed, 16.5% divorced; Foreign born: 1.6%; Speak English only: 96.8%; With disability: 22.0%; Veterans: 7.7%; Ancestry: 15.4% American, 11.3% Irish, 7.5% German, 3.7% English, 1.3% Scotch-Irish
Employment: 2.4% management, business, and financial, 2.1% computer, engineering, and science, 2.0% education, legal, community service, arts, and media, 2.7% healthcare practitioners, 24.9% service, 20.7% sales and office, 16.3% natural resources, construction, and maintenance, 28.9% production, transportation, and material moving
Income: Per capita: $13,453; Median household: $25,182; Average household: $32,762; Households with income of $100,000 or more: 2.2%; Poverty rate: 32.6%
Educational Attainment: High school diploma or higher: 65.9%; Bachelor's degree or higher: 2.8%; Graduate/professional degree or higher: 1.1%
Housing: Homeownership rate: 57.3%; Median home value: $68,500; Median year structure built: 1966; Homeowner vacancy rate: 3.5%; Median gross rent: $681 per month; Rental vacancy rate: 11.8%
Health Insurance: 78.4% have insurance; 40.3% have private insurance; 50.5% have public insurance; 21.6% do not have insurance; 9.5% of children under 18 do not have insurance
Transportation: Commute: 91.7% car, 3.0% public transportation, 2.1% walk, 2.0% work from home; Median travel time to work: 21.9 minutes

HONEA PATH (town).
Covers a land area of 3.618 square miles and a water area of 0.002 square miles. Located at 34.45° N. Lat; 82.39° W. Long. Elevation is 791 feet.
History: Honea is the Indian word for path, which makes Honea Path literally "path path."
Population: 3,597; Growth (since 2000): 2.7%; Density: 994.1 persons per square mile; Race: 77.0% White, 19.6% Black/African American, 0.3% Asian, 0.2% American Indian/Alaska Native, 0.0% Native Hawaiian/Other Pacific Islander, 2.4% Two or more races, 1.4% Hispanic of any race; Average household size: 2.31; Median age: 40.5; Age under 18: 23.7%; Age 65 and over: 19.3%; Males per 100 females: 81.6; Marriage status: 31.3% never married, 51.6% now married, 1.1% separated, 10.6% widowed, 6.5% divorced; Foreign born: 0.0%; Speak English only: 99.7%; With disability: 21.9%; Veterans: 12.1%; Ancestry: 32.6% American, 8.1% German, 5.5% English, 4.1% Irish, 2.2% Polish
Employment: 14.5% management, business, and financial, 2.4% computer, engineering, and science, 15.2% education, legal, community service, arts, and media, 3.2% healthcare practitioners, 17.1% service,

25.4% sales and office, 3.1% natural resources, construction, and maintenance, 19.0% production, transportation, and material moving
Income: Per capita: $17,280; Median household: $24,019; Average household: $40,736; Households with income of $100,000 or more: 10.8%; Poverty rate: 25.8%
Educational Attainment: High school diploma or higher: 75.3%; Bachelor's degree or higher: 14.0%; Graduate/professional degree or higher: 5.5%

School District(s)
Anderson 02 (PK-12)
    2012-13 Enrollment: 3,706 . . . . (864) 369-7364
Housing: Homeownership rate: 64.9%; Median home value: $79,800; Median year structure built: 1963; Homeowner vacancy rate: 4.5%; Median gross rent: $337 per month; Rental vacancy rate: 13.8%
Health Insurance: 83.6% have insurance; 54.1% have private insurance; 47.2% have public insurance; 16.4% do not have insurance; 8.3% of children under 18 do not have insurance
Safety: Violent crime rate: 33.2 per 10,000 population; Property crime rate: 431.8 per 10,000 population
Transportation: Commute: 99.0% car, 0.0% public transportation, 0.0% walk, 1.0% work from home; Median travel time to work: 22.8 minutes
Additional Information Contacts
Town of Honea Path . . . . (864) 369-2466
    http://www.townofhoneapath.com

IVA (town).
Covers a land area of 0.893 square miles and a water area of 0.002 square miles. Located at 34.31° N. Lat; 82.66° W. Long. Elevation is 712 feet.
History: Iva is said to be one of many towns named by railroad officials for pretty girls. Established between the Savannah and Rocky Rivers about 1884, the chief industry in Iva was the Jackson Mill which manufactured sheeting.
Population: 1,218; Growth (since 2000): 5.4%; Density: 1,364.0 persons per square mile; Race: 91.3% White, 6.4% Black/African American, 0.8% Asian, 0.7% American Indian/Alaska Native, 0.0% Native Hawaiian/Other Pacific Islander, 0.7% Two or more races, 0.2% Hispanic of any race; Average household size: 2.50; Median age: 40.9; Age under 18: 23.7%; Age 65 and over: 22.5%; Males per 100 females: 79.6

School District(s)
Anderson 03 (PK-12)
    2012-13 Enrollment: 2,563 . . . . (864) 348-6196
Housing: Homeownership rate: 61.0%; Homeowner vacancy rate: 2.4%; Rental vacancy rate: 15.7%

NORTHLAKE (CDP).
Covers a land area of 4.128 square miles and a water area of 1.059 square miles. Located at 34.57° N. Lat; 82.69° W. Long. Elevation is 659 feet.
History: named for the 55,950-acre (226 sq. km.) Lake Hartwell, a U.S. Army Corps of Engineers lake with nearly 1,000 miles (2,000 km) of shoreline for residential and recreational use. The area is a growing industrial, commercial and tourist center.
Population: 3,745; Growth (since 2000): 2.4%; Density: 907.2 persons per square mile; Race: 85.8% White, 9.2% Black/African American, 1.8% Asian, 0.5% American Indian/Alaska Native, 0.0% Native Hawaiian/Other Pacific Islander, 1.8% Two or more races, 2.0% Hispanic of any race; Average household size: 2.37; Median age: 44.7; Age under 18: 20.3%; Age 65 and over: 17.7%; Males per 100 females: 92.7; Marriage status: 20.3% never married, 59.9% now married, 1.4% separated, 6.4% widowed, 13.4% divorced; Foreign born: 5.9%; Speak English only: 91.2%; With disability: 9.0%; Veterans: 11.3%; Ancestry: 16.3% Irish, 15.6% English, 14.5% American, 12.6% German, 8.0% Scottish
Employment: 19.2% management, business, and financial, 6.4% computer, engineering, and science, 10.1% education, legal, community service, arts, and media, 6.1% healthcare practitioners, 10.4% service, 28.6% sales and office, 7.2% natural resources, construction, and maintenance, 12.1% production, transportation, and material moving
Income: Per capita: $32,775; Median household: $63,158; Average household: $78,465; Households with income of $100,000 or more: 23.6%; Poverty rate: 6.0%
Educational Attainment: High school diploma or higher: 93.1%; Bachelor's degree or higher: 36.9%; Graduate/professional degree or higher: 12.6%
Housing: Homeownership rate: 74.5%; Median home value: $165,700; Median year structure built: 1986; Homeowner vacancy rate: 3.7%; Median gross rent: $849 per month; Rental vacancy rate: 14.2%

Health Insurance: 89.5% have insurance; 77.8% have private insurance; 26.0% have public insurance; 10.5% do not have insurance; 2.3% of children under 18 do not have insurance
Transportation: Commute: 95.6% car, 0.0% public transportation, 0.4% walk, 4.0% work from home; Median travel time to work: 23.1 minutes

PELZER (town).
Covers a land area of 0.184 square miles and a water area of 0.006 square miles. Located at 34.64° N. Lat; 82.46° W. Long. Elevation is 745 feet.
History: Pelzer, an early textile town, was named for Francis J. Pelzer who established the Pelzer Manufacturing Company in 1881.
Population: 89; Growth (since 2000): -8.2%; Density: 482.8 persons per square mile; Race: 94.4% White, 2.2% Black/African American, 0.0% Asian, 1.1% American Indian/Alaska Native, 0.0% Native Hawaiian/Other Pacific Islander, 2.2% Two or more races, 4.5% Hispanic of any race; Average household size: 2.70; Median age: 43.5; Age under 18: 23.6%; Age 65 and over: 14.6%; Males per 100 females: 97.8
School District(s)
Dept of Correction N04 (09-12)
    2012-13 Enrollment: 752 . . . . (803) 896-8556
Greenville 01 (PK-12)
    2012-13 Enrollment: 73,649 . . . . (864) 355-8860
Housing: Homeownership rate: 81.8%; Homeowner vacancy rate: 0.0%; Rental vacancy rate: 0.0%

PENDLETON (town).
Covers a land area of 3.790 square miles and a water area of 0.027 square miles. Located at 34.65° N. Lat; 82.78° W. Long. Elevation is 853 feet.
History: Planned in 1790 as the seat of the Pendleton District, the town was named for Judge Henry Pendleton of Culpeper, Virginia, who organized the Culpeper Minute Men. Pendleton was noted for its fine cabinet and carriage makers.
Population: 2,964; Growth (since 2000): -0.1%; Density: 782.1 persons per square mile; Race: 72.3% White, 23.3% Black/African American, 1.2% Asian, 0.3% American Indian/Alaska Native, 0.1% Native Hawaiian/Other Pacific Islander, 2.6% Two or more races, 1.6% Hispanic of any race; Average household size: 2.10; Median age: 40.4; Age under 18: 18.2%; Age 65 and over: 19.8%; Males per 100 females: 88.5; Marriage status: 29.3% never married, 47.5% now married, 4.1% separated, 6.1% widowed, 17.1% divorced; Foreign born: 4.2%; Speak English only: 98.1%; With disability: 19.3%; Veterans: 11.2%; Ancestry: 12.4% Irish, 11.4% German, 9.2% English, 6.5% Scotch-Irish, 5.3% American
Employment: 12.2% management, business, and financial, 3.5% computer, engineering, and science, 25.7% education, legal, community service, arts, and media, 4.7% healthcare practitioners, 20.5% service, 18.0% sales and office, 5.7% natural resources, construction, and maintenance, 9.8% production, transportation, and material moving
Income: Per capita: $20,236; Median household: $27,188; Average household: $38,015; Households with income of $100,000 or more: 5.7%; Poverty rate: 34.9%
Educational Attainment: High school diploma or higher: 85.7%; Bachelor's degree or higher: 30.5%; Graduate/professional degree or higher: 15.6%
School District(s)
Anderson 04 (PK-12)
    2012-13 Enrollment: 2,914 . . . . (864) 403-2000
Two-year College(s)
Tri-County Technical College (Public)
    Fall 2013 Enrollment: 6,553 . . . . (864) 646-1500
    2013-14 Tuition: In-state $4,872; Out-of-state $8,328
Housing: Homeownership rate: 58.8%; Median home value: $112,500; Median year structure built: 1975; Homeowner vacancy rate: 3.9%; Median gross rent: $530 per month; Rental vacancy rate: 20.3%
Health Insurance: 82.7% have insurance; 63.7% have private insurance; 39.0% have public insurance; 17.3% do not have insurance; 8.4% of children under 18 do not have insurance
Transportation: Commute: 94.8% car, 1.3% public transportation, 0.0% walk, 3.9% work from home; Median travel time to work: 21.9 minutes
Additional Information Contacts
Town of Pendleton . . . . (864) 646-9409
    http://www.townofpendleton.org

PIEDMONT (CDP).
Covers a land area of 8.596 square miles and a water area of 0.169 square miles. Located at 34.71° N. Lat; 82.47° W. Long. Elevation is 791 feet.
Population: 5,103; Growth (since 2000): 8.9%; Density: 593.7 persons per square mile; Race: 89.1% White, 7.8% Black/African American, 0.2% Asian, 0.3% American Indian/Alaska Native, 0.0% Native Hawaiian/Other Pacific Islander, 1.7% Two or more races, 2.5% Hispanic of any race; Average household size: 2.56; Median age: 39.5; Age under 18: 24.2%; Age 65 and over: 14.9%; Males per 100 females: 94.5; Marriage status: 27.0% never married, 51.8% now married, 1.7% separated, 8.2% widowed, 12.9% divorced; Foreign born: 0.9%; Speak English only: 99.5%; With disability: 18.4%; Veterans: 7.1%; Ancestry: 21.3% American, 13.4% Irish, 10.4% English, 7.5% German, 2.3% French
Employment: 8.8% management, business, and financial, 0.4% computer, engineering, and science, 4.3% education, legal, community service, arts, and media, 4.9% healthcare practitioners, 25.4% service, 26.2% sales and office, 8.8% natural resources, construction, and maintenance, 21.1% production, transportation, and material moving
Income: Per capita: $18,199; Median household: $40,754; Average household: $45,162; Households with income of $100,000 or more: 6.0%; Poverty rate: 13.4%
Educational Attainment: High school diploma or higher: 80.3%; Bachelor's degree or higher: 8.7%; Graduate/professional degree or higher: 1.8%
School District(s)
Anderson 01 (PK-12)
    2012-13 Enrollment: 9,402 . . . . (864) 847-7344
Greenville 01 (PK-12)
    2012-13 Enrollment: 73,649 . . . . (864) 355-8860
Housing: Homeownership rate: 75.4%; Median home value: $97,300; Median year structure built: 1979; Homeowner vacancy rate: 2.9%; Median gross rent: $685 per month; Rental vacancy rate: 11.8%
Health Insurance: 82.8% have insurance; 56.5% have private insurance; 35.6% have public insurance; 17.2% do not have insurance; 4.9% of children under 18 do not have insurance
Transportation: Commute: 98.6% car, 0.0% public transportation, 0.0% walk, 1.4% work from home; Median travel time to work: 23.2 minutes

POWDERSVILLE (CDP).
Note: Statistics that would complete this profile are not available because the CDP was created after the 2010 Census was released.

STARR (town).
Covers a land area of 1.476 square miles and a water area of 0.002 square miles. Located at 34.37° N. Lat; 82.70° W. Long. Elevation is 768 feet.
Population: 173; Growth (since 2000): 0.0%; Density: 117.2 persons per square mile; Race: 92.5% White, 5.8% Black/African American, 0.0% Asian, 0.0% American Indian/Alaska Native, 0.6% Native Hawaiian/Other Pacific Islander, 1.2% Two or more races, 1.7% Hispanic of any race; Average household size: 2.54; Median age: 42.8; Age under 18: 26.0%; Age 65 and over: 14.5%; Males per 100 females: 106.0
School District(s)
Anderson 03 (PK-12)
    2012-13 Enrollment: 2,563 . . . . (864) 348-6196
Housing: Homeownership rate: 70.6%; Homeowner vacancy rate: 4.0%; Rental vacancy rate: 9.1%

TOWNVILLE (unincorporated postal area)
ZCTA: 29689
    Covers a land area of 35.613 square miles and a water area of 12.272 square miles. Located at 34.53° N. Lat; 82.87° W. Long. Elevation is 817 feet.
    Population: 3,889; Growth (since 2000): 3.1%; Density: 109.2 persons per square mile; Race: 93.3% White, 4.0% Black/African American, 0.2% Asian, 0.2% American Indian/Alaska Native, 0.0% Native Hawaiian/Other Pacific Islander, 1.9% Two or more races, 1.3% Hispanic of any race; Average household size: 2.31; Median age: 47.5; Age under 18: 19.2%; Age 65 and over: 17.3%; Males per 100 females: 101.7; Marriage status: 18.2% never married, 63.7% now married, 0.4% separated, 5.9% widowed, 12.2% divorced; Foreign born: 1.2%; Speak English only: 97.3%; With disability: 17.7%; Veterans: 11.6%; Ancestry: 19.3% American, 16.0% Irish, 8.7% German, 7.6% English, 3.5% Italian
    Employment: 8.8% management, business, and financial, 4.3% computer, engineering, and science, 8.6% education, legal, community service, arts, and media, 5.0% healthcare practitioners, 24.3% service,

18.2% sales and office, 8.3% natural resources, construction, and maintenance, 22.5% production, transportation, and material moving
Income: Per capita: $22,252; Median household: $55,943; Average household: $57,130; Households with income of $100,000 or more: 13.6%; Poverty rate: 13.3%
Educational Attainment: High school diploma or higher: 84.2%; Bachelor's degree or higher: 17.4%; Graduate/professional degree or higher: 5.2%
School District(s)
Anderson 04 (PK-12)
    2012-13 Enrollment: 2,914 . . . . (864) 403-2000
Housing: Homeownership rate: 82.6%; Median home value: $159,800; Median year structure built: 1988; Homeowner vacancy rate: 5.8%; Median gross rent: $831 per month; Rental vacancy rate: 15.3%
Health Insurance: 78.0% have insurance; 62.3% have private insurance; 33.3% have public insurance; 22.0% do not have insurance; 16.5% of children under 18 do not have insurance
Transportation: Commute: 88.9% car, 0.0% public transportation, 3.9% walk, 0.9% work from home; Median travel time to work: 30.5 minutes

WEST PELZER (town). Covers a land area of 0.510 square miles and a water area of <.001 square miles. Located at 34.64° N. Lat; 82.47° W. Long. Elevation is 846 feet.
Population: 880; Growth (since 2000): 0.1%; Density: 1,724.5 persons per square mile; Race: 92.4% White, 5.1% Black/African American, 0.1% Asian, 0.0% American Indian/Alaska Native, 0.0% Native Hawaiian/Other Pacific Islander, 1.6% Two or more races, 3.5% Hispanic of any race; Average household size: 2.29; Median age: 38.2; Age under 18: 22.6%; Age 65 and over: 16.0%; Males per 100 females: 95.6
School District(s)
Anderson 01 (PK-12)
    2012-13 Enrollment: 9,402 . . . . (864) 847-7344
Housing: Homeownership rate: 57.9%; Homeowner vacancy rate: 3.0%; Rental vacancy rate: 15.2%
Safety: Violent crime rate: 22.7 per 10,000 population; Property crime rate: 1,404.3 per 10,000 population

WILLIAMSTON (town). Covers a land area of 3.642 square miles and a water area of 0.037 square miles. Located at 34.62° N. Lat; 82.48° W. Long. Elevation is 807 feet.
Population: 3,934; Growth (since 2000): 3.8%; Density: 1,080.3 persons per square mile; Race: 83.4% White, 13.2% Black/African American, 0.1% Asian, 0.1% American Indian/Alaska Native, 0.0% Native Hawaiian/Other Pacific Islander, 1.3% Two or more races, 2.8% Hispanic of any race; Average household size: 2.44; Median age: 39.3; Age under 18: 23.8%; Age 65 and over: 17.0%; Males per 100 females: 85.6; Marriage status: 22.6% never married, 50.3% now married, 1.5% separated, 14.3% widowed, 12.8% divorced; Foreign born: 2.2%; Speak English only: 93.8%; With disability: 12.1%; Veterans: 8.0%; Ancestry: 14.8% American, 9.7% German, 9.1% Irish, 7.1% English, 4.8% French Canadian
Employment: 4.1% management, business, and financial, 3.5% computer, engineering, and science, 10.7% education, legal, community service, arts, and media, 4.2% healthcare practitioners, 28.0% service, 26.7% sales and office, 11.0% natural resources, construction, and maintenance, 11.8% production, transportation, and material moving
Income: Per capita: $19,412; Median household: $40,664; Average household: $50,512; Households with income of $100,000 or more: 11.7%; Poverty rate: 7.7%
Educational Attainment: High school diploma or higher: 83.4%; Bachelor's degree or higher: 17.6%; Graduate/professional degree or higher: 3.3%
School District(s)
Anderson 01 (PK-12)
    2012-13 Enrollment: 9,402 . . . . (864) 847-7344
Anderson 80 (09-12)
    2012-13 Enrollment: n/a . . . . (864) 847-4121
Housing: Homeownership rate: 67.3%; Median home value: $87,400; Median year structure built: 1969; Homeowner vacancy rate: 3.3%; Median gross rent: $675 per month; Rental vacancy rate: 10.9%
Health Insurance: 85.0% have insurance; 66.4% have private insurance; 31.6% have public insurance; 15.0% do not have insurance; 7.3% of children under 18 do not have insurance
Safety: Violent crime rate: 57.4 per 10,000 population; Property crime rate: 451.6 per 10,000 population
Newspapers: The Journal (weekly circulation 4100)

Transportation: Commute: 94.2% car, 0.0% public transportation, 1.3% walk, 3.7% work from home; Median travel time to work: 25.7 minutes
Additional Information Contacts
Town of Williamston . . . . (864) 847-7473
    http://www.williamstonsc.us

Bamberg County

Located in south central South Carolina; bounded on the north by the South Fork of the Edisto River. Covers a land area of 393.370 square miles, a water area of 2.193 square miles, and is located in the Eastern Time Zone at 33.20° N. Lat., 81.05° W. Long. The county was founded in 1897. County seat is Bamberg.

Weather Station: Bamberg   Elevation: 165 feet

	Jan	Feb	Mar	Apr	May	Jun	Jul	Aug	Sep	Oct	Nov	Dec
High	58	62	70	77	84	89	92	90	84	75	67	59
Low	36	39	44	51	59	67	71	70	65	54	45	38
Precip	3.8	3.5	4.5	3.0	3.1	5.1	4.8	5.2	4.2	3.1	2.9	3.1
Snow	0.3	tr	tr	0.0	0.0	0.0	0.0	0.0	0.0	0.0	0.0	0.1

High and Low temperatures in degrees Fahrenheit; Precipitation and Snow in inches

Population: 15,987; Growth (since 2000): -4.0%; Density: 40.6 persons per square mile; Race: 36.1% White, 61.5% Black/African American, 0.4% Asian, 0.3% American Indian/Alaska Native, 0.0% Native Hawaiian/Other Pacific Islander, 1.0% two or more races, 1.6% Hispanic of any race; Average household size: 2.44; Median age: 39.3; Age under 18: 22.3%; Age 65 and over: 16.0%; Males per 100 females: 90.7; Marriage status: 37.3% never married, 44.1% now married, 5.0% separated, 11.8% widowed, 6.8% divorced; Foreign born: 1.8%; Speak English only: 98.2%; With disability: 21.6%; Veterans: 10.7%; Ancestry: 14.1% American, 5.0% German, 3.7% Irish, 3.5% English, 1.2% Scottish
Religion: Six largest groups: 20.1% Baptist, 13.7% Methodist/Pietist, 2.9% Pentecostal, 2.1% Non-denominational Protestant, 0.6% Other Groups, 0.5% Episcopalianism/Anglicanism
Economy: Unemployment rate: 11.1%; Leading industries: 20.4% retail trade; 16.0% other services (except public administration); 14.5% health care and social assistance; Farms: 315 totaling 92,524 acres; Company size: 0 employ 1,000 or more persons, 0 employ 500 to 999 persons, 7 employ 100 to 499 persons, 268 employ less than 100 persons; Business ownership: n/a women-owned, 71 Black-owned, n/a Hispanic-owned, n/a Asian-owned
Employment: 10.7% management, business, and financial, 2.1% computer, engineering, and science, 7.7% education, legal, community service, arts, and media, 5.6% healthcare practitioners, 23.4% service, 20.9% sales and office, 10.3% natural resources, construction, and maintenance, 19.1% production, transportation, and material moving
Income: Per capita: $18,902; Median household: $31,483; Average household: $47,786; Households with income of $100,000 or more: 8.5%; Poverty rate: 27.6%
Educational Attainment: High school diploma or higher: 75.5%; Bachelor's degree or higher: 17.5%; Graduate/professional degree or higher: 5.4%
Housing: Homeownership rate: 70.9%; Median home value: $74,700; Median year structure built: 1977; Homeowner vacancy rate: 2.1%; Median gross rent: $567 per month; Rental vacancy rate: 11.9%
Vital Statistics: Birth rate: 101.7 per 10,000 population; Death rate: 112.8 per 10,000 population; Age-adjusted cancer mortality rate: 188.9 deaths per 100,000 population
Health Insurance: 80.6% have insurance; 50.4% have private insurance; 41.6% have public insurance; 19.4% do not have insurance; 7.8% of children under 18 do not have insurance
Health Care: Physicians: 3.8 per 10,000 population; Hospital beds: 15.1 per 10,000 population; Hospital admissions: 370.5 per 10,000 population
Transportation: Commute: 91.4% car, 0.4% public transportation, 5.2% walk, 2.2% work from home; Median travel time to work: 23.6 minutes
Presidential Election: 67.2% Obama, 31.9% Romney (2012)
National and State Parks: Rivers Bridge State Park
Additional Information Contacts
Bamberg Government . . . . (803) 245-3025
    http://www.bambergcountysc.gov

Bamberg County Communities

BAMBERG (town). County seat. Covers a land area of 3.582 square miles and a water area of 0.012 square miles. Located at 33.30° N. Lat; 81.03° W. Long. Elevation is 164 feet.

Population: 3,607; Growth (since 2000): -3.4%; Density: 1,007.0 persons per square mile; Race: 41.3% White, 55.3% Black/African American, 1.1% Asian, 0.4% American Indian/Alaska Native, 0.0% Native Hawaiian/Other Pacific Islander, 1.3% Two or more races, 1.6% Hispanic of any race; Average household size: 2.38; Median age: 38.7; Age under 18: 22.8%; Age 65 and over: 17.4%; Males per 100 females: 84.8; Marriage status: 36.0% never married, 43.3% now married, 4.9% separated, 13.2% widowed, 7.6% divorced; Foreign born: 2.3%; Speak English only: 98.8%; With disability: 16.8%; Veterans: 9.9%; Ancestry: 14.2% American, 8.2% Irish, 4.8% English, 4.5% German, 3.6% European

Employment: 14.9% management, business, and financial, 2.5% computer, engineering, and science, 10.4% education, legal, community service, arts, and media, 8.0% healthcare practitioners, 26.2% service, 12.9% sales and office, 10.5% natural resources, construction, and maintenance, 14.7% production, transportation, and material moving

Income: Per capita: $22,713; Median household: $39,531; Average household: $52,960; Households with income of $100,000 or more: 17.0%; Poverty rate: 26.8%

Educational Attainment: High school diploma or higher: 82.7%; Bachelor's degree or higher: 22.9%; Graduate/professional degree or higher: 9.5%

School District(s)
Bamberg 01 (PK-12)
    2012-13 Enrollment: 1,434 . . . . (803) 245-3053

Housing: Homeownership rate: 64.0%; Median home value: $104,200; Median year structure built: 1967; Homeowner vacancy rate: 2.6%; Median gross rent: $633 per month; Rental vacancy rate: 7.6%

Health Insurance: 84.2% have insurance; 62.5% have private insurance; 41.4% have public insurance; 15.8% do not have insurance; 0.0% of children under 18 do not have insurance

Safety: Violent crime rate: 64.7 per 10,000 population; Property crime rate: 376.8 per 10,000 population

Newspapers: Advertizer-Herald (weekly circulation 5800)

Transportation: Commute: 90.4% car, 0.6% public transportation, 8.0% walk, 0.2% work from home; Median travel time to work: 17.6 minutes

Additional Information Contacts
Town of Bamberg . . . . (803) 245-5128
    http://www.bambergsc.com

DENMARK (city). Covers a land area of 3.836 square miles and a water area of 0.003 square miles. Located at 33.31° N. Lat; 81.13° W. Long. Elevation is 246 feet.

History: Denmark was an early communications center for the state, with main lines of the American Telegraph and Telephone Company and the Southern Bell Company.

Population: 3,538; Growth (since 2000): 6.3%; Density: 922.4 persons per square mile; Race: 8.6% White, 90.1% Black/African American, 0.3% Asian, 0.1% American Indian/Alaska Native, 0.1% Native Hawaiian/Other Pacific Islander, 0.5% Two or more races, 0.9% Hispanic of any race; Average household size: 2.34; Median age: 32.7; Age under 18: 21.7%; Age 65 and over: 13.6%; Males per 100 females: 84.5; Marriage status: 50.1% never married, 32.1% now married, 8.2% separated, 12.5% widowed, 5.4% divorced; Foreign born: 0.4%; Speak English only: 99.2%; With disability: 22.4%; Veterans: 7.2%; Ancestry: 3.4% American, 2.9% Irish, 2.4% German, 0.4% African, 0.3% Norwegian

Employment: 7.1% management, business, and financial, 0.0% computer, engineering, and science, 3.2% education, legal, community service, arts, and media, 2.4% healthcare practitioners, 34.3% service, 27.1% sales and office, 2.3% natural resources, construction, and maintenance, 23.7% production, transportation, and material moving

Income: Per capita: $15,776; Median household: $17,931; Average household: $46,795; Households with income of $100,000 or more: 3.1%; Poverty rate: 49.4%

Educational Attainment: High school diploma or higher: 69.7%; Bachelor's degree or higher: 17.1%; Graduate/professional degree or higher: 2.3%

School District(s)
Bamberg 02 (PK-12)
    2012-13 Enrollment: 810 . . . . (803) 793-3346

Four-year College(s)
Voorhees College (Private, Not-for-profit, Historically black, Protestant Episcopal)
    Fall 2013 Enrollment: 536 . . . . (803) 780-1234
    2013-14 Tuition: In-state $10,780; Out-of-state $10,780

Two-year College(s)
Denmark Technical College (Public, Historically black)
    Fall 2013 Enrollment: 1,838 . . . . (803) 793-5100
    2013-14 Tuition: In-state $2,662; Out-of-state $5,014

Housing: Homeownership rate: 53.4%; Median home value: $59,500; Median year structure built: 1973; Homeowner vacancy rate: 2.3%; Median gross rent: $377 per month; Rental vacancy rate: 10.1%

Health Insurance: 79.2% have insurance; 37.8% have private insurance; 48.0% have public insurance; 20.8% do not have insurance; 4.2% of children under 18 do not have insurance

Safety: Violent crime rate: 69.1 per 10,000 population; Property crime rate: 555.4 per 10,000 population

Transportation: Commute: 88.9% car, 0.0% public transportation, 8.8% walk, 0.0% work from home; Median travel time to work: 23.4 minutes; Amtrak: Train service available.

Additional Information Contacts
City of Denmark. . . . . (803) 793-3734
    http://www.bambergcountychamber.org

EHRHARDT (town). Covers a land area of 3.112 square miles and a water area of 0 square miles. Located at 33.10° N. Lat; 81.01° W. Long. Elevation is 141 feet.

Population: 545; Growth (since 2000): -11.2%; Density: 175.2 persons per square mile; Race: 46.8% White, 49.4% Black/African American, 0.7% Asian, 0.4% American Indian/Alaska Native, 0.0% Native Hawaiian/Other Pacific Islander, 0.9% Two or more races, 2.0% Hispanic of any race; Average household size: 2.32; Median age: 48.6; Age under 18: 20.2%; Age 65 and over: 21.1%; Males per 100 females: 85.4

Housing: Homeownership rate: 70.5%; Homeowner vacancy rate: 6.1%; Rental vacancy rate: 27.8%

Safety: Violent crime rate: 92.9 per 10,000 population; Property crime rate: 632.0 per 10,000 population

GOVAN (town). Covers a land area of 0.752 square miles and a water area of 0 square miles. Located at 33.22° N. Lat; 81.17° W. Long. Elevation is 239 feet.

Population: 65; Growth (since 2000): -3.0%; Density: 86.4 persons per square mile; Race: 60.0% White, 35.4% Black/African American, 0.0% Asian, 1.5% American Indian/Alaska Native, 0.0% Native Hawaiian/Other Pacific Islander, 3.1% Two or more races, 3.1% Hispanic of any race; Average household size: 2.32; Median age: 49.3; Age under 18: 15.4%; Age 65 and over: 18.5%; Males per 100 females: 116.7

Housing: Homeownership rate: 64.3%; Homeowner vacancy rate: 5.3%; Rental vacancy rate: 0.0%

OLAR (town). Covers a land area of 0.785 square miles and a water area of 0 square miles. Located at 33.18° N. Lat; 81.19° W. Long. Elevation is 203 feet.

Population: 257; Growth (since 2000): 8.4%; Density: 327.3 persons per square mile; Race: 52.9% White, 43.6% Black/African American, 0.4% Asian, 0.4% American Indian/Alaska Native, 0.0% Native Hawaiian/Other Pacific Islander, 2.7% Two or more races, 0.4% Hispanic of any race; Average household size: 2.09; Median age: 51.5; Age under 18: 12.8%; Age 65 and over: 26.5%; Males per 100 females: 87.6

Housing: Homeownership rate: 76.5%; Homeowner vacancy rate: 3.0%; Rental vacancy rate: 14.7%

Barnwell County

Located in western South Carolina; bounded on the west by the Savannah River, and on the northeast by the South Fork of the Edisto River. Covers a land area of 548.393 square miles, a water area of 8.870 square miles, and is located in the Eastern Time Zone at 33.26° N. Lat., 81.43° W. Long. The county was founded in 1798. County seat is Barnwell.

Population: 22,621; Growth (since 2000): -3.7%; Density: 41.2 persons per square mile; Race: 52.6% White, 44.3% Black/African American, 0.6% Asian, 0.4% American Indian/Alaska Native, 0.0% Native Hawaiian/Other Pacific Islander, 1.5% two or more races, 1.8% Hispanic of any race; Average household size: 2.50; Median age: 38.8; Age under 18: 25.6%; Age 65 and over: 14.0%; Males per 100 females: 91.5; Marriage status:

32.3% never married, 49.0% now married, 4.4% separated, 8.0% widowed, 10.8% divorced; Foreign born: 1.3%; Speak English only: 97.5%; With disability: 22.6%; Veterans: 9.2%; Ancestry: 19.6% American, 6.8% German, 4.7% English, 4.1% Irish, 1.6% Scotch-Irish
Religion: Six largest groups: 43.8% Baptist, 4.4% Methodist/Pietist, 4.0% Pentecostal, 1.6% Non-denominational Protestant, 1.4% Presbyterian-Reformed, 1.0% Latter-day Saints
Economy: Unemployment rate: 9.7%; Leading industries: 21.8% retail trade; 16.7% other services (except public administration); 9.2% health care and social assistance; Farms: 397 totaling 87,837 acres; Company size: 0 employ 1,000 or more persons, 1 employs 500 to 999 persons, 8 employ 100 to 499 persons, 339 employ less than 100 persons; Business ownership: 477 women-owned, 302 Black-owned, n/a Hispanic-owned, n/a Asian-owned
Employment: 9.2% management, business, and financial, 2.6% computer, engineering, and science, 10.6% education, legal, community service, arts, and media, 3.8% healthcare practitioners, 19.0% service, 18.2% sales and office, 11.2% natural resources, construction, and maintenance, 25.4% production, transportation, and material moving
Income: Per capita: $18,862; Median household: $35,231; Average household: $47,861; Households with income of $100,000 or more: 8.9%; Poverty rate: 29.1%
Educational Attainment: High school diploma or higher: 79.7%; Bachelor's degree or higher: 11.2%; Graduate/professional degree or higher: 3.1%
Housing: Homeownership rate: 70.3%; Median home value: $72,400; Median year structure built: 1981; Homeowner vacancy rate: 1.9%; Median gross rent: $625 per month; Rental vacancy rate: 11.5%
Vital Statistics: Birth rate: 139.2 per 10,000 population; Death rate: 123.9 per 10,000 population; Age-adjusted cancer mortality rate: 225.0 deaths per 100,000 population
Health Insurance: 84.6% have insurance; 56.5% have private insurance; 42.7% have public insurance; 15.4% do not have insurance; 4.2% of children under 18 do not have insurance
Health Care: Physicians: 4.9 per 10,000 population; Hospital beds: 14.7 per 10,000 population; Hospital admissions: 389.6 per 10,000 population
Transportation: Commute: 94.6% car, 0.2% public transportation, 2.9% walk, 1.4% work from home; Median travel time to work: 25.3 minutes
Presidential Election: 52.3% Obama, 47.0% Romney (2012)
National and State Parks: Barnwell State Park; Ernest Rand Memorial State Forest
Additional Information Contacts
Barnwell Government . . . . (803) 541-1000
   http://www.barnwellcounty.sc.gov

Barnwell County Communities

BARNWELL (city). County seat. Covers a land area of 7.850 square miles and a water area of 0.148 square miles. Located at 33.24° N. Lat; 81.37° W. Long. Elevation is 217 feet.
History: Barnwell was taken over by Sherman's men on his famous march, and burned down. The community's contribution to the Confederacy was General Johnson Hagood, governor from 1880 to 1882.
Population: 4,750; Growth (since 2000): -5.7%; Density: 605.1 persons per square mile; Race: 44.5% White, 51.5% Black/African American, 1.5% Asian, 0.2% American Indian/Alaska Native, 0.1% Native Hawaiian/Other Pacific Islander, 1.7% Two or more races, 1.0% Hispanic of any race; Average household size: 2.39; Median age: 36.7; Age under 18: 26.5%; Age 65 and over: 15.2%; Males per 100 females: 89.5; Marriage status: 32.6% never married, 49.2% now married, 6.7% separated, 6.8% widowed, 11.4% divorced; Foreign born: 1.7%; Speak English only: 98.4%; With disability: 18.9%; Veterans: 7.5%; Ancestry: 13.0% American, 6.5% German, 4.3% English, 4.1% Irish, 2.6% Scotch-Irish
Employment: 18.9% management, business, and financial, 1.8% computer, engineering, and science, 17.5% education, legal, community service, arts, and media, 2.4% healthcare practitioners, 12.9% service, 19.8% sales and office, 6.4% natural resources, construction, and maintenance, 20.3% production, transportation, and material moving
Income: Per capita: $15,313; Median household: $31,490; Average household: $39,223; Households with income of $100,000 or more: 5.2%; Poverty rate: 42.3%
Educational Attainment: High school diploma or higher: 83.1%; Bachelor's degree or higher: 15.5%; Graduate/professional degree or higher: 5.3%

School District(s)
Barnwell 45 (PK-12)
   2012-13 Enrollment: 2,441 . . . . (803) 541-1300
Housing: Homeownership rate: 56.0%; Median home value: $99,400; Median year structure built: 1969; Homeowner vacancy rate: 3.8%; Median gross rent: $668 per month; Rental vacancy rate: 10.9%
Health Insurance: 88.1% have insurance; 51.1% have private insurance; 51.1% have public insurance; 11.9% do not have insurance; 0.0% of children under 18 do not have insurance
Hospitals: Barnwell County Hospital (56 beds)
Safety: Violent crime rate: 96.6 per 10,000 population; Property crime rate: 783.8 per 10,000 population
Newspapers: People Sentinel (weekly circulation 8500)
Transportation: Commute: 94.8% car, 0.0% public transportation, 3.4% walk, 1.1% work from home; Median travel time to work: 20.8 minutes
Additional Information Contacts
City of Barnwell . . . . (803) 259-3266
   http://www.cityofbarnwell.com

BLACKVILLE (town). Covers a land area of 8.932 square miles and a water area of 0.102 square miles. Located at 33.35° N. Lat; 81.29° W. Long. Elevation is 292 feet.
History: Blackville was named for Alexander Black, an early railroad executive. Cucumbers was an early money-making crop for Blackville farmers. Blackville was in the path of Sherman's march to the sea in 1865, and shared in the devastation.
Population: 2,406; Growth (since 2000): -19.1%; Density: 269.4 persons per square mile; Race: 19.2% White, 78.0% Black/African American, 0.1% Asian, 0.2% American Indian/Alaska Native, 0.0% Native Hawaiian/Other Pacific Islander, 1.4% Two or more races, 3.4% Hispanic of any race; Average household size: 2.59; Median age: 36.9; Age under 18: 27.7%; Age 65 and over: 13.4%; Males per 100 females: 85.8
School District(s)
Barnwell 19 (PK-12)
   2012-13 Enrollment: 825 . . . . (803) 284-5605
Barnwell 80 (09-12)
   2012-13 Enrollment: n/a . . . . (803) 259-5512
Housing: Homeownership rate: 61.3%; Homeowner vacancy rate: 2.2%; Rental vacancy rate: 17.8%
Safety: Violent crime rate: 68.3 per 10,000 population; Property crime rate: 379.7 per 10,000 population
Additional Information Contacts
Town of Blackville . . . . (803) 284-2444
   http://townofblackville.com

ELKO (town). Covers a land area of 1.049 square miles and a water area of 0 square miles. Located at 33.38° N. Lat; 81.38° W. Long. Elevation is 338 feet.
Population: 193; Growth (since 2000): -9.0%; Density: 184.0 persons per square mile; Race: 40.4% White, 59.1% Black/African American, 0.0% Asian, 0.0% American Indian/Alaska Native, 0.0% Native Hawaiian/Other Pacific Islander, 0.5% Two or more races, 0.5% Hispanic of any race; Average household size: 2.38; Median age: 39.9; Age under 18: 24.4%; Age 65 and over: 16.6%; Males per 100 females: 103.2
Housing: Homeownership rate: 72.9%; Homeowner vacancy rate: 0.0%; Rental vacancy rate: 26.7%

HILDA (town). Covers a land area of 3.070 square miles and a water area of 0.038 square miles. Located at 33.28° N. Lat; 81.24° W. Long. Elevation is 259 feet.
Population: 447; Growth (since 2000): 2.5%; Density: 145.6 persons per square mile; Race: 87.9% White, 10.7% Black/African American, 0.0% Asian, 0.4% American Indian/Alaska Native, 0.0% Native Hawaiian/Other Pacific Islander, 0.9% Two or more races, 1.6% Hispanic of any race; Average household size: 2.42; Median age: 39.6; Age under 18: 24.4%; Age 65 and over: 15.4%; Males per 100 females: 86.3
Housing: Homeownership rate: 85.4%; Homeowner vacancy rate: 1.2%; Rental vacancy rate: 12.5%

KLINE (town). Covers a land area of 3.106 square miles and a water area of 0.025 square miles. Located at 33.12° N. Lat; 81.34° W. Long. Elevation is 243 feet.
Population: 197; Growth (since 2000): -17.2%; Density: 63.4 persons per square mile; Race: 49.7% White, 44.7% Black/African American, 0.0% Asian, 0.0% American Indian/Alaska Native, 0.0% Native Hawaiian/Other

Pacific Islander, 1.0% Two or more races, 9.1% Hispanic of any race; Average household size: 2.56; Median age: 43.6; Age under 18: 21.3%; Age 65 and over: 14.2%; Males per 100 females: 99.0
Housing: Homeownership rate: 71.5%; Homeowner vacancy rate: 3.5%; Rental vacancy rate: 8.0%

SNELLING (town).
Covers a land area of 4.036 square miles and a water area of 0.049 square miles. Located at 33.24° N. Lat; 81.47° W. Long. Elevation is 230 feet.
Population: 274; Growth (since 2000): 11.4%; Density: 67.9 persons per square mile; Race: 81.8% White, 16.4% Black/African American, 0.0% Asian, 0.0% American Indian/Alaska Native, 0.0% Native Hawaiian/Other Pacific Islander, 1.1% Two or more races, 0.7% Hispanic of any race; Average household size: 2.58; Median age: 41.5; Age under 18: 21.5%; Age 65 and over: 7.7%; Males per 100 females: 110.8
Housing: Homeownership rate: 76.4%; Homeowner vacancy rate: 0.0%; Rental vacancy rate: 3.3%

WILLISTON (town).
Covers a land area of 8.953 square miles and a water area of 0.063 square miles. Located at 33.40° N. Lat; 81.42° W. Long. Elevation is 354 feet.
History: Williston was known as an asparagus-marketing center.
Population: 3,139; Growth (since 2000): -5.1%; Density: 350.6 persons per square mile; Race: 43.3% White, 54.0% Black/African American, 0.2% Asian, 0.8% American Indian/Alaska Native, 0.0% Native Hawaiian/Other Pacific Islander, 1.4% Two or more races, 1.1% Hispanic of any race; Average household size: 2.35; Median age: 39.5; Age under 18: 25.9%; Age 65 and over: 16.8%; Males per 100 females: 88.2; Marriage status: 33.6% never married, 47.1% now married, 3.6% separated, 7.7% widowed, 11.6% divorced; Foreign born: 0.0%; Speak English only: 100.0%; With disability: 23.8%; Veterans: 11.1%; Ancestry: 15.7% American, 5.7% German, 5.2% English, 3.8% Scotch-Irish, 2.8% Irish
Employment: 11.3% management, business, and financial, 5.3% computer, engineering, and science, 10.8% education, legal, community service, arts, and media, 9.8% healthcare practitioners, 18.7% service, 15.6% sales and office, 10.0% natural resources, construction, and maintenance, 18.5% production, transportation, and material moving
Income: Per capita: $14,516; Median household: $29,041; Average household: $40,920; Households with income of $100,000 or more: 6.9%; Poverty rate: 38.9%
Educational Attainment: High school diploma or higher: 73.2%; Bachelor's degree or higher: 16.1%; Graduate/professional degree or higher: 5.5%

School District(s)
Barnwell 29 (PK-12)
    2012-13 Enrollment: 936. . . . . (803) 266-7878
Housing: Homeownership rate: 59.2%; Median home value: $66,400; Median year structure built: 1977; Homeowner vacancy rate: 1.8%; Median gross rent: $644 per month; Rental vacancy rate: 8.9%
Health Insurance: 87.1% have insurance; 49.1% have private insurance; 50.9% have public insurance; 12.9% do not have insurance; 1.0% of children under 18 do not have insurance
Safety: Violent crime rate: 52.2 per 10,000 population; Property crime rate: 365.2 per 10,000 population
Transportation: Commute: 88.2% car, 1.9% public transportation, 8.2% walk, 1.7% work from home; Median travel time to work: 21.8 minutes
Additional Information Contacts
Town of Williston . . . . (803) 266-7015
    http://www.williston-sc.com

Beaufort County

Located in southern South Carolina, along the Atlantic coast; bounded on the north by the Combahee River, on the northeast by Saint Helena River, and on the south by the Savannah River; includes Port Royal, Parris, Saint Helena, and Hilton Head Islan Covers a land area of 576.280 square miles, a water area of 347.116 square miles, and is located in the Eastern Time Zone at 32.36° N. Lat., 80.69° W. Long. The county was founded in 1764. County seat is Beaufort.

Beaufort County is part of the Hilton Head Island-Bluffton-Beaufort, SC Metropolitan Statistical Area. The entire metro area includes: Beaufort County, SC; Jasper County, SC

Weather Station: Beaufort 7 SW										Elevation: 20 feet		
	Jan	Feb	Mar	Apr	May	Jun	Jul	Aug	Sep	Oct	Nov	Dec
High	60	63	70	76	83	88	91	89	85	77	69	61
Low	41	43	49	56	64	71	75	74	69	60	51	43
Precip	4.0	3.3	3.8	3.2	2.7	6.1	5.4	6.9	4.9	3.9	2.8	2.8
Snow	tr	tr	tr	0.0	0.0	0.0	0.0	0.0	0.0	0.0	0.0	0.2

High and Low temperatures in degrees Fahrenheit; Precipitation and Snow in inches

Weather Station: Yemassee										Elevation: 24 feet		
	Jan	Feb	Mar	Apr	May	Jun	Jul	Aug	Sep	Oct	Nov	Dec
High	61	66	73	79	86	91	93	91	87	79	71	64
Low	35	38	43	49	57	65	68	68	63	51	43	36
Precip	3.8	3.5	4.2	3.4	3.1	6.5	6.0	6.7	5.2	3.7	2.7	3.3
Snow	0.0	tr	tr	0.0	0.0	0.0	0.0	0.0	0.0	0.0	0.0	0.1

High and Low temperatures in degrees Fahrenheit; Precipitation and Snow in inches

Population: 162,233; Growth (since 2000): 34.1%; Density: 281.5 persons per square mile; Race: 71.9% White, 19.3% Black/African American, 1.2% Asian, 0.3% American Indian/Alaska Native, 0.1% Native Hawaiian/Other Pacific Islander, 2.1% two or more races, 12.1% Hispanic of any race; Average household size: 2.42; Median age: 40.6; Age under 18: 21.2%; Age 65 and over: 20.4%; Males per 100 females: 97.5; Marriage status: 24.8% never married, 58.8% now married, 2.5% separated, 6.4% widowed, 10.0% divorced; Foreign born: 10.3%; Speak English only: 86.1%; With disability: 11.9%; Veterans: 15.2%; Ancestry: 14.8% German, 12.9% Irish, 11.3% English, 5.9% American, 5.6% Italian
Religion: Six largest groups: 9.9% Catholicism, 8.4% Baptist, 5.2% Non-denominational Protestant, 3.3% Presbyterian-Reformed, 3.1% Episcopalianism/Anglicanism, 2.9% Methodist/Pietist
Economy: Unemployment rate: 6.0%; Leading industries: 15.3% retail trade; 11.7% construction; 11.6% professional, scientific, and technical services; Farms: 137 totaling 42,177 acres; Company size: 1 employs 1,000 or more persons, 2 employ 500 to 999 persons, 56 employ 100 to 499 persons, 4,729 employ less than 100 persons; Business ownership: 4,176 women-owned, 1,217 Black-owned, 328 Hispanic-owned, 286 Asian-owned
Employment: 14.8% management, business, and financial, 1.9% computer, engineering, and science, 10.3% education, legal, community service, arts, and media, 5.0% healthcare practitioners, 24.5% service, 25.6% sales and office, 10.8% natural resources, construction, and maintenance, 7.2% production, transportation, and material moving
Income: Per capita: $32,503; Median household: $57,316; Average household: $80,008; Households with income of $100,000 or more: 24.0%; Poverty rate: 12.5%
Educational Attainment: High school diploma or higher: 91.3%; Bachelor's degree or higher: 37.6%; Graduate/professional degree or higher: 14.9%
Housing: Homeownership rate: 70.6%; Median home value: $275,500; Median year structure built: 1992; Homeowner vacancy rate: 4.1%; Median gross rent: $1,039 per month; Rental vacancy rate: 30.7%
Vital Statistics: Birth rate: 117.8 per 10,000 population; Death rate: 77.5 per 10,000 population; Age-adjusted cancer mortality rate: 156.0 deaths per 100,000 population
Health Insurance: 82.9% have insurance; 66.5% have private insurance; 35.7% have public insurance; 17.1% do not have insurance; 13.8% of children under 18 do not have insurance
Health Care: Physicians: 19.9 per 10,000 population; Hospital beds: 18.9 per 10,000 population; Hospital admissions: 963.3 per 10,000 population
Transportation: Commute: 86.8% car, 0.6% public transportation, 3.4% walk, 6.4% work from home; Median travel time to work: 20.9 minutes
Presidential Election: 40.7% Obama, 58.2% Romney (2012)
National and State Parks: Hunting Island State Park
Additional Information Contacts
Beaufort Government . . . . (843) 255-2000
    http://www.bcgov.net

Beaufort County Communities

BEAUFORT (city).
County seat. Covers a land area of 27.600 square miles and a water area of 5.979 square miles. Located at 32.45° N. Lat; 80.71° W. Long. Elevation is 10 feet.
History: Beaufort, a seacoast town on Port Royal Island, was laid out in 1710 and named for Henry, Duke of Beaufort. The harbor had been visited by the Spanish and French in the 1500's. The area was settled briefly by a Scotch group in 1684, and then by planters from Barbados and other

British colonies in 1710. Beaufort was occupied by Union soldiers in 1861, and most of the families living there at the time lost their homes.
Population: 12,361; Growth (since 2000): -4.5%; Density: 447.9 persons per square mile; Race: 67.1% White, 25.7% Black/African American, 1.4% Asian, 0.3% American Indian/Alaska Native, 0.1% Native Hawaiian/Other Pacific Islander, 2.6% Two or more races, 6.7% Hispanic of any race; Average household size: 2.28; Median age: 34.2; Age under 18: 22.3%; Age 65 and over: 15.5%; Males per 100 females: 95.6; Marriage status: 29.9% never married, 52.5% now married, 4.0% separated, 6.1% widowed, 11.5% divorced; Foreign born: 7.6%; Speak English only: 89.8%; With disability: 15.1%; Veterans: 18.2%; Ancestry: 13.2% German, 12.3% English, 10.0% Irish, 9.0% American, 4.0% Italian
Employment: 18.0% management, business, and financial, 1.9% computer, engineering, and science, 11.4% education, legal, community service, arts, and media, 5.8% healthcare practitioners, 19.0% service, 25.3% sales and office, 11.3% natural resources, construction, and maintenance, 7.2% production, transportation, and material moving
Income: Per capita: $27,719; Median household: $50,801; Average household: $69,177; Households with income of $100,000 or more: 20.7%; Poverty rate: 19.4%
Educational Attainment: High school diploma or higher: 89.3%; Bachelor's degree or higher: 40.7%; Graduate/professional degree or higher: 16.4%

School District(s)
Beaufort 01 (PK-12)
    2012-13 Enrollment: 20,443 . . . . (843) 322-2300
Two-year College(s)
Technical College of the Lowcountry (Public)
    Fall 2013 Enrollment: 2,427 . . . . (800) 768-8252
    2013-14 Tuition: In-state $4,540; Out-of-state $8,548
Housing: Homeownership rate: 53.8%; Median home value: $252,700; Median year structure built: 1978; Homeowner vacancy rate: 4.9%; Median gross rent: $819 per month; Rental vacancy rate: 11.0%
Health Insurance: 84.6% have insurance; 65.9% have private insurance; 35.9% have public insurance; 15.4% do not have insurance; 15.9% of children under 18 do not have insurance
Hospitals: Beaufort County Memorial Hospital (197 beds)
Safety: Violent crime rate: 118.4 per 10,000 population; Property crime rate: 622.4 per 10,000 population
Newspapers: Beaufort Gazette (daily circulation 12400)
Transportation: Commute: 85.1% car, 0.0% public transportation, 4.8% walk, 6.2% work from home; Median travel time to work: 19.9 minutes
Airports: Beaufort County (general aviation); Beaufort MCAS /Merritt Field (general aviation)
Additional Information Contacts
City of Beaufort . . . . (843) 525-7070
    http://www.cityofbeaufort.org

BLUFFTON (town). Covers a land area of 51.301 square miles and a water area of 2.210 square miles. Located at 32.21° N. Lat; 80.93° W. Long. Elevation is 20 feet.
History: Bluffton has been a popular spot for writers and artists. Here the poet Henry Timrod taught school in the 1860's, and here the botanist Dr. Joseph Mellichamp is buried.
Population: 12,530; Growth (since 2000): 882.7%; Density: 244.2 persons per square mile; Race: 71.4% White, 16.2% Black/African American, 2.0% Asian, 0.3% American Indian/Alaska Native, 0.0% Native Hawaiian/Other Pacific Islander, 2.9% Two or more races, 18.8% Hispanic of any race; Average household size: 2.84; Median age: 32.7; Age under 18: 28.9%; Age 65 and over: 7.3%; Males per 100 females: 95.5; Marriage status: 26.6% never married, 56.1% now married, 1.8% separated, 4.3% widowed, 13.0% divorced; Foreign born: 16.1%; Speak English only: 77.9%; With disability: 9.3%; Veterans: 10.4%; Ancestry: 13.4% Irish, 12.6% German, 9.1% Italian, 8.8% English, 4.6% American
Employment: 16.7% management, business, and financial, 1.6% computer, engineering, and science, 9.6% education, legal, community service, arts, and media, 5.9% healthcare practitioners, 22.0% service, 27.8% sales and office, 9.4% natural resources, construction, and maintenance, 7.0% production, transportation, and material moving
Income: Per capita: $26,034; Median household: $60,038; Average household: $74,026; Households with income of $100,000 or more: 23.9%; Poverty rate: 16.1%
Educational Attainment: High school diploma or higher: 90.0%; Bachelor's degree or higher: 30.9%; Graduate/professional degree or higher: 11.0%

School District(s)
Beaufort 01 (PK-12)
    2012-13 Enrollment: 20,443 . . . . (843) 322-2300
Four-year College(s)
University of South Carolina-Beaufort (Public)
    Fall 2013 Enrollment: 1,724 . . . . (843) 208-8000
    2013-14 Tuition: In-state $8,972; Out-of-state $18,824
Housing: Homeownership rate: 74.6%; Median home value: $216,500; Median year structure built: 2004; Homeowner vacancy rate: 6.4%; Median gross rent: $1,310 per month; Rental vacancy rate: 14.7%
Health Insurance: 75.0% have insurance; 62.1% have private insurance; 21.4% have public insurance; 25.0% do not have insurance; 20.3% of children under 18 do not have insurance
Safety: Violent crime rate: 37.6 per 10,000 population; Property crime rate: 290.5 per 10,000 population
Newspapers: Bluffton Today (daily circulation 19200)
Transportation: Commute: 92.1% car, 0.2% public transportation, 2.3% walk, 4.5% work from home; Median travel time to work: 23.6 minutes
Additional Information Contacts
Town of Bluffton . . . . (843) 706-4500
    http://www.townofbluffton.com

BURTON (CDP). Covers a land area of 8.536 square miles and a water area of 0.020 square miles. Located at 32.42° N. Lat; 80.74° W. Long. Elevation is 33 feet.
Population: 6,976; Growth (since 2000): -2.8%; Density: 817.2 persons per square mile; Race: 48.1% White, 43.1% Black/African American, 1.3% Asian, 0.4% American Indian/Alaska Native, 0.2% Native Hawaiian/Other Pacific Islander, 2.7% Two or more races, 9.9% Hispanic of any race; Average household size: 2.62; Median age: 31.3; Age under 18: 26.4%; Age 65 and over: 9.1%; Males per 100 females: 94.6; Marriage status: 26.2% never married, 52.5% now married, 2.5% separated, 4.7% widowed, 16.5% divorced; Foreign born: 2.6%; Speak English only: 95.1%; With disability: 13.7%; Veterans: 19.2%; Ancestry: 8.0% German, 4.9% Scottish, 4.6% American, 4.3% Dutch, 4.2% Irish
Employment: 7.9% management, business, and financial, 1.2% computer, engineering, and science, 11.6% education, legal, community service, arts, and media, 2.8% healthcare practitioners, 25.4% service, 21.5% sales and office, 18.6% natural resources, construction, and maintenance, 11.0% production, transportation, and material moving
Income: Per capita: $19,233; Median household: $42,238; Average household: $50,693; Households with income of $100,000 or more: 9.4%; Poverty rate: 10.6%
Educational Attainment: High school diploma or higher: 89.1%; Bachelor's degree or higher: 14.4%; Graduate/professional degree or higher: 4.8%
Housing: Homeownership rate: 57.2%; Median home value: $132,400; Median year structure built: 1986; Homeowner vacancy rate: 2.5%; Median gross rent: $905 per month; Rental vacancy rate: 14.8%
Health Insurance: 77.8% have insurance; 60.5% have private insurance; 29.1% have public insurance; 22.2% do not have insurance; 16.0% of children under 18 do not have insurance
Transportation: Commute: 92.5% car, 0.0% public transportation, 2.3% walk, 0.8% work from home; Median travel time to work: 20.9 minutes

---

DAUFUSKIE ISLAND (unincorporated postal area)
ZCTA: 29915
    Covers a land area of 10.770 square miles and a water area of 2.414 square miles. Located at 32.12° N. Lat; 80.87° W. Long..
    Population: 416; Growth (since 2000): n/a; Density: 38.6 persons per square mile; Race: 93.5% White, 5.3% Black/African American, 0.5% Asian, 0.0% American Indian/Alaska Native, 0.0% Native Hawaiian/Other Pacific Islander, 0.7% Two or more races, 1.9% Hispanic of any race; Average household size: 2.04; Median age: 58.5; Age under 18: 11.3%; Age 65 and over: 29.1%; Males per 100 females: 102.9
    Housing: Homeownership rate: 89.7%; Homeowner vacancy rate: 6.5%; Rental vacancy rate: 68.6%

HILTON HEAD ISLAND (town). Covers a land area of 41.363 square miles and a water area of 27.771 square miles. Located at 32.19° N. Lat; 80.74° W. Long. Elevation is 10 feet.
History: Hilton Head Island, sometimes referred to as simply Hilton Head, is a low country resort town located on an island of the same name in Beaufort County, South Carolina. The island gets its name from Captain

William Hilton who, in 1663, discovered a headland near the entrance to Port Royal Sound, which he then named.

Population: 37,099; Growth (since 2000): 9.6%; Density: 896.9 persons per square mile; Race: 82.9% White, 7.5% Black/African American, 0.9% Asian, 0.2% American Indian/Alaska Native, 0.1% Native Hawaiian/Other Pacific Islander, 1.2% Two or more races, 15.8% Hispanic of any race; Average household size: 2.23; Median age: 50.9; Age under 18: 16.6%; Age 65 and over: 28.8%; Males per 100 females: 96.4; Marriage status: 20.9% never married, 63.1% now married, 2.4% separated, 7.3% widowed, 8.7% divorced; Foreign born: 15.1%; Speak English only: 81.4%; With disability: 10.8%; Veterans: 14.0%; Ancestry: 16.2% German, 14.7% English, 14.5% Irish, 7.1% Italian, 4.8% American

Employment: 17.5% management, business, and financial, 2.5% computer, engineering, and science, 8.9% education, legal, community service, arts, and media, 4.7% healthcare practitioners, 23.8% service, 27.5% sales and office, 11.5% natural resources, construction, and maintenance, 3.5% production, transportation, and material moving

Income: Per capita: $46,091; Median household: $69,772; Average household: $101,114; Households with income of $100,000 or more: 32.9%; Poverty rate: 8.5%

Educational Attainment: High school diploma or higher: 92.3%; Bachelor's degree or higher: 48.5%; Graduate/professional degree or higher: 18.1%

School District(s)

Beaufort 01 (PK-12)
    2012-13 Enrollment: 20,443 . . . . (843) 322-2300

Housing: Homeownership rate: 72.8%; Median home value: $447,900; Median year structure built: 1986; Homeowner vacancy rate: 4.9%; Median gross rent: $1,092 per month; Rental vacancy rate: 55.1%

Health Insurance: 82.6% have insurance; 68.9% have private insurance; 37.6% have public insurance; 17.4% do not have insurance; 17.3% of children under 18 do not have insurance

Hospitals: Hilton Head Regional Medical Center (93 beds)

Newspapers: Island Packet (daily circulation 19300)

Transportation: Commute: 85.6% car, 1.0% public transportation, 2.2% walk, 7.9% work from home; Median travel time to work: 17.9 minutes

Airports: Hilton Head (primary service/non-hub)

Additional Information Contacts

Town of Hilton Head Island . . . . (843) 341-4600
    http://www.hiltonheadislandsc.gov

LAUREL BAY (CDP).

Covers a land area of 4.500 square miles and a water area of 0.889 square miles. Located at 32.46° N. Lat; 80.79° W. Long. Elevation is 36 feet.

Population: 5,891; Growth (since 2000): -11.1%; Density: 1,309.2 persons per square mile; Race: 66.9% White, 23.9% Black/African American, 1.3% Asian, 0.9% American Indian/Alaska Native, 0.1% Native Hawaiian/Other Pacific Islander, 3.8% Two or more races, 11.1% Hispanic of any race; Average household size: 3.04; Median age: 23.6; Age under 18: 37.3%; Age 65 and over: 2.2%; Males per 100 females: 93.5; Marriage status: 16.8% never married, 70.3% now married, 0.5% separated, 3.7% widowed, 9.1% divorced; Foreign born: 1.8%; Speak English only: 94.0%; With disability: 8.5%; Veterans: 22.4%; Ancestry: 17.0% German, 10.7% Irish, 6.4% Italian, 5.2% English, 5.1% Scotch-Irish

Employment: 5.7% management, business, and financial, 1.8% computer, engineering, and science, 6.2% education, legal, community service, arts, and media, 1.8% healthcare practitioners, 29.6% service, 34.1% sales and office, 14.0% natural resources, construction, and maintenance, 6.7% production, transportation, and material moving

Income: Per capita: $17,872; Median household: $42,733; Average household: $54,795; Households with income of $100,000 or more: 6.5%; Poverty rate: 14.8%

Educational Attainment: High school diploma or higher: 93.9%; Bachelor's degree or higher: 13.3%; Graduate/professional degree or higher: 1.1%

Housing: Homeownership rate: 24.2%; Median home value: $149,500; Median year structure built: 1979; Homeowner vacancy rate: 4.3%; Median gross rent: $1,069 per month; Rental vacancy rate: 10.6%

Health Insurance: 85.9% have insurance; 79.4% have private insurance; 11.5% have public insurance; 14.1% do not have insurance; 8.7% of children under 18 do not have insurance

Transportation: Commute: 97.2% car, 0.0% public transportation, 0.0% walk, 1.4% work from home; Median travel time to work: 19.2 minutes

OKATIE (unincorporated postal area)
ZCTA: 29909

Covers a land area of 55.193 square miles and a water area of 27.277 square miles. Located at 32.34° N. Lat; 80.85° W. Long..

Population: 16,394; Growth (since 2000): n/a; Density: 297.0 persons per square mile; Race: 92.9% White, 5.0% Black/African American, 0.6% Asian, 0.1% American Indian/Alaska Native, 0.0% Native Hawaiian/Other Pacific Islander, 0.7% Two or more races, 3.2% Hispanic of any race; Average household size: 1.96; Median age: 66.0; Age under 18: 7.0%; Age 65 and over: 53.8%; Males per 100 females: 87.7; Marriage status: 9.6% never married, 72.5% now married, 0.7% separated, 10.2% widowed, 7.7% divorced; Foreign born: 7.5%; Speak English only: 94.4%; With disability: 15.5%; Veterans: 19.6%; Ancestry: 24.0% German, 18.6% Irish, 17.6% English, 9.8% Italian, 7.6% American

Employment: 16.9% management, business, and financial, 2.9% computer, engineering, and science, 10.6% education, legal, community service, arts, and media, 4.7% healthcare practitioners, 15.5% service, 39.4% sales and office, 5.0% natural resources, construction, and maintenance, 5.0% production, transportation, and material moving

Income: Per capita: $41,003; Median household: $65,487; Average household: $81,090; Households with income of $100,000 or more: 25.8%; Poverty rate: 3.5%

Educational Attainment: High school diploma or higher: 96.8%; Bachelor's degree or higher: 47.2%; Graduate/professional degree or higher: 21.6%

School District(s)

Beaufort 01 (PK-12)
    2012-13 Enrollment: 20,443 . . . . (843) 322-2300

Housing: Homeownership rate: 92.1%; Median home value: $262,700; Median year structure built: 2002; Homeowner vacancy rate: 2.8%; Median gross rent: $1,097 per month; Rental vacancy rate: 27.2%

Health Insurance: 97.5% have insurance; 81.0% have private insurance; 61.9% have public insurance; 2.5% do not have insurance; 0.0% of children under 18 do not have insurance

Transportation: Commute: 88.0% car, 0.0% public transportation, 1.2% walk, 5.7% work from home; Median travel time to work: 24.8 minutes

PARRIS ISLAND (unincorporated postal area)
ZCTA: 29905

Covers a land area of 2.768 square miles and a water area of 0.802 square miles. Located at 32.35° N. Lat; 80.68° W. Long..

Population: 3,054; Growth (since 2000): n/a; Density: 1,103.5 persons per square mile; Race: 77.2% White, 13.2% Black/African American, 2.4% Asian, 0.7% American Indian/Alaska Native, 0.1% Native Hawaiian/Other Pacific Islander, 3.7% Two or more races, 15.4% Hispanic of any race; Average household size: 3.64; Median age: 20.3; Age under 18: 1.6%; Age 65 and over: 0.0%; Males per 100 females: 384.0; Marriage status: 85.6% never married, 11.3% now married, 1.5% separated, 0.0% widowed, 3.2% divorced; Foreign born: 6.6%; Speak English only: 80.5%; With disability: 1.8%; Veterans: 45.9%; Ancestry: 18.5% German, 15.4% Irish, 9.6% Italian, 8.0% English, 6.1% American

Employment: 6.4% management, business, and financial, 7.5% computer, engineering, and science, 0.9% education, legal, community service, arts, and media, 0.0% healthcare practitioners, 49.8% service, 26.5% sales and office, 3.4% natural resources, construction, and maintenance, 5.5% production, transportation, and material moving

Income: Per capita: $14,275; Median household: $85,769; Average household: $78,177; Households with income of $100,000 or more: 7.7%; Poverty rate: n/a

Educational Attainment: High school diploma or higher: 98.4%; Bachelor's degree or higher: 22.5%; Graduate/professional degree or higher: 2.0%

Housing: Homeownership rate: n/a; Median home value: n/a; Median year structure built: 2002; Homeowner vacancy rate: 0.0%; Median gross rent: $1,633 per month; Rental vacancy rate: 8.3%

Health Insurance: 81.7% have insurance; 53.2% have private insurance; 28.4% have public insurance; 18.3% do not have insurance; 0.0% of children under 18 do not have insurance

Transportation: Commute: 24.7% car, 0.0% public transportation, 30.2% walk, 31.6% work from home; Median travel time to work: 11.7 minutes

PORT ROYAL (town). Covers a land area of 18.945 square miles and a water area of 3.065 square miles. Located at 32.36° N. Lat; 80.70° W. Long. Elevation is 23 feet.

History: Port Royal has one of the names surviving from early French attempts at settlement. The English considered settling here in 1670, but moved on to the site of Charleston. Activity here increased when the Parris Island Bridge was completed in 1939.

Population: 10,678; Growth (since 2000): 170.3%; Density: 563.6 persons per square mile; Race: 68.8% White, 20.7% Black/African American, 2.5% Asian, 0.6% American Indian/Alaska Native, 0.1% Native Hawaiian/Other Pacific Islander, 3.7% Two or more races, 13.3% Hispanic of any race; Average household size: 2.35; Median age: 22.9; Age under 18: 18.0%; Age 65 and over: 5.3%; Males per 100 females: 146.1; Marriage status: 57.1% never married, 32.2% now married, 3.3% separated, 3.2% widowed, 7.4% divorced; Foreign born: 5.3%; Speak English only: 86.6%; With disability: 9.0%; Veterans: 28.7%; Ancestry: 14.7% Irish, 13.9% German, 7.2% English, 6.3% American, 5.5% Italian

Employment: 9.3% management, business, and financial, 4.5% computer, engineering, and science, 19.2% education, legal, community service, arts, and media, 5.2% healthcare practitioners, 22.4% service, 24.0% sales and office, 8.0% natural resources, construction, and maintenance, 7.3% production, transportation, and material moving

Income: Per capita: $19,657; Median household: $45,381; Average household: $56,743; Households with income of $100,000 or more: 12.7%; Poverty rate: 9.7%

Educational Attainment: High school diploma or higher: 92.6%; Bachelor's degree or higher: 34.6%; Graduate/professional degree or higher: 17.8%

School District(s)

Beaufort 01 (PK-12)
    2012-13 Enrollment: 20,443 . . . . (843) 322-2300

Housing: Homeownership rate: 35.1%; Median home value: $197,100; Median year structure built: 1996; Homeowner vacancy rate: 8.5%; Median gross rent: $970 per month; Rental vacancy rate: 12.1%

Health Insurance: 90.8% have insurance; 74.6% have private insurance; 30.2% have public insurance; 9.2% do not have insurance; 3.5% of children under 18 do not have insurance

Safety: Violent crime rate: 12.2 per 10,000 population; Property crime rate: 256.9 per 10,000 population

Transportation: Commute: 55.7% car, 0.0% public transportation, 17.4% walk, 19.1% work from home; Median travel time to work: 13.2 minutes

Additional Information Contacts

Town of Port Royal . . . . (843) 986-2205
    http://www.portroyal.org

SAINT HELENA ISLAND (unincorporated postal area)

ZCTA: 29920
    Covers a land area of 97.687 square miles and a water area of 46.543 square miles. Located at 32.37° N. Lat; 80.54° W. Long..

Population: 9,481; Growth (since 2000): -0.1%; Density: 97.1 persons per square mile; Race: 41.1% White, 54.8% Black/African American, 0.2% Asian, 0.2% American Indian/Alaska Native, 0.1% Native Hawaiian/Other Pacific Islander, 1.5% Two or more races, 3.9% Hispanic of any race; Average household size: 2.36; Median age: 49.7; Age under 18: 20.5%; Age 65 and over: 24.1%; Males per 100 females: 91.3; Marriage status: 31.6% never married, 51.1% now married, 2.1% separated, 7.1% widowed, 10.2% divorced; Foreign born: 3.5%; Speak English only: 94.5%; With disability: 18.4%; Veterans: 13.5%; Ancestry: 8.4% German, 7.6% English, 7.5% Irish, 5.0% American, 2.0% African

Employment: 15.0% management, business, and financial, 1.0% computer, engineering, and science, 14.1% education, legal, community service, arts, and media, 5.3% healthcare practitioners, 27.5% service, 13.5% sales and office, 6.9% natural resources, construction, and maintenance, 16.7% production, transportation, and material moving

Income: Per capita: $27,774; Median household: $48,668; Average household: $66,510; Households with income of $100,000 or more: 18.6%; Poverty rate: 18.5%

Educational Attainment: High school diploma or higher: 88.2%; Bachelor's degree or higher: 34.0%; Graduate/professional degree or higher: 17.8%

School District(s)

Beaufort 01 (PK-12)
    2012-13 Enrollment: 20,443 . . . . (843) 322-2300

Housing: Homeownership rate: 83.5%; Median home value: $194,300; Median year structure built: 1992; Homeowner vacancy rate: 3.0%; Median gross rent: $776 per month; Rental vacancy rate: 45.8%

Health Insurance: 81.8% have insurance; 55.9% have private insurance; 46.4% have public insurance; 18.2% do not have insurance; 9.3% of children under 18 do not have insurance

Transportation: Commute: 86.7% car, 2.3% public transportation, 2.0% walk, 5.8% work from home; Median travel time to work: 27.5 minutes

SEABROOK (unincorporated postal area)

ZCTA: 29940
    Covers a land area of 57.120 square miles and a water area of 10.990 square miles. Located at 32.55° N. Lat; 80.70° W. Long. Elevation is 16 feet.

Population: 3,967; Growth (since 2000): -8.8%; Density: 69.5 persons per square mile; Race: 33.3% White, 63.8% Black/African American, 0.2% Asian, 0.1% American Indian/Alaska Native, 0.0% Native Hawaiian/Other Pacific Islander, 1.7% Two or more races, 2.6% Hispanic of any race; Average household size: 2.68; Median age: 40.1; Age under 18: 25.4%; Age 65 and over: 12.9%; Males per 100 females: 89.1; Marriage status: 31.8% never married, 47.7% now married, 6.1% separated, 7.9% widowed, 12.6% divorced; Foreign born: 0.9%; Speak English only: 97.8%; With disability: 11.2%; Veterans: 12.4%; Ancestry: 9.2% American, 7.1% Irish, 6.6% German, 5.9% English, 1.7% Scottish

Employment: 10.6% management, business, and financial, 0.0% computer, engineering, and science, 4.4% education, legal, community service, arts, and media, 9.3% healthcare practitioners, 32.9% service, 17.8% sales and office, 11.3% natural resources, construction, and maintenance, 13.8% production, transportation, and material moving

Income: Per capita: $17,492; Median household: $35,049; Average household: $47,057; Households with income of $100,000 or more: 11.7%; Poverty rate: 34.0%

Educational Attainment: High school diploma or higher: 80.3%; Bachelor's degree or higher: 12.7%; Graduate/professional degree or higher: 3.0%

School District(s)

Beaufort 01 (PK-12)
    2012-13 Enrollment: 20,443 . . . . (843) 322-2300

Housing: Homeownership rate: 83.5%; Median home value: $98,900; Median year structure built: 1992; Homeowner vacancy rate: 1.1%; Median gross rent: $1,128 per month; Rental vacancy rate: 12.1%

Health Insurance: 81.0% have insurance; 43.7% have private insurance; 43.8% have public insurance; 19.0% do not have insurance; 6.8% of children under 18 do not have insurance

Transportation: Commute: 92.6% car, 0.0% public transportation, 3.5% walk, 2.6% work from home; Median travel time to work: 28.4 minutes

SHELDON (unincorporated postal area)

ZCTA: 29941
    Covers a land area of 16.146 square miles and a water area of 3.126 square miles. Located at 32.55° N. Lat; 80.81° W. Long. Elevation is 26 feet.

Population: 497; Growth (since 2000): 2,060.9%; Density: 30.8 persons per square mile; Race: 47.5% White, 50.1% Black/African American, 0.0% Asian, 0.0% American Indian/Alaska Native, 0.0% Native Hawaiian/Other Pacific Islander, 0.8% Two or more races, 2.4% Hispanic of any race; Average household size: 2.22; Median age: 57.6; Age under 18: 13.1%; Age 65 and over: 33.2%; Males per 100 females: 94.1

Housing: Homeownership rate: 89.8%; Homeowner vacancy rate: 1.5%; Rental vacancy rate: 8.0%

SHELL POINT (CDP). Covers a land area of 3.932 square miles and a water area of 1.619 square miles. Located at 32.38° N. Lat; 80.75° W. Long. Elevation is 16 feet.

Population: 2,336; Growth (since 2000): -18.2%; Density: 594.2 persons per square mile; Race: 73.5% White, 18.1% Black/African American, 2.1% Asian, 0.4% American Indian/Alaska Native, 0.2% Native Hawaiian/Other Pacific Islander, 2.7% Two or more races, 8.4% Hispanic of any race; Average household size: 2.68; Median age: 36.5; Age under 18: 26.0%; Age 65 and over: 13.4%; Males per 100 females: 94.5

Housing: Homeownership rate: 74.7%; Homeowner vacancy rate: 2.7%; Rental vacancy rate: 10.4%

Berkeley County

Located in southeastern South Carolina; bounded on the north by the Santee River; includes part of Francis Marion National Forest. Covers a land area of 1,098.857 square miles, a water area of 130.380 square miles, and is located in the Eastern Time Zone at 33.21° N. Lat., 79.95° W. Long. The county was founded in 1882. County seat is Moncks Corner.

Berkeley County is part of the Charleston-North Charleston, SC Metropolitan Statistical Area. The entire metro area includes: Berkeley County, SC; Charleston County, SC; Dorchester County, SC

Population: 177,843; Growth (since 2000): 24.7%; Density: 161.8 persons per square mile; Race: 66.5% White, 25.0% Black/African American, 2.3% Asian, 0.6% American Indian/Alaska Native, 0.1% Native Hawaiian/Other Pacific Islander, 2.7% two or more races, 6.0% Hispanic of any race; Average household size: 2.66; Median age: 34.5; Age under 18: 25.3%; Age 65 and over: 10.0%; Males per 100 females: 99.6; Marriage status: 30.7% never married, 53.9% now married, 3.2% separated, 5.2% widowed, 10.3% divorced; Foreign born: 5.8%; Speak English only: 92.2%; With disability: 12.2%; Veterans: 15.5%; Ancestry: 12.0% German, 11.5% American, 10.2% Irish, 7.5% English, 3.2% Italian
Religion: Six largest groups: 10.0% Baptist, 6.3% Methodist/Pietist, 4.2% Pentecostal, 4.1% Catholicism, 2.7% Non-denominational Protestant, 0.8% Presbyterian-Reformed
Economy: Unemployment rate: 6.0%; Leading industries: 14.6% retail trade; 11.3% construction; 11.0% other services (except public administration); Farms: 373 totaling 75,063 acres; Company size: 1 employs 1,000 or more persons, 2 employ 500 to 999 persons, 61 employs 100 to 499 persons, 2,606 employ less than 100 persons; Business ownership: 3,412 women-owned, 1,615 Black-owned, n/a Hispanic-owned, 292 Asian-owned
Employment: 12.6% management, business, and financial, 5.0% computer, engineering, and science, 8.6% education, legal, community service, arts, and media, 4.8% healthcare practitioners, 17.1% service, 25.5% sales and office, 11.9% natural resources, construction, and maintenance, 14.5% production, transportation, and material moving
Income: Per capita: $24,165; Median household: $52,427; Average household: $64,596; Households with income of $100,000 or more: 17.6%; Poverty rate: 14.4%
Educational Attainment: High school diploma or higher: 86.7%; Bachelor's degree or higher: 21.3%; Graduate/professional degree or higher: 7.1%
Housing: Homeownership rate: 72.5%; Median home value: $150,400; Median year structure built: 1990; Homeowner vacancy rate: 2.7%; Median gross rent: $960 per month; Rental vacancy rate: 11.4%
Vital Statistics: Birth rate: 135.4 per 10,000 population; Death rate: 63.4 per 10,000 population; Age-adjusted cancer mortality rate: 183.2 deaths per 100,000 population
Health Insurance: 82.1% have insurance; 65.6% have private insurance; 27.3% have public insurance; 17.9% do not have insurance; 11.9% of children under 18 do not have insurance
Health Care: Physicians: 8.7 per 10,000 population; Hospital beds: 0.0 per 10,000 population; Hospital admissions: 0.0 per 10,000 population
Air Quality Index: 99.2% good, 0.8% moderate, 0.0% unhealthy for sensitive individuals, 0.0% unhealthy (percent of days)
Transportation: Commute: 91.8% car, 0.8% public transportation, 3.2% walk, 2.9% work from home; Median travel time to work: 25.5 minutes
Presidential Election: 41.9% Obama, 56.4% Romney (2012)
National and State Parks: Francis Marion National Forest; Old Santee Canal State Park
Additional Information Contacts
Berkeley Government . . . . (843) 761-6900
    http://www.berkeleycountysc.gov

Berkeley County Communities

BONNEAU (town). Covers a land area of 3.013 square miles and a water area of 0.053 square miles. Located at 33.31° N. Lat; 79.95° W. Long. Elevation is 59 feet.
History: Bonneau was named for the Huguenot ancestors of Mrs. John C. Calhoun.
Population: 487; Growth (since 2000): 37.6%; Density: 161.6 persons per square mile; Race: 83.6% White, 12.3% Black/African American, 1.4% Asian, 0.2% American Indian/Alaska Native, 0.0% Native Hawaiian/Other

Pacific Islander, 1.4% Two or more races, 1.6% Hispanic of any race; Average household size: 2.56; Median age: 36.9; Age under 18: 26.9%; Age 65 and over: 12.9%; Males per 100 females: 85.2
Housing: Homeownership rate: 72.6%; Homeowner vacancy rate: 0.7%; Rental vacancy rate: 8.8%

BONNEAU BEACH (CDP). Covers a land area of 2.346 square miles and a water area of 0.041 square miles. Located at 33.32° N. Lat; 79.99° W. Long. Elevation is 75 feet.
Population: 1,929; Growth (since 2000): n/a; Density: 822.4 persons per square mile; Race: 88.4% White, 8.6% Black/African American, 0.0% Asian, 1.2% American Indian/Alaska Native, 0.0% Native Hawaiian/Other Pacific Islander, 1.2% Two or more races, 1.1% Hispanic of any race; Average household size: 2.47; Median age: 47.0; Age under 18: 19.7%; Age 65 and over: 18.5%; Males per 100 females: 104.1
Housing: Homeownership rate: 84.6%; Homeowner vacancy rate: 5.4%; Rental vacancy rate: 11.2%

CORDESVILLE (unincorporated postal area)
ZCTA: 29434
    Covers a land area of 55.504 square miles and a water area of 0.830 square miles. Located at 33.14° N. Lat; 79.84° W. Long. Elevation is 49 feet.
    Population: 537; Growth (since 2000): -6.3%; Density: 9.7 persons per square mile; Race: 78.6% White, 18.2% Black/African American, 0.0% Asian, 0.0% American Indian/Alaska Native, 0.9% Native Hawaiian/Other Pacific Islander, 1.1% Two or more races, 1.3% Hispanic of any race; Average household size: 2.53; Median age: 45.4; Age under 18: 22.9%; Age 65 and over: 12.8%; Males per 100 females: 96.0
    Housing: Homeownership rate: 80.2%; Homeowner vacancy rate: 1.7%; Rental vacancy rate: 12.5%

CROSS (unincorporated postal area)
ZCTA: 29436
    Covers a land area of 80.646 square miles and a water area of 32.733 square miles. Located at 33.32° N. Lat; 80.19° W. Long. Elevation is 79 feet.
    Population: 4,471; Growth (since 2000): 0.4%; Density: 55.4 persons per square mile; Race: 40.9% White, 55.7% Black/African American, 0.2% Asian, 1.2% American Indian/Alaska Native, 0.0% Native Hawaiian/Other Pacific Islander, 1.5% Two or more races, 1.2% Hispanic of any race; Average household size: 2.52; Median age: 43.4; Age under 18: 22.7%; Age 65 and over: 16.1%; Males per 100 females: 95.3; Marriage status: 31.5% never married, 48.3% now married, 3.8% separated, 9.7% widowed, 10.5% divorced; Foreign born: 0.7%; Speak English only: 98.7%; With disability: 20.2%; Veterans: 12.2%; Ancestry: 10.9% American, 7.8% German, 6.1% Irish, 3.8% English, 1.7% Scottish
    Employment: 2.8% management, business, and financial, 6.8% computer, engineering, and science, 14.7% education, legal, community service, arts, and media, 5.3% healthcare practitioners, 14.1% service, 21.2% sales and office, 21.3% natural resources, construction, and maintenance, 13.7% production, transportation, and material moving
    Income: Per capita: $19,070; Median household: $42,500; Average household: $47,966; Households with income of $100,000 or more: 7.8%; Poverty rate: 15.9%
    Educational Attainment: High school diploma or higher: 82.4%; Bachelor's degree or higher: 12.5%; Graduate/professional degree or higher: 5.9%
School District(s)
Berkeley 01 (PK-12)
    2012-13 Enrollment: 30,942 . . . . (843) 899-8601
    Housing: Homeownership rate: 79.7%; Median home value: $95,500; Median year structure built: 1991; Homeowner vacancy rate: 1.8%; Median gross rent: $854 per month; Rental vacancy rate: 12.4%
    Health Insurance: 78.5% have insurance; 54.1% have private insurance; 40.2% have public insurance; 21.5% do not have insurance; 19.7% of children under 18 do not have insurance
    Transportation: Commute: 96.7% car, 2.1% public transportation, 0.5% walk, 0.7% work from home; Median travel time to work: 37.2 minutes

GOOSE CREEK (city). Covers a land area of 40.086 square miles and a water area of 0.768 square miles. Located at 32.99° N. Lat; 80.01° W. Long. Elevation is 30 feet.

History: Goose Creek was settled prior to 1680 by wealthy Barbadian planters known as the Goose Creek Men. The property of Goose Creek had been granted in 1674 to Lady Margaret after the death of her husband, Sir John Yeamans, Landgrave.

Population: 35,938; Growth (since 2000): 23.0%; Density: 896.5 persons per square mile; Race: 71.2% White, 18.3% Black/African American, 3.7% Asian, 0.5% American Indian/Alaska Native, 0.1% Native Hawaiian/Other Pacific Islander, 3.6% Two or more races, 6.1% Hispanic of any race; Average household size: 2.72; Median age: 30.2; Age under 18: 24.9%; Age 65 and over: 7.3%; Males per 100 females: 106.8; Marriage status: 31.4% never married, 56.9% now married, 2.6% separated, 3.5% widowed, 8.2% divorced; Foreign born: 5.4%; Speak English only: 91.8%; With disability: 9.2%; Veterans: 17.8%; Ancestry: 14.8% German, 13.6% Irish, 12.6% American, 8.4% English, 4.5% Italian

Employment: 15.6% management, business, and financial, 5.4% computer, engineering, and science, 11.2% education, legal, community service, arts, and media, 3.7% healthcare practitioners, 14.9% service, 30.2% sales and office, 8.2% natural resources, construction, and maintenance, 11.0% production, transportation, and material moving

Income: Per capita: $25,244; Median household: $62,466; Average household: $70,000; Households with income of $100,000 or more: 20.2%; Poverty rate: 9.7%

Educational Attainment: High school diploma or higher: 92.7%; Bachelor's degree or higher: 26.8%; Graduate/professional degree or higher: 7.2%

School District(s)
Berkeley 01 (PK-12)
    2012-13 Enrollment: 30,942 . . . . (843) 899-8601
Vocational/Technical School(s)
Lacy Cosmetology School-Goose Creek (Private, For-profit)
    Fall 2013 Enrollment: 38 . . . . (843) 572-8705
    2013-14 Tuition: $17,065

Housing: Homeownership rate: 71.1%; Median home value: $168,800; Median year structure built: 1995; Homeowner vacancy rate: 2.1%; Median gross rent: $1,084 per month; Rental vacancy rate: 13.8%

Health Insurance: 87.7% have insurance; 76.0% have private insurance; 22.9% have public insurance; 12.3% do not have insurance; 5.6% of children under 18 do not have insurance

Safety: Violent crime rate: 21.6 per 10,000 population; Property crime rate: 244.0 per 10,000 population

Transportation: Commute: 85.0% car, 1.2% public transportation, 11.1% walk, 1.7% work from home; Median travel time to work: 23.3 minutes

Additional Information Contacts
City of Goose Creek . . . . (843) 797-6220
    http://www.cityofgoosecreek.com

HANAHAN (city). Covers a land area of 10.688 square miles and a water area of 0.822 square miles. Located at 32.93° N. Lat; 80.01° W. Long. Elevation is 36 feet.

Population: 17,997; Growth (since 2000): 39.1%; Density: 1,683.9 persons per square mile; Race: 74.7% White, 13.9% Black/African American, 3.4% Asian, 0.6% American Indian/Alaska Native, 0.1% Native Hawaiian/Other Pacific Islander, 2.9% Two or more races, 9.1% Hispanic of any race; Average household size: 2.52; Median age: 34.2; Age under 18: 24.3%; Age 65 and over: 10.8%; Males per 100 females: 101.1; Marriage status: 30.8% never married, 52.2% now married, 3.8% separated, 5.3% widowed, 11.7% divorced; Foreign born: 12.1%; Speak English only: 84.3%; With disability: 9.3%; Veterans: 15.3%; Ancestry: 12.8% German, 11.1% Irish, 10.8% American, 9.0% English, 4.9% French

Employment: 13.7% management, business, and financial, 5.0% computer, engineering, and science, 7.4% education, legal, community service, arts, and media, 4.9% healthcare practitioners, 18.7% service, 26.8% sales and office, 10.6% natural resources, construction, and maintenance, 12.9% production, transportation, and material moving

Income: Per capita: $25,507; Median household: $48,403; Average household: $62,006; Households with income of $100,000 or more: 18.8%; Poverty rate: 15.6%

Educational Attainment: High school diploma or higher: 86.6%; Bachelor's degree or higher: 25.1%; Graduate/professional degree or higher: 7.9%

School District(s)
Berkeley 01 (PK-12)
    2012-13 Enrollment: 30,942 . . . . (843) 899-8601

Housing: Homeownership rate: 64.7%; Median home value: $180,800; Median year structure built: 1980; Homeowner vacancy rate: 2.3%; Median gross rent: $860 per month; Rental vacancy rate: 13.7%

Health Insurance: 76.1% have insurance; 62.4% have private insurance; 23.3% have public insurance; 23.9% do not have insurance; 19.3% of children under 18 do not have insurance

Safety: Violent crime rate: 16.4 per 10,000 population; Property crime rate: 226.2 per 10,000 population

Transportation: Commute: 93.3% car, 0.7% public transportation, 1.0% walk, 3.3% work from home; Median travel time to work: 20.4 minutes

Additional Information Contacts
City of Hanahan . . . . (843) 554-4221
    http://www.cityofhanahan.com

HUGER (unincorporated postal area)
ZCTA: 29450

Covers a land area of 144.433 square miles and a water area of 2.060 square miles. Located at 33.07° N. Lat; 79.78° W. Long. Elevation is 30 feet.

Population: 3,105; Growth (since 2000): 8.0%; Density: 21.5 persons per square mile; Race: 31.4% White, 65.8% Black/African American, 0.2% Asian, 0.3% American Indian/Alaska Native, 0.0% Native Hawaiian/Other Pacific Islander, 1.0% Two or more races, 2.1% Hispanic of any race; Average household size: 2.71; Median age: 38.7; Age under 18: 25.4%; Age 65 and over: 10.7%; Males per 100 females: 92.5; Marriage status: 36.4% never married, 50.4% now married, 7.0% separated, 6.5% widowed, 6.8% divorced; Foreign born: 0.0%; Speak English only: 100.0%; With disability: 16.0%; Veterans: 12.8%; Ancestry: 12.6% American, 5.8% German, 4.2% French, 2.2% Irish, 2.2% African

Employment: 10.7% management, business, and financial, 1.8% computer, engineering, and science, 5.6% education, legal, community service, arts, and media, 7.3% healthcare practitioners, 26.0% service, 20.7% sales and office, 12.9% natural resources, construction, and maintenance, 15.0% production, transportation, and material moving

Income: Per capita: $18,745; Median household: $34,762; Average household: $48,050; Households with income of $100,000 or more: 10.9%; Poverty rate: 16.2%

Educational Attainment: High school diploma or higher: 79.3%; Bachelor's degree or higher: 11.9%; Graduate/professional degree or higher: 6.6%

School District(s)
Berkeley 01 (PK-12)
    2012-13 Enrollment: 30,942 . . . . (843) 899-8601

Housing: Homeownership rate: 82.6%; Median home value: $186,100; Median year structure built: 1985; Homeowner vacancy rate: 0.8%; Median gross rent: $952 per month; Rental vacancy rate: 5.7%

Health Insurance: 81.2% have insurance; 46.9% have private insurance; 50.7% have public insurance; 18.8% do not have insurance; 8.3% of children under 18 do not have insurance

Transportation: Commute: 93.5% car, 1.4% public transportation, 0.0% walk, 3.9% work from home; Median travel time to work: 31.5 minutes

JAMESTOWN (town). Covers a land area of 0.606 square miles and a water area of 0 square miles. Located at 33.29° N. Lat; 79.69° W. Long. Elevation is 30 feet.

Population: 72; Growth (since 2000): -25.8%; Density: 118.9 persons per square mile; Race: 43.1% White, 55.6% Black/African American, 0.0% Asian, 0.0% American Indian/Alaska Native, 0.0% Native Hawaiian/Other Pacific Islander, 1.4% Two or more races, 0.0% Hispanic of any race; Average household size: 2.40; Median age: 32.0; Age under 18: 22.2%; Age 65 and over: 11.1%; Males per 100 females: 94.6

Housing: Homeownership rate: 80.0%; Homeowner vacancy rate: 0.0%; Rental vacancy rate: 0.0%

LADSON (CDP). Covers a land area of 7.023 square miles and a water area of 0 square miles. Located at 33.01° N. Lat; 80.11° W. Long. Elevation is 46 feet.

Population: 13,790; Growth (since 2000): 4.0%; Density: 1,963.5 persons per square mile; Race: 61.5% White, 26.3% Black/African American, 2.2% Asian, 0.8% American Indian/Alaska Native, 0.1% Native Hawaiian/Other Pacific Islander, 3.6% Two or more races, 11.3% Hispanic of any race;

Average household size: 2.95; Median age: 32.2; Age under 18: 29.5%; Age 65 and over: 7.3%; Males per 100 females: 96.5; Marriage status: 32.6% never married, 52.0% now married, 4.6% separated, 5.3% widowed, 10.1% divorced; Foreign born: 6.0%; Speak English only: 92.0%; With disability: 12.5%; Veterans: 17.3%; Ancestry: 11.7% American, 11.5% German, 7.6% English, 7.4% Irish, 4.3% Polish

Employment: 7.9% management, business, and financial, 5.2% computer, engineering, and science, 5.1% education, legal, community service, arts, and media, 3.9% healthcare practitioners, 20.5% service, 26.4% sales and office, 10.4% natural resources, construction, and maintenance, 20.6% production, transportation, and material moving

Income: Per capita: $20,161; Median household: $48,669; Average household: $58,298; Households with income of $100,000 or more: 14.3%; Poverty rate: 12.5%

Educational Attainment: High school diploma or higher: 84.3%; Bachelor's degree or higher: 14.2%; Graduate/professional degree or higher: 4.5%

School District(s)
Berkeley 01 (PK-12)
   2012-13 Enrollment: 30,942 . . . . (843) 899-8601
Charleston 01 (PK-12)
   2012-13 Enrollment: 44,599 . . . . (843) 937-6318
Dorchester 02 (PK-12)
   2012-13 Enrollment: 23,741 . . . . (843) 873-2901
Housing: Homeownership rate: 73.3%; Median home value: $123,700; Median year structure built: 1984; Homeowner vacancy rate: 2.7%; Median gross rent: $1,034 per month; Rental vacancy rate: 8.4%
Health Insurance: 79.6% have insurance; 64.1% have private insurance; 25.2% have public insurance; 20.4% do not have insurance; 11.6% of children under 18 do not have insurance
Transportation: Commute: 94.3% car, 0.0% public transportation, 1.1% walk, 3.6% work from home; Median travel time to work: 26.2 minutes

MONCKS CORNER (town). County seat. Covers a land area of
7.285 square miles and a water area of 0.134 square miles. Located at 33.20° N. Lat; 79.98° W. Long. Elevation is 52 feet.
History: Monck's store, in the corner formed by the roads from Charleston to Murray's Ferry and to the Congarees, provided the name of Moncks Corner for the community.
Population: 7,885; Growth (since 2000): 32.5%; Density: 1,082.3 persons per square mile; Race: 57.7% White, 36.0% Black/African American, 0.5% Asian, 0.5% American Indian/Alaska Native, 0.0% Native Hawaiian/Other Pacific Islander, 2.0% Two or more races, 5.1% Hispanic of any race; Average household size: 2.60; Median age: 33.1; Age under 18: 27.4%; Age 65 and over: 10.6%; Males per 100 females: 94.5; Marriage status: 32.6% never married, 48.5% now married, 2.8% separated, 5.8% widowed, 13.1% divorced; Foreign born: 4.5%; Speak English only: 94.3%; With disability: 15.1%; Veterans: 13.2%; Ancestry: 10.9% American, 10.0% Irish, 9.3% German, 8.5% English, 2.7% Italian
Employment: 11.6% management, business, and financial, 4.0% computer, engineering, and science, 7.0% education, legal, community service, arts, and media, 2.6% healthcare practitioners, 21.8% service, 24.4% sales and office, 17.3% natural resources, construction, and maintenance, 11.4% production, transportation, and material moving
Income: Per capita: $21,199; Median household: $45,852; Average household: $54,093; Households with income of $100,000 or more: 10.7%; Poverty rate: 16.8%
Educational Attainment: High school diploma or higher: 85.0%; Bachelor's degree or higher: 12.9%; Graduate/professional degree or higher: 3.7%

School District(s)
Berkeley 01 (PK-12)
   2012-13 Enrollment: 30,942 . . . . (843) 899-8601
Housing: Homeownership rate: 63.7%; Median home value: $153,200; Median year structure built: 1985; Homeowner vacancy rate: 8.8%; Median gross rent: $743 per month; Rental vacancy rate: 13.0%
Health Insurance: 74.3% have insurance; 56.2% have private insurance; 29.0% have public insurance; 25.7% do not have insurance; 16.5% of children under 18 do not have insurance
Safety: Violent crime rate: 42.6 per 10,000 population; Property crime rate: 608.1 per 10,000 population
Newspapers: Berkeley Independent (weekly circulation 9500)
Transportation: Commute: 94.1% car, 0.9% public transportation, 1.1% walk, 2.5% work from home; Median travel time to work: 23.1 minutes
Airports: Berkeley County (general aviation)

Additional Information Contacts
Town of Moncks Corner . . . . (843) 719-7900
   http://townofmonckscorner.sc.gov

PINEVILLE (unincorporated postal area)
ZCTA: 29468
   Covers a land area of 74.738 square miles and a water area of 36.610 square miles. Located at 33.42° N. Lat; 80.06° W. Long. Elevation is 79 feet.
   Population: 2,107; Growth (since 2000): -9.1%; Density: 28.2 persons per square mile; Race: 15.5% White, 83.5% Black/African American, 0.1% Asian, 0.2% American Indian/Alaska Native, 0.0% Native Hawaiian/Other Pacific Islander, 0.4% Two or more races, 0.9% Hispanic of any race; Average household size: 2.48; Median age: 43.9; Age under 18: 22.7%; Age 65 and over: 18.3%; Males per 100 females: 89.8

School District(s)
Berkeley 01 (PK-12)
   2012-13 Enrollment: 30,942 . . . . (843) 899-8601
   Housing: Homeownership rate: 82.4%; Homeowner vacancy rate: 1.5%; Rental vacancy rate: 11.7%

PINOPOLIS (CDP). Covers a land area of 1.432 square miles and a
water area of 0 square miles. Located at 33.23° N. Lat; 80.04° W. Long. Elevation is 89 feet.
Population: 948; Growth (since 2000): n/a; Density: 662.0 persons per square mile; Race: 93.0% White, 5.6% Black/African American, 0.4% Asian, 0.5% American Indian/Alaska Native, 0.1% Native Hawaiian/Other Pacific Islander, 0.3% Two or more races, 0.7% Hispanic of any race; Average household size: 2.38; Median age: 51.9; Age under 18: 16.8%; Age 65 and over: 21.3%; Males per 100 females: 102.6
Housing: Homeownership rate: 89.2%; Homeowner vacancy rate: 2.2%; Rental vacancy rate: 12.2%

RUSSELLVILLE (CDP). Covers a land area of 3.753 square miles
and a water area of 0 square miles. Located at 33.40° N. Lat; 79.96° W. Long. Elevation is 79 feet.
Population: 488; Growth (since 2000): n/a; Density: 130.0 persons per square mile; Race: 25.6% White, 72.5% Black/African American, 0.2% Asian, 0.0% American Indian/Alaska Native, 0.0% Native Hawaiian/Other Pacific Islander, 0.8% Two or more races, 0.8% Hispanic of any race; Average household size: 2.82; Median age: 39.1; Age under 18: 26.4%; Age 65 and over: 14.3%; Males per 100 females: 92.9
Housing: Homeownership rate: 76.9%; Homeowner vacancy rate: 1.5%; Rental vacancy rate: 11.1%

SAINT STEPHEN (town). Covers a land area of 2.388 square miles
and a water area of 0 square miles. Located at 33.40° N. Lat; 79.93° W. Long. Elevation is 79 feet.
Population: 1,697; Growth (since 2000): -4.4%; Density: 710.7 persons per square mile; Race: 41.4% White, 55.4% Black/African American, 0.1% Asian, 0.3% American Indian/Alaska Native, 0.0% Native Hawaiian/Other Pacific Islander, 1.6% Two or more races, 2.2% Hispanic of any race; Average household size: 2.46; Median age: 36.8; Age under 18: 28.3%; Age 65 and over: 17.9%; Males per 100 females: 82.5

School District(s)
Berkeley 01 (PK-12)
   2012-13 Enrollment: 30,942 . . . . (843) 899-8601
Housing: Homeownership rate: 56.5%; Homeowner vacancy rate: 2.6%; Rental vacancy rate: 4.4%

SANGAREE (CDP). Covers a land area of 2.031 square miles and a
water area of 0 square miles. Located at 33.03° N. Lat; 80.13° W. Long. Elevation is 72 feet.
Population: 8,220; Growth (since 2000): n/a; Density: 4,047.6 persons per square mile; Race: 70.4% White, 23.6% Black/African American, 1.1% Asian, 0.8% American Indian/Alaska Native, 0.2% Native Hawaiian/Other Pacific Islander, 2.8% Two or more races, 4.8% Hispanic of any race; Average household size: 2.84; Median age: 33.6; Age under 18: 28.0%; Age 65 and over: 6.9%; Males per 100 females: 93.4; Marriage status: 28.8% never married, 53.5% now married, 3.1% separated, 5.1% widowed, 12.6% divorced; Foreign born: 2.8%; Speak English only: 95.9%; With disability: 13.7%; Veterans: 23.1%; Ancestry: 16.6% Irish, 13.4% German, 13.3% American, 4.1% English, 3.5% Italian

Employment: 8.7% management, business, and financial, 5.4% computer, engineering, and science, 9.1% education, legal, community service, arts, and media, 2.1% healthcare practitioners, 16.3% service, 28.6% sales and office, 10.9% natural resources, construction, and maintenance, 18.8% production, transportation, and material moving
Income: Per capita: $21,450; Median household: $54,761; Average household: $62,411; Households with income of $100,000 or more: 17.7%; Poverty rate: 13.2%
Educational Attainment: High school diploma or higher: 85.8%; Bachelor's degree or higher: 17.0%; Graduate/professional degree or higher: 5.4%
Housing: Homeownership rate: 74.7%; Median home value: $132,400; Median year structure built: 1984; Homeowner vacancy rate: 2.1%; Median gross rent: $1,031 per month; Rental vacancy rate: 4.8%
Health Insurance: 80.9% have insurance; 63.4% have private insurance; 26.9% have public insurance; 19.1% do not have insurance; 13.3% of children under 18 do not have insurance
Transportation: Commute: 93.8% car, 0.6% public transportation, 0.2% walk, 4.5% work from home; Median travel time to work: 28.5 minutes

Calhoun County

Located in central South Carolina; bounded on the north by the Congaree River, and on the northeast by Lake Marion. Covers a land area of 381.151 square miles, a water area of 11.332 square miles, and is located in the Eastern Time Zone at 33.67° N. Lat., 80.78° W. Long. The county was founded in 1908. County seat is Saint Matthews.

Calhoun County is part of the Columbia, SC Metropolitan Statistical Area. The entire metro area includes: Calhoun County, SC; Fairfield County, SC; Kershaw County, SC; Lexington County, SC; Richland County, SC; Saluda County, SC

Population: 15,175; Growth (since 2000): -0.1%; Density: 39.8 persons per square mile; Race: 53.9% White, 42.6% Black/African American, 0.2% Asian, 0.3% American Indian/Alaska Native, 0.1% Native Hawaiian/Other Pacific Islander, 1.2% two or more races, 3.0% Hispanic of any race; Average household size: 2.47; Median age: 43.4; Age under 18: 21.7%; Age 65 and over: 16.3%; Males per 100 females: 95.1; Marriage status: 27.7% never married, 55.6% now married, 4.3% separated, 7.3% widowed, 9.4% divorced; Foreign born: 2.0%; Speak English only: 97.1%; With disability: 17.7%; Veterans: 10.8%; Ancestry: 12.2% American, 11.0% German, 7.7% Irish, 7.0% English, 2.3% Scotch-Irish
Religion: Six largest groups: 23.7% Methodist/Pietist, 4.1% Baptist, 3.7% Lutheran, 2.8% Non-denominational Protestant, 1.0% Pentecostal, 0.7% Episcopalianism/Anglicanism
Economy: Unemployment rate: 8.6%; Leading industries: 15.7% retail trade; 14.9% other services (except public administration); 14.0% construction; Farms: 412 totaling 118,382 acres; Company size: 0 employ 1,000 or more persons, 0 employ 500 to 999 persons, 7 employ 100 to 499 persons, 235 employ less than 100 persons; Business ownership: n/a women-owned, n/a Black-owned, n/a Hispanic-owned, n/a Asian-owned
Employment: 11.0% management, business, and financial, 3.1% computer, engineering, and science, 8.5% education, legal, community service, arts, and media, 5.1% healthcare practitioners, 15.1% service, 21.2% sales and office, 12.0% natural resources, construction, and maintenance, 24.1% production, transportation, and material moving
Income: Per capita: $23,023; Median household: $40,704; Average household: $55,479; Households with income of $100,000 or more: 13.3%; Poverty rate: 18.2%
Educational Attainment: High school diploma or higher: 82.8%; Bachelor's degree or higher: 16.9%; Graduate/professional degree or higher: 5.7%
Housing: Homeownership rate: 78.7%; Median home value: $100,600; Median year structure built: 1984; Homeowner vacancy rate: 1.4%; Median gross rent: $674 per month; Rental vacancy rate: 8.7%
Vital Statistics: Birth rate: 98.3 per 10,000 population; Death rate: 115.6 per 10,000 population; Age-adjusted cancer mortality rate: 150.7 deaths per 100,000 population
Health Insurance: 83.6% have insurance; 59.4% have private insurance; 37.5% have public insurance; 16.4% do not have insurance; 6.8% of children under 18 do not have insurance
Health Care: Physicians: 1.3 per 10,000 population; Hospital beds: 0.0 per 10,000 population; Hospital admissions: 0.0 per 10,000 population

Transportation: Commute: 90.1% car, 0.3% public transportation, 1.4% walk, 3.3% work from home; Median travel time to work: 27.1 minutes
Presidential Election: 51.6% Obama, 47.3% Romney (2012)
Additional Information Contacts
Calhoun Government . . . . (803) 874-2435
  http://www.calhouncounty.sc.gov

Calhoun County Communities

CAMERON (town). Covers a land area of 3.125 square miles and a water area of 0 square miles. Located at 33.56° N. Lat; 80.72° W. Long. Elevation is 177 feet.
Population: 424; Growth (since 2000): -5.6%; Density: 135.7 persons per square mile; Race: 63.2% White, 33.7% Black/African American, 0.2% Asian, 0.0% American Indian/Alaska Native, 0.0% Native Hawaiian/Other Pacific Islander, 1.7% Two or more races, 1.2% Hispanic of any race; Average household size: 2.51; Median age: 45.0; Age under 18: 21.2%; Age 65 and over: 17.0%; Males per 100 females: 92.7
Housing: Homeownership rate: 84.4%; Homeowner vacancy rate: 2.0%; Rental vacancy rate: 18.8%

SAINT MATTHEWS (town). County seat. Covers a land area of 1.921 square miles and a water area of 0.007 square miles. Located at 33.66° N. Lat; 80.78° W. Long. Elevation is 276 feet.
History: St. Matthews, taking its name from an early parish, was first the site of a trading post on the Cherokee Path. Palatine Germans arrived between 1730 and 1740, clearing small patches for cattle enclosures and food crops. By the onset of the Revolution, many large plantations had been established and cotton was a favorite crop.
Population: 2,021; Growth (since 2000): -4.1%; Density: 1,052.3 persons per square mile; Race: 35.7% White, 60.9% Black/African American, 0.4% Asian, 0.2% American Indian/Alaska Native, 0.0% Native Hawaiian/Other Pacific Islander, 0.9% Two or more races, 2.6% Hispanic of any race; Average household size: 2.32; Median age: 46.1; Age under 18: 22.2%; Age 65 and over: 22.1%; Males per 100 females: 81.7
School District(s)
Calhoun 01 (PK-12)
    2012-13 Enrollment: 1,720 . . . . (803) 655-7310
Housing: Homeownership rate: 63.2%; Homeowner vacancy rate: 2.8%; Rental vacancy rate: 7.6%
Safety: Violent crime rate: 66.0 per 10,000 population; Property crime rate: 390.7 per 10,000 population
Newspapers: Calhoun Times (weekly circulation 2000)

Charleston County

Located in southeastern South Carolina, on the Atlantic coast; bounded on the southwest by the mouth of the South Edisto River, and on the northeast by the mouth of the South Santee River. Covers a land area of 916.089 square miles, a water area of 441.907 square miles, and is located in the Eastern Time Zone at 32.80° N. Lat., 79.94° W. Long. The county was founded in 1769. County seat is Charleston.

Charleston County is part of the Charleston-North Charleston, SC Metropolitan Statistical Area. The entire metro area includes: Berkeley County, SC; Charleston County, SC; Dorchester County, SC

Weather Station: Charleston City   Elevation: 9 feet

	Jan	Feb	Mar	Apr	May	Jun	Jul	Aug	Sep	Oct	Nov	Dec
High	57	60	66	72	79	85	88	87	83	75	68	60
Low	43	46	52	59	67	74	77	76	72	62	53	46
Precip	2.9	2.4	3.4	2.6	2.3	4.6	5.4	6.3	5.7	3.7	2.1	2.6
Snow	na	na	na	na	na	na	na	na	na	na	na	na

High and Low temperatures in degrees Fahrenheit; Precipitation and Snow in inches

Weather Station: Charleston Intl Arpt   Elevation: 40 feet

	Jan	Feb	Mar	Apr	May	Jun	Jul	Aug	Sep	Oct	Nov	Dec
High	59	63	69	76	83	88	91	90	85	77	70	62
Low	38	41	47	54	62	70	74	73	68	57	48	41
Precip	3.6	2.9	3.8	3.0	3.1	5.5	6.4	6.8	5.6	3.8	2.5	3.1
Snow	0.1	tr	0.1	tr	tr	tr	tr	0.0	0.0	0.0	tr	0.5

High and Low temperatures in degrees Fahrenheit; Precipitation and Snow in inches

Weather Station: Sullivans Island										Elevation: 2 feet	
	Jan	Feb	Mar	Apr	May	Jun	Jul	Aug	Sep	Oct	Nov	Dec
High	59	61	67	74	81	87	90	89	84	77	70	62
Low	39	41	48	55	64	71	74	73	69	59	51	43
Precip	3.9	3.1	4.0	3.2	2.4	4.4	5.3	6.3	4.4	4.4	2.9	3.3
Snow	tr	tr	tr	0.0	0.0	0.0	0.0	0.0	0.0	0.0	0.0	0.1

High and Low temperatures in degrees Fahrenheit; Precipitation and Snow in inches

Population: 350,209; Growth (since 2000): 13.0%; Density: 382.3 persons per square mile; Race: 64.2% White, 29.8% Black/African American, 1.3% Asian, 0.3% American Indian/Alaska Native, 0.1% Native Hawaiian/Other Pacific Islander, 1.6% two or more races, 5.4% Hispanic of any race; Average household size: 2.36; Median age: 35.9; Age under 18: 20.7%; Age 65 and over: 12.8%; Males per 100 females: 94.2; Marriage status: 37.5% never married, 45.5% now married, 3.1% separated, 5.9% widowed, 11.1% divorced; Foreign born: 5.4%; Speak English only: 92.8%; With disability: 10.8%; Veterans: 11.1%; Ancestry: 11.5% German, 11.2% American, 10.7% Irish, 10.5% English, 3.6% Italian
Religion: Six largest groups: 12.9% Baptist, 11.4% Methodist/Pietist, 10.7% Non-denominational Protestant, 7.4% Catholicism, 4.3% Episcopalianism/Anglicanism, 3.7% Presbyterian-Reformed
Economy: Unemployment rate: 5.3%; Leading industries: 16.3% retail trade; 13.1% professional, scientific, and technical services; 10.5% health care and social assistance; Farms: 359 totaling 35,436 acres; Company size: 11 employs 1,000 or more persons, 10 employ 500 to 999 persons, 216 employ 100 to 499 persons, 11,674 employ less than 100 persons; Business ownership: 10,506 women-owned, 3,793 Black-owned, 536 Hispanic-owned, 509 Asian-owned
Employment: 14.8% management, business, and financial, 5.6% computer, engineering, and science, 10.7% education, legal, community service, arts, and media, 7.3% healthcare practitioners, 19.5% service, 24.7% sales and office, 8.0% natural resources, construction, and maintenance, 9.4% production, transportation, and material moving
Income: Per capita: $30,158; Median household: $50,792; Average household: $72,569; Households with income of $100,000 or more: 22.0%; Poverty rate: 18.2%
Educational Attainment: High school diploma or higher: 88.3%; Bachelor's degree or higher: 39.4%; Graduate/professional degree or higher: 14.1%
Housing: Homeownership rate: 60.3%; Median home value: $236,100; Median year structure built: 1983; Homeowner vacancy rate: 3.2%; Median gross rent: $950 per month; Rental vacancy rate: 15.2%
Vital Statistics: Birth rate: 129.6 per 10,000 population; Death rate: 81.5 per 10,000 population; Age-adjusted cancer mortality rate: 183.3 deaths per 100,000 population
Health Insurance: 83.7% have insurance; 67.5% have private insurance; 27.9% have public insurance; 16.3% do not have insurance; 8.1% of children under 18 do not have insurance
Health Care: Physicians: 70.9 per 10,000 population; Hospital beds: 59.8 per 10,000 population; Hospital admissions: 2,554.3 per 10,000 population
Air Quality Index: 83.3% good, 16.7% moderate, 0.0% unhealthy for sensitive individuals, 0.0% unhealthy (percent of days)
Transportation: Commute: 88.0% car, 2.1% public transportation, 3.0% walk, 4.5% work from home; Median travel time to work: 22.4 minutes
Presidential Election: 50.4% Obama, 48.0% Romney (2012)
National and State Parks: Cape Romain National Wildlife Refuge; Charles Pinckney National Historic Site; Charles Towne Landing State Historic Site; Edisto Beach State Park; Ernest F Hollings Ace Basin National Wildlife Refuge; Fort Sumter National Monument; Hampton Plantation State Park; USS Yorktown State Park
Additional Information Contacts
Charleston Government . . . . (843) 958-5000
  http://www.charlestoncounty.org

Charleston County Communities

ADAMS RUN (unincorporated postal area)
ZCTA: 29426
  Covers a land area of 67.297 square miles and a water area of 0.499 square miles. Located at 32.80° N. Lat; 80.37° W. Long. Elevation is 30 feet.
  Population: 1,741; Growth (since 2000): -5.1%; Density: 25.9 persons per square mile; Race: 34.3% White, 62.8% Black/African American, 0.2% Asian, 0.6% American Indian/Alaska Native, 0.1% Native Hawaiian/Other Pacific Islander, 0.8% Two or more races, 2.3%

Hispanic of any race; Average household size: 2.61; Median age: 40.9; Age under 18: 24.1%; Age 65 and over: 14.6%; Males per 100 females: 93.9
  Housing: Homeownership rate: 82.2%; Homeowner vacancy rate: 1.6%; Rental vacancy rate: 11.2%

AWENDAW (town). Covers a land area of 9.470 square miles and a water area of 0.206 square miles. Located at 32.98° N. Lat; 79.64° W. Long. Elevation is 20 feet.
Population: 1,294; Growth (since 2000): 8.3%; Density: 136.6 persons per square mile; Race: 40.9% White, 57.7% Black/African American, 0.3% Asian, 0.0% American Indian/Alaska Native, 0.0% Native Hawaiian/Other Pacific Islander, 1.0% Two or more races, 0.9% Hispanic of any race; Average household size: 2.56; Median age: 45.3; Age under 18: 19.4%; Age 65 and over: 15.4%; Males per 100 females: 97.6
Housing: Homeownership rate: 83.6%; Homeowner vacancy rate: 1.8%; Rental vacancy rate: 6.7%
Additional Information Contacts
Town of Awendaw . . . . (843) 928-3100
  http://www.awendawsc.org

CHARLESTON (city). County seat. Covers a land area of 108.979 square miles and a water area of 18.513 square miles. Located at 32.82° N. Lat; 79.96° W. Long. Elevation is 10 feet.
History: Charles Town, as it was originally called, was settled in 1670 by English pioneers who established themselves on Albemarle Point, westward across the Ashley River from the present location. Oyster Point was higher and better adapted for defense, and was selected for the site of the town laid out in 1672. For many years Charleston's history was the history of South Carolina. It was the center from which colonization radiated and the capital of the province until 1786. The influx of French Huguenots and French Catholics from Acadia in the 17th century, the arrival of Scots and South Germans in the 18th century, and immigration of North Germans and Irish in the 19th century gave Charleston a cosmopolitan atmosphere. The name was changed from Charles Town to Charleston in 1783 after more than two years of British occupation. The long siege of the city during the Civil War took its toll on Charleston, which was the center of blockade running for the Confederates and the place where submarine warfare was introduced. Recovery after the war was slowed by a devastating earthquake in 1886.
Population: 120,083; Growth (since 2000): 24.2%; Density: 1,101.9 persons per square mile; Race: 70.2% White, 25.4% Black/African American, 1.6% Asian, 0.2% American Indian/Alaska Native, 0.1% Native Hawaiian/Other Pacific Islander, 1.5% Two or more races, 2.9% Hispanic of any race; Average household size: 2.18; Median age: 32.5; Age under 18: 18.0%; Age 65 and over: 12.2%; Males per 100 females: 89.6; Marriage status: 43.5% never married, 41.0% now married, 2.5% separated, 5.4% widowed, 10.2% divorced; Foreign born: 4.2%; Speak English only: 94.7%; With disability: 9.6%; Veterans: 9.5%; Ancestry: 12.4% German, 11.9% English, 11.7% Irish, 11.5% American, 4.0% Italian
Employment: 15.8% management, business, and financial, 6.1% computer, engineering, and science, 13.4% education, legal, community service, arts, and media, 9.4% healthcare practitioners, 20.2% service, 23.7% sales and office, 4.8% natural resources, construction, and maintenance, 6.6% production, transportation, and material moving
Income: Per capita: $32,131; Median household: $51,737; Average household: $74,242; Households with income of $100,000 or more: 22.8%; Poverty rate: 19.5%
Educational Attainment: High school diploma or higher: 92.6%; Bachelor's degree or higher: 48.9%; Graduate/professional degree or higher: 18.5%

School District(s)
Berkeley 01 (PK-12)
  2012-13 Enrollment: 30,942 . . . . (843) 899-8601
Charleston 01 (PK-12)
  2012-13 Enrollment: 44,599 . . . . (843) 937-6318
Four-year College(s)
Charleston School of Law (Private, For-profit)
  Fall 2013 Enrollment: 542 . . . . (843) 329-1000
Charleston Southern University (Private, Not-for-profit, Baptist)
  Fall 2013 Enrollment: 3,269 . . . . (843) 863-7000
  2013-14 Tuition: In-state $22,090; Out-of-state $22,090
Citadel Military College of South Carolina (Public)
  Fall 2013 Enrollment: 3,598 . . . . (843) 225-3294
  2013-14 Tuition: In-state $10,838; Out-of-state $29,639

College of Charleston (Public)
    Fall 2013 Enrollment: 11,619 . . . . (843) 953-5500
    2013-14 Tuition: In-state $10,626; Out-of-state $27,090
Medical University of South Carolina (Public)
    Fall 2013 Enrollment: 2,775 . . . . (843) 792-2300
The Art Institute of Charleston (Private, For-profit)
    Fall 2013 Enrollment: 643 . . . . (843) 727-3500
    2013-14 Tuition: In-state $17,596; Out-of-state $17,596

Two-year College(s)

Miller-Motte Technical College-North Charleston (Private, For-profit)
    Fall 2013 Enrollment: 704 . . . . (843) 574-0101
    2013-14 Tuition: In-state $10,360; Out-of-state $10,360
Trident Technical College (Public)
    Fall 2013 Enrollment: 17,489 . . . . (843) 574-6111
    2013-14 Tuition: In-state $4,238; Out-of-state $7,210

Vocational/Technical School(s)

Charleston Cosmetology Institute (Private, For-profit)
    Fall 2013 Enrollment: 106 . . . . (843) 552-3670
    2013-14 Tuition: $17,500
Lacy Cosmetology School-West Ashley (Private, For-profit)
    Fall 2013 Enrollment: 9 . . . . (803) 648-6181
    2013-14 Tuition: $16,900
Housing: Homeownership rate: 52.1%; Median home value: $253,800; Median year structure built: 1982; Homeowner vacancy rate: 4.1%; Median gross rent: $968 per month; Rental vacancy rate: 10.8%
Health Insurance: 87.4% have insurance; 73.8% have private insurance; 24.8% have public insurance; 12.6% do not have insurance; 7.6% of children under 18 do not have insurance
Hospitals: Bon Secours - Saint Francis Xavier Hospital (141 beds); Charleston VA Medical Center (145 beds); Musc Medical Center (596 beds); Roper Hospital (453 beds); Trident Medical Center (296 beds)
Safety: Violent crime rate: 18.2 per 10,000 population; Property crime rate: 250.9 per 10,000 population
Newspapers: Charleston City Paper (weekly circulation 40000); Post & Courier (daily circulation 95700)
Transportation: Commute: 83.7% car, 2.8% public transportation, 5.2% walk, 4.4% work from home; Median travel time to work: 21.0 minutes
Airports: Charleston AFB/International (primary service/small hub); Charleston Executive (general aviation)
Additional Information Contacts
City of Charleston . . . . (843) 577-6970
    http://www.charlestoncity.info

CHARLESTON AFB (unincorporated postal area)
ZCTA: 29404
    Covers a land area of 5.086 square miles and a water area of 0.019 square miles. Located at 32.90° N. Lat; 80.05° W. Long..
Population: 1,348; Growth (since 2000): -69.3%; Density: 265.1 persons per square mile; Race: 73.1% White, 17.3% Black/African American, 1.5% Asian, 0.4% American Indian/Alaska Native, 0.0% Native Hawaiian/Other Pacific Islander, 5.3% Two or more races, 7.4% Hispanic of any race; Average household size: 3.21; Median age: 21.9; Age under 18: 25.7%; Age 65 and over: 0.1%; Males per 100 females: 154.8
Housing: Homeownership rate: 1.1%; Homeowner vacancy rate: 0.0%; Rental vacancy rate: 26.6%

FOLLY BEACH (city). Covers a land area of 12.507 square miles and a water area of 6.362 square miles. Located at 32.67° N. Lat; 79.96° W. Long. Elevation is 10 feet.
Population: 2,617; Growth (since 2000): 23.7%; Density: 209.2 persons per square mile; Race: 96.3% White, 1.5% Black/African American, 0.5% Asian, 0.3% American Indian/Alaska Native, 0.1% Native Hawaiian/Other Pacific Islander, 0.8% Two or more races, 1.7% Hispanic of any race; Average household size: 1.92; Median age: 47.7; Age under 18: 10.2%; Age 65 and over: 18.1%; Males per 100 females: 105.3; Marriage status: 36.9% never married, 41.3% now married, 1.6% separated, 1.2% widowed, 20.5% divorced; Foreign born: 2.7%; Speak English only: 96.2%; With disability: 11.0%; Veterans: 16.7%; Ancestry: 16.0% English, 15.6% German, 12.5% Irish, 11.5% Scottish, 5.6% American
Employment: 14.1% management, business, and financial, 9.9% computer, engineering, and science, 6.0% education, legal, community service, arts, and media, 5.5% healthcare practitioners, 35.7% service, 15.0% sales and office, 9.2% natural resources, construction, and maintenance, 4.6% production, transportation, and material moving

Income: Per capita: $49,743; Median household: $76,607; Average household: $98,681; Households with income of $100,000 or more: 42.3%; Poverty rate: 13.1%
Educational Attainment: High school diploma or higher: 96.9%; Bachelor's degree or higher: 54.8%; Graduate/professional degree or higher: 21.0%
Housing: Homeownership rate: 59.0%; Median home value: $607,700; Median year structure built: 1985; Homeowner vacancy rate: 5.7%; Median gross rent: $1,333 per month; Rental vacancy rate: 42.6%
Health Insurance: 80.6% have insurance; 75.7% have private insurance; 17.9% have public insurance; 19.4% do not have insurance; 4.0% of children under 18 do not have insurance
Safety: Violent crime rate: 59.2 per 10,000 population; Property crime rate: 547.7 per 10,000 population
Transportation: Commute: 68.5% car, 0.0% public transportation, 14.3% walk, 12.2% work from home; Median travel time to work: 21.2 minutes

HOLLYWOOD (town). Covers a land area of 23.132 square miles and a water area of 1.383 square miles. Located at 32.75° N. Lat; 80.20° W. Long. Elevation is 30 feet.
Population: 4,714; Growth (since 2000): 19.5%; Density: 203.8 persons per square mile; Race: 41.0% White, 55.4% Black/African American, 0.3% Asian, 0.2% American Indian/Alaska Native, 0.1% Native Hawaiian/Other Pacific Islander, 0.8% Two or more races, 4.0% Hispanic of any race; Average household size: 2.60; Median age: 45.7; Age under 18: 20.2%; Age 65 and over: 15.0%; Males per 100 females: 97.3; Marriage status: 26.9% never married, 53.8% now married, 1.9% separated, 7.6% widowed, 11.6% divorced; Foreign born: 1.5%; Speak English only: 99.2%; With disability: 17.2%; Veterans: 12.2%; Ancestry: 12.0% American, 10.1% English, 5.1% German, 4.7% Irish, 3.4% Italian
Employment: 12.2% management, business, and financial, 1.5% computer, engineering, and science, 10.0% education, legal, community service, arts, and media, 6.2% healthcare practitioners, 14.8% service, 25.7% sales and office, 9.7% natural resources, construction, and maintenance, 19.8% production, transportation, and material moving
Income: Per capita: $39,381; Median household: $53,799; Average household: $94,605; Households with income of $100,000 or more: 24.7%; Poverty rate: 7.9%
Educational Attainment: High school diploma or higher: 82.4%; Bachelor's degree or higher: 28.4%; Graduate/professional degree or higher: 11.9%

School District(s)

Charleston 01 (PK-12)
    2012-13 Enrollment: 44,599 . . . . (843) 937-6318
Housing: Homeownership rate: 82.5%; Median home value: $200,600; Median year structure built: 1990; Homeowner vacancy rate: 2.5%; Median gross rent: $832 per month; Rental vacancy rate: 12.2%
Health Insurance: 83.6% have insurance; 65.2% have private insurance; 33.0% have public insurance; 16.4% do not have insurance; 16.8% of children under 18 do not have insurance
Transportation: Commute: 93.7% car, 0.0% public transportation, 1.8% walk, 3.7% work from home; Median travel time to work: 27.2 minutes
Additional Information Contacts
Town of Hollywood . . . . (843) 889-3222
    http://www.townofhollywood.org

ISLE OF PALMS (city). Covers a land area of 4.436 square miles and a water area of 1.000 square miles. Located at 32.80° N. Lat; 79.75° W. Long. Elevation is 3 feet.
History: Destroyed by Hurricane Hugo (1989); since rebuilt.
Population: 4,133; Growth (since 2000): -9.8%; Density: 931.7 persons per square mile; Race: 97.7% White, 0.6% Black/African American, 0.8% Asian, 0.1% American Indian/Alaska Native, 0.0% Native Hawaiian/Other Pacific Islander, 0.7% Two or more races, 1.1% Hispanic of any race; Average household size: 2.26; Median age: 52.6; Age under 18: 17.0%; Age 65 and over: 22.6%; Males per 100 females: 98.1; Marriage status: 24.3% never married, 62.6% now married, 1.2% separated, 2.9% widowed, 10.1% divorced; Foreign born: 3.5%; Speak English only: 95.5%; With disability: 7.4%; Veterans: 15.4%; Ancestry: 20.5% German, 20.2% English, 18.7% Irish, 9.5% American, 6.1% French
Employment: 26.8% management, business, and financial, 8.2% computer, engineering, and science, 20.2% education, legal, community service, arts, and media, 9.2% healthcare practitioners, 4.8% service, 17.5% sales and office, 5.7% natural resources, construction, and maintenance, 7.7% production, transportation, and material moving

Income: Per capita: $54,203; Median household: $80,556; Average household: $128,674; Households with income of $100,000 or more: 44.7%; Poverty rate: 18.9%

Educational Attainment: High school diploma or higher: 99.0%; Bachelor's degree or higher: 65.8%; Graduate/professional degree or higher: 25.2%

Housing: Homeownership rate: 81.0%; Median home value: $792,200; Median year structure built: 1986; Homeowner vacancy rate: 4.2%; Median gross rent: $1,563 per month; Rental vacancy rate: 75.7%

Health Insurance: 92.8% have insurance; 84.7% have private insurance; 29.0% have public insurance; 7.2% do not have insurance; 5.0% of children under 18 do not have insurance

Safety: Violent crime rate: 4.7 per 10,000 population; Property crime rate: 326.9 per 10,000 population

Transportation: Commute: 88.5% car, 0.0% public transportation, 2.6% walk, 8.0% work from home; Median travel time to work: 33.9 minutes

Additional Information Contacts
City of Isle of Palms. . . . . (843) 886-6428
  http://www.iop.net

JAMES ISLAND (town).
Note: Statistics that would complete this profile are not available because the town was incorporated after the 2010 Census was released.

JOHNS ISLAND (unincorporated postal area)
ZCTA: 29455

Covers a land area of 107.093 square miles and a water area of 11.018 square miles. Located at 32.62° N. Lat; 80.04° W. Long. Elevation is 10 feet.

Population: 20,478; Growth (since 2000): 49.6%; Density: 191.2 persons per square mile; Race: 68.1% White, 24.5% Black/African American, 0.7% Asian, 0.3% American Indian/Alaska Native, 0.1% Native Hawaiian/Other Pacific Islander, 1.4% Two or more races, 9.0% Hispanic of any race; Average household size: 2.42; Median age: 44.2; Age under 18: 18.5%; Age 65 and over: 18.0%; Males per 100 females: 98.2; Marriage status: 26.9% never married, 57.3% now married, 2.1% separated, 5.4% widowed, 10.4% divorced; Foreign born: 6.6%; Speak English only: 88.9%; With disability: 12.6%; Veterans: 11.1%; Ancestry: 14.4% Irish, 14.1% American, 10.7% English, 9.9% German, 4.7% Italian

Employment: 15.3% management, business, and financial, 3.2% computer, engineering, and science, 8.4% education, legal, community service, arts, and media, 6.9% healthcare practitioners, 26.1% service, 21.1% sales and office, 10.4% natural resources, construction, and maintenance, 8.6% production, transportation, and material moving

Income: Per capita: $36,676; Median household: $60,954; Average household: $95,722; Households with income of $100,000 or more: 29.9%; Poverty rate: 15.6%

Educational Attainment: High school diploma or higher: 87.4%; Bachelor's degree or higher: 40.6%; Graduate/professional degree or higher: 15.5%

School District(s)
Charleston 01 (PK-12)
  2012-13 Enrollment: 44,599 . . . . (843) 937-6318

Housing: Homeownership rate: 78.9%; Median home value: $261,500; Median year structure built: 1990; Homeowner vacancy rate: 3.7%; Median gross rent: $869 per month; Rental vacancy rate: 45.8%

Health Insurance: 79.2% have insurance; 61.8% have private insurance; 30.8% have public insurance; 20.8% do not have insurance; 12.8% of children under 18 do not have insurance

Transportation: Commute: 90.5% car, 0.2% public transportation, 0.7% walk, 5.9% work from home; Median travel time to work: 25.5 minutes

KIAWAH ISLAND (town). Covers a land area of 10.980 square miles and a water area of 2.469 square miles. Located at 32.62° N. Lat; 80.06° W. Long. Elevation is 3 feet.
Population: 1,626; Growth (since 2000): 39.8%; Density: 148.1 persons per square mile; Race: 96.9% White, 2.2% Black/African American, 0.3% Asian, 0.0% American Indian/Alaska Native, 0.0% Native Hawaiian/Other Pacific Islander, 0.3% Two or more races, 0.9% Hispanic of any race; Average household size: 2.00; Median age: 63.6; Age under 18: 5.6%; Age 65 and over: 43.8%; Males per 100 females: 92.4

Housing: Homeownership rate: 95.1%; Homeowner vacancy rate: 2.4%; Rental vacancy rate: 90.6%

Additional Information Contacts
Town of Kiawah Island . . . . (843) 768-9166
  http://www.kiawahisland.org

LINCOLNVILLE (town). Covers a land area of 1.190 square miles and a water area of 0 square miles. Located at 33.01° N. Lat; 80.16° W. Long. Elevation is 66 feet.
Population: 1,139; Growth (since 2000): 26.0%; Density: 957.2 persons per square mile; Race: 44.6% White, 48.5% Black/African American, 0.2% Asian, 0.4% American Indian/Alaska Native, 0.0% Native Hawaiian/Other Pacific Islander, 2.5% Two or more races, 6.0% Hispanic of any race; Average household size: 2.64; Median age: 39.0; Age under 18: 24.2%; Age 65 and over: 15.6%; Males per 100 females: 91.8

Housing: Homeownership rate: 55.1%; Homeowner vacancy rate: 0.8%; Rental vacancy rate: 6.8%

MCCLELLANVILLE (town). Covers a land area of 2.236 square miles and a water area of 0.118 square miles. Located at 33.09° N. Lat; 79.47° W. Long. Elevation is 3 feet.
History: Nearby are Harrietta House and Gardens.

Population: 499; Growth (since 2000): 8.7%; Density: 223.2 persons per square mile; Race: 88.0% White, 11.4% Black/African American, 0.4% Asian, 0.2% American Indian/Alaska Native, 0.0% Native Hawaiian/Other Pacific Islander, 0.0% Two or more races, 0.6% Hispanic of any race; Average household size: 2.22; Median age: 53.8; Age under 18: 16.4%; Age 65 and over: 23.8%; Males per 100 females: 94.9

School District(s)
Charleston 01 (PK-12)
  2012-13 Enrollment: 44,599 . . . . (843) 937-6318
Sc Public Charter SD (PK-12)
  2012-13 Enrollment: 11,500 . . . . (803) 734-8322

Housing: Homeownership rate: 86.7%; Homeowner vacancy rate: 4.4%; Rental vacancy rate: 9.1%

MEGGETT (town). Covers a land area of 17.848 square miles and a water area of 0.572 square miles. Located at 32.70° N. Lat; 80.27° W. Long. Elevation is 10 feet.
History: Meggett has been known as the Cabbage Patch. Reports in the past tell of fortunes made and lost on the price fluctuations of the cabbage.

Population: 1,226; Growth (since 2000): -0.3%; Density: 68.7 persons per square mile; Race: 84.5% White, 13.5% Black/African American, 0.4% Asian, 0.2% American Indian/Alaska Native, 0.0% Native Hawaiian/Other Pacific Islander, 1.0% Two or more races, 1.1% Hispanic of any race; Average household size: 2.31; Median age: 51.3; Age under 18: 16.1%; Age 65 and over: 19.7%; Males per 100 females: 102.3

Housing: Homeownership rate: 89.2%; Homeowner vacancy rate: 1.6%; Rental vacancy rate: 3.4%

MOUNT PLEASANT (town). Covers a land area of 45.082 square miles and a water area of 7.524 square miles. Located at 32.85° N. Lat; 79.83° W. Long. Elevation is 23 feet.
History: Mount Pleasant originated as a summer resort for the island planters. Andrew Hibben operated the first direct ferry from Hadrell's Point in 1770.

Population: 67,843; Growth (since 2000): 42.5%; Density: 1,504.9 persons per square mile; Race: 91.3% White, 5.1% Black/African American, 1.6% Asian, 0.2% American Indian/Alaska Native, 0.0% Native Hawaiian/Other Pacific Islander, 1.1% Two or more races, 2.7% Hispanic of any race; Average household size: 2.43; Median age: 39.1; Age under 18: 24.1%; Age 65 and over: 12.2%; Males per 100 females: 92.6; Marriage status: 26.5% never married, 58.5% now married, 2.3% separated, 4.9% widowed, 10.1% divorced; Foreign born: 4.3%; Speak English only: 94.8%; With disability: 7.1%; Veterans: 10.9%; Ancestry: 18.2% German, 16.5% Irish, 14.8% English, 10.5% American, 6.4% Italian

Employment: 22.9% management, business, and financial, 7.2% computer, engineering, and science, 12.8% education, legal, community service, arts, and media, 9.4% healthcare practitioners, 13.2% service, 24.7% sales and office, 4.6% natural resources, construction, and maintenance, 5.3% production, transportation, and material moving

Income: Per capita: $40,870; Median household: $76,085; Average household: $100,185; Households with income of $100,000 or more: 37.8%; Poverty rate: 8.1%

Educational Attainment: High school diploma or higher: 97.1%; Bachelor's degree or higher: 59.5%; Graduate/professional degree or higher: 21.5%

School District(s)

Charleston 01 (PK-12)
    2012-13 Enrollment: 44,599 . . . . (843) 937-6318
Housing: Homeownership rate: 72.6%; Median home value: $349,200; Median year structure built: 1994; Homeowner vacancy rate: 3.1%; Median gross rent: $1,238 per month; Rental vacancy rate: 10.3%
Health Insurance: 91.5% have insurance; 85.4% have private insurance; 16.7% have public insurance; 8.5% do not have insurance; 5.6% of children under 18 do not have insurance
Hospitals: East Cooper Medical Center (100 beds); Mount Pleasant Hospital
Safety: Violent crime rate: 16.0 per 10,000 population; Property crime rate: 195.1 per 10,000 population
Newspapers: Moultrie News (weekly circulation 32000)
Transportation: Commute: 89.5% car, 0.2% public transportation, 1.0% walk, 7.9% work from home; Median travel time to work: 21.9 minutes
Additional Information Contacts
Town of Mount Pleasant . . . . (843) 884-8517
    http://www.townofmountpleasant.com

NORTH CHARLESTON (city).
Covers a land area of 73.187 square miles and a water area of 3.461 square miles. Located at 32.92° N. Lat; 80.07° W. Long. Elevation is 20 feet.
History: North Charleston is the third-largest city in South Carolina. From the 17th century until the Civil War, the area was developed primarily for plantations to cultivate commodity crops, such as rice and indigo.
Population: 97,471; Growth (since 2000): 22.4%; Density: 1,331.8 persons per square mile; Race: 41.6% White, 47.2% Black/African American, 1.9% Asian, 0.5% American Indian/Alaska Native, 0.2% Native Hawaiian/Other Pacific Islander, 2.5% Two or more races, 10.9% Hispanic of any race; Average household size: 2.54; Median age: 30.6; Age under 18: 25.5%; Age 65 and over: 8.4%; Males per 100 females: 98.4; Marriage status: 40.9% never married, 42.5% now married, 4.7% separated, 5.1% widowed, 11.5% divorced; Foreign born: 9.2%; Speak English only: 87.7%; With disability: 10.5%; Veterans: 12.6%; Ancestry: 8.9% American, 7.4% German, 6.0% Irish, 4.8% English, 2.1% Italian
Employment: 9.2% management, business, and financial, 4.9% computer, engineering, and science, 6.7% education, legal, community service, arts, and media, 4.3% healthcare practitioners, 22.2% service, 24.8% sales and office, 12.7% natural resources, construction, and maintenance, 15.3% production, transportation, and material moving
Income: Per capita: $19,717; Median household: $39,322; Average household: $50,445; Households with income of $100,000 or more: 11.1%; Poverty rate: 23.4%
Educational Attainment: High school diploma or higher: 79.7%; Bachelor's degree or higher: 19.0%; Graduate/professional degree or higher: 5.5%

School District(s)

Charleston 01 (PK-12)
    2012-13 Enrollment: 44,599 . . . . (843) 937-6318
Dorchester 02 (PK-12)
    2012-13 Enrollment: 23,741 . . . . (843) 873-2901
Sc Public Charter SD (PK-12)
    2012-13 Enrollment: 11,500 . . . . (803) 734-8322

Four-year College(s)

ITT Technical Institute-North Charleston (Private, For-profit)
    Fall 2013 Enrollment: 265 . . . . (843) 745-5700
    2013-14 Tuition: In-state $18,048; Out-of-state $18,048
Virginia College-Charleston (Private, For-profit)
    Fall 2013 Enrollment: 425 . . . . (843) 614-4300
    2013-14 Tuition: In-state $13,330; Out-of-state $13,330

Vocational/Technical School(s)

Centura College-North Charleston (Private, For-profit)
    Fall 2013 Enrollment: 43 . . . . (843) 569-0889
    2013-14 Tuition: In-state $15,547; Out-of-state $15,547
Paul Mitchell The School-Charleston (Private, For-profit)
    Fall 2013 Enrollment: 196 . . . . (843) 725-0246
    2013-14 Tuition: $14,400
Southeastern Institute-Charleston (Private, For-profit)
    Fall 2013 Enrollment: 229 . . . . (843) 747-1279
    2013-14 Tuition: $15,584
Housing: Homeownership rate: 47.9%; Median home value: $138,300; Median year structure built: 1983; Homeowner vacancy rate: 4.2%; Median gross rent: $855 per month; Rental vacancy rate: 14.2%

Health Insurance: 76.9% have insurance; 53.9% have private insurance; 32.0% have public insurance; 23.1% do not have insurance; 9.1% of children under 18 do not have insurance
Safety: Violent crime rate: 67.1 per 10,000 population; Property crime rate: 561.7 per 10,000 population
Newspapers: North Charleston News (weekly circulation 12000)
Transportation: Commute: 90.5% car, 3.3% public transportation, 1.8% walk, 2.2% work from home; Median travel time to work: 22.0 minutes; Amtrak: Train service available.
Additional Information Contacts
City of North Charleston . . . . (843) 554-5700
    http://www.northcharleston.org

RAVENEL (town).
Covers a land area of 12.642 square miles and a water area of 0 square miles. Located at 32.78° N. Lat; 80.23° W. Long. Elevation is 36 feet.
History: Formerly Ravenels.
Population: 2,465; Growth (since 2000): 11.3%; Density: 195.0 persons per square mile; Race: 50.1% White, 44.3% Black/African American, 0.1% Asian, 0.2% American Indian/Alaska Native, 0.0% Native Hawaiian/Other Pacific Islander, 1.9% Two or more races, 7.1% Hispanic of any race; Average household size: 2.74; Median age: 39.4; Age under 18: 24.5%; Age 65 and over: 12.6%; Males per 100 females: 98.5

School District(s)

Charleston 01 (PK-12)
    2012-13 Enrollment: 44,599 . . . . (843) 937-6318
Housing: Homeownership rate: 76.6%; Homeowner vacancy rate: 2.1%; Rental vacancy rate: 12.8%

ROCKVILLE (town).
Covers a land area of 0.424 square miles and a water area of 0.090 square miles. Located at 32.60° N. Lat; 80.19° W. Long. Elevation is 10 feet.
Population: 134; Growth (since 2000): -2.2%; Density: 316.3 persons per square mile; Race: 87.3% White, 11.2% Black/African American, 0.0% Asian, 1.5% American Indian/Alaska Native, 0.0% Native Hawaiian/Other Pacific Islander, 0.0% Two or more races, 1.5% Hispanic of any race; Average household size: 2.06; Median age: 60.0; Age under 18: 13.4%; Age 65 and over: 31.3%; Males per 100 females: 103.0
Housing: Homeownership rate: 81.5%; Homeowner vacancy rate: 5.4%; Rental vacancy rate: 14.3%

SEABROOK ISLAND (town).
Covers a land area of 5.971 square miles and a water area of 1.032 square miles. Located at 32.59° N. Lat; 80.18° W. Long. Elevation is 7 feet.
Population: 1,714; Growth (since 2000): 37.1%; Density: 287.0 persons per square mile; Race: 97.2% White, 2.0% Black/African American, 0.4% Asian, 0.1% American Indian/Alaska Native, 0.1% Native Hawaiian/Other Pacific Islander, 0.2% Two or more races, 1.1% Hispanic of any race; Average household size: 1.87; Median age: 65.0; Age under 18: 4.2%; Age 65 and over: 50.2%; Males per 100 females: 95.9
Housing: Homeownership rate: 90.1%; Homeowner vacancy rate: 4.3%; Rental vacancy rate: 74.0%
Additional Information Contacts
Town of Seabrook Island. . . . . (843) 768-9121
    http://www.townofseabrookisland.org

SULLIVAN'S ISLAND (town).
Covers a land area of 2.498 square miles and a water area of 0.941 square miles. Located at 32.77° N. Lat; 79.84° W. Long. Elevation is 13 feet.
History: Sullivan's Island was a seashore resort before the Civil War. It was named for Captain Florence O'Sullivan, captain of the first English ship to bring settlers here in 1670.
Population: 1,791; Growth (since 2000): -6.3%; Density: 717.0 persons per square mile; Race: 98.4% White, 0.8% Black/African American, 0.2% Asian, 0.0% American Indian/Alaska Native, 0.0% Native Hawaiian/Other Pacific Islander, 0.6% Two or more races, 1.1% Hispanic of any race; Average household size: 2.34; Median age: 47.1; Age under 18: 21.7%; Age 65 and over: 14.7%; Males per 100 females: 97.5
Housing: Homeownership rate: 72.9%; Homeowner vacancy rate: 1.6%; Rental vacancy rate: 11.3%
Safety: Violent crime rate: 10.8 per 10,000 population; Property crime rate: 306.8 per 10,000 population

WADMALAW ISLAND (unincorporated postal area)
ZCTA: 29487

Covers a land area of 41.897 square miles and a water area of 8.726 square miles. Located at 32.66° N. Lat; 80.18° W. Long. Elevation is 3 feet.

Population: 2,725; Growth (since 2000): 4.4%; Density: 65.0 persons per square mile; Race: 45.1% White, 52.4% Black/African American, 0.1% Asian, 0.1% American Indian/Alaska Native, 0.0% Native Hawaiian/Other Pacific Islander, 0.6% Two or more races, 2.6% Hispanic of any race; Average household size: 2.48; Median age: 47.8; Age under 18: 20.1%; Age 65 and over: 19.4%; Males per 100 females: 92.2; Marriage status: 31.1% never married, 52.7% now married, 1.7% separated, 8.1% widowed, 8.1% divorced; Foreign born: 1.5%; Speak English only: 98.2%; With disability: 11.6%; Veterans: 12.6%; Ancestry: 12.4% English, 8.5% American, 5.4% German, 4.6% French, 3.9% Scottish

Employment: 19.9% management, business, and financial, 3.2% computer, engineering, and science, 6.2% education, legal, community service, arts, and media, 6.0% healthcare practitioners, 22.0% service, 27.4% sales and office, 4.2% natural resources, construction, and maintenance, 11.0% production, transportation, and material moving

Income: Per capita: $32,758; Median household: $47,068; Average household: $83,985; Households with income of $100,000 or more: 26.5%; Poverty rate: 22.5%

Educational Attainment: High school diploma or higher: 80.2%; Bachelor's degree or higher: 36.9%; Graduate/professional degree or higher: 17.2%

School District(s)
Charleston 01 (PK-12)
    2012-13 Enrollment: 44,599 . . . . (843) 937-6318

Housing: Homeownership rate: 86.3%; Median home value: $270,600; Median year structure built: 1987; Homeowner vacancy rate: 2.1%; Median gross rent: $867 per month; Rental vacancy rate: 7.9%

Health Insurance: 86.1% have insurance; 68.2% have private insurance; 32.3% have public insurance; 13.9% do not have insurance; 8.2% of children under 18 do not have insurance

Transportation: Commute: 94.4% car, 1.1% public transportation, 0.0% walk, 3.6% work from home; Median travel time to work: 37.0 minutes

Cherokee County

Located in northern South Carolina; bounded on the north by North Carolina, and on the south by the Pacolet River; drained by the Broad River. Covers a land area of 392.659 square miles, a water area of 4.519 square miles, and is located in the Eastern Time Zone at 35.05° N. Lat., 81.61° W. Long. The county was founded in 1897. County seat is Gaffney.

Cherokee County is part of the Gaffney, SC Micropolitan Statistical Area. The entire metro area includes: Cherokee County, SC

Weather Station: Ninety Nine Islands   Elevation: 500 feet

	Jan	Feb	Mar	Apr	May	Jun	Jul	Aug	Sep	Oct	Nov	Dec
High	52	56	64	72	79	85	89	88	81	72	63	54
Low	27	30	36	43	53	62	66	66	58	46	36	29
Precip	3.7	3.7	4.6	3.1	3.5	3.6	3.7	4.8	3.7	3.5	3.5	3.8
Snow	0.7	0.5	0.3	0.0	0.0	0.0	0.0	0.0	0.0	0.0	tr	tr

High and Low temperatures in degrees Fahrenheit; Precipitation and Snow in inches

Population: 55,342; Growth (since 2000): 5.3%; Density: 140.9 persons per square mile; Race: 75.0% White, 20.4% Black/African American, 0.6% Asian, 0.4% American Indian/Alaska Native, 0.0% Native Hawaiian/Other Pacific Islander, 1.4% two or more races, 3.7% Hispanic of any race; Average household size: 2.54; Median age: 38.3; Age under 18: 24.7%; Age 65 and over: 13.4%; Males per 100 females: 94.3; Marriage status: 30.7% never married, 50.4% now married, 3.8% separated, 7.3% widowed, 11.5% divorced; Foreign born: 2.5%; Speak English only: 95.6%; With disability: 17.7%; Veterans: 8.6%; Ancestry: 15.7% American, 9.0% Irish, 7.3% German, 6.3% English, 2.2% Scotch-Irish

Religion: Six largest groups: 45.8% Baptist, 5.3% Methodist/Pietist, 4.0% Non-denominational Protestant, 2.4% Pentecostal, 2.0% Catholicism, 1.1% Latter-day Saints

Economy: Unemployment rate: 7.0%; Leading industries: 24.2% retail trade; 16.7% other services (except public administration); 8.9% accommodation and food services; Farms: 490 totaling 64,601 acres; Company size: 1 employs 1,000 or more persons, 2 employ 500 to 999

persons, 25 employ 100 to 499 persons, 942 employ less than 100 persons; Business ownership: 903 women-owned, n/a Black-owned, n/a Hispanic-owned, 36 Asian-owned

Employment: 9.8% management, business, and financial, 2.8% computer, engineering, and science, 8.6% education, legal, community service, arts, and media, 4.3% healthcare practitioners, 16.0% service, 23.1% sales and office, 8.7% natural resources, construction, and maintenance, 26.6% production, transportation, and material moving

Income: Per capita: $18,240; Median household: $34,202; Average household: $46,702; Households with income of $100,000 or more: 8.9%; Poverty rate: 23.0%

Educational Attainment: High school diploma or higher: 75.0%; Bachelor's degree or higher: 14.3%; Graduate/professional degree or higher: 3.9%

Housing: Homeownership rate: 68.9%; Median home value: $83,600; Median year structure built: 1981; Homeowner vacancy rate: 2.0%; Median gross rent: $615 per month; Rental vacancy rate: 10.3%

Vital Statistics: Birth rate: 125.8 per 10,000 population; Death rate: 97.9 per 10,000 population; Age-adjusted cancer mortality rate: 196.5 deaths per 100,000 population

Health Insurance: 82.2% have insurance; 55.9% have private insurance; 37.5% have public insurance; 17.8% do not have insurance; 8.7% of children under 18 do not have insurance

Health Care: Physicians: 6.3 per 10,000 population; Hospital beds: 22.5 per 10,000 population; Hospital admissions: 600.1 per 10,000 population

Air Quality Index: 93.9% good, 6.1% moderate, 0.0% unhealthy for sensitive individuals, 0.0% unhealthy (percent of days)

Transportation: Commute: 95.6% car, 0.0% public transportation, 1.4% walk, 1.6% work from home; Median travel time to work: 20.4 minutes

Presidential Election: 34.8% Obama, 64.1% Romney (2012)

National and State Parks: Cowpens National Battlefield

Additional Information Contacts
Cherokee Government . . . . (864) 487-2571
    http://www.cherokeecountysc.com

Cherokee County Communities

BLACKSBURG (town). Covers a land area of 1.872 square miles and a water area of 0 square miles. Located at 35.12° N. Lat; 81.52° W. Long. Elevation is 761 feet.

History: When pioneer Stark established his trading post on the site that is now Blacksburg, it was called Stark's Folly, for the vicinity was desolate and the land appeared worthless. Stark was a good salesman, however, and soon persuaded others to settle. In 1886 a railroad line was brought in, and the settlement grew.

Population: 1,848; Growth (since 2000): -1.7%; Density: 987.3 persons per square mile; Race: 74.5% White, 21.4% Black/African American, 0.5% Asian, 0.4% American Indian/Alaska Native, 0.1% Native Hawaiian/Other Pacific Islander, 2.5% Two or more races, 1.0% Hispanic of any race; Average household size: 2.47; Median age: 35.1; Age under 18: 28.5%; Age 65 and over: 13.7%; Males per 100 females: 81.2

School District(s)
Cherokee 01 (PK-12)
    2012-13 Enrollment: 9,033 . . . . (864) 206-2233

Housing: Homeownership rate: 53.2%; Homeowner vacancy rate: 2.7%; Rental vacancy rate: 9.1%

Safety: Violent crime rate: 53.6 per 10,000 population; Property crime rate: 509.1 per 10,000 population

Newspapers: Blacksburg Times (weekly circulation 2800)

EAST GAFFNEY (CDP). Covers a land area of 3.056 square miles and a water area of 0.007 square miles. Located at 35.09° N. Lat; 81.62° W. Long. Elevation is 771 feet.

Population: 3,085; Growth (since 2000): -7.9%; Density: 1,009.6 persons per square mile; Race: 68.2% White, 25.6% Black/African American, 0.3% Asian, 0.4% American Indian/Alaska Native, 0.1% Native Hawaiian/Other Pacific Islander, 1.8% Two or more races, 5.5% Hispanic of any race; Average household size: 2.50; Median age: 37.0; Age under 18: 24.2%; Age 65 and over: 13.0%; Males per 100 females: 96.7; Marriage status: 37.4% never married, 32.1% now married, 5.6% separated, 12.8% widowed, 17.7% divorced; Foreign born: 6.3%; Speak English only: 91.6%; With disability: 16.9%; Veterans: 2.9%; Ancestry: 10.0% American, 8.8% English, 4.6% Irish, 3.1% German, 2.6% Scottish

Employment: 2.6% management, business, and financial, 2.2% computer, engineering, and science, 4.3% education, legal, community service, arts,

and media, 2.5% healthcare practitioners, 12.8% service, 28.2% sales and office, 11.6% natural resources, construction, and maintenance, 35.8% production, transportation, and material moving

Income: Per capita: $12,882; Median household: $22,024; Average household: $30,929; Households with income of $100,000 or more: 1.4%; Poverty rate: 35.4%

Educational Attainment: High school diploma or higher: 62.6%; Bachelor's degree or higher: 7.0%; Graduate/professional degree or higher: 1.8%

Housing: Homeownership rate: 58.9%; Median home value: $53,700; Median year structure built: 1969; Homeowner vacancy rate: 4.2%; Median gross rent: $531 per month; Rental vacancy rate: 13.5%

Health Insurance: 72.4% have insurance; 39.0% have private insurance; 43.4% have public insurance; 27.6% do not have insurance; 16.2% of children under 18 do not have insurance

Transportation: Commute: 97.3% car, 0.0% public transportation, 0.0% walk, 0.7% work from home; Median travel time to work: 15.9 minutes

---

GAFFNEY (city). County seat. Covers a land area of 8.324 square miles and a water area of 0.026 square miles. Located at 35.08° N. Lat; 81.66° W. Long. Elevation is 784 feet.

History: Previously called Gaffney's Old Field, the town was named for an Irishman, Michael Gaffney, who settled here in 1804. Soon promoters extolled the nearby Limestone Springs as therapeutic, a large hotel was built, and the community of Gaffney became a resort.

Population: 12,414; Growth (since 2000): -4.3%; Density: 1,491.3 persons per square mile; Race: 50.1% White, 45.7% Black/African American, 0.9% Asian, 0.2% American Indian/Alaska Native, 0.1% Native Hawaiian/Other Pacific Islander, 1.6% Two or more races, 3.1% Hispanic of any race; Average household size: 2.34; Median age: 38.6; Age under 18: 22.4%; Age 65 and over: 17.4%; Males per 100 females: 85.2; Marriage status: 43.2% never married, 36.8% now married, 4.9% separated, 8.7% widowed, 11.4% divorced; Foreign born: 2.1%; Speak English only: 95.1%; With disability: 17.1%; Veterans: 10.5%; Ancestry: 8.3% American, 5.5% German, 5.1% English, 3.4% Irish, 2.0% Scotch-Irish

Employment: 9.2% management, business, and financial, 2.5% computer, engineering, and science, 11.8% education, legal, community service, arts, and media, 1.7% healthcare practitioners, 18.1% service, 26.0% sales and office, 4.5% natural resources, construction, and maintenance, 26.3% production, transportation, and material moving

Income: Per capita: $18,549; Median household: $28,598; Average household: $43,952; Households with income of $100,000 or more: 9.0%; Poverty rate: 26.6%

Educational Attainment: High school diploma or higher: 77.9%; Bachelor's degree or higher: 18.6%; Graduate/professional degree or higher: 5.3%

School District(s)

Cherokee 01 (PK-12)
    2012-13 Enrollment: 9,033 . . . . (864) 206-2233

Four-year College(s)

Limestone College (Private, Not-for-profit)
    Fall 2013 Enrollment: 3,307 . . . . (800) 795-7151
    2013-14 Tuition: In-state $22,080; Out-of-state $22,080

Housing: Homeownership rate: 53.7%; Median home value: $86,800; Median year structure built: 1968; Homeowner vacancy rate: 4.2%; Median gross rent: $581 per month; Rental vacancy rate: 11.8%

Health Insurance: 84.3% have insurance; 56.1% have private insurance; 42.4% have public insurance; 15.7% do not have insurance; 6.6% of children under 18 do not have insurance

Hospitals: Novant Health Gaffney Medical Center (125 beds)

Safety: Violent crime rate: 52.1 per 10,000 population; Property crime rate: 297.4 per 10,000 population

Newspapers: Cherokee Chronicle Inc. (weekly circulation 7000); Gaffney Ledger (weekly circulation 9500)

Transportation: Commute: 92.9% car, 0.0% public transportation, 1.5% walk, 1.5% work from home; Median travel time to work: 15.4 minutes

Additional Information Contacts

City of Gaffney. . . . . (864) 487-6244
    http://www.getintogaffney-sc.com

Chester County

Located in northern South Carolina; bounded on the west by the Broad River, and on the east by the Catawba River; includes part of Sumter National Forest. Covers a land area of 580.657 square miles, a water area

of 5.507 square miles, and is located in the Eastern Time Zone at 34.69° N. Lat., 81.16° W. Long. The county was founded in 1785. County seat is Chester.

Chester County is part of the Charlotte-Concord-Gastonia, NC-SC Metropolitan Statistical Area. The entire metro area includes: Cabarrus County, NC; Gaston County, NC; Iredell County, NC; Lincoln County, NC; Mecklenburg County, NC; Rowan County, NC; Union County, NC; Chester County, SC; Lancaster County, SC; York County, SC

Weather Station: Chester 1 NW								Elevation: 520 feet			
	Jan	Feb	Mar	Apr	May	Jun	Jul	Aug	Sep	Oct	Nov	Dec
High	53	57	65	74	81	88	91	89	83	73	64	55
Low	29	31	38	45	54	64	68	67	60	47	38	31
Precip	4.1	3.7	4.4	3.3	2.9	4.2	3.9	4.7	3.7	3.4	3.6	3.5
Snow	1.0	0.5	0.5	0.0	0.0	0.0	0.0	0.0	0.0	0.0	0.0	0.1

High and Low temperatures in degrees Fahrenheit; Precipitation and Snow in inches

Population: 33,140; Growth (since 2000): -2.7%; Density: 57.1 persons per square mile; Race: 59.8% White, 37.4% Black/African American, 0.3% Asian, 0.4% American Indian/Alaska Native, 0.0% Native Hawaiian/Other Pacific Islander, 1.5% two or more races, 1.4% Hispanic of any race; Average household size: 2.56; Median age: 40.3; Age under 18: 23.9%; Age 65 and over: 14.6%; Males per 100 females: 93.6; Marriage status: 32.7% never married, 47.3% now married, 4.5% separated, 9.4% widowed, 10.6% divorced; Foreign born: 1.0%; Speak English only: 98.8%; With disability: 17.9%; Veterans: 10.5%; Ancestry: 18.8% American, 7.2% Irish, 5.6% English, 5.5% German, 5.1% African

Religion: Six largest groups: 24.1% Baptist, 15.8% Methodist/Pietist, 4.4% Presbyterian-Reformed, 2.9% Non-denominational Protestant, 2.9% Pentecostal, 1.4% Holiness

Economy: Unemployment rate: 8.2%; Leading industries: 18.8% retail trade; 15.2% other services (except public administration); 9.7% health care and social assistance; Farms: 477 totaling 95,506 acres; Company size: 0 employ 1,000 or more persons, 0 employ 500 to 999 persons, 11 employs 100 to 499 persons, 516 employ less than 100 persons; Business ownership: 396 women-owned, n/a Black-owned, n/a Hispanic-owned, n/a Asian-owned

Employment: 7.5% management, business, and financial, 2.6% computer, engineering, and science, 6.1% education, legal, community service, arts, and media, 4.4% healthcare practitioners, 15.9% service, 25.7% sales and office, 12.2% natural resources, construction, and maintenance, 25.6% production, transportation, and material moving

Income: Per capita: $18,098; Median household: $33,103; Average household: $45,683; Households with income of $100,000 or more: 9.0%; Poverty rate: 24.5%

Educational Attainment: High school diploma or higher: 78.0%; Bachelor's degree or higher: 12.4%; Graduate/professional degree or higher: 3.6%

Housing: Homeownership rate: 74.2%; Median home value: $82,500; Median year structure built: 1976; Homeowner vacancy rate: 2.1%; Median gross rent: $606 per month; Rental vacancy rate: 8.8%

Vital Statistics: Birth rate: 125.5 per 10,000 population; Death rate: 120.0 per 10,000 population; Age-adjusted cancer mortality rate: 243.6 deaths per 100,000 population

Health Insurance: 83.6% have insurance; 55.0% have private insurance; 41.3% have public insurance; 16.4% do not have insurance; 7.0% of children under 18 do not have insurance

Health Care: Physicians: 4.9 per 10,000 population; Hospital beds: 41.4 per 10,000 population; Hospital admissions: 551.0 per 10,000 population

Transportation: Commute: 93.5% car, 0.8% public transportation, 1.5% walk, 2.2% work from home; Median travel time to work: 31.0 minutes

Presidential Election: 54.8% Obama, 44.2% Romney (2012)

National and State Parks: Chester State Park; Landsford Canal State Park

Additional Information Contacts

Chester Government . . . . (803) 385-2605
    http://www.chestercounty.org

Chester County Communities

BLACKSTOCK (unincorporated postal area)

ZCTA: 29014
    Covers a land area of 164.590 square miles and a water area of 0.140 square miles. Located at 34.52° N. Lat; 81.11° W. Long. Elevation is 620 feet.

Population: 1,891; Growth (since 2000): 8.6%; Density: 11.5 persons per square mile; Race: 67.7% White, 30.2% Black/African American, 0.1% Asian, 0.3% American Indian/Alaska Native, 0.0% Native Hawaiian/Other Pacific Islander, 0.8% Two or more races, 1.7% Hispanic of any race; Average household size: 2.53; Median age: 42.8; Age under 18: 20.6%; Age 65 and over: 15.5%; Males per 100 females: 100.3

Housing: Homeownership rate: 85.3%; Homeowner vacancy rate: 1.4%; Rental vacancy rate: 6.0%

CHESTER (city). County seat. Covers a land area of 3.267 square miles and a water area of 0 square miles. Located at 34.70° N. Lat; 81.21° W. Long. Elevation is 541 feet.

History: Chester is one of three South Carolina towns named by settlers who came from Pennsylvania soon after 1755. In 1807, Aaron Burr, while under arrest for treason here, broke away from his guards, climbed on a big rock, and harangued a curious crowd before he was recaptured. In 1904, Dr. Gill Wylie, a native of Chester who became a prominent New York physician, helped to launch the hydroelectric development that brought many mills to the area.

Population: 5,607; Growth (since 2000): -13.4%; Density: 1,716.2 persons per square mile; Race: 31.9% White, 65.5% Black/African American, 0.2% Asian, 0.3% American Indian/Alaska Native, 0.1% Native Hawaiian/Other Pacific Islander, 1.7% Two or more races, 1.2% Hispanic of any race; Average household size: 2.53; Median age: 36.4; Age under 18: 27.0%; Age 65 and over: 13.6%; Males per 100 females: 91.9; Marriage status: 43.8% never married, 33.4% now married, 5.5% separated, 10.1% widowed, 12.7% divorced; Foreign born: 1.1%; Speak English only: 99.0%; With disability: 17.7%; Veterans: 9.1%; Ancestry: 10.5% American, 7.8% African, 4.7% English, 3.1% Irish, 2.7% German

Employment: 6.6% management, business, and financial, 1.0% computer, engineering, and science, 8.6% education, legal, community service, arts, and media, 4.3% healthcare practitioners, 23.2% service, 23.8% sales and office, 10.8% natural resources, construction, and maintenance, 21.7% production, transportation, and material moving

Income: Per capita: $14,529; Median household: $22,237; Average household: $36,295; Households with income of $100,000 or more: 6.7%; Poverty rate: 38.0%

Educational Attainment: High school diploma or higher: 75.7%; Bachelor's degree or higher: 15.9%; Graduate/professional degree or higher: 5.5%

School District(s)

Chester 01 (PK-12)
    2012-13 Enrollment: 5,520 . . . . (803) 385-6122

Housing: Homeownership rate: 55.3%; Median home value: $66,100; Median year structure built: 1967; Homeowner vacancy rate: 4.5%; Median gross rent: $544 per month; Rental vacancy rate: 13.3%

Health Insurance: 82.7% have insurance; 44.8% have private insurance; 51.9% have public insurance; 17.3% do not have insurance; 5.8% of children under 18 do not have insurance

Hospitals: Chester Regional Medical Center (182 beds)

Safety: Violent crime rate: 125.7 per 10,000 population; Property crime rate: 672.3 per 10,000 population

Newspapers: The News & Reporter (weekly circulation 7000)

Transportation: Commute: 91.3% car, 0.9% public transportation, 2.5% walk, 3.5% work from home; Median travel time to work: 25.5 minutes

Additional Information Contacts

City of Chester. . . . . (803) 581-2123
    http://www.chestersc.org

EDGEMOOR (unincorporated postal area)
ZCTA: 29712

Covers a land area of 27.909 square miles and a water area of 0.036 square miles. Located at 34.80° N. Lat; 80.98° W. Long. Elevation is 594 feet.

Population: 2,317; Growth (since 2000): -0.5%; Density: 83.0 persons per square mile; Race: 79.5% White, 17.7% Black/African American, 0.2% Asian, 0.9% American Indian/Alaska Native, 0.0% Native Hawaiian/Other Pacific Islander, 1.4% Two or more races, 1.3% Hispanic of any race; Average household size: 2.57; Median age: 42.8; Age under 18: 22.4%; Age 65 and over: 13.9%; Males per 100 females: 101.0

Housing: Homeownership rate: 85.3%; Homeowner vacancy rate: 1.2%; Rental vacancy rate: 6.9%

EUREKA MILL (CDP). Covers a land area of 1.291 square miles and a water area of 0 square miles. Located at 34.72° N. Lat; 81.19° W. Long. Elevation is 518 feet.

Population: 1,476; Growth (since 2000): -15.0%; Density: 1,143.4 persons per square mile; Race: 42.3% White, 56.0% Black/African American, 0.4% Asian, 0.1% American Indian/Alaska Native, 0.1% Native Hawaiian/Other Pacific Islander, 0.7% Two or more races, 0.7% Hispanic of any race; Average household size: 2.59; Median age: 38.1; Age under 18: 23.2%; Age 65 and over: 12.2%; Males per 100 females: 82.0

Housing: Homeownership rate: 66.4%; Homeowner vacancy rate: 4.0%; Rental vacancy rate: 8.9%

FORT LAWN (town). Covers a land area of 1.393 square miles and a water area of 0 square miles. Located at 34.70° N. Lat; 80.90° W. Long. Elevation is 531 feet.

History: Fort Lawn was named for the Fort family.

Population: 895; Growth (since 2000): 3.6%; Density: 642.7 persons per square mile; Race: 58.2% White, 38.4% Black/African American, 0.4% Asian, 0.7% American Indian/Alaska Native, 0.0% Native Hawaiian/Other Pacific Islander, 2.1% Two or more races, 1.0% Hispanic of any race; Average household size: 2.62; Median age: 36.3; Age under 18: 25.9%; Age 65 and over: 10.9%; Males per 100 females: 90.8

Housing: Homeownership rate: 65.5%; Homeowner vacancy rate: 1.8%; Rental vacancy rate: 9.2%

Safety: Violent crime rate: 34.4 per 10,000 population; Property crime rate: 367.4 per 10,000 population

GAYLE MILL (CDP). Covers a land area of 0.654 square miles and a water area of 0 square miles. Located at 34.70° N. Lat; 81.24° W. Long. Elevation is 466 feet.

Population: 913; Growth (since 2000): -16.5%; Density: 1,396.4 persons per square mile; Race: 42.1% White, 55.3% Black/African American, 0.5% Asian, 0.5% American Indian/Alaska Native, 0.0% Native Hawaiian/Other Pacific Islander, 1.2% Two or more races, 1.0% Hispanic of any race; Average household size: 2.56; Median age: 32.5; Age under 18: 29.9%; Age 65 and over: 11.2%; Males per 100 females: 84.1

Housing: Homeownership rate: 48.0%; Homeowner vacancy rate: 0.6%; Rental vacancy rate: 8.8%

GREAT FALLS (town). Covers a land area of 4.239 square miles and a water area of 0.140 square miles. Located at 34.57° N. Lat; 80.91° W. Long. Elevation is 466 feet.

History: In the early 1800's, Great Falls was an important power center, using the Catawba River as a source. The first cotton mill here was destroyed during the Civil War.

Population: 1,979; Growth (since 2000): -9.8%; Density: 466.9 persons per square mile; Race: 66.4% White, 31.3% Black/African American, 0.0% Asian, 0.0% American Indian/Alaska Native, 0.0% Native Hawaiian/Other Pacific Islander, 2.0% Two or more races, 0.8% Hispanic of any race; Average household size: 2.51; Median age: 37.0; Age under 18: 26.1%; Age 65 and over: 15.3%; Males per 100 females: 86.5

School District(s)

Chester 01 (PK-12)
    2012-13 Enrollment: 5,520 . . . . (803) 385-6122

Housing: Homeownership rate: 65.7%; Homeowner vacancy rate: 3.2%; Rental vacancy rate: 9.3%

Safety: Violent crime rate: 51.7 per 10,000 population; Property crime rate: 599.2 per 10,000 population

LANDO (unincorporated postal area)
ZCTA: 29724

Covers a land area of 0.248 square miles and a water area of 0 square miles. Located at 34.77° N. Lat; 81.01° W. Long. Elevation is 509 feet.

Population: 43; Growth (since 2000): -51.7%; Density: 173.3 persons per square mile; Race: 90.7% White, 2.3% Black/African American, 0.0% Asian, 0.0% American Indian/Alaska Native, 0.0% Native Hawaiian/Other Pacific Islander, 7.0% Two or more races, 0.0% Hispanic of any race; Average household size: 2.69; Median age: 35.5; Age under 18: 34.9%; Age 65 and over: 16.3%; Males per 100 females: 115.0

Housing: Homeownership rate: 6.3%; Homeowner vacancy rate: 0.0%; Rental vacancy rate: 0.0%

LOWRYS (town). Covers a land area of 3.161 square miles and a water area of 0 square miles. Located at 34.80° N. Lat; 81.24° W. Long. Elevation is 725 feet.
Population: 200; Growth (since 2000): -3.4%; Density: 63.3 persons per square mile; Race: 81.5% White, 16.5% Black/African American, 0.5% Asian, 0.0% American Indian/Alaska Native, 0.0% Native Hawaiian/Other Pacific Islander, 1.5% Two or more races, 2.5% Hispanic of any race; Average household size: 2.60; Median age: 40.5; Age under 18: 23.0%; Age 65 and over: 15.5%; Males per 100 females: 96.1
Housing: Homeownership rate: 76.6%; Homeowner vacancy rate: 1.7%; Rental vacancy rate: 0.0%

RICHBURG (town). Covers a land area of 0.876 square miles and a water area of 0 square miles. Located at 34.72° N. Lat; 81.02° W. Long. Elevation is 584 feet.
Population: 275; Growth (since 2000): -17.2%; Density: 313.8 persons per square mile; Race: 33.1% White, 66.2% Black/African American, 0.0% Asian, 0.0% American Indian/Alaska Native, 0.0% Native Hawaiian/Other Pacific Islander, 0.7% Two or more races, 0.0% Hispanic of any race; Average household size: 2.46; Median age: 45.6; Age under 18: 17.5%; Age 65 and over: 19.6%; Males per 100 females: 82.1
School District(s)
Chester 01 (PK-12)
　2012-13 Enrollment: 5,520 . . . . (803) 385-6122
Housing: Homeownership rate: 77.7%; Homeowner vacancy rate: 2.2%; Rental vacancy rate: 3.8%

Chesterfield County

Located in northern South Carolina; bounded on the east by the Pee Dee River, on the west by the Lynches River, and on the north by North Carolina. Covers a land area of 799.075 square miles, a water area of 6.670 square miles, and is located in the Eastern Time Zone at 34.64° N. Lat., 80.16° W. Long. The county was founded in 1798. County seat is Chesterfield.

Weather Station: Cheraw　　　　　　　　　　　　Elevation: 140 feet

	Jan	Feb	Mar	Apr	May	Jun	Jul	Aug	Sep	Oct	Nov	Dec
High	53	57	65	74	81	88	91	89	83	74	65	56
Low	31	33	39	47	56	65	70	69	62	49	40	33
Precip	3.7	3.1	4.0	2.8	3.0	4.7	5.1	5.5	3.9	3.7	2.9	3.1
Snow	0.4	0.3	0.4	0.0	0.0	0.0	0.0	0.0	0.0	0.0	0.0	tr

High and Low temperatures in degrees Fahrenheit; Precipitation and Snow in inches

Weather Station: Pageland　　　　　　　　　　　　Elevation: 620 feet

	Jan	Feb	Mar	Apr	May	Jun	Jul	Aug	Sep	Oct	Nov	Dec
High	55	59	67	75	82	88	91	90	84	75	66	57
Low	33	36	42	49	58	66	70	68	62	51	42	36
Precip	4.1	3.6	4.2	3.1	2.7	3.9	4.9	4.7	3.6	3.9	3.4	3.4
Snow	0.9	0.3	0.4	0.0	0.0	0.0	0.0	0.0	0.0	0.0	0.0	0.1

High and Low temperatures in degrees Fahrenheit; Precipitation and Snow in inches

Population: 46,734; Growth (since 2000): 9.3%; Density: 58.5 persons per square mile; Race: 62.8% White, 32.6% Black/African American, 0.4% Asian, 0.5% American Indian/Alaska Native, 0.0% Native Hawaiian/Other Pacific Islander, 1.6% two or more races, 3.6% Hispanic of any race; Average household size: 2.52; Median age: 39.3; Age under 18: 24.7%; Age 65 and over: 13.5%; Males per 100 females: 94.4; Marriage status: 29.5% never married, 51.1% now married, 4.1% separated, 8.2% widowed, 11.1% divorced; Foreign born: 2.3%; Speak English only: 96.5%; With disability: 15.1%; Veterans: 9.0%; Ancestry: 16.7% American, 6.8% Irish, 5.8% English, 5.6% German, 3.2% Scotch-Irish
Religion: Six largest groups: 25.8% Baptist, 14.5% Methodist/Pietist, 3.7% Pentecostal, 2.2% Presbyterian-Reformed, 1.2% Non-denominational Protestant, 1.0% Latter-day Saints
Economy: Unemployment rate: 7.3%; Leading industries: 20.1% retail trade; 13.1% health care and social assistance; 12.2% other services (except public administration); Farms: 717 totaling 131,021 acres; Company size: 0 employ 1,000 or more persons, 3 employ 500 to 999 persons, 17 employ 100 to 499 persons, 667 employ less than 100 persons; Business ownership: n/a women-owned, 497 Black-owned, 25 Hispanic-owned, n/a Asian-owned
Employment: 8.4% management, business, and financial, 1.4% computer, engineering, and science, 9.8% education, legal, community service, arts, and media, 3.6% healthcare practitioners, 17.0% service, 23.5% sales and office, 13.1% natural resources, construction, and maintenance, 23.3% production, transportation, and material moving
Income: Per capita: $17,140; Median household: $31,252; Average household: $42,640; Households with income of $100,000 or more: 8.8%; Poverty rate: 26.8%
Educational Attainment: High school diploma or higher: 74.9%; Bachelor's degree or higher: 12.6%; Graduate/professional degree or higher: 4.3%
Housing: Homeownership rate: 72.9%; Median home value: $79,400; Median year structure built: 1979; Homeowner vacancy rate: 1.7%; Median gross rent: $592 per month; Rental vacancy rate: 13.6%
Vital Statistics: Birth rate: 109.1 per 10,000 population; Death rate: 111.3 per 10,000 population; Age-adjusted cancer mortality rate: 180.3 deaths per 100,000 population
Health Insurance: 80.9% have insurance; 52.6% have private insurance; 39.1% have public insurance; 19.1% do not have insurance; 6.9% of children under 18 do not have insurance
Health Care: Physicians: 5.4 per 10,000 population; Hospital beds: 23.8 per 10,000 population; Hospital admissions: 950.6 per 10,000 population
Air Quality Index: 69.4% good, 30.6% moderate, 0.0% unhealthy for sensitive individuals, 0.0% unhealthy (percent of days)
Transportation: Commute: 92.7% car, 0.2% public transportation, 1.2% walk, 4.1% work from home; Median travel time to work: 23.9 minutes
Presidential Election: 48.0% Obama, 51.2% Romney (2012)
National and State Parks: Carolina Sandhills National Wildlife Refuge; Cheraw State Park; Sand Hills State Forest; Sandhills State Forest
Additional Information Contacts
Chesterfield Government . . . . (843) 623-2574
　http://www.chesterfieldcountysc.com

Chesterfield County Communities

CHERAW (town). Covers a land area of 5.422 square miles and a water area of 0.035 square miles. Located at 34.70° N. Lat; 79.90° W. Long. Elevation is 154 feet.
History: Cheraw was settled about 1752 by Welsh folk from Pennsylvania. When the Big Pee Dee River was opened for traffic, Cheraw's population and prosperity increased. An early resident here was Captain Moses Rogers, who in 1819 made the first transatlantic crossing using steam power in the sailing packet "Savannah."
Population: 5,851; Growth (since 2000): 5.9%; Density: 1,079.1 persons per square mile; Race: 40.2% White, 56.0% Black/African American, 0.6% Asian, 0.8% American Indian/Alaska Native, 0.0% Native Hawaiian/Other Pacific Islander, 1.8% Two or more races, 1.1% Hispanic of any race; Average household size: 2.36; Median age: 40.6; Age under 18: 26.0%; Age 65 and over: 18.6%; Males per 100 females: 78.2; Marriage status: 30.8% never married, 39.7% now married, 4.7% separated, 13.2% widowed, 16.3% divorced; Foreign born: 1.8%; Speak English only: 98.5%; With disability: 20.3%; Veterans: 12.9%; Ancestry: 12.9% American, 9.2% English, 4.0% Scottish, 3.1% Scotch-Irish, 3.0% Jamaican
Employment: 11.3% management, business, and financial, 0.0% computer, engineering, and science, 10.2% education, legal, community service, arts, and media, 4.4% healthcare practitioners, 24.7% service, 32.3% sales and office, 4.7% natural resources, construction, and maintenance, 12.4% production, transportation, and material moving
Income: Per capita: $18,581; Median household: $22,876; Average household: $37,479; Households with income of $100,000 or more: 6.3%; Poverty rate: 36.8%
Educational Attainment: High school diploma or higher: 73.1%; Bachelor's degree or higher: 19.5%; Graduate/professional degree or higher: 8.3%
School District(s)
Chesterfield 01 (PK-12)
　2012-13 Enrollment: 7,476 . . . . (843) 623-2175
Two-year College(s)
Northeastern Technical College (Public)
　Fall 2013 Enrollment: 1,153 . . . . (843) 921-6900
　2013-14 Tuition: In-state $3,846; Out-of-state $6,174
Housing: Homeownership rate: 51.2%; Median home value: $87,500; Median year structure built: 1965; Homeowner vacancy rate: 3.2%; Median gross rent: $470 per month; Rental vacancy rate: 7.7%
Health Insurance: 84.2% have insurance; 42.9% have private insurance; 57.5% have public insurance; 15.8% do not have insurance; 0.0% of children under 18 do not have insurance
Hospitals: Chesterfield General Hospital (59 beds)

Safety: Violent crime rate: 88.4 per 10,000 population; Property crime rate: 632.9 per 10,000 population
Newspapers: The Cheraw Chronicle (weekly circulation 8000)
Transportation: Commute: 89.7% car, 0.0% public transportation, 4.2% walk, 6.1% work from home; Median travel time to work: 10.6 minutes
Airports: Cheraw Municipal/Lynch Bellinger Field (general aviation)
Additional Information Contacts
Town of Cheraw . . . . (843) 537-8400
    http://www.cheraw.com

CHESTERFIELD (town). County seat. Covers a land area of 4.045
square miles and a water area of 0 square miles. Located at 34.73° N. Lat; 80.08° W. Long. Elevation is 292 feet.
History: Chesterfield was organized in 1798 and named for Lord Chesterfield. Most of its early citizens were Welsh Baptists from Delaware, or Scotch-Irish and English from other states.
Population: 1,472; Growth (since 2000): 11.7%; Density: 363.9 persons per square mile; Race: 59.4% White, 38.1% Black/African American, 0.6% Asian, 0.2% American Indian/Alaska Native, 0.0% Native Hawaiian/Other Pacific Islander, 0.7% Two or more races, 1.6% Hispanic of any race; Average household size: 2.32; Median age: 37.6; Age under 18: 23.3%; Age 65 and over: 14.9%; Males per 100 females: 97.8
School District(s)
Chesterfield 01 (PK-12)
    2012-13 Enrollment: 7,476 . . . . (843) 623-2175
Housing: Homeownership rate: 64.7%; Homeowner vacancy rate: 4.1%; Rental vacancy rate: 9.7%
Safety: Violent crime rate: 48.4 per 10,000 population; Property crime rate: 345.8 per 10,000 population
Additional Information Contacts
Town of Chesterfield . . . . (843) 623-2131
    http://www.chesterfield-sc.com

JEFFERSON (town). Covers a land area of 1.795 square miles and a
water area of 0.012 square miles. Located at 34.65° N. Lat; 80.38° W. Long. Elevation is 443 feet.
Population: 753; Growth (since 2000): 7.0%; Density: 419.4 persons per square mile; Race: 62.0% White, 30.9% Black/African American, 1.6% Asian, 0.0% American Indian/Alaska Native, 0.0% Native Hawaiian/Other Pacific Islander, 3.9% Two or more races, 1.5% Hispanic of any race; Average household size: 2.51; Median age: 37.8; Age under 18: 27.0%; Age 65 and over: 16.5%; Males per 100 females: 83.7
School District(s)
Chesterfield 01 (PK-12)
    2012-13 Enrollment: 7,476 . . . . (843) 623-2175
Housing: Homeownership rate: 69.2%; Homeowner vacancy rate: 0.5%; Rental vacancy rate: 8.0%

MCBEE (town). Covers a land area of 1.277 square miles and a water
area of 0 square miles. Located at 34.47° N. Lat; 80.26° W. Long. Elevation is 472 feet.
History: McBee came into existence in 1900 when a barbecue was held and lots sold at auction.
Population: 867; Growth (since 2000): 21.4%; Density: 678.9 persons per square mile; Race: 56.5% White, 40.4% Black/African American, 0.0% Asian, 0.6% American Indian/Alaska Native, 0.0% Native Hawaiian/Other Pacific Islander, 1.3% Two or more races, 2.7% Hispanic of any race; Average household size: 2.50; Median age: 38.2; Age under 18: 25.0%; Age 65 and over: 14.9%; Males per 100 females: 84.9
School District(s)
Chesterfield 01 (PK-12)
    2012-13 Enrollment: 7,476 . . . . (843) 623-2175
Housing: Homeownership rate: 75.9%; Homeowner vacancy rate: 2.2%; Rental vacancy rate: 8.7%
Safety: Violent crime rate: 11.7 per 10,000 population; Property crime rate: 408.4 per 10,000 population

MOUNT CROGHAN (town). Covers a land area of 0.759 square
miles and a water area of 0 square miles. Located at 34.77° N. Lat; 80.23° W. Long. Elevation is 446 feet.
Population: 195; Growth (since 2000): 25.8%; Density: 257.0 persons per square mile; Race: 82.1% White, 7.7% Black/African American, 0.0% Asian, 0.0% American Indian/Alaska Native, 0.0% Native Hawaiian/Other Pacific Islander, 4.6% Two or more races, 7.7% Hispanic of any race;

Average household size: 2.60; Median age: 40.4; Age under 18: 26.7%; Age 65 and over: 17.4%; Males per 100 females: 95.0
Housing: Homeownership rate: 81.4%; Homeowner vacancy rate: 3.1%; Rental vacancy rate: 6.3%

PAGELAND (town). Covers a land area of 4.368 square miles and a
water area of 0.043 square miles. Located at 34.77° N. Lat; 80.39° W. Long. Elevation is 650 feet.
History: Pageland was called Old Store until the Cheraw & Lancaster Railroad placed a depot here in 1904 and named the stop for the railroad president, S.H. Page.
Population: 2,760; Growth (since 2000): 9.5%; Density: 631.9 persons per square mile; Race: 52.5% White, 32.9% Black/African American, 0.7% Asian, 0.5% American Indian/Alaska Native, 0.0% Native Hawaiian/Other Pacific Islander, 2.1% Two or more races, 13.9% Hispanic of any race; Average household size: 2.55; Median age: 37.1; Age under 18: 23.7%; Age 65 and over: 14.7%; Males per 100 females: 97.6; Marriage status: 35.4% never married, 41.8% now married, 4.7% separated, 10.4% widowed, 12.4% divorced; Foreign born: 14.1%; Speak English only: 81.0%; With disability: 12.0%; Veterans: 3.6%; Ancestry: 13.4% American, 4.9% German, 4.8% Irish, 2.9% African, 2.8% English
Employment: 3.6% management, business, and financial, 0.2% computer, engineering, and science, 4.0% education, legal, community service, arts, and media, 2.2% healthcare practitioners, 28.4% service, 21.6% sales and office, 20.5% natural resources, construction, and maintenance, 19.4% production, transportation, and material moving
Income: Per capita: $14,788; Median household: $26,627; Average household: $34,850; Households with income of $100,000 or more: 6.2%; Poverty rate: 30.6%
Educational Attainment: High school diploma or higher: 71.7%; Bachelor's degree or higher: 7.6%; Graduate/professional degree or higher: 2.8%
School District(s)
Chesterfield 01 (PK-12)
    2012-13 Enrollment: 7,476 . . . . (843) 623-2175
Housing: Homeownership rate: 54.3%; Median home value: $91,600; Median year structure built: 1977; Homeowner vacancy rate: 3.0%; Median gross rent: $669 per month; Rental vacancy rate: 14.0%
Health Insurance: 69.3% have insurance; 42.1% have private insurance; 36.5% have public insurance; 30.7% do not have insurance; 21.6% of children under 18 do not have insurance
Safety: Violent crime rate: 95.7 per 10,000 population; Property crime rate: 622.2 per 10,000 population
Newspapers: Pageland Progressive-Journal (weekly circulation 3200)
Transportation: Commute: 79.0% car, 0.7% public transportation, 6.7% walk, 5.2% work from home; Median travel time to work: 23.7 minutes

PATRICK (town). Covers a land area of 0.959 square miles and a
water area of 0 square miles. Located at 34.58° N. Lat; 80.04° W. Long. Elevation is 220 feet.
Population: 351; Growth (since 2000): -0.8%; Density: 365.9 persons per square mile; Race: 75.5% White, 22.8% Black/African American, 0.0% Asian, 0.6% American Indian/Alaska Native, 0.0% Native Hawaiian/Other Pacific Islander, 1.1% Two or more races, 0.3% Hispanic of any race; Average household size: 2.15; Median age: 45.4; Age under 18: 17.4%; Age 65 and over: 20.5%; Males per 100 females: 85.7
School District(s)
Chesterfield 01 (PK-12)
    2012-13 Enrollment: 7,476 . . . . (843) 623-2175
Housing: Homeownership rate: 79.2%; Homeowner vacancy rate: 7.7%; Rental vacancy rate: 8.1%

RUBY (town). Covers a land area of 2.469 square miles and a water
area of <.001 square miles. Located at 34.75° N. Lat; 80.18° W. Long. Elevation is 384 feet.
Population: 360; Growth (since 2000): 3.4%; Density: 145.8 persons per square mile; Race: 90.6% White, 7.8% Black/African American, 0.0% Asian, 0.3% American Indian/Alaska Native, 0.0% Native Hawaiian/Other Pacific Islander, 0.3% Two or more races, 0.8% Hispanic of any race; Average household size: 2.43; Median age: 42.0; Age under 18: 25.6%; Age 65 and over: 18.1%; Males per 100 females: 82.7
School District(s)
Chesterfield 01 (PK-12)
    2012-13 Enrollment: 7,476 . . . . (843) 623-2175

Housing: Homeownership rate: 82.4%; Homeowner vacancy rate: 4.7%; Rental vacancy rate: 16.1%

Clarendon County

Located in eastern South Carolina; bounded on the south by Lake Marion; drained by the Black River. Covers a land area of 606.936 square miles, a water area of 88.713 square miles, and is located in the Eastern Time Zone at 33.66° N. Lat., 80.22° W. Long. The county was founded in 1855. County seat is Manning.

Weather Station: Manning										Elevation: 100 feet	
	Jan	Feb	Mar	Apr	May	Jun	Jul	Aug	Sep	Oct	Nov	Dec
High	57	61	69	78	85	91	93	92	86	77	69	60
Low	34	36	42	49	58	66	69	69	62	51	43	36
Precip	4.2	3.7	4.0	3.3	3.8	5.3	5.5	5.8	4.4	3.5	2.9	3.6
Snow	0.6	0.2	0.2	0.0	0.0	0.0	0.0	0.0	0.0	0.0	0.0	0.1

High and Low temperatures in degrees Fahrenheit; Precipitation and Snow in inches

Population: 34,971; Growth (since 2000): 7.6%; Density: 57.6 persons per square mile; Race: 47.0% White, 50.1% Black/African American, 0.6% Asian, 0.2% American Indian/Alaska Native, 0.0% Native Hawaiian/Other Pacific Islander, 0.8% two or more races, 2.6% Hispanic of any race; Average household size: 2.54; Median age: 41.4; Age under 18: 22.3%; Age 65 and over: 16.8%; Males per 100 females: 97.6; Marriage status: 34.5% never married, 48.0% now married, 5.0% separated, 8.5% widowed, 9.0% divorced; Foreign born: 1.5%; Speak English only: 96.6%; With disability: 22.0%; Veterans: 10.7%; Ancestry: 11.2% American, 7.2% Irish, 5.9% English, 5.4% German, 1.7% Scotch-Irish

Religion: Six largest groups: 16.2% Methodist/Pietist, 9.8% Baptist, 5.4% Non-denominational Protestant, 5.3% Presbyterian-Reformed, 2.4% Pentecostal, 1.0% Catholicism

Economy: Unemployment rate: 8.9%; Leading industries: 24.9% retail trade; 13.8% other services (except public administration); 11.7% accommodation and food services; Farms: 422 totaling 173,865 acres; Company size: 0 employ 1,000 or more persons, 1 employs 500 to 999 persons, 4 employ 100 to 499 persons, 489 employ less than 100 persons; Business ownership: 967 women-owned, 821 Black-owned, n/a Hispanic-owned, 51 Asian-owned

Employment: 10.1% management, business, and financial, 1.8% computer, engineering, and science, 10.4% education, legal, community service, arts, and media, 6.1% healthcare practitioners, 20.4% service, 22.1% sales and office, 9.3% natural resources, construction, and maintenance, 19.8% production, transportation, and material moving

Income: Per capita: $17,665; Median household: $31,410; Average household: $45,609; Households with income of $100,000 or more: 9.4%; Poverty rate: 24.9%

Educational Attainment: High school diploma or higher: 77.7%; Bachelor's degree or higher: 13.0%; Graduate/professional degree or higher: 4.7%

Housing: Homeownership rate: 74.7%; Median home value: $85,900; Median year structure built: 1987; Homeowner vacancy rate: 3.7%; Median gross rent: $584 per month; Rental vacancy rate: 9.3%

Vital Statistics: Birth rate: 99.5 per 10,000 population; Death rate: 101.3 per 10,000 population; Age-adjusted cancer mortality rate: 202.1 deaths per 100,000 population

Health Insurance: 79.8% have insurance; 50.2% have private insurance; 44.7% have public insurance; 20.2% do not have insurance; 10.4% of children under 18 do not have insurance

Health Care: Physicians: 9.3 per 10,000 population; Hospital beds: 16.2 per 10,000 population; Hospital admissions: 741.7 per 10,000 population

Transportation: Commute: 92.8% car, 0.3% public transportation, 2.1% walk, 3.4% work from home; Median travel time to work: 28.3 minutes

Presidential Election: 55.8% Obama, 43.4% Romney (2012)

National and State Parks: Santee National Wildlife Refuge

Additional Information Contacts

Clarendon Government . . . . (803) 435-4443
    http://www.clarendoncountygov.org

Clarendon County Communities

ALCOLU (CDP). Covers a land area of 4.549 square miles and a water area of 0.021 square miles. Located at 33.76° N. Lat; 80.22° W. Long. Elevation is 125 feet.

Population: 429; Growth (since 2000): n/a; Density: 94.3 persons per square mile; Race: 45.2% White, 52.0% Black/African American, 0.7% Asian, 0.0% American Indian/Alaska Native, 0.0% Native Hawaiian/Other Pacific Islander, 0.9% Two or more races, 3.3% Hispanic of any race; Average household size: 2.60; Median age: 39.5; Age under 18: 24.5%; Age 65 and over: 14.9%; Males per 100 females: 79.5

School District(s)

Clarendon 02 (PK-12)
    2012-13 Enrollment: 3,049 . . . . (803) 435-4435

Housing: Homeownership rate: 66.1%; Homeowner vacancy rate: 1.8%; Rental vacancy rate: 13.8%

GABLE (unincorporated postal area)
ZCTA: 29051

Covers a land area of 42.447 square miles and a water area of 0.097 square miles. Located at 33.86° N. Lat; 80.13° W. Long. Elevation is 105 feet.

Population: 951; Growth (since 2000): 9.6%; Density: 22.4 persons per square mile; Race: 40.2% White, 57.5% Black/African American, 0.0% Asian, 0.1% American Indian/Alaska Native, 0.0% Native Hawaiian/Other Pacific Islander, 1.2% Two or more races, 2.1% Hispanic of any race; Average household size: 2.77; Median age: 44.1; Age under 18: 23.4%; Age 65 and over: 17.2%; Males per 100 females: 88.3

Housing: Homeownership rate: 81.3%; Homeowner vacancy rate: 1.1%; Rental vacancy rate: 3.0%

MANNING (city). County seat. Covers a land area of 2.762 square miles and a water area of 0 square miles. Located at 33.69° N. Lat; 80.22° W. Long. Elevation is 128 feet.

History: Manning was named for Richard I. Manning, second of six South Carolina governors, all related, five of whom came from Clarendon County.

Population: 4,108; Growth (since 2000): 2.1%; Density: 1,487.6 persons per square mile; Race: 33.1% White, 62.7% Black/African American, 2.4% Asian, 0.1% American Indian/Alaska Native, 0.0% Native Hawaiian/Other Pacific Islander, 1.0% Two or more races, 1.9% Hispanic of any race; Average household size: 2.37; Median age: 39.2; Age under 18: 23.4%; Age 65 and over: 16.7%; Males per 100 females: 82.8; Marriage status: 38.6% never married, 40.0% now married, 5.1% separated, 12.4% widowed, 9.0% divorced; Foreign born: 1.0%; Speak English only: 99.0%; With disability: 27.9%; Veterans: 8.7%; Ancestry: 10.1% American, 6.7% Irish, 3.4% English, 2.3% German, 2.2% African

Employment: 9.7% management, business, and financial, 0.0% computer, engineering, and science, 9.0% education, legal, community service, arts, and media, 12.1% healthcare practitioners, 31.4% service, 22.1% sales and office, 2.9% natural resources, construction, and maintenance, 12.8% production, transportation, and material moving

Income: Per capita: $14,244; Median household: $20,761; Average household: $35,215; Households with income of $100,000 or more: 5.7%; Poverty rate: 35.4%

Educational Attainment: High school diploma or higher: 70.9%; Bachelor's degree or higher: 11.9%; Graduate/professional degree or higher: 5.2%

School District(s)

Clarendon 02 (PK-12)
    2012-13 Enrollment: 3,049 . . . . (803) 435-4435
Clarendon 80 (09-12)
    2012-13 Enrollment: n/a . . . . (843) 473-2531

Housing: Homeownership rate: 53.7%; Median home value: $86,600; Median year structure built: 1972; Homeowner vacancy rate: 4.0%; Median gross rent: $523 per month; Rental vacancy rate: 5.0%

Health Insurance: 79.6% have insurance; 45.3% have private insurance; 47.1% have public insurance; 20.4% do not have insurance; 13.4% of children under 18 do not have insurance

Hospitals: Clarendon Memorial Hospital (56 beds)

Safety: Violent crime rate: 143.8 per 10,000 population; Property crime rate: 1,023.8 per 10,000 population

Newspapers: Manning Times (weekly circulation 3700)

Transportation: Commute: 86.4% car, 0.0% public transportation, 8.3% walk, 3.7% work from home; Median travel time to work: 23.4 minutes
Additional Information Contacts
City of Manning . . . . (803) 435-8477
   http://www.cityofmanning.org

NEW ZION (unincorporated postal area)
ZCTA: 29111
   Covers a land area of 64.650 square miles and a water area of 0.041 square miles. Located at 33.79° N. Lat; 80.01° W. Long. Elevation is 102 feet.
   Population: 1,632; Growth (since 2000): -39.8%; Density: 25.2 persons per square mile; Race: 54.2% White, 44.4% Black/African American, 0.2% Asian, 0.4% American Indian/Alaska Native, 0.0% Native Hawaiian/Other Pacific Islander, 0.1% Two or more races, 1.4% Hispanic of any race; Average household size: 2.85; Median age: 37.3; Age under 18: 25.9%; Age 65 and over: 14.3%; Males per 100 females: 94.1

School District(s)
Clarendon 03 (PK-12)
   2012-13 Enrollment: 1,213 . . . . (843) 659-2188
   Housing: Homeownership rate: 80.8%; Homeowner vacancy rate: 1.3%; Rental vacancy rate: 6.8%

PAXVILLE (town). Covers a land area of 1.051 square miles and a water area of 0 square miles. Located at 33.74° N. Lat; 80.36° W. Long. Elevation is 184 feet.
Population: 185; Growth (since 2000): -25.4%; Density: 176.1 persons per square mile; Race: 54.1% White, 45.9% Black/African American, 0.0% Asian, 0.0% American Indian/Alaska Native, 0.0% Native Hawaiian/Other Pacific Islander, 0.0% Two or more races, 1.6% Hispanic of any race; Average household size: 2.68; Median age: 44.8; Age under 18: 19.5%; Age 65 and over: 18.4%; Males per 100 females: 88.8
Housing: Homeownership rate: 73.9%; Homeowner vacancy rate: 1.9%; Rental vacancy rate: 14.3%

SUMMERTON (town). Covers a land area of 1.283 square miles and a water area of 0 square miles. Located at 33.60° N. Lat; 80.35° W. Long. Elevation is 138 feet.
History: Summerton served as a place of refuge for residents of Charleston who had to flee from the Union forces.
Population: 1,000; Growth (since 2000): -5.7%; Density: 779.4 persons per square mile; Race: 34.9% White, 62.0% Black/African American, 1.4% Asian, 0.1% American Indian/Alaska Native, 0.1% Native Hawaiian/Other Pacific Islander, 0.5% Two or more races, 1.6% Hispanic of any race; Average household size: 2.23; Median age: 43.7; Age under 18: 22.1%; Age 65 and over: 19.6%; Males per 100 females: 75.4

School District(s)
Clarendon 01 (PK-12)
   2012-13 Enrollment: 831. . . . . (803) 485-2325
Housing: Homeownership rate: 60.8%; Homeowner vacancy rate: 2.5%; Rental vacancy rate: 8.8%
Safety: Violent crime rate: 102.9 per 10,000 population; Property crime rate: 535.0 per 10,000 population

TURBEVILLE (town). Covers a land area of 1.301 square miles and a water area of 0 square miles. Located at 33.89° N. Lat; 80.02° W. Long. Elevation is 128 feet.
Population: 766; Growth (since 2000): 27.2%; Density: 588.7 persons per square mile; Race: 60.7% White, 36.2% Black/African American, 0.5% Asian, 0.4% American Indian/Alaska Native, 0.0% Native Hawaiian/Other Pacific Islander, 0.4% Two or more races, 2.9% Hispanic of any race; Average household size: 2.47; Median age: 37.7; Age under 18: 26.4%; Age 65 and over: 14.0%; Males per 100 females: 94.9

School District(s)
Clarendon 03 (PK-12)
   2012-13 Enrollment: 1,213 . . . . (843) 659-2188
Dept of Correction N04 (09-12)
   2012-13 Enrollment: 752. . . . . (803) 896-8556
Housing: Homeownership rate: 55.4%; Homeowner vacancy rate: 2.3%; Rental vacancy rate: 7.9%
Safety: Violent crime rate: 24.5 per 10,000 population; Property crime rate: 343.1 per 10,000 population

Colleton County

Located in southern South Carolina; bounded on the northeast and east by the Edisto River, on the southwest by the Combahee River, and on the south by Saint Helena Sound. Covers a land area of 1,056.491 square miles, a water area of 76.795 square miles, and is located in the Eastern Time Zone at 32.83° N. Lat., 80.66° W. Long. The county was founded in 1798. County seat is Walterboro.
Population: 38,892; Growth (since 2000): 1.6%; Density: 36.8 persons per square mile; Race: 57.0% White, 39.0% Black/African American, 0.3% Asian, 0.8% American Indian/Alaska Native, 0.0% Native Hawaiian/Other Pacific Islander, 1.5% two or more races, 2.8% Hispanic of any race; Average household size: 2.54; Median age: 40.7; Age under 18: 24.4%; Age 65 and over: 15.6%; Males per 100 females: 93.1; Marriage status: 29.3% never married, 50.3% now married, 4.7% separated, 8.9% widowed, 11.5% divorced; Foreign born: 1.9%; Speak English only: 96.7%; With disability: 18.5%; Veterans: 13.8%; Ancestry: 23.7% American, 6.3% German, 6.2% English, 4.4% Irish, 1.4% Scotch-Irish
Religion: Six largest groups: 22.3% Baptist, 17.6% Methodist/Pietist, 6.3% Non-denominational Protestant, 2.0% Pentecostal, 1.7% Catholicism, 1.2% Other Groups
Economy: Unemployment rate: 6.8%; Leading industries: 20.9% retail trade; 9.5% health care and social assistance; 9.2% accommodation and food services; Farms: 530 totaling 187,722 acres; Company size: 0 employ 1,000 or more persons, 0 employ 500 to 999 persons, 10 employ 100 to 499 persons, 747 employ less than 100 persons; Business ownership: 765 women-owned, 666 Black-owned, n/a Hispanic-owned, n/a Asian-owned
Employment: 9.6% management, business, and financial, 2.0% computer, engineering, and science, 7.9% education, legal, community service, arts, and media, 5.2% healthcare practitioners, 20.5% service, 23.6% sales and office, 13.3% natural resources, construction, and maintenance, 17.8% production, transportation, and material moving
Income: Per capita: $18,769; Median household: $33,233; Average household: $47,044; Households with income of $100,000 or more: 9.2%; Poverty rate: 20.6%
Educational Attainment: High school diploma or higher: 78.8%; Bachelor's degree or higher: 14.7%; Graduate/professional degree or higher: 5.3%
Housing: Homeownership rate: 75.0%; Median home value: $89,900; Median year structure built: 1984; Homeowner vacancy rate: 2.3%; Median gross rent: $702 per month; Rental vacancy rate: 29.7%
Vital Statistics: Birth rate: 119.9 per 10,000 population; Death rate: 139.5 per 10,000 population; Age-adjusted cancer mortality rate: 205.7 deaths per 100,000 population
Health Insurance: 80.8% have insurance; 50.3% have private insurance; 43.7% have public insurance; 19.2% do not have insurance; 6.7% of children under 18 do not have insurance
Health Care: Physicians: 11.5 per 10,000 population; Hospital beds: 34.0 per 10,000 population; Hospital admissions: 1,167.9 per 10,000 population
Air Quality Index: 86.0% good, 14.0% moderate, 0.0% unhealthy for sensitive individuals, 0.0% unhealthy (percent of days)
Transportation: Commute: 94.6% car, 0.2% public transportation, 1.9% walk, 1.4% work from home; Median travel time to work: 33.4 minutes
Presidential Election: 49.6% Obama, 49.4% Romney (2012)
National and State Parks: Colleton State Park; Givhans Ferry State Park
Additional Information Contacts
Colleton Government . . . . (843) 549-5791
   http://www.colletoncounty.org

Colleton County Communities

COTTAGEVILLE (town). Covers a land area of 3.416 square miles and a water area of 0 square miles. Located at 32.94° N. Lat; 80.48° W. Long. Elevation is 46 feet.
Population: 762; Growth (since 2000): 7.8%; Density: 223.1 persons per square mile; Race: 89.2% White, 7.3% Black/African American, 0.5% Asian, 1.4% American Indian/Alaska Native, 0.0% Native Hawaiian/Other Pacific Islander, 1.4% Two or more races, 2.1% Hispanic of any race; Average household size: 2.43; Median age: 43.3; Age under 18: 21.4%; Age 65 and over: 15.0%; Males per 100 females: 90.5

School District(s)
Colleton 01 (PK-12)
   2012-13 Enrollment: 6,122 . . . . (843) 782-4525
Housing: Homeownership rate: 77.9%; Homeowner vacancy rate: 3.6%; Rental vacancy rate: 8.0%

Safety: Violent crime rate: 0.0 per 10,000 population; Property crime rate: 187.7 per 10,000 population

EDISTO BEACH (town).
Covers a land area of 2.127 square miles and a water area of 0.223 square miles. Located at 32.50° N. Lat; 80.31° W. Long. Elevation is 10 feet.

Population: 414; Growth (since 2000): -35.4%; Density: 194.7 persons per square mile; Race: 98.8% White, 1.0% Black/African American, 0.0% Asian, 0.0% American Indian/Alaska Native, 0.0% Native Hawaiian/Other Pacific Islander, 0.0% Two or more races, 0.5% Hispanic of any race; Average household size: 1.78; Median age: 63.8; Age under 18: 3.4%; Age 65 and over: 45.4%; Males per 100 females: 96.2

School District(s)
Colleton 01 (PK-12)
    2012-13 Enrollment: 6,122 . . . . (843) 782-4525
Housing: Homeownership rate: 89.7%; Homeowner vacancy rate: 7.9%; Rental vacancy rate: 97.6%
Safety: Violent crime rate: 0.0 per 10,000 population; Property crime rate: 1,605.8 per 10,000 population

EDISTO ISLAND (unincorporated postal area)
ZCTA: 29438
    Covers a land area of 74.662 square miles and a water area of 18.434 square miles. Located at 32.56° N. Lat; 80.32° W. Long..
Population: 2,408; Growth (since 2000): 4.7%; Density: 32.3 persons per square mile; Race: 63.7% White, 34.0% Black/African American, 0.0% Asian, 0.3% American Indian/Alaska Native, 0.0% Native Hawaiian/Other Pacific Islander, 0.5% Two or more races, 3.6% Hispanic of any race; Average household size: 2.26; Median age: 54.1; Age under 18: 15.6%; Age 65 and over: 25.4%; Males per 100 females: 95.8

School District(s)
Charleston 01 (PK-12)
    2012-13 Enrollment: 44,599 . . . . (843) 937-6318
    Housing: Homeownership rate: 83.2%; Homeowner vacancy rate: 4.5%; Rental vacancy rate: 86.8%

GREEN POND (unincorporated postal area)
ZCTA: 29446
    Covers a land area of 169.557 square miles and a water area of 23.637 square miles. Located at 32.63° N. Lat; 80.55° W. Long. Elevation is 30 feet.
Population: 1,138; Growth (since 2000): -19.4%; Density: 6.7 persons per square mile; Race: 24.6% White, 74.3% Black/African American, 0.0% Asian, 0.4% American Indian/Alaska Native, 0.0% Native Hawaiian/Other Pacific Islander, 0.6% Two or more races, 0.4% Hispanic of any race; Average household size: 2.53; Median age: 45.7; Age under 18: 20.7%; Age 65 and over: 15.8%; Males per 100 females: 93.9
Housing: Homeownership rate: 81.8%; Homeowner vacancy rate: 1.3%; Rental vacancy rate: 7.7%

ISLANDTON (CDP).
Covers a land area of 2.769 square miles and a water area of 0 square miles. Located at 32.91° N. Lat; 80.94° W. Long. Elevation is 62 feet.
Population: 70; Growth (since 2000): n/a; Density: 25.3 persons per square mile; Race: 62.9% White, 35.7% Black/African American, 0.0% Asian, 0.0% American Indian/Alaska Native, 0.0% Native Hawaiian/Other Pacific Islander, 0.0% Two or more races, 1.4% Hispanic of any race; Average household size: 2.00; Median age: 52.3; Age under 18: 10.0%; Age 65 and over: 22.9%; Males per 100 females: 70.7
Housing: Homeownership rate: 88.5%; Homeowner vacancy rate: 0.0%; Rental vacancy rate: 0.0%

JACKSONBORO (CDP).
Covers a land area of 14.465 square miles and a water area of 0 square miles. Located at 32.77° N. Lat; 80.48° W. Long. Elevation is 23 feet.
Population: 478; Growth (since 2000): n/a; Density: 33.0 persons per square mile; Race: 32.4% White, 66.5% Black/African American, 0.0% Asian, 0.0% American Indian/Alaska Native, 0.0% Native Hawaiian/Other Pacific Islander, 1.0% Two or more races, 0.6% Hispanic of any race; Average household size: 2.49; Median age: 43.8; Age under 18: 22.0%; Age 65 and over: 16.5%; Males per 100 females: 87.5
Housing: Homeownership rate: 81.3%; Homeowner vacancy rate: 0.6%; Rental vacancy rate: 2.6%

LODGE (town).
Covers a land area of 3.144 square miles and a water area of 0 square miles. Located at 33.07° N. Lat; 80.95° W. Long. Elevation is 108 feet.
Population: 120; Growth (since 2000): 5.3%; Density: 38.2 persons per square mile; Race: 80.8% White, 3.3% Black/African American, 0.0% Asian, 0.0% American Indian/Alaska Native, 0.0% Native Hawaiian/Other Pacific Islander, 0.0% Two or more races, 15.8% Hispanic of any race; Average household size: 2.26; Median age: 48.5; Age under 18: 18.3%; Age 65 and over: 14.2%; Males per 100 females: 122.2
Housing: Homeownership rate: 77.3%; Homeowner vacancy rate: 8.9%; Rental vacancy rate: 7.7%

ROUND O (unincorporated postal area)
ZCTA: 29474
    Covers a land area of 112.272 square miles and a water area of 0.110 square miles. Located at 32.88° N. Lat; 80.52° W. Long. Elevation is 36 feet.
Population: 2,176; Growth (since 2000): 19.9%; Density: 19.4 persons per square mile; Race: 68.2% White, 27.2% Black/African American, 0.3% Asian, 1.1% American Indian/Alaska Native, 0.0% Native Hawaiian/Other Pacific Islander, 2.3% Two or more races, 1.7% Hispanic of any race; Average household size: 2.50; Median age: 44.0; Age under 18: 22.2%; Age 65 and over: 16.0%; Males per 100 females: 90.4
Housing: Homeownership rate: 84.6%; Homeowner vacancy rate: 0.9%; Rental vacancy rate: 5.5%

RUFFIN (unincorporated postal area)
ZCTA: 29475
    Covers a land area of 107.243 square miles and a water area of 0.140 square miles. Located at 32.96° N. Lat; 80.81° W. Long. Elevation is 72 feet.
Population: 2,874; Growth (since 2000): 13.0%; Density: 26.8 persons per square mile; Race: 63.2% White, 33.0% Black/African American, 0.1% Asian, 0.3% American Indian/Alaska Native, 0.0% Native Hawaiian/Other Pacific Islander, 1.3% Two or more races, 4.3% Hispanic of any race; Average household size: 2.55; Median age: 41.4; Age under 18: 24.2%; Age 65 and over: 15.4%; Males per 100 females: 95.0; Marriage status: 21.6% never married, 62.4% now married, 7.5% separated, 6.9% widowed, 9.0% divorced; Foreign born: 3.2%; Speak English only: 95.8%; With disability: 28.1%; Veterans: 15.6%; Ancestry: 30.1% American, 11.4% English, 9.5% German, 3.2% Irish, 2.6% Italian
Employment: 3.1% management, business, and financial, 0.0% computer, engineering, and science, 7.9% education, legal, community service, arts, and media, 4.8% healthcare practitioners, 24.9% service, 20.7% sales and office, 19.7% natural resources, construction, and maintenance, 18.9% production, transportation, and material moving
Income: Per capita: $17,334; Median household: $27,245; Average household: $40,376; Households with income of $100,000 or more: 6.2%; Poverty rate: 23.8%
Educational Attainment: High school diploma or higher: 77.2%; Bachelor's degree or higher: 6.3%; Graduate/professional degree or higher: 2.2%

School District(s)
Colleton 01 (PK-12)
    2012-13 Enrollment: 6,122 . . . . (843) 782-4525
Housing: Homeownership rate: 79.7%; Median home value: $70,700; Median year structure built: 1981; Homeowner vacancy rate: 1.9%; Median gross rent: $630 per month; Rental vacancy rate: 10.8%
Health Insurance: 83.8% have insurance; 55.3% have private insurance; 47.9% have public insurance; 16.2% do not have insurance; 10.6% of children under 18 do not have insurance
Transportation: Commute: 95.1% car, 0.0% public transportation, 4.1% walk, 0.0% work from home; Median travel time to work: 29.3 minutes

SMOAKS (town).
Covers a land area of 1.630 square miles and a water area of 0 square miles. Located at 33.09° N. Lat; 80.81° W. Long. Elevation is 102 feet.
Population: 126; Growth (since 2000): -10.0%; Density: 77.3 persons per square mile; Race: 99.2% White, 0.0% Black/African American, 0.0% Asian, 0.8% American Indian/Alaska Native, 0.0% Native Hawaiian/Other Pacific Islander, 0.0% Two or more races, 0.0% Hispanic of any race; Average household size: 2.33; Median age: 41.0; Age under 18: 22.2%; Age 65 and over: 21.4%; Males per 100 females: 96.9

Housing: Homeownership rate: 79.6%; Homeowner vacancy rate: 2.3%; Rental vacancy rate: 8.3%

WALTERBORO (city). County seat. Covers a land area of 6.488 square miles and a water area of 0 square miles. Located at 32.90° N. Lat; 80.68° W. Long. Elevation is 69 feet.

History: Walterboro was settled early in the 18th century by rice planters. It was first named Ireland Creek. Two citizens, one named Walter and the other Smith, each insisted that the town be named for him. They ended the dispute by a tree-felling contest in which Smith was vanquished and the town became Walterboro.

Population: 5,398; Growth (since 2000): 4.8%; Density: 832.0 persons per square mile; Race: 45.2% White, 50.5% Black/African American, 1.0% Asian, 0.3% American Indian/Alaska Native, 0.0% Native Hawaiian/Other Pacific Islander, 1.5% Two or more races, 2.9% Hispanic of any race; Average household size: 2.38; Median age: 38.9; Age under 18: 25.8%; Age 65 and over: 17.9%; Males per 100 females: 80.3; Marriage status: 36.1% never married, 35.8% now married, 7.5% separated, 14.0% widowed, 14.1% divorced; Foreign born: 0.5%; Speak English only: 99.4%; With disability: 17.1%; Veterans: 12.0%; Ancestry: 8.7% American, 7.1% German, 6.0% Irish, 5.9% English, 4.3% Scotch-Irish

Employment: 6.6% management, business, and financial, 1.2% computer, engineering, and science, 9.0% education, legal, community service, arts, and media, 9.7% healthcare practitioners, 33.4% service, 26.3% sales and office, 6.7% natural resources, construction, and maintenance, 7.2% production, transportation, and material moving

Income: Per capita: $20,223; Median household: $24,135; Average household: $46,290; Households with income of $100,000 or more: 11.2%; Poverty rate: 30.1%

Educational Attainment: High school diploma or higher: 81.7%; Bachelor's degree or higher: 24.1%; Graduate/professional degree or higher: 11.0%

School District(s)

Colleton 01 (PK-12)
    2012-13 Enrollment: 6,122 . . . . (843) 782-4525

Vocational/Technical School(s)

Cosmetic Arts Institute (Private, For-profit)
    Fall 2013 Enrollment: 34 . . . . (843) 549-8587
    2013-14 Tuition: $16,400

Housing: Homeownership rate: 54.2%; Median home value: $131,200; Median year structure built: 1970; Homeowner vacancy rate: 4.3%; Median gross rent: $626 per month; Rental vacancy rate: 11.8%

Health Insurance: 86.9% have insurance; 47.5% have private insurance; 51.1% have public insurance; 13.1% do not have insurance; 6.6% of children under 18 do not have insurance

Hospitals: Colleton Medical Center (131 beds)

Safety: Violent crime rate: 87.1 per 10,000 population; Property crime rate: 1,037.7 per 10,000 population

Newspapers: Press & Standard (weekly circulation 29000); The Dispatch (weekly circulation 2100)

Transportation: Commute: 87.0% car, 1.4% public transportation, 4.4% walk, 3.6% work from home; Median travel time to work: 24.4 minutes

Airports: Lowcountry Regional (general aviation)

Additional Information Contacts

City of Walterboro . . . . (843) 549-2545
    http://www.walterborosc.org

WILLIAMS (town). Covers a land area of 0.847 square miles and a water area of 0 square miles. Located at 33.03° N. Lat; 80.84° W. Long. Elevation is 102 feet.

Population: 117; Growth (since 2000): 0.9%; Density: 138.1 persons per square mile; Race: 59.0% White, 31.6% Black/African American, 0.0% Asian, 0.0% American Indian/Alaska Native, 0.0% Native Hawaiian/Other Pacific Islander, 4.3% Two or more races, 6.0% Hispanic of any race; Average household size: 2.60; Median age: 51.1; Age under 18: 19.7%; Age 65 and over: 29.9%; Males per 100 females: 88.7

Housing: Homeownership rate: 73.3%; Homeowner vacancy rate: 0.0%; Rental vacancy rate: 0.0%

Darlington County

Located in northeastern South Carolina; bounded on the east by the Pee Dee River. Covers a land area of 561.153 square miles, a water area of 5.652 square miles, and is located in the Eastern Time Zone at 34.33° N.

Lat., 79.96° W. Long. The county was founded in 1785. County seat is Darlington.

Darlington County is part of the Florence, SC Metropolitan Statistical Area. The entire metro area includes: Darlington County, SC; Florence County, SC

Weather Station: Darlington   Elevation: 149 feet

	Jan	Feb	Mar	Apr	May	Jun	Jul	Aug	Sep	Oct	Nov	Dec
High	56	61	69	77	84	89	92	90	85	76	67	59
Low	34	37	43	50	59	67	71	70	63	52	43	36
Precip	3.8	3.3	4.2	2.7	3.3	4.5	5.0	5.5	4.0	3.4	2.8	3.2
Snow	0.1	tr	0.2	0.0	0.0	0.0	0.0	0.0	0.0	0.0	0.0	0.0

High and Low temperatures in degrees Fahrenheit; Precipitation and Snow in inches

Weather Station: Florence 8 NE   Elevation: 120 feet

	Jan	Feb	Mar	Apr	May	Jun	Jul	Aug	Sep	Oct	Nov	Dec
High	55	59	67	75	83	89	92	90	85	76	67	58
Low	33	35	42	50	59	67	71	69	63	51	42	35
Precip	3.9	3.2	4.1	2.9	3.6	4.2	5.1	5.6	4.0	3.4	3.1	3.5
Snow	tr	tr	0.4	0.0	0.0	0.0	0.0	0.0	0.0	0.0	0.0	0.1

High and Low temperatures in degrees Fahrenheit; Precipitation and Snow in inches

Population: 68,681; Growth (since 2000): 1.9%; Density: 122.4 persons per square mile; Race: 55.9% White, 41.6% Black/African American, 0.3% Asian, 0.3% American Indian/Alaska Native, 0.0% Native Hawaiian/Other Pacific Islander, 1.1% two or more races, 1.7% Hispanic of any race; Average household size: 2.54; Median age: 39.6; Age under 18: 24.3%; Age 65 and over: 14.3%; Males per 100 females: 90.1; Marriage status: 31.0% never married, 50.1% now married, 3.7% separated, 8.4% widowed, 10.5% divorced; Foreign born: 1.9%; Speak English only: 97.4%; With disability: 17.2%; Veterans: 9.2%; Ancestry: 10.8% American, 7.5% Irish, 6.5% English, 6.0% German, 2.3% Scottish

Religion: Six largest groups: 22.1% Baptist, 11.3% Methodist/Pietist, 4.0% Non-denominational Protestant, 2.2% Presbyterian-Reformed, 2.1% Pentecostal, 1.7% Other Groups

Economy: Unemployment rate: 7.5%; Leading industries: 20.8% retail trade; 13.6% other services (except public administration); 8.6% health care and social assistance; Farms: 385 totaling 176,848 acres; Company size: 0 employ 1,000 or more persons, 3 employ 500 to 999 persons, 31 employs 100 to 499 persons, 1,091 employs less than 100 persons; Business ownership: 1,347 women-owned, n/a Black-owned, n/a Hispanic-owned, n/a Asian-owned

Employment: 9.0% management, business, and financial, 3.2% computer, engineering, and science, 10.7% education, legal, community service, arts, and media, 5.0% healthcare practitioners, 18.4% service, 25.1% sales and office, 9.4% natural resources, construction, and maintenance, 19.2% production, transportation, and material moving

Income: Per capita: $20,105; Median household: $36,323; Average household: $50,535; Households with income of $100,000 or more: 10.4%; Poverty rate: 24.0%

Educational Attainment: High school diploma or higher: 79.2%; Bachelor's degree or higher: 17.0%; Graduate/professional degree or higher: 5.0%

Housing: Homeownership rate: 71.6%; Median home value: $87,200; Median year structure built: 1980; Homeowner vacancy rate: 2.4%; Median gross rent: $601 per month; Rental vacancy rate: 11.7%

Vital Statistics: Birth rate: 117.8 per 10,000 population; Death rate: 114.5 per 10,000 population; Age-adjusted cancer mortality rate: 216.1 deaths per 100,000 population

Health Insurance: 82.5% have insurance; 55.7% have private insurance; 38.7% have public insurance; 17.5% do not have insurance; 7.8% of children under 18 do not have insurance

Health Care: Physicians: 8.8 per 10,000 population; Hospital beds: 14.5 per 10,000 population; Hospital admissions: 779.6 per 10,000 population

Air Quality Index: 98.7% good, 1.3% moderate, 0.0% unhealthy for sensitive individuals, 0.0% unhealthy (percent of days)

Transportation: Commute: 94.1% car, 0.0% public transportation, 1.3% walk, 3.2% work from home; Median travel time to work: 22.9 minutes

Presidential Election: 51.3% Obama, 47.9% Romney (2012)

Additional Information Contacts

Darlington Government . . . . (843) 398-4330
    http://www.darcosc.com

Darlington County Communities

DARLINGTON (city). County seat. Covers a land area of 4.547 square miles and a water area of 0 square miles. Located at 34.30° N. Lat; 79.87° W. Long. Elevation is 151 feet.

History: Darlington was settled in 1798 and incorporated in 1835. A constable and two citizens were killed and others wounded in the Darlington War of 1894, an outbreak aroused by Governor B.R. Tillmans' liquor regulations permitting private homes to be searched without warrants.

Population: 6,289; Growth (since 2000): -6.4%; Density: 1,383.2 persons per square mile; Race: 37.9% White, 60.6% Black/African American, 0.4% Asian, 0.2% American Indian/Alaska Native, 0.0% Native Hawaiian/Other Pacific Islander, 0.7% Two or more races, 0.7% Hispanic of any race; Average household size: 2.32; Median age: 41.6; Age under 18: 23.8%; Age 65 and over: 19.0%; Males per 100 females: 76.5; Marriage status: 31.1% never married, 44.6% now married, 4.3% separated, 10.2% widowed, 14.1% divorced; Foreign born: 4.4%; Speak English only: 96.1%; With disability: 16.1%; Veterans: 8.0%; Ancestry: 9.6% Irish, 6.1% American, 5.4% English, 3.8% German, 2.7% Scotch-Irish

Employment: 10.2% management, business, and financial, 2.8% computer, engineering, and science, 17.2% education, legal, community service, arts, and media, 4.6% healthcare practitioners, 19.5% service, 24.8% sales and office, 4.7% natural resources, construction, and maintenance, 16.3% production, transportation, and material moving

Income: Per capita: $20,208; Median household: $27,270; Average household: $46,399; Households with income of $100,000 or more: 11.6%; Poverty rate: 32.6%

Educational Attainment: High school diploma or higher: 77.4%; Bachelor's degree or higher: 24.6%; Graduate/professional degree or higher: 10.8%

School District(s)
Darlington 01 (PK-12)
   2012-13 Enrollment: 10,269 . . . . (843) 398-2267

Housing: Homeownership rate: 52.2%; Median home value: $87,800; Median year structure built: 1968; Homeowner vacancy rate: 3.4%; Median gross rent: $546 per month; Rental vacancy rate: 7.7%

Health Insurance: 80.5% have insurance; 50.9% have private insurance; 41.4% have public insurance; 19.5% do not have insurance; 5.2% of children under 18 do not have insurance

Hospitals: Mcleod Medical Center - Darlington (49 beds)

Safety: Violent crime rate: 77.4 per 10,000 population; Property crime rate: 740.3 per 10,000 population

Newspapers: News & Press (weekly circulation 6000)

Transportation: Commute: 93.2% car, 0.0% public transportation, 1.3% walk, 3.5% work from home; Median travel time to work: 19.6 minutes

Airports: Darlington County Jetport (general aviation)

Additional Information Contacts
City of Darlington. . . . . (843) 398-4000
   http://darlingtonsconline.com

HARTSVILLE (city). Covers a land area of 5.723 square miles and a water area of 0.438 square miles. Located at 34.36° N. Lat; 80.08° W. Long. Elevation is 217 feet.

History: Hartsville was named for Thomas Edward Hart, on whose plantation the community developed. Here in 1866 Major James Lide Coker, connected with the Hart family through marriage, opened a store.

Population: 7,764; Growth (since 2000): 2.8%; Density: 1,356.7 persons per square mile; Race: 51.0% White, 46.3% Black/African American, 0.8% Asian, 0.2% American Indian/Alaska Native, 0.1% Native Hawaiian/Other Pacific Islander, 1.0% Two or more races, 1.5% Hispanic of any race; Average household size: 2.32; Median age: 36.7; Age under 18: 24.3%; Age 65 and over: 16.2%; Males per 100 females: 79.8; Marriage status: 38.2% never married, 38.5% now married, 4.5% separated, 13.5% widowed, 9.9% divorced; Foreign born: 2.6%; Speak English only: 97.3%; With disability: 20.0%; Veterans: 9.8%; Ancestry: 12.7% Irish, 8.8% German, 8.5% English, 7.5% American, 3.1% Scotch-Irish

Employment: 10.0% management, business, and financial, 7.6% computer, engineering, and science, 22.6% education, legal, community service, arts, and media, 3.7% healthcare practitioners, 19.7% service, 19.6% sales and office, 4.3% natural resources, construction, and maintenance, 12.7% production, transportation, and material moving

Income: Per capita: $24,365; Median household: $29,956; Average household: $58,737; Households with income of $100,000 or more: 13.5%; Poverty rate: 22.8%

Educational Attainment: High school diploma or higher: 84.0%; Bachelor's degree or higher: 30.8%; Graduate/professional degree or higher: 10.5%

School District(s)
Darlington 01 (PK-12)
   2012-13 Enrollment: 10,269 . . . . (843) 398-2267
Governor' School for Science and Mathematics (09-12)
   2012-13 Enrollment: 171. . . . . (843) 383-3900

Four-year College(s)
Coker College (Private, Not-for-profit)
   Fall 2013 Enrollment: 1,172 . . . . (843) 383-8000
   2013-14 Tuition: In-state $24,579; Out-of-state $24,579

Housing: Homeownership rate: 52.5%; Median home value: $112,000; Median year structure built: 1967; Homeowner vacancy rate: 8.4%; Median gross rent: $596 per month; Rental vacancy rate: 9.9%

Health Insurance: 83.5% have insurance; 56.4% have private insurance; 40.5% have public insurance; 16.5% do not have insurance; 8.8% of children under 18 do not have insurance

Hospitals: Carolina Pines Regional Medical Center (116 beds)

Safety: Violent crime rate: 110.4 per 10,000 population; Property crime rate: 1,005.5 per 10,000 population

Newspapers: The Messenger (weekly circulation 7500)

Transportation: Commute: 85.7% car, 0.0% public transportation, 4.7% walk, 6.5% work from home; Median travel time to work: 18.3 minutes

Additional Information Contacts
City of Hartsville . . . . (843) 383-3018
   http://www.hartsvillesc.com

LAMAR (town). Covers a land area of 1.170 square miles and a water area of 0 square miles. Located at 34.17° N. Lat; 80.06° W. Long. Elevation is 174 feet.

Population: 989; Growth (since 2000): -2.6%; Density: 845.1 persons per square mile; Race: 48.3% White, 49.4% Black/African American, 0.4% Asian, 0.6% American Indian/Alaska Native, 0.0% Native Hawaiian/Other Pacific Islander, 0.7% Two or more races, 0.7% Hispanic of any race; Average household size: 2.51; Median age: 43.1; Age under 18: 23.4%; Age 65 and over: 17.7%; Males per 100 females: 89.5

School District(s)
Darlington 01 (PK-12)
   2012-13 Enrollment: 10,269 . . . . (843) 398-2267

Housing: Homeownership rate: 76.2%; Homeowner vacancy rate: 1.3%; Rental vacancy rate: 13.5%

Safety: Violent crime rate: 51.1 per 10,000 population; Property crime rate: 368.1 per 10,000 population

LYDIA (CDP). Covers a land area of 2.643 square miles and a water area of 0 square miles. Located at 34.29° N. Lat; 80.12° W. Long. Elevation is 210 feet.

Population: 642; Growth (since 2000): n/a; Density: 242.9 persons per square mile; Race: 32.4% White, 65.7% Black/African American, 0.0% Asian, 0.0% American Indian/Alaska Native, 0.0% Native Hawaiian/Other Pacific Islander, 0.9% Two or more races, 2.0% Hispanic of any race; Average household size: 2.56; Median age: 39.1; Age under 18: 26.6%; Age 65 and over: 10.7%; Males per 100 females: 91.1

Housing: Homeownership rate: 82.5%; Homeowner vacancy rate: 3.2%; Rental vacancy rate: 10.0%

NORTH HARTSVILLE (CDP). Covers a land area of 4.562 square miles and a water area of 0.006 square miles. Located at 34.40° N. Lat; 80.07° W. Long. Elevation is 207 feet.

Population: 3,251; Growth (since 2000): 3.7%; Density: 712.6 persons per square mile; Race: 73.4% White, 22.6% Black/African American, 0.3% Asian, 0.7% American Indian/Alaska Native, 0.0% Native Hawaiian/Other Pacific Islander, 1.4% Two or more races, 3.3% Hispanic of any race; Average household size: 2.62; Median age: 39.9; Age under 18: 24.9%; Age 65 and over: 14.5%; Males per 100 females: 97.3; Marriage status: 33.7% never married, 50.9% now married, 3.1% separated, 4.6% widowed, 10.8% divorced; Foreign born: 4.8%; Speak English only: 94.5%; With disability: 21.0%; Veterans: 13.6%; Ancestry: 12.0% American, 8.6% German, 8.3% English, 2.7% Scotch-Irish, 2.0% Irish

Employment: 13.9% management, business, and financial, 3.3% computer, engineering, and science, 12.1% education, legal, community

service, arts, and media, 3.2% healthcare practitioners, 11.7% service, 16.5% sales and office, 12.5% natural resources, construction, and maintenance, 26.9% production, transportation, and material moving
Income: Per capita: $25,247; Median household: $43,409; Average household: $63,274; Households with income of $100,000 or more: 9.7%; Poverty rate: 19.0%
Educational Attainment: High school diploma or higher: 81.0%; Bachelor's degree or higher: 20.2%; Graduate/professional degree or higher: 5.3%
Housing: Homeownership rate: 75.8%; Median home value: $103,800; Median year structure built: 1978; Homeowner vacancy rate: 1.7%; Median gross rent: $552 per month; Rental vacancy rate: 7.0%
Health Insurance: 85.6% have insurance; 55.8% have private insurance; 41.8% have public insurance; 14.4% do not have insurance; 1.5% of children under 18 do not have insurance
Transportation: Commute: 92.5% car, 0.0% public transportation, 0.0% walk, 2.2% work from home; Median travel time to work: 26.1 minutes

SOCIETY HILL (town). Covers a land area of 2.192 square miles and a water area of 0 square miles. Located at 34.51° N. Lat; 79.85° W. Long. Elevation is 157 feet.
History: Society Hill was the core of the Welsh Neck settlement, a tract on both sides of the Big Pee Dee River granted by George II to Baptists from Delaware, who came here about 1736.
Population: 563; Growth (since 2000): -19.6%; Density: 256.8 persons per square mile; Race: 44.0% White, 52.0% Black/African American, 0.0% Asian, 0.7% American Indian/Alaska Native, 0.0% Native Hawaiian/Other Pacific Islander, 2.3% Two or more races, 2.1% Hispanic of any race; Average household size: 2.46; Median age: 43.1; Age under 18: 20.1%; Age 65 and over: 13.5%; Males per 100 females: 88.9
School District(s)
Darlington 01 (PK-12)
    2012-13 Enrollment: 10,269 . . . . (843) 398-2267
Housing: Homeownership rate: 73.8%; Homeowner vacancy rate: 2.3%; Rental vacancy rate: 17.7%

Dillon County

Located in northeastern South Carolina; bounded on the northeast by North Carolina; drained by the Little Pee Dee River. Covers a land area of 404.872 square miles, a water area of 1.720 square miles, and is located in the Eastern Time Zone at 34.39° N. Lat., 79.37° W. Long. The county was founded in 1910. County seat is Dillon.

Weather Station: Dillon   Elevation: 115 feet

	Jan	Feb	Mar	Apr	May	Jun	Jul	Aug	Sep	Oct	Nov	Dec
High	54	58	66	74	82	88	91	89	84	75	66	57
Low	32	35	40	48	57	66	71	69	63	51	41	34
Precip	3.6	3.2	4.0	3.1	3.3	4.4	5.2	5.1	4.1	3.2	3.1	3.0
Snow	0.7	0.2	0.5	0.0	0.0	0.0	0.0	0.0	0.0	0.0	0.0	0.2

High and Low temperatures in degrees Fahrenheit; Precipitation and Snow in inches

Population: 32,062; Growth (since 2000): 4.4%; Density: 79.2 persons per square mile; Race: 48.0% White, 46.1% Black/African American, 0.2% Asian, 2.5% American Indian/Alaska Native, 0.0% Native Hawaiian/Other Pacific Islander, 1.6% two or more races, 2.6% Hispanic of any race; Average household size: 2.65; Median age: 36.7; Age under 18: 26.7%; Age 65 and over: 13.0%; Males per 100 females: 88.8; Marriage status: 34.1% never married, 46.8% now married, 5.3% separated, 8.7% widowed, 10.4% divorced; Foreign born: 2.5%; Speak English only: 96.9%; With disability: 18.6%; Veterans: 8.8%; Ancestry: 14.8% American, 9.3% English, 5.0% Irish, 3.1% German, 2.0% Scotch-Irish
Religion: Six largest groups: 24.6% Baptist, 15.2% Methodist/Pietist, 7.5% Pentecostal, 3.6% Other Groups, 3.5% Non-denominational Protestant, 2.1% Presbyterian-Reformed
Economy: Unemployment rate: 9.3%; Leading industries: 24.6% retail trade; 13.6% other services (except public administration); 11.3% accommodation and food services; Farms: 228 totaling 106,749 acres; Company size: 1 employs 1,000 or more persons, 1 employs 500 to 999 persons, 16 employ 100 to 499 persons, 469 employ less than 100 persons; Business ownership: 332 women-owned, n/a Black-owned, n/a Hispanic-owned, n/a Asian-owned
Employment: 7.9% management, business, and financial, 0.9% computer, engineering, and science, 5.2% education, legal, community service, arts, and media, 5.1% healthcare practitioners, 20.8% service, 25.0% sales and

office, 12.1% natural resources, construction, and maintenance, 23.0% production, transportation, and material moving
Income: Per capita: $14,988; Median household: $28,817; Average household: $39,244; Households with income of $100,000 or more: 6.3%; Poverty rate: 31.5%
Educational Attainment: High school diploma or higher: 70.6%; Bachelor's degree or higher: 8.2%; Graduate/professional degree or higher: 2.9%
Housing: Homeownership rate: 66.3%; Median home value: $64,400; Median year structure built: 1979; Homeowner vacancy rate: 1.9%; Median gross rent: $546 per month; Rental vacancy rate: 10.8%
Vital Statistics: Birth rate: 133.2 per 10,000 population; Death rate: 111.8 per 10,000 population; Age-adjusted cancer mortality rate: 219.9 deaths per 100,000 population
Health Insurance: 81.8% have insurance; 45.5% have private insurance; 47.1% have public insurance; 18.2% do not have insurance; 4.1% of children under 18 do not have insurance
Health Care: Physicians: 7.6 per 10,000 population; Hospital beds: 19.9 per 10,000 population; Hospital admissions: 880.2 per 10,000 population
Transportation: Commute: 94.1% car, 1.1% public transportation, 1.6% walk, 2.6% work from home; Median travel time to work: 23.0 minutes
Presidential Election: 57.7% Obama, 41.6% Romney (2012)
National and State Parks: Little Pee Dee State Park
Additional Information Contacts
Dillon Government. . . . . (843) 774-5611
    http://www.dilloncounty.sc.gov

Dillon County Communities

DILLON (city). County seat. Covers a land area of 5.225 square miles and a water area of 0.011 square miles. Located at 34.42° N. Lat; 79.37° W. Long. Elevation is 112 feet.
History: Dillon was built up about 1887 when the Atlantic Coast Line Railroad came through. It was named for J.W. Dillon, an Irish immigrant and head of the local railroad movement.
Population: 6,788; Growth (since 2000): 7.5%; Density: 1,299.2 persons per square mile; Race: 42.8% White, 53.1% Black/African American, 0.6% Asian, 1.6% American Indian/Alaska Native, 0.0% Native Hawaiian/Other Pacific Islander, 1.2% Two or more races, 1.2% Hispanic of any race; Average household size: 2.51; Median age: 36.2; Age under 18: 27.4%; Age 65 and over: 16.2%; Males per 100 females: 85.8; Marriage status: 34.6% never married, 46.7% now married, 5.1% separated, 11.7% widowed, 7.1% divorced; Foreign born: 1.8%; Speak English only: 95.6%; With disability: 18.2%; Veterans: 10.0%; Ancestry: 9.8% American, 4.0% English, 4.0% German, 2.3% Irish, 1.8% Scottish
Employment: 11.4% management, business, and financial, 0.6% computer, engineering, and science, 7.4% education, legal, community service, arts, and media, 5.7% healthcare practitioners, 24.6% service, 19.6% sales and office, 9.7% natural resources, construction, and maintenance, 21.0% production, transportation, and material moving
Income: Per capita: $15,916; Median household: $26,503; Average household: $38,630; Households with income of $100,000 or more: 8.2%; Poverty rate: 37.5%
Educational Attainment: High school diploma or higher: 63.1%; Bachelor's degree or higher: 7.1%; Graduate/professional degree or higher: 2.1%
School District(s)
Dillon 04 (PK-12)
    2012-13 Enrollment: 4,287 . . . . (843) 774-1200
Dillon 80 (09-12)
    2012-13 Enrollment: n/a . . . . (843) 774-5143
Housing: Homeownership rate: 51.5%; Median home value: $102,700; Median year structure built: 1970; Homeowner vacancy rate: 3.0%; Median gross rent: $537 per month; Rental vacancy rate: 7.6%
Health Insurance: 85.3% have insurance; 43.7% have private insurance; 57.0% have public insurance; 14.7% do not have insurance; 6.5% of children under 18 do not have insurance
Hospitals: Mcleod Medical Center - Dillon (79 beds)
Safety: Violent crime rate: 161.5 per 10,000 population; Property crime rate: 1,273.6 per 10,000 population
Newspapers: Dillon Herald (weekly circulation 7400)
Transportation: Commute: 87.1% car, 5.5% public transportation, 2.6% walk, 3.7% work from home; Median travel time to work: 22.4 minutes; Amtrak: Train service available.

Additional Information Contacts
City of Dillon . . . . (843) 774-2227
   http://www.dilloncitysc.com

FORK (unincorporated postal area)
ZCTA: 29543

Covers a land area of 18.478 square miles and a water area of 0 square miles. Located at 34.29° N. Lat; 79.27° W. Long. Elevation is 98 feet.
Population: 606; Growth (since 2000): -8.7%; Density: 32.8 persons per square mile; Race: 72.6% White, 25.2% Black/African American, 0.0% Asian, 1.2% American Indian/Alaska Native, 0.0% Native Hawaiian/Other Pacific Islander, 0.7% Two or more races, 0.5% Hispanic of any race; Average household size: 2.23; Median age: 54.4; Age under 18: 12.7%; Age 65 and over: 30.4%; Males per 100 females: 87.6
Housing: Homeownership rate: 82.6%; Homeowner vacancy rate: 2.1%; Rental vacancy rate: 7.1%

HAMER (unincorporated postal area)
ZCTA: 29547

Covers a land area of 39.782 square miles and a water area of 0.083 square miles. Located at 34.50° N. Lat; 79.33° W. Long. Elevation is 148 feet.
Population: 2,917; Growth (since 2000): 14.7%; Density: 73.3 persons per square mile; Race: 47.1% White, 44.3% Black/African American, 0.2% Asian, 3.7% American Indian/Alaska Native, 0.1% Native Hawaiian/Other Pacific Islander, 2.0% Two or more races, 3.5% Hispanic of any race; Average household size: 2.95; Median age: 33.7; Age under 18: 29.4%; Age 65 and over: 8.4%; Males per 100 females: 92.9; Marriage status: 37.0% never married, 46.2% now married, 3.9% separated, 5.9% widowed, 10.8% divorced; Foreign born: 1.0%; Speak English only: 97.8%; With disability: 20.4%; Veterans: 6.1%; Ancestry: 12.0% American, 8.7% English, 4.4% Scotch-Irish, 3.2% Irish, 2.3% German
Employment: 5.9% management, business, and financial, 2.2% computer, engineering, and science, 1.3% education, legal, community service, arts, and media, 4.6% healthcare practitioners, 14.8% service, 17.6% sales and office, 19.5% natural resources, construction, and maintenance, 34.1% production, transportation, and material moving
Income: Per capita: $14,556; Median household: $32,595; Average household: $36,846; Households with income of $100,000 or more: 1.5%; Poverty rate: 28.2%
Educational Attainment: High school diploma or higher: 72.1%; Bachelor's degree or higher: 5.3%; Graduate/professional degree or higher: 2.3%
Housing: Homeownership rate: 75.8%; Median home value: $57,400; Median year structure built: 1980; Homeowner vacancy rate: 0.4%; Median gross rent: $630 per month; Rental vacancy rate: 19.3%
Health Insurance: 83.8% have insurance; 47.7% have private insurance; 45.8% have public insurance; 16.2% do not have insurance; 0.2% of children under 18 do not have insurance
Transportation: Commute: 98.3% car, 0.0% public transportation, 0.1% walk, 0.1% work from home; Median travel time to work: 26.7 minutes

LAKE VIEW (town).
Covers a land area of 1.688 square miles and a water area of <.001 square miles. Located at 34.34° N. Lat; 79.17° W. Long. Elevation is 89 feet.
History: Formerly called Pages Mill.
Population: 807; Growth (since 2000): 2.3%; Density: 478.2 persons per square mile; Race: 65.2% White, 33.0% Black/African American, 0.1% Asian, 0.5% American Indian/Alaska Native, 0.0% Native Hawaiian/Other Pacific Islander, 0.2% Two or more races, 1.5% Hispanic of any race; Average household size: 2.16; Median age: 49.5; Age under 18: 19.6%; Age 65 and over: 27.1%; Males per 100 females: 75.8
School District(s)
Dillon 04 (PK-12)
   2012-13 Enrollment: 4,287 . . . . (843) 774-1200
Housing: Homeownership rate: 62.4%; Homeowner vacancy rate: 3.6%; Rental vacancy rate: 8.5%
Safety: Violent crime rate: 50.5 per 10,000 population; Property crime rate: 530.3 per 10,000 population

LATTA (town).
Covers a land area of 1.096 square miles and a water area of 0 square miles. Located at 34.34° N. Lat; 79.43° W. Long. Elevation is 105 feet.
History: Latta preserves the name of the construction engineer who in 1888 had charge of the Atlantic Coast Line branch on which the town was laid out.
Population: 1,379; Growth (since 2000): -2.2%; Density: 1,258.5 persons per square mile; Race: 59.2% White, 38.4% Black/African American, 0.1% Asian, 0.4% American Indian/Alaska Native, 0.0% Native Hawaiian/Other Pacific Islander, 1.5% Two or more races, 1.2% Hispanic of any race; Average household size: 2.46; Median age: 41.0; Age under 18: 23.6%; Age 65 and over: 17.4%; Males per 100 females: 81.9
School District(s)
Dillon 03 (PK-12)
   2012-13 Enrollment: 1,648 . . . . (843) 752-7101
Housing: Homeownership rate: 68.0%; Homeowner vacancy rate: 2.8%; Rental vacancy rate: 2.7%
Safety: Violent crime rate: 274.3 per 10,000 population; Property crime rate: 719.1 per 10,000 population

LITTLE ROCK (unincorporated postal area)
ZCTA: 29567

Covers a land area of 21.336 square miles and a water area of 0.009 square miles. Located at 34.56° N. Lat; 79.43° W. Long. Elevation is 131 feet.
Population: 564; Growth (since 2000): -13.2%; Density: 26.4 persons per square mile; Race: 30.9% White, 43.6% Black/African American, 0.2% Asian, 18.8% American Indian/Alaska Native, 0.2% Native Hawaiian/Other Pacific Islander, 3.7% Two or more races, 5.3% Hispanic of any race; Average household size: 2.89; Median age: 35.5; Age under 18: 28.5%; Age 65 and over: 11.3%; Males per 100 females: 95.8
Housing: Homeownership rate: 66.1%; Homeowner vacancy rate: 2.3%; Rental vacancy rate: 12.0%

Dorchester County

Located in southeastern South Carolina; bounded on the west by the Eisto River; drained by the Ashley River. Covers a land area of 573.233 square miles, a water area of 2.573 square miles, and is located in the Eastern Time Zone at 33.08° N. Lat., 80.40° W. Long. The county was founded in 1868. County seat is Saint George.

Dorchester County is part of the Charleston-North Charleston, SC Metropolitan Statistical Area. The entire metro area includes: Berkeley County, SC; Charleston County, SC; Dorchester County, SC

Weather Station: Summerville   Elevation: 35 feet

	Jan	Feb	Mar	Apr	May	Jun	Jul	Aug	Sep	Oct	Nov	Dec
High	59	62	70	76	83	88	91	90	85	77	69	61
Low	35	37	43	49	59	67	71	70	65	53	44	37
Precip	4.3	3.2	4.0	3.4	3.4	5.7	6.0	6.6	5.5	3.9	3.3	3.3
Snow	0.1	0.1	0.0	0.0	0.0	0.0	0.0	0.0	0.0	0.0	0.0	0.3

High and Low temperatures in degrees Fahrenheit; Precipitation and Snow in inches

Population: 136,555; Growth (since 2000): 41.6%; Density: 238.2 persons per square mile; Race: 67.8% White, 25.8% Black/African American, 1.5% Asian, 0.7% American Indian/Alaska Native, 0.1% Native Hawaiian/Other Pacific Islander, 2.6% two or more races, 4.4% Hispanic of any race; Average household size: 2.68; Median age: 35.6; Age under 18: 27.1%; Age 65 and over: 10.1%; Males per 100 females: 94.6; Marriage status: 27.6% never married, 55.4% now married, 3.2% separated, 5.8% widowed, 11.1% divorced; Foreign born: 4.3%; Speak English only: 93.8%; With disability: 11.3%; Veterans: 14.5%; Ancestry: 17.5% American, 12.8% German, 10.8% Irish, 8.8% English, 3.6% Italian
Religion: Six largest groups: 14.6% Baptist, 11.2% Methodist/Pietist, 5.8% Catholicism, 3.5% Non-denominational Protestant, 1.1% Lutheran, 1.1% Latter-day Saints
Economy: Unemployment rate: 5.6%; Leading industries: 13.9% retail trade; 11.3% construction; 11.1% other services (except public administration); Farms: 411 totaling 74,529 acres; Company size: 1 employs 1,000 or more persons, 2 employ 500 to 999 persons, 26 employ 100 to 499 persons, 2,084 employ less than 100 persons; Business ownership: 2,866 women-owned, 1,516 Black-owned, 197 Hispanic-owned, n/a Asian-owned

Employment: 15.0% management, business, and financial, 5.5% computer, engineering, and science, 8.3% education, legal, community service, arts, and media, 5.4% healthcare practitioners, 17.1% service, 25.9% sales and office, 10.4% natural resources, construction, and maintenance, 12.3% production, transportation, and material moving
Income: Per capita: $24,495; Median household: $53,857; Average household: $65,457; Households with income of $100,000 or more: 20.1%; Poverty rate: 12.1%
Educational Attainment: High school diploma or higher: 89.4%; Bachelor's degree or higher: 24.5%; Graduate/professional degree or higher: 8.7%
Housing: Homeownership rate: 71.8%; Median home value: $167,400; Median year structure built: 1992; Homeowner vacancy rate: 2.7%; Median gross rent: $957 per month; Rental vacancy rate: 11.0%
Vital Statistics: Birth rate: 123.2 per 10,000 population; Death rate: 65.3 per 10,000 population; Age-adjusted cancer mortality rate: 179.3 deaths per 100,000 population
Health Insurance: 85.3% have insurance; 69.7% have private insurance; 26.7% have public insurance; 14.7% do not have insurance; 8.0% of children under 18 do not have insurance
Health Care: Physicians: 7.9 per 10,000 population; Hospital beds: 0.0 per 10,000 population; Hospital admissions: 0.0 per 10,000 population
Transportation: Commute: 93.5% car, 0.4% public transportation, 1.0% walk, 4.0% work from home; Median travel time to work: 28.1 minutes
Presidential Election: 41.2% Obama, 57.2% Romney (2012)
National and State Parks: Old Fort Dorchester State Historical Park
Additional Information Contacts
Dorchester Government . . . . (843) 563-0160
   http://www.dorchestercounty.net

Dorchester County Communities

DORCHESTER (unincorporated postal area)
ZCTA: 29437
   Covers a land area of 93.146 square miles and a water area of 0.262 square miles. Located at 33.14° N. Lat; 80.43° W. Long. Elevation is 105 feet.
   Population: 2,380; Growth (since 2000): 13.0%; Density: 25.6 persons per square mile; Race: 57.4% White, 40.0% Black/African American, 0.4% Asian, 0.4% American Indian/Alaska Native, 0.0% Native Hawaiian/Other Pacific Islander, 1.3% Two or more races, 2.2% Hispanic of any race; Average household size: 2.52; Median age: 43.2; Age under 18: 21.2%; Age 65 and over: 13.4%; Males per 100 females: 94.4
   School District(s)
Dorchester 04 (PK-12)
   2012-13 Enrollment: 2,208 . . . . (843) 563-5910
Dorchester 80 (09-12)
   2012-13 Enrollment: n/a . . . . (843) 563-2123
   Housing: Homeownership rate: 82.7%; Homeowner vacancy rate: 1.0%; Rental vacancy rate: 3.6%

HARLEYVILLE (town). Covers a land area of 1.152 square miles and a water area of 0 square miles. Located at 33.21° N. Lat; 80.45° W. Long. Elevation is 89 feet.
Population: 677; Growth (since 2000): 14.0%; Density: 587.7 persons per square mile; Race: 65.3% White, 32.2% Black/African American, 0.6% Asian, 0.4% American Indian/Alaska Native, 0.0% Native Hawaiian/Other Pacific Islander, 1.2% Two or more races, 1.3% Hispanic of any race; Average household size: 2.45; Median age: 37.2; Age under 18: 27.2%; Age 65 and over: 14.6%; Males per 100 females: 88.1
Housing: Homeownership rate: 63.2%; Homeowner vacancy rate: 0.6%; Rental vacancy rate: 6.5%
Safety: Violent crime rate: 114.9 per 10,000 population; Property crime rate: 704.0 per 10,000 population

REEVESVILLE (town). Covers a land area of 1.609 square miles and a water area of 0.019 square miles. Located at 33.20° N. Lat; 80.64° W. Long. Elevation is 108 feet.
Population: 196; Growth (since 2000): -5.3%; Density: 121.8 persons per square mile; Race: 82.1% White, 14.8% Black/African American, 0.5% Asian, 0.0% American Indian/Alaska Native, 0.0% Native Hawaiian/Other Pacific Islander, 2.6% Two or more races, 0.0% Hispanic of any race; Average household size: 2.33; Median age: 44.0; Age under 18: 21.9%; Age 65 and over: 21.9%; Males per 100 females: 79.8

Housing: Homeownership rate: 89.3%; Homeowner vacancy rate: 0.0%; Rental vacancy rate: 0.0%

RIDGEVILLE (town). Covers a land area of 1.796 square miles and a water area of 0 square miles. Located at 33.09° N. Lat; 80.31° W. Long. Elevation is 75 feet.
Population: 1,979; Growth (since 2000): 17.1%; Density: 1,101.7 persons per square mile; Race: 33.0% White, 63.8% Black/African American, 0.1% Asian, 0.6% American Indian/Alaska Native, 0.0% Native Hawaiian/Other Pacific Islander, 0.3% Two or more races, 2.5% Hispanic of any race; Average household size: 2.82; Median age: 36.1; Age under 18: 6.9%; Age 65 and over: 4.6%; Males per 100 females: 559.7
School District(s)
Dept of Correction N04 (09-12)
   2012-13 Enrollment: 752 . . . . (803) 896-8556
Dorchester 04 (PK-12)
   2012-13 Enrollment: 2,208 . . . . (843) 563-5910
Housing: Homeownership rate: 70.6%; Homeowner vacancy rate: 0.0%; Rental vacancy rate: 11.4%

SAINT GEORGE (town). County seat. Covers a land area of 2.703 square miles and a water area of 0 square miles. Located at 33.19° N. Lat; 80.58° W. Long. Elevation is 105 feet.
History: St. George was settled in 1788. Its name is an abbreviated form of St. George's Parish, in which the community began.
Population: 2,084; Growth (since 2000): -0.4%; Density: 771.0 persons per square mile; Race: 51.6% White, 46.7% Black/African American, 0.5% Asian, 0.3% American Indian/Alaska Native, 0.0% Native Hawaiian/Other Pacific Islander, 0.4% Two or more races, 0.8% Hispanic of any race; Average household size: 2.31; Median age: 41.3; Age under 18: 22.0%; Age 65 and over: 18.5%; Males per 100 females: 100.2
School District(s)
Dorchester 04 (PK-12)
   2012-13 Enrollment: 2,208 . . . . (843) 563-5910
Housing: Homeownership rate: 57.4%; Homeowner vacancy rate: 3.0%; Rental vacancy rate: 6.0%
Safety: Violent crime rate: 70.1 per 10,000 population; Property crime rate: 612.4 per 10,000 population
Newspapers: The Eagle-Record (weekly circulation 3100)

SUMMERVILLE (town). Covers a land area of 18.045 square miles and a water area of 0.113 square miles. Located at 33.01° N. Lat; 80.18° W. Long. Elevation is 72 feet.
History: Summerville was established as a winter resort.
Population: 43,392; Growth (since 2000): 56.4%; Density: 2,404.7 persons per square mile; Race: 72.1% White, 21.4% Black/African American, 1.5% Asian, 0.4% American Indian/Alaska Native, 0.1% Native Hawaiian/Other Pacific Islander, 2.9% Two or more races, 5.0% Hispanic of any race; Average household size: 2.55; Median age: 34.7; Age under 18: 27.0%; Age 65 and over: 10.5%; Males per 100 females: 89.2; Marriage status: 26.4% never married, 55.6% now married, 2.7% separated, 6.0% widowed, 12.0% divorced; Foreign born: 3.8%; Speak English only: 94.1%; With disability: 10.5%; Veterans: 15.2%; Ancestry: 17.4% German, 15.9% American, 13.5% Irish, 10.9% English, 4.9% Italian
Employment: 17.5% management, business, and financial, 4.9% computer, engineering, and science, 10.0% education, legal, community service, arts, and media, 5.6% healthcare practitioners, 18.0% service, 25.0% sales and office, 8.3% natural resources, construction, and maintenance, 10.7% production, transportation, and material moving
Income: Per capita: $25,766; Median household: $55,256; Average household: $66,765; Households with income of $100,000 or more: 20.5%; Poverty rate: 11.5%
Educational Attainment: High school diploma or higher: 93.0%; Bachelor's degree or higher: 29.9%; Graduate/professional degree or higher: 10.6%
School District(s)
Berkeley 01 (PK-12)
   2012-13 Enrollment: 30,942 . . . . (843) 899-8601
Dorchester 02 (PK-12)
   2012-13 Enrollment: 23,741 . . . . (843) 873-2901
Housing: Homeownership rate: 63.7%; Median home value: $180,600; Median year structure built: 1993; Homeowner vacancy rate: 2.7%; Median gross rent: $964 per month; Rental vacancy rate: 12.4%

Health Insurance: 85.2% have insurance; 72.1% have private insurance; 24.7% have public insurance; 14.8% do not have insurance; 8.5% of children under 18 do not have insurance

Safety: Violent crime rate: 23.0 per 10,000 population; Property crime rate: 341.3 per 10,000 population

Newspapers: Goose Creek Gazette (weekly circulation 13000); Journal-Scene (weekly circulation 9000)

Transportation: Commute: 93.3% car, 0.3% public transportation, 1.2% walk, 4.4% work from home; Median travel time to work: 28.0 minutes

Airports: Summerville (general aviation)

Additional Information Contacts

Town of Summerville . . . . (843) 871-6000
    http://www.summerville.sc.us

Edgefield County

Located in western South Carolina; bounded on the southwest by the Savannah River and the Georgia border; includes part of Sumter National Forest. Covers a land area of 500.406 square miles, a water area of 6.294 square miles, and is located in the Eastern Time Zone at 33.78° N. Lat., 81.97° W. Long. The county was founded in 1785. County seat is Edgefield.

Edgefield County is part of the Augusta-Richmond County, GA-SC Metropolitan Statistical Area. The entire metro area includes: Burke County, GA; Columbia County, GA; Lincoln County, GA; McDuffie County, GA; Richmond County, GA; Aiken County, SC; Edgefield County, SC

Weather Station: Johnston 4 SW   Elevation: 620 feet

	Jan	Feb	Mar	Apr	May	Jun	Jul	Aug	Sep	Oct	Nov	Dec
High	54	59	66	75	83	90	93	91	85	75	66	57
Low	31	34	40	47	55	64	67	66	61	49	40	33
Precip	4.2	4.2	4.9	3.0	3.1	4.6	4.1	4.8	3.9	3.4	3.4	3.5
Snow	0.8	0.5	0.2	0.0	0.0	0.0	0.0	0.0	0.0	0.0	0.0	0.1

High and Low temperatures in degrees Fahrenheit; Precipitation and Snow in inches

Population: 26,985; Growth (since 2000): 9.7%; Density: 53.9 persons per square mile; Race: 58.6% White, 37.2% Black/African American, 0.4% Asian, 0.2% American Indian/Alaska Native, 0.0% Native Hawaiian/Other Pacific Islander, 1.3% two or more races, 5.2% Hispanic of any race; Average household size: 2.56; Median age: 40.3; Age under 18: 21.4%; Age 65 and over: 13.1%; Males per 100 females: 117.3; Marriage status: 30.9% never married, 50.7% now married, 4.7% separated, 7.8% widowed, 10.6% divorced; Foreign born: 4.6%; Speak English only: 94.1%; With disability: 14.4%; Veterans: 10.2%; Ancestry: 15.9% American, 8.8% English, 7.4% Irish, 5.5% German, 2.7% Scotch-Irish

Religion: Six largest groups: 23.5% Baptist, 6.8% Catholicism, 4.6% Methodist/Pietist, 1.4% Lutheran, 0.9% Pentecostal, 0.7% Non-denominational Protestant

Economy: Unemployment rate: 7.2%; Leading industries: 17.1% retail trade; 15.6% other services (except public administration); 11.1% construction; Farms: 389 totaling 81,499 acres; Company size: 0 employ 1,000 or more persons, 1 employs 500 to 999 persons, 9 employ 100 to 499 persons, 305 employ less than 100 persons; Business ownership: n/a women-owned, n/a Black-owned, n/a Hispanic-owned, n/a Asian-owned

Employment: 8.8% management, business, and financial, 3.4% computer, engineering, and science, 7.8% education, legal, community service, arts, and media, 5.2% healthcare practitioners, 15.0% service, 23.2% sales and office, 14.6% natural resources, construction, and maintenance, 22.0% production, transportation, and material moving

Income: Per capita: $20,753; Median household: $43,861; Average household: $57,414; Households with income of $100,000 or more: 15.5%; Poverty rate: 19.9%

Educational Attainment: High school diploma or higher: 81.3%; Bachelor's degree or higher: 17.2%; Graduate/professional degree or higher: 5.8%

Housing: Homeownership rate: 76.1%; Median home value: $109,500; Median year structure built: 1985; Homeowner vacancy rate: 1.5%; Median gross rent: $597 per month; Rental vacancy rate: 8.0%

Vital Statistics: Birth rate: 65.8 per 10,000 population; Death rate: 87.4 per 10,000 population; Age-adjusted cancer mortality rate: 147.5 deaths per 100,000 population

Health Insurance: 85.8% have insurance; 62.2% have private insurance; 35.5% have public insurance; 14.2% do not have insurance; 7.9% of children under 18 do not have insurance

Health Care: Physicians: 9.9 per 10,000 population; Hospital beds: 9.4 per 10,000 population; Hospital admissions: 168.8 per 10,000 population

Air Quality Index: 81.6% good, 18.4% moderate, 0.0% unhealthy for sensitive individuals, 0.0% unhealthy (percent of days)

Transportation: Commute: 94.8% car, 0.6% public transportation, 0.8% walk, 2.7% work from home; Median travel time to work: 25.5 minutes

Presidential Election: 42.9% Obama, 56.2% Romney (2012)

Additional Information Contacts

Edgefield Government . . . . (803) 637-4080
    http://www.edgefieldcounty.sc.gov

Edgefield County Communities

EDGEFIELD (town). County seat. Covers a land area of 4.183 square miles and a water area of 0.116 square miles. Located at 33.79° N. Lat; 81.93° W. Long. Elevation is 531 feet.

History: From its beginnings in the 18th century, Edgefield was a center of political discussion and unrest. Nine state governors, five lieutenant governors, and numerous other leaders launched their political careers here.

Population: 4,750; Growth (since 2000): 6.8%; Density: 1,135.5 persons per square mile; Race: 38.9% White, 54.1% Black/African American, 0.4% Asian, 0.3% American Indian/Alaska Native, 0.1% Native Hawaiian/Other Pacific Islander, 2.4% Two or more races, 11.9% Hispanic of any race; Average household size: 2.24; Median age: 38.7; Age under 18: 13.5%; Age 65 and over: 12.0%; Males per 100 females: 228.9; Marriage status: 38.9% never married, 34.9% now married, 7.6% separated, 9.7% widowed, 16.4% divorced; Foreign born: 10.1%; Speak English only: 85.9%; With disability: 11.9%; Veterans: 8.4%; Ancestry: 7.8% American, 5.9% English, 4.8% Irish, 3.6% German, 3.0% African

Employment: 4.6% management, business, and financial, 1.8% computer, engineering, and science, 9.2% education, legal, community service, arts, and media, 2.0% healthcare practitioners, 18.4% service, 26.0% sales and office, 8.1% natural resources, construction, and maintenance, 29.9% production, transportation, and material moving

Income: Per capita: $12,195; Median household: $22,804; Average household: $41,890; Households with income of $100,000 or more: 7.2%; Poverty rate: 24.8%

Educational Attainment: High school diploma or higher: 75.7%; Bachelor's degree or higher: 8.9%; Graduate/professional degree or higher: 3.6%

School District(s)

Edgefield 01 (PK-12)
    2012-13 Enrollment: 3,508 . . . . (803) 275-4601

Housing: Homeownership rate: 50.4%; Median home value: $82,900; Median year structure built: 1967; Homeowner vacancy rate: 2.1%; Median gross rent: $561 per month; Rental vacancy rate: 7.2%

Health Insurance: 90.7% have insurance; 57.1% have private insurance; 44.1% have public insurance; 9.3% do not have insurance; 1.7% of children under 18 do not have insurance

Hospitals: Edgefield County Hospital (20 beds)

Safety: Violent crime rate: 23.6 per 10,000 population; Property crime rate: 100.6 per 10,000 population

Newspapers: Edgefield Advertiser (weekly circulation 2600); Edgefield Citizen-News (weekly circulation 3300)

Transportation: Commute: 95.0% car, 0.3% public transportation, 0.0% walk, 0.5% work from home; Median travel time to work: 17.9 minutes

Additional Information Contacts

Town of Edgefield . . . . (803) 637-4014
    http://www.edgefieldsc.net

JOHNSTON (town). Covers a land area of 2.648 square miles and a water area of 0.086 square miles. Located at 33.83° N. Lat; 81.80° W. Long. Elevation is 663 feet.

Population: 2,362; Growth (since 2000): 1.1%; Density: 892.1 persons per square mile; Race: 35.8% White, 62.7% Black/African American, 0.2% Asian, 0.1% American Indian/Alaska Native, 0.0% Native Hawaiian/Other Pacific Islander, 0.8% Two or more races, 1.8% Hispanic of any race; Average household size: 2.48; Median age: 41.8; Age under 18: 23.8%; Age 65 and over: 15.1%; Males per 100 females: 86.0

School District(s)

Edgefield 01 (PK-12)
    2012-13 Enrollment: 3,508 . . . . (803) 275-4601

Housing: Homeownership rate: 58.4%; Homeowner vacancy rate: 2.4%; Rental vacancy rate: 10.1%

Safety: Violent crime rate: 91.9 per 10,000 population; Property crime rate: 301.8 per 10,000 population

MURPHYS ESTATES (CDP). Covers a land area of 2.083 square miles and a water area of 0.003 square miles. Located at 33.60° N. Lat; 81.95° W. Long. Elevation is 571 feet.

Population: 1,441; Growth (since 2000): -5.1%; Density: 691.9 persons per square mile; Race: 89.6% White, 8.5% Black/African American, 0.5% Asian, 0.4% American Indian/Alaska Native, 0.0% Native Hawaiian/Other Pacific Islander, 0.6% Two or more races, 1.3% Hispanic of any race; Average household size: 2.86; Median age: 36.3; Age under 18: 25.0%; Age 65 and over: 11.8%; Males per 100 females: 92.6
Housing: Homeownership rate: 84.5%; Homeowner vacancy rate: 0.5%; Rental vacancy rate: 8.2%

TRENTON (town). Covers a land area of 1.261 square miles and a water area of 0.015 square miles. Located at 33.74° N. Lat; 81.84° W. Long. Elevation is 620 feet.

History: Trenton was the home of Benjamin R. Tillman (1847-1918), who introduced the commercial growing of asparagus and served as governor and U.S. senator.
Population: 196; Growth (since 2000): -13.3%; Density: 155.4 persons per square mile; Race: 65.8% White, 31.6% Black/African American, 0.0% Asian, 0.0% American Indian/Alaska Native, 0.0% Native Hawaiian/Other Pacific Islander, 0.0% Two or more races, 4.1% Hispanic of any race; Average household size: 2.00; Median age: 51.8; Age under 18: 16.8%; Age 65 and over: 19.9%; Males per 100 females: 98.0

School District(s)

Dept of Correction N04 (09-12)
    2012-13 Enrollment: 752 . . . . (803) 896-8556
Edgefield 01 (PK-12)
    2012-13 Enrollment: 3,508 . . . . (803) 275-4601
Housing: Homeownership rate: 67.4%; Homeowner vacancy rate: 0.0%; Rental vacancy rate: 5.9%

Fairfield County

Located in north central South Carolina; bounded on the west by the Broad River, and on the east by Wateree Pond; includes part of Sumter National Forest. Covers a land area of 686.277 square miles, a water area of 23.604 square miles, and is located in the Eastern Time Zone at 34.40° N. Lat., 81.13° W. Long. The county was founded in 1785. County seat is Winnsboro.

Fairfield County is part of the Columbia, SC Metropolitan Statistical Area. The entire metro area includes: Calhoun County, SC; Fairfield County, SC; Kershaw County, SC; Lexington County, SC; Richland County, SC; Saluda County, SC

Weather Station: Winnsboro										Elevation: 560 feet	
	Jan	Feb	Mar	Apr	May	Jun	Jul	Aug	Sep	Oct	Nov	Dec
High	53	58	66	74	82	89	91	89	83	74	65	55
Low	32	34	41	49	58	66	70	69	62	51	41	34
Precip	4.1	3.8	4.4	3.0	2.8	4.2	3.9	4.4	3.4	3.4	3.2	3.3
Snow	0.4	0.1	0.1	0.0	0.0	0.0	0.0	0.0	0.0	0.0	0.0	0.0

High and Low temperatures in degrees Fahrenheit; Precipitation and Snow in inches

Population: 23,956; Growth (since 2000): 2.1%; Density: 34.9 persons per square mile; Race: 38.6% White, 59.1% Black/African American, 0.2% Asian, 0.2% American Indian/Alaska Native, 0.0% Native Hawaiian/Other Pacific Islander, 1.1% two or more races, 1.6% Hispanic of any race; Average household size: 2.50; Median age: 42.4; Age under 18: 22.7%; Age 65 and over: 14.9%; Males per 100 females: 91.9; Marriage status: 32.0% never married, 48.0% now married, 4.6% separated, 9.2% widowed, 10.8% divorced; Foreign born: 1.8%; Speak English only: 96.6%; With disability: 17.2%; Veterans: 11.3%; Ancestry: 21.4% American, 4.8% English, 4.1% German, 3.5% Irish, 3.5% African
Religion: Six largest groups: 26.7% Baptist, 14.6% Methodist/Pietist, 5.7% Presbyterian-Reformed, 3.6% Non-denominational Protestant, 1.9% Latter-day Saints, 1.8% Pentecostal
Economy: Unemployment rate: 6.7%; Leading industries: 18.4% retail trade; 13.3% other services (except public administration); 9.2% health care and social assistance; Farms: 194 totaling 44,512 acres; Company size: 0 employ 1,000 or more persons, 1 employs 500 to 999 persons, 10 employ 100 to 499 persons, 283 employ less than 100 persons; Business

ownership: 391 women-owned, 374 Black-owned, n/a Hispanic-owned, n/a Asian-owned
Employment: 9.4% management, business, and financial, 2.7% computer, engineering, and science, 8.7% education, legal, community service, arts, and media, 4.0% healthcare practitioners, 19.8% service, 21.5% sales and office, 10.4% natural resources, construction, and maintenance, 23.5% production, transportation, and material moving
Income: Per capita: $20,257; Median household: $36,120; Average household: $48,165; Households with income of $100,000 or more: 10.8%; Poverty rate: 22.7%
Educational Attainment: High school diploma or higher: 81.4%; Bachelor's degree or higher: 15.5%; Graduate/professional degree or higher: 6.1%
Housing: Homeownership rate: 74.2%; Median home value: $91,900; Median year structure built: 1982; Homeowner vacancy rate: 2.0%; Median gross rent: $633 per month; Rental vacancy rate: 12.3%
Vital Statistics: Birth rate: 102.1 per 10,000 population; Death rate: 122.5 per 10,000 population; Age-adjusted cancer mortality rate: 196.3 deaths per 100,000 population
Health Insurance: 84.4% have insurance; 55.6% have private insurance; 39.4% have public insurance; 15.6% do not have insurance; 6.7% of children under 18 do not have insurance
Health Care: Physicians: 7.7 per 10,000 population; Hospital beds: 17.0 per 10,000 population; Hospital admissions: 513.1 per 10,000 population
Transportation: Commute: 94.2% car, 0.1% public transportation, 1.8% walk, 3.3% work from home; Median travel time to work: 28.2 minutes
Presidential Election: 65.4% Obama, 33.6% Romney (2012)
National and State Parks: Lake Wateree State Park
Additional Information Contacts
Fairfield Government . . . . (803) 712-6526
   http://www.fairfieldsc.com

Fairfield County Communities

BLAIR (unincorporated postal area)

ZCTA: 29015
   Covers a land area of 121.379 square miles and a water area of 9.225 square miles. Located at 34.44° N. Lat; 81.33° W. Long. Elevation is 387 feet.
   Population: 1,738; Growth (since 2000): -2.0%; Density: 14.3 persons per square mile; Race: 16.5% White, 82.6% Black/African American, 0.0% Asian, 0.5% American Indian/Alaska Native, 0.0% Native Hawaiian/Other Pacific Islander, 0.3% Two or more races, 0.3% Hispanic of any race; Average household size: 2.71; Median age: 42.2; Age under 18: 23.0%; Age 65 and over: 15.8%; Males per 100 females: 89.3

School District(s)

Fairfield 01 (PK-12)
   2012-13 Enrollment: 3,026 . . . . (803) 635-4607
   Housing: Homeownership rate: 81.4%; Homeowner vacancy rate: 0.8%; Rental vacancy rate: 15.6%

JENKINSVILLE (town). Covers a land area of 0.089 square miles and a water area of 0 square miles. Located at 34.31° N. Lat; 81.29° W. Long. Elevation is 466 feet.

Population: 46; Growth (since 2000): n/a; Density: 515.7 persons per square mile; Race: 0.0% White, 100.0% Black/African American, 0.0% Asian, 0.0% American Indian/Alaska Native, 0.0% Native Hawaiian/Other Pacific Islander, 0.0% Two or more races, 0.0% Hispanic of any race; Average household size: 2.42; Median age: 40.0; Age under 18: 23.9%; Age 65 and over: 19.6%; Males per 100 females: 91.7
Housing: Homeownership rate: 84.2%; Homeowner vacancy rate: 20.0%; Rental vacancy rate: 0.0%

RIDGEWAY (town). Covers a land area of 0.485 square miles and a water area of 0 square miles. Located at 34.31° N. Lat; 80.96° W. Long. Elevation is 614 feet.

Population: 319; Growth (since 2000): -2.7%; Density: 658.2 persons per square mile; Race: 53.3% White, 45.5% Black/African American, 0.0% Asian, 0.0% American Indian/Alaska Native, 0.0% Native Hawaiian/Other Pacific Islander, 0.6% Two or more races, 0.9% Hispanic of any race; Average household size: 2.33; Median age: 46.3; Age under 18: 21.3%; Age 65 and over: 16.9%; Males per 100 females: 87.6

School District(s)

Fairfield 01 (PK-12)
    2012-13 Enrollment: 3,026 . . . . (803) 635-4607
Housing: Homeownership rate: 70.8%; Homeowner vacancy rate: 3.0%; Rental vacancy rate: 7.0%

WINNSBORO (town). County seat. Covers a land area of 3.228

square miles and a water area of 0 square miles. Located at 34.37° N. Lat; 81.09° W. Long. Elevation is 535 feet.
History: Winnsboro was settled about 1755 and incorporated in 1785. It was named for Colonel Richard Winn, Revolutionary officer and early town father. The first settlers came from the coastal states. In 1780, when British troops occupied the settlement, Cornwallis's supposed comment on the outlying "fair fields" gave Fairfield County, of which Winnsboro was the seat, its name.
Population: 3,550; Growth (since 2000): -1.4%; Density: 1,099.8 persons per square mile; Race: 36.9% White, 60.6% Black/African American, 0.3% Asian, 0.2% American Indian/Alaska Native, 0.0% Native Hawaiian/Other Pacific Islander, 1.1% Two or more races, 2.0% Hispanic of any race; Average household size: 2.34; Median age: 40.0; Age under 18: 24.2%; Age 65 and over: 16.9%; Males per 100 females: 82.4; Marriage status: 43.2% never married, 39.6% now married, 6.0% separated, 8.2% widowed, 9.0% divorced; Foreign born: 5.2%; Speak English only: 90.9%; With disability: 11.4%; Veterans: 8.6%; Ancestry: 20.6% American, 4.2% Irish, 3.6% English, 3.2% Scotch-Irish, 1.2% European
Employment: 12.8% management, business, and financial, 0.0% computer, engineering, and science, 12.2% education, legal, community service, arts, and media, 1.0% healthcare practitioners, 32.6% service, 19.6% sales and office, 1.8% natural resources, construction, and maintenance, 20.1% production, transportation, and material moving
Income: Per capita: $18,596; Median household: $31,102; Average household: $42,611; Households with income of $100,000 or more: 9.0%; Poverty rate: 26.4%
Educational Attainment: High school diploma or higher: 87.7%; Bachelor's degree or higher: 14.0%; Graduate/professional degree or higher: 6.2%

School District(s)

Fairfield 01 (PK-12)
    2012-13 Enrollment: 3,026 . . . . (803) 635-4607
Housing: Homeownership rate: 55.5%; Median home value: $90,700; Median year structure built: 1972; Homeowner vacancy rate: 3.3%; Median gross rent: $598 per month; Rental vacancy rate: 16.0%
Health Insurance: 81.5% have insurance; 54.6% have private insurance; 40.6% have public insurance; 18.5% do not have insurance; 0.0% of children under 18 do not have insurance
Hospitals: Fairfield Memorial Hospital (25 beds)
Safety: Violent crime rate: 40.8 per 10,000 population; Property crime rate: 609.7 per 10,000 population
Newspapers: Herald-Independent (weekly circulation 5000)
Transportation: Commute: 89.2% car, 0.8% public transportation, 7.7% walk, 2.3% work from home; Median travel time to work: 25.7 minutes
Airports: Fairfield County (general aviation)
Additional Information Contacts
Town of Winnsboro . . . . (803) 635-4041
    http://www.townofwinnsboro.com

WINNSBORO MILLS (CDP). Covers a land area of 2.634 square

miles and a water area of 0 square miles. Located at 34.36° N. Lat; 81.07° W. Long. Elevation is 561 feet.
Population: 1,898; Growth (since 2000): -16.1%; Density: 720.6 persons per square mile; Race: 34.0% White, 57.9% Black/African American, 0.9% Asian, 0.4% American Indian/Alaska Native, 0.0% Native Hawaiian/Other Pacific Islander, 2.7% Two or more races, 6.6% Hispanic of any race; Average household size: 2.60; Median age: 35.1; Age under 18: 27.1%; Age 65 and over: 9.9%; Males per 100 females: 92.1
Housing: Homeownership rate: 49.8%; Homeowner vacancy rate: 2.7%; Rental vacancy rate: 18.0%

Florence County

Located in east central South Carolina; bounded on the east by the Pee Dee River; drained by the Lynches River. Covers a land area of 799.964 square miles, a water area of 3.761 square miles, and is located in the Eastern Time Zone at 34.03° N. Lat., 79.71° W. Long. The county was founded in 1888. County seat is Florence.

Florence County is part of the Florence, SC Metropolitan Statistical Area. The entire metro area includes: Darlington County, SC; Florence County, SC

Weather Station: Florence City County Arpt   Elevation: 145 feet

	Jan	Feb	Mar	Apr	May	Jun	Jul	Aug	Sep	Oct	Nov	Dec
High	56	60	68	76	83	89	91	90	85	76	67	58
Low	35	38	44	51	59	68	71	71	64	53	44	37
Precip	3.3	2.8	3.5	2.7	3.2	4.4	5.1	5.3	3.5	3.1	2.7	3.0
Snow	na	na	na	na	na	na	na	na	na	na	na	na

High and Low temperatures in degrees Fahrenheit; Precipitation and Snow in inches

Weather Station: Lake City 2 SE   Elevation: 75 feet

	Jan	Feb	Mar	Apr	May	Jun	Jul	Aug	Sep	Oct	Nov	Dec
High	57	60	68	76	83	89	92	90	85	76	69	59
Low	33	35	42	48	57	66	70	69	63	51	42	35
Precip	3.8	3.3	4.3	2.8	2.9	4.4	5.2	5.9	4.4	3.1	2.7	3.4
Snow	0.4	0.4	0.3	0.0	0.0	0.0	0.0	0.0	0.0	0.0	0.0	0.3

High and Low temperatures in degrees Fahrenheit; Precipitation and Snow in inches

Population: 136,885; Growth (since 2000): 8.8%; Density: 171.1 persons per square mile; Race: 54.9% White, 41.3% Black/African American, 1.2% Asian, 0.3% American Indian/Alaska Native, 0.0% Native Hawaiian/Other Pacific Islander, 1.1% two or more races, 2.2% Hispanic of any race; Average household size: 2.54; Median age: 37.6; Age under 18: 24.6%; Age 65 and over: 13.2%; Males per 100 females: 88.6; Marriage status: 33.6% never married, 48.5% now married, 3.9% separated, 8.1% widowed, 9.8% divorced; Foreign born: 2.6%; Speak English only: 96.3%; With disability: 16.0%; Veterans: 9.0%; Ancestry: 8.9% American, 7.5% Irish, 7.3% English, 6.5% German, 2.6% Scotch-Irish
Religion: Six largest groups: 22.4% Baptist, 10.6% Methodist/Pietist, 7.6% Non-denominational Protestant, 5.1% Pentecostal, 2.4% Catholicism, 1.8% Presbyterian-Reformed
Economy: Unemployment rate: 7.4%; Leading industries: 22.5% retail trade; 11.5% health care and social assistance; 10.8% other services (except public administration); Farms: 632 totaling 156,014 acres; Company size: 4 employ 1,000 or more persons, 8 employ 500 to 999 persons, 68 employ 100 to 499 persons, 3,022 employ less than 100 persons; Business ownership: 2,921 women-owned, 1,981 Black-owned, 110 Hispanic-owned, 234 Asian-owned
Employment: 11.8% management, business, and financial, 3.3% computer, engineering, and science, 11.0% education, legal, community service, arts, and media, 7.5% healthcare practitioners, 19.0% service, 26.1% sales and office, 7.8% natural resources, construction, and maintenance, 13.5% production, transportation, and material moving
Income: Per capita: $22,432; Median household: $41,910; Average household: $57,895; Households with income of $100,000 or more: 14.4%; Poverty rate: 19.8%
Educational Attainment: High school diploma or higher: 82.6%; Bachelor's degree or higher: 21.3%; Graduate/professional degree or higher: 8.0%
Housing: Homeownership rate: 67.5%; Median home value: $114,900; Median year structure built: 1982; Homeowner vacancy rate: 2.4%; Median gross rent: $647 per month; Rental vacancy rate: 11.1%
Vital Statistics: Birth rate: 131.6 per 10,000 population; Death rate: 101.7 per 10,000 population; Age-adjusted cancer mortality rate: 204.2 deaths per 100,000 population
Health Insurance: 85.3% have insurance; 59.4% have private insurance; 36.8% have public insurance; 14.7% do not have insurance; 5.1% of children under 18 do not have insurance
Health Care: Physicians: 28.5 per 10,000 population; Hospital beds: 84.3 per 10,000 population; Hospital admissions: 2,874.4 per 10,000 population
Air Quality Index: 67.7% good, 32.3% moderate, 0.0% unhealthy for sensitive individuals, 0.0% unhealthy (percent of days)
Transportation: Commute: 93.2% car, 0.4% public transportation, 1.1% walk, 4.1% work from home; Median travel time to work: 22.5 minutes
Presidential Election: 49.2% Obama, 49.8% Romney (2012)
National and State Parks: Lynches River State Park
Additional Information Contacts
Florence Government . . . . (843) 665-3031
    http://www.florenceco.org

Florence County Communities

COWARD (town). Covers a land area of 3.531 square miles and a water area of <.001 square miles. Located at 33.97° N. Lat; 79.75° W. Long. Elevation is 82 feet.
Population: 752; Growth (since 2000): 15.7%; Density: 212.9 persons per square mile; Race: 80.6% White, 14.1% Black/African American, 0.0% Asian, 0.7% American Indian/Alaska Native, 0.0% Native Hawaiian/Other Pacific Islander, 1.6% Two or more races, 4.4% Hispanic of any race; Average household size: 2.52; Median age: 35.1; Age under 18: 25.0%; Age 65 and over: 12.1%; Males per 100 females: 91.3

School District(s)
Florence 03 (PK-12)
    2012-13 Enrollment: 3,761 . . . . (843) 374-8652
Housing: Homeownership rate: 69.8%; Homeowner vacancy rate: 1.4%; Rental vacancy rate: 6.3%
Safety: Violent crime rate: 0.0 per 10,000 population; Property crime rate: 252.7 per 10,000 population

EFFINGHAM (unincorporated postal area)
ZCTA: 29541
    Covers a land area of 78.554 square miles and a water area of 0.049 square miles. Located at 34.06° N. Lat; 79.74° W. Long. Elevation is 102 feet.
Population: 9,465; Growth (since 2000): 17.3%; Density: 120.5 persons per square mile; Race: 56.9% White, 39.8% Black/African American, 0.5% Asian, 0.3% American Indian/Alaska Native, 0.0% Native Hawaiian/Other Pacific Islander, 1.2% Two or more races, 2.1% Hispanic of any race; Average household size: 2.64; Median age: 38.0; Age under 18: 24.0%; Age 65 and over: 10.4%; Males per 100 females: 100.3; Marriage status: 31.3% never married, 56.1% now married, 5.0% separated, 5.1% widowed, 7.5% divorced; Foreign born: 3.0%; Speak English only: 95.3%; With disability: 13.9%; Veterans: 6.4%; Ancestry: 10.3% American, 10.2% Irish, 8.9% German, 5.1% English, 2.1% Polish
Employment: 7.6% management, business, and financial, 1.5% computer, engineering, and science, 7.9% education, legal, community service, arts, and media, 7.0% healthcare practitioners, 17.2% service, 26.0% sales and office, 12.5% natural resources, construction, and maintenance, 20.3% production, transportation, and material moving
Income: Per capita: $23,049; Median household: $43,512; Average household: $62,018; Households with income of $100,000 or more: 11.4%; Poverty rate: 20.6%
Educational Attainment: High school diploma or higher: 79.2%; Bachelor's degree or higher: 12.4%; Graduate/professional degree or higher: 3.2%

School District(s)
Florence 01 (PK-12)
    2012-13 Enrollment: 16,146 . . . . (843) 673-1106
Housing: Homeownership rate: 80.1%; Median home value: $103,700; Median year structure built: 1990; Homeowner vacancy rate: 1.4%; Median gross rent: $629 per month; Rental vacancy rate: 9.1%
Health Insurance: 83.5% have insurance; 61.9% have private insurance; 32.0% have public insurance; 16.5% do not have insurance; 5.8% of children under 18 do not have insurance
Transportation: Commute: 92.1% car, 0.6% public transportation, 1.0% walk, 4.8% work from home; Median travel time to work: 26.3 minutes

FLORENCE (city). County seat. Covers a land area of 20.888 square miles and a water area of 0.046 square miles. Located at 34.18° N. Lat; 79.78° W. Long. Elevation is 138 feet.
History: Florence owes its existence to the eccentricity of Colonel Eli Gregg who, in the 1850's, owned the largest store at Mars bluff, seven miles eastward. Due to his prejudice against railroad workmen, Colonel Gregg refused to allow a depot in his neighborhood, and consequently the Wilmington & Manchester Railroad was forced to locate its station some distance away in an uninhabited forest of virgin pines. First called Wilds, the name was changed to Florence in 1859, in honor of the baby daughter of General William Harllee, head of the railroad. During the Civil War, Florence rose to importance as a shipping center and point of embarkation for troops, as a hospital town, and finally as a prison where some 8,000 Federal prisoners were held.
Population: 37,056; Growth (since 2000): 22.5%; Density: 1,774.0 persons per square mile; Race: 50.0% White, 46.0% Black/African American, 1.8% Asian, 0.3% American Indian/Alaska Native, 0.0% Native

Hawaiian/Other Pacific Islander, 1.3% Two or more races, 1.5% Hispanic of any race; Average household size: 2.43; Median age: 37.4; Age under 18: 24.5%; Age 65 and over: 13.9%; Males per 100 females: 83.5; Marriage status: 35.1% never married, 46.1% now married, 4.4% separated, 8.1% widowed, 10.7% divorced; Foreign born: 2.3%; Speak English only: 96.3%; With disability: 15.1%; Veterans: 9.4%; Ancestry: 8.4% American, 7.7% English, 7.4% German, 5.6% Irish, 3.6% Scotch-Irish
Employment: 13.9% management, business, and financial, 3.6% computer, engineering, and science, 14.1% education, legal, community service, arts, and media, 10.7% healthcare practitioners, 19.6% service, 24.3% sales and office, 4.2% natural resources, construction, and maintenance, 9.5% production, transportation, and material moving
Income: Per capita: $25,481; Median household: $41,663; Average household: $61,368; Households with income of $100,000 or more: 16.1%; Poverty rate: 19.5%
Educational Attainment: High school diploma or higher: 86.7%; Bachelor's degree or higher: 29.8%; Graduate/professional degree or higher: 12.2%

School District(s)
Darlington 01 (PK-12)
    2012-13 Enrollment: 10,269 . . . . (843) 398-2267
Florence 01 (PK-12)
    2012-13 Enrollment: 16,146 . . . . (843) 673-1106
Four-year College(s)
Francis Marion University (Public)
    Fall 2013 Enrollment: 4,058 . . . . (843) 661-1362
    2013-14 Tuition: In-state $9,386; Out-of-state $18,364
Two-year College(s)
Florence-Darlington Technical College (Public)
    Fall 2013 Enrollment: 5,991 . . . . (843) 661-8324
    2013-14 Tuition: In-state $4,100; Out-of-state $5,934
Virginia College-Florence (Private, For-profit)
    Fall 2013 Enrollment: 458 . . . . (843) 407-2200
    2013-14 Tuition: In-state $13,429; Out-of-state $13,429
Vocational/Technical School(s)
Kenneth Shuler School of Cosmetology-Florence (Private, For-profit)
    Fall 2013 Enrollment: 146 . . . . (843) 679-3778
    2013-14 Tuition: $16,750
Housing: Homeownership rate: 59.9%; Median home value: $148,700; Median year structure built: 1976; Homeowner vacancy rate: 3.4%; Median gross rent: $659 per month; Rental vacancy rate: 10.4%
Health Insurance: 87.4% have insurance; 62.1% have private insurance; 37.0% have public insurance; 12.6% do not have insurance; 4.3% of children under 18 do not have insurance
Hospitals: Carolinas Hospital System (420 beds); Mcleod Regional Medical Center - Pee Dee (371 beds)
Safety: Violent crime rate: 77.9 per 10,000 population; Property crime rate: 780.6 per 10,000 population
Newspapers: Morning News (daily circulation 30600); The News Journal (weekly circulation 26000)
Transportation: Commute: 91.7% car, 1.0% public transportation, 0.8% walk, 4.5% work from home; Median travel time to work: 19.1 minutes; Amtrak: Train service available.
Airports: Florence Regional (primary service/non-hub)
Additional Information Contacts
City of Florence . . . . (843) 665-3113
    http://www.cityofflorence.com

JOHNSONVILLE (city). Covers a land area of 2.058 square miles and a water area of 0.028 square miles. Located at 33.81° N. Lat; 79.44° W. Long. Elevation is 89 feet.
History: Johnsonville, first established as a crossroads settlement, was laid out and sold in town lots in the early 1900's. Its nickname was Ashboro, because everything in town was said to have burned at one time or another.
Population: 1,480; Growth (since 2000): 4.4%; Density: 719.0 persons per square mile; Race: 74.1% White, 21.8% Black/African American, 1.6% Asian, 0.2% American Indian/Alaska Native, 0.3% Native Hawaiian/Other Pacific Islander, 1.4% Two or more races, 2.6% Hispanic of any race; Average household size: 2.62; Median age: 37.8; Age under 18: 26.4%; Age 65 and over: 14.4%; Males per 100 females: 90.7

School District(s)
Florence 05 (PK-12)
    2012-13 Enrollment: 1,468 . . . . (843) 386-2358

Housing: Homeownership rate: 77.4%; Homeowner vacancy rate: 1.6%; Rental vacancy rate: 18.5%
Safety: Violent crime rate: 20.0 per 10,000 population; Property crime rate: 193.6 per 10,000 population

LAKE CITY (city). Covers a land area of 5.223 square miles and a water area of 0.008 square miles. Located at 33.87° N. Lat; 79.75° W. Long. Elevation is 75 feet.

History: Lake City takes its name from Lake Swamp, a nearby lagoon of the Lynches River.
Population: 6,675; Growth (since 2000): 3.0%; Density: 1,278.1 persons per square mile; Race: 19.4% White, 77.5% Black/African American, 0.3% Asian, 0.3% American Indian/Alaska Native, 0.0% Native Hawaiian/Other Pacific Islander, 0.9% Two or more races, 3.0% Hispanic of any race; Average household size: 2.63; Median age: 34.0; Age under 18: 29.2%; Age 65 and over: 13.8%; Males per 100 females: 82.2; Marriage status: 39.0% never married, 41.6% now married, 5.8% separated, 12.9% widowed, 6.5% divorced; Foreign born: 0.2%; Speak English only: 98.7%; With disability: 24.6%; Veterans: 9.5%; Ancestry: 5.3% English, 3.8% American, 3.6% Scotch-Irish, 2.5% Irish, 1.6% Haitian
Employment: 8.1% management, business, and financial, 0.0% computer, engineering, and science, 10.5% education, legal, community service, arts, and media, 3.1% healthcare practitioners, 24.8% service, 29.8% sales and office, 7.1% natural resources, construction, and maintenance, 16.7% production, transportation, and material moving
Income: Per capita: $17,002; Median household: $30,174; Average household: $44,663; Households with income of $100,000 or more: 7.9%; Poverty rate: 27.8%
Educational Attainment: High school diploma or higher: 72.1%; Bachelor's degree or higher: 12.5%; Graduate/professional degree or higher: 2.9%
School District(s)
Florence 03 (PK-12)
    2012-13 Enrollment: 3,761 . . . . (843) 374-8652
Sc Public Charter SD (PK-12)
    2012-13 Enrollment: 11,500 . . . . (803) 734-8322
Housing: Homeownership rate: 53.9%; Median home value: $83,100; Median year structure built: 1970; Homeowner vacancy rate: 2.6%; Median gross rent: $601 per month; Rental vacancy rate: 7.7%
Health Insurance: 85.8% have insurance; 48.0% have private insurance; 47.2% have public insurance; 14.2% do not have insurance; 0.0% of children under 18 do not have insurance
Hospitals: Lake City Community Hospital (48 beds)
Safety: Violent crime rate: 101.1 per 10,000 population; Property crime rate: 875.7 per 10,000 population
Newspapers: Lake City News & Post (weekly circulation 3300)
Transportation: Commute: 90.0% car, 1.3% public transportation, 5.0% walk, 3.7% work from home; Median travel time to work: 20.2 minutes
Additional Information Contacts
City of Lake City . . . . (843) 374-8611
    http://www.lakecitysc.orgindex.php

OLANTA (town). Covers a land area of 0.995 square miles and a water area of 0.004 square miles. Located at 33.94° N. Lat; 79.93° W. Long. Elevation is 112 feet.

Population: 563; Growth (since 2000): -8.2%; Density: 566.0 persons per square mile; Race: 58.4% White, 37.8% Black/African American, 0.4% Asian, 0.0% American Indian/Alaska Native, 0.0% Native Hawaiian/Other Pacific Islander, 1.8% Two or more races, 2.1% Hispanic of any race; Average household size: 2.51; Median age: 42.7; Age under 18: 24.2%; Age 65 and over: 21.3%; Males per 100 females: 78.2
School District(s)
Florence 03 (PK-12)
    2012-13 Enrollment: 3,761 . . . . (843) 374-8652
Vocational/Technical School(s)
Jolei's Hair Institute (Private, For-profit)
    Fall 2013 Enrollment: 41 . . . . (843) 396-9010
    2013-14 Tuition: $14,265
Housing: Homeownership rate: 68.3%; Homeowner vacancy rate: 10.9%; Rental vacancy rate: 14.3%

PAMPLICO (town). Covers a land area of 1.607 square miles and a water area of 0.011 square miles. Located at 34.00° N. Lat; 79.57° W. Long. Elevation is 82 feet.

Population: 1,226; Growth (since 2000): 7.6%; Density: 762.8 persons per square mile; Race: 40.2% White, 55.7% Black/African American, 0.2% Asian, 0.3% American Indian/Alaska Native, 0.0% Native Hawaiian/Other Pacific Islander, 1.2% Two or more races, 3.5% Hispanic of any race; Average household size: 2.68; Median age: 35.6; Age under 18: 29.1%; Age 65 and over: 14.0%; Males per 100 females: 82.7
School District(s)
Florence 02 (PK-12)
    2012-13 Enrollment: 1,215 . . . . (843) 493-2502
Housing: Homeownership rate: 58.0%; Homeowner vacancy rate: 1.1%; Rental vacancy rate: 5.0%

QUINBY (town). Covers a land area of 1.348 square miles and a water area of 0 square miles. Located at 34.23° N. Lat; 79.74° W. Long. Elevation is 118 feet.

Population: 932; Growth (since 2000): 10.7%; Density: 691.4 persons per square mile; Race: 29.8% White, 68.3% Black/African American, 0.1% Asian, 0.0% American Indian/Alaska Native, 0.0% Native Hawaiian/Other Pacific Islander, 1.6% Two or more races, 0.3% Hispanic of any race; Average household size: 2.52; Median age: 45.6; Age under 18: 22.4%; Age 65 and over: 19.7%; Males per 100 females: 91.4
Housing: Homeownership rate: 83.8%; Homeowner vacancy rate: 2.5%; Rental vacancy rate: 13.0%

SCRANTON (town). Covers a land area of 0.844 square miles and a water area of 0 square miles. Located at 33.92° N. Lat; 79.74° W. Long. Elevation is 95 feet.

Population: 932; Growth (since 2000): -1.1%; Density: 1,104.8 persons per square mile; Race: 39.3% White, 58.5% Black/African American, 0.1% Asian, 0.3% American Indian/Alaska Native, 0.0% Native Hawaiian/Other Pacific Islander, 1.2% Two or more races, 1.7% Hispanic of any race; Average household size: 2.66; Median age: 40.6; Age under 18: 23.5%; Age 65 and over: 18.8%; Males per 100 females: 79.2
School District(s)
Florence 03 (PK-12)
    2012-13 Enrollment: 3,761 . . . . (843) 374-8652
Housing: Homeownership rate: 61.0%; Homeowner vacancy rate: 2.0%; Rental vacancy rate: 4.6%
Safety: Violent crime rate: 0.0 per 10,000 population; Property crime rate: 166.1 per 10,000 population

TIMMONSVILLE (town). Covers a land area of 2.589 square miles and a water area of 0 square miles. Located at 34.13° N. Lat; 79.94° W. Long. Elevation is 148 feet.

History: Timmonsville was the birthplace and home of Melvin Purvis, one of the "G-men" who ran down Dillinger.
Population: 2,320; Growth (since 2000): 0.2%; Density: 896.2 persons per square mile; Race: 16.6% White, 81.8% Black/African American, 0.6% Asian, 0.2% American Indian/Alaska Native, 0.0% Native Hawaiian/Other Pacific Islander, 0.6% Two or more races, 1.3% Hispanic of any race; Average household size: 2.67; Median age: 36.7; Age under 18: 25.7%; Age 65 and over: 12.3%; Males per 100 females: 80.8
School District(s)
Florence 04 (PK-12)
    2012-13 Enrollment: 649 . . . . (843) 346-3956
Housing: Homeownership rate: 54.3%; Homeowner vacancy rate: 4.5%; Rental vacancy rate: 8.3%

Georgetown County

Located in eastern South Carolina; bounded on the east by the Atlantic Ocean, on the northeast by the Pee Dee River, and on the south by the Santee River; watered by the Waccamaw and Black Rivers. Covers a land area of 813.547 square miles, a water area of 221.100 square miles, and is located in the Eastern Time Zone at 33.42° N. Lat., 79.30° W. Long. The county was founded in 1769. County seat is Georgetown.

Georgetown County is part of the Georgetown, SC Micropolitan Statistical Area. The entire metro area includes: Georgetown County, SC

Weather Station: Andrews — Elevation: 35 feet

	Jan	Feb	Mar	Apr	May	Jun	Jul	Aug	Sep	Oct	Nov	Dec
High	58	62	69	77	83	88	91	89	84	77	69	61
Low	36	38	44	51	59	67	71	71	65	54	45	38
Precip	4.1	3.3	3.6	3.1	3.7	5.0	5.7	6.1	5.2	3.9	3.0	3.2
Snow	0.2	tr	0.1	0.0	0.0	0.0	0.0	0.0	0.0	0.0	0.0	0.4

High and Low temperatures in degrees Fahrenheit; Precipitation and Snow in inches

Weather Station: Brookgreen Gardens — Elevation: 20 feet

	Jan	Feb	Mar	Apr	May	Jun	Jul	Aug	Sep	Oct	Nov	Dec
High	57	61	68	75	82	87	90	89	84	77	68	60
Low	37	40	45	52	60	68	72	71	66	56	47	39
Precip	4.1	3.4	4.3	3.3	3.2	4.9	5.8	6.3	6.5	4.5	3.2	3.9
Snow	0.2	tr	0.2	0.0	0.0	0.0	0.0	0.0	0.0	0.0	0.0	0.4

High and Low temperatures in degrees Fahrenheit; Precipitation and Snow in inches

Population: 60,158; Growth (since 2000): 7.8%; Density: 73.9 persons per square mile; Race: 63.2% White, 33.6% Black/African American, 0.5% Asian, 0.2% American Indian/Alaska Native, 0.0% Native Hawaiian/Other Pacific Islander, 0.9% two or more races, 3.1% Hispanic of any race; Average household size: 2.43; Median age: 45.4; Age under 18: 21.6%; Age 65 and over: 19.8%; Males per 100 females: 90.9; Marriage status: 27.8% never married, 53.4% now married, 3.6% separated, 8.8% widowed, 10.0% divorced; Foreign born: 3.0%; Speak English only: 96.3%; With disability: 16.3%; Veterans: 12.8%; Ancestry: 10.6% English, 10.2% American, 8.7% Irish, 7.1% German, 3.7% Italian
Religion: Six largest groups: 20.7% Methodist/Pietist, 15.6% Baptist, 6.6% Catholicism, 5.2% Pentecostal, 4.5% Non-denominational Protestant, 2.6% Presbyterian-Reformed
Economy: Unemployment rate: 6.5%; Leading industries: 17.3% retail trade; 12.4% health care and social assistance; 11.0% other services (except public administration); Farms: 209 totaling 66,359 acres; Company size: 1 employs 1,000 or more persons, 1 employs 500 to 999 persons, 15 employ 100 to 499 persons, 1,733 employ less than 100 persons; Business ownership: 2,056 women-owned, 683 Black-owned, n/a Hispanic-owned, 31 Asian-owned
Employment: 12.1% management, business, and financial, 1.8% computer, engineering, and science, 9.1% education, legal, community service, arts, and media, 5.8% healthcare practitioners, 24.4% service, 22.5% sales and office, 9.7% natural resources, construction, and maintenance, 14.5% production, transportation, and material moving
Income: Per capita: $24,437; Median household: $40,131; Average household: $60,198; Households with income of $100,000 or more: 15.5%; Poverty rate: 21.2%
Educational Attainment: High school diploma or higher: 84.5%; Bachelor's degree or higher: 22.7%; Graduate/professional degree or higher: 9.6%
Housing: Homeownership rate: 77.8%; Median home value: $158,800; Median year structure built: 1989; Homeowner vacancy rate: 3.1%; Median gross rent: $803 per month; Rental vacancy rate: 26.5%
Vital Statistics: Birth rate: 97.5 per 10,000 population; Death rate: 120.9 per 10,000 population; Age-adjusted cancer mortality rate: 207.1 deaths per 100,000 population
Health Insurance: 78.9% have insurance; 55.5% have private insurance; 39.7% have public insurance; 21.1% do not have insurance; 17.4% of children under 18 do not have insurance
Health Care: Physicians: 19.4 per 10,000 population; Hospital beds: 50.7 per 10,000 population; Hospital admissions: 2,349.4 per 10,000 population
Air Quality Index: 99.4% good, 0.6% moderate, 0.0% unhealthy for sensitive individuals, 0.0% unhealthy (percent of days)
Transportation: Commute: 91.0% car, 0.8% public transportation, 1.0% walk, 4.1% work from home; Median travel time to work: 25.2 minutes
Presidential Election: 45.7% Obama, 53.4% Romney (2012)
National and State Parks: Huntington Beach State Park
Additional Information Contacts
Georgetown Government . . . . (843) 545-3215
   http://www.georgetowncountysc.org

Georgetown County Communities

ANDREWS (town). Covers a land area of 2.205 square miles and a water area of 0 square miles. Located at 33.45° N. Lat; 79.57° W. Long. Elevation is 26 feet.
History: First called Rosemary, Andrews was renamed for the lumber mill owner who made the settlement a boom town during a brief period of prosperity.

Population: 2,861; Growth (since 2000): -6.7%; Density: 1,297.6 persons per square mile; Race: 31.6% White, 64.9% Black/African American, 0.8% Asian, 0.5% American Indian/Alaska Native, 0.0% Native Hawaiian/Other Pacific Islander, 0.8% Two or more races, 3.6% Hispanic of any race; Average household size: 2.67; Median age: 36.0; Age under 18: 27.9%; Age 65 and over: 13.9%; Males per 100 females: 84.0; Marriage status: 39.2% never married, 43.9% now married, 7.0% separated, 5.9% widowed, 11.0% divorced; Foreign born: 6.0%; Speak English only: 91.7%; With disability: 22.3%; Veterans: 7.4%; Ancestry: 6.7% American, 5.5% English, 3.7% Irish, 2.5% Scotch-Irish, 1.1% Lebanese
Employment: 13.7% management, business, and financial, 0.0% computer, engineering, and science, 6.0% education, legal, community service, arts, and media, 6.8% healthcare practitioners, 21.4% service, 25.4% sales and office, 3.2% natural resources, construction, and maintenance, 23.5% production, transportation, and material moving
Income: Per capita: $12,576; Median household: $26,852; Average household: $35,980; Households with income of $100,000 or more: 4.0%; Poverty rate: 43.2%
Educational Attainment: High school diploma or higher: 69.4%; Bachelor's degree or higher: 6.0%; Graduate/professional degree or higher: 2.2%

School District(s)
Georgetown 01 (PK-12)
   2012-13 Enrollment: 9,725 . . . . (843) 436-7178
Housing: Homeownership rate: 62.0%; Median home value: $77,800; Median year structure built: 1974; Homeowner vacancy rate: 2.5%; Median gross rent: $600 per month; Rental vacancy rate: 13.3%
Health Insurance: 72.6% have insurance; 36.4% have private insurance; 47.9% have public insurance; 27.4% do not have insurance; 22.7% of children under 18 do not have insurance
Safety: Violent crime rate: 92.1 per 10,000 population; Property crime rate: 683.7 per 10,000 population
Transportation: Commute: 91.3% car, 3.4% public transportation, 0.0% walk, 0.0% work from home; Median travel time to work: 29.0 minutes
Additional Information Contacts
Town of Andrews . . . . (843) 264-8666
   http://www.townofandrews.org

GEORGETOWN (city). County seat. Covers a land area of 6.910 square miles and a water area of 0.606 square miles. Located at 33.37° N. Lat; 79.28° W. Long. Elevation is 16 feet.
History: Georgetown was established in 1735, named for the Prince of Wales (later George II of England), and laid out on a tract donated by the Reverend William Screven. Most of the settlers were English, and the town flourished as a port, shipping rice and indigo to the West Indies and Great Britain.
Population: 9,163; Growth (since 2000): 2.4%; Density: 1,326.0 persons per square mile; Race: 37.8% White, 56.7% Black/African American, 0.7% Asian, 0.2% American Indian/Alaska Native, 0.1% Native Hawaiian/Other Pacific Islander, 1.3% Two or more races, 5.3% Hispanic of any race; Average household size: 2.53; Median age: 36.7; Age under 18: 27.1%; Age 65 and over: 14.7%; Males per 100 females: 81.6; Marriage status: 37.0% never married, 41.5% now married, 2.7% separated, 9.8% widowed, 11.7% divorced; Foreign born: 3.3%; Speak English only: 95.4%; With disability: 18.1%; Veterans: 11.9%; Ancestry: 7.2% American, 5.2% English, 4.5% Irish, 3.9% German, 1.0% French
Employment: 14.4% management, business, and financial, 0.0% computer, engineering, and science, 14.0% education, legal, community service, arts, and media, 2.1% healthcare practitioners, 27.0% service, 21.7% sales and office, 6.2% natural resources, construction, and maintenance, 14.6% production, transportation, and material moving
Income: Per capita: $18,839; Median household: $26,330; Average household: $45,730; Households with income of $100,000 or more: 8.7%; Poverty rate: 29.5%
Educational Attainment: High school diploma or higher: 81.2%; Bachelor's degree or higher: 17.7%; Graduate/professional degree or higher: 8.2%

School District(s)
Georgetown 01 (PK-12)
   2012-13 Enrollment: 9,725 . . . . (843) 436-7178
Housing: Homeownership rate: 53.6%; Median home value: $114,500; Median year structure built: 1966; Homeowner vacancy rate: 4.1%; Median gross rent: $683 per month; Rental vacancy rate: 9.7%

Health Insurance: 79.7% have insurance; 50.5% have private insurance; 43.0% have public insurance; 20.3% do not have insurance; 19.7% of children under 18 do not have insurance
Hospitals: Georgetown Memorial Hospital (131 beds)
Safety: Violent crime rate: 122.4 per 10,000 population; Property crime rate: 566.6 per 10,000 population
Newspapers: Georgetown Times (weekly circulation 9000)
Transportation: Commute: 88.5% car, 4.1% public transportation, 0.7% walk, 2.3% work from home; Median travel time to work: 19.8 minutes
Airports: Georgetown County (general aviation)
Additional Information Contacts
City of Georgetown . . . . (843) 545-4001
   http://www.cityofgeorgetownsc.com

MURRELLS INLET (CDP).
Covers a land area of 7.360 square miles and a water area of 0.167 square miles. Located at 33.56° N. Lat; 79.06° W. Long. Elevation is 16 feet.
History: According to local legend, Captain Murrell, a pirate, often took shelter here along the marshes.
Population: 7,547; Growth (since 2000): 36.7%; Density: 1,025.5 persons per square mile; Race: 90.7% White, 6.5% Black/African American, 0.9% Asian, 0.3% American Indian/Alaska Native, 0.0% Native Hawaiian/Other Pacific Islander, 0.8% Two or more races, 2.2% Hispanic of any race; Average household size: 2.12; Median age: 53.6; Age under 18: 13.7%; Age 65 and over: 26.4%; Males per 100 females: 94.9; Marriage status: 20.3% never married, 62.6% now married, 1.8% separated, 7.0% widowed, 10.0% divorced; Foreign born: 0.9%; Speak English only: 98.0%; With disability: 14.3%; Veterans: 15.9%; Ancestry: 20.8% Irish, 13.2% English, 12.8% German, 12.4% American, 9.3% Italian
Employment: 14.8% management, business, and financial, 1.9% computer, engineering, and science, 10.3% education, legal, community service, arts, and media, 9.2% healthcare practitioners, 21.5% service, 26.4% sales and office, 9.7% natural resources, construction, and maintenance, 6.2% production, transportation, and material moving
Income: Per capita: $35,176; Median household: $48,118; Average household: $75,607; Households with income of $100,000 or more: 19.0%; Poverty rate: 8.1%
Educational Attainment: High school diploma or higher: 92.3%; Bachelor's degree or higher: 28.1%; Graduate/professional degree or higher: 10.4%
School District(s)
Horry 01 (PK-12)
   2012-13 Enrollment: 39,998 . . . . (843) 488-6700
Housing: Homeownership rate: 82.6%; Median home value: $226,800; Median year structure built: 1996; Homeowner vacancy rate: 3.5%; Median gross rent: $934 per month; Rental vacancy rate: 15.5%
Health Insurance: 71.7% have insurance; 58.9% have private insurance; 35.9% have public insurance; 28.3% do not have insurance; 39.2% of children under 18 do not have insurance
Hospitals: Waccamaw Community Hospital (111 beds)
Transportation: Commute: 91.0% car, 0.0% public transportation, 0.0% walk, 7.9% work from home; Median travel time to work: 20.0 minutes

PAWLEYS ISLAND (town).
Covers a land area of 0.701 square miles and a water area of 0.291 square miles. Located at 33.43° N. Lat; 79.12° W. Long. Elevation is 3 feet.
History: Pawley's Island was one of the first resorts established along the sand dunes.
Population: 103; Growth (since 2000): -25.4%; Density: 146.9 persons per square mile; Race: 98.1% White, 0.0% Black/African American, 0.0% Asian, 0.0% American Indian/Alaska Native, 0.0% Native Hawaiian/Other Pacific Islander, 1.9% Two or more races, 0.0% Hispanic of any race; Average household size: 1.78; Median age: 63.9; Age under 18: 3.9%; Age 65 and over: 47.6%; Males per 100 females: 102.0
School District(s)
Georgetown 01 (PK-12)
   2012-13 Enrollment: 9,725 . . . . (843) 436-7178
Housing: Homeownership rate: 86.3%; Homeowner vacancy rate: 15.3%; Rental vacancy rate: 96.6%
Newspapers: The Coastal Observer (weekly circulation 5000)

Greenville County

Located in northwestern South Carolina; bounded on the north by North Carolina, and on the west by the Saluda River; drained by the Enoree and Reedy Rivers. Covers a land area of 785.120 square miles, a water area of 9.746 square miles, and is located in the Eastern Time Zone at 34.89° N. Lat., 82.37° W. Long. The county was founded in 1798. County seat is Greenville.

Greenville County is part of the Greenville-Anderson-Mauldin, SC Metropolitan Statistical Area. The entire metro area includes: Anderson County, SC; Greenville County, SC; Laurens County, SC; Pickens County, SC

Weather Station: Caesars Head | | | | | | | | | Elevation: 3,200 feet
	Jan	Feb	Mar	Apr	May	Jun	Jul	Aug	Sep	Oct	Nov	Dec
High	45	48	56	65	71	77	79	78	72	63	55	47
Low	28	30	36	44	52	60	64	63	57	47	38	30
Precip	5.2	5.1	5.8	5.1	5.5	6.8	6.5	5.8	5.9	5.0	5.9	5.9
Snow	3.7	1.6	1.1	0.1	0.1	0.0	0.0	0.0	0.0	0.0	tr	1.4

High and Low temperatures in degrees Fahrenheit; Precipitation and Snow in inches

Population: 451,225; Growth (since 2000): 18.9%; Density: 574.7 persons per square mile; Race: 73.8% White, 18.1% Black/African American, 2.0% Asian, 0.3% American Indian/Alaska Native, 0.1% Native Hawaiian/Other Pacific Islander, 1.9% two or more races, 8.1% Hispanic of any race; Average household size: 2.49; Median age: 37.2; Age under 18: 24.2%; Age 65 and over: 12.8%; Males per 100 females: 94.1; Marriage status: 30.3% never married, 53.3% now married, 2.7% separated, 6.1% widowed, 10.3% divorced; Foreign born: 8.0%; Speak English only: 88.6%; With disability: 11.2%; Veterans: 9.3%; Ancestry: 11.5% English, 11.3% German, 11.2% American, 10.8% Irish, 3.0% Scotch-Irish
Religion: Six largest groups: 24.5% Baptist, 8.3% Pentecostal, 7.7% Non-denominational Protestant, 5.6% Catholicism, 5.4% Methodist/Pietist, 3.7% Presbyterian-Reformed
Economy: Unemployment rate: 5.2%; Leading industries: 14.5% retail trade; 12.6% professional, scientific, and technical services; 9.7% other services (except public administration); Farms: 1,101 totaling 72,863 acres; Company size: 16 employ 1,000 or more persons, 26 employ 500 to 999 persons, 284 employ 100 to 499 persons, 11,793 employ less than 100 persons; Business ownership: 11,184 women-owned, 3,289 Black-owned, 1,326 Hispanic-owned, 920 Asian-owned
Employment: 14.5% management, business, and financial, 6.2% computer, engineering, and science, 9.9% education, legal, community service, arts, and media, 5.9% healthcare practitioners, 16.9% service, 25.2% sales and office, 7.8% natural resources, construction, and maintenance, 13.5% production, transportation, and material moving
Income: Per capita: $26,643; Median household: $49,022; Average household: $67,633; Households with income of $100,000 or more: 20.0%; Poverty rate: 15.8%
Educational Attainment: High school diploma or higher: 85.7%; Bachelor's degree or higher: 31.2%; Graduate/professional degree or higher: 11.1%
Housing: Homeownership rate: 67.4%; Median home value: $153,600; Median year structure built: 1984; Homeowner vacancy rate: 3.0%; Median gross rent: $747 per month; Rental vacancy rate: 11.2%
Vital Statistics: Birth rate: 131.0 per 10,000 population; Death rate: 80.0 per 10,000 population; Age-adjusted cancer mortality rate: 184.6 deaths per 100,000 population
Health Insurance: 83.5% have insurance; 65.8% have private insurance; 28.4% have public insurance; 16.5% do not have insurance; 8.6% of children under 18 do not have insurance
Health Care: Physicians: 31.2 per 10,000 population; Hospital beds: 32.7 per 10,000 population; Hospital admissions: 1,446.3 per 10,000 population
Air Quality Index: 77.3% good, 22.7% moderate, 0.0% unhealthy for sensitive individuals, 0.0% unhealthy (percent of days)
Transportation: Commute: 93.2% car, 0.3% public transportation, 1.8% walk, 3.8% work from home; Median travel time to work: 21.5 minutes
Presidential Election: 35.2% Obama, 63.0% Romney (2012)
National and State Parks: Caesars Head State Park; Paris Mountain State Park; Pleasant Ridge State Park
Additional Information Contacts
Greenville Government . . . . (864) 467-8551
   http://www.greenvillecounty.org

Greenville County Communities

BEREA (CDP). Covers a land area of 7.704 square miles and a water area of 0.295 square miles. Located at 34.88° N. Lat; 82.47° W. Long. Elevation is 1,040 feet.

Population: 14,295; Growth (since 2000): 1.0%; Density: 1,855.6 persons per square mile; Race: 60.6% White, 18.1% Black/African American, 1.2% Asian, 0.5% American Indian/Alaska Native, 0.0% Native Hawaiian/Other Pacific Islander, 2.7% Two or more races, 25.4% Hispanic of any race; Average household size: 2.58; Median age: 36.2; Age under 18: 24.1%; Age 65 and over: 15.9%; Males per 100 females: 94.9; Marriage status: 27.1% never married, 48.7% now married, 3.6% separated, 9.1% widowed, 15.2% divorced; Foreign born: 13.2%; Speak English only: 77.1%; With disability: 12.8%; Veterans: 7.9%; Ancestry: 12.2% American, 9.9% Irish, 6.5% German, 6.2% English, 2.9% Scotch-Irish

Employment: 6.1% management, business, and financial, 3.8% computer, engineering, and science, 5.3% education, legal, community service, arts, and media, 2.4% healthcare practitioners, 22.7% service, 28.4% sales and office, 12.9% natural resources, construction, and maintenance, 18.3% production, transportation, and material moving

Income: Per capita: $16,209; Median household: $30,610; Average household: $39,868; Households with income of $100,000 or more: 5.1%; Poverty rate: 31.8%

Educational Attainment: High school diploma or higher: 73.3%; Bachelor's degree or higher: 11.7%; Graduate/professional degree or higher: 3.9%

Housing: Homeownership rate: 60.2%; Median home value: $111,800; Median year structure built: 1974; Homeowner vacancy rate: 2.4%; Median gross rent: $639 per month; Rental vacancy rate: 16.0%

Health Insurance: 78.8% have insurance; 47.3% have private insurance; 43.8% have public insurance; 21.2% do not have insurance; 7.4% of children under 18 do not have insurance

Transportation: Commute: 94.7% car, 0.4% public transportation, 1.5% walk, 1.5% work from home; Median travel time to work: 23.6 minutes

CITY VIEW (CDP). Covers a land area of 0.518 square miles and a water area of 0.006 square miles. Located at 34.86° N. Lat; 82.42° W. Long. Elevation is 981 feet.

Population: 1,345; Growth (since 2000): 7.3%; Density: 2,596.9 persons per square mile; Race: 48.0% White, 28.0% Black/African American, 0.1% Asian, 0.6% American Indian/Alaska Native, 0.4% Native Hawaiian/Other Pacific Islander, 2.9% Two or more races, 33.4% Hispanic of any race; Average household size: 3.08; Median age: 29.6; Age under 18: 28.9%; Age 65 and over: 7.4%; Males per 100 females: 101.6

Housing: Homeownership rate: 31.9%; Homeowner vacancy rate: 13.5%; Rental vacancy rate: 12.7%

CLEVELAND (unincorporated postal area)

ZCTA: 29635

Covers a land area of 69.225 square miles and a water area of 0.898 square miles. Located at 35.08° N. Lat; 82.63° W. Long. Elevation is 1,001 feet.

Population: 1,254; Growth (since 2000): 10.2%; Density: 18.1 persons per square mile; Race: 97.3% White, 0.6% Black/African American, 0.2% Asian, 0.1% American Indian/Alaska Native, 0.1% Native Hawaiian/Other Pacific Islander, 1.0% Two or more races, 1.4% Hispanic of any race; Average household size: 2.31; Median age: 48.4; Age under 18: 18.8%; Age 65 and over: 18.6%; Males per 100 females: 108.0

Housing: Homeownership rate: 87.9%; Homeowner vacancy rate: 2.4%; Rental vacancy rate: 6.9%

DUNEAN (CDP). Covers a land area of 1.575 square miles and a water area of 0.003 square miles. Located at 34.82° N. Lat; 82.42° W. Long. Elevation is 978 feet.

Population: 3,671; Growth (since 2000): -11.7%; Density: 2,330.9 persons per square mile; Race: 56.1% White, 35.0% Black/African American, 0.3% Asian, 0.3% American Indian/Alaska Native, 0.0% Native Hawaiian/Other Pacific Islander, 2.5% Two or more races, 10.2% Hispanic of any race; Average household size: 2.33; Median age: 39.5; Age under 18: 21.0%; Age 65 and over: 15.9%; Males per 100 females: 96.8; Marriage status: 42.7% never married, 42.1% now married, 2.8% separated, 6.4% widowed, 8.8% divorced; Foreign born: 11.1%; Speak English only: 87.4%;

With disability: 13.5%; Veterans: 6.0%; Ancestry: 9.8% German, 9.6% American, 8.2% Irish, 3.4% English, 2.1% Scotch-Irish

Employment: 11.8% management, business, and financial, 1.9% computer, engineering, and science, 4.1% education, legal, community service, arts, and media, 4.4% healthcare practitioners, 31.0% service, 25.7% sales and office, 4.2% natural resources, construction, and maintenance, 16.9% production, transportation, and material moving

Income: Per capita: $15,463; Median household: $35,638; Average household: $39,787; Households with income of $100,000 or more: 3.3%; Poverty rate: 23.4%

Educational Attainment: High school diploma or higher: 76.3%; Bachelor's degree or higher: 10.1%; Graduate/professional degree or higher: 1.8%

Housing: Homeownership rate: 53.9%; Median home value: $89,800; Median year structure built: 1958; Homeowner vacancy rate: 5.0%; Median gross rent: $767 per month; Rental vacancy rate: 15.5%

Health Insurance: 72.6% have insurance; 46.0% have private insurance; 35.2% have public insurance; 27.4% do not have insurance; 17.7% of children under 18 do not have insurance

Transportation: Commute: 93.6% car, 0.0% public transportation, 0.4% walk, 1.6% work from home; Median travel time to work: 15.6 minutes

FIVE FORKS (CDP). Covers a land area of 7.568 square miles and a water area of 0.045 square miles. Located at 34.81° N. Lat; 82.23° W. Long. Elevation is 876 feet.

History: Known as "Five Forks Plantation", it is an upscale neighborhood located within the area of Simpsonville, South Carolina. This neighborhood was developed by Clifton Land and Timber, who also developed other Simpsonville Subdivisions like Waverly Hall, Asheton Lakes, Savannah and Shellbrook Plantation.

Population: 14,140; Growth (since 2000): 75.3%; Density: 1,868.4 persons per square mile; Race: 87.5% White, 5.5% Black/African American, 4.4% Asian, 0.2% American Indian/Alaska Native, 0.0% Native Hawaiian/Other Pacific Islander, 1.5% Two or more races, 4.2% Hispanic of any race; Average household size: 3.05; Median age: 37.3; Age under 18: 33.3%; Age 65 and over: 6.9%; Males per 100 females: 97.1; Marriage status: 21.1% never married, 69.3% now married, 1.3% separated, 4.4% widowed, 5.2% divorced; Foreign born: 7.9%; Speak English only: 91.4%; With disability: 4.3%; Veterans: 8.4%; Ancestry: 18.8% German, 16.5% English, 13.5% Irish, 10.0% American, 8.2% Italian

Employment: 26.5% management, business, and financial, 12.1% computer, engineering, and science, 10.7% education, legal, community service, arts, and media, 9.0% healthcare practitioners, 10.5% service, 21.5% sales and office, 4.0% natural resources, construction, and maintenance, 5.8% production, transportation, and material moving

Income: Per capita: $41,815; Median household: $114,556; Average household: $129,286; Households with income of $100,000 or more: 60.1%; Poverty rate: 1.6%

Educational Attainment: High school diploma or higher: 96.1%; Bachelor's degree or higher: 59.8%; Graduate/professional degree or higher: 20.8%

Housing: Homeownership rate: 93.1%; Median home value: $258,300; Median year structure built: 1998; Homeowner vacancy rate: 2.1%; Median gross rent: $1,520 per month; Rental vacancy rate: 3.0%

Health Insurance: 96.0% have insurance; 92.7% have private insurance; 10.7% have public insurance; 4.0% do not have insurance; 0.6% of children under 18 do not have insurance

Transportation: Commute: 94.2% car, 0.3% public transportation, 0.0% walk, 5.0% work from home; Median travel time to work: 24.4 minutes

FOUNTAIN INN (city). Covers a land area of 7.887 square miles and a water area of 0.034 square miles. Located at 34.70° N. Lat; 82.20° W. Long. Elevation is 866 feet.

History: Fountain Inn took its name from an inn where stagecoaches stopped overnight on trips between Greenville and Charleston. The inn was named for a fountain in its yard.

Population: 7,799; Growth (since 2000): 29.6%; Density: 988.9 persons per square mile; Race: 63.7% White, 31.2% Black/African American, 0.3% Asian, 0.3% American Indian/Alaska Native, 0.2% Native Hawaiian/Other Pacific Islander, 2.0% Two or more races, 6.0% Hispanic of any race; Average household size: 2.67; Median age: 35.0; Age under 18: 27.2%; Age 65 and over: 11.4%; Males per 100 females: 88.4; Marriage status: 31.1% never married, 48.7% now married, 2.9% separated, 7.8% widowed, 12.4% divorced; Foreign born: 3.4%; Speak English only: 96.7%;

With disability: 14.0%; Veterans: 11.5%; Ancestry: 10.1% German, 9.9% American, 9.6% English, 7.6% Irish, 4.6% Italian
Employment: 12.8% management, business, and financial, 4.4% computer, engineering, and science, 12.1% education, legal, community service, arts, and media, 1.5% healthcare practitioners, 19.8% service, 24.1% sales and office, 6.6% natural resources, construction, and maintenance, 18.7% production, transportation, and material moving
Income: Per capita: $20,713; Median household: $46,152; Average household: $52,960; Households with income of $100,000 or more: 12.6%; Poverty rate: 14.7%
Educational Attainment: High school diploma or higher: 90.5%; Bachelor's degree or higher: 19.7%; Graduate/professional degree or higher: 7.1%

School District(s)
Greenville 01 (PK-12)
    2012-13 Enrollment: 73,649 . . . . (864) 355-8860
Housing: Homeownership rate: 73.3%; Median home value: $115,900; Median year structure built: 1989; Homeowner vacancy rate: 2.1%; Median gross rent: $645 per month; Rental vacancy rate: 8.9%
Health Insurance: 85.8% have insurance; 67.7% have private insurance; 30.2% have public insurance; 14.2% do not have insurance; 10.0% of children under 18 do not have insurance
Safety: Violent crime rate: 51.4 per 10,000 population; Property crime rate: 181.8 per 10,000 population
Transportation: Commute: 96.6% car, 0.0% public transportation, 1.6% walk, 1.4% work from home; Median travel time to work: 22.4 minutes
Additional Information Contacts
City of Fountain Inn . . . . (864) 862-4421
    http://www.fountaininn.org

GANTT (CDP). Covers a land area of 9.913 square miles and a water area of 0.016 square miles. Located at 34.79° N. Lat; 82.40° W. Long. Elevation is 988 feet.
Population: 14,229; Growth (since 2000): 1.9%; Density: 1,435.4 persons per square mile; Race: 29.1% White, 59.2% Black/African American, 0.3% Asian, 0.4% American Indian/Alaska Native, 0.0% Native Hawaiian/Other Pacific Islander, 1.8% Two or more races, 13.2% Hispanic of any race; Average household size: 2.68; Median age: 36.4; Age under 18: 26.0%; Age 65 and over: 13.0%; Males per 100 females: 92.3; Marriage status: 42.9% never married, 40.2% now married, 5.4% separated, 8.4% widowed, 8.6% divorced; Foreign born: 7.3%; Speak English only: 89.3%; With disability: 13.2%; Veterans: 7.7%; Ancestry: 6.2% American, 3.5% English, 3.1% Irish, 2.8% German, 1.3% Scottish
Employment: 7.6% management, business, and financial, 2.5% computer, engineering, and science, 5.8% education, legal, community service, arts, and media, 6.4% healthcare practitioners, 16.0% service, 24.8% sales and office, 9.7% natural resources, construction, and maintenance, 27.2% production, transportation, and material moving
Income: Per capita: $18,941; Median household: $31,428; Average household: $48,953; Households with income of $100,000 or more: 9.7%; Poverty rate: 26.6%
Educational Attainment: High school diploma or higher: 74.7%; Bachelor's degree or higher: 15.3%; Graduate/professional degree or higher: 5.0%
Housing: Homeownership rate: 59.2%; Median home value: $88,000; Median year structure built: 1974; Homeowner vacancy rate: 2.8%; Median gross rent: $706 per month; Rental vacancy rate: 15.5%
Health Insurance: 78.7% have insurance; 42.7% have private insurance; 45.3% have public insurance; 21.3% do not have insurance; 4.5% of children under 18 do not have insurance
Transportation: Commute: 94.4% car, 1.0% public transportation, 0.0% walk, 3.2% work from home; Median travel time to work: 20.5 minutes

GOLDEN GROVE (CDP). Covers a land area of 5.715 square miles and a water area of 0.081 square miles. Located at 34.73° N. Lat; 82.44° W. Long. Elevation is 866 feet.
Population: 2,467; Growth (since 2000): 5.1%; Density: 431.7 persons per square mile; Race: 73.5% White, 21.6% Black/African American, 0.4% Asian, 0.2% American Indian/Alaska Native, 0.0% Native Hawaiian/Other Pacific Islander, 2.3% Two or more races, 3.8% Hispanic of any race; Average household size: 2.56; Median age: 38.4; Age under 18: 24.1%; Age 65 and over: 13.9%; Males per 100 females: 93.9
Housing: Homeownership rate: 78.8%; Homeowner vacancy rate: 1.9%; Rental vacancy rate: 12.1%

GREENVILLE (city). County seat. Covers a land area of 28.669 square miles and a water area of 0.148 square miles. Located at 34.84° N. Lat; 82.36° W. Long. Elevation is 984 feet.
History: Greenville stands on the tract of land presented to Richard Pearis, an Irishman who came from Virginia about 1765 as a trader. The first village, laid out in 1797, was called Pleasantburg. Pleasantburg flourished as a resort, and the falls of the Reedy River were soon utilized to furnish power for iron works, corn, and cotton mills. In 1831 the community was incorporated as Greenville, taking the name of the county. The Southern Railway was completed to Greenville in 1874, and about the same time the modern textile industry had its start.
Population: 58,409; Growth (since 2000): 4.3%; Density: 2,037.4 persons per square mile; Race: 64.0% White, 30.0% Black/African American, 1.4% Asian, 0.3% American Indian/Alaska Native, 0.1% Native Hawaiian/Other Pacific Islander, 1.8% Two or more races, 5.9% Hispanic of any race; Average household size: 2.08; Median age: 34.6; Age under 18: 19.4%; Age 65 and over: 12.8%; Males per 100 females: 92.7; Marriage status: 42.1% never married, 39.9% now married, 3.9% separated, 6.3% widowed, 11.7% divorced; Foreign born: 6.5%; Speak English only: 91.7%; With disability: 11.0%; Veterans: 7.0%; Ancestry: 12.2% English, 10.9% German, 9.3% Irish, 9.1% American, 3.5% Scotch-Irish
Employment: 16.3% management, business, and financial, 6.0% computer, engineering, and science, 14.3% education, legal, community service, arts, and media, 7.4% healthcare practitioners, 17.6% service, 24.0% sales and office, 5.0% natural resources, construction, and maintenance, 9.5% production, transportation, and material moving
Income: Per capita: $30,829; Median household: $40,793; Average household: $69,300; Households with income of $100,000 or more: 19.5%; Poverty rate: 20.0%
Educational Attainment: High school diploma or higher: 85.9%; Bachelor's degree or higher: 41.3%; Graduate/professional degree or higher: 16.2%

School District(s)
Anderson 01 (PK-12)
    2012-13 Enrollment: 9,402 . . . . (864) 847-7344
Governor's School for the Arts and Humanities (09-12)
    2012-13 Enrollment: 231. . . . . (864) 282-3777
Greenville 01 (PK-12)
    2012-13 Enrollment: 73,649 . . . . (864) 355-8860
Four-year College(s)
Bob Jones University (Private, For-profit)
    Fall 2013 Enrollment: 3,364 . . . . (864) 242-5100
    2013-14 Tuition: In-state $13,460; Out-of-state $13,460
Brown Mackie College-Greenville (Private, For-profit)
    Fall 2013 Enrollment: 845. . . . . (864) 239-5300
    2013-14 Tuition: In-state $12,114; Out-of-state $12,114
Furman University (Private, Not-for-profit)
    Fall 2013 Enrollment: 2,953 . . . . (864) 294-2000
    2013-14 Tuition: In-state $43,164; Out-of-state $43,164
ITT Technical Institute-Greenville (Private, For-profit)
    Fall 2013 Enrollment: 353. . . . . (864) 288-0777
    2013-14 Tuition: In-state $18,048; Out-of-state $18,048
Strayer University-South Carolina (Private, For-profit)
    Fall 2013 Enrollment: 2,051 . . . . (864) 250-7000
    2013-14 Tuition: In-state $15,495; Out-of-state $15,495
Two-year College(s)
Greenville Technical College (Public)
    Fall 2013 Enrollment: 13,448 . . . . (864) 250-8000
    2013-14 Tuition: In-state $4,310; Out-of-state $8,150
Virginia College-Greenville (Private, For-profit)
    Fall 2013 Enrollment: 460. . . . . (864) 679-4922
    2013-14 Tuition: In-state $11,895; Out-of-state $11,895
Vocational/Technical School(s)
Academy of Hair Technology (Private, For-profit)
    Fall 2013 Enrollment: 84. . . . . (864) 322-0300
    2013-14 Tuition: $14,000
Kenneth Shuler School of Cosmetology-Greenville (Private, For-profit)
    Fall 2013 Enrollment: 175. . . . . (864) 269-6886
    2013-14 Tuition: $16,750
Salon 496 Barber Academy (Private, For-profit)
    Fall 2013 Enrollment: 30. . . . . (864) 242-0800
    2013-14 Tuition: $17,150
Housing: Homeownership rate: 45.3%; Median home value: $200,500; Median year structure built: 1973; Homeowner vacancy rate: 5.7%; Median gross rent: $749 per month; Rental vacancy rate: 11.9%

Health Insurance: 83.3% have insurance; 63.5% have private insurance; 29.1% have public insurance; 16.7% do not have insurance; 8.5% of children under 18 do not have insurance
Hospitals: GHS Greenville Memorial Medical Center (710 beds); GHS Patewood Memorial Hospital; Saint Francis - Downtown (257 beds)
Safety: Violent crime rate: 74.4 per 10,000 population; Property crime rate: 533.0 per 10,000 population
Newspapers: Greenville News (daily circulation 82700); Journal Watchdog (weekly circulation 45000); The Beat (weekly circulation 15000); Tribune Times (weekly circulation 37000)
Transportation: Commute: 87.5% car, 0.5% public transportation, 6.1% walk, 4.9% work from home; Median travel time to work: 17.0 minutes; Amtrak: Train service available.
Airports: Donaldson Center (general aviation); Greenville Downtown (general aviation)
Additional Information Contacts
City of Greenville. . . . . (864) 232-2273
    http://www.greatergreenville.com

GREER (city). Covers a land area of 20.637 square miles and a water area of 2.087 square miles. Located at 34.93° N. Lat; 82.23° W. Long. Elevation is 1,014 feet.
History: Greer grew up on an old cotton patch. In 1873 the Richmond & Danville Railroad established a flag station on the land of Manning Greer. Development of the village was slow until industrialists selected Greer as a site for a textile mill.
Population: 25,515; Growth (since 2000): 51.5%; Density: 1,236.4 persons per square mile; Race: 70.8% White, 17.3% Black/African American, 2.2% Asian, 0.3% American Indian/Alaska Native, 0.1% Native Hawaiian/Other Pacific Islander, 2.1% Two or more races, 14.5% Hispanic of any race; Average household size: 2.52; Median age: 33.9; Age under 18: 26.6%; Age 65 and over: 10.9%; Males per 100 females: 90.5; Marriage status: 32.5% never married, 49.2% now married, 2.8% separated, 6.6% widowed, 11.7% divorced; Foreign born: 11.8%; Speak English only: 80.5%; With disability: 12.7%; Veterans: 7.9%; Ancestry: 11.2% German, 10.0% Irish, 7.9% American, 7.8% English, 3.4% Italian
Employment: 14.1% management, business, and financial, 5.9% computer, engineering, and science, 8.2% education, legal, community service, arts, and media, 6.3% healthcare practitioners, 16.9% service, 23.2% sales and office, 9.0% natural resources, construction, and maintenance, 16.4% production, transportation, and material moving
Income: Per capita: $24,429; Median household: $42,991; Average household: $60,180; Households with income of $100,000 or more: 17.9%; Poverty rate: 19.4%
Educational Attainment: High school diploma or higher: 83.4%; Bachelor's degree or higher: 26.9%; Graduate/professional degree or higher: 9.7%

School District(s)
Greenville 01 (PK-12)
    2012-13 Enrollment: 73,649 . . . . (864) 355-8860
Housing: Homeownership rate: 63.2%; Median home value: $141,200; Median year structure built: 1995; Homeowner vacancy rate: 3.6%; Median gross rent: $747 per month; Rental vacancy rate: 12.8%
Health Insurance: 82.2% have insurance; 63.1% have private insurance; 28.7% have public insurance; 17.8% do not have insurance; 4.5% of children under 18 do not have insurance
Hospitals: GHS Greer Memorial Hospital; Village Hospital (48 beds)
Safety: Violent crime rate: 46.4 per 10,000 population; Property crime rate: 284.9 per 10,000 population
Newspapers: Greer Citizen (weekly circulation 11000)
Transportation: Commute: 95.6% car, 0.2% public transportation, 2.1% walk, 1.7% work from home; Median travel time to work: 21.4 minutes
Airports: Greenville Spartanburg International (primary service/small hub)
Additional Information Contacts
City of Greer . . . . (864) 848-2150
    http://www.cityofgreer.org

JUDSON (CDP). Covers a land area of 0.792 square miles and a water area of 0 square miles. Located at 34.83° N. Lat; 82.43° W. Long. Elevation is 981 feet.
Population: 2,050; Growth (since 2000): -16.5%; Density: 2,587.6 persons per square mile; Race: 30.5% White, 59.2% Black/African American, 0.1% Asian, 0.5% American Indian/Alaska Native, 0.0% Native Hawaiian/Other Pacific Islander, 4.0% Two or more races, 13.1% Hispanic of any race;

Average household size: 2.68; Median age: 34.5; Age under 18: 27.0%; Age 65 and over: 9.1%; Males per 100 females: 99.8
Housing: Homeownership rate: 45.4%; Homeowner vacancy rate: 9.7%; Rental vacancy rate: 19.6%

MAULDIN (city). Covers a land area of 9.954 square miles and a water area of 0.046 square miles. Located at 34.79° N. Lat; 82.30° W. Long. Elevation is 942 feet.
History: The name of Mauldin was given to the town almost accidentally in 1820 thanks to South Carolina's Lieutenant Governor, W. L. Mauldin. The train station was called "Mauldin" because the Lt. Governor had assisted in getting the Greenville Laurens Railroad Company to come through the village. Over time, the entire area took the name of Mauldin.
Population: 22,889; Growth (since 2000): 50.3%; Density: 2,299.5 persons per square mile; Race: 68.7% White, 22.5% Black/African American, 3.5% Asian, 0.3% American Indian/Alaska Native, 0.1% Native Hawaiian/Other Pacific Islander, 2.2% Two or more races, 7.7% Hispanic of any race; Average household size: 2.42; Median age: 37.1; Age under 18: 24.5%; Age 65 and over: 11.8%; Males per 100 females: 88.9; Marriage status: 30.1% never married, 53.2% now married, 1.9% separated, 6.9% widowed, 9.8% divorced; Foreign born: 7.2%; Speak English only: 90.7%; With disability: 9.0%; Veterans: 11.8%; Ancestry: 15.1% English, 12.8% German, 11.5% Irish, 10.4% American, 3.4% Scottish
Employment: 13.7% management, business, and financial, 9.8% computer, engineering, and science, 10.3% education, legal, community service, arts, and media, 6.7% healthcare practitioners, 12.8% service, 29.0% sales and office, 5.2% natural resources, construction, and maintenance, 12.4% production, transportation, and material moving
Income: Per capita: $27,197; Median household: $57,551; Average household: $66,026; Households with income of $100,000 or more: 19.4%; Poverty rate: 5.9%
Educational Attainment: High school diploma or higher: 91.0%; Bachelor's degree or higher: 35.9%; Graduate/professional degree or higher: 13.9%

School District(s)
Greenville 01 (PK-12)
    2012-13 Enrollment: 73,649 . . . . (864) 355-8860
Housing: Homeownership rate: 67.6%; Median home value: $148,500; Median year structure built: 1991; Homeowner vacancy rate: 2.8%; Median gross rent: $878 per month; Rental vacancy rate: 6.7%
Health Insurance: 85.6% have insurance; 73.2% have private insurance; 22.8% have public insurance; 14.4% do not have insurance; 6.5% of children under 18 do not have insurance
Safety: Violent crime rate: 16.6 per 10,000 population; Property crime rate: 170.1 per 10,000 population
Transportation: Commute: 96.1% car, 0.1% public transportation, 0.7% walk, 3.0% work from home; Median travel time to work: 18.5 minutes
Additional Information Contacts
City of Mauldin. . . . . (864) 289-8892
    http://www.cityofmauldin.org

PARKER (CDP). Covers a land area of 6.822 square miles and a water area of 0.046 square miles. Located at 34.85° N. Lat; 82.45° W. Long. Elevation is 1,020 feet.
Population: 11,431; Growth (since 2000): 6.2%; Density: 1,675.7 persons per square mile; Race: 62.0% White, 21.7% Black/African American, 0.4% Asian, 0.5% American Indian/Alaska Native, 0.0% Native Hawaiian/Other Pacific Islander, 2.6% Two or more races, 20.8% Hispanic of any race; Average household size: 2.65; Median age: 34.0; Age under 18: 25.5%; Age 65 and over: 12.2%; Males per 100 females: 99.4; Marriage status: 36.9% never married, 44.7% now married, 4.4% separated, 6.2% widowed, 12.1% divorced; Foreign born: 9.6%; Speak English only: 80.0%; With disability: 17.6%; Veterans: 8.4%; Ancestry: 12.5% American, 9.9% Irish, 8.0% English, 4.2% German, 2.3% Italian
Employment: 5.1% management, business, and financial, 0.3% computer, engineering, and science, 5.3% education, legal, community service, arts, and media, 1.4% healthcare practitioners, 25.3% service, 18.5% sales and office, 20.0% natural resources, construction, and maintenance, 24.2% production, transportation, and material moving
Income: Per capita: $12,234; Median household: $25,293; Average household: $32,603; Households with income of $100,000 or more: 3.5%; Poverty rate: 37.8%

Educational Attainment: High school diploma or higher: 64.3%; Bachelor's degree or higher: 6.8%; Graduate/professional degree or higher: 1.8%

Housing: Homeownership rate: 52.7%; Median home value: $67,600; Median year structure built: 1959; Homeowner vacancy rate: 4.2%; Median gross rent: $718 per month; Rental vacancy rate: 13.9%

Health Insurance: 68.2% have insurance; 34.7% have private insurance; 42.1% have public insurance; 31.8% do not have insurance; 16.3% of children under 18 do not have insurance

Transportation: Commute: 91.8% car, 0.9% public transportation, 3.1% walk, 0.6% work from home; Median travel time to work: 22.1 minutes

---

SANS SOUCI (CDP). Covers a land area of 3.311 square miles and a water area of 0.048 square miles. Located at 34.89° N. Lat; 82.42° W. Long. Elevation is 1,014 feet.

Population: 7,869; Growth (since 2000): 0.4%; Density: 2,376.9 persons per square mile; Race: 69.5% White, 15.3% Black/African American, 1.0% Asian, 1.7% American Indian/Alaska Native, 0.1% Native Hawaiian/Other Pacific Islander, 2.7% Two or more races, 17.1% Hispanic of any race; Average household size: 2.42; Median age: 35.2; Age under 18: 23.4%; Age 65 and over: 13.8%; Males per 100 females: 91.0; Marriage status: 32.4% never married, 46.7% now married, 2.3% separated, 7.2% widowed, 13.7% divorced; Foreign born: 15.7%; Speak English only: 76.0%; With disability: 14.2%; Veterans: 10.5%; Ancestry: 12.4% Irish, 10.8% American, 8.6% English, 7.8% German, 2.7% French

Employment: 7.8% management, business, and financial, 5.3% computer, engineering, and science, 5.8% education, legal, community service, arts, and media, 3.3% healthcare practitioners, 21.0% service, 25.4% sales and office, 12.8% natural resources, construction, and maintenance, 18.7% production, transportation, and material moving

Income: Per capita: $15,299; Median household: $28,323; Average household: $35,659; Households with income of $100,000 or more: 2.7%; Poverty rate: 27.7%

Educational Attainment: High school diploma or higher: 72.9%; Bachelor's degree or higher: 15.5%; Graduate/professional degree or higher: 4.6%

Housing: Homeownership rate: 55.2%; Median home value: $90,800; Median year structure built: 1966; Homeowner vacancy rate: 4.0%; Median gross rent: $661 per month; Rental vacancy rate: 17.1%

Health Insurance: 66.5% have insurance; 42.8% have private insurance; 33.5% have public insurance; 33.5% do not have insurance; 24.1% of children under 18 do not have insurance

Transportation: Commute: 92.2% car, 1.1% public transportation, 1.6% walk, 3.6% work from home; Median travel time to work: 20.1 minutes

---

SIMPSONVILLE (city). Covers a land area of 8.809 square miles and a water area of 0.025 square miles. Located at 34.73° N. Lat; 82.26° W. Long. Elevation is 866 feet.

History: At Simpsonville is one of the oldest roads in South Carolina. It was utilized for stagecoaches between Georgia and North Carolina.

Population: 18,238; Growth (since 2000): 27.1%; Density: 2,070.3 persons per square mile; Race: 75.7% White, 16.4% Black/African American, 1.3% Asian, 0.3% American Indian/Alaska Native, 0.1% Native Hawaiian/Other Pacific Islander, 2.3% Two or more races, 8.9% Hispanic of any race; Average household size: 2.57; Median age: 36.5; Age under 18: 26.0%; Age 65 and over: 11.0%; Males per 100 females: 93.9; Marriage status: 25.6% never married, 57.6% now married, 2.4% separated, 4.8% widowed, 11.9% divorced; Foreign born: 9.1%; Speak English only: 85.1%; With disability: 11.7%; Veterans: 9.9%; Ancestry: 14.4% American, 10.7% Irish, 9.2% German, 9.1% English, 3.3% Scotch-Irish

Employment: 12.8% management, business, and financial, 6.9% computer, engineering, and science, 8.1% education, legal, community service, arts, and media, 3.4% healthcare practitioners, 16.5% service, 24.0% sales and office, 7.9% natural resources, construction, and maintenance, 20.4% production, transportation, and material moving

Income: Per capita: $26,143; Median household: $50,604; Average household: $63,867; Households with income of $100,000 or more: 15.3%; Poverty rate: 8.3%

Educational Attainment: High school diploma or higher: 88.5%; Bachelor's degree or higher: 26.5%; Graduate/professional degree or higher: 9.2%

School District(s)

Greenville 01 (PK-12)
    2012-13 Enrollment: 73,649 . . . . (864) 355-8860

Housing: Homeownership rate: 66.1%; Median home value: $136,200; Median year structure built: 1988; Homeowner vacancy rate: 3.3%; Median gross rent: $875 per month; Rental vacancy rate: 8.7%

Health Insurance: 83.3% have insurance; 69.7% have private insurance; 24.3% have public insurance; 16.7% do not have insurance; 10.2% of children under 18 do not have insurance

Hospitals: GHS - Hillcrest Memorial Hospital (43 beds)

Transportation: Commute: 96.7% car, 0.0% public transportation, 0.1% walk, 2.3% work from home; Median travel time to work: 21.1 minutes

Additional Information Contacts

City of Simpsonville . . . . (864) 967-9526
   http://www.simpsonville.com

SLATER-MARIETTA (CDP). Covers a land area of 4.308 square miles and a water area of 0.006 square miles. Located at 35.04° N. Lat; 82.49° W. Long. Elevation is 1,024 feet.

Population: 2,176; Growth (since 2000): -2.3%; Density: 505.1 persons per square mile; Race: 88.6% White, 0.7% Black/African American, 0.1% Asian, 0.6% American Indian/Alaska Native, 0.0% Native Hawaiian/Other Pacific Islander, 1.1% Two or more races, 10.9% Hispanic of any race; Average household size: 2.60; Median age: 38.8; Age under 18: 24.3%; Age 65 and over: 15.9%; Males per 100 females: 98.9

School District(s)

Greenville 01 (PK-12)
    2012-13 Enrollment: 73,649 . . . . (864) 355-8860

Housing: Homeownership rate: 67.3%; Homeowner vacancy rate: 2.3%; Rental vacancy rate: 20.5%

TAYLORS (CDP). Covers a land area of 10.701 square miles and a water area of 0.040 square miles. Located at 34.91° N. Lat; 82.31° W. Long. Elevation is 925 feet.

History: Taylors was formerly Chick Springs, a summer resort.

Population: 21,617; Growth (since 2000): 7.4%; Density: 2,020.2 persons per square mile; Race: 76.9% White, 14.9% Black/African American, 2.5% Asian, 0.2% American Indian/Alaska Native, 0.1% Native Hawaiian/Other Pacific Islander, 2.0% Two or more races, 8.3% Hispanic of any race; Average household size: 2.50; Median age: 36.9; Age under 18: 24.6%; Age 65 and over: 13.6%; Males per 100 females: 89.7; Marriage status: 27.6% never married, 51.8% now married, 2.2% separated, 6.0% widowed, 14.6% divorced; Foreign born: 8.0%; Speak English only: 90.2%; With disability: 13.1%; Veterans: 9.4%; Ancestry: 12.9% German, 12.3% Irish, 11.9% English, 10.6% American, 3.1% Scotch-Irish

Employment: 12.1% management, business, and financial, 6.3% computer, engineering, and science, 9.0% education, legal, community service, arts, and media, 6.7% healthcare practitioners, 18.3% service, 27.7% sales and office, 5.4% natural resources, construction, and maintenance, 14.5% production, transportation, and material moving

Income: Per capita: $23,242; Median household: $47,149; Average household: $59,113; Households with income of $100,000 or more: 14.9%; Poverty rate: 17.6%

Educational Attainment: High school diploma or higher: 86.8%; Bachelor's degree or higher: 26.8%; Graduate/professional degree or higher: 9.0%

School District(s)

Greenville 01 (PK-12)
    2012-13 Enrollment: 73,649 . . . . (864) 355-8860

Housing: Homeownership rate: 69.4%; Median home value: $137,000; Median year structure built: 1978; Homeowner vacancy rate: 2.0%; Median gross rent: $761 per month; Rental vacancy rate: 8.1%

Health Insurance: 81.3% have insurance; 61.2% have private insurance; 32.3% have public insurance; 18.7% do not have insurance; 12.2% of children under 18 do not have insurance

Transportation: Commute: 97.0% car, 0.0% public transportation, 0.0% walk, 2.0% work from home; Median travel time to work: 20.8 minutes

---

TIGERVILLE (CDP). Covers a land area of 1.329 square miles and a water area of 0.017 square miles. Located at 35.07° N. Lat; 82.37° W. Long. Elevation is 1,004 feet.

Population: 1,312; Growth (since 2000): n/a; Density: 987.5 persons per square mile; Race: 87.2% White, 8.0% Black/African American, 0.5% Asian, 0.2% American Indian/Alaska Native, 0.0% Native Hawaiian/Other Pacific Islander, 0.4% Two or more races, 1.4% Hispanic of any race; Average household size: 2.83; Median age: 20.5; Age under 18: 2.8%; Age 65 and over: 1.6%; Males per 100 females: 89.9

Four-year College(s)

North Greenville University (Private, Not-for-profit, Southern Baptist)
Fall 2013 Enrollment: 2,466 .... (864) 977-7000
2013-14 Tuition: In-state $14,772; Out-of-state $14,772

Housing: Homeownership rate: 65.0%; Homeowner vacancy rate: 3.7%; Rental vacancy rate: 12.5%

TRAVELERS REST (city).

Covers a land area of 4.521 square miles and a water area of 0.025 square miles. Located at 34.97° N. Lat; 82.44° W. Long. Elevation is 1,099 feet.

History: Travelers Rest began as an overnight stop for stagecoaches, the last pause for northbound passengers before the steep climb into the Blue Ridge.

Population: 4,576; Growth (since 2000): 11.6%; Density: 1,012.1 persons per square mile; Race: 79.9% White, 15.3% Black/African American, 1.1% Asian, 0.2% American Indian/Alaska Native, 0.0% Native Hawaiian/Other Pacific Islander, 1.6% Two or more races, 4.5% Hispanic of any race; Average household size: 2.60; Median age: 34.4; Age under 18: 29.3%; Age 65 and over: 12.1%; Males per 100 females: 89.8; Marriage status: 29.2% never married, 54.2% now married, 4.6% separated, 6.1% widowed, 10.5% divorced; Foreign born: 2.6%; Speak English only: 95.0%; With disability: 10.4%; Veterans: 9.0%; Ancestry: 19.0% English, 8.7% Scotch-Irish, 8.5% American, 8.0% Irish, 7.6% German

Employment: 11.5% management, business, and financial, 4.4% computer, engineering, and science, 9.7% education, legal, community service, arts, and media, 4.3% healthcare practitioners, 24.4% service, 25.1% sales and office, 10.0% natural resources, construction, and maintenance, 10.6% production, transportation, and material moving

Income: Per capita: $20,901; Median household: $50,768; Average household: $57,583; Households with income of $100,000 or more: 14.3%; Poverty rate: 19.9%

Educational Attainment: High school diploma or higher: 81.6%; Bachelor's degree or higher: 20.5%; Graduate/professional degree or higher: 9.8%

School District(s)

Greenville 01 (PK-12)
2012-13 Enrollment: 73,649 .... (864) 355-8860

Housing: Homeownership rate: 64.1%; Median home value: $154,100; Median year structure built: 1989; Homeowner vacancy rate: 2.4%; Median gross rent: $704 per month; Rental vacancy rate: 11.8%

Health Insurance: 83.3% have insurance; 63.6% have private insurance; 32.9% have public insurance; 16.7% do not have insurance; 11.6% of children under 18 do not have insurance

Safety: Violent crime rate: 18.7 per 10,000 population; Property crime rate: 643.3 per 10,000 population

Newspapers: Travelers Rest Monitor (weekly circulation 3000)

Transportation: Commute: 97.8% car, 0.0% public transportation, 0.5% walk, 1.7% work from home; Median travel time to work: 20.8 minutes

Additional Information Contacts

City of Travelers Rest .... (864) 834-7958
http://travelersrestsc.com

WADE HAMPTON (CDP).

Covers a land area of 8.959 square miles and a water area of 0.050 square miles. Located at 34.88° N. Lat; 82.33° W. Long. Elevation is 1,024 feet.

Population: 20,622; Growth (since 2000): 0.8%; Density: 2,301.9 persons per square mile; Race: 78.0% White, 10.2% Black/African American, 3.2% Asian, 0.4% American Indian/Alaska Native, 0.1% Native Hawaiian/Other Pacific Islander, 2.1% Two or more races, 11.2% Hispanic of any race; Average household size: 2.26; Median age: 39.8; Age under 18: 20.5%; Age 65 and over: 18.1%; Males per 100 females: 91.7; Marriage status: 27.4% never married, 53.4% now married, 3.5% separated, 7.6% widowed, 11.6% divorced; Foreign born: 10.4%; Speak English only: 84.4%; With disability: 11.8%; Veterans: 11.7%; Ancestry: 14.0% English, 12.3% German, 11.8% Irish, 10.5% American, 4.8% Scotch-Irish

Employment: 13.3% management, business, and financial, 7.2% computer, engineering, and science, 12.2% education, legal, community service, arts, and media, 6.4% healthcare practitioners, 17.6% service, 25.7% sales and office, 5.6% natural resources, construction, and maintenance, 11.9% production, transportation, and material moving

Income: Per capita: $28,593; Median household: $44,386; Average household: $62,546; Households with income of $100,000 or more: 18.2%; Poverty rate: 14.0%

Educational Attainment: High school diploma or higher: 87.7%; Bachelor's degree or higher: 37.8%; Graduate/professional degree or higher: 11.9%

Housing: Homeownership rate: 60.8%; Median home value: $161,400; Median year structure built: 1972; Homeowner vacancy rate: 2.6%; Median gross rent: $701 per month; Rental vacancy rate: 10.0%

Health Insurance: 81.2% have insurance; 65.4% have private insurance; 31.1% have public insurance; 18.8% do not have insurance; 15.5% of children under 18 do not have insurance

Transportation: Commute: 92.8% car, 0.7% public transportation, 1.3% walk, 4.2% work from home; Median travel time to work: 18.3 minutes

WARE PLACE (CDP).

Covers a land area of 0.917 square miles and a water area of <.001 square miles. Located at 34.62° N. Lat; 82.38° W. Long. Elevation is 886 feet.

Population: 228; Growth (since 2000): n/a; Density: 248.5 persons per square mile; Race: 83.8% White, 12.7% Black/African American, 0.0% Asian, 0.9% American Indian/Alaska Native, 0.0% Native Hawaiian/Other Pacific Islander, 1.3% Two or more races, 1.3% Hispanic of any race; Average household size: 2.38; Median age: 46.4; Age under 18: 19.7%; Age 65 and over: 16.2%; Males per 100 females: 105.4

Housing: Homeownership rate: 69.8%; Homeowner vacancy rate: 0.0%; Rental vacancy rate: 27.5%

WELCOME (CDP).

Covers a land area of 4.636 square miles and a water area of 0.049 square miles. Located at 34.81° N. Lat; 82.47° W. Long. Elevation is 984 feet.

Population: 6,668; Growth (since 2000): 4.4%; Density: 1,438.2 persons per square mile; Race: 58.6% White, 27.9% Black/African American, 0.4% Asian, 0.6% American Indian/Alaska Native, 0.0% Native Hawaiian/Other Pacific Islander, 1.8% Two or more races, 16.3% Hispanic of any race; Average household size: 2.54; Median age: 36.8; Age under 18: 24.8%; Age 65 and over: 13.9%; Males per 100 females: 90.9; Marriage status: 28.3% never married, 45.4% now married, 3.2% separated, 10.8% widowed, 15.5% divorced; Foreign born: 10.8%; Speak English only: 86.3%; With disability: 11.6%; Veterans: 9.4%; Ancestry: 14.6% American, 8.8% Irish, 5.7% English, 3.3% German, 2.9% Scotch-Irish

Employment: 7.5% management, business, and financial, 1.9% computer, engineering, and science, 3.8% education, legal, community service, arts, and media, 5.0% healthcare practitioners, 21.7% service, 26.0% sales and office, 19.2% natural resources, construction, and maintenance, 15.0% production, transportation, and material moving

Income: Per capita: $16,188; Median household: $29,163; Average household: $37,765; Households with income of $100,000 or more: 3.7%; Poverty rate: 27.4%

Educational Attainment: High school diploma or higher: 75.5%; Bachelor's degree or higher: 11.1%; Graduate/professional degree or higher: 3.4%

Housing: Homeownership rate: 62.0%; Median home value: $79,900; Median year structure built: 1969; Homeowner vacancy rate: 3.4%; Median gross rent: $682 per month; Rental vacancy rate: 10.8%

Health Insurance: 70.2% have insurance; 40.4% have private insurance; 42.2% have public insurance; 29.8% do not have insurance; 13.9% of children under 18 do not have insurance

Transportation: Commute: 96.6% car, 0.0% public transportation, 1.2% walk, 1.8% work from home; Median travel time to work: 21.9 minutes

Greenwood County

Located in western South Carolina; bounded on the northeast by the Saluda River; includes part of Sumter National Forest. Covers a land area of 454.726 square miles, a water area of 8.200 square miles, and is located in the Eastern Time Zone at 34.16° N. Lat., 82.13° W. Long. The county was founded in 1897. County seat is Greenwood.

Greenwood County is part of the Greenwood, SC Micropolitan Statistical Area. The entire metro area includes: Abbeville County, SC; Greenwood County, SC

Weather Station: Greenwood 3 SW											Elevation: 615 feet	
	Jan	Feb	Mar	Apr	May	Jun	Jul	Aug	Sep	Oct	Nov	Dec
High	53	58	65	74	81	88	91	89	83	73	64	55
Low	30	33	39	46	55	65	68	68	60	49	39	32
Precip	4.2	4.1	4.7	2.9	2.9	3.8	3.6	3.6	3.2	3.4	3.7	3.7
Snow	1.1	0.5	0.4	0.0	0.0	0.0	0.0	0.0	0.0	0.0	0.0	0.2

High and Low temperatures in degrees Fahrenheit; Precipitation and Snow in inches

Population: 69,661; Growth (since 2000): 5.1%; Density: 153.2 persons per square mile; Race: 62.9% White, 31.4% Black/African American, 0.8% Asian, 0.3% American Indian/Alaska Native, 0.0% Native Hawaiian/Other Pacific Islander, 1.2% two or more races, 5.4% Hispanic of any race; Average household size: 2.43; Median age: 37.9; Age under 18: 23.7%; Age 65 and over: 15.1%; Males per 100 females: 88.2; Marriage status: 33.6% never married, 48.3% now married, 3.3% separated, 7.4% widowed, 10.8% divorced; Foreign born: 3.9%; Speak English only: 93.7%; With disability: 14.9%; Veterans: 9.4%; Ancestry: 18.4% American, 8.2% Irish, 7.7% English, 7.4% German, 3.0% Scotch-Irish
Religion: Six largest groups: 29.6% Baptist, 12.8% Methodist/Pietist, 5.8% Pentecostal, 4.0% Non-denominational Protestant, 3.9% Presbyterian-Reformed, 2.9% Catholicism
Economy: Unemployment rate: 6.9%; Leading industries: 20.2% retail trade; 11.7% other services (except public administration); 10.5% health care and social assistance; Farms: 476 totaling 85,521 acres; Company size: 2 employ 1,000 or more persons, 5 employ 500 to 999 persons, 19 employ 100 to 499 persons, 1,331 employs less than 100 persons; Business ownership: 1,356 women-owned, 702 Black-owned, 85 Hispanic-owned, 67 Asian-owned
Employment: 9.0% management, business, and financial, 4.3% computer, engineering, and science, 9.7% education, legal, community service, arts, and media, 7.1% healthcare practitioners, 16.0% service, 23.9% sales and office, 9.3% natural resources, construction, and maintenance, 20.9% production, transportation, and material moving
Income: Per capita: $21,053; Median household: $36,540; Average household: $52,446; Households with income of $100,000 or more: 13.1%; Poverty rate: 23.1%
Educational Attainment: High school diploma or higher: 80.4%; Bachelor's degree or higher: 22.1%; Graduate/professional degree or higher: 6.7%
Housing: Homeownership rate: 65.4%; Median home value: $104,900; Median year structure built: 1977; Homeowner vacancy rate: 2.5%; Median gross rent: $637 per month; Rental vacancy rate: 10.7%
Vital Statistics: Birth rate: 126.2 per 10,000 population; Death rate: 102.5 per 10,000 population; Age-adjusted cancer mortality rate: 160.8 deaths per 100,000 population
Health Insurance: 82.4% have insurance; 57.0% have private insurance; 37.7% have public insurance; 17.6% do not have insurance; 7.4% of children under 18 do not have insurance
Health Care: Physicians: 28.7 per 10,000 population; Hospital beds: 53.3 per 10,000 population; Hospital admissions: 2,060.2 per 10,000 population
Transportation: Commute: 94.9% car, 0.4% public transportation, 2.0% walk, 2.4% work from home; Median travel time to work: 21.2 minutes
Presidential Election: 41.8% Obama, 57.0% Romney (2012)
National and State Parks: Greenwood State Park; Ninety Six National Historic Site
Additional Information Contacts
Greenwood Government . . . . (864) 942-8546
  http://www.co.greenwood.sc.us

Greenwood County Communities

BRADLEY (CDP). Covers a land area of 7.858 square miles and a water area of 0.003 square miles. Located at 34.03° N. Lat; 82.25° W. Long. Elevation is 581 feet.
History: Bradley was named for the family of Irish Patrick Bradley, ardent supporters of the Presbyterian reform movement.
Population: 170; Growth (since 2000): -0.6%; Density: 21.6 persons per square mile; Race: 66.5% White, 33.5% Black/African American, 0.0% Asian, 0.0% American Indian/Alaska Native, 0.0% Native Hawaiian/Other Pacific Islander, 0.0% Two or more races, 1.8% Hispanic of any race; Average household size: 2.62; Median age: 40.0; Age under 18: 27.6%; Age 65 and over: 16.5%; Males per 100 females: 95.4
Housing: Homeownership rate: 90.8%; Homeowner vacancy rate: 4.8%; Rental vacancy rate: 25.0%

COKESBURY (CDP). Covers a land area of 0.593 square miles and a water area of 0 square miles. Located at 34.29° N. Lat; 82.21° W. Long. Elevation is 630 feet.
Population: 215; Growth (since 2000): -22.9%; Density: 362.5 persons per square mile; Race: 24.2% White, 74.9% Black/African American, 0.0% Asian, 0.0% American Indian/Alaska Native, 0.0% Native Hawaiian/Other

Pacific Islander, 0.9% Two or more races, 0.0% Hispanic of any race; Average household size: 2.44; Median age: 42.8; Age under 18: 20.9%; Age 65 and over: 11.6%; Males per 100 females: 95.5
Housing: Homeownership rate: 85.3%; Homeowner vacancy rate: 3.8%; Rental vacancy rate: 7.1%

CORONACA (CDP). Covers a land area of 1.690 square miles and a water area of 0.006 square miles. Located at 34.25° N. Lat; 82.11° W. Long. Elevation is 558 feet.
Population: 191; Growth (since 2000): 12.4%; Density: 113.0 persons per square mile; Race: 76.4% White, 19.4% Black/African American, 0.0% Asian, 0.0% American Indian/Alaska Native, 0.0% Native Hawaiian/Other Pacific Islander, 2.6% Two or more races, 3.7% Hispanic of any race; Average household size: 2.27; Median age: 42.5; Age under 18: 20.9%; Age 65 and over: 15.7%; Males per 100 females: 99.0
Housing: Homeownership rate: 77.4%; Homeowner vacancy rate: 1.5%; Rental vacancy rate: 16.7%

GREENWOOD (city). County seat. Covers a land area of 16.232 square miles and a water area of 0.118 square miles. Located at 34.19° N. Lat; 82.15° W. Long. Elevation is 663 feet.
History: The name of Greenwood dates from 1823, when Judge John McGehee built his log cabin on a tract of forest land and his wife named the plantation Green Wood. When the McGehees sold the tract in 1829 to J.Y. Jones, he parceled it off and sold lots. Although the residents called their settlement Green Wood, the first post office, established in 1837, was Woodville. The Post Office Department finally conformed to local custom in 1850, making the name Greenwood. The Southern Railway reached Greenwood in 1852, and the town was incorporated in 1857. In 1897 Greenwood was made the seat of the new county of Greenwood created from parts of Edgefield and Abbeville Counties.
Population: 23,222; Growth (since 2000): 5.2%; Density: 1,430.6 persons per square mile; Race: 44.6% White, 44.7% Black/African American, 1.0% Asian, 0.4% American Indian/Alaska Native, 0.1% Native Hawaiian/Other Pacific Islander, 1.4% Two or more races, 11.0% Hispanic of any race; Average household size: 2.38; Median age: 31.6; Age under 18: 24.2%; Age 65 and over: 14.5%; Males per 100 females: 84.2; Marriage status: 43.4% never married, 34.8% now married, 3.5% separated, 9.7% widowed, 12.2% divorced; Foreign born: 5.8%; Speak English only: 89.8%; With disability: 15.2%; Veterans: 7.3%; Ancestry: 14.2% American, 5.7% German, 5.6% Irish, 5.5% English, 2.7% Scotch-Irish
Employment: 4.8% management, business, and financial, 3.2% computer, engineering, and science, 10.1% education, legal, community service, arts, and media, 7.0% healthcare practitioners, 19.8% service, 23.6% sales and office, 8.5% natural resources, construction, and maintenance, 23.0% production, transportation, and material moving
Income: Per capita: $16,589; Median household: $24,584; Average household: $41,310; Households with income of $100,000 or more: 7.4%; Poverty rate: 34.5%
Educational Attainment: High school diploma or higher: 73.5%; Bachelor's degree or higher: 19.2%; Graduate/professional degree or higher: 6.5%

School District(s)

Dept of Correction N04 (09-12)
    2012-13 Enrollment: 752 . . . . (803) 896-8556
Greenwood 50 (PK-12)
    2012-13 Enrollment: 9,029 . . . . (864) 941-5424
Greenwood 80 (09-12)
    2012-13 Enrollment: n/a . . . . (864) 941-5750
Four-year College(s)
Lander University (Public)
    Fall 2013 Enrollment: 2,877 . . . . (864) 388-8000
    2013-14 Tuition: In-state $10,100; Out-of-state $19,136
Two-year College(s)
Piedmont Technical College (Public)
    Fall 2013 Enrollment: 6,171 . . . . (864) 941-8324
    2013-14 Tuition: In-state $4,208; Out-of-state $5,408
Vocational/Technical School(s)
Charzanne Beauty College (Private, For-profit)
    Fall 2013 Enrollment: 59 . . . . (864) 223-7321
    2013-14 Tuition: $16,000
Housing: Homeownership rate: 46.4%; Median home value: $89,200; Median year structure built: 1967; Homeowner vacancy rate: 3.4%; Median gross rent: $636 per month; Rental vacancy rate: 12.6%

Health Insurance: 80.2% have insurance; 46.9% have private insurance; 43.3% have public insurance; 19.8% do not have insurance; 8.7% of children under 18 do not have insurance
Hospitals: Self Regional Healthcare (421 beds)
Safety: Violent crime rate: 128.6 per 10,000 population; Property crime rate: 639.8 per 10,000 population
Newspapers: Index-Journal (daily circulation 14000)
Transportation: Commute: 93.3% car, 0.3% public transportation, 3.7% walk, 2.0% work from home; Median travel time to work: 20.8 minutes
Airports: Greenwood County (general aviation)
Additional Information Contacts
City of Greenwood. . . . . (864) 942-8412
   http://www.cityofgreenwoodsc.com

HODGES (town). Covers a land area of 0.781 square miles and a water area of 0.002 square miles. Located at 34.29° N. Lat; 82.25° W. Long. Elevation is 696 feet.
Population: 155; Growth (since 2000): -1.9%; Density: 198.6 persons per square mile; Race: 89.0% White, 7.7% Black/African American, 0.0% Asian, 0.6% American Indian/Alaska Native, 0.0% Native Hawaiian/Other Pacific Islander, 1.9% Two or more races, 1.3% Hispanic of any race; Average household size: 2.54; Median age: 44.8; Age under 18: 20.6%; Age 65 and over: 18.7%; Males per 100 females: 106.7
School District(s)
Greenwood 50 (PK-12)
   2012-13 Enrollment: 9,029 . . . . (864) 941-5424
Housing: Homeownership rate: 85.2%; Homeowner vacancy rate: 5.5%; Rental vacancy rate: 0.0%

NINETY SIX (town). Covers a land area of 1.498 square miles and a water area of 0 square miles. Located at 34.17° N. Lat; 82.02° W. Long. Elevation is 551 feet.
History: Ninety Six began around the trading post established about 1730 by Captain John Francis at the convergence of several country paths. The numerical name was given by traders erroneously calculating the mileage from Keowee.
Population: 1,998; Growth (since 2000): 3.2%; Density: 1,334.2 persons per square mile; Race: 78.2% White, 19.7% Black/African American, 0.4% Asian, 0.3% American Indian/Alaska Native, 0.0% Native Hawaiian/Other Pacific Islander, 1.0% Two or more races, 1.2% Hispanic of any race; Average household size: 2.46; Median age: 37.6; Age under 18: 29.0%; Age 65 and over: 17.2%; Males per 100 females: 84.5
School District(s)
Greenwood 52 (PK-12)
   2012-13 Enrollment: 1,721 . . . . (864) 543-3100
Housing: Homeownership rate: 73.1%; Homeowner vacancy rate: 3.4%; Rental vacancy rate: 6.4%
Newspapers: Star & Beacon (weekly circulation 3000)

PROMISED LAND (CDP). Covers a land area of 1.559 square miles and a water area of 0 square miles. Located at 34.13° N. Lat; 82.23° W. Long. Elevation is 623 feet.
Population: 511; Growth (since 2000): -8.6%; Density: 327.7 persons per square mile; Race: 4.1% White, 94.1% Black/African American, 0.4% Asian, 0.0% American Indian/Alaska Native, 0.0% Native Hawaiian/Other Pacific Islander, 0.2% Two or more races, 0.8% Hispanic of any race; Average household size: 2.75; Median age: 44.8; Age under 18: 19.6%; Age 65 and over: 16.8%; Males per 100 females: 102.0
Housing: Homeownership rate: 86.6%; Homeowner vacancy rate: 1.2%; Rental vacancy rate: 3.8%

TROY (town). Covers a land area of 0.799 square miles and a water area of <.001 square miles. Located at 33.99° N. Lat; 82.30° W. Long. Elevation is 515 feet.
History: Troy, once known as Indian Hill, was the home of Patrick Noble (1787-1840), who died while serving as governor of the state.
Population: 93; Growth (since 2000): -11.4%; Density: 116.4 persons per square mile; Race: 86.0% White, 10.8% Black/African American, 0.0% Asian, 1.1% American Indian/Alaska Native, 0.0% Native Hawaiian/Other Pacific Islander, 0.0% Two or more races, 3.2% Hispanic of any race; Average household size: 2.21; Median age: 46.5; Age under 18: 21.5%; Age 65 and over: 24.7%; Males per 100 females: 102.2
Housing: Homeownership rate: 88.1%; Homeowner vacancy rate: 5.1%; Rental vacancy rate: 0.0%

WARE SHOALS (town). Covers a land area of 3.896 square miles and a water area of 0.120 square miles. Located at 34.39° N. Lat; 82.24° W. Long. Elevation is 633 feet.
Population: 2,170; Growth (since 2000): -8.2%; Density: 557.0 persons per square mile; Race: 76.7% White, 20.9% Black/African American, 0.1% Asian, 0.1% American Indian/Alaska Native, 0.0% Native Hawaiian/Other Pacific Islander, 1.4% Two or more races, 1.4% Hispanic of any race; Average household size: 2.38; Median age: 42.2; Age under 18: 22.2%; Age 65 and over: 18.0%; Males per 100 females: 87.2
School District(s)
Greenwood 51 (PK-12)
   2012-13 Enrollment: 1,016 . . . . (864) 456-7496
Housing: Homeownership rate: 60.9%; Homeowner vacancy rate: 3.4%; Rental vacancy rate: 17.2%
Safety: Violent crime rate: 115.6 per 10,000 population; Property crime rate: 740.1 per 10,000 population
Newspapers: The Observer (weekly circulation 3000)

Hampton County

Located in southern South Carolina; bounded on the southwest by the Savannah River and the Georgia border; drained by the Coosawhatchie River. Covers a land area of 559.896 square miles, a water area of 2.810 square miles, and is located in the Eastern Time Zone at 32.78° N. Lat., 81.14° W. Long. The county was founded in 1787. County seat is Hampton.

Weather Station: Hampton										Elevation: 95 feet		
	Jan	Feb	Mar	Apr	May	Jun	Jul	Aug	Sep	Oct	Nov	Dec
High	60	65	71	78	85	90	93	91	86	78	70	62
Low	38	41	47	53	61	68	72	71	66	55	47	40
Precip	4.2	3.2	4.4	3.1	2.7	5.5	4.8	5.9	3.9	3.1	2.8	3.1
Snow	0.2	0.1	tr	0.0	0.0	0.0	0.0	0.0	0.0	0.0	tr	0.2

High and Low temperatures in degrees Fahrenheit; Precipitation and Snow in inches

Population: 21,090; Growth (since 2000): -1.4%; Density: 37.7 persons per square mile; Race: 42.7% White, 53.9% Black/African American, 0.5% Asian, 0.3% American Indian/Alaska Native, 0.0% Native Hawaiian/Other Pacific Islander, 1.3% two or more races, 3.5% Hispanic of any race; Average household size: 2.57; Median age: 38.4; Age under 18: 24.1%; Age 65 and over: 13.4%; Males per 100 females: 105.1; Marriage status: 32.0% never married, 50.0% now married, 4.3% separated, 3.7% widowed, 9.9% divorced; Foreign born: 1.9%; Speak English only: 95.7%; With disability: 20.6%; Veterans: 8.4%; Ancestry: 9.9% American, 6.9% Irish, 6.6% German, 3.9% English, 1.7% African
Religion: Six largest groups: 34.1% Baptist, 11.8% Methodist/Pietist, 6.3% Non-denominational Protestant, 1.7% Pentecostal, 0.6% Presbyterian-Reformed, 0.4% Catholicism
Economy: Unemployment rate: 8.0%; Leading industries: 27.0% retail trade; 14.4% other services (except public administration); 9.1% accommodation and food services; Farms: 323 totaling 139,090 acres; Company size: 0 employ 1,000 or more persons, 0 employ 500 to 999 persons, 5 employ 100 to 499 persons, 336 employ less than 100 persons; Business ownership: 499 women-owned, 532 Black-owned, n/a Hispanic-owned, n/a Asian-owned
Employment: 8.0% management, business, and financial, 2.1% computer, engineering, and science, 11.4% education, legal, community service, arts, and media, 4.0% healthcare practitioners, 21.9% service, 21.4% sales and office, 11.7% natural resources, construction, and maintenance, 19.5% production, transportation, and material moving
Income: Per capita: $19,332; Median household: $34,233; Average household: $48,479; Households with income of $100,000 or more: 9.1%; Poverty rate: 25.2%
Educational Attainment: High school diploma or higher: 75.8%; Bachelor's degree or higher: 11.4%; Graduate/professional degree or higher: 4.3%
Housing: Homeownership rate: 73.7%; Median home value: $79,400; Median year structure built: 1979; Homeowner vacancy rate: 1.8%; Median gross rent: $633 per month; Rental vacancy rate: 11.3%
Vital Statistics: Birth rate: 106.8 per 10,000 population; Death rate: 112.2 per 10,000 population; Age-adjusted cancer mortality rate: 178.6 deaths per 100,000 population
Health Insurance: 83.2% have insurance; 53.0% have private insurance; 40.7% have public insurance; 16.8% do not have insurance; 10.0% of children under 18 do not have insurance

Health Care: Physicians: 6.3 per 10,000 population; Hospital beds: 15.4 per 10,000 population; Hospital admissions: 467.5 per 10,000 population
Transportation: Commute: 91.5% car, 2.7% public transportation, 2.8% walk, 2.1% work from home; Median travel time to work: 28.9 minutes
Presidential Election: 63.4% Obama, 36.0% Romney (2012)
National and State Parks: Lake Warren State Park
Additional Information Contacts
Hampton Government . . . . (803) 914-2250
    http://www.hamptoncountysc.org

Hampton County Communities

BRUNSON (town). Covers a land area of 1.017 square miles and a water area of 0 square miles. Located at 32.92° N. Lat; 81.19° W. Long. Elevation is 135 feet.
Population: 554; Growth (since 2000): -5.9%; Density: 544.8 persons per square mile; Race: 56.5% White, 42.1% Black/African American, 0.0% Asian, 0.2% American Indian/Alaska Native, 0.0% Native Hawaiian/Other Pacific Islander, 0.7% Two or more races, 0.9% Hispanic of any race; Average household size: 2.30; Median age: 40.4; Age under 18: 22.2%; Age 65 and over: 13.4%; Males per 100 females: 97.2
School District(s)
Hampton 01 (PK-12)
    2012-13 Enrollment: 2,487 . . . . (803) 943-4576
Housing: Homeownership rate: 63.1%; Homeowner vacancy rate: 3.7%; Rental vacancy rate: 10.0%

EARLY BRANCH (unincorporated postal area)
ZCTA: 29916
    Covers a land area of 73.072 square miles and a water area of 0.070 square miles. Located at 32.72° N. Lat; 80.97° W. Long. Elevation is 69 feet.
    Population: 1,533; Growth (since 2000): -1.7%; Density: 21.0 persons per square mile; Race: 62.4% White, 34.8% Black/African American, 0.3% Asian, 0.0% American Indian/Alaska Native, 0.0% Native Hawaiian/Other Pacific Islander, 1.8% Two or more races, 1.9% Hispanic of any race; Average household size: 2.55; Median age: 42.4; Age under 18: 23.6%; Age 65 and over: 16.2%; Males per 100 females: 94.1
    Housing: Homeownership rate: 81.2%; Homeowner vacancy rate: 0.8%; Rental vacancy rate: 13.0%

ESTILL (town). Covers a land area of 3.230 square miles and a water area of 0 square miles. Located at 32.75° N. Lat; 81.24° W. Long. Elevation is 112 feet.
Population: 2,040; Growth (since 2000): -15.9%; Density: 631.6 persons per square mile; Race: 17.7% White, 78.1% Black/African American, 0.1% Asian, 0.6% American Indian/Alaska Native, 0.0% Native Hawaiian/Other Pacific Islander, 0.9% Two or more races, 4.8% Hispanic of any race; Average household size: 2.69; Median age: 37.3; Age under 18: 27.3%; Age 65 and over: 15.5%; Males per 100 females: 89.9
School District(s)
Hampton 02 (PK-12)
    2012-13 Enrollment: 949 . . . . (803) 625-5001
Housing: Homeownership rate: 60.6%; Homeowner vacancy rate: 3.7%; Rental vacancy rate: 10.2%
Safety: Violent crime rate: 155.3 per 10,000 population; Property crime rate: 486.0 per 10,000 population
Additional Information Contacts
Town of Estill . . . . (803) 625-3243

FURMAN (town). Covers a land area of 3.118 square miles and a water area of 0 square miles. Located at 32.68° N. Lat; 81.19° W. Long. Elevation is 112 feet.
Population: 239; Growth (since 2000): -16.4%; Density: 76.7 persons per square mile; Race: 25.9% White, 73.2% Black/African American, 0.0% Asian, 0.0% American Indian/Alaska Native, 0.0% Native Hawaiian/Other Pacific Islander, 0.8% Two or more races, 1.3% Hispanic of any race; Average household size: 2.41; Median age: 49.1; Age under 18: 17.6%; Age 65 and over: 19.7%; Males per 100 females: 83.8
Housing: Homeownership rate: 84.9%; Homeowner vacancy rate: 1.2%; Rental vacancy rate: 29.2%

GARNETT (unincorporated postal area)
ZCTA: 29922
    Covers a land area of 133.969 square miles and a water area of 1.551 square miles. Located at 32.63° N. Lat; 81.28° W. Long. Elevation is 75 feet.
    Population: 1,214; Growth (since 2000): 42.8%; Density: 9.1 persons per square mile; Race: 11.5% White, 87.5% Black/African American, 0.0% Asian, 0.0% American Indian/Alaska Native, 0.1% Native Hawaiian/Other Pacific Islander, 0.8% Two or more races, 1.6% Hispanic of any race; Average household size: 2.64; Median age: 36.4; Age under 18: 27.0%; Age 65 and over: 11.8%; Males per 100 females: 92.4
    Housing: Homeownership rate: 85.4%; Homeowner vacancy rate: 1.0%; Rental vacancy rate: 16.0%

GIFFORD (town). Covers a land area of 0.967 square miles and a water area of 0 square miles. Located at 32.86° N. Lat; 81.24° W. Long. Elevation is 138 feet.
Population: 288; Growth (since 2000): -22.2%; Density: 297.8 persons per square mile; Race: 4.2% White, 94.1% Black/African American, 0.0% Asian, 0.0% American Indian/Alaska Native, 0.0% Native Hawaiian/Other Pacific Islander, 1.4% Two or more races, 0.0% Hispanic of any race; Average household size: 2.80; Median age: 35.6; Age under 18: 24.7%; Age 65 and over: 12.8%; Males per 100 females: 93.3
Housing: Homeownership rate: 79.6%; Homeowner vacancy rate: 0.0%; Rental vacancy rate: 21.4%

HAMPTON (town). County seat. Covers a land area of 4.513 square miles and a water area of 0.014 square miles. Located at 32.87° N. Lat; 81.11° W. Long. Elevation is 108 feet.
History: Hampton was named for General Wade Hampton, who laid the cornerstone for the new courthouse of Hampton County in 1878.
Population: 2,808; Growth (since 2000): -1.0%; Density: 622.3 persons per square mile; Race: 50.4% White, 45.6% Black/African American, 2.0% Asian, 0.5% American Indian/Alaska Native, 0.0% Native Hawaiian/Other Pacific Islander, 0.9% Two or more races, 1.7% Hispanic of any race; Average household size: 2.33; Median age: 40.6; Age under 18: 25.0%; Age 65 and over: 17.8%; Males per 100 females: 84.7; Marriage status: 25.1% never married, 55.4% now married, 4.1% separated, 7.9% widowed, 11.7% divorced; Foreign born: 1.4%; Speak English only: 95.6%; With disability: 11.9%; Veterans: 12.9%; Ancestry: 13.6% American, 5.5% English, 4.7% Irish, 4.4% German, 2.8% French
Employment: 11.2% management, business, and financial, 0.7% computer, engineering, and science, 16.4% education, legal, community service, arts, and media, 3.7% healthcare practitioners, 27.9% service, 20.1% sales and office, 5.1% natural resources, construction, and maintenance, 14.9% production, transportation, and material moving
Income: Per capita: $18,718; Median household: $38,938; Average household: $54,863; Households with income of $100,000 or more: 15.5%; Poverty rate: 26.5%
Educational Attainment: High school diploma or higher: 82.7%; Bachelor's degree or higher: 19.2%; Graduate/professional degree or higher: 5.0%
School District(s)
Hampton 01 (PK-12)
    2012-13 Enrollment: 2,487 . . . . (803) 943-4576
Housing: Homeownership rate: 61.2%; Median home value: $88,700; Median year structure built: 1974; Homeowner vacancy rate: 3.5%; Median gross rent: $644 per month; Rental vacancy rate: 10.3%
Health Insurance: 78.6% have insurance; 65.6% have private insurance; 25.8% have public insurance; 21.4% do not have insurance; 18.6% of children under 18 do not have insurance
Safety: Violent crime rate: 36.5 per 10,000 population; Property crime rate: 591.2 per 10,000 population
Newspapers: Hampton County Guardian (weekly circulation 4500)
Transportation: Commute: 86.2% car, 4.8% public transportation, 7.2% walk, 1.8% work from home; Median travel time to work: 22.8 minutes

LURAY (town). Covers a land area of 1.033 square miles and a water area of 0 square miles. Located at 32.81° N. Lat; 81.24° W. Long. Elevation is 138 feet.
History: Luray prospered as the center of peanut and strawberry growing.
Population: 127; Growth (since 2000): 10.4%; Density: 122.9 persons per square mile; Race: 45.7% White, 43.3% Black/African American, 0.0% Asian, 0.0% American Indian/Alaska Native, 0.0% Native Hawaiian/Other

Pacific Islander, 2.4% Two or more races, 22.0% Hispanic of any race; Average household size: 2.89; Median age: 42.1; Age under 18: 26.8%; Age 65 and over: 11.8%; Males per 100 females: 98.4
Housing: Homeownership rate: 79.6%; Homeowner vacancy rate: 2.8%; Rental vacancy rate: 0.0%

SCOTIA (town). Covers a land area of 3.165 square miles and a water area of 0 square miles. Located at 32.68° N. Lat; 81.24° W. Long. Elevation is 92 feet.
Population: 215; Growth (since 2000): -5.3%; Density: 67.9 persons per square mile; Race: 28.8% White, 71.2% Black/African American, 0.0% Asian, 0.0% American Indian/Alaska Native, 0.0% Native Hawaiian/Other Pacific Islander, 0.0% Two or more races, 0.0% Hispanic of any race; Average household size: 3.03; Median age: 39.3; Age under 18: 25.6%; Age 65 and over: 13.0%; Males per 100 females: 90.3
Housing: Homeownership rate: 83.1%; Homeowner vacancy rate: 0.0%; Rental vacancy rate: 18.8%

VARNVILLE (town). Covers a land area of 3.832 square miles and a water area of 0 square miles. Located at 32.85° N. Lat; 81.08° W. Long. Elevation is 108 feet.
Population: 2,162; Growth (since 2000): 4.2%; Density: 564.2 persons per square mile; Race: 34.6% White, 63.1% Black/African American, 0.8% Asian, 0.1% American Indian/Alaska Native, 0.0% Native Hawaiian/Other Pacific Islander, 1.3% Two or more races, 0.4% Hispanic of any race; Average household size: 2.62; Median age: 35.4; Age under 18: 29.1%; Age 65 and over: 13.6%; Males per 100 females: 91.3
School District(s)
Hampton 01 (PK-12)
    2012-13 Enrollment: 2,487 . . . . (803) 943-4576
Housing: Homeownership rate: 66.4%; Homeowner vacancy rate: 2.9%; Rental vacancy rate: 10.8%
Hospitals: Hampton Regional Medical Center (68 beds)
Additional Information Contacts
Town of Varnville. . . . . (803) 943-2979
    http://www.varnville.orgindex.html

YEMASSEE (town). Covers a land area of 4.510 square miles and a water area of 0 square miles. Located at 32.69° N. Lat; 80.85° W. Long. Elevation is 43 feet.
Population: 1,027; Growth (since 2000): 27.3%; Density: 227.7 persons per square mile; Race: 41.3% White, 54.5% Black/African American, 1.4% Asian, 0.5% American Indian/Alaska Native, 0.1% Native Hawaiian/Other Pacific Islander, 1.9% Two or more races, 2.4% Hispanic of any race; Average household size: 2.58; Median age: 33.4; Age under 18: 30.3%; Age 65 and over: 11.1%; Males per 100 females: 83.4
School District(s)
Hampton 01 (PK-12)
    2012-13 Enrollment: 2,487 . . . . (803) 943-4576
Housing: Homeownership rate: 66.8%; Homeowner vacancy rate: 1.1%; Rental vacancy rate: 6.3%

Horry County

Located in eastern South Carolina; bounded on the west by Little Pee Dee River, on the southeast by the Atlantic Ocean, and on the northeast by North Carolina; drained by the Waccamaw River. Covers a land area of 1,133.896 square miles, a water area of 121.106 square miles, and is located in the Eastern Time Zone at 33.91° N. Lat., 78.98° W. Long. The county was founded in 1802. County seat is Conway.

Horry County is part of the Myrtle Beach-Conway-North Myrtle Beach, SC-NC Metropolitan Statistical Area. The entire metro area includes: Brunswick County, NC; Horry County, SC

Weather Station: Conway | | | | | | | | | | Elevation: 20 feet
	Jan	Feb	Mar	Apr	May	Jun	Jul	Aug	Sep	Oct	Nov	Dec
High	58	61	68	76	83	88	91	90	85	77	69	60
Low	35	37	44	51	60	68	72	71	65	54	45	37
Precip	4.1	3.4	4.1	3.1	3.6	4.9	6.9	7.3	5.4	3.3	2.8	3.5
Snow	0.2	tr	0.0	0.0	0.0	0.0	0.0	0.0	0.0	0.0	0.0	0.5

High and Low temperatures in degrees Fahrenheit; Precipitation and Snow in inches

Weather Station: Loris 1 S | | | | | | | | | | Elevation: 89 feet
	Jan	Feb	Mar	Apr	May	Jun	Jul	Aug	Sep	Oct	Nov	Dec
High	56	60	67	75	82	87	90	89	84	76	68	58
Low	33	35	40	48	56	65	70	69	62	51	41	34
Precip	4.0	3.6	4.1	3.1	3.7	5.3	6.1	6.9	5.8	3.0	2.7	2.9
Snow	0.3	0.3	0.6	0.0	0.0	0.0	0.0	0.0	0.0	0.0	0.0	0.6

High and Low temperatures in degrees Fahrenheit; Precipitation and Snow in inches

Population: 269,291; Growth (since 2000): 37.0%; Density: 237.5 persons per square mile; Race: 79.9% White, 13.4% Black/African American, 1.0% Asian, 0.5% American Indian/Alaska Native, 0.1% Native Hawaiian/Other Pacific Islander, 2.0% two or more races, 6.2% Hispanic of any race; Average household size: 2.37; Median age: 41.1; Age under 18: 20.1%; Age 65 and over: 17.1%; Males per 100 females: 95.7; Marriage status: 28.1% never married, 53.9% now married, 2.8% separated, 7.1% widowed, 10.9% divorced; Foreign born: 6.7%; Speak English only: 91.7%; With disability: 14.6%; Veterans: 12.6%; Ancestry: 14.5% American, 13.9% English, 13.7% Irish, 13.7% German, 6.7% Italian
Religion: Six largest groups: 16.6% Baptist, 6.7% Catholicism, 6.1% Methodist/Pietist, 4.7% Non-denominational Protestant, 1.8% Presbyterian-Reformed, 1.5% Pentecostal
Economy: Unemployment rate: 6.8%; Leading industries: 20.2% retail trade; 15.0% accommodation and food services; 9.7% construction; Farms: 938 totaling 177,569 acres; Company size: 2 employ 1,000 or more persons, 4 employ 500 to 999 persons, 115 employ 100 to 499 persons, 8,066 employ less than 100 persons; Business ownership: 6,624 women-owned, 1,328 Black-owned, 431 Hispanic-owned, 530 Asian-owned
Employment: 11.5% management, business, and financial, 1.8% computer, engineering, and science, 9.1% education, legal, community service, arts, and media, 5.2% healthcare practitioners, 25.6% service, 29.5% sales and office, 10.6% natural resources, construction, and maintenance, 6.8% production, transportation, and material moving
Income: Per capita: $24,002; Median household: $42,431; Average household: $56,988; Households with income of $100,000 or more: 12.8%; Poverty rate: 18.6%
Educational Attainment: High school diploma or higher: 87.7%; Bachelor's degree or higher: 22.7%; Graduate/professional degree or higher: 7.4%
Housing: Homeownership rate: 68.6%; Median home value: $159,600; Median year structure built: 1992; Homeowner vacancy rate: 4.9%; Median gross rent: $833 per month; Rental vacancy rate: 29.2%
Vital Statistics: Birth rate: 105.7 per 10,000 population; Death rate: 95.2 per 10,000 population; Age-adjusted cancer mortality rate: 183.7 deaths per 100,000 population
Health Insurance: 78.0% have insurance; 58.6% have private insurance; 35.0% have public insurance; 22.0% do not have insurance; 13.3% of children under 18 do not have insurance
Health Care: Physicians: 18.3 per 10,000 population; Hospital beds: 24.5 per 10,000 population; Hospital admissions: 988.1 per 10,000 population
Transportation: Commute: 93.0% car, 0.3% public transportation, 1.5% walk, 3.1% work from home; Median travel time to work: 21.2 minutes
Presidential Election: 34.6% Obama, 64.2% Romney (2012)
National and State Parks: Myrtle Beach State Park
Additional Information Contacts
Horry Government. . . . . (843) 915-5080
    http://www.horrycounty.org

Horry County Communities

ATLANTIC BEACH (town). Covers a land area of 0.160 square miles and a water area of 0 square miles. Located at 33.80° N. Lat; 78.72° W. Long. Elevation is 30 feet.
Population: 334; Growth (since 2000): -4.8%; Density: 2,085.2 persons per square mile; Race: 29.3% White, 54.5% Black/African American, 0.0% Asian, 0.9% American Indian/Alaska Native, 0.0% Native Hawaiian/Other Pacific Islander, 4.5% Two or more races, 16.5% Hispanic of any race; Average household size: 2.24; Median age: 31.7; Age under 18: 25.1%; Age 65 and over: 11.4%; Males per 100 females: 90.9
Housing: Homeownership rate: 19.6%; Homeowner vacancy rate: 3.3%; Rental vacancy rate: 34.6%

AYNOR (town). Covers a land area of 1.857 square miles and a water area of 0 square miles. Located at 34.00° N. Lat; 79.21° W. Long. Elevation is 112 feet.
Population: 560; Growth (since 2000): -4.6%; Density: 301.6 persons per square mile; Race: 81.6% White, 15.7% Black/African American, 0.4% Asian, 0.9% American Indian/Alaska Native, 0.0% Native Hawaiian/Other Pacific Islander, 1.4% Two or more races, 0.7% Hispanic of any race; Average household size: 2.40; Median age: 41.2; Age under 18: 24.8%; Age 65 and over: 18.8%; Males per 100 females: 87.9
School District(s)
Horry 01 (PK-12)
    2012-13 Enrollment: 39,998 . . . . (843) 488-6700
Housing: Homeownership rate: 70.4%; Homeowner vacancy rate: 1.8%; Rental vacancy rate: 19.8%
Safety: Violent crime rate: 16.3 per 10,000 population; Property crime rate: 114.2 per 10,000 population

BRIARCLIFFE ACRES (town). Covers a land area of 0.655 square miles and a water area of 0 square miles. Located at 33.79° N. Lat; 78.75° W. Long. Elevation is 10 feet.
Population: 457; Growth (since 2000): -2.8%; Density: 697.8 persons per square mile; Race: 95.8% White, 1.1% Black/African American, 0.7% Asian, 0.0% American Indian/Alaska Native, 0.9% Native Hawaiian/Other Pacific Islander, 1.5% Two or more races, 1.1% Hispanic of any race; Average household size: 2.23; Median age: 59.5; Age under 18: 13.3%; Age 65 and over: 33.0%; Males per 100 females: 85.0
Housing: Homeownership rate: 95.1%; Homeowner vacancy rate: 3.0%; Rental vacancy rate: 23.1%
Additional Information Contacts
Town of Briarcliffe Acres . . . . (843) 272-8863
    http://www.townofbriarcliffe.us

BUCKSPORT (CDP). Covers a land area of 4.204 square miles and a water area of 0.020 square miles. Located at 33.67° N. Lat; 79.11° W. Long. Elevation is 20 feet.
Population: 876; Growth (since 2000): -21.6%; Density: 208.4 persons per square mile; Race: 8.0% White, 90.2% Black/African American, 0.0% Asian, 0.0% American Indian/Alaska Native, 0.0% Native Hawaiian/Other Pacific Islander, 1.0% Two or more races, 1.9% Hispanic of any race; Average household size: 2.59; Median age: 43.0; Age under 18: 24.0%; Age 65 and over: 14.5%; Males per 100 females: 80.6
Housing: Homeownership rate: 80.4%; Homeowner vacancy rate: 2.5%; Rental vacancy rate: 25.0%

CONWAY (city). County seat. Covers a land area of 21.942 square miles and a water area of 0.841 square miles. Located at 33.85° N. Lat; 79.04° W. Long. Elevation is 36 feet.
History: Early settlers to Conway came from North Carolina to work in lumber operations and the naval stores industry. The first inhabitants were connected to the outside world only by the rivers down which they shipped their logs and turpentine to the coast. Conway was established on land granted by George II of England. In 1801 it was named in honor of General Robert Conway.
Population: 17,103; Growth (since 2000): 45.1%; Density: 779.5 persons per square mile; Race: 59.6% White, 37.0% Black/African American, 0.7% Asian, 0.2% American Indian/Alaska Native, 0.0% Native Hawaiian/Other Pacific Islander, 1.5% Two or more races, 2.9% Hispanic of any race; Average household size: 2.49; Median age: 29.3; Age under 18: 20.0%; Age 65 and over: 13.2%; Males per 100 females: 84.3; Marriage status: 47.4% never married, 37.9% now married, 2.9% separated, 8.1% widowed, 6.7% divorced; Foreign born: 2.3%; Speak English only: 96.7%; With disability: 14.2%; Veterans: 10.0%; Ancestry: 11.2% American, 9.1% Irish, 8.2% German, 8.0% English, 4.6% Italian
Employment: 10.1% management, business, and financial, 1.8% computer, engineering, and science, 11.6% education, legal, community service, arts, and media, 4.5% healthcare practitioners, 31.5% service, 29.4% sales and office, 4.9% natural resources, construction, and maintenance, 6.3% production, transportation, and material moving
Income: Per capita: $19,036; Median household: $34,732; Average household: $51,292; Households with income of $100,000 or more: 9.2%; Poverty rate: 32.7%
Educational Attainment: High school diploma or higher: 84.8%; Bachelor's degree or higher: 23.8%; Graduate/professional degree or higher: 9.5%

School District(s)
Horry 01 (PK-12)
    2012-13 Enrollment: 39,998 . . . . (843) 488-6700
Four-year College(s)
Coastal Carolina University (Public)
    Fall 2013 Enrollment: 9,478 . . . . (843) 347-3161
    2013-14 Tuition: In-state $9,760; Out-of-state $22,770
Two-year College(s)
Horry-Georgetown Technical College (Public)
    Fall 2013 Enrollment: 7,660 . . . . (843) 347-3186
    2013-14 Tuition: In-state $4,504; Out-of-state $6,294
Miller-Motte Technical College-Conway (Private, For-profit)
    Fall 2013 Enrollment: 752 . . . . (843) 591-1100
    2013-14 Tuition: In-state $10,422; Out-of-state $10,422
Housing: Homeownership rate: 56.4%; Median home value: $149,700; Median year structure built: 1984; Homeowner vacancy rate: 5.8%; Median gross rent: $687 per month; Rental vacancy rate: 10.9%
Health Insurance: 83.4% have insurance; 60.1% have private insurance; 34.3% have public insurance; 16.6% do not have insurance; 9.4% of children under 18 do not have insurance
Hospitals: Conway Medical Center (248 beds)
Safety: Violent crime rate: 59.1 per 10,000 population; Property crime rate: 460.2 per 10,000 population
Newspapers: Horry Independent (weekly circulation 6000); Myrtle Beach Herald (weekly circulation 4000)
Transportation: Commute: 89.3% car, 2.3% public transportation, 3.0% walk, 3.3% work from home; Median travel time to work: 20.5 minutes
Additional Information Contacts
City of Conway . . . . (843) 248-1760
    http://www.cityofconway.com

FORESTBROOK (CDP). Covers a land area of 3.737 square miles and a water area of 0 square miles. Located at 33.72° N. Lat; 78.97° W. Long. Elevation is 13 feet.
Population: 4,612; Growth (since 2000): 36.0%; Density: 1,234.2 persons per square mile; Race: 85.9% White, 7.6% Black/African American, 1.3% Asian, 0.3% American Indian/Alaska Native, 0.1% Native Hawaiian/Other Pacific Islander, 2.5% Two or more races, 5.8% Hispanic of any race; Average household size: 2.65; Median age: 39.9; Age under 18: 23.3%; Age 65 and over: 13.0%; Males per 100 females: 99.1; Marriage status: 27.2% never married, 58.2% now married, 4.2% separated, 5.0% widowed, 9.6% divorced; Foreign born: 3.0%; Speak English only: 96.1%; With disability: 12.0%; Veterans: 10.9%; Ancestry: 20.8% German, 15.0% American, 13.4% Irish, 13.1% English, 7.4% Italian
Employment: 10.1% management, business, and financial, 7.5% computer, engineering, and science, 5.7% education, legal, community service, arts, and media, 8.1% healthcare practitioners, 24.2% service, 33.2% sales and office, 7.9% natural resources, construction, and maintenance, 3.3% production, transportation, and material moving
Income: Per capita: $26,441; Median household: $58,858; Average household: $63,914; Households with income of $100,000 or more: 22.3%; Poverty rate: 14.2%
Educational Attainment: High school diploma or higher: 93.9%; Bachelor's degree or higher: 20.5%; Graduate/professional degree or higher: 6.6%
Housing: Homeownership rate: 77.9%; Median home value: $162,000; Median year structure built: 1991; Homeowner vacancy rate: 4.3%; Median gross rent: $738 per month; Rental vacancy rate: 14.5%
Health Insurance: 79.7% have insurance; 68.6% have private insurance; 26.6% have public insurance; 20.3% do not have insurance; 18.2% of children under 18 do not have insurance
Transportation: Commute: 98.6% car, 0.0% public transportation, 0.0% walk, 1.0% work from home; Median travel time to work: 20.7 minutes

GALIVANTS FERRY (unincorporated postal area)
ZCTA: 29544
    Covers a land area of 113.969 square miles and a water area of 0.934 square miles. Located at 33.93° N. Lat; 79.26° W. Long. Elevation is 43 feet.
    Population: 4,909; Growth (since 2000): 12.5%; Density: 43.1 persons per square mile; Race: 91.1% White, 6.5% Black/African American, 0.0% Asian, 0.8% American Indian/Alaska Native, 0.0% Native Hawaiian/Other Pacific Islander, 0.9% Two or more races, 2.1% Hispanic of any race; Average household size: 2.66; Median age: 37.2; Age under 18: 26.1%; Age 65 and over: 12.0%; Males per 100 females:

95.3; Marriage status: 25.0% never married, 60.9% now married, 2.2% separated, 4.9% widowed, 9.1% divorced; Foreign born: 1.0%; Speak English only: 97.2%; With disability: 23.4%; Veterans: 10.1%; Ancestry: 26.3% American, 18.9% English, 14.5% Irish, 3.5% German, 1.3% Italian

Employment: 9.5% management, business, and financial, 3.1% computer, engineering, and science, 8.0% education, legal, community service, arts, and media, 5.5% healthcare practitioners, 24.9% service, 24.2% sales and office, 14.7% natural resources, construction, and maintenance, 10.1% production, transportation, and material moving

Income: Per capita: $15,950; Median household: $39,757; Average household: $46,526; Households with income of $100,000 or more: 9.2%; Poverty rate: 20.2%

Educational Attainment: High school diploma or higher: 72.1%; Bachelor's degree or higher: 12.5%; Graduate/professional degree or higher: 4.3%

School District(s)

Horry 01 (PK-12)
    2012-13 Enrollment: 39,998 . . . . (843) 488-6700
    Housing: Homeownership rate: 74.7%; Median home value: $102,000; Median year structure built: 1988; Homeowner vacancy rate: 1.4%; Median gross rent: $667 per month; Rental vacancy rate: 19.6%
    Health Insurance: 88.9% have insurance; 56.9% have private insurance; 43.0% have public insurance; 11.1% do not have insurance; 1.2% of children under 18 do not have insurance
    Transportation: Commute: 91.4% car, 0.6% public transportation, 0.4% walk, 6.5% work from home; Median travel time to work: 27.5 minutes

GARDEN CITY (CDP). Covers a land area of 5.368 square miles and a water area of 0.080 square miles. Located at 33.59° N. Lat; 79.01° W. Long. Elevation is 20 feet.

Population: 9,209; Growth (since 2000): -1.6%; Density: 1,715.6 persons per square mile; Race: 95.3% White, 1.7% Black/African American, 0.3% Asian, 0.3% American Indian/Alaska Native, 0.1% Native Hawaiian/Other Pacific Islander, 1.4% Two or more races, 2.9% Hispanic of any race; Average household size: 1.99; Median age: 56.1; Age under 18: 13.0%; Age 65 and over: 35.2%; Males per 100 females: 87.4; Marriage status: 19.2% never married, 52.6% now married, 1.5% separated, 15.5% widowed, 12.8% divorced; Foreign born: 3.7%; Speak English only: 96.6%; With disability: 17.1%; Veterans: 17.6%; Ancestry: 19.9% German, 19.5% American, 14.5% Irish, 12.3% English, 6.0% Italian

Employment: 14.9% management, business, and financial, 1.4% computer, engineering, and science, 8.5% education, legal, community service, arts, and media, 3.6% healthcare practitioners, 23.0% service, 33.4% sales and office, 9.8% natural resources, construction, and maintenance, 5.4% production, transportation, and material moving

Income: Per capita: $28,339; Median household: $37,173; Average household: $54,620; Households with income of $100,000 or more: 8.2%; Poverty rate: 14.4%

Educational Attainment: High school diploma or higher: 90.7%; Bachelor's degree or higher: 23.5%; Graduate/professional degree or higher: 7.1%

School District(s)

Horry 01 (PK-12)
    2012-13 Enrollment: 39,998 . . . . (843) 488-6700
    Housing: Homeownership rate: 75.8%; Median home value: $125,200; Median year structure built: 1990; Homeowner vacancy rate: 5.5%; Median gross rent: $860 per month; Rental vacancy rate: 50.6%
    Health Insurance: 80.9% have insurance; 67.1% have private insurance; 44.6% have public insurance; 19.1% do not have insurance; 28.8% of children under 18 do not have insurance
    Transportation: Commute: 95.9% car, 0.0% public transportation, 0.4% walk, 3.2% work from home; Median travel time to work: 21.1 minutes

GREEN SEA (unincorporated postal area)
ZCTA: 29545
    Covers a land area of 35.932 square miles and a water area of 0.062 square miles. Located at 34.16° N. Lat; 78.97° W. Long. Elevation is 85 feet.
    Population: 1,657; Growth (since 2000): 15.1%; Density: 46.1 persons per square mile; Race: 74.1% White, 22.4% Black/African American, 0.2% Asian, 0.7% American Indian/Alaska Native, 0.0% Native Hawaiian/Other Pacific Islander, 1.1% Two or more races, 2.2% Hispanic of any race; Average household size: 2.63; Median age: 36.0;

Age under 18: 27.6%; Age 65 and over: 13.6%; Males per 100 females: 96.1

School District(s)

Horry 01 (PK-12)
    2012-13 Enrollment: 39,998 . . . . (843) 488-6700
    Housing: Homeownership rate: 74.2%; Homeowner vacancy rate: 1.7%; Rental vacancy rate: 9.9%

LITTLE RIVER (CDP). Covers a land area of 10.480 square miles and a water area of 0.346 square miles. Located at 33.88° N. Lat; 78.64° W. Long. Elevation is 36 feet.

History: Little River was once known as Yankee Town because of its numerous North Carolina settlers.

Population: 8,960; Growth (since 2000): 27.5%; Density: 855.0 persons per square mile; Race: 89.0% White, 6.6% Black/African American, 0.9% Asian, 0.5% American Indian/Alaska Native, 0.0% Native Hawaiian/Other Pacific Islander, 1.3% Two or more races, 3.2% Hispanic of any race; Average household size: 2.02; Median age: 54.1; Age under 18: 13.1%; Age 65 and over: 29.0%; Males per 100 females: 92.9; Marriage status: 16.2% never married, 58.7% now married, 1.5% separated, 9.1% widowed, 16.0% divorced; Foreign born: 4.1%; Speak English only: 93.0%; With disability: 14.9%; Veterans: 15.2%; Ancestry: 19.6% English, 17.4% German, 14.9% Irish, 11.9% American, 7.0% Italian

Employment: 12.9% management, business, and financial, 3.0% computer, engineering, and science, 6.6% education, legal, community service, arts, and media, 2.1% healthcare practitioners, 25.6% service, 35.5% sales and office, 8.9% natural resources, construction, and maintenance, 5.3% production, transportation, and material moving

Income: Per capita: $27,237; Median household: $44,606; Average household: $53,035; Households with income of $100,000 or more: 13.3%; Poverty rate: 9.8%

Educational Attainment: High school diploma or higher: 90.0%; Bachelor's degree or higher: 26.3%; Graduate/professional degree or higher: 6.6%

School District(s)

Horry 01 (PK-12)
    2012-13 Enrollment: 39,998 . . . . (843) 488-6700
    Housing: Homeownership rate: 73.1%; Median home value: $172,400; Median year structure built: 1991; Homeowner vacancy rate: 4.6%; Median gross rent: $845 per month; Rental vacancy rate: 20.9%
    Health Insurance: 81.7% have insurance; 67.5% have private insurance; 39.0% have public insurance; 18.3% do not have insurance; 0.0% of children under 18 do not have insurance
    Transportation: Commute: 92.7% car, 0.0% public transportation, 1.2% walk, 6.1% work from home; Median travel time to work: 18.5 minutes

LONGS (unincorporated postal area)
ZCTA: 29568
    Covers a land area of 92.071 square miles and a water area of 0.276 square miles. Located at 33.91° N. Lat; 78.75° W. Long. Elevation is 36 feet.
    Population: 12,224; Growth (since 2000): 57.2%; Density: 132.8 persons per square mile; Race: 65.1% White, 30.8% Black/African American, 0.9% Asian, 0.5% American Indian/Alaska Native, 0.0% Native Hawaiian/Other Pacific Islander, 1.8% Two or more races, 3.4% Hispanic of any race; Average household size: 2.46; Median age: 43.8; Age under 18: 21.8%; Age 65 and over: 18.3%; Males per 100 females: 93.8; Marriage status: 25.4% never married, 57.7% now married, 3.0% separated, 7.1% widowed, 9.8% divorced; Foreign born: 3.7%; Speak English only: 96.2%; With disability: 15.8%; Veterans: 13.8%; Ancestry: 16.4% German, 14.4% English, 13.6% Irish, 6.8% American, 5.2% Italian

Employment: 9.7% management, business, and financial, 3.0% computer, engineering, and science, 8.7% education, legal, community service, arts, and media, 4.0% healthcare practitioners, 23.5% service, 32.2% sales and office, 7.0% natural resources, construction, and maintenance, 11.8% production, transportation, and material moving

Income: Per capita: $23,184; Median household: $43,304; Average household: $56,596; Households with income of $100,000 or more: 12.8%; Poverty rate: 16.8%

Educational Attainment: High school diploma or higher: 90.8%; Bachelor's degree or higher: 16.9%; Graduate/professional degree or higher: 3.3%

Housing: Homeownership rate: 82.0%; Median home value: $139,200; Median year structure built: 1998; Homeowner vacancy rate: 3.9%; Median gross rent: $860 per month; Rental vacancy rate: 19.9%
Health Insurance: 85.2% have insurance; 61.8% have private insurance; 38.1% have public insurance; 14.8% do not have insurance; 2.7% of children under 18 do not have insurance
Transportation: Commute: 95.0% car, 0.0% public transportation, 1.5% walk, 2.5% work from home; Median travel time to work: 23.6 minutes

---

LORIS (city).
Covers a land area of 4.547 square miles and a water area of 0.020 square miles. Located at 34.06° N. Lat; 78.89° W. Long. Elevation is 98 feet.
History: Loris gained recognition as a strawberry market as well as one of the principal tobacco markets.
Population: 2,396; Growth (since 2000): 15.2%; Density: 527.0 persons per square mile; Race: 53.9% White, 39.7% Black/African American, 1.2% Asian, 0.3% American Indian/Alaska Native, 0.1% Native Hawaiian/Other Pacific Islander, 2.1% Two or more races, 4.4% Hispanic of any race; Average household size: 2.39; Median age: 42.7; Age under 18: 22.0%; Age 65 and over: 19.7%; Males per 100 females: 78.8
School District(s)
Horry 01 (PK-12)
    2012-13 Enrollment: 39,998 . . . . (843) 488-6700
Housing: Homeownership rate: 58.8%; Homeowner vacancy rate: 3.5%; Rental vacancy rate: 12.5%
Hospitals: Mcleod Loris Seacoast Hospital
Safety: Violent crime rate: 76.4 per 10,000 population; Property crime rate: 579.2 per 10,000 population
Newspapers: Loris Scene (weekly circulation 6500)

MYRTLE BEACH (city).
Covers a land area of 23.324 square miles and a water area of 0.242 square miles. Located at 33.71° N. Lat; 78.89° W. Long. Elevation is 26 feet.
History: Incorporated 1938.
Population: 27,109; Growth (since 2000): 19.1%; Density: 1,162.3 persons per square mile; Race: 72.3% White, 13.9% Black/African American, 1.5% Asian, 0.7% American Indian/Alaska Native, 0.3% Native Hawaiian/Other Pacific Islander, 2.7% Two or more races, 13.7% Hispanic of any race; Average household size: 2.22; Median age: 39.2; Age under 18: 18.5%; Age 65 and over: 15.1%; Males per 100 females: 103.2; Marriage status: 34.8% never married, 46.2% now married, 2.9% separated, 6.8% widowed, 12.1% divorced; Foreign born: 18.4%; Speak English only: 77.4%; With disability: 14.4%; Veterans: 9.4%; Ancestry: 13.0% Irish, 12.5% English, 9.6% American, 9.6% German, 6.9% Italian
Employment: 9.2% management, business, and financial, 2.3% computer, engineering, and science, 8.9% education, legal, community service, arts, and media, 6.1% healthcare practitioners, 28.1% service, 26.8% sales and office, 13.4% natural resources, construction, and maintenance, 5.2% production, transportation, and material moving
Income: Per capita: $27,178; Median household: $36,293; Average household: $62,405; Households with income of $100,000 or more: 15.1%; Poverty rate: 26.6%
Educational Attainment: High school diploma or higher: 84.4%; Bachelor's degree or higher: 27.3%; Graduate/professional degree or higher: 9.2%
School District(s)
Horry 01 (PK-12)
    2012-13 Enrollment: 39,998 . . . . (843) 488-6700
Four-year College(s)
Cathedral Bible College (Private, Not-for-profit, Other Protestant)
    Fall 2013 Enrollment: 156 . . . . (843) 477-1503
    2013-14 Tuition: In-state $2,600; Out-of-state $2,600
ITT Technical Institute-Myrtle Beach (Private, For-profit)
    Fall 2013 Enrollment: 216 . . . . (843) 497-7820
    2013-14 Tuition: In-state $18,048; Out-of-state $18,048
Two-year College(s)
Golf Academy of America-Myrtle Beach (Private, For-profit)
    Fall 2013 Enrollment: 299 . . . . (800) 342-7342
    2013-14 Tuition: In-state $16,670; Out-of-state $16,670
Vocational/Technical School(s)
Strand College of Hair Design (Private, For-profit)
    Fall 2013 Enrollment: 58 . . . . (843) 467-2397
    2013-14 Tuition: $14,300

Housing: Homeownership rate: 48.7%; Median home value: $167,100; Median year structure built: 1985; Homeowner vacancy rate: 6.7%; Median gross rent: $822 per month; Rental vacancy rate: 23.1%
Health Insurance: 66.2% have insurance; 46.6% have private insurance; 33.4% have public insurance; 33.8% do not have insurance; 20.8% of children under 18 do not have insurance
Hospitals: Grand Strand Regional Medical Center (219 beds)
Safety: Violent crime rate: 165.7 per 10,000 population; Property crime rate: 1,596.1 per 10,000 population
Newspapers: Sun News (daily circulation 48100)
Transportation: Commute: 87.8% car, 0.4% public transportation, 4.9% walk, 2.2% work from home; Median travel time to work: 16.9 minutes
Airports: Myrtle Beach International (primary service/small hub)
Additional Information Contacts
City of Myrtle Beach . . . . (843) 918-1000
    http://www.cityofmyrtlebeach.com

NORTH MYRTLE BEACH (city).
Covers a land area of 17.094 square miles and a water area of 0.599 square miles. Located at 33.80° N. Lat; 78.75° W. Long. Elevation is 7 feet.
History: North Myrtle Beach is a coastal resort city in Horry County, South Carolina. It was created in 1968 from four existing municipalities north of Myrtle Beach, and serves as one of the primary tourist towns along the Grand Strand.
Population: 13,752; Growth (since 2000): 25.3%; Density: 804.5 persons per square mile; Race: 90.4% White, 3.3% Black/African American, 0.9% Asian, 0.5% American Indian/Alaska Native, 0.1% Native Hawaiian/Other Pacific Islander, 1.4% Two or more races, 6.3% Hispanic of any race; Average household size: 2.04; Median age: 54.7; Age under 18: 11.8%; Age 65 and over: 27.2%; Males per 100 females: 97.7; Marriage status: 18.6% never married, 58.5% now married, 3.7% separated, 8.6% widowed, 14.3% divorced; Foreign born: 7.5%; Speak English only: 93.1%; With disability: 16.0%; Veterans: 15.6%; Ancestry: 23.3% English, 16.6% German, 16.1% Irish, 9.5% American, 7.0% Italian
Employment: 13.0% management, business, and financial, 1.5% computer, engineering, and science, 12.0% education, legal, community service, arts, and media, 4.4% healthcare practitioners, 27.8% service, 31.6% sales and office, 5.9% natural resources, construction, and maintenance, 3.7% production, transportation, and material moving
Income: Per capita: $35,046; Median household: $47,679; Average household: $67,644; Households with income of $100,000 or more: 16.4%; Poverty rate: 10.2%
Educational Attainment: High school diploma or higher: 92.5%; Bachelor's degree or higher: 31.9%; Graduate/professional degree or higher: 12.7%
School District(s)
Horry 01 (PK-12)
    2012-13 Enrollment: 39,998 . . . . (843) 488-6700
Housing: Homeownership rate: 69.5%; Median home value: $248,000; Median year structure built: 1993; Homeowner vacancy rate: 11.3%; Median gross rent: $827 per month; Rental vacancy rate: 57.4%
Health Insurance: 80.4% have insurance; 67.2% have private insurance; 38.5% have public insurance; 19.6% do not have insurance; 9.1% of children under 18 do not have insurance
Safety: Violent crime rate: 81.8 per 10,000 population; Property crime rate: 1,068.7 per 10,000 population
Newspapers: North Myrtle Beach Times (weekly circulation 16000)
Transportation: Commute: 87.9% car, 0.2% public transportation, 2.6% walk, 4.1% work from home; Median travel time to work: 18.7 minutes
Airports: Grand Strand (general aviation)
Additional Information Contacts
City of North Myrtle Beach . . . . (843) 280-5555
    http://www.n-myrtle-beach.sc.us

RED HILL (CDP).
Covers a land area of 11.290 square miles and a water area of 0.059 square miles. Located at 33.78° N. Lat; 79.01° W. Long. Elevation is 33 feet.
Population: 13,223; Growth (since 2000): 25.8%; Density: 1,171.2 persons per square mile; Race: 81.5% White, 9.9% Black/African American, 1.2% Asian, 0.5% American Indian/Alaska Native, 0.1% Native Hawaiian/Other Pacific Islander, 2.2% Two or more races, 8.5% Hispanic of any race; Average household size: 2.43; Median age: 40.0; Age under 18: 19.3%; Age 65 and over: 18.6%; Males per 100 females: 96.7; Marriage status: 31.9% never married, 52.9% now married, 3.7% separated, 6.8% widowed, 8.4% divorced; Foreign born: 10.1%; Speak

English only: 87.3%; With disability: 13.8%; Veterans: 10.8%; Ancestry: 19.3% American, 16.6% German, 13.2% Irish, 11.9% English, 6.8% Italian
Employment: 11.3% management, business, and financial, 1.2% computer, engineering, and science, 9.3% education, legal, community service, arts, and media, 2.8% healthcare practitioners, 21.9% service, 30.8% sales and office, 16.6% natural resources, construction, and maintenance, 6.0% production, transportation, and material moving
Income: Per capita: $22,234; Median household: $41,939; Average household: $53,319; Households with income of $100,000 or more: 11.1%; Poverty rate: 22.0%
Educational Attainment: High school diploma or higher: 87.0%; Bachelor's degree or higher: 20.5%; Graduate/professional degree or higher: 7.9%
Housing: Homeownership rate: 70.5%; Median home value: $158,900; Median year structure built: 1994; Homeowner vacancy rate: 3.8%; Median gross rent: $822 per month; Rental vacancy rate: 18.9%
Health Insurance: 76.8% have insurance; 58.1% have private insurance; 34.6% have public insurance; 23.2% do not have insurance; 25.7% of children under 18 do not have insurance
Transportation: Commute: 95.4% car, 0.1% public transportation, 1.0% walk, 1.8% work from home; Median travel time to work: 21.1 minutes

SOCASTEE (CDP). Covers a land area of 13.345 square miles and a water area of 0.524 square miles. Located at 33.69° N. Lat; 79.01° W. Long. Elevation is 20 feet.
Population: 19,952; Growth (since 2000): 39.6%; Density: 1,495.0 persons per square mile; Race: 81.8% White, 7.6% Black/African American, 1.8% Asian, 0.6% American Indian/Alaska Native, 0.2% Native Hawaiian/Other Pacific Islander, 2.9% Two or more races, 10.8% Hispanic of any race; Average household size: 2.50; Median age: 36.3; Age under 18: 22.5%; Age 65 and over: 11.6%; Males per 100 females: 97.9; Marriage status: 29.3% never married, 52.7% now married, 2.1% separated, 4.9% widowed, 13.2% divorced; Foreign born: 9.3%; Speak English only: 89.9%; With disability: 12.5%; Veterans: 15.2%; Ancestry: 17.3% American, 15.0% Irish, 14.1% German, 10.1% English, 7.0% Italian
Employment: 10.3% management, business, and financial, 1.4% computer, engineering, and science, 6.5% education, legal, community service, arts, and media, 5.6% healthcare practitioners, 30.0% service, 30.2% sales and office, 10.5% natural resources, construction, and maintenance, 5.5% production, transportation, and material moving
Income: Per capita: $19,536; Median household: $39,558; Average household: $48,890; Households with income of $100,000 or more: 7.5%; Poverty rate: 18.9%
Educational Attainment: High school diploma or higher: 89.0%; Bachelor's degree or higher: 16.3%; Graduate/professional degree or higher: 5.6%
Housing: Homeownership rate: 60.7%; Median home value: $143,800; Median year structure built: 1993; Homeowner vacancy rate: 4.0%; Median gross rent: $847 per month; Rental vacancy rate: 14.7%
Health Insurance: 73.7% have insurance; 53.3% have private insurance; 31.7% have public insurance; 26.3% do not have insurance; 21.7% of children under 18 do not have insurance
Transportation: Commute: 92.5% car, 0.0% public transportation, 0.5% walk, 3.7% work from home; Median travel time to work: 19.8 minutes

SURFSIDE BEACH (town). Covers a land area of 1.932 square miles and a water area of 0.022 square miles. Located at 33.61° N. Lat; 78.98° W. Long. Elevation is 10 feet.
Population: 3,837; Growth (since 2000): -13.3%; Density: 1,986.2 persons per square mile; Race: 96.1% White, 0.9% Black/African American, 0.6% Asian, 0.4% American Indian/Alaska Native, 0.0% Native Hawaiian/Other Pacific Islander, 1.3% Two or more races, 2.0% Hispanic of any race; Average household size: 2.06; Median age: 50.3; Age under 18: 13.3%; Age 65 and over: 22.6%; Males per 100 females: 92.3; Marriage status: 24.9% never married, 49.9% now married, 1.8% separated, 8.8% widowed, 16.4% divorced; Foreign born: 4.5%; Speak English only: 94.1%; With disability: 14.0%; Veterans: 13.8%; Ancestry: 26.9% English, 16.2% Irish, 14.2% German, 7.7% American, 5.8% Italian
Employment: 7.2% management, business, and financial, 1.3% computer, engineering, and science, 12.1% education, legal, community service, arts, and media, 7.1% healthcare practitioners, 26.3% service, 30.5% sales and office, 9.3% natural resources, construction, and maintenance, 6.3% production, transportation, and material moving

Income: Per capita: $24,980; Median household: $42,044; Average household: $50,932; Households with income of $100,000 or more: 8.8%; Poverty rate: 10.5%
Educational Attainment: High school diploma or higher: 89.9%; Bachelor's degree or higher: 31.9%; Graduate/professional degree or higher: 11.7%
Housing: Homeownership rate: 63.3%; Median home value: $246,100; Median year structure built: 1987; Homeowner vacancy rate: 7.3%; Median gross rent: $903 per month; Rental vacancy rate: 55.5%
Health Insurance: 82.4% have insurance; 71.5% have private insurance; 33.0% have public insurance; 17.6% do not have insurance; 24.2% of children under 18 do not have insurance
Safety: Violent crime rate: 46.8 per 10,000 population; Property crime rate: 640.2 per 10,000 population
Transportation: Commute: 88.7% car, 0.0% public transportation, 1.1% walk, 4.4% work from home; Median travel time to work: 19.6 minutes
Additional Information Contacts
Town of Surfside Beach . . . . (843) 913-6111
  http://www.surfsidebeach.org

Jasper County

Located in southern South Carolina; bounded on the west by the Savannah River and the Georgia border, on the northeast by the Coosawhatchie River, and on the southeast by the Broad River. Covers a land area of 655.318 square miles, a water area of 44.044 square miles, and is located in the Eastern Time Zone at 32.43° N. Lat., 81.02° W. Long. The county was founded in 1912. County seat is Ridgeland.

Jasper County is part of the Hilton Head Island-Bluffton-Beaufort, SC Metropolitan Statistical Area. The entire metro area includes: Beaufort County, SC; Jasper County, SC

Population: 24,777; Growth (since 2000): 19.8%; Density: 37.8 persons per square mile; Race: 43.0% White, 46.0% Black/African American, 0.7% Asian, 0.5% American Indian/Alaska Native, 0.1% Native Hawaiian/Other Pacific Islander, 1.4% two or more races, 15.1% Hispanic of any race; Average household size: 2.73; Median age: 34.6; Age under 18: 24.8%; Age 65 and over: 11.2%; Males per 100 females: 108.7; Marriage status: 38.1% never married, 45.9% now married, 4.5% separated, 8.3% widowed, 7.6% divorced; Foreign born: 9.1%; Speak English only: 87.2%; With disability: 15.1%; Veterans: 8.4%; Ancestry: 7.4% Irish, 6.1% American, 5.8% English, 5.2% German, 1.7% Italian
Religion: Six largest groups: 13.5% Baptist, 4.6% Methodist/Pietist, 3.9% Catholicism, 2.6% Latter-day Saints, 1.8% Pentecostal, 0.9% Adventist
Economy: Unemployment rate: 5.8%; Leading industries: 19.4% retail trade; 14.7% construction; 11.7% other services (except public administration); Farms: 115 totaling 68,602 acres; Company size: 0 employ 1,000 or more persons, 0 employ 500 to 999 persons, 6 employ 100 to 499 persons, 531 employs less than 100 persons; Business ownership: 407 women-owned, 369 Black-owned, n/a Hispanic-owned, n/a Asian-owned
Employment: 8.6% management, business, and financial, 1.2% computer, engineering, and science, 8.4% education, legal, community service, arts, and media, 3.3% healthcare practitioners, 27.1% service, 22.2% sales and office, 14.5% natural resources, construction, and maintenance, 14.8% production, transportation, and material moving
Income: Per capita: $17,350; Median household: $36,413; Average household: $46,044; Households with income of $100,000 or more: 6.7%; Poverty rate: 23.7%
Educational Attainment: High school diploma or higher: 78.8%; Bachelor's degree or higher: 12.5%; Graduate/professional degree or higher: 3.4%
Housing: Homeownership rate: 68.9%; Median home value: $90,200; Median year structure built: 1990; Homeowner vacancy rate: 3.0%; Median gross rent: $758 per month; Rental vacancy rate: 14.6%
Vital Statistics: Birth rate: 126.2 per 10,000 population; Death rate: 74.7 per 10,000 population; Age-adjusted cancer mortality rate: 195.5 deaths per 100,000 population
Health Insurance: 74.6% have insurance; 49.6% have private insurance; 35.8% have public insurance; 25.4% do not have insurance; 15.9% of children under 18 do not have insurance
Health Care: Physicians: 4.6 per 10,000 population; Hospital beds: 16.2 per 10,000 population; Hospital admissions: 584.8 per 10,000 population

Transportation: Commute: 94.2% car, 0.0% public transportation, 1.2% walk, 3.3% work from home; Median travel time to work: 27.6 minutes
Presidential Election: 57.4% Obama, 41.6% Romney (2012)
National and State Parks: Savannah National Wildlife Refuge; Tybee National Wildlife Refuge
Additional Information Contacts
Jasper Government. . . . . (843) 726-7710
    http://www.jaspercountysc.org

Jasper County Communities

HARDEEVILLE (city). Covers a land area of 45.161 square miles and a water area of 0.109 square miles. Located at 32.29° N. Lat; 81.04° W. Long. Elevation is 26 feet.
Population: 2,952; Growth (since 2000): 64.6%; Density: 65.4 persons per square mile; Race: 43.7% White, 34.7% Black/African American, 2.0% Asian, 0.8% American Indian/Alaska Native, 0.0% Native Hawaiian/Other Pacific Islander, 2.7% Two or more races, 28.4% Hispanic of any race; Average household size: 2.76; Median age: 29.3; Age under 18: 25.4%; Age 65 and over: 7.9%; Males per 100 females: 107.2; Marriage status: 44.7% never married, 42.5% now married, 6.4% separated, 6.7% widowed, 6.0% divorced; Foreign born: 13.4%; Speak English only: 78.4%; With disability: 8.1%; Veterans: 6.3%; Ancestry: 8.5% English, 8.3% Irish, 8.0% German, 5.9% Italian, 3.6% American
Employment: 7.2% management, business, and financial, 1.9% computer, engineering, and science, 10.6% education, legal, community service, arts, and media, 2.9% healthcare practitioners, 25.2% service, 25.6% sales and office, 14.9% natural resources, construction, and maintenance, 11.7% production, transportation, and material moving
Income: Per capita: $17,142; Median household: $35,594; Average household: $43,489; Households with income of $100,000 or more: 8.2%; Poverty rate: 30.3%
Educational Attainment: High school diploma or higher: 76.5%; Bachelor's degree or higher: 18.5%; Graduate/professional degree or higher: 4.9%
School District(s)
Jasper 01 (PK-12)
    2012-13 Enrollment: 2,908 . . . . (843) 717-1110
Sc Public Charter SD (PK-12)
    2012-13 Enrollment: 11,500 . . . . (803) 734-8322
Housing: Homeownership rate: 42.3%; Median home value: $117,400; Median year structure built: 1992; Homeowner vacancy rate: 7.3%; Median gross rent: $945 per month; Rental vacancy rate: 13.1%
Health Insurance: 68.6% have insurance; 46.3% have private insurance; 30.1% have public insurance; 31.4% do not have insurance; 21.2% of children under 18 do not have insurance
Hospitals: Coastal Carolina Hospital
Safety: Violent crime rate: 88.6 per 10,000 population; Property crime rate: 605.3 per 10,000 population
Transportation: Commute: 94.5% car, 0.0% public transportation, 1.4% walk, 4.1% work from home; Median travel time to work: 23.5 minutes

PINELAND (unincorporated postal area)
ZCTA: 29934
    Covers a land area of 69.635 square miles and a water area of 0.001 square miles. Located at 32.59° N. Lat; 81.11° W. Long. Elevation is 69 feet.
    Population: 1,172; Growth (since 2000): 5.8%; Density: 16.8 persons per square mile; Race: 16.6% White, 81.1% Black/African American, 0.1% Asian, 0.3% American Indian/Alaska Native, 0.0% Native Hawaiian/Other Pacific Islander, 1.0% Two or more races, 2.4% Hispanic of any race; Average household size: 2.70; Median age: 40.4; Age under 18: 25.9%; Age 65 and over: 14.1%; Males per 100 females: 90.9
    Housing: Homeownership rate: 82.1%; Homeowner vacancy rate: 2.2%; Rental vacancy rate: 14.3%

RIDGELAND (town). County seat. Covers a land area of 44.451 square miles and a water area of 0.262 square miles. Located at 32.47° N. Lat; 80.93° W. Long. Elevation is 59 feet.
History: Ridgeland was known as the scene of numerous marriages because of its proximity to the Georgia border and the more lenient South Carolina marriage license laws. The turpentine-yielding pines here were the basis for a lumber industry.

Population: 4,036; Growth (since 2000): 60.3%; Density: 90.8 persons per square mile; Race: 39.7% White, 51.2% Black/African American, 0.5% Asian, 1.2% American Indian/Alaska Native, 0.1% Native Hawaiian/Other Pacific Islander, 1.0% Two or more races, 15.1% Hispanic of any race; Average household size: 2.79; Median age: 31.6; Age under 18: 19.5%; Age 65 and over: 8.5%; Males per 100 females: 179.1; Marriage status: 47.9% never married, 38.5% now married, 6.1% separated, 5.6% widowed, 8.0% divorced; Foreign born: 8.8%; Speak English only: 87.0%; With disability: 12.2%; Veterans: 9.5%; Ancestry: 8.6% Irish, 5.1% English, 4.2% German, 2.2% Scottish, 1.5% American
Employment: 16.2% management, business, and financial, 0.3% computer, engineering, and science, 1.9% education, legal, community service, arts, and media, 4.0% healthcare practitioners, 31.0% service, 20.6% sales and office, 16.9% natural resources, construction, and maintenance, 9.0% production, transportation, and material moving
Income: Per capita: $16,578; Median household: $35,495; Average household: $50,721; Households with income of $100,000 or more: 8.1%; Poverty rate: 35.1%
Educational Attainment: High school diploma or higher: 76.3%; Bachelor's degree or higher: 8.8%; Graduate/professional degree or higher: 2.4%
School District(s)
Beaufort 80 (09-12)
    2012-13 Enrollment: n/a . . . . (843) 987-8107
Jasper 01 (PK-12)
    2012-13 Enrollment: 2,908 . . . . (843) 717-1110
Housing: Homeownership rate: 46.5%; Median home value: $157,900; Median year structure built: 1987; Homeowner vacancy rate: 7.5%; Median gross rent: $692 per month; Rental vacancy rate: 15.9%
Health Insurance: 79.0% have insurance; 52.2% have private insurance; 35.1% have public insurance; 21.0% do not have insurance; 16.1% of children under 18 do not have insurance
Safety: Violent crime rate: 36.8 per 10,000 population; Property crime rate: 368.4 per 10,000 population
Newspapers: Sun Times Inc (weekly circulation 2400)
Transportation: Commute: 85.1% car, 0.0% public transportation, 7.1% walk, 5.5% work from home; Median travel time to work: 27.7 minutes
Additional Information Contacts
Town of Ridgeland . . . . (843) 726-7500
    http://www.ridgelandsc.gov

TILLMAN (unincorporated postal area)
ZCTA: 29943
    Covers a land area of 45.820 square miles and a water area of 1.022 square miles. Located at 32.48° N. Lat; 81.19° W. Long. Elevation is 56 feet.
    Population: 477; Growth (since 2000): 240.7%; Density: 10.4 persons per square mile; Race: 32.5% White, 65.8% Black/African American, 0.0% Asian, 0.0% American Indian/Alaska Native, 0.0% Native Hawaiian/Other Pacific Islander, 0.4% Two or more races, 1.3% Hispanic of any race; Average household size: 2.52; Median age: 41.5; Age under 18: 21.8%; Age 65 and over: 12.6%; Males per 100 females: 97.9
    Housing: Homeownership rate: 80.4%; Homeowner vacancy rate: 1.3%; Rental vacancy rate: 9.8%

Kershaw County

Located in north central South Carolina; bounded on the east by the Lynches River; includes part of Wateree River and Pond. Covers a land area of 726.562 square miles, a water area of 13.833 square miles, and is located in the Eastern Time Zone at 34.34° N. Lat., 80.59° W. Long. The county was founded in 1798. County seat is Camden.

Kershaw County is part of the Columbia, SC Metropolitan Statistical Area. The entire metro area includes: Calhoun County, SC; Fairfield County, SC; Kershaw County, SC; Lexington County, SC; Richland County, SC; Saluda County, SC

Population: 61,697; Growth (since 2000): 17.2%; Density: 84.9 persons per square mile; Race: 71.3% White, 24.6% Black/African American, 0.5% Asian, 0.3% American Indian/Alaska Native, 0.0% Native Hawaiian/Other Pacific Islander, 1.6% two or more races, 3.7% Hispanic of any race; Average household size: 2.56; Median age: 40.2; Age under 18: 24.5%; Age 65 and over: 14.3%; Males per 100 females: 94.8; Marriage status:

24.9% never married, 57.3% now married, 3.6% separated, 7.4% widowed, 10.4% divorced; Foreign born: 2.9%; Speak English only: 95.4%; With disability: 14.3%; Veterans: 11.7%; Ancestry: 31.2% American, 7.3% Irish, 7.1% English, 6.0% German, 2.1% Scotch-Irish
Religion: Six largest groups: 28.8% Baptist, 8.8% Methodist/Pietist, 4.2% Pentecostal, 2.8% Catholicism, 2.5% Non-denominational Protestant, 2.0% Presbyterian-Reformed
Economy: Unemployment rate: 6.2%; Leading industries: 16.8% retail trade; 13.6% other services (except public administration); 11.1% construction; Farms: 483 totaling 82,877 acres; Company size: 2 employ 1,000 or more persons, 2 employ 500 to 999 persons, 14 employ 100 to 499 persons, 1,040 employ less than 100 persons; Business ownership: 1,357 women-owned, n/a Black-owned, n/a Hispanic-owned, 77 Asian-owned
Employment: 11.8% management, business, and financial, 3.0% computer, engineering, and science, 9.2% education, legal, community service, arts, and media, 5.8% healthcare practitioners, 17.7% service, 24.4% sales and office, 11.5% natural resources, construction, and maintenance, 16.6% production, transportation, and material moving
Income: Per capita: $22,638; Median household: $43,765; Average household: $57,561; Households with income of $100,000 or more: 13.6%; Poverty rate: 16.7%
Educational Attainment: High school diploma or higher: 84.9%; Bachelor's degree or higher: 19.3%; Graduate/professional degree or higher: 6.9%
Housing: Homeownership rate: 78.4%; Median home value: $116,000; Median year structure built: 1987; Homeowner vacancy rate: 2.3%; Median gross rent: $679 per month; Rental vacancy rate: 8.5%
Vital Statistics: Birth rate: 113.3 per 10,000 population; Death rate: 108.8 per 10,000 population; Age-adjusted cancer mortality rate: 207.0 deaths per 100,000 population
Health Insurance: 83.6% have insurance; 62.5% have private insurance; 34.1% have public insurance; 16.4% do not have insurance; 7.4% of children under 18 do not have insurance
Health Care: Physicians: 16.7 per 10,000 population; Hospital beds: 34.7 per 10,000 population; Hospital admissions: 961.9 per 10,000 population
Transportation: Commute: 94.8% car, 0.2% public transportation, 1.1% walk, 2.9% work from home; Median travel time to work: 27.8 minutes
Presidential Election: 40.3% Obama, 58.4% Romney (2012)
National and State Parks: N R Goodale State Park
Additional Information Contacts
Kershaw Government . . . . (803) 425-7223
    http://www.kershaw.sc.gov

Kershaw County Communities

BETHUNE (town). Covers a land area of 1.100 square miles and a water area of 0 square miles. Located at 34.41° N. Lat; 80.35° W. Long. Elevation is 279 feet.
Population: 334; Growth (since 2000): -5.1%; Density: 303.7 persons per square mile; Race: 87.1% White, 11.4% Black/African American, 0.0% Asian, 1.2% American Indian/Alaska Native, 0.0% Native Hawaiian/Other Pacific Islander, 0.3% Two or more races, 2.1% Hispanic of any race; Average household size: 2.27; Median age: 49.2; Age under 18: 18.0%; Age 65 and over: 25.4%; Males per 100 females: 79.6
School District(s)
Kershaw 01 (PK-12)
    2012-13 Enrollment: 10,401 . . . . (803) 432-8416
Housing: Homeownership rate: 87.1%; Homeowner vacancy rate: 5.9%; Rental vacancy rate: 13.6%

BOYKIN (CDP). Covers a land area of 6.881 square miles and a water area of 0.188 square miles. Located at 34.12° N. Lat; 80.58° W. Long. Elevation is 164 feet.
Population: 100; Growth (since 2000): n/a; Density: 14.5 persons per square mile; Race: 80.0% White, 6.0% Black/African American, 0.0% Asian, 0.0% American Indian/Alaska Native, 0.0% Native Hawaiian/Other Pacific Islander, 4.0% Two or more races, 16.0% Hispanic of any race; Average household size: 2.86; Median age: 36.8; Age under 18: 27.0%; Age 65 and over: 8.0%; Males per 100 females: 81.8
Housing: Homeownership rate: 80.0%; Homeowner vacancy rate: 0.0%; Rental vacancy rate: 0.0%

CAMDEN (city). County seat. Covers a land area of 10.681 square miles and a water area of 0.707 square miles. Located at 34.26° N. Lat; 80.61° W. Long. Elevation is 190 feet.
History: Settlement began here in 1733 when a few English families built homes along the Wateree River. In 1758 a store was established by Joseph Kershaw and the settlement became known as Pine Tree Hill. By 1760 Kershaw was milling flour, operating saw and gristmills, indigo works, a tobacco warehouse, and a distillery. Camden's name was selected in 1768 to honor Charles Pratt, Earl of Camden, who championed colonial rights. Camden was incorporated in 1791. Fourteen Revolutionary War battles were waged in Camden, the most important being the Battle of Camden on August 16, 1780, called America's most disastrous defeat. Camden was again torn by war between 1861 and 1865, and was burned by Sherman in February 1865. For nearly a century Camden, noted for its duels, was the mecca for gentlemen seeking instruction in the code of honor, until the Cash-Shannon duel in 1880 caused the adoption of the antidueling law in the State constitution.
Population: 6,838; Growth (since 2000): 2.3%; Density: 640.2 persons per square mile; Race: 62.2% White, 35.1% Black/African American, 0.7% Asian, 0.2% American Indian/Alaska Native, 0.0% Native Hawaiian/Other Pacific Islander, 1.1% Two or more races, 2.4% Hispanic of any race; Average household size: 2.26; Median age: 45.3; Age under 18: 21.9%; Age 65 and over: 21.6%; Males per 100 females: 81.7; Marriage status: 27.6% never married, 49.1% now married, 2.9% separated, 10.5% widowed, 12.8% divorced; Foreign born: 4.0%; Speak English only: 94.7%; With disability: 10.9%; Veterans: 10.3%; Ancestry: 25.6% American, 7.7% German, 7.5% Irish, 7.4% English, 3.8% Scotch-Irish
Employment: 15.4% management, business, and financial, 2.2% computer, engineering, and science, 13.5% education, legal, community service, arts, and media, 10.8% healthcare practitioners, 17.4% service, 19.2% sales and office, 11.7% natural resources, construction, and maintenance, 9.7% production, transportation, and material moving
Income: Per capita: $31,304; Median household: $50,974; Average household: $74,147; Households with income of $100,000 or more: 26.5%; Poverty rate: 15.3%
Educational Attainment: High school diploma or higher: 85.4%; Bachelor's degree or higher: 36.5%; Graduate/professional degree or higher: 13.8%
School District(s)
Kershaw 01 (PK-12)
    2012-13 Enrollment: 10,401 . . . . (803) 432-8416
Vocational/Technical School(s)
LeGrand Institute of Cosmetology Inc (Private, For-profit)
    Fall 2013 Enrollment: 31 . . . . (803) 425-8449
    2013-14 Tuition: $12,500
Housing: Homeownership rate: 68.0%; Median home value: $166,700; Median year structure built: 1960; Homeowner vacancy rate: 4.4%; Median gross rent: $855 per month; Rental vacancy rate: 12.7%
Health Insurance: 87.0% have insurance; 68.9% have private insurance; 36.2% have public insurance; 13.0% do not have insurance; 7.7% of children under 18 do not have insurance
Hospitals: Kershaw Health (201 beds)
Safety: Violent crime rate: 140.1 per 10,000 population; Property crime rate: 668.8 per 10,000 population
Newspapers: Chronicle-Independent (weekly circulation 8800)
Transportation: Commute: 89.0% car, 0.4% public transportation, 1.8% walk, 6.7% work from home; Median travel time to work: 21.2 minutes; Amtrak: Train service available.
Airports: Woodward Field (general aviation)
Additional Information Contacts
City of Camden . . . . (803) 432-2421
    http://www.cityofcamden.org

CASSATT (unincorporated postal area)
ZCTA: 29032
    Covers a land area of 78.989 square miles and a water area of 0.308 square miles. Located at 34.35° N. Lat; 80.45° W. Long. Elevation is 390 feet.
    Population: 4,424; Growth (since 2000): 4.9%; Density: 56.0 persons per square mile; Race: 64.2% White, 30.0% Black/African American, 0.4% Asian, 0.2% American Indian/Alaska Native, 0.1% Native Hawaiian/Other Pacific Islander, 1.6% Two or more races, 6.0% Hispanic of any race; Average household size: 2.74; Median age: 36.3; Age under 18: 26.0%; Age 65 and over: 10.3%; Males per 100 females: 100.0; Marriage status: 24.3% never married, 58.6% now married, 5.5%

separated, 7.2% widowed, 9.9% divorced; Foreign born: 1.4%; Speak English only: 96.5%; With disability: 15.3%; Veterans: 10.6%; Ancestry: 44.8% American, 5.3% English, 4.8% Irish, 3.6% African, 1.7% German
Employment: 5.5% management, business, and financial, 0.6% computer, engineering, and science, 6.9% education, legal, community service, arts, and media, 2.3% healthcare practitioners, 21.8% service, 17.1% sales and office, 19.9% natural resources, construction, and maintenance, 26.0% production, transportation, and material moving
Income: Per capita: $13,367; Median household: $26,467; Average household: $35,329; Households with income of $100,000 or more: 1.6%; Poverty rate: 23.5%
Educational Attainment: High school diploma or higher: 80.1%; Bachelor's degree or higher: 7.1%; Graduate/professional degree or higher: 2.9%

School District(s)
Kershaw 01 (PK-12)
    2012-13 Enrollment: 10,401 . . . . (803) 432-8416
Housing: Homeownership rate: 74.2%; Median home value: $67,500; Median year structure built: 1992; Homeowner vacancy rate: 1.5%; Median gross rent: $634 per month; Rental vacancy rate: 9.5%
Health Insurance: 77.7% have insurance; 42.3% have private insurance; 43.1% have public insurance; 22.3% do not have insurance; 6.9% of children under 18 do not have insurance
Transportation: Commute: 95.9% car, 0.0% public transportation, 2.3% walk, 1.2% work from home; Median travel time to work: 30.0 minutes

ELGIN (town).
Covers a land area of 1.060 square miles and a water area of 0 square miles. Located at 34.17° N. Lat; 80.79° W. Long. Elevation is 407 feet.
Population: 1,311; Growth (since 2000): 62.7%; Density: 1,237.1 persons per square mile; Race: 83.5% White, 11.1% Black/African American, 0.2% Asian, 0.5% American Indian/Alaska Native, 0.0% Native Hawaiian/Other Pacific Islander, 2.2% Two or more races, 5.9% Hispanic of any race; Average household size: 2.71; Median age: 36.8; Age under 18: 28.1%; Age 65 and over: 9.2%; Males per 100 females: 94.8
School District(s)
Kershaw 01 (PK-12)
    2012-13 Enrollment: 10,401 . . . . (803) 432-8416
Richland 02 (PK-12)
    2012-13 Enrollment: 26,564 . . . . (803) 738-3236
Housing: Homeownership rate: 86.8%; Homeowner vacancy rate: 4.1%; Rental vacancy rate: 6.9%
Safety: Violent crime rate: 111.1 per 10,000 population; Property crime rate: 592.6 per 10,000 population

LIBERTY HILL (unincorporated postal area)
ZCTA: 29074
Covers a land area of 20.215 square miles and a water area of 3.660 square miles. Located at 34.44° N. Lat; 80.82° W. Long. Elevation is 561 feet.
Population: 241; Growth (since 2000): -30.9%; Density: 11.9 persons per square mile; Race: 91.3% White, 7.5% Black/African American, 0.4% Asian, 0.0% American Indian/Alaska Native, 0.0% Native Hawaiian/Other Pacific Islander, 0.4% Two or more races, 0.8% Hispanic of any race; Average household size: 1.79; Median age: 60.5; Age under 18: 5.8%; Age 65 and over: 38.2%; Males per 100 females: 102.5
Housing: Homeownership rate: 96.3%; Homeowner vacancy rate: 5.1%; Rental vacancy rate: 37.5%

LUGOFF (CDP).
Covers a land area of 15.035 square miles and a water area of 0.250 square miles. Located at 34.22° N. Lat; 80.69° W. Long. Elevation is 269 feet.
Population: 7,434; Growth (since 2000): 18.4%; Density: 494.4 persons per square mile; Race: 79.9% White, 16.9% Black/African American, 0.5% Asian, 0.2% American Indian/Alaska Native, 0.1% Native Hawaiian/Other Pacific Islander, 1.4% Two or more races, 2.7% Hispanic of any race; Average household size: 2.59; Median age: 39.2; Age under 18: 26.3%; Age 65 and over: 13.3%; Males per 100 females: 92.8; Marriage status: 23.4% never married, 58.5% now married, 2.6% separated, 6.0% widowed, 12.2% divorced; Foreign born: 3.2%; Speak English only: 94.5%; With disability: 12.1%; Veterans: 11.2%; Ancestry: 22.9% American, 11.7% Irish, 8.8% German, 8.3% English, 2.9% Scottish
Employment: 15.4% management, business, and financial, 2.4% computer, engineering, and science, 10.2% education, legal, community

service, arts, and media, 7.1% healthcare practitioners, 16.3% service, 27.4% sales and office, 8.1% natural resources, construction, and maintenance, 13.0% production, transportation, and material moving
Income: Per capita: $28,541; Median household: $55,456; Average household: $70,545; Households with income of $100,000 or more: 15.2%; Poverty rate: 8.7%
Educational Attainment: High school diploma or higher: 92.3%; Bachelor's degree or higher: 29.9%; Graduate/professional degree or higher: 11.6%
School District(s)
Kershaw 01 (PK-12)
    2012-13 Enrollment: 10,401 . . . . (803) 432-8416
Housing: Homeownership rate: 81.0%; Median home value: $132,300; Median year structure built: 1990; Homeowner vacancy rate: 1.7%; Median gross rent: $587 per month; Rental vacancy rate: 3.7%
Health Insurance: 83.8% have insurance; 72.4% have private insurance; 25.8% have public insurance; 16.2% do not have insurance; 11.5% of children under 18 do not have insurance
Transportation: Commute: 96.0% car, 0.0% public transportation, 0.0% walk, 2.5% work from home; Median travel time to work: 23.9 minutes

WESTVILLE (unincorporated postal area)
ZCTA: 29175
Covers a land area of 7.506 square miles and a water area of 0 square miles. Located at 34.44° N. Lat; 80.60° W. Long. Elevation is 453 feet.
Population: 378; Growth (since 2000): 11.5%; Density: 50.4 persons per square mile; Race: 71.4% White, 26.5% Black/African American, 0.0% Asian, 0.3% American Indian/Alaska Native, 0.0% Native Hawaiian/Other Pacific Islander, 1.6% Two or more races, 0.0% Hispanic of any race; Average household size: 2.32; Median age: 47.4; Age under 18: 22.2%; Age 65 and over: 16.7%; Males per 100 females: 89.9
Housing: Homeownership rate: 85.9%; Homeowner vacancy rate: 0.0%; Rental vacancy rate: 0.0%

Lancaster County

Located in northern South Carolina; bounded on the west by the Catawba River, and on the north by North Carolina. Covers a land area of 549.160 square miles, a water area of 5.962 square miles, and is located in the Eastern Time Zone at 34.69° N. Lat., 80.70° W. Long. The county was founded in 1798. County seat is Lancaster.

Lancaster County is part of the Charlotte-Concord-Gastonia, NC-SC Metropolitan Statistical Area. The entire metro area includes: Cabarrus County, NC; Gaston County, NC; Iredell County, NC; Lincoln County, NC; Mecklenburg County, NC; Rowan County, NC; Union County, NC; Chester County, SC; Lancaster County, SC; York County, SC

Population: 76,652; Growth (since 2000): 24.9%; Density: 139.6 persons per square mile; Race: 71.5% White, 23.8% Black/African American, 0.6% Asian, 0.3% American Indian/Alaska Native, 0.0% Native Hawaiian/Other Pacific Islander, 1.3% two or more races, 4.4% Hispanic of any race; Average household size: 2.51; Median age: 39.7; Age under 18: 23.3%; Age 65 and over: 15.3%; Males per 100 females: 97.1; Marriage status: 28.5% never married, 52.0% now married, 3.6% separated, 7.3% widowed, 12.2% divorced; Foreign born: 3.1%; Speak English only: 94.8%; With disability: 13.7%; Veterans: 10.5%; Ancestry: 20.3% American, 8.6% Irish, 7.9% German, 7.2% English, 3.9% Scotch-Irish
Religion: Six largest groups: 31.4% Baptist, 12.6% Methodist/Pietist, 2.3% Presbyterian-Reformed, 2.2% Non-denominational Protestant, 1.1% Pentecostal, 1.0% Catholicism
Economy: Unemployment rate: 7.0%; Leading industries: 19.4% retail trade; 15.5% other services (except public administration); 11.0% health care and social assistance; Farms: 577 totaling 65,079 acres; Company size: 0 employ 1,000 or more persons, 2 employ 500 to 999 persons, 20 employ 100 to 499 persons, 1,203 employ less than 100 persons; Business ownership: 1,199 women-owned, 476 Black-owned, 85 Hispanic-owned, 81 Asian-owned
Employment: 11.0% management, business, and financial, 2.7% computer, engineering, and science, 8.1% education, legal, community service, arts, and media, 4.3% healthcare practitioners, 16.2% service, 29.8% sales and office, 9.6% natural resources, construction, and maintenance, 18.2% production, transportation, and material moving

Income: Per capita: $21,003; Median household: $42,217; Average household: $53,222; Households with income of $100,000 or more: 12.2%; Poverty rate: 21.0%

Educational Attainment: High school diploma or higher: 82.3%; Bachelor's degree or higher: 18.7%; Graduate/professional degree or higher: 5.8%

Housing: Homeownership rate: 75.6%; Median home value: $142,200; Median year structure built: 1984; Homeowner vacancy rate: 2.3%; Median gross rent: $654 per month; Rental vacancy rate: 9.9%

Vital Statistics: Birth rate: 111.1 per 10,000 population; Death rate: 94.7 per 10,000 population; Age-adjusted cancer mortality rate: 195.5 deaths per 100,000 population

Health Insurance: 82.5% have insurance; 60.0% have private insurance; 36.1% have public insurance; 17.5% do not have insurance; 7.4% of children under 18 do not have insurance

Health Care: Physicians: 9.3 per 10,000 population; Hospital beds: 23.9 per 10,000 population; Hospital admissions: 1,014.7 per 10,000 population

Transportation: Commute: 94.2% car, 0.2% public transportation, 0.9% walk, 3.0% work from home; Median travel time to work: 27.5 minutes

Presidential Election: 40.5% Obama, 58.3% Romney (2012)

National and State Parks: Andrew Jackson State Park

Additional Information Contacts

Lancaster Government . . . . (803) 285-1581
   http://www.lancastercountysc.net

Lancaster County Communities

ELGIN (CDP). Covers a land area of 4.859 square miles and a water area of 0.017 square miles. Located at 34.67° N. Lat; 80.72° W. Long. Elevation is 600 feet.

Population: 2,607; Growth (since 2000): 7.5%; Density: 536.5 persons per square mile; Race: 70.2% White, 20.0% Black/African American, 0.0% Asian, 0.1% American Indian/Alaska Native, 0.0% Native Hawaiian/Other Pacific Islander, 0.9% Two or more races, 10.4% Hispanic of any race; Average household size: 2.65; Median age: 37.7; Age under 18: 24.3%; Age 65 and over: 12.5%; Males per 100 females: 96.3; Marriage status: 38.6% never married, 41.9% now married, 4.9% separated, 10.7% widowed, 8.7% divorced; Foreign born: 9.0%; Speak English only: 90.0%; With disability: 11.9%; Veterans: 8.2%; Ancestry: 18.6% American, 9.1% English, 9.0% African, 7.9% Irish, 7.7% Scotch-Irish

Employment: 4.2% management, business, and financial, 10.0% computer, engineering, and science, 7.3% education, legal, community service, arts, and media, 0.0% healthcare practitioners, 16.1% service, 29.3% sales and office, 9.1% natural resources, construction, and maintenance, 24.1% production, transportation, and material moving

Income: Per capita: $17,289; Median household: $26,084; Average household: $40,527; Households with income of $100,000 or more: 9.5%; Poverty rate: 36.7%

Educational Attainment: High school diploma or higher: 74.5%; Bachelor's degree or higher: 11.0%; Graduate/professional degree or higher: 2.5%

Housing: Homeownership rate: 75.8%; Median home value: $119,000; Median year structure built: 1978; Homeowner vacancy rate: 1.8%; Median gross rent: $637 per month; Rental vacancy rate: 8.8%

Health Insurance: 89.5% have insurance; 59.6% have private insurance; 42.5% have public insurance; 10.5% do not have insurance; 5.5% of children under 18 do not have insurance

Transportation: Commute: 97.3% car, 0.0% public transportation, 1.4% walk, 1.3% work from home; Median travel time to work: 23.2 minutes

HEATH SPRINGS (town). Covers a land area of 1.625 square miles and a water area of 0 square miles. Located at 34.59° N. Lat; 80.68° W. Long. Elevation is 686 feet.

History: B.D. Heath laid out the town of Heath's Spring, but in 1910 its name was changed to Heath Springs to honor Colonel Leroy Springs, Heath's business partner.

Population: 790; Growth (since 2000): -8.6%; Density: 486.1 persons per square mile; Race: 45.1% White, 52.9% Black/African American, 0.3% Asian, 0.1% American Indian/Alaska Native, 0.1% Native Hawaiian/Other Pacific Islander, 0.8% Two or more races, 0.1% Hispanic of any race; Average household size: 2.42; Median age: 42.3; Age under 18: 22.9%; Age 65 and over: 17.8%; Males per 100 females: 91.3

School District(s)

Lancaster 01 (PK-12)
   2012-13 Enrollment: 11,804 . . . . (803) 416-8806

Housing: Homeownership rate: 70.4%; Homeowner vacancy rate: 2.5%; Rental vacancy rate: 6.7%

IRWIN (CDP). Covers a land area of 2.985 square miles and a water area of 0.004 square miles. Located at 34.69° N. Lat; 80.82° W. Long. Elevation is 492 feet.

Population: 1,405; Growth (since 2000): 4.6%; Density: 470.6 persons per square mile; Race: 67.8% White, 28.9% Black/African American, 0.1% Asian, 0.3% American Indian/Alaska Native, 0.0% Native Hawaiian/Other Pacific Islander, 0.9% Two or more races, 3.6% Hispanic of any race; Average household size: 2.65; Median age: 37.2; Age under 18: 25.2%; Age 65 and over: 15.0%; Males per 100 females: 88.3

Housing: Homeownership rate: 80.5%; Homeowner vacancy rate: 0.9%; Rental vacancy rate: 1.9%

KERSHAW (town). Covers a land area of 1.857 square miles and a water area of 0 square miles. Located at 34.54° N. Lat; 80.59° W. Long. Elevation is 522 feet.

History: Kershaw was named for Colonel Joseph Kershaw, a solider in the Revolutionary War.

Population: 1,803; Growth (since 2000): 9.6%; Density: 970.7 persons per square mile; Race: 70.6% White, 26.5% Black/African American, 0.4% Asian, 0.7% American Indian/Alaska Native, 0.0% Native Hawaiian/Other Pacific Islander, 1.3% Two or more races, 1.3% Hispanic of any race; Average household size: 2.42; Median age: 38.8; Age under 18: 25.6%; Age 65 and over: 18.1%; Males per 100 females: 88.6

School District(s)

Dept of Correction N04 (09-12)
   2012-13 Enrollment: 752 . . . . (803) 896-8556
Kershaw 01 (PK-12)
   2012-13 Enrollment: 10,401 . . . . (803) 432-8416
Lancaster 01 (PK-12)
   2012-13 Enrollment: 11,804 . . . . (803) 416-8806

Housing: Homeownership rate: 67.2%; Homeowner vacancy rate: 3.8%; Rental vacancy rate: 7.9%

Newspapers: Kershaw News-Era (weekly circulation 3200)

LANCASTER (city). County seat. Covers a land area of 6.415 square miles and a water area of 0.083 square miles. Located at 34.72° N. Lat; 80.78° W. Long. Elevation is 545 feet.

History: Lancaster's history has been tinged with many religious vagaries, including legal recognition of witchcraft, and the Waxhaw Revival, an offshoot of the nation-wide Great Revival.

Population: 8,526; Growth (since 2000): 4.3%; Density: 1,329.1 persons per square mile; Race: 43.0% White, 51.3% Black/African American, 0.9% Asian, 0.2% American Indian/Alaska Native, 0.0% Native Hawaiian/Other Pacific Islander, 1.1% Two or more races, 5.7% Hispanic of any race; Average household size: 2.40; Median age: 36.9; Age under 18: 25.3%; Age 65 and over: 16.3%; Males per 100 females: 85.0; Marriage status: 39.9% never married, 37.9% now married, 5.2% separated, 9.0% widowed, 13.2% divorced; Foreign born: 1.4%; Speak English only: 95.9%; With disability: 15.9%; Veterans: 8.1%; Ancestry: 11.5% American, 5.1% German, 5.0% Scotch-Irish, 3.6% Irish, 3.5% English

Employment: 4.8% management, business, and financial, 0.8% computer, engineering, and science, 12.1% education, legal, community service, arts, and media, 3.7% healthcare practitioners, 22.8% service, 28.3% sales and office, 4.4% natural resources, construction, and maintenance, 23.2% production, transportation, and material moving

Income: Per capita: $16,711; Median household: $29,845; Average household: $40,918; Households with income of $100,000 or more: 6.2%; Poverty rate: 32.2%

Educational Attainment: High school diploma or higher: 78.6%; Bachelor's degree or higher: 17.7%; Graduate/professional degree or higher: 6.7%

School District(s)

Lancaster 01 (PK-12)
   2012-13 Enrollment: 11,804 . . . . (803) 416-8806

Two-year College(s)

University of South Carolina-Lancaster (Public)
   Fall 2013 Enrollment: 1,811 . . . . (803) 313-7000
   2013-14 Tuition: In-state $6,482; Out-of-state $15,632

Housing: Homeownership rate: 45.8%; Median home value: $97,600; Median year structure built: 1968; Homeowner vacancy rate: 3.9%; Median gross rent: $648 per month; Rental vacancy rate: 11.7%

Health Insurance: 75.5% have insurance; 42.2% have private insurance; 44.6% have public insurance; 24.5% do not have insurance; 13.1% of children under 18 do not have insurance
Hospitals: Springs Memorial Hospital (200 beds)
Safety: Violent crime rate: 123.5 per 10,000 population; Property crime rate: 701.5 per 10,000 population
Newspapers: Lancaster News (weekly circulation 13500)
Transportation: Commute: 95.6% car, 0.2% public transportation, 1.5% walk, 1.7% work from home; Median travel time to work: 24.3 minutes
Airports: Lancaster County-Mc Whirter Field (general aviation)
Additional Information Contacts
City of Lancaster . . . . (803) 286-8414
   http://www.lancastercitysc.com

SPRINGDALE (CDP). Covers a land area of 4.225 square miles and a water area of 0.016 square miles. Located at 34.69° N. Lat; 80.78° W. Long. Elevation is 538 feet.
Population: 2,574; Growth (since 2000): -10.1%; Density: 609.3 persons per square mile; Race: 62.5% White, 27.7% Black/African American, 0.3% Asian, 0.4% American Indian/Alaska Native, 0.0% Native Hawaiian/Other Pacific Islander, 2.6% Two or more races, 10.0% Hispanic of any race; Average household size: 2.65; Median age: 34.6; Age under 18: 26.1%; Age 65 and over: 14.0%; Males per 100 females: 97.7; Marriage status: 33.1% never married, 45.2% now married, 6.9% separated, 7.8% widowed, 13.9% divorced; Foreign born: 0.0%; Speak English only: 91.1%; With disability: 15.8%; Veterans: 9.1%; Ancestry: 24.4% American, 4.3% English, 3.7% Scotch-Irish, 2.9% Irish, 1.9% Scottish
Employment: 8.4% management, business, and financial, 1.4% computer, engineering, and science, 6.0% education, legal, community service, arts, and media, 7.2% healthcare practitioners, 18.8% service, 24.2% sales and office, 9.2% natural resources, construction, and maintenance, 24.8% production, transportation, and material moving
Income: Per capita: $13,299; Median household: $24,372; Average household: $33,119; Households with income of $100,000 or more: 2.1%; Poverty rate: 37.0%
Educational Attainment: High school diploma or higher: 65.0%; Bachelor's degree or higher: 11.2%; Graduate/professional degree or higher: n/a
Housing: Homeownership rate: 55.3%; Median home value: $78,900; Median year structure built: 1974; Homeowner vacancy rate: 3.2%; Median gross rent: $619 per month; Rental vacancy rate: 16.5%
Health Insurance: 73.1% have insurance; 40.9% have private insurance; 37.3% have public insurance; 26.9% do not have insurance; 7.8% of children under 18 do not have insurance
Transportation: Commute: 87.4% car, 0.0% public transportation, 0.0% walk, 1.2% work from home; Median travel time to work: 21.4 minutes

Laurens County

Located in northwestern South Carolina; bounded on the southwest by the Saluda River, and on the northeast by the Enoree River; includes part of Lake Greenwood, and part of Sumter National Forest. Covers a land area of 713.804 square miles, a water area of 10.035 square miles, and is located in the Eastern Time Zone at 34.48° N. Lat., 82.01° W. Long. The county was founded in 1785. County seat is Laurens.

Laurens County is part of the Greenville-Anderson-Mauldin, SC Metropolitan Statistical Area. The entire metro area includes: Anderson County, SC; Greenville County, SC; Laurens County, SC; Pickens County, SC

Weather Station: Laurens									Elevation: 588 feet		
	Jan	Feb	Mar	Apr	May	Jun	Jul	Aug	Sep	Oct	Nov	Dec
High	53	57	65	74	82	89	92	90	84	74	65	56
Low	28	31	38	45	55	64	67	66	59	46	37	30
Precip	4.2	4.0	4.9	3.3	3.1	4.0	3.6	3.7	3.5	3.6	3.6	3.9
Snow	0.7	0.4	0.3	0.0	0.0	0.0	0.0	0.0	0.0	0.0	tr	0.1

High and Low temperatures in degrees Fahrenheit; Precipitation and Snow in inches

Population: 66,537; Growth (since 2000): -4.4%; Density: 93.2 persons per square mile; Race: 70.4% White, 25.4% Black/African American, 0.3% Asian, 0.2% American Indian/Alaska Native, 0.1% Native Hawaiian/Other Pacific Islander, 1.3% two or more races, 4.1% Hispanic of any race; Average household size: 2.51; Median age: 39.9; Age under 18: 23.2%; Age 65 and over: 15.0%; Males per 100 females: 94.3; Marriage status: 30.1% never married, 50.5% now married, 4.0% separated, 8.1%

widowed, 11.2% divorced; Foreign born: 2.5%; Speak English only: 95.4%; With disability: 19.0%; Veterans: 9.7%; Ancestry: 12.7% American, 10.3% Irish, 8.2% English, 7.8% German, 2.4% Scotch-Irish
Religion: Six largest groups: 42.9% Baptist, 8.3% Methodist/Pietist, 3.9% Presbyterian-Reformed, 3.8% Pentecostal, 0.6% Catholicism, 0.6% Non-denominational Protestant
Economy: Unemployment rate: 6.9%; Leading industries: 19.4% retail trade; 14.6% other services (except public administration); 9.5% health care and social assistance; Farms: 826 totaling 122,659 acres; Company size: 0 employ 1,000 or more persons, 4 employ 500 to 999 persons, 29 employ 100 to 499 persons, 906 employ less than 100 persons; Business ownership: 1,132 women-owned, 466 Black-owned, n/a Hispanic-owned, 65 Asian-owned
Employment: 8.3% management, business, and financial, 2.8% computer, engineering, and science, 7.6% education, legal, community service, arts, and media, 3.9% healthcare practitioners, 18.1% service, 22.8% sales and office, 10.8% natural resources, construction, and maintenance, 25.6% production, transportation, and material moving
Income: Per capita: $19,153; Median household: $37,383; Average household: $48,125; Households with income of $100,000 or more: 8.8%; Poverty rate: 20.6%
Educational Attainment: High school diploma or higher: 78.2%; Bachelor's degree or higher: 14.5%; Graduate/professional degree or higher: 4.5%
Housing: Homeownership rate: 72.0%; Median home value: $81,800; Median year structure built: 1981; Homeowner vacancy rate: 2.3%; Median gross rent: $663 per month; Rental vacancy rate: 12.2%
Vital Statistics: Birth rate: 119.0 per 10,000 population; Death rate: 115.7 per 10,000 population; Age-adjusted cancer mortality rate: 208.7 deaths per 100,000 population
Health Insurance: 82.8% have insurance; 59.8% have private insurance; 36.0% have public insurance; 17.2% do not have insurance; 11.3% of children under 18 do not have insurance
Health Care: Physicians: 8.6 per 10,000 population; Hospital beds: 16.4 per 10,000 population; Hospital admissions: 448.1 per 10,000 population
Transportation: Commute: 94.0% car, 0.4% public transportation, 2.6% walk, 2.3% work from home; Median travel time to work: 24.6 minutes
Presidential Election: 40.6% Obama, 58.0% Romney (2012)
Additional Information Contacts
Laurens Government. . . . . (864) 984-3538
   http://www.laurenscountysc.org

Laurens County Communities

CLINTON (city). Covers a land area of 9.875 square miles and a water area of 0.068 square miles. Located at 34.48° N. Lat; 81.86° W. Long. Elevation is 676 feet.
History: The town of Clinton is a monument to the zeal of the Reverend William Plumer Jacobs (1842-1917) who brought a church, a library, a school, an orphanage, and a monthly magazine to the community.
Population: 8,490; Growth (since 2000): 4.9%; Density: 859.7 persons per square mile; Race: 59.4% White, 37.0% Black/African American, 0.6% Asian, 0.2% American Indian/Alaska Native, 0.0% Native Hawaiian/Other Pacific Islander, 1.5% Two or more races, 2.2% Hispanic of any race; Average household size: 2.40; Median age: 32.7; Age under 18: 21.7%; Age 65 and over: 16.1%; Males per 100 females: 85.2; Marriage status: 54.2% never married, 24.8% now married, 3.9% separated, 10.2% widowed, 10.9% divorced; Foreign born: 1.6%; Speak English only: 97.2%; With disability: 19.1%; Veterans: 5.8%; Ancestry: 8.2% American, 7.8% Irish, 7.4% English, 6.2% German, 2.6% Scotch-Irish
Employment: 6.0% management, business, and financial, 0.8% computer, engineering, and science, 15.6% education, legal, community service, arts, and media, 2.6% healthcare practitioners, 24.7% service, 25.1% sales and office, 5.8% natural resources, construction, and maintenance, 19.2% production, transportation, and material moving
Income: Per capita: $13,566; Median household: $29,411; Average household: $37,625; Households with income of $100,000 or more: 4.2%; Poverty rate: 37.7%
Educational Attainment: High school diploma or higher: 67.6%; Bachelor's degree or higher: 17.1%; Graduate/professional degree or higher: 6.9%

School District(s)
Laurens 56 (PK-12)
   2012-13 Enrollment: 3,066 . . . . (864) 833-0800

Four-year College(s)
Presbyterian College (Private, Not-for-profit, Presbyterian Church (USA))
  Fall 2013 Enrollment: 1,433 . . . . (864) 833-2820
  2013-14 Tuition: In-state $33,650; Out-of-state $33,650
Housing: Homeownership rate: 48.4%; Median home value: $76,900; Median year structure built: 1966; Homeowner vacancy rate: 4.3%; Median gross rent: $662 per month; Rental vacancy rate: 12.5%
Health Insurance: 81.9% have insurance; 50.9% have private insurance; 41.9% have public insurance; 18.1% do not have insurance; 10.3% of children under 18 do not have insurance
Hospitals: GHS Laurens County Memorial Hospital (90 beds)
Safety: Violent crime rate: 62.5 per 10,000 population; Property crime rate: 522.5 per 10,000 population
Newspapers: Clinton Chronicle (weekly circulation 3500)
Transportation: Commute: 79.5% car, 2.1% public transportation, 11.6% walk, 3.4% work from home; Median travel time to work: 18.9 minutes
Additional Information Contacts
City of Clinton . . . . (864) 833-7505
  http://www.cityofclintonsc.com

CROSS HILL (town). Covers a land area of 3.091 square miles and a water area of 0 square miles. Located at 34.30° N. Lat; 81.98° W. Long. Elevation is 587 feet.
Population: 507; Growth (since 2000): -15.6%; Density: 164.0 persons per square mile; Race: 38.5% White, 59.4% Black/African American, 0.2% Asian, 0.0% American Indian/Alaska Native, 0.0% Native Hawaiian/Other Pacific Islander, 1.2% Two or more races, 2.0% Hispanic of any race; Average household size: 2.45; Median age: 42.5; Age under 18: 20.7%; Age 65 and over: 14.2%; Males per 100 females: 85.7
Housing: Homeownership rate: 84.5%; Homeowner vacancy rate: 2.2%; Rental vacancy rate: 8.1%

GRAY COURT (town). Covers a land area of 1.871 square miles and a water area of 0.003 square miles. Located at 34.61° N. Lat; 82.11° W. Long. Elevation is 801 feet.
Population: 795; Growth (since 2000): -22.1%; Density: 425.0 persons per square mile; Race: 45.0% White, 41.8% Black/African American, 0.0% Asian, 0.3% American Indian/Alaska Native, 0.1% Native Hawaiian/Other Pacific Islander, 1.8% Two or more races, 15.3% Hispanic of any race; Average household size: 2.62; Median age: 40.7; Age under 18: 23.4%; Age 65 and over: 15.1%; Males per 100 females: 99.7
School District(s)
Laurens 55 (PK-12)
  2012-13 Enrollment: 5,881 . . . . (864) 984-3568
Housing: Homeownership rate: 74.2%; Homeowner vacancy rate: 2.6%; Rental vacancy rate: 8.2%

JOANNA (CDP). Covers a land area of 3.137 square miles and a water area of 0.006 square miles. Located at 34.42° N. Lat; 81.80° W. Long. Elevation is 607 feet.
Population: 1,539; Growth (since 2000): -4.4%; Density: 490.5 persons per square mile; Race: 79.3% White, 16.4% Black/African American, 0.3% Asian, 0.6% American Indian/Alaska Native, 0.0% Native Hawaiian/Other Pacific Islander, 0.7% Two or more races, 4.7% Hispanic of any race; Average household size: 2.44; Median age: 40.0; Age under 18: 22.4%; Age 65 and over: 16.3%; Males per 100 females: 92.6
School District(s)
Laurens 56 (PK-12)
  2012-13 Enrollment: 3,066 . . . . (864) 833-0800
Housing: Homeownership rate: 67.3%; Homeowner vacancy rate: 3.8%; Rental vacancy rate: 17.1%

LAURENS (city). County seat. Covers a land area of 10.386 square miles and a water area of 0 square miles. Located at 34.50° N. Lat; 82.02° W. Long. Elevation is 614 feet.
History: Laurens was settled by people of Scotch-Irish descent, who came here before the Revolution.
Population: 9,139; Growth (since 2000): -7.8%; Density: 879.9 persons per square mile; Race: 52.5% White, 42.8% Black/African American, 0.3% Asian, 0.3% American Indian/Alaska Native, 0.0% Native Hawaiian/Other Pacific Islander, 1.2% Two or more races, 5.7% Hispanic of any race; Average household size: 2.34; Median age: 39.9; Age under 18: 24.0%; Age 65 and over: 19.5%; Males per 100 females: 84.9; Marriage status: 35.6% never married, 42.9% now married, 2.2% separated, 11.6% widowed, 10.0% divorced; Foreign born: 5.1%; Speak English only: 92.0%;

With disability: 22.1%; Veterans: 9.1%; Ancestry: 8.3% English, 8.2% American, 7.2% Irish, 4.4% German, 1.6% Scottish
Employment: 9.3% management, business, and financial, 1.6% computer, engineering, and science, 7.4% education, legal, community service, arts, and media, 4.6% healthcare practitioners, 29.3% service, 22.5% sales and office, 7.7% natural resources, construction, and maintenance, 17.7% production, transportation, and material moving
Income: Per capita: $17,860; Median household: $24,583; Average household: $39,513; Households with income of $100,000 or more: 5.2%; Poverty rate: 22.7%
Educational Attainment: High school diploma or higher: 78.2%; Bachelor's degree or higher: 18.9%; Graduate/professional degree or higher: 5.9%
School District(s)
Laurens 55 (PK-12)
  2012-13 Enrollment: 5,881 . . . . (864) 984-3568
Housing: Homeownership rate: 53.3%; Median home value: $80,700; Median year structure built: 1967; Homeowner vacancy rate: 2.9%; Median gross rent: $591 per month; Rental vacancy rate: 13.1%
Health Insurance: 80.5% have insurance; 60.5% have private insurance; 38.6% have public insurance; 19.5% do not have insurance; 10.7% of children under 18 do not have insurance
Safety: Violent crime rate: 99.3 per 10,000 population; Property crime rate: 662.8 per 10,000 population
Newspapers: Laurens County Advertiser (weekly circulation 8000)
Transportation: Commute: 94.5% car, 0.5% public transportation, 3.7% walk, 0.9% work from home; Median travel time to work: 23.2 minutes
Additional Information Contacts
City of Laurens . . . . (864) 984-3933
  http://www.cityoflaurenssc.comindex.html

MOUNTVILLE (CDP). Covers a land area of 2.845 square miles and a water area of 0.015 square miles. Located at 34.37° N. Lat; 81.98° W. Long. Elevation is 627 feet.
Population: 108; Growth (since 2000): -16.9%; Density: 38.0 persons per square mile; Race: 80.6% White, 13.0% Black/African American, 0.9% Asian, 0.0% American Indian/Alaska Native, 0.0% Native Hawaiian/Other Pacific Islander, 0.0% Two or more races, 5.6% Hispanic of any race; Average household size: 2.45; Median age: 40.5; Age under 18: 21.3%; Age 65 and over: 17.6%; Males per 100 females: 61.2
Housing: Homeownership rate: 88.6%; Homeowner vacancy rate: 4.9%; Rental vacancy rate: 28.6%

PRINCETON (CDP). Covers a land area of 0.749 square miles and a water area of 0 square miles. Located at 34.49° N. Lat; 82.30° W. Long. Elevation is 761 feet.
Population: 62; Growth (since 2000): -4.6%; Density: 82.8 persons per square mile; Race: 72.6% White, 11.3% Black/African American, 0.0% Asian, 0.0% American Indian/Alaska Native, 0.0% Native Hawaiian/Other Pacific Islander, 16.1% Two or more races, 0.0% Hispanic of any race; Average household size: 2.82; Median age: 37.8; Age under 18: 32.3%; Age 65 and over: 9.7%; Males per 100 females: 100.0
Housing: Homeownership rate: 81.9%; Homeowner vacancy rate: 5.3%; Rental vacancy rate: 0.0%

WATERLOO (town). Covers a land area of 1.398 square miles and a water area of 0 square miles. Located at 34.35° N. Lat; 82.06° W. Long. Elevation is 614 feet.
History: Near Waterloo was the site of Rosemont Manor, built by Patrick Cuningham in 1769 on lands granted him by King George. During the Revolution the family remained loyal, and for a while were exiled to the West Indies, but later returned to their home and to serve in the State legislature.
Population: 166; Growth (since 2000): -18.2%; Density: 118.7 persons per square mile; Race: 45.8% White, 52.4% Black/African American, 0.0% Asian, 0.0% American Indian/Alaska Native, 0.0% Native Hawaiian/Other Pacific Islander, 1.8% Two or more races, 0.0% Hispanic of any race; Average household size: 2.31; Median age: 44.0; Age under 18: 19.3%; Age 65 and over: 18.7%; Males per 100 females: 100.0
School District(s)
Laurens 55 (PK-12)
  2012-13 Enrollment: 5,881 . . . . (864) 984-3568
Housing: Homeownership rate: 70.8%; Homeowner vacancy rate: 0.0%; Rental vacancy rate: 22.2%

WATTS MILLS (CDP). Covers a land area of 2.268 square miles and a water area of 0 square miles. Located at 34.52° N. Lat; 81.99° W. Long. Elevation is 702 feet.

History: Formerly known as Wattsville.

Population: 1,635; Growth (since 2000): 10.5%; Density: 721.0 persons per square mile; Race: 57.9% White, 20.9% Black/African American, 0.4% Asian, 0.2% American Indian/Alaska Native, 0.2% Native Hawaiian/Other Pacific Islander, 2.3% Two or more races, 29.3% Hispanic of any race; Average household size: 2.90; Median age: 30.5; Age under 18: 30.3%; Age 65 and over: 9.8%; Males per 100 females: 104.1

Housing: Homeownership rate: 49.1%; Homeowner vacancy rate: 4.0%; Rental vacancy rate: 14.2%

Lee County

Located in northeast central South Carolina; drained by the Lynches and Black Rivers. Covers a land area of 410.184 square miles, a water area of 1.048 square miles, and is located in the Eastern Time Zone at 34.16° N. Lat., 80.25° W. Long. The county was founded in 1902. County seat is Bishopville.

Weather Station: Bishopville 8 NNW   Elevation: 249 feet

	Jan	Feb	Mar	Apr	May	Jun	Jul	Aug	Sep	Oct	Nov	Dec
High	54	59	66	75	82	89	91	90	84	75	67	58
Low	31	34	40	48	57	66	69	68	62	51	41	34
Precip	3.7	3.4	3.9	2.8	3.2	4.2	4.4	5.0	3.8	3.3	3.0	3.2
Snow	0.2	0.2	0.2	0.0	0.0	0.0	0.0	0.0	0.0	0.0	0.0	0.1

High and Low temperatures in degrees Fahrenheit; Precipitation and Snow in inches

Population: 19,220; Growth (since 2000): -4.5%; Density: 46.9 persons per square mile; Race: 33.4% White, 64.3% Black/African American, 0.3% Asian, 0.3% American Indian/Alaska Native, 0.0% Native Hawaiian/Other Pacific Islander, 0.9% two or more races, 1.7% Hispanic of any race; Average household size: 2.54; Median age: 38.9; Age under 18: 22.2%; Age 65 and over: 13.5%; Males per 100 females: 107.3; Marriage status: 42.2% never married, 38.5% now married, 5.8% separated, 10.2% widowed, 9.1% divorced; Foreign born: 1.4%; Speak English only: 96.7%; With disability: 17.7%; Veterans: 7.7%; Ancestry: 31.5% American, 5.8% English, 3.9% Irish, 3.4% German, 2.2% African

Religion: Six largest groups: 17.7% Methodist/Pietist, 9.5% Baptist, 2.2% Presbyterian-Reformed, 1.6% Non-denominational Protestant, 1.4% Holiness, 1.0% Other Groups

Economy: Unemployment rate: 7.6%; Leading industries: 20.3% retail trade; 13.5% other services (except public administration); 12.1% health care and social assistance; Farms: 386 totaling 142,449 acres; Company size: 0 employ 1,000 or more persons, 0 employ 500 to 999 persons, 1 employs 100 to 499 persons, 206 employ less than 100 persons; Business ownership: 111 women-owned, n/a Black-owned, n/a Hispanic-owned, n/a Asian-owned

Employment: 9.8% management, business, and financial, 2.3% computer, engineering, and science, 9.1% education, legal, community service, arts, and media, 4.3% healthcare practitioners, 22.4% service, 23.6% sales and office, 8.9% natural resources, construction, and maintenance, 19.5% production, transportation, and material moving

Income: Per capita: $14,740; Median household: $27,373; Average household: $39,486; Households with income of $100,000 or more: 6.0%; Poverty rate: 28.0%

Educational Attainment: High school diploma or higher: 72.8%; Bachelor's degree or higher: 9.1%; Graduate/professional degree or higher: 3.4%

Housing: Homeownership rate: 71.9%; Median home value: $65,000; Median year structure built: 1981; Homeowner vacancy rate: 1.7%; Median gross rent: $561 per month; Rental vacancy rate: 6.9%

Vital Statistics: Birth rate: 90.5 per 10,000 population; Death rate: 142.3 per 10,000 population; Age-adjusted cancer mortality rate: 295.4 deaths per 100,000 population

Health Insurance: 82.8% have insurance; 46.7% have private insurance; 49.3% have public insurance; 17.2% do not have insurance; 4.7% of children under 18 do not have insurance

Health Care: Physicians: 2.7 per 10,000 population; Hospital beds: 0.0 per 10,000 population; Hospital admissions: 0.0 per 10,000 population

Transportation: Commute: 94.2% car, 0.0% public transportation, 1.8% walk, 2.8% work from home; Median travel time to work: 28.9 minutes

Presidential Election: 67.1% Obama, 31.8% Romney (2012)

National and State Parks: Lee State Park

Additional Information Contacts
Lee Government . . . . (803) 484-5341
   http://www.leecountysc.com

Lee County Communities

BISHOPVILLE (city). County seat. Covers a land area of 2.337 square miles and a water area of 0.032 square miles. Located at 34.22° N. Lat; 80.25° W. Long. Elevation is 223 feet.

History: Bishopville was named about 1825 for Dr. Jacques Bishop. Bishopville was the home of U.S. Senator E.D. "Cotton Ed" Smith.

Population: 3,471; Growth (since 2000): -5.4%; Density: 1,485.0 persons per square mile; Race: 26.2% White, 71.3% Black/African American, 0.8% Asian, 0.3% American Indian/Alaska Native, 0.0% Native Hawaiian/Other Pacific Islander, 1.0% Two or more races, 1.2% Hispanic of any race; Average household size: 2.33; Median age: 40.0; Age under 18: 25.4%; Age 65 and over: 18.2%; Males per 100 females: 77.3; Marriage status: 51.6% never married, 29.2% now married, 5.9% separated, 9.5% widowed, 9.7% divorced; Foreign born: 0.8%; Speak English only: 98.9%; With disability: 18.4%; Veterans: 5.2%; Ancestry: 27.5% American, 6.8% African, 2.0% English, 1.8% German, 1.6% Irish

Employment: 3.6% management, business, and financial, 3.0% computer, engineering, and science, 8.6% education, legal, community service, arts, and media, 10.6% healthcare practitioners, 26.4% service, 32.6% sales and office, 3.2% natural resources, construction, and maintenance, 12.1% production, transportation, and material moving

Income: Per capita: $9,885; Median household: $17,642; Average household: $28,920; Households with income of $100,000 or more: 0.4%; Poverty rate: 48.8%

Educational Attainment: High school diploma or higher: 72.8%; Bachelor's degree or higher: 9.6%; Graduate/professional degree or higher: 2.3%

School District(s)
Dept of Correction N04 (09-12)
   2012-13 Enrollment: 752 . . . . (803) 896-8556
Lee 01 (PK-12)
   2012-13 Enrollment: 2,249 . . . . (803) 484-5327
Sc Public Charter SD (PK-12)
   2012-13 Enrollment: 11,500 . . . . (803) 734-8322

Housing: Homeownership rate: 50.1%; Median home value: $74,000; Median year structure built: 1970; Homeowner vacancy rate: 2.9%; Median gross rent: $444 per month; Rental vacancy rate: 4.3%

Health Insurance: 84.3% have insurance; 35.6% have private insurance; 57.2% have public insurance; 15.7% do not have insurance; 2.4% of children under 18 do not have insurance

Safety: Violent crime rate: 173.9 per 10,000 population; Property crime rate: 725.4 per 10,000 population

Newspapers: Lee County Observer (weekly circulation 3500)

Transportation: Commute: 91.0% car, 0.0% public transportation, 8.2% walk, 0.9% work from home; Median travel time to work: 21.5 minutes

Additional Information Contacts
City of Bishopville . . . . (803) 484-9418
   http://cityofbishopvillesc.com

ELLIOTT (unincorporated postal area)
ZCTA: 29046
   Covers a land area of 2.493 square miles and a water area of 0.010 square miles. Located at 34.10° N. Lat; 80.15° W. Long. Elevation is 174 feet.
   Population: 237; Growth (since 2000): -17.1%; Density: 95.1 persons per square mile; Race: 7.2% White, 92.4% Black/African American, 0.0% Asian, 0.0% American Indian/Alaska Native, 0.0% Native Hawaiian/Other Pacific Islander, 0.4% Two or more races, 0.0% Hispanic of any race; Average household size: 2.47; Median age: 47.2; Age under 18: 19.4%; Age 65 and over: 23.2%; Males per 100 females: 88.1
   Housing: Homeownership rate: 86.5%; Homeowner vacancy rate: 0.0%; Rental vacancy rate: 0.0%

LYNCHBURG (town). Covers a land area of 1.132 square miles and a water area of 0 square miles. Located at 34.06° N. Lat; 80.08° W. Long. Elevation is 151 feet.

History: Lynchburg was known during Revolutionary days as Willow Grove. Here, under cover of a thick growth of willows, General Marion's army defeated British troops in 1781.

Population: 373; Growth (since 2000): -36.6%; Density: 329.6 persons per square mile; Race: 15.5% White, 84.5% Black/African American, 0.0% Asian, 0.0% American Indian/Alaska Native, 0.0% Native Hawaiian/Other Pacific Islander, 0.0% Two or more races, 2.1% Hispanic of any race; Average household size: 2.30; Median age: 45.9; Age under 18: 22.0%; Age 65 and over: 19.6%; Males per 100 females: 75.9
Housing: Homeownership rate: 69.2%; Homeowner vacancy rate: 1.7%; Rental vacancy rate: 3.8%
Safety: Violent crime rate: 84.5 per 10,000 population; Property crime rate: 535.2 per 10,000 population

Lexington County

Located in central South Carolina; bounded on the northeast by the Congaree River, and on the southwest by the North Fork of the Edisto River; in the Sand Hill belt, drained by the Saluda River and Lake Murray. Covers a land area of 698.913 square miles, a water area of 58.816 square miles, and is located in the Eastern Time Zone at 33.89° N. Lat., 81.27° W. Long. The county was founded in 1804. County seat is Lexington.

Lexington County is part of the Columbia, SC Metropolitan Statistical Area. The entire metro area includes: Calhoun County, SC; Fairfield County, SC; Kershaw County, SC; Lexington County, SC; Richland County, SC; Saluda County, SC

Weather Station: Columbia Metro Arpt										Elevation: 212 feet		
	Jan	Feb	Mar	Apr	May	Jun	Jul	Aug	Sep	Oct	Nov	Dec
High	56	60	68	76	84	90	93	91	85	76	67	58
Low	34	36	43	50	59	68	71	71	64	52	42	35
Precip	3.6	3.6	4.0	2.7	3.1	4.6	5.3	5.2	3.7	3.2	2.8	3.2
Snow	0.6	0.4	0.2	tr	tr	tr	0.0	tr	0.0	0.0	tr	0.1

High and Low temperatures in degrees Fahrenheit; Precipitation and Snow in inches

Weather Station: Pelion 4 NW										Elevation: 450 feet		
	Jan	Feb	Mar	Apr	May	Jun	Jul	Aug	Sep	Oct	Nov	Dec
High	57	61	69	77	84	89	92	90	85	76	67	59
Low	33	35	41	48	57	66	70	69	62	50	41	34
Precip	4.4	4.1	4.6	3.0	3.0	5.3	5.6	5.4	4.2	3.5	3.4	3.8
Snow	0.5	0.1	tr	0.0	0.0	0.0	0.0	0.0	0.0	0.0	0.0	tr

High and Low temperatures in degrees Fahrenheit; Precipitation and Snow in inches

Population: 262,391; Growth (since 2000): 21.5%; Density: 375.4 persons per square mile; Race: 79.3% White, 14.3% Black/African American, 1.4% Asian, 0.4% American Indian/Alaska Native, 0.0% Native Hawaiian/Other Pacific Islander, 1.9% two or more races, 5.5% Hispanic of any race; Average household size: 2.53; Median age: 37.9; Age under 18: 24.5%; Age 65 and over: 12.2%; Males per 100 females: 95.4; Marriage status: 27.4% never married, 55.5% now married, 2.9% separated, 6.2% widowed, 10.9% divorced; Foreign born: 4.9%; Speak English only: 93.0%; With disability: 11.3%; Veterans: 11.5%; Ancestry: 15.6% German, 12.1% American, 11.6% Irish, 10.4% English, 3.5% Italian
Religion: Six largest groups: 16.8% Baptist, 10.2% Methodist/Pietist, 6.4% Lutheran, 3.8% Pentecostal, 3.5% Non-denominational Protestant, 2.2% Catholicism
Economy: Unemployment rate: 5.1%; Leading industries: 17.1% retail trade; 11.9% other services (except public administration); 10.4% construction; Farms: 1,011 totaling 107,700 acres; Company size: 2 employ 1,000 or more persons, 7 employ 500 to 999 persons, 109 employ 100 to 499 persons, 5,991 employs less than 100 persons; Business ownership: 5,524 women-owned, 1,257 Black-owned, 340 Hispanic-owned, 429 Asian-owned
Employment: 14.5% management, business, and financial, 4.7% computer, engineering, and science, 10.7% education, legal, community service, arts, and media, 6.2% healthcare practitioners, 15.2% service, 27.0% sales and office, 11.3% natural resources, construction, and maintenance, 10.4% production, transportation, and material moving
Income: Per capita: $26,886; Median household: $54,061; Average household: $67,779; Households with income of $100,000 or more: 20.0%; Poverty rate: 13.2%
Educational Attainment: High school diploma or higher: 88.4%; Bachelor's degree or higher: 28.7%; Graduate/professional degree or higher: 10.3%
Housing: Homeownership rate: 73.7%; Median home value: $140,100; Median year structure built: 1987; Homeowner vacancy rate: 2.5%; Median gross rent: $820 per month; Rental vacancy rate: 11.7%

Vital Statistics: Birth rate: 119.6 per 10,000 population; Death rate: 77.8 per 10,000 population; Age-adjusted cancer mortality rate: 180.9 deaths per 100,000 population
Health Insurance: 85.7% have insurance; 70.5% have private insurance; 26.7% have public insurance; 14.3% do not have insurance; 6.8% of children under 18 do not have insurance
Health Care: Physicians: 16.7 per 10,000 population; Hospital beds: 17.8 per 10,000 population; Hospital admissions: 787.7 per 10,000 population
Air Quality Index: 75.1% good, 24.9% moderate, 0.0% unhealthy for sensitive individuals, 0.0% unhealthy (percent of days)
Transportation: Commute: 92.2% car, 0.2% public transportation, 0.6% walk, 4.0% work from home; Median travel time to work: 25.2 minutes
Presidential Election: 30.3% Obama, 68.1% Romney (2012)
Additional Information Contacts
Lexington Government . . . . (803) 785-8212
   http://www.lex-co.com

Lexington County Communities

BATESBURG-LEESVILLE (town). Covers a land area of 7.785 square miles and a water area of 0.104 square miles. Located at 33.91° N. Lat; 81.53° W. Long. Elevation is 643 feet.
Population: 5,362; Growth (since 2000): -2.8%; Density: 688.7 persons per square mile; Race: 49.5% White, 46.6% Black/African American, 0.7% Asian, 0.1% American Indian/Alaska Native, 0.0% Native Hawaiian/Other Pacific Islander, 1.2% Two or more races, 3.6% Hispanic of any race; Average household size: 2.46; Median age: 39.8; Age under 18: 24.7%; Age 65 and over: 16.6%; Males per 100 females: 85.1; Marriage status: 30.0% never married, 49.1% now married, 5.1% separated, 9.6% widowed, 11.3% divorced; Foreign born: 2.4%; Speak English only: 96.8%; With disability: 23.1%; Veterans: 9.2%; Ancestry: 11.0% American, 9.5% German, 7.0% Irish, 5.9% English, 1.3% Scotch-Irish
Employment: 13.2% management, business, and financial, 3.0% computer, engineering, and science, 11.9% education, legal, community service, arts, and media, 1.1% healthcare practitioners, 19.4% service, 28.7% sales and office, 7.2% natural resources, construction, and maintenance, 15.5% production, transportation, and material moving
Income: Per capita: $19,435; Median household: $25,887; Average household: $47,967; Households with income of $100,000 or more: 6.9%; Poverty rate: 31.9%
Educational Attainment: High school diploma or higher: 80.9%; Bachelor's degree or higher: 13.1%; Graduate/professional degree or higher: 4.2%

School District(s)
Lexington 03 (PK-12)
   2012-13 Enrollment: 1,984 . . . . (803) 532-4423
Housing: Homeownership rate: 63.3%; Median home value: $96,900; Median year structure built: 1967; Homeowner vacancy rate: 3.8%; Median gross rent: $664 per month; Rental vacancy rate: 8.5%
Health Insurance: 86.7% have insurance; 58.0% have private insurance; 47.6% have public insurance; 13.3% do not have insurance; 4.9% of children under 18 do not have insurance
Safety: Violent crime rate: 92.5 per 10,000 population; Property crime rate: 490.0 per 10,000 population
Newspapers: The Twin City News (weekly circulation 4800)
Transportation: Commute: 90.6% car, 0.0% public transportation, 0.0% walk, 7.4% work from home; Median travel time to work: 26.8 minutes
Additional Information Contacts
Town of Batesburg-Leesville . . . . (803) 532-4601
   http://www.batesburg-leesville.org

CAYCE (city). Covers a land area of 16.648 square miles and a water area of 0.770 square miles. Located at 33.95° N. Lat; 81.04° W. Long. Elevation is 239 feet.
History: Cayce, named for a local family, prospered from a lumber mill, granite quarry, and surrounding fields of cotton and corn. The Cayce House, built in 1765 as a trading post, was alternately a British and American stronghold, finally captured and held by General Nathanael Greene.
Population: 12,528; Growth (since 2000): 3.1%; Density: 752.5 persons per square mile; Race: 68.0% White, 25.1% Black/African American, 1.9% Asian, 0.4% American Indian/Alaska Native, 0.1% Native Hawaiian/Other Pacific Islander, 2.1% Two or more races, 4.3% Hispanic of any race; Average household size: 2.34; Median age: 34.9; Age under 18: 18.6%; Age 65 and over: 14.0%; Males per 100 females: 92.1; Marriage status:

40.0% never married, 42.2% now married, 3.6% separated, 7.4% widowed, 10.4% divorced; Foreign born: 5.3%; Speak English only: 94.0%; With disability: 13.5%; Veterans: 10.9%; Ancestry: 13.0% German, 9.3% Irish, 8.4% American, 7.9% English, 3.8% Scotch-Irish

Employment: 12.1% management, business, and financial, 5.1% computer, engineering, and science, 9.7% education, legal, community service, arts, and media, 6.9% healthcare practitioners, 20.2% service, 26.4% sales and office, 9.4% natural resources, construction, and maintenance, 10.3% production, transportation, and material moving

Income: Per capita: $23,523; Median household: $43,776; Average household: $54,429; Households with income of $100,000 or more: 11.6%; Poverty rate: 21.2%

Educational Attainment: High school diploma or higher: 88.1%; Bachelor's degree or higher: 23.9%; Graduate/professional degree or higher: 8.8%

School District(s)
Lexington 02 (PK-12)
    2012-13 Enrollment: 8,850 . . . . (803) 739-8399
Sc Public Charter SD (PK-12)
    2012-13 Enrollment: 11,500 . . . . (803) 734-8322

Housing: Homeownership rate: 60.6%; Median home value: $120,500; Median year structure built: 1964; Homeowner vacancy rate: 2.4%; Median gross rent: $849 per month; Rental vacancy rate: 8.2%

Health Insurance: 82.6% have insurance; 65.8% have private insurance; 28.8% have public insurance; 17.4% do not have insurance; 10.3% of children under 18 do not have insurance

Transportation: Commute: 95.2% car, 0.3% public transportation, 0.5% walk, 2.2% work from home; Median travel time to work: 18.1 minutes

Additional Information Contacts
City of Cayce . . . . (803) 796-9020
    http://www.cityofcayce-sc.gov

CHAPIN (town). Covers a land area of 2.011 square miles and a water area of 0.011 square miles. Located at 34.16° N. Lat; 81.34° W. Long. Elevation is 466 feet.

Population: 1,445; Growth (since 2000): 130.1%; Density: 718.7 persons per square mile; Race: 83.1% White, 11.7% Black/African American, 1.3% Asian, 0.3% American Indian/Alaska Native, 0.0% Native Hawaiian/Other Pacific Islander, 1.7% Two or more races, 5.2% Hispanic of any race; Average household size: 2.41; Median age: 36.4; Age under 18: 26.2%; Age 65 and over: 16.8%; Males per 100 females: 85.3

School District(s)
Lexington 05 (PK-12)
    2012-13 Enrollment: 16,435 . . . . (803) 476-6800
Sc Public Charter SD (PK-12)
    2012-13 Enrollment: 11,500 . . . . (803) 734-8322

Housing: Homeownership rate: 80.2%; Homeowner vacancy rate: 4.6%; Rental vacancy rate: 6.3%

Safety: Violent crime rate: 59.8 per 10,000 population; Property crime rate: 239.0 per 10,000 population

Additional Information Contacts
Town of Chapin . . . . (803) 345-2444
    http://www.chapinsc.com

GASTON (town). Covers a land area of 5.314 square miles and a water area of 0 square miles. Located at 33.82° N. Lat; 81.10° W. Long. Elevation is 499 feet.

Population: 1,645; Growth (since 2000): 26.2%; Density: 309.5 persons per square mile; Race: 84.3% White, 9.2% Black/African American, 0.4% Asian, 0.4% American Indian/Alaska Native, 0.1% Native Hawaiian/Other Pacific Islander, 3.2% Two or more races, 5.5% Hispanic of any race; Average household size: 2.60; Median age: 37.2; Age under 18: 25.3%; Age 65 and over: 11.2%; Males per 100 females: 105.6

School District(s)
Lexington 04 (PK-12)
    2012-13 Enrollment: 3,502 . . . . (803) 568-1000

Housing: Homeownership rate: 71.8%; Homeowner vacancy rate: 2.6%; Rental vacancy rate: 11.7%

Safety: Violent crime rate: 30.1 per 10,000 population; Property crime rate: 535.5 per 10,000 population

GILBERT (town). Covers a land area of 2.710 square miles and a water area of 0.062 square miles. Located at 33.92° N. Lat; 81.39° W. Long. Elevation is 538 feet.

Population: 565; Growth (since 2000): 13.0%; Density: 208.5 persons per square mile; Race: 89.2% White, 3.4% Black/African American, 0.0% Asian, 0.4% American Indian/Alaska Native, 0.0% Native Hawaiian/Other Pacific Islander, 0.2% Two or more races, 8.8% Hispanic of any race; Average household size: 2.76; Median age: 36.6; Age under 18: 28.1%; Age 65 and over: 9.4%; Males per 100 females: 99.6

School District(s)
Lexington 01 (PK-12)
    2012-13 Enrollment: 23,556 . . . . (803) 321-1002

Housing: Homeownership rate: 77.1%; Homeowner vacancy rate: 1.8%; Rental vacancy rate: 12.7%

LEXINGTON (town). County seat. Covers a land area of 8.871 square miles and a water area of 0.077 square miles. Located at 33.99° N. Lat; 81.21° W. Long. Elevation is 394 feet.

History: Lexington was settled by pioneers of German descent, who established farms here.

Population: 17,870; Growth (since 2000): 82.5%; Density: 2,014.5 persons per square mile; Race: 80.8% White, 12.7% Black/African American, 3.7% Asian, 0.3% American Indian/Alaska Native, 0.0% Native Hawaiian/Other Pacific Islander, 1.5% Two or more races, 3.5% Hispanic of any race; Average household size: 2.31; Median age: 34.8; Age under 18: 24.6%; Age 65 and over: 10.3%; Males per 100 females: 93.0; Marriage status: 28.9% never married, 53.7% now married, 3.7% separated, 5.2% widowed, 12.2% divorced; Foreign born: 5.3%; Speak English only: 92.1%; With disability: 11.7%; Veterans: 9.4%; Ancestry: 16.6% Irish, 12.9% German, 12.6% English, 11.5% American, 4.4% Italian

Employment: 21.9% management, business, and financial, 5.9% computer, engineering, and science, 15.4% education, legal, community service, arts, and media, 8.2% healthcare practitioners, 11.3% service, 27.4% sales and office, 5.1% natural resources, construction, and maintenance, 5.0% production, transportation, and material moving

Income: Per capita: $30,574; Median household: $61,477; Average household: $76,519; Households with income of $100,000 or more: 26.8%; Poverty rate: 11.7%

Educational Attainment: High school diploma or higher: 93.9%; Bachelor's degree or higher: 41.7%; Graduate/professional degree or higher: 16.5%

School District(s)
Lexington 01 (PK-12)
    2012-13 Enrollment: 23,556 . . . . (803) 321-1002
Vocational/Technical School(s)
Lacy Cosmetology School-Lexington (Private, For-profit)
    Fall 2013 Enrollment: 18 . . . . (803) 951-2236
    2013-14 Tuition: $17,065

Housing: Homeownership rate: 60.1%; Median home value: $175,500; Median year structure built: 1999; Homeowner vacancy rate: 3.9%; Median gross rent: $910 per month; Rental vacancy rate: 11.6%

Health Insurance: 91.7% have insurance; 80.9% have private insurance; 22.4% have public insurance; 8.3% do not have insurance; 6.2% of children under 18 do not have insurance

Safety: Violent crime rate: 23.0 per 10,000 population; Property crime rate: 356.6 per 10,000 population

Newspapers: Lexington County Chronicle (weekly circulation 8000)

Transportation: Commute: 92.6% car, 0.1% public transportation, 1.0% walk, 4.7% work from home; Median travel time to work: 23.2 minutes

Additional Information Contacts
Town of Lexington . . . . (803) 359-4164
    http://www.lexsc.com

OAK GROVE (CDP). Covers a land area of 6.650 square miles and a water area of 0.037 square miles. Located at 33.98° N. Lat; 81.14° W. Long. Elevation is 338 feet.

Population: 10,291; Growth (since 2000): 25.8%; Density: 1,547.4 persons per square mile; Race: 78.8% White, 11.3% Black/African American, 1.6% Asian, 0.4% American Indian/Alaska Native, 0.0% Native Hawaiian/Other Pacific Islander, 1.8% Two or more races, 10.7% Hispanic of any race; Average household size: 2.45; Median age: 36.0; Age under 18: 24.4%; Age 65 and over: 11.8%; Males per 100 females: 97.8; Marriage status: 27.9% never married, 54.1% now married, 3.1% separated, 6.1% widowed, 11.8% divorced; Foreign born: 6.0%; Speak

English only: 92.3%; With disability: 12.4%; Veterans: 11.0%; Ancestry: 10.9% German, 10.2% American, 8.3% Irish, 5.3% English, 4.5% Italian
Employment: 12.3% management, business, and financial, 2.8% computer, engineering, and science, 8.4% education, legal, community service, arts, and media, 5.9% healthcare practitioners, 13.0% service, 30.6% sales and office, 16.9% natural resources, construction, and maintenance, 10.1% production, transportation, and material moving
Income: Per capita: $24,752; Median household: $47,881; Average household: $58,803; Households with income of $100,000 or more: 13.5%; Poverty rate: 8.0%
Educational Attainment: High school diploma or higher: 89.8%; Bachelor's degree or higher: 24.3%; Graduate/professional degree or higher: 8.9%
Housing: Homeownership rate: 74.4%; Median home value: $129,000; Median year structure built: 1984; Homeowner vacancy rate: 1.7%; Median gross rent: $910 per month; Rental vacancy rate: 12.5%
Health Insurance: 84.4% have insurance; 70.5% have private insurance; 24.1% have public insurance; 15.6% do not have insurance; 12.0% of children under 18 do not have insurance
Transportation: Commute: 92.0% car, 0.0% public transportation, 0.8% walk, 4.7% work from home; Median travel time to work: 22.1 minutes

PELION (town). Covers a land area of 3.598 square miles and a water area of 0.089 square miles. Located at 33.78° N. Lat; 81.26° W. Long. Elevation is 387 feet.
Population: 674; Growth (since 2000): 21.9%; Density: 187.3 persons per square mile; Race: 93.2% White, 1.5% Black/African American, 0.7% Asian, 0.0% American Indian/Alaska Native, 0.0% Native Hawaiian/Other Pacific Islander, 1.2% Two or more races, 5.6% Hispanic of any race; Average household size: 2.92; Median age: 34.8; Age under 18: 28.9%; Age 65 and over: 12.3%; Males per 100 females: 89.3
School District(s)
Lexington 01 (PK-12)
    2012-13 Enrollment: 23,556 . . . . (803) 321-1002
Housing: Homeownership rate: 84.9%; Homeowner vacancy rate: 2.6%; Rental vacancy rate: 2.9%
Safety: Violent crime rate: 72.6 per 10,000 population; Property crime rate: 449.9 per 10,000 population

PINE RIDGE (town). Covers a land area of 4.722 square miles and a water area of 0.035 square miles. Located at 33.91° N. Lat; 81.10° W. Long. Elevation is 262 feet.
Population: 2,064; Growth (since 2000): 29.6%; Density: 437.1 persons per square mile; Race: 86.6% White, 9.7% Black/African American, 1.3% Asian, 0.3% American Indian/Alaska Native, 0.0% Native Hawaiian/Other Pacific Islander, 1.4% Two or more races, 1.8% Hispanic of any race; Average household size: 2.60; Median age: 39.6; Age under 18: 22.9%; Age 65 and over: 13.2%; Males per 100 females: 93.1
Housing: Homeownership rate: 81.7%; Homeowner vacancy rate: 2.6%; Rental vacancy rate: 11.4%

RED BANK (CDP). Covers a land area of 11.805 square miles and a water area of 0.231 square miles. Located at 33.93° N. Lat; 81.23° W. Long. Elevation is 341 feet.
Population: 9,617; Growth (since 2000): 9.1%; Density: 814.6 persons per square mile; Race: 84.6% White, 10.3% Black/African American, 0.6% Asian, 0.5% American Indian/Alaska Native, 0.0% Native Hawaiian/Other Pacific Islander, 1.9% Two or more races, 4.0% Hispanic of any race; Average household size: 2.59; Median age: 35.8; Age under 18: 25.5%; Age 65 and over: 8.6%; Males per 100 females: 94.1; Marriage status: 26.7% never married, 51.5% now married, 1.9% separated, 6.4% widowed, 15.4% divorced; Foreign born: 1.5%; Speak English only: 97.0%; With disability: 12.9%; Veterans: 9.0%; Ancestry: 18.2% German, 13.9% Irish, 13.1% American, 6.5% English, 6.2% Italian
Employment: 11.4% management, business, and financial, 3.8% computer, engineering, and science, 11.0% education, legal, community service, arts, and media, 7.3% healthcare practitioners, 9.8% service, 30.3% sales and office, 14.8% natural resources, construction, and maintenance, 11.6% production, transportation, and material moving
Income: Per capita: $23,616; Median household: $46,216; Average household: $55,510; Households with income of $100,000 or more: 14.3%; Poverty rate: 16.7%
Educational Attainment: High school diploma or higher: 84.7%; Bachelor's degree or higher: 19.9%; Graduate/professional degree or higher: 5.0%

Housing: Homeownership rate: 78.2%; Median home value: $117,000; Median year structure built: 1989; Homeowner vacancy rate: 1.9%; Median gross rent: $816 per month; Rental vacancy rate: 7.6%
Health Insurance: 83.2% have insurance; 68.6% have private insurance; 24.6% have public insurance; 16.8% do not have insurance; 5.5% of children under 18 do not have insurance
Transportation: Commute: 96.4% car, 0.0% public transportation, 1.3% walk, 1.6% work from home; Median travel time to work: 26.3 minutes

SEVEN OAKS (CDP). Covers a land area of 7.584 square miles and a water area of 0.117 square miles. Located at 34.05° N. Lat; 81.14° W. Long. Elevation is 217 feet.
History: Seven Oaks is on the fall line from the Appalachian Mountains. The fall line is the spot where rivers usually become unnavigable when sailing upstream, and is also the spot farthest downstream where falling water can usefully power a mill.
Population: 15,144; Growth (since 2000): -3.9%; Density: 1,996.7 persons per square mile; Race: 60.4% White, 32.0% Black/African American, 2.8% Asian, 0.3% American Indian/Alaska Native, 0.2% Native Hawaiian/Other Pacific Islander, 2.8% Two or more races, 3.8% Hispanic of any race; Average household size: 2.32; Median age: 38.3; Age under 18: 22.1%; Age 65 and over: 15.4%; Males per 100 females: 89.3; Marriage status: 31.5% never married, 50.4% now married, 3.4% separated, 7.2% widowed, 10.9% divorced; Foreign born: 4.3%; Speak English only: 93.5%; With disability: 11.3%; Veterans: 13.4%; Ancestry: 13.9% German, 13.6% English, 10.4% Irish, 10.0% American, 3.6% Italian
Employment: 16.2% management, business, and financial, 6.0% computer, engineering, and science, 15.2% education, legal, community service, arts, and media, 3.9% healthcare practitioners, 16.7% service, 27.8% sales and office, 5.9% natural resources, construction, and maintenance, 8.4% production, transportation, and material moving
Income: Per capita: $26,446; Median household: $48,802; Average household: $61,130; Households with income of $100,000 or more: 16.3%; Poverty rate: 13.5%
Educational Attainment: High school diploma or higher: 93.3%; Bachelor's degree or higher: 35.6%; Graduate/professional degree or higher: 14.4%
Housing: Homeownership rate: 60.3%; Median home value: $142,300; Median year structure built: 1975; Homeowner vacancy rate: 2.6%; Median gross rent: $792 per month; Rental vacancy rate: 12.1%
Health Insurance: 87.2% have insurance; 73.7% have private insurance; 29.6% have public insurance; 12.8% do not have insurance; 6.8% of children under 18 do not have insurance
Transportation: Commute: 92.6% car, 0.2% public transportation, 0.4% walk, 3.5% work from home; Median travel time to work: 20.7 minutes

SOUTH CONGAREE (town). Covers a land area of 3.285 square miles and a water area of 0.045 square miles. Located at 33.91° N. Lat; 81.14° W. Long. Elevation is 190 feet.
Population: 2,306; Growth (since 2000): 1.8%; Density: 702.0 persons per square mile; Race: 85.3% White, 9.6% Black/African American, 1.5% Asian, 0.5% American Indian/Alaska Native, 0.0% Native Hawaiian/Other Pacific Islander, 1.7% Two or more races, 2.8% Hispanic of any race; Average household size: 2.51; Median age: 40.2; Age under 18: 22.1%; Age 65 and over: 13.8%; Males per 100 females: 99.1
Housing: Homeownership rate: 67.8%; Homeowner vacancy rate: 1.4%; Rental vacancy rate: 18.4%

SPRINGDALE (town). Covers a land area of 2.729 square miles and a water area of 0.029 square miles. Located at 33.96° N. Lat; 81.11° W. Long. Elevation is 230 feet.
Population: 2,636; Growth (since 2000): -8.4%; Density: 966.0 persons per square mile; Race: 84.2% White, 10.7% Black/African American, 1.7% Asian, 0.3% American Indian/Alaska Native, 0.0% Native Hawaiian/Other Pacific Islander, 1.6% Two or more races, 3.6% Hispanic of any race; Average household size: 2.28; Median age: 46.0; Age under 18: 19.1%; Age 65 and over: 23.8%; Males per 100 females: 91.0; Marriage status: 28.5% never married, 54.5% now married, 4.3% separated, 7.8% widowed, 9.2% divorced; Foreign born: 5.6%; Speak English only: 93.1%; With disability: 10.2%; Veterans: 12.1%; Ancestry: 18.2% German, 9.4% Irish, 9.0% American, 8.3% English, 3.9% Scotch-Irish
Employment: 11.7% management, business, and financial, 3.6% computer, engineering, and science, 9.6% education, legal, community service, arts, and media, 6.0% healthcare practitioners, 20.4% service,

24.8% sales and office, 9.5% natural resources, construction, and maintenance, 14.4% production, transportation, and material moving
Income: Per capita: $28,088; Median household: $58,750; Average household: $66,346; Households with income of $100,000 or more: 19.1%; Poverty rate: 9.3%
Educational Attainment: High school diploma or higher: 94.4%; Bachelor's degree or higher: 22.7%; Graduate/professional degree or higher: 6.6%
Housing: Homeownership rate: 74.3%; Median home value: $147,600; Median year structure built: 1967; Homeowner vacancy rate: 2.5%; Median gross rent: $913 per month; Rental vacancy rate: 6.0%
Health Insurance: 87.5% have insurance; 79.5% have private insurance; 29.1% have public insurance; 12.5% do not have insurance; 9.9% of children under 18 do not have insurance
Safety: Violent crime rate: 33.4 per 10,000 population; Property crime rate: 463.3 per 10,000 population
Transportation: Commute: 95.0% car, 0.3% public transportation, 0.4% walk, 2.1% work from home; Median travel time to work: 19.4 minutes
Additional Information Contacts
Town of Springdale . . . . (803) 794-0408
  http://www.springdalesc.com

SUMMIT (town). Covers a land area of 1.489 square miles and a water area of 0 square miles. Located at 33.92° N. Lat; 81.42° W. Long. Elevation is 607 feet.
Population: 402; Growth (since 2000): 83.6%; Density: 270.0 persons per square mile; Race: 91.0% White, 8.0% Black/African American, 0.0% Asian, 0.2% American Indian/Alaska Native, 0.0% Native Hawaiian/Other Pacific Islander, 0.7% Two or more races, 1.7% Hispanic of any race; Average household size: 2.75; Median age: 35.4; Age under 18: 25.6%; Age 65 and over: 11.9%; Males per 100 females: 91.4
Housing: Homeownership rate: 83.5%; Homeowner vacancy rate: 1.6%; Rental vacancy rate: 11.1%

SWANSEA (town). Covers a land area of 2.033 square miles and a water area of 0.054 square miles. Located at 33.74° N. Lat; 81.10° W. Long. Elevation is 358 feet.
History: The name of Swansea is said to be a corruption of the German "zwanzig," meaning twenty, as the town was sited about 20 miles from Columbia.
Population: 827; Growth (since 2000): 55.2%; Density: 406.7 persons per square mile; Race: 40.3% White, 54.1% Black/African American, 0.1% Asian, 1.7% American Indian/Alaska Native, 0.0% Native Hawaiian/Other Pacific Islander, 2.2% Two or more races, 1.9% Hispanic of any race; Average household size: 2.36; Median age: 39.3; Age under 18: 25.2%; Age 65 and over: 16.2%; Males per 100 females: 85.0
School District(s)
Calhoun 01 (PK-12)
  2012-13 Enrollment: 1,720 . . . . (803) 655-7310
Lexington 04 (PK-12)
  2012-13 Enrollment: 3,502 . . . . (803) 568-1000
Housing: Homeownership rate: 60.4%; Homeowner vacancy rate: 1.9%; Rental vacancy rate: 8.5%
Safety: Violent crime rate: 186.5 per 10,000 population; Property crime rate: 594.4 per 10,000 population
Additional Information Contacts
Town of Swansea . . . . (803) 568-2835
  http://www.swanseatown.net

WEST COLUMBIA (city). Covers a land area of 6.992 square miles and a water area of 0.211 square miles. Located at 33.99° N. Lat; 81.10° W. Long. Elevation is 285 feet.
History: West Columbia, settled across the Congaree River from Columbia, was known as New Brookland until 1938.
Population: 14,988; Growth (since 2000): 14.7%; Density: 2,143.6 persons per square mile; Race: 68.0% White, 18.5% Black/African American, 1.8% Asian, 0.8% American Indian/Alaska Native, 0.0% Native Hawaiian/Other Pacific Islander, 2.3% Two or more races, 14.5% Hispanic of any race; Average household size: 2.23; Median age: 37.4; Age under 18: 18.5%; Age 65 and over: 16.3%; Males per 100 females: 95.7; Marriage status: 35.3% never married, 44.0% now married, 2.9% separated, 9.8% widowed, 10.9% divorced; Foreign born: 13.5%; Speak English only: 85.6%; With disability: 12.2%; Veterans: 10.1%; Ancestry: 12.4% German, 10.7% American, 9.1% Irish, 7.0% English, 3.0% Italian

Employment: 11.5% management, business, and financial, 3.7% computer, engineering, and science, 14.5% education, legal, community service, arts, and media, 5.5% healthcare practitioners, 16.7% service, 24.9% sales and office, 14.2% natural resources, construction, and maintenance, 9.0% production, transportation, and material moving
Income: Per capita: $25,124; Median household: $40,594; Average household: $53,024; Households with income of $100,000 or more: 13.2%; Poverty rate: 18.7%
Educational Attainment: High school diploma or higher: 85.5%; Bachelor's degree or higher: 33.8%; Graduate/professional degree or higher: 12.9%
School District(s)
Lexington 01 (PK-12)
  2012-13 Enrollment: 23,556 . . . . (803) 321-1002
Lexington 02 (PK-12)
  2012-13 Enrollment: 8,850 . . . . (803) 739-8399
Two-year College(s)
Midlands Technical College (Public)
  Fall 2013 Enrollment: 11,634 . . . . (803) 738-8324
  2013-14 Tuition: In-state $4,750; Out-of-state $11,086
Vocational/Technical School(s)
Columbia Academy of Cosmetology (Private, For-profit)
  Fall 2013 Enrollment: 37 . . . . (803) 796-9986
  2013-14 Tuition: $13,575
Housing: Homeownership rate: 50.8%; Median home value: $132,000; Median year structure built: 1973; Homeowner vacancy rate: 2.7%; Median gross rent: $811 per month; Rental vacancy rate: 16.2%
Health Insurance: 78.2% have insurance; 61.1% have private insurance; 31.1% have public insurance; 21.8% do not have insurance; 12.8% of children under 18 do not have insurance
Hospitals: Lexington Medical Center (380 beds)
Safety: Violent crime rate: 70.6 per 10,000 population; Property crime rate: 490.6 per 10,000 population
Transportation: Commute: 91.4% car, 0.0% public transportation, 1.5% walk, 2.5% work from home; Median travel time to work: 19.5 minutes
Additional Information Contacts
City of West Columbia . . . . (803) 791-1880
  http://www.westcolumbiasc.gov

Marion County

Located in eastern South Carolina; bounded on the west by the Pee Dee River, and on the east by the Little Pee Dee River. Covers a land area of 489.227 square miles, a water area of 4.908 square miles, and is located in the Eastern Time Zone at 34.08° N. Lat., 79.36° W. Long. The county was founded in 1800. County seat is Marion.
Population: 33,062; Growth (since 2000): -6.8%; Density: 67.6 persons per square mile; Race: 40.6% White, 55.9% Black/African American, 0.5% Asian, 0.4% American Indian/Alaska Native, 0.0% Native Hawaiian/Other Pacific Islander, 1.2% two or more races, 2.4% Hispanic of any race; Average household size: 2.52; Median age: 39.9; Age under 18: 24.4%; Age 65 and over: 14.7%; Males per 100 females: 84.2; Marriage status: 34.1% never married, 45.7% now married, 6.3% separated, 9.5% widowed, 10.6% divorced; Foreign born: 2.1%; Speak English only: 96.8%; With disability: 18.0%; Veterans: 8.6%; Ancestry: 10.6% American, 9.3% English, 4.2% Irish, 2.5% German, 1.5% Scotch-Irish
Religion: Six largest groups: 26.5% Baptist, 15.1% Methodist/Pietist, 5.5% Other Groups, 2.3% Non-denominational Protestant, 1.8% Pentecostal, 1.7% Presbyterian-Reformed
Economy: Unemployment rate: 11.3%; Leading industries: 25.4% retail trade; 13.4% other services (except public administration); 11.6% health care and social assistance; Farms: 275 totaling 80,213 acres; Company size: 1 employs 1,000 or more persons, 0 employ 500 to 999 persons, 7 employ 100 to 499 persons, 508 employ less than 100 persons; Business ownership: 491 women-owned, 396 Black-owned, n/a Hispanic-owned, 40 Asian-owned
Employment: 9.2% management, business, and financial, 2.1% computer, engineering, and science, 7.9% education, legal, community service, arts, and media, 6.6% healthcare practitioners, 19.7% service, 23.9% sales and office, 9.9% natural resources, construction, and maintenance, 20.7% production, transportation, and material moving
Income: Per capita: $16,531; Median household: $29,149; Average household: $41,719; Households with income of $100,000 or more: 8.2%; Poverty rate: 27.4%

Educational Attainment: High school diploma or higher: 81.8%; Bachelor's degree or higher: 13.6%; Graduate/professional degree or higher: 4.8%

Housing: Homeownership rate: 68.8%; Median home value: $77,800; Median year structure built: 1978; Homeowner vacancy rate: 2.0%; Median gross rent: $544 per month; Rental vacancy rate: 8.4%

Vital Statistics: Birth rate: 124.7 per 10,000 population; Death rate: 131.0 per 10,000 population; Age-adjusted cancer mortality rate: 161.1 deaths per 100,000 population

Health Insurance: 80.8% have insurance; 46.5% have private insurance; 44.8% have public insurance; 19.2% do not have insurance; 4.3% of children under 18 do not have insurance

Health Care: Physicians: 8.6 per 10,000 population; Hospital beds: 37.9 per 10,000 population; Hospital admissions: 1,045.8 per 10,000 population

Transportation: Commute: 93.8% car, 1.0% public transportation, 0.9% walk, 3.6% work from home; Median travel time to work: 26.0 minutes

Presidential Election: 64.6% Obama, 34.5% Romney (2012)

Additional Information Contacts

Marion Government. . . . . (843) 423-8240
  http://www.marionsc.org

Marion County Communities

CENTENARY (unincorporated postal area)

ZCTA: 29519

Covers a land area of 4.290 square miles and a water area of 0 square miles. Located at 34.02° N. Lat; 79.36° W. Long. Elevation is 56 feet.

Population: 285; Growth (since 2000): 68.6%; Density: 66.4 persons per square mile; Race: 19.3% White, 79.3% Black/African American, 0.0% Asian, 0.0% American Indian/Alaska Native, 0.0% Native Hawaiian/Other Pacific Islander, 1.4% Two or more races, 1.8% Hispanic of any race; Average household size: 2.52; Median age: 42.4; Age under 18: 18.2%; Age 65 and over: 14.7%; Males per 100 females: 79.2

Housing: Homeownership rate: 79.6%; Homeowner vacancy rate: 2.2%; Rental vacancy rate: 14.8%

GRESHAM (unincorporated postal area)

ZCTA: 29546

Covers a land area of 145.712 square miles and a water area of 3.194 square miles. Located at 33.88° N. Lat; 79.35° W. Long. Elevation is 52 feet.

Population: 2,834; Growth (since 2000): -7.1%; Density: 19.4 persons per square mile; Race: 36.7% White, 55.5% Black/African American, 0.1% Asian, 0.1% American Indian/Alaska Native, 0.0% Native Hawaiian/Other Pacific Islander, 1.7% Two or more races, 7.8% Hispanic of any race; Average household size: 2.69; Median age: 38.5; Age under 18: 24.1%; Age 65 and over: 12.9%; Males per 100 females: 91.6; Marriage status: 32.0% never married, 48.5% now married, 10.4% separated, 9.1% widowed, 10.4% divorced; Foreign born: 8.5%; Speak English only: 85.8%; With disability: 14.7%; Veterans: 7.5%; Ancestry: 15.3% English, 10.8% American, 5.7% Irish, 2.6% German, 2.0% Italian

Employment: 4.6% management, business, and financial, 2.4% computer, engineering, and science, 8.2% education, legal, community service, arts, and media, 3.9% healthcare practitioners, 19.9% service, 31.3% sales and office, 16.6% natural resources, construction, and maintenance, 13.1% production, transportation, and material moving

Income: Per capita: $18,302; Median household: $25,578; Average household: $43,315; Households with income of $100,000 or more: 13.2%; Poverty rate: 30.2%

Educational Attainment: High school diploma or higher: 81.3%; Bachelor's degree or higher: 15.4%; Graduate/professional degree or higher: 7.4%

Housing: Homeownership rate: 79.5%; Median home value: $58,100; Median year structure built: 1981; Homeowner vacancy rate: 1.4%; Median gross rent: $632 per month; Rental vacancy rate: 11.0%

Health Insurance: 73.7% have insurance; 38.4% have private insurance; 44.9% have public insurance; 26.3% do not have insurance; 3.0% of children under 18 do not have insurance

Transportation: Commute: 96.3% car, 0.0% public transportation, 1.4% walk, 2.3% work from home; Median travel time to work: 37.6 minutes

MARION (city). County seat. Covers a land area of 4.421 square miles and a water area of 0 square miles. Located at 34.18° N. Lat; 79.40° W. Long. Elevation is 75 feet.

History: Marion, first called Gilesboro for Colonel Hugh Giles, began as a courthouse town in 1800. During the 1830's it followed the county in honoring General Francis Marion, the Swamp Fox of the Revolution.

Population: 6,939; Growth (since 2000): -1.5%; Density: 1,569.7 persons per square mile; Race: 27.8% White, 69.2% Black/African American, 1.1% Asian, 0.2% American Indian/Alaska Native, 0.0% Native Hawaiian/Other Pacific Islander, 1.4% Two or more races, 1.3% Hispanic of any race; Average household size: 2.48; Median age: 35.3; Age under 18: 27.6%; Age 65 and over: 14.6%; Males per 100 females: 78.2; Marriage status: 41.2% never married, 37.1% now married, 6.2% separated, 10.9% widowed, 10.9% divorced; Foreign born: 1.5%; Speak English only: 97.9%; With disability: 16.4%; Veterans: 8.7%; Ancestry: 6.2% English, 3.4% Scotch-Irish, 2.9% American, 2.8% German, 2.7% Irish

Employment: 5.4% management, business, and financial, 2.7% computer, engineering, and science, 13.1% education, legal, community service, arts, and media, 7.7% healthcare practitioners, 24.8% service, 21.6% sales and office, 1.6% natural resources, construction, and maintenance, 23.0% production, transportation, and material moving

Income: Per capita: $14,634; Median household: $21,392; Average household: $37,344; Households with income of $100,000 or more: 5.3%; Poverty rate: 41.1%

Educational Attainment: High school diploma or higher: 83.5%; Bachelor's degree or higher: 16.5%; Graduate/professional degree or higher: 6.0%

Housing: Homeownership rate: 52.4%; Median home value: $104,200; Median year structure built: 1971; Homeowner vacancy rate: 3.5%; Median gross rent: $503 per month; Rental vacancy rate: 4.1%

Health Insurance: 81.4% have insurance; 35.2% have private insurance; 55.2% have public insurance; 18.6% do not have insurance; 1.2% of children under 18 do not have insurance

Safety: Violent crime rate: 133.6 per 10,000 population; Property crime rate: 873.3 per 10,000 population

Newspapers: The Star & Enterprise (weekly circulation 12000)

Transportation: Commute: 91.4% car, 2.9% public transportation, 0.0% walk, 3.2% work from home; Median travel time to work: 22.6 minutes

Additional Information Contacts

City of Marion . . . . (843) 423-5961
  http://www.marionsc.gov

MULLINS (city). Covers a land area of 3.064 square miles and a water area of 0 square miles. Located at 34.20° N. Lat; 79.25° W. Long. Elevation is 98 feet.

History: Mullins was known as the largest tobacco market in South Carolina.

Population: 4,663; Growth (since 2000): -7.3%; Density: 1,521.7 persons per square mile; Race: 31.2% White, 65.8% Black/African American, 1.0% Asian, 0.4% American Indian/Alaska Native, 0.0% Native Hawaiian/Other Pacific Islander, 1.4% Two or more races, 0.8% Hispanic of any race; Average household size: 2.44; Median age: 39.9; Age under 18: 25.3%; Age 65 and over: 18.3%; Males per 100 females: 73.9; Marriage status: 33.9% never married, 45.5% now married, 8.7% separated, 12.1% widowed, 8.5% divorced; Foreign born: 0.8%; Speak English only: 99.2%; With disability: 23.0%; Veterans: 8.6%; Ancestry: 16.1% American, 8.0% English, 2.6% European, 2.1% Irish, 0.9% West Indian

Employment: 8.7% management, business, and financial, 2.4% computer, engineering, and science, 6.3% education, legal, community service, arts, and media, 3.0% healthcare practitioners, 29.0% service, 23.4% sales and office, 3.7% natural resources, construction, and maintenance, 23.5% production, transportation, and material moving

Income: Per capita: $16,525; Median household: $28,117; Average household: $40,930; Households with income of $100,000 or more: 8.4%; Poverty rate: 31.0%

Educational Attainment: High school diploma or higher: 80.4%; Bachelor's degree or higher: 13.3%; Graduate/professional degree or higher: 4.3%

School District(s)

Marion 80 (09-12)
    2012-13 Enrollment: n/a . . . . (843) 423-1941

Vocational/Technical School(s)

Academy for Careers and Technology (Public)
    Fall 2013 Enrollment: 50 . . . . (843) 423-1941
    2013-14 Tuition: $6,300

Housing: Homeownership rate: 54.8%; Median home value: $80,100; Median year structure built: 1967; Homeowner vacancy rate: 3.8%; Median gross rent: $474 per month; Rental vacancy rate: 8.8%
Health Insurance: 79.1% have insurance; 40.3% have private insurance; 50.7% have public insurance; 20.9% do not have insurance; 8.6% of children under 18 do not have insurance
Hospitals: Carolinas Hospital System Marion (124 beds)
Safety: Violent crime rate: 139.9 per 10,000 population; Property crime rate: 977.3 per 10,000 population
Transportation: Commute: 89.3% car, 1.1% public transportation, 3.4% walk, 6.2% work from home; Median travel time to work: 25.3 minutes
Additional Information Contacts
City of Mullins . . . . (843) 464-9583
    http://www.mullinssc.us

NICHOLS (town). Covers a land area of 1.406 square miles and a water area of 0 square miles. Located at 34.24° N. Lat; 79.15° W. Long. Elevation is 56 feet.
Population: 368; Growth (since 2000): -9.8%; Density: 261.8 persons per square mile; Race: 59.0% White, 40.5% Black/African American, 0.3% Asian, 0.0% American Indian/Alaska Native, 0.0% Native Hawaiian/Other Pacific Islander, 0.0% Two or more races, 0.3% Hispanic of any race; Average household size: 2.04; Median age: 51.6; Age under 18: 16.6%; Age 65 and over: 22.3%; Males per 100 females: 72.8
Housing: Homeownership rate: 74.4%; Homeowner vacancy rate: 1.5%; Rental vacancy rate: 13.2%
Safety: Violent crime rate: 27.6 per 10,000 population; Property crime rate: 469.6 per 10,000 population

SELLERS (town). Covers a land area of 0.693 square miles and a water area of 0 square miles. Located at 34.28° N. Lat; 79.47° W. Long. Elevation is 82 feet.
Population: 219; Growth (since 2000): -20.9%; Density: 315.9 persons per square mile; Race: 18.7% White, 79.9% Black/African American, 0.0% Asian, 0.0% American Indian/Alaska Native, 0.0% Native Hawaiian/Other Pacific Islander, 0.9% Two or more races, 1.4% Hispanic of any race; Average household size: 2.35; Median age: 44.3; Age under 18: 19.2%; Age 65 and over: 14.2%; Males per 100 females: 81.0
Housing: Homeownership rate: 72.0%; Homeowner vacancy rate: 1.4%; Rental vacancy rate: 6.5%

Marlboro County

Located in northeastern South Carolina; bounded on the southwest by the Pee Dee River, and on the north and northeast by North Carolina. Covers a land area of 479.674 square miles, a water area of 5.600 square miles, and is located in the Eastern Time Zone at 34.60° N. Lat., 79.68° W. Long. The county was founded in 1798. County seat is Bennettsville.

Marlboro County is part of the Bennettsville, SC Micropolitan Statistical Area. The entire metro area includes: Marlboro County, SC

Weather Station: Mccoll 3 NNW								Elevation: 189 feet			
	Jan	Feb	Mar	Apr	May	Jun	Jul	Aug	Sep	Oct	Nov	Dec
High	54	59	67	76	83	89	92	90	83	75	66	57
Low	33	36	42	49	58	66	70	69	63	51	42	35
Precip	2.8	3.1	3.3	2.2	2.4	3.4	3.9	3.9	3.5	2.7	2.7	2.6
Snow	0.3	0.8	0.4	0.0	0.0	0.0	0.0	0.0	0.0	0.0	tr	0.1

High and Low temperatures in degrees Fahrenheit; Precipitation and Snow in inches

Population: 28,933; Growth (since 2000): 0.4%; Density: 60.3 persons per square mile; Race: 41.4% White, 50.9% Black/African American, 0.3% Asian, 4.5% American Indian/Alaska Native, 0.0% Native Hawaiian/Other Pacific Islander, 1.8% two or more races, 2.8% Hispanic of any race; Average household size: 2.47; Median age: 38.8; Age under 18: 21.9%; Age 65 and over: 13.1%; Males per 100 females: 111.6; Marriage status: 40.4% never married, 40.5% now married, 5.5% separated, 8.2% widowed, 10.9% divorced; Foreign born: 1.9%; Speak English only: 97.0%; With disability: 20.4%; Veterans: 8.4%; Ancestry: 8.9% American, 5.0% Irish, 4.2% English, 3.8% German, 2.9% Scotch-Irish
Religion: Six largest groups: 15.1% Methodist/Pietist, 10.6% Baptist, 4.9% Non-denominational Protestant, 3.5% Pentecostal, 1.0% Holiness, 1.0% Presbyterian-Reformed
Economy: Unemployment rate: 9.3%; Leading industries: 28.7% retail trade; 12.6% health care and social assistance; 10.9% other services (except public administration); Farms: 224 totaling 113,301 acres;

Company size: 0 employ 1,000 or more persons, 1 employs 500 to 999 persons, 10 employ 100 to 499 persons, 330 employ less than 100 persons; Business ownership: 139 women-owned, n/a Black-owned, n/a Hispanic-owned, n/a Asian-owned
Employment: 6.7% management, business, and financial, 1.3% computer, engineering, and science, 7.2% education, legal, community service, arts, and media, 5.5% healthcare practitioners, 18.8% service, 20.6% sales and office, 10.1% natural resources, construction, and maintenance, 29.6% production, transportation, and material moving
Income: Per capita: $14,577; Median household: $28,297; Average household: $39,077; Households with income of $100,000 or more: 5.7%; Poverty rate: 30.7%
Educational Attainment: High school diploma or higher: 69.9%; Bachelor's degree or higher: 8.7%; Graduate/professional degree or higher: 3.2%
Housing: Homeownership rate: 65.5%; Median home value: $58,200; Median year structure built: 1976; Homeowner vacancy rate: 1.4%; Median gross rent: $590 per month; Rental vacancy rate: 12.0%
Vital Statistics: Birth rate: 112.8 per 10,000 population; Death rate: 102.8 per 10,000 population; Age-adjusted cancer mortality rate: 232.4 deaths per 100,000 population
Health Insurance: 81.5% have insurance; 45.5% have private insurance; 47.2% have public insurance; 18.5% do not have insurance; 7.0% of children under 18 do not have insurance
Health Care: Physicians: 6.0 per 10,000 population; Hospital beds: 35.8 per 10,000 population; Hospital admissions: 537.1 per 10,000 population
Transportation: Commute: 95.8% car, 0.5% public transportation, 1.3% walk, 1.2% work from home; Median travel time to work: 23.1 minutes
Presidential Election: 61.9% Obama, 37.3% Romney (2012)
Additional Information Contacts
Marlboro Government . . . . (843) 479-5613
    http://www.marlborocounty.sc.gov

Marlboro County Communities

BENNETTSVILLE (city). County seat. Covers a land area of 6.116 square miles and a water area of 0.633 square miles. Located at 34.63° N. Lat; 79.69° W. Long. Elevation is 154 feet.
History: Bennettsville was settled by Baptists from Delaware, and became the seat of Marlboro County, a prime land for cotton and corn. In 1889 Zachariah J. Drake topped the world's record with 255 bushels of shelled corn from one acre, winning the American Agriculturist prize.
Population: 9,069; Growth (since 2000): -3.8%; Density: 1,482.9 persons per square mile; Race: 32.7% White, 64.2% Black/African American, 0.4% Asian, 0.8% American Indian/Alaska Native, 0.0% Native Hawaiian/Other Pacific Islander, 1.2% Two or more races, 1.6% Hispanic of any race; Average household size: 2.34; Median age: 38.7; Age under 18: 20.5%; Age 65 and over: 14.7%; Males per 100 females: 121.2; Marriage status: 43.8% never married, 32.6% now married, 4.4% separated, 11.4% widowed, 12.1% divorced; Foreign born: 1.9%; Speak English only: 97.5%; With disability: 17.9%; Veterans: 8.5%; Ancestry: 5.8% American, 4.6% German, 4.5% English, 3.6% Irish, 1.6% Scotch-Irish
Employment: 11.5% management, business, and financial, 0.9% computer, engineering, and science, 10.8% education, legal, community service, arts, and media, 7.9% healthcare practitioners, 13.6% service, 15.4% sales and office, 5.5% natural resources, construction, and maintenance, 34.4% production, transportation, and material moving
Income: Per capita: $15,344; Median household: $27,104; Average household: $42,219; Households with income of $100,000 or more: 6.9%; Poverty rate: 33.2%
Educational Attainment: High school diploma or higher: 70.5%; Bachelor's degree or higher: 14.9%; Graduate/professional degree or higher: 5.7%
School District(s)
Marlboro 01 (PK-12)
    2012-13 Enrollment: 4,312 . . . . (843) 479-4016
Housing: Homeownership rate: 53.2%; Median home value: $79,400; Median year structure built: 1969; Homeowner vacancy rate: 2.0%; Median gross rent: $572 per month; Rental vacancy rate: 13.1%
Health Insurance: 85.3% have insurance; 43.4% have private insurance; 54.6% have public insurance; 14.7% do not have insurance; 6.3% of children under 18 do not have insurance
Hospitals: Marlboro Park Hospital (102 beds)
Safety: Violent crime rate: 130.5 per 10,000 population; Property crime rate: 515.4 per 10,000 population

Newspapers: Marlboro Herald Advocate (weekly circulation 6800)
Transportation: Commute: 95.7% car, 0.7% public transportation, 1.3% walk, 0.8% work from home; Median travel time to work: 22.6 minutes
Additional Information Contacts
City of Bennettsville . . . . (843) 479-9001
   http://www.bennettsvillesc.com

BLENHEIM (town). Covers a land area of 0.653 square miles and a water area of 0 square miles. Located at 34.51° N. Lat; 79.65° W. Long. Elevation is 118 feet.
History: At Blenheim during the Revolution, Tristram Thomas, with a battery of wooden guns erected at a bend of the river, captured 100 Tories and a boatload of supplies.
Population: 154; Growth (since 2000): 12.4%; Density: 235.7 persons per square mile; Race: 56.5% White, 37.7% Black/African American, 0.0% Asian, 1.9% American Indian/Alaska Native, 0.0% Native Hawaiian/Other Pacific Islander, 3.9% Two or more races, 0.0% Hispanic of any race; Average household size: 2.30; Median age: 45.0; Age under 18: 23.4%; Age 65 and over: 14.9%; Males per 100 females: 79.1
School District(s)
Marlboro 01 (PK-12)
   2012-13 Enrollment: 4,312 . . . . (843) 479-4016
Housing: Homeownership rate: 70.2%; Homeowner vacancy rate: 0.0%; Rental vacancy rate: 0.0%

CLIO (town). Covers a land area of 0.856 square miles and a water area of 0 square miles. Located at 34.58° N. Lat; 79.55° W. Long. Elevation is 194 feet.
Population: 726; Growth (since 2000): -6.2%; Density: 848.0 persons per square mile; Race: 26.9% White, 64.3% Black/African American, 0.0% Asian, 7.9% American Indian/Alaska Native, 0.0% Native Hawaiian/Other Pacific Islander, 1.0% Two or more races, 1.1% Hispanic of any race; Average household size: 2.44; Median age: 43.7; Age under 18: 21.1%; Age 65 and over: 17.5%; Males per 100 females: 79.7
School District(s)
Marlboro 01 (PK-12)
   2012-13 Enrollment: 4,312 . . . . (843) 479-4016
Housing: Homeownership rate: 57.6%; Homeowner vacancy rate: 3.9%; Rental vacancy rate: 11.7%

MCCOLL (town). Covers a land area of 1.050 square miles and a water area of 0.001 square miles. Located at 34.67° N. Lat; 79.54° W. Long. Elevation is 184 feet.
History: McColl was first a cotton depot on the railroad.
Population: 2,174; Growth (since 2000): -13.0%; Density: 2,070.4 persons per square mile; Race: 56.8% White, 22.7% Black/African American, 0.1% Asian, 16.7% American Indian/Alaska Native, 0.0% Native Hawaiian/Other Pacific Islander, 3.0% Two or more races, 1.9% Hispanic of any race; Average household size: 2.46; Median age: 37.3; Age under 18: 25.3%; Age 65 and over: 13.3%; Males per 100 females: 92.0
School District(s)
Marlboro 01 (PK-12)
   2012-13 Enrollment: 4,312 . . . . (843) 479-4016
Housing: Homeownership rate: 59.1%; Homeowner vacancy rate: 1.1%; Rental vacancy rate: 11.0%
Safety: Violent crime rate: 91.1 per 10,000 population; Property crime rate: 292.4 per 10,000 population

TATUM (town). Covers a land area of 0.908 square miles and a water area of 0 square miles. Located at 34.64° N. Lat; 79.59° W. Long. Elevation is 197 feet.
Population: 75; Growth (since 2000): 8.7%; Density: 82.6 persons per square mile; Race: 73.3% White, 17.3% Black/African American, 0.0% Asian, 9.3% American Indian/Alaska Native, 0.0% Native Hawaiian/Other Pacific Islander, 0.0% Two or more races, 1.3% Hispanic of any race; Average household size: 2.34; Median age: 44.8; Age under 18: 20.0%; Age 65 and over: 12.0%; Males per 100 females: 120.6
Housing: Homeownership rate: 75.0%; Homeowner vacancy rate: 0.0%; Rental vacancy rate: 11.1%

WALLACE (CDP). Covers a land area of 6.569 square miles and a water area of 0.123 square miles. Located at 34.72° N. Lat; 79.84° W. Long. Elevation is 151 feet.
Population: 892; Growth (since 2000): n/a; Density: 135.8 persons per square mile; Race: 55.4% White, 38.9% Black/African American, 0.0%

Asian, 2.8% American Indian/Alaska Native, 0.0% Native Hawaiian/Other Pacific Islander, 2.5% Two or more races, 1.1% Hispanic of any race; Average household size: 2.43; Median age: 42.1; Age under 18: 22.5%; Age 65 and over: 15.0%; Males per 100 females: 92.2
School District(s)
Marlboro 01 (PK-12)
   2012-13 Enrollment: 4,312 . . . . (843) 479-4016
Housing: Homeownership rate: 73.5%; Homeowner vacancy rate: 1.8%; Rental vacancy rate: 3.0%

McCormick County

Located in western South Carolina; bounded on the west by the Savannah River and the Georgia border; includes part of Sumter National Forest. Covers a land area of 359.130 square miles, a water area of 34.743 square miles, and is located in the Eastern Time Zone at 33.90° N. Lat., 82.32° W. Long. The county was founded in 1914. County seat is McCormick.

Weather Station: Clark Hill 1 W									Elevation: 379 feet		
	Jan	Feb	Mar	Apr	May	Jun	Jul	Aug	Sep	Oct	Nov	Dec
High	56	60	68	76	84	90	94	92	87	77	68	58
Low	30	33	40	47	55	64	68	67	60	48	40	33
Precip	4.2	4.1	4.7	2.8	2.8	4.4	4.2	4.2	3.5	3.8	3.1	3.4
Snow	0.0	0.3	0.0	0.0	0.0	0.0	0.0	0.0	0.0	0.0	0.0	0.0

High and Low temperatures in degrees Fahrenheit; Precipitation and Snow in inches

Population: 10,233; Growth (since 2000): 2.8%; Density: 28.5 persons per square mile; Race: 48.7% White, 49.7% Black/African American, 0.3% Asian, 0.1% American Indian/Alaska Native, 0.1% Native Hawaiian/Other Pacific Islander, 0.9% two or more races, 0.8% Hispanic of any race; Average household size: 2.22; Median age: 50.0; Age under 18: 14.5%; Age 65 and over: 23.9%; Males per 100 females: 118.9; Marriage status: 28.4% never married, 55.7% now married, 4.0% separated, 6.8% widowed, 9.2% divorced; Foreign born: 1.5%; Speak English only: 97.1%; With disability: 18.9%; Veterans: 13.3%; Ancestry: 11.4% German, 10.6% American, 10.3% English, 7.4% Irish, 3.3% Scotch-Irish
Religion: Six largest groups: 19.4% Methodist/Pietist, 13.5% Baptist, 2.8% Catholicism, 2.8% Lutheran, 0.5% Presbyterian-Reformed, 0.1% Other Groups
Economy: Unemployment rate: 8.6%; Leading industries: 23.4% retail trade; 16.0% other services (except public administration); 10.6% health care and social assistance; Farms: 93 totaling 30,043 acres; Company size: 0 employ 1,000 or more persons, 0 employ 500 to 999 persons, 2 employ 100 to 499 persons, 92 employ less than 100 persons; Business ownership: n/a women-owned, 249 Black-owned, n/a Hispanic-owned, n/a Asian-owned
Employment: 6.7% management, business, and financial, 0.7% computer, engineering, and science, 10.5% education, legal, community service, arts, and media, 4.6% healthcare practitioners, 24.7% service, 20.8% sales and office, 13.2% natural resources, construction, and maintenance, 18.8% production, transportation, and material moving
Income: Per capita: $22,150; Median household: $40,028; Average household: $54,877; Households with income of $100,000 or more: 11.5%; Poverty rate: 17.2%
Educational Attainment: High school diploma or higher: 78.8%; Bachelor's degree or higher: 18.2%; Graduate/professional degree or higher: 7.4%
Housing: Homeownership rate: 79.9%; Median home value: $112,500; Median year structure built: 1985; Homeowner vacancy rate: 2.3%; Median gross rent: $514 per month; Rental vacancy rate: 16.4%
Vital Statistics: Birth rate: 50.3 per 10,000 population; Death rate: 133.7 per 10,000 population; Age-adjusted cancer mortality rate: 168.3 deaths per 100,000 population
Health Insurance: 90.9% have insurance; 64.7% have private insurance; 45.5% have public insurance; 9.1% do not have insurance; 6.6% of children under 18 do not have insurance
Health Care: Physicians: 5.0 per 10,000 population; Hospital beds: 0.0 per 10,000 population; Hospital admissions: 0.0 per 10,000 population
Transportation: Commute: 95.5% car, 0.1% public transportation, 0.0% walk, 4.3% work from home; Median travel time to work: 29.4 minutes
Presidential Election: 51.4% Obama, 47.8% Romney (2012)
National and State Parks: Baker Creek State Park; Hamilton Branch State Park; Hickory Knob State Park; Sumter National Forest

Additional Information Contacts

McCormick Government . . . . (864) 852-2195
  http://mccormickcountysc.org

McCormick County Communities

CLARKS HILL (CDP). Covers a land area of 3.196 square miles and a water area of 0 square miles. Located at 33.66° N. Lat; 82.17° W. Long. Elevation is 466 feet.

History: Clarks Hill recalls pre-Revolutionary Blacksmith Clark, whose forge and farm were just below the present settlement. This was the home of congressman George Tillman, brother of "Pitchfork Ben" Tillman.

Population: 381; Growth (since 2000): 1.3%; Density: 119.2 persons per square mile; Race: 18.4% White, 78.5% Black/African American, 0.0% Asian, 0.0% American Indian/Alaska Native, 0.0% Native Hawaiian/Other Pacific Islander, 3.1% Two or more races, 0.0% Hispanic of any race; Average household size: 2.86; Median age: 40.1; Age under 18: 23.6%; Age 65 and over: 15.2%; Males per 100 females: 85.9

Housing: Homeownership rate: 85.7%; Homeowner vacancy rate: 0.0%; Rental vacancy rate: 5.0%

MCCORMICK (town). County seat. Covers a land area of 4.052 square miles and a water area of 0 square miles. Located at 33.91° N. Lat; 82.29° W. Long. Elevation is 535 feet.

History: McCormick was named for Cyrus McCormick, inventor of the reaper, who gave to the town a large part of the land on which it was built. Gold was first taken in 1852 from Dorn's Gold Mine, which Dorn discovered while on a fox hunt. His hounds, digging into a burrow, unearthed the vein.

Population: 2,783; Growth (since 2000): 86.9%; Density: 686.9 persons per square mile; Race: 29.5% White, 68.3% Black/African American, 0.5% Asian, 0.2% American Indian/Alaska Native, 0.2% Native Hawaiian/Other Pacific Islander, 0.9% Two or more races, 1.6% Hispanic of any race; Average household size: 2.16; Median age: 39.4; Age under 18: 13.1%; Age 65 and over: 11.1%; Males per 100 females: 234.5; Marriage status: 50.1% never married, 29.4% now married, 5.2% separated, 4.5% widowed, 15.9% divorced; Foreign born: 2.0%; Speak English only: 96.3%; With disability: 24.8%; Veterans: 8.5%; Ancestry: 11.0% American, 5.7% German, 4.9% English, 3.9% Irish, 1.2% European

Employment: 8.0% management, business, and financial, 0.0% computer, engineering, and science, 11.6% education, legal, community service, arts, and media, 2.4% healthcare practitioners, 24.4% service, 12.6% sales and office, 11.8% natural resources, construction, and maintenance, 29.2% production, transportation, and material moving

Income: Per capita: $9,326; Median household: $22,656; Average household: $35,764; Households with income of $100,000 or more: 6.4%; Poverty rate: 25.8%

Educational Attainment: High school diploma or higher: 69.4%; Bachelor's degree or higher: 8.8%; Graduate/professional degree or higher: 2.0%

School District(s)

Dept of Correction N04 (09-12)
  2012-13 Enrollment: 752 . . . . (803) 896-8556
John De La Howe (06-11)
  2012-13 Enrollment: 38 . . . . (864) 391-0413
Mccormick 01 (PK-12)
  2012-13 Enrollment: 820 . . . . (864) 852-2435

Housing: Homeownership rate: 49.0%; Median home value: $93,800; Median year structure built: 1969; Homeowner vacancy rate: 2.8%; Median gross rent: $500 per month; Rental vacancy rate: 7.4%

Health Insurance: 86.7% have insurance; 55.2% have private insurance; 47.9% have public insurance; 13.3% do not have insurance; 3.7% of children under 18 do not have insurance

Safety: Violent crime rate: 33.1 per 10,000 population; Property crime rate: 286.8 per 10,000 population

Newspapers: McCormick Messenger (weekly circulation 2700)

Transportation: Commute: 94.9% car, 0.5% public transportation, 0.0% walk, 4.5% work from home; Median travel time to work: 27.4 minutes

MODOC (CDP). Covers a land area of 3.984 square miles and a water area of 3.188 square miles. Located at 33.72° N. Lat; 82.22° W. Long. Elevation is 400 feet.

History: Modoc was named in the early 1870's when the Augusta-Knoxville railroad was laid through this area, which was a time that the Modoc Indians in Oregon were in the national news.

Population: 218; Growth (since 2000): -14.8%; Density: 54.7 persons per square mile; Race: 95.9% White, 2.3% Black/African American, 0.0% Asian, 0.9% American Indian/Alaska Native, 0.0% Native Hawaiian/Other Pacific Islander, 0.9% Two or more races, 0.9% Hispanic of any race; Average household size: 2.08; Median age: 53.8; Age under 18: 10.6%; Age 65 and over: 21.6%; Males per 100 females: 115.8

Housing: Homeownership rate: 89.5%; Homeowner vacancy rate: 6.0%; Rental vacancy rate: 40.9%

MOUNT CARMEL (CDP). Covers a land area of 9.189 square miles and a water area of 0 square miles. Located at 34.02° N. Lat; 82.50° W. Long. Elevation is 541 feet.

Population: 216; Growth (since 2000): -8.9%; Density: 23.5 persons per square mile; Race: 8.8% White, 88.9% Black/African American, 1.9% Asian, 0.0% American Indian/Alaska Native, 0.0% Native Hawaiian/Other Pacific Islander, 0.5% Two or more races, 0.0% Hispanic of any race; Average household size: 2.54; Median age: 44.4; Age under 18: 21.3%; Age 65 and over: 20.8%; Males per 100 females: 78.5

Housing: Homeownership rate: 75.3%; Homeowner vacancy rate: 1.5%; Rental vacancy rate: 4.5%

PARKSVILLE (town). Covers a land area of 0.728 square miles and a water area of <.001 square miles. Located at 33.79° N. Lat; 82.22° W. Long. Elevation is 348 feet.

History: Parksville was named in 1758 for Anthony Park, a trader.

Population: 117; Growth (since 2000): -2.5%; Density: 160.7 persons per square mile; Race: 94.0% White, 2.6% Black/African American, 0.0% Asian, 0.0% American Indian/Alaska Native, 0.0% Native Hawaiian/Other Pacific Islander, 3.4% Two or more races, 0.9% Hispanic of any race; Average household size: 2.09; Median age: 48.9; Age under 18: 12.8%; Age 65 and over: 19.7%; Males per 100 females: 108.9

Housing: Homeownership rate: 83.9%; Homeowner vacancy rate: 2.0%; Rental vacancy rate: 0.0%

PLUM BRANCH (town). Covers a land area of 0.362 square miles and a water area of 0 square miles. Located at 33.85° N. Lat; 82.26° W. Long. Elevation is 459 feet.

Population: 82; Growth (since 2000): -16.3%; Density: 226.3 persons per square mile; Race: 72.0% White, 24.4% Black/African American, 0.0% Asian, 0.0% American Indian/Alaska Native, 0.0% Native Hawaiian/Other Pacific Islander, 3.7% Two or more races, 0.0% Hispanic of any race; Average household size: 2.34; Median age: 46.3; Age under 18: 17.1%; Age 65 and over: 17.1%; Males per 100 females: 115.8

Housing: Homeownership rate: 94.3%; Homeowner vacancy rate: 2.9%; Rental vacancy rate: 0.0%

WILLINGTON (CDP). Covers a land area of 5.955 square miles and a water area of 0.042 square miles. Located at 33.97° N. Lat; 82.45° W. Long. Elevation is 486 feet.

Population: 142; Growth (since 2000): -19.8%; Density: 23.8 persons per square mile; Race: 14.1% White, 85.9% Black/African American, 0.0% Asian, 0.0% American Indian/Alaska Native, 0.0% Native Hawaiian/Other Pacific Islander, 0.0% Two or more races, 0.0% Hispanic of any race; Average household size: 2.33; Median age: 47.0; Age under 18: 16.2%; Age 65 and over: 21.1%; Males per 100 females: 97.2

Housing: Homeownership rate: 77.0%; Homeowner vacancy rate: 4.1%; Rental vacancy rate: 6.7%

Newberry County

Located in northwest central South Carolina; bounded on the east by the Broad River, on the south by the Saluda River, and on the north by the Enoree River; includes part of Lake Murray, and part of Sumter National Forest. Covers a land area of 630.037 square miles, a water area of 17.249 square miles, and is located in the Eastern Time Zone at 34.29° N. Lat., 81.60° W. Long. The county was founded in 1785. County seat is Newberry.

Newberry County is part of the Newberry, SC Micropolitan Statistical Area. The entire metro area includes: Newberry County, SC

Weather Station: Little Mountain   Elevation: 710 feet

	Jan	Feb	Mar	Apr	May	Jun	Jul	Aug	Sep	Oct	Nov	Dec
High	54	58	66	74	81	87	90	88	83	73	64	56
Low	35	37	43	50	58	66	69	69	62	52	44	36
Precip	4.1	3.9	4.5	3.0	2.8	4.2	4.6	4.6	3.9	3.5	3.3	3.6
Snow	1.1	0.5	0.5	0.0	0.0	0.0	0.0	0.0	0.0	0.0	tr	0.2

High and Low temperatures in degrees Fahrenheit; Precipitation and Snow in inches

Population: 37,508; Growth (since 2000): 3.9%; Density: 59.5 persons per square mile; Race: 62.1% White, 31.0% Black/African American, 0.3% Asian, 0.3% American Indian/Alaska Native, 0.1% Native Hawaiian/Other Pacific Islander, 1.2% two or more races, 7.2% Hispanic of any race; Average household size: 2.47; Median age: 39.9; Age under 18: 22.8%; Age 65 and over: 15.9%; Males per 100 females: 94.8; Marriage status: 31.3% never married, 52.3% now married, 4.2% separated, 8.2% widowed, 8.2% divorced; Foreign born: 5.4%; Speak English only: 92.3%; With disability: 13.9%; Veterans: 9.2%; Ancestry: 16.9% American, 15.3% German, 7.3% Irish, 6.4% English, 2.8% Scotch-Irish
Religion: Six largest groups: 20.7% Methodist/Pietist, 17.6% Lutheran, 15.8% Baptist, 3.0% Presbyterian-Reformed, 2.0% Pentecostal, 1.5% Non-denominational Protestant
Economy: Unemployment rate: 5.4%; Leading industries: 19.0% retail trade; 14.3% other services (except public administration); 9.5% construction; Farms: 594 totaling 104,493 acres; Company size: 1 employs 1,000 or more persons, 0 employ 500 to 999 persons, 13 employ 100 to 499 persons, 693 employ less than 100 persons; Business ownership: 625 women-owned, n/a Black-owned, n/a Hispanic-owned, n/a Asian-owned
Employment: 8.5% management, business, and financial, 3.0% computer, engineering, and science, 9.1% education, legal, community service, arts, and media, 7.2% healthcare practitioners, 16.0% service, 23.2% sales and office, 13.5% natural resources, construction, and maintenance, 19.5% production, transportation, and material moving
Income: Per capita: $21,591; Median household: $41,718; Average household: $54,951; Households with income of $100,000 or more: 13.8%; Poverty rate: 17.2%
Educational Attainment: High school diploma or higher: 76.9%; Bachelor's degree or higher: 18.9%; Graduate/professional degree or higher: 6.3%
Housing: Homeownership rate: 72.5%; Median home value: $107,400; Median year structure built: 1979; Homeowner vacancy rate: 2.4%; Median gross rent: $637 per month; Rental vacancy rate: 10.6%
Vital Statistics: Birth rate: 113.0 per 10,000 population; Death rate: 108.5 per 10,000 population; Age-adjusted cancer mortality rate: 188.1 deaths per 100,000 population
Health Insurance: 85.8% have insurance; 62.0% have private insurance; 36.7% have public insurance; 14.2% do not have insurance; 3.0% of children under 18 do not have insurance
Health Care: Physicians: 9.3 per 10,000 population; Hospital beds: 8.5 per 10,000 population; Hospital admissions: 611.5 per 10,000 population
Transportation: Commute: 96.2% car, 0.5% public transportation, 0.9% walk, 1.8% work from home; Median travel time to work: 24.4 minutes
Presidential Election: 42.3% Obama, 56.6% Romney (2012)
National and State Parks: Billy Dreher Island State Park
Additional Information Contacts
Newberry Government . . . . (803) 321-2110
    http://www.newberrycounty.net

Newberry County Communities

CHAPPELLS (unincorporated postal area)
ZCTA: 29037
    Covers a land area of 67.208 square miles and a water area of 1.825 square miles. Located at 34.19° N. Lat; 81.87° W. Long. Elevation is 436 feet.
    Population: 824; Growth (since 2000): -10.5%; Density: 12.3 persons per square mile; Race: 79.1% White, 18.0% Black/African American, 0.4% Asian, 0.4% American Indian/Alaska Native, 0.0% Native Hawaiian/Other Pacific Islander, 1.2% Two or more races, 2.1% Hispanic of any race; Average household size: 2.37; Median age: 47.3; Age under 18: 19.5%; Age 65 and over: 21.2%; Males per 100 females: 99.5
    Housing: Homeownership rate: 81.2%; Homeowner vacancy rate: 1.7%; Rental vacancy rate: 8.5%

KINARDS (unincorporated postal area)
ZCTA: 29355
    Covers a land area of 68.453 square miles and a water area of 0.085 square miles. Located at 34.29° N. Lat; 81.83° W. Long. Elevation is 591 feet.
    Population: 810; Growth (since 2000): 1.1%; Density: 11.8 persons per square mile; Race: 82.5% White, 14.2% Black/African American, 0.0% Asian, 0.0% American Indian/Alaska Native, 0.0% Native Hawaiian/Other Pacific Islander, 0.6% Two or more races, 4.0% Hispanic of any race; Average household size: 2.50; Median age: 42.8; Age under 18: 21.0%; Age 65 and over: 16.0%; Males per 100 females: 95.2
    Housing: Homeownership rate: 81.8%; Homeowner vacancy rate: 1.1%; Rental vacancy rate: 17.8%

LITTLE MOUNTAIN (town). Covers a land area of 1.417 square miles and a water area of 0 square miles. Located at 34.20° N. Lat; 81.41° W. Long. Elevation is 614 feet.
Population: 291; Growth (since 2000): 14.1%; Density: 205.3 persons per square mile; Race: 81.8% White, 16.5% Black/African American, 0.3% Asian, 0.7% American Indian/Alaska Native, 0.0% Native Hawaiian/Other Pacific Islander, 0.7% Two or more races, 0.0% Hispanic of any race; Average household size: 2.33; Median age: 40.9; Age under 18: 22.7%; Age 65 and over: 17.5%; Males per 100 females: 81.9
School District(s)
Newberry 01 (PK-12)
    2012-13 Enrollment: 5,919 . . . . (803) 321-2600
Housing: Homeownership rate: 61.6%; Homeowner vacancy rate: 2.5%; Rental vacancy rate: 4.0%

NEWBERRY (city). County seat. Covers a land area of 8.574 square miles and a water area of 0.004 square miles. Located at 34.28° N. Lat; 81.60° W. Long. Elevation is 492 feet.
History: Seat of Newberry College.
Population: 10,277; Growth (since 2000): -2.9%; Density: 1,198.7 persons per square mile; Race: 45.4% White, 45.6% Black/African American, 0.6% Asian, 0.4% American Indian/Alaska Native, 0.1% Native Hawaiian/Other Pacific Islander, 1.8% Two or more races, 8.6% Hispanic of any race; Average household size: 2.36; Median age: 33.2; Age under 18: 22.7%; Age 65 and over: 16.4%; Males per 100 females: 85.8; Marriage status: 44.3% never married, 37.5% now married, 4.8% separated, 10.9% widowed, 7.3% divorced; Foreign born: 10.2%; Speak English only: 83.5%; With disability: 15.1%; Veterans: 6.1%; Ancestry: 16.0% American, 8.7% German, 6.1% Irish, 5.7% English, 2.3% Scotch-Irish
Employment: 7.1% management, business, and financial, 1.8% computer, engineering, and science, 12.5% education, legal, community service, arts, and media, 5.5% healthcare practitioners, 16.9% service, 25.0% sales and office, 10.0% natural resources, construction, and maintenance, 21.1% production, transportation, and material moving
Income: Per capita: $17,033; Median household: $29,333; Average household: $42,375; Households with income of $100,000 or more: 10.2%; Poverty rate: 30.5%
Educational Attainment: High school diploma or higher: 70.4%; Bachelor's degree or higher: 26.2%; Graduate/professional degree or higher: 9.8%
School District(s)
Newberry 01 (PK-12)
    2012-13 Enrollment: 5,919 . . . . (803) 321-2600
Four-year College(s)
Newberry College (Private, Not-for-profit, Evangelical Lutheran Church)
    Fall 2013 Enrollment: 1,039 . . . . (803) 276-5010
    2013-14 Tuition: In-state $23,800; Out-of-state $23,800
Housing: Homeownership rate: 49.5%; Median home value: $116,300; Median year structure built: 1963; Homeowner vacancy rate: 4.3%; Median gross rent: $635 per month; Rental vacancy rate: 8.8%
Health Insurance: 83.3% have insurance; 50.7% have private insurance; 42.8% have public insurance; 16.7% do not have insurance; 0.0% of children under 18 do not have insurance
Hospitals: Newberry County Memorial Hospital (102 beds)
Safety: Violent crime rate: 66.4 per 10,000 population; Property crime rate: 481.2 per 10,000 population
Newspapers: Observer-Herald-News (weekly circulation 6200)
Transportation: Commute: 94.7% car, 0.0% public transportation, 2.8% walk, 2.2% work from home; Median travel time to work: 15.4 minutes

Additional Information Contacts
City of Newberry . . . . (803) 321-1000
http://www.cityofnewberry.com

PEAK (town). Covers a land area of 0.389 square miles and a water area of 0.001 square miles. Located at 34.24° N. Lat; 81.33° W. Long. Elevation is 292 feet.
Population: 64; Growth (since 2000): 4.9%; Density: 164.5 persons per square mile; Race: 70.3% White, 28.1% Black/African American, 0.0% Asian, 0.0% American Indian/Alaska Native, 0.0% Native Hawaiian/Other Pacific Islander, 1.6% Two or more races, 0.0% Hispanic of any race; Average household size: 2.21; Median age: 45.5; Age under 18: 18.7%; Age 65 and over: 21.9%; Males per 100 females: 64.1
Housing: Homeownership rate: 68.9%; Homeowner vacancy rate: 4.8%; Rental vacancy rate: 25.0%

POMARIA (town). Covers a land area of 1.041 square miles and a water area of 0.006 square miles. Located at 34.27° N. Lat; 81.42° W. Long. Elevation is 404 feet.
Population: 179; Growth (since 2000): 1.1%; Density: 171.9 persons per square mile; Race: 61.5% White, 38.0% Black/African American, 0.0% Asian, 0.0% American Indian/Alaska Native, 0.0% Native Hawaiian/Other Pacific Islander, 0.6% Two or more races, 0.6% Hispanic of any race; Average household size: 2.80; Median age: 41.1; Age under 18: 27.4%; Age 65 and over: 11.7%; Males per 100 females: 90.4
School District(s)
Newberry 01 (PK-12)
2012-13 Enrollment: 5,919 . . . . (803) 321-2600
Housing: Homeownership rate: 81.3%; Homeowner vacancy rate: 1.9%; Rental vacancy rate: 25.0%

PROSPERITY (town). Covers a land area of 1.870 square miles and a water area of 0.002 square miles. Located at 34.21° N. Lat; 81.53° W. Long. Elevation is 541 feet.
History: Prosperity was originally named Frog Level.
Population: 1,180; Growth (since 2000): 12.7%; Density: 631.2 persons per square mile; Race: 55.6% White, 42.0% Black/African American, 0.1% Asian, 0.3% American Indian/Alaska Native, 0.0% Native Hawaiian/Other Pacific Islander, 0.8% Two or more races, 3.1% Hispanic of any race; Average household size: 2.54; Median age: 38.8; Age under 18: 25.3%; Age 65 and over: 12.1%; Males per 100 females: 80.4
School District(s)
Newberry 01 (PK-12)
2012-13 Enrollment: 5,919 . . . . (803) 321-2600
Housing: Homeownership rate: 69.2%; Homeowner vacancy rate: 0.9%; Rental vacancy rate: 15.2%
Safety: Violent crime rate: 8.4 per 10,000 population; Property crime rate: 211.0 per 10,000 population
Additional Information Contacts
Town of Prosperity . . . . (803) 364-2622
http://www.prosperitysc.com

SILVERSTREET (town). Covers a land area of 3.347 square miles and a water area of 0 square miles. Located at 34.22° N. Lat; 81.71° W. Long. Elevation is 489 feet.
Population: 162; Growth (since 2000): -25.0%; Density: 48.4 persons per square mile; Race: 75.9% White, 19.8% Black/African American, 0.0% Asian, 0.0% American Indian/Alaska Native, 0.0% Native Hawaiian/Other Pacific Islander, 0.0% Two or more races, 4.3% Hispanic of any race; Average household size: 2.38; Median age: 45.3; Age under 18: 22.2%; Age 65 and over: 20.4%; Males per 100 females: 90.6
Housing: Homeownership rate: 89.7%; Homeowner vacancy rate: 1.6%; Rental vacancy rate: 0.0%

WHITMIRE (town). Covers a land area of 1.236 square miles and a water area of 0 square miles. Located at 34.50° N. Lat; 81.61° W. Long. Elevation is 436 feet.
History: In 1801 George Frederick Whitmire, ancestor of publisher William Randolph Hearst, built a trading post here.
Population: 1,441; Growth (since 2000): -4.7%; Density: 1,166.1 persons per square mile; Race: 77.9% White, 19.3% Black/African American, 0.3% Asian, 0.7% American Indian/Alaska Native, 0.0% Native Hawaiian/Other Pacific Islander, 1.2% Two or more races, 1.7% Hispanic of any race; Average household size: 2.41; Median age: 39.5; Age under 18: 25.1%; Age 65 and over: 16.2%; Males per 100 females: 95.5

School District(s)
Newberry 01 (PK-12)
2012-13 Enrollment: 5,919 . . . . (803) 321-2600
Housing: Homeownership rate: 66.2%; Homeowner vacancy rate: 2.8%; Rental vacancy rate: 9.7%
Safety: Violent crime rate: 41.7 per 10,000 population; Property crime rate: 347.5 per 10,000 population

Oconee County

Located in northwestern South Carolina, in the Blue Ridge; bounded on the north by North Carolina, on the northwest by the Chattanooga River and the Georgia border, on the southwest by the Tugaloo River and the Georgia border, and on the east by the Keowee and Seneca Rivers. Covers a land area of 626.334 square miles, a water area of 47.179 square miles, and is located in the Eastern Time Zone at 34.75° N. Lat., 83.06° W. Long. The county was founded in 1868. County seat is Walhalla.

Oconee County is part of the Seneca, SC Micropolitan Statistical Area. The entire metro area includes: Oconee County, SC

Weather Station: Walhalla   Elevation: 979 feet

	Jan	Feb	Mar	Apr	May	Jun	Jul	Aug	Sep	Oct	Nov	Dec
High	53	57	65	73	79	86	89	88	82	72	63	55
Low	30	32	38	44	53	62	65	65	59	48	38	32
Precip	4.9	4.8	5.5	4.0	4.5	4.7	5.1	5.4	5.1	4.2	4.6	5.1
Snow	1.8	0.9	0.4	tr	0.0	0.0	0.0	0.0	0.0	0.0	tr	0.2

High and Low temperatures in degrees Fahrenheit; Precipitation and Snow in inches

Population: 74,273; Growth (since 2000): 12.2%; Density: 118.6 persons per square mile; Race: 87.8% White, 7.6% Black/African American, 0.6% Asian, 0.2% American Indian/Alaska Native, 0.0% Native Hawaiian/Other Pacific Islander, 1.6% two or more races, 4.5% Hispanic of any race; Average household size: 2.40; Median age: 43.4; Age under 18: 21.1%; Age 65 and over: 19.0%; Males per 100 females: 97.6; Marriage status: 24.2% never married, 57.3% now married, 3.2% separated, 7.6% widowed, 10.9% divorced; Foreign born: 3.2%; Speak English only: 95.3%; With disability: 18.3%; Veterans: 12.4%; Ancestry: 13.7% Irish, 13.4% German, 12.6% American, 11.4% English, 3.1% Scotch-Irish
Religion: Six largest groups: 37.7% Baptist, 4.9% Pentecostal, 3.4% Catholicism, 3.1% Methodist/Pietist, 2.7% Non-denominational Protestant, 1.4% Presbyterian-Reformed
Economy: Unemployment rate: 6.3%; Leading industries: 17.2% retail trade; 13.5% other services (except public administration); 12.4% construction; Farms: 884 totaling 67,871 acres; Company size: 1 employs 1,000 or more persons, 4 employ 500 to 999 persons, 28 employ 100 to 499 persons, 1,439 employ less than 100 persons; Business ownership: 1,671 women-owned, 158 Black-owned, 71 Hispanic-owned, n/a Asian-owned
Employment: 11.2% management, business, and financial, 4.2% computer, engineering, and science, 10.2% education, legal, community service, arts, and media, 5.7% healthcare practitioners, 18.9% service, 22.3% sales and office, 10.3% natural resources, construction, and maintenance, 17.1% production, transportation, and material moving
Income: Per capita: $23,904; Median household: $41,394; Average household: $57,692; Households with income of $100,000 or more: 13.3%; Poverty rate: 19.1%
Educational Attainment: High school diploma or higher: 83.1%; Bachelor's degree or higher: 21.7%; Graduate/professional degree or higher: 8.9%
Housing: Homeownership rate: 75.1%; Median home value: $136,300; Median year structure built: 1986; Homeowner vacancy rate: 3.1%; Median gross rent: $665 per month; Rental vacancy rate: 14.2%
Vital Statistics: Birth rate: 109.8 per 10,000 population; Death rate: 112.3 per 10,000 population; Age-adjusted cancer mortality rate: 186.6 deaths per 100,000 population
Health Insurance: 83.3% have insurance; 60.9% have private insurance; 39.6% have public insurance; 16.7% do not have insurance; 9.8% of children under 18 do not have insurance
Health Care: Physicians: 16.7 per 10,000 population; Hospital beds: 33.4 per 10,000 population; Hospital admissions: 1,044.1 per 10,000 population
Air Quality Index: 99.7% good, 0.3% moderate, 0.0% unhealthy for sensitive individuals, 0.0% unhealthy (percent of days)
Transportation: Commute: 93.5% car, 0.6% public transportation, 1.2% walk, 3.6% work from home; Median travel time to work: 24.3 minutes

Presidential Election: 27.9% Obama, 70.5% Romney (2012)
National and State Parks: Oconee State Park
Additional Information Contacts
Oconee Government . . . . (864) 638-4280
   http://www.oconeesc.com

Oconee County Communities

FAIR PLAY (CDP).
Covers a land area of 6.737 square miles and a water area of 0.023 square miles. Located at 34.51° N. Lat; 82.99° W. Long. Elevation is 814 feet.
Population: 687; Growth (since 2000): n/a; Density: 102.0 persons per square mile; Race: 95.1% White, 0.4% Black/African American, 0.9% Asian, 0.4% American Indian/Alaska Native, 0.0% Native Hawaiian/Other Pacific Islander, 1.9% Two or more races, 2.2% Hispanic of any race; Average household size: 2.39; Median age: 46.6; Age under 18: 20.5%; Age 65 and over: 19.7%; Males per 100 females: 106.9
Housing: Homeownership rate: 77.7%; Homeowner vacancy rate: 4.3%; Rental vacancy rate: 8.5%

LONG CREEK (unincorporated postal area)
ZCTA: 29658
   Covers a land area of 24.921 square miles and a water area of 0.476 square miles. Located at 34.76° N. Lat; 83.28° W. Long..
   Population: 333; Growth (since 2000): 62.4%; Density: 13.4 persons per square mile; Race: 96.1% White, 0.9% Black/African American, 0.3% Asian, 0.6% American Indian/Alaska Native, 0.0% Native Hawaiian/Other Pacific Islander, 0.6% Two or more races, 4.8% Hispanic of any race; Average household size: 2.23; Median age: 42.8; Age under 18: 21.9%; Age 65 and over: 14.4%; Males per 100 females: 104.3
   Housing: Homeownership rate: 91.1%; Homeowner vacancy rate: 0.7%; Rental vacancy rate: 0.0%

MOUNTAIN REST (unincorporated postal area)
ZCTA: 29664
   Covers a land area of 95.830 square miles and a water area of 0.440 square miles. Located at 34.86° N. Lat; 83.16° W. Long..
   Population: 1,808; Growth (since 2000): 28.3%; Density: 18.9 persons per square mile; Race: 97.9% White, 0.4% Black/African American, 0.1% Asian, 0.4% American Indian/Alaska Native, 0.1% Native Hawaiian/Other Pacific Islander, 1.1% Two or more races, 0.9% Hispanic of any race; Average household size: 2.32; Median age: 47.9; Age under 18: 19.2%; Age 65 and over: 19.4%; Males per 100 females: 102.2
   Housing: Homeownership rate: 83.7%; Homeowner vacancy rate: 2.2%; Rental vacancy rate: 10.5%

NEWRY (CDP).
Covers a land area of 0.295 square miles and a water area of <.001 square miles. Located at 34.73° N. Lat; 82.91° W. Long. Elevation is 735 feet.
Population: 172; Growth (since 2000): n/a; Density: 582.6 persons per square mile; Race: 96.5% White, 0.0% Black/African American, 0.6% Asian, 0.0% American Indian/Alaska Native, 0.0% Native Hawaiian/Other Pacific Islander, 2.9% Two or more races, 0.6% Hispanic of any race; Average household size: 2.07; Median age: 39.0; Age under 18: 18.0%; Age 65 and over: 18.0%; Males per 100 females: 107.2
Housing: Homeownership rate: 69.9%; Homeowner vacancy rate: 1.7%; Rental vacancy rate: 18.8%

SALEM (town).
Covers a land area of 0.829 square miles and a water area of 0 square miles. Located at 34.89° N. Lat; 82.98° W. Long. Elevation is 1,070 feet.
Population: 135; Growth (since 2000): 7.1%; Density: 162.9 persons per square mile; Race: 99.3% White, 0.0% Black/African American, 0.0% Asian, 0.0% American Indian/Alaska Native, 0.0% Native Hawaiian/Other Pacific Islander, 0.7% Two or more races, 0.0% Hispanic of any race; Average household size: 2.25; Median age: 45.3; Age under 18: 21.5%; Age 65 and over: 18.5%; Males per 100 females: 98.5
School District(s)
Oconee 01 (PK-12)
   2012-13 Enrollment: 10,558 . . . . (864) 886-4500
Housing: Homeownership rate: 65.0%; Homeowner vacancy rate: 2.5%; Rental vacancy rate: 8.7%

SENECA (city).
Covers a land area of 7.552 square miles and a water area of 0.054 square miles. Located at 34.68° N. Lat; 82.97° W. Long. Elevation is 955 feet.
History: Seneca was established in 1873, when a second railroad arrived and intersected an older line to form the town's site.
Population: 8,102; Growth (since 2000): 5.9%; Density: 1,072.9 persons per square mile; Race: 65.3% White, 29.0% Black/African American, 0.9% Asian, 0.3% American Indian/Alaska Native, 0.0% Native Hawaiian/Other Pacific Islander, 2.3% Two or more races, 4.5% Hispanic of any race; Average household size: 2.27; Median age: 41.4; Age under 18: 22.2%; Age 65 and over: 18.9%; Males per 100 females: 87.1; Marriage status: 29.6% never married, 40.8% now married, 3.3% separated, 11.2% widowed, 18.4% divorced; Foreign born: 5.6%; Speak English only: 91.8%; With disability: 17.2%; Veterans: 10.5%; Ancestry: 11.1% German, 8.9% Irish, 7.8% English, 6.9% American, 4.4% Scotch-Irish
Employment: 14.1% management, business, and financial, 5.3% computer, engineering, and science, 9.1% education, legal, community service, arts, and media, 8.1% healthcare practitioners, 19.6% service, 22.7% sales and office, 6.5% natural resources, construction, and maintenance, 14.6% production, transportation, and material moving
Income: Per capita: $24,397; Median household: $34,917; Average household: $50,752; Households with income of $100,000 or more: 13.8%; Poverty rate: 21.2%
Educational Attainment: High school diploma or higher: 84.5%; Bachelor's degree or higher: 24.0%; Graduate/professional degree or higher: 9.0%
School District(s)
Oconee 01 (PK-12)
   2012-13 Enrollment: 10,558 . . . . (864) 886-4500
Housing: Homeownership rate: 56.3%; Median home value: $122,600; Median year structure built: 1978; Homeowner vacancy rate: 4.5%; Median gross rent: $618 per month; Rental vacancy rate: 10.9%
Health Insurance: 82.4% have insurance; 63.9% have private insurance; 35.1% have public insurance; 17.6% do not have insurance; 11.7% of children under 18 do not have insurance
Hospitals: Oconee Medical Center (160 beds)
Safety: Violent crime rate: 74.1 per 10,000 population; Property crime rate: 322.4 per 10,000 population
Newspapers: Daily Journal (daily circulation 9000)
Transportation: Commute: 93.5% car, 1.3% public transportation, 4.0% walk, 0.9% work from home; Median travel time to work: 20.7 minutes
Airports: Oconee County Regional (general aviation)
Additional Information Contacts
City of Seneca . . . . (864) 885-2700
   http://www.seneca.sc.us

TAMASSEE (unincorporated postal area)
ZCTA: 29686
   Covers a land area of 30.602 square miles and a water area of 0.400 square miles. Located at 34.96° N. Lat; 83.05° W. Long. Elevation is 1,063 feet.
   Population: 1,027; Growth (since 2000): 11.1%; Density: 33.6 persons per square mile; Race: 95.2% White, 3.1% Black/African American, 0.0% Asian, 0.3% American Indian/Alaska Native, 0.0% Native Hawaiian/Other Pacific Islander, 1.2% Two or more races, 1.5% Hispanic of any race; Average household size: 2.27; Median age: 48.2; Age under 18: 23.0%; Age 65 and over: 20.5%; Males per 100 females: 94.5
School District(s)
Oconee 01 (PK-12)
   2012-13 Enrollment: 10,558 . . . . (864) 886-4500
   Housing: Homeownership rate: 85.2%; Homeowner vacancy rate: 1.6%; Rental vacancy rate: 11.1%

UTICA (CDP).
Covers a land area of 1.358 square miles and a water area of 0.001 square miles. Located at 34.68° N. Lat; 82.93° W. Long. Elevation is 879 feet.
Population: 1,489; Growth (since 2000): 12.6%; Density: 1,096.2 persons per square mile; Race: 72.9% White, 20.9% Black/African American, 0.5% Asian, 0.3% American Indian/Alaska Native, 0.0% Native Hawaiian/Other Pacific Islander, 3.1% Two or more races, 5.3% Hispanic of any race; Average household size: 2.56; Median age: 34.5; Age under 18: 24.5%; Age 65 and over: 11.6%; Males per 100 females: 98.3
Housing: Homeownership rate: 64.4%; Homeowner vacancy rate: 3.1%; Rental vacancy rate: 24.2%

WALHALLA (city). County seat. Covers a land area of 3.958 square miles and a water area of 0.062 square miles. Located at 34.77° N. Lat; 83.06° W. Long. Elevation is 1,033 feet.

History: Walhalla was founded in 1850 by General John A. Wagener of the German Colonization Society of Charleston. The community was named by settlers who declared the site as beautiful as the Valhalla, garden of Norse immortals.

Population: 4,263; Growth (since 2000): 12.2%; Density: 1,077.0 persons per square mile; Race: 76.2% White, 6.0% Black/African American, 0.8% Asian, 0.4% American Indian/Alaska Native, 0.0% Native Hawaiian/Other Pacific Islander, 2.2% Two or more races, 22.5% Hispanic of any race; Average household size: 2.52; Median age: 34.7; Age under 18: 27.8%; Age 65 and over: 14.4%; Males per 100 females: 95.8; Marriage status: 26.5% never married, 44.5% now married, 3.0% separated, 12.0% widowed, 16.9% divorced; Foreign born: 14.1%; Speak English only: 81.3%; With disability: 20.4%; Veterans: 7.4%; Ancestry: 13.9% English, 12.8% German, 9.3% Irish, 7.1% American, 4.4% European

Employment: 7.4% management, business, and financial, 0.6% computer, engineering, and science, 11.2% education, legal, community service, arts, and media, 2.7% healthcare practitioners, 17.9% service, 19.0% sales and office, 17.9% natural resources, construction, and maintenance, 23.3% production, transportation, and material moving

Income: Per capita: $15,234; Median household: $33,098; Average household: $43,001; Households with income of $100,000 or more: 9.1%; Poverty rate: 33.5%

Educational Attainment: High school diploma or higher: 68.5%; Bachelor's degree or higher: 12.1%; Graduate/professional degree or higher: 6.0%

School District(s)

Oconee 01 (PK-12)
    2012-13 Enrollment: 10,558 . . . . (864) 886-4500

Housing: Homeownership rate: 55.9%; Median home value: $89,400; Median year structure built: 1968; Homeowner vacancy rate: 2.5%; Median gross rent: $386 per month; Rental vacancy rate: 10.8%

Health Insurance: 79.4% have insurance; 34.1% have private insurance; 58.0% have public insurance; 20.6% do not have insurance; 11.7% of children under 18 do not have insurance

Safety: Violent crime rate: 54.2 per 10,000 population; Property crime rate: 242.8 per 10,000 population

Newspapers: Keowee Courier (weekly circulation 2500)

Transportation: Commute: 99.9% car, 0.0% public transportation, 0.1% walk, 0.0% work from home; Median travel time to work: 19.8 minutes

Additional Information Contacts

City of Walhalla . . . . (864) 638-4343
    http://www.walhallasc.com

WEST UNION (town). Covers a land area of 0.765 square miles and a water area of <.001 square miles. Located at 34.76° N. Lat; 83.04° W. Long. Elevation is 994 feet.

History: A reform movement was responsible for the name of West Union. Colonel Joseph Greshim, a Baptist minister, moved here, formed a temperance union, and named it West Union because of its geographic relation to his former home.

Population: 291; Growth (since 2000): -2.0%; Density: 380.3 persons per square mile; Race: 85.2% White, 2.4% Black/African American, 0.3% Asian, 2.7% American Indian/Alaska Native, 0.0% Native Hawaiian/Other Pacific Islander, 1.0% Two or more races, 14.8% Hispanic of any race; Average household size: 2.22; Median age: 42.5; Age under 18: 19.9%; Age 65 and over: 20.3%; Males per 100 females: 95.3

Housing: Homeownership rate: 60.3%; Homeowner vacancy rate: 0.0%; Rental vacancy rate: 10.2%

Safety: Violent crime rate: 68.5 per 10,000 population; Property crime rate: 1,438.4 per 10,000 population

WESTMINSTER (city). Covers a land area of 3.407 square miles and a water area of 0.004 square miles. Located at 34.67° N. Lat; 83.09° W. Long. Elevation is 932 feet.

History: Westminster was a railroad stop of the 1870's whose economy was later boosted by textile mills utilizing waterpower.

Population: 2,418; Growth (since 2000): -11.8%; Density: 709.6 persons per square mile; Race: 83.9% White, 10.7% Black/African American, 0.3% Asian, 0.1% American Indian/Alaska Native, 0.0% Native Hawaiian/Other Pacific Islander, 1.9% Two or more races, 6.2% Hispanic of any race; Average household size: 2.34; Median age: 41.3; Age under 18: 24.4%; Age 65 and over: 19.1%; Males per 100 females: 84.7

School District(s)

Oconee 01 (PK-12)
    2012-13 Enrollment: 10,558 . . . . (864) 886-4500

Housing: Homeownership rate: 63.2%; Homeowner vacancy rate: 4.5%; Rental vacancy rate: 12.8%

Safety: Violent crime rate: 49.3 per 10,000 population; Property crime rate: 423.3 per 10,000 population

Newspapers: Westminster News (weekly circulation 2500)

Orangeburg County

Located in south central South Carolina; bounded on the southwest by the South Fork of the Edisto River, and on the east by Lake Marion. Covers a land area of 1,106.101 square miles, a water area of 21.801 square miles, and is located in the Eastern Time Zone at 33.44° N. Lat., 80.80° W. Long. The county was founded in 1769. County seat is Orangeburg.

Orangeburg County is part of the Orangeburg, SC Micropolitan Statistical Area. The entire metro area includes: Orangeburg County, SC

Weather Station: Orangeburg 2   Elevation: 180 feet

	Jan	Feb	Mar	Apr	May	Jun	Jul	Aug	Sep	Oct	Nov	Dec
High	58	62	69	77	84	90	93	91	86	77	69	61
Low	34	37	44	50	58	67	70	70	64	52	43	36
Precip	4.0	3.6	4.2	2.7	3.3	5.2	5.5	5.0	3.8	3.6	2.9	3.1
Snow	0.1	0.3	0.1	0.0	0.0	0.0	0.0	0.0	0.0	0.0	0.0	0.1

High and Low temperatures in degrees Fahrenheit; Precipitation and Snow in inches

Population: 92,501; Growth (since 2000): 1.0%; Density: 83.6 persons per square mile; Race: 34.3% White, 62.2% Black/African American, 0.8% Asian, 0.5% American Indian/Alaska Native, 0.0% Native Hawaiian/Other Pacific Islander, 1.2% two or more races, 1.9% Hispanic of any race; Average household size: 2.49; Median age: 38.1; Age under 18: 23.2%; Age 65 and over: 14.8%; Males per 100 females: 88.6; Marriage status: 37.8% never married, 45.1% now married, 5.7% separated, 9.0% widowed, 8.2% divorced; Foreign born: 2.0%; Speak English only: 96.7%; With disability: 16.6%; Veterans: 9.2%; Ancestry: 9.7% American, 4.8% German, 3.8% English, 2.8% Irish, 1.0% African

Religion: Six largest groups: 25.2% Baptist, 21.6% Methodist/Pietist, 4.2% Non-denominational Protestant, 1.4% Pentecostal, 1.2% Catholicism, 1.1% Hindu

Economy: Unemployment rate: 10.7%; Leading industries: 22.5% retail trade; 12.9% health care and social assistance; 12.4% other services (except public administration); Farms: 1,056 totaling 283,128 acres; Company size: 2 employ 1,000 or more persons, 2 employ 500 to 999 persons, 28 employ 100 to 499 persons, 1,636 employ less than 100 persons; Business ownership: 2,151 women-owned, 2,216 Black-owned, 33 Hispanic-owned, 80 Asian-owned

Employment: 9.8% management, business, and financial, 2.3% computer, engineering, and science, 11.5% education, legal, community service, arts, and media, 5.0% healthcare practitioners, 19.6% service, 23.4% sales and office, 8.3% natural resources, construction, and maintenance, 20.1% production, transportation, and material moving

Income: Per capita: $17,687; Median household: $34,110; Average household: $45,181; Households with income of $100,000 or more: 8.4%; Poverty rate: 23.7%

Educational Attainment: High school diploma or higher: 79.3%; Bachelor's degree or higher: 18.6%; Graduate/professional degree or higher: 7.4%

Housing: Homeownership rate: 68.6%; Median home value: $84,700; Median year structure built: 1981; Homeowner vacancy rate: 2.2%; Median gross rent: $661 per month; Rental vacancy rate: 10.5%

Vital Statistics: Birth rate: 125.0 per 10,000 population; Death rate: 115.9 per 10,000 population; Age-adjusted cancer mortality rate: 193.1 deaths per 100,000 population

Health Insurance: 79.9% have insurance; 53.7% have private insurance; 38.0% have public insurance; 20.1% do not have insurance; 9.1% of children under 18 do not have insurance

Health Care: Physicians: 12.7 per 10,000 population; Hospital beds: 32.8 per 10,000 population; Hospital admissions: 1,195.0 per 10,000 population

Transportation: Commute: 94.4% car, 0.0% public transportation, 1.5% walk, 2.1% work from home; Median travel time to work: 24.3 minutes

Presidential Election: 71.4% Obama, 27.9% Romney (2012)

National and State Parks: Santee State Park

Additional Information Contacts

Orangeburg Government . . . . (803) 533-6243
   http://www.orangeburgcounty.org

Orangeburg County Communities

BOWMAN (town). Covers a land area of 1.197 square miles and a water area of 0 square miles. Located at 33.35° N. Lat; 80.68° W. Long. Elevation is 144 feet.

Population: 968; Growth (since 2000): -19.2%; Density: 809.0 persons per square mile; Race: 28.8% White, 69.7% Black/African American, 0.1% Asian, 0.0% American Indian/Alaska Native, 0.0% Native Hawaiian/Other Pacific Islander, 0.3% Two or more races, 1.8% Hispanic of any race; Average household size: 2.42; Median age: 41.3; Age under 18: 24.0%; Age 65 and over: 17.4%; Males per 100 females: 89.4

Housing: Homeownership rate: 63.6%; Homeowner vacancy rate: 2.3%; Rental vacancy rate: 8.8%

Additional Information Contacts

Town of Bowman. . . . . (803) 829-2666
   http://www.bowmansc.com

BRANCHVILLE (town). Covers a land area of 3.142 square miles and a water area of 0 square miles. Located at 33.25° N. Lat; 80.82° W. Long. Elevation is 125 feet.

History: Branchville owes its existence and name to the first branch railroad in the state. It was the point from which a connecting line to Columbia was begun in 1840 and completed in 1842, when a wood-burning engine made the first run.

Population: 1,024; Growth (since 2000): -5.4%; Density: 325.9 persons per square mile; Race: 51.4% White, 45.7% Black/African American, 0.2% Asian, 1.1% American Indian/Alaska Native, 0.0% Native Hawaiian/Other Pacific Islander, 1.0% Two or more races, 1.6% Hispanic of any race; Average household size: 2.50; Median age: 38.7; Age under 18: 25.7%; Age 65 and over: 17.8%; Males per 100 females: 87.2

School District(s)

Orangeburg 04 (PK-12)
   2012-13 Enrollment: 3,925 . . . . (803) 534-8081

Housing: Homeownership rate: 68.3%; Homeowner vacancy rate: 1.8%; Rental vacancy rate: 13.9%

BROOKDALE (CDP). Covers a land area of 3.637 square miles and a water area of 0.003 square miles. Located at 33.52° N. Lat; 80.84° W. Long. Elevation is 220 feet.

Population: 4,873; Growth (since 2000): 3.2%; Density: 1,339.8 persons per square mile; Race: 0.8% White, 98.1% Black/African American, 0.2% Asian, 0.1% American Indian/Alaska Native, 0.0% Native Hawaiian/Other Pacific Islander, 0.8% Two or more races, 0.7% Hispanic of any race; Average household size: 2.48; Median age: 27.7; Age under 18: 21.3%; Age 65 and over: 14.6%; Males per 100 females: 81.6; Marriage status: 52.7% never married, 31.6% now married, 10.4% separated, 9.6% widowed, 6.0% divorced; Foreign born: 0.9%; Speak English only: 97.7%; With disability: 16.9%; Veterans: 9.4%; Ancestry: 1.2% American, 1.0% African, 0.4% English, 0.3% Kenyan, 0.2% Dutch

Employment: 6.0% management, business, and financial, 3.0% computer, engineering, and science, 10.2% education, legal, community service, arts, and media, 0.0% healthcare practitioners, 20.0% service, 37.2% sales and office, 3.4% natural resources, construction, and maintenance, 20.2% production, transportation, and material moving

Income: Per capita: $11,700; Median household: $17,045; Average household: $28,488; Households with income of $100,000 or more: 5.0%; Poverty rate: 46.0%

Educational Attainment: High school diploma or higher: 75.8%; Bachelor's degree or higher: 21.0%; Graduate/professional degree or higher: 10.9%

Housing: Homeownership rate: 46.1%; Median home value: $83,500; Median year structure built: 1975; Homeowner vacancy rate: 3.7%; Median gross rent: $525 per month; Rental vacancy rate: 13.9%

Health Insurance: 74.0% have insurance; 45.7% have private insurance; 42.7% have public insurance; 26.0% do not have insurance; 29.5% of children under 18 do not have insurance

Transportation: Commute: 86.8% car, 0.0% public transportation, 2.6% walk, 5.4% work from home; Median travel time to work: 16.6 minutes

COPE (town). Covers a land area of 0.250 square miles and a water area of 0 square miles. Located at 33.38° N. Lat; 81.01° W. Long. Elevation is 197 feet.

Population: 77; Growth (since 2000): -28.0%; Density: 308.4 persons per square mile; Race: 57.1% White, 40.3% Black/African American, 0.0% Asian, 0.0% American Indian/Alaska Native, 0.0% Native Hawaiian/Other Pacific Islander, 2.6% Two or more races, 0.0% Hispanic of any race; Average household size: 1.97; Median age: 45.8; Age under 18: 20.8%; Age 65 and over: 20.8%; Males per 100 females: 79.1

School District(s)

Orangeburg 80 (07-12)
   2012-13 Enrollment: n/a . . . . (803) 534-7661

Housing: Homeownership rate: 77.0%; Homeowner vacancy rate: 6.3%; Rental vacancy rate: 30.8%

CORDOVA (town). Covers a land area of 0.436 square miles and a water area of 0 square miles. Located at 33.43° N. Lat; 80.92° W. Long. Elevation is 253 feet.

Population: 169; Growth (since 2000): 7.6%; Density: 387.7 persons per square mile; Race: 84.6% White, 12.4% Black/African American, 0.0% Asian, 1.8% American Indian/Alaska Native, 0.0% Native Hawaiian/Other Pacific Islander, 1.2% Two or more races, 1.8% Hispanic of any race; Average household size: 2.96; Median age: 33.5; Age under 18: 30.8%; Age 65 and over: 10.7%; Males per 100 females: 79.8

School District(s)

Orangeburg 04 (PK-12)
   2012-13 Enrollment: 3,925 . . . . (803) 534-8081

Housing: Homeownership rate: 61.4%; Homeowner vacancy rate: 7.9%; Rental vacancy rate: 4.3%

EDISTO (CDP). Covers a land area of 5.418 square miles and a water area of 0.040 square miles. Located at 33.48° N. Lat; 80.90° W. Long. Elevation is 220 feet.

Population: 2,559; Growth (since 2000): -2.8%; Density: 472.3 persons per square mile; Race: 23.4% White, 74.0% Black/African American, 0.2% Asian, 0.2% American Indian/Alaska Native, 0.0% Native Hawaiian/Other Pacific Islander, 0.7% Two or more races, 2.7% Hispanic of any race; Average household size: 2.53; Median age: 36.3; Age under 18: 25.3%; Age 65 and over: 11.8%; Males per 100 females: 92.0; Marriage status: 33.7% never married, 48.8% now married, 6.5% separated, 9.1% widowed, 8.4% divorced; Foreign born: 3.5%; Speak English only: 91.8%; With disability: 15.0%; Veterans: 11.2%; Ancestry: 11.8% American, 2.9% Polish, 2.6% German, 2.3% Italian, 1.8% Irish

Employment: 7.5% management, business, and financial, 2.4% computer, engineering, and science, 19.7% education, legal, community service, arts, and media, 4.0% healthcare practitioners, 26.6% service, 15.2% sales and office, 2.1% natural resources, construction, and maintenance, 22.6% production, transportation, and material moving

Income: Per capita: $13,378; Median household: $27,664; Average household: $32,850; Households with income of $100,000 or more: 1.2%; Poverty rate: 33.0%

Educational Attainment: High school diploma or higher: 77.5%; Bachelor's degree or higher: 19.1%; Graduate/professional degree or higher: 5.9%

Housing: Homeownership rate: 60.5%; Median home value: $69,800; Median year structure built: 1971; Homeowner vacancy rate: 1.8%; Median gross rent: $640 per month; Rental vacancy rate: 7.6%

Health Insurance: 76.0% have insurance; 41.4% have private insurance; 45.7% have public insurance; 24.0% do not have insurance; 14.5% of children under 18 do not have insurance

Transportation: Commute: 92.3% car, 0.2% public transportation, 0.0% walk, 0.0% work from home; Median travel time to work: 19.4 minutes

ELLOREE (town). Covers a land area of 0.955 square miles and a water area of 0 square miles. Located at 33.53° N. Lat; 80.57° W. Long. Elevation is 164 feet.

Population: 692; Growth (since 2000): -6.7%; Density: 724.9 persons per square mile; Race: 55.3% White, 41.0% Black/African American, 1.0% Asian, 0.3% American Indian/Alaska Native, 0.0% Native Hawaiian/Other Pacific Islander, 1.6% Two or more races, 0.9% Hispanic of any race; Average household size: 2.20; Median age: 47.8; Age under 18: 19.9%; Age 65 and over: 23.6%; Males per 100 females: 77.9

School District(s)

Orangeburg 03 (PK-12)
   2012-13 Enrollment: 3,028 . . . . (803) 496-3288

Housing: Homeownership rate: 70.8%; Homeowner vacancy rate: 2.2%; Rental vacancy rate: 8.9%
Additional Information Contacts
Town of Elloree . . . . (803) 897-2821
   http://www.elloreesc.com

EUTAWVILLE (town). Covers a land area of 0.952 square miles and a water area of 0 square miles. Located at 33.40° N. Lat; 80.34° W. Long. Elevation is 108 feet.

History: Nearby was fought the Revolutionary battle of Eutaw Springs (Sept. 8, 1781).
Population: 315; Growth (since 2000): -8.4%; Density: 330.8 persons per square mile; Race: 61.3% White, 36.2% Black/African American, 0.0% Asian, 0.0% American Indian/Alaska Native, 0.0% Native Hawaiian/Other Pacific Islander, 0.6% Two or more races, 3.5% Hispanic of any race; Average household size: 2.48; Median age: 43.7; Age under 18: 23.8%; Age 65 and over: 20.0%; Males per 100 females: 92.1
School District(s)
Orangeburg 03 (PK-12)
   2012-13 Enrollment: 3,028 . . . . (803) 496-3288
Housing: Homeownership rate: 78.7%; Homeowner vacancy rate: 1.0%; Rental vacancy rate: 10.0%

HOLLY HILL (town). Covers a land area of 1.307 square miles and a water area of 0.005 square miles. Located at 33.33° N. Lat; 80.41° W. Long. Elevation is 105 feet.

History: Incorporated 1887.
Population: 1,277; Growth (since 2000): -0.3%; Density: 977.4 persons per square mile; Race: 40.4% White, 55.1% Black/African American, 0.9% Asian, 0.6% American Indian/Alaska Native, 0.0% Native Hawaiian/Other Pacific Islander, 1.3% Two or more races, 2.7% Hispanic of any race; Average household size: 2.46; Median age: 43.0; Age under 18: 24.0%; Age 65 and over: 20.1%; Males per 100 females: 81.1
School District(s)
Orangeburg 03 (PK-12)
   2012-13 Enrollment: 3,028 . . . . (803) 496-3288
Housing: Homeownership rate: 63.4%; Homeowner vacancy rate: 2.9%; Rental vacancy rate: 9.5%
Safety: Violent crime rate: 127.1 per 10,000 population; Property crime rate: 1,024.6 per 10,000 population

LIVINGSTON (town). Covers a land area of 0.815 square miles and a water area of 0 square miles. Located at 33.55° N. Lat; 81.12° W. Long. Elevation is 328 feet.

Population: 136; Growth (since 2000): -8.1%; Density: 166.8 persons per square mile; Race: 74.3% White, 25.0% Black/African American, 0.0% Asian, 0.0% American Indian/Alaska Native, 0.0% Native Hawaiian/Other Pacific Islander, 0.7% Two or more races, 0.0% Hispanic of any race; Average household size: 2.16; Median age: 43.6; Age under 18: 15.4%; Age 65 and over: 19.9%; Males per 100 females: 97.1
Housing: Homeownership rate: 71.4%; Homeowner vacancy rate: 0.0%; Rental vacancy rate: 5.3%

NEESES (town). Covers a land area of 1.753 square miles and a water area of 0 square miles. Located at 33.54° N. Lat; 81.12° W. Long. Elevation is 341 feet.

Population: 374; Growth (since 2000): -9.4%; Density: 213.3 persons per square mile; Race: 76.2% White, 20.1% Black/African American, 0.8% Asian, 0.5% American Indian/Alaska Native, 0.0% Native Hawaiian/Other Pacific Islander, 0.8% Two or more races, 1.6% Hispanic of any race; Average household size: 2.63; Median age: 37.3; Age under 18: 27.0%; Age 65 and over: 14.4%; Males per 100 females: 92.8
School District(s)
Orangeburg 04 (PK-12)
   2012-13 Enrollment: 3,925 . . . . (803) 534-8081
Housing: Homeownership rate: 73.2%; Homeowner vacancy rate: 0.0%; Rental vacancy rate: 11.6%

NORTH (town). Covers a land area of 0.824 square miles and a water area of 0 square miles. Located at 33.62° N. Lat; 81.10° W. Long. Elevation is 276 feet.

Population: 754; Growth (since 2000): -7.3%; Density: 915.1 persons per square mile; Race: 48.5% White, 47.2% Black/African American, 0.1% Asian, 0.8% American Indian/Alaska Native, 0.0% Native Hawaiian/Other Pacific Islander, 3.3% Two or more races, 0.8% Hispanic of any race;

Average household size: 2.27; Median age: 42.5; Age under 18: 22.1%; Age 65 and over: 17.4%; Males per 100 females: 88.0
School District(s)
Orangeburg 05 (PK-12)
   2012-13 Enrollment: 6,947 . . . . (803) 533-7930
Housing: Homeownership rate: 61.4%; Homeowner vacancy rate: 5.5%; Rental vacancy rate: 14.1%
Safety: Violent crime rate: 26.6 per 10,000 population; Property crime rate: 491.4 per 10,000 population
Additional Information Contacts
Town of North . . . . (803) 247-2101
   http://www.townofnorth-sc.gov

NORWAY (town). Covers a land area of 0.795 square miles and a water area of 0.005 square miles. Located at 33.45° N. Lat; 81.13° W. Long. Elevation is 239 feet.

Population: 337; Growth (since 2000): -13.4%; Density: 423.7 persons per square mile; Race: 40.1% White, 54.0% Black/African American, 0.0% Asian, 0.6% American Indian/Alaska Native, 0.0% Native Hawaiian/Other Pacific Islander, 1.8% Two or more races, 3.9% Hispanic of any race; Average household size: 2.39; Median age: 45.9; Age under 18: 16.3%; Age 65 and over: 20.5%; Males per 100 females: 106.7
Housing: Homeownership rate: 73.0%; Homeowner vacancy rate: 3.7%; Rental vacancy rate: 22.0%

ORANGEBURG (city). County seat. Covers a land area of 8.469 square miles and a water area of 0.010 square miles. Located at 33.49° N. Lat; 80.87° W. Long. Elevation is 243 feet.

History: Orangeburg, settled in the 1730's and named for William, Prince of Orange, became the head of old Amelia Township. The community was an early trade center and the scene of both Whig and Tory Revolutionary victories.
Population: 13,964; Growth (since 2000): 9.4%; Density: 1,648.9 persons per square mile; Race: 21.3% White, 75.0% Black/African American, 1.7% Asian, 0.2% American Indian/Alaska Native, 0.1% Native Hawaiian/Other Pacific Islander, 1.1% Two or more races, 1.9% Hispanic of any race; Average household size: 2.27; Median age: 28.8; Age under 18: 18.9%; Age 65 and over: 14.2%; Males per 100 females: 84.7; Marriage status: 52.0% never married, 31.1% now married, 4.0% separated, 8.7% widowed, 8.2% divorced; Foreign born: 2.6%; Speak English only: 94.9%; With disability: 13.6%; Veterans: 8.8%; Ancestry: 4.9% English, 4.3% American, 3.0% Irish, 2.9% German, 0.6% French
Employment: 10.0% management, business, and financial, 3.4% computer, engineering, and science, 16.6% education, legal, community service, arts, and media, 3.1% healthcare practitioners, 23.7% service, 21.4% sales and office, 3.2% natural resources, construction, and maintenance, 18.6% production, transportation, and material moving
Income: Per capita: $15,862; Median household: $32,645; Average household: $41,271; Households with income of $100,000 or more: 7.6%; Poverty rate: 31.1%
Educational Attainment: High school diploma or higher: 83.9%; Bachelor's degree or higher: 28.7%; Graduate/professional degree or higher: 12.7%
School District(s)
Felton Lab Sch Sc H24 (KG-08)
   2012-13 Enrollment: 110 . . . . (803) 536-7034
Orangeburg 05 (PK-12)
   2012-13 Enrollment: 6,947 . . . . (803) 533-7930
Four-year College(s)
Claflin University (Private, Not-for-profit, Historically black, United Methodist)
   Fall 2013 Enrollment: 1,884 . . . . (803) 535-5000
   2013-14 Tuition: In-state $15,010; Out-of-state $15,010
South Carolina State University (Public, Historically black)
   Fall 2013 Enrollment: 3,463 . . . . (803) 536-7000
   2013-14 Tuition: In-state $9,776; Out-of-state $18,910
Two-year College(s)
Orangeburg Calhoun Technical College (Public)
   Fall 2013 Enrollment: 2,718 . . . . (803) 536-0311
   2013-14 Tuition: In-state $4,717; Out-of-state $6,493
Housing: Homeownership rate: 45.6%; Median home value: $130,600; Median year structure built: 1970; Homeowner vacancy rate: 4.0%; Median gross rent: $642 per month; Rental vacancy rate: 9.2%

Health Insurance: 78.8% have insurance; 54.3% have private insurance; 35.9% have public insurance; 21.2% do not have insurance; 9.4% of children under 18 do not have insurance
Hospitals: Trmc of Orangeburg & Calhoun (286 beds)
Safety: Violent crime rate: 71.6 per 10,000 population; Property crime rate: 618.4 per 10,000 population
Newspapers: Times & Democrat (daily circulation 17100)
Transportation: Commute: 96.5% car, 0.0% public transportation, 2.6% walk, 0.8% work from home; Median travel time to work: 16.1 minutes
Airports: Dry Swamp (general aviation); Orangeburg Municipal (general aviation)
Additional Information Contacts
City of Orangeburg . . . . (803) 533-6000
  http://www.orangeburg.sc.us

ROWESVILLE (town). Covers a land area of 0.832 square miles and a water area of 0 square miles. Located at 33.37° N. Lat; 80.84° W. Long. Elevation is 167 feet.

Population: 304; Growth (since 2000): -19.6%; Density: 365.5 persons per square mile; Race: 39.8% White, 57.6% Black/African American, 0.0% Asian, 0.7% American Indian/Alaska Native, 0.0% Native Hawaiian/Other Pacific Islander, 0.7% Two or more races, 1.3% Hispanic of any race; Average household size: 2.65; Median age: 40.0; Age under 18: 22.4%; Age 65 and over: 14.1%; Males per 100 females: 100.0
School District(s)
Orangeburg 05 (PK-12)
  2012-13 Enrollment: 6,947 . . . . (803) 533-7930
Housing: Homeownership rate: 73.4%; Homeowner vacancy rate: 1.2%; Rental vacancy rate: 3.2%

SANTEE (town). Covers a land area of 2.110 square miles and a water area of 0.009 square miles. Located at 33.49° N. Lat; 80.49° W. Long. Elevation is 138 feet.

Population: 961; Growth (since 2000): 29.9%; Density: 455.4 persons per square mile; Race: 27.4% White, 65.9% Black/African American, 2.7% Asian, 0.0% American Indian/Alaska Native, 0.0% Native Hawaiian/Other Pacific Islander, 2.1% Two or more races, 3.3% Hispanic of any race; Average household size: 2.26; Median age: 44.1; Age under 18: 22.1%; Age 65 and over: 25.9%; Males per 100 females: 77.3
School District(s)
Orangeburg 03 (PK-12)
  2012-13 Enrollment: 3,028 . . . . (803) 496-3288
Housing: Homeownership rate: 60.2%; Homeowner vacancy rate: 4.1%; Rental vacancy rate: 16.7%
Safety: Violent crime rate: 136.6 per 10,000 population; Property crime rate: 1,407.6 per 10,000 population

SPRINGFIELD (town). Covers a land area of 1.739 square miles and a water area of 0 square miles. Located at 33.50° N. Lat; 81.28° W. Long. Elevation is 299 feet.

Population: 524; Growth (since 2000): 4.0%; Density: 301.3 persons per square mile; Race: 60.3% White, 35.5% Black/African American, 0.8% Asian, 2.3% American Indian/Alaska Native, 0.0% Native Hawaiian/Other Pacific Islander, 1.0% Two or more races, 0.8% Hispanic of any race; Average household size: 2.30; Median age: 47.8; Age under 18: 21.2%; Age 65 and over: 25.6%; Males per 100 females: 81.9
Housing: Homeownership rate: 82.9%; Homeowner vacancy rate: 4.5%; Rental vacancy rate: 4.9%

VANCE (town). Covers a land area of 0.505 square miles and a water area of 0 square miles. Located at 33.44° N. Lat; 80.42° W. Long. Elevation is 131 feet.

Population: 170; Growth (since 2000): -18.3%; Density: 336.5 persons per square mile; Race: 10.0% White, 80.0% Black/African American, 6.5% Asian, 2.9% American Indian/Alaska Native, 0.0% Native Hawaiian/Other Pacific Islander, 0.6% Two or more races, 0.6% Hispanic of any race; Average household size: 2.74; Median age: 38.5; Age under 18: 30.0%; Age 65 and over: 14.1%; Males per 100 females: 70.0
School District(s)
Orangeburg 03 (PK-12)
  2012-13 Enrollment: 3,028 . . . . (803) 496-3288
Housing: Homeownership rate: 83.8%; Homeowner vacancy rate: 0.0%; Rental vacancy rate: 16.7%

WILKINSON HEIGHTS (CDP). Covers a land area of 2.995 square miles and a water area of 0 square miles. Located at 33.49° N. Lat; 80.83° W. Long. Elevation is 226 feet.

Population: 2,493; Growth (since 2000): -18.7%; Density: 832.3 persons per square mile; Race: 3.0% White, 92.5% Black/African American, 0.2% Asian, 0.1% American Indian/Alaska Native, 0.0% Native Hawaiian/Other Pacific Islander, 1.2% Two or more races, 4.1% Hispanic of any race; Average household size: 2.50; Median age: 35.1; Age under 18: 22.8%; Age 65 and over: 16.9%; Males per 100 females: 88.6
Housing: Homeownership rate: 54.1%; Homeowner vacancy rate: 5.6%; Rental vacancy rate: 11.9%

WOODFORD (town). Covers a land area of 0.785 square miles and a water area of 0 square miles. Located at 33.67° N. Lat; 81.11° W. Long. Elevation is 381 feet.

Population: 185; Growth (since 2000): -5.6%; Density: 235.6 persons per square mile; Race: 43.8% White, 52.4% Black/African American, 0.0% Asian, 1.6% American Indian/Alaska Native, 0.0% Native Hawaiian/Other Pacific Islander, 0.0% Two or more races, 5.4% Hispanic of any race; Average household size: 2.53; Median age: 41.9; Age under 18: 24.9%; Age 65 and over: 16.8%; Males per 100 females: 117.6
Housing: Homeownership rate: 74.0%; Homeowner vacancy rate: 0.0%; Rental vacancy rate: 9.5%

Pickens County

Located in northwestern South Carolina; bounded on the east by the Saluda River, on the west by the Keowee and Seneca Rivers, and on the north by North Carolina; includes parts of the Blue Ridge, and Sumter National Forest. Covers a land area of 496.407 square miles, a water area of 15.622 square miles, and is located in the Eastern Time Zone at 34.89° N. Lat., 82.73° W. Long. The county was founded in 1826. County seat is Pickens.

Pickens County is part of the Greenville-Anderson-Mauldin, SC Metropolitan Statistical Area. The entire metro area includes: Anderson County, SC; Greenville County, SC; Laurens County, SC; Pickens County, SC

Weather Station: Clemson University									Elevation: 824 feet		
	Jan	Feb	Mar	Apr	May	Jun	Jul	Aug	Sep	Oct	Nov	Dec
High	53	57	64	72	80	87	90	89	83	73	64	55
Low	31	33	40	47	56	64	68	68	61	49	40	33
Precip	4.7	4.6	5.3	3.6	3.6	3.8	4.1	4.8	3.9	3.8	3.9	4.7
Snow	1.0	0.9	0.5	0.0	0.0	0.0	0.0	0.0	0.0	0.0	0.0	0.1

High and Low temperatures in degrees Fahrenheit; Precipitation and Snow in inches

Weather Station: Pickens									Elevation: 1,162 feet		
	Jan	Feb	Mar	Apr	May	Jun	Jul	Aug	Sep	Oct	Nov	Dec
High	52	56	65	73	80	87	89	88	82	72	63	54
Low	30	33	40	47	56	64	68	67	60	49	40	33
Precip	4.9	4.5	5.1	3.8	4.0	4.3	4.8	5.0	4.4	4.0	4.2	4.9
Snow	0.8	0.6	tr	tr	0.0	0.0	0.0	0.0	0.0	0.0	tr	0.1

High and Low temperatures in degrees Fahrenheit; Precipitation and Snow in inches

Population: 119,224; Growth (since 2000): 7.6%; Density: 240.2 persons per square mile; Race: 88.7% White, 6.6% Black/African American, 1.6% Asian, 0.2% American Indian/Alaska Native, 0.0% Native Hawaiian/Other Pacific Islander, 1.5% two or more races, 3.1% Hispanic of any race; Average household size: 2.48; Median age: 34.9; Age under 18: 20.4%; Age 65 and over: 13.4%; Males per 100 females: 99.8; Marriage status: 35.3% never married, 49.7% now married, 2.2% separated, 6.0% widowed, 9.0% divorced; Foreign born: 4.0%; Speak English only: 94.9%; With disability: 14.2%; Veterans: 8.9%; Ancestry: 14.3% Irish, 13.0% American, 11.9% German, 10.8% English, 3.5% Italian
Religion: Six largest groups: 29.6% Baptist, 5.2% Methodist/Pietist, 3.5% Pentecostal, 3.1% Non-denominational Protestant, 2.9% Presbyterian-Reformed, 2.4% Catholicism
Economy: Unemployment rate: 5.7%; Leading industries: 16.1% retail trade; 13.1% other services (except public administration); 11.5% construction; Farms: 727 totaling 44,975 acres; Company size: 0 employ 1,000 or more persons, 2 employ 500 to 999 persons, 32 employ 100 to 499 persons, 1,990 employ less than 100 persons; Business ownership: 2,378 women-owned, 423 Black-owned, 70 Hispanic-owned, 157 Asian-owned

Employment: 11.0% management, business, and financial, 5.2% computer, engineering, and science, 12.5% education, legal, community service, arts, and media, 5.1% healthcare practitioners, 18.2% service, 22.8% sales and office, 10.1% natural resources, construction, and maintenance, 15.2% production, transportation, and material moving
Income: Per capita: $21,182; Median household: $41,788; Average household: $55,504; Households with income of $100,000 or more: 12.9%; Poverty rate: 18.9%
Educational Attainment: High school diploma or higher: 82.2%; Bachelor's degree or higher: 23.0%; Graduate/professional degree or higher: 9.4%
Housing: Homeownership rate: 68.9%; Median home value: $123,900; Median year structure built: 1985; Homeowner vacancy rate: 2.4%; Median gross rent: $713 per month; Rental vacancy rate: 10.2%
Vital Statistics: Birth rate: 101.3 per 10,000 population; Death rate: 87.5 per 10,000 population; Age-adjusted cancer mortality rate: 166.6 deaths per 100,000 population
Health Insurance: 86.4% have insurance; 68.3% have private insurance; 29.2% have public insurance; 13.6% do not have insurance; 5.7% of children under 18 do not have insurance
Health Care: Physicians: 12.6 per 10,000 population; Hospital beds: 11.0 per 10,000 population; Hospital admissions: 478.5 per 10,000 population
Air Quality Index: 96.3% good, 3.7% moderate, 0.0% unhealthy for sensitive individuals, 0.0% unhealthy (percent of days)
Transportation: Commute: 93.1% car, 0.6% public transportation, 3.1% walk, 2.2% work from home; Median travel time to work: 23.2 minutes
Presidential Election: 24.5% Obama, 73.5% Romney (2012)
National and State Parks: Keowee Toxaway State Park; South Carolina State Botanical Gardens; Table Rock State Park
Additional Information Contacts
Pickens Government . . . . (864) 898-5856
http://www.co.pickens.sc.us

Pickens County Communities

ARIAL (CDP). Covers a land area of 4.678 square miles and a water area of 0.016 square miles. Located at 34.85° N. Lat; 82.64° W. Long. Elevation is 1,037 feet.
Population: 2,543; Growth (since 2000): -2.5%; Density: 543.6 persons per square mile; Race: 92.6% White, 3.5% Black/African American, 0.2% Asian, 0.4% American Indian/Alaska Native, 0.0% Native Hawaiian/Other Pacific Islander, 1.6% Two or more races, 5.1% Hispanic of any race; Average household size: 2.48; Median age: 38.8; Age under 18: 24.3%; Age 65 and over: 18.2%; Males per 100 females: 97.3; Marriage status: 24.7% never married, 52.4% now married, 2.0% separated, 7.0% widowed, 15.8% divorced; Foreign born: 0.2%; Speak English only: 99.6%; With disability: 24.3%; Veterans: 8.4%; Ancestry: 16.8% Irish, 15.8% American, 10.6% German, 8.1% English, 7.5% Scotch-Irish
Employment: 9.1% management, business, and financial, 3.3% computer, engineering, and science, 3.0% education, legal, community service, arts, and media, 5.2% healthcare practitioners, 15.1% service, 32.6% sales and office, 9.0% natural resources, construction, and maintenance, 22.8% production, transportation, and material moving
Income: Per capita: $16,701; Median household: $34,046; Average household: $46,598; Households with income of $100,000 or more: 10.8%; Poverty rate: 28.1%
Educational Attainment: High school diploma or higher: 69.4%; Bachelor's degree or higher: 7.4%; Graduate/professional degree or higher: 2.0%
Housing: Homeownership rate: 76.5%; Median home value: $97,900; Median year structure built: 1978; Homeowner vacancy rate: 2.3%; Median gross rent: $750 per month; Rental vacancy rate: 16.7%
Health Insurance: 88.9% have insurance; 48.5% have private insurance; 51.1% have public insurance; 11.1% do not have insurance; 0.0% of children under 18 do not have insurance
Transportation: Commute: 93.2% car, 0.0% public transportation, 2.5% walk, 3.2% work from home; Median travel time to work: 28.4 minutes

CENTRAL (town). Covers a land area of 2.694 square miles and a water area of 0.003 square miles. Located at 34.72° N. Lat; 82.78° W. Long. Elevation is 912 feet.
History: So named because it was halfway between Atlanta and Charlotte, Central was famed as an eating stop for Southern Railway passengers before the days of dining cars.

Population: 5,159; Growth (since 2000): 46.5%; Density: 1,914.7 persons per square mile; Race: 75.8% White, 15.3% Black/African American, 3.3% Asian, 0.2% American Indian/Alaska Native, 0.0% Native Hawaiian/Other Pacific Islander, 1.9% Two or more races, 5.1% Hispanic of any race; Average household size: 2.43; Median age: 22.5; Age under 18: 11.1%; Age 65 and over: 6.8%; Males per 100 females: 105.2; Marriage status: 72.3% never married, 19.9% now married, 0.9% separated, 3.4% widowed, 4.4% divorced; Foreign born: 5.4%; Speak English only: 93.5%; With disability: 10.1%; Veterans: 3.0%; Ancestry: 16.7% German, 14.5% English, 12.7% Irish, 8.1% American, 4.8% Italian
Employment: 9.7% management, business, and financial, 7.6% computer, engineering, and science, 21.6% education, legal, community service, arts, and media, 0.4% healthcare practitioners, 31.5% service, 19.1% sales and office, 3.3% natural resources, construction, and maintenance, 7.0% production, transportation, and material moving
Income: Per capita: $12,516; Median household: $24,630; Average household: $29,465; Households with income of $100,000 or more: 2.0%; Poverty rate: 43.8%
Educational Attainment: High school diploma or higher: 84.3%; Bachelor's degree or higher: 37.0%; Graduate/professional degree or higher: 21.1%

School District(s)
Pickens 01 (PK-12)
   2012-13 Enrollment: 16,735 . . . . (864) 397-1000
Four-year College(s)
Southern Wesleyan University (Private, Not-for-profit, Wesleyan)
   Fall 2013 Enrollment: 1,701 . . . . (864) 644-5000
   2013-14 Tuition: In-state $22,200; Out-of-state $22,200
Housing: Homeownership rate: 22.2%; Median home value: $103,400; Median year structure built: 1990; Homeowner vacancy rate: 3.5%; Median gross rent: $912 per month; Rental vacancy rate: 8.3%
Health Insurance: 87.9% have insurance; 81.6% have private insurance; 11.9% have public insurance; 12.1% do not have insurance; 0.0% of children under 18 do not have insurance
Safety: Violent crime rate: 13.6 per 10,000 population; Property crime rate: 347.4 per 10,000 population
Transportation: Commute: 94.2% car, 1.8% public transportation, 2.1% walk, 0.4% work from home; Median travel time to work: 15.6 minutes
Additional Information Contacts
Town of Central . . . . (864) 639-6381
http://www.cityofcentral.org

CLEMSON (city). Covers a land area of 7.440 square miles and a water area of 0.462 square miles. Located at 34.68° N. Lat; 82.81° W. Long. Elevation is 722 feet.
History: Clemson developed when Clemson Agricultural College was founded here in 1889 on land bequeathed by Thomas G. Clemson.
Population: 13,905; Growth (since 2000): 16.5%; Density: 1,868.9 persons per square mile; Race: 79.1% White, 10.3% Black/African American, 8.1% Asian, 0.1% American Indian/Alaska Native, 0.0% Native Hawaiian/Other Pacific Islander, 1.6% Two or more races, 2.2% Hispanic of any race; Average household size: 2.33; Median age: 24.3; Age under 18: 13.8%; Age 65 and over: 11.6%; Males per 100 females: 111.9; Marriage status: 56.0% never married, 34.8% now married, 1.0% separated, 4.8% widowed, 4.5% divorced; Foreign born: 13.4%; Speak English only: 87.3%; With disability: 7.3%; Veterans: 7.4%; Ancestry: 16.7% German, 13.3% English, 11.7% Irish, 4.5% Italian, 4.5% American
Employment: 13.0% management, business, and financial, 8.7% computer, engineering, and science, 27.4% education, legal, community service, arts, and media, 5.5% healthcare practitioners, 15.0% service, 18.7% sales and office, 5.4% natural resources, construction, and maintenance, 6.4% production, transportation, and material moving
Income: Per capita: $23,235; Median household: $37,851; Average household: $54,924; Households with income of $100,000 or more: 17.3%; Poverty rate: 36.3%
Educational Attainment: High school diploma or higher: 97.3%; Bachelor's degree or higher: 63.6%; Graduate/professional degree or higher: 34.6%

School District(s)
Pickens 01 (PK-12)
   2012-13 Enrollment: 16,735 . . . . (864) 397-1000
Four-year College(s)
Clemson University (Public)
   Fall 2013 Enrollment: 21,303 . . . . (864) 656-4636
   2013-14 Tuition: In-state $13,054; Out-of-state $30,488

Housing: Homeownership rate: 43.0%; Median home value: $200,300; Median year structure built: 1983; Homeowner vacancy rate: 3.2%; Median gross rent: $697 per month; Rental vacancy rate: 7.5%
Health Insurance: 94.3% have insurance; 87.7% have private insurance; 19.6% have public insurance; 5.7% do not have insurance; 4.4% of children under 18 do not have insurance
Safety: Violent crime rate: 14.9 per 10,000 population; Property crime rate: 349.5 per 10,000 population
Transportation: Commute: 84.4% car, 4.0% public transportation, 5.4% walk, 3.2% work from home; Median travel time to work: 17.1 minutes; Amtrak: Train service available.
Additional Information Contacts
City of Clemson . . . . (864) 653-2030
  http://www.cityofclemson.org

EASLEY (city). Covers a land area of 12.257 square miles and a water area of 0.021 square miles. Located at 34.82° N. Lat; 82.59° W. Long. Elevation is 1,066 feet.

History: Easley was established as a railroad station in 1874, The first of its mills was built in 1900 and the village grew rapidly.
Population: 19,993; Growth (since 2000): 12.6%; Density: 1,631.1 persons per square mile; Race: 83.1% White, 11.4% Black/African American, 0.8% Asian, 0.2% American Indian/Alaska Native, 0.0% Native Hawaiian/Other Pacific Islander, 1.8% Two or more races, 5.6% Hispanic of any race; Average household size: 2.39; Median age: 40.5; Age under 18: 22.8%; Age 65 and over: 18.0%; Males per 100 females: 89.7; Marriage status: 24.2% never married, 56.7% now married, 3.4% separated, 7.6% widowed, 11.5% divorced; Foreign born: 4.9%; Speak English only: 93.3%; With disability: 15.6%; Veterans: 11.8%; Ancestry: 13.1% American, 12.8% Irish, 11.6% English, 10.7% German, 2.9% Scotch-Irish
Employment: 11.5% management, business, and financial, 4.9% computer, engineering, and science, 9.8% education, legal, community service, arts, and media, 5.9% healthcare practitioners, 16.5% service, 28.6% sales and office, 8.9% natural resources, construction, and maintenance, 13.8% production, transportation, and material moving
Income: Per capita: $23,158; Median household: $42,494; Average household: $55,930; Households with income of $100,000 or more: 13.1%; Poverty rate: 12.7%
Educational Attainment: High school diploma or higher: 82.8%; Bachelor's degree or higher: 23.1%; Graduate/professional degree or higher: 7.8%

School District(s)
Anderson 01 (PK-12)
  2012-13 Enrollment: 9,402 . . . . (864) 847-7344
Pickens 01 (PK-12)
  2012-13 Enrollment: 16,735 . . . . (864) 397-1000
Housing: Homeownership rate: 65.3%; Median home value: $136,400; Median year structure built: 1979; Homeowner vacancy rate: 3.2%; Median gross rent: $703 per month; Rental vacancy rate: 9.9%
Health Insurance: 85.4% have insurance; 64.4% have private insurance; 33.7% have public insurance; 14.6% do not have insurance; 3.7% of children under 18 do not have insurance
Hospitals: Baptist Easley Hospital (109 beds)
Safety: Violent crime rate: 37.3 per 10,000 population; Property crime rate: 641.8 per 10,000 population
Newspapers: Easley Progress (weekly circulation 9500); Pickens Sentinel (weekly circulation 7000); Powdersville Post (weekly circulation 6700)
Transportation: Commute: 96.3% car, 0.0% public transportation, 0.8% walk, 2.1% work from home; Median travel time to work: 23.5 minutes
Additional Information Contacts
City of Easley . . . . (864) 855-7900
  http://www.cityofeasley.com

LIBERTY (city). Covers a land area of 4.451 square miles and a water area of 0.013 square miles. Located at 34.79° N. Lat; 82.70° W. Long. Elevation is 981 feet.

History: Liberty was once called Salubrity because of its location in the Blue Ridge foothills. Tradition maintains that the name was changed in 1776 when residents learned that the Liberty Bell had rung.
Population: 3,269; Growth (since 2000): 8.6%; Density: 734.5 persons per square mile; Race: 86.7% White, 9.1% Black/African American, 0.4% Asian, 0.1% American Indian/Alaska Native, 0.0% Native Hawaiian/Other Pacific Islander, 2.1% Two or more races, 4.0% Hispanic of any race; Average household size: 2.37; Median age: 39.6; Age under 18: 23.4%;

Age 65 and over: 16.9%; Males per 100 females: 93.1; Marriage status: 31.2% never married, 47.1% now married, 3.2% separated, 8.5% widowed, 13.1% divorced; Foreign born: 4.0%; Speak English only: 93.2%; With disability: 19.0%; Veterans: 5.9%; Ancestry: 25.0% American, 13.7% Irish, 9.3% English, 5.8% German, 4.3% Scotch-Irish
Employment: 5.7% management, business, and financial, 0.0% computer, engineering, and science, 10.0% education, legal, community service, arts, and media, 6.0% healthcare practitioners, 19.8% service, 22.1% sales and office, 15.3% natural resources, construction, and maintenance, 21.1% production, transportation, and material moving
Income: Per capita: $16,966; Median household: $33,393; Average household: $39,613; Households with income of $100,000 or more: 4.3%; Poverty rate: 20.6%
Educational Attainment: High school diploma or higher: 82.9%; Bachelor's degree or higher: 15.4%; Graduate/professional degree or higher: 5.1%

School District(s)
Pickens 01 (PK-12)
  2012-13 Enrollment: 16,735 . . . . (864) 397-1000
Housing: Homeownership rate: 70.7%; Median home value: $96,900; Median year structure built: 1967; Homeowner vacancy rate: 2.3%; Median gross rent: $575 per month; Rental vacancy rate: 9.0%
Health Insurance: 86.2% have insurance; 58.5% have private insurance; 38.6% have public insurance; 13.8% do not have insurance; 0.0% of children under 18 do not have insurance
Safety: Violent crime rate: 27.7 per 10,000 population; Property crime rate: 384.0 per 10,000 population
Transportation: Commute: 95.0% car, 0.0% public transportation, 0.0% walk, 3.8% work from home; Median travel time to work: 21.3 minutes

NORRIS (town). Covers a land area of 1.884 square miles and a water area of 0 square miles. Located at 34.77° N. Lat; 82.75° W. Long. Elevation is 1,004 feet.

Population: 813; Growth (since 2000): -4.0%; Density: 431.6 persons per square mile; Race: 91.0% White, 6.4% Black/African American, 0.0% Asian, 0.5% American Indian/Alaska Native, 0.0% Native Hawaiian/Other Pacific Islander, 0.6% Two or more races, 3.1% Hispanic of any race; Average household size: 2.49; Median age: 39.8; Age under 18: 24.1%; Age 65 and over: 16.4%; Males per 100 females: 95.9
Housing: Homeownership rate: 77.9%; Homeowner vacancy rate: 0.8%; Rental vacancy rate: 2.6%

PICKENS (city). County seat. Covers a land area of 2.828 square miles and a water area of 0.022 square miles. Located at 34.89° N. Lat; 82.71° W. Long. Elevation is 1,093 feet.

History: The town of Pickens as well as the county were named in honor of General Andrew Pickens (1739-1817) of Revolutionary War fame.
Population: 3,126; Growth (since 2000): 3.8%; Density: 1,105.3 persons per square mile; Race: 80.5% White, 15.3% Black/African American, 0.6% Asian, 0.2% American Indian/Alaska Native, 0.0% Native Hawaiian/Other Pacific Islander, 2.3% Two or more races, 3.4% Hispanic of any race; Average household size: 2.33; Median age: 39.8; Age under 18: 22.2%; Age 65 and over: 18.0%; Males per 100 females: 88.9; Marriage status: 32.0% never married, 40.5% now married, 1.4% separated, 8.6% widowed, 19.0% divorced; Foreign born: 1.4%; Speak English only: 97.9%; With disability: 21.0%; Veterans: 9.0%; Ancestry: 17.0% Irish, 15.1% American, 10.4% German, 7.0% English, 2.7% Scotch-Irish
Employment: 13.2% management, business, and financial, 3.4% computer, engineering, and science, 8.0% education, legal, community service, arts, and media, 2.1% healthcare practitioners, 21.9% service, 24.5% sales and office, 6.7% natural resources, construction, and maintenance, 20.1% production, transportation, and material moving
Income: Per capita: $18,405; Median household: $32,800; Average household: $43,532; Households with income of $100,000 or more: 5.4%; Poverty rate: 28.4%
Educational Attainment: High school diploma or higher: 69.2%; Bachelor's degree or higher: 13.2%; Graduate/professional degree or higher: 3.0%

School District(s)
Pickens 01 (PK-12)
  2012-13 Enrollment: 16,735 . . . . (864) 397-1000
Sc Public Charter SD (PK-12)
  2012-13 Enrollment: 11,500 . . . . (803) 734-8322

Housing: Homeownership rate: 57.3%; Median home value: $86,400; Median year structure built: 1969; Homeowner vacancy rate: 3.6%; Median gross rent: $658 per month; Rental vacancy rate: 15.2%
Health Insurance: 80.5% have insurance; 46.4% have private insurance; 46.9% have public insurance; 19.5% do not have insurance; 9.5% of children under 18 do not have insurance
Hospitals: Cannon Memorial Hospital (55 beds)
Safety: Violent crime rate: 41.3 per 10,000 population; Property crime rate: 667.1 per 10,000 population
Transportation: Commute: 97.8% car, 0.0% public transportation, 0.5% walk, 0.0% work from home; Median travel time to work: 24.9 minutes
Airports: Pickens County (general aviation)

SIX MILE (town). Covers a land area of 2.038 square miles and a water area of 0.012 square miles. Located at 34.81° N. Lat; 82.81° W. Long. Elevation is 1,024 feet.
Population: 675; Growth (since 2000): 22.1%; Density: 331.2 persons per square mile; Race: 96.9% White, 1.2% Black/African American, 0.6% Asian, 0.0% American Indian/Alaska Native, 0.0% Native Hawaiian/Other Pacific Islander, 0.7% Two or more races, 0.7% Hispanic of any race; Average household size: 2.44; Median age: 43.2; Age under 18: 22.5%; Age 65 and over: 18.1%; Males per 100 females: 95.7

School District(s)
Pickens 01 (PK-12)
  2012-13 Enrollment: 16,735 . . . . (864) 397-1000
Housing: Homeownership rate: 73.3%; Homeowner vacancy rate: 1.4%; Rental vacancy rate: 7.5%

SUNSET (unincorporated postal area)
ZCTA: 29685
  Covers a land area of 86.190 square miles and a water area of 6.530 square miles. Located at 34.99° N. Lat; 82.84° W. Long. Elevation is 1,017 feet.
Population: 1,230; Growth (since 2000): 24.1%; Density: 14.3 persons per square mile; Race: 97.4% White, 0.5% Black/African American, 0.4% Asian, 0.1% American Indian/Alaska Native, 0.0% Native Hawaiian/Other Pacific Islander, 0.8% Two or more races, 1.4% Hispanic of any race; Average household size: 2.22; Median age: 52.7; Age under 18: 17.6%; Age 65 and over: 20.6%; Males per 100 females: 97.1
Housing: Homeownership rate: 88.6%; Homeowner vacancy rate: 7.9%; Rental vacancy rate: 4.5%

Richland County

Located in central South Carolina, in the Sand Hills belt; bounded partly on the southwest by the Congaree River, and on the east by the Wateree River; includes parts of Lake Murray and the Broad River. Covers a land area of 757.068 square miles, a water area of 14.643 square miles, and is located in the Eastern Time Zone at 34.03° N. Lat., 80.90° W. Long. The county was founded in 1799. County seat is Columbia.

Richland County is part of the Columbia, SC Metropolitan Statistical Area. The entire metro area includes: Calhoun County, SC; Fairfield County, SC; Kershaw County, SC; Lexington County, SC; Richland County, SC; Saluda County, SC

Weather Station: Columbia — Elevation: 387 feet

	Jan	Feb	Mar	Apr	May	Jun	Jul	Aug	Sep	Oct	Nov	Dec
High	58	63	71	79	86	92	95	93	88	78	69	60
Low	37	40	46	53	61	69	72	71	65	54	45	39
Precip	3.9	3.7	4.6	2.8	2.9	5.3	5.4	4.6	3.5	3.2	3.1	3.4
Snow	0.4	0.3	0.1	0.0	0.0	0.0	0.0	0.0	0.0	0.0	0.0	tr

High and Low temperatures in degrees Fahrenheit; Precipitation and Snow in inches

Weather Station: Sandhill Research Elgin — Elevation: 439 feet

	Jan	Feb	Mar	Apr	May	Jun	Jul	Aug	Sep	Oct	Nov	Dec
High	54	59	67	75	82	89	92	90	84	75	66	57
Low	33	36	42	50	59	67	70	69	63	52	43	35
Precip	3.8	3.7	4.2	3.1	2.9	3.9	4.8	4.9	3.8	3.3	3.1	3.4
Snow	0.3	0.0	0.1	0.0	0.0	0.0	0.0	0.0	0.0	0.0	0.0	0.0

High and Low temperatures in degrees Fahrenheit; Precipitation and Snow in inches

Population: 384,504; Growth (since 2000): 19.9%; Density: 507.9 persons per square mile; Race: 47.3% White, 45.9% Black/African American, 2.2% Asian, 0.3% American Indian/Alaska Native, 0.1% Native Hawaiian/Other

Pacific Islander, 2.2% two or more races, 4.8% Hispanic of any race; Average household size: 2.43; Median age: 32.6; Age under 18: 22.8%; Age 65 and over: 9.8%; Males per 100 females: 95.0; Marriage status: 42.0% never married, 42.7% now married, 3.2% separated, 5.2% widowed, 10.1% divorced; Foreign born: 5.2%; Speak English only: 92.3%; With disability: 11.3%; Veterans: 11.5%; Ancestry: 9.4% German, 7.9% Irish, 7.9% American, 7.8% English, 2.3% Italian
Religion: Six largest groups: 17.4% Baptist, 7.9% Methodist/Pietist, 7.3% Non-denominational Protestant, 4.7% Presbyterian-Reformed, 4.2% Catholicism, 2.2% Episcopalianism/Anglicanism
Economy: Unemployment rate: 6.4%; Leading industries: 14.5% retail trade; 13.5% professional, scientific, and technical services; 11.1% other services (except public administration); Farms: 398 totaling 60,836 acres; Company size: 11 employs 1,000 or more persons, 13 employ 500 to 999 persons, 201 employs 100 to 499 persons, 8,456 employ less than 100 persons; Business ownership: 7,519 women-owned, 6,315 Black-owned, 321 Hispanic-owned, 747 Asian-owned
Employment: 14.6% management, business, and financial, 5.2% computer, engineering, and science, 13.3% education, legal, community service, arts, and media, 6.1% healthcare practitioners, 19.0% service, 26.4% sales and office, 6.1% natural resources, construction, and maintenance, 9.3% production, transportation, and material moving
Income: Per capita: $25,763; Median household: $48,359; Average household: $65,720; Households with income of $100,000 or more: 18.8%; Poverty rate: 17.2%
Educational Attainment: High school diploma or higher: 89.7%; Bachelor's degree or higher: 36.1%; Graduate/professional degree or higher: 14.1%
Housing: Homeownership rate: 61.3%; Median home value: $149,800; Median year structure built: 1981; Homeowner vacancy rate: 3.1%; Median gross rent: $849 per month; Rental vacancy rate: 12.2%
Vital Statistics: Birth rate: 121.9 per 10,000 population; Death rate: 70.8 per 10,000 population; Age-adjusted cancer mortality rate: 191.4 deaths per 100,000 population
Health Insurance: 86.5% have insurance; 70.1% have private insurance; 27.5% have public insurance; 13.5% do not have insurance; 5.7% of children under 18 do not have insurance
Health Care: Physicians: 32.6 per 10,000 population; Hospital beds: 54.0 per 10,000 population; Hospital admissions: 1,834.2 per 10,000 population
Air Quality Index: 76.2% good, 23.8% moderate, 0.0% unhealthy for sensitive individuals, 0.0% unhealthy (percent of days)
Transportation: Commute: 86.8% car, 1.0% public transportation, 5.1% walk, 5.0% work from home; Median travel time to work: 21.0 minutes
Presidential Election: 65.3% Obama, 33.4% Romney (2012)
National and State Parks: Congaree National Park; Congaree National Park Wilderness; Harrison State Forest; Sesquicentennial State Park
Additional Information Contacts
Richland Government . . . . (803) 576-1950
  http://www.rcgov.us

Richland County Communities

ARCADIA LAKES (town). Covers a land area of 0.547 square miles and a water area of 0.123 square miles. Located at 34.05° N. Lat; 80.96° W. Long. Elevation is 226 feet.
Population: 861; Growth (since 2000): -2.4%; Density: 1,574.5 persons per square mile; Race: 90.5% White, 4.9% Black/African American, 3.5% Asian, 0.0% American Indian/Alaska Native, 0.0% Native Hawaiian/Other Pacific Islander, 0.8% Two or more races, 1.9% Hispanic of any race; Average household size: 2.20; Median age: 55.4; Age under 18: 15.4%; Age 65 and over: 27.9%; Males per 100 females: 99.3
Housing: Homeownership rate: 92.3%; Homeowner vacancy rate: 1.1%; Rental vacancy rate: 21.1%

BLYTHEWOOD (town). Covers a land area of 9.681 square miles and a water area of 0.077 square miles. Located at 34.21° N. Lat; 81.00° W. Long. Elevation is 499 feet.
History: Blythewood was called Doko (of Indian origin meaning watering place) until postal authorities changed its name. It had been a watering station for locomotives.
Population: 2,034; Growth (since 2000): 1,096.5%; Density: 210.1 persons per square mile; Race: 69.8% White, 27.0% Black/African American, 1.0% Asian, 0.4% American Indian/Alaska Native, 0.1% Native Hawaiian/Other Pacific Islander, 1.5% Two or more races, 2.8% Hispanic

of any race; Average household size: 2.81; Median age: 40.6; Age under 18: 27.6%; Age 65 and over: 8.8%; Males per 100 females: 93.9

School District(s)

Richland 02 (PK-12)

2012-13 Enrollment: 26,564 . . . . (803) 738-3236

Housing: Homeownership rate: 90.9%; Homeowner vacancy rate: 3.7%; Rental vacancy rate: 8.2%

COLUMBIA (city). State capital. County seat. Covers a land area of 132.213 square miles and a water area of 2.716 square miles. Located at 34.03° N. Lat; 80.90° W. Long. Elevation is 289 feet.

History: Columbia was founded as the capital of South Carolina in 1786, the site chosen as a compromise between the small farmers of the Up Country and the wealthier Low Country planters. Colonel Thomas Taylor's plantation, The Plains, and parts of the surrounding farms near Friday's Ferry were selected for the location of the capital. Columbia's business boomed after the invention of the cotton gin in 1801, and the textile industry flourished with the establishment of cotton factories. Columbia was incorporated in 1805. When the Civil War began, Columbia was believed safe from invasion, but Sherman led 40,000 troops into the city on February 16, 1865. Though the city surrendered, it was burned to the ground. Reconstruction was a hard time, but Columbia emerged to continue its textile industry.

Population: 129,272; Growth (since 2000): 11.2%; Density: 977.8 persons per square mile; Race: 51.7% White, 42.2% Black/African American, 2.2% Asian, 0.3% American Indian/Alaska Native, 0.1% Native Hawaiian/Other Pacific Islander, 2.0% Two or more races, 4.3% Hispanic of any race; Average household size: 2.18; Median age: 28.1; Age under 18: 17.0%; Age 65 and over: 8.7%; Males per 100 females: 106.0; Marriage status: 54.2% never married, 32.3% now married, 3.5% separated, 4.7% widowed, 8.8% divorced; Foreign born: 5.2%; Speak English only: 92.3%; With disability: 11.3%; Veterans: 8.8%; Ancestry: 9.1% English, 9.0% German, 8.8% Irish, 7.7% American, 2.9% Scottish

Employment: 14.0% management, business, and financial, 4.9% computer, engineering, and science, 16.7% education, legal, community service, arts, and media, 6.2% healthcare practitioners, 21.1% service, 23.6% sales and office, 5.8% natural resources, construction, and maintenance, 7.7% production, transportation, and material moving

Income: Per capita: $24,779; Median household: $41,344; Average household: $64,281; Households with income of $100,000 or more: 17.5%; Poverty rate: 23.8%

Educational Attainment: High school diploma or higher: 86.7%; Bachelor's degree or higher: 39.5%; Graduate/professional degree or higher: 16.8%

School District(s)

Dept of Correction N04 (09-12)

2012-13 Enrollment: 752 . . . . (803) 896-8556

Dept of Juvenile Justice (04-12)

2012-13 Enrollment: 681 . . . . (803) 896-9110

Lexington 05 (PK-12)

2012-13 Enrollment: 16,435 . . . . (803) 476-6800

Richland 01 (PK-12)

2012-13 Enrollment: 24,138 . . . . (803) 231-7500

Richland 02 (PK-12)

2012-13 Enrollment: 26,564 . . . . (803) 738-3236

Sc Public Charter SD (PK-12)

2012-13 Enrollment: 11,500 . . . . (803) 734-8322

Four-year College(s)

Allen University (Private, Not-for-profit, Historically black, African Methodist Episcopal)

Fall 2013 Enrollment: 651 . . . . (803) 376-5700

2013-14 Tuition: In-state $11,940; Out-of-state $11,940

Benedict College (Private, Not-for-profit, Historically black, Baptist)

Fall 2013 Enrollment: 2,512 . . . . (803) 256-4220

2013-14 Tuition: In-state $18,254; Out-of-state $18,254

Columbia College (Private, Not-for-profit, United Methodist)

Fall 2013 Enrollment: 1,169 . . . . (803) 786-3012

2013-14 Tuition: In-state $26,800; Out-of-state $26,800

Columbia International University (Private, Not-for-profit)

Fall 2013 Enrollment: 1,154 . . . . (803) 754-4100

2013-14 Tuition: In-state $18,930; Out-of-state $18,930

ITT Technical Institute-Columbia (Private, For-profit)

Fall 2013 Enrollment: 357 . . . . (803) 216-6600

2013-14 Tuition: In-state $18,048; Out-of-state $18,048

Lenoir-Rhyne University-Lutheran Theological Southern Seminary (Private, Not-for-profit, Evangelical Lutheran Church)

Fall 2013 Enrollment: 107 . . . . (803) 786-5150

South University-Columbia (Private, For-profit)

Fall 2013 Enrollment: 1,627 . . . . (803) 799-9082

2013-14 Tuition: In-state $16,360; Out-of-state $16,360

University of Phoenix-Columbia Campus (Private, For-profit)

Fall 2013 Enrollment: 784 . . . . (866) 766-0766

2013-14 Tuition: In-state $10,231; Out-of-state $10,231

University of South Carolina-Columbia (Public)

Fall 2013 Enrollment: 31,964 . . . . (803) 777-7000

2013-14 Tuition: In-state $10,816; Out-of-state $28,528

W L Bonner College (Private, Not-for-profit, Pentecostal Holiness Church)

Fall 2013 Enrollment: n/a . . . . (803) 754-3950

2013-14 Tuition: In-state $5,436; Out-of-state $5,436

Two-year College(s)

Centura College-Columbia (Private, For-profit)

Fall 2013 Enrollment: 64 . . . . (803) 754-7544

2013-14 Tuition: In-state $15,547; Out-of-state $15,547

Fortis College-Columbia (Private, For-profit)

Fall 2013 Enrollment: 543 . . . . (803) 678-4800

2013-14 Tuition: In-state $15,772; Out-of-state $15,772

Virginia College-Columbia (Private, For-profit)

Fall 2013 Enrollment: 550 . . . . (803) 509-7100

2013-14 Tuition: In-state $17,620; Out-of-state $17,620

Vocational/Technical School(s)

Kenneth Shuler School of Cosmetology and Nails-Columbia (Private, For-profit)

Fall 2013 Enrollment: 83 . . . . (803) 772-6042

2013-14 Tuition: $16,750

Kenneth Shuler School of Cosmetology-Columbia (Private, For-profit)

Fall 2013 Enrollment: 119 . . . . (803) 776-9100

2013-14 Tuition: $16,750

Paul Mitchell The School-Columbia (Private, For-profit)

Fall 2013 Enrollment: 179 . . . . (803) 772-2232

2013-14 Tuition: $14,400

Regency Beauty Institute-Columbia (Private, For-profit)

Fall 2013 Enrollment: 39 . . . . (800) 787-6456

2013-14 Tuition: $16,200

Remington College-Columbia Campus (Private, Not-for-profit)

Fall 2013 Enrollment: 336 . . . . (803) 214-9000

2013-14 Tuition: $15,995

Southeastern Institute-Columbia (Private, For-profit)

Fall 2013 Enrollment: 177 . . . . (803) 798-8800

2013-14 Tuition: $15,584

Housing: Homeownership rate: 47.4%; Median home value: $163,500; Median year structure built: 1969; Homeowner vacancy rate: 4.2%; Median gross rent: $819 per month; Rental vacancy rate: 13.3%

Health Insurance: 86.7% have insurance; 68.8% have private insurance; 27.2% have public insurance; 13.3% do not have insurance; 4.3% of children under 18 do not have insurance

Hospitals: Columbia SC VA Medical Center (216 beds); Palmetto Health Baptist (489 beds); Palmetto Health Richland (649 beds); Sisters of Charity Providence Hospitals (239 beds)

Safety: Violent crime rate: 72.0 per 10,000 population; Property crime rate: 604.1 per 10,000 population

Newspapers: Columbia Star (weekly circulation 14500); Free Times (weekly circulation 35000); Northeast News (weekly circulation 10000); The State (daily circulation 105000)

Transportation: Commute: 73.3% car, 1.8% public transportation, 13.7% walk, 9.2% work from home; Median travel time to work: 16.2 minutes; Amtrak: Train service available.

Airports: Columbia Metropolitan (primary service/small hub); Jim Hamilton L.B. Owens (general aviation)

Additional Information Contacts

City of Columbia . . . . (803) 545-3000

　http://www.columbiasc.net

DENTSVILLE (CDP). Covers a land area of 6.767 square miles and a water area of 0.133 square miles. Located at 34.08° N. Lat; 80.96° W. Long. Elevation is 236 feet.

Population: 14,062; Growth (since 2000): 8.1%; Density: 2,078.0 persons per square mile; Race: 22.6% White, 69.3% Black/African American, 2.8% Asian, 0.3% American Indian/Alaska Native, 0.1% Native Hawaiian/Other Pacific Islander, 2.5% Two or more races, 5.3% Hispanic of any race;

Average household size: 2.25; Median age: 33.6; Age under 18: 23.0%; Age 65 and over: 13.1%; Males per 100 females: 81.8; Marriage status: 46.0% never married, 32.8% now married, 3.5% separated, 7.9% widowed, 13.4% divorced; Foreign born: 6.2%; Speak English only: 91.8%; With disability: 13.1%; Veterans: 11.8%; Ancestry: 3.8% Irish, 3.6% American, 2.8% German, 2.2% English, 2.2% African
Employment: 8.2% management, business, and financial, 7.6% computer, engineering, and science, 9.9% education, legal, community service, arts, and media, 6.0% healthcare practitioners, 15.0% service, 35.4% sales and office, 8.2% natural resources, construction, and maintenance, 9.7% production, transportation, and material moving
Income: Per capita: $21,258; Median household: $37,802; Average household: $47,358; Households with income of $100,000 or more: 8.4%; Poverty rate: 16.1%
Educational Attainment: High school diploma or higher: 89.1%; Bachelor's degree or higher: 31.8%; Graduate/professional degree or higher: 14.0%
Housing: Homeownership rate: 37.4%; Median home value: $109,600; Median year structure built: 1979; Homeowner vacancy rate: 2.4%; Median gross rent: $827 per month; Rental vacancy rate: 10.5%
Health Insurance: 79.0% have insurance; 57.9% have private insurance; 32.7% have public insurance; 21.0% do not have insurance; 12.2% of children under 18 do not have insurance
Transportation: Commute: 92.3% car, 1.8% public transportation, 1.1% walk, 3.5% work from home; Median travel time to work: 18.7 minutes

EASTOVER (town). Covers a land area of 1.214 square miles and a water area of 0 square miles. Located at 33.88° N. Lat; 80.69° W. Long. Elevation is 187 feet.
Population: 813; Growth (since 2000): -2.0%; Density: 669.5 persons per square mile; Race: 5.0% White, 93.4% Black/African American, 0.0% Asian, 0.4% American Indian/Alaska Native, 0.0% Native Hawaiian/Other Pacific Islander, 1.2% Two or more races, 1.1% Hispanic of any race; Average household size: 2.53; Median age: 34.0; Age under 18: 28.2%; Age 65 and over: 13.3%; Males per 100 females: 84.8
School District(s)
Richland 01 (PK-12)
    2012-13 Enrollment: 24,138 . . . . (803) 231-7500
Housing: Homeownership rate: 51.1%; Homeowner vacancy rate: 0.6%; Rental vacancy rate: 6.1%

FOREST ACRES (city). Covers a land area of 4.596 square miles and a water area of 0.371 square miles. Located at 34.03° N. Lat; 80.97° W. Long. Elevation is 246 feet.
History: Nestled among old-growth pines and hardwoods, the City of Forest Acres was incorporated in 1935 in part to encourage the residential qualities that will always be cherished as imparting a small town feel in urban surroundings.
Population: 10,361; Growth (since 2000): -1.9%; Density: 2,254.3 persons per square mile; Race: 76.0% White, 19.4% Black/African American, 1.5% Asian, 0.2% American Indian/Alaska Native, 0.1% Native Hawaiian/Other Pacific Islander, 1.9% Two or more races, 3.0% Hispanic of any race; Average household size: 2.11; Median age: 43.0; Age under 18: 21.0%; Age 65 and over: 19.1%; Males per 100 females: 84.8; Marriage status: 29.5% never married, 47.0% now married, 2.0% separated, 9.7% widowed, 13.8% divorced; Foreign born: 5.0%; Speak English only: 92.6%; With disability: 10.6%; Veterans: 12.4%; Ancestry: 16.1% English, 12.7% German, 10.6% American, 10.4% Irish, 7.9% Scotch-Irish
Employment: 16.0% management, business, and financial, 4.8% computer, engineering, and science, 23.9% education, legal, community service, arts, and media, 6.0% healthcare practitioners, 14.1% service, 28.0% sales and office, 3.5% natural resources, construction, and maintenance, 3.6% production, transportation, and material moving
Income: Per capita: $35,694; Median household: $52,271; Average household: $72,684; Households with income of $100,000 or more: 26.0%; Poverty rate: 12.7%
Educational Attainment: High school diploma or higher: 97.6%; Bachelor's degree or higher: 56.5%; Graduate/professional degree or higher: 24.1%
Housing: Homeownership rate: 70.3%; Median home value: $180,600; Median year structure built: 1964; Homeowner vacancy rate: 3.0%; Median gross rent: $851 per month; Rental vacancy rate: 14.0%
Health Insurance: 91.4% have insurance; 79.5% have private insurance; 30.4% have public insurance; 8.6% do not have insurance; 4.0% of children under 18 do not have insurance

Safety: Violent crime rate: 68.5 per 10,000 population; Property crime rate: 573.4 per 10,000 population
Transportation: Commute: 94.4% car, 0.0% public transportation, 1.1% walk, 4.0% work from home; Median travel time to work: 17.3 minutes
Additional Information Contacts
City of Forest Acres. . . . . (803) 782-9475
    http://www.forestacres.net/index.php

GADSDEN (CDP). Covers a land area of 11.500 square miles and a water area of 0.007 square miles. Located at 33.85° N. Lat; 80.77° W. Long. Elevation is 148 feet.
Population: 1,632; Growth (since 2000): n/a; Density: 141.9 persons per square mile; Race: 4.3% White, 94.4% Black/African American, 0.1% Asian, 0.2% American Indian/Alaska Native, 0.0% Native Hawaiian/Other Pacific Islander, 0.9% Two or more races, 1.2% Hispanic of any race; Average household size: 2.72; Median age: 38.8; Age under 18: 25.7%; Age 65 and over: 11.6%; Males per 100 females: 86.9
School District(s)
Richland 01 (PK-12)
    2012-13 Enrollment: 24,138 . . . . (803) 231-7500
Housing: Homeownership rate: 76.1%; Homeowner vacancy rate: 0.2%; Rental vacancy rate: 3.4%

HOPKINS (CDP). Covers a land area of 16.508 square miles and a water area of 0.022 square miles. Located at 33.90° N. Lat; 80.86° W. Long. Elevation is 164 feet.
Population: 2,882; Growth (since 2000): n/a; Density: 174.6 persons per square mile; Race: 14.1% White, 82.7% Black/African American, 0.2% Asian, 0.2% American Indian/Alaska Native, 0.0% Native Hawaiian/Other Pacific Islander, 1.5% Two or more races, 2.6% Hispanic of any race; Average household size: 2.75; Median age: 41.4; Age under 18: 23.8%; Age 65 and over: 13.2%; Males per 100 females: 86.5; Marriage status: 47.3% never married, 35.4% now married, 3.7% separated, 9.2% widowed, 8.1% divorced; Foreign born: 3.0%; Speak English only: 96.6%; With disability: 22.2%; Veterans: 11.7%; Ancestry: 12.5% English, 6.6% American, 5.4% African, 3.3% German, 0.7% Irish
Employment: 7.2% management, business, and financial, 0.0% computer, engineering, and science, 6.6% education, legal, community service, arts, and media, 0.5% healthcare practitioners, 23.1% service, 30.6% sales and office, 9.7% natural resources, construction, and maintenance, 22.4% production, transportation, and material moving
Income: Per capita: $19,060; Median household: $45,047; Average household: $49,554; Households with income of $100,000 or more: 8.4%; Poverty rate: 25.4%
Educational Attainment: High school diploma or higher: 76.6%; Bachelor's degree or higher: 12.5%; Graduate/professional degree or higher: 3.9%
School District(s)
Richland 01 (PK-12)
    2012-13 Enrollment: 24,138 . . . . (803) 231-7500
Housing: Homeownership rate: 80.9%; Median home value: $88,300; Median year structure built: 1978; Homeowner vacancy rate: 1.2%; Median gross rent: $848 per month; Rental vacancy rate: 8.2%
Health Insurance: 79.4% have insurance; 46.7% have private insurance; 47.9% have public insurance; 20.6% do not have insurance; 0.0% of children under 18 do not have insurance
Transportation: Commute: 85.5% car, 1.6% public transportation, 0.0% walk, 1.1% work from home; Median travel time to work: 25.8 minutes

IRMO (town). Covers a land area of 6.261 square miles and a water area of 0 square miles. Located at 34.10° N. Lat; 81.19° W. Long. Elevation is 354 feet.
Population: 11,097; Growth (since 2000): 0.5%; Density: 1,772.3 persons per square mile; Race: 64.6% White, 29.9% Black/African American, 1.6% Asian, 0.4% American Indian/Alaska Native, 0.0% Native Hawaiian/Other Pacific Islander, 2.5% Two or more races, 3.3% Hispanic of any race; Average household size: 2.56; Median age: 36.6; Age under 18: 25.2%; Age 65 and over: 10.2%; Males per 100 females: 89.7; Marriage status: 31.9% never married, 50.0% now married, 3.1% separated, 4.5% widowed, 13.5% divorced; Foreign born: 2.8%; Speak English only: 94.9%; With disability: 9.5%; Veterans: 14.2%; Ancestry: 16.3% German, 14.2% Irish, 9.3% American, 8.7% English, 3.2% Scottish
Employment: 14.8% management, business, and financial, 7.1% computer, engineering, and science, 12.9% education, legal, community service, arts, and media, 4.8% healthcare practitioners, 15.7% service,

27.8% sales and office, 7.6% natural resources, construction, and maintenance, 9.3% production, transportation, and material moving
Income: Per capita: $25,159; Median household: $58,242; Average household: $64,013; Households with income of $100,000 or more: 16.0%; Poverty rate: 17.1%
Educational Attainment: High school diploma or higher: 92.8%; Bachelor's degree or higher: 36.4%; Graduate/professional degree or higher: 11.0%

School District(s)

Lexington 05 (PK-12)
    2012-13 Enrollment: 16,435 . . . . (803) 476-6800
Housing: Homeownership rate: 82.1%; Median home value: $125,900; Median year structure built: 1982; Homeowner vacancy rate: 3.0%; Median gross rent: $1,056 per month; Rental vacancy rate: 7.5%
Health Insurance: 82.7% have insurance; 68.2% have private insurance; 24.7% have public insurance; 17.3% do not have insurance; 8.2% of children under 18 do not have insurance
Safety: Violent crime rate: 45.6 per 10,000 population; Property crime rate: 292.7 per 10,000 population
Newspapers: Lake Murray News (weekly circulation 9000)
Transportation: Commute: 92.1% car, 0.0% public transportation, 0.5% walk, 5.1% work from home; Median travel time to work: 22.7 minutes
Additional Information Contacts
Town of Irmo . . . . (803) 781-7050
    http://www.townofirmosc.com

LAKE MURRAY OF RICHLAND (CDP). Covers a land area of 5.584 square miles and a water area of 3.114 square miles. Located at 34.12° N. Lat; 81.27° W. Long. Elevation is 449 feet.
History: Lake Murray is named after William Murray, the engineer who, with his partner T. C. Williams, conceived and persevered until "the world's largest earthen dam" at that time was finished.
Population: 5,484; Growth (since 2000): 55.5%; Density: 982.0 persons per square mile; Race: 96.1% White, 1.3% Black/African American, 1.1% Asian, 0.2% American Indian/Alaska Native, 0.0% Native Hawaiian/Other Pacific Islander, 0.9% Two or more races, 1.7% Hispanic of any race; Average household size: 2.65; Median age: 45.9; Age under 18: 23.5%; Age 65 and over: 18.2%; Males per 100 females: 90.8; Marriage status: 20.0% never married, 69.0% now married, 1.4% separated, 6.0% widowed, 5.0% divorced; Foreign born: 2.8%; Speak English only: 96.6%; With disability: 8.8%; Veterans: 11.8%; Ancestry: 23.9% German, 18.4% American, 14.4% Irish, 6.7% English, 5.8% Scottish
Employment: 21.5% management, business, and financial, 7.8% computer, engineering, and science, 13.8% education, legal, community service, arts, and media, 11.6% healthcare practitioners, 6.1% service, 24.7% sales and office, 6.9% natural resources, construction, and maintenance, 7.6% production, transportation, and material moving
Income: Per capita: $50,027; Median household: $106,768; Average household: $140,072; Households with income of $100,000 or more: 53.8%; Poverty rate: 3.4%
Educational Attainment: High school diploma or higher: 92.3%; Bachelor's degree or higher: 51.2%; Graduate/professional degree or higher: 15.0%
Housing: Homeownership rate: 93.0%; Median home value: $312,500; Median year structure built: 1996; Homeowner vacancy rate: 2.3%; Median gross rent: $1,200 per month; Rental vacancy rate: 20.6%
Health Insurance: 95.9% have insurance; 88.8% have private insurance; 21.5% have public insurance; 4.1% do not have insurance; 0.0% of children under 18 do not have insurance
Transportation: Commute: 91.9% car, 0.9% public transportation, 0.0% walk, 1.1% work from home; Median travel time to work: 26.8 minutes

SAINT ANDREWS (CDP). Covers a land area of 6.346 square miles and a water area of 0.021 square miles. Located at 34.05° N. Lat; 81.11° W. Long. Elevation is 322 feet.
Population: 20,493; Growth (since 2000): -6.1%; Density: 3,229.5 persons per square mile; Race: 28.3% White, 65.7% Black/African American, 2.0% Asian, 0.3% American Indian/Alaska Native, 0.1% Native Hawaiian/Other Pacific Islander, 2.2% Two or more races, 3.7% Hispanic of any race; Average household size: 2.09; Median age: 31.0; Age under 18: 22.2%; Age 65 and over: 9.4%; Males per 100 females: 85.2; Marriage status: 49.7% never married, 33.2% now married, 4.6% separated, 5.4% widowed, 11.6% divorced; Foreign born: 4.3%; Speak English only: 93.6%; With disability: 13.6%; Veterans: 9.1%; Ancestry: 5.7% German, 5.2% Irish, 4.5% English, 4.1% American, 2.2% French

Employment: 9.7% management, business, and financial, 3.4% computer, engineering, and science, 12.6% education, legal, community service, arts, and media, 5.2% healthcare practitioners, 22.6% service, 32.5% sales and office, 3.9% natural resources, construction, and maintenance, 10.2% production, transportation, and material moving
Income: Per capita: $18,469; Median household: $32,537; Average household: $40,320; Households with income of $100,000 or more: 5.2%; Poverty rate: 27.3%
Educational Attainment: High school diploma or higher: 89.8%; Bachelor's degree or higher: 27.8%; Graduate/professional degree or higher: 9.0%
Housing: Homeownership rate: 35.3%; Median home value: $107,400; Median year structure built: 1976; Homeowner vacancy rate: 3.5%; Median gross rent: $732 per month; Rental vacancy rate: 13.0%
Health Insurance: 79.7% have insurance; 53.9% have private insurance; 36.1% have public insurance; 20.3% do not have insurance; 7.2% of children under 18 do not have insurance
Transportation: Commute: 88.6% car, 1.9% public transportation, 1.3% walk, 2.0% work from home; Median travel time to work: 19.9 minutes

WOODFIELD (CDP). Covers a land area of 2.743 square miles and a water area of 0.038 square miles. Located at 34.06° N. Lat; 80.93° W. Long. Elevation is 341 feet.
Population: 9,303; Growth (since 2000): 0.7%; Density: 3,391.0 persons per square mile; Race: 30.9% White, 51.4% Black/African American, 3.1% Asian, 0.7% American Indian/Alaska Native, 0.3% Native Hawaiian/Other Pacific Islander, 3.8% Two or more races, 19.3% Hispanic of any race; Average household size: 2.58; Median age: 34.3; Age under 18: 24.3%; Age 65 and over: 13.2%; Males per 100 females: 87.0; Marriage status: 36.5% never married, 46.2% now married, 5.2% separated, 7.3% widowed, 10.0% divorced; Foreign born: 20.6%; Speak English only: 76.5%; With disability: 14.3%; Veterans: 15.7%; Ancestry: 5.0% American, 4.4% German, 3.2% English, 2.0% Irish, 1.8% French
Employment: 8.7% management, business, and financial, 2.0% computer, engineering, and science, 6.1% education, legal, community service, arts, and media, 3.7% healthcare practitioners, 31.3% service, 25.7% sales and office, 13.6% natural resources, construction, and maintenance, 8.9% production, transportation, and material moving
Income: Per capita: $19,244; Median household: $43,549; Average household: $49,910; Households with income of $100,000 or more: 7.7%; Poverty rate: 19.1%
Educational Attainment: High school diploma or higher: 84.1%; Bachelor's degree or higher: 18.0%; Graduate/professional degree or higher: 4.1%
Housing: Homeownership rate: 53.3%; Median home value: $99,200; Median year structure built: 1972; Homeowner vacancy rate: 4.8%; Median gross rent: $949 per month; Rental vacancy rate: 11.0%
Health Insurance: 78.0% have insurance; 57.7% have private insurance; 33.6% have public insurance; 22.0% do not have insurance; 10.1% of children under 18 do not have insurance
Transportation: Commute: 96.2% car, 0.5% public transportation, 0.2% walk, 2.8% work from home; Median travel time to work: 18.9 minutes

Saluda County

Located in west central South Carolina; bounded on the north by the Saluda River and Lake Murray; includes part of Sumter National Forest. Covers a land area of 452.778 square miles, a water area of 9.042 square miles, and is located in the Eastern Time Zone at 34.01° N. Lat., 81.73° W. Long. The county was founded in 1896. County seat is Saluda.

Saluda County is part of the Columbia, SC Metropolitan Statistical Area. The entire metro area includes: Calhoun County, SC; Fairfield County, SC; Kershaw County, SC; Lexington County, SC; Richland County, SC; Saluda County, SC

Weather Station: Saluda										Elevation: 479 feet	
	Jan	Feb	Mar	Apr	May	Jun	Jul	Aug	Sep	Oct	Nov	Dec
High	54	59	67	75	83	90	93	91	85	75	65	56
Low	31	34	40	48	57	66	69	68	61	49	40	33
Precip	4.3	4.1	4.8	2.9	3.4	4.5	4.5	4.2	3.6	3.4	3.4	3.7
Snow	0.2	0.2	0.3	0.0	0.0	0.0	0.0	0.0	0.0	0.0	0.0	0.1

High and Low temperatures in degrees Fahrenheit; Precipitation and Snow in inches

Population: 19,875; Growth (since 2000): 3.6%; Density: 43.9 persons per square mile; Race: 61.1% White, 26.3% Black/African American, 0.2%

Asian, 0.4% American Indian/Alaska Native, 0.3% Native Hawaiian/Other Pacific Islander, 1.4% two or more races, 14.4% Hispanic of any race; Average household size: 2.61; Median age: 39.6; Age under 18: 23.0%; Age 65 and over: 16.1%; Males per 100 females: 101.0; Marriage status: 28.9% never married, 53.2% now married, 3.2% separated, 7.7% widowed, 10.2% divorced; Foreign born: 9.4%; Speak English only: 86.6%; With disability: 15.4%; Veterans: 9.4%; Ancestry: 19.6% American, 11.0% German, 10.2% Irish, 6.7% English, 1.1% Italian

Religion: Six largest groups: 15.0% Baptist, 11.2% Methodist/Pietist, 3.4% Pentecostal, 3.3% Lutheran, 1.5% Catholicism, 1.2% Non-denominational Protestant

Economy: Unemployment rate: 5.1%; Leading industries: 19.0% retail trade; 14.7% other services (except public administration); 12.8% construction; Farms: 587 totaling 107,948 acres; Company size: 1 employs 1,000 or more persons, 0 employ 500 to 999 persons, 3 employ 100 to 499 persons, 254 employ less than 100 persons; Business ownership: 256 women-owned, 157 Black-owned, n/a Hispanic-owned, n/a Asian-owned

Employment: 8.0% management, business, and financial, 2.9% computer, engineering, and science, 8.4% education, legal, community service, arts, and media, 4.0% healthcare practitioners, 14.1% service, 21.8% sales and office, 19.8% natural resources, construction, and maintenance, 21.0% production, transportation, and material moving

Income: Per capita: $19,725; Median household: $38,514; Average household: $50,955; Households with income of $100,000 or more: 10.7%; Poverty rate: 21.5%

Educational Attainment: High school diploma or higher: 76.8%; Bachelor's degree or higher: 12.4%; Graduate/professional degree or higher: 3.2%

Housing: Homeownership rate: 75.0%; Median home value: $90,400; Median year structure built: 1979; Homeowner vacancy rate: 1.5%; Median gross rent: $589 per month; Rental vacancy rate: 6.6%

Vital Statistics: Birth rate: 123.9 per 10,000 population; Death rate: 89.6 per 10,000 population; Age-adjusted cancer mortality rate: 173.2 deaths per 100,000 population

Health Insurance: 78.7% have insurance; 56.4% have private insurance; 35.2% have public insurance; 21.3% do not have insurance; 5.9% of children under 18 do not have insurance

Health Care: Physicians: 1.5 per 10,000 population; Hospital beds: 0.0 per 10,000 population; Hospital admissions: 0.0 per 10,000 population

Transportation: Commute: 90.5% car, 1.5% public transportation, 2.4% walk, 3.7% work from home; Median travel time to work: 29.0 minutes

Presidential Election: 38.9% Obama, 60.0% Romney (2012)

Additional Information Contacts

Saluda Government . . . . (864) 445-4500
   http://www.saludacounty.sc.gov

Saluda County Communities

RIDGE SPRING (town). Covers a land area of 1.822 square miles and a water area of 0.027 square miles. Located at 33.85° N. Lat; 81.66° W. Long. Elevation is 636 feet.

Population: 737; Growth (since 2000): -10.4%; Density: 404.6 persons per square mile; Race: 36.2% White, 59.0% Black/African American, 0.1% Asian, 0.3% American Indian/Alaska Native, 0.1% Native Hawaiian/Other Pacific Islander, 2.2% Two or more races, 3.0% Hispanic of any race; Average household size: 2.45; Median age: 43.0; Age under 18: 22.8%; Age 65 and over: 18.2%; Males per 100 females: 83.3

School District(s)

Aiken 01 (PK-12)
   2012-13 Enrollment: 24,686 . . . . (803) 641-2430

Housing: Homeownership rate: 67.7%; Homeowner vacancy rate: 4.2%; Rental vacancy rate: 9.3%

SALUDA (town). County seat. Covers a land area of 3.249 square miles and a water area of 0.042 square miles. Located at 34.00° N. Lat; 81.77° W. Long. Elevation is 479 feet.

History: The Red Bank Church in Saluda was originally a brush arbor, replaced in 1784 by a log hut, in 1855 by a frame building, and in 1913 by a brick church. The name of Saluda is a Indian term meaning "river of corn."

Population: 3,565; Growth (since 2000): 16.3%; Density: 1,097.4 persons per square mile; Race: 30.4% White, 39.4% Black/African American, 0.4% Asian, 0.8% American Indian/Alaska Native, 0.9% Native Hawaiian/Other Pacific Islander, 1.8% Two or more races, 33.9% Hispanic of any race; Average household size: 2.87; Median age: 29.9; Age under 18: 27.8%;

Age 65 and over: 11.8%; Males per 100 females: 97.3; Marriage status: 41.4% never married, 47.7% now married, 3.5% separated, 3.7% widowed, 7.1% divorced; Foreign born: 21.2%; Speak English only: 69.5%; With disability: 11.6%; Veterans: 6.4%; Ancestry: 6.5% American, 5.2% Irish, 5.1% German, 1.6% English, 1.2% French

Employment: 9.4% management, business, and financial, 0.1% computer, engineering, and science, 4.8% education, legal, community service, arts, and media, 0.8% healthcare practitioners, 12.7% service, 23.6% sales and office, 21.0% natural resources, construction, and maintenance, 27.5% production, transportation, and material moving

Income: Per capita: $17,022; Median household: $27,021; Average household: $43,121; Households with income of $100,000 or more: 10.9%; Poverty rate: 36.0%

Educational Attainment: High school diploma or higher: 68.3%; Bachelor's degree or higher: 11.7%; Graduate/professional degree or higher: 2.4%

School District(s)

Saluda 01 (PK-12)
   2012-13 Enrollment: 2,185 . . . . (864) 445-8441

Housing: Homeownership rate: 47.2%; Median home value: $82,900; Median year structure built: 1972; Homeowner vacancy rate: 0.5%; Median gross rent: $536 per month; Rental vacancy rate: 3.8%

Health Insurance: 70.2% have insurance; 39.8% have private insurance; 40.3% have public insurance; 29.8% do not have insurance; 4.0% of children under 18 do not have insurance

Safety: Violent crime rate: 61.7 per 10,000 population; Property crime rate: 241.2 per 10,000 population

Newspapers: Saluda Standard-Sentinel (weekly circulation 4500)

Transportation: Commute: 88.8% car, 2.6% public transportation, 0.7% walk, 5.2% work from home; Median travel time to work: 28.1 minutes

WARD (town). Covers a land area of 0.776 square miles and a water area of 0 square miles. Located at 33.86° N. Lat; 81.73° W. Long. Elevation is 666 feet.

Population: 91; Growth (since 2000): -17.3%; Density: 117.3 persons per square mile; Race: 69.2% White, 19.8% Black/African American, 0.0% Asian, 0.0% American Indian/Alaska Native, 0.0% Native Hawaiian/Other Pacific Islander, 1.1% Two or more races, 9.9% Hispanic of any race; Average household size: 2.12; Median age: 39.6; Age under 18: 15.4%; Age 65 and over: 16.5%; Males per 100 females: 111.6

Housing: Homeownership rate: 65.1%; Homeowner vacancy rate: 3.4%; Rental vacancy rate: 6.3%

Spartanburg County

Located in northwestern South Carolina; bounded on the north by North Carolina, and on the southwest by the Enoree River; drained by the Tyger River. Covers a land area of 807.926 square miles, a water area of 11.317 square miles, and is located in the Eastern Time Zone at 34.93° N. Lat., 81.99° W. Long. The county was founded in 1785. County seat is Spartanburg.

Spartanburg County is part of the Spartanburg, SC Metropolitan Statistical Area. The entire metro area includes: Spartanburg County, SC; Union County, SC

Weather Station: Greer Greenville-Spartanbrg Arpt										Elevation: 957 feet		
	Jan	Feb	Mar	Apr	May	Jun	Jul	Aug	Sep	Oct	Nov	Dec
High	52	56	64	72	79	86	89	88	81	72	63	54
Low	32	35	41	48	57	65	69	68	61	50	41	34
Precip	3.8	3.9	4.8	3.4	3.8	4.0	4.6	4.4	3.6	3.5	3.7	4.1
Snow	2.4	1.2	1.0	tr	tr	tr	tr	tr	0.0	0.0	0.1	0.3

High and Low temperatures in degrees Fahrenheit; Precipitation and Snow in inches

Weather Station: Spartanburg 3 SSE										Elevation: 609 feet		
	Jan	Feb	Mar	Apr	May	Jun	Jul	Aug	Sep	Oct	Nov	Dec
High	55	59	67	76	82	88	91	90	84	75	65	56
Low	30	32	38	45	54	63	67	66	59	47	38	31
Precip	4.2	3.9	4.9	3.6	3.5	4.7	3.9	4.2	3.6	4.2	3.7	4.3
Snow	0.9	0.1	0.2	0.0	0.0	0.0	0.0	0.0	0.0	0.0	0.0	0.1

High and Low temperatures in degrees Fahrenheit; Precipitation and Snow in inches

Population: 284,307; Growth (since 2000): 12.0%; Density: 351.9 persons per square mile; Race: 72.3% White, 20.6% Black/African American, 2.0% Asian, 0.3% American Indian/Alaska Native, 0.0% Native Hawaiian/Other Pacific Islander, 1.7% two or more races, 5.9% Hispanic of any race;

Average household size: 2.53; Median age: 38.0; Age under 18: 24.4%; Age 65 and over: 13.4%; Males per 100 females: 94.0; Marriage status: 29.6% never married, 53.4% now married, 3.4% separated, 7.2% widowed, 9.9% divorced; Foreign born: 6.4%; Speak English only: 90.6%; With disability: 15.0%; Veterans: 9.6%; Ancestry: 12.6% American, 10.2% Irish, 9.7% English, 8.5% German, 2.7% Scottish

Religion: Six largest groups: 33.9% Baptist, 6.3% Methodist/Pietist, 4.0% Non-denominational Protestant, 2.5% Presbyterian-Reformed, 2.1% Pentecostal, 1.9% Catholicism

Economy: Unemployment rate: 5.8%; Leading industries: 17.3% retail trade; 12.0% other services (except public administration); 9.4% health care and social assistance; Farms: 1,338 totaling 101,849 acres; Company size: 6 employ 1,000 or more persons, 13 employ 500 to 999 persons, 158 employ 100 to 499 persons, 6,013 employ less than 100 persons; Business ownership: 5,518 women-owned, 1,528 Black-owned, 506 Hispanic-owned, 429 Asian-owned

Employment: 11.2% management, business, and financial, 4.2% computer, engineering, and science, 9.6% education, legal, community service, arts, and media, 5.4% healthcare practitioners, 16.8% service, 25.2% sales and office, 8.3% natural resources, construction, and maintenance, 19.3% production, transportation, and material moving

Income: Per capita: $21,889; Median household: $42,919; Average household: $56,606; Households with income of $100,000 or more: 14.3%; Poverty rate: 17.9%

Educational Attainment: High school diploma or higher: 82.2%; Bachelor's degree or higher: 21.3%; Graduate/professional degree or higher: 7.5%

Housing: Homeownership rate: 69.8%; Median home value: $121,300; Median year structure built: 1981; Homeowner vacancy rate: 2.9%; Median gross rent: $686 per month; Rental vacancy rate: 12.6%

Vital Statistics: Birth rate: 122.7 per 10,000 population; Death rate: 94.6 per 10,000 population; Age-adjusted cancer mortality rate: 179.3 deaths per 100,000 population

Health Insurance: 82.3% have insurance; 61.4% have private insurance; 32.0% have public insurance; 17.7% do not have insurance; 10.2% of children under 18 do not have insurance

Health Care: Physicians: 21.3 per 10,000 population; Hospital beds: 28.3 per 10,000 population; Hospital admissions: 1,229.9 per 10,000 population

Air Quality Index: 75.1% good, 24.9% moderate, 0.0% unhealthy for sensitive individuals, 0.0% unhealthy (percent of days)

Transportation: Commute: 94.9% car, 0.3% public transportation, 1.6% walk, 2.6% work from home; Median travel time to work: 21.9 minutes

Presidential Election: 37.7% Obama, 60.9% Romney (2012)

National and State Parks: Croft State Park

Additional Information Contacts
Spartanburg Government . . . . (864) 596-2591
  http://www.spartanburgcounty.org

Spartanburg County Communities

ARCADIA (CDP). Covers a land area of 1.960 square miles and a water area of 0.005 square miles. Located at 34.96° N. Lat; 81.99° W. Long. Elevation is 807 feet.
Population: 2,634; Growth (since 2000): n/a; Density: 1,343.7 persons per square mile; Race: 56.8% White, 16.1% Black/African American, 3.3% Asian, 1.0% American Indian/Alaska Native, 0.2% Native Hawaiian/Other Pacific Islander, 3.4% Two or more races, 34.5% Hispanic of any race; Average household size: 2.65; Median age: 29.9; Age under 18: 26.3%; Age 65 and over: 9.1%; Males per 100 females: 103.1; Marriage status: 29.4% never married, 63.9% now married, 5.8% separated, 3.1% widowed, 3.5% divorced; Foreign born: 26.2%; Speak English only: 52.1%; With disability: 11.0%; Veterans: 12.3%; Ancestry: 11.7% American, 3.9% Irish, 2.7% Scottish, 1.9% English, 1.4% Pennsylvania German
Employment: 5.3% management, business, and financial, 0.0% computer, engineering, and science, 5.3% education, legal, community service, arts, and media, 1.3% healthcare practitioners, 21.5% service, 14.7% sales and office, 13.1% natural resources, construction, and maintenance, 38.9% production, transportation, and material moving
Income: Per capita: $13,828; Median household: $31,439; Average household: $42,373; Households with income of $100,000 or more: 12.1%; Poverty rate: 39.8%
Educational Attainment: High school diploma or higher: 72.3%; Bachelor's degree or higher: 25.3%; Graduate/professional degree or higher: 2.6%

Housing: Homeownership rate: 39.2%; Median home value: $58,900; Median year structure built: 1981; Homeowner vacancy rate: 1.8%; Median gross rent: $721 per month; Rental vacancy rate: 13.7%
Health Insurance: 66.7% have insurance; 30.4% have private insurance; 38.2% have public insurance; 33.3% do not have insurance; 0.0% of children under 18 do not have insurance
Transportation: Commute: 98.3% car, 0.2% public transportation, 0.0% walk, 1.5% work from home; Median travel time to work: 25.4 minutes

BOILING SPRINGS (CDP). Covers a land area of 6.837 square miles and a water area of 0 square miles. Located at 35.05° N. Lat; 81.98° W. Long. Elevation is 919 feet.
History: Boiling Springs was an attraction to visitors as early as 1780. Local historians tell that the springs once spouted upward more than four feet, depositing clean white sand on the surrounding banks. For a time in the early 1900's, pipe lines were run to several nearby houses to supply hot running water.
Population: 8,219; Growth (since 2000): 80.9%; Density: 1,202.2 persons per square mile; Race: 81.9% White, 10.4% Black/African American, 3.7% Asian, 0.3% American Indian/Alaska Native, 0.0% Native Hawaiian/Other Pacific Islander, 1.5% Two or more races, 4.3% Hispanic of any race; Average household size: 2.60; Median age: 35.3; Age under 18: 27.3%; Age 65 and over: 10.7%; Males per 100 females: 92.7; Marriage status: 24.3% never married, 67.7% now married, 1.9% separated, 2.9% widowed, 5.0% divorced; Foreign born: 10.9%; Speak English only: 86.0%; With disability: 8.3%; Veterans: 8.4%; Ancestry: 13.2% American, 11.9% English, 11.5% Irish, 8.5% German, 5.3% Scottish
Employment: 11.9% management, business, and financial, 5.2% computer, engineering, and science, 16.1% education, legal, community service, arts, and media, 7.6% healthcare practitioners, 11.7% service, 26.2% sales and office, 6.0% natural resources, construction, and maintenance, 15.1% production, transportation, and material moving
Income: Per capita: $28,120; Median household: $67,515; Average household: $77,715; Households with income of $100,000 or more: 27.3%; Poverty rate: 7.9%
Educational Attainment: High school diploma or higher: 90.2%; Bachelor's degree or higher: 36.1%; Graduate/professional degree or higher: 15.3%

School District(s)
Spartanburg 02 (PK-12)
  2012-13 Enrollment: 10,074 . . . . (864) 578-0128
Housing: Homeownership rate: 72.0%; Median home value: $149,000; Median year structure built: 2001; Homeowner vacancy rate: 2.7%; Median gross rent: $810 per month; Rental vacancy rate: 9.5%
Health Insurance: 83.0% have insurance; 74.8% have private insurance; 18.4% have public insurance; 17.0% do not have insurance; 21.6% of children under 18 do not have insurance
Transportation: Commute: 93.8% car, 0.0% public transportation, 1.6% walk, 3.0% work from home; Median travel time to work: 21.1 minutes

CAMPOBELLO (town). Covers a land area of 2.792 square miles and a water area of 0 square miles. Located at 35.13° N. Lat; 82.15° W. Long. Elevation is 915 feet.
Population: 502; Growth (since 2000): 11.8%; Density: 179.8 persons per square mile; Race: 86.7% White, 9.4% Black/African American, 2.2% Asian, 0.0% American Indian/Alaska Native, 0.0% Native Hawaiian/Other Pacific Islander, 0.8% Two or more races, 1.6% Hispanic of any race; Average household size: 2.52; Median age: 45.5; Age under 18: 19.9%; Age 65 and over: 16.7%; Males per 100 females: 101.6
School District(s)
Spartanburg 01 (PK-12)
  2012-13 Enrollment: 5,018 . . . . (864) 472-2846
Housing: Homeownership rate: 81.4%; Homeowner vacancy rate: 5.1%; Rental vacancy rate: 15.9%

CENTRAL PACOLET (town). Covers a land area of 0.250 square miles and a water area of 0 square miles. Located at 34.91° N. Lat; 81.75° W. Long. Elevation is 686 feet.
Population: 216; Growth (since 2000): -19.1%; Density: 864.0 persons per square mile; Race: 93.1% White, 4.2% Black/African American, 1.9% Asian, 0.0% American Indian/Alaska Native, 0.0% Native Hawaiian/Other Pacific Islander, 0.5% Two or more races, 0.5% Hispanic of any race; Average household size: 2.30; Median age: 46.0; Age under 18: 23.1%; Age 65 and over: 17.6%; Males per 100 females: 98.2

Housing: Homeownership rate: 69.1%; Homeowner vacancy rate: 3.0%; Rental vacancy rate: 6.5%

CHESNEE (city).
Covers a land area of 1.137 square miles and a water area of 0 square miles. Located at 35.15° N. Lat; 81.86° W. Long. Elevation is 892 feet.
History: Chesnee was named for the Chesney family who had land grants here in 1750 and who remained loyalists through the Revolution.
Population: 868; Growth (since 2000): -13.5%; Density: 763.5 persons per square mile; Race: 66.0% White, 27.1% Black/African American, 0.2% Asian, 0.6% American Indian/Alaska Native, 0.0% Native Hawaiian/Other Pacific Islander, 3.6% Two or more races, 4.4% Hispanic of any race; Average household size: 2.31; Median age: 37.9; Age under 18: 24.8%; Age 65 and over: 15.0%; Males per 100 females: 91.2
School District(s)
Spartanburg 02 (PK-12)
   2012-13 Enrollment: 10,074 . . . . (864) 578-0128
Housing: Homeownership rate: 52.4%; Homeowner vacancy rate: 9.5%; Rental vacancy rate: 14.0%
Safety: Violent crime rate: 112.9 per 10,000 population; Property crime rate: 643.3 per 10,000 population

CLIFTON (CDP).
Covers a land area of 1.073 square miles and a water area of 0.065 square miles. Located at 34.99° N. Lat; 81.82° W. Long. Elevation is 607 feet.
Population: 541; Growth (since 2000): n/a; Density: 504.3 persons per square mile; Race: 91.7% White, 5.4% Black/African American, 0.9% Asian, 0.0% American Indian/Alaska Native, 0.0% Native Hawaiian/Other Pacific Islander, 1.8% Two or more races, 0.9% Hispanic of any race; Average household size: 2.65; Median age: 38.8; Age under 18: 24.4%; Age 65 and over: 11.6%; Males per 100 females: 100.4
Housing: Homeownership rate: 74.0%; Homeowner vacancy rate: 5.0%; Rental vacancy rate: 24.3%

CONVERSE (CDP).
Covers a land area of 0.690 square miles and a water area of 0.011 square miles. Located at 35.00° N. Lat; 81.84° W. Long. Elevation is 709 feet.
Population: 608; Growth (since 2000): n/a; Density: 880.9 persons per square mile; Race: 91.9% White, 5.9% Black/African American, 0.3% Asian, 0.3% American Indian/Alaska Native, 0.0% Native Hawaiian/Other Pacific Islander, 1.0% Two or more races, 2.1% Hispanic of any race; Average household size: 2.40; Median age: 39.2; Age under 18: 24.3%; Age 65 and over: 14.5%; Males per 100 females: 93.6
Housing: Homeownership rate: 67.2%; Homeowner vacancy rate: 2.3%; Rental vacancy rate: 7.7%

COWPENS (town).
Covers a land area of 2.358 square miles and a water area of 0 square miles. Located at 35.02° N. Lat; 81.80° W. Long. Elevation is 860 feet.
History: Cowpens was named for the cow pens of Tory cattleman Hanna. In the early days when cattle raising was lucrative, the pens were maintained commercially for the convenience of herdsmen driving their stock to market.
Population: 2,162; Growth (since 2000): -5.1%; Density: 917.0 persons per square mile; Race: 73.9% White, 21.2% Black/African American, 0.1% Asian, 0.3% American Indian/Alaska Native, 0.0% Native Hawaiian/Other Pacific Islander, 2.0% Two or more races, 4.3% Hispanic of any race; Average household size: 2.44; Median age: 38.4; Age under 18: 25.3%; Age 65 and over: 15.5%; Males per 100 females: 90.7
School District(s)
Spartanburg 03 (PK-12)
   2012-13 Enrollment: 2,937 . . . . (864) 279-6000
Housing: Homeownership rate: 67.2%; Homeowner vacancy rate: 2.8%; Rental vacancy rate: 3.1%
Safety: Violent crime rate: 22.6 per 10,000 population; Property crime rate: 271.6 per 10,000 population
Additional Information Contacts
Town of Cowpens . . . . (864) 463-3201
   http://www.mycowpensgov.com

CROSS ANCHOR (CDP).
Covers a land area of 0.774 square miles and a water area of 0.004 square miles. Located at 34.64° N. Lat; 81.86° W. Long. Elevation is 669 feet.
Population: 126; Growth (since 2000): n/a; Density: 162.8 persons per square mile; Race: 71.4% White, 23.8% Black/African American, 0.8%

Asian, 0.8% American Indian/Alaska Native, 0.0% Native Hawaiian/Other Pacific Islander, 3.2% Two or more races, 4.0% Hispanic of any race; Average household size: 2.03; Median age: 51.0; Age under 18: 18.3%; Age 65 and over: 18.3%; Males per 100 females: 72.6
Housing: Homeownership rate: 83.8%; Homeowner vacancy rate: 0.0%; Rental vacancy rate: 9.1%

DRAYTON (unincorporated postal area)
ZCTA: 29333
   Covers a land area of 0.380 square miles and a water area of 0 square miles. Located at 34.97° N. Lat; 81.91° W. Long. Elevation is 741 feet.
   Population: 374; Growth (since 2000): n/a; Density: 983.5 persons per square mile; Race: 84.0% White, 12.6% Black/African American, 0.3% Asian, 0.0% American Indian/Alaska Native, 0.0% Native Hawaiian/Other Pacific Islander, 3.2% Two or more races, 2.4% Hispanic of any race; Average household size: 2.29; Median age: 42.4; Age under 18: 19.8%; Age 65 and over: 17.9%; Males per 100 females: 97.9
   Housing: Homeownership rate: 63.8%; Homeowner vacancy rate: 0.0%; Rental vacancy rate: 14.5%

DUNCAN (town).
Covers a land area of 4.674 square miles and a water area of 0.103 square miles. Located at 34.94° N. Lat; 82.14° W. Long. Elevation is 863 feet.
Population: 3,181; Growth (since 2000): 10.8%; Density: 680.5 persons per square mile; Race: 60.9% White, 30.5% Black/African American, 1.0% Asian, 0.2% American Indian/Alaska Native, 0.0% Native Hawaiian/Other Pacific Islander, 3.2% Two or more races, 9.2% Hispanic of any race; Average household size: 2.56; Median age: 31.4; Age under 18: 30.6%; Age 65 and over: 9.8%; Males per 100 females: 81.5; Marriage status: 36.7% never married, 50.0% now married, 3.3% separated, 2.5% widowed, 10.8% divorced; Foreign born: 5.4%; Speak English only: 91.5%; With disability: 24.6%; Veterans: 9.6%; Ancestry: 17.9% Irish, 10.8% German, 10.0% English, 5.8% American, 3.1% French
Employment: 11.0% management, business, and financial, 0.0% computer, engineering, and science, 3.9% education, legal, community service, arts, and media, 6.1% healthcare practitioners, 19.1% service, 30.3% sales and office, 2.4% natural resources, construction, and maintenance, 27.3% production, transportation, and material moving
Income: Per capita: $17,881; Median household: $34,417; Average household: $41,268; Households with income of $100,000 or more: 4.6%; Poverty rate: 18.5%
Educational Attainment: High school diploma or higher: 86.6%; Bachelor's degree or higher: 18.5%; Graduate/professional degree or higher: 3.2%
School District(s)
Spartanburg 05 (PK-12)
   2012-13 Enrollment: 7,809 . . . . (864) 949-2350
Housing: Homeownership rate: 49.4%; Median home value: $106,100; Median year structure built: 1990; Homeowner vacancy rate: 5.2%; Median gross rent: $645 per month; Rental vacancy rate: 9.2%
Health Insurance: 86.4% have insurance; 64.6% have private insurance; 31.3% have public insurance; 13.6% do not have insurance; 2.9% of children under 18 do not have insurance
Safety: Violent crime rate: 12.3 per 10,000 population; Property crime rate: 252.1 per 10,000 population
Transportation: Commute: 92.4% car, 0.0% public transportation, 3.7% walk, 1.3% work from home; Median travel time to work: 20.3 minutes
Additional Information Contacts
Town of Duncan . . . . (864) 439-2664
   http://www.cityofspartanburg.org

ENOREE (CDP).
Covers a land area of 1.548 square miles and a water area of 0.036 square miles. Located at 34.66° N. Lat; 81.96° W. Long. Elevation is 584 feet.
Population: 665; Growth (since 2000): n/a; Density: 429.5 persons per square mile; Race: 78.9% White, 13.8% Black/African American, 1.2% Asian, 0.2% American Indian/Alaska Native, 0.0% Native Hawaiian/Other Pacific Islander, 2.6% Two or more races, 5.6% Hispanic of any race; Average household size: 2.47; Median age: 40.6; Age under 18: 22.1%; Age 65 and over: 16.1%; Males per 100 females: 93.3
School District(s)
Dept of Correction N04 (09-12)
   2012-13 Enrollment: 752. . . . . (803) 896-8556

Housing: Homeownership rate: 68.8%; Homeowner vacancy rate: 6.5%; Rental vacancy rate: 4.5%

FAIRFOREST (CDP).
Covers a land area of 2.092 square miles and a water area of 0.006 square miles. Located at 34.95° N. Lat; 82.02° W. Long. Elevation is 850 feet.
Population: 1,693; Growth (since 2000): n/a; Density: 809.3 persons per square mile; Race: 62.0% White, 17.2% Black/African American, 5.8% Asian, 0.3% American Indian/Alaska Native, 0.0% Native Hawaiian/Other Pacific Islander, 2.5% Two or more races, 35.4% Hispanic of any race; Average household size: 2.78; Median age: 30.8; Age under 18: 28.7%; Age 65 and over: 10.8%; Males per 100 females: 106.5
Housing: Homeownership rate: 63.6%; Homeowner vacancy rate: 2.0%; Rental vacancy rate: 7.5%

FINGERVILLE (CDP).
Covers a land area of 0.244 square miles and a water area of 0 square miles. Located at 35.14° N. Lat; 82.00° W. Long. Elevation is 889 feet.
Population: 134; Growth (since 2000): n/a; Density: 548.2 persons per square mile; Race: 93.3% White, 3.7% Black/African American, 0.0% Asian, 1.5% American Indian/Alaska Native, 0.0% Native Hawaiian/Other Pacific Islander, 1.5% Two or more races, 0.7% Hispanic of any race; Average household size: 2.44; Median age: 38.0; Age under 18: 28.4%; Age 65 and over: 9.7%; Males per 100 females: 100.0
Housing: Homeownership rate: 60.0%; Homeowner vacancy rate: 10.8%; Rental vacancy rate: 8.3%

GLENDALE (CDP).
Covers a land area of 0.212 square miles and a water area of 0 square miles. Located at 34.95° N. Lat; 81.84° W. Long. Elevation is 692 feet.
Population: 307; Growth (since 2000): n/a; Density: 1,444.8 persons per square mile; Race: 94.5% White, 2.9% Black/African American, 0.7% Asian, 0.0% American Indian/Alaska Native, 0.0% Native Hawaiian/Other Pacific Islander, 0.7% Two or more races, 3.6% Hispanic of any race; Average household size: 2.77; Median age: 34.8; Age under 18: 27.4%; Age 65 and over: 11.4%; Males per 100 females: 99.4
Housing: Homeownership rate: 65.7%; Homeowner vacancy rate: 8.8%; Rental vacancy rate: 0.0%

INMAN (city).
Covers a land area of 1.436 square miles and a water area of 0.004 square miles. Located at 35.05° N. Lat; 82.09° W. Long. Elevation is 981 feet.
History: Painter Henry Inman and others in South Carolina created some of the earliest genre painting done in the U.S. (1825-1850).
Population: 2,321; Growth (since 2000): 23.2%; Density: 1,616.6 persons per square mile; Race: 68.9% White, 24.4% Black/African American, 2.7% Asian, 0.1% American Indian/Alaska Native, 0.0% Native Hawaiian/Other Pacific Islander, 2.2% Two or more races, 3.3% Hispanic of any race; Average household size: 2.26; Median age: 39.2; Age under 18: 23.6%; Age 65 and over: 19.8%; Males per 100 females: 80.5
School District(s)
Spartanburg 01 (PK-12)
    2012-13 Enrollment: 5,018 . . . . (864) 472-2846
Spartanburg 02 (PK-12)
    2012-13 Enrollment: 10,074 . . . . (864) 578-0128
Spartanburg 82 (09-12)
    2012-13 Enrollment: n/a . . . . (864) 592-2790
Housing: Homeownership rate: 55.3%; Homeowner vacancy rate: 7.8%; Rental vacancy rate: 5.9%
Safety: Violent crime rate: 41.8 per 10,000 population; Property crime rate: 292.6 per 10,000 population

INMAN MILLS (CDP).
Covers a land area of 1.139 square miles and a water area of 0 square miles. Located at 35.04° N. Lat; 82.10° W. Long. Elevation is 919 feet.
Population: 1,050; Growth (since 2000): -8.8%; Density: 922.0 persons per square mile; Race: 88.9% White, 7.7% Black/African American, 1.3% Asian, 0.3% American Indian/Alaska Native, 0.0% Native Hawaiian/Other Pacific Islander, 1.1% Two or more races, 1.8% Hispanic of any race; Average household size: 2.28; Median age: 52.1; Age under 18: 17.5%; Age 65 and over: 34.8%; Males per 100 females: 65.1
Housing: Homeownership rate: 69.1%; Homeowner vacancy rate: 3.9%; Rental vacancy rate: 12.8%

LANDRUM (city).
Covers a land area of 2.678 square miles and a water area of 0.008 square miles. Located at 35.18° N. Lat; 82.19° W. Long. Elevation is 1,047 feet.
History: Landrum, once a popular summer resort, was named for Baptist minister J.G. Landrum, founder of many churches in this area.
Population: 2,376; Growth (since 2000): -3.9%; Density: 887.1 persons per square mile; Race: 81.5% White, 13.0% Black/African American, 0.9% Asian, 0.3% American Indian/Alaska Native, 0.0% Native Hawaiian/Other Pacific Islander, 2.3% Two or more races, 4.3% Hispanic of any race; Average household size: 2.28; Median age: 44.0; Age under 18: 22.3%; Age 65 and over: 19.4%; Males per 100 females: 89.6
School District(s)
Spartanburg 01 (PK-12)
    2012-13 Enrollment: 5,018 . . . . (864) 472-2846
Housing: Homeownership rate: 70.2%; Homeowner vacancy rate: 4.4%; Rental vacancy rate: 11.1%
Safety: Violent crime rate: 24.7 per 10,000 population; Property crime rate: 263.1 per 10,000 population
Newspapers: The News Leader (weekly circulation 2400)

LYMAN (town).
Covers a land area of 5.976 square miles and a water area of 0.585 square miles. Located at 34.97° N. Lat; 82.14° W. Long. Elevation is 856 feet.
Population: 3,243; Growth (since 2000): 22.0%; Density: 542.6 persons per square mile; Race: 84.9% White, 10.7% Black/African American, 0.8% Asian, 0.3% American Indian/Alaska Native, 0.0% Native Hawaiian/Other Pacific Islander, 1.8% Two or more races, 3.7% Hispanic of any race; Average household size: 2.38; Median age: 39.8; Age under 18: 21.6%; Age 65 and over: 16.2%; Males per 100 females: 90.8; Marriage status: 17.4% never married, 64.5% now married, 3.4% separated, 8.7% widowed, 9.4% divorced; Foreign born: 7.6%; Speak English only: 91.3%; With disability: 8.5%; Veterans: 19.9%; Ancestry: 17.4% Irish, 10.5% German, 8.8% Polish, 7.8% English, 7.6% American
Employment: 6.5% management, business, and financial, 3.9% computer, engineering, and science, 11.5% education, legal, community service, arts, and media, 2.2% healthcare practitioners, 13.8% service, 33.1% sales and office, 4.1% natural resources, construction, and maintenance, 25.0% production, transportation, and material moving
Income: Per capita: $19,449; Median household: $44,444; Average household: $47,689; Households with income of $100,000 or more: 7.0%; Poverty rate: 10.7%
Educational Attainment: High school diploma or higher: 87.9%; Bachelor's degree or higher: 20.9%; Graduate/professional degree or higher: 3.7%
School District(s)
Spartanburg 05 (PK-12)
    2012-13 Enrollment: 7,809 . . . . (864) 949-2350
Housing: Homeownership rate: 75.0%; Median home value: $113,000; Median year structure built: 1973; Homeowner vacancy rate: 3.7%; Median gross rent: $640 per month; Rental vacancy rate: 6.8%
Health Insurance: 78.3% have insurance; 64.5% have private insurance; 24.0% have public insurance; 21.7% do not have insurance; 4.4% of children under 18 do not have insurance
Safety: Violent crime rate: 9.0 per 10,000 population; Property crime rate: 431.0 per 10,000 population
Transportation: Commute: 94.1% car, 0.0% public transportation, 3.9% walk, 1.9% work from home; Median travel time to work: 15.9 minutes

MAYO (CDP).
Covers a land area of 3.041 square miles and a water area of 0 square miles. Located at 35.09° N. Lat; 81.85° W. Long. Elevation is 889 feet.
Population: 1,592; Growth (since 2000): -13.6%; Density: 523.6 persons per square mile; Race: 94.2% White, 3.1% Black/African American, 0.3% Asian, 0.1% American Indian/Alaska Native, 0.0% Native Hawaiian/Other Pacific Islander, 1.4% Two or more races, 2.6% Hispanic of any race; Average household size: 2.48; Median age: 41.3; Age under 18: 22.0%; Age 65 and over: 16.1%; Males per 100 females: 95.6
School District(s)
Spartanburg 02 (PK-12)
    2012-13 Enrollment: 10,074 . . . . (864) 578-0128
Housing: Homeownership rate: 72.2%; Homeowner vacancy rate: 1.7%; Rental vacancy rate: 5.8%

MOORE (unincorporated postal area)
ZCTA: 29369
Covers a land area of 28.513 square miles and a water area of 0.391 square miles. Located at 34.87° N. Lat; 82.02° W. Long. Elevation is 715 feet.
Population: 13,044; Growth (since 2000): 44.3%; Density: 457.5 persons per square mile; Race: 74.7% White, 20.0% Black/African American, 1.9% Asian, 0.1% American Indian/Alaska Native, 0.0% Native Hawaiian/Other Pacific Islander, 1.5% Two or more races, 4.0% Hispanic of any race; Average household size: 2.66; Median age: 39.4; Age under 18: 26.6%; Age 65 and over: 11.4%; Males per 100 females: 92.2; Marriage status: 25.5% never married, 62.5% now married, 2.9% separated, 4.7% widowed, 7.3% divorced; Foreign born: 4.8%; Speak English only: 92.8%; With disability: 9.5%; Veterans: 10.3%; Ancestry: 12.2% English, 11.0% German, 8.6% Irish, 8.5% American, 3.1% Italian
Employment: 18.5% management, business, and financial, 9.4% computer, engineering, and science, 13.4% education, legal, community service, arts, and media, 5.0% healthcare practitioners, 14.9% service, 21.4% sales and office, 4.3% natural resources, construction, and maintenance, 13.0% production, transportation, and material moving
Income: Per capita: $27,940; Median household: $61,831; Average household: $77,303; Households with income of $100,000 or more: 25.6%; Poverty rate: 13.5%
Educational Attainment: High school diploma or higher: 91.2%; Bachelor's degree or higher: 34.3%; Graduate/professional degree or higher: 12.1%
School District(s)
Spartanburg 05 (PK-12)
  2012-13 Enrollment: 7,809 . . . . (864) 949-2350
Spartanburg 06 (PK-12)
  2012-13 Enrollment: 11,023 . . . . (864) 576-4212
Spartanburg 81 (10-12)
  2012-13 Enrollment: n/a . . . . (864) 576-5020
Housing: Homeownership rate: 85.3%; Median home value: $160,800; Median year structure built: 1992; Homeowner vacancy rate: 2.8%; Median gross rent: $859 per month; Rental vacancy rate: 7.3%
Health Insurance: 88.4% have insurance; 74.8% have private insurance; 23.7% have public insurance; 11.6% do not have insurance; 6.7% of children under 18 do not have insurance
Transportation: Commute: 96.3% car, 0.5% public transportation, 0.3% walk, 2.7% work from home; Median travel time to work: 22.3 minutes

PACOLET (town). Covers a land area of 3.510 square miles and a water area of 0.023 square miles. Located at 34.91° N. Lat; 81.76° W. Long. Elevation is 771 feet.
Population: 2,235; Growth (since 2000): -16.9%; Density: 636.7 persons per square mile; Race: 75.7% White, 21.7% Black/African American, 1.2% Asian, 0.2% American Indian/Alaska Native, 0.1% Native Hawaiian/Other Pacific Islander, 1.0% Two or more races, 1.1% Hispanic of any race; Average household size: 2.31; Median age: 43.9; Age under 18: 20.9%; Age 65 and over: 21.7%; Males per 100 females: 88.1
School District(s)
Spartanburg 03 (PK-12)
  2012-13 Enrollment: 2,937 . . . . (864) 279-6000
Housing: Homeownership rate: 73.0%; Homeowner vacancy rate: 3.8%; Rental vacancy rate: 10.0%
Safety: Violent crime rate: 39.5 per 10,000 population; Property crime rate: 509.0 per 10,000 population

PACOLET MILLS (unincorporated postal area)
ZCTA: 29373
Covers a land area of 0.661 square miles and a water area of 0.068 square miles. Located at 34.92° N. Lat; 81.75° W. Long. Elevation is 541 feet.
Population: 297; Growth (since 2000): 49.2%; Density: 449.0 persons per square mile; Race: 92.3% White, 5.4% Black/African American, 0.3% Asian, 0.3% American Indian/Alaska Native, 0.0% Native Hawaiian/Other Pacific Islander, 1.7% Two or more races, 0.3% Hispanic of any race; Average household size: 2.56; Median age: 39.8; Age under 18: 22.2%; Age 65 and over: 19.9%; Males per 100 females: 82.2
Housing: Homeownership rate: 66.4%; Homeowner vacancy rate: 4.7%; Rental vacancy rate: 7.0%

PAULINE (unincorporated postal area)
ZCTA: 29374
Covers a land area of 51.730 square miles and a water area of 0.283 square miles. Located at 34.78° N. Lat; 81.85° W. Long. Elevation is 761 feet.
Population: 3,534; Growth (since 2000): -22.7%; Density: 68.3 persons per square mile; Race: 93.1% White, 4.0% Black/African American, 0.5% Asian, 0.2% American Indian/Alaska Native, 0.0% Native Hawaiian/Other Pacific Islander, 0.8% Two or more races, 2.4% Hispanic of any race; Average household size: 2.51; Median age: 42.9; Age under 18: 23.8%; Age 65 and over: 14.3%; Males per 100 females: 104.2; Marriage status: 23.6% never married, 63.8% now married, 2.3% separated, 6.5% widowed, 6.2% divorced; Foreign born: 2.2%; Speak English only: 98.0%; With disability: 13.6%; Veterans: 15.0%; Ancestry: 18.1% American, 15.4% Irish, 9.5% English, 7.1% Scotch-Irish, 6.9% German
Employment: 11.6% management, business, and financial, 4.3% computer, engineering, and science, 11.3% education, legal, community service, arts, and media, 9.2% healthcare practitioners, 9.0% service, 21.6% sales and office, 20.9% natural resources, construction, and maintenance, 12.0% production, transportation, and material moving
Income: Per capita: $25,134; Median household: $50,859; Average household: $63,038; Households with income of $100,000 or more: 20.7%; Poverty rate: 12.2%
Educational Attainment: High school diploma or higher: 86.6%; Bachelor's degree or higher: 19.5%; Graduate/professional degree or higher: 7.2%
School District(s)
Spartanburg 06 (PK-12)
  2012-13 Enrollment: 11,023 . . . . (864) 576-4212
Housing: Homeownership rate: 82.9%; Median home value: $155,100; Median year structure built: 1982; Homeowner vacancy rate: 1.9%; Median gross rent: $834 per month; Rental vacancy rate: 3.6%
Health Insurance: 85.2% have insurance; 69.3% have private insurance; 29.3% have public insurance; 14.8% do not have insurance; 10.2% of children under 18 do not have insurance
Transportation: Commute: 99.0% car, 0.0% public transportation, 0.0% walk, 1.0% work from home; Median travel time to work: 32.0 minutes

REIDVILLE (town). Covers a land area of 1.684 square miles and a water area of 0.019 square miles. Located at 34.87° N. Lat; 82.10° W. Long. Elevation is 820 feet.
Population: 601; Growth (since 2000): 25.7%; Density: 356.8 persons per square mile; Race: 86.7% White, 7.0% Black/African American, 1.8% Asian, 0.5% American Indian/Alaska Native, 1.0% Native Hawaiian/Other Pacific Islander, 0.7% Two or more races, 3.0% Hispanic of any race; Average household size: 2.53; Median age: 38.3; Age under 18: 25.8%; Age 65 and over: 11.8%; Males per 100 females: 89.0
School District(s)
Spartanburg 05 (PK-12)
  2012-13 Enrollment: 7,809 . . . . (864) 949-2350
Housing: Homeownership rate: 79.0%; Homeowner vacancy rate: 2.6%; Rental vacancy rate: 9.1%

ROEBUCK (CDP). Covers a land area of 4.292 square miles and a water area of 0.018 square miles. Located at 34.88° N. Lat; 81.96° W. Long. Elevation is 748 feet.
History: Roebuck was named for Colonel Benjamin Roebuck, commander of the First Spartan Regiment during the last months of the Revolution.
Population: 2,200; Growth (since 2000): 27.5%; Density: 512.6 persons per square mile; Race: 78.7% White, 16.0% Black/African American, 2.4% Asian, 0.0% American Indian/Alaska Native, 0.0% Native Hawaiian/Other Pacific Islander, 1.2% Two or more races, 3.7% Hispanic of any race; Average household size: 2.64; Median age: 39.6; Age under 18: 25.0%; Age 65 and over: 16.0%; Males per 100 females: 93.3
School District(s)
Spartanburg 06 (PK-12)
  2012-13 Enrollment: 11,023 . . . . (864) 576-4212
Housing: Homeownership rate: 77.1%; Homeowner vacancy rate: 1.8%; Rental vacancy rate: 6.3%

SAXON (CDP). Covers a land area of 2.387 square miles and a water area of 0.007 square miles. Located at 34.96° N. Lat; 81.97° W. Long. Elevation is 856 feet.
History: Spartanburg Methodist College here.

Population: 3,424; Growth (since 2000): -7.6%; Density: 1,434.3 persons per square mile; Race: 45.6% White, 34.6% Black/African American, 1.0% Asian, 1.4% American Indian/Alaska Native, 0.0% Native Hawaiian/Other Pacific Islander, 2.5% Two or more races, 22.4% Hispanic of any race; Average household size: 2.71; Median age: 28.4; Age under 18: 23.3%; Age 65 and over: 10.2%; Males per 100 females: 104.3; Marriage status: 53.5% never married, 32.7% now married, 6.5% separated, 2.6% widowed, 11.3% divorced; Foreign born: 9.3%; Speak English only: 87.2%; With disability: 15.7%; Veterans: 7.5%; Ancestry: 12.4% English, 8.9% American, 4.6% Irish, 2.8% German, 2.6% African

Employment: 3.4% management, business, and financial, 0.2% computer, engineering, and science, 6.6% education, legal, community service, arts, and media, 2.7% healthcare practitioners, 31.0% service, 24.1% sales and office, 8.4% natural resources, construction, and maintenance, 23.6% production, transportation, and material moving

Income: Per capita: $10,767; Median household: $22,207; Average household: $33,074; Households with income of $100,000 or more: 2.5%; Poverty rate: 37.3%

Educational Attainment: High school diploma or higher: 62.6%; Bachelor's degree or higher: 5.2%; Graduate/professional degree or higher: 1.5%

Housing: Homeownership rate: 52.2%; Median home value: $43,900; Median year structure built: 1968; Homeowner vacancy rate: 4.8%; Median gross rent: $638 per month; Rental vacancy rate: 17.3%

Health Insurance: 69.4% have insurance; 35.2% have private insurance; 41.6% have public insurance; 30.6% do not have insurance; 9.8% of children under 18 do not have insurance

Transportation: Commute: 92.2% car, 0.0% public transportation, 5.6% walk, 1.6% work from home; Median travel time to work: 19.6 minutes

SOUTHERN SHOPS (CDP). Covers a land area of 3.564 square miles and a water area of 0.011 square miles. Located at 34.98° N. Lat; 81.99° W. Long. Elevation is 876 feet.

Population: 3,767; Growth (since 2000): 1.6%; Density: 1,057.0 persons per square mile; Race: 51.8% White, 17.0% Black/African American, 1.2% Asian, 0.8% American Indian/Alaska Native, 0.0% Native Hawaiian/Other Pacific Islander, 2.9% Two or more races, 40.7% Hispanic of any race; Average household size: 3.08; Median age: 30.4; Age under 18: 26.9%; Age 65 and over: 7.0%; Males per 100 females: 139.8; Marriage status: 43.4% never married, 35.2% now married, 5.3% separated, 5.4% widowed, 16.1% divorced; Foreign born: 27.7%; Speak English only: 57.1%; With disability: 11.3%; Veterans: 8.2%; Ancestry: 9.1% Irish, 6.1% American, 4.9% English, 4.3% German, 3.8% Scotch-Irish

Employment: 1.5% management, business, and financial, 0.6% computer, engineering, and science, 2.5% education, legal, community service, arts, and media, 1.2% healthcare practitioners, 31.7% service, 7.4% sales and office, 20.7% natural resources, construction, and maintenance, 34.5% production, transportation, and material moving

Income: Per capita: $9,600; Median household: $20,378; Average household: $27,130; Households with income of $100,000 or more: 0.8%; Poverty rate: 60.6%

Educational Attainment: High school diploma or higher: 50.2%; Bachelor's degree or higher: 3.9%; Graduate/professional degree or higher: 0.5%

Housing: Homeownership rate: 45.7%; Median home value: $43,600; Median year structure built: 1969; Homeowner vacancy rate: 2.4%; Median gross rent: $638 per month; Rental vacancy rate: 14.3%

Health Insurance: 57.3% have insurance; 19.6% have private insurance; 40.4% have public insurance; 42.7% do not have insurance; 26.1% of children under 18 do not have insurance

Transportation: Commute: 94.1% car, 0.0% public transportation, 3.7% walk, 0.0% work from home; Median travel time to work: 18.8 minutes

SPARTANBURG (city). County seat. Covers a land area of 19.769 square miles and a water area of 0.117 square miles. Located at 34.94° N. Lat; 81.93° W. Long. Elevation is 797 feet.

History: The city and county of Spartanburg derive their name from the Spartan Regiment, a body of South Carolina militia which was formed here in 1776 and served throughout the Revolution. The site for the new county seat was selected in 1785, when Thomas Williamson gave two acres of virgin forest on his plantation for the purpose. Spartanburg was incorporated in 1831. Transportation was an early problem, as the site was not on any established roads or waterways, making the railroad's arrival in 1859 an important event. Spartanburg boomed during the Civil War, supplying provisions and tools for the Confederate forces. The city profited

by war for the second time in 1917, when it became nationally important as the site of Camp Wadsworth.

Population: 37,013; Growth (since 2000): -6.7%; Density: 1,872.2 persons per square mile; Race: 45.6% White, 49.3% Black/African American, 1.8% Asian, 0.2% American Indian/Alaska Native, 0.0% Native Hawaiian/Other Pacific Islander, 1.8% Two or more races, 3.4% Hispanic of any race; Average household size: 2.27; Median age: 35.5; Age under 18: 23.5%; Age 65 and over: 14.6%; Males per 100 females: 79.0; Marriage status: 41.0% never married, 36.8% now married, 4.1% separated, 10.4% widowed, 11.8% divorced; Foreign born: 3.9%; Speak English only: 94.9%; With disability: 16.5%; Veterans: 8.9%; Ancestry: 10.0% English, 7.7% Irish, 7.0% American, 6.6% German, 4.0% Scottish

Employment: 10.4% management, business, and financial, 2.8% computer, engineering, and science, 14.3% education, legal, community service, arts, and media, 6.5% healthcare practitioners, 18.0% service, 26.1% sales and office, 4.7% natural resources, construction, and maintenance, 17.1% production, transportation, and material moving

Income: Per capita: $20,143; Median household: $33,129; Average household: $46,737; Households with income of $100,000 or more: 9.6%; Poverty rate: 26.4%

Educational Attainment: High school diploma or higher: 82.0%; Bachelor's degree or higher: 27.7%; Graduate/professional degree or higher: 12.0%

School District(s)
Deaf & Blind School (PK-12)
 2012-13 Enrollment: 266 . . . . (864) 585-7711
Sc Public Charter SD (PK-12)
 2012-13 Enrollment: 11,500 . . . . (803) 734-8322
Spartanburg 03 (PK-12)
 2012-13 Enrollment: 2,937 . . . . (864) 279-6000
Spartanburg 06 (PK-12)
 2012-13 Enrollment: 11,023 . . . . (864) 576-4212
Spartanburg 07 (PK-12)
 2012-13 Enrollment: 7,175 . . . . (864) 594-4405
Spartanburg 80 (10-12)
 2012-13 Enrollment: n/a . . . . (864) 579-2810

Four-year College(s)
Converse College (Private, Not-for-profit)
 Fall 2013 Enrollment: 1,333 . . . . (864) 596-9000
 2013-14 Tuition: In-state $29,124; Out-of-state $29,124
Sherman College of Straight Chiropractic (Private, Not-for-profit)
 Fall 2013 Enrollment: 286 . . . . (864) 578-8770
University of South Carolina-Upstate (Public)
 Fall 2013 Enrollment: 5,445 . . . . (864) 503-5000
 2013-14 Tuition: In-state $10,198; Out-of-state $20,226
Wofford College (Private, Not-for-profit, United Methodist)
 Fall 2013 Enrollment: 1,615 . . . . (864) 597-4000
 2013-14 Tuition: In-state $35,515; Out-of-state $35,515

Two-year College(s)
Spartanburg Community College (Public)
 Fall 2013 Enrollment: 5,864 . . . . (864) 592-4600
 2013-14 Tuition: In-state $4,830; Out-of-state $7,844
Spartanburg Methodist College (Private, Not-for-profit, United Methodist)
 Fall 2013 Enrollment: 818 . . . . (864) 587-4000
 2013-14 Tuition: In-state $15,745; Out-of-state $15,745
Virginia College-Spartanburg (Private, For-profit)
 Fall 2013 Enrollment: 495 . . . . (864) 504-3200
 2013-14 Tuition: In-state $12,250; Out-of-state $12,250

Vocational/Technical School(s)
Kenneth Shuler School of Cosmetology-Spartanburg (Private, For-profit)
 Fall 2013 Enrollment: 113 . . . . (864) 587-6000
 2013-14 Tuition: $16,750
Palmetto Beauty School (Private, For-profit)
 Fall 2013 Enrollment: 65 . . . . (864) 579-2550
 2013-14 Tuition: $14,600
Regency Beauty Institute-Spartanburg (Private, For-profit)
 Fall 2013 Enrollment: 50 . . . . (800) 787-6456
 2013-14 Tuition: $16,200

Housing: Homeownership rate: 49.1%; Median home value: $121,100; Median year structure built: 1966; Homeowner vacancy rate: 4.9%; Median gross rent: $644 per month; Rental vacancy rate: 13.8%

Health Insurance: 83.3% have insurance; 57.2% have private insurance; 38.0% have public insurance; 16.7% do not have insurance; 6.7% of children under 18 do not have insurance

Hospitals: Mary Black Memorial Hospital (226 beds); Spartanburg Regional Medical Center (588 beds)
Safety: Violent crime rate: 140.5 per 10,000 population; Property crime rate: 711.1 per 10,000 population
Newspapers: Herald-Journal (daily circulation 45400); Inman Times (weekly circulation 3800)
Transportation: Commute: 90.8% car, 1.1% public transportation, 4.2% walk, 2.8% work from home; Median travel time to work: 17.9 minutes; Amtrak: Train service available.
Airports: Spartanburg Downtown Memorial (general aviation)
Additional Information Contacts
City of Spartanburg . . . . (864) 596-2905
  http://www.cityofspartanburg.org

STARTEX (CDP). Covers a land area of 1.531 square miles and a water area of 0.024 square miles. Located at 34.93° N. Lat; 82.10° W. Long. Elevation is 794 feet.
Population: 859; Growth (since 2000): -13.1%; Density: 561.2 persons per square mile; Race: 89.2% White, 6.4% Black/African American, 0.8% Asian, 0.5% American Indian/Alaska Native, 0.0% Native Hawaiian/Other Pacific Islander, 0.8% Two or more races, 4.4% Hispanic of any race; Average household size: 2.53; Median age: 37.8; Age under 18: 24.4%; Age 65 and over: 15.7%; Males per 100 females: 83.9
Housing: Homeownership rate: 69.0%; Homeowner vacancy rate: 4.8%; Rental vacancy rate: 9.3%

UNA (unincorporated postal area)
ZCTA: 29378
  Covers a land area of 0.087 square miles and a water area of 0 square miles. Located at 34.97° N. Lat; 81.97° W. Long. Elevation is 886 feet.
Population: 207; Growth (since 2000): n/a; Density: 2,379.4 persons per square mile; Race: 28.5% White, 41.5% Black/African American, 2.9% Asian, 1.9% American Indian/Alaska Native, 0.0% Native Hawaiian/Other Pacific Islander, 6.3% Two or more races, 34.3% Hispanic of any race; Average household size: 3.00; Median age: 27.5; Age under 18: 31.4%; Age 65 and over: 4.8%; Males per 100 females: 97.1
Housing: Homeownership rate: 26.1%; Homeowner vacancy rate: 0.0%; Rental vacancy rate: 17.7%

VALLEY FALLS (CDP). Covers a land area of 5.183 square miles and a water area of 0.033 square miles. Located at 35.01° N. Lat; 81.97° W. Long. Elevation is 797 feet.
Population: 6,299; Growth (since 2000): 57.9%; Density: 1,215.4 persons per square mile; Race: 68.8% White, 24.6% Black/African American, 1.7% Asian, 0.3% American Indian/Alaska Native, 0.0% Native Hawaiian/Other Pacific Islander, 1.4% Two or more races, 6.6% Hispanic of any race; Average household size: 2.22; Median age: 23.0; Age under 18: 16.5%; Age 65 and over: 9.2%; Males per 100 females: 77.6; Marriage status: 53.3% never married, 36.2% now married, 0.9% separated, 5.0% widowed, 5.5% divorced; Foreign born: 6.7%; Speak English only: 96.0%; With disability: 8.3%; Veterans: 6.2%; Ancestry: 14.2% Irish, 11.4% American, 10.1% German, 7.9% English, 2.5% Scotch-Irish
Employment: 6.1% management, business, and financial, 0.6% computer, engineering, and science, 13.4% education, legal, community service, arts, and media, 5.7% healthcare practitioners, 26.8% service, 29.9% sales and office, 5.9% natural resources, construction, and maintenance, 11.7% production, transportation, and material moving
Income: Per capita: $15,960; Median household: $36,661; Average household: $42,112; Households with income of $100,000 or more: 8.7%; Poverty rate: 24.1%
Educational Attainment: High school diploma or higher: 83.5%; Bachelor's degree or higher: 25.2%; Graduate/professional degree or higher: 7.4%
Housing: Homeownership rate: 40.7%; Median home value: $125,500; Median year structure built: 1994; Homeowner vacancy rate: 3.4%; Median gross rent: $653 per month; Rental vacancy rate: 14.3%
Health Insurance: 82.0% have insurance; 67.2% have private insurance; 23.9% have public insurance; 18.0% do not have insurance; 22.4% of children under 18 do not have insurance
Transportation: Commute: 92.4% car, 0.0% public transportation, 3.7% walk, 3.5% work from home; Median travel time to work: 20.6 minutes

WELLFORD (city). Covers a land area of 4.323 square miles and a water area of 0.018 square miles. Located at 34.95° N. Lat; 82.10° W. Long. Elevation is 863 feet.
Population: 2,378; Growth (since 2000): 17.1%; Density: 550.1 persons per square mile; Race: 47.7% White, 46.5% Black/African American, 0.8% Asian, 0.4% American Indian/Alaska Native, 0.0% Native Hawaiian/Other Pacific Islander, 2.8% Two or more races, 4.2% Hispanic of any race; Average household size: 2.42; Median age: 40.3; Age under 18: 22.3%; Age 65 and over: 15.6%; Males per 100 females: 87.2
School District(s)
Spartanburg 05 (PK-12)
  2012-13 Enrollment: 7,809 . . . . (864) 949-2350
Housing: Homeownership rate: 64.7%; Homeowner vacancy rate: 2.8%; Rental vacancy rate: 9.2%
Safety: Violent crime rate: 12.4 per 10,000 population; Property crime rate: 123.6 per 10,000 population

WOODRUFF (city). Covers a land area of 3.912 square miles and a water area of 0.021 square miles. Located at 34.74° N. Lat; 82.03° W. Long. Elevation is 787 feet.
History: Woodruff was variously known as The Hill, Cross Roads, and Woodruff Tavern until 1876, when it was surveyed and incorporated under the present name.
Population: 4,090; Growth (since 2000): -3.3%; Density: 1,045.6 persons per square mile; Race: 66.5% White, 25.2% Black/African American, 0.4% Asian, 0.1% American Indian/Alaska Native, 0.0% Native Hawaiian/Other Pacific Islander, 3.0% Two or more races, 7.7% Hispanic of any race; Average household size: 2.51; Median age: 38.0; Age under 18: 25.9%; Age 65 and over: 16.9%; Males per 100 females: 89.2; Marriage status: 26.9% never married, 51.4% now married, 9.8% separated, 12.6% widowed, 9.0% divorced; Foreign born: 2.3%; Speak English only: 94.7%; With disability: 15.4%; Veterans: 7.1%; Ancestry: 12.6% Irish, 6.9% English, 6.4% Italian, 6.0% American, 5.3% German
Employment: 7.7% management, business, and financial, 2.2% computer, engineering, and science, 6.7% education, legal, community service, arts, and media, 1.1% healthcare practitioners, 26.7% service, 13.7% sales and office, 22.5% natural resources, construction, and maintenance, 19.4% production, transportation, and material moving
Income: Per capita: $13,925; Median household: $31,997; Average household: $38,541; Households with income of $100,000 or more: 4.7%; Poverty rate: 30.2%
Educational Attainment: High school diploma or higher: 58.7%; Bachelor's degree or higher: 8.4%; Graduate/professional degree or higher: 2.8%
School District(s)
Spartanburg 04 (PK-12)
  2012-13 Enrollment: 2,838 . . . . (864) 476-3186
Housing: Homeownership rate: 56.2%; Median home value: $65,400; Median year structure built: 1964; Homeowner vacancy rate: 3.5%; Median gross rent: $573 per month; Rental vacancy rate: 10.1%
Health Insurance: 75.2% have insurance; 31.3% have private insurance; 50.8% have public insurance; 24.8% do not have insurance; 8.3% of children under 18 do not have insurance
Safety: Violent crime rate: 60.7 per 10,000 population; Property crime rate: 235.3 per 10,000 population
Newspapers: Hometown News (weekly circulation 35000)
Transportation: Commute: 96.9% car, 0.0% public transportation, 0.0% walk, 0.0% work from home; Median travel time to work: 28.0 minutes
Additional Information Contacts
City of Woodruff . . . . (864) 476-8154
  http://www.cityofwoodruff.com

Sumter County

Located in central South Carolina; bounded on the west by the Wateree River, and on the northeast by the Lynches River; drained by the Black River; includes part of Lake Marion. Covers a land area of 665.066 square miles, a water area of 17.019 square miles, and is located in the Eastern Time Zone at 33.92° N. Lat., 80.38° W. Long. The county was founded in 1798. County seat is Sumter.

Sumter County is part of the Sumter, SC Metropolitan Statistical Area. The entire metro area includes: Sumter County, SC

Weather Station: Sumter   Elevation: 176 feet

	Jan	Feb	Mar	Apr	May	Jun	Jul	Aug	Sep	Oct	Nov	Dec
High	56	60	67	76	83	89	92	90	85	75	67	58
Low	33	35	41	49	57	66	70	69	63	51	42	35
Precip	4.0	3.5	4.0	3.1	3.3	5.1	5.1	4.8	3.9	3.4	3.0	3.3
Snow	0.1	0.2	tr	0.0	0.0	0.0	0.0	0.0	0.0	0.0	0.0	tr

High and Low temperatures in degrees Fahrenheit; Precipitation and Snow in inches

Population: 107,456; Growth (since 2000): 2.7%; Density: 161.6 persons per square mile; Race: 48.2% White, 46.9% Black/African American, 1.1% Asian, 0.4% American Indian/Alaska Native, 0.1% Native Hawaiian/Other Pacific Islander, 1.9% two or more races, 3.3% Hispanic of any race; Average household size: 2.59; Median age: 35.4; Age under 18: 25.5%; Age 65 and over: 13.0%; Males per 100 females: 92.8; Marriage status: 34.0% never married, 48.7% now married, 3.6% separated, 7.2% widowed, 10.1% divorced; Foreign born: 3.5%; Speak English only: 95.2%; With disability: 16.8%; Veterans: 15.4%; Ancestry: 11.6% American, 6.3% Irish, 6.3% German, 6.0% English, 5.4% African
Religion: Six largest groups: 23.3% Baptist, 14.3% Methodist/Pietist, 6.0% Non-denominational Protestant, 2.7% Presbyterian-Reformed, 2.1% Pentecostal, 1.8% Catholicism
Economy: Unemployment rate: 7.0%; Leading industries: 22.5% retail trade; 12.9% other services (except public administration); 10.8% health care and social assistance; Farms: 515 totaling 176,002 acres; Company size: 1 employs 1,000 or more persons, 7 employ 500 to 999 persons, 36 employ 100 to 499 persons, 1,729 employ less than 100 persons; Business ownership: 2,157 women-owned, 1,668 Black-owned, 137 Hispanic-owned, 230 Asian-owned
Employment: 10.0% management, business, and financial, 3.5% computer, engineering, and science, 10.2% education, legal, community service, arts, and media, 5.7% healthcare practitioners, 19.0% service, 23.5% sales and office, 9.8% natural resources, construction, and maintenance, 18.2% production, transportation, and material moving
Income: Per capita: $20,340; Median household: $41,366; Average household: $53,133; Households with income of $100,000 or more: 11.6%; Poverty rate: 17.9%
Educational Attainment: High school diploma or higher: 82.3%; Bachelor's degree or higher: 19.2%; Graduate/professional degree or higher: 7.1%
Housing: Homeownership rate: 66.8%; Median home value: $107,300; Median year structure built: 1982; Homeowner vacancy rate: 2.4%; Median gross rent: $726 per month; Rental vacancy rate: 10.3%
Vital Statistics: Birth rate: 141.4 per 10,000 population; Death rate: 90.6 per 10,000 population; Age-adjusted cancer mortality rate: 202.6 deaths per 100,000 population
Health Insurance: 83.4% have insurance; 57.3% have private insurance; 38.3% have public insurance; 16.6% do not have insurance; 6.5% of children under 18 do not have insurance
Health Care: Physicians: 14.1 per 10,000 population; Hospital beds: 24.2 per 10,000 population; Hospital admissions: 823.8 per 10,000 population
Transportation: Commute: 95.3% car, 0.2% public transportation, 1.7% walk, 1.7% work from home; Median travel time to work: 21.9 minutes
Presidential Election: 58.3% Obama, 40.7% Romney (2012)
National and State Parks: Manchester State Forest; Poinsett State Forest; Poinsett State Park; Woods Bay State Park
Additional Information Contacts
Sumter Government . . . . (803) 436-2227
    http://www.sumtercountysc.org

Sumter County Communities

CANE SAVANNAH (CDP). Covers a land area of 3.618 square miles and a water area of 0.070 square miles. Located at 33.89° N. Lat; 80.44° W. Long. Elevation is 184 feet.
Population: 1,117; Growth (since 2000): -23.1%; Density: 308.7 persons per square mile; Race: 60.8% White, 35.7% Black/African American, 0.2% Asian, 0.4% American Indian/Alaska Native, 0.2% Native Hawaiian/Other Pacific Islander, 2.6% Two or more races, 1.3% Hispanic of any race; Average household size: 2.69; Median age: 39.8; Age under 18: 23.4%; Age 65 and over: 11.3%; Males per 100 females: 91.9
Housing: Homeownership rate: 81.8%; Homeowner vacancy rate: 1.7%; Rental vacancy rate: 9.4%

CHERRYVALE (CDP). Covers a land area of 1.809 square miles and a water area of 0.031 square miles. Located at 33.95° N. Lat; 80.46° W. Long. Elevation is 207 feet.
Population: 2,496; Growth (since 2000): 1.4%; Density: 1,379.9 persons per square mile; Race: 35.9% White, 56.5% Black/African American, 1.3% Asian, 0.6% American Indian/Alaska Native, 0.1% Native Hawaiian/Other Pacific Islander, 3.7% Two or more races, 4.2% Hispanic of any race; Average household size: 2.55; Median age: 29.2; Age under 18: 29.3%; Age 65 and over: 8.9%; Males per 100 females: 89.8
Housing: Homeownership rate: 41.9%; Homeowner vacancy rate: 6.1%; Rental vacancy rate: 17.4%

DALZELL (CDP). Covers a land area of 5.886 square miles and a water area of 0.048 square miles. Located at 34.02° N. Lat; 80.43° W. Long. Elevation is 217 feet.
History: Dalzell may be the home of descendants of two pirates, a Turk and a Frenchman, who joined the Revolution as scouts under General Sumter.
Population: 3,059; Growth (since 2000): 35.4%; Density: 519.7 persons per square mile; Race: 55.0% White, 39.3% Black/African American, 1.3% Asian, 0.5% American Indian/Alaska Native, 0.2% Native Hawaiian/Other Pacific Islander, 2.7% Two or more races, 2.8% Hispanic of any race; Average household size: 2.68; Median age: 29.4; Age under 18: 30.1%; Age 65 and over: 8.3%; Males per 100 females: 93.5; Marriage status: 40.2% never married, 53.1% now married, 2.3% separated, 2.1% widowed, 4.6% divorced; Foreign born: 2.4%; Speak English only: 89.9%; With disability: 13.8%; Veterans: 32.1%; Ancestry: 21.3% American, 17.3% German, 8.9% African, 6.9% Irish, 4.2% Serbian
Employment: 16.1% management, business, and financial, 1.6% computer, engineering, and science, 14.5% education, legal, community service, arts, and media, 8.2% healthcare practitioners, 22.2% service, 15.1% sales and office, 11.8% natural resources, construction, and maintenance, 10.5% production, transportation, and material moving
Income: Per capita: $19,554; Median household: $51,783; Average household: $56,205; Households with income of $100,000 or more: 9.2%; Poverty rate: 15.0%
Educational Attainment: High school diploma or higher: 87.5%; Bachelor's degree or higher: 21.9%; Graduate/professional degree or higher: 7.4%
School District(s)
Sumter 01 (PK-12)
    2012-13 Enrollment: 16,796 . . . . (803) 469-6900
Housing: Homeownership rate: 73.3%; Median home value: $114,300; Median year structure built: 1994; Homeowner vacancy rate: 2.0%; Median gross rent: $736 per month; Rental vacancy rate: 9.1%
Health Insurance: 96.5% have insurance; 70.0% have private insurance; 34.8% have public insurance; 3.5% do not have insurance; 0.0% of children under 18 do not have insurance
Transportation: Commute: 99.1% car, 0.0% public transportation, 0.0% walk, 0.9% work from home; Median travel time to work: 24.1 minutes

EAST SUMTER (CDP). Covers a land area of 3.318 square miles and a water area of 0.005 square miles. Located at 33.93° N. Lat; 80.29° W. Long. Elevation is 144 feet.
Population: 1,343; Growth (since 2000): 10.1%; Density: 404.8 persons per square mile; Race: 43.3% White, 51.2% Black/African American, 0.6% Asian, 0.4% American Indian/Alaska Native, 0.0% Native Hawaiian/Other Pacific Islander, 0.4% Two or more races, 6.0% Hispanic of any race; Average household size: 2.56; Median age: 37.8; Age under 18: 24.9%; Age 65 and over: 14.7%; Males per 100 females: 85.2
Housing: Homeownership rate: 74.3%; Homeowner vacancy rate: 1.7%; Rental vacancy rate: 8.2%

HORATIO (unincorporated postal area)
ZCTA: 29062
    Covers a land area of 16.192 square miles and a water area of 0.433 square miles. Located at 34.00° N. Lat; 80.61° W. Long. Elevation is 144 feet.
    Population: 176; Growth (since 2000): 89.2%; Density: 10.9 persons per square mile; Race: 31.8% White, 65.9% Black/African American, 1.7% Asian, 0.0% American Indian/Alaska Native, 0.0% Native Hawaiian/Other Pacific Islander, 0.6% Two or more races, 0.0% Hispanic of any race; Average household size: 2.32; Median age: 47.0; Age under 18: 17.6%; Age 65 and over: 18.2%; Males per 100 females: 107.1

Housing: Homeownership rate: 82.8%; Homeowner vacancy rate: 1.6%; Rental vacancy rate: 0.0%

LAKEWOOD (CDP). Covers a land area of 7.558 square miles and a water area of 0.174 square miles. Located at 33.84° N. Lat; 80.35° W. Long. Elevation is 177 feet.
Population: 3,032; Growth (since 2000): 16.5%; Density: 401.2 persons per square mile; Race: 61.5% White, 34.1% Black/African American, 0.8% Asian, 0.2% American Indian/Alaska Native, 0.0% Native Hawaiian/Other Pacific Islander, 1.8% Two or more races, 3.7% Hispanic of any race; Average household size: 2.68; Median age: 39.0; Age under 18: 26.5%; Age 65 and over: 11.0%; Males per 100 females: 95.7; Marriage status: 25.6% never married, 60.7% now married, 1.1% separated, 5.1% widowed, 8.5% divorced; Foreign born: 3.2%; Speak English only: 96.8%; With disability: 7.8%; Veterans: 6.0%; Ancestry: 17.0% American, 7.5% German, 7.4% English, 7.3% Irish, 2.4% African
Employment: 16.0% management, business, and financial, 3.6% computer, engineering, and science, 8.9% education, legal, community service, arts, and media, 9.8% healthcare practitioners, 12.0% service, 16.2% sales and office, 10.9% natural resources, construction, and maintenance, 22.7% production, transportation, and material moving
Income: Per capita: $20,532; Median household: $51,094; Average household: $59,603; Households with income of $100,000 or more: 17.4%; Poverty rate: 12.3%
Educational Attainment: High school diploma or higher: 85.0%; Bachelor's degree or higher: 17.5%; Graduate/professional degree or higher: 6.1%
Housing: Homeownership rate: 76.3%; Median home value: $122,500; Median year structure built: 1987; Homeowner vacancy rate: 2.0%; Median gross rent: $769 per month; Rental vacancy rate: 5.9%
Health Insurance: 91.5% have insurance; 66.8% have private insurance; 31.9% have public insurance; 8.5% do not have insurance; 0.0% of children under 18 do not have insurance
Transportation: Commute: 96.9% car, 0.0% public transportation, 1.2% walk, 1.9% work from home; Median travel time to work: 22.4 minutes

---

MAYESVILLE (town). Covers a land area of 1.024 square miles and a water area of 0 square miles. Located at 33.98° N. Lat; 80.20° W. Long. Elevation is 144 feet.
History: Mayesville is the birthplace of Mary McLeod Bethune, who worked as a teacher and missionary in South Carolina for many years.
Population: 731; Growth (since 2000): -27.0%; Density: 714.0 persons per square mile; Race: 14.9% White, 83.0% Black/African American, 0.1% Asian, 0.0% American Indian/Alaska Native, 0.0% Native Hawaiian/Other Pacific Islander, 1.0% Two or more races, 2.2% Hispanic of any race; Average household size: 2.66; Median age: 45.3; Age under 18: 21.8%; Age 65 and over: 15.3%; Males per 100 females: 83.2
School District(s)
Lee 01 (PK-12)
    2012-13 Enrollment: 2,249 . . . . (803) 484-5327
Housing: Homeownership rate: 79.6%; Homeowner vacancy rate: 1.3%; Rental vacancy rate: 4.9%

MULBERRY (CDP). Covers a land area of 1.964 square miles and a water area of 0.017 square miles. Located at 33.96° N. Lat; 80.33° W. Long. Elevation is 144 feet.
Population: 529; Growth (since 2000): -37.1%; Density: 269.3 persons per square mile; Race: 46.9% White, 40.3% Black/African American, 0.0% Asian, 0.0% American Indian/Alaska Native, 0.0% Native Hawaiian/Other Pacific Islander, 1.7% Two or more races, 13.0% Hispanic of any race; Average household size: 2.56; Median age: 39.4; Age under 18: 22.9%; Age 65 and over: 17.2%; Males per 100 females: 94.5
Housing: Homeownership rate: 62.9%; Homeowner vacancy rate: 1.6%; Rental vacancy rate: 7.4%

OAKLAND (CDP). Covers a land area of 0.680 square miles and a water area of 0.006 square miles. Located at 33.99° N. Lat; 80.50° W. Long. Elevation is 338 feet.
Population: 1,232; Growth (since 2000): -3.1%; Density: 1,811.2 persons per square mile; Race: 55.7% White, 36.7% Black/African American, 2.4% Asian, 0.5% American Indian/Alaska Native, 0.2% Native Hawaiian/Other Pacific Islander, 3.7% Two or more races, 5.3% Hispanic of any race; Average household size: 2.44; Median age: 35.1; Age under 18: 26.1%; Age 65 and over: 19.0%; Males per 100 females: 86.9

Housing: Homeownership rate: 63.1%; Homeowner vacancy rate: 3.0%; Rental vacancy rate: 5.0%

OSWEGO (CDP). Covers a land area of 1.205 square miles and a water area of 0 square miles. Located at 34.01° N. Lat; 80.29° W. Long. Elevation is 154 feet.
Population: 84; Growth (since 2000): -11.6%; Density: 69.7 persons per square mile; Race: 86.9% White, 13.1% Black/African American, 0.0% Asian, 0.0% American Indian/Alaska Native, 0.0% Native Hawaiian/Other Pacific Islander, 0.0% Two or more races, 2.4% Hispanic of any race; Average household size: 2.27; Median age: 50.7; Age under 18: 21.4%; Age 65 and over: 26.2%; Males per 100 females: 104.9
Housing: Homeownership rate: 83.8%; Homeowner vacancy rate: 6.1%; Rental vacancy rate: 14.3%

PINEWOOD (town). Covers a land area of 1.071 square miles and a water area of 0 square miles. Located at 33.74° N. Lat; 80.46° W. Long. Elevation is 190 feet.
Population: 538; Growth (since 2000): 17.2%; Density: 502.4 persons per square mile; Race: 38.8% White, 59.7% Black/African American, 0.6% Asian, 0.2% American Indian/Alaska Native, 0.0% Native Hawaiian/Other Pacific Islander, 0.2% Two or more races, 0.6% Hispanic of any race; Average household size: 2.32; Median age: 40.7; Age under 18: 24.9%; Age 65 and over: 18.6%; Males per 100 females: 71.9
School District(s)
Sumter 01 (PK-12)
    2012-13 Enrollment: 16,796 . . . . (803) 469-6900
Housing: Homeownership rate: 59.0%; Homeowner vacancy rate: 2.8%; Rental vacancy rate: 8.7%

PRIVATEER (CDP). Covers a land area of 8.164 square miles and a water area of 0.061 square miles. Located at 33.82° N. Lat; 80.39° W. Long. Elevation is 171 feet.
Population: 2,349; Growth (since 2000): 10.9%; Density: 287.7 persons per square mile; Race: 83.3% White, 11.9% Black/African American, 0.2% Asian, 0.4% American Indian/Alaska Native, 0.0% Native Hawaiian/Other Pacific Islander, 2.3% Two or more races, 4.8% Hispanic of any race; Average household size: 2.83; Median age: 35.5; Age under 18: 26.5%; Age 65 and over: 10.9%; Males per 100 females: 94.9
Housing: Homeownership rate: 76.7%; Homeowner vacancy rate: 0.6%; Rental vacancy rate: 7.1%

REMBERT (CDP). Covers a land area of 3.836 square miles and a water area of 0 square miles. Located at 34.10° N. Lat; 80.53° W. Long. Elevation is 213 feet.
Population: 306; Growth (since 2000): -24.6%; Density: 79.8 persons per square mile; Race: 24.5% White, 65.7% Black/African American, 0.0% Asian, 0.7% American Indian/Alaska Native, 0.0% Native Hawaiian/Other Pacific Islander, 3.3% Two or more races, 7.2% Hispanic of any race; Average household size: 2.83; Median age: 42.4; Age under 18: 22.2%; Age 65 and over: 14.7%; Males per 100 females: 87.7
School District(s)
Dept of Correction N04 (09-12)
    2012-13 Enrollment: 752 . . . . (803) 896-8556
Lee 01 (PK-12)
    2012-13 Enrollment: 2,249 . . . . (803) 484-5327
Sumter 01 (PK-12)
    2012-13 Enrollment: 16,796 . . . . (803) 469-6900
Housing: Homeownership rate: 80.5%; Homeowner vacancy rate: 2.2%; Rental vacancy rate: 8.7%

SHAW AFB (unincorporated postal area)
ZCTA: 29152
    Covers a land area of 4.648 square miles and a water area of 0.025 square miles. Located at 33.97° N. Lat; 80.47° W. Long..
    Population: 2,393; Growth (since 2000): -61.5%; Density: 514.8 persons per square mile; Race: 70.8% White, 16.4% Black/African American, 1.8% Asian, 0.3% American Indian/Alaska Native, 0.6% Native Hawaiian/Other Pacific Islander, 7.0% Two or more races, 9.6% Hispanic of any race; Average household size: 3.23; Median age: 21.7; Age under 18: 31.1%; Age 65 and over: 0.4%; Males per 100 females: 140.0
School District(s)
Sumter 01 (PK-12)
    2012-13 Enrollment: 16,796 . . . . (803) 469-6900

Housing: Homeownership rate: 2.8%; Homeowner vacancy rate: 0.0%; Rental vacancy rate: 13.8%

SHILOH (CDP). Covers a land area of 9.732 square miles and a water area of 0.022 square miles. Located at 33.95° N. Lat; 80.02° W. Long. Elevation is 121 feet.
Population: 214; Growth (since 2000): -17.4%; Density: 22.0 persons per square mile; Race: 41.1% White, 55.1% Black/African American, 0.0% Asian, 0.0% American Indian/Alaska Native, 0.0% Native Hawaiian/Other Pacific Islander, 1.4% Two or more races, 5.1% Hispanic of any race; Average household size: 2.74; Median age: 40.3; Age under 18: 23.8%; Age 65 and over: 18.2%; Males per 100 females: 76.9
Housing: Homeownership rate: 82.0%; Homeowner vacancy rate: 0.0%; Rental vacancy rate: 12.5%

SOUTH SUMTER (CDP). Covers a land area of 2.398 square miles and a water area of 0 square miles. Located at 33.89° N. Lat; 80.34° W. Long. Elevation is 161 feet.
Population: 2,411; Growth (since 2000): -28.4%; Density: 1,005.5 persons per square mile; Race: 9.0% White, 89.0% Black/African American, 0.0% Asian, 0.2% American Indian/Alaska Native, 0.1% Native Hawaiian/Other Pacific Islander, 0.7% Two or more races, 2.2% Hispanic of any race; Average household size: 2.72; Median age: 34.6; Age under 18: 27.7%; Age 65 and over: 12.4%; Males per 100 females: 81.4
Housing: Homeownership rate: 58.3%; Homeowner vacancy rate: 1.5%; Rental vacancy rate: 4.8%

STATEBURG (CDP). Covers a land area of 4.649 square miles and a water area of 0.031 square miles. Located at 33.97° N. Lat; 80.53° W. Long. Elevation is 305 feet.
Population: 1,380; Growth (since 2000): 9.2%; Density: 296.8 persons per square mile; Race: 74.7% White, 20.1% Black/African American, 2.0% Asian, 0.7% American Indian/Alaska Native, 0.0% Native Hawaiian/Other Pacific Islander, 2.2% Two or more races, 1.3% Hispanic of any race; Average household size: 2.54; Median age: 44.6; Age under 18: 22.1%; Age 65 and over: 15.4%; Males per 100 females: 99.7
Housing: Homeownership rate: 85.7%; Homeowner vacancy rate: 0.9%; Rental vacancy rate: 11.2%

SUMTER (city). County seat. Covers a land area of 32.086 square miles and a water area of 0.203 square miles. Located at 33.94° N. Lat; 80.40° W. Long. Elevation is 171 feet.
History: The city of Sumter was first called Sumterville after Revolutionary General Thomas Sumter, whose home was nearby. In 1798 the village was selected for the courthouse of old Sumter District, and town lines were laid out in 1800. With no access to waterways or railroad, development was slow. The Camden branch of the South Carolina Railroad reached the town in 1843, followed by other railroads and a system of highways, and the town was incorporated in 1845. It is recorded that a Sumter soldier, George E. Haynesworth, fired the first shot of the Civil War on January 9, 1861. In 1912 Sumter was first in the U.S. to adopt the commission-city-manager form of government.
Population: 40,524; Growth (since 2000): 2.2%; Density: 1,263.0 persons per square mile; Race: 45.3% White, 49.1% Black/African American, 1.6% Asian, 0.3% American Indian/Alaska Native, 0.1% Native Hawaiian/Other Pacific Islander, 2.1% Two or more races, 3.6% Hispanic of any race; Average household size: 2.48; Median age: 32.5; Age under 18: 25.9%; Age 65 and over: 13.9%; Males per 100 females: 88.9; Marriage status: 35.4% never married, 46.6% now married, 4.0% separated, 8.2% widowed, 9.8% divorced; Foreign born: 3.7%; Speak English only: 95.2%; With disability: 16.6%; Veterans: 15.6%; Ancestry: 9.3% American, 6.8% German, 6.2% Irish, 6.1% English, 6.0% African
Employment: 9.8% management, business, and financial, 4.7% computer, engineering, and science, 13.2% education, legal, community service, arts, and media, 7.1% healthcare practitioners, 20.1% service, 22.8% sales and office, 8.5% natural resources, construction, and maintenance, 13.8% production, transportation, and material moving
Income: Per capita: $22,572; Median household: $39,429; Average household: $54,769; Households with income of $100,000 or more: 13.1%; Poverty rate: 20.2%
Educational Attainment: High school diploma or higher: 85.7%; Bachelor's degree or higher: 24.7%; Graduate/professional degree or higher: 9.8%

School District(s)
Sumter 01 (PK-12)
    2012-13 Enrollment: 16,796 . . . . (803) 469-6900
Four-year College(s)
Morris College (Private, Not-for-profit, Historically black, Baptist)
    Fall 2013 Enrollment: 824 . . . . (803) 934-3200
    2013-14 Tuition: In-state $11,087; Out-of-state $11,087
Two-year College(s)
Central Carolina Technical College (Public)
    Fall 2013 Enrollment: 4,456 . . . . (803) 778-1961
    2013-14 Tuition: In-state $4,361; Out-of-state $6,400
University of South Carolina-Sumter (Public)
    Fall 2013 Enrollment: 924 . . . . (803) 775-8727
    2013-14 Tuition: In-state $6,482; Out-of-state $15,632
Vocational/Technical School(s)
Sumter Beauty College (Private, For-profit)
    Fall 2013 Enrollment: 28 . . . . (803) 773-7311
    2013-14 Tuition: $9,750
Housing: Homeownership rate: 53.3%; Median home value: $133,900; Median year structure built: 1977; Homeowner vacancy rate: 3.8%; Median gross rent: $718 per month; Rental vacancy rate: 10.4%
Health Insurance: 85.6% have insurance; 59.6% have private insurance; 39.4% have public insurance; 14.4% do not have insurance; 4.1% of children under 18 do not have insurance
Hospitals: Tuomey Healthcare System (266 beds)
Safety: Violent crime rate: 94.6 per 10,000 population; Property crime rate: 492.1 per 10,000 population
Newspapers: The Item (daily circulation 19100)
Transportation: Commute: 93.1% car, 0.3% public transportation, 3.2% walk, 1.7% work from home; Median travel time to work: 19.2 minutes
Airports: Shaw AFB (general aviation); Sumter (general aviation)
Additional Information Contacts
City of Sumter . . . . (803) 436-2500
    http://www.sumter-sc.com

WEDGEFIELD (CDP). Covers a land area of 8.480 square miles and a water area of 0.113 square miles. Located at 33.88° N. Lat; 80.52° W. Long. Elevation is 249 feet.
Population: 1,615; Growth (since 2000): n/a; Density: 190.4 persons per square mile; Race: 63.7% White, 32.1% Black/African American, 1.2% Asian, 0.2% American Indian/Alaska Native, 0.0% Native Hawaiian/Other Pacific Islander, 2.4% Two or more races, 1.8% Hispanic of any race; Average household size: 2.77; Median age: 37.5; Age under 18: 27.8%; Age 65 and over: 12.6%; Males per 100 females: 101.4
School District(s)
Sumter 01 (PK-12)
    2012-13 Enrollment: 16,796 . . . . (803) 469-6900
Housing: Homeownership rate: 73.5%; Homeowner vacancy rate: 2.5%; Rental vacancy rate: 10.5%

Union County

Located in northern South Carolina; bounded on the north by the Pacolet River, on the south by the Enoree River, and on the east by the Broad River; drained by the Tyger River; includes part of Sumter National Forest. Covers a land area of 514.171 square miles, a water area of 1.855 square miles, and is located in the Eastern Time Zone at 34.69° N. Lat., 81.62° W. Long. The county was founded in 1798. County seat is Union.

Union County is part of the Spartanburg, SC Metropolitan Statistical Area. The entire metro area includes: Spartanburg County, SC; Union County, SC

Weather Station: Santuck										Elevation: 520 feet		
	Jan	Feb	Mar	Apr	May	Jun	Jul	Aug	Sep	Oct	Nov	Dec
High	54	58	66	75	82	88	91	89	82	72	64	55
Low	33	36	41	49	58	66	70	69	62	51	42	35
Precip	4.0	3.9	4.5	3.0	2.7	3.9	3.4	4.2	4.1	3.6	3.5	3.6
Snow	1.7	1.3	0.7	tr	tr	0.0	0.0	0.0	0.0	0.0	tr	0.2

High and Low temperatures in degrees Fahrenheit; Precipitation and Snow in inches

Weather Station: Union 8 SW | | | | | | | | | Elevation: 560 feet

	Jan	Feb	Mar	Apr	May	Jun	Jul	Aug	Sep	Oct	Nov	Dec
High	52	57	65	73	81	87	90	89	82	73	64	54
Low	28	30	36	44	53	63	67	66	59	46	37	29
Precip	4.4	4.0	4.9	3.5	3.0	4.1	3.4	4.0	3.5	3.8	3.6	3.6
Snow	1.3	0.7	0.1	0.0	0.0	0.0	0.0	0.0	0.0	0.0	0.0	0.1

High and Low temperatures in degrees Fahrenheit; Precipitation and Snow in inches

Population: 28,961; Growth (since 2000): -3.1%; Density: 56.3 persons per square mile; Race: 66.6% White, 31.3% Black/African American, 0.3% Asian, 0.2% American Indian/Alaska Native, 0.0% Native Hawaiian/Other Pacific Islander, 1.2% two or more races, 1.0% Hispanic of any race; Average household size: 2.38; Median age: 41.9; Age under 18: 22.8%; Age 65 and over: 16.5%; Males per 100 females: 90.8; Marriage status: 29.0% never married, 50.3% now married, 4.2% separated, 8.8% widowed, 11.9% divorced; Foreign born: 0.7%; Speak English only: 98.3%; With disability: 20.4%; Veterans: 9.3%; Ancestry: 13.7% American, 7.9% Irish, 6.8% English, 6.2% German, 2.5% Scottish
Religion: Six largest groups: 57.9% Baptist, 16.4% Methodist/Pietist, 2.0% Non-denominational Protestant, 1.7% Pentecostal, 1.3% Presbyterian-Reformed, 0.6% Latter-day Saints
Economy: Unemployment rate: 7.9%; Leading industries: 21.7% retail trade; 18.0% other services (except public administration); 8.6% finance and insurance; Farms: 264 totaling 47,312 acres; Company size: 0 employ 1,000 or more persons, 2 employ 500 to 999 persons, 10 employ 100 to 499 persons, 444 employ less than 100 persons; Business ownership: 522 women-owned, 298 Black-owned, n/a Hispanic-owned, n/a Asian-owned
Employment: 7.0% management, business, and financial, 1.2% computer, engineering, and science, 10.2% education, legal, community service, arts, and media, 5.3% healthcare practitioners, 16.2% service, 23.8% sales and office, 10.8% natural resources, construction, and maintenance, 25.7% production, transportation, and material moving
Income: Per capita: $19,037; Median household: $32,556; Average household: $44,480; Households with income of $100,000 or more: 9.0%; Poverty rate: 20.1%
Educational Attainment: High school diploma or higher: 78.1%; Bachelor's degree or higher: 12.9%; Graduate/professional degree or higher: 4.3%
Housing: Homeownership rate: 71.8%; Median home value: $74,000; Median year structure built: 1973; Homeowner vacancy rate: 2.0%; Median gross rent: $610 per month; Rental vacancy rate: 10.3%
Vital Statistics: Birth rate: 102.0 per 10,000 population; Death rate: 126.7 per 10,000 population; Age-adjusted cancer mortality rate: 219.1 deaths per 100,000 population
Health Insurance: 83.8% have insurance; 58.5% have private insurance; 40.5% have public insurance; 16.2% do not have insurance; 9.9% of children under 18 do not have insurance
Health Care: Physicians: 7.1 per 10,000 population; Hospital beds: 60.0 per 10,000 population; Hospital admissions: 951.5 per 10,000 population
Transportation: Commute: 95.8% car, 0.2% public transportation, 1.3% walk, 1.7% work from home; Median travel time to work: 26.4 minutes
Presidential Election: 46.2% Obama, 52.5% Romney (2012)
National and State Parks: Rose Hill State Park
Additional Information Contacts
Union Government . . . . (864) 429-1630
    http://www.countyofunion.com

Union County Communities

BUFFALO (CDP). Covers a land area of 4.025 square miles and a water area of 0 square miles. Located at 34.72° N. Lat; 81.68° W. Long. Elevation is 591 feet.
History: Buffalo, which began as a mill town, preserves in its name the memory of the wild buffalo that once roamed the country and used the salt licks nearby.
Population: 1,266; Growth (since 2000): -11.2%; Density: 314.5 persons per square mile; Race: 84.6% White, 14.1% Black/African American, 0.2% Asian, 0.1% American Indian/Alaska Native, 0.1% Native Hawaiian/Other Pacific Islander, 0.8% Two or more races, 0.6% Hispanic of any race; Average household size: 2.44; Median age: 38.8; Age under 18: 22.3%; Age 65 and over: 15.3%; Males per 100 females: 96.3
School District(s)
Union 01 (PK-12)
    2012-13 Enrollment: 4,140 . . . . (864) 429-1740

Housing: Homeownership rate: 67.9%; Homeowner vacancy rate: 1.9%; Rental vacancy rate: 8.6%

CARLISLE (town). Covers a land area of 1.416 square miles and a water area of 0 square miles. Located at 34.59° N. Lat; 81.46° W. Long. Elevation is 456 feet.
History: Called Fish Dam until 1890, Carlisle was named for the Reverend Coleman Carlisle, a Methodist minister.
Population: 436; Growth (since 2000): -12.1%; Density: 307.9 persons per square mile; Race: 8.9% White, 87.8% Black/African American, 0.2% Asian, 0.0% American Indian/Alaska Native, 0.0% Native Hawaiian/Other Pacific Islander, 3.0% Two or more races, 0.0% Hispanic of any race; Average household size: 2.44; Median age: 43.0; Age under 18: 23.9%; Age 65 and over: 16.3%; Males per 100 females: 94.6
Housing: Homeownership rate: 85.5%; Homeowner vacancy rate: 1.9%; Rental vacancy rate: 43.5%

JONESVILLE (town). Covers a land area of 1.015 square miles and a water area of 0.008 square miles. Located at 34.83° N. Lat; 81.68° W. Long. Elevation is 686 feet.
History: Named for Charles Jones, its first postmaster and school teacher, Jonesville developed on the site of a blockhouse built before the Revolution by John Haile.
Population: 911; Growth (since 2000): -7.2%; Density: 897.7 persons per square mile; Race: 65.4% White, 32.6% Black/African American, 0.0% Asian, 0.2% American Indian/Alaska Native, 0.0% Native Hawaiian/Other Pacific Islander, 1.2% Two or more races, 1.9% Hispanic of any race; Average household size: 2.15; Median age: 44.7; Age under 18: 20.0%; Age 65 and over: 18.2%; Males per 100 females: 84.0
School District(s)
Union 01 (PK-12)
    2012-13 Enrollment: 4,140 . . . . (864) 429-1740
Housing: Homeownership rate: 61.5%; Homeowner vacancy rate: 4.4%; Rental vacancy rate: 3.6%

LOCKHART (town). Covers a land area of 0.305 square miles and a water area of 0.104 square miles. Located at 34.80° N. Lat; 81.47° W. Long. Elevation is 453 feet.
Population: 488; Growth (since 2000): 1,151.3%; Density: 1,598.6 persons per square mile; Race: 91.2% White, 5.9% Black/African American, 0.0% Asian, 0.8% American Indian/Alaska Native, 0.0% Native Hawaiian/Other Pacific Islander, 1.8% Two or more races, 0.6% Hispanic of any race; Average household size: 2.39; Median age: 43.6; Age under 18: 21.5%; Age 65 and over: 17.4%; Males per 100 females: 95.2
School District(s)
Union 01 (PK-12)
    2012-13 Enrollment: 4,140 . . . . (864) 429-1740
Housing: Homeownership rate: 73.1%; Homeowner vacancy rate: 2.0%; Rental vacancy rate: 9.8%

MONARCH MILL (CDP). Covers a land area of 5.613 square miles and a water area of 0 square miles. Located at 34.72° N. Lat; 81.58° W. Long. Elevation is 627 feet.
Population: 1,811; Growth (since 2000): -6.2%; Density: 322.6 persons per square mile; Race: 81.7% White, 16.5% Black/African American, 0.2% Asian, 0.1% American Indian/Alaska Native, 0.1% Native Hawaiian/Other Pacific Islander, 1.4% Two or more races, 0.8% Hispanic of any race; Average household size: 2.41; Median age: 41.5; Age under 18: 21.8%; Age 65 and over: 16.6%; Males per 100 females: 91.4
Housing: Homeownership rate: 74.1%; Homeowner vacancy rate: 1.9%; Rental vacancy rate: 13.7%

UNION (city). County seat. Covers a land area of 8.084 square miles and a water area of 0 square miles. Located at 34.72° N. Lat; 81.62° W. Long. Elevation is 640 feet.
History: Union was settled in 1791 around the Union Church where Episcopalian and Presbyterian congregations worshiped. Before the Civil War, Union prospered as a crossroad where stagecoach and produce wagons met near the Broad and Tiger Rivers.
Population: 8,393; Growth (since 2000): -4.5%; Density: 1,038.2 persons per square mile; Race: 50.5% White, 47.0% Black/African American, 0.4% Asian, 0.3% American Indian/Alaska Native, 0.0% Native Hawaiian/Other Pacific Islander, 1.4% Two or more races, 1.2% Hispanic of any race; Average household size: 2.24; Median age: 41.3; Age under 18: 23.5%; Age 65 and over: 18.0%; Males per 100 females: 80.5; Marriage status:

33.2% never married, 41.7% now married, 5.6% separated, 11.7% widowed, 13.3% divorced; Foreign born: 0.2%; Speak English only: 98.8%; With disability: 21.3%; Veterans: 10.5%; Ancestry: 8.5% American, 6.5% German, 6.4% Irish, 3.9% English, 3.2% Scottish

Employment: 9.0% management, business, and financial, 0.3% computer, engineering, and science, 18.0% education, legal, community service, arts, and media, 4.7% healthcare practitioners, 13.9% service, 28.8% sales and office, 9.5% natural resources, construction, and maintenance, 15.8% production, transportation, and material moving

Income: Per capita: $19,080; Median household: $26,438; Average household: $41,377; Households with income of $100,000 or more: 8.5%; Poverty rate: 24.3%

Educational Attainment: High school diploma or higher: 79.5%; Bachelor's degree or higher: 21.4%; Graduate/professional degree or higher: 6.4%

School District(s)
Union 01 (PK-12)
    2012-13 Enrollment: 4,140 . . . . (864) 429-1740

Two-year College(s)
University of South Carolina-Union (Public)
    Fall 2013 Enrollment: 484 . . . . (864) 429-8728
    2013-14 Tuition: In-state $6,482; Out-of-state $15,632

Housing: Homeownership rate: 54.3%; Median home value: $81,600; Median year structure built: 1965; Homeowner vacancy rate: 3.8%; Median gross rent: $539 per month; Rental vacancy rate: 8.8%

Health Insurance: 84.6% have insurance; 56.5% have private insurance; 42.9% have public insurance; 15.4% do not have insurance; 3.9% of children under 18 do not have insurance

Hospitals: Wallace Thomson Hospital (143 beds)

Safety: Violent crime rate: 94.8 per 10,000 population; Property crime rate: 459.1 per 10,000 population

Newspapers: Union Daily Times (daily circulation 6400)

Transportation: Commute: 92.3% car, 0.0% public transportation, 2.3% walk, 3.2% work from home; Median travel time to work: 23.2 minutes

Additional Information Contacts
City of Union . . . . (864) 429-1700
    http://www.cityofunion.net

Williamsburg County

Located in east central South Carolina; bounded on the south by the Santee River; drained by the Black River. Covers a land area of 934.159 square miles, a water area of 2.884 square miles, and is located in the Eastern Time Zone at 33.63° N. Lat., 79.72° W. Long. The county was founded in 1802. County seat is Kingstree.

Population: 34,423; Growth (since 2000): -7.5%; Density: 36.8 persons per square mile; Race: 31.8% White, 65.8% Black/African American, 0.4% Asian, 0.3% American Indian/Alaska Native, 0.0% Native Hawaiian/Other Pacific Islander, 0.8% two or more races, 2.0% Hispanic of any race; Average household size: 2.53; Median age: 40.2; Age under 18: 23.6%; Age 65 and over: 14.6%; Males per 100 females: 94.6; Marriage status: 37.4% never married, 41.6% now married, 5.3% separated, 11.0% widowed, 10.0% divorced; Foreign born: 1.4%; Speak English only: 97.4%; With disability: 19.7%; Veterans: 7.9%; Ancestry: 6.9% American, 3.4% English, 2.0% Irish, 1.7% Scotch-Irish, 0.9% German

Religion: Six largest groups: 36.5% Methodist/Pietist, 9.1% Baptist, 4.5% Other Groups, 4.1% Pentecostal, 4.0% Non-denominational Protestant, 3.2% Presbyterian-Reformed

Economy: Unemployment rate: 7.6%; Leading industries: 22.6% retail trade; 13.6% other services (except public administration); 10.8% health care and social assistance; Farms: 679 totaling 224,437 acres; Company size: 0 employ 1,000 or more persons, 1 employs 500 to 999 persons, 10 employ 100 to 499 persons, 497 employ less than 100 persons; Business ownership: 590 women-owned, 702 Black-owned, n/a Hispanic-owned, n/a Asian-owned

Employment: 7.8% management, business, and financial, 1.9% computer, engineering, and science, 8.7% education, legal, community service, arts, and media, 4.8% healthcare practitioners, 18.9% service, 27.5% sales and office, 9.8% natural resources, construction, and maintenance, 20.6% production, transportation, and material moving

Income: Per capita: $14,845; Median household: $25,849; Average household: $38,787; Households with income of $100,000 or more: 6.7%; Poverty rate: 30.8%

Educational Attainment: High school diploma or higher: 77.6%; Bachelor's degree or higher: 12.2%; Graduate/professional degree or higher: 4.6%

Housing: Homeownership rate: 75.2%; Median home value: $67,100; Median year structure built: 1979; Homeowner vacancy rate: 1.0%; Median gross rent: $576 per month; Rental vacancy rate: 7.2%

Vital Statistics: Birth rate: 101.9 per 10,000 population; Death rate: 114.6 per 10,000 population; Age-adjusted cancer mortality rate: 219.3 deaths per 100,000 population

Health Insurance: 75.3% have insurance; 44.0% have private insurance; 41.0% have public insurance; 24.7% do not have insurance; 21.2% of children under 18 do not have insurance

Health Care: Physicians: 2.4 per 10,000 population; Hospital beds: 7.3 per 10,000 population; Hospital admissions: 282.0 per 10,000 population

Transportation: Commute: 93.3% car, 1.4% public transportation, 2.1% walk, 2.6% work from home; Median travel time to work: 28.6 minutes

Presidential Election: 69.5% Obama, 29.6% Romney (2012)

Additional Information Contacts
Williamsburg Government . . . . (843) 355-9321
    http://www.williamsburgcounty.sc.gov

Williamsburg County Communities

CADES (unincorporated postal area)
ZCTA: 29518
    Covers a land area of 48.635 square miles and a water area of 0 square miles. Located at 33.79° N. Lat; 79.85° W. Long. Elevation is 69 feet.
    Population: 1,232; Growth (since 2000): -9.9%; Density: 25.3 persons per square mile; Race: 57.3% White, 41.3% Black/African American, 0.2% Asian, 0.1% American Indian/Alaska Native, 0.0% Native Hawaiian/Other Pacific Islander, 0.5% Two or more races, 1.1% Hispanic of any race; Average household size: 2.58; Median age: 43.8; Age under 18: 22.4%; Age 65 and over: 16.2%; Males per 100 females: 90.7
    Housing: Homeownership rate: 84.6%; Homeowner vacancy rate: 0.5%; Rental vacancy rate: 10.8%

GREELEYVILLE (town). Covers a land area of 1.223 square miles and a water area of 0 square miles. Located at 33.58° N. Lat; 79.99° W. Long. Elevation is 79 feet.
History: Formerly spelled Greelyville.
Population: 438; Growth (since 2000): -3.1%; Density: 358.0 persons per square mile; Race: 28.3% White, 68.9% Black/African American, 0.0% Asian, 0.0% American Indian/Alaska Native, 0.0% Native Hawaiian/Other Pacific Islander, 2.3% Two or more races, 2.7% Hispanic of any race; Average household size: 2.39; Median age: 41.3; Age under 18: 26.3%; Age 65 and over: 20.8%; Males per 100 females: 86.4

School District(s)
Williamsburg 01 (PK-12)
    2012-13 Enrollment: 4,619 . . . . (843) 355-5571
Housing: Homeownership rate: 69.4%; Homeowner vacancy rate: 0.8%; Rental vacancy rate: 5.0%

HEMINGWAY (town). Covers a land area of 0.851 square miles and a water area of 0 square miles. Located at 33.75° N. Lat; 79.45° W. Long. Elevation is 52 feet.
Population: 459; Growth (since 2000): -19.9%; Density: 539.5 persons per square mile; Race: 57.7% White, 34.6% Black/African American, 1.7% Asian, 0.0% American Indian/Alaska Native, 0.0% Native Hawaiian/Other Pacific Islander, 2.2% Two or more races, 7.2% Hispanic of any race; Average household size: 2.27; Median age: 47.1; Age under 18: 20.3%; Age 65 and over: 22.4%; Males per 100 females: 80.7

School District(s)
Georgetown 01 (PK-12)
    2012-13 Enrollment: 9,725 . . . . (843) 436-7178
Williamsburg 01 (PK-12)
    2012-13 Enrollment: 4,619 . . . . (843) 355-5571
Housing: Homeownership rate: 68.8%; Homeowner vacancy rate: 2.8%; Rental vacancy rate: 10.0%
Safety: Violent crime rate: 113.1 per 10,000 population; Property crime rate: 701.4 per 10,000 population
Newspapers: The Weekly Observer (weekly circulation 3400)

KINGSTREE (town). County seat. Covers a land area of 3.154 square miles and a water area of 0.024 square miles. Located at 33.67° N. Lat; 79.83° W. Long. Elevation is 62 feet.

History: Kingstree dates from 1732 when Irish immigrants sailed up the Black River to build their clay shelters around the King's Tree, a white pine on the river bank. An early explorer had marked the tree with an arrow, as white pines farther north were marked for masts in His Majesty's ships.

Population: 3,328; Growth (since 2000): -4.8%; Density: 1,055.0 persons per square mile; Race: 29.4% White, 67.5% Black/African American, 2.4% Asian, 0.1% American Indian/Alaska Native, 0.0% Native Hawaiian/Other Pacific Islander, 0.5% Two or more races, 0.6% Hispanic of any race; Average household size: 2.36; Median age: 36.5; Age under 18: 27.9%; Age 65 and over: 16.9%; Males per 100 females: 80.3; Marriage status: 34.8% never married, 47.1% now married, 3.6% separated, 5.2% widowed, 12.9% divorced; Foreign born: 3.5%; Speak English only: 97.6%; With disability: 17.0%; Veterans: 14.3%; Ancestry: 9.7% American, 2.8% English, 2.4% Scotch-Irish, 1.6% Scottish, 1.2% French

Employment: 6.6% management, business, and financial, 0.0% computer, engineering, and science, 10.0% education, legal, community service, arts, and media, 4.2% healthcare practitioners, 31.4% service, 26.4% sales and office, 3.6% natural resources, construction, and maintenance, 17.8% production, transportation, and material moving

Income: Per capita: $15,727; Median household: $26,618; Average household: $43,602; Households with income of $100,000 or more: 8.3%; Poverty rate: 37.9%

Educational Attainment: High school diploma or higher: 82.2%; Bachelor's degree or higher: 23.9%; Graduate/professional degree or higher: 5.6%

School District(s)
Williamsburg 01 (PK-12)
    2012-13 Enrollment: 4,619 . . . . (843) 355-5571
Two-year College(s)
Williamsburg Technical College (Public)
    Fall 2013 Enrollment: 729 . . . . (843) 355-4110
    2013-14 Tuition: In-state $3,770; Out-of-state $7,056
Housing: Homeownership rate: 46.9%; Median home value: $96,200; Median year structure built: 1974; Homeowner vacancy rate: 4.1%; Median gross rent: $609 per month; Rental vacancy rate: 5.0%
Health Insurance: 75.5% have insurance; 43.6% have private insurance; 45.3% have public insurance; 24.5% do not have insurance; 28.6% of children under 18 do not have insurance
Hospitals: Williamsburg Regional Hospital (25 beds)
Safety: Violent crime rate: 126.6 per 10,000 population; Property crime rate: 923.1 per 10,000 population
Newspapers: The News (weekly circulation 4800)
Transportation: Commute: 92.5% car, 5.0% public transportation, 1.7% walk, 0.9% work from home; Median travel time to work: 23.4 minutes; Amtrak: Train service available.
Additional Information Contacts
Town of Kingstree . . . . (843) 355-7484
    http://www.kingstree.org

LANE (town). Covers a land area of 3.950 square miles and a water area of 0 square miles. Located at 33.53° N. Lat; 79.88° W. Long. Elevation is 66 feet.
Population: 508; Growth (since 2000): -13.2%; Density: 128.6 persons per square mile; Race: 8.7% White, 90.6% Black/African American, 0.0% Asian, 0.0% American Indian/Alaska Native, 0.0% Native Hawaiian/Other Pacific Islander, 0.8% Two or more races, 0.2% Hispanic of any race; Average household size: 2.51; Median age: 41.7; Age under 18: 24.2%; Age 65 and over: 16.3%; Males per 100 females: 77.6
Housing: Homeownership rate: 77.8%; Homeowner vacancy rate: 0.6%; Rental vacancy rate: 22.4%

NESMITH (unincorporated postal area)
ZCTA: 29580
    Covers a land area of 69.596 square miles and a water area of 0.125 square miles. Located at 33.65° N. Lat; 79.55° W. Long. Elevation is 39 feet.
    Population: 1,450; Growth (since 2000): -18.2%; Density: 20.8 persons per square mile; Race: 9.5% White, 88.9% Black/African American, 0.0% Asian, 0.3% American Indian/Alaska Native, 0.0% Native Hawaiian/Other Pacific Islander, 0.6% Two or more races, 0.8% Hispanic of any race; Average household size: 2.48; Median age: 44.2;

Age under 18: 22.8%; Age 65 and over: 14.9%; Males per 100 females: 89.0
    Housing: Homeownership rate: 81.5%; Homeowner vacancy rate: 0.6%; Rental vacancy rate: 2.7%

SALTERS (unincorporated postal area)
ZCTA: 29590
    Covers a land area of 99.263 square miles and a water area of 0.087 square miles. Located at 33.57° N. Lat; 79.85° W. Long. Elevation is 62 feet.
    Population: 3,677; Growth (since 2000): 15.7%; Density: 37.0 persons per square mile; Race: 17.0% White, 76.3% Black/African American, 0.4% Asian, 0.7% American Indian/Alaska Native, 0.1% Native Hawaiian/Other Pacific Islander, 1.3% Two or more races, 10.0% Hispanic of any race; Average household size: 2.47; Median age: 37.8; Age under 18: 15.9%; Age 65 and over: 11.2%; Males per 100 females: 172.8; Marriage status: 49.9% never married, 32.9% now married, 7.8% separated, 5.9% widowed, 11.3% divorced; Foreign born: 7.0%; Speak English only: 87.2%; With disability: 22.5%; Veterans: 6.0%; Ancestry: 2.9% American, 2.7% German, 2.0% English, 1.3% Irish, 1.1% African
    Employment: 6.4% management, business, and financial, 0.0% computer, engineering, and science, 8.4% education, legal, community service, arts, and media, 0.7% healthcare practitioners, 20.0% service, 23.5% sales and office, 13.4% natural resources, construction, and maintenance, 27.8% production, transportation, and material moving
    Income: Per capita: $10,254; Median household: $20,911; Average household: $34,167; Households with income of $100,000 or more: 2.1%; Poverty rate: 38.9%
    Educational Attainment: High school diploma or higher: 72.3%; Bachelor's degree or higher: 4.8%; Graduate/professional degree or higher: 0.7%
School District(s)
Williamsburg 01 (PK-12)
    2012-13 Enrollment: 4,619 . . . . (843) 355-5571
    Housing: Homeownership rate: 81.2%; Median home value: $39,300; Median year structure built: 1978; Homeowner vacancy rate: 0.4%; Median gross rent: $480 per month; Rental vacancy rate: 3.5%
    Health Insurance: 67.4% have insurance; 36.6% have private insurance; 39.3% have public insurance; 32.6% do not have insurance; 5.8% of children under 18 do not have insurance
    Transportation: Commute: 98.4% car, 0.0% public transportation, 0.0% walk, 0.9% work from home; Median travel time to work: 40.9 minutes

STUCKEY (town). Covers a land area of 0.935 square miles and a water area of 0 square miles. Located at 33.73° N. Lat; 79.51° W. Long. Elevation is 49 feet.
Population: 245; Growth (since 2000): -6.8%; Density: 262.1 persons per square mile; Race: 18.0% White, 81.2% Black/African American, 0.0% Asian, 0.0% American Indian/Alaska Native, 0.0% Native Hawaiian/Other Pacific Islander, 0.8% Two or more races, 0.4% Hispanic of any race; Average household size: 2.78; Median age: 39.4; Age under 18: 25.7%; Age 65 and over: 11.8%; Males per 100 females: 85.6
Housing: Homeownership rate: 84.1%; Homeowner vacancy rate: 0.0%; Rental vacancy rate: 0.0%

York County

Located in northern South Carolina; bounded on the west by the Broad River, on the east by the Catawba River, and on the north by North Carolina; includes part of Catawba Lake. Covers a land area of 680.595 square miles, a water area of 15.213 square miles, and is located in the Eastern Time Zone at 34.97° N. Lat., 81.18° W. Long. The county was founded in 1798. County seat is York.

York County is part of the Charlotte-Concord-Gastonia, NC-SC Metropolitan Statistical Area. The entire metro area includes: Cabarrus County, NC; Gaston County, NC; Iredell County, NC; Lincoln County, NC; Mecklenburg County, NC; Rowan County, NC; Union County, NC; Chester County, SC; Lancaster County, SC; York County, SC

Weather Station: Winthrop University   Elevation: 689 feet

	Jan	Feb	Mar	Apr	May	Jun	Jul	Aug	Sep	Oct	Nov	Dec
High	52	57	65	74	80	87	90	89	82	73	64	55
Low	33	35	42	50	58	67	70	69	63	52	42	35
Precip	3.7	3.7	4.4	3.2	2.8	4.2	3.8	4.0	3.6	3.5	3.5	3.4
Snow	1.8	1.4	0.5	tr	0.0	0.0	0.0	0.0	0.0	0.0	0.1	0.1

High and Low temperatures in degrees Fahrenheit; Precipitation and Snow in inches

Population: 226,073; Growth (since 2000): 37.3%; Density: 332.2 persons per square mile; Race: 74.8% White, 19.0% Black/African American, 1.5% Asian, 0.9% American Indian/Alaska Native, 0.1% Native Hawaiian/Other Pacific Islander, 1.8% two or more races, 4.5% Hispanic of any race; Average household size: 2.59; Median age: 37.2; Age under 18: 25.5%; Age 65 and over: 11.3%; Males per 100 females: 93.3; Marriage status: 27.3% never married, 57.7% now married, 3.1% separated, 5.3% widowed, 9.8% divorced; Foreign born: 4.6%; Speak English only: 93.5%; With disability: 11.2%; Veterans: 9.8%; Ancestry: 13.0% German, 11.5% Irish, 9.6% English, 9.3% American, 4.2% Scotch-Irish
Religion: Six largest groups: 17.2% Baptist, 7.4% Methodist/Pietist, 6.2% Presbyterian-Reformed, 6.2% Catholicism, 4.9% Non-denominational Protestant, 3.8% Pentecostal
Economy: Unemployment rate: 6.8%; Leading industries: 14.7% retail trade; 11.4% other services (except public administration); 10.3% professional, scientific, and technical services; Farms: 1,004 totaling 123,929 acres; Company size: 5 employ 1,000 or more persons, 5 employ 500 to 999 persons, 104 employ 100 to 499 persons, 4,356 employ less than 100 persons; Business ownership: 4,904 women-owned, 1,456 Black-owned, 229 Hispanic-owned, 216 Asian-owned
Employment: 16.2% management, business, and financial, 5.2% computer, engineering, and science, 10.0% education, legal, community service, arts, and media, 4.7% healthcare practitioners, 16.0% service, 26.2% sales and office, 8.5% natural resources, construction, and maintenance, 13.3% production, transportation, and material moving
Income: Per capita: $26,553; Median household: $53,740; Average household: $69,888; Households with income of $100,000 or more: 22.2%; Poverty rate: 13.4%
Educational Attainment: High school diploma or higher: 87.5%; Bachelor's degree or higher: 28.5%; Graduate/professional degree or higher: 9.2%
Housing: Homeownership rate: 72.4%; Median home value: $159,300; Median year structure built: 1992; Homeowner vacancy rate: 2.4%; Median gross rent: $796 per month; Rental vacancy rate: 12.3%
Vital Statistics: Birth rate: 121.3 per 10,000 population; Death rate: 74.1 per 10,000 population; Age-adjusted cancer mortality rate: 186.5 deaths per 100,000 population
Health Insurance: 86.3% have insurance; 70.3% have private insurance; 25.9% have public insurance; 13.7% do not have insurance; 5.7% of children under 18 do not have insurance
Health Care: Physicians: 13.5 per 10,000 population; Hospital beds: 14.2 per 10,000 population; Hospital admissions: 691.0 per 10,000 population
Air Quality Index: 97.3% good, 2.7% moderate, 0.0% unhealthy for sensitive individuals, 0.0% unhealthy (percent of days)
Transportation: Commute: 92.3% car, 0.4% public transportation, 1.2% walk, 5.0% work from home; Median travel time to work: 25.1 minutes
Presidential Election: 39.0% Obama, 59.4% Romney (2012)
National and State Parks: Kings Mountain National Military Park; Kings Mountain State Park
Additional Information Contacts
York Government . . . . (803) 628-3036
   http://www.yorkcountygov.com

York County Communities

CATAWBA (CDP). Covers a land area of 9.948 square miles and a water area of 0.405 square miles. Located at 34.84° N. Lat; 80.90° W. Long. Elevation is 571 feet.
Population: 1,343; Growth (since 2000): n/a; Density: 135.0 persons per square mile; Race: 78.5% White, 17.1% Black/African American, 0.3% Asian, 1.4% American Indian/Alaska Native, 0.0% Native Hawaiian/Other Pacific Islander, 1.5% Two or more races, 3.4% Hispanic of any race; Average household size: 2.75; Median age: 40.4; Age under 18: 21.7%; Age 65 and over: 12.7%; Males per 100 females: 103.5
Housing: Homeownership rate: 68.8%; Homeowner vacancy rate: 1.2%; Rental vacancy rate: 8.4%

CLOVER (town). Covers a land area of 4.459 square miles and a water area of 0.011 square miles. Located at 35.11° N. Lat; 81.22° W. Long. Elevation is 814 feet.
Population: 5,094; Growth (since 2000): 26.9%; Density: 1,142.5 persons per square mile; Race: 76.5% White, 19.2% Black/African American, 0.6% Asian, 0.5% American Indian/Alaska Native, 0.0% Native Hawaiian/Other Pacific Islander, 1.9% Two or more races, 4.4% Hispanic of any race; Average household size: 2.65; Median age: 33.8; Age under 18: 29.1%; Age 65 and over: 10.1%; Males per 100 females: 92.4; Marriage status: 24.2% never married, 55.8% now married, 3.1% separated, 7.0% widowed, 13.0% divorced; Foreign born: 2.0%; Speak English only: 95.8%; With disability: 10.8%; Veterans: 8.4%; Ancestry: 18.2% American, 13.5% German, 7.9% Irish, 6.1% English, 5.3% African
Employment: 16.5% management, business, and financial, 2.8% computer, engineering, and science, 10.1% education, legal, community service, arts, and media, 4.3% healthcare practitioners, 12.4% service, 26.5% sales and office, 12.1% natural resources, construction, and maintenance, 15.3% production, transportation, and material moving
Income: Per capita: $19,978; Median household: $44,561; Average household: $54,716; Households with income of $100,000 or more: 13.6%; Poverty rate: 22.7%
Educational Attainment: High school diploma or higher: 83.2%; Bachelor's degree or higher: 16.4%; Graduate/professional degree or higher: 4.7%
School District(s)
York 02 (PK-12)
   2012-13 Enrollment: 6,742 . . . . (803) 810-8000
Housing: Homeownership rate: 62.9%; Median home value: $118,400; Median year structure built: 1987; Homeowner vacancy rate: 4.1%; Median gross rent: $848 per month; Rental vacancy rate: 7.5%
Health Insurance: 86.1% have insurance; 65.8% have private insurance; 30.5% have public insurance; 13.9% do not have insurance; 6.0% of children under 18 do not have insurance
Safety: Violent crime rate: 277.1 per 10,000 population; Property crime rate: 280.8 per 10,000 population
Transportation: Commute: 96.2% car, 0.9% public transportation, 1.0% walk, 0.0% work from home; Median travel time to work: 27.8 minutes
Additional Information Contacts
Town of Clover . . . . (803) 222-9495
   http://www.cloversc.info/

FORT MILL (town). Covers a land area of 16.341 square miles and a water area of 0.254 square miles. Located at 35.01° N. Lat; 80.94° W. Long. Elevation is 623 feet.
History: Fort Mill was established as a textile mill village for employees of the Springs mills.
Population: 10,811; Growth (since 2000): 42.5%; Density: 661.6 persons per square mile; Race: 77.6% White, 17.6% Black/African American, 1.3% Asian, 0.4% American Indian/Alaska Native, 0.0% Native Hawaiian/Other Pacific Islander, 2.1% Two or more races, 2.9% Hispanic of any race; Average household size: 2.58; Median age: 36.3; Age under 18: 29.8%; Age 65 and over: 10.0%; Males per 100 females: 87.5; Marriage status: 26.4% never married, 60.5% now married, 2.5% separated, 4.5% widowed, 8.7% divorced; Foreign born: 3.9%; Speak English only: 93.8%; With disability: 9.5%; Veterans: 10.5%; Ancestry: 16.9% German, 15.9% English, 15.2% Irish, 7.2% American, 4.2% Scottish
Employment: 21.9% management, business, and financial, 5.2% computer, engineering, and science, 10.8% education, legal, community service, arts, and media, 4.5% healthcare practitioners, 10.5% service, 33.7% sales and office, 5.1% natural resources, construction, and maintenance, 8.3% production, transportation, and material moving
Income: Per capita: $34,030; Median household: $64,596; Average household: $86,190; Households with income of $100,000 or more: 31.2%; Poverty rate: 8.6%
Educational Attainment: High school diploma or higher: 91.0%; Bachelor's degree or higher: 36.4%; Graduate/professional degree or higher: 10.0%
School District(s)
York 04 (PK-12)
   2012-13 Enrollment: 11,069 . . . . (803) 548-2527
Housing: Homeownership rate: 68.0%; Median home value: $193,600; Median year structure built: 1994; Homeowner vacancy rate: 2.3%; Median gross rent: $870 per month; Rental vacancy rate: 7.6%

Health Insurance: 90.2% have insurance; 77.5% have private insurance; 22.6% have public insurance; 9.8% do not have insurance; 4.2% of children under 18 do not have insurance
Safety: Violent crime rate: 19.9 per 10,000 population; Property crime rate: 175.2 per 10,000 population
Newspapers: Ft. Mill Times (weekly circulation 6800)
Transportation: Commute: 89.9% car, 0.7% public transportation, 0.6% walk, 7.9% work from home; Median travel time to work: 25.5 minutes
Additional Information Contacts
Town of Fort Mill . . . . (803) 547-2116
    http://www.fortmillsc.org

HICKORY GROVE (town). Covers a land area of 1.671 square miles and a water area of 0 square miles. Located at 34.98° N. Lat; 81.42° W. Long. Elevation is 682 feet.

Population: 440; Growth (since 2000): 30.6%; Density: 263.4 persons per square mile; Race: 70.0% White, 25.9% Black/African American, 0.2% Asian, 0.9% American Indian/Alaska Native, 0.0% Native Hawaiian/Other Pacific Islander, 3.0% Two or more races, 0.9% Hispanic of any race; Average household size: 2.70; Median age: 40.0; Age under 18: 26.6%; Age 65 and over: 12.3%; Males per 100 females: 92.1

School District(s)
York 01 (PK-12)
    2012-13 Enrollment: 5,137 . . . . (803) 818-6337
Housing: Homeownership rate: 81.0%; Homeowner vacancy rate: 1.5%; Rental vacancy rate: 6.1%

INDIA HOOK (CDP). Covers a land area of 2.637 square miles and a water area of 0.902 square miles. Located at 35.01° N. Lat; 81.04° W. Long. Elevation is 636 feet.

Population: 3,328; Growth (since 2000): 106.2%; Density: 1,262.1 persons per square mile; Race: 88.0% White, 6.3% Black/African American, 1.4% Asian, 0.4% American Indian/Alaska Native, 0.1% Native Hawaiian/Other Pacific Islander, 2.1% Two or more races, 4.9% Hispanic of any race; Average household size: 2.38; Median age: 40.2; Age under 18: 21.9%; Age 65 and over: 12.7%; Males per 100 females: 94.4; Marriage status: 12.5% never married, 64.2% now married, 0.0% separated, 5.9% widowed, 17.4% divorced; Foreign born: 1.3%; Speak English only: 92.0%; With disability: 17.8%; Veterans: 18.1%; Ancestry: 17.5% Irish, 11.4% German, 11.1% American, 9.1% English, 4.9% French
Employment: 14.0% management, business, and financial, 7.9% computer, engineering, and science, 4.9% education, legal, community service, arts, and media, 12.4% healthcare practitioners, 12.6% service, 28.8% sales and office, 5.8% natural resources, construction, and maintenance, 13.5% production, transportation, and material moving
Income: Per capita: $33,845; Median household: $67,392; Average household: $81,979; Households with income of $100,000 or more: 31.0%; Poverty rate: 11.8%
Educational Attainment: High school diploma or higher: 94.9%; Bachelor's degree or higher: 30.0%; Graduate/professional degree or higher: 9.7%
Housing: Homeownership rate: 89.0%; Median home value: $143,800; Median year structure built: 1998; Homeowner vacancy rate: 2.3%; Median gross rent: $1,605 per month; Rental vacancy rate: 10.3%
Health Insurance: 91.8% have insurance; 84.7% have private insurance; 20.0% have public insurance; 8.2% do not have insurance; 1.7% of children under 18 do not have insurance
Transportation: Commute: 94.5% car, 0.0% public transportation, 0.0% walk, 4.8% work from home; Median travel time to work: 24.1 minutes

LAKE WYLIE (CDP). Covers a land area of 7.844 square miles and a water area of 2.743 square miles. Located at 35.10° N. Lat; 81.07° W. Long. Elevation is 584 feet.

History: Lake Wylie is a census-designated place (CDP) in York County, South Carolina, United States. Lake Wylie derives its name from Lake Wylie (the body of water), which was named after Dr. W. Gil Wylie in 1960.
Population: 8,841; Growth (since 2000): 188.8%; Density: 1,127.1 persons per square mile; Race: 88.7% White, 7.1% Black/African American, 1.4% Asian, 0.3% American Indian/Alaska Native, 0.1% Native Hawaiian/Other Pacific Islander, 1.4% Two or more races, 3.9% Hispanic of any race; Average household size: 2.51; Median age: 40.4; Age under 18: 26.3%; Age 65 and over: 14.3%; Males per 100 females: 97.3; Marriage status: 20.1% never married, 64.6% now married, 0.9% separated, 4.7% widowed, 10.6% divorced; Foreign born: 3.4%; Speak

English only: 95.7%; With disability: 8.4%; Veterans: 11.2%; Ancestry: 23.8% German, 13.5% Irish, 12.4% English, 11.2% American, 9.3% Italian
Employment: 24.8% management, business, and financial, 9.4% computer, engineering, and science, 9.2% education, legal, community service, arts, and media, 3.8% healthcare practitioners, 13.1% service, 29.0% sales and office, 2.0% natural resources, construction, and maintenance, 8.7% production, transportation, and material moving
Income: Per capita: $38,267; Median household: $75,915; Average household: $98,983; Households with income of $100,000 or more: 37.4%; Poverty rate: 4.0%
Educational Attainment: High school diploma or higher: 95.8%; Bachelor's degree or higher: 47.4%; Graduate/professional degree or higher: 14.5%
Housing: Homeownership rate: 78.5%; Median home value: $286,200; Median year structure built: 2000; Homeowner vacancy rate: 3.1%; Median gross rent: $916 per month; Rental vacancy rate: 18.3%
Health Insurance: 90.4% have insurance; 82.6% have private insurance; 17.9% have public insurance; 9.6% do not have insurance; 6.5% of children under 18 do not have insurance
Newspapers: Lake Wylie Pilot (weekly circulation 11000)
Transportation: Commute: 92.8% car, 0.4% public transportation, 0.9% walk, 4.0% work from home; Median travel time to work: 29.5 minutes

LESSLIE (CDP). Covers a land area of 6.082 square miles and a water area of 0.049 square miles. Located at 34.88° N. Lat; 80.95° W. Long. Elevation is 699 feet.

Population: 3,112; Growth (since 2000): 37.2%; Density: 511.6 persons per square mile; Race: 84.9% White, 10.3% Black/African American, 1.7% Asian, 0.7% American Indian/Alaska Native, 0.0% Native Hawaiian/Other Pacific Islander, 1.7% Two or more races, 2.9% Hispanic of any race; Average household size: 2.71; Median age: 38.5; Age under 18: 25.2%; Age 65 and over: 11.9%; Males per 100 females: 95.6; Marriage status: 29.2% never married, 50.2% now married, 1.0% separated, 7.6% widowed, 13.0% divorced; Foreign born: 0.6%; Speak English only: 99.4%; With disability: 14.7%; Veterans: 5.7%; Ancestry: 21.9% Irish, 9.9% German, 9.5% English, 8.2% Italian, 6.5% American
Employment: 12.8% management, business, and financial, 4.4% computer, engineering, and science, 8.6% education, legal, community service, arts, and media, 3.1% healthcare practitioners, 21.5% service, 32.9% sales and office, 4.4% natural resources, construction, and maintenance, 12.2% production, transportation, and material moving
Income: Per capita: $21,226; Median household: $48,846; Average household: $56,449; Households with income of $100,000 or more: 14.1%; Poverty rate: 18.2%
Educational Attainment: High school diploma or higher: 84.2%; Bachelor's degree or higher: 10.7%; Graduate/professional degree or higher: 2.9%
Housing: Homeownership rate: 83.8%; Median home value: $163,000; Median year structure built: 1989; Homeowner vacancy rate: 2.0%; Median gross rent: $616 per month; Rental vacancy rate: 13.1%
Health Insurance: 73.3% have insurance; 57.2% have private insurance; 24.6% have public insurance; 26.7% do not have insurance; 14.9% of children under 18 do not have insurance
Transportation: Commute: 94.4% car, 0.0% public transportation, 0.0% walk, 4.8% work from home; Median travel time to work: 31.9 minutes

MCCONNELLS (town). Covers a land area of 3.390 square miles and a water area of 0.030 square miles. Located at 34.88° N. Lat; 81.23° W. Long. Elevation is 682 feet.

History: Formerly called McConnellsville.
Population: 255; Growth (since 2000): -11.1%; Density: 75.2 persons per square mile; Race: 74.1% White, 25.5% Black/African American, 0.0% Asian, 0.0% American Indian/Alaska Native, 0.0% Native Hawaiian/Other Pacific Islander, 0.4% Two or more races, 0.8% Hispanic of any race; Average household size: 2.55; Median age: 44.9; Age under 18: 21.2%; Age 65 and over: 11.8%; Males per 100 females: 112.5
Housing: Homeownership rate: 82.0%; Homeowner vacancy rate: 1.2%; Rental vacancy rate: 14.3%

NEWPORT (CDP). Covers a land area of 8.711 square miles and a water area of 0.061 square miles. Located at 34.98° N. Lat; 81.10° W. Long. Elevation is 699 feet.

Population: 4,136; Growth (since 2000): 2.6%; Density: 474.8 persons per square mile; Race: 84.1% White, 11.9% Black/African American, 1.3% Asian, 0.6% American Indian/Alaska Native, 0.0% Native Hawaiian/Other

Pacific Islander, 1.8% Two or more races, 2.3% Hispanic of any race; Average household size: 2.73; Median age: 41.6; Age under 18: 24.2%; Age 65 and over: 11.2%; Males per 100 females: 93.2; Marriage status: 17.7% never married, 67.0% now married, 2.1% separated, 3.8% widowed, 11.4% divorced; Foreign born: 4.0%; Speak English only: 90.1%; With disability: 6.4%; Veterans: 15.0%; Ancestry: 18.0% German, 14.8% English, 13.4% Irish, 10.6% Scotch-Irish, 8.7% American
Employment: 9.9% management, business, and financial, 6.0% computer, engineering, and science, 16.4% education, legal, community service, arts, and media, 13.9% healthcare practitioners, 14.5% service, 29.7% sales and office, 5.7% natural resources, construction, and maintenance, 3.9% production, transportation, and material moving
Income: Per capita: $27,501; Median household: $57,907; Average household: $72,052; Households with income of $100,000 or more: 24.2%; Poverty rate: 5.9%
Educational Attainment: High school diploma or higher: 94.8%; Bachelor's degree or higher: 34.3%; Graduate/professional degree or higher: 14.6%
Housing: Homeownership rate: 86.8%; Median home value: $193,000; Median year structure built: 1984; Homeowner vacancy rate: 2.3%; Median gross rent: $746 per month; Rental vacancy rate: 5.7%
Health Insurance: 89.7% have insurance; 80.9% have private insurance; 17.7% have public insurance; 10.3% do not have insurance; 8.2% of children under 18 do not have insurance
Transportation: Commute: 91.7% car, 0.0% public transportation, 0.8% walk, 7.5% work from home; Median travel time to work: 24.0 minutes

RIVERVIEW (CDP). Covers a land area of 1.520 square miles and a water area of 0.004 square miles. Located at 35.01° N. Lat; 80.99° W. Long. Elevation is 643 feet.
Population: 681; Growth (since 2000): -3.8%; Density: 448.1 persons per square mile; Race: 93.4% White, 1.8% Black/African American, 1.8% Asian, 0.3% American Indian/Alaska Native, 0.0% Native Hawaiian/Other Pacific Islander, 1.8% Two or more races, 2.8% Hispanic of any race; Average household size: 2.49; Median age: 42.9; Age under 18: 21.3%; Age 65 and over: 16.4%; Males per 100 females: 107.6
Housing: Homeownership rate: 77.0%; Homeowner vacancy rate: 1.9%; Rental vacancy rate: 1.5%

ROCK HILL (city). Covers a land area of 35.722 square miles and a water area of 0.161 square miles. Located at 34.94° N. Lat; 81.02° W. Long. Elevation is 679 feet.
History: Named for the flint-rock hill that slowed area railroad construction crews. Rock Hill derives its name from a small hill in the vicinity. In 1852 just a depot on the new Southern Railway line, during the Civil War Rock Hill became a point of transfer for Confederate troops and military supplies. Rock Hill was incorporated in 1870; its growth came with the spread of cotton mills and the development of hydroelectric power.
Population: 66,154; Growth (since 2000): 32.9%; Density: 1,851.9 persons per square mile; Race: 54.6% White, 38.3% Black/African American, 1.7% Asian, 0.5% American Indian/Alaska Native, 0.1% Native Hawaiian/Other Pacific Islander, 2.1% Two or more races, 5.7% Hispanic of any race; Average household size: 2.43; Median age: 31.9; Age under 18: 24.4%; Age 65 and over: 10.4%; Males per 100 females: 85.3; Marriage status: 38.4% never married, 45.1% now married, 3.9% separated, 6.3% widowed, 10.2% divorced; Foreign born: 4.8%; Speak English only: 92.8%; With disability: 11.5%; Veterans: 8.8%; Ancestry: 9.9% Irish, 9.7% German, 9.0% African, 8.2% English, 5.8% American
Employment: 12.4% management, business, and financial, 4.2% computer, engineering, and science, 11.4% education, legal, community service, arts, and media, 4.4% healthcare practitioners, 19.0% service, 26.1% sales and office, 6.7% natural resources, construction, and maintenance, 15.8% production, transportation, and material moving
Income: Per capita: $22,416; Median household: $42,550; Average household: $55,955; Households with income of $100,000 or more: 13.3%; Poverty rate: 18.7%
Educational Attainment: High school diploma or higher: 86.9%; Bachelor's degree or higher: 28.7%; Graduate/professional degree or higher: 9.5%

School District(s)
Sc Public Charter SD (PK-12)
    2012-13 Enrollment: 11,500 . . . . (803) 734-8322
York 03 (PK-12)
    2012-13 Enrollment: 17,524 . . . . (803) 981-1000

Four-year College(s)
Clinton College (Private, Not-for-profit, Historically black, African Methodist Episcopal Zion Church)
    Fall 2013 Enrollment: 185 . . . . (803) 327-7402
    2013-14 Tuition: In-state $4,900; Out-of-state $4,900
Winthrop University (Public)
    Fall 2013 Enrollment: 6,130 . . . . (803) 323-2211
    2013-14 Tuition: In-state $13,670; Out-of-state $26,240
Two-year College(s)
York Technical College (Public)
    Fall 2013 Enrollment: 5,030 . . . . (803) 327-8000
    2013-14 Tuition: In-state $4,493; Out-of-state $8,921
Vocational/Technical School(s)
Kenneth Shuler School of Cosmetology-Rock Hill (Private, For-profit)
    Fall 2013 Enrollment: 110 . . . . (803) 315-4904
    2013-14 Tuition: $16,750
Styletrends Barber and Hairstyling Academy (Private, For-profit)
    Fall 2013 Enrollment: 17 . . . . (803) 328-0807
    2013-14 Tuition: $13,990
Housing: Homeownership rate: 53.4%; Median home value: $133,100; Median year structure built: 1990; Homeowner vacancy rate: 3.1%; Median gross rent: $770 per month; Rental vacancy rate: 13.7%
Health Insurance: 84.1% have insurance; 66.2% have private insurance; 26.8% have public insurance; 15.9% do not have insurance; 5.9% of children under 18 do not have insurance
Hospitals: Piedmont Medical Center (268 beds)
Safety: Violent crime rate: 54.2 per 10,000 population; Property crime rate: 376.4 per 10,000 population
Newspapers: The Herald (daily circulation 30100)
Transportation: Commute: 93.7% car, 0.3% public transportation, 2.5% walk, 2.4% work from home; Median travel time to work: 22.2 minutes
Airports: Rock Hill/York County/Bryant Field (general aviation)
Additional Information Contacts
City of Rock Hill. . . . . (803) 329-7011
    http://www.ci.rock-hill.sc.us

SHARON (town). Covers a land area of 1.310 square miles and a water area of 0 square miles. Located at 34.95° N. Lat; 81.34° W. Long. Elevation is 653 feet.
History: Sharon grew up around a church of the same name, whose congregation split off from Bullock's Creek Church.
Population: 494; Growth (since 2000): 17.3%; Density: 377.0 persons per square mile; Race: 93.7% White, 2.4% Black/African American, 0.0% Asian, 1.8% American Indian/Alaska Native, 0.0% Native Hawaiian/Other Pacific Islander, 2.0% Two or more races, 1.2% Hispanic of any race; Average household size: 2.67; Median age: 36.7; Age under 18: 27.3%; Age 65 and over: 13.2%; Males per 100 females: 98.4
Housing: Homeownership rate: 73.0%; Homeowner vacancy rate: 2.9%; Rental vacancy rate: 0.0%

SMYRNA (town). Covers a land area of 0.706 square miles and a water area of 0 square miles. Located at 35.04° N. Lat; 81.41° W. Long. Elevation is 761 feet.
History: At Smyrna, gold was formerly extracted by the shaft method from the Bar Kat and Terry mines.
Population: 45; Growth (since 2000): -23.7%; Density: 63.7 persons per square mile; Race: 100.0% White, 0.0% Black/African American, 0.0% Asian, 0.0% American Indian/Alaska Native, 0.0% Native Hawaiian/Other Pacific Islander, 0.0% Two or more races, 0.0% Hispanic of any race; Average household size: 2.05; Median age: 48.5; Age under 18: 13.3%; Age 65 and over: 20.0%; Males per 100 females: 95.7
Housing: Homeownership rate: 81.9%; Homeowner vacancy rate: 21.7%; Rental vacancy rate: 0.0%

TEGA CAY (city). Covers a land area of 3.870 square miles and a water area of 0.694 square miles. Located at 35.04° N. Lat; 81.01° W. Long. Elevation is 630 feet.
History: The name Tega Cay is Polynesian for "Beautiful Peninsula." The city's slogan is "The Good Life."
Population: 7,620; Growth (since 2000): 88.4%; Density: 1,969.1 persons per square mile; Race: 92.6% White, 3.0% Black/African American, 2.0% Asian, 0.2% American Indian/Alaska Native, 0.1% Native Hawaiian/Other Pacific Islander, 1.4% Two or more races, 3.3% Hispanic of any race; Average household size: 2.77; Median age: 40.2; Age under 18: 29.2%; Age 65 and over: 10.5%; Males per 100 females: 97.8; Marriage status:

19.4% never married, 72.5% now married, 1.1% separated, 2.2% widowed, 5.9% divorced; Foreign born: 6.8%; Speak English only: 90.1%; With disability: 4.9%; Veterans: 7.6%; Ancestry: 16.2% German, 15.6% English, 15.0% Irish, 12.5% Italian, 11.6% American

Employment: 33.5% management, business, and financial, 8.3% computer, engineering, and science, 14.3% education, legal, community service, arts, and media, 5.0% healthcare practitioners, 7.1% service, 26.3% sales and office, 1.5% natural resources, construction, and maintenance, 3.9% production, transportation, and material moving

Income: Per capita: $39,780; Median household: $108,958; Average household: $116,679; Households with income of $100,000 or more: 55.1%; Poverty rate: 2.2%

Educational Attainment: High school diploma or higher: 97.7%; Bachelor's degree or higher: 59.2%; Graduate/professional degree or higher: 17.4%

Housing: Homeownership rate: 93.2%; Median home value: $276,900; Median year structure built: 2000; Homeowner vacancy rate: 2.9%; Median gross rent: $1,653 per month; Rental vacancy rate: 5.0%

Health Insurance: 93.2% have insurance; 89.6% have private insurance; 12.7% have public insurance; 6.8% do not have insurance; 7.6% of children under 18 do not have insurance

Safety: Violent crime rate: 2.5 per 10,000 population; Property crime rate: 157.0 per 10,000 population

Transportation: Commute: 90.7% car, 0.9% public transportation, 0.0% walk, 6.1% work from home; Median travel time to work: 29.3 minutes

Additional Information Contacts

City of Tega Cay . . . . (803) 548-3512
  http://www.tegacaysc.org

YORK (city). County seat. Covers a land area of 8.210 square miles and a water area of 0.118 square miles. Located at 35.00° N. Lat; 81.24° W. Long. Elevation is 758 feet.

History: Formerly Yorkville, York was settled when some Scotch-Irish people from Pennsylvania came here about 1757 and took up land around Fergus Cross, a stagecoach tavern.

Population: 7,736; Growth (since 2000): 10.8%; Density: 942.3 persons per square mile; Race: 54.4% White, 38.4% Black/African American, 0.6% Asian, 0.8% American Indian/Alaska Native, 0.0% Native Hawaiian/Other Pacific Islander, 2.1% Two or more races, 7.3% Hispanic of any race; Average household size: 2.57; Median age: 34.6; Age under 18: 27.5%; Age 65 and over: 14.3%; Males per 100 females: 86.0; Marriage status: 36.9% never married, 43.6% now married, 3.9% separated, 8.6% widowed, 10.9% divorced; Foreign born: 6.1%; Speak English only: 90.3%; With disability: 18.4%; Veterans: 8.9%; Ancestry: 11.3% American, 4.8% Scotch-Irish, 4.3% Irish, 4.0% German, 3.9% African

Employment: 8.9% management, business, and financial, 0.3% computer, engineering, and science, 3.4% education, legal, community service, arts, and media, 2.1% healthcare practitioners, 24.0% service, 26.4% sales and office, 7.4% natural resources, construction, and maintenance, 27.5% production, transportation, and material moving

Income: Per capita: $15,007; Median household: $29,789; Average household: $41,763; Households with income of $100,000 or more: 8.5%; Poverty rate: 31.3%

Educational Attainment: High school diploma or higher: 71.8%; Bachelor's degree or higher: 13.1%; Graduate/professional degree or higher: 6.0%

School District(s)

York 01 (PK-12)
  2012-13 Enrollment: 5,137 . . . . (803) 818-6337

Housing: Homeownership rate: 57.1%; Median home value: $110,300; Median year structure built: 1978; Homeowner vacancy rate: 3.6%; Median gross rent: $685 per month; Rental vacancy rate: 14.5%

Health Insurance: 82.3% have insurance; 46.0% have private insurance; 47.5% have public insurance; 17.7% do not have insurance; 4.4% of children under 18 do not have insurance

Safety: Violent crime rate: 79.5 per 10,000 population; Property crime rate: 430.2 per 10,000 population

Newspapers: Enquirer-Herald (weekly circulation 3000)

Transportation: Commute: 95.5% car, 0.0% public transportation, 0.0% walk, 3.6% work from home; Median travel time to work: 25.3 minutes

Additional Information Contacts

City of York . . . . (803) 684-2341
  http://www.yorkcitysc.com

Place Name Index

Abbeville (city) Abbeville County, 667
Abbeville County, 667
Adams Run (unincorporated) Charleston County, 688
Aiken (city) Aiken County, 669
Aiken County, 668
Alcolu (CDP) Clarendon County, 697
Allendale (town) Allendale County, 672
Allendale County, 672
Anderson (city) Anderson County, 674
Anderson County, 673
Andrews (town) Georgetown County, 710
Antreville (CDP) Abbeville County, 667
Arcadia (CDP) Spartanburg County, 754
Arcadia Lakes (town) Richland County, 749
Arial (CDP) Pickens County, 747
Atlantic Beach (town) Horry County, 720
Awendaw (town) Charleston County, 688
Aynor (town) Horry County, 721
Bamberg (town) Bamberg County, 678
Bamberg County, 677
Barnwell (city) Barnwell County, 679
Barnwell County, 678
Batesburg-Leesville (town) Lexington County, 732
Bath (unincorporated) Aiken County, 669
Beaufort (city) Beaufort County, 680
Beaufort County, 680
Beech Island (unincorporated) Aiken County, 669
Belton (city) Anderson County, 674
Belvedere (CDP) Aiken County, 669
Bennettsville (city) Marlboro County, 737
Berea (CDP) Greenville County, 712
Berkeley County, 684
Bethune (town) Kershaw County, 726
Bishopville (city) Lee County, 731
Blacksburg (town) Cherokee County, 692
Blackstock (unincorporated) Chester County, 693
Blackville (town) Barnwell County, 679
Blair (unincorporated) Fairfield County, 706
Blenheim (town) Marlboro County, 738
Bluffton (town) Beaufort County, 681
Blythewood (town) Richland County, 749
Boiling Springs (CDP) Spartanburg County, 754
Bonneau (town) Berkeley County, 684
Bonneau Beach (CDP) Berkeley County, 684
Bowman (town) Orangeburg County, 744
Boykin (CDP) Kershaw County, 726
Bradley (CDP) Greenwood County, 717
Branchville (town) Orangeburg County, 744
Briarcliffe Acres (town) Horry County, 721
Brookdale (CDP) Orangeburg County, 744
Brunson (town) Hampton County, 719
Bucksport (CDP) Horry County, 721
Buffalo (CDP) Union County, 763
Burnettown (town) Aiken County, 670
Burton (CDP) Beaufort County, 681
Cades (unincorporated) Williamsburg County, 764
Calhoun County, 687
Calhoun Falls (town) Abbeville County, 667
Camden (city) Kershaw County, 726
Cameron (town) Calhoun County, 687
Campobello (town) Spartanburg County, 754
Cane Savannah (CDP) Sumter County, 760
Carlisle (town) Union County, 763
Cassatt (unincorporated) Kershaw County, 726
Catawba (CDP) York County, 766
Cayce (city) Lexington County, 732
Centenary (unincorporated) Marion County, 736
Centerville (CDP) Anderson County, 674
Central (town) Pickens County, 747

Central Pacolet (town) Spartanburg County, 754
Chapin (town) Lexington County, 733
Chappells (unincorporated) Newberry County, 740
Charleston (city) Charleston County, 688
Charleston AFB (unincorporated) Charleston County, 689
Charleston County, 687
Cheraw (town) Chesterfield County, 695
Cherokee County, 692
Cherryvale (CDP) Sumter County, 760
Chesnee (city) Spartanburg County, 755
Chester (city) Chester County, 694
Chester County, 693
Chesterfield (town) Chesterfield County, 696
Chesterfield County, 695
City View (CDP) Greenville County, 712
Clarendon County, 697
Clarks Hill (CDP) McCormick County, 739
Clearwater (CDP) Aiken County, 670
Clemson (city) Pickens County, 747
Cleveland (unincorporated) Greenville County, 712
Clifton (CDP) Spartanburg County, 755
Clinton (city) Laurens County, 729
Clio (town) Marlboro County, 738
Clover (town) York County, 766
Cokesbury (CDP) Greenwood County, 717
Colleton County, 698
Columbia (city) Richland County, 750
Converse (CDP) Spartanburg County, 755
Conway (city) Horry County, 721
Cope (town) Orangeburg County, 744
Cordesville (unincorporated) Berkeley County, 684
Cordova (town) Orangeburg County, 744
Coronaca (CDP) Greenwood County, 717
Cottageville (town) Colleton County, 698
Coward (town) Florence County, 708
Cowpens (town) Spartanburg County, 755
Cross (unincorporated) Berkeley County, 684
Cross Anchor (CDP) Spartanburg County, 755
Cross Hill (town) Laurens County, 730
Dalzell (CDP) Sumter County, 760
Darlington (city) Darlington County, 701
Darlington County, 700
Daufuskie Island (unincorporated) Beaufort County, 681
Denmark (city) Bamberg County, 678
Dentsville (CDP) Richland County, 750
Dillon (city) Dillon County, 702
Dillon County, 702
Donalds (town) Abbeville County, 668
Dorchester (unincorporated) Dorchester County, 704
Dorchester County, 703
Drayton (unincorporated) Spartanburg County, 755
Due West (town) Abbeville County, 668
Duncan (town) Spartanburg County, 755
Dunean (CDP) Greenville County, 712
Early Branch (unincorporated) Hampton County, 719
Easley (city) Pickens County, 748
East Gaffney (CDP) Cherokee County, 692
East Sumter (CDP) Sumter County, 760
Eastover (town) Richland County, 751
Edgefield (town) Edgefield County, 705
Edgefield County, 705
Edgemoor (unincorporated) Chester County, 694
Edisto (CDP) Orangeburg County, 744
Edisto Beach (town) Colleton County, 699
Edisto Island (unincorporated) Colleton County, 699

Effingham (unincorporated) Florence County, 708
Ehrhardt (town) Bamberg County, 678
Elgin (town) Kershaw County, 727
Elgin (CDP) Lancaster County, 728
Elko (town) Barnwell County, 679
Elliott (unincorporated) Lee County, 731
Elloree (town) Orangeburg County, 744
Enoree (CDP) Spartanburg County, 755
Estill (town) Hampton County, 719
Eureka Mill (CDP) Chester County, 694
Eutawville (town) Orangeburg County, 745
Fair Play (CDP) Oconee County, 742
Fairfax (town) Allendale County, 673
Fairfield County, 706
Fairforest (CDP) Spartanburg County, 756
Fingerville (CDP) Spartanburg County, 756
Five Forks (CDP) Greenville County, 712
Florence (city) Florence County, 708
Florence County, 707
Folly Beach (city) Charleston County, 689
Forest Acres (city) Richland County, 751
Forestbrook (CDP) Horry County, 721
Fork (unincorporated) Dillon County, 703
Fort Lawn (town) Chester County, 694
Fort Mill (town) York County, 766
Fountain Inn (city) Greenville County, 712
Furman (town) Hampton County, 719
Gable (unincorporated) Clarendon County, 697
Gadsden (CDP) Richland County, 751
Gaffney (city) Cherokee County, 693
Galivants Ferry (unincorporated) Horry County, 721
Gantt (CDP) Greenville County, 713
Garden City (CDP) Horry County, 722
Garnett (unincorporated) Hampton County, 719
Gaston (town) Lexington County, 733
Gayle Mill (CDP) Chester County, 694
Georgetown (city) Georgetown County, 710
Georgetown County, 709
Gifford (town) Hampton County, 719
Gilbert (town) Lexington County, 733
Glendale (CDP) Spartanburg County, 756
Gloverville (CDP) Aiken County, 670
Golden Grove (CDP) Greenville County, 713
Goose Creek (city) Berkeley County, 685
Govan (town) Bamberg County, 678
Graniteville (CDP) Aiken County, 670
Gray Court (town) Laurens County, 730
Great Falls (town) Chester County, 694
Greeleyville (town) Williamsburg County, 764
Green Pond (unincorporated) Colleton County, 699
Green Sea (unincorporated) Horry County, 722
Greenville (city) Greenville County, 713
Greenville County, 711
Greenwood (city) Greenwood County, 717
Greenwood County, 716
Greer (city) Greenville County, 714
Gresham (unincorporated) Marion County, 736
Hamer (unincorporated) Dillon County, 703
Hampton (town) Hampton County, 719
Hampton County, 718
Hanahan (city) Berkeley County, 685
Hardeeville (city) Jasper County, 725
Harleyville (town) Dorchester County, 704
Hartsville (city) Darlington County, 701
Heath Springs (town) Lancaster County, 728
Hemingway (town) Williamsburg County, 764
Hickory Grove (town) York County, 767
Hilda (town) Barnwell County, 679
Hilton Head Island (town) Beaufort County, 681
Hodges (town) Greenwood County, 718
Holly Hill (town) Orangeburg County, 745

CDP = Census Designated Place

Hollywood (town) Charleston County, 689
Homeland Park (CDP) Anderson County, 675
Honea Path (town) Anderson County, 675
Hopkins (CDP) Richland County, 751
Horatio (unincorporated) Sumter County, 760
Horry County, 720
Huger (unincorporated) Berkeley County, 685
India Hook (CDP) York County, 767
Inman (city) Spartanburg County, 756
Inman Mills (CDP) Spartanburg County, 756
Irmo (town) Richland County, 751
Irwin (CDP) Lancaster County, 728
Islandton (CDP) Colleton County, 699
Isle of Palms (city) Charleston County, 689
Iva (town) Anderson County, 675
Jackson (town) Aiken County, 671
Jacksonboro (CDP) Colleton County, 699
James Island (town) Charleston County, 690
Jamestown (town) Berkeley County, 685
Jasper County, 724
Jefferson (town) Chesterfield County, 696
Jenkinsville (town) Fairfield County, 706
Joanna (CDP) Laurens County, 730
Johns Island (unincorporated) Charleston
   County, 690
Johnsonville (city) Florence County, 708
Johnston (town) Edgefield County, 705
Jonesville (town) Union County, 763
Judson (CDP) Greenville County, 714
Kershaw (town) Lancaster County, 728
Kershaw County, 725
Kiawah Island (town) Charleston County, 690
Kinards (unincorporated) Newberry County, 740
Kingstree (town) Williamsburg County, 765
Kline (town) Barnwell County, 679
Ladson (CDP) Berkeley County, 685
Lake City (city) Florence County, 709
Lake Murray of Richland (CDP) Richland
   County, 752
Lake Secession (CDP) Abbeville County, 668
Lake View (town) Dillon County, 703
Lake Wylie (CDP) York County, 767
Lakewood (CDP) Sumter County, 761
Lamar (town) Darlington County, 701
Lancaster (city) Lancaster County, 728
Lancaster County, 727
Lando (unincorporated) Chester County, 694
Landrum (city) Spartanburg County, 756
Lane (town) Williamsburg County, 765
Langley (CDP) Aiken County, 671
Latta (town) Dillon County, 703
Laurel Bay (CDP) Beaufort County, 682
Laurens (city) Laurens County, 730
Laurens County, 729
Lee County, 731
Lesslie (CDP) York County, 767
Lexington (town) Lexington County, 733
Lexington County, 732
Liberty (city) Pickens County, 748
Liberty Hill (unincorporated) Kershaw County,
   727
Lincolnville (town) Charleston County, 690
Little Mountain (town) Newberry County, 740
Little River (CDP) Horry County, 722
Little Rock (unincorporated) Dillon County, 703
Livingston (town) Orangeburg County, 745
Lockhart (town) Union County, 763
Lodge (town) Colleton County, 699
Long Creek (unincorporated) Oconee County,
   742
Longs (unincorporated) Horry County, 722
Loris (city) Horry County, 723
Lowndesville (town) Abbeville County, 668
Lowrys (town) Chester County, 695

Lugoff (CDP) Kershaw County, 727
Luray (town) Hampton County, 719
Lydia (CDP) Darlington County, 701
Lyman (town) Spartanburg County, 756
Lynchburg (town) Lee County, 731
Manning (city) Clarendon County, 697
Marion (city) Marion County, 736
Marion County, 735
Marlboro County, 737
Martin (unincorporated) Allendale County, 673
Mauldin (city) Greenville County, 714
Mayesville (town) Sumter County, 761
Mayo (CDP) Spartanburg County, 756
McBee (town) Chesterfield County, 696
McClellanville (town) Charleston County, 690
McColl (town) Marlboro County, 738
McConnells (town) York County, 767
McCormick (town) McCormick County, 739
McCormick County, 738
Meggett (town) Charleston County, 690
Modoc (CDP) McCormick County, 739
Monarch Mill (CDP) Union County, 763
Moncks Corner (town) Berkeley County, 686
Monetta (town) Aiken County, 671
Moore (unincorporated) Spartanburg County,
   757
Mount Carmel (CDP) McCormick County, 739
Mount Croghan (town) Chesterfield County, 696
Mount Pleasant (town) Charleston County, 690
Mountain Rest (unincorporated) Oconee County,
   742
Mountville (CDP) Laurens County, 730
Mulberry (CDP) Sumter County, 761
Mullins (city) Marion County, 736
Murphys Estates (CDP) Edgefield County, 706
Murrells Inlet (CDP) Georgetown County, 711
Myrtle Beach (city) Horry County, 723
Neeses (town) Orangeburg County, 745
Nesmith (unincorporated) Williamsburg County,
   765
New Ellenton (town) Aiken County, 671
New Zion (unincorporated) Clarendon County,
   698
Newberry (city) Newberry County, 740
Newberry County, 739
Newport (CDP) York County, 767
Newry (CDP) Oconee County, 742
Nichols (town) Marion County, 737
Ninety Six (town) Greenwood County, 718
Norris (town) Pickens County, 748
North (town) Orangeburg County, 745
North Augusta (city) Aiken County, 671
North Charleston (city) Charleston County, 691
North Hartsville (CDP) Darlington County, 701
North Myrtle Beach (city) Horry County, 723
Northlake (CDP) Anderson County, 675
Norway (town) Orangeburg County, 745
Oak Grove (CDP) Lexington County, 733
Oakland (CDP) Sumter County, 761
Oconee County, 741
Okatie (unincorporated) Beaufort County, 682
Olanta (town) Florence County, 709
Olar (town) Bamberg County, 678
Orangeburg (city) Orangeburg County, 745
Orangeburg County, 743
Oswego (CDP) Sumter County, 761
Pacolet (town) Spartanburg County, 757
Pacolet Mills (unincorporated) Spartanburg
   County, 757
Pageland (town) Chesterfield County, 696
Pamplico (town) Florence County, 709
Parker (CDP) Greenville County, 714
Parksville (town) McCormick County, 739

Parris Island (unincorporated) Beaufort County,
   682
Patrick (town) Chesterfield County, 696
Pauline (unincorporated) Spartanburg County,
   757
Pawleys Island (town) Georgetown County, 711
Paxville (town) Clarendon County, 698
Peak (town) Newberry County, 741
Pelion (town) Lexington County, 734
Pelzer (town) Anderson County, 676
Pendleton (town) Anderson County, 676
Perry (town) Aiken County, 671
Pickens (city) Pickens County, 748
Pickens County, 746
Piedmont (CDP) Anderson County, 676
Pine Ridge (town) Lexington County, 734
Pineland (unincorporated) Jasper County, 725
Pineville (unincorporated) Berkeley County, 686
Pinewood (town) Sumter County, 761
Pinopolis (CDP) Berkeley County, 686
Plum Branch (town) McCormick County, 739
Pomaria (town) Newberry County, 741
Port Royal (town) Beaufort County, 683
Powdersville (CDP) Anderson County, 676
Princeton (CDP) Laurens County, 730
Privateer (CDP) Sumter County, 761
Promised Land (CDP) Greenwood County, 718
Prosperity (town) Newberry County, 741
Quinby (town) Florence County, 709
Ravenel (town) Charleston County, 691
Red Bank (CDP) Lexington County, 734
Red Hill (CDP) Horry County, 723
Reevesville (town) Dorchester County, 704
Reidville (town) Spartanburg County, 757
Rembert (CDP) Sumter County, 761
Richburg (town) Chester County, 695
Richland County, 749
Ridge Spring (town) Saluda County, 753
Ridgeland (town) Jasper County, 725
Ridgeville (town) Dorchester County, 704
Ridgeway (town) Fairfield County, 706
Riverview (CDP) York County, 768
Rock Hill (city) York County, 768
Rockville (town) Charleston County, 691
Roebuck (CDP) Spartanburg County, 757
Round O (unincorporated) Colleton County, 699
Rowesville (town) Orangeburg County, 746
Ruby (town) Chesterfield County, 696
Ruffin (unincorporated) Colleton County, 699
Russellville (CDP) Berkeley County, 686
Saint Andrews (CDP) Richland County, 752
Saint George (town) Dorchester County, 704
Saint Helena Island (unincorporated) Beaufort
   County, 683
Saint Matthews (town) Calhoun County, 687
Saint Stephen (town) Berkeley County, 686
Salem (town) Oconee County, 742
Salley (town) Aiken County, 671
Salters (unincorporated) Williamsburg County,
   765
Saluda (town) Saluda County, 753
Saluda County, 752
Sangaree (CDP) Berkeley County, 686
Sans Souci (CDP) Greenville County, 715
Santee (town) Orangeburg County, 746
Saxon (CDP) Spartanburg County, 757
Scotia (town) Hampton County, 720
Scranton (town) Florence County, 709
Seabrook (unincorporated) Beaufort County, 683
Seabrook Island (town) Charleston County, 691
Sellers (town) Marion County, 737
Seneca (city) Oconee County, 742
Seven Oaks (CDP) Lexington County, 734
Sharon (town) York County, 768

CDP = Census Designated Place

CDP = Census Designated Place

CDP = Census Designated Place

Comparative Statistics

This section compares the 100 largest cities by population in the state, by the following data points:

Population

Place	2000 Census	2010 Census	Growth 2000–2010 (%)
Abbeville city *Abbeville Co.*	5,840	5,237	-10.3
Aiken city *Aiken Co.*	25,337	29,524	16.5
Anderson city *Anderson Co.*	25,514	26,686	4.5
Barnwell city *Barnwell Co.*	5,035	4,750	-5.6
Batesburg-Leesville town *Lexington Co.*	5,517	5,362	-2.8
Beaufort city *Beaufort Co.*	12,950	12,361	-4.5
Belvedere cdp *Aiken Co.*	5,631	5,792	2.8
Bennettsville city *Marlboro Co.*	9,425	9,069	-3.7
Berea cdp *Greenville Co.*	14,158	14,295	0.9
Bluffton town *Beaufort Co.*	1,275	12,530	882.7
Boiling Springs cdp *Spartanburg Co.*	4,544	8,219	80.8
Brookdale cdp *Orangeburg Co.*	4,724	4,873	3.1
Burton cdp *Beaufort Co.*	7,180	6,976	-2.8
Camden city *Kershaw Co.*	6,682	6,838	2.3
Cayce city *Lexington Co.*	12,150	12,528	3.1
Centerville cdp *Anderson Co.*	5,181	6,586	27.1
Central town *Pickens Co.*	3,522	5,159	46.4
Charleston city *Charleston Co.*	96,650	120,083	24.2
Cheraw town *Chesterfield Co.*	5,524	5,851	5.9
Chester city *Chester Co.*	6,476	5,607	-13.4
Clemson city *Pickens Co.*	11,939	13,905	16.4
Clinton city *Laurens Co.*	8,091	8,490	4.9
Clover town *York Co.*	4,014	5,094	26.9
Columbia city *Richland Co.*	116,278	129,272	11.1
Conway city *Horry Co.*	11,788	17,103	45.0
Darlington city *Darlington Co.*	6,720	6,289	-6.4
Dentsville cdp *Richland Co.*	13,009	14,062	8.0
Dillon city *Dillon Co.*	6,316	6,788	7.4
Easley city *Pickens Co.*	17,754	19,993	12.6
Edgefield town *Edgefield Co.*	4,449	4,750	6.7
Five Forks cdp *Greenville Co.*	8,064	14,140	75.3
Florence city *Florence Co.*	30,248	37,056	22.5
Forest Acres city *Richland Co.*	10,558	10,361	-1.8
Forestbrook cdp *Horry Co.*	3,391	4,612	36.0
Fort Mill town *York Co.*	7,587	10,811	42.4
Fountain Inn city *Greenville Co.*	6,017	7,799	29.6
Gaffney city *Cherokee Co.*	12,968	12,414	-4.2
Gantt cdp *Greenville Co.*	13,962	14,229	1.9
Garden City cdp *Horry Co.*	9,357	9,209	-1.5
Georgetown city *Georgetown Co.*	8,950	9,163	2.3
Goose Creek city *Berkeley Co.*	29,208	35,938	23.0
Greenville city *Greenville Co.*	56,002	58,409	4.3
Greenwood city *Greenwood Co.*	22,071	23,222	5.2
Greer city *Greenville Co.*	16,843	25,515	51.4
Hanahan city *Berkeley Co.*	12,937	17,997	39.1
Hartsville city *Darlington Co.*	7,556	7,764	2.7
Hilton Head Island town *Beaufort Co.*	33,862	37,099	9.5
Hollywood town *Charleston Co.*	3,946	4,714	19.4
Homeland Park cdp *Anderson Co.*	6,337	6,296	-0.6
Irmo town *Richland Co.*	11,039	11,097	0.5

Place	2000 Census	2010 Census	Growth 2000–2010 (%)
Ladson cdp *Berkeley Co.*	13,264	13,790	3.9
Lake City city *Florence Co.*	6,478	6,675	3.0
Lake Murray of Richland cdp *Richland Co.*	3,526	5,484	55.5
Lake Wylie cdp *York Co.*	3,061	8,841	188.8
Lancaster city *Lancaster Co.*	8,177	8,526	4.2
Laurel Bay cdp *Beaufort Co.*	6,625	5,891	-11.0
Laurens city *Laurens Co.*	9,916	9,139	-7.8
Lexington town *Lexington Co.*	9,793	17,870	82.4
Little River cdp *Horry Co.*	7,027	8,960	27.5
Lugoff cdp *Kershaw Co.*	6,278	7,434	18.4
Marion city *Marion Co.*	7,042	6,939	-1.4
Mauldin city *Greenville Co.*	15,224	22,889	50.3
Moncks Corner town *Berkeley Co.*	5,952	7,885	32.4
Mount Pleasant town *Charleston Co.*	47,609	67,843	42.5
Mullins city *Marion Co.*	5,029	4,663	-7.2
Murrells Inlet cdp *Georgetown Co.*	5,519	7,547	36.7
Myrtle Beach city *Horry Co.*	22,759	27,109	19.1
Newberry city *Newberry Co.*	10,580	10,277	-2.8
North Augusta city *Aiken Co.*	17,574	21,348	21.4
North Charleston city *Charleston Co.*	79,641	97,471	22.3
North Myrtle Beach city *Horry Co.*	10,974	13,752	25.3
Oak Grove cdp *Lexington Co.*	8,183	10,291	25.7
Orangeburg city *Orangeburg Co.*	12,765	13,964	9.3
Parker cdp *Greenville Co.*	10,760	11,431	6.2
Piedmont cdp *Anderson Co.*	4,684	5,103	8.9
Port Royal town *Beaufort Co.*	3,950	10,678	170.3
Red Bank cdp *Lexington Co.*	8,811	9,617	9.1
Red Hill cdp *Horry Co.*	10,509	13,223	25.8
Rock Hill city *York Co.*	49,765	66,154	32.9
Saint Andrews cdp *Richland Co.*	21,814	20,493	-6.0
Sangaree cdp *Berkeley Co.*	n/a	8,220	n/a
Sans Souci cdp *Greenville Co.*	7,836	7,869	0.4
Seneca city *Oconee Co.*	7,652	8,102	5.8
Seven Oaks cdp *Lexington Co.*	15,755	15,144	-3.8
Simpsonville city *Greenville Co.*	14,352	18,238	27.0
Socastee cdp *Horry Co.*	14,295	19,952	39.5
Spartanburg city *Spartanburg Co.*	39,673	37,013	-6.7
Summerville town *Dorchester Co.*	27,752	43,392	56.3
Sumter city *Sumter Co.*	39,643	40,524	2.2
Taylors cdp *Greenville Co.*	20,125	21,617	7.4
Tega Cay city *York Co.*	4,044	7,620	88.4
Travelers Rest city *Greenville Co.*	4,099	4,576	11.6
Union city *Union Co.*	8,793	8,393	-4.5
Valley Falls cdp *Spartanburg Co.*	3,990	6,299	57.8
Wade Hampton cdp *Greenville Co.*	20,458	20,622	0.8
Walterboro city *Colleton Co.*	5,153	5,398	4.7
Welcome cdp *Greenville Co.*	6,390	6,668	4.3
West Columbia city *Lexington Co.*	13,064	14,988	14.7
Woodfield cdp *Richland Co.*	9,238	9,303	0.7
York city *York Co.*	6,985	7,736	10.7

SOURCE: U.S. Census Bureau, Census 2010, Census 2000

Physical Characteristics

Place	Density (persons per square mile)	Land Area (square miles)	Water Area (square miles)	Elevation (feet)
Abbeville city *Abbeville Co.*	856.3	6.12	0.01	591
Aiken city *Aiken Co.*	1,426.5	20.70	0.14	515
Anderson city *Anderson Co.*	1,828.5	14.59	0.04	787
Barnwell city *Barnwell Co.*	605.1	7.85	0.15	217
Batesburg-Leesville town *Lexington Co.*	688.7	7.79	0.10	643
Beaufort city *Beaufort Co.*	447.9	27.60	5.98	10
Belvedere cdp *Aiken Co.*	1,653.1	3.50	0.01	486
Bennettsville city *Marlboro Co.*	1,482.9	6.12	0.63	154
Berea cdp *Greenville Co.*	1,855.6	7.70	0.29	1,040
Bluffton town *Beaufort Co.*	244.2	51.30	2.21	20
Boiling Springs cdp *Spartanburg Co.*	1,202.2	6.84	0.00	919
Brookdale cdp *Orangeburg Co.*	1,339.8	3.64	0.00	220
Burton cdp *Beaufort Co.*	817.2	8.54	0.02	33
Camden city *Kershaw Co.*	640.2	10.68	0.71	190
Cayce city *Lexington Co.*	752.5	16.65	0.77	239
Centerville cdp *Anderson Co.*	1,115.4	5.90	0.03	833
Central town *Pickens Co.*	1,914.7	2.69	0.00	912
Charleston city *Charleston Co.*	1,101.9	108.98	18.51	10
Cheraw town *Chesterfield Co.*	1,079.1	5.42	0.03	154
Chester city *Chester Co.*	1,716.2	3.27	0.00	541
Clemson city *Pickens Co.*	1,868.9	7.44	0.46	722
Clinton city *Laurens Co.*	859.7	9.88	0.07	676
Clover town *York Co.*	1,142.5	4.46	0.01	814
Columbia city *Richland Co.*	977.8	132.21	2.72	289
Conway city *Horry Co.*	779.5	21.94	0.84	36
Darlington city *Darlington Co.*	1,383.2	4.55	0.00	151
Dentsville cdp *Richland Co.*	2,078.0	6.77	0.13	236
Dillon city *Dillon Co.*	1,299.2	5.22	0.01	112
Easley city *Pickens Co.*	1,631.1	12.26	0.02	1,066
Edgefield town *Edgefield Co.*	1,135.5	4.18	0.12	531
Five Forks cdp *Greenville Co.*	1,868.4	7.57	0.04	876
Florence city *Florence Co.*	1,774.0	20.89	0.05	138
Forest Acres city *Richland Co.*	2,254.3	4.60	0.37	246
Forestbrook cdp *Horry Co.*	1,234.2	3.74	0.00	13
Fort Mill town *York Co.*	661.6	16.34	0.25	623
Fountain Inn city *Greenville Co.*	988.9	7.89	0.03	866
Gaffney city *Cherokee Co.*	1,491.3	8.32	0.03	784
Gantt cdp *Greenville Co.*	1,435.4	9.91	0.02	988
Garden City cdp *Horry Co.*	1,715.6	5.37	0.08	20
Georgetown city *Georgetown Co.*	1,326.0	6.91	0.61	16
Goose Creek city *Berkeley Co.*	896.5	40.09	0.77	30
Greenville city *Greenville Co.*	2,037.4	28.67	0.15	984
Greenwood city *Greenwood Co.*	1,430.6	16.23	0.12	663
Greer city *Greenville Co.*	1,236.4	20.64	2.09	1,014
Hanahan city *Berkeley Co.*	1,683.9	10.69	0.82	36
Hartsville city *Darlington Co.*	1,356.7	5.72	0.44	217
Hilton Head Island town *Beaufort Co.*	896.9	41.36	27.77	10
Hollywood town *Charleston Co.*	203.8	23.13	1.38	30
Homeland Park cdp *Anderson Co.*	1,335.7	4.71	0.01	784
Irmo town *Richland Co.*	1,772.3	6.26	0.00	354

Place	Density (persons per square mile)	Land Area (square miles)	Water Area (square miles)	Elevation (feet)
Ladson cdp *Berkeley Co.*	1,963.5	7.02	0.00	46
Lake City city *Florence Co.*	1,278.1	5.22	0.01	75
Lake Murray of Richland cdp *Richland Co.*	982.0	5.58	3.11	449
Lake Wylie cdp *York Co.*	1,127.1	7.84	2.74	584
Lancaster city *Lancaster Co.*	1,329.1	6.41	0.08	545
Laurel Bay cdp *Beaufort Co.*	1,309.2	4.50	0.89	36
Laurens city *Laurens Co.*	879.9	10.39	0.00	614
Lexington town *Lexington Co.*	2,014.5	8.87	0.08	394
Little River cdp *Horry Co.*	855.0	10.48	0.35	36
Lugoff cdp *Kershaw Co.*	494.4	15.03	0.25	269
Marion city *Marion Co.*	1,569.7	4.42	0.00	75
Mauldin city *Greenville Co.*	2,299.5	9.95	0.05	942
Moncks Corner town *Berkeley Co.*	1,082.3	7.29	0.13	52
Mount Pleasant town *Charleston Co.*	1,504.9	45.08	7.52	23
Mullins city *Marion Co.*	1,521.7	3.06	0.00	98
Murrells Inlet cdp *Georgetown Co.*	1,025.5	7.36	0.17	16
Myrtle Beach city *Horry Co.*	1,162.3	23.32	0.24	26
Newberry city *Newberry Co.*	1,198.7	8.57	0.00	492
North Augusta city *Aiken Co.*	1,065.7	20.03	0.46	387
North Charleston city *Charleston Co.*	1,331.8	73.19	3.46	20
North Myrtle Beach city *Horry Co.*	804.5	17.09	0.60	7
Oak Grove cdp *Lexington Co.*	1,547.4	6.65	0.04	338
Orangeburg city *Orangeburg Co.*	1,648.9	8.47	0.01	243
Parker cdp *Greenville Co.*	1,675.7	6.82	0.05	1,020
Piedmont cdp *Anderson Co.*	593.7	8.60	0.17	791
Port Royal town *Beaufort Co.*	563.6	18.95	3.06	23
Red Bank cdp *Lexington Co.*	814.6	11.81	0.23	341
Red Hill cdp *Horry Co.*	1,171.2	11.29	0.06	33
Rock Hill city *York Co.*	1,851.9	35.72	0.16	679
Saint Andrews cdp *Richland Co.*	3,229.5	6.35	0.02	322
Sangaree cdp *Berkeley Co.*	4,047.6	2.03	0.00	72
Sans Souci cdp *Greenville Co.*	2,376.9	3.31	0.05	1,014
Seneca city *Oconee Co.*	1,072.9	7.55	0.05	955
Seven Oaks cdp *Lexington Co.*	1,996.7	7.58	0.12	217
Simpsonville city *Greenville Co.*	2,070.3	8.81	0.02	866
Socastee cdp *Horry Co.*	1,495.0	13.35	0.52	20
Spartanburg city *Spartanburg Co.*	1,872.2	19.77	0.12	797
Summerville town *Dorchester Co.*	2,404.7	18.04	0.11	72
Sumter city *Sumter Co.*	1,263.0	32.09	0.20	171
Taylors cdp *Greenville Co.*	2,020.2	10.70	0.04	925
Tega Cay city *York Co.*	1,969.1	3.87	0.69	630
Travelers Rest city *Greenville Co.*	1,012.1	4.52	0.02	1,099
Union city *Union Co.*	1,038.2	8.08	0.00	640
Valley Falls cdp *Spartanburg Co.*	1,215.4	5.18	0.03	797
Wade Hampton cdp *Greenville Co.*	2,301.9	8.96	0.05	1,024
Walterboro city *Colleton Co.*	832.0	6.49	0.00	69
Welcome cdp *Greenville Co.*	1,438.2	4.64	0.05	984
West Columbia city *Lexington Co.*	2,143.6	6.99	0.21	285
Woodfield cdp *Richland Co.*	3,391.0	2.74	0.04	341
York city *York Co.*	942.3	8.21	0.12	758

SOURCE: *U.S. Census Bureau, Census 2010*

Population by Race/Hispanic Origin

Place	White[1] (%)	Black[1] (%)	Asian[1] (%)	AIAN[1,2] (%)	NHOPI[1,3] (%)	Two or More Races (%)	Hispanic[4] (%)
Abbeville city *Abbeville Co.*	46.9	50.5	0.4	0.2	0.0	1.5	0.9
Aiken city *Aiken Co.*	66.8	28.5	1.9	0.4	0.1	1.5	2.6
Anderson city *Anderson Co.*	61.4	33.6	1.0	0.3	0.0	2.1	4.1
Barnwell city *Barnwell Co.*	44.5	51.5	1.5	0.2	0.1	1.7	1.0
Batesburg-Leesville town *Lexington Co.*	49.5	46.6	0.7	0.1	0.0	1.2	3.6
Beaufort city *Beaufort Co.*	67.1	25.7	1.4	0.3	0.1	2.6	6.7
Belvedere cdp *Aiken Co.*	66.8	26.2	0.4	0.3	0.1	2.6	6.0
Bennettsville city *Marlboro Co.*	32.7	64.2	0.4	0.8	0.0	1.2	1.6
Berea cdp *Greenville Co.*	60.6	18.1	1.2	0.5	0.0	2.7	25.4
Bluffton town *Beaufort Co.*	71.4	16.2	2.0	0.3	0.0	2.9	18.8
Boiling Springs cdp *Spartanburg Co.*	81.9	10.4	3.7	0.3	0.0	1.5	4.3
Brookdale cdp *Orangeburg Co.*	0.8	98.1	0.2	0.1	0.0	0.8	0.7
Burton cdp *Beaufort Co.*	48.1	43.1	1.3	0.4	0.2	2.7	9.9
Camden city *Kershaw Co.*	62.2	35.1	0.7	0.2	0.0	1.1	2.4
Cayce city *Lexington Co.*	68.0	25.1	1.9	0.4	0.1	2.1	4.3
Centerville cdp *Anderson Co.*	83.3	13.3	1.1	0.2	0.0	1.3	2.7
Central town *Pickens Co.*	75.8	15.3	3.3	0.2	0.0	1.9	5.1
Charleston city *Charleston Co.*	70.2	25.4	1.6	0.2	0.1	1.5	2.9
Cheraw town *Chesterfield Co.*	40.2	56.0	0.6	0.8	0.0	1.8	1.1
Chester city *Chester Co.*	31.9	65.5	0.2	0.3	0.1	1.7	1.2
Clemson city *Pickens Co.*	79.1	10.3	8.1	0.1	0.0	1.6	2.2
Clinton city *Laurens Co.*	59.4	37.0	0.6	0.2	0.0	1.5	2.2
Clover town *York Co.*	76.5	19.2	0.6	0.5	0.0	1.9	4.4
Columbia city *Richland Co.*	51.7	42.2	2.2	0.3	0.1	2.0	4.3
Conway city *Horry Co.*	59.6	37.0	0.7	0.2	0.0	1.5	2.9
Darlington city *Darlington Co.*	37.9	60.6	0.4	0.2	0.0	0.7	0.7
Dentsville cdp *Richland Co.*	22.6	69.3	2.8	0.3	0.1	2.5	5.3
Dillon city *Dillon Co.*	42.8	53.1	0.6	1.6	0.0	1.2	1.2
Easley city *Pickens Co.*	83.1	11.4	0.8	0.2	0.0	1.8	5.6
Edgefield town *Edgefield Co.*	38.9	54.1	0.4	0.3	0.1	2.4	11.9
Five Forks cdp *Greenville Co.*	87.5	5.5	4.4	0.2	0.0	1.5	4.2
Florence city *Florence Co.*	50.0	46.0	1.8	0.3	0.0	1.3	1.5
Forest Acres city *Richland Co.*	76.0	19.4	1.5	0.2	0.1	1.9	3.0
Forestbrook cdp *Horry Co.*	85.9	7.6	1.3	0.3	0.1	2.5	5.8
Fort Mill town *York Co.*	77.6	17.6	1.3	0.4	0.0	2.1	2.9
Fountain Inn city *Greenville Co.*	63.7	31.2	0.3	0.3	0.2	2.0	6.0
Gaffney city *Cherokee Co.*	50.1	45.7	0.9	0.2	0.1	1.6	3.1
Gantt cdp *Greenville Co.*	29.1	59.2	0.3	0.4	0.0	1.8	13.2
Garden City cdp *Horry Co.*	95.3	1.7	0.3	0.3	0.1	1.4	2.9
Georgetown city *Georgetown Co.*	37.8	56.7	0.7	0.2	0.1	1.3	5.3
Goose Creek city *Berkeley Co.*	71.2	18.3	3.7	0.5	0.1	3.6	6.1
Greenville city *Greenville Co.*	64.0	30.0	1.4	0.3	0.1	1.8	5.9
Greenwood city *Greenwood Co.*	44.6	44.7	1.0	0.4	0.1	1.4	11.0
Greer city *Greenville Co.*	70.8	17.3	2.2	0.3	0.1	2.1	14.5
Hanahan city *Berkeley Co.*	74.7	13.9	3.4	0.6	0.1	2.9	9.1
Hartsville city *Darlington Co.*	51.0	46.3	0.8	0.2	0.1	1.0	1.5
Hilton Head Island town *Beaufort Co.*	82.9	7.5	0.9	0.2	0.1	1.2	15.8
Hollywood town *Charleston Co.*	41.0	55.4	0.3	0.2	0.1	0.8	4.0
Homeland Park cdp *Anderson Co.*	62.5	31.8	0.3	0.2	0.0	2.3	5.6
Irmo town *Richland Co.*	64.6	29.9	1.6	0.4	0.0	2.5	3.3

Place	White[1] (%)	Black[1] (%)	Asian[1] (%)	AIAN[1,2] (%)	NHOPI[1,3] (%)	Two or More Races (%)	Hispanic[4] (%)
Ladson cdp *Berkeley Co.*	61.5	26.3	2.2	0.8	0.1	3.6	11.3
Lake City city *Florence Co.*	19.4	77.5	0.3	0.3	0.0	0.9	3.0
Lake Murray of Richland cdp *Richland Co.*	96.1	1.3	1.1	0.2	0.0	0.9	1.7
Lake Wylie cdp *York Co.*	88.7	7.1	1.4	0.3	0.1	1.4	3.9
Lancaster city *Lancaster Co.*	43.0	51.3	0.9	0.2	0.0	1.1	5.7
Laurel Bay cdp *Beaufort Co.*	66.9	23.9	1.3	0.9	0.1	3.8	11.1
Laurens city *Laurens Co.*	52.5	42.8	0.3	0.3	0.0	1.2	5.7
Lexington town *Lexington Co.*	80.8	12.7	3.7	0.3	0.0	1.5	3.5
Little River cdp *Horry Co.*	89.0	6.6	0.9	0.5	0.0	1.3	3.2
Lugoff cdp *Kershaw Co.*	79.9	16.9	0.5	0.2	0.1	1.4	2.7
Marion city *Marion Co.*	27.8	69.2	1.1	0.2	0.0	1.4	1.3
Mauldin city *Greenville Co.*	68.7	22.5	3.5	0.3	0.1	2.2	7.7
Moncks Corner town *Berkeley Co.*	57.7	36.0	0.5	0.5	0.0	2.0	5.1
Mount Pleasant town *Charleston Co.*	91.3	5.1	1.6	0.2	0.0	1.1	2.7
Mullins city *Marion Co.*	31.2	65.8	1.0	0.4	0.0	1.4	0.8
Murrells Inlet cdp *Georgetown Co.*	90.7	6.5	0.9	0.3	0.0	0.8	2.2
Myrtle Beach city *Horry Co.*	72.3	13.9	1.5	0.7	0.3	2.7	13.7
Newberry city *Newberry Co.*	45.4	45.6	0.6	0.4	0.1	1.8	8.6
North Augusta city *Aiken Co.*	74.2	20.4	1.1	0.3	0.0	2.0	4.2
North Charleston city *Charleston Co.*	41.6	47.2	1.9	0.5	0.2	2.5	10.9
North Myrtle Beach city *Horry Co.*	90.4	3.3	0.9	0.5	0.1	1.4	6.3
Oak Grove cdp *Lexington Co.*	78.8	11.3	1.6	0.4	0.0	1.8	10.7
Orangeburg city *Orangeburg Co.*	21.3	75.0	1.7	0.2	0.1	1.1	1.9
Parker cdp *Greenville Co.*	62.0	21.7	0.4	0.5	0.0	2.6	20.8
Piedmont cdp *Anderson Co.*	89.1	7.8	0.2	0.3	0.0	1.7	2.5
Port Royal town *Beaufort Co.*	68.8	20.7	2.5	0.6	0.1	3.7	13.3
Red Bank cdp *Lexington Co.*	84.6	10.3	0.6	0.5	0.0	1.9	4.0
Red Hill cdp *Horry Co.*	81.5	9.9	1.2	0.5	0.1	2.2	8.5
Rock Hill city *York Co.*	54.6	38.3	1.7	0.5	0.1	2.1	5.7
Saint Andrews cdp *Richland Co.*	28.3	65.7	2.0	0.3	0.1	2.2	3.7
Sangaree cdp *Berkeley Co.*	70.4	23.6	1.1	0.8	0.2	2.8	4.8
Sans Souci cdp *Greenville Co.*	69.5	15.3	1.0	1.7	0.1	2.7	17.1
Seneca city *Oconee Co.*	65.3	29.0	0.9	0.3	0.0	2.3	4.5
Seven Oaks cdp *Lexington Co.*	60.4	32.0	2.8	0.3	0.2	2.8	3.8
Simpsonville city *Greenville Co.*	75.7	16.4	1.3	0.3	0.1	2.3	8.9
Socastee cdp *Horry Co.*	81.8	7.6	1.8	0.6	0.2	2.9	10.8
Spartanburg city *Spartanburg Co.*	45.6	49.3	1.8	0.2	0.0	1.8	3.4
Summerville town *Dorchester Co.*	72.1	21.4	1.5	0.4	0.1	2.9	5.0
Sumter city *Sumter Co.*	45.3	49.1	1.6	0.3	0.1	2.1	3.6
Taylors cdp *Greenville Co.*	76.9	14.9	2.5	0.2	0.1	2.0	8.3
Tega Cay city *York Co.*	92.6	3.0	2.0	0.2	0.1	1.4	3.3
Travelers Rest city *Greenville Co.*	79.9	15.3	1.1	0.2	0.0	1.6	4.5
Union city *Union Co.*	50.5	47.0	0.4	0.3	0.0	1.4	1.2
Valley Falls cdp *Spartanburg Co.*	68.8	24.6	1.7	0.3	0.0	1.4	6.6
Wade Hampton cdp *Greenville Co.*	78.0	10.2	3.2	0.4	0.1	2.1	11.2
Walterboro city *Colleton Co.*	45.2	50.5	1.0	0.3	0.0	1.5	2.9
Welcome cdp *Greenville Co.*	58.6	27.9	0.4	0.6	0.0	1.8	16.3
West Columbia city *Lexington Co.*	68.0	18.5	1.8	0.8	0.0	2.3	14.5
Woodfield cdp *Richland Co.*	30.9	51.4	3.1	0.7	0.3	3.8	19.3
York city *York Co.*	54.4	38.4	0.6	0.8	0.0	2.1	7.3

NOTE: (1) Exclude multiple race combinations; (2) American Indian/Alaska Native; (3) Native Hawaiian/Other Pacific Islander; (4) May be of any race
SOURCE: U.S. Census Bureau, Census 2010

Average Household Size, Age, and Male/Female Ratio

Place	Average Household Size (persons)	Median Age (years)	Age Under 18 (%)	Age 65 and Over (%)	Males per 100 Females
Abbeville city Abbeville Co.	2.30	40.4	24.0	17.5	81.3
Aiken city Aiken Co.	2.20	44.8	19.6	21.9	85.3
Anderson city Anderson Co.	2.25	36.8	23.4	17.9	80.2
Barnwell city Barnwell Co.	2.39	36.7	26.5	15.2	89.5
Batesburg-Leesville town Lexington Co.	2.46	39.8	24.7	16.6	85.1
Beaufort city Beaufort Co.	2.28	34.2	22.3	15.5	95.6
Belvedere cdp Aiken Co.	2.54	36.2	25.0	15.0	94.0
Bennettsville city Marlboro Co.	2.34	38.7	20.5	14.7	121.2
Berea cdp Greenville Co.	2.58	36.2	24.1	15.9	94.9
Bluffton town Beaufort Co.	2.84	32.7	28.9	7.3	95.5
Boiling Springs cdp Spartanburg Co.	2.60	35.3	27.3	10.7	92.7
Brookdale cdp Orangeburg Co.	2.48	27.7	21.3	14.6	81.6
Burton cdp Beaufort Co.	2.62	31.3	26.4	9.1	94.6
Camden city Kershaw Co.	2.26	45.3	21.9	21.6	81.7
Cayce city Lexington Co.	2.34	34.9	18.6	14.0	92.1
Centerville cdp Anderson Co.	2.46	39.3	23.1	15.7	90.6
Central town Pickens Co.	2.43	22.5	11.1	6.8	105.2
Charleston city Charleston Co.	2.18	32.5	18.0	12.2	89.6
Cheraw town Chesterfield Co.	2.36	40.6	26.0	18.6	78.2
Chester city Chester Co.	2.53	36.4	27.0	13.6	91.9
Clemson city Pickens Co.	2.33	24.3	13.8	11.6	111.9
Clinton city Laurens Co.	2.40	32.7	21.7	16.1	85.2
Clover town York Co.	2.65	33.8	29.1	10.1	92.4
Columbia city Richland Co.	2.18	28.1	17.0	8.7	106.0
Conway city Horry Co.	2.49	29.3	20.0	13.2	84.3
Darlington city Darlington Co.	2.32	41.6	23.8	19.0	76.5
Dentsville cdp Richland Co.	2.25	33.6	23.0	13.1	81.8
Dillon city Dillon Co.	2.51	36.2	27.4	16.2	85.8
Easley city Pickens Co.	2.39	40.5	22.8	18.0	89.7
Edgefield town Edgefield Co.	2.24	38.7	13.5	12.0	228.9
Five Forks cdp Greenville Co.	3.05	37.3	33.3	6.9	97.1
Florence city Florence Co.	2.43	37.4	24.5	13.9	83.5
Forest Acres city Richland Co.	2.11	43.0	21.0	19.1	84.8
Forestbrook cdp Horry Co.	2.65	39.9	23.3	13.0	99.1
Fort Mill town York Co.	2.58	36.3	29.8	10.0	87.5
Fountain Inn city Greenville Co.	2.67	35.0	27.2	11.4	88.4
Gaffney city Cherokee Co.	2.34	38.6	22.4	17.4	85.2
Gantt cdp Greenville Co.	2.68	36.4	26.0	13.0	92.3
Garden City cdp Horry Co.	1.99	56.1	13.0	35.2	87.4
Georgetown city Georgetown Co.	2.53	36.7	27.1	14.7	81.6
Goose Creek city Berkeley Co.	2.72	30.2	24.9	7.3	106.8
Greenville city Greenville Co.	2.08	34.6	19.4	12.8	92.7
Greenwood city Greenwood Co.	2.38	31.6	24.2	14.5	84.2
Greer city Greenville Co.	2.52	33.9	26.6	10.9	90.5
Hanahan city Berkeley Co.	2.52	34.2	24.3	10.8	101.1
Hartsville city Darlington Co.	2.32	36.7	24.3	16.2	79.8
Hilton Head Island town Beaufort Co.	2.23	50.9	16.6	28.8	96.4
Hollywood town Charleston Co.	2.60	45.7	20.2	15.0	97.3
Homeland Park cdp Anderson Co.	2.45	36.1	25.8	14.9	91.4
Irmo town Richland Co.	2.56	36.6	25.2	10.2	89.7

Place	Average Household Size (persons)	Median Age (years)	Age Under 18 (%)	Age 65 and Over (%)	Males per 100 Females
Ladson cdp *Berkeley Co.*	2.95	32.2	29.5	7.3	96.5
Lake City city *Florence Co.*	2.63	34.0	29.2	13.8	82.2
Lake Murray of Richland cdp *Richland Co.*	2.65	45.9	23.5	18.2	90.8
Lake Wylie cdp *York Co.*	2.51	40.4	26.3	14.3	97.3
Lancaster city *Lancaster Co.*	2.40	36.9	25.3	16.3	85.0
Laurel Bay cdp *Beaufort Co.*	3.04	23.6	37.3	2.2	93.5
Laurens city *Laurens Co.*	2.34	39.9	24.0	19.5	84.9
Lexington town *Lexington Co.*	2.31	34.8	24.6	10.3	93.0
Little River cdp *Horry Co.*	2.02	54.1	13.1	29.0	92.9
Lugoff cdp *Kershaw Co.*	2.59	39.2	26.3	13.3	92.8
Marion city *Marion Co.*	2.48	35.3	27.6	14.6	78.2
Mauldin city *Greenville Co.*	2.42	37.1	24.5	11.8	88.9
Moncks Corner town *Berkeley Co.*	2.60	33.1	27.4	10.6	94.5
Mount Pleasant town *Charleston Co.*	2.43	39.1	24.1	12.2	92.6
Mullins city *Marion Co.*	2.44	39.9	25.3	18.3	73.9
Murrells Inlet cdp *Georgetown Co.*	2.12	53.6	13.7	26.4	94.9
Myrtle Beach city *Horry Co.*	2.22	39.2	18.5	15.1	103.2
Newberry city *Newberry Co.*	2.36	33.2	22.7	16.4	85.8
North Augusta city *Aiken Co.*	2.34	37.9	23.4	14.7	88.5
North Charleston city *Charleston Co.*	2.54	30.6	25.5	8.4	98.4
North Myrtle Beach city *Horry Co.*	2.04	54.7	11.8	27.2	97.7
Oak Grove cdp *Lexington Co.*	2.45	36.0	24.4	11.8	97.8
Orangeburg city *Orangeburg Co.*	2.27	28.8	18.9	14.2	84.7
Parker cdp *Greenville Co.*	2.65	34.0	25.5	12.2	99.4
Piedmont cdp *Anderson Co.*	2.56	39.5	24.2	14.9	94.5
Port Royal town *Beaufort Co.*	2.35	22.9	18.0	5.3	146.1
Red Bank cdp *Lexington Co.*	2.59	35.8	25.5	8.6	94.1
Red Hill cdp *Horry Co.*	2.43	40.0	19.3	18.6	96.7
Rock Hill city *York Co.*	2.43	31.9	24.4	10.4	85.3
Saint Andrews cdp *Richland Co.*	2.09	31.0	22.2	9.4	85.2
Sangaree cdp *Berkeley Co.*	2.84	33.6	28.0	6.9	93.4
Sans Souci cdp *Greenville Co.*	2.42	35.2	23.4	13.8	91.0
Seneca city *Oconee Co.*	2.27	41.4	22.2	18.9	87.1
Seven Oaks cdp *Lexington Co.*	2.32	38.3	22.1	15.4	89.3
Simpsonville city *Greenville Co.*	2.57	36.5	26.0	11.0	93.9
Socastee cdp *Horry Co.*	2.50	36.3	22.5	11.6	97.9
Spartanburg city *Spartanburg Co.*	2.27	35.5	23.5	14.6	79.0
Summerville town *Dorchester Co.*	2.55	34.7	27.0	10.5	89.2
Sumter city *Sumter Co.*	2.48	32.5	25.9	13.9	88.9
Taylors cdp *Greenville Co.*	2.50	36.9	24.6	13.6	89.7
Tega Cay city *York Co.*	2.77	40.2	29.2	10.5	97.8
Travelers Rest city *Greenville Co.*	2.60	34.4	29.3	12.1	89.8
Union city *Union Co.*	2.24	41.3	23.5	18.0	80.5
Valley Falls cdp *Spartanburg Co.*	2.22	23.0	16.5	9.2	77.6
Wade Hampton cdp *Greenville Co.*	2.26	39.8	20.5	18.1	91.7
Walterboro city *Colleton Co.*	2.38	38.9	25.8	17.9	80.3
Welcome cdp *Greenville Co.*	2.54	36.8	24.8	13.9	90.9
West Columbia city *Lexington Co.*	2.23	37.4	18.5	16.3	95.7
Woodfield cdp *Richland Co.*	2.58	34.3	24.3	13.2	87.0
York city *York Co.*	2.57	34.6	27.5	14.3	86.0

SOURCE: *U.S. Census Bureau, Census 2010*

Foreign Born, Language Spoken, Disabled Persons, and Veterans

Place	Foreign Born (%)	Speak English Only at Home (%)	With a Disability (%)	Veterans (%)
Abbeville city *Abbeville Co.*	0.50	98.0	24.5	9.4
Aiken city *Aiken Co.*	4.00	96.0	12.0	12.5
Anderson city *Anderson Co.*	3.70	94.5	17.2	8.9
Barnwell city *Barnwell Co.*	1.70	98.4	18.9	7.5
Batesburg-Leesville town *Lexington Co.*	2.40	96.8	23.1	9.2
Beaufort city *Beaufort Co.*	7.60	89.8	15.1	18.2
Belvedere cdp *Aiken Co.*	5.60	91.3	14.4	14.8
Bennettsville city *Marlboro Co.*	1.90	97.5	17.9	8.5
Berea cdp *Greenville Co.*	13.20	77.1	12.8	7.9
Bluffton town *Beaufort Co.*	16.10	77.9	9.3	10.4
Boiling Springs cdp *Spartanburg Co.*	10.90	86.0	8.3	8.4
Brookdale cdp *Orangeburg Co.*	0.90	97.7	16.9	9.4
Burton cdp *Beaufort Co.*	2.60	95.1	13.7	19.2
Camden city *Kershaw Co.*	4.00	94.7	10.9	10.3
Cayce city *Lexington Co.*	5.30	94.0	13.5	10.9
Centerville cdp *Anderson Co.*	2.90	96.5	12.4	9.1
Central town *Pickens Co.*	5.40	93.5	10.1	3.0
Charleston city *Charleston Co.*	4.20	94.7	9.6	9.5
Cheraw town *Chesterfield Co.*	1.80	98.5	20.3	15.3
Chester city *Chester Co.*	1.10	99.0	17.7	9.1
Clemson city *Pickens Co.*	13.40	87.3	7.3	7.4
Clinton city *Laurens Co.*	1.60	97.2	19.1	5.8
Clover town *York Co.*	2.00	95.8	10.8	8.4
Columbia city *Richland Co.*	5.20	92.3	11.3	8.8
Conway city *Horry Co.*	2.30	96.7	14.2	10.0
Darlington city *Darlington Co.*	4.40	96.1	16.1	8.0
Dentsville cdp *Richland Co.*	6.20	91.8	13.1	11.8
Dillon city *Dillon Co.*	1.80	95.6	18.2	10.0
Easley city *Pickens Co.*	4.90	93.3	15.6	11.8
Edgefield town *Edgefield Co.*	10.10	85.9	11.9	8.4
Five Forks cdp *Greenville Co.*	7.90	91.4	4.3	8.4
Florence city *Florence Co.*	2.30	96.3	15.1	9.4
Forest Acres city *Richland Co.*	5.00	92.6	10.6	12.4
Forestbrook cdp *Horry Co.*	3.00	96.1	12.0	10.9
Fort Mill town *York Co.*	3.90	93.8	9.5	10.5
Fountain Inn city *Greenville Co.*	3.40	96.7	14.0	11.5
Gaffney city *Cherokee Co.*	2.10	95.1	17.1	10.5
Gantt cdp *Greenville Co.*	7.30	89.3	13.2	7.7
Garden City cdp *Horry Co.*	3.70	96.6	17.1	17.6
Georgetown city *Georgetown Co.*	3.30	95.4	18.1	11.9
Goose Creek city *Berkeley Co.*	5.40	91.8	9.2	17.8
Greenville city *Greenville Co.*	6.50	91.7	11.0	7.0
Greenwood city *Greenwood Co.*	5.80	89.8	15.2	7.3
Greer city *Greenville Co.*	11.80	80.5	12.7	7.9
Hanahan city *Berkeley Co.*	12.10	84.3	9.3	15.3
Hartsville city *Darlington Co.*	2.60	97.3	20.0	9.8
Hilton Head Island town *Beaufort Co.*	15.10	81.4	10.8	14.0
Hollywood town *Charleston Co.*	1.50	99.2	17.2	12.2
Homeland Park cdp *Anderson Co.*	1.60	96.8	22.0	7.7
Irmo town *Richland Co.*	2.80	94.9	9.5	14.2

Place	Foreign Born (%)	Speak English Only at Home (%)	With a Disability (%)	Veterans (%)
Ladson cdp *Berkeley Co.*	6.00	92.0	12.5	17.3
Lake City city *Florence Co.*	0.20	98.7	24.6	9.5
Lake Murray of Richland cdp *Richland Co.*	2.80	96.6	8.8	11.8
Lake Wylie cdp *York Co.*	3.40	95.7	8.4	11.2
Lancaster city *Lancaster Co.*	1.40	95.9	15.9	8.1
Laurel Bay cdp *Beaufort Co.*	1.80	94.0	8.5	22.4
Laurens city *Laurens Co.*	5.10	92.0	22.1	9.1
Lexington town *Lexington Co.*	5.30	92.1	11.7	9.4
Little River cdp *Horry Co.*	4.10	93.0	14.9	15.2
Lugoff cdp *Kershaw Co.*	3.20	94.5	12.1	11.2
Marion city *Marion Co.*	1.50	97.9	16.4	8.7
Mauldin city *Greenville Co.*	7.20	90.7	9.0	11.8
Moncks Corner town *Berkeley Co.*	4.50	94.3	15.1	13.2
Mount Pleasant town *Charleston Co.*	4.30	94.8	7.1	10.9
Mullins city *Marion Co.*	0.80	99.2	23.0	8.6
Murrells Inlet cdp *Georgetown Co.*	0.90	98.0	14.3	15.9
Myrtle Beach city *Horry Co.*	18.40	77.4	14.4	9.4
Newberry city *Newberry Co.*	10.20	83.5	15.1	6.1
North Augusta city *Aiken Co.*	3.60	94.9	12.7	12.6
North Charleston city *Charleston Co.*	9.20	87.7	10.5	12.6
North Myrtle Beach city *Horry Co.*	7.50	93.1	16.0	15.6
Oak Grove cdp *Lexington Co.*	6.00	92.3	12.4	11.0
Orangeburg city *Orangeburg Co.*	2.60	94.9	13.6	8.8
Parker cdp *Greenville Co.*	9.60	80.0	17.6	8.4
Piedmont cdp *Anderson Co.*	0.90	99.5	18.4	7.1
Port Royal town *Beaufort Co.*	5.30	86.6	9.0	28.7
Red Bank cdp *Lexington Co.*	1.50	97.0	12.9	9.0
Red Hill cdp *Horry Co.*	10.10	87.3	13.8	10.8
Rock Hill city *York Co.*	4.80	92.8	11.5	8.8
Saint Andrews cdp *Richland Co.*	4.30	93.6	13.6	9.1
Sangaree cdp *Berkeley Co.*	2.80	95.9	13.7	23.1
Sans Souci cdp *Greenville Co.*	15.70	76.0	14.2	10.5
Seneca city *Oconee Co.*	5.60	91.8	17.2	10.5
Seven Oaks cdp *Lexington Co.*	4.30	93.5	11.3	13.4
Simpsonville city *Greenville Co.*	9.10	85.1	11.7	9.9
Socastee cdp *Horry Co.*	9.30	89.9	12.5	15.2
Spartanburg city *Spartanburg Co.*	3.90	94.9	16.5	8.9
Summerville town *Dorchester Co.*	3.80	94.1	10.5	15.2
Sumter city *Sumter Co.*	3.70	95.2	16.6	15.6
Taylors cdp *Greenville Co.*	8.00	90.2	13.1	9.4
Tega Cay city *York Co.*	6.80	90.1	4.9	7.6
Travelers Rest city *Greenville Co.*	2.60	95.0	10.4	9.0
Union city *Union Co.*	0.20	98.8	21.3	10.5
Valley Falls cdp *Spartanburg Co.*	6.70	96.0	8.3	6.2
Wade Hampton cdp *Greenville Co.*	10.40	84.4	11.8	11.7
Walterboro city *Colleton Co.*	0.50	99.4	17.1	12.0
Welcome cdp *Greenville Co.*	10.80	86.3	11.6	9.4
West Columbia city *Lexington Co.*	13.50	85.6	12.2	10.1
Woodfield cdp *Richland Co.*	20.60	76.5	14.3	15.7
York city *York Co.*	6.10	90.3	18.4	8.9

SOURCE: U.S. Census Bureau, American Community Survey, 2009-2013 Five-Year Estimates

Five Largest Ancestry Groups

Place	Group 1	Group 2	Group 3	Group 4	Group 5
Abbeville city *Abbeville Co.*	American (14.6%)	Irish (6.2%)	Scotch-Irish (5.1%)	Scottish (3.6%)	English (3.3%)
Aiken city *Aiken Co.*	American (14.7%)	German (11.2%)	English (10.5%)	Irish (9.5%)	Italian (3.5%)
Anderson city *Anderson Co.*	American (12.7%)	English (10.0%)	Irish (9.7%)	German (6.7%)	Scotch-Irish (3.8%)
Barnwell city *Barnwell Co.*	American (13.0%)	German (6.5%)	English (4.3%)	Irish (4.1%)	Scotch-Irish (2.6%)
Batesburg-Leesville town *Lexington Co.*	American (11.0%)	German (9.5%)	Irish (7.0%)	English (5.9%)	Scotch-Irish (1.3%)
Beaufort city *Beaufort Co.*	German (13.2%)	English (12.3%)	Irish (10.0%)	American (9.0%)	Italian (4.0%)
Belvedere cdp *Aiken Co.*	American (18.4%)	Irish (7.2%)	German (5.3%)	English (5.3%)	Scotch-Irish (1.3%)
Bennettsville city *Marlboro Co.*	American (5.8%)	German (4.6%)	English (4.5%)	Irish (3.6%)	Scotch-Irish (1.6%)
Berea cdp *Greenville Co.*	American (12.2%)	Irish (9.9%)	German (6.5%)	English (6.2%)	Scotch-Irish (2.9%)
Bluffton town *Beaufort Co.*	Irish (13.4%)	German (12.6%)	Italian (9.1%)	English (8.8%)	American (4.6%)
Boiling Springs cdp *Spartanburg Co.*	American (13.2%)	English (11.9%)	Irish (11.5%)	German (8.5%)	Scottish (5.3%)
Brookdale cdp *Orangeburg Co.*	American (1.2%)	African (1.0%)	English (0.4%)	Kenyan (0.3%)	Dutch (0.2%)
Burton cdp *Beaufort Co.*	German (8.0%)	Scottish (4.9%)	American (4.6%)	Dutch (4.3%)	Irish (4.2%)
Camden city *Kershaw Co.*	American (25.6%)	German (7.7%)	Irish (7.5%)	English (7.4%)	Scotch-Irish (3.8%)
Cayce city *Lexington Co.*	German (13.0%)	Irish (9.3%)	American (8.4%)	English (7.9%)	Scotch-Irish (3.8%)
Centerville cdp *Anderson Co.*	Irish (13.6%)	American (12.9%)	German (11.7%)	English (11.4%)	Scotch-Irish (5.1%)
Central town *Pickens Co.*	German (16.7%)	English (14.5%)	Irish (12.7%)	American (8.1%)	Italian (4.8%)
Charleston city *Charleston Co.*	German (12.4%)	English (11.9%)	Irish (11.7%)	American (11.5%)	Italian (4.0%)
Cheraw town *Chesterfield Co.*	American (12.9%)	English (9.2%)	Scottish (4.0%)	Scotch-Irish (3.1%)	Jamaican (3.0%)
Chester city *Chester Co.*	American (10.5%)	African (7.8%)	English (4.7%)	Irish (3.1%)	German (2.7%)
Clemson city *Pickens Co.*	German (16.7%)	English (13.3%)	Irish (11.7%)	Italian (4.5%)	American (4.5%)
Clinton city *Laurens Co.*	American (8.2%)	Irish (7.8%)	English (7.4%)	German (6.2%)	Scotch-Irish (2.6%)
Clover town *York Co.*	American (18.2%)	German (13.5%)	Irish (7.9%)	English (6.1%)	African (5.3%)
Columbia city *Richland Co.*	English (9.1%)	German (9.0%)	Irish (8.8%)	American (7.7%)	Scottish (2.9%)
Conway city *Horry Co.*	American (11.2%)	Irish (9.1%)	German (8.2%)	English (8.0%)	Italian (4.6%)
Darlington city *Darlington Co.*	Irish (9.6%)	American (6.1%)	English (5.4%)	German (3.8%)	Scotch-Irish (2.7%)
Dentsville cdp *Richland Co.*	Irish (3.8%)	American (3.6%)	German (2.8%)	English (2.2%)	African (2.2%)
Dillon city *Dillon Co.*	American (9.8%)	English (4.0%)	German (4.0%)	Irish (2.3%)	Scottish (1.8%)
Easley city *Pickens Co.*	American (13.1%)	Irish (12.8%)	English (11.6%)	German (10.7%)	Scotch-Irish (2.9%)
Edgefield town *Edgefield Co.*	American (7.8%)	English (5.9%)	Irish (4.8%)	German (3.6%)	African (3.0%)
Five Forks cdp *Greenville Co.*	German (18.8%)	English (16.5%)	Irish (13.5%)	American (10.0%)	Italian (8.2%)
Florence city *Florence Co.*	American (8.4%)	English (7.7%)	German (7.4%)	Irish (5.6%)	Scotch-Irish (3.6%)
Forest Acres city *Richland Co.*	English (16.1%)	German (12.7%)	American (10.6%)	Irish (10.4%)	Scotch-Irish (7.9%)
Forestbrook cdp *Horry Co.*	German (20.8%)	American (15.0%)	Irish (13.4%)	English (13.1%)	Italian (7.4%)
Fort Mill town *York Co.*	German (16.9%)	English (15.9%)	Irish (15.2%)	American (7.2%)	Scottish (4.2%)
Fountain Inn city *Greenville Co.*	German (10.1%)	American (9.9%)	English (9.6%)	Irish (7.6%)	Italian (4.6%)
Gaffney city *Cherokee Co.*	American (8.3%)	German (5.5%)	English (5.1%)	Irish (3.4%)	Scotch-Irish (2.0%)
Gantt cdp *Greenville Co.*	American (6.2%)	English (3.5%)	Irish (3.1%)	German (2.8%)	Scottish (1.3%)
Garden City cdp *Horry Co.*	German (19.9%)	American (19.5%)	Irish (14.5%)	English (12.3%)	Italian (6.0%)
Georgetown city *Georgetown Co.*	American (7.2%)	English (5.2%)	Irish (4.5%)	German (3.9%)	French (1.0%)
Goose Creek city *Berkeley Co.*	German (14.8%)	Irish (13.6%)	American (12.6%)	English (8.4%)	Italian (4.5%)
Greenville city *Greenville Co.*	English (12.2%)	German (10.9%)	Irish (9.3%)	American (9.1%)	Scotch-Irish (3.5%)
Greenwood city *Greenwood Co.*	American (14.2%)	German (5.7%)	Irish (5.6%)	English (5.5%)	Scotch-Irish (2.7%)
Greer city *Greenville Co.*	German (11.2%)	Irish (10.0%)	American (7.9%)	English (7.8%)	Italian (3.4%)
Hanahan city *Berkeley Co.*	German (12.8%)	Irish (11.1%)	American (10.8%)	English (9.0%)	French (4.9%)
Hartsville city *Darlington Co.*	Irish (12.7%)	German (8.8%)	English (8.5%)	American (7.5%)	Scotch-Irish (3.1%)
Hilton Head Island town *Beaufort Co.*	German (16.2%)	English (14.7%)	Irish (14.5%)	Italian (7.1%)	American (4.8%)
Hollywood town *Charleston Co.*	American (12.0%)	English (10.1%)	German (5.1%)	Irish (4.7%)	Italian (3.4%)
Homeland Park cdp *Anderson Co.*	American (15.4%)	Irish (11.3%)	German (7.5%)	English (3.7%)	Scotch-Irish (1.3%)
Irmo town *Richland Co.*	German (16.3%)	Irish (14.2%)	American (9.3%)	English (8.7%)	Scottish (3.2%)

Place	Group 1	Group 2	Group 3	Group 4	Group 5
Ladson cdp *Berkeley Co.*	American (11.7%)	German (11.5%)	English (7.6%)	Irish (7.4%)	Polish (4.3%)
Lake City city *Florence Co.*	English (5.3%)	American (3.8%)	Scotch-Irish (3.6%)	Irish (2.5%)	Haitian (1.6%)
Lake Murray of Richland cdp *Richland Co.*	German (23.9%)	American (18.4%)	Irish (14.4%)	English (6.7%)	Scottish (5.8%)
Lake Wylie cdp *York Co.*	German (23.8%)	Irish (13.5%)	English (12.4%)	American (11.2%)	Italian (9.3%)
Lancaster city *Lancaster Co.*	American (11.5%)	German (5.1%)	Scotch-Irish (5.0%)	Irish (3.6%)	English (3.5%)
Laurel Bay cdp *Beaufort Co.*	German (17.0%)	Irish (10.7%)	Italian (6.4%)	English (5.2%)	Scotch-Irish (5.1%)
Laurens city *Laurens Co.*	English (8.3%)	American (8.2%)	Irish (7.2%)	German (4.4%)	Scottish (1.6%)
Lexington town *Lexington Co.*	Irish (16.6%)	German (12.9%)	English (12.6%)	American (11.5%)	Italian (4.4%)
Little River cdp *Horry Co.*	English (19.6%)	German (17.4%)	Irish (14.9%)	American (11.9%)	Italian (7.0%)
Lugoff cdp *Kershaw Co.*	American (22.9%)	Irish (11.7%)	German (8.8%)	English (8.3%)	Scottish (2.9%)
Marion city *Marion Co.*	English (6.2%)	Scotch-Irish (3.4%)	American (2.9%)	German (2.8%)	Irish (2.7%)
Mauldin city *Greenville Co.*	English (15.1%)	German (12.8%)	Irish (11.5%)	American (10.4%)	Scottish (3.4%)
Moncks Corner town *Berkeley Co.*	American (10.9%)	Irish (10.0%)	German (9.3%)	English (8.5%)	Italian (2.7%)
Mount Pleasant town *Charleston Co.*	German (18.2%)	Irish (16.5%)	English (14.8%)	American (10.5%)	Italian (6.4%)
Mullins city *Marion Co.*	American (16.1%)	English (8.0%)	European (2.6%)	Irish (2.1%)	West Indian (0.9%)
Murrells Inlet cdp *Georgetown Co.*	Irish (20.8%)	English (13.2%)	German (12.8%)	American (12.4%)	Italian (9.3%)
Myrtle Beach city *Horry Co.*	Irish (13.0%)	English (12.5%)	American (9.6%)	German (9.6%)	Italian (6.9%)
Newberry city *Newberry Co.*	American (16.0%)	German (8.7%)	Irish (6.1%)	English (5.7%)	Scotch-Irish (2.3%)
North Augusta city *Aiken Co.*	American (20.7%)	English (12.3%)	Irish (10.5%)	German (10.2%)	French (3.0%)
North Charleston city *Charleston Co.*	American (8.9%)	German (7.4%)	Irish (6.0%)	English (4.8%)	Italian (2.1%)
North Myrtle Beach city *Horry Co.*	English (23.3%)	German (16.6%)	Irish (16.1%)	American (9.5%)	Italian (7.0%)
Oak Grove cdp *Lexington Co.*	German (10.9%)	American (10.2%)	Irish (8.3%)	English (5.3%)	Italian (4.5%)
Orangeburg city *Orangeburg Co.*	English (4.9%)	American (4.3%)	Irish (3.0%)	German (2.9%)	French (0.6%)
Parker cdp *Greenville Co.*	American (12.5%)	Irish (9.9%)	English (8.0%)	German (4.2%)	Italian (2.3%)
Piedmont cdp *Anderson Co.*	American (21.3%)	Irish (13.4%)	English (10.4%)	Irish (7.5%)	French (2.3%)
Port Royal town *Beaufort Co.*	Irish (14.7%)	German (13.9%)	English (7.2%)	American (6.3%)	Italian (5.5%)
Red Bank cdp *Lexington Co.*	German (18.2%)	Irish (13.9%)	American (13.1%)	English (6.5%)	Italian (6.2%)
Red Hill cdp *Horry Co.*	American (19.3%)	German (16.6%)	Irish (13.2%)	English (11.9%)	Italian (6.8%)
Rock Hill city *York Co.*	Irish (9.9%)	German (9.7%)	African (9.0%)	English (8.2%)	American (5.8%)
Saint Andrews cdp *Richland Co.*	German (5.7%)	Irish (5.2%)	English (4.5%)	American (4.1%)	French (2.2%)
Sangaree cdp *Berkeley Co.*	Irish (16.6%)	German (13.4%)	American (13.3%)	English (4.1%)	Italian (3.5%)
Sans Souci cdp *Greenville Co.*	Irish (12.4%)	American (10.8%)	English (8.6%)	German (7.8%)	French (2.7%)
Seneca city *Oconee Co.*	German (11.1%)	Irish (8.9%)	English (7.8%)	American (6.9%)	Scotch-Irish (4.4%)
Seven Oaks cdp *Lexington Co.*	German (13.9%)	English (13.6%)	Irish (10.4%)	American (10.0%)	Italian (3.6%)
Simpsonville city *Greenville Co.*	American (14.4%)	Irish (10.7%)	German (9.2%)	English (9.1%)	Scotch-Irish (3.3%)
Socastee cdp *Horry Co.*	American (17.3%)	Irish (15.0%)	German (14.1%)	English (10.1%)	Italian (7.0%)
Spartanburg city *Spartanburg Co.*	English (10.0%)	Irish (7.7%)	American (7.0%)	German (6.6%)	Scottish (4.0%)
Summerville town *Dorchester Co.*	German (17.4%)	American (15.9%)	Irish (13.5%)	English (10.9%)	Italian (4.9%)
Sumter city *Sumter Co.*	American (9.3%)	German (6.8%)	Irish (6.2%)	English (6.1%)	African (6.0%)
Taylors cdp *Greenville Co.*	German (12.9%)	Irish (12.3%)	English (11.9%)	American (10.6%)	Scotch-Irish (3.1%)
Tega Cay city *York Co.*	German (16.2%)	English (15.6%)	Irish (15.0%)	Italian (12.5%)	American (11.6%)
Travelers Rest city *Greenville Co.*	English (19.0%)	Scotch-Irish (8.7%)	American (8.5%)	Irish (8.0%)	German (7.6%)
Union city *Union Co.*	American (8.5%)	German (6.5%)	Irish (6.4%)	English (3.9%)	Scottish (3.2%)
Valley Falls cdp *Spartanburg Co.*	Irish (14.2%)	American (11.4%)	German (10.1%)	English (7.9%)	Scotch-Irish (2.5%)
Wade Hampton cdp *Greenville Co.*	English (14.0%)	German (12.3%)	Irish (11.8%)	American (10.5%)	Scotch-Irish (4.8%)
Walterboro city *Colleton Co.*	American (8.7%)	German (7.1%)	Irish (6.0%)	English (5.9%)	Scotch-Irish (4.3%)
Welcome cdp *Greenville Co.*	American (14.6%)	Irish (8.8%)	English (5.7%)	German (3.3%)	Scotch-Irish (2.9%)
West Columbia city *Lexington Co.*	German (12.4%)	American (10.7%)	Irish (9.1%)	English (7.0%)	Italian (3.0%)
Woodfield cdp *Richland Co.*	American (5.0%)	German (4.4%)	English (3.2%)	Irish (2.0%)	French (1.8%)
York city *York Co.*	American (11.3%)	Scotch-Irish (4.8%)	Irish (4.3%)	German (4.0%)	African (3.9%)

NOTE: "French" excludes Basque; Please refer to the User Guide for more information.
SOURCE: U.S. Census Bureau, American Community Survey, 2009-2013 Five-Year Estimates

Marriage Status

Place	Never Married (%)	Now Married[1] (%)	Separated (%)	Widowed (%)	Divorced (%)
Abbeville city *Abbeville Co.*	34.8	45.3	4.1	10.3	9.6
Aiken city *Aiken Co.*	34.4	47.3	1.5	10.2	8.2
Anderson city *Anderson Co.*	37.1	41.5	4.8	11.6	9.8
Barnwell city *Barnwell Co.*	32.6	49.2	6.7	6.8	11.4
Batesburg-Leesville town *Lexington Co.*	30.0	49.1	5.1	9.6	11.3
Beaufort city *Beaufort Co.*	29.9	52.5	4.0	6.1	11.5
Belvedere cdp *Aiken Co.*	24.2	49.9	6.0	9.9	16.0
Bennettsville city *Marlboro Co.*	43.8	32.6	4.4	11.4	12.1
Berea cdp *Greenville Co.*	27.1	48.7	3.6	9.1	15.2
Bluffton town *Beaufort Co.*	26.6	56.1	1.8	4.3	13.0
Boiling Springs cdp *Spartanburg Co.*	24.3	67.7	1.9	2.9	5.0
Brookdale cdp *Orangeburg Co.*	52.7	31.6	10.4	9.6	6.0
Burton cdp *Beaufort Co.*	26.2	52.5	2.5	4.7	16.5
Camden city *Kershaw Co.*	27.6	49.1	2.9	10.5	12.8
Cayce city *Lexington Co.*	40.0	42.2	3.6	7.4	10.4
Centerville cdp *Anderson Co.*	24.7	61.4	4.5	4.8	9.1
Central town *Pickens Co.*	72.3	19.9	0.9	3.4	4.4
Charleston city *Charleston Co.*	43.5	41.0	2.5	5.4	10.2
Cheraw town *Chesterfield Co.*	30.8	39.7	4.7	13.2	16.3
Chester city *Chester Co.*	43.8	33.4	5.5	10.1	12.7
Clemson city *Pickens Co.*	56.0	34.8	1.0	4.8	4.5
Clinton city *Laurens Co.*	54.2	24.8	3.9	10.2	10.9
Clover town *York Co.*	24.2	55.8	3.1	7.0	13.0
Columbia city *Richland Co.*	54.2	32.3	3.5	4.7	8.8
Conway city *Horry Co.*	47.4	37.9	2.9	8.1	6.7
Darlington city *Darlington Co.*	31.1	44.6	4.3	10.2	14.1
Dentsville cdp *Richland Co.*	46.0	32.8	3.5	7.9	13.4
Dillon city *Dillon Co.*	34.6	46.7	5.1	11.7	7.1
Easley city *Pickens Co.*	24.2	56.7	3.4	7.6	11.5
Edgefield town *Edgefield Co.*	38.9	34.9	7.6	9.7	16.4
Five Forks cdp *Greenville Co.*	21.1	69.3	1.3	4.4	5.2
Florence city *Florence Co.*	35.1	46.1	4.4	8.1	10.7
Forest Acres city *Richland Co.*	29.5	47.0	2.0	9.7	13.8
Forestbrook cdp *Horry Co.*	27.2	58.2	4.2	5.0	9.6
Fort Mill town *York Co.*	26.4	60.5	2.5	4.5	8.7
Fountain Inn city *Greenville Co.*	31.1	48.7	2.9	7.8	12.4
Gaffney city *Cherokee Co.*	43.2	36.8	4.9	8.7	11.4
Gantt cdp *Greenville Co.*	42.9	40.2	5.4	8.4	8.6
Garden City cdp *Horry Co.*	19.2	52.6	1.5	15.5	12.8
Georgetown city *Georgetown Co.*	37.0	41.5	2.7	9.8	11.7
Goose Creek city *Berkeley Co.*	31.4	56.9	2.6	3.5	8.2
Greenville city *Greenville Co.*	42.1	39.9	3.9	6.3	11.7
Greenwood city *Greenwood Co.*	43.4	34.8	3.5	9.7	12.2
Greer city *Greenville Co.*	32.5	49.2	2.8	6.6	11.7
Hanahan city *Berkeley Co.*	30.8	52.2	3.8	5.3	11.7
Hartsville city *Darlington Co.*	38.2	38.5	4.5	13.5	9.9
Hilton Head Island town *Beaufort Co.*	20.9	63.1	2.4	7.3	8.7
Hollywood town *Charleston Co.*	26.9	53.8	1.9	7.6	11.6
Homeland Park cdp *Anderson Co.*	32.6	41.8	4.7	9.0	16.5
Irmo town *Richland Co.*	31.9	50.0	3.1	4.5	13.5

Place	Never Married (%)	Now Married[1] (%)	Separated (%)	Widowed (%)	Divorced (%)
Ladson cdp *Berkeley Co.*	32.6	52.0	4.6	5.3	10.1
Lake City city *Florence Co.*	39.0	41.6	5.8	12.9	6.5
Lake Murray of Richland cdp *Richland Co.*	20.0	69.0	1.4	6.0	5.0
Lake Wylie cdp *York Co.*	20.1	64.6	0.9	4.7	10.6
Lancaster city *Lancaster Co.*	39.9	37.9	5.2	9.0	13.2
Laurel Bay cdp *Beaufort Co.*	16.8	70.3	0.5	3.7	9.1
Laurens city *Laurens Co.*	35.6	42.9	2.2	11.6	10.0
Lexington town *Lexington Co.*	28.9	53.7	3.7	5.2	12.2
Little River cdp *Horry Co.*	16.2	58.7	1.5	9.1	16.0
Lugoff cdp *Kershaw Co.*	23.4	58.5	2.6	6.0	12.2
Marion city *Marion Co.*	41.2	37.1	6.2	10.9	10.9
Mauldin city *Greenville Co.*	30.1	53.2	1.9	6.9	9.8
Moncks Corner town *Berkeley Co.*	32.6	48.5	2.8	5.8	13.1
Mount Pleasant town *Charleston Co.*	26.5	58.5	2.3	4.9	10.1
Mullins city *Marion Co.*	33.9	45.5	8.7	12.1	8.5
Murrells Inlet cdp *Georgetown Co.*	20.3	62.6	1.8	7.0	10.0
Myrtle Beach city *Horry Co.*	34.8	46.2	2.9	6.8	12.1
Newberry city *Newberry Co.*	44.3	37.5	4.8	10.9	7.3
North Augusta city *Aiken Co.*	27.9	51.0	4.1	7.7	13.4
North Charleston city *Charleston Co.*	40.9	42.5	4.7	5.1	11.5
North Myrtle Beach city *Horry Co.*	18.6	58.5	3.7	8.6	14.3
Oak Grove cdp *Lexington Co.*	27.9	54.1	3.1	6.1	11.8
Orangeburg city *Orangeburg Co.*	52.0	31.1	4.0	8.7	8.2
Parker cdp *Greenville Co.*	36.9	44.7	4.4	6.2	12.1
Piedmont cdp *Anderson Co.*	27.0	51.8	1.7	8.2	12.9
Port Royal town *Beaufort Co.*	57.1	32.2	3.3	3.2	7.4
Red Bank cdp *Lexington Co.*	26.7	51.5	1.9	6.4	15.4
Red Hill cdp *Horry Co.*	31.9	52.9	3.7	6.8	8.4
Rock Hill city *York Co.*	38.4	45.1	3.9	6.3	10.2
Saint Andrews cdp *Richland Co.*	49.7	33.2	4.6	5.4	11.6
Sangaree cdp *Berkeley Co.*	28.8	53.5	3.1	5.1	12.6
Sans Souci cdp *Greenville Co.*	32.4	46.7	2.3	7.2	13.7
Seneca city *Oconee Co.*	29.6	40.8	3.3	11.2	18.4
Seven Oaks cdp *Lexington Co.*	31.5	50.4	3.4	7.2	10.9
Simpsonville city *Greenville Co.*	25.6	57.6	2.4	4.8	11.9
Socastee cdp *Horry Co.*	29.3	52.7	2.1	4.9	13.2
Spartanburg city *Spartanburg Co.*	41.0	36.8	4.1	10.4	11.8
Summerville town *Dorchester Co.*	26.4	55.6	2.7	6.0	12.0
Sumter city *Sumter Co.*	35.4	46.6	4.0	8.2	9.8
Taylors cdp *Greenville Co.*	27.6	51.8	2.2	6.0	14.6
Tega Cay city *York Co.*	19.4	72.5	1.1	2.2	5.9
Travelers Rest city *Greenville Co.*	29.2	54.2	4.6	6.1	10.5
Union city *Union Co.*	33.2	41.7	5.6	11.7	13.3
Valley Falls cdp *Spartanburg Co.*	53.3	36.2	0.9	5.0	5.5
Wade Hampton cdp *Greenville Co.*	27.4	53.4	3.5	7.6	11.6
Walterboro city *Colleton Co.*	36.1	35.8	7.5	14.0	14.1
Welcome cdp *Greenville Co.*	28.3	45.4	3.2	10.8	15.5
West Columbia city *Lexington Co.*	35.3	44.0	2.9	9.8	10.9
Woodfield cdp *Richland Co.*	36.5	46.2	5.2	7.3	10.0
York city *York Co.*	36.9	43.6	3.9	8.6	10.9

NOTE: (1) Includes separated.
SOURCE: U.S. Census Bureau, American Community Survey, 2009-2013 Five-Year Estimates

Employment by Occupation

Place	MBF[1] (%)	CES[2] (%)	ELCAM[3] (%)	HPT[4] (%)	S[5] (%)	SO[6] (%)	NRCM[7] (%)	PTMM[8] (%)
Abbeville city *Abbeville Co.*	9.5	1.1	11.7	3.8	26.4	24.6	4.9	18.0
Aiken city *Aiken Co.*	17.2	9.7	12.1	6.3	18.5	21.9	5.1	9.2
Anderson city *Anderson Co.*	10.7	2.6	10.0	6.2	21.7	23.5	8.1	17.1
Barnwell city *Barnwell Co.*	18.9	1.8	17.5	2.4	12.9	19.8	6.4	20.3
Batesburg-Leesville town *Lexington Co.*	13.2	3.0	11.9	1.1	19.4	28.7	7.2	15.5
Beaufort city *Beaufort Co.*	18.0	1.9	11.4	5.8	19.0	25.3	11.3	7.2
Belvedere cdp *Aiken Co.*	10.6	2.1	9.6	6.9	16.5	22.2	11.4	20.7
Bennettsville city *Marlboro Co.*	11.5	0.9	10.8	7.9	13.6	15.4	5.5	34.4
Berea cdp *Greenville Co.*	6.1	3.8	5.3	2.4	22.7	28.4	12.9	18.3
Bluffton town *Beaufort Co.*	16.7	1.6	9.6	5.9	22.0	27.8	9.4	7.0
Boiling Springs cdp *Spartanburg Co.*	11.9	5.2	16.1	7.6	11.7	26.2	6.0	15.1
Brookdale cdp *Orangeburg Co.*	6.0	3.0	10.2	0.0	20.0	37.2	3.4	20.2
Burton cdp *Beaufort Co.*	7.9	1.2	11.6	2.8	25.4	21.5	18.6	11.0
Camden city *Kershaw Co.*	15.4	2.2	13.5	10.8	17.4	19.2	11.7	9.7
Cayce city *Lexington Co.*	12.1	5.1	9.7	6.9	20.2	26.4	9.4	10.3
Centerville cdp *Anderson Co.*	11.2	5.3	11.1	8.3	14.3	21.3	6.0	22.5
Central town *Pickens Co.*	9.7	7.6	21.6	0.4	31.5	19.1	3.3	7.0
Charleston city *Charleston Co.*	15.8	6.1	13.4	9.4	20.2	23.7	4.8	6.6
Cheraw town *Chesterfield Co.*	11.3	0.0	10.2	4.4	24.7	32.3	4.7	12.4
Chester city *Chester Co.*	6.6	1.0	8.6	4.3	23.2	23.8	10.8	21.7
Clemson city *Pickens Co.*	13.0	8.7	27.4	5.5	15.0	18.7	5.4	6.4
Clinton city *Laurens Co.*	6.0	0.8	15.6	2.6	24.7	25.1	5.8	19.2
Clover town *York Co.*	16.5	2.8	10.1	4.3	12.4	26.5	12.1	15.3
Columbia city *Richland Co.*	14.0	4.9	16.7	6.2	21.1	23.6	5.8	7.7
Conway city *Horry Co.*	10.1	1.8	11.6	4.5	31.5	29.4	4.9	6.3
Darlington city *Darlington Co.*	10.2	2.8	17.2	4.6	19.5	24.8	4.7	16.3
Dentsville cdp *Richland Co.*	8.2	7.6	9.9	6.0	15.0	35.4	8.2	9.7
Dillon city *Dillon Co.*	11.4	0.6	7.4	5.7	24.6	19.6	9.7	21.0
Easley city *Pickens Co.*	11.5	4.9	9.8	5.9	16.5	28.6	8.9	13.8
Edgefield town *Edgefield Co.*	4.6	1.8	9.2	2.0	18.4	26.0	8.1	29.9
Five Forks cdp *Greenville Co.*	26.5	12.1	10.7	9.0	10.5	21.5	4.0	5.8
Florence city *Florence Co.*	13.9	3.6	14.1	10.7	19.6	24.3	4.2	9.5
Forest Acres city *Richland Co.*	16.0	4.8	23.9	6.0	14.1	28.0	3.5	3.6
Forestbrook cdp *Horry Co.*	10.1	7.5	5.7	8.1	24.2	33.2	7.9	3.3
Fort Mill town *York Co.*	21.9	5.2	10.8	4.5	10.5	33.7	5.1	8.3
Fountain Inn city *Greenville Co.*	12.8	4.4	12.1	1.5	19.8	24.1	6.6	18.7
Gaffney city *Cherokee Co.*	9.2	2.5	11.8	1.7	18.1	26.0	4.5	26.3
Gantt cdp *Greenville Co.*	7.6	2.5	5.8	6.4	16.0	24.8	9.7	27.2
Garden City cdp *Horry Co.*	14.9	1.4	8.5	3.6	23.0	33.4	9.8	5.4
Georgetown city *Georgetown Co.*	14.4	0.0	14.0	2.1	27.0	21.7	6.2	14.6
Goose Creek city *Berkeley Co.*	15.6	5.4	11.2	3.7	14.9	30.2	8.2	11.0
Greenville city *Greenville Co.*	16.3	6.0	14.3	7.4	17.6	24.0	5.0	9.5
Greenwood city *Greenwood Co.*	4.8	3.2	10.1	7.0	19.8	23.6	8.5	23.0
Greer city *Greenville Co.*	14.1	5.9	8.2	6.3	16.9	23.2	9.0	16.4
Hanahan city *Berkeley Co.*	13.7	5.0	7.4	4.9	18.7	26.8	10.6	12.9
Hartsville city *Darlington Co.*	10.0	7.6	22.6	3.7	19.7	19.6	4.3	12.7
Hilton Head Island town *Beaufort Co.*	17.5	2.5	8.9	4.7	23.8	27.5	11.5	3.5
Hollywood town *Charleston Co.*	12.2	1.5	10.0	6.2	14.8	25.7	9.7	19.8
Homeland Park cdp *Anderson Co.*	2.4	2.1	2.0	2.7	24.9	20.7	16.3	28.9
Irmo town *Richland Co.*	14.8	7.1	12.9	4.8	15.7	27.8	7.6	9.3

Place	MBF[1] (%)	CES[2] (%)	ELCAM[3] (%)	HPT[4] (%)	S[5] (%)	SO[6] (%)	NRCM[7] (%)	PTMM[8] (%)
Ladson cdp *Berkeley Co.*	7.9	5.2	5.1	3.9	20.5	26.4	10.4	20.6
Lake City city *Florence Co.*	8.1	0.0	10.5	3.1	24.8	29.8	7.1	16.7
Lake Murray of Richland cdp *Richland Co.*	21.5	7.8	13.8	11.6	6.1	24.7	6.9	7.6
Lake Wylie cdp *York Co.*	24.8	9.4	9.2	3.8	13.1	29.0	2.0	8.7
Lancaster city *Lancaster Co.*	4.8	0.8	12.1	3.7	22.8	28.3	4.4	23.2
Laurel Bay cdp *Beaufort Co.*	5.7	1.8	6.2	1.8	29.6	34.1	14.0	6.7
Laurens city *Laurens Co.*	9.3	1.6	7.4	4.6	29.3	22.5	7.7	17.7
Lexington town *Lexington Co.*	21.9	5.9	15.4	8.2	11.3	27.4	5.1	5.0
Little River cdp *Horry Co.*	12.9	3.0	6.6	2.1	25.6	35.5	8.9	5.3
Lugoff cdp *Kershaw Co.*	15.4	2.4	10.2	7.1	16.3	27.4	8.1	13.0
Marion city *Marion Co.*	5.4	2.7	13.1	7.7	24.8	21.6	1.6	23.0
Mauldin city *Greenville Co.*	13.7	9.8	10.3	6.7	12.8	29.0	5.2	12.4
Moncks Corner town *Berkeley Co.*	11.6	4.0	7.0	2.6	21.8	24.4	17.3	11.4
Mount Pleasant town *Charleston Co.*	22.9	7.2	12.8	9.4	13.2	24.7	4.6	5.3
Mullins city *Marion Co.*	8.7	2.4	6.3	3.0	29.0	23.4	3.7	23.5
Murrells Inlet cdp *Georgetown Co.*	14.8	1.9	10.3	9.2	21.5	26.4	9.7	6.2
Myrtle Beach city *Horry Co.*	9.2	2.3	8.9	6.1	28.1	26.8	13.4	5.2
Newberry city *Newberry Co.*	7.1	1.8	12.5	5.5	16.9	25.0	10.0	21.1
North Augusta city *Aiken Co.*	15.8	7.3	12.6	11.4	15.8	22.6	4.7	9.7
North Charleston city *Charleston Co.*	9.2	4.9	6.7	4.3	22.2	24.8	12.7	15.3
North Myrtle Beach city *Horry Co.*	13.0	1.5	12.0	4.4	27.8	31.6	5.9	3.7
Oak Grove cdp *Lexington Co.*	12.3	2.8	8.4	5.9	13.0	30.6	16.9	10.1
Orangeburg city *Orangeburg Co.*	10.0	3.4	16.6	3.1	23.7	21.4	3.2	18.6
Parker cdp *Greenville Co.*	5.1	0.3	5.3	1.4	25.3	18.5	20.0	24.2
Piedmont cdp *Anderson Co.*	8.8	0.4	4.3	4.9	25.4	26.2	8.8	21.1
Port Royal town *Beaufort Co.*	9.3	4.5	19.2	5.2	22.4	24.0	8.0	7.3
Red Bank cdp *Lexington Co.*	11.4	3.8	11.0	7.3	9.8	30.3	14.8	11.6
Red Hill cdp *Horry Co.*	11.3	1.2	9.3	2.8	21.9	30.8	16.6	6.0
Rock Hill city *York Co.*	12.4	4.2	11.4	4.4	19.0	26.1	6.7	15.8
Saint Andrews cdp *Richland Co.*	9.7	3.4	12.6	5.2	22.6	32.5	3.9	10.2
Sangaree cdp *Berkeley Co.*	8.7	5.4	9.1	2.1	16.3	28.6	10.9	18.8
Sans Souci cdp *Greenville Co.*	7.8	5.3	5.8	3.3	21.0	25.4	12.8	18.7
Seneca city *Oconee Co.*	14.1	5.3	9.1	8.1	19.6	22.7	6.5	14.6
Seven Oaks cdp *Lexington Co.*	16.2	6.0	15.2	3.9	16.7	27.8	5.9	8.4
Simpsonville city *Greenville Co.*	12.8	6.9	8.1	3.4	16.5	24.0	7.9	20.4
Socastee cdp *Horry Co.*	10.3	1.4	6.5	5.6	30.0	30.2	10.5	5.5
Spartanburg city *Spartanburg Co.*	10.4	2.8	14.3	6.5	18.0	26.1	4.7	17.1
Summerville town *Dorchester Co.*	17.5	4.9	10.0	5.6	18.0	25.0	8.3	10.7
Sumter city *Sumter Co.*	9.8	4.7	13.2	7.1	20.1	22.8	8.5	13.8
Taylors cdp *Greenville Co.*	12.1	6.3	9.0	6.7	18.3	27.7	5.4	14.5
Tega Cay city *York Co.*	33.5	8.3	14.3	5.0	7.1	26.3	1.5	3.9
Travelers Rest city *Greenville Co.*	11.5	4.4	9.7	4.3	24.4	25.1	10.0	10.6
Union city *Union Co.*	9.0	0.3	18.0	4.7	13.9	28.8	9.5	15.8
Valley Falls cdp *Spartanburg Co.*	6.1	0.6	13.4	5.7	26.8	29.9	5.9	11.7
Wade Hampton cdp *Greenville Co.*	13.3	7.2	12.2	6.4	17.6	25.7	5.6	11.9
Walterboro city *Colleton Co.*	6.6	1.2	9.0	9.7	33.4	26.3	6.7	7.2
Welcome cdp *Greenville Co.*	7.5	1.9	3.8	5.0	21.7	26.0	19.2	15.0
West Columbia city *Lexington Co.*	11.5	3.7	14.5	5.5	16.7	24.9	14.2	9.0
Woodfield cdp *Richland Co.*	8.7	2.0	6.1	3.7	31.3	25.7	13.6	8.9
York city *York Co.*	8.9	0.3	3.4	2.1	24.0	26.4	7.4	27.5

NOTES: (1) Management, business, and financial occupations; (2) Computer, engineering, and science occupations; (3) Education, legal, community service, arts, and media occupations; (4) Healthcare practitioners and technical occupations; (5) Service occupations; (6) Sales and office occupations; (7) Natural resources, construction, and maintenance occupations; (8) Production, transportation, and material moving occupations
SOURCE: U.S. Census Bureau, American Community Survey, 2009-2013 Five-Year Estimates

Educational Attainment

Place	Percent of Population 25 Years and Over with:		
	High School Diploma or Higher[1]	Bachelor's Degree or Higher	Graduate/Professional Degree or Higher
Abbeville city *Abbeville Co.*	74.6	11.6	4.5
Aiken city *Aiken Co.*	90.8	43.1	18.7
Anderson city *Anderson Co.*	78.9	21.8	7.6
Barnwell city *Barnwell Co.*	83.1	15.5	5.3
Batesburg-Leesville town *Lexington Co.*	80.9	13.1	4.2
Beaufort city *Beaufort Co.*	89.3	40.7	16.4
Belvedere cdp *Aiken Co.*	82.2	11.8	5.6
Bennettsville city *Marlboro Co.*	70.5	14.9	5.7
Berea cdp *Greenville Co.*	73.3	11.7	3.9
Bluffton town *Beaufort Co.*	90.0	30.9	11.0
Boiling Springs cdp *Spartanburg Co.*	90.2	36.1	15.3
Brookdale cdp *Orangeburg Co.*	75.8	21.0	10.9
Burton cdp *Beaufort Co.*	89.1	14.4	4.8
Camden city *Kershaw Co.*	85.4	36.5	13.8
Cayce city *Lexington Co.*	88.1	23.9	8.8
Centerville cdp *Anderson Co.*	85.8	19.4	6.4
Central town *Pickens Co.*	84.3	37.0	21.1
Charleston city *Charleston Co.*	92.6	48.9	18.5
Cheraw town *Chesterfield Co.*	73.1	19.5	8.3
Chester city *Chester Co.*	75.7	15.9	5.5
Clemson city *Pickens Co.*	97.3	63.6	34.6
Clinton city *Laurens Co.*	67.6	17.1	6.9
Clover town *York Co.*	83.2	16.4	4.7
Columbia city *Richland Co.*	86.7	39.5	16.8
Conway city *Horry Co.*	84.8	23.8	9.5
Darlington city *Darlington Co.*	77.4	24.6	10.8
Dentsville cdp *Richland Co.*	89.1	31.8	14.0
Dillon city *Dillon Co.*	63.1	7.1	2.1
Easley city *Pickens Co.*	82.8	23.1	7.8
Edgefield town *Edgefield Co.*	75.7	8.9	3.6
Five Forks cdp *Greenville Co.*	96.1	59.8	20.8
Florence city *Florence Co.*	86.7	29.8	12.2
Forest Acres city *Richland Co.*	97.6	56.5	24.1
Forestbrook cdp *Horry Co.*	93.9	20.5	6.6
Fort Mill town *York Co.*	91.0	36.4	10.0
Fountain Inn city *Greenville Co.*	90.5	19.7	7.1
Gaffney city *Cherokee Co.*	77.9	18.6	5.3
Gantt cdp *Greenville Co.*	74.7	15.3	5.0
Garden City cdp *Horry Co.*	90.7	23.5	7.1
Georgetown city *Georgetown Co.*	81.2	17.7	8.2
Goose Creek city *Berkeley Co.*	92.7	26.8	7.2
Greenville city *Greenville Co.*	85.9	41.3	16.2
Greenwood city *Greenwood Co.*	73.5	19.2	6.5
Greer city *Greenville Co.*	83.4	26.9	9.7
Hanahan city *Berkeley Co.*	86.6	25.1	7.9
Hartsville city *Darlington Co.*	84.0	30.8	10.5
Hilton Head Island town *Beaufort Co.*	92.3	48.5	18.1
Hollywood town *Charleston Co.*	82.4	28.4	11.9
Homeland Park cdp *Anderson Co.*	65.9	2.8	1.1
Irmo town *Richland Co.*	92.8	36.4	11.0

Place	Percent of Population 25 Years and Over with:		
	High School Diploma or Higher[1]	Bachelor's Degree or Higher	Graduate/Professional Degree or Higher
Ladson cdp Berkeley Co.	84.3	14.2	4.5
Lake City city Florence Co.	72.1	12.5	2.9
Lake Murray of Richland cdp Richland Co.	92.3	51.2	15.0
Lake Wylie cdp York Co.	95.8	47.4	14.5
Lancaster city Lancaster Co.	78.6	17.7	6.7
Laurel Bay cdp Beaufort Co.	93.9	13.3	1.1
Laurens city Laurens Co.	78.2	18.9	5.9
Lexington town Lexington Co.	93.9	41.7	16.5
Little River cdp Horry Co.	90.0	26.3	6.6
Lugoff cdp Kershaw Co.	92.3	29.9	11.6
Marion city Marion Co.	83.5	16.5	6.0
Mauldin city Greenville Co.	91.0	35.9	13.9
Moncks Corner town Berkeley Co.	85.0	12.9	3.7
Mount Pleasant town Charleston Co.	97.1	59.5	21.5
Mullins city Marion Co.	80.4	13.3	4.3
Murrells Inlet cdp Georgetown Co.	92.3	28.1	10.4
Myrtle Beach city Horry Co.	84.4	27.3	9.2
Newberry city Newberry Co.	70.4	26.2	9.8
North Augusta city Aiken Co.	92.0	33.6	13.1
North Charleston city Charleston Co.	79.7	19.0	5.5
North Myrtle Beach city Horry Co.	92.5	31.9	12.7
Oak Grove cdp Lexington Co.	89.8	24.3	8.9
Orangeburg city Orangeburg Co.	83.9	28.7	12.7
Parker cdp Greenville Co.	64.3	6.8	1.8
Piedmont cdp Anderson Co.	80.3	8.7	1.8
Port Royal town Beaufort Co.	92.6	34.6	17.8
Red Bank cdp Lexington Co.	84.7	19.9	5.0
Red Hill cdp Horry Co.	87.0	20.5	7.9
Rock Hill city York Co.	86.9	28.7	9.5
Saint Andrews cdp Richland Co.	89.8	27.8	9.0
Sangaree cdp Berkeley Co.	85.8	17.0	5.4
Sans Souci cdp Greenville Co.	72.9	15.5	4.6
Seneca city Oconee Co.	84.5	24.0	9.0
Seven Oaks cdp Lexington Co.	93.3	35.6	14.4
Simpsonville city Greenville Co.	88.5	26.5	9.2
Socastee cdp Horry Co.	89.0	16.3	5.6
Spartanburg city Spartanburg Co.	82.0	27.7	12.0
Summerville town Dorchester Co.	93.0	29.9	10.6
Sumter city Sumter Co.	85.7	24.7	9.8
Taylors cdp Greenville Co.	86.8	26.8	9.0
Tega Cay city York Co.	97.7	59.2	17.4
Travelers Rest city Greenville Co.	81.6	20.5	9.8
Union city Union Co.	79.5	21.4	6.4
Valley Falls cdp Spartanburg Co.	83.5	25.2	7.4
Wade Hampton cdp Greenville Co.	87.7	37.8	11.9
Walterboro city Colleton Co.	81.7	24.1	11.0
Welcome cdp Greenville Co.	75.5	11.1	3.4
West Columbia city Lexington Co.	85.5	33.8	12.9
Woodfield cdp Richland Co.	84.1	18.0	4.1
York city York Co.	71.8	13.1	6.0

NOTE: (1) Includes General Equivalency Diploma (GED)
SOURCE: U.S. Census Bureau, American Community Survey, 2009-2013 Five-Year Estimates

Health Insurance

Place	Percent of Total Population with:				Percent of Population[1] Under Age 18 without Health Insurance
	Any Insurance	Private Insurance	Public Insurance	No Insurance	
Abbeville city *Abbeville Co.*	86.9	52.8	49.0	13.1	1.0
Aiken city *Aiken Co.*	90.1	71.5	36.8	9.9	5.8
Anderson city *Anderson Co.*	82.0	53.8	40.7	18.0	8.7
Barnwell city *Barnwell Co.*	88.1	51.1	51.1	11.9	0.0
Batesburg-Leesville town *Lexington Co.*	86.7	58.0	47.6	13.3	4.9
Beaufort city *Beaufort Co.*	84.6	65.9	35.9	15.4	15.9
Belvedere cdp *Aiken Co.*	83.1	56.1	40.8	16.9	5.3
Bennettsville city *Marlboro Co.*	85.3	43.4	54.6	14.7	6.3
Berea cdp *Greenville Co.*	78.8	47.3	43.8	21.2	7.4
Bluffton town *Beaufort Co.*	75.0	62.1	21.4	25.0	20.3
Boiling Springs cdp *Spartanburg Co.*	83.0	74.8	18.4	17.0	21.6
Brookdale cdp *Orangeburg Co.*	74.0	45.7	42.7	26.0	29.5
Burton cdp *Beaufort Co.*	77.8	60.5	29.1	22.2	16.0
Camden city *Kershaw Co.*	87.0	68.9	36.2	13.0	7.7
Cayce city *Lexington Co.*	82.6	65.8	28.8	17.4	10.3
Centerville cdp *Anderson Co.*	85.7	70.4	28.9	14.3	12.4
Central town *Pickens Co.*	87.9	81.6	11.9	12.1	0.0
Charleston city *Charleston Co.*	87.4	73.8	24.8	12.6	7.6
Cheraw town *Chesterfield Co.*	84.2	42.9	57.5	15.8	0.0
Chester city *Chester Co.*	82.7	44.8	51.9	17.3	5.8
Clemson city *Pickens Co.*	94.3	87.7	19.6	5.7	4.4
Clinton city *Laurens Co.*	81.9	50.9	41.9	18.1	10.3
Clover town *York Co.*	86.1	65.8	30.5	13.9	6.0
Columbia city *Richland Co.*	86.7	68.8	27.2	13.3	4.3
Conway city *Horry Co.*	83.4	60.1	34.3	16.6	9.4
Darlington city *Darlington Co.*	80.5	50.9	41.4	19.5	5.2
Dentsville cdp *Richland Co.*	79.0	57.9	32.7	21.0	12.2
Dillon city *Dillon Co.*	85.3	43.7	57.0	14.7	6.5
Easley city *Pickens Co.*	85.4	64.4	33.7	14.6	3.7
Edgefield town *Edgefield Co.*	90.7	57.1	44.1	9.3	1.7
Five Forks cdp *Greenville Co.*	96.0	92.7	10.7	4.0	0.6
Florence city *Florence Co.*	87.4	62.1	37.0	12.6	4.3
Forest Acres city *Richland Co.*	91.4	79.5	30.4	8.6	4.0
Forestbrook cdp *Horry Co.*	79.7	68.6	26.6	20.3	18.2
Fort Mill town *York Co.*	90.2	77.5	22.6	9.8	4.2
Fountain Inn city *Greenville Co.*	85.8	67.7	30.2	14.2	10.0
Gaffney city *Cherokee Co.*	84.3	56.1	42.4	15.7	6.6
Gantt cdp *Greenville Co.*	78.7	42.7	45.3	21.3	4.5
Garden City cdp *Horry Co.*	80.9	67.1	44.6	19.1	28.8
Georgetown city *Georgetown Co.*	79.7	50.5	43.0	20.3	19.7
Goose Creek city *Berkeley Co.*	87.7	76.0	22.9	12.3	5.6
Greenville city *Greenville Co.*	83.3	63.5	29.1	16.7	8.5
Greenwood city *Greenwood Co.*	80.2	46.9	43.3	19.8	8.7
Greer city *Greenville Co.*	82.2	63.1	28.7	17.8	4.5
Hanahan city *Berkeley Co.*	76.1	62.4	23.3	23.9	19.3
Hartsville city *Darlington Co.*	83.5	56.4	40.5	16.5	8.8
Hilton Head Island town *Beaufort Co.*	82.6	68.9	37.6	17.4	17.3
Hollywood town *Charleston Co.*	83.6	65.2	33.0	16.4	16.8
Homeland Park cdp *Anderson Co.*	78.4	40.3	50.5	21.6	9.5
Irmo town *Richland Co.*	82.7	68.2	24.7	17.3	8.2

Place	Percent of Total Population with:				Percent of Population[1] Under Age 18 without Health Insurance
	Any Insurance	Private Insurance	Public Insurance	No Insurance	
Ladson cdp *Berkeley Co.*	79.6	64.1	25.2	20.4	11.6
Lake City city *Florence Co.*	85.8	48.0	47.2	14.2	0.0
Lake Murray of Richland cdp *Richland Co.*	95.9	88.8	21.5	4.1	0.0
Lake Wylie cdp *York Co.*	90.4	82.6	17.9	9.6	6.5
Lancaster city *Lancaster Co.*	75.5	42.2	44.6	24.5	13.1
Laurel Bay cdp *Beaufort Co.*	85.9	79.4	11.5	14.1	8.7
Laurens city *Laurens Co.*	80.5	60.5	38.6	19.5	10.7
Lexington town *Lexington Co.*	91.7	80.9	22.4	8.3	6.2
Little River cdp *Horry Co.*	81.7	67.5	39.0	18.3	0.0
Lugoff cdp *Kershaw Co.*	83.8	72.4	25.8	16.2	11.5
Marion city *Marion Co.*	81.4	35.2	55.2	18.6	1.2
Mauldin city *Greenville Co.*	85.6	73.2	22.8	14.4	6.5
Moncks Corner town *Berkeley Co.*	74.3	56.2	29.0	25.7	16.5
Mount Pleasant town *Charleston Co.*	91.5	85.4	16.7	8.5	5.6
Mullins city *Marion Co.*	79.1	40.3	50.7	20.9	8.6
Murrells Inlet cdp *Georgetown Co.*	71.7	58.9	35.9	28.3	39.2
Myrtle Beach city *Horry Co.*	66.2	46.6	33.4	33.8	20.8
Newberry city *Newberry Co.*	83.3	50.7	42.8	16.7	0.0
North Augusta city *Aiken Co.*	88.8	74.6	27.0	11.2	6.6
North Charleston city *Charleston Co.*	76.9	53.9	32.0	23.1	9.1
North Myrtle Beach city *Horry Co.*	80.4	67.2	38.5	19.6	9.1
Oak Grove cdp *Lexington Co.*	84.4	70.5	24.1	15.6	12.0
Orangeburg city *Orangeburg Co.*	78.8	54.3	35.9	21.2	9.4
Parker cdp *Greenville Co.*	68.2	34.7	42.1	31.8	16.3
Piedmont cdp *Anderson Co.*	82.8	56.5	35.6	17.2	4.9
Port Royal town *Beaufort Co.*	90.8	74.6	30.2	9.2	3.5
Red Bank cdp *Lexington Co.*	83.2	68.6	24.6	16.8	5.5
Red Hill cdp *Horry Co.*	76.8	58.1	34.6	23.2	25.7
Rock Hill city *York Co.*	84.1	66.2	26.8	15.9	5.9
Saint Andrews cdp *Richland Co.*	79.7	53.9	36.1	20.3	7.2
Sangaree cdp *Berkeley Co.*	80.9	63.4	26.9	19.1	13.3
Sans Souci cdp *Greenville Co.*	66.5	42.8	33.5	33.5	24.1
Seneca city *Oconee Co.*	82.4	63.9	35.1	17.6	11.7
Seven Oaks cdp *Lexington Co.*	87.2	73.7	29.6	12.8	6.8
Simpsonville city *Greenville Co.*	83.3	69.7	24.3	16.7	10.2
Socastee cdp *Horry Co.*	73.7	53.3	31.7	26.3	21.7
Spartanburg city *Spartanburg Co.*	83.3	57.2	38.0	16.7	6.7
Summerville town *Dorchester Co.*	85.2	72.1	24.7	14.8	8.5
Sumter city *Sumter Co.*	85.6	59.6	39.4	14.4	4.1
Taylors cdp *Greenville Co.*	81.3	61.2	32.3	18.7	12.2
Tega Cay city *York Co.*	93.2	89.6	12.7	6.8	7.6
Travelers Rest city *Greenville Co.*	83.3	63.6	32.9	16.7	11.6
Union city *Union Co.*	84.6	56.5	42.9	15.4	3.9
Valley Falls cdp *Spartanburg Co.*	82.0	67.2	23.9	18.0	22.4
Wade Hampton cdp *Greenville Co.*	81.2	65.4	31.1	18.8	15.5
Walterboro city *Colleton Co.*	86.9	47.5	51.1	13.1	6.6
Welcome cdp *Greenville Co.*	70.2	40.4	42.2	29.8	13.9
West Columbia city *Lexington Co.*	78.2	61.1	31.1	21.8	12.8
Woodfield cdp *Richland Co.*	78.0	57.7	33.6	22.0	10.1
York city *York Co.*	82.3	46.0	47.5	17.7	4.4

NOTE: (1) Civilian noninstitutionalized population.
SOURCE: U.S. Census Bureau, American Community Survey, 2009-2013 Five-Year Estimates

Income and Poverty

Place	Average Household Income ($)	Median Household Income ($)	Per Capita Income ($)	Households w/$100,000+ Income (%)	Poverty Rate (%)
Abbeville city *Abbeville Co.*	35,608	23,027	14,771	5.1	37.4
Aiken city *Aiken Co.*	74,298	53,127	31,853	25.7	17.0
Anderson city *Anderson Co.*	44,150	30,032	18,845	10.0	27.5
Barnwell city *Barnwell Co.*	39,223	31,490	15,313	5.2	42.3
Batesburg-Leesville town *Lexington Co.*	47,967	25,887	19,435	6.9	31.9
Beaufort city *Beaufort Co.*	69,177	50,801	27,719	20.7	19.4
Belvedere cdp *Aiken Co.*	53,782	42,208	20,229	9.4	24.2
Bennettsville city *Marlboro Co.*	42,219	27,104	15,344	6.9	33.2
Berea cdp *Greenville Co.*	39,868	30,610	16,209	5.1	31.8
Bluffton town *Beaufort Co.*	74,026	60,038	26,034	23.9	16.1
Boiling Springs cdp *Spartanburg Co.*	77,715	67,515	28,120	27.3	7.9
Brookdale cdp *Orangeburg Co.*	28,488	17,045	11,700	5.0	46.0
Burton cdp *Beaufort Co.*	50,693	42,238	19,233	9.4	10.6
Camden city *Kershaw Co.*	74,147	50,974	31,304	26.5	15.3
Cayce city *Lexington Co.*	54,429	43,776	23,523	11.6	21.2
Centerville cdp *Anderson Co.*	53,958	43,004	21,925	12.8	7.1
Central town *Pickens Co.*	29,465	24,630	12,516	2.0	43.8
Charleston city *Charleston Co.*	74,242	51,737	32,131	22.8	19.5
Cheraw town *Chesterfield Co.*	37,479	22,876	18,581	6.3	36.8
Chester city *Chester Co.*	36,295	22,237	14,529	6.7	38.0
Clemson city *Pickens Co.*	54,924	37,851	23,235	17.3	36.3
Clinton city *Laurens Co.*	37,625	29,411	13,566	4.2	37.7
Clover town *York Co.*	54,716	44,561	19,978	13.6	22.7
Columbia city *Richland Co.*	64,281	41,344	24,779	17.5	23.8
Conway city *Horry Co.*	51,292	34,732	19,036	9.2	32.7
Darlington city *Darlington Co.*	46,399	27,270	20,208	11.6	32.6
Dentsville cdp *Richland Co.*	47,358	37,802	21,258	8.4	16.1
Dillon city *Dillon Co.*	38,630	26,503	15,916	8.2	37.5
Easley city *Pickens Co.*	55,930	42,494	23,158	13.1	12.7
Edgefield town *Edgefield Co.*	41,890	22,804	12,195	7.2	24.8
Five Forks cdp *Greenville Co.*	129,286	114,556	41,815	60.1	1.6
Florence city *Florence Co.*	61,368	41,663	25,481	16.1	19.5
Forest Acres city *Richland Co.*	72,684	52,271	35,694	26.0	12.7
Forestbrook cdp *Horry Co.*	63,914	58,858	26,441	22.3	14.2
Fort Mill town *York Co.*	86,190	64,596	34,030	31.2	8.6
Fountain Inn city *Greenville Co.*	52,960	46,152	20,713	12.6	14.7
Gaffney city *Cherokee Co.*	43,952	28,598	18,549	9.0	26.6
Gantt cdp *Greenville Co.*	48,953	31,428	18,941	9.7	26.6
Garden City cdp *Horry Co.*	54,620	37,173	28,339	8.2	14.4
Georgetown city *Georgetown Co.*	45,730	26,330	18,839	8.7	29.5
Goose Creek city *Berkeley Co.*	70,000	62,466	25,244	20.2	9.7
Greenville city *Greenville Co.*	69,300	40,793	30,829	19.5	20.0
Greenwood city *Greenwood Co.*	41,310	24,584	16,589	7.4	34.5
Greer city *Greenville Co.*	60,180	42,991	24,429	17.9	19.4
Hanahan city *Berkeley Co.*	62,006	48,403	25,507	18.8	15.6
Hartsville city *Darlington Co.*	58,737	29,956	24,365	13.5	22.8
Hilton Head Island town *Beaufort Co.*	101,114	69,772	46,091	32.9	8.5
Hollywood town *Charleston Co.*	94,605	53,799	39,381	24.7	7.9
Homeland Park cdp *Anderson Co.*	32,762	25,182	13,453	2.2	32.6
Irmo town *Richland Co.*	64,013	58,242	25,159	16.0	17.1

Place	Average Household Income ($)	Median Household Income ($)	Per Capita Income ($)	Households w/$100,000+ Income (%)	Poverty Rate (%)
Ladson cdp *Berkeley Co.*	58,298	48,669	20,161	14.3	12.5
Lake City city *Florence Co.*	44,663	30,174	17,002	7.9	27.8
Lake Murray of Richland cdp *Richland Co.*	140,072	106,768	50,027	53.8	3.4
Lake Wylie cdp *York Co.*	98,983	75,915	38,267	37.4	4.0
Lancaster city *Lancaster Co.*	40,918	29,845	16,711	6.2	32.2
Laurel Bay cdp *Beaufort Co.*	54,795	42,733	17,872	6.5	14.8
Laurens city *Laurens Co.*	39,513	24,583	17,860	5.2	22.7
Lexington town *Lexington Co.*	76,519	61,477	30,574	26.8	11.7
Little River cdp *Horry Co.*	53,035	44,606	27,237	13.3	9.8
Lugoff cdp *Kershaw Co.*	70,545	55,456	28,541	15.2	8.7
Marion city *Marion Co.*	37,344	21,392	14,634	5.3	41.1
Mauldin city *Greenville Co.*	66,026	57,551	27,197	19.4	5.9
Moncks Corner town *Berkeley Co.*	54,093	45,852	21,199	10.7	16.8
Mount Pleasant town *Charleston Co.*	100,185	76,085	40,870	37.8	8.1
Mullins city *Marion Co.*	40,930	28,117	16,525	8.4	31.0
Murrells Inlet cdp *Georgetown Co.*	75,607	48,118	35,176	19.0	8.1
Myrtle Beach city *Horry Co.*	62,405	36,293	27,178	15.1	26.6
Newberry city *Newberry Co.*	42,375	29,333	17,033	10.2	30.5
North Augusta city *Aiken Co.*	66,181	49,027	29,025	18.7	11.6
North Charleston city *Charleston Co.*	50,445	39,322	19,717	11.1	23.4
North Myrtle Beach city *Horry Co.*	67,644	47,679	35,046	16.4	10.2
Oak Grove cdp *Lexington Co.*	58,803	47,881	24,752	13.5	8.0
Orangeburg city *Orangeburg Co.*	41,271	32,645	15,862	7.6	31.1
Parker cdp *Greenville Co.*	32,603	25,293	12,234	3.5	37.8
Piedmont cdp *Anderson Co.*	45,162	40,754	18,199	6.0	13.4
Port Royal town *Beaufort Co.*	56,743	45,381	19,657	12.7	9.7
Red Bank cdp *Lexington Co.*	55,510	46,216	23,616	14.3	16.7
Red Hill cdp *Horry Co.*	53,319	41,939	22,234	11.1	22.0
Rock Hill city *York Co.*	55,955	42,550	22,416	13.3	18.7
Saint Andrews cdp *Richland Co.*	40,320	32,537	18,469	5.2	27.3
Sangaree cdp *Berkeley Co.*	62,411	54,761	21,450	17.7	13.2
Sans Souci cdp *Greenville Co.*	35,659	28,323	15,299	2.7	27.7
Seneca city *Oconee Co.*	50,752	34,917	24,397	13.8	21.2
Seven Oaks cdp *Lexington Co.*	61,130	48,802	26,446	16.3	13.5
Simpsonville city *Greenville Co.*	63,867	50,604	26,143	15.3	8.3
Socastee cdp *Horry Co.*	48,890	39,558	19,536	7.5	18.9
Spartanburg city *Spartanburg Co.*	46,737	33,129	20,143	9.6	26.4
Summerville town *Dorchester Co.*	66,765	55,256	25,766	20.5	11.5
Sumter city *Sumter Co.*	54,769	39,429	22,572	13.1	20.2
Taylors cdp *Greenville Co.*	59,113	47,149	23,242	14.9	17.6
Tega Cay city *York Co.*	116,679	108,958	39,780	55.1	2.2
Travelers Rest city *Greenville Co.*	57,583	50,768	20,901	14.3	19.9
Union city *Union Co.*	41,377	26,438	19,080	8.5	24.3
Valley Falls cdp *Spartanburg Co.*	42,112	36,661	15,960	8.7	24.1
Wade Hampton cdp *Greenville Co.*	62,546	44,386	28,593	18.2	14.0
Walterboro city *Colleton Co.*	46,290	24,135	20,223	11.2	30.1
Welcome cdp *Greenville Co.*	37,765	29,163	16,188	3.7	27.4
West Columbia city *Lexington Co.*	53,024	40,594	25,124	13.2	18.7
Woodfield cdp *Richland Co.*	49,910	43,549	19,244	7.7	19.1
York city *York Co.*	41,763	29,789	15,007	8.5	31.3

SOURCE: U.S. Census Bureau, American Community Survey, 2009-2013 Five-Year Estimates

Housing

Place	Homeownership Rate (%)	Median Home Value ($)	Median Year Structure Built	Homeowner Vacancy Rate (%)	Median Gross Rent ($/month)	Rental Vacancy Rate (%)
Abbeville city Abbeville Co.	59.3	$87,200	1962	3.4	$678	13.2
Aiken city Aiken Co.	66.0	$179,100	1986	3.5	$839	6.8
Anderson city Anderson Co.	49.3	$122,100	1969	4.7	$629	12.4
Barnwell city Barnwell Co.	56.0	$99,400	1969	3.8	$668	10.9
Batesburg-Leesville town Lexington Co.	63.3	$96,900	1967	3.8	$664	8.5
Beaufort city Beaufort Co.	53.8	$252,700	1978	4.9	$819	11.0
Belvedere cdp Aiken Co.	69.2	$95,100	1969	2.8	$704	7.5
Bennettsville city Marlboro Co.	53.2	$79,400	1969	2.0	$572	13.1
Berea cdp Greenville Co.	60.2	$111,800	1974	2.4	$639	16.0
Bluffton town Beaufort Co.	74.6	$216,500	2004	6.4	$1,310	14.7
Boiling Springs cdp Spartanburg Co.	72.0	$149,000	2001	2.7	$810	9.5
Brookdale cdp Orangeburg Co.	46.1	$83,500	1975	3.7	$525	13.9
Burton cdp Beaufort Co.	57.2	$132,400	1986	2.5	$905	14.8
Camden city Kershaw Co.	68.0	$166,700	1960	4.4	$855	12.7
Cayce city Lexington Co.	60.6	$120,500	1964	2.4	$849	8.2
Centerville cdp Anderson Co.	76.1	$132,500	1988	5.6	$561	8.0
Central town Pickens Co.	22.2	$103,400	1990	3.5	$912	8.3
Charleston city Charleston Co.	52.1	$253,800	1982	4.1	$968	10.8
Cheraw town Chesterfield Co.	51.2	$87,500	1965	3.2	$470	7.7
Chester city Chester Co.	55.3	$66,100	1967	4.5	$544	13.3
Clemson city Pickens Co.	43.0	$200,300	1983	3.2	$697	7.5
Clinton city Laurens Co.	48.4	$76,900	1966	4.3	$662	12.5
Clover town York Co.	62.9	$118,400	1987	4.1	$848	7.5
Columbia city Richland Co.	47.4	$163,500	1969	4.2	$819	13.3
Conway city Horry Co.	56.4	$149,700	1984	5.8	$687	10.9
Darlington city Darlington Co.	52.2	$87,800	1968	3.4	$546	7.7
Dentsville cdp Richland Co.	37.4	$109,600	1979	2.4	$827	10.5
Dillon city Dillon Co.	51.5	$102,700	1970	3.0	$537	7.6
Easley city Pickens Co.	65.3	$136,400	1979	3.2	$703	9.9
Edgefield town Edgefield Co.	50.4	$82,900	1967	2.1	$561	7.2
Five Forks cdp Greenville Co.	93.1	$258,300	1998	2.1	$1,520	3.0
Florence city Florence Co.	59.9	$148,700	1976	3.4	$659	10.4
Forest Acres city Richland Co.	70.3	$180,600	1964	3.0	$851	14.0
Forestbrook cdp Horry Co.	77.9	$162,000	1991	4.3	$738	14.5
Fort Mill town York Co.	68.0	$193,600	1994	2.3	$870	7.6
Fountain Inn city Greenville Co.	73.3	$115,900	1989	2.1	$645	8.9
Gaffney city Cherokee Co.	53.7	$86,800	1968	4.2	$581	11.8
Gantt cdp Greenville Co.	59.2	$88,000	1974	2.8	$706	15.5
Garden City cdp Horry Co.	75.8	$125,200	1990	5.5	$860	50.6
Georgetown city Georgetown Co.	53.6	$114,500	1966	4.1	$683	9.7
Goose Creek city Berkeley Co.	71.1	$168,800	1995	2.1	$1,084	13.8
Greenville city Greenville Co.	45.3	$200,500	1973	5.7	$749	11.9
Greenwood city Greenwood Co.	46.4	$89,200	1967	3.4	$636	12.6
Greer city Greenville Co.	63.2	$141,200	1995	3.6	$747	12.8
Hanahan city Berkeley Co.	64.7	$180,800	1980	2.3	$860	13.7
Hartsville city Darlington Co.	52.5	$112,000	1967	8.4	$596	9.9
Hilton Head Island town Beaufort Co.	72.8	$447,900	1986	4.9	$1,092	55.1
Hollywood town Charleston Co.	82.5	$200,600	1990	2.5	$832	12.2
Homeland Park cdp Anderson Co.	57.3	$68,500	1966	3.5	$681	11.8
Irmo town Richland Co.	82.1	$125,900	1982	3.0	$1,056	7.5

Place	Homeownership Rate (%)	Median Home Value ($)	Median Year Structure Built	Homeowner Vacancy Rate (%)	Median Gross Rent ($/month)	Rental Vacancy Rate (%)
Ladson cdp *Berkeley Co.*	73.3	$123,700	1984	2.7	$1,034	8.4
Lake City city *Florence Co.*	53.9	$83,100	1970	2.6	$601	7.7
Lake Murray of Richland cdp *Richland Co.*	93.0	$312,500	1996	2.3	$1,200	20.6
Lake Wylie cdp *York Co.*	78.5	$286,200	2000	3.1	$916	18.3
Lancaster city *Lancaster Co.*	45.8	$97,600	1968	3.9	$648	11.7
Laurel Bay cdp *Beaufort Co.*	24.2	$149,500	1979	4.3	$1,069	10.6
Laurens city *Laurens Co.*	53.3	$80,700	1967	2.9	$591	13.1
Lexington town *Lexington Co.*	60.1	$175,500	1999	3.9	$910	11.6
Little River cdp *Horry Co.*	73.1	$172,400	1991	4.6	$845	20.9
Lugoff cdp *Kershaw Co.*	81.0	$132,300	1990	1.7	$587	3.7
Marion city *Marion Co.*	52.4	$104,200	1971	3.5	$503	4.1
Mauldin city *Greenville Co.*	67.6	$148,500	1991	2.8	$878	6.7
Moncks Corner town *Berkeley Co.*	63.7	$153,200	1985	8.8	$743	13.0
Mount Pleasant town *Charleston Co.*	72.6	$349,200	1994	3.1	$1,238	10.3
Mullins city *Marion Co.*	54.8	$80,100	1967	3.8	$474	8.8
Murrells Inlet cdp *Georgetown Co.*	82.6	$226,800	1996	3.5	$934	15.5
Myrtle Beach city *Horry Co.*	48.7	$167,100	1985	6.7	$822	23.1
Newberry city *Newberry Co.*	49.5	$116,300	1963	4.3	$635	8.8
North Augusta city *Aiken Co.*	66.8	$147,200	1979	2.7	$688	7.3
North Charleston city *Charleston Co.*	47.9	$138,300	1983	4.2	$855	14.2
North Myrtle Beach city *Horry Co.*	69.5	$248,000	1993	11.3	$827	57.4
Oak Grove cdp *Lexington Co.*	74.4	$129,000	1984	1.7	$910	12.5
Orangeburg city *Orangeburg Co.*	45.6	$130,600	1970	4.0	$642	9.2
Parker cdp *Greenville Co.*	52.7	$67,600	1959	4.2	$718	13.9
Piedmont cdp *Anderson Co.*	75.4	$97,300	1979	2.9	$685	11.8
Port Royal town *Beaufort Co.*	35.1	$197,100	1996	8.5	$970	12.1
Red Bank cdp *Lexington Co.*	78.2	$117,000	1989	1.9	$816	7.6
Red Hill cdp *Horry Co.*	70.5	$158,900	1994	3.8	$822	18.9
Rock Hill city *York Co.*	53.4	$133,100	1990	3.1	$770	13.7
Saint Andrews cdp *Richland Co.*	35.3	$107,400	1976	3.5	$732	13.0
Sangaree cdp *Berkeley Co.*	74.7	$132,400	1984	2.1	$1,031	4.8
Sans Souci cdp *Greenville Co.*	55.2	$90,800	1966	4.0	$661	17.1
Seneca city *Oconee Co.*	56.3	$122,600	1978	4.5	$618	10.9
Seven Oaks cdp *Lexington Co.*	60.3	$142,300	1975	2.6	$792	12.1
Simpsonville city *Greenville Co.*	66.1	$136,200	1988	3.3	$875	8.7
Socastee cdp *Horry Co.*	60.7	$143,800	1993	4.0	$847	14.7
Spartanburg city *Spartanburg Co.*	49.1	$121,100	1966	4.9	$644	13.8
Summerville town *Dorchester Co.*	63.7	$180,600	1993	2.7	$964	12.4
Sumter city *Sumter Co.*	53.3	$133,900	1977	3.8	$718	10.4
Taylors cdp *Greenville Co.*	69.4	$137,000	1978	2.0	$761	8.1
Tega Cay city *York Co.*	93.2	$276,900	2000	2.9	$1,653	5.0
Travelers Rest city *Greenville Co.*	64.1	$154,100	1989	2.4	$704	11.8
Union city *Union Co.*	54.3	$81,600	1965	3.8	$539	8.8
Valley Falls cdp *Spartanburg Co.*	40.7	$125,500	1994	3.4	$653	14.3
Wade Hampton cdp *Greenville Co.*	60.8	$161,400	1972	2.6	$701	10.0
Walterboro city *Colleton Co.*	54.2	$131,200	1970	4.3	$626	11.8
Welcome cdp *Greenville Co.*	62.0	$79,900	1969	3.4	$682	10.8
West Columbia city *Lexington Co.*	50.8	$132,000	1973	2.7	$811	16.2
Woodfield cdp *Richland Co.*	53.3	$99,200	1972	4.8	$949	11.0
York city *York Co.*	57.1	$110,300	1978	3.6	$685	14.5

SOURCE: U.S. Census Bureau, Census 2010; U.S. Census Bureau, American Community Survey, 2009-2013 Five-Year Estimates

Commute to Work

Place	Automobile (%)	Public Trans-portation (%)	Walk (%)	Work from Home (%)	Median Travel Time to Work (minutes)
Abbeville city Abbeville Co.	94.8	0.0	2.1	1.9	24.9
Aiken city Aiken Co.	91.0	0.3	2.1	4.7	21.4
Anderson city Anderson Co.	91.5	2.6	2.9	1.6	18.9
Barnwell city Barnwell Co.	94.8	0.0	3.4	1.1	20.8
Batesburg-Leesville town Lexington Co.	90.6	0.0	0.0	7.4	26.8
Beaufort city Beaufort Co.	85.1	0.0	4.8	6.2	19.9
Belvedere cdp Aiken Co.	93.5	0.0	2.7	1.2	25.2
Bennettsville city Marlboro Co.	95.7	0.7	1.3	0.8	22.6
Berea cdp Greenville Co.	94.7	0.4	1.5	1.5	23.6
Bluffton town Beaufort Co.	92.1	0.2	2.3	4.5	23.6
Boiling Springs cdp Spartanburg Co.	93.8	0.0	1.6	3.0	21.1
Brookdale cdp Orangeburg Co.	86.8	0.0	2.6	5.4	16.6
Burton cdp Beaufort Co.	92.5	0.0	2.3	0.8	20.9
Camden city Kershaw Co.	89.0	0.4	1.8	6.7	21.2
Cayce city Lexington Co.	95.2	0.3	0.5	2.2	18.1
Centerville cdp Anderson Co.	96.8	0.0	0.4	2.0	19.1
Central town Pickens Co.	94.2	1.8	2.1	0.4	15.6
Charleston city Charleston Co.	83.7	2.8	5.2	4.4	21.0
Cheraw town Chesterfield Co.	89.7	0.0	4.2	6.1	10.6
Chester city Chester Co.	91.3	0.9	2.5	3.5	25.5
Clemson city Pickens Co.	84.4	4.0	5.4	3.2	17.1
Clinton city Laurens Co.	79.5	2.1	11.6	3.4	18.9
Clover town York Co.	96.2	0.9	1.0	0.0	27.8
Columbia city Richland Co.	73.3	1.8	13.7	9.2	16.2
Conway city Horry Co.	89.3	2.3	3.0	3.3	20.5
Darlington city Darlington Co.	93.2	0.0	1.3	3.5	19.6
Dentsville cdp Richland Co.	92.3	1.8	1.1	3.5	18.7
Dillon city Dillon Co.	87.1	5.5	2.6	3.7	22.4
Easley city Pickens Co.	96.3	0.0	0.8	2.1	23.5
Edgefield town Edgefield Co.	95.0	0.3	0.0	0.5	17.9
Five Forks cdp Greenville Co.	94.2	0.3	0.0	5.0	24.4
Florence city Florence Co.	91.7	1.0	0.8	4.5	19.1
Forest Acres city Richland Co.	94.4	0.0	1.1	4.0	17.3
Forestbrook cdp Horry Co.	98.6	0.0	0.0	1.0	20.7
Fort Mill town York Co.	89.9	0.7	0.6	7.9	25.5
Fountain Inn city Greenville Co.	96.6	0.0	1.6	1.4	22.4
Gaffney city Cherokee Co.	92.9	0.0	1.5	1.5	15.4
Gantt cdp Greenville Co.	94.4	1.0	0.0	3.2	20.5
Garden City cdp Horry Co.	95.9	0.0	0.4	3.2	21.1
Georgetown city Georgetown Co.	88.5	4.1	0.7	2.3	19.8
Goose Creek city Berkeley Co.	85.0	1.2	11.1	1.7	23.3
Greenville city Greenville Co.	87.5	0.5	6.1	4.9	17.0
Greenwood city Greenwood Co.	93.3	0.3	3.7	2.0	20.8
Greer city Greenville Co.	95.6	0.2	2.1	1.7	21.4
Hanahan city Berkeley Co.	93.3	0.7	1.0	3.3	20.4
Hartsville city Darlington Co.	85.7	0.0	4.7	6.5	18.3
Hilton Head Island town Beaufort Co.	85.6	1.0	2.2	7.9	17.9
Hollywood town Charleston Co.	93.7	0.0	1.8	3.7	27.2
Homeland Park cdp Anderson Co.	91.7	3.0	2.1	2.0	21.9
Irmo town Richland Co.	92.1	0.0	0.5	5.1	22.7

Place	Automobile (%)	Public Transportation (%)	Walk (%)	Work from Home (%)	Median Travel Time to Work (minutes)
Ladson cdp *Berkeley Co.*	94.3	0.0	1.1	3.6	26.2
Lake City city *Florence Co.*	90.0	1.3	5.0	3.7	20.2
Lake Murray of Richland cdp *Richland Co.*	91.9	0.9	0.0	1.1	26.8
Lake Wylie cdp *York Co.*	92.8	0.4	0.9	4.0	29.5
Lancaster city *Lancaster Co.*	95.6	0.2	1.5	1.7	24.3
Laurel Bay cdp *Beaufort Co.*	97.2	0.0	0.0	1.4	19.2
Laurens city *Laurens Co.*	94.5	0.5	3.7	0.9	23.2
Lexington town *Lexington Co.*	92.6	0.1	1.0	4.7	23.2
Little River cdp *Horry Co.*	92.7	0.0	1.2	6.1	18.5
Lugoff cdp *Kershaw Co.*	96.0	0.0	0.0	2.5	23.9
Marion city *Marion Co.*	91.4	2.9	0.0	3.2	22.6
Mauldin city *Greenville Co.*	96.1	0.1	0.7	3.0	18.5
Moncks Corner town *Berkeley Co.*	94.1	0.9	1.1	2.5	23.1
Mount Pleasant town *Charleston Co.*	89.5	0.2	1.0	7.9	21.9
Mullins city *Marion Co.*	89.3	1.1	3.4	6.2	25.3
Murrells Inlet cdp *Georgetown Co.*	91.0	0.0	0.0	7.9	20.0
Myrtle Beach city *Horry Co.*	87.8	0.4	4.9	2.2	16.9
Newberry city *Newberry Co.*	94.7	0.0	2.8	2.2	15.4
North Augusta city *Aiken Co.*	94.2	0.1	1.7	3.0	24.4
North Charleston city *Charleston Co.*	90.5	3.3	1.8	2.2	22.0
North Myrtle Beach city *Horry Co.*	87.9	0.2	2.6	4.1	18.7
Oak Grove cdp *Lexington Co.*	92.0	0.0	0.8	4.7	22.1
Orangeburg city *Orangeburg Co.*	96.5	0.0	2.6	0.8	16.1
Parker cdp *Greenville Co.*	91.8	0.9	3.1	0.6	22.1
Piedmont cdp *Anderson Co.*	98.6	0.0	0.0	1.4	23.2
Port Royal town *Beaufort Co.*	55.7	0.0	17.4	19.1	13.2
Red Bank cdp *Lexington Co.*	96.4	0.0	1.3	1.6	26.3
Red Hill cdp *Horry Co.*	95.4	0.1	1.0	1.8	21.1
Rock Hill city *York Co.*	93.7	0.3	2.5	2.4	22.2
Saint Andrews cdp *Richland Co.*	88.6	1.9	1.3	2.0	19.9
Sangaree cdp *Berkeley Co.*	93.8	0.6	0.2	4.5	28.5
Sans Souci cdp *Greenville Co.*	92.2	1.1	1.6	3.6	20.1
Seneca city *Oconee Co.*	93.5	1.3	4.0	0.9	20.7
Seven Oaks cdp *Lexington Co.*	92.6	0.2	0.4	3.5	20.7
Simpsonville city *Greenville Co.*	96.7	0.0	0.1	2.3	21.1
Socastee cdp *Horry Co.*	92.5	0.0	0.5	3.7	19.8
Spartanburg city *Spartanburg Co.*	90.8	1.1	4.2	2.8	17.9
Summerville town *Dorchester Co.*	93.3	0.3	1.2	4.4	28.0
Sumter city *Sumter Co.*	93.1	0.3	3.2	1.7	19.2
Taylors cdp *Greenville Co.*	97.0	0.0	0.0	2.0	20.8
Tega Cay city *York Co.*	90.7	0.9	0.0	6.1	29.3
Travelers Rest city *Greenville Co.*	97.8	0.0	0.5	1.7	20.8
Union city *Union Co.*	92.3	0.0	2.3	3.2	23.2
Valley Falls cdp *Spartanburg Co.*	92.4	0.0	3.7	3.5	20.6
Wade Hampton cdp *Greenville Co.*	92.8	0.7	1.3	4.2	18.3
Walterboro city *Colleton Co.*	87.0	1.4	4.4	3.6	24.4
Welcome cdp *Greenville Co.*	96.6	0.0	1.2	1.8	21.9
West Columbia city *Lexington Co.*	91.4	0.0	1.5	2.5	19.5
Woodfield cdp *Richland Co.*	96.2	0.5	0.2	2.8	18.9
York city *York Co.*	95.5	0.0	0.0	3.6	25.3

SOURCE: U.S. Census Bureau, American Community Survey, 2009-2013 Five-Year Estimates

Crime

Place	Violent Crime Rate (crimes per 10,000 population)	Property Crime Rate (crimes per 10,000 population)
Abbeville city *Abbeville Co.*	77.5	416.4
Aiken city *Aiken Co.*	32.0	493.6
Anderson city *Anderson Co.*	103.7	901.5
Barnwell city *Barnwell Co.*	96.6	783.8
Batesburg-Leesville town *Lexington Co.*	92.5	490.0
Beaufort city *Beaufort Co.*	118.4	622.4
Belvedere cdp *Aiken Co.*	n/a	n/a
Bennettsville city *Marlboro Co.*	130.5	515.4
Berea cdp *Greenville Co.*	n/a	n/a
Bluffton town *Beaufort Co.*	37.6	290.5
Boiling Springs cdp *Spartanburg Co.*	n/a	n/a
Brookdale cdp *Orangeburg Co.*	n/a	n/a
Burton cdp *Beaufort Co.*	n/a	n/a
Camden city *Kershaw Co.*	140.1	668.8
Cayce city *Lexington Co.*	n/a	n/a
Centerville cdp *Anderson Co.*	n/a	n/a
Central town *Pickens Co.*	13.6	347.4
Charleston city *Charleston Co.*	18.2	250.9
Cheraw town *Chesterfield Co.*	88.4	632.9
Chester city *Chester Co.*	125.7	672.3
Clemson city *Pickens Co.*	14.9	349.5
Clinton city *Laurens Co.*	62.5	522.5
Clover town *York Co.*	277.1	280.8
Columbia city *Richland Co.*	72.0	604.1
Conway city *Horry Co.*	59.1	460.2
Darlington city *Darlington Co.*	77.4	740.3
Dentsville cdp *Richland Co.*	n/a	n/a
Dillon city *Dillon Co.*	161.5	1,273.6
Easley city *Pickens Co.*	37.3	641.8
Edgefield town *Edgefield Co.*	23.6	100.6
Five Forks cdp *Greenville Co.*	n/a	n/a
Florence city *Florence Co.*	77.9	780.6
Forest Acres city *Richland Co.*	68.5	573.4
Forestbrook cdp *Horry Co.*	n/a	n/a
Fort Mill town *York Co.*	19.9	175.2
Fountain Inn city *Greenville Co.*	51.4	181.8
Gaffney city *Cherokee Co.*	52.1	297.4
Gantt cdp *Greenville Co.*	n/a	n/a
Garden City cdp *Horry Co.*	n/a	n/a
Georgetown city *Georgetown Co.*	122.4	566.6
Goose Creek city *Berkeley Co.*	21.6	244.0
Greenville city *Greenville Co.*	74.4	533.0
Greenwood city *Greenwood Co.*	128.6	639.8
Greer city *Greenville Co.*	46.4	284.9
Hanahan city *Berkeley Co.*	16.4	226.2
Hartsville city *Darlington Co.*	110.4	1,005.5
Hilton Head Island town *Beaufort Co.*	n/a	n/a
Hollywood town *Charleston Co.*	n/a	n/a
Homeland Park cdp *Anderson Co.*	n/a	n/a
Irmo town *Richland Co.*	45.6	292.7

Place	Violent Crime Rate (crimes per 10,000 population)	Property Crime Rate (crimes per 10,000 population)
Ladson cdp *Berkeley Co.*	n/a	n/a
Lake City city *Florence Co.*	101.1	875.7
Lake Murray of Richland cdp *Richland Co.*	n/a	n/a
Lake Wylie cdp *York Co.*	n/a	n/a
Lancaster city *Lancaster Co.*	123.5	701.5
Laurel Bay cdp *Beaufort Co.*	n/a	n/a
Laurens city *Laurens Co.*	99.3	662.8
Lexington town *Lexington Co.*	23.0	356.6
Little River cdp *Horry Co.*	n/a	n/a
Lugoff cdp *Kershaw Co.*	n/a	n/a
Marion city *Marion Co.*	133.6	873.3
Mauldin city *Greenville Co.*	16.6	170.1
Moncks Corner town *Berkeley Co.*	42.6	608.1
Mount Pleasant town *Charleston Co.*	16.0	195.1
Mullins city *Marion Co.*	139.9	977.3
Murrells Inlet cdp *Georgetown Co.*	n/a	n/a
Myrtle Beach city *Horry Co.*	165.7	1,596.1
Newberry city *Newberry Co.*	66.4	481.2
North Augusta city *Aiken Co.*	18.6	376.3
North Charleston city *Charleston Co.*	67.1	561.7
North Myrtle Beach city *Horry Co.*	81.8	1,068.7
Oak Grove cdp *Lexington Co.*	n/a	n/a
Orangeburg city *Orangeburg Co.*	71.6	618.4
Parker cdp *Greenville Co.*	n/a	n/a
Piedmont cdp *Anderson Co.*	n/a	n/a
Port Royal town *Beaufort Co.*	12.2	256.9
Red Bank cdp *Lexington Co.*	n/a	n/a
Red Hill cdp *Horry Co.*	n/a	n/a
Rock Hill city *York Co.*	54.2	376.4
Saint Andrews cdp *Richland Co.*	n/a	n/a
Sangaree cdp *Berkeley Co.*	n/a	n/a
Sans Souci cdp *Greenville Co.*	n/a	n/a
Seneca city *Oconee Co.*	74.1	322.4
Seven Oaks cdp *Lexington Co.*	n/a	n/a
Simpsonville city *Greenville Co.*	n/a	n/a
Socastee cdp *Horry Co.*	n/a	n/a
Spartanburg city *Spartanburg Co.*	140.5	711.1
Summerville town *Dorchester Co.*	23.0	341.3
Sumter city *Sumter Co.*	94.6	492.1
Taylors cdp *Greenville Co.*	n/a	n/a
Tega Cay city *York Co.*	2.5	157.0
Travelers Rest city *Greenville Co.*	18.7	643.3
Union city *Union Co.*	94.8	459.1
Valley Falls cdp *Spartanburg Co.*	n/a	n/a
Wade Hampton cdp *Greenville Co.*	n/a	n/a
Walterboro city *Colleton Co.*	87.1	1,037.7
Welcome cdp *Greenville Co.*	n/a	n/a
West Columbia city *Lexington Co.*	70.6	490.6
Woodfield cdp *Richland Co.*	n/a	n/a
York city *York Co.*	79.5	430.2

NOTE: n/a not available.
SOURCE: Federal Bureau of Investigation, Uniform Crime Reports, 2013

Community Rankings

This section ranks incorporated places and CDPs (Census Designated Places) with populations of 2,500 or more. Unincorporated postal areas were not considered. For each topic below, you will find two tables, one in Descending Order—highest to lowest, and one in Ascending Order—lowest to highest. Four topics are exceptions to this rule, and only include Descending Order—Water Area, Ancestry (five tables), Native Hawaiian/Other Pacific Islander, and Commute to Work: Public Transportation. This is because there are an extraordinarily large number of places that place at the bottom of these topics with zero numbers.

Land Area

Top 150 Places Ranked in *Descending* Order

State Rank	Nat'l Rank	Sq. Miles	Place	State Rank	Nat'l Rank	Sq. Miles	Place
1	71	132.213	**Columbia** (city) Richland County	76	n/a	6.415	**Lancaster** (city) Lancaster County
2	93	108.979	**Charleston** (city) Charleston County	77	3549	6.346	**Saint Andrews** (CDP) Richland County
3	177	73.187	**North Charleston** (city) Charleston County	78	3568	6.261	**Irmo** (town) Richland County
4	350	51.301	**Bluffton** (town) Beaufort County	79	n/a	6.116	**Abbeville** (city) Abbeville County
5	n/a	45.161	**Hardeeville** (city) Jasper County	80	n/a	6.116	**Bennettsville** (city) Marlboro County
6	442	45.082	**Mount Pleasant** (town) Charleston County	81	n/a	6.082	**Lesslie** (CDP) York County
7	n/a	44.451	**Ridgeland** (town) Jasper County	82	n/a	5.976	**Lyman** (town) Spartanburg County
8	528	41.363	**Hilton Head Island** (town) Beaufort County	83	n/a	5.905	**Centerville** (CDP) Anderson County
9	555	40.086	**Goose Creek** (city) Berkeley County	84	n/a	5.886	**Dalzell** (CDP) Sumter County
10	690	35.722	**Rock Hill** (city) York County	85	n/a	5.723	**Hartsville** (city) Darlington County
11	884	32.086	**Sumter** (city) Sumter County	86	n/a	5.584	**Lake Murray of Richland** (CDP) Richland County
12	1042	28.669	**Greenville** (city) Greenville County	87	n/a	5.477	**Burnettown** (town) Aiken County
13	1105	27.600	**Beaufort** (city) Beaufort County	88	n/a	5.422	**Cheraw** (town) Chesterfield County
14	1349	23.324	**Myrtle Beach** (city) Horry County	89	n/a	5.418	**Edisto** (CDP) Orangeburg County
15	n/a	23.132	**Hollywood** (town) Charleston County	90	n/a	5.368	**Garden City** (CDP) Horry County
16	1463	21.942	**Conway** (city) Horry County	91	n/a	5.225	**Dillon** (city) Dillon County
17	1528	20.888	**Florence** (city) Florence County	92	n/a	5.223	**Lake City** (city) Florence County
18	1548	20.697	**Aiken** (city) Aiken County	93	n/a	5.183	**Valley Falls** (CDP) Spartanburg County
19	1551	20.637	**Greer** (city) Greenville County	94	n/a	4.859	**Elgin** (CDP) Lancaster County
20	1598	20.032	**North Augusta** (city) Aiken County	95	n/a	4.714	**Homeland Park** (CDP) Anderson County
21	1630	19.769	**Spartanburg** (city) Spartanburg County	96	n/a	4.678	**Arial** (CDP) Pickens County
22	1689	18.945	**Port Royal** (town) Beaufort County	97	n/a	4.674	**Duncan** (town) Spartanburg County
23	1766	18.045	**Summerville** (town) Dorchester County	98	n/a	4.636	**Welcome** (CDP) Greenville County
24	1848	17.094	**North Myrtle Beach** (city) Horry County	99	3970	4.596	**Forest Acres** (city) Richland County
25	1890	16.648	**Cayce** (city) Lexington County	100	n/a	4.562	**North Hartsville** (CDP) Darlington County
26	n/a	16.508	**Hopkins** (CDP) Richland County	101	n/a	4.547	**Darlington** (city) Darlington County
27	1917	16.341	**Fort Mill** (town) York County	102	n/a	4.521	**Travelers Rest** (city) Greenville County
28	1932	16.232	**Greenwood** (city) Greenwood County	103	n/a	4.513	**Hampton** (town) Hampton County
29	n/a	15.035	**Lugoff** (CDP) Kershaw County	104	n/a	4.500	**Laurel Bay** (CDP) Beaufort County
30	2136	14.595	**Anderson** (city) Anderson County	105	n/a	4.459	**Clover** (town) York County
31	2284	13.345	**Socastee** (CDP) Horry County	106	n/a	4.451	**Liberty** (city) Pickens County
32	n/a	12.507	**Folly Beach** (city) Charleston County	107	n/a	4.436	**Isle of Palms** (city) Charleston County
33	2428	12.257	**Easley** (city) Pickens County	108	n/a	4.421	**Marion** (city) Marion County
34	n/a	11.805	**Red Bank** (CDP) Lexington County	109	n/a	4.368	**Pageland** (town) Chesterfield County
35	2572	11.290	**Red Hill** (CDP) Horry County	110	n/a	4.225	**Springdale** (CDP) Lancaster County
36	2658	10.701	**Taylors** (CDP) Greenville County	111	n/a	4.189	**Clearwater** (CDP) Aiken County
37	2662	10.688	**Hanahan** (city) Berkeley County	112	n/a	4.183	**Edgefield** (town) Edgefield County
38	n/a	10.681	**Camden** (city) Kershaw County	113	n/a	4.128	**Northlake** (CDP) Anderson County
39	n/a	10.480	**Little River** (CDP) Horry County	114	n/a	4.052	**McCormick** (town) McCormick County
40	n/a	10.386	**Laurens** (city) Laurens County	115	n/a	3.958	**Walhalla** (city) Oconee County
41	2795	9.954	**Mauldin** (city) Greenville County	116	n/a	3.912	**Woodruff** (city) Spartanburg County
42	2809	9.913	**Gantt** (CDP) Greenville County	117	n/a	3.870	**Tega Cay** (city) York County
43	n/a	9.875	**Clinton** (city) Laurens County	118	n/a	3.842	**Belton** (city) Anderson County
44	2989	8.959	**Wade Hampton** (CDP) Greenville County	119	n/a	3.836	**Denmark** (city) Bamberg County
45	n/a	8.953	**Williston** (town) Barnwell County	120	n/a	3.790	**Pendleton** (town) Anderson County
46	3008	8.871	**Lexington** (town) Lexington County	121	n/a	3.737	**Forestbrook** (CDP) Horry County
47	3024	8.809	**Simpsonville** (city) Greenville County	122	n/a	3.642	**Williamston** (town) Anderson County
48	n/a	8.711	**Newport** (CDP) York County	123	n/a	3.637	**Brookdale** (CDP) Orangeburg County
49	n/a	8.596	**Piedmont** (CDP) Anderson County	124	n/a	3.628	**Gloverville** (CDP) Aiken County
50	3070	8.574	**Newberry** (city) Newberry County	125	n/a	3.618	**Honea Path** (town) Anderson County
51	n/a	8.536	**Burton** (CDP) Beaufort County	126	n/a	3.582	**Bamberg** (town) Bamberg County
52	3086	8.469	**Orangeburg** (city) Orangeburg County	127	n/a	3.564	**Southern Shops** (CDP) Spartanburg County
53	3113	8.324	**Gaffney** (city) Cherokee County	128	n/a	3.504	**Belvedere** (CDP) Aiken County
54	n/a	8.210	**York** (city) York County	129	n/a	3.311	**Sans Souci** (CDP) Greenville County
55	n/a	8.084	**Union** (city) Union County	130	n/a	3.310	**Allendale** (town) Allendale County
56	n/a	7.887	**Fountain Inn** (city) Greenville County	131	n/a	3.307	**Graniteville** (CDP) Aiken County
57	n/a	7.850	**Barnwell** (city) Barnwell County	132	n/a	3.267	**Chester** (city) Chester County
58	n/a	7.844	**Lake Wylie** (CDP) York County	133	n/a	3.249	**Saluda** (town) Saluda County
59	n/a	7.785	**Batesburg-Leesville** (town) Lexington County	134	n/a	3.228	**Winnsboro** (town) Fairfield County
60	3242	7.704	**Berea** (CDP) Greenville County	135	n/a	3.154	**Kingstree** (town) Williamsburg County
61	3266	7.584	**Seven Oaks** (CDP) Lexington County	136	n/a	3.064	**Mullins** (city) Marion County
62	3270	7.568	**Five Forks** (CDP) Greenville County	137	n/a	3.056	**East Gaffney** (CDP) Cherokee County
63	n/a	7.558	**Lakewood** (CDP) Sumter County	138	n/a	2.828	**Pickens** (city) Pickens County
64	n/a	7.552	**Seneca** (city) Oconee County	139	n/a	2.762	**Manning** (city) Clarendon County
65	3295	7.440	**Clemson** (city) Pickens County	140	n/a	2.743	**Woodfield** (CDP) Richland County
66	n/a	7.360	**Murrells Inlet** (CDP) Georgetown County	141	n/a	2.729	**Springdale** (town) Lexington County
67	n/a	7.285	**Moncks Corner** (town) Berkeley County	142	n/a	2.694	**Central** (town) Pickens County
68	3383	7.023	**Ladson** (CDP) Berkeley County	143	n/a	2.637	**India Hook** (CDP) York County
69	3394	6.992	**West Columbia** (city) Lexington County	144	n/a	2.387	**Saxon** (CDP) Spartanburg County
70	n/a	6.910	**Georgetown** (city) Georgetown County	145	n/a	2.337	**Bishopville** (city) Lee County
71	n/a	6.837	**Boiling Springs** (CDP) Spartanburg County	146	n/a	2.205	**Andrews** (town) Georgetown County
72	3441	6.822	**Parker** (CDP) Greenville County	147	n/a	2.031	**Sangaree** (CDP) Berkeley County
73	3452	6.767	**Dentsville** (CDP) Richland County	148	n/a	1.960	**Arcadia** (CDP) Spartanburg County
74	3481	6.650	**Oak Grove** (CDP) Lexington County	149	n/a	1.932	**Surfside Beach** (town) Horry County
75	n/a	6.488	**Walterboro** (city) Colleton County	150	n/a	1.575	**Dunean** (CDP) Greenville County

Note: *The state column ranks the top/bottom 150 places in the state with population of 2,500 or more. The national column ranks the top/bottom places in the country with population of 10,000 or more. Places that are unincorporated were not considered in the rankings. n/a indicates data not available. Please refer to the User Guide for additional information.*

Land Area

Top 150 Places Ranked in *Ascending* Order

State Rank	Nat'l Rank	Sq. Miles	Place
1	n/a	1.575	**Dunean** (CDP) Greenville County
2	n/a	1.932	**Surfside Beach** (town) Horry County
3	n/a	1.960	**Arcadia** (CDP) Spartanburg County
4	n/a	2.031	**Sangaree** (CDP) Berkeley County
5	n/a	2.205	**Andrews** (town) Georgetown County
6	n/a	2.337	**Bishopville** (city) Lee County
7	n/a	2.387	**Saxon** (CDP) Spartanburg County
8	n/a	2.637	**India Hook** (CDP) York County
9	n/a	2.694	**Central** (town) Pickens County
10	n/a	2.729	**Springdale** (town) Lexington County
11	n/a	2.743	**Woodfield** (CDP) Richland County
12	n/a	2.762	**Manning** (city) Clarendon County
13	n/a	2.828	**Pickens** (city) Pickens County
14	n/a	3.056	**East Gaffney** (CDP) Cherokee County
15	n/a	3.064	**Mullins** (city) Marion County
16	n/a	3.154	**Kingstree** (town) Williamsburg County
17	n/a	3.228	**Winnsboro** (town) Fairfield County
18	n/a	3.249	**Saluda** (town) Saluda County
19	n/a	3.267	**Chester** (city) Chester County
20	n/a	3.307	**Graniteville** (CDP) Aiken County
21	n/a	3.310	**Allendale** (town) Allendale County
22	n/a	3.311	**Sans Souci** (CDP) Greenville County
23	n/a	3.504	**Belvedere** (CDP) Aiken County
24	n/a	3.564	**Southern Shops** (CDP) Spartanburg County
25	n/a	3.582	**Bamberg** (town) Bamberg County
26	n/a	3.618	**Honea Path** (town) Anderson County
27	n/a	3.628	**Gloverville** (CDP) Aiken County
28	n/a	3.637	**Brookdale** (CDP) Orangeburg County
29	n/a	3.642	**Williamston** (town) Anderson County
30	n/a	3.737	**Forestbrook** (CDP) Horry County
31	n/a	3.790	**Pendleton** (town) Anderson County
32	n/a	3.836	**Denmark** (city) Bamberg County
33	n/a	3.842	**Belton** (city) Anderson County
34	n/a	3.870	**Tega Cay** (city) York County
35	n/a	3.912	**Woodruff** (city) Spartanburg County
36	n/a	3.958	**Walhalla** (city) Oconee County
37	n/a	4.052	**McCormick** (town) McCormick County
38	n/a	4.128	**Northlake** (CDP) Anderson County
39	n/a	4.183	**Edgefield** (town) Edgefield County
40	n/a	4.189	**Clearwater** (CDP) Aiken County
41	n/a	4.225	**Springdale** (CDP) Lancaster County
42	n/a	4.368	**Pageland** (town) Chesterfield County
43	n/a	4.421	**Marion** (city) Marion County
44	n/a	4.436	**Isle of Palms** (city) Charleston County
45	n/a	4.451	**Liberty** (city) Pickens County
46	n/a	4.459	**Clover** (town) York County
47	n/a	4.500	**Laurel Bay** (CDP) Beaufort County
48	n/a	4.513	**Hampton** (town) Hampton County
49	n/a	4.521	**Travelers Rest** (city) Greenville County
50	n/a	4.547	**Darlington** (city) Darlington County
51	n/a	4.562	**North Hartsville** (CDP) Darlington County
52	686	4.596	**Forest Acres** (city) Richland County
53	n/a	4.636	**Welcome** (CDP) Greenville County
54	n/a	4.674	**Duncan** (town) Spartanburg County
55	n/a	4.678	**Arial** (CDP) Pickens County
56	n/a	4.714	**Homeland Park** (CDP) Anderson County
57	n/a	4.859	**Elgin** (CDP) Lancaster County
58	n/a	5.183	**Valley Falls** (CDP) Spartanburg County
59	n/a	5.223	**Lake City** (city) Florence County
60	n/a	5.225	**Dillon** (city) Dillon County
61	n/a	5.368	**Garden City** (CDP) Horry County
62	n/a	5.418	**Edisto** (CDP) Orangeburg County
63	n/a	5.422	**Cheraw** (town) Chesterfield County
64	n/a	5.477	**Burnettown** (town) Aiken County
65	n/a	5.584	**Lake Murray of Richland** (CDP) Richland County
66	n/a	5.723	**Hartsville** (city) Darlington County
67	n/a	5.886	**Dalzell** (CDP) Sumter County
68	n/a	5.905	**Centerville** (CDP) Anderson County
69	n/a	5.976	**Lyman** (town) Spartanburg County
70	n/a	6.082	**Lesslie** (CDP) York County
71	n/a	6.116	**Bennettsville** (city) Marlboro County
72	n/a	6.116	**Abbeville** (city) Abbeville County
73	1088	6.261	**Irmo** (town) Richland County
74	1107	6.346	**Saint Andrews** (CDP) Richland County
75	n/a	6.415	**Lancaster** (city) Lancaster County
76	n/a	6.488	**Walterboro** (city) Colleton County
77	1175	6.650	**Oak Grove** (CDP) Lexington County
78	1204	6.767	**Dentsville** (CDP) Richland County
79	1215	6.822	**Parker** (CDP) Greenville County
80	n/a	6.837	**Boiling Springs** (CDP) Spartanburg County
81	n/a	6.910	**Georgetown** (city) Georgetown County
82	1262	6.992	**West Columbia** (city) Lexington County
83	1273	7.023	**Ladson** (CDP) Berkeley County
84	n/a	7.285	**Moncks Corner** (town) Berkeley County
85	n/a	7.360	**Murrells Inlet** (CDP) Georgetown County
86	1361	7.440	**Clemson** (city) Pickens County
87	n/a	7.552	**Seneca** (city) Oconee County
88	n/a	7.558	**Lakewood** (CDP) Sumter County
89	1386	7.568	**Five Forks** (CDP) Greenville County
90	1390	7.584	**Seven Oaks** (CDP) Lexington County
91	1414	7.704	**Berea** (CDP) Greenville County
92	n/a	7.785	**Batesburg-Leesville** (town) Lexington County
93	n/a	7.844	**Lake Wylie** (CDP) York County
94	n/a	7.850	**Barnwell** (city) Barnwell County
95	n/a	7.887	**Fountain Inn** (city) Greenville County
96	n/a	8.084	**Union** (city) Union County
97	n/a	8.210	**York** (city) York County
98	1543	8.324	**Gaffney** (city) Cherokee County
99	1570	8.469	**Orangeburg** (city) Orangeburg County
100	n/a	8.536	**Burton** (CDP) Beaufort County
101	1586	8.574	**Newberry** (city) Newberry County
102	n/a	8.596	**Piedmont** (CDP) Anderson County
103	n/a	8.711	**Newport** (CDP) York County
104	1632	8.809	**Simpsonville** (city) Greenville County
105	1648	8.871	**Lexington** (town) Lexington County
106	n/a	8.953	**Williston** (town) Barnwell County
107	1667	8.959	**Wade Hampton** (CDP) Greenville County
108	n/a	9.875	**Clinton** (city) Laurens County
109	1847	9.913	**Gantt** (CDP) Greenville County
110	1861	9.954	**Mauldin** (city) Greenville County
111	n/a	10.386	**Laurens** (city) Laurens County
112	n/a	10.480	**Little River** (CDP) Horry County
113	n/a	10.681	**Camden** (city) Kershaw County
114	1994	10.688	**Hanahan** (city) Berkeley County
115	1998	10.701	**Taylors** (CDP) Greenville County
116	2084	11.290	**Red Hill** (CDP) Horry County
117	n/a	11.805	**Red Bank** (CDP) Lexington County
118	2228	12.257	**Easley** (city) Pickens County
119	n/a	12.507	**Folly Beach** (city) Charleston County
120	2372	13.345	**Socastee** (CDP) Horry County
121	2520	14.595	**Anderson** (city) Anderson County
122	n/a	15.035	**Lugoff** (CDP) Kershaw County
123	2724	16.232	**Greenwood** (city) Greenwood County
124	2739	16.341	**Fort Mill** (town) York County
125	n/a	16.508	**Hopkins** (CDP) Richland County
126	2766	16.648	**Cayce** (city) Lexington County
127	2808	17.094	**North Myrtle Beach** (city) Horry County
128	2890	18.045	**Summerville** (town) Dorchester County
129	2967	18.945	**Port Royal** (town) Beaufort County
130	3026	19.769	**Spartanburg** (city) Spartanburg County
131	3058	20.032	**North Augusta** (city) Aiken County
132	3105	20.637	**Greer** (city) Greenville County
133	3108	20.697	**Aiken** (city) Aiken County
134	3128	20.888	**Florence** (city) Florence County
135	3193	21.942	**Conway** (city) Horry County
136	n/a	23.132	**Hollywood** (town) Charleston County
137	3307	23.324	**Myrtle Beach** (city) Horry County
138	3551	27.600	**Beaufort** (city) Beaufort County
139	3614	28.669	**Greenville** (city) Greenville County
140	3772	32.086	**Sumter** (city) Sumter County
141	3966	35.722	**Rock Hill** (city) York County
142	4101	40.086	**Goose Creek** (city) Berkeley County
143	4128	41.363	**Hilton Head Island** (town) Beaufort County
144	n/a	44.451	**Ridgeland** (town) Jasper County
145	4214	45.082	**Mount Pleasant** (town) Charleston County
146	n/a	45.161	**Hardeeville** (city) Jasper County
147	4306	51.301	**Bluffton** (town) Beaufort County
148	4479	73.187	**North Charleston** (city) Charleston County
149	4563	108.979	**Charleston** (city) Charleston County
150	4585	132.213	**Columbia** (city) Richland County

Note: *The state column ranks the top/bottom 150 places in the state with population of 2,500 or more. The national column ranks the top/bottom places in the country with population of 10,000 or more. Places that are unincorporated were not considered in the rankings. n/a indicates data not available. Please refer to the User Guide for additional information.*

Water Area

Top 150 Places Ranked in *Descending* Order

State Rank	Nat'l Rank	Sq. Miles	Place	State Rank	Nat'l Rank	Sq. Miles	Place
1	52	27.771	**Hilton Head Island** (town) Beaufort County	76	3195	0.046	**Florence** (city) Florence County
2	78	18.513	**Charleston** (city) Charleston County	77	3202	0.046	**Mauldin** (city) Greenville County
3	196	7.524	**Mount Pleasant** (town) Charleston County	78	3207	0.046	**Parker** (CDP) Greenville County
4	n/a	6.362	**Folly Beach** (city) Charleston County	79	3214	0.045	**Five Forks** (CDP) Greenville County
5	242	5.979	**Beaufort** (city) Beaufort County	80	3222	0.044	**Anderson** (city) Anderson County
6	371	3.461	**North Charleston** (city) Charleston County	81	n/a	0.043	**Pageland** (town) Chesterfield County
7	n/a	3.114	**Lake Murray of Richland** (CDP) Richland County	82	n/a	0.042	**Saluda** (town) Saluda County
8	415	3.065	**Port Royal** (town) Beaufort County	83	n/a	0.040	**Edisto** (CDP) Orangeburg County
9	n/a	2.743	**Lake Wylie** (CDP) York County	84	3280	0.040	**Taylors** (CDP) Greenville County
10	451	2.716	**Columbia** (city) Richland County	85	n/a	0.038	**Woodfield** (CDP) Richland County
11	537	2.210	**Bluffton** (town) Beaufort County	86	n/a	0.037	**Williamston** (town) Anderson County
12	557	2.087	**Greer** (city) Greenville County	87	3328	0.037	**Oak Grove** (CDP) Lexington County
13	n/a	1.383	**Hollywood** (town) Charleston County	88	n/a	0.035	**Cheraw** (town) Chesterfield County
14	n/a	1.059	**Northlake** (CDP) Anderson County	89	n/a	0.034	**Fountain Inn** (city) Greenville County
15	n/a	1.000	**Isle of Palms** (city) Charleston County	90	n/a	0.033	**Valley Falls** (CDP) Spartanburg County
16	n/a	0.902	**India Hook** (CDP) York County	91	n/a	0.032	**Bishopville** (city) Lee County
17	n/a	0.889	**Laurel Bay** (CDP) Beaufort County	92	n/a	0.031	**Centerville** (CDP) Anderson County
18	1076	0.841	**Conway** (city) Horry County	93	n/a	0.029	**Springdale** (town) Lexington County
19	1091	0.822	**Hanahan** (city) Berkeley County	94	n/a	0.027	**Pendleton** (town) Anderson County
20	1135	0.770	**Cayce** (city) Lexington County	95	3471	0.026	**Gaffney** (city) Cherokee County
21	1137	0.768	**Goose Creek** (city) Berkeley County	96	3485	0.025	**Simpsonville** (city) Greenville County
22	n/a	0.707	**Camden** (city) Kershaw County	97	n/a	0.025	**Travelers Rest** (city) Greenville County
23	n/a	0.694	**Tega Cay** (city) York County	98	n/a	0.024	**Kingstree** (town) Williamsburg County
24	n/a	0.633	**Bennettsville** (city) Marlboro County	99	n/a	0.022	**Pickens** (city) Pickens County
25	n/a	0.606	**Georgetown** (city) Georgetown County	100	n/a	0.022	**Surfside Beach** (town) Horry County
26	1293	0.599	**North Myrtle Beach** (city) Horry County	101	n/a	0.022	**Hopkins** (CDP) Richland County
27	n/a	0.585	**Lyman** (town) Spartanburg County	102	n/a	0.021	**Woodruff** (city) Spartanburg County
28	n/a	0.553	**Burnettown** (town) Aiken County	103	3560	0.021	**Easley** (city) Pickens County
29	1392	0.524	**Socastee** (CDP) Horry County	104	3573	0.021	**Saint Andrews** (CDP) Richland County
30	1479	0.462	**Clemson** (city) Pickens County	105	n/a	0.020	**Burton** (CDP) Beaufort County
31	1481	0.461	**North Augusta** (city) Aiken County	106	n/a	0.018	**Graniteville** (CDP) Aiken County
32	n/a	0.438	**Hartsville** (city) Darlington County	107	n/a	0.017	**Elgin** (CDP) Lancaster County
33	1626	0.371	**Forest Acres** (city) Richland County	108	3668	0.016	**Gantt** (CDP) Greenville County
34	n/a	0.346	**Little River** (CDP) Horry County	109	n/a	0.016	**Arial** (CDP) Pickens County
35	1815	0.295	**Berea** (CDP) Greenville County	110	n/a	0.016	**Springdale** (CDP) Lancaster County
36	n/a	0.262	**Ridgeland** (town) Jasper County	111	n/a	0.014	**Hampton** (town) Hampton County
37	1934	0.254	**Fort Mill** (town) York County	112	n/a	0.013	**Liberty** (city) Pickens County
38	n/a	0.250	**Lugoff** (CDP) Kershaw County	113	n/a	0.013	**Belton** (city) Anderson County
39	1982	0.242	**Myrtle Beach** (city) Horry County	114	n/a	0.012	**Bamberg** (town) Bamberg County
40	n/a	0.231	**Red Bank** (CDP) Lexington County	115	n/a	0.012	**Abbeville** (city) Abbeville County
41	2084	0.211	**West Columbia** (city) Lexington County	116	n/a	0.011	**Clover** (town) York County
42	2124	0.203	**Sumter** (city) Sumter County	117	n/a	0.011	**Dillon** (city) Dillon County
43	n/a	0.174	**Lakewood** (CDP) Sumter County	118	n/a	0.011	**Homeland Park** (CDP) Anderson County
44	n/a	0.169	**Piedmont** (CDP) Anderson County	119	n/a	0.011	**Southern Shops** (CDP) Spartanburg County
45	n/a	0.167	**Murrells Inlet** (CDP) Georgetown County	120	3818	0.010	**Orangeburg** (city) Orangeburg County
46	2314	0.161	**Rock Hill** (city) York County	121	n/a	0.009	**Gloverville** (CDP) Aiken County
47	n/a	0.148	**Barnwell** (city) Barnwell County	122	n/a	0.008	**Lake City** (city) Florence County
48	2370	0.148	**Greenville** (city) Greenville County	123	n/a	0.007	**East Gaffney** (CDP) Cherokee County
49	2397	0.142	**Aiken** (city) Aiken County	124	n/a	0.007	**Saxon** (CDP) Spartanburg County
50	n/a	0.134	**Moncks Corner** (town) Berkeley County	125	n/a	0.006	**Belvedere** (CDP) Aiken County
51	2461	0.133	**Dentsville** (CDP) Richland County	126	n/a	0.006	**North Hartsville** (CDP) Darlington County
52	n/a	0.122	**Clearwater** (CDP) Aiken County	127	n/a	0.005	**Arcadia** (CDP) Spartanburg County
53	2557	0.118	**Greenwood** (city) Greenwood County	128	3981	0.004	**Newberry** (city) Newberry County
54	n/a	0.118	**York** (city) York County	129	n/a	0.003	**Denmark** (city) Bamberg County
55	2570	0.117	**Spartanburg** (city) Spartanburg County	130	n/a	0.003	**Dunean** (CDP) Greenville County
56	2574	0.117	**Seven Oaks** (CDP) Lexington County	131	n/a	0.003	**Brookdale** (CDP) Orangeburg County
57	n/a	0.116	**Edgefield** (town) Edgefield County	132	n/a	0.003	**Central** (town) Pickens County
58	2601	0.113	**Summerville** (town) Dorchester County	133	n/a	0.002	**Honea Path** (town) Anderson County
59	n/a	0.109	**Hardeeville** (city) Jasper County	134	n/a	0.000	**Allendale** (town) Allendale County
60	n/a	0.104	**Batesburg-Leesville** (town) Lexington County	134	n/a	0.000	**Andrews** (town) Georgetown County
61	n/a	0.103	**Duncan** (town) Spartanburg County	134	n/a	0.000	**Boiling Springs** (CDP) Spartanburg County
62	n/a	0.083	**Lancaster** (city) Lancaster County	134	n/a	0.000	**Chester** (city) Chester County
63	n/a	0.080	**Garden City** (CDP) Horry County	134	n/a	0.000	**Darlington** (city) Darlington County
64	2874	0.077	**Lexington** (town) Lexington County	134	n/a	0.000	**Forestbrook** (CDP) Horry County
65	n/a	0.068	**Clinton** (city) Laurens County	134	4158	0.000	**Irmo** (town) Richland County
66	n/a	0.063	**Williston** (town) Barnwell County	134	4158	0.000	**Ladson** (CDP) Berkeley County
67	n/a	0.062	**Walhalla** (city) Oconee County	134	n/a	0.000	**Laurens** (city) Laurens County
68	n/a	0.061	**Newport** (CDP) York County	134	n/a	0.000	**Manning** (city) Clarendon County
69	3054	0.059	**Red Hill** (CDP) Horry County	134	n/a	0.000	**Marion** (city) Marion County
70	n/a	0.054	**Seneca** (city) Oconee County	134	n/a	0.000	**McCormick** (town) McCormick County
71	3158	0.050	**Wade Hampton** (CDP) Greenville County	134	n/a	0.000	**Mullins** (city) Marion County
72	n/a	0.049	**Welcome** (CDP) Greenville County	134	n/a	0.000	**Sangaree** (CDP) Berkeley County
73	n/a	0.049	**Lesslie** (CDP) York County	134	n/a	0.000	**Union** (city) Union County
74	n/a	0.048	**Sans Souci** (CDP) Greenville County	134	n/a	0.000	**Walterboro** (city) Colleton County
75	n/a	0.048	**Dalzell** (CDP) Sumter County	134	n/a	0.000	**Winnsboro** (town) Fairfield County

Note: The state column ranks the top/bottom 150 places in the state with population of 2,500 or more. The national column ranks the top/bottom places in the country with population of 10,000 or more. Places that are unincorporated were not considered in the rankings. n/a indicates data not available. Please refer to the User Guide for additional information.

Elevation

Top 150 Places Ranked in *Descending* Order

State Rank	Nat'l Rank	Feet	Place
1	n/a	1,099	**Travelers Rest** (city) Greenville County
2	n/a	1,093	**Pickens** (city) Pickens County
3	580	1,066	**Easley** (city) Pickens County
4	624	1,040	**Berea** (CDP) Greenville County
5	n/a	1,037	**Arial** (CDP) Pickens County
6	n/a	1,033	**Walhalla** (city) Oconee County
7	655	1,024	**Wade Hampton** (CDP) Greenville County
8	660	1,020	**Parker** (CDP) Greenville County
9	670	1,014	**Greer** (city) Greenville County
9	n/a	1,014	**Sans Souci** (CDP) Greenville County
11	710	988	**Gantt** (CDP) Greenville County
12	714	984	**Greenville** (city) Greenville County
12	n/a	984	**Welcome** (CDP) Greenville County
14	n/a	981	**Liberty** (city) Pickens County
15	n/a	978	**Dunean** (CDP) Greenville County
16	n/a	955	**Seneca** (city) Oconee County
17	793	942	**Mauldin** (city) Greenville County
18	831	925	**Taylors** (CDP) Greenville County
19	n/a	919	**Boiling Springs** (CDP) Spartanburg County
20	n/a	912	**Central** (town) Pickens County
21	n/a	883	**Belton** (city) Anderson County
22	955	876	**Five Forks** (CDP) Greenville County
22	n/a	876	**Southern Shops** (CDP) Spartanburg County
24	n/a	866	**Fountain Inn** (city) Greenville County
24	981	866	**Simpsonville** (city) Greenville County
26	n/a	863	**Duncan** (town) Spartanburg County
27	n/a	856	**Lyman** (town) Spartanburg County
27	n/a	856	**Saxon** (CDP) Spartanburg County
29	n/a	853	**Pendleton** (town) Anderson County
30	n/a	833	**Centerville** (CDP) Anderson County
31	n/a	814	**Clover** (town) York County
32	n/a	807	**Arcadia** (CDP) Spartanburg County
32	n/a	807	**Williamston** (town) Anderson County
34	1140	797	**Spartanburg** (city) Spartanburg County
34	n/a	797	**Valley Falls** (CDP) Spartanburg County
36	n/a	791	**Honea Path** (town) Anderson County
36	n/a	791	**Piedmont** (CDP) Anderson County
38	1163	787	**Anderson** (city) Anderson County
38	n/a	787	**Woodruff** (city) Spartanburg County
40	1174	784	**Gaffney** (city) Cherokee County
40	n/a	784	**Homeland Park** (CDP) Anderson County
42	n/a	771	**East Gaffney** (CDP) Cherokee County
43	n/a	758	**York** (city) York County
44	1354	722	**Clemson** (city) Pickens County
45	n/a	699	**Lesslie** (CDP) York County
45	n/a	699	**Newport** (CDP) York County
47	1479	679	**Rock Hill** (city) York County
48	n/a	676	**Clinton** (city) Laurens County
49	1538	663	**Greenwood** (city) Greenwood County
50	n/a	659	**Northlake** (CDP) Anderson County
51	n/a	650	**Pageland** (town) Chesterfield County
52	n/a	643	**Batesburg-Leesville** (town) Lexington County
53	n/a	640	**Union** (city) Union County
54	n/a	636	**India Hook** (CDP) York County
55	n/a	630	**Tega Cay** (city) York County
56	1686	623	**Fort Mill** (town) York County
57	n/a	614	**Laurens** (city) Laurens County
58	n/a	600	**Elgin** (CDP) Lancaster County
59	n/a	591	**Abbeville** (city) Abbeville County
60	n/a	584	**Lake Wylie** (CDP) York County
61	n/a	545	**Lancaster** (city) Lancaster County
62	n/a	541	**Chester** (city) Chester County
63	n/a	538	**Springdale** (CDP) Lancaster County
64	n/a	535	**McCormick** (town) McCormick County
64	n/a	535	**Winnsboro** (town) Fairfield County
66	n/a	531	**Edgefield** (town) Edgefield County
67	2026	515	**Aiken** (city) Aiken County
68	2085	492	**Newberry** (city) Newberry County
69	n/a	486	**Belvedere** (CDP) Aiken County
70	n/a	479	**Saluda** (town) Saluda County
71	n/a	449	**Lake Murray of Richland** (CDP) Richland County
72	2296	394	**Lexington** (town) Lexington County
73	2312	387	**North Augusta** (city) Aiken County
74	2398	354	**Irmo** (town) Richland County
74	n/a	354	**Williston** (town) Barnwell County

State Rank	Nat'l Rank	Feet	Place
76	n/a	341	**Red Bank** (CDP) Lexington County
76	n/a	341	**Woodfield** (CDP) Richland County
78	2447	338	**Oak Grove** (CDP) Lexington County
79	2498	322	**Saint Andrews** (CDP) Richland County
80	2588	289	**Columbia** (city) Richland County
81	2595	285	**West Columbia** (city) Lexington County
82	n/a	269	**Lugoff** (CDP) Kershaw County
83	n/a	246	**Denmark** (city) Bamberg County
83	2703	246	**Forest Acres** (city) Richland County
85	2712	243	**Orangeburg** (city) Orangeburg County
86	2723	239	**Cayce** (city) Lexington County
87	2734	236	**Dentsville** (CDP) Richland County
88	n/a	233	**Graniteville** (CDP) Aiken County
89	n/a	230	**Springdale** (town) Lexington County
90	n/a	223	**Bishopville** (city) Lee County
91	n/a	220	**Brookdale** (CDP) Orangeburg County
91	n/a	220	**Edisto** (CDP) Orangeburg County
93	n/a	217	**Barnwell** (city) Barnwell County
93	n/a	217	**Dalzell** (CDP) Sumter County
93	n/a	217	**Hartsville** (city) Darlington County
93	2797	217	**Seven Oaks** (CDP) Lexington County
97	n/a	207	**North Hartsville** (CDP) Darlington County
98	n/a	203	**Gloverville** (CDP) Aiken County
99	n/a	190	**Camden** (city) Kershaw County
100	n/a	187	**Allendale** (town) Allendale County
101	n/a	177	**Burnettown** (town) Aiken County
101	n/a	177	**Lakewood** (CDP) Sumter County
103	2947	171	**Sumter** (city) Sumter County
104	n/a	164	**Bamberg** (town) Bamberg County
104	n/a	164	**Hopkins** (CDP) Richland County
106	n/a	154	**Bennettsville** (city) Marlboro County
106	n/a	154	**Cheraw** (town) Chesterfield County
108	n/a	151	**Darlington** (city) Darlington County
109	n/a	148	**Clearwater** (CDP) Aiken County
110	3082	138	**Florence** (city) Florence County
111	n/a	128	**Manning** (city) Clarendon County
112	n/a	112	**Dillon** (city) Dillon County
113	n/a	108	**Hampton** (town) Hampton County
114	n/a	98	**Mullins** (city) Marion County
115	n/a	75	**Lake City** (city) Florence County
115	n/a	75	**Marion** (city) Marion County
117	n/a	72	**Sangaree** (CDP) Berkeley County
117	3460	72	**Summerville** (town) Dorchester County
119	n/a	69	**Walterboro** (city) Colleton County
120	n/a	62	**Kingstree** (town) Williamsburg County
121	n/a	59	**Ridgeland** (town) Jasper County
122	n/a	52	**Moncks Corner** (town) Berkeley County
123	3681	46	**Ladson** (CDP) Berkeley County
124	3784	36	**Conway** (city) Horry County
124	3784	36	**Hanahan** (city) Berkeley County
124	n/a	36	**Laurel Bay** (CDP) Beaufort County
124	n/a	36	**Little River** (CDP) Horry County
128	n/a	33	**Burton** (CDP) Beaufort County
128	3815	33	**Red Hill** (CDP) Horry County
130	3855	30	**Goose Creek** (city) Berkeley County
130	n/a	30	**Hollywood** (town) Charleston County
132	n/a	26	**Andrews** (town) Georgetown County
132	n/a	26	**Hardeeville** (city) Jasper County
132	3902	26	**Myrtle Beach** (city) Horry County
135	3932	23	**Mount Pleasant** (town) Charleston County
135	3932	23	**Port Royal** (town) Beaufort County
137	3978	20	**Bluffton** (town) Beaufort County
137	n/a	20	**Garden City** (CDP) Horry County
137	3978	20	**North Charleston** (city) Charleston County
137	3978	20	**Socastee** (CDP) Horry County
141	n/a	16	**Georgetown** (city) Georgetown County
141	n/a	16	**Murrells Inlet** (CDP) Georgetown County
143	n/a	13	**Forestbrook** (CDP) Horry County
144	4152	10	**Beaufort** (city) Beaufort County
144	4152	10	**Charleston** (city) Charleston County
144	n/a	10	**Folly Beach** (city) Charleston County
144	4152	10	**Hilton Head Island** (town) Beaufort County
144	n/a	10	**Surfside Beach** (town) Horry County
149	4230	7	**North Myrtle Beach** (city) Horry County
150	n/a	3	**Isle of Palms** (city) Charleston County

Note: The state column ranks the top/bottom 150 places in the state with population of 2,500 or more. The national column ranks the top/bottom places in the country with population of 10,000 or more. Places that are unincorporated were not considered in the rankings. n/a indicates data not available. Please refer to the User Guide for additional information.

Elevation

Top 150 Places Ranked in *Ascending* Order

State Rank	Nat'l Rank	Feet	Place		State Rank	Nat'l Rank	Feet	Place
1	n/a	3	Isle of Palms (city) Charleston County		76	1958	354	Irmo (town) Richland County
2	62	7	North Myrtle Beach (city) Horry County		76	n/a	354	Williston (town) Barnwell County
3	139	10	Beaufort (city) Beaufort County		78	2048	387	North Augusta (city) Aiken County
3	139	10	Charleston (city) Charleston County		79	2064	394	Lexington (town) Lexington County
3	n/a	10	Folly Beach (city) Charleston County		80	n/a	449	Lake Murray of Richland (CDP) Richland County
3	139	10	Hilton Head Island (town) Beaufort County		81	n/a	479	Saluda (town) Saluda County
3	n/a	10	Surfside Beach (town) Horry County		82	n/a	486	Belvedere (CDP) Aiken County
8	n/a	13	Forestbrook (CDP) Horry County		83	2275	492	Newberry (city) Newberry County
9	n/a	16	Georgetown (city) Georgetown County		84	2332	515	Aiken (city) Aiken County
9	n/a	16	Murrells Inlet (CDP) Georgetown County		85	n/a	531	Edgefield (town) Edgefield County
11	318	20	Bluffton (town) Beaufort County		86	n/a	535	McCormick (town) McCormick County
11	n/a	20	Garden City (CDP) Horry County		86	n/a	535	Winnsboro (town) Fairfield County
11	318	20	North Charleston (city) Charleston County		88	n/a	538	Springdale (CDP) Lancaster County
11	318	20	Socastee (CDP) Horry County		89	n/a	541	Chester (city) Chester County
15	390	23	Mount Pleasant (town) Charleston County		90	n/a	545	Lancaster (city) Lancaster County
15	390	23	Port Royal (town) Beaufort County		91	n/a	584	Lake Wylie (CDP) York County
17	n/a	26	Andrews (town) Georgetown County		92	n/a	591	Abbeville (city) Abbeville County
17	n/a	26	Hardeeville (city) Jasper County		93	n/a	600	Elgin (CDP) Lancaster County
17	436	26	Myrtle Beach (city) Horry County		94	n/a	614	Laurens (city) Laurens County
20	466	30	Goose Creek (city) Berkeley County		95	2665	623	Fort Mill (town) York County
20	n/a	30	Hollywood (town) Charleston County		96	n/a	630	Tega Cay (city) York County
22	n/a	33	Burton (CDP) Beaufort County		97	n/a	636	India Hook (CDP) York County
22	513	33	Red Hill (CDP) Horry County		98	n/a	640	Union (city) Union County
24	553	36	Conway (city) Horry County		99	n/a	643	Batesburg-Leesville (town) Lexington County
24	553	36	Hanahan (city) Berkeley County		100	n/a	650	Pageland (town) Chesterfield County
24	n/a	36	Laurel Bay (CDP) Beaufort County		101	n/a	659	Northlake (CDP) Anderson County
24	n/a	36	Little River (CDP) Horry County		102	2822	663	Greenwood (city) Greenwood County
28	655	46	Ladson (CDP) Berkeley County		103	n/a	676	Clinton (city) Laurens County
29	n/a	52	Moncks Corner (town) Berkeley County		104	2877	679	Rock Hill (city) York County
30	n/a	59	Ridgeland (town) Jasper County		105	n/a	699	Lesslie (CDP) York County
31	n/a	62	Kingstree (town) Williamsburg County		105	n/a	699	Newport (CDP) York County
32	n/a	69	Walterboro (city) Colleton County		107	3005	722	Clemson (city) Pickens County
33	n/a	72	Sangaree (CDP) Berkeley County		108	n/a	758	York (city) York County
33	880	72	Summerville (town) Dorchester County		109	n/a	771	East Gaffney (CDP) Cherokee County
35	n/a	75	Lake City (city) Florence County		110	3185	784	Gaffney (city) Cherokee County
35	n/a	75	Marion (city) Marion County		110	n/a	784	Homeland Park (CDP) Anderson County
37	n/a	98	Mullins (city) Marion County		112	3194	787	Anderson (city) Anderson County
38	n/a	108	Hampton (town) Hampton County		112	n/a	787	Woodruff (city) Spartanburg County
39	n/a	112	Dillon (city) Dillon County		114	n/a	791	Honea Path (town) Anderson County
40	n/a	128	Manning (city) Clarendon County		114	n/a	791	Piedmont (CDP) Anderson County
41	1279	138	Florence (city) Florence County		116	3218	797	Spartanburg (city) Spartanburg County
42	n/a	148	Clearwater (CDP) Aiken County		116	n/a	797	Valley Falls (CDP) Spartanburg County
43	n/a	151	Darlington (city) Darlington County		118	n/a	807	Arcadia (CDP) Spartanburg County
44	n/a	154	Bennettsville (city) Marlboro County		118	n/a	807	Williamston (town) Anderson County
44	n/a	154	Cheraw (town) Chesterfield County		120	n/a	814	Clover (town) York County
46	n/a	164	Bamberg (town) Bamberg County		121	n/a	833	Centerville (CDP) Anderson County
46	n/a	164	Hopkins (CDP) Richland County		122	n/a	853	Pendleton (town) Anderson County
48	1412	171	Sumter (city) Sumter County		123	n/a	856	Lyman (town) Spartanburg County
49	n/a	177	Burnettown (town) Aiken County		123	n/a	856	Saxon (CDP) Spartanburg County
49	n/a	177	Lakewood (CDP) Sumter County		125	n/a	863	Duncan (town) Spartanburg County
51	n/a	187	Allendale (town) Allendale County		126	n/a	866	Fountain Inn (city) Greenville County
52	n/a	190	Camden (city) Kershaw County		126	3378	866	Simpsonville (city) Greenville County
53	n/a	203	Gloverville (CDP) Aiken County		128	3407	876	Five Forks (CDP) Greenville County
54	n/a	207	North Hartsville (CDP) Darlington County		128	n/a	876	Southern Shops (CDP) Spartanburg County
55	n/a	217	Barnwell (city) Barnwell County		130	n/a	883	Belton (city) Anderson County
55	n/a	217	Dalzell (CDP) Sumter County		131	n/a	912	Central (town) Pickens County
55	n/a	217	Hartsville (city) Darlington County		132	n/a	919	Boiling Springs (CDP) Spartanburg County
55	1561	217	Seven Oaks (CDP) Lexington County		133	3530	925	Taylors (CDP) Greenville County
59	n/a	220	Brookdale (CDP) Orangeburg County		134	3562	942	Mauldin (city) Greenville County
59	n/a	220	Edisto (CDP) Orangeburg County		135	n/a	955	Seneca (city) Oconee County
61	n/a	223	Bishopville (city) Lee County		136	n/a	978	Dunean (CDP) Greenville County
62	n/a	230	Springdale (town) Lexington County		137	n/a	981	Liberty (city) Pickens County
63	n/a	233	Graniteville (CDP) Aiken County		138	3649	984	Greenville (city) Greenville County
64	1624	236	Dentsville (CDP) Richland County		138	n/a	984	Welcome (CDP) Greenville County
65	1634	239	Cayce (city) Lexington County		140	3654	988	Gantt (CDP) Greenville County
66	1645	243	Orangeburg (city) Orangeburg County		141	3695	1,014	Greer (city) Greenville County
67	n/a	246	Denmark (city) Bamberg County		141	n/a	1,014	Sans Souci (CDP) Greenville County
67	1656	246	Forest Acres (city) Richland County		143	3704	1,020	Parker (CDP) Greenville County
69	n/a	269	Lugoff (CDP) Kershaw County		144	3708	1,024	Wade Hampton (CDP) Greenville County
70	1766	285	West Columbia (city) Lexington County		145	n/a	1,033	Walhalla (city) Oconee County
71	1773	289	Columbia (city) Richland County		146	n/a	1,037	Arial (CDP) Pickens County
72	1862	322	Saint Andrews (CDP) Richland County		147	3740	1,040	Berea (CDP) Greenville County
73	1908	338	Oak Grove (CDP) Lexington County		148	3781	1,066	Easley (city) Pickens County
74	n/a	341	Red Bank (CDP) Lexington County		149	n/a	1,093	Pickens (city) Pickens County
74	n/a	341	Woodfield (CDP) Richland County		150	n/a	1,099	Travelers Rest (city) Greenville County

Note: The state column ranks the top/bottom 150 places in the state with population of 2,500 or more. The national column ranks the top/bottom places in the country with population of 10,000 or more. Places that are unincorporated were not considered in the rankings. n/a indicates data not available. Please refer to the User Guide for additional information.

Population

Top 150 Places Ranked in *Descending* Order

State Rank	Nat'l Rank	Number	Place
1	208	129,272	**Columbia** (city) Richland County
2	229	120,083	**Charleston** (city) Charleston County
3	316	97,471	**North Charleston** (city) Charleston County
4	537	67,843	**Mount Pleasant** (town) Charleston County
5	559	66,154	**Rock Hill** (city) York County
6	672	58,409	**Greenville** (city) Greenville County
7	987	43,392	**Summerville** (town) Dorchester County
8	1076	40,524	**Sumter** (city) Sumter County
9	1180	37,099	**Hilton Head Island** (town) Beaufort County
10	1183	37,056	**Florence** (city) Florence County
11	1186	37,013	**Spartanburg** (city) Spartanburg County
12	1231	35,938	**Goose Creek** (city) Berkeley County
13	1560	29,524	**Aiken** (city) Aiken County
14	1736	27,109	**Myrtle Beach** (city) Horry County
15	1767	26,686	**Anderson** (city) Anderson County
16	1862	25,515	**Greer** (city) Greenville County
17	2072	23,222	**Greenwood** (city) Greenwood County
18	2110	22,889	**Mauldin** (city) Greenville County
19	2233	21,617	**Taylors** (CDP) Greenville County
20	2267	21,348	**North Augusta** (city) Aiken County
21	2342	20,622	**Wade Hampton** (CDP) Greenville County
22	2355	20,493	**Saint Andrews** (CDP) Richland County
23	2421	19,993	**Easley** (city) Pickens County
24	2423	19,952	**Socastee** (CDP) Horry County
25	2684	18,238	**Simpsonville** (city) Greenville County
26	2725	17,997	**Hanahan** (city) Berkeley County
27	2741	17,870	**Lexington** (town) Lexington County
28	2866	17,103	**Conway** (city) Horry County
29	3223	15,144	**Seven Oaks** (CDP) Lexington County
30	3255	14,988	**West Columbia** (city) Lexington County
31	3408	14,295	**Berea** (CDP) Greenville County
32	3422	14,229	**Gantt** (CDP) Greenville County
33	3448	14,140	**Five Forks** (CDP) Greenville County
34	3461	14,062	**Dentsville** (CDP) Richland County
35	3487	13,964	**Orangeburg** (city) Orangeburg County
36	3503	13,905	**Clemson** (city) Pickens County
37	3528	13,790	**Ladson** (CDP) Berkeley County
38	3537	13,752	**North Myrtle Beach** (city) Horry County
39	3679	13,223	**Red Hill** (CDP) Horry County
40	3844	12,530	**Bluffton** (town) Beaufort County
41	3846	12,528	**Cayce** (city) Lexington County
42	3870	12,414	**Gaffney** (city) Cherokee County
43	3881	12,361	**Beaufort** (city) Beaufort County
44	4149	11,431	**Parker** (CDP) Greenville County
45	4267	11,097	**Irmo** (town) Richland County
46	4359	10,811	**Fort Mill** (town) York County
47	4405	10,678	**Port Royal** (town) Beaufort County
48	4525	10,361	**Forest Acres** (city) Richland County
49	4556	10,291	**Oak Grove** (CDP) Lexington County
50	4557	10,277	**Newberry** (city) Newberry County
51	n/a	9,617	**Red Bank** (CDP) Lexington County
52	n/a	9,303	**Woodfield** (CDP) Richland County
53	n/a	9,209	**Garden City** (CDP) Horry County
54	n/a	9,163	**Georgetown** (city) Georgetown County
55	n/a	9,139	**Laurens** (city) Laurens County
56	n/a	9,069	**Bennettsville** (city) Marlboro County
57	n/a	8,960	**Little River** (CDP) Horry County
58	n/a	8,841	**Lake Wylie** (CDP) York County
59	n/a	8,526	**Lancaster** (city) Lancaster County
60	n/a	8,490	**Clinton** (city) Laurens County
61	n/a	8,393	**Union** (city) Union County
62	n/a	8,220	**Sangaree** (CDP) Berkeley County
63	n/a	8,219	**Boiling Springs** (CDP) Spartanburg County
64	n/a	8,102	**Seneca** (city) Oconee County
65	n/a	7,885	**Moncks Corner** (town) Berkeley County
66	n/a	7,869	**Sans Souci** (CDP) Greenville County
67	n/a	7,799	**Fountain Inn** (city) Greenville County
68	n/a	7,764	**Hartsville** (city) Darlington County
69	n/a	7,736	**York** (city) York County
70	n/a	7,620	**Tega Cay** (city) York County
71	n/a	7,547	**Murrells Inlet** (CDP) Georgetown County
72	n/a	7,434	**Lugoff** (CDP) Kershaw County
73	n/a	6,976	**Burton** (CDP) Beaufort County
74	n/a	6,939	**Marion** (city) Marion County
75	n/a	6,838	**Camden** (city) Kershaw County
76	n/a	6,788	**Dillon** (city) Dillon County
77	n/a	6,675	**Lake City** (city) Florence County
78	n/a	6,668	**Welcome** (CDP) Greenville County
79	n/a	6,586	**Centerville** (CDP) Anderson County
80	n/a	6,299	**Valley Falls** (CDP) Spartanburg County
81	n/a	6,296	**Homeland Park** (CDP) Anderson County
82	n/a	6,289	**Darlington** (city) Darlington County
83	n/a	5,891	**Laurel Bay** (CDP) Beaufort County
84	n/a	5,851	**Cheraw** (town) Chesterfield County
85	n/a	5,792	**Belvedere** (CDP) Aiken County
86	n/a	5,607	**Chester** (city) Chester County
87	n/a	5,484	**Lake Murray of Richland** (CDP) Richland County
88	n/a	5,398	**Walterboro** (city) Colleton County
89	n/a	5,362	**Batesburg-Leesville** (town) Lexington County
90	n/a	5,237	**Abbeville** (city) Abbeville County
91	n/a	5,159	**Central** (town) Pickens County
92	n/a	5,103	**Piedmont** (CDP) Anderson County
93	n/a	5,094	**Clover** (town) York County
94	n/a	4,873	**Brookdale** (CDP) Orangeburg County
95	n/a	4,750	**Barnwell** (city) Barnwell County
95	n/a	4,750	**Edgefield** (town) Edgefield County
97	n/a	4,714	**Hollywood** (town) Charleston County
98	n/a	4,663	**Mullins** (city) Marion County
99	n/a	4,612	**Forestbrook** (CDP) Horry County
100	n/a	4,576	**Travelers Rest** (city) Greenville County
101	n/a	4,370	**Clearwater** (CDP) Aiken County
102	n/a	4,263	**Walhalla** (city) Oconee County
103	n/a	4,136	**Newport** (CDP) York County
104	n/a	4,134	**Belton** (city) Anderson County
105	n/a	4,133	**Isle of Palms** (city) Charleston County
106	n/a	4,108	**Manning** (city) Clarendon County
107	n/a	4,090	**Woodruff** (city) Spartanburg County
108	n/a	4,036	**Ridgeland** (town) Jasper County
109	n/a	3,934	**Williamston** (town) Anderson County
110	n/a	3,837	**Surfside Beach** (town) Horry County
111	n/a	3,767	**Southern Shops** (CDP) Spartanburg County
112	n/a	3,745	**Northlake** (CDP) Anderson County
113	n/a	3,671	**Dunean** (CDP) Greenville County
114	n/a	3,607	**Bamberg** (town) Bamberg County
115	n/a	3,597	**Honea Path** (town) Anderson County
116	n/a	3,565	**Saluda** (town) Saluda County
117	n/a	3,550	**Winnsboro** (town) Fairfield County
118	n/a	3,538	**Denmark** (city) Bamberg County
119	n/a	3,482	**Allendale** (town) Allendale County
120	n/a	3,471	**Bishopville** (city) Lee County
121	n/a	3,424	**Saxon** (CDP) Spartanburg County
122	n/a	3,328	**India Hook** (CDP) York County
122	n/a	3,328	**Kingstree** (town) Williamsburg County
124	n/a	3,269	**Liberty** (city) Pickens County
125	n/a	3,251	**North Hartsville** (CDP) Darlington County
126	n/a	3,243	**Lyman** (town) Spartanburg County
127	n/a	3,181	**Duncan** (town) Spartanburg County
128	n/a	3,139	**Williston** (town) Barnwell County
129	n/a	3,126	**Pickens** (city) Pickens County
130	n/a	3,112	**Lesslie** (CDP) York County
131	n/a	3,085	**East Gaffney** (CDP) Cherokee County
132	n/a	3,059	**Dalzell** (CDP) Sumter County
133	n/a	3,032	**Lakewood** (CDP) Sumter County
134	n/a	2,964	**Pendleton** (town) Anderson County
135	n/a	2,952	**Hardeeville** (city) Jasper County
136	n/a	2,882	**Hopkins** (CDP) Richland County
137	n/a	2,861	**Andrews** (town) Georgetown County
138	n/a	2,831	**Gloverville** (CDP) Aiken County
139	n/a	2,808	**Hampton** (town) Hampton County
140	n/a	2,783	**McCormick** (town) McCormick County
141	n/a	2,760	**Pageland** (town) Chesterfield County
142	n/a	2,673	**Burnettown** (town) Aiken County
143	n/a	2,636	**Springdale** (town) Lexington County
144	n/a	2,634	**Arcadia** (CDP) Spartanburg County
145	n/a	2,617	**Folly Beach** (city) Charleston County
146	n/a	2,614	**Graniteville** (CDP) Aiken County
147	n/a	2,607	**Elgin** (CDP) Lancaster County
148	n/a	2,574	**Springdale** (town) Lancaster County
149	n/a	2,559	**Edisto** (CDP) Orangeburg County
150	n/a	2,543	**Arial** (CDP) Pickens County

Note: The state column ranks the top/bottom 150 places in the state with population of 2,500 or more. The national column ranks the top/bottom places in the country with population of 10,000 or more. Places that are unincorporated were not considered in the rankings. n/a indicates data not available. Please refer to the User Guide for additional information.

Population

Top 150 Places Ranked in *Ascending* Order

State Rank	Nat'l Rank	Number	Place	State Rank	Nat'l Rank	Number	Place
1	n/a	2,543	**Arial** (CDP) Pickens County	76	n/a	6,838	**Camden** (city) Kershaw County
2	n/a	2,559	**Edisto** (CDP) Orangeburg County	77	n/a	6,939	**Marion** (city) Marion County
3	n/a	2,574	**Springdale** (CDP) Lancaster County	78	n/a	6,976	**Burton** (CDP) Beaufort County
4	n/a	2,607	**Elgin** (CDP) Lancaster County	79	n/a	7,434	**Lugoff** (CDP) Kershaw County
5	n/a	2,614	**Graniteville** (CDP) Aiken County	80	n/a	7,547	**Murrells Inlet** (CDP) Georgetown County
6	n/a	2,617	**Folly Beach** (city) Charleston County	81	n/a	7,620	**Tega Cay** (city) York County
7	n/a	2,634	**Arcadia** (CDP) Spartanburg County	82	n/a	7,736	**York** (city) York County
8	n/a	2,636	**Springdale** (town) Lexington County	83	n/a	7,764	**Hartsville** (city) Darlington County
9	n/a	2,673	**Burnettown** (town) Aiken County	84	n/a	7,799	**Fountain Inn** (city) Greenville County
10	n/a	2,760	**Pageland** (town) Chesterfield County	85	n/a	7,869	**Sans Souci** (CDP) Greenville County
11	n/a	2,783	**McCormick** (town) McCormick County	86	n/a	7,885	**Moncks Corner** (town) Berkeley County
12	n/a	2,808	**Hampton** (town) Hampton County	87	n/a	8,102	**Seneca** (city) Oconee County
13	n/a	2,831	**Gloverville** (CDP) Aiken County	88	n/a	8,219	**Boiling Springs** (CDP) Spartanburg County
14	n/a	2,861	**Andrews** (town) Georgetown County	89	n/a	8,220	**Sangaree** (CDP) Berkeley County
15	n/a	2,882	**Hopkins** (CDP) Richland County	90	n/a	8,393	**Union** (city) Union County
16	n/a	2,952	**Hardeeville** (city) Jasper County	91	n/a	8,490	**Clinton** (city) Laurens County
17	n/a	2,964	**Pendleton** (town) Anderson County	92	n/a	8,526	**Lancaster** (city) Lancaster County
18	n/a	3,032	**Lakewood** (CDP) Sumter County	93	n/a	8,841	**Lake Wylie** (CDP) York County
19	n/a	3,059	**Dalzell** (CDP) Sumter County	94	n/a	8,960	**Little River** (CDP) Horry County
20	n/a	3,085	**East Gaffney** (CDP) Cherokee County	95	n/a	9,069	**Bennettsville** (city) Marlboro County
21	n/a	3,112	**Lesslie** (CDP) York County	96	n/a	9,139	**Laurens** (city) Laurens County
22	n/a	3,126	**Pickens** (city) Pickens County	97	n/a	9,163	**Georgetown** (city) Georgetown County
23	n/a	3,139	**Williston** (town) Barnwell County	98	n/a	9,209	**Garden City** (CDP) Horry County
24	n/a	3,181	**Duncan** (town) Spartanburg County	99	n/a	9,303	**Woodfield** (CDP) Richland County
25	n/a	3,243	**Lyman** (town) Spartanburg County	100	n/a	9,617	**Red Bank** (CDP) Lexington County
26	n/a	3,251	**North Hartsville** (CDP) Darlington County	101	99	10,277	**Newberry** (city) Newberry County
27	n/a	3,269	**Liberty** (city) Pickens County	102	100	10,291	**Oak Grove** (CDP) Lexington County
28	n/a	3,328	**India Hook** (CDP) York County	103	131	10,361	**Forest Acres** (city) Richland County
28	n/a	3,328	**Kingstree** (town) Williamsburg County	104	251	10,678	**Port Royal** (town) Beaufort County
30	n/a	3,424	**Saxon** (CDP) Spartanburg County	105	296	10,811	**Fort Mill** (town) York County
31	n/a	3,471	**Bishopville** (city) Lee County	106	388	11,097	**Irmo** (town) Richland County
32	n/a	3,482	**Allendale** (town) Allendale County	107	507	11,431	**Parker** (CDP) Greenville County
33	n/a	3,538	**Denmark** (city) Bamberg County	108	774	12,361	**Beaufort** (city) Beaufort County
34	n/a	3,550	**Winnsboro** (town) Fairfield County	109	786	12,414	**Gaffney** (city) Cherokee County
35	n/a	3,565	**Saluda** (town) Saluda County	110	810	12,528	**Cayce** (city) Lexington County
36	n/a	3,597	**Honea Path** (town) Anderson County	111	812	12,530	**Bluffton** (town) Beaufort County
37	n/a	3,607	**Bamberg** (town) Bamberg County	112	977	13,223	**Red Hill** (CDP) Horry County
38	n/a	3,671	**Dunean** (CDP) Greenville County	113	1119	13,752	**North Myrtle Beach** (city) Horry County
39	n/a	3,745	**Northlake** (CDP) Anderson County	114	1127	13,790	**Ladson** (CDP) Berkeley County
40	n/a	3,767	**Southern Shops** (CDP) Spartanburg County	115	1153	13,905	**Clemson** (city) Pickens County
41	n/a	3,837	**Surfside Beach** (town) Horry County	116	1169	13,964	**Orangeburg** (city) Orangeburg County
42	n/a	3,934	**Williamston** (town) Anderson County	117	1195	14,062	**Dentsville** (CDP) Richland County
43	n/a	4,036	**Ridgeland** (town) Jasper County	118	1208	14,140	**Five Forks** (CDP) Greenville County
44	n/a	4,090	**Woodruff** (city) Spartanburg County	119	1234	14,229	**Gantt** (CDP) Greenville County
45	n/a	4,108	**Manning** (city) Clarendon County	120	1248	14,295	**Berea** (CDP) Greenville County
46	n/a	4,133	**Isle of Palms** (city) Charleston County	121	1401	14,988	**West Columbia** (city) Lexington County
47	n/a	4,134	**Belton** (city) Anderson County	122	1433	15,144	**Seven Oaks** (CDP) Lexington County
48	n/a	4,136	**Newport** (CDP) York County	123	1790	17,103	**Conway** (city) Horry County
49	n/a	4,263	**Walhalla** (city) Oconee County	124	1915	17,870	**Lexington** (town) Lexington County
50	n/a	4,370	**Clearwater** (CDP) Aiken County	125	1931	17,997	**Hanahan** (city) Berkeley County
51	n/a	4,576	**Travelers Rest** (city) Greenville County	126	1972	18,238	**Simpsonville** (city) Greenville County
52	n/a	4,612	**Forestbrook** (CDP) Horry County	127	2233	19,952	**Socastee** (CDP) Horry County
53	n/a	4,663	**Mullins** (city) Marion County	128	2235	19,993	**Easley** (city) Pickens County
54	n/a	4,714	**Hollywood** (town) Charleston County	129	2301	20,493	**Saint Andrews** (CDP) Richland County
55	n/a	4,750	**Barnwell** (city) Barnwell County	130	2314	20,622	**Wade Hampton** (CDP) Greenville County
55	n/a	4,750	**Edgefield** (town) Edgefield County	131	2388	21,348	**North Augusta** (city) Aiken County
57	n/a	4,873	**Brookdale** (CDP) Orangeburg County	132	2423	21,617	**Taylors** (CDP) Greenville County
58	n/a	5,094	**Clover** (town) York County	133	2546	22,889	**Mauldin** (city) Greenville County
59	n/a	5,103	**Piedmont** (CDP) Anderson County	134	2584	23,222	**Greenwood** (city) Greenwood County
60	n/a	5,159	**Central** (town) Pickens County	135	2794	25,515	**Greer** (city) Greenville County
61	n/a	5,237	**Abbeville** (city) Abbeville County	136	2889	26,686	**Anderson** (city) Anderson County
62	n/a	5,362	**Batesburg-Leesville** (town) Lexington County	137	2920	27,109	**Myrtle Beach** (city) Horry County
63	n/a	5,398	**Walterboro** (city) Colleton County	138	3095	29,524	**Aiken** (city) Aiken County
64	n/a	5,484	**Lake Murray of Richland** (CDP) Richland County	139	3425	35,938	**Goose Creek** (city) Berkeley County
65	n/a	5,607	**Chester** (city) Chester County	140	3470	37,013	**Spartanburg** (city) Spartanburg County
66	n/a	5,792	**Belvedere** (CDP) Aiken County	141	3473	37,056	**Florence** (city) Florence County
67	n/a	5,851	**Cheraw** (town) Chesterfield County	142	3476	37,099	**Hilton Head Island** (town) Beaufort County
68	n/a	5,891	**Laurel Bay** (CDP) Beaufort County	143	3580	40,524	**Sumter** (city) Sumter County
69	n/a	6,289	**Darlington** (city) Darlington County	144	3669	43,392	**Summerville** (town) Dorchester County
70	n/a	6,296	**Homeland Park** (CDP) Anderson County	145	3984	58,409	**Greenville** (city) Greenville County
71	n/a	6,299	**Valley Falls** (CDP) Spartanburg County	146	4097	66,154	**Rock Hill** (city) York County
72	n/a	6,586	**Centerville** (CDP) Anderson County	147	4119	67,843	**Mount Pleasant** (town) Charleston County
73	n/a	6,668	**Welcome** (CDP) Greenville County	148	4340	97,471	**North Charleston** (city) Charleston County
74	n/a	6,675	**Lake City** (city) Florence County	149	4427	120,083	**Charleston** (city) Charleston County
75	n/a	6,788	**Dillon** (city) Dillon County	150	4448	129,272	**Columbia** (city) Richland County

Note: The state column ranks the top/bottom 150 places in the state with population of 2,500 or more. The national column ranks the top/bottom places in the country with population of 10,000 or more. Places that are unincorporated were not considered in the rankings. n/a indicates data not available. Please refer to the User Guide for additional information.

Population Growth

Top 150 Places Ranked in *Descending* Order

State Rank	Nat'l Rank	Percent	Place
1	7	882.7	**Bluffton** (town) Beaufort County
2	n/a	188.8	**Lake Wylie** (CDP) York County
3	79	170.3	**Port Royal** (town) Beaufort County
4	n/a	106.2	**India Hook** (CDP) York County
5	n/a	88.4	**Tega Cay** (city) York County
6	n/a	86.9	**McCormick** (town) McCormick County
7	210	82.5	**Lexington** (town) Lexington County
8	n/a	80.9	**Boiling Springs** (CDP) Spartanburg County
9	235	75.3	**Five Forks** (CDP) Greenville County
10	n/a	64.6	**Hardeeville** (city) Jasper County
11	n/a	60.3	**Ridgeland** (town) Jasper County
12	n/a	57.9	**Valley Falls** (CDP) Spartanburg County
13	353	56.4	**Summerville** (town) Dorchester County
14	n/a	55.5	**Lake Murray of Richland** (CDP) Richland County
15	400	51.5	**Greer** (city) Greenville County
16	407	50.3	**Mauldin** (city) Greenville County
17	n/a	46.5	**Central** (town) Pickens County
18	458	45.1	**Conway** (city) Horry County
19	496	42.5	**Fort Mill** (town) York County
19	496	42.5	**Mount Pleasant** (town) Charleston County
21	543	39.6	**Socastee** (CDP) Horry County
22	555	39.1	**Hanahan** (city) Berkeley County
23	n/a	37.2	**Lesslie** (CDP) York County
24	n/a	36.7	**Murrells Inlet** (CDP) Georgetown County
25	n/a	36.0	**Forestbrook** (CDP) Horry County
26	n/a	35.4	**Dalzell** (CDP) Sumter County
27	681	32.9	**Rock Hill** (city) York County
28	n/a	32.5	**Moncks Corner** (town) Berkeley County
29	n/a	29.6	**Fountain Inn** (city) Greenville County
30	n/a	27.5	**Little River** (CDP) Horry County
31	n/a	27.1	**Centerville** (CDP) Anderson County
31	827	27.1	**Simpsonville** (city) Greenville County
33	n/a	26.9	**Clover** (town) York County
34	858	25.8	**Oak Grove** (CDP) Lexington County
34	858	25.8	**Red Hill** (CDP) Horry County
36	872	25.3	**North Myrtle Beach** (city) Horry County
37	916	24.2	**Charleston** (city) Charleston County
38	n/a	23.7	**Folly Beach** (city) Charleston County
39	963	23.0	**Goose Creek** (city) Berkeley County
40	982	22.5	**Florence** (city) Florence County
41	987	22.4	**North Charleston** (city) Charleston County
42	n/a	22.0	**Lyman** (town) Spartanburg County
43	1023	21.5	**North Augusta** (city) Aiken County
44	n/a	19.5	**Hollywood** (town) Charleston County
45	1124	19.1	**Myrtle Beach** (city) Horry County
46	n/a	18.4	**Lugoff** (CDP) Kershaw County
47	1250	16.5	**Aiken** (city) Aiken County
47	1250	16.5	**Clemson** (city) Pickens County
47	n/a	16.5	**Lakewood** (CDP) Sumter County
50	n/a	16.3	**Saluda** (town) Saluda County
51	1373	14.7	**West Columbia** (city) Lexington County
52	1536	12.6	**Easley** (city) Pickens County
53	n/a	12.2	**Walhalla** (city) Oconee County
54	n/a	11.6	**Travelers Rest** (city) Greenville County
55	1634	11.2	**Columbia** (city) Richland County
56	n/a	10.8	**Duncan** (town) Spartanburg County
56	n/a	10.8	**York** (city) York County
58	1782	9.6	**Hilton Head Island** (town) Beaufort County
59	n/a	9.5	**Pageland** (town) Chesterfield County
60	1802	9.4	**Orangeburg** (city) Orangeburg County
61	n/a	9.1	**Red Bank** (CDP) Lexington County
62	n/a	8.9	**Piedmont** (CDP) Anderson County
63	n/a	8.6	**Liberty** (city) Pickens County
64	1953	8.1	**Dentsville** (CDP) Richland County
65	n/a	7.5	**Dillon** (city) Dillon County
65	n/a	7.5	**Elgin** (CDP) Lancaster County
67	2037	7.4	**Taylors** (CDP) Greenville County
68	n/a	6.8	**Edgefield** (town) Edgefield County
69	n/a	6.3	**Denmark** (city) Bamberg County
70	2204	6.2	**Parker** (CDP) Greenville County
71	n/a	5.9	**Cheraw** (town) Chesterfield County
71	n/a	5.9	**Seneca** (city) Oconee County
73	2341	5.2	**Greenwood** (city) Greenwood County
74	n/a	4.9	**Clinton** (city) Laurens County
75	n/a	4.8	**Walterboro** (city) Colleton County
76	2452	4.6	**Anderson** (city) Anderson County
77	n/a	4.4	**Welcome** (CDP) Greenville County
78	2501	4.3	**Greenville** (city) Greenville County
78	n/a	4.3	**Lancaster** (city) Lancaster County
80	n/a	4.1	**Clearwater** (CDP) Aiken County
81	2547	4.0	**Ladson** (CDP) Berkeley County
82	n/a	3.8	**Pickens** (city) Pickens County
82	n/a	3.8	**Williamston** (town) Anderson County
84	n/a	3.7	**North Hartsville** (CDP) Darlington County
85	n/a	3.2	**Brookdale** (CDP) Orangeburg County
86	2747	3.1	**Cayce** (city) Lexington County
87	n/a	3.0	**Lake City** (city) Florence County
88	n/a	2.9	**Belvedere** (CDP) Aiken County
89	n/a	2.8	**Hartsville** (city) Darlington County
90	n/a	2.7	**Honea Path** (town) Anderson County
91	n/a	2.6	**Newport** (CDP) York County
92	n/a	2.4	**Georgetown** (city) Georgetown County
92	n/a	2.4	**Northlake** (CDP) Anderson County
94	n/a	2.3	**Camden** (city) Kershaw County
95	2948	2.2	**Sumter** (city) Sumter County
96	n/a	2.1	**Manning** (city) Clarendon County
97	3013	1.9	**Gantt** (CDP) Greenville County
98	n/a	1.6	**Southern Shops** (CDP) Spartanburg County
99	3190	1.0	**Berea** (CDP) Greenville County
100	n/a	0.9	**Gloverville** (CDP) Aiken County
101	3237	0.8	**Wade Hampton** (CDP) Greenville County
102	n/a	0.7	**Woodfield** (CDP) Richland County
103	3296	0.5	**Irmo** (town) Richland County
104	n/a	0.4	**Sans Souci** (CDP) Greenville County
105	n/a	-0.1	**Pendleton** (town) Anderson County
106	n/a	-0.6	**Homeland Park** (CDP) Anderson County
107	n/a	-1.0	**Arcadia** (CDP) Spartanburg County
107	n/a	-1.0	**Graniteville** (CDP) Aiken County
107	n/a	-1.0	**Hampton** (town) Hampton County
107	n/a	-1.0	**Hopkins** (CDP) Richland County
107	n/a	-1.0	**Sangaree** (CDP) Berkeley County
112	n/a	-1.4	**Winnsboro** (town) Fairfield County
113	n/a	-1.5	**Marion** (city) Marion County
114	n/a	-1.6	**Garden City** (CDP) Horry County
115	n/a	-1.7	**Burnettown** (town) Aiken County
116	3913	-1.9	**Forest Acres** (city) Richland County
117	n/a	-2.5	**Arial** (CDP) Pickens County
118	n/a	-2.8	**Batesburg-Leesville** (town) Lexington County
118	n/a	-2.8	**Burton** (CDP) Beaufort County
118	n/a	-2.8	**Edisto** (CDP) Orangeburg County
121	4053	-2.9	**Newberry** (city) Newberry County
122	n/a	-3.3	**Woodruff** (city) Spartanburg County
123	n/a	-3.4	**Bamberg** (town) Bamberg County
124	n/a	-3.8	**Bennettsville** (city) Marlboro County
125	4172	-3.9	**Seven Oaks** (CDP) Lexington County
126	4215	-4.3	**Gaffney** (city) Cherokee County
127	4236	-4.5	**Beaufort** (city) Beaufort County
127	n/a	-4.5	**Union** (city) Union County
129	n/a	-4.8	**Kingstree** (town) Williamsburg County
130	n/a	-5.1	**Williston** (town) Barnwell County
131	n/a	-5.4	**Bishopville** (city) Lee County
132	n/a	-5.7	**Barnwell** (city) Barnwell County
133	4373	-6.1	**Saint Andrews** (CDP) Richland County
134	n/a	-6.4	**Darlington** (city) Darlington County
135	n/a	-6.7	**Andrews** (town) Georgetown County
135	4414	-6.7	**Spartanburg** (city) Spartanburg County
137	n/a	-7.3	**Belton** (city) Anderson County
137	n/a	-7.3	**Mullins** (city) Marion County
139	n/a	-7.6	**Saxon** (CDP) Spartanburg County
140	n/a	-7.8	**Laurens** (city) Laurens County
141	n/a	-7.9	**East Gaffney** (CDP) Cherokee County
142	n/a	-8.4	**Springdale** (town) Lexington County
143	n/a	-9.8	**Isle of Palms** (city) Charleston County
144	n/a	-10.1	**Springdale** (CDP) Lancaster County
145	n/a	-10.3	**Abbeville** (city) Abbeville County
146	n/a	-11.1	**Laurel Bay** (CDP) Beaufort County
147	n/a	-11.7	**Dunean** (CDP) Greenville County
148	n/a	-13.3	**Surfside Beach** (town) Horry County
149	n/a	-13.4	**Chester** (city) Chester County
150	n/a	-14.1	**Allendale** (town) Allendale County

Note: The state column ranks the top/bottom 150 places in the state with population of 2,500 or more. The national column ranks the top/bottom places in the country with population of 10,000 or more. Places that are unincorporated were not considered in the rankings. n/a indicates data not available. Please refer to the User Guide for additional information.

Population Growth

Top 150 Places Ranked in *Ascending* Order

State Rank	Nat'l Rank	Percent	Place
1	n/a	-14.1	**Allendale** (town) Allendale County
2	n/a	-13.4	**Chester** (city) Chester County
3	n/a	-13.3	**Surfside Beach** (town) Horry County
4	n/a	-11.7	**Dunean** (CDP) Greenville County
5	n/a	-11.1	**Laurel Bay** (CDP) Beaufort County
6	n/a	-10.3	**Abbeville** (city) Abbeville County
7	n/a	-10.1	**Springdale** (CDP) Lancaster County
8	n/a	-9.8	**Isle of Palms** (city) Charleston County
9	n/a	-8.4	**Springdale** (town) Lexington County
10	n/a	-7.9	**East Gaffney** (CDP) Cherokee County
11	n/a	-7.8	**Laurens** (city) Laurens County
12	n/a	-7.6	**Saxon** (CDP) Spartanburg County
13	n/a	-7.3	**Belton** (city) Anderson County
13	n/a	-7.3	**Mullins** (city) Marion County
15	n/a	-6.7	**Andrews** (town) Georgetown County
15	238	-6.7	**Spartanburg** (city) Spartanburg County
17	n/a	-6.4	**Darlington** (city) Darlington County
18	275	-6.1	**Saint Andrews** (CDP) Richland County
19	n/a	-5.7	**Barnwell** (city) Barnwell County
20	n/a	-5.4	**Bishopville** (city) Lee County
21	n/a	-5.1	**Williston** (town) Barnwell County
22	n/a	-4.8	**Kingstree** (town) Williamsburg County
23	407	-4.5	**Beaufort** (city) Beaufort County
23	n/a	-4.5	**Union** (city) Union County
25	431	-4.3	**Gaffney** (city) Cherokee County
26	477	-3.9	**Seven Oaks** (CDP) Lexington County
27	n/a	-3.8	**Bennettsville** (city) Marlboro County
28	n/a	-3.4	**Bamberg** (town) Bamberg County
29	n/a	-3.3	**Woodruff** (city) Spartanburg County
30	593	-2.9	**Newberry** (city) Newberry County
31	n/a	-2.8	**Batesburg-Leesville** (town) Lexington County
31	n/a	-2.8	**Burton** (CDP) Beaufort County
31	n/a	-2.8	**Edisto** (CDP) Orangeburg County
34	n/a	-2.5	**Arial** (CDP) Pickens County
35	724	-1.9	**Forest Acres** (city) Richland County
36	n/a	-1.7	**Burnettown** (town) Aiken County
37	n/a	-1.6	**Garden City** (CDP) Horry County
38	n/a	-1.5	**Marion** (city) Marion County
39	n/a	-1.4	**Winnsboro** (town) Fairfield County
40	n/a	-1.0	**Hampton** (town) Hampton County
41	n/a	-0.6	**Homeland Park** (CDP) Anderson County
42	n/a	-0.1	**Pendleton** (town) Anderson County
43	n/a	0.4	**Sans Souci** (CDP) Greenville County
44	1175	0.5	**Irmo** (town) Richland County
45	n/a	0.7	**Woodfield** (CDP) Richland County
46	1237	0.8	**Wade Hampton** (CDP) Greenville County
47	n/a	0.9	**Gloverville** (CDP) Aiken County
48	1282	1.0	**Berea** (CDP) Greenville County
49	n/a	1.6	**Southern Shops** (CDP) Spartanburg County
50	1463	1.9	**Gantt** (CDP) Greenville County
51	n/a	2.1	**Manning** (city) Clarendon County
52	1529	2.2	**Sumter** (city) Sumter County
53	n/a	2.3	**Camden** (city) Kershaw County
54	n/a	2.4	**Georgetown** (city) Georgetown County
54	n/a	2.4	**Northlake** (CDP) Anderson County
56	n/a	2.6	**Newport** (CDP) York County
57	n/a	2.7	**Honea Path** (town) Anderson County
58	n/a	2.8	**Hartsville** (city) Darlington County
59	n/a	2.9	**Belvedere** (CDP) Aiken County
60	n/a	3.0	**Lake City** (city) Florence County
61	1720	3.1	**Cayce** (city) Lexington County
62	n/a	3.2	**Brookdale** (CDP) Orangeburg County
63	n/a	3.7	**North Hartsville** (CDP) Darlington County
64	n/a	3.8	**Pickens** (city) Pickens County
64	n/a	3.8	**Williamston** (town) Anderson County
66	1920	4.0	**Ladson** (CDP) Berkeley County
67	n/a	4.1	**Clearwater** (CDP) Aiken County
68	1978	4.3	**Greenville** (city) Greenville County
68	n/a	4.3	**Lancaster** (city) Lancaster County
70	n/a	4.4	**Welcome** (CDP) Greenville County
71	2024	4.6	**Anderson** (city) Anderson County
72	n/a	4.8	**Walterboro** (city) Colleton County
73	n/a	4.9	**Clinton** (city) Laurens County
74	2129	5.2	**Greenwood** (city) Greenwood County
75	n/a	5.9	**Cheraw** (town) Chesterfield County
75	n/a	5.9	**Seneca** (city) Oconee County
77	2275	6.2	**Parker** (CDP) Greenville County
78	n/a	6.3	**Denmark** (city) Bamberg County
79	n/a	6.8	**Edgefield** (town) Edgefield County
80	2446	7.4	**Taylors** (CDP) Greenville County
81	n/a	7.5	**Dillon** (city) Dillon County
81	n/a	7.5	**Elgin** (CDP) Lancaster County
83	2525	8.1	**Dentsville** (CDP) Richland County
84	n/a	8.6	**Liberty** (city) Pickens County
85	n/a	8.9	**Piedmont** (CDP) Anderson County
86	n/a	9.1	**Red Bank** (CDP) Lexington County
87	2677	9.4	**Orangeburg** (city) Orangeburg County
88	n/a	9.5	**Pageland** (town) Chesterfield County
89	2701	9.6	**Hilton Head Island** (town) Beaufort County
90	n/a	10.8	**Duncan** (town) Spartanburg County
90	n/a	10.8	**York** (city) York County
92	2851	11.2	**Columbia** (city) Richland County
93	n/a	11.6	**Travelers Rest** (city) Greenville County
94	n/a	12.2	**Walhalla** (city) Oconee County
95	2949	12.6	**Easley** (city) Pickens County
96	3113	14.7	**West Columbia** (city) Lexington County
97	n/a	16.3	**Saluda** (town) Saluda County
98	3237	16.5	**Aiken** (city) Aiken County
98	3237	16.5	**Clemson** (city) Pickens County
98	n/a	16.5	**Lakewood** (CDP) Sumter County
101	n/a	18.4	**Lugoff** (CDP) Kershaw County
102	3359	19.1	**Myrtle Beach** (city) Horry County
103	n/a	19.5	**Hollywood** (town) Charleston County
104	3466	21.5	**North Augusta** (city) Aiken County
105	n/a	22.0	**Lyman** (town) Spartanburg County
106	3502	22.4	**North Charleston** (city) Charleston County
107	3506	22.5	**Florence** (city) Florence County
108	3528	23.0	**Goose Creek** (city) Berkeley County
109	n/a	23.7	**Folly Beach** (city) Charleston County
110	3567	24.2	**Charleston** (city) Charleston County
111	3618	25.3	**North Myrtle Beach** (city) Horry County
112	3627	25.8	**Oak Grove** (CDP) Lexington County
112	3627	25.8	**Red Hill** (CDP) Horry County
114	n/a	26.9	**Clover** (town) York County
115	n/a	27.1	**Centerville** (CDP) Anderson County
115	3662	27.1	**Simpsonville** (city) Greenville County
117	n/a	27.5	**Little River** (CDP) Horry County
118	n/a	29.6	**Fountain Inn** (city) Greenville County
119	n/a	32.5	**Moncks Corner** (town) Berkeley County
120	3810	32.9	**Rock Hill** (city) York County
121	n/a	35.4	**Dalzell** (CDP) Sumter County
122	n/a	36.0	**Forestbrook** (CDP) Horry County
123	n/a	36.7	**Murrells Inlet** (CDP) Georgetown County
124	n/a	37.2	**Lesslie** (CDP) York County
125	3934	39.1	**Hanahan** (city) Berkeley County
126	3947	39.6	**Socastee** (CDP) Horry County
127	3995	42.5	**Fort Mill** (town) York County
127	3995	42.5	**Mount Pleasant** (town) Charleston County
129	4033	45.1	**Conway** (city) Horry County
130	n/a	46.5	**Central** (town) Pickens County
131	4085	50.3	**Mauldin** (city) Greenville County
132	4092	51.5	**Greer** (city) Greenville County
133	n/a	55.5	**Lake Murray of Richland** (CDP) Richland County
134	4136	56.4	**Summerville** (town) Dorchester County
135	n/a	57.9	**Valley Falls** (CDP) Spartanburg County
136	n/a	60.3	**Ridgeland** (town) Jasper County
137	n/a	64.6	**Hardeeville** (city) Jasper County
138	4256	75.3	**Five Forks** (CDP) Greenville County
139	n/a	80.9	**Boiling Springs** (CDP) Spartanburg County
140	4282	82.5	**Lexington** (town) Lexington County
141	n/a	86.9	**McCormick** (town) McCormick County
142	n/a	88.4	**Tega Cay** (city) York County
143	n/a	106.2	**India Hook** (CDP) York County
144	4412	170.3	**Port Royal** (town) Beaufort County
145	n/a	188.8	**Lake Wylie** (CDP) York County
146	4485	882.7	**Bluffton** (town) Beaufort County

Note: The state column ranks the top/bottom 150 places in the state with population of 2,500 or more. The national column ranks the top/bottom places in the country with population of 10,000 or more. Places that are unincorporated were not considered in the rankings. n/a indicates data not available. Please refer to the User Guide for additional information.

Population Density

Top 150 Places Ranked in *Descending* Order

State Rank	Nat'l Rank	Pop./ Sq. Mi.	Place
1	n/a	4,047.6	**Sangaree** (CDP) Berkeley County
2	n/a	3,391.0	**Woodfield** (CDP) Richland County
3	1327	3,229.5	**Saint Andrews** (CDP) Richland County
4	1943	2,404.7	**Summerville** (town) Dorchester County
5	n/a	2,376.9	**Sans Souci** (CDP) Greenville County
6	n/a	2,330.9	**Dunean** (CDP) Greenville County
7	2053	2,301.9	**Wade Hampton** (CDP) Greenville County
8	2056	2,299.5	**Mauldin** (city) Greenville County
9	2103	2,254.3	**Forest Acres** (city) Richland County
10	2204	2,143.6	**West Columbia** (city) Lexington County
11	2282	2,078.0	**Dentsville** (CDP) Richland County
12	2290	2,070.3	**Simpsonville** (city) Greenville County
13	2321	2,037.4	**Greenville** (city) Greenville County
14	2339	2,020.2	**Taylors** (CDP) Greenville County
15	2344	2,014.5	**Lexington** (town) Lexington County
16	2360	1,996.7	**Seven Oaks** (CDP) Lexington County
17	n/a	1,986.2	**Surfside Beach** (town) Horry County
18	n/a	1,969.1	**Tega Cay** (city) York County
19	2390	1,963.5	**Ladson** (CDP) Berkeley County
20	n/a	1,914.7	**Central** (town) Pickens County
21	2499	1,872.2	**Spartanburg** (city) Spartanburg County
22	2503	1,868.9	**Clemson** (city) Pickens County
23	2504	1,868.4	**Five Forks** (CDP) Greenville County
24	2517	1,855.6	**Berea** (CDP) Greenville County
25	2521	1,851.9	**Rock Hill** (city) York County
26	2547	1,828.5	**Anderson** (city) Anderson County
27	2621	1,774.0	**Florence** (city) Florence County
28	2622	1,772.3	**Irmo** (town) Richland County
29	n/a	1,716.2	**Chester** (city) Chester County
30	n/a	1,715.6	**Garden City** (CDP) Horry County
31	2738	1,683.9	**Hanahan** (city) Berkeley County
32	2750	1,675.7	**Parker** (CDP) Greenville County
33	n/a	1,653.1	**Belvedere** (CDP) Aiken County
34	2793	1,648.9	**Orangeburg** (city) Orangeburg County
35	2814	1,631.1	**Easley** (city) Pickens County
36	n/a	1,569.7	**Marion** (city) Marion County
37	2912	1,547.4	**Oak Grove** (CDP) Lexington County
38	n/a	1,521.7	**Mullins** (city) Marion County
39	2975	1,504.9	**Mount Pleasant** (town) Charleston County
40	2987	1,495.0	**Socastee** (CDP) Horry County
41	2990	1,491.3	**Gaffney** (city) Cherokee County
42	n/a	1,487.6	**Manning** (city) Clarendon County
43	n/a	1,485.0	**Bishopville** (city) Lee County
44	n/a	1,482.9	**Bennettsville** (city) Marlboro County
45	n/a	1,438.2	**Welcome** (CDP) Greenville County
46	3065	1,435.4	**Gantt** (CDP) Greenville County
47	n/a	1,434.3	**Saxon** (CDP) Spartanburg County
48	3072	1,430.6	**Greenwood** (city) Greenwood County
49	3083	1,426.5	**Aiken** (city) Aiken County
50	n/a	1,383.2	**Darlington** (city) Darlington County
51	n/a	1,356.7	**Hartsville** (city) Darlington County
52	n/a	1,343.7	**Arcadia** (CDP) Spartanburg County
53	n/a	1,339.8	**Brookdale** (CDP) Orangeburg County
54	n/a	1,335.7	**Homeland Park** (CDP) Anderson County
55	3210	1,331.8	**North Charleston** (city) Charleston County
56	n/a	1,329.1	**Lancaster** (city) Lancaster County
57	n/a	1,326.0	**Georgetown** (city) Georgetown County
58	n/a	1,309.2	**Laurel Bay** (CDP) Beaufort County
59	n/a	1,299.2	**Dillon** (city) Dillon County
60	n/a	1,297.6	**Andrews** (town) Georgetown County
61	n/a	1,278.1	**Lake City** (city) Florence County
62	3303	1,263.0	**Sumter** (city) Sumter County
63	n/a	1,262.1	**India Hook** (CDP) York County
64	3336	1,236.4	**Greer** (city) Greenville County
65	n/a	1,234.2	**Forestbrook** (CDP) Horry County
66	n/a	1,215.4	**Valley Falls** (CDP) Spartanburg County
67	n/a	1,202.2	**Boiling Springs** (CDP) Spartanburg County
68	3396	1,198.7	**Newberry** (city) Newberry County
69	3439	1,171.2	**Red Hill** (CDP) Horry County
70	3451	1,162.3	**Myrtle Beach** (city) Horry County
71	n/a	1,142.5	**Clover** (town) York County
72	n/a	1,135.5	**Edgefield** (town) Edgefield County
73	n/a	1,127.1	**Lake Wylie** (CDP) York County
74	n/a	1,115.4	**Centerville** (CDP) Anderson County
75	n/a	1,105.3	**Pickens** (city) Pickens County
76	3539	1,101.9	**Charleston** (city) Charleston County
77	n/a	1,099.8	**Winnsboro** (town) Fairfield County
78	n/a	1,097.4	**Saluda** (town) Saluda County
79	n/a	1,082.3	**Moncks Corner** (town) Berkeley County
80	n/a	1,080.3	**Williamston** (town) Anderson County
81	n/a	1,079.1	**Cheraw** (town) Chesterfield County
82	n/a	1,077.0	**Walhalla** (city) Oconee County
83	n/a	1,076.0	**Belton** (city) Anderson County
84	n/a	1,072.9	**Seneca** (city) Oconee County
85	3587	1,065.7	**North Augusta** (city) Aiken County
86	n/a	1,057.0	**Southern Shops** (CDP) Spartanburg County
87	n/a	1,055.0	**Kingstree** (town) Williamsburg County
88	n/a	1,051.9	**Allendale** (town) Allendale County
89	n/a	1,045.6	**Woodruff** (city) Spartanburg County
90	n/a	1,043.2	**Clearwater** (CDP) Aiken County
91	n/a	1,038.2	**Union** (city) Union County
92	n/a	1,025.5	**Murrells Inlet** (CDP) Georgetown County
93	n/a	1,012.1	**Travelers Rest** (city) Greenville County
94	n/a	1,009.6	**East Gaffney** (CDP) Cherokee County
95	n/a	1,007.0	**Bamberg** (town) Bamberg County
96	n/a	994.1	**Honea Path** (town) Anderson County
97	n/a	988.9	**Fountain Inn** (city) Greenville County
98	n/a	982.0	**Lake Murray of Richland** (CDP) Richland County
99	3712	977.8	**Columbia** (city) Richland County
100	n/a	966.0	**Springdale** (town) Lexington County
101	n/a	942.3	**York** (city) York County
102	n/a	931.7	**Isle of Palms** (city) Charleston County
103	n/a	922.4	**Denmark** (city) Bamberg County
104	n/a	907.2	**Northlake** (CDP) Anderson County
105	3814	896.9	**Hilton Head Island** (town) Beaufort County
106	3816	896.5	**Goose Creek** (city) Berkeley County
107	n/a	879.9	**Laurens** (city) Laurens County
108	n/a	859.7	**Clinton** (city) Laurens County
109	n/a	856.3	**Abbeville** (city) Abbeville County
110	n/a	855.0	**Little River** (CDP) Horry County
111	n/a	832.0	**Walterboro** (city) Colleton County
112	n/a	817.2	**Burton** (CDP) Beaufort County
113	n/a	814.6	**Red Bank** (CDP) Lexington County
114	3927	804.5	**North Myrtle Beach** (city) Horry County
115	n/a	790.5	**Graniteville** (CDP) Aiken County
116	n/a	782.1	**Pendleton** (town) Anderson County
117	n/a	780.2	**Gloverville** (CDP) Aiken County
118	3961	779.5	**Conway** (city) Horry County
119	4000	752.5	**Cayce** (city) Lexington County
120	n/a	734.5	**Liberty** (city) Pickens County
121	n/a	712.6	**North Hartsville** (CDP) Darlington County
122	n/a	688.7	**Batesburg-Leesville** (town) Lexington County
123	n/a	686.9	**McCormick** (town) McCormick County
124	n/a	680.5	**Duncan** (town) Spartanburg County
125	4118	661.6	**Fort Mill** (town) York County
126	n/a	640.2	**Camden** (city) Kershaw County
127	n/a	631.9	**Pageland** (town) Chesterfield County
128	n/a	622.3	**Hampton** (town) Hampton County
129	n/a	609.3	**Springdale** (CDP) Lancaster County
130	n/a	605.1	**Barnwell** (city) Barnwell County
131	n/a	593.7	**Piedmont** (CDP) Anderson County
132	4227	563.6	**Port Royal** (town) Beaufort County
133	n/a	543.6	**Arial** (CDP) Pickens County
134	n/a	542.6	**Lyman** (town) Spartanburg County
135	n/a	536.5	**Elgin** (CDP) Lancaster County
136	n/a	519.7	**Dalzell** (CDP) Sumter County
137	n/a	511.6	**Lesslie** (CDP) York County
138	n/a	494.4	**Lugoff** (CDP) Kershaw County
139	n/a	488.1	**Burnettown** (town) Aiken County
140	n/a	474.8	**Newport** (CDP) York County
141	n/a	472.3	**Edisto** (CDP) Orangeburg County
142	4383	447.9	**Beaufort** (city) Beaufort County
143	n/a	401.2	**Lakewood** (CDP) Sumter County
144	n/a	350.6	**Williston** (town) Barnwell County
145	4591	244.2	**Bluffton** (town) Beaufort County
146	n/a	209.2	**Folly Beach** (city) Charleston County
147	n/a	203.8	**Hollywood** (town) Charleston County
148	n/a	174.6	**Hopkins** (CDP) Richland County
149	n/a	90.8	**Ridgeland** (town) Jasper County
150	n/a	65.4	**Hardeeville** (city) Jasper County

Note: The state column ranks the top/bottom 150 places in the state with population of 2,500 or more. The national column ranks the top/bottom places in the country with population of 10,000 or more. Places that are unincorporated were not considered in the rankings. n/a indicates data not available. Please refer to the User Guide for additional information.

Population Density

Top 150 Places Ranked in *Ascending* Order

State Rank	Nat'l Rank	Pop./ Sq. Mi.	Place
1	n/a	65.4	Hardeeville (city) Jasper County
2	n/a	90.8	Ridgeland (town) Jasper County
3	n/a	174.6	Hopkins (CDP) Richland County
4	n/a	203.8	Hollywood (town) Charleston County
5	n/a	209.2	Folly Beach (city) Charleston County
6	65	244.2	Bluffton (town) Beaufort County
7	n/a	350.6	Williston (town) Barnwell County
8	n/a	401.2	Lakewood (CDP) Sumter County
9	273	447.9	Beaufort (city) Beaufort County
10	n/a	472.3	Edisto (CDP) Orangeburg County
11	n/a	474.8	Newport (CDP) York County
12	n/a	488.1	Burnettown (town) Aiken County
13	n/a	494.4	Lugoff (CDP) Kershaw County
14	n/a	511.6	Lesslie (CDP) York County
15	n/a	519.7	Dalzell (CDP) Sumter County
16	n/a	536.5	Elgin (CDP) Lancaster County
17	n/a	542.6	Lyman (town) Spartanburg County
18	n/a	543.6	Arial (CDP) Pickens County
19	427	563.6	Port Royal (town) Beaufort County
20	n/a	593.7	Piedmont (CDP) Anderson County
21	n/a	605.1	Barnwell (city) Barnwell County
22	n/a	609.3	Springdale (CDP) Lancaster County
23	n/a	622.3	Hampton (town) Hampton County
24	n/a	631.9	Pageland (town) Chesterfield County
25	n/a	640.2	Camden (city) Kershaw County
26	538	661.6	Fort Mill (town) York County
27	n/a	680.5	Duncan (town) Spartanburg County
28	n/a	686.9	McCormick (town) McCormick County
29	n/a	688.7	Batesburg-Leesville (town) Lexington County
30	n/a	712.6	North Hartsville (CDP) Darlington County
31	n/a	734.5	Liberty (city) Pickens County
32	656	752.5	Cayce (city) Lexington County
33	695	779.5	Conway (city) Horry County
34	n/a	780.2	Gloverville (CDP) Aiken County
35	n/a	782.1	Pendleton (town) Anderson County
36	n/a	790.5	Graniteville (CDP) Aiken County
37	729	804.5	North Myrtle Beach (city) Horry County
38	n/a	814.6	Red Bank (CDP) Lexington County
39	n/a	817.2	Burton (CDP) Beaufort County
40	n/a	832.0	Walterboro (city) Colleton County
41	n/a	855.0	Little River (CDP) Horry County
42	n/a	856.3	Abbeville (city) Abbeville County
43	n/a	859.7	Clinton (city) Laurens County
44	n/a	879.9	Laurens (city) Laurens County
45	840	896.5	Goose Creek (city) Berkeley County
46	842	896.9	Hilton Head Island (town) Beaufort County
47	n/a	907.2	Northlake (CDP) Anderson County
48	n/a	922.4	Denmark (city) Bamberg County
49	n/a	931.7	Isle of Palms (city) Charleston County
50	n/a	942.3	York (city) York County
51	n/a	966.0	Springdale (town) Lexington County
52	944	977.8	Columbia (city) Richland County
53	n/a	982.0	Lake Murray of Richland (CDP) Richland County
54	n/a	988.9	Fountain Inn (city) Greenville County
55	n/a	994.1	Honea Path (town) Anderson County
56	n/a	1,007.0	Bamberg (town) Bamberg County
57	n/a	1,009.6	East Gaffney (CDP) Cherokee County
58	n/a	1,012.1	Travelers Rest (city) Greenville County
59	n/a	1,025.5	Murrells Inlet (CDP) Georgetown County
60	n/a	1,038.2	Union (city) Union County
61	n/a	1,043.2	Clearwater (CDP) Aiken County
62	n/a	1,045.6	Woodruff (city) Spartanburg County
63	n/a	1,051.9	Allendale (town) Allendale County
64	n/a	1,055.0	Kingstree (town) Williamsburg County
65	n/a	1,057.0	Southern Shops (CDP) Spartanburg County
66	1069	1,065.7	North Augusta (city) Aiken County
67	n/a	1,072.9	Seneca (city) Oconee County
68	n/a	1,076.0	Belton (city) Anderson County
69	n/a	1,077.0	Walhalla (city) Oconee County
70	n/a	1,079.1	Cheraw (town) Chesterfield County
71	n/a	1,080.3	Williamston (town) Anderson County
72	n/a	1,082.3	Moncks Corner (town) Berkeley County
73	n/a	1,097.4	Saluda (town) Saluda County
74	n/a	1,099.8	Winnsboro (town) Fairfield County
75	1117	1,101.9	Charleston (city) Charleston County
76	n/a	1,105.3	Pickens (city) Pickens County
77	n/a	1,115.4	Centerville (CDP) Anderson County
78	n/a	1,127.1	Lake Wylie (CDP) York County
79	n/a	1,135.5	Edgefield (town) Edgefield County
80	n/a	1,142.5	Clover (town) York County
81	1205	1,162.3	Myrtle Beach (city) Horry County
82	1217	1,171.2	Red Hill (CDP) Horry County
83	1260	1,198.7	Newberry (city) Newberry County
84	n/a	1,202.2	Boiling Springs (CDP) Spartanburg County
85	n/a	1,215.4	Valley Falls (CDP) Spartanburg County
86	n/a	1,234.2	Forestbrook (CDP) Horry County
87	1320	1,236.4	Greer (city) Greenville County
88	n/a	1,262.1	India Hook (CDP) York County
89	1353	1,263.0	Sumter (city) Sumter County
90	n/a	1,278.1	Lake City (city) Florence County
91	n/a	1,297.6	Andrews (town) Georgetown County
92	n/a	1,299.2	Dillon (city) Dillon County
93	n/a	1,309.2	Laurel Bay (CDP) Beaufort County
94	n/a	1,326.0	Georgetown (city) Georgetown County
95	n/a	1,329.1	Lancaster (city) Lancaster County
96	1446	1,331.8	North Charleston (city) Charleston County
97	n/a	1,335.7	Homeland Park (CDP) Anderson County
98	n/a	1,339.8	Brookdale (CDP) Orangeburg County
99	n/a	1,343.7	Arcadia (CDP) Spartanburg County
100	n/a	1,356.7	Hartsville (city) Darlington County
101	n/a	1,383.2	Darlington (city) Darlington County
102	1573	1,426.5	Aiken (city) Aiken County
103	1584	1,430.6	Greenwood (city) Greenwood County
104	n/a	1,434.3	Saxon (CDP) Spartanburg County
105	1590	1,435.4	Gantt (CDP) Greenville County
106	n/a	1,438.2	Welcome (CDP) Greenville County
107	n/a	1,482.9	Bennettsville (city) Marlboro County
108	n/a	1,485.0	Bishopville (city) Lee County
109	n/a	1,487.6	Manning (city) Clarendon County
110	1666	1,491.3	Gaffney (city) Cherokee County
111	1669	1,495.0	Socastee (CDP) Horry County
112	1681	1,504.9	Mount Pleasant (town) Charleston County
113	n/a	1,521.7	Mullins (city) Marion County
114	1744	1,547.4	Oak Grove (CDP) Lexington County
115	n/a	1,569.7	Marion (city) Marion County
116	1842	1,631.1	Easley (city) Pickens County
117	1863	1,648.9	Orangeburg (city) Orangeburg County
118	n/a	1,653.1	Belvedere (CDP) Aiken County
119	1905	1,675.7	Parker (CDP) Greenville County
120	1918	1,683.9	Hanahan (city) Berkeley County
121	n/a	1,715.6	Garden City (CDP) Horry County
122	n/a	1,716.2	Chester (city) Chester County
123	2034	1,772.3	Irmo (town) Richland County
124	2035	1,774.0	Florence (city) Florence County
125	2109	1,828.5	Anderson (city) Anderson County
126	2135	1,851.9	Rock Hill (city) York County
127	2139	1,855.6	Berea (CDP) Greenville County
128	2151	1,868.4	Five Forks (CDP) Greenville County
129	2153	1,868.9	Clemson (city) Pickens County
130	2157	1,872.2	Spartanburg (city) Spartanburg County
131	n/a	1,914.7	Central (town) Pickens County
132	2266	1,963.5	Ladson (CDP) Berkeley County
133	n/a	1,969.1	Tega Cay (city) York County
134	n/a	1,986.2	Surfside Beach (town) Horry County
135	2296	1,996.7	Seven Oaks (CDP) Lexington County
136	2312	2,014.5	Lexington (town) Lexington County
137	2317	2,020.2	Taylors (CDP) Greenville County
138	2335	2,037.4	Greenville (city) Greenville County
139	2366	2,070.3	Simpsonville (city) Greenville County
140	2374	2,078.0	Dentsville (CDP) Richland County
141	2452	2,143.6	West Columbia (city) Lexington County
142	2553	2,254.3	Forest Acres (city) Richland County
143	2600	2,299.5	Mauldin (city) Greenville County
144	2603	2,301.9	Wade Hampton (CDP) Greenville County
145	n/a	2,330.9	Dunean (CDP) Greenville County
146	n/a	2,376.9	Sans Souci (CDP) Greenville County
147	2713	2,404.7	Summerville (town) Dorchester County
148	3329	3,229.5	Saint Andrews (CDP) Richland County
149	n/a	3,391.0	Woodfield (CDP) Richland County
150	n/a	4,047.6	Sangaree (CDP) Berkeley County

Note: The state column ranks the top/bottom 150 places in the state with population of 2,500 or more. The national column ranks the top/bottom places in the country with population of 10,000 or more. Places that are unincorporated were not considered in the rankings. n/a indicates data not available. Please refer to the User Guide for additional information.

White Population

Top 150 Places Ranked in *Descending* Order

State Rank	Nat'l Rank	Percent	Place
1	n/a	97.7	**Isle of Palms** (city) Charleston County
2	n/a	96.3	**Folly Beach** (city) Charleston County
3	n/a	96.1	**Lake Murray of Richland** (CDP) Richland County
3	n/a	96.1	**Surfside Beach** (town) Horry County
5	n/a	95.3	**Garden City** (CDP) Horry County
6	n/a	92.6	**Arial** (CDP) Pickens County
6	n/a	92.6	**Tega Cay** (city) York County
8	1024	91.3	**Mount Pleasant** (town) Charleston County
9	n/a	90.7	**Murrells Inlet** (CDP) Georgetown County
10	1173	90.4	**North Myrtle Beach** (city) Horry County
11	n/a	89.1	**Piedmont** (CDP) Anderson County
12	n/a	89.0	**Little River** (CDP) Horry County
13	n/a	88.7	**Lake Wylie** (CDP) York County
14	n/a	88.0	**India Hook** (CDP) York County
15	1608	87.5	**Five Forks** (CDP) Greenville County
16	n/a	86.7	**Liberty** (city) Pickens County
17	n/a	85.9	**Forestbrook** (CDP) Horry County
18	n/a	85.8	**Northlake** (CDP) Anderson County
19	n/a	84.9	**Lesslie** (CDP) York County
19	n/a	84.9	**Lyman** (town) Spartanburg County
21	n/a	84.6	**Red Bank** (CDP) Lexington County
22	n/a	84.2	**Springdale** (town) Lexington County
23	n/a	84.1	**Newport** (CDP) York County
24	n/a	83.4	**Williamston** (town) Anderson County
25	n/a	83.3	**Centerville** (CDP) Anderson County
26	2165	83.1	**Easley** (city) Pickens County
27	2188	82.9	**Hilton Head Island** (town) Beaufort County
28	n/a	81.9	**Boiling Springs** (CDP) Spartanburg County
29	2304	81.8	**Socastee** (CDP) Horry County
30	2332	81.5	**Red Hill** (CDP) Horry County
31	n/a	80.9	**Gloverville** (CDP) Aiken County
32	2397	80.8	**Lexington** (town) Lexington County
33	n/a	80.7	**Belton** (city) Anderson County
34	n/a	80.5	**Pickens** (city) Pickens County
35	n/a	79.9	**Lugoff** (CDP) Kershaw County
35	n/a	79.9	**Travelers Rest** (city) Greenville County
37	2561	79.1	**Clemson** (city) Pickens County
38	2585	78.8	**Oak Grove** (CDP) Lexington County
39	n/a	78.3	**Burnettown** (town) Aiken County
40	2653	78.0	**Wade Hampton** (CDP) Greenville County
41	2682	77.6	**Fort Mill** (town) York County
42	n/a	77.0	**Honea Path** (town) Anderson County
43	2751	76.9	**Taylors** (CDP) Greenville County
44	n/a	76.5	**Clover** (town) York County
45	n/a	76.2	**Walhalla** (city) Oconee County
46	2810	76.0	**Forest Acres** (city) Richland County
47	n/a	75.8	**Central** (town) Pickens County
48	2842	75.7	**Simpsonville** (city) Greenville County
49	2922	74.7	**Hanahan** (city) Berkeley County
50	2960	74.2	**North Augusta** (city) Aiken County
51	n/a	73.4	**North Hartsville** (CDP) Darlington County
52	3078	72.3	**Myrtle Beach** (city) Horry County
52	n/a	72.3	**Pendleton** (town) Anderson County
54	3090	72.1	**Summerville** (town) Dorchester County
55	3143	71.4	**Bluffton** (town) Beaufort County
56	3157	71.2	**Goose Creek** (city) Berkeley County
57	3189	70.8	**Greer** (city) Greenville County
58	n/a	70.4	**Sangaree** (CDP) Berkeley County
59	3224	70.2	**Charleston** (city) Charleston County
59	n/a	70.2	**Elgin** (CDP) Lancaster County
61	n/a	69.6	**Clearwater** (CDP) Aiken County
62	n/a	69.5	**Sans Souci** (CDP) Greenville County
63	3317	68.8	**Port Royal** (town) Beaufort County
63	n/a	68.8	**Valley Falls** (CDP) Spartanburg County
65	3322	68.7	**Mauldin** (city) Greenville County
66	n/a	68.2	**East Gaffney** (CDP) Cherokee County
67	3364	68.0	**Cayce** (city) Lexington County
67	3364	68.0	**West Columbia** (city) Lexington County
69	3421	67.1	**Beaufort** (city) Beaufort County
70	n/a	66.9	**Laurel Bay** (CDP) Beaufort County
71	3443	66.8	**Aiken** (city) Aiken County
71	n/a	66.8	**Belvedere** (CDP) Aiken County
73	n/a	66.5	**Woodruff** (city) Spartanburg County
74	n/a	65.3	**Graniteville** (CDP) Aiken County
74	n/a	65.3	**Seneca** (city) Oconee County
76	3553	64.6	**Irmo** (town) Richland County
77	3584	64.0	**Greenville** (city) Greenville County
78	n/a	63.7	**Fountain Inn** (city) Greenville County
79	n/a	62.5	**Homeland Park** (CDP) Anderson County
79	n/a	62.5	**Springdale** (CDP) Lancaster County
81	n/a	62.2	**Camden** (city) Kershaw County
82	3682	62.0	**Parker** (CDP) Greenville County
83	3708	61.5	**Ladson** (CDP) Berkeley County
83	n/a	61.5	**Lakewood** (CDP) Sumter County
85	3713	61.4	**Anderson** (city) Anderson County
86	n/a	60.9	**Duncan** (town) Spartanburg County
87	3740	60.6	**Berea** (CDP) Greenville County
88	3750	60.4	**Seven Oaks** (CDP) Lexington County
89	3781	59.6	**Conway** (city) Horry County
90	n/a	59.4	**Clinton** (city) Laurens County
91	n/a	58.6	**Welcome** (CDP) Greenville County
92	n/a	57.7	**Moncks Corner** (town) Berkeley County
93	n/a	56.8	**Arcadia** (CDP) Spartanburg County
94	n/a	56.1	**Dunean** (CDP) Greenville County
95	n/a	55.0	**Dalzell** (CDP) Sumter County
96	3961	54.6	**Rock Hill** (city) York County
97	n/a	54.4	**York** (city) York County
98	n/a	52.5	**Laurens** (city) Laurens County
98	n/a	52.5	**Pageland** (town) Chesterfield County
100	n/a	51.8	**Southern Shops** (CDP) Spartanburg County
101	4055	51.7	**Columbia** (city) Richland County
102	n/a	51.0	**Hartsville** (city) Darlington County
103	n/a	50.5	**Union** (city) Union County
104	n/a	50.4	**Hampton** (town) Hampton County
105	4100	50.1	**Gaffney** (city) Cherokee County
106	4101	50.0	**Florence** (city) Florence County
107	n/a	49.5	**Batesburg-Leesville** (town) Lexington County
108	n/a	48.1	**Burton** (CDP) Beaufort County
109	n/a	46.9	**Abbeville** (city) Abbeville County
110	n/a	45.6	**Saxon** (CDP) Spartanburg County
110	4215	45.6	**Spartanburg** (city) Spartanburg County
112	4222	45.4	**Newberry** (city) Newberry County
113	4226	45.3	**Sumter** (city) Sumter County
114	n/a	45.2	**Walterboro** (city) Colleton County
115	4248	44.6	**Greenwood** (city) Greenwood County
116	n/a	44.5	**Barnwell** (city) Barnwell County
117	n/a	43.7	**Hardeeville** (city) Jasper County
118	n/a	43.3	**Williston** (town) Barnwell County
119	n/a	43.0	**Lancaster** (city) Lancaster County
120	n/a	42.8	**Dillon** (city) Dillon County
121	4306	41.6	**North Charleston** (city) Charleston County
122	n/a	41.3	**Bamberg** (town) Bamberg County
123	n/a	41.0	**Hollywood** (town) Charleston County
124	n/a	40.2	**Cheraw** (town) Chesterfield County
125	n/a	39.7	**Ridgeland** (town) Jasper County
126	n/a	38.9	**Edgefield** (town) Edgefield County
127	n/a	37.9	**Darlington** (city) Darlington County
128	n/a	37.8	**Georgetown** (city) Georgetown County
129	n/a	36.9	**Winnsboro** (town) Fairfield County
130	n/a	33.1	**Manning** (city) Clarendon County
131	n/a	32.7	**Bennettsville** (city) Marlboro County
132	n/a	31.9	**Chester** (city) Chester County
133	n/a	31.6	**Andrews** (town) Georgetown County
134	n/a	31.2	**Mullins** (city) Marion County
135	n/a	30.9	**Woodfield** (CDP) Richland County
136	n/a	30.4	**Saluda** (town) Saluda County
137	n/a	29.5	**McCormick** (town) McCormick County
138	n/a	29.4	**Kingstree** (town) Williamsburg County
139	4473	29.1	**Gantt** (CDP) Greenville County
140	4483	28.3	**Saint Andrews** (CDP) Richland County
141	n/a	27.8	**Marion** (city) Marion County
142	n/a	26.2	**Bishopville** (city) Lee County
143	n/a	23.4	**Edisto** (CDP) Orangeburg County
144	4536	22.6	**Dentsville** (CDP) Richland County
145	4543	21.3	**Orangeburg** (city) Orangeburg County
146	n/a	19.4	**Lake City** (city) Florence County
147	n/a	14.1	**Hopkins** (CDP) Richland County
148	n/a	12.8	**Allendale** (town) Allendale County
149	n/a	8.6	**Denmark** (city) Bamberg County
150	n/a	0.8	**Brookdale** (CDP) Orangeburg County

Note: *The state column ranks the top/bottom 150 places in the state with population of 2,500 or more. The national column ranks the top/bottom places in the country with population of 10,000 or more. Places that are unincorporated were not considered in the rankings. n/a indicates data not available. Please refer to the User Guide for additional information.*

White Population

Top 150 Places Ranked in *Ascending* Order

State Rank	Nat'l Rank	Percent	Place
1	n/a	0.8	Brookdale (CDP) Orangeburg County
2	n/a	8.6	Denmark (city) Bamberg County
3	n/a	12.8	Allendale (town) Allendale County
4	n/a	14.1	Hopkins (CDP) Richland County
5	n/a	19.4	Lake City (city) Florence County
6	113	21.3	Orangeburg (city) Orangeburg County
7	120	22.6	Dentsville (CDP) Richland County
8	n/a	23.4	Edisto (CDP) Orangeburg County
9	n/a	26.2	Bishopville (city) Lee County
10	n/a	27.8	Marion (city) Marion County
11	171	28.3	Saint Andrews (CDP) Richland County
12	183	29.1	Gantt (CDP) Greenville County
13	n/a	29.4	Kingstree (town) Williamsburg County
14	n/a	29.5	McCormick (town) McCormick County
15	n/a	30.4	Saluda (town) Saluda County
16	n/a	30.9	Woodfield (CDP) Richland County
17	n/a	31.2	Mullins (city) Marion County
18	n/a	31.6	Andrews (town) Georgetown County
19	n/a	31.9	Chester (city) Chester County
20	n/a	32.7	Bennettsville (city) Marlboro County
21	n/a	33.1	Manning (city) Clarendon County
22	n/a	36.9	Winnsboro (town) Fairfield County
23	n/a	37.8	Georgetown (city) Georgetown County
24	n/a	37.9	Darlington (city) Darlington County
25	n/a	38.9	Edgefield (town) Edgefield County
26	n/a	39.7	Ridgeland (town) Jasper County
27	n/a	40.2	Cheraw (town) Chesterfield County
28	n/a	41.0	Hollywood (town) Charleston County
29	n/a	41.3	Bamberg (town) Bamberg County
30	346	41.6	North Charleston (city) Charleston County
31	n/a	42.8	Dillon (city) Dillon County
32	n/a	43.0	Lancaster (city) Lancaster County
33	n/a	43.3	Williston (town) Barnwell County
34	n/a	43.7	Hardeeville (city) Jasper County
35	n/a	44.5	Barnwell (city) Barnwell County
36	408	44.6	Greenwood (city) Greenwood County
37	n/a	45.2	Walterboro (city) Colleton County
38	425	45.3	Sumter (city) Sumter County
39	431	45.4	Newberry (city) Newberry County
40	n/a	45.6	Saxon (CDP) Spartanburg County
40	437	45.6	Spartanburg (city) Spartanburg County
42	n/a	46.9	Abbeville (city) Abbeville County
43	n/a	48.1	Burton (CDP) Beaufort County
44	n/a	49.5	Batesburg-Leesville (town) Lexington County
45	549	50.0	Florence (city) Florence County
46	556	50.1	Gaffney (city) Cherokee County
47	n/a	50.4	Hampton (town) Hampton County
48	n/a	50.5	Union (city) Union County
49	n/a	51.0	Hartsville (city) Darlington County
50	598	51.7	Columbia (city) Richland County
51	n/a	51.8	Southern Shops (CDP) Spartanburg County
52	n/a	52.5	Laurens (city) Laurens County
52	n/a	52.5	Pageland (town) Chesterfield County
54	n/a	54.4	York (city) York County
55	689	54.6	Rock Hill (city) York County
56	n/a	55.0	Dalzell (CDP) Sumter County
57	n/a	56.1	Dunean (CDP) Greenville County
58	n/a	56.8	Arcadia (CDP) Spartanburg County
59	n/a	57.7	Moncks Corner (town) Berkeley County
60	n/a	58.6	Welcome (CDP) Greenville County
61	n/a	59.4	Clinton (city) Laurens County
62	869	59.6	Conway (city) Horry County
63	897	60.4	Seven Oaks (CDP) Lexington County
64	914	60.6	Berea (CDP) Greenville County
65	n/a	60.9	Duncan (town) Spartanburg County
66	941	61.4	Anderson (city) Anderson County
67	944	61.5	Ladson (CDP) Berkeley County
67	n/a	61.5	Lakewood (CDP) Sumter County
69	970	62.0	Parker (CDP) Greenville County
70	n/a	62.2	Camden (city) Kershaw County
71	n/a	62.5	Homeland Park (CDP) Anderson County
71	n/a	62.5	Springdale (CDP) Lancaster County
73	n/a	63.7	Fountain Inn (city) Greenville County
74	1069	64.0	Greenville (city) Greenville County
75	1097	64.6	Irmo (town) Richland County
76	n/a	65.3	Graniteville (CDP) Aiken County
76	n/a	65.3	Seneca (city) Oconee County
78	n/a	66.5	Woodruff (city) Spartanburg County
79	1212	66.8	Aiken (city) Aiken County
79	n/a	66.8	Belvedere (CDP) Aiken County
81	n/a	66.9	Laurel Bay (CDP) Beaufort County
82	1230	67.1	Beaufort (city) Beaufort County
83	1284	68.0	Cayce (city) Lexington County
83	1284	68.0	West Columbia (city) Lexington County
85	n/a	68.2	East Gaffney (CDP) Cherokee County
86	1328	68.7	Mauldin (city) Greenville County
87	1335	68.8	Port Royal (town) Beaufort County
87	n/a	68.8	Valley Falls (CDP) Spartanburg County
89	n/a	69.5	Sans Souci (CDP) Greenville County
90	n/a	69.6	Clearwater (CDP) Aiken County
91	1425	70.2	Charleston (city) Charleston County
91	n/a	70.2	Elgin (CDP) Lancaster County
93	n/a	70.4	Sangaree (CDP) Berkeley County
94	1459	70.8	Greer (city) Greenville County
95	1496	71.2	Goose Creek (city) Berkeley County
96	1504	71.4	Bluffton (town) Beaufort County
97	1560	72.1	Summerville (town) Dorchester County
98	1570	72.3	Myrtle Beach (city) Horry County
98	n/a	72.3	Pendleton (town) Anderson County
100	n/a	73.4	North Hartsville (CDP) Darlington County
101	1684	74.2	North Augusta (city) Aiken County
102	1721	74.7	Hanahan (city) Berkeley County
103	1806	75.7	Simpsonville (city) Greenville County
104	n/a	75.8	Central (town) Pickens County
105	1837	76.0	Forest Acres (city) Richland County
106	n/a	76.2	Walhalla (city) Oconee County
107	n/a	76.5	Clover (town) York County
108	1901	76.9	Taylors (CDP) Greenville County
109	n/a	77.0	Honea Path (town) Anderson County
110	1963	77.6	Fort Mill (town) York County
111	1994	78.0	Wade Hampton (CDP) Greenville County
112	n/a	78.3	Burnettown (town) Aiken County
113	2063	78.8	Oak Grove (CDP) Lexington County
114	2089	79.1	Clemson (city) Pickens County
115	n/a	79.9	Lugoff (CDP) Kershaw County
115	n/a	79.9	Travelers Rest (city) Greenville County
117	n/a	80.5	Pickens (city) Pickens County
118	n/a	80.7	Belton (city) Anderson County
119	2249	80.8	Lexington (town) Lexington County
120	n/a	80.9	Gloverville (CDP) Aiken County
121	2318	81.5	Red Hill (CDP) Horry County
122	2343	81.8	Socastee (CDP) Horry County
123	n/a	81.9	Boiling Springs (CDP) Spartanburg County
124	2459	82.9	Hilton Head Island (town) Beaufort County
125	2480	83.1	Easley (city) Pickens County
126	n/a	83.3	Centerville (CDP) Anderson County
127	n/a	83.4	Williamston (town) Anderson County
128	n/a	84.1	Newport (CDP) York County
129	n/a	84.2	Springdale (town) Lexington County
130	n/a	84.6	Red Bank (CDP) Lexington County
131	n/a	84.9	Lesslie (CDP) York County
131	n/a	84.9	Lyman (town) Spartanburg County
133	n/a	85.8	Northlake (CDP) Anderson County
134	n/a	85.9	Forestbrook (CDP) Horry County
135	n/a	86.7	Liberty (city) Pickens County
136	3031	87.5	Five Forks (CDP) Greenville County
137	n/a	88.0	India Hook (CDP) York County
138	n/a	88.7	Lake Wylie (CDP) York County
139	n/a	89.0	Little River (CDP) Horry County
140	n/a	89.1	Piedmont (CDP) Anderson County
141	3469	90.4	North Myrtle Beach (city) Horry County
142	n/a	90.7	Murrells Inlet (CDP) Georgetown County
143	3621	91.3	Mount Pleasant (town) Charleston County
144	n/a	92.6	Arial (CDP) Pickens County
144	n/a	92.6	Tega Cay (city) York County
146	n/a	95.3	Garden City (CDP) Horry County
147	n/a	96.1	Lake Murray of Richland (CDP) Richland County
147	n/a	96.1	Surfside Beach (town) Horry County
149	n/a	96.3	Folly Beach (city) Charleston County
150	n/a	97.7	Isle of Palms (city) Charleston County

Note: The state column ranks the top/bottom 150 places in the state with population of 2,500 or more. The national column ranks the top/bottom places in the country with population of 10,000 or more. Places that are unincorporated were not considered in the rankings. n/a indicates data not available. Please refer to the User Guide for additional information.

Black/African American Population

Top 150 Places Ranked in *Descending* Order

State Rank	Nat'l Rank	Percent	Place
1	n/a	98.1	**Brookdale** (CDP) Orangeburg County
2	n/a	90.1	**Denmark** (city) Bamberg County
3	n/a	83.4	**Allendale** (town) Allendale County
4	n/a	82.7	**Hopkins** (CDP) Richland County
5	n/a	77.5	**Lake City** (city) Florence County
6	68	75.0	**Orangeburg** (city) Orangeburg County
7	n/a	74.0	**Edisto** (CDP) Orangeburg County
8	n/a	71.3	**Bishopville** (city) Lee County
9	91	69.3	**Dentsville** (CDP) Richland County
10	n/a	69.2	**Marion** (city) Marion County
11	n/a	68.3	**McCormick** (town) McCormick County
12	n/a	67.5	**Kingstree** (town) Williamsburg County
13	n/a	65.8	**Mullins** (city) Marion County
14	110	65.7	**Saint Andrews** (CDP) Richland County
15	n/a	65.5	**Chester** (city) Chester County
16	n/a	64.9	**Andrews** (town) Georgetown County
17	n/a	64.2	**Bennettsville** (city) Marlboro County
18	n/a	62.7	**Manning** (city) Clarendon County
19	n/a	60.6	**Darlington** (city) Darlington County
19	n/a	60.6	**Winnsboro** (town) Fairfield County
21	142	59.2	**Gantt** (CDP) Greenville County
22	n/a	56.7	**Georgetown** (city) Georgetown County
23	n/a	56.0	**Cheraw** (town) Chesterfield County
24	n/a	55.4	**Hollywood** (town) Charleston County
25	n/a	55.3	**Bamberg** (town) Bamberg County
26	n/a	54.1	**Edgefield** (town) Edgefield County
27	n/a	54.0	**Williston** (town) Barnwell County
28	n/a	53.1	**Dillon** (city) Dillon County
29	n/a	51.5	**Barnwell** (city) Barnwell County
30	n/a	51.4	**Woodfield** (CDP) Richland County
31	n/a	51.3	**Lancaster** (city) Lancaster County
32	n/a	51.2	**Ridgeland** (town) Jasper County
33	n/a	50.5	**Abbeville** (city) Abbeville County
33	n/a	50.5	**Walterboro** (city) Colleton County
35	217	49.3	**Spartanburg** (city) Spartanburg County
36	221	49.1	**Sumter** (city) Sumter County
37	245	47.2	**North Charleston** (city) Charleston County
38	n/a	47.0	**Union** (city) Union County
39	n/a	46.6	**Batesburg-Leesville** (town) Lexington County
40	n/a	46.3	**Hartsville** (city) Darlington County
41	250	46.0	**Florence** (city) Florence County
42	252	45.7	**Gaffney** (city) Cherokee County
43	n/a	45.6	**Hampton** (town) Hampton County
43	255	45.6	**Newberry** (city) Newberry County
45	264	44.7	**Greenwood** (city) Greenwood County
46	n/a	43.1	**Burton** (CDP) Beaufort County
47	n/a	42.8	**Laurens** (city) Laurens County
48	283	42.2	**Columbia** (city) Richland County
49	n/a	39.4	**Saluda** (town) Saluda County
50	n/a	39.3	**Dalzell** (CDP) Sumter County
51	n/a	38.4	**York** (city) York County
52	327	38.3	**Rock Hill** (city) York County
53	n/a	37.0	**Clinton** (city) Laurens County
53	343	37.0	**Conway** (city) Horry County
55	n/a	36.0	**Moncks Corner** (town) Berkeley County
56	n/a	35.1	**Camden** (city) Kershaw County
57	n/a	35.0	**Dunean** (CDP) Greenville County
58	n/a	34.7	**Hardeeville** (city) Jasper County
59	n/a	34.6	**Saxon** (CDP) Spartanburg County
60	n/a	34.1	**Lakewood** (CDP) Sumter County
61	393	33.6	**Anderson** (city) Anderson County
62	n/a	32.9	**Pageland** (town) Chesterfield County
63	424	32.0	**Seven Oaks** (CDP) Lexington County
64	n/a	31.8	**Homeland Park** (CDP) Anderson County
65	n/a	31.2	**Fountain Inn** (city) Greenville County
66	n/a	30.5	**Duncan** (town) Spartanburg County
67	471	30.0	**Greenville** (city) Greenville County
68	474	29.9	**Irmo** (town) Richland County
69	n/a	29.0	**Seneca** (city) Oconee County
70	n/a	28.6	**Graniteville** (CDP) Aiken County
71	502	28.5	**Aiken** (city) Aiken County
72	n/a	27.9	**Welcome** (CDP) Greenville County
73	n/a	27.7	**Springdale** (CDP) Lancaster County
74	563	26.3	**Ladson** (CDP) Berkeley County
75	n/a	26.2	**Belvedere** (CDP) Aiken County
76	574	25.7	**Beaufort** (city) Beaufort County
77	n/a	25.6	**East Gaffney** (CDP) Cherokee County
78	584	25.4	**Charleston** (city) Charleston County
79	n/a	25.2	**Woodruff** (city) Spartanburg County
80	595	25.1	**Cayce** (city) Lexington County
81	n/a	24.6	**Valley Falls** (CDP) Spartanburg County
82	n/a	23.9	**Laurel Bay** (CDP) Beaufort County
83	n/a	23.6	**Sangaree** (CDP) Berkeley County
84	n/a	23.3	**Pendleton** (town) Anderson County
85	n/a	22.6	**North Hartsville** (CDP) Darlington County
86	663	22.5	**Mauldin** (city) Greenville County
87	696	21.7	**Parker** (CDP) Greenville County
88	705	21.4	**Summerville** (town) Dorchester County
89	718	20.7	**Port Royal** (town) Beaufort County
90	728	20.4	**North Augusta** (city) Aiken County
91	n/a	20.0	**Elgin** (CDP) Lancaster County
92	n/a	19.6	**Honea Path** (town) Anderson County
93	767	19.4	**Forest Acres** (city) Richland County
94	n/a	19.2	**Clover** (town) York County
95	804	18.5	**West Columbia** (city) Lexington County
96	818	18.3	**Goose Creek** (city) Berkeley County
97	827	18.1	**Berea** (CDP) Greenville County
98	849	17.6	**Fort Mill** (town) York County
99	861	17.3	**Greer** (city) Greenville County
100	n/a	17.0	**Southern Shops** (CDP) Spartanburg County
101	n/a	16.9	**Lugoff** (CDP) Kershaw County
102	n/a	16.6	**Belton** (city) Anderson County
103	907	16.4	**Simpsonville** (city) Greenville County
104	n/a	16.3	**Clearwater** (CDP) Aiken County
105	924	16.2	**Bluffton** (town) Beaufort County
106	n/a	16.1	**Arcadia** (CDP) Spartanburg County
107	n/a	15.3	**Central** (town) Pickens County
107	n/a	15.3	**Pickens** (city) Pickens County
107	n/a	15.3	**Sans Souci** (CDP) Greenville County
107	n/a	15.3	**Travelers Rest** (city) Greenville County
111	1001	14.9	**Taylors** (CDP) Greenville County
112	n/a	14.2	**Burnettown** (town) Aiken County
113	1063	13.9	**Hanahan** (city) Berkeley County
113	1063	13.9	**Myrtle Beach** (city) Horry County
115	n/a	13.5	**Gloverville** (CDP) Aiken County
116	n/a	13.3	**Centerville** (CDP) Anderson County
117	n/a	13.2	**Williamston** (town) Anderson County
118	1143	12.7	**Lexington** (town) Lexington County
119	n/a	11.9	**Newport** (CDP) York County
120	1244	11.4	**Easley** (city) Pickens County
121	1256	11.3	**Oak Grove** (CDP) Lexington County
122	n/a	10.7	**Lyman** (town) Spartanburg County
122	n/a	10.7	**Springdale** (town) Lexington County
124	n/a	10.4	**Boiling Springs** (CDP) Spartanburg County
125	1352	10.3	**Clemson** (city) Pickens County
125	n/a	10.3	**Lesslie** (CDP) York County
125	n/a	10.3	**Red Bank** (CDP) Lexington County
128	1363	10.2	**Wade Hampton** (CDP) Greenville County
129	1408	9.9	**Red Hill** (CDP) Horry County
130	n/a	9.2	**Northlake** (CDP) Anderson County
131	n/a	9.1	**Liberty** (city) Pickens County
132	n/a	7.8	**Piedmont** (CDP) Anderson County
133	n/a	7.6	**Forestbrook** (CDP) Horry County
133	1653	7.6	**Socastee** (CDP) Horry County
135	1669	7.5	**Hilton Head Island** (town) Beaufort County
136	n/a	7.1	**Lake Wylie** (CDP) York County
137	n/a	6.6	**Little River** (CDP) Horry County
138	n/a	6.5	**Murrells Inlet** (CDP) Georgetown County
139	n/a	6.3	**India Hook** (CDP) York County
140	n/a	6.0	**Walhalla** (city) Oconee County
141	2026	5.5	**Five Forks** (CDP) Greenville County
142	2116	5.1	**Mount Pleasant** (town) Charleston County
143	n/a	3.5	**Arial** (CDP) Pickens County
144	2602	3.3	**North Myrtle Beach** (city) Horry County
145	n/a	3.0	**Tega Cay** (city) York County
146	n/a	1.7	**Garden City** (CDP) Horry County
147	n/a	1.5	**Folly Beach** (city) Charleston County
148	n/a	1.3	**Lake Murray of Richland** (CDP) Richland County
149	n/a	0.9	**Surfside Beach** (town) Horry County
150	n/a	0.6	**Isle of Palms** (city) Charleston County

Note: The state column ranks the top/bottom 150 places in the state with population of 2,500 or more. The national column ranks the top/bottom places in the country with population of 10,000 or more. Places that are unincorporated were not considered in the rankings. n/a indicates data not available. Please refer to the User Guide for additional information.

Black/African American Population

Top 150 Places Ranked in *Ascending* Order

State Rank	Nat'l Rank	Percent	Place
1	n/a	0.6	**Isle of Palms** (city) Charleston County
2	n/a	0.9	**Surfside Beach** (town) Horry County
3	n/a	1.3	**Lake Murray of Richland** (CDP) Richland County
4	n/a	1.5	**Folly Beach** (city) Charleston County
5	n/a	1.7	**Garden City** (CDP) Horry County
6	n/a	3.0	**Tega Cay** (city) York County
7	2003	3.3	**North Myrtle Beach** (city) Horry County
8	n/a	3.5	**Arial** (CDP) Pickens County
9	2518	5.1	**Mount Pleasant** (town) Charleston County
10	2607	5.5	**Five Forks** (CDP) Greenville County
11	n/a	6.0	**Walhalla** (city) Oconee County
12	n/a	6.3	**India Hook** (CDP) York County
13	n/a	6.5	**Murrells Inlet** (CDP) Georgetown County
14	n/a	6.6	**Little River** (CDP) Horry County
15	n/a	7.1	**Lake Wylie** (CDP) York County
16	2973	7.5	**Hilton Head Island** (town) Beaufort County
17	n/a	7.6	**Forestbrook** (CDP) Horry County
17	2988	7.6	**Socastee** (CDP) Horry County
19	n/a	7.8	**Piedmont** (CDP) Anderson County
20	n/a	9.1	**Liberty** (city) Pickens County
21	n/a	9.2	**Northlake** (CDP) Anderson County
22	3242	9.9	**Red Hill** (CDP) Horry County
23	3276	10.2	**Wade Hampton** (CDP) Greenville County
24	3294	10.3	**Clemson** (city) Pickens County
24	n/a	10.3	**Lesslie** (CDP) York County
24	n/a	10.3	**Red Bank** (CDP) Lexington County
27	n/a	10.4	**Boiling Springs** (CDP) Spartanburg County
28	n/a	10.7	**Lyman** (town) Spartanburg County
28	n/a	10.7	**Springdale** (town) Lexington County
30	3394	11.3	**Oak Grove** (CDP) Lexington County
31	3401	11.4	**Easley** (city) Pickens County
32	n/a	11.9	**Newport** (CDP) York County
33	3503	12.7	**Lexington** (town) Lexington County
34	n/a	13.2	**Williamston** (town) Anderson County
35	n/a	13.3	**Centerville** (CDP) Anderson County
36	n/a	13.5	**Gloverville** (CDP) Aiken County
37	3587	13.9	**Hanahan** (city) Berkeley County
37	3587	13.9	**Myrtle Beach** (city) Horry County
39	n/a	14.2	**Burnettown** (town) Aiken County
40	3649	14.9	**Taylors** (CDP) Greenville County
41	n/a	15.3	**Central** (town) Pickens County
41	n/a	15.3	**Pickens** (city) Pickens County
41	n/a	15.3	**Sans Souci** (CDP) Greenville County
41	n/a	15.3	**Travelers Rest** (city) Greenville County
45	n/a	16.1	**Arcadia** (CDP) Spartanburg County
46	3726	16.2	**Bluffton** (town) Beaufort County
47	n/a	16.3	**Clearwater** (CDP) Aiken County
48	3738	16.4	**Simpsonville** (city) Greenville County
49	n/a	16.6	**Belton** (city) Anderson County
50	n/a	16.9	**Lugoff** (CDP) Kershaw County
51	n/a	17.0	**Southern Shops** (CDP) Spartanburg County
52	3793	17.3	**Greer** (city) Greenville County
53	3806	17.6	**Fort Mill** (town) York County
54	3821	18.1	**Berea** (CDP) Greenville County
55	3833	18.3	**Goose Creek** (city) Berkeley County
56	3844	18.5	**West Columbia** (city) Lexington County
57	n/a	19.2	**Clover** (town) York County
58	3886	19.4	**Forest Acres** (city) Richland County
59	n/a	19.6	**Honea Path** (town) Anderson County
60	n/a	20.0	**Elgin** (CDP) Lancaster County
61	3924	20.4	**North Augusta** (city) Aiken County
62	3933	20.7	**Port Royal** (town) Beaufort County
63	3950	21.4	**Summerville** (town) Dorchester County
64	3956	21.7	**Parker** (CDP) Greenville County
65	3990	22.5	**Mauldin** (city) Greenville County
66	n/a	22.6	**North Hartsville** (CDP) Darlington County
67	n/a	23.3	**Pendleton** (town) Anderson County
68	n/a	23.6	**Sangaree** (CDP) Berkeley County
69	n/a	23.9	**Laurel Bay** (CDP) Beaufort County
70	n/a	24.6	**Valley Falls** (CDP) Spartanburg County
71	4059	25.1	**Cayce** (city) Lexington County
72	n/a	25.2	**Woodruff** (city) Spartanburg County
73	4066	25.4	**Charleston** (city) Charleston County
74	n/a	25.6	**East Gaffney** (CDP) Cherokee County
75	4081	25.7	**Beaufort** (city) Beaufort County
76	n/a	26.2	**Belvedere** (CDP) Aiken County
77	4093	26.3	**Ladson** (CDP) Berkeley County
78	n/a	27.7	**Springdale** (CDP) Lancaster County
79	n/a	27.9	**Welcome** (CDP) Greenville County
80	4152	28.5	**Aiken** (city) Aiken County
81	n/a	28.6	**Graniteville** (CDP) Aiken County
82	n/a	29.0	**Seneca** (city) Oconee County
83	4177	29.9	**Irmo** (town) Richland County
84	4183	30.0	**Greenville** (city) Greenville County
85	n/a	30.5	**Duncan** (town) Spartanburg County
86	n/a	31.2	**Fountain Inn** (city) Greenville County
87	n/a	31.8	**Homeland Park** (CDP) Anderson County
88	4230	32.0	**Seven Oaks** (CDP) Lexington County
89	n/a	32.9	**Pageland** (town) Chesterfield County
90	4261	33.6	**Anderson** (city) Anderson County
91	n/a	34.1	**Lakewood** (CDP) Sumter County
92	n/a	34.6	**Saxon** (CDP) Spartanburg County
93	n/a	34.7	**Hardeeville** (city) Jasper County
94	n/a	35.0	**Dunean** (CDP) Greenville County
95	n/a	35.1	**Camden** (city) Kershaw County
96	n/a	36.0	**Moncks Corner** (town) Berkeley County
97	n/a	37.0	**Clinton** (city) Laurens County
97	4311	37.0	**Conway** (city) Horry County
99	4323	38.3	**Rock Hill** (city) York County
100	n/a	38.4	**York** (city) York County
101	n/a	39.3	**Dalzell** (CDP) Sumter County
102	n/a	39.4	**Saluda** (town) Saluda County
103	4370	42.2	**Columbia** (city) Richland County
104	n/a	42.8	**Laurens** (city) Laurens County
105	n/a	43.1	**Burton** (CDP) Beaufort County
106	4392	44.7	**Greenwood** (city) Greenwood County
107	4400	45.6	**Hampton** (town) Hampton County
107	4400	45.6	**Newberry** (city) Newberry County
109	4402	45.7	**Gaffney** (city) Cherokee County
110	4406	46.0	**Florence** (city) Florence County
111	n/a	46.3	**Hartsville** (city) Darlington County
112	n/a	46.6	**Batesburg-Leesville** (town) Lexington County
113	n/a	47.0	**Union** (city) Union County
114	4411	47.2	**North Charleston** (city) Charleston County
115	4435	49.1	**Sumter** (city) Sumter County
116	4438	49.3	**Spartanburg** (city) Spartanburg County
117	n/a	50.5	**Abbeville** (city) Abbeville County
117	n/a	50.5	**Walterboro** (city) Colleton County
119	n/a	51.2	**Ridgeland** (town) Jasper County
120	n/a	51.3	**Lancaster** (city) Lancaster County
121	n/a	51.4	**Woodfield** (CDP) Richland County
122	n/a	51.5	**Barnwell** (city) Barnwell County
123	n/a	53.1	**Dillon** (city) Dillon County
124	n/a	54.0	**Williston** (town) Barnwell County
125	n/a	54.1	**Edgefield** (town) Edgefield County
126	n/a	55.3	**Bamberg** (town) Bamberg County
127	n/a	55.4	**Hollywood** (town) Charleston County
128	n/a	56.0	**Cheraw** (town) Chesterfield County
129	n/a	56.7	**Georgetown** (city) Georgetown County
130	4512	59.2	**Gantt** (CDP) Greenville County
131	n/a	60.6	**Darlington** (city) Darlington County
131	n/a	60.6	**Winnsboro** (town) Fairfield County
133	n/a	62.7	**Manning** (city) Clarendon County
134	n/a	64.2	**Bennettsville** (city) Marlboro County
135	n/a	64.9	**Andrews** (town) Georgetown County
136	n/a	65.5	**Chester** (city) Chester County
137	4546	65.7	**Saint Andrews** (CDP) Richland County
138	n/a	65.8	**Mullins** (city) Marion County
139	n/a	67.5	**Kingstree** (town) Williamsburg County
140	n/a	68.3	**McCormick** (town) McCormick County
141	n/a	69.2	**Marion** (city) Marion County
142	4565	69.3	**Dentsville** (CDP) Richland County
143	n/a	71.3	**Bishopville** (city) Lee County
144	n/a	74.0	**Edisto** (CDP) Orangeburg County
145	4588	75.0	**Orangeburg** (city) Orangeburg County
146	n/a	77.5	**Lake City** (city) Florence County
147	n/a	82.7	**Hopkins** (CDP) Richland County
148	n/a	83.4	**Allendale** (town) Allendale County
149	n/a	90.1	**Denmark** (city) Bamberg County
150	n/a	98.1	**Brookdale** (CDP) Orangeburg County

Note: The state column ranks the top/bottom 150 places in the state with population of 2,500 or more. The national column ranks the top/bottom places in the country with population of 10,000 or more. Places that are unincorporated were not considered in the rankings. n/a indicates data not available. Please refer to the User Guide for additional information.

Asian Population

Top 150 Places Ranked in *Descending* Order

State Rank	Nat'l Rank	Percent	Place
1	706	8.1	**Clemson** (city) Pickens County
2	1326	4.4	**Five Forks** (CDP) Greenville County
3	n/a	3.7	**Boiling Springs** (CDP) Spartanburg County
3	1569	3.7	**Goose Creek** (city) Berkeley County
3	1569	3.7	**Lexington** (town) Lexington County
6	1659	3.5	**Mauldin** (city) Greenville County
7	1700	3.4	**Hanahan** (city) Berkeley County
8	n/a	3.3	**Arcadia** (CDP) Spartanburg County
8	n/a	3.3	**Central** (town) Pickens County
10	1787	3.2	**Wade Hampton** (CDP) Greenville County
11	n/a	3.1	**Woodfield** (CDP) Richland County
12	2010	2.8	**Dentsville** (CDP) Richland County
12	2010	2.8	**Seven Oaks** (CDP) Lexington County
14	2173	2.5	**Port Royal** (town) Beaufort County
14	2173	2.5	**Taylors** (CDP) Greenville County
16	n/a	2.4	**Kingstree** (town) Williamsburg County
16	n/a	2.4	**Manning** (city) Clarendon County
18	2384	2.2	**Columbia** (city) Richland County
18	2384	2.2	**Greer** (city) Greenville County
18	2384	2.2	**Ladson** (CDP) Berkeley County
21	2527	2.0	**Bluffton** (town) Beaufort County
21	n/a	2.0	**Hampton** (town) Hampton County
21	n/a	2.0	**Hardeeville** (city) Jasper County
21	2527	2.0	**Saint Andrews** (CDP) Richland County
21	n/a	2.0	**Tega Cay** (city) York County
26	2598	1.9	**Aiken** (city) Aiken County
26	2598	1.9	**Cayce** (city) Lexington County
26	2598	1.9	**North Charleston** (city) Charleston County
29	2688	1.8	**Florence** (city) Florence County
29	n/a	1.8	**Northlake** (CDP) Anderson County
29	2688	1.8	**Socastee** (CDP) Horry County
29	2688	1.8	**Spartanburg** (city) Spartanburg County
29	2688	1.8	**West Columbia** (city) Lexington County
34	n/a	1.7	**Lesslie** (CDP) York County
34	2801	1.7	**Orangeburg** (city) Orangeburg County
34	2801	1.7	**Rock Hill** (city) York County
34	n/a	1.7	**Springdale** (town) Lexington County
34	n/a	1.7	**Valley Falls** (CDP) Spartanburg County
39	2898	1.6	**Charleston** (city) Charleston County
39	2898	1.6	**Irmo** (town) Richland County
39	2898	1.6	**Mount Pleasant** (town) Charleston County
39	2898	1.6	**Oak Grove** (CDP) Lexington County
39	2898	1.6	**Sumter** (city) Sumter County
44	n/a	1.5	**Barnwell** (city) Barnwell County
44	3009	1.5	**Forest Acres** (city) Richland County
44	3009	1.5	**Myrtle Beach** (city) Horry County
44	3009	1.5	**Summerville** (town) Dorchester County
48	3111	1.4	**Beaufort** (city) Beaufort County
48	3111	1.4	**Greenville** (city) Greenville County
48	n/a	1.4	**India Hook** (CDP) York County
48	n/a	1.4	**Lake Wylie** (CDP) York County
52	n/a	1.3	**Burton** (CDP) Beaufort County
52	n/a	1.3	**Dalzell** (CDP) Sumter County
52	n/a	1.3	**Forestbrook** (CDP) Horry County
52	3229	1.3	**Fort Mill** (town) York County
52	n/a	1.3	**Laurel Bay** (CDP) Beaufort County
52	n/a	1.3	**Newport** (CDP) York County
52	3229	1.3	**Simpsonville** (city) Greenville County
59	3327	1.2	**Berea** (CDP) Greenville County
59	n/a	1.2	**Pendleton** (town) Anderson County
59	3327	1.2	**Red Hill** (CDP) Horry County
59	n/a	1.2	**Southern Shops** (CDP) Spartanburg County
63	n/a	1.1	**Bamberg** (town) Bamberg County
63	n/a	1.1	**Centerville** (CDP) Anderson County
63	n/a	1.1	**Lake Murray of Richland** (CDP) Richland County
63	n/a	1.1	**Marion** (city) Marion County
63	3443	1.1	**North Augusta** (city) Aiken County
63	n/a	1.1	**Sangaree** (CDP) Berkeley County
63	n/a	1.1	**Travelers Rest** (city) Greenville County
70	3560	1.0	**Anderson** (city) Anderson County
70	n/a	1.0	**Duncan** (town) Spartanburg County
70	3560	1.0	**Greenwood** (city) Greenwood County
70	n/a	1.0	**Mullins** (city) Marion County
70	n/a	1.0	**Sans Souci** (CDP) Greenville County
70	n/a	1.0	**Saxon** (CDP) Spartanburg County
70	n/a	1.0	**Walterboro** (city) Colleton County
77	3694	0.9	**Gaffney** (city) Cherokee County
77	3694	0.9	**Hilton Head Island** (town) Beaufort County
77	n/a	0.9	**Lancaster** (city) Lancaster County
77	n/a	0.9	**Little River** (CDP) Horry County
77	n/a	0.9	**Murrells Inlet** (CDP) Georgetown County
77	3694	0.9	**North Myrtle Beach** (city) Horry County
77	n/a	0.9	**Seneca** (city) Oconee County
84	n/a	0.8	**Andrews** (town) Georgetown County
84	n/a	0.8	**Bishopville** (city) Lee County
84	3856	0.8	**Easley** (city) Pickens County
84	n/a	0.8	**Hartsville** (city) Darlington County
84	n/a	0.8	**Isle of Palms** (city) Charleston County
84	n/a	0.8	**Lakewood** (CDP) Sumter County
84	n/a	0.8	**Lyman** (town) Spartanburg County
84	n/a	0.8	**Walhalla** (city) Oconee County
92	n/a	0.7	**Allendale** (town) Allendale County
92	n/a	0.7	**Batesburg-Leesville** (town) Lexington County
92	n/a	0.7	**Burnettown** (town) Aiken County
92	n/a	0.7	**Camden** (city) Kershaw County
92	4028	0.7	**Conway** (city) Horry County
92	n/a	0.7	**Georgetown** (city) Georgetown County
92	n/a	0.7	**Pageland** (town) Chesterfield County
99	n/a	0.6	**Cheraw** (town) Chesterfield County
99	n/a	0.6	**Clinton** (city) Laurens County
99	n/a	0.6	**Clover** (town) York County
99	n/a	0.6	**Dillon** (city) Dillon County
99	4205	0.6	**Newberry** (city) Newberry County
99	n/a	0.6	**Pickens** (city) Pickens County
99	n/a	0.6	**Red Bank** (CDP) Lexington County
99	n/a	0.6	**Surfside Beach** (town) Horry County
99	n/a	0.6	**York** (city) York County
108	n/a	0.5	**Folly Beach** (city) Charleston County
108	n/a	0.5	**Lugoff** (CDP) Kershaw County
108	n/a	0.5	**McCormick** (town) McCormick County
108	n/a	0.5	**Moncks Corner** (town) Berkeley County
108	n/a	0.5	**Ridgeland** (town) Jasper County
113	n/a	0.4	**Abbeville** (city) Abbeville County
113	n/a	0.4	**Belvedere** (CDP) Aiken County
113	n/a	0.4	**Bennettsville** (city) Marlboro County
113	n/a	0.4	**Darlington** (city) Darlington County
113	n/a	0.4	**Edgefield** (town) Edgefield County
113	n/a	0.4	**Liberty** (city) Pickens County
113	4459	0.4	**Parker** (CDP) Greenville County
113	n/a	0.4	**Saluda** (town) Saluda County
113	n/a	0.4	**Union** (city) Union County
113	n/a	0.4	**Welcome** (CDP) Greenville County
113	n/a	0.4	**Woodruff** (city) Spartanburg County
124	n/a	0.3	**Belton** (city) Anderson County
124	n/a	0.3	**Denmark** (city) Bamberg County
124	n/a	0.3	**Dunean** (CDP) Greenville County
124	n/a	0.3	**East Gaffney** (CDP) Cherokee County
124	n/a	0.3	**Fountain Inn** (city) Greenville County
124	4549	0.3	**Gantt** (CDP) Greenville County
124	n/a	0.3	**Garden City** (CDP) Horry County
124	n/a	0.3	**Hollywood** (town) Charleston County
124	n/a	0.3	**Homeland Park** (CDP) Anderson County
124	n/a	0.3	**Honea Path** (town) Anderson County
124	n/a	0.3	**Lake City** (city) Florence County
124	n/a	0.3	**Laurens** (city) Laurens County
124	n/a	0.3	**North Hartsville** (CDP) Darlington County
124	n/a	0.3	**Springdale** (CDP) Lancaster County
124	n/a	0.3	**Winnsboro** (town) Fairfield County
139	n/a	0.2	**Arial** (CDP) Pickens County
139	n/a	0.2	**Brookdale** (CDP) Orangeburg County
139	n/a	0.2	**Chester** (city) Chester County
139	n/a	0.2	**Clearwater** (CDP) Aiken County
139	n/a	0.2	**Edisto** (CDP) Orangeburg County
139	n/a	0.2	**Gloverville** (CDP) Aiken County
139	n/a	0.2	**Hopkins** (CDP) Richland County
139	n/a	0.2	**Piedmont** (CDP) Anderson County
139	n/a	0.2	**Williston** (town) Barnwell County
148	n/a	0.1	**Williamston** (town) Anderson County
149	n/a	0.0	**Elgin** (CDP) Lancaster County
149	n/a	0.0	**Graniteville** (CDP) Aiken County

Note: The state column ranks the top/bottom 150 places in the state with population of 2,500 or more. The national column ranks the top/bottom places in the country with population of 10,000 or more. Places that are unincorporated were not considered in the rankings. n/a indicates data not available. Please refer to the User Guide for additional information.

Asian Population

Top 150 Places Ranked in *Ascending* Order

State Rank	Nat'l Rank	Percent	Place
1	n/a	0.0	Elgin (CDP) Lancaster County
1	n/a	0.0	Graniteville (CDP) Aiken County
3	n/a	0.1	Williamston (town) Anderson County
4	n/a	0.2	Arial (CDP) Pickens County
4	n/a	0.2	Brookdale (CDP) Orangeburg County
4	n/a	0.2	Chester (city) Chester County
4	n/a	0.2	Clearwater (CDP) Aiken County
4	n/a	0.2	Edisto (CDP) Orangeburg County
4	n/a	0.2	Gloverville (CDP) Aiken County
4	n/a	0.2	Hopkins (CDP) Richland County
4	n/a	0.2	Piedmont (CDP) Anderson County
4	n/a	0.2	Williston (town) Barnwell County
13	n/a	0.3	Belton (city) Anderson County
13	n/a	0.3	Denmark (city) Bamberg County
13	n/a	0.3	Dunean (CDP) Greenville County
13	n/a	0.3	East Gaffney (CDP) Cherokee County
13	n/a	0.3	Fountain Inn (city) Greenville County
13	61	0.3	Gantt (CDP) Greenville County
13	n/a	0.3	Garden City (CDP) Horry County
13	n/a	0.3	Hollywood (town) Charleston County
13	n/a	0.3	Homeland Park (CDP) Anderson County
13	n/a	0.3	Honea Path (town) Anderson County
13	n/a	0.3	Lake City (city) Florence County
13	n/a	0.3	Laurens (city) Laurens County
13	n/a	0.3	North Hartsville (CDP) Darlington County
13	n/a	0.3	Springdale (CDP) Lancaster County
13	n/a	0.3	Winnsboro (town) Fairfield County
28	n/a	0.4	Abbeville (city) Abbeville County
28	n/a	0.4	Belvedere (CDP) Aiken County
28	n/a	0.4	Bennettsville (city) Marlboro County
28	n/a	0.4	Darlington (city) Darlington County
28	n/a	0.4	Edgefield (town) Edgefield County
28	n/a	0.4	Liberty (city) Pickens County
28	108	0.4	Parker (CDP) Greenville County
28	n/a	0.4	Saluda (town) Saluda County
28	n/a	0.4	Union (city) Union County
28	n/a	0.4	Welcome (CDP) Greenville County
28	n/a	0.4	Woodruff (city) Spartanburg County
39	n/a	0.5	Folly Beach (city) Charleston County
39	n/a	0.5	Lugoff (CDP) Kershaw County
39	n/a	0.5	McCormick (town) McCormick County
39	n/a	0.5	Moncks Corner (town) Berkeley County
39	n/a	0.5	Ridgeland (town) Jasper County
44	n/a	0.6	Cheraw (town) Chesterfield County
44	n/a	0.6	Clinton (city) Laurens County
44	n/a	0.6	Clover (town) York County
44	n/a	0.6	Dillon (city) Dillon County
44	321	0.6	Newberry (city) Newberry County
44	n/a	0.6	Pickens (city) Pickens County
44	n/a	0.6	Red Bank (CDP) Lexington County
44	n/a	0.6	Surfside Beach (town) Horry County
44	n/a	0.6	York (city) York County
53	n/a	0.7	Allendale (town) Allendale County
53	n/a	0.7	Batesburg-Leesville (town) Lexington County
53	n/a	0.7	Burnettown (town) Aiken County
53	n/a	0.7	Camden (city) Kershaw County
53	452	0.7	Conway (city) Horry County
53	n/a	0.7	Georgetown (city) Georgetown County
53	n/a	0.7	Pageland (town) Chesterfield County
60	n/a	0.8	Andrews (town) Georgetown County
60	n/a	0.8	Bishopville (city) Lee County
60	629	0.8	Easley (city) Pickens County
60	n/a	0.8	Hartsville (city) Darlington County
60	n/a	0.8	Isle of Palms (city) Charleston County
60	n/a	0.8	Lakewood (CDP) Sumter County
60	n/a	0.8	Lyman (town) Spartanburg County
60	n/a	0.8	Walhalla (city) Oconee County
68	801	0.9	Gaffney (city) Cherokee County
68	801	0.9	Hilton Head Island (town) Beaufort County
68	n/a	0.9	Lancaster (city) Lancaster County
68	n/a	0.9	Little River (CDP) Horry County
68	n/a	0.9	Murrells Inlet (CDP) Georgetown County
68	801	0.9	North Myrtle Beach (city) Horry County
68	n/a	0.9	Seneca (city) Oconee County
75	963	1.0	Anderson (city) Anderson County
75	n/a	1.0	Duncan (town) Spartanburg County
75	963	1.0	Greenwood (city) Greenwood County
75	n/a	1.0	Mullins (city) Marion County
75	n/a	1.0	Sans Souci (CDP) Greenville County
75	n/a	1.0	Saxon (CDP) Spartanburg County
75	n/a	1.0	Walterboro (city) Colleton County
82	n/a	1.1	Bamberg (town) Bamberg County
82	n/a	1.1	Centerville (CDP) Anderson County
82	n/a	1.1	Lake Murray of Richland (CDP) Richland County
82	n/a	1.1	Marion (city) Marion County
82	1097	1.1	North Augusta (city) Aiken County
82	n/a	1.1	Sangaree (CDP) Berkeley County
82	n/a	1.1	Travelers Rest (city) Greenville County
89	1214	1.2	Berea (CDP) Greenville County
89	n/a	1.2	Pendleton (town) Anderson County
89	1214	1.2	Red Hill (CDP) Horry County
89	n/a	1.2	Southern Shops (CDP) Spartanburg County
93	n/a	1.3	Burton (CDP) Beaufort County
93	n/a	1.3	Dalzell (CDP) Sumter County
93	n/a	1.3	Forestbrook (CDP) Horry County
93	1330	1.3	Fort Mill (town) York County
93	n/a	1.3	Laurel Bay (CDP) Beaufort County
93	n/a	1.3	Newport (CDP) York County
93	1330	1.3	Simpsonville (city) Greenville County
100	1428	1.4	Beaufort (city) Beaufort County
100	1428	1.4	Greenville (city) Greenville County
100	n/a	1.4	India Hook (CDP) York County
100	n/a	1.4	Lake Wylie (CDP) York County
104	n/a	1.5	Barnwell (city) Barnwell County
104	1546	1.5	Forest Acres (city) Richland County
104	1546	1.5	Myrtle Beach (city) Horry County
104	1546	1.5	Summerville (town) Dorchester County
108	1648	1.6	Charleston (city) Charleston County
108	1648	1.6	Irmo (town) Richland County
108	1648	1.6	Mount Pleasant (town) Charleston County
108	1648	1.6	Oak Grove (CDP) Lexington County
108	1648	1.6	Sumter (city) Sumter County
113	n/a	1.7	Lesslie (CDP) York County
113	1759	1.7	Orangeburg (city) Orangeburg County
113	1759	1.7	Rock Hill (city) York County
113	n/a	1.7	Springdale (town) Lexington County
113	n/a	1.7	Valley Falls (CDP) Spartanburg County
118	1856	1.8	Florence (city) Florence County
118	n/a	1.8	Northlake (CDP) Anderson County
118	1856	1.8	Socastee (CDP) Horry County
118	1856	1.8	Spartanburg (city) Spartanburg County
118	1856	1.8	West Columbia (city) Lexington County
123	1969	1.9	Aiken (city) Aiken County
123	1969	1.9	Cayce (city) Lexington County
123	1969	1.9	North Charleston (city) Charleston County
126	2059	2.0	Bluffton (town) Beaufort County
126	n/a	2.0	Hampton (town) Hampton County
126	n/a	2.0	Hardeeville (city) Jasper County
126	2059	2.0	Saint Andrews (CDP) Richland County
126	n/a	2.0	Tega Cay (city) York County
131	2192	2.2	Columbia (city) Richland County
131	2192	2.2	Greer (city) Greenville County
131	2192	2.2	Ladson (CDP) Berkeley County
134	n/a	2.4	Kingstree (town) Williamsburg County
134	n/a	2.4	Manning (city) Clarendon County
136	2420	2.5	Port Royal (town) Beaufort County
136	2420	2.5	Taylors (CDP) Greenville County
138	2593	2.8	Dentsville (CDP) Richland County
138	2593	2.8	Seven Oaks (CDP) Lexington County
140	n/a	3.1	Woodfield (CDP) Richland County
141	2807	3.2	Wade Hampton (CDP) Greenville County
142	n/a	3.3	Arcadia (CDP) Spartanburg County
142	n/a	3.3	Central (town) Pickens County
144	2912	3.4	Hanahan (city) Berkeley County
145	2957	3.5	Mauldin (city) Greenville County
146	n/a	3.7	Boiling Springs (CDP) Spartanburg County
146	3039	3.7	Goose Creek (city) Berkeley County
146	3039	3.7	Lexington (town) Lexington County
149	3296	4.4	Five Forks (CDP) Greenville County
150	3941	8.1	Clemson (city) Pickens County

Note: The state column ranks the top/bottom 150 places in the state with population of 2,500 or more. The national column ranks the top/bottom places in the country with population of 10,000 or more. Places that are unincorporated were not considered in the rankings. n/a indicates data not available. Please refer to the User Guide for additional information.

American Indian/Alaska Native Population

Top 150 Places Ranked in *Descending* Order

State Rank	Nat'l Rank	Percent	Place		State Rank	Nat'l Rank	Percent	Place
1	n/a	1.7	**Sans Souci** (CDP) Greenville County		65	2288	0.3	**Florence** (city) Florence County
2	n/a	1.6	**Dillon** (city) Dillon County		65	n/a	0.3	**Folly Beach** (city) Charleston County
3	n/a	1.4	**Saxon** (CDP) Spartanburg County		65	n/a	0.3	**Forestbrook** (CDP) Horry County
4	n/a	1.2	**Ridgeland** (town) Jasper County		65	n/a	0.3	**Fountain Inn** (city) Greenville County
5	n/a	1.0	**Arcadia** (CDP) Spartanburg County		65	n/a	0.3	**Garden City** (CDP) Horry County
6	n/a	0.9	**Laurel Bay** (CDP) Beaufort County		65	2288	0.3	**Greenville** (city) Greenville County
7	n/a	0.8	**Bennettsville** (city) Marlboro County		65	2288	0.3	**Greer** (city) Greenville County
7	n/a	0.8	**Cheraw** (town) Chesterfield County		65	n/a	0.3	**Lake City** (city) Florence County
7	n/a	0.8	**Hardeeville** (city) Jasper County		65	n/a	0.3	**Lake Wylie** (CDP) York County
7	795	0.8	**Ladson** (CDP) Berkeley County		65	n/a	0.3	**Laurens** (city) Laurens County
7	n/a	0.8	**Saluda** (town) Saluda County		65	2288	0.3	**Lexington** (town) Lexington County
7	n/a	0.8	**Sangaree** (CDP) Berkeley County		65	n/a	0.3	**Lyman** (town) Spartanburg County
7	n/a	0.8	**Southern Shops** (CDP) Spartanburg County		65	2288	0.3	**Mauldin** (city) Greenville County
7	795	0.8	**West Columbia** (city) Lexington County		65	n/a	0.3	**Murrells Inlet** (CDP) Georgetown County
7	n/a	0.8	**Williston** (town) Barnwell County		65	2288	0.3	**North Augusta** (city) Aiken County
7	n/a	0.8	**York** (city) York County		65	n/a	0.3	**Pendleton** (town) Anderson County
17	n/a	0.7	**Gloverville** (CDP) Aiken County		65	n/a	0.3	**Piedmont** (CDP) Anderson County
17	n/a	0.7	**Graniteville** (CDP) Aiken County		65	2288	0.3	**Saint Andrews** (CDP) Richland County
17	n/a	0.7	**Lesslie** (CDP) York County		65	n/a	0.3	**Seneca** (city) Oconee County
17	954	0.7	**Myrtle Beach** (city) Horry County		65	2288	0.3	**Seven Oaks** (CDP) Lexington County
17	n/a	0.7	**North Hartsville** (CDP) Darlington County		65	2288	0.3	**Simpsonville** (city) Greenville County
17	n/a	0.7	**Woodfield** (CDP) Richland County		65	n/a	0.3	**Springdale** (town) Lexington County
23	n/a	0.6	**Burnettown** (town) Aiken County		65	2288	0.3	**Sumter** (city) Sumter County
23	n/a	0.6	**Clearwater** (CDP) Aiken County		65	n/a	0.3	**Union** (city) Union County
23	1134	0.6	**Hanahan** (city) Berkeley County		65	n/a	0.3	**Valley Falls** (CDP) Spartanburg County
23	n/a	0.6	**Newport** (CDP) York County		65	n/a	0.3	**Walterboro** (city) Colleton County
23	1134	0.6	**Port Royal** (town) Beaufort County		102	n/a	0.2	**Abbeville** (city) Abbeville County
23	1134	0.6	**Socastee** (CDP) Horry County		102	n/a	0.2	**Allendale** (town) Allendale County
23	n/a	0.6	**Welcome** (CDP) Greenville County		102	n/a	0.2	**Barnwell** (city) Barnwell County
30	n/a	0.5	**Andrews** (town) Georgetown County		102	n/a	0.2	**Belton** (city) Anderson County
30	1413	0.5	**Berea** (CDP) Greenville County		102	n/a	0.2	**Camden** (city) Kershaw County
30	n/a	0.5	**Clover** (town) York County		102	n/a	0.2	**Centerville** (CDP) Anderson County
30	n/a	0.5	**Dalzell** (CDP) Sumter County		102	n/a	0.2	**Central** (town) Pickens County
30	1413	0.5	**Goose Creek** (city) Berkeley County		102	3031	0.2	**Charleston** (city) Charleston County
30	n/a	0.5	**Hampton** (town) Hampton County		102	n/a	0.2	**Clinton** (city) Laurens County
30	n/a	0.5	**Little River** (CDP) Horry County		102	3031	0.2	**Conway** (city) Horry County
30	n/a	0.5	**Moncks Corner** (town) Berkeley County		102	n/a	0.2	**Darlington** (city) Darlington County
30	1413	0.5	**North Charleston** (city) Charleston County		102	n/a	0.2	**Duncan** (town) Spartanburg County
30	1413	0.5	**North Myrtle Beach** (city) Horry County		102	3031	0.2	**Easley** (city) Pickens County
30	n/a	0.5	**Northlake** (CDP) Anderson County		102	n/a	0.2	**Edisto** (CDP) Orangeburg County
30	n/a	0.5	**Pageland** (town) Chesterfield County		102	3031	0.2	**Five Forks** (CDP) Greenville County
30	1413	0.5	**Parker** (CDP) Greenville County		102	3031	0.2	**Forest Acres** (city) Richland County
30	n/a	0.5	**Red Bank** (CDP) Lexington County		102	3031	0.2	**Gaffney** (city) Cherokee County
30	1413	0.5	**Red Hill** (CDP) Horry County		102	n/a	0.2	**Georgetown** (city) Georgetown County
30	1413	0.5	**Rock Hill** (city) York County		102	n/a	0.2	**Hartsville** (city) Darlington County
46	n/a	0.4	**Aiken** (city) Aiken County		102	3031	0.2	**Hilton Head Island** (town) Beaufort County
46	n/a	0.4	**Arial** (CDP) Pickens County		102	n/a	0.2	**Hollywood** (town) Charleston County
46	n/a	0.4	**Bamberg** (town) Bamberg County		102	n/a	0.2	**Homeland Park** (CDP) Anderson County
46	n/a	0.4	**Burton** (CDP) Beaufort County		102	n/a	0.2	**Honea Path** (town) Anderson County
46	1783	0.4	**Cayce** (city) Lexington County		102	n/a	0.2	**Hopkins** (CDP) Richland County
46	n/a	0.4	**East Gaffney** (CDP) Cherokee County		102	n/a	0.2	**Lake Murray of Richland** (CDP) Richland County
46	1783	0.4	**Fort Mill** (town) York County		102	n/a	0.2	**Lakewood** (CDP) Sumter County
46	1783	0.4	**Gantt** (CDP) Greenville County		102	n/a	0.2	**Lancaster** (city) Lancaster County
46	1783	0.4	**Greenwood** (city) Greenwood County		102	n/a	0.2	**Lugoff** (CDP) Kershaw County
46	n/a	0.4	**India Hook** (CDP) York County		102	n/a	0.2	**Marion** (city) Marion County
46	1783	0.4	**Irmo** (town) Richland County		102	n/a	0.2	**McCormick** (town) McCormick County
46	n/a	0.4	**Mullins** (city) Marion County		102	3031	0.2	**Mount Pleasant** (town) Charleston County
46	1783	0.4	**Newberry** (city) Newberry County		102	3031	0.2	**Orangeburg** (city) Orangeburg County
46	1783	0.4	**Oak Grove** (CDP) Lexington County		102	n/a	0.2	**Pickens** (city) Pickens County
46	n/a	0.4	**Springdale** (CDP) Lancaster County		102	3031	0.2	**Spartanburg** (city) Spartanburg County
46	1783	0.4	**Summerville** (town) Dorchester County		102	3031	0.2	**Taylors** (CDP) Greenville County
46	n/a	0.4	**Surfside Beach** (town) Horry County		102	n/a	0.2	**Tega Cay** (city) York County
46	1783	0.4	**Wade Hampton** (CDP) Greenville County		102	n/a	0.2	**Travelers Rest** (city) Greenville County
46	n/a	0.4	**Walhalla** (city) Oconee County		102	n/a	0.2	**Winnsboro** (town) Fairfield County
65	2288	0.3	**Anderson** (city) Anderson County		140	n/a	0.1	**Batesburg-Leesville** (town) Lexington County
65	2288	0.3	**Beaufort** (city) Beaufort County		140	n/a	0.1	**Brookdale** (CDP) Orangeburg County
65	n/a	0.3	**Belvedere** (CDP) Aiken County		140	3935	0.1	**Clemson** (city) Pickens County
65	n/a	0.3	**Bishopville** (city) Lee County		140	n/a	0.1	**Denmark** (city) Bamberg County
65	2288	0.3	**Bluffton** (town) Beaufort County		140	n/a	0.1	**Elgin** (CDP) Lancaster County
65	n/a	0.3	**Boiling Springs** (CDP) Spartanburg County		140	n/a	0.1	**Isle of Palms** (city) Charleston County
65	n/a	0.3	**Chester** (city) Chester County		140	n/a	0.1	**Kingstree** (town) Williamsburg County
65	2288	0.3	**Columbia** (city) Richland County		140	n/a	0.1	**Liberty** (city) Pickens County
65	2288	0.3	**Dentsville** (CDP) Richland County		140	n/a	0.1	**Manning** (city) Clarendon County
65	n/a	0.3	**Dunean** (CDP) Greenville County		140	n/a	0.1	**Williamston** (town) Anderson County
65	n/a	0.3	**Edgefield** (town) Edgefield County		140	n/a	0.1	**Woodruff** (city) Spartanburg County

Note: The state column ranks the top/bottom 150 places in the state with population of 2,500 or more. The national column ranks the top/bottom places in the country with population of 10,000 or more. Places that are unincorporated were not considered in the rankings. n/a indicates data not available. Please refer to the User Guide for additional information.

American Indian/Alaska Native Population

Top 150 Places Ranked in *Ascending* Order

State Rank	Nat'l Rank	Percent	Place
1	n/a	0.1	Batesburg-Leesville (town) Lexington County
1	n/a	0.1	Brookdale (CDP) Orangeburg County
1	61	0.1	Clemson (city) Pickens County
1	n/a	0.1	Denmark (city) Bamberg County
1	n/a	0.1	Elgin (CDP) Lancaster County
1	n/a	0.1	Isle of Palms (city) Charleston County
1	n/a	0.1	Kingstree (town) Williamsburg County
1	n/a	0.1	Liberty (city) Pickens County
1	n/a	0.1	Manning (city) Clarendon County
1	n/a	0.1	Williamston (town) Anderson County
1	n/a	0.1	Woodruff (city) Spartanburg County
12	n/a	0.2	Abbeville (city) Abbeville County
12	n/a	0.2	Allendale (town) Allendale County
12	n/a	0.2	Barnwell (city) Barnwell County
12	n/a	0.2	Belton (city) Anderson County
12	n/a	0.2	Camden (city) Kershaw County
12	n/a	0.2	Centerville (CDP) Anderson County
12	n/a	0.2	Central (town) Pickens County
12	722	0.2	Charleston (city) Charleston County
12	n/a	0.2	Clinton (city) Laurens County
12	722	0.2	Conway (city) Horry County
12	n/a	0.2	Darlington (city) Darlington County
12	n/a	0.2	Duncan (town) Spartanburg County
12	722	0.2	Easley (city) Pickens County
12	n/a	0.2	Edisto (CDP) Orangeburg County
12	722	0.2	Five Forks (CDP) Greenville County
12	722	0.2	Forest Acres (city) Richland County
12	722	0.2	Gaffney (city) Cherokee County
12	n/a	0.2	Georgetown (city) Georgetown County
12	n/a	0.2	Hartsville (city) Darlington County
12	722	0.2	Hilton Head Island (town) Beaufort County
12	n/a	0.2	Hollywood (town) Charleston County
12	n/a	0.2	Homeland Park (CDP) Anderson County
12	n/a	0.2	Honea Path (town) Anderson County
12	n/a	0.2	Hopkins (CDP) Richland County
12	n/a	0.2	Lake Murray of Richland (CDP) Richland County
12	n/a	0.2	Lakewood (CDP) Sumter County
12	n/a	0.2	Lancaster (city) Lancaster County
12	n/a	0.2	Lugoff (CDP) Kershaw County
12	n/a	0.2	Marion (city) Marion County
12	n/a	0.2	McCormick (town) McCormick County
12	722	0.2	Mount Pleasant (town) Charleston County
12	722	0.2	Orangeburg (city) Orangeburg County
12	n/a	0.2	Pickens (city) Pickens County
12	722	0.2	Spartanburg (city) Spartanburg County
12	722	0.2	Taylors (CDP) Greenville County
12	n/a	0.2	Tega Cay (city) York County
12	n/a	0.2	Travelers Rest (city) Greenville County
12	n/a	0.2	Winnsboro (town) Fairfield County
50	1626	0.3	Anderson (city) Anderson County
50	1626	0.3	Beaufort (city) Beaufort County
50	n/a	0.3	Belvedere (CDP) Aiken County
50	n/a	0.3	Bishopville (city) Lee County
50	1626	0.3	Bluffton (town) Beaufort County
50	n/a	0.3	Boiling Springs (CDP) Spartanburg County
50	n/a	0.3	Chester (city) Chester County
50	1626	0.3	Columbia (city) Richland County
50	1626	0.3	Dentsville (CDP) Richland County
50	n/a	0.3	Dunean (CDP) Greenville County
50	n/a	0.3	Edgefield (town) Edgefield County
50	1626	0.3	Florence (city) Florence County
50	n/a	0.3	Folly Beach (city) Charleston County
50	n/a	0.3	Forestbrook (CDP) Horry County
50	n/a	0.3	Fountain Inn (city) Greenville County
50	n/a	0.3	Garden City (CDP) Horry County
50	1626	0.3	Greenville (city) Greenville County
50	1626	0.3	Greer (city) Greenville County
50	n/a	0.3	Lake City (city) Florence County
50	n/a	0.3	Lake Wylie (CDP) York County
50	n/a	0.3	Laurens (city) Laurens County
50	1626	0.3	Lexington (town) Lexington County
50	n/a	0.3	Lyman (town) Spartanburg County
50	1626	0.3	Mauldin (city) Greenville County
50	n/a	0.3	Murrells Inlet (CDP) Georgetown County
50	1626	0.3	North Augusta (city) Aiken County
50	n/a	0.3	Pendleton (town) Anderson County
50	n/a	0.3	Piedmont (CDP) Anderson County
50	1626	0.3	Saint Andrews (CDP) Richland County
50	n/a	0.3	Seneca (city) Oconee County
50	1626	0.3	Seven Oaks (CDP) Lexington County
50	1626	0.3	Simpsonville (city) Greenville County
50	n/a	0.3	Springdale (town) Lexington County
50	1626	0.3	Sumter (city) Sumter County
50	n/a	0.3	Union (city) Union County
50	n/a	0.3	Valley Falls (CDP) Spartanburg County
50	n/a	0.3	Walterboro (city) Colleton County
87	2369	0.4	Aiken (city) Aiken County
87	n/a	0.4	Arial (CDP) Pickens County
87	n/a	0.4	Bamberg (town) Bamberg County
87	n/a	0.4	Burton (CDP) Beaufort County
87	2369	0.4	Cayce (city) Lexington County
87	n/a	0.4	East Gaffney (CDP) Cherokee County
87	2369	0.4	Fort Mill (town) York County
87	2369	0.4	Gantt (CDP) Greenville County
87	2369	0.4	Greenwood (city) Greenwood County
87	n/a	0.4	India Hook (CDP) York County
87	2369	0.4	Irmo (town) Richland County
87	n/a	0.4	Mullins (city) Marion County
87	2369	0.4	Newberry (city) Newberry County
87	2369	0.4	Oak Grove (CDP) Lexington County
87	n/a	0.4	Springdale (CDP) Lancaster County
87	2369	0.4	Summerville (town) Dorchester County
87	n/a	0.4	Surfside Beach (town) Horry County
87	2369	0.4	Wade Hampton (CDP) Greenville County
87	n/a	0.4	Walhalla (city) Oconee County
106	n/a	0.5	Andrews (town) Georgetown County
106	2874	0.5	Berea (CDP) Greenville County
106	n/a	0.5	Clover (town) York County
106	n/a	0.5	Dalzell (CDP) Sumter County
106	2874	0.5	Goose Creek (city) Berkeley County
106	n/a	0.5	Hampton (town) Hampton County
106	n/a	0.5	Little River (CDP) Horry County
106	n/a	0.5	Moncks Corner (town) Berkeley County
106	2874	0.5	North Charleston (city) Charleston County
106	2874	0.5	North Myrtle Beach (city) Horry County
106	n/a	0.5	Northlake (CDP) Anderson County
106	n/a	0.5	Pageland (town) Chesterfield County
106	2874	0.5	Parker (CDP) Greenville County
106	n/a	0.5	Red Bank (CDP) Lexington County
106	n/a	0.5	Red Hill (CDP) Horry County
106	2874	0.5	Rock Hill (city) York County
122	n/a	0.6	Burnettown (town) Aiken County
122	n/a	0.6	Clearwater (CDP) Aiken County
122	3244	0.6	Hanahan (city) Berkeley County
122	n/a	0.6	Newport (CDP) York County
122	3244	0.6	Port Royal (town) Beaufort County
122	3244	0.6	Socastee (CDP) Horry County
122	n/a	0.6	Welcome (CDP) Greenville County
129	n/a	0.7	Gloverville (CDP) Aiken County
129	n/a	0.7	Graniteville (CDP) Aiken County
129	n/a	0.7	Lesslie (CDP) York County
129	3523	0.7	Myrtle Beach (city) Horry County
129	n/a	0.7	North Hartsville (CDP) Darlington County
129	n/a	0.7	Woodfield (CDP) Richland County
135	n/a	0.8	Bennettsville (city) Marlboro County
135	n/a	0.8	Cheraw (town) Chesterfield County
135	n/a	0.8	Hardeeville (city) Jasper County
135	3703	0.8	Ladson (CDP) Berkeley County
135	n/a	0.8	Saluda (town) Saluda County
135	n/a	0.8	Sangaree (CDP) Berkeley County
135	n/a	0.8	Southern Shops (CDP) Spartanburg County
135	3703	0.8	West Columbia (city) Lexington County
135	n/a	0.8	Williston (town) Barnwell County
135	n/a	0.8	York (city) York County
145	n/a	0.9	Laurel Bay (CDP) Beaufort County
146	n/a	1.0	Arcadia (CDP) Spartanburg County
147	n/a	1.2	Ridgeland (town) Jasper County
148	n/a	1.4	Saxon (CDP) Spartanburg County
149	n/a	1.6	Dillon (city) Dillon County
150	n/a	1.7	Sans Souci (CDP) Greenville County

Note: The state column ranks the top/bottom 150 places in the state with population of 2,500 or more. The national column ranks the top/bottom places in the country with population of 10,000 or more. Places that are unincorporated were not considered in the rankings. n/a indicates data not available. Please refer to the User Guide for additional information.

Native Hawaiian/Other Pacific Islander Population

Top 150 Places Ranked in *Descending* Order

State Rank	Nat'l Rank	Percent	Place
1	n/a	0.9	**Saluda** (town) Saluda County
2	374	0.3	**Myrtle Beach** (city) Horry County
2	n/a	0.3	**Woodfield** (CDP) Richland County
4	n/a	0.2	**Arcadia** (CDP) Spartanburg County
4	n/a	0.2	**Burton** (CDP) Beaufort County
4	n/a	0.2	**Dalzell** (CDP) Sumter County
4	n/a	0.2	**Fountain Inn** (city) Greenville County
4	n/a	0.2	**McCormick** (town) McCormick County
4	510	0.2	**North Charleston** (city) Charleston County
4	n/a	0.2	**Sangaree** (CDP) Berkeley County
4	510	0.2	**Seven Oaks** (CDP) Lexington County
4	510	0.2	**Socastee** (CDP) Horry County
13	820	0.1	**Aiken** (city) Aiken County
13	n/a	0.1	**Allendale** (town) Allendale County
13	n/a	0.1	**Barnwell** (city) Barnwell County
13	820	0.1	**Beaufort** (city) Beaufort County
13	n/a	0.1	**Belvedere** (CDP) Aiken County
13	820	0.1	**Cayce** (city) Lexington County
13	820	0.1	**Charleston** (city) Charleston County
13	n/a	0.1	**Chester** (city) Chester County
13	820	0.1	**Columbia** (city) Richland County
13	n/a	0.1	**Denmark** (city) Bamberg County
13	820	0.1	**Dentsville** (CDP) Richland County
13	n/a	0.1	**East Gaffney** (CDP) Cherokee County
13	n/a	0.1	**Edgefield** (town) Edgefield County
13	n/a	0.1	**Folly Beach** (city) Charleston County
13	820	0.1	**Forest Acres** (city) Richland County
13	n/a	0.1	**Forestbrook** (CDP) Horry County
13	820	0.1	**Gaffney** (city) Cherokee County
13	n/a	0.1	**Garden City** (CDP) Horry County
13	n/a	0.1	**Georgetown** (city) Georgetown County
13	820	0.1	**Goose Creek** (city) Berkeley County
13	n/a	0.1	**Graniteville** (CDP) Aiken County
13	820	0.1	**Greenville** (city) Greenville County
13	820	0.1	**Greenwood** (city) Greenwood County
13	820	0.1	**Greer** (city) Greenville County
13	820	0.1	**Hanahan** (city) Berkeley County
13	n/a	0.1	**Hartsville** (city) Darlington County
13	820	0.1	**Hilton Head Island** (town) Beaufort County
13	n/a	0.1	**Hollywood** (town) Charleston County
13	n/a	0.1	**India Hook** (CDP) York County
13	820	0.1	**Ladson** (CDP) Berkeley County
13	n/a	0.1	**Lake Wylie** (CDP) York County
13	n/a	0.1	**Laurel Bay** (CDP) Beaufort County
13	n/a	0.1	**Lugoff** (CDP) Kershaw County
13	820	0.1	**Mauldin** (city) Greenville County
13	820	0.1	**Newberry** (city) Newberry County
13	820	0.1	**North Myrtle Beach** (city) Horry County
13	820	0.1	**Orangeburg** (city) Orangeburg County
13	n/a	0.1	**Pendleton** (town) Anderson County
13	820	0.1	**Port Royal** (town) Beaufort County
13	820	0.1	**Red Hill** (CDP) Horry County
13	n/a	0.1	**Ridgeland** (town) Jasper County
13	820	0.1	**Rock Hill** (city) York County
13	820	0.1	**Saint Andrews** (CDP) Richland County
13	n/a	0.1	**Sans Souci** (CDP) Greenville County
13	820	0.1	**Simpsonville** (city) Greenville County
13	820	0.1	**Summerville** (town) Dorchester County
13	820	0.1	**Sumter** (city) Sumter County
13	820	0.1	**Taylors** (CDP) Greenville County
13	n/a	0.1	**Tega Cay** (city) York County
13	820	0.1	**Wade Hampton** (CDP) Greenville County
63	n/a	0.0	**Abbeville** (city) Abbeville County
63	2061	0.0	**Anderson** (city) Anderson County
63	n/a	0.0	**Andrews** (town) Georgetown County
63	n/a	0.0	**Arial** (CDP) Pickens County
63	n/a	0.0	**Bamberg** (town) Bamberg County
63	n/a	0.0	**Batesburg-Leesville** (town) Lexington County
63	n/a	0.0	**Belton** (city) Anderson County
63	n/a	0.0	**Bennettsville** (city) Marlboro County
63	2061	0.0	**Berea** (CDP) Greenville County
63	n/a	0.0	**Bishopville** (city) Lee County
63	2061	0.0	**Bluffton** (town) Beaufort County
63	n/a	0.0	**Boiling Springs** (CDP) Spartanburg County
63	n/a	0.0	**Brookdale** (CDP) Orangeburg County
63	n/a	0.0	**Burnettown** (town) Aiken County
63	n/a	0.0	**Camden** (city) Kershaw County
63	n/a	0.0	**Centerville** (CDP) Anderson County
63	n/a	0.0	**Central** (town) Pickens County
63	n/a	0.0	**Cheraw** (town) Chesterfield County
63	n/a	0.0	**Clearwater** (CDP) Aiken County
63	2061	0.0	**Clemson** (city) Pickens County
63	n/a	0.0	**Clinton** (city) Laurens County
63	n/a	0.0	**Clover** (town) York County
63	2061	0.0	**Conway** (city) Horry County
63	n/a	0.0	**Darlington** (city) Darlington County
63	n/a	0.0	**Dillon** (city) Dillon County
63	n/a	0.0	**Duncan** (town) Spartanburg County
63	n/a	0.0	**Dunean** (CDP) Greenville County
63	2061	0.0	**Easley** (city) Pickens County
63	n/a	0.0	**Edisto** (CDP) Orangeburg County
63	n/a	0.0	**Elgin** (CDP) Lancaster County
63	2061	0.0	**Five Forks** (CDP) Greenville County
63	2061	0.0	**Florence** (city) Florence County
63	2061	0.0	**Fort Mill** (town) York County
63	2061	0.0	**Gantt** (CDP) Greenville County
63	n/a	0.0	**Gloverville** (CDP) Aiken County
63	n/a	0.0	**Hampton** (town) Hampton County
63	n/a	0.0	**Hardeeville** (city) Jasper County
63	n/a	0.0	**Homeland Park** (CDP) Anderson County
63	n/a	0.0	**Honea Path** (town) Anderson County
63	n/a	0.0	**Hopkins** (CDP) Richland County
63	2061	0.0	**Irmo** (town) Richland County
63	n/a	0.0	**Isle of Palms** (city) Charleston County
63	n/a	0.0	**Kingstree** (town) Williamsburg County
63	n/a	0.0	**Lake City** (city) Florence County
63	n/a	0.0	**Lake Murray of Richland** (CDP) Richland County
63	n/a	0.0	**Lakewood** (CDP) Sumter County
63	n/a	0.0	**Lancaster** (city) Lancaster County
63	n/a	0.0	**Laurens** (city) Laurens County
63	n/a	0.0	**Lesslie** (CDP) York County
63	2061	0.0	**Lexington** (town) Lexington County
63	n/a	0.0	**Liberty** (city) Pickens County
63	n/a	0.0	**Little River** (CDP) Horry County
63	n/a	0.0	**Lyman** (town) Spartanburg County
63	n/a	0.0	**Manning** (city) Clarendon County
63	n/a	0.0	**Marion** (city) Marion County
63	n/a	0.0	**Moncks Corner** (town) Berkeley County
63	2061	0.0	**Mount Pleasant** (town) Charleston County
63	n/a	0.0	**Mullins** (city) Marion County
63	n/a	0.0	**Murrells Inlet** (CDP) Georgetown County
63	n/a	0.0	**Newport** (CDP) York County
63	2061	0.0	**North Augusta** (city) Aiken County
63	n/a	0.0	**North Hartsville** (CDP) Darlington County
63	n/a	0.0	**Northlake** (CDP) Anderson County
63	2061	0.0	**Oak Grove** (CDP) Lexington County
63	n/a	0.0	**Pageland** (town) Chesterfield County
63	2061	0.0	**Parker** (CDP) Greenville County
63	n/a	0.0	**Pickens** (city) Pickens County
63	n/a	0.0	**Piedmont** (CDP) Anderson County
63	n/a	0.0	**Red Bank** (CDP) Lexington County
63	n/a	0.0	**Saxon** (CDP) Spartanburg County
63	n/a	0.0	**Seneca** (city) Oconee County
63	n/a	0.0	**Southern Shops** (CDP) Spartanburg County
63	2061	0.0	**Spartanburg** (city) Spartanburg County
63	n/a	0.0	**Springdale** (CDP) Lancaster County
63	n/a	0.0	**Springdale** (town) Lexington County
63	n/a	0.0	**Surfside Beach** (town) Horry County
63	n/a	0.0	**Travelers Rest** (city) Greenville County
63	n/a	0.0	**Union** (city) Union County
63	n/a	0.0	**Valley Falls** (CDP) Spartanburg County
63	n/a	0.0	**Walhalla** (city) Oconee County
63	n/a	0.0	**Walterboro** (city) Colleton County
63	n/a	0.0	**Welcome** (CDP) Greenville County
63	2061	0.0	**West Columbia** (city) Lexington County
63	n/a	0.0	**Williamston** (town) Anderson County
63	n/a	0.0	**Williston** (town) Barnwell County
63	n/a	0.0	**Winnsboro** (town) Fairfield County
63	n/a	0.0	**Woodruff** (city) Spartanburg County
63	n/a	0.0	**York** (city) York County

Note: The state column ranks the top/bottom 150 places in the state with population of 2,500 or more. The national column ranks the top/bottom places in the country with population of 10,000 or more. Places that are unincorporated were not considered in the rankings. n/a indicates data not available. Please refer to the User Guide for additional information.

Two or More Races

Top 150 Places Ranked in *Descending* Order

State Rank	Nat'l Rank	Percent	Place	State Rank	Nat'l Rank	Percent	Place
1	n/a	3.8	**Laurel Bay** (CDP) Beaufort County	68	3250	1.8	**Newberry** (city) Newberry County
1	n/a	3.8	**Woodfield** (CDP) Richland County	68	n/a	1.8	**Newport** (CDP) York County
3	1030	3.7	**Port Royal** (town) Beaufort County	68	n/a	1.8	**Northlake** (CDP) Anderson County
4	1109	3.6	**Goose Creek** (city) Berkeley County	68	3250	1.8	**Oak Grove** (CDP) Lexington County
4	1109	3.6	**Ladson** (CDP) Berkeley County	68	n/a	1.8	**Saluda** (town) Saluda County
6	n/a	3.4	**Arcadia** (CDP) Spartanburg County	68	3250	1.8	**Spartanburg** (city) Spartanburg County
7	n/a	3.2	**Duncan** (town) Spartanburg County	68	n/a	1.8	**Welcome** (CDP) Greenville County
8	n/a	3.0	**Gloverville** (CDP) Aiken County	83	n/a	1.7	**Barnwell** (city) Barnwell County
8	n/a	3.0	**Woodruff** (city) Spartanburg County	83	n/a	1.7	**Chester** (city) Chester County
10	1717	2.9	**Bluffton** (town) Beaufort County	83	n/a	1.7	**Lesslie** (CDP) York County
10	1717	2.9	**Hanahan** (city) Berkeley County	83	n/a	1.7	**Piedmont** (CDP) Anderson County
10	1717	2.9	**Socastee** (CDP) Horry County	87	n/a	1.6	**Arial** (CDP) Pickens County
10	n/a	2.9	**Southern Shops** (CDP) Spartanburg County	87	3607	1.6	**Clemson** (city) Pickens County
10	1717	2.9	**Summerville** (town) Dorchester County	87	3607	1.6	**Gaffney** (city) Cherokee County
15	n/a	2.8	**Sangaree** (CDP) Berkeley County	87	n/a	1.6	**Springdale** (town) Lexington County
15	1828	2.8	**Seven Oaks** (CDP) Lexington County	87	n/a	1.6	**Travelers Rest** (city) Greenville County
17	1935	2.7	**Berea** (CDP) Greenville County	92	n/a	1.5	**Abbeville** (city) Abbeville County
17	n/a	2.7	**Burton** (CDP) Beaufort County	92	3796	1.5	**Aiken** (city) Aiken County
17	n/a	2.7	**Dalzell** (CDP) Sumter County	92	n/a	1.5	**Boiling Springs** (CDP) Spartanburg County
17	n/a	2.7	**Hardeeville** (city) Jasper County	92	3796	1.5	**Charleston** (city) Charleston County
17	1935	2.7	**Myrtle Beach** (city) Horry County	92	n/a	1.5	**Clinton** (city) Laurens County
17	n/a	2.7	**Sans Souci** (CDP) Greenville County	92	3796	1.5	**Conway** (city) Horry County
23	2062	2.6	**Beaufort** (city) Beaufort County	92	3796	1.5	**Five Forks** (CDP) Greenville County
23	n/a	2.6	**Belvedere** (CDP) Aiken County	92	n/a	1.5	**Hopkins** (CDP) Richland County
23	2062	2.6	**Parker** (CDP) Greenville County	92	3796	1.5	**Lexington** (town) Lexington County
23	n/a	2.6	**Pendleton** (town) Anderson County	92	n/a	1.5	**Walterboro** (city) Colleton County
23	n/a	2.6	**Springdale** (CDP) Lancaster County	102	n/a	1.4	**Allendale** (town) Allendale County
28	2209	2.5	**Dentsville** (CDP) Richland County	102	n/a	1.4	**Garden City** (CDP) Horry County
28	n/a	2.5	**Dunean** (CDP) Greenville County	102	3933	1.4	**Greenwood** (city) Greenwood County
28	n/a	2.5	**Forestbrook** (CDP) Horry County	102	n/a	1.4	**Lake Wylie** (CDP) York County
28	n/a	2.5	**Graniteville** (CDP) Aiken County	102	n/a	1.4	**Lugoff** (CDP) Kershaw County
28	2209	2.5	**Irmo** (town) Richland County	102	n/a	1.4	**Marion** (city) Marion County
28	2209	2.5	**North Charleston** (city) Charleston County	102	n/a	1.4	**Mullins** (city) Marion County
28	n/a	2.5	**Saxon** (CDP) Spartanburg County	102	n/a	1.4	**North Hartsville** (CDP) Darlington County
35	n/a	2.4	**Edgefield** (town) Edgefield County	102	3933	1.4	**North Myrtle Beach** (city) Horry County
35	n/a	2.4	**Honea Path** (town) Anderson County	102	n/a	1.4	**Tega Cay** (city) York County
37	n/a	2.3	**Homeland Park** (CDP) Anderson County	102	n/a	1.4	**Union** (city) Union County
37	n/a	2.3	**Pickens** (city) Pickens County	102	n/a	1.4	**Valley Falls** (CDP) Spartanburg County
37	n/a	2.3	**Seneca** (city) Oconee County	102	n/a	1.4	**Williston** (town) Barnwell County
37	2489	2.3	**Simpsonville** (city) Greenville County	115	n/a	1.3	**Bamberg** (town) Bamberg County
37	2489	2.3	**West Columbia** (city) Lexington County	115	n/a	1.3	**Centerville** (CDP) Anderson County
42	2642	2.2	**Mauldin** (city) Greenville County	115	4108	1.3	**Florence** (city) Florence County
42	2642	2.2	**Red Hill** (CDP) Horry County	115	n/a	1.3	**Georgetown** (city) Georgetown County
42	2642	2.2	**Saint Andrews** (CDP) Richland County	115	n/a	1.3	**Little River** (CDP) Horry County
42	n/a	2.2	**Walhalla** (city) Oconee County	115	n/a	1.3	**Surfside Beach** (town) Horry County
46	2791	2.1	**Anderson** (city) Anderson County	115	n/a	1.3	**Williamston** (town) Anderson County
46	n/a	2.1	**Burnettown** (town) Aiken County	122	n/a	1.2	**Batesburg-Leesville** (town) Lexington County
46	2791	2.1	**Cayce** (city) Lexington County	122	n/a	1.2	**Bennettsville** (city) Marlboro County
46	2791	2.1	**Fort Mill** (town) York County	122	n/a	1.2	**Dillon** (city) Dillon County
46	2791	2.1	**Greer** (city) Greenville County	122	4242	1.2	**Hilton Head Island** (town) Beaufort County
46	n/a	2.1	**India Hook** (CDP) York County	122	n/a	1.2	**Laurens** (city) Laurens County
46	n/a	2.1	**Liberty** (city) Pickens County	127	n/a	1.1	**Camden** (city) Kershaw County
46	n/a	2.1	**Pageland** (town) Chesterfield County	127	n/a	1.1	**Lancaster** (city) Lancaster County
46	2791	2.1	**Rock Hill** (city) York County	127	4362	1.1	**Mount Pleasant** (town) Charleston County
46	2791	2.1	**Sumter** (city) Sumter County	127	4362	1.1	**Orangeburg** (city) Orangeburg County
46	2791	2.1	**Wade Hampton** (CDP) Greenville County	127	n/a	1.1	**Winnsboro** (town) Fairfield County
46	n/a	2.1	**York** (city) York County	132	n/a	1.0	**Bishopville** (city) Lee County
58	2950	2.0	**Columbia** (city) Richland County	132	n/a	1.0	**Hartsville** (city) Darlington County
58	n/a	2.0	**Fountain Inn** (city) Greenville County	132	n/a	1.0	**Manning** (city) Clarendon County
58	n/a	2.0	**Moncks Corner** (town) Berkeley County	132	n/a	1.0	**Ridgeland** (town) Jasper County
58	2950	2.0	**North Augusta** (city) Aiken County	136	n/a	0.9	**Elgin** (CDP) Lancaster County
58	2950	2.0	**Taylors** (CDP) Greenville County	136	n/a	0.9	**Hampton** (town) Hampton County
63	n/a	1.9	**Central** (town) Pickens County	136	n/a	0.9	**Lake City** (city) Florence County
63	n/a	1.9	**Clearwater** (CDP) Aiken County	136	n/a	0.9	**Lake Murray of Richland** (CDP) Richland County
63	n/a	1.9	**Clover** (town) York County	136	n/a	0.9	**McCormick** (town) McCormick County
63	3098	1.9	**Forest Acres** (city) Richland County	141	n/a	0.8	**Andrews** (town) Georgetown County
63	n/a	1.9	**Red Bank** (CDP) Lexington County	141	n/a	0.8	**Brookdale** (CDP) Orangeburg County
68	n/a	1.8	**Belton** (city) Anderson County	141	n/a	0.8	**Folly Beach** (city) Charleston County
68	n/a	1.8	**Cheraw** (town) Chesterfield County	141	n/a	0.8	**Hollywood** (town) Charleston County
68	3250	1.8	**Easley** (city) Pickens County	141	n/a	0.8	**Murrells Inlet** (CDP) Georgetown County
68	n/a	1.8	**East Gaffney** (CDP) Cherokee County	146	n/a	0.7	**Darlington** (city) Darlington County
68	3250	1.8	**Gantt** (CDP) Greenville County	146	n/a	0.7	**Edisto** (CDP) Orangeburg County
68	3250	1.8	**Greenville** (city) Greenville County	146	n/a	0.7	**Isle of Palms** (city) Charleston County
68	n/a	1.8	**Lakewood** (CDP) Sumter County	149	n/a	0.5	**Denmark** (city) Bamberg County
68	n/a	1.8	**Lyman** (town) Spartanburg County	149	n/a	0.5	**Kingstree** (town) Williamsburg County

Note: The state column ranks the top/bottom 150 places in the state with population of 2,500 or more. The national column ranks the top/bottom places in the country with population of 10,000 or more. Places that are unincorporated were not considered in the rankings. n/a indicates data not available. Please refer to the User Guide for additional information.

Two or More Races

Top 150 Places Ranked in *Ascending* Order

State Rank	Nat'l Rank	Percent	Place
1	n/a	0.5	**Denmark** (city) Bamberg County
1	n/a	0.5	**Kingstree** (town) Williamsburg County
3	n/a	0.7	**Darlington** (city) Darlington County
3	n/a	0.7	**Edisto** (CDP) Orangeburg County
3	n/a	0.7	**Isle of Palms** (city) Charleston County
6	n/a	0.8	**Andrews** (town) Georgetown County
6	n/a	0.8	**Brookdale** (CDP) Orangeburg County
6	n/a	0.8	**Folly Beach** (city) Charleston County
6	n/a	0.8	**Hollywood** (town) Charleston County
6	n/a	0.8	**Murrells Inlet** (CDP) Georgetown County
11	n/a	0.9	**Elgin** (CDP) Lancaster County
11	n/a	0.9	**Hampton** (town) Hampton County
11	n/a	0.9	**Lake City** (city) Florence County
11	n/a	0.9	**Lake Murray of Richland** (CDP) Richland County
11	n/a	0.9	**McCormick** (town) McCormick County
16	n/a	1.0	**Bishopville** (city) Lee County
16	n/a	1.0	**Hartsville** (city) Darlington County
16	n/a	1.0	**Manning** (city) Clarendon County
16	n/a	1.0	**Ridgeland** (town) Jasper County
20	n/a	1.1	**Camden** (city) Kershaw County
20	n/a	1.1	**Lancaster** (city) Lancaster County
20	192	1.1	**Mount Pleasant** (town) Charleston County
20	192	1.1	**Orangeburg** (city) Orangeburg County
20	n/a	1.1	**Winnsboro** (town) Fairfield County
25	n/a	1.2	**Batesburg-Leesville** (town) Lexington County
25	n/a	1.2	**Bennettsville** (city) Marlboro County
25	n/a	1.2	**Dillon** (city) Dillon County
25	295	1.2	**Hilton Head Island** (town) Beaufort County
25	n/a	1.2	**Laurens** (city) Laurens County
30	n/a	1.3	**Bamberg** (town) Bamberg County
30	n/a	1.3	**Centerville** (CDP) Anderson County
30	415	1.3	**Florence** (city) Florence County
30	n/a	1.3	**Georgetown** (city) Georgetown County
30	n/a	1.3	**Little River** (CDP) Horry County
30	n/a	1.3	**Surfside Beach** (town) Horry County
30	n/a	1.3	**Williamston** (town) Anderson County
37	n/a	1.4	**Allendale** (town) Allendale County
37	n/a	1.4	**Garden City** (CDP) Horry County
37	549	1.4	**Greenwood** (city) Greenwood County
37	n/a	1.4	**Lake Wylie** (CDP) York County
37	n/a	1.4	**Lugoff** (CDP) Kershaw County
37	n/a	1.4	**Marion** (city) Marion County
37	n/a	1.4	**Mullins** (city) Marion County
37	n/a	1.4	**North Hartsville** (CDP) Darlington County
37	549	1.4	**North Myrtle Beach** (city) Horry County
37	n/a	1.4	**Tega Cay** (city) York County
37	n/a	1.4	**Union** (city) Union County
37	n/a	1.4	**Valley Falls** (CDP) Spartanburg County
37	n/a	1.4	**Williston** (town) Barnwell County
50	n/a	1.5	**Abbeville** (city) Abbeville County
50	724	1.5	**Aiken** (city) Aiken County
50	n/a	1.5	**Boiling Springs** (CDP) Spartanburg County
50	724	1.5	**Charleston** (city) Charleston County
50	n/a	1.5	**Clinton** (city) Laurens County
50	724	1.5	**Conway** (city) Horry County
50	724	1.5	**Five Forks** (CDP) Greenville County
50	n/a	1.5	**Hopkins** (CDP) Richland County
50	724	1.5	**Lexington** (town) Lexington County
50	n/a	1.5	**Walterboro** (city) Colleton County
60	n/a	1.6	**Arial** (CDP) Pickens County
60	861	1.6	**Clemson** (city) Pickens County
60	861	1.6	**Gaffney** (city) Cherokee County
60	n/a	1.6	**Springdale** (town) Lexington County
60	n/a	1.6	**Travelers Rest** (city) Greenville County
65	n/a	1.7	**Barnwell** (city) Barnwell County
65	n/a	1.7	**Chester** (city) Chester County
65	n/a	1.7	**Lesslie** (CDP) York County
65	n/a	1.7	**Piedmont** (CDP) Anderson County
69	n/a	1.8	**Belton** (city) Anderson County
69	n/a	1.8	**Cheraw** (town) Chesterfield County
69	1219	1.8	**Easley** (city) Pickens County
69	n/a	1.8	**East Gaffney** (CDP) Cherokee County
69	1219	1.8	**Gantt** (CDP) Greenville County
69	1219	1.8	**Greenville** (city) Greenville County
69	n/a	1.8	**Lakewood** (CDP) Sumter County
69	n/a	1.8	**Lyman** (town) Spartanburg County
69	1219	1.8	**Newberry** (city) Newberry County
69	n/a	1.8	**Newport** (CDP) York County
69	n/a	1.8	**Northlake** (CDP) Anderson County
69	1219	1.8	**Oak Grove** (CDP) Lexington County
69	n/a	1.8	**Saluda** (town) Saluda County
69	1219	1.8	**Spartanburg** (city) Spartanburg County
69	n/a	1.8	**Welcome** (CDP) Greenville County
84	n/a	1.9	**Central** (town) Pickens County
84	n/a	1.9	**Clearwater** (CDP) Aiken County
84	n/a	1.9	**Clover** (town) York County
84	1407	1.9	**Forest Acres** (city) Richland County
84	n/a	1.9	**Red Bank** (CDP) Lexington County
89	1559	2.0	**Columbia** (city) Richland County
89	n/a	2.0	**Fountain Inn** (city) Greenville County
89	n/a	2.0	**Moncks Corner** (town) Berkeley County
89	1559	2.0	**North Augusta** (city) Aiken County
89	1559	2.0	**Taylors** (CDP) Greenville County
94	1707	2.1	**Anderson** (city) Anderson County
94	n/a	2.1	**Burnettown** (town) Aiken County
94	1707	2.1	**Cayce** (city) Lexington County
94	1707	2.1	**Fort Mill** (town) York County
94	1707	2.1	**Greer** (city) Greenville County
94	n/a	2.1	**India Hook** (CDP) York County
94	n/a	2.1	**Liberty** (city) Pickens County
94	n/a	2.1	**Pageland** (town) Chesterfield County
94	1707	2.1	**Rock Hill** (city) York County
94	1707	2.1	**Sumter** (city) Sumter County
94	1707	2.1	**Wade Hampton** (CDP) Greenville County
94	n/a	2.1	**York** (city) York County
106	1866	2.2	**Mauldin** (city) Greenville County
106	1866	2.2	**Red Hill** (CDP) Horry County
106	1866	2.2	**Saint Andrews** (CDP) Richland County
106	n/a	2.2	**Walhalla** (city) Oconee County
110	n/a	2.3	**Homeland Park** (CDP) Anderson County
110	n/a	2.3	**Pickens** (city) Pickens County
110	n/a	2.3	**Seneca** (city) Oconee County
110	2015	2.3	**Simpsonville** (city) Greenville County
110	2015	2.3	**West Columbia** (city) Lexington County
115	n/a	2.4	**Edgefield** (town) Edgefield County
115	n/a	2.4	**Honea Path** (town) Anderson County
117	2300	2.5	**Dentsville** (CDP) Richland County
117	n/a	2.5	**Dunean** (CDP) Greenville County
117	n/a	2.5	**Forestbrook** (CDP) Horry County
117	n/a	2.5	**Graniteville** (CDP) Aiken County
117	2300	2.5	**Irmo** (town) Richland County
117	2300	2.5	**North Charleston** (city) Charleston County
117	n/a	2.5	**Saxon** (CDP) Spartanburg County
124	2448	2.6	**Beaufort** (city) Beaufort County
124	n/a	2.6	**Belvedere** (CDP) Aiken County
124	2448	2.6	**Parker** (CDP) Greenville County
124	n/a	2.6	**Pendleton** (town) Anderson County
124	n/a	2.6	**Springdale** (CDP) Lancaster County
129	2595	2.7	**Berea** (CDP) Greenville County
129	n/a	2.7	**Burton** (CDP) Beaufort County
129	n/a	2.7	**Dalzell** (CDP) Sumter County
129	n/a	2.7	**Hardeeville** (city) Jasper County
129	2595	2.7	**Myrtle Beach** (city) Horry County
129	n/a	2.7	**Sans Souci** (CDP) Greenville County
135	n/a	2.8	**Sangaree** (CDP) Berkeley County
135	2722	2.8	**Seven Oaks** (CDP) Lexington County
137	2829	2.9	**Bluffton** (town) Beaufort County
137	2829	2.9	**Hanahan** (city) Berkeley County
137	2829	2.9	**Socastee** (CDP) Horry County
137	n/a	2.9	**Southern Shops** (CDP) Spartanburg County
137	2829	2.9	**Summerville** (town) Dorchester County
142	n/a	3.0	**Gloverville** (CDP) Aiken County
142	n/a	3.0	**Woodruff** (city) Spartanburg County
144	n/a	3.2	**Duncan** (town) Spartanburg County
145	n/a	3.4	**Arcadia** (CDP) Spartanburg County
146	3466	3.6	**Goose Creek** (city) Berkeley County
146	3466	3.6	**Ladson** (CDP) Berkeley County
148	3548	3.7	**Port Royal** (town) Beaufort County
149	n/a	3.8	**Laurel Bay** (CDP) Beaufort County
149	n/a	3.8	**Woodfield** (CDP) Richland County

Note: The state column ranks the top/bottom 150 places in the state with population of 2,500 or more. The national column ranks the top/bottom places in the country with population of 10,000 or more. Places that are unincorporated were not considered in the rankings. n/a indicates data not available. Please refer to the User Guide for additional information.

Hispanic Population

Top 150 Places Ranked in *Descending* Order

State Rank	Nat'l Rank	Percent	Place
1	n/a	40.7	**Southern Shops** (CDP) Spartanburg County
2	n/a	34.5	**Arcadia** (CDP) Spartanburg County
3	n/a	33.9	**Saluda** (town) Saluda County
4	n/a	28.4	**Hardeeville** (city) Jasper County
5	782	25.4	**Berea** (CDP) Greenville County
6	n/a	22.5	**Walhalla** (city) Oconee County
7	n/a	22.4	**Saxon** (CDP) Spartanburg County
8	968	20.8	**Parker** (CDP) Greenville County
9	n/a	19.3	**Woodfield** (CDP) Richland County
10	1056	18.8	**Bluffton** (town) Beaufort County
11	n/a	17.1	**Sans Souci** (CDP) Greenville County
12	n/a	16.3	**Welcome** (CDP) Greenville County
13	1243	15.8	**Hilton Head Island** (town) Beaufort County
14	n/a	15.1	**Ridgeland** (town) Jasper County
15	1349	14.5	**Greer** (city) Greenville County
15	1349	14.5	**West Columbia** (city) Lexington County
17	n/a	13.9	**Pageland** (town) Chesterfield County
18	1429	13.7	**Myrtle Beach** (city) Horry County
19	n/a	13.6	**Clearwater** (CDP) Aiken County
20	1465	13.3	**Port Royal** (town) Beaufort County
21	1475	13.2	**Gantt** (CDP) Greenville County
22	n/a	11.9	**Edgefield** (town) Edgefield County
23	1677	11.3	**Ladson** (CDP) Berkeley County
24	1690	11.2	**Wade Hampton** (CDP) Greenville County
25	n/a	11.1	**Laurel Bay** (CDP) Beaufort County
26	1713	11.0	**Greenwood** (city) Greenwood County
27	1725	10.9	**North Charleston** (city) Charleston County
28	1734	10.8	**Socastee** (CDP) Horry County
29	1746	10.7	**Oak Grove** (CDP) Lexington County
30	n/a	10.4	**Elgin** (CDP) Lancaster County
31	n/a	10.2	**Dunean** (CDP) Greenville County
32	n/a	10.0	**Springdale** (CDP) Lancaster County
33	n/a	9.9	**Burton** (CDP) Beaufort County
34	n/a	9.2	**Duncan** (town) Spartanburg County
35	1942	9.1	**Hanahan** (city) Berkeley County
36	1974	8.9	**Simpsonville** (city) Greenville County
37	2021	8.6	**Newberry** (city) Newberry County
38	2034	8.5	**Red Hill** (CDP) Horry County
39	2067	8.3	**Taylors** (CDP) Greenville County
40	2166	7.7	**Mauldin** (city) Greenville County
40	n/a	7.7	**Woodruff** (city) Spartanburg County
42	n/a	7.3	**York** (city) York County
43	2382	6.7	**Beaufort** (city) Beaufort County
44	n/a	6.6	**Valley Falls** (CDP) Spartanburg County
45	n/a	6.4	**Burnettown** (town) Aiken County
46	2495	6.3	**North Myrtle Beach** (city) Horry County
47	2544	6.1	**Goose Creek** (city) Berkeley County
48	n/a	6.0	**Belvedere** (CDP) Aiken County
48	n/a	6.0	**Fountain Inn** (city) Greenville County
50	n/a	5.9	**Graniteville** (CDP) Aiken County
50	2586	5.9	**Greenville** (city) Greenville County
52	n/a	5.8	**Forestbrook** (CDP) Horry County
53	n/a	5.7	**Lancaster** (city) Lancaster County
53	n/a	5.7	**Laurens** (city) Laurens County
53	2640	5.7	**Rock Hill** (city) York County
56	2661	5.6	**Easley** (city) Pickens County
56	n/a	5.6	**Homeland Park** (CDP) Anderson County
58	n/a	5.5	**East Gaffney** (CDP) Cherokee County
59	2736	5.3	**Dentsville** (CDP) Richland County
59	n/a	5.3	**Georgetown** (city) Georgetown County
61	n/a	5.1	**Arial** (CDP) Pickens County
61	n/a	5.1	**Central** (town) Pickens County
61	n/a	5.1	**Moncks Corner** (town) Berkeley County
64	2832	5.0	**Summerville** (town) Dorchester County
65	n/a	4.9	**India Hook** (CDP) York County
66	n/a	4.8	**Sangaree** (CDP) Berkeley County
67	n/a	4.5	**Seneca** (city) Oconee County
67	n/a	4.5	**Travelers Rest** (city) Greenville County
69	n/a	4.4	**Clover** (town) York County
70	n/a	4.3	**Boiling Springs** (CDP) Spartanburg County
70	3060	4.3	**Cayce** (city) Lexington County
70	3060	4.3	**Columbia** (city) Richland County
73	3098	4.2	**Five Forks** (CDP) Greenville County
73	3098	4.2	**North Augusta** (city) Aiken County
75	3122	4.1	**Anderson** (city) Anderson County
76	n/a	4.0	**Hollywood** (town) Charleston County
76	n/a	4.0	**Liberty** (city) Pickens County
76	n/a	4.0	**Red Bank** (CDP) Lexington County
79	n/a	3.9	**Lake Wylie** (CDP) York County
80	3229	3.8	**Seven Oaks** (CDP) Lexington County
81	n/a	3.7	**Lakewood** (CDP) Sumter County
81	n/a	3.7	**Lyman** (town) Spartanburg County
81	3261	3.7	**Saint Andrews** (CDP) Richland County
84	n/a	3.6	**Andrews** (town) Georgetown County
84	n/a	3.6	**Batesburg-Leesville** (town) Lexington County
84	n/a	3.6	**Springdale** (town) Lexington County
84	3297	3.6	**Sumter** (city) Sumter County
88	3334	3.5	**Lexington** (town) Lexington County
89	n/a	3.4	**Pickens** (city) Pickens County
89	3377	3.4	**Spartanburg** (city) Spartanburg County
91	3421	3.3	**Irmo** (town) Richland County
91	n/a	3.3	**North Hartsville** (CDP) Darlington County
91	n/a	3.3	**Tega Cay** (city) York County
94	n/a	3.2	**Little River** (CDP) Horry County
95	3505	3.1	**Gaffney** (city) Cherokee County
95	n/a	3.1	**Gloverville** (CDP) Aiken County
97	3560	3.0	**Forest Acres** (city) Richland County
97	n/a	3.0	**Lake City** (city) Florence County
99	3607	2.9	**Charleston** (city) Charleston County
99	3607	2.9	**Conway** (city) Horry County
99	3607	2.9	**Fort Mill** (town) York County
99	n/a	2.9	**Garden City** (CDP) Horry County
99	n/a	2.9	**Lesslie** (CDP) York County
99	n/a	2.9	**Walterboro** (city) Colleton County
105	n/a	2.8	**Allendale** (town) Allendale County
105	n/a	2.8	**Dalzell** (CDP) Sumter County
105	n/a	2.8	**Williamston** (town) Anderson County
108	n/a	2.7	**Centerville** (CDP) Anderson County
108	n/a	2.7	**Edisto** (CDP) Orangeburg County
108	n/a	2.7	**Lugoff** (CDP) Kershaw County
108	3711	2.7	**Mount Pleasant** (town) Charleston County
112	3754	2.6	**Aiken** (city) Aiken County
112	n/a	2.6	**Hopkins** (CDP) Richland County
114	n/a	2.5	**Piedmont** (CDP) Anderson County
115	n/a	2.4	**Camden** (city) Kershaw County
116	n/a	2.3	**Newport** (CDP) York County
117	3988	2.2	**Clemson** (city) Pickens County
117	n/a	2.2	**Clinton** (city) Laurens County
117	n/a	2.2	**Murrells Inlet** (CDP) Georgetown County
120	n/a	2.0	**Northlake** (CDP) Anderson County
120	n/a	2.0	**Surfside Beach** (town) Horry County
120	n/a	2.0	**Winnsboro** (town) Fairfield County
123	n/a	1.9	**Belton** (city) Anderson County
123	n/a	1.9	**Manning** (city) Clarendon County
123	4156	1.9	**Orangeburg** (city) Orangeburg County
126	n/a	1.7	**Folly Beach** (city) Charleston County
126	n/a	1.7	**Hampton** (town) Hampton County
126	n/a	1.7	**Lake Murray of Richland** (CDP) Richland County
129	n/a	1.6	**Bamberg** (town) Bamberg County
129	n/a	1.6	**Bennettsville** (city) Marlboro County
129	n/a	1.6	**McCormick** (town) McCormick County
129	n/a	1.6	**Pendleton** (town) Anderson County
133	4394	1.5	**Florence** (city) Florence County
133	n/a	1.5	**Hartsville** (city) Darlington County
135	n/a	1.4	**Honea Path** (town) Anderson County
136	n/a	1.3	**Marion** (city) Marion County
137	n/a	1.2	**Bishopville** (city) Lee County
137	n/a	1.2	**Chester** (city) Chester County
137	n/a	1.2	**Dillon** (city) Dillon County
137	n/a	1.2	**Union** (city) Union County
141	n/a	1.1	**Cheraw** (town) Chesterfield County
141	n/a	1.1	**Isle of Palms** (city) Charleston County
141	n/a	1.1	**Williston** (town) Barnwell County
144	n/a	1.0	**Barnwell** (city) Barnwell County
145	n/a	0.9	**Abbeville** (city) Abbeville County
145	n/a	0.9	**Denmark** (city) Bamberg County
147	n/a	0.8	**Mullins** (city) Marion County
148	n/a	0.7	**Brookdale** (CDP) Orangeburg County
148	n/a	0.7	**Darlington** (city) Darlington County
150	n/a	0.6	**Kingstree** (town) Williamsburg County

Note: The state column ranks the top/bottom 150 places in the state with population of 2,500 or more. The national column ranks the top/bottom places in the country with population of 10,000 or more. Places that are unincorporated were not considered in the rankings. n/a indicates data not available. Please refer to the User Guide for additional information.

Hispanic Population

Top 150 Places Ranked in *Ascending* Order

State Rank	Nat'l Rank	Percent	Place
1	n/a	0.6	**Kingstree** (town) Williamsburg County
2	n/a	0.7	**Brookdale** (CDP) Orangeburg County
2	n/a	0.7	**Darlington** (city) Darlington County
4	n/a	0.8	**Mullins** (city) Marion County
5	n/a	0.9	**Abbeville** (city) Abbeville County
5	n/a	0.9	**Denmark** (city) Bamberg County
7	n/a	1.0	**Barnwell** (city) Barnwell County
8	n/a	1.1	**Cheraw** (town) Chesterfield County
8	n/a	1.1	**Isle of Palms** (city) Charleston County
8	n/a	1.1	**Williston** (town) Barnwell County
11	n/a	1.2	**Bishopville** (city) Lee County
11	n/a	1.2	**Chester** (city) Chester County
11	n/a	1.2	**Dillon** (city) Dillon County
11	n/a	1.2	**Union** (city) Union County
15	n/a	1.3	**Marion** (city) Marion County
16	n/a	1.4	**Honea Path** (town) Anderson County
17	215	1.5	**Florence** (city) Florence County
17	n/a	1.5	**Hartsville** (city) Darlington County
19	n/a	1.6	**Bamberg** (town) Bamberg County
19	n/a	1.6	**Bennettsville** (city) Marlboro County
19	n/a	1.6	**McCormick** (town) McCormick County
19	n/a	1.6	**Pendleton** (town) Anderson County
23	n/a	1.7	**Folly Beach** (city) Charleston County
23	n/a	1.7	**Hampton** (town) Hampton County
23	n/a	1.7	**Lake Murray of Richland** (CDP) Richland County
26	n/a	1.9	**Belton** (city) Anderson County
26	n/a	1.9	**Manning** (city) Clarendon County
26	444	1.9	**Orangeburg** (city) Orangeburg County
29	n/a	2.0	**Northlake** (CDP) Anderson County
29	n/a	2.0	**Surfside Beach** (town) Horry County
29	n/a	2.0	**Winnsboro** (town) Fairfield County
32	612	2.2	**Clemson** (city) Pickens County
32	n/a	2.2	**Clinton** (city) Laurens County
32	n/a	2.2	**Murrells Inlet** (CDP) Georgetown County
35	n/a	2.3	**Newport** (CDP) York County
36	n/a	2.4	**Camden** (city) Kershaw County
37	n/a	2.5	**Piedmont** (CDP) Anderson County
38	845	2.6	**Aiken** (city) Aiken County
38	n/a	2.6	**Hopkins** (CDP) Richland County
40	n/a	2.7	**Centerville** (CDP) Anderson County
40	n/a	2.7	**Edisto** (CDP) Orangeburg County
40	n/a	2.7	**Lugoff** (CDP) Kershaw County
40	903	2.7	**Mount Pleasant** (town) Charleston County
44	n/a	2.8	**Allendale** (town) Allendale County
44	n/a	2.8	**Dalzell** (CDP) Sumter County
44	n/a	2.8	**Williamston** (town) Anderson County
47	997	2.9	**Charleston** (city) Charleston County
47	997	2.9	**Conway** (city) Horry County
47	997	2.9	**Fort Mill** (town) York County
47	n/a	2.9	**Garden City** (CDP) Horry County
47	n/a	2.9	**Lesslie** (CDP) York County
47	n/a	2.9	**Walterboro** (city) Colleton County
53	1050	3.0	**Forest Acres** (city) Richland County
53	n/a	3.0	**Lake City** (city) Florence County
55	1097	3.1	**Gaffney** (city) Cherokee County
55	n/a	3.1	**Gloverville** (CDP) Aiken County
57	n/a	3.2	**Little River** (CDP) Horry County
58	1195	3.3	**Irmo** (town) Richland County
58	n/a	3.3	**North Hartsville** (CDP) Darlington County
58	n/a	3.3	**Tega Cay** (city) York County
61	n/a	3.4	**Pickens** (city) Pickens County
61	1236	3.4	**Spartanburg** (city) Spartanburg County
63	1280	3.5	**Lexington** (town) Lexington County
64	n/a	3.6	**Andrews** (town) Georgetown County
64	n/a	3.6	**Batesburg-Leesville** (town) Lexington County
64	n/a	3.6	**Springdale** (town) Lexington County
64	1323	3.6	**Sumter** (city) Sumter County
68	n/a	3.7	**Lakewood** (CDP) Sumter County
68	n/a	3.7	**Lyman** (town) Spartanburg County
68	1360	3.7	**Saint Andrews** (CDP) Richland County
71	1396	3.8	**Seven Oaks** (CDP) Lexington County
72	n/a	3.9	**Lake Wylie** (CDP) York County
73	n/a	4.0	**Hollywood** (town) Charleston County
73	n/a	4.0	**Liberty** (city) Pickens County
73	n/a	4.0	**Red Bank** (CDP) Lexington County
76	1488	4.1	**Anderson** (city) Anderson County
77	1535	4.2	**Five Forks** (CDP) Greenville County
77	1535	4.2	**North Augusta** (city) Aiken County
79	n/a	4.3	**Boiling Springs** (CDP) Spartanburg County
79	1559	4.3	**Cayce** (city) Lexington County
79	1559	4.3	**Columbia** (city) Richland County
82	n/a	4.4	**Clover** (town) York County
83	n/a	4.5	**Seneca** (city) Oconee County
83	n/a	4.5	**Travelers Rest** (city) Greenville County
85	n/a	4.8	**Sangaree** (CDP) Berkeley County
86	n/a	4.9	**India Hook** (CDP) York County
87	1787	5.0	**Summerville** (town) Dorchester County
88	n/a	5.1	**Arial** (CDP) Pickens County
88	n/a	5.1	**Central** (town) Pickens County
88	n/a	5.1	**Moncks Corner** (town) Berkeley County
91	1887	5.3	**Dentsville** (CDP) Richland County
91	n/a	5.3	**Georgetown** (city) Georgetown County
93	n/a	5.5	**East Gaffney** (CDP) Cherokee County
94	1970	5.6	**Easley** (city) Pickens County
94	n/a	5.6	**Homeland Park** (CDP) Anderson County
96	n/a	5.7	**Lancaster** (city) Lancaster County
96	n/a	5.7	**Laurens** (city) Laurens County
96	1996	5.7	**Rock Hill** (city) York County
99	n/a	5.8	**Forestbrook** (CDP) Horry County
100	n/a	5.9	**Graniteville** (CDP) Aiken County
100	2044	5.9	**Greenville** (city) Greenville County
102	n/a	6.0	**Belvedere** (CDP) Aiken County
102	n/a	6.0	**Fountain Inn** (city) Greenville County
104	2093	6.1	**Goose Creek** (city) Berkeley County
105	2135	6.3	**North Myrtle Beach** (city) Horry County
106	n/a	6.4	**Burnettown** (town) Aiken County
107	n/a	6.6	**Valley Falls** (CDP) Spartanburg County
108	2251	6.7	**Beaufort** (city) Beaufort County
109	n/a	7.3	**York** (city) York County
110	2472	7.7	**Mauldin** (city) Greenville County
110	n/a	7.7	**Woodruff** (city) Spartanburg County
112	2576	8.3	**Taylors** (CDP) Greenville County
113	2605	8.5	**Red Hill** (CDP) Horry County
114	2623	8.6	**Newberry** (city) Newberry County
115	2668	8.9	**Simpsonville** (city) Greenville County
116	2706	9.1	**Hanahan** (city) Berkeley County
117	n/a	9.2	**Duncan** (town) Spartanburg County
118	n/a	9.9	**Burton** (CDP) Beaufort County
119	n/a	10.0	**Springdale** (CDP) Lancaster County
120	n/a	10.2	**Dunean** (CDP) Greenville County
121	n/a	10.4	**Elgin** (CDP) Lancaster County
122	2895	10.7	**Oak Grove** (CDP) Lexington County
123	2911	10.8	**Socastee** (CDP) Horry County
124	2923	10.9	**North Charleston** (city) Charleston County
125	2932	11.0	**Greenwood** (city) Greenwood County
126	n/a	11.1	**Laurel Bay** (CDP) Beaufort County
127	2952	11.2	**Wade Hampton** (CDP) Greenville County
128	2967	11.3	**Ladson** (CDP) Berkeley County
129	n/a	11.9	**Edgefield** (town) Edgefield County
130	3176	13.2	**Gantt** (CDP) Greenville County
131	3182	13.3	**Port Royal** (town) Beaufort County
132	n/a	13.6	**Clearwater** (CDP) Aiken County
133	3221	13.7	**Myrtle Beach** (city) Horry County
134	n/a	13.9	**Pageland** (town) Chesterfield County
135	3296	14.5	**Greer** (city) Greenville County
135	3296	14.5	**West Columbia** (city) Lexington County
137	n/a	15.1	**Ridgeland** (town) Jasper County
138	3408	15.8	**Hilton Head Island** (town) Beaufort County
139	n/a	16.3	**Welcome** (CDP) Greenville County
140	n/a	17.1	**Sans Souci** (CDP) Greenville County
141	3598	18.8	**Bluffton** (town) Beaufort County
142	n/a	19.3	**Woodfield** (CDP) Richland County
143	3681	20.8	**Parker** (CDP) Greenville County
144	n/a	22.4	**Saxon** (CDP) Spartanburg County
145	n/a	22.5	**Walhalla** (city) Oconee County
146	3867	25.4	**Berea** (CDP) Greenville County
147	n/a	28.4	**Hardeeville** (city) Jasper County
148	n/a	33.9	**Saluda** (town) Saluda County
149	n/a	34.5	**Arcadia** (CDP) Spartanburg County
150	n/a	40.7	**Southern Shops** (CDP) Spartanburg County

Note: The state column ranks the top/bottom 150 places in the state with population of 2,500 or more. The national column ranks the top/bottom places in the country with population of 10,000 or more. Places that are unincorporated were not considered in the rankings. n/a indicates data not available. Please refer to the User Guide for additional information.

Average Household Size

Top 150 Places Ranked in *Descending* Order

State Rank	Nat'l Rank	Persons	Place	State Rank	Nat'l Rank	Persons	Place
1	n/a	3.0	**Southern Shops** (CDP) Spartanburg County	75	n/a	2.4	**Williamston** (town) Anderson County
2	499	3.0	**Five Forks** (CDP) Greenville County	77	n/a	2.4	**Central** (town) Pickens County
3	n/a	3.0	**Laurel Bay** (CDP) Beaufort County	77	3032	2.4	**Florence** (city) Florence County
4	704	2.9	**Ladson** (CDP) Berkeley County	77	n/a	2.4	**Gloverville** (CDP) Aiken County
5	n/a	2.8	**Saluda** (town) Saluda County	77	3032	2.4	**Mount Pleasant** (town) Charleston County
6	1018	2.8	**Bluffton** (town) Beaufort County	77	3032	2.4	**Red Hill** (CDP) Horry County
6	n/a	2.8	**Sangaree** (CDP) Berkeley County	77	3032	2.4	**Rock Hill** (city) York County
8	n/a	2.7	**Ridgeland** (town) Jasper County	83	3107	2.4	**Mauldin** (city) Greenville County
9	n/a	2.7	**Tega Cay** (city) York County	83	n/a	2.4	**Sans Souci** (CDP) Greenville County
10	n/a	2.7	**Hardeeville** (city) Jasper County	85	n/a	2.4	**Clinton** (city) Laurens County
11	n/a	2.7	**Hopkins** (CDP) Richland County	85	n/a	2.4	**Lancaster** (city) Lancaster County
12	n/a	2.7	**Newport** (CDP) York County	87	n/a	2.3	**Barnwell** (city) Barnwell County
13	1433	2.7	**Goose Creek** (city) Berkeley County	87	3296	2.3	**Easley** (city) Pickens County
14	n/a	2.7	**Lesslie** (CDP) York County	89	n/a	2.3	**Bamberg** (town) Bamberg County
14	n/a	2.7	**Saxon** (CDP) Spartanburg County	89	3347	2.3	**Greenwood** (city) Greenwood County
16	n/a	2.6	**Dalzell** (CDP) Sumter County	89	n/a	2.3	**India Hook** (CDP) York County
16	1617	2.6	**Gantt** (CDP) Greenville County	89	n/a	2.3	**Lyman** (town) Spartanburg County
16	n/a	2.6	**Lakewood** (CDP) Sumter County	89	n/a	2.3	**Walterboro** (city) Colleton County
19	n/a	2.6	**Andrews** (town) Georgetown County	94	n/a	2.3	**Liberty** (city) Pickens County
19	n/a	2.6	**Fountain Inn** (city) Greenville County	94	n/a	2.3	**Manning** (city) Clarendon County
21	n/a	2.6	**Arcadia** (CDP) Spartanburg County	94	n/a	2.3	**Northlake** (CDP) Anderson County
21	n/a	2.6	**Clover** (town) York County	97	n/a	2.3	**Cheraw** (town) Chesterfield County
21	n/a	2.6	**Elgin** (CDP) Lancaster County	97	n/a	2.3	**Kingstree** (town) Williamsburg County
21	n/a	2.6	**Forestbrook** (CDP) Horry County	97	3485	2.3	**Newberry** (city) Newberry County
21	n/a	2.6	**Lake Murray of Richland** (CDP) Richland County	100	3550	2.3	**Port Royal** (town) Beaufort County
21	1788	2.6	**Parker** (CDP) Greenville County	100	n/a	2.3	**Williston** (town) Barnwell County
21	n/a	2.6	**Springdale** (CDP) Lancaster County	102	n/a	2.3	**Bennettsville** (city) Marlboro County
28	n/a	2.6	**Lake City** (city) Florence County	102	3608	2.3	**Cayce** (city) Lexington County
29	n/a	2.6	**Burton** (CDP) Beaufort County	102	n/a	2.3	**Denmark** (city) Bamberg County
29	n/a	2.6	**North Hartsville** (CDP) Darlington County	102	3608	2.3	**Gaffney** (city) Cherokee County
31	n/a	2.6	**Boiling Springs** (CDP) Spartanburg County	102	n/a	2.3	**Laurens** (city) Laurens County
31	n/a	2.6	**Hollywood** (town) Charleston County	102	3608	2.3	**North Augusta** (city) Aiken County
31	n/a	2.6	**Moncks Corner** (town) Berkeley County	102	n/a	2.3	**Winnsboro** (town) Fairfield County
31	n/a	2.6	**Travelers Rest** (city) Greenville County	109	n/a	2.3	**Bishopville** (city) Lee County
35	n/a	2.5	**Lugoff** (CDP) Kershaw County	109	3660	2.3	**Clemson** (city) Pickens County
35	n/a	2.5	**Red Bank** (CDP) Lexington County	109	n/a	2.3	**Dunean** (CDP) Greenville County
37	2136	2.5	**Berea** (CDP) Greenville County	109	n/a	2.3	**Hampton** (town) Hampton County
37	2136	2.5	**Fort Mill** (town) York County	109	n/a	2.3	**Pickens** (city) Pickens County
37	n/a	2.5	**Woodfield** (CDP) Richland County	114	n/a	2.3	**Darlington** (city) Darlington County
40	2188	2.5	**Simpsonville** (city) Greenville County	114	n/a	2.3	**Hartsville** (city) Darlington County
40	n/a	2.5	**York** (city) York County	114	3713	2.3	**Seven Oaks** (CDP) Lexington County
42	n/a	2.5	**Burnettown** (town) Aiken County	117	n/a	2.3	**Belton** (city) Anderson County
42	n/a	2.5	**Duncan** (town) Spartanburg County	117	n/a	2.3	**Honea Path** (town) Anderson County
42	2234	2.5	**Irmo** (town) Richland County	117	3765	2.3	**Lexington** (town) Lexington County
42	n/a	2.5	**Piedmont** (CDP) Anderson County	120	n/a	2.3	**Abbeville** (city) Abbeville County
46	n/a	2.5	**Pageland** (town) Chesterfield County	121	3937	2.2	**Beaufort** (city) Beaufort County
46	2282	2.5	**Summerville** (town) Dorchester County	121	n/a	2.2	**Springdale** (town) Lexington County
48	n/a	2.5	**Belvedere** (CDP) Aiken County	123	3984	2.2	**Orangeburg** (city) Orangeburg County
48	2334	2.5	**North Charleston** (city) Charleston County	123	n/a	2.2	**Seneca** (city) Oconee County
48	n/a	2.5	**Welcome** (CDP) Greenville County	123	3984	2.2	**Spartanburg** (city) Spartanburg County
51	n/a	2.5	**Chester** (city) Chester County	126	n/a	2.2	**Camden** (city) Kershaw County
51	n/a	2.5	**Edisto** (CDP) Orangeburg County	126	n/a	2.2	**Isle of Palms** (city) Charleston County
51	n/a	2.5	**Georgetown** (city) Georgetown County	126	4034	2.2	**Wade Hampton** (CDP) Greenville County
54	n/a	2.5	**Clearwater** (CDP) Aiken County	129	4084	2.2	**Anderson** (city) Anderson County
54	2464	2.5	**Greer** (city) Greenville County	129	4084	2.2	**Dentsville** (CDP) Richland County
54	2464	2.5	**Hanahan** (city) Berkeley County	131	n/a	2.2	**Edgefield** (town) Edgefield County
54	n/a	2.5	**Walhalla** (city) Oconee County	131	n/a	2.2	**Union** (city) Union County
58	n/a	2.5	**Allendale** (town) Allendale County	133	4164	2.2	**Hilton Head Island** (town) Beaufort County
58	n/a	2.5	**Dillon** (city) Dillon County	133	4164	2.2	**West Columbia** (city) Lexington County
58	n/a	2.5	**Lake Wylie** (CDP) York County	135	4204	2.2	**Myrtle Beach** (city) Horry County
58	n/a	2.5	**Woodruff** (city) Spartanburg County	135	n/a	2.2	**Valley Falls** (CDP) Spartanburg County
62	n/a	2.5	**East Gaffney** (CDP) Cherokee County	137	4293	2.2	**Aiken** (city) Aiken County
62	2568	2.5	**Socastee** (CDP) Horry County	138	4345	2.1	**Charleston** (city) Charleston County
62	2568	2.5	**Taylors** (CDP) Greenville County	138	4345	2.1	**Columbia** (city) Richland County
65	2630	2.4	**Conway** (city) Horry County	140	n/a	2.1	**McCormick** (town) McCormick County
65	n/a	2.4	**Graniteville** (CDP) Aiken County	141	n/a	2.1	**Murrells Inlet** (CDP) Georgetown County
67	n/a	2.4	**Arial** (CDP) Pickens County	142	4498	2.1	**Forest Acres** (city) Richland County
67	n/a	2.4	**Brookdale** (CDP) Orangeburg County	143	n/a	2.1	**Pendleton** (town) Anderson County
67	n/a	2.4	**Marion** (city) Marion County	144	4528	2.0	**Saint Andrews** (CDP) Richland County
67	2698	2.4	**Sumter** (city) Sumter County	145	4543	2.0	**Greenville** (city) Greenville County
71	n/a	2.4	**Batesburg-Leesville** (town) Lexington County	146	n/a	2.0	**Surfside Beach** (town) Horry County
71	n/a	2.4	**Centerville** (CDP) Anderson County	147	4577	2.0	**North Myrtle Beach** (city) Horry County
73	n/a	2.4	**Homeland Park** (CDP) Anderson County	148	n/a	2.0	**Little River** (CDP) Horry County
73	2893	2.4	**Oak Grove** (CDP) Lexington County	149	n/a	1.9	**Garden City** (CDP) Horry County
75	n/a	2.4	**Mullins** (city) Marion County	150	n/a	1.9	**Folly Beach** (city) Charleston County

Note: The state column ranks the top/bottom 150 places in the state with population of 2,500 or more. The national column ranks the top/bottom places in the country with population of 10,000 or more. Places that are unincorporated were not considered in the rankings. n/a indicates data not available. Please refer to the User Guide for additional information.

Average Household Size

Top 150 Places Ranked in *Ascending* Order

State Rank	Nat'l Rank	Persons	Place	State Rank	Nat'l Rank	Persons	Place
1	n/a	1.9	**Folly Beach** (city) Charleston County	75	n/a	2.4	**Williamston** (town) Anderson County
2	n/a	1.9	**Garden City** (CDP) Horry County	77	n/a	2.4	**Homeland Park** (CDP) Anderson County
3	n/a	2.0	**Little River** (CDP) Horry County	77	1689	2.4	**Oak Grove** (CDP) Lexington County
4	72	2.0	**North Myrtle Beach** (city) Horry County	79	n/a	2.4	**Batesburg-Leesville** (town) Lexington County
5	n/a	2.0	**Surfside Beach** (town) Horry County	79	n/a	2.4	**Centerville** (CDP) Anderson County
6	102	2.0	**Greenville** (city) Greenville County	81	n/a	2.4	**Arial** (CDP) Pickens County
7	114	2.0	**Saint Andrews** (CDP) Richland County	81	n/a	2.4	**Brookdale** (CDP) Orangeburg County
8	n/a	2.1	**Pendleton** (town) Anderson County	81	n/a	2.4	**Marion** (city) Marion County
9	144	2.1	**Forest Acres** (city) Richland County	81	1889	2.4	**Sumter** (city) Sumter County
10	n/a	2.1	**Murrells Inlet** (CDP) Georgetown County	85	1959	2.4	**Conway** (city) Horry County
11	n/a	2.1	**McCormick** (town) McCormick County	85	n/a	2.4	**Graniteville** (CDP) Aiken County
12	278	2.1	**Charleston** (city) Charleston County	87	n/a	2.5	**East Gaffney** (CDP) Cherokee County
12	278	2.1	**Columbia** (city) Richland County	87	2027	2.5	**Socastee** (CDP) Horry County
14	337	2.2	**Aiken** (city) Aiken County	87	2027	2.5	**Taylors** (CDP) Greenville County
15	405	2.2	**Myrtle Beach** (city) Horry County	90	n/a	2.5	**Allendale** (town) Allendale County
15	n/a	2.2	**Valley Falls** (CDP) Spartanburg County	90	n/a	2.5	**Dillon** (city) Dillon County
17	453	2.2	**Hilton Head Island** (town) Beaufort County	90	n/a	2.5	**Lake Wylie** (CDP) York County
17	453	2.2	**West Columbia** (city) Lexington County	90	n/a	2.5	**Woodruff** (city) Spartanburg County
19	n/a	2.2	**Edgefield** (town) Edgefield County	94	n/a	2.5	**Clearwater** (CDP) Aiken County
19	n/a	2.2	**Union** (city) Union County	94	2139	2.5	**Greer** (city) Greenville County
21	531	2.2	**Anderson** (city) Anderson County	94	2139	2.5	**Hanahan** (city) Berkeley County
21	531	2.2	**Dentsville** (CDP) Richland County	94	n/a	2.5	**Walhalla** (city) Oconee County
23	n/a	2.2	**Camden** (city) Kershaw County	98	n/a	2.5	**Chester** (city) Chester County
23	n/a	2.2	**Isle of Palms** (city) Charleston County	98	n/a	2.5	**Edisto** (CDP) Orangeburg County
23	573	2.2	**Wade Hampton** (CDP) Greenville County	98	n/a	2.5	**Georgetown** (city) Georgetown County
26	623	2.2	**Orangeburg** (city) Orangeburg County	101	n/a	2.5	**Belvedere** (CDP) Aiken County
26	n/a	2.2	**Seneca** (city) Oconee County	101	2259	2.5	**North Charleston** (city) Charleston County
26	623	2.2	**Spartanburg** (city) Spartanburg County	101	n/a	2.5	**Welcome** (CDP) Greenville County
29	673	2.2	**Beaufort** (city) Beaufort County	104	n/a	2.5	**Pageland** (town) Chesterfield County
29	n/a	2.2	**Springdale** (town) Lexington County	104	2323	2.5	**Summerville** (town) Dorchester County
31	n/a	2.3	**Abbeville** (city) Abbeville County	106	n/a	2.5	**Burnettown** (town) Aiken County
32	n/a	2.3	**Belton** (city) Anderson County	106	n/a	2.5	**Duncan** (town) Spartanburg County
32	n/a	2.3	**Honea Path** (town) Anderson County	106	2375	2.5	**Irmo** (town) Richland County
32	837	2.3	**Lexington** (town) Lexington County	106	n/a	2.5	**Piedmont** (CDP) Anderson County
35	n/a	2.3	**Darlington** (city) Darlington County	110	2423	2.5	**Simpsonville** (city) Greenville County
35	n/a	2.3	**Hartsville** (city) Darlington County	110	n/a	2.5	**York** (city) York County
35	892	2.3	**Seven Oaks** (CDP) Lexington County	112	2469	2.5	**Berea** (CDP) Greenville County
38	n/a	2.3	**Bishopville** (city) Lee County	112	2469	2.5	**Fort Mill** (town) York County
38	944	2.3	**Clemson** (city) Pickens County	112	n/a	2.5	**Woodfield** (CDP) Richland County
38	n/a	2.3	**Dunean** (CDP) Greenville County	115	n/a	2.5	**Lugoff** (CDP) Kershaw County
38	n/a	2.3	**Hampton** (town) Hampton County	115	n/a	2.5	**Red Bank** (CDP) Lexington County
38	n/a	2.3	**Pickens** (city) Pickens County	117	n/a	2.6	**Boiling Springs** (CDP) Spartanburg County
43	n/a	2.3	**Bennettsville** (city) Marlboro County	117	n/a	2.6	**Hollywood** (town) Charleston County
43	997	2.3	**Cayce** (city) Lexington County	117	n/a	2.6	**Moncks Corner** (town) Berkeley County
43	n/a	2.3	**Denmark** (city) Bamberg County	117	n/a	2.6	**Travelers Rest** (city) Greenville County
43	997	2.3	**Gaffney** (city) Cherokee County	121	n/a	2.6	**Burton** (CDP) Beaufort County
43	n/a	2.3	**Laurens** (city) Laurens County	121	n/a	2.6	**North Hartsville** (CDP) Darlington County
43	997	2.3	**North Augusta** (city) Aiken County	123	n/a	2.6	**Lake City** (city) Florence County
43	n/a	2.3	**Winnsboro** (town) Fairfield County	124	n/a	2.6	**Arcadia** (CDP) Spartanburg County
50	1049	2.3	**Port Royal** (town) Beaufort County	124	n/a	2.6	**Clover** (town) York County
50	n/a	2.3	**Williston** (town) Barnwell County	124	n/a	2.6	**Elgin** (CDP) Lancaster County
52	n/a	2.3	**Cheraw** (town) Chesterfield County	124	n/a	2.6	**Forestbrook** (CDP) Horry County
52	n/a	2.3	**Kingstree** (town) Williamsburg County	124	n/a	2.6	**Lake Murray of Richland** (CDP) Richland County
52	1107	2.3	**Newberry** (city) Newberry County	124	2824	2.6	**Parker** (CDP) Greenville County
55	n/a	2.3	**Liberty** (city) Pickens County	124	n/a	2.6	**Springdale** (CDP) Lancaster County
55	n/a	2.3	**Manning** (city) Clarendon County	131	n/a	2.6	**Andrews** (town) Georgetown County
55	n/a	2.3	**Northlake** (CDP) Anderson County	131	n/a	2.6	**Fountain Inn** (city) Greenville County
58	n/a	2.3	**Bamberg** (town) Bamberg County	133	n/a	2.6	**Dalzell** (CDP) Sumter County
58	1234	2.3	**Greenwood** (city) Greenwood County	133	2975	2.6	**Gantt** (CDP) Greenville County
58	n/a	2.3	**India Hook** (CDP) York County	133	n/a	2.6	**Lakewood** (CDP) Sumter County
58	n/a	2.3	**Lyman** (town) Spartanburg County	136	n/a	2.7	**Lesslie** (CDP) York County
58	n/a	2.3	**Walterboro** (city) Colleton County	136	n/a	2.7	**Saxon** (CDP) Spartanburg County
63	n/a	2.3	**Barnwell** (city) Barnwell County	138	3174	2.7	**Goose Creek** (city) Berkeley County
63	1310	2.3	**Easley** (city) Pickens County	139	n/a	2.7	**Newport** (CDP) York County
65	n/a	2.4	**Clinton** (city) Laurens County	140	n/a	2.7	**Hopkins** (CDP) Richland County
65	n/a	2.4	**Lancaster** (city) Lancaster County	141	n/a	2.7	**Hardeeville** (city) Jasper County
67	1478	2.4	**Mauldin** (city) Greenville County	142	n/a	2.7	**Tega Cay** (city) York County
67	n/a	2.4	**Sans Souci** (CDP) Greenville County	143	n/a	2.7	**Ridgeland** (town) Jasper County
69	n/a	2.4	**Central** (town) Pickens County	144	3608	2.8	**Bluffton** (town) Beaufort County
69	1550	2.4	**Florence** (city) Florence County	144	n/a	2.8	**Sangaree** (CDP) Berkeley County
69	n/a	2.4	**Gloverville** (CDP) Aiken County	146	n/a	2.8	**Saluda** (town) Saluda County
69	1550	2.4	**Mount Pleasant** (town) Charleston County	147	3921	2.9	**Ladson** (CDP) Berkeley County
69	1550	2.4	**Red Hill** (CDP) Horry County	148	n/a	3.0	**Laurel Bay** (CDP) Beaufort County
69	1550	2.4	**Rock Hill** (city) York County	149	4141	3.0	**Five Forks** (CDP) Greenville County
75	n/a	2.4	**Mullins** (city) Marion County	150	n/a	3.0	**Southern Shops** (CDP) Spartanburg County

Note: The state column ranks the top/bottom 150 places in the state with population of 2,500 or more. The national column ranks the top/bottom places in the country with population of 10,000 or more. Places that are unincorporated were not considered in the rankings. n/a indicates data not available. Please refer to the User Guide for additional information.

Median Age

Top 150 Places Ranked in *Descending* Order

State Rank	Nat'l Rank	Years	Place
1	n/a	56.1	**Garden City** (CDP) Horry County
2	32	54.7	**North Myrtle Beach** (city) Horry County
3	n/a	54.1	**Little River** (CDP) Horry County
4	n/a	53.6	**Murrells Inlet** (CDP) Georgetown County
5	n/a	52.6	**Isle of Palms** (city) Charleston County
6	57	50.9	**Hilton Head Island** (town) Beaufort County
7	n/a	50.3	**Surfside Beach** (town) Horry County
8	n/a	47.7	**Folly Beach** (city) Charleston County
9	n/a	46.0	**Springdale** (town) Lexington County
10	n/a	45.9	**Lake Murray of Richland** (CDP) Richland County
11	n/a	45.7	**Hollywood** (town) Charleston County
12	n/a	45.3	**Camden** (city) Kershaw County
13	380	44.8	**Aiken** (city) Aiken County
14	n/a	44.7	**Northlake** (CDP) Anderson County
15	699	43.0	**Forest Acres** (city) Richland County
16	n/a	41.6	**Darlington** (city) Darlington County
16	n/a	41.6	**Newport** (CDP) York County
18	n/a	41.4	**Hopkins** (CDP) Richland County
18	n/a	41.4	**Seneca** (city) Oconee County
20	n/a	41.3	**Burnettown** (town) Aiken County
20	n/a	41.3	**Union** (city) Union County
22	n/a	40.8	**Belton** (city) Anderson County
23	n/a	40.6	**Cheraw** (town) Chesterfield County
23	n/a	40.6	**Hampton** (town) Hampton County
25	1437	40.5	**Easley** (city) Pickens County
25	n/a	40.5	**Honea Path** (town) Anderson County
27	n/a	40.4	**Abbeville** (city) Abbeville County
27	n/a	40.4	**Lake Wylie** (CDP) York County
27	n/a	40.4	**Pendleton** (town) Anderson County
30	n/a	40.2	**India Hook** (CDP) York County
30	n/a	40.2	**Tega Cay** (city) York County
32	n/a	40.0	**Bishopville** (city) Lee County
32	1610	40.0	**Red Hill** (CDP) Horry County
32	n/a	40.0	**Winnsboro** (town) Fairfield County
35	n/a	39.9	**Forestbrook** (CDP) Horry County
35	n/a	39.9	**Laurens** (city) Laurens County
35	n/a	39.9	**Mullins** (city) Marion County
35	n/a	39.9	**North Hartsville** (CDP) Darlington County
39	n/a	39.8	**Batesburg-Leesville** (town) Lexington County
39	n/a	39.8	**Lyman** (town) Spartanburg County
39	n/a	39.8	**Pickens** (city) Pickens County
39	1673	39.8	**Wade Hampton** (CDP) Greenville County
43	n/a	39.6	**Liberty** (city) Pickens County
44	n/a	39.5	**Dunean** (CDP) Greenville County
44	n/a	39.5	**Piedmont** (CDP) Anderson County
44	n/a	39.5	**Williston** (town) Barnwell County
47	n/a	39.4	**McCormick** (town) McCormick County
48	n/a	39.3	**Centerville** (CDP) Anderson County
48	n/a	39.3	**Williamston** (town) Anderson County
50	n/a	39.2	**Lugoff** (CDP) Kershaw County
50	n/a	39.2	**Manning** (city) Clarendon County
50	1872	39.2	**Myrtle Beach** (city) Horry County
53	1904	39.1	**Mount Pleasant** (town) Charleston County
54	n/a	39.0	**Lakewood** (CDP) Sumter County
55	n/a	38.9	**Walterboro** (city) Colleton County
56	n/a	38.8	**Arial** (CDP) Pickens County
57	n/a	38.7	**Bamberg** (town) Bamberg County
57	n/a	38.7	**Bennettsville** (city) Marlboro County
57	n/a	38.7	**Edgefield** (town) Edgefield County
60	2042	38.6	**Gaffney** (city) Cherokee County
61	n/a	38.5	**Lesslie** (CDP) York County
62	2137	38.3	**Seven Oaks** (CDP) Lexington County
63	n/a	38.0	**Gloverville** (CDP) Aiken County
63	n/a	38.0	**Woodruff** (city) Spartanburg County
65	2272	37.9	**North Augusta** (city) Aiken County
66	n/a	37.7	**Elgin** (CDP) Lancaster County
67	2432	37.4	**Florence** (city) Florence County
67	2432	37.4	**West Columbia** (city) Lexington County
69	2466	37.3	**Five Forks** (CDP) Greenville County
70	2534	37.1	**Mauldin** (city) Greenville County
70	n/a	37.1	**Pageland** (town) Chesterfield County
72	n/a	37.0	**East Gaffney** (CDP) Cherokee County
73	n/a	36.9	**Lancaster** (city) Lancaster County
73	2615	36.9	**Taylors** (CDP) Greenville County
75	2641	36.8	**Anderson** (city) Anderson County
75	n/a	36.8	**Welcome** (CDP) Greenville County
77	n/a	36.7	**Barnwell** (city) Barnwell County
77	n/a	36.7	**Georgetown** (city) Georgetown County
77	n/a	36.7	**Hartsville** (city) Darlington County
80	2716	36.6	**Irmo** (town) Richland County
81	n/a	36.5	**Kingstree** (town) Williamsburg County
81	2742	36.5	**Simpsonville** (city) Greenville County
83	n/a	36.4	**Chester** (city) Chester County
83	2768	36.4	**Gantt** (CDP) Greenville County
85	n/a	36.3	**Edisto** (CDP) Orangeburg County
85	2802	36.3	**Fort Mill** (town) York County
85	2802	36.3	**Socastee** (CDP) Horry County
88	n/a	36.2	**Belvedere** (CDP) Aiken County
88	2826	36.2	**Berea** (CDP) Greenville County
88	n/a	36.2	**Dillon** (city) Dillon County
91	n/a	36.1	**Homeland Park** (CDP) Anderson County
92	n/a	36.0	**Andrews** (town) Georgetown County
92	n/a	36.0	**Clearwater** (CDP) Aiken County
92	2893	36.0	**Oak Grove** (CDP) Lexington County
95	n/a	35.8	**Red Bank** (CDP) Lexington County
96	3039	35.5	**Spartanburg** (city) Spartanburg County
97	n/a	35.4	**Allendale** (town) Allendale County
98	n/a	35.3	**Boiling Springs** (CDP) Spartanburg County
98	n/a	35.3	**Marion** (city) Marion County
100	n/a	35.2	**Sans Souci** (CDP) Greenville County
101	n/a	35.0	**Fountain Inn** (city) Greenville County
102	3192	34.9	**Cayce** (city) Lexington County
103	3218	34.8	**Lexington** (town) Lexington County
104	3247	34.7	**Summerville** (town) Dorchester County
104	n/a	34.7	**Walhalla** (city) Oconee County
106	3280	34.6	**Greenville** (city) Greenville County
106	n/a	34.6	**Springdale** (CDP) Lancaster County
106	n/a	34.6	**York** (city) York County
109	n/a	34.5	**Graniteville** (CDP) Aiken County
110	n/a	34.4	**Travelers Rest** (city) Greenville County
111	n/a	34.3	**Woodfield** (CDP) Richland County
112	3378	34.2	**Beaufort** (city) Beaufort County
112	3378	34.2	**Hanahan** (city) Berkeley County
114	n/a	34.0	**Lake City** (city) Florence County
114	3432	34.0	**Parker** (CDP) Greenville County
116	3462	33.9	**Greer** (city) Greenville County
117	n/a	33.8	**Clover** (town) York County
118	3554	33.6	**Dentsville** (CDP) Richland County
118	n/a	33.6	**Sangaree** (CDP) Berkeley County
120	3651	33.2	**Newberry** (city) Newberry County
121	n/a	33.1	**Moncks Corner** (town) Berkeley County
122	3763	32.7	**Bluffton** (town) Beaufort County
122	n/a	32.7	**Clinton** (city) Laurens County
122	n/a	32.7	**Denmark** (city) Bamberg County
125	3806	32.5	**Charleston** (city) Charleston County
125	3806	32.5	**Sumter** (city) Sumter County
127	3880	32.2	**Ladson** (CDP) Berkeley County
128	3942	31.9	**Rock Hill** (city) York County
129	3999	31.6	**Greenwood** (city) Greenwood County
129	n/a	31.6	**Ridgeland** (town) Jasper County
131	n/a	31.4	**Duncan** (town) Spartanburg County
132	n/a	31.3	**Burton** (CDP) Beaufort County
133	4092	31.0	**Saint Andrews** (CDP) Richland County
134	4164	30.6	**North Charleston** (city) Charleston County
135	n/a	30.4	**Southern Shops** (CDP) Spartanburg County
136	4211	30.2	**Goose Creek** (city) Berkeley County
137	n/a	29.9	**Arcadia** (CDP) Spartanburg County
137	n/a	29.9	**Saluda** (town) Saluda County
139	n/a	29.4	**Dalzell** (CDP) Sumter County
140	4308	29.3	**Conway** (city) Horry County
140	n/a	29.3	**Hardeeville** (city) Jasper County
142	4350	28.8	**Orangeburg** (city) Orangeburg County
143	n/a	28.4	**Saxon** (CDP) Spartanburg County
144	4410	28.1	**Columbia** (city) Richland County
145	n/a	27.7	**Brookdale** (CDP) Orangeburg County
146	4554	24.3	**Clemson** (city) Pickens County
147	n/a	23.6	**Laurel Bay** (CDP) Beaufort County
148	n/a	23.0	**Valley Falls** (CDP) Spartanburg County
149	4591	22.9	**Port Royal** (town) Beaufort County
150	n/a	22.5	**Central** (town) Pickens County

Note: The state column ranks the top/bottom 150 places in the state with population of 2,500 or more. The national column ranks the top/bottom places in the country with population of 10,000 or more. Places that are unincorporated were not considered in the rankings. n/a indicates data not available. Please refer to the User Guide for additional information.

Median Age

Top 150 Places Ranked in *Ascending* Order

State Rank	Nat'l Rank	Years	Place
1	n/a	22.5	**Central** (town) Pickens County
2	62	22.9	**Port Royal** (town) Beaufort County
3	n/a	23.0	**Valley Falls** (CDP) Spartanburg County
4	n/a	23.6	**Laurel Bay** (CDP) Beaufort County
5	101	24.3	**Clemson** (city) Pickens County
6	n/a	27.7	**Brookdale** (CDP) Orangeburg County
7	238	28.1	**Columbia** (city) Richland County
8	n/a	28.4	**Saxon** (CDP) Spartanburg County
9	292	28.8	**Orangeburg** (city) Orangeburg County
10	342	29.3	**Conway** (city) Horry County
10	n/a	29.3	**Hardeeville** (city) Jasper County
12	n/a	29.4	**Dalzell** (CDP) Sumter County
13	n/a	29.9	**Arcadia** (CDP) Spartanburg County
13	n/a	29.9	**Saluda** (town) Saluda County
15	430	30.2	**Goose Creek** (city) Berkeley County
16	n/a	30.4	**Southern Shops** (CDP) Spartanburg County
17	483	30.6	**North Charleston** (city) Charleston County
18	548	31.0	**Saint Andrews** (CDP) Richland County
19	n/a	31.3	**Burton** (CDP) Beaufort County
20	n/a	31.4	**Duncan** (town) Spartanburg County
21	640	31.6	**Greenwood** (city) Greenwood County
21	n/a	31.6	**Ridgeland** (town) Jasper County
23	687	31.9	**Rock Hill** (city) York County
24	755	32.2	**Ladson** (CDP) Berkeley County
25	818	32.5	**Charleston** (city) Charleston County
25	818	32.5	**Sumter** (city) Sumter County
27	870	32.7	**Bluffton** (town) Beaufort County
27	n/a	32.7	**Clinton** (city) Laurens County
27	n/a	32.7	**Denmark** (city) Bamberg County
30	n/a	33.1	**Moncks Corner** (town) Berkeley County
31	982	33.2	**Newberry** (city) Newberry County
32	1080	33.6	**Dentsville** (CDP) Richland County
32	n/a	33.6	**Sangaree** (CDP) Berkeley County
34	n/a	33.8	**Clover** (town) York County
35	1167	33.9	**Greer** (city) Greenville County
36	n/a	34.0	**Lake City** (city) Florence County
36	n/a	34.0	**Parker** (CDP) Greenville County
38	1249	34.2	**Beaufort** (city) Beaufort County
38	1249	34.2	**Hanahan** (city) Berkeley County
40	n/a	34.3	**Woodfield** (CDP) Richland County
41	n/a	34.4	**Travelers Rest** (city) Greenville County
42	n/a	34.5	**Graniteville** (CDP) Aiken County
43	1339	34.6	**Greenville** (city) Greenville County
43	n/a	34.6	**Springdale** (CDP) Lancaster County
43	n/a	34.6	**York** (city) York County
46	1377	34.7	**Summerville** (town) Dorchester County
46	n/a	34.7	**Walhalla** (city) Oconee County
48	1410	34.8	**Lexington** (town) Lexington County
49	1439	34.9	**Cayce** (city) Lexington County
50	n/a	35.0	**Fountain Inn** (city) Greenville County
51	n/a	35.2	**Sans Souci** (CDP) Greenville County
52	n/a	35.3	**Boiling Springs** (CDP) Spartanburg County
52	n/a	35.3	**Marion** (city) Marion County
54	n/a	35.4	**Allendale** (town) Allendale County
55	1588	35.5	**Spartanburg** (city) Spartanburg County
56	n/a	35.8	**Red Bank** (CDP) Lexington County
57	n/a	36.0	**Andrews** (town) Georgetown County
57	n/a	36.0	**Clearwater** (CDP) Aiken County
57	1728	36.0	**Oak Grove** (CDP) Lexington County
60	n/a	36.1	**Homeland Park** (CDP) Anderson County
61	n/a	36.2	**Belvedere** (CDP) Aiken County
61	1796	36.2	**Berea** (CDP) Greenville County
61	n/a	36.2	**Dillon** (city) Dillon County
64	n/a	36.3	**Edisto** (CDP) Orangeburg County
64	1831	36.3	**Fort Mill** (town) York County
64	1831	36.3	**Socastee** (CDP) Horry County
67	n/a	36.4	**Chester** (city) Chester County
67	1855	36.4	**Gantt** (CDP) Greenville County
69	n/a	36.5	**Kingstree** (town) Williamsburg County
69	1889	36.5	**Simpsonville** (city) Greenville County
71	1915	36.6	**Irmo** (town) Richland County
72	n/a	36.7	**Barnwell** (city) Barnwell County
72	n/a	36.7	**Georgetown** (city) Georgetown County
72	n/a	36.7	**Hartsville** (city) Darlington County
75	1976	36.8	**Anderson** (city) Anderson County
75	n/a	36.8	**Welcome** (CDP) Greenville County
77	n/a	36.9	**Lancaster** (city) Lancaster County
77	2016	36.9	**Taylors** (CDP) Greenville County
79	n/a	37.0	**East Gaffney** (CDP) Cherokee County
80	2082	37.1	**Mauldin** (city) Greenville County
80	n/a	37.1	**Pageland** (town) Chesterfield County
82	2161	37.3	**Five Forks** (CDP) Greenville County
83	2191	37.4	**Florence** (city) Florence County
83	2191	37.4	**West Columbia** (city) Lexington County
85	n/a	37.7	**Elgin** (CDP) Lancaster County
86	2348	37.9	**North Augusta** (city) Aiken County
87	n/a	38.0	**Gloverville** (CDP) Aiken County
87	n/a	38.0	**Woodruff** (city) Spartanburg County
89	2482	38.3	**Seven Oaks** (CDP) Lexington County
90	n/a	38.5	**Lesslie** (CDP) York County
91	2591	38.6	**Gaffney** (city) Cherokee County
92	n/a	38.7	**Bamberg** (town) Bamberg County
92	n/a	38.7	**Bennettsville** (city) Marlboro County
92	n/a	38.7	**Edgefield** (town) Edgefield County
95	n/a	38.8	**Arial** (CDP) Pickens County
96	n/a	38.9	**Walterboro** (city) Colleton County
97	n/a	39.0	**Lakewood** (CDP) Sumter County
98	2723	39.1	**Mount Pleasant** (town) Charleston County
99	n/a	39.2	**Lugoff** (CDP) Kershaw County
99	n/a	39.2	**Manning** (city) Clarendon County
99	2753	39.2	**Myrtle Beach** (city) Horry County
102	n/a	39.3	**Centerville** (CDP) Anderson County
102	n/a	39.3	**Williamston** (town) Anderson County
104	n/a	39.4	**McCormick** (town) McCormick County
105	n/a	39.5	**Dunean** (CDP) Greenville County
105	n/a	39.5	**Piedmont** (CDP) Anderson County
105	n/a	39.5	**Williston** (town) Barnwell County
108	n/a	39.6	**Liberty** (city) Pickens County
109	n/a	39.8	**Batesburg-Leesville** (town) Lexington County
109	n/a	39.8	**Lyman** (town) Spartanburg County
109	n/a	39.8	**Pickens** (city) Pickens County
109	2947	39.8	**Wade Hampton** (CDP) Greenville County
113	n/a	39.9	**Forestbrook** (CDP) Horry County
113	n/a	39.9	**Laurens** (city) Laurens County
113	n/a	39.9	**Mullins** (city) Marion County
113	n/a	39.9	**North Hartsville** (CDP) Darlington County
117	n/a	40.0	**Bishopville** (city) Lee County
117	3022	40.0	**Red Hill** (CDP) Horry County
117	n/a	40.0	**Winnsboro** (town) Fairfield County
120	n/a	40.2	**India Hook** (CDP) York County
120	n/a	40.2	**Tega Cay** (city) York County
122	n/a	40.4	**Abbeville** (city) Abbeville County
122	n/a	40.4	**Lake Wylie** (CDP) York County
122	n/a	40.4	**Pendleton** (town) Anderson County
125	3185	40.5	**Easley** (city) Pickens County
125	n/a	40.5	**Honea Path** (town) Anderson County
127	n/a	40.6	**Cheraw** (town) Chesterfield County
127	n/a	40.6	**Hampton** (town) Hampton County
129	n/a	40.8	**Belton** (city) Anderson County
130	n/a	41.3	**Burnettown** (town) Aiken County
130	n/a	41.3	**Union** (city) Union County
132	n/a	41.4	**Hopkins** (CDP) Richland County
132	n/a	41.4	**Seneca** (city) Oconee County
134	n/a	41.6	**Darlington** (city) Darlington County
134	n/a	41.6	**Newport** (CDP) York County
136	3937	43.0	**Forest Acres** (city) Richland County
137	n/a	44.7	**Northlake** (CDP) Anderson County
138	4259	44.8	**Aiken** (city) Aiken County
139	n/a	45.3	**Camden** (city) Kershaw County
140	n/a	45.7	**Hollywood** (town) Charleston County
141	n/a	45.9	**Lake Murray of Richland** (CDP) Richland County
142	n/a	46.0	**Springdale** (town) Lexington County
143	n/a	47.7	**Folly Beach** (city) Charleston County
144	n/a	50.3	**Surfside Beach** (town) Horry County
145	4596	50.9	**Hilton Head Island** (town) Beaufort County
146	n/a	52.6	**Isle of Palms** (city) Charleston County
147	n/a	53.6	**Murrells Inlet** (CDP) Georgetown County
148	n/a	54.1	**Little River** (CDP) Horry County
149	4624	54.7	**North Myrtle Beach** (city) Horry County
150	n/a	56.1	**Garden City** (CDP) Horry County

Note: The state column ranks the top/bottom 150 places in the state with population of 2,500 or more. The national column ranks the top/bottom places in the country with population of 10,000 or more. Places that are unincorporated were not considered in the rankings. n/a indicates data not available. Please refer to the User Guide for additional information.

Population Under Age 18

Top 150 Places Ranked in *Descending* Order

State Rank	Nat'l Rank	Percent	Place
1	n/a	37.3	**Laurel Bay** (CDP) Beaufort County
2	149	33.3	**Five Forks** (CDP) Greenville County
3	n/a	30.6	**Duncan** (town) Spartanburg County
4	n/a	30.1	**Dalzell** (CDP) Sumter County
5	522	29.8	**Fort Mill** (town) York County
6	572	29.5	**Ladson** (CDP) Berkeley County
7	n/a	29.3	**Travelers Rest** (city) Greenville County
8	n/a	29.2	**Lake City** (city) Florence County
8	n/a	29.2	**Tega Cay** (city) York County
10	n/a	29.1	**Clover** (town) York County
11	663	28.9	**Bluffton** (town) Beaufort County
12	n/a	28.0	**Allendale** (town) Allendale County
12	n/a	28.0	**Sangaree** (CDP) Berkeley County
14	n/a	27.9	**Andrews** (town) Georgetown County
14	n/a	27.9	**Kingstree** (town) Williamsburg County
16	n/a	27.8	**Saluda** (town) Saluda County
16	n/a	27.8	**Walhalla** (city) Oconee County
18	n/a	27.6	**Marion** (city) Marion County
19	n/a	27.5	**Graniteville** (CDP) Aiken County
19	n/a	27.5	**York** (city) York County
21	n/a	27.4	**Dillon** (city) Dillon County
21	n/a	27.4	**Moncks Corner** (town) Berkeley County
23	n/a	27.3	**Boiling Springs** (CDP) Spartanburg County
24	n/a	27.2	**Fountain Inn** (city) Greenville County
25	n/a	27.1	**Georgetown** (city) Georgetown County
26	n/a	27.0	**Chester** (city) Chester County
26	1125	27.0	**Summerville** (town) Dorchester County
28	n/a	26.9	**Southern Shops** (CDP) Spartanburg County
29	1251	26.6	**Greer** (city) Greenville County
30	n/a	26.5	**Barnwell** (city) Barnwell County
30	n/a	26.5	**Lakewood** (CDP) Sumter County
32	n/a	26.4	**Burton** (CDP) Beaufort County
33	n/a	26.3	**Arcadia** (CDP) Spartanburg County
33	n/a	26.3	**Lake Wylie** (CDP) York County
33	n/a	26.3	**Lugoff** (CDP) Kershaw County
36	n/a	26.1	**Springdale** (CDP) Lancaster County
37	n/a	26.0	**Cheraw** (town) Chesterfield County
37	1461	26.0	**Gantt** (CDP) Greenville County
37	1461	26.0	**Simpsonville** (city) Greenville County
40	1496	25.9	**Sumter** (city) Sumter County
40	n/a	25.9	**Williston** (town) Barnwell County
40	n/a	25.9	**Woodruff** (city) Spartanburg County
43	n/a	25.8	**Homeland Park** (CDP) Anderson County
43	n/a	25.8	**Walterboro** (city) Colleton County
45	1643	25.5	**North Charleston** (city) Charleston County
45	1643	25.5	**Parker** (CDP) Greenville County
45	n/a	25.5	**Red Bank** (CDP) Lexington County
48	n/a	25.4	**Bishopville** (city) Lee County
48	n/a	25.4	**Hardeeville** (city) Jasper County
50	n/a	25.3	**Edisto** (CDP) Orangeburg County
50	n/a	25.3	**Gloverville** (CDP) Aiken County
50	n/a	25.3	**Lancaster** (city) Lancaster County
50	n/a	25.3	**Mullins** (city) Marion County
54	1762	25.2	**Irmo** (town) Richland County
54	n/a	25.2	**Lesslie** (CDP) York County
56	n/a	25.0	**Belvedere** (CDP) Aiken County
56	n/a	25.0	**Hampton** (town) Hampton County
58	1891	24.9	**Goose Creek** (city) Berkeley County
58	n/a	24.9	**North Hartsville** (CDP) Darlington County
60	n/a	24.8	**Welcome** (CDP) Greenville County
61	n/a	24.7	**Batesburg-Leesville** (town) Lexington County
62	n/a	24.6	**Clearwater** (CDP) Aiken County
62	2025	24.6	**Lexington** (town) Lexington County
62	2025	24.6	**Taylors** (CDP) Greenville County
65	2075	24.5	**Florence** (city) Florence County
65	2075	24.5	**Mauldin** (city) Greenville County
67	2122	24.4	**Oak Grove** (CDP) Lexington County
67	2122	24.4	**Rock Hill** (city) York County
69	n/a	24.3	**Arial** (CDP) Pickens County
69	n/a	24.3	**Elgin** (CDP) Lancaster County
69	2158	24.3	**Hanahan** (city) Berkeley County
69	n/a	24.3	**Hartsville** (city) Darlington County
69	n/a	24.3	**Woodfield** (CDP) Richland County
74	n/a	24.2	**East Gaffney** (CDP) Cherokee County
74	2205	24.2	**Greenwood** (city) Greenwood County
74	n/a	24.2	**Newport** (CDP) York County
74	n/a	24.2	**Piedmont** (CDP) Anderson County
74	n/a	24.2	**Winnsboro** (town) Fairfield County
79	2255	24.1	**Berea** (CDP) Greenville County
79	2255	24.1	**Mount Pleasant** (town) Charleston County
81	n/a	24.0	**Abbeville** (city) Abbeville County
81	n/a	24.0	**Laurens** (city) Laurens County
83	n/a	23.8	**Darlington** (city) Darlington County
83	n/a	23.8	**Hopkins** (CDP) Richland County
83	n/a	23.8	**Williamston** (town) Anderson County
86	n/a	23.7	**Honea Path** (town) Anderson County
86	n/a	23.7	**Pageland** (town) Chesterfield County
88	n/a	23.5	**Lake Murray of Richland** (CDP) Richland County
88	2525	23.5	**Spartanburg** (city) Spartanburg County
88	n/a	23.5	**Union** (city) Union County
91	2577	23.4	**Anderson** (city) Anderson County
91	n/a	23.4	**Liberty** (city) Pickens County
91	n/a	23.4	**Manning** (city) Clarendon County
91	2577	23.4	**North Augusta** (city) Aiken County
91	n/a	23.4	**Sans Souci** (CDP) Greenville County
96	n/a	23.3	**Belton** (city) Anderson County
96	n/a	23.3	**Forestbrook** (CDP) Horry County
96	n/a	23.3	**Saxon** (CDP) Spartanburg County
99	n/a	23.1	**Burnettown** (town) Aiken County
99	n/a	23.1	**Centerville** (CDP) Anderson County
101	2776	23.0	**Dentsville** (CDP) Richland County
102	n/a	22.8	**Bamberg** (town) Bamberg County
102	2870	22.8	**Easley** (city) Pickens County
104	2913	22.7	**Newberry** (city) Newberry County
105	3007	22.5	**Socastee** (CDP) Horry County
106	3047	22.4	**Gaffney** (city) Cherokee County
107	3092	22.3	**Beaufort** (city) Beaufort County
108	n/a	22.2	**Pickens** (city) Pickens County
108	3141	22.2	**Saint Andrews** (CDP) Richland County
108	n/a	22.2	**Seneca** (city) Oconee County
111	3185	22.1	**Seven Oaks** (CDP) Lexington County
112	n/a	21.9	**Camden** (city) Kershaw County
112	n/a	21.9	**India Hook** (CDP) York County
114	n/a	21.7	**Clinton** (city) Laurens County
114	n/a	21.7	**Denmark** (city) Bamberg County
116	n/a	21.6	**Lyman** (town) Spartanburg County
117	n/a	21.3	**Brookdale** (CDP) Orangeburg County
118	n/a	21.0	**Dunean** (CDP) Greenville County
118	3606	21.0	**Forest Acres** (city) Richland County
120	n/a	20.5	**Bennettsville** (city) Marlboro County
120	3790	20.5	**Wade Hampton** (CDP) Greenville County
122	n/a	20.3	**Northlake** (CDP) Anderson County
123	n/a	20.2	**Hollywood** (town) Charleston County
124	3938	20.0	**Conway** (city) Horry County
125	4026	19.6	**Aiken** (city) Aiken County
126	n/a	19.5	**Ridgeland** (town) Jasper County
127	4074	19.4	**Greenville** (city) Greenville County
128	4102	19.3	**Red Hill** (CDP) Horry County
129	n/a	19.1	**Springdale** (town) Lexington County
130	4186	18.9	**Orangeburg** (city) Orangeburg County
131	4238	18.6	**Cayce** (city) Lexington County
132	4259	18.5	**Myrtle Beach** (city) Horry County
132	4259	18.5	**West Columbia** (city) Lexington County
134	n/a	18.2	**Pendleton** (town) Anderson County
135	4312	18.0	**Charleston** (city) Charleston County
135	4312	18.0	**Port Royal** (town) Beaufort County
137	4405	17.0	**Columbia** (city) Richland County
137	n/a	17.0	**Isle of Palms** (city) Charleston County
139	4431	16.6	**Hilton Head Island** (town) Beaufort County
140	n/a	16.5	**Valley Falls** (CDP) Spartanburg County
141	4553	13.8	**Clemson** (city) Pickens County
142	n/a	13.7	**Murrells Inlet** (CDP) Georgetown County
143	n/a	13.5	**Edgefield** (town) Edgefield County
144	n/a	13.3	**Surfside Beach** (town) Horry County
145	n/a	13.1	**Little River** (CDP) Horry County
145	n/a	13.1	**McCormick** (town) McCormick County
147	n/a	13.0	**Garden City** (CDP) Horry County
148	4596	11.8	**North Myrtle Beach** (city) Horry County
149	n/a	11.1	**Central** (town) Pickens County
150	n/a	10.2	**Folly Beach** (city) Charleston County

Note: The state column ranks the top/bottom 150 places in the state with population of 2,500 or more. The national column ranks the top/bottom places in the country with population of 10,000 or more. Places that are unincorporated were not considered in the rankings. n/a indicates data not available. Please refer to the User Guide for additional information.

Population Under Age 18

Top 150 Places Ranked in *Ascending* Order

State Rank	Nat'l Rank	Percent	Place
1	n/a	10.2	**Folly Beach** (city) Charleston County
2	n/a	11.1	**Central** (town) Pickens County
3	59	11.8	**North Myrtle Beach** (city) Horry County
4	n/a	13.0	**Garden City** (CDP) Horry County
5	n/a	13.1	**Little River** (CDP) Horry County
5	n/a	13.1	**McCormick** (town) McCormick County
7	n/a	13.3	**Surfside Beach** (town) Horry County
8	n/a	13.5	**Edgefield** (town) Edgefield County
9	n/a	13.7	**Murrells Inlet** (CDP) Georgetown County
10	100	13.8	**Clemson** (city) Pickens County
11	n/a	16.5	**Valley Falls** (CDP) Spartanburg County
12	221	16.6	**Hilton Head Island** (town) Beaufort County
13	244	17.0	**Columbia** (city) Richland County
13	n/a	17.0	**Isle of Palms** (city) Charleston County
15	334	18.0	**Charleston** (city) Charleston County
15	334	18.0	**Port Royal** (town) Beaufort County
17	n/a	18.2	**Pendleton** (town) Anderson County
18	383	18.5	**Myrtle Beach** (city) Horry County
18	383	18.5	**West Columbia** (city) Lexington County
20	398	18.6	**Cayce** (city) Lexington County
21	453	18.9	**Orangeburg** (city) Orangeburg County
22	n/a	19.1	**Springdale** (town) Lexington County
23	533	19.3	**Red Hill** (CDP) Horry County
24	555	19.4	**Greenville** (city) Greenville County
25	n/a	19.5	**Ridgeland** (town) Jasper County
26	605	19.6	**Aiken** (city) Aiken County
27	696	20.0	**Conway** (city) Horry County
28	n/a	20.2	**Hollywood** (town) Charleston County
29	n/a	20.3	**Northlake** (CDP) Anderson County
30	n/a	20.5	**Bennettsville** (city) Marlboro County
30	840	20.5	**Wade Hampton** (CDP) Greenville County
32	n/a	21.0	**Dunean** (CDP) Greenville County
32	1007	21.0	**Forest Acres** (city) Richland County
34	n/a	21.3	**Brookdale** (CDP) Orangeburg County
35	n/a	21.6	**Lyman** (town) Spartanburg County
36	n/a	21.7	**Clinton** (city) Laurens County
36	n/a	21.7	**Denmark** (city) Bamberg County
38	n/a	21.9	**Camden** (city) Kershaw County
38	n/a	21.9	**India Hook** (CDP) York County
40	1435	22.1	**Seven Oaks** (CDP) Lexington County
41	n/a	22.2	**Pickens** (city) Pickens County
41	1472	22.2	**Saint Andrews** (CDP) Richland County
41	n/a	22.2	**Seneca** (city) Oconee County
44	1516	22.3	**Beaufort** (city) Beaufort County
45	1565	22.4	**Gaffney** (city) Cherokee County
46	1610	22.5	**Socastee** (CDP) Horry County
47	1700	22.7	**Newberry** (city) Newberry County
48	n/a	22.8	**Bamberg** (town) Bamberg County
48	1744	22.8	**Easley** (city) Pickens County
50	1833	23.0	**Dentsville** (CDP) Richland County
51	n/a	23.1	**Burnettown** (town) Aiken County
51	n/a	23.1	**Centerville** (CDP) Anderson County
53	n/a	23.3	**Belton** (city) Anderson County
53	n/a	23.3	**Forestbrook** (CDP) Horry County
53	n/a	23.3	**Saxon** (CDP) Spartanburg County
56	2033	23.4	**Anderson** (city) Anderson County
56	n/a	23.4	**Liberty** (city) Pickens County
56	n/a	23.4	**Manning** (city) Clarendon County
56	2033	23.4	**North Augusta** (city) Aiken County
56	n/a	23.4	**Sans Souci** (CDP) Greenville County
61	n/a	23.5	**Lake Murray of Richland** (CDP) Richland County
61	2080	23.5	**Spartanburg** (city) Spartanburg County
61	n/a	23.5	**Union** (city) Union County
64	n/a	23.7	**Honea Path** (town) Anderson County
64	n/a	23.7	**Pageland** (town) Chesterfield County
66	n/a	23.8	**Darlington** (city) Darlington County
66	n/a	23.8	**Hopkins** (CDP) Richland County
66	n/a	23.8	**Williamston** (town) Anderson County
69	n/a	24.0	**Abbeville** (city) Abbeville County
69	n/a	24.0	**Laurens** (city) Laurens County
71	2355	24.1	**Berea** (CDP) Greenville County
71	2355	24.1	**Mount Pleasant** (town) Charleston County
73	n/a	24.2	**East Gaffney** (CDP) Cherokee County
73	2402	24.2	**Greenwood** (city) Greenwood County
73	n/a	24.2	**Newport** (CDP) York County
73	n/a	24.2	**Piedmont** (CDP) Anderson County
73	n/a	24.2	**Winnsboro** (town) Fairfield County
78	n/a	24.3	**Arial** (CDP) Pickens County
78	n/a	24.3	**Elgin** (CDP) Lancaster County
78	2452	24.3	**Hanahan** (city) Berkeley County
78	n/a	24.3	**Hartsville** (city) Darlington County
78	n/a	24.3	**Woodfield** (CDP) Richland County
83	2499	24.4	**Oak Grove** (CDP) Lexington County
83	2499	24.4	**Rock Hill** (city) York County
85	2535	24.5	**Florence** (city) Florence County
85	2535	24.5	**Mauldin** (city) Greenville County
87	n/a	24.6	**Clearwater** (CDP) Aiken County
87	2582	24.6	**Lexington** (town) Lexington County
87	2582	24.6	**Taylors** (CDP) Greenville County
90	n/a	24.7	**Batesburg-Leesville** (town) Lexington County
91	n/a	24.8	**Welcome** (CDP) Greenville County
92	2723	24.9	**Goose Creek** (city) Berkeley County
92	n/a	24.9	**North Hartsville** (CDP) Darlington County
94	n/a	25.0	**Belvedere** (CDP) Aiken County
94	n/a	25.0	**Hampton** (town) Hampton County
96	2860	25.2	**Irmo** (town) Richland County
96	n/a	25.2	**Lesslie** (CDP) York County
98	n/a	25.3	**Edisto** (CDP) Orangeburg County
98	n/a	25.3	**Gloverville** (CDP) Aiken County
98	n/a	25.3	**Lancaster** (city) Lancaster County
98	n/a	25.3	**Mullins** (city) Marion County
102	n/a	25.4	**Bishopville** (city) Lee County
102	n/a	25.4	**Hardeeville** (city) Jasper County
104	2975	25.5	**North Charleston** (city) Charleston County
104	2975	25.5	**Parker** (CDP) Greenville County
104	n/a	25.5	**Red Bank** (CDP) Lexington County
107	n/a	25.8	**Homeland Park** (CDP) Anderson County
107	n/a	25.8	**Walterboro** (city) Colleton County
109	3127	25.9	**Sumter** (city) Sumter County
109	n/a	25.9	**Williston** (town) Barnwell County
109	n/a	25.9	**Woodruff** (city) Spartanburg County
112	n/a	26.0	**Cheraw** (town) Chesterfield County
112	3161	26.0	**Gantt** (CDP) Greenville County
112	3161	26.0	**Simpsonville** (city) Greenville County
115	n/a	26.1	**Springdale** (CDP) Lancaster County
116	n/a	26.3	**Arcadia** (CDP) Spartanburg County
116	n/a	26.3	**Lake Wylie** (CDP) York County
116	n/a	26.3	**Lugoff** (CDP) Kershaw County
119	n/a	26.4	**Burton** (CDP) Beaufort County
120	n/a	26.5	**Barnwell** (city) Barnwell County
120	n/a	26.5	**Lakewood** (CDP) Sumter County
122	3367	26.6	**Greer** (city) Greenville County
123	n/a	26.9	**Southern Shops** (CDP) Spartanburg County
124	n/a	27.0	**Chester** (city) Chester County
124	3501	27.0	**Summerville** (town) Dorchester County
126	n/a	27.1	**Georgetown** (city) Georgetown County
127	n/a	27.2	**Fountain Inn** (city) Greenville County
128	n/a	27.3	**Boiling Springs** (CDP) Spartanburg County
129	n/a	27.4	**Dillon** (city) Dillon County
129	n/a	27.4	**Moncks Corner** (town) Berkeley County
131	n/a	27.5	**Graniteville** (CDP) Aiken County
131	n/a	27.5	**York** (city) York County
133	n/a	27.6	**Marion** (city) Marion County
134	n/a	27.8	**Saluda** (town) Saluda County
134	n/a	27.8	**Walhalla** (city) Oconee County
136	n/a	27.9	**Andrews** (town) Georgetown County
136	n/a	27.9	**Kingstree** (town) Williamsburg County
138	n/a	28.0	**Allendale** (town) Allendale County
138	n/a	28.0	**Sangaree** (CDP) Berkeley County
140	3983	28.9	**Bluffton** (town) Beaufort County
141	n/a	29.1	**Clover** (town) York County
142	n/a	29.2	**Lake City** (city) Florence County
142	n/a	29.2	**Tega Cay** (city) York County
144	n/a	29.3	**Travelers Rest** (city) Greenville County
145	4074	29.5	**Ladson** (CDP) Berkeley County
146	4118	29.8	**Fort Mill** (town) York County
147	n/a	30.1	**Dalzell** (CDP) Sumter County
148	n/a	30.6	**Duncan** (town) Spartanburg County
149	4499	33.3	**Five Forks** (CDP) Greenville County
150	n/a	37.3	**Laurel Bay** (CDP) Beaufort County

Note: The state column ranks the top/bottom 150 places in the state with population of 2,500 or more. The national column ranks the top/bottom places in the country with population of 10,000 or more. Places that are unincorporated were not considered in the rankings. n/a indicates data not available. Please refer to the User Guide for additional information.

Population Age 65 and Over

Top 150 Places Ranked in *Descending* Order

State Rank	Nat'l Rank	Percent	Place
1	n/a	35.2	**Garden City** (CDP) Horry County
2	n/a	29.0	**Little River** (CDP) Horry County
3	58	28.8	**Hilton Head Island** (town) Beaufort County
4	72	27.2	**North Myrtle Beach** (city) Horry County
5	n/a	26.4	**Murrells Inlet** (CDP) Georgetown County
6	n/a	23.8	**Springdale** (town) Lexington County
7	n/a	22.6	**Isle of Palms** (city) Charleston County
7	n/a	22.6	**Surfside Beach** (town) Horry County
9	197	21.9	**Aiken** (city) Aiken County
10	n/a	21.6	**Camden** (city) Kershaw County
11	n/a	19.8	**Pendleton** (town) Anderson County
12	n/a	19.5	**Laurens** (city) Laurens County
13	n/a	19.3	**Honea Path** (town) Anderson County
14	404	19.1	**Forest Acres** (city) Richland County
15	n/a	19.0	**Darlington** (city) Darlington County
16	n/a	18.9	**Seneca** (city) Oconee County
17	n/a	18.6	**Cheraw** (town) Chesterfield County
17	495	18.6	**Red Hill** (CDP) Horry County
19	n/a	18.3	**Mullins** (city) Marion County
20	n/a	18.2	**Arial** (CDP) Pickens County
20	n/a	18.2	**Bishopville** (city) Lee County
20	n/a	18.2	**Lake Murray of Richland** (CDP) Richland County
23	n/a	18.1	**Belton** (city) Anderson County
23	n/a	18.1	**Folly Beach** (city) Charleston County
23	574	18.1	**Wade Hampton** (CDP) Greenville County
26	595	18.0	**Easley** (city) Pickens County
26	n/a	18.0	**Pickens** (city) Pickens County
26	n/a	18.0	**Union** (city) Union County
29	616	17.9	**Anderson** (city) Anderson County
29	n/a	17.9	**Walterboro** (city) Colleton County
31	n/a	17.8	**Hampton** (town) Hampton County
32	n/a	17.7	**Northlake** (CDP) Anderson County
33	n/a	17.5	**Abbeville** (city) Abbeville County
34	n/a	17.4	**Bamberg** (town) Bamberg County
34	741	17.4	**Gaffney** (city) Cherokee County
36	n/a	17.0	**Williamston** (town) Anderson County
37	n/a	16.9	**Kingstree** (town) Williamsburg County
37	n/a	16.9	**Liberty** (city) Pickens County
37	n/a	16.9	**Winnsboro** (town) Fairfield County
37	n/a	16.9	**Woodruff** (city) Spartanburg County
41	n/a	16.8	**Williston** (town) Barnwell County
42	n/a	16.7	**Manning** (city) Clarendon County
43	n/a	16.6	**Batesburg-Leesville** (town) Lexington County
44	1004	16.4	**Newberry** (city) Newberry County
45	n/a	16.3	**Lancaster** (city) Lancaster County
45	1033	16.3	**West Columbia** (city) Lexington County
47	n/a	16.2	**Burnettown** (town) Aiken County
47	n/a	16.2	**Dillon** (city) Dillon County
47	n/a	16.2	**Hartsville** (city) Darlington County
47	n/a	16.2	**Lyman** (town) Spartanburg County
51	n/a	16.1	**Clinton** (city) Laurens County
52	1150	15.9	**Berea** (CDP) Greenville County
52	n/a	15.9	**Dunean** (CDP) Greenville County
54	n/a	15.7	**Centerville** (CDP) Anderson County
55	1295	15.5	**Beaufort** (city) Beaufort County
56	1326	15.4	**Seven Oaks** (CDP) Lexington County
57	n/a	15.2	**Barnwell** (city) Barnwell County
58	1433	15.1	**Myrtle Beach** (city) Horry County
59	n/a	15.0	**Belvedere** (CDP) Aiken County
59	n/a	15.0	**Graniteville** (CDP) Aiken County
59	n/a	15.0	**Hollywood** (town) Charleston County
62	n/a	14.9	**Homeland Park** (CDP) Anderson County
62	n/a	14.9	**Piedmont** (CDP) Anderson County
64	n/a	14.7	**Bennettsville** (city) Marlboro County
64	n/a	14.7	**Georgetown** (city) Georgetown County
64	1574	14.7	**North Augusta** (city) Aiken County
64	n/a	14.7	**Pageland** (town) Chesterfield County
68	n/a	14.6	**Brookdale** (CDP) Orangeburg County
68	n/a	14.6	**Marion** (city) Marion County
68	1615	14.6	**Spartanburg** (city) Spartanburg County
71	1653	14.5	**Greenwood** (city) Greenwood County
71	n/a	14.5	**North Hartsville** (CDP) Darlington County
73	n/a	14.4	**Walhalla** (city) Oconee County
74	n/a	14.3	**Lake Wylie** (CDP) York County
74	n/a	14.3	**York** (city) York County
76	n/a	14.2	**Clearwater** (CDP) Aiken County
76	1781	14.2	**Orangeburg** (city) Orangeburg County
78	n/a	14.1	**Gloverville** (CDP) Aiken County
79	1865	14.0	**Cayce** (city) Lexington County
79	n/a	14.0	**Springdale** (CDP) Lancaster County
81	n/a	13.9	**Andrews** (town) Georgetown County
81	1911	13.9	**Florence** (city) Florence County
81	1911	13.9	**Sumter** (city) Sumter County
81	n/a	13.9	**Welcome** (CDP) Greenville County
85	n/a	13.8	**Lake City** (city) Florence County
85	n/a	13.8	**Sans Souci** (CDP) Greenville County
87	n/a	13.6	**Chester** (city) Chester County
87	n/a	13.6	**Denmark** (city) Bamberg County
87	2052	13.6	**Taylors** (CDP) Greenville County
90	n/a	13.3	**Lugoff** (CDP) Kershaw County
91	2220	13.2	**Conway** (city) Horry County
91	n/a	13.2	**Hopkins** (CDP) Richland County
91	n/a	13.2	**Woodfield** (CDP) Richland County
94	2260	13.1	**Dentsville** (CDP) Richland County
95	n/a	13.0	**East Gaffney** (CDP) Cherokee County
95	n/a	13.0	**Forestbrook** (CDP) Horry County
95	2304	13.0	**Gantt** (CDP) Greenville County
98	n/a	12.8	**Allendale** (town) Allendale County
98	2390	12.8	**Greenville** (city) Greenville County
100	n/a	12.7	**India Hook** (CDP) York County
101	n/a	12.5	**Elgin** (CDP) Lancaster County
102	2665	12.2	**Charleston** (city) Charleston County
102	2665	12.2	**Mount Pleasant** (town) Charleston County
102	2665	12.2	**Parker** (CDP) Greenville County
105	n/a	12.1	**Travelers Rest** (city) Greenville County
106	n/a	12.0	**Edgefield** (town) Edgefield County
107	n/a	11.9	**Lesslie** (CDP) York County
108	n/a	11.8	**Edisto** (CDP) Orangeburg County
108	2823	11.8	**Mauldin** (city) Greenville County
108	2823	11.8	**Oak Grove** (CDP) Lexington County
108	n/a	11.8	**Saluda** (town) Saluda County
112	2924	11.6	**Clemson** (city) Pickens County
112	2924	11.6	**Socastee** (CDP) Horry County
114	n/a	11.4	**Fountain Inn** (city) Greenville County
115	n/a	11.2	**Newport** (CDP) York County
116	n/a	11.1	**McCormick** (town) McCormick County
117	n/a	11.0	**Lakewood** (CDP) Sumter County
117	3159	11.0	**Simpsonville** (city) Greenville County
119	3190	10.9	**Greer** (city) Greenville County
120	3230	10.8	**Hanahan** (city) Berkeley County
121	n/a	10.7	**Boiling Springs** (CDP) Spartanburg County
122	n/a	10.6	**Moncks Corner** (town) Berkeley County
123	3351	10.5	**Summerville** (town) Dorchester County
123	n/a	10.5	**Tega Cay** (city) York County
125	3388	10.4	**Rock Hill** (city) York County
126	3427	10.3	**Lexington** (town) Lexington County
127	3462	10.2	**Irmo** (town) Richland County
127	n/a	10.2	**Saxon** (CDP) Spartanburg County
129	n/a	10.1	**Clover** (town) York County
130	3520	10.0	**Fort Mill** (town) York County
131	n/a	9.8	**Duncan** (town) Spartanburg County
132	3681	9.4	**Saint Andrews** (CDP) Richland County
133	n/a	9.2	**Valley Falls** (CDP) Spartanburg County
134	n/a	9.1	**Arcadia** (CDP) Spartanburg County
134	n/a	9.1	**Burton** (CDP) Beaufort County
136	3890	8.7	**Columbia** (city) Richland County
137	n/a	8.6	**Red Bank** (CDP) Lexington County
138	n/a	8.5	**Ridgeland** (town) Jasper County
139	3986	8.4	**North Charleston** (city) Charleston County
140	n/a	8.3	**Dalzell** (CDP) Sumter County
141	n/a	7.9	**Hardeeville** (city) Jasper County
142	4232	7.3	**Bluffton** (town) Beaufort County
142	4232	7.3	**Goose Creek** (city) Berkeley County
142	4232	7.3	**Ladson** (CDP) Berkeley County
145	n/a	7.0	**Southern Shops** (CDP) Spartanburg County
146	4309	6.9	**Five Forks** (CDP) Greenville County
146	n/a	6.9	**Sangaree** (CDP) Berkeley County
148	n/a	6.8	**Central** (town) Pickens County
149	4529	5.3	**Port Royal** (town) Beaufort County
150	n/a	2.2	**Laurel Bay** (CDP) Beaufort County

Note: *The state column ranks the top/bottom 150 places in the state with population of 2,500 or more. The national column ranks the top/bottom places in the country with population of 10,000 or more. Places that are unincorporated were not considered in the rankings. n/a indicates data not available. Please refer to the User Guide for additional information.*

Population Age 65 and Over

Top 150 Places Ranked in *Ascending* Order

State Rank	Nat'l Rank	Percent	Place
1	n/a	2.2	**Laurel Bay** (CDP) Beaufort County
2	112	5.3	**Port Royal** (town) Beaufort County
3	n/a	6.8	**Central** (town) Pickens County
4	331	6.9	**Five Forks** (CDP) Greenville County
4	n/a	6.9	**Sangaree** (CDP) Berkeley County
6	n/a	7.0	**Southern Shops** (CDP) Spartanburg County
7	408	7.3	**Bluffton** (town) Beaufort County
7	408	7.3	**Goose Creek** (city) Berkeley County
7	408	7.3	**Ladson** (CDP) Berkeley County
10	n/a	7.9	**Hardeeville** (city) Jasper County
11	n/a	8.3	**Dalzell** (CDP) Sumter County
12	644	8.4	**North Charleston** (city) Charleston County
13	n/a	8.5	**Ridgeland** (town) Jasper County
14	n/a	8.6	**Red Bank** (CDP) Lexington County
15	733	8.7	**Columbia** (city) Richland County
16	n/a	9.1	**Arcadia** (CDP) Spartanburg County
16	n/a	9.1	**Burton** (CDP) Beaufort County
18	n/a	9.2	**Valley Falls** (CDP) Spartanburg County
19	944	9.4	**Saint Andrews** (CDP) Richland County
20	n/a	9.8	**Duncan** (town) Spartanburg County
21	1094	10.0	**Fort Mill** (town) York County
22	n/a	10.1	**Clover** (town) York County
23	1170	10.2	**Irmo** (town) Richland County
23	n/a	10.2	**Saxon** (CDP) Spartanburg County
25	1195	10.3	**Lexington** (town) Lexington County
26	1230	10.4	**Rock Hill** (city) York County
27	1269	10.5	**Summerville** (town) Dorchester County
27	n/a	10.5	**Tega Cay** (city) York County
29	n/a	10.6	**Moncks Corner** (town) Berkeley County
30	n/a	10.7	**Boiling Springs** (CDP) Spartanburg County
31	1391	10.8	**Hanahan** (city) Berkeley County
32	1427	10.9	**Greer** (city) Greenville County
33	n/a	11.0	**Lakewood** (CDP) Sumter County
33	1467	11.0	**Simpsonville** (city) Greenville County
35	n/a	11.1	**McCormick** (town) McCormick County
36	n/a	11.2	**Newport** (CDP) York County
37	n/a	11.4	**Fountain Inn** (city) Greenville County
38	1700	11.6	**Clemson** (city) Pickens County
38	1700	11.6	**Socastee** (CDP) Horry County
40	n/a	11.8	**Edisto** (CDP) Orangeburg County
40	1789	11.8	**Mauldin** (city) Greenville County
40	1789	11.8	**Oak Grove** (CDP) Lexington County
40	n/a	11.8	**Saluda** (town) Saluda County
44	n/a	11.9	**Lesslie** (CDP) York County
45	n/a	12.0	**Edgefield** (town) Edgefield County
46	n/a	12.1	**Travelers Rest** (city) Greenville County
47	1958	12.2	**Charleston** (city) Charleston County
47	1958	12.2	**Mount Pleasant** (town) Charleston County
47	1958	12.2	**Parker** (CDP) Greenville County
50	n/a	12.5	**Elgin** (CDP) Lancaster County
51	n/a	12.7	**India Hook** (CDP) York County
52	n/a	12.8	**Allendale** (town) Allendale County
52	2221	12.8	**Greenville** (city) Greenville County
54	n/a	13.0	**East Gaffney** (CDP) Cherokee County
54	n/a	13.0	**Forestbrook** (CDP) Horry County
54	2313	13.0	**Gantt** (CDP) Greenville County
57	2353	13.1	**Dentsville** (CDP) Richland County
58	2397	13.2	**Conway** (city) Horry County
58	n/a	13.2	**Hopkins** (CDP) Richland County
58	n/a	13.2	**Woodfield** (CDP) Richland County
61	n/a	13.3	**Lugoff** (CDP) Kershaw County
62	n/a	13.6	**Chester** (city) Chester County
62	n/a	13.6	**Denmark** (city) Bamberg County
62	2562	13.6	**Taylors** (CDP) Greenville County
65	n/a	13.8	**Lake City** (city) Florence County
65	n/a	13.8	**Sans Souci** (CDP) Greenville County
67	n/a	13.9	**Andrews** (town) Georgetown County
67	2693	13.9	**Florence** (city) Florence County
67	2693	13.9	**Sumter** (city) Sumter County
67	n/a	13.9	**Welcome** (CDP) Greenville County
71	2746	14.0	**Cayce** (city) Lexington County
71	n/a	14.0	**Springdale** (town) Lancaster County
73	n/a	14.1	**Gloverville** (CDP) Aiken County
74	n/a	14.2	**Clearwater** (CDP) Aiken County
74	2825	14.2	**Orangeburg** (city) Orangeburg County
76	n/a	14.3	**Lake Wylie** (CDP) York County
76	n/a	14.3	**York** (city) York County
78	n/a	14.4	**Walhalla** (city) Oconee County
79	2966	14.5	**Greenwood** (city) Greenwood County
79	n/a	14.5	**North Hartsville** (CDP) Darlington County
81	n/a	14.6	**Brookdale** (CDP) Orangeburg County
81	n/a	14.6	**Marion** (city) Marion County
81	3004	14.6	**Spartanburg** (city) Spartanburg County
84	n/a	14.7	**Bennettsville** (city) Marlboro County
84	n/a	14.7	**Georgetown** (city) Georgetown County
84	3042	14.7	**North Augusta** (city) Aiken County
84	n/a	14.7	**Pageland** (town) Chesterfield County
88	n/a	14.9	**Homeland Park** (CDP) Anderson County
88	n/a	14.9	**Piedmont** (CDP) Anderson County
90	n/a	15.0	**Belvedere** (CDP) Aiken County
90	n/a	15.0	**Graniteville** (CDP) Aiken County
90	n/a	15.0	**Hollywood** (town) Charleston County
93	3191	15.1	**Myrtle Beach** (city) Horry County
94	n/a	15.2	**Barnwell** (city) Barnwell County
95	3302	15.4	**Seven Oaks** (CDP) Lexington County
96	3331	15.5	**Beaufort** (city) Beaufort County
97	n/a	15.7	**Centerville** (CDP) Anderson County
98	3477	15.9	**Berea** (CDP) Greenville County
98	n/a	15.9	**Dunean** (CDP) Greenville County
100	n/a	16.1	**Clinton** (city) Laurens County
101	n/a	16.2	**Burnettown** (town) Aiken County
101	n/a	16.2	**Dillon** (city) Dillon County
101	n/a	16.2	**Hartsville** (city) Darlington County
101	n/a	16.2	**Lyman** (town) Spartanburg County
105	n/a	16.3	**Lancaster** (city) Lancaster County
105	3595	16.3	**West Columbia** (city) Lexington County
107	3624	16.4	**Newberry** (city) Newberry County
108	n/a	16.6	**Batesburg-Leesville** (town) Lexington County
109	n/a	16.7	**Manning** (city) Clarendon County
110	n/a	16.8	**Williston** (town) Barnwell County
111	n/a	16.9	**Kingstree** (town) Williamsburg County
111	n/a	16.9	**Liberty** (city) Pickens County
111	n/a	16.9	**Winnsboro** (town) Fairfield County
111	n/a	16.9	**Woodruff** (city) Spartanburg County
115	n/a	17.0	**Williamston** (town) Anderson County
116	n/a	17.4	**Bamberg** (town) Bamberg County
116	3895	17.4	**Gaffney** (city) Cherokee County
118	n/a	17.5	**Abbeville** (city) Abbeville County
119	n/a	17.7	**Northlake** (CDP) Anderson County
120	n/a	17.8	**Hampton** (town) Hampton County
121	4022	17.9	**Anderson** (city) Anderson County
121	n/a	17.9	**Walterboro** (city) Colleton County
123	4041	18.0	**Easley** (city) Pickens County
123	n/a	18.0	**Pickens** (city) Pickens County
123	n/a	18.0	**Union** (city) Union County
126	n/a	18.1	**Belton** (city) Anderson County
126	n/a	18.1	**Folly Beach** (city) Charleston County
126	4062	18.1	**Wade Hampton** (CDP) Greenville County
129	n/a	18.2	**Arial** (CDP) Pickens County
129	n/a	18.2	**Bishopville** (city) Lee County
129	n/a	18.2	**Lake Murray of Richland** (CDP) Richland County
132	n/a	18.3	**Mullins** (city) Marion County
133	n/a	18.6	**Cheraw** (town) Chesterfield County
133	4149	18.6	**Red Hill** (CDP) Horry County
135	n/a	18.9	**Seneca** (city) Oconee County
136	n/a	19.0	**Darlington** (city) Darlington County
137	4222	19.1	**Forest Acres** (city) Richland County
138	n/a	19.3	**Honea Path** (town) Anderson County
139	n/a	19.5	**Laurens** (city) Laurens County
140	n/a	19.8	**Pendleton** (town) Anderson County
141	n/a	21.6	**Camden** (city) Kershaw County
142	4454	21.9	**Aiken** (city) Aiken County
143	n/a	22.6	**Isle of Palms** (city) Charleston County
143	n/a	22.6	**Surfside Beach** (town) Horry County
145	n/a	23.8	**Springdale** (town) Lexington County
146	n/a	26.4	**Murrells Inlet** (CDP) Georgetown County
147	4582	27.2	**North Myrtle Beach** (city) Horry County
148	4598	28.8	**Hilton Head Island** (town) Beaufort County
149	n/a	29.0	**Little River** (CDP) Horry County
150	n/a	35.2	**Garden City** (CDP) Horry County

Note: The state column ranks the top/bottom 150 places in the state with population of 2,500 or more. The national column ranks the top/bottom places in the country with population of 10,000 or more. Places that are unincorporated were not considered in the rankings. n/a indicates data not available. Please refer to the User Guide for additional information.

Males per 100 Females

Top 150 Places Ranked in *Descending* Order

State Rank	Nat'l Rank	Ratio	Place
1	n/a	234.5	**McCormick** (town) McCormick County
2	n/a	228.9	**Edgefield** (town) Edgefield County
3	n/a	179.1	**Ridgeland** (town) Jasper County
4	32	146.1	**Port Royal** (town) Beaufort County
5	n/a	139.8	**Southern Shops** (CDP) Spartanburg County
6	n/a	121.2	**Bennettsville** (city) Marlboro County
7	122	111.9	**Clemson** (city) Pickens County
8	n/a	107.2	**Hardeeville** (city) Jasper County
9	197	106.8	**Goose Creek** (city) Berkeley County
10	218	106.0	**Columbia** (city) Richland County
11	n/a	105.3	**Folly Beach** (city) Charleston County
12	n/a	105.2	**Central** (town) Pickens County
13	n/a	104.3	**Saxon** (CDP) Spartanburg County
14	338	103.2	**Myrtle Beach** (city) Horry County
15	n/a	103.1	**Arcadia** (CDP) Spartanburg County
16	501	101.1	**Hanahan** (city) Berkeley County
17	n/a	100.7	**Burnettown** (town) Aiken County
18	n/a	99.4	**Clearwater** (CDP) Aiken County
18	753	99.4	**Parker** (CDP) Greenville County
20	n/a	99.1	**Forestbrook** (CDP) Horry County
21	974	98.4	**North Charleston** (city) Charleston County
22	n/a	98.1	**Isle of Palms** (city) Charleston County
23	1086	97.9	**Socastee** (CDP) Horry County
24	1115	97.8	**Oak Grove** (CDP) Lexington County
24	n/a	97.8	**Tega Cay** (city) York County
26	1140	97.7	**North Myrtle Beach** (city) Horry County
26	n/a	97.7	**Springdale** (CDP) Lancaster County
28	n/a	97.6	**Pageland** (town) Chesterfield County
29	n/a	97.4	**Gloverville** (CDP) Aiken County
30	n/a	97.3	**Arial** (CDP) Pickens County
30	n/a	97.3	**Hollywood** (town) Charleston County
30	n/a	97.3	**Lake Wylie** (CDP) York County
30	n/a	97.3	**North Hartsville** (CDP) Darlington County
30	n/a	97.3	**Saluda** (town) Saluda County
35	1311	97.1	**Five Forks** (CDP) Greenville County
36	n/a	96.8	**Dunean** (CDP) Greenville County
37	n/a	96.7	**East Gaffney** (CDP) Cherokee County
37	1441	96.7	**Red Hill** (CDP) Horry County
39	1504	96.5	**Ladson** (CDP) Berkeley County
40	1532	96.4	**Hilton Head Island** (town) Beaufort County
41	n/a	96.3	**Elgin** (CDP) Lancaster County
42	n/a	95.8	**Walhalla** (city) Oconee County
43	n/a	95.7	**Lakewood** (CDP) Sumter County
43	1809	95.7	**West Columbia** (city) Lexington County
45	1839	95.6	**Beaufort** (city) Beaufort County
45	n/a	95.6	**Lesslie** (CDP) York County
47	1882	95.5	**Bluffton** (town) Beaufort County
48	2117	94.9	**Berea** (CDP) Greenville County
48	n/a	94.9	**Murrells Inlet** (CDP) Georgetown County
50	n/a	94.6	**Burton** (CDP) Beaufort County
51	n/a	94.5	**Moncks Corner** (town) Berkeley County
51	n/a	94.5	**Piedmont** (CDP) Anderson County
53	n/a	94.4	**India Hook** (CDP) York County
54	n/a	94.1	**Red Bank** (CDP) Lexington County
55	n/a	94.0	**Belvedere** (CDP) Aiken County
56	2526	93.9	**Simpsonville** (city) Greenville County
57	n/a	93.5	**Dalzell** (CDP) Sumter County
57	n/a	93.5	**Laurel Bay** (CDP) Beaufort County
59	n/a	93.4	**Sangaree** (CDP) Berkeley County
60	n/a	93.2	**Newport** (CDP) York County
61	n/a	93.1	**Liberty** (city) Pickens County
62	2929	93.0	**Lexington** (town) Lexington County
63	n/a	92.9	**Little River** (CDP) Horry County
64	n/a	92.8	**Lugoff** (CDP) Kershaw County
65	n/a	92.7	**Boiling Springs** (CDP) Spartanburg County
65	3028	92.7	**Greenville** (city) Greenville County
65	n/a	92.7	**Northlake** (CDP) Anderson County
68	3076	92.6	**Mount Pleasant** (town) Charleston County
69	n/a	92.4	**Clover** (town) York County
70	3170	92.3	**Gantt** (CDP) Greenville County
70	n/a	92.3	**Surfside Beach** (town) Horry County
72	3243	92.1	**Cayce** (city) Lexington County
73	n/a	92.0	**Edisto** (CDP) Orangeburg County
74	n/a	91.9	**Chester** (city) Chester County
75	3393	91.7	**Wade Hampton** (CDP) Greenville County
76	n/a	91.4	**Homeland Park** (CDP) Anderson County
77	n/a	91.0	**Sans Souci** (CDP) Greenville County
77	n/a	91.0	**Springdale** (town) Lexington County
79	n/a	90.9	**Welcome** (CDP) Greenville County
80	n/a	90.8	**Graniteville** (CDP) Aiken County
80	n/a	90.8	**Lake Murray of Richland** (CDP) Richland County
80	n/a	90.8	**Lyman** (town) Spartanburg County
83	n/a	90.6	**Centerville** (CDP) Anderson County
84	3736	90.5	**Greer** (city) Greenville County
85	n/a	89.8	**Travelers Rest** (city) Greenville County
86	3923	89.7	**Easley** (city) Pickens County
86	3923	89.7	**Irmo** (town) Richland County
86	3923	89.7	**Taylors** (CDP) Greenville County
89	3944	89.6	**Charleston** (city) Charleston County
90	n/a	89.5	**Barnwell** (city) Barnwell County
91	4002	89.3	**Seven Oaks** (CDP) Lexington County
92	4016	89.2	**Summerville** (town) Dorchester County
92	n/a	89.2	**Woodruff** (city) Spartanburg County
94	4070	88.9	**Mauldin** (city) Greenville County
94	n/a	88.9	**Pickens** (city) Pickens County
94	4070	88.9	**Sumter** (city) Sumter County
97	4136	88.5	**North Augusta** (city) Aiken County
97	n/a	88.5	**Pendleton** (town) Anderson County
99	n/a	88.4	**Fountain Inn** (city) Greenville County
100	n/a	88.2	**Williston** (town) Barnwell County
101	n/a	87.7	**Allendale** (town) Allendale County
102	4262	87.5	**Fort Mill** (town) York County
103	n/a	87.4	**Garden City** (CDP) Horry County
104	n/a	87.1	**Seneca** (city) Oconee County
105	n/a	87.0	**Woodfield** (CDP) Richland County
106	n/a	86.5	**Hopkins** (CDP) Richland County
107	n/a	86.0	**York** (city) York County
108	n/a	85.8	**Dillon** (city) Dillon County
108	4420	85.8	**Newberry** (city) Newberry County
110	n/a	85.6	**Williamston** (town) Anderson County
111	4452	85.3	**Aiken** (city) Aiken County
111	4452	85.3	**Rock Hill** (city) York County
113	n/a	85.2	**Clinton** (city) Laurens County
113	4460	85.2	**Gaffney** (city) Cherokee County
113	4460	85.2	**Saint Andrews** (CDP) Richland County
116	n/a	85.1	**Batesburg-Leesville** (town) Lexington County
117	n/a	85.0	**Lancaster** (city) Lancaster County
118	n/a	84.9	**Laurens** (city) Laurens County
119	n/a	84.8	**Bamberg** (town) Bamberg County
119	n/a	84.8	**Belton** (city) Anderson County
119	4484	84.8	**Forest Acres** (city) Richland County
122	n/a	84.7	**Hampton** (town) Hampton County
122	4492	84.7	**Orangeburg** (city) Orangeburg County
124	n/a	84.5	**Denmark** (city) Bamberg County
125	4520	84.3	**Conway** (city) Horry County
126	4526	84.2	**Greenwood** (city) Greenwood County
127	n/a	84.0	**Andrews** (town) Georgetown County
128	4552	83.5	**Florence** (city) Florence County
129	n/a	82.8	**Manning** (city) Clarendon County
130	n/a	82.4	**Winnsboro** (town) Fairfield County
131	n/a	82.2	**Lake City** (city) Florence County
132	4594	81.8	**Dentsville** (CDP) Richland County
133	n/a	81.7	**Camden** (city) Kershaw County
134	n/a	81.6	**Brookdale** (CDP) Orangeburg County
134	n/a	81.6	**Georgetown** (city) Georgetown County
134	n/a	81.6	**Honea Path** (town) Anderson County
137	n/a	81.5	**Duncan** (town) Spartanburg County
138	n/a	81.3	**Abbeville** (city) Abbeville County
139	n/a	80.5	**Union** (city) Union County
140	n/a	80.3	**Kingstree** (town) Williamsburg County
140	n/a	80.3	**Walterboro** (city) Colleton County
142	4624	80.2	**Anderson** (city) Anderson County
143	n/a	79.8	**Hartsville** (city) Darlington County
144	4632	79.0	**Spartanburg** (city) Spartanburg County
145	n/a	78.2	**Cheraw** (town) Chesterfield County
145	n/a	78.2	**Marion** (city) Marion County
147	n/a	77.6	**Valley Falls** (CDP) Spartanburg County
148	n/a	77.3	**Bishopville** (city) Lee County
149	n/a	76.5	**Darlington** (city) Darlington County
150	n/a	73.9	**Mullins** (city) Marion County

Note: The state column ranks the top/bottom 150 places in the state with population of 2,500 or more. The national column ranks the top/bottom places in the country with population of 10,000 or more. Places that are unincorporated were not considered in the rankings. n/a indicates data not available. Please refer to the User Guide for additional information.

Males per 100 Females

Top 150 Places Ranked in *Ascending* Order

State Rank	Nat'l Rank	Ratio	Place
1	n/a	73.9	**Mullins** (city) Marion County
2	n/a	76.5	**Darlington** (city) Darlington County
3	n/a	77.3	**Bishopville** (city) Lee County
4	n/a	77.6	**Valley Falls** (CDP) Spartanburg County
5	n/a	78.2	**Cheraw** (town) Chesterfield County
5	n/a	78.2	**Marion** (city) Marion County
7	23	79.0	**Spartanburg** (city) Spartanburg County
8	n/a	79.8	**Hartsville** (city) Darlington County
9	31	80.2	**Anderson** (city) Anderson County
10	n/a	80.3	**Kingstree** (town) Williamsburg County
10	n/a	80.3	**Walterboro** (city) Colleton County
12	n/a	80.5	**Union** (city) Union County
13	n/a	81.3	**Abbeville** (city) Abbeville County
14	n/a	81.5	**Duncan** (town) Spartanburg County
15	n/a	81.6	**Brookdale** (CDP) Orangeburg County
15	n/a	81.6	**Georgetown** (city) Georgetown County
15	n/a	81.6	**Honea Path** (town) Anderson County
18	n/a	81.7	**Camden** (city) Kershaw County
19	62	81.8	**Dentsville** (CDP) Richland County
20	n/a	82.2	**Lake City** (city) Florence County
21	n/a	82.4	**Winnsboro** (town) Fairfield County
22	n/a	82.8	**Manning** (city) Clarendon County
23	103	83.5	**Florence** (city) Florence County
24	n/a	84.0	**Andrews** (town) Georgetown County
25	127	84.2	**Greenwood** (city) Greenwood County
26	131	84.3	**Conway** (city) Horry County
27	n/a	84.5	**Denmark** (city) Bamberg County
28	n/a	84.7	**Hampton** (town) Hampton County
28	159	84.7	**Orangeburg** (city) Orangeburg County
30	n/a	84.8	**Bamberg** (town) Bamberg County
30	n/a	84.8	**Belton** (city) Anderson County
30	165	84.8	**Forest Acres** (city) Richland County
33	n/a	84.9	**Laurens** (city) Laurens County
34	n/a	85.0	**Lancaster** (city) Lancaster County
35	n/a	85.1	**Batesburg-Leesville** (town) Lexington County
36	n/a	85.2	**Clinton** (city) Laurens County
36	186	85.2	**Gaffney** (city) Cherokee County
36	186	85.2	**Saint Andrews** (CDP) Richland County
39	197	85.3	**Aiken** (city) Aiken County
39	197	85.3	**Rock Hill** (city) York County
41	n/a	85.6	**Williamston** (town) Anderson County
42	n/a	85.8	**Dillon** (city) Dillon County
42	229	85.8	**Newberry** (city) Newberry County
44	n/a	86.0	**York** (city) York County
45	n/a	86.5	**Hopkins** (CDP) Richland County
46	n/a	87.0	**Woodfield** (CDP) Richland County
47	n/a	87.1	**Seneca** (city) Oconee County
48	n/a	87.4	**Garden City** (CDP) Horry County
49	387	87.5	**Fort Mill** (town) York County
50	n/a	87.7	**Allendale** (town) Allendale County
51	n/a	88.2	**Williston** (town) Barnwell County
52	n/a	88.4	**Fountain Inn** (city) Greenville County
53	504	88.5	**North Augusta** (city) Aiken County
53	n/a	88.5	**Pendleton** (town) Anderson County
55	568	88.9	**Mauldin** (city) Greenville County
55	n/a	88.9	**Pickens** (city) Pickens County
55	568	88.9	**Sumter** (city) Sumter County
58	631	89.2	**Summerville** (town) Dorchester County
58	n/a	89.2	**Woodruff** (city) Spartanburg County
60	641	89.3	**Seven Oaks** (CDP) Lexington County
61	n/a	89.5	**Barnwell** (city) Barnwell County
62	689	89.6	**Charleston** (city) Charleston County
63	713	89.7	**Easley** (city) Pickens County
63	713	89.7	**Irmo** (town) Richland County
63	713	89.7	**Taylors** (CDP) Greenville County
66	n/a	89.8	**Travelers Rest** (city) Greenville County
67	893	90.5	**Greer** (city) Greenville County
68	n/a	90.6	**Centerville** (CDP) Anderson County
69	n/a	90.8	**Graniteville** (CDP) Aiken County
69	n/a	90.8	**Lake Murray of Richland** (CDP) Richland County
69	n/a	90.8	**Lyman** (town) Spartanburg County
72	n/a	90.9	**Welcome** (CDP) Greenville County
73	n/a	91.0	**Sans Souci** (CDP) Greenville County
73	n/a	91.0	**Springdale** (town) Lexington County
75	n/a	91.4	**Homeland Park** (CDP) Anderson County
76	1233	91.7	**Wade Hampton** (CDP) Greenville County
77	n/a	91.9	**Chester** (city) Chester County
78	n/a	92.0	**Edisto** (CDP) Orangeburg County
79	1381	92.1	**Cayce** (city) Lexington County
80	1458	92.3	**Gantt** (CDP) Greenville County
80	n/a	92.3	**Surfside Beach** (town) Horry County
82	n/a	92.4	**Clover** (town) York County
83	1546	92.6	**Mount Pleasant** (town) Charleston County
84	n/a	92.7	**Boiling Springs** (CDP) Spartanburg County
84	1581	92.7	**Greenville** (city) Greenville County
84	n/a	92.7	**Northlake** (CDP) Anderson County
87	n/a	92.8	**Lugoff** (CDP) Kershaw County
88	n/a	92.9	**Little River** (CDP) Horry County
89	1695	93.0	**Lexington** (town) Lexington County
90	n/a	93.1	**Liberty** (city) Pickens County
91	n/a	93.2	**Newport** (CDP) York County
92	n/a	93.4	**Sangaree** (CDP) Berkeley County
93	n/a	93.5	**Dalzell** (CDP) Sumter County
93	n/a	93.5	**Laurel Bay** (CDP) Beaufort County
95	2082	93.9	**Simpsonville** (city) Greenville County
96	n/a	94.0	**Belvedere** (CDP) Aiken County
97	n/a	94.1	**Red Bank** (CDP) Lexington County
98	n/a	94.4	**India Hook** (CDP) York County
99	n/a	94.5	**Moncks Corner** (town) Berkeley County
99	n/a	94.5	**Piedmont** (CDP) Anderson County
101	n/a	94.6	**Burton** (CDP) Beaufort County
102	2486	94.9	**Berea** (CDP) Greenville County
102	n/a	94.9	**Murrells Inlet** (CDP) Georgetown County
104	2734	95.5	**Bluffton** (town) Beaufort County
105	2775	95.6	**Beaufort** (city) Beaufort County
105	n/a	95.6	**Lesslie** (CDP) York County
107	n/a	95.7	**Lakewood** (CDP) Sumter County
107	2818	95.7	**West Columbia** (city) Lexington County
109	n/a	95.8	**Walhalla** (city) Oconee County
110	n/a	96.3	**Elgin** (CDP) Lancaster County
111	3083	96.4	**Hilton Head Island** (town) Beaufort County
112	3125	96.5	**Ladson** (CDP) Berkeley County
113	n/a	96.7	**East Gaffney** (CDP) Cherokee County
113	3186	96.7	**Red Hill** (CDP) Horry County
115	n/a	96.8	**Dunean** (CDP) Greenville County
116	3312	97.1	**Five Forks** (CDP) Greenville County
117	n/a	97.3	**Arial** (CDP) Pickens County
117	n/a	97.3	**Hollywood** (town) Charleston County
117	n/a	97.3	**Lake Wylie** (CDP) York County
117	n/a	97.3	**North Hartsville** (CDP) Darlington County
117	n/a	97.3	**Saluda** (town) Saluda County
122	n/a	97.4	**Gloverville** (CDP) Aiken County
123	n/a	97.6	**Pageland** (town) Chesterfield County
124	3492	97.7	**North Myrtle Beach** (city) Horry County
124	n/a	97.7	**Springdale** (CDP) Lancaster County
126	3517	97.8	**Oak Grove** (CDP) Lexington County
126	n/a	97.8	**Tega Cay** (city) York County
128	3542	97.9	**Socastee** (CDP) Horry County
129	n/a	98.1	**Isle of Palms** (city) Charleston County
130	3662	98.4	**North Charleston** (city) Charleston County
131	n/a	99.1	**Forestbrook** (CDP) Horry County
132	n/a	99.4	**Clearwater** (CDP) Aiken County
132	3881	99.4	**Parker** (CDP) Greenville County
134	n/a	100.7	**Burnettown** (town) Aiken County
135	4141	101.1	**Hanahan** (city) Berkeley County
136	n/a	103.1	**Arcadia** (CDP) Spartanburg County
137	4311	103.2	**Myrtle Beach** (city) Horry County
138	n/a	104.3	**Saxon** (CDP) Spartanburg County
139	n/a	105.2	**Central** (town) Pickens County
140	n/a	105.3	**Folly Beach** (city) Charleston County
141	4434	106.0	**Columbia** (city) Richland County
142	4455	106.8	**Goose Creek** (city) Berkeley County
143	n/a	107.2	**Hardeeville** (city) Jasper County
144	4534	111.9	**Clemson** (city) Pickens County
145	n/a	121.2	**Bennettsville** (city) Marlboro County
146	n/a	139.8	**Southern Shops** (CDP) Spartanburg County
147	4624	146.1	**Port Royal** (town) Beaufort County
148	n/a	179.1	**Ridgeland** (town) Jasper County
149	n/a	228.9	**Edgefield** (town) Edgefield County
150	n/a	234.5	**McCormick** (town) McCormick County

Note: The state column ranks the top/bottom 150 places in the state with population of 2,500 or more. The national column ranks the top/bottom places in the country with population of 10,000 or more. Places that are unincorporated were not considered in the rankings. n/a indicates data not available. Please refer to the User Guide for additional information.

Marriage Status: Never Married

Top 150 Places Ranked in *Descending* Order

State Rank	Nat'l Rank	Percent	Place
1	n/a	72.3	Central (town) Pickens County
2	74	57.1	Port Royal (town) Beaufort County
3	90	56.0	Clemson (city) Pickens County
4	n/a	54.2	Clinton (city) Laurens County
4	113	54.2	Columbia (city) Richland County
6	n/a	53.5	Saxon (CDP) Spartanburg County
7	n/a	53.3	Valley Falls (CDP) Spartanburg County
8	n/a	52.7	Brookdale (CDP) Orangeburg County
9	153	52.0	Orangeburg (city) Orangeburg County
10	n/a	51.6	Bishopville (city) Lee County
11	n/a	50.1	Denmark (city) Bamberg County
11	n/a	50.1	McCormick (town) McCormick County
13	n/a	49.8	Allendale (town) Allendale County
14	194	49.7	Saint Andrews (CDP) Richland County
15	n/a	47.9	Ridgeland (town) Jasper County
16	254	47.4	Conway (city) Horry County
17	n/a	47.3	Hopkins (CDP) Richland County
18	294	46.0	Dentsville (CDP) Richland County
19	n/a	44.7	Hardeeville (city) Jasper County
20	359	44.3	Newberry (city) Newberry County
21	n/a	43.8	Bennettsville (city) Marlboro County
21	n/a	43.8	Chester (city) Chester County
23	401	43.5	Charleston (city) Charleston County
24	406	43.4	Greenwood (city) Greenwood County
24	n/a	43.4	Southern Shops (CDP) Spartanburg County
26	416	43.2	Gaffney (city) Cherokee County
26	n/a	43.2	Winnsboro (town) Fairfield County
28	439	42.9	Gantt (CDP) Greenville County
29	n/a	42.7	Dunean (CDP) Greenville County
30	491	42.1	Greenville (city) Greenville County
31	n/a	41.4	Saluda (town) Saluda County
32	n/a	41.3	Graniteville (CDP) Aiken County
33	n/a	41.2	Marion (city) Marion County
34	553	41.0	Spartanburg (city) Spartanburg County
35	566	40.9	North Charleston (city) Charleston County
36	n/a	40.2	Dalzell (CDP) Sumter County
37	640	40.0	Cayce (city) Lexington County
38	n/a	39.9	Lancaster (city) Lancaster County
39	n/a	39.2	Andrews (town) Georgetown County
40	n/a	39.0	Lake City (city) Florence County
41	n/a	38.9	Edgefield (town) Edgefield County
42	n/a	38.6	Elgin (CDP) Lancaster County
42	n/a	38.6	Manning (city) Clarendon County
44	783	38.4	Rock Hill (city) York County
45	n/a	38.2	Hartsville (city) Darlington County
46	n/a	37.4	East Gaffney (CDP) Cherokee County
47	924	37.1	Anderson (city) Anderson County
48	n/a	37.0	Georgetown (city) Georgetown County
49	n/a	36.9	Folly Beach (city) Charleston County
49	947	36.9	Parker (CDP) Greenville County
49	n/a	36.9	York (city) York County
52	n/a	36.7	Duncan (town) Spartanburg County
53	n/a	36.5	Woodfield (CDP) Richland County
54	n/a	36.1	Walterboro (city) Colleton County
55	n/a	36.0	Bamberg (town) Bamberg County
56	n/a	35.6	Laurens (city) Laurens County
57	n/a	35.4	Pageland (town) Chesterfield County
57	1141	35.4	Sumter (city) Sumter County
59	1158	35.3	West Columbia (city) Lexington County
60	1192	35.1	Florence (city) Florence County
61	n/a	34.8	Abbeville (city) Abbeville County
61	n/a	34.8	Kingstree (town) Williamsburg County
61	1245	34.8	Myrtle Beach (city) Horry County
64	n/a	34.6	Dillon (city) Dillon County
65	1312	34.4	Aiken (city) Aiken County
66	n/a	33.9	Mullins (city) Marion County
67	n/a	33.7	Edisto (CDP) Orangeburg County
67	n/a	33.7	North Hartsville (CDP) Darlington County
69	n/a	33.6	Williston (town) Barnwell County
70	n/a	33.2	Union (city) Union County
71	n/a	33.1	Springdale (CDP) Lancaster County
72	n/a	32.6	Barnwell (city) Barnwell County
72	n/a	32.6	Homeland Park (CDP) Anderson County
72	1661	32.6	Ladson (CDP) Berkeley County
72	n/a	32.6	Moncks Corner (town) Berkeley County
76	1679	32.5	Greer (city) Greenville County
77	n/a	32.4	Sans Souci (CDP) Greenville County
78	n/a	32.0	Pickens (city) Pickens County
79	1810	31.9	Irmo (town) Richland County
79	1810	31.9	Red Hill (CDP) Horry County
81	1929	31.5	Seven Oaks (CDP) Lexington County
82	1963	31.4	Goose Creek (city) Berkeley County
83	n/a	31.3	Honea Path (town) Anderson County
84	n/a	31.2	Liberty (city) Pickens County
85	n/a	31.1	Darlington (city) Darlington County
85	n/a	31.1	Fountain Inn (city) Greenville County
87	n/a	30.8	Cheraw (town) Chesterfield County
87	n/a	30.8	Gloverville (CDP) Aiken County
87	2102	30.8	Hanahan (city) Berkeley County
90	2277	30.1	Mauldin (city) Greenville County
91	n/a	30.0	Batesburg-Leesville (town) Lexington County
92	2337	29.9	Beaufort (city) Beaufort County
93	n/a	29.6	Seneca (city) Oconee County
94	2423	29.5	Forest Acres (city) Richland County
95	n/a	29.4	Arcadia (CDP) Spartanburg County
96	n/a	29.3	Pendleton (town) Anderson County
96	2491	29.3	Socastee (CDP) Horry County
98	n/a	29.2	Lesslie (CDP) York County
98	n/a	29.2	Travelers Rest (city) Greenville County
100	n/a	29.0	Belton (city) Anderson County
101	2587	28.9	Lexington (town) Lexington County
102	n/a	28.8	Sangaree (CDP) Berkeley County
103	n/a	28.5	Clearwater (CDP) Aiken County
103	n/a	28.5	Springdale (town) Lexington County
105	n/a	28.3	Welcome (CDP) Greenville County
106	2901	27.9	North Augusta (city) Aiken County
106	2901	27.9	Oak Grove (CDP) Lexington County
108	n/a	27.6	Camden (city) Kershaw County
108	2984	27.6	Taylors (CDP) Greenville County
110	3042	27.4	Wade Hampton (CDP) Greenville County
111	n/a	27.2	Forestbrook (CDP) Horry County
112	3134	27.1	Berea (CDP) Greenville County
113	n/a	27.0	Piedmont (CDP) Anderson County
114	n/a	26.9	Hollywood (town) Charleston County
114	n/a	26.9	Woodruff (city) Spartanburg County
116	n/a	26.7	Red Bank (CDP) Lexington County
117	3265	26.6	Bluffton (town) Beaufort County
118	n/a	26.5	Burnettown (town) Aiken County
118	3302	26.5	Mount Pleasant (town) Charleston County
118	n/a	26.5	Walhalla (city) Oconee County
121	3330	26.4	Fort Mill (town) York County
121	3330	26.4	Summerville (town) Dorchester County
123	n/a	26.2	Burton (CDP) Beaufort County
124	n/a	25.6	Lakewood (CDP) Sumter County
124	3516	25.6	Simpsonville (city) Greenville County
126	n/a	25.1	Hampton (town) Hampton County
127	n/a	24.9	Surfside Beach (town) Horry County
128	n/a	24.7	Arial (CDP) Pickens County
128	n/a	24.7	Centerville (CDP) Anderson County
130	n/a	24.3	Boiling Springs (CDP) Spartanburg County
130	n/a	24.3	Isle of Palms (city) Charleston County
132	n/a	24.2	Belvedere (CDP) Aiken County
132	n/a	24.2	Clover (town) York County
132	3849	24.2	Easley (city) Pickens County
135	n/a	23.4	Lugoff (CDP) Kershaw County
136	n/a	22.6	Williamston (town) Anderson County
137	4414	21.1	Five Forks (CDP) Greenville County
138	4431	20.9	Hilton Head Island (town) Beaufort County
139	n/a	20.3	Murrells Inlet (CDP) Georgetown County
139	n/a	20.3	Northlake (CDP) Anderson County
141	n/a	20.1	Lake Wylie (CDP) York County
142	n/a	20.0	Lake Murray of Richland (CDP) Richland County
143	n/a	19.4	Tega Cay (city) York County
144	n/a	19.2	Garden City (CDP) Horry County
145	4578	18.6	North Myrtle Beach (city) Horry County
146	n/a	17.7	Newport (CDP) York County
147	n/a	17.4	Lyman (town) Spartanburg County
148	n/a	16.8	Laurel Bay (CDP) Beaufort County
149	n/a	16.2	Little River (CDP) Horry County
150	n/a	12.5	India Hook (CDP) York County

Note: The state column ranks the top/bottom 150 places in the state with population of 2,500 or more. The national column ranks the top/bottom places in the country with population of 10,000 or more. Places that are unincorporated were not considered in the rankings. n/a indicates data not available. Please refer to the User Guide for additional information.

Marriage Status: Never Married

Top 150 Places Ranked in *Ascending* Order

State Rank	Nat'l Rank	Percent	Place
1	n/a	12.5	**India Hook** (CDP) York County
2	n/a	16.2	**Little River** (CDP) Horry County
3	n/a	16.8	**Laurel Bay** (CDP) Beaufort County
4	n/a	17.4	**Lyman** (town) Spartanburg County
5	n/a	17.7	**Newport** (CDP) York County
6	76	18.6	**North Myrtle Beach** (city) Horry County
7	n/a	19.2	**Garden City** (CDP) Horry County
8	n/a	19.4	**Tega Cay** (city) York County
9	n/a	20.0	**Lake Murray of Richland** (CDP) Richland County
10	n/a	20.1	**Lake Wylie** (CDP) York County
11	n/a	20.3	**Murrells Inlet** (CDP) Georgetown County
11	n/a	20.3	**Northlake** (CDP) Anderson County
13	213	20.9	**Hilton Head Island** (town) Beaufort County
14	234	21.1	**Five Forks** (CDP) Greenville County
15	n/a	22.6	**Williamston** (town) Anderson County
16	n/a	23.4	**Lugoff** (CDP) Kershaw County
17	n/a	24.2	**Belvedere** (CDP) Aiken County
17	n/a	24.2	**Clover** (town) York County
17	794	24.2	**Easley** (city) Pickens County
20	n/a	24.3	**Boiling Springs** (CDP) Spartanburg County
20	n/a	24.3	**Isle of Palms** (city) Charleston County
22	n/a	24.7	**Arial** (CDP) Pickens County
22	n/a	24.7	**Centerville** (CDP) Anderson County
24	n/a	24.9	**Surfside Beach** (town) Horry County
25	n/a	25.1	**Hampton** (town) Hampton County
26	n/a	25.6	**Lakewood** (CDP) Sumter County
26	1106	25.6	**Simpsonville** (city) Greenville County
28	n/a	26.2	**Burton** (CDP) Beaufort County
29	1298	26.4	**Fort Mill** (town) York County
29	1298	26.4	**Summerville** (town) Dorchester County
31	n/a	26.5	**Burnettown** (town) Aiken County
31	1327	26.5	**Mount Pleasant** (town) Charleston County
31	n/a	26.5	**Walhalla** (city) Oconee County
34	1355	26.6	**Bluffton** (town) Beaufort County
35	n/a	26.7	**Red Bank** (CDP) Lexington County
36	n/a	26.9	**Hollywood** (town) Charleston County
36	n/a	26.9	**Woodruff** (city) Spartanburg County
38	n/a	27.0	**Piedmont** (CDP) Anderson County
39	1502	27.1	**Berea** (CDP) Greenville County
40	n/a	27.2	**Forestbrook** (CDP) Horry County
41	1589	27.4	**Wade Hampton** (CDP) Greenville County
42	n/a	27.6	**Camden** (city) Kershaw County
42	1635	27.6	**Taylors** (CDP) Greenville County
44	1728	27.9	**North Augusta** (city) Aiken County
44	1728	27.9	**Oak Grove** (CDP) Lexington County
46	n/a	28.3	**Welcome** (CDP) Greenville County
47	n/a	28.5	**Clearwater** (CDP) Aiken County
47	n/a	28.5	**Springdale** (town) Lexington County
49	n/a	28.8	**Sangaree** (CDP) Berkeley County
50	2039	28.9	**Lexington** (town) Lexington County
51	n/a	29.0	**Belton** (city) Anderson County
52	n/a	29.2	**Lesslie** (CDP) York County
52	n/a	29.2	**Travelers Rest** (city) Greenville County
54	n/a	29.3	**Pendleton** (town) Anderson County
54	2145	29.3	**Socastee** (CDP) Horry County
56	n/a	29.4	**Arcadia** (CDP) Spartanburg County
57	2198	29.5	**Forest Acres** (city) Richland County
58	n/a	29.6	**Seneca** (city) Oconee County
59	2300	29.9	**Beaufort** (city) Beaufort County
60	n/a	30.0	**Batesburg-Leesville** (town) Lexington County
61	2350	30.1	**Mauldin** (city) Greenville County
62	n/a	30.8	**Cheraw** (town) Chesterfield County
62	n/a	30.8	**Gloverville** (CDP) Aiken County
62	2527	30.8	**Hanahan** (city) Berkeley County
65	n/a	31.1	**Darlington** (city) Darlington County
65	n/a	31.1	**Fountain Inn** (city) Greenville County
67	n/a	31.2	**Liberty** (city) Pickens County
68	n/a	31.3	**Honea Path** (town) Anderson County
69	2673	31.4	**Goose Creek** (city) Berkeley County
70	2694	31.5	**Seven Oaks** (CDP) Lexington County
71	2810	31.9	**Irmo** (town) Richland County
71	2810	31.9	**Red Hill** (CDP) Horry County
73	n/a	32.0	**Pickens** (city) Pickens County
74	n/a	32.4	**Sans Souci** (CDP) Greenville County
75	2951	32.5	**Greer** (city) Greenville County
76	n/a	32.6	**Barnwell** (city) Barnwell County
76	n/a	32.6	**Homeland Park** (CDP) Anderson County
76	2978	32.6	**Ladson** (CDP) Berkeley County
76	n/a	32.6	**Moncks Corner** (town) Berkeley County
80	n/a	33.1	**Springdale** (CDP) Lancaster County
81	n/a	33.2	**Union** (city) Union County
82	n/a	33.6	**Williston** (town) Barnwell County
83	n/a	33.7	**Edisto** (CDP) Orangeburg County
83	n/a	33.7	**North Hartsville** (CDP) Darlington County
85	n/a	33.9	**Mullins** (city) Marion County
86	3315	34.4	**Aiken** (city) Aiken County
87	n/a	34.6	**Dillon** (city) Dillon County
88	n/a	34.8	**Abbeville** (city) Abbeville County
88	n/a	34.8	**Kingstree** (town) Williamsburg County
88	3403	34.8	**Myrtle Beach** (city) Horry County
91	3445	35.1	**Florence** (city) Florence County
92	3477	35.3	**West Columbia** (city) Lexington County
93	n/a	35.4	**Pageland** (town) Chesterfield County
93	3499	35.4	**Sumter** (city) Sumter County
95	n/a	35.6	**Laurens** (city) Laurens County
96	n/a	36.0	**Bamberg** (town) Bamberg County
97	n/a	36.1	**Walterboro** (city) Colleton County
98	n/a	36.5	**Woodfield** (CDP) Richland County
99	n/a	36.7	**Duncan** (town) Spartanburg County
100	n/a	36.9	**Folly Beach** (city) Charleston County
100	3691	36.9	**Parker** (CDP) Greenville County
100	n/a	36.9	**York** (city) York County
103	n/a	37.0	**Georgetown** (city) Georgetown County
104	3721	37.1	**Anderson** (city) Anderson County
105	n/a	37.4	**East Gaffney** (CDP) Cherokee County
106	n/a	38.2	**Hartsville** (city) Darlington County
107	3864	38.4	**Rock Hill** (city) York County
108	n/a	38.6	**Elgin** (CDP) Lancaster County
108	n/a	38.6	**Manning** (city) Clarendon County
110	n/a	38.9	**Edgefield** (town) Edgefield County
111	n/a	39.0	**Lake City** (city) Florence County
112	n/a	39.2	**Andrews** (town) Georgetown County
113	n/a	39.9	**Lancaster** (city) Lancaster County
114	4009	40.0	**Cayce** (city) Lexington County
115	n/a	40.2	**Dalzell** (CDP) Sumter County
116	4081	40.9	**North Charleston** (city) Charleston County
117	4091	41.0	**Spartanburg** (city) Spartanburg County
118	n/a	41.2	**Marion** (city) Marion County
119	n/a	41.3	**Graniteville** (CDP) Aiken County
120	n/a	41.4	**Saluda** (town) Saluda County
121	4162	42.1	**Greenville** (city) Greenville County
122	n/a	42.7	**Dunean** (CDP) Greenville County
123	4206	42.9	**Gantt** (CDP) Greenville County
124	4230	43.2	**Gaffney** (city) Cherokee County
124	n/a	43.2	**Winnsboro** (town) Fairfield County
126	4245	43.4	**Greenwood** (city) Greenwood County
126	n/a	43.4	**Southern Shops** (CDP) Spartanburg County
128	4251	43.5	**Charleston** (city) Charleston County
129	n/a	43.8	**Bennettsville** (city) Marlboro County
129	n/a	43.8	**Chester** (city) Chester County
131	4293	44.3	**Newberry** (city) Newberry County
132	n/a	44.7	**Hardeeville** (city) Jasper County
133	4358	46.0	**Dentsville** (CDP) Richland County
134	n/a	47.3	**Hopkins** (CDP) Richland County
135	4396	47.4	**Conway** (city) Horry County
136	n/a	47.9	**Ridgeland** (town) Jasper County
137	4462	49.7	**Saint Andrews** (CDP) Richland County
138	n/a	49.8	**Allendale** (town) Allendale County
139	n/a	50.1	**Denmark** (city) Bamberg County
139	n/a	50.1	**McCormick** (town) McCormick County
141	n/a	51.6	**Bishopville** (city) Lee County
142	4502	52.0	**Orangeburg** (city) Orangeburg County
143	n/a	52.7	**Brookdale** (CDP) Orangeburg County
144	n/a	53.3	**Valley Falls** (CDP) Spartanburg County
145	n/a	53.5	**Saxon** (CDP) Spartanburg County
146	n/a	54.2	**Clinton** (city) Laurens County
146	4541	54.2	**Columbia** (city) Richland County
148	4565	56.0	**Clemson** (city) Pickens County
149	4581	57.1	**Port Royal** (town) Beaufort County
150	n/a	72.3	**Central** (town) Pickens County

Note: The state column ranks the top/bottom 150 places in the state with population of 2,500 or more. The national column ranks the top/bottom places in the country with population of 10,000 or more. Places that are unincorporated were not considered in the rankings. n/a indicates data not available. Please refer to the User Guide for additional information.

Marriage Status: Now Married

Top 150 Places Ranked in *Descending* Order

State Rank	Nat'l Rank	Percent	Place
1	n/a	72.5	**Tega Cay** (city) York County
2	n/a	70.3	**Laurel Bay** (CDP) Beaufort County
3	66	69.3	**Five Forks** (CDP) Greenville County
4	n/a	69.0	**Lake Murray of Richland** (CDP) Richland County
5	n/a	67.7	**Boiling Springs** (CDP) Spartanburg County
6	n/a	67.0	**Newport** (CDP) York County
7	n/a	64.6	**Lake Wylie** (CDP) York County
8	n/a	64.5	**Lyman** (town) Spartanburg County
9	n/a	64.2	**India Hook** (CDP) York County
10	n/a	63.9	**Arcadia** (CDP) Spartanburg County
11	452	63.1	**Hilton Head Island** (town) Beaufort County
12	n/a	62.6	**Isle of Palms** (city) Charleston County
12	n/a	62.6	**Murrells Inlet** (CDP) Georgetown County
14	n/a	61.4	**Centerville** (CDP) Anderson County
15	n/a	60.7	**Lakewood** (CDP) Sumter County
16	764	60.5	**Fort Mill** (town) York County
17	n/a	59.9	**Northlake** (CDP) Anderson County
18	n/a	58.7	**Little River** (CDP) Horry County
19	n/a	58.5	**Lugoff** (CDP) Kershaw County
19	1073	58.5	**Mount Pleasant** (town) Charleston County
19	1073	58.5	**North Myrtle Beach** (city) Horry County
22	n/a	58.2	**Forestbrook** (CDP) Horry County
23	1211	57.6	**Simpsonville** (city) Greenville County
24	n/a	57.5	**Burnettown** (town) Aiken County
25	1323	56.9	**Goose Creek** (city) Berkeley County
26	1352	56.7	**Easley** (city) Pickens County
27	1476	56.1	**Bluffton** (town) Beaufort County
28	n/a	55.8	**Clover** (town) York County
29	1587	55.6	**Summerville** (town) Dorchester County
30	n/a	55.4	**Hampton** (town) Hampton County
31	n/a	54.5	**Springdale** (town) Lexington County
32	n/a	54.2	**Travelers Rest** (city) Greenville County
33	1871	54.1	**Oak Grove** (CDP) Lexington County
34	n/a	53.8	**Hollywood** (town) Charleston County
35	1958	53.7	**Lexington** (town) Lexington County
36	n/a	53.5	**Sangaree** (CDP) Berkeley County
37	2032	53.4	**Wade Hampton** (CDP) Greenville County
38	2070	53.2	**Mauldin** (city) Greenville County
39	n/a	53.1	**Dalzell** (CDP) Sumter County
40	2131	52.9	**Red Hill** (CDP) Horry County
41	2170	52.7	**Socastee** (CDP) Horry County
42	n/a	52.6	**Garden City** (CDP) Horry County
43	2206	52.5	**Beaufort** (city) Beaufort County
43	n/a	52.5	**Burton** (CDP) Beaufort County
45	n/a	52.4	**Arial** (CDP) Pickens County
46	2264	52.2	**Hanahan** (city) Berkeley County
47	2306	52.0	**Ladson** (CDP) Berkeley County
48	n/a	51.8	**Piedmont** (CDP) Anderson County
48	2347	51.8	**Taylors** (CDP) Greenville County
50	n/a	51.7	**Belton** (city) Anderson County
51	n/a	51.6	**Honea Path** (town) Anderson County
52	n/a	51.5	**Red Bank** (CDP) Lexington County
53	n/a	51.4	**Woodruff** (city) Spartanburg County
54	2500	51.0	**North Augusta** (city) Aiken County
55	n/a	50.9	**North Hartsville** (CDP) Darlington County
56	2631	50.4	**Seven Oaks** (CDP) Lexington County
57	n/a	50.3	**Williamston** (town) Anderson County
58	n/a	50.2	**Lesslie** (CDP) York County
59	n/a	50.0	**Duncan** (town) Spartanburg County
59	2720	50.0	**Irmo** (town) Richland County
61	n/a	49.9	**Belvedere** (CDP) Aiken County
61	n/a	49.9	**Clearwater** (CDP) Aiken County
61	n/a	49.9	**Surfside Beach** (town) Horry County
64	n/a	49.2	**Barnwell** (city) Barnwell County
64	2884	49.2	**Greer** (city) Greenville County
66	n/a	49.1	**Batesburg-Leesville** (town) Lexington County
66	n/a	49.1	**Camden** (city) Kershaw County
68	n/a	48.8	**Edisto** (CDP) Orangeburg County
69	2982	48.7	**Berea** (CDP) Greenville County
69	n/a	48.7	**Fountain Inn** (city) Greenville County
71	n/a	48.5	**Moncks Corner** (town) Berkeley County
72	n/a	47.7	**Saluda** (town) Saluda County
73	n/a	47.5	**Pendleton** (town) Anderson County
74	3253	47.3	**Aiken** (city) Aiken County
75	n/a	47.1	**Kingstree** (town) Williamsburg County
75	n/a	47.1	**Liberty** (city) Pickens County
75	n/a	47.1	**Williston** (town) Barnwell County
78	3296	47.0	**Forest Acres** (city) Richland County
79	n/a	46.7	**Dillon** (city) Dillon County
79	n/a	46.7	**Sans Souci** (CDP) Greenville County
81	3370	46.6	**Sumter** (city) Sumter County
82	3444	46.2	**Myrtle Beach** (city) Horry County
82	n/a	46.2	**Woodfield** (CDP) Richland County
84	3459	46.1	**Florence** (city) Florence County
85	n/a	45.5	**Mullins** (city) Marion County
86	n/a	45.4	**Welcome** (CDP) Greenville County
87	n/a	45.3	**Abbeville** (city) Abbeville County
88	n/a	45.2	**Springdale** (CDP) Lancaster County
89	3614	45.1	**Rock Hill** (city) York County
90	3659	44.7	**Parker** (CDP) Greenville County
91	n/a	44.6	**Darlington** (city) Darlington County
92	n/a	44.5	**Walhalla** (city) Oconee County
93	n/a	44.3	**Graniteville** (CDP) Aiken County
94	3761	44.0	**West Columbia** (city) Lexington County
95	n/a	43.9	**Andrews** (town) Georgetown County
96	n/a	43.7	**Gloverville** (CDP) Aiken County
97	n/a	43.6	**York** (city) York County
98	n/a	43.3	**Bamberg** (town) Bamberg County
99	n/a	42.9	**Laurens** (city) Laurens County
100	n/a	42.5	**Hardeeville** (city) Jasper County
100	3945	42.5	**North Charleston** (city) Charleston County
102	3981	42.2	**Cayce** (city) Lexington County
103	n/a	42.1	**Dunean** (CDP) Greenville County
104	n/a	41.9	**Elgin** (CDP) Lancaster County
105	n/a	41.8	**Homeland Park** (CDP) Anderson County
105	n/a	41.8	**Pageland** (town) Chesterfield County
107	n/a	41.7	**Union** (city) Union County
108	n/a	41.6	**Lake City** (city) Florence County
109	4039	41.5	**Anderson** (city) Anderson County
109	n/a	41.5	**Georgetown** (city) Georgetown County
111	n/a	41.3	**Folly Beach** (city) Charleston County
112	4080	41.0	**Charleston** (city) Charleston County
113	n/a	40.8	**Seneca** (city) Oconee County
114	n/a	40.5	**Pickens** (city) Pickens County
115	4146	40.2	**Gantt** (CDP) Greenville County
116	n/a	40.0	**Manning** (city) Clarendon County
117	4168	39.9	**Greenville** (city) Greenville County
118	n/a	39.7	**Cheraw** (town) Chesterfield County
119	n/a	39.6	**Winnsboro** (town) Fairfield County
120	n/a	38.5	**Hartsville** (city) Darlington County
120	n/a	38.5	**Ridgeland** (town) Jasper County
122	4296	37.9	**Conway** (city) Horry County
122	n/a	37.9	**Lancaster** (city) Lancaster County
124	4320	37.5	**Newberry** (city) Newberry County
125	n/a	37.1	**Marion** (city) Marion County
126	4353	36.8	**Gaffney** (city) Cherokee County
126	4353	36.8	**Spartanburg** (city) Spartanburg County
128	n/a	36.2	**Valley Falls** (CDP) Spartanburg County
129	n/a	35.8	**Walterboro** (city) Colleton County
130	n/a	35.4	**Hopkins** (CDP) Richland County
131	n/a	35.2	**Allendale** (town) Allendale County
131	n/a	35.2	**Southern Shops** (CDP) Spartanburg County
133	n/a	34.9	**Edgefield** (town) Edgefield County
134	4431	34.8	**Clemson** (city) Pickens County
134	4431	34.8	**Greenwood** (city) Greenwood County
136	n/a	33.4	**Chester** (city) Chester County
137	4489	33.2	**Saint Andrews** (CDP) Richland County
138	4503	32.8	**Dentsville** (CDP) Richland County
139	n/a	32.7	**Saxon** (CDP) Spartanburg County
140	n/a	32.6	**Bennettsville** (city) Marlboro County
141	4514	32.3	**Columbia** (city) Richland County
142	4517	32.2	**Port Royal** (town) Beaufort County
143	n/a	32.1	**Denmark** (city) Bamberg County
143	n/a	32.1	**East Gaffney** (CDP) Cherokee County
145	n/a	31.6	**Brookdale** (CDP) Orangeburg County
146	4542	31.1	**Orangeburg** (city) Orangeburg County
147	n/a	29.4	**McCormick** (town) McCormick County
148	n/a	29.2	**Bishopville** (city) Lee County
149	n/a	24.8	**Clinton** (city) Laurens County
150	n/a	19.9	**Central** (town) Pickens County

Note: The state column ranks the top/bottom 150 places in the state with population of 2,500 or more. The national column ranks the top/bottom places in the country with population of 10,000 or more. Places that are unincorporated were not considered in the rankings. n/a indicates data not available. Please refer to the User Guide for additional information.

Marriage Status: Now Married

Top 150 Places Ranked in *Ascending* Order

State Rank	Nat'l Rank	Percent	Place
1	n/a	19.9	Central (town) Pickens County
2	n/a	24.8	Clinton (city) Laurens County
3	n/a	29.2	Bishopville (city) Lee County
4	n/a	29.4	McCormick (town) McCormick County
5	112	31.1	Orangeburg (city) Orangeburg County
6	n/a	31.6	Brookdale (CDP) Orangeburg County
7	n/a	32.1	Denmark (city) Bamberg County
7	n/a	32.1	East Gaffney (CDP) Cherokee County
9	136	32.2	Port Royal (town) Beaufort County
10	140	32.3	Columbia (city) Richland County
11	n/a	32.6	Bennettsville (city) Marlboro County
12	n/a	32.7	Saxon (CDP) Spartanburg County
13	149	32.8	Dentsville (CDP) Richland County
14	164	33.2	Saint Andrews (CDP) Richland County
15	n/a	33.4	Chester (city) Chester County
16	220	34.8	Clemson (city) Pickens County
16	220	34.8	Greenwood (city) Greenwood County
18	n/a	34.9	Edgefield (town) Edgefield County
19	n/a	35.2	Allendale (town) Allendale County
19	n/a	35.2	Southern Shops (CDP) Spartanburg County
21	n/a	35.4	Hopkins (CDP) Richland County
22	n/a	35.8	Walterboro (city) Colleton County
23	n/a	36.2	Valley Falls (CDP) Spartanburg County
24	296	36.8	Gaffney (city) Cherokee County
24	296	36.8	Spartanburg (city) Spartanburg County
26	n/a	37.1	Marion (city) Marion County
27	331	37.5	Newberry (city) Newberry County
28	353	37.9	Conway (city) Horry County
28	n/a	37.9	Lancaster (city) Lancaster County
30	n/a	38.5	Hartsville (city) Darlington County
30	n/a	38.5	Ridgeland (town) Jasper County
32	n/a	39.6	Winnsboro (town) Fairfield County
33	n/a	39.7	Cheraw (town) Chesterfield County
34	481	39.9	Greenville (city) Greenville County
35	n/a	40.0	Manning (city) Clarendon County
36	505	40.2	Gantt (CDP) Greenville County
37	n/a	40.5	Pickens (city) Pickens County
38	n/a	40.8	Seneca (city) Oconee County
39	571	41.0	Charleston (city) Charleston County
40	n/a	41.3	Folly Beach (city) Charleston County
41	612	41.5	Anderson (city) Anderson County
41	n/a	41.5	Georgetown (city) Georgetown County
43	n/a	41.6	Lake City (city) Florence County
44	n/a	41.7	Union (city) Union County
45	n/a	41.8	Homeland Park (CDP) Anderson County
45	n/a	41.8	Pageland (town) Chesterfield County
47	n/a	41.9	Elgin (CDP) Lancaster County
48	n/a	42.1	Dunean (CDP) Greenville County
49	666	42.2	Cayce (city) Lexington County
50	n/a	42.5	Hardeeville (city) Jasper County
50	701	42.5	North Charleston (city) Charleston County
52	n/a	42.9	Laurens (city) Laurens County
53	n/a	43.3	Bamberg (town) Bamberg County
54	n/a	43.6	York (city) York County
55	n/a	43.7	Gloverville (CDP) Aiken County
56	n/a	43.9	Andrews (town) Georgetown County
57	883	44.0	West Columbia (city) Lexington County
58	n/a	44.3	Graniteville (CDP) Aiken County
59	n/a	44.5	Walhalla (city) Oconee County
60	n/a	44.6	Darlington (city) Darlington County
61	975	44.7	Parker (CDP) Greenville County
62	1031	45.1	Rock Hill (city) York County
63	n/a	45.2	Springdale (CDP) Lancaster County
64	n/a	45.3	Abbeville (city) Abbeville County
65	n/a	45.4	Welcome (CDP) Greenville County
66	n/a	45.5	Mullins (city) Marion County
67	1179	46.1	Florence (city) Florence County
68	1198	46.2	Myrtle Beach (city) Horry County
68	n/a	46.2	Woodfield (CDP) Richland County
70	1264	46.6	Sumter (city) Sumter County
71	n/a	46.7	Dillon (city) Dillon County
71	n/a	46.7	Sans Souci (CDP) Greenville County
73	1346	47.0	Forest Acres (city) Richland County
74	n/a	47.1	Kingstree (town) Williamsburg County
74	n/a	47.1	Liberty (city) Pickens County
74	n/a	47.1	Williston (town) Barnwell County
77	1389	47.3	Aiken (city) Aiken County
78	n/a	47.5	Pendleton (town) Anderson County
79	n/a	47.7	Saluda (town) Saluda County
80	n/a	48.5	Moncks Corner (town) Berkeley County
81	1652	48.7	Berea (CDP) Greenville County
81	n/a	48.7	Fountain Inn (city) Greenville County
83	n/a	48.8	Edisto (CDP) Orangeburg County
84	n/a	49.1	Batesburg-Leesville (town) Lexington County
84	n/a	49.1	Camden (city) Kershaw County
86	n/a	49.2	Barnwell (city) Barnwell County
86	1756	49.2	Greer (city) Greenville County
88	n/a	49.9	Belvedere (CDP) Aiken County
88	n/a	49.9	Clearwater (CDP) Aiken County
88	n/a	49.9	Surfside Beach (town) Horry County
91	n/a	50.0	Duncan (town) Spartanburg County
91	1918	50.0	Irmo (town) Richland County
93	n/a	50.2	Lesslie (CDP) York County
94	n/a	50.3	Williamston (town) Anderson County
95	2006	50.4	Seven Oaks (CDP) Lexington County
96	n/a	50.9	North Hartsville (CDP) Darlington County
97	2139	51.0	North Augusta (city) Aiken County
98	n/a	51.4	Woodruff (city) Spartanburg County
99	n/a	51.5	Red Bank (CDP) Lexington County
100	n/a	51.6	Honea Path (town) Anderson County
101	n/a	51.7	Belton (city) Anderson County
102	n/a	51.8	Piedmont (CDP) Anderson County
102	2282	51.8	Taylors (CDP) Greenville County
104	2332	52.0	Ladson (CDP) Berkeley County
105	2366	52.2	Hanahan (city) Berkeley County
106	n/a	52.4	Arial (CDP) Pickens County
107	2437	52.5	Beaufort (city) Beaufort County
107	n/a	52.5	Burton (CDP) Beaufort County
109	n/a	52.6	Garden City (CDP) Horry County
110	2467	52.7	Socastee (CDP) Horry County
111	2509	52.9	Red Hill (CDP) Horry County
112	n/a	53.1	Dalzell (CDP) Sumter County
113	2570	53.2	Mauldin (city) Greenville County
114	2604	53.4	Wade Hampton (CDP) Greenville County
115	n/a	53.5	Sangaree (CDP) Berkeley County
116	2681	53.7	Lexington (town) Lexington County
117	n/a	53.8	Hollywood (town) Charleston County
118	2762	54.1	Oak Grove (CDP) Lexington County
119	n/a	54.2	Travelers Rest (city) Greenville County
120	n/a	54.5	Springdale (town) Lexington County
121	n/a	55.4	Hampton (town) Hampton County
122	3062	55.6	Summerville (town) Dorchester County
123	n/a	55.8	Clover (town) York County
124	3162	56.1	Bluffton (town) Beaufort County
125	3281	56.7	Easley (city) Pickens County
126	3318	56.9	Goose Creek (city) Berkeley County
127	n/a	57.5	Burnettown (town) Aiken County
128	3428	57.6	Simpsonville (city) Greenville County
129	n/a	58.2	Forestbrook (CDP) Horry County
130	n/a	58.5	Lugoff (CDP) Kershaw County
130	3568	58.5	Mount Pleasant (town) Charleston County
130	3568	58.5	North Myrtle Beach (city) Horry County
133	n/a	58.7	Little River (CDP) Horry County
134	n/a	59.9	Northlake (CDP) Anderson County
135	3874	60.5	Fort Mill (town) York County
136	n/a	60.7	Lakewood (CDP) Sumter County
137	n/a	61.4	Centerville (CDP) Anderson County
138	n/a	62.6	Isle of Palms (city) Charleston County
138	n/a	62.6	Murrells Inlet (CDP) Georgetown County
140	4197	63.1	Hilton Head Island (town) Beaufort County
141	n/a	63.9	Arcadia (CDP) Spartanburg County
142	n/a	64.2	India Hook (CDP) York County
143	n/a	64.5	Lyman (town) Spartanburg County
144	n/a	64.6	Lake Wylie (CDP) York County
145	n/a	67.0	Newport (CDP) York County
146	n/a	67.7	Boiling Springs (CDP) Spartanburg County
147	n/a	69.0	Lake Murray of Richland (CDP) Richland County
148	4587	69.3	Five Forks (CDP) Greenville County
149	n/a	70.3	Laurel Bay (CDP) Beaufort County
150	n/a	72.5	Tega Cay (city) York County

Note: The state column ranks the top/bottom 150 places in the state with population of 2,500 or more. The national column ranks the top/bottom places in the country with population of 10,000 or more. Places that are unincorporated were not considered in the rankings. n/a indicates data not available. Please refer to the User Guide for additional information.

Marriage Status: Separated

Top 150 Places Ranked in *Descending* Order

State Rank	Nat'l Rank	Percent	Place
1	n/a	10.4	**Brookdale** (CDP) Orangeburg County
2	n/a	9.8	**Woodruff** (city) Spartanburg County
3	n/a	8.7	**Mullins** (city) Marion County
4	n/a	8.2	**Denmark** (city) Bamberg County
5	n/a	7.6	**Edgefield** (town) Edgefield County
5	n/a	7.6	**Graniteville** (CDP) Aiken County
7	n/a	7.5	**Walterboro** (city) Colleton County
8	n/a	7.0	**Andrews** (town) Georgetown County
9	n/a	6.9	**Springdale** (CDP) Lancaster County
10	n/a	6.7	**Barnwell** (city) Barnwell County
11	n/a	6.5	**Edisto** (CDP) Orangeburg County
11	n/a	6.5	**Saxon** (CDP) Spartanburg County
13	n/a	6.4	**Hardeeville** (city) Jasper County
14	n/a	6.2	**Marion** (city) Marion County
15	n/a	6.1	**Belton** (city) Anderson County
15	n/a	6.1	**Ridgeland** (town) Jasper County
17	n/a	6.0	**Belvedere** (CDP) Aiken County
17	n/a	6.0	**Winnsboro** (town) Fairfield County
19	n/a	5.9	**Bishopville** (city) Lee County
20	n/a	5.8	**Arcadia** (CDP) Spartanburg County
20	n/a	5.8	**Lake City** (city) Florence County
22	n/a	5.6	**East Gaffney** (CDP) Cherokee County
22	n/a	5.6	**Union** (city) Union County
24	n/a	5.5	**Chester** (city) Chester County
25	44	5.4	**Gantt** (CDP) Greenville County
26	n/a	5.3	**Southern Shops** (CDP) Spartanburg County
27	n/a	5.2	**Lancaster** (city) Lancaster County
27	n/a	5.2	**McCormick** (town) McCormick County
27	n/a	5.2	**Woodfield** (CDP) Richland County
30	n/a	5.1	**Batesburg-Leesville** (town) Lexington County
30	n/a	5.1	**Dillon** (city) Dillon County
30	n/a	5.1	**Manning** (city) Clarendon County
33	n/a	4.9	**Bamberg** (town) Bamberg County
33	n/a	4.9	**Elgin** (CDP) Lancaster County
33	87	4.9	**Gaffney** (city) Cherokee County
36	98	4.8	**Anderson** (city) Anderson County
36	98	4.8	**Newberry** (city) Newberry County
38	n/a	4.7	**Cheraw** (town) Chesterfield County
38	n/a	4.7	**Homeland Park** (CDP) Anderson County
38	112	4.7	**North Charleston** (city) Charleston County
38	n/a	4.7	**Pageland** (town) Chesterfield County
42	n/a	4.6	**Clearwater** (CDP) Aiken County
42	126	4.6	**Ladson** (CDP) Berkeley County
42	126	4.6	**Saint Andrews** (CDP) Richland County
42	n/a	4.6	**Travelers Rest** (city) Greenville County
46	n/a	4.5	**Centerville** (CDP) Anderson County
46	n/a	4.5	**Hartsville** (city) Darlington County
48	n/a	4.4	**Bennettsville** (city) Marlboro County
48	165	4.4	**Florence** (city) Florence County
48	165	4.4	**Parker** (CDP) Greenville County
51	n/a	4.3	**Darlington** (city) Darlington County
51	n/a	4.3	**Springdale** (town) Lexington County
53	n/a	4.2	**Forestbrook** (CDP) Horry County
54	n/a	4.1	**Abbeville** (city) Abbeville County
54	n/a	4.1	**Hampton** (town) Hampton County
54	236	4.1	**North Augusta** (city) Aiken County
54	n/a	4.1	**Pendleton** (town) Anderson County
54	236	4.1	**Spartanburg** (city) Spartanburg County
59	267	4.0	**Beaufort** (city) Beaufort County
59	267	4.0	**Orangeburg** (city) Orangeburg County
59	267	4.0	**Sumter** (city) Sumter County
62	n/a	3.9	**Clinton** (city) Laurens County
62	305	3.9	**Greenville** (city) Greenville County
62	305	3.9	**Rock Hill** (city) York County
62	n/a	3.9	**York** (city) York County
66	342	3.8	**Hanahan** (city) Berkeley County
67	n/a	3.7	**Hopkins** (CDP) Richland County
67	387	3.7	**Lexington** (town) Lexington County
67	387	3.7	**North Myrtle Beach** (city) Horry County
67	387	3.7	**Red Hill** (CDP) Horry County
71	438	3.6	**Berea** (CDP) Greenville County
71	438	3.6	**Cayce** (city) Lexington County
71	n/a	3.6	**Kingstree** (town) Williamsburg County
71	n/a	3.6	**Williston** (town) Barnwell County
75	487	3.5	**Columbia** (city) Richland County
75	487	3.5	**Dentsville** (CDP) Richland County
75	487	3.5	**Greenwood** (city) Greenwood County
75	n/a	3.5	**Saluda** (town) Saluda County
75	487	3.5	**Wade Hampton** (CDP) Greenville County
80	554	3.4	**Easley** (city) Pickens County
80	n/a	3.4	**Gloverville** (CDP) Aiken County
80	n/a	3.4	**Lyman** (town) Spartanburg County
80	554	3.4	**Seven Oaks** (CDP) Lexington County
84	n/a	3.3	**Duncan** (town) Spartanburg County
84	615	3.3	**Port Royal** (town) Beaufort County
84	n/a	3.3	**Seneca** (city) Oconee County
87	n/a	3.2	**Liberty** (city) Pickens County
87	n/a	3.2	**Welcome** (CDP) Greenville County
89	n/a	3.1	**Clover** (town) York County
89	747	3.1	**Irmo** (town) Richland County
89	n/a	3.1	**North Hartsville** (CDP) Darlington County
89	747	3.1	**Oak Grove** (CDP) Lexington County
89	n/a	3.1	**Sangaree** (CDP) Berkeley County
94	n/a	3.0	**Allendale** (town) Allendale County
94	n/a	3.0	**Walhalla** (city) Oconee County
96	n/a	2.9	**Camden** (city) Kershaw County
96	906	2.9	**Conway** (city) Horry County
96	n/a	2.9	**Fountain Inn** (city) Greenville County
96	906	2.9	**Myrtle Beach** (city) Horry County
96	906	2.9	**West Columbia** (city) Lexington County
101	n/a	2.8	**Dunean** (CDP) Greenville County
101	1005	2.8	**Greer** (city) Greenville County
101	n/a	2.8	**Moncks Corner** (town) Berkeley County
104	n/a	2.7	**Georgetown** (city) Georgetown County
104	1100	2.7	**Summerville** (town) Dorchester County
106	1195	2.6	**Goose Creek** (city) Berkeley County
106	n/a	2.6	**Lugoff** (CDP) Kershaw County
108	n/a	2.5	**Burton** (CDP) Beaufort County
108	1300	2.5	**Charleston** (city) Charleston County
108	1300	2.5	**Fort Mill** (town) York County
111	1419	2.4	**Hilton Head Island** (town) Beaufort County
111	1419	2.4	**Simpsonville** (city) Greenville County
113	n/a	2.3	**Dalzell** (CDP) Sumter County
113	1550	2.3	**Mount Pleasant** (town) Charleston County
113	n/a	2.3	**Sans Souci** (CDP) Greenville County
116	n/a	2.2	**Laurens** (city) Laurens County
116	1676	2.2	**Taylors** (CDP) Greenville County
118	n/a	2.1	**Newport** (CDP) York County
118	1816	2.1	**Socastee** (CDP) Horry County
120	n/a	2.0	**Arial** (CDP) Pickens County
120	n/a	2.0	**Burnettown** (town) Aiken County
120	1961	2.0	**Forest Acres** (city) Richland County
123	n/a	1.9	**Boiling Springs** (CDP) Spartanburg County
123	n/a	1.9	**Hollywood** (town) Charleston County
123	2118	1.9	**Mauldin** (city) Greenville County
123	n/a	1.9	**Red Bank** (CDP) Lexington County
127	2275	1.8	**Bluffton** (town) Beaufort County
127	n/a	1.8	**Murrells Inlet** (CDP) Georgetown County
127	n/a	1.8	**Surfside Beach** (town) Horry County
130	n/a	1.7	**Piedmont** (CDP) Anderson County
131	n/a	1.6	**Folly Beach** (city) Charleston County
132	2791	1.5	**Aiken** (city) Aiken County
132	n/a	1.5	**Garden City** (CDP) Horry County
132	n/a	1.5	**Little River** (CDP) Horry County
132	n/a	1.5	**Williamston** (town) Anderson County
136	n/a	1.4	**Lake Murray of Richland** (CDP) Richland County
136	n/a	1.4	**Northlake** (CDP) Anderson County
136	n/a	1.4	**Pickens** (city) Pickens County
139	3167	1.3	**Five Forks** (CDP) Greenville County
140	n/a	1.2	**Isle of Palms** (city) Charleston County
141	n/a	1.1	**Honea Path** (town) Anderson County
141	n/a	1.1	**Lakewood** (CDP) Sumter County
141	n/a	1.1	**Tega Cay** (city) York County
144	3734	1.0	**Clemson** (city) Pickens County
144	n/a	1.0	**Lesslie** (CDP) York County
146	n/a	0.9	**Central** (town) Pickens County
146	n/a	0.9	**Lake Wylie** (CDP) York County
146	n/a	0.9	**Valley Falls** (CDP) Spartanburg County
149	n/a	0.5	**Laurel Bay** (CDP) Beaufort County
150	n/a	0.0	**India Hook** (CDP) York County

Note: The state column ranks the top/bottom 150 places in the state with population of 2,500 or more. The national column ranks the top/bottom places in the country with population of 10,000 or more. Places that are unincorporated were not considered in the rankings. n/a indicates data not available. Please refer to the User Guide for additional information.

Marriage Status: Separated

Top 150 Places Ranked in *Ascending* Order

State Rank	Nat'l Rank	Percent	Place
1	n/a	0.0	**India Hook** (CDP) York County
2	n/a	0.5	**Laurel Bay** (CDP) Beaufort County
3	n/a	0.9	**Central** (town) Pickens County
3	n/a	0.9	**Lake Wylie** (CDP) York County
3	n/a	0.9	**Valley Falls** (CDP) Spartanburg County
6	763	1.0	**Clemson** (city) Pickens County
6	n/a	1.0	**Lesslie** (CDP) York County
8	n/a	1.1	**Honea Path** (town) Anderson County
8	n/a	1.1	**Lakewood** (CDP) Sumter County
8	n/a	1.1	**Tega Cay** (city) York County
11	n/a	1.2	**Isle of Palms** (city) Charleston County
12	1281	1.3	**Five Forks** (CDP) Greenville County
13	n/a	1.4	**Lake Murray of Richland** (CDP) Richland County
13	n/a	1.4	**Northlake** (CDP) Anderson County
13	n/a	1.4	**Pickens** (city) Pickens County
16	1674	1.5	**Aiken** (city) Aiken County
16	n/a	1.5	**Garden City** (CDP) Horry County
16	n/a	1.5	**Little River** (CDP) Horry County
16	n/a	1.5	**Williamston** (town) Anderson County
20	n/a	1.6	**Folly Beach** (city) Charleston County
21	n/a	1.7	**Piedmont** (CDP) Anderson County
22	2235	1.8	**Bluffton** (town) Beaufort County
22	n/a	1.8	**Murrells Inlet** (CDP) Georgetown County
22	n/a	1.8	**Surfside Beach** (town) Horry County
25	n/a	1.9	**Boiling Springs** (CDP) Spartanburg County
25	n/a	1.9	**Hollywood** (town) Charleston County
25	2382	1.9	**Mauldin** (city) Greenville County
25	n/a	1.9	**Red Bank** (CDP) Lexington County
29	n/a	2.0	**Arial** (CDP) Pickens County
29	n/a	2.0	**Burnettown** (town) Aiken County
29	2539	2.0	**Forest Acres** (city) Richland County
32	n/a	2.1	**Newport** (CDP) York County
32	2696	2.1	**Socastee** (CDP) Horry County
34	n/a	2.2	**Laurens** (city) Laurens County
34	2841	2.2	**Taylors** (CDP) Greenville County
36	n/a	2.3	**Dalzell** (CDP) Sumter County
36	2981	2.3	**Mount Pleasant** (town) Charleston County
36	n/a	2.3	**Sans Souci** (CDP) Greenville County
39	3107	2.4	**Hilton Head Island** (town) Beaufort County
39	3107	2.4	**Simpsonville** (city) Greenville County
41	n/a	2.5	**Burton** (CDP) Beaufort County
41	3238	2.5	**Charleston** (city) Charleston County
41	3238	2.5	**Fort Mill** (town) York County
44	3357	2.6	**Goose Creek** (city) Berkeley County
44	n/a	2.6	**Lugoff** (CDP) Kershaw County
46	n/a	2.7	**Georgetown** (city) Georgetown County
46	3462	2.7	**Summerville** (town) Dorchester County
48	n/a	2.8	**Dunean** (CDP) Greenville County
48	3557	2.8	**Greer** (city) Greenville County
48	n/a	2.8	**Moncks Corner** (town) Berkeley County
51	n/a	2.9	**Camden** (city) Kershaw County
51	3652	2.9	**Conway** (city) Horry County
51	n/a	2.9	**Fountain Inn** (city) Greenville County
51	3652	2.9	**Myrtle Beach** (city) Horry County
51	3652	2.9	**West Columbia** (city) Lexington County
56	n/a	3.0	**Allendale** (town) Allendale County
56	n/a	3.0	**Walhalla** (city) Oconee County
58	n/a	3.1	**Clover** (town) York County
58	3842	3.1	**Irmo** (town) Richland County
58	n/a	3.1	**North Hartsville** (CDP) Darlington County
58	3842	3.1	**Oak Grove** (CDP) Lexington County
58	n/a	3.1	**Sangaree** (CDP) Berkeley County
63	n/a	3.2	**Liberty** (city) Pickens County
63	n/a	3.2	**Welcome** (CDP) Greenville County
65	n/a	3.3	**Duncan** (town) Spartanburg County
65	3971	3.3	**Port Royal** (town) Beaufort County
65	n/a	3.3	**Seneca** (city) Oconee County
68	4042	3.4	**Easley** (city) Pickens County
68	n/a	3.4	**Gloverville** (CDP) Aiken County
68	n/a	3.4	**Lyman** (town) Spartanburg County
68	4042	3.4	**Seven Oaks** (CDP) Lexington County
72	4103	3.5	**Columbia** (city) Richland County
72	4103	3.5	**Dentsville** (CDP) Richland County
72	4103	3.5	**Greenwood** (city) Greenwood County
72	n/a	3.5	**Saluda** (town) Saluda County
72	4103	3.5	**Wade Hampton** (CDP) Greenville County
77	4170	3.6	**Berea** (CDP) Greenville County
77	4170	3.6	**Cayce** (city) Lexington County
77	n/a	3.6	**Kingstree** (town) Williamsburg County
77	n/a	3.6	**Williston** (town) Barnwell County
81	n/a	3.7	**Hopkins** (CDP) Richland County
81	4219	3.7	**Lexington** (town) Lexington County
81	4219	3.7	**North Myrtle Beach** (city) Horry County
81	4219	3.7	**Red Hill** (CDP) Horry County
85	4270	3.8	**Hanahan** (city) Berkeley County
86	n/a	3.9	**Clinton** (city) Laurens County
86	4315	3.9	**Greenville** (city) Greenville County
86	4315	3.9	**Rock Hill** (city) York County
86	n/a	3.9	**York** (city) York County
90	4352	4.0	**Beaufort** (city) Beaufort County
90	4352	4.0	**Orangeburg** (city) Orangeburg County
90	4352	4.0	**Sumter** (city) Sumter County
93	n/a	4.1	**Abbeville** (city) Abbeville County
93	n/a	4.1	**Hampton** (town) Hampton County
93	4390	4.1	**North Augusta** (city) Aiken County
93	n/a	4.1	**Pendleton** (town) Anderson County
93	4390	4.1	**Spartanburg** (city) Spartanburg County
98	n/a	4.2	**Forestbrook** (CDP) Horry County
99	n/a	4.3	**Darlington** (city) Darlington County
99	n/a	4.3	**Springdale** (town) Lexington County
101	n/a	4.4	**Bennettsville** (city) Marlboro County
101	4472	4.4	**Florence** (city) Florence County
101	4472	4.4	**Parker** (CDP) Greenville County
104	n/a	4.5	**Centerville** (CDP) Anderson County
104	n/a	4.5	**Hartsville** (city) Darlington County
106	n/a	4.6	**Clearwater** (CDP) Aiken County
106	4508	4.6	**Ladson** (CDP) Berkeley County
106	4508	4.6	**Saint Andrews** (CDP) Richland County
106	n/a	4.6	**Travelers Rest** (city) Greenville County
110	n/a	4.7	**Cheraw** (town) Chesterfield County
110	n/a	4.7	**Homeland Park** (CDP) Anderson County
110	4531	4.7	**North Charleston** (city) Charleston County
110	n/a	4.7	**Pageland** (town) Chesterfield County
114	4545	4.8	**Anderson** (city) Anderson County
114	4545	4.8	**Newberry** (city) Newberry County
116	n/a	4.9	**Bamberg** (town) Bamberg County
116	n/a	4.9	**Elgin** (CDP) Lancaster County
116	4559	4.9	**Gaffney** (city) Cherokee County
119	n/a	5.1	**Batesburg-Leesville** (town) Lexington County
119	n/a	5.1	**Dillon** (city) Dillon County
119	n/a	5.1	**Manning** (city) Clarendon County
122	n/a	5.2	**Lancaster** (city) Lancaster County
122	n/a	5.2	**McCormick** (town) McCormick County
122	n/a	5.2	**Woodfield** (CDP) Richland County
125	n/a	5.3	**Southern Shops** (CDP) Spartanburg County
126	4610	5.4	**Gantt** (CDP) Greenville County
127	n/a	5.5	**Chester** (city) Chester County
128	n/a	5.6	**East Gaffney** (CDP) Cherokee County
128	n/a	5.6	**Union** (city) Union County
130	n/a	5.8	**Arcadia** (CDP) Spartanburg County
130	n/a	5.8	**Lake City** (city) Florence County
132	n/a	5.9	**Bishopville** (city) Lee County
133	n/a	6.0	**Belvedere** (CDP) Aiken County
133	n/a	6.0	**Winnsboro** (town) Fairfield County
135	n/a	6.1	**Belton** (city) Anderson County
135	n/a	6.1	**Ridgeland** (town) Jasper County
137	n/a	6.2	**Marion** (city) Marion County
138	n/a	6.4	**Hardeeville** (city) Jasper County
139	n/a	6.5	**Edisto** (CDP) Orangeburg County
139	n/a	6.5	**Saxon** (CDP) Spartanburg County
141	n/a	6.7	**Barnwell** (city) Barnwell County
142	n/a	6.9	**Springdale** (CDP) Lancaster County
143	n/a	7.0	**Andrews** (town) Georgetown County
144	n/a	7.5	**Walterboro** (city) Colleton County
145	n/a	7.6	**Edgefield** (town) Edgefield County
145	n/a	7.6	**Graniteville** (CDP) Aiken County
147	n/a	8.2	**Denmark** (city) Bamberg County
148	n/a	8.7	**Mullins** (city) Marion County
149	n/a	9.8	**Woodruff** (city) Spartanburg County
150	n/a	10.4	**Brookdale** (CDP) Orangeburg County

Note: The state column ranks the top/bottom 150 places in the state with population of 2,500 or more. The national column ranks the top/bottom places in the country with population of 10,000 or more. Places that are unincorporated were not considered in the rankings. n/a indicates data not available. Please refer to the User Guide for additional information.

Marriage Status: Widowed

Top 150 Places Ranked in *Descending* Order

State Rank	Nat'l Rank	Percent	Place	State Rank	Nat'l Rank	Percent	Place
1	n/a	15.5	**Garden City** (CDP) Horry County	76	1250	7.3	**Hilton Head Island** (town) Beaufort County
2	n/a	14.3	**Williamston** (town) Anderson County	76	n/a	7.3	**Woodfield** (CDP) Richland County
3	n/a	14.0	**Walterboro** (city) Colleton County	78	n/a	7.2	**Sans Souci** (CDP) Greenville County
4	n/a	13.5	**Hartsville** (city) Darlington County	78	1323	7.2	**Seven Oaks** (CDP) Lexington County
5	n/a	13.2	**Bamberg** (town) Bamberg County	80	n/a	7.0	**Arial** (CDP) Pickens County
5	n/a	13.2	**Cheraw** (town) Chesterfield County	80	n/a	7.0	**Clover** (town) York County
7	n/a	12.9	**Lake City** (city) Florence County	80	n/a	7.0	**Murrells Inlet** (CDP) Georgetown County
8	n/a	12.8	**East Gaffney** (CDP) Cherokee County	83	n/a	6.9	**Belton** (city) Anderson County
9	n/a	12.6	**Woodruff** (city) Spartanburg County	83	1553	6.9	**Mauldin** (city) Greenville County
10	n/a	12.5	**Denmark** (city) Bamberg County	85	n/a	6.8	**Barnwell** (city) Barnwell County
11	n/a	12.4	**Manning** (city) Clarendon County	85	1628	6.8	**Myrtle Beach** (city) Horry County
12	n/a	12.1	**Mullins** (city) Marion County	85	1628	6.8	**Red Hill** (CDP) Horry County
13	n/a	12.0	**Walhalla** (city) Oconee County	88	n/a	6.7	**Hardeeville** (city) Jasper County
14	n/a	11.7	**Dillon** (city) Dillon County	89	n/a	6.6	**Burnettown** (town) Aiken County
14	n/a	11.7	**Union** (city) Union County	89	1779	6.6	**Greer** (city) Greenville County
16	56	11.6	**Anderson** (city) Anderson County	91	n/a	6.4	**Dunean** (CDP) Greenville County
16	n/a	11.6	**Laurens** (city) Laurens County	91	n/a	6.4	**Northlake** (CDP) Anderson County
18	n/a	11.4	**Bennettsville** (city) Marlboro County	91	n/a	6.4	**Red Bank** (CDP) Lexington County
18	n/a	11.4	**Gloverville** (CDP) Aiken County	94	2038	6.3	**Greenville** (city) Greenville County
20	n/a	11.2	**Seneca** (city) Oconee County	94	2038	6.3	**Rock Hill** (city) York County
21	n/a	10.9	**Marion** (city) Marion County	96	2119	6.2	**Parker** (CDP) Greenville County
21	85	10.9	**Newberry** (city) Newberry County	97	2198	6.1	**Beaufort** (city) Beaufort County
23	n/a	10.8	**Welcome** (CDP) Greenville County	97	2198	6.1	**Oak Grove** (CDP) Lexington County
24	n/a	10.7	**Elgin** (CDP) Lancaster County	97	n/a	6.1	**Pendleton** (town) Anderson County
25	n/a	10.6	**Honea Path** (town) Anderson County	97	n/a	6.1	**Travelers Rest** (city) Greenville County
26	n/a	10.5	**Camden** (city) Kershaw County	101	n/a	6.0	**Lake Murray of Richland** (CDP) Richland County
27	n/a	10.4	**Pageland** (town) Chesterfield County	101	n/a	6.0	**Lugoff** (CDP) Kershaw County
27	132	10.4	**Spartanburg** (city) Spartanburg County	101	2296	6.0	**Summerville** (town) Dorchester County
29	n/a	10.3	**Abbeville** (city) Abbeville County	101	2296	6.0	**Taylors** (CDP) Greenville County
30	160	10.2	**Aiken** (city) Aiken County	105	n/a	5.9	**Andrews** (town) Georgetown County
30	n/a	10.2	**Clinton** (city) Laurens County	105	n/a	5.9	**Graniteville** (CDP) Aiken County
30	n/a	10.2	**Darlington** (city) Darlington County	105	n/a	5.9	**India Hook** (CDP) York County
33	n/a	10.1	**Chester** (city) Chester County	108	n/a	5.8	**Moncks Corner** (town) Berkeley County
34	n/a	9.9	**Belvedere** (CDP) Aiken County	109	n/a	5.6	**Ridgeland** (town) Jasper County
35	n/a	9.8	**Georgetown** (city) Georgetown County	110	2863	5.4	**Charleston** (city) Charleston County
35	234	9.8	**West Columbia** (city) Lexington County	110	2863	5.4	**Saint Andrews** (CDP) Richland County
37	n/a	9.7	**Edgefield** (town) Edgefield County	110	n/a	5.4	**Southern Shops** (CDP) Spartanburg County
37	250	9.7	**Forest Acres** (city) Richland County	113	2953	5.3	**Hanahan** (city) Berkeley County
37	250	9.7	**Greenwood** (city) Greenwood County	113	2953	5.3	**Ladson** (CDP) Berkeley County
40	n/a	9.6	**Batesburg-Leesville** (town) Lexington County	115	n/a	5.2	**Kingstree** (town) Williamsburg County
40	n/a	9.6	**Brookdale** (CDP) Orangeburg County	115	3051	5.2	**Lexington** (town) Lexington County
42	n/a	9.5	**Bishopville** (city) Lee County	117	n/a	5.1	**Lakewood** (CDP) Sumter County
43	n/a	9.2	**Hopkins** (CDP) Richland County	117	3126	5.1	**North Charleston** (city) Charleston County
44	403	9.1	**Berea** (CDP) Greenville County	117	n/a	5.1	**Sangaree** (CDP) Berkeley County
44	n/a	9.1	**Edisto** (CDP) Orangeburg County	120	n/a	5.0	**Forestbrook** (CDP) Horry County
44	n/a	9.1	**Little River** (CDP) Horry County	120	n/a	5.0	**Valley Falls** (CDP) Spartanburg County
47	n/a	9.0	**Homeland Park** (CDP) Anderson County	122	n/a	4.9	**Clearwater** (CDP) Aiken County
47	n/a	9.0	**Lancaster** (city) Lancaster County	122	3273	4.9	**Mount Pleasant** (town) Charleston County
49	n/a	8.8	**Allendale** (town) Allendale County	122	3273	4.9	**Socastee** (CDP) Horry County
49	n/a	8.8	**Surfside Beach** (town) Horry County	125	n/a	4.8	**Centerville** (CDP) Anderson County
51	514	8.7	**Gaffney** (city) Cherokee County	125	3362	4.8	**Clemson** (city) Pickens County
51	n/a	8.7	**Lyman** (town) Spartanburg County	125	3362	4.8	**Simpsonville** (city) Greenville County
51	514	8.7	**Orangeburg** (city) Orangeburg County	128	n/a	4.7	**Burton** (CDP) Beaufort County
54	560	8.6	**North Myrtle Beach** (city) Horry County	128	3439	4.7	**Columbia** (city) Richland County
54	n/a	8.6	**Pickens** (city) Pickens County	128	n/a	4.7	**Lake Wylie** (CDP) York County
54	n/a	8.6	**York** (city) York County	131	n/a	4.6	**North Hartsville** (CDP) Darlington County
57	n/a	8.5	**Liberty** (city) Pickens County	132	3618	4.5	**Fort Mill** (town) York County
58	648	8.4	**Gantt** (CDP) Greenville County	132	3618	4.5	**Irmo** (town) Richland County
59	n/a	8.2	**Piedmont** (CDP) Anderson County	132	n/a	4.5	**McCormick** (town) McCormick County
59	743	8.2	**Sumter** (city) Sumter County	135	3692	4.4	**Five Forks** (CDP) Greenville County
59	n/a	8.2	**Winnsboro** (town) Fairfield County	136	3753	4.3	**Bluffton** (town) Beaufort County
62	786	8.1	**Conway** (city) Horry County	137	n/a	3.8	**Newport** (CDP) York County
62	786	8.1	**Florence** (city) Florence County	138	n/a	3.7	**Laurel Bay** (CDP) Beaufort County
64	881	7.9	**Dentsville** (CDP) Richland County	138	n/a	3.7	**Saluda** (town) Saluda County
64	n/a	7.9	**Hampton** (town) Hampton County	140	4179	3.5	**Goose Creek** (city) Berkeley County
66	n/a	7.8	**Fountain Inn** (city) Greenville County	141	n/a	3.4	**Central** (town) Pickens County
66	n/a	7.8	**Springdale** (CDP) Lancaster County	142	4310	3.2	**Port Royal** (town) Beaufort County
66	n/a	7.8	**Springdale** (town) Lexington County	143	n/a	3.1	**Arcadia** (CDP) Spartanburg County
69	986	7.7	**North Augusta** (city) Aiken County	144	n/a	2.9	**Boiling Springs** (CDP) Spartanburg County
69	n/a	7.7	**Williston** (town) Barnwell County	144	n/a	2.9	**Isle of Palms** (city) Charleston County
71	1048	7.6	**Easley** (city) Pickens County	146	n/a	2.6	**Saxon** (CDP) Spartanburg County
71	n/a	7.6	**Hollywood** (town) Charleston County	147	n/a	2.5	**Duncan** (town) Spartanburg County
71	n/a	7.6	**Lesslie** (CDP) York County	148	n/a	2.2	**Tega Cay** (city) York County
71	1048	7.6	**Wade Hampton** (CDP) Greenville County	149	n/a	2.1	**Dalzell** (CDP) Sumter County
75	1177	7.4	**Cayce** (city) Lexington County	150	n/a	1.2	**Folly Beach** (city) Charleston County

Note: *The state column ranks the top/bottom 150 places in the state with population of 2,500 or more. The national column ranks the top/bottom places in the country with population of 10,000 or more. Places that are unincorporated were not considered in the rankings. n/a indicates data not available. Please refer to the User Guide for additional information.*

Marriage Status: Widowed

Top 150 Places Ranked in *Ascending* Order

State Rank	Nat'l Rank	Percent	Place
1	n/a	1.2	**Folly Beach** (city) Charleston County
2	n/a	2.1	**Dalzell** (CDP) Sumter County
3	n/a	2.2	**Tega Cay** (city) York County
4	n/a	2.5	**Duncan** (town) Spartanburg County
5	n/a	2.6	**Saxon** (CDP) Spartanburg County
6	n/a	2.9	**Boiling Springs** (CDP) Spartanburg County
6	n/a	2.9	**Isle of Palms** (city) Charleston County
8	n/a	3.1	**Arcadia** (CDP) Spartanburg County
9	307	3.2	**Port Royal** (town) Beaufort County
10	n/a	3.4	**Central** (town) Pickens County
11	424	3.5	**Goose Creek** (city) Berkeley County
12	n/a	3.7	**Laurel Bay** (CDP) Beaufort County
12	n/a	3.7	**Saluda** (town) Saluda County
14	n/a	3.8	**Newport** (CDP) York County
15	840	4.3	**Bluffton** (town) Beaufort County
16	904	4.4	**Five Forks** (CDP) Greenville County
17	965	4.5	**Fort Mill** (town) York County
17	965	4.5	**Irmo** (town) Richland County
17	n/a	4.5	**McCormick** (town) McCormick County
20	n/a	4.6	**North Hartsville** (CDP) Darlington County
21	n/a	4.7	**Burton** (CDP) Beaufort County
21	1132	4.7	**Columbia** (city) Richland County
21	n/a	4.7	**Lake Wylie** (CDP) York County
24	n/a	4.8	**Centerville** (CDP) Anderson County
24	1218	4.8	**Clemson** (city) Pickens County
24	1218	4.8	**Simpsonville** (city) Greenville County
27	n/a	4.9	**Clearwater** (CDP) Aiken County
27	1295	4.9	**Mount Pleasant** (town) Charleston County
27	1295	4.9	**Socastee** (CDP) Horry County
30	n/a	5.0	**Forestbrook** (CDP) Horry County
30	n/a	5.0	**Valley Falls** (CDP) Spartanburg County
32	n/a	5.1	**Lakewood** (CDP) Sumter County
32	1457	5.1	**North Charleston** (city) Charleston County
32	n/a	5.1	**Sangaree** (CDP) Berkeley County
35	n/a	5.2	**Kingstree** (town) Williamsburg County
35	1531	5.2	**Lexington** (town) Lexington County
37	1606	5.3	**Hanahan** (city) Berkeley County
37	1606	5.3	**Ladson** (CDP) Berkeley County
39	1704	5.4	**Charleston** (city) Charleston County
39	1704	5.4	**Saint Andrews** (CDP) Richland County
39	n/a	5.4	**Southern Shops** (CDP) Spartanburg County
42	n/a	5.6	**Ridgeland** (town) Jasper County
43	n/a	5.8	**Moncks Corner** (town) Berkeley County
44	n/a	5.9	**Andrews** (town) Georgetown County
44	n/a	5.9	**Graniteville** (CDP) Aiken County
44	n/a	5.9	**India Hook** (CDP) York County
47	n/a	6.0	**Lake Murray of Richland** (CDP) Richland County
47	n/a	6.0	**Lugoff** (CDP) Kershaw County
47	2274	6.0	**Summerville** (town) Dorchester County
47	2274	6.0	**Taylors** (CDP) Greenville County
51	2361	6.1	**Beaufort** (city) Beaufort County
51	2361	6.1	**Oak Grove** (CDP) Lexington County
51	n/a	6.1	**Pendleton** (town) Anderson County
51	n/a	6.1	**Travelers Rest** (city) Greenville County
55	2459	6.2	**Parker** (CDP) Greenville County
56	2538	6.3	**Greenville** (city) Greenville County
56	2538	6.3	**Rock Hill** (city) York County
58	n/a	6.4	**Dunean** (CDP) Greenville County
58	n/a	6.4	**Northlake** (CDP) Anderson County
58	n/a	6.4	**Red Bank** (CDP) Lexington County
61	n/a	6.6	**Burnettown** (town) Aiken County
61	2799	6.6	**Greer** (city) Greenville County
63	n/a	6.7	**Hardeeville** (city) Jasper County
64	n/a	6.8	**Barnwell** (city) Barnwell County
64	2951	6.8	**Myrtle Beach** (city) Horry County
64	2951	6.8	**Red Hill** (CDP) Horry County
67	n/a	6.9	**Belton** (city) Anderson County
67	3029	6.9	**Mauldin** (city) Greenville County
69	n/a	7.0	**Arial** (CDP) Pickens County
69	n/a	7.0	**Clover** (town) York County
69	n/a	7.0	**Murrells Inlet** (CDP) Georgetown County
72	n/a	7.2	**Sans Souci** (CDP) Greenville County
72	3259	7.2	**Seven Oaks** (CDP) Lexington County
74	3334	7.3	**Hilton Head Island** (town) Beaufort County
74	n/a	7.3	**Woodfield** (CDP) Richland County
76	3407	7.4	**Cayce** (city) Lexington County
77	3547	7.6	**Easley** (city) Pickens County
77	n/a	7.6	**Hollywood** (town) Charleston County
77	n/a	7.6	**Lesslie** (CDP) York County
77	3547	7.6	**Wade Hampton** (CDP) Greenville County
81	3609	7.7	**North Augusta** (city) Aiken County
81	n/a	7.7	**Williston** (town) Barnwell County
83	n/a	7.8	**Fountain Inn** (city) Greenville County
83	n/a	7.8	**Springdale** (CDP) Lancaster County
83	n/a	7.8	**Springdale** (town) Lexington County
86	3715	7.9	**Dentsville** (CDP) Richland County
86	n/a	7.9	**Hampton** (town) Hampton County
88	3824	8.1	**Conway** (city) Horry County
88	3824	8.1	**Florence** (city) Florence County
90	n/a	8.2	**Piedmont** (CDP) Anderson County
90	3871	8.2	**Sumter** (city) Sumter County
90	n/a	8.2	**Winnsboro** (town) Fairfield County
93	3961	8.4	**Gantt** (CDP) Greenville County
94	n/a	8.5	**Liberty** (city) Pickens County
95	4055	8.6	**North Myrtle Beach** (city) Horry County
95	n/a	8.6	**Pickens** (city) Pickens County
95	n/a	8.6	**York** (city) York County
98	4097	8.7	**Gaffney** (city) Cherokee County
98	n/a	8.7	**Lyman** (town) Spartanburg County
98	4097	8.7	**Orangeburg** (city) Orangeburg County
101	n/a	8.8	**Allendale** (town) Allendale County
101	n/a	8.8	**Surfside Beach** (town) Horry County
103	n/a	9.0	**Homeland Park** (CDP) Anderson County
103	n/a	9.0	**Lancaster** (city) Lancaster County
105	4224	9.1	**Berea** (CDP) Greenville County
105	n/a	9.1	**Edisto** (CDP) Orangeburg County
105	n/a	9.1	**Little River** (CDP) Horry County
108	n/a	9.2	**Hopkins** (CDP) Richland County
109	n/a	9.5	**Bishopville** (city) Lee County
110	n/a	9.6	**Batesburg-Leesville** (town) Lexington County
110	n/a	9.6	**Brookdale** (CDP) Orangeburg County
112	n/a	9.7	**Edgefield** (town) Edgefield County
112	4375	9.7	**Forest Acres** (city) Richland County
112	4375	9.7	**Greenwood** (city) Greenwood County
115	n/a	9.8	**Georgetown** (city) Georgetown County
115	4407	9.8	**West Columbia** (city) Lexington County
117	n/a	9.9	**Belvedere** (CDP) Aiken County
118	n/a	10.1	**Chester** (city) Chester County
119	4478	10.2	**Aiken** (city) Aiken County
119	n/a	10.2	**Clinton** (city) Laurens County
119	n/a	10.2	**Darlington** (city) Darlington County
122	n/a	10.3	**Abbeville** (city) Abbeville County
123	n/a	10.4	**Pageland** (town) Chesterfield County
123	4513	10.4	**Spartanburg** (city) Spartanburg County
125	n/a	10.5	**Camden** (city) Kershaw County
126	n/a	10.6	**Honea Path** (town) Anderson County
127	n/a	10.7	**Elgin** (CDP) Lancaster County
128	n/a	10.8	**Welcome** (CDP) Greenville County
129	n/a	10.9	**Marion** (city) Marion County
129	4567	10.9	**Newberry** (city) Newberry County
131	n/a	11.2	**Seneca** (city) Oconee County
132	n/a	11.4	**Bennettsville** (city) Marlboro County
132	n/a	11.4	**Gloverville** (CDP) Aiken County
134	4598	11.6	**Anderson** (city) Anderson County
134	n/a	11.6	**Laurens** (city) Laurens County
136	n/a	11.7	**Dillon** (city) Dillon County
136	n/a	11.7	**Union** (city) Union County
138	n/a	12.0	**Walhalla** (city) Oconee County
139	n/a	12.1	**Mullins** (city) Marion County
140	n/a	12.4	**Manning** (city) Clarendon County
141	n/a	12.5	**Denmark** (city) Bamberg County
142	n/a	12.6	**Woodruff** (city) Spartanburg County
143	n/a	12.8	**East Gaffney** (CDP) Cherokee County
144	n/a	12.9	**Lake City** (city) Florence County
145	n/a	13.2	**Bamberg** (town) Bamberg County
145	n/a	13.2	**Cheraw** (town) Chesterfield County
147	n/a	13.5	**Hartsville** (city) Darlington County
148	n/a	14.0	**Walterboro** (city) Colleton County
149	n/a	14.3	**Williamston** (town) Anderson County
150	n/a	15.5	**Garden City** (CDP) Horry County

Note: The state column ranks the top/bottom 150 places in the state with population of 2,500 or more. The national column ranks the top/bottom places in the country with population of 10,000 or more. Places that are unincorporated were not considered in the rankings. n/a indicates data not available. Please refer to the User Guide for additional information.

Marriage Status: Divorced

Top 150 Places Ranked in *Descending* Order

State Rank	Nat'l Rank	Percent	Place
1	n/a	20.5	**Folly Beach** (city) Charleston County
2	n/a	19.0	**Pickens** (city) Pickens County
3	n/a	18.4	**Seneca** (city) Oconee County
4	n/a	17.7	**East Gaffney** (CDP) Cherokee County
5	n/a	17.4	**India Hook** (CDP) York County
6	n/a	17.1	**Pendleton** (town) Anderson County
7	n/a	16.9	**Walhalla** (city) Oconee County
8	n/a	16.8	**Clearwater** (CDP) Aiken County
9	n/a	16.5	**Burton** (CDP) Beaufort County
9	n/a	16.5	**Homeland Park** (CDP) Anderson County
11	n/a	16.4	**Edgefield** (town) Edgefield County
11	n/a	16.4	**Surfside Beach** (town) Horry County
13	n/a	16.3	**Cheraw** (town) Chesterfield County
14	n/a	16.1	**Southern Shops** (CDP) Spartanburg County
15	n/a	16.0	**Belvedere** (CDP) Aiken County
15	n/a	16.0	**Little River** (CDP) Horry County
17	n/a	15.9	**McCormick** (town) McCormick County
18	n/a	15.8	**Arial** (CDP) Pickens County
19	n/a	15.5	**Welcome** (CDP) Greenville County
20	n/a	15.4	**Red Bank** (CDP) Lexington County
21	386	15.2	**Berea** (CDP) Greenville County
22	543	14.6	**Taylors** (CDP) Greenville County
23	637	14.3	**North Myrtle Beach** (city) Horry County
24	n/a	14.1	**Darlington** (city) Darlington County
24	n/a	14.1	**Walterboro** (city) Colleton County
26	n/a	14.0	**Gloverville** (CDP) Aiken County
27	n/a	13.9	**Springdale** (CDP) Lancaster County
28	809	13.8	**Forest Acres** (city) Richland County
29	n/a	13.7	**Sans Souci** (CDP) Greenville County
30	920	13.5	**Irmo** (town) Richland County
31	969	13.4	**Dentsville** (CDP) Richland County
31	969	13.4	**North Augusta** (city) Aiken County
31	n/a	13.4	**Northlake** (CDP) Anderson County
34	n/a	13.3	**Union** (city) Union County
35	n/a	13.2	**Lancaster** (city) Lancaster County
35	1051	13.2	**Socastee** (CDP) Horry County
37	n/a	13.1	**Liberty** (city) Pickens County
37	n/a	13.1	**Moncks Corner** (town) Berkeley County
39	1134	13.0	**Bluffton** (town) Beaufort County
39	n/a	13.0	**Clover** (town) York County
39	n/a	13.0	**Lesslie** (CDP) York County
42	n/a	12.9	**Kingstree** (town) Williamsburg County
42	n/a	12.9	**Piedmont** (CDP) Anderson County
44	n/a	12.8	**Camden** (city) Kershaw County
44	n/a	12.8	**Garden City** (CDP) Horry County
44	n/a	12.8	**Williamston** (town) Anderson County
47	n/a	12.7	**Chester** (city) Chester County
48	n/a	12.6	**Sangaree** (CDP) Berkeley County
49	n/a	12.4	**Belton** (city) Anderson County
49	n/a	12.4	**Fountain Inn** (city) Greenville County
49	n/a	12.4	**Pageland** (town) Chesterfield County
52	1497	12.2	**Greenwood** (city) Greenwood County
52	1497	12.2	**Lexington** (town) Lexington County
52	n/a	12.2	**Lugoff** (CDP) Kershaw County
55	n/a	12.1	**Bennettsville** (city) Marlboro County
55	1545	12.1	**Myrtle Beach** (city) Horry County
55	1545	12.1	**Parker** (CDP) Greenville County
58	1604	12.0	**Summerville** (town) Dorchester County
59	1646	11.9	**Simpsonville** (city) Greenville County
60	1695	11.8	**Oak Grove** (CDP) Lexington County
60	1695	11.8	**Spartanburg** (city) Spartanburg County
62	n/a	11.7	**Georgetown** (city) Georgetown County
62	1750	11.7	**Greenville** (city) Greenville County
62	1750	11.7	**Greer** (city) Greenville County
62	n/a	11.7	**Hampton** (town) Hampton County
62	1750	11.7	**Hanahan** (city) Berkeley County
67	n/a	11.6	**Hollywood** (town) Charleston County
67	1804	11.6	**Saint Andrews** (CDP) Richland County
67	1804	11.6	**Wade Hampton** (CDP) Greenville County
67	n/a	11.6	**Williston** (town) Barnwell County
71	1859	11.5	**Beaufort** (city) Beaufort County
71	1859	11.5	**Easley** (city) Pickens County
71	1859	11.5	**North Charleston** (city) Charleston County
74	n/a	11.4	**Barnwell** (city) Barnwell County
74	1910	11.4	**Gaffney** (city) Cherokee County
74	n/a	11.4	**Newport** (CDP) York County
77	n/a	11.3	**Batesburg-Leesville** (town) Lexington County
77	n/a	11.3	**Saxon** (CDP) Spartanburg County
79	n/a	11.0	**Andrews** (town) Georgetown County
80	n/a	10.9	**Clinton** (city) Laurens County
80	n/a	10.9	**Marion** (city) Marion County
80	2168	10.9	**Seven Oaks** (CDP) Lexington County
80	2168	10.9	**West Columbia** (city) Lexington County
80	n/a	10.9	**York** (city) York County
85	n/a	10.8	**Duncan** (town) Spartanburg County
85	n/a	10.8	**North Hartsville** (CDP) Darlington County
87	2277	10.7	**Florence** (city) Florence County
88	n/a	10.6	**Lake Wylie** (CDP) York County
89	n/a	10.5	**Travelers Rest** (city) Greenville County
90	2441	10.4	**Cayce** (city) Lexington County
91	2536	10.2	**Charleston** (city) Charleston County
91	2536	10.2	**Rock Hill** (city) York County
93	n/a	10.1	**Isle of Palms** (city) Charleston County
93	2602	10.1	**Ladson** (CDP) Berkeley County
93	2602	10.1	**Mount Pleasant** (town) Charleston County
96	n/a	10.0	**Laurens** (city) Laurens County
96	n/a	10.0	**Murrells Inlet** (CDP) Georgetown County
96	n/a	10.0	**Woodfield** (CDP) Richland County
99	n/a	9.9	**Hartsville** (city) Darlington County
100	2779	9.8	**Anderson** (city) Anderson County
100	2779	9.8	**Mauldin** (city) Greenville County
100	2779	9.8	**Sumter** (city) Sumter County
103	n/a	9.7	**Bishopville** (city) Lee County
104	n/a	9.6	**Abbeville** (city) Abbeville County
104	n/a	9.6	**Forestbrook** (CDP) Horry County
106	n/a	9.4	**Burnettown** (town) Aiken County
106	n/a	9.4	**Lyman** (town) Spartanburg County
108	n/a	9.2	**Springdale** (town) Lexington County
109	n/a	9.1	**Centerville** (CDP) Anderson County
109	n/a	9.1	**Laurel Bay** (CDP) Beaufort County
111	n/a	9.0	**Manning** (city) Clarendon County
111	n/a	9.0	**Winnsboro** (town) Fairfield County
111	n/a	9.0	**Woodruff** (city) Spartanburg County
114	3285	8.8	**Columbia** (city) Richland County
114	n/a	8.8	**Dunean** (CDP) Greenville County
116	n/a	8.7	**Elgin** (CDP) Lancaster County
116	3333	8.7	**Fort Mill** (town) York County
116	3333	8.7	**Hilton Head Island** (town) Beaufort County
119	3384	8.6	**Gantt** (CDP) Greenville County
120	n/a	8.5	**Lakewood** (CDP) Sumter County
120	n/a	8.5	**Mullins** (city) Marion County
122	n/a	8.4	**Edisto** (CDP) Orangeburg County
122	n/a	8.4	**Graniteville** (CDP) Aiken County
122	3479	8.4	**Red Hill** (CDP) Horry County
125	3565	8.2	**Aiken** (city) Aiken County
125	3565	8.2	**Goose Creek** (city) Berkeley County
125	3565	8.2	**Orangeburg** (city) Orangeburg County
128	n/a	8.1	**Hopkins** (CDP) Richland County
129	n/a	8.0	**Ridgeland** (town) Jasper County
130	n/a	7.6	**Bamberg** (town) Bamberg County
131	3928	7.4	**Port Royal** (town) Beaufort County
132	3968	7.3	**Newberry** (city) Newberry County
133	n/a	7.1	**Dillon** (city) Dillon County
133	n/a	7.1	**Saluda** (town) Saluda County
135	4164	6.7	**Conway** (city) Horry County
136	n/a	6.5	**Honea Path** (town) Anderson County
136	n/a	6.5	**Lake City** (city) Florence County
138	n/a	6.2	**Allendale** (town) Allendale County
139	n/a	6.0	**Brookdale** (CDP) Orangeburg County
139	n/a	6.0	**Hardeeville** (city) Jasper County
141	n/a	5.9	**Tega Cay** (city) York County
142	n/a	5.5	**Valley Falls** (CDP) Spartanburg County
143	n/a	5.4	**Denmark** (city) Bamberg County
144	4484	5.2	**Five Forks** (CDP) Greenville County
145	n/a	5.0	**Boiling Springs** (CDP) Spartanburg County
145	n/a	5.0	**Lake Murray of Richland** (CDP) Richland County
147	n/a	4.6	**Dalzell** (CDP) Sumter County
148	4565	4.5	**Clemson** (city) Pickens County
149	n/a	4.4	**Central** (town) Pickens County
150	n/a	3.5	**Arcadia** (CDP) Spartanburg County

Note: The state column ranks the top/bottom 150 places in the state with population of 2,500 or more. The national column ranks the top/bottom places in the country with population of 10,000 or more. Places that are unincorporated were not considered in the rankings. n/a indicates data not available. Please refer to the User Guide for additional information.

Marriage Status: Divorced

Top 150 Places Ranked in *Ascending* Order

State Rank	Nat'l Rank	Percent	Place
1	n/a	3.5	**Arcadia** (CDP) Spartanburg County
2	n/a	4.4	**Central** (town) Pickens County
3	85	4.5	**Clemson** (city) Pickens County
4	n/a	4.6	**Dalzell** (CDP) Sumter County
5	n/a	5.0	**Boiling Springs** (CDP) Spartanburg County
5	n/a	5.0	**Lake Murray of Richland** (CDP) Richland County
7	156	5.2	**Five Forks** (CDP) Greenville County
8	n/a	5.4	**Denmark** (city) Bamberg County
9	n/a	5.5	**Valley Falls** (CDP) Spartanburg County
10	n/a	5.9	**Tega Cay** (city) York County
11	n/a	6.0	**Brookdale** (CDP) Orangeburg County
11	n/a	6.0	**Hardeeville** (city) Jasper County
13	n/a	6.2	**Allendale** (town) Allendale County
14	n/a	6.5	**Honea Path** (town) Anderson County
14	n/a	6.5	**Lake City** (city) Florence County
16	466	6.7	**Conway** (city) Horry County
17	n/a	7.1	**Dillon** (city) Dillon County
17	n/a	7.1	**Saluda** (town) Saluda County
19	655	7.3	**Newberry** (city) Newberry County
20	689	7.4	**Port Royal** (town) Beaufort County
21	n/a	7.6	**Bamberg** (town) Bamberg County
22	n/a	8.0	**Ridgeland** (town) Jasper County
23	n/a	8.1	**Hopkins** (CDP) Richland County
24	1044	8.2	**Aiken** (city) Aiken County
24	1044	8.2	**Goose Creek** (city) Berkeley County
24	1044	8.2	**Orangeburg** (city) Orangeburg County
27	n/a	8.4	**Edisto** (CDP) Orangeburg County
27	n/a	8.4	**Graniteville** (CDP) Aiken County
27	1135	8.4	**Red Hill** (CDP) Horry County
30	n/a	8.5	**Lakewood** (CDP) Sumter County
30	n/a	8.5	**Mullins** (city) Marion County
32	1228	8.6	**Gantt** (CDP) Greenville County
33	n/a	8.7	**Elgin** (CDP) Lancaster County
33	1273	8.7	**Fort Mill** (town) York County
33	1273	8.7	**Hilton Head Island** (town) Beaufort County
36	1324	8.8	**Columbia** (city) Richland County
36	n/a	8.8	**Dunean** (CDP) Greenville County
38	n/a	9.0	**Manning** (city) Clarendon County
38	n/a	9.0	**Winnsboro** (town) Fairfield County
38	n/a	9.0	**Woodruff** (city) Spartanburg County
41	n/a	9.1	**Centerville** (CDP) Anderson County
41	n/a	9.1	**Laurel Bay** (CDP) Beaufort County
43	n/a	9.2	**Springdale** (town) Lexington County
44	n/a	9.4	**Burnettown** (town) Aiken County
44	n/a	9.4	**Lyman** (town) Spartanburg County
46	n/a	9.6	**Abbeville** (city) Abbeville County
46	n/a	9.6	**Forestbrook** (CDP) Horry County
48	n/a	9.7	**Bishopville** (city) Lee County
49	1823	9.8	**Anderson** (city) Anderson County
49	1823	9.8	**Mauldin** (city) Greenville County
49	1823	9.8	**Sumter** (city) Sumter County
52	n/a	9.9	**Hartsville** (city) Darlington County
53	n/a	10.0	**Laurens** (city) Laurens County
53	n/a	10.0	**Murrells Inlet** (CDP) Georgetown County
53	n/a	10.0	**Woodfield** (CDP) Richland County
56	n/a	10.1	**Isle of Palms** (city) Charleston County
56	1982	10.1	**Ladson** (CDP) Berkeley County
56	1982	10.1	**Mount Pleasant** (town) Charleston County
59	2055	10.2	**Charleston** (city) Charleston County
59	2055	10.2	**Rock Hill** (city) York County
61	2170	10.4	**Cayce** (city) Lexington County
62	n/a	10.5	**Travelers Rest** (city) Greenville County
63	n/a	10.6	**Lake Wylie** (CDP) York County
64	2318	10.7	**Florence** (city) Florence County
65	n/a	10.8	**Duncan** (town) Spartanburg County
65	n/a	10.8	**North Hartsville** (CDP) Darlington County
67	n/a	10.9	**Clinton** (city) Laurens County
67	n/a	10.9	**Marion** (city) Marion County
67	2441	10.9	**Seven Oaks** (CDP) Lexington County
67	2441	10.9	**West Columbia** (city) Lexington County
67	n/a	10.9	**York** (city) York County
72	n/a	11.0	**Andrews** (town) Georgetown County
73	n/a	11.3	**Batesburg-Leesville** (town) Lexington County
73	n/a	11.3	**Saxon** (CDP) Spartanburg County
75	n/a	11.4	**Barnwell** (city) Barnwell County
75	2703	11.4	**Gaffney** (city) Cherokee County
75	n/a	11.4	**Newport** (CDP) York County
78	2747	11.5	**Beaufort** (city) Beaufort County
78	2747	11.5	**Easley** (city) Pickens County
78	2747	11.5	**North Charleston** (city) Charleston County
81	n/a	11.6	**Hollywood** (town) Charleston County
81	2798	11.6	**Saint Andrews** (CDP) Richland County
81	2798	11.6	**Wade Hampton** (CDP) Greenville County
81	n/a	11.6	**Williston** (town) Barnwell County
85	n/a	11.7	**Georgetown** (city) Georgetown County
85	2853	11.7	**Greenville** (city) Greenville County
85	2853	11.7	**Greer** (city) Greenville County
85	n/a	11.7	**Hampton** (town) Hampton County
85	2853	11.7	**Hanahan** (city) Berkeley County
90	2907	11.8	**Oak Grove** (CDP) Lexington County
90	2907	11.8	**Spartanburg** (city) Spartanburg County
92	2962	11.9	**Simpsonville** (city) Greenville County
93	3011	12.0	**Summerville** (town) Dorchester County
94	n/a	12.1	**Bennettsville** (city) Marlboro County
94	3053	12.1	**Myrtle Beach** (city) Horry County
94	3053	12.1	**Parker** (CDP) Greenville County
97	3112	12.2	**Greenwood** (city) Greenwood County
97	3112	12.2	**Lexington** (town) Lexington County
97	n/a	12.2	**Lugoff** (CDP) Kershaw County
100	n/a	12.4	**Belton** (city) Anderson County
100	n/a	12.4	**Fountain Inn** (city) Greenville County
100	n/a	12.4	**Pageland** (town) Chesterfield County
103	n/a	12.6	**Sangaree** (CDP) Berkeley County
104	n/a	12.7	**Chester** (city) Chester County
105	n/a	12.8	**Camden** (city) Kershaw County
105	n/a	12.8	**Garden City** (CDP) Horry County
105	n/a	12.8	**Williamston** (town) Anderson County
108	n/a	12.9	**Kingstree** (town) Williamsburg County
108	n/a	12.9	**Piedmont** (CDP) Anderson County
110	3471	13.0	**Bluffton** (town) Beaufort County
110	n/a	13.0	**Clover** (town) York County
110	n/a	13.0	**Lesslie** (CDP) York County
113	n/a	13.1	**Liberty** (city) Pickens County
113	n/a	13.1	**Moncks Corner** (town) Berkeley County
115	n/a	13.2	**Lancaster** (city) Lancaster County
115	3567	13.2	**Socastee** (CDP) Horry County
117	n/a	13.3	**Union** (city) Union County
118	3632	13.4	**Dentsville** (CDP) Richland County
118	3632	13.4	**North Augusta** (city) Aiken County
118	n/a	13.4	**Northlake** (CDP) Anderson County
121	3688	13.5	**Irmo** (town) Richland County
122	n/a	13.7	**Sans Souci** (CDP) Greenville County
123	3807	13.8	**Forest Acres** (city) Richland County
124	n/a	13.9	**Springdale** (CDP) Lancaster County
125	n/a	14.0	**Gloverville** (CDP) Aiken County
126	n/a	14.1	**Darlington** (city) Darlington County
126	n/a	14.1	**Walterboro** (city) Colleton County
128	3990	14.3	**North Myrtle Beach** (city) Horry County
129	4084	14.6	**Taylors** (CDP) Greenville County
130	4244	15.2	**Berea** (CDP) Greenville County
131	n/a	15.4	**Red Bank** (CDP) Lexington County
132	n/a	15.5	**Welcome** (CDP) Greenville County
133	n/a	15.8	**Arial** (CDP) Pickens County
134	n/a	15.9	**McCormick** (town) McCormick County
135	n/a	16.0	**Belvedere** (CDP) Aiken County
135	n/a	16.0	**Little River** (CDP) Horry County
137	n/a	16.1	**Southern Shops** (CDP) Spartanburg County
138	n/a	16.3	**Cheraw** (town) Chesterfield County
139	n/a	16.4	**Edgefield** (town) Edgefield County
139	n/a	16.4	**Surfside Beach** (town) Horry County
141	n/a	16.5	**Burton** (CDP) Beaufort County
141	n/a	16.5	**Homeland Park** (CDP) Anderson County
143	n/a	16.8	**Clearwater** (CDP) Aiken County
144	n/a	16.9	**Walhalla** (city) Oconee County
145	n/a	17.1	**Pendleton** (town) Anderson County
146	n/a	17.4	**India Hook** (CDP) York County
147	n/a	17.7	**East Gaffney** (CDP) Cherokee County
148	n/a	18.4	**Seneca** (city) Oconee County
149	n/a	19.0	**Pickens** (city) Pickens County
150	n/a	20.5	**Folly Beach** (city) Charleston County

Note: The state column ranks the top/bottom 150 places in the state with population of 2,500 or more. The national column ranks the top/bottom places in the country with population of 10,000 or more. Places that are unincorporated were not considered in the rankings. n/a indicates data not available. Please refer to the User Guide for additional information.

Foreign Born

Top 150 Places Ranked in *Descending* Order

State Rank	Nat'l Rank	Percent	Place
1	n/a	27.7	**Southern Shops** (CDP) Spartanburg County
2	n/a	26.2	**Arcadia** (CDP) Spartanburg County
3	n/a	21.2	**Saluda** (town) Saluda County
4	n/a	20.6	**Woodfield** (CDP) Richland County
5	1018	18.4	**Myrtle Beach** (city) Horry County
6	1200	16.1	**Bluffton** (town) Beaufort County
7	n/a	15.7	**Sans Souci** (CDP) Greenville County
8	1296	15.1	**Hilton Head Island** (town) Beaufort County
9	n/a	14.1	**Pageland** (town) Chesterfield County
9	n/a	14.1	**Walhalla** (city) Oconee County
11	1479	13.5	**West Columbia** (city) Lexington County
12	1489	13.4	**Clemson** (city) Pickens County
12	n/a	13.4	**Hardeeville** (city) Jasper County
14	1520	13.2	**Berea** (CDP) Greenville County
15	1645	12.1	**Hanahan** (city) Berkeley County
16	1690	11.8	**Greer** (city) Greenville County
17	n/a	11.1	**Dunean** (CDP) Greenville County
18	n/a	10.9	**Boiling Springs** (CDP) Spartanburg County
19	n/a	10.8	**Welcome** (CDP) Greenville County
20	1931	10.4	**Wade Hampton** (CDP) Greenville County
21	1968	10.2	**Newberry** (city) Newberry County
22	n/a	10.1	**Edgefield** (town) Edgefield County
22	1987	10.1	**Red Hill** (CDP) Horry County
24	2099	9.6	**Parker** (CDP) Greenville County
25	n/a	9.3	**Saxon** (CDP) Spartanburg County
25	2153	9.3	**Socastee** (CDP) Horry County
27	2178	9.2	**North Charleston** (city) Charleston County
28	2201	9.1	**Simpsonville** (city) Greenville County
29	n/a	9.0	**Elgin** (CDP) Lancaster County
30	n/a	8.8	**Ridgeland** (town) Jasper County
31	2429	8.0	**Taylors** (CDP) Greenville County
32	2455	7.9	**Five Forks** (CDP) Greenville County
33	2528	7.6	**Beaufort** (city) Beaufort County
33	n/a	7.6	**Lyman** (town) Spartanburg County
35	2565	7.5	**North Myrtle Beach** (city) Horry County
36	2615	7.3	**Gantt** (CDP) Greenville County
37	2648	7.2	**Mauldin** (city) Greenville County
38	n/a	6.8	**Tega Cay** (city) York County
39	n/a	6.7	**Valley Falls** (CDP) Spartanburg County
40	2839	6.5	**Greenville** (city) Greenville County
41	n/a	6.3	**East Gaffney** (CDP) Cherokee County
42	2929	6.2	**Dentsville** (CDP) Richland County
43	n/a	6.1	**York** (city) York County
44	n/a	6.0	**Andrews** (town) Georgetown County
44	2990	6.0	**Ladson** (CDP) Berkeley County
44	2990	6.0	**Oak Grove** (CDP) Lexington County
47	n/a	5.9	**Northlake** (CDP) Anderson County
48	3039	5.8	**Greenwood** (city) Greenwood County
49	n/a	5.6	**Belvedere** (CDP) Aiken County
49	n/a	5.6	**Seneca** (city) Oconee County
49	n/a	5.6	**Springdale** (town) Lexington County
52	n/a	5.4	**Central** (town) Pickens County
52	n/a	5.4	**Duncan** (town) Spartanburg County
52	3165	5.4	**Goose Creek** (city) Berkeley County
55	3191	5.3	**Cayce** (city) Lexington County
55	3191	5.3	**Lexington** (town) Lexington County
55	3191	5.3	**Port Royal** (town) Beaufort County
58	3225	5.2	**Columbia** (city) Richland County
58	n/a	5.2	**Winnsboro** (town) Fairfield County
60	n/a	5.1	**Laurens** (city) Laurens County
61	3295	5.0	**Forest Acres** (city) Richland County
62	3329	4.9	**Easley** (city) Pickens County
63	n/a	4.8	**North Hartsville** (CDP) Darlington County
63	3363	4.8	**Rock Hill** (city) York County
65	n/a	4.5	**Moncks Corner** (town) Berkeley County
65	n/a	4.5	**Surfside Beach** (town) Horry County
67	n/a	4.4	**Darlington** (city) Darlington County
68	3522	4.3	**Mount Pleasant** (town) Charleston County
68	3522	4.3	**Saint Andrews** (CDP) Richland County
68	3522	4.3	**Seven Oaks** (CDP) Lexington County
71	3554	4.2	**Charleston** (city) Charleston County
71	n/a	4.2	**Pendleton** (town) Anderson County
73	n/a	4.1	**Little River** (CDP) Horry County
74	3625	4.0	**Aiken** (city) Aiken County
74	n/a	4.0	**Camden** (city) Kershaw County
74	n/a	4.0	**Liberty** (city) Pickens County
74	n/a	4.0	**Newport** (CDP) York County
78	3661	3.9	**Fort Mill** (town) York County
78	3661	3.9	**Spartanburg** (city) Spartanburg County
80	3689	3.8	**Summerville** (town) Dorchester County
81	3723	3.7	**Anderson** (city) Anderson County
81	n/a	3.7	**Garden City** (CDP) Horry County
81	3723	3.7	**Sumter** (city) Sumter County
84	3755	3.6	**North Augusta** (city) Aiken County
85	n/a	3.5	**Clearwater** (CDP) Aiken County
85	n/a	3.5	**Edisto** (CDP) Orangeburg County
85	n/a	3.5	**Isle of Palms** (city) Charleston County
85	n/a	3.5	**Kingstree** (town) Williamsburg County
89	n/a	3.4	**Fountain Inn** (city) Greenville County
89	n/a	3.4	**Lake Wylie** (CDP) York County
91	n/a	3.3	**Georgetown** (city) Georgetown County
92	n/a	3.2	**Lakewood** (CDP) Sumter County
92	n/a	3.2	**Lugoff** (CDP) Kershaw County
94	n/a	3.0	**Forestbrook** (CDP) Horry County
94	n/a	3.0	**Hopkins** (CDP) Richland County
96	n/a	2.9	**Centerville** (CDP) Anderson County
97	4035	2.8	**Irmo** (town) Richland County
97	n/a	2.8	**Lake Murray of Richland** (CDP) Richland County
97	n/a	2.8	**Sangaree** (CDP) Berkeley County
100	n/a	2.7	**Folly Beach** (city) Charleston County
101	n/a	2.6	**Burton** (CDP) Beaufort County
101	n/a	2.6	**Hartsville** (city) Darlington County
101	4119	2.6	**Orangeburg** (city) Orangeburg County
101	n/a	2.6	**Travelers Rest** (city) Greenville County
105	n/a	2.4	**Batesburg-Leesville** (town) Lexington County
105	n/a	2.4	**Dalzell** (CDP) Sumter County
107	n/a	2.3	**Bamberg** (town) Bamberg County
107	4198	2.3	**Conway** (city) Horry County
107	4198	2.3	**Florence** (city) Florence County
107	n/a	2.3	**Woodruff** (city) Spartanburg County
111	n/a	2.2	**Williamston** (town) Anderson County
112	4276	2.1	**Gaffney** (city) Cherokee County
113	n/a	2.0	**Clover** (town) York County
113	n/a	2.0	**McCormick** (town) McCormick County
115	n/a	1.9	**Bennettsville** (city) Marlboro County
116	n/a	1.8	**Cheraw** (town) Chesterfield County
116	n/a	1.8	**Dillon** (city) Dillon County
116	n/a	1.8	**Laurel Bay** (CDP) Beaufort County
119	n/a	1.7	**Barnwell** (city) Barnwell County
120	n/a	1.6	**Burnettown** (town) Aiken County
120	n/a	1.6	**Clinton** (city) Laurens County
120	n/a	1.6	**Homeland Park** (CDP) Anderson County
123	n/a	1.5	**Hollywood** (town) Charleston County
123	n/a	1.5	**Marion** (city) Marion County
123	n/a	1.5	**Red Bank** (CDP) Lexington County
126	n/a	1.4	**Hampton** (town) Hampton County
126	n/a	1.4	**Lancaster** (city) Lancaster County
126	n/a	1.4	**Pickens** (city) Pickens County
129	n/a	1.3	**India Hook** (CDP) York County
130	n/a	1.1	**Chester** (city) Chester County
131	n/a	1.0	**Belton** (city) Anderson County
131	n/a	1.0	**Manning** (city) Clarendon County
133	n/a	0.9	**Brookdale** (CDP) Orangeburg County
133	n/a	0.9	**Murrells Inlet** (CDP) Georgetown County
133	n/a	0.9	**Piedmont** (CDP) Anderson County
136	n/a	0.8	**Bishopville** (city) Lee County
136	n/a	0.8	**Mullins** (city) Marion County
138	n/a	0.6	**Lesslie** (CDP) York County
139	n/a	0.5	**Abbeville** (city) Abbeville County
139	n/a	0.5	**Walterboro** (city) Colleton County
141	n/a	0.4	**Allendale** (town) Allendale County
141	n/a	0.4	**Denmark** (city) Bamberg County
143	n/a	0.2	**Arial** (CDP) Pickens County
143	n/a	0.2	**Lake City** (city) Florence County
143	n/a	0.2	**Union** (city) Union County
146	n/a	0.0	**Gloverville** (CDP) Aiken County
146	n/a	0.0	**Graniteville** (CDP) Aiken County
146	n/a	0.0	**Honea Path** (town) Anderson County
146	n/a	0.0	**Springdale** (CDP) Lancaster County
146	n/a	0.0	**Williston** (town) Barnwell County

Note: The state column ranks the top/bottom 150 places in the state with population of 2,500 or more. The national column ranks the top/bottom places in the country with population of 10,000 or more. Places that are unincorporated were not considered in the rankings. n/a indicates data not available. Please refer to the User Guide for additional information.

Foreign Born

Top 150 Places Ranked in *Ascending* Order

State Rank	Nat'l Rank	Percent	Place
1	n/a	0.0	**Gloverville** (CDP) Aiken County
1	n/a	0.0	**Graniteville** (CDP) Aiken County
1	n/a	0.0	**Honea Path** (town) Anderson County
1	n/a	0.0	**Springdale** (CDP) Lancaster County
1	n/a	0.0	**Williston** (town) Barnwell County
6	n/a	0.2	**Arial** (CDP) Pickens County
6	n/a	0.2	**Lake City** (city) Florence County
6	n/a	0.2	**Union** (city) Union County
9	n/a	0.4	**Allendale** (town) Allendale County
9	n/a	0.4	**Denmark** (city) Bamberg County
11	n/a	0.5	**Abbeville** (city) Abbeville County
11	n/a	0.5	**Walterboro** (city) Colleton County
13	n/a	0.6	**Lesslie** (CDP) York County
14	n/a	0.8	**Bishopville** (city) Lee County
14	n/a	0.8	**Mullins** (city) Marion County
16	n/a	0.9	**Brookdale** (CDP) Orangeburg County
16	n/a	0.9	**Murrells Inlet** (CDP) Georgetown County
16	n/a	0.9	**Piedmont** (CDP) Anderson County
19	n/a	1.0	**Belton** (city) Anderson County
19	n/a	1.0	**Manning** (city) Clarendon County
21	n/a	1.1	**Chester** (city) Chester County
22	n/a	1.3	**India Hook** (CDP) York County
23	n/a	1.4	**Hampton** (town) Hampton County
23	n/a	1.4	**Lancaster** (city) Lancaster County
23	n/a	1.4	**Pickens** (city) Pickens County
26	n/a	1.5	**Hollywood** (town) Charleston County
26	n/a	1.5	**Marion** (city) Marion County
26	n/a	1.5	**Red Bank** (CDP) Lexington County
29	n/a	1.6	**Burnettown** (town) Aiken County
29	n/a	1.6	**Clinton** (city) Laurens County
29	n/a	1.6	**Homeland Park** (CDP) Anderson County
32	n/a	1.7	**Barnwell** (city) Barnwell County
33	n/a	1.8	**Cheraw** (town) Chesterfield County
33	n/a	1.8	**Dillon** (city) Dillon County
33	n/a	1.8	**Laurel Bay** (CDP) Beaufort County
36	n/a	1.9	**Bennettsville** (city) Marlboro County
37	n/a	2.0	**Clover** (town) York County
37	n/a	2.0	**McCormick** (town) McCormick County
39	352	2.1	**Gaffney** (city) Cherokee County
40	n/a	2.2	**Williamston** (town) Anderson County
41	n/a	2.3	**Bamberg** (town) Bamberg County
41	418	2.3	**Conway** (city) Horry County
41	418	2.3	**Florence** (city) Florence County
41	n/a	2.3	**Woodruff** (city) Spartanburg County
45	n/a	2.4	**Batesburg-Leesville** (town) Lexington County
45	n/a	2.4	**Dalzell** (CDP) Sumter County
47	n/a	2.6	**Burton** (CDP) Beaufort County
47	n/a	2.6	**Hartsville** (city) Darlington County
47	506	2.6	**Orangeburg** (city) Orangeburg County
47	n/a	2.6	**Travelers Rest** (city) Greenville County
51	n/a	2.7	**Folly Beach** (city) Charleston County
52	572	2.8	**Irmo** (town) Richland County
52	n/a	2.8	**Lake Murray of Richland** (CDP) Richland County
52	n/a	2.8	**Sangaree** (CDP) Berkeley County
55	n/a	2.9	**Centerville** (CDP) Anderson County
56	n/a	3.0	**Forestbrook** (CDP) Horry County
56	n/a	3.0	**Hopkins** (CDP) Richland County
58	n/a	3.2	**Lakewood** (CDP) Sumter County
58	n/a	3.2	**Lugoff** (CDP) Kershaw County
60	n/a	3.3	**Georgetown** (city) Georgetown County
61	n/a	3.4	**Fountain Inn** (city) Greenville County
61	n/a	3.4	**Lake Wylie** (CDP) York County
63	n/a	3.5	**Clearwater** (CDP) Aiken County
63	n/a	3.5	**Edisto** (CDP) Orangeburg County
63	n/a	3.5	**Isle of Palms** (city) Charleston County
63	n/a	3.5	**Kingstree** (town) Williamsburg County
67	865	3.6	**North Augusta** (city) Aiken County
68	902	3.7	**Anderson** (city) Anderson County
68	n/a	3.7	**Garden City** (CDP) Horry County
68	902	3.7	**Sumter** (city) Sumter County
71	934	3.8	**Summerville** (town) Dorchester County
72	968	3.9	**Fort Mill** (town) York County
72	968	3.9	**Spartanburg** (city) Spartanburg County
74	996	4.0	**Aiken** (city) Aiken County
74	n/a	4.0	**Camden** (city) Kershaw County
74	n/a	4.0	**Liberty** (city) Pickens County
74	n/a	4.0	**Newport** (CDP) York County
78	n/a	4.1	**Little River** (CDP) Horry County
79	1065	4.2	**Charleston** (city) Charleston County
79	n/a	4.2	**Pendleton** (town) Anderson County
81	1103	4.3	**Mount Pleasant** (town) Charleston County
81	1103	4.3	**Saint Andrews** (CDP) Richland County
81	1103	4.3	**Seven Oaks** (CDP) Lexington County
84	n/a	4.4	**Darlington** (city) Darlington County
85	n/a	4.5	**Moncks Corner** (town) Berkeley County
85	n/a	4.5	**Surfside Beach** (town) Horry County
87	n/a	4.8	**North Hartsville** (CDP) Darlington County
87	1256	4.8	**Rock Hill** (city) York County
89	1294	4.9	**Easley** (city) Pickens County
90	1328	5.0	**Forest Acres** (city) Richland County
91	n/a	5.1	**Laurens** (city) Laurens County
92	1400	5.2	**Columbia** (city) Richland County
92	n/a	5.2	**Winnsboro** (town) Fairfield County
94	1432	5.3	**Cayce** (city) Lexington County
94	1432	5.3	**Lexington** (town) Lexington County
94	1432	5.3	**Port Royal** (town) Beaufort County
97	n/a	5.4	**Central** (town) Pickens County
97	n/a	5.4	**Duncan** (town) Spartanburg County
97	1466	5.4	**Goose Creek** (city) Berkeley County
100	n/a	5.6	**Belvedere** (CDP) Aiken County
100	n/a	5.6	**Seneca** (city) Oconee County
100	n/a	5.6	**Springdale** (town) Lexington County
103	1587	5.8	**Greenwood** (city) Greenwood County
104	n/a	5.9	**Northlake** (CDP) Anderson County
105	n/a	6.0	**Andrews** (town) Georgetown County
105	1646	6.0	**Ladson** (CDP) Berkeley County
105	1646	6.0	**Oak Grove** (CDP) Lexington County
108	n/a	6.1	**York** (city) York County
109	1702	6.2	**Dentsville** (CDP) Richland County
110	n/a	6.3	**East Gaffney** (CDP) Cherokee County
111	1788	6.5	**Greenville** (city) Greenville County
112	n/a	6.7	**Valley Falls** (CDP) Spartanburg County
113	n/a	6.8	**Tega Cay** (city) York County
114	1988	7.2	**Mauldin** (city) Greenville County
115	2009	7.3	**Gantt** (CDP) Greenville County
116	2069	7.5	**North Myrtle Beach** (city) Horry County
117	2092	7.6	**Beaufort** (city) Beaufort County
117	n/a	7.6	**Lyman** (town) Spartanburg County
119	2182	7.9	**Five Forks** (CDP) Greenville County
120	2202	8.0	**Taylors** (CDP) Greenville County
121	n/a	8.8	**Ridgeland** (town) Jasper County
122	n/a	9.0	**Elgin** (CDP) Lancaster County
123	2439	9.1	**Simpsonville** (city) Greenville County
124	2456	9.2	**North Charleston** (city) Charleston County
125	n/a	9.3	**Saxon** (CDP) Spartanburg County
125	2479	9.3	**Socastee** (CDP) Horry County
127	2535	9.6	**Parker** (CDP) Greenville County
128	n/a	10.1	**Edgefield** (town) Edgefield County
128	2648	10.1	**Red Hill** (CDP) Horry County
130	2670	10.2	**Newberry** (city) Newberry County
131	2709	10.4	**Wade Hampton** (CDP) Greenville County
132	n/a	10.8	**Welcome** (CDP) Greenville County
133	n/a	10.9	**Boiling Springs** (CDP) Spartanburg County
134	n/a	11.1	**Dunean** (CDP) Greenville County
135	2950	11.8	**Greer** (city) Greenville County
136	2999	12.1	**Hanahan** (city) Berkeley County
137	3129	13.2	**Berea** (CDP) Greenville County
138	3154	13.4	**Clemson** (city) Pickens County
138	n/a	13.4	**Hardeeville** (city) Jasper County
140	3168	13.5	**West Columbia** (city) Lexington County
141	n/a	14.1	**Pageland** (town) Chesterfield County
141	n/a	14.1	**Walhalla** (city) Oconee County
143	3348	15.1	**Hilton Head Island** (town) Beaufort County
144	n/a	15.7	**Sans Souci** (CDP) Greenville County
145	3448	16.1	**Bluffton** (town) Beaufort County
146	3633	18.4	**Myrtle Beach** (city) Horry County
147	n/a	20.6	**Woodfield** (CDP) Richland County
148	n/a	21.2	**Saluda** (town) Saluda County
149	n/a	26.2	**Arcadia** (CDP) Spartanburg County
150	n/a	27.7	**Southern Shops** (CDP) Spartanburg County

Note: The state column ranks the top/bottom 150 places in the state with population of 2,500 or more. The national column ranks the top/bottom places in the country with population of 10,000 or more. Places that are unincorporated were not considered in the rankings. n/a indicates data not available. Please refer to the User Guide for additional information.

Speak English Only at Home

Top 150 Places Ranked in *Descending* Order

State Rank	Nat'l Rank	Percent	Place
1	n/a	100.0	Gloverville (CDP) Aiken County
1	n/a	100.0	Williston (town) Barnwell County
3	n/a	99.7	Honea Path (town) Anderson County
4	n/a	99.6	Arial (CDP) Pickens County
5	n/a	99.5	Piedmont (CDP) Anderson County
6	n/a	99.4	Allendale (town) Allendale County
6	n/a	99.4	Lesslie (CDP) York County
6	n/a	99.4	Walterboro (city) Colleton County
9	n/a	99.2	Denmark (city) Bamberg County
9	n/a	99.2	Hollywood (town) Charleston County
9	n/a	99.2	Mullins (city) Marion County
12	n/a	99.0	Chester (city) Chester County
12	n/a	99.0	Manning (city) Clarendon County
14	n/a	98.9	Bishopville (city) Lee County
15	n/a	98.8	Bamberg (town) Bamberg County
15	n/a	98.8	Union (city) Union County
17	n/a	98.7	Lake City (city) Florence County
18	n/a	98.5	Cheraw (town) Chesterfield County
19	n/a	98.4	Barnwell (city) Barnwell County
20	n/a	98.1	Graniteville (CDP) Aiken County
20	n/a	98.1	Pendleton (town) Anderson County
22	n/a	98.0	Abbeville (city) Abbeville County
22	n/a	98.0	Murrells Inlet (CDP) Georgetown County
24	n/a	97.9	Marion (city) Marion County
24	n/a	97.9	Pickens (city) Pickens County
26	n/a	97.7	Brookdale (CDP) Orangeburg County
27	n/a	97.6	Kingstree (town) Williamsburg County
28	n/a	97.5	Bennettsville (city) Marlboro County
29	n/a	97.3	Hartsville (city) Darlington County
30	n/a	97.2	Clinton (city) Laurens County
31	n/a	97.0	Red Bank (CDP) Lexington County
32	n/a	96.8	Batesburg-Leesville (town) Lexington County
32	n/a	96.8	Homeland Park (CDP) Anderson County
32	n/a	96.8	Lakewood (CDP) Sumter County
35	254	96.7	Conway (city) Horry County
35	n/a	96.7	Fountain Inn (city) Greenville County
37	n/a	96.6	Garden City (CDP) Horry County
37	n/a	96.6	Hopkins (CDP) Richland County
37	n/a	96.6	Lake Murray of Richland (CDP) Richland County
40	n/a	96.5	Centerville (CDP) Anderson County
41	n/a	96.4	Burnettown (town) Aiken County
42	338	96.3	Florence (city) Florence County
42	n/a	96.3	McCormick (town) McCormick County
44	n/a	96.2	Folly Beach (city) Charleston County
45	n/a	96.1	Darlington (city) Darlington County
45	n/a	96.1	Forestbrook (CDP) Horry County
47	412	96.0	Aiken (city) Aiken County
47	n/a	96.0	Belton (city) Anderson County
47	n/a	96.0	Valley Falls (CDP) Spartanburg County
50	n/a	95.9	Lancaster (city) Lancaster County
50	n/a	95.9	Sangaree (CDP) Berkeley County
52	n/a	95.8	Clover (town) York County
53	n/a	95.7	Lake Wylie (CDP) York County
54	n/a	95.6	Dillon (city) Dillon County
54	n/a	95.6	Hampton (town) Hampton County
56	n/a	95.5	Isle of Palms (city) Charleston County
57	n/a	95.4	Georgetown (city) Georgetown County
58	629	95.2	Sumter (city) Sumter County
59	n/a	95.1	Burton (CDP) Beaufort County
59	658	95.1	Gaffney (city) Cherokee County
61	n/a	95.0	Travelers Rest (city) Greenville County
62	714	94.9	Irmo (town) Richland County
62	714	94.9	North Augusta (city) Aiken County
62	714	94.9	Orangeburg (city) Orangeburg County
62	714	94.9	Spartanburg (city) Spartanburg County
66	742	94.8	Mount Pleasant (town) Charleston County
67	n/a	94.7	Camden (city) Kershaw County
67	768	94.7	Charleston (city) Charleston County
67	n/a	94.7	Woodruff (city) Spartanburg County
70	814	94.5	Anderson (city) Anderson County
70	n/a	94.5	Lugoff (CDP) Kershaw County
70	n/a	94.5	North Hartsville (CDP) Darlington County
73	n/a	94.3	Moncks Corner (town) Berkeley County
74	904	94.1	Summerville (town) Dorchester County
74	n/a	94.1	Surfside Beach (town) Horry County
76	931	94.0	Cayce (city) Lexington County
76	n/a	94.0	Laurel Bay (CDP) Beaufort County
78	975	93.8	Fort Mill (town) York County
78	n/a	93.8	Williamston (town) Anderson County
80	1025	93.6	Saint Andrews (CDP) Richland County
81	n/a	93.5	Central (town) Pickens County
81	1047	93.5	Seven Oaks (CDP) Lexington County
83	1097	93.3	Easley (city) Pickens County
84	n/a	93.2	Liberty (city) Pickens County
85	1144	93.1	North Myrtle Beach (city) Horry County
85	n/a	93.1	Springdale (town) Lexington County
87	n/a	93.0	Little River (CDP) Horry County
88	1210	92.8	Rock Hill (city) York County
89	1271	92.6	Forest Acres (city) Richland County
90	1346	92.3	Columbia (city) Richland County
90	1346	92.3	Oak Grove (CDP) Lexington County
92	1395	92.1	Lexington (town) Lexington County
93	n/a	92.0	India Hook (CDP) York County
93	1416	92.0	Ladson (CDP) Berkeley County
93	n/a	92.0	Laurens (city) Laurens County
96	1457	91.8	Dentsville (CDP) Richland County
96	n/a	91.8	Edisto (CDP) Orangeburg County
96	1457	91.8	Goose Creek (city) Berkeley County
96	n/a	91.8	Seneca (city) Oconee County
100	n/a	91.7	Andrews (town) Georgetown County
100	1481	91.7	Greenville (city) Greenville County
102	n/a	91.6	East Gaffney (CDP) Cherokee County
103	n/a	91.5	Duncan (town) Spartanburg County
104	1547	91.4	Five Forks (CDP) Greenville County
105	n/a	91.3	Belvedere (CDP) Aiken County
105	n/a	91.3	Lyman (town) Spartanburg County
107	n/a	91.2	Northlake (CDP) Anderson County
108	n/a	91.1	Springdale (CDP) Lancaster County
109	n/a	90.9	Winnsboro (town) Fairfield County
110	1674	90.7	Mauldin (city) Greenville County
111	n/a	90.3	York (city) York County
112	1780	90.2	Taylors (CDP) Greenville County
113	n/a	90.1	Newport (CDP) York County
113	n/a	90.1	Tega Cay (city) York County
115	n/a	90.0	Elgin (CDP) Lancaster County
116	n/a	89.9	Dalzell (CDP) Sumter County
116	1848	89.9	Socastee (CDP) Horry County
118	1863	89.8	Beaufort (city) Beaufort County
118	1863	89.8	Greenwood (city) Greenwood County
120	n/a	89.7	Clearwater (CDP) Aiken County
121	1949	89.3	Gantt (CDP) Greenville County
122	2227	87.7	North Charleston (city) Charleston County
123	n/a	87.4	Dunean (CDP) Greenville County
124	2285	87.3	Clemson (city) Pickens County
124	2285	87.3	Red Hill (CDP) Horry County
126	n/a	87.2	Saxon (CDP) Spartanburg County
127	n/a	87.0	Ridgeland (town) Jasper County
128	2375	86.6	Port Royal (town) Beaufort County
129	n/a	86.3	Welcome (CDP) Greenville County
130	n/a	86.0	Boiling Springs (CDP) Spartanburg County
131	n/a	85.9	Edgefield (town) Edgefield County
132	2528	85.6	West Columbia (city) Lexington County
133	2588	85.1	Simpsonville (city) Greenville County
134	2684	84.4	Wade Hampton (CDP) Greenville County
135	2692	84.3	Hanahan (city) Berkeley County
136	2785	83.5	Newberry (city) Newberry County
137	3009	81.4	Hilton Head Island (town) Beaufort County
138	n/a	81.3	Walhalla (city) Oconee County
139	n/a	81.0	Pageland (town) Chesterfield County
140	3093	80.5	Greer (city) Greenville County
141	3142	80.0	Parker (CDP) Greenville County
142	n/a	78.4	Hardeeville (city) Jasper County
143	3297	77.9	Bluffton (town) Beaufort County
144	3325	77.4	Myrtle Beach (city) Horry County
145	3341	77.1	Berea (CDP) Greenville County
146	n/a	76.5	Woodfield (CDP) Richland County
147	n/a	76.0	Sans Souci (CDP) Greenville County
148	n/a	69.5	Saluda (town) Saluda County
149	n/a	57.1	Southern Shops (CDP) Spartanburg County
150	n/a	52.1	Arcadia (CDP) Spartanburg County

Note: The state column ranks the top/bottom 150 places in the state with population of 2,500 or more. The national column ranks the top/bottom places in the country with population of 10,000 or more. Places that are unincorporated were not considered in the rankings. n/a indicates data not available. Please refer to the User Guide for additional information.

Speak English Only at Home
Top 150 Places Ranked in *Ascending* Order

State Rank	Nat'l Rank	Percent	Place
1	n/a	52.1	**Arcadia** (CDP) Spartanburg County
2	n/a	57.1	**Southern Shops** (CDP) Spartanburg County
3	n/a	69.5	**Saluda** (town) Saluda County
4	n/a	76.0	**Sans Souci** (CDP) Greenville County
5	n/a	76.5	**Woodfield** (CDP) Richland County
6	1309	77.1	**Berea** (CDP) Greenville County
7	1327	77.4	**Myrtle Beach** (city) Horry County
8	1357	77.9	**Bluffton** (town) Beaufort County
9	n/a	78.4	**Hardeeville** (city) Jasper County
10	1510	80.0	**Parker** (CDP) Greenville County
11	1551	80.5	**Greer** (city) Greenville County
12	n/a	81.0	**Pageland** (town) Chesterfield County
13	n/a	81.3	**Walhalla** (city) Oconee County
14	1640	81.4	**Hilton Head Island** (town) Beaufort County
15	1864	83.5	**Newberry** (city) Newberry County
16	1949	84.3	**Hanahan** (city) Berkeley County
17	1965	84.4	**Wade Hampton** (CDP) Greenville County
18	2052	85.1	**Simpsonville** (city) Greenville County
19	2117	85.6	**West Columbia** (city) Lexington County
20	n/a	85.9	**Edgefield** (town) Edgefield County
21	n/a	86.0	**Boiling Springs** (CDP) Spartanburg County
22	n/a	86.3	**Welcome** (CDP) Greenville County
23	2266	86.6	**Port Royal** (town) Beaufort County
24	n/a	87.0	**Ridgeland** (town) Jasper County
25	n/a	87.2	**Saxon** (CDP) Spartanburg County
26	2360	87.3	**Clemson** (city) Pickens County
26	2360	87.3	**Red Hill** (CDP) Horry County
28	n/a	87.4	**Dunean** (CDP) Greenville County
29	2410	87.7	**North Charleston** (city) Charleston County
30	2689	89.3	**Gantt** (CDP) Greenville County
31	n/a	89.7	**Clearwater** (CDP) Aiken County
32	2779	89.8	**Beaufort** (city) Beaufort County
32	2779	89.8	**Greenwood** (city) Greenwood County
34	n/a	89.9	**Dalzell** (CDP) Sumter County
34	2794	89.9	**Socastee** (CDP) Horry County
36	n/a	90.0	**Elgin** (CDP) Lancaster County
37	n/a	90.1	**Newport** (CDP) York County
37	n/a	90.1	**Tega Cay** (city) York County
39	2849	90.2	**Taylors** (CDP) Greenville County
40	n/a	90.3	**York** (city) York County
41	2963	90.7	**Mauldin** (city) Greenville County
42	n/a	90.9	**Winnsboro** (town) Fairfield County
43	n/a	91.1	**Springdale** (CDP) Lancaster County
44	n/a	91.2	**Northlake** (CDP) Anderson County
45	n/a	91.3	**Belvedere** (CDP) Aiken County
45	n/a	91.3	**Lyman** (town) Spartanburg County
47	3091	91.4	**Five Forks** (CDP) Greenville County
48	n/a	91.5	**Duncan** (town) Spartanburg County
49	n/a	91.6	**East Gaffney** (CDP) Cherokee County
50	n/a	91.7	**Andrews** (town) Georgetown County
50	3155	91.7	**Greenville** (city) Greenville County
52	3176	91.8	**Dentsville** (CDP) Richland County
52	n/a	91.8	**Edisto** (CDP) Orangeburg County
52	3176	91.8	**Goose Creek** (city) Berkeley County
52	n/a	91.8	**Seneca** (city) Oconee County
56	n/a	92.0	**India Hook** (CDP) York County
56	3216	92.0	**Ladson** (CDP) Berkeley County
56	n/a	92.0	**Laurens** (city) Laurens County
59	3241	92.1	**Lexington** (town) Lexington County
60	3287	92.3	**Columbia** (city) Richland County
60	3287	92.3	**Oak Grove** (CDP) Lexington County
62	3361	92.6	**Forest Acres** (city) Richland County
63	3417	92.8	**Rock Hill** (city) York County
64	n/a	93.0	**Little River** (CDP) Horry County
65	3489	93.1	**North Myrtle Beach** (city) Horry County
65	n/a	93.1	**Springdale** (town) Lexington County
67	n/a	93.2	**Liberty** (city) Pickens County
68	3533	93.3	**Easley** (city) Pickens County
69	n/a	93.5	**Central** (town) Pickens County
69	3586	93.5	**Seven Oaks** (CDP) Lexington County
71	3610	93.6	**Saint Andrews** (CDP) Richland County
72	3659	93.8	**Fort Mill** (town) York County
72	n/a	93.8	**Williamston** (town) Anderson County
74	3703	94.0	**Cayce** (city) Lexington County
74	n/a	94.0	**Laurel Bay** (CDP) Beaufort County
76	3726	94.1	**Summerville** (town) Dorchester County
76	n/a	94.1	**Surfside Beach** (town) Horry County
78	n/a	94.3	**Moncks Corner** (town) Berkeley County
79	3825	94.5	**Anderson** (city) Anderson County
79	n/a	94.5	**Lugoff** (CDP) Kershaw County
79	n/a	94.5	**North Hartsville** (CDP) Darlington County
82	n/a	94.7	**Camden** (city) Kershaw County
82	3863	94.7	**Charleston** (city) Charleston County
82	n/a	94.7	**Woodruff** (city) Spartanburg County
85	3889	94.8	**Mount Pleasant** (town) Charleston County
86	3915	94.9	**Irmo** (town) Richland County
86	3915	94.9	**North Augusta** (city) Aiken County
86	3915	94.9	**Orangeburg** (city) Orangeburg County
86	3915	94.9	**Spartanburg** (city) Spartanburg County
90	n/a	95.0	**Travelers Rest** (city) Greenville County
91	n/a	95.1	**Burton** (CDP) Beaufort County
91	3969	95.1	**Gaffney** (city) Cherokee County
93	3999	95.2	**Sumter** (city) Sumter County
94	n/a	95.4	**Georgetown** (city) Georgetown County
95	n/a	95.5	**Isle of Palms** (city) Charleston County
96	n/a	95.6	**Dillon** (city) Dillon County
96	n/a	95.6	**Hampton** (town) Hampton County
98	n/a	95.7	**Lake Wylie** (CDP) York County
99	n/a	95.8	**Clover** (town) York County
100	n/a	95.9	**Lancaster** (city) Lancaster County
100	n/a	95.9	**Sangaree** (CDP) Berkeley County
102	4221	96.0	**Aiken** (city) Aiken County
102	n/a	96.0	**Belton** (city) Anderson County
102	n/a	96.0	**Valley Falls** (CDP) Spartanburg County
105	n/a	96.1	**Darlington** (city) Darlington County
105	n/a	96.1	**Forestbrook** (CDP) Horry County
107	n/a	96.2	**Folly Beach** (city) Charleston County
108	4294	96.3	**Florence** (city) Florence County
108	n/a	96.3	**McCormick** (town) McCormick County
110	n/a	96.4	**Burnettown** (town) Aiken County
111	n/a	96.5	**Centerville** (CDP) Anderson County
112	n/a	96.6	**Garden City** (CDP) Horry County
112	n/a	96.6	**Hopkins** (CDP) Richland County
112	n/a	96.6	**Lake Murray of Richland** (CDP) Richland County
115	4375	96.7	**Conway** (city) Horry County
115	n/a	96.7	**Fountain Inn** (city) Greenville County
117	n/a	96.8	**Batesburg-Leesville** (town) Lexington County
117	n/a	96.8	**Homeland Park** (CDP) Anderson County
117	n/a	96.8	**Lakewood** (CDP) Sumter County
120	n/a	97.0	**Red Bank** (CDP) Lexington County
121	n/a	97.2	**Clinton** (city) Laurens County
122	n/a	97.3	**Hartsville** (city) Darlington County
123	n/a	97.5	**Bennettsville** (city) Marlboro County
124	n/a	97.6	**Kingstree** (town) Williamsburg County
125	n/a	97.7	**Brookdale** (CDP) Orangeburg County
126	n/a	97.9	**Marion** (city) Marion County
126	n/a	97.9	**Pickens** (city) Pickens County
128	n/a	98.0	**Abbeville** (city) Abbeville County
128	n/a	98.0	**Murrells Inlet** (CDP) Georgetown County
130	n/a	98.1	**Graniteville** (CDP) Aiken County
130	n/a	98.1	**Pendleton** (town) Anderson County
132	n/a	98.4	**Barnwell** (city) Barnwell County
133	n/a	98.5	**Cheraw** (town) Chesterfield County
134	n/a	98.7	**Lake City** (city) Florence County
135	n/a	98.8	**Bamberg** (town) Bamberg County
135	n/a	98.8	**Union** (city) Union County
137	n/a	98.9	**Bishopville** (city) Lee County
138	n/a	99.0	**Chester** (city) Chester County
138	n/a	99.0	**Manning** (city) Clarendon County
140	n/a	99.2	**Denmark** (city) Bamberg County
140	n/a	99.2	**Hollywood** (town) Charleston County
140	n/a	99.2	**Mullins** (city) Marion County
143	n/a	99.4	**Allendale** (town) Allendale County
143	n/a	99.4	**Lesslie** (CDP) York County
143	n/a	99.4	**Walterboro** (city) Colleton County
146	n/a	99.5	**Piedmont** (CDP) Anderson County
147	n/a	99.6	**Arial** (CDP) Pickens County
148	n/a	99.7	**Honea Path** (town) Anderson County
149	n/a	100.0	**Gloverville** (CDP) Aiken County
149	n/a	100.0	**Williston** (town) Barnwell County

Note: The state column ranks the top/bottom 150 places in the state with population of 2,500 or more. The national column ranks the top/bottom places in the country with population of 10,000 or more. Places that are unincorporated were not considered in the rankings. n/a indicates data not available. Please refer to the User Guide for additional information.

Individuals with a Disability

Top 150 Places Ranked in *Descending* Order

State Rank	Nat'l Rank	Percent	Place
1	n/a	27.9	Manning (city) Clarendon County
2	n/a	24.8	McCormick (town) McCormick County
3	n/a	24.6	Duncan (town) Spartanburg County
3	n/a	24.6	Lake City (city) Florence County
5	n/a	24.5	Abbeville (city) Abbeville County
6	n/a	24.3	Arial (CDP) Pickens County
7	n/a	23.8	Williston (town) Barnwell County
8	n/a	23.4	Clearwater (CDP) Aiken County
9	n/a	23.1	Batesburg-Leesville (town) Lexington County
10	n/a	23.0	Belton (city) Anderson County
10	n/a	23.0	Mullins (city) Marion County
12	n/a	22.4	Denmark (city) Bamberg County
13	n/a	22.3	Andrews (town) Georgetown County
14	n/a	22.2	Hopkins (CDP) Richland County
15	n/a	22.1	Laurens (city) Laurens County
16	n/a	22.0	Homeland Park (CDP) Anderson County
17	n/a	21.9	Honea Path (town) Anderson County
18	n/a	21.7	Allendale (town) Allendale County
19	n/a	21.3	Union (city) Union County
20	n/a	21.0	Gloverville (CDP) Aiken County
20	n/a	21.0	North Hartsville (CDP) Darlington County
20	n/a	21.0	Pickens (city) Pickens County
23	n/a	20.4	Walhalla (city) Oconee County
24	n/a	20.3	Cheraw (town) Chesterfield County
25	n/a	20.0	Hartsville (city) Darlington County
26	n/a	19.3	Pendleton (town) Anderson County
27	n/a	19.1	Clinton (city) Laurens County
28	n/a	19.0	Liberty (city) Pickens County
29	n/a	18.9	Barnwell (city) Barnwell County
30	n/a	18.4	Bishopville (city) Lee County
30	n/a	18.4	Piedmont (CDP) Anderson County
30	n/a	18.4	York (city) York County
33	n/a	18.2	Dillon (city) Dillon County
34	n/a	18.1	Georgetown (city) Georgetown County
35	n/a	17.9	Bennettsville (city) Marlboro County
36	n/a	17.8	India Hook (CDP) York County
37	n/a	17.7	Chester (city) Chester County
38	n/a	17.6	Burnettown (town) Aiken County
38	384	17.6	Parker (CDP) Greenville County
40	436	17.2	Anderson (city) Anderson County
40	n/a	17.2	Hollywood (town) Charleston County
40	n/a	17.2	Seneca (city) Oconee County
43	451	17.1	Gaffney (city) Cherokee County
43	n/a	17.1	Garden City (CDP) Horry County
43	n/a	17.1	Walterboro (city) Colleton County
46	n/a	17.0	Kingstree (town) Williamsburg County
47	n/a	16.9	Brookdale (CDP) Orangeburg County
47	n/a	16.9	East Gaffney (CDP) Cherokee County
49	n/a	16.8	Bamberg (town) Bamberg County
50	536	16.6	Sumter (city) Sumter County
51	555	16.5	Spartanburg (city) Spartanburg County
52	n/a	16.4	Marion (city) Marion County
53	n/a	16.1	Darlington (city) Darlington County
54	658	16.0	North Myrtle Beach (city) Horry County
55	n/a	15.9	Lancaster (city) Lancaster County
56	n/a	15.8	Springdale (CDP) Lancaster County
57	n/a	15.7	Saxon (CDP) Spartanburg County
58	740	15.6	Easley (city) Pickens County
59	n/a	15.4	Woodruff (city) Spartanburg County
60	839	15.2	Greenwood (city) Greenwood County
61	869	15.1	Beaufort (city) Beaufort County
61	869	15.1	Florence (city) Florence County
61	n/a	15.1	Moncks Corner (town) Berkeley County
61	869	15.1	Newberry (city) Newberry County
65	n/a	15.0	Edisto (CDP) Orangeburg County
66	n/a	14.9	Little River (CDP) Horry County
67	n/a	14.7	Lesslie (CDP) York County
68	n/a	14.4	Belvedere (CDP) Aiken County
68	1031	14.4	Myrtle Beach (city) Horry County
70	n/a	14.3	Murrells Inlet (CDP) Georgetown County
70	n/a	14.3	Woodfield (CDP) Richland County
72	1086	14.2	Conway (city) Horry County
72	n/a	14.2	Sans Souci (CDP) Greenville County
74	n/a	14.0	Fountain Inn (city) Greenville County
74	n/a	14.0	Surfside Beach (town) Horry County
76	n/a	13.8	Dalzell (CDP) Sumter County
76	1201	13.8	Red Hill (CDP) Horry County
78	n/a	13.7	Burton (CDP) Beaufort County
78	n/a	13.7	Sangaree (CDP) Berkeley County
80	1258	13.6	Orangeburg (city) Orangeburg County
80	1258	13.6	Saint Andrews (CDP) Richland County
82	1298	13.5	Cayce (city) Lexington County
82	n/a	13.5	Dunean (CDP) Greenville County
84	1393	13.2	Gantt (CDP) Greenville County
85	1426	13.1	Dentsville (CDP) Richland County
85	1426	13.1	Taylors (CDP) Greenville County
87	n/a	12.9	Red Bank (CDP) Lexington County
88	1522	12.8	Berea (CDP) Greenville County
89	1554	12.7	Greer (city) Greenville County
89	1554	12.7	North Augusta (city) Aiken County
91	1618	12.5	Ladson (CDP) Berkeley County
91	1618	12.5	Socastee (CDP) Horry County
93	n/a	12.4	Centerville (CDP) Anderson County
93	1655	12.4	Oak Grove (CDP) Lexington County
95	n/a	12.2	Ridgeland (town) Jasper County
95	1744	12.2	West Columbia (city) Lexington County
97	n/a	12.1	Lugoff (CDP) Kershaw County
97	n/a	12.1	Williamston (town) Anderson County
99	1824	12.0	Aiken (city) Aiken County
99	n/a	12.0	Forestbrook (CDP) Horry County
99	n/a	12.0	Pageland (town) Chesterfield County
102	n/a	11.9	Edgefield (town) Edgefield County
102	n/a	11.9	Elgin (CDP) Lancaster County
102	n/a	11.9	Hampton (town) Hampton County
105	1912	11.8	Wade Hampton (CDP) Greenville County
106	1952	11.7	Lexington (town) Lexington County
106	1952	11.7	Simpsonville (city) Greenville County
108	n/a	11.6	Saluda (town) Saluda County
108	n/a	11.6	Welcome (CDP) Greenville County
110	2049	11.5	Rock Hill (city) York County
111	n/a	11.4	Winnsboro (town) Fairfield County
112	2134	11.3	Columbia (city) Richland County
112	2134	11.3	Seven Oaks (CDP) Lexington County
112	n/a	11.3	Southern Shops (CDP) Spartanburg County
115	n/a	11.0	Arcadia (CDP) Spartanburg County
115	n/a	11.0	Folly Beach (city) Charleston County
115	2256	11.0	Greenville (city) Greenville County
118	n/a	10.9	Camden (city) Kershaw County
119	n/a	10.8	Clover (town) York County
119	2352	10.8	Hilton Head Island (town) Beaufort County
121	n/a	10.7	Graniteville (CDP) Aiken County
122	2439	10.6	Forest Acres (city) Richland County
123	2495	10.5	North Charleston (city) Charleston County
123	2495	10.5	Summerville (town) Dorchester County
125	n/a	10.4	Travelers Rest (city) Greenville County
126	n/a	10.2	Springdale (town) Lexington County
127	n/a	10.1	Central (town) Pickens County
128	2917	9.6	Charleston (city) Charleston County
129	2977	9.5	Fort Mill (town) York County
129	2977	9.5	Irmo (town) Richland County
131	3090	9.3	Bluffton (town) Beaufort County
131	3090	9.3	Hanahan (city) Berkeley County
133	3130	9.2	Goose Creek (city) Berkeley County
134	3232	9.0	Mauldin (city) Greenville County
134	n/a	9.0	Northlake (CDP) Anderson County
134	3232	9.0	Port Royal (town) Beaufort County
137	n/a	8.8	Lake Murray of Richland (CDP) Richland County
138	n/a	8.5	Laurel Bay (CDP) Beaufort County
138	n/a	8.5	Lyman (town) Spartanburg County
140	n/a	8.4	Lake Wylie (CDP) York County
141	n/a	8.3	Boiling Springs (CDP) Spartanburg County
141	n/a	8.3	Valley Falls (CDP) Spartanburg County
143	n/a	8.1	Hardeeville (city) Jasper County
144	n/a	7.8	Lakewood (CDP) Sumter County
145	n/a	7.4	Isle of Palms (city) Charleston County
146	4033	7.3	Clemson (city) Pickens County
147	4107	7.1	Mount Pleasant (town) Charleston County
148	n/a	6.4	Newport (CDP) York County
149	n/a	4.9	Tega Cay (city) York County
150	4615	4.3	Five Forks (CDP) Greenville County

Note: *The state column ranks the top/bottom 150 places in the state with population of 2,500 or more. The national column ranks the top/bottom places in the country with population of 10,000 or more. Places that are unincorporated were not considered in the rankings. n/a indicates data not available. Please refer to the User Guide for additional information.*

Individuals with a Disability

Top 150 Places Ranked in *Ascending* Order

State Rank	Nat'l Rank	Percent	Place
1	34	4.3	**Five Forks** (CDP) Greenville County
2	n/a	4.9	**Tega Cay** (city) York County
3	n/a	6.4	**Newport** (CDP) York County
4	520	7.1	**Mount Pleasant** (town) Charleston County
5	589	7.3	**Clemson** (city) Pickens County
6	n/a	7.4	**Isle of Palms** (city) Charleston County
7	n/a	7.8	**Lakewood** (CDP) Sumter County
8	n/a	8.1	**Hardeeville** (city) Jasper County
9	n/a	8.3	**Boiling Springs** (CDP) Spartanburg County
9	n/a	8.3	**Valley Falls** (CDP) Spartanburg County
11	n/a	8.4	**Lake Wylie** (CDP) York County
12	n/a	8.5	**Laurel Bay** (CDP) Beaufort County
12	n/a	8.5	**Lyman** (town) Spartanburg County
14	n/a	8.8	**Lake Murray of Richland** (CDP) Richland County
15	1373	9.0	**Mauldin** (city) Greenville County
15	n/a	9.0	**Northlake** (CDP) Anderson County
15	1373	9.0	**Port Royal** (town) Beaufort County
18	1468	9.2	**Goose Creek** (city) Berkeley County
19	1527	9.3	**Bluffton** (town) Beaufort County
19	1527	9.3	**Hanahan** (city) Berkeley County
21	1625	9.5	**Fort Mill** (town) York County
21	1625	9.5	**Irmo** (town) Richland County
23	1680	9.6	**Charleston** (city) Charleston County
24	n/a	10.1	**Central** (town) Pickens County
25	n/a	10.2	**Springdale** (town) Lexington County
26	n/a	10.4	**Travelers Rest** (city) Greenville County
27	2113	10.5	**North Charleston** (city) Charleston County
27	2113	10.5	**Summerville** (town) Dorchester County
29	2162	10.6	**Forest Acres** (city) Richland County
30	n/a	10.7	**Graniteville** (CDP) Aiken County
31	n/a	10.8	**Clover** (town) York County
31	2262	10.8	**Hilton Head Island** (town) Beaufort County
33	n/a	10.9	**Camden** (city) Kershaw County
34	n/a	11.0	**Arcadia** (CDP) Spartanburg County
34	n/a	11.0	**Folly Beach** (city) Charleston County
34	2350	11.0	**Greenville** (city) Greenville County
37	2479	11.3	**Columbia** (city) Richland County
37	2479	11.3	**Seven Oaks** (CDP) Lexington County
37	n/a	11.3	**Southern Shops** (CDP) Spartanburg County
40	n/a	11.4	**Winnsboro** (town) Fairfield County
41	2575	11.5	**Rock Hill** (city) York County
42	n/a	11.6	**Saluda** (town) Saluda County
42	n/a	11.6	**Welcome** (CDP) Greenville County
44	2661	11.7	**Lexington** (town) Lexington County
44	2661	11.7	**Simpsonville** (city) Greenville County
46	2705	11.8	**Wade Hampton** (CDP) Greenville County
47	n/a	11.9	**Edgefield** (town) Edgefield County
47	n/a	11.9	**Elgin** (CDP) Lancaster County
47	n/a	11.9	**Hampton** (town) Hampton County
50	2785	12.0	**Aiken** (city) Aiken County
50	n/a	12.0	**Forestbrook** (CDP) Horry County
50	n/a	12.0	**Pageland** (town) Chesterfield County
53	n/a	12.1	**Lugoff** (CDP) Kershaw County
53	n/a	12.1	**Williamston** (town) Anderson County
55	n/a	12.2	**Ridgeland** (town) Jasper County
55	2869	12.2	**West Columbia** (city) Lexington County
57	n/a	12.4	**Centerville** (CDP) Anderson County
57	2952	12.4	**Oak Grove** (CDP) Lexington County
59	3002	12.5	**Ladson** (CDP) Berkeley County
59	3002	12.5	**Socastee** (CDP) Horry County
61	3077	12.7	**Greer** (city) Greenville County
61	3077	12.7	**North Augusta** (city) Aiken County
63	3103	12.8	**Berea** (CDP) Greenville County
64	n/a	12.9	**Red Bank** (CDP) Lexington County
65	3199	13.1	**Dentsville** (CDP) Richland County
65	3199	13.1	**Taylors** (CDP) Greenville County
67	3231	13.2	**Gantt** (CDP) Greenville County
68	3333	13.5	**Cayce** (city) Lexington County
68	n/a	13.5	**Dunean** (CDP) Greenville County
70	3359	13.6	**Orangeburg** (city) Orangeburg County
70	3359	13.6	**Saint Andrews** (CDP) Richland County
72	n/a	13.7	**Burton** (CDP) Beaufort County
72	n/a	13.7	**Sangaree** (CDP) Berkeley County
74	n/a	13.8	**Dalzell** (CDP) Sumter County
74	3429	13.8	**Red Hill** (CDP) Horry County
76	n/a	14.0	**Fountain Inn** (city) Greenville County
76	n/a	14.0	**Surfside Beach** (town) Horry County
78	3538	14.2	**Conway** (city) Horry County
78	n/a	14.2	**Sans Souci** (CDP) Greenville County
80	n/a	14.3	**Murrells Inlet** (CDP) Georgetown County
80	n/a	14.3	**Woodfield** (CDP) Richland County
82	n/a	14.4	**Belvedere** (CDP) Aiken County
82	3599	14.4	**Myrtle Beach** (city) Horry County
84	n/a	14.7	**Lesslie** (CDP) York County
85	n/a	14.9	**Little River** (CDP) Horry County
86	n/a	15.0	**Edisto** (CDP) Orangeburg County
87	3758	15.1	**Beaufort** (city) Beaufort County
87	3758	15.1	**Florence** (city) Florence County
87	n/a	15.1	**Moncks Corner** (town) Berkeley County
87	3758	15.1	**Newberry** (city) Newberry County
91	3788	15.2	**Greenwood** (city) Greenwood County
92	n/a	15.4	**Woodruff** (city) Spartanburg County
93	3883	15.6	**Easley** (city) Pickens County
94	n/a	15.7	**Saxon** (CDP) Spartanburg County
95	n/a	15.8	**Springdale** (CDP) Lancaster County
96	n/a	15.9	**Lancaster** (city) Lancaster County
97	3976	16.0	**North Myrtle Beach** (city) Horry County
98	n/a	16.1	**Darlington** (city) Darlington County
99	n/a	16.4	**Marion** (city) Marion County
100	4081	16.5	**Spartanburg** (city) Spartanburg County
101	4102	16.6	**Sumter** (city) Sumter County
102	n/a	16.8	**Bamberg** (town) Bamberg County
103	n/a	16.9	**Brookdale** (CDP) Orangeburg County
103	n/a	16.9	**East Gaffney** (CDP) Cherokee County
105	n/a	17.0	**Kingstree** (town) Williamsburg County
106	4191	17.1	**Gaffney** (city) Cherokee County
106	n/a	17.1	**Garden City** (CDP) Horry County
106	n/a	17.1	**Walterboro** (city) Colleton County
109	4206	17.2	**Anderson** (city) Anderson County
109	n/a	17.2	**Hollywood** (town) Charleston County
109	n/a	17.2	**Seneca** (city) Oconee County
112	n/a	17.6	**Burnettown** (town) Aiken County
112	4258	17.6	**Parker** (CDP) Greenville County
114	n/a	17.7	**Chester** (city) Chester County
115	n/a	17.8	**India Hook** (CDP) York County
116	n/a	17.9	**Bennettsville** (city) Marlboro County
117	n/a	18.1	**Georgetown** (city) Georgetown County
118	n/a	18.2	**Dillon** (city) Dillon County
119	n/a	18.4	**Bishopville** (city) Lee County
119	n/a	18.4	**Piedmont** (CDP) Anderson County
119	n/a	18.4	**York** (city) York County
122	n/a	18.9	**Barnwell** (city) Barnwell County
123	n/a	19.0	**Liberty** (city) Pickens County
124	n/a	19.1	**Clinton** (city) Laurens County
125	n/a	19.3	**Pendleton** (town) Anderson County
126	n/a	20.0	**Hartsville** (city) Darlington County
127	n/a	20.3	**Cheraw** (town) Chesterfield County
128	n/a	20.4	**Walhalla** (city) Oconee County
129	n/a	21.0	**Gloverville** (CDP) Aiken County
129	n/a	21.0	**North Hartsville** (CDP) Darlington County
129	n/a	21.0	**Pickens** (city) Pickens County
132	n/a	21.3	**Union** (city) Union County
133	n/a	21.7	**Allendale** (town) Allendale County
134	n/a	21.9	**Honea Path** (town) Anderson County
135	n/a	22.0	**Homeland Park** (CDP) Anderson County
136	n/a	22.1	**Laurens** (city) Laurens County
137	n/a	22.2	**Hopkins** (CDP) Richland County
138	n/a	22.3	**Andrews** (town) Georgetown County
139	n/a	22.4	**Denmark** (city) Bamberg County
140	n/a	23.0	**Belton** (city) Anderson County
140	n/a	23.0	**Mullins** (city) Marion County
142	n/a	23.1	**Batesburg-Leesville** (town) Lexington County
143	n/a	23.4	**Clearwater** (CDP) Aiken County
144	n/a	23.8	**Williston** (town) Barnwell County
145	n/a	24.3	**Arial** (CDP) Pickens County
146	n/a	24.5	**Abbeville** (city) Abbeville County
147	n/a	24.6	**Duncan** (town) Spartanburg County
147	n/a	24.6	**Lake City** (city) Florence County
149	n/a	24.8	**McCormick** (town) McCormick County
150	n/a	27.9	**Manning** (city) Clarendon County

Note: *The state column ranks the top/bottom 150 places in the state with population of 2,500 or more. The national column ranks the top/bottom places in the country with population of 10,000 or more. Places that are unincorporated were not considered in the rankings. n/a indicates data not available. Please refer to the User Guide for additional information.*

Veterans

Top 150 Places Ranked in *Descending* Order

State Rank	Nat'l Rank	Percent	Place
1	n/a	32.1	**Dalzell** (CDP) Sumter County
2	7	28.7	**Port Royal** (town) Beaufort County
3	n/a	23.1	**Sangaree** (CDP) Berkeley County
4	n/a	22.4	**Laurel Bay** (CDP) Beaufort County
5	n/a	19.9	**Lyman** (town) Spartanburg County
6	n/a	19.2	**Burton** (CDP) Beaufort County
7	102	18.2	**Beaufort** (city) Beaufort County
8	n/a	18.1	**India Hook** (CDP) York County
9	118	17.8	**Goose Creek** (city) Berkeley County
10	n/a	17.6	**Garden City** (CDP) Horry County
11	136	17.3	**Ladson** (CDP) Berkeley County
12	n/a	16.7	**Folly Beach** (city) Charleston County
13	n/a	15.9	**Murrells Inlet** (CDP) Georgetown County
14	n/a	15.7	**Woodfield** (CDP) Richland County
15	207	15.6	**North Myrtle Beach** (city) Horry County
15	207	15.6	**Sumter** (city) Sumter County
17	n/a	15.4	**Isle of Palms** (city) Charleston County
18	n/a	15.3	**Cheraw** (town) Chesterfield County
18	228	15.3	**Hanahan** (city) Berkeley County
20	n/a	15.2	**Little River** (CDP) Horry County
20	234	15.2	**Socastee** (CDP) Horry County
20	234	15.2	**Summerville** (town) Dorchester County
23	n/a	15.0	**Newport** (CDP) York County
24	n/a	14.8	**Belvedere** (CDP) Aiken County
25	n/a	14.3	**Kingstree** (town) Williamsburg County
26	n/a	14.2	**Irmo** (town) Richland County
27	n/a	14.1	**Belton** (city) Anderson County
28	331	14.0	**Hilton Head Island** (town) Beaufort County
29	n/a	13.8	**Surfside Beach** (town) Horry County
30	n/a	13.6	**North Hartsville** (CDP) Darlington County
31	388	13.4	**Seven Oaks** (CDP) Lexington County
32	n/a	13.2	**Moncks Corner** (town) Berkeley County
33	n/a	12.9	**Hampton** (town) Hampton County
34	518	12.6	**North Augusta** (city) Aiken County
34	518	12.6	**North Charleston** (city) Charleston County
36	542	12.5	**Aiken** (city) Aiken County
37	566	12.4	**Forest Acres** (city) Richland County
38	n/a	12.3	**Arcadia** (CDP) Spartanburg County
39	n/a	12.2	**Hollywood** (town) Charleston County
40	n/a	12.1	**Honea Path** (town) Anderson County
40	n/a	12.1	**Springdale** (town) Lexington County
42	n/a	12.0	**Walterboro** (city) Colleton County
43	n/a	11.9	**Georgetown** (city) Georgetown County
44	n/a	11.8	**Burnettown** (town) Aiken County
44	697	11.8	**Dentsville** (CDP) Richland County
44	697	11.8	**Easley** (city) Pickens County
44	n/a	11.8	**Lake Murray of Richland** (CDP) Richland County
44	697	11.8	**Mauldin** (city) Greenville County
49	n/a	11.7	**Hopkins** (CDP) Richland County
49	720	11.7	**Wade Hampton** (CDP) Greenville County
51	n/a	11.5	**Fountain Inn** (city) Greenville County
52	n/a	11.3	**Northlake** (CDP) Anderson County
53	n/a	11.2	**Edisto** (CDP) Orangeburg County
53	n/a	11.2	**Lake Wylie** (CDP) York County
53	n/a	11.2	**Lugoff** (CDP) Kershaw County
53	n/a	11.2	**Pendleton** (town) Anderson County
57	n/a	11.1	**Williston** (town) Barnwell County
58	976	11.0	**Oak Grove** (CDP) Lexington County
59	1016	10.9	**Cayce** (city) Lexington County
59	n/a	10.9	**Forestbrook** (CDP) Horry County
59	1016	10.9	**Mount Pleasant** (town) Charleston County
62	1065	10.8	**Red Hill** (CDP) Horry County
63	1222	10.5	**Fort Mill** (town) York County
63	1222	10.5	**Gaffney** (city) Cherokee County
63	n/a	10.5	**Sans Souci** (CDP) Greenville County
63	n/a	10.5	**Seneca** (city) Oconee County
63	n/a	10.5	**Union** (city) Union County
68	1272	10.4	**Bluffton** (town) Beaufort County
69	n/a	10.3	**Camden** (city) Kershaw County
70	1445	10.1	**West Columbia** (city) Lexington County
71	1492	10.0	**Conway** (city) Horry County
71	n/a	10.0	**Dillon** (city) Dillon County
73	n/a	9.9	**Bamberg** (town) Bamberg County
73	1565	9.9	**Simpsonville** (city) Greenville County
75	n/a	9.8	**Hartsville** (city) Darlington County
76	n/a	9.6	**Duncan** (town) Spartanburg County
77	1832	9.5	**Charleston** (city) Charleston County
77	n/a	9.5	**Lake City** (city) Florence County
77	n/a	9.5	**Ridgeland** (town) Jasper County
80	n/a	9.4	**Abbeville** (city) Abbeville County
80	n/a	9.4	**Brookdale** (CDP) Orangeburg County
80	1897	9.4	**Florence** (city) Florence County
80	1897	9.4	**Lexington** (town) Lexington County
80	1897	9.4	**Myrtle Beach** (city) Horry County
80	1897	9.4	**Taylors** (CDP) Greenville County
80	n/a	9.4	**Welcome** (CDP) Greenville County
87	n/a	9.2	**Batesburg-Leesville** (town) Lexington County
88	n/a	9.1	**Centerville** (CDP) Anderson County
88	n/a	9.1	**Chester** (city) Chester County
88	n/a	9.1	**Laurens** (city) Laurens County
88	2103	9.1	**Saint Andrews** (CDP) Richland County
88	n/a	9.1	**Springdale** (CDP) Lancaster County
93	n/a	9.0	**Pickens** (city) Pickens County
93	n/a	9.0	**Red Bank** (CDP) Lexington County
93	n/a	9.0	**Travelers Rest** (city) Greenville County
96	2253	8.9	**Anderson** (city) Anderson County
96	2253	8.9	**Spartanburg** (city) Spartanburg County
96	n/a	8.9	**York** (city) York County
99	2312	8.8	**Columbia** (city) Richland County
99	2312	8.8	**Orangeburg** (city) Orangeburg County
99	2312	8.8	**Rock Hill** (city) York County
102	n/a	8.7	**Manning** (city) Clarendon County
102	n/a	8.7	**Marion** (city) Marion County
104	n/a	8.6	**Mullins** (city) Marion County
104	n/a	8.6	**Winnsboro** (town) Fairfield County
106	n/a	8.5	**Bennettsville** (city) Marlboro County
106	n/a	8.5	**Clearwater** (CDP) Aiken County
106	n/a	8.5	**McCormick** (town) McCormick County
109	n/a	8.4	**Arial** (CDP) Pickens County
109	n/a	8.4	**Boiling Springs** (CDP) Spartanburg County
109	n/a	8.4	**Clover** (town) York County
109	n/a	8.4	**Edgefield** (town) Edgefield County
109	2599	8.4	**Five Forks** (CDP) Greenville County
109	2599	8.4	**Parker** (CDP) Greenville County
115	n/a	8.2	**Elgin** (CDP) Lancaster County
115	n/a	8.2	**Southern Shops** (CDP) Spartanburg County
117	n/a	8.1	**Lancaster** (city) Lancaster County
118	n/a	8.0	**Darlington** (city) Darlington County
118	n/a	8.0	**Williamston** (town) Anderson County
120	2894	7.9	**Berea** (CDP) Greenville County
120	2894	7.9	**Greer** (city) Greenville County
122	2996	7.7	**Gantt** (CDP) Greenville County
122	n/a	7.7	**Homeland Park** (CDP) Anderson County
124	n/a	7.6	**Allendale** (town) Allendale County
124	n/a	7.6	**Tega Cay** (city) York County
126	n/a	7.5	**Barnwell** (city) Barnwell County
126	n/a	7.5	**Saxon** (CDP) Spartanburg County
128	n/a	7.4	**Andrews** (town) Georgetown County
128	3150	7.4	**Clemson** (city) Pickens County
128	n/a	7.4	**Walhalla** (city) Oconee County
131	3214	7.3	**Greenwood** (city) Greenwood County
132	n/a	7.2	**Denmark** (city) Bamberg County
133	n/a	7.1	**Graniteville** (CDP) Aiken County
133	n/a	7.1	**Piedmont** (CDP) Anderson County
133	n/a	7.1	**Woodruff** (city) Spartanburg County
136	n/a	7.0	**Gloverville** (CDP) Aiken County
136	3371	7.0	**Greenville** (city) Greenville County
138	n/a	6.4	**Saluda** (town) Saluda County
139	n/a	6.3	**Hardeeville** (city) Jasper County
140	n/a	6.2	**Valley Falls** (CDP) Spartanburg County
141	3789	6.1	**Newberry** (city) Newberry County
142	n/a	6.0	**Dunean** (CDP) Greenville County
142	n/a	6.0	**Lakewood** (CDP) Sumter County
144	n/a	5.9	**Liberty** (city) Pickens County
145	n/a	5.8	**Clinton** (city) Laurens County
146	n/a	5.7	**Lesslie** (CDP) York County
147	n/a	5.2	**Bishopville** (city) Lee County
148	n/a	3.6	**Pageland** (town) Chesterfield County
149	n/a	3.0	**Central** (town) Pickens County
150	n/a	2.9	**East Gaffney** (CDP) Cherokee County

Note: The state column ranks the top/bottom 150 places in the state with population of 2,500 or more. The national column ranks the top/bottom places in the country with population of 10,000 or more. Places that are unincorporated were not considered in the rankings. n/a indicates data not available. Please refer to the User Guide for additional information.

Veterans

Top 150 Places Ranked in *Ascending* Order

State Rank	Nat'l Rank	Percent	Place
1	n/a	2.9	**East Gaffney** (CDP) Cherokee County
2	n/a	3.0	**Central** (town) Pickens County
3	n/a	3.6	**Pageland** (town) Chesterfield County
4	n/a	5.2	**Bishopville** (city) Lee County
5	n/a	5.7	**Lesslie** (CDP) York County
6	n/a	5.8	**Clinton** (city) Laurens County
7	n/a	5.9	**Liberty** (city) Pickens County
8	n/a	6.0	**Dunean** (CDP) Greenville County
8	n/a	6.0	**Lakewood** (CDP) Sumter County
10	826	6.1	**Newberry** (city) Newberry County
11	n/a	6.2	**Valley Falls** (CDP) Spartanburg County
12	n/a	6.3	**Hardeeville** (city) Jasper County
13	n/a	6.4	**Saluda** (town) Saluda County
14	n/a	7.0	**Gloverville** (CDP) Aiken County
14	1230	7.0	**Greenville** (city) Greenville County
16	n/a	7.1	**Graniteville** (CDP) Aiken County
16	n/a	7.1	**Piedmont** (CDP) Anderson County
16	n/a	7.1	**Woodruff** (city) Spartanburg County
19	n/a	7.2	**Denmark** (city) Bamberg County
20	1398	7.3	**Greenwood** (city) Greenwood County
21	n/a	7.4	**Andrews** (town) Georgetown County
21	1443	7.4	**Clemson** (city) Pickens County
21	n/a	7.4	**Walhalla** (city) Oconee County
24	n/a	7.5	**Barnwell** (city) Barnwell County
24	n/a	7.5	**Saxon** (CDP) Spartanburg County
26	n/a	7.6	**Allendale** (town) Allendale County
26	n/a	7.6	**Tega Cay** (city) York County
28	1599	7.7	**Gantt** (CDP) Greenville County
28	n/a	7.7	**Homeland Park** (CDP) Anderson County
30	1710	7.9	**Berea** (CDP) Greenville County
30	1710	7.9	**Greer** (city) Greenville County
32	n/a	8.0	**Darlington** (city) Darlington County
32	n/a	8.0	**Williamston** (town) Anderson County
34	n/a	8.1	**Lancaster** (city) Lancaster County
35	n/a	8.2	**Elgin** (CDP) Lancaster County
35	n/a	8.2	**Southern Shops** (CDP) Spartanburg County
37	n/a	8.4	**Arial** (CDP) Pickens County
37	n/a	8.4	**Boiling Springs** (CDP) Spartanburg County
37	n/a	8.4	**Clover** (town) York County
37	n/a	8.4	**Edgefield** (town) Edgefield County
37	1991	8.4	**Five Forks** (CDP) Greenville County
37	1991	8.4	**Parker** (CDP) Greenville County
43	n/a	8.5	**Bennettsville** (city) Marlboro County
43	n/a	8.5	**Clearwater** (CDP) Aiken County
43	n/a	8.5	**McCormick** (town) McCormick County
46	n/a	8.6	**Mullins** (city) Marion County
46	n/a	8.6	**Winnsboro** (town) Fairfield County
48	n/a	8.7	**Manning** (city) Clarendon County
48	n/a	8.7	**Marion** (city) Marion County
50	2274	8.8	**Columbia** (city) Richland County
50	2274	8.8	**Orangeburg** (city) Orangeburg County
50	2274	8.8	**Rock Hill** (city) York County
53	2345	8.9	**Anderson** (city) Anderson County
53	2345	8.9	**Spartanburg** (city) Spartanburg County
53	n/a	8.9	**York** (city) York County
56	n/a	9.0	**Pickens** (city) Pickens County
56	n/a	9.0	**Red Bank** (CDP) Lexington County
56	n/a	9.0	**Travelers Rest** (city) Greenville County
59	n/a	9.1	**Centerville** (CDP) Anderson County
59	n/a	9.1	**Chester** (city) Chester County
59	n/a	9.1	**Laurens** (city) Laurens County
59	2479	9.1	**Saint Andrews** (CDP) Richland County
59	n/a	9.1	**Springdale** (town) Lancaster County
64	n/a	9.2	**Batesburg-Leesville** (town) Lexington County
65	n/a	9.4	**Abbeville** (city) Abbeville County
65	n/a	9.4	**Brookdale** (CDP) Orangeburg County
65	2680	9.4	**Florence** (city) Florence County
65	2680	9.4	**Lexington** (town) Lexington County
65	2680	9.4	**Myrtle Beach** (city) Horry County
65	2680	9.4	**Taylors** (CDP) Greenville County
65	n/a	9.4	**Welcome** (CDP) Greenville County
72	2760	9.5	**Charleston** (city) Charleston County
72	n/a	9.5	**Lake City** (city) Florence County
72	n/a	9.5	**Ridgeland** (town) Jasper County
75	n/a	9.6	**Duncan** (town) Spartanburg County
76	n/a	9.8	**Hartsville** (city) Darlington County
77	n/a	9.9	**Bamberg** (town) Bamberg County
77	3017	9.9	**Simpsonville** (city) Greenville County
79	3092	10.0	**Conway** (city) Horry County
79	n/a	10.0	**Dillon** (city) Dillon County
81	3165	10.1	**West Columbia** (city) Lexington County
82	n/a	10.3	**Camden** (city) Kershaw County
83	3329	10.4	**Bluffton** (town) Beaufort County
84	3385	10.5	**Fort Mill** (town) York County
84	3385	10.5	**Gaffney** (city) Cherokee County
84	n/a	10.5	**Sans Souci** (CDP) Greenville County
84	n/a	10.5	**Seneca** (city) Oconee County
84	n/a	10.5	**Union** (city) Union County
89	3539	10.8	**Red Hill** (CDP) Horry County
90	3592	10.9	**Cayce** (city) Lexington County
90	n/a	10.9	**Forestbrook** (CDP) Horry County
90	3592	10.9	**Mount Pleasant** (town) Charleston County
93	3641	11.0	**Oak Grove** (CDP) Lexington County
94	n/a	11.1	**Williston** (town) Barnwell County
95	n/a	11.2	**Edisto** (CDP) Orangeburg County
95	n/a	11.2	**Lake Wylie** (CDP) York County
95	n/a	11.2	**Lugoff** (CDP) Kershaw County
95	n/a	11.2	**Pendleton** (town) Anderson County
99	n/a	11.3	**Northlake** (CDP) Anderson County
100	n/a	11.5	**Fountain Inn** (city) Greenville County
101	n/a	11.7	**Hopkins** (CDP) Richland County
101	3901	11.7	**Wade Hampton** (CDP) Greenville County
103	n/a	11.8	**Burnettown** (town) Aiken County
103	3937	11.8	**Dentsville** (CDP) Richland County
103	3937	11.8	**Easley** (city) Pickens County
103	n/a	11.8	**Lake Murray of Richland** (CDP) Richland County
103	3937	11.8	**Mauldin** (city) Greenville County
108	n/a	11.9	**Georgetown** (city) Georgetown County
109	n/a	12.0	**Walterboro** (city) Colleton County
110	n/a	12.1	**Honea Path** (town) Anderson County
110	n/a	12.1	**Springdale** (town) Lexington County
112	n/a	12.2	**Hollywood** (town) Charleston County
113	n/a	12.3	**Arcadia** (CDP) Spartanburg County
114	4071	12.4	**Forest Acres** (city) Richland County
115	4091	12.5	**Aiken** (city) Aiken County
116	4115	12.6	**North Augusta** (city) Aiken County
116	4115	12.6	**North Charleston** (city) Charleston County
118	n/a	12.9	**Hampton** (town) Hampton County
119	n/a	13.2	**Moncks Corner** (town) Berkeley County
120	4256	13.4	**Seven Oaks** (CDP) Lexington County
121	n/a	13.6	**North Hartsville** (CDP) Darlington County
122	n/a	13.8	**Surfside Beach** (town) Horry County
123	4318	14.0	**Hilton Head Island** (town) Beaufort County
124	n/a	14.1	**Belton** (city) Anderson County
125	4340	14.2	**Irmo** (town) Richland County
126	n/a	14.3	**Kingstree** (town) Williamsburg County
127	n/a	14.8	**Belvedere** (CDP) Aiken County
128	n/a	15.0	**Newport** (CDP) York County
129	n/a	15.2	**Little River** (CDP) Horry County
129	4417	15.2	**Socastee** (CDP) Horry County
129	4417	15.2	**Summerville** (town) Dorchester County
132	n/a	15.3	**Cheraw** (town) Chesterfield County
132	4423	15.3	**Hanahan** (city) Berkeley County
134	n/a	15.4	**Isle of Palms** (city) Charleston County
135	4443	15.6	**North Myrtle Beach** (city) Horry County
135	4443	15.6	**Sumter** (city) Sumter County
137	n/a	15.7	**Woodfield** (CDP) Richland County
138	n/a	15.9	**Murrells Inlet** (CDP) Georgetown County
139	n/a	16.7	**Folly Beach** (city) Charleston County
140	4519	17.3	**Ladson** (CDP) Berkeley County
141	n/a	17.6	**Garden City** (CDP) Horry County
142	4533	17.8	**Goose Creek** (city) Berkeley County
143	n/a	18.1	**India Hook** (CDP) York County
144	4551	18.2	**Beaufort** (city) Beaufort County
145	n/a	19.2	**Burton** (CDP) Beaufort County
146	n/a	19.9	**Lyman** (town) Spartanburg County
147	n/a	22.4	**Laurel Bay** (CDP) Beaufort County
148	n/a	23.1	**Sangaree** (CDP) Berkeley County
149	4649	28.7	**Port Royal** (town) Beaufort County
150	n/a	32.1	**Dalzell** (CDP) Sumter County

Note: The state column ranks the top/bottom 150 places in the state with population of 2,500 or more. The national column ranks the top/bottom places in the country with population of 10,000 or more. Places that are unincorporated were not considered in the rankings. n/a indicates data not available. Please refer to the User Guide for additional information.

Ancestry: German

Top 150 Places Ranked in *Descending* Order

State Rank	Nat'l Rank	Percent	Place
1	1	76.8	Chilton (city) Calumet County
2	2	73.3	Barton (town) Washington County
3	3	73.0	Addison (town) Washington County
4	4	72.6	Dyersville (city) Dubuque County
5	5	70.9	Jackson (town) Washington County
6	6	70.5	Howards Grove (village) Sheboygan County
7	7	70.3	Mayville (city) Dodge County
8	8	69.9	Minster (village) Auglaize County
9	9	69.1	Hartford (town) Washington County
9	9	69.1	Polk (town) Washington County
11	11	68.4	Medford (town) Taylor County
12	12	68.1	Brillion (city) Calumet County
13	13	67.8	Kiel (city) Manitowoc County
14	14	67.7	Hortonville (village) Outagamie County
15	15	66.9	Wakefield (township) Stearns County
16	16	66.1	Center (town) Outagamie County
17	17	66.0	Plymouth (town) Sheboygan County
17	17	66.0	Sheboygan (town) Sheboygan County
17	17	66.0	Trenton (town) Washington County
20	20	65.8	Fayette (township) Juniata County
20	20	65.8	Wheatland (town) Kenosha County
22	22	65.5	Kewaskum (village) Washington County
23	23	65.4	Springfield (town) Dane County
24	24	65.2	Empire (town) Fond du Lac County
25	25	64.8	Mukwa (town) Waupaca County
26	26	64.2	Albany (city) Stearns County
27	27	64.0	Jackson (village) Washington County
28	28	63.9	New Bremen (village) Auglaize County
29	29	63.8	New Ulm (city) Brown County
30	30	63.0	Coldwater (village) Mercer County
30	30	63.0	West Bend (town) Washington County
32	32	62.3	Breese (city) Clinton County
33	33	61.9	Taycheedah (town) Fond du Lac County
34	34	61.4	Merrill (town) Lincoln County
34	34	61.4	New Holstein (city) Calumet County
36	36	60.9	Beaver Dam (town) Dodge County
36	36	60.9	Friendship (town) Fond du Lac County
36	36	60.9	Mandan (city) Morton County
39	39	60.8	Miami Heights (CDP) Hamilton County
40	40	60.6	Plymouth (city) Sheboygan County
40	40	60.6	Sheboygan Falls (city) Sheboygan County
42	42	60.4	Medford (city) Taylor County
43	43	60.3	Merrill (city) Lincoln County
43	43	60.3	Saint Marys (city) Elk County
45	45	60.2	Elizabeth (township) Lancaster County
46	46	59.7	Stettin (town) Marathon County
47	47	59.6	Merton (village) Waukesha County
48	48	59.5	Wales (village) Waukesha County
49	49	59.4	Dale (town) Outagamie County
49	49	59.4	Germantown (village) Washington County
49	49	59.4	Grundy Center (city) Grundy County
49	49	59.4	Saint Augusta (city) Stearns County
53	53	59.3	Columbus (city) Columbia County
53	53	59.3	Farmington (town) Washington County
55	55	59.2	Fond du Lac (town) Fond du Lac County
55	55	59.2	Wayne (city) Wayne County
57	57	59.1	Caledonia (city) Houston County
58	58	58.9	Ixonia (town) Jefferson County
58	58	58.9	Lodi (town) Columbia County
60	60	58.3	Horicon (city) Dodge County
61	61	58.2	Johnson Creek (village) Jefferson County
62	62	58.0	Oakland (town) Jefferson County
62	62	58.0	Sauk Centre (city) Stearns County
64	64	57.8	Richfield (village) Washington County
65	65	57.7	Harrison (town) Calumet County
65	65	57.7	Sebewaing (township) Huron County
67	67	57.6	Fox (township) Elk County
67	67	57.6	West Bend (city) Washington County
69	69	57.4	Grafton (town) Ozaukee County
69	69	57.4	Ripon (city) Fond du Lac County
71	71	57.3	Harrison (city) Hamilton County
72	72	57.2	Carroll (city) Carroll County
72	72	57.2	Washington (township) Schuylkill County
74	74	57.1	Kronenwetter (village) Marathon County
75	75	56.9	Ellington (town) Outagamie County
76	76	56.8	Norwood Young America (city) Carver County
76	76	56.8	Saukville (village) Ozaukee County
78	78	56.5	Sherwood (village) Calumet County
78	78	56.5	Slinger (village) Washington County
80	80	56.4	Delphos (city) Allen County
80	80	56.4	Oregon (town) Dane County
80	80	56.4	Shelby (town) La Crosse County
83	83	56.3	Lisbon (town) Waukesha County
83	83	56.3	Sussex (village) Waukesha County
85	85	56.2	Bismarck (city) Burleigh County
85	85	56.2	Poynette (village) Columbia County
87	87	56.0	Alsace (township) Berks County
87	87	56.0	Jordan (city) Scott County
89	89	55.9	Eagle (town) Waukesha County
90	90	55.8	Waukesha (town) Waukesha County
91	91	55.7	Clayton (town) Winnebago County
91	91	55.7	Pine Grove (township) Schuylkill County
93	93	55.6	Ashippun (town) Dodge County
93	93	55.6	Rockland (township) Berks County
95	95	55.5	Clintonville (city) Waupaca County
95	95	55.5	Pewaukee (city) Waukesha County
95	95	55.5	Sevastopol (town) Door County
98	98	55.3	Lake Crystal (city) Blue Earth County
98	98	55.3	Plainview (city) Wabasha County
98	98	55.3	Rock Rapids (city) Lyon County
101	101	55.2	De Witt (city) Clinton County
101	101	55.2	Merton (town) Waukesha County
101	101	55.2	Watertown (city) Jefferson County
104	104	55.1	Hartford (city) Washington County
105	105	55.0	Upper Augusta (township) Northumberland County
106	106	54.9	Delhi Hills (CDP) Hamilton County
107	107	54.8	Aberdeen (city) Brown County
107	107	54.8	Delafield (town) Waukesha County
109	109	54.7	Jamestown (city) Stutsman County
110	110	54.6	Cottage Grove (town) Dane County
110	110	54.6	Hallam (borough) York County
110	110	54.6	Vernon (town) Waukesha County
113	113	54.5	Monticello (city) Jones County
113	113	54.5	Mukwonago (town) Waukesha County
115	115	54.4	Milbank (city) Grant County
116	116	54.3	Beulah (city) Mercer County
116	116	54.3	Cross Plains (village) Dane County
116	116	54.3	Lima (town) Sheboygan County
119	119	54.2	Algoma (city) Kewaunee County
119	119	54.2	Cold Spring (city) Stearns County
119	119	54.2	Lodi (city) Columbia County
119	119	54.2	Monfort Heights (CDP) Hamilton County
123	123	54.1	Mack (CDP) Hamilton County
123	123	54.1	North Mankato (city) Nicollet County
125	125	54.0	Menasha (town) Winnebago County
125	125	54.0	Rome (town) Adams County
127	127	53.9	Hays (city) Ellis County
128	128	53.8	Brockway (township) Stearns County
128	128	53.8	Dent (CDP) Hamilton County
128	128	53.8	Lake Wazeecha (CDP) Wood County
128	128	53.8	Sleepy Eye (city) Brown County
132	132	53.7	Zumbrota (city) Goodhue County
133	133	53.6	Dickinson (city) Stark County
134	134	53.5	Beaver Dam (city) Dodge County
134	134	53.5	Fond du Lac (city) Fond du Lac County
134	134	53.5	Wescott (town) Shawano County
137	137	53.4	Eagle Point (town) Chippewa County
137	137	53.4	Grafton (village) Ozaukee County
139	139	53.3	Freeburg (village) Saint Clair County
140	140	53.2	Lake Wisconsin (CDP) Columbia County
140	140	53.2	Marshfield (city) Wood County
142	142	53.1	Dell Rapids (city) Minnehaha County
142	142	53.1	Lake Mills (city) Jefferson County
142	142	53.1	Muskego (city) Waukesha County
142	142	53.1	Oregon (village) Dane County
142	142	53.1	Portage (city) Columbia County
147	147	53.0	Hereford (township) Berks County
147	147	53.0	Marysville (city) Marshall County
147	147	53.0	North Fond du Lac (village) Fond du Lac County
150	150	52.9	Blackhawk (CDP) Meade County

Note: *The state column ranks the top/bottom 150 places in the state with population of 2,500 or more. The national column ranks the top/bottom places in the country with population of 10,000 or more. Places that are unincorporated were not considered in the rankings. n/a indicates data not available. Please refer to the User Guide for additional information.*

Ancestry: English

Top 150 Places Ranked in *Descending* Order

State Rank	Nat'l Rank	Percent	Place
1	1	84.4	**Hildale** (city) Washington County
2	2	66.2	**Colorado City** (town) Mohave County
3	3	42.2	**Alpine** (city) Utah County
4	4	41.5	**Fruit Heights** (city) Davis County
4	4	41.5	**Manti** (city) Sanpete County
6	6	40.8	**Highland** (city) Utah County
7	7	40.5	**Mapleton** (city) Utah County
8	8	39.1	**Beaver** (city) Beaver County
9	9	38.4	**Centerville** (city) Davis County
10	10	38.2	**Hooper** (city) Weber County
10	10	38.2	**Hopkinton** (town) Merrimack County
12	12	37.8	**Sheridan** (city) Grant County
13	13	36.9	**Santa Clara** (city) Washington County
14	14	36.0	**Saint George** (town) Knox County
15	15	35.9	**Farmingdale** (town) Kennebec County
16	16	35.7	**Bountiful** (city) Davis County
17	17	35.6	**Rockport** (town) Knox County
18	18	35.4	**Kanab** (city) Kane County
18	18	35.4	**McCall** (city) Valley County
20	20	35.0	**Wolfeboro** (CDP) Carroll County
21	21	34.8	**Farr West** (city) Weber County
21	21	34.8	**Providence** (city) Cache County
23	23	34.6	**Bristol** (town) Lincoln County
23	23	34.6	**Rexburg** (city) Madison County
25	25	34.5	**North Logan** (city) Cache County
26	26	34.3	**Boothbay** (town) Lincoln County
26	26	34.3	**Parowan** (city) Iron County
28	28	34.2	**Pleasant View** (city) Weber County
29	29	33.8	**Wellsville** (city) Cache County
30	30	33.6	**Monmouth** (city) Kennebec County
31	31	33.5	**Holladay** (city) Salt Lake County
32	32	33.4	**Hyde Park** (city) Cache County
32	32	33.4	**Trent Woods** (town) Craven County
34	34	33.0	**Salem** (city) Utah County
35	35	32.9	**Delta** (city) Millard County
36	36	32.8	**Freeport** (town) Cumberland County
36	36	32.8	**Midway** (city) Wasatch County
36	36	32.8	**West Bountiful** (city) Davis County
39	39	32.6	**Farmington** (city) Davis County
39	39	32.6	**Kaysville** (city) Davis County
41	41	32.5	**Kennebunkport** (town) York County
42	42	32.4	**Wolfeboro** (town) Carroll County
43	43	32.2	**Woodstock** (town) Windsor County
44	44	32.0	**Santaquin** (city) Utah County
45	45	31.9	**Chichester** (town) Merrimack County
46	46	31.8	**American Fork** (city) Utah County
46	46	31.8	**Anson** (town) Somerset County
46	46	31.8	**Camden** (town) Knox County
46	46	31.8	**Hyrum** (city) Cache County
50	50	31.6	**Spring Arbor** (township) Jackson County
51	51	31.5	**Poland** (town) Androscoggin County
52	52	31.4	**Herriman** (city) Salt Lake County
53	53	31.3	**Morgan** (city) Morgan County
54	54	31.1	**Alamo** (town) Wheeler County
54	54	31.1	**Charlestown** (town) Sullivan County
56	56	31.0	**Spanish Fork** (city) Utah County
56	56	31.0	**Waldoboro** (town) Lincoln County
58	58	30.9	**Ivins** (city) Washington County
59	59	30.8	**Yarmouth** (town) Cumberland County
60	60	30.7	**Cedar Hills** (city) Utah County
61	61	30.6	**Bethel** (town) Oxford County
61	61	30.6	**Bridgton** (town) Cumberland County
61	61	30.6	**Lake San Marcos** (CDP) San Diego County
61	61	30.6	**Rockland** (city) Knox County
61	61	30.6	**Saint George** (city) Washington County
61	61	30.6	**Woods Cross** (city) Davis County
67	67	30.5	**Cedar City** (city) Iron County
68	68	30.3	**North Salt Lake** (city) Davis County
68	68	30.3	**South Jordan** (city) Salt Lake County
70	70	30.2	**Eagle Mountain** (city) Utah County
71	71	30.1	**Preston** (city) Franklin County
72	72	29.9	**Camden** (CDP) Knox County
73	73	29.8	**South Beach** (CDP) Indian River County
74	74	29.7	**Harpswell** (town) Cumberland County
74	74	29.7	**Indian River Shores** (town) Indian River County
76	76	29.5	**Helena** (city) Telfair County
76	76	29.5	**Manchester** (town) Kennebec County
76	76	29.5	**Nephi** (city) Juab County
76	76	29.5	**Washington Terrace** (city) Weber County
80	80	29.4	**Yarmouth** (CDP) Cumberland County
81	81	29.3	**Springville** (city) Utah County
82	82	29.2	**Clinton** (town) Kennebec County
82	82	29.2	**Grantsville** (city) Tooele County
84	84	29.1	**Little Compton** (town) Newport County
84	84	29.1	**Plain City** (city) Weber County
86	86	29.0	**Cottonwood Heights** (city) Salt Lake County
86	86	29.0	**Warren** (town) Knox County
88	88	28.9	**Madison** (town) Carroll County
88	88	28.9	**Washington** (city) Washington County
90	90	28.8	**Lindon** (city) Utah County
90	90	28.8	**Livermore Falls** (town) Androscoggin County
90	90	28.8	**Nibley** (city) Cache County
93	93	28.7	**Orem** (city) Utah County
93	93	28.7	**Woolwich** (town) Sagadahoc County
95	95	28.6	**Pleasant Grove** (city) Utah County
96	96	28.5	**Arundel** (town) York County
96	96	28.5	**China** (town) Kennebec County
98	98	28.4	**Lehi** (city) Utah County
98	98	28.4	**Tamworth** (town) Carroll County
100	100	28.3	**Bradford** (town) Orange County
100	100	28.3	**Enoch** (city) Iron County
102	102	28.2	**Oneida** (town) Scott County
102	102	28.2	**Oxford** (town) Oxford County
102	102	28.2	**South Weber** (city) Davis County
105	105	28.1	**Maeser** (CDP) Uintah County
105	105	28.1	**Walpole** (town) Cheshire County
107	107	28.0	**Hampden** (CDP) Penobscot County
107	107	28.0	**Sandy** (city) Salt Lake County
109	109	27.9	**Northfield** (town) Franklin County
109	109	27.9	**Perry** (city) Box Elder County
111	111	27.8	**Limerick** (town) York County
111	111	27.8	**Orleans** (town) Barnstable County
111	111	27.8	**Riverton** (city) Salt Lake County
114	114	27.7	**Draper** (city) Salt Lake County
114	114	27.7	**Hartland** (town) Windsor County
114	114	27.7	**Otisco** (town) Onondaga County
114	114	27.7	**Saratoga Springs** (city) Utah County
114	114	27.7	**Smithfield** (city) Cache County
119	119	27.6	**Bluffdale** (city) Salt Lake County
119	119	27.6	**Bowdoin** (town) Sagadahoc County
119	119	27.6	**East Bloomfield** (town) Ontario County
119	119	27.6	**North Yarmouth** (town) Cumberland County
119	119	27.6	**Syracuse** (city) Davis County
124	124	27.5	**Harrison** (town) Cumberland County
124	124	27.5	**Highland Park** (town) Dallas County
124	124	27.5	**South Eliot** (CDP) York County
127	127	27.4	**Hampden** (town) Penobscot County
127	127	27.4	**Montpelier** (city) Bear Lake County
127	127	27.4	**Winston** (city) Douglas County
130	130	27.3	**Buxton** (town) York County
130	130	27.3	**North Ogden** (city) Weber County
130	130	27.3	**White Hall** (city) Jefferson County
133	133	27.2	**Thetford** (town) Orange County
134	134	27.1	**Greene** (town) Chenango County
134	134	27.1	**Wakefield** (town) Carroll County
136	136	26.9	**New Durham** (town) Strafford County
136	136	26.9	**Stansbury Park** (CDP) Tooele County
136	136	26.9	**Surfside Beach** (town) Horry County
139	139	26.8	**Stratham** (town) Rockingham County
140	140	26.6	**Concord** (township) Jackson County
140	140	26.6	**Millcreek** (CDP) Salt Lake County
140	140	26.6	**Peterborough** (CDP) Hillsborough County
140	140	26.6	**Turner** (town) Androscoggin County
144	144	26.5	**Foster** (town) Providence County
144	144	26.5	**Hope** (township) Barry County
144	144	26.5	**Norwich** (town) Windsor County
147	147	26.4	**Belle Meade** (city) Davidson County
148	148	26.3	**Belfast** (city) Waldo County
149	149	26.2	**Richfield** (city) Sevier County
149	149	26.2	**South Duxbury** (CDP) Plymouth County

Note: The state column ranks the top/bottom 150 places in the state with population of 2,500 or more. The national column ranks the top/bottom places in the country with population of 10,000 or more. Places that are unincorporated were not considered in the rankings. n/a indicates data not available. Please refer to the User Guide for additional information.

Ancestry: American

Top 150 Places Ranked in *Descending* Order

State Rank	Nat'l Rank	Percent	Place
1	1	66.4	**La Follette** (city) Campbell County
2	2	60.0	**Gloverville** (CDP) Aiken County
3	3	54.6	**Clearwater** (CDP) Aiken County
4	4	54.4	**Treasure Lake** (CDP) Clearfield County
5	5	51.7	**Healdton** (city) Carter County
6	6	45.9	**Bonifay** (city) Holmes County
7	7	45.8	**Harlem** (CDP) Hendry County
8	8	45.5	**Bean Station** (city) Grainger County
8	8	45.5	**Stanford** (city) Lincoln County
10	10	44.5	**Pell City** (city) Saint Clair County
11	11	44.3	**New Tazewell** (town) Claiborne County
12	12	43.9	**Dresden** (town) Weakley County
13	13	43.6	**Hartford** (city) Ohio County
14	14	43.2	**Blue Hill** (town) Hancock County
15	15	43.1	**Eaton** (town) Madison County
16	16	43.0	**Church Hill** (city) Hawkins County
17	17	42.6	**Middlesborough** (city) Bell County
18	18	42.1	**Temple** (city) Carroll County
19	19	41.1	**Georgetown** (city) Vermilion County
20	20	40.9	**Grantville** (city) Coweta County
20	20	40.9	**Summerville** (city) Chattooga County
22	22	40.6	**Morehead** (city) Rowan County
23	23	40.5	**Bayou Vista** (CDP) Saint Mary Parish
24	24	40.4	**Lone Grove** (city) Carter County
24	24	40.4	**Wilkesboro** (town) Wilkes County
26	26	39.9	**Chincoteague** (town) Accomack County
27	27	39.8	**Bremen** (city) Haralson County
28	28	39.7	**Cullowhee** (CDP) Jackson County
29	29	39.4	**Nassau Village-Ratliff** (CDP) Nassau County
30	30	38.8	**Crab Orchard** (CDP) Raleigh County
31	31	38.7	**Stanton** (city) Powell County
32	32	38.4	**Rogersville** (town) Hawkins County
33	33	38.2	**Cookeville** (city) Putnam County
34	34	38.0	**Livingston** (town) Overton County
35	35	37.6	**Gray Summit** (CDP) Franklin County
35	35	37.6	**Harrogate** (city) Claiborne County
37	37	37.4	**North Terre Haute** (CDP) Vigo County
38	38	37.3	**Mount Carmel** (CDP) Clermont County
39	39	36.9	**Atkins** (city) Pope County
39	39	36.9	**Burnettown** (town) Aiken County
39	39	36.9	**De Funiak Springs** (city) Walton County
42	42	36.8	**Lake of the Woods** (CDP) Champaign County
42	42	36.8	**Suncoast Estates** (CDP) Lee County
44	44	36.7	**Lancaster** (city) Garrard County
44	44	36.7	**Sandy** (township) Clearfield County
46	46	36.6	**Donalsonville** (city) Seminole County
47	47	36.3	**Bradford** (township) Clearfield County
47	47	36.3	**Broadway** (town) Rockingham County
47	47	36.3	**Jena** (town) La Salle Parish
50	50	36.2	**Algood** (city) Putnam County
50	50	36.2	**Sylva** (town) Jackson County
52	52	36.0	**Unicoi** (town) Unicoi County
53	53	35.6	**Bloomingdale** (CDP) Sullivan County
53	53	35.6	**Somerset** (city) Pulaski County
53	53	35.6	**Timberville** (town) Rockingham County
56	56	35.5	**Beaver Dam** (city) Ohio County
56	56	35.5	**Oliver Springs** (town) Anderson County
58	58	35.4	**Bucksport** (CDP) Hancock County
59	59	35.1	**England** (city) Lonoke County
59	59	35.1	**Fairview** (CDP) Walker County
59	59	35.1	**LaFayette** (city) Walker County
62	62	34.9	**Bucksport** (town) Hancock County
62	62	34.9	**Mountain City** (town) Johnson County
62	62	34.9	**Shepherdsville** (city) Bullitt County
65	65	34.8	**Blennerhassett** (CDP) Wood County
66	66	34.7	**South Lebanon** (village) Warren County
67	67	34.5	**Mount Carmel** (town) Hawkins County
68	68	34.3	**Hannahs Mill** (CDP) Upson County
69	69	34.2	**Mills** (town) Natrona County
69	69	34.2	**Rockwood** (city) Roane County
71	71	33.5	**North Wilkesboro** (town) Wilkes County
71	71	33.5	**Odenville** (town) Saint Clair County
73	73	33.3	**Ward** (city) Lonoke County
74	74	33.2	**Bawcomville** (CDP) Ouachita Parish
75	75	33.1	**Bethel** (village) Clermont County
75	75	33.1	**Grottoes** (town) Rockingham County
77	77	33.0	**Shelbyville** (city) Bedford County
78	78	32.7	**Dawson Springs** (city) Hopkins County
78	78	32.7	**Galena** (city) Cherokee County
78	78	32.7	**Pike Road** (town) Montgomery County
81	81	32.6	**Erwin** (town) Unicoi County
81	81	32.6	**Honea Path** (town) Anderson County
83	83	32.5	**West Tisbury** (town) Dukes County
84	84	32.3	**Pearisburg** (town) Giles County
85	85	32.2	**Evansville** (town) Natrona County
86	86	32.0	**Moody** (city) Saint Clair County
86	86	32.0	**Pittsburg** (city) Crawford County
88	88	31.9	**Woodbury** (town) Cannon County
89	89	31.8	**Dandridge** (town) Jefferson County
90	90	31.7	**Withamsville** (CDP) Clermont County
91	91	31.5	**Margaret** (town) Saint Clair County
92	92	31.4	**Pigeon Forge** (city) Sevier County
93	93	31.3	**Alva** (CDP) Lee County
94	94	31.1	**Hilliard** (town) Nassau County
95	95	30.8	**Monterey** (town) Putnam County
96	96	30.7	**Icard** (CDP) Burke County
97	97	30.5	**Flemingsburg** (city) Fleming County
97	97	30.5	**Shady Spring** (CDP) Raleigh County
99	99	30.4	**Irvine** (city) Estill County
100	100	30.3	**Cloverdale** (CDP) Botetourt County
100	100	30.3	**Hamilton** (town) Madison County
100	100	30.3	**Sylacauga** (city) Talladega County
100	100	30.3	**Underwood-Petersville** (CDP) Lauderdale County
104	104	30.2	**Central City** (city) Muhlenberg County
104	104	30.2	**Harriman** (city) Roane County
104	104	30.2	**Prestonsburg** (city) Floyd County
107	107	30.1	**Stuarts Draft** (CDP) Augusta County
108	108	30.0	**Madison** (town) Madison County
108	108	30.0	**Verona** (CDP) Augusta County
108	108	30.0	**Waynesville** (town) Haywood County
111	111	29.8	**Granville** (town) Washington County
111	111	29.8	**Paris** (city) Bourbon County
111	111	29.8	**Winchester** (city) Clark County
114	114	29.7	**Byron** (city) Peach County
114	114	29.7	**Emmett** (city) Gem County
114	114	29.7	**Hillview** (city) Bullitt County
114	114	29.7	**Oak Grove** (CDP) Washington County
114	114	29.7	**Sunnyvale** (town) Dallas County
114	114	29.7	**Wickenburg** (town) Maricopa County
120	120	29.6	**Jefferson City** (city) Jefferson County
121	121	29.5	**Ball** (town) Rapides Parish
121	121	29.5	**Corinth** (town) Penobscot County
121	121	29.5	**Lincoln** (city) Talladega County
124	124	29.4	**Manchester** (city) Coffee County
124	124	29.4	**Owensboro** (city) Daviess County
126	126	29.3	**Kings Mountain** (city) Cleveland County
127	127	29.2	**Buckner** (CDP) Oldham County
127	127	29.2	**Malabar** (town) Brevard County
129	129	29.1	**Baxter Springs** (city) Cherokee County
130	130	28.9	**Kingston** (city) Roane County
130	130	28.9	**Morristown** (city) Hamblen County
132	132	28.8	**Bayshore** (CDP) New Hanover County
132	132	28.8	**Buena Vista** (independent city)
134	134	28.7	**Grissom AFB** (CDP) Miami County
134	134	28.7	**Hodgenville** (city) Larue County
136	136	28.5	**Claiborne** (CDP) Ouachita Parish
136	136	28.5	**Inwood** (CDP) Polk County
136	136	28.5	**Moyock** (CDP) Currituck County
136	136	28.5	**Richlands** (town) Tazewell County
136	136	28.5	**Tabor City** (town) Columbus County
141	141	28.4	**Dundee** (town) Polk County
141	141	28.4	**Jan Phyl Village** (CDP) Polk County
141	141	28.4	**Morgan** (city) Morgan County
144	144	28.3	**West Liberty** (city) Morgan County
145	145	28.2	**Bicknell** (city) Knox County
145	145	28.2	**Fort Scott** (city) Bourbon County
145	145	28.2	**Putney** (CDP) Dougherty County
148	148	28.1	**Berwick** (town) Saint Mary Parish
148	148	28.1	**Corinth** (town) Saratoga County
148	148	28.1	**Middleton** (city) Canyon County

Note: *The state column ranks the top/bottom 150 places in the state with population of 2,500 or more. The national column ranks the top/bottom places in the country with population of 10,000 or more. Places that are unincorporated were not considered in the rankings. n/a indicates data not available. Please refer to the User Guide for additional information.*

Ancestry: Irish

Top 150 Places Ranked in *Descending* Order

State Rank	Nat'l Rank	Percent	Place
1	1	52.0	**Pearl River** (CDP) Rockland County
2	2	51.7	**Ocean Bluff-Brant Rock** (CDP) Plymouth County
3	3	50.6	**Green Harbor-Cedar Crest** (CDP) Plymouth County
4	4	49.4	**Rockledge** (borough) Montgomery County
5	5	48.3	**Walpole** (CDP) Norfolk County
6	6	47.4	**North Scituate** (CDP) Plymouth County
7	7	47.0	**Scituate** (CDP) Plymouth County
8	8	46.9	**Marshfield** (town) Plymouth County
9	9	46.2	**Scituate** (town) Plymouth County
10	10	45.8	**Ridley Park** (borough) Delaware County
11	11	45.5	**Spring Lake Heights** (borough) Monmouth County
12	12	45.3	**Oak Valley** (CDP) Gloucester County
13	13	45.2	**Hanover** (town) Plymouth County
14	14	44.7	**Norwell** (town) Plymouth County
15	15	44.2	**Glenside** (CDP) Montgomery County
15	15	44.2	**Manasquan** (borough) Monmouth County
17	17	43.8	**Norwood** (borough) Delaware County
18	18	42.9	**Walpole** (town) Norfolk County
18	18	42.9	**Wynantskill** (CDP) Rensselaer County
20	20	42.8	**Springfield** (township) Delaware County
21	21	42.6	**Folsom** (CDP) Delaware County
21	21	42.6	**Glenolden** (borough) Delaware County
21	21	42.6	**Highlands** (borough) Monmouth County
24	24	42.2	**Marshfield** (CDP) Plymouth County
25	25	41.7	**North Middletown** (CDP) Monmouth County
26	26	41.6	**Braintree Town** (city) Norfolk County
27	27	41.4	**Weymouth Town** (city) Norfolk County
28	28	41.1	**Littleton Common** (CDP) Middlesex County
28	28	41.1	**North Wildwood** (city) Cape May County
30	30	41.0	**Bridgewater** (CDP) Plymouth County
31	31	40.9	**Abington** (cdp/town) Plymouth County
31	31	40.9	**Nahant** (cdp/town) Essex County
31	31	40.9	**Spring Lake** (borough) Monmouth County
34	34	40.6	**Whitman** (town) Plymouth County
35	35	40.5	**Cohasset** (town) Norfolk County
35	35	40.5	**Hopedale** (CDP) Worcester County
35	35	40.5	**Sayville** (CDP) Suffolk County
38	38	40.4	**Brielle** (borough) Monmouth County
39	39	40.3	**Hull** (cdp/town) Plymouth County
40	40	40.2	**Gloucester City** (city) Camden County
41	41	39.9	**Churchville** (CDP) Bucks County
42	42	39.7	**Haddon Heights** (borough) Camden County
43	43	39.6	**Notre Dame** (CDP) Saint Joseph County
44	44	39.5	**Ashland** (borough) Schuylkill County
44	44	39.5	**Hingham** (town) Plymouth County
46	46	39.4	**Avon** (town) Norfolk County
47	47	39.3	**Garden City** (village) Nassau County
47	47	39.3	**Tinicum** (township) Delaware County
49	49	39.2	**Milton** (cdp/town) Norfolk County
49	49	39.2	**Ramtown** (CDP) Monmouth County
51	51	39.1	**Ridley** (township) Delaware County
52	52	38.8	**Bridgewater** (town) Plymouth County
53	53	38.5	**Hanson** (town) Plymouth County
53	53	38.5	**North Reading** (town) Middlesex County
53	53	38.5	**Prospect Park** (borough) Delaware County
53	53	38.5	**Rockland** (town) Plymouth County
57	57	38.4	**Hingham** (CDP) Plymouth County
58	58	38.3	**Foxborough** (town) Norfolk County
59	59	38.1	**Foxborough** (CDP) Norfolk County
60	60	38.0	**Barrington** (borough) Camden County
61	61	37.9	**Aldan** (borough) Delaware County
61	61	37.9	**Mansfield Center** (CDP) Bristol County
61	61	37.9	**National Park** (borough) Gloucester County
64	64	37.8	**East Sandwich** (CDP) Barnstable County
65	65	37.6	**Haverford** (township) Delaware County
65	65	37.6	**West Brandywine** (township) Chester County
67	67	37.5	**East Bridgewater** (town) Plymouth County
68	68	37.4	**Buzzards Bay** (CDP) Barnstable County
69	69	37.3	**Blauvelt** (CDP) Rockland County
69	69	37.3	**East Quogue** (CDP) Suffolk County
71	71	37.2	**Canton** (town) Norfolk County
71	71	37.2	**North Falmouth** (CDP) Barnstable County
73	73	37.1	**Pembroke** (town) Plymouth County
73	73	37.1	**Upton** (CDP) Worcester County
73	73	37.1	**Woodbury Heights** (borough) Gloucester County
76	76	36.9	**Fair Haven** (borough) Monmouth County
77	77	36.8	**Clementon** (borough) Camden County
77	77	36.8	**Duxbury** (town) Plymouth County
79	79	36.7	**Fairview** (CDP) Monmouth County
79	79	36.7	**Folcroft** (borough) Delaware County
79	79	36.7	**Newtown** (township) Delaware County
82	82	36.6	**Rockville Centre** (village) Nassau County
83	83	36.5	**Oceanport** (borough) Monmouth County
83	83	36.5	**West Bridgewater** (town) Plymouth County
85	85	36.2	**Audubon** (borough) Camden County
85	85	36.2	**Campo** (CDP) San Diego County
87	87	36.0	**Orleans** (town) Jefferson County
87	87	36.0	**Shark River Hills** (CDP) Monmouth County
89	89	35.8	**Drexel Hill** (CDP) Delaware County
89	89	35.8	**Trappe** (borough) Montgomery County
89	89	35.8	**West Sayville** (CDP) Suffolk County
92	92	35.5	**Leonardo** (CDP) Monmouth County
92	92	35.5	**Little Silver** (borough) Monmouth County
94	94	35.3	**Bethlehem** (township) Hunterdon County
95	95	35.2	**East Islip** (CDP) Suffolk County
95	95	35.2	**Kingston** (town) Plymouth County
97	97	35.1	**Dedham** (cdp/town) Norfolk County
97	97	35.1	**Hopedale** (town) Worcester County
97	97	35.1	**Wilmington** (cdp/town) Middlesex County
100	100	35.0	**Green Island** (town/village) Albany County
100	100	35.0	**Medford Lakes** (borough) Burlington County
102	102	34.9	**Holbrook** (cdp/town) Norfolk County
102	102	34.9	**Mansfield** (town) Bristol County
104	104	34.8	**LaFayette** (town) Onondaga County
104	104	34.8	**North Plymouth** (CDP) Plymouth County
104	104	34.8	**Norton** (town) Bristol County
104	104	34.8	**Tuckerton** (borough) Ocean County
104	104	34.8	**Wakefield** (cdp/town) Middlesex County
109	109	34.7	**Cape Neddick** (CDP) York County
109	109	34.7	**Tewksbury** (town) Middlesex County
109	109	34.7	**Woodlyn** (CDP) Delaware County
109	109	34.7	**Woolwich** (township) Gloucester County
113	113	34.6	**Wanamassa** (CDP) Monmouth County
114	114	34.5	**East Shoreham** (CDP) Suffolk County
114	114	34.5	**Horsham** (CDP) Montgomery County
114	114	34.5	**Skippack** (CDP) Montgomery County
117	117	34.4	**Plymouth** (town) Plymouth County
117	117	34.4	**Western Springs** (village) Cook County
119	119	34.3	**Bethel** (township) Delaware County
119	119	34.3	**Melrose** (city) Middlesex County
119	119	34.3	**Point Pleasant** (borough) Ocean County
122	122	34.2	**Aston** (township) Delaware County
122	122	34.2	**North Seekonk** (CDP) Bristol County
122	122	34.2	**Wanakah** (CDP) Erie County
122	122	34.2	**Westvale** (CDP) Onondaga County
126	126	34.1	**Reading** (cdp/town) Middlesex County
126	126	34.1	**Winthrop Town** (city) Suffolk County
128	128	34.0	**Atkinson** (town) Rockingham County
128	128	34.0	**Bella Vista** (CDP) Shasta County
128	128	34.0	**Hopkinton** (CDP) Middlesex County
128	128	34.0	**Plymouth** (CDP) Plymouth County
128	128	34.0	**Washington** (town) Dutchess County
128	128	34.0	**Williston Park** (village) Nassau County
134	134	33.9	**Norwood** (cdp/town) Norfolk County
135	135	33.8	**Clinton** (town) Worcester County
135	135	33.8	**Halifax** (town) Plymouth County
135	135	33.8	**Mystic Island** (CDP) Ocean County
135	135	33.8	**Wall** (township) Monmouth County
139	139	33.7	**Massapequa Park** (village) Nassau County
140	140	33.6	**Cold Spring Harbor** (CDP) Suffolk County
140	140	33.6	**Dalton** (town) Berkshire County
142	142	33.5	**Colonie** (village) Albany County
142	142	33.5	**Middletown** (township) Monmouth County
142	142	33.5	**Seabrook** (town) Rockingham County
142	142	33.5	**Waterford** (township) Camden County
146	146	33.4	**Medfield** (CDP) Norfolk County
146	146	33.4	**Montgomery** (village) Orange County
146	146	33.4	**Mount Ephraim** (borough) Camden County
149	149	33.3	**Dover** (town) Dutchess County
149	149	33.3	**Fort Salonga** (CDP) Suffolk County

Note: The state column ranks the top/bottom 150 places in the state with population of 2,500 or more. The national column ranks the top/bottom places in the country with population of 10,000 or more. Places that are unincorporated were not considered in the rankings. n/a indicates data not available. Please refer to the User Guide for additional information.

Ancestry: Italian

Top 150 Places Ranked in *Descending* Order

State Rank	Nat'l Rank	Percent	Place
1	1	51.2	Johnston (town) Providence County
2	2	50.9	Fairfield (township) Essex County
3	3	49.0	North Massapequa (CDP) Nassau County
4	4	47.7	East Haven (cdp/town) New Haven County
5	5	47.3	Watertown (CDP) Litchfield County
6	6	46.3	Massapequa (CDP) Nassau County
7	7	45.4	Eastchester (CDP) Westchester County
8	8	45.3	Thornwood (CDP) Westchester County
9	9	44.4	Glendora (CDP) Camden County
10	10	44.0	Frankfort (village) Herkimer County
11	11	43.5	Hawthorne (CDP) Westchester County
12	12	43.4	Hammonton (town) Atlantic County
13	13	43.3	North Branford (town) New Haven County
13	13	43.3	Turnersville (CDP) Gloucester County
15	15	42.8	West Islip (CDP) Suffolk County
16	16	42.6	Massapequa Park (village) Nassau County
17	17	42.1	Franklin Square (CDP) Nassau County
18	18	41.9	Islip Terrace (CDP) Suffolk County
19	19	41.6	Watertown (town) Litchfield County
20	20	41.4	Nesconset (CDP) Suffolk County
21	21	41.1	Lake Grove (village) Suffolk County
22	22	40.4	North Haven (cdp/town) New Haven County
23	23	40.3	Gibbstown (CDP) Gloucester County
24	24	40.2	Saint James (CDP) Suffolk County
24	24	40.2	Seaford (CDP) Nassau County
26	26	40.1	East Hanover (township) Morris County
26	26	40.1	Saugus (cdp/town) Essex County
28	28	39.9	Marlboro (CDP) Ulster County
29	29	39.7	Beach Haven West (CDP) Ocean County
30	30	39.5	East Islip (CDP) Suffolk County
30	30	39.5	Smithtown (CDP) Suffolk County
32	32	39.3	Jefferson Valley-Yorktown (CDP) Westchester County
33	33	39.2	Jessup (borough) Lackawanna County
33	33	39.2	Monmouth Beach (borough) Monmouth County
35	35	39.0	Brightwaters (village) Suffolk County
36	36	38.7	South Farmingdale (CDP) Nassau County
37	37	38.1	Frankfort (town) Herkimer County
37	37	38.1	Richwood (CDP) Gloucester County
39	39	38.0	Bayville (village) Nassau County
39	39	38.0	Malverne (village) Nassau County
39	39	38.0	North Providence (town) Providence County
42	42	37.9	Cedar Grove (township) Essex County
43	43	37.8	Plainedge (CDP) Nassau County
44	44	37.7	Holtsville (CDP) Suffolk County
44	44	37.7	Oakville (CDP) Litchfield County
46	46	37.6	Blackwood (CDP) Camden County
46	46	37.6	Holbrook (CDP) Suffolk County
48	48	37.4	Center Moriches (CDP) Suffolk County
48	48	37.4	Dunmore (borough) Lackawanna County
48	48	37.4	Smithtown (town) Suffolk County
51	51	37.2	North Great River (CDP) Suffolk County
52	52	37.1	Blue Point (CDP) Suffolk County
52	52	37.1	East Norwich (CDP) Nassau County
52	52	37.1	Ronkonkoma (CDP) Suffolk County
52	52	37.1	West Pittston (borough) Luzerne County
56	56	36.9	Hauppauge (CDP) Suffolk County
57	57	36.8	Bohemia (CDP) Suffolk County
57	57	36.8	Farmingville (CDP) Suffolk County
57	57	36.8	Old Forge (borough) Lackawanna County
57	57	36.8	Pemberwick (CDP) Fairfield County
61	61	36.7	Mechanicville (city) Saratoga County
61	61	36.7	Miller Place (CDP) Suffolk County
61	61	36.7	Nutley (township) Essex County
61	61	36.7	Selden (CDP) Suffolk County
61	61	36.7	Wood-Ridge (borough) Bergen County
66	66	36.6	Glen Head (CDP) Nassau County
67	67	36.5	Pittston (city) Luzerne County
68	68	36.4	Centerport (CDP) Suffolk County
69	69	36.2	Barnegat (CDP) Ocean County
70	70	36.1	Mahopac (CDP) Putnam County
70	70	36.1	Ocean Acres (CDP) Ocean County
72	72	36.0	Lindenhurst (village) Suffolk County
72	72	36.0	Lyncourt (CDP) Onondaga County
72	72	36.0	Union Vale (town) Dutchess County
72	72	36.0	Washington (township) Gloucester County
76	76	35.9	Eastchester (town) Westchester County
77	77	35.8	Garden City South (CDP) Nassau County
77	77	35.8	Greenwich (township) Gloucester County
77	77	35.8	Manorville (CDP) Suffolk County
80	80	35.7	Lake Pocotopaug (CDP) Middlesex County
80	80	35.7	Moonachie (borough) Bergen County
80	80	35.7	Oyster Bay (CDP) Nassau County
83	83	35.6	East Freehold (CDP) Monmouth County
83	83	35.6	Oakdale (CDP) Suffolk County
83	83	35.6	Ramtown (CDP) Monmouth County
86	86	35.5	Kensington (CDP) Hartford County
86	86	35.5	Pelham Manor (village) Westchester County
88	88	35.4	Holiday City-Berkeley (CDP) Ocean County
88	88	35.4	Yaphank (CDP) Suffolk County
90	90	35.2	Carmel (town) Putnam County
91	91	35.1	Commack (CDP) Suffolk County
92	92	34.9	Hazlet (township) Monmouth County
92	92	34.9	Somers (town) Westchester County
94	94	34.5	Bethpage (CDP) Nassau County
94	94	34.5	Middle Island (CDP) Suffolk County
94	94	34.5	Port Jefferson Station (CDP) Suffolk County
97	97	34.4	Lynnfield (cdp/town) Essex County
98	98	34.3	Kings Park (CDP) Suffolk County
98	98	34.3	North Babylon (CDP) Suffolk County
98	98	34.3	West Babylon (CDP) Suffolk County
101	101	34.2	Totowa (borough) Passaic County
102	102	34.1	Ellwood City (borough) Lawrence County
102	102	34.1	Stoneham (cdp/town) Middlesex County
104	104	34.0	Cranston (city) Providence County
104	104	34.0	Shirley (CDP) Suffolk County
106	106	33.9	Pequannock (township) Morris County
106	106	33.9	Pine Lake Park (CDP) Ocean County
108	108	33.8	East Fishkill (town) Dutchess County
108	108	33.8	Montrose (CDP) Westchester County
110	110	33.7	Locust Valley (CDP) Nassau County
110	110	33.7	Neshannock (township) Lawrence County
110	110	33.7	West Bay Shore (CDP) Suffolk County
110	110	33.7	Yorktown (town) Westchester County
114	114	33.6	Holiday City South (CDP) Ocean County
114	114	33.6	Kenmore (village) Erie County
114	114	33.6	Lacey (township) Ocean County
114	114	33.6	Prospect (town) New Haven County
114	114	33.6	Roseland (borough) Essex County
114	114	33.6	Wantagh (CDP) Nassau County
120	120	33.5	Waldwick (borough) Bergen County
120	120	33.5	Wolcott (town) New Haven County
122	122	33.4	East Shoreham (CDP) Suffolk County
122	122	33.4	South Huntington (CDP) Suffolk County
122	122	33.4	West Sayville (CDP) Suffolk County
125	125	33.3	Exeter (borough) Luzerne County
125	125	33.3	Toms River (township) Ocean County
127	127	33.2	East Williston (village) Nassau County
127	127	33.2	Lyndhurst (township) Bergen County
129	129	33.1	Lake Ronkonkoma (CDP) Suffolk County
129	129	33.1	Toms River (CDP) Ocean County
129	129	33.1	Westerly (CDP) Washington County
132	132	33.0	Cold Spring Harbor (CDP) Suffolk County
132	132	33.0	Mount Sinai (CDP) Suffolk County
134	134	32.9	Hasbrouck Heights (borough) Bergen County
134	134	32.9	Stafford (township) Ocean County
136	136	32.8	Berlin (town) Hartford County
136	136	32.8	Galeville (CDP) Onondaga County
136	136	32.8	West Caldwell (township) Essex County
139	139	32.7	Putnam Valley (town) Putnam County
139	139	32.7	Sound Beach (CDP) Suffolk County
141	141	32.6	Babylon (village) Suffolk County
141	141	32.6	Centereach (CDP) Suffolk County
141	141	32.6	Elwood (CDP) Suffolk County
141	141	32.6	Middletown (township) Monmouth County
141	141	32.6	North Patchogue (CDP) Suffolk County
146	146	32.5	Lincroft (CDP) Monmouth County
147	147	32.4	Barnegat (township) Ocean County
147	147	32.4	Caldwell (borough) Essex County
147	147	32.4	Levittown (CDP) Nassau County
147	147	32.4	Oceanport (borough) Monmouth County

Note: The state column ranks the top/bottom 150 places in the state with population of 2,500 or more. The national column ranks the top/bottom places in the country with population of 10,000 or more. Places that are unincorporated were not considered in the rankings. n/a indicates data not available. Please refer to the User Guide for additional information.

Employment: Management, Business, and Financial Occupations

Top 150 Places Ranked in *Descending* Order

State Rank	Nat'l Rank	Percent	Place
1	n/a	33.5	**Tega Cay** (city) York County
2	n/a	26.8	**Isle of Palms** (city) Charleston County
3	239	26.5	**Five Forks** (CDP) Greenville County
4	n/a	24.8	**Lake Wylie** (CDP) York County
5	515	22.9	**Mount Pleasant** (town) Charleston County
6	619	21.9	**Fort Mill** (town) York County
6	619	21.9	**Lexington** (town) Lexington County
8	n/a	21.5	**Lake Murray of Richland** (CDP) Richland County
9	n/a	19.2	**Northlake** (CDP) Anderson County
10	n/a	18.9	**Barnwell** (city) Barnwell County
11	1214	18.0	**Beaufort** (city) Beaufort County
12	1311	17.5	**Hilton Head Island** (town) Beaufort County
12	1311	17.5	**Summerville** (town) Dorchester County
14	1375	17.2	**Aiken** (city) Aiken County
15	1479	16.7	**Bluffton** (town) Beaufort County
16	n/a	16.5	**Clover** (town) York County
17	1577	16.3	**Greenville** (city) Greenville County
18	n/a	16.2	**Ridgeland** (town) Jasper County
18	1600	16.2	**Seven Oaks** (CDP) Lexington County
20	n/a	16.1	**Dalzell** (CDP) Sumter County
21	1644	16.0	**Forest Acres** (city) Richland County
21	n/a	16.0	**Lakewood** (CDP) Sumter County
23	1695	15.8	**Charleston** (city) Charleston County
23	1695	15.8	**North Augusta** (city) Aiken County
25	1749	15.6	**Goose Creek** (city) Berkeley County
26	n/a	15.4	**Camden** (city) Kershaw County
26	n/a	15.4	**Lugoff** (CDP) Kershaw County
28	n/a	14.9	**Bamberg** (town) Bamberg County
28	n/a	14.9	**Garden City** (CDP) Horry County
30	1957	14.8	**Irmo** (town) Richland County
30	n/a	14.8	**Murrells Inlet** (CDP) Georgetown County
32	n/a	14.5	**Honea Path** (town) Anderson County
33	n/a	14.4	**Georgetown** (city) Georgetown County
34	n/a	14.3	**Belton** (city) Anderson County
35	n/a	14.1	**Folly Beach** (city) Charleston County
35	2155	14.1	**Greer** (city) Greenville County
35	n/a	14.1	**Seneca** (city) Oconee County
38	2195	14.0	**Columbia** (city) Richland County
38	n/a	14.0	**India Hook** (CDP) York County
40	2224	13.9	**Florence** (city) Florence County
40	n/a	13.9	**North Hartsville** (CDP) Darlington County
42	n/a	13.7	**Andrews** (town) Georgetown County
42	2274	13.7	**Hanahan** (city) Berkeley County
42	2274	13.7	**Mauldin** (city) Greenville County
45	2393	13.3	**Wade Hampton** (CDP) Greenville County
46	n/a	13.2	**Batesburg-Leesville** (town) Lexington County
46	n/a	13.2	**Pickens** (city) Pickens County
48	2520	13.0	**Clemson** (city) Pickens County
48	2520	13.0	**North Myrtle Beach** (city) Horry County
50	n/a	12.9	**Little River** (CDP) Horry County
51	n/a	12.8	**Fountain Inn** (city) Greenville County
51	n/a	12.8	**Lesslie** (CDP) York County
51	2579	12.8	**Simpsonville** (city) Greenville County
51	n/a	12.8	**Winnsboro** (town) Fairfield County
55	2697	12.4	**Rock Hill** (city) York County
56	2733	12.3	**Oak Grove** (CDP) Lexington County
57	n/a	12.2	**Hollywood** (town) Charleston County
57	n/a	12.2	**Pendleton** (town) Anderson County
59	2808	12.1	**Cayce** (city) Lexington County
59	2808	12.1	**Taylors** (CDP) Greenville County
61	n/a	11.9	**Boiling Springs** (CDP) Spartanburg County
62	n/a	11.8	**Dunean** (CDP) Greenville County
63	n/a	11.7	**Springdale** (town) Lexington County
64	n/a	11.6	**Moncks Corner** (town) Berkeley County
65	n/a	11.5	**Bennettsville** (city) Marlboro County
65	3023	11.5	**Easley** (city) Pickens County
65	n/a	11.5	**Travelers Rest** (city) Greenville County
65	3023	11.5	**West Columbia** (city) Lexington County
69	n/a	11.4	**Dillon** (city) Dillon County
69	n/a	11.4	**Red Bank** (CDP) Lexington County
71	n/a	11.3	**Cheraw** (town) Chesterfield County
71	3101	11.3	**Red Hill** (CDP) Horry County
71	n/a	11.3	**Williston** (town) Barnwell County
74	n/a	11.2	**Centerville** (CDP) Anderson County
74	n/a	11.2	**Hampton** (town) Hampton County
76	n/a	11.1	**Allendale** (town) Allendale County
77	n/a	11.0	**Duncan** (town) Spartanburg County
78	3303	10.7	**Anderson** (city) Anderson County
79	n/a	10.6	**Belvedere** (CDP) Aiken County
80	3397	10.4	**Spartanburg** (city) Spartanburg County
81	3433	10.3	**Socastee** (CDP) Horry County
82	n/a	10.2	**Darlington** (city) Darlington County
83	3512	10.1	**Conway** (city) Horry County
83	n/a	10.1	**Forestbrook** (CDP) Horry County
85	n/a	10.0	**Hartsville** (city) Darlington County
85	3549	10.0	**Orangeburg** (city) Orangeburg County
87	n/a	9.9	**Newport** (CDP) York County
88	3616	9.8	**Sumter** (city) Sumter County
89	n/a	9.7	**Central** (town) Pickens County
89	n/a	9.7	**Manning** (city) Clarendon County
89	3653	9.7	**Saint Andrews** (CDP) Richland County
92	n/a	9.5	**Abbeville** (city) Abbeville County
93	n/a	9.4	**Saluda** (town) Saluda County
94	n/a	9.3	**Laurens** (city) Laurens County
94	3794	9.3	**Port Royal** (town) Beaufort County
96	3825	9.2	**Gaffney** (city) Cherokee County
96	3825	9.2	**Myrtle Beach** (city) Horry County
96	3825	9.2	**North Charleston** (city) Charleston County
99	n/a	9.1	**Arial** (CDP) Pickens County
100	n/a	9.0	**Union** (city) Union County
101	n/a	8.9	**York** (city) York County
102	n/a	8.8	**Piedmont** (CDP) Anderson County
103	n/a	8.7	**Mullins** (city) Marion County
103	n/a	8.7	**Sangaree** (CDP) Berkeley County
103	n/a	8.7	**Woodfield** (CDP) Richland County
106	n/a	8.4	**Springdale** (CDP) Lancaster County
107	4138	8.2	**Dentsville** (CDP) Richland County
108	n/a	8.1	**Lake City** (city) Florence County
109	n/a	8.0	**Burnettown** (town) Aiken County
109	n/a	8.0	**McCormick** (town) McCormick County
111	n/a	7.9	**Burton** (CDP) Beaufort County
111	4201	7.9	**Ladson** (CDP) Berkeley County
113	n/a	7.8	**Sans Souci** (CDP) Greenville County
114	n/a	7.7	**Woodruff** (city) Spartanburg County
115	4251	7.6	**Gantt** (CDP) Greenville County
116	n/a	7.5	**Edisto** (CDP) Orangeburg County
116	n/a	7.5	**Welcome** (CDP) Greenville County
118	n/a	7.4	**Walhalla** (city) Oconee County
119	n/a	7.2	**Hardeeville** (city) Jasper County
119	n/a	7.2	**Hopkins** (CDP) Richland County
119	n/a	7.2	**Surfside Beach** (town) Horry County
122	n/a	7.1	**Denmark** (city) Bamberg County
122	4346	7.1	**Newberry** (city) Newberry County
124	n/a	6.6	**Chester** (city) Chester County
124	n/a	6.6	**Kingstree** (town) Williamsburg County
124	n/a	6.6	**Walterboro** (city) Colleton County
127	n/a	6.5	**Lyman** (town) Spartanburg County
128	4491	6.1	**Berea** (CDP) Greenville County
128	n/a	6.1	**Valley Falls** (CDP) Spartanburg County
130	n/a	6.0	**Brookdale** (CDP) Orangeburg County
130	n/a	6.0	**Clinton** (city) Laurens County
132	n/a	5.7	**Laurel Bay** (CDP) Beaufort County
132	n/a	5.7	**Liberty** (city) Pickens County
134	n/a	5.5	**Graniteville** (CDP) Aiken County
135	n/a	5.4	**Marion** (city) Marion County
136	n/a	5.3	**Arcadia** (CDP) Spartanburg County
137	4572	5.1	**Parker** (CDP) Greenville County
138	4590	4.8	**Greenwood** (city) Greenwood County
138	n/a	4.8	**Lancaster** (city) Lancaster County
140	n/a	4.7	**Gloverville** (CDP) Aiken County
141	n/a	4.6	**Edgefield** (town) Edgefield County
142	n/a	4.2	**Elgin** (CDP) Lancaster County
143	n/a	4.1	**Williamston** (town) Anderson County
144	n/a	3.6	**Bishopville** (city) Lee County
144	n/a	3.6	**Pageland** (town) Chesterfield County
146	n/a	3.4	**Saxon** (CDP) Spartanburg County
147	n/a	3.2	**Clearwater** (CDP) Aiken County
148	n/a	2.6	**East Gaffney** (CDP) Cherokee County
149	n/a	2.4	**Homeland Park** (CDP) Anderson County
150	n/a	1.5	**Southern Shops** (CDP) Spartanburg County

Note: The state column ranks the top/bottom 150 places in the state with population of 2,500 or more. The national column ranks the top/bottom places in the country with population of 10,000 or more. Places that are unincorporated were not considered in the rankings. n/a indicates data not available. Please refer to the User Guide for additional information.

Employment: Management, Business, and Financial Occupations

Top 150 Places Ranked in *Ascending* Order

State Rank	Nat'l Rank	Percent	Place
1	n/a	1.5	**Southern Shops** (CDP) Spartanburg County
2	n/a	2.4	**Homeland Park** (CDP) Anderson County
3	n/a	2.6	**East Gaffney** (CDP) Cherokee County
4	n/a	3.2	**Clearwater** (CDP) Aiken County
5	n/a	3.4	**Saxon** (CDP) Spartanburg County
6	n/a	3.6	**Bishopville** (city) Lee County
6	n/a	3.6	**Pageland** (town) Chesterfield County
8	n/a	4.1	**Williamston** (town) Anderson County
9	n/a	4.2	**Elgin** (CDP) Lancaster County
10	n/a	4.6	**Edgefield** (town) Edgefield County
11	n/a	4.7	**Gloverville** (CDP) Aiken County
12	62	4.8	**Greenwood** (city) Greenwood County
12	n/a	4.8	**Lancaster** (city) Lancaster County
14	74	5.1	**Parker** (CDP) Greenville County
15	n/a	5.3	**Arcadia** (CDP) Spartanburg County
16	n/a	5.4	**Marion** (city) Marion County
17	n/a	5.5	**Graniteville** (CDP) Aiken County
18	n/a	5.7	**Laurel Bay** (CDP) Beaufort County
18	n/a	5.7	**Liberty** (city) Pickens County
20	n/a	6.0	**Brookdale** (CDP) Orangeburg County
20	n/a	6.0	**Clinton** (city) Laurens County
22	157	6.1	**Berea** (CDP) Greenville County
22	n/a	6.1	**Valley Falls** (CDP) Spartanburg County
24	n/a	6.5	**Lyman** (town) Spartanburg County
25	n/a	6.6	**Chester** (city) Chester County
25	n/a	6.6	**Kingstree** (town) Williamsburg County
25	n/a	6.6	**Walterboro** (city) Colleton County
28	n/a	7.1	**Denmark** (city) Bamberg County
28	288	7.1	**Newberry** (city) Newberry County
30	n/a	7.2	**Hardeeville** (city) Jasper County
30	n/a	7.2	**Hopkins** (CDP) Richland County
30	n/a	7.2	**Surfside Beach** (town) Horry County
33	n/a	7.4	**Walhalla** (city) Oconee County
34	n/a	7.5	**Edisto** (CDP) Orangeburg County
34	n/a	7.5	**Welcome** (CDP) Greenville County
36	380	7.6	**Gantt** (CDP) Greenville County
37	n/a	7.7	**Woodruff** (city) Spartanburg County
38	n/a	7.8	**Sans Souci** (CDP) Greenville County
39	n/a	7.9	**Burton** (CDP) Beaufort County
39	439	7.9	**Ladson** (CDP) Berkeley County
41	n/a	8.0	**Burnettown** (town) Aiken County
41	n/a	8.0	**McCormick** (town) McCormick County
43	n/a	8.1	**Lake City** (city) Florence County
44	497	8.2	**Dentsville** (CDP) Richland County
45	n/a	8.4	**Springdale** (CDP) Lancaster County
46	n/a	8.7	**Mullins** (city) Marion County
46	n/a	8.7	**Sangaree** (CDP) Berkeley County
46	n/a	8.7	**Woodfield** (CDP) Richland County
49	n/a	8.8	**Piedmont** (CDP) Anderson County
50	n/a	8.9	**York** (city) York County
51	n/a	9.0	**Union** (city) Union County
52	n/a	9.1	**Arial** (CDP) Pickens County
53	789	9.2	**Gaffney** (city) Cherokee County
53	789	9.2	**Myrtle Beach** (city) Horry County
53	789	9.2	**North Charleston** (city) Charleston County
56	n/a	9.3	**Laurens** (city) Laurens County
56	832	9.3	**Port Royal** (town) Beaufort County
58	n/a	9.4	**Saluda** (town) Saluda County
59	n/a	9.5	**Abbeville** (city) Abbeville County
60	n/a	9.7	**Central** (town) Pickens County
60	n/a	9.7	**Manning** (city) Clarendon County
60	977	9.7	**Saint Andrews** (CDP) Richland County
63	1004	9.8	**Sumter** (city) Sumter County
64	n/a	9.9	**Newport** (CDP) York County
65	n/a	10.0	**Hartsville** (city) Darlington County
65	1067	10.0	**Orangeburg** (city) Orangeburg County
67	1108	10.1	**Conway** (city) Horry County
67	n/a	10.1	**Forestbrook** (CDP) Horry County
69	n/a	10.2	**Darlington** (city) Darlington County
70	1177	10.3	**Socastee** (CDP) Horry County
71	1224	10.4	**Spartanburg** (city) Spartanburg County
72	n/a	10.6	**Belvedere** (CDP) Aiken County
73	1321	10.7	**Anderson** (city) Anderson County
74	n/a	11.0	**Duncan** (town) Spartanburg County
75	n/a	11.1	**Allendale** (town) Allendale County
76	n/a	11.2	**Centerville** (CDP) Anderson County
76	n/a	11.2	**Hampton** (town) Hampton County
78	n/a	11.3	**Cheraw** (town) Chesterfield County
78	1524	11.3	**Red Hill** (CDP) Horry County
78	n/a	11.3	**Williston** (town) Barnwell County
81	n/a	11.4	**Dillon** (city) Dillon County
81	n/a	11.4	**Red Bank** (CDP) Lexington County
83	n/a	11.5	**Bennettsville** (city) Marlboro County
83	1596	11.5	**Easley** (city) Pickens County
83	n/a	11.5	**Travelers Rest** (city) Greenville County
83	1596	11.5	**West Columbia** (city) Lexington County
87	n/a	11.6	**Moncks Corner** (town) Berkeley County
88	n/a	11.7	**Springdale** (town) Lexington County
89	n/a	11.8	**Dunean** (CDP) Greenville County
90	n/a	11.9	**Boiling Springs** (CDP) Spartanburg County
91	1815	12.1	**Cayce** (city) Lexington County
91	1815	12.1	**Taylors** (CDP) Greenville County
93	n/a	12.2	**Hollywood** (town) Charleston County
93	n/a	12.2	**Pendleton** (town) Anderson County
95	1886	12.3	**Oak Grove** (CDP) Lexington County
96	1924	12.4	**Rock Hill** (city) York County
97	n/a	12.8	**Fountain Inn** (city) Greenville County
97	n/a	12.8	**Lesslie** (CDP) York County
97	2044	12.8	**Simpsonville** (city) Greenville County
97	n/a	12.8	**Winnsboro** (town) Fairfield County
101	n/a	12.9	**Little River** (CDP) Horry County
102	2106	13.0	**Clemson** (city) Pickens County
102	2106	13.0	**North Myrtle Beach** (city) Horry County
104	n/a	13.2	**Batesburg-Leesville** (town) Lexington County
104	n/a	13.2	**Pickens** (city) Pickens County
106	2221	13.3	**Wade Hampton** (CDP) Greenville County
107	n/a	13.7	**Andrews** (town) Georgetown County
107	2346	13.7	**Hanahan** (city) Berkeley County
107	2346	13.7	**Mauldin** (city) Greenville County
110	2412	13.9	**Florence** (city) Florence County
110	n/a	13.9	**North Hartsville** (CDP) Darlington County
112	2433	14.0	**Columbia** (city) Richland County
112	n/a	14.0	**India Hook** (CDP) York County
114	n/a	14.1	**Folly Beach** (city) Charleston County
114	2462	14.1	**Greer** (city) Greenville County
114	n/a	14.1	**Seneca** (city) Oconee County
117	n/a	14.3	**Belton** (city) Anderson County
118	n/a	14.4	**Georgetown** (city) Georgetown County
119	n/a	14.5	**Honea Path** (town) Anderson County
120	2674	14.8	**Irmo** (town) Richland County
120	n/a	14.8	**Murrells Inlet** (CDP) Georgetown County
122	n/a	14.9	**Bamberg** (town) Bamberg County
122	n/a	14.9	**Garden City** (CDP) Horry County
124	n/a	15.4	**Camden** (city) Kershaw County
124	n/a	15.4	**Lugoff** (CDP) Kershaw County
126	2885	15.6	**Goose Creek** (city) Berkeley County
127	2935	15.8	**Charleston** (city) Charleston County
127	2935	15.8	**North Augusta** (city) Aiken County
129	2986	16.0	**Forest Acres** (city) Richland County
129	n/a	16.0	**Lakewood** (CDP) Sumter County
131	n/a	16.1	**Dalzell** (CDP) Sumter County
132	n/a	16.2	**Ridgeland** (town) Jasper County
132	3039	16.2	**Seven Oaks** (CDP) Lexington County
134	3057	16.3	**Greenville** (city) Greenville County
135	n/a	16.5	**Clover** (town) York County
136	3150	16.7	**Bluffton** (town) Beaufort County
137	3256	17.2	**Aiken** (city) Aiken County
138	3321	17.5	**Hilton Head Island** (town) Beaufort County
138	3321	17.5	**Summerville** (town) Dorchester County
140	3426	18.0	**Beaufort** (city) Beaufort County
141	n/a	18.9	**Barnwell** (city) Barnwell County
142	n/a	19.2	**Northlake** (CDP) Anderson County
143	n/a	21.5	**Lake Murray of Richland** (CDP) Richland County
144	4023	21.9	**Fort Mill** (town) York County
144	4023	21.9	**Lexington** (town) Lexington County
146	4129	22.9	**Mount Pleasant** (town) Charleston County
147	n/a	24.8	**Lake Wylie** (CDP) York County
148	4413	26.5	**Five Forks** (CDP) Greenville County
149	n/a	26.8	**Isle of Palms** (city) Charleston County
150	n/a	33.5	**Tega Cay** (city) York County

Note: *The state column ranks the top/bottom 150 places in the state with population of 2,500 or more. The national column ranks the top/bottom places in the country with population of 10,000 or more. Places that are unincorporated were not considered in the rankings. n/a indicates data not available. Please refer to the User Guide for additional information.*

Employment: Computer, Engineering, and Science Occupations

Top 150 Places Ranked in *Descending* Order

State Rank	Nat'l Rank	Percent	Place
1	239	12.1	**Five Forks** (CDP) Greenville County
2	n/a	10.0	**Elgin** (CDP) Lancaster County
3	n/a	9.9	**Folly Beach** (city) Charleston County
4	478	9.8	**Mauldin** (city) Greenville County
5	490	9.7	**Aiken** (city) Aiken County
6	n/a	9.4	**Lake Wylie** (CDP) York County
7	667	8.7	**Clemson** (city) Pickens County
8	n/a	8.3	**Tega Cay** (city) York County
9	n/a	8.2	**Isle of Palms** (city) Charleston County
10	n/a	7.9	**India Hook** (CDP) York County
11	n/a	7.8	**Lake Murray of Richland** (CDP) Richland County
12	n/a	7.6	**Central** (town) Pickens County
12	957	7.6	**Dentsville** (CDP) Richland County
12	n/a	7.6	**Hartsville** (city) Darlington County
15	n/a	7.5	**Forestbrook** (CDP) Horry County
16	1061	7.3	**North Augusta** (city) Aiken County
17	1097	7.2	**Mount Pleasant** (town) Charleston County
17	1097	7.2	**Wade Hampton** (CDP) Greenville County
19	1137	7.1	**Irmo** (town) Richland County
20	1224	6.9	**Simpsonville** (city) Greenville County
21	n/a	6.4	**Northlake** (CDP) Anderson County
22	1484	6.3	**Taylors** (CDP) Greenville County
23	1579	6.1	**Charleston** (city) Charleston County
24	1624	6.0	**Greenville** (city) Greenville County
24	n/a	6.0	**Newport** (CDP) York County
24	1624	6.0	**Seven Oaks** (CDP) Lexington County
27	1682	5.9	**Greer** (city) Greenville County
27	1682	5.9	**Lexington** (town) Lexington County
29	1952	5.4	**Goose Creek** (city) Berkeley County
29	n/a	5.4	**Sangaree** (CDP) Berkeley County
31	n/a	5.3	**Centerville** (CDP) Anderson County
31	n/a	5.3	**Sans Souci** (CDP) Greenville County
31	n/a	5.3	**Seneca** (city) Oconee County
31	n/a	5.3	**Williston** (town) Barnwell County
35	n/a	5.2	**Boiling Springs** (CDP) Spartanburg County
35	2067	5.2	**Fort Mill** (town) York County
35	2067	5.2	**Ladson** (CDP) Berkeley County
38	2126	5.1	**Cayce** (city) Lexington County
39	2178	5.0	**Hanahan** (city) Berkeley County
40	2244	4.9	**Columbia** (city) Richland County
40	2244	4.9	**Easley** (city) Pickens County
40	2244	4.9	**North Charleston** (city) Charleston County
40	2244	4.9	**Summerville** (town) Dorchester County
44	2311	4.8	**Forest Acres** (city) Richland County
45	2376	4.7	**Sumter** (city) Sumter County
46	n/a	4.6	**Clearwater** (CDP) Aiken County
47	2496	4.5	**Port Royal** (town) Beaufort County
48	n/a	4.4	**Fountain Inn** (city) Greenville County
48	n/a	4.4	**Lesslie** (CDP) York County
48	n/a	4.4	**Travelers Rest** (city) Greenville County
51	2703	4.2	**Rock Hill** (city) York County
52	n/a	4.0	**Burnettown** (town) Aiken County
52	n/a	4.0	**Moncks Corner** (town) Berkeley County
54	n/a	3.9	**Lyman** (town) Spartanburg County
55	2972	3.8	**Berea** (CDP) Greenville County
55	n/a	3.8	**Red Bank** (CDP) Lexington County
57	3030	3.7	**West Columbia** (city) Lexington County
58	3093	3.6	**Florence** (city) Florence County
58	n/a	3.6	**Lakewood** (CDP) Sumter County
58	n/a	3.6	**Springdale** (town) Lexington County
61	n/a	3.5	**Pendleton** (town) Anderson County
61	n/a	3.5	**Williamston** (town) Anderson County
63	3220	3.4	**Orangeburg** (city) Orangeburg County
63	n/a	3.4	**Pickens** (city) Pickens County
63	3220	3.4	**Saint Andrews** (CDP) Richland County
66	n/a	3.3	**Arial** (CDP) Pickens County
66	n/a	3.3	**North Hartsville** (CDP) Darlington County
68	3358	3.2	**Greenwood** (city) Greenwood County
69	n/a	3.0	**Batesburg-Leesville** (town) Lexington County
69	n/a	3.0	**Bishopville** (city) Lee County
69	n/a	3.0	**Brookdale** (CDP) Orangeburg County
69	n/a	3.0	**Little River** (CDP) Horry County
73	n/a	2.9	**Belton** (city) Anderson County
74	n/a	2.8	**Clover** (town) York County
74	n/a	2.8	**Darlington** (city) Darlington County
74	3632	2.8	**Oak Grove** (CDP) Lexington County
74	3632	2.8	**Spartanburg** (city) Spartanburg County
78	n/a	2.7	**Marion** (city) Marion County
79	3764	2.6	**Anderson** (city) Anderson County
80	n/a	2.5	**Bamberg** (town) Bamberg County
80	3837	2.5	**Gaffney** (city) Cherokee County
80	3837	2.5	**Gantt** (CDP) Greenville County
80	3837	2.5	**Hilton Head Island** (town) Beaufort County
84	n/a	2.4	**Edisto** (CDP) Orangeburg County
84	n/a	2.4	**Honea Path** (town) Anderson County
84	n/a	2.4	**Lugoff** (CDP) Kershaw County
84	n/a	2.4	**Mullins** (city) Marion County
88	3953	2.3	**Myrtle Beach** (city) Horry County
89	n/a	2.2	**Camden** (city) Kershaw County
89	n/a	2.2	**East Gaffney** (CDP) Cherokee County
89	n/a	2.2	**Woodruff** (city) Spartanburg County
92	n/a	2.1	**Belvedere** (CDP) Aiken County
92	n/a	2.1	**Homeland Park** (CDP) Anderson County
94	n/a	2.0	**Woodfield** (CDP) Richland County
95	4178	1.9	**Beaufort** (city) Beaufort County
95	n/a	1.9	**Dunean** (CDP) Greenville County
95	n/a	1.9	**Hardeeville** (city) Jasper County
95	n/a	1.9	**Murrells Inlet** (CDP) Georgetown County
95	n/a	1.9	**Welcome** (CDP) Greenville County
100	n/a	1.8	**Barnwell** (city) Barnwell County
100	4232	1.8	**Conway** (city) Horry County
100	n/a	1.8	**Edgefield** (town) Edgefield County
100	n/a	1.8	**Laurel Bay** (CDP) Beaufort County
100	4232	1.8	**Newberry** (city) Newberry County
105	4332	1.6	**Bluffton** (town) Beaufort County
105	n/a	1.6	**Dalzell** (CDP) Sumter County
105	n/a	1.6	**Laurens** (city) Laurens County
108	n/a	1.5	**Hollywood** (town) Charleston County
108	4374	1.5	**North Myrtle Beach** (city) Horry County
110	n/a	1.4	**Garden City** (CDP) Horry County
110	4418	1.4	**Socastee** (CDP) Horry County
110	n/a	1.4	**Springdale** (CDP) Lancaster County
113	n/a	1.3	**Surfside Beach** (town) Horry County
114	n/a	1.2	**Burton** (CDP) Beaufort County
114	4485	1.2	**Red Hill** (CDP) Horry County
114	n/a	1.2	**Walterboro** (city) Colleton County
117	n/a	1.1	**Abbeville** (city) Abbeville County
118	n/a	1.0	**Chester** (city) Chester County
119	n/a	0.9	**Bennettsville** (city) Marlboro County
119	n/a	0.9	**Graniteville** (CDP) Aiken County
121	n/a	0.8	**Clinton** (city) Laurens County
121	n/a	0.8	**Lancaster** (city) Lancaster County
123	n/a	0.7	**Hampton** (town) Hampton County
124	n/a	0.6	**Dillon** (city) Dillon County
124	n/a	0.6	**Southern Shops** (CDP) Spartanburg County
124	n/a	0.6	**Valley Falls** (CDP) Spartanburg County
124	n/a	0.6	**Walhalla** (city) Oconee County
128	n/a	0.4	**Piedmont** (CDP) Anderson County
129	4636	0.3	**Parker** (CDP) Greenville County
129	n/a	0.3	**Ridgeland** (town) Jasper County
129	n/a	0.3	**Union** (city) Union County
129	n/a	0.3	**York** (city) York County
133	n/a	0.2	**Pageland** (town) Chesterfield County
133	n/a	0.2	**Saxon** (CDP) Spartanburg County
135	n/a	0.1	**Saluda** (town) Saluda County
136	n/a	0.0	**Allendale** (town) Allendale County
136	n/a	0.0	**Andrews** (town) Georgetown County
136	n/a	0.0	**Arcadia** (CDP) Spartanburg County
136	n/a	0.0	**Cheraw** (town) Chesterfield County
136	n/a	0.0	**Denmark** (city) Bamberg County
136	n/a	0.0	**Duncan** (town) Spartanburg County
136	n/a	0.0	**Georgetown** (city) Georgetown County
136	n/a	0.0	**Gloverville** (CDP) Aiken County
136	n/a	0.0	**Hopkins** (CDP) Richland County
136	n/a	0.0	**Kingstree** (town) Williamsburg County
136	n/a	0.0	**Lake City** (city) Florence County
136	n/a	0.0	**Liberty** (city) Pickens County
136	n/a	0.0	**Manning** (city) Clarendon County
136	n/a	0.0	**McCormick** (town) McCormick County
136	n/a	0.0	**Winnsboro** (town) Fairfield County

Note: The state column ranks the top/bottom 150 places in the state with population of 2,500 or more. The national column ranks the top/bottom places in the country with population of 10,000 or more. Places that are unincorporated were not considered in the rankings. n/a indicates data not available. Please refer to the User Guide for additional information.

Employment: Computer, Engineering, and Science Occupations

Top 150 Places Ranked in *Ascending* Order

State Rank	Nat'l Rank	Percent	Place		State Rank	Nat'l Rank	Percent	Place
1	n/a	0.0	Allendale (town) Allendale County		74	952	2.8	Oak Grove (CDP) Lexington County
1	n/a	0.0	Andrews (town) Georgetown County		74	952	2.8	Spartanburg (city) Spartanburg County
1	n/a	0.0	Arcadia (CDP) Spartanburg County		78	n/a	2.9	Belton (city) Anderson County
1	n/a	0.0	Cheraw (town) Chesterfield County		79	n/a	3.0	Batesburg-Leesville (town) Lexington County
1	n/a	0.0	Denmark (city) Bamberg County		79	n/a	3.0	Bishopville (city) Lee County
1	n/a	0.0	Duncan (town) Spartanburg County		79	n/a	3.0	Brookdale (CDP) Orangeburg County
1	n/a	0.0	Georgetown (city) Georgetown County		79	n/a	3.0	Little River (CDP) Horry County
1	n/a	0.0	Gloverville (CDP) Aiken County		83	1222	3.2	Greenwood (city) Greenwood County
1	n/a	0.0	Hopkins (CDP) Richland County		84	n/a	3.3	Arial (CDP) Pickens County
1	n/a	0.0	Kingstree (town) Williamsburg County		84	n/a	3.3	North Hartsville (CDP) Darlington County
1	n/a	0.0	Lake City (city) Florence County		86	1360	3.4	Orangeburg (city) Orangeburg County
1	n/a	0.0	Liberty (city) Pickens County		86	n/a	3.4	Pickens (city) Pickens County
1	n/a	0.0	Manning (city) Clarendon County		86	1360	3.4	Saint Andrews (CDP) Richland County
1	n/a	0.0	McCormick (town) McCormick County		89	n/a	3.5	Pendleton (town) Anderson County
1	n/a	0.0	Winnsboro (town) Fairfield County		89	n/a	3.5	Williamston (town) Anderson County
16	n/a	0.1	Saluda (town) Saluda County		91	1500	3.6	Florence (city) Florence County
17	n/a	0.2	Pageland (town) Chesterfield County		91	n/a	3.6	Lakewood (CDP) Sumter County
17	n/a	0.2	Saxon (CDP) Spartanburg County		91	n/a	3.6	Springdale (town) Lexington County
19	13	0.3	Parker (CDP) Greenville County		94	1564	3.7	West Columbia (city) Lexington County
19	n/a	0.3	Ridgeland (town) Jasper County		95	1627	3.8	Berea (CDP) Greenville County
19	n/a	0.3	Union (city) Union County		95	n/a	3.8	Red Bank (CDP) Lexington County
19	n/a	0.3	York (city) York County		97	n/a	3.9	Lyman (town) Spartanburg County
23	n/a	0.4	Piedmont (CDP) Anderson County		98	n/a	4.0	Burnettown (town) Aiken County
24	n/a	0.6	Dillon (city) Dillon County		98	n/a	4.0	Moncks Corner (town) Berkeley County
24	n/a	0.6	Southern Shops (CDP) Spartanburg County		100	1880	4.2	Rock Hill (city) York County
24	n/a	0.6	Valley Falls (CDP) Spartanburg County		101	n/a	4.4	Fountain Inn (city) Greenville County
24	n/a	0.6	Walhalla (city) Oconee County		101	n/a	4.4	Lesslie (CDP) York County
28	n/a	0.7	Hampton (town) Hampton County		101	n/a	4.4	Travelers Rest (city) Greenville County
29	n/a	0.8	Clinton (city) Laurens County		104	2074	4.5	Port Royal (town) Beaufort County
29	n/a	0.8	Lancaster (city) Lancaster County		105	n/a	4.6	Clearwater (CDP) Aiken County
31	n/a	0.9	Bennettsville (city) Marlboro County		106	2229	4.7	Sumter (city) Sumter County
31	n/a	0.9	Graniteville (CDP) Aiken County		107	2281	4.8	Forest Acres (city) Richland County
33	n/a	1.0	Chester (city) Chester County		108	2346	4.9	Columbia (city) Richland County
34	n/a	1.1	Abbeville (city) Abbeville County		108	2346	4.9	Easley (city) Pickens County
35	n/a	1.2	Burton (CDP) Beaufort County		108	2346	4.9	North Charleston (city) Charleston County
35	150	1.2	Red Hill (CDP) Horry County		108	2346	4.9	Summerville (town) Dorchester County
35	n/a	1.2	Walterboro (city) Colleton County		112	2413	5.0	Hanahan (city) Berkeley County
38	n/a	1.3	Surfside Beach (town) Horry County		113	2479	5.1	Cayce (city) Lexington County
39	n/a	1.4	Garden City (CDP) Horry County		114	n/a	5.2	Boiling Springs (CDP) Spartanburg County
39	202	1.4	Socastee (CDP) Horry County		114	2531	5.2	Fort Mill (town) York County
39	n/a	1.4	Springdale (CDP) Lancaster County		114	2531	5.2	Ladson (CDP) Berkeley County
42	n/a	1.5	Hollywood (town) Charleston County		117	n/a	5.3	Centerville (CDP) Anderson County
42	239	1.5	North Myrtle Beach (city) Horry County		117	n/a	5.3	Sans Souci (CDP) Greenville County
44	283	1.6	Bluffton (town) Beaufort County		117	n/a	5.3	Seneca (city) Oconee County
44	n/a	1.6	Dalzell (CDP) Sumter County		117	n/a	5.3	Williston (town) Barnwell County
44	n/a	1.6	Laurens (city) Laurens County		121	2646	5.4	Goose Creek (city) Berkeley County
47	n/a	1.8	Barnwell (city) Barnwell County		121	n/a	5.4	Sangaree (CDP) Berkeley County
47	360	1.8	Conway (city) Horry County		123	2922	5.9	Greer (city) Greenville County
47	n/a	1.8	Edgefield (town) Edgefield County		123	2922	5.9	Lexington (town) Lexington County
47	n/a	1.8	Laurel Bay (CDP) Beaufort County		125	2975	6.0	Greenville (city) Greenville County
47	360	1.8	Newberry (city) Newberry County		125	n/a	6.0	Newport (CDP) York County
52	425	1.9	Beaufort (city) Beaufort County		125	2975	6.0	Seven Oaks (CDP) Lexington County
52	n/a	1.9	Dunean (CDP) Greenville County		128	3033	6.1	Charleston (city) Charleston County
52	n/a	1.9	Hardeeville (city) Jasper County		129	3122	6.3	Taylors (CDP) Greenville County
52	n/a	1.9	Murrells Inlet (CDP) Georgetown County		130	n/a	6.4	Northlake (CDP) Anderson County
52	n/a	1.9	Welcome (CDP) Greenville County		131	3390	6.9	Simpsonville (city) Greenville County
57	n/a	2.0	Woodfield (CDP) Richland County		132	3467	7.1	Irmo (town) Richland County
58	n/a	2.1	Belvedere (CDP) Aiken County		133	3520	7.2	Mount Pleasant (town) Charleston County
58	n/a	2.1	Homeland Park (CDP) Anderson County		133	3520	7.2	Wade Hampton (CDP) Greenville County
60	n/a	2.2	Camden (city) Kershaw County		135	3560	7.3	North Augusta (city) Aiken County
60	n/a	2.2	East Gaffney (CDP) Cherokee County		136	n/a	7.5	Forestbrook (CDP) Horry County
60	n/a	2.2	Woodruff (city) Spartanburg County		137	n/a	7.6	Central (town) Pickens County
63	649	2.3	Myrtle Beach (city) Horry County		137	3665	7.6	Dentsville (CDP) Richland County
64	n/a	2.4	Edisto (CDP) Orangeburg County		137	n/a	7.6	Hartsville (city) Darlington County
64	n/a	2.4	Honea Path (town) Anderson County		140	n/a	7.8	Lake Murray of Richland (CDP) Richland County
64	n/a	2.4	Lugoff (CDP) Kershaw County		141	n/a	7.9	India Hook (CDP) York County
64	n/a	2.4	Mullins (city) Marion County		142	n/a	8.2	Isle of Palms (city) Charleston County
68	n/a	2.5	Bamberg (town) Bamberg County		143	n/a	8.3	Tega Cay (city) York County
68	754	2.5	Gaffney (city) Cherokee County		144	3962	8.7	Clemson (city) Pickens County
68	754	2.5	Gantt (CDP) Greenville County		145	n/a	9.4	Lake Wylie (CDP) York County
68	754	2.5	Hilton Head Island (town) Beaufort County		146	4143	9.7	Aiken (city) Aiken County
72	820	2.6	Anderson (city) Anderson County		147	4167	9.8	Mauldin (city) Greenville County
73	n/a	2.7	Marion (city) Marion County		148	n/a	9.9	Folly Beach (city) Charleston County
74	n/a	2.8	Clover (town) York County		149	n/a	10.0	Elgin (CDP) Lancaster County
74	n/a	2.8	Darlington (city) Darlington County		150	4411	12.1	Five Forks (CDP) Greenville County

Note: *The state column ranks the top/bottom 150 places in the state with population of 2,500 or more. The national column ranks the top/bottom places in the country with population of 10,000 or more. Places that are unincorporated were not considered in the rankings. n/a indicates data not available. Please refer to the User Guide for additional information.*

Employment: Education, Legal, Community Service, Arts, and Media Occupations
Top 150 Places Ranked in *Descending* Order

State Rank	Nat'l Rank	Percent	Place
1	16	27.4	**Clemson** (city) Pickens County
2	n/a	25.7	**Pendleton** (town) Anderson County
3	53	23.9	**Forest Acres** (city) Richland County
4	n/a	22.6	**Hartsville** (city) Darlington County
5	n/a	21.6	**Central** (town) Pickens County
6	n/a	20.2	**Isle of Palms** (city) Charleston County
7	n/a	19.7	**Edisto** (CDP) Orangeburg County
8	205	19.2	**Port Royal** (town) Beaufort County
9	n/a	19.1	**Allendale** (town) Allendale County
10	n/a	18.0	**Union** (city) Union County
11	n/a	17.5	**Barnwell** (city) Barnwell County
12	n/a	17.2	**Darlington** (city) Darlington County
13	376	16.7	**Columbia** (city) Richland County
14	386	16.6	**Orangeburg** (city) Orangeburg County
15	n/a	16.4	**Hampton** (town) Hampton County
15	n/a	16.4	**Newport** (CDP) York County
17	n/a	16.1	**Boiling Springs** (CDP) Spartanburg County
18	n/a	15.6	**Clinton** (city) Laurens County
19	550	15.4	**Lexington** (town) Lexington County
20	n/a	15.2	**Honea Path** (town) Anderson County
20	583	15.2	**Seven Oaks** (CDP) Lexington County
22	n/a	14.5	**Dalzell** (CDP) Sumter County
22	718	14.5	**West Columbia** (city) Lexington County
24	771	14.3	**Greenville** (city) Greenville County
24	771	14.3	**Spartanburg** (city) Spartanburg County
24	n/a	14.3	**Tega Cay** (city) York County
27	824	14.1	**Florence** (city) Florence County
28	n/a	14.0	**Georgetown** (city) Georgetown County
29	n/a	13.8	**Lake Murray of Richland** (CDP) Richland County
30	n/a	13.5	**Camden** (city) Kershaw County
31	1021	13.4	**Charleston** (city) Charleston County
31	n/a	13.4	**Valley Falls** (CDP) Spartanburg County
33	1079	13.2	**Sumter** (city) Sumter County
34	n/a	13.1	**Marion** (city) Marion County
35	1188	12.9	**Irmo** (town) Richland County
36	1228	12.8	**Mount Pleasant** (town) Charleston County
37	1307	12.6	**North Augusta** (city) Aiken County
37	1307	12.6	**Saint Andrews** (CDP) Richland County
39	1346	12.5	**Newberry** (city) Newberry County
40	1460	12.2	**Wade Hampton** (CDP) Greenville County
40	n/a	12.2	**Winnsboro** (town) Fairfield County
42	1505	12.1	**Aiken** (city) Aiken County
42	n/a	12.1	**Fountain Inn** (city) Greenville County
42	n/a	12.1	**Lancaster** (city) Lancaster County
42	n/a	12.1	**North Hartsville** (CDP) Darlington County
42	n/a	12.1	**Surfside Beach** (town) Horry County
47	1552	12.0	**North Myrtle Beach** (city) Horry County
48	n/a	11.9	**Batesburg-Leesville** (town) Lexington County
49	1642	11.8	**Gaffney** (city) Cherokee County
50	n/a	11.7	**Abbeville** (city) Abbeville County
51	n/a	11.6	**Burton** (CDP) Beaufort County
51	1745	11.6	**Conway** (city) Horry County
51	n/a	11.6	**McCormick** (town) McCormick County
54	n/a	11.5	**Lyman** (town) Spartanburg County
55	1841	11.4	**Beaufort** (city) Beaufort County
55	1841	11.4	**Rock Hill** (city) York County
57	1945	11.2	**Goose Creek** (city) Berkeley County
57	n/a	11.2	**Walhalla** (city) Oconee County
59	n/a	11.1	**Centerville** (CDP) Anderson County
60	n/a	11.0	**Red Bank** (CDP) Lexington County
61	n/a	10.8	**Bennettsville** (city) Marlboro County
61	2158	10.8	**Fort Mill** (town) York County
61	n/a	10.8	**Williston** (town) Barnwell County
64	2211	10.7	**Five Forks** (CDP) Greenville County
64	n/a	10.7	**Williamston** (town) Anderson County
66	n/a	10.6	**Hardeeville** (city) Jasper County
67	n/a	10.5	**Lake City** (city) Florence County
68	n/a	10.4	**Bamberg** (town) Bamberg County
69	2466	10.3	**Mauldin** (city) Greenville County
69	n/a	10.3	**Murrells Inlet** (CDP) Georgetown County
71	n/a	10.2	**Brookdale** (CDP) Orangeburg County
71	n/a	10.2	**Cheraw** (town) Chesterfield County
71	n/a	10.2	**Lugoff** (CDP) Kershaw County
74	n/a	10.1	**Clover** (town) York County
74	2588	10.1	**Greenwood** (city) Greenwood County
74	n/a	10.1	**Northlake** (CDP) Anderson County
77	2650	10.0	**Anderson** (city) Anderson County
77	n/a	10.0	**Hollywood** (town) Charleston County
77	n/a	10.0	**Kingstree** (town) Williamsburg County
77	n/a	10.0	**Liberty** (city) Pickens County
77	2650	10.0	**Summerville** (town) Dorchester County
82	2719	9.9	**Dentsville** (CDP) Richland County
83	2775	9.8	**Easley** (city) Pickens County
84	2823	9.7	**Cayce** (city) Lexington County
84	n/a	9.7	**Travelers Rest** (city) Greenville County
86	n/a	9.6	**Belvedere** (CDP) Aiken County
86	2888	9.6	**Bluffton** (town) Beaufort County
86	n/a	9.6	**Springdale** (town) Lexington County
89	3049	9.3	**Red Hill** (CDP) Horry County
90	n/a	9.2	**Edgefield** (town) Edgefield County
90	n/a	9.2	**Lake Wylie** (CDP) York County
92	n/a	9.1	**Sangaree** (CDP) Berkeley County
92	n/a	9.1	**Seneca** (city) Oconee County
94	n/a	9.0	**Manning** (city) Clarendon County
94	3217	9.0	**Taylors** (CDP) Greenville County
94	n/a	9.0	**Walterboro** (city) Colleton County
97	3269	8.9	**Hilton Head Island** (town) Beaufort County
97	n/a	8.9	**Lakewood** (CDP) Sumter County
97	3269	8.9	**Myrtle Beach** (city) Horry County
100	n/a	8.6	**Bishopville** (city) Lee County
100	n/a	8.6	**Chester** (city) Chester County
100	n/a	8.6	**Lesslie** (CDP) York County
103	n/a	8.5	**Belton** (city) Anderson County
103	n/a	8.5	**Garden City** (CDP) Horry County
105	3539	8.4	**Oak Grove** (CDP) Lexington County
106	3634	8.2	**Greer** (city) Greenville County
107	3680	8.1	**Simpsonville** (city) Greenville County
108	n/a	8.0	**Graniteville** (CDP) Aiken County
108	n/a	8.0	**Pickens** (city) Pickens County
110	n/a	7.4	**Dillon** (city) Dillon County
110	3975	7.4	**Hanahan** (city) Berkeley County
110	n/a	7.4	**Laurens** (city) Laurens County
113	n/a	7.3	**Elgin** (CDP) Lancaster County
114	n/a	7.0	**Moncks Corner** (town) Berkeley County
115	4224	6.7	**North Charleston** (city) Charleston County
115	n/a	6.7	**Woodruff** (city) Spartanburg County
117	n/a	6.6	**Hopkins** (CDP) Richland County
117	n/a	6.6	**Little River** (CDP) Horry County
117	n/a	6.6	**Saxon** (CDP) Spartanburg County
120	4273	6.5	**Socastee** (CDP) Horry County
121	n/a	6.3	**Mullins** (city) Marion County
122	n/a	6.2	**Burnettown** (town) Aiken County
122	n/a	6.2	**Laurel Bay** (CDP) Beaufort County
124	n/a	6.1	**Woodfield** (CDP) Richland County
125	n/a	6.0	**Andrews** (town) Georgetown County
125	n/a	6.0	**Folly Beach** (city) Charleston County
125	n/a	6.0	**Springdale** (CDP) Lancaster County
128	4437	5.8	**Gantt** (CDP) Greenville County
128	n/a	5.8	**Sans Souci** (CDP) Greenville County
130	n/a	5.7	**Forestbrook** (CDP) Horry County
131	n/a	5.4	**Gloverville** (CDP) Aiken County
132	n/a	5.3	**Arcadia** (CDP) Spartanburg County
132	4510	5.3	**Berea** (CDP) Greenville County
132	4510	5.3	**Parker** (CDP) Greenville County
135	4535	5.1	**Ladson** (CDP) Berkeley County
136	n/a	4.9	**India Hook** (CDP) York County
137	n/a	4.8	**Saluda** (town) Saluda County
138	n/a	4.3	**East Gaffney** (CDP) Cherokee County
138	n/a	4.3	**Piedmont** (CDP) Anderson County
140	n/a	4.1	**Dunean** (CDP) Greenville County
141	n/a	4.0	**Clearwater** (CDP) Aiken County
141	n/a	4.0	**Pageland** (town) Chesterfield County
143	n/a	3.9	**Duncan** (town) Spartanburg County
144	n/a	3.8	**Welcome** (CDP) Greenville County
145	n/a	3.4	**York** (city) York County
146	n/a	3.2	**Denmark** (city) Bamberg County
147	n/a	3.0	**Arial** (CDP) Pickens County
148	n/a	2.5	**Southern Shops** (CDP) Spartanburg County
149	n/a	2.0	**Homeland Park** (CDP) Anderson County
150	n/a	1.9	**Ridgeland** (town) Jasper County

Note: The state column ranks the top/bottom 150 places in the state with population of 2,500 or more. The national column ranks the top/bottom places in the country with population of 10,000 or more. Places that are unincorporated were not considered in the rankings. n/a indicates data not available. Please refer to the User Guide for additional information.

Employment: Education, Legal, Community Service, Arts, and Media Occupations

Top 150 Places Ranked in *Ascending* Order

State Rank	Nat'l Rank	Percent	Place
1	n/a	1.9	**Ridgeland** (town) Jasper County
2	n/a	2.0	**Homeland Park** (CDP) Anderson County
3	n/a	2.5	**Southern Shops** (CDP) Spartanburg County
4	n/a	3.0	**Arial** (CDP) Pickens County
5	n/a	3.2	**Denmark** (city) Bamberg County
6	n/a	3.4	**York** (city) York County
7	n/a	3.8	**Welcome** (CDP) Greenville County
8	n/a	3.9	**Duncan** (town) Spartanburg County
9	n/a	4.0	**Clearwater** (CDP) Aiken County
9	n/a	4.0	**Pageland** (town) Chesterfield County
11	n/a	4.1	**Dunean** (CDP) Greenville County
12	n/a	4.3	**East Gaffney** (CDP) Cherokee County
12	n/a	4.3	**Piedmont** (CDP) Anderson County
14	n/a	4.8	**Saluda** (town) Saluda County
15	n/a	4.9	**India Hook** (CDP) York County
16	110	5.1	**Ladson** (CDP) Berkeley County
17	136	5.3	**Arcadia** (CDP) Spartanburg County
17	136	5.3	**Berea** (CDP) Greenville County
17	136	5.3	**Parker** (CDP) Greenville County
20	n/a	5.4	**Gloverville** (CDP) Aiken County
21	n/a	5.7	**Forestbrook** (CDP) Horry County
22	203	5.8	**Gantt** (CDP) Greenville County
22	n/a	5.8	**Sans Souci** (CDP) Greenville County
24	n/a	6.0	**Andrews** (town) Georgetown County
24	n/a	6.0	**Folly Beach** (city) Charleston County
24	n/a	6.0	**Springdale** (CDP) Lancaster County
27	n/a	6.1	**Woodfield** (CDP) Richland County
28	n/a	6.2	**Burnettown** (town) Aiken County
28	n/a	6.2	**Laurel Bay** (CDP) Beaufort County
30	n/a	6.3	**Mullins** (city) Marion County
31	353	6.5	**Socastee** (CDP) Horry County
32	n/a	6.6	**Hopkins** (CDP) Richland County
32	n/a	6.6	**Little River** (CDP) Horry County
32	n/a	6.6	**Saxon** (CDP) Spartanburg County
35	409	6.7	**North Charleston** (city) Charleston County
35	n/a	6.7	**Woodruff** (city) Spartanburg County
37	n/a	7.0	**Moncks Corner** (town) Berkeley County
38	n/a	7.3	**Elgin** (CDP) Lancaster County
39	n/a	7.4	**Dillon** (city) Dillon County
39	646	7.4	**Hanahan** (city) Berkeley County
39	n/a	7.4	**Laurens** (city) Laurens County
42	n/a	8.0	**Graniteville** (CDP) Aiken County
42	n/a	8.0	**Pickens** (city) Pickens County
44	936	8.1	**Simpsonville** (city) Greenville County
45	977	8.2	**Greer** (city) Greenville County
46	1067	8.4	**Oak Grove** (CDP) Lexington County
47	n/a	8.5	**Belton** (city) Anderson County
47	n/a	8.5	**Garden City** (CDP) Horry County
49	n/a	8.6	**Bishopville** (city) Lee County
49	n/a	8.6	**Chester** (city) Chester County
49	n/a	8.6	**Lesslie** (CDP) York County
52	1329	8.9	**Hilton Head Island** (town) Beaufort County
52	n/a	8.9	**Lakewood** (CDP) Sumter County
52	1329	8.9	**Myrtle Beach** (city) Horry County
55	n/a	9.0	**Manning** (city) Clarendon County
55	1388	9.0	**Taylors** (CDP) Greenville County
55	n/a	9.0	**Walterboro** (city) Colleton County
58	n/a	9.1	**Sangaree** (CDP) Berkeley County
58	n/a	9.1	**Seneca** (city) Oconee County
60	n/a	9.2	**Edgefield** (town) Edgefield County
60	n/a	9.2	**Lake Wylie** (CDP) York County
62	1546	9.3	**Red Hill** (CDP) Horry County
63	n/a	9.6	**Belvedere** (CDP) Aiken County
63	1715	9.6	**Bluffton** (town) Beaufort County
63	n/a	9.6	**Springdale** (town) Lexington County
66	1769	9.7	**Cayce** (city) Lexington County
66	n/a	9.7	**Travelers Rest** (city) Greenville County
68	1834	9.8	**Easley** (city) Pickens County
69	1882	9.9	**Dentsville** (CDP) Richland County
70	1938	10.0	**Anderson** (city) Anderson County
70	n/a	10.0	**Hollywood** (town) Charleston County
70	n/a	10.0	**Kingstree** (town) Williamsburg County
70	n/a	10.0	**Liberty** (city) Pickens County
70	1938	10.0	**Summerville** (town) Dorchester County
75	n/a	10.1	**Clover** (town) York County
75	2007	10.1	**Greenwood** (city) Greenwood County
75	n/a	10.1	**Northlake** (CDP) Anderson County
78	n/a	10.2	**Brookdale** (CDP) Orangeburg County
78	n/a	10.2	**Cheraw** (town) Chesterfield County
78	n/a	10.2	**Lugoff** (CDP) Kershaw County
81	2128	10.3	**Mauldin** (city) Greenville County
81	n/a	10.3	**Murrells Inlet** (CDP) Georgetown County
83	n/a	10.4	**Bamberg** (town) Bamberg County
84	n/a	10.5	**Lake City** (city) Florence County
85	n/a	10.6	**Hardeeville** (city) Jasper County
86	2374	10.7	**Five Forks** (CDP) Greenville County
86	n/a	10.7	**Williamston** (town) Anderson County
88	n/a	10.8	**Bennettsville** (city) Marlboro County
88	2446	10.8	**Fort Mill** (town) York County
88	n/a	10.8	**Williston** (town) Barnwell County
91	n/a	11.0	**Red Bank** (CDP) Lexington County
92	n/a	11.1	**Centerville** (CDP) Anderson County
93	2659	11.2	**Goose Creek** (city) Berkeley County
93	n/a	11.2	**Walhalla** (city) Oconee County
95	2760	11.4	**Beaufort** (city) Beaufort County
95	2760	11.4	**Rock Hill** (city) York County
97	n/a	11.5	**Lyman** (town) Spartanburg County
98	n/a	11.6	**Burton** (CDP) Beaufort County
98	2854	11.6	**Conway** (city) Horry County
98	n/a	11.6	**McCormick** (town) McCormick County
101	n/a	11.7	**Abbeville** (city) Abbeville County
102	2959	11.8	**Gaffney** (city) Cherokee County
103	n/a	11.9	**Batesburg-Leesville** (town) Lexington County
104	3071	12.0	**North Myrtle Beach** (city) Horry County
105	3105	12.1	**Aiken** (city) Aiken County
105	n/a	12.1	**Fountain Inn** (city) Greenville County
105	n/a	12.1	**Lancaster** (city) Lancaster County
105	n/a	12.1	**North Hartsville** (CDP) Darlington County
105	n/a	12.1	**Surfside Beach** (town) Horry County
110	3152	12.2	**Wade Hampton** (CDP) Greenville County
110	n/a	12.2	**Winnsboro** (town) Fairfield County
112	3277	12.5	**Newberry** (city) Newberry County
113	3311	12.6	**North Augusta** (city) Aiken County
113	3311	12.6	**Saint Andrews** (CDP) Richland County
115	3394	12.8	**Mount Pleasant** (town) Charleston County
116	3429	12.9	**Irmo** (town) Richland County
117	n/a	13.1	**Marion** (city) Marion County
118	3540	13.2	**Sumter** (city) Sumter County
119	3612	13.4	**Charleston** (city) Charleston County
119	n/a	13.4	**Valley Falls** (CDP) Spartanburg County
121	n/a	13.5	**Camden** (city) Kershaw County
122	n/a	13.8	**Lake Murray of Richland** (CDP) Richland County
123	n/a	14.0	**Georgetown** (city) Georgetown County
124	3806	14.1	**Florence** (city) Florence County
125	3862	14.3	**Greenville** (city) Greenville County
125	3862	14.3	**Spartanburg** (city) Spartanburg County
125	n/a	14.3	**Tega Cay** (city) York County
128	n/a	14.5	**Dalzell** (CDP) Sumter County
128	3913	14.5	**West Columbia** (city) Lexington County
130	n/a	15.2	**Honea Path** (town) Anderson County
130	4053	15.2	**Seven Oaks** (CDP) Lexington County
132	4091	15.4	**Lexington** (town) Lexington County
133	n/a	15.6	**Clinton** (city) Laurens County
134	n/a	16.1	**Boiling Springs** (CDP) Spartanburg County
135	n/a	16.4	**Hampton** (town) Hampton County
135	n/a	16.4	**Newport** (CDP) York County
137	4260	16.6	**Orangeburg** (city) Orangeburg County
138	4271	16.7	**Columbia** (city) Richland County
139	n/a	17.2	**Darlington** (city) Darlington County
140	n/a	17.5	**Barnwell** (city) Barnwell County
141	n/a	18.0	**Union** (city) Union County
142	n/a	19.1	**Allendale** (town) Allendale County
143	4446	19.2	**Port Royal** (town) Beaufort County
144	n/a	19.7	**Edisto** (CDP) Orangeburg County
145	n/a	20.2	**Isle of Palms** (city) Charleston County
146	n/a	21.6	**Central** (town) Pickens County
147	n/a	22.6	**Hartsville** (city) Darlington County
148	4602	23.9	**Forest Acres** (city) Richland County
149	n/a	25.7	**Pendleton** (town) Anderson County
150	4640	27.4	**Clemson** (city) Pickens County

Note: The state column ranks the top/bottom 150 places in the state with population of 2,500 or more. The national column ranks the top/bottom places in the country with population of 10,000 or more. Places that are unincorporated were not considered in the rankings. n/a indicates data not available. Please refer to the User Guide for additional information.

Employment: Healthcare Practitioners

Top 150 Places Ranked in *Descending* Order

State Rank	Nat'l Rank	Percent	Place	State Rank	Nat'l Rank	Percent	Place
1	n/a	13.9	**Newport** (CDP) York County	75	n/a	4.9	**Piedmont** (CDP) Anderson County
2	n/a	12.4	**India Hook** (CDP) York County	77	3071	4.8	**Irmo** (town) Richland County
3	n/a	12.1	**Manning** (city) Clarendon County	78	3155	4.7	**Hilton Head Island** (town) Beaufort County
4	n/a	11.6	**Lake Murray of Richland** (CDP) Richland County	78	n/a	4.7	**Pendleton** (town) Anderson County
5	79	11.4	**North Augusta** (city) Aiken County	78	n/a	4.7	**Union** (city) Union County
6	n/a	10.8	**Camden** (city) Kershaw County	81	n/a	4.6	**Darlington** (city) Darlington County
7	118	10.7	**Florence** (city) Florence County	81	n/a	4.6	**Laurens** (city) Laurens County
8	n/a	10.6	**Bishopville** (city) Lee County	83	3312	4.5	**Conway** (city) Horry County
9	n/a	9.8	**Lakewood** (CDP) Sumter County	83	3312	4.5	**Fort Mill** (town) York County
9	n/a	9.8	**Williston** (town) Barnwell County	85	n/a	4.4	**Cheraw** (town) Chesterfield County
11	n/a	9.7	**Walterboro** (city) Colleton County	85	n/a	4.4	**Dunean** (CDP) Greenville County
12	279	9.4	**Charleston** (city) Charleston County	85	3409	4.4	**North Myrtle Beach** (city) Horry County
12	279	9.4	**Mount Pleasant** (town) Charleston County	85	3409	4.4	**Rock Hill** (city) York County
14	n/a	9.2	**Isle of Palms** (city) Charleston County	89	n/a	4.3	**Chester** (city) Chester County
14	n/a	9.2	**Murrells Inlet** (CDP) Georgetown County	89	n/a	4.3	**Clover** (town) York County
16	356	9.0	**Five Forks** (CDP) Greenville County	89	3506	4.3	**North Charleston** (city) Charleston County
17	n/a	8.3	**Centerville** (CDP) Anderson County	89	n/a	4.3	**Travelers Rest** (city) Greenville County
18	n/a	8.2	**Dalzell** (CDP) Sumter County	93	n/a	4.2	**Kingstree** (town) Williamsburg County
18	559	8.2	**Lexington** (town) Lexington County	93	n/a	4.2	**Williamston** (town) Anderson County
20	n/a	8.1	**Forestbrook** (CDP) Horry County	95	n/a	4.0	**Edisto** (CDP) Orangeburg County
20	n/a	8.1	**Seneca** (city) Oconee County	95	n/a	4.0	**Ridgeland** (town) Jasper County
22	n/a	8.0	**Bamberg** (town) Bamberg County	97	3781	3.9	**Ladson** (CDP) Berkeley County
23	n/a	7.9	**Bennettsville** (city) Marlboro County	97	3781	3.9	**Seven Oaks** (CDP) Lexington County
24	n/a	7.7	**Marion** (city) Marion County	99	n/a	3.8	**Abbeville** (city) Abbeville County
25	n/a	7.6	**Boiling Springs** (CDP) Spartanburg County	99	n/a	3.8	**Lake Wylie** (CDP) York County
26	903	7.4	**Greenville** (city) Greenville County	101	3897	3.7	**Goose Creek** (city) Berkeley County
27	n/a	7.3	**Red Bank** (CDP) Lexington County	101	n/a	3.7	**Hampton** (town) Hampton County
28	n/a	7.2	**Springdale** (CDP) Lancaster County	101	n/a	3.7	**Hartsville** (city) Darlington County
29	n/a	7.1	**Lugoff** (CDP) Kershaw County	101	n/a	3.7	**Lancaster** (city) Lancaster County
29	1083	7.1	**Sumter** (city) Sumter County	101	n/a	3.7	**Woodfield** (CDP) Richland County
29	n/a	7.1	**Surfside Beach** (town) Horry County	106	n/a	3.6	**Garden City** (CDP) Horry County
32	n/a	7.0	**Gloverville** (CDP) Aiken County	107	4062	3.4	**Simpsonville** (city) Greenville County
32	1138	7.0	**Greenwood** (city) Greenwood County	108	n/a	3.3	**Burnettown** (town) Aiken County
34	n/a	6.9	**Belvedere** (CDP) Aiken County	108	n/a	3.3	**Sans Souci** (CDP) Greenville County
34	1192	6.9	**Cayce** (city) Lexington County	110	n/a	3.2	**Honea Path** (town) Anderson County
36	n/a	6.8	**Andrews** (town) Georgetown County	110	n/a	3.2	**North Hartsville** (CDP) Darlington County
36	n/a	6.8	**Clearwater** (CDP) Aiken County	112	n/a	3.1	**Lake City** (city) Florence County
38	1339	6.7	**Mauldin** (city) Greenville County	112	n/a	3.1	**Lesslie** (CDP) York County
38	1339	6.7	**Taylors** (CDP) Greenville County	112	4220	3.1	**Orangeburg** (city) Orangeburg County
40	1488	6.5	**Spartanburg** (city) Spartanburg County	115	n/a	3.0	**Mullins** (city) Marion County
41	1560	6.4	**Gantt** (CDP) Greenville County	116	n/a	2.9	**Hardeeville** (city) Jasper County
41	1560	6.4	**Wade Hampton** (CDP) Greenville County	117	n/a	2.8	**Burton** (CDP) Beaufort County
43	1625	6.3	**Aiken** (city) Aiken County	117	4337	2.8	**Red Hill** (CDP) Horry County
43	1625	6.3	**Greer** (city) Greenville County	119	n/a	2.7	**Homeland Park** (CDP) Anderson County
45	1723	6.2	**Anderson** (city) Anderson County	119	n/a	2.7	**Saxon** (CDP) Spartanburg County
45	1723	6.2	**Columbia** (city) Richland County	119	n/a	2.7	**Walhalla** (city) Oconee County
45	n/a	6.2	**Hollywood** (town) Charleston County	122	n/a	2.6	**Clinton** (city) Laurens County
48	n/a	6.1	**Duncan** (town) Spartanburg County	122	n/a	2.6	**Moncks Corner** (town) Berkeley County
48	n/a	6.1	**Graniteville** (CDP) Aiken County	124	n/a	2.5	**East Gaffney** (CDP) Cherokee County
48	1812	6.1	**Myrtle Beach** (city) Horry County	125	n/a	2.4	**Barnwell** (city) Barnwell County
48	n/a	6.1	**Northlake** (CDP) Anderson County	125	4459	2.4	**Berea** (CDP) Greenville County
52	1919	6.0	**Dentsville** (CDP) Richland County	125	n/a	2.4	**Denmark** (city) Bamberg County
52	1919	6.0	**Forest Acres** (city) Richland County	125	n/a	2.4	**McCormick** (town) McCormick County
52	n/a	6.0	**Liberty** (city) Pickens County	129	n/a	2.2	**Lyman** (town) Spartanburg County
52	n/a	6.0	**Springdale** (town) Lexington County	129	n/a	2.2	**Pageland** (town) Chesterfield County
56	2017	5.9	**Bluffton** (town) Beaufort County	131	n/a	2.1	**Georgetown** (city) Georgetown County
56	2017	5.9	**Easley** (city) Pickens County	131	n/a	2.1	**Little River** (CDP) Horry County
56	2017	5.9	**Oak Grove** (CDP) Lexington County	131	n/a	2.1	**Pickens** (city) Pickens County
59	2114	5.8	**Beaufort** (city) Beaufort County	131	n/a	2.1	**Sangaree** (CDP) Berkeley County
60	n/a	5.7	**Dillon** (city) Dillon County	131	n/a	2.1	**York** (city) York County
60	n/a	5.7	**Valley Falls** (CDP) Spartanburg County	136	n/a	2.0	**Edgefield** (town) Edgefield County
62	2328	5.6	**Socastee** (CDP) Horry County	137	n/a	1.8	**Laurel Bay** (CDP) Beaufort County
62	2328	5.6	**Summerville** (town) Dorchester County	138	4577	1.7	**Gaffney** (city) Cherokee County
64	2423	5.5	**Clemson** (city) Pickens County	139	n/a	1.5	**Fountain Inn** (city) Greenville County
64	· n/a	5.5	**Folly Beach** (city) Charleston County	140	4608	1.4	**Parker** (CDP) Greenville County
64	2423	5.5	**Newberry** (city) Newberry County	141	n/a	1.3	**Arcadia** (CDP) Spartanburg County
64	2423	5.5	**West Columbia** (city) Lexington County	142	n/a	1.2	**Southern Shops** (CDP) Spartanburg County
68	n/a	5.3	**Allendale** (town) Allendale County	143	n/a	1.1	**Batesburg-Leesville** (town) Lexington County
69	n/a	5.2	**Arial** (CDP) Pickens County	143	n/a	1.1	**Woodruff** (city) Spartanburg County
69	n/a	5.2	**Belton** (city) Anderson County	145	n/a	1.0	**Winnsboro** (town) Fairfield County
69	2696	5.2	**Port Royal** (town) Beaufort County	146	n/a	0.8	**Saluda** (town) Saluda County
69	2696	5.2	**Saint Andrews** (CDP) Richland County	147	n/a	0.5	**Hopkins** (CDP) Richland County
73	n/a	5.0	**Tega Cay** (city) York County	148	n/a	0.4	**Central** (town) Pickens County
73	n/a	5.0	**Welcome** (CDP) Greenville County	149	n/a	0.0	**Brookdale** (CDP) Orangeburg County
75	2977	4.9	**Hanahan** (city) Berkeley County	149	n/a	0.0	**Elgin** (CDP) Lancaster County

Note: The state column ranks the top/bottom 150 places in the state with population of 2,500 or more. The national column ranks the top/bottom places in the country with population of 10,000 or more. Places that are unincorporated were not considered in the rankings. n/a indicates data not available. Please refer to the User Guide for additional information.

Employment: Healthcare Practitioners

Top 150 Places Ranked in *Ascending* Order

State Rank	Nat'l Rank	Percent	Place
1	n/a	0.0	Brookdale (CDP) Orangeburg County
1	n/a	0.0	Elgin (CDP) Lancaster County
3	n/a	0.4	Central (town) Pickens County
4	n/a	0.5	Hopkins (CDP) Richland County
5	n/a	0.8	Saluda (town) Saluda County
6	n/a	1.0	Winnsboro (town) Fairfield County
7	n/a	1.1	Batesburg-Leesville (town) Lexington County
7	n/a	1.1	Woodruff (city) Spartanburg County
9	n/a	1.2	Southern Shops (CDP) Spartanburg County
10	n/a	1.3	Arcadia (CDP) Spartanburg County
11	41	1.4	Parker (CDP) Greenville County
12	n/a	1.5	Fountain Inn (city) Greenville County
13	71	1.7	Gaffney (city) Cherokee County
14	n/a	1.8	Laurel Bay (CDP) Beaufort County
15	n/a	2.0	Edgefield (town) Edgefield County
16	n/a	2.1	Georgetown (city) Georgetown County
16	n/a	2.1	Little River (CDP) Horry County
16	n/a	2.1	Pickens (city) Pickens County
16	n/a	2.1	Sangaree (CDP) Berkeley County
16	n/a	2.1	York (city) York County
21	n/a	2.2	Lyman (town) Spartanburg County
21	n/a	2.2	Pageland (town) Chesterfield County
23	n/a	2.4	Barnwell (city) Barnwell County
23	177	2.4	Berea (CDP) Greenville County
23	n/a	2.4	Denmark (city) Bamberg County
23	n/a	2.4	McCormick (town) McCormick County
27	n/a	2.5	East Gaffney (CDP) Cherokee County
28	n/a	2.6	Clinton (city) Laurens County
28	n/a	2.6	Moncks Corner (town) Berkeley County
30	n/a	2.7	Homeland Park (CDP) Anderson County
30	n/a	2.7	Saxon (CDP) Spartanburg County
30	n/a	2.7	Walhalla (city) Oconee County
33	n/a	2.8	Burton (CDP) Beaufort County
33	280	2.8	Red Hill (CDP) Horry County
35	n/a	2.9	Hardeeville (city) Jasper County
36	n/a	3.0	Mullins (city) Marion County
37	n/a	3.1	Lake City (city) Florence County
37	n/a	3.1	Lesslie (CDP) York County
37	396	3.1	Orangeburg (city) Orangeburg County
40	n/a	3.2	Honea Path (town) Anderson County
40	n/a	3.2	North Hartsville (CDP) Darlington County
42	n/a	3.3	Burnettown (town) Aiken County
42	n/a	3.3	Sans Souci (CDP) Greenville County
44	529	3.4	Simpsonville (city) Greenville County
45	n/a	3.6	Garden City (CDP) Horry County
46	706	3.7	Goose Creek (city) Berkeley County
46	n/a	3.7	Hampton (town) Hampton County
46	n/a	3.7	Hartsville (city) Darlington County
46	n/a	3.7	Lancaster (city) Lancaster County
46	n/a	3.7	Woodfield (CDP) Richland County
51	n/a	3.8	Abbeville (city) Abbeville County
51	n/a	3.8	Lake Wylie (CDP) York County
53	823	3.9	Ladson (CDP) Berkeley County
53	823	3.9	Seven Oaks (CDP) Lexington County
55	n/a	4.0	Edisto (CDP) Orangeburg County
55	n/a	4.0	Ridgeland (town) Jasper County
57	n/a	4.2	Kingstree (town) Williamsburg County
57	n/a	4.2	Williamston (town) Anderson County
59	n/a	4.3	Chester (city) Chester County
59	n/a	4.3	Clover (town) York County
59	1076	4.3	North Charleston (city) Charleston County
59	n/a	4.3	Travelers Rest (city) Greenville County
63	n/a	4.4	Cheraw (town) Chesterfield County
63	n/a	4.4	Dunean (CDP) Greenville County
63	1151	4.4	North Myrtle Beach (city) Horry County
63	1151	4.4	Rock Hill (city) York County
67	1248	4.5	Conway (city) Horry County
67	1248	4.5	Fort Mill (town) York County
69	n/a	4.6	Darlington (city) Darlington County
69	n/a	4.6	Laurens (city) Laurens County
71	1418	4.7	Hilton Head Island (town) Beaufort County
71	n/a	4.7	Pendleton (town) Anderson County
71	n/a	4.7	Union (city) Union County
74	1502	4.8	Irmo (town) Richland County
75	1586	4.9	Hanahan (city) Berkeley County
75	n/a	4.9	Piedmont (CDP) Anderson County
77	n/a	5.0	Tega Cay (city) York County
77	n/a	5.0	Welcome (CDP) Greenville County
79	n/a	5.2	Arial (CDP) Pickens County
79	n/a	5.2	Belton (city) Anderson County
79	1868	5.2	Port Royal (town) Beaufort County
79	1868	5.2	Saint Andrews (CDP) Richland County
83	n/a	5.3	Allendale (town) Allendale County
84	2138	5.5	Clemson (city) Pickens County
84	n/a	5.5	Folly Beach (city) Charleston County
84	2138	5.5	Newberry (city) Newberry County
84	2138	5.5	West Columbia (city) Lexington County
88	2234	5.6	Socastee (CDP) Horry County
88	2234	5.6	Summerville (town) Dorchester County
90	n/a	5.7	Dillon (city) Dillon County
90	n/a	5.7	Valley Falls (CDP) Spartanburg County
92	2446	5.8	Beaufort (city) Beaufort County
93	2543	5.9	Bluffton (town) Beaufort County
93	2543	5.9	Easley (city) Pickens County
93	2543	5.9	Oak Grove (CDP) Lexington County
96	2640	6.0	Dentsville (CDP) Richland County
96	2640	6.0	Forest Acres (city) Richland County
96	n/a	6.0	Liberty (city) Pickens County
96	n/a	6.0	Springdale (town) Lexington County
100	n/a	6.1	Duncan (town) Spartanburg County
100	n/a	6.1	Graniteville (CDP) Aiken County
100	2738	6.1	Myrtle Beach (city) Horry County
100	n/a	6.1	Northlake (CDP) Anderson County
104	2845	6.2	Anderson (city) Anderson County
104	2845	6.2	Columbia (city) Richland County
104	n/a	6.2	Hollywood (town) Charleston County
107	2934	6.3	Aiken (city) Aiken County
107	2934	6.3	Greer (city) Greenville County
109	3032	6.4	Gantt (CDP) Greenville County
109	3032	6.4	Wade Hampton (CDP) Greenville County
111	3097	6.5	Spartanburg (city) Spartanburg County
112	3253	6.7	Mauldin (city) Greenville County
112	3253	6.7	Taylors (CDP) Greenville County
114	n/a	6.8	Andrews (town) Georgetown County
114	n/a	6.8	Clearwater (CDP) Aiken County
116	n/a	6.9	Belvedere (CDP) Aiken County
116	3404	6.9	Cayce (city) Lexington County
118	n/a	7.0	Gloverville (CDP) Aiken County
118	3465	7.0	Greenwood (city) Greenwood County
120	n/a	7.1	Lugoff (CDP) Kershaw County
120	3519	7.1	Sumter (city) Sumter County
120	n/a	7.1	Surfside Beach (town) Horry County
123	n/a	7.2	Springdale (CDP) Lancaster County
124	n/a	7.3	Red Bank (CDP) Lexington County
125	3703	7.4	Greenville (city) Greenville County
126	n/a	7.6	Boiling Springs (CDP) Spartanburg County
127	n/a	7.7	Marion (city) Marion County
128	n/a	7.9	Bennettsville (city) Marlboro County
129	n/a	8.0	Bamberg (town) Bamberg County
130	n/a	8.1	Forestbrook (CDP) Horry County
130	n/a	8.1	Seneca (city) Oconee County
132	n/a	8.2	Dalzell (CDP) Sumter County
132	4060	8.2	Lexington (town) Lexington County
134	n/a	8.3	Centerville (CDP) Anderson County
135	4280	9.0	Five Forks (CDP) Greenville County
136	n/a	9.2	Isle of Palms (city) Charleston County
136	n/a	9.2	Murrells Inlet (CDP) Georgetown County
138	4363	9.4	Charleston (city) Charleston County
138	4363	9.4	Mount Pleasant (town) Charleston County
140	n/a	9.7	Walterboro (city) Colleton County
141	n/a	9.8	Lakewood (CDP) Sumter County
141	n/a	9.8	Williston (town) Barnwell County
143	n/a	10.6	Bishopville (city) Lee County
144	4528	10.7	Florence (city) Florence County
145	n/a	10.8	Camden (city) Kershaw County
146	4568	11.4	North Augusta (city) Aiken County
147	n/a	11.6	Lake Murray of Richland (CDP) Richland County
148	n/a	12.1	Manning (city) Clarendon County
149	n/a	12.4	India Hook (CDP) York County
150	n/a	13.9	Newport (CDP) York County

Note: *The state column ranks the top/bottom 150 places in the state with population of 2,500 or more. The national column ranks the top/bottom places in the country with population of 10,000 or more. Places that are unincorporated were not considered in the rankings. n/a indicates data not available. Please refer to the User Guide for additional information.*

Employment: Service Occupations

Top 150 Places Ranked in *Descending* Order

State Rank	Nat'l Rank	Percent	Place
1	n/a	35.7	**Folly Beach** (city) Charleston County
2	n/a	34.3	**Denmark** (city) Bamberg County
3	n/a	33.4	**Walterboro** (city) Colleton County
4	n/a	32.6	**Winnsboro** (town) Fairfield County
5	n/a	31.7	**Southern Shops** (CDP) Spartanburg County
6	n/a	31.5	**Central** (town) Pickens County
6	86	31.5	**Conway** (city) Horry County
8	n/a	31.4	**Kingstree** (town) Williamsburg County
8	n/a	31.4	**Manning** (city) Clarendon County
10	n/a	31.3	**Woodfield** (CDP) Richland County
11	n/a	31.0	**Dunean** (CDP) Greenville County
11	n/a	31.0	**Ridgeland** (town) Jasper County
11	n/a	31.0	**Saxon** (CDP) Spartanburg County
14	117	30.0	**Socastee** (CDP) Horry County
15	n/a	29.6	**Laurel Bay** (CDP) Beaufort County
16	n/a	29.3	**Laurens** (city) Laurens County
17	n/a	29.0	**Mullins** (city) Marion County
18	n/a	28.4	**Pageland** (town) Chesterfield County
19	205	28.1	**Myrtle Beach** (city) Horry County
20	n/a	28.0	**Williamston** (town) Anderson County
21	n/a	27.9	**Hampton** (town) Hampton County
22	220	27.8	**North Myrtle Beach** (city) Horry County
23	n/a	27.0	**Georgetown** (city) Georgetown County
24	n/a	26.8	**Valley Falls** (CDP) Spartanburg County
25	n/a	26.7	**Woodruff** (city) Spartanburg County
26	n/a	26.6	**Edisto** (CDP) Orangeburg County
27	n/a	26.4	**Abbeville** (city) Abbeville County
27	n/a	26.4	**Bishopville** (city) Lee County
29	n/a	26.3	**Surfside Beach** (town) Horry County
30	n/a	26.2	**Bamberg** (town) Bamberg County
31	n/a	25.6	**Little River** (CDP) Horry County
32	n/a	25.4	**Burton** (CDP) Beaufort County
32	n/a	25.4	**Piedmont** (CDP) Anderson County
34	407	25.3	**Parker** (CDP) Greenville County
35	n/a	25.2	**Hardeeville** (city) Jasper County
36	n/a	24.9	**Homeland Park** (CDP) Anderson County
37	n/a	24.8	**Lake City** (city) Florence County
37	n/a	24.8	**Marion** (city) Marion County
39	n/a	24.7	**Cheraw** (town) Chesterfield County
39	n/a	24.7	**Clinton** (city) Laurens County
41	n/a	24.6	**Dillon** (city) Dillon County
42	n/a	24.4	**Burnettown** (town) Aiken County
42	n/a	24.4	**McCormick** (town) McCormick County
42	n/a	24.4	**Travelers Rest** (city) Greenville County
45	n/a	24.2	**Forestbrook** (CDP) Horry County
46	n/a	24.0	**York** (city) York County
47	634	23.8	**Hilton Head Island** (town) Beaufort County
48	651	23.7	**Orangeburg** (city) Orangeburg County
49	n/a	23.5	**Allendale** (town) Allendale County
50	n/a	23.2	**Chester** (city) Chester County
51	n/a	23.1	**Hopkins** (CDP) Richland County
52	n/a	23.0	**Garden City** (CDP) Horry County
53	n/a	22.9	**Graniteville** (CDP) Aiken County
54	n/a	22.8	**Lancaster** (city) Lancaster County
55	841	22.7	**Berea** (CDP) Greenville County
56	859	22.6	**Saint Andrews** (CDP) Richland County
57	892	22.4	**Port Royal** (town) Beaufort County
58	n/a	22.2	**Dalzell** (CDP) Sumter County
58	940	22.2	**North Charleston** (city) Charleston County
60	983	22.0	**Bluffton** (town) Beaufort County
61	n/a	21.9	**Pickens** (city) Pickens County
61	1007	21.9	**Red Hill** (CDP) Horry County
63	n/a	21.8	**Moncks Corner** (town) Berkeley County
64	1060	21.7	**Anderson** (city) Anderson County
64	n/a	21.7	**Welcome** (CDP) Greenville County
66	n/a	21.5	**Arcadia** (CDP) Spartanburg County
66	n/a	21.5	**Lesslie** (CDP) York County
66	n/a	21.5	**Murrells Inlet** (CDP) Georgetown County
69	n/a	21.4	**Andrews** (town) Georgetown County
70	1222	21.1	**Columbia** (city) Richland County
71	n/a	21.0	**Sans Souci** (CDP) Greenville County
72	1386	20.5	**Ladson** (CDP) Berkeley County
72	n/a	20.5	**Pendleton** (town) Anderson County
74	n/a	20.4	**Springdale** (town) Lexington County
75	1475	20.2	**Cayce** (city) Lexington County
75	1475	20.2	**Charleston** (city) Charleston County
77	1505	20.1	**Sumter** (city) Sumter County
78	n/a	20.0	**Brookdale** (CDP) Orangeburg County
79	n/a	19.8	**Fountain Inn** (city) Greenville County
79	1592	19.8	**Greenwood** (city) Greenwood County
79	n/a	19.8	**Liberty** (city) Pickens County
82	n/a	19.7	**Hartsville** (city) Darlington County
83	1662	19.6	**Florence** (city) Florence County
83	n/a	19.6	**Seneca** (city) Oconee County
85	n/a	19.5	**Darlington** (city) Darlington County
86	n/a	19.4	**Batesburg-Leesville** (town) Lexington County
87	n/a	19.1	**Duncan** (town) Spartanburg County
88	1875	19.0	**Beaufort** (city) Beaufort County
88	1875	19.0	**Rock Hill** (city) York County
90	n/a	18.8	**Springdale** (CDP) Lancaster County
91	1971	18.7	**Hanahan** (city) Berkeley County
91	n/a	18.7	**Williston** (town) Barnwell County
93	2037	18.5	**Aiken** (city) Aiken County
94	n/a	18.4	**Edgefield** (town) Edgefield County
95	2095	18.3	**Taylors** (CDP) Greenville County
96	2158	18.1	**Gaffney** (city) Cherokee County
97	2185	18.0	**Spartanburg** (city) Spartanburg County
97	2185	18.0	**Summerville** (town) Dorchester County
99	n/a	17.9	**Walhalla** (city) Oconee County
100	2317	17.6	**Greenville** (city) Greenville County
100	2317	17.6	**Wade Hampton** (CDP) Greenville County
102	n/a	17.4	**Camden** (city) Kershaw County
103	n/a	17.1	**Honea Path** (town) Anderson County
104	2554	16.9	**Greer** (city) Greenville County
104	2554	16.9	**Newberry** (city) Newberry County
106	2607	16.7	**Seven Oaks** (CDP) Lexington County
106	2607	16.7	**West Columbia** (city) Lexington County
108	n/a	16.5	**Belvedere** (CDP) Aiken County
108	2692	16.5	**Easley** (city) Pickens County
108	2692	16.5	**Simpsonville** (city) Greenville County
111	n/a	16.3	**Lugoff** (CDP) Kershaw County
111	n/a	16.3	**Sangaree** (CDP) Berkeley County
113	n/a	16.1	**Elgin** (CDP) Lancaster County
114	2865	16.0	**Gantt** (CDP) Greenville County
115	2929	15.8	**North Augusta** (city) Aiken County
116	n/a	15.7	**Belton** (city) Anderson County
116	2962	15.7	**Irmo** (town) Richland County
118	n/a	15.1	**Arial** (CDP) Pickens County
119	3182	15.0	**Clemson** (city) Pickens County
119	3182	15.0	**Dentsville** (CDP) Richland County
121	3215	14.9	**Goose Creek** (city) Berkeley County
122	n/a	14.8	**Hollywood** (town) Charleston County
123	n/a	14.5	**Newport** (CDP) York County
124	n/a	14.3	**Centerville** (CDP) Anderson County
125	3458	14.1	**Forest Acres** (city) Richland County
126	n/a	13.9	**Union** (city) Union County
127	n/a	13.8	**Lyman** (town) Spartanburg County
128	n/a	13.6	**Bennettsville** (city) Marlboro County
129	3687	13.2	**Mount Pleasant** (town) Charleston County
130	n/a	13.1	**Lake Wylie** (CDP) York County
131	3733	13.0	**Oak Grove** (CDP) Lexington County
132	n/a	12.9	**Barnwell** (city) Barnwell County
133	n/a	12.8	**East Gaffney** (CDP) Cherokee County
133	3793	12.8	**Mauldin** (city) Greenville County
135	n/a	12.7	**Saluda** (town) Saluda County
136	n/a	12.6	**India Hook** (CDP) York County
137	n/a	12.4	**Clover** (town) York County
137	n/a	12.4	**Gloverville** (CDP) Aiken County
139	n/a	12.0	**Lakewood** (CDP) Sumter County
140	n/a	11.7	**Boiling Springs** (CDP) Spartanburg County
140	n/a	11.7	**North Hartsville** (CDP) Darlington County
142	4101	11.3	**Lexington** (town) Lexington County
143	n/a	10.6	**Clearwater** (CDP) Aiken County
144	4249	10.5	**Five Forks** (CDP) Greenville County
144	4249	10.5	**Fort Mill** (town) York County
146	n/a	10.4	**Northlake** (CDP) Anderson County
147	n/a	9.8	**Red Bank** (CDP) Lexington County
148	n/a	7.1	**Tega Cay** (city) York County
149	n/a	6.1	**Lake Murray of Richland** (CDP) Richland County
150	n/a	4.8	**Isle of Palms** (city) Charleston County

Note: The state column ranks the top/bottom 150 places in the state with population of 2,500 or more. The national column ranks the top/bottom places in the country with population of 10,000 or more. Places that are unincorporated were not considered in the rankings. n/a indicates data not available. Please refer to the User Guide for additional information.

Employment: Service Occupations

Top 150 Places Ranked in *Ascending* Order

State Rank	Nat'l Rank	Percent	Place
1	n/a	4.8	**Isle of Palms** (city) Charleston County
2	n/a	6.1	**Lake Murray of Richland** (CDP) Richland County
3	n/a	7.1	**Tega Cay** (city) York County
4	n/a	9.8	**Red Bank** (CDP) Lexington County
5	n/a	10.4	**Northlake** (CDP) Anderson County
6	396	10.5	**Five Forks** (CDP) Greenville County
6	396	10.5	**Fort Mill** (town) York County
8	n/a	10.6	**Clearwater** (CDP) Aiken County
9	535	11.3	**Lexington** (town) Lexington County
10	n/a	11.7	**Boiling Springs** (CDP) Spartanburg County
10	n/a	11.7	**North Hartsville** (CDP) Darlington County
12	n/a	12.0	**Lakewood** (CDP) Sumter County
13	n/a	12.4	**Clover** (town) York County
13	n/a	12.4	**Gloverville** (CDP) Aiken County
15	n/a	12.6	**India Hook** (CDP) York County
16	n/a	12.7	**Saluda** (town) Saluda County
17	n/a	12.8	**East Gaffney** (CDP) Cherokee County
17	846	12.8	**Mauldin** (city) Greenville County
19	n/a	12.9	**Barnwell** (city) Barnwell County
20	895	13.0	**Oak Grove** (CDP) Lexington County
21	n/a	13.1	**Lake Wylie** (CDP) York County
22	947	13.2	**Mount Pleasant** (town) Charleston County
23	n/a	13.6	**Bennettsville** (city) Marlboro County
24	n/a	13.8	**Lyman** (town) Spartanburg County
25	n/a	13.9	**Union** (city) Union County
26	1167	14.1	**Forest Acres** (city) Richland County
27	n/a	14.3	**Centerville** (CDP) Anderson County
28	n/a	14.5	**Newport** (CDP) York County
29	n/a	14.8	**Hollywood** (town) Charleston County
30	1407	14.9	**Goose Creek** (city) Berkeley County
31	1442	15.0	**Clemson** (city) Pickens County
31	1442	15.0	**Dentsville** (CDP) Richland County
33	n/a	15.1	**Arial** (CDP) Pickens County
34	n/a	15.7	**Belton** (city) Anderson County
34	1657	15.7	**Irmo** (town) Richland County
36	1695	15.8	**North Augusta** (city) Aiken County
37	1764	16.0	**Gantt** (CDP) Greenville County
38	n/a	16.1	**Elgin** (CDP) Lancaster County
39	n/a	16.3	**Lugoff** (CDP) Kershaw County
39	n/a	16.3	**Sangaree** (CDP) Berkeley County
41	n/a	16.5	**Belvedere** (CDP) Aiken County
41	1935	16.5	**Easley** (city) Pickens County
41	1935	16.5	**Simpsonville** (city) Greenville County
44	2006	16.7	**Seven Oaks** (CDP) Lexington County
44	2006	16.7	**West Columbia** (city) Lexington County
46	2072	16.9	**Greer** (city) Greenville County
46	2072	16.9	**Newberry** (city) Newberry County
48	n/a	17.1	**Honea Path** (town) Anderson County
49	n/a	17.4	**Camden** (city) Kershaw County
50	2296	17.6	**Greenville** (city) Greenville County
50	2296	17.6	**Wade Hampton** (CDP) Greenville County
52	n/a	17.9	**Walhalla** (city) Oconee County
53	2436	18.0	**Spartanburg** (city) Spartanburg County
53	2436	18.0	**Summerville** (town) Dorchester County
55	2472	18.1	**Gaffney** (city) Cherokee County
56	2523	18.3	**Taylors** (CDP) Greenville County
57	n/a	18.4	**Edgefield** (town) Edgefield County
58	2590	18.5	**Aiken** (city) Aiken County
59	2652	18.7	**Hanahan** (city) Berkeley County
59	n/a	18.7	**Williston** (town) Barnwell County
61	n/a	18.8	**Springdale** (CDP) Lancaster County
62	2747	19.0	**Beaufort** (city) Beaufort County
62	2747	19.0	**Rock Hill** (city) York County
64	n/a	19.1	**Duncan** (town) Spartanburg County
65	n/a	19.4	**Batesburg-Leesville** (town) Lexington County
66	n/a	19.5	**Darlington** (city) Darlington County
67	2961	19.6	**Florence** (city) Florence County
67	n/a	19.6	**Seneca** (city) Oconee County
69	n/a	19.7	**Hartsville** (city) Darlington County
70	n/a	19.8	**Fountain Inn** (city) Greenville County
70	3031	19.8	**Greenwood** (city) Greenwood County
70	n/a	19.8	**Liberty** (city) Pickens County
73	n/a	20.0	**Brookdale** (CDP) Orangeburg County
74	3127	20.1	**Sumter** (city) Sumter County
75	3152	20.2	**Cayce** (city) Lexington County
75	3152	20.2	**Charleston** (city) Charleston County
77	n/a	20.4	**Springdale** (town) Lexington County
78	3244	20.5	**Ladson** (CDP) Berkeley County
78	n/a	20.5	**Pendleton** (town) Anderson County
80	n/a	21.0	**Sans Souci** (CDP) Greenville County
81	3405	21.1	**Columbia** (city) Richland County
82	n/a	21.4	**Andrews** (town) Georgetown County
83	n/a	21.5	**Arcadia** (CDP) Spartanburg County
83	n/a	21.5	**Lesslie** (CDP) York County
83	n/a	21.5	**Murrells Inlet** (CDP) Georgetown County
86	3574	21.7	**Anderson** (city) Anderson County
86	n/a	21.7	**Welcome** (CDP) Greenville County
88	n/a	21.8	**Moncks Corner** (town) Berkeley County
89	n/a	21.9	**Pickens** (city) Pickens County
89	3622	21.9	**Red Hill** (CDP) Horry County
91	3650	22.0	**Bluffton** (town) Beaufort County
92	n/a	22.2	**Dalzell** (CDP) Sumter County
92	3694	22.2	**North Charleston** (city) Charleston County
94	3742	22.4	**Port Royal** (town) Beaufort County
95	3778	22.6	**Saint Andrews** (CDP) Richland County
96	3798	22.7	**Berea** (CDP) Greenville County
97	n/a	22.8	**Lancaster** (city) Lancaster County
98	n/a	22.9	**Graniteville** (CDP) Aiken County
99	n/a	23.0	**Garden City** (CDP) Horry County
100	n/a	23.1	**Hopkins** (CDP) Richland County
101	n/a	23.2	**Chester** (city) Chester County
102	n/a	23.5	**Allendale** (town) Allendale County
103	3990	23.7	**Orangeburg** (city) Orangeburg County
104	4006	23.8	**Hilton Head Island** (town) Beaufort County
105	n/a	24.0	**York** (city) York County
106	n/a	24.2	**Forestbrook** (CDP) Horry County
107	n/a	24.4	**Burnettown** (town) Aiken County
107	n/a	24.4	**McCormick** (town) McCormick County
107	n/a	24.4	**Travelers Rest** (city) Greenville County
110	n/a	24.6	**Dillon** (city) Dillon County
111	n/a	24.7	**Cheraw** (town) Chesterfield County
111	n/a	24.7	**Clinton** (city) Laurens County
113	n/a	24.8	**Lake City** (city) Florence County
113	n/a	24.8	**Marion** (city) Marion County
115	n/a	24.9	**Homeland Park** (CDP) Anderson County
116	n/a	25.2	**Hardeeville** (city) Jasper County
117	4236	25.3	**Parker** (CDP) Greenville County
118	n/a	25.4	**Burton** (CDP) Beaufort County
118	n/a	25.4	**Piedmont** (CDP) Anderson County
120	n/a	25.6	**Little River** (CDP) Horry County
121	n/a	26.2	**Bamberg** (town) Bamberg County
122	n/a	26.3	**Surfside Beach** (town) Horry County
123	n/a	26.4	**Abbeville** (city) Abbeville County
123	n/a	26.4	**Bishopville** (city) Lee County
125	n/a	26.6	**Edisto** (CDP) Orangeburg County
126	n/a	26.7	**Woodruff** (city) Spartanburg County
127	n/a	26.8	**Valley Falls** (CDP) Spartanburg County
128	n/a	27.0	**Georgetown** (city) Georgetown County
129	4433	27.8	**North Myrtle Beach** (city) Horry County
130	n/a	27.9	**Hampton** (town) Hampton County
131	n/a	28.0	**Williamston** (town) Anderson County
132	4446	28.1	**Myrtle Beach** (city) Horry County
133	n/a	28.4	**Pageland** (town) Chesterfield County
134	n/a	29.0	**Mullins** (city) Marion County
135	n/a	29.3	**Laurens** (city) Laurens County
136	n/a	29.6	**Laurel Bay** (CDP) Beaufort County
137	4534	30.0	**Socastee** (CDP) Horry County
138	n/a	31.0	**Dunean** (CDP) Greenville County
138	n/a	31.0	**Ridgeland** (town) Jasper County
138	n/a	31.0	**Saxon** (CDP) Spartanburg County
141	n/a	31.3	**Woodfield** (CDP) Richland County
142	n/a	31.4	**Kingstree** (town) Williamsburg County
142	n/a	31.4	**Manning** (city) Clarendon County
144	n/a	31.5	**Central** (town) Pickens County
144	4568	31.5	**Conway** (city) Horry County
146	n/a	31.7	**Southern Shops** (CDP) Spartanburg County
147	n/a	32.6	**Winnsboro** (town) Fairfield County
148	n/a	33.4	**Walterboro** (city) Colleton County
149	n/a	34.3	**Denmark** (city) Bamberg County
150	n/a	35.7	**Folly Beach** (city) Charleston County

Note: The state column ranks the top/bottom 150 places in the state with population of 2,500 or more. The national column ranks the top/bottom places in the country with population of 10,000 or more. Places that are unincorporated were not considered in the rankings. n/a indicates data not available. Please refer to the User Guide for additional information.

Employment: Sales and Office Occupations

Top 150 Places Ranked in *Descending* Order

State Rank	Nat'l Rank	Percent	Place
1	n/a	37.2	**Brookdale** (CDP) Orangeburg County
2	n/a	36.2	**Graniteville** (CDP) Aiken County
3	n/a	35.5	**Little River** (CDP) Horry County
4	17	35.4	**Dentsville** (CDP) Richland County
5	n/a	34.1	**Laurel Bay** (CDP) Beaufort County
6	51	33.7	**Fort Mill** (town) York County
7	n/a	33.4	**Garden City** (CDP) Horry County
8	n/a	33.2	**Forestbrook** (CDP) Horry County
9	n/a	33.1	**Lyman** (town) Spartanburg County
10	n/a	32.9	**Lesslie** (CDP) York County
11	n/a	32.6	**Arial** (CDP) Pickens County
11	n/a	32.6	**Bishopville** (city) Lee County
13	91	32.5	**Saint Andrews** (CDP) Richland County
14	n/a	32.3	**Cheraw** (town) Chesterfield County
15	164	31.6	**North Myrtle Beach** (city) Horry County
16	252	30.8	**Red Hill** (CDP) Horry County
17	n/a	30.6	**Hopkins** (CDP) Richland County
17	277	30.6	**Oak Grove** (CDP) Lexington County
19	n/a	30.5	**Surfside Beach** (town) Horry County
20	n/a	30.3	**Duncan** (town) Spartanburg County
20	n/a	30.3	**Red Bank** (CDP) Lexington County
22	329	30.2	**Goose Creek** (city) Berkeley County
22	329	30.2	**Socastee** (CDP) Horry County
24	n/a	29.9	**Valley Falls** (CDP) Spartanburg County
25	n/a	29.8	**Lake City** (city) Florence County
26	n/a	29.7	**Newport** (CDP) York County
27	492	29.4	**Conway** (city) Horry County
28	n/a	29.3	**Elgin** (CDP) Lancaster County
29	n/a	29.0	**Lake Wylie** (CDP) York County
29	604	29.0	**Mauldin** (city) Greenville County
31	n/a	28.8	**India Hook** (CDP) York County
31	n/a	28.8	**Union** (city) Union County
33	n/a	28.7	**Batesburg-Leesville** (town) Lexington County
34	701	28.6	**Easley** (city) Pickens County
34	n/a	28.6	**Northlake** (CDP) Anderson County
34	n/a	28.6	**Sangaree** (CDP) Berkeley County
37	771	28.4	**Berea** (CDP) Greenville County
38	n/a	28.3	**Clearwater** (CDP) Aiken County
38	n/a	28.3	**Lancaster** (city) Lancaster County
40	n/a	28.2	**East Gaffney** (CDP) Cherokee County
41	904	28.0	**Forest Acres** (city) Richland County
42	972	27.8	**Bluffton** (town) Beaufort County
42	972	27.8	**Irmo** (town) Richland County
42	972	27.8	**Seven Oaks** (CDP) Lexington County
45	1015	27.7	**Taylors** (CDP) Greenville County
46	1110	27.5	**Hilton Head Island** (town) Beaufort County
47	1156	27.4	**Lexington** (town) Lexington County
47	n/a	27.4	**Lugoff** (CDP) Kershaw County
49	n/a	27.1	**Denmark** (city) Bamberg County
50	1464	26.8	**Hanahan** (city) Berkeley County
50	1464	26.8	**Myrtle Beach** (city) Horry County
52	n/a	26.7	**Williamston** (town) Anderson County
53	n/a	26.5	**Clover** (town) York County
54	1681	26.4	**Cayce** (city) Lexington County
54	n/a	26.4	**Kingstree** (town) Williamsburg County
54	1681	26.4	**Ladson** (CDP) Berkeley County
54	n/a	26.4	**Murrells Inlet** (CDP) Georgetown County
54	n/a	26.4	**York** (city) York County
59	n/a	26.3	**Tega Cay** (city) York County
59	n/a	26.3	**Walterboro** (city) Colleton County
61	n/a	26.2	**Boiling Springs** (CDP) Spartanburg County
61	n/a	26.2	**Piedmont** (CDP) Anderson County
63	1873	26.1	**Rock Hill** (city) York County
63	1873	26.1	**Spartanburg** (city) Spartanburg County
65	n/a	26.0	**Edgefield** (town) Edgefield County
65	1930	26.0	**Gaffney** (city) Cherokee County
65	n/a	26.0	**Welcome** (CDP) Greenville County
68	n/a	25.7	**Dunean** (CDP) Greenville County
68	n/a	25.7	**Hollywood** (town) Charleston County
68	2116	25.7	**Wade Hampton** (CDP) Greenville County
68	n/a	25.7	**Woodfield** (CDP) Richland County
72	n/a	25.6	**Hardeeville** (city) Jasper County
73	n/a	25.4	**Andrews** (town) Georgetown County
73	n/a	25.4	**Honea Path** (town) Anderson County
73	n/a	25.4	**Sans Souci** (CDP) Greenville County
76	2327	25.3	**Beaufort** (city) Beaufort County
77	n/a	25.1	**Clinton** (city) Laurens County
77	n/a	25.1	**Travelers Rest** (city) Greenville County
79	2489	25.0	**Newberry** (city) Newberry County
79	2489	25.0	**Summerville** (town) Dorchester County
81	2554	24.9	**West Columbia** (city) Lexington County
82	n/a	24.8	**Darlington** (city) Darlington County
82	2612	24.8	**Gantt** (CDP) Greenville County
82	2612	24.8	**North Charleston** (city) Charleston County
82	n/a	24.8	**Springdale** (town) Lexington County
86	n/a	24.7	**Lake Murray of Richland** (CDP) Richland County
86	2671	24.7	**Mount Pleasant** (town) Charleston County
88	n/a	24.6	**Abbeville** (city) Abbeville County
89	n/a	24.5	**Pickens** (city) Pickens County
90	n/a	24.4	**Moncks Corner** (town) Berkeley County
91	2911	24.3	**Florence** (city) Florence County
92	n/a	24.2	**Springdale** (CDP) Lancaster County
93	n/a	24.1	**Fountain Inn** (city) Greenville County
93	n/a	24.1	**Saxon** (CDP) Spartanburg County
95	3051	24.0	**Greenville** (city) Greenville County
95	3051	24.0	**Port Royal** (town) Beaufort County
95	3051	24.0	**Simpsonville** (city) Greenville County
98	n/a	23.8	**Chester** (city) Chester County
99	3190	23.7	**Charleston** (city) Charleston County
100	3236	23.6	**Columbia** (city) Richland County
100	3236	23.6	**Greenwood** (city) Greenwood County
100	n/a	23.6	**Saluda** (town) Saluda County
103	3282	23.5	**Anderson** (city) Anderson County
104	n/a	23.4	**Mullins** (city) Marion County
105	3418	23.2	**Greer** (city) Greenville County
106	n/a	22.8	**Burnettown** (town) Aiken County
106	3577	22.8	**Sumter** (city) Sumter County
108	n/a	22.7	**Seneca** (city) Oconee County
109	3653	22.6	**North Augusta** (city) Aiken County
110	n/a	22.5	**Laurens** (city) Laurens County
111	n/a	22.2	**Belvedere** (CDP) Aiken County
112	n/a	22.1	**Liberty** (city) Pickens County
112	n/a	22.1	**Manning** (city) Clarendon County
114	3870	21.9	**Aiken** (city) Aiken County
115	n/a	21.7	**Georgetown** (city) Georgetown County
116	n/a	21.6	**Marion** (city) Marion County
116	n/a	21.6	**Pageland** (town) Chesterfield County
118	n/a	21.5	**Burton** (CDP) Beaufort County
118	3982	21.5	**Five Forks** (CDP) Greenville County
120	4014	21.4	**Orangeburg** (city) Orangeburg County
121	n/a	21.3	**Centerville** (CDP) Anderson County
122	n/a	20.9	**Gloverville** (CDP) Aiken County
123	n/a	20.7	**Homeland Park** (CDP) Anderson County
124	n/a	20.6	**Ridgeland** (town) Jasper County
125	n/a	20.1	**Hampton** (town) Hampton County
126	n/a	19.8	**Barnwell** (city) Barnwell County
126	n/a	19.8	**Belton** (city) Anderson County
128	n/a	19.6	**Dillon** (city) Dillon County
128	n/a	19.6	**Hartsville** (city) Darlington County
128	n/a	19.6	**Winnsboro** (town) Fairfield County
131	n/a	19.2	**Camden** (city) Kershaw County
132	n/a	19.1	**Central** (town) Pickens County
133	n/a	19.0	**Walhalla** (city) Oconee County
134	4458	18.7	**Clemson** (city) Pickens County
135	4476	18.5	**Parker** (CDP) Greenville County
136	n/a	18.0	**Pendleton** (town) Anderson County
137	n/a	17.5	**Isle of Palms** (city) Charleston County
138	n/a	16.5	**North Hartsville** (CDP) Darlington County
139	n/a	16.2	**Lakewood** (CDP) Sumter County
140	n/a	15.6	**Williston** (town) Barnwell County
141	n/a	15.4	**Bennettsville** (city) Marlboro County
142	n/a	15.2	**Edisto** (CDP) Orangeburg County
143	n/a	15.1	**Dalzell** (CDP) Sumter County
144	n/a	15.0	**Folly Beach** (city) Charleston County
145	n/a	14.7	**Arcadia** (CDP) Spartanburg County
146	n/a	14.6	**Allendale** (town) Allendale County
147	n/a	13.7	**Woodruff** (city) Spartanburg County
148	n/a	12.9	**Bamberg** (town) Bamberg County
149	n/a	12.6	**McCormick** (town) McCormick County
150	n/a	7.4	**Southern Shops** (CDP) Spartanburg County

Note: The state column ranks the top/bottom 150 places in the state with population of 2,500 or more. The national column ranks the top/bottom places in the country with population of 10,000 or more. Places that are unincorporated were not considered in the rankings. n/a indicates data not available. Please refer to the User Guide for additional information.

Employment: Sales and Office Occupations

Top 150 Places Ranked in *Ascending* Order

State Rank	Nat'l Rank	Percent	Place
1	n/a	7.4	**Southern Shops** (CDP) Spartanburg County
2	n/a	12.6	**McCormick** (town) McCormick County
3	n/a	12.9	**Bamberg** (town) Bamberg County
4	n/a	13.7	**Woodruff** (city) Spartanburg County
5	n/a	14.6	**Allendale** (town) Allendale County
6	n/a	14.7	**Arcadia** (CDP) Spartanburg County
7	n/a	15.0	**Folly Beach** (city) Charleston County
8	n/a	15.1	**Dalzell** (CDP) Sumter County
9	n/a	15.2	**Edisto** (CDP) Orangeburg County
10	n/a	15.4	**Bennettsville** (city) Marlboro County
11	n/a	15.6	**Williston** (town) Barnwell County
12	n/a	16.2	**Lakewood** (CDP) Sumter County
13	n/a	16.5	**North Hartsville** (CDP) Darlington County
14	n/a	17.5	**Isle of Palms** (city) Charleston County
15	n/a	18.0	**Pendleton** (town) Anderson County
16	174	18.5	**Parker** (CDP) Greenville County
17	186	18.7	**Clemson** (city) Pickens County
18	n/a	19.0	**Walhalla** (city) Oconee County
19	n/a	19.1	**Central** (town) Pickens County
20	n/a	19.2	**Camden** (city) Kershaw County
21	n/a	19.6	**Dillon** (city) Dillon County
21	n/a	19.6	**Hartsville** (city) Darlington County
21	n/a	19.6	**Winnsboro** (town) Fairfield County
24	n/a	19.8	**Barnwell** (city) Barnwell County
24	n/a	19.8	**Belton** (city) Anderson County
26	n/a	20.1	**Hampton** (town) Hampton County
27	n/a	20.6	**Ridgeland** (town) Jasper County
28	n/a	20.7	**Homeland Park** (CDP) Anderson County
29	n/a	20.9	**Gloverville** (CDP) Aiken County
30	n/a	21.3	**Centerville** (CDP) Anderson County
31	618	21.4	**Orangeburg** (city) Orangeburg County
32	n/a	21.5	**Burton** (CDP) Beaufort County
32	643	21.5	**Five Forks** (CDP) Greenville County
34	n/a	21.6	**Marion** (city) Marion County
34	n/a	21.6	**Pageland** (town) Chesterfield County
36	n/a	21.7	**Georgetown** (city) Georgetown County
37	762	21.9	**Aiken** (city) Aiken County
38	n/a	22.1	**Liberty** (city) Pickens County
38	n/a	22.1	**Manning** (city) Clarendon County
40	n/a	22.2	**Belvedere** (CDP) Aiken County
41	n/a	22.5	**Laurens** (city) Laurens County
42	974	22.6	**North Augusta** (city) Aiken County
43	n/a	22.7	**Seneca** (city) Oconee County
44	n/a	22.8	**Burnettown** (town) Aiken County
44	1041	22.8	**Sumter** (city) Sumter County
46	1198	23.2	**Greer** (city) Greenville County
47	n/a	23.4	**Mullins** (city) Marion County
48	1320	23.5	**Anderson** (city) Anderson County
49	1375	23.6	**Columbia** (city) Richland County
49	1375	23.6	**Greenwood** (city) Greenwood County
49	n/a	23.6	**Saluda** (town) Saluda County
52	1421	23.7	**Charleston** (city) Charleston County
53	n/a	23.8	**Chester** (city) Chester County
54	1555	24.0	**Greenville** (city) Greenville County
54	1555	24.0	**Port Royal** (town) Beaufort County
54	1555	24.0	**Simpsonville** (city) Greenville County
57	n/a	24.1	**Fountain Inn** (city) Greenville County
57	n/a	24.1	**Saxon** (CDP) Spartanburg County
59	n/a	24.2	**Springdale** (CDP) Lancaster County
60	1693	24.3	**Florence** (city) Florence County
61	n/a	24.4	**Moncks Corner** (town) Berkeley County
62	n/a	24.5	**Pickens** (city) Pickens County
63	n/a	24.6	**Abbeville** (city) Abbeville County
64	n/a	24.7	**Lake Murray of Richland** (CDP) Richland County
64	1933	24.7	**Mount Pleasant** (town) Charleston County
66	n/a	24.8	**Darlington** (city) Darlington County
66	1986	24.8	**Gantt** (CDP) Greenville County
66	1986	24.8	**North Charleston** (city) Charleston County
66	n/a	24.8	**Springdale** (town) Lexington County
70	2045	24.9	**West Columbia** (city) Lexington County
71	2103	25.0	**Newberry** (city) Newberry County
71	2103	25.0	**Summerville** (town) Dorchester County
73	n/a	25.1	**Clinton** (city) Laurens County
73	n/a	25.1	**Travelers Rest** (city) Greenville County
75	2272	25.3	**Beaufort** (city) Beaufort County
76	n/a	25.4	**Andrews** (town) Georgetown County
76	n/a	25.4	**Honea Path** (town) Anderson County
76	n/a	25.4	**Sans Souci** (CDP) Greenville County
79	n/a	25.6	**Hardeeville** (city) Jasper County
80	n/a	25.7	**Dunean** (CDP) Greenville County
80	n/a	25.7	**Hollywood** (town) Charleston County
80	2485	25.7	**Wade Hampton** (CDP) Greenville County
80	n/a	25.7	**Woodfield** (CDP) Richland County
84	n/a	26.0	**Edgefield** (town) Edgefield County
84	2660	26.0	**Gaffney** (city) Cherokee County
84	n/a	26.0	**Welcome** (CDP) Greenville County
87	2727	26.1	**Rock Hill** (city) York County
87	2727	26.1	**Spartanburg** (city) Spartanburg County
89	n/a	26.2	**Boiling Springs** (CDP) Spartanburg County
89	n/a	26.2	**Piedmont** (CDP) Anderson County
91	n/a	26.3	**Tega Cay** (city) York County
91	n/a	26.3	**Walterboro** (city) Colleton County
93	2919	26.4	**Cayce** (city) Lexington County
93	n/a	26.4	**Kingstree** (town) Williamsburg County
93	2919	26.4	**Ladson** (CDP) Berkeley County
93	n/a	26.4	**Murrells Inlet** (CDP) Georgetown County
93	n/a	26.4	**York** (city) York County
98	n/a	26.5	**Clover** (town) York County
99	n/a	26.7	**Williamston** (town) Anderson County
100	3142	26.8	**Hanahan** (city) Berkeley County
100	3142	26.8	**Myrtle Beach** (city) Horry County
102	n/a	27.1	**Denmark** (city) Bamberg County
103	3459	27.4	**Lexington** (town) Lexington County
103	n/a	27.4	**Lugoff** (CDP) Kershaw County
105	3501	27.5	**Hilton Head Island** (town) Beaufort County
106	3595	27.7	**Taylors** (CDP) Greenville County
107	3642	27.8	**Bluffton** (town) Beaufort County
107	3642	27.8	**Irmo** (town) Richland County
107	3642	27.8	**Seven Oaks** (CDP) Lexington County
110	3718	28.0	**Forest Acres** (city) Richland County
111	n/a	28.2	**East Gaffney** (CDP) Cherokee County
112	n/a	28.3	**Clearwater** (CDP) Aiken County
112	n/a	28.3	**Lancaster** (city) Lancaster County
114	3857	28.4	**Berea** (CDP) Greenville County
115	3924	28.6	**Easley** (city) Pickens County
115	n/a	28.6	**Northlake** (CDP) Anderson County
115	n/a	28.6	**Sangaree** (CDP) Berkeley County
118	n/a	28.7	**Batesburg-Leesville** (town) Lexington County
119	n/a	28.8	**India Hook** (CDP) York County
119	n/a	28.8	**Union** (city) Union County
121	n/a	29.0	**Lake Wylie** (CDP) York County
121	4033	29.0	**Mauldin** (city) Greenville County
123	n/a	29.3	**Elgin** (CDP) Lancaster County
124	4133	29.4	**Conway** (city) Horry County
125	n/a	29.7	**Newport** (CDP) York County
126	n/a	29.8	**Lake City** (city) Florence County
127	n/a	29.9	**Valley Falls** (CDP) Spartanburg County
128	4313	30.2	**Goose Creek** (city) Berkeley County
128	4313	30.2	**Socastee** (CDP) Horry County
130	n/a	30.3	**Duncan** (town) Spartanburg County
130	n/a	30.3	**Red Bank** (CDP) Lexington County
132	n/a	30.5	**Surfside Beach** (town) Horry County
133	n/a	30.6	**Hopkins** (CDP) Richland County
133	4363	30.6	**Oak Grove** (CDP) Lexington County
135	4395	30.8	**Red Hill** (CDP) Horry County
136	4488	31.6	**North Myrtle Beach** (city) Horry County
137	n/a	32.3	**Cheraw** (town) Chesterfield County
138	4561	32.5	**Saint Andrews** (CDP) Richland County
139	n/a	32.6	**Arial** (CDP) Pickens County
139	n/a	32.6	**Bishopville** (city) Lee County
141	n/a	32.9	**Lesslie** (CDP) York County
142	n/a	33.1	**Lyman** (town) Spartanburg County
143	n/a	33.2	**Forestbrook** (CDP) Horry County
144	n/a	33.4	**Garden City** (CDP) Horry County
145	4603	33.7	**Fort Mill** (town) York County
146	n/a	34.1	**Laurel Bay** (CDP) Beaufort County
147	4638	35.4	**Dentsville** (CDP) Richland County
148	n/a	35.5	**Little River** (CDP) Horry County
149	n/a	36.2	**Graniteville** (CDP) Aiken County
150	n/a	37.2	**Brookdale** (CDP) Orangeburg County

Note: The state column ranks the top/bottom 150 places in the state with population of 2,500 or more. The national column ranks the top/bottom places in the country with population of 10,000 or more. Places that are unincorporated were not considered in the rankings. n/a indicates data not available. Please refer to the User Guide for additional information.

Employment: Natural Resources, Construction, and Maintenance Occupations

Top 150 Places Ranked in *Descending* Order

State Rank	Nat'l Rank	Percent	Place
1	n/a	22.5	**Woodruff** (city) Spartanburg County
2	n/a	21.0	**Saluda** (town) Saluda County
3	n/a	20.7	**Southern Shops** (CDP) Spartanburg County
4	n/a	20.5	**Pageland** (town) Chesterfield County
5	78	20.0	**Parker** (CDP) Greenville County
6	n/a	19.3	**Burnettown** (town) Aiken County
7	n/a	19.2	**Welcome** (CDP) Greenville County
8	n/a	18.6	**Burton** (CDP) Beaufort County
9	n/a	17.9	**Walhalla** (city) Oconee County
10	n/a	17.3	**Moncks Corner** (town) Berkeley County
11	135	16.9	**Oak Grove** (CDP) Lexington County
11	n/a	16.9	**Ridgeland** (town) Jasper County
13	n/a	16.6	**Clearwater** (CDP) Aiken County
13	144	16.6	**Red Hill** (CDP) Horry County
15	n/a	16.3	**Gloverville** (CDP) Aiken County
15	n/a	16.3	**Homeland Park** (CDP) Anderson County
17	n/a	15.3	**Liberty** (city) Pickens County
18	n/a	14.9	**Hardeeville** (city) Jasper County
19	n/a	14.8	**Red Bank** (CDP) Lexington County
20	282	14.2	**West Columbia** (city) Lexington County
21	n/a	14.0	**Laurel Bay** (CDP) Beaufort County
22	n/a	13.6	**Woodfield** (CDP) Richland County
23	n/a	13.5	**Belton** (city) Anderson County
24	355	13.4	**Myrtle Beach** (city) Horry County
25	n/a	13.1	**Arcadia** (CDP) Spartanburg County
26	413	12.9	**Berea** (CDP) Greenville County
27	n/a	12.8	**Sans Souci** (CDP) Greenville County
28	444	12.7	**North Charleston** (city) Charleston County
29	n/a	12.5	**North Hartsville** (CDP) Darlington County
30	n/a	12.1	**Clover** (town) York County
31	n/a	11.9	**Graniteville** (CDP) Aiken County
32	n/a	11.8	**Dalzell** (CDP) Sumter County
32	n/a	11.8	**McCormick** (town) McCormick County
34	n/a	11.7	**Camden** (city) Kershaw County
35	n/a	11.6	**East Gaffney** (CDP) Cherokee County
36	678	11.5	**Hilton Head Island** (town) Beaufort County
37	n/a	11.4	**Belvedere** (CDP) Aiken County
38	715	11.3	**Beaufort** (city) Beaufort County
39	n/a	11.0	**Williamston** (town) Anderson County
40	n/a	10.9	**Lakewood** (CDP) Sumter County
40	n/a	10.9	**Sangaree** (CDP) Berkeley County
42	n/a	10.8	**Chester** (city) Chester County
43	904	10.6	**Hanahan** (city) Berkeley County
44	n/a	10.5	**Bamberg** (town) Bamberg County
44	938	10.5	**Socastee** (CDP) Horry County
46	977	10.4	**Ladson** (CDP) Berkeley County
47	1124	10.0	**Newberry** (city) Newberry County
47	n/a	10.0	**Travelers Rest** (city) Greenville County
47	n/a	10.0	**Williston** (town) Barnwell County
50	n/a	9.8	**Garden City** (CDP) Horry County
51	n/a	9.7	**Dillon** (city) Dillon County
51	1245	9.7	**Gantt** (CDP) Greenville County
51	n/a	9.7	**Hollywood** (town) Charleston County
51	n/a	9.7	**Hopkins** (CDP) Richland County
51	n/a	9.7	**Murrells Inlet** (CDP) Georgetown County
56	n/a	9.5	**Springdale** (town) Lexington County
56	n/a	9.5	**Union** (city) Union County
58	1370	9.4	**Bluffton** (town) Beaufort County
58	1370	9.4	**Cayce** (city) Lexington County
60	n/a	9.3	**Surfside Beach** (town) Horry County
61	n/a	9.2	**Folly Beach** (city) Charleston County
61	n/a	9.2	**Springdale** (CDP) Lancaster County
63	n/a	9.1	**Elgin** (CDP) Lancaster County
64	n/a	9.0	**Arial** (CDP) Pickens County
64	1566	9.0	**Greer** (city) Greenville County
66	1624	8.9	**Easley** (city) Pickens County
66	n/a	8.9	**Little River** (CDP) Horry County
68	n/a	8.8	**Piedmont** (CDP) Anderson County
69	1835	8.5	**Greenwood** (city) Greenwood County
69	1835	8.5	**Sumter** (city) Sumter County
71	n/a	8.4	**Saxon** (CDP) Spartanburg County
72	1931	8.3	**Summerville** (town) Dorchester County
73	1984	8.2	**Dentsville** (CDP) Richland County
73	1984	8.2	**Goose Creek** (city) Berkeley County
75	2041	8.1	**Anderson** (city) Anderson County
75	n/a	8.1	**Edgefield** (town) Edgefield County
75	n/a	8.1	**Lugoff** (CDP) Kershaw County
78	n/a	8.0	**Allendale** (town) Allendale County
78	2093	8.0	**Port Royal** (town) Beaufort County
80	n/a	7.9	**Forestbrook** (CDP) Horry County
80	2142	7.9	**Simpsonville** (city) Greenville County
82	n/a	7.7	**Laurens** (city) Laurens County
83	2306	7.6	**Irmo** (town) Richland County
84	n/a	7.4	**York** (city) York County
85	n/a	7.2	**Batesburg-Leesville** (town) Lexington County
85	n/a	7.2	**Northlake** (CDP) Anderson County
87	n/a	7.1	**Lake City** (city) Florence County
88	n/a	6.9	**Lake Murray of Richland** (CDP) Richland County
89	n/a	6.7	**Pickens** (city) Pickens County
89	2855	6.7	**Rock Hill** (city) York County
89	n/a	6.7	**Walterboro** (city) Colleton County
92	n/a	6.6	**Fountain Inn** (city) Greenville County
93	n/a	6.5	**Seneca** (city) Oconee County
94	n/a	6.4	**Barnwell** (city) Barnwell County
95	n/a	6.2	**Georgetown** (city) Georgetown County
96	n/a	6.0	**Boiling Springs** (CDP) Spartanburg County
96	n/a	6.0	**Centerville** (CDP) Anderson County
98	3341	5.9	**North Myrtle Beach** (city) Horry County
98	3341	5.9	**Seven Oaks** (CDP) Lexington County
98	n/a	5.9	**Valley Falls** (CDP) Spartanburg County
101	n/a	5.8	**Clinton** (city) Laurens County
101	3411	5.8	**Columbia** (city) Richland County
101	n/a	5.8	**India Hook** (CDP) York County
104	n/a	5.7	**Isle of Palms** (city) Charleston County
104	n/a	5.7	**Newport** (CDP) York County
104	n/a	5.7	**Pendleton** (town) Anderson County
107	3508	5.6	**Wade Hampton** (CDP) Greenville County
108	n/a	5.5	**Bennettsville** (city) Marlboro County
109	3584	5.4	**Clemson** (city) Pickens County
109	3584	5.4	**Taylors** (CDP) Greenville County
111	3670	5.2	**Mauldin** (city) Greenville County
112	3710	5.1	**Aiken** (city) Aiken County
112	3710	5.1	**Fort Mill** (town) York County
112	n/a	5.1	**Hampton** (town) Hampton County
112	3710	5.1	**Lexington** (town) Lexington County
116	3766	5.0	**Greenville** (city) Greenville County
117	n/a	4.9	**Abbeville** (city) Abbeville County
117	3811	4.9	**Conway** (city) Horry County
119	3844	4.8	**Charleston** (city) Charleston County
120	n/a	4.7	**Cheraw** (town) Chesterfield County
120	n/a	4.7	**Darlington** (city) Darlington County
120	3892	4.7	**North Augusta** (city) Aiken County
120	3892	4.7	**Spartanburg** (city) Spartanburg County
124	3928	4.6	**Mount Pleasant** (town) Charleston County
125	3965	4.5	**Gaffney** (city) Cherokee County
126	n/a	4.4	**Lancaster** (city) Lancaster County
126	n/a	4.4	**Lesslie** (CDP) York County
128	n/a	4.3	**Hartsville** (city) Darlington County
129	n/a	4.2	**Dunean** (CDP) Greenville County
129	4073	4.2	**Florence** (city) Florence County
131	n/a	4.1	**Lyman** (town) Spartanburg County
132	4139	4.0	**Five Forks** (CDP) Greenville County
133	4157	3.9	**Saint Andrews** (CDP) Richland County
134	n/a	3.7	**Mullins** (city) Marion County
135	n/a	3.6	**Kingstree** (town) Williamsburg County
136	4280	3.5	**Forest Acres** (city) Richland County
137	n/a	3.4	**Brookdale** (CDP) Orangeburg County
138	n/a	3.3	**Central** (town) Pickens County
139	n/a	3.2	**Andrews** (town) Georgetown County
139	n/a	3.2	**Bishopville** (city) Lee County
139	4349	3.2	**Orangeburg** (city) Orangeburg County
142	n/a	3.1	**Honea Path** (town) Anderson County
143	n/a	2.9	**Manning** (city) Clarendon County
144	n/a	2.4	**Duncan** (town) Spartanburg County
145	n/a	2.3	**Denmark** (city) Bamberg County
146	n/a	2.1	**Edisto** (CDP) Orangeburg County
147	n/a	2.0	**Lake Wylie** (CDP) York County
148	n/a	1.8	**Winnsboro** (town) Fairfield County
149	n/a	1.6	**Marion** (city) Marion County
150	n/a	1.5	**Tega Cay** (city) York County

Note: *The state column ranks the top/bottom 150 places in the state with population of 2,500 or more. The national column ranks the top/bottom places in the country with population of 10,000 or more. Places that are unincorporated were not considered in the rankings. n/a indicates data not available. Please refer to the User Guide for additional information.*

Employment: Natural Resources, Construction, and Maintenance Occupations

Top 150 Places Ranked in *Ascending* Order

State Rank	Nat'l Rank	Percent	Place	State Rank	Nat'l Rank	Percent	Place
1	n/a	1.5	Tega Cay (city) York County	74	n/a	8.1	Lugoff (CDP) Kershaw County
2	n/a	1.6	Marion (city) Marion County	77	2616	8.2	Dentsville (CDP) Richland County
3	n/a	1.8	Winnsboro (town) Fairfield County	77	2616	8.2	Goose Creek (city) Berkeley County
4	n/a	2.0	Lake Wylie (CDP) York County	79	2673	8.3	Summerville (town) Dorchester County
5	n/a	2.1	Edisto (CDP) Orangeburg County	80	n/a	8.4	Saxon (CDP) Spartanburg County
6	n/a	2.3	Denmark (city) Bamberg County	81	2770	8.5	Greenwood (city) Greenwood County
7	n/a	2.4	Duncan (town) Spartanburg County	81	2770	8.5	Sumter (city) Sumter County
8	n/a	2.9	Manning (city) Clarendon County	83	n/a	8.8	Piedmont (CDP) Anderson County
9	n/a	3.1	Honea Path (town) Anderson County	84	2974	8.9	Easley (city) Pickens County
10	n/a	3.2	Andrews (town) Georgetown County	84	n/a	8.9	Little River (CDP) Horry County
10	n/a	3.2	Bishopville (city) Lee County	86	n/a	9.0	Arial (CDP) Pickens County
10	281	3.2	Orangeburg (city) Orangeburg County	86	3033	9.0	Greer (city) Greenville County
13	n/a	3.3	Central (town) Pickens County	88	n/a	9.1	Elgin (CDP) Lancaster County
14	n/a	3.4	Brookdale (CDP) Orangeburg County	89	n/a	9.2	Folly Beach (city) Charleston County
15	355	3.5	Forest Acres (city) Richland County	89	n/a	9.2	Springdale (CDP) Lancaster County
16	n/a	3.6	Kingstree (town) Williamsburg County	91	n/a	9.3	Surfside Beach (town) Horry County
17	n/a	3.7	Mullins (city) Marion County	92	3239	9.4	Bluffton (town) Beaufort County
18	466	3.9	Saint Andrews (CDP) Richland County	92	3239	9.4	Cayce (city) Lexington County
19	500	4.0	Five Forks (CDP) Greenville County	94	n/a	9.5	Springdale (town) Lexington County
20	n/a	4.1	Lyman (town) Spartanburg County	94	n/a	9.5	Union (city) Union County
21	n/a	4.2	Dunean (CDP) Greenville County	96	n/a	9.7	Dillon (city) Dillon County
21	553	4.2	Florence (city) Florence County	96	3368	9.7	Gantt (CDP) Greenville County
23	n/a	4.3	Hartsville (city) Darlington County	96	n/a	9.7	Hollywood (town) Charleston County
24	n/a	4.4	Lancaster (city) Lancaster County	96	n/a	9.7	Hopkins (CDP) Richland County
24	n/a	4.4	Lesslie (CDP) York County	96	n/a	9.7	Murrells Inlet (CDP) Georgetown County
26	641	4.5	Gaffney (city) Cherokee County	101	n/a	9.8	Garden City (CDP) Horry County
27	692	4.6	Mount Pleasant (town) Charleston County	102	3494	10.0	Newberry (city) Newberry County
28	n/a	4.7	Cheraw (town) Chesterfield County	102	n/a	10.0	Travelers Rest (city) Greenville County
28	n/a	4.7	Darlington (city) Darlington County	102	n/a	10.0	Williston (town) Barnwell County
28	729	4.7	North Augusta (city) Aiken County	105	3648	10.4	Ladson (CDP) Berkeley County
28	729	4.7	Spartanburg (city) Spartanburg County	106	n/a	10.5	Bamberg (town) Bamberg County
32	765	4.8	Charleston (city) Charleston County	106	3680	10.5	Socastee (CDP) Horry County
33	n/a	4.9	Abbeville (city) Abbeville County	108	3719	10.6	Hanahan (city) Berkeley County
33	813	4.9	Conway (city) Horry County	109	n/a	10.8	Chester (city) Chester County
35	846	5.0	Greenville (city) Greenville County	110	n/a	10.9	Lakewood (CDP) Sumter County
36	891	5.1	Aiken (city) Aiken County	110	n/a	10.9	Sangaree (CDP) Berkeley County
36	891	5.1	Fort Mill (town) York County	112	n/a	11.0	Williamston (town) Anderson County
36	n/a	5.1	Hampton (town) Hampton County	113	3921	11.3	Beaufort (city) Beaufort County
36	891	5.1	Lexington (town) Lexington County	114	n/a	11.4	Belvedere (CDP) Aiken County
40	947	5.2	Mauldin (city) Greenville County	115	3962	11.5	Hilton Head Island (town) Beaufort County
41	1023	5.4	Clemson (city) Pickens County	116	n/a	11.6	East Gaffney (CDP) Cherokee County
41	1023	5.4	Taylors (CDP) Greenville County	117	n/a	11.7	Camden (city) Kershaw County
43	n/a	5.5	Bennettsville (city) Marlboro County	118	n/a	11.8	Dalzell (CDP) Sumter County
44	1109	5.6	Wade Hampton (CDP) Greenville County	118	n/a	11.8	McCormick (town) McCormick County
45	n/a	5.7	Isle of Palms (city) Charleston County	120	n/a	11.9	Graniteville (CDP) Aiken County
45	n/a	5.7	Newport (CDP) York County	121	n/a	12.1	Clover (town) York County
45	n/a	5.7	Pendleton (town) Anderson County	122	n/a	12.5	North Hartsville (CDP) Darlington County
48	n/a	5.8	Clinton (city) Laurens County	123	4199	12.7	North Charleston (city) Charleston County
48	1199	5.8	Columbia (city) Richland County	124	n/a	12.8	Sans Souci (CDP) Greenville County
48	n/a	5.8	India Hook (CDP) York County	125	4230	12.9	Berea (CDP) Greenville County
51	1246	5.9	North Myrtle Beach (city) Horry County	126	n/a	13.1	Arcadia (CDP) Spartanburg County
51	1246	5.9	Seven Oaks (CDP) Lexington County	127	4286	13.4	Myrtle Beach (city) Horry County
51	n/a	5.9	Valley Falls (CDP) Spartanburg County	128	n/a	13.5	Belton (city) Anderson County
54	n/a	6.0	Boiling Springs (CDP) Spartanburg County	129	n/a	13.6	Woodfield (CDP) Richland County
54	n/a	6.0	Centerville (CDP) Anderson County	130	n/a	14.0	Laurel Bay (CDP) Beaufort County
56	n/a	6.2	Georgetown (city) Georgetown County	131	4362	14.2	West Columbia (city) Lexington County
57	n/a	6.4	Barnwell (city) Barnwell County	132	n/a	14.8	Red Bank (CDP) Lexington County
58	n/a	6.5	Seneca (city) Oconee County	133	n/a	14.9	Hardeeville (city) Jasper County
59	n/a	6.6	Fountain Inn (city) Greenville County	134	n/a	15.3	Liberty (city) Pickens County
60	n/a	6.7	Pickens (city) Pickens County	135	n/a	16.3	Gloverville (CDP) Aiken County
60	1753	6.7	Rock Hill (city) York County	135	n/a	16.3	Homeland Park (CDP) Anderson County
60	n/a	6.7	Walterboro (city) Colleton County	137	n/a	16.6	Clearwater (CDP) Aiken County
63	n/a	6.9	Lake Murray of Richland (CDP) Richland County	137	4507	16.6	Red Hill (CDP) Horry County
64	n/a	7.1	Lake City (city) Florence County	139	4519	16.9	Oak Grove (CDP) Lexington County
65	n/a	7.2	Batesburg-Leesville (town) Lexington County	139	n/a	16.9	Ridgeland (town) Jasper County
65	n/a	7.2	Northlake (CDP) Anderson County	141	n/a	17.3	Moncks Corner (town) Berkeley County
67	n/a	7.4	York (city) York County	142	n/a	17.9	Walhalla (city) Oconee County
68	2285	7.6	Irmo (town) Richland County	143	n/a	18.6	Burton (CDP) Beaufort County
69	n/a	7.7	Laurens (city) Laurens County	144	n/a	19.2	Welcome (CDP) Greenville County
70	n/a	7.9	Forestbrook (CDP) Horry County	145	n/a	19.3	Burnettown (town) Aiken County
70	2468	7.9	Simpsonville (city) Greenville County	146	4578	20.0	Parker (CDP) Greenville County
72	n/a	8.0	Allendale (town) Allendale County	147	n/a	20.5	Pageland (town) Chesterfield County
72	2515	8.0	Port Royal (town) Beaufort County	148	n/a	20.7	Southern Shops (CDP) Spartanburg County
74	2564	8.1	Anderson (city) Anderson County	149	n/a	21.0	Saluda (town) Saluda County
74	n/a	8.1	Edgefield (town) Edgefield County	150	n/a	22.5	Woodruff (city) Spartanburg County

Note: The state column ranks the top/bottom 150 places in the state with population of 2,500 or more. The national column ranks the top/bottom places in the country with population of 10,000 or more. Places that are unincorporated were not considered in the rankings. n/a indicates data not available. Please refer to the User Guide for additional information.

Employment: Production, Transportation, and Material Moving Occupations

Top 150 Places Ranked in *Descending* Order

State Rank	Nat'l Rank	Percent	Place	State Rank	Nat'l Rank	Percent	Place
1	n/a	38.9	**Arcadia** (CDP) Spartanburg County	76	n/a	14.6	**Georgetown** (city) Georgetown County
2	n/a	35.8	**East Gaffney** (CDP) Cherokee County	76	n/a	14.6	**Seneca** (city) Oconee County
3	n/a	34.5	**Southern Shops** (CDP) Spartanburg County	78	1203	14.5	**Taylors** (CDP) Greenville County
4	n/a	34.4	**Bennettsville** (city) Marlboro County	79	n/a	14.4	**Springdale** (town) Lexington County
5	n/a	33.3	**Gloverville** (CDP) Aiken County	80	1363	13.8	**Easley** (city) Pickens County
6	n/a	29.9	**Edgefield** (town) Edgefield County	80	1363	13.8	**Sumter** (city) Sumter County
7	n/a	29.2	**McCormick** (town) McCormick County	82	n/a	13.5	**India Hook** (CDP) York County
8	n/a	28.9	**Homeland Park** (CDP) Anderson County	83	n/a	13.0	**Lugoff** (CDP) Kershaw County
9	n/a	27.5	**Saluda** (town) Saluda County	84	1582	12.9	**Hanahan** (city) Berkeley County
9	n/a	27.5	**York** (city) York County	85	n/a	12.8	**Manning** (city) Clarendon County
11	n/a	27.3	**Duncan** (town) Spartanburg County	86	n/a	12.7	**Hartsville** (city) Darlington County
12	81	27.2	**Gantt** (CDP) Greenville County	87	n/a	12.4	**Cheraw** (town) Chesterfield County
13	n/a	26.9	**North Hartsville** (CDP) Darlington County	87	1723	12.4	**Mauldin** (city) Greenville County
14	99	26.3	**Gaffney** (city) Cherokee County	89	n/a	12.2	**Lesslie** (CDP) York County
15	n/a	26.0	**Clearwater** (CDP) Aiken County	90	n/a	12.1	**Bishopville** (city) Lee County
16	n/a	25.0	**Lyman** (town) Spartanburg County	90	n/a	12.1	**Northlake** (CDP) Anderson County
17	n/a	24.8	**Springdale** (CDP) Lancaster County	92	n/a	12.0	**Burnettown** (town) Aiken County
18	161	24.2	**Parker** (CDP) Greenville County	93	1868	11.9	**Wade Hampton** (CDP) Greenville County
19	n/a	24.1	**Elgin** (CDP) Lancaster County	94	n/a	11.8	**Williamston** (town) Anderson County
20	n/a	23.7	**Denmark** (city) Bamberg County	95	n/a	11.7	**Hardeeville** (city) Jasper County
21	n/a	23.6	**Saxon** (CDP) Spartanburg County	95	n/a	11.7	**Valley Falls** (CDP) Spartanburg County
22	n/a	23.5	**Andrews** (town) Georgetown County	97	n/a	11.6	**Red Bank** (CDP) Lexington County
22	n/a	23.5	**Mullins** (city) Marion County	98	n/a	11.4	**Moncks Corner** (town) Berkeley County
24	n/a	23.3	**Walhalla** (city) Oconee County	99	n/a	11.0	**Burton** (CDP) Beaufort County
25	n/a	23.2	**Lancaster** (city) Lancaster County	99	2146	11.0	**Goose Creek** (city) Berkeley County
26	201	23.0	**Greenwood** (city) Greenwood County	101	2253	10.7	**Summerville** (town) Dorchester County
26	n/a	23.0	**Marion** (city) Marion County	102	n/a	10.6	**Travelers Rest** (city) Greenville County
28	n/a	22.8	**Arial** (CDP) Pickens County	103	n/a	10.5	**Dalzell** (CDP) Sumter County
29	n/a	22.7	**Lakewood** (CDP) Sumter County	104	2389	10.3	**Cayce** (city) Lexington County
30	n/a	22.6	**Edisto** (CDP) Orangeburg County	105	2415	10.2	**Saint Andrews** (CDP) Richland County
31	n/a	22.5	**Centerville** (CDP) Anderson County	106	2450	10.1	**Oak Grove** (CDP) Lexington County
32	n/a	22.4	**Hopkins** (CDP) Richland County	107	n/a	9.8	**Pendleton** (town) Anderson County
33	n/a	21.7	**Chester** (city) Chester County	108	n/a	9.7	**Camden** (city) Kershaw County
34	n/a	21.1	**Liberty** (city) Pickens County	108	2581	9.7	**Dentsville** (CDP) Richland County
34	301	21.1	**Newberry** (city) Newberry County	108	2581	9.7	**North Augusta** (city) Aiken County
34	n/a	21.1	**Piedmont** (CDP) Anderson County	111	2660	9.5	**Florence** (city) Florence County
37	n/a	21.0	**Dillon** (city) Dillon County	111	2660	9.5	**Greenville** (city) Greenville County
38	n/a	20.7	**Belvedere** (CDP) Aiken County	113	2731	9.3	**Irmo** (town) Richland County
39	346	20.6	**Ladson** (CDP) Berkeley County	114	2759	9.2	**Aiken** (city) Aiken County
40	368	20.4	**Simpsonville** (city) Greenville County	115	n/a	9.0	**Ridgeland** (town) Jasper County
41	n/a	20.3	**Barnwell** (city) Barnwell County	115	2827	9.0	**West Columbia** (city) Lexington County
42	n/a	20.2	**Brookdale** (CDP) Orangeburg County	117	n/a	8.9	**Woodfield** (CDP) Richland County
43	n/a	20.1	**Belton** (city) Anderson County	118	n/a	8.7	**Lake Wylie** (CDP) York County
43	n/a	20.1	**Pickens** (city) Pickens County	119	n/a	8.4	**Graniteville** (CDP) Aiken County
43	n/a	20.1	**Winnsboro** (town) Fairfield County	119	3040	8.4	**Seven Oaks** (CDP) Lexington County
46	n/a	19.8	**Hollywood** (town) Charleston County	121	3071	8.3	**Fort Mill** (town) York County
47	n/a	19.4	**Pageland** (town) Chesterfield County	122	3295	7.7	**Columbia** (city) Richland County
47	n/a	19.4	**Woodruff** (city) Spartanburg County	122	n/a	7.7	**Isle of Palms** (city) Charleston County
49	n/a	19.2	**Clinton** (city) Laurens County	124	n/a	7.6	**Lake Murray of Richland** (CDP) Richland County
50	n/a	19.0	**Honea Path** (town) Anderson County	125	3424	7.3	**Port Royal** (town) Beaufort County
51	n/a	18.8	**Sangaree** (CDP) Berkeley County	126	3464	7.2	**Beaufort** (city) Beaufort County
52	n/a	18.7	**Fountain Inn** (city) Greenville County	126	n/a	7.2	**Walterboro** (city) Colleton County
52	n/a	18.7	**Sans Souci** (CDP) Greenville County	128	3511	7.0	**Bluffton** (town) Beaufort County
54	522	18.6	**Orangeburg** (city) Orangeburg County	128	n/a	7.0	**Central** (town) Pickens County
55	n/a	18.5	**Allendale** (town) Allendale County	130	n/a	6.7	**Laurel Bay** (CDP) Beaufort County
55	n/a	18.5	**Williston** (town) Barnwell County	131	3637	6.6	**Charleston** (city) Charleston County
57	556	18.3	**Berea** (CDP) Greenville County	132	3687	6.4	**Clemson** (city) Pickens County
58	n/a	18.0	**Abbeville** (city) Abbeville County	133	3715	6.3	**Conway** (city) Horry County
59	n/a	17.8	**Kingstree** (town) Williamsburg County	133	n/a	6.3	**Surfside Beach** (town) Horry County
60	n/a	17.7	**Laurens** (city) Laurens County	135	n/a	6.2	**Murrells Inlet** (CDP) Georgetown County
61	739	17.1	**Anderson** (city) Anderson County	136	3804	6.0	**Red Hill** (CDP) Horry County
61	739	17.1	**Spartanburg** (city) Spartanburg County	137	3865	5.8	**Five Forks** (CDP) Greenville County
63	n/a	16.9	**Dunean** (CDP) Greenville County	138	3945	5.5	**Socastee** (CDP) Horry County
64	n/a	16.7	**Lake City** (city) Florence County	139	n/a	5.4	**Garden City** (CDP) Horry County
65	839	16.4	**Greer** (city) Greenville County	140	n/a	5.3	**Little River** (CDP) Horry County
66	n/a	16.3	**Darlington** (city) Darlington County	140	3993	5.3	**Mount Pleasant** (town) Charleston County
67	949	15.8	**Rock Hill** (city) York County	142	4024	5.2	**Myrtle Beach** (city) Horry County
67	n/a	15.8	**Union** (city) Union County	143	4088	5.0	**Lexington** (town) Lexington County
69	n/a	15.5	**Batesburg-Leesville** (town) Lexington County	144	n/a	4.6	**Folly Beach** (city) Charleston County
70	n/a	15.3	**Clover** (town) York County	145	n/a	3.9	**Newport** (CDP) York County
70	1050	15.3	**North Charleston** (city) Charleston County	145	n/a	3.9	**Tega Cay** (city) York County
72	n/a	15.1	**Boiling Springs** (CDP) Spartanburg County	147	4388	3.7	**North Myrtle Beach** (city) Horry County
73	n/a	15.0	**Welcome** (CDP) Greenville County	148	4403	3.6	**Forest Acres** (city) Richland County
74	n/a	14.9	**Hampton** (town) Hampton County	149	4422	3.5	**Hilton Head Island** (town) Beaufort County
75	n/a	14.7	**Bamberg** (town) Bamberg County	150	n/a	3.3	**Forestbrook** (CDP) Horry County

Note: The state column ranks the top/bottom 150 places in the state with population of 2,500 or more. The national column ranks the top/bottom places in the country with population of 10,000 or more. Places that are unincorporated were not considered in the rankings. n/a indicates data not available. Please refer to the User Guide for additional information.

Employment: Production, Transportation, and Material Moving Occupations

Top 150 Places Ranked in *Ascending* Order

State Rank	Nat'l Rank	Percent	Place
1	n/a	3.3	Forestbrook (CDP) Horry County
2	214	3.5	Hilton Head Island (town) Beaufort County
3	235	3.6	Forest Acres (city) Richland County
4	254	3.7	North Myrtle Beach (city) Horry County
5	n/a	3.9	Newport (CDP) York County
5	n/a	3.9	Tega Cay (city) York County
7	n/a	4.6	Folly Beach (city) Charleston County
8	548	5.0	Lexington (town) Lexington County
9	602	5.2	Myrtle Beach (city) Horry County
10	n/a	5.3	Little River (CDP) Horry County
10	633	5.3	Mount Pleasant (town) Charleston County
12	n/a	5.4	Garden City (CDP) Horry County
13	691	5.5	Socastee (CDP) Horry County
14	764	5.8	Five Forks (CDP) Greenville County
15	817	6.0	Red Hill (CDP) Horry County
16	n/a	6.2	Murrells Inlet (CDP) Georgetown County
17	916	6.3	Conway (city) Horry County
17	n/a	6.3	Surfside Beach (town) Horry County
19	942	6.4	Clemson (city) Pickens County
20	993	6.6	Charleston (city) Charleston County
21	n/a	6.7	Laurel Bay (CDP) Beaufort County
22	1123	7.0	Bluffton (town) Beaufort County
22	n/a	7.0	Central (town) Pickens County
24	1168	7.2	Beaufort (city) Beaufort County
24	n/a	7.2	Walterboro (city) Colleton County
26	1193	7.3	Port Royal (town) Beaufort County
27	n/a	7.6	Lake Murray of Richland (CDP) Richland County
28	1325	7.7	Columbia (city) Richland County
28	n/a	7.7	Isle of Palms (city) Charleston County
30	1547	8.3	Fort Mill (town) York County
31	n/a	8.4	Graniteville (CDP) Aiken County
31	1586	8.4	Seven Oaks (CDP) Lexington County
33	n/a	8.7	Lake Wylie (CDP) York County
34	n/a	8.9	Woodfield (CDP) Richland County
35	n/a	9.0	Ridgeland (town) Jasper County
35	1789	9.0	West Columbia (city) Lexington County
37	1862	9.2	Aiken (city) Aiken County
38	1898	9.3	Irmo (town) Richland County
39	1957	9.5	Florence (city) Florence County
39	1957	9.5	Greenville (city) Greenville County
41	n/a	9.7	Camden (city) Kershaw County
41	2032	9.7	Dentsville (CDP) Richland County
41	2032	9.7	North Augusta (city) Aiken County
44	n/a	9.8	Pendleton (town) Anderson County
45	2173	10.1	Oak Grove (CDP) Lexington County
46	2207	10.2	Saint Andrews (CDP) Richland County
47	2242	10.3	Cayce (city) Lexington County
48	n/a	10.5	Dalzell (CDP) Sumter County
49	n/a	10.6	Travelers Rest (city) Greenville County
50	2369	10.7	Summerville (town) Dorchester County
51	n/a	11.0	Burton (CDP) Beaufort County
51	2477	11.0	Goose Creek (city) Berkeley County
53	n/a	11.4	Moncks Corner (town) Berkeley County
54	n/a	11.6	Red Bank (CDP) Lexington County
55	n/a	11.7	Hardeeville (city) Jasper County
55	n/a	11.7	Valley Falls (CDP) Spartanburg County
57	n/a	11.8	Williamston (town) Anderson County
58	2764	11.9	Wade Hampton (CDP) Greenville County
59	n/a	12.0	Burnettown (town) Aiken County
60	n/a	12.1	Bishopville (city) Lee County
60	n/a	12.1	Northlake (CDP) Anderson County
62	n/a	12.2	Lesslie (CDP) York County
63	n/a	12.4	Cheraw (town) Chesterfield County
63	2898	12.4	Mauldin (city) Greenville County
65	n/a	12.7	Hartsville (city) Darlington County
66	n/a	12.8	Manning (city) Clarendon County
67	3049	12.9	Hanahan (city) Berkeley County
68	n/a	13.0	Lugoff (CDP) Kershaw County
69	n/a	13.5	India Hook (CDP) York County
70	3265	13.8	Easley (city) Pickens County
70	3265	13.8	Sumter (city) Sumter County
72	n/a	14.4	Springdale (town) Lexington County
73	3433	14.5	Taylors (CDP) Greenville County
74	n/a	14.6	Georgetown (city) Georgetown County
74	n/a	14.6	Seneca (city) Oconee County
76	n/a	14.7	Bamberg (town) Bamberg County
77	n/a	14.9	Hampton (town) Hampton County
78	n/a	15.0	Welcome (CDP) Greenville County
79	n/a	15.1	Boiling Springs (CDP) Spartanburg County
80	n/a	15.3	Clover (town) York County
80	3589	15.3	North Charleston (city) Charleston County
82	n/a	15.5	Batesburg-Leesville (town) Lexington County
83	3685	15.8	Rock Hill (city) York County
83	n/a	15.8	Union (city) Union County
85	n/a	16.3	Darlington (city) Darlington County
86	3797	16.4	Greer (city) Greenville County
87	n/a	16.7	Lake City (city) Florence County
88	n/a	16.9	Dunean (CDP) Greenville County
89	3903	17.1	Anderson (city) Anderson County
89	3903	17.1	Spartanburg (city) Spartanburg County
91	n/a	17.7	Laurens (city) Laurens County
92	n/a	17.8	Kingstree (town) Williamsburg County
93	n/a	18.0	Abbeville (city) Abbeville County
94	4084	18.3	Berea (CDP) Greenville County
95	n/a	18.5	Allendale (town) Allendale County
95	n/a	18.5	Williston (town) Barnwell County
97	4116	18.6	Orangeburg (city) Orangeburg County
98	n/a	18.7	Fountain Inn (city) Greenville County
98	n/a	18.7	Sans Souci (CDP) Greenville County
100	n/a	18.8	Sangaree (CDP) Berkeley County
101	n/a	19.0	Honea Path (town) Anderson County
102	n/a	19.2	Clinton (city) Laurens County
103	n/a	19.4	Pageland (town) Chesterfield County
103	n/a	19.4	Woodruff (city) Spartanburg County
105	n/a	19.8	Hollywood (town) Charleston County
106	n/a	20.1	Belton (city) Anderson County
106	n/a	20.1	Pickens (city) Pickens County
106	n/a	20.1	Winnsboro (town) Fairfield County
109	n/a	20.2	Brookdale (CDP) Orangeburg County
110	n/a	20.3	Barnwell (city) Barnwell County
111	4280	20.4	Simpsonville (city) Greenville County
112	4301	20.6	Ladson (CDP) Berkeley County
113	n/a	20.7	Belvedere (CDP) Aiken County
114	n/a	21.0	Dillon (city) Dillon County
115	n/a	21.1	Liberty (city) Pickens County
115	4344	21.1	Newberry (city) Newberry County
115	n/a	21.1	Piedmont (CDP) Anderson County
118	n/a	21.7	Chester (city) Chester County
119	n/a	22.4	Hopkins (CDP) Richland County
120	n/a	22.5	Centerville (CDP) Anderson County
121	n/a	22.6	Edisto (CDP) Orangeburg County
122	n/a	22.7	Lakewood (CDP) Sumter County
123	n/a	22.8	Arial (CDP) Pickens County
124	4449	23.0	Greenwood (city) Greenwood County
124	n/a	23.0	Marion (city) Marion County
126	n/a	23.2	Lancaster (city) Lancaster County
127	n/a	23.3	Walhalla (city) Oconee County
128	n/a	23.5	Andrews (town) Georgetown County
128	n/a	23.5	Mullins (city) Marion County
130	n/a	23.6	Saxon (CDP) Spartanburg County
131	n/a	23.7	Denmark (city) Bamberg County
132	n/a	24.1	Elgin (CDP) Lancaster County
133	4494	24.2	Parker (CDP) Greenville County
134	n/a	24.8	Springdale (CDP) Lancaster County
135	n/a	25.0	Lyman (town) Spartanburg County
136	n/a	26.0	Clearwater (CDP) Aiken County
137	4556	26.3	Gaffney (city) Cherokee County
138	n/a	26.9	North Hartsville (CDP) Darlington County
139	4572	27.2	Gantt (CDP) Greenville County
140	n/a	27.3	Duncan (town) Spartanburg County
141	n/a	27.5	Saluda (town) Saluda County
141	n/a	27.5	York (city) York County
143	n/a	28.9	Homeland Park (CDP) Anderson County
144	n/a	29.2	McCormick (town) McCormick County
145	n/a	29.9	Edgefield (town) Edgefield County
146	n/a	33.3	Gloverville (CDP) Aiken County
147	n/a	34.4	Bennettsville (city) Marlboro County
148	n/a	34.5	Southern Shops (CDP) Spartanburg County
149	n/a	35.8	East Gaffney (CDP) Cherokee County
150	n/a	38.9	Arcadia (CDP) Spartanburg County

Note: *The state column ranks the top/bottom 150 places in the state with population of 2,500 or more. The national column ranks the top/bottom places in the country with population of 10,000 or more. Places that are unincorporated were not considered in the rankings. n/a indicates data not available. Please refer to the User Guide for additional information.*

Per Capita Income

Top 150 Places Ranked in *Descending* Order

State Rank	Nat'l Rank	Dollars	Place
1	n/a	54,203	**Isle of Palms** (city) Charleston County
2	n/a	50,027	**Lake Murray of Richland** (CDP) Richland County
3	n/a	49,743	**Folly Beach** (city) Charleston County
4	436	46,091	**Hilton Head Island** (town) Beaufort County
5	663	41,815	**Five Forks** (CDP) Greenville County
6	720	40,870	**Mount Pleasant** (town) Charleston County
7	n/a	39,780	**Tega Cay** (city) York County
8	n/a	39,381	**Hollywood** (town) Charleston County
9	n/a	38,267	**Lake Wylie** (CDP) York County
10	1159	35,694	**Forest Acres** (city) Richland County
11	n/a	35,176	**Murrells Inlet** (CDP) Georgetown County
12	1231	35,046	**North Myrtle Beach** (city) Horry County
13	1363	34,030	**Fort Mill** (town) York County
14	n/a	33,845	**India Hook** (CDP) York County
15	n/a	32,775	**Northlake** (CDP) Anderson County
16	1605	32,131	**Charleston** (city) Charleston County
17	1648	31,853	**Aiken** (city) Aiken County
18	n/a	31,304	**Camden** (city) Kershaw County
19	1796	30,829	**Greenville** (city) Greenville County
20	1842	30,574	**Lexington** (town) Lexington County
21	2081	29,025	**North Augusta** (city) Aiken County
22	2161	28,593	**Wade Hampton** (CDP) Greenville County
23	n/a	28,541	**Lugoff** (CDP) Kershaw County
24	n/a	28,339	**Garden City** (CDP) Horry County
25	n/a	28,120	**Boiling Springs** (CDP) Spartanburg County
26	n/a	28,088	**Springdale** (town) Lexington County
27	2321	27,719	**Beaufort** (city) Beaufort County
28	n/a	27,501	**Newport** (CDP) York County
29	n/a	27,237	**Little River** (CDP) Horry County
30	2403	27,197	**Mauldin** (city) Greenville County
31	2406	27,178	**Myrtle Beach** (city) Horry County
32	2548	26,446	**Seven Oaks** (CDP) Lexington County
33	n/a	26,441	**Forestbrook** (CDP) Horry County
34	2599	26,143	**Simpsonville** (city) Greenville County
35	2622	26,034	**Bluffton** (town) Beaufort County
36	2670	25,766	**Summerville** (town) Dorchester County
37	2720	25,507	**Hanahan** (city) Berkeley County
38	2727	25,481	**Florence** (city) Florence County
39	n/a	25,247	**North Hartsville** (CDP) Darlington County
40	2774	25,244	**Goose Creek** (city) Berkeley County
41	2787	25,159	**Irmo** (town) Richland County
42	2793	25,124	**West Columbia** (city) Lexington County
43	n/a	24,980	**Surfside Beach** (town) Horry County
44	2864	24,779	**Columbia** (city) Richland County
45	2871	24,752	**Oak Grove** (CDP) Lexington County
46	2922	24,429	**Greer** (city) Greenville County
47	n/a	24,397	**Seneca** (city) Oconee County
48	n/a	24,365	**Hartsville** (city) Darlington County
49	n/a	23,616	**Red Bank** (CDP) Lexington County
50	3091	23,523	**Cayce** (city) Lexington County
51	3155	23,242	**Taylors** (CDP) Greenville County
52	3158	23,235	**Clemson** (city) Pickens County
53	3174	23,158	**Easley** (city) Pickens County
54	n/a	22,713	**Bamberg** (town) Bamberg County
55	3295	22,572	**Sumter** (city) Sumter County
56	3330	22,416	**Rock Hill** (city) York County
57	3367	22,234	**Red Hill** (CDP) Horry County
58	n/a	21,925	**Centerville** (CDP) Anderson County
59	n/a	21,450	**Sangaree** (CDP) Berkeley County
60	3572	21,258	**Dentsville** (CDP) Richland County
61	n/a	21,226	**Lesslie** (CDP) York County
62	n/a	21,199	**Moncks Corner** (town) Berkeley County
63	n/a	20,901	**Travelers Rest** (city) Greenville County
64	n/a	20,713	**Fountain Inn** (city) Greenville County
65	n/a	20,532	**Lakewood** (CDP) Sumter County
66	n/a	20,491	**Belton** (city) Anderson County
67	n/a	20,236	**Pendleton** (town) Anderson County
68	n/a	20,229	**Belvedere** (CDP) Aiken County
69	n/a	20,223	**Walterboro** (city) Colleton County
70	n/a	20,208	**Darlington** (city) Darlington County
71	3798	20,161	**Ladson** (CDP) Berkeley County
72	3804	20,143	**Spartanburg** (city) Spartanburg County
73	n/a	19,978	**Clover** (town) York County
74	3890	19,717	**North Charleston** (city) Charleston County
75	3901	19,657	**Port Royal** (town) Beaufort County
76	n/a	19,554	**Dalzell** (CDP) Sumter County
77	3926	19,536	**Socastee** (CDP) Horry County
78	n/a	19,449	**Lyman** (town) Spartanburg County
79	n/a	19,435	**Batesburg-Leesville** (town) Lexington County
80	n/a	19,412	**Williamston** (town) Anderson County
81	n/a	19,244	**Woodfield** (CDP) Richland County
82	n/a	19,233	**Burton** (CDP) Beaufort County
83	n/a	19,080	**Union** (city) Union County
84	n/a	19,060	**Hopkins** (CDP) Richland County
85	4014	19,036	**Conway** (city) Horry County
86	4024	18,941	**Gantt** (CDP) Greenville County
87	4041	18,845	**Anderson** (city) Anderson County
88	n/a	18,839	**Georgetown** (city) Georgetown County
89	n/a	18,718	**Hampton** (town) Hampton County
90	n/a	18,596	**Winnsboro** (town) Fairfield County
91	n/a	18,581	**Cheraw** (town) Chesterfield County
92	4104	18,549	**Gaffney** (city) Cherokee County
93	n/a	18,470	**Burnettown** (town) Aiken County
94	4116	18,469	**Saint Andrews** (CDP) Richland County
95	n/a	18,405	**Pickens** (city) Pickens County
96	n/a	18,199	**Piedmont** (CDP) Anderson County
97	n/a	17,881	**Duncan** (town) Spartanburg County
98	n/a	17,872	**Laurel Bay** (CDP) Beaufort County
99	n/a	17,860	**Laurens** (city) Laurens County
100	n/a	17,289	**Elgin** (CDP) Lancaster County
101	n/a	17,280	**Honea Path** (town) Anderson County
102	n/a	17,142	**Hardeeville** (city) Jasper County
103	4328	17,033	**Newberry** (city) Newberry County
104	n/a	17,022	**Saluda** (town) Saluda County
105	n/a	17,002	**Lake City** (city) Florence County
106	n/a	16,966	**Liberty** (city) Pickens County
107	n/a	16,711	**Lancaster** (city) Lancaster County
108	n/a	16,701	**Arial** (CDP) Pickens County
109	4372	16,589	**Greenwood** (city) Greenwood County
110	n/a	16,578	**Ridgeland** (town) Jasper County
111	n/a	16,525	**Mullins** (city) Marion County
112	n/a	16,524	**Graniteville** (CDP) Aiken County
113	4412	16,209	**Berea** (CDP) Greenville County
114	n/a	16,188	**Welcome** (CDP) Greenville County
115	n/a	15,960	**Valley Falls** (CDP) Spartanburg County
116	n/a	15,916	**Dillon** (city) Dillon County
117	4445	15,862	**Orangeburg** (city) Orangeburg County
118	n/a	15,776	**Denmark** (city) Bamberg County
119	n/a	15,727	**Kingstree** (town) Williamsburg County
120	n/a	15,463	**Dunean** (CDP) Greenville County
121	n/a	15,344	**Bennettsville** (city) Marlboro County
122	n/a	15,313	**Barnwell** (city) Barnwell County
123	n/a	15,299	**Sans Souci** (CDP) Greenville County
124	n/a	15,234	**Walhalla** (city) Oconee County
125	n/a	15,007	**York** (city) York County
126	n/a	14,788	**Pageland** (town) Chesterfield County
127	n/a	14,771	**Abbeville** (city) Abbeville County
128	n/a	14,672	**Clearwater** (CDP) Aiken County
129	n/a	14,634	**Marion** (city) Marion County
130	n/a	14,529	**Chester** (city) Chester County
131	n/a	14,516	**Williston** (town) Barnwell County
132	n/a	14,382	**Gloverville** (CDP) Aiken County
133	n/a	14,244	**Manning** (city) Clarendon County
134	n/a	13,925	**Woodruff** (city) Spartanburg County
135	n/a	13,828	**Arcadia** (CDP) Spartanburg County
136	n/a	13,566	**Clinton** (city) Laurens County
137	n/a	13,453	**Homeland Park** (CDP) Anderson County
138	n/a	13,378	**Edisto** (CDP) Orangeburg County
139	n/a	13,299	**Springdale** (CDP) Lancaster County
140	n/a	12,882	**East Gaffney** (CDP) Cherokee County
141	n/a	12,576	**Andrews** (town) Georgetown County
142	n/a	12,516	**Central** (town) Pickens County
143	4595	12,234	**Parker** (CDP) Greenville County
144	n/a	12,195	**Edgefield** (town) Edgefield County
145	n/a	11,700	**Brookdale** (CDP) Orangeburg County
146	n/a	11,182	**Allendale** (town) Allendale County
147	n/a	10,767	**Saxon** (CDP) Spartanburg County
148	n/a	9,885	**Bishopville** (city) Lee County
149	n/a	9,600	**Southern Shops** (CDP) Spartanburg County
150	n/a	9,326	**McCormick** (town) McCormick County

Note: The state column ranks the top/bottom 150 places in the state with population of 2,500 or more. The national column ranks the top/bottom places in the country with population of 10,000 or more. Places that are unincorporated were not considered in the rankings. n/a indicates data not available. Please refer to the User Guide for additional information.

Per Capita Income

Top 150 Places Ranked in *Ascending* Order

State Rank	Nat'l Rank	Dollars	Place
1	n/a	9,326	**McCormick** (town) McCormick County
2	n/a	9,600	**Southern Shops** (CDP) Spartanburg County
3	n/a	9,885	**Bishopville** (city) Lee County
4	n/a	10,767	**Saxon** (CDP) Spartanburg County
5	n/a	11,182	**Allendale** (town) Allendale County
6	n/a	11,700	**Brookdale** (CDP) Orangeburg County
7	n/a	12,195	**Edgefield** (town) Edgefield County
8	60	12,234	**Parker** (CDP) Greenville County
9	n/a	12,516	**Central** (town) Pickens County
10	n/a	12,576	**Andrews** (town) Georgetown County
11	n/a	12,882	**East Gaffney** (CDP) Cherokee County
12	n/a	13,299	**Springdale** (CDP) Lancaster County
13	n/a	13,378	**Edisto** (CDP) Orangeburg County
14	n/a	13,453	**Homeland Park** (CDP) Anderson County
15	n/a	13,566	**Clinton** (city) Laurens County
16	n/a	13,828	**Arcadia** (CDP) Spartanburg County
17	n/a	13,925	**Woodruff** (city) Spartanburg County
18	n/a	14,244	**Manning** (city) Clarendon County
19	n/a	14,382	**Gloverville** (CDP) Aiken County
20	n/a	14,516	**Williston** (town) Barnwell County
21	n/a	14,529	**Chester** (city) Chester County
22	n/a	14,634	**Marion** (city) Marion County
23	n/a	14,672	**Clearwater** (CDP) Aiken County
24	n/a	14,771	**Abbeville** (city) Abbeville County
25	n/a	14,788	**Pageland** (town) Chesterfield County
26	n/a	15,007	**York** (city) York County
27	n/a	15,234	**Walhalla** (city) Oconee County
28	n/a	15,299	**Sans Souci** (CDP) Greenville County
29	n/a	15,313	**Barnwell** (city) Barnwell County
30	n/a	15,344	**Bennettsville** (city) Marlboro County
31	n/a	15,463	**Dunean** (CDP) Greenville County
32	n/a	15,727	**Kingstree** (town) Williamsburg County
33	n/a	15,776	**Denmark** (city) Bamberg County
34	211	15,862	**Orangeburg** (city) Orangeburg County
35	n/a	15,916	**Dillon** (city) Dillon County
36	n/a	15,960	**Valley Falls** (CDP) Spartanburg County
37	n/a	16,188	**Welcome** (CDP) Greenville County
38	244	16,209	**Berea** (CDP) Greenville County
39	n/a	16,524	**Graniteville** (CDP) Aiken County
40	n/a	16,525	**Mullins** (city) Marion County
41	n/a	16,578	**Ridgeland** (town) Jasper County
42	284	16,589	**Greenwood** (city) Greenwood County
43	n/a	16,701	**Arial** (CDP) Pickens County
44	n/a	16,711	**Lancaster** (city) Lancaster County
45	n/a	16,966	**Liberty** (city) Pickens County
46	n/a	17,002	**Lake City** (city) Florence County
47	n/a	17,022	**Saluda** (town) Saluda County
48	328	17,033	**Newberry** (city) Newberry County
49	n/a	17,142	**Hardeeville** (city) Jasper County
50	n/a	17,280	**Honea Path** (town) Anderson County
51	n/a	17,289	**Elgin** (CDP) Lancaster County
52	n/a	17,860	**Laurens** (city) Laurens County
53	n/a	17,872	**Laurel Bay** (CDP) Beaufort County
54	n/a	17,881	**Duncan** (town) Spartanburg County
55	n/a	18,199	**Piedmont** (CDP) Anderson County
56	n/a	18,405	**Pickens** (city) Pickens County
57	540	18,469	**Saint Andrews** (CDP) Richland County
58	n/a	18,470	**Burnettown** (town) Aiken County
59	552	18,549	**Gaffney** (city) Cherokee County
60	n/a	18,581	**Cheraw** (town) Chesterfield County
61	n/a	18,596	**Winnsboro** (town) Fairfield County
62	n/a	18,718	**Hampton** (town) Hampton County
63	n/a	18,839	**Georgetown** (city) Georgetown County
64	615	18,845	**Anderson** (city) Anderson County
65	632	18,941	**Gantt** (CDP) Greenville County
66	642	19,036	**Conway** (city) Horry County
67	n/a	19,060	**Hopkins** (CDP) Richland County
68	n/a	19,080	**Union** (city) Union County
69	n/a	19,233	**Burton** (CDP) Beaufort County
70	n/a	19,244	**Woodfield** (CDP) Richland County
71	n/a	19,412	**Williamston** (town) Anderson County
72	n/a	19,435	**Batesburg-Leesville** (town) Lexington County
73	n/a	19,449	**Lyman** (town) Spartanburg County
74	730	19,536	**Socastee** (CDP) Horry County
75	n/a	19,554	**Dalzell** (CDP) Sumter County
76	754	19,657	**Port Royal** (town) Beaufort County
77	766	19,717	**North Charleston** (city) Charleston County
78	n/a	19,978	**Clover** (town) York County
79	852	20,143	**Spartanburg** (city) Spartanburg County
80	858	20,161	**Ladson** (CDP) Berkeley County
81	n/a	20,208	**Darlington** (city) Darlington County
82	n/a	20,223	**Walterboro** (city) Colleton County
83	n/a	20,229	**Belvedere** (CDP) Aiken County
84	n/a	20,236	**Pendleton** (town) Anderson County
85	n/a	20,491	**Belton** (city) Anderson County
86	n/a	20,532	**Lakewood** (CDP) Sumter County
87	n/a	20,713	**Fountain Inn** (city) Greenville County
88	n/a	20,901	**Travelers Rest** (city) Greenville County
89	n/a	21,199	**Moncks Corner** (town) Berkeley County
90	n/a	21,226	**Lesslie** (CDP) York County
91	1084	21,258	**Dentsville** (CDP) Richland County
92	n/a	21,450	**Sangaree** (CDP) Berkeley County
93	n/a	21,925	**Centerville** (CDP) Anderson County
94	1289	22,234	**Red Hill** (CDP) Horry County
95	1326	22,416	**Rock Hill** (city) York County
96	1361	22,572	**Sumter** (city) Sumter County
97	n/a	22,713	**Bamberg** (town) Bamberg County
98	1482	23,158	**Easley** (city) Pickens County
99	1498	23,235	**Clemson** (city) Pickens County
100	1501	23,242	**Taylors** (CDP) Greenville County
101	1565	23,523	**Cayce** (city) Lexington County
102	n/a	23,616	**Red Bank** (CDP) Lexington County
103	n/a	24,365	**Hartsville** (city) Darlington County
104	n/a	24,397	**Seneca** (city) Oconee County
105	1734	24,429	**Greer** (city) Greenville County
106	1785	24,752	**Oak Grove** (CDP) Lexington County
107	1791	24,779	**Columbia** (city) Richland County
108	n/a	24,980	**Surfside Beach** (town) Horry County
109	1863	25,124	**West Columbia** (city) Lexington County
110	1869	25,159	**Irmo** (town) Richland County
111	1882	25,244	**Goose Creek** (city) Berkeley County
112	n/a	25,247	**North Hartsville** (CDP) Darlington County
113	1929	25,481	**Florence** (city) Florence County
114	1936	25,507	**Hanahan** (city) Berkeley County
115	1986	25,766	**Summerville** (town) Dorchester County
116	2034	26,034	**Bluffton** (town) Beaufort County
117	2057	26,143	**Simpsonville** (city) Greenville County
118	n/a	26,441	**Forestbrook** (CDP) Horry County
119	2107	26,446	**Seven Oaks** (CDP) Lexington County
120	2250	27,178	**Myrtle Beach** (city) Horry County
121	2253	27,197	**Mauldin** (city) Greenville County
122	n/a	27,237	**Little River** (CDP) Horry County
123	n/a	27,501	**Newport** (CDP) York County
124	2334	27,719	**Beaufort** (city) Beaufort County
125	n/a	28,088	**Springdale** (town) Lexington County
126	n/a	28,120	**Boiling Springs** (CDP) Spartanburg County
127	n/a	28,339	**Garden City** (CDP) Horry County
128	n/a	28,541	**Lugoff** (CDP) Kershaw County
129	2495	28,593	**Wade Hampton** (CDP) Greenville County
130	2575	29,025	**North Augusta** (city) Aiken County
131	2814	30,574	**Lexington** (town) Lexington County
132	2860	30,829	**Greenville** (city) Greenville County
133	n/a	31,304	**Camden** (city) Kershaw County
134	3006	31,853	**Aiken** (city) Aiken County
135	3051	32,131	**Charleston** (city) Charleston County
136	n/a	32,775	**Northlake** (CDP) Anderson County
137	n/a	33,845	**India Hook** (CDP) York County
138	3293	34,030	**Fort Mill** (town) York County
139	3425	35,046	**North Myrtle Beach** (city) Horry County
140	n/a	35,176	**Murrells Inlet** (CDP) Georgetown County
141	3497	35,694	**Forest Acres** (city) Richland County
142	n/a	38,267	**Lake Wylie** (CDP) York County
143	n/a	39,381	**Hollywood** (town) Charleston County
144	n/a	39,780	**Tega Cay** (city) York County
145	3936	40,870	**Mount Pleasant** (town) Charleston County
146	3992	41,815	**Five Forks** (CDP) Greenville County
147	4220	46,091	**Hilton Head Island** (town) Beaufort County
148	n/a	49,743	**Folly Beach** (city) Charleston County
149	n/a	50,027	**Lake Murray of Richland** (CDP) Richland County
150	n/a	54,203	**Isle of Palms** (city) Charleston County

Note: The state column ranks the top/bottom 150 places in the state with population of 2,500 or more. The national column ranks the top/bottom places in the country with population of 10,000 or more. Places that are unincorporated were not considered in the rankings. n/a indicates data not available. Please refer to the User Guide for additional information.

Median Household Income

Top 150 Places Ranked in *Descending* Order

State Rank	Nat'l Rank	Dollars	Place
1	214	114,556	**Five Forks** (CDP) Greenville County
2	n/a	108,958	**Tega Cay** (city) York County
3	n/a	106,768	**Lake Murray of Richland** (CDP) Richland County
4	n/a	80,556	**Isle of Palms** (city) Charleston County
5	n/a	76,607	**Folly Beach** (city) Charleston County
6	1214	76,085	**Mount Pleasant** (town) Charleston County
7	n/a	75,915	**Lake Wylie** (CDP) York County
8	1536	69,772	**Hilton Head Island** (town) Beaufort County
9	n/a	67,515	**Boiling Springs** (CDP) Spartanburg County
10	n/a	67,392	**India Hook** (CDP) York County
11	1829	64,596	**Fort Mill** (town) York County
12	n/a	63,158	**Northlake** (CDP) Anderson County
13	1961	62,466	**Goose Creek** (city) Berkeley County
14	2026	61,477	**Lexington** (town) Lexington County
15	2145	60,038	**Bluffton** (town) Beaufort County
16	n/a	58,858	**Forestbrook** (CDP) Horry County
17	n/a	58,750	**Springdale** (town) Lexington County
18	2251	58,242	**Irmo** (town) Richland County
19	n/a	57,907	**Newport** (CDP) York County
20	2298	57,551	**Mauldin** (city) Greenville County
21	n/a	55,456	**Lugoff** (CDP) Kershaw County
22	2444	55,256	**Summerville** (town) Dorchester County
23	n/a	54,761	**Sangaree** (CDP) Berkeley County
24	n/a	53,799	**Hollywood** (town) Charleston County
25	2625	53,127	**Aiken** (city) Aiken County
26	2700	52,271	**Forest Acres** (city) Richland County
27	n/a	51,783	**Dalzell** (CDP) Sumter County
28	2742	51,737	**Charleston** (city) Charleston County
29	n/a	51,094	**Lakewood** (CDP) Sumter County
30	n/a	50,974	**Camden** (city) Kershaw County
31	2805	50,801	**Beaufort** (city) Beaufort County
32	n/a	50,768	**Travelers Rest** (city) Greenville County
33	2825	50,604	**Simpsonville** (city) Greenville County
34	2948	49,027	**North Augusta** (city) Aiken County
35	n/a	48,846	**Lesslie** (CDP) York County
36	2970	48,802	**Seven Oaks** (CDP) Lexington County
37	2982	48,669	**Ladson** (CDP) Berkeley County
38	3012	48,403	**Hanahan** (city) Berkeley County
39	n/a	48,118	**Murrells Inlet** (CDP) Georgetown County
40	3061	47,881	**Oak Grove** (CDP) Lexington County
41	3078	47,679	**North Myrtle Beach** (city) Horry County
42	3117	47,149	**Taylors** (CDP) Greenville County
43	n/a	46,216	**Red Bank** (CDP) Lexington County
44	n/a	46,152	**Fountain Inn** (city) Greenville County
45	n/a	45,852	**Moncks Corner** (town) Berkeley County
46	3260	45,381	**Port Royal** (town) Beaufort County
47	n/a	45,047	**Hopkins** (CDP) Richland County
48	n/a	44,606	**Little River** (CDP) Horry County
49	n/a	44,561	**Clover** (town) York County
50	n/a	44,444	**Lyman** (town) Spartanburg County
51	3341	44,386	**Wade Hampton** (CDP) Greenville County
52	3396	43,776	**Cayce** (city) Lexington County
53	n/a	43,549	**Woodfield** (CDP) Richland County
54	n/a	43,409	**North Hartsville** (CDP) Darlington County
55	n/a	43,004	**Centerville** (CDP) Anderson County
56	3481	42,991	**Greer** (city) Greenville County
57	n/a	42,733	**Laurel Bay** (CDP) Beaufort County
58	3519	42,550	**Rock Hill** (city) York County
59	3523	42,494	**Easley** (city) Pickens County
60	n/a	42,238	**Burton** (CDP) Beaufort County
61	n/a	42,208	**Belvedere** (CDP) Aiken County
62	n/a	42,044	**Surfside Beach** (town) Horry County
63	3583	41,939	**Red Hill** (CDP) Horry County
64	3606	41,663	**Florence** (city) Florence County
65	3635	41,344	**Columbia** (city) Richland County
66	3697	40,793	**Greenville** (city) Greenville County
67	n/a	40,754	**Piedmont** (CDP) Anderson County
68	n/a	40,664	**Williamston** (town) Anderson County
69	3722	40,594	**West Columbia** (city) Lexington County
70	3803	39,558	**Socastee** (CDP) Horry County
71	n/a	39,531	**Bamberg** (town) Bamberg County
72	3818	39,429	**Sumter** (city) Sumter County
73	3829	39,322	**North Charleston** (city) Charleston County
74	n/a	38,938	**Hampton** (town) Hampton County
75	3957	37,851	**Clemson** (city) Pickens County
76	3964	37,802	**Dentsville** (CDP) Richland County
77	n/a	37,173	**Garden City** (CDP) Horry County
78	n/a	36,739	**Burnettown** (town) Aiken County
79	n/a	36,661	**Valley Falls** (CDP) Spartanburg County
80	4077	36,293	**Myrtle Beach** (city) Horry County
81	n/a	35,638	**Dunean** (CDP) Greenville County
82	n/a	35,594	**Hardeeville** (city) Jasper County
83	n/a	35,495	**Ridgeland** (town) Jasper County
84	n/a	34,917	**Seneca** (city) Oconee County
85	4192	34,732	**Conway** (city) Horry County
86	n/a	34,417	**Duncan** (town) Spartanburg County
87	n/a	34,046	**Arial** (CDP) Pickens County
88	n/a	33,393	**Liberty** (city) Pickens County
89	4298	33,129	**Spartanburg** (city) Spartanburg County
90	n/a	33,098	**Walhalla** (city) Oconee County
91	n/a	32,800	**Pickens** (city) Pickens County
92	4328	32,645	**Orangeburg** (city) Orangeburg County
93	4334	32,537	**Saint Andrews** (CDP) Richland County
94	n/a	31,997	**Woodruff** (city) Spartanburg County
95	n/a	31,490	**Barnwell** (city) Barnwell County
96	n/a	31,439	**Arcadia** (CDP) Spartanburg County
97	4397	31,428	**Gantt** (CDP) Greenville County
98	n/a	31,102	**Winnsboro** (town) Fairfield County
99	4445	30,610	**Berea** (CDP) Greenville County
100	n/a	30,263	**Belton** (city) Anderson County
101	n/a	30,174	**Lake City** (city) Florence County
102	4468	30,032	**Anderson** (city) Anderson County
103	n/a	29,956	**Hartsville** (city) Darlington County
104	n/a	29,845	**Lancaster** (city) Lancaster County
105	n/a	29,789	**York** (city) York County
106	n/a	29,411	**Clinton** (city) Laurens County
107	4491	29,333	**Newberry** (city) Newberry County
108	n/a	29,163	**Welcome** (CDP) Greenville County
109	n/a	29,041	**Williston** (town) Barnwell County
110	4514	28,598	**Gaffney** (city) Cherokee County
111	n/a	28,323	**Sans Souci** (CDP) Greenville County
112	n/a	28,117	**Mullins** (city) Marion County
113	n/a	27,664	**Edisto** (CDP) Orangeburg County
114	n/a	27,270	**Darlington** (city) Darlington County
115	n/a	27,188	**Pendleton** (town) Anderson County
116	n/a	27,104	**Bennettsville** (city) Marlboro County
117	n/a	27,021	**Saluda** (town) Saluda County
118	n/a	26,852	**Andrews** (town) Georgetown County
119	n/a	26,627	**Pageland** (town) Chesterfield County
120	n/a	26,618	**Kingstree** (town) Williamsburg County
121	n/a	26,555	**Clearwater** (CDP) Aiken County
122	n/a	26,503	**Dillon** (city) Dillon County
123	n/a	26,438	**Union** (city) Union County
124	n/a	26,330	**Georgetown** (city) Georgetown County
125	n/a	26,084	**Elgin** (CDP) Lancaster County
126	n/a	25,887	**Batesburg-Leesville** (town) Lexington County
127	4610	25,293	**Parker** (CDP) Greenville County
128	n/a	25,182	**Homeland Park** (CDP) Anderson County
129	n/a	24,630	**Central** (town) Pickens County
130	4625	24,584	**Greenwood** (city) Greenwood County
131	n/a	24,583	**Laurens** (city) Laurens County
132	n/a	24,372	**Springdale** (CDP) Lancaster County
133	n/a	24,135	**Walterboro** (city) Colleton County
134	n/a	24,019	**Honea Path** (town) Anderson County
135	n/a	23,798	**Gloverville** (CDP) Aiken County
136	n/a	23,790	**Graniteville** (CDP) Aiken County
137	n/a	23,027	**Abbeville** (city) Abbeville County
138	n/a	22,946	**Allendale** (town) Allendale County
139	n/a	22,876	**Cheraw** (town) Chesterfield County
140	n/a	22,804	**Edgefield** (town) Edgefield County
141	n/a	22,656	**McCormick** (town) McCormick County
142	n/a	22,237	**Chester** (city) Chester County
143	n/a	22,207	**Saxon** (CDP) Spartanburg County
144	n/a	22,024	**East Gaffney** (CDP) Cherokee County
145	n/a	21,392	**Marion** (city) Marion County
146	n/a	20,761	**Manning** (city) Clarendon County
147	n/a	20,378	**Southern Shops** (CDP) Spartanburg County
148	n/a	17,931	**Denmark** (city) Bamberg County
149	n/a	17,642	**Bishopville** (city) Lee County
150	n/a	17,045	**Brookdale** (CDP) Orangeburg County

Note: The state column ranks the top/bottom 150 places in the state with population of 2,500 or more. The national column ranks the top/bottom places in the country with population of 10,000 or more. Places that are unincorporated were not considered in the rankings. n/a indicates data not available. Please refer to the User Guide for additional information.

Median Household Income

Top 150 Places Ranked in *Ascending* Order

State Rank	Nat'l Rank	Dollars	Place
1	n/a	17,045	**Brookdale** (CDP) Orangeburg County
2	n/a	17,642	**Bishopville** (city) Lee County
3	n/a	17,931	**Denmark** (city) Bamberg County
4	n/a	20,378	**Southern Shops** (CDP) Spartanburg County
5	n/a	20,761	**Manning** (city) Clarendon County
6	n/a	21,392	**Marion** (city) Marion County
7	n/a	22,024	**East Gaffney** (CDP) Cherokee County
8	n/a	22,207	**Saxon** (CDP) Spartanburg County
9	n/a	22,237	**Chester** (city) Chester County
10	n/a	22,656	**McCormick** (town) McCormick County
11	n/a	22,804	**Edgefield** (town) Edgefield County
12	n/a	22,876	**Cheraw** (town) Chesterfield County
13	n/a	22,946	**Allendale** (town) Allendale County
14	n/a	23,027	**Abbeville** (city) Abbeville County
15	n/a	23,790	**Graniteville** (CDP) Aiken County
16	n/a	23,798	**Gloverville** (CDP) Aiken County
17	n/a	24,019	**Honea Path** (town) Anderson County
18	n/a	24,135	**Walterboro** (city) Colleton County
19	n/a	24,372	**Springdale** (CDP) Lancaster County
20	n/a	24,583	**Laurens** (city) Laurens County
21	31	24,584	**Greenwood** (city) Greenwood County
22	n/a	24,630	**Central** (town) Pickens County
23	n/a	25,182	**Homeland Park** (CDP) Anderson County
24	46	25,293	**Parker** (CDP) Greenville County
25	n/a	25,887	**Batesburg-Leesville** (town) Lexington County
26	n/a	26,084	**Elgin** (CDP) Lancaster County
27	n/a	26,330	**Georgetown** (city) Georgetown County
28	n/a	26,438	**Union** (city) Union County
29	n/a	26,503	**Dillon** (city) Dillon County
30	n/a	26,555	**Clearwater** (CDP) Aiken County
31	n/a	26,618	**Kingstree** (town) Williamsburg County
32	n/a	26,627	**Pageland** (town) Chesterfield County
33	n/a	26,852	**Andrews** (town) Georgetown County
34	n/a	27,021	**Saluda** (town) Saluda County
35	n/a	27,104	**Bennettsville** (city) Marlboro County
36	n/a	27,188	**Pendleton** (town) Anderson County
37	n/a	27,270	**Darlington** (city) Darlington County
38	n/a	27,664	**Edisto** (CDP) Orangeburg County
39	n/a	28,117	**Mullins** (city) Marion County
40	n/a	28,323	**Sans Souci** (CDP) Greenville County
41	142	28,598	**Gaffney** (city) Cherokee County
42	n/a	29,041	**Williston** (town) Barnwell County
43	n/a	29,163	**Welcome** (CDP) Greenville County
44	165	29,333	**Newberry** (city) Newberry County
45	n/a	29,411	**Clinton** (city) Laurens County
46	n/a	29,789	**York** (city) York County
47	n/a	29,845	**Lancaster** (city) Lancaster County
48	n/a	29,956	**Hartsville** (city) Darlington County
49	188	30,032	**Anderson** (city) Anderson County
50	n/a	30,174	**Lake City** (city) Florence County
51	n/a	30,263	**Belton** (city) Anderson County
52	211	30,610	**Berea** (CDP) Greenville County
53	n/a	31,102	**Winnsboro** (town) Fairfield County
54	259	31,428	**Gantt** (CDP) Greenville County
55	n/a	31,439	**Arcadia** (CDP) Spartanburg County
56	n/a	31,490	**Barnwell** (city) Barnwell County
57	n/a	31,997	**Woodruff** (city) Spartanburg County
58	322	32,537	**Saint Andrews** (CDP) Richland County
59	328	32,645	**Orangeburg** (city) Orangeburg County
60	n/a	32,800	**Pickens** (city) Pickens County
61	n/a	33,098	**Walhalla** (city) Oconee County
62	358	33,129	**Spartanburg** (city) Spartanburg County
63	n/a	33,393	**Liberty** (city) Pickens County
64	n/a	34,046	**Arial** (CDP) Pickens County
65	n/a	34,417	**Duncan** (town) Spartanburg County
66	464	34,732	**Conway** (city) Horry County
67	n/a	34,917	**Seneca** (city) Oconee County
68	n/a	35,495	**Ridgeland** (town) Jasper County
69	n/a	35,594	**Hardeeville** (city) Jasper County
70	n/a	35,638	**Dunean** (CDP) Greenville County
71	579	36,293	**Myrtle Beach** (city) Horry County
72	n/a	36,661	**Valley Falls** (CDP) Spartanburg County
73	n/a	36,739	**Burnettown** (town) Aiken County
74	n/a	37,173	**Garden City** (CDP) Horry County
75	692	37,802	**Dentsville** (CDP) Richland County
76	699	37,851	**Clemson** (city) Pickens County
77	n/a	38,938	**Hampton** (town) Hampton County
78	827	39,322	**North Charleston** (city) Charleston County
79	837	39,429	**Sumter** (city) Sumter County
80	n/a	39,531	**Bamberg** (town) Bamberg County
81	853	39,558	**Socastee** (CDP) Horry County
82	934	40,594	**West Columbia** (city) Lexington County
83	n/a	40,664	**Williamston** (town) Anderson County
84	n/a	40,754	**Piedmont** (CDP) Anderson County
85	958	40,793	**Greenville** (city) Greenville County
86	1021	41,344	**Columbia** (city) Richland County
87	1049	41,663	**Florence** (city) Florence County
88	1073	41,939	**Red Hill** (CDP) Horry County
89	n/a	42,044	**Surfside Beach** (town) Horry County
90	n/a	42,208	**Belvedere** (CDP) Aiken County
91	n/a	42,238	**Burton** (CDP) Beaufort County
92	1133	42,494	**Easley** (city) Pickens County
93	1137	42,550	**Rock Hill** (city) York County
94	n/a	42,733	**Laurel Bay** (CDP) Beaufort County
95	1175	42,991	**Greer** (city) Greenville County
96	n/a	43,004	**Centerville** (CDP) Anderson County
97	n/a	43,409	**North Hartsville** (CDP) Darlington County
98	n/a	43,549	**Woodfield** (CDP) Richland County
99	1260	43,776	**Cayce** (city) Lexington County
100	1315	44,386	**Wade Hampton** (CDP) Greenville County
101	n/a	44,444	**Lyman** (town) Spartanburg County
102	n/a	44,561	**Clover** (town) York County
103	n/a	44,606	**Little River** (CDP) Horry County
104	n/a	45,047	**Hopkins** (CDP) Richland County
105	1396	45,381	**Port Royal** (town) Beaufort County
106	n/a	45,852	**Moncks Corner** (town) Berkeley County
107	n/a	46,152	**Fountain Inn** (city) Greenville County
108	n/a	46,216	**Red Bank** (CDP) Lexington County
109	1539	47,149	**Taylors** (CDP) Greenville County
110	1578	47,679	**North Myrtle Beach** (city) Horry County
111	1595	47,881	**Oak Grove** (CDP) Lexington County
112	n/a	48,118	**Murrells Inlet** (CDP) Georgetown County
113	1644	48,403	**Hanahan** (city) Berkeley County
114	1674	48,669	**Ladson** (CDP) Berkeley County
115	1686	48,802	**Seven Oaks** (CDP) Lexington County
116	n/a	48,846	**Lesslie** (CDP) York County
117	1708	49,027	**North Augusta** (city) Aiken County
118	1831	50,604	**Simpsonville** (city) Greenville County
119	n/a	50,768	**Travelers Rest** (city) Greenville County
120	1851	50,801	**Beaufort** (city) Beaufort County
121	n/a	50,974	**Camden** (city) Kershaw County
122	n/a	51,094	**Lakewood** (CDP) Sumter County
123	1914	51,737	**Charleston** (city) Charleston County
124	n/a	51,783	**Dalzell** (CDP) Sumter County
125	1956	52,271	**Forest Acres** (city) Richland County
126	2031	53,127	**Aiken** (city) Aiken County
127	n/a	53,799	**Hollywood** (town) Charleston County
128	n/a	54,761	**Sangaree** (CDP) Berkeley County
129	2212	55,256	**Summerville** (town) Dorchester County
130	n/a	55,456	**Lugoff** (CDP) Kershaw County
131	2358	57,551	**Mauldin** (city) Greenville County
132	n/a	57,907	**Newport** (CDP) York County
133	2405	58,242	**Irmo** (town) Richland County
134	n/a	58,750	**Springdale** (town) Lexington County
135	n/a	58,858	**Forestbrook** (CDP) Horry County
136	2511	60,038	**Bluffton** (town) Beaufort County
137	2630	61,477	**Lexington** (town) Lexington County
138	2695	62,466	**Goose Creek** (city) Berkeley County
139	n/a	63,158	**Northlake** (CDP) Anderson County
140	2827	64,596	**Fort Mill** (town) York County
141	n/a	67,392	**India Hook** (CDP) York County
142	n/a	67,515	**Boiling Springs** (CDP) Spartanburg County
143	3120	69,772	**Hilton Head Island** (town) Beaufort County
144	n/a	75,915	**Lake Wylie** (CDP) York County
145	3442	76,085	**Mount Pleasant** (town) Charleston County
146	n/a	76,607	**Folly Beach** (city) Charleston County
147	n/a	80,556	**Isle of Palms** (city) Charleston County
148	n/a	106,768	**Lake Murray of Richland** (CDP) Richland County
149	n/a	108,958	**Tega Cay** (city) York County
150	4442	114,556	**Five Forks** (CDP) Greenville County

Note: The state column ranks the top/bottom 150 places in the state with population of 2,500 or more. The national column ranks the top/bottom places in the country with population of 10,000 or more. Places that are unincorporated were not considered in the rankings. n/a indicates data not available. Please refer to the User Guide for additional information.

Average Household Income

Top 150 Places Ranked in *Descending* Order

State Rank	Nat'l Rank	Dollars	Place
1	n/a	140,072	**Lake Murray of Richland** (CDP) Richland County
2	377	129,286	**Five Forks** (CDP) Greenville County
3	n/a	128,674	**Isle of Palms** (city) Charleston County
4	n/a	116,679	**Tega Cay** (city) York County
5	931	101,114	**Hilton Head Island** (town) Beaufort County
6	961	100,185	**Mount Pleasant** (town) Charleston County
7	n/a	98,983	**Lake Wylie** (CDP) York County
8	n/a	98,681	**Folly Beach** (city) Charleston County
9	n/a	94,605	**Hollywood** (town) Charleston County
10	1505	86,190	**Fort Mill** (town) York County
11	n/a	81,979	**India Hook** (CDP) York County
12	n/a	78,465	**Northlake** (CDP) Anderson County
13	n/a	77,715	**Boiling Springs** (CDP) Spartanburg County
14	2010	76,519	**Lexington** (town) Lexington County
15	n/a	75,607	**Murrells Inlet** (CDP) Georgetown County
16	2135	74,298	**Aiken** (city) Aiken County
17	2137	74,242	**Charleston** (city) Charleston County
18	n/a	74,147	**Camden** (city) Kershaw County
19	2153	74,026	**Bluffton** (town) Beaufort County
20	2221	72,684	**Forest Acres** (city) Richland County
21	n/a	72,052	**Newport** (CDP) York County
22	n/a	70,545	**Lugoff** (CDP) Kershaw County
23	2401	70,000	**Goose Creek** (city) Berkeley County
24	2440	69,300	**Greenville** (city) Greenville County
25	2445	69,177	**Beaufort** (city) Beaufort County
26	2557	67,644	**North Myrtle Beach** (city) Horry County
27	2632	66,765	**Summerville** (town) Dorchester County
28	n/a	66,346	**Springdale** (town) Lexington County
29	2682	66,181	**North Augusta** (city) Aiken County
30	2697	66,026	**Mauldin** (city) Greenville County
31	2818	64,281	**Columbia** (city) Richland County
32	2835	64,013	**Irmo** (town) Richland County
33	n/a	63,914	**Forestbrook** (CDP) Horry County
34	2845	63,867	**Simpsonville** (city) Greenville County
35	n/a	63,274	**North Hartsville** (CDP) Darlington County
36	2938	62,546	**Wade Hampton** (CDP) Greenville County
37	n/a	62,411	**Sangaree** (CDP) Berkeley County
38	2950	62,405	**Myrtle Beach** (city) Horry County
39	2989	62,006	**Hanahan** (city) Berkeley County
40	3033	61,368	**Florence** (city) Florence County
41	3054	61,130	**Seven Oaks** (CDP) Lexington County
42	3126	60,180	**Greer** (city) Greenville County
43	n/a	59,603	**Lakewood** (CDP) Sumter County
44	3206	59,113	**Taylors** (CDP) Greenville County
45	3225	58,803	**Oak Grove** (CDP) Lexington County
46	n/a	58,737	**Hartsville** (city) Darlington County
47	3269	58,298	**Ladson** (CDP) Berkeley County
48	n/a	57,583	**Travelers Rest** (city) Greenville County
49	3408	56,743	**Port Royal** (town) Beaufort County
50	n/a	56,449	**Lesslie** (CDP) York County
51	n/a	56,205	**Dalzell** (CDP) Sumter County
52	3476	55,955	**Rock Hill** (city) York County
53	3479	55,930	**Easley** (city) Pickens County
54	n/a	55,510	**Red Bank** (CDP) Lexington County
55	3562	54,924	**Clemson** (city) Pickens County
56	n/a	54,863	**Hampton** (town) Hampton County
57	n/a	54,795	**Laurel Bay** (CDP) Beaufort County
58	3572	54,769	**Sumter** (city) Sumter County
59	n/a	54,716	**Clover** (town) York County
60	n/a	54,620	**Garden City** (CDP) Horry County
61	3612	54,429	**Cayce** (city) Lexington County
62	n/a	54,093	**Moncks Corner** (town) Berkeley County
63	n/a	53,958	**Centerville** (CDP) Anderson County
64	n/a	53,782	**Belvedere** (CDP) Aiken County
65	3704	53,319	**Red Hill** (CDP) Horry County
66	n/a	53,035	**Little River** (CDP) Horry County
67	3732	53,024	**West Columbia** (city) Lexington County
68	n/a	52,960	**Bamberg** (town) Bamberg County
68	n/a	52,960	**Fountain Inn** (city) Greenville County
70	3869	51,292	**Conway** (city) Horry County
71	n/a	50,932	**Surfside Beach** (town) Horry County
72	n/a	50,752	**Seneca** (city) Oconee County
73	n/a	50,721	**Ridgeland** (town) Jasper County
74	n/a	50,693	**Burton** (CDP) Beaufort County
75	n/a	50,512	**Williamston** (town) Anderson County
76	3932	50,445	**North Charleston** (city) Charleston County
77	n/a	49,910	**Woodfield** (CDP) Richland County
78	n/a	49,554	**Hopkins** (CDP) Richland County
79	4039	48,953	**Gantt** (CDP) Greenville County
80	4047	48,890	**Socastee** (CDP) Horry County
81	n/a	47,967	**Batesburg-Leesville** (town) Lexington County
82	n/a	47,689	**Lyman** (town) Spartanburg County
83	4170	47,358	**Dentsville** (CDP) Richland County
84	n/a	46,795	**Denmark** (city) Bamberg County
85	n/a	46,744	**Belton** (city) Anderson County
86	4220	46,737	**Spartanburg** (city) Spartanburg County
87	n/a	46,598	**Arial** (CDP) Pickens County
88	n/a	46,399	**Darlington** (city) Darlington County
89	n/a	46,290	**Walterboro** (city) Colleton County
90	n/a	45,730	**Georgetown** (city) Georgetown County
91	n/a	45,162	**Piedmont** (CDP) Anderson County
92	n/a	44,795	**Burnettown** (town) Aiken County
93	n/a	44,663	**Lake City** (city) Florence County
94	4396	44,150	**Anderson** (city) Anderson County
95	4404	43,952	**Gaffney** (city) Cherokee County
96	n/a	43,602	**Kingstree** (town) Williamsburg County
97	n/a	43,532	**Pickens** (city) Pickens County
98	n/a	43,489	**Hardeeville** (city) Jasper County
99	n/a	43,121	**Saluda** (town) Saluda County
100	n/a	43,001	**Walhalla** (city) Oconee County
101	n/a	42,611	**Winnsboro** (town) Fairfield County
102	4466	42,375	**Newberry** (city) Newberry County
103	n/a	42,373	**Arcadia** (CDP) Spartanburg County
104	n/a	42,219	**Bennettsville** (city) Marlboro County
105	n/a	42,112	**Valley Falls** (CDP) Spartanburg County
106	n/a	41,890	**Edgefield** (town) Edgefield County
107	n/a	41,763	**York** (city) York County
108	n/a	41,377	**Union** (city) Union County
109	4502	41,310	**Greenwood** (city) Greenwood County
110	4505	41,271	**Orangeburg** (city) Orangeburg County
111	n/a	41,268	**Duncan** (town) Spartanburg County
112	n/a	40,930	**Mullins** (city) Marion County
113	n/a	40,920	**Williston** (town) Barnwell County
114	n/a	40,918	**Lancaster** (city) Lancaster County
115	n/a	40,736	**Honea Path** (town) Anderson County
116	n/a	40,527	**Elgin** (CDP) Lancaster County
117	4534	40,320	**Saint Andrews** (CDP) Richland County
118	4551	39,868	**Berea** (CDP) Greenville County
119	n/a	39,787	**Dunean** (CDP) Greenville County
120	n/a	39,613	**Liberty** (city) Pickens County
121	n/a	39,513	**Laurens** (city) Laurens County
122	n/a	39,223	**Barnwell** (city) Barnwell County
123	n/a	38,630	**Dillon** (city) Dillon County
124	n/a	38,541	**Woodruff** (city) Spartanburg County
125	n/a	38,015	**Pendleton** (town) Anderson County
126	n/a	37,765	**Welcome** (CDP) Greenville County
127	n/a	37,625	**Clinton** (city) Laurens County
128	n/a	37,479	**Cheraw** (town) Chesterfield County
129	n/a	37,344	**Marion** (city) Marion County
130	n/a	36,295	**Chester** (city) Chester County
131	n/a	35,980	**Andrews** (town) Georgetown County
132	n/a	35,764	**McCormick** (town) McCormick County
133	n/a	35,681	**Clearwater** (CDP) Aiken County
134	n/a	35,659	**Sans Souci** (CDP) Greenville County
135	n/a	35,633	**Graniteville** (CDP) Aiken County
136	n/a	35,608	**Abbeville** (city) Abbeville County
137	n/a	35,215	**Manning** (city) Clarendon County
138	n/a	34,850	**Pageland** (town) Chesterfield County
139	n/a	33,119	**Springdale** (CDP) Lancaster County
140	n/a	33,074	**Saxon** (CDP) Spartanburg County
141	n/a	32,850	**Edisto** (CDP) Orangeburg County
142	n/a	32,762	**Homeland Park** (CDP) Anderson County
143	4640	32,603	**Parker** (CDP) Greenville County
144	n/a	31,314	**Gloverville** (CDP) Aiken County
145	n/a	30,929	**East Gaffney** (CDP) Cherokee County
146	n/a	30,134	**Allendale** (town) Allendale County
147	n/a	29,465	**Central** (town) Pickens County
148	n/a	28,920	**Bishopville** (city) Lee County
149	n/a	28,488	**Brookdale** (CDP) Orangeburg County
150	n/a	27,130	**Southern Shops** (CDP) Spartanburg County

Note: The state column ranks the top/bottom 150 places in the state with population of 2,500 or more. The national column ranks the top/bottom places in the country with population of 10,000 or more. Places that are unincorporated were not considered in the rankings. n/a indicates data not available. Please refer to the User Guide for additional information.

Average Household Income

Top 150 Places Ranked in *Ascending* Order

State Rank	Nat'l Rank	Dollars	Place
1	n/a	27,130	Southern Shops (CDP) Spartanburg County
2	n/a	28,488	Brookdale (CDP) Orangeburg County
3	n/a	28,920	Bishopville (city) Lee County
4	n/a	29,465	Central (town) Pickens County
5	n/a	30,134	Allendale (town) Allendale County
6	n/a	30,929	East Gaffney (CDP) Cherokee County
7	n/a	31,314	Gloverville (CDP) Aiken County
8	16	32,603	Parker (CDP) Greenville County
9	n/a	32,762	Homeland Park (CDP) Anderson County
10	n/a	32,850	Edisto (CDP) Orangeburg County
11	n/a	33,074	Saxon (CDP) Spartanburg County
12	n/a	33,119	Springdale (CDP) Lancaster County
13	n/a	34,850	Pageland (town) Chesterfield County
14	n/a	35,215	Manning (city) Clarendon County
15	n/a	35,608	Abbeville (city) Abbeville County
16	n/a	35,633	Graniteville (CDP) Aiken County
17	n/a	35,659	Sans Souci (CDP) Greenville County
18	n/a	35,681	Clearwater (CDP) Aiken County
19	n/a	35,764	McCormick (town) McCormick County
20	n/a	35,980	Andrews (town) Georgetown County
21	n/a	36,295	Chester (city) Chester County
22	n/a	37,344	Marion (city) Marion County
23	n/a	37,479	Cheraw (town) Chesterfield County
24	n/a	37,625	Clinton (city) Laurens County
25	n/a	37,765	Welcome (CDP) Greenville County
26	n/a	38,015	Pendleton (town) Anderson County
27	n/a	38,541	Woodruff (city) Spartanburg County
28	n/a	38,630	Dillon (city) Dillon County
29	n/a	39,223	Barnwell (city) Barnwell County
30	n/a	39,513	Laurens (city) Laurens County
31	n/a	39,613	Liberty (city) Pickens County
32	n/a	39,787	Dunean (CDP) Greenville County
33	105	39,868	Berea (CDP) Greenville County
34	122	40,320	Saint Andrews (CDP) Richland County
35	n/a	40,527	Elgin (CDP) Lancaster County
36	n/a	40,736	Honea Path (town) Anderson County
37	n/a	40,918	Lancaster (city) Lancaster County
38	n/a	40,920	Williston (town) Barnwell County
39	n/a	40,930	Mullins (city) Marion County
40	n/a	41,268	Duncan (town) Spartanburg County
41	151	41,271	Orangeburg (city) Orangeburg County
42	154	41,310	Greenwood (city) Greenwood County
43	n/a	41,377	Union (city) Union County
44	n/a	41,763	York (city) York County
45	n/a	41,890	Edgefield (town) Edgefield County
46	n/a	42,112	Valley Falls (CDP) Spartanburg County
47	n/a	42,219	Bennettsville (city) Marlboro County
48	n/a	42,373	Arcadia (CDP) Spartanburg County
49	190	42,375	Newberry (city) Newberry County
50	n/a	42,611	Winnsboro (town) Fairfield County
51	n/a	43,001	Walhalla (city) Oconee County
52	n/a	43,121	Saluda (town) Saluda County
53	n/a	43,489	Hardeeville (city) Jasper County
54	n/a	43,532	Pickens (city) Pickens County
55	n/a	43,602	Kingstree (town) Williamsburg County
56	252	43,952	Gaffney (city) Cherokee County
57	260	44,150	Anderson (city) Anderson County
58	n/a	44,663	Lake City (city) Florence County
59	n/a	44,795	Burnettown (town) Aiken County
60	n/a	45,162	Piedmont (CDP) Anderson County
61	n/a	45,730	Georgetown (city) Georgetown County
62	n/a	46,290	Walterboro (city) Colleton County
63	n/a	46,399	Darlington (city) Darlington County
64	n/a	46,598	Arial (CDP) Pickens County
65	436	46,737	Spartanburg (city) Spartanburg County
66	n/a	46,744	Belton (city) Anderson County
67	n/a	46,795	Denmark (city) Bamberg County
68	486	47,358	Dentsville (CDP) Richland County
69	n/a	47,689	Lyman (town) Spartanburg County
70	n/a	47,967	Batesburg-Leesville (town) Lexington County
71	609	48,890	Socastee (CDP) Horry County
72	617	48,953	Gantt (CDP) Greenville County
73	n/a	49,554	Hopkins (CDP) Richland County
74	n/a	49,910	Woodfield (CDP) Richland County
75	724	50,445	North Charleston (city) Charleston County
76	n/a	50,512	Williamston (town) Anderson County
77	n/a	50,693	Burton (CDP) Beaufort County
78	n/a	50,721	Ridgeland (town) Jasper County
79	n/a	50,752	Seneca (city) Oconee County
80	n/a	50,932	Surfside Beach (town) Horry County
81	787	51,292	Conway (city) Horry County
82	n/a	52,960	Bamberg (town) Bamberg County
82	n/a	52,960	Fountain Inn (city) Greenville County
84	924	53,024	West Columbia (city) Lexington County
85	n/a	53,035	Little River (CDP) Horry County
86	952	53,319	Red Hill (CDP) Horry County
87	n/a	53,782	Belvedere (CDP) Aiken County
88	n/a	53,958	Centerville (CDP) Anderson County
89	n/a	54,093	Moncks Corner (town) Berkeley County
90	1044	54,429	Cayce (city) Lexington County
91	n/a	54,620	Garden City (CDP) Horry County
92	n/a	54,716	Clover (town) York County
93	1084	54,769	Sumter (city) Sumter County
94	n/a	54,795	Laurel Bay (CDP) Beaufort County
95	n/a	54,863	Hampton (town) Hampton County
96	1094	54,924	Clemson (city) Pickens County
97	n/a	55,510	Red Bank (CDP) Lexington County
98	1177	55,930	Easley (city) Pickens County
99	1180	55,955	Rock Hill (city) York County
100	n/a	56,205	Dalzell (CDP) Sumter County
101	n/a	56,449	Lesslie (CDP) York County
102	1248	56,743	Port Royal (town) Beaufort County
103	n/a	57,583	Travelers Rest (city) Greenville County
104	1387	58,298	Ladson (CDP) Berkeley County
105	n/a	58,737	Hartsville (city) Darlington County
106	1431	58,803	Oak Grove (CDP) Lexington County
107	1450	59,113	Taylors (CDP) Greenville County
108	n/a	59,603	Lakewood (CDP) Sumter County
109	1530	60,180	Greer (city) Greenville County
110	1602	61,130	Seven Oaks (CDP) Lexington County
111	1623	61,368	Florence (city) Florence County
112	1667	62,006	Hanahan (city) Berkeley County
113	1706	62,405	Myrtle Beach (city) Horry County
114	n/a	62,411	Sangaree (CDP) Berkeley County
115	1718	62,546	Wade Hampton (CDP) Greenville County
116	n/a	63,274	North Hartsville (CDP) Darlington County
117	1811	63,867	Simpsonville (city) Greenville County
118	n/a	63,914	Forestbrook (CDP) Horry County
119	1821	64,013	Irmo (town) Richland County
120	1838	64,281	Columbia (city) Richland County
121	1959	66,026	Mauldin (city) Greenville County
122	1974	66,181	North Augusta (city) Aiken County
123	n/a	66,346	Springdale (town) Lexington County
124	2023	66,765	Summerville (town) Dorchester County
125	2099	67,644	North Myrtle Beach (city) Horry County
126	2211	69,177	Beaufort (city) Beaufort County
127	2216	69,300	Greenville (city) Greenville County
128	2255	70,000	Goose Creek (city) Berkeley County
129	n/a	70,545	Lugoff (CDP) Kershaw County
130	n/a	72,052	Newport (CDP) York County
131	2435	72,684	Forest Acres (city) Richland County
132	2503	74,026	Bluffton (town) Beaufort County
133	n/a	74,147	Camden (city) Kershaw County
134	2519	74,242	Charleston (city) Charleston County
135	2521	74,298	Aiken (city) Aiken County
136	n/a	75,607	Murrells Inlet (CDP) Georgetown County
137	2646	76,519	Lexington (town) Lexington County
138	n/a	77,715	Boiling Springs (CDP) Spartanburg County
139	n/a	78,465	Northlake (CDP) Anderson County
140	n/a	81,979	India Hook (CDP) York County
141	3151	86,190	Fort Mill (town) York County
142	n/a	94,605	Hollywood (town) Charleston County
143	n/a	98,681	Folly Beach (city) Charleston County
144	n/a	98,983	Lake Wylie (CDP) York County
145	3695	100,185	Mount Pleasant (town) Charleston County
146	3725	101,114	Hilton Head Island (town) Beaufort County
147	n/a	116,679	Tega Cay (city) York County
148	n/a	128,674	Isle of Palms (city) Charleston County
149	4279	129,286	Five Forks (CDP) Greenville County
150	n/a	140,072	Lake Murray of Richland (CDP) Richland County

Note: *The state column ranks the top/bottom 150 places in the state with population of 2,500 or more. The national column ranks the top/bottom places in the country with population of 10,000 or more. Places that are unincorporated were not considered in the rankings. n/a indicates data not available. Please refer to the User Guide for additional information.*

Households with Income of $100,000 or More

Top 150 Places Ranked in *Descending* Order

State Rank	Nat'l Rank	Percent	Place
1	149	60.1	**Five Forks** (CDP) Greenville County
2	n/a	55.1	**Tega Cay** (city) York County
3	n/a	53.8	**Lake Murray of Richland** (CDP) Richland County
4	n/a	44.7	**Isle of Palms** (city) Charleston County
5	n/a	42.3	**Folly Beach** (city) Charleston County
6	1067	37.8	**Mount Pleasant** (town) Charleston County
7	n/a	37.4	**Lake Wylie** (CDP) York County
8	1419	32.9	**Hilton Head Island** (town) Beaufort County
9	1523	31.2	**Fort Mill** (town) York County
10	n/a	31.0	**India Hook** (CDP) York County
11	n/a	27.3	**Boiling Springs** (CDP) Spartanburg County
12	1861	26.8	**Lexington** (town) Lexington County
13	n/a	26.5	**Camden** (city) Kershaw County
14	1940	26.0	**Forest Acres** (city) Richland County
15	1974	25.7	**Aiken** (city) Aiken County
16	n/a	24.7	**Hollywood** (town) Charleston County
17	n/a	24.2	**Newport** (CDP) York County
18	2149	23.9	**Bluffton** (town) Beaufort County
19	n/a	23.6	**Northlake** (CDP) Anderson County
20	2254	22.8	**Charleston** (city) Charleston County
21	n/a	22.3	**Forestbrook** (CDP) Horry County
22	2466	20.7	**Beaufort** (city) Beaufort County
23	2492	20.5	**Summerville** (town) Dorchester County
24	2531	20.2	**Goose Creek** (city) Berkeley County
25	2633	19.5	**Greenville** (city) Greenville County
26	2644	19.4	**Mauldin** (city) Greenville County
27	n/a	19.1	**Springdale** (town) Lexington County
28	n/a	19.0	**Murrells Inlet** (CDP) Georgetown County
29	2710	18.8	**Hanahan** (city) Berkeley County
30	2722	18.7	**North Augusta** (city) Aiken County
31	2784	18.2	**Wade Hampton** (CDP) Greenville County
32	2823	17.9	**Greer** (city) Greenville County
33	n/a	17.7	**Sangaree** (CDP) Berkeley County
34	2876	17.5	**Columbia** (city) Richland County
35	n/a	17.4	**Lakewood** (CDP) Sumter County
36	2901	17.3	**Clemson** (city) Pickens County
37	n/a	17.0	**Bamberg** (town) Bamberg County
38	3014	16.4	**North Myrtle Beach** (city) Horry County
39	3023	16.3	**Seven Oaks** (CDP) Lexington County
40	3047	16.1	**Florence** (city) Florence County
41	3057	16.0	**Irmo** (town) Richland County
42	n/a	15.5	**Hampton** (town) Hampton County
43	3153	15.3	**Simpsonville** (city) Greenville County
44	n/a	15.2	**Lugoff** (CDP) Kershaw County
45	3178	15.1	**Myrtle Beach** (city) Horry County
46	3205	14.9	**Taylors** (CDP) Greenville County
47	3295	14.3	**Ladson** (CDP) Berkeley County
47	n/a	14.3	**Red Bank** (CDP) Lexington County
47	n/a	14.3	**Travelers Rest** (city) Greenville County
50	n/a	14.1	**Lesslie** (CDP) York County
51	n/a	13.8	**Seneca** (city) Oconee County
52	n/a	13.6	**Clover** (town) York County
53	n/a	13.5	**Hartsville** (city) Darlington County
53	3392	13.5	**Oak Grove** (CDP) Lexington County
55	n/a	13.3	**Little River** (CDP) Horry County
55	3434	13.3	**Rock Hill** (city) York County
57	3448	13.2	**West Columbia** (city) Lexington County
58	3463	13.1	**Easley** (city) Pickens County
58	3463	13.1	**Sumter** (city) Sumter County
60	n/a	12.8	**Centerville** (CDP) Anderson County
61	3512	12.7	**Port Royal** (town) Beaufort County
62	n/a	12.6	**Fountain Inn** (city) Greenville County
63	n/a	12.1	**Arcadia** (CDP) Spartanburg County
64	n/a	11.9	**Belton** (city) Anderson County
65	n/a	11.7	**Williamston** (town) Anderson County
66	3720	11.6	**Cayce** (city) Lexington County
66	n/a	11.6	**Darlington** (city) Darlington County
68	n/a	11.2	**Walterboro** (city) Colleton County
69	3810	11.1	**North Charleston** (city) Charleston County
69	3810	11.1	**Red Hill** (CDP) Horry County
71	n/a	10.9	**Saluda** (town) Saluda County
72	n/a	10.8	**Arial** (CDP) Pickens County
72	n/a	10.8	**Honea Path** (town) Anderson County
74	n/a	10.7	**Moncks Corner** (town) Berkeley County
75	3968	10.2	**Newberry** (city) Newberry County
76	4007	10.0	**Anderson** (city) Anderson County
77	4058	9.7	**Gantt** (CDP) Greenville County
77	n/a	9.7	**North Hartsville** (CDP) Darlington County
79	4071	9.6	**Spartanburg** (city) Spartanburg County
80	n/a	9.5	**Elgin** (CDP) Lancaster County
81	n/a	9.4	**Belvedere** (CDP) Aiken County
81	n/a	9.4	**Burton** (CDP) Beaufort County
83	4138	9.2	**Conway** (city) Horry County
83	n/a	9.2	**Dalzell** (CDP) Sumter County
85	n/a	9.1	**Walhalla** (city) Oconee County
86	4169	9.0	**Gaffney** (city) Cherokee County
86	n/a	9.0	**Winnsboro** (town) Fairfield County
88	n/a	8.8	**Surfside Beach** (town) Horry County
89	n/a	8.7	**Georgetown** (city) Georgetown County
89	n/a	8.7	**Valley Falls** (CDP) Spartanburg County
91	n/a	8.5	**Union** (city) Union County
91	n/a	8.5	**York** (city) York County
93	4256	8.4	**Dentsville** (CDP) Richland County
93	n/a	8.4	**Hopkins** (CDP) Richland County
93	n/a	8.4	**Mullins** (city) Marion County
96	n/a	8.3	**Graniteville** (CDP) Aiken County
96	n/a	8.3	**Kingstree** (town) Williamsburg County
98	n/a	8.2	**Dillon** (city) Dillon County
98	n/a	8.2	**Garden City** (CDP) Horry County
98	n/a	8.2	**Hardeeville** (city) Jasper County
101	n/a	8.1	**Ridgeland** (town) Jasper County
102	n/a	7.9	**Lake City** (city) Florence County
103	n/a	7.7	**Woodfield** (CDP) Richland County
104	4363	7.6	**Orangeburg** (city) Orangeburg County
105	4376	7.5	**Socastee** (CDP) Horry County
106	4387	7.4	**Greenwood** (city) Greenwood County
107	n/a	7.2	**Burnettown** (town) Aiken County
107	n/a	7.2	**Edgefield** (town) Edgefield County
109	n/a	7.0	**Lyman** (town) Spartanburg County
110	n/a	6.9	**Batesburg-Leesville** (town) Lexington County
110	n/a	6.9	**Bennettsville** (city) Marlboro County
110	n/a	6.9	**Williston** (town) Barnwell County
113	n/a	6.7	**Chester** (city) Chester County
114	n/a	6.5	**Laurel Bay** (CDP) Beaufort County
115	n/a	6.4	**McCormick** (town) McCormick County
116	n/a	6.3	**Cheraw** (town) Chesterfield County
117	n/a	6.2	**Lancaster** (city) Lancaster County
117	n/a	6.2	**Pageland** (town) Chesterfield County
119	n/a	6.0	**Piedmont** (CDP) Anderson County
120	n/a	5.7	**Manning** (city) Clarendon County
120	n/a	5.7	**Pendleton** (town) Anderson County
122	n/a	5.4	**Pickens** (city) Pickens County
123	n/a	5.3	**Marion** (city) Marion County
124	n/a	5.2	**Barnwell** (city) Barnwell County
124	n/a	5.2	**Laurens** (city) Laurens County
124	4570	5.2	**Saint Andrews** (CDP) Richland County
127	n/a	5.1	**Abbeville** (city) Abbeville County
127	4574	5.1	**Berea** (CDP) Greenville County
129	n/a	5.0	**Brookdale** (CDP) Orangeburg County
130	n/a	4.8	**Allendale** (town) Allendale County
131	n/a	4.7	**Woodruff** (city) Spartanburg County
132	n/a	4.6	**Duncan** (town) Spartanburg County
133	n/a	4.3	**Liberty** (city) Pickens County
134	n/a	4.2	**Clinton** (city) Laurens County
135	n/a	4.0	**Andrews** (town) Georgetown County
136	n/a	3.7	**Clearwater** (CDP) Aiken County
136	n/a	3.7	**Welcome** (CDP) Greenville County
138	4625	3.5	**Parker** (CDP) Greenville County
139	n/a	3.3	**Dunean** (CDP) Greenville County
140	n/a	3.1	**Denmark** (city) Bamberg County
141	n/a	2.8	**Gloverville** (CDP) Aiken County
142	n/a	2.7	**Sans Souci** (CDP) Greenville County
143	n/a	2.5	**Saxon** (CDP) Spartanburg County
144	n/a	2.2	**Homeland Park** (CDP) Anderson County
145	n/a	2.1	**Springdale** (CDP) Lancaster County
146	n/a	2.0	**Central** (town) Pickens County
147	n/a	1.4	**East Gaffney** (CDP) Cherokee County
148	n/a	1.2	**Edisto** (CDP) Orangeburg County
149	n/a	0.8	**Southern Shops** (CDP) Spartanburg County
150	n/a	0.4	**Bishopville** (city) Lee County

Note: The state column ranks the top/bottom 150 places in the state with population of 2,500 or more. The national column ranks the top/bottom places in the country with population of 10,000 or more. Places that are unincorporated were not considered in the rankings. n/a indicates data not available. Please refer to the User Guide for additional information.

Households with Income of $100,000 or More

Top 150 Places Ranked in *Ascending* Order

State Rank	Nat'l Rank	Percent	Place
1	n/a	0.4	**Bishopville** (city) Lee County
2	n/a	0.8	**Southern Shops** (CDP) Spartanburg County
3	n/a	1.2	**Edisto** (CDP) Orangeburg County
4	n/a	1.4	**East Gaffney** (CDP) Cherokee County
5	n/a	2.0	**Central** (town) Pickens County
6	n/a	2.1	**Springdale** (CDP) Lancaster County
7	n/a	2.2	**Homeland Park** (CDP) Anderson County
8	n/a	2.5	**Saxon** (CDP) Spartanburg County
9	n/a	2.7	**Sans Souci** (CDP) Greenville County
10	n/a	2.8	**Gloverville** (CDP) Aiken County
11	n/a	3.1	**Denmark** (city) Bamberg County
12	n/a	3.3	**Dunean** (CDP) Greenville County
13	28	3.5	**Parker** (CDP) Greenville County
14	n/a	3.7	**Clearwater** (CDP) Aiken County
14	n/a	3.7	**Welcome** (CDP) Greenville County
16	n/a	4.0	**Andrews** (town) Georgetown County
17	n/a	4.2	**Clinton** (city) Laurens County
18	n/a	4.3	**Liberty** (city) Pickens County
19	n/a	4.6	**Duncan** (town) Spartanburg County
20	n/a	4.7	**Woodruff** (city) Spartanburg County
21	n/a	4.8	**Allendale** (town) Allendale County
22	n/a	5.0	**Brookdale** (CDP) Orangeburg County
23	n/a	5.1	**Abbeville** (city) Abbeville County
23	74	5.1	**Berea** (CDP) Greenville County
25	n/a	5.2	**Barnwell** (city) Barnwell County
25	n/a	5.2	**Laurens** (city) Laurens County
25	83	5.2	**Saint Andrews** (CDP) Richland County
28	n/a	5.3	**Marion** (city) Marion County
29	n/a	5.4	**Pickens** (city) Pickens County
30	n/a	5.7	**Manning** (city) Clarendon County
30	n/a	5.7	**Pendleton** (town) Anderson County
32	n/a	6.0	**Piedmont** (CDP) Anderson County
33	n/a	6.2	**Lancaster** (city) Lancaster County
33	n/a	6.2	**Pageland** (town) Chesterfield County
35	n/a	6.3	**Cheraw** (town) Chesterfield County
36	n/a	6.4	**McCormick** (town) McCormick County
37	n/a	6.5	**Laurel Bay** (CDP) Beaufort County
38	n/a	6.7	**Chester** (city) Chester County
39	n/a	6.9	**Batesburg-Leesville** (town) Lexington County
39	n/a	6.9	**Bennettsville** (city) Marlboro County
39	n/a	6.9	**Williston** (town) Barnwell County
42	n/a	7.0	**Lyman** (town) Spartanburg County
43	n/a	7.2	**Burnettown** (town) Aiken County
43	n/a	7.2	**Edgefield** (town) Edgefield County
45	257	7.4	**Greenwood** (city) Greenwood County
46	270	7.5	**Socastee** (CDP) Horry County
47	281	7.6	**Orangeburg** (city) Orangeburg County
48	n/a	7.7	**Woodfield** (CDP) Richland County
49	n/a	7.9	**Lake City** (city) Florence County
50	n/a	8.1	**Ridgeland** (town) Jasper County
51	n/a	8.2	**Dillon** (city) Dillon County
51	n/a	8.2	**Garden City** (CDP) Horry County
51	n/a	8.2	**Hardeeville** (city) Jasper County
54	n/a	8.3	**Graniteville** (CDP) Aiken County
54	n/a	8.3	**Kingstree** (town) Williamsburg County
56	386	8.4	**Dentsville** (CDP) Richland County
56	n/a	8.4	**Hopkins** (CDP) Richland County
56	n/a	8.4	**Mullins** (city) Marion County
59	n/a	8.5	**Union** (city) Union County
59	n/a	8.5	**York** (city) York County
61	n/a	8.7	**Georgetown** (city) Georgetown County
61	n/a	8.7	**Valley Falls** (CDP) Spartanburg County
63	n/a	8.8	**Surfside Beach** (town) Horry County
64	478	9.0	**Gaffney** (city) Cherokee County
64	n/a	9.0	**Winnsboro** (town) Fairfield County
66	n/a	9.1	**Walhalla** (city) Oconee County
67	504	9.2	**Conway** (city) Horry County
67	n/a	9.2	**Dalzell** (CDP) Sumter County
69	n/a	9.4	**Belvedere** (CDP) Aiken County
69	n/a	9.4	**Burton** (CDP) Beaufort County
71	n/a	9.5	**Elgin** (CDP) Lancaster County
72	567	9.6	**Spartanburg** (city) Spartanburg County
73	586	9.7	**Gantt** (CDP) Greenville County
73	n/a	9.7	**North Hartsville** (CDP) Darlington County
75	633	10.0	**Anderson** (city) Anderson County
76	666	10.2	**Newberry** (city) Newberry County
77	n/a	10.7	**Moncks Corner** (town) Berkeley County
78	n/a	10.8	**Arial** (CDP) Pickens County
78	n/a	10.8	**Honea Path** (town) Anderson County
80	n/a	10.9	**Saluda** (town) Saluda County
81	826	11.1	**North Charleston** (city) Charleston County
81	826	11.1	**Red Hill** (CDP) Horry County
83	n/a	11.2	**Walterboro** (city) Colleton County
84	919	11.6	**Cayce** (city) Lexington County
84	n/a	11.6	**Darlington** (city) Darlington County
86	n/a	11.7	**Williamston** (town) Anderson County
87	n/a	11.9	**Belton** (city) Anderson County
88	n/a	12.1	**Arcadia** (CDP) Spartanburg County
89	n/a	12.6	**Fountain Inn** (city) Greenville County
90	1126	12.7	**Port Royal** (town) Beaufort County
91	n/a	12.8	**Centerville** (CDP) Anderson County
92	1179	13.1	**Easley** (city) Pickens County
92	1179	13.1	**Sumter** (city) Sumter County
94	1194	13.2	**West Columbia** (city) Lexington County
95	n/a	13.3	**Little River** (CDP) Horry County
95	1209	13.3	**Rock Hill** (city) York County
97	n/a	13.5	**Hartsville** (city) Darlington County
97	1243	13.5	**Oak Grove** (CDP) Lexington County
99	n/a	13.6	**Clover** (town) York County
100	n/a	13.8	**Seneca** (city) Oconee County
101	n/a	14.1	**Lesslie** (CDP) York County
102	1354	14.3	**Ladson** (CDP) Berkeley County
102	n/a	14.3	**Red Bank** (CDP) Lexington County
102	n/a	14.3	**Travelers Rest** (city) Greenville County
105	1437	14.9	**Taylors** (CDP) Greenville County
106	1465	15.1	**Myrtle Beach** (city) Horry County
107	n/a	15.2	**Lugoff** (CDP) Kershaw County
108	1490	15.3	**Simpsonville** (city) Greenville County
109	n/a	15.5	**Hampton** (town) Hampton County
110	1583	16.0	**Irmo** (town) Richland County
111	1600	16.1	**Florence** (city) Florence County
112	1626	16.3	**Seven Oaks** (CDP) Lexington County
113	1634	16.4	**North Myrtle Beach** (city) Horry County
114	n/a	17.0	**Bamberg** (town) Bamberg County
115	1743	17.3	**Clemson** (city) Pickens County
116	n/a	17.4	**Lakewood** (CDP) Sumter County
117	1769	17.5	**Columbia** (city) Richland County
118	n/a	17.7	**Sangaree** (CDP) Berkeley County
119	1815	17.9	**Greer** (city) Greenville County
120	1856	18.2	**Wade Hampton** (CDP) Greenville County
121	1927	18.7	**North Augusta** (city) Aiken County
122	1935	18.8	**Hanahan** (city) Berkeley County
123	n/a	19.0	**Murrells Inlet** (CDP) Georgetown County
124	n/a	19.1	**Springdale** (town) Lexington County
125	2005	19.4	**Mauldin** (city) Greenville County
126	2013	19.5	**Greenville** (city) Greenville County
127	2110	20.2	**Goose Creek** (city) Berkeley County
128	2153	20.5	**Summerville** (town) Dorchester County
129	2178	20.7	**Beaufort** (city) Beaufort County
130	n/a	22.3	**Forestbrook** (CDP) Horry County
131	2398	22.8	**Charleston** (city) Charleston County
132	n/a	23.6	**Northlake** (CDP) Anderson County
133	2500	23.9	**Bluffton** (town) Beaufort County
134	n/a	24.2	**Newport** (CDP) York County
135	n/a	24.7	**Hollywood** (town) Charleston County
136	2671	25.7	**Aiken** (city) Aiken County
137	2704	26.0	**Forest Acres** (city) Richland County
138	n/a	26.5	**Camden** (city) Kershaw County
139	2784	26.8	**Lexington** (town) Lexington County
140	n/a	27.3	**Boiling Springs** (CDP) Spartanburg County
141	n/a	31.0	**India Hook** (CDP) York County
142	3129	31.2	**Fort Mill** (town) York County
143	3233	32.9	**Hilton Head Island** (town) Beaufort County
144	n/a	37.4	**Lake Wylie** (CDP) York County
145	3586	37.8	**Mount Pleasant** (town) Charleston County
146	n/a	42.3	**Folly Beach** (city) Charleston County
147	n/a	44.7	**Isle of Palms** (city) Charleston County
148	n/a	53.8	**Lake Murray of Richland** (CDP) Richland County
149	n/a	55.1	**Tega Cay** (city) York County
150	4506	60.1	**Five Forks** (CDP) Greenville County

Note: The state column ranks the top/bottom 150 places in the state with population of 2,500 or more. The national column ranks the top/bottom places in the country with population of 10,000 or more. Places that are unincorporated were not considered in the rankings. n/a indicates data not available. Please refer to the User Guide for additional information.

Poverty Rate

Top 150 Places Ranked in *Descending* Order

State Rank	Nat'l Rank	Percent	Place
1	n/a	60.6	**Southern Shops** (CDP) Spartanburg County
2	n/a	49.4	**Denmark** (city) Bamberg County
3	n/a	48.8	**Bishopville** (city) Lee County
4	n/a	46.0	**Brookdale** (CDP) Orangeburg County
5	n/a	43.8	**Central** (town) Pickens County
6	n/a	43.2	**Andrews** (town) Georgetown County
7	n/a	42.3	**Barnwell** (city) Barnwell County
8	n/a	41.1	**Marion** (city) Marion County
9	n/a	40.4	**Clearwater** (CDP) Aiken County
10	n/a	39.8	**Arcadia** (CDP) Spartanburg County
11	n/a	39.3	**Allendale** (town) Allendale County
12	n/a	38.9	**Williston** (town) Barnwell County
13	n/a	38.0	**Chester** (city) Chester County
14	n/a	37.9	**Kingstree** (town) Williamsburg County
15	71	37.8	**Parker** (CDP) Greenville County
16	n/a	37.7	**Clinton** (city) Laurens County
17	n/a	37.5	**Dillon** (city) Dillon County
18	n/a	37.4	**Abbeville** (city) Abbeville County
19	n/a	37.3	**Saxon** (CDP) Spartanburg County
20	n/a	37.0	**Springdale** (CDP) Lancaster County
21	n/a	36.8	**Cheraw** (town) Chesterfield County
22	n/a	36.7	**Elgin** (CDP) Lancaster County
23	95	36.3	**Clemson** (city) Pickens County
24	n/a	36.0	**Saluda** (town) Saluda County
25	n/a	35.4	**East Gaffney** (CDP) Cherokee County
25	n/a	35.4	**Manning** (city) Clarendon County
27	n/a	35.1	**Ridgeland** (town) Jasper County
28	n/a	34.9	**Pendleton** (town) Anderson County
29	132	34.5	**Greenwood** (city) Greenwood County
30	n/a	33.5	**Walhalla** (city) Oconee County
31	n/a	33.4	**Gloverville** (CDP) Aiken County
32	n/a	33.2	**Bennettsville** (city) Marlboro County
33	n/a	33.0	**Edisto** (CDP) Orangeburg County
34	179	32.7	**Conway** (city) Horry County
35	n/a	32.6	**Darlington** (city) Darlington County
35	n/a	32.6	**Homeland Park** (CDP) Anderson County
37	n/a	32.2	**Lancaster** (city) Lancaster County
38	n/a	31.9	**Batesburg-Leesville** (town) Lexington County
39	214	31.8	**Berea** (CDP) Greenville County
40	n/a	31.3	**York** (city) York County
41	232	31.1	**Orangeburg** (city) Orangeburg County
42	n/a	31.0	**Mullins** (city) Marion County
43	n/a	30.6	**Pageland** (town) Chesterfield County
44	251	30.5	**Newberry** (city) Newberry County
45	n/a	30.3	**Hardeeville** (city) Jasper County
46	n/a	30.2	**Woodruff** (city) Spartanburg County
47	n/a	30.1	**Walterboro** (city) Colleton County
48	n/a	29.5	**Georgetown** (city) Georgetown County
49	n/a	28.8	**Graniteville** (CDP) Aiken County
50	n/a	28.4	**Pickens** (city) Pickens County
51	n/a	28.1	**Arial** (CDP) Pickens County
52	n/a	27.8	**Lake City** (city) Florence County
53	n/a	27.7	**Sans Souci** (CDP) Greenville County
54	391	27.5	**Anderson** (city) Anderson County
55	n/a	27.4	**Welcome** (CDP) Greenville County
56	405	27.3	**Saint Andrews** (CDP) Richland County
57	n/a	26.8	**Bamberg** (town) Bamberg County
58	443	26.6	**Gaffney** (city) Cherokee County
58	443	26.6	**Gantt** (CDP) Greenville County
58	443	26.6	**Myrtle Beach** (city) Horry County
61	n/a	26.5	**Hampton** (town) Hampton County
62	459	26.4	**Spartanburg** (city) Spartanburg County
62	n/a	26.4	**Winnsboro** (town) Fairfield County
64	n/a	25.8	**Honea Path** (town) Anderson County
64	n/a	25.8	**McCormick** (town) McCormick County
66	n/a	25.4	**Hopkins** (CDP) Richland County
67	n/a	24.8	**Edgefield** (town) Edgefield County
68	n/a	24.3	**Union** (city) Union County
69	n/a	24.2	**Belvedere** (CDP) Aiken County
70	n/a	24.1	**Valley Falls** (CDP) Spartanburg County
71	662	23.8	**Columbia** (city) Richland County
72	n/a	23.4	**Dunean** (CDP) Greenville County
72	700	23.4	**North Charleston** (city) Charleston County
74	n/a	22.8	**Hartsville** (city) Darlington County
75	n/a	22.7	**Clover** (town) York County
75	n/a	22.7	**Laurens** (city) Laurens County
77	844	22.0	**Red Hill** (CDP) Horry County
78	n/a	21.5	**Belton** (city) Anderson County
79	924	21.2	**Cayce** (city) Lexington County
79	n/a	21.2	**Seneca** (city) Oconee County
81	n/a	20.6	**Liberty** (city) Pickens County
82	1028	20.2	**Sumter** (city) Sumter County
83	1052	20.0	**Greenville** (city) Greenville County
84	n/a	19.9	**Travelers Rest** (city) Greenville County
85	1115	19.5	**Charleston** (city) Charleston County
85	1115	19.5	**Florence** (city) Florence County
87	1131	19.4	**Beaufort** (city) Beaufort County
87	1131	19.4	**Greer** (city) Greenville County
89	n/a	19.1	**Woodfield** (CDP) Richland County
90	n/a	19.0	**North Hartsville** (CDP) Darlington County
91	n/a	18.9	**Isle of Palms** (city) Charleston County
91	1205	18.9	**Socastee** (CDP) Horry County
93	1222	18.7	**Rock Hill** (city) York County
93	1222	18.7	**West Columbia** (city) Lexington County
95	n/a	18.5	**Duncan** (town) Spartanburg County
96	n/a	18.2	**Lesslie** (CDP) York County
97	n/a	17.6	**Burnettown** (town) Aiken County
97	1368	17.6	**Taylors** (CDP) Greenville County
99	1437	17.1	**Irmo** (town) Richland County
100	1451	17.0	**Aiken** (city) Aiken County
101	n/a	16.8	**Moncks Corner** (town) Berkeley County
102	n/a	16.7	**Red Bank** (CDP) Lexington County
103	1573	16.1	**Bluffton** (town) Beaufort County
103	1573	16.1	**Dentsville** (CDP) Richland County
105	1638	15.6	**Hanahan** (city) Berkeley County
106	n/a	15.3	**Camden** (city) Kershaw County
107	n/a	15.0	**Dalzell** (CDP) Sumter County
108	n/a	14.8	**Laurel Bay** (CDP) Beaufort County
109	n/a	14.7	**Fountain Inn** (city) Greenville County
110	n/a	14.4	**Garden City** (CDP) Horry County
111	n/a	14.2	**Forestbrook** (CDP) Horry County
112	1886	14.0	**Wade Hampton** (CDP) Greenville County
113	1954	13.5	**Seven Oaks** (CDP) Lexington County
114	n/a	13.4	**Piedmont** (CDP) Anderson County
115	n/a	13.2	**Sangaree** (CDP) Berkeley County
116	n/a	13.1	**Folly Beach** (city) Charleston County
117	2071	12.7	**Easley** (city) Pickens County
117	2071	12.7	**Forest Acres** (city) Richland County
119	2092	12.5	**Ladson** (CDP) Berkeley County
120	n/a	12.3	**Lakewood** (CDP) Sumter County
121	n/a	11.8	**India Hook** (CDP) York County
122	2230	11.7	**Lexington** (town) Lexington County
123	2255	11.6	**North Augusta** (city) Aiken County
124	2274	11.5	**Summerville** (town) Dorchester County
125	n/a	10.7	**Lyman** (town) Spartanburg County
126	n/a	10.6	**Burton** (CDP) Beaufort County
127	n/a	10.5	**Surfside Beach** (town) Horry County
128	2521	10.2	**North Myrtle Beach** (city) Horry County
129	n/a	9.8	**Little River** (CDP) Horry County
130	2626	9.7	**Goose Creek** (city) Berkeley County
130	2626	9.7	**Port Royal** (town) Beaufort County
132	n/a	9.3	**Springdale** (town) Lexington County
133	n/a	8.7	**Lugoff** (CDP) Kershaw County
134	2853	8.6	**Fort Mill** (town) York County
135	2875	8.5	**Hilton Head Island** (town) Beaufort County
136	2927	8.3	**Simpsonville** (city) Greenville County
137	2973	8.1	**Mount Pleasant** (town) Charleston County
137	n/a	8.1	**Murrells Inlet** (CDP) Georgetown County
139	3006	8.0	**Oak Grove** (CDP) Lexington County
140	n/a	7.9	**Boiling Springs** (CDP) Spartanburg County
140	n/a	7.9	**Hollywood** (town) Charleston County
142	n/a	7.7	**Williamston** (town) Anderson County
143	n/a	7.1	**Centerville** (CDP) Anderson County
144	n/a	6.0	**Northlake** (CDP) Anderson County
145	3586	5.9	**Mauldin** (city) Greenville County
145	n/a	5.9	**Newport** (CDP) York County
147	n/a	4.0	**Lake Wylie** (CDP) York County
148	n/a	3.4	**Lake Murray of Richland** (CDP) Richland County
149	n/a	2.2	**Tega Cay** (city) York County
150	4626	1.6	**Five Forks** (CDP) Greenville County

Note: The state column ranks the top/bottom 150 places in the state with population of 2,500 or more. The national column ranks the top/bottom places in the country with population of 10,000 or more. Places that are unincorporated were not considered in the rankings. n/a indicates data not available. Please refer to the User Guide for additional information.

Poverty Rate

Top 150 Places Ranked in *Ascending* Order

State Rank	Nat'l Rank	Percent	Place
1	23	1.6	Five Forks (CDP) Greenville County
2	n/a	2.2	Tega Cay (city) York County
3	n/a	3.4	Lake Murray of Richland (CDP) Richland County
4	n/a	4.0	Lake Wylie (CDP) York County
5	1048	5.9	Mauldin (city) Greenville County
5	n/a	5.9	Newport (CDP) York County
7	n/a	6.0	Northlake (CDP) Anderson County
8	n/a	7.1	Centerville (CDP) Anderson County
9	n/a	7.7	Williamston (town) Anderson County
10	n/a	7.9	Boiling Springs (CDP) Spartanburg County
10	n/a	7.9	Hollywood (town) Charleston County
12	1629	8.0	Oak Grove (CDP) Lexington County
13	1651	8.1	Mount Pleasant (town) Charleston County
13	n/a	8.1	Murrells Inlet (CDP) Georgetown County
15	1705	8.3	Simpsonville (city) Greenville County
16	1754	8.5	Hilton Head Island (town) Beaufort County
17	1782	8.6	Fort Mill (town) York County
18	n/a	8.7	Lugoff (CDP) Kershaw County
19	n/a	9.3	Springdale (town) Lexington County
20	2009	9.7	Goose Creek (city) Berkeley County
20	2009	9.7	Port Royal (town) Beaufort County
22	n/a	9.8	Little River (CDP) Horry County
23	2117	10.2	North Myrtle Beach (city) Horry County
24	n/a	10.5	Surfside Beach (town) Horry County
25	n/a	10.6	Burton (CDP) Beaufort County
26	n/a	10.7	Lyman (town) Spartanburg County
27	2362	11.5	Summerville (town) Dorchester County
28	2383	11.6	North Augusta (city) Aiken County
29	2402	11.7	Lexington (town) Lexington County
30	n/a	11.8	India Hook (CDP) York County
31	n/a	12.3	Lakewood (CDP) Sumter County
32	2548	12.5	Ladson (CDP) Berkeley County
33	2574	12.7	Easley (city) Pickens County
33	2574	12.7	Forest Acres (city) Richland County
35	n/a	13.1	Folly Beach (city) Charleston County
36	n/a	13.2	Sangaree (CDP) Berkeley County
37	n/a	13.4	Piedmont (CDP) Anderson County
38	2678	13.5	Seven Oaks (CDP) Lexington County
39	2756	14.0	Wade Hampton (CDP) Greenville County
40	n/a	14.2	Forestbrook (CDP) Horry County
41	n/a	14.4	Garden City (CDP) Horry County
42	n/a	14.7	Fountain Inn (city) Greenville County
43	n/a	14.8	Laurel Bay (CDP) Beaufort County
44	n/a	15.0	Dalzell (CDP) Sumter County
45	n/a	15.3	Camden (city) Kershaw County
46	3005	15.6	Hanahan (city) Berkeley County
47	3068	16.1	Bluffton (town) Beaufort County
47	3068	16.1	Dentsville (CDP) Richland County
49	n/a	16.7	Red Bank (CDP) Lexington County
50	n/a	16.8	Moncks Corner (town) Berkeley County
51	3194	17.0	Aiken (city) Aiken County
52	3206	17.1	Irmo (town) Richland County
53	n/a	17.6	Burnettown (town) Aiken County
53	3270	17.6	Taylors (CDP) Greenville County
55	n/a	18.2	Lesslie (CDP) York County
56	n/a	18.5	Duncan (town) Spartanburg County
57	3427	18.7	Rock Hill (city) York County
57	3427	18.7	West Columbia (city) Lexington County
59	n/a	18.9	Isle of Palms (city) Charleston County
59	3442	18.9	Socastee (CDP) Horry County
61	n/a	19.0	North Hartsville (CDP) Darlington County
62	n/a	19.1	Woodfield (CDP) Richland County
63	3512	19.4	Beaufort (city) Beaufort County
63	3512	19.4	Greer (city) Greenville County
65	3526	19.5	Charleston (city) Charleston County
65	3526	19.5	Florence (city) Florence County
67	n/a	19.9	Travelers Rest (city) Greenville County
68	3592	20.0	Greenville (city) Greenville County
69	3616	20.2	Sumter (city) Sumter County
70	n/a	20.6	Liberty (city) Pickens County
71	3722	21.2	Cayce (city) Lexington County
71	n/a	21.2	Seneca (city) Oconee County
73	n/a	21.5	Belton (city) Anderson County
74	3804	22.0	Red Hill (CDP) Horry County
75	n/a	22.7	Clover (town) York County
75	n/a	22.7	Laurens (city) Laurens County
77	n/a	22.8	Hartsville (city) Darlington County
78	n/a	23.4	Dunean (CDP) Greenville County
78	3947	23.4	North Charleston (city) Charleston County
80	3986	23.8	Columbia (city) Richland County
81	n/a	24.1	Valley Falls (CDP) Spartanburg County
82	n/a	24.2	Belvedere (CDP) Aiken County
83	n/a	24.3	Union (city) Union County
84	n/a	24.8	Edgefield (town) Edgefield County
85	n/a	25.4	Hopkins (CDP) Richland County
86	n/a	25.8	Honea Path (town) Anderson County
86	n/a	25.8	McCormick (town) McCormick County
88	4191	26.4	Spartanburg (city) Spartanburg County
88	n/a	26.4	Winnsboro (town) Fairfield County
90	n/a	26.5	Hampton (town) Hampton County
91	4207	26.6	Gaffney (city) Cherokee County
91	4207	26.6	Gantt (CDP) Greenville County
91	4207	26.6	Myrtle Beach (city) Horry County
94	n/a	26.8	Bamberg (town) Bamberg County
95	4246	27.3	Saint Andrews (CDP) Richland County
96	n/a	27.4	Welcome (CDP) Greenville County
97	4259	27.5	Anderson (city) Anderson County
98	n/a	27.7	Sans Souci (CDP) Greenville County
99	n/a	27.8	Lake City (city) Florence County
100	n/a	28.1	Arial (CDP) Pickens County
101	n/a	28.4	Pickens (city) Pickens County
102	n/a	28.8	Graniteville (CDP) Aiken County
103	n/a	29.5	Georgetown (city) Georgetown County
104	n/a	30.1	Walterboro (city) Colleton County
105	n/a	30.2	Woodruff (city) Spartanburg County
106	n/a	30.3	Hardeeville (city) Jasper County
107	4404	30.5	Newberry (city) Newberry County
108	n/a	30.6	Pageland (town) Chesterfield County
109	n/a	31.0	Mullins (city) Marion County
110	4424	31.1	Orangeburg (city) Orangeburg County
111	n/a	31.3	York (city) York County
112	4438	31.8	Berea (CDP) Greenville County
113	n/a	31.9	Batesburg-Leesville (town) Lexington County
114	n/a	32.2	Lancaster (city) Lancaster County
115	n/a	32.6	Darlington (city) Darlington County
115	n/a	32.6	Homeland Park (CDP) Anderson County
117	4470	32.7	Conway (city) Horry County
118	n/a	33.0	Edisto (CDP) Orangeburg County
119	n/a	33.2	Bennettsville (city) Marlboro County
120	n/a	33.4	Gloverville (CDP) Aiken County
121	n/a	33.5	Walhalla (city) Oconee County
122	4524	34.5	Greenwood (city) Greenwood County
123	n/a	34.9	Pendleton (town) Anderson County
124	n/a	35.1	Ridgeland (town) Jasper County
125	n/a	35.4	East Gaffney (CDP) Cherokee County
125	n/a	35.4	Manning (city) Clarendon County
127	n/a	36.0	Saluda (town) Saluda County
128	4559	36.3	Clemson (city) Pickens County
129	n/a	36.7	Elgin (CDP) Lancaster County
130	n/a	36.8	Cheraw (town) Chesterfield County
131	n/a	37.0	Springdale (CDP) Lancaster County
132	n/a	37.3	Saxon (CDP) Spartanburg County
133	n/a	37.4	Abbeville (city) Abbeville County
134	n/a	37.5	Dillon (city) Dillon County
135	n/a	37.7	Clinton (city) Laurens County
136	4582	37.8	Parker (CDP) Greenville County
137	n/a	37.9	Kingstree (town) Williamsburg County
138	n/a	38.0	Chester (city) Chester County
139	n/a	38.9	Williston (town) Barnwell County
140	n/a	39.3	Allendale (town) Allendale County
141	n/a	39.8	Arcadia (CDP) Spartanburg County
142	n/a	40.4	Clearwater (CDP) Aiken County
143	n/a	41.1	Marion (city) Marion County
144	n/a	42.3	Barnwell (city) Barnwell County
145	n/a	43.2	Andrews (town) Georgetown County
146	n/a	43.8	Central (town) Pickens County
147	n/a	46.0	Brookdale (CDP) Orangeburg County
148	n/a	48.8	Bishopville (city) Lee County
149	n/a	49.4	Denmark (city) Bamberg County
150	n/a	60.6	Southern Shops (CDP) Spartanburg County

Note: *The state column ranks the top/bottom 150 places in the state with population of 2,500 or more. The national column ranks the top/bottom places in the country with population of 10,000 or more. Places that are unincorporated were not considered in the rankings. n/a indicates data not available. Please refer to the User Guide for additional information.*

Educational Attainment: High School Diploma or Higher

Top 150 Places Ranked in *Descending* Order

State Rank	Nat'l Rank	Percent	Place
1	n/a	99.0	**Isle of Palms** (city) Charleston County
2	n/a	97.7	**Tega Cay** (city) York County
3	148	97.6	**Forest Acres** (city) Richland County
4	202	97.3	**Clemson** (city) Pickens County
5	252	97.1	**Mount Pleasant** (town) Charleston County
6	n/a	96.9	**Folly Beach** (city) Charleston County
7	474	96.1	**Five Forks** (CDP) Greenville County
8	n/a	95.8	**Lake Wylie** (CDP) York County
9	n/a	94.9	**India Hook** (CDP) York County
10	n/a	94.8	**Newport** (CDP) York County
11	n/a	94.4	**Springdale** (town) Lexington County
12	n/a	93.9	**Forestbrook** (CDP) Horry County
12	n/a	93.9	**Laurel Bay** (CDP) Beaufort County
12	1160	93.9	**Lexington** (town) Lexington County
15	1369	93.3	**Seven Oaks** (CDP) Lexington County
16	n/a	93.1	**Northlake** (CDP) Anderson County
17	1468	93.0	**Summerville** (town) Dorchester County
18	1532	92.8	**Irmo** (town) Richland County
19	1569	92.7	**Goose Creek** (city) Berkeley County
20	1595	92.6	**Charleston** (city) Charleston County
20	1595	92.6	**Port Royal** (town) Beaufort County
22	1629	92.5	**North Myrtle Beach** (city) Horry County
23	1702	92.3	**Hilton Head Island** (town) Beaufort County
23	n/a	92.3	**Lake Murray of Richland** (CDP) Richland County
23	n/a	92.3	**Lugoff** (CDP) Kershaw County
23	n/a	92.3	**Murrells Inlet** (CDP) Georgetown County
27	1799	92.0	**North Augusta** (city) Aiken County
28	2071	91.0	**Fort Mill** (town) York County
28	2071	91.0	**Mauldin** (city) Greenville County
30	2137	90.8	**Aiken** (city) Aiken County
31	n/a	90.7	**Garden City** (CDP) Horry County
32	n/a	90.5	**Fountain Inn** (city) Greenville County
33	n/a	90.2	**Boiling Springs** (CDP) Spartanburg County
34	2342	90.0	**Bluffton** (town) Beaufort County
34	n/a	90.0	**Little River** (CDP) Horry County
36	n/a	89.9	**Surfside Beach** (town) Horry County
37	2389	89.8	**Oak Grove** (CDP) Lexington County
37	2389	89.8	**Saint Andrews** (CDP) Richland County
39	2501	89.3	**Beaufort** (city) Beaufort County
40	n/a	89.1	**Burton** (CDP) Beaufort County
40	2551	89.1	**Dentsville** (CDP) Richland County
42	2571	89.0	**Socastee** (CDP) Horry County
43	2684	88.5	**Simpsonville** (city) Greenville County
44	2785	88.1	**Cayce** (city) Lexington County
45	n/a	87.9	**Lyman** (town) Spartanburg County
46	2873	87.7	**Wade Hampton** (CDP) Greenville County
46	n/a	87.7	**Winnsboro** (town) Fairfield County
48	n/a	87.5	**Dalzell** (CDP) Sumter County
49	3008	87.0	**Red Hill** (CDP) Horry County
50	3031	86.9	**Rock Hill** (city) York County
51	3042	86.8	**Taylors** (CDP) Greenville County
52	3057	86.7	**Columbia** (city) Richland County
52	3057	86.7	**Florence** (city) Florence County
54	n/a	86.6	**Duncan** (town) Spartanburg County
54	3077	86.6	**Hanahan** (city) Berkeley County
56	3194	85.9	**Greenville** (city) Greenville County
57	n/a	85.8	**Centerville** (CDP) Anderson County
57	n/a	85.8	**Sangaree** (CDP) Berkeley County
59	n/a	85.7	**Pendleton** (town) Anderson County
59	3233	85.7	**Sumter** (city) Sumter County
61	3271	85.5	**West Columbia** (city) Lexington County
62	n/a	85.4	**Camden** (city) Kershaw County
63	n/a	85.0	**Lakewood** (CDP) Sumter County
63	n/a	85.0	**Moncks Corner** (town) Berkeley County
65	3385	84.8	**Conway** (city) Horry County
66	n/a	84.7	**Red Bank** (CDP) Lexington County
67	n/a	84.5	**Seneca** (city) Oconee County
68	3451	84.4	**Myrtle Beach** (city) Horry County
69	n/a	84.3	**Central** (town) Pickens County
69	3461	84.3	**Ladson** (CDP) Berkeley County
71	n/a	84.2	**Lesslie** (CDP) York County
72	n/a	84.1	**Woodfield** (CDP) Richland County
73	n/a	84.0	**Hartsville** (city) Darlington County
74	n/a	83.9	**Graniteville** (CDP) Aiken County
74	3516	83.9	**Orangeburg** (city) Orangeburg County
76	n/a	83.5	**Marion** (city) Marion County
76	n/a	83.5	**Valley Falls** (CDP) Spartanburg County
78	3609	83.4	**Greer** (city) Greenville County
78	n/a	83.4	**Williamston** (town) Anderson County
80	n/a	83.2	**Clover** (town) York County
81	n/a	83.1	**Barnwell** (city) Barnwell County
82	n/a	82.9	**Liberty** (city) Pickens County
83	3683	82.8	**Easley** (city) Pickens County
84	n/a	82.7	**Bamberg** (town) Bamberg County
84	n/a	82.7	**Hampton** (town) Hampton County
86	n/a	82.4	**Hollywood** (town) Charleston County
87	n/a	82.2	**Belvedere** (CDP) Aiken County
87	n/a	82.2	**Kingstree** (town) Williamsburg County
89	3775	82.0	**Spartanburg** (city) Spartanburg County
90	n/a	81.7	**Walterboro** (city) Colleton County
91	n/a	81.6	**Travelers Rest** (city) Greenville County
92	n/a	81.2	**Georgetown** (city) Georgetown County
93	n/a	81.0	**North Hartsville** (CDP) Darlington County
94	n/a	80.9	**Batesburg-Leesville** (town) Lexington County
95	n/a	80.4	**Mullins** (city) Marion County
96	n/a	80.3	**Piedmont** (CDP) Anderson County
97	n/a	80.0	**Burnettown** (town) Aiken County
98	3996	79.7	**North Charleston** (city) Charleston County
99	n/a	79.5	**Union** (city) Union County
100	n/a	79.3	**Clearwater** (CDP) Aiken County
101	4062	78.9	**Anderson** (city) Anderson County
102	n/a	78.6	**Lancaster** (city) Lancaster County
103	n/a	78.2	**Laurens** (city) Laurens County
104	4138	77.9	**Gaffney** (city) Cherokee County
105	n/a	77.6	**Belton** (city) Anderson County
106	n/a	77.5	**Edisto** (CDP) Orangeburg County
107	n/a	77.4	**Darlington** (city) Darlington County
108	n/a	76.6	**Hopkins** (CDP) Richland County
109	n/a	76.5	**Hardeeville** (city) Jasper County
110	n/a	76.3	**Dunean** (CDP) Greenville County
110	n/a	76.3	**Ridgeland** (town) Jasper County
112	n/a	75.8	**Brookdale** (CDP) Orangeburg County
113	n/a	75.7	**Chester** (city) Chester County
113	n/a	75.7	**Edgefield** (town) Edgefield County
115	n/a	75.5	**Welcome** (CDP) Greenville County
116	n/a	75.3	**Honea Path** (town) Anderson County
117	4298	74.7	**Gantt** (CDP) Greenville County
118	n/a	74.6	**Abbeville** (city) Abbeville County
119	n/a	74.5	**Elgin** (CDP) Lancaster County
120	4356	73.5	**Greenwood** (city) Greenwood County
121	4361	73.3	**Berea** (CDP) Greenville County
122	n/a	73.2	**Williston** (town) Barnwell County
123	n/a	73.1	**Cheraw** (town) Chesterfield County
124	n/a	72.9	**Sans Souci** (CDP) Greenville County
125	n/a	72.8	**Bishopville** (city) Lee County
126	n/a	72.3	**Arcadia** (CDP) Spartanburg County
127	n/a	72.1	**Lake City** (city) Florence County
128	n/a	71.8	**York** (city) York County
129	n/a	71.7	**Pageland** (town) Chesterfield County
130	n/a	70.9	**Manning** (city) Clarendon County
131	n/a	70.5	**Bennettsville** (city) Marlboro County
132	4439	70.4	**Newberry** (city) Newberry County
133	n/a	69.7	**Denmark** (city) Bamberg County
134	n/a	69.5	**Allendale** (town) Allendale County
135	n/a	69.4	**Andrews** (town) Georgetown County
135	n/a	69.4	**Arial** (CDP) Pickens County
135	n/a	69.4	**McCormick** (town) McCormick County
138	n/a	69.2	**Pickens** (city) Pickens County
139	n/a	68.5	**Walhalla** (city) Oconee County
140	n/a	68.3	**Saluda** (town) Saluda County
141	n/a	67.6	**Clinton** (city) Laurens County
142	n/a	65.9	**Homeland Park** (CDP) Anderson County
143	n/a	65.0	**Springdale** (CDP) Lancaster County
144	4540	64.3	**Parker** (CDP) Greenville County
145	n/a	63.1	**Dillon** (city) Dillon County
146	n/a	62.6	**East Gaffney** (CDP) Cherokee County
146	n/a	62.6	**Saxon** (CDP) Spartanburg County
148	n/a	59.3	**Gloverville** (CDP) Aiken County
149	n/a	58.7	**Woodruff** (city) Spartanburg County
150	n/a	50.2	**Southern Shops** (CDP) Spartanburg County

Note: The state column ranks the top/bottom 150 places in the state with population of 2,500 or more. The national column ranks the top/bottom places in the country with population of 10,000 or more. Places that are unincorporated were not considered in the rankings. n/a indicates data not available. Please refer to the User Guide for additional information.

Educational Attainment: High School Diploma or Higher

Top 150 Places Ranked in *Ascending* Order

State Rank	Nat'l Rank	Percent	Place
1	n/a	50.2	Southern Shops (CDP) Spartanburg County
2	n/a	58.7	Woodruff (city) Spartanburg County
3	n/a	59.3	Gloverville (CDP) Aiken County
4	n/a	62.6	East Gaffney (CDP) Cherokee County
4	n/a	62.6	Saxon (CDP) Spartanburg County
6	n/a	63.1	Dillon (city) Dillon County
7	114	64.3	Parker (CDP) Greenville County
8	n/a	65.0	Springdale (CDP) Lancaster County
9	n/a	65.9	Homeland Park (CDP) Anderson County
10	n/a	67.6	Clinton (city) Laurens County
11	n/a	68.3	Saluda (town) Saluda County
12	n/a	68.5	Walhalla (city) Oconee County
13	n/a	69.2	Pickens (city) Pickens County
14	n/a	69.4	Andrews (town) Georgetown County
14	n/a	69.4	Arial (CDP) Pickens County
14	n/a	69.4	McCormick (town) McCormick County
17	n/a	69.5	Allendale (town) Allendale County
18	n/a	69.7	Denmark (city) Bamberg County
19	217	70.4	Newberry (city) Newberry County
20	n/a	70.5	Bennettsville (city) Marlboro County
21	n/a	70.9	Manning (city) Clarendon County
22	n/a	71.7	Pageland (town) Chesterfield County
23	n/a	71.8	York (city) York County
24	n/a	72.1	Lake City (city) Florence County
25	n/a	72.3	Arcadia (CDP) Spartanburg County
26	n/a	72.8	Bishopville (city) Lee County
27	n/a	72.9	Sans Souci (CDP) Greenville County
28	n/a	73.1	Cheraw (town) Chesterfield County
29	n/a	73.2	Williston (town) Barnwell County
30	293	73.3	Berea (CDP) Greenville County
31	299	73.5	Greenwood (city) Greenwood County
32	n/a	74.5	Elgin (CDP) Lancaster County
33	n/a	74.6	Abbeville (city) Abbeville County
34	354	74.7	Gantt (CDP) Greenville County
35	n/a	75.3	Honea Path (town) Anderson County
36	n/a	75.5	Welcome (CDP) Greenville County
37	n/a	75.7	Chester (city) Chester County
37	n/a	75.7	Edgefield (town) Edgefield County
39	n/a	75.8	Brookdale (CDP) Orangeburg County
40	n/a	76.3	Dunean (CDP) Greenville County
40	n/a	76.3	Ridgeland (town) Jasper County
42	n/a	76.5	Hardeeville (city) Jasper County
43	n/a	76.6	Hopkins (CDP) Richland County
44	n/a	77.4	Darlington (city) Darlington County
45	n/a	77.5	Edisto (CDP) Orangeburg County
46	n/a	77.6	Belton (city) Anderson County
47	515	77.9	Gaffney (city) Cherokee County
48	n/a	78.2	Laurens (city) Laurens County
49	n/a	78.6	Lancaster (city) Lancaster County
50	585	78.9	Anderson (city) Anderson County
51	n/a	79.3	Clearwater (CDP) Aiken County
52	n/a	79.5	Union (city) Union County
53	651	79.7	North Charleston (city) Charleston County
54	n/a	80.0	Burnettown (town) Aiken County
55	n/a	80.3	Piedmont (CDP) Anderson County
56	n/a	80.4	Mullins (city) Marion County
57	n/a	80.9	Batesburg-Leesville (town) Lexington County
58	n/a	81.0	North Hartsville (CDP) Darlington County
59	n/a	81.2	Georgetown (city) Georgetown County
60	n/a	81.6	Travelers Rest (city) Greenville County
61	n/a	81.7	Walterboro (city) Colleton County
62	870	82.0	Spartanburg (city) Spartanburg County
63	n/a	82.2	Belvedere (CDP) Aiken County
63	n/a	82.2	Kingstree (town) Williamsburg County
65	n/a	82.4	Hollywood (town) Charleston County
66	n/a	82.7	Bamberg (town) Bamberg County
66	n/a	82.7	Hampton (town) Hampton County
68	962	82.8	Easley (city) Pickens County
69	n/a	82.9	Liberty (city) Pickens County
70	n/a	83.1	Barnwell (city) Barnwell County
71	n/a	83.2	Clover (town) York County
72	1027	83.4	Greer (city) Greenville County
72	n/a	83.4	Williamston (town) Anderson County
74	n/a	83.5	Marion (city) Marion County
74	n/a	83.5	Valley Falls (CDP) Spartanburg County
76	n/a	83.9	Graniteville (CDP) Aiken County
76	1121	83.9	Orangeburg (city) Orangeburg County
78	n/a	84.0	Hartsville (city) Darlington County
79	n/a	84.1	Woodfield (CDP) Richland County
80	n/a	84.2	Lesslie (CDP) York County
81	n/a	84.3	Central (town) Pickens County
81	1181	84.3	Ladson (CDP) Berkeley County
83	1196	84.4	Myrtle Beach (city) Horry County
84	n/a	84.5	Seneca (city) Oconee County
85	n/a	84.7	Red Bank (CDP) Lexington County
86	1250	84.8	Conway (city) Horry County
87	n/a	85.0	Lakewood (CDP) Sumter County
87	n/a	85.0	Moncks Corner (town) Berkeley County
89	n/a	85.4	Camden (city) Kershaw County
90	1372	85.5	West Columbia (city) Lexington County
91	n/a	85.7	Pendleton (town) Anderson County
91	1403	85.7	Sumter (city) Sumter County
93	n/a	85.8	Centerville (CDP) Anderson County
93	n/a	85.8	Sangaree (CDP) Berkeley County
95	1445	85.9	Greenville (city) Greenville County
96	n/a	86.6	Duncan (town) Spartanburg County
96	1569	86.6	Hanahan (city) Berkeley County
98	1580	86.7	Columbia (city) Richland County
98	1580	86.7	Florence (city) Florence County
100	1600	86.8	Taylors (CDP) Greenville County
101	1615	86.9	Rock Hill (city) York County
102	1626	87.0	Red Hill (CDP) Horry County
103	n/a	87.5	Dalzell (CDP) Sumter County
104	1758	87.7	Wade Hampton (CDP) Greenville County
104	n/a	87.7	Winnsboro (town) Fairfield County
106	n/a	87.9	Lyman (town) Spartanburg County
107	1852	88.1	Cayce (city) Lexington County
108	1947	88.5	Simpsonville (city) Greenville County
109	2061	89.0	Socastee (CDP) Horry County
110	n/a	89.1	Burton (CDP) Beaufort County
110	2086	89.1	Dentsville (CDP) Richland County
112	2132	89.3	Beaufort (city) Beaufort County
113	2250	89.8	Oak Grove (CDP) Lexington County
113	2250	89.8	Saint Andrews (CDP) Richland County
115	n/a	89.9	Surfside Beach (town) Horry County
116	2288	90.0	Bluffton (town) Beaufort County
116	n/a	90.0	Little River (CDP) Horry County
118	n/a	90.2	Boiling Springs (CDP) Spartanburg County
119	n/a	90.5	Fountain Inn (city) Greenville County
120	n/a	90.7	Garden City (CDP) Horry County
121	2497	90.8	Aiken (city) Aiken County
122	2555	91.0	Fort Mill (town) York County
122	2555	91.0	Mauldin (city) Greenville County
124	2827	92.0	North Augusta (city) Aiken County
125	2923	92.3	Hilton Head Island (town) Beaufort County
125	n/a	92.3	Lake Murray of Richland (CDP) Richland County
125	n/a	92.3	Lugoff (CDP) Kershaw County
125	n/a	92.3	Murrells Inlet (CDP) Georgetown County
129	2987	92.5	North Myrtle Beach (city) Horry County
130	3028	92.6	Charleston (city) Charleston County
130	3028	92.6	Port Royal (town) Beaufort County
132	3062	92.7	Goose Creek (city) Berkeley County
133	3088	92.8	Irmo (town) Richland County
134	3163	93.0	Summerville (town) Dorchester County
135	n/a	93.1	Northlake (CDP) Anderson County
136	3258	93.3	Seven Oaks (CDP) Lexington County
137	n/a	93.9	Forestbrook (CDP) Horry County
137	n/a	93.9	Laurel Bay (CDP) Beaufort County
137	3465	93.9	Lexington (town) Lexington County
140	n/a	94.4	Springdale (town) Lexington County
141	n/a	94.8	Newport (CDP) York County
142	n/a	94.9	India Hook (CDP) York County
143	n/a	95.8	Lake Wylie (CDP) York County
144	4156	96.1	Five Forks (CDP) Greenville County
145	n/a	96.9	Folly Beach (city) Charleston County
146	4387	97.1	Mount Pleasant (town) Charleston County
147	4428	97.3	Clemson (city) Pickens County
148	4494	97.6	Forest Acres (city) Richland County
149	n/a	97.7	Tega Cay (city) York County
150	n/a	99.0	Isle of Palms (city) Charleston County

Note: The state column ranks the top/bottom 150 places in the state with population of 2,500 or more. The national column ranks the top/bottom places in the country with population of 10,000 or more. Places that are unincorporated were not considered in the rankings. n/a indicates data not available. Please refer to the User Guide for additional information.

Educational Attainment: Bachelor's Degree or Higher

Top 150 Places Ranked in *Descending* Order

State Rank	Nat'l Rank	Percent	Place
1	n/a	65.8	**Isle of Palms** (city) Charleston County
2	245	63.6	**Clemson** (city) Pickens County
3	337	59.8	**Five Forks** (CDP) Greenville County
4	346	59.5	**Mount Pleasant** (town) Charleston County
5	n/a	59.2	**Tega Cay** (city) York County
6	423	56.5	**Forest Acres** (city) Richland County
7	n/a	54.8	**Folly Beach** (city) Charleston County
8	n/a	51.2	**Lake Murray of Richland** (CDP) Richland County
9	735	48.9	**Charleston** (city) Charleston County
10	767	48.5	**Hilton Head Island** (town) Beaufort County
11	n/a	47.4	**Lake Wylie** (CDP) York County
12	1051	43.1	**Aiken** (city) Aiken County
13	1125	41.7	**Lexington** (town) Lexington County
14	1150	41.3	**Greenville** (city) Greenville County
15	1187	40.7	**Beaufort** (city) Beaufort County
16	1281	39.5	**Columbia** (city) Richland County
17	1408	37.8	**Wade Hampton** (CDP) Greenville County
18	n/a	37.0	**Central** (town) Pickens County
19	n/a	36.9	**Northlake** (CDP) Anderson County
20	n/a	36.5	**Camden** (city) Kershaw County
21	1514	36.4	**Fort Mill** (town) York County
21	1514	36.4	**Irmo** (town) Richland County
23	n/a	36.1	**Boiling Springs** (CDP) Spartanburg County
24	1555	35.9	**Mauldin** (city) Greenville County
25	1585	35.6	**Seven Oaks** (CDP) Lexington County
26	1685	34.6	**Port Royal** (town) Beaufort County
27	n/a	34.3	**Newport** (CDP) York County
28	1763	33.8	**West Columbia** (city) Lexington County
29	1789	33.6	**North Augusta** (city) Aiken County
30	1948	31.9	**North Myrtle Beach** (city) Horry County
30	n/a	31.9	**Surfside Beach** (town) Horry County
32	1962	31.8	**Dentsville** (CDP) Richland County
33	2046	30.9	**Bluffton** (town) Beaufort County
34	n/a	30.8	**Hartsville** (city) Darlington County
35	n/a	30.5	**Pendleton** (town) Anderson County
36	n/a	30.0	**India Hook** (CDP) York County
37	n/a	29.9	**Lugoff** (CDP) Kershaw County
37	2158	29.9	**Summerville** (town) Dorchester County
39	2174	29.8	**Florence** (city) Florence County
40	2297	28.7	**Orangeburg** (city) Orangeburg County
40	2297	28.7	**Rock Hill** (city) York County
42	n/a	28.4	**Hollywood** (town) Charleston County
43	n/a	28.1	**Murrells Inlet** (CDP) Georgetown County
44	2387	27.8	**Saint Andrews** (CDP) Richland County
45	2404	27.7	**Spartanburg** (city) Spartanburg County
46	2442	27.3	**Myrtle Beach** (city) Horry County
47	2497	26.9	**Greer** (city) Greenville County
48	2514	26.8	**Goose Creek** (city) Berkeley County
48	2514	26.8	**Taylors** (CDP) Greenville County
50	2542	26.5	**Simpsonville** (city) Greenville County
51	n/a	26.3	**Little River** (CDP) Horry County
52	2582	26.2	**Newberry** (city) Newberry County
53	n/a	25.3	**Arcadia** (CDP) Spartanburg County
54	n/a	25.2	**Valley Falls** (CDP) Spartanburg County
55	2711	25.1	**Hanahan** (city) Berkeley County
56	2759	24.7	**Sumter** (city) Sumter County
57	n/a	24.6	**Darlington** (city) Darlington County
58	2807	24.3	**Oak Grove** (CDP) Lexington County
59	n/a	24.1	**Walterboro** (city) Colleton County
60	n/a	24.0	**Seneca** (city) Oconee County
61	2852	23.9	**Cayce** (city) Lexington County
61	n/a	23.9	**Kingstree** (town) Williamsburg County
63	2867	23.8	**Conway** (city) Horry County
64	n/a	23.5	**Garden City** (CDP) Horry County
65	2953	23.1	**Easley** (city) Pickens County
66	n/a	22.9	**Bamberg** (town) Bamberg County
67	n/a	22.7	**Springdale** (town) Lexington County
68	n/a	21.9	**Dalzell** (CDP) Sumter County
69	3111	21.8	**Anderson** (city) Anderson County
70	n/a	21.4	**Union** (city) Union County
71	n/a	21.0	**Brookdale** (CDP) Orangeburg County
72	n/a	20.9	**Lyman** (town) Spartanburg County
73	n/a	20.8	**Allendale** (town) Allendale County
74	n/a	20.5	**Forestbrook** (CDP) Horry County
74	3301	20.5	**Red Hill** (CDP) Horry County
74	n/a	20.5	**Travelers Rest** (city) Greenville County
77	n/a	20.2	**North Hartsville** (CDP) Darlington County
78	n/a	19.9	**Red Bank** (CDP) Lexington County
79	n/a	19.7	**Fountain Inn** (city) Greenville County
80	n/a	19.5	**Cheraw** (town) Chesterfield County
81	n/a	19.4	**Centerville** (CDP) Anderson County
82	3472	19.2	**Greenwood** (city) Greenwood County
82	n/a	19.2	**Hampton** (town) Hampton County
84	n/a	19.1	**Edisto** (CDP) Orangeburg County
85	3507	19.0	**North Charleston** (city) Charleston County
86	n/a	18.9	**Laurens** (city) Laurens County
87	3557	18.6	**Gaffney** (city) Cherokee County
88	n/a	18.5	**Duncan** (town) Spartanburg County
88	n/a	18.5	**Hardeeville** (city) Jasper County
90	n/a	18.0	**Woodfield** (CDP) Richland County
91	n/a	17.7	**Georgetown** (city) Georgetown County
91	n/a	17.7	**Lancaster** (city) Lancaster County
93	n/a	17.6	**Williamston** (town) Anderson County
94	n/a	17.5	**Lakewood** (CDP) Sumter County
95	n/a	17.1	**Clinton** (city) Laurens County
95	n/a	17.1	**Denmark** (city) Bamberg County
97	n/a	17.0	**Sangaree** (CDP) Berkeley County
98	n/a	16.5	**Marion** (city) Marion County
99	n/a	16.4	**Clover** (town) York County
100	3870	16.3	**Socastee** (CDP) Horry County
101	n/a	16.1	**Williston** (town) Barnwell County
102	n/a	15.9	**Chester** (city) Chester County
103	n/a	15.6	**Belton** (city) Anderson County
104	n/a	15.5	**Barnwell** (city) Barnwell County
104	n/a	15.5	**Sans Souci** (CDP) Greenville County
106	n/a	15.4	**Liberty** (city) Pickens County
107	4008	15.3	**Gantt** (CDP) Greenville County
108	n/a	14.9	**Bennettsville** (city) Marlboro County
109	n/a	14.4	**Burton** (CDP) Beaufort County
110	4147	14.2	**Ladson** (CDP) Berkeley County
111	n/a	14.0	**Honea Path** (town) Anderson County
111	n/a	14.0	**Winnsboro** (town) Fairfield County
113	n/a	13.3	**Laurel Bay** (CDP) Beaufort County
113	n/a	13.3	**Mullins** (city) Marion County
115	n/a	13.2	**Pickens** (city) Pickens County
116	n/a	13.1	**Batesburg-Leesville** (town) Lexington County
116	n/a	13.1	**York** (city) York County
118	n/a	12.9	**Moncks Corner** (town) Berkeley County
119	n/a	12.5	**Hopkins** (CDP) Richland County
119	n/a	12.5	**Lake City** (city) Florence County
121	n/a	12.1	**Walhalla** (city) Oconee County
122	n/a	11.9	**Manning** (city) Clarendon County
123	n/a	11.8	**Belvedere** (CDP) Aiken County
124	4362	11.7	**Berea** (CDP) Greenville County
124	n/a	11.7	**Saluda** (town) Saluda County
126	n/a	11.6	**Abbeville** (city) Abbeville County
127	n/a	11.5	**Burnettown** (town) Aiken County
128	n/a	11.2	**Springdale** (CDP) Lancaster County
129	n/a	11.1	**Welcome** (CDP) Greenville County
130	n/a	11.0	**Elgin** (CDP) Lancaster County
131	n/a	10.9	**Clearwater** (CDP) Aiken County
132	n/a	10.7	**Lesslie** (CDP) York County
133	n/a	10.1	**Dunean** (CDP) Greenville County
134	n/a	9.6	**Bishopville** (city) Lee County
135	n/a	9.4	**Graniteville** (CDP) Aiken County
136	n/a	8.9	**Edgefield** (town) Edgefield County
137	n/a	8.8	**McCormick** (town) McCormick County
137	n/a	8.8	**Ridgeland** (town) Jasper County
139	n/a	8.7	**Piedmont** (CDP) Anderson County
140	n/a	8.4	**Woodruff** (city) Spartanburg County
141	n/a	7.6	**Pageland** (town) Chesterfield County
142	n/a	7.4	**Arial** (CDP) Pickens County
143	n/a	7.1	**Dillon** (city) Dillon County
144	n/a	7.0	**East Gaffney** (CDP) Cherokee County
145	4597	6.8	**Parker** (CDP) Greenville County
146	n/a	6.6	**Gloverville** (CDP) Aiken County
147	n/a	6.0	**Andrews** (town) Georgetown County
148	n/a	5.2	**Saxon** (CDP) Spartanburg County
149	n/a	3.9	**Southern Shops** (CDP) Spartanburg County
150	n/a	2.8	**Homeland Park** (CDP) Anderson County

Note: The state column ranks the top/bottom 150 places in the state with population of 2,500 or more. The national column ranks the top/bottom places in the country with population of 10,000 or more. Places that are unincorporated were not considered in the rankings. n/a indicates data not available. Please refer to the User Guide for additional information.

Educational Attainment: Bachelor's Degree or Higher

Top 150 Places Ranked in *Ascending* Order

State Rank	Nat'l Rank	Percent	Place
1	n/a	2.8	**Homeland Park** (CDP) Anderson County
2	n/a	3.9	**Southern Shops** (CDP) Spartanburg County
3	n/a	5.2	**Saxon** (CDP) Spartanburg County
4	n/a	6.0	**Andrews** (town) Georgetown County
5	n/a	6.6	**Gloverville** (CDP) Aiken County
6	57	6.8	**Parker** (CDP) Greenville County
7	n/a	7.0	**East Gaffney** (CDP) Cherokee County
8	n/a	7.1	**Dillon** (city) Dillon County
9	n/a	7.4	**Arial** (CDP) Pickens County
10	n/a	7.6	**Pageland** (town) Chesterfield County
11	n/a	8.4	**Woodruff** (city) Spartanburg County
12	n/a	8.7	**Piedmont** (CDP) Anderson County
13	n/a	8.8	**McCormick** (town) McCormick County
13	n/a	8.8	**Ridgeland** (town) Jasper County
15	n/a	8.9	**Edgefield** (town) Edgefield County
16	n/a	9.4	**Graniteville** (CDP) Aiken County
17	n/a	9.6	**Bishopville** (city) Lee County
18	n/a	10.1	**Dunean** (CDP) Greenville County
19	n/a	10.7	**Lesslie** (CDP) York County
20	n/a	10.9	**Clearwater** (CDP) Aiken County
21	n/a	11.0	**Elgin** (CDP) Lancaster County
22	n/a	11.1	**Welcome** (CDP) Greenville County
23	n/a	11.2	**Springdale** (CDP) Lancaster County
24	n/a	11.5	**Burnettown** (town) Aiken County
25	n/a	11.6	**Abbeville** (city) Abbeville County
26	286	11.7	**Berea** (CDP) Greenville County
26	n/a	11.7	**Saluda** (town) Saluda County
28	n/a	11.8	**Belvedere** (CDP) Aiken County
29	n/a	11.9	**Manning** (city) Clarendon County
30	n/a	12.1	**Walhalla** (city) Oconee County
31	n/a	12.5	**Hopkins** (CDP) Richland County
31	n/a	12.5	**Lake City** (city) Florence County
33	n/a	12.9	**Moncks Corner** (town) Berkeley County
34	n/a	13.1	**Batesburg-Leesville** (town) Lexington County
34	n/a	13.1	**York** (city) York County
36	n/a	13.2	**Pickens** (city) Pickens County
37	n/a	13.3	**Laurel Bay** (CDP) Beaufort County
37	n/a	13.3	**Mullins** (city) Marion County
39	n/a	14.0	**Honea Path** (town) Anderson County
39	n/a	14.0	**Winnsboro** (town) Fairfield County
41	499	14.2	**Ladson** (CDP) Berkeley County
42	n/a	14.4	**Burton** (CDP) Beaufort County
43	n/a	14.9	**Bennettsville** (city) Marlboro County
44	636	15.3	**Gantt** (CDP) Greenville County
45	n/a	15.4	**Liberty** (city) Pickens County
46	n/a	15.5	**Barnwell** (city) Barnwell County
46	n/a	15.5	**Sans Souci** (CDP) Greenville County
48	n/a	15.6	**Belton** (city) Anderson County
49	n/a	15.9	**Chester** (city) Chester County
50	n/a	16.1	**Williston** (town) Barnwell County
51	774	16.3	**Socastee** (CDP) Horry County
52	n/a	16.4	**Clover** (town) York County
53	n/a	16.5	**Marion** (city) Marion County
54	n/a	17.0	**Sangaree** (CDP) Berkeley County
55	n/a	17.1	**Clinton** (city) Laurens County
55	n/a	17.1	**Denmark** (city) Bamberg County
57	n/a	17.5	**Lakewood** (CDP) Sumter County
58	n/a	17.6	**Williamston** (town) Anderson County
59	n/a	17.7	**Georgetown** (city) Georgetown County
59	n/a	17.7	**Lancaster** (city) Lancaster County
61	n/a	18.0	**Woodfield** (CDP) Richland County
62	n/a	18.5	**Duncan** (town) Spartanburg County
62	n/a	18.5	**Hardeeville** (city) Jasper County
64	1080	18.6	**Gaffney** (city) Cherokee County
65	n/a	18.9	**Laurens** (city) Laurens County
66	1141	19.0	**North Charleston** (city) Charleston County
67	n/a	19.1	**Edisto** (CDP) Orangeburg County
68	1169	19.2	**Greenwood** (city) Greenwood County
68	n/a	19.2	**Hampton** (town) Hampton County
70	n/a	19.4	**Centerville** (CDP) Anderson County
71	n/a	19.5	**Cheraw** (town) Chesterfield County
72	n/a	19.7	**Fountain Inn** (city) Greenville County
73	n/a	19.9	**Red Bank** (CDP) Lexington County
74	n/a	20.2	**North Hartsville** (CDP) Darlington County
75	n/a	20.5	**Forestbrook** (CDP) Horry County
75	1343	20.5	**Red Hill** (CDP) Horry County
75	n/a	20.5	**Travelers Rest** (city) Greenville County
78	n/a	20.8	**Allendale** (town) Allendale County
79	n/a	20.9	**Lyman** (town) Spartanburg County
80	n/a	21.0	**Brookdale** (CDP) Orangeburg County
81	n/a	21.4	**Union** (city) Union County
82	1537	21.8	**Anderson** (city) Anderson County
83	n/a	21.9	**Dalzell** (CDP) Sumter County
84	n/a	22.7	**Springdale** (town) Lexington County
85	n/a	22.9	**Bamberg** (town) Bamberg County
86	1689	23.1	**Easley** (city) Pickens County
87	n/a	23.5	**Garden City** (CDP) Horry County
88	1780	23.8	**Conway** (city) Horry County
89	1790	23.9	**Cayce** (city) Lexington County
89	n/a	23.9	**Kingstree** (town) Williamsburg County
91	n/a	24.0	**Seneca** (city) Oconee County
92	n/a	24.1	**Walterboro** (city) Colleton County
93	1838	24.3	**Oak Grove** (CDP) Lexington County
94	n/a	24.6	**Darlington** (city) Darlington County
95	1883	24.7	**Sumter** (city) Sumter County
96	1935	25.1	**Hanahan** (city) Berkeley County
97	n/a	25.2	**Valley Falls** (CDP) Spartanburg County
98	n/a	25.3	**Arcadia** (CDP) Spartanburg County
99	2060	26.2	**Newberry** (city) Newberry County
100	n/a	26.3	**Little River** (CDP) Horry County
101	2095	26.5	**Simpsonville** (city) Greenville County
102	2134	26.8	**Goose Creek** (city) Berkeley County
102	2134	26.8	**Taylors** (CDP) Greenville County
104	2143	26.9	**Greer** (city) Greenville County
105	2197	27.3	**Myrtle Beach** (city) Horry County
106	2239	27.7	**Spartanburg** (city) Spartanburg County
107	2253	27.8	**Saint Andrews** (CDP) Richland County
108	n/a	28.1	**Murrells Inlet** (CDP) Georgetown County
109	n/a	28.4	**Hollywood** (town) Charleston County
110	2349	28.7	**Orangeburg** (city) Orangeburg County
110	2349	28.7	**Rock Hill** (city) York County
112	2470	29.8	**Florence** (city) Florence County
113	n/a	29.9	**Lugoff** (CDP) Kershaw County
113	2483	29.9	**Summerville** (town) Dorchester County
115	n/a	30.0	**India Hook** (CDP) York County
116	n/a	30.5	**Pendleton** (town) Anderson County
117	n/a	30.8	**Hartsville** (city) Darlington County
118	2601	30.9	**Bluffton** (town) Beaufort County
119	2685	31.8	**Dentsville** (CDP) Richland County
120	2695	31.9	**North Myrtle Beach** (city) Horry County
120	n/a	31.9	**Surfside Beach** (town) Horry County
122	2857	33.6	**North Augusta** (city) Aiken County
123	2882	33.8	**West Columbia** (city) Lexington County
124	n/a	34.3	**Newport** (CDP) York County
125	2961	34.6	**Port Royal** (town) Beaufort County
126	3065	35.6	**Seven Oaks** (CDP) Lexington County
127	3093	35.9	**Mauldin** (city) Greenville County
128	n/a	36.1	**Boiling Springs** (CDP) Spartanburg County
129	3133	36.4	**Fort Mill** (town) York County
129	3133	36.4	**Irmo** (town) Richland County
131	n/a	36.5	**Camden** (city) Kershaw County
132	n/a	36.9	**Northlake** (CDP) Anderson County
133	n/a	37.0	**Central** (town) Pickens County
134	3239	37.8	**Wade Hampton** (CDP) Greenville County
135	3369	39.5	**Columbia** (city) Richland County
136	3461	40.7	**Beaufort** (city) Beaufort County
137	3497	41.3	**Greenville** (city) Greenville County
138	3521	41.7	**Lexington** (town) Lexington County
139	3602	43.1	**Aiken** (city) Aiken County
140	n/a	47.4	**Lake Wylie** (CDP) York County
141	3883	48.5	**Hilton Head Island** (town) Beaufort County
142	3912	48.9	**Charleston** (city) Charleston County
143	n/a	51.2	**Lake Murray of Richland** (CDP) Richland County
144	n/a	54.8	**Folly Beach** (city) Charleston County
145	4224	56.5	**Forest Acres** (city) Richland County
146	n/a	59.2	**Tega Cay** (city) York County
147	4309	59.5	**Mount Pleasant** (town) Charleston County
148	4316	59.8	**Five Forks** (CDP) Greenville County
149	4409	63.6	**Clemson** (city) Pickens County
150	n/a	65.8	**Isle of Palms** (city) Charleston County

Note: The state column ranks the top/bottom 150 places in the state with population of 2,500 or more. The national column ranks the top/bottom places in the country with population of 10,000 or more. Places that are unincorporated were not considered in the rankings. n/a indicates data not available. Please refer to the User Guide for additional information.

Educational Attainment: Graduate/Professional Degree

Top 150 Places Ranked in *Descending* Order

State Rank	Nat'l Rank	Percent	Place
1	130	34.6	**Clemson** (city) Pickens County
2	n/a	25.2	**Isle of Palms** (city) Charleston County
3	458	24.1	**Forest Acres** (city) Richland County
4	586	21.5	**Mount Pleasant** (town) Charleston County
5	n/a	21.1	**Central** (town) Pickens County
6	n/a	21.0	**Folly Beach** (city) Charleston County
7	643	20.8	**Five Forks** (CDP) Greenville County
8	835	18.7	**Aiken** (city) Aiken County
9	850	18.5	**Charleston** (city) Charleston County
10	886	18.1	**Hilton Head Island** (town) Beaufort County
11	919	17.8	**Port Royal** (town) Beaufort County
12	n/a	17.4	**Tega Cay** (city) York County
13	1045	16.8	**Columbia** (city) Richland County
14	1071	16.5	**Lexington** (town) Lexington County
15	1088	16.4	**Beaufort** (city) Beaufort County
16	1114	16.2	**Greenville** (city) Greenville County
17	n/a	15.6	**Pendleton** (town) Anderson County
18	n/a	15.3	**Boiling Springs** (CDP) Spartanburg County
19	n/a	15.0	**Lake Murray of Richland** (CDP) Richland County
20	n/a	14.6	**Newport** (CDP) York County
21	n/a	14.5	**Lake Wylie** (CDP) York County
22	1326	14.4	**Seven Oaks** (CDP) Lexington County
23	1389	14.0	**Dentsville** (CDP) Richland County
24	1412	13.9	**Mauldin** (city) Greenville County
25	n/a	13.8	**Camden** (city) Kershaw County
26	1543	13.1	**North Augusta** (city) Aiken County
27	1579	12.9	**West Columbia** (city) Lexington County
28	1617	12.7	**North Myrtle Beach** (city) Horry County
28	1617	12.7	**Orangeburg** (city) Orangeburg County
30	n/a	12.6	**Northlake** (CDP) Anderson County
31	1719	12.2	**Florence** (city) Florence County
32	1765	12.0	**Spartanburg** (city) Spartanburg County
33	n/a	11.9	**Hollywood** (town) Charleston County
33	1791	11.9	**Wade Hampton** (CDP) Greenville County
35	n/a	11.7	**Surfside Beach** (town) Horry County
36	n/a	11.6	**Lugoff** (CDP) Kershaw County
37	1985	11.0	**Bluffton** (town) Beaufort County
37	1985	11.0	**Irmo** (town) Richland County
37	n/a	11.0	**Walterboro** (city) Colleton County
40	n/a	10.9	**Brookdale** (CDP) Orangeburg County
41	n/a	10.8	**Darlington** (city) Darlington County
42	2082	10.6	**Summerville** (town) Dorchester County
43	n/a	10.5	**Hartsville** (city) Darlington County
44	n/a	10.4	**Murrells Inlet** (CDP) Georgetown County
45	2241	10.0	**Fort Mill** (town) York County
46	2294	9.8	**Newberry** (city) Newberry County
46	2294	9.8	**Sumter** (city) Sumter County
46	n/a	9.8	**Travelers Rest** (city) Greenville County
49	2317	9.7	**Greer** (city) Greenville County
49	n/a	9.7	**India Hook** (CDP) York County
51	n/a	9.5	**Bamberg** (town) Bamberg County
51	2374	9.5	**Conway** (city) Horry County
51	2374	9.5	**Rock Hill** (city) York County
54	2471	9.2	**Myrtle Beach** (city) Horry County
54	2471	9.2	**Simpsonville** (city) Greenville County
56	2534	9.0	**Saint Andrews** (CDP) Richland County
56	n/a	9.0	**Seneca** (city) Oconee County
56	2534	9.0	**Taylors** (CDP) Greenville County
59	2565	8.9	**Oak Grove** (CDP) Lexington County
60	2586	8.8	**Cayce** (city) Lexington County
61	n/a	8.3	**Cheraw** (town) Chesterfield County
62	n/a	8.2	**Georgetown** (city) Georgetown County
63	2882	7.9	**Hanahan** (city) Berkeley County
63	2882	7.9	**Red Hill** (CDP) Horry County
65	2917	7.8	**Easley** (city) Pickens County
66	2997	7.6	**Anderson** (city) Anderson County
67	n/a	7.4	**Dalzell** (CDP) Sumter County
67	n/a	7.4	**Valley Falls** (CDP) Spartanburg County
69	3128	7.2	**Goose Creek** (city) Berkeley County
70	n/a	7.1	**Fountain Inn** (city) Greenville County
70	n/a	7.1	**Garden City** (CDP) Horry County
72	n/a	6.9	**Clinton** (city) Laurens County
73	n/a	6.7	**Lancaster** (city) Lancaster County
74	n/a	6.6	**Forestbrook** (CDP) Horry County
74	n/a	6.6	**Little River** (CDP) Horry County
74	n/a	6.6	**Springdale** (town) Lexington County
77	3373	6.5	**Greenwood** (city) Greenwood County
78	n/a	6.4	**Belton** (city) Anderson County
78	n/a	6.4	**Centerville** (CDP) Anderson County
78	n/a	6.4	**Union** (city) Union County
81	n/a	6.2	**Winnsboro** (town) Fairfield County
82	n/a	6.1	**Lakewood** (CDP) Sumter County
83	n/a	6.0	**Marion** (city) Marion County
83	n/a	6.0	**Walhalla** (city) Oconee County
83	n/a	6.0	**York** (city) York County
86	n/a	5.9	**Edisto** (CDP) Orangeburg County
86	n/a	5.9	**Laurens** (city) Laurens County
88	n/a	5.7	**Bennettsville** (city) Marlboro County
89	n/a	5.6	**Belvedere** (CDP) Aiken County
89	n/a	5.6	**Kingstree** (town) Williamsburg County
89	3697	5.6	**Socastee** (CDP) Horry County
92	n/a	5.5	**Chester** (city) Chester County
92	n/a	5.5	**Honea Path** (town) Anderson County
92	3735	5.5	**North Charleston** (city) Charleston County
92	n/a	5.5	**Williston** (town) Barnwell County
96	n/a	5.4	**Sangaree** (CDP) Berkeley County
97	n/a	5.3	**Barnwell** (city) Barnwell County
97	3794	5.3	**Gaffney** (city) Cherokee County
97	n/a	5.3	**North Hartsville** (CDP) Darlington County
100	n/a	5.2	**Manning** (city) Clarendon County
101	n/a	5.1	**Liberty** (city) Pickens County
102	3899	5.0	**Gantt** (CDP) Greenville County
102	n/a	5.0	**Hampton** (town) Hampton County
102	n/a	5.0	**Red Bank** (CDP) Lexington County
105	n/a	4.9	**Hardeeville** (city) Jasper County
106	n/a	4.8	**Burton** (CDP) Beaufort County
107	n/a	4.7	**Clover** (town) York County
108	n/a	4.6	**Sans Souci** (CDP) Greenville County
109	n/a	4.5	**Abbeville** (city) Abbeville County
109	n/a	4.5	**Allendale** (town) Allendale County
109	4067	4.5	**Ladson** (CDP) Berkeley County
112	n/a	4.3	**Mullins** (city) Marion County
113	n/a	4.2	**Batesburg-Leesville** (town) Lexington County
114	n/a	4.1	**Woodfield** (CDP) Richland County
115	n/a	4.0	**Clearwater** (CDP) Aiken County
116	4242	3.9	**Berea** (CDP) Greenville County
116	n/a	3.9	**Hopkins** (CDP) Richland County
118	n/a	3.8	**Burnettown** (town) Aiken County
119	n/a	3.7	**Lyman** (town) Spartanburg County
119	n/a	3.7	**Moncks Corner** (town) Berkeley County
121	n/a	3.6	**Edgefield** (town) Edgefield County
122	n/a	3.4	**Welcome** (CDP) Greenville County
123	n/a	3.3	**Williamston** (town) Anderson County
124	n/a	3.2	**Duncan** (town) Spartanburg County
125	n/a	3.0	**Pickens** (city) Pickens County
126	n/a	2.9	**Lake City** (city) Florence County
126	n/a	2.9	**Lesslie** (CDP) York County
128	n/a	2.8	**Pageland** (town) Chesterfield County
128	n/a	2.8	**Woodruff** (city) Spartanburg County
130	n/a	2.6	**Arcadia** (CDP) Spartanburg County
131	n/a	2.5	**Elgin** (CDP) Lancaster County
132	n/a	2.4	**Gloverville** (CDP) Aiken County
132	n/a	2.4	**Ridgeland** (town) Jasper County
132	n/a	2.4	**Saluda** (town) Saluda County
135	n/a	2.3	**Bishopville** (city) Lee County
135	n/a	2.3	**Denmark** (city) Bamberg County
137	n/a	2.2	**Andrews** (town) Georgetown County
138	n/a	2.1	**Dillon** (city) Dillon County
139	n/a	2.0	**Arial** (CDP) Pickens County
139	n/a	2.0	**McCormick** (town) McCormick County
141	n/a	1.8	**Dunean** (CDP) Greenville County
141	n/a	1.8	**East Gaffney** (CDP) Cherokee County
141	n/a	1.8	**Graniteville** (CDP) Aiken County
141	4582	1.8	**Parker** (CDP) Greenville County
141	n/a	1.8	**Piedmont** (CDP) Anderson County
146	n/a	1.5	**Saxon** (CDP) Spartanburg County
147	n/a	1.1	**Homeland Park** (CDP) Anderson County
147	n/a	1.1	**Laurel Bay** (CDP) Beaufort County
149	n/a	0.5	**Southern Shops** (CDP) Spartanburg County
150	n/a	0.0	**Springdale** (CDP) Lancaster County

Note: The state column ranks the top/bottom 150 places in the state with population of 2,500 or more. The national column ranks the top/bottom places in the country with population of 10,000 or more. Places that are unincorporated were not considered in the rankings. n/a indicates data not available. Please refer to the User Guide for additional information.

Educational Attainment: Graduate/Professional Degree

Top 150 Places Ranked in *Ascending* Order

State Rank	Nat'l Rank	Percent	Place
1	n/a	0.0	Springdale (CDP) Lancaster County
2	n/a	0.5	Southern Shops (CDP) Spartanburg County
3	n/a	1.1	Homeland Park (CDP) Anderson County
3	n/a	1.1	Laurel Bay (CDP) Beaufort County
5	n/a	1.5	Saxon (CDP) Spartanburg County
6	n/a	1.8	Dunean (CDP) Greenville County
6	n/a	1.8	East Gaffney (CDP) Cherokee County
6	n/a	1.8	Graniteville (CDP) Aiken County
6	70	1.8	Parker (CDP) Greenville County
6	n/a	1.8	Piedmont (CDP) Anderson County
11	n/a	2.0	Arial (CDP) Pickens County
11	n/a	2.0	McCormick (town) McCormick County
13	n/a	2.1	Dillon (city) Dillon County
14	n/a	2.2	Andrews (town) Georgetown County
15	n/a	2.3	Bishopville (city) Lee County
15	n/a	2.3	Denmark (city) Bamberg County
17	n/a	2.4	Gloverville (CDP) Aiken County
17	n/a	2.4	Ridgeland (town) Jasper County
17	n/a	2.4	Saluda (town) Saluda County
20	n/a	2.5	Elgin (CDP) Lancaster County
21	n/a	2.6	Arcadia (CDP) Spartanburg County
22	n/a	2.8	Pageland (town) Chesterfield County
22	n/a	2.8	Woodruff (city) Spartanburg County
24	n/a	2.9	Lake City (city) Florence County
24	n/a	2.9	Lesslie (CDP) York County
26	n/a	3.0	Pickens (city) Pickens County
27	n/a	3.2	Duncan (town) Spartanburg County
28	n/a	3.3	Williamston (town) Anderson County
29	n/a	3.4	Welcome (CDP) Greenville County
30	n/a	3.6	Edgefield (town) Edgefield County
31	n/a	3.7	Lyman (town) Spartanburg County
31	n/a	3.7	Moncks Corner (town) Berkeley County
33	n/a	3.8	Burnettown (town) Aiken County
34	398	3.9	Berea (CDP) Greenville County
34	n/a	3.9	Hopkins (CDP) Richland County
36	n/a	4.0	Clearwater (CDP) Aiken County
37	n/a	4.1	Woodfield (CDP) Richland County
38	n/a	4.2	Batesburg-Leesville (town) Lexington County
39	n/a	4.3	Mullins (city) Marion County
40	n/a	4.5	Abbeville (city) Abbeville County
40	n/a	4.5	Allendale (town) Allendale County
40	551	4.5	Ladson (CDP) Berkeley County
43	n/a	4.6	Sans Souci (CDP) Greenville County
44	n/a	4.7	Clover (town) York County
45	n/a	4.8	Burton (CDP) Beaufort County
46	n/a	4.9	Hardeeville (city) Jasper County
47	726	5.0	Gantt (CDP) Greenville County
47	n/a	5.0	Hampton (town) Hampton County
47	n/a	5.0	Red Bank (CDP) Lexington County
50	n/a	5.1	Liberty (city) Pickens County
51	n/a	5.2	Manning (city) Clarendon County
52	n/a	5.3	Barnwell (city) Barnwell County
52	828	5.3	Gaffney (city) Cherokee County
52	n/a	5.3	North Hartsville (CDP) Darlington County
55	n/a	5.4	Sangaree (CDP) Berkeley County
56	n/a	5.5	Chester (city) Chester County
56	n/a	5.5	Honea Path (town) Anderson County
56	892	5.5	North Charleston (city) Charleston County
56	n/a	5.5	Williston (town) Barnwell County
60	n/a	5.6	Belvedere (CDP) Aiken County
60	n/a	5.6	Kingstree (town) Williamsburg County
60	922	5.6	Socastee (CDP) Horry County
63	n/a	5.7	Bennettsville (city) Marlboro County
64	n/a	5.9	Edisto (CDP) Orangeburg County
64	n/a	5.9	Laurens (city) Laurens County
66	n/a	6.0	Marion (city) Marion County
66	n/a	6.0	Walhalla (city) Oconee County
66	n/a	6.0	York (city) York County
69	n/a	6.1	Lakewood (CDP) Sumter County
70	n/a	6.2	Winnsboro (town) Fairfield County
71	n/a	6.4	Belton (city) Anderson County
71	n/a	6.4	Centerville (CDP) Anderson County
71	n/a	6.4	Union (city) Union County
74	1246	6.5	Greenwood (city) Greenwood County
75	n/a	6.6	Forestbrook (CDP) Horry County
75	n/a	6.6	Little River (CDP) Horry County
75	n/a	6.6	Springdale (town) Lexington County
78	n/a	6.7	Lancaster (city) Lancaster County
79	n/a	6.9	Clinton (city) Laurens County
80	n/a	7.1	Fountain Inn (city) Greenville County
80	n/a	7.1	Garden City (CDP) Horry County
82	1486	7.2	Goose Creek (city) Berkeley County
83	n/a	7.4	Dalzell (CDP) Sumter County
83	n/a	7.4	Valley Falls (CDP) Spartanburg County
85	1635	7.6	Anderson (city) Anderson County
86	1697	7.8	Easley (city) Pickens County
87	1740	7.9	Hanahan (city) Berkeley County
87	1740	7.9	Red Hill (CDP) Horry County
89	n/a	8.2	Georgetown (city) Georgetown County
90	n/a	8.3	Cheraw (town) Chesterfield County
91	2042	8.8	Cayce (city) Lexington County
92	2071	8.9	Oak Grove (CDP) Lexington County
93	2092	9.0	Saint Andrews (CDP) Richland County
93	n/a	9.0	Seneca (city) Oconee County
93	2092	9.0	Taylors (CDP) Greenville County
96	2156	9.2	Myrtle Beach (city) Horry County
96	2156	9.2	Simpsonville (city) Greenville County
98	n/a	9.5	Bamberg (town) Bamberg County
98	2245	9.5	Conway (city) Horry County
98	2245	9.5	Rock Hill (city) York County
101	2312	9.7	Greer (city) Greenville County
101	n/a	9.7	India Hook (CDP) York County
103	2340	9.8	Newberry (city) Newberry County
103	2340	9.8	Sumter (city) Sumter County
103	n/a	9.8	Travelers Rest (city) Greenville County
106	2386	10.0	Fort Mill (town) York County
107	n/a	10.4	Murrells Inlet (CDP) Georgetown County
108	n/a	10.5	Hartsville (city) Darlington County
109	2556	10.6	Summerville (town) Dorchester County
110	n/a	10.8	Darlington (city) Darlington County
111	n/a	10.9	Brookdale (CDP) Orangeburg County
112	2649	11.0	Bluffton (town) Beaufort County
112	2649	11.0	Irmo (town) Richland County
112	n/a	11.0	Walterboro (city) Colleton County
115	n/a	11.6	Lugoff (CDP) Kershaw County
116	n/a	11.7	Surfside Beach (town) Horry County
117	n/a	11.9	Hollywood (town) Charleston County
117	2844	11.9	Wade Hampton (CDP) Greenville County
119	2866	12.0	Spartanburg (city) Spartanburg County
120	2916	12.2	Florence (city) Florence County
121	n/a	12.6	Northlake (CDP) Anderson County
122	3014	12.7	North Myrtle Beach (city) Horry County
122	3014	12.7	Orangeburg (city) Orangeburg County
124	3059	12.9	West Columbia (city) Lexington County
125	3096	13.1	North Augusta (city) Aiken County
126	n/a	13.8	Camden (city) Kershaw County
127	3229	13.9	Mauldin (city) Greenville County
128	3245	14.0	Dentsville (CDP) Richland County
129	3315	14.4	Seven Oaks (CDP) Lexington County
130	n/a	14.5	Lake Wylie (CDP) York County
131	n/a	14.6	Newport (CDP) York County
132	n/a	15.0	Lake Murray of Richland (CDP) Richland County
133	n/a	15.3	Boiling Springs (CDP) Spartanburg County
134	n/a	15.6	Pendleton (town) Anderson County
135	3535	16.2	Greenville (city) Greenville County
136	3556	16.4	Beaufort (city) Beaufort County
137	3569	16.5	Lexington (town) Lexington County
138	3602	16.8	Columbia (city) Richland County
139	n/a	17.4	Tega Cay (city) York County
140	3729	17.8	Port Royal (town) Beaufort County
141	3757	18.1	Hilton Head Island (town) Beaufort County
142	3798	18.5	Charleston (city) Charleston County
143	3815	18.7	Aiken (city) Aiken County
144	4004	20.8	Five Forks (CDP) Greenville County
145	n/a	21.0	Folly Beach (city) Charleston County
146	n/a	21.1	Central (town) Pickens County
147	4063	21.5	Mount Pleasant (town) Charleston County
148	4195	24.1	Forest Acres (city) Richland County
149	n/a	25.2	Isle of Palms (city) Charleston County
150	4526	34.6	Clemson (city) Pickens County

Note: The state column ranks the top/bottom 150 places in the state with population of 2,500 or more. The national column ranks the top/bottom places in the country with population of 10,000 or more. Places that are unincorporated were not considered in the rankings. n/a indicates data not available. Please refer to the User Guide for additional information.

Homeownership Rate

Top 150 Places Ranked in *Descending* Order

State Rank	Nat'l Rank	Percent	Place
1	n/a	93.2	**Tega Cay** (city) York County
2	70	93.1	**Five Forks** (CDP) Greenville County
3	n/a	93.0	**Lake Murray of Richland** (CDP) Richland County
4	n/a	89.0	**India Hook** (CDP) York County
5	n/a	86.8	**Newport** (CDP) York County
6	n/a	83.8	**Lesslie** (CDP) York County
7	n/a	82.6	**Murrells Inlet** (CDP) Georgetown County
8	n/a	82.5	**Hollywood** (town) Charleston County
9	774	82.1	**Irmo** (town) Richland County
10	n/a	81.0	**Isle of Palms** (city) Charleston County
10	n/a	81.0	**Lugoff** (CDP) Kershaw County
12	n/a	80.9	**Hopkins** (CDP) Richland County
13	n/a	79.8	**Burnettown** (town) Aiken County
14	n/a	78.5	**Lake Wylie** (CDP) York County
15	n/a	78.2	**Red Bank** (CDP) Lexington County
16	n/a	77.9	**Forestbrook** (CDP) Horry County
17	n/a	76.5	**Arial** (CDP) Pickens County
18	n/a	76.3	**Lakewood** (CDP) Sumter County
19	n/a	76.1	**Centerville** (CDP) Anderson County
20	n/a	75.8	**Elgin** (CDP) Lancaster County
20	n/a	75.8	**Garden City** (CDP) Horry County
20	n/a	75.8	**North Hartsville** (CDP) Darlington County
23	n/a	75.4	**Piedmont** (CDP) Anderson County
24	n/a	75.0	**Lyman** (town) Spartanburg County
25	n/a	74.7	**Sangaree** (CDP) Berkeley County
26	1480	74.6	**Bluffton** (town) Beaufort County
27	n/a	74.5	**Northlake** (CDP) Anderson County
28	1505	74.4	**Oak Grove** (CDP) Lexington County
29	n/a	74.3	**Springdale** (town) Lexington County
30	n/a	73.3	**Dalzell** (CDP) Sumter County
30	n/a	73.3	**Fountain Inn** (city) Greenville County
30	1605	73.3	**Ladson** (CDP) Berkeley County
33	n/a	73.1	**Little River** (CDP) Horry County
34	1655	72.8	**Hilton Head Island** (town) Beaufort County
35	1678	72.6	**Mount Pleasant** (town) Charleston County
36	n/a	72.0	**Boiling Springs** (CDP) Spartanburg County
37	1865	71.1	**Goose Creek** (city) Berkeley County
38	n/a	70.7	**Liberty** (city) Pickens County
39	1923	70.5	**Red Hill** (CDP) Horry County
40	1942	70.3	**Forest Acres** (city) Richland County
41	2019	69.5	**North Myrtle Beach** (city) Horry County
42	2032	69.4	**Taylors** (CDP) Greenville County
43	n/a	69.2	**Belvedere** (CDP) Aiken County
44	n/a	68.0	**Camden** (city) Kershaw County
44	2182	68.0	**Fort Mill** (town) York County
46	2225	67.6	**Mauldin** (city) Greenville County
47	n/a	67.3	**Williamston** (town) Anderson County
48	2320	66.8	**North Augusta** (city) Aiken County
49	2393	66.1	**Simpsonville** (city) Greenville County
50	2404	66.0	**Aiken** (city) Aiken County
51	2483	65.3	**Easley** (city) Pickens County
52	n/a	64.9	**Honea Path** (town) Anderson County
53	2546	64.7	**Hanahan** (city) Berkeley County
54	n/a	64.1	**Travelers Rest** (city) Greenville County
55	n/a	64.0	**Bamberg** (town) Bamberg County
56	n/a	63.7	**Moncks Corner** (town) Berkeley County
56	2628	63.7	**Summerville** (town) Dorchester County
58	n/a	63.6	**Graniteville** (CDP) Aiken County
59	n/a	63.3	**Batesburg-Leesville** (town) Lexington County
59	n/a	63.3	**Surfside Beach** (town) Horry County
61	2682	63.2	**Greer** (city) Greenville County
62	n/a	63.1	**Belton** (city) Anderson County
63	n/a	62.9	**Clover** (town) York County
64	n/a	62.1	**Clearwater** (CDP) Aiken County
64	n/a	62.1	**Gloverville** (CDP) Aiken County
66	n/a	62.0	**Andrews** (town) Georgetown County
66	n/a	62.0	**Welcome** (CDP) Greenville County
68	n/a	61.2	**Hampton** (town) Hampton County
69	2944	60.8	**Wade Hampton** (CDP) Greenville County
70	2961	60.7	**Socastee** (CDP) Horry County
71	2983	60.6	**Cayce** (city) Lexington County
72	n/a	60.5	**Edisto** (CDP) Orangeburg County
73	3024	60.3	**Seven Oaks** (CDP) Lexington County
74	3043	60.2	**Berea** (CDP) Greenville County
75	3053	60.1	**Lexington** (town) Lexington County
76	3074	59.9	**Florence** (city) Florence County
77	n/a	59.3	**Abbeville** (city) Abbeville County
78	3153	59.2	**Gantt** (CDP) Greenville County
78	n/a	59.2	**Williston** (town) Barnwell County
80	n/a	59.0	**Folly Beach** (city) Charleston County
81	n/a	58.9	**East Gaffney** (CDP) Cherokee County
82	n/a	58.8	**Pendleton** (town) Anderson County
83	n/a	57.3	**Homeland Park** (CDP) Anderson County
83	n/a	57.3	**Pickens** (city) Pickens County
85	n/a	57.2	**Burton** (CDP) Beaufort County
86	n/a	57.1	**York** (city) York County
87	n/a	57.0	**Allendale** (town) Allendale County
88	3479	56.4	**Conway** (city) Horry County
89	n/a	56.3	**Seneca** (city) Oconee County
90	n/a	56.2	**Woodruff** (city) Spartanburg County
91	n/a	56.0	**Barnwell** (city) Barnwell County
92	n/a	55.9	**Walhalla** (city) Oconee County
93	n/a	55.5	**Winnsboro** (town) Fairfield County
94	n/a	55.3	**Chester** (city) Chester County
94	n/a	55.3	**Springdale** (CDP) Lancaster County
96	n/a	55.2	**Sans Souci** (CDP) Greenville County
97	n/a	54.8	**Mullins** (city) Marion County
98	n/a	54.3	**Pageland** (town) Chesterfield County
98	n/a	54.3	**Union** (city) Union County
100	n/a	54.2	**Walterboro** (city) Colleton County
101	n/a	53.9	**Dunean** (CDP) Greenville County
101	n/a	53.9	**Lake City** (city) Florence County
103	3740	53.8	**Beaufort** (city) Beaufort County
104	3750	53.7	**Gaffney** (city) Cherokee County
104	n/a	53.7	**Manning** (city) Clarendon County
106	n/a	53.6	**Georgetown** (city) Georgetown County
107	n/a	53.4	**Denmark** (city) Bamberg County
107	3782	53.4	**Rock Hill** (city) York County
109	n/a	53.3	**Laurens** (city) Laurens County
109	3793	53.3	**Sumter** (city) Sumter County
109	n/a	53.3	**Woodfield** (CDP) Richland County
112	n/a	53.2	**Bennettsville** (city) Marlboro County
113	3834	52.7	**Parker** (CDP) Greenville County
114	n/a	52.5	**Hartsville** (city) Darlington County
115	n/a	52.4	**Marion** (city) Marion County
116	n/a	52.2	**Darlington** (city) Darlington County
116	n/a	52.2	**Saxon** (CDP) Spartanburg County
118	3898	52.1	**Charleston** (city) Charleston County
119	n/a	51.5	**Dillon** (city) Dillon County
120	n/a	51.2	**Cheraw** (town) Chesterfield County
121	3986	50.8	**West Columbia** (city) Lexington County
122	n/a	50.4	**Edgefield** (town) Edgefield County
123	n/a	50.1	**Bishopville** (city) Lee County
124	4063	49.5	**Newberry** (city) Newberry County
125	n/a	49.4	**Duncan** (town) Spartanburg County
126	4075	49.3	**Anderson** (city) Anderson County
127	4093	49.1	**Spartanburg** (city) Spartanburg County
128	n/a	49.0	**McCormick** (town) McCormick County
129	4121	48.7	**Myrtle Beach** (city) Horry County
130	n/a	48.4	**Clinton** (city) Laurens County
131	4165	47.9	**North Charleston** (city) Charleston County
132	4195	47.4	**Columbia** (city) Richland County
133	n/a	47.2	**Saluda** (town) Saluda County
134	n/a	46.9	**Kingstree** (town) Williamsburg County
135	n/a	46.5	**Ridgeland** (town) Jasper County
136	4231	46.4	**Greenwood** (city) Greenwood County
137	n/a	46.1	**Brookdale** (CDP) Orangeburg County
138	n/a	45.8	**Lancaster** (city) Lancaster County
139	n/a	45.7	**Southern Shops** (CDP) Spartanburg County
140	4273	45.6	**Orangeburg** (city) Orangeburg County
141	4285	45.3	**Greenville** (city) Greenville County
142	4359	43.0	**Clemson** (city) Pickens County
143	n/a	42.3	**Hardeeville** (city) Jasper County
144	n/a	40.7	**Valley Falls** (CDP) Spartanburg County
145	n/a	39.2	**Arcadia** (CDP) Spartanburg County
146	4515	37.4	**Dentsville** (CDP) Richland County
147	4543	35.3	**Saint Andrews** (CDP) Richland County
148	4545	35.1	**Port Royal** (town) Beaufort County
149	n/a	24.2	**Laurel Bay** (CDP) Beaufort County
150	n/a	22.2	**Central** (town) Pickens County

Note: The state column ranks the top/bottom 150 places in the state with population of 2,500 or more. The national column ranks the top/bottom places in the country with population of 10,000 or more. Places that are unincorporated were not considered in the rankings. n/a indicates data not available. Please refer to the User Guide for additional information.

Homeownership Rate

Top 150 Places Ranked in *Ascending* Order

State Rank	Nat'l Rank	Percent	Place
1	n/a	22.2	**Central** (town) Pickens County
2	n/a	24.2	**Laurel Bay** (CDP) Beaufort County
3	111	35.1	**Port Royal** (town) Beaufort County
4	113	35.3	**Saint Andrews** (CDP) Richland County
5	138	37.4	**Dentsville** (CDP) Richland County
6	n/a	39.2	**Arcadia** (CDP) Spartanburg County
7	n/a	40.7	**Valley Falls** (CDP) Spartanburg County
8	n/a	42.3	**Hardeeville** (city) Jasper County
9	292	43.0	**Clemson** (city) Pickens County
10	367	45.3	**Greenville** (city) Greenville County
11	380	45.6	**Orangeburg** (city) Orangeburg County
12	n/a	45.7	**Southern Shops** (CDP) Spartanburg County
13	n/a	45.8	**Lancaster** (city) Lancaster County
14	n/a	46.1	**Brookdale** (CDP) Orangeburg County
15	422	46.4	**Greenwood** (city) Greenwood County
16	n/a	46.5	**Ridgeland** (town) Jasper County
17	n/a	46.9	**Kingstree** (town) Williamsburg County
18	n/a	47.2	**Saluda** (town) Saluda County
19	455	47.4	**Columbia** (city) Richland County
20	483	47.9	**North Charleston** (city) Charleston County
21	n/a	48.4	**Clinton** (city) Laurens County
22	533	48.7	**Myrtle Beach** (city) Horry County
23	n/a	49.0	**McCormick** (town) McCormick County
24	558	49.1	**Spartanburg** (city) Spartanburg County
25	574	49.3	**Anderson** (city) Anderson County
26	n/a	49.4	**Duncan** (town) Spartanburg County
27	586	49.5	**Newberry** (city) Newberry County
28	n/a	50.1	**Bishopville** (city) Lee County
29	n/a	50.4	**Edgefield** (town) Edgefield County
30	661	50.8	**West Columbia** (city) Lexington County
31	n/a	51.2	**Cheraw** (town) Chesterfield County
32	n/a	51.5	**Dillon** (city) Dillon County
33	750	52.1	**Charleston** (city) Charleston County
34	n/a	52.2	**Darlington** (city) Darlington County
34	n/a	52.2	**Saxon** (CDP) Spartanburg County
36	n/a	52.4	**Marion** (city) Marion County
37	n/a	52.5	**Hartsville** (city) Darlington County
38	813	52.7	**Parker** (CDP) Greenville County
39	n/a	53.2	**Bennettsville** (city) Marlboro County
40	n/a	53.3	**Laurens** (city) Laurens County
40	853	53.3	**Sumter** (city) Sumter County
40	n/a	53.3	**Woodfield** (CDP) Richland County
43	n/a	53.4	**Denmark** (city) Bamberg County
43	864	53.4	**Rock Hill** (city) York County
45	n/a	53.6	**Georgetown** (city) Georgetown County
46	896	53.7	**Gaffney** (city) Cherokee County
46	n/a	53.7	**Manning** (city) Clarendon County
48	907	53.8	**Beaufort** (city) Beaufort County
49	n/a	53.9	**Dunean** (CDP) Greenville County
49	n/a	53.9	**Lake City** (city) Florence County
51	n/a	54.2	**Walterboro** (city) Colleton County
52	n/a	54.3	**Pageland** (town) Chesterfield County
52	n/a	54.3	**Union** (city) Union County
54	n/a	54.8	**Mullins** (city) Marion County
55	n/a	55.2	**Sans Souci** (CDP) Greenville County
56	n/a	55.3	**Chester** (city) Chester County
56	n/a	55.3	**Springdale** (CDP) Lancaster County
58	n/a	55.5	**Winnsboro** (town) Fairfield County
59	n/a	55.9	**Walhalla** (city) Oconee County
60	n/a	56.0	**Barnwell** (city) Barnwell County
61	n/a	56.2	**Woodruff** (city) Spartanburg County
62	n/a	56.3	**Seneca** (city) Oconee County
63	1162	56.4	**Conway** (city) Horry County
64	n/a	57.0	**Allendale** (town) Allendale County
65	n/a	57.1	**York** (city) York County
66	n/a	57.2	**Burton** (CDP) Beaufort County
67	n/a	57.3	**Homeland Park** (CDP) Anderson County
67	n/a	57.3	**Pickens** (city) Pickens County
69	n/a	58.8	**Pendleton** (town) Anderson County
70	n/a	58.9	**East Gaffney** (CDP) Cherokee County
71	n/a	59.0	**Folly Beach** (city) Charleston County
72	1493	59.2	**Gantt** (CDP) Greenville County
72	n/a	59.2	**Williston** (town) Barnwell County
74	n/a	59.3	**Abbeville** (city) Abbeville County
75	1566	59.9	**Florence** (city) Florence County
76	1595	60.1	**Lexington** (town) Lexington County
77	1604	60.2	**Berea** (CDP) Greenville County
78	1614	60.3	**Seven Oaks** (CDP) Lexington County
79	n/a	60.5	**Edisto** (CDP) Orangeburg County
80	1659	60.6	**Cayce** (city) Lexington County
81	1674	60.7	**Socastee** (CDP) Horry County
82	1696	60.8	**Wade Hampton** (CDP) Greenville County
83	n/a	61.2	**Hampton** (town) Hampton County
84	n/a	62.0	**Andrews** (town) Georgetown County
84	n/a	62.0	**Welcome** (CDP) Greenville County
86	n/a	62.1	**Clearwater** (CDP) Aiken County
86	n/a	62.1	**Gloverville** (CDP) Aiken County
88	n/a	62.9	**Clover** (town) York County
89	n/a	63.1	**Belton** (city) Anderson County
90	1960	63.2	**Greer** (city) Greenville County
91	n/a	63.3	**Batesburg-Leesville** (town) Lexington County
91	n/a	63.3	**Surfside Beach** (town) Horry County
93	n/a	63.6	**Graniteville** (CDP) Aiken County
94	n/a	63.7	**Moncks Corner** (town) Berkeley County
94	2018	63.7	**Summerville** (town) Dorchester County
96	n/a	64.0	**Bamberg** (town) Bamberg County
97	n/a	64.1	**Travelers Rest** (city) Greenville County
98	2106	64.7	**Hanahan** (city) Berkeley County
99	n/a	64.9	**Honea Path** (town) Anderson County
100	2158	65.3	**Easley** (city) Pickens County
101	2241	66.0	**Aiken** (city) Aiken County
102	2253	66.1	**Simpsonville** (city) Greenville County
103	2329	66.8	**North Augusta** (city) Aiken County
104	n/a	67.3	**Williamston** (town) Anderson County
105	2425	67.6	**Mauldin** (city) Greenville County
106	n/a	68.0	**Camden** (city) Kershaw County
106	2467	68.0	**Fort Mill** (town) York County
108	n/a	69.2	**Belvedere** (CDP) Aiken County
109	2615	69.4	**Taylors** (CDP) Greenville County
110	2625	69.5	**North Myrtle Beach** (city) Horry County
111	2710	70.3	**Forest Acres** (city) Richland County
112	2720	70.5	**Red Hill** (CDP) Horry County
113	n/a	70.7	**Liberty** (city) Pickens County
114	2779	71.1	**Goose Creek** (city) Berkeley County
115	n/a	72.0	**Boiling Springs** (CDP) Spartanburg County
116	2967	72.6	**Mount Pleasant** (town) Charleston County
117	2989	72.8	**Hilton Head Island** (town) Beaufort County
118	n/a	73.1	**Little River** (CDP) Horry County
119	n/a	73.3	**Dalzell** (CDP) Sumter County
119	n/a	73.3	**Fountain Inn** (city) Greenville County
119	3038	73.3	**Ladson** (CDP) Berkeley County
122	n/a	74.3	**Springdale** (town) Lexington County
123	3142	74.4	**Oak Grove** (CDP) Lexington County
124	n/a	74.5	**Northlake** (CDP) Anderson County
125	3165	74.6	**Bluffton** (town) Beaufort County
126	n/a	74.7	**Sangaree** (CDP) Berkeley County
127	n/a	75.0	**Lyman** (town) Spartanburg County
128	n/a	75.4	**Piedmont** (CDP) Anderson County
129	n/a	75.8	**Elgin** (CDP) Lancaster County
129	n/a	75.8	**Garden City** (CDP) Horry County
129	n/a	75.8	**North Hartsville** (CDP) Darlington County
132	n/a	76.1	**Centerville** (CDP) Anderson County
133	n/a	76.3	**Lakewood** (CDP) Sumter County
134	n/a	76.5	**Arial** (CDP) Pickens County
135	n/a	77.9	**Forestbrook** (CDP) Horry County
136	n/a	78.2	**Red Bank** (CDP) Lexington County
137	n/a	78.5	**Lake Wylie** (CDP) York County
138	n/a	79.8	**Burnettown** (town) Aiken County
139	n/a	80.9	**Hopkins** (CDP) Richland County
140	n/a	81.0	**Isle of Palms** (city) Charleston County
140	n/a	81.0	**Lugoff** (CDP) Kershaw County
142	3871	82.1	**Irmo** (town) Richland County
143	n/a	82.5	**Hollywood** (town) Charleston County
144	n/a	82.6	**Murrells Inlet** (CDP) Georgetown County
145	n/a	83.8	**Lesslie** (CDP) York County
146	n/a	86.8	**Newport** (CDP) York County
147	n/a	89.0	**India Hook** (CDP) York County
148	n/a	93.0	**Lake Murray of Richland** (CDP) Richland County
149	4584	93.1	**Five Forks** (CDP) Greenville County
150	n/a	93.2	**Tega Cay** (city) York County

Note: The state column ranks the top/bottom 150 places in the state with population of 2,500 or more. The national column ranks the top/bottom places in the country with population of 10,000 or more. Places that are unincorporated were not considered in the rankings. n/a indicates data not available. Please refer to the User Guide for additional information.

Median Home Value

Top 150 Places Ranked in *Descending* Order

State Rank	Nat'l Rank	Dollars	Place		State Rank	Nat'l Rank	Dollars	Place
1	n/a	792,200	**Isle of Palms** (city) Charleston County		76	n/a	117,000	**Red Bank** (CDP) Lexington County
2	n/a	607,700	**Folly Beach** (city) Charleston County		77	3762	116,300	**Newberry** (city) Newberry County
3	421	447,900	**Hilton Head Island** (town) Beaufort County		78	n/a	115,900	**Fountain Inn** (city) Greenville County
4	826	349,200	**Mount Pleasant** (town) Charleston County		79	n/a	114,500	**Georgetown** (city) Georgetown County
5	n/a	312,500	**Lake Murray of Richland** (CDP) Richland County		80	n/a	114,300	**Dalzell** (CDP) Sumter County
6	n/a	286,200	**Lake Wylie** (CDP) York County		81	n/a	113,000	**Lyman** (town) Spartanburg County
7	n/a	276,900	**Tega Cay** (city) York County		82	n/a	112,500	**Clearwater** (CDP) Aiken County
8	1538	258,300	**Five Forks** (CDP) Greenville County		82	n/a	112,500	**Pendleton** (town) Anderson County
9	1565	253,800	**Charleston** (city) Charleston County		84	n/a	112,000	**Hartsville** (city) Darlington County
10	1571	252,700	**Beaufort** (city) Beaufort County		85	3866	111,800	**Berea** (CDP) Greenville County
11	1611	248,000	**North Myrtle Beach** (city) Horry County		86	n/a	110,300	**York** (city) York County
12	n/a	246,100	**Surfside Beach** (town) Horry County		87	3909	109,600	**Dentsville** (CDP) Richland County
13	n/a	226,800	**Murrells Inlet** (CDP) Georgetown County		88	3949	107,400	**Saint Andrews** (CDP) Richland County
14	1975	216,500	**Bluffton** (town) Beaufort County		89	n/a	106,100	**Duncan** (town) Spartanburg County
15	n/a	200,600	**Hollywood** (town) Charleston County		90	n/a	104,200	**Bamberg** (town) Bamberg County
16	2178	200,500	**Greenville** (city) Greenville County		90	n/a	104,200	**Marion** (city) Marion County
17	2181	200,300	**Clemson** (city) Pickens County		92	n/a	103,800	**North Hartsville** (CDP) Darlington County
18	2224	197,100	**Port Royal** (town) Beaufort County		93	n/a	103,400	**Central** (town) Pickens County
19	2279	193,600	**Fort Mill** (town) York County		94	n/a	102,700	**Dillon** (city) Dillon County
20	n/a	193,000	**Newport** (CDP) York County		95	n/a	99,400	**Barnwell** (city) Barnwell County
21	2454	180,800	**Hanahan** (city) Berkeley County		96	n/a	99,200	**Woodfield** (CDP) Richland County
22	2460	180,600	**Forest Acres** (city) Richland County		97	n/a	97,900	**Arial** (CDP) Pickens County
22	2460	180,600	**Summerville** (town) Dorchester County		98	n/a	97,600	**Lancaster** (city) Lancaster County
24	2492	179,100	**Aiken** (city) Aiken County		99	n/a	97,300	**Piedmont** (CDP) Anderson County
25	2540	175,500	**Lexington** (town) Lexington County		100	n/a	96,900	**Batesburg-Leesville** (town) Lexington County
26	n/a	172,400	**Little River** (CDP) Horry County		100	n/a	96,900	**Liberty** (city) Pickens County
27	2669	168,800	**Goose Creek** (city) Berkeley County		102	n/a	96,200	**Kingstree** (town) Williamsburg County
28	2714	167,100	**Myrtle Beach** (city) Horry County		103	n/a	95,100	**Belvedere** (CDP) Aiken County
29	n/a	166,700	**Camden** (city) Kershaw County		104	n/a	93,800	**McCormick** (town) McCormick County
30	n/a	165,700	**Northlake** (CDP) Anderson County		105	n/a	91,600	**Pageland** (town) Chesterfield County
31	2783	163,500	**Columbia** (city) Richland County		106	n/a	90,800	**Sans Souci** (CDP) Greenville County
32	n/a	163,000	**Lesslie** (CDP) York County		107	n/a	90,700	**Winnsboro** (town) Fairfield County
33	n/a	162,000	**Forestbrook** (CDP) Horry County		108	n/a	89,800	**Dunean** (CDP) Greenville County
34	2822	161,400	**Wade Hampton** (CDP) Greenville County		109	n/a	89,400	**Walhalla** (city) Oconee County
35	2879	158,900	**Red Hill** (CDP) Horry County		110	4276	89,200	**Greenwood** (city) Greenwood County
36	n/a	157,900	**Ridgeland** (town) Jasper County		111	n/a	88,700	**Hampton** (town) Hampton County
37	n/a	154,100	**Travelers Rest** (city) Greenville County		112	n/a	88,300	**Hopkins** (CDP) Richland County
38	n/a	153,200	**Moncks Corner** (town) Berkeley County		113	n/a	88,200	**Burnettown** (town) Aiken County
39	3084	149,700	**Conway** (city) Horry County		114	4301	88,000	**Gantt** (CDP) Greenville County
40	n/a	149,500	**Laurel Bay** (CDP) Beaufort County		115	n/a	87,800	**Darlington** (city) Darlington County
41	n/a	149,000	**Boiling Springs** (CDP) Spartanburg County		116	n/a	87,500	**Cheraw** (town) Chesterfield County
42	3109	148,700	**Florence** (city) Florence County		117	n/a	87,400	**Williamston** (town) Anderson County
43	3119	148,500	**Mauldin** (city) Greenville County		118	n/a	87,200	**Abbeville** (city) Abbeville County
44	n/a	147,600	**Springdale** (town) Lexington County		119	4326	86,800	**Gaffney** (city) Cherokee County
45	3147	147,200	**North Augusta** (city) Aiken County		120	n/a	86,600	**Manning** (city) Clarendon County
46	n/a	143,800	**India Hook** (CDP) York County		121	n/a	86,400	**Pickens** (city) Pickens County
46	3204	143,800	**Socastee** (CDP) Horry County		122	n/a	83,500	**Brookdale** (CDP) Orangeburg County
48	3237	142,300	**Seven Oaks** (CDP) Lexington County		123	n/a	83,100	**Lake City** (city) Florence County
49	3257	141,200	**Greer** (city) Greenville County		124	n/a	82,900	**Edgefield** (town) Edgefield County
50	3306	138,300	**North Charleston** (city) Charleston County		124	n/a	82,900	**Saluda** (town) Saluda County
51	3332	137,000	**Taylors** (CDP) Greenville County		126	n/a	82,100	**Belton** (city) Anderson County
52	3345	136,400	**Easley** (city) Pickens County		127	n/a	81,600	**Union** (city) Union County
53	3349	136,200	**Simpsonville** (city) Greenville County		128	n/a	80,700	**Laurens** (city) Laurens County
54	3392	133,900	**Sumter** (city) Sumter County		129	n/a	80,100	**Mullins** (city) Marion County
55	3408	133,100	**Rock Hill** (city) York County		130	n/a	79,900	**Welcome** (CDP) Greenville County
56	n/a	132,500	**Centerville** (CDP) Anderson County		131	n/a	79,800	**Honea Path** (town) Anderson County
57	n/a	132,400	**Burton** (CDP) Beaufort County		132	n/a	79,400	**Bennettsville** (city) Marlboro County
57	n/a	132,400	**Sangaree** (CDP) Berkeley County		133	n/a	78,900	**Springdale** (CDP) Lancaster County
59	n/a	132,300	**Lugoff** (CDP) Kershaw County		134	n/a	78,100	**Graniteville** (CDP) Aiken County
60	3436	132,000	**West Columbia** (city) Lexington County		135	n/a	77,800	**Andrews** (town) Georgetown County
61	n/a	131,200	**Walterboro** (city) Colleton County		136	n/a	76,900	**Clinton** (city) Laurens County
62	3464	130,500	**Orangeburg** (city) Orangeburg County		137	n/a	75,100	**Allendale** (town) Allendale County
63	3510	129,000	**Oak Grove** (CDP) Lexington County		138	n/a	74,000	**Bishopville** (city) Lee County
64	3561	125,900	**Irmo** (town) Richland County		139	n/a	69,800	**Edisto** (CDP) Orangeburg County
65	n/a	125,500	**Valley Falls** (CDP) Spartanburg County		140	n/a	68,500	**Homeland Park** (CDP) Anderson County
66	n/a	125,200	**Garden City** (CDP) Horry County		141	4570	67,600	**Parker** (CDP) Greenville County
67	3597	123,700	**Ladson** (CDP) Berkeley County		142	n/a	66,400	**Williston** (town) Barnwell County
68	n/a	122,600	**Seneca** (city) Oconee County		143	n/a	66,100	**Chester** (city) Chester County
69	n/a	122,500	**Lakewood** (CDP) Sumter County		144	n/a	65,400	**Woodruff** (city) Spartanburg County
70	3624	122,100	**Anderson** (city) Anderson County		145	n/a	65,000	**Gloverville** (CDP) Aiken County
71	3650	121,100	**Spartanburg** (city) Spartanburg County		146	n/a	59,500	**Denmark** (city) Bamberg County
72	3663	120,500	**Cayce** (city) Lexington County		147	n/a	58,900	**Arcadia** (CDP) Spartanburg County
73	n/a	119,000	**Elgin** (CDP) Lancaster County		148	n/a	53,700	**East Gaffney** (CDP) Cherokee County
74	n/a	118,400	**Clover** (town) York County		149	n/a	43,900	**Saxon** (CDP) Spartanburg County
75	n/a	117,400	**Hardeeville** (city) Jasper County		150	n/a	43,600	**Southern Shops** (CDP) Spartanburg County

Note: The state column ranks the top/bottom 150 places in the state with population of 2,500 or more. The national column ranks the top/bottom places in the country with population of 10,000 or more. Places that are unincorporated were not considered in the rankings. n/a indicates data not available. Please refer to the User Guide for additional information.

Median Home Value

Top 150 Places Ranked in *Ascending* Order

State Rank	Nat'l Rank	Dollars	Place
1	n/a	43,600	**Southern Shops** (CDP) Spartanburg County
2	n/a	43,900	**Saxon** (CDP) Spartanburg County
3	n/a	53,700	**East Gaffney** (CDP) Cherokee County
4	n/a	58,900	**Arcadia** (CDP) Spartanburg County
5	n/a	59,500	**Denmark** (city) Bamberg County
6	n/a	65,000	**Gloverville** (CDP) Aiken County
7	n/a	65,400	**Woodruff** (city) Spartanburg County
8	n/a	66,100	**Chester** (city) Chester County
9	n/a	66,400	**Williston** (town) Barnwell County
10	78	67,600	**Parker** (CDP) Greenville County
11	n/a	68,500	**Homeland Park** (CDP) Anderson County
12	n/a	69,800	**Edisto** (CDP) Orangeburg County
13	n/a	74,000	**Bishopville** (city) Lee County
14	n/a	75,100	**Allendale** (town) Allendale County
15	n/a	76,900	**Clinton** (city) Laurens County
16	n/a	77,800	**Andrews** (town) Georgetown County
17	n/a	78,100	**Graniteville** (CDP) Aiken County
18	n/a	78,900	**Springdale** (CDP) Lancaster County
19	n/a	79,400	**Bennettsville** (city) Marlboro County
20	n/a	79,800	**Honea Path** (town) Anderson County
21	n/a	79,900	**Welcome** (CDP) Greenville County
22	n/a	80,100	**Mullins** (city) Marion County
23	n/a	80,700	**Laurens** (city) Laurens County
24	n/a	81,600	**Union** (city) Union County
25	n/a	82,100	**Belton** (city) Anderson County
26	n/a	82,900	**Edgefield** (town) Edgefield County
26	n/a	82,900	**Saluda** (town) Saluda County
28	n/a	83,100	**Lake City** (city) Florence County
29	n/a	83,500	**Brookdale** (CDP) Orangeburg County
30	n/a	86,400	**Pickens** (city) Pickens County
31	n/a	86,600	**Manning** (city) Clarendon County
32	320	86,800	**Gaffney** (city) Cherokee County
33	n/a	87,200	**Abbeville** (city) Abbeville County
34	n/a	87,400	**Williamston** (town) Anderson County
35	n/a	87,500	**Cheraw** (town) Chesterfield County
36	n/a	87,800	**Darlington** (city) Darlington County
37	347	88,000	**Gantt** (CDP) Greenville County
38	n/a	88,200	**Burnettown** (town) Aiken County
39	n/a	88,300	**Hopkins** (CDP) Richland County
40	n/a	88,700	**Hampton** (town) Hampton County
41	371	89,200	**Greenwood** (city) Greenwood County
42	n/a	89,400	**Walhalla** (city) Oconee County
43	n/a	89,800	**Dunean** (CDP) Greenville County
44	n/a	90,700	**Winnsboro** (town) Fairfield County
45	n/a	90,800	**Sans Souci** (CDP) Greenville County
46	n/a	91,600	**Pageland** (town) Chesterfield County
47	n/a	93,800	**McCormick** (town) McCormick County
48	n/a	95,100	**Belvedere** (CDP) Aiken County
49	n/a	96,200	**Kingstree** (town) Williamsburg County
50	n/a	96,900	**Batesburg-Leesville** (town) Lexington County
50	n/a	96,900	**Liberty** (city) Pickens County
52	n/a	97,300	**Piedmont** (CDP) Anderson County
53	n/a	97,600	**Lancaster** (city) Lancaster County
54	n/a	97,900	**Arial** (CDP) Pickens County
55	n/a	99,200	**Woodfield** (CDP) Richland County
56	n/a	99,400	**Barnwell** (city) Barnwell County
57	n/a	102,700	**Dillon** (city) Dillon County
58	n/a	103,400	**Central** (town) Pickens County
59	n/a	103,800	**North Hartsville** (CDP) Darlington County
60	n/a	104,200	**Bamberg** (city) Bamberg County
60	n/a	104,200	**Marion** (city) Marion County
62	n/a	106,100	**Duncan** (town) Spartanburg County
63	699	107,400	**Saint Andrews** (CDP) Richland County
64	737	109,600	**Dentsville** (CDP) Richland County
65	n/a	110,300	**York** (city) York County
66	780	111,800	**Berea** (CDP) Greenville County
67	n/a	112,000	**Hartsville** (city) Darlington County
68	n/a	112,500	**Clearwater** (CDP) Aiken County
68	n/a	112,500	**Pendleton** (town) Anderson County
70	n/a	113,000	**Lyman** (town) Spartanburg County
71	n/a	114,300	**Dalzell** (CDP) Sumter County
72	n/a	114,500	**Georgetown** (city) Georgetown County
73	n/a	115,900	**Fountain Inn** (city) Greenville County
74	882	116,300	**Newberry** (city) Newberry County
75	n/a	117,000	**Red Bank** (CDP) Lexington County
76	n/a	117,400	**Hardeeville** (city) Jasper County
77	n/a	118,400	**Clover** (town) York County
78	n/a	119,000	**Elgin** (CDP) Lancaster County
79	983	120,500	**Cayce** (city) Lexington County
80	995	121,100	**Spartanburg** (city) Spartanburg County
81	1020	122,100	**Anderson** (city) Anderson County
82	n/a	122,500	**Lakewood** (CDP) Sumter County
83	n/a	122,600	**Seneca** (city) Oconee County
84	1049	123,700	**Ladson** (CDP) Berkeley County
85	n/a	125,200	**Garden City** (CDP) Horry County
86	n/a	125,500	**Valley Falls** (CDP) Spartanburg County
87	1087	125,900	**Irmo** (town) Richland County
88	1137	129,000	**Oak Grove** (CDP) Lexington County
89	1184	130,600	**Orangeburg** (city) Orangeburg County
90	n/a	131,200	**Walterboro** (city) Colleton County
91	1209	132,000	**West Columbia** (city) Lexington County
92	n/a	132,300	**Lugoff** (CDP) Kershaw County
93	n/a	132,400	**Burton** (CDP) Beaufort County
93	n/a	132,400	**Sangaree** (CDP) Berkeley County
95	n/a	132,500	**Centerville** (CDP) Anderson County
96	1237	133,100	**Rock Hill** (city) York County
97	1254	133,900	**Sumter** (city) Sumter County
98	1297	136,200	**Simpsonville** (city) Greenville County
99	1301	136,400	**Easley** (city) Pickens County
100	1313	137,000	**Taylors** (CDP) Greenville County
101	1341	138,300	**North Charleston** (city) Charleston County
102	1390	141,200	**Greer** (city) Greenville County
103	1409	142,300	**Seven Oaks** (CDP) Lexington County
104	n/a	143,800	**India Hook** (CDP) York County
104	1441	143,800	**Socastee** (CDP) Horry County
106	1500	147,200	**North Augusta** (city) Aiken County
107	n/a	147,600	**Springdale** (town) Lexington County
108	1528	148,500	**Mauldin** (city) Greenville County
109	1538	148,700	**Florence** (city) Florence County
110	n/a	149,000	**Boiling Springs** (CDP) Spartanburg County
111	n/a	149,500	**Laurel Bay** (CDP) Beaufort County
112	1560	149,700	**Conway** (city) Horry County
113	n/a	153,200	**Moncks Corner** (town) Berkeley County
114	n/a	154,100	**Travelers Rest** (city) Greenville County
115	n/a	157,900	**Ridgeland** (town) Jasper County
116	1767	158,900	**Red Hill** (CDP) Horry County
117	1825	161,400	**Wade Hampton** (CDP) Greenville County
118	n/a	162,000	**Forestbrook** (CDP) Horry County
119	n/a	163,000	**Lesslie** (CDP) York County
120	1861	163,500	**Columbia** (city) Richland County
121	n/a	165,700	**Northlake** (CDP) Anderson County
122	n/a	166,700	**Camden** (city) Kershaw County
123	1932	167,100	**Myrtle Beach** (city) Horry County
124	1975	168,800	**Goose Creek** (city) Berkeley County
125	n/a	172,400	**Little River** (CDP) Horry County
126	2106	175,500	**Lexington** (town) Lexington County
127	2156	179,100	**Aiken** (city) Aiken County
128	2187	180,600	**Forest Acres** (city) Richland County
128	2187	180,600	**Summerville** (town) Dorchester County
130	2191	180,800	**Hanahan** (city) Berkeley County
131	n/a	193,000	**Newport** (CDP) York County
132	2369	193,600	**Fort Mill** (town) York County
133	2423	197,100	**Port Royal** (town) Beaufort County
134	2467	200,300	**Clemson** (city) Pickens County
135	2469	200,500	**Greenville** (city) Greenville County
136	n/a	200,600	**Hollywood** (town) Charleston County
137	2672	216,500	**Bluffton** (town) Beaufort County
138	n/a	226,800	**Murrells Inlet** (CDP) Georgetown County
139	n/a	246,100	**Surfside Beach** (town) Horry County
140	3036	248,000	**North Myrtle Beach** (city) Horry County
141	3076	252,700	**Beaufort** (city) Beaufort County
142	3083	253,800	**Charleston** (city) Charleston County
143	3110	258,300	**Five Forks** (CDP) Greenville County
144	n/a	276,900	**Tega Cay** (city) York County
145	n/a	286,200	**Lake Wylie** (CDP) York County
146	n/a	312,500	**Lake Murray of Richland** (CDP) Richland County
147	3822	349,200	**Mount Pleasant** (town) Charleston County
148	4227	447,900	**Hilton Head Island** (town) Beaufort County
149	n/a	607,700	**Folly Beach** (city) Charleston County
150	n/a	792,200	**Isle of Palms** (city) Charleston County

Note: The state column ranks the top/bottom 150 places in the state with population of 2,500 or more. The national column ranks the top/bottom places in the country with population of 10,000 or more. Places that are unincorporated were not considered in the rankings. n/a indicates data not available. Please refer to the User Guide for additional information.

Median Year Structure Built

Top 150 Places Ranked in *Descending* Order

State Rank	Nat'l Rank	Year	Place
1	8	2004	**Bluffton** (town) Beaufort County
2	n/a	2001	**Boiling Springs** (CDP) Spartanburg County
3	n/a	2000	**Lake Wylie** (CDP) York County
3	n/a	2000	**Tega Cay** (city) York County
5	153	1999	**Lexington** (town) Lexington County
6	181	1998	**Five Forks** (CDP) Greenville County
6	n/a	1998	**India Hook** (CDP) York County
8	n/a	1996	**Lake Murray of Richland** (CDP) Richland County
8	n/a	1996	**Murrells Inlet** (CDP) Georgetown County
8	266	1996	**Port Royal** (town) Beaufort County
11	312	1995	**Goose Creek** (city) Berkeley County
11	312	1995	**Greer** (city) Greenville County
13	n/a	1994	**Dalzell** (CDP) Sumter County
13	369	1994	**Fort Mill** (town) York County
13	369	1994	**Mount Pleasant** (town) Charleston County
13	369	1994	**Red Hill** (CDP) Horry County
13	n/a	1994	**Valley Falls** (CDP) Spartanburg County
18	435	1993	**North Myrtle Beach** (city) Horry County
18	435	1993	**Socastee** (CDP) Horry County
18	435	1993	**Summerville** (town) Dorchester County
21	n/a	1992	**Hardeeville** (city) Jasper County
22	n/a	1991	**Forestbrook** (CDP) Horry County
22	n/a	1991	**Little River** (CDP) Horry County
22	566	1991	**Mauldin** (city) Greenville County
25	n/a	1990	**Central** (town) Pickens County
25	n/a	1990	**Duncan** (town) Spartanburg County
25	n/a	1990	**Garden City** (CDP) Horry County
25	n/a	1990	**Hollywood** (town) Charleston County
25	n/a	1990	**Lugoff** (CDP) Kershaw County
25	651	1990	**Rock Hill** (city) York County
31	n/a	1989	**Fountain Inn** (city) Greenville County
31	n/a	1989	**Lesslie** (CDP) York County
31	n/a	1989	**Red Bank** (CDP) Lexington County
31	n/a	1989	**Travelers Rest** (city) Greenville County
35	n/a	1988	**Centerville** (CDP) Anderson County
35	778	1988	**Simpsonville** (city) Greenville County
37	n/a	1987	**Clover** (town) York County
37	n/a	1987	**Lakewood** (CDP) Sumter County
37	n/a	1987	**Ridgeland** (town) Jasper County
37	n/a	1987	**Surfside Beach** (town) Horry County
41	933	1986	**Aiken** (city) Aiken County
41	n/a	1986	**Burton** (CDP) Beaufort County
41	933	1986	**Hilton Head Island** (town) Beaufort County
41	n/a	1986	**Isle of Palms** (city) Charleston County
41	n/a	1986	**Northlake** (CDP) Anderson County
46	n/a	1985	**Folly Beach** (city) Charleston County
46	n/a	1985	**Moncks Corner** (town) Berkeley County
46	1031	1985	**Myrtle Beach** (city) Horry County
49	1133	1984	**Conway** (city) Horry County
49	1133	1984	**Ladson** (CDP) Berkeley County
49	n/a	1984	**Newport** (CDP) York County
49	1133	1984	**Oak Grove** (CDP) Lexington County
49	n/a	1984	**Sangaree** (CDP) Berkeley County
54	1238	1983	**Clemson** (city) Pickens County
54	1238	1983	**North Charleston** (city) Charleston County
56	1344	1982	**Charleston** (city) Charleston County
56	1344	1982	**Irmo** (town) Richland County
58	n/a	1981	**Arcadia** (CDP) Spartanburg County
59	n/a	1980	**Gloverville** (CDP) Aiken County
59	1563	1980	**Hanahan** (city) Berkeley County
61	1668	1979	**Dentsville** (CDP) Richland County
61	1668	1979	**Easley** (city) Pickens County
61	n/a	1979	**Laurel Bay** (CDP) Beaufort County
61	1668	1979	**North Augusta** (city) Aiken County
61	n/a	1979	**Piedmont** (CDP) Anderson County
66	n/a	1978	**Arial** (CDP) Pickens County
66	1795	1978	**Beaufort** (city) Beaufort County
66	n/a	1978	**Clearwater** (CDP) Aiken County
66	n/a	1978	**Elgin** (CDP) Lancaster County
66	n/a	1978	**Hopkins** (CDP) Richland County
66	n/a	1978	**North Hartsville** (CDP) Darlington County
66	n/a	1978	**Seneca** (city) Oconee County
66	1795	1978	**Taylors** (CDP) Greenville County
66	n/a	1978	**York** (city) York County
75	n/a	1977	**Pageland** (town) Chesterfield County
75	1932	1977	**Sumter** (city) Sumter County
75	n/a	1977	**Williston** (town) Barnwell County
78	2051	1976	**Florence** (city) Florence County
78	2051	1976	**Saint Andrews** (CDP) Richland County
80	n/a	1975	**Brookdale** (CDP) Orangeburg County
80	n/a	1975	**Pendleton** (town) Anderson County
80	2191	1975	**Seven Oaks** (CDP) Lexington County
83	n/a	1974	**Andrews** (town) Georgetown County
83	2330	1974	**Berea** (CDP) Greenville County
83	2330	1974	**Gantt** (CDP) Greenville County
83	n/a	1974	**Hampton** (town) Hampton County
83	n/a	1974	**Kingstree** (town) Williamsburg County
83	n/a	1974	**Springdale** (CDP) Lancaster County
89	n/a	1973	**Denmark** (city) Bamberg County
89	2449	1973	**Greenville** (city) Greenville County
89	n/a	1973	**Lyman** (town) Spartanburg County
89	2449	1973	**West Columbia** (city) Lexington County
93	n/a	1972	**Manning** (city) Clarendon County
93	n/a	1972	**Saluda** (town) Saluda County
93	2560	1972	**Wade Hampton** (CDP) Greenville County
93	n/a	1972	**Winnsboro** (town) Fairfield County
93	n/a	1972	**Woodfield** (CDP) Richland County
98	n/a	1971	**Allendale** (town) Allendale County
98	n/a	1971	**Edisto** (CDP) Orangeburg County
98	n/a	1971	**Marion** (city) Marion County
101	n/a	1970	**Bishopville** (city) Lee County
101	n/a	1970	**Dillon** (city) Dillon County
101	n/a	1970	**Graniteville** (CDP) Aiken County
101	n/a	1970	**Lake City** (city) Florence County
101	2810	1970	**Orangeburg** (city) Orangeburg County
101	n/a	1970	**Walterboro** (city) Colleton County
107	2903	1969	**Anderson** (city) Anderson County
107	n/a	1969	**Barnwell** (city) Barnwell County
107	n/a	1969	**Belvedere** (CDP) Aiken County
107	n/a	1969	**Bennettsville** (city) Marlboro County
107	2903	1969	**Columbia** (city) Richland County
107	n/a	1969	**East Gaffney** (CDP) Cherokee County
107	n/a	1969	**McCormick** (town) McCormick County
107	n/a	1969	**Pickens** (city) Pickens County
107	n/a	1969	**Southern Shops** (CDP) Spartanburg County
107	n/a	1969	**Welcome** (CDP) Greenville County
107	n/a	1969	**Williamston** (town) Anderson County
118	n/a	1968	**Darlington** (city) Darlington County
118	3015	1968	**Gaffney** (city) Cherokee County
118	n/a	1968	**Lancaster** (city) Lancaster County
118	n/a	1968	**Saxon** (CDP) Spartanburg County
118	n/a	1968	**Walhalla** (city) Oconee County
123	n/a	1967	**Bamberg** (town) Bamberg County
123	n/a	1967	**Batesburg-Leesville** (town) Lexington County
123	n/a	1967	**Burnettown** (town) Aiken County
123	n/a	1967	**Chester** (city) Chester County
123	n/a	1967	**Edgefield** (town) Edgefield County
123	3117	1967	**Greenwood** (city) Greenwood County
123	n/a	1967	**Hartsville** (city) Darlington County
123	n/a	1967	**Laurens** (city) Laurens County
123	n/a	1967	**Liberty** (city) Pickens County
123	n/a	1967	**Mullins** (city) Marion County
123	n/a	1967	**Springdale** (town) Lexington County
134	n/a	1966	**Clinton** (city) Laurens County
134	n/a	1966	**Georgetown** (city) Georgetown County
134	n/a	1966	**Homeland Park** (CDP) Anderson County
134	n/a	1966	**Sans Souci** (CDP) Greenville County
134	3213	1966	**Spartanburg** (city) Spartanburg County
139	n/a	1965	**Cheraw** (town) Chesterfield County
139	n/a	1965	**Union** (city) Union County
141	3399	1964	**Cayce** (city) Lexington County
141	3399	1964	**Forest Acres** (city) Richland County
141	n/a	1964	**Woodruff** (city) Spartanburg County
144	n/a	1963	**Honea Path** (town) Anderson County
144	3485	1963	**Newberry** (city) Newberry County
146	n/a	1962	**Abbeville** (city) Abbeville County
147	n/a	1960	**Belton** (city) Anderson County
147	n/a	1960	**Camden** (city) Kershaw County
149	3771	1959	**Parker** (CDP) Greenville County
150	n/a	1958	**Dunean** (CDP) Greenville County

Note: The state column ranks the top/bottom 150 places in the state with population of 2,500 or more. The national column ranks the top/bottom places in the country with population of 10,000 or more. Places that are unincorporated were not considered in the rankings. n/a indicates data not available. Please refer to the User Guide for additional information.

Median Year Structure Built

Top 150 Places Ranked in *Ascending* Order

State Rank	Nat'l Rank	Year	Place
1	n/a	1958	**Dunean** (CDP) Greenville County
2	808	1959	**Parker** (CDP) Greenville County
3	n/a	1960	**Belton** (city) Anderson County
3	n/a	1960	**Camden** (city) Kershaw County
5	n/a	1962	**Abbeville** (city) Abbeville County
6	n/a	1963	**Honea Path** (town) Anderson County
6	1097	1963	**Newberry** (city) Newberry County
8	1172	1964	**Cayce** (city) Lexington County
8	1172	1964	**Forest Acres** (city) Richland County
8	n/a	1964	**Woodruff** (city) Spartanburg County
11	n/a	1965	**Cheraw** (town) Chesterfield County
11	n/a	1965	**Union** (city) Union County
13	n/a	1966	**Clinton** (city) Laurens County
13	n/a	1966	**Georgetown** (city) Georgetown County
13	n/a	1966	**Homeland Park** (CDP) Anderson County
13	n/a	1966	**Sans Souci** (CDP) Greenville County
13	1334	1966	**Spartanburg** (city) Spartanburg County
18	n/a	1967	**Bamberg** (town) Bamberg County
18	n/a	1967	**Batesburg-Leesville** (town) Lexington County
18	n/a	1967	**Burnettown** (town) Aiken County
18	n/a	1967	**Chester** (city) Chester County
18	n/a	1967	**Edgefield** (town) Edgefield County
18	1444	1967	**Greenwood** (city) Greenwood County
18	n/a	1967	**Hartsville** (city) Darlington County
18	n/a	1967	**Laurens** (city) Laurens County
18	n/a	1967	**Liberty** (city) Pickens County
18	n/a	1967	**Mullins** (city) Marion County
18	n/a	1967	**Springdale** (town) Lexington County
29	n/a	1968	**Darlington** (city) Darlington County
29	1540	1968	**Gaffney** (city) Cherokee County
29	n/a	1968	**Lancaster** (city) Lancaster County
29	n/a	1968	**Saxon** (CDP) Spartanburg County
29	n/a	1968	**Walhalla** (city) Oconee County
34	1642	1969	**Anderson** (city) Anderson County
34	n/a	1969	**Barnwell** (city) Barnwell County
34	n/a	1969	**Belvedere** (CDP) Aiken County
34	n/a	1969	**Bennettsville** (city) Marlboro County
34	1642	1969	**Columbia** (city) Richland County
34	n/a	1969	**East Gaffney** (CDP) Cherokee County
34	n/a	1969	**McCormick** (town) McCormick County
34	n/a	1969	**Pickens** (city) Pickens County
34	n/a	1969	**Southern Shops** (CDP) Spartanburg County
34	n/a	1969	**Welcome** (CDP) Greenville County
34	n/a	1969	**Williamston** (town) Anderson County
45	n/a	1970	**Bishopville** (city) Lee County
45	n/a	1970	**Dillon** (city) Dillon County
45	n/a	1970	**Graniteville** (CDP) Aiken County
45	n/a	1970	**Lake City** (city) Florence County
45	1754	1970	**Orangeburg** (city) Orangeburg County
45	n/a	1970	**Walterboro** (city) Colleton County
51	n/a	1971	**Allendale** (town) Allendale County
51	n/a	1971	**Edisto** (CDP) Orangeburg County
51	n/a	1971	**Marion** (city) Marion County
54	n/a	1972	**Manning** (city) Clarendon County
54	n/a	1972	**Saluda** (town) Saluda County
54	1989	1972	**Wade Hampton** (CDP) Greenville County
54	n/a	1972	**Winnsboro** (town) Fairfield County
54	n/a	1972	**Woodfield** (CDP) Richland County
59	n/a	1973	**Denmark** (city) Bamberg County
59	2097	1973	**Greenville** (city) Greenville County
59	n/a	1973	**Lyman** (town) Spartanburg County
59	2097	1973	**West Columbia** (city) Lexington County
63	n/a	1974	**Andrews** (town) Georgetown County
63	2208	1974	**Berea** (CDP) Greenville County
63	2208	1974	**Gantt** (CDP) Greenville County
63	n/a	1974	**Hampton** (town) Hampton County
63	n/a	1974	**Kingstree** (town) Williamsburg County
63	n/a	1974	**Springdale** (CDP) Lancaster County
69	n/a	1975	**Brookdale** (CDP) Orangeburg County
69	n/a	1975	**Pendleton** (town) Anderson County
69	2327	1975	**Seven Oaks** (CDP) Lexington County
72	2466	1976	**Florence** (city) Florence County
72	2466	1976	**Saint Andrews** (CDP) Richland County
74	n/a	1977	**Pageland** (town) Chesterfield County
74	2606	1977	**Sumter** (city) Sumter County
74	n/a	1977	**Williston** (town) Barnwell County
77	n/a	1978	**Arial** (CDP) Pickens County
77	2725	1978	**Beaufort** (city) Beaufort County
77	n/a	1978	**Clearwater** (CDP) Aiken County
77	n/a	1978	**Elgin** (CDP) Lancaster County
77	n/a	1978	**Hopkins** (CDP) Richland County
77	n/a	1978	**North Hartsville** (CDP) Darlington County
77	n/a	1978	**Seneca** (city) Oconee County
77	2725	1978	**Taylors** (CDP) Greenville County
77	n/a	1978	**York** (city) York County
86	2862	1979	**Dentsville** (CDP) Richland County
86	2862	1979	**Easley** (city) Pickens County
86	n/a	1979	**Laurel Bay** (CDP) Beaufort County
86	2862	1979	**North Augusta** (city) Aiken County
86	n/a	1979	**Piedmont** (CDP) Anderson County
91	n/a	1980	**Gloverville** (CDP) Aiken County
91	2989	1980	**Hanahan** (city) Berkeley County
93	n/a	1981	**Arcadia** (CDP) Spartanburg County
94	3194	1982	**Charleston** (city) Charleston County
94	3194	1982	**Irmo** (town) Richland County
96	3313	1983	**Clemson** (city) Pickens County
96	3313	1983	**North Charleston** (city) Charleston County
98	3419	1984	**Conway** (city) Horry County
98	3419	1984	**Ladson** (CDP) Berkeley County
98	n/a	1984	**Newport** (CDP) York County
98	3419	1984	**Oak Grove** (CDP) Lexington County
98	n/a	1984	**Sangaree** (CDP) Berkeley County
103	n/a	1985	**Folly Beach** (city) Charleston County
103	n/a	1985	**Moncks Corner** (town) Berkeley County
103	3524	1985	**Myrtle Beach** (city) Horry County
106	3626	1986	**Aiken** (city) Aiken County
106	n/a	1986	**Burton** (CDP) Beaufort County
106	3626	1986	**Hilton Head Island** (town) Beaufort County
106	n/a	1986	**Isle of Palms** (city) Charleston County
106	n/a	1986	**Northlake** (CDP) Anderson County
111	n/a	1987	**Clover** (town) York County
111	n/a	1987	**Lakewood** (CDP) Sumter County
111	n/a	1987	**Ridgeland** (town) Jasper County
111	n/a	1987	**Surfside Beach** (town) Horry County
115	n/a	1988	**Centerville** (CDP) Anderson County
115	3806	1988	**Simpsonville** (city) Greenville County
117	n/a	1989	**Fountain Inn** (city) Greenville County
117	n/a	1989	**Lesslie** (CDP) York County
117	n/a	1989	**Red Bank** (CDP) Lexington County
117	n/a	1989	**Travelers Rest** (city) Greenville County
121	n/a	1990	**Central** (town) Pickens County
121	n/a	1990	**Duncan** (town) Spartanburg County
121	n/a	1990	**Garden City** (CDP) Horry County
121	n/a	1990	**Hollywood** (town) Charleston County
121	n/a	1990	**Lugoff** (CDP) Kershaw County
121	3942	1990	**Rock Hill** (city) York County
127	n/a	1991	**Forestbrook** (CDP) Horry County
127	n/a	1991	**Little River** (CDP) Horry County
127	4006	1991	**Mauldin** (city) Greenville County
130	n/a	1992	**Hardeeville** (city) Jasper County
131	4156	1993	**North Myrtle Beach** (city) Horry County
131	4156	1993	**Socastee** (CDP) Horry County
131	4156	1993	**Summerville** (town) Dorchester County
134	n/a	1994	**Dalzell** (CDP) Sumter County
134	4222	1994	**Fort Mill** (town) York County
134	4222	1994	**Mount Pleasant** (town) Charleston County
134	4222	1994	**Red Hill** (CDP) Horry County
134	n/a	1994	**Valley Falls** (CDP) Spartanburg County
139	4288	1995	**Goose Creek** (city) Berkeley County
139	4288	1995	**Greer** (city) Greenville County
141	n/a	1996	**Lake Murray of Richland** (CDP) Richland County
141	n/a	1996	**Murrells Inlet** (CDP) Georgetown County
141	4345	1996	**Port Royal** (town) Beaufort County
144	4437	1998	**Five Forks** (CDP) Greenville County
144	n/a	1998	**India Hook** (CDP) York County
146	4476	1999	**Lexington** (town) Lexington County
147	n/a	2000	**Lake Wylie** (CDP) York County
147	n/a	2000	**Tega Cay** (city) York County
149	n/a	2001	**Boiling Springs** (CDP) Spartanburg County
150	4626	2004	**Bluffton** (town) Beaufort County

Note: *The state column ranks the top/bottom 150 places in the state with population of 2,500 or more. The national column ranks the top/bottom places in the country with population of 10,000 or more. Places that are unincorporated were not considered in the rankings. n/a indicates data not available. Please refer to the User Guide for additional information.*

Homeowner Vacancy Rate

Top 150 Places Ranked in *Descending* Order

State Rank	Nat'l Rank	Percent	Place
1	6	11.3	**North Myrtle Beach** (city) Horry County
2	n/a	8.8	**Moncks Corner** (town) Berkeley County
3	17	8.5	**Port Royal** (town) Beaufort County
4	n/a	8.4	**Hartsville** (city) Darlington County
5	n/a	7.5	**Ridgeland** (town) Jasper County
6	n/a	7.3	**Hardeeville** (city) Jasper County
6	n/a	7.3	**Surfside Beach** (town) Horry County
8	51	6.7	**Myrtle Beach** (city) Horry County
9	67	6.4	**Bluffton** (town) Beaufort County
10	104	5.8	**Conway** (city) Horry County
11	n/a	5.7	**Folly Beach** (city) Charleston County
11	109	5.7	**Greenville** (city) Greenville County
13	n/a	5.6	**Centerville** (CDP) Anderson County
14	n/a	5.5	**Garden City** (CDP) Horry County
15	n/a	5.2	**Duncan** (town) Spartanburg County
16	n/a	5.0	**Dunean** (CDP) Greenville County
17	206	4.9	**Beaufort** (city) Beaufort County
17	206	4.9	**Hilton Head Island** (town) Beaufort County
17	206	4.9	**Spartanburg** (city) Spartanburg County
20	n/a	4.8	**Saxon** (CDP) Spartanburg County
20	n/a	4.8	**Woodfield** (CDP) Richland County
22	242	4.7	**Anderson** (city) Anderson County
23	n/a	4.6	**Little River** (CDP) Horry County
24	n/a	4.5	**Chester** (city) Chester County
24	n/a	4.5	**Honea Path** (town) Anderson County
24	n/a	4.5	**Seneca** (city) Oconee County
27	n/a	4.4	**Camden** (city) Kershaw County
28	n/a	4.3	**Clinton** (city) Laurens County
28	n/a	4.3	**Forestbrook** (CDP) Horry County
28	n/a	4.3	**Laurel Bay** (CDP) Beaufort County
28	340	4.3	**Newberry** (city) Newberry County
28	n/a	4.3	**Walterboro** (city) Colleton County
33	367	4.2	**Columbia** (city) Richland County
33	n/a	4.2	**East Gaffney** (CDP) Cherokee County
33	367	4.2	**Gaffney** (city) Cherokee County
33	n/a	4.2	**Isle of Palms** (city) Charleston County
33	367	4.2	**North Charleston** (city) Charleston County
33	367	4.2	**Parker** (CDP) Greenville County
39	403	4.1	**Charleston** (city) Charleston County
39	n/a	4.1	**Clover** (town) York County
39	n/a	4.1	**Georgetown** (city) Georgetown County
39	n/a	4.1	**Kingstree** (town) Williamsburg County
43	n/a	4.0	**Manning** (city) Clarendon County
43	444	4.0	**Orangeburg** (city) Orangeburg County
43	n/a	4.0	**Sans Souci** (CDP) Greenville County
43	444	4.0	**Socastee** (CDP) Horry County
47	n/a	3.9	**Belton** (city) Anderson County
47	n/a	3.9	**Lancaster** (city) Lancaster County
47	485	3.9	**Lexington** (town) Lexington County
47	n/a	3.9	**Pendleton** (town) Anderson County
51	n/a	3.8	**Barnwell** (city) Barnwell County
51	n/a	3.8	**Batesburg-Leesville** (town) Lexington County
51	n/a	3.8	**Mullins** (city) Marion County
51	539	3.8	**Red Hill** (CDP) Horry County
51	539	3.8	**Sumter** (city) Sumter County
51	n/a	3.8	**Union** (city) Union County
57	n/a	3.7	**Brookdale** (CDP) Orangeburg County
57	n/a	3.7	**Lyman** (town) Spartanburg County
57	n/a	3.7	**Northlake** (CDP) Anderson County
60	641	3.6	**Greer** (city) Greenville County
60	n/a	3.6	**Pickens** (city) Pickens County
60	n/a	3.6	**York** (city) York County
63	702	3.5	**Aiken** (city) Aiken County
63	n/a	3.5	**Central** (city) Pickens County
63	n/a	3.5	**Hampton** (town) Hampton County
63	n/a	3.5	**Homeland Park** (CDP) Anderson County
63	n/a	3.5	**Marion** (city) Marion County
63	n/a	3.5	**Murrells Inlet** (CDP) Georgetown County
63	702	3.5	**Saint Andrews** (CDP) Richland County
63	n/a	3.5	**Woodruff** (city) Spartanburg County
71	n/a	3.4	**Abbeville** (city) Abbeville County
71	n/a	3.4	**Darlington** (city) Darlington County
71	765	3.4	**Florence** (city) Florence County
71	765	3.4	**Greenwood** (city) Greenwood County
71	n/a	3.4	**Valley Falls** (CDP) Spartanburg County
71	n/a	3.4	**Welcome** (CDP) Greenville County
77	n/a	3.3	**Clearwater** (CDP) Aiken County
77	841	3.3	**Simpsonville** (city) Greenville County
77	n/a	3.3	**Williamston** (town) Anderson County
77	n/a	3.3	**Winnsboro** (town) Fairfield County
81	n/a	3.2	**Cheraw** (town) Chesterfield County
81	932	3.2	**Clemson** (city) Pickens County
81	932	3.2	**Easley** (city) Pickens County
81	n/a	3.2	**Graniteville** (CDP) Aiken County
81	n/a	3.2	**Springdale** (CDP) Lancaster County
86	n/a	3.1	**Allendale** (town) Allendale County
86	n/a	3.1	**Lake Wylie** (CDP) York County
86	1014	3.1	**Mount Pleasant** (town) Charleston County
86	1014	3.1	**Rock Hill** (city) York County
90	n/a	3.0	**Dillon** (city) Dillon County
90	1083	3.0	**Forest Acres** (city) Richland County
90	1083	3.0	**Irmo** (town) Richland County
90	n/a	3.0	**Pageland** (town) Chesterfield County
94	n/a	2.9	**Bishopville** (city) Lee County
94	n/a	2.9	**Laurens** (city) Laurens County
94	n/a	2.9	**Piedmont** (CDP) Anderson County
94	n/a	2.9	**Tega Cay** (city) York County
98	n/a	2.8	**Belvedere** (CDP) Aiken County
98	1296	2.8	**Gantt** (CDP) Greenville County
98	1296	2.8	**Mauldin** (city) Greenville County
98	n/a	2.8	**McCormick** (town) McCormick County
102	n/a	2.7	**Boiling Springs** (CDP) Spartanburg County
102	1413	2.7	**Ladson** (CDP) Berkeley County
102	1413	2.7	**North Augusta** (city) Aiken County
102	1413	2.7	**Summerville** (town) Dorchester County
102	1413	2.7	**West Columbia** (city) Lexington County
107	n/a	2.6	**Bamberg** (town) Bamberg County
107	n/a	2.6	**Lake City** (city) Florence County
107	1548	2.6	**Seven Oaks** (CDP) Lexington County
107	1548	2.6	**Wade Hampton** (CDP) Greenville County
111	n/a	2.5	**Andrews** (town) Georgetown County
111	n/a	2.5	**Burton** (CDP) Beaufort County
111	n/a	2.5	**Hollywood** (town) Charleston County
111	n/a	2.5	**Springdale** (town) Lexington County
111	n/a	2.5	**Walhalla** (city) Oconee County
116	1799	2.4	**Berea** (CDP) Greenville County
116	1799	2.4	**Cayce** (city) Lexington County
116	1799	2.4	**Dentsville** (CDP) Richland County
116	n/a	2.4	**Southern Shops** (CDP) Spartanburg County
116	n/a	2.4	**Travelers Rest** (city) Greenville County
121	n/a	2.3	**Arial** (CDP) Pickens County
121	n/a	2.3	**Denmark** (city) Bamberg County
121	1955	2.3	**Fort Mill** (town) York County
121	1955	2.3	**Hanahan** (city) Berkeley County
121	n/a	2.3	**India Hook** (CDP) York County
121	n/a	2.3	**Lake Murray of Richland** (CDP) Richland County
121	n/a	2.3	**Liberty** (city) Pickens County
121	n/a	2.3	**Newport** (CDP) York County
129	n/a	2.1	**Edgefield** (town) Edgefield County
129	2268	2.1	**Five Forks** (CDP) Greenville County
129	n/a	2.1	**Fountain Inn** (city) Greenville County
129	2268	2.1	**Goose Creek** (city) Berkeley County
129	n/a	2.1	**Sangaree** (CDP) Berkeley County
134	n/a	2.0	**Bennettsville** (city) Marlboro County
134	n/a	2.0	**Burnettown** (town) Aiken County
134	n/a	2.0	**Dalzell** (CDP) Sumter County
134	n/a	2.0	**Lakewood** (CDP) Sumter County
134	n/a	2.0	**Lesslie** (CDP) York County
134	2443	2.0	**Taylors** (CDP) Greenville County
140	n/a	1.9	**Red Bank** (CDP) Lexington County
141	n/a	1.8	**Arcadia** (CDP) Spartanburg County
141	n/a	1.8	**Edisto** (CDP) Orangeburg County
141	n/a	1.8	**Elgin** (CDP) Lancaster County
141	n/a	1.8	**Williston** (town) Barnwell County
145	n/a	1.7	**Lugoff** (CDP) Kershaw County
145	n/a	1.7	**North Hartsville** (CDP) Darlington County
145	2963	1.7	**Oak Grove** (CDP) Lexington County
148	n/a	1.5	**Gloverville** (CDP) Aiken County
149	n/a	1.2	**Hopkins** (CDP) Richland County
150	n/a	0.5	**Saluda** (town) Saluda County

Note: The state column ranks the top/bottom 150 places in the state with population of 2,500 or more. The national column ranks the top/bottom places in the country with population of 10,000 or more. Places that are unincorporated were not considered in the rankings. n/a indicates data not available. Please refer to the User Guide for additional information.

Homeowner Vacancy Rate

Top 150 Places Ranked in *Ascending* Order

State Rank	Nat'l Rank	Percent	Place
1	n/a	0.5	**Saluda** (town) Saluda County
2	n/a	1.2	**Hopkins** (CDP) Richland County
3	n/a	1.5	**Gloverville** (CDP) Aiken County
4	n/a	1.7	**Lugoff** (CDP) Kershaw County
4	n/a	1.7	**North Hartsville** (CDP) Darlington County
4	1503	1.7	**Oak Grove** (CDP) Lexington County
7	n/a	1.8	**Arcadia** (CDP) Spartanburg County
7	n/a	1.8	**Edisto** (CDP) Orangeburg County
7	n/a	1.8	**Elgin** (CDP) Lancaster County
7	n/a	1.8	**Williston** (town) Barnwell County
11	n/a	1.9	**Red Bank** (CDP) Lexington County
12	n/a	2.0	**Bennettsville** (city) Marlboro County
12	n/a	2.0	**Burnettown** (town) Aiken County
12	n/a	2.0	**Dalzell** (CDP) Sumter County
12	n/a	2.0	**Lakewood** (CDP) Sumter County
12	n/a	2.0	**Lesslie** (CDP) York County
12	2036	2.0	**Taylors** (CDP) Greenville County
18	n/a	2.1	**Edgefield** (town) Edgefield County
18	2214	2.1	**Five Forks** (CDP) Greenville County
18	n/a	2.1	**Fountain Inn** (city) Greenville County
18	2214	2.1	**Goose Creek** (city) Berkeley County
18	n/a	2.1	**Sangaree** (CDP) Berkeley County
23	n/a	2.3	**Arial** (CDP) Pickens County
23	n/a	2.3	**Denmark** (city) Bamberg County
23	2531	2.3	**Fort Mill** (town) York County
23	2531	2.3	**Hanahan** (city) Berkeley County
23	n/a	2.3	**India Hook** (CDP) York County
23	n/a	2.3	**Lake Murray of Richland** (CDP) Richland County
23	n/a	2.3	**Liberty** (city) Pickens County
23	n/a	2.3	**Newport** (CDP) York County
31	2702	2.4	**Berea** (CDP) Greenville County
31	2702	2.4	**Cayce** (city) Lexington County
31	2702	2.4	**Dentsville** (CDP) Richland County
31	n/a	2.4	**Southern Shops** (CDP) Spartanburg County
31	n/a	2.4	**Travelers Rest** (city) Greenville County
36	n/a	2.5	**Andrews** (town) Georgetown County
36	n/a	2.5	**Burton** (CDP) Beaufort County
36	n/a	2.5	**Hollywood** (town) Charleston County
36	n/a	2.5	**Springdale** (town) Lexington County
36	n/a	2.5	**Walhalla** (city) Oconee County
41	n/a	2.6	**Bamberg** (town) Bamberg County
41	n/a	2.6	**Lake City** (city) Florence County
41	2992	2.6	**Seven Oaks** (CDP) Lexington County
41	2992	2.6	**Wade Hampton** (CDP) Greenville County
45	n/a	2.7	**Boiling Springs** (CDP) Spartanburg County
45	3109	2.7	**Ladson** (CDP) Berkeley County
45	3109	2.7	**North Augusta** (city) Aiken County
45	3109	2.7	**Summerville** (town) Dorchester County
45	3109	2.7	**West Columbia** (city) Lexington County
50	n/a	2.8	**Belvedere** (CDP) Aiken County
50	3244	2.8	**Gantt** (CDP) Greenville County
50	3244	2.8	**Mauldin** (city) Greenville County
50	n/a	2.8	**McCormick** (town) McCormick County
54	n/a	2.9	**Bishopville** (city) Lee County
54	n/a	2.9	**Laurens** (city) Laurens County
54	n/a	2.9	**Piedmont** (CDP) Anderson County
54	n/a	2.9	**Tega Cay** (city) York County
58	n/a	3.0	**Dillon** (city) Dillon County
58	3466	3.0	**Forest Acres** (city) Richland County
58	3466	3.0	**Irmo** (town) Richland County
58	n/a	3.0	**Pageland** (town) Chesterfield County
62	n/a	3.1	**Allendale** (town) Allendale County
62	n/a	3.1	**Lake Wylie** (CDP) York County
62	3574	3.1	**Mount Pleasant** (town) Charleston County
62	3574	3.1	**Rock Hill** (city) York County
66	n/a	3.2	**Cheraw** (town) Chesterfield County
66	3643	3.2	**Clemson** (city) Pickens County
66	3643	3.2	**Easley** (city) Pickens County
66	n/a	3.2	**Graniteville** (CDP) Aiken County
66	n/a	3.2	**Springdale** (CDP) Lancaster County
71	n/a	3.3	**Clearwater** (CDP) Aiken County
71	3725	3.3	**Simpsonville** (city) Greenville County
71	n/a	3.3	**Williamston** (town) Anderson County
71	n/a	3.3	**Winnsboro** (town) Fairfield County
75	n/a	3.4	**Abbeville** (city) Abbeville County
75	n/a	3.4	**Darlington** (city) Darlington County
75	3816	3.4	**Florence** (city) Florence County
75	3816	3.4	**Greenwood** (city) Greenwood County
75	n/a	3.4	**Valley Falls** (CDP) Spartanburg County
75	n/a	3.4	**Welcome** (CDP) Greenville County
81	3892	3.5	**Aiken** (city) Aiken County
81	n/a	3.5	**Central** (town) Pickens County
81	n/a	3.5	**Hampton** (town) Hampton County
81	n/a	3.5	**Homeland Park** (CDP) Anderson County
81	n/a	3.5	**Marion** (city) Marion County
81	n/a	3.5	**Murrells Inlet** (CDP) Georgetown County
81	3892	3.5	**Saint Andrews** (CDP) Richland County
81	n/a	3.5	**Woodruff** (city) Spartanburg County
89	3955	3.6	**Greer** (city) Greenville County
89	n/a	3.6	**Pickens** (city) Pickens County
89	n/a	3.6	**York** (city) York County
92	n/a	3.7	**Brookdale** (CDP) Orangeburg County
92	n/a	3.7	**Lyman** (town) Spartanburg County
92	n/a	3.7	**Northlake** (CDP) Anderson County
95	n/a	3.8	**Barnwell** (city) Barnwell County
95	n/a	3.8	**Batesburg-Leesville** (town) Lexington County
95	n/a	3.8	**Mullins** (city) Marion County
95	4068	3.8	**Red Hill** (CDP) Horry County
95	4068	3.8	**Sumter** (city) Sumter County
95	n/a	3.8	**Union** (city) Union County
101	n/a	3.9	**Belton** (city) Anderson County
101	n/a	3.9	**Lancaster** (city) Lancaster County
101	4118	3.9	**Lexington** (town) Lexington County
101	n/a	3.9	**Pendleton** (town) Anderson County
105	n/a	4.0	**Manning** (city) Clarendon County
105	4172	4.0	**Orangeburg** (city) Orangeburg County
105	n/a	4.0	**Sans Souci** (CDP) Greenville County
105	4172	4.0	**Socastee** (CDP) Horry County
109	4213	4.1	**Charleston** (city) Charleston County
109	n/a	4.1	**Clover** (town) York County
109	n/a	4.1	**Georgetown** (city) Georgetown County
109	n/a	4.1	**Kingstree** (town) Williamsburg County
113	4254	4.2	**Columbia** (city) Richland County
113	n/a	4.2	**East Gaffney** (CDP) Cherokee County
113	4254	4.2	**Gaffney** (city) Cherokee County
113	n/a	4.2	**Isle of Palms** (city) Charleston County
113	4254	4.2	**North Charleston** (city) Charleston County
113	4254	4.2	**Parker** (CDP) Greenville County
119	n/a	4.3	**Clinton** (city) Laurens County
119	n/a	4.3	**Forestbrook** (CDP) Horry County
119	n/a	4.3	**Laurel Bay** (CDP) Beaufort County
119	4290	4.3	**Newberry** (city) Newberry County
119	n/a	4.3	**Walterboro** (city) Colleton County
124	n/a	4.4	**Camden** (city) Kershaw County
125	n/a	4.5	**Chester** (city) Chester County
125	n/a	4.5	**Honea Path** (town) Anderson County
125	n/a	4.5	**Seneca** (city) Oconee County
128	n/a	4.6	**Little River** (CDP) Horry County
129	4394	4.7	**Anderson** (city) Anderson County
130	n/a	4.8	**Saxon** (CDP) Spartanburg County
130	n/a	4.8	**Woodfield** (CDP) Richland County
132	4430	4.9	**Beaufort** (city) Beaufort County
132	4430	4.9	**Hilton Head Island** (town) Beaufort County
132	4430	4.9	**Spartanburg** (city) Spartanburg County
135	n/a	5.0	**Dunean** (CDP) Greenville County
136	n/a	5.2	**Duncan** (town) Spartanburg County
137	n/a	5.5	**Garden City** (CDP) Horry County
138	n/a	5.6	**Centerville** (CDP) Anderson County
139	n/a	5.7	**Folly Beach** (city) Charleston County
139	4534	5.7	**Greenville** (city) Greenville County
141	4548	5.8	**Conway** (city) Horry County
142	4584	6.4	**Bluffton** (town) Beaufort County
143	4599	6.7	**Myrtle Beach** (city) Horry County
144	n/a	7.3	**Hardeeville** (city) Jasper County
144	n/a	7.3	**Surfside Beach** (town) Horry County
146	n/a	7.5	**Ridgeland** (town) Jasper County
147	n/a	8.4	**Hartsville** (city) Darlington County
148	4637	8.5	**Port Royal** (town) Beaufort County
149	n/a	8.8	**Moncks Corner** (town) Berkeley County
150	4650	11.3	**North Myrtle Beach** (city) Horry County

Note: *The state column ranks the top/bottom 150 places in the state with population of 2,500 or more. The national column ranks the top/bottom places in the country with population of 10,000 or more. Places that are unincorporated were not considered in the rankings. n/a indicates data not available. Please refer to the User Guide for additional information.*

Median Gross Rent

Top 150 Places Ranked in *Descending* Order

State Rank	Nat'l Rank	Dollars	Place
1	n/a	1,653	**Tega Cay** (city) York County
2	n/a	1,605	**India Hook** (CDP) York County
3	n/a	1,563	**Isle of Palms** (city) Charleston County
4	455	1,520	**Five Forks** (CDP) Greenville County
5	n/a	1,333	**Folly Beach** (city) Charleston County
6	892	1,310	**Bluffton** (town) Beaufort County
7	1084	1,238	**Mount Pleasant** (town) Charleston County
8	n/a	1,200	**Lake Murray of Richland** (CDP) Richland County
9	1649	1,092	**Hilton Head Island** (town) Beaufort County
10	1687	1,084	**Goose Creek** (city) Berkeley County
11	n/a	1,069	**Laurel Bay** (CDP) Beaufort County
12	1827	1,056	**Irmo** (town) Richland County
13	1907	1,034	**Ladson** (CDP) Berkeley County
14	n/a	1,031	**Sangaree** (CDP) Berkeley County
15	2237	970	**Port Royal** (town) Beaufort County
16	2250	968	**Charleston** (city) Charleston County
17	2284	964	**Summerville** (town) Dorchester County
18	n/a	949	**Woodfield** (CDP) Richland County
19	n/a	945	**Hardeeville** (city) Jasper County
20	n/a	934	**Murrells Inlet** (CDP) Georgetown County
21	n/a	916	**Lake Wylie** (CDP) York County
22	n/a	913	**Springdale** (town) Lexington County
23	n/a	912	**Central** (town) Pickens County
24	2603	910	**Lexington** (town) Lexington County
24	2603	910	**Oak Grove** (CDP) Lexington County
26	n/a	905	**Burton** (CDP) Beaufort County
27	n/a	903	**Surfside Beach** (town) Horry County
28	2814	878	**Mauldin** (city) Greenville County
29	2835	875	**Simpsonville** (city) Greenville County
30	2863	870	**Fort Mill** (town) York County
31	n/a	860	**Garden City** (CDP) Horry County
31	2923	860	**Hanahan** (city) Berkeley County
33	n/a	855	**Camden** (city) Kershaw County
33	2961	855	**North Charleston** (city) Charleston County
35	2987	851	**Forest Acres** (city) Richland County
36	3003	849	**Cayce** (city) Lexington County
36	n/a	849	**Northlake** (CDP) Anderson County
38	n/a	848	**Clover** (town) York County
38	n/a	848	**Hopkins** (CDP) Richland County
40	3016	847	**Socastee** (CDP) Horry County
41	n/a	845	**Little River** (CDP) Horry County
42	3066	839	**Aiken** (city) Aiken County
43	n/a	832	**Hollywood** (town) Charleston County
44	3140	827	**Dentsville** (CDP) Richland County
44	3140	827	**North Myrtle Beach** (city) Horry County
46	3169	822	**Myrtle Beach** (city) Horry County
46	3169	822	**Red Hill** (CDP) Horry County
48	3190	819	**Beaufort** (city) Beaufort County
48	3190	819	**Columbia** (city) Richland County
50	n/a	816	**Red Bank** (CDP) Lexington County
51	3229	811	**West Columbia** (city) Lexington County
52	n/a	810	**Boiling Springs** (CDP) Spartanburg County
53	3334	792	**Seven Oaks** (CDP) Lexington County
54	3463	770	**Rock Hill** (city) York County
55	n/a	769	**Lakewood** (CDP) Sumter County
56	n/a	767	**Dunean** (CDP) Greenville County
57	3517	761	**Taylors** (CDP) Greenville County
58	n/a	750	**Arial** (CDP) Pickens County
59	3591	749	**Greenville** (city) Greenville County
60	3603	747	**Greer** (city) Greenville County
61	n/a	746	**Newport** (CDP) York County
62	n/a	743	**Moncks Corner** (town) Berkeley County
63	n/a	738	**Forestbrook** (CDP) Horry County
64	n/a	736	**Dalzell** (CDP) Sumter County
65	3700	732	**Saint Andrews** (CDP) Richland County
66	n/a	721	**Arcadia** (CDP) Spartanburg County
67	3787	718	**Parker** (CDP) Greenville County
67	3787	718	**Sumter** (city) Sumter County
69	n/a	706	**Burnettown** (town) Aiken County
69	3859	706	**Gantt** (CDP) Greenville County
71	n/a	704	**Belvedere** (CDP) Aiken County
71	n/a	704	**Travelers Rest** (city) Greenville County
73	3875	703	**Easley** (city) Pickens County
74	3886	701	**Wade Hampton** (CDP) Greenville County
75	3904	697	**Clemson** (city) Pickens County
76	n/a	692	**Ridgeland** (town) Jasper County
77	3959	688	**North Augusta** (city) Aiken County
78	3966	687	**Conway** (city) Horry County
79	n/a	685	**Piedmont** (CDP) Anderson County
79	n/a	685	**York** (city) York County
81	n/a	683	**Georgetown** (city) Georgetown County
82	n/a	682	**Welcome** (CDP) Greenville County
83	n/a	681	**Homeland Park** (CDP) Anderson County
84	n/a	678	**Abbeville** (city) Abbeville County
85	n/a	675	**Williamston** (town) Anderson County
86	n/a	669	**Pageland** (town) Chesterfield County
87	n/a	668	**Barnwell** (city) Barnwell County
88	n/a	664	**Batesburg-Leesville** (town) Lexington County
89	n/a	662	**Clinton** (city) Laurens County
90	n/a	661	**Sans Souci** (CDP) Greenville County
91	4116	659	**Florence** (city) Florence County
92	n/a	658	**Pickens** (city) Pickens County
93	n/a	653	**Valley Falls** (CDP) Spartanburg County
94	n/a	648	**Lancaster** (city) Lancaster County
95	n/a	645	**Duncan** (town) Spartanburg County
95	n/a	645	**Fountain Inn** (city) Greenville County
95	n/a	645	**Graniteville** (CDP) Aiken County
98	n/a	644	**Hampton** (town) Hampton County
98	4196	644	**Spartanburg** (city) Spartanburg County
98	n/a	644	**Williston** (town) Barnwell County
101	4209	642	**Orangeburg** (city) Orangeburg County
102	n/a	640	**Edisto** (CDP) Orangeburg County
102	n/a	640	**Lyman** (town) Spartanburg County
104	4232	639	**Berea** (CDP) Greenville County
105	n/a	638	**Saxon** (CDP) Spartanburg County
105	n/a	638	**Southern Shops** (CDP) Spartanburg County
107	n/a	637	**Elgin** (CDP) Lancaster County
108	4251	636	**Greenwood** (city) Greenwood County
109	4259	635	**Newberry** (city) Newberry County
110	n/a	633	**Bamberg** (town) Bamberg County
111	4291	629	**Anderson** (city) Anderson County
112	n/a	626	**Walterboro** (city) Colleton County
113	n/a	619	**Springdale** (CDP) Lancaster County
114	n/a	618	**Seneca** (city) Oconee County
115	n/a	616	**Lesslie** (CDP) York County
116	n/a	615	**Gloverville** (CDP) Aiken County
117	n/a	609	**Kingstree** (town) Williamsburg County
118	n/a	601	**Lake City** (city) Florence County
119	n/a	600	**Andrews** (town) Georgetown County
120	n/a	598	**Winnsboro** (town) Fairfield County
121	n/a	596	**Hartsville** (city) Darlington County
122	n/a	591	**Laurens** (city) Laurens County
123	n/a	587	**Lugoff** (CDP) Kershaw County
124	4508	581	**Gaffney** (city) Cherokee County
125	n/a	575	**Liberty** (city) Pickens County
126	n/a	573	**Woodruff** (city) Spartanburg County
127	n/a	572	**Bennettsville** (city) Marlboro County
128	n/a	563	**Belton** (city) Anderson County
129	n/a	561	**Centerville** (CDP) Anderson County
129	n/a	561	**Edgefield** (town) Edgefield County
131	n/a	552	**North Hartsville** (CDP) Darlington County
132	n/a	549	**Clearwater** (CDP) Aiken County
133	n/a	546	**Darlington** (city) Darlington County
134	n/a	544	**Chester** (city) Chester County
135	n/a	539	**Union** (city) Union County
136	n/a	537	**Dillon** (city) Dillon County
137	n/a	536	**Saluda** (town) Saluda County
138	n/a	531	**East Gaffney** (CDP) Cherokee County
139	n/a	530	**Pendleton** (town) Anderson County
140	n/a	525	**Brookdale** (CDP) Orangeburg County
141	n/a	523	**Manning** (city) Clarendon County
142	n/a	503	**Marion** (city) Marion County
143	n/a	500	**McCormick** (town) McCormick County
144	n/a	474	**Mullins** (city) Marion County
145	n/a	470	**Cheraw** (town) Chesterfield County
146	n/a	444	**Bishopville** (city) Lee County
147	n/a	417	**Allendale** (town) Allendale County
148	n/a	386	**Walhalla** (city) Oconee County
149	n/a	377	**Denmark** (city) Bamberg County
150	n/a	337	**Honea Path** (town) Anderson County

Note: *The state column ranks the top/bottom 150 places in the state with population of 2,500 or more. The national column ranks the top/bottom places in the country with population of 10,000 or more. Places that are unincorporated were not considered in the rankings. n/a indicates data not available. Please refer to the User Guide for additional information.*

Median Gross Rent

Top 150 Places Ranked in *Ascending* Order

State Rank	Nat'l Rank	Dollars	Place
1	n/a	337	**Honea Path** (town) Anderson County
2	n/a	377	**Denmark** (city) Bamberg County
3	n/a	386	**Walhalla** (city) Oconee County
4	n/a	417	**Allendale** (town) Allendale County
5	n/a	444	**Bishopville** (city) Lee County
6	n/a	470	**Cheraw** (town) Chesterfield County
7	n/a	474	**Mullins** (city) Marion County
8	n/a	500	**McCormick** (town) McCormick County
9	n/a	503	**Marion** (city) Marion County
10	n/a	523	**Manning** (city) Clarendon County
11	n/a	525	**Brookdale** (CDP) Orangeburg County
12	n/a	530	**Pendleton** (town) Anderson County
13	n/a	531	**East Gaffney** (CDP) Cherokee County
14	n/a	536	**Saluda** (town) Saluda County
15	n/a	537	**Dillon** (city) Dillon County
16	n/a	539	**Union** (city) Union County
17	n/a	544	**Chester** (city) Chester County
18	n/a	546	**Darlington** (city) Darlington County
19	n/a	549	**Clearwater** (CDP) Aiken County
20	n/a	552	**North Hartsville** (CDP) Darlington County
21	n/a	561	**Centerville** (CDP) Anderson County
21	n/a	561	**Edgefield** (town) Edgefield County
23	n/a	563	**Belton** (city) Anderson County
24	n/a	572	**Bennettsville** (city) Marlboro County
25	n/a	573	**Woodruff** (city) Spartanburg County
26	n/a	575	**Liberty** (city) Pickens County
27	144	581	**Gaffney** (city) Cherokee County
28	n/a	587	**Lugoff** (CDP) Kershaw County
29	n/a	591	**Laurens** (city) Laurens County
30	n/a	596	**Hartsville** (city) Darlington County
31	n/a	598	**Winnsboro** (town) Fairfield County
32	n/a	600	**Andrews** (town) Georgetown County
33	n/a	601	**Lake City** (city) Florence County
34	n/a	609	**Kingstree** (town) Williamsburg County
35	n/a	615	**Gloverville** (CDP) Aiken County
36	n/a	616	**Lesslie** (CDP) York County
37	n/a	618	**Seneca** (city) Oconee County
38	n/a	619	**Springdale** (CDP) Lancaster County
39	n/a	626	**Walterboro** (city) Colleton County
40	361	629	**Anderson** (city) Anderson County
41	n/a	633	**Bamberg** (town) Bamberg County
42	393	635	**Newberry** (city) Newberry County
43	398	636	**Greenwood** (city) Greenwood County
44	n/a	637	**Elgin** (CDP) Lancaster County
45	n/a	638	**Saxon** (CDP) Spartanburg County
45	n/a	638	**Southern Shops** (CDP) Spartanburg County
47	418	639	**Berea** (CDP) Greenville County
48	n/a	640	**Edisto** (CDP) Orangeburg County
48	n/a	640	**Lyman** (town) Spartanburg County
50	439	642	**Orangeburg** (city) Orangeburg County
51	n/a	644	**Hampton** (town) Hampton County
51	452	644	**Spartanburg** (city) Spartanburg County
51	n/a	644	**Williston** (town) Barnwell County
54	n/a	645	**Duncan** (town) Spartanburg County
54	n/a	645	**Fountain Inn** (city) Greenville County
54	n/a	645	**Graniteville** (CDP) Aiken County
57	n/a	648	**Lancaster** (city) Lancaster County
58	n/a	653	**Valley Falls** (CDP) Spartanburg County
59	n/a	658	**Pickens** (city) Pickens County
60	537	659	**Florence** (city) Florence County
61	n/a	661	**Sans Souci** (CDP) Greenville County
62	n/a	662	**Clinton** (city) Laurens County
63	n/a	664	**Batesburg-Leesville** (town) Lexington County
64	n/a	668	**Barnwell** (city) Barnwell County
65	n/a	669	**Pageland** (town) Chesterfield County
66	n/a	675	**Williamston** (town) Anderson County
67	n/a	678	**Abbeville** (city) Abbeville County
68	n/a	681	**Homeland Park** (CDP) Anderson County
69	n/a	682	**Welcome** (CDP) Greenville County
70	n/a	683	**Georgetown** (city) Georgetown County
71	n/a	685	**Piedmont** (CDP) Anderson County
71	n/a	685	**York** (city) York County
73	683	687	**Conway** (city) Horry County
74	691	688	**North Augusta** (city) Aiken County
75	n/a	692	**Ridgeland** (town) Jasper County
76	744	697	**Clemson** (city) Pickens County
77	769	701	**Wade Hampton** (CDP) Greenville County
78	775	703	**Easley** (city) Pickens County
79	n/a	704	**Belvedere** (CDP) Aiken County
79	n/a	704	**Travelers Rest** (city) Greenville County
81	n/a	706	**Burnettown** (town) Aiken County
81	789	706	**Gantt** (CDP) Greenville County
83	864	718	**Parker** (CDP) Greenville County
83	864	718	**Sumter** (city) Sumter County
85	n/a	721	**Arcadia** (CDP) Spartanburg County
86	945	732	**Saint Andrews** (CDP) Richland County
87	n/a	736	**Dalzell** (CDP) Sumter County
88	n/a	738	**Forestbrook** (CDP) Horry County
89	n/a	743	**Moncks Corner** (town) Berkeley County
90	n/a	746	**Newport** (CDP) York County
91	1046	747	**Greer** (city) Greenville County
92	1059	749	**Greenville** (city) Greenville County
93	n/a	750	**Arial** (CDP) Pickens County
94	1135	761	**Taylors** (CDP) Greenville County
95	n/a	767	**Dunean** (CDP) Greenville County
96	n/a	769	**Lakewood** (CDP) Sumter County
97	1184	770	**Rock Hill** (city) York County
98	1318	792	**Seven Oaks** (CDP) Lexington County
99	n/a	810	**Boiling Springs** (CDP) Spartanburg County
100	1423	811	**West Columbia** (city) Lexington County
101	n/a	816	**Red Bank** (CDP) Lexington County
102	1460	819	**Beaufort** (city) Beaufort County
102	1460	819	**Columbia** (city) Richland County
104	1480	822	**Myrtle Beach** (city) Horry County
104	1480	822	**Red Hill** (CDP) Horry County
106	1512	827	**Dentsville** (CDP) Richland County
106	1512	827	**North Myrtle Beach** (city) Horry County
108	n/a	832	**Hollywood** (town) Charleston County
109	1582	839	**Aiken** (city) Aiken County
110	n/a	845	**Little River** (CDP) Horry County
111	1631	847	**Socastee** (CDP) Horry County
112	n/a	848	**Clover** (town) York County
112	n/a	848	**Hopkins** (CDP) Richland County
114	1651	849	**Cayce** (city) Lexington County
114	n/a	849	**Northlake** (CDP) Anderson County
116	1664	851	**Forest Acres** (city) Richland County
117	n/a	855	**Camden** (city) Kershaw County
117	1689	855	**North Charleston** (city) Charleston County
119	n/a	860	**Garden City** (CDP) Horry County
119	1727	860	**Hanahan** (city) Berkeley County
121	1781	870	**Fort Mill** (town) York County
122	1814	875	**Simpsonville** (city) Greenville County
123	1835	878	**Mauldin** (city) Greenville County
124	n/a	903	**Surfside Beach** (town) Horry County
125	n/a	905	**Burton** (CDP) Beaufort County
126	2043	910	**Lexington** (town) Lexington County
126	2043	910	**Oak Grove** (CDP) Lexington County
128	n/a	912	**Central** (town) Pickens County
129	n/a	913	**Springdale** (town) Lexington County
130	n/a	916	**Lake Wylie** (CDP) York County
131	n/a	934	**Murrells Inlet** (CDP) Georgetown County
132	n/a	945	**Hardeeville** (city) Jasper County
133	n/a	949	**Woodfield** (CDP) Richland County
134	2367	964	**Summerville** (town) Dorchester County
135	2393	968	**Charleston** (city) Charleston County
136	2414	970	**Port Royal** (town) Beaufort County
137	n/a	1,031	**Sangaree** (CDP) Berkeley County
138	2746	1,034	**Ladson** (CDP) Berkeley County
139	2824	1,056	**Irmo** (town) Richland County
140	n/a	1,069	**Laurel Bay** (CDP) Beaufort County
141	2962	1,084	**Goose Creek** (city) Berkeley County
142	3003	1,092	**Hilton Head Island** (town) Beaufort County
143	n/a	1,200	**Lake Murray of Richland** (CDP) Richland County
144	3568	1,238	**Mount Pleasant** (town) Charleston County
145	3760	1,310	**Bluffton** (town) Beaufort County
146	n/a	1,333	**Folly Beach** (city) Charleston County
147	4200	1,520	**Five Forks** (CDP) Greenville County
148	n/a	1,563	**Isle of Palms** (city) Charleston County
149	n/a	1,605	**India Hook** (CDP) York County
150	n/a	1,653	**Tega Cay** (city) York County

Note: The state column ranks the top/bottom 150 places in the state with population of 2,500 or more. The national column ranks the top/bottom places in the country with population of 10,000 or more. Places that are unincorporated were not considered in the rankings. n/a indicates data not available. Please refer to the User Guide for additional information.

Rental Vacancy Rate

Top 150 Places Ranked in *Descending* Order

State Rank	Nat'l Rank	Percent	Place
1	n/a	75.7	**Isle of Palms** (city) Charleston County
2	3	57.4	**North Myrtle Beach** (city) Horry County
3	n/a	55.5	**Surfside Beach** (town) Horry County
4	4	55.1	**Hilton Head Island** (town) Beaufort County
5	n/a	50.6	**Garden City** (CDP) Horry County
6	n/a	42.6	**Folly Beach** (city) Charleston County
7	23	23.1	**Myrtle Beach** (city) Horry County
8	n/a	20.9	**Little River** (CDP) Horry County
9	n/a	20.6	**Lake Murray of Richland** (CDP) Richland County
10	n/a	20.3	**Pendleton** (town) Anderson County
11	69	18.9	**Red Hill** (CDP) Horry County
12	n/a	18.3	**Lake Wylie** (CDP) York County
13	n/a	17.3	**Saxon** (CDP) Spartanburg County
14	n/a	17.1	**Sans Souci** (CDP) Greenville County
15	n/a	16.7	**Arial** (CDP) Pickens County
16	n/a	16.5	**Springdale** (CDP) Lancaster County
17	152	16.2	**West Columbia** (city) Lexington County
18	159	16.0	**Berea** (CDP) Greenville County
18	n/a	16.0	**Winnsboro** (town) Fairfield County
20	n/a	15.9	**Ridgeland** (town) Jasper County
21	n/a	15.5	**Dunean** (CDP) Greenville County
21	193	15.5	**Gantt** (CDP) Greenville County
21	n/a	15.5	**Murrells Inlet** (CDP) Georgetown County
24	n/a	15.2	**Pickens** (city) Pickens County
25	n/a	14.8	**Burton** (CDP) Beaufort County
26	239	14.7	**Bluffton** (town) Beaufort County
26	239	14.7	**Socastee** (CDP) Horry County
28	n/a	14.5	**Forestbrook** (CDP) Horry County
28	n/a	14.5	**York** (city) York County
30	n/a	14.3	**Southern Shops** (CDP) Spartanburg County
30	n/a	14.3	**Valley Falls** (CDP) Spartanburg County
32	283	14.2	**North Charleston** (city) Charleston County
32	n/a	14.2	**Northlake** (CDP) Anderson County
34	303	14.0	**Forest Acres** (city) Richland County
34	n/a	14.0	**Pageland** (town) Chesterfield County
36	n/a	13.9	**Brookdale** (CDP) Orangeburg County
36	316	13.9	**Parker** (CDP) Greenville County
38	321	13.8	**Goose Creek** (city) Berkeley County
38	n/a	13.8	**Honea Path** (town) Anderson County
38	321	13.8	**Spartanburg** (city) Spartanburg County
41	n/a	13.7	**Arcadia** (CDP) Spartanburg County
41	335	13.7	**Hanahan** (city) Berkeley County
41	335	13.7	**Rock Hill** (city) York County
44	n/a	13.5	**East Gaffney** (CDP) Cherokee County
45	n/a	13.3	**Andrews** (town) Georgetown County
45	n/a	13.3	**Chester** (city) Chester County
45	385	13.3	**Columbia** (city) Richland County
48	n/a	13.2	**Abbeville** (city) Abbeville County
49	n/a	13.1	**Bennettsville** (city) Marlboro County
49	n/a	13.1	**Hardeeville** (city) Jasper County
49	n/a	13.1	**Laurens** (city) Laurens County
49	n/a	13.1	**Lesslie** (CDP) York County
53	n/a	13.0	**Moncks Corner** (town) Berkeley County
53	428	13.0	**Saint Andrews** (CDP) Richland County
55	459	12.8	**Greer** (city) Greenville County
56	n/a	12.7	**Camden** (city) Kershaw County
57	493	12.6	**Greenwood** (city) Greenwood County
58	n/a	12.5	**Belton** (city) Anderson County
58	n/a	12.5	**Clinton** (city) Laurens County
58	512	12.5	**Oak Grove** (CDP) Lexington County
61	530	12.4	**Anderson** (city) Anderson County
61	530	12.4	**Summerville** (town) Dorchester County
63	n/a	12.2	**Gloverville** (CDP) Aiken County
63	n/a	12.2	**Hollywood** (town) Charleston County
65	582	12.1	**Port Royal** (town) Beaufort County
65	582	12.1	**Seven Oaks** (CDP) Lexington County
67	635	11.9	**Greenville** (city) Greenville County
68	656	11.8	**Gaffney** (city) Cherokee County
68	n/a	11.8	**Homeland Park** (CDP) Anderson County
68	n/a	11.8	**Piedmont** (CDP) Anderson County
68	n/a	11.8	**Travelers Rest** (city) Greenville County
68	n/a	11.8	**Walterboro** (city) Colleton County
73	n/a	11.7	**Lancaster** (city) Lancaster County
74	706	11.6	**Lexington** (town) Lexington County
75	860	11.0	**Beaufort** (city) Beaufort County
75	n/a	11.0	**Woodfield** (CDP) Richland County
77	n/a	10.9	**Barnwell** (city) Barnwell County
77	896	10.9	**Conway** (city) Horry County
77	n/a	10.9	**Seneca** (city) Oconee County
77	n/a	10.9	**Williamston** (town) Anderson County
81	930	10.8	**Charleston** (city) Charleston County
81	n/a	10.8	**Walhalla** (city) Oconee County
81	n/a	10.8	**Welcome** (CDP) Greenville County
84	n/a	10.6	**Laurel Bay** (CDP) Beaufort County
85	1024	10.5	**Dentsville** (CDP) Richland County
86	1061	10.4	**Florence** (city) Florence County
86	1061	10.4	**Sumter** (city) Sumter County
88	n/a	10.3	**Hampton** (town) Hampton County
88	n/a	10.3	**India Hook** (CDP) York County
88	1107	10.3	**Mount Pleasant** (town) Charleston County
91	n/a	10.1	**Denmark** (city) Bamberg County
91	n/a	10.1	**Woodruff** (city) Spartanburg County
93	1220	10.0	**Wade Hampton** (CDP) Greenville County
94	1258	9.9	**Easley** (city) Pickens County
94	n/a	9.9	**Hartsville** (city) Darlington County
96	n/a	9.7	**Clearwater** (CDP) Aiken County
96	n/a	9.7	**Georgetown** (city) Georgetown County
98	n/a	9.5	**Boiling Springs** (CDP) Spartanburg County
99	n/a	9.2	**Duncan** (town) Spartanburg County
99	1541	9.2	**Orangeburg** (city) Orangeburg County
101	n/a	9.1	**Dalzell** (CDP) Sumter County
102	n/a	9.0	**Liberty** (city) Pickens County
103	n/a	8.9	**Fountain Inn** (city) Greenville County
103	n/a	8.9	**Williston** (town) Barnwell County
105	n/a	8.8	**Elgin** (CDP) Lancaster County
105	n/a	8.8	**Mullins** (city) Marion County
105	1710	8.8	**Newberry** (city) Newberry County
105	n/a	8.8	**Union** (city) Union County
109	1755	8.7	**Simpsonville** (city) Greenville County
110	n/a	8.6	**Allendale** (town) Allendale County
111	n/a	8.5	**Batesburg-Leesville** (town) Lexington County
112	1892	8.4	**Ladson** (CDP) Berkeley County
113	n/a	8.3	**Central** (town) Pickens County
114	1993	8.2	**Cayce** (city) Lexington County
114	n/a	8.2	**Hopkins** (CDP) Richland County
116	2058	8.1	**Taylors** (CDP) Greenville County
117	n/a	8.0	**Centerville** (CDP) Anderson County
117	n/a	8.0	**Graniteville** (CDP) Aiken County
119	n/a	7.9	**Burnettown** (town) Aiken County
120	n/a	7.7	**Cheraw** (town) Chesterfield County
120	n/a	7.7	**Darlington** (city) Darlington County
120	n/a	7.7	**Lake City** (city) Florence County
123	n/a	7.6	**Bamberg** (town) Bamberg County
123	n/a	7.6	**Dillon** (city) Dillon County
123	n/a	7.6	**Edisto** (CDP) Orangeburg County
123	2325	7.6	**Fort Mill** (town) York County
123	n/a	7.6	**Red Bank** (CDP) Lexington County
128	n/a	7.5	**Belvedere** (CDP) Aiken County
128	2389	7.5	**Clemson** (city) Pickens County
128	n/a	7.5	**Clover** (town) York County
128	2389	7.5	**Irmo** (town) Richland County
132	n/a	7.4	**McCormick** (town) McCormick County
133	2504	7.3	**North Augusta** (city) Aiken County
134	n/a	7.2	**Edgefield** (town) Edgefield County
135	n/a	7.0	**North Hartsville** (CDP) Darlington County
136	2810	6.8	**Aiken** (city) Aiken County
136	n/a	6.8	**Lyman** (town) Spartanburg County
138	2865	6.7	**Mauldin** (city) Greenville County
139	n/a	6.0	**Springdale** (town) Lexington County
140	n/a	5.9	**Lakewood** (CDP) Sumter County
141	n/a	5.7	**Newport** (CDP) York County
142	n/a	5.0	**Kingstree** (town) Williamsburg County
142	n/a	5.0	**Manning** (city) Clarendon County
142	n/a	5.0	**Tega Cay** (city) York County
145	n/a	4.8	**Sangaree** (CDP) Berkeley County
146	n/a	4.3	**Bishopville** (city) Lee County
147	n/a	4.1	**Marion** (city) Marion County
148	n/a	3.8	**Saluda** (town) Saluda County
149	n/a	3.7	**Lugoff** (CDP) Kershaw County
150	4572	3.0	**Five Forks** (CDP) Greenville County

Note: The state column ranks the top/bottom 150 places in the state with population of 2,500 or more. The national column ranks the top/bottom places in the country with population of 10,000 or more. Places that are unincorporated were not considered in the rankings. n/a indicates data not available. Please refer to the User Guide for additional information.

Rental Vacancy Rate

Top 150 Places Ranked in *Ascending* Order

State Rank	Nat'l Rank	Percent	Place
1	74	3.0	Five Forks (CDP) Greenville County
2	n/a	3.7	Lugoff (CDP) Kershaw County
3	n/a	3.8	Saluda (town) Saluda County
4	n/a	4.1	Marion (city) Marion County
5	n/a	4.3	Bishopville (city) Lee County
6	n/a	4.8	Sangaree (CDP) Berkeley County
7	n/a	5.0	Kingstree (town) Williamsburg County
7	n/a	5.0	Manning (city) Clarendon County
7	n/a	5.0	Tega Cay (city) York County
10	n/a	5.7	Newport (CDP) York County
11	n/a	5.9	Lakewood (CDP) Sumter County
12	n/a	6.0	Springdale (town) Lexington County
13	1726	6.7	Mauldin (city) Greenville County
14	1792	6.8	Aiken (city) Aiken County
14	n/a	6.8	Lyman (town) Spartanburg County
16	n/a	7.0	North Hartsville (CDP) Darlington County
17	n/a	7.2	Edgefield (town) Edgefield County
18	2099	7.3	North Augusta (city) Aiken County
19	n/a	7.4	McCormick (town) McCormick County
20	n/a	7.5	Belvedere (CDP) Aiken County
20	2217	7.5	Clemson (city) Pickens County
20	n/a	7.5	Clover (town) York County
20	2217	7.5	Irmo (town) Richland County
24	n/a	7.6	Bamberg (town) Bamberg County
24	n/a	7.6	Dillon (city) Dillon County
24	n/a	7.6	Edisto (CDP) Orangeburg County
24	2268	7.6	Fort Mill (town) York County
24	n/a	7.6	Red Bank (CDP) Lexington County
29	n/a	7.7	Cheraw (town) Chesterfield County
29	n/a	7.7	Darlington (city) Darlington County
29	n/a	7.7	Lake City (city) Florence County
32	n/a	7.9	Burnettown (town) Aiken County
33	n/a	8.0	Centerville (CDP) Anderson County
33	n/a	8.0	Graniteville (CDP) Aiken County
35	2542	8.1	Taylors (CDP) Greenville County
36	2599	8.2	Cayce (city) Lexington County
36	n/a	8.2	Hopkins (CDP) Richland County
38	n/a	8.3	Central (town) Pickens County
39	2717	8.4	Ladson (CDP) Berkeley County
40	n/a	8.5	Batesburg-Leesville (town) Lexington County
41	n/a	8.6	Allendale (town) Allendale County
42	2865	8.7	Simpsonville (city) Greenville County
43	n/a	8.8	Elgin (CDP) Lancaster County
43	n/a	8.8	Mullins (city) Marion County
43	2902	8.8	Newberry (city) Newberry County
43	n/a	8.8	Union (city) Union County
47	n/a	8.9	Fountain Inn (city) Greenville County
47	n/a	8.9	Williston (town) Barnwell County
49	n/a	9.0	Liberty (city) Pickens County
50	n/a	9.1	Dalzell (CDP) Sumter County
51	n/a	9.2	Duncan (town) Spartanburg County
51	3074	9.2	Orangeburg (city) Orangeburg County
53	n/a	9.5	Boiling Springs (CDP) Spartanburg County
54	n/a	9.7	Clearwater (CDP) Aiken County
54	n/a	9.7	Georgetown (city) Georgetown County
56	3366	9.9	Easley (city) Pickens County
56	n/a	9.9	Hartsville (city) Darlington County
58	3399	10.0	Wade Hampton (CDP) Greenville County
59	n/a	10.1	Denmark (city) Bamberg County
59	n/a	10.1	Woodruff (city) Spartanburg County
61	n/a	10.3	Hampton (town) Hampton County
61	n/a	10.3	India Hook (CDP) York County
61	3506	10.3	Mount Pleasant (town) Charleston County
64	3550	10.4	Florence (city) Florence County
64	3550	10.4	Sumter (city) Sumter County
66	3596	10.5	Dentsville (CDP) Richland County
67	n/a	10.6	Laurel Bay (CDP) Beaufort County
68	3697	10.8	Charleston (city) Charleston County
68	n/a	10.8	Walhalla (city) Oconee County
68	n/a	10.8	Welcome (CDP) Greenville County
71	n/a	10.9	Barnwell (city) Barnwell County
71	3727	10.9	Conway (city) Horry County
71	n/a	10.9	Seneca (city) Oconee County
71	n/a	10.9	Williamston (town) Anderson County
75	3761	11.0	Beaufort (city) Beaufort County
75	n/a	11.0	Woodfield (CDP) Richland County
77	3926	11.6	Lexington (town) Lexington County
78	n/a	11.7	Lancaster (city) Lancaster County
79	3975	11.8	Gaffney (city) Cherokee County
79	n/a	11.8	Homeland Park (CDP) Anderson County
79	n/a	11.8	Piedmont (CDP) Anderson County
79	n/a	11.8	Travelers Rest (city) Greenville County
79	n/a	11.8	Walterboro (city) Colleton County
84	4001	11.9	Greenville (city) Greenville County
85	4052	12.1	Port Royal (town) Beaufort County
85	4052	12.1	Seven Oaks (CDP) Lexington County
87	n/a	12.2	Gloverville (CDP) Aiken County
87	n/a	12.2	Hollywood (town) Charleston County
89	4114	12.4	Anderson (city) Anderson County
89	4114	12.4	Summerville (town) Dorchester County
91	n/a	12.5	Belton (city) Anderson County
91	n/a	12.5	Clinton (city) Laurens County
91	4127	12.5	Oak Grove (CDP) Lexington County
94	4145	12.6	Greenwood (city) Greenwood County
95	n/a	12.7	Camden (city) Kershaw County
96	4177	12.8	Greer (city) Greenville County
97	n/a	13.0	Moncks Corner (town) Berkeley County
97	4211	13.0	Saint Andrews (CDP) Richland County
99	n/a	13.1	Bennettsville (city) Marlboro County
99	n/a	13.1	Hardeeville (city) Jasper County
99	n/a	13.1	Laurens (city) Laurens County
99	n/a	13.1	Lesslie (CDP) York County
103	n/a	13.2	Abbeville (city) Abbeville County
104	n/a	13.3	Andrews (town) Georgetown County
104	n/a	13.3	Chester (city) Chester County
104	4257	13.3	Columbia (city) Richland County
107	n/a	13.5	East Gaffney (CDP) Cherokee County
108	n/a	13.7	Arcadia (CDP) Spartanburg County
108	4305	13.7	Hanahan (city) Berkeley County
108	4305	13.7	Rock Hill (city) York County
111	4322	13.8	Goose Creek (city) Berkeley County
111	n/a	13.8	Honea Path (town) Anderson County
111	4322	13.8	Spartanburg (city) Spartanburg County
114	n/a	13.9	Brookdale (CDP) Orangeburg County
114	4336	13.9	Parker (CDP) Greenville County
116	4341	14.0	Forest Acres (city) Richland County
116	n/a	14.0	Pageland (town) Chesterfield County
118	4362	14.2	North Charleston (city) Charleston County
118	n/a	14.2	Northlake (CDP) Anderson County
120	n/a	14.3	Southern Shops (CDP) Spartanburg County
120	n/a	14.3	Valley Falls (CDP) Spartanburg County
122	n/a	14.5	Forestbrook (CDP) Horry County
122	n/a	14.5	York (city) York County
124	4411	14.7	Bluffton (town) Beaufort County
124	4411	14.7	Socastee (CDP) Horry County
126	n/a	14.8	Burton (CDP) Beaufort County
127	n/a	15.2	Pickens (city) Pickens County
128	n/a	15.5	Dunean (CDP) Greenville County
128	4455	15.5	Gantt (CDP) Greenville County
128	n/a	15.5	Murrells Inlet (CDP) Georgetown County
131	n/a	15.9	Ridgeland (town) Jasper County
132	4489	16.0	Berea (CDP) Greenville County
132	n/a	16.0	Winnsboro (town) Fairfield County
134	4500	16.2	West Columbia (city) Lexington County
135	n/a	16.5	Springdale (CDP) Lancaster County
136	n/a	16.7	Arial (CDP) Pickens County
137	n/a	17.1	Sans Souci (CDP) Greenville County
138	n/a	17.3	Saxon (CDP) Spartanburg County
139	n/a	18.3	Lake Wylie (CDP) York County
140	4587	18.9	Red Hill (CDP) Horry County
141	n/a	20.3	Pendleton (town) Anderson County
142	n/a	20.6	Lake Murray of Richland (CDP) Richland County
143	n/a	20.9	Little River (CDP) Horry County
144	4632	23.1	Myrtle Beach (city) Horry County
145	n/a	42.6	Folly Beach (city) Charleston County
146	n/a	50.6	Garden City (CDP) Horry County
147	4652	55.1	Hilton Head Island (town) Beaufort County
148	n/a	55.5	Surfside Beach (town) Horry County
149	4653	57.4	North Myrtle Beach (city) Horry County
150	n/a	75.7	Isle of Palms (city) Charleston County

Note: The state column ranks the top/bottom 150 places in the state with population of 2,500 or more. The national column ranks the top/bottom places in the country with population of 10,000 or more. Places that are unincorporated were not considered in the rankings. n/a indicates data not available. Please refer to the User Guide for additional information.

Population with Health Insurance

Top 150 Places Ranked in *Descending* Order

State Rank	Nat'l Rank	Percent	Place
1	n/a	96.5	**Dalzell** (CDP) Sumter County
2	361	96.0	**Five Forks** (CDP) Greenville County
3	n/a	95.9	**Lake Murray of Richland** (CDP) Richland County
4	779	94.3	**Clemson** (city) Pickens County
5	n/a	93.2	**Tega Cay** (city) York County
6	n/a	92.8	**Isle of Palms** (city) Charleston County
7	n/a	91.8	**India Hook** (CDP) York County
8	1478	91.7	**Lexington** (town) Lexington County
9	1525	91.5	**Lakewood** (CDP) Sumter County
9	1525	91.5	**Mount Pleasant** (town) Charleston County
11	1552	91.4	**Forest Acres** (city) Richland County
12	1703	90.8	**Port Royal** (town) Beaufort County
13	n/a	90.7	**Edgefield** (town) Edgefield County
14	n/a	90.4	**Lake Wylie** (CDP) York County
15	1847	90.2	**Fort Mill** (town) York County
16	1876	90.1	**Aiken** (city) Aiken County
17	n/a	89.7	**Newport** (CDP) York County
18	n/a	89.5	**Elgin** (CDP) Lancaster County
18	n/a	89.5	**Northlake** (CDP) Anderson County
20	n/a	88.9	**Arial** (CDP) Pickens County
21	2194	88.8	**North Augusta** (city) Aiken County
22	n/a	88.1	**Barnwell** (city) Barnwell County
23	n/a	87.9	**Central** (town) Pickens County
24	2456	87.7	**Goose Creek** (city) Berkeley County
25	n/a	87.5	**Springdale** (town) Lexington County
26	2527	87.4	**Charleston** (city) Charleston County
26	2527	87.4	**Florence** (city) Florence County
28	2574	87.2	**Seven Oaks** (CDP) Lexington County
29	n/a	87.1	**Williston** (town) Barnwell County
30	n/a	87.0	**Camden** (city) Kershaw County
31	n/a	86.9	**Abbeville** (city) Abbeville County
31	n/a	86.9	**Walterboro** (city) Colleton County
33	n/a	86.7	**Batesburg-Leesville** (town) Lexington County
33	2685	86.7	**Columbia** (city) Richland County
33	n/a	86.7	**McCormick** (town) McCormick County
36	n/a	86.4	**Duncan** (town) Spartanburg County
37	n/a	86.2	**Liberty** (city) Pickens County
38	n/a	86.1	**Clover** (town) York County
39	n/a	85.9	**Laurel Bay** (CDP) Beaufort County
40	n/a	85.8	**Fountain Inn** (city) Greenville County
40	n/a	85.8	**Lake City** (city) Florence County
42	n/a	85.7	**Centerville** (CDP) Anderson County
43	2944	85.6	**Mauldin** (city) Greenville County
43	n/a	85.6	**North Hartsville** (CDP) Darlington County
43	2944	85.6	**Sumter** (city) Sumter County
46	2994	85.4	**Easley** (city) Pickens County
47	n/a	85.3	**Bennettsville** (city) Marlboro County
47	n/a	85.3	**Dillon** (city) Dillon County
49	3033	85.2	**Summerville** (town) Dorchester County
50	n/a	85.0	**Williamston** (town) Anderson County
51	3128	84.6	**Beaufort** (city) Beaufort County
51	n/a	84.6	**Union** (city) Union County
53	3167	84.4	**Oak Grove** (CDP) Lexington County
54	n/a	84.3	**Bishopville** (city) Lee County
54	3185	84.3	**Gaffney** (city) Cherokee County
56	n/a	84.2	**Bamberg** (town) Bamberg County
56	n/a	84.2	**Cheraw** (town) Chesterfield County
58	3228	84.1	**Rock Hill** (city) York County
59	n/a	83.8	**Lugoff** (CDP) Kershaw County
60	n/a	83.6	**Hollywood** (town) Charleston County
60	n/a	83.6	**Honea Path** (town) Anderson County
62	n/a	83.5	**Hartsville** (city) Darlington County
63	3371	83.4	**Conway** (city) Horry County
64	3392	83.3	**Greenville** (city) Greenville County
64	3392	83.3	**Newberry** (city) Newberry County
64	3392	83.3	**Simpsonville** (city) Greenville County
64	3392	83.3	**Spartanburg** (city) Spartanburg County
64	n/a	83.3	**Travelers Rest** (city) Greenville County
69	n/a	83.2	**Red Bank** (CDP) Lexington County
70	n/a	83.1	**Belvedere** (CDP) Aiken County
71	n/a	83.0	**Boiling Springs** (CDP) Spartanburg County
72	n/a	82.8	**Piedmont** (CDP) Anderson County
73	n/a	82.7	**Chester** (city) Chester County
73	3498	82.7	**Irmo** (town) Richland County
73	n/a	82.7	**Pendleton** (town) Anderson County
76	3520	82.6	**Cayce** (city) Lexington County
76	3520	82.6	**Hilton Head Island** (town) Beaufort County
78	n/a	82.4	**Seneca** (city) Oconee County
78	n/a	82.4	**Surfside Beach** (town) Horry County
80	n/a	82.3	**York** (city) York County
81	3600	82.2	**Greer** (city) Greenville County
82	3624	82.0	**Anderson** (city) Anderson County
82	n/a	82.0	**Valley Falls** (CDP) Spartanburg County
84	n/a	81.9	**Clinton** (city) Laurens County
85	n/a	81.7	**Little River** (CDP) Horry County
86	n/a	81.5	**Winnsboro** (town) Fairfield County
87	n/a	81.4	**Marion** (city) Marion County
88	3735	81.3	**Taylors** (CDP) Greenville County
89	3753	81.2	**Wade Hampton** (CDP) Greenville County
90	n/a	80.9	**Garden City** (CDP) Horry County
90	n/a	80.9	**Sangaree** (CDP) Berkeley County
92	n/a	80.8	**Burnettown** (town) Aiken County
93	n/a	80.6	**Folly Beach** (city) Charleston County
94	n/a	80.5	**Darlington** (city) Darlington County
94	n/a	80.5	**Laurens** (city) Laurens County
94	n/a	80.5	**Pickens** (city) Pickens County
97	3866	80.4	**North Myrtle Beach** (city) Horry County
98	3904	80.2	**Greenwood** (city) Greenwood County
99	n/a	79.7	**Forestbrook** (CDP) Horry County
99	n/a	79.7	**Georgetown** (city) Georgetown County
99	3960	79.7	**Saint Andrews** (CDP) Richland County
102	3978	79.6	**Ladson** (CDP) Berkeley County
102	n/a	79.6	**Manning** (city) Clarendon County
104	n/a	79.4	**Hopkins** (CDP) Richland County
104	n/a	79.4	**Walhalla** (city) Oconee County
106	n/a	79.2	**Denmark** (city) Bamberg County
107	n/a	79.1	**Mullins** (city) Marion County
108	4033	79.0	**Dentsville** (CDP) Richland County
108	n/a	79.0	**Graniteville** (CDP) Aiken County
108	n/a	79.0	**Ridgeland** (town) Jasper County
111	4058	78.8	**Berea** (CDP) Greenville County
111	4058	78.8	**Orangeburg** (city) Orangeburg County
113	4067	78.7	**Gantt** (CDP) Greenville County
114	n/a	78.6	**Hampton** (town) Hampton County
115	n/a	78.4	**Homeland Park** (CDP) Anderson County
116	n/a	78.3	**Lyman** (town) Spartanburg County
117	4119	78.2	**West Columbia** (city) Lexington County
118	n/a	78.0	**Gloverville** (CDP) Aiken County
118	n/a	78.0	**Woodfield** (CDP) Richland County
120	n/a	77.8	**Burton** (CDP) Beaufort County
121	4217	76.9	**North Charleston** (city) Charleston County
122	4221	76.8	**Red Hill** (CDP) Horry County
123	4277	76.1	**Hanahan** (city) Berkeley County
124	n/a	76.0	**Edisto** (CDP) Orangeburg County
125	n/a	75.5	**Kingstree** (town) Williamsburg County
125	n/a	75.5	**Lancaster** (city) Lancaster County
127	n/a	75.3	**Belton** (city) Anderson County
128	n/a	75.2	**Woodruff** (city) Spartanburg County
129	4340	75.0	**Bluffton** (town) Beaufort County
130	n/a	74.3	**Moncks Corner** (town) Berkeley County
131	n/a	74.0	**Brookdale** (CDP) Orangeburg County
132	4409	73.7	**Socastee** (CDP) Horry County
133	n/a	73.3	**Lesslie** (CDP) York County
134	n/a	73.1	**Springdale** (CDP) Lancaster County
135	n/a	72.6	**Andrews** (town) Georgetown County
135	n/a	72.6	**Dunean** (CDP) Greenville County
137	n/a	72.4	**East Gaffney** (CDP) Cherokee County
138	n/a	71.9	**Allendale** (town) Allendale County
139	n/a	71.7	**Murrells Inlet** (CDP) Georgetown County
140	n/a	70.2	**Saluda** (town) Saluda County
140	n/a	70.2	**Welcome** (CDP) Greenville County
142	n/a	69.4	**Saxon** (CDP) Spartanburg County
143	n/a	69.3	**Pageland** (town) Chesterfield County
144	n/a	68.6	**Hardeeville** (city) Jasper County
145	4560	68.2	**Parker** (CDP) Greenville County
146	n/a	67.6	**Clearwater** (CDP) Aiken County
147	n/a	66.7	**Arcadia** (CDP) Spartanburg County
148	n/a	66.5	**Sans Souci** (CDP) Greenville County
149	4582	66.2	**Myrtle Beach** (city) Horry County
150	n/a	57.3	**Southern Shops** (CDP) Spartanburg County

Note: The state column ranks the top/bottom 150 places in the state with population of 2,500 or more. The national column ranks the top/bottom places in the country with population of 10,000 or more. Places that are unincorporated were not considered in the rankings. n/a indicates data not available. Please refer to the User Guide for additional information.

Population with Health Insurance

Top 150 Places Ranked in *Ascending* Order

State Rank	Nat'l Rank	Percent	Place
1	n/a	57.3	Southern Shops (CDP) Spartanburg County
2	72	66.2	Myrtle Beach (city) Horry County
3	n/a	66.5	Sans Souci (CDP) Greenville County
4	n/a	66.7	Arcadia (CDP) Spartanburg County
5	n/a	67.6	Clearwater (CDP) Aiken County
6	94	68.2	Parker (CDP) Greenville County
7	n/a	68.6	Hardeeville (city) Jasper County
8	n/a	69.3	Pageland (town) Chesterfield County
9	n/a	69.4	Saxon (CDP) Spartanburg County
10	n/a	70.2	Saluda (town) Saluda County
10	n/a	70.2	Welcome (CDP) Greenville County
12	n/a	71.7	Murrells Inlet (CDP) Georgetown County
13	n/a	71.9	Allendale (town) Allendale County
14	n/a	72.4	East Gaffney (CDP) Cherokee County
15	n/a	72.6	Andrews (town) Georgetown County
15	n/a	72.6	Dunean (CDP) Greenville County
17	n/a	73.1	Springdale (CDP) Lancaster County
18	n/a	73.3	Lesslie (CDP) York County
19	243	73.7	Socastee (CDP) Horry County
20	n/a	74.0	Brookdale (CDP) Orangeburg County
21	n/a	74.3	Moncks Corner (town) Berkeley County
22	306	75.0	Bluffton (town) Beaufort County
23	n/a	75.2	Woodruff (city) Spartanburg County
24	n/a	75.3	Belton (city) Anderson County
25	n/a	75.5	Kingstree (town) Williamsburg County
25	n/a	75.5	Lancaster (city) Lancaster County
27	n/a	76.0	Edisto (CDP) Orangeburg County
28	373	76.1	Hanahan (city) Berkeley County
29	430	76.8	Red Hill (CDP) Horry County
30	436	76.9	North Charleston (city) Charleston County
31	n/a	77.8	Burton (CDP) Beaufort County
32	n/a	78.0	Gloverville (CDP) Aiken County
32	n/a	78.0	Woodfield (CDP) Richland County
34	525	78.2	West Columbia (city) Lexington County
35	n/a	78.3	Lyman (town) Spartanburg County
36	n/a	78.4	Homeland Park (CDP) Anderson County
37	n/a	78.6	Hampton (town) Hampton County
38	577	78.7	Gantt (CDP) Greenville County
39	590	78.8	Berea (CDP) Greenville County
39	590	78.8	Orangeburg (city) Orangeburg County
41	615	79.0	Dentsville (CDP) Richland County
41	n/a	79.0	Graniteville (CDP) Aiken County
41	n/a	79.0	Ridgeland (town) Jasper County
44	n/a	79.1	Mullins (city) Marion County
45	n/a	79.2	Denmark (city) Bamberg County
46	n/a	79.4	Hopkins (CDP) Richland County
46	n/a	79.4	Walhalla (city) Oconee County
48	673	79.6	Ladson (CDP) Berkeley County
48	n/a	79.6	Manning (city) Clarendon County
50	n/a	79.7	Forestbrook (CDP) Horry County
50	n/a	79.7	Georgetown (city) Georgetown County
50	679	79.7	Saint Andrews (CDP) Richland County
53	739	80.2	Greenwood (city) Greenwood County
54	774	80.4	North Myrtle Beach (city) Horry County
55	n/a	80.5	Darlington (city) Darlington County
55	n/a	80.5	Laurens (city) Laurens County
55	n/a	80.5	Pickens (city) Pickens County
58	n/a	80.6	Folly Beach (city) Charleston County
59	n/a	80.8	Burnettown (town) Aiken County
60	n/a	80.9	Garden City (CDP) Horry County
60	n/a	80.9	Sangaree (CDP) Berkeley County
62	884	81.2	Wade Hampton (CDP) Greenville County
63	904	81.3	Taylors (CDP) Greenville County
64	n/a	81.4	Marion (city) Marion County
65	n/a	81.5	Winnsboro (town) Fairfield County
66	n/a	81.7	Little River (CDP) Horry County
67	n/a	81.9	Clinton (city) Laurens County
68	1020	82.0	Anderson (city) Anderson County
68	n/a	82.0	Valley Falls (CDP) Spartanburg County
70	1039	82.2	Greer (city) Greenville County
71	n/a	82.3	York (city) York County
72	n/a	82.4	Seneca (city) Oconee County
72	n/a	82.4	Surfside Beach (town) Horry County
74	1115	82.6	Cayce (city) Lexington County
74	1115	82.6	Hilton Head Island (town) Beaufort County
76	n/a	82.7	Chester (city) Chester County
76	1137	82.7	Irmo (town) Richland County
76	n/a	82.7	Pendleton (town) Anderson County
79	n/a	82.8	Piedmont (CDP) Anderson County
80	n/a	83.0	Boiling Springs (CDP) Spartanburg County
81	n/a	83.1	Belvedere (CDP) Aiken County
82	n/a	83.2	Red Bank (CDP) Lexington County
83	1242	83.3	Greenville (city) Greenville County
83	1242	83.3	Newberry (city) Newberry County
83	1242	83.3	Simpsonville (city) Greenville County
83	1242	83.3	Spartanburg (city) Spartanburg County
83	n/a	83.3	Travelers Rest (city) Greenville County
88	1265	83.4	Conway (city) Horry County
89	n/a	83.5	Hartsville (city) Darlington County
90	n/a	83.6	Hollywood (town) Charleston County
90	n/a	83.6	Honea Path (town) Anderson County
92	n/a	83.8	Lugoff (CDP) Kershaw County
93	1412	84.1	Rock Hill (city) York County
94	n/a	84.2	Bamberg (town) Bamberg County
94	n/a	84.2	Cheraw (town) Chesterfield County
96	n/a	84.3	Bishopville (city) Lee County
96	1452	84.3	Gaffney (city) Cherokee County
98	1472	84.4	Oak Grove (CDP) Lexington County
99	1511	84.6	Beaufort (city) Beaufort County
99	n/a	84.6	Union (city) Union County
101	n/a	85.0	Williamston (town) Anderson County
102	1603	85.2	Summerville (town) Dorchester County
103	n/a	85.3	Bennettsville (city) Marlboro County
103	n/a	85.3	Dillon (city) Dillon County
105	1643	85.4	Easley (city) Pickens County
106	1683	85.6	Mauldin (city) Greenville County
106	n/a	85.6	North Hartsville (CDP) Darlington County
106	1683	85.6	Sumter (city) Sumter County
109	n/a	85.7	Centerville (CDP) Anderson County
110	n/a	85.8	Fountain Inn (city) Greenville County
110	n/a	85.8	Lake City (city) Florence County
112	n/a	85.9	Laurel Bay (CDP) Beaufort County
113	n/a	86.1	Clover (town) York County
114	n/a	86.2	Liberty (city) Pickens County
115	n/a	86.4	Duncan (town) Spartanburg County
116	n/a	86.7	Batesburg-Leesville (town) Lexington County
116	1942	86.7	Columbia (city) Richland County
116	n/a	86.7	McCormick (town) McCormick County
119	n/a	86.9	Abbeville (city) Abbeville County
119	n/a	86.9	Walterboro (city) Colleton County
121	n/a	87.0	Camden (city) Kershaw County
122	n/a	87.1	Williston (town) Barnwell County
123	2063	87.2	Seven Oaks (CDP) Lexington County
124	2111	87.4	Charleston (city) Charleston County
124	2111	87.4	Florence (city) Florence County
126	n/a	87.5	Springdale (town) Lexington County
127	2175	87.7	Goose Creek (city) Berkeley County
128	n/a	87.9	Central (town) Pickens County
129	n/a	88.1	Barnwell (city) Barnwell County
130	2434	88.8	North Augusta (city) Aiken County
131	n/a	88.9	Arial (CDP) Pickens County
132	n/a	89.5	Elgin (CDP) Lancaster County
132	n/a	89.5	Northlake (CDP) Anderson County
134	n/a	89.7	Newport (CDP) York County
135	2759	90.1	Aiken (city) Aiken County
136	2781	90.2	Fort Mill (town) York County
137	n/a	90.4	Lake Wylie (CDP) York County
138	n/a	90.7	Edgefield (town) Edgefield County
139	2929	90.8	Port Royal (town) Beaufort County
140	3078	91.4	Forest Acres (city) Richland County
141	n/a	91.5	Lakewood (CDP) Sumter County
141	3105	91.5	Mount Pleasant (town) Charleston County
143	3158	91.7	Lexington (town) Lexington County
144	n/a	91.8	India Hook (CDP) York County
145	n/a	92.8	Isle of Palms (city) Charleston County
146	n/a	93.2	Tega Cay (city) York County
147	3856	94.3	Clemson (city) Pickens County
148	n/a	95.9	Lake Murray of Richland (CDP) Richland County
149	4270	96.0	Five Forks (CDP) Greenville County
150	n/a	96.5	Dalzell (CDP) Sumter County

Note: The state column ranks the top/bottom 150 places in the state with population of 2,500 or more. The national column ranks the top/bottom places in the country with population of 10,000 or more. Places that are unincorporated were not considered in the rankings. n/a indicates data not available. Please refer to the User Guide for additional information.

Population with Private Health Insurance

Top 150 Places Ranked in *Descending* Order

State Rank	Nat'l Rank	Percent	Place
1	69	92.7	**Five Forks** (CDP) Greenville County
2	n/a	89.6	**Tega Cay** (city) York County
3	n/a	88.8	**Lake Murray of Richland** (CDP) Richland County
4	475	87.7	**Clemson** (city) Pickens County
5	764	85.4	**Mount Pleasant** (town) Charleston County
6	n/a	84.7	**India Hook** (CDP) York County
6	n/a	84.7	**Isle of Palms** (city) Charleston County
8	n/a	82.6	**Lake Wylie** (CDP) York County
9	n/a	81.6	**Central** (town) Pickens County
10	1321	80.9	**Lexington** (town) Lexington County
10	n/a	80.9	**Newport** (CDP) York County
12	1514	79.5	**Forest Acres** (city) Richland County
12	n/a	79.5	**Springdale** (town) Lexington County
14	n/a	79.4	**Laurel Bay** (CDP) Beaufort County
15	n/a	77.8	**Northlake** (CDP) Anderson County
16	1736	77.5	**Fort Mill** (town) York County
17	1912	76.0	**Goose Creek** (city) Berkeley County
18	n/a	75.7	**Folly Beach** (city) Charleston County
19	n/a	74.8	**Boiling Springs** (CDP) Spartanburg County
20	2068	74.6	**North Augusta** (city) Aiken County
20	2068	74.6	**Port Royal** (town) Beaufort County
22	2162	73.8	**Charleston** (city) Charleston County
23	2172	73.7	**Seven Oaks** (CDP) Lexington County
24	2217	73.2	**Mauldin** (city) Greenville County
25	n/a	72.4	**Lugoff** (CDP) Kershaw County
26	2319	72.1	**Summerville** (town) Dorchester County
27	2384	71.5	**Aiken** (city) Aiken County
27	n/a	71.5	**Surfside Beach** (town) Horry County
29	2483	70.5	**Oak Grove** (CDP) Lexington County
30	n/a	70.4	**Centerville** (CDP) Anderson County
31	n/a	70.0	**Dalzell** (CDP) Sumter County
32	2578	69.7	**Simpsonville** (city) Greenville County
33	n/a	68.9	**Camden** (city) Kershaw County
33	2650	68.9	**Hilton Head Island** (town) Beaufort County
35	2662	68.8	**Columbia** (city) Richland County
36	n/a	68.6	**Forestbrook** (CDP) Horry County
36	n/a	68.6	**Red Bank** (CDP) Lexington County
38	2726	68.2	**Irmo** (town) Richland County
39	n/a	67.7	**Fountain Inn** (city) Greenville County
40	n/a	67.5	**Little River** (CDP) Horry County
41	2817	67.2	**North Myrtle Beach** (city) Horry County
41	n/a	67.2	**Valley Falls** (CDP) Spartanburg County
43	n/a	67.1	**Garden City** (CDP) Horry County
44	n/a	66.8	**Lakewood** (CDP) Sumter County
45	n/a	66.4	**Williamston** (town) Anderson County
46	2921	66.2	**Rock Hill** (city) York County
47	2941	65.9	**Beaufort** (city) Beaufort County
48	2949	65.8	**Cayce** (city) Lexington County
48	n/a	65.8	**Clover** (town) York County
50	n/a	65.6	**Hampton** (town) Hampton County
51	2985	65.4	**Wade Hampton** (CDP) Greenville County
52	n/a	65.2	**Hollywood** (town) Charleston County
53	n/a	64.6	**Duncan** (town) Spartanburg County
54	n/a	64.5	**Lyman** (town) Spartanburg County
55	3086	64.4	**Easley** (city) Pickens County
56	3113	64.1	**Ladson** (CDP) Berkeley County
57	n/a	63.9	**Seneca** (city) Oconee County
58	n/a	63.7	**Pendleton** (town) Anderson County
59	n/a	63.6	**Travelers Rest** (city) Greenville County
60	3169	63.5	**Greenville** (city) Greenville County
61	n/a	63.4	**Sangaree** (CDP) Berkeley County
62	3216	63.1	**Greer** (city) Greenville County
63	n/a	62.5	**Bamberg** (town) Bamberg County
64	3279	62.4	**Hanahan** (city) Berkeley County
65	3312	62.1	**Bluffton** (town) Beaufort County
65	3312	62.1	**Florence** (city) Florence County
67	3378	61.2	**Taylors** (CDP) Greenville County
68	3386	61.1	**West Columbia** (city) Lexington County
69	n/a	60.5	**Burton** (CDP) Beaufort County
69	n/a	60.5	**Laurens** (city) Laurens County
71	3458	60.1	**Conway** (city) Horry County
72	n/a	59.6	**Elgin** (CDP) Lancaster County
72	3505	59.6	**Sumter** (city) Sumter County
74	n/a	58.9	**Murrells Inlet** (CDP) Georgetown County
75	n/a	58.5	**Liberty** (city) Pickens County
76	3616	58.1	**Red Hill** (CDP) Horry County
77	n/a	58.0	**Batesburg-Leesville** (town) Lexington County
78	3637	57.9	**Dentsville** (CDP) Richland County
79	n/a	57.7	**Woodfield** (CDP) Richland County
80	n/a	57.2	**Lesslie** (CDP) York County
80	3704	57.2	**Spartanburg** (city) Spartanburg County
82	n/a	57.1	**Edgefield** (town) Edgefield County
83	n/a	56.5	**Piedmont** (CDP) Anderson County
83	n/a	56.5	**Union** (city) Union County
85	n/a	56.4	**Hartsville** (city) Darlington County
86	n/a	56.2	**Moncks Corner** (town) Berkeley County
87	n/a	56.1	**Belvedere** (CDP) Aiken County
87	3794	56.1	**Gaffney** (city) Cherokee County
89	n/a	55.8	**North Hartsville** (CDP) Darlington County
90	n/a	55.2	**McCormick** (town) McCormick County
91	n/a	54.8	**Burnettown** (town) Aiken County
92	n/a	54.6	**Winnsboro** (town) Fairfield County
93	3934	54.3	**Orangeburg** (city) Orangeburg County
94	n/a	54.1	**Honea Path** (town) Anderson County
95	3956	53.9	**North Charleston** (city) Charleston County
95	3956	53.9	**Saint Andrews** (CDP) Richland County
97	3963	53.8	**Anderson** (city) Anderson County
98	3989	53.3	**Socastee** (CDP) Horry County
99	n/a	52.8	**Abbeville** (city) Abbeville County
100	n/a	52.2	**Ridgeland** (town) Jasper County
101	n/a	51.1	**Barnwell** (city) Barnwell County
102	n/a	50.9	**Clinton** (city) Laurens County
102	n/a	50.9	**Darlington** (city) Darlington County
104	4122	50.7	**Newberry** (city) Newberry County
105	n/a	50.5	**Georgetown** (city) Georgetown County
106	n/a	50.3	**Belton** (city) Anderson County
107	n/a	49.1	**Williston** (town) Barnwell County
108	n/a	48.5	**Arial** (CDP) Pickens County
109	n/a	48.0	**Lake City** (city) Florence County
110	n/a	47.5	**Walterboro** (city) Colleton County
111	4281	47.3	**Berea** (CDP) Greenville County
112	4295	46.9	**Greenwood** (city) Greenwood County
113	n/a	46.7	**Hopkins** (CDP) Richland County
114	4309	46.6	**Myrtle Beach** (city) Horry County
115	n/a	46.4	**Pickens** (city) Pickens County
116	n/a	46.3	**Hardeeville** (city) Jasper County
117	n/a	46.0	**Dunean** (CDP) Greenville County
117	n/a	46.0	**Graniteville** (CDP) Aiken County
117	n/a	46.0	**York** (city) York County
120	n/a	45.7	**Brookdale** (CDP) Orangeburg County
121	n/a	45.3	**Manning** (city) Clarendon County
122	n/a	44.8	**Chester** (city) Chester County
123	n/a	43.7	**Dillon** (city) Dillon County
124	n/a	43.6	**Kingstree** (town) Williamsburg County
125	n/a	43.4	**Bennettsville** (city) Marlboro County
126	n/a	42.9	**Cheraw** (town) Chesterfield County
127	n/a	42.8	**Sans Souci** (CDP) Greenville County
128	4438	42.7	**Gantt** (CDP) Greenville County
129	n/a	42.2	**Lancaster** (city) Lancaster County
130	n/a	42.1	**Pageland** (town) Chesterfield County
131	n/a	41.4	**Edisto** (CDP) Orangeburg County
132	n/a	40.9	**Clearwater** (CDP) Aiken County
132	n/a	40.9	**Springdale** (CDP) Lancaster County
134	n/a	40.8	**Allendale** (town) Allendale County
135	n/a	40.4	**Welcome** (CDP) Greenville County
136	n/a	40.3	**Homeland Park** (CDP) Anderson County
136	n/a	40.3	**Mullins** (city) Marion County
138	n/a	39.8	**Saluda** (town) Saluda County
139	n/a	39.0	**East Gaffney** (CDP) Cherokee County
140	n/a	37.8	**Denmark** (city) Bamberg County
141	n/a	36.9	**Gloverville** (CDP) Aiken County
142	n/a	36.4	**Andrews** (town) Georgetown County
143	n/a	35.6	**Bishopville** (city) Lee County
144	n/a	35.2	**Marion** (city) Marion County
144	n/a	35.2	**Saxon** (CDP) Spartanburg County
146	4565	34.7	**Parker** (CDP) Greenville County
147	n/a	34.1	**Walhalla** (city) Oconee County
148	n/a	31.3	**Woodruff** (city) Spartanburg County
149	n/a	30.4	**Arcadia** (CDP) Spartanburg County
150	n/a	19.6	**Southern Shops** (CDP) Spartanburg County

Note: The state column ranks the top/bottom 150 places in the state with population of 2,500 or more. The national column ranks the top/bottom places in the country with population of 10,000 or more. Places that are unincorporated were not considered in the rankings. n/a indicates data not available. Please refer to the User Guide for additional information.

Population with Private Health Insurance

Top 150 Places Ranked in *Ascending* Order

State Rank	Nat'l Rank	Percent	Place
1	n/a	19.6	Southern Shops (CDP) Spartanburg County
2	n/a	30.4	Arcadia (CDP) Spartanburg County
3	n/a	31.3	Woodruff (city) Spartanburg County
4	n/a	34.1	Walhalla (city) Oconee County
5	89	34.7	Parker (CDP) Greenville County
6	n/a	35.2	Marion (city) Marion County
6	n/a	35.2	Saxon (CDP) Spartanburg County
8	n/a	35.6	Bishopville (city) Lee County
9	n/a	36.4	Andrews (town) Georgetown County
10	n/a	36.9	Gloverville (CDP) Aiken County
11	n/a	37.8	Denmark (city) Bamberg County
12	n/a	39.0	East Gaffney (CDP) Cherokee County
13	n/a	39.8	Saluda (town) Saluda County
14	n/a	40.3	Homeland Park (CDP) Anderson County
14	n/a	40.3	Mullins (city) Marion County
16	n/a	40.4	Welcome (CDP) Greenville County
17	n/a	40.8	Allendale (town) Allendale County
18	n/a	40.9	Clearwater (CDP) Aiken County
18	n/a	40.9	Springdale (CDP) Lancaster County
20	n/a	41.4	Edisto (CDP) Orangeburg County
21	n/a	42.1	Pageland (town) Chesterfield County
22	n/a	42.2	Lancaster (city) Lancaster County
23	216	42.7	Gantt (CDP) Greenville County
24	n/a	42.8	Sans Souci (CDP) Greenville County
25	n/a	42.9	Cheraw (town) Chesterfield County
26	n/a	43.4	Bennettsville (city) Marlboro County
27	n/a	43.6	Kingstree (town) Williamsburg County
28	n/a	43.7	Dillon (city) Dillon County
29	n/a	44.8	Chester (city) Chester County
30	n/a	45.3	Manning (city) Clarendon County
31	n/a	45.7	Brookdale (CDP) Orangeburg County
32	n/a	46.0	Dunean (CDP) Greenville County
32	n/a	46.0	Graniteville (CDP) Aiken County
32	n/a	46.0	York (city) York County
35	n/a	46.3	Hardeeville (city) Jasper County
36	n/a	46.4	Pickens (city) Pickens County
37	342	46.6	Myrtle Beach (city) Horry County
38	n/a	46.7	Hopkins (CDP) Richland County
39	356	46.9	Greenwood (city) Greenwood County
40	372	47.3	Berea (CDP) Greenville County
41	n/a	47.5	Walterboro (city) Colleton County
42	n/a	48.0	Lake City (city) Florence County
43	n/a	48.5	Arial (CDP) Pickens County
44	n/a	49.1	Williston (town) Barnwell County
45	n/a	50.3	Belton (city) Anderson County
46	n/a	50.5	Georgetown (city) Georgetown County
47	529	50.7	Newberry (city) Newberry County
48	n/a	50.9	Clinton (city) Laurens County
48	n/a	50.9	Darlington (city) Darlington County
50	n/a	51.1	Barnwell (city) Barnwell County
51	n/a	52.2	Ridgeland (town) Jasper County
52	n/a	52.8	Abbeville (city) Abbeville County
53	660	53.3	Socastee (CDP) Horry County
54	683	53.8	Anderson (city) Anderson County
55	694	53.9	North Charleston (city) Charleston County
55	694	53.9	Saint Andrews (CDP) Richland County
57	n/a	54.1	Honea Path (town) Anderson County
58	717	54.3	Orangeburg (city) Orangeburg County
59	n/a	54.6	Winnsboro (town) Fairfield County
60	n/a	54.8	Burnettown (town) Aiken County
61	n/a	55.2	McCormick (town) McCormick County
62	n/a	55.8	North Hartsville (CDP) Darlington County
63	n/a	56.1	Belvedere (CDP) Aiken County
63	852	56.1	Gaffney (city) Cherokee County
65	n/a	56.2	Moncks Corner (town) Berkeley County
66	n/a	56.4	Hartsville (city) Darlington County
67	n/a	56.5	Piedmont (CDP) Anderson County
67	n/a	56.5	Union (city) Union County
69	n/a	57.1	Edgefield (town) Edgefield County
70	n/a	57.2	Lesslie (CDP) York County
70	946	57.2	Spartanburg (city) Spartanburg County
72	n/a	57.7	Woodfield (CDP) Richland County
73	1011	57.9	Dentsville (CDP) Richland County
74	n/a	58.0	Batesburg-Leesville (town) Lexington County
75	1028	58.1	Red Hill (CDP) Horry County
76	n/a	58.5	Liberty (city) Pickens County
77	n/a	58.9	Murrells Inlet (CDP) Georgetown County
78	n/a	59.6	Elgin (CDP) Lancaster County
78	1146	59.6	Sumter (city) Sumter County
80	1186	60.1	Conway (city) Horry County
81	n/a	60.5	Burton (CDP) Beaufort County
81	n/a	60.5	Laurens (city) Laurens County
83	1265	61.1	West Columbia (city) Lexington County
84	1271	61.2	Taylors (CDP) Greenville County
85	1341	62.1	Bluffton (town) Beaufort County
85	1341	62.1	Florence (city) Florence County
87	1366	62.4	Hanahan (city) Berkeley County
88	n/a	62.5	Bamberg (town) Bamberg County
89	1429	63.1	Greer (city) Greenville County
90	n/a	63.4	Sangaree (CDP) Berkeley County
91	1475	63.5	Greenville (city) Greenville County
92	n/a	63.6	Travelers Rest (city) Greenville County
93	n/a	63.7	Pendleton (town) Anderson County
94	n/a	63.9	Seneca (city) Oconee County
95	1537	64.1	Ladson (CDP) Berkeley County
96	1559	64.4	Easley (city) Pickens County
97	n/a	64.5	Lyman (town) Spartanburg County
98	n/a	64.6	Duncan (town) Spartanburg County
99	n/a	65.2	Hollywood (town) Charleston County
100	1661	65.4	Wade Hampton (CDP) Greenville County
101	n/a	65.6	Hampton (town) Hampton County
102	1697	65.8	Cayce (city) Lexington County
102	n/a	65.8	Clover (town) York County
104	1708	65.9	Beaufort (city) Beaufort County
105	1726	66.2	Rock Hill (city) York County
106	n/a	66.4	Williamston (town) Anderson County
107	n/a	66.8	Lakewood (CDP) Sumter County
108	n/a	67.1	Garden City (CDP) Horry County
109	1829	67.2	North Myrtle Beach (city) Horry County
109	n/a	67.2	Valley Falls (CDP) Spartanburg County
111	n/a	67.5	Little River (CDP) Horry County
112	n/a	67.7	Fountain Inn (city) Greenville County
113	1922	68.2	Irmo (town) Richland County
114	n/a	68.6	Forestbrook (CDP) Horry County
114	n/a	68.6	Red Bank (CDP) Lexington County
116	1979	68.8	Columbia (city) Richland County
117	n/a	68.9	Camden (city) Kershaw County
117	1995	68.9	Hilton Head Island (town) Beaufort County
119	2063	69.7	Simpsonville (city) Greenville County
120	n/a	70.0	Dalzell (CDP) Sumter County
121	n/a	70.4	Centerville (CDP) Anderson County
122	2163	70.5	Oak Grove (CDP) Lexington County
123	2263	71.5	Aiken (city) Aiken County
123	n/a	71.5	Surfside Beach (town) Horry County
125	2328	72.1	Summerville (town) Dorchester County
126	n/a	72.4	Lugoff (CDP) Kershaw County
127	2430	73.2	Mauldin (city) Greenville County
128	2473	73.7	Seven Oaks (CDP) Lexington County
129	2485	73.8	Charleston (city) Charleston County
130	2568	74.6	North Augusta (city) Aiken County
130	2568	74.6	Port Royal (town) Beaufort County
132	n/a	74.8	Boiling Springs (CDP) Spartanburg County
133	n/a	75.7	Folly Beach (city) Charleston County
134	2736	76.0	Goose Creek (city) Berkeley County
135	2912	77.5	Fort Mill (town) York County
136	n/a	77.8	Northlake (CDP) Anderson County
137	n/a	79.4	Laurel Bay (CDP) Beaufort County
138	3124	79.5	Forest Acres (city) Richland County
138	n/a	79.5	Springdale (town) Lexington County
140	3323	80.9	Lexington (town) Lexington County
140	n/a	80.9	Newport (CDP) York County
142	n/a	81.6	Central (town) Pickens County
143	n/a	82.6	Lake Wylie (CDP) York County
144	n/a	84.7	India Hook (CDP) York County
144	n/a	84.7	Isle of Palms (city) Charleston County
146	3878	85.4	Mount Pleasant (town) Charleston County
147	4164	87.7	Clemson (city) Pickens County
148	n/a	88.8	Lake Murray of Richland (CDP) Richland County
149	n/a	89.6	Tega Cay (city) York County
150	4585	92.7	Five Forks (CDP) Greenville County

Note: The state column ranks the top/bottom 150 places in the state with population of 2,500 or more. The national column ranks the top/bottom places in the country with population of 10,000 or more. Places that are unincorporated were not considered in the rankings. n/a indicates data not available. Please refer to the User Guide for additional information.

Population with Public Health Insurance

Top 150 Places Ranked in *Descending* Order

State Rank	Nat'l Rank	Percent	Place
1	n/a	58.0	**Walhalla** (city) Oconee County
2	n/a	57.5	**Cheraw** (town) Chesterfield County
3	n/a	57.2	**Bishopville** (city) Lee County
4	n/a	57.0	**Dillon** (city) Dillon County
5	n/a	55.2	**Marion** (city) Marion County
6	n/a	54.6	**Bennettsville** (city) Marlboro County
7	n/a	51.9	**Chester** (city) Chester County
8	n/a	51.1	**Arial** (CDP) Pickens County
8	n/a	51.1	**Barnwell** (city) Barnwell County
8	n/a	51.1	**Walterboro** (city) Colleton County
11	n/a	50.9	**Williston** (town) Barnwell County
12	n/a	50.8	**Woodruff** (city) Spartanburg County
13	n/a	50.7	**Mullins** (city) Marion County
14	n/a	50.5	**Homeland Park** (CDP) Anderson County
15	n/a	49.0	**Abbeville** (city) Abbeville County
16	n/a	48.3	**Gloverville** (CDP) Aiken County
17	n/a	48.0	**Denmark** (city) Bamberg County
18	n/a	47.9	**Andrews** (town) Georgetown County
18	n/a	47.9	**Hopkins** (CDP) Richland County
18	n/a	47.9	**McCormick** (town) McCormick County
21	n/a	47.6	**Batesburg-Leesville** (town) Lexington County
22	n/a	47.5	**York** (city) York County
23	n/a	47.2	**Honea Path** (town) Anderson County
23	n/a	47.2	**Lake City** (city) Florence County
25	n/a	47.1	**Manning** (city) Clarendon County
26	n/a	46.9	**Pickens** (city) Pickens County
27	n/a	45.7	**Edisto** (CDP) Orangeburg County
28	260	45.3	**Gantt** (CDP) Greenville County
28	n/a	45.3	**Kingstree** (town) Williamsburg County
30	n/a	44.6	**Garden City** (CDP) Horry County
30	n/a	44.6	**Lancaster** (city) Lancaster County
32	n/a	44.1	**Edgefield** (town) Edgefield County
33	348	43.8	**Berea** (CDP) Greenville County
34	n/a	43.4	**East Gaffney** (CDP) Cherokee County
35	380	43.3	**Greenwood** (city) Greenwood County
36	n/a	43.0	**Georgetown** (city) Georgetown County
37	n/a	42.9	**Graniteville** (CDP) Aiken County
37	n/a	42.9	**Union** (city) Union County
39	414	42.8	**Newberry** (city) Newberry County
40	n/a	42.7	**Brookdale** (CDP) Orangeburg County
41	n/a	42.5	**Elgin** (CDP) Lancaster County
42	433	42.4	**Gaffney** (city) Cherokee County
43	n/a	42.2	**Welcome** (CDP) Greenville County
44	457	42.1	**Parker** (CDP) Greenville County
45	n/a	41.9	**Allendale** (town) Allendale County
45	n/a	41.9	**Clinton** (city) Laurens County
47	n/a	41.8	**North Hartsville** (CDP) Darlington County
48	n/a	41.6	**Saxon** (CDP) Spartanburg County
49	n/a	41.4	**Bamberg** (town) Bamberg County
49	n/a	41.4	**Darlington** (city) Darlington County
51	n/a	40.8	**Belvedere** (CDP) Aiken County
52	560	40.7	**Anderson** (city) Anderson County
53	n/a	40.6	**Winnsboro** (town) Fairfield County
54	n/a	40.5	**Hartsville** (city) Darlington County
55	n/a	40.4	**Southern Shops** (CDP) Spartanburg County
56	n/a	40.3	**Saluda** (town) Saluda County
57	666	39.4	**Sumter** (city) Sumter County
58	n/a	39.0	**Little River** (CDP) Horry County
58	n/a	39.0	**Pendleton** (town) Anderson County
60	n/a	38.6	**Laurens** (city) Laurens County
60	n/a	38.6	**Liberty** (city) Pickens County
62	746	38.5	**North Myrtle Beach** (city) Horry County
63	n/a	38.4	**Burnettown** (town) Aiken County
64	n/a	38.2	**Arcadia** (CDP) Spartanburg County
64	n/a	38.2	**Belton** (city) Anderson County
66	791	38.0	**Spartanburg** (city) Spartanburg County
67	834	37.6	**Hilton Head Island** (town) Beaufort County
68	n/a	37.3	**Springdale** (CDP) Lancaster County
69	907	37.0	**Florence** (city) Florence County
70	924	36.8	**Aiken** (city) Aiken County
71	n/a	36.5	**Pageland** (town) Chesterfield County
72	n/a	36.4	**Clearwater** (CDP) Aiken County
73	n/a	36.2	**Camden** (city) Kershaw County
74	994	36.1	**Saint Andrews** (CDP) Richland County
75	1025	35.9	**Beaufort** (city) Beaufort County
75	n/a	35.9	**Murrells Inlet** (CDP) Georgetown County
75	1025	35.9	**Orangeburg** (city) Orangeburg County
78	n/a	35.6	**Piedmont** (CDP) Anderson County
79	n/a	35.2	**Dunean** (CDP) Greenville County
80	n/a	35.1	**Ridgeland** (town) Jasper County
80	n/a	35.1	**Seneca** (city) Oconee County
82	n/a	34.8	**Dalzell** (CDP) Sumter County
83	1189	34.6	**Red Hill** (CDP) Horry County
84	1235	34.3	**Conway** (city) Horry County
85	1330	33.7	**Easley** (city) Pickens County
86	n/a	33.6	**Woodfield** (CDP) Richland County
87	n/a	33.5	**Sans Souci** (CDP) Greenville County
88	1376	33.4	**Myrtle Beach** (city) Horry County
89	n/a	33.0	**Hollywood** (town) Charleston County
89	n/a	33.0	**Surfside Beach** (town) Horry County
91	n/a	32.9	**Travelers Rest** (city) Greenville County
92	1484	32.7	**Dentsville** (CDP) Richland County
93	1547	32.3	**Taylors** (CDP) Greenville County
94	1579	32.0	**North Charleston** (city) Charleston County
95	n/a	31.9	**Lakewood** (CDP) Sumter County
96	1627	31.7	**Socastee** (CDP) Horry County
97	n/a	31.6	**Williamston** (town) Anderson County
98	n/a	31.3	**Duncan** (town) Spartanburg County
99	1713	31.1	**Wade Hampton** (CDP) Greenville County
99	1713	31.1	**West Columbia** (city) Lexington County
101	n/a	30.5	**Clover** (town) York County
102	1830	30.4	**Forest Acres** (city) Richland County
103	n/a	30.2	**Fountain Inn** (city) Greenville County
103	1857	30.2	**Port Royal** (town) Beaufort County
105	n/a	30.1	**Hardeeville** (city) Jasper County
106	1966	29.6	**Seven Oaks** (CDP) Lexington County
107	n/a	29.1	**Burton** (CDP) Beaufort County
107	2040	29.1	**Greenville** (city) Greenville County
107	n/a	29.1	**Springdale** (town) Lexington County
110	n/a	29.0	**Isle of Palms** (city) Charleston County
110	n/a	29.0	**Moncks Corner** (town) Berkeley County
112	n/a	28.9	**Centerville** (CDP) Anderson County
113	2094	28.8	**Cayce** (city) Lexington County
114	2112	28.7	**Greer** (city) Greenville County
115	2371	27.2	**Columbia** (city) Richland County
116	2410	27.0	**North Augusta** (city) Aiken County
117	n/a	26.9	**Sangaree** (CDP) Berkeley County
118	2451	26.8	**Rock Hill** (city) York County
119	n/a	26.6	**Forestbrook** (CDP) Horry County
120	n/a	26.0	**Northlake** (CDP) Anderson County
121	n/a	25.8	**Hampton** (town) Hampton County
121	n/a	25.8	**Lugoff** (CDP) Kershaw County
123	2774	25.2	**Ladson** (CDP) Berkeley County
124	2843	24.8	**Charleston** (city) Charleston County
125	2865	24.7	**Irmo** (town) Richland County
125	2865	24.7	**Summerville** (town) Dorchester County
127	n/a	24.6	**Lesslie** (CDP) York County
127	n/a	24.6	**Red Bank** (CDP) Lexington County
129	2934	24.3	**Simpsonville** (city) Greenville County
130	2974	24.1	**Oak Grove** (CDP) Lexington County
131	n/a	24.0	**Lyman** (town) Spartanburg County
132	n/a	23.9	**Valley Falls** (CDP) Spartanburg County
133	3142	23.3	**Hanahan** (city) Berkeley County
134	3222	22.9	**Goose Creek** (city) Berkeley County
135	3236	22.8	**Mauldin** (city) Greenville County
136	3277	22.6	**Fort Mill** (town) York County
137	3305	22.4	**Lexington** (town) Lexington County
138	n/a	21.5	**Lake Murray of Richland** (CDP) Richland County
139	3487	21.4	**Bluffton** (town) Beaufort County
140	n/a	20.0	**India Hook** (CDP) York County
141	3807	19.6	**Clemson** (city) Pickens County
142	n/a	18.4	**Boiling Springs** (CDP) Spartanburg County
143	n/a	17.9	**Folly Beach** (city) Charleston County
143	n/a	17.9	**Lake Wylie** (CDP) York County
145	n/a	17.7	**Newport** (CDP) York County
146	4216	16.7	**Mount Pleasant** (town) Charleston County
147	n/a	12.7	**Tega Cay** (city) York County
148	n/a	11.9	**Central** (town) Pickens County
149	n/a	11.5	**Laurel Bay** (CDP) Beaufort County
150	4583	10.7	**Five Forks** (CDP) Greenville County

Note: The state column ranks the top/bottom 150 places in the state with population of 2,500 or more. The national column ranks the top/bottom places in the country with population of 10,000 or more. Places that are unincorporated were not considered in the rankings. n/a indicates data not available. Please refer to the User Guide for additional information.

Population with Public Health Insurance

Top 150 Places Ranked in *Ascending* Order

State Rank	Nat'l Rank	Percent	Place	State Rank	Nat'l Rank	Percent	Place
1	71	10.7	**Five Forks** (CDP) Greenville County	74	3617	35.9	**Orangeburg** (city) Orangeburg County
2	n/a	11.5	**Laurel Bay** (CDP) Beaufort County	77	3647	36.1	**Saint Andrews** (CDP) Richland County
3	n/a	11.9	**Central** (town) Pickens County	78	n/a	36.2	**Camden** (city) Kershaw County
4	n/a	12.7	**Tega Cay** (city) York County	79	n/a	36.4	**Clearwater** (CDP) Aiken County
5	430	16.7	**Mount Pleasant** (town) Charleston County	80	n/a	36.5	**Pageland** (town) Chesterfield County
6	n/a	17.7	**Newport** (CDP) York County	81	3726	36.8	**Aiken** (city) Aiken County
7	n/a	17.9	**Folly Beach** (city) Charleston County	82	3743	37.0	**Florence** (city) Florence County
7	n/a	17.9	**Lake Wylie** (CDP) York County	83	n/a	37.3	**Springdale** (CDP) Lancaster County
9	n/a	18.4	**Boiling Springs** (CDP) Spartanburg County	84	3810	37.6	**Hilton Head Island** (town) Beaufort County
10	834	19.6	**Clemson** (city) Pickens County	85	3854	38.0	**Spartanburg** (city) Spartanburg County
11	n/a	20.0	**India Hook** (CDP) York County	86	n/a	38.2	**Arcadia** (CDP) Spartanburg County
12	1151	21.4	**Bluffton** (town) Beaufort County	86	n/a	38.2	**Belton** (city) Anderson County
13	n/a	21.5	**Lake Murray of Richland** (CDP) Richland County	88	n/a	38.4	**Burnettown** (town) Aiken County
14	1336	22.4	**Lexington** (town) Lexington County	89	3903	38.5	**North Myrtle Beach** (city) Horry County
15	1364	22.6	**Fort Mill** (town) York County	90	n/a	38.6	**Laurens** (city) Laurens County
16	1404	22.8	**Mauldin** (city) Greenville County	90	n/a	38.6	**Liberty** (city) Pickens County
17	1421	22.9	**Goose Creek** (city) Berkeley County	92	n/a	39.0	**Little River** (CDP) Horry County
18	1491	23.3	**Hanahan** (city) Berkeley County	92	n/a	39.0	**Pendleton** (town) Anderson County
19	n/a	23.9	**Valley Falls** (CDP) Spartanburg County	94	3980	39.4	**Sumter** (city) Sumter County
20	n/a	24.0	**Lyman** (town) Spartanburg County	95	n/a	40.3	**Saluda** (town) Saluda County
21	1653	24.1	**Oak Grove** (CDP) Lexington County	96	n/a	40.4	**Southern Shops** (CDP) Spartanburg County
22	1703	24.3	**Simpsonville** (city) Greenville County	97	n/a	40.5	**Hartsville** (city) Darlington County
23	n/a	24.6	**Lesslie** (CDP) York County	98	n/a	40.6	**Winnsboro** (town) Fairfield County
23	n/a	24.6	**Red Bank** (CDP) Lexington County	99	4093	40.7	**Anderson** (city) Anderson County
25	1768	24.7	**Irmo** (town) Richland County	100	n/a	40.8	**Belvedere** (CDP) Aiken County
25	1768	24.7	**Summerville** (town) Dorchester County	101	n/a	41.4	**Bamberg** (town) Bamberg County
27	1792	24.8	**Charleston** (city) Charleston County	101	n/a	41.4	**Darlington** (city) Darlington County
28	1866	25.2	**Ladson** (CDP) Berkeley County	103	n/a	41.6	**Saxon** (CDP) Spartanburg County
29	n/a	25.8	**Hampton** (town) Hampton County	104	n/a	41.8	**North Hartsville** (CDP) Darlington County
29	n/a	25.8	**Lugoff** (CDP) Kershaw County	105	n/a	41.9	**Allendale** (town) Allendale County
31	n/a	26.0	**Northlake** (CDP) Anderson County	105	n/a	41.9	**Clinton** (city) Laurens County
32	n/a	26.6	**Forestbrook** (CDP) Horry County	107	4189	42.1	**Parker** (CDP) Greenville County
33	2174	26.8	**Rock Hill** (city) York County	108	n/a	42.2	**Welcome** (CDP) Greenville County
34	n/a	26.9	**Sangaree** (CDP) Berkeley County	109	4214	42.4	**Gaffney** (city) Cherokee County
35	2232	27.0	**North Augusta** (city) Aiken County	110	n/a	42.5	**Elgin** (CDP) Lancaster County
36	2262	27.2	**Columbia** (city) Richland County	111	n/a	42.7	**Brookdale** (CDP) Orangeburg County
37	2530	28.7	**Greer** (city) Greenville County	112	4238	42.8	**Newberry** (city) Newberry County
38	2545	28.8	**Cayce** (city) Lexington County	113	n/a	42.9	**Graniteville** (CDP) Aiken County
39	n/a	28.9	**Centerville** (CDP) Anderson County	113	n/a	42.9	**Union** (city) Union County
40	n/a	29.0	**Isle of Palms** (city) Charleston County	115	n/a	43.0	**Georgetown** (city) Georgetown County
40	n/a	29.0	**Moncks Corner** (town) Berkeley County	116	4266	43.3	**Greenwood** (city) Greenwood County
42	n/a	29.1	**Burton** (CDP) Beaufort County	117	n/a	43.4	**East Gaffney** (CDP) Cherokee County
42	2601	29.1	**Greenville** (city) Greenville County	118	4303	43.8	**Berea** (CDP) Greenville County
42	n/a	29.1	**Springdale** (town) Lexington County	119	n/a	44.1	**Edgefield** (town) Edgefield County
45	2671	29.6	**Seven Oaks** (CDP) Lexington County	120	n/a	44.6	**Garden City** (CDP) Horry County
46	n/a	30.1	**Hardeeville** (city) Jasper County	120	n/a	44.6	**Lancaster** (city) Lancaster County
47	n/a	30.2	**Fountain Inn** (city) Greenville County	122	4394	45.3	**Gantt** (CDP) Greenville County
47	2779	30.2	**Port Royal** (town) Beaufort County	122	n/a	45.3	**Kingstree** (town) Williamsburg County
49	2813	30.4	**Forest Acres** (city) Richland County	124	n/a	45.7	**Edisto** (CDP) Orangeburg County
50	n/a	30.5	**Clover** (town) York County	125	n/a	46.9	**Pickens** (city) Pickens County
51	2930	31.1	**Wade Hampton** (CDP) Greenville County	126	n/a	47.1	**Manning** (city) Clarendon County
51	2930	31.1	**West Columbia** (city) Lexington County	127	n/a	47.2	**Honea Path** (town) Anderson County
53	n/a	31.3	**Duncan** (town) Spartanburg County	127	n/a	47.2	**Lake City** (city) Florence County
54	n/a	31.6	**Williamston** (town) Anderson County	129	n/a	47.5	**York** (city) York County
55	3018	31.7	**Socastee** (CDP) Horry County	130	n/a	47.6	**Batesburg-Leesville** (town) Lexington County
56	n/a	31.9	**Lakewood** (CDP) Sumter County	131	n/a	47.9	**Andrews** (town) Georgetown County
57	3069	32.0	**North Charleston** (city) Charleston County	131	n/a	47.9	**Hopkins** (CDP) Richland County
58	3100	32.3	**Taylors** (CDP) Greenville County	131	n/a	47.9	**McCormick** (town) McCormick County
59	3152	32.7	**Dentsville** (CDP) Richland County	134	n/a	48.0	**Denmark** (city) Bamberg County
60	n/a	32.9	**Travelers Rest** (city) Greenville County	135	n/a	48.3	**Gloverville** (CDP) Aiken County
61	n/a	33.0	**Hollywood** (town) Charleston County	136	n/a	49.0	**Abbeville** (city) Abbeville County
61	n/a	33.0	**Surfside Beach** (town) Horry County	137	n/a	50.5	**Homeland Park** (CDP) Anderson County
63	3262	33.4	**Myrtle Beach** (city) Horry County	138	n/a	50.7	**Mullins** (city) Marion County
64	n/a	33.5	**Sans Souci** (CDP) Greenville County	139	n/a	50.8	**Woodruff** (city) Spartanburg County
65	n/a	33.6	**Woodfield** (CDP) Richland County	140	n/a	50.9	**Williston** (town) Barnwell County
66	3309	33.7	**Easley** (city) Pickens County	141	n/a	51.1	**Arial** (CDP) Pickens County
67	3404	34.3	**Conway** (city) Horry County	141	n/a	51.1	**Barnwell** (city) Barnwell County
68	3453	34.6	**Red Hill** (CDP) Horry County	141	n/a	51.1	**Walterboro** (city) Colleton County
69	n/a	34.8	**Dalzell** (CDP) Sumter County	144	n/a	51.9	**Chester** (city) Chester County
70	n/a	35.1	**Ridgeland** (town) Jasper County	145	n/a	54.6	**Bennettsville** (city) Marlboro County
70	n/a	35.1	**Seneca** (city) Oconee County	146	n/a	55.2	**Marion** (city) Marion County
72	n/a	35.2	**Dunean** (CDP) Greenville County	147	n/a	57.0	**Dillon** (city) Dillon County
73	n/a	35.6	**Piedmont** (CDP) Anderson County	148	n/a	57.2	**Bishopville** (city) Lee County
74	3617	35.9	**Beaufort** (city) Beaufort County	149	n/a	57.5	**Cheraw** (town) Chesterfield County
74	n/a	35.9	**Murrells Inlet** (CDP) Georgetown County	150	n/a	58.0	**Walhalla** (city) Oconee County

Note: *The state column ranks the top/bottom 150 places in the state with population of 2,500 or more. The national column ranks the top/bottom places in the country with population of 10,000 or more. Places that are unincorporated were not considered in the rankings. n/a indicates data not available. Please refer to the User Guide for additional information.*

Population with No Health Insurance

Top 150 Places Ranked in *Descending* Order

State Rank	Nat'l Rank	Percent	Place
1	n/a	42.7	**Southern Shops** (CDP) Spartanburg County
2	72	33.8	**Myrtle Beach** (city) Horry County
3	n/a	33.5	**Sans Souci** (CDP) Greenville County
4	n/a	33.3	**Arcadia** (CDP) Spartanburg County
5	n/a	32.4	**Clearwater** (CDP) Aiken County
6	94	31.8	**Parker** (CDP) Greenville County
7	n/a	31.4	**Hardeeville** (city) Jasper County
8	n/a	30.7	**Pageland** (town) Chesterfield County
9	n/a	30.6	**Saxon** (CDP) Spartanburg County
10	n/a	29.8	**Saluda** (town) Saluda County
10	n/a	29.8	**Welcome** (CDP) Greenville County
12	n/a	28.3	**Murrells Inlet** (CDP) Georgetown County
13	n/a	28.1	**Allendale** (town) Allendale County
14	n/a	27.6	**East Gaffney** (CDP) Cherokee County
15	n/a	27.4	**Andrews** (town) Georgetown County
15	n/a	27.4	**Dunean** (CDP) Greenville County
17	n/a	26.9	**Springdale** (CDP) Lancaster County
18	n/a	26.7	**Lesslie** (CDP) York County
19	243	26.3	**Socastee** (CDP) Horry County
20	n/a	26.0	**Brookdale** (CDP) Orangeburg County
21	n/a	25.7	**Moncks Corner** (town) Berkeley County
22	306	25.0	**Bluffton** (town) Beaufort County
23	n/a	24.8	**Woodruff** (city) Spartanburg County
24	n/a	24.7	**Belton** (city) Anderson County
25	n/a	24.5	**Kingstree** (town) Williamsburg County
25	n/a	24.5	**Lancaster** (city) Lancaster County
27	n/a	24.0	**Edisto** (CDP) Orangeburg County
28	373	23.9	**Hanahan** (city) Berkeley County
29	430	23.2	**Red Hill** (CDP) Horry County
30	436	23.1	**North Charleston** (city) Charleston County
31	n/a	22.2	**Burton** (CDP) Beaufort County
32	n/a	22.0	**Gloverville** (CDP) Aiken County
32	n/a	22.0	**Woodfield** (CDP) Richland County
34	525	21.8	**West Columbia** (city) Lexington County
35	n/a	21.7	**Lyman** (town) Spartanburg County
36	n/a	21.6	**Homeland Park** (CDP) Anderson County
37	n/a	21.4	**Hampton** (town) Hampton County
38	577	21.3	**Gantt** (CDP) Greenville County
39	590	21.2	**Berea** (CDP) Greenville County
39	590	21.2	**Orangeburg** (city) Orangeburg County
41	615	21.0	**Dentsville** (CDP) Richland County
41	n/a	21.0	**Graniteville** (CDP) Aiken County
41	n/a	21.0	**Ridgeland** (town) Jasper County
44	n/a	20.9	**Mullins** (city) Marion County
45	n/a	20.8	**Denmark** (city) Bamberg County
46	n/a	20.6	**Hopkins** (CDP) Richland County
46	n/a	20.6	**Walhalla** (city) Oconee County
48	673	20.4	**Ladson** (CDP) Berkeley County
48	n/a	20.4	**Manning** (city) Clarendon County
50	n/a	20.3	**Forestbrook** (CDP) Horry County
50	n/a	20.3	**Georgetown** (city) Georgetown County
50	679	20.3	**Saint Andrews** (CDP) Richland County
53	739	19.8	**Greenwood** (city) Greenwood County
54	774	19.6	**North Myrtle Beach** (city) Horry County
55	n/a	19.5	**Darlington** (city) Darlington County
55	n/a	19.5	**Laurens** (city) Laurens County
55	n/a	19.5	**Pickens** (city) Pickens County
58	n/a	19.4	**Folly Beach** (city) Charleston County
59	n/a	19.2	**Burnettown** (town) Aiken County
60	n/a	19.1	**Garden City** (CDP) Horry County
60	n/a	19.1	**Sangaree** (CDP) Berkeley County
62	884	18.8	**Wade Hampton** (CDP) Greenville County
63	904	18.7	**Taylors** (CDP) Greenville County
64	n/a	18.6	**Marion** (city) Marion County
65	n/a	18.5	**Winnsboro** (town) Fairfield County
66	n/a	18.3	**Little River** (CDP) Horry County
67	n/a	18.1	**Clinton** (city) Laurens County
68	1020	18.0	**Anderson** (city) Anderson County
68	n/a	18.0	**Valley Falls** (CDP) Spartanburg County
70	1039	17.8	**Greer** (city) Greenville County
71	n/a	17.7	**York** (city) York County
72	n/a	17.6	**Seneca** (city) Oconee County
72	n/a	17.6	**Surfside Beach** (town) Horry County
74	1115	17.4	**Cayce** (city) Lexington County
74	1115	17.4	**Hilton Head Island** (town) Beaufort County
76	n/a	17.3	**Chester** (city) Chester County
76	1137	17.3	**Irmo** (town) Richland County
76	n/a	17.3	**Pendleton** (town) Anderson County
79	n/a	17.2	**Piedmont** (CDP) Anderson County
80	n/a	17.0	**Boiling Springs** (CDP) Spartanburg County
81	n/a	16.9	**Belvedere** (CDP) Aiken County
82	n/a	16.8	**Red Bank** (CDP) Lexington County
83	1242	16.7	**Greenville** (city) Greenville County
83	1242	16.7	**Newberry** (city) Newberry County
83	1242	16.7	**Simpsonville** (city) Greenville County
83	1242	16.7	**Spartanburg** (city) Spartanburg County
83	n/a	16.7	**Travelers Rest** (city) Greenville County
88	1265	16.6	**Conway** (city) Horry County
89	n/a	16.5	**Hartsville** (city) Darlington County
90	n/a	16.4	**Hollywood** (town) Charleston County
90	n/a	16.4	**Honea Path** (town) Anderson County
92	n/a	16.2	**Lugoff** (CDP) Kershaw County
93	1412	15.9	**Rock Hill** (city) York County
94	n/a	15.8	**Bamberg** (town) Bamberg County
94	n/a	15.8	**Cheraw** (town) Chesterfield County
96	n/a	15.7	**Bishopville** (city) Lee County
96	1452	15.7	**Gaffney** (city) Cherokee County
98	1472	15.6	**Oak Grove** (CDP) Lexington County
99	1511	15.4	**Beaufort** (city) Beaufort County
99	n/a	15.4	**Union** (city) Union County
101	n/a	15.0	**Williamston** (town) Anderson County
102	1603	14.8	**Summerville** (town) Dorchester County
103	n/a	14.7	**Bennettsville** (city) Marlboro County
103	n/a	14.7	**Dillon** (city) Dillon County
105	1643	14.6	**Easley** (city) Pickens County
106	1683	14.4	**Mauldin** (city) Greenville County
106	n/a	14.4	**North Hartsville** (CDP) Darlington County
106	1683	14.4	**Sumter** (city) Sumter County
109	n/a	14.3	**Centerville** (CDP) Anderson County
110	n/a	14.2	**Fountain Inn** (city) Greenville County
110	n/a	14.2	**Lake City** (city) Florence County
112	n/a	14.1	**Laurel Bay** (CDP) Beaufort County
113	n/a	13.9	**Clover** (town) York County
114	n/a	13.8	**Liberty** (city) Pickens County
115	n/a	13.6	**Duncan** (town) Spartanburg County
116	n/a	13.3	**Batesburg-Leesville** (town) Lexington County
116	1942	13.3	**Columbia** (city) Richland County
116	n/a	13.3	**McCormick** (town) McCormick County
119	n/a	13.1	**Abbeville** (city) Abbeville County
119	n/a	13.1	**Walterboro** (city) Colleton County
121	n/a	13.0	**Camden** (city) Kershaw County
122	n/a	12.9	**Williston** (town) Barnwell County
123	2063	12.8	**Seven Oaks** (CDP) Lexington County
124	2111	12.6	**Charleston** (city) Charleston County
124	2111	12.6	**Florence** (city) Florence County
126	n/a	12.5	**Springdale** (town) Lexington County
127	2175	12.3	**Goose Creek** (city) Berkeley County
128	n/a	12.1	**Central** (town) Pickens County
129	n/a	11.9	**Barnwell** (city) Barnwell County
130	2434	11.2	**North Augusta** (city) Aiken County
131	n/a	11.1	**Arial** (CDP) Pickens County
132	n/a	10.5	**Elgin** (CDP) Lancaster County
132	n/a	10.5	**Northlake** (CDP) Anderson County
134	n/a	10.3	**Newport** (CDP) York County
135	2759	9.9	**Aiken** (city) Aiken County
136	2781	9.8	**Fort Mill** (town) York County
137	n/a	9.6	**Lake Wylie** (CDP) York County
138	n/a	9.3	**Edgefield** (town) Edgefield County
139	2929	9.2	**Port Royal** (town) Beaufort County
140	3078	8.6	**Forest Acres** (city) Richland County
141	n/a	8.5	**Lakewood** (CDP) Sumter County
141	3105	8.5	**Mount Pleasant** (town) Charleston County
143	3158	8.3	**Lexington** (town) Lexington County
144	n/a	8.2	**India Hook** (CDP) York County
145	n/a	7.2	**Isle of Palms** (city) Charleston County
146	n/a	6.8	**Tega Cay** (city) York County
147	3856	5.7	**Clemson** (city) Pickens County
148	n/a	4.1	**Lake Murray of Richland** (CDP) Richland County
149	4270	4.0	**Five Forks** (CDP) Greenville County
150	n/a	3.5	**Dalzell** (CDP) Sumter County

Note: The state column ranks the top/bottom 150 places in the state with population of 2,500 or more. The national column ranks the top/bottom places in the country with population of 10,000 or more. Places that are unincorporated were not considered in the rankings. n/a indicates data not available. Please refer to the User Guide for additional information.

Population with No Health Insurance

Top 150 Places Ranked in *Ascending* Order

State Rank	Nat'l Rank	Percent	Place
1	n/a	3.5	Dalzell (CDP) Sumter County
2	361	4.0	Five Forks (CDP) Greenville County
3	n/a	4.1	Lake Murray of Richland (CDP) Richland County
4	779	5.7	Clemson (city) Pickens County
5	n/a	6.8	Tega Cay (city) York County
6	n/a	7.2	Isle of Palms (city) Charleston County
7	n/a	8.2	India Hook (CDP) York County
8	1478	8.3	Lexington (town) Lexington County
9	n/a	8.5	Lakewood (CDP) Sumter County
9	1525	8.5	Mount Pleasant (town) Charleston County
11	1552	8.6	Forest Acres (city) Richland County
12	1703	9.2	Port Royal (town) Beaufort County
13	n/a	9.3	Edgefield (town) Edgefield County
14	n/a	9.6	Lake Wylie (CDP) York County
15	1847	9.8	Fort Mill (town) York County
16	1876	9.9	Aiken (city) Aiken County
17	n/a	10.3	Newport (CDP) York County
18	n/a	10.5	Elgin (CDP) Lancaster County
18	n/a	10.5	Northlake (CDP) Anderson County
20	n/a	11.1	Arial (CDP) Pickens County
21	2194	11.2	North Augusta (city) Aiken County
22	n/a	11.9	Barnwell (city) Barnwell County
23	n/a	12.1	Central (town) Pickens County
24	2456	12.3	Goose Creek (city) Berkeley County
25	n/a	12.5	Springdale (town) Lexington County
26	2527	12.6	Charleston (city) Charleston County
26	2527	12.6	Florence (city) Florence County
28	2574	12.8	Seven Oaks (CDP) Lexington County
29	n/a	12.9	Williston (town) Barnwell County
30	n/a	13.0	Camden (city) Kershaw County
31	n/a	13.1	Abbeville (city) Abbeville County
31	n/a	13.1	Walterboro (city) Colleton County
33	n/a	13.3	Batesburg-Leesville (town) Lexington County
33	2685	13.3	Columbia (city) Richland County
33	n/a	13.3	McCormick (town) McCormick County
36	n/a	13.6	Duncan (town) Spartanburg County
37	n/a	13.8	Liberty (city) Pickens County
38	n/a	13.9	Clover (town) York County
39	n/a	14.1	Laurel Bay (CDP) Beaufort County
40	n/a	14.2	Fountain Inn (city) Greenville County
40	n/a	14.2	Lake City (city) Florence County
42	n/a	14.3	Centerville (CDP) Anderson County
43	2944	14.4	Mauldin (city) Greenville County
43	n/a	14.4	North Hartsville (CDP) Darlington County
43	2944	14.4	Sumter (city) Sumter County
46	2994	14.6	Easley (city) Pickens County
47	n/a	14.7	Bennettsville (city) Marlboro County
47	n/a	14.7	Dillon (city) Dillon County
49	3033	14.8	Summerville (town) Dorchester County
50	n/a	15.0	Williamston (town) Anderson County
51	3128	15.4	Beaufort (city) Beaufort County
51	n/a	15.4	Union (city) Union County
53	3167	15.6	Oak Grove (CDP) Lexington County
54	n/a	15.7	Bishopville (city) Lee County
54	3185	15.7	Gaffney (city) Cherokee County
56	n/a	15.8	Bamberg (town) Bamberg County
56	n/a	15.8	Cheraw (town) Chesterfield County
58	3228	15.9	Rock Hill (city) York County
59	n/a	16.2	Lugoff (CDP) Kershaw County
60	n/a	16.4	Hollywood (town) Charleston County
60	n/a	16.4	Honea Path (town) Anderson County
62	n/a	16.5	Hartsville (city) Darlington County
63	3371	16.6	Conway (city) Horry County
64	3392	16.7	Greenville (city) Greenville County
64	3392	16.7	Newberry (city) Newberry County
64	3392	16.7	Simpsonville (city) Greenville County
64	3392	16.7	Spartanburg (city) Spartanburg County
64	n/a	16.7	Travelers Rest (city) Greenville County
69	n/a	16.8	Red Bank (CDP) Lexington County
70	n/a	16.9	Belvedere (CDP) Aiken County
71	n/a	17.0	Boiling Springs (CDP) Spartanburg County
72	n/a	17.2	Piedmont (CDP) Anderson County
73	n/a	17.3	Chester (city) Chester County
73	3498	17.3	Irmo (town) Richland County
73	n/a	17.3	Pendleton (town) Anderson County
76	3520	17.4	Cayce (city) Lexington County
76	3520	17.4	Hilton Head Island (town) Beaufort County
78	n/a	17.6	Seneca (city) Oconee County
78	n/a	17.6	Surfside Beach (town) Horry County
80	n/a	17.7	York (city) York County
81	3600	17.8	Greer (city) Greenville County
82	3624	18.0	Anderson (city) Anderson County
82	n/a	18.0	Valley Falls (CDP) Spartanburg County
84	n/a	18.1	Clinton (city) Laurens County
85	n/a	18.3	Little River (CDP) Horry County
86	n/a	18.5	Winnsboro (town) Fairfield County
87	n/a	18.6	Marion (city) Marion County
88	3735	18.7	Taylors (CDP) Greenville County
89	3753	18.8	Wade Hampton (CDP) Greenville County
90	n/a	19.1	Garden City (CDP) Horry County
90	n/a	19.1	Sangaree (CDP) Berkeley County
92	n/a	19.2	Burnettown (town) Aiken County
93	n/a	19.4	Folly Beach (city) Charleston County
94	n/a	19.5	Darlington (city) Darlington County
94	n/a	19.5	Laurens (city) Laurens County
94	n/a	19.5	Pickens (city) Pickens County
97	3866	19.6	North Myrtle Beach (city) Horry County
98	3904	19.8	Greenwood (city) Greenwood County
99	n/a	20.3	Forestbrook (CDP) Horry County
99	n/a	20.3	Georgetown (city) Georgetown County
99	3960	20.3	Saint Andrews (CDP) Richland County
102	3978	20.4	Ladson (CDP) Berkeley County
102	n/a	20.4	Manning (city) Clarendon County
104	n/a	20.6	Hopkins (CDP) Richland County
104	n/a	20.6	Walhalla (city) Oconee County
106	n/a	20.8	Denmark (city) Bamberg County
107	n/a	20.9	Mullins (city) Marion County
108	4033	21.0	Dentsville (CDP) Richland County
108	n/a	21.0	Graniteville (CDP) Aiken County
108	n/a	21.0	Ridgeland (town) Jasper County
111	4058	21.2	Berea (CDP) Greenville County
111	4058	21.2	Orangeburg (city) Orangeburg County
113	4067	21.3	Gantt (CDP) Greenville County
114	n/a	21.4	Hampton (town) Hampton County
115	n/a	21.6	Homeland Park (CDP) Anderson County
116	n/a	21.7	Lyman (town) Spartanburg County
117	4119	21.8	West Columbia (city) Lexington County
118	n/a	22.0	Gloverville (CDP) Aiken County
118	n/a	22.0	Woodfield (CDP) Richland County
120	n/a	22.2	Burton (CDP) Beaufort County
121	4217	23.1	North Charleston (city) Charleston County
122	4221	23.2	Red Hill (CDP) Horry County
123	4277	23.9	Hanahan (city) Berkeley County
124	n/a	24.0	Edisto (CDP) Orangeburg County
125	n/a	24.5	Kingstree (town) Williamsburg County
125	n/a	24.5	Lancaster (city) Lancaster County
127	n/a	24.7	Belton (city) Anderson County
128	n/a	24.8	Woodruff (city) Spartanburg County
129	4340	25.0	Bluffton (town) Beaufort County
130	n/a	25.7	Moncks Corner (town) Berkeley County
131	n/a	26.0	Brookdale (CDP) Orangeburg County
132	4409	26.3	Socastee (CDP) Horry County
133	n/a	26.7	Lesslie (CDP) York County
134	n/a	26.9	Springdale (CDP) Lancaster County
135	n/a	27.4	Andrews (town) Georgetown County
135	n/a	27.4	Dunean (CDP) Greenville County
137	n/a	27.6	East Gaffney (CDP) Cherokee County
138	n/a	28.1	Allendale (town) Allendale County
139	n/a	28.3	Murrells Inlet (CDP) Georgetown County
140	n/a	29.8	Saluda (town) Saluda County
140	n/a	29.8	Welcome (CDP) Greenville County
142	n/a	30.6	Saxon (CDP) Spartanburg County
143	n/a	30.7	Pageland (town) Chesterfield County
144	n/a	31.4	Hardeeville (city) Jasper County
145	4560	31.8	Parker (CDP) Greenville County
146	n/a	32.4	Clearwater (CDP) Aiken County
147	n/a	33.3	Arcadia (CDP) Spartanburg County
148	n/a	33.5	Sans Souci (CDP) Greenville County
149	4582	33.8	Myrtle Beach (city) Horry County
150	n/a	42.7	Southern Shops (CDP) Spartanburg County

Note: The state column ranks the top/bottom 150 places in the state with population of 2,500 or more. The national column ranks the top/bottom places in the country with population of 10,000 or more. Places that are unincorporated were not considered in the rankings. n/a indicates data not available. Please refer to the User Guide for additional information.

Population Under 18 Years Old with No Health Insurance

Top 150 Places Ranked in *Descending* Order

State Rank	Nat'l Rank	Percent	Place
1	n/a	39.2	**Murrells Inlet** (CDP) Georgetown County
2	n/a	29.5	**Brookdale** (CDP) Orangeburg County
3	n/a	28.8	**Garden City** (CDP) Horry County
4	n/a	28.6	**Kingstree** (town) Williamsburg County
5	n/a	26.4	**Clearwater** (CDP) Aiken County
6	n/a	26.1	**Southern Shops** (CDP) Spartanburg County
7	17	25.7	**Red Hill** (CDP) Horry County
8	n/a	24.2	**Surfside Beach** (town) Horry County
9	n/a	24.1	**Sans Souci** (CDP) Greenville County
10	n/a	22.7	**Andrews** (town) Georgetown County
11	n/a	22.4	**Valley Falls** (CDP) Spartanburg County
12	49	21.7	**Socastee** (CDP) Horry County
13	n/a	21.6	**Boiling Springs** (CDP) Spartanburg County
13	n/a	21.6	**Pageland** (town) Chesterfield County
15	n/a	21.2	**Hardeeville** (city) Jasper County
16	60	20.8	**Myrtle Beach** (city) Horry County
17	74	20.3	**Bluffton** (town) Beaufort County
18	n/a	19.7	**Georgetown** (city) Georgetown County
19	105	19.3	**Hanahan** (city) Berkeley County
20	n/a	18.6	**Hampton** (town) Hampton County
21	n/a	18.2	**Forestbrook** (CDP) Horry County
22	n/a	17.7	**Dunean** (CDP) Greenville County
23	n/a	17.3	**Burnettown** (town) Aiken County
23	155	17.3	**Hilton Head Island** (town) Beaufort County
25	n/a	16.8	**Hollywood** (town) Charleston County
26	n/a	16.5	**Moncks Corner** (town) Berkeley County
27	204	16.3	**Parker** (CDP) Greenville County
28	n/a	16.2	**East Gaffney** (CDP) Cherokee County
29	n/a	16.1	**Gloverville** (CDP) Aiken County
29	n/a	16.1	**Ridgeland** (town) Jasper County
31	n/a	16.0	**Burton** (CDP) Beaufort County
32	226	15.9	**Beaufort** (city) Beaufort County
33	n/a	15.5	**Belton** (city) Anderson County
33	253	15.5	**Wade Hampton** (CDP) Greenville County
35	n/a	14.9	**Lesslie** (CDP) York County
36	n/a	14.5	**Edisto** (CDP) Orangeburg County
37	n/a	13.9	**Welcome** (CDP) Greenville County
38	n/a	13.4	**Manning** (city) Clarendon County
39	n/a	13.3	**Sangaree** (CDP) Berkeley County
40	n/a	13.1	**Lancaster** (city) Lancaster County
41	466	12.8	**West Columbia** (city) Lexington County
42	n/a	12.4	**Centerville** (CDP) Anderson County
43	522	12.2	**Dentsville** (CDP) Richland County
43	522	12.2	**Taylors** (CDP) Greenville County
45	549	12.0	**Oak Grove** (CDP) Lexington County
46	n/a	11.7	**Seneca** (city) Oconee County
46	n/a	11.7	**Walhalla** (city) Oconee County
48	598	11.6	**Ladson** (CDP) Berkeley County
48	n/a	11.6	**Travelers Rest** (city) Greenville County
50	n/a	11.5	**Lugoff** (CDP) Kershaw County
51	n/a	10.7	**Laurens** (city) Laurens County
52	790	10.3	**Cayce** (city) Lexington County
52	n/a	10.3	**Clinton** (city) Laurens County
54	806	10.2	**Simpsonville** (city) Greenville County
55	n/a	10.1	**Woodfield** (CDP) Richland County
56	n/a	10.0	**Fountain Inn** (city) Greenville County
57	n/a	9.9	**Springdale** (town) Lexington County
58	n/a	9.8	**Saxon** (CDP) Spartanburg County
59	n/a	9.5	**Homeland Park** (CDP) Anderson County
59	n/a	9.5	**Pickens** (city) Pickens County
61	976	9.4	**Conway** (city) Horry County
61	976	9.4	**Orangeburg** (city) Orangeburg County
63	1040	9.1	**North Charleston** (city) Charleston County
63	1040	9.1	**North Myrtle Beach** (city) Horry County
65	n/a	8.8	**Hartsville** (city) Darlington County
66	1119	8.7	**Anderson** (city) Anderson County
66	1119	8.7	**Greenwood** (city) Greenwood County
66	n/a	8.7	**Laurel Bay** (CDP) Beaufort County
69	n/a	8.6	**Mullins** (city) Marion County
70	1164	8.5	**Greenville** (city) Greenville County
70	1164	8.5	**Summerville** (town) Dorchester County
72	n/a	8.4	**Pendleton** (town) Anderson County
73	n/a	8.3	**Honea Path** (town) Anderson County
73	n/a	8.3	**Woodruff** (city) Spartanburg County
75	1227	8.2	**Irmo** (town) Richland County
75	n/a	8.2	**Newport** (CDP) York County
77	n/a	7.8	**Springdale** (CDP) Lancaster County
78	n/a	7.7	**Camden** (city) Kershaw County
79	1393	7.6	**Charleston** (city) Charleston County
79	n/a	7.6	**Tega Cay** (city) York County
81	1456	7.4	**Berea** (CDP) Greenville County
82	n/a	7.3	**Williamston** (town) Anderson County
83	1516	7.2	**Saint Andrews** (CDP) Richland County
84	1650	6.8	**Seven Oaks** (CDP) Lexington County
85	1687	6.7	**Spartanburg** (city) Spartanburg County
86	1719	6.6	**Gaffney** (city) Cherokee County
86	1719	6.6	**North Augusta** (city) Aiken County
86	n/a	6.6	**Walterboro** (city) Colleton County
89	n/a	6.5	**Dillon** (city) Dillon County
89	n/a	6.5	**Lake Wylie** (CDP) York County
89	1752	6.5	**Mauldin** (city) Greenville County
92	n/a	6.3	**Bennettsville** (city) Marlboro County
93	1849	6.2	**Lexington** (town) Lexington County
94	n/a	6.0	**Clover** (town) York County
95	1955	5.9	**Rock Hill** (city) York County
96	1989	5.8	**Aiken** (city) Aiken County
96	n/a	5.8	**Chester** (city) Chester County
98	2056	5.6	**Goose Creek** (city) Berkeley County
98	2056	5.6	**Mount Pleasant** (town) Charleston County
100	n/a	5.5	**Elgin** (CDP) Lancaster County
100	n/a	5.5	**Red Bank** (CDP) Lexington County
102	n/a	5.4	**Allendale** (town) Allendale County
103	n/a	5.3	**Belvedere** (CDP) Aiken County
104	n/a	5.2	**Darlington** (city) Darlington County
105	n/a	5.0	**Isle of Palms** (city) Charleston County
106	n/a	4.9	**Batesburg-Leesville** (town) Lexington County
106	n/a	4.9	**Piedmont** (CDP) Anderson County
108	2540	4.5	**Gantt** (CDP) Greenville County
108	2540	4.5	**Greer** (city) Greenville County
110	2578	4.4	**Clemson** (city) Pickens County
110	n/a	4.4	**Lyman** (town) Spartanburg County
110	n/a	4.4	**York** (city) York County
113	2616	4.3	**Columbia** (city) Richland County
113	2616	4.3	**Florence** (city) Florence County
113	n/a	4.3	**Graniteville** (CDP) Aiken County
116	n/a	4.2	**Denmark** (city) Bamberg County
116	2675	4.2	**Fort Mill** (town) York County
118	2719	4.1	**Sumter** (city) Sumter County
119	n/a	4.0	**Folly Beach** (city) Charleston County
119	2765	4.0	**Forest Acres** (city) Richland County
119	n/a	4.0	**Saluda** (town) Saluda County
122	n/a	3.9	**Union** (city) Union County
123	2926	3.7	**Easley** (city) Pickens County
123	n/a	3.7	**McCormick** (town) McCormick County
125	3036	3.5	**Port Royal** (town) Beaufort County
126	n/a	2.9	**Duncan** (town) Spartanburg County
127	n/a	2.4	**Bishopville** (city) Lee County
128	n/a	2.3	**Northlake** (CDP) Anderson County
129	n/a	1.7	**Edgefield** (town) Edgefield County
129	n/a	1.7	**India Hook** (CDP) York County
131	n/a	1.5	**North Hartsville** (CDP) Darlington County
132	n/a	1.2	**Marion** (city) Marion County
133	n/a	1.0	**Abbeville** (city) Abbeville County
133	n/a	1.0	**Williston** (town) Barnwell County
135	4447	0.6	**Five Forks** (CDP) Greenville County
136	n/a	0.0	**Arcadia** (CDP) Spartanburg County
136	n/a	0.0	**Arial** (CDP) Pickens County
136	n/a	0.0	**Bamberg** (town) Bamberg County
136	n/a	0.0	**Barnwell** (city) Barnwell County
136	n/a	0.0	**Central** (town) Pickens County
136	n/a	0.0	**Cheraw** (town) Chesterfield County
136	n/a	0.0	**Dalzell** (CDP) Sumter County
136	n/a	0.0	**Hopkins** (CDP) Richland County
136	n/a	0.0	**Lake City** (city) Florence County
136	n/a	0.0	**Lake Murray of Richland** (CDP) Richland County
136	n/a	0.0	**Lakewood** (CDP) Sumter County
136	n/a	0.0	**Liberty** (city) Pickens County
136	n/a	0.0	**Little River** (CDP) Horry County
136	4574	0.0	**Newberry** (city) Newberry County
136	n/a	0.0	**Winnsboro** (town) Fairfield County

Note: The state column ranks the top/bottom 150 places in the state with population of 2,500 or more. The national column ranks the top/bottom places in the country with population of 10,000 or more. Places that are unincorporated were not considered in the rankings. n/a indicates data not available. Please refer to the User Guide for additional information.

Population Under 18 Years Old with No Health Insurance

Top 150 Places Ranked in *Ascending* Order

State Rank	Nat'l Rank	Percent	Place
1	n/a	0.0	Arcadia (CDP) Spartanburg County
1	n/a	0.0	Arial (CDP) Pickens County
1	n/a	0.0	Bamberg (town) Bamberg County
1	n/a	0.0	Barnwell (city) Barnwell County
1	n/a	0.0	Central (town) Pickens County
1	n/a	0.0	Cheraw (town) Chesterfield County
1	n/a	0.0	Dalzell (CDP) Sumter County
1	n/a	0.0	Hopkins (CDP) Richland County
1	n/a	0.0	Lake City (city) Florence County
1	n/a	0.0	Lake Murray of Richland (CDP) Richland County
1	n/a	0.0	Lakewood (CDP) Sumter County
1	n/a	0.0	Liberty (city) Pickens County
1	n/a	0.0	Little River (CDP) Horry County
1	1	0.0	Newberry (city) Newberry County
1	n/a	0.0	Winnsboro (town) Fairfield County
16	177	0.6	Five Forks (CDP) Greenville County
17	n/a	1.0	Abbeville (city) Abbeville County
17	n/a	1.0	Williston (town) Barnwell County
19	n/a	1.2	Marion (city) Marion County
20	n/a	1.5	North Hartsville (CDP) Darlington County
21	n/a	1.7	Edgefield (town) Edgefield County
21	n/a	1.7	India Hook (CDP) York County
23	n/a	2.3	Northlake (CDP) Anderson County
24	n/a	2.4	Bishopville (city) Lee County
25	n/a	2.9	Duncan (town) Spartanburg County
26	1573	3.5	Port Royal (town) Beaufort County
27	1682	3.7	Easley (city) Pickens County
27	n/a	3.7	McCormick (town) McCormick County
29	n/a	3.9	Union (city) Union County
30	n/a	4.0	Folly Beach (city) Charleston County
30	1832	4.0	Forest Acres (city) Richland County
30	n/a	4.0	Saluda (town) Saluda County
33	1892	4.1	Sumter (city) Sumter County
34	n/a	4.2	Denmark (city) Bamberg County
34	1938	4.2	Fort Mill (town) York County
36	1982	4.3	Columbia (city) Richland County
36	1982	4.3	Florence (city) Florence County
36	n/a	4.3	Graniteville (CDP) Aiken County
39	2041	4.4	Clemson (city) Pickens County
39	n/a	4.4	Lyman (town) Spartanburg County
39	n/a	4.4	York (city) York County
42	2079	4.5	Gantt (CDP) Greenville County
42	2079	4.5	Greer (city) Greenville County
44	n/a	4.9	Batesburg-Leesville (town) Lexington County
44	n/a	4.9	Piedmont (CDP) Anderson County
46	n/a	5.0	Isle of Palms (city) Charleston County
47	n/a	5.2	Darlington (city) Darlington County
48	n/a	5.3	Belvedere (CDP) Aiken County
49	n/a	5.4	Allendale (town) Allendale County
50	n/a	5.5	Elgin (CDP) Lancaster County
50	n/a	5.5	Red Bank (CDP) Lexington County
52	2564	5.6	Goose Creek (city) Berkeley County
52	2564	5.6	Mount Pleasant (town) Charleston County
54	2632	5.8	Aiken (city) Aiken County
54	n/a	5.8	Chester (city) Chester County
56	2668	5.9	Rock Hill (city) York County
57	n/a	6.0	Clover (town) York County
58	2775	6.2	Lexington (town) Lexington County
59	n/a	6.3	Bennettsville (city) Marlboro County
60	n/a	6.5	Dillon (city) Dillon County
60	n/a	6.5	Lake Wylie (CDP) York County
60	2872	6.5	Mauldin (city) Greenville County
63	2905	6.6	Gaffney (city) Cherokee County
63	2905	6.6	North Augusta (city) Aiken County
63	n/a	6.6	Walterboro (city) Colleton County
66	2938	6.7	Spartanburg (city) Spartanburg County
67	2970	6.8	Seven Oaks (CDP) Lexington County
68	3106	7.2	Saint Andrews (CDP) Richland County
69	n/a	7.3	Williamston (town) Anderson County
70	3173	7.4	Berea (CDP) Greenville County
71	3228	7.6	Charleston (city) Charleston County
71	n/a	7.6	Tega Cay (city) York County
73	n/a	7.7	Camden (city) Kershaw County
74	n/a	7.8	Springdale (CDP) Lancaster County
75	3400	8.2	Irmo (town) Richland County
75	n/a	8.2	Newport (CDP) York County
77	n/a	8.3	Honea Path (town) Anderson County
77	n/a	8.3	Woodruff (city) Spartanburg County
79	n/a	8.4	Pendleton (town) Anderson County
80	3475	8.5	Greenville (city) Greenville County
80	3475	8.5	Summerville (town) Dorchester County
82	n/a	8.6	Mullins (city) Marion County
83	3519	8.7	Anderson (city) Anderson County
83	3519	8.7	Greenwood (city) Greenwood County
83	n/a	8.7	Laurel Bay (CDP) Beaufort County
86	n/a	8.8	Hartsville (city) Darlington County
87	3596	9.1	North Charleston (city) Charleston County
87	3596	9.1	North Myrtle Beach (city) Horry County
89	3653	9.4	Conway (city) Horry County
89	3653	9.4	Orangeburg (city) Orangeburg County
91	n/a	9.5	Homeland Park (CDP) Anderson County
91	n/a	9.5	Pickens (city) Pickens County
93	n/a	9.8	Saxon (CDP) Spartanburg County
94	n/a	9.9	Springdale (town) Lexington County
95	n/a	10.0	Fountain Inn (city) Greenville County
96	n/a	10.1	Woodfield (CDP) Richland County
97	3834	10.2	Simpsonville (city) Greenville County
98	3851	10.3	Cayce (city) Lexington County
98	n/a	10.3	Clinton (city) Laurens County
100	n/a	10.7	Laurens (city) Laurens County
101	n/a	11.5	Lugoff (CDP) Kershaw County
102	4039	11.6	Ladson (CDP) Berkeley County
102	n/a	11.6	Travelers Rest (city) Greenville County
104	n/a	11.7	Seneca (city) Oconee County
104	n/a	11.7	Walhalla (city) Oconee County
106	4094	12.0	Oak Grove (CDP) Lexington County
107	4125	12.2	Dentsville (CDP) Richland County
107	4125	12.2	Taylors (CDP) Greenville County
109	n/a	12.4	Centerville (CDP) Anderson County
110	4185	12.8	West Columbia (city) Lexington County
111	n/a	13.1	Lancaster (city) Lancaster County
112	n/a	13.3	Sangaree (CDP) Berkeley County
113	n/a	13.4	Manning (city) Clarendon County
114	n/a	13.9	Welcome (CDP) Greenville County
115	n/a	14.5	Edisto (CDP) Orangeburg County
116	n/a	14.9	Lesslie (CDP) York County
117	n/a	15.5	Belton (city) Anderson County
117	4399	15.5	Wade Hampton (CDP) Greenville County
119	4422	15.9	Beaufort (city) Beaufort County
120	n/a	16.0	Burton (CDP) Beaufort County
121	n/a	16.1	Gloverville (CDP) Aiken County
121	n/a	16.1	Ridgeland (town) Jasper County
123	n/a	16.2	East Gaffney (CDP) Cherokee County
124	4447	16.3	Parker (CDP) Greenville County
125	n/a	16.5	Moncks Corner (town) Berkeley County
126	n/a	16.8	Hollywood (town) Charleston County
127	n/a	17.3	Burnettown (town) Aiken County
127	4495	17.3	Hilton Head Island (town) Beaufort County
129	n/a	17.7	Dunean (CDP) Greenville County
130	n/a	18.2	Forestbrook (CDP) Horry County
131	n/a	18.6	Hampton (town) Hampton County
132	4549	19.3	Hanahan (city) Berkeley County
133	n/a	19.7	Georgetown (city) Georgetown County
134	4578	20.3	Bluffton (town) Beaufort County
135	4594	20.8	Myrtle Beach (city) Horry County
136	n/a	21.2	Hardeeville (city) Jasper County
137	n/a	21.6	Boiling Springs (CDP) Spartanburg County
137	n/a	21.6	Pageland (town) Chesterfield County
139	4607	21.7	Socastee (CDP) Horry County
140	n/a	22.4	Valley Falls (CDP) Spartanburg County
141	n/a	22.7	Andrews (town) Georgetown County
142	n/a	24.1	Sans Souci (CDP) Greenville County
143	n/a	24.2	Surfside Beach (town) Horry County
144	4639	25.7	Red Hill (CDP) Horry County
145	n/a	26.1	Southern Shops (CDP) Spartanburg County
146	n/a	26.4	Clearwater (CDP) Aiken County
147	n/a	28.6	Kingstree (town) Williamsburg County
148	n/a	28.8	Garden City (CDP) Horry County
149	n/a	29.5	Brookdale (CDP) Orangeburg County
150	n/a	39.2	Murrells Inlet (CDP) Georgetown County

Note: The state column ranks the top/bottom 150 places in the state with population of 2,500 or more. The national column ranks the top/bottom places in the country with population of 10,000 or more. Places that are unincorporated were not considered in the rankings. n/a indicates data not available. Please refer to the User Guide for additional information.

Commute to Work: Car

Top 150 Places Ranked in *Descending* Order

State Rank	Nat'l Rank	Percent	Place
1	n/a	100.0	**Gloverville** (CDP) Aiken County
2	n/a	99.9	**Walhalla** (city) Oconee County
3	n/a	99.1	**Dalzell** (CDP) Sumter County
4	n/a	99.0	**Honea Path** (town) Anderson County
5	n/a	98.6	**Forestbrook** (CDP) Horry County
5	n/a	98.6	**Piedmont** (CDP) Anderson County
7	n/a	98.3	**Arcadia** (CDP) Spartanburg County
8	n/a	97.8	**Pickens** (city) Pickens County
8	n/a	97.8	**Travelers Rest** (city) Greenville County
10	n/a	97.5	**Graniteville** (CDP) Aiken County
11	n/a	97.3	**East Gaffney** (CDP) Cherokee County
11	n/a	97.3	**Elgin** (CDP) Lancaster County
13	n/a	97.2	**Laurel Bay** (CDP) Beaufort County
14	46	97.0	**Taylors** (CDP) Greenville County
15	n/a	96.9	**Lakewood** (CDP) Sumter County
15	n/a	96.9	**Woodruff** (city) Spartanburg County
17	n/a	96.8	**Centerville** (CDP) Anderson County
18	73	96.7	**Simpsonville** (city) Greenville County
19	n/a	96.6	**Fountain Inn** (city) Greenville County
19	n/a	96.6	**Welcome** (CDP) Greenville County
21	102	96.5	**Orangeburg** (city) Orangeburg County
22	n/a	96.4	**Red Bank** (CDP) Lexington County
23	123	96.3	**Easley** (city) Pickens County
24	n/a	96.2	**Clover** (town) York County
24	n/a	96.2	**Woodfield** (CDP) Richland County
26	150	96.1	**Mauldin** (city) Greenville County
27	n/a	96.0	**Lugoff** (CDP) Kershaw County
28	n/a	95.9	**Garden City** (CDP) Horry County
29	n/a	95.7	**Bennettsville** (city) Marlboro County
30	252	95.6	**Greer** (city) Greenville County
30	n/a	95.6	**Lancaster** (city) Lancaster County
30	n/a	95.6	**Northlake** (CDP) Anderson County
33	n/a	95.5	**York** (city) York County
34	306	95.4	**Red Hill** (CDP) Horry County
35	365	95.2	**Cayce** (city) Lexington County
36	n/a	95.0	**Edgefield** (town) Edgefield County
36	n/a	95.0	**Liberty** (city) Pickens County
36	n/a	95.0	**Springdale** (town) Lexington County
39	n/a	94.9	**McCormick** (town) McCormick County
40	n/a	94.8	**Abbeville** (city) Abbeville County
40	n/a	94.8	**Barnwell** (city) Barnwell County
40	n/a	94.8	**Pendleton** (town) Anderson County
43	500	94.7	**Berea** (CDP) Greenville County
43	500	94.7	**Newberry** (city) Newberry County
45	n/a	94.5	**Hardeeville** (city) Jasper County
45	n/a	94.5	**India Hook** (CDP) York County
45	n/a	94.5	**Laurens** (city) Laurens County
48	609	94.4	**Forest Acres** (city) Richland County
48	609	94.4	**Gantt** (CDP) Greenville County
48	n/a	94.4	**Lesslie** (CDP) York County
51	649	94.3	**Ladson** (CDP) Berkeley County
52	n/a	94.2	**Central** (town) Pickens County
52	678	94.2	**Five Forks** (CDP) Greenville County
52	678	94.2	**North Augusta** (city) Aiken County
52	n/a	94.2	**Williamston** (town) Anderson County
56	n/a	94.1	**Belton** (city) Anderson County
56	n/a	94.1	**Lyman** (town) Spartanburg County
56	n/a	94.1	**Moncks Corner** (town) Berkeley County
56	n/a	94.1	**Southern Shops** (CDP) Spartanburg County
60	n/a	94.0	**Burnettown** (town) Aiken County
61	n/a	93.8	**Boiling Springs** (CDP) Spartanburg County
61	n/a	93.8	**Sangaree** (CDP) Berkeley County
63	n/a	93.7	**Hollywood** (town) Charleston County
63	917	93.7	**Rock Hill** (city) York County
65	n/a	93.6	**Dunean** (CDP) Greenville County
66	n/a	93.5	**Belvedere** (CDP) Aiken County
66	n/a	93.5	**Seneca** (city) Oconee County
68	1086	93.3	**Greenwood** (city) Greenwood County
68	1086	93.3	**Hanahan** (city) Berkeley County
68	1086	93.3	**Summerville** (town) Dorchester County
71	n/a	93.2	**Arial** (CDP) Pickens County
71	n/a	93.2	**Darlington** (city) Darlington County
73	1193	93.1	**Sumter** (city) Sumter County
74	n/a	92.9	**Allendale** (town) Allendale County
74	1277	92.9	**Gaffney** (city) Cherokee County
76	n/a	92.8	**Lake Wylie** (CDP) York County
76	1322	92.8	**Wade Hampton** (CDP) Greenville County
78	n/a	92.7	**Little River** (CDP) Horry County
79	1416	92.6	**Lexington** (town) Lexington County
79	1416	92.6	**Seven Oaks** (CDP) Lexington County
81	n/a	92.5	**Burton** (CDP) Beaufort County
81	n/a	92.5	**Kingstree** (town) Williamsburg County
81	n/a	92.5	**North Hartsville** (CDP) Darlington County
81	1466	92.5	**Socastee** (CDP) Horry County
85	n/a	92.4	**Duncan** (town) Spartanburg County
85	n/a	92.4	**Valley Falls** (CDP) Spartanburg County
87	1563	92.3	**Dentsville** (CDP) Richland County
87	n/a	92.3	**Edisto** (CDP) Orangeburg County
87	n/a	92.3	**Union** (city) Union County
90	n/a	92.2	**Sans Souci** (CDP) Greenville County
90	n/a	92.2	**Saxon** (CDP) Spartanburg County
92	1644	92.1	**Bluffton** (town) Beaufort County
92	1644	92.1	**Irmo** (town) Richland County
94	1695	92.0	**Oak Grove** (CDP) Lexington County
95	n/a	91.9	**Lake Murray of Richland** (CDP) Richland County
96	1782	91.8	**Parker** (CDP) Greenville County
97	1819	91.7	**Florence** (city) Florence County
97	n/a	91.7	**Homeland Park** (CDP) Anderson County
97	n/a	91.7	**Newport** (CDP) York County
100	1892	91.5	**Anderson** (city) Anderson County
101	n/a	91.4	**Marion** (city) Marion County
101	1937	91.4	**West Columbia** (city) Lexington County
103	n/a	91.3	**Andrews** (town) Georgetown County
103	n/a	91.3	**Chester** (city) Chester County
105	2112	91.0	**Aiken** (city) Aiken County
105	n/a	91.0	**Bishopville** (city) Lee County
105	n/a	91.0	**Murrells Inlet** (CDP) Georgetown County
108	2200	90.8	**Spartanburg** (city) Spartanburg County
109	n/a	90.7	**Tega Cay** (city) York County
110	n/a	90.6	**Batesburg-Leesville** (town) Lexington County
110	n/a	90.6	**Clearwater** (CDP) Aiken County
112	2308	90.5	**North Charleston** (city) Charleston County
113	n/a	90.4	**Bamberg** (town) Bamberg County
114	n/a	90.0	**Lake City** (city) Florence County
115	2530	89.9	**Fort Mill** (town) York County
116	n/a	89.7	**Cheraw** (town) Chesterfield County
117	2657	89.5	**Mount Pleasant** (town) Charleston County
118	2741	89.3	**Conway** (city) Horry County
118	n/a	89.3	**Mullins** (city) Marion County
120	n/a	89.2	**Winnsboro** (town) Fairfield County
121	n/a	89.0	**Camden** (city) Kershaw County
122	n/a	88.9	**Denmark** (city) Bamberg County
123	n/a	88.8	**Saluda** (town) Saluda County
124	n/a	88.7	**Surfside Beach** (town) Horry County
125	2942	88.6	**Saint Andrews** (CDP) Richland County
126	n/a	88.5	**Georgetown** (city) Georgetown County
126	n/a	88.5	**Isle of Palms** (city) Charleston County
128	n/a	88.2	**Williston** (town) Barnwell County
129	3148	87.9	**North Myrtle Beach** (city) Horry County
130	3175	87.8	**Myrtle Beach** (city) Horry County
131	3250	87.5	**Greenville** (city) Greenville County
132	n/a	87.4	**Springdale** (CDP) Lancaster County
133	n/a	87.1	**Dillon** (city) Dillon County
134	n/a	87.0	**Walterboro** (city) Colleton County
135	n/a	86.8	**Brookdale** (CDP) Orangeburg County
136	n/a	86.4	**Manning** (city) Clarendon County
137	n/a	86.2	**Hampton** (town) Hampton County
138	n/a	85.7	**Hartsville** (city) Darlington County
139	3597	85.6	**Hilton Head Island** (town) Beaufort County
140	n/a	85.5	**Hopkins** (CDP) Richland County
141	3672	85.1	**Beaufort** (city) Beaufort County
141	n/a	85.1	**Ridgeland** (town) Jasper County
143	3685	85.0	**Goose Creek** (city) Berkeley County
144	3763	84.4	**Clemson** (city) Pickens County
145	3848	83.7	**Charleston** (city) Charleston County
146	n/a	79.5	**Clinton** (city) Laurens County
147	n/a	79.0	**Pageland** (town) Chesterfield County
148	4398	73.3	**Columbia** (city) Richland County
149	n/a	68.5	**Folly Beach** (city) Charleston County
150	4609	55.7	**Port Royal** (town) Beaufort County

Note: The state column ranks the top/bottom 150 places in the state with population of 2,500 or more. The national column ranks the top/bottom places in the country with population of 10,000 or more. Places that are unincorporated were not considered in the rankings. n/a indicates data not available. Please refer to the User Guide for additional information.

Commute to Work: Car

Top 150 Places Ranked in *Ascending* Order

State Rank	Nat'l Rank	Percent	Place
1	47	55.7	**Port Royal** (town) Beaufort County
2	n/a	68.5	**Folly Beach** (city) Charleston County
3	258	73.3	**Columbia** (city) Richland County
4	n/a	79.0	**Pageland** (town) Chesterfield County
5	n/a	79.5	**Clinton** (city) Laurens County
6	796	83.7	**Charleston** (city) Charleston County
7	884	84.4	**Clemson** (city) Pickens County
8	962	85.0	**Goose Creek** (city) Berkeley County
9	972	85.1	**Beaufort** (city) Beaufort County
9	n/a	85.1	**Ridgeland** (town) Jasper County
11	n/a	85.5	**Hopkins** (CDP) Richland County
12	1041	85.6	**Hilton Head Island** (town) Beaufort County
13	n/a	85.7	**Hartsville** (city) Darlington County
14	n/a	86.2	**Hampton** (town) Hampton County
15	n/a	86.4	**Manning** (city) Clarendon County
16	n/a	86.8	**Brookdale** (CDP) Orangeburg County
17	n/a	87.0	**Walterboro** (city) Colleton County
18	n/a	87.1	**Dillon** (city) Dillon County
19	n/a	87.4	**Springdale** (CDP) Lancaster County
20	1393	87.5	**Greenville** (city) Greenville County
21	1459	87.8	**Myrtle Beach** (city) Horry County
22	1482	87.9	**North Myrtle Beach** (city) Horry County
23	n/a	88.2	**Williston** (town) Barnwell County
24	n/a	88.5	**Georgetown** (city) Georgetown County
24	n/a	88.5	**Isle of Palms** (city) Charleston County
26	1685	88.6	**Saint Andrews** (CDP) Richland County
27	n/a	88.7	**Surfside Beach** (town) Horry County
28	n/a	88.8	**Saluda** (town) Saluda County
29	n/a	88.9	**Denmark** (city) Bamberg County
30	n/a	89.0	**Camden** (city) Kershaw County
31	n/a	89.2	**Winnsboro** (town) Fairfield County
32	1887	89.3	**Conway** (city) Horry County
32	n/a	89.3	**Mullins** (city) Marion County
34	1953	89.5	**Mount Pleasant** (town) Charleston County
35	n/a	89.7	**Cheraw** (town) Chesterfield County
36	2086	89.9	**Fort Mill** (town) York County
37	n/a	90.0	**Lake City** (city) Florence County
38	n/a	90.4	**Bamberg** (town) Bamberg County
39	2310	90.5	**North Charleston** (city) Charleston County
40	n/a	90.6	**Batesburg-Leesville** (town) Lexington County
40	n/a	90.6	**Clearwater** (CDP) Aiken County
42	n/a	90.7	**Tega Cay** (city) York County
43	2417	90.8	**Spartanburg** (city) Spartanburg County
44	2508	91.0	**Aiken** (city) Aiken County
44	n/a	91.0	**Bishopville** (city) Lee County
44	n/a	91.0	**Murrells Inlet** (CDP) Georgetown County
47	n/a	91.3	**Andrews** (town) Georgetown County
47	n/a	91.3	**Chester** (city) Chester County
49	n/a	91.4	**Marion** (city) Marion County
49	2676	91.4	**West Columbia** (city) Lexington County
51	2720	91.5	**Anderson** (city) Anderson County
52	2800	91.7	**Florence** (city) Florence County
52	n/a	91.7	**Homeland Park** (CDP) Anderson County
52	n/a	91.7	**Newport** (CDP) York County
55	2838	91.8	**Parker** (CDP) Greenville County
56	n/a	91.9	**Lake Murray of Richland** (CDP) Richland County
57	2913	92.0	**Oak Grove** (CDP) Lexington County
58	2962	92.1	**Bluffton** (town) Beaufort County
58	2962	92.1	**Irmo** (town) Richland County
60	n/a	92.2	**Sans Souci** (CDP) Greenville County
60	n/a	92.2	**Saxon** (CDP) Spartanburg County
62	3049	92.3	**Dentsville** (CDP) Richland County
62	n/a	92.3	**Edisto** (CDP) Orangeburg County
62	n/a	92.3	**Union** (city) Union County
65	n/a	92.4	**Duncan** (town) Spartanburg County
65	n/a	92.4	**Valley Falls** (CDP) Spartanburg County
67	n/a	92.5	**Burton** (CDP) Beaufort County
67	n/a	92.5	**Kingstree** (town) Williamsburg County
67	n/a	92.5	**North Hartsville** (CDP) Darlington County
67	3143	92.5	**Socastee** (CDP) Horry County
71	3191	92.6	**Lexington** (town) Lexington County
71	3191	92.6	**Seven Oaks** (CDP) Lexington County
73	n/a	92.7	**Little River** (CDP) Horry County
74	n/a	92.8	**Lake Wylie** (CDP) York County
74	3286	92.8	**Wade Hampton** (CDP) Greenville County
76	n/a	92.9	**Allendale** (town) Allendale County
76	3335	92.9	**Gaffney** (city) Cherokee County
78	3420	93.1	**Sumter** (city) Sumter County
79	n/a	93.2	**Arial** (CDP) Pickens County
79	n/a	93.2	**Darlington** (city) Darlington County
81	3510	93.3	**Greenwood** (city) Greenwood County
81	3510	93.3	**Hanahan** (city) Berkeley County
81	3510	93.3	**Summerville** (town) Dorchester County
84	n/a	93.5	**Belvedere** (CDP) Aiken County
84	n/a	93.5	**Seneca** (city) Oconee County
86	n/a	93.6	**Dunean** (CDP) Greenville County
87	n/a	93.7	**Hollywood** (town) Charleston County
87	3693	93.7	**Rock Hill** (city) York County
89	n/a	93.8	**Boiling Springs** (CDP) Spartanburg County
89	n/a	93.8	**Sangaree** (CDP) Berkeley County
91	n/a	94.0	**Burnettown** (town) Aiken County
92	n/a	94.1	**Belton** (city) Anderson County
92	n/a	94.1	**Lyman** (town) Spartanburg County
92	n/a	94.1	**Moncks Corner** (town) Berkeley County
92	n/a	94.1	**Southern Shops** (CDP) Spartanburg County
96	n/a	94.2	**Central** (town) Pickens County
96	3935	94.2	**Five Forks** (CDP) Greenville County
96	3935	94.2	**North Augusta** (city) Aiken County
96	n/a	94.2	**Williamston** (town) Anderson County
100	3979	94.3	**Ladson** (CDP) Berkeley County
101	4008	94.4	**Forest Acres** (city) Richland County
101	4008	94.4	**Gantt** (CDP) Greenville County
101	n/a	94.4	**Lesslie** (CDP) York County
104	n/a	94.5	**Hardeeville** (city) Jasper County
104	n/a	94.5	**India Hook** (CDP) York County
104	n/a	94.5	**Laurens** (city) Laurens County
107	4118	94.7	**Berea** (CDP) Greenville County
107	4118	94.7	**Newberry** (city) Newberry County
109	n/a	94.8	**Abbeville** (city) Abbeville County
109	n/a	94.8	**Barnwell** (city) Barnwell County
109	n/a	94.8	**Pendleton** (town) Anderson County
112	n/a	94.9	**McCormick** (town) McCormick County
113	n/a	95.0	**Edgefield** (town) Edgefield County
113	n/a	95.0	**Liberty** (city) Pickens County
113	n/a	95.0	**Springdale** (town) Lexington County
116	4267	95.2	**Cayce** (city) Lexington County
117	4324	95.4	**Red Hill** (CDP) Horry County
118	n/a	95.5	**York** (city) York County
119	4379	95.6	**Greer** (city) Greenville County
119	n/a	95.6	**Lancaster** (city) Lancaster County
119	n/a	95.6	**Northlake** (CDP) Anderson County
122	n/a	95.7	**Bennettsville** (city) Marlboro County
123	n/a	95.9	**Garden City** (CDP) Horry County
124	n/a	96.0	**Lugoff** (CDP) Kershaw County
125	4489	96.1	**Mauldin** (city) Greenville County
126	n/a	96.2	**Clover** (town) York County
126	n/a	96.2	**Woodfield** (CDP) Richland County
128	4519	96.3	**Easley** (city) Pickens County
129	n/a	96.4	**Red Bank** (CDP) Lexington County
130	4542	96.5	**Orangeburg** (city) Orangeburg County
131	n/a	96.6	**Fountain Inn** (city) Greenville County
131	n/a	96.6	**Welcome** (CDP) Greenville County
133	4571	96.7	**Simpsonville** (city) Greenville County
134	n/a	96.8	**Centerville** (CDP) Anderson County
135	n/a	96.9	**Lakewood** (CDP) Sumter County
135	n/a	96.9	**Woodruff** (city) Spartanburg County
137	4604	97.0	**Taylors** (CDP) Greenville County
138	n/a	97.2	**Laurel Bay** (CDP) Beaufort County
139	n/a	97.3	**East Gaffney** (CDP) Cherokee County
139	n/a	97.3	**Elgin** (CDP) Lancaster County
141	n/a	97.5	**Graniteville** (CDP) Aiken County
142	n/a	97.8	**Pickens** (city) Pickens County
142	n/a	97.8	**Travelers Rest** (city) Greenville County
144	n/a	98.3	**Arcadia** (CDP) Spartanburg County
145	n/a	98.6	**Forestbrook** (CDP) Horry County
145	n/a	98.6	**Piedmont** (CDP) Anderson County
147	n/a	99.0	**Honea Path** (town) Anderson County
148	n/a	99.1	**Dalzell** (CDP) Sumter County
149	n/a	99.9	**Walhalla** (city) Oconee County
150	n/a	100.0	**Gloverville** (CDP) Aiken County

Note: *The state column ranks the top/bottom 150 places in the state with population of 2,500 or more. The national column ranks the top/bottom places in the country with population of 10,000 or more. Places that are unincorporated were not considered in the rankings. n/a indicates data not available. Please refer to the User Guide for additional information.*

Commute to Work: Public Transportation

Top 150 Places Ranked in *Descending* Order

State Rank	Nat'l Rank	Percent	Place
1	n/a	5.5	**Dillon** (city) Dillon County
2	n/a	5.0	**Kingstree** (town) Williamsburg County
3	n/a	4.8	**Hampton** (town) Hampton County
4	n/a	4.1	**Georgetown** (city) Georgetown County
5	1149	4.0	**Clemson** (city) Pickens County
6	n/a	3.4	**Andrews** (town) Georgetown County
7	1376	3.3	**North Charleston** (city) Charleston County
8	n/a	3.0	**Homeland Park** (CDP) Anderson County
9	n/a	2.9	**Marion** (city) Marion County
10	1549	2.8	**Charleston** (city) Charleston County
11	1635	2.6	**Anderson** (city) Anderson County
11	n/a	2.6	**Saluda** (town) Saluda County
13	1801	2.3	**Conway** (city) Horry County
14	n/a	2.1	**Clinton** (city) Laurens County
15	2005	1.9	**Saint Andrews** (CDP) Richland County
15	n/a	1.9	**Williston** (town) Barnwell County
17	n/a	1.8	**Central** (town) Pickens County
17	2054	1.8	**Columbia** (city) Richland County
17	2054	1.8	**Dentsville** (CDP) Richland County
20	n/a	1.6	**Hopkins** (CDP) Richland County
21	n/a	1.4	**Walterboro** (city) Colleton County
22	n/a	1.3	**Lake City** (city) Florence County
22	n/a	1.3	**Pendleton** (town) Anderson County
22	n/a	1.3	**Seneca** (city) Oconee County
25	2496	1.2	**Goose Creek** (city) Berkeley County
26	n/a	1.1	**Allendale** (town) Allendale County
26	n/a	1.1	**Mullins** (city) Marion County
26	n/a	1.1	**Sans Souci** (CDP) Greenville County
26	2599	1.1	**Spartanburg** (city) Spartanburg County
30	2684	1.0	**Florence** (city) Florence County
30	2684	1.0	**Gantt** (CDP) Greenville County
30	2684	1.0	**Hilton Head Island** (town) Beaufort County
33	n/a	0.9	**Chester** (city) Chester County
33	n/a	0.9	**Clover** (town) York County
33	n/a	0.9	**Lake Murray of Richland** (CDP) Richland County
33	n/a	0.9	**Moncks Corner** (town) Berkeley County
33	2793	0.9	**Parker** (CDP) Greenville County
33	n/a	0.9	**Tega Cay** (city) York County
39	n/a	0.8	**Winnsboro** (town) Fairfield County
40	n/a	0.7	**Bennettsville** (city) Marlboro County
40	3031	0.7	**Fort Mill** (town) York County
40	3031	0.7	**Hanahan** (city) Berkeley County
40	n/a	0.7	**Pageland** (town) Chesterfield County
40	3031	0.7	**Wade Hampton** (CDP) Greenville County
45	n/a	0.6	**Bamberg** (town) Bamberg County
45	n/a	0.6	**Sangaree** (CDP) Berkeley County
47	3338	0.5	**Greenville** (city) Greenville County
47	n/a	0.5	**Laurens** (city) Laurens County
47	n/a	0.5	**McCormick** (town) McCormick County
47	n/a	0.5	**Woodfield** (CDP) Richland County
51	3488	0.4	**Berea** (CDP) Greenville County
51	n/a	0.4	**Camden** (city) Kershaw County
51	n/a	0.4	**Lake Wylie** (CDP) York County
51	3488	0.4	**Myrtle Beach** (city) Horry County
55	3669	0.3	**Aiken** (city) Aiken County
55	3669	0.3	**Cayce** (city) Lexington County
55	n/a	0.3	**Edgefield** (town) Edgefield County
55	3669	0.3	**Five Forks** (CDP) Greenville County
55	3669	0.3	**Greenwood** (city) Greenwood County
55	3669	0.3	**Rock Hill** (city) York County
55	n/a	0.3	**Springdale** (town) Lexington County
55	3669	0.3	**Summerville** (town) Dorchester County
55	n/a	0.3	**Sumter** (city) Sumter County
64	n/a	0.2	**Arcadia** (CDP) Spartanburg County
64	3876	0.2	**Bluffton** (town) Beaufort County
64	n/a	0.2	**Edisto** (CDP) Orangeburg County
64	3876	0.2	**Greer** (city) Greenville County
64	n/a	0.2	**Lancaster** (city) Lancaster County
64	3876	0.2	**Mount Pleasant** (town) Charleston County
64	3876	0.2	**North Myrtle Beach** (city) Horry County
64	3876	0.2	**Seven Oaks** (CDP) Lexington County
72	4109	0.1	**Lexington** (town) Lexington County
72	4109	0.1	**Mauldin** (city) Greenville County
72	4109	0.1	**North Augusta** (city) Aiken County
72	4109	0.1	**Red Hill** (CDP) Horry County
76	n/a	0.0	**Abbeville** (city) Abbeville County
76	n/a	0.0	**Arial** (CDP) Pickens County
76	n/a	0.0	**Barnwell** (city) Barnwell County
76	n/a	0.0	**Batesburg-Leesville** (town) Lexington County
76	4278	0.0	**Beaufort** (city) Beaufort County
76	n/a	0.0	**Belton** (city) Anderson County
76	n/a	0.0	**Belvedere** (CDP) Aiken County
76	n/a	0.0	**Bishopville** (city) Lee County
76	n/a	0.0	**Boiling Springs** (CDP) Spartanburg County
76	n/a	0.0	**Brookdale** (CDP) Orangeburg County
76	n/a	0.0	**Burnettown** (town) Aiken County
76	n/a	0.0	**Burton** (CDP) Beaufort County
76	n/a	0.0	**Centerville** (CDP) Anderson County
76	n/a	0.0	**Cheraw** (town) Chesterfield County
76	n/a	0.0	**Clearwater** (CDP) Aiken County
76	n/a	0.0	**Dalzell** (CDP) Sumter County
76	n/a	0.0	**Darlington** (city) Darlington County
76	n/a	0.0	**Denmark** (city) Bamberg County
76	n/a	0.0	**Duncan** (town) Spartanburg County
76	n/a	0.0	**Dunean** (CDP) Greenville County
76	4278	0.0	**Easley** (city) Pickens County
76	n/a	0.0	**East Gaffney** (CDP) Cherokee County
76	n/a	0.0	**Elgin** (CDP) Lancaster County
76	n/a	0.0	**Folly Beach** (city) Charleston County
76	4278	0.0	**Forest Acres** (city) Richland County
76	n/a	0.0	**Forestbrook** (CDP) Horry County
76	n/a	0.0	**Fountain Inn** (city) Greenville County
76	4278	0.0	**Gaffney** (city) Cherokee County
76	n/a	0.0	**Garden City** (CDP) Horry County
76	n/a	0.0	**Gloverville** (CDP) Aiken County
76	n/a	0.0	**Graniteville** (CDP) Aiken County
76	n/a	0.0	**Hardeeville** (city) Jasper County
76	n/a	0.0	**Hartsville** (city) Darlington County
76	n/a	0.0	**Hollywood** (town) Charleston County
76	n/a	0.0	**Honea Path** (town) Anderson County
76	n/a	0.0	**India Hook** (CDP) York County
76	4278	0.0	**Irmo** (town) Richland County
76	n/a	0.0	**Isle of Palms** (city) Charleston County
76	4278	0.0	**Ladson** (CDP) Berkeley County
76	n/a	0.0	**Lakewood** (CDP) Sumter County
76	n/a	0.0	**Laurel Bay** (CDP) Beaufort County
76	n/a	0.0	**Lesslie** (CDP) York County
76	n/a	0.0	**Liberty** (city) Pickens County
76	n/a	0.0	**Little River** (CDP) Horry County
76	n/a	0.0	**Lugoff** (CDP) Kershaw County
76	n/a	0.0	**Lyman** (town) Spartanburg County
76	n/a	0.0	**Manning** (city) Clarendon County
76	n/a	0.0	**Murrells Inlet** (CDP) Georgetown County
76	4278	0.0	**Newberry** (city) Newberry County
76	n/a	0.0	**Newport** (CDP) York County
76	n/a	0.0	**North Hartsville** (CDP) Darlington County
76	n/a	0.0	**Northlake** (CDP) Anderson County
76	4278	0.0	**Oak Grove** (CDP) Lexington County
76	4278	0.0	**Orangeburg** (city) Orangeburg County
76	n/a	0.0	**Pickens** (city) Pickens County
76	n/a	0.0	**Piedmont** (CDP) Anderson County
76	4278	0.0	**Port Royal** (town) Beaufort County
76	n/a	0.0	**Red Bank** (CDP) Lexington County
76	n/a	0.0	**Ridgeland** (town) Jasper County
76	n/a	0.0	**Saxon** (CDP) Spartanburg County
76	4278	0.0	**Simpsonville** (city) Greenville County
76	4278	0.0	**Socastee** (CDP) Horry County
76	n/a	0.0	**Southern Shops** (CDP) Spartanburg County
76	n/a	0.0	**Springdale** (CDP) Lancaster County
76	n/a	0.0	**Surfside Beach** (town) Horry County
76	4278	0.0	**Taylors** (CDP) Greenville County
76	n/a	0.0	**Travelers Rest** (city) Greenville County
76	n/a	0.0	**Union** (city) Union County
76	n/a	0.0	**Valley Falls** (CDP) Spartanburg County
76	n/a	0.0	**Walhalla** (city) Oconee County
76	n/a	0.0	**Welcome** (CDP) Greenville County
76	4278	0.0	**West Columbia** (city) Lexington County
76	n/a	0.0	**Williamston** (town) Anderson County
76	n/a	0.0	**Woodruff** (city) Spartanburg County
76	n/a	0.0	**York** (city) York County

Note: The state column ranks the top/bottom 150 places in the state with population of 2,500 or more. The national column ranks the top/bottom places in the country with population of 10,000 or more. Places that are unincorporated were not considered in the rankings. n/a indicates data not available. Please refer to the User Guide for additional information.

Commute to Work: Walk

Top 150 Places Ranked in *Descending* Order

State Rank	Nat'l Rank	Percent	Place
1	49	17.4	**Port Royal** (town) Beaufort County
2	n/a	14.3	**Folly Beach** (city) Charleston County
3	81	13.7	**Columbia** (city) Richland County
4	n/a	11.6	**Clinton** (city) Laurens County
5	122	11.1	**Goose Creek** (city) Berkeley County
6	n/a	8.8	**Denmark** (city) Bamberg County
7	n/a	8.3	**Manning** (city) Clarendon County
8	n/a	8.2	**Bishopville** (city) Lee County
8	n/a	8.2	**Williston** (town) Barnwell County
10	n/a	8.0	**Bamberg** (town) Bamberg County
11	n/a	7.7	**Winnsboro** (town) Fairfield County
12	n/a	7.2	**Hampton** (town) Hampton County
13	n/a	7.1	**Ridgeland** (town) Jasper County
14	n/a	6.7	**Pageland** (town) Chesterfield County
15	373	6.1	**Greenville** (city) Greenville County
16	n/a	5.6	**Saxon** (CDP) Spartanburg County
17	438	5.4	**Clemson** (city) Pickens County
18	471	5.2	**Charleston** (city) Charleston County
19	n/a	5.0	**Lake City** (city) Florence County
20	n/a	4.9	**Belton** (city) Anderson County
20	506	4.9	**Myrtle Beach** (city) Horry County
22	520	4.8	**Beaufort** (city) Beaufort County
23	n/a	4.7	**Hartsville** (city) Darlington County
24	n/a	4.4	**Walterboro** (city) Colleton County
25	n/a	4.2	**Cheraw** (town) Chesterfield County
25	637	4.2	**Spartanburg** (city) Spartanburg County
27	n/a	4.0	**Seneca** (city) Oconee County
28	n/a	3.9	**Lyman** (town) Spartanburg County
29	n/a	3.7	**Duncan** (town) Spartanburg County
29	766	3.7	**Greenwood** (city) Greenwood County
29	n/a	3.7	**Laurens** (city) Laurens County
29	n/a	3.7	**Southern Shops** (CDP) Spartanburg County
29	n/a	3.7	**Valley Falls** (CDP) Spartanburg County
34	n/a	3.4	**Barnwell** (city) Barnwell County
34	n/a	3.4	**Mullins** (city) Marion County
36	965	3.2	**Sumter** (city) Sumter County
37	1009	3.1	**Parker** (CDP) Greenville County
38	1053	3.0	**Conway** (city) Horry County
39	1105	2.9	**Anderson** (city) Anderson County
40	1164	2.8	**Newberry** (city) Newberry County
41	n/a	2.7	**Belvedere** (CDP) Aiken County
42	n/a	2.6	**Brookdale** (CDP) Orangeburg County
42	n/a	2.6	**Dillon** (city) Dillon County
42	n/a	2.6	**Isle of Palms** (city) Charleston County
42	1289	2.6	**North Myrtle Beach** (city) Horry County
42	1289	2.6	**Orangeburg** (city) Orangeburg County
47	n/a	2.5	**Arial** (CDP) Pickens County
47	n/a	2.5	**Chester** (city) Chester County
47	1347	2.5	**Rock Hill** (city) York County
50	1513	2.3	**Bluffton** (town) Beaufort County
50	n/a	2.3	**Burton** (CDP) Beaufort County
50	n/a	2.3	**Union** (city) Union County
53	1584	2.2	**Hilton Head Island** (town) Beaufort County
54	n/a	2.1	**Abbeville** (city) Abbeville County
54	1686	2.1	**Aiken** (city) Aiken County
54	n/a	2.1	**Central** (town) Pickens County
54	1686	2.1	**Greer** (city) Greenville County
54	n/a	2.1	**Homeland Park** (CDP) Anderson County
59	n/a	2.0	**Clearwater** (CDP) Aiken County
60	n/a	1.8	**Camden** (city) Kershaw County
60	n/a	1.8	**Hollywood** (town) Charleston County
60	1994	1.8	**North Charleston** (city) Charleston County
63	n/a	1.7	**Kingstree** (town) Williamsburg County
63	2120	1.7	**North Augusta** (city) Aiken County
65	n/a	1.6	**Boiling Springs** (CDP) Spartanburg County
65	n/a	1.6	**Fountain Inn** (city) Greenville County
65	n/a	1.6	**Sans Souci** (CDP) Greenville County
68	2367	1.5	**Berea** (CDP) Greenville County
68	2367	1.5	**Gaffney** (city) Cherokee County
68	n/a	1.5	**Lancaster** (city) Lancaster County
68	2367	1.5	**West Columbia** (city) Lexington County
72	n/a	1.4	**Elgin** (CDP) Lancaster County
72	n/a	1.4	**Hardeeville** (city) Jasper County
74	n/a	1.3	**Bennettsville** (city) Marlboro County
74	n/a	1.3	**Darlington** (city) Darlington County
74	n/a	1.3	**Red Bank** (CDP) Lexington County
74	2661	1.3	**Saint Andrews** (CDP) Richland County
74	2661	1.3	**Wade Hampton** (CDP) Greenville County
74	n/a	1.3	**Williamston** (town) Anderson County
80	n/a	1.2	**Allendale** (town) Allendale County
80	n/a	1.2	**Lakewood** (CDP) Sumter County
80	n/a	1.2	**Little River** (CDP) Horry County
80	2817	1.2	**Summerville** (town) Dorchester County
80	n/a	1.2	**Welcome** (CDP) Greenville County
85	2976	1.1	**Dentsville** (CDP) Richland County
85	2976	1.1	**Forest Acres** (city) Richland County
85	2976	1.1	**Ladson** (CDP) Berkeley County
85	n/a	1.1	**Moncks Corner** (town) Berkeley County
85	n/a	1.1	**Surfside Beach** (town) Horry County
90	n/a	1.0	**Clover** (town) York County
90	3154	1.0	**Hanahan** (city) Berkeley County
90	3154	1.0	**Lexington** (town) Lexington County
90	3154	1.0	**Mount Pleasant** (town) Charleston County
90	3154	1.0	**Red Hill** (CDP) Horry County
95	n/a	0.9	**Lake Wylie** (CDP) York County
96	3503	0.8	**Easley** (city) Pickens County
96	3503	0.8	**Florence** (city) Florence County
96	n/a	0.8	**Newport** (CDP) York County
96	3503	0.8	**Oak Grove** (CDP) Lexington County
100	n/a	0.7	**Georgetown** (city) Georgetown County
100	3687	0.7	**Mauldin** (city) Greenville County
100	n/a	0.7	**Saluda** (town) Saluda County
103	3855	0.6	**Fort Mill** (town) York County
104	4006	0.5	**Cayce** (city) Lexington County
104	4006	0.5	**Irmo** (town) Richland County
104	n/a	0.5	**Pickens** (city) Pickens County
104	4006	0.5	**Socastee** (CDP) Horry County
104	n/a	0.5	**Travelers Rest** (city) Greenville County
109	n/a	0.4	**Burnettown** (town) Aiken County
109	n/a	0.4	**Centerville** (CDP) Anderson County
109	n/a	0.4	**Dunean** (CDP) Greenville County
109	n/a	0.4	**Garden City** (CDP) Horry County
109	n/a	0.4	**Northlake** (CDP) Anderson County
109	4160	0.4	**Seven Oaks** (CDP) Lexington County
109	n/a	0.4	**Springdale** (town) Lexington County
116	n/a	0.2	**Sangaree** (CDP) Berkeley County
116	n/a	0.2	**Woodfield** (CDP) Richland County
118	4506	0.1	**Simpsonville** (city) Greenville County
118	n/a	0.1	**Walhalla** (city) Oconee County
120	n/a	0.0	**Andrews** (town) Georgetown County
120	n/a	0.0	**Arcadia** (CDP) Spartanburg County
120	n/a	0.0	**Batesburg-Leesville** (town) Lexington County
120	n/a	0.0	**Dalzell** (CDP) Sumter County
120	n/a	0.0	**East Gaffney** (CDP) Cherokee County
120	n/a	0.0	**Edgefield** (town) Edgefield County
120	n/a	0.0	**Edisto** (CDP) Orangeburg County
120	4564	0.0	**Five Forks** (CDP) Greenville County
120	n/a	0.0	**Forestbrook** (CDP) Horry County
120	4564	0.0	**Gantt** (CDP) Greenville County
120	n/a	0.0	**Gloverville** (CDP) Aiken County
120	n/a	0.0	**Graniteville** (CDP) Aiken County
120	n/a	0.0	**Honea Path** (town) Anderson County
120	n/a	0.0	**Hopkins** (CDP) Richland County
120	n/a	0.0	**India Hook** (CDP) York County
120	n/a	0.0	**Lake Murray of Richland** (CDP) Richland County
120	n/a	0.0	**Laurel Bay** (CDP) Beaufort County
120	n/a	0.0	**Lesslie** (CDP) York County
120	n/a	0.0	**Liberty** (city) Pickens County
120	n/a	0.0	**Lugoff** (CDP) Kershaw County
120	n/a	0.0	**Marion** (city) Marion County
120	n/a	0.0	**McCormick** (town) McCormick County
120	n/a	0.0	**Murrells Inlet** (CDP) Georgetown County
120	n/a	0.0	**North Hartsville** (CDP) Darlington County
120	n/a	0.0	**Pendleton** (town) Anderson County
120	n/a	0.0	**Piedmont** (CDP) Anderson County
120	n/a	0.0	**Springdale** (CDP) Lancaster County
120	4564	0.0	**Taylors** (CDP) Greenville County
120	n/a	0.0	**Tega Cay** (city) York County
120	n/a	0.0	**Woodruff** (city) Spartanburg County
120	n/a	0.0	**York** (city) York County

Note: The state column ranks the top/bottom 150 places in the state with population of 2,500 or more. The national column ranks the top/bottom places in the country with population of 10,000 or more. Places that are unincorporated were not considered in the rankings. n/a indicates data not available. Please refer to the User Guide for additional information.

Commute to Work: Walk

Top 150 Places Ranked in *Ascending* Order

State Rank	Nat'l Rank	Percent	Place
1	n/a	0.0	**Andrews** (town) Georgetown County
1	n/a	0.0	**Arcadia** (CDP) Spartanburg County
1	n/a	0.0	**Batesburg-Leesville** (town) Lexington County
1	n/a	0.0	**Dalzell** (CDP) Sumter County
1	n/a	0.0	**East Gaffney** (CDP) Cherokee County
1	n/a	0.0	**Edgefield** (town) Edgefield County
1	n/a	0.0	**Edisto** (CDP) Orangeburg County
1	1	0.0	**Five Forks** (CDP) Greenville County
1	n/a	0.0	**Forestbrook** (CDP) Horry County
1	1	0.0	**Gantt** (CDP) Greenville County
1	n/a	0.0	**Gloverville** (CDP) Aiken County
1	n/a	0.0	**Graniteville** (CDP) Aiken County
1	n/a	0.0	**Honea Path** (town) Anderson County
1	n/a	0.0	**Hopkins** (CDP) Richland County
1	n/a	0.0	**India Hook** (CDP) York County
1	n/a	0.0	**Lake Murray of Richland** (CDP) Richland County
1	n/a	0.0	**Laurel Bay** (CDP) Beaufort County
1	n/a	0.0	**Lesslie** (CDP) York County
1	n/a	0.0	**Liberty** (city) Pickens County
1	n/a	0.0	**Lugoff** (CDP) Kershaw County
1	n/a	0.0	**Marion** (city) Marion County
1	n/a	0.0	**McCormick** (town) McCormick County
1	n/a	0.0	**Murrells Inlet** (CDP) Georgetown County
1	n/a	0.0	**North Hartsville** (CDP) Darlington County
1	n/a	0.0	**Pendleton** (town) Anderson County
1	n/a	0.0	**Piedmont** (CDP) Anderson County
1	n/a	0.0	**Springdale** (CDP) Lancaster County
1	1	0.0	**Taylors** (CDP) Greenville County
1	n/a	0.0	**Tega Cay** (city) York County
1	n/a	0.0	**Woodruff** (city) Spartanburg County
1	n/a	0.0	**York** (city) York County
32	93	0.1	**Simpsonville** (city) Greenville County
32	n/a	0.1	**Walhalla** (city) Oconee County
34	n/a	0.2	**Sangaree** (CDP) Berkeley County
34	n/a	0.2	**Woodfield** (CDP) Richland County
36	n/a	0.4	**Burnettown** (town) Aiken County
36	n/a	0.4	**Centerville** (CDP) Anderson County
36	n/a	0.4	**Dunean** (CDP) Greenville County
36	n/a	0.4	**Garden City** (CDP) Horry County
36	n/a	0.4	**Northlake** (CDP) Anderson County
36	358	0.4	**Seven Oaks** (CDP) Lexington County
36	n/a	0.4	**Springdale** (town) Lexington County
43	497	0.5	**Cayce** (city) Lexington County
43	497	0.5	**Irmo** (town) Richland County
43	n/a	0.5	**Pickens** (city) Pickens County
43	497	0.5	**Socastee** (CDP) Horry County
43	n/a	0.5	**Travelers Rest** (city) Greenville County
48	651	0.6	**Fort Mill** (town) York County
49	n/a	0.7	**Georgetown** (city) Georgetown County
49	802	0.7	**Mauldin** (city) Greenville County
49	n/a	0.7	**Saluda** (city) Saluda County
52	970	0.8	**Easley** (city) Pickens County
52	970	0.8	**Florence** (city) Florence County
52	n/a	0.8	**Newport** (CDP) York County
52	970	0.8	**Oak Grove** (CDP) Lexington County
56	n/a	0.9	**Lake Wylie** (CDP) York County
57	n/a	1.0	**Clover** (town) York County
57	1324	1.0	**Hanahan** (city) Berkeley County
57	1324	1.0	**Lexington** (town) Lexington County
57	1324	1.0	**Mount Pleasant** (town) Charleston County
57	1324	1.0	**Red Hill** (CDP) Horry County
62	1503	1.1	**Dentsville** (CDP) Richland County
62	1503	1.1	**Forest Acres** (city) Richland County
62	1503	1.1	**Ladson** (CDP) Berkeley County
62	n/a	1.1	**Moncks Corner** (town) Berkeley County
62	n/a	1.1	**Surfside Beach** (town) Horry County
67	n/a	1.2	**Allendale** (town) Allendale County
67	n/a	1.2	**Lakewood** (CDP) Sumter County
67	n/a	1.2	**Little River** (CDP) Horry County
67	1681	1.2	**Summerville** (town) Dorchester County
67	n/a	1.2	**Welcome** (CDP) Greenville County
72	n/a	1.3	**Bennettsville** (city) Marlboro County
72	n/a	1.3	**Darlington** (city) Darlington County
72	n/a	1.3	**Red Bank** (CDP) Lexington County
72	1840	1.3	**Saint Andrews** (CDP) Richland County
72	1840	1.3	**Wade Hampton** (CDP) Greenville County
72	n/a	1.3	**Williamston** (town) Anderson County
78	n/a	1.4	**Elgin** (CDP) Lancaster County
78	n/a	1.4	**Hardeeville** (city) Jasper County
80	2157	1.5	**Berea** (CDP) Greenville County
80	2157	1.5	**Gaffney** (city) Cherokee County
80	n/a	1.5	**Lancaster** (city) Lancaster County
80	2157	1.5	**West Columbia** (city) Lexington County
84	n/a	1.6	**Boiling Springs** (CDP) Spartanburg County
84	n/a	1.6	**Fountain Inn** (city) Greenville County
84	n/a	1.6	**Sans Souci** (CDP) Greenville County
87	n/a	1.7	**Kingstree** (town) Williamsburg County
87	2427	1.7	**North Augusta** (city) Aiken County
89	n/a	1.8	**Camden** (city) Kershaw County
89	n/a	1.8	**Hollywood** (town) Charleston County
89	2537	1.8	**North Charleston** (city) Charleston County
92	n/a	2.0	**Clearwater** (CDP) Aiken County
93	n/a	2.1	**Abbeville** (city) Abbeville County
93	2876	2.1	**Aiken** (city) Aiken County
93	n/a	2.1	**Central** (town) Pickens County
93	2876	2.1	**Greer** (city) Greenville County
93	n/a	2.1	**Homeland Park** (CDP) Anderson County
98	2971	2.2	**Hilton Head Island** (town) Beaufort County
99	3073	2.3	**Bluffton** (town) Beaufort County
99	n/a	2.3	**Burton** (CDP) Beaufort County
99	n/a	2.3	**Union** (city) Union County
102	n/a	2.5	**Arial** (CDP) Pickens County
102	n/a	2.5	**Chester** (city) Chester County
102	3218	2.5	**Rock Hill** (city) York County
105	n/a	2.6	**Brookdale** (CDP) Orangeburg County
105	n/a	2.6	**Dillon** (city) Dillon County
105	n/a	2.6	**Isle of Palms** (city) Charleston County
105	3310	2.6	**North Myrtle Beach** (city) Horry County
105	3310	2.6	**Orangeburg** (city) Orangeburg County
110	n/a	2.7	**Belvedere** (CDP) Aiken County
111	3439	2.8	**Newberry** (city) Newberry County
112	3493	2.9	**Anderson** (city) Anderson County
113	3552	3.0	**Conway** (city) Horry County
114	3604	3.1	**Parker** (CDP) Greenville County
115	3648	3.2	**Sumter** (city) Sumter County
116	n/a	3.4	**Barnwell** (city) Barnwell County
116	n/a	3.4	**Mullins** (city) Marion County
118	n/a	3.7	**Duncan** (town) Spartanburg County
118	3858	3.7	**Greenwood** (city) Greenwood County
118	n/a	3.7	**Laurens** (city) Laurens County
118	n/a	3.7	**Southern Shops** (CDP) Spartanburg County
118	n/a	3.7	**Valley Falls** (CDP) Spartanburg County
123	n/a	3.9	**Lyman** (town) Spartanburg County
124	n/a	4.0	**Seneca** (city) Oconee County
125	n/a	4.2	**Cheraw** (town) Chesterfield County
125	3997	4.2	**Spartanburg** (city) Spartanburg County
127	n/a	4.4	**Walterboro** (city) Colleton County
128	n/a	4.7	**Hartsville** (city) Darlington County
129	4119	4.8	**Beaufort** (city) Beaufort County
130	n/a	4.9	**Belton** (city) Anderson County
130	4137	4.9	**Myrtle Beach** (city) Horry County
132	n/a	5.0	**Lake City** (city) Florence County
133	4174	5.2	**Charleston** (city) Charleston County
134	4199	5.4	**Clemson** (city) Pickens County
135	n/a	5.6	**Saxon** (CDP) Spartanburg County
136	4276	6.1	**Greenville** (city) Greenville County
137	n/a	6.7	**Pageland** (town) Chesterfield County
138	n/a	7.1	**Ridgeland** (town) Jasper County
139	n/a	7.2	**Hampton** (town) Hampton County
140	n/a	7.7	**Winnsboro** (town) Fairfield County
141	n/a	8.0	**Bamberg** (town) Bamberg County
142	n/a	8.2	**Bishopville** (city) Lee County
142	n/a	8.2	**Williston** (town) Barnwell County
144	n/a	8.3	**Manning** (city) Clarendon County
145	n/a	8.8	**Denmark** (city) Bamberg County
146	4533	11.1	**Goose Creek** (city) Berkeley County
147	n/a	11.6	**Clinton** (city) Laurens County
148	4573	13.7	**Columbia** (city) Richland County
149	n/a	14.3	**Folly Beach** (city) Charleston County
150	4606	17.4	**Port Royal** (town) Beaufort County

Note: The state column ranks the top/bottom 150 places in the state with population of 2,500 or more. The national column ranks the top/bottom places in the country with population of 10,000 or more. Places that are unincorporated were not considered in the rankings. n/a indicates data not available. Please refer to the User Guide for additional information.

Commute to Work: Work from Home

Top 150 Places Ranked in *Descending* Order

State Rank	Nat'l Rank	Percent	Place
1	7	19.1	**Port Royal** (town) Beaufort County
2	n/a	12.2	**Folly Beach** (city) Charleston County
3	187	9.2	**Columbia** (city) Richland County
4	313	8.0	**Isle of Palms** (city) Charleston County
5	313	7.9	**Fort Mill** (town) York County
5	313	7.9	**Hilton Head Island** (town) Beaufort County
5	313	7.9	**Mount Pleasant** (town) Charleston County
5	n/a	7.9	**Murrells Inlet** (CDP) Georgetown County
9	n/a	7.5	**Newport** (CDP) York County
10	n/a	7.4	**Batesburg-Leesville** (town) Lexington County
11	n/a	6.7	**Camden** (city) Kershaw County
12	n/a	6.5	**Hartsville** (city) Darlington County
13	701	6.2	**Beaufort** (city) Beaufort County
13	n/a	6.2	**Mullins** (city) Marion County
15	n/a	6.1	**Cheraw** (town) Chesterfield County
15	n/a	6.1	**Little River** (CDP) Horry County
15	n/a	6.1	**Tega Cay** (city) York County
18	n/a	5.7	**Clearwater** (CDP) Aiken County
19	n/a	5.5	**Ridgeland** (town) Jasper County
20	n/a	5.4	**Brookdale** (CDP) Orangeburg County
21	n/a	5.2	**Pageland** (town) Chesterfield County
21	n/a	5.2	**Saluda** (town) Saluda County
23	1163	5.1	**Irmo** (town) Richland County
24	n/a	5.0	**Burnettown** (town) Aiken County
24	1209	5.0	**Five Forks** (CDP) Greenville County
26	1254	4.9	**Greenville** (city) Greenville County
27	n/a	4.8	**Allendale** (town) Allendale County
27	n/a	4.8	**India Hook** (CDP) York County
27	n/a	4.8	**Lesslie** (CDP) York County
30	1372	4.7	**Aiken** (city) Aiken County
30	1372	4.7	**Lexington** (town) Lexington County
30	1372	4.7	**Oak Grove** (CDP) Lexington County
33	1495	4.5	**Bluffton** (town) Beaufort County
33	1495	4.5	**Florence** (city) Florence County
33	n/a	4.5	**McCormick** (town) McCormick County
33	n/a	4.5	**Sangaree** (CDP) Berkeley County
37	1566	4.4	**Charleston** (city) Charleston County
37	1566	4.4	**Summerville** (town) Dorchester County
37	n/a	4.4	**Surfside Beach** (town) Horry County
40	1720	4.2	**Wade Hampton** (CDP) Greenville County
41	n/a	4.1	**Hardeeville** (city) Jasper County
41	1790	4.1	**North Myrtle Beach** (city) Horry County
43	1884	4.0	**Forest Acres** (city) Richland County
43	n/a	4.0	**Lake Wylie** (CDP) York County
43	n/a	4.0	**Northlake** (CDP) Anderson County
46	n/a	3.9	**Pendleton** (town) Anderson County
47	n/a	3.8	**Liberty** (city) Pickens County
48	n/a	3.7	**Dillon** (city) Dillon County
48	n/a	3.7	**Hollywood** (town) Charleston County
48	n/a	3.7	**Lake City** (city) Florence County
48	n/a	3.7	**Manning** (city) Clarendon County
48	2137	3.7	**Socastee** (CDP) Horry County
48	n/a	3.7	**Williamston** (town) Anderson County
54	2227	3.6	**Ladson** (CDP) Berkeley County
54	n/a	3.6	**Sans Souci** (CDP) Greenville County
54	n/a	3.6	**Walterboro** (city) Colleton County
54	n/a	3.6	**York** (city) York County
58	n/a	3.5	**Chester** (city) Chester County
58	n/a	3.5	**Darlington** (city) Darlington County
58	2321	3.5	**Dentsville** (CDP) Richland County
58	2321	3.5	**Seven Oaks** (CDP) Lexington County
58	n/a	3.5	**Valley Falls** (CDP) Spartanburg County
63	n/a	3.4	**Clinton** (city) Laurens County
64	2522	3.3	**Conway** (city) Horry County
64	2522	3.3	**Hanahan** (city) Berkeley County
66	n/a	3.2	**Arial** (CDP) Pickens County
66	2621	3.2	**Clemson** (city) Pickens County
66	2621	3.2	**Gantt** (CDP) Greenville County
66	n/a	3.2	**Garden City** (CDP) Horry County
66	n/a	3.2	**Marion** (city) Marion County
66	n/a	3.2	**Union** (city) Union County
72	n/a	3.0	**Boiling Springs** (CDP) Spartanburg County
72	2821	3.0	**Mauldin** (city) Greenville County
72	2821	3.0	**North Augusta** (city) Aiken County
75	3026	2.8	**Spartanburg** (city) Spartanburg County
75	n/a	2.8	**Woodfield** (CDP) Richland County
77	n/a	2.5	**Lugoff** (CDP) Kershaw County
77	n/a	2.5	**Moncks Corner** (town) Berkeley County
77	3336	2.5	**West Columbia** (city) Lexington County
80	3451	2.4	**Rock Hill** (city) York County
81	n/a	2.3	**Georgetown** (city) Georgetown County
81	3553	2.3	**Simpsonville** (city) Greenville County
81	n/a	2.3	**Winnsboro** (town) Fairfield County
84	3645	2.2	**Cayce** (city) Lexington County
84	3645	2.2	**Myrtle Beach** (city) Horry County
84	3645	2.2	**Newberry** (city) Newberry County
84	3645	2.2	**North Charleston** (city) Charleston County
84	n/a	2.2	**North Hartsville** (CDP) Darlington County
89	3752	2.1	**Easley** (city) Pickens County
89	n/a	2.1	**Springdale** (town) Lexington County
91	n/a	2.0	**Centerville** (CDP) Anderson County
91	3839	2.0	**Greenwood** (city) Greenwood County
91	n/a	2.0	**Homeland Park** (CDP) Anderson County
91	3839	2.0	**Saint Andrews** (CDP) Richland County
91	3839	2.0	**Taylors** (CDP) Greenville County
96	n/a	1.9	**Abbeville** (city) Abbeville County
96	n/a	1.9	**Graniteville** (CDP) Aiken County
96	n/a	1.9	**Lakewood** (CDP) Sumter County
96	n/a	1.9	**Lyman** (town) Spartanburg County
100	n/a	1.8	**Hampton** (town) Hampton County
100	4023	1.8	**Red Hill** (CDP) Horry County
100	n/a	1.8	**Welcome** (CDP) Greenville County
103	4118	1.7	**Goose Creek** (city) Berkeley County
103	4118	1.7	**Greer** (city) Greenville County
103	n/a	1.7	**Lancaster** (city) Lancaster County
103	4118	1.7	**Sumter** (city) Sumter County
103	n/a	1.7	**Travelers Rest** (city) Greenville County
103	n/a	1.7	**Williston** (town) Barnwell County
109	4190	1.6	**Anderson** (city) Anderson County
109	n/a	1.6	**Dunean** (CDP) Greenville County
109	n/a	1.6	**Red Bank** (CDP) Lexington County
109	n/a	1.6	**Saxon** (CDP) Spartanburg County
113	n/a	1.5	**Arcadia** (CDP) Spartanburg County
113	4259	1.5	**Berea** (CDP) Greenville County
113	4259	1.5	**Gaffney** (city) Cherokee County
116	n/a	1.4	**Fountain Inn** (city) Greenville County
116	n/a	1.4	**Laurel Bay** (CDP) Beaufort County
116	n/a	1.4	**Piedmont** (CDP) Anderson County
119	n/a	1.3	**Duncan** (town) Spartanburg County
119	n/a	1.3	**Elgin** (CDP) Lancaster County
121	n/a	1.2	**Belvedere** (CDP) Aiken County
121	n/a	1.2	**Springdale** (CDP) Lancaster County
123	n/a	1.1	**Barnwell** (city) Barnwell County
123	n/a	1.1	**Hopkins** (CDP) Richland County
123	n/a	1.1	**Lake Murray of Richland** (CDP) Richland County
126	n/a	1.0	**Forestbrook** (CDP) Horry County
126	n/a	1.0	**Honea Path** (town) Anderson County
128	n/a	0.9	**Bishopville** (city) Lee County
128	n/a	0.9	**Dalzell** (CDP) Sumter County
128	n/a	0.9	**Kingstree** (town) Williamsburg County
128	n/a	0.9	**Laurens** (city) Laurens County
128	n/a	0.9	**Seneca** (city) Oconee County
133	n/a	0.8	**Bennettsville** (city) Marlboro County
133	n/a	0.8	**Burton** (CDP) Beaufort County
133	4571	0.8	**Orangeburg** (city) Orangeburg County
136	n/a	0.7	**East Gaffney** (CDP) Cherokee County
137	4617	0.6	**Parker** (CDP) Greenville County
138	n/a	0.5	**Belton** (city) Anderson County
138	n/a	0.5	**Edgefield** (town) Edgefield County
140	n/a	0.4	**Central** (town) Pickens County
141	n/a	0.2	**Bamberg** (town) Bamberg County
142	n/a	0.0	**Andrews** (town) Georgetown County
142	n/a	0.0	**Clover** (town) York County
142	n/a	0.0	**Denmark** (city) Bamberg County
142	n/a	0.0	**Edisto** (CDP) Orangeburg County
142	n/a	0.0	**Gloverville** (CDP) Aiken County
142	n/a	0.0	**Pickens** (city) Pickens County
142	n/a	0.0	**Southern Shops** (CDP) Spartanburg County
142	n/a	0.0	**Walhalla** (city) Oconee County
142	n/a	0.0	**Woodruff** (city) Spartanburg County

Note: The state column ranks the top/bottom 150 places in the state with population of 2,500 or more. The national column ranks the top/bottom places in the country with population of 10,000 or more. Places that are unincorporated were not considered in the rankings. n/a indicates data not available. Please refer to the User Guide for additional information.

Commute to Work: Work from Home

Top 150 Places Ranked in *Ascending* Order

State Rank	Nat'l Rank	Percent	Place
1	n/a	0.0	**Andrews** (town) Georgetown County
1	n/a	0.0	**Clover** (town) York County
1	n/a	0.0	**Denmark** (city) Bamberg County
1	n/a	0.0	**Edisto** (town) Orangeburg County
1	n/a	0.0	**Gloverville** (CDP) Aiken County
1	n/a	0.0	**Pickens** (city) Pickens County
1	n/a	0.0	**Southern Shops** (CDP) Spartanburg County
1	n/a	0.0	**Walhalla** (city) Oconee County
1	n/a	0.0	**Woodruff** (city) Spartanburg County
10	n/a	0.2	**Bamberg** (town) Bamberg County
11	n/a	0.4	**Central** (town) Pickens County
12	n/a	0.5	**Belton** (city) Anderson County
12	n/a	0.5	**Edgefield** (town) Edgefield County
14	29	0.6	**Parker** (CDP) Greenville County
15	n/a	0.7	**East Gaffney** (CDP) Cherokee County
16	n/a	0.8	**Bennettsville** (city) Marlboro County
16	n/a	0.8	**Burton** (CDP) Beaufort County
16	59	0.8	**Orangeburg** (city) Orangeburg County
19	n/a	0.9	**Bishopville** (city) Lee County
19	n/a	0.9	**Dalzell** (CDP) Sumter County
19	n/a	0.9	**Kingstree** (town) Williamsburg County
19	n/a	0.9	**Laurens** (city) Laurens County
19	n/a	0.9	**Seneca** (city) Oconee County
24	n/a	1.0	**Forestbrook** (CDP) Horry County
24	n/a	1.0	**Honea Path** (town) Anderson County
26	n/a	1.1	**Barnwell** (city) Barnwell County
26	n/a	1.1	**Hopkins** (CDP) Richland County
26	n/a	1.1	**Lake Murray of Richland** (CDP) Richland County
29	n/a	1.2	**Belvedere** (CDP) Aiken County
29	n/a	1.2	**Springdale** (CDP) Lancaster County
31	n/a	1.3	**Duncan** (town) Spartanburg County
31	n/a	1.3	**Elgin** (CDP) Lancaster County
33	n/a	1.4	**Fountain Inn** (city) Greenville County
33	n/a	1.4	**Laurel Bay** (CDP) Beaufort County
33	n/a	1.4	**Piedmont** (CDP) Anderson County
36	n/a	1.5	**Arcadia** (CDP) Spartanburg County
36	327	1.5	**Berea** (CDP) Greenville County
36	327	1.5	**Gaffney** (city) Cherokee County
39	398	1.6	**Anderson** (city) Anderson County
39	n/a	1.6	**Dunean** (CDP) Greenville County
39	n/a	1.6	**Red Bank** (CDP) Lexington County
39	n/a	1.6	**Saxon** (CDP) Spartanburg County
43	467	1.7	**Goose Creek** (city) Berkeley County
43	467	1.7	**Greer** (city) Greenville County
43	n/a	1.7	**Lancaster** (city) Lancaster County
43	467	1.7	**Sumter** (city) Sumter County
43	n/a	1.7	**Travelers Rest** (city) Greenville County
43	n/a	1.7	**Williston** (town) Barnwell County
49	n/a	1.8	**Hampton** (town) Hampton County
49	539	1.8	**Red Hill** (CDP) Horry County
49	n/a	1.8	**Welcome** (CDP) Greenville County
52	n/a	1.9	**Abbeville** (city) Abbeville County
52	n/a	1.9	**Graniteville** (CDP) Aiken County
52	n/a	1.9	**Lakewood** (CDP) Sumter County
52	n/a	1.9	**Lyman** (town) Spartanburg County
56	n/a	2.0	**Centerville** (CDP) Anderson County
56	710	2.0	**Greenwood** (city) Greenwood County
56	n/a	2.0	**Homeland Park** (CDP) Anderson County
56	710	2.0	**Saint Andrews** (CDP) Richland County
56	710	2.0	**Taylors** (CDP) Greenville County
61	818	2.1	**Easley** (city) Pickens County
61	n/a	2.1	**Springdale** (town) Lexington County
63	905	2.2	**Cayce** (city) Lexington County
63	905	2.2	**Myrtle Beach** (city) Horry County
63	905	2.2	**Newberry** (city) Newberry County
63	905	2.2	**North Charleston** (city) Charleston County
63	n/a	2.2	**North Hartsville** (CDP) Darlington County
68	n/a	2.3	**Georgetown** (city) Georgetown County
68	1012	2.3	**Simpsonville** (city) Greenville County
68	n/a	2.3	**Winnsboro** (town) Fairfield County
71	1104	2.4	**Rock Hill** (city) York County
72	n/a	2.5	**Lugoff** (CDP) Kershaw County
72	n/a	2.5	**Moncks Corner** (town) Berkeley County
72	1206	2.5	**West Columbia** (city) Lexington County
75	1547	2.8	**Spartanburg** (city) Spartanburg County
75	n/a	2.8	**Woodfield** (CDP) Richland County
77	n/a	3.0	**Boiling Springs** (CDP) Spartanburg County
77	1744	3.0	**Mauldin** (city) Greenville County
77	1744	3.0	**North Augusta** (city) Aiken County
80	n/a	3.2	**Arial** (CDP) Pickens County
80	1928	3.2	**Clemson** (city) Pickens County
80	1928	3.2	**Gantt** (CDP) Greenville County
80	n/a	3.2	**Garden City** (CDP) Horry County
80	n/a	3.2	**Marion** (city) Marion County
80	n/a	3.2	**Union** (city) Union County
86	2036	3.3	**Conway** (city) Horry County
86	2036	3.3	**Hanahan** (city) Berkeley County
88	n/a	3.4	**Clinton** (city) Laurens County
89	n/a	3.5	**Chester** (city) Chester County
89	n/a	3.5	**Darlington** (city) Darlington County
89	2224	3.5	**Dentsville** (CDP) Richland County
89	2224	3.5	**Seven Oaks** (CDP) Lexington County
89	n/a	3.5	**Valley Falls** (CDP) Spartanburg County
94	2336	3.6	**Ladson** (CDP) Berkeley County
94	n/a	3.6	**Sans Souci** (CDP) Greenville County
94	n/a	3.6	**Walterboro** (city) Colleton County
94	n/a	3.6	**York** (city) York County
98	n/a	3.7	**Dillon** (city) Dillon County
98	n/a	3.7	**Hollywood** (town) Charleston County
98	n/a	3.7	**Lake City** (city) Florence County
98	n/a	3.7	**Manning** (city) Clarendon County
98	2430	3.7	**Socastee** (CDP) Horry County
98	n/a	3.7	**Williamston** (town) Anderson County
104	n/a	3.8	**Liberty** (city) Pickens County
105	n/a	3.9	**Pendleton** (town) Anderson County
106	2705	4.0	**Forest Acres** (city) Richland County
106	n/a	4.0	**Lake Wylie** (CDP) York County
106	n/a	4.0	**Northlake** (CDP) Anderson County
109	n/a	4.1	**Hardeeville** (city) Jasper County
109	2773	4.1	**North Myrtle Beach** (city) Horry County
111	2867	4.2	**Wade Hampton** (CDP) Greenville County
112	3007	4.4	**Charleston** (city) Charleston County
112	3007	4.4	**Summerville** (town) Dorchester County
112	n/a	4.4	**Surfside Beach** (town) Horry County
115	3091	4.5	**Bluffton** (town) Beaufort County
115	3091	4.5	**Florence** (city) Florence County
115	n/a	4.5	**McCormick** (town) McCormick County
115	n/a	4.5	**Sangaree** (CDP) Berkeley County
119	3228	4.7	**Aiken** (city) Aiken County
119	3228	4.7	**Lexington** (town) Lexington County
119	3228	4.7	**Oak Grove** (CDP) Lexington County
122	n/a	4.8	**Allendale** (town) Allendale County
122	n/a	4.8	**India Hook** (CDP) York County
122	n/a	4.8	**Lesslie** (CDP) York County
125	3341	4.9	**Greenville** (city) Greenville County
126	n/a	5.0	**Burnettown** (town) Aiken County
126	3403	5.0	**Five Forks** (CDP) Greenville County
128	3448	5.1	**Irmo** (town) Richland County
129	n/a	5.2	**Pageland** (town) Chesterfield County
129	n/a	5.2	**Saluda** (town) Saluda County
131	n/a	5.4	**Brookdale** (CDP) Orangeburg County
132	n/a	5.5	**Ridgeland** (town) Jasper County
133	n/a	5.7	**Clearwater** (CDP) Aiken County
134	n/a	6.1	**Cheraw** (town) Chesterfield County
134	n/a	6.1	**Little River** (CDP) Horry County
134	n/a	6.1	**Tega Cay** (city) York County
137	3918	6.2	**Beaufort** (city) Beaufort County
137	n/a	6.2	**Mullins** (city) Marion County
139	n/a	6.5	**Hartsville** (city) Darlington County
140	n/a	6.7	**Camden** (city) Kershaw County
141	n/a	7.4	**Batesburg-Leesville** (town) Lexington County
142	n/a	7.5	**Newport** (CDP) York County
143	4329	7.9	**Fort Mill** (town) York County
143	4329	7.9	**Hilton Head Island** (town) Beaufort County
143	4329	7.9	**Mount Pleasant** (town) Charleston County
143	n/a	7.9	**Murrells Inlet** (CDP) Georgetown County
147	n/a	8.0	**Isle of Palms** (city) Charleston County
148	4467	9.2	**Columbia** (city) Richland County
149	n/a	12.2	**Folly Beach** (city) Charleston County
150	4649	19.1	**Port Royal** (town) Beaufort County

Note: The state column ranks the top/bottom 150 places in the state with population of 2,500 or more. The national column ranks the top/bottom places in the country with population of 10,000 or more. Places that are unincorporated were not considered in the rankings. n/a indicates data not available. Please refer to the User Guide for additional information.

Median Travel Time to Work

Top 150 Places Ranked in *Descending* Order

State Rank	Nat'l Rank	Minutes	Place
1	n/a	33.9	**Isle of Palms** (city) Charleston County
2	n/a	31.9	**Lesslie** (CDP) York County
3	n/a	29.5	**Lake Wylie** (CDP) York County
4	n/a	29.3	**Tega Cay** (city) York County
5	n/a	29.0	**Andrews** (town) Georgetown County
6	n/a	28.5	**Sangaree** (CDP) Berkeley County
7	n/a	28.4	**Arial** (CDP) Pickens County
8	n/a	28.1	**Saluda** (town) Saluda County
9	1399	28.0	**Summerville** (town) Dorchester County
9	n/a	28.0	**Woodruff** (city) Spartanburg County
11	n/a	27.8	**Clover** (town) York County
12	n/a	27.7	**Ridgeland** (town) Jasper County
13	n/a	27.4	**McCormick** (town) McCormick County
14	n/a	27.2	**Hollywood** (town) Charleston County
15	n/a	26.8	**Batesburg-Leesville** (town) Lexington County
15	n/a	26.8	**Lake Murray of Richland** (CDP) Richland County
17	n/a	26.3	**Red Bank** (CDP) Lexington County
18	1824	26.2	**Ladson** (CDP) Berkeley County
19	n/a	26.1	**North Hartsville** (CDP) Darlington County
20	n/a	25.8	**Hopkins** (CDP) Richland County
21	n/a	25.7	**Williamston** (town) Anderson County
21	n/a	25.7	**Winnsboro** (town) Fairfield County
23	n/a	25.5	**Allendale** (town) Allendale County
23	n/a	25.5	**Chester** (city) Chester County
23	2014	25.5	**Fort Mill** (town) York County
26	n/a	25.4	**Arcadia** (CDP) Spartanburg County
27	n/a	25.3	**Mullins** (city) Marion County
27	n/a	25.3	**York** (city) York County
29	n/a	25.2	**Belvedere** (CDP) Aiken County
30	n/a	24.9	**Abbeville** (city) Abbeville County
30	n/a	24.9	**Pickens** (city) Pickens County
32	2313	24.4	**Five Forks** (CDP) Greenville County
32	2313	24.4	**North Augusta** (city) Aiken County
32	n/a	24.4	**Walterboro** (city) Colleton County
35	n/a	24.3	**Lancaster** (city) Lancaster County
36	n/a	24.1	**Dalzell** (CDP) Sumter County
36	n/a	24.1	**India Hook** (CDP) York County
38	n/a	24.0	**Newport** (CDP) York County
39	n/a	23.9	**Lugoff** (CDP) Kershaw County
40	n/a	23.7	**Pageland** (town) Chesterfield County
41	2577	23.6	**Berea** (CDP) Greenville County
41	2577	23.6	**Bluffton** (town) Beaufort County
43	2614	23.5	**Easley** (city) Pickens County
43	n/a	23.5	**Graniteville** (CDP) Aiken County
43	n/a	23.5	**Hardeeville** (city) Jasper County
46	n/a	23.4	**Denmark** (city) Bamberg County
46	n/a	23.4	**Kingstree** (town) Williamsburg County
46	n/a	23.4	**Manning** (city) Clarendon County
49	2664	23.3	**Goose Creek** (city) Berkeley County
50	n/a	23.2	**Elgin** (CDP) Lancaster County
50	n/a	23.2	**Laurens** (city) Laurens County
50	2697	23.2	**Lexington** (town) Lexington County
50	n/a	23.2	**Piedmont** (CDP) Anderson County
50	n/a	23.2	**Union** (city) Union County
55	n/a	23.1	**Moncks Corner** (town) Berkeley County
55	n/a	23.1	**Northlake** (CDP) Anderson County
57	n/a	22.8	**Burnettown** (town) Aiken County
57	n/a	22.8	**Gloverville** (CDP) Aiken County
57	n/a	22.8	**Hampton** (town) Hampton County
57	n/a	22.8	**Honea Path** (town) Anderson County
61	2818	22.7	**Irmo** (town) Richland County
62	n/a	22.6	**Bennettsville** (city) Marlboro County
62	n/a	22.6	**Marion** (city) Marion County
64	n/a	22.4	**Dillon** (city) Dillon County
64	n/a	22.4	**Fountain Inn** (city) Greenville County
64	n/a	22.4	**Lakewood** (CDP) Sumter County
67	2977	22.2	**Rock Hill** (city) York County
68	3005	22.1	**Oak Grove** (CDP) Lexington County
68	3005	22.1	**Parker** (CDP) Greenville County
70	3038	22.0	**North Charleston** (city) Charleston County
71	n/a	21.9	**Homeland Park** (CDP) Anderson County
71	3064	21.9	**Mount Pleasant** (town) Charleston County
71	n/a	21.9	**Pendleton** (town) Anderson County
71	n/a	21.9	**Welcome** (CDP) Greenville County
75	n/a	21.8	**Williston** (town) Barnwell County
76	n/a	21.5	**Bishopville** (city) Lee County
77	3200	21.4	**Aiken** (city) Aiken County
77	3200	21.4	**Greer** (city) Greenville County
77	n/a	21.4	**Springdale** (CDP) Lancaster County
80	n/a	21.3	**Liberty** (city) Pickens County
81	n/a	21.2	**Camden** (city) Kershaw County
81	n/a	21.2	**Folly Beach** (city) Charleston County
83	n/a	21.1	**Boiling Springs** (CDP) Spartanburg County
83	n/a	21.1	**Garden City** (CDP) Horry County
83	3272	21.1	**Red Hill** (CDP) Horry County
83	3272	21.1	**Simpsonville** (city) Greenville County
87	3309	21.0	**Charleston** (city) Charleston County
88	n/a	20.9	**Burton** (CDP) Beaufort County
89	n/a	20.8	**Barnwell** (city) Barnwell County
89	3359	20.8	**Greenwood** (city) Greenwood County
89	3359	20.8	**Taylors** (CDP) Greenville County
89	n/a	20.8	**Travelers Rest** (city) Greenville County
93	n/a	20.7	**Belton** (city) Anderson County
93	n/a	20.7	**Forestbrook** (CDP) Horry County
93	n/a	20.7	**Seneca** (city) Oconee County
93	3391	20.7	**Seven Oaks** (CDP) Lexington County
97	n/a	20.6	**Valley Falls** (CDP) Spartanburg County
98	3434	20.5	**Conway** (city) Horry County
98	3434	20.5	**Gantt** (CDP) Greenville County
100	3453	20.4	**Hanahan** (city) Berkeley County
101	n/a	20.3	**Duncan** (town) Spartanburg County
102	n/a	20.2	**Lake City** (city) Florence County
103	n/a	20.1	**Sans Souci** (CDP) Greenville County
104	n/a	20.0	**Murrells Inlet** (CDP) Georgetown County
105	3592	19.9	**Beaufort** (city) Beaufort County
105	3592	19.9	**Saint Andrews** (CDP) Richland County
107	n/a	19.8	**Georgetown** (city) Georgetown County
107	3612	19.8	**Socastee** (CDP) Horry County
107	n/a	19.8	**Walhalla** (city) Oconee County
110	n/a	19.6	**Darlington** (city) Darlington County
110	n/a	19.6	**Saxon** (CDP) Spartanburg County
110	n/a	19.6	**Surfside Beach** (town) Horry County
113	3684	19.5	**West Columbia** (city) Lexington County
114	n/a	19.4	**Edisto** (CDP) Orangeburg County
114	n/a	19.4	**Springdale** (town) Lexington County
116	n/a	19.2	**Clearwater** (CDP) Aiken County
116	n/a	19.2	**Laurel Bay** (CDP) Beaufort County
116	3774	19.2	**Sumter** (city) Sumter County
119	n/a	19.1	**Centerville** (CDP) Anderson County
119	3795	19.1	**Florence** (city) Florence County
121	3846	18.9	**Anderson** (city) Anderson County
121	n/a	18.9	**Clinton** (city) Laurens County
121	n/a	18.9	**Woodfield** (CDP) Richland County
124	n/a	18.8	**Southern Shops** (CDP) Spartanburg County
125	3876	18.7	**Dentsville** (CDP) Richland County
125	3876	18.7	**North Myrtle Beach** (city) Horry County
127	n/a	18.5	**Little River** (CDP) Horry County
127	3922	18.5	**Mauldin** (city) Greenville County
129	n/a	18.3	**Hartsville** (city) Darlington County
129	3956	18.3	**Wade Hampton** (CDP) Greenville County
131	3991	18.1	**Cayce** (city) Lexington County
132	n/a	17.9	**Edgefield** (town) Edgefield County
132	4027	17.9	**Hilton Head Island** (town) Beaufort County
132	4027	17.9	**Spartanburg** (city) Spartanburg County
135	n/a	17.6	**Bamberg** (town) Bamberg County
136	4135	17.3	**Forest Acres** (city) Richland County
137	4173	17.1	**Clemson** (city) Pickens County
138	4189	17.0	**Greenville** (city) Greenville County
139	4202	16.9	**Myrtle Beach** (city) Horry County
140	n/a	16.6	**Brookdale** (CDP) Orangeburg County
141	4307	16.2	**Columbia** (city) Richland County
142	4321	16.1	**Orangeburg** (city) Orangeburg County
143	n/a	15.9	**East Gaffney** (CDP) Cherokee County
143	n/a	15.9	**Lyman** (town) Spartanburg County
145	n/a	15.6	**Central** (town) Pickens County
145	n/a	15.6	**Dunean** (CDP) Greenville County
147	4416	15.4	**Gaffney** (city) Cherokee County
147	4416	15.4	**Newberry** (city) Newberry County
149	4594	13.2	**Port Royal** (town) Beaufort County
150	n/a	10.6	**Cheraw** (town) Chesterfield County

Note: *The state column ranks the top/bottom 150 places in the state with population of 2,500 or more. The national column ranks the top/bottom places in the country with population of 10,000 or more. Places that are unincorporated were not considered in the rankings. n/a indicates data not available. Please refer to the User Guide for additional information.*

Median Travel Time to Work

Top 150 Places Ranked in *Ascending* Order

State Rank	Nat'l Rank	Minutes	Place
1	n/a	10.6	**Cheraw** (town) Chesterfield County
2	58	13.2	**Port Royal** (town) Beaufort County
3	233	15.4	**Gaffney** (city) Cherokee County
3	233	15.4	**Newberry** (city) Newberry County
5	n/a	15.6	**Central** (town) Pickens County
5	n/a	15.6	**Dunean** (CDP) Greenville County
7	n/a	15.9	**East Gaffney** (CDP) Cherokee County
7	n/a	15.9	**Lyman** (town) Spartanburg County
9	325	16.1	**Orangeburg** (city) Orangeburg County
10	336	16.2	**Columbia** (city) Richland County
11	n/a	16.6	**Brookdale** (CDP) Orangeburg County
12	441	16.9	**Myrtle Beach** (city) Horry County
13	455	17.0	**Greenville** (city) Greenville County
14	468	17.1	**Clemson** (city) Pickens County
15	507	17.3	**Forest Acres** (city) Richland County
16	n/a	17.6	**Bamberg** (town) Bamberg County
17	n/a	17.9	**Edgefield** (town) Edgefield County
17	611	17.9	**Hilton Head Island** (town) Beaufort County
17	611	17.9	**Spartanburg** (city) Spartanburg County
20	643	18.1	**Cayce** (city) Lexington County
21	n/a	18.3	**Hartsville** (city) Darlington County
21	686	18.3	**Wade Hampton** (CDP) Greenville County
23	n/a	18.5	**Little River** (CDP) Horry County
23	716	18.5	**Mauldin** (city) Greenville County
25	756	18.7	**Dentsville** (CDP) Richland County
25	756	18.7	**North Myrtle Beach** (city) Horry County
27	n/a	18.8	**Southern Shops** (CDP) Spartanburg County
28	798	18.9	**Anderson** (city) Anderson County
28	n/a	18.9	**Clinton** (city) Laurens County
28	n/a	18.9	**Woodfield** (CDP) Richland County
31	n/a	19.1	**Centerville** (CDP) Anderson County
31	833	19.1	**Florence** (city) Florence County
33	n/a	19.2	**Clearwater** (CDP) Aiken County
33	n/a	19.2	**Laurel Bay** (CDP) Beaufort County
33	862	19.2	**Sumter** (city) Sumter County
36	n/a	19.4	**Edisto** (CDP) Orangeburg County
36	n/a	19.4	**Springdale** (town) Lexington County
38	937	19.5	**West Columbia** (city) Lexington County
39	n/a	19.6	**Darlington** (city) Darlington County
39	n/a	19.6	**Saxon** (CDP) Spartanburg County
39	n/a	19.6	**Surfside Beach** (town) Horry County
42	n/a	19.8	**Georgetown** (city) Georgetown County
42	1019	19.8	**Socastee** (CDP) Horry County
42	n/a	19.8	**Walhalla** (city) Oconee County
45	1045	19.9	**Beaufort** (city) Beaufort County
45	1045	19.9	**Saint Andrews** (CDP) Richland County
47	n/a	20.0	**Murrells Inlet** (CDP) Georgetown County
48	n/a	20.1	**Sans Souci** (CDP) Greenville County
49	n/a	20.2	**Lake City** (city) Florence County
50	n/a	20.3	**Duncan** (town) Spartanburg County
51	1179	20.4	**Hanahan** (city) Berkeley County
52	1204	20.5	**Conway** (city) Horry County
52	1204	20.5	**Gantt** (CDP) Greenville County
54	n/a	20.6	**Valley Falls** (CDP) Spartanburg County
55	n/a	20.7	**Belton** (city) Anderson County
55	n/a	20.7	**Forestbrook** (CDP) Horry County
55	n/a	20.7	**Seneca** (city) Oconee County
55	1247	20.7	**Seven Oaks** (CDP) Lexington County
59	n/a	20.8	**Barnwell** (city) Barnwell County
59	1266	20.8	**Greenwood** (city) Greenwood County
59	1266	20.8	**Taylors** (CDP) Greenville County
59	n/a	20.8	**Travelers Rest** (city) Greenville County
63	n/a	20.9	**Burton** (CDP) Beaufort County
64	1323	21.0	**Charleston** (city) Charleston County
65	n/a	21.1	**Boiling Springs** (CDP) Spartanburg County
65	n/a	21.1	**Garden City** (CDP) Horry County
65	1348	21.1	**Red Hill** (CDP) Horry County
65	1348	21.1	**Simpsonville** (city) Greenville County
69	n/a	21.2	**Camden** (city) Kershaw County
69	n/a	21.2	**Folly Beach** (city) Charleston County
71	n/a	21.3	**Liberty** (city) Pickens County
72	1435	21.4	**Aiken** (city) Aiken County
72	1435	21.4	**Greer** (city) Greenville County
72	n/a	21.4	**Springdale** (CDP) Lancaster County
75	n/a	21.5	**Bishopville** (city) Lee County
76	n/a	21.8	**Williston** (town) Barnwell County
77	n/a	21.9	**Homeland Park** (CDP) Anderson County
77	1562	21.9	**Mount Pleasant** (town) Charleston County
77	n/a	21.9	**Pendleton** (town) Anderson County
77	n/a	21.9	**Welcome** (CDP) Greenville County
81	1593	22.0	**North Charleston** (city) Charleston County
82	1619	22.1	**Oak Grove** (CDP) Lexington County
82	1619	22.1	**Parker** (CDP) Greenville County
84	1652	22.2	**Rock Hill** (city) York County
85	n/a	22.4	**Dillon** (city) Dillon County
85	n/a	22.4	**Fountain Inn** (city) Greenville County
85	n/a	22.4	**Lakewood** (CDP) Sumter County
88	n/a	22.6	**Bennettsville** (city) Marlboro County
88	n/a	22.6	**Marion** (city) Marion County
90	1812	22.7	**Irmo** (town) Richland County
91	n/a	22.8	**Burnettown** (town) Aiken County
91	n/a	22.8	**Gloverville** (CDP) Aiken County
91	n/a	22.8	**Hampton** (town) Hampton County
91	n/a	22.8	**Honea Path** (town) Anderson County
95	n/a	23.1	**Moncks Corner** (town) Berkeley County
95	n/a	23.1	**Northlake** (CDP) Anderson County
97	n/a	23.2	**Elgin** (CDP) Lancaster County
97	n/a	23.2	**Laurens** (city) Laurens County
97	1932	23.2	**Lexington** (town) Lexington County
97	n/a	23.2	**Piedmont** (CDP) Anderson County
97	n/a	23.2	**Union** (city) Union County
102	1960	23.3	**Goose Creek** (city) Berkeley County
103	n/a	23.4	**Denmark** (city) Bamberg County
103	n/a	23.4	**Kingstree** (town) Williamsburg County
103	n/a	23.4	**Manning** (city) Clarendon County
106	2016	23.5	**Easley** (city) Pickens County
106	n/a	23.5	**Graniteville** (CDP) Aiken County
106	n/a	23.5	**Hardeeville** (city) Jasper County
109	2043	23.6	**Berea** (CDP) Greenville County
109	2043	23.6	**Bluffton** (town) Beaufort County
111	n/a	23.7	**Pageland** (town) Chesterfield County
112	n/a	23.9	**Lugoff** (CDP) Kershaw County
113	n/a	24.0	**Newport** (CDP) York County
114	n/a	24.1	**Dalzell** (CDP) Sumter County
114	n/a	24.1	**India Hook** (CDP) York County
116	n/a	24.3	**Lancaster** (city) Lancaster County
117	2307	24.4	**Five Forks** (CDP) Greenville County
117	2307	24.4	**North Augusta** (city) Aiken County
117	n/a	24.4	**Walterboro** (city) Colleton County
120	n/a	24.9	**Abbeville** (city) Abbeville County
120	n/a	24.9	**Pickens** (city) Pickens County
122	n/a	25.2	**Belvedere** (CDP) Aiken County
123	n/a	25.3	**Mullins** (city) Marion County
123	n/a	25.3	**York** (city) York County
125	n/a	25.4	**Arcadia** (CDP) Spartanburg County
126	n/a	25.5	**Allendale** (town) Allendale County
126	n/a	25.5	**Chester** (city) Chester County
126	2620	25.5	**Fort Mill** (town) York County
129	n/a	25.7	**Williamston** (town) Anderson County
129	n/a	25.7	**Winnsboro** (town) Fairfield County
131	n/a	25.8	**Hopkins** (CDP) Richland County
132	n/a	26.1	**North Hartsville** (CDP) Darlington County
133	2806	26.2	**Ladson** (CDP) Berkeley County
134	n/a	26.3	**Red Bank** (CDP) Lexington County
135	n/a	26.8	**Batesburg-Leesville** (town) Lexington County
135	n/a	26.8	**Lake Murray of Richland** (CDP) Richland County
137	n/a	27.2	**Hollywood** (town) Charleston County
138	n/a	27.4	**McCormick** (town) McCormick County
139	n/a	27.7	**Ridgeland** (town) Jasper County
140	n/a	27.8	**Clover** (town) York County
141	3240	28.0	**Summerville** (town) Dorchester County
141	n/a	28.0	**Woodruff** (city) Spartanburg County
143	n/a	28.1	**Saluda** (town) Saluda County
144	n/a	28.4	**Arial** (CDP) Pickens County
145	n/a	28.5	**Sangaree** (CDP) Berkeley County
146	n/a	29.0	**Andrews** (town) Georgetown County
147	n/a	29.3	**Tega Cay** (city) York County
148	n/a	29.5	**Lake Wylie** (CDP) York County
149	n/a	31.9	**Lesslie** (CDP) York County
150	n/a	33.9	**Isle of Palms** (city) Charleston County

Note: The state column ranks the top/bottom 150 places in the state with population of 2,500 or more. The national column ranks the top/bottom places in the country with population of 10,000 or more. Places that are unincorporated were not considered in the rankings. n/a indicates data not available. Please refer to the User Guide for additional information.

Violent Crime Rate per 10,000 Population

Top 150 Places Ranked in *Descending* Order

State Rank	Nat'l Rank	Rate	Place
1	n/a	277.1	**Clover** (town) York County
2	n/a	173.9	**Bishopville** (city) Lee County
3	25	165.7	**Myrtle Beach** (city) Horry County
4	n/a	161.5	**Dillon** (city) Dillon County
5	n/a	149.8	**Allendale** (town) Allendale County
6	n/a	143.8	**Manning** (city) Clarendon County
7	49	140.5	**Spartanburg** (city) Spartanburg County
8	n/a	140.1	**Camden** (city) Kershaw County
9	n/a	139.9	**Mullins** (city) Marion County
10	n/a	133.6	**Marion** (city) Marion County
11	n/a	130.5	**Bennettsville** (city) Marlboro County
12	62	128.6	**Greenwood** (city) Greenwood County
13	n/a	126.6	**Kingstree** (town) Williamsburg County
14	n/a	125.7	**Chester** (city) Chester County
15	n/a	123.5	**Lancaster** (city) Lancaster County
16	n/a	122.4	**Georgetown** (city) Georgetown County
17	88	118.4	**Beaufort** (city) Beaufort County
18	n/a	110.4	**Hartsville** (city) Darlington County
19	117	103.7	**Anderson** (city) Anderson County
20	n/a	101.1	**Lake City** (city) Florence County
21	n/a	99.3	**Laurens** (city) Laurens County
22	n/a	96.6	**Barnwell** (city) Barnwell County
23	n/a	95.7	**Pageland** (town) Chesterfield County
24	n/a	94.8	**Union** (city) Union County
25	157	94.6	**Sumter** (city) Sumter County
26	n/a	92.5	**Batesburg-Leesville** (town) Lexington County
27	n/a	92.1	**Andrews** (town) Georgetown County
28	n/a	88.6	**Hardeeville** (city) Jasper County
29	n/a	88.4	**Cheraw** (town) Chesterfield County
30	n/a	87.1	**Walterboro** (city) Colleton County
31	222	81.8	**North Myrtle Beach** (city) Horry County
32	n/a	79.5	**York** (city) York County
33	n/a	78.2	**Belton** (city) Anderson County
34	255	77.9	**Florence** (city) Florence County
35	n/a	77.5	**Abbeville** (city) Abbeville County
36	n/a	77.4	**Darlington** (city) Darlington County
37	279	74.4	**Greenville** (city) Greenville County
38	n/a	74.1	**Seneca** (city) Oconee County
39	299	72.0	**Columbia** (city) Richland County
40	303	71.6	**Orangeburg** (city) Orangeburg County
41	313	70.6	**West Columbia** (city) Lexington County
42	n/a	69.1	**Denmark** (city) Bamberg County
43	337	68.5	**Forest Acres** (city) Richland County
44	354	67.1	**North Charleston** (city) Charleston County
45	361	66.4	**Newberry** (city) Newberry County
46	n/a	64.7	**Bamberg** (town) Bamberg County
47	n/a	62.5	**Clinton** (city) Laurens County
48	n/a	61.7	**Saluda** (town) Saluda County
49	n/a	60.7	**Woodruff** (city) Spartanburg County
50	n/a	59.2	**Folly Beach** (city) Charleston County
51	457	59.1	**Conway** (city) Horry County
52	n/a	57.4	**Williamston** (town) Anderson County
53	522	54.2	**Rock Hill** (city) York County
53	n/a	54.2	**Walhalla** (city) Oconee County
55	n/a	52.2	**Williston** (town) Barnwell County
56	558	52.1	**Gaffney** (city) Cherokee County
57	n/a	51.4	**Fountain Inn** (city) Greenville County
58	n/a	46.8	**Surfside Beach** (town) Horry County
59	678	46.4	**Greer** (city) Greenville County
60	704	45.6	**Irmo** (town) Richland County
61	n/a	42.6	**Moncks Corner** (town) Berkeley County
62	n/a	41.3	**Pickens** (city) Pickens County
63	n/a	40.8	**Winnsboro** (town) Fairfield County
64	901	37.6	**Bluffton** (town) Beaufort County
65	914	37.3	**Easley** (city) Pickens County
66	n/a	36.8	**Ridgeland** (town) Jasper County
67	n/a	36.6	**Burnettown** (town) Aiken County
68	n/a	36.5	**Hampton** (town) Hampton County
69	n/a	33.4	**Springdale** (town) Lexington County
70	n/a	33.2	**Honea Path** (town) Anderson County
71	n/a	33.1	**McCormick** (town) McCormick County
72	1099	32.0	**Aiken** (city) Aiken County
73	n/a	27.7	**Liberty** (city) Pickens County
74	n/a	23.6	**Edgefield** (town) Edgefield County
75	1500	23.0	**Lexington** (town) Lexington County
75	1500	23.0	**Summerville** (town) Dorchester County
77	1565	21.6	**Goose Creek** (city) Berkeley County
78	1679	19.9	**Fort Mill** (town) York County
79	n/a	18.7	**Travelers Rest** (city) Greenville County
80	1764	18.6	**North Augusta** (city) Aiken County
81	1796	18.2	**Charleston** (city) Charleston County
82	1893	16.6	**Mauldin** (city) Greenville County
83	1912	16.4	**Hanahan** (city) Berkeley County
84	1940	16.0	**Mount Pleasant** (town) Charleston County
85	2029	14.9	**Clemson** (city) Pickens County
86	n/a	13.6	**Central** (town) Pickens County
87	n/a	12.3	**Duncan** (town) Spartanburg County
88	2247	12.2	**Port Royal** (town) Beaufort County
89	n/a	9.0	**Lyman** (town) Spartanburg County
90	n/a	4.7	**Isle of Palms** (city) Charleston County
91	n/a	2.5	**Tega Cay** (city) York County

Note: The state column ranks the top/bottom 150 places in the state with population of 2,500 or more. The national column ranks the top/bottom places in the country with population of 10,000 or more. Places that are unincorporated were not considered in the rankings. n/a indicates data not available. Please refer to the User Guide for additional information.

Violent Crime Rate per 10,000 Population

Top 150 Places Ranked in *Ascending* Order

State Rank	Nat'l Rank	Rate	Place
1	n/a	2.5	**Tega Cay** (city) York County
2	n/a	4.7	**Isle of Palms** (city) Charleston County
3	n/a	9.0	**Lyman** (town) Spartanburg County
4	1013	12.2	**Port Royal** (town) Beaufort County
5	n/a	12.3	**Duncan** (town) Spartanburg County
6	n/a	13.6	**Central** (town) Pickens County
7	1238	14.9	**Clemson** (city) Pickens County
8	1321	16.0	**Mount Pleasant** (town) Charleston County
9	1354	16.4	**Hanahan** (city) Berkeley County
10	1370	16.6	**Mauldin** (city) Greenville County
11	1469	18.2	**Charleston** (city) Charleston County
12	1503	18.6	**North Augusta** (city) Aiken County
13	n/a	18.7	**Travelers Rest** (city) Greenville County
14	1587	19.9	**Fort Mill** (town) York County
15	1700	21.6	**Goose Creek** (city) Berkeley County
16	1769	23.0	**Lexington** (town) Lexington County
16	1769	23.0	**Summerville** (town) Dorchester County
18	n/a	23.6	**Edgefield** (town) Edgefield County
19	n/a	27.7	**Liberty** (city) Pickens County
20	2161	32.0	**Aiken** (city) Aiken County
21	n/a	33.1	**McCormick** (town) McCormick County
22	n/a	33.2	**Honea Path** (town) Anderson County
23	n/a	33.4	**Springdale** (town) Lexington County
24	n/a	36.5	**Hampton** (town) Hampton County
25	n/a	36.6	**Burnettown** (town) Aiken County
26	n/a	36.8	**Ridgeland** (town) Jasper County
27	2352	37.3	**Easley** (city) Pickens County
28	2366	37.6	**Bluffton** (town) Beaufort County
29	n/a	40.8	**Winnsboro** (town) Fairfield County
30	n/a	41.3	**Pickens** (city) Pickens County
31	n/a	42.6	**Moncks Corner** (town) Berkeley County
32	2563	45.6	**Irmo** (town) Richland County
33	2590	46.4	**Greer** (city) Greenville County
34	n/a	46.8	**Surfside Beach** (town) Horry County
35	n/a	51.4	**Fountain Inn** (city) Greenville County
36	2710	52.1	**Gaffney** (city) Cherokee County
37	n/a	52.2	**Williston** (town) Barnwell County
38	2749	54.2	**Rock Hill** (city) York County
38	n/a	54.2	**Walhalla** (city) Oconee County
40	n/a	57.4	**Williamston** (town) Anderson County
41	2812	59.1	**Conway** (city) Horry County
42	n/a	59.2	**Folly Beach** (city) Charleston County
43	n/a	60.7	**Woodruff** (city) Spartanburg County
44	n/a	61.7	**Saluda** (town) Saluda County
45	n/a	62.5	**Clinton** (city) Laurens County
46	n/a	64.7	**Bamberg** (town) Bamberg County
47	2908	66.4	**Newberry** (city) Newberry County
48	2917	67.1	**North Charleston** (city) Charleston County
49	2933	68.5	**Forest Acres** (city) Richland County
50	n/a	69.1	**Denmark** (city) Bamberg County
51	2957	70.6	**West Columbia** (city) Lexington County
52	2968	71.6	**Orangeburg** (city) Orangeburg County
53	2971	72.0	**Columbia** (city) Richland County
54	n/a	74.1	**Seneca** (city) Oconee County
55	2991	74.4	**Greenville** (city) Greenville County
56	n/a	77.4	**Darlington** (city) Darlington County
57	n/a	77.5	**Abbeville** (city) Abbeville County
58	3014	77.9	**Florence** (city) Florence County
59	n/a	78.2	**Belton** (city) Anderson County
60	n/a	79.5	**York** (city) York County
61	3048	81.8	**North Myrtle Beach** (city) Horry County
62	n/a	87.1	**Walterboro** (city) Colleton County
63	n/a	88.4	**Cheraw** (town) Chesterfield County
64	n/a	88.6	**Hardeeville** (city) Jasper County
65	n/a	92.1	**Andrews** (town) Georgetown County
66	n/a	92.5	**Batesburg-Leesville** (town) Lexington County
67	3114	94.6	**Sumter** (city) Sumter County
68	n/a	94.8	**Union** (city) Union County
69	n/a	95.7	**Pageland** (town) Chesterfield County
70	n/a	96.6	**Barnwell** (city) Barnwell County
71	n/a	99.3	**Laurens** (city) Laurens County
72	n/a	101.1	**Lake City** (city) Florence County
73	3153	103.7	**Anderson** (city) Anderson County
74	n/a	110.4	**Hartsville** (city) Darlington County
75	3183	118.4	**Beaufort** (city) Beaufort County
76	n/a	122.4	**Georgetown** (city) Georgetown County
77	n/a	123.5	**Lancaster** (city) Lancaster County
78	n/a	125.7	**Chester** (city) Chester County
79	n/a	126.6	**Kingstree** (town) Williamsburg County
80	3209	128.6	**Greenwood** (city) Greenwood County
81	n/a	130.5	**Bennettsville** (city) Marlboro County
82	n/a	133.6	**Marion** (city) Marion County
83	n/a	139.9	**Mullins** (city) Marion County
84	n/a	140.1	**Camden** (city) Kershaw County
85	3222	140.5	**Spartanburg** (city) Spartanburg County
86	n/a	143.8	**Manning** (city) Clarendon County
87	n/a	149.8	**Allendale** (town) Allendale County
88	n/a	161.5	**Dillon** (city) Dillon County
89	3246	165.7	**Myrtle Beach** (city) Horry County
90	n/a	173.9	**Bishopville** (city) Lee County
91	n/a	277.1	**Clover** (town) York County

Note: The state column ranks the top/bottom 150 places in the state with population of 2,500 or more. The national column ranks the top/bottom places in the country with population of 10,000 or more. Places that are unincorporated were not considered in the rankings. n/a indicates data not available. Please refer to the User Guide for additional information.

Property Crime Rate per 10,000 Population

Top 150 Places Ranked in *Descending* Order

State Rank	Nat'l Rank	Rate	Place
1	2	1,596.1	**Myrtle Beach** (city) Horry County
2	n/a	1,273.6	**Dillon** (city) Dillon County
3	12	1,068.7	**North Myrtle Beach** (city) Horry County
4	n/a	1,037.7	**Walterboro** (city) Colleton County
5	n/a	1,023.8	**Manning** (city) Clarendon County
6	n/a	1,005.5	**Hartsville** (city) Darlington County
7	n/a	977.3	**Mullins** (city) Marion County
8	n/a	923.1	**Kingstree** (town) Williamsburg County
9	22	901.5	**Anderson** (city) Anderson County
10	n/a	875.7	**Lake City** (city) Florence County
11	n/a	873.3	**Marion** (city) Marion County
12	n/a	783.8	**Barnwell** (city) Barnwell County
13	52	780.6	**Florence** (city) Florence County
14	n/a	740.3	**Darlington** (city) Darlington County
15	n/a	725.4	**Bishopville** (city) Lee County
16	77	711.1	**Spartanburg** (city) Spartanburg County
17	n/a	701.5	**Lancaster** (city) Lancaster County
18	n/a	683.7	**Andrews** (town) Georgetown County
19	n/a	672.3	**Chester** (city) Chester County
20	n/a	668.8	**Camden** (city) Kershaw County
21	n/a	667.1	**Pickens** (city) Pickens County
22	n/a	662.8	**Laurens** (city) Laurens County
23	n/a	643.3	**Travelers Rest** (city) Greenville County
24	130	641.8	**Easley** (city) Pickens County
25	n/a	640.2	**Surfside Beach** (town) Horry County
26	132	639.8	**Greenwood** (city) Greenwood County
27	n/a	632.9	**Cheraw** (town) Chesterfield County
28	156	622.4	**Beaufort** (city) Beaufort County
29	n/a	622.2	**Pageland** (town) Chesterfield County
30	160	618.4	**Orangeburg** (city) Orangeburg County
31	n/a	609.7	**Winnsboro** (town) Fairfield County
32	n/a	608.1	**Moncks Corner** (town) Berkeley County
33	n/a	605.3	**Hardeeville** (city) Jasper County
34	178	604.1	**Columbia** (city) Richland County
35	n/a	591.2	**Hampton** (town) Hampton County
36	216	573.4	**Forest Acres** (city) Richland County
37	n/a	566.6	**Georgetown** (city) Georgetown County
38	236	561.7	**North Charleston** (city) Charleston County
39	n/a	555.4	**Denmark** (city) Bamberg County
40	n/a	547.7	**Folly Beach** (city) Charleston County
41	291	533.0	**Greenville** (city) Greenville County
42	n/a	522.5	**Clinton** (city) Laurens County
43	n/a	518.7	**Belton** (city) Anderson County
44	n/a	515.4	**Bennettsville** (city) Marlboro County
45	392	493.6	**Aiken** (city) Aiken County
46	396	492.1	**Sumter** (city) Sumter County
47	401	490.6	**West Columbia** (city) Lexington County
48	n/a	490.0	**Batesburg-Leesville** (town) Lexington County
49	437	481.2	**Newberry** (city) Newberry County
50	n/a	463.3	**Springdale** (town) Lexington County
51	502	460.2	**Conway** (city) Horry County
52	n/a	459.1	**Union** (city) Union County
53	n/a	458.4	**Allendale** (town) Allendale County
54	n/a	451.6	**Williamston** (town) Anderson County
55	n/a	431.8	**Honea Path** (town) Anderson County
56	n/a	431.0	**Lyman** (town) Spartanburg County
57	n/a	430.2	**York** (city) York County
58	n/a	416.4	**Abbeville** (city) Abbeville County
59	n/a	384.0	**Liberty** (city) Pickens County
60	n/a	376.8	**Bamberg** (town) Bamberg County
61	819	376.4	**Rock Hill** (city) York County
62	820	376.3	**North Augusta** (city) Aiken County
63	n/a	368.4	**Ridgeland** (town) Jasper County
64	n/a	365.2	**Williston** (town) Barnwell County
65	919	356.6	**Lexington** (town) Lexington County
66	955	349.5	**Clemson** (city) Pickens County
67	n/a	347.4	**Central** (town) Pickens County
68	988	341.3	**Summerville** (town) Dorchester County
69	n/a	326.9	**Isle of Palms** (city) Charleston County
70	n/a	322.4	**Seneca** (city) Oconee County
71	1262	297.4	**Gaffney** (city) Cherokee County
72	1289	292.7	**Irmo** (town) Richland County
73	1312	290.5	**Bluffton** (town) Beaufort County
74	n/a	286.8	**McCormick** (town) McCormick County
75	1347	284.9	**Greer** (city) Greenville County
76	n/a	280.8	**Clover** (town) York County
77	1584	256.9	**Port Royal** (town) Beaufort County
78	n/a	252.1	**Duncan** (town) Spartanburg County
79	1635	250.9	**Charleston** (city) Charleston County
80	1684	244.0	**Goose Creek** (city) Berkeley County
81	n/a	242.8	**Walhalla** (city) Oconee County
82	n/a	241.2	**Saluda** (town) Saluda County
83	n/a	235.3	**Woodruff** (city) Spartanburg County
84	1827	226.2	**Hanahan** (city) Berkeley County
85	2131	195.1	**Mount Pleasant** (town) Charleston County
86	n/a	181.8	**Fountain Inn** (city) Greenville County
87	2309	175.2	**Fort Mill** (town) York County
88	2347	170.1	**Mauldin** (city) Greenville County
89	n/a	157.0	**Tega Cay** (city) York County
90	n/a	124.4	**Burnettown** (town) Aiken County
91	n/a	100.6	**Edgefield** (town) Edgefield County

Note: The state column ranks the top/bottom 150 places in the state with population of 2,500 or more. The national column ranks the top/bottom places in the country with population of 10,000 or more. Places that are unincorporated were not considered in the rankings. n/a indicates data not available. Please refer to the User Guide for additional information.

Property Crime Rate per 10,000 Population

Top 150 Places Ranked in *Ascending* Order

State Rank	Nat'l Rank	Rate	Place
1	n/a	100.6	**Edgefield** (town) Edgefield County
2	n/a	124.4	**Burnettown** (town) Aiken County
3	n/a	157.0	**Tega Cay** (city) York County
4	922	170.1	**Mauldin** (city) Greenville County
5	961	175.2	**Fort Mill** (town) York County
6	n/a	181.8	**Fountain Inn** (city) Greenville County
7	1139	195.1	**Mount Pleasant** (town) Charleston County
8	1442	226.2	**Hanahan** (city) Berkeley County
9	n/a	235.3	**Woodruff** (city) Spartanburg County
10	n/a	241.2	**Saluda** (town) Saluda County
11	n/a	242.8	**Walhalla** (city) Oconee County
12	1585	244.0	**Goose Creek** (city) Berkeley County
13	1634	250.9	**Charleston** (city) Charleston County
14	n/a	252.1	**Duncan** (town) Spartanburg County
15	1685	256.9	**Port Royal** (town) Beaufort County
16	n/a	280.8	**Clover** (town) York County
17	1923	284.9	**Greer** (city) Greenville County
18	n/a	286.8	**McCormick** (town) McCormick County
19	1958	290.5	**Bluffton** (town) Beaufort County
20	1981	292.7	**Irmo** (town) Richland County
21	2008	297.4	**Gaffney** (city) Cherokee County
22	n/a	322.4	**Seneca** (city) Oconee County
23	n/a	326.9	**Isle of Palms** (city) Charleston County
24	2281	341.3	**Summerville** (town) Dorchester County
25	n/a	347.4	**Central** (town) Pickens County
26	2315	349.5	**Clemson** (city) Pickens County
27	2351	356.6	**Lexington** (town) Lexington County
28	n/a	365.2	**Williston** (town) Barnwell County
29	n/a	368.4	**Ridgeland** (town) Jasper County
30	2450	376.3	**North Augusta** (city) Aiken County
31	2451	376.4	**Rock Hill** (city) York County
32	n/a	376.8	**Bamberg** (town) Bamberg County
33	n/a	384.0	**Liberty** (city) Pickens County
34	n/a	416.4	**Abbeville** (city) Abbeville County
35	n/a	430.2	**York** (city) York County
36	n/a	431.0	**Lyman** (town) Spartanburg County
37	n/a	431.8	**Honea Path** (town) Anderson County
38	n/a	451.6	**Williamston** (town) Anderson County
39	n/a	458.4	**Allendale** (town) Allendale County
40	n/a	459.1	**Union** (city) Union County
41	2768	460.2	**Conway** (city) Horry County
42	n/a	463.3	**Springdale** (town) Lexington County
43	2832	481.2	**Newberry** (city) Newberry County
44	n/a	490.0	**Batesburg-Leesville** (town) Lexington County
45	2869	490.6	**West Columbia** (city) Lexington County
46	2873	492.1	**Sumter** (city) Sumter County
47	2878	493.6	**Aiken** (city) Aiken County
48	n/a	515.4	**Bennettsville** (city) Marlboro County
49	n/a	518.7	**Belton** (city) Anderson County
50	n/a	522.5	**Clinton** (city) Laurens County
51	2979	533.0	**Greenville** (city) Greenville County
52	n/a	547.7	**Folly Beach** (city) Charleston County
53	n/a	555.4	**Denmark** (city) Bamberg County
54	3034	561.7	**North Charleston** (city) Charleston County
55	n/a	566.6	**Georgetown** (city) Georgetown County
56	3054	573.4	**Forest Acres** (city) Richland County
57	n/a	591.2	**Hampton** (town) Hampton County
58	3092	604.1	**Columbia** (city) Richland County
59	n/a	605.3	**Hardeeville** (city) Jasper County
60	n/a	608.1	**Moncks Corner** (town) Berkeley County
61	n/a	609.7	**Winnsboro** (town) Fairfield County
62	3110	618.4	**Orangeburg** (city) Orangeburg County
63	n/a	622.2	**Pageland** (town) Chesterfield County
64	3114	622.4	**Beaufort** (city) Beaufort County
65	n/a	632.9	**Cheraw** (town) Chesterfield County
66	3137	639.8	**Greenwood** (city) Greenwood County
67	n/a	640.2	**Surfside Beach** (town) Horry County
68	3140	641.8	**Easley** (city) Pickens County
69	n/a	643.3	**Travelers Rest** (city) Greenville County
70	n/a	662.8	**Laurens** (city) Laurens County
71	n/a	667.1	**Pickens** (city) Pickens County
72	n/a	668.8	**Camden** (city) Kershaw County
73	n/a	672.3	**Chester** (city) Chester County
74	n/a	683.7	**Andrews** (town) Georgetown County
75	n/a	701.5	**Lancaster** (city) Lancaster County
76	3193	711.1	**Spartanburg** (city) Spartanburg County
77	n/a	725.4	**Bishopville** (city) Lee County
78	n/a	740.3	**Darlington** (city) Darlington County
79	3218	780.6	**Florence** (city) Florence County
80	n/a	783.8	**Barnwell** (city) Barnwell County
81	n/a	873.3	**Marion** (city) Marion County
82	n/a	875.7	**Lake City** (city) Florence County
83	3248	901.5	**Anderson** (city) Anderson County
84	n/a	923.1	**Kingstree** (town) Williamsburg County
85	n/a	977.3	**Mullins** (city) Marion County
86	n/a	1,005.5	**Hartsville** (city) Darlington County
87	n/a	1,023.8	**Manning** (city) Clarendon County
88	n/a	1,037.7	**Walterboro** (city) Colleton County
89	3258	1,068.7	**North Myrtle Beach** (city) Horry County
90	n/a	1,273.6	**Dillon** (city) Dillon County
91	3268	1,596.1	**Myrtle Beach** (city) Horry County

Note: The state column ranks the top/bottom 150 places in the state with population of 2,500 or more. The national column ranks the top/bottom places in the country with population of 10,000 or more. Places that are unincorporated were not considered in the rankings. n/a indicates data not available. Please refer to the User Guide for additional information.

Education

South Carolina Public School Educational Profile

Category	Value	Category	Value
Schools *(2011-2012)*	1,231	**Diploma Recipients** *(2009-2010)*	40,438
Instructional Level		White, Non-Hispanic	22,985
Primary	672	Black, Non-Hispanic	15,125
Middle	255	Asian/Pacific Islander, Non-Hispanic	699
High	250	American Indian/Alaskan Native, Non-Hispanic	109
Other/Not Reported	54	Hawaiian Native/Pacific Islander, Non-Hispanic	n/a
Curriculum		Two or More Races, Non-Hispanic	n/a
Regular	1,161	Hispanic of Any Race	1,394
Special Education	10	**Staff** *(2011-2012)*	
Vocational	39	Teachers (FTE)	46,782.2
Alternative	21	Salary[1] ($)	48,425
Type		Librarians/Media Specialists (FTE)	1,099.8
Magnet	137	Guidance Counselors (FTE)	1,828.6
Charter	52	**Ratios** *(2011-2012)*	
Title I Eligible	1,039	Number of Students per Teacher	15.5 to 1
School-wide Title I	988	Number of Students per Librarian	661.2 to 1
Students *(2011-2012)*	727,186	Number of Students per Guidance Counselor	397.7 to 1
Gender (%)		**Finances** *(2010-2011)*	
Male	51.4	Current Expenditures ($ per student)	
Female	48.6	Total	8,903
Race/Ethnicity (%)		Instruction	5,082
White, Non-Hispanic	53.2	Support Services	3,333
Black, Non-Hispanic	35.6	Other	488
Asian, Non-Hispanic	1.4	General Revenue ($ per student)	
American Indian/Alaskan Native, Non-Hisp.	0.3	Total	10,847
Hawaiian Native/Pacific Islander, Non-Hisp.	0.1	From Federal Sources	1,496
Two or More Races, Non-Hispanic	2.7	From State Sources	4,705
Hispanic of Any Race	6.7	From Local Sources	4,647
Special Programs (%)		Long-Term Debt Outstanding ($ per student)	
Individual Education Program (IEP)	13.7	At Beginning of Fiscal Year	14,145
English Language Learner (ELL)	5.4	Issued During Fiscal Year	1,263
Eligible for Free Lunch Program	50.2	Retired During Fiscal Year	755
Eligible for Reduced-Price Lunch Program	6.6	At End of Fiscal Year	14,641
Average Freshman Grad. Rate (%) *(2009-2010)*	68.2	**College Entrance Exam Scores**	
White, Non-Hispanic	72.8	SAT Reasoning Test™ *(2013)*	
Black, Non-Hispanic	61.5	Participation Rate (%)	64
Asian/Pacific Islander, Non-Hispanic	97.1	Mean Critical Reading Score	484
American Indian/Alaskan Native, Non-Hispanic	59.6	Mean Math Score	487
Hispanic of Any Race	65.7	Mean Writing Score	465
High School Drop-out Rate (%) *(2009-2010)*	3.0	ACT *(2013)*	
White, Non-Hispanic	2.7	Participation Rate (%)	51
Black, Non-Hispanic	3.3	Mean Composite Score	20.4
Asian/Pacific Islander, Non-Hispanic	1.3	Mean English Score	19.7
American Indian/Alaskan Native, Non-Hispanic	5.6	Mean Math Score	20.3
Hawaiian Native/Pacific Islander, Non-Hispanic	n/a	Mean Reading Score	20.8
Two or More Races, Non-Hispanic	n/a	Mean Science Score	20.3
Hispanic of Any Race	3.6		

Note: *For an explanation of data, please refer to the User's Guide in the front of the book; (1) Average salary for classroom teachers in 2013-14*

Number of Schools

Rank	Number	District Name	City
1	96	Greenville 01	Greenville
2	78	Charleston 01	Charleston
3	51	Horry 01	Conway
4	50	Richland 01	Columbia
5	40	Aiken 01	Aiken
6	39	Berkeley 01	Moncks Corner
7	31	Beaufort 01	Beaufort
8	30	Richland 02	Columbia
9	28	Lexington 01	Lexington
9	28	York 03	Rock Hill
11	27	Sumter 01	Sumter
12	26	Pickens 01	Easley
13	23	Darlington 01	Darlington
14	22	Florence 01	Florence
15	21	Dorchester 02	Summerville
16	20	Anderson 05	Anderson
16	20	Lancaster 01	Lancaster
18	19	Cherokee 01	Gaffney
18	19	Kershaw 01	Camden
18	19	Lexington 05	Irmo
18	19	Oconee 01	Walhalla
22	18	Georgetown 01	Georgetown
22	18	Sc Public Charter SD	Columbia
24	16	Chesterfield 01	Chesterfield
25	15	Lexington 02	West Columbia
26	14	Anderson 01	Williamston
26	14	Greenwood 50	Greenwood
26	14	Newberry 01	Newberry
26	14	Orangeburg 05	Orangeburg
26	14	Spartanburg 02	Spartanburg
26	14	Spartanburg 06	Roebuck
32	13	Spartanburg 07	Spartanburg
32	13	Williamston 01	Kingstree
32	13	York 04	Fort Mill
35	12	Chester 01	Chester
35	12	Spartanburg 05	Duncan
37	11	Laurens 55	Laurens
38	10	Colleton 01	Walterboro
38	10	Spartanburg 01	Campobello
40	9	Abbeville 60	Abbeville
40	9	Dillon 04	Dillon
40	9	Edgefield 01	Edgefield
40	9	Florence 03	Lake City
40	9	Marlboro 01	Bennettsville
40	9	York 01	York
40	9	York 02	Clover
47	8	Fairfield 01	Winnsboro
47	8	Orangeburg 04	Cope
49	7	Anderson 02	Honea Path
49	7	Hampton 01	Hampton
49	7	Lexington 04	Swansea
49	7	Orangeburg 03	Holly Hill
49	7	Spartanburg 03	Glendale
49	7	Union 01	Union
55	6	Anderson 04	Pendleton
55	6	Clarendon 02	Manning
55	6	Laurens 56	Clinton
55	6	Lee 01	Bishopville
59	5	Anderson 03	Iva
59	5	Dorchester 04	Saint George
59	5	Jasper 01	Ridgeland
59	5	Saluda 01	Saluda
63	4	Barnwell 45	Barnwell
63	4	Dillon 03	Latta
63	4	Greenwood 52	Ninety Six
63	4	Lexington 03	Batesburg
63	4	Marion 01	Marion
63	4	Marion 02	Mullins
63	4	Spartanburg 04	Woodruff
70	3	Calhoun 01	Saint Matthews

Number of Teachers

Rank	Number	District Name	City
1	4,375.7	Greenville 01	Greenville
2	3,221.5	Charleston 01	Charleston
3	2,564.3	Horry 01	Conway
4	1,787.6	Berkeley 01	Moncks Corner
5	1,760.2	Richland 01	Columbia
6	1,684.3	Richland 02	Columbia
7	1,511.7	Lexington 01	Lexington

Rank	Number	District Name	City
8	1,507.8	Aiken 01	Aiken
9	1,393.0	Beaufort 01	Beaufort
10	1,355.1	Dorchester 02	Summerville
11	1,146.6	Lexington 05	Irmo
12	1,124.4	York 03	Rock Hill
13	1,031.6	Florence 01	Florence
14	1,005.9	Sumter 01	Sumter
15	989.1	Pickens 01	Easley
16	820.4	Anderson 05	Anderson
17	761.7	Oconee 01	Walhalla
18	713.0	Lancaster 01	Lancaster
19	662.5	York 04	Fort Mill
20	662.1	Spartanburg 06	Roebuck
21	653.3	Georgetown 01	Georgetown
22	632.1	Kershaw 01	Camden
23	622.1	Darlington 01	Darlington
24	594.8	Spartanburg 02	Spartanburg
25	593.4	Spartanburg 07	Spartanburg
26	588.4	Cherokee 01	Gaffney
27	571.0	Lexington 02	West Columbia
28	521.9	Greenwood 50	Greenwood
29	511.6	Spartanburg 05	Duncan
30	504.7	Anderson 01	Williamston
31	481.3	Chesterfield 01	Chesterfield
32	461.5	Orangeburg 05	Orangeburg
33	447.0	York 02	Clover
34	404.5	Newberry 01	Newberry
35	370.1	Colleton 01	Walterboro
36	355.3	Chester 01	Chester
37	349.9	Spartanburg 01	Campobello
38	336.6	York 01	York
39	330.7	Laurens 55	Laurens
40	323.4	Sc Public Charter SD	Columbia
41	282.0	Williamston 01	Kingstree
42	280.5	Union 01	Union
43	278.9	Marlboro 01	Bennettsville
44	272.0	Edgefield 01	Edgefield
45	268.5	Fairfield 01	Winnsboro
46	242.0	Orangeburg 04	Cope
47	236.5	Dillon 04	Dillon
48	229.7	Florence 03	Lake City
49	222.1	Abbeville 60	Abbeville
50	220.5	Orangeburg 03	Holly Hill
51	207.4	Anderson 02	Honea Path
52	200.0	Jasper 01	Ridgeland
53	195.7	Spartanburg 03	Glendale
54	188.6	Anderson 04	Pendleton
55	188.2	Laurens 56	Clinton
56	185.1	Lexington 04	Swansea
57	178.1	Hampton 01	Hampton
58	165.6	Marion 01	Marion
59	162.0	Dorchester 04	Saint George
60	161.8	Clarendon 02	Manning
61	160.5	Anderson 03	Iva
62	157.0	Barnwell 45	Barnwell
63	149.2	Spartanburg 04	Woodruff
64	139.7	Saluda 01	Saluda
65	135.0	Lee 01	Bishopville
66	128.8	Lexington 03	Batesburg
67	113.0	Calhoun 01	Saint Matthews
68	110.0	Marion 02	Mullins
69	102.0	Greenwood 52	Ninety Six
70	88.9	Dillon 03	Latta

Number of Students

Rank	Number	District Name	City
1	72,153	Greenville 01	Greenville
2	44,058	Charleston 01	Charleston
3	38,957	Horry 01	Conway
4	30,085	Berkeley 01	Moncks Corner
5	25,954	Richland 02	Columbia
6	24,729	Aiken 01	Aiken
7	23,942	Richland 01	Columbia
8	23,346	Dorchester 02	Summerville
9	22,990	Lexington 01	Lexington
10	19,992	Beaufort 01	Beaufort
11	17,217	York 03	Rock Hill
12	16,915	Sumter 01	Sumter
13	16,560	Lexington 05	Irmo
14	16,546	Pickens 01	Easley
15	16,027	Florence 01	Florence
16	12,559	Anderson 05	Anderson
17	11,745	Lancaster 01	Lancaster
18	10,742	York 04	Fort Mill

Rank	Number	District Name	City
19	10,658	Spartanburg 06	Roebuck
20	10,546	Oconee 01	Walhalla
21	10,423	Darlington 01	Darlington
22	10,345	Kershaw 01	Camden
23	9,978	Sc Public Charter SD	Columbia
24	9,969	Spartanburg 02	Spartanburg
25	9,680	Georgetown 01	Georgetown
26	9,275	Anderson 01	Williamston
27	9,094	Greenwood 50	Greenwood
28	9,087	Cherokee 01	Gaffney
29	8,854	Lexington 02	West Columbia
30	7,695	Spartanburg 05	Duncan
31	7,572	Chesterfield 01	Chesterfield
32	7,159	Spartanburg 07	Spartanburg
33	6,855	Orangeburg 05	Orangeburg
34	6,615	York 02	Clover
35	6,221	Colleton 01	Walterboro
36	5,941	Laurens 55	Laurens
37	5,804	Newberry 01	Newberry
38	5,499	Chester 01	Chester
39	5,166	York 01	York
40	5,100	Spartanburg 01	Campobello
41	4,737	Williamsburg 01	Kingstree
42	4,317	Marlboro 01	Bennettsville
43	4,310	Dillon 04	Dillon
44	4,193	Union 01	Union
45	3,921	Edgefield 01	Edgefield
46	3,913	Orangeburg 04	Cope
47	3,659	Anderson 02	Honea Path
48	3,608	Florence 03	Lake City
49	3,493	Lexington 04	Swansea
50	3,316	Jasper 01	Ridgeland
51	3,146	Abbeville 60	Abbeville
52	3,108	Fairfield 01	Winnsboro
53	3,060	Clarendon 02	Manning
54	3,058	Orangeburg 03	Holly Hill
55	3,050	Laurens 56	Clinton
56	2,956	Spartanburg 03	Glendale
57	2,866	Anderson 04	Pendleton
58	2,860	Spartanburg 04	Woodruff
59	2,797	Marion 01	Marion
60	2,584	Anderson 03	Iva
61	2,547	Hampton 01	Hampton
62	2,406	Barnwell 45	Barnwell
63	2,248	Lee 01	Bishopville
64	2,193	Dorchester 04	Saint George
65	2,151	Saluda 01	Saluda
66	2,021	Lexington 03	Batesburg
67	1,809	Marion 02	Mullins
68	1,721	Calhoun 01	Saint Matthews
69	1,712	Greenwood 52	Ninety Six
70	1,660	Dillon 03	Latta

Male Students

Rank	Percent	District Name	City
1	53.0	Abbeville 60	Abbeville
1	53.0	Spartanburg 02	Spartanburg
3	52.8	Chester 01	Chester
3	52.8	Spartanburg 07	Spartanburg
5	52.7	Spartanburg 03	Glendale
6	52.6	Dorchester 04	Saint George
7	52.5	Greenwood 52	Ninety Six
7	52.5	Williamsburg 01	Kingstree
9	52.4	Edgefield 01	Edgefield
10	52.3	Georgetown 01	Georgetown
10	52.3	Jasper 01	Ridgeland
10	52.3	Orangeburg 04	Cope
10	52.3	Saluda 01	Saluda
14	52.2	Kershaw 01	Camden
15	52.1	Laurens 55	Laurens
16	52.0	Spartanburg 04	Woodruff
16	52.0	Spartanburg 05	Duncan
16	52.0	York 02	Clover
19	51.9	Anderson 01	Williamston
19	51.9	Marion 01	Marion
19	51.9	Marlboro 01	Bennettsville
22	51.8	Aiken 01	Aiken
22	51.8	Greenwood 50	Greenwood
22	51.8	Lancaster 01	Lancaster
22	51.8	Spartanburg 06	Roebuck
26	51.7	Anderson 04	Pendleton
26	51.7	York 04	Fort Mill
28	51.6	Berkeley 01	Moncks Corner

Note: This section only includes districts with 1,500 or more students; All categories are ranked from high to low

Rank	Percent	District Name	City
28	51.6	Hampton 01	Hampton
28	51.6	Lexington 04	Swansea
31	51.5	Horry 01	Conway
31	51.5	Oconee 01	Walhalla
33	51.4	Anderson 05	Anderson
33	51.4	Greenville 01	Greenville
33	51.4	Lexington 01	Lexington
33	51.4	Orangeburg 05	Orangeburg
37	51.3	Cherokee 01	Gaffney
37	51.3	Dorchester 02	Summerville
37	51.3	Pickens 01	Easley
37	51.3	Union 01	Union
41	51.2	Anderson 02	Honea Path
41	51.2	Anderson 03	Iva
41	51.2	Beaufort 01	Beaufort
41	51.2	Calhoun 01	Saint Matthews
41	51.2	Spartanburg 01	Campobello
41	51.2	York 03	Rock Hill
47	51.1	Charleston 01	Charleston
47	51.1	Florence 03	Lake City
49	51.0	Barnwell 45	Barnwell
49	51.0	Laurens 56	Clinton
51	50.9	Darlington 01	Darlington
51	50.9	Lexington 05	Irmo
51	50.9	Orangeburg 03	Holly Hill
51	50.9	Sumter 01	Sumter
51	50.9	York 01	York
56	50.8	Clarendon 02	Manning
56	50.8	Fairfield 01	Winnsboro
56	50.8	Florence 01	Florence
56	50.8	Newberry 01	Newberry
56	50.8	Richland 02	Columbia
61	50.6	Colleton 01	Walterboro
61	50.6	Richland 01	Columbia
63	50.5	Dillon 04	Dillon
63	50.5	Lexington 03	Batesburg
65	50.4	Lexington 02	West Columbia
65	50.4	Marion 02	Mullins
67	50.2	Chesterfield 01	Chesterfield
68	50.0	Lee 01	Bishopville
69	49.5	Dillon 03	Latta
70	47.0	Sc Public Charter SD	Columbia

Female Students

Rank	Percent	District Name	City
1	53.0	Sc Public Charter SD	Columbia
2	50.5	Dillon 03	Latta
3	50.0	Lee 01	Bishopville
4	49.8	Chesterfield 01	Chesterfield
5	49.6	Lexington 02	West Columbia
5	49.6	Marion 02	Mullins
7	49.5	Dillon 04	Dillon
7	49.5	Lexington 03	Batesburg
9	49.4	Colleton 01	Walterboro
9	49.4	Richland 01	Columbia
11	49.2	Clarendon 02	Manning
11	49.2	Fairfield 01	Winnsboro
11	49.2	Florence 01	Florence
11	49.2	Newberry 01	Newberry
11	49.2	Richland 02	Columbia
16	49.1	Darlington 01	Darlington
16	49.1	Lexington 05	Irmo
16	49.1	Orangeburg 03	Holly Hill
16	49.1	Sumter 01	Sumter
16	49.1	York 01	York
21	49.0	Barnwell 45	Barnwell
21	49.0	Laurens 56	Clinton
23	48.9	Charleston 01	Charleston
23	48.9	Florence 03	Lake City
25	48.8	Anderson 02	Honea Path
25	48.8	Anderson 03	Iva
25	48.8	Beaufort 01	Beaufort
25	48.8	Calhoun 01	Saint Matthews
25	48.8	Spartanburg 01	Campobello
25	48.8	York 03	Rock Hill
31	48.7	Cherokee 01	Gaffney
31	48.7	Dorchester 02	Summerville
31	48.7	Pickens 01	Easley
31	48.7	Union 01	Union
35	48.6	Anderson 05	Anderson
35	48.6	Greenville 01	Greenville
35	48.6	Lexington 01	Lexington
35	48.6	Orangeburg 05	Orangeburg

Rank	Percent	District Name	City
39	48.5	Horry 01	Conway
39	48.5	Oconee 01	Walhalla
41	48.4	Berkeley 01	Moncks Corner
41	48.4	Hampton 01	Hampton
41	48.4	Lexington 04	Swansea
44	48.3	Anderson 04	Pendleton
44	48.3	York 04	Fort Mill
46	48.2	Aiken 01	Aiken
46	48.2	Greenwood 50	Greenwood
46	48.2	Lancaster 01	Lancaster
46	48.2	Spartanburg 06	Roebuck
50	48.1	Anderson 01	Williamston
50	48.1	Marion 01	Marion
50	48.1	Marlboro 01	Bennettsville
53	48.0	Spartanburg 04	Woodruff
53	48.0	Spartanburg 05	Duncan
53	48.0	York 02	Clover
56	47.9	Laurens 55	Laurens
57	47.8	Kershaw 01	Camden
58	47.7	Georgetown 01	Georgetown
58	47.7	Jasper 01	Ridgeland
58	47.7	Orangeburg 04	Cope
58	47.7	Saluda 01	Saluda
62	47.6	Edgefield 01	Edgefield
63	47.5	Greenwood 52	Ninety Six
63	47.5	Williamsburg 01	Kingstree
65	47.4	Dorchester 04	Saint George
66	47.3	Spartanburg 03	Glendale
67	47.2	Chester 01	Chester
67	47.2	Spartanburg 07	Spartanburg
69	47.0	Abbeville 60	Abbeville
69	47.0	Spartanburg 02	Spartanburg

Individual Education Program Students

Rank	Percent	District Name	City
1	21.9	Anderson 02	Honea Path
2	19.9	Laurens 56	Clinton
3	19.8	Laurens 55	Laurens
4	19.2	Florence 03	Lake City
5	19.0	Spartanburg 03	Glendale
6	18.9	Clarendon 02	Manning
7	18.8	Lexington 03	Batesburg
8	18.2	Marlboro 01	Bennettsville
8	18.2	Williamsburg 01	Kingstree
10	18.1	Edgefield 01	Edgefield
11	17.9	Lexington 04	Swansea
12	17.5	Union 01	Union
13	17.1	Barnwell 45	Barnwell
14	16.8	Anderson 03	Iva
15	16.6	Florence 01	Florence
16	16.5	Colleton 01	Walterboro
16	16.5	Oconee 01	Walhalla
16	16.5	Spartanburg 07	Spartanburg
19	16.4	Marion 02	Mullins
20	16.3	Fairfield 01	Winnsboro
21	16.2	Lexington 02	West Columbia
22	15.9	Dorchester 04	Saint George
22	15.9	Lee 01	Bishopville
24	15.8	Abbeville 60	Abbeville
24	15.8	Orangeburg 05	Orangeburg
26	15.7	Darlington 01	Darlington
27	15.4	Horry 01	Conway
28	15.2	Richland 01	Columbia
29	15.0	Marion 01	Marion
29	15.0	Newberry 01	Newberry
31	14.5	Lexington 05	Irmo
32	14.4	Calhoun 01	Saint Matthews
33	14.3	Berkeley 01	Moncks Corner
33	14.3	Orangeburg 03	Holly Hill
33	14.3	Saluda 01	Saluda
36	14.1	Anderson 04	Pendleton
36	14.1	Sumter 01	Sumter
38	14.0	York 03	Rock Hill
39	13.8	Lancaster 01	Lancaster
40	13.7	Anderson 05	Anderson
41	13.6	Greenwood 50	Greenwood
42	13.5	Greenville 01	Greenville
43	13.4	York 01	York
44	13.3	Chester 01	Chester
45	13.2	Spartanburg 06	Roebuck
46	13.1	Orangeburg 04	Cope
47	12.8	Kershaw 01	Camden
48	12.5	Hampton 01	Hampton

Rank	Percent	District Name	City
49	12.4	Jasper 01	Ridgeland
49	12.4	Pickens 01	Easley
51	12.3	Spartanburg 02	Spartanburg
52	12.2	Dillon 03	Latta
52	12.2	Richland 02	Columbia
52	12.2	Spartanburg 04	Woodruff
55	12.1	Georgetown 01	Georgetown
56	11.9	Aiken 01	Aiken
57	11.8	Anderson 01	Williamston
58	11.6	Spartanburg 05	Duncan
59	11.5	Dorchester 02	Summerville
59	11.5	Spartanburg 01	Campobello
61	11.3	Lexington 01	Lexington
62	11.0	Beaufort 01	Beaufort
62	11.0	Cherokee 01	Gaffney
64	10.7	Sc Public Charter SD	Columbia
65	10.5	Greenwood 52	Ninety Six
66	10.3	Chesterfield 01	Chesterfield
67	10.2	Charleston 01	Charleston
68	10.1	Dillon 04	Dillon
69	10.0	York 04	Fort Mill
70	8.8	York 02	Clover

English Language Learner Students

Rank	Percent	District Name	City
1	22.1	Jasper 01	Ridgeland
2	20.9	Saluda 01	Saluda
3	15.9	Beaufort 01	Beaufort
4	14.1	Spartanburg 06	Roebuck
5	11.6	Spartanburg 02	Spartanburg
6	10.3	Greenville 01	Greenville
7	10.2	Greenwood 50	Greenwood
8	9.3	Lexington 02	West Columbia
8	9.3	Newberry 01	Newberry
10	9.0	Spartanburg 01	Campobello
11	7.2	Laurens 55	Laurens
12	6.6	Horry 01	Conway
13	6.0	Lexington 03	Batesburg
14	5.9	Dillon 04	Dillon
14	5.9	Oconee 01	Walhalla
16	5.8	Spartanburg 05	Duncan
17	5.7	Berkeley 01	Moncks Corner
18	5.4	Aiken 01	Aiken
18	5.4	Lancaster 01	Lancaster
18	5.4	Lexington 04	Swansea
21	5.3	Charleston 01	Charleston
21	5.3	Richland 02	Columbia
21	5.3	Spartanburg 07	Spartanburg
24	5.0	York 03	Rock Hill
25	4.7	Cherokee 01	Gaffney
25	4.7	Spartanburg 03	Glendale
27	4.6	Spartanburg 04	Woodruff
28	4.4	York 01	York
29	4.1	Anderson 05	Anderson
30	3.9	Lexington 01	Lexington
31	3.6	Florence 03	Lake City
32	3.4	Pickens 01	Easley
33	3.3	Calhoun 01	Saint Matthews
34	3.2	Chesterfield 01	Chesterfield
35	3.1	Georgetown 01	Georgetown
36	3.0	Anderson 01	Williamston
36	3.0	Clarendon 02	Manning
38	2.9	Kershaw 01	Camden
39	2.8	Dorchester 02	Summerville
39	2.8	Lexington 05	Irmo
39	2.8	Richland 01	Columbia
42	2.7	Colleton 01	Walterboro
42	2.7	York 02	Clover
44	2.5	Laurens 56	Clinton
45	2.1	York 04	Fort Mill
46	2.0	Florence 01	Florence
47	1.9	Abbeville 60	Abbeville
47	1.9	Orangeburg 05	Orangeburg
49	1.7	Barnwell 45	Barnwell
50	1.6	Fairfield 01	Winnsboro
50	1.6	Orangeburg 04	Cope
52	1.5	Hampton 01	Hampton
52	1.5	Lee 01	Bishopville
54	1.4	Anderson 04	Pendleton
54	1.4	Darlington 01	Darlington
54	1.4	Edgefield 01	Edgefield
57	1.3	Dorchester 04	Saint George
57	1.3	Marion 01	Marion

Note: This section only includes districts with 1,500 or more students; All categories are ranked from high to low

Rank	Percent	District Name	City
59	1.2	Anderson 03	Iva
59	1.2	Sumter 01	Sumter
61	1.1	Anderson 02	Honea Path
61	1.1	Chester 01	Chester
63	0.9	Marion 02	Mullins
63	0.9	Orangeburg 03	Holly Hill
65	0.7	Union 01	Union
66	0.5	Greenwood 52	Ninety Six
66	0.5	Marlboro 01	Bennettsville
68	0.4	Dillon 03	Latta
69	0.2	Sc Public Charter SD	Columbia
69	0.2	Williamsburg 01	Kingstree

Students Eligible for Free Lunch

Rank	Percent	District Name	City
1	86.4	Williamsburg 01	Kingstree
2	83.6	Dillon 04	Dillon
3	80.4	Florence 03	Lake City
4	80.1	Lee 01	Bishopville
5	79.9	Fairfield 01	Winnsboro
6	79.7	Orangeburg 03	Holly Hill
7	78.7	Calhoun 01	Saint Matthews
8	78.6	Marion 02	Mullins
9	77.6	Orangeburg 05	Orangeburg
10	77.0	Marion 01	Marion
11	75.9	Clarendon 02	Manning
12	70.1	Marlboro 01	Bennettsville
13	69.6	Colleton 01	Walterboro
14	69.5	Dorchester 04	Saint George
15	68.2	Lexington 04	Swansea
16	66.5	Laurens 56	Clinton
17	66.2	Darlington 01	Darlington
18	66.0	Orangeburg 04	Cope
19	63.9	Richland 01	Columbia
20	63.6	Hampton 01	Hampton
21	63.4	Sumter 01	Sumter
22	63.3	Chester 01	Chester
23	62.7	Spartanburg 07	Spartanburg
24	62.4	Saluda 01	Saluda
25	62.3	Cherokee 01	Gaffney
26	60.3	Laurens 55	Laurens
27	59.8	Jasper 01	Ridgeland
28	59.5	Chesterfield 01	Chesterfield
29	59.1	Lexington 03	Batesburg
30	58.6	Georgetown 01	Georgetown
31	58.0	Union 01	Union
32	57.6	Barnwell 45	Barnwell
33	57.4	Newberry 01	Newberry
34	57.2	Dillon 03	Latta
34	57.2	Horry 01	Conway
36	56.3	Abbeville 60	Abbeville
37	56.2	Lexington 02	West Columbia
38	55.6	Florence 01	Florence
39	55.5	Greenwood 50	Greenwood
40	55.3	Anderson 03	Iva
41	55.0	Spartanburg 03	Glendale
42	54.4	Edgefield 01	Edgefield
43	51.7	Aiken 01	Aiken
43	51.7	York 01	York
45	50.0	Oconee 01	Walhalla
46	49.6	Lancaster 01	Lancaster
47	49.2	Anderson 05	Anderson
48	49.0	Berkeley 01	Moncks Corner
49	47.3	York 03	Rock Hill
50	46.7	Kershaw 01	Camden
51	46.4	Spartanburg 06	Roebuck
52	46.3	Beaufort 01	Beaufort
53	46.1	Charleston 01	Charleston
54	44.3	Anderson 04	Pendleton
55	44.2	Greenwood 52	Ninety Six
56	44.0	Spartanburg 01	Campobello
57	43.9	Anderson 02	Honea Path
58	42.9	Spartanburg 02	Spartanburg
59	42.2	Greenville 01	Greenville
60	41.9	Spartanburg 05	Duncan
61	39.7	Pickens 01	Easley
62	39.3	Spartanburg 04	Woodruff
63	37.6	Sc Public Charter SD	Columbia
64	36.6	Richland 02	Columbia
65	33.6	Dorchester 02	Summerville
66	33.1	Anderson 01	Williamston
67	29.9	Lexington 01	Lexington
68	27.0	Lexington 05	Irmo
69	25.7	York 02	Clover
70	15.8	York 04	Fort Mill

Students Eligible for Reduced-Price Lunch

Rank	Percent	District Name	City
1	13.3	Sc Public Charter SD	Columbia
2	10.0	Abbeville 60	Abbeville
3	9.5	Spartanburg 05	Duncan
4	9.3	Hampton 01	Hampton
5	9.2	Dillon 03	Latta
6	9.1	Richland 02	Columbia
7	9.0	Orangeburg 04	Cope
8	8.9	Union 01	Union
9	8.8	Anderson 03	Iva
10	8.7	Anderson 04	Pendleton
11	8.4	Berkeley 01	Moncks Corner
11	8.4	Greenwood 52	Ninety Six
13	8.3	Laurens 55	Laurens
14	8.1	Anderson 02	Honea Path
15	8.0	Chesterfield 01	Chesterfield
15	8.0	Spartanburg 04	Woodruff
17	7.8	Anderson 01	Williamston
17	7.8	Spartanburg 01	Campobello
19	7.7	Lexington 03	Batesburg
20	7.6	Marlboro 01	Bennettsville
20	7.6	York 01	York
22	7.5	Newberry 01	Newberry
22	7.5	Orangeburg 05	Orangeburg
24	7.4	Laurens 56	Clinton
24	7.4	Oconee 01	Walhalla
24	7.4	Spartanburg 02	Spartanburg
27	7.2	Colleton 01	Walterboro
27	7.2	Fairfield 01	Winnsboro
27	7.2	Lexington 01	Lexington
27	7.2	Lexington 02	West Columbia
31	7.1	Lexington 04	Swansea
31	7.1	Sumter 01	Sumter
33	7.0	Edgefield 01	Edgefield
34	6.9	Barnwell 45	Barnwell
34	6.9	Cherokee 01	Gaffney
34	6.9	Dorchester 02	Summerville
34	6.9	Georgetown 01	Georgetown
38	6.8	Pickens 01	Easley
39	6.7	Dorchester 04	Saint George
39	6.7	Spartanburg 03	Glendale
41	6.6	Aiken 01	Aiken
42	6.5	Spartanburg 06	Roebuck
43	6.4	Beaufort 01	Beaufort
43	6.4	York 03	Rock Hill
45	6.2	Chester 01	Chester
45	6.2	Lancaster 01	Lancaster
47	6.1	Florence 01	Florence
47	6.1	Greenwood 50	Greenwood
47	6.1	Horry 01	Conway
50	6.0	Marion 01	Marion
50	6.0	Spartanburg 07	Spartanburg
52	5.9	Calhoun 01	Saint Matthews
52	5.9	Greenville 01	Greenville
54	5.8	Dillon 04	Dillon
54	5.8	Lexington 05	Irmo
56	5.7	Darlington 01	Darlington
56	5.7	York 02	Clover
58	5.6	Charleston 01	Charleston
58	5.6	Saluda 01	Saluda
60	5.4	Clarendon 02	Manning
61	5.2	Kershaw 01	Camden
62	5.0	Anderson 05	Anderson
62	5.0	Jasper 01	Ridgeland
64	4.9	Lee 01	Bishopville
65	4.8	Orangeburg 03	Holly Hill
66	4.7	Williamsburg 01	Kingstree
67	4.6	Marion 02	Mullins
68	4.5	Florence 03	Lake City
69	3.9	York 04	Fort Mill
70	3.7	Richland 01	Columbia

Student/Teacher Ratio
(number of students per teacher)

Rank	Number	District Name	City
1	11.6	Fairfield 01	Winnsboro
2	12.1	Spartanburg 07	Spartanburg
3	13.5	Dorchester 04	Saint George
4	13.6	Richland 01	Columbia
5	13.7	Charleston 01	Charleston
6	13.8	Oconee 01	Walhalla
7	13.9	Orangeburg 03	Holly Hill
8	14.2	Abbeville 60	Abbeville
9	14.3	Hampton 01	Hampton
9	14.3	Newberry 01	Newberry
11	14.4	Beaufort 01	Beaufort
11	14.4	Edgefield 01	Edgefield
11	14.4	Lexington 05	Irmo
14	14.6	Spartanburg 01	Campobello
15	14.8	Georgetown 01	Georgetown
15	14.8	York 02	Clover
17	14.9	Orangeburg 05	Orangeburg
17	14.9	Union 01	Union
19	15.0	Spartanburg 05	Duncan
20	15.1	Spartanburg 03	Glendale
21	15.2	Anderson 04	Pendleton
21	15.2	Calhoun 01	Saint Matthews
21	15.2	Horry 01	Conway
21	15.2	Lexington 01	Lexington
25	15.3	Anderson 05	Anderson
25	15.3	Barnwell 45	Barnwell
25	15.3	York 01	York
25	15.3	York 03	Rock Hill
29	15.4	Cherokee 01	Gaffney
29	15.4	Richland 02	Columbia
29	15.4	Saluda 01	Saluda
32	15.5	Chester 01	Chester
32	15.5	Florence 01	Florence
32	15.5	Lexington 02	West Columbia
32	15.5	Marlboro 01	Bennettsville
36	15.7	Chesterfield 01	Chesterfield
36	15.7	Florence 03	Lake City
36	15.7	Lexington 03	Batesburg
39	16.1	Anderson 03	Iva
39	16.1	Spartanburg 06	Roebuck
41	16.2	Laurens 56	Clinton
41	16.2	Orangeburg 04	Cope
41	16.2	York 04	Fort Mill
44	16.4	Aiken 01	Aiken
44	16.4	Kershaw 01	Camden
44	16.4	Marion 02	Mullins
47	16.5	Greenville 01	Greenville
47	16.5	Lancaster 01	Lancaster
49	16.6	Jasper 01	Ridgeland
50	16.7	Lee 01	Bishopville
50	16.7	Pickens 01	Easley
52	16.8	Berkeley 01	Moncks Corner
52	16.8	Colleton 01	Walterboro
52	16.8	Darlington 01	Darlington
52	16.8	Greenwood 52	Ninety Six
52	16.8	Spartanburg 02	Spartanburg
52	16.8	Sumter 01	Sumter
52	16.8	Williamsburg 01	Kingstree
59	16.9	Marion 01	Marion
60	17.2	Dorchester 02	Summerville
61	17.4	Greenwood 50	Greenwood
62	17.6	Anderson 02	Honea Path
63	18.0	Laurens 55	Laurens
64	18.2	Dillon 04	Dillon
65	18.4	Anderson 01	Williamston
66	18.7	Dillon 03	Latta
67	18.9	Clarendon 02	Manning
67	18.9	Lexington 04	Swansea
69	19.2	Spartanburg 04	Woodruff
70	30.9	Sc Public Charter SD	Columbia

Student/Librarian Ratio
(number of students per librarian)

Rank	Number	District Name	City
1	388.5	Fairfield 01	Winnsboro
2	393.3	Abbeville 60	Abbeville
3	407.6	Greenwood 52	Ninety Six
4	422.3	Spartanburg 03	Glendale
5	430.2	Saluda 01	Saluda
6	430.3	Calhoun 01	Saint Matthews
7	438.6	Dorchester 04	Saint George
8	452.3	Marion 02	Mullins
9	477.7	Anderson 04	Pendleton
10	483.7	Newberry 01	Newberry
11	489.6	Orangeburg 05	Orangeburg
12	502.2	Oconee 01	Walhalla

Note: This section only includes districts with 1,500 or more students; All categories are ranked from high to low

Rank	Number	District Name	City
13	505.3	Lexington 03	Batesburg
14	510.0	Spartanburg 01	Campobello
15	515.4	Florence 03	Lake City
16	516.8	Anderson 03	Iva
17	522.8	Richland 01	Columbia
18	526.3	Williamsburg 01	Kingstree
19	534.5	Cherokee 01	Gaffney
20	537.8	Georgetown 01	Georgetown
21	538.8	Dillon 04	Dillon
22	539.6	Marlboro 01	Bennettsville
23	540.1	Laurens 55	Laurens
24	553.3	Dillon 03	Latta
25	553.4	Lexington 02	West Columbia
26	560.1	Edgefield 01	Edgefield
27	562.0	Lee 01	Bishopville
28	562.9	Anderson 02	Honea Path
29	574.0	York 01	York
30	587.3	Lancaster 01	Lancaster
31	591.9	Spartanburg 05	Duncan
32	596.6	Spartanburg 07	Spartanburg
33	599.0	Union 01	Union
34	601.4	York 02	Clover
35	601.5	Barnwell 45	Barnwell
36	603.1	Aiken 01	Aiken
37	610.0	Laurens 56	Clinton
38	611.6	Orangeburg 03	Holly Hill
39	612.0	Clarendon 02	Manning
40	618.3	Anderson 01	Williamston
41	627.0	Kershaw 01	Camden
42	631.2	Charleston 01	Charleston
43	636.8	Hampton 01	Hampton
44	651.4	Darlington 01	Darlington
45	652.2	Orangeburg 04	Cope
46	658.4	Chesterfield 01	Chesterfield
47	663.2	Jasper 01	Ridgeland
48	666.4	Beaufort 01	Beaufort
49	675.2	York 03	Rock Hill
50	676.6	Sumter 01	Sumter
51	687.4	Chester 01	Chester
52	691.2	Colleton 01	Walterboro
53	699.3	Marion 01	Marion
54	710.5	Spartanburg 06	Roebuck
55	715.0	Spartanburg 04	Woodruff
56	716.3	Berkeley 01	Moncks Corner
57	719.4	Pickens 01	Easley
58	720.0	Lexington 05	Irmo
59	727.5	Greenwood 50	Greenwood
60	747.7	Greenville 01	Greenville
61	763.2	Florence 01	Florence
62	811.1	Richland 02	Columbia
63	826.3	York 04	Fort Mill
64	828.9	Horry 01	Conway
65	830.8	Spartanburg 02	Spartanburg
66	837.3	Anderson 05	Anderson
67	873.3	Lexington 04	Swansea
68	884.2	Lexington 01	Lexington
69	972.8	Dorchester 02	Summerville
70	9,978.0	Sc Public Charter SD	Columbia

Student/Counselor Ratio
(number of students per counselor)

Rank	Number	District Name	City
1	239.1	Fairfield 01	Winnsboro
2	274.2	Edgefield 01	Edgefield
3	279.6	Spartanburg 07	Spartanburg
4	286.6	Anderson 04	Pendleton
5	286.8	Calhoun 01	Saint Matthews
6	290.2	Newberry 01	Newberry
7	302.5	Lexington 01	Lexington
8	310.8	Marion 01	Marion
9	313.3	Cherokee 01	Gaffney
10	323.5	Richland 01	Columbia
11	326.7	Williamsburg 01	Kingstree
12	331.2	Abbeville 60	Abbeville
13	331.6	Jasper 01	Ridgeland
14	332.1	Marlboro 01	Bennettsville
15	335.9	Spartanburg 03	Glendale
16	342.4	Greenwood 52	Ninety Six
17	342.8	Orangeburg 05	Orangeburg
18	344.3	York 03	Rock Hill
19	349.1	York 01	York
20	351.5	Oconee 01	Walhalla
21	355.7	Orangeburg 04	Cope

Rank	Number	District Name	City
22	360.8	Florence 03	Lake City
23	362.0	Charleston 01	Charleston
24	365.3	Georgetown 01	Georgetown
25	365.5	Dorchester 04	Saint George
26	374.7	Lee 01	Bishopville
27	376.2	Kershaw 01	Camden
28	378.6	Beaufort 01	Beaufort
29	381.2	Union 01	Union
30	382.3	Orangeburg 03	Holly Hill
31	384.8	Spartanburg 05	Duncan
32	386.0	Darlington 01	Darlington
33	389.1	York 02	Clover
34	390.3	Richland 02	Columbia
35	402.7	Sumter 01	Sumter
36	404.8	Spartanburg 01	Campobello
37	405.1	Anderson 05	Anderson
38	407.3	Chester 01	Chester
39	409.9	Spartanburg 06	Roebuck
40	424.5	Hampton 01	Hampton
41	424.6	Lexington 05	Irmo
42	425.5	Lancaster 01	Lancaster
43	429.7	York 04	Fort Mill
44	430.2	Saluda 01	Saluda
45	430.7	Anderson 03	Iva
46	431.4	Anderson 01	Williamston
47	435.4	Pickens 01	Easley
48	442.7	Horry 01	Conway
48	442.7	Lexington 02	West Columbia
50	444.7	Dorchester 02	Summerville
51	445.4	Chesterfield 01	Chesterfield
52	457.0	Laurens 55	Laurens
53	457.4	Anderson 02	Honea Path
54	474.6	Aiken 01	Aiken
55	476.7	Spartanburg 04	Woodruff
56	481.2	Barnwell 45	Barnwell
57	482.6	Greenville 01	Greenville
58	485.7	Florence 01	Florence
59	498.5	Spartanburg 02	Spartanburg
60	505.2	Greenwood 50	Greenwood
61	505.3	Lexington 03	Batesburg
62	505.6	Berkeley 01	Moncks Corner
63	510.0	Clarendon 02	Manning
64	516.9	Laurens 56	Clinton
64	516.9	Marion 02	Mullins
66	518.4	Colleton 01	Walterboro
67	538.8	Dillon 04	Dillon
68	553.3	Dillon 03	Latta
69	623.6	Sc Public Charter SD	Columbia
70	698.6	Lexington 04	Swansea

Current Expenditures per Student

Rank	Dollars	District Name	City
1	12,975	Fairfield 01	Winnsboro
2	12,323	Spartanburg 07	Spartanburg
3	11,988	Dorchester 04	Saint George
4	11,943	Richland 01	Columbia
5	11,391	Orangeburg 05	Orangeburg
6	11,203	Beaufort 01	Beaufort
7	10,712	Orangeburg 03	Holly Hill
8	10,511	Jasper 01	Ridgeland
9	10,432	Williamsburg 01	Kingstree
10	10,397	Lexington 03	Batesburg
11	10,295	Calhoun 01	Saint Matthews
12	10,284	Lee 01	Bishopville
13	10,165	Lexington 05	Irmo
14	10,139	Florence 03	Lake City
15	10,060	Oconee 01	Walhalla
16	9,956	York 02	Clover
17	9,823	Charleston 01	Charleston
18	9,791	Anderson 04	Pendleton
19	9,728	Horry 01	Conway
20	9,726	Marlboro 01	Bennettsville
21	9,665	Richland 02	Columbia
22	9,646	Newberry 01	Newberry
23	9,605	Georgetown 01	Georgetown
24	9,495	Abbeville 60	Abbeville
25	9,454	Spartanburg 03	Glendale
26	9,364	Hampton 01	Hampton
27	9,205	Lexington 01	Lexington
28	9,203	Barnwell 45	Barnwell
29	9,146	Saluda 01	Saluda
30	9,075	Laurens 56	Clinton
31	9,048	Lexington 02	West Columbia

Rank	Dollars	District Name	City
32	8,940	York 01	York
33	8,837	Edgefield 01	Edgefield
34	8,827	Spartanburg 05	Duncan
35	8,795	Marion 02	Mullins
36	8,785	Florence 01	Florence
37	8,752	Orangeburg 04	Cope
38	8,748	Chester 01	Chester
39	8,741	Colleton 01	Walterboro
40	8,721	Greenwood 52	Ninety Six
41	8,650	Spartanburg 01	Campobello
42	8,508	York 03	Rock Hill
43	8,457	Darlington 01	Darlington
44	8,431	Chesterfield 01	Chesterfield
45	8,326	Lexington 04	Swansea
46	8,299	Anderson 05	Anderson
47	8,211	Laurens 55	Laurens
48	8,188	Marion 01	Marion
49	8,186	Berkeley 01	Moncks Corner
49	8,186	Cherokee 01	Gaffney
51	8,182	Greenwood 50	Greenwood
52	8,095	Spartanburg 06	Roebuck
53	8,065	Anderson 03	Iva
54	8,030	Union 01	Union
55	8,019	Lancaster 01	Lancaster
56	8,007	Kershaw 01	Camden
57	7,803	Aiken 01	Aiken
58	7,800	York 04	Fort Mill
59	7,718	Anderson 02	Honea Path
60	7,681	Dillon 04	Dillon
61	7,672	Pickens 01	Easley
62	7,634	Clarendon 02	Manning
63	7,515	Greenville 01	Greenville
64	7,354	Spartanburg 04	Woodruff
65	7,346	Dillon 03	Latta
66	7,272	Spartanburg 02	Spartanburg
67	7,117	Dorchester 02	Summerville
68	6,734	Anderson 01	Williamston
69	4,724	Sc Public Charter SD	Columbia
n/a	n/a	Sumter 01	Sumter

Total General Revenue per Student

Rank	Dollars	District Name	City
1	15,704	Spartanburg 07	Spartanburg
2	14,802	Richland 01	Columbia
3	13,997	Fairfield 01	Winnsboro
4	13,839	Beaufort 01	Beaufort
5	13,517	Charleston 01	Charleston
6	13,411	Dorchester 04	Saint George
7	13,161	Calhoun 01	Saint Matthews
8	13,140	York 02	Clover
9	12,721	Lee 01	Bishopville
10	12,262	Jasper 01	Ridgeland
11	12,186	Orangeburg 03	Holly Hill
12	12,094	Orangeburg 05	Orangeburg
13	12,077	Horry 01	Conway
14	11,998	Richland 02	Columbia
15	11,969	Oconee 01	Walhalla
16	11,936	Lexington 05	Irmo
17	11,862	Lexington 03	Batesburg
18	11,722	Georgetown 01	Georgetown
19	11,667	Anderson 04	Pendleton
20	11,482	Greenwood 52	Ninety Six
21	11,315	Newberry 01	Newberry
22	11,220	Williamsburg 01	Kingstree
23	11,192	Lexington 01	Lexington
24	10,896	Spartanburg 01	Campobello
25	10,760	Spartanburg 05	Duncan
26	10,716	York 04	Fort Mill
27	10,659	Spartanburg 03	Glendale
28	10,626	Marlboro 01	Bennettsville
29	10,576	Edgefield 01	Edgefield
30	10,574	Darlington 01	Darlington
31	10,563	York 01	York
32	10,537	Colleton 01	Walterboro
33	10,383	Laurens 56	Clinton
34	10,275	Lexington 02	West Columbia
35	10,140	Florence 03	Lake City
36	10,127	York 03	Rock Hill
37	10,084	Florence 01	Florence
38	10,064	Chester 01	Chester
39	10,027	Greenwood 50	Greenwood
40	9,966	Cherokee 01	Gaffney
41	9,941	Abbeville 60	Abbeville
42	9,897	Orangeburg 04	Cope

Note: This section only includes districts with 1,500 or more students; All categories are ranked from high to low

Rank		District Name	City
43	9,761	Kershaw 01	Camden
44	9,747	Greenville 01	Greenville
45	9,714	Saluda 01	Saluda
46	9,708	Lancaster 01	Lancaster
47	9,697	Berkeley 01	Moncks Corner
48	9,668	Spartanburg 06	Roebuck
49	9,632	Pickens 01	Easley
50	9,608	Anderson 05	Anderson
51	9,528	Hampton 01	Hampton
52	9,365	Barnwell 45	Barnwell
53	9,356	Chesterfield 01	Chesterfield
54	9,283	Clarendon 02	Manning
55	9,260	Laurens 55	Laurens
56	9,208	Lexington 04	Swansea
57	9,151	Sc Public Charter SD	Columbia
58	9,094	Anderson 03	Iva
59	9,052	Aiken 01	Aiken
60	8,958	Marion 02	Mullins
61	8,937	Union 01	Union
62	8,876	Anderson 02	Honea Path
63	8,779	Spartanburg 02	Spartanburg
64	8,681	Marion 01	Marion
65	8,523	Dorchester 02	Summerville
66	8,156	Anderson 01	Williamston
67	7,910	Dillon 04	Dillon
68	7,631	Spartanburg 04	Woodruff
69	7,301	Dillon 03	Latta
n/a	n/a	Sumter 01	Sumter

Long-Term Debt per Student (end of FY)

Rank	Dollars	District Name	City
1	33,503	York 01	York
2	32,146	Beaufort 01	Beaufort
3	26,966	Richland 01	Columbia
4	26,518	York 04	Fort Mill
5	25,435	Greenville 01	Greenville
6	24,378	Pickens 01	Easley
7	23,701	Lee 01	Bishopville
8	23,483	Richland 02	Columbia
9	22,950	Calhoun 01	Saint Matthews
10	22,602	Charleston 01	Charleston
11	21,467	Berkeley 01	Moncks Corner
12	19,471	Georgetown 01	Georgetown
13	17,350	Greenwood 52	Ninety Six
14	17,144	Spartanburg 01	Campobello
15	17,120	Chesterfield 01	Chesterfield
16	17,022	Kershaw 01	Camden
17	16,861	Lexington 01	Lexington
18	16,813	Greenwood 50	Greenwood
19	16,312	Colleton 01	Walterboro
20	15,469	Jasper 01	Ridgeland
21	14,302	Horry 01	Conway
22	13,736	Anderson 04	Pendleton
23	13,693	York 02	Clover
24	13,578	York 03	Rock Hill
25	13,353	Lexington 04	Swansea
26	13,197	Spartanburg 05	Duncan
27	13,111	Lexington 03	Batesburg
28	13,049	Newberry 01	Newberry
29	12,454	Orangeburg 05	Orangeburg
30	12,246	Dorchester 02	Summerville
31	12,178	Lancaster 01	Lancaster
32	12,143	Anderson 02	Honea Path
33	11,439	Orangeburg 04	Cope
34	11,412	Cherokee 01	Gaffney
35	11,338	Anderson 01	Williamston
36	11,271	Saluda 01	Saluda
37	10,961	Anderson 05	Anderson
38	10,726	Laurens 55	Laurens
39	10,200	Orangeburg 03	Holly Hill
40	10,073	Marlboro 01	Bennettsville
41	9,891	Oconee 01	Walhalla
42	9,673	Union 01	Union
43	9,660	Anderson 03	Iva
44	8,848	Barnwell 45	Barnwell
45	8,640	Dorchester 04	Saint George
46	8,386	Williamsburg 01	Kingstree
47	8,236	Spartanburg 03	Glendale
48	7,213	Lexington 05	Irmo
49	6,895	Chester 01	Chester
50	6,411	Hampton 01	Hampton
51	5,435	Laurens 56	Clinton
52	4,054	Darlington 01	Darlington

Rank		District Name	City
53	3,016	Abbeville 60	Abbeville
54	2,977	Edgefield 01	Edgefield
55	2,905	Lexington 02	West Columbia
56	2,353	Clarendon 02	Manning
57	2,131	Fairfield 01	Winnsboro
58	1,240	Florence 03	Lake City
59	1,239	Spartanburg 06	Roebuck
60	1,186	Florence 01	Florence
61	1,163	Aiken 01	Aiken
62	883	Spartanburg 02	Spartanburg
63	819	Dillon 03	Latta
64	681	Spartanburg 07	Spartanburg
65	525	Marion 01	Marion
66	284	Spartanburg 04	Woodruff
67	0	Dillon 04	Dillon
67	0	Marion 02	Mullins
67	0	Sc Public Charter SD	Columbia
n/a	n/a	Sumter 01	Sumter

Number of Diploma Recipients

Rank	Number	District Name	City
1	3,805	Greenville 01	Greenville
2	2,158	Charleston 01	Charleston
3	2,091	Horry 01	Conway
4	1,422	Berkeley 01	Moncks Corner
5	1,347	Richland 02	Columbia
6	1,276	Aiken 01	Aiken
7	1,251	Richland 01	Columbia
8	1,206	Lexington 01	Lexington
9	1,186	Lexington 05	Irmo
10	1,136	Dorchester 02	Summerville
11	997	York 03	Rock Hill
12	995	Beaufort 01	Beaufort
13	900	Florence 01	Florence
14	855	Pickens 01	Easley
15	747	Lancaster 01	Lancaster
16	640	Anderson 05	Anderson
17	636	Georgetown 01	Georgetown
18	621	Spartanburg 06	Roebuck
19	609	Kershaw 01	Camden
20	599	Oconee 01	Walhalla
21	569	Darlington 01	Darlington
22	558	Greenwood 50	Greenwood
22	558	Spartanburg 02	Spartanburg
24	548	Anderson 01	Williamston
25	542	York 04	Fort Mill
26	498	Cherokee 01	Gaffney
27	483	Lexington 02	West Columbia
28	463	Spartanburg 05	Duncan
29	423	Chesterfield 01	Chesterfield
30	376	Orangeburg 05	Orangeburg
31	370	Spartanburg 07	Spartanburg
32	366	Chester 01	Chester
32	366	York 02	Clover
34	365	Newberry 01	Newberry
35	309	Williamsburg 01	Kingstree
36	290	Spartanburg 01	Campobello
37	269	Laurens 55	Laurens
38	266	York 01	York
39	259	Orangeburg 04	Cope
40	248	Union 01	Union
41	246	Colleton 01	Walterboro
42	239	Edgefield 01	Edgefield
43	220	Marlboro 01	Bennettsville
44	210	Anderson 02	Honea Path
45	205	Fairfield 01	Winnsboro
46	193	Spartanburg 03	Glendale
47	190	Laurens 56	Clinton
48	184	Clarendon 02	Manning
49	181	Dillon 04	Dillon
50	180	Anderson 04	Pendleton
51	177	Hampton 01	Hampton
52	173	Abbeville 60	Abbeville
53	160	Lexington 04	Swansea
53	160	Orangeburg 03	Holly Hill
55	158	Jasper 01	Ridgeland
56	148	Spartanburg 04	Woodruff
57	147	Barnwell 45	Barnwell
58	144	Florence 03	Lake City
59	131	Lexington 03	Batesburg
59	131	Marion 01	Marion
61	126	Dorchester 04	Saint George
62	125	Lee 01	Bishopville

Rank		District Name	City
63	122	Marion 02	Mullins
64	114	Anderson 03	Iva
65	111	Saluda 01	Saluda
66	107	Greenwood 52	Ninety Six
67	85	Dillon 03	Latta
68	81	Calhoun 01	Saint Matthews
69	54	Sc Public Charter SD	Columbia
n/a	n/a	Sumter 01	Sumter

High School Drop-out Rate

Rank	Percent	District Name	City
1	9.8	Colleton 01	Walterboro
2	9.6	Laurens 55	Laurens
3	8.6	Sc Public Charter SD	Columbia
4	7.8	Orangeburg 05	Orangeburg
5	6.9	Dillon 04	Dillon
6	6.6	Marion 02	Mullins
7	6.2	Marion 01	Marion
8	5.8	Anderson 04	Pendleton
8	5.8	Hampton 01	Hampton
10	5.6	Spartanburg 07	Spartanburg
11	5.5	Berkeley 01	Moncks Corner
12	4.8	Horry 01	Conway
13	4.7	Aiken 01	Aiken
14	4.6	Chester 01	Chester
15	4.3	Lexington 04	Swansea
15	4.3	Oconee 01	Walhalla
17	4.2	Dorchester 02	Summerville
17	4.2	Spartanburg 05	Duncan
19	4.1	Anderson 05	Anderson
20	4.0	Pickens 01	Easley
21	3.9	Lexington 02	West Columbia
21	3.9	Richland 01	Columbia
23	3.8	York 02	Clover
24	3.6	Laurens 56	Clinton
25	3.5	Anderson 02	Honea Path
25	3.5	Greenville 01	Greenville
25	3.5	Lancaster 01	Lancaster
28	3.4	Anderson 03	Iva
28	3.4	Greenwood 50	Greenwood
28	3.4	Spartanburg 01	Campobello
31	3.3	Orangeburg 04	Cope
32	3.2	Abbeville 60	Abbeville
33	3.0	York 01	York
34	2.9	Richland 02	Columbia
35	2.8	Charleston 01	Charleston
35	2.8	Kershaw 01	Camden
35	2.8	Marlboro 01	Bennettsville
35	2.8	Saluda 01	Saluda
35	2.8	York 03	Rock Hill
40	2.6	Clarendon 02	Manning
40	2.6	Jasper 01	Ridgeland
42	2.5	Dorchester 04	Saint George
42	2.5	Lexington 03	Batesburg
42	2.5	Orangeburg 03	Holly Hill
42	2.5	Spartanburg 02	Spartanburg
42	2.5	Spartanburg 06	Roebuck
47	2.4	Chesterfield 01	Chesterfield
48	2.2	Anderson 01	Williamston
48	2.2	Cherokee 01	Gaffney
48	2.2	Florence 01	Florence
51	2.1	Georgetown 01	Georgetown
51	2.1	Newberry 01	Newberry
53	1.9	Florence 03	Lake City
53	1.9	Spartanburg 03	Glendale
55	1.7	Greenwood 52	Ninety Six
55	1.7	Lexington 05	Irmo
57	1.4	Darlington 01	Darlington
57	1.4	Fairfield 01	Winnsboro
57	1.4	Lexington 01	Lexington
60	1.3	Williamsburg 01	Kingstree
61	1.1	Dillon 03	Latta
61	1.1	York 04	Fort Mill
63	1.0	Barnwell 45	Barnwell
63	1.0	Calhoun 01	Saint Matthews
65	0.9	Beaufort 01	Beaufort
65	0.9	Union 01	Union
67	0.8	Lee 01	Bishopville
68	0.7	Edgefield 01	Edgefield
69	0.5	Spartanburg 04	Woodruff
n/a	n/a	Sumter 01	Sumter

Note: This section only includes districts with 1,500 or more students; All categories are ranked from high to low

Average Freshman Graduation Rate

Rank	Percent	District Name	City
1	93.3	York 04	Fort Mill
2	80.8	Lexington 05	Irmo
3	79.9	Greenwood 52	Ninety Six
4	79.6	Anderson 04	Pendleton
5	76.8	Spartanburg 06	Roebuck
6	76.7	York 02	Clover
7	74.8	Spartanburg 05	Duncan
8	74.7	Anderson 01	Williamston
9	74.4	Richland 02	Columbia
10	74.3	Spartanburg 02	Spartanburg
11	74.2	Newberry 01	Newberry
12	73.7	Lancaster 01	Lancaster
12	73.7	Lexington 01	Lexington
14	72.6	Spartanburg 03	Glendale
15	72.5	Spartanburg 01	Campobello
16	72.4	Edgefield 01	Edgefield
17	72.1	Horry 01	Conway
18	71.1	Greenwood 50	Greenwood
19	69.5	Chesterfield 01	Chesterfield
20	69.3	York 01	York
21	69.0	Greenville 01	Greenville
22	68.8	Georgetown 01	Georgetown
23	68.7	Orangeburg 04	Cope
24	68.2	Anderson 02	Honea Path
25	67.5	York 03	Rock Hill
26	67.4	Clarendon 02	Manning
26	67.4	Dorchester 02	Summerville
28	67.3	Florence 01	Florence
28	67.3	Saluda 01	Saluda
30	67.2	Lexington 02	West Columbia
31	67.1	Kershaw 01	Camden
32	66.8	Hampton 01	Hampton
33	66.5	Oconee 01	Walhalla
34	65.9	Anderson 05	Anderson
34	65.9	Chester 01	Chester
36	65.6	Williamsburg 01	Kingstree
37	65.5	Lexington 03	Batesburg
38	64.6	Berkeley 01	Moncks Corner
39	64.4	Cherokee 01	Gaffney
40	64.1	Spartanburg 04	Woodruff
41	63.7	Beaufort 01	Beaufort
42	63.5	Laurens 56	Clinton
43	62.9	Marion 02	Mullins
43	62.9	Pickens 01	Easley
45	62.7	Jasper 01	Ridgeland
46	62.5	Aiken 01	Aiken
46	62.5	Dillon 03	Latta
48	61.6	Fairfield 01	Winnsboro
49	61.5	Barnwell 45	Barnwell
50	60.5	Orangeburg 05	Orangeburg
51	60.2	Charleston 01	Charleston
51	60.2	Union 01	Union
53	58.8	Richland 01	Columbia
54	58.4	Laurens 55	Laurens
55	58.3	Calhoun 01	Saint Matthews
56	57.5	Dorchester 04	Saint George
57	56.0	Darlington 01	Darlington
58	55.2	Dillon 04	Dillon
59	55.1	Marlboro 01	Bennettsville
60	55.0	Marion 01	Marion
61	54.3	Lee 01	Bishopville
62	54.1	Abbeville 60	Abbeville
63	53.9	Spartanburg 07	Spartanburg
64	53.5	Anderson 03	Iva
65	51.6	Lexington 04	Swansea
66	49.8	Orangeburg 03	Holly Hill
67	44.4	Florence 03	Lake City
68	44.3	Colleton 01	Walterboro
n/a	n/a	Sc Public Charter SD	Columbia
n/a	n/a	Sumter 01	Sumter

Note: This section only includes districts with 1,500 or more students; All categories are ranked from high to low

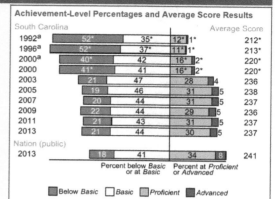

The Nation's Report Card — **Mathematics** 2013 State Snapshot Report

South Carolina
Grade 4
Public Schools

Overall Results

- In 2013, the average score of fourth-grade students in South Carolina was 237. This was lower than the average score of 241 for public school students in the nation.
- The average score for students in South Carolina in 2013 (237) was not significantly different from their average score in 2011 (237) and was higher than their average score in 1992 (212).
- The score gap between higher performing students in South Carolina (those at the 75th percentile) and lower performing students (those at the 25th percentile) was 39 points in 2013. This performance gap was not significantly different from that in 1992 (43 points).
- The percentage of students in South Carolina who performed at or above the NAEP *Proficient* level was 35 percent in 2013. This percentage was not significantly different from that in 2011 (36 percent) and was greater than that in 1992 (13 percent).
- The percentage of students in South Carolina who performed at or above the NAEP *Basic* level was 79 percent in 2013. This percentage was not significantly different from that in 2011 (79 percent) and was greater than that in 1992 (48 percent).

Achievement-Level Percentages and Average Score Results

South Carolina				Average Score
1992[a]	52*	35*	12* 1*	212*
1996[a]	52*	37*	11* 1*	213*
2000[a]	40*	42	16* 2*	220*
2000	41*	41	16* 2*	220*
2003	21	47	28 4	236
2005	19	46	31 5	238
2007	20	44	31 5	237
2009	22	44	29 5	236
2011	21	43	31 5	237
2013	21	44	30 5	237
Nation (public)				
2013	18	41	34 8	241

Percent below *Basic* or at *Basic* — Percent at *Proficient* or *Advanced*

■ Below *Basic*   ☐ *Basic*   ▨ *Proficient*   ■ *Advanced*

* Significantly different (*p* < .05) from state's results in 2013. Significance tests were performed using unrounded numbers.
[a] Accommodations not permitted. For information about NAEP accommodations, see http://nces.ed.gov/nationsreportcard/about/inclusion.aspx.

NOTE: Detail may not sum to totals because of rounding.

Compare the Average Score in 2013 to Other States/Jurisdictions

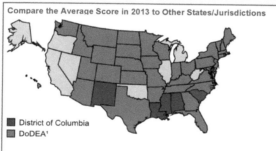

■ District of Columbia
■ DoDEA[1]

[1] Department of Defense Education Activity (overseas and domestic schools).

In 2013, the average score in South Carolina (237) was
- lower than those in 38 states/jurisdictions
- higher than those in 5 states/jurisdictions
- not significantly different from those in 8 states/jurisdictions

Average Scores for State/Jurisdiction and Nation (public)

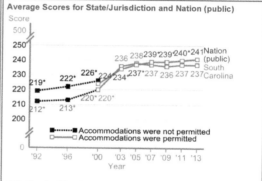

■ Accommodations were not permitted
☐ Accommodations were permitted

* Significantly different (*p* < .05) from 2013. Significance tests were performed using unrounded numbers.

NOTE: For information about NAEP accommodations, see http://nces.ed.gov/nationsreportcard/about/inclusion.aspx.

Results for Student Groups in 2013

Reporting Groups	Percent of students	Avg. score	Percentages at or above Basic	Percentages at or above Proficient	Percent at Advanced
Race/Ethnicity					
White	53	247	89	49	8
Black	35	222	64	15	1
Hispanic	7	229	73	25	2
Asian	1	‡	‡	‡	‡
American Indian/Alaska Native	#	‡	‡	‡	‡
Native Hawaiian/Pacific Islander	#	‡	‡	‡	‡
Two or more races	3	239	85	36	3
Gender					
Male	51	236	77	36	6
Female	49	238	81	35	5
National School Lunch Program					
Eligible	62	227	69	22	2
Not eligible	38	252	94	57	11

\# Rounds to zero.   ‡ Reporting standards not met.

NOTE: Detail may not sum to totals because of rounding, and because the "Information not available" category for the National School Lunch Program, which provides free/reduced-price lunches, is not displayed. Black includes African American and Hispanic includes Latino. Race categories exclude Hispanic origin.

Score Gaps for Student Groups

- In 2013, Black students had an average score that was 25 points lower than White students. This performance gap was narrower than that in 1992 (31 points).
- In 2013, Hispanic students had an average score that was 18 points lower than White students. Data are not reported for Hispanic students in 1992, because reporting standards were not met.
- In 2013, male students in South Carolina had an average score that was not significantly different from female students.
- In 2013, students who were eligible for free/reduced-price school lunch, an indicator of low family income, had an average score that was 25 points lower than students who were not eligible for free/reduced-price school lunch. This performance gap was not significantly different from that in 1996 (25 points).

NOTE: Statistical comparisons are calculated on the basis of unrounded scale scores or percentages.
SOURCE: U.S. Department of Education, Institute of Education Sciences, National Center for Education Statistics, National Assessment of Educational Progress (NAEP), various years, 1992–2013 Mathematics Assessments.

The Nation's Report Card
Mathematics
2013 State Snapshot Report

South Carolina
Grade 8
Public Schools

Overall Results

- In 2013, the average score of eighth-grade students in South Carolina was 280. This was lower than the average score of 284 for public school students in the nation.
- The average score for students in South Carolina in 2013 (280) was not significantly different from their average score in 2011 (281) and was higher than their average score in 1992 (261).
- The score gap between higher performing students in South Carolina (those at the 75th percentile) and lower performing students (those at the 25th percentile) was 51 points in 2013. This performance gap was not significantly different from that in 1992 (49 points).
- The percentage of students in South Carolina who performed at or above the NAEP *Proficient* level was 31 percent in 2013. This percentage was not significantly different from that in 2011 (32 percent) and was greater than that in 1992 (15 percent).
- The percentage of students in South Carolina who performed at or above the NAEP *Basic* level was 69 percent in 2013. This percentage was not significantly different from that in 2011 (70 percent) and was greater than that in 1992 (48 percent).

Achievement-Level Percentages and Average Score Results

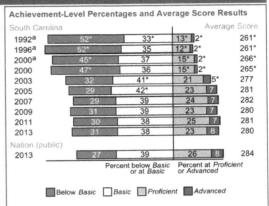

* Significantly different (*p* < .05) from state's results in 2013. Significance tests were performed using unrounded numbers.
a Accommodations not permitted. For information about NAEP accommodations, see http://nces.ed.gov/nationsreportcard/about/inclusion.aspx.

NOTE: Detail may not sum to totals because of rounding.

Compare the Average Score in 2013 to Other States/Jurisdictions

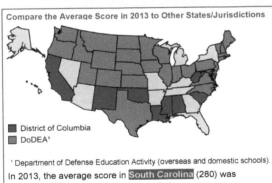

- District of Columbia
- DoDEA[1]

[1] Department of Defense Education Activity (overseas and domestic schools).

In 2013, the average score in **South Carolina** (280) was
- lower than those in 30 states/jurisdictions
- higher than those in 8 states/jurisdictions
- not significantly different from those in 13 states/jurisdictions

Average Scores for State/Jurisdiction and Nation (public)

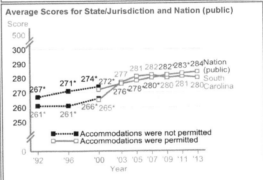

* Significantly different (*p* < .05) from 2013. Significance tests were performed using unrounded numbers.

NOTE: For information about NAEP accommodations, see http://nces.ed.gov/nationsreportcard/about/inclusion.aspx.

Results for Student Groups in 2013

Reporting Groups	Percent of students	Avg. score	Percentages at or above *Basic*	*Proficient*	Percent at *Advanced*
Race/Ethnicity					
White	55	292	81	43	11
Black	36	261	48	13	2
Hispanic	5	272	62	23	4
Asian	2	‡	‡	‡	‡
American Indian/Alaska Native	#	‡	‡	‡	‡
Native Hawaiian/Pacific Islander	#	‡	‡	‡	‡
Two or more races	2	286	79	31	6
Gender					
Male	50	281	69	32	8
Female	50	279	68	29	7
National School Lunch Program					
Eligible	54	266	55	17	3
Not eligible	46	296	84	47	13

Rounds to zero.   ‡ Reporting standards not met.
NOTE: Detail may not sum to totals because of rounding, and because the "Information not available" category for the National School Lunch Program, which provides free/reduced-price lunches, is not displayed. Black includes African American and Hispanic includes Latino. Race categories exclude Hispanic origin.

Score Gaps for Student Groups

- In 2013, Black students had an average score that was 31 points lower than White students. This performance gap was not significantly different from that in 1992 (33 points).
- In 2013, Hispanic students had an average score that was 20 points lower than White students. Data are not reported for Hispanic students in 1992, because reporting standards were not met.
- In 2013, male students in South Carolina had an average score that was not significantly different from female students.
- In 2013, students who were eligible for free/reduced-price school lunch, an indicator of low family income, had an average score that was 30 points lower than students who were not eligible for free/reduced-price school lunch. This performance gap was not significantly different from that in 1996 (26 points).

 NATIONAL CENTER FOR EDUCATION STATISTICS
Institute of Education Sciences

NOTE: Statistical comparisons are calculated on the basis of unrounded scale scores or percentages.
SOURCE: U.S. Department of Education, Institute of Education Sciences, National Center for Education Statistics, National Assessment of Educational Progress (NAEP), various years, 1992–2013 Mathematics Assessments.

The Nation's Report Card — Reading — 2013 State Snapshot Report

South Carolina
Grade 4
Public Schools

Overall Results

- In 2013, the average score of fourth-grade students in South Carolina was 214. This was lower than the average score of 221 for public school students in the nation.
- The average score for students in South Carolina in 2013 (214) was not significantly different from their average score in 2011 (215) and was higher than their average score in 1992 (210).
- The score gap between higher performing students in South Carolina (those at the 75th percentile) and lower performing students (those at the 25th percentile) was 49 points in 2013. This performance gap was not significantly different from that in 1992 (47 points).
- The percentage of students in South Carolina who performed at or above the NAEP *Proficient* level was 28 percent in 2013. This percentage was not significantly different from that in 2011 (28 percent) and was greater than that in 1992 (22 percent).
- The percentage of students in South Carolina who performed at or above the NAEP *Basic* level was 60 percent in 2013. This percentage was not significantly different from that in 2011 (61 percent) and was greater than that in 1992 (53 percent).

Achievement-Level Percentages and Average Score Results

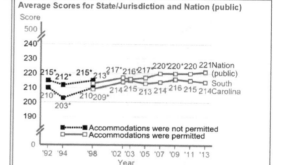

South Carolina				Average Score
1992a	47*	31	18* 4*	210*
1994a	52*	28*	16* 4*	203*
1998a	45*	32	19* 4*	210
1998	47*	31	18* 4*	209*
2002	42	33	20 5	214
2003	41	34	20 5	215
2005	43	32	20 6	213
2007	41	33	20 5	214
2009	38	34	22 6	216
2011	39	33	22 6	215
2013	40	32	22 6	214
Nation (public)				
2013	33	33	26 8	221

Percent below *Basic* or at *Basic*   Percent at *Proficient* or *Advanced*

☐ Below *Basic*   ☐ *Basic*   ☐ *Proficient*   ■ *Advanced*

* Significantly different (*p* < .05) from state's results in 2013. Significance tests were performed using unrounded numbers.
a Accommodations not permitted. For information about NAEP accommodations, see http://nces.ed.gov/nationsreportcard/about/inclusion.aspx.

NOTE: Detail may not sum to totals because of rounding.

Compare the Average Score in 2013 to Other States/Jurisdictions

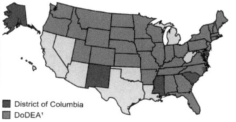

■ District of Columbia
■ DoDEA¹

¹ Department of Defense Education Activity (overseas and domestic schools).

In 2013, the average score in South Carolina (214) was
- lower than those in 38 states/jurisdictions
- higher than those in 4 states/jurisdictions
- not significantly different from those in 9 states/jurisdictions

Average Scores for State/Jurisdiction and Nation (public)

Score

Nation (public): 215* 212* 215* 213* 217* 216* 217* 220* 220* 220 221
South Carolina: 210 203* 210 209* 214 215 213 214 216 215 214

■ Accommodations were not permitted
□ Accommodations were permitted

'92 '94   '98   '02 '03 '05 '07 '09 '11 '13
Year

* Significantly different (*p* < .05) from 2013. Significance tests were performed using unrounded numbers.

NOTE: For information about NAEP accommodations, see http://nces.ed.gov/nationsreportcard/about/inclusion.aspx.

Results for Student Groups in 2013

Reporting Groups	Percent of students	Avg. score	Percentages at or above *Basic*	*Proficient*	Percent at *Advanced*
Race/Ethnicity					
White	53	224	72	39	9
Black	35	197	43	13	1
Hispanic	7	211	60	21	3
Asian	1	‡	‡	‡	‡
American Indian/Alaska Native	#	‡	‡	‡	‡
Native Hawaiian/Pacific Islander	#	‡	‡	‡	‡
Two or more races	3	218	67	30	5
Gender					
Male	51	209	57	25	5
Female	49	218	65	31	7
National School Lunch Program					
Eligible	62	202	49	17	2
Not eligible	38	232	79	46	12

Rounds to zero.   ‡ Reporting standards not met.

NOTE: Detail may not sum to totals because of rounding, and because the "Information not available" category for the National School Lunch Program, which provides free/reduced-price lunches, is not displayed. Black includes African American and Hispanic includes Latino. Race categories exclude Hispanic origin.

Score Gaps for Student Groups

- In 2013, Black students had an average score that was 27 points lower than White students. This performance gap was not significantly different from that in 1992 (27 points).
- In 2013, Hispanic students had an average score that was 13 points lower than White students. Data are not reported for Hispanic students in 1992, because reporting standards were not met.
- In 2013, female students in South Carolina had an average score that was higher than male students by 9 points.
- In 2013, students who were eligible for free/reduced-price school lunch, an indicator of low family income, had an average score that was 29 points lower than students who were not eligible for free/reduced-price school lunch. This performance gap was not significantly different from that in 1998 (29 points).

ies NATIONAL CENTER FOR EDUCATION STATISTICS — Institute of Education Sciences

NOTE: Statistical comparisons are calculated on the basis of unrounded scale scores or percentages.
SOURCE: U.S. Department of Education, Institute of Education Sciences, National Center for Education Statistics, National Assessment of Educational Progress (NAEP), various years, 1992–2013 Reading Assessments.

The Nation's Report Card   Reading   2013 State Snapshot Report

South Carolina
Grade 8
Public Schools

Overall Results

- In 2013, the average score of eighth-grade students in South Carolina was 261. This was lower than the average score of 266 for public school students in the nation.
- The average score for students in South Carolina in 2013 (261) was not significantly different from their average score in 2011 (260) and was higher than their average score in 1998 (255).
- The score gap between higher performing students in South Carolina (those at the 75th percentile) and lower performing students (those at the 25th percentile) was 45 points in 2013. This performance gap was not significantly different from that in 1998 (45 points).
- The percentage of students in South Carolina who performed at or above the NAEP *Proficient* level was 29 percent in 2013. This percentage was not significantly different from that in 2011 (27 percent) and was greater than that in 1998 (22 percent).
- The percentage of students in South Carolina who performed at or above the NAEP *Basic* level was 73 percent in 2013. This percentage was not significantly different from that in 2011 (72 percent) and was greater than that in 1998 (66 percent).

Achievement-Level Percentages and Average Score Results

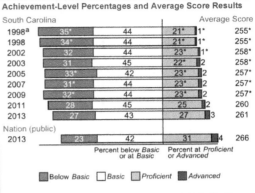

* Significantly different (*p* < .05) from state's results in 2013. Significance tests were performed using unrounded numbers.
a Accommodations not permitted. For information about NAEP accommodations, see http://nces.ed.gov/nationsreportcard/about/inclusion.aspx.

NOTE: Detail may not sum to totals because of rounding.

Compare the Average Score in 2013 to Other States/Jurisdictions

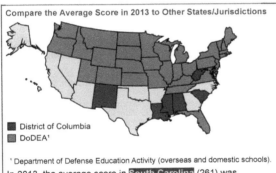

- District of Columbia
- DoDEA[1]

[1] Department of Defense Education Activity (overseas and domestic schools).

In 2013, the average score in South Carolina (261) was
- lower than those in 35 states/jurisdictions
- higher than those in 6 states/jurisdictions
- not significantly different from those in 10 states/jurisdictions

Average Scores for State/Jurisdiction and Nation (public)

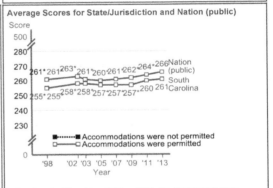

* Significantly different (*p* < .05) from 2013. Significance tests were performed using unrounded numbers.

NOTE: For information about NAEP accommodations, see http://nces.ed.gov/nationsreportcard/about/inclusion.aspx.

Results for Student Groups in 2013

Reporting Groups	Percent of students	Avg. score	Percentages at or above Basic	Percentages at or above Proficient	Percent at Advanced
Race/Ethnicity					
White	55	271	82	39	4
Black	36	247	58	14	#
Hispanic	5	257	70	24	2
Asian	2	‡	‡	‡	‡
American Indian/Alaska Native	#	‡	‡	‡	‡
Native Hawaiian/Pacific Islander	#	‡	‡	‡	‡
Two or more races	2	‡	‡	‡	‡
Gender					
Male	50	256	67	23	2
Female	50	267	78	35	3
National School Lunch Program					
Eligible	54	250	62	17	1
Not eligible	46	275	86	44	5

Rounds to zero.   ‡ Reporting standards not met.

NOTE: Detail may not sum to totals because of rounding, and because the "Information not available" category for the National School Lunch Program, which provides free/reduced-price lunches, is not displayed. Black includes African American and Hispanic includes Latino. Race categories exclude Hispanic origin.

Score Gaps for Student Groups

- In 2013, Black students had an average score that was 24 points lower than White students. This performance gap was not significantly different from that in 1998 (25 points).
- In 2013, Hispanic students had an average score that was 14 points lower than White students. Data are not reported for Hispanic students in 1998, because reporting standards were not met.
- In 2013, female students in South Carolina had an average score that was higher than male students by 12 points.
- In 2013, students who were eligible for free/reduced-price school lunch, an indicator of low family income, had an average score that was 25 points lower than students who were not eligible for free/reduced-price school lunch. This performance gap was not significantly different from that in 1998 (26 points).

South Carolina
Grade 4
Public Schools

The Nation's Report Card — Science 2009 — State Snapshot Report

2009 Science Assessment Content

Guided by a new framework, the NAEP science assessment was updated in 2009 to keep the content current with key developments in science, curriculum standards, assessments, and research. The 2009 framework organizes science content into three broad content areas. **Physical science** includes concepts related to properties and changes of matter, forms of energy, energy transfer and conservation, position and motion of objects, and forces affecting motion. **Life science** includes concepts related to organization and development, matter and energy transformations, interdependence, heredity and reproduction, and evolution and diversity. **Earth and space sciences** includes concepts related to objects in the universe, the history of the Earth, properties of Earth materials, tectonics, energy in Earth systems, climate and weather, and biogeochemical cycles.

The 2009 science assessment was composed of 143 questions at grade 4, 162 at grade 8, and 179 at grade 12. Students responded to only a portion of the questions, which included both multiple-choice questions and questions that required a written response.

Compare the Average Score in 2009 to Other States/Jurisdictions

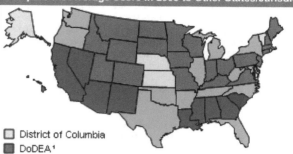

☐ District of Columbia
■ DoDEA[1]

[1] Department of Defense Education Activity (overseas and domestic schools).

In 2009, the average score in **South Carolina** was
- lower than those in 23 states/jurisdictions
- higher than those in 9 states/jurisdictions
- not significantly different from those in 14 states/jurisdictions
- 5 states/jurisdictions did not participate

Overall Results

- In 2009, the average score of fourth-grade students in South Carolina was 149. This was not significantly different from the average score of 149 for public school students in the nation.
- The percentage of students in South Carolina who performed at or above the NAEP *Proficient* level was 33 percent in 2009. This percentage was not significantly different from the nation (32 percent).
- The percentage of students in South Carolina who performed at or above the NAEP *Basic* level was 72 percent in 2009. This percentage was not significantly different from the nation (71 percent).

Achievement-Level Percentages and Average Score Results

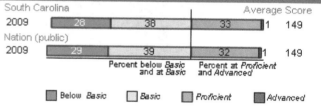

	Average Score
South Carolina 2009	149
Nation (public) 2009	149

Percent below *Basic* and at *Basic* / Percent at *Proficient* and *Advanced*

■ Below *Basic* ☐ *Basic* ▨ *Proficient* ■ *Advanced*

NOTE: Detail may not sum to totals because of rounding.

Results for Student Groups in 2009

Reporting Groups	Percent of students	Avg. score	Percentages at or above Basic	Percentages at or above Proficient	Percent at Advanced
Gender					
Male	51	150	72	34	1
Female	49	149	71	33	#
Race/Ethnicity					
White	55	163	87	49	1
Black	35	128	47	10	#
Hispanic	6	140	65	23	#
Asian/Pacific Islander	1	‡	‡	‡	‡
American Indian/Alaska Native	#	‡	‡	‡	‡
National School Lunch Program					
Eligible	56	137	59	19	#
Not eligible	44	165	88	52	1

Rounds to zero.   ‡ Reporting standards not met.

NOTE: Detail may not sum to totals because of rounding, and because the "Information not available" category for the National School Lunch Program, which provides free/reduced-price lunches, and the "Unclassified" category for race/ethnicity are not displayed.

Score Gaps for Student Groups

- In 2009, male students in South Carolina had an average score that was not significantly different from female students.
- In 2009, Black students had an average score that was 35 points lower than White students. This performance gap was not significantly different from the nation (35 points).
- In 2009, Hispanic students had an average score that was 24 points lower than White students. This performance gap was not significantly different from the nation (32 points).
- In 2009, students who were eligible for free/reduced-price school lunch, an indicator of low family income, had an average score that was 29 points lower than students who were not eligible for free/reduced-price school lunch. This performance gap was not significantly different from the nation (29 points).

NOTE: Statistical comparisons are calculated on the basis of unrounded scale scores or percentages.
SOURCE: U.S. Department of Education, Institute of Education Sciences, National Center for Education Statistics, National Assessment of Educational Progress (NAEP), 2009 Science Assessment.

The Nation's Science Report Card 2011 State Snapshot Report

South Carolina
Grade 8
Public Schools

Overall Results

- In 2011, the average score of eighth-grade students in South Carolina was 149. This was not significantly different from the average score of 151 for public school students in the nation.
- The average score for students in South Carolina in 2011 (149) was higher than their average score in 2009 (143).
- In 2011, the score gap between students in South Carolina at the 75th percentile and students at the 25th percentile was 46 points. This performance gap was not significantly different from that of 2009 (47 points).
- The percentage of students in South Carolina who performed at or above the NAEP *Proficient* level was 28 percent in 2011. This percentage was greater than that in 2009 (23 percent).
- The percentage of students in South Carolina who performed at or above the NAEP *Basic* level was 61 percent in 2011. This percentage was greater than that in 2009 (55 percent).

Achievement-Level Percentages and Average Score Results

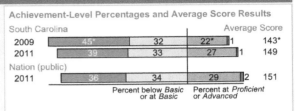

Percent below *Basic* or at *Basic* | Percent at *Proficient* or *Advanced*

Below *Basic* | Basic | Proficient | Advanced

* Significantly different (*p* < .05) from state's results in 2011. Significance tests were performed using unrounded numbers.

NOTE: Detail may not sum to totals because of rounding.

Compare the Average Score in 2011 to Other States/Jurisdictions

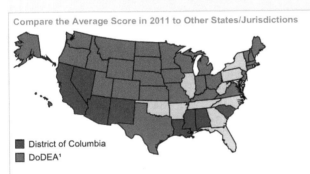

- District of Columbia
- DoDEA[1]

[1] Department of Defense Education Activity (overseas and domestic schools).

In 2011, the average score in South Carolina (149) was
- lower than those in 29 states/jurisdictions
- higher than those in 9 states/jurisdictions
- not significantly different from those in 13 states/jurisdictions

Average Scores for State/Jurisdiction and Nation (public)

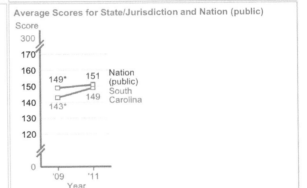

* Significantly different (*p* < .05) from 2011. Significance tests were performed using unrounded numbers.

Results for Student Groups in 2011

Reporting Groups	Percent of students	Avg. score	Percentages at or above Basic	Proficient	Percent at Advanced
Race/Ethnicity					
White	55	163	78	42	2
Black	36	128	36	8	#
Hispanic	5	139	50	16	#
Asian	1	‡	‡	‡	‡
American Indian/Alaska Native	#	‡	‡	‡	‡
Native Hawaiian/Pacific Islander	#	‡	‡	‡	‡
Two or more races	2	‡	‡	‡	‡
Gender					
Male	51	150	62	32	2
Female	49	147	61	24	1
National School Lunch Program					
Eligible	52	137	47	15	#
Not eligible	48	162	77	42	3

Rounds to zero. ‡ Reporting standards not met.

NOTE: Detail may not sum to totals because of rounding, and because the "Information not available" category for the National School Lunch Program, which provides free/reduced-price lunches, is not displayed. Black includes African American and Hispanic includes Latino. Race categories exclude Hispanic origin.

Score Gaps for Student Groups

- In 2011, Black students had an average score that was 35 points lower than White students. This performance gap was not significantly different from that in 2009 (34 points).
- In 2011, Hispanic students had an average score that was 24 points lower than White students. This performance gap was not significantly different from that in 2009 (29 points).
- In 2011, male students in South Carolina had an average score that was not significantly different from female students.
- In 2011, students who were eligible for free/reduced-price school lunch, an indicator of low family income, had an average score that was 26 points lower than students who were not eligible for free/reduced-price school lunch. This performance gap was not significantly different from that in 2009 (29 points).

NOTE: Statistical comparisons are calculated on the basis of unrounded scale scores or percentages.
SOURCE: U.S. Department of Education, Institute of Education Sciences, National Center for Education Statistics, National Assessment of Educational Progress (NAEP), 2009 and 2011 Science Assessments.

ies NATIONAL CENTER FOR EDUCATION STATISTICS
Institute of Education Sciences

NCES National Center for Education Statistics

The Nation's Report Card
State **Writing** 2002
Snapshot Report

South Carolina
Grade 4
Public School

NCES 2003-532SC4

The writing assessment of the National Assessment of Educational Progress (NAEP) measures narrative, informative, and persuasive writing–three purposes identified in the NAEP framework. The NAEP writing scale ranges from 0 to 300.

Overall Writing Results for South Carolina

- The average scale score for fourth-grade students in South Carolina was 145.

- South Carolina's average score (145) was lower[1] than that of the nation's public schools (153).

- Students' average scale scores in South Carolina were higher than those in 5 jurisdictions[2], not significantly different from those in 14 jurisdictions, and lower than those in 28 jurisdictions.

- The percentage of students who performed at or above the NAEP *Proficient* level was 17 percent. The percentage of students who performed at or above the *Basic* level was 82 percent.

Student Percentage at Each Achievement Level

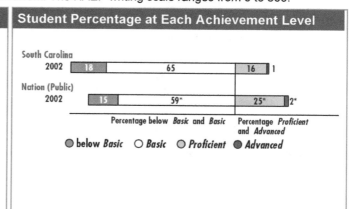

South Carolina
2002   18   65   16   1

Nation (Public)
2002   15   59*   25*   2*

Percentage below *Basic* and *Basic*   Percentage *Proficient* and *Advanced*

● below *Basic*   ○ *Basic*   ○ *Proficient*   ● *Advanced*

Performance of NAEP Reporting Groups in South Carolina

Reporting groups	Percentage of students	Average Score	Percentage of students at			
			Below *Basic*	*Basic*	*Proficient*	*Advanced*
Male	51	136 ↓	25	65	10 ↓	#
Female	49	154 ↓	11	64 ↑	24 ↓	1 ↓
White	55	153 ↓	13	64 ↑	22 ↓	1 ↓
Black	42	135 ↓	25	66	9 ↓	#
Hispanic	2	---	---	---	---	---
Asian/Pacific Islander	1	---	---	---	---	---
American Indian/Alaska Native	#	---	---	---	---	---
Free/reduced-priced school lunch						
Eligible	54	136 ↓	24	66	10 ↓	#
Not eligible	40	155 ↓	11	63 ↑	24 ↓	2 ↓
Information not available	5	158	8	65	25	1

Average Score Gaps Between Selected Groups

- Female students in South Carolina had an average score that was higher than that of male students (18 points). This performance gap was not significantly different from that of the Nation (18 points).

- White students had an average score that was higher than that of Black students (17 points). This performance gap was not significantly different from that of the Nation (20 points).

- The sample size was not sufficient to permit a reliable estimate for Hispanic students in South Carolina.

- Students who were not eligible for free/reduced-price school lunch had an average score that was higher than that of students who were eligible (19 points). This performance gap was not significantly different from that of the Nation (22 points).

Writing Scale Scores at Selected Percentiles

Scale Score Distribution

	25th Percentile	50th Percentile	75th Percentile
South Carolina	123 ↓	145 ↓	167 ↓
Nation (Public)	128	153	178

An examination of scores at different percentiles on the 0-300 NAEP writing scale at each grade indicates how well students at lower, middle, and higher levels of the distribution performed. For example, the data above shows that 75 percent of students in public schools nationally scored below *178*, while 75 percent of students in South Carolina scored below *167*.

Percentage rounds to zero.   --- Reporting standards not met; sample size insufficient to permit a reliable estimate.
* Significantly different from South Carolina.   ↑ Significantly higher than, ↓ lower than appropriate subgroup in the nation (public).
[1] Comparisons (higher/lower/not different) are based on statistical tests. The .05 level was used for testing statistical significance.
[2] "Jurisdictions" includes participating states and other jurisdictions (such as Guam or the District of Columbia).
NOTE: Detail may not sum to totals because of rounding. Score gaps are calculated based on differences between unrounded average scale scores.
Visit http://nces.ed.gov/nationsreportcard/states/ for additional results and detailed information.
SOURCE: U.S. Department of Education, Institute of Education Sciences, National Center for Education Statistics, National Assessment of Educational Progress (NAEP), 2002 Writing Assessment.

The National Assessment of Educational Progress (NAEP) assesses writing for three purposes identified in the NAEP framework: narrative, informative, and persuasive. The NAEP writing scale ranges from 0 to 300.

Overall Writing Results for South Carolina

- In 2007, the average scale score for eighth-grade students in South Carolina was 148. This was not significantly different from their average score in 2002 (146) and was higher than their average score in 1998 (140).[1]
- South Carolina's average score (148) in 2007 was lower than that of the nation's public schools (154).
- Of the 45 states and one other jurisdiction that participated in the 2007 eighth-grade assessment, students' average scale score in South Carolina was higher than those in 4 jurisdictions, not significantly different from those in 9 jurisdictions, and lower than those in 32 jurisdictions.[2]
- The percentage of students in South Carolina who performed at or above the NAEP Proficient level was 23 percent in 2007. This percentage was not significantly different from that in 2002 (20 percent) and was greater than that in 1998 (15 percent).
- The percentage of students in South Carolina who performed at or above the NAEP Basic level was 85 percent in 2007. This percentage was not significantly different from that in 2002 (84 percent) and was greater than that in 1998 (79 percent).

Percentages at NAEP Achievement Levels and Average Score

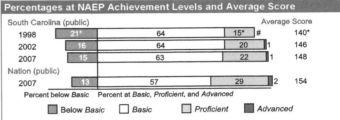

NOTE: The NAEP grade 8 writing achievement levels correspond to the following scale points: Below Basic, 113 or lower; Basic, 114–172; Proficient, 173–223; Advanced, 224 or above.

Performance of NAEP Reporting Groups in South Carolina: 2007

Reporting groups	Percent of students	Average score	Percent below Basic	Percent of students at or above Basic	Proficient	Percent Advanced
Male	49	137	22	78	12	#
Female	51	159	7	93	32	1
White	55	156	9	91	30	1
Black	39	137	21	79	12	#
Hispanic	4↑	140	23	77	18	#
Asian/Pacific Islander	1	‡	‡	‡	‡	‡
American Indian/Alaska Native	#	‡	‡	‡	‡	‡
Eligible for National School Lunch Program	50↑	139	21	79	13	#
Not eligible for National School Lunch Program	50	157	8	92	32	1

Average Score Gaps Between Selected Groups

- In 2007, male students in South Carolina had an average score that was lower than that of female students by 22 points. This performance gap was not significantly different from that of 1998 (21 points).
- In 2007, Black students had an average score that was lower than that of White students by 18 points. This performance gap was not significantly different from that of 1998 (22 points).
- In 2007, Hispanic students had an average score that was lower than that of White students by 16 points. Data are not reported for Hispanic students in 1998, because reporting standards were not met.
- In 2007, students who were eligible for free/reduced-price school lunch, an indicator of poverty, had an average score that was lower than that of students who were not eligible for free/reduced-price school lunch by 19 points. This performance gap was not significantly different from that of 1998 (23 points).
- In 2007, the score gap between students at the 75th percentile and students at the 25th percentile was 44 points. This performance gap was not significantly different from that of 1998 (43 points).

Writing Scores at Selected Percentiles in South Carolina

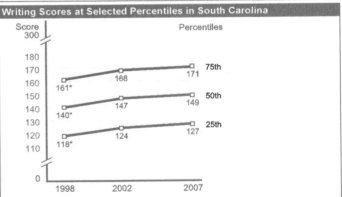

NOTE: Scores at selected percentiles on the NAEP writing scale indicate how well students at lower, middle, and higher levels performed.

Rounds to zero.
* Significantly different from 2007.
‡ Reporting standards not met.
↑ Significantly higher than 2002. ↓ Significantly lower than 2002.
[1] Comparisons (higher/lower/narrower/wider/not different) are based on statistical tests. The .05 level with appropriate adjustments for multiple comparisons was used for testing statistical significance. Statistical comparisons are calculated on the basis of unrounded scale scores or percentages. Comparisons across jurisdictions and comparisons with the nation or within a jurisdiction across years may be affected by differences in exclusion rates for students with disabilities (SD) and English language learners (ELL). The exclusion rates for SD and ELL in South Carolina were 3 percent and "percentage rounds to zero" in 2007, respectively. For more information on NAEP significance testing, see http://nces.ed.gov/nationsreportcard/writing/interpret-results.asp#statistical.
[2] "Jurisdiction" refers to states, the District of Columbia, and the Department of Defense Education Activity schools.
NOTE: Detail may not sum to totals because of rounding and because the "Information not available" category for the National School Lunch Program, which provides free and reduced-price lunches, and the "Unclassified" category for race/ethnicity are not displayed. Visit http://nces.ed.gov/nationsreportcard/states/ for additional results and detailed information.
SOURCE: U.S. Department of Education, Institute of Education Sciences, National Center for Education Statistics, National Assessment of Educational Progress (NAEP), 1998, 2002, and 2007 Writing Assessments.

South Carolina Federal Report Card

ESEA/Federal Accountability System

Overall Weighted Points Total	**B**
Overall Grade Conversion	**85.4**
Points Total - Elementary Grades	87.9
Points Total - Middle Grades	82.3
Points Total - High School Grades	87.3

South Carolina uses Annual Measurable Objectives (AMOs) that are based on actual school performance as measured by student test scores on the state standards assessments and end-of-course exams.

Index Score	Grade	Description
90-100	A	Performance substantially exceeds the state's expectations.
80-89.9	B	Performance exceeds the state's expectations.
70-79.9	C	Performance meets the state's expectations.
60-69.9	D	Performance does not meet the state's expectations.
Less than 60	F	Performance is substantially below the state's expectations.

Elementary School Matrix

Title	ELA Proficiency Met/Improved	Math Proficiency Met/Improved	Science Proficiency Met/Improved	Social Studies* Proficiency Met/Improved	ELA Percent Tested	Math Percent Tested
All Students	1	1	0.8	1	1	1
Male	0.9	1	0.8	1	1	1
Female	1	1	0.8	1	1	1
White	1	1	1	1	1	1
African-American	0.8	0.7	0.6	0.8	1	1
Asian/Pacific Islander	1	1	1	1	1	1
Hispanic	0.9	0.9	0.7	0.9	1	1
American Indian/Alaskan	1	1	0.8	1	1	1
Disabled	0.1	0.5	0	0.6	1	1
LEP	0.9	0.9	0.7	0.9	1	1
Subsidized Meals	0.8	0.8	0.6	0.8	1	1
Migrant**	0.6	0.7	0	0.8	1	1
Total Number of Points	9.4	9.8	7.8	10	11	11
Total Number of Objectives Met	11	11	11	11	11	11
Percent of Objectives Met	85.45	89.09	70.91	90.91	100	100
Weight	0.4	0.4	0.05	0.05	0.05	0.05
Weighted Points Subtotal	34.18	35.64	3.55	4.55	5	5
Points Total	87.9					

0 = Did Not Meet State Objective	0.1 - 0.5 = Level of Improvement Between Previous Year and Current Year	0.6-0.9 = Level of Proximity to the AMO (quartile between percent and AMO)	1 = Met State Objective

Middle School Matrix

Title	ELA Proficiency Met/Improved	Math Proficiency Met/Improved	Science Proficiency Met/Improved	Social Studies* Proficiency Met/Improved	ELA Percent Tested	Math Percent Tested
All Students	0.9	1	1	1	1	1
Male	0.8	0.9	1	1	1	1
Female	1	1	1	1	1	1
White	1	1	1	1	1	1
African-American	0.6	0.7	0.7	0.7	1	1
Asian/Pacific Islander	1	1	1	1	1	1
Hispanic	0.8	0.9	0.9	0.9	1	1
American Indian/Alaskan	0.9	0.9	1	1	1	1
Disabled	0	0.1	0.3	0.2	1	1
LEP	0.7	0.9	0.8	0.9	1	1
Subsidized Meals	0.7	0.7	0.8	0.8	1	1
Migrant**	0	0.6	0.6	0.6	1	1
Total Number of Points	8.4	9.1	9.5	9.5	11	11
Total Number of Objectives Met	11	11	11	11	11	11
Percent of Objectives Met	76.36	82.73	86.36	86.36	100	100
Weight	0.4	0.4	0.05	0.05	0.05	0.05
Weighted Points Subtotal	30.54	33.09	4.32	4.32	5	5
Points Total	82.3					

0 = Did Not Meet State Objective	0.1 - 0.5 = Level of Improvement Between Previous Year and Current Year	0.6-0.9 = Level of Proximity to the AMO (quartile between percent and AMO)	1 = Met State Objective

* Social Studies used as "Other Academic Indicator" for elementary and middle schools.

**Due to low N-Size the Migrant subgroup was not included in ESEA calculations.

High School Matrix

Title	ELA Proficiency Met/Improved	Math Proficiency Met/Improved	Science Proficiency Met/Improved	History Proficiency Met/Improved	Graduation Rate	ELA Percent Tested	Math Percent Tested
All Students	1	0.9	1	1	1	1	1
Male	0.9	0.9	1	1	1	1	1
Female	1	0.9	1	0.9	1	1	1
White	1	1	1	1	1	1	1
African-American	0.8	0.7	0.8	0.2	1	1	1
Asian/Pacific Islander	1	1	1	1	1	1	1
Hispanic	0.9	0.8	1	0.8	1	1	1
American Indian/Alaskan	1	0.9	1	1	0.9	1	1
Disabled	0.6	0	0.1	0.1	0.1	1	1
LEP	0.8	0.8	0.9	0.7	0.9	1	1
Subsidized Meals	0.8	0.7	0.9	0.6	0.8	1	1
Migrant	N/A	N/A	N/A	N/A	0	N/A	N/A
Total Number of Points	9.8	8.6	9.7	8.3	9.7	11	11
Total Number of Objectives Met	11	11	11	11	11	11	11
Percent of Objectives Met	89.09	78.18	88.18	75.45	88.18	100	100
Weight	0.225	0.225	0.05	0.05	0.3	0.075	0.075
Weighted Points Subtotal	20.05	17.59	4.41	3.77	26.45	7.5	7.5
Points Total	87.3						

0 = Did Not Meet State Objective	0.1 - 0.5 = Level of Improvement Between Previous Year and Current Year	0.6-0.9 = Level of Proximity to the AMO (quartile between percent and AMO)	1 = Met State Objective

Performance By Group

Subgroups	ELA Mean	Math Mean	Science Mean	Soc Studies*/ History Mean	ELA % Tested	Math % Tested	Science % Tested	Graduation Rate
Grades 3 - 5								
All Students	643.8	644.3	626.4	645.0	99.7	99.8	99.8	N/A
Male	638.9	643.9	627.0	646.5	99.7	99.8	99.8	N/A
Female	649.0	644.6	625.8	643.4	99.8	99.9	99.8	N/A
White	659.5	662.7	644.4	659.5	99.8	99.9	99.8	N/A
African American	622.3	617.3	601.2	624.1	99.7	99.8	99.7	N/A
Asian/Pacific Islander	669.9	686.6	655.9	673.4	99.9	100.0	99.8	N/A
Hispanic	631.7	634.6	614.5	636.5	99.7	99.9	99.9	N/A
American Indian/Alaskan	642.1	640.4	627.1	641.8	99.7	99.9	99.5	N/A
Disabled	599.3	596.5	587.6	609.2	98.9	99.5	99.5	N/A
Limited English Proficient	631.2	638.6	615.0	638.1	99.7	99.9	99.9	N/A
Subsidized Meals	627.7	625.2	609.4	628.7	99.7	99.8	99.7	N/A
Migrant	608.2	615.1	590.4	623.4	100.0	100.0	100.0	N/A
Annual Measurable Objective (AMO)	640.0	640.0	640.0	640.0	95.0	95.0	95.0	N/A
Grades 6 - 8								
All Students	627.8	632.2	634.7	637.4	99.7	99.7	99.7	N/A
Male	620.6	630.1	634.4	639.8	99.7	99.7	99.6	N/A
Female	635.4	634.3	635.0	634.9	99.8	99.8	99.7	N/A
White	644.3	647.7	652.3	652.3	99.8	99.8	99.7	N/A
African American	604.3	608.5	608.9	615.2	99.7	99.7	99.6	N/A
Asian/Pacific Islander	658.5	680.2	673.0	677.3	99.9	99.9	99.9	N/A
Hispanic	617.3	625.4	625.0	630.5	99.7	99.7	99.7	N/A
American Indian/Alaskan	629.4	631.2	637.2	638.3	99.9	99.8	99.7	N/A
Disabled	574.5	584.3	584.9	592.8	99.4	99.4	99.2	N/A
Limited English Proficient	612.5	625.8	622.5	629.8	99.6	99.7	99.8	N/A
Subsidized Meals	610.0	614.6	616.3	619.9	99.7	99.7	99.6	N/A
Migrant	586.4	606.8	600.8	607.7	98.2	98.2	100.0	N/A
Annual Measurable Objective (AMO)	632.0	632.0	632.0	632.0	95.0	95.0	95.0	N/A
Grades 9 - 12								
All Students	229.3	222.6	81.8	74.9	98.7	98.7	100.0	80.0
Male	225.6	222.4	81.8	75.9	98.3	98.3	100.0	75.7
Female	233.2	222.9	81.9	74.0	99.2	99.1	100.0	84.5
White	235.9	230.8	86.1	78.1	99.0	98.9	100.0	82.8
African American	219.6	209.6	75.2	69.9	98.3	98.3	100.0	76.0
Asian/Pacific Islander	240.2	245.8	89.4	80.3	99.3	99.3	100.0	88.0
Hispanic	225.1	219.4	79.5	73.5	98.9	99.0	100.0	76.9
American Indian/Alaskan	228.8	220.3	81.9	77.2	98.9	99.3	100.0	74.3
Disabled	204.3	196.5	68.4	66.2	96.6	96.5	100.0	43.2
Limited English Proficient	218.0	214.7	76.6	71.3	99.3	99.3	100.0	73.4
Subsidized Meals	221.1	212.6	76.8	70.8	98.3	98.2	100.0	72.5
Migrant	N/A	N/A	N/A	N/A	N/A	N/A	100.0	61.5
Annual Measurable Objective (AMO)	229.0	226.0	78.0	75.0	95.0	95.0	95.0	75.1

* Social Studies used as "Other Academic Indicator" for elementary and middle schools.

NAEP* Average Scale Scores

*Performance reported for SC and nation, data not available at school level.

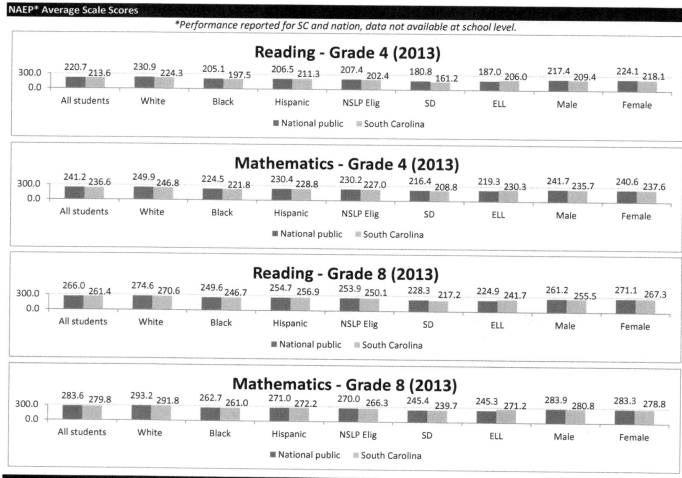

Key	
NSLP	National school lunch program
SD	Student with disabilities
ELL	English language learner
NAEP	National Association of Education Progress

	SD Participation Rate	ELL Participation Rate
Reading, Grade 4	89.0%	96.0%
Reading, Grade 8	85.0%	96.0%
Mathematics, Grade 4	93.0%	99.0%
Mathematics, Grade 8	90.0%	95.0%

Teacher Quality and Student Attendance

	State
Classes in low poverty schools not taught by highly qualified teachers	3.2%
Classes in high poverty schools not taught by highly qualified teachers	7.3%

	State	State Objective	Met Objective
Classes not taught by highly qualified teachers	4.5%	0.0%	No
Student attendance rate, grades K-8	95.3%	94.0%*	Yes

	State
Professional qualifications of all elementary and secondary teachers in the State (Advanced Degrees)	61.9%
Percentage of all elementary and secondary teachers in the State with emergency or provisional credentials	0.0%

	State
Number of recently arrived ELL students exempted from ELA in state assessments	729

*Or greater than last year.

Two-Year SC PASS Performance By Grade Level Trend Data

	Grade	SC PASS ELA			SC PASS Math		
		N	Mean	%Tested	N	Mean	%Tested
2013	3	54,247	651.1	99.7	54,328	629.7	99.7
	4	53,984	639.6	99.7	54,055	646.5	99.7
	5	54,506	647.3	99.8	54,512	639.7	99.7
	6	56,184	633.3	99.8	56,180	634.6	99.6
	7	56,323	628.3	99.8	56,321	631.9	99.6
	8	54,460	629.8	99.6	54,462	629.1	99.5

	Grade	SC PASS Science			SC PASS Social Studies*/History		
		N	Mean	%Tested	N	Mean	%Tested
	3	27,325	617.8	100.0	27,238	639.4	100.0
	4	53,984	628.9	99.7	53,968	654.1	99.7
	5	27,389	627.4	100.0	27,237	637.3	99.8
	6	28,173	622.9	99.8	28,234	646.5	99.9
	7	56,220	634.1	99.6	56,220	630.3	99.6
	8	27,293	627.7	99.7	27,212	641.3	99.6

	Grade	SC PASS ELA			SC PASS Math		
		N	Mean	%Tested	N	Mean	%Tested
2014	3	54,936	649.1	99.6	55,045	636.9	99.6
	4	54,433	640.6	99.7	54,515	646.2	99.7
	5	54,526	641.8	99.9	54,519	650.1	99.7
	6	54,950	631.0	99.8	54,955	630.9	99.6
	7	56,530	626.4	99.8	56,537	635.0	99.6
	8	55,992	626.2	99.7	55,991	630.5	99.5

	Grade	SC PASS Science			SC PASS Social Studies*/History		
		N	Mean	%Tested	N	Mean	%Tested
	3	27,587	617.4	99.5	27,407	639.2	99.3
	4	54,448	627.9	99.7	54,424	652.2	99.7
	5	27,291	633.1	99.5	27,107	636.6	99.4
	6	27,446	624.6	99.4	27,486	646.5	99.2
	7	56,429	639.5	99.5	56,400	630.7	99.5
	8	27,982	635.0	99.3	27,826	642.0	99.2

* Social Studies used as "Other Academic Indicator" for elementary and middle schools.

NOTE: Results include the SC-ALT test.

Two-Year High School Trend Data

	Grade	HSAP ELA			HASP Math		
		N	Mean	%Tested	N	Mean	%Tested
2013	9	3,905	210.0	90.6	3,876	200.9	89.9
	10	46,805	230.8	99.4	46,782	226.3	99.3
	11	105	227.3	72.5	107	222.7	73.1
	12	6	I/S	I/S	7	I/S	I/S
	Grade	End-of-Coursce Science			End-of-Course Social Studies*/History		
		N	Mean	%Tested	N	Mean	%Tested
	9	20,206	81.5	100.0	528	65.8	100.0
	10	29,615	81.8	100.0	5,368	69.0	100.0
	11	1,970	74.7	100.0	38,376	73.5	100.0
	12	822	75.2	100.0	3,053	71.1	100.0

	Grade	HSAP ELA			HASP Math		
		N	Mean	%Tested	N	Mean	%Tested
2014	9	3,999	209.0	91.6	3,992	199.0	91.3
	10	47,946	231.1	99.4	47,939	224.6	99.4
	11	90	223.0	73.1	89	218.2	72.2
	12	11	N/A	61.1	11	194.9	61.1
	Grade	End-of-Coursce Science			End-of-Course Social Studies*/History		
		N	Mean	%Tested	N	Mean	%Tested
	9	20,986	82.9	100.0	542	66.3	100.0
	10	30,634	81.6	100.0	5,429	70.7	100.0
	11	1,402	75.4	100.0	38,505	75.8	100.0
	12	583	74.4	100.0	3,062	72.8	100.0

* Social Studies used as "Other Academic Indicator" for elementary and middle schools.

NOTE: ELA and Math N-counts are based on number of students. Science and History N-counts are based on number of End-of-Course Biology 1 and US History and the Constitution tests administered. Results include the SC-ALT test.

Ancestry and Ethnicity

South Carolina State Profile

Population: 4,625,364

Ancestry	Population	%
Afghan (0)	0	<0.01
African, Sub-Saharan (34,418)	39,304	0.87
African (31,294)	35,276	0.78
Cape Verdean (284)	378	0.01
Ethiopian (396)	429	0.01
Ghanaian (149)	192	<0.01
Kenyan (190)	294	0.01
Liberian (120)	274	0.01
Nigerian (684)	699	0.02
Senegalese (40)	40	<0.01
Sierra Leonean (12)	12	<0.01
Somalian (149)	149	<0.01
South African (529)	853	0.02
Sudanese (123)	145	<0.01
Ugandan (28)	28	<0.01
Zimbabwean (12)	12	<0.01
Other Sub-Saharan African (408)	523	0.01
Albanian (666)	808	0.02
Alsatian (41)	113	<0.01
American (563,469)	563,469	12.49
Arab (6,867)	10,632	0.24
Arab (840)	1,113	0.02
Egyptian (1,310)	1,759	0.04
Iraqi (53)	64	<0.01
Jordanian (600)	615	0.01
Lebanese (2,240)	4,408	0.10
Moroccan (246)	395	0.01
Palestinian (302)	320	0.01
Syrian (453)	995	0.02
Other Arab (823)	963	0.02
Armenian (449)	1,024	0.02
Assyrian/Chaldean/Syriac (29)	94	<0.01
Australian (403)	684	0.02
Austrian (1,553)	5,711	0.13
Basque (81)	110	<0.01
Belgian (829)	2,062	0.05
Brazilian (1,883)	2,413	0.05
British (10,309)	18,348	0.41
Bulgarian (545)	769	0.02
Cajun (293)	768	0.02
Canadian (3,489)	6,175	0.14
Carpatho Rusyn (0)	27	<0.01
Celtic (457)	727	0.02
Croatian (716)	2,097	0.05
Cypriot (40)	40	<0.01
Czech (2,068)	7,444	0.17
Czechoslovakian (1,030)	2,098	0.05
Danish (1,792)	6,353	0.14
Dutch (10,485)	45,122	1.00
Eastern European (1,128)	1,405	0.03
English (206,463)	423,815	9.39
Estonian (84)	104	<0.01
European (32,834)	36,969	0.82
Finnish (1,799)	4,080	0.09
French, ex. Basque (23,340)	89,148	1.98
French Canadian (7,618)	15,434	0.34
German (163,825)	464,530	10.30
German Russian (106)	134	<0.01
Greek (6,918)	13,475	0.30
Guyanese (157)	365	0.01
Hungarian (3,699)	10,608	0.24
Icelander (128)	270	0.01
Iranian (1,167)	1,406	0.03
Irish (164,713)	435,909	9.66
Israeli (423)	596	0.01
Italian (47,931)	120,326	2.67
Latvian (388)	625	0.01
Lithuanian (1,248)	3,690	0.08
Luxemburger (11)	79	<0.01
Macedonian (79)	182	<0.01
Maltese (99)	210	<0.01
New Zealander (87)	116	<0.01
Northern European (1,703)	1,865	0.04

Ancestry (cont.)	Population	%
Norwegian (6,282)	17,246	0.38
Pennsylvania German (1,180)	1,877	0.04
Polish (20,963)	58,211	1.29
Portuguese (2,431)	5,466	0.12
Romanian (1,356)	2,497	0.06
Russian (6,201)	15,467	0.34
Scandinavian (1,900)	3,863	0.09
Scotch-Irish (91,658)	151,637	3.36
Scottish (39,005)	97,162	2.15
Serbian (425)	1,084	0.02
Slavic (478)	1,340	0.03
Slovak (1,943)	4,937	0.11
Slovene (407)	855	0.02
Soviet Union (12)	26	<0.01
Swedish (6,377)	23,186	0.51
Swiss (2,577)	8,780	0.19
Turkish (1,211)	1,758	0.04
Ukrainian (4,082)	7,313	0.16
Welsh (5,976)	22,370	0.50
West Indian, ex. Hispanic (7,193)	10,670	0.24
Bahamian (391)	581	0.01
Barbadian (193)	253	0.01
Belizean (103)	152	<0.01
Bermudan (171)	215	<0.01
British West Indian (174)	242	0.01
Dutch West Indian (109)	259	0.01
Haitian (1,029)	1,548	0.03
Jamaican (3,233)	4,323	0.10
Trinidadian/Tobagonian (888)	1,111	0.02
U.S. Virgin Islander (33)	38	<0.01
West Indian (836)	1,884	0.04
Other West Indian (33)	64	<0.01
Yugoslavian (427)	1,058	0.02

Hispanic Origin	Population	%
Hispanic or Latino (of any race)	235,682	5.10
Central American, ex. Mexican	26,290	0.57
Costa Rican	1,943	0.04
Guatemalan	8,883	0.19
Honduran	8,091	0.17
Nicaraguan	1,303	0.03
Panamanian	2,104	0.05
Salvadoran	3,830	0.08
Other Central American	136	<0.01
Cuban	5,955	0.13
Dominican Republic	3,018	0.07
Mexican	138,358	2.99
Puerto Rican	26,493	0.57
South American	17,856	0.39
Argentinean	1,439	0.03
Bolivian	493	0.01
Chilean	567	0.01
Colombian	9,436	0.20
Ecuadorian	1,602	0.03
Paraguayan	111	<0.01
Peruvian	1,908	0.04
Uruguayan	853	0.02
Venezuelan	1,315	0.03
Other South American	132	<0.01
Other Hispanic or Latino	17,712	0.38

Race*	Population	%
African-American/Black (1,290,684)	1,332,188	28.80
Not Hispanic (1,279,998)	1,316,691	28.47
Hispanic (10,686)	15,497	0.34
American Indian/Alaska Native (19,524)	42,171	0.91
Not Hispanic (16,614)	36,942	0.80
Hispanic (2,910)	5,229	0.11
Alaska Athabascan (Ala. Nat.) (26)	50	<0.01
Aleut (Alaska Native) (17)	40	<0.01
Apache (144)	366	0.01
Arapaho (3)	8	<0.01
Blackfeet (134)	937	0.02
Canadian/French Am. Ind. (34)	88	<0.01
Central American Ind. (114)	166	<0.01
Cherokee (3,126)	10,675	0.23

Race* (cont.)	Population	%
Cheyenne (13)	47	<0.01
Chickasaw (108)	201	<0.01
Chippewa (204)	388	0.01
Choctaw (218)	481	0.01
Colville (1)	2	<0.01
Comanche (46)	99	<0.01
Cree (19)	50	<0.01
Creek (196)	415	0.01
Crow (12)	63	<0.01
Delaware (26)	76	<0.01
Hopi (7)	18	<0.01
Houma (18)	26	<0.01
Inupiat (Alaska Native) (30)	63	<0.01
Iroquois (280)	575	0.01
Kiowa (12)	23	<0.01
Lumbee (1,585)	2,212	0.05
Menominee (6)	15	<0.01
Mexican American Ind. (936)	1,248	0.03
Navajo (152)	297	0.01
Osage (24)	45	<0.01
Ottawa (13)	25	<0.01
Paiute (3)	10	<0.01
Pima (7)	11	<0.01
Potawatomi (57)	83	<0.01
Pueblo (49)	72	<0.01
Puget Sound Salish (15)	25	<0.01
Seminole (51)	230	<0.01
Shoshone (4)	32	<0.01
Sioux (319)	688	0.01
South American Ind. (67)	186	<0.01
Spanish American Ind. (76)	97	<0.01
Tlingit-Haida (Alaska Native) (39)	62	<0.01
Tohono O'Odham (16)	20	<0.01
Tsimshian (Alaska Native) (3)	8	<0.01
Ute (8)	18	<0.01
Yakama (2)	9	<0.01
Yaqui (19)	32	<0.01
Yuman (4)	8	<0.01
Yup'ik (Alaska Native) (7)	12	<0.01
Asian (59,051)	75,674	1.64
Not Hispanic (58,307)	73,426	1.59
Hispanic (744)	2,248	0.05
Bangladeshi (214)	234	0.01
Bhutanese (5)	5	<0.01
Burmese (405)	425	0.01
Cambodian (1,334)	1,617	0.03
Chinese, ex. Taiwanese (9,279)	11,271	0.24
Filipino (10,053)	15,228	0.33
Hmong (1,135)	1,218	0.03
Indian (15,941)	17,961	0.39
Indonesian (177)	286	0.01
Japanese (2,413)	4,745	0.10
Korean (4,876)	7,162	0.15
Laotian (1,157)	1,432	0.03
Malaysian (56)	122	<0.01
Nepalese (140)	154	<0.01
Pakistani (986)	1,127	0.02
Sri Lankan (177)	212	<0.01
Taiwanese (369)	477	0.01
Thai (1,070)	1,797	0.04
Vietnamese (6,801)	7,840	0.17
Hawaii Native/Pacific Islander (2,706)	5,880	0.13
Not Hispanic (2,113)	4,709	0.10
Hispanic (593)	1,171	0.03
Fijian (12)	40	<0.01
Guamanian/Chamorro (1,046)	1,568	0.03
Marshallese (14)	18	<0.01
Native Hawaiian (570)	1,654	0.04
Samoan (225)	555	0.01
Tongan (27)	61	<0.01
White (3,060,000)	3,127,075	67.61
Not Hispanic (2,962,740)	3,017,747	65.24
Hispanic (97,260)	109,328	2.36

Notes: † The Census 2010 population figure is used to calculate the percentages in the Hispanic Origin and Race categories. Ancestry percentages are based on the 2006-2010 American Community Survey population (not shown); ‡ Numbers in parentheses indicate the number of people reporting a single ancestry; * Numbers in parentheses indicate the number of persons reporting this race alone, not in combination with any other race; Please refer to the Explanation of Data for more information.

County Profiles

Aiken County

Population: 160,099

Ancestry	Population	%
Afghan (0)	0	<0.01
African, Sub-Saharan (780)	889	0.57
African (774)	872	0.56
Cape Verdean (0)	0	<0.01
Ethiopian (0)	0	<0.01
Ghanaian (0)	0	<0.01
Kenyan (0)	0	<0.01
Liberian (0)	0	<0.01
Nigerian (0)	0	<0.01
Senegalese (0)	0	<0.01
Sierra Leonean (0)	0	<0.01
Somalian (0)	0	<0.01
South African (0)	11	0.01
Sudanese (6)	6	<0.01
Ugandan (0)	0	<0.01
Zimbabwean (0)	0	<0.01
Other Sub-Saharan African (0)	0	<0.01
Albanian (39)	39	0.02
Alsatian (0)	0	<0.01
American (32,327)	32,327	20.63
Arab (79)	196	0.13
Arab (25)	25	0.02
Egyptian (12)	61	0.04
Iraqi (0)	0	<0.01
Jordanian (0)	0	<0.01
Lebanese (37)	83	0.05
Moroccan (0)	0	<0.01
Palestinian (0)	0	<0.01
Syrian (5)	27	0.02
Other Arab (0)	0	<0.01
Armenian (0)	80	0.05
Assyrian/Chaldean/Syriac (0)	0	<0.01
Australian (0)	8	0.01
Austrian (53)	205	0.13
Basque (0)	0	<0.01
Belgian (33)	54	0.03
Brazilian (23)	45	0.03
British (406)	621	0.40
Bulgarian (12)	12	0.01
Cajun (0)	0	<0.01
Canadian (141)	349	0.22
Carpatho Rusyn (0)	0	<0.01
Celtic (41)	50	0.03
Croatian (30)	109	0.07
Cypriot (0)	0	<0.01
Czech (54)	223	0.14
Czechoslovakian (22)	34	0.02
Danish (51)	245	0.16
Dutch (283)	1,373	0.88
Eastern European (0)	10	0.01
English (7,888)	15,738	10.05
Estonian (7)	7	<0.01
European (1,120)	1,278	0.82
Finnish (66)	66	0.04
French, ex. Basque (810)	3,096	1.98
French Canadian (180)	488	0.31
German (5,820)	15,552	9.93
German Russian (17)	30	0.02
Greek (154)	369	0.24
Guyanese (0)	9	0.01
Hungarian (120)	285	0.18
Icelander (0)	0	<0.01
Iranian (14)	14	0.01
Irish (4,591)	13,543	8.64
Israeli (0)	0	<0.01
Italian (1,829)	4,276	2.73
Latvian (0)	25	0.02
Lithuanian (45)	115	0.07
Luxemburger (0)	0	<0.01
Macedonian (0)	0	<0.01
Maltese (0)	0	<0.01
New Zealander (0)	0	<0.01
Northern European (42)	42	0.03
Norwegian (171)	460	0.29
Pennsylvania German (51)	117	0.07
Polish (775)	1,900	1.21
Portuguese (34)	93	0.06
Romanian (76)	97	0.06
Russian (155)	429	0.27
Scandinavian (65)	167	0.11
Scotch-Irish (1,716)	3,613	2.31
Scottish (1,082)	2,751	1.76
Serbian (0)	20	0.01
Slavic (25)	72	0.05
Slovak (53)	157	0.10
Slovene (10)	18	0.01
Soviet Union (0)	0	<0.01
Swedish (76)	664	0.42
Swiss (144)	292	0.19
Turkish (0)	0	<0.01
Ukrainian (165)	212	0.14
Welsh (181)	905	0.58
West Indian, ex. Hispanic (291)	346	0.22
Bahamian (0)	0	<0.01
Barbadian (26)	26	0.02
Belizean (30)	30	0.02
Bermudan (0)	0	<0.01
British West Indian (0)	0	<0.01
Dutch West Indian (0)	0	<0.01
Haitian (116)	163	0.10
Jamaican (72)	72	0.05
Trinidadian/Tobagonian (0)	0	<0.01
U.S. Virgin Islander (3)	3	<0.01
West Indian (44)	52	0.03
Other West Indian (0)	0	<0.01
Yugoslavian (12)	12	0.01

Hispanic Origin	Population	%
Hispanic or Latino (of any race)	7,824	4.89
Central American, ex. Mexican	898	0.56
Costa Rican	264	0.16
Guatemalan	196	0.12
Honduran	154	0.10
Nicaraguan	30	0.02
Panamanian	74	0.05
Salvadoran	178	0.11
Other Central American	2	<0.01
Cuban	170	0.11
Dominican Republic	48	0.03
Mexican	5,139	3.21
Puerto Rican	800	0.50
South American	239	0.15
Argentinean	42	0.03
Bolivian	5	<0.01
Chilean	27	0.02
Colombian	82	0.05
Ecuadorian	30	0.02
Paraguayan	2	<0.01
Peruvian	27	0.02
Uruguayan	6	<0.01
Venezuelan	16	0.01
Other South American	2	<0.01
Other Hispanic or Latino	530	0.33

Race*	Population	%
African-American/Black (39,354)	40,846	25.51
Not Hispanic (39,043)	40,424	25.25
Hispanic (311)	422	0.26
American Indian/Alaska Native (682)	1,703	1.06
Not Hispanic (589)	1,508	0.94
Hispanic (93)	195	0.12
Alaska Athabascan (Ala. Nat.) (1)	1	<0.01
Aleut (Alaska Native) (0)	0	<0.01
Apache (9)	29	0.02
Arapaho (0)	0	<0.01
Blackfeet (4)	44	0.03
Canadian/French Am. Ind. (0)	1	<0.01
Central American Ind. (0)	2	<0.01
Cherokee (147)	545	0.34
Cheyenne (2)	2	<0.01
Chickasaw (9)	11	<0.01
Chippewa (15)	18	0.01
Choctaw (15)	30	0.02
Colville (0)	1	<0.01
Comanche (6)	8	<0.01
Cree (0)	0	<0.01
Creek (11)	33	0.02
Crow (0)	0	<0.01
Delaware (1)	3	<0.01
Hopi (0)	0	<0.01
Houma (0)	0	<0.01
Inupiat (Alaska Native) (1)	2	<0.01
Iroquois (11)	15	0.01
Kiowa (0)	0	<0.01
Lumbee (40)	61	0.04
Menominee (2)	5	<0.01
Mexican American Ind. (13)	27	0.02
Navajo (10)	21	0.01
Osage (1)	2	<0.01
Ottawa (4)	4	<0.01
Paiute (0)	0	<0.01
Pima (1)	1	<0.01
Potawatomi (0)	0	<0.01
Pueblo (2)	4	<0.01
Puget Sound Salish (0)	1	<0.01
Seminole (2)	11	0.01
Shoshone (0)	3	<0.01
Sioux (4)	24	0.01
South American Ind. (2)	3	<0.01
Spanish American Ind. (3)	4	<0.01
Tlingit-Haida (Alaska Native) (2)	2	<0.01
Tohono O'Odham (0)	0	<0.01
Tsimshian (Alaska Native) (0)	0	<0.01
Ute (0)	1	<0.01
Yakama (1)	1	<0.01
Yaqui (0)	6	<0.01
Yuman (0)	0	<0.01
Yup'ik (Alaska Native) (0)	1	<0.01
Asian (1,329)	1,858	1.16
Not Hispanic (1,318)	1,793	1.12
Hispanic (11)	65	0.04
Bangladeshi (3)	8	<0.01
Bhutanese (0)	0	<0.01
Burmese (8)	8	<0.01
Cambodian (4)	10	0.01
Chinese, ex. Taiwanese (218)	278	0.17
Filipino (252)	382	0.24
Hmong (0)	0	<0.01
Indian (363)	440	0.27
Indonesian (2)	6	<0.01
Japanese (92)	183	0.11
Korean (94)	191	0.12
Laotian (8)	15	0.01
Malaysian (2)	2	<0.01
Nepalese (12)	12	0.01
Pakistani (6)	6	<0.01
Sri Lankan (0)	0	<0.01
Taiwanese (18)	22	0.01
Thai (17)	26	0.02
Vietnamese (174)	208	0.13
Hawaii Native/Pacific Islander (61)	159	0.10
Not Hispanic (52)	129	0.08
Hispanic (9)	30	0.02
Fijian (0)	0	<0.01
Guamanian/Chamorro (13)	32	0.02
Marshallese (0)	0	<0.01
Native Hawaiian (36)	75	0.05
Samoan (1)	8	<0.01
Tongan (0)	0	<0.01
White (111,457)	114,155	71.30
Not Hispanic (108,566)	110,782	69.20
Hispanic (2,891)	3,373	2.11

Notes: † The Census 2010 population figure is used to calculate the percentages in the Hispanic Origin and Race categories. Ancestry percentages are based on the 2006-2010 American Community Survey population (not shown); ‡ Numbers in parentheses indicate the number of people reporting a single ancestry; * Numbers in parentheses indicate the number of persons reporting this race alone, not in combination with any other race; Please refer to the Explanation of Data for more information.

Anderson County

Population: 187,126

Ancestry	Population	%
Afghan (0)	0	<0.01
African, Sub-Saharan (495)	594	0.32
African (245)	318	0.17
Cape Verdean (41)	67	0.04
Ethiopian (13)	13	0.01
Ghanaian (0)	0	<0.01
Kenyan (0)	0	<0.01
Liberian (0)	0	<0.01
Nigerian (196)	196	0.11
Senegalese (0)	0	<0.01
Sierra Leonean (0)	0	<0.01
Somalian (0)	0	<0.01
South African (0)	0	<0.01
Sudanese (0)	0	<0.01
Ugandan (0)	0	<0.01
Zimbabwean (0)	0	<0.01
Other Sub-Saharan African (0)	0	<0.01
Albanian (0)	0	<0.01
Alsatian (27)	27	0.01
American (29,203)	29,203	15.90
Arab (356)	569	0.31
Arab (62)	106	0.06
Egyptian (74)	74	0.04
Iraqi (0)	0	<0.01
Jordanian (50)	50	0.03
Lebanese (58)	169	0.09
Moroccan (25)	25	0.01
Palestinian (20)	20	0.01
Syrian (14)	28	0.02
Other Arab (53)	97	0.05
Armenian (14)	14	0.01
Assyrian/Chaldean/Syriac (0)	0	<0.01
Australian (10)	44	0.02
Austrian (58)	149	0.08
Basque (0)	0	<0.01
Belgian (15)	50	0.03
Brazilian (0)	0	<0.01
British (404)	933	0.51
Bulgarian (0)	0	<0.01
Cajun (15)	15	0.01
Canadian (160)	312	0.17
Carpatho Rusyn (0)	0	<0.01
Celtic (37)	51	0.03
Croatian (11)	73	0.04
Cypriot (0)	0	<0.01
Czech (73)	240	0.13
Czechoslovakian (116)	218	0.12
Danish (110)	195	0.11
Dutch (419)	2,199	1.20
Eastern European (0)	0	<0.01
English (11,281)	19,855	10.81
Estonian (0)	0	<0.01
European (1,292)	1,430	0.78
Finnish (64)	160	0.09
French, ex. Basque (1,065)	3,675	2.00
French Canadian (269)	475	0.26
German (6,541)	18,808	10.24
German Russian (0)	0	<0.01
Greek (181)	334	0.18
Guyanese (0)	0	<0.01
Hungarian (163)	580	0.32
Icelander (0)	0	<0.01
Iranian (131)	155	0.08
Irish (11,390)	24,931	13.57
Israeli (0)	0	<0.01
Italian (1,845)	4,583	2.49
Latvian (0)	0	<0.01
Lithuanian (13)	76	0.04
Luxemburger (0)	0	<0.01
Macedonian (0)	0	<0.01
Maltese (0)	0	<0.01
New Zealander (0)	0	<0.01
Northern European (89)	89	0.05
Norwegian (234)	629	0.34
Pennsylvania German (21)	70	0.04

Ancestry	Population	%
Polish (628)	1,660	0.90
Portuguese (128)	292	0.16
Romanian (97)	180	0.10
Russian (205)	379	0.21
Scandinavian (56)	105	0.06
Scotch-Irish (4,698)	7,789	4.24
Scottish (2,063)	4,049	2.20
Serbian (0)	0	<0.01
Slavic (25)	38	0.02
Slovak (67)	189	0.10
Slovene (0)	9	<0.01
Soviet Union (0)	0	<0.01
Swedish (76)	546	0.30
Swiss (68)	301	0.16
Turkish (0)	14	0.01
Ukrainian (258)	436	0.24
Welsh (227)	892	0.49
West Indian, ex. Hispanic (311)	336	0.18
Bahamian (59)	59	0.03
Barbadian (0)	0	<0.01
Belizean (0)	0	<0.01
Bermudan (0)	0	<0.01
British West Indian (14)	14	0.01
Dutch West Indian (9)	21	0.01
Haitian (207)	207	0.11
Jamaican (22)	22	0.01
Trinidadian/Tobagonian (0)	0	<0.01
U.S. Virgin Islander (0)	0	<0.01
West Indian (0)	13	0.01
Other West Indian (0)	0	<0.01
Yugoslavian (0)	0	<0.01

Hispanic Origin	Population	%
Hispanic or Latino (of any race)	5,447	2.91
Central American, ex. Mexican	567	0.30
Costa Rican	33	0.02
Guatemalan	132	0.07
Honduran	115	0.06
Nicaraguan	47	0.03
Panamanian	35	0.02
Salvadoran	188	0.10
Other Central American	17	0.01
Cuban	201	0.11
Dominican Republic	50	0.03
Mexican	2,991	1.60
Puerto Rican	737	0.39
South American	402	0.21
Argentinean	14	0.01
Bolivian	5	<0.01
Chilean	5	<0.01
Colombian	210	0.11
Ecuadorian	16	0.01
Paraguayan	5	<0.01
Peruvian	95	0.05
Uruguayan	5	<0.01
Venezuelan	44	0.02
Other South American	3	<0.01
Other Hispanic or Latino	499	0.27

Race*	Population	%
African-American/Black (30,020)	31,652	16.91
Not Hispanic (29,810)	31,343	16.75
Hispanic (210)	309	0.17
American Indian/Alaska Native (478)	1,255	0.67
Not Hispanic (420)	1,155	0.62
Hispanic (58)	100	0.05
Alaska Athabascan (Ala. Nat.) (1)	1	<0.01
Aleut (Alaska Native) (1)	3	<0.01
Apache (2)	8	<0.01
Arapaho (0)	1	<0.01
Blackfeet (1)	17	0.01
Canadian/French Am. Ind. (2)	6	<0.01
Central American Ind. (1)	1	<0.01
Cherokee (121)	455	0.24
Cheyenne (0)	0	<0.01
Chickasaw (1)	3	<0.01
Chippewa (5)	14	0.01
Choctaw (16)	31	0.02
Colville (0)	0	<0.01

	Population	%
Comanche (5)	7	<0.01
Cree (1)	1	<0.01
Creek (12)	27	0.01
Crow (2)	3	<0.01
Delaware (1)	4	<0.01
Hopi (0)	0	<0.01
Houma (0)	0	<0.01
Inupiat (Alaska Native) (0)	0	<0.01
Iroquois (13)	22	0.01
Kiowa (1)	1	<0.01
Lumbee (21)	27	0.01
Menominee (0)	0	<0.01
Mexican American Ind. (13)	15	0.01
Navajo (4)	10	0.01
Osage (1)	1	<0.01
Ottawa (0)	1	<0.01
Paiute (0)	0	<0.01
Pima (0)	1	<0.01
Potawatomi (3)	4	<0.01
Pueblo (1)	1	<0.01
Puget Sound Salish (1)	1	<0.01
Seminole (4)	8	<0.01
Shoshone (0)	0	<0.01
Sioux (2)	16	0.01
South American Ind. (1)	4	<0.01
Spanish American Ind. (1)	1	<0.01
Tlingit-Haida (Alaska Native) (0)	0	<0.01
Tohono O'Odham (0)	1	<0.01
Tsimshian (Alaska Native) (0)	1	<0.01
Ute (0)	0	<0.01
Yakama (0)	0	<0.01
Yaqui (1)	1	<0.01
Yuman (2)	2	<0.01
Yup'ik (Alaska Native) (0)	0	<0.01
Asian (1,405)	1,816	0.97
Not Hispanic (1,384)	1,770	0.95
Hispanic (21)	46	0.02
Bangladeshi (5)	5	<0.01
Bhutanese (0)	0	<0.01
Burmese (0)	0	<0.01
Cambodian (3)	3	<0.01
Chinese, ex. Taiwanese (202)	234	0.13
Filipino (165)	262	0.14
Hmong (0)	0	<0.01
Indian (532)	603	0.32
Indonesian (17)	23	0.01
Japanese (34)	89	0.05
Korean (152)	208	0.11
Laotian (5)	8	<0.01
Malaysian (3)	6	<0.01
Nepalese (1)	4	<0.01
Pakistani (46)	50	0.03
Sri Lankan (8)	8	<0.01
Taiwanese (1)	1	<0.01
Thai (27)	46	0.02
Vietnamese (132)	153	0.08
Hawaii Native/Pacific Islander (43)	121	0.06
Not Hispanic (29)	99	0.05
Hispanic (14)	22	0.01
Fijian (0)	0	<0.01
Guamanian/Chamorro (15)	19	0.01
Marshallese (0)	0	<0.01
Native Hawaiian (17)	41	0.02
Samoan (4)	17	0.01
Tongan (0)	0	<0.01
White (149,818)	152,398	81.44
Not Hispanic (147,362)	149,645	79.97
Hispanic (2,456)	2,753	1.47

Notes: † The Census 2010 population figure is used to calculate the percentages in the Hispanic Origin and Race categories. Ancestry percentages are based on the 2006-2010 American Community Survey population (not shown); ‡ Numbers in parentheses indicate the number of people reporting a single ancestry; * Numbers in parentheses indicate the number of persons reporting this race alone, not in combination with any other race; Please refer to the Explanation of Data for more information.

Beaufort County

Population: 162,233

Ancestry	Population	%
Afghan (0)	0	<0.01
African, Sub-Saharan (1,452)	1,665	1.07
African (1,193)	1,329	0.85
Cape Verdean (132)	149	0.10
Ethiopian (0)	0	<0.01
Ghanaian (0)	0	<0.01
Kenyan (11)	20	0.01
Liberian (0)	0	<0.01
Nigerian (0)	0	<0.01
Senegalese (0)	0	<0.01
Sierra Leonean (0)	0	<0.01
Somalian (0)	0	<0.01
South African (116)	159	0.10
Sudanese (0)	0	<0.01
Ugandan (0)	0	<0.01
Zimbabwean (0)	0	<0.01
Other Sub-Saharan African (0)	8	0.01
Albanian (33)	48	0.03
Alsatian (0)	25	0.02
American (7,840)	7,840	5.04
Arab (125)	276	0.18
Arab (7)	36	0.02
Egyptian (10)	10	0.01
Iraqi (12)	12	0.01
Jordanian (0)	0	<0.01
Lebanese (80)	141	0.09
Moroccan (0)	0	<0.01
Palestinian (0)	18	0.01
Syrian (11)	54	0.03
Other Arab (5)	5	<0.01
Armenian (90)	155	0.10
Assyrian/Chaldean/Syriac (0)	0	<0.01
Australian (23)	162	0.10
Austrian (148)	496	0.32
Basque (58)	58	0.04
Belgian (74)	183	0.12
Brazilian (222)	231	0.15
British (481)	757	0.49
Bulgarian (98)	98	0.06
Cajun (25)	55	0.04
Canadian (147)	540	0.35
Carpatho Rusyn (0)	0	<0.01
Celtic (12)	17	0.01
Croatian (13)	95	0.06
Cypriot (0)	0	<0.01
Czech (168)	723	0.46
Czechoslovakian (57)	94	0.06
Danish (69)	439	0.28
Dutch (597)	2,525	1.62
Eastern European (106)	106	0.07
English (8,553)	20,451	13.15
Estonian (22)	22	0.01
European (602)	660	0.42
Finnish (137)	321	0.21
French, ex. Basque (1,225)	4,996	3.21
French Canadian (677)	1,254	0.81
German (7,901)	24,071	15.47
German Russian (0)	0	<0.01
Greek (152)	638	0.41
Guyanese (40)	40	0.03
Hungarian (241)	935	0.60
Icelander (9)	9	0.01
Iranian (42)	71	0.05
Irish (7,213)	20,891	13.43
Israeli (34)	63	0.04
Italian (3,599)	8,358	5.37
Latvian (128)	140	0.09
Lithuanian (134)	329	0.21
Luxemburger (0)	0	<0.01
Macedonian (11)	45	0.03
Maltese (13)	16	0.01
New Zealander (0)	0	<0.01
Northern European (50)	50	0.03
Norwegian (736)	1,384	0.89
Pennsylvania German (41)	51	0.03

Ancestry (cont.)	Population	%
Polish (1,780)	5,388	3.46
Portuguese (135)	245	0.16
Romanian (39)	141	0.09
Russian (534)	1,267	0.81
Scandinavian (63)	131	0.08
Scotch-Irish (2,065)	4,047	2.60
Scottish (1,500)	4,804	3.09
Serbian (30)	30	0.02
Slavic (31)	116	0.07
Slovak (291)	425	0.27
Slovene (32)	32	0.02
Soviet Union (0)	0	<0.01
Swedish (520)	1,703	1.09
Swiss (169)	437	0.28
Turkish (70)	70	0.05
Ukrainian (226)	387	0.25
Welsh (328)	1,424	0.92
West Indian, ex. Hispanic (539)	657	0.42
Bahamian (46)	46	0.03
Barbadian (33)	43	0.03
Belizean (0)	10	0.01
Bermudan (16)	16	0.01
British West Indian (0)	0	<0.01
Dutch West Indian (8)	28	0.02
Haitian (42)	59	0.04
Jamaican (305)	356	0.23
Trinidadian/Tobagonian (79)	81	0.05
U.S. Virgin Islander (10)	10	0.01
West Indian (0)	8	0.01
Other West Indian (0)	0	<0.01
Yugoslavian (73)	123	0.08

Hispanic Origin	Population	%
Hispanic or Latino (of any race)	19,567	12.06
Central American, ex. Mexican	3,053	1.88
Costa Rican	310	0.19
Guatemalan	365	0.22
Honduran	1,689	1.04
Nicaraguan	243	0.15
Panamanian	123	0.08
Salvadoran	313	0.19
Other Central American	10	0.01
Cuban	318	0.20
Dominican Republic	246	0.15
Mexican	11,135	6.86
Puerto Rican	1,578	0.97
South American	1,947	1.20
Argentinean	435	0.27
Bolivian	151	0.09
Chilean	34	0.02
Colombian	464	0.29
Ecuadorian	106	0.07
Paraguayan	9	0.01
Peruvian	144	0.09
Uruguayan	417	0.26
Venezuelan	177	0.11
Other South American	10	0.01
Other Hispanic or Latino	1,290	0.80

Race*	Population	%
African-American/Black (31,290)	32,868	20.26
Not Hispanic (30,662)	31,948	19.69
Hispanic (628)	920	0.57
American Indian/Alaska Native (481)	1,225	0.76
Not Hispanic (338)	960	0.59
Hispanic (143)	265	0.16
Alaska Athabascan (Ala. Nat.) (0)	0	<0.01
Aleut (Alaska Native) (0)	7	<0.01
Apache (6)	19	0.01
Arapaho (0)	0	<0.01
Blackfeet (0)	49	0.03
Canadian/French Am. Ind. (0)	1	<0.01
Central American Ind. (6)	8	<0.01
Cherokee (50)	264	0.16
Cheyenne (0)	0	<0.01
Chickasaw (1)	5	<0.01
Chippewa (12)	17	0.01
Choctaw (9)	19	0.01
Colville (1)	1	<0.01

Race* (cont.)	Population	%
Comanche (3)	6	<0.01
Cree (0)	5	<0.01
Creek (11)	25	0.02
Crow (0)	3	<0.01
Delaware (0)	4	<0.01
Hopi (0)	2	<0.01
Houma (1)	1	<0.01
Inupiat (Alaska Native) (0)	4	<0.01
Iroquois (13)	33	0.02
Kiowa (0)	2	<0.01
Lumbee (23)	28	0.02
Menominee (2)	2	<0.01
Mexican American Ind. (40)	51	0.03
Navajo (17)	25	0.02
Osage (0)	1	<0.01
Ottawa (0)	6	<0.01
Paiute (0)	0	<0.01
Pima (0)	0	<0.01
Potawatomi (2)	2	<0.01
Pueblo (1)	1	<0.01
Puget Sound Salish (1)	1	<0.01
Seminole (0)	16	0.01
Shoshone (0)	1	<0.01
Sioux (4)	12	0.01
South American Ind. (7)	12	0.01
Spanish American Ind. (10)	10	0.01
Tlingit-Haida (Alaska Native) (0)	1	<0.01
Tohono O'Odham (0)	0	<0.01
Tsimshian (Alaska Native) (0)	0	<0.01
Ute (0)	0	<0.01
Yakama (0)	0	<0.01
Yaqui (1)	2	<0.01
Yuman (1)	2	<0.01
Yup'ik (Alaska Native) (0)	1	<0.01
Asian (1,889)	2,668	1.64
Not Hispanic (1,822)	2,487	1.53
Hispanic (67)	181	0.11
Bangladeshi (5)	5	<0.01
Bhutanese (0)	0	<0.01
Burmese (18)	23	0.01
Cambodian (7)	12	0.01
Chinese, ex. Taiwanese (349)	449	0.28
Filipino (460)	796	0.49
Hmong (3)	4	<0.01
Indian (244)	294	0.18
Indonesian (9)	10	0.01
Japanese (175)	338	0.21
Korean (146)	213	0.13
Laotian (15)	31	0.02
Malaysian (7)	11	0.01
Nepalese (2)	3	<0.01
Pakistani (17)	24	0.01
Sri Lankan (4)	4	<0.01
Taiwanese (5)	11	0.01
Thai (50)	75	0.05
Vietnamese (282)	320	0.20
Hawaii Native/Pacific Islander (119)	313	0.19
Not Hispanic (78)	230	0.14
Hispanic (41)	83	0.05
Fijian (2)	5	<0.01
Guamanian/Chamorro (56)	85	0.05
Marshallese (1)	1	<0.01
Native Hawaiian (24)	121	0.07
Samoan (12)	28	0.02
Tongan (0)	0	<0.01
White (116,606)	119,399	73.60
Not Hispanic (107,279)	109,224	67.33
Hispanic (9,327)	10,175	6.27

*Notes: † The Census 2010 population figure is used to calculate the percentages in the Hispanic Origin and Race categories. Ancestry percentages are based on the 2006-2010 American Community Survey population (not shown); ‡ Numbers in parentheses indicate the number of people reporting a single ancestry; * Numbers in parentheses indicate the number of persons reporting this race alone, not in combination with any other race; Please refer to the Explanation of Data for more information.*

Berkeley County

Population: 177,843

Ancestry	Population	%
Afghan (0)	0	<0.01
African, Sub-Saharan (510)	575	0.34
African (452)	511	0.30
Cape Verdean (0)	0	<0.01
Ethiopian (0)	0	<0.01
Ghanaian (0)	0	<0.01
Kenyan (0)	0	<0.01
Liberian (0)	0	<0.01
Nigerian (49)	49	0.03
Senegalese (0)	0	<0.01
Sierra Leonean (0)	0	<0.01
Somalian (0)	0	<0.01
South African (9)	9	0.01
Sudanese (0)	0	<0.01
Ugandan (0)	0	<0.01
Zimbabwean (0)	0	<0.01
Other Sub-Saharan African (0)	6	<0.01
Albanian (0)	0	<0.01
Alsatian (0)	0	<0.01
American (17,595)	17,595	10.36
Arab (380)	433	0.25
Arab (0)	16	0.01
Egyptian (274)	274	0.16
Iraqi (0)	0	<0.01
Jordanian (0)	0	<0.01
Lebanese (12)	34	0.02
Moroccan (0)	15	0.01
Palestinian (0)	0	<0.01
Syrian (29)	29	0.02
Other Arab (65)	65	0.04
Armenian (0)	5	<0.01
Assyrian/Chaldean/Syriac (0)	0	<0.01
Australian (0)	0	<0.01
Austrian (59)	131	0.08
Basque (0)	0	<0.01
Belgian (36)	124	0.07
Brazilian (498)	594	0.35
British (221)	583	0.34
Bulgarian (0)	9	0.01
Cajun (49)	79	0.05
Canadian (96)	254	0.15
Carpatho Rusyn (0)	0	<0.01
Celtic (9)	9	0.01
Croatian (0)	19	0.01
Cypriot (0)	0	<0.01
Czech (160)	388	0.23
Czechoslovakian (9)	32	0.02
Danish (147)	194	0.11
Dutch (409)	1,815	1.07
Eastern European (2)	2	<0.01
English (6,121)	13,082	7.70
Estonian (0)	0	<0.01
European (1,516)	1,584	0.93
Finnish (56)	68	0.04
French, ex. Basque (987)	4,693	2.76
French Canadian (503)	924	0.54
German (7,368)	21,239	12.50
German Russian (0)	0	<0.01
Greek (185)	390	0.23
Guyanese (0)	0	<0.01
Hungarian (63)	336	0.20
Icelander (0)	13	0.01
Iranian (0)	0	<0.01
Irish (5,638)	16,387	9.65
Israeli (6)	6	<0.01
Italian (1,856)	5,420	3.19
Latvian (0)	0	<0.01
Lithuanian (65)	112	0.07
Luxemburger (0)	8	<0.01
Macedonian (0)	0	<0.01
Maltese (0)	0	<0.01
New Zealander (0)	0	<0.01
Northern European (33)	45	0.03
Norwegian (327)	856	0.50
Pennsylvania German (0)	0	<0.01

Ancestry	Population	%
Polish (1,171)	2,850	1.68
Portuguese (197)	348	0.20
Romanian (20)	54	0.03
Russian (128)	563	0.33
Scandinavian (70)	152	0.09
Scotch-Irish (2,200)	4,346	2.56
Scottish (1,244)	3,873	2.28
Serbian (13)	51	0.03
Slavic (31)	105	0.06
Slovak (86)	208	0.12
Slovene (13)	13	0.01
Soviet Union (0)	0	<0.01
Swedish (297)	812	0.48
Swiss (51)	267	0.16
Turkish (0)	0	<0.01
Ukrainian (141)	199	0.12
Welsh (283)	1,281	0.75
West Indian, ex. Hispanic (278)	449	0.26
Bahamian (0)	0	<0.01
Barbadian (0)	0	<0.01
Belizean (0)	10	0.01
Bermudan (0)	0	<0.01
British West Indian (0)	0	<0.01
Dutch West Indian (0)	0	<0.01
Haitian (0)	43	0.03
Jamaican (263)	315	0.19
Trinidadian/Tobagonian (1)	1	<0.01
U.S. Virgin Islander (0)	0	<0.01
West Indian (14)	80	0.05
Other West Indian (0)	0	<0.01
Yugoslavian (9)	16	0.01

Hispanic Origin	Population	%
Hispanic or Latino (of any race)	10,755	6.05
Central American, ex. Mexican	1,445	0.81
Costa Rican	57	0.03
Guatemalan	380	0.21
Honduran	499	0.28
Nicaraguan	58	0.03
Panamanian	127	0.07
Salvadoran	313	0.18
Other Central American	11	0.01
Cuban	260	0.15
Dominican Republic	200	0.11
Mexican	5,564	3.13
Puerto Rican	1,658	0.93
South American	639	0.36
Argentinean	76	0.04
Bolivian	13	0.01
Chilean	25	0.01
Colombian	253	0.14
Ecuadorian	102	0.06
Paraguayan	2	<0.01
Peruvian	98	0.06
Uruguayan	19	0.01
Venezuelan	40	0.02
Other South American	11	0.01
Other Hispanic or Latino	989	0.56

Race*	Population	%
African-American/Black (44,514)	46,562	26.18
Not Hispanic (44,023)	45,821	25.76
Hispanic (491)	741	0.42
American Indian/Alaska Native (1,067)	2,338	1.31
Not Hispanic (910)	2,072	1.17
Hispanic (157)	266	0.15
Alaska Athabascan (Ala. Nat.) (0)	1	<0.01
Aleut (Alaska Native) (4)	8	<0.01
Apache (7)	20	0.01
Arapaho (0)	0	<0.01
Blackfeet (12)	58	0.03
Canadian/French Am. Ind. (4)	5	<0.01
Central American Ind. (9)	13	0.01
Cherokee (206)	588	0.33
Cheyenne (0)	1	<0.01
Chickasaw (7)	15	0.01
Chippewa (15)	33	0.02
Choctaw (13)	29	0.02
Colville (0)	0	<0.01

Race* (cont.)	Population	%
Comanche (8)	13	0.01
Cree (1)	5	<0.01
Creek (17)	37	0.02
Crow (2)	3	<0.01
Delaware (3)	6	<0.01
Hopi (0)	0	<0.01
Houma (4)	5	<0.01
Inupiat (Alaska Native) (1)	2	<0.01
Iroquois (15)	32	0.02
Kiowa (2)	2	<0.01
Lumbee (53)	73	0.04
Menominee (0)	0	<0.01
Mexican American Ind. (41)	47	0.03
Navajo (5)	14	0.01
Osage (1)	10	0.01
Ottawa (0)	0	<0.01
Paiute (1)	1	<0.01
Pima (0)	0	<0.01
Potawatomi (3)	4	<0.01
Pueblo (7)	11	0.01
Puget Sound Salish (1)	3	<0.01
Seminole (4)	17	0.01
Shoshone (0)	0	<0.01
Sioux (18)	39	0.02
South American Ind. (4)	7	<0.01
Spanish American Ind. (8)	8	<0.01
Tlingit-Haida (Alaska Native) (0)	1	<0.01
Tohono O'Odham (0)	0	<0.01
Tsimshian (Alaska Native) (0)	0	<0.01
Ute (1)	1	<0.01
Yakama (0)	1	<0.01
Yaqui (0)	0	<0.01
Yuman (0)	0	<0.01
Yup'ik (Alaska Native) (1)	1	<0.01
Asian (4,046)	5,497	3.09
Not Hispanic (3,981)	5,328	3.00
Hispanic (65)	169	0.10
Bangladeshi (4)	4	<0.01
Bhutanese (0)	0	<0.01
Burmese (0)	0	<0.01
Cambodian (27)	31	0.02
Chinese, ex. Taiwanese (376)	519	0.29
Filipino (2,489)	3,395	1.91
Hmong (5)	7	<0.01
Indian (317)	398	0.22
Indonesian (1)	4	<0.01
Japanese (136)	309	0.17
Korean (124)	227	0.13
Laotian (14)	23	0.01
Malaysian (0)	13	0.01
Nepalese (5)	5	<0.01
Pakistani (26)	29	0.02
Sri Lankan (11)	12	0.01
Taiwanese (9)	18	0.01
Thai (42)	83	0.05
Vietnamese (332)	402	0.23
Hawaii Native/Pacific Islander (184)	415	0.23
Not Hispanic (146)	355	0.20
Hispanic (38)	60	0.03
Fijian (0)	1	<0.01
Guamanian/Chamorro (65)	114	0.06
Marshallese (0)	0	<0.01
Native Hawaiian (52)	133	0.07
Samoan (12)	35	0.02
Tongan (0)	0	<0.01
White (118,232)	122,387	68.82
Not Hispanic (113,553)	117,019	65.80
Hispanic (4,679)	5,368	3.02

Notes: † The Census 2010 population figure is used to calculate the percentages in the Hispanic Origin and Race categories. Ancestry percentages are based on the 2006-2010 American Community Survey population (not shown); ‡ Numbers in parentheses indicate the number of people reporting a single ancestry; * Numbers in parentheses indicate the number of persons reporting this race alone, not in combination with any other race; Please refer to the Explanation of Data for more information.

Charleston County

Population: 350,209

Ancestry	Population	%
Afghan (0)	0	<0.01
African, Sub-Saharan (1,641)	2,183	0.64
African (1,396)	1,806	0.53
Cape Verdean (7)	7	<0.01
Ethiopian (32)	32	0.01
Ghanaian (0)	0	<0.01
Kenyan (0)	0	<0.01
Liberian (0)	0	<0.01
Nigerian (94)	94	0.03
Senegalese (0)	0	<0.01
Sierra Leonean (0)	0	<0.01
Somalian (0)	0	<0.01
South African (60)	181	0.05
Sudanese (9)	9	<0.01
Ugandan (0)	0	<0.01
Zimbabwean (12)	12	<0.01
Other Sub-Saharan African (31)	42	0.01
Albanian (14)	74	0.02
Alsatian (0)	22	0.01
American (33,568)	33,568	9.80
Arab (837)	1,441	0.42
Arab (63)	86	0.03
Egyptian (163)	175	0.05
Iraqi (10)	21	0.01
Jordanian (129)	140	0.04
Lebanese (367)	718	0.21
Moroccan (25)	62	0.02
Palestinian (0)	0	<0.01
Syrian (67)	191	0.06
Other Arab (13)	48	0.01
Armenian (76)	143	0.04
Assyrian/Chaldean/Syriac (0)	0	<0.01
Australian (7)	15	<0.01
Austrian (169)	664	0.19
Basque (0)	0	<0.01
Belgian (92)	160	0.05
Brazilian (83)	200	0.06
British (953)	1,683	0.49
Bulgarian (69)	69	0.02
Cajun (0)	17	<0.01
Canadian (272)	447	0.13
Carpatho Rusyn (0)	0	<0.01
Celtic (17)	34	0.01
Croatian (15)	129	0.04
Cypriot (0)	0	<0.01
Czech (214)	962	0.28
Czechoslovakian (45)	239	0.07
Danish (186)	544	0.16
Dutch (960)	3,382	0.99
Eastern European (172)	192	0.06
English (15,296)	37,501	10.95
Estonian (26)	46	0.01
European (3,545)	3,944	1.15
Finnish (89)	244	0.07
French, ex. Basque (2,164)	9,181	2.68
French Canadian (550)	1,052	0.31
German (12,137)	38,787	11.33
German Russian (0)	0	<0.01
Greek (836)	1,876	0.55
Guyanese (22)	22	0.01
Hungarian (265)	976	0.29
Icelander (0)	0	<0.01
Iranian (131)	143	0.04
Irish (13,019)	34,851	10.18
Israeli (26)	34	0.01
Italian (4,761)	12,492	3.65
Latvian (42)	96	0.03
Lithuanian (233)	512	0.15
Luxemburger (11)	11	<0.01
Macedonian (12)	26	0.01
Maltese (0)	0	<0.01
New Zealander (18)	33	0.01
Northern European (341)	359	0.10
Norwegian (441)	1,644	0.48
Pennsylvania German (13)	78	0.02

Ancestry (cont.)	Population	%
Polish (2,012)	5,800	1.69
Portuguese (312)	642	0.19
Romanian (152)	335	0.10
Russian (994)	2,276	0.66
Scandinavian (209)	588	0.17
Scotch-Irish (6,132)	11,151	3.26
Scottish (3,997)	10,628	3.10
Serbian (0)	84	0.02
Slavic (13)	75	0.02
Slovak (123)	349	0.10
Slovene (44)	81	0.02
Soviet Union (0)	14	<0.01
Swedish (626)	2,596	0.76
Swiss (218)	799	0.23
Turkish (177)	213	0.06
Ukrainian (374)	929	0.27
Welsh (691)	2,167	0.63
West Indian, ex. Hispanic (545)	671	0.20
Bahamian (15)	15	<0.01
Barbadian (13)	13	<0.01
Belizean (0)	0	<0.01
Bermudan (0)	0	<0.01
British West Indian (5)	5	<0.01
Dutch West Indian (46)	46	0.01
Haitian (27)	27	0.01
Jamaican (220)	237	0.07
Trinidadian/Tobagonian (29)	39	0.01
U.S. Virgin Islander (0)	0	<0.01
West Indian (190)	289	0.08
Other West Indian (0)	0	<0.01
Yugoslavian (14)	76	0.02

Hispanic Origin	Population	%
Hispanic or Latino (of any race)	18,877	5.39
Central American, ex. Mexican	1,677	0.48
Costa Rican	75	0.02
Guatemalan	796	0.23
Honduran	370	0.11
Nicaraguan	94	0.03
Panamanian	146	0.04
Salvadoran	191	0.05
Other Central American	5	<0.01
Cuban	490	0.14
Dominican Republic	198	0.06
Mexican	12,106	3.46
Puerto Rican	1,637	0.47
South American	1,207	0.34
Argentinean	184	0.05
Bolivian	111	0.03
Chilean	85	0.02
Colombian	342	0.10
Ecuadorian	179	0.05
Paraguayan	12	<0.01
Peruvian	163	0.05
Uruguayan	31	0.01
Venezuelan	93	0.03
Other South American	7	<0.01
Other Hispanic or Latino	1,562	0.45

Race*	Population	%
African-American/Black (104,239)	106,887	30.52
Not Hispanic (103,479)	105,753	30.20
Hispanic (760)	1,134	0.32
American Indian/Alaska Native (1,068)	2,607	0.74
Not Hispanic (838)	2,177	0.62
Hispanic (230)	430	0.12
Alaska Athabascan (Ala. Nat.) (0)	2	<0.01
Aleut (Alaska Native) (1)	1	<0.01
Apache (6)	14	<0.01
Arapaho (0)	0	<0.01
Blackfeet (4)	68	0.02
Canadian/French Am. Ind. (1)	9	<0.01
Central American Ind. (7)	13	<0.01
Cherokee (177)	680	0.19
Cheyenne (0)	1	<0.01
Chickasaw (2)	8	<0.01
Chippewa (20)	33	0.01
Choctaw (8)	26	0.01
Colville (0)	0	<0.01

Race* (cont.)	Population	%
Comanche (4)	11	<0.01
Cree (2)	5	<0.01
Creek (10)	33	0.01
Crow (0)	7	<0.01
Delaware (2)	3	<0.01
Hopi (0)	1	<0.01
Houma (1)	4	<0.01
Inupiat (Alaska Native) (2)	9	<0.01
Iroquois (12)	39	0.01
Kiowa (5)	5	<0.01
Lumbee (56)	73	0.02
Menominee (0)	0	<0.01
Mexican American Ind. (93)	110	0.03
Navajo (4)	16	<0.01
Osage (3)	6	<0.01
Ottawa (0)	0	<0.01
Paiute (0)	1	<0.01
Pima (0)	0	<0.01
Potawatomi (3)	10	<0.01
Pueblo (1)	1	<0.01
Puget Sound Salish (2)	3	<0.01
Seminole (0)	12	<0.01
Shoshone (0)	6	<0.01
Sioux (34)	67	0.02
South American Ind. (4)	8	<0.01
Spanish American Ind. (3)	3	<0.01
Tlingit-Haida (Alaska Native) (2)	2	<0.01
Tohono O'Odham (0)	0	<0.01
Tsimshian (Alaska Native) (3)	3	<0.01
Ute (1)	2	<0.01
Yakama (0)	0	<0.01
Yaqui (1)	2	<0.01
Yuman (0)	1	<0.01
Yup'ik (Alaska Native) (0)	0	<0.01
Asian (4,719)	6,178	1.76
Not Hispanic (4,660)	5,997	1.71
Hispanic (59)	181	0.05
Bangladeshi (10)	11	<0.01
Bhutanese (1)	1	<0.01
Burmese (35)	35	0.01
Cambodian (32)	35	0.01
Chinese, ex. Taiwanese (968)	1,152	0.33
Filipino (1,110)	1,634	0.47
Hmong (4)	4	<0.01
Indian (1,061)	1,228	0.35
Indonesian (15)	27	0.01
Japanese (209)	402	0.11
Korean (351)	538	0.15
Laotian (13)	14	<0.01
Malaysian (3)	17	<0.01
Nepalese (11)	12	<0.01
Pakistani (58)	62	0.02
Sri Lankan (21)	31	0.01
Taiwanese (52)	64	0.02
Thai (67)	116	0.03
Vietnamese (499)	585	0.17
Hawaii Native/Pacific Islander (299)	543	0.16
Not Hispanic (246)	449	0.13
Hispanic (53)	94	0.03
Fijian (1)	2	<0.01
Guamanian/Chamorro (105)	146	0.04
Marshallese (0)	1	<0.01
Native Hawaiian (43)	119	0.03
Samoan (19)	43	0.01
Tongan (2)	3	<0.01
White (224,910)	229,462	65.52
Not Hispanic (217,260)	220,975	63.10
Hispanic (7,650)	8,487	2.42

*Notes: † The Census 2010 population figure is used to calculate the percentages in the Hispanic Origin and Race categories. Ancestry percentages are based on the 2006-2010 American Community Survey population (not shown); ‡ Numbers in parentheses indicate the number of people reporting a single ancestry; * Numbers in parentheses indicate the number of persons reporting this race alone, not in combination with any other race; Please refer to the Explanation of Data for more information.*

Cherokee County

Population: 55,342

Ancestry	Population	%
Afghan (0)	0	<0.01
African, Sub-Saharan (116)	208	0.38
African (112)	204	0.37
Cape Verdean (0)	0	<0.01
Ethiopian (0)	0	<0.01
Ghanaian (0)	0	<0.01
Kenyan (0)	0	<0.01
Liberian (0)	0	<0.01
Nigerian (0)	0	<0.01
Senegalese (0)	0	<0.01
Sierra Leonean (4)	4	0.01
Somalian (0)	0	<0.01
South African (0)	0	<0.01
Sudanese (0)	0	<0.01
Ugandan (0)	0	<0.01
Zimbabwean (0)	0	<0.01
Other Sub-Saharan African (0)	0	<0.01
Albanian (0)	0	<0.01
Alsatian (0)	0	<0.01
American (8,035)	8,035	14.65
Arab (76)	76	0.14
Arab (0)	0	<0.01
Egyptian (0)	0	<0.01
Iraqi (0)	0	<0.01
Jordanian (26)	26	0.05
Lebanese (27)	27	0.05
Moroccan (0)	0	<0.01
Palestinian (0)	0	<0.01
Syrian (23)	23	0.04
Other Arab (0)	0	<0.01
Armenian (0)	0	<0.01
Assyrian/Chaldean/Syriac (0)	0	<0.01
Australian (0)	0	<0.01
Austrian (7)	7	0.01
Basque (13)	13	0.02
Belgian (0)	0	<0.01
Brazilian (0)	0	<0.01
British (35)	112	0.20
Bulgarian (5)	5	0.01
Cajun (10)	10	0.02
Canadian (0)	0	<0.01
Carpatho Rusyn (0)	0	<0.01
Celtic (0)	0	<0.01
Croatian (0)	0	<0.01
Cypriot (0)	0	<0.01
Czech (6)	17	0.03
Czechoslovakian (0)	0	<0.01
Danish (0)	10	0.02
Dutch (71)	540	0.98
Eastern European (0)	0	<0.01
English (2,041)	3,607	6.58
Estonian (0)	0	<0.01
European (95)	171	0.31
Finnish (0)	0	<0.01
French, ex. Basque (276)	877	1.60
French Canadian (0)	8	0.01
German (1,336)	3,543	6.46
German Russian (0)	0	<0.01
Greek (88)	102	0.19
Guyanese (0)	0	<0.01
Hungarian (20)	28	0.05
Icelander (0)	0	<0.01
Iranian (0)	0	<0.01
Irish (2,233)	5,305	9.68
Israeli (0)	0	<0.01
Italian (260)	529	0.96
Latvian (0)	0	<0.01
Lithuanian (0)	0	<0.01
Luxemburger (0)	0	<0.01
Macedonian (0)	0	<0.01
Maltese (0)	0	<0.01
New Zealander (0)	0	<0.01
Northern European (0)	0	<0.01
Norwegian (27)	77	0.14
Pennsylvania German (6)	6	0.01

Ancestry (cont.)	Population	%
Polish (67)	167	0.30
Portuguese (78)	78	0.14
Romanian (17)	17	0.03
Russian (57)	57	0.10
Scandinavian (0)	0	<0.01
Scotch-Irish (1,019)	1,600	2.92
Scottish (454)	733	1.34
Serbian (19)	27	0.05
Slavic (0)	0	<0.01
Slovak (0)	0	<0.01
Slovene (0)	0	<0.01
Soviet Union (0)	0	<0.01
Swedish (50)	117	0.21
Swiss (7)	7	0.01
Turkish (0)	15	0.03
Ukrainian (0)	0	<0.01
Welsh (51)	237	0.43
West Indian, ex. Hispanic (24)	36	0.07
Bahamian (0)	0	<0.01
Barbadian (0)	0	<0.01
Belizean (0)	0	<0.01
Bermudan (0)	0	<0.01
British West Indian (0)	0	<0.01
Dutch West Indian (0)	0	<0.01
Haitian (0)	0	<0.01
Jamaican (0)	0	<0.01
Trinidadian/Tobagonian (0)	0	<0.01
U.S. Virgin Islander (0)	0	<0.01
West Indian (24)	36	0.07
Other West Indian (0)	0	<0.01
Yugoslavian (0)	8	0.01

Hispanic Origin	Population	%
Hispanic or Latino (of any race)	2,032	3.67
Central American, ex. Mexican	155	0.28
Costa Rican	5	0.01
Guatemalan	98	0.18
Honduran	27	0.05
Nicaraguan	6	0.01
Panamanian	8	0.01
Salvadoran	8	0.01
Other Central American	3	0.01
Cuban	14	0.03
Dominican Republic	22	0.04
Mexican	1,480	2.67
Puerto Rican	160	0.29
South American	29	0.05
Argentinean	1	<0.01
Bolivian	0	<0.01
Chilean	0	<0.01
Colombian	12	0.02
Ecuadorian	2	<0.01
Paraguayan	1	<0.01
Peruvian	7	0.01
Uruguayan	0	<0.01
Venezuelan	5	0.01
Other South American	1	<0.01
Other Hispanic or Latino	172	0.31

Race*	Population	%
African-American/Black (11,278)	11,708	21.16
Not Hispanic (11,214)	11,624	21.00
Hispanic (64)	84	0.15
American Indian/Alaska Native (199)	431	0.78
Not Hispanic (129)	353	0.64
Hispanic (70)	78	0.14
Alaska Athabascan (Ala. Nat.) (0)	0	<0.01
Aleut (Alaska Native) (0)	0	<0.01
Apache (1)	1	<0.01
Arapaho (0)	0	<0.01
Blackfeet (5)	7	0.01
Canadian/French Am. Ind. (0)	0	<0.01
Central American Ind. (0)	0	<0.01
Cherokee (35)	156	0.28
Cheyenne (2)	2	<0.01
Chickasaw (0)	0	<0.01
Chippewa (0)	0	<0.01
Choctaw (3)	4	0.01
Colville (0)	0	<0.01

Race* (cont.)	Population	%
Comanche (2)	2	<0.01
Cree (0)	0	<0.01
Creek (3)	6	0.01
Crow (0)	1	<0.01
Delaware (0)	0	<0.01
Hopi (0)	0	<0.01
Houma (0)	2	<0.01
Inupiat (Alaska Native) (2)	2	<0.01
Iroquois (2)	2	<0.01
Kiowa (0)	0	<0.01
Lumbee (9)	15	0.03
Menominee (0)	0	<0.01
Mexican American Ind. (5)	7	0.01
Navajo (2)	2	<0.01
Osage (0)	0	<0.01
Ottawa (0)	0	<0.01
Paiute (0)	0	<0.01
Pima (0)	0	<0.01
Potawatomi (0)	0	<0.01
Pueblo (0)	4	0.01
Puget Sound Salish (0)	0	<0.01
Seminole (0)	0	<0.01
Shoshone (0)	0	<0.01
Sioux (2)	2	<0.01
South American Ind. (0)	0	<0.01
Spanish American Ind. (0)	1	<0.01
Tlingit-Haida (Alaska Native) (0)	0	<0.01
Tohono O'Odham (0)	0	<0.01
Tsimshian (Alaska Native) (0)	0	<0.01
Ute (2)	2	<0.01
Yakama (0)	0	<0.01
Yaqui (0)	0	<0.01
Yuman (0)	0	<0.01
Yup'ik (Alaska Native) (0)	0	<0.01
Asian (313)	366	0.66
Not Hispanic (308)	359	0.65
Hispanic (5)	7	0.01
Bangladeshi (0)	0	<0.01
Bhutanese (0)	0	<0.01
Burmese (0)	0	<0.01
Cambodian (2)	4	0.01
Chinese, ex. Taiwanese (49)	51	0.09
Filipino (35)	42	0.08
Hmong (14)	18	0.03
Indian (118)	130	0.23
Indonesian (1)	3	0.01
Japanese (7)	13	0.02
Korean (11)	16	0.03
Laotian (10)	10	0.02
Malaysian (0)	0	<0.01
Nepalese (0)	0	<0.01
Pakistani (23)	24	0.04
Sri Lankan (0)	0	<0.01
Taiwanese (2)	2	<0.01
Thai (7)	10	0.02
Vietnamese (22)	25	0.05
Hawaii Native/Pacific Islander (17)	33	0.06
Not Hispanic (6)	16	0.03
Hispanic (11)	17	0.03
Fijian (0)	0	<0.01
Guamanian/Chamorro (10)	16	0.03
Marshallese (0)	0	<0.01
Native Hawaiian (2)	3	0.01
Samoan (2)	4	0.01
Tongan (0)	1	<0.01
White (41,525)	42,256	76.35
Not Hispanic (40,939)	41,567	75.11
Hispanic (586)	689	1.24

Notes: † The Census 2010 population figure is used to calculate the percentages in the Hispanic Origin and Race categories. Ancestry percentages are based on the 2006-2010 American Community Survey population (not shown); ‡ Numbers in parentheses indicate the number of people reporting a single ancestry; * Numbers in parentheses indicate the number of persons reporting this race alone, not in combination with any other race; Please refer to the Explanation of Data for more information.

Darlington County

Population: 68,681

Ancestry	Population	%
Afghan (0)	0	<0.01
African, Sub-Saharan (144)	144	0.21
African (144)	144	0.21
Cape Verdean (0)	0	<0.01
Ethiopian (0)	0	<0.01
Ghanaian (0)	0	<0.01
Kenyan (0)	0	<0.01
Liberian (0)	0	<0.01
Nigerian (0)	0	<0.01
Senegalese (0)	0	<0.01
Sierra Leonean (0)	0	<0.01
Somalian (0)	0	<0.01
South African (0)	0	<0.01
Sudanese (0)	0	<0.01
Ugandan (0)	0	<0.01
Zimbabwean (0)	0	<0.01
Other Sub-Saharan African (0)	0	<0.01
Albanian (0)	0	<0.01
Alsatian (0)	0	<0.01
American (6,532)	6,532	9.52
Arab (48)	92	0.13
Arab (0)	0	<0.01
Egyptian (0)	0	<0.01
Iraqi (0)	0	<0.01
Jordanian (0)	0	<0.01
Lebanese (25)	25	0.04
Moroccan (0)	0	<0.01
Palestinian (0)	0	<0.01
Syrian (23)	67	0.10
Other Arab (0)	0	<0.01
Armenian (8)	30	0.04
Assyrian/Chaldean/Syriac (0)	0	<0.01
Australian (0)	0	<0.01
Austrian (0)	109	0.16
Basque (0)	0	<0.01
Belgian (0)	0	<0.01
Brazilian (0)	0	<0.01
British (23)	175	0.26
Bulgarian (0)	0	<0.01
Cajun (0)	0	<0.01
Canadian (85)	92	0.13
Carpatho Rusyn (0)	0	<0.01
Celtic (15)	33	0.05
Croatian (0)	7	0.01
Cypriot (0)	0	<0.01
Czech (0)	20	0.03
Czechoslovakian (0)	0	<0.01
Danish (0)	28	0.04
Dutch (101)	362	0.53
Eastern European (3)	3	<0.01
English (3,077)	4,797	6.99
Estonian (0)	0	<0.01
European (363)	375	0.55
Finnish (0)	13	0.02
French, ex. Basque (255)	562	0.82
French Canadian (100)	124	0.18
German (1,237)	3,017	4.40
German Russian (0)	0	<0.01
Greek (40)	50	0.07
Guyanese (0)	20	0.03
Hungarian (61)	96	0.14
Icelander (0)	0	<0.01
Iranian (0)	22	0.03
Irish (1,705)	3,627	5.29
Israeli (0)	0	<0.01
Italian (228)	547	0.80
Latvian (0)	0	<0.01
Lithuanian (0)	0	<0.01
Luxemburger (0)	0	<0.01
Macedonian (0)	0	<0.01
Maltese (0)	0	<0.01
New Zealander (0)	0	<0.01
Northern European (0)	0	<0.01
Norwegian (101)	140	0.20
Pennsylvania German (7)	7	0.01

Ancestry	Population	%
Polish (37)	238	0.35
Portuguese (0)	0	<0.01
Romanian (0)	0	<0.01
Russian (52)	88	0.13
Scandinavian (9)	9	0.01
Scotch-Irish (1,328)	1,797	2.62
Scottish (512)	1,154	1.68
Serbian (0)	18	0.03
Slavic (0)	5	0.01
Slovak (15)	43	0.06
Slovene (0)	0	<0.01
Soviet Union (0)	0	<0.01
Swedish (30)	137	0.20
Swiss (32)	128	0.19
Turkish (0)	0	<0.01
Ukrainian (13)	24	0.03
Welsh (131)	189	0.28
West Indian, ex. Hispanic (69)	109	0.16
Bahamian (0)	0	<0.01
Barbadian (0)	0	<0.01
Belizean (0)	0	<0.01
Bermudan (0)	0	<0.01
British West Indian (0)	0	<0.01
Dutch West Indian (0)	0	<0.01
Haitian (0)	20	0.03
Jamaican (0)	0	<0.01
Trinidadian/Tobagonian (0)	0	<0.01
U.S. Virgin Islander (11)	11	0.02
West Indian (58)	78	0.11
Other West Indian (0)	0	<0.01
Yugoslavian (0)	0	<0.01

Hispanic Origin	Population	%
Hispanic or Latino (of any race)	1,140	1.66
Central American, ex. Mexican	49	0.07
Costa Rican	2	<0.01
Guatemalan	14	0.02
Honduran	24	0.03
Nicaraguan	1	<0.01
Panamanian	4	0.01
Salvadoran	4	0.01
Other Central American	0	<0.01
Cuban	16	0.02
Dominican Republic	9	0.01
Mexican	748	1.09
Puerto Rican	147	0.21
South American	32	0.05
Argentinean	2	<0.01
Bolivian	0	<0.01
Chilean	3	<0.01
Colombian	5	0.01
Ecuadorian	6	0.01
Paraguayan	2	<0.01
Peruvian	4	0.01
Uruguayan	0	<0.01
Venezuelan	8	0.01
Other South American	2	<0.01
Other Hispanic or Latino	139	0.20

Race*	Population	%
African-American/Black (28,573)	29,036	42.28
Not Hispanic (28,463)	28,885	42.06
Hispanic (110)	151	0.22
American Indian/Alaska Native (194)	457	0.67
Not Hispanic (184)	439	0.64
Hispanic (10)	18	0.03
Alaska Athabascan (Ala. Nat.) (1)	1	<0.01
Aleut (Alaska Native) (0)	0	<0.01
Apache (0)	2	<0.01
Arapaho (0)	0	<0.01
Blackfeet (4)	14	0.02
Canadian/French Am. Ind. (0)	0	<0.01
Central American Ind. (0)	0	<0.01
Cherokee (33)	117	0.17
Cheyenne (0)	1	<0.01
Chickasaw (2)	2	<0.01
Chippewa (1)	2	<0.01
Choctaw (0)	0	<0.01
Colville (0)	0	<0.01

	Population	%
Comanche (0)	1	<0.01
Cree (0)	0	<0.01
Creek (2)	2	<0.01
Crow (1)	1	<0.01
Delaware (0)	1	<0.01
Hopi (0)	0	<0.01
Houma (0)	0	<0.01
Inupiat (Alaska Native) (0)	0	<0.01
Iroquois (4)	7	0.01
Kiowa (0)	0	<0.01
Lumbee (15)	33	0.05
Menominee (0)	0	<0.01
Mexican American Ind. (5)	5	0.01
Navajo (1)	1	<0.01
Osage (0)	0	<0.01
Ottawa (0)	0	<0.01
Paiute (0)	0	<0.01
Pima (0)	0	<0.01
Potawatomi (0)	0	<0.01
Pueblo (0)	0	<0.01
Puget Sound Salish (4)	4	0.01
Seminole (0)	0	<0.01
Shoshone (0)	0	<0.01
Sioux (1)	5	0.01
South American Ind. (1)	2	<0.01
Spanish American Ind. (0)	1	<0.01
Tlingit-Haida (Alaska Native) (0)	0	<0.01
Tohono O'Odham (0)	0	<0.01
Tsimshian (Alaska Native) (0)	0	<0.01
Ute (0)	1	<0.01
Yakama (0)	0	<0.01
Yaqui (0)	0	<0.01
Yuman (0)	0	<0.01
Yup'ik (Alaska Native) (0)	0	<0.01
Asian (203)	289	0.42
Not Hispanic (201)	285	0.41
Hispanic (2)	4	0.01
Bangladeshi (0)	0	<0.01
Bhutanese (0)	0	<0.01
Burmese (0)	0	<0.01
Cambodian (0)	0	<0.01
Chinese, ex. Taiwanese (49)	58	0.08
Filipino (35)	61	0.09
Hmong (0)	0	<0.01
Indian (75)	92	0.13
Indonesian (0)	0	<0.01
Japanese (9)	15	0.02
Korean (9)	18	0.03
Laotian (0)	0	<0.01
Malaysian (0)	0	<0.01
Nepalese (0)	0	<0.01
Pakistani (8)	9	0.01
Sri Lankan (0)	0	<0.01
Taiwanese (0)	0	<0.01
Thai (6)	10	0.01
Vietnamese (7)	12	0.02
Hawaii Native/Pacific Islander (8)	31	0.05
Not Hispanic (6)	24	0.03
Hispanic (2)	7	0.01
Fijian (0)	0	<0.01
Guamanian/Chamorro (1)	6	0.01
Marshallese (0)	0	<0.01
Native Hawaiian (2)	6	0.01
Samoan (2)	5	0.01
Tongan (0)	0	<0.01
White (38,366)	38,965	56.73
Not Hispanic (37,993)	38,548	56.13
Hispanic (373)	417	0.61

Dorchester County

Population: 136,555

Ancestry	Population	%
Afghan (0)	0	<0.01
African, Sub-Saharan (375)	672	0.52
African (340)	605	0.47
Cape Verdean (0)	0	<0.01
Ethiopian (0)	0	<0.01
Ghanaian (5)	5	<0.01
Kenyan (0)	0	<0.01
Liberian (0)	0	<0.01
Nigerian (0)	0	<0.01
Senegalese (0)	0	<0.01
Sierra Leonean (0)	0	<0.01
Somalian (0)	0	<0.01
South African (15)	47	0.04
Sudanese (0)	0	<0.01
Ugandan (0)	0	<0.01
Zimbabwean (0)	0	<0.01
Other Sub-Saharan African (15)	15	0.01
Albanian (14)	14	0.01
Alsatian (0)	0	<0.01
American (19,352)	19,352	14.93
Arab (13)	83	0.06
Arab (0)	0	<0.01
Egyptian (13)	13	0.01
Iraqi (0)	0	<0.01
Jordanian (0)	0	<0.01
Lebanese (0)	70	0.05
Moroccan (0)	0	<0.01
Palestinian (0)	0	<0.01
Syrian (0)	0	<0.01
Other Arab (0)	0	<0.01
Armenian (0)	20	0.02
Assyrian/Chaldean/Syriac (20)	20	0.02
Australian (56)	56	0.04
Austrian (14)	277	0.21
Basque (0)	0	<0.01
Belgian (175)	325	0.25
Brazilian (20)	36	0.03
British (196)	539	0.42
Bulgarian (29)	29	0.02
Cajun (0)	7	0.01
Canadian (149)	276	0.21
Carpatho Rusyn (0)	0	<0.01
Celtic (0)	0	<0.01
Croatian (35)	89	0.07
Cypriot (0)	0	<0.01
Czech (97)	379	0.29
Czechoslovakian (120)	160	0.12
Danish (70)	281	0.22
Dutch (398)	1,701	1.31
Eastern European (26)	26	0.02
English (5,091)	12,388	9.56
Estonian (0)	0	<0.01
European (1,653)	1,845	1.42
Finnish (8)	49	0.04
French, ex. Basque (816)	3,706	2.86
French Canadian (314)	652	0.50
German (5,644)	17,670	13.63
German Russian (0)	0	<0.01
Greek (114)	516	0.40
Guyanese (17)	23	0.02
Hungarian (145)	333	0.26
Icelander (0)	0	<0.01
Iranian (0)	0	<0.01
Irish (3,753)	14,443	11.14
Israeli (23)	23	0.02
Italian (1,868)	4,824	3.72
Latvian (0)	0	<0.01
Lithuanian (29)	143	0.11
Luxemburger (0)	0	<0.01
Macedonian (0)	0	<0.01
Maltese (0)	21	0.02
New Zealander (0)	0	<0.01
Northern European (26)	26	0.02
Norwegian (245)	666	0.51
Pennsylvania German (0)	13	0.01

Ancestry	Population	%
Polish (874)	2,489	1.92
Portuguese (74)	317	0.24
Romanian (20)	29	0.02
Russian (179)	612	0.47
Scandinavian (88)	237	0.18
Scotch-Irish (1,867)	3,153	2.43
Scottish (1,149)	2,814	2.17
Serbian (8)	8	0.01
Slavic (30)	116	0.09
Slovak (138)	313	0.24
Slovene (31)	82	0.06
Soviet Union (0)	0	<0.01
Swedish (320)	1,023	0.79
Swiss (110)	313	0.24
Turkish (0)	0	<0.01
Ukrainian (16)	199	0.15
Welsh (192)	623	0.48
West Indian, ex. Hispanic (255)	346	0.27
Bahamian (0)	0	<0.01
Barbadian (0)	0	<0.01
Belizean (34)	34	0.03
Bermudan (0)	0	<0.01
British West Indian (53)	53	0.04
Dutch West Indian (0)	29	0.02
Haitian (14)	14	0.01
Jamaican (16)	78	0.06
Trinidadian/Tobagonian (138)	138	0.11
U.S. Virgin Islander (0)	0	<0.01
West Indian (0)	0	<0.01
Other West Indian (0)	0	<0.01
Yugoslavian (15)	43	0.03

Hispanic Origin	Population	%
Hispanic or Latino (of any race)	6,075	4.45
Central American, ex. Mexican	576	0.42
Costa Rican	25	0.02
Guatemalan	160	0.12
Honduran	96	0.07
Nicaraguan	80	0.06
Panamanian	132	0.10
Salvadoran	79	0.06
Other Central American	4	<0.01
Cuban	244	0.18
Dominican Republic	132	0.10
Mexican	2,762	2.02
Puerto Rican	1,247	0.91
South American	546	0.40
Argentinean	55	0.04
Bolivian	27	0.02
Chilean	22	0.02
Colombian	204	0.15
Ecuadorian	55	0.04
Paraguayan	3	<0.01
Peruvian	120	0.09
Uruguayan	6	<0.01
Venezuelan	51	0.04
Other South American	3	<0.01
Other Hispanic or Latino	568	0.42

Race*	Population	%
African-American/Black (35,266)	37,069	27.15
Not Hispanic (34,861)	36,465	26.70
Hispanic (405)	604	0.44
American Indian/Alaska Native (904)	1,885	1.38
Not Hispanic (853)	1,736	1.27
Hispanic (51)	149	0.11
Alaska Athabascan (Ala. Nat.) (7)	13	0.01
Aleut (Alaska Native) (2)	3	<0.01
Apache (12)	18	0.01
Arapaho (0)	0	<0.01
Blackfeet (10)	66	0.05
Canadian/French Am. Ind. (1)	5	<0.01
Central American Ind. (1)	2	<0.01
Cherokee (110)	384	0.28
Cheyenne (0)	0	<0.01
Chickasaw (6)	12	0.01
Chippewa (6)	10	0.01
Choctaw (15)	38	0.03
Colville (0)	0	<0.01

Race*	Population	%
Comanche (5)	7	0.01
Cree (0)	1	<0.01
Creek (2)	15	0.01
Crow (0)	3	<0.01
Delaware (1)	5	<0.01
Hopi (0)	0	<0.01
Houma (2)	2	<0.01
Inupiat (Alaska Native) (3)	4	<0.01
Iroquois (15)	29	0.02
Kiowa (0)	0	<0.01
Lumbee (27)	51	0.04
Menominee (1)	1	<0.01
Mexican American Ind. (10)	13	0.01
Navajo (7)	12	0.01
Osage (0)	0	<0.01
Ottawa (2)	2	<0.01
Paiute (0)	0	<0.01
Pima (1)	1	<0.01
Potawatomi (0)	1	<0.01
Pueblo (2)	2	<0.01
Puget Sound Salish (2)	2	<0.01
Seminole (3)	18	0.01
Shoshone (0)	1	<0.01
Sioux (20)	54	0.04
South American Ind. (2)	2	<0.01
Spanish American Ind. (2)	6	<0.01
Tlingit-Haida (Alaska Native) (2)	4	<0.01
Tohono O'Odham (1)	1	<0.01
Tsimshian (Alaska Native) (0)	0	<0.01
Ute (0)	0	<0.01
Yakama (0)	0	<0.01
Yaqui (1)	1	<0.01
Yuman (0)	0	<0.01
Yup'ik (Alaska Native) (0)	0	<0.01
Asian (2,052)	3,069	2.25
Not Hispanic (2,016)	2,956	2.16
Hispanic (36)	113	0.08
Bangladeshi (14)	14	0.01
Bhutanese (0)	0	<0.01
Burmese (8)	8	0.01
Cambodian (4)	7	0.01
Chinese, ex. Taiwanese (265)	351	0.26
Filipino (750)	1,259	0.92
Hmong (0)	0	<0.01
Indian (334)	402	0.29
Indonesian (8)	14	0.01
Japanese (98)	281	0.21
Korean (137)	235	0.17
Laotian (7)	14	0.01
Malaysian (2)	3	<0.01
Nepalese (0)	0	<0.01
Pakistani (13)	16	0.01
Sri Lankan (3)	5	<0.01
Taiwanese (7)	10	0.01
Thai (49)	98	0.07
Vietnamese (281)	323	0.24
Hawaii Native/Pacific Islander (146)	304	0.22
Not Hispanic (127)	276	0.20
Hispanic (19)	28	0.02
Fijian (0)	0	<0.01
Guamanian/Chamorro (65)	102	0.07
Marshallese (1)	1	<0.01
Native Hawaiian (37)	110	0.08
Samoan (2)	9	0.01
Tongan (12)	12	0.01
White (92,621)	95,677	70.06
Not Hispanic (89,427)	92,047	67.41
Hispanic (3,194)	3,630	2.66

*Notes: † The Census 2010 population figure is used to calculate the percentages in the Hispanic Origin and Race categories. Ancestry percentages are based on the 2006-2010 American Community Survey population (not shown); ‡ Numbers in parentheses indicate the number of people reporting a single ancestry; * Numbers in parentheses indicate the number of persons reporting this race alone, not in combination with any other race; Please refer to the Explanation of Data for more information.*

Florence County

Population: 136,885

Ancestry	Population	%
Afghan (0)	0	<0.01
African, Sub-Saharan (611)	672	0.50
African (561)	622	0.46
Cape Verdean (0)	0	<0.01
Ethiopian (32)	32	0.02
Ghanaian (0)	0	<0.01
Kenyan (0)	0	<0.01
Liberian (0)	0	<0.01
Nigerian (0)	0	<0.01
Senegalese (0)	0	<0.01
Sierra Leonean (0)	0	<0.01
Somalian (0)	0	<0.01
South African (0)	0	<0.01
Sudanese (0)	0	<0.01
Ugandan (0)	0	<0.01
Zimbabwean (0)	0	<0.01
Other Sub-Saharan African (18)	18	0.01
Albanian (0)	0	<0.01
Alsatian (0)	0	<0.01
American (11,397)	11,397	8.45
Arab (134)	224	0.17
Arab (0)	0	<0.01
Egyptian (9)	19	0.01
Iraqi (0)	0	<0.01
Jordanian (0)	0	<0.01
Lebanese (46)	70	0.05
Moroccan (0)	0	<0.01
Palestinian (79)	79	0.06
Syrian (0)	56	0.04
Other Arab (0)	0	<0.01
Armenian (0)	0	<0.01
Assyrian/Chaldean/Syriac (0)	0	<0.01
Australian (0)	0	<0.01
Austrian (38)	114	0.08
Basque (0)	0	<0.01
Belgian (0)	0	<0.01
Brazilian (18)	18	0.01
British (283)	396	0.29
Bulgarian (0)	0	<0.01
Cajun (0)	0	<0.01
Canadian (67)	84	0.06
Carpatho Rusyn (0)	0	<0.01
Celtic (10)	19	0.01
Croatian (0)	114	0.08
Cypriot (0)	0	<0.01
Czech (83)	147	0.11
Czechoslovakian (78)	78	0.06
Danish (12)	87	0.06
Dutch (133)	947	0.70
Eastern European (0)	0	<0.01
English (6,055)	10,456	7.75
Estonian (0)	0	<0.01
European (789)	789	0.58
Finnish (9)	9	0.01
French, ex. Basque (589)	1,819	1.35
French Canadian (111)	270	0.20
German (2,777)	8,300	6.15
German Russian (0)	0	<0.01
Greek (344)	520	0.39
Guyanese (0)	0	<0.01
Hungarian (6)	61	0.05
Icelander (0)	0	<0.01
Iranian (42)	42	0.03
Irish (4,662)	9,049	6.71
Israeli (0)	0	<0.01
Italian (920)	1,856	1.38
Latvian (0)	24	0.02
Lithuanian (12)	12	0.01
Luxemburger (0)	0	<0.01
Macedonian (0)	0	<0.01
Maltese (0)	0	<0.01
New Zealander (0)	0	<0.01
Northern European (33)	33	0.02
Norwegian (152)	316	0.23
Pennsylvania German (0)	0	<0.01

Ancestry	Population	%
Polish (309)	1,164	0.86
Portuguese (0)	17	0.01
Romanian (11)	80	0.06
Russian (124)	222	0.16
Scandinavian (0)	13	0.01
Scotch-Irish (3,909)	5,842	4.33
Scottish (1,032)	2,297	1.70
Serbian (40)	109	0.08
Slavic (0)	31	0.02
Slovak (38)	183	0.14
Slovene (0)	0	<0.01
Soviet Union (0)	0	<0.01
Swedish (26)	290	0.21
Swiss (34)	157	0.12
Turkish (23)	23	0.02
Ukrainian (28)	81	0.06
Welsh (74)	727	0.54
West Indian, ex. Hispanic (215)	277	0.21
Bahamian (0)	15	0.01
Barbadian (0)	0	<0.01
Belizean (0)	0	<0.01
Bermudan (0)	0	<0.01
British West Indian (0)	0	<0.01
Dutch West Indian (14)	14	0.01
Haitian (21)	21	0.02
Jamaican (143)	167	0.12
Trinidadian/Tobagonian (0)	10	0.01
U.S. Virgin Islander (0)	0	<0.01
West Indian (37)	50	0.04
Other West Indian (0)	0	<0.01
Yugoslavian (17)	17	0.01

Hispanic Origin	Population	%
Hispanic or Latino (of any race)	3,030	2.21
Central American, ex. Mexican	178	0.13
Costa Rican	19	0.01
Guatemalan	36	0.03
Honduran	48	0.04
Nicaraguan	1	<0.01
Panamanian	15	0.01
Salvadoran	59	0.04
Other Central American	0	<0.01
Cuban	84	0.06
Dominican Republic	53	0.04
Mexican	1,837	1.34
Puerto Rican	471	0.34
South American	107	0.08
Argentinean	7	0.01
Bolivian	9	0.01
Chilean	0	<0.01
Colombian	42	0.03
Ecuadorian	8	0.01
Paraguayan	0	<0.01
Peruvian	23	0.02
Uruguayan	5	<0.01
Venezuelan	13	0.01
Other South American	0	<0.01
Other Hispanic or Latino	300	0.22

Race*	Population	%
African-American/Black (56,506)	57,495	42.00
Not Hispanic (56,204)	57,082	41.70
Hispanic (302)	413	0.30
American Indian/Alaska Native (464)	990	0.72
Not Hispanic (424)	902	0.66
Hispanic (40)	88	0.06
Alaska Athabascan (Ala. Nat.) (1)	1	<0.01
Aleut (Alaska Native) (0)	0	<0.01
Apache (3)	10	0.01
Arapaho (0)	0	<0.01
Blackfeet (1)	23	0.02
Canadian/French Am. Ind. (2)	2	<0.01
Central American Ind. (0)	0	<0.01
Cherokee (59)	199	0.15
Cheyenne (0)	0	<0.01
Chickasaw (25)	31	0.02
Chippewa (4)	13	0.01
Choctaw (1)	5	<0.01
Colville (0)	0	<0.01

	Population	%
Comanche (0)	0	<0.01
Cree (0)	0	<0.01
Creek (6)	7	0.01
Crow (0)	0	<0.01
Delaware (0)	5	<0.01
Hopi (0)	0	<0.01
Houma (0)	0	<0.01
Inupiat (Alaska Native) (0)	0	<0.01
Iroquois (3)	7	0.01
Kiowa (0)	0	<0.01
Lumbee (83)	121	0.09
Menominee (0)	0	<0.01
Mexican American Ind. (9)	13	0.01
Navajo (1)	1	<0.01
Osage (2)	2	<0.01
Ottawa (0)	0	<0.01
Paiute (0)	0	<0.01
Pima (1)	1	<0.01
Potawatomi (0)	0	<0.01
Pueblo (1)	1	<0.01
Puget Sound Salish (0)	0	<0.01
Seminole (0)	2	<0.01
Shoshone (0)	0	<0.01
Sioux (2)	11	0.01
South American Ind. (1)	4	<0.01
Spanish American Ind. (3)	4	<0.01
Tlingit-Haida (Alaska Native) (0)	0	<0.01
Tohono O'Odham (1)	1	<0.01
Tsimshian (Alaska Native) (0)	0	<0.01
Ute (0)	0	<0.01
Yakama (0)	0	<0.01
Yaqui (0)	0	<0.01
Yuman (0)	0	<0.01
Yup'ik (Alaska Native) (0)	0	<0.01
Asian (1,671)	1,936	1.41
Not Hispanic (1,660)	1,895	1.38
Hispanic (11)	41	0.03
Bangladeshi (0)	0	<0.01
Bhutanese (0)	0	<0.01
Burmese (3)	3	<0.01
Cambodian (2)	3	<0.01
Chinese, ex. Taiwanese (323)	365	0.27
Filipino (258)	320	0.23
Hmong (0)	0	<0.01
Indian (518)	571	0.42
Indonesian (4)	6	<0.01
Japanese (94)	135	0.10
Korean (134)	173	0.13
Laotian (13)	13	0.01
Malaysian (2)	3	<0.01
Nepalese (11)	12	0.01
Pakistani (35)	48	0.04
Sri Lankan (13)	13	0.01
Taiwanese (41)	46	0.03
Thai (18)	31	0.02
Vietnamese (155)	163	0.12
Hawaii Native/Pacific Islander (23)	76	0.06
Not Hispanic (23)	72	0.05
Hispanic (0)	4	<0.01
Fijian (0)	3	<0.01
Guamanian/Chamorro (4)	9	0.01
Marshallese (0)	0	<0.01
Native Hawaiian (6)	19	0.01
Samoan (9)	16	0.01
Tongan (0)	0	<0.01
White (75,116)	76,297	55.74
Not Hispanic (74,105)	75,132	54.89
Hispanic (1,011)	1,165	0.85

Notes: † The Census 2010 population figure is used to calculate the percentages in the Hispanic Origin and Race categories. Ancestry percentages are based on the 2006-2010 American Community Survey population (not shown); ‡ Numbers in parentheses indicate the number of people reporting a single ancestry; * Numbers in parentheses indicate the number of persons reporting this race alone, not in combination with any other race; Please refer to the Explanation of Data for more information.

Georgetown County

Population: 60,158

Ancestry	Population	%
Afghan (0)	0	<0.01
African, Sub-Saharan (102)	164	0.27
African (29)	91	0.15
Cape Verdean (0)	0	<0.01
Ethiopian (0)	0	<0.01
Ghanaian (0)	0	<0.01
Kenyan (0)	0	<0.01
Liberian (0)	0	<0.01
Nigerian (0)	0	<0.01
Senegalese (0)	0	<0.01
Sierra Leonean (0)	0	<0.01
Somalian (0)	0	<0.01
South African (73)	73	0.12
Sudanese (0)	0	<0.01
Ugandan (0)	0	<0.01
Zimbabwean (0)	0	<0.01
Other Sub-Saharan African (0)	0	<0.01
Albanian (0)	0	<0.01
Alsatian (0)	0	<0.01
American (5,224)	5,224	8.67
Arab (59)	106	0.18
Arab (0)	0	<0.01
Egyptian (0)	0	<0.01
Iraqi (0)	0	<0.01
Jordanian (0)	0	<0.01
Lebanese (59)	106	0.18
Moroccan (0)	0	<0.01
Palestinian (0)	0	<0.01
Syrian (0)	0	<0.01
Other Arab (0)	0	<0.01
Armenian (8)	8	0.01
Assyrian/Chaldean/Syriac (0)	0	<0.01
Australian (9)	9	0.01
Austrian (45)	172	0.29
Basque (0)	0	<0.01
Belgian (0)	5	0.01
Brazilian (0)	13	0.02
British (184)	266	0.44
Bulgarian (0)	0	<0.01
Cajun (0)	0	<0.01
Canadian (0)	10	0.02
Carpatho Rusyn (0)	0	<0.01
Celtic (0)	0	<0.01
Croatian (0)	0	<0.01
Cypriot (0)	0	<0.01
Czech (11)	32	0.05
Czechoslovakian (15)	24	0.04
Danish (35)	61	0.10
Dutch (178)	459	0.76
Eastern European (33)	33	0.05
English (5,471)	8,126	13.49
Estonian (0)	0	<0.01
European (294)	294	0.49
Finnish (8)	8	0.01
French, ex. Basque (284)	1,000	1.66
French Canadian (77)	219	0.36
German (1,770)	4,568	7.58
German Russian (0)	0	<0.01
Greek (18)	152	0.25
Guyanese (0)	0	<0.01
Hungarian (62)	280	0.46
Icelander (0)	0	<0.01
Iranian (0)	0	<0.01
Irish (2,408)	5,393	8.95
Israeli (0)	0	<0.01
Italian (944)	1,711	2.84
Latvian (0)	0	<0.01
Lithuanian (11)	31	0.05
Luxemburger (0)	0	<0.01
Macedonian (0)	0	<0.01
Maltese (0)	0	<0.01
New Zealander (0)	0	<0.01
Northern European (25)	25	0.04
Norwegian (151)	264	0.44
Pennsylvania German (10)	37	0.06

Ancestry	Population	%
Polish (376)	1,082	1.80
Portuguese (38)	48	0.08
Romanian (0)	0	<0.01
Russian (40)	125	0.21
Scandinavian (0)	0	<0.01
Scotch-Irish (1,394)	2,133	3.54
Scottish (287)	820	1.36
Serbian (10)	10	0.02
Slavic (0)	12	0.02
Slovak (44)	81	0.13
Slovene (10)	55	0.09
Soviet Union (0)	0	<0.01
Swedish (62)	214	0.36
Swiss (52)	141	0.23
Turkish (0)	0	<0.01
Ukrainian (28)	61	0.10
Welsh (152)	273	0.45
West Indian, ex. Hispanic (58)	66	0.11
Bahamian (0)	0	<0.01
Barbadian (0)	0	<0.01
Belizean (0)	0	<0.01
Bermudan (0)	0	<0.01
British West Indian (0)	0	<0.01
Dutch West Indian (0)	0	<0.01
Haitian (7)	7	0.01
Jamaican (8)	8	0.01
Trinidadian/Tobagonian (0)	0	<0.01
U.S. Virgin Islander (0)	0	<0.01
West Indian (43)	51	0.08
Other West Indian (0)	0	<0.01
Yugoslavian (0)	11	0.02

Hispanic Origin	Population	%
Hispanic or Latino (of any race)	1,867	3.10
Central American, ex. Mexican	133	0.22
Costa Rican	4	0.01
Guatemalan	44	0.07
Honduran	30	0.05
Nicaraguan	4	0.01
Panamanian	9	0.01
Salvadoran	41	0.07
Other Central American	1	<0.01
Cuban	51	0.08
Dominican Republic	15	0.02
Mexican	1,279	2.13
Puerto Rican	198	0.33
South American	66	0.11
Argentinean	4	0.01
Bolivian	3	<0.01
Chilean	4	0.01
Colombian	25	0.04
Ecuadorian	3	<0.01
Paraguayan	3	<0.01
Peruvian	5	0.01
Uruguayan	6	0.01
Venezuelan	5	0.01
Other South American	8	0.01
Other Hispanic or Latino	125	0.21

Race*	Population	%
African-American/Black (20,214)	20,525	34.12
Not Hispanic (20,128)	20,395	33.90
Hispanic (86)	130	0.22
American Indian/Alaska Native (136)	328	0.55
Not Hispanic (128)	304	0.51
Hispanic (8)	24	0.04
Alaska Athabascan (Ala. Nat.) (0)	0	<0.01
Aleut (Alaska Native) (0)	0	<0.01
Apache (1)	5	0.01
Arapaho (0)	0	<0.01
Blackfeet (3)	10	0.02
Canadian/French Am. Ind. (0)	0	<0.01
Central American Ind. (0)	2	<0.01
Cherokee (41)	117	0.19
Cheyenne (0)	0	<0.01
Chickasaw (2)	2	<0.01
Chippewa (1)	1	<0.01
Choctaw (0)	2	<0.01
Colville (0)	0	<0.01

	Population	%
Comanche (0)	1	<0.01
Cree (1)	2	<0.01
Creek (3)	3	<0.01
Crow (0)	0	<0.01
Delaware (0)	0	<0.01
Hopi (0)	0	<0.01
Houma (0)	0	<0.01
Inupiat (Alaska Native) (0)	0	<0.01
Iroquois (1)	9	0.01
Kiowa (0)	0	<0.01
Lumbee (14)	25	0.04
Menominee (0)	0	<0.01
Mexican American Ind. (1)	1	<0.01
Navajo (1)	3	<0.01
Osage (0)	0	<0.01
Ottawa (0)	0	<0.01
Paiute (0)	0	<0.01
Pima (0)	0	<0.01
Potawatomi (0)	0	<0.01
Pueblo (0)	0	<0.01
Puget Sound Salish (0)	0	<0.01
Seminole (3)	4	0.01
Shoshone (0)	0	<0.01
Sioux (0)	5	0.01
South American Ind. (0)	0	<0.01
Spanish American Ind. (0)	0	<0.01
Tlingit-Haida (Alaska Native) (0)	1	<0.01
Tohono O'Odham (0)	0	<0.01
Tsimshian (Alaska Native) (0)	0	<0.01
Ute (0)	0	<0.01
Yakama (0)	0	<0.01
Yaqui (0)	0	<0.01
Yuman (0)	0	<0.01
Yup'ik (Alaska Native) (0)	0	<0.01
Asian (271)	339	0.56
Not Hispanic (269)	332	0.55
Hispanic (2)	7	0.01
Bangladeshi (0)	0	<0.01
Bhutanese (0)	0	<0.01
Burmese (0)	0	<0.01
Cambodian (0)	0	<0.01
Chinese, ex. Taiwanese (65)	75	0.12
Filipino (55)	72	0.12
Hmong (1)	1	<0.01
Indian (69)	80	0.13
Indonesian (0)	0	<0.01
Japanese (11)	20	0.03
Korean (30)	47	0.08
Laotian (0)	1	<0.01
Malaysian (0)	0	<0.01
Nepalese (0)	0	<0.01
Pakistani (1)	1	<0.01
Sri Lankan (1)	1	<0.01
Taiwanese (0)	0	<0.01
Thai (5)	10	0.02
Vietnamese (13)	14	0.02
Hawaii Native/Pacific Islander (14)	33	0.05
Not Hispanic (6)	20	0.03
Hispanic (8)	13	0.02
Fijian (0)	0	<0.01
Guamanian/Chamorro (3)	8	0.01
Marshallese (0)	0	<0.01
Native Hawaiian (9)	13	0.02
Samoan (1)	4	0.01
Tongan (0)	0	<0.01
White (38,005)	38,417	63.86
Not Hispanic (37,311)	37,628	62.55
Hispanic (694)	789	1.31

*Notes: † The Census 2010 population figure is used to calculate the percentages in the Hispanic Origin and Race categories. Ancestry percentages are based on the 2006-2010 American Community Survey population (not shown); ‡ Numbers in parentheses indicate the number of people reporting a single ancestry; * Numbers in parentheses indicate the number of persons reporting this race alone, not in combination with any other race; Please refer to the Explanation of Data for more information.*

Greenville County

Population: 451,225

Ancestry	Population	%
Afghan (0)	0	<0.01
African, Sub-Saharan (1,857)	2,108	0.48
African (1,219)	1,390	0.32
Cape Verdean (30)	81	0.02
Ethiopian (225)	225	0.05
Ghanaian (14)	14	<0.01
Kenyan (0)	0	<0.01
Liberian (24)	24	0.01
Nigerian (108)	108	0.02
Senegalese (0)	0	<0.01
Sierra Leonean (0)	0	<0.01
Somalian (149)	149	0.03
South African (68)	88	0.02
Sudanese (0)	0	<0.01
Ugandan (0)	0	<0.01
Zimbabwean (0)	0	<0.01
Other Sub-Saharan African (20)	29	0.01
Albanian (48)	68	0.02
Alsatian (0)	0	<0.01
American (56,684)	56,684	12.99
Arab (1,743)	2,147	0.49
Arab (238)	255	0.06
Egyptian (347)	364	0.08
Iraqi (0)	0	<0.01
Jordanian (321)	325	0.07
Lebanese (516)	839	0.19
Moroccan (0)	0	<0.01
Palestinian (42)	42	0.01
Syrian (11)	39	0.01
Other Arab (268)	283	0.06
Armenian (19)	74	0.02
Assyrian/Chaldean/Syriac (0)	14	<0.01
Australian (17)	39	0.01
Austrian (148)	698	0.16
Basque (10)	39	0.01
Belgian (54)	239	0.05
Brazilian (374)	394	0.09
British (1,763)	2,686	0.62
Bulgarian (38)	38	0.01
Cajun (19)	29	0.01
Canadian (497)	954	0.22
Carpatho Rusyn (0)	0	<0.01
Celtic (55)	55	0.01
Croatian (110)	258	0.06
Cypriot (14)	14	<0.01
Czech (206)	812	0.19
Czechoslovakian (101)	219	0.05
Danish (194)	748	0.17
Dutch (1,213)	4,682	1.07
Eastern European (235)	323	0.07
English (20,828)	47,767	10.94
Estonian (6)	6	<0.01
European (4,652)	5,088	1.17
Finnish (565)	979	0.22
French, ex. Basque (2,197)	9,268	2.12
French Canadian (973)	2,091	0.48
German (17,144)	50,726	11.62
German Russian (0)	0	<0.01
Greek (1,541)	2,375	0.54
Guyanese (26)	26	0.01
Hungarian (304)	1,080	0.25
Icelander (17)	70	0.02
Iranian (313)	362	0.08
Irish (15,924)	46,750	10.71
Israeli (86)	119	0.03
Italian (4,108)	13,181	3.02
Latvian (41)	55	0.01
Lithuanian (84)	374	0.09
Luxemburger (0)	0	<0.01
Macedonian (24)	79	0.02
Maltese (0)	14	<0.01
New Zealander (0)	0	<0.01
Northern European (227)	240	0.05
Norwegian (742)	2,447	0.56
Pennsylvania German (109)	221	0.05

Ancestry (cont.)	Population	%
Polish (2,562)	6,976	1.60
Portuguese (258)	702	0.16
Romanian (234)	406	0.09
Russian (668)	1,732	0.40
Scandinavian (288)	401	0.09
Scotch-Irish (8,947)	15,852	3.63
Scottish (4,408)	11,537	2.64
Serbian (80)	184	0.04
Slavic (79)	93	0.02
Slovak (339)	718	0.16
Slovene (111)	191	0.04
Soviet Union (0)	0	<0.01
Swedish (758)	2,979	0.68
Swiss (266)	973	0.22
Turkish (163)	303	0.07
Ukrainian (225)	598	0.14
Welsh (694)	2,486	0.57
West Indian, ex. Hispanic (514)	744	0.17
Bahamian (24)	24	0.01
Barbadian (0)	0	<0.01
Belizean (0)	0	<0.01
Bermudan (0)	0	<0.01
British West Indian (21)	21	<0.01
Dutch West Indian (0)	38	0.01
Haitian (131)	173	0.04
Jamaican (219)	275	0.06
Trinidadian/Tobagonian (79)	96	0.02
U.S. Virgin Islander (0)	0	<0.01
West Indian (40)	107	0.02
Other West Indian (0)	10	<0.01
Yugoslavian (53)	203	0.05

Hispanic Origin	Population	%
Hispanic or Latino (of any race)	36,495	8.09
Central American, ex. Mexican	5,158	1.14
Costa Rican	552	0.12
Guatemalan	1,935	0.43
Honduran	1,510	0.33
Nicaraguan	224	0.05
Panamanian	126	0.03
Salvadoran	794	0.18
Other Central American	17	<0.01
Cuban	1,022	0.23
Dominican Republic	625	0.14
Mexican	17,869	3.96
Puerto Rican	3,150	0.70
South American	6,343	1.41
Argentinean	162	0.04
Bolivian	35	0.01
Chilean	99	0.02
Colombian	4,943	1.10
Ecuadorian	255	0.06
Paraguayan	24	0.01
Peruvian	400	0.09
Uruguayan	148	0.03
Venezuelan	250	0.06
Other South American	27	0.01
Other Hispanic or Latino	2,328	0.52

Race*	Population	%
African-American/Black (81,497)	85,558	18.96
Not Hispanic (80,569)	84,118	18.64
Hispanic (928)	1,440	0.32
American Indian/Alaska Native (1,401)	3,226	0.71
Not Hispanic (915)	2,491	0.55
Hispanic (486)	735	0.16
Alaska Athabascan (Ala. Nat.) (4)	5	<0.01
Aleut (Alaska Native) (0)	0	<0.01
Apache (24)	43	0.01
Arapaho (0)	0	<0.01
Blackfeet (13)	67	0.01
Canadian/French Am. Ind. (4)	15	<0.01
Central American Ind. (43)	46	0.01
Cherokee (242)	863	0.19
Cheyenne (1)	9	<0.01
Chickasaw (8)	21	<0.01
Chippewa (11)	30	0.01
Choctaw (22)	47	0.01
Colville (0)	0	<0.01

Race* (cont.)	Population	%
Comanche (2)	5	<0.01
Cree (0)	1	<0.01
Creek (7)	22	<0.01
Crow (0)	1	<0.01
Delaware (0)	5	<0.01
Hopi (1)	1	<0.01
Houma (0)	0	<0.01
Inupiat (Alaska Native) (5)	7	<0.01
Iroquois (21)	44	0.01
Kiowa (1)	3	<0.01
Lumbee (80)	114	0.03
Menominee (0)	0	<0.01
Mexican American Ind. (265)	305	0.07
Navajo (15)	27	0.01
Osage (4)	4	<0.01
Ottawa (2)	5	<0.01
Paiute (0)	0	<0.01
Pima (1)	1	<0.01
Potawatomi (10)	10	<0.01
Pueblo (6)	7	<0.01
Puget Sound Salish (0)	0	<0.01
Seminole (3)	16	<0.01
Shoshone (0)	0	<0.01
Sioux (17)	40	0.01
South American Ind. (4)	14	<0.01
Spanish American Ind. (10)	11	<0.01
Tlingit-Haida (Alaska Native) (0)	2	<0.01
Tohono O'Odham (0)	0	<0.01
Tsimshian (Alaska Native) (0)	0	<0.01
Ute (2)	3	<0.01
Yakama (0)	2	<0.01
Yaqui (5)	7	<0.01
Yuman (0)	0	<0.01
Yup'ik (Alaska Native) (0)	0	<0.01
Asian (8,849)	10,786	2.39
Not Hispanic (8,772)	10,514	2.33
Hispanic (77)	272	0.06
Bangladeshi (17)	21	<0.01
Bhutanese (0)	0	<0.01
Burmese (100)	102	0.02
Cambodian (43)	62	0.01
Chinese, ex. Taiwanese (1,341)	1,627	0.36
Filipino (733)	1,207	0.27
Hmong (16)	23	0.01
Indian (2,953)	3,242	0.72
Indonesian (19)	33	0.01
Japanese (375)	610	0.14
Korean (777)	1,023	0.23
Laotian (21)	28	0.01
Malaysian (7)	12	<0.01
Nepalese (25)	25	0.01
Pakistani (241)	267	0.06
Sri Lankan (26)	34	0.01
Taiwanese (53)	69	0.02
Thai (108)	166	0.04
Vietnamese (1,749)	1,862	0.41
Hawaii Native/Pacific Islander (257)	575	0.13
Not Hispanic (217)	468	0.10
Hispanic (40)	107	0.02
Fijian (3)	9	<0.01
Guamanian/Chamorro (61)	104	0.02
Marshallese (2)	2	<0.01
Native Hawaiian (44)	158	0.04
Samoan (25)	58	0.01
Tongan (1)	7	<0.01
White (333,084)	340,376	75.43
Not Hispanic (317,197)	322,819	71.54
Hispanic (15,887)	17,557	3.89

*Notes: † The Census 2010 population figure is used to calculate the percentages in the Hispanic Origin and Race categories. Ancestry percentages are based on the 2006-2010 American Community Survey population (not shown); ‡ Numbers in parentheses indicate the number of people reporting a single ancestry; * Numbers in parentheses indicate the number of persons reporting this race alone, not in combination with any other race; Please refer to the Explanation of Data for more information.*

Greenwood County

Population: 69,661

Ancestry	Population	%
Afghan (0)	0	<0.01
African, Sub-Saharan (310)	344	0.50
African (286)	300	0.44
Cape Verdean (0)	0	<0.01
Ethiopian (16)	16	0.02
Ghanaian (0)	0	<0.01
Kenyan (0)	0	<0.01
Liberian (0)	0	<0.01
Nigerian (0)	0	<0.01
Senegalese (0)	0	<0.01
Sierra Leonean (0)	0	<0.01
Somalian (0)	0	<0.01
South African (8)	28	0.04
Sudanese (0)	0	<0.01
Ugandan (0)	0	<0.01
Zimbabwean (0)	0	<0.01
Other Sub-Saharan African (0)	0	<0.01
Albanian (0)	0	<0.01
Alsatian (0)	0	<0.01
American (12,286)	12,286	17.83
Arab (0)	0	<0.01
Arab (0)	0	<0.01
Egyptian (0)	0	<0.01
Iraqi (0)	0	<0.01
Jordanian (0)	0	<0.01
Lebanese (0)	0	<0.01
Moroccan (0)	0	<0.01
Palestinian (0)	0	<0.01
Syrian (0)	0	<0.01
Other Arab (0)	0	<0.01
Armenian (0)	0	<0.01
Assyrian/Chaldean/Syriac (0)	0	<0.01
Australian (0)	0	<0.01
Austrian (0)	0	<0.01
Basque (0)	0	<0.01
Belgian (0)	0	<0.01
Brazilian (0)	0	<0.01
British (108)	210	0.30
Bulgarian (9)	9	0.01
Cajun (11)	11	0.02
Canadian (6)	6	0.01
Carpatho Rusyn (0)	0	<0.01
Celtic (0)	16	0.02
Croatian (14)	80	0.12
Cypriot (0)	0	<0.01
Czech (22)	22	0.03
Czechoslovakian (14)	26	0.04
Danish (71)	108	0.16
Dutch (148)	689	1.00
Eastern European (0)	13	0.02
English (3,414)	5,974	8.67
Estonian (0)	0	<0.01
European (410)	421	0.61
Finnish (0)	19	0.03
French, ex. Basque (227)	996	1.45
French Canadian (72)	88	0.13
German (2,045)	5,517	8.01
German Russian (0)	0	<0.01
Greek (56)	227	0.33
Guyanese (0)	0	<0.01
Hungarian (0)	35	0.05
Icelander (0)	0	<0.01
Iranian (0)	0	<0.01
Irish (2,292)	5,628	8.17
Israeli (0)	0	<0.01
Italian (663)	1,119	1.62
Latvian (0)	0	<0.01
Lithuanian (17)	69	0.10
Luxemburger (0)	0	<0.01
Macedonian (0)	0	<0.01
Maltese (0)	0	<0.01
New Zealander (0)	0	<0.01
Northern European (3)	3	<0.01
Norwegian (48)	240	0.35
Pennsylvania German (22)	22	0.03

Ancestry	Population	%
Polish (93)	376	0.55
Portuguese (0)	0	<0.01
Romanian (0)	11	0.02
Russian (32)	503	0.73
Scandinavian (62)	75	0.11
Scotch-Irish (1,823)	2,842	4.13
Scottish (408)	1,081	1.57
Serbian (0)	0	<0.01
Slavic (14)	28	0.04
Slovak (8)	8	0.01
Slovene (0)	0	<0.01
Soviet Union (0)	0	<0.01
Swedish (17)	212	0.31
Swiss (23)	41	0.06
Turkish (0)	0	<0.01
Ukrainian (0)	14	0.02
Welsh (32)	182	0.26
West Indian, ex. Hispanic (50)	66	0.10
Bahamian (0)	0	<0.01
Barbadian (0)	0	<0.01
Belizean (0)	0	<0.01
Bermudan (0)	0	<0.01
British West Indian (0)	0	<0.01
Dutch West Indian (0)	0	<0.01
Haitian (0)	0	<0.01
Jamaican (35)	35	0.05
Trinidadian/Tobagonian (0)	0	<0.01
U.S. Virgin Islander (0)	0	<0.01
West Indian (15)	31	0.04
Other West Indian (0)	0	<0.01
Yugoslavian (0)	0	<0.01

Hispanic Origin	Population	%
Hispanic or Latino (of any race)	3,789	5.44
Central American, ex. Mexican	286	0.41
Costa Rican	40	0.06
Guatemalan	167	0.24
Honduran	62	0.09
Nicaraguan	4	0.01
Panamanian	5	0.01
Salvadoran	8	0.01
Other Central American	0	<0.01
Cuban	58	0.08
Dominican Republic	19	0.03
Mexican	2,922	4.19
Puerto Rican	181	0.26
South American	78	0.11
Argentinean	5	0.01
Bolivian	0	<0.01
Chilean	8	0.01
Colombian	30	0.04
Ecuadorian	15	0.02
Paraguayan	4	0.01
Peruvian	7	0.01
Uruguayan	0	<0.01
Venezuelan	9	0.01
Other South American	0	<0.01
Other Hispanic or Latino	245	0.35

Race*	Population	%
African-American/Black (21,846)	22,250	31.94
Not Hispanic (21,728)	22,087	31.71
Hispanic (118)	163	0.23
American Indian/Alaska Native (196)	393	0.56
Not Hispanic (139)	313	0.45
Hispanic (57)	80	0.11
Alaska Athabascan (Ala. Nat.) (4)	4	0.01
Aleut (Alaska Native) (1)	1	<0.01
Apache (0)	4	0.01
Arapaho (0)	0	<0.01
Blackfeet (0)	8	0.01
Canadian/French Am. Ind. (0)	0	<0.01
Central American Ind. (0)	0	<0.01
Cherokee (30)	100	0.14
Cheyenne (0)	0	<0.01
Chickasaw (0)	1	<0.01
Chippewa (1)	1	<0.01
Choctaw (4)	4	0.01
Colville (0)	0	<0.01

Race* (cont.)	Population	%
Comanche (0)	0	<0.01
Cree (0)	0	<0.01
Creek (2)	4	0.01
Crow (0)	0	<0.01
Delaware (0)	0	<0.01
Hopi (0)	0	<0.01
Houma (0)	0	<0.01
Inupiat (Alaska Native) (0)	0	<0.01
Iroquois (3)	4	0.01
Kiowa (3)	3	<0.01
Lumbee (5)	10	0.01
Menominee (0)	0	<0.01
Mexican American Ind. (20)	31	0.04
Navajo (0)	1	<0.01
Osage (0)	0	<0.01
Ottawa (0)	0	<0.01
Paiute (0)	0	<0.01
Pima (0)	0	<0.01
Potawatomi (6)	6	0.01
Pueblo (0)	0	<0.01
Puget Sound Salish (0)	0	<0.01
Seminole (1)	2	<0.01
Shoshone (0)	0	<0.01
Sioux (4)	5	0.01
South American Ind. (0)	0	<0.01
Spanish American Ind. (0)	0	<0.01
Tlingit-Haida (Alaska Native) (2)	2	<0.01
Tohono O'Odham (0)	0	<0.01
Tsimshian (Alaska Native) (0)	0	<0.01
Ute (0)	0	<0.01
Yakama (0)	0	<0.01
Yaqui (1)	1	<0.01
Yuman (0)	0	<0.01
Yup'ik (Alaska Native) (0)	0	<0.01
Asian (572)	737	1.06
Not Hispanic (568)	730	1.05
Hispanic (4)	7	0.01
Bangladeshi (1)	1	<0.01
Bhutanese (0)	0	<0.01
Burmese (0)	0	<0.01
Cambodian (11)	15	0.02
Chinese, ex. Taiwanese (56)	76	0.11
Filipino (130)	162	0.23
Hmong (0)	0	<0.01
Indian (115)	140	0.20
Indonesian (4)	5	0.01
Japanese (78)	107	0.15
Korean (38)	62	0.09
Laotian (1)	1	<0.01
Malaysian (0)	0	<0.01
Nepalese (0)	0	<0.01
Pakistani (10)	12	0.02
Sri Lankan (0)	0	<0.01
Taiwanese (1)	1	<0.01
Thai (15)	18	0.03
Vietnamese (72)	95	0.14
Hawaii Native/Pacific Islander (25)	41	0.06
Not Hispanic (11)	25	0.04
Hispanic (14)	16	0.02
Fijian (0)	0	<0.01
Guamanian/Chamorro (13)	14	0.02
Marshallese (3)	6	0.01
Native Hawaiian (6)	9	0.01
Samoan (3)	5	0.01
Tongan (0)	0	<0.01
White (43,783)	44,475	63.84
Not Hispanic (42,709)	43,241	62.07
Hispanic (1,074)	1,234	1.77

*Notes: † The Census 2010 population figure is used to calculate the percentages in the Hispanic Origin and Race categories. Ancestry percentages are based on the 2006-2010 American Community Survey population (not shown); ‡ Numbers in parentheses indicate the number of people reporting a single ancestry; * Numbers in parentheses indicate the number of persons reporting this race alone, not in combination with any other race; Please refer to the Explanation of Data for more information.*

Horry County

Population: 269,291

Ancestry	Population	%
Afghan (0)	0	<0.01
African, Sub-Saharan (291)	418	0.16
African (275)	386	0.15
Cape Verdean (0)	0	<0.01
Ethiopian (0)	0	<0.01
Ghanaian (0)	0	<0.01
Kenyan (0)	0	<0.01
Liberian (0)	0	<0.01
Nigerian (0)	0	<0.01
Senegalese (0)	0	<0.01
Sierra Leonean (0)	0	<0.01
Somalian (0)	0	<0.01
South African (16)	16	0.01
Sudanese (0)	0	<0.01
Ugandan (0)	0	<0.01
Zimbabwean (0)	0	<0.01
Other Sub-Saharan African (0)	16	0.01
Albanian (347)	382	0.15
Alsatian (0)	25	0.01
American (39,456)	39,456	15.28
Arab (428)	677	0.26
Arab (40)	55	0.02
Egyptian (54)	79	0.03
Iraqi (0)	0	<0.01
Jordanian (0)	0	<0.01
Lebanese (195)	342	0.13
Moroccan (111)	111	0.04
Palestinian (0)	0	<0.01
Syrian (28)	68	0.03
Other Arab (0)	22	0.01
Armenian (97)	176	0.07
Assyrian/Chaldean/Syriac (9)	9	<0.01
Australian (155)	155	0.06
Austrian (143)	467	0.18
Basque (0)	0	<0.01
Belgian (78)	219	0.08
Brazilian (78)	125	0.05
British (687)	1,084	0.42
Bulgarian (73)	89	0.03
Cajun (0)	19	0.01
Canadian (409)	598	0.23
Carpatho Rusyn (0)	14	0.01
Celtic (19)	59	0.02
Croatian (154)	397	0.15
Cypriot (0)	0	<0.01
Czech (229)	676	0.26
Czechoslovakian (168)	297	0.11
Danish (116)	263	0.10
Dutch (1,293)	4,334	1.68
Eastern European (142)	142	0.05
English (13,305)	29,277	11.34
Estonian (0)	0	<0.01
European (1,577)	1,718	0.67
Finnish (63)	232	0.09
French, ex. Basque (2,315)	7,950	3.08
French Canadian (665)	1,470	0.57
German (11,167)	33,185	12.85
German Russian (0)	0	<0.01
Greek (675)	1,159	0.45
Guyanese (17)	17	0.01
Hungarian (709)	1,430	0.55
Icelander (78)	94	0.04
Iranian (6)	21	0.01
Irish (12,696)	34,399	13.32
Israeli (142)	186	0.07
Italian (7,365)	15,853	6.14
Latvian (27)	61	0.02
Lithuanian (161)	398	0.15
Luxemburger (0)	0	<0.01
Macedonian (0)	0	<0.01
Maltese (0)	0	<0.01
New Zealander (17)	17	0.01
Northern European (43)	43	0.02
Norwegian (345)	995	0.39
Pennsylvania German (125)	182	0.07

Ancestry	Population	%
Polish (2,846)	6,974	2.70
Portuguese (503)	863	0.33
Romanian (195)	241	0.09
Russian (548)	1,377	0.53
Scandinavian (52)	118	0.05
Scotch-Irish (4,685)	7,783	3.01
Scottish (2,924)	7,045	2.73
Serbian (17)	75	0.03
Slavic (30)	183	0.07
Slovak (247)	613	0.24
Slovene (34)	103	0.04
Soviet Union (12)	12	<0.01
Swedish (624)	2,003	0.78
Swiss (171)	579	0.22
Turkish (39)	57	0.02
Ukrainian (376)	585	0.23
Welsh (406)	1,957	0.76
West Indian, ex. Hispanic (761)	1,069	0.41
Bahamian (52)	140	0.05
Barbadian (0)	0	<0.01
Belizean (0)	0	<0.01
Bermudan (57)	57	0.02
British West Indian (25)	25	0.01
Dutch West Indian (0)	0	<0.01
Haitian (32)	153	0.06
Jamaican (500)	525	0.20
Trinidadian/Tobagonian (65)	113	0.04
U.S. Virgin Islander (0)	0	<0.01
West Indian (30)	56	0.02
Other West Indian (0)	0	<0.01
Yugoslavian (0)	124	0.05

Hispanic Origin	Population	%
Hispanic or Latino (of any race)	16,683	6.20
Central American, ex. Mexican	2,085	0.77
Costa Rican	65	0.02
Guatemalan	1,022	0.38
Honduran	579	0.22
Nicaraguan	40	0.01
Panamanian	57	0.02
Salvadoran	314	0.12
Other Central American	8	<0.01
Cuban	336	0.12
Dominican Republic	142	0.05
Mexican	10,106	3.75
Puerto Rican	1,781	0.66
South American	856	0.32
Argentinean	80	0.03
Bolivian	20	0.01
Chilean	42	0.02
Colombian	318	0.12
Ecuadorian	181	0.07
Paraguayan	5	<0.01
Peruvian	100	0.04
Uruguayan	22	0.01
Venezuelan	80	0.03
Other South American	8	<0.01
Other Hispanic or Latino	1,377	0.51

Race*	Population	%
African-American/Black (36,202)	38,764	14.39
Not Hispanic (35,753)	38,039	14.13
Hispanic (449)	725	0.27
American Indian/Alaska Native (1,279)	2,857	1.06
Not Hispanic (1,075)	2,515	0.93
Hispanic (204)	342	0.13
Alaska Athabascan (Ala. Nat.) (0)	0	<0.01
Aleut (Alaska Native) (0)	1	<0.01
Apache (15)	35	0.01
Arapaho (0)	0	<0.01
Blackfeet (10)	69	0.03
Canadian/French Am. Ind. (4)	10	<0.01
Central American Ind. (3)	9	<0.01
Cherokee (225)	751	0.28
Cheyenne (0)	7	<0.01
Chickasaw (3)	5	<0.01
Chippewa (8)	23	0.01
Choctaw (11)	32	0.01
Colville (0)	0	<0.01

	Population	%
Comanche (0)	4	<0.01
Cree (2)	8	<0.01
Creek (14)	20	0.01
Crow (2)	6	<0.01
Delaware (0)	5	<0.01
Hopi (0)	1	<0.01
Houma (1)	2	<0.01
Inupiat (Alaska Native) (2)	2	<0.01
Iroquois (39)	86	0.03
Kiowa (0)	0	<0.01
Lumbee (151)	228	0.08
Menominee (2)	2	<0.01
Mexican American Ind. (31)	46	0.02
Navajo (14)	24	0.01
Osage (2)	2	<0.01
Ottawa (0)	0	<0.01
Paiute (0)	0	<0.01
Pima (0)	0	<0.01
Potawatomi (3)	6	<0.01
Pueblo (1)	1	<0.01
Puget Sound Salish (0)	0	<0.01
Seminole (1)	2	<0.01
Shoshone (1)	6	<0.01
Sioux (34)	61	0.02
South American Ind. (5)	13	<0.01
Spanish American Ind. (2)	4	<0.01
Tlingit-Haida (Alaska Native) (1)	5	<0.01
Tohono O'Odham (0)	0	<0.01
Tsimshian (Alaska Native) (0)	1	<0.01
Ute (0)	4	<0.01
Yakama (0)	0	<0.01
Yaqui (1)	1	<0.01
Yuman (0)	0	<0.01
Yup'ik (Alaska Native) (0)	0	<0.01
Asian (2,816)	3,799	1.41
Not Hispanic (2,774)	3,682	1.37
Hispanic (42)	117	0.04
Bangladeshi (6)	6	<0.01
Bhutanese (0)	0	<0.01
Burmese (11)	13	<0.01
Cambodian (28)	33	0.01
Chinese, ex. Taiwanese (480)	580	0.22
Filipino (573)	820	0.30
Hmong (0)	0	<0.01
Indian (525)	638	0.24
Indonesian (18)	26	0.01
Japanese (163)	287	0.11
Korean (195)	309	0.11
Laotian (40)	51	0.02
Malaysian (3)	3	<0.01
Nepalese (5)	5	<0.01
Pakistani (16)	18	0.01
Sri Lankan (5)	13	<0.01
Taiwanese (8)	11	<0.01
Thai (149)	226	0.08
Vietnamese (463)	536	0.20
Hawaii Native/Pacific Islander (305)	486	0.18
Not Hispanic (232)	373	0.14
Hispanic (73)	113	0.04
Fijian (0)	0	<0.01
Guamanian/Chamorro (104)	116	0.04
Marshallese (0)	0	<0.01
Native Hawaiian (37)	100	0.04
Samoan (13)	29	0.01
Tongan (3)	6	<0.01
White (215,071)	219,728	81.60
Not Hispanic (208,096)	211,962	78.71
Hispanic (6,975)	7,766	2.88

*Notes: † The Census 2010 population figure is used to calculate the percentages in the Hispanic Origin and Race categories. Ancestry percentages are based on the 2006-2010 American Community Survey population (not shown); ‡ Numbers in parentheses indicate the number of people reporting a single ancestry; * Numbers in parentheses indicate the number of persons reporting this race alone, not in combination with any other race; Please refer to the Explanation of Data for more information.*

Kershaw County

Population: 61,697

Ancestry	Population	%
Afghan (0)	0	<0.01
African, Sub-Saharan (254)	254	0.42
African (254)	254	0.42
Cape Verdean (0)	0	<0.01
Ethiopian (0)	0	<0.01
Ghanaian (0)	0	<0.01
Kenyan (0)	0	<0.01
Liberian (0)	0	<0.01
Nigerian (0)	0	<0.01
Senegalese (0)	0	<0.01
Sierra Leonean (0)	0	<0.01
Somalian (0)	0	<0.01
South African (0)	0	<0.01
Sudanese (0)	0	<0.01
Ugandan (0)	0	<0.01
Zimbabwean (0)	0	<0.01
Other Sub-Saharan African (0)	0	<0.01
Albanian (0)	0	<0.01
Alsatian (0)	0	<0.01
American (16,878)	16,878	28.05
Arab (47)	163	0.27
Arab (0)	0	<0.01
Egyptian (30)	95	0.16
Iraqi (0)	0	<0.01
Jordanian (0)	0	<0.01
Lebanese (17)	68	0.11
Moroccan (0)	0	<0.01
Palestinian (0)	0	<0.01
Syrian (0)	0	<0.01
Other Arab (0)	0	<0.01
Armenian (0)	0	<0.01
Assyrian/Chaldean/Syriac (0)	0	<0.01
Australian (0)	0	<0.01
Austrian (7)	7	0.01
Basque (0)	0	<0.01
Belgian (73)	94	0.16
Brazilian (0)	0	<0.01
British (133)	263	0.44
Bulgarian (12)	12	0.02
Cajun (0)	0	<0.01
Canadian (13)	29	0.05
Carpatho Rusyn (0)	0	<0.01
Celtic (0)	0	<0.01
Croatian (0)	12	0.02
Cypriot (0)	0	<0.01
Czech (0)	15	0.02
Czechoslovakian (27)	27	0.04
Danish (17)	53	0.09
Dutch (135)	435	0.72
Eastern European (14)	14	0.02
English (2,590)	4,693	7.80
Estonian (0)	0	<0.01
European (672)	697	1.16
Finnish (53)	53	0.09
French, ex. Basque (339)	910	1.51
French Canadian (159)	270	0.45
German (1,453)	3,762	6.25
German Russian (0)	0	<0.01
Greek (22)	79	0.13
Guyanese (0)	0	<0.01
Hungarian (5)	146	0.24
Icelander (0)	0	<0.01
Iranian (0)	0	<0.01
Irish (2,470)	4,622	7.68
Israeli (0)	0	<0.01
Italian (579)	1,375	2.29
Latvian (0)	0	<0.01
Lithuanian (0)	40	0.07
Luxemburger (0)	0	<0.01
Macedonian (0)	0	<0.01
Maltese (0)	0	<0.01
New Zealander (0)	14	0.02
Northern European (17)	17	0.03
Norwegian (78)	277	0.46
Pennsylvania German (0)	0	<0.01

Ancestry	Population	%
Polish (197)	419	0.70
Portuguese (18)	52	0.09
Romanian (0)	0	<0.01
Russian (13)	26	0.04
Scandinavian (0)	25	0.04
Scotch-Irish (938)	1,694	2.82
Scottish (636)	1,290	2.14
Serbian (14)	23	0.04
Slavic (0)	0	<0.01
Slovak (10)	42	0.07
Slovene (0)	0	<0.01
Soviet Union (0)	0	<0.01
Swedish (16)	128	0.21
Swiss (4)	58	0.10
Turkish (0)	0	<0.01
Ukrainian (20)	20	0.03
Welsh (134)	208	0.35
West Indian, ex. Hispanic (30)	56	0.09
Bahamian (0)	0	<0.01
Barbadian (0)	0	<0.01
Belizean (0)	0	<0.01
Bermudan (0)	0	<0.01
British West Indian (0)	0	<0.01
Dutch West Indian (0)	0	<0.01
Haitian (0)	0	<0.01
Jamaican (30)	56	0.09
Trinidadian/Tobagonian (0)	0	<0.01
U.S. Virgin Islander (0)	0	<0.01
West Indian (0)	0	<0.01
Other West Indian (0)	0	<0.01
Yugoslavian (0)	0	<0.01

Hispanic Origin	Population	%
Hispanic or Latino (of any race)	2,298	3.72
Central American, ex. Mexican	300	0.49
Costa Rican	3	<0.01
Guatemalan	31	0.05
Honduran	198	0.32
Nicaraguan	23	0.04
Panamanian	32	0.05
Salvadoran	12	0.02
Other Central American	1	<0.01
Cuban	48	0.08
Dominican Republic	17	0.03
Mexican	1,263	2.05
Puerto Rican	427	0.69
South American	65	0.11
Argentinean	1	<0.01
Bolivian	2	<0.01
Chilean	4	0.01
Colombian	25	0.04
Ecuadorian	6	0.01
Paraguayan	1	<0.01
Peruvian	8	0.01
Uruguayan	0	<0.01
Venezuelan	17	0.03
Other South American	1	<0.01
Other Hispanic or Latino	178	0.29

Race*	Population	%
African-American/Black (15,188)	15,694	25.44
Not Hispanic (15,057)	15,512	25.14
Hispanic (131)	182	0.29
American Indian/Alaska Native (197)	440	0.71
Not Hispanic (182)	398	0.65
Hispanic (15)	42	0.07
Alaska Athabascan (Ala. Nat.) (0)	0	<0.01
Aleut (Alaska Native) (0)	0	<0.01
Apache (1)	2	<0.01
Arapaho (0)	1	<0.01
Blackfeet (0)	9	0.01
Canadian/French Am. Ind. (0)	0	<0.01
Central American Ind. (0)	0	<0.01
Cherokee (60)	158	0.26
Cheyenne (0)	0	<0.01
Chickasaw (3)	3	<0.01
Chippewa (0)	2	<0.01
Choctaw (3)	5	0.01
Colville (0)	0	<0.01

Race*	Population	%
Comanche (0)	0	<0.01
Cree (1)	1	<0.01
Creek (9)	11	0.02
Crow (0)	4	0.01
Delaware (2)	2	<0.01
Hopi (0)	0	<0.01
Houma (1)	1	<0.01
Inupiat (Alaska Native) (0)	0	<0.01
Iroquois (6)	10	0.02
Kiowa (0)	0	<0.01
Lumbee (11)	19	0.03
Menominee (0)	1	<0.01
Mexican American Ind. (1)	2	<0.01
Navajo (0)	3	<0.01
Osage (0)	0	<0.01
Ottawa (0)	0	<0.01
Paiute (0)	3	<0.01
Pima (0)	0	<0.01
Potawatomi (0)	0	<0.01
Pueblo (0)	0	<0.01
Puget Sound Salish (0)	0	<0.01
Seminole (1)	9	0.01
Shoshone (0)	0	<0.01
Sioux (2)	7	0.01
South American Ind. (0)	0	<0.01
Spanish American Ind. (0)	1	<0.01
Tlingit-Haida (Alaska Native) (0)	0	<0.01
Tohono O'Odham (0)	0	<0.01
Tsimshian (Alaska Native) (0)	0	<0.01
Ute (0)	0	<0.01
Yakama (0)	0	<0.01
Yaqui (0)	0	<0.01
Yuman (0)	0	<0.01
Yup'ik (Alaska Native) (1)	1	<0.01
Asian (302)	490	0.79
Not Hispanic (296)	466	0.76
Hispanic (6)	24	0.04
Bangladeshi (7)	12	0.02
Bhutanese (0)	0	<0.01
Burmese (0)	1	<0.01
Cambodian (7)	10	0.02
Chinese, ex. Taiwanese (47)	67	0.11
Filipino (52)	93	0.15
Hmong (0)	0	<0.01
Indian (49)	73	0.12
Indonesian (1)	1	<0.01
Japanese (15)	37	0.06
Korean (51)	101	0.16
Laotian (7)	7	0.01
Malaysian (0)	0	<0.01
Nepalese (0)	0	<0.01
Pakistani (8)	14	0.02
Sri Lankan (0)	0	<0.01
Taiwanese (1)	3	<0.01
Thai (11)	18	0.03
Vietnamese (24)	33	0.05
Hawaii Native/Pacific Islander (29)	47	0.08
Not Hispanic (26)	43	0.07
Hispanic (3)	4	0.01
Fijian (0)	0	<0.01
Guamanian/Chamorro (16)	23	0.04
Marshallese (0)	0	<0.01
Native Hawaiian (10)	17	0.03
Samoan (0)	1	<0.01
Tongan (1)	1	<0.01
White (43,965)	44,812	72.63
Not Hispanic (43,009)	43,703	70.83
Hispanic (956)	1,109	1.80

*Notes: † The Census 2010 population figure is used to calculate the percentages in the Hispanic Origin and Race categories. Ancestry percentages are based on the 2006-2010 American Community Survey population (not shown); ‡ Numbers in parentheses indicate the number of people reporting a single ancestry; * Numbers in parentheses indicate the number of persons reporting this race alone, not in combination with any other race; Please refer to the Explanation of Data for more information.*

Lancaster County

Population: 76,652

Ancestry	Population	%
Afghan (0)	0	<0.01
African, Sub-Saharan (540)	616	0.85
African (471)	520	0.72
Cape Verdean (0)	0	<0.01
Ethiopian (0)	0	<0.01
Ghanaian (0)	0	<0.01
Kenyan (0)	0	<0.01
Liberian (55)	82	0.11
Nigerian (14)	14	0.02
Senegalese (0)	0	<0.01
Sierra Leonean (0)	0	<0.01
Somalian (0)	0	<0.01
South African (0)	0	<0.01
Sudanese (0)	0	<0.01
Ugandan (0)	0	<0.01
Zimbabwean (0)	0	<0.01
Other Sub-Saharan African (0)	0	<0.01
Albanian (0)	0	<0.01
Alsatian (0)	0	<0.01
American (17,289)	17,289	23.91
Arab (50)	134	0.19
Arab (0)	0	<0.01
Egyptian (41)	70	0.10
Iraqi (0)	0	<0.01
Jordanian (0)	0	<0.01
Lebanese (9)	51	0.07
Moroccan (0)	13	0.02
Palestinian (0)	0	<0.01
Syrian (0)	0	<0.01
Other Arab (0)	0	<0.01
Armenian (0)	10	0.01
Assyrian/Chaldean/Syriac (0)	0	<0.01
Australian (0)	0	<0.01
Austrian (5)	40	0.06
Basque (0)	0	<0.01
Belgian (0)	0	<0.01
Brazilian (0)	0	<0.01
British (149)	269	0.37
Bulgarian (0)	0	<0.01
Cajun (0)	0	<0.01
Canadian (24)	55	0.08
Carpatho Rusyn (0)	0	<0.01
Celtic (0)	0	<0.01
Croatian (0)	13	0.02
Cypriot (0)	0	<0.01
Czech (17)	103	0.14
Czechoslovakian (0)	11	0.02
Danish (24)	32	0.04
Dutch (56)	413	0.57
Eastern European (0)	0	<0.01
English (2,900)	5,488	7.59
Estonian (0)	0	<0.01
European (168)	190	0.26
Finnish (16)	16	0.02
French, ex. Basque (260)	956	1.32
French Canadian (13)	47	0.07
German (2,216)	5,231	7.23
German Russian (0)	0	<0.01
Greek (30)	62	0.09
Guyanese (0)	0	<0.01
Hungarian (38)	48	0.07
Icelander (0)	0	<0.01
Iranian (0)	0	<0.01
Irish (2,979)	5,766	7.97
Israeli (21)	21	0.03
Italian (607)	1,173	1.62
Latvian (8)	20	0.03
Lithuanian (35)	171	0.24
Luxemburger (0)	0	<0.01
Macedonian (0)	0	<0.01
Maltese (0)	0	<0.01
New Zealander (0)	0	<0.01
Northern European (30)	30	0.04
Norwegian (53)	115	0.16
Pennsylvania German (22)	34	0.05

Ancestry	Population	%
Polish (151)	474	0.66
Portuguese (0)	0	<0.01
Romanian (0)	0	<0.01
Russian (71)	162	0.22
Scandinavian (0)	0	<0.01
Scotch-Irish (2,278)	3,110	4.30
Scottish (493)	1,193	1.65
Serbian (0)	0	<0.01
Slavic (0)	9	0.01
Slovak (34)	105	0.15
Slovene (0)	0	<0.01
Soviet Union (0)	0	<0.01
Swedish (279)	420	0.58
Swiss (6)	30	0.04
Turkish (0)	10	0.01
Ukrainian (10)	98	0.14
Welsh (33)	122	0.17
West Indian, ex. Hispanic (59)	137	0.19
Bahamian (0)	0	<0.01
Barbadian (0)	0	<0.01
Belizean (0)	0	<0.01
Bermudan (50)	68	0.09
British West Indian (0)	0	<0.01
Dutch West Indian (0)	18	0.02
Haitian (0)	11	0.02
Jamaican (0)	11	0.02
Trinidadian/Tobagonian (0)	0	<0.01
U.S. Virgin Islander (0)	0	<0.01
West Indian (9)	29	0.04
Other West Indian (0)	0	<0.01
Yugoslavian (0)	13	0.02

Hispanic Origin	Population	%
Hispanic or Latino (of any race)	3,384	4.41
Central American, ex. Mexican	404	0.53
Costa Rican	18	0.02
Guatemalan	43	0.06
Honduran	238	0.31
Nicaraguan	24	0.03
Panamanian	30	0.04
Salvadoran	50	0.07
Other Central American	1	<0.01
Cuban	85	0.11
Dominican Republic	48	0.06
Mexican	1,934	2.52
Puerto Rican	308	0.40
South American	346	0.45
Argentinean	44	0.06
Bolivian	1	<0.01
Chilean	4	0.01
Colombian	159	0.21
Ecuadorian	83	0.11
Paraguayan	2	<0.01
Peruvian	29	0.04
Uruguayan	4	0.01
Venezuelan	20	0.03
Other South American	0	<0.01
Other Hispanic or Latino	259	0.34

Race*	Population	%
African-American/Black (18,278)	18,811	24.54
Not Hispanic (18,162)	18,630	24.30
Hispanic (116)	181	0.24
American Indian/Alaska Native (235)	504	0.66
Not Hispanic (214)	468	0.61
Hispanic (21)	36	0.05
Alaska Athabascan (Ala. Nat.) (0)	0	<0.01
Aleut (Alaska Native) (1)	1	<0.01
Apache (3)	5	0.01
Arapaho (0)	0	<0.01
Blackfeet (7)	14	0.02
Canadian/French Am. Ind. (0)	0	<0.01
Central American Ind. (1)	1	<0.01
Cherokee (44)	119	0.16
Cheyenne (0)	0	<0.01
Chickasaw (1)	1	<0.01
Chippewa (2)	3	<0.01
Choctaw (3)	3	<0.01
Colville (0)	0	<0.01

Race*	Population	%
Comanche (0)	1	<0.01
Cree (0)	1	<0.01
Creek (2)	3	<0.01
Crow (0)	2	<0.01
Delaware (0)	0	<0.01
Hopi (0)	1	<0.01
Houma (0)	0	<0.01
Inupiat (Alaska Native) (0)	0	<0.01
Iroquois (5)	9	0.01
Kiowa (0)	0	<0.01
Lumbee (35)	56	0.07
Menominee (0)	0	<0.01
Mexican American Ind. (5)	5	0.01
Navajo (1)	2	<0.01
Osage (0)	0	<0.01
Ottawa (0)	0	<0.01
Paiute (0)	0	<0.01
Pima (1)	1	<0.01
Potawatomi (0)	0	<0.01
Pueblo (0)	0	<0.01
Puget Sound Salish (0)	0	<0.01
Seminole (0)	2	<0.01
Shoshone (0)	0	<0.01
Sioux (2)	6	0.01
South American Ind. (3)	4	0.01
Spanish American Ind. (0)	0	<0.01
Tlingit-Haida (Alaska Native) (0)	0	<0.01
Tohono O'Odham (0)	0	<0.01
Tsimshian (Alaska Native) (0)	0	<0.01
Ute (0)	0	<0.01
Yakama (0)	0	<0.01
Yaqui (0)	0	<0.01
Yuman (0)	0	<0.01
Yup'ik (Alaska Native) (0)	0	<0.01
Asian (494)	613	0.80
Not Hispanic (492)	601	0.78
Hispanic (2)	12	0.02
Bangladeshi (0)	0	<0.01
Bhutanese (0)	0	<0.01
Burmese (0)	0	<0.01
Cambodian (9)	16	0.02
Chinese, ex. Taiwanese (72)	89	0.12
Filipino (78)	102	0.13
Hmong (0)	0	<0.01
Indian (205)	221	0.29
Indonesian (1)	2	<0.01
Japanese (21)	41	0.05
Korean (34)	55	0.07
Laotian (4)	4	0.01
Malaysian (0)	0	<0.01
Nepalese (0)	0	<0.01
Pakistani (7)	7	0.01
Sri Lankan (1)	1	<0.01
Taiwanese (1)	5	0.01
Thai (5)	8	0.01
Vietnamese (36)	47	0.06
Hawaii Native/Pacific Islander (17)	43	0.06
Not Hispanic (15)	33	0.04
Hispanic (2)	10	0.01
Fijian (0)	0	<0.01
Guamanian/Chamorro (6)	16	0.02
Marshallese (0)	0	<0.01
Native Hawaiian (2)	8	0.01
Samoan (3)	9	0.01
Tongan (0)	0	<0.01
White (54,844)	55,697	72.66
Not Hispanic (53,490)	54,182	70.69
Hispanic (1,354)	1,515	1.98

*Notes: † The Census 2010 population figure is used to calculate the percentages in the Hispanic Origin and Race categories. Ancestry percentages are based on the 2006-2010 American Community Survey population (not shown); ‡ Numbers in parentheses indicate the number of people reporting a single ancestry; * Numbers in parentheses indicate the number of persons reporting this race alone, not in combination with any other race; Please refer to the Explanation of Data for more information.*

Laurens County
Population: 66,537

Ancestry	Population	%
Afghan (0)	0	<0.01
African, Sub-Saharan (142)	161	0.24
African (142)	161	0.24
Cape Verdean (0)	0	<0.01
Ethiopian (0)	0	<0.01
Ghanaian (0)	0	<0.01
Kenyan (0)	0	<0.01
Liberian (0)	0	<0.01
Nigerian (0)	0	<0.01
Senegalese (0)	0	<0.01
Sierra Leonean (0)	0	<0.01
Somalian (0)	0	<0.01
South African (0)	0	<0.01
Sudanese (0)	0	<0.01
Ugandan (0)	0	<0.01
Zimbabwean (0)	0	<0.01
Other Sub-Saharan African (0)	0	<0.01
Albanian (0)	0	<0.01
Alsatian (0)	0	<0.01
American (7,888)	7,888	11.77
Arab (16)	38	0.06
Arab (0)	0	<0.01
Egyptian (0)	0	<0.01
Iraqi (0)	0	<0.01
Jordanian (0)	0	<0.01
Lebanese (5)	17	0.03
Moroccan (0)	0	<0.01
Palestinian (0)	0	<0.01
Syrian (11)	21	0.03
Other Arab (0)	0	<0.01
Armenian (0)	0	<0.01
Assyrian/Chaldean/Syriac (0)	0	<0.01
Australian (16)	16	0.02
Austrian (0)	51	0.08
Basque (0)	0	<0.01
Belgian (0)	0	<0.01
Brazilian (12)	37	0.06
British (96)	158	0.24
Bulgarian (0)	0	<0.01
Cajun (0)	0	<0.01
Canadian (10)	21	0.03
Carpatho Rusyn (0)	0	<0.01
Celtic (0)	0	<0.01
Croatian (0)	0	<0.01
Cypriot (0)	0	<0.01
Czech (37)	57	0.09
Czechoslovakian (20)	30	0.04
Danish (9)	212	0.32
Dutch (75)	607	0.91
Eastern European (0)	0	<0.01
English (2,712)	5,886	8.78
Estonian (0)	0	<0.01
European (437)	489	0.73
Finnish (27)	27	0.04
French, ex. Basque (316)	1,056	1.58
French Canadian (141)	219	0.33
German (2,619)	6,478	9.66
German Russian (0)	0	<0.01
Greek (0)	49	0.07
Guyanese (0)	0	<0.01
Hungarian (120)	131	0.20
Icelander (0)	0	<0.01
Iranian (2)	2	<0.01
Irish (2,378)	6,579	9.82
Israeli (0)	0	<0.01
Italian (255)	932	1.39
Latvian (0)	0	<0.01
Lithuanian (0)	18	0.03
Luxemburger (0)	0	<0.01
Macedonian (0)	0	<0.01
Maltese (0)	0	<0.01
New Zealander (0)	0	<0.01
Northern European (0)	0	<0.01
Norwegian (16)	122	0.18
Pennsylvania German (399)	399	0.60

	Population	%
Polish (228)	444	0.66
Portuguese (0)	7	0.01
Romanian (12)	12	0.02
Russian (0)	61	0.09
Scandinavian (14)	81	0.12
Scotch-Irish (1,379)	2,448	3.65
Scottish (549)	1,149	1.71
Serbian (0)	0	<0.01
Slavic (0)	0	<0.01
Slovak (11)	11	0.02
Slovene (0)	0	<0.01
Soviet Union (0)	0	<0.01
Swedish (70)	150	0.22
Swiss (19)	42	0.06
Turkish (0)	0	<0.01
Ukrainian (0)	43	0.06
Welsh (50)	272	0.41
West Indian, ex. Hispanic (31)	117	0.17
Bahamian (0)	0	<0.01
Barbadian (0)	0	<0.01
Belizean (0)	0	<0.01
Bermudan (0)	0	<0.01
British West Indian (0)	59	0.09
Dutch West Indian (0)	0	<0.01
Haitian (0)	0	<0.01
Jamaican (31)	31	0.05
Trinidadian/Tobagonian (0)	0	<0.01
U.S. Virgin Islander (0)	0	<0.01
West Indian (0)	27	0.04
Other West Indian (0)	0	<0.01
Yugoslavian (0)	0	<0.01

Hispanic Origin	Population	%
Hispanic or Latino (of any race)	2,729	4.10
Central American, ex. Mexican	397	0.60
Costa Rican	5	0.01
Guatemalan	275	0.41
Honduran	86	0.13
Nicaraguan	2	<0.01
Panamanian	11	0.02
Salvadoran	18	0.03
Other Central American	0	<0.01
Cuban	37	0.06
Dominican Republic	20	0.03
Mexican	1,760	2.65
Puerto Rican	196	0.29
South American	95	0.14
Argentinean	3	<0.01
Bolivian	0	<0.01
Chilean	3	<0.01
Colombian	60	0.09
Ecuadorian	9	0.01
Paraguayan	3	<0.01
Peruvian	4	0.01
Uruguayan	7	0.01
Venezuelan	4	0.01
Other South American	2	<0.01
Other Hispanic or Latino	224	0.34

Race*	Population	%
African-American/Black (16,933)	17,406	26.16
Not Hispanic (16,808)	17,255	25.93
Hispanic (125)	151	0.23
American Indian/Alaska Native (153)	369	0.55
Not Hispanic (137)	342	0.51
Hispanic (16)	27	0.04
Alaska Athabascan (Ala. Nat.) (0)	0	<0.01
Aleut (Alaska Native) (0)	1	<0.01
Apache (2)	7	0.01
Arapaho (0)	0	<0.01
Blackfeet (3)	13	0.02
Canadian/French Am. Ind. (0)	0	<0.01
Central American Ind. (0)	0	<0.01
Cherokee (52)	150	0.23
Cheyenne (0)	0	<0.01
Chickasaw (0)	0	<0.01
Chippewa (1)	4	0.01
Choctaw (1)	3	<0.01
Colville (0)	0	<0.01

	Population	%
Comanche (0)	0	<0.01
Cree (1)	1	<0.01
Creek (0)	0	<0.01
Crow (1)	3	<0.01
Delaware (0)	0	<0.01
Hopi (0)	1	<0.01
Houma (0)	0	<0.01
Inupiat (Alaska Native) (1)	1	<0.01
Iroquois (1)	5	0.01
Kiowa (0)	0	<0.01
Lumbee (12)	12	0.02
Menominee (0)	0	<0.01
Mexican American Ind. (2)	3	<0.01
Navajo (1)	3	<0.01
Osage (0)	0	<0.01
Ottawa (0)	0	<0.01
Paiute (0)	0	<0.01
Pima (0)	0	<0.01
Potawatomi (0)	1	<0.01
Pueblo (0)	0	<0.01
Puget Sound Salish (0)	1	<0.01
Seminole (0)	0	<0.01
Shoshone (0)	0	<0.01
Sioux (2)	8	0.01
South American Ind. (0)	0	<0.01
Spanish American Ind. (1)	1	<0.01
Tlingit-Haida (Alaska Native) (0)	0	<0.01
Tohono O'Odham (0)	0	<0.01
Tsimshian (Alaska Native) (0)	2	<0.01
Ute (0)	0	<0.01
Yakama (0)	0	<0.01
Yaqui (0)	0	<0.01
Yuman (0)	0	<0.01
Yup'ik (Alaska Native) (0)	0	<0.01
Asian (183)	303	0.46
Not Hispanic (175)	283	0.43
Hispanic (8)	20	0.03
Bangladeshi (0)	0	<0.01
Bhutanese (0)	0	<0.01
Burmese (0)	0	<0.01
Cambodian (4)	5	0.01
Chinese, ex. Taiwanese (20)	26	0.04
Filipino (34)	72	0.11
Hmong (1)	1	<0.01
Indian (67)	91	0.14
Indonesian (0)	0	<0.01
Japanese (9)	26	0.04
Korean (12)	24	0.04
Laotian (0)	0	<0.01
Malaysian (0)	0	<0.01
Nepalese (0)	0	<0.01
Pakistani (2)	2	<0.01
Sri Lankan (0)	0	<0.01
Taiwanese (0)	0	<0.01
Thai (3)	5	0.01
Vietnamese (12)	29	0.04
Hawaii Native/Pacific Islander (34)	66	0.10
Not Hispanic (25)	46	0.07
Hispanic (9)	20	0.03
Fijian (0)	0	<0.01
Guamanian/Chamorro (13)	24	0.04
Marshallese (0)	0	<0.01
Native Hawaiian (4)	10	0.02
Samoan (3)	5	0.01
Tongan (0)	3	<0.01
White (46,848)	47,613	71.56
Not Hispanic (45,900)	46,553	69.97
Hispanic (948)	1,060	1.59

*Notes: † The Census 2010 population figure is used to calculate the percentages in the Hispanic Origin and Race categories. Ancestry percentages are based on the 2006-2010 American Community Survey population (not shown); ‡ Numbers in parentheses indicate the number of people reporting a single ancestry; * Numbers in parentheses indicate the number of persons reporting this race alone, not in combination with any other race; Please refer to the Explanation of Data for more information.*

Lexington County

Population: 262,391

Ancestry	Population	%
Afghan (0)	0	<0.01
African, Sub-Saharan (2,011)	2,216	0.88
African (1,903)	2,058	0.81
Cape Verdean (0)	0	<0.01
Ethiopian (0)	0	<0.01
Ghanaian (17)	25	0.01
Kenyan (0)	42	0.02
Liberian (0)	0	<0.01
Nigerian (0)	0	<0.01
Senegalese (0)	0	<0.01
Sierra Leonean (0)	0	<0.01
Somalian (0)	0	<0.01
South African (30)	30	0.01
Sudanese (39)	39	0.02
Ugandan (0)	0	<0.01
Zimbabwean (0)	0	<0.01
Other Sub-Saharan African (22)	22	0.01
Albanian (0)	0	<0.01
Alsatian (0)	0	<0.01
American (35,404)	35,404	14.02
Arab (336)	474	0.19
Arab (96)	96	0.04
Egyptian (24)	58	0.02
Iraqi (0)	0	<0.01
Jordanian (0)	0	<0.01
Lebanese (152)	219	0.09
Moroccan (0)	12	<0.01
Palestinian (50)	50	0.02
Syrian (14)	32	0.01
Other Arab (0)	7	<0.01
Armenian (12)	69	0.03
Assyrian/Chaldean/Syriac (0)	0	<0.01
Australian (9)	9	<0.01
Austrian (52)	211	0.08
Basque (0)	0	<0.01
Belgian (21)	36	0.01
Brazilian (71)	110	0.04
British (605)	1,207	0.48
Bulgarian (68)	173	0.07
Cajun (0)	13	0.01
Canadian (236)	323	0.13
Carpatho Rusyn (0)	0	<0.01
Celtic (73)	73	0.03
Croatian (12)	52	0.02
Cypriot (0)	0	<0.01
Czech (187)	573	0.23
Czechoslovakian (0)	69	0.03
Danish (121)	569	0.23
Dutch (757)	3,177	1.26
Eastern European (19)	28	0.01
English (15,788)	31,576	12.50
Estonian (0)	0	<0.01
European (2,285)	2,519	1.00
Finnish (70)	318	0.13
French, ex. Basque (1,761)	5,776	2.29
French Canadian (643)	1,061	0.42
German (16,528)	43,455	17.21
German Russian (0)	0	<0.01
Greek (491)	880	0.35
Guyanese (6)	6	<0.01
Hungarian (336)	673	0.27
Icelander (0)	0	<0.01
Iranian (205)	221	0.09
Irish (9,910)	29,928	11.85
Israeli (58)	110	0.04
Italian (3,056)	8,031	3.18
Latvian (42)	42	0.02
Lithuanian (54)	107	0.04
Luxemburger (0)	0	<0.01
Macedonian (18)	18	0.01
Maltese (0)	38	0.02
New Zealander (0)	0	<0.01
Northern European (160)	160	0.06
Norwegian (353)	941	0.37
Pennsylvania German (8)	15	0.01

Ancestry (cont.)	Population	%
Polish (1,309)	3,633	1.44
Portuguese (138)	371	0.15
Romanian (55)	104	0.04
Russian (432)	990	0.39
Scandinavian (101)	366	0.14
Scotch-Irish (5,334)	9,197	3.64
Scottish (2,290)	6,077	2.41
Serbian (41)	69	0.03
Slavic (6)	26	0.01
Slovak (31)	148	0.06
Slovene (31)	49	0.02
Soviet Union (0)	0	<0.01
Swedish (479)	1,734	0.69
Swiss (187)	679	0.27
Turkish (81)	143	0.06
Ukrainian (151)	344	0.14
Welsh (296)	1,282	0.51
West Indian, ex. Hispanic (348)	609	0.24
Bahamian (14)	47	0.02
Barbadian (0)	0	<0.01
Belizean (39)	39	0.02
Bermudan (20)	20	0.01
British West Indian (0)	0	<0.01
Dutch West Indian (10)	10	<0.01
Haitian (0)	8	<0.01
Jamaican (129)	177	0.07
Trinidadian/Tobagonian (100)	100	0.04
U.S. Virgin Islander (0)	0	<0.01
West Indian (18)	190	0.08
Other West Indian (18)	18	0.01
Yugoslavian (92)	130	0.05

Hispanic Origin	Population	%
Hispanic or Latino (of any race)	14,529	5.54
Central American, ex. Mexican	1,518	0.58
Costa Rican	52	0.02
Guatemalan	719	0.27
Honduran	426	0.16
Nicaraguan	65	0.02
Panamanian	101	0.04
Salvadoran	149	0.06
Other Central American	6	<0.01
Cuban	444	0.17
Dominican Republic	154	0.06
Mexican	9,036	3.44
Puerto Rican	1,796	0.68
South American	640	0.24
Argentinean	78	0.03
Bolivian	13	<0.01
Chilean	23	0.01
Colombian	204	0.08
Ecuadorian	92	0.04
Paraguayan	6	<0.01
Peruvian	127	0.05
Uruguayan	11	<0.01
Venezuelan	79	0.03
Other South American	7	<0.01
Other Hispanic or Latino	941	0.36

Race*	Population	%
African-American/Black (37,522)	39,819	15.18
Not Hispanic (36,995)	38,968	14.85
Hispanic (527)	851	0.32
American Indian/Alaska Native (1,134)	2,674	1.02
Not Hispanic (957)	2,338	0.89
Hispanic (177)	336	0.13
Alaska Athabascan (Ala. Nat.) (1)	1	<0.01
Aleut (Alaska Native) (2)	4	<0.01
Apache (3)	12	<0.01
Arapaho (0)	0	<0.01
Blackfeet (8)	63	0.02
Canadian/French Am. Ind. (0)	0	<0.01
Central American Ind. (3)	3	<0.01
Cherokee (208)	717	0.27
Cheyenne (4)	5	<0.01
Chickasaw (5)	13	<0.01
Chippewa (14)	25	0.01
Choctaw (10)	26	0.01
Colville (0)	0	<0.01

Race* (cont.)	Population	%
Comanche (4)	14	0.01
Cree (1)	2	<0.01
Creek (15)	30	0.01
Crow (0)	3	<0.01
Delaware (1)	6	<0.01
Hopi (0)	0	<0.01
Houma (2)	2	<0.01
Inupiat (Alaska Native) (3)	5	<0.01
Iroquois (25)	37	0.01
Kiowa (0)	0	<0.01
Lumbee (68)	115	0.04
Menominee (0)	0	<0.01
Mexican American Ind. (64)	102	0.04
Navajo (5)	14	0.01
Osage (0)	2	<0.01
Ottawa (0)	0	<0.01
Paiute (0)	1	<0.01
Pima (0)	0	<0.01
Potawatomi (7)	10	<0.01
Pueblo (13)	15	0.01
Puget Sound Salish (0)	0	<0.01
Seminole (7)	17	0.01
Shoshone (0)	0	<0.01
Sioux (18)	43	0.02
South American Ind. (10)	25	0.01
Spanish American Ind. (5)	6	<0.01
Tlingit-Haida (Alaska Native) (5)	11	<0.01
Tohono O'Odham (0)	0	<0.01
Tsimshian (Alaska Native) (0)	1	<0.01
Ute (0)	0	<0.01
Yakama (0)	0	<0.01
Yaqui (1)	1	<0.01
Yuman (0)	0	<0.01
Yup'ik (Alaska Native) (1)	1	<0.01
Asian (3,729)	4,646	1.77
Not Hispanic (3,693)	4,545	1.73
Hispanic (36)	101	0.04
Bangladeshi (39)	41	0.02
Bhutanese (0)	0	<0.01
Burmese (27)	31	0.01
Cambodian (8)	16	0.01
Chinese, ex. Taiwanese (776)	941	0.36
Filipino (284)	497	0.19
Hmong (6)	8	<0.01
Indian (1,500)	1,628	0.62
Indonesian (4)	11	<0.01
Japanese (120)	243	0.09
Korean (272)	418	0.16
Laotian (69)	90	0.03
Malaysian (0)	5	<0.01
Nepalese (0)	0	<0.01
Pakistani (52)	65	0.02
Sri Lankan (9)	9	<0.01
Taiwanese (27)	30	0.01
Thai (37)	88	0.03
Vietnamese (334)	433	0.17
Hawaii Native/Pacific Islander (130)	303	0.12
Not Hispanic (105)	244	0.09
Hispanic (25)	59	0.02
Fijian (0)	2	<0.01
Guamanian/Chamorro (48)	80	0.03
Marshallese (0)	0	<0.01
Native Hawaiian (28)	80	0.03
Samoan (8)	26	0.01
Tongan (1)	6	<0.01
White (208,023)	212,168	80.86
Not Hispanic (201,946)	205,316	78.25
Hispanic (6,077)	6,852	2.61

Oconee County

Population: 74,273

Ancestry	Population	%
Afghan (0)	0	<0.01
African, Sub-Saharan (94)	117	0.16
African (86)	96	0.13
Cape Verdean (0)	0	<0.01
Ethiopian (0)	0	<0.01
Ghanaian (0)	0	<0.01
Kenyan (0)	0	<0.01
Liberian (0)	0	<0.01
Nigerian (0)	0	<0.01
Senegalese (0)	0	<0.01
Sierra Leonean (0)	0	<0.01
Somalian (0)	0	<0.01
South African (0)	0	<0.01
Sudanese (0)	13	0.02
Ugandan (0)	0	<0.01
Zimbabwean (0)	0	<0.01
Other Sub-Saharan African (8)	8	0.01
Albanian (0)	12	0.02
Alsatian (0)	0	<0.01
American (10,525)	10,525	14.41
Arab (214)	214	0.29
Arab (70)	70	0.10
Egyptian (40)	40	0.05
Iraqi (0)	0	<0.01
Jordanian (0)	0	<0.01
Lebanese (26)	26	0.04
Moroccan (0)	0	<0.01
Palestinian (78)	78	0.11
Syrian (0)	0	<0.01
Other Arab (0)	0	<0.01
Armenian (0)	12	0.02
Assyrian/Chaldean/Syriac (0)	0	<0.01
Australian (11)	29	0.04
Austrian (26)	162	0.22
Basque (0)	0	<0.01
Belgian (26)	97	0.13
Brazilian (11)	11	0.02
British (218)	344	0.47
Bulgarian (0)	0	<0.01
Cajun (0)	0	<0.01
Canadian (61)	125	0.17
Carpatho Rusyn (0)	0	<0.01
Celtic (0)	13	0.02
Croatian (34)	53	0.07
Cypriot (0)	0	<0.01
Czech (39)	91	0.12
Czechoslovakian (0)	25	0.03
Danish (45)	213	0.29
Dutch (293)	961	1.32
Eastern European (0)	11	0.02
English (3,992)	7,949	10.88
Estonian (0)	0	<0.01
European (450)	546	0.75
Finnish (26)	61	0.08
French, ex. Basque (316)	1,373	1.88
French Canadian (15)	293	0.40
German (3,726)	9,879	13.53
German Russian (0)	0	<0.01
Greek (11)	156	0.21
Guyanese (0)	0	<0.01
Hungarian (74)	184	0.25
Icelander (0)	0	<0.01
Iranian (0)	0	<0.01
Irish (4,129)	10,252	14.04
Israeli (0)	0	<0.01
Italian (526)	1,102	1.51
Latvian (0)	0	<0.01
Lithuanian (22)	32	0.04
Luxemburger (0)	0	<0.01
Macedonian (0)	0	<0.01
Maltese (0)	0	<0.01
New Zealander (0)	0	<0.01
Northern European (0)	0	<0.01
Norwegian (108)	394	0.54
Pennsylvania German (0)	12	0.02
Polish (356)	856	1.17
Portuguese (17)	64	0.09
Romanian (18)	30	0.04
Russian (114)	208	0.28
Scandinavian (64)	74	0.10
Scotch-Irish (1,820)	2,870	3.93
Scottish (814)	2,029	2.78
Serbian (0)	0	<0.01
Slavic (12)	23	0.03
Slovak (54)	62	0.08
Slovene (14)	28	0.04
Soviet Union (0)	0	<0.01
Swedish (119)	514	0.70
Swiss (37)	179	0.25
Turkish (28)	52	0.07
Ukrainian (15)	29	0.04
Welsh (75)	572	0.78
West Indian, ex. Hispanic (78)	95	0.13
Bahamian (0)	0	<0.01
Barbadian (0)	0	<0.01
Belizean (0)	0	<0.01
Bermudan (0)	0	<0.01
British West Indian (0)	0	<0.01
Dutch West Indian (0)	3	<0.01
Haitian (68)	68	0.09
Jamaican (10)	24	0.03
Trinidadian/Tobagonian (0)	0	<0.01
U.S. Virgin Islander (0)	0	<0.01
West Indian (0)	0	<0.01
Other West Indian (0)	0	<0.01
Yugoslavian (0)	0	<0.01

Hispanic Origin	Population	%
Hispanic or Latino (of any race)	3,349	4.51
Central American, ex. Mexican	215	0.29
Costa Rican	12	0.02
Guatemalan	39	0.05
Honduran	41	0.06
Nicaraguan	10	0.01
Panamanian	5	0.01
Salvadoran	108	0.15
Other Central American	0	<0.01
Cuban	41	0.06
Dominican Republic	10	0.01
Mexican	2,542	3.42
Puerto Rican	163	0.22
South American	91	0.12
Argentinean	8	0.01
Bolivian	4	0.01
Chilean	4	0.01
Colombian	28	0.04
Ecuadorian	19	0.03
Paraguayan	7	0.01
Peruvian	6	0.01
Uruguayan	13	0.02
Venezuelan	1	<0.01
Other South American	1	<0.01
Other Hispanic or Latino	287	0.39

Race*	Population	%
African-American/Black (5,613)	6,203	8.35
Not Hispanic (5,550)	6,091	8.20
Hispanic (63)	112	0.15
American Indian/Alaska Native (176)	529	0.71
Not Hispanic (152)	473	0.64
Hispanic (24)	56	0.08
Alaska Athabascan (Ala. Nat.) (0)	0	<0.01
Aleut (Alaska Native) (0)	0	<0.01
Apache (1)	1	<0.01
Arapaho (0)	0	<0.01
Blackfeet (1)	8	0.01
Canadian/French Am. Ind. (1)	4	0.01
Central American Ind. (1)	1	<0.01
Cherokee (57)	230	0.31
Cheyenne (0)	2	<0.01
Chickasaw (1)	1	<0.01
Chippewa (7)	12	0.02
Choctaw (3)	3	<0.01
Colville (0)	0	<0.01
Comanche (0)	0	<0.01
Cree (0)	2	<0.01
Creek (8)	9	0.01
Crow (0)	0	<0.01
Delaware (3)	3	<0.01
Hopi (1)	1	<0.01
Houma (0)	0	<0.01
Inupiat (Alaska Native) (0)	0	<0.01
Iroquois (1)	3	<0.01
Kiowa (0)	0	<0.01
Lumbee (11)	17	0.02
Menominee (0)	0	<0.01
Mexican American Ind. (3)	3	<0.01
Navajo (0)	1	<0.01
Osage (0)	0	<0.01
Ottawa (0)	0	<0.01
Paiute (0)	0	<0.01
Pima (0)	0	<0.01
Potawatomi (1)	1	<0.01
Pueblo (0)	0	<0.01
Puget Sound Salish (0)	0	<0.01
Seminole (0)	4	0.01
Shoshone (0)	2	<0.01
Sioux (9)	10	0.01
South American Ind. (2)	8	0.01
Spanish American Ind. (3)	3	<0.01
Tlingit-Haida (Alaska Native) (2)	2	<0.01
Tohono O'Odham (1)	3	<0.01
Tsimshian (Alaska Native) (0)	0	<0.01
Ute (0)	0	<0.01
Yakama (0)	0	<0.01
Yaqui (0)	0	<0.01
Yuman (0)	0	<0.01
Yup'ik (Alaska Native) (0)	0	<0.01
Asian (436)	584	0.79
Not Hispanic (421)	549	0.74
Hispanic (15)	35	0.05
Bangladeshi (0)	0	<0.01
Bhutanese (0)	0	<0.01
Burmese (0)	1	<0.01
Cambodian (1)	3	<0.01
Chinese, ex. Taiwanese (79)	96	0.13
Filipino (60)	81	0.11
Hmong (0)	0	<0.01
Indian (117)	124	0.17
Indonesian (4)	5	0.01
Japanese (40)	69	0.09
Korean (36)	61	0.08
Laotian (1)	2	<0.01
Malaysian (0)	0	<0.01
Nepalese (0)	0	<0.01
Pakistani (11)	11	0.01
Sri Lankan (3)	3	<0.01
Taiwanese (11)	12	0.02
Thai (7)	16	0.02
Vietnamese (40)	41	0.06
Hawaii Native/Pacific Islander (10)	49	0.07
Not Hispanic (8)	39	0.05
Hispanic (2)	10	0.01
Fijian (0)	0	<0.01
Guamanian/Chamorro (2)	5	0.01
Marshallese (0)	0	<0.01
Native Hawaiian (5)	24	0.03
Samoan (2)	5	0.01
Tongan (0)	0	<0.01
White (65,177)	66,271	89.23
Not Hispanic (63,807)	64,693	87.10
Hispanic (1,370)	1,578	2.12

Notes: † The Census 2010 population figure is used to calculate the percentages in the Hispanic Origin and Race categories. Ancestry percentages are based on the 2006-2010 American Community Survey population (not shown); ‡ Numbers in parentheses indicate the number of people reporting a single ancestry; * Numbers in parentheses indicate the number of persons reporting this race alone, not in combination with any other race; Please refer to the Explanation of Data for more information.

Orangeburg County

Population: 92,501

Ancestry	Population	%
Afghan (0)	0	<0.01
African, Sub-Saharan (650)	713	0.77
African (515)	557	0.60
Cape Verdean (0)	0	<0.01
Ethiopian (0)	0	<0.01
Ghanaian (0)	0	<0.01
Kenyan (0)	0	<0.01
Liberian (0)	21	0.02
Nigerian (13)	13	0.01
Senegalese (40)	40	0.04
Sierra Leonean (0)	0	<0.01
Somalian (0)	0	<0.01
South African (0)	0	<0.01
Sudanese (0)	0	<0.01
Ugandan (28)	28	0.03
Zimbabwean (0)	0	<0.01
Other Sub-Saharan African (54)	54	0.06
Albanian (0)	0	<0.01
Alsatian (0)	0	<0.01
American (7,121)	7,121	7.70
Arab (34)	45	0.05
Arab (0)	0	<0.01
Egyptian (0)	0	<0.01
Iraqi (0)	0	<0.01
Jordanian (0)	0	<0.01
Lebanese (0)	11	0.01
Moroccan (0)	0	<0.01
Palestinian (0)	0	<0.01
Syrian (34)	34	0.04
Other Arab (0)	0	<0.01
Armenian (0)	0	<0.01
Assyrian/Chaldean/Syriac (0)	0	<0.01
Australian (0)	0	<0.01
Austrian (7)	18	0.02
Basque (0)	0	<0.01
Belgian (0)	11	0.01
Brazilian (18)	18	0.02
British (77)	80	0.09
Bulgarian (19)	19	0.02
Cajun (9)	9	0.01
Canadian (0)	27	0.03
Carpatho Rusyn (0)	0	<0.01
Celtic (0)	0	<0.01
Croatian (0)	15	0.02
Cypriot (0)	0	<0.01
Czech (50)	61	0.07
Czechoslovakian (0)	0	<0.01
Danish (14)	86	0.09
Dutch (165)	454	0.49
Eastern European (13)	13	0.01
English (2,103)	3,541	3.83
Estonian (0)	0	<0.01
European (409)	433	0.47
Finnish (11)	11	0.01
French, ex. Basque (177)	658	0.71
French Canadian (33)	79	0.09
German (2,207)	4,739	5.12
German Russian (0)	15	0.02
Greek (20)	58	0.06
Guyanese (9)	9	0.01
Hungarian (0)	66	0.07
Icelander (2)	2	<0.01
Iranian (0)	0	<0.01
Irish (1,302)	3,621	3.92
Israeli (0)	0	<0.01
Italian (201)	603	0.65
Latvian (0)	0	<0.01
Lithuanian (10)	10	0.01
Luxemburger (0)	0	<0.01
Macedonian (0)	0	<0.01
Maltese (0)	0	<0.01
New Zealander (0)	0	<0.01
Northern European (16)	16	0.02
Norwegian (33)	104	0.11
Pennsylvania German (0)	11	0.01

	Population	%
Polish (154)	272	0.29
Portuguese (2)	10	0.01
Romanian (67)	82	0.09
Russian (7)	29	0.03
Scandinavian (2)	2	<0.01
Scotch-Irish (477)	831	0.90
Scottish (181)	397	0.43
Serbian (0)	0	<0.01
Slavic (0)	4	<0.01
Slovak (0)	9	0.01
Slovene (0)	0	<0.01
Soviet Union (0)	0	<0.01
Swedish (39)	98	0.11
Swiss (14)	90	0.10
Turkish (24)	37	0.04
Ukrainian (2)	2	<0.01
Welsh (3)	59	0.06
West Indian, ex. Hispanic (261)	380	0.41
Bahamian (0)	15	0.02
Barbadian (16)	16	0.02
Belizean (0)	0	<0.01
Bermudan (0)	0	<0.01
British West Indian (0)	0	<0.01
Dutch West Indian (0)	0	<0.01
Haitian (0)	6	0.01
Jamaican (192)	242	0.26
Trinidadian/Tobagonian (42)	42	0.05
U.S. Virgin Islander (0)	0	<0.01
West Indian (11)	59	0.06
Other West Indian (0)	0	<0.01
Yugoslavian (0)	0	<0.01

Hispanic Origin	Population	%
Hispanic or Latino (of any race)	1,767	1.91
Central American, ex. Mexican	120	0.13
Costa Rican	6	0.01
Guatemalan	15	0.02
Honduran	33	0.04
Nicaraguan	5	0.01
Panamanian	27	0.03
Salvadoran	25	0.03
Other Central American	9	0.01
Cuban	87	0.09
Dominican Republic	15	0.02
Mexican	1,051	1.14
Puerto Rican	204	0.22
South American	44	0.05
Argentinean	5	0.01
Bolivian	0	<0.01
Chilean	1	<0.01
Colombian	24	0.03
Ecuadorian	2	<0.01
Paraguayan	0	<0.01
Peruvian	6	0.01
Uruguayan	1	<0.01
Venezuelan	1	<0.01
Other South American	4	<0.01
Other Hispanic or Latino	246	0.27

Race*	Population	%
African-American/Black (57,535)	58,197	62.91
Not Hispanic (57,286)	57,878	62.57
Hispanic (249)	319	0.34
American Indian/Alaska Native (491)	910	0.98
Not Hispanic (468)	859	0.93
Hispanic (23)	51	0.06
Alaska Athabascan (Ala. Nat.) (0)	0	<0.01
Aleut (Alaska Native) (0)	0	<0.01
Apache (0)	4	<0.01
Arapaho (0)	0	<0.01
Blackfeet (5)	22	0.02
Canadian/French Am. Ind. (0)	0	<0.01
Central American Ind. (0)	1	<0.01
Cherokee (58)	178	0.19
Cheyenne (0)	0	<0.01
Chickasaw (2)	9	0.01
Chippewa (5)	6	0.01
Choctaw (0)	2	<0.01
Colville (0)	0	<0.01

	Population	%
Comanche (0)	0	<0.01
Cree (1)	2	<0.01
Creek (11)	20	0.02
Crow (0)	0	<0.01
Delaware (1)	1	<0.01
Hopi (1)	1	<0.01
Houma (0)	0	<0.01
Inupiat (Alaska Native) (0)	0	<0.01
Iroquois (0)	1	<0.01
Kiowa (0)	0	<0.01
Lumbee (9)	13	0.01
Menominee (0)	0	<0.01
Mexican American Ind. (9)	21	0.02
Navajo (0)	4	<0.01
Osage (0)	0	<0.01
Ottawa (0)	0	<0.01
Paiute (0)	0	<0.01
Pima (0)	0	<0.01
Potawatomi (0)	0	<0.01
Pueblo (0)	0	<0.01
Puget Sound Salish (0)	0	<0.01
Seminole (0)	2	<0.01
Shoshone (0)	0	<0.01
Sioux (71)	79	0.09
South American Ind. (0)	1	<0.01
Spanish American Ind. (0)	0	<0.01
Tlingit-Haida (Alaska Native) (1)	2	<0.01
Tohono O'Odham (0)	0	<0.01
Tsimshian (Alaska Native) (0)	0	<0.01
Ute (0)	0	<0.01
Yakama (0)	0	<0.01
Yaqui (0)	0	<0.01
Yuman (0)	0	<0.01
Yup'ik (Alaska Native) (0)	0	<0.01
Asian (752)	941	1.02
Not Hispanic (751)	926	1.00
Hispanic (1)	15	0.02
Bangladeshi (17)	19	0.02
Bhutanese (0)	0	<0.01
Burmese (0)	0	<0.01
Cambodian (0)	0	<0.01
Chinese, ex. Taiwanese (126)	149	0.16
Filipino (49)	95	0.10
Hmong (0)	0	<0.01
Indian (385)	428	0.46
Indonesian (11)	11	0.01
Japanese (34)	48	0.05
Korean (23)	39	0.04
Laotian (3)	3	<0.01
Malaysian (1)	4	<0.01
Nepalese (0)	0	<0.01
Pakistani (20)	23	0.02
Sri Lankan (10)	10	0.01
Taiwanese (4)	8	0.01
Thai (12)	16	0.02
Vietnamese (39)	54	0.06
Hawaii Native/Pacific Islander (14)	61	0.07
Not Hispanic (12)	59	0.06
Hispanic (2)	2	<0.01
Fijian (0)	0	<0.01
Guamanian/Chamorro (6)	17	0.02
Marshallese (0)	0	<0.01
Native Hawaiian (3)	17	0.02
Samoan (1)	3	<0.01
Tongan (0)	0	<0.01
White (31,770)	32,562	35.20
Not Hispanic (31,206)	31,907	34.49
Hispanic (564)	655	0.71

Pickens County

Population: 119,224

Ancestry	Population	%
Afghan (0)	0	<0.01
African, Sub-Saharan (272)	330	0.28
African (140)	165	0.14
Cape Verdean (0)	0	<0.01
Ethiopian (0)	0	<0.01
Ghanaian (93)	93	0.08
Kenyan (0)	0	<0.01
Liberian (0)	0	<0.01
Nigerian (9)	12	0.01
Senegalese (0)	0	<0.01
Sierra Leonean (0)	0	<0.01
Somalian (0)	0	<0.01
South African (30)	60	0.05
Sudanese (0)	0	<0.01
Ugandan (0)	0	<0.01
Zimbabwean (0)	0	<0.01
Other Sub-Saharan African (0)	0	<0.01
Albanian (13)	13	0.01
Alsatian (0)	0	<0.01
American (18,970)	18,970	16.10
Arab (482)	547	0.46
Arab (85)	95	0.08
Egyptian (62)	62	0.05
Iraqi (0)	0	<0.01
Jordanian (11)	11	0.01
Lebanese (13)	68	0.06
Moroccan (0)	0	<0.01
Palestinian (12)	12	0.01
Syrian (81)	81	0.07
Other Arab (218)	218	0.19
Armenian (10)	10	0.01
Assyrian/Chaldean/Syriac (0)	0	<0.01
Australian (0)	0	<0.01
Austrian (102)	257	0.22
Basque (0)	0	<0.01
Belgian (12)	26	0.02
Brazilian (159)	177	0.15
British (588)	867	0.74
Bulgarian (0)	0	<0.01
Cajun (0)	28	0.02
Canadian (99)	171	0.15
Carpatho Rusyn (0)	13	0.01
Celtic (8)	18	0.02
Croatian (8)	28	0.02
Cypriot (0)	0	<0.01
Czech (20)	121	0.10
Czechoslovakian (45)	91	0.08
Danish (52)	198	0.17
Dutch (190)	1,186	1.01
Eastern European (0)	0	<0.01
English (6,033)	12,074	10.25
Estonian (0)	0	<0.01
European (817)	1,039	0.88
Finnish (74)	216	0.18
French, ex. Basque (568)	2,611	2.22
French Canadian (190)	332	0.28
German (4,762)	14,302	12.14
German Russian (0)	0	<0.01
Greek (174)	302	0.26
Guyanese (0)	0	<0.01
Hungarian (26)	223	0.19
Icelander (0)	0	<0.01
Iranian (27)	37	0.03
Irish (6,125)	15,152	12.86
Israeli (0)	0	<0.01
Italian (1,284)	3,637	3.09
Latvian (0)	13	0.01
Lithuanian (35)	143	0.12
Luxemburger (0)	0	<0.01
Macedonian (0)	0	<0.01
Maltese (0)	0	<0.01
New Zealander (0)	0	<0.01
Northern European (24)	33	0.03
Norwegian (160)	442	0.38
Pennsylvania German (31)	131	0.11

	Population	%
Polish (500)	1,541	1.31
Portuguese (34)	109	0.09
Romanian (10)	82	0.07
Russian (78)	408	0.35
Scandinavian (70)	244	0.21
Scotch-Irish (3,306)	5,612	4.76
Scottish (1,395)	3,162	2.68
Serbian (0)	0	<0.01
Slavic (34)	74	0.06
Slovak (53)	127	0.11
Slovene (19)	31	0.03
Soviet Union (0)	0	<0.01
Swedish (249)	867	0.74
Swiss (100)	327	0.28
Turkish (116)	141	0.12
Ukrainian (147)	287	0.24
Welsh (295)	809	0.69
West Indian, ex. Hispanic (65)	65	0.06
Bahamian (0)	0	<0.01
Barbadian (0)	0	<0.01
Belizean (0)	0	<0.01
Bermudan (0)	0	<0.01
British West Indian (0)	0	<0.01
Dutch West Indian (10)	10	0.01
Haitian (0)	0	<0.01
Jamaican (17)	17	0.01
Trinidadian/Tobagonian (26)	26	0.02
U.S. Virgin Islander (0)	0	<0.01
West Indian (12)	12	0.01
Other West Indian (0)	0	<0.01
Yugoslavian (0)	0	<0.01

Hispanic Origin	Population	%
Hispanic or Latino (of any race)	3,743	3.14
Central American, ex. Mexican	252	0.21
Costa Rican	39	0.03
Guatemalan	30	0.03
Honduran	58	0.05
Nicaraguan	36	0.03
Panamanian	26	0.02
Salvadoran	56	0.05
Other Central American	7	0.01
Cuban	160	0.13
Dominican Republic	37	0.03
Mexican	2,311	1.94
Puerto Rican	356	0.30
South American	344	0.29
Argentinean	15	0.01
Bolivian	4	<0.01
Chilean	9	0.01
Colombian	224	0.19
Ecuadorian	20	0.02
Paraguayan	4	<0.01
Peruvian	40	0.03
Uruguayan	1	<0.01
Venezuelan	27	0.02
Other South American	0	<0.01
Other Hispanic or Latino	283	0.24

Race*	Population	%
African-American/Black (7,854)	8,622	7.23
Not Hispanic (7,792)	8,518	7.14
Hispanic (62)	104	0.09
American Indian/Alaska Native (230)	761	0.64
Not Hispanic (210)	713	0.60
Hispanic (20)	48	0.04
Alaska Athabascan (Ala. Nat.) (0)	4	<0.01
Aleut (Alaska Native) (0)	2	<0.01
Apache (5)	8	0.01
Arapaho (0)	0	<0.01
Blackfeet (3)	18	0.02
Canadian/French Am. Ind. (0)	2	<0.01
Central American Ind. (0)	0	<0.01
Cherokee (69)	308	0.26
Cheyenne (0)	1	<0.01
Chickasaw (1)	3	<0.01
Chippewa (3)	6	0.01
Choctaw (6)	11	0.01
Colville (0)	0	<0.01

	Population	%
Comanche (0)	0	<0.01
Cree (1)	1	<0.01
Creek (2)	7	0.01
Crow (1)	2	<0.01
Delaware (0)	0	<0.01
Hopi (0)	0	<0.01
Houma (0)	0	<0.01
Inupiat (Alaska Native) (0)	2	<0.01
Iroquois (4)	7	0.01
Kiowa (0)	0	<0.01
Lumbee (18)	26	0.02
Menominee (0)	0	<0.01
Mexican American Ind. (2)	5	<0.01
Navajo (8)	13	0.01
Osage (0)	1	<0.01
Ottawa (0)	0	<0.01
Paiute (0)	0	<0.01
Pima (0)	0	<0.01
Potawatomi (1)	4	<0.01
Pueblo (0)	0	<0.01
Puget Sound Salish (0)	0	<0.01
Seminole (2)	7	0.01
Shoshone (0)	1	<0.01
Sioux (0)	12	0.01
South American Ind. (0)	4	<0.01
Spanish American Ind. (3)	3	<0.01
Tlingit-Haida (Alaska Native) (0)	2	<0.01
Tohono O'Odham (0)	0	<0.01
Tsimshian (Alaska Native) (0)	0	<0.01
Ute (0)	0	<0.01
Yakama (1)	1	<0.01
Yaqui (0)	0	<0.01
Yuman (0)	0	<0.01
Yup'ik (Alaska Native) (0)	0	<0.01
Asian (1,913)	2,255	1.89
Not Hispanic (1,900)	2,209	1.85
Hispanic (13)	46	0.04
Bangladeshi (7)	7	0.01
Bhutanese (0)	0	<0.01
Burmese (3)	3	<0.01
Cambodian (13)	16	0.01
Chinese, ex. Taiwanese (673)	726	0.61
Filipino (102)	176	0.15
Hmong (2)	4	<0.01
Indian (656)	700	0.59
Indonesian (8)	11	0.01
Japanese (47)	116	0.10
Korean (151)	192	0.16
Laotian (1)	11	0.01
Malaysian (1)	3	<0.01
Nepalese (12)	12	0.01
Pakistani (27)	34	0.03
Sri Lankan (29)	31	0.03
Taiwanese (33)	39	0.03
Thai (30)	43	0.04
Vietnamese (52)	71	0.06
Hawaii Native/Pacific Islander (14)	66	0.06
Not Hispanic (14)	49	0.04
Hispanic (0)	17	0.01
Fijian (0)	0	<0.01
Guamanian/Chamorro (5)	10	0.01
Marshallese (0)	0	<0.01
Native Hawaiian (7)	36	0.03
Samoan (1)	2	<0.01
Tongan (0)	2	<0.01
White (105,747)	107,396	90.08
Not Hispanic (103,958)	105,353	88.37
Hispanic (1,789)	2,043	1.71

*Notes: † The Census 2010 population figure is used to calculate the percentages in the Hispanic Origin and Race categories. Ancestry percentages are based on the 2006-2010 American Community Survey population (not shown); ‡ Numbers in parentheses indicate the number of people reporting a single ancestry; * Numbers in parentheses indicate the number of persons reporting this race alone, not in combination with any other race; Please refer to the Explanation of Data for more information.*

Richland County

Population: 384,504

Ancestry	Population	%
Afghan (0)	0	<0.01
African, Sub-Saharan (7,289)	8,403	2.26
African (6,830)	7,737	2.08
Cape Verdean (9)	9	<0.01
Ethiopian (64)	97	0.03
Ghanaian (5)	40	0.01
Kenyan (33)	86	0.02
Liberian (0)	51	0.01
Nigerian (73)	73	0.02
Senegalese (0)	0	<0.01
Sierra Leonean (0)	0	<0.01
Somalian (0)	0	<0.01
South African (7)	7	<0.01
Sudanese (69)	69	0.02
Ugandan (0)	0	<0.01
Zimbabwean (0)	0	<0.01
Other Sub-Saharan African (199)	234	0.06
Albanian (28)	28	0.01
Alsatian (14)	14	<0.01
American (26,531)	26,531	7.12
Arab (741)	1,359	0.36
Arab (111)	131	0.04
Egyptian (51)	184	0.05
Iraqi (23)	23	0.01
Jordanian (39)	39	0.01
Lebanese (288)	643	0.17
Moroccan (0)	54	0.01
Palestinian (0)	0	<0.01
Syrian (41)	97	0.03
Other Arab (188)	188	0.05
Armenian (34)	34	0.01
Assyrian/Chaldean/Syriac (0)	51	0.01
Australian (17)	30	0.01
Austrian (176)	476	0.13
Basque (0)	0	<0.01
Belgian (79)	250	0.07
Brazilian (73)	113	0.03
British (931)	1,787	0.48
Bulgarian (22)	57	0.02
Cajun (61)	130	0.03
Canadian (395)	624	0.17
Carpatho Rusyn (0)	0	<0.01
Celtic (25)	76	0.02
Croatian (84)	234	0.06
Cypriot (11)	11	<0.01
Czech (111)	544	0.15
Czechoslovakian (68)	168	0.05
Danish (152)	584	0.16
Dutch (673)	2,830	0.76
Eastern European (168)	212	0.06
English (14,512)	32,004	8.59
Estonian (9)	9	<0.01
European (3,100)	3,704	0.99
Finnish (112)	344	0.09
French, ex. Basque (1,397)	7,036	1.89
French Canadian (572)	1,286	0.35
German (12,581)	35,661	9.57
German Russian (60)	60	0.02
Greek (895)	1,468	0.39
Guyanese (0)	173	0.05
Hungarian (403)	1,056	0.28
Icelander (0)	24	0.01
Iranian (77)	112	0.03
Irish (9,919)	28,198	7.57
Israeli (12)	19	0.01
Italian (2,790)	7,720	2.07
Latvian (29)	42	0.01
Lithuanian (35)	202	0.05
Luxemburger (0)	51	0.01
Macedonian (0)	0	<0.01
Maltese (0)	0	<0.01
New Zealander (28)	28	0.01
Northern European (348)	396	0.11
Norwegian (699)	1,849	0.50
Pennsylvania German (12)	71	0.02

Ancestry (cont.)	Population	%
Polish (1,253)	4,124	1.11
Portuguese (114)	347	0.09
Romanian (136)	301	0.08
Russian (500)	1,415	0.38
Scandinavian (219)	411	0.11
Scotch-Irish (6,671)	11,933	3.20
Scottish (2,907)	7,947	2.13
Serbian (94)	104	0.03
Slavic (81)	171	0.05
Slovak (58)	193	0.05
Slovene (48)	101	0.03
Soviet Union (0)	0	<0.01
Swedish (339)	1,765	0.47
Swiss (115)	622	0.17
Turkish (165)	186	0.05
Ukrainian (191)	459	0.12
Welsh (449)	1,602	0.43
West Indian, ex. Hispanic (1,545)	2,315	0.62
Bahamian (155)	194	0.05
Barbadian (23)	23	0.01
Belizean (0)	29	0.01
Bermudan (13)	13	<0.01
British West Indian (38)	38	0.01
Dutch West Indian (0)	0	<0.01
Haitian (325)	482	0.13
Jamaican (574)	817	0.22
Trinidadian/Tobagonian (156)	247	0.07
U.S. Virgin Islander (9)	14	<0.01
West Indian (237)	443	0.12
Other West Indian (15)	15	<0.01
Yugoslavian (47)	109	0.03

Hispanic Origin	Population	%
Hispanic or Latino (of any race)	18,637	4.85
Central American, ex. Mexican	2,210	0.57
Costa Rican	94	0.02
Guatemalan	550	0.14
Honduran	570	0.15
Nicaraguan	81	0.02
Panamanian	688	0.18
Salvadoran	223	0.06
Other Central American	4	<0.01
Cuban	608	0.16
Dominican Republic	421	0.11
Mexican	8,242	2.14
Puerto Rican	4,421	1.15
South American	1,140	0.30
Argentinean	78	0.02
Bolivian	43	0.01
Chilean	51	0.01
Colombian	486	0.13
Ecuadorian	111	0.03
Paraguayan	7	<0.01
Peruvian	162	0.04
Uruguayan	17	<0.01
Venezuelan	172	0.04
Other South American	13	<0.01
Other Hispanic or Latino	1,595	0.41

Race*	Population	%
African-American/Black (176,538)	181,673	47.25
Not Hispanic (174,549)	178,894	46.53
Hispanic (1,989)	2,779	0.72
American Indian/Alaska Native (1,230)	3,366	0.88
Not Hispanic (987)	2,811	0.73
Hispanic (243)	555	0.14
Alaska Athabascan (Ala. Nat.) (2)	3	<0.01
Aleut (Alaska Native) (3)	3	<0.01
Apache (13)	41	0.01
Arapaho (2)	2	<0.01
Blackfeet (3)	98	0.03
Canadian/French Am. Ind. (2)	4	<0.01
Central American Ind. (10)	21	0.01
Cherokee (169)	796	0.21
Cheyenne (1)	7	<0.01
Chickasaw (6)	13	<0.01
Chippewa (6)	30	0.01
Choctaw (24)	58	0.02
Colville (0)	0	<0.01

Race* (cont.)	Population	%
Comanche (1)	4	<0.01
Cree (6)	6	<0.01
Creek (3)	14	<0.01
Crow (2)	9	<0.01
Delaware (6)	7	<0.01
Hopi (2)	4	<0.01
Houma (0)	1	<0.01
Inupiat (Alaska Native) (2)	7	<0.01
Iroquois (13)	38	0.01
Kiowa (0)	5	<0.01
Lumbee (63)	94	0.02
Menominee (0)	0	<0.01
Mexican American Ind. (64)	115	0.03
Navajo (22)	41	0.01
Osage (2)	3	<0.01
Ottawa (1)	1	<0.01
Paiute (1)	2	<0.01
Pima (0)	0	<0.01
Potawatomi (10)	13	<0.01
Pueblo (8)	13	<0.01
Puget Sound Salish (0)	0	<0.01
Seminole (8)	26	0.01
Shoshone (2)	2	<0.01
Sioux (24)	56	0.01
South American Ind. (6)	28	0.01
Spanish American Ind. (8)	14	<0.01
Tlingit-Haida (Alaska Native) (1)	1	<0.01
Tohono O'Odham (5)	5	<0.01
Tsimshian (Alaska Native) (0)	0	<0.01
Ute (1)	1	<0.01
Yakama (0)	0	<0.01
Yaqui (1)	1	<0.01
Yuman (0)	0	<0.01
Yup'ik (Alaska Native) (2)	2	<0.01
Asian (8,548)	10,872	2.83
Not Hispanic (8,433)	10,524	2.74
Hispanic (115)	348	0.09
Bangladeshi (67)	68	0.02
Bhutanese (4)	4	<0.01
Burmese (179)	183	0.05
Cambodian (45)	71	0.02
Chinese, ex. Taiwanese (1,413)	1,677	0.44
Filipino (976)	1,585	0.41
Hmong (56)	59	0.02
Indian (2,523)	2,790	0.73
Indonesian (20)	36	0.01
Japanese (348)	714	0.19
Korean (1,415)	1,941	0.50
Laotian (39)	59	0.02
Malaysian (9)	14	<0.01
Nepalese (35)	39	0.01
Pakistani (213)	231	0.06
Sri Lankan (15)	16	<0.01
Taiwanese (63)	69	0.02
Thai (149)	241	0.06
Vietnamese (641)	774	0.20
Hawaii Native/Pacific Islander (425)	875	0.23
Not Hispanic (372)	752	0.20
Hispanic (53)	123	0.03
Fijian (3)	9	<0.01
Guamanian/Chamorro (146)	222	0.06
Marshallese (3)	3	<0.01
Native Hawaiian (95)	263	0.07
Samoan (59)	119	0.03
Tongan (7)	7	<0.01
White (181,974)	188,191	48.94
Not Hispanic (174,267)	179,310	46.63
Hispanic (7,707)	8,881	2.31

Notes: † The Census 2010 population figure is used to calculate the percentages in the Hispanic Origin and Race categories. Ancestry percentages are based on the 2006-2010 American Community Survey population (not shown); ‡ Numbers in parentheses indicate the number of people reporting a single ancestry; * Numbers in parentheses indicate the number of persons reporting this race alone, not in combination with any other race; Please refer to the Explanation of Data for more information.

Spartanburg County

Population: 284,307

Ancestry	Population	%
Afghan (0)	0	<0.01
African, Sub-Saharan (701)	919	0.33
African (540)	758	0.27
Cape Verdean (0)	0	<0.01
Ethiopian (0)	0	<0.01
Ghanaian (0)	0	<0.01
Kenyan (82)	82	0.03
Liberian (0)	0	<0.01
Nigerian (10)	10	<0.01
Senegalese (0)	0	<0.01
Sierra Leonean (0)	0	<0.01
Somalian (0)	0	<0.01
South African (46)	46	0.02
Sudanese (0)	0	<0.01
Ugandan (0)	0	<0.01
Zimbabwean (0)	0	<0.01
Other Sub-Saharan African (23)	23	0.01
Albanian (25)	25	0.01
Alsatian (0)	0	<0.01
American (37,738)	37,738	13.57
Arab (241)	453	0.16
Arab (35)	131	0.05
Egyptian (0)	0	<0.01
Iraqi (0)	0	<0.01
Jordanian (0)	0	<0.01
Lebanese (186)	302	0.11
Moroccan (0)	0	<0.01
Palestinian (10)	10	<0.01
Syrian (10)	10	<0.01
Other Arab (0)	0	<0.01
Armenian (38)	102	0.04
Assyrian/Chaldean/Syriac (0)	0	<0.01
Australian (0)	0	<0.01
Austrian (104)	383	0.14
Basque (0)	0	<0.01
Belgian (10)	23	0.01
Brazilian (80)	93	0.03
British (712)	1,151	0.41
Bulgarian (91)	150	0.05
Cajun (27)	51	0.02
Canadian (248)	297	0.11
Carpatho Rusyn (0)	0	<0.01
Celtic (44)	77	0.03
Croatian (51)	99	0.04
Cypriot (0)	0	<0.01
Czech (92)	379	0.14
Czechoslovakian (38)	50	0.02
Danish (42)	365	0.13
Dutch (378)	2,680	0.96
Eastern European (74)	74	0.03
English (13,402)	26,686	9.59
Estonian (0)	0	<0.01
European (1,972)	2,449	0.88
Finnish (206)	507	0.18
French, ex. Basque (1,315)	4,282	1.54
French Canadian (199)	678	0.24
German (8,000)	24,375	8.76
German Russian (29)	29	0.01
Greek (380)	775	0.28
Guyanese (7)	7	<0.01
Hungarian (222)	633	0.23
Icelander (12)	12	<0.01
Iranian (49)	76	0.03
Irish (11,371)	29,088	10.46
Israeli (8)	8	<0.01
Italian (2,033)	5,775	2.08
Latvian (26)	26	0.01
Lithuanian (39)	225	0.08
Luxemburger (0)	0	<0.01
Macedonian (0)	0	<0.01
Maltese (0)	0	<0.01
New Zealander (0)	0	<0.01
Northern European (43)	43	0.02
Norwegian (286)	707	0.25
Pennsylvania German (177)	220	0.08

Ancestry	Population	%
Polish (977)	2,560	0.92
Portuguese (167)	372	0.13
Romanian (14)	14	0.01
Russian (680)	1,168	0.42
Scandinavian (201)	248	0.09
Scotch-Irish (7,079)	10,794	3.88
Scottish (2,540)	6,374	2.29
Serbian (10)	49	0.02
Slavic (0)	31	0.01
Slovak (49)	186	0.07
Slovene (0)	5	<0.01
Soviet Union (0)	0	<0.01
Swedish (402)	1,399	0.50
Swiss (385)	821	0.30
Turkish (14)	14	0.01
Ukrainian (1,309)	1,587	0.57
Welsh (342)	973	0.35
West Indian, ex. Hispanic (254)	382	0.14
Bahamian (0)	0	<0.01
Barbadian (58)	58	0.02
Belizean (0)	0	<0.01
Bermudan (0)	0	<0.01
British West Indian (0)	0	<0.01
Dutch West Indian (0)	18	0.01
Haitian (13)	13	<0.01
Jamaican (112)	148	0.05
Trinidadian/Tobagonian (52)	97	0.03
U.S. Virgin Islander (0)	0	<0.01
West Indian (19)	48	0.02
Other West Indian (0)	0	<0.01
Yugoslavian (68)	108	0.04

Hispanic Origin	Population	%
Hispanic or Latino (of any race)	16,658	5.86
Central American, ex. Mexican	1,187	0.42
Costa Rican	84	0.03
Guatemalan	302	0.11
Honduran	381	0.13
Nicaraguan	57	0.02
Panamanian	63	0.02
Salvadoran	282	0.10
Other Central American	18	0.01
Cuban	281	0.10
Dominican Republic	128	0.05
Mexican	11,544	4.06
Puerto Rican	1,338	0.47
South American	1,091	0.38
Argentinean	53	0.02
Bolivian	17	0.01
Chilean	39	0.01
Colombian	657	0.23
Ecuadorian	119	0.04
Paraguayan	0	<0.01
Peruvian	108	0.04
Uruguayan	21	0.01
Venezuelan	70	0.02
Other South American	7	<0.01
Other Hispanic or Latino	1,089	0.38

Race*	Population	%
African-American/Black (58,565)	61,037	21.47
Not Hispanic (58,115)	60,308	21.21
Hispanic (450)	729	0.26
American Indian/Alaska Native (764)	1,991	0.70
Not Hispanic (562)	1,620	0.57
Hispanic (202)	371	0.13
Alaska Athabascan (Ala. Nat.) (1)	2	<0.01
Aleut (Alaska Native) (0)	1	<0.01
Apache (8)	20	0.01
Arapaho (0)	0	<0.01
Blackfeet (9)	45	0.02
Canadian/French Am. Ind. (4)	8	<0.01
Central American Ind. (3)	3	<0.01
Cherokee (155)	640	0.23
Cheyenne (1)	2	<0.01
Chickasaw (0)	6	<0.01
Chippewa (18)	23	0.01
Choctaw (16)	25	0.01
Colville (0)	0	<0.01

	Population	%
Comanche (1)	3	<0.01
Cree (1)	3	<0.01
Creek (7)	12	<0.01
Crow (1)	6	<0.01
Delaware (1)	6	<0.01
Hopi (1)	4	<0.01
Houma (3)	3	<0.01
Inupiat (Alaska Native) (3)	5	<0.01
Iroquois (12)	17	0.01
Kiowa (0)	0	<0.01
Lumbee (70)	93	0.03
Menominee (0)	1	<0.01
Mexican American Ind. (103)	141	0.05
Navajo (2)	6	<0.01
Osage (3)	3	<0.01
Ottawa (1)	1	<0.01
Paiute (0)	1	<0.01
Pima (0)	0	<0.01
Potawatomi (4)	4	<0.01
Pueblo (4)	5	<0.01
Puget Sound Salish (0)	1	<0.01
Seminole (2)	2	<0.01
Shoshone (0)	3	<0.01
Sioux (7)	20	0.01
South American Ind. (0)	19	0.01
Spanish American Ind. (1)	2	<0.01
Tlingit-Haida (Alaska Native) (7)	7	<0.01
Tohono O'Odham (0)	0	<0.01
Tsimshian (Alaska Native) (0)	0	<0.01
Ute (0)	0	<0.01
Yakama (0)	0	<0.01
Yaqui (5)	7	<0.01
Yuman (0)	0	<0.01
Yup'ik (Alaska Native) (1)	1	<0.01
Asian (5,746)	6,639	2.34
Not Hispanic (5,680)	6,488	2.28
Hispanic (66)	151	0.05
Bangladeshi (4)	4	<0.01
Bhutanese (0)	0	<0.01
Burmese (4)	4	<0.01
Cambodian (972)	1,123	0.39
Chinese, ex. Taiwanese (384)	485	0.17
Filipino (357)	549	0.19
Hmong (769)	799	0.28
Indian (1,233)	1,382	0.49
Indonesian (9)	20	0.01
Japanese (95)	169	0.06
Korean (188)	277	0.10
Laotian (750)	883	0.31
Malaysian (5)	5	<0.01
Nepalese (18)	21	0.01
Pakistani (79)	88	0.03
Sri Lankan (11)	13	<0.01
Taiwanese (12)	12	<0.01
Thai (60)	137	0.05
Vietnamese (397)	465	0.16
Hawaii Native/Pacific Islander (86)	260	0.09
Not Hispanic (69)	208	0.07
Hispanic (17)	52	0.02
Fijian (1)	2	<0.01
Guamanian/Chamorro (34)	50	0.02
Marshallese (0)	0	<0.01
Native Hawaiian (25)	69	0.02
Samoan (11)	23	0.01
Tongan (0)	0	<0.01
White (205,680)	209,733	73.77
Not Hispanic (199,184)	202,437	71.20
Hispanic (6,496)	7,296	2.57

Notes: † The Census 2010 population figure is used to calculate the percentages in the Hispanic Origin and Race categories. Ancestry percentages are based on the 2006-2010 American Community Survey population (not shown); ‡ Numbers in parentheses indicate the number of people reporting a single ancestry; * Numbers in parentheses indicate the number of persons reporting this race alone, not in combination with any other race; Please refer to the Explanation of Data for more information.

Sumter County

Population: 107,456

Ancestry	Population	%
Afghan (0)	0	<0.01
African, Sub-Saharan (7,502)	7,722	7.24
African (7,445)	7,610	7.14
Cape Verdean (0)	0	<0.01
Ethiopian (5)	5	<0.01
Ghanaian (0)	0	<0.01
Kenyan (0)	0	<0.01
Liberian (41)	96	0.09
Nigerian (11)	11	0.01
Senegalese (0)	0	<0.01
Sierra Leonean (0)	0	<0.01
Somalian (0)	0	<0.01
South African (0)	0	<0.01
Sudanese (0)	0	<0.01
Ugandan (0)	0	<0.01
Zimbabwean (0)	0	<0.01
Other Sub-Saharan African (0)	0	<0.01
Albanian (0)	0	<0.01
Alsatian (0)	0	<0.01
American (7,351)	7,351	6.90
Arab (0)	81	0.08
Arab (0)	0	<0.01
Egyptian (0)	0	<0.01
Iraqi (0)	0	<0.01
Jordanian (0)	0	<0.01
Lebanese (0)	70	0.07
Moroccan (0)	0	<0.01
Palestinian (0)	0	<0.01
Syrian (0)	11	0.01
Other Arab (0)	0	<0.01
Armenian (0)	0	<0.01
Assyrian/Chaldean/Syriac (0)	0	<0.01
Australian (39)	39	0.04
Austrian (13)	53	0.05
Basque (0)	0	<0.01
Belgian (0)	0	<0.01
Brazilian (0)	0	<0.01
British (85)	338	0.32
Bulgarian (0)	0	<0.01
Cajun (46)	46	0.04
Canadian (11)	26	0.02
Carpatho Rusyn (0)	0	<0.01
Celtic (60)	60	0.06
Croatian (10)	30	0.03
Cypriot (0)	0	<0.01
Czech (12)	90	0.08
Czechoslovakian (0)	10	0.01
Danish (31)	48	0.05
Dutch (186)	647	0.61
Eastern European (41)	41	0.04
English (3,066)	6,489	6.09
Estonian (14)	14	0.01
European (550)	711	0.67
Finnish (0)	31	0.03
French, ex. Basque (333)	1,317	1.24
French Canadian (220)	446	0.42
German (2,331)	6,286	5.90
German Russian (0)	0	<0.01
Greek (63)	144	0.14
Guyanese (0)	0	<0.01
Hungarian (68)	125	0.12
Icelander (0)	0	<0.01
Iranian (0)	0	<0.01
Irish (2,231)	6,090	5.71
Israeli (0)	0	<0.01
Italian (679)	1,807	1.70
Latvian (11)	11	0.01
Lithuanian (15)	46	0.04
Luxemburger (0)	0	<0.01
Macedonian (0)	0	<0.01
Maltese (0)	9	0.01
New Zealander (0)	0	<0.01
Northern European (0)	17	0.02
Norwegian (73)	170	0.16
Pennsylvania German (37)	37	0.03

Ancestry	Population	%
Polish (295)	954	0.89
Portuguese (19)	70	0.07
Romanian (12)	35	0.03
Russian (90)	155	0.15
Scandinavian (0)	54	0.05
Scotch-Irish (1,438)	2,258	2.12
Scottish (574)	1,579	1.48
Serbian (49)	191	0.18
Slavic (0)	8	0.01
Slovak (0)	22	0.02
Slovene (0)	0	<0.01
Soviet Union (0)	0	<0.01
Swedish (90)	261	0.24
Swiss (0)	0	<0.01
Turkish (222)	355	0.33
Ukrainian (7)	7	0.01
Welsh (205)	396	0.37
West Indian, ex. Hispanic (177)	346	0.32
Bahamian (0)	0	<0.01
Barbadian (24)	24	0.02
Belizean (0)	0	<0.01
Bermudan (0)	0	<0.01
British West Indian (0)	0	<0.01
Dutch West Indian (0)	0	<0.01
Haitian (0)	0	<0.01
Jamaican (83)	157	0.15
Trinidadian/Tobagonian (58)	58	0.05
U.S. Virgin Islander (0)	0	<0.01
West Indian (12)	107	0.10
Other West Indian (0)	0	<0.01
Yugoslavian (0)	13	0.01

Hispanic Origin	Population	%
Hispanic or Latino (of any race)	3,532	3.29
Central American, ex. Mexican	334	0.31
Costa Rican	8	0.01
Guatemalan	123	0.11
Honduran	78	0.07
Nicaraguan	16	0.01
Panamanian	71	0.07
Salvadoran	38	0.04
Other Central American	0	<0.01
Cuban	87	0.08
Dominican Republic	48	0.04
Mexican	1,959	1.82
Puerto Rican	681	0.63
South American	86	0.08
Argentinean	5	<0.01
Bolivian	0	<0.01
Chilean	4	<0.01
Colombian	40	0.04
Ecuadorian	8	0.01
Paraguayan	0	<0.01
Peruvian	16	0.01
Uruguayan	3	<0.01
Venezuelan	10	0.01
Other South American	0	<0.01
Other Hispanic or Latino	337	0.31

Race*	Population	%
African-American/Black (50,414)	51,456	47.89
Not Hispanic (50,110)	51,027	47.49
Hispanic (304)	429	0.40
American Indian/Alaska Native (389)	977	0.91
Not Hispanic (334)	844	0.79
Hispanic (55)	133	0.12
Alaska Athabascan (Ala. Nat.) (0)	0	<0.01
Aleut (Alaska Native) (0)	1	<0.01
Apache (7)	15	0.01
Arapaho (1)	2	<0.01
Blackfeet (9)	17	0.02
Canadian/French Am. Ind. (2)	2	<0.01
Central American Ind. (3)	6	0.01
Cherokee (44)	235	0.22
Cheyenne (0)	0	<0.01
Chickasaw (1)	5	<0.01
Chippewa (3)	9	0.01
Choctaw (6)	11	0.01
Colville (0)	0	<0.01

	Population	%
Comanche (1)	1	<0.01
Cree (0)	1	<0.01
Creek (4)	10	0.01
Crow (0)	2	<0.01
Delaware (0)	1	<0.01
Hopi (0)	0	<0.01
Houma (0)	0	<0.01
Inupiat (Alaska Native) (0)	0	<0.01
Iroquois (4)	9	0.01
Kiowa (0)	0	<0.01
Lumbee (78)	98	0.09
Menominee (0)	1	<0.01
Mexican American Ind. (9)	26	0.02
Navajo (2)	7	0.01
Osage (0)	2	<0.01
Ottawa (0)	0	<0.01
Paiute (1)	1	<0.01
Pima (1)	1	<0.01
Potawatomi (0)	1	<0.01
Pueblo (1)	2	<0.01
Puget Sound Salish (0)	0	<0.01
Seminole (1)	5	<0.01
Shoshone (1)	1	<0.01
Sioux (4)	10	0.01
South American Ind. (5)	5	<0.01
Spanish American Ind. (0)	0	<0.01
Tlingit-Haida (Alaska Native) (3)	4	<0.01
Tohono O'Odham (0)	0	<0.01
Tsimshian (Alaska Native) (0)	0	<0.01
Ute (1)	1	<0.01
Yakama (0)	4	<0.01
Yaqui (1)	1	<0.01
Yuman (0)	0	<0.01
Yup'ik (Alaska Native) (0)	0	<0.01
Asian (1,188)	1,769	1.65
Not Hispanic (1,167)	1,698	1.58
Hispanic (21)	71	0.07
Bangladeshi (1)	1	<0.01
Bhutanese (0)	0	<0.01
Burmese (3)	3	<0.01
Cambodian (2)	5	<0.01
Chinese, ex. Taiwanese (108)	149	0.14
Filipino (400)	608	0.57
Hmong (5)	7	0.01
Indian (202)	239	0.22
Indonesian (4)	10	0.01
Japanese (78)	173	0.16
Korean (139)	228	0.21
Laotian (7)	11	0.01
Malaysian (0)	1	<0.01
Nepalese (0)	0	<0.01
Pakistani (8)	9	0.01
Sri Lankan (0)	0	<0.01
Taiwanese (4)	13	0.01
Thai (101)	154	0.14
Vietnamese (79)	99	0.09
Hawaii Native/Pacific Islander (99)	191	0.18
Not Hispanic (93)	169	0.16
Hispanic (6)	22	0.02
Fijian (0)	0	<0.01
Guamanian/Chamorro (53)	68	0.06
Marshallese (0)	0	<0.01
Native Hawaiian (22)	49	0.05
Samoan (7)	20	0.02
Tongan (0)	1	<0.01
White (51,825)	53,470	49.76
Not Hispanic (50,423)	51,806	48.21
Hispanic (1,402)	1,664	1.55

Notes: † The Census 2010 population figure is used to calculate the percentages in the Hispanic Origin and Race categories. Ancestry percentages are based on the 2006-2010 American Community Survey population (not shown); ‡ Numbers in parentheses indicate the number of people reporting a single ancestry; * Numbers in parentheses indicate the number of persons reporting this race alone, not in combination with any other race; Please refer to the Explanation of Data for more information.

York County

Population: 226,073

Ancestry	Population	%
Afghan (0)	0	<0.01
African, Sub-Saharan (772)	929	0.43
African (677)	815	0.38
Cape Verdean (65)	65	0.03
Ethiopian (0)	0	<0.01
Ghanaian (0)	0	<0.01
Kenyan (0)	0	<0.01
Liberian (0)	0	<0.01
Nigerian (0)	0	<0.01
Senegalese (0)	0	<0.01
Sierra Leonean (0)	0	<0.01
Somalian (0)	0	<0.01
South African (12)	31	0.01
Sudanese (0)	0	<0.01
Ugandan (0)	0	<0.01
Zimbabwean (0)	0	<0.01
Other Sub-Saharan African (18)	18	0.01
Albanian (105)	105	0.05
Alsatian (0)	0	<0.01
American (19,706)	19,706	9.17
Arab (265)	584	0.27
Arab (0)	0	<0.01
Egyptian (89)	164	0.08
Iraqi (8)	8	<0.01
Jordanian (24)	24	0.01
Lebanese (84)	253	0.12
Moroccan (0)	0	<0.01
Palestinian (11)	11	0.01
Syrian (36)	94	0.04
Other Arab (13)	30	0.01
Armenian (18)	42	0.02
Assyrian/Chaldean/Syriac (0)	0	<0.01
Australian (30)	30	0.01
Austrian (168)	457	0.21
Basque (0)	0	<0.01
Belgian (40)	120	0.06
Brazilian (37)	92	0.04
British (614)	1,005	0.47
Bulgarian (0)	0	<0.01
Cajun (0)	36	0.02
Canadian (282)	369	0.17
Carpatho Rusyn (0)	0	<0.01
Celtic (0)	0	<0.01
Croatian (114)	157	0.07
Cypriot (15)	15	0.01
Czech (104)	527	0.25
Czechoslovakian (34)	119	0.06
Danish (200)	439	0.20
Dutch (665)	3,413	1.59
Eastern European (71)	141	0.07
English (10,805)	22,002	10.24
Estonian (0)	0	<0.01
European (2,021)	2,271	1.06
Finnish (84)	137	0.06
French, ex. Basque (1,169)	4,755	2.21
French Canadian (436)	950	0.44
German (10,139)	30,160	14.03
German Russian (0)	0	<0.01
Greek (87)	296	0.14
Guyanese (13)	13	0.01
Hungarian (174)	582	0.27
Icelander (10)	46	0.02
Iranian (39)	39	0.02
Irish (10,046)	26,398	12.28
Israeli (0)	0	<0.01
Italian (3,311)	8,612	4.01
Latvian (15)	51	0.02
Lithuanian (89)	312	0.15
Luxemburger (0)	9	<0.01
Macedonian (14)	14	0.01
Maltese (86)	86	0.04
New Zealander (24)	24	0.01
Northern European (88)	127	0.06
Norwegian (378)	1,208	0.56
Pennsylvania German (79)	127	0.06

Ancestry	Population	%
Polish (1,144)	3,693	1.72
Portuguese (79)	173	0.08
Romanian (20)	55	0.03
Russian (270)	703	0.33
Scandinavian (108)	142	0.07
Scotch-Irish (8,181)	12,825	5.97
Scottish (2,122)	5,274	2.45
Serbian (0)	0	<0.01
Slavic (12)	12	0.01
Slovak (141)	616	0.29
Slovene (10)	41	0.02
Soviet Union (0)	0	<0.01
Swedish (295)	1,458	0.68
Swiss (75)	590	0.27
Turkish (16)	23	0.01
Ukrainian (152)	403	0.19
Welsh (290)	1,276	0.59
West Indian, ex. Hispanic (71)	185	0.09
Bahamian (7)	7	<0.01
Barbadian (0)	0	<0.01
Belizean (0)	0	<0.01
Bermudan (0)	15	0.01
British West Indian (18)	18	0.01
Dutch West Indian (0)	0	<0.01
Haitian (0)	0	<0.01
Jamaican (24)	87	0.04
Trinidadian/Tobagonian (12)	12	0.01
U.S. Virgin Islander (0)	0	<0.01
West Indian (10)	46	0.02
Other West Indian (0)	0	<0.01
Yugoslavian (27)	39	0.02

Hispanic Origin	Population	%
Hispanic or Latino (of any race)	10,075	4.46
Central American, ex. Mexican	994	0.44
Costa Rican	106	0.05
Guatemalan	168	0.07
Honduran	343	0.15
Nicaraguan	47	0.02
Panamanian	88	0.04
Salvadoran	235	0.10
Other Central American	7	<0.01
Cuban	389	0.17
Dominican Republic	239	0.11
Mexican	5,365	2.37
Puerto Rican	1,347	0.60
South American	1,089	0.48
Argentinean	54	0.02
Bolivian	18	0.01
Chilean	61	0.03
Colombian	466	0.21
Ecuadorian	152	0.07
Paraguayan	8	<0.01
Peruvian	154	0.07
Uruguayan	98	0.04
Venezuelan	65	0.03
Other South American	13	0.01
Other Hispanic or Latino	652	0.29

Race*	Population	%
African-American/Black (43,003)	45,106	19.95
Not Hispanic (42,608)	44,508	19.69
Hispanic (395)	598	0.26
American Indian/Alaska Native (1,934)	3,240	1.43
Not Hispanic (1,777)	2,982	1.32
Hispanic (157)	258	0.11
Alaska Athabascan (Ala. Nat.) (1)	2	<0.01
Aleut (Alaska Native) (1)	2	<0.01
Apache (9)	20	0.01
Arapaho (0)	1	<0.01
Blackfeet (2)	46	0.02
Canadian/French Am. Ind. (3)	4	<0.01
Central American Ind. (3)	13	0.01
Cherokee (151)	510	0.23
Cheyenne (1)	3	<0.01
Chickasaw (0)	2	<0.01
Chippewa (9)	17	0.01
Choctaw (15)	42	0.02
Colville (0)	0	<0.01

Race*	Population	%
Comanche (2)	6	<0.01
Cree (0)	1	<0.01
Creek (23)	35	0.02
Crow (0)	3	<0.01
Delaware (4)	4	<0.01
Hopi (0)	0	<0.01
Houma (1)	1	<0.01
Inupiat (Alaska Native) (2)	5	<0.01
Iroquois (19)	41	0.02
Kiowa (0)	1	<0.01
Lumbee (75)	109	0.05
Menominee (0)	0	<0.01
Mexican American Ind. (39)	49	0.02
Navajo (12)	18	0.01
Osage (5)	5	<0.01
Ottawa (0)	2	<0.01
Paiute (0)	0	<0.01
Pima (0)	0	<0.01
Potawatomi (0)	1	<0.01
Pueblo (1)	1	<0.01
Puget Sound Salish (1)	1	<0.01
Seminole (3)	20	0.01
Shoshone (1)	1	<0.01
Sioux (13)	31	0.01
South American Ind. (3)	15	0.01
Spanish American Ind. (2)	2	<0.01
Tlingit-Haida (Alaska Native) (7)	7	<0.01
Tohono O'Odham (5)	5	<0.01
Tsimshian (Alaska Native) (0)	0	<0.01
Ute (0)	2	<0.01
Yakama (0)	0	<0.01
Yaqui (0)	0	<0.01
Yuman (0)	0	<0.01
Yup'ik (Alaska Native) (1)	1	<0.01
Asian (3,413)	4,190	1.85
Not Hispanic (3,394)	4,120	1.82
Hispanic (19)	70	0.03
Bangladeshi (7)	7	<0.01
Bhutanese (0)	0	<0.01
Burmese (2)	3	<0.01
Cambodian (100)	120	0.05
Chinese, ex. Taiwanese (428)	541	0.24
Filipino (320)	488	0.22
Hmong (239)	269	0.12
Indian (882)	977	0.43
Indonesian (10)	14	0.01
Japanese (57)	144	0.06
Korean (218)	334	0.15
Laotian (100)	114	0.05
Malaysian (7)	15	0.01
Nepalese (0)	0	<0.01
Pakistani (39)	49	0.02
Sri Lankan (2)	3	<0.01
Taiwanese (13)	21	0.01
Thai (35)	73	0.03
Vietnamese (783)	875	0.39
Hawaii Native/Pacific Islander (126)	270	0.12
Not Hispanic (72)	191	0.08
Hispanic (54)	79	0.03
Fijian (0)	5	<0.01
Guamanian/Chamorro (71)	88	0.04
Marshallese (1)	1	<0.01
Native Hawaiian (13)	44	0.02
Samoan (9)	31	0.01
Tongan (4)	11	<0.01
White (169,158)	172,828	76.45
Not Hispanic (164,371)	167,499	74.09
Hispanic (4,787)	5,329	2.36

Notes: † The Census 2010 population figure is used to calculate the percentages in the Hispanic Origin and Race categories. Ancestry percentages are based on the 2006-2010 American Community Survey population (not shown); ‡ Numbers in parentheses indicate the number of people reporting a single ancestry; * Numbers in parentheses indicate the number of persons reporting this race alone, not in combination with any other race; Please refer to the Explanation of Data for more information.

Place Profiles

Charleston

Place Type: City
County: Charleston
Population: 120,083

Ancestry	Population	%
Afghan (0)	0	<0.01
African, Sub-Saharan (661)	754	0.65
African (544)	577	0.50
Cape Verdean (0)	0	<0.01
Ethiopian (11)	11	0.01
Ghanaian (0)	0	<0.01
Kenyan (0)	0	<0.01
Liberian (0)	0	<0.01
Nigerian (94)	94	0.08
Senegalese (0)	0	<0.01
Sierra Leonean (0)	0	<0.01
Somalian (0)	0	<0.01
South African (0)	49	0.04
Sudanese (0)	0	<0.01
Ugandan (0)	0	<0.01
Zimbabwean (12)	12	0.01
Other Sub-Saharan African (0)	11	0.01
Albanian (14)	14	0.01
Alsatian (0)	0	<0.01
American (12,018)	12,018	10.33
Arab (636)	878	0.75
Arab (37)	37	0.03
Egyptian (134)	134	0.12
Iraqi (10)	21	0.02
Jordanian (129)	140	0.12
Lebanese (243)	312	0.27
Moroccan (25)	53	0.05
Palestinian (0)	0	<0.01
Syrian (58)	146	0.13
Other Arab (0)	35	0.03
Armenian (46)	61	0.05
Assyrian/Chaldean/Syriac (0)	0	<0.01
Australian (7)	15	0.01
Austrian (24)	182	0.16
Basque (0)	0	<0.01
Belgian (35)	57	0.05
Brazilian (10)	42	0.04
British (422)	801	0.69
Bulgarian (40)	40	0.03
Cajun (12)	45	0.04
Canadian (120)	194	0.17
Carpatho Rusyn (0)	0	<0.01
Celtic (0)	0	<0.01
Croatian (4)	12	0.01
Cypriot (0)	0	<0.01
Czech (81)	393	0.34
Czechoslovakian (13)	148	0.13
Danish (84)	204	0.18
Dutch (392)	1,301	1.12
Eastern European (42)	42	0.04
English (5,522)	14,530	12.49
Estonian (13)	26	0.02
European (1,287)	1,434	1.23
Finnish (35)	44	0.04
French, ex. Basque (735)	3,182	2.73
French Canadian (211)	397	0.34
German (4,276)	14,321	12.31
German Russian (0)	0	<0.01
Greek (414)	882	0.76
Guyanese (0)	0	<0.01
Hungarian (36)	327	0.28
Icelander (0)	0	<0.01
Iranian (93)	105	0.09
Irish (4,375)	12,396	10.65
Israeli (16)	16	0.01
Italian (1,692)	4,553	3.91
Latvian (0)	7	0.01
Lithuanian (108)	214	0.18
Luxemburger (0)	0	<0.01
Macedonian (0)	14	0.01

	Population	%
Maltese (0)	0	<0.01
New Zealander (0)	15	0.01
Northern European (132)	132	0.11
Norwegian (211)	734	0.63
Pennsylvania German (0)	19	0.02
Polish (835)	2,127	1.83
Portuguese (18)	109	0.09
Romanian (33)	94	0.08
Russian (512)	1,267	1.09
Scandinavian (109)	239	0.21
Scotch-Irish (2,233)	4,145	3.56
Scottish (1,610)	4,177	3.59
Serbian (0)	26	0.02
Slavic (0)	30	0.03
Slovak (48)	193	0.17
Slovene (9)	35	0.03
Soviet Union (0)	0	<0.01
Swedish (325)	993	0.85
Swiss (82)	297	0.26
Turkish (39)	39	0.03
Ukrainian (263)	408	0.35
Welsh (318)	909	0.78
West Indian, ex. Hispanic (172)	199	0.17
Bahamian (15)	15	0.01
Barbadian (0)	0	<0.01
Belizean (0)	0	<0.01
Bermudan (0)	0	<0.01
British West Indian (0)	0	<0.01
Dutch West Indian (0)	0	<0.01
Haitian (0)	0	<0.01
Jamaican (132)	132	0.11
Trinidadian/Tobagonian (14)	14	0.01
U.S. Virgin Islander (0)	0	<0.01
West Indian (11)	38	0.03
Other West Indian (0)	0	<0.01
Yugoslavian (14)	43	0.04

Hispanic Origin	Population	%
Hispanic or Latino (of any race)	3,451	2.87
Central American, ex. Mexican	296	0.25
Costa Rican	26	0.02
Guatemalan	93	0.08
Honduran	57	0.05
Nicaraguan	20	0.02
Panamanian	72	0.06
Salvadoran	25	0.02
Other Central American	3	<0.01
Cuban	150	0.12
Dominican Republic	55	0.05
Mexican	1,590	1.32
Puerto Rican	528	0.44
South American	477	0.40
Argentinean	83	0.07
Bolivian	62	0.05
Chilean	27	0.02
Colombian	126	0.10
Ecuadorian	83	0.07
Paraguayan	4	<0.01
Peruvian	51	0.04
Uruguayan	8	0.01
Venezuelan	30	0.02
Other South American	3	<0.01
Other Hispanic or Latino	355	0.30

Race*	Population	%
African-American/Black (30,491)	31,268	26.04
Not Hispanic (30,288)	30,973	25.79
Hispanic (203)	295	0.25
American Indian/Alaska Native (271)	753	0.63
Not Hispanic (235)	665	0.55
Hispanic (36)	88	0.07
Alaska Athabascan (Ala. Nat.) (0)	1	<0.01
Aleut (Alaska Native) (0)	1	<0.01
Apache (2)	6	<0.01
Arapaho (0)	0	<0.01
Blackfeet (2)	24	0.02

	Population	%
Canadian/French Am. Ind. (1)	4	<0.01
Central American Ind. (4)	7	0.01
Cherokee (54)	199	0.17
Cheyenne (0)	1	<0.01
Chickasaw (2)	5	<0.01
Chippewa (2)	6	<0.01
Choctaw (1)	12	0.01
Colville (0)	0	<0.01
Comanche (0)	0	<0.01
Cree (0)	3	<0.01
Creek (6)	11	0.01
Crow (0)	2	<0.01
Delaware (0)	0	<0.01
Hopi (0)	0	<0.01
Houma (0)	0	<0.01
Inupiat (Alaska Native) (2)	7	0.01
Iroquois (4)	10	0.01
Kiowa (4)	4	<0.01
Lumbee (15)	19	0.02
Menominee (0)	0	<0.01
Mexican American Ind. (6)	14	0.01
Navajo (1)	2	<0.01
Osage (0)	1	<0.01
Ottawa (0)	0	<0.01
Paiute (0)	0	<0.01
Pima (0)	0	<0.01
Potawatomi (2)	5	<0.01
Pueblo (1)	1	<0.01
Puget Sound Salish (2)	3	<0.01
Seminole (0)	5	<0.01
Shoshone (0)	4	<0.01
Sioux (2)	9	0.01
South American Ind. (3)	6	<0.01
Spanish American Ind. (0)	0	<0.01
Tlingit-Haida (Alaska Native) (0)	0	<0.01
Tohono O'Odham (0)	0	<0.01
Tsimshian (Alaska Native) (0)	0	<0.01
Ute (1)	2	<0.01
Yakama (0)	0	<0.01
Yaqui (0)	0	<0.01
Yuman (0)	0	<0.01
Yup'ik (Alaska Native) (0)	0	<0.01
Asian (1,971)	2,557	2.13
Not Hispanic (1,950)	2,491	2.07
Hispanic (21)	66	0.05
Bangladeshi (6)	7	0.01
Bhutanese (1)	1	<0.01
Burmese (16)	16	0.01
Cambodian (10)	10	0.01
Chinese, ex. Taiwanese (405)	484	0.40
Filipino (316)	522	0.43
Hmong (1)	1	<0.01
Indian (564)	637	0.53
Indonesian (5)	7	0.01
Japanese (85)	158	0.13
Korean (162)	244	0.20
Laotian (0)	0	<0.01
Malaysian (1)	4	<0.01
Nepalese (4)	5	<0.01
Pakistani (18)	20	0.02
Sri Lankan (18)	22	0.02
Taiwanese (36)	39	0.03
Thai (28)	49	0.04
Vietnamese (203)	243	0.20
Hawaii Native/Pacific Islander (122)	213	0.18
Not Hispanic (111)	192	0.16
Hispanic (11)	21	0.02
Fijian (1)	1	<0.01
Guamanian/Chamorro (21)	28	0.02
Marshallese (0)	1	<0.01
Native Hawaiian (17)	44	0.04
Samoan (6)	14	0.01
Tongan (0)	0	<0.01
White (84,258)	85,755	71.41
Not Hispanic (82,427)	83,699	69.70
Hispanic (1,831)	2,056	1.71

*Notes: † The Census 2010 population figure is used to calculate the percentages in the Hispanic Origin and Race categories. Ancestry percentages are based on the 2006-2010 American Community Survey population (not shown); ‡ Numbers in parentheses indicate the number of people reporting a single ancestry; * Numbers in parentheses indicate the number of persons reporting this race alone, not in combination with any other race; Please refer to the Explanation of Data for more information.*

Columbia

Place Type: City
County: Richland
Population: 129,272

Ancestry	Population	%
Afghan (0)	0	<0.01
African, Sub-Saharan (1,871)	2,206	1.73
African (1,606)	1,837	1.44
Cape Verdean (9)	9	0.01
Ethiopian (64)	64	0.05
Ghanaian (5)	5	<0.01
Kenyan (19)	72	0.06
Liberian (0)	51	0.04
Nigerian (39)	39	0.03
Senegalese (0)	0	<0.01
Sierra Leonean (0)	0	<0.01
Somalian (0)	0	<0.01
South African (0)	0	<0.01
Sudanese (47)	47	0.04
Ugandan (0)	0	<0.01
Zimbabwean (0)	0	<0.01
Other Sub-Saharan African (82)	82	0.06
Albanian (0)	0	<0.01
Alsatian (0)	0	<0.01
American (7,637)	7,637	5.98
Arab (321)	547	0.43
Arab (18)	38	0.03
Egyptian (24)	107	0.08
Iraqi (12)	12	0.01
Jordanian (0)	0	<0.01
Lebanese (104)	208	0.16
Moroccan (0)	12	0.01
Palestinian (0)	0	<0.01
Syrian (29)	36	0.03
Other Arab (134)	134	0.11
Armenian (25)	25	0.02
Assyrian/Chaldean/Syriac (0)	31	0.02
Australian (17)	30	0.02
Austrian (68)	154	0.12
Basque (0)	0	<0.01
Belgian (0)	60	0.05
Brazilian (11)	33	0.03
British (380)	762	0.60
Bulgarian (22)	57	0.04
Cajun (61)	130	0.10
Canadian (102)	214	0.17
Carpatho Rusyn (0)	0	<0.01
Celtic (12)	39	0.03
Croatian (35)	55	0.04
Cypriot (11)	11	0.01
Czech (52)	246	0.19
Czechoslovakian (49)	107	0.08
Danish (106)	201	0.16
Dutch (271)	1,053	0.83
Eastern European (51)	76	0.06
English (5,522)	12,269	9.61
Estonian (9)	9	0.01
European (1,334)	1,415	1.11
Finnish (61)	149	0.12
French, ex. Basque (573)	2,527	1.98
French Canadian (139)	442	0.35
German (3,693)	12,047	9.44
German Russian (0)	0	<0.01
Greek (566)	603	0.47
Guyanese (0)	0	<0.01
Hungarian (97)	311	0.24
Icelander (0)	0	<0.01
Iranian (64)	81	0.06
Irish (4,142)	10,384	8.14
Israeli (12)	12	0.01
Italian (1,075)	2,784	2.18
Latvian (14)	27	0.02
Lithuanian (11)	113	0.09
Luxemburger (0)	51	0.04
Macedonian (0)	0	<0.01
Maltese (0)	0	<0.01
New Zealander (13)	13	0.01
Northern European (99)	147	0.12

Ancestry (continued)	Population	%
Norwegian (314)	742	0.58
Pennsylvania German (0)	0	<0.01
Polish (547)	1,762	1.38
Portuguese (20)	113	0.09
Romanian (56)	82	0.06
Russian (217)	602	0.47
Scandinavian (56)	102	0.08
Scotch-Irish (2,850)	4,743	3.72
Scottish (1,294)	3,524	2.76
Serbian (83)	83	0.07
Slavic (71)	119	0.09
Slovak (49)	79	0.06
Slovene (28)	64	0.05
Soviet Union (0)	0	<0.01
Swedish (140)	504	0.39
Swiss (11)	308	0.24
Turkish (34)	34	0.03
Ukrainian (75)	142	0.11
Welsh (234)	697	0.55
West Indian, ex. Hispanic (413)	643	0.50
Bahamian (97)	97	0.08
Barbadian (0)	0	<0.01
Belizean (0)	10	0.01
Bermudan (0)	0	<0.01
British West Indian (0)	0	<0.01
Dutch West Indian (0)	0	<0.01
Haitian (53)	53	0.04
Jamaican (125)	227	0.18
Trinidadian/Tobagonian (54)	98	0.08
U.S. Virgin Islander (9)	9	0.01
West Indian (60)	134	0.11
Other West Indian (15)	15	0.01
Yugoslavian (47)	74	0.06

Hispanic Origin	Population	%
Hispanic or Latino (of any race)	5,622	4.35
Central American, ex. Mexican	473	0.37
Costa Rican	17	0.01
Guatemalan	136	0.11
Honduran	99	0.08
Nicaraguan	17	0.01
Panamanian	132	0.10
Salvadoran	72	0.06
Other Central American	0	<0.01
Cuban	208	0.16
Dominican Republic	154	0.12
Mexican	2,423	1.87
Puerto Rican	1,337	1.03
South American	428	0.33
Argentinean	41	0.03
Bolivian	10	0.01
Chilean	15	0.01
Colombian	188	0.15
Ecuadorian	50	0.04
Paraguayan	4	<0.01
Peruvian	60	0.05
Uruguayan	5	<0.01
Venezuelan	53	0.04
Other South American	2	<0.01
Other Hispanic or Latino	599	0.46

Race*	Population	%
African-American/Black (54,537)	55,929	43.26
Not Hispanic (53,948)	55,158	42.67
Hispanic (589)	771	0.60
American Indian/Alaska Native (434)	1,141	0.88
Not Hispanic (363)	962	0.74
Hispanic (71)	179	0.14
Alaska Athabascan (Ala. Nat.) (0)	0	<0.01
Aleut (Alaska Native) (1)	1	<0.01
Apache (10)	19	0.01
Arapaho (1)	1	<0.01
Blackfeet (1)	39	0.03
Canadian/French Am. Ind. (1)	1	<0.01
Central American Ind. (3)	8	0.01
Cherokee (52)	256	0.20
Cheyenne (1)	5	<0.01
Chickasaw (4)	4	<0.01
Chippewa (5)	10	0.01

Race* (continued)	Population	%
Choctaw (15)	34	0.03
Colville (0)	0	<0.01
Comanche (0)	0	<0.01
Cree (0)	0	<0.01
Creek (1)	3	<0.01
Crow (1)	5	<0.01
Delaware (2)	2	<0.01
Hopi (1)	1	<0.01
Houma (0)	1	<0.01
Inupiat (Alaska Native) (0)	5	<0.01
Iroquois (1)	11	0.01
Kiowa (0)	0	<0.01
Lumbee (16)	26	0.02
Menominee (0)	0	<0.01
Mexican American Ind. (13)	25	0.02
Navajo (13)	20	0.02
Osage (2)	3	<0.01
Ottawa (1)	1	<0.01
Paiute (1)	1	<0.01
Pima (0)	0	<0.01
Potawatomi (0)	2	<0.01
Pueblo (3)	4	<0.01
Puget Sound Salish (0)	0	<0.01
Seminole (5)	11	0.01
Shoshone (1)	1	<0.01
Sioux (15)	26	0.02
South American Ind. (2)	9	0.01
Spanish American Ind. (0)	3	<0.01
Tlingit-Haida (Alaska Native) (1)	1	<0.01
Tohono O'Odham (0)	0	<0.01
Tsimshian (Alaska Native) (0)	0	<0.01
Ute (0)	0	<0.01
Yakama (0)	0	<0.01
Yaqui (1)	1	<0.01
Yuman (0)	0	<0.01
Yup'ik (Alaska Native) (2)	2	<0.01
Asian (2,879)	3,707	2.87
Not Hispanic (2,846)	3,610	2.79
Hispanic (33)	97	0.08
Bangladeshi (21)	21	0.02
Bhutanese (0)	0	<0.01
Burmese (10)	11	0.01
Cambodian (20)	27	0.02
Chinese, ex. Taiwanese (685)	800	0.62
Filipino (292)	519	0.40
Hmong (18)	20	0.02
Indian (878)	953	0.74
Indonesian (15)	20	0.02
Japanese (95)	231	0.18
Korean (359)	536	0.41
Laotian (15)	21	0.02
Malaysian (1)	4	<0.01
Nepalese (20)	24	0.02
Pakistani (39)	44	0.03
Sri Lankan (13)	14	0.01
Taiwanese (32)	33	0.03
Thai (54)	70	0.05
Vietnamese (150)	196	0.15
Hawaii Native/Pacific Islander (164)	338	0.26
Not Hispanic (150)	304	0.24
Hispanic (14)	34	0.03
Fijian (2)	6	<0.01
Guamanian/Chamorro (50)	71	0.05
Marshallese (1)	1	<0.01
Native Hawaiian (40)	116	0.09
Samoan (32)	56	0.04
Tongan (2)	5	<0.01
White (66,777)	68,681	53.13
Not Hispanic (64,062)	65,644	50.78
Hispanic (2,715)	3,037	2.35

Notes: † The Census 2010 population figure is used to calculate the percentages in the Hispanic Origin and Race categories. Ancestry percentages are based on the 2006-2010 American Community Survey population (not shown); ‡ Numbers in parentheses indicate the number of people reporting a single ancestry; * Numbers in parentheses indicate the number of persons reporting this race alone, not in combination with any other race; Please refer to the Explanation of Data for more information.

Greenville

Place Type: City
County: Greenville
Population: 58,409

Ancestry	Population	%
Afghan (0)	0	<0.01
African, Sub-Saharan (275)	331	0.57
African (192)	228	0.39
Cape Verdean (30)	30	0.05
Ethiopian (0)	0	<0.01
Ghanaian (0)	0	<0.01
Kenyan (0)	0	<0.01
Liberian (0)	0	<0.01
Nigerian (53)	53	0.09
Senegalese (0)	0	<0.01
Sierra Leonean (0)	0	<0.01
Somalian (0)	0	<0.01
South African (0)	20	0.03
Sudanese (0)	0	<0.01
Ugandan (0)	0	<0.01
Zimbabwean (0)	0	<0.01
Other Sub-Saharan African (0)	0	<0.01
Albanian (0)	0	<0.01
Alsatian (0)	0	<0.01
American (6,496)	6,496	11.23
Arab (281)	420	0.73
Arab (95)	95	0.16
Egyptian (5)	5	0.01
Iraqi (0)	0	<0.01
Jordanian (98)	98	0.17
Lebanese (83)	222	0.38
Moroccan (0)	0	<0.01
Palestinian (0)	0	<0.01
Syrian (0)	0	<0.01
Other Arab (0)	0	<0.01
Armenian (0)	0	<0.01
Assyrian/Chaldean/Syriac (0)	0	<0.01
Australian (0)	0	<0.01
Austrian (0)	64	0.11
Basque (0)	15	0.03
Belgian (0)	0	<0.01
Brazilian (31)	31	0.05
British (197)	337	0.58
Bulgarian (6)	6	0.01
Cajun (0)	0	<0.01
Canadian (84)	132	0.23
Carpatho Rusyn (0)	0	<0.01
Celtic (29)	29	0.05
Croatian (13)	13	0.02
Cypriot (0)	0	<0.01
Czech (36)	114	0.20
Czechoslovakian (0)	0	<0.01
Danish (31)	92	0.16
Dutch (257)	813	1.41
Eastern European (11)	11	0.02
English (3,230)	7,396	12.79
Estonian (6)	6	0.01
European (549)	601	1.04
Finnish (0)	0	<0.01
French, ex. Basque (375)	1,290	2.23
French Canadian (133)	290	0.50
German (2,350)	6,981	12.07
German Russian (0)	0	<0.01
Greek (107)	201	0.35
Guyanese (0)	0	<0.01
Hungarian (50)	117	0.20
Icelander (12)	12	0.02
Iranian (31)	51	0.09
Irish (1,602)	4,691	8.11
Israeli (0)	0	<0.01
Italian (414)	1,445	2.50
Latvian (8)	22	0.04
Lithuanian (0)	12	0.02
Luxemburger (0)	0	<0.01
Macedonian (6)	6	0.01
Maltese (0)	14	0.02
New Zealander (0)	0	<0.01
Northern European (24)	24	0.04
Norwegian (169)	494	0.85
Pennsylvania German (17)	17	0.03
Polish (262)	862	1.49
Portuguese (0)	22	0.04
Romanian (54)	79	0.14
Russian (74)	205	0.35
Scandinavian (58)	95	0.16
Scotch-Irish (1,520)	2,731	4.72
Scottish (718)	1,782	3.08
Serbian (7)	42	0.07
Slavic (41)	41	0.07
Slovak (10)	19	0.03
Slovene (0)	7	0.01
Soviet Union (0)	0	<0.01
Swedish (148)	449	0.78
Swiss (74)	262	0.45
Turkish (0)	125	0.22
Ukrainian (32)	89	0.15
Welsh (106)	417	0.72
West Indian, ex. Hispanic (112)	182	0.31
Bahamian (2)	2	<0.01
Barbadian (0)	0	<0.01
Belizean (0)	0	<0.01
Bermudan (0)	0	<0.01
British West Indian (0)	0	<0.01
Dutch West Indian (0)	0	<0.01
Haitian (15)	24	0.04
Jamaican (61)	93	0.16
Trinidadian/Tobagonian (18)	18	0.03
U.S. Virgin Islander (0)	0	<0.01
West Indian (16)	35	0.06
Other West Indian (0)	10	0.02
Yugoslavian (9)	18	0.03

Hispanic Origin	Population	%
Hispanic or Latino (of any race)	3,443	5.89
Central American, ex. Mexican	394	0.67
Costa Rican	42	0.07
Guatemalan	199	0.34
Honduran	80	0.14
Nicaraguan	15	0.03
Panamanian	7	0.01
Salvadoran	49	0.08
Other Central American	2	<0.01
Cuban	75	0.13
Dominican Republic	84	0.14
Mexican	1,692	2.90
Puerto Rican	337	0.58
South American	600	1.03
Argentinean	33	0.06
Bolivian	2	<0.01
Chilean	18	0.03
Colombian	427	0.73
Ecuadorian	18	0.03
Paraguayan	6	0.01
Peruvian	45	0.08
Uruguayan	15	0.03
Venezuelan	36	0.06
Other South American	0	<0.01
Other Hispanic or Latino	261	0.45

Race*	Population	%
African-American/Black (17,519)	18,069	30.94
Not Hispanic (17,377)	17,855	30.57
Hispanic (142)	214	0.37
American Indian/Alaska Native (148)	425	0.73
Not Hispanic (91)	334	0.57
Hispanic (57)	91	0.16
Alaska Athabascan (Ala. Nat.) (0)	0	<0.01
Aleut (Alaska Native) (0)	0	<0.01
Apache (2)	6	0.01
Arapaho (0)	0	<0.01
Blackfeet (0)	10	0.02
Canadian/French Am. Ind. (0)	0	<0.01
Central American Ind. (0)	0	<0.01
Cherokee (15)	113	0.19
Cheyenne (0)	0	<0.01
Chickasaw (0)	2	<0.01
Chippewa (0)	1	<0.01
Choctaw (8)	11	0.02
Colville (0)	0	<0.01
Comanche (0)	1	<0.01
Cree (0)	1	<0.01
Creek (0)	1	<0.01
Crow (0)	0	<0.01
Delaware (0)	1	<0.01
Hopi (0)	0	<0.01
Houma (0)	0	<0.01
Inupiat (Alaska Native) (0)	0	<0.01
Iroquois (1)	4	0.01
Kiowa (0)	1	<0.01
Lumbee (3)	5	0.01
Menominee (0)	0	<0.01
Mexican American Ind. (43)	47	0.08
Navajo (0)	2	<0.01
Osage (0)	0	<0.01
Ottawa (0)	0	<0.01
Paiute (0)	0	<0.01
Pima (0)	0	<0.01
Potawatomi (0)	0	<0.01
Pueblo (0)	0	<0.01
Puget Sound Salish (0)	0	<0.01
Seminole (0)	6	0.01
Shoshone (0)	0	<0.01
Sioux (4)	12	0.02
South American Ind. (0)	4	0.01
Spanish American Ind. (2)	2	<0.01
Tlingit-Haida (Alaska Native) (0)	0	<0.01
Tohono O'Odham (0)	0	<0.01
Tsimshian (Alaska Native) (0)	0	<0.01
Ute (0)	0	<0.01
Yakama (0)	1	<0.01
Yaqui (2)	2	<0.01
Yuman (0)	0	<0.01
Yup'ik (Alaska Native) (0)	0	<0.01
Asian (793)	1,045	1.79
Not Hispanic (782)	1,006	1.72
Hispanic (11)	39	0.07
Bangladeshi (2)	5	0.01
Bhutanese (0)	0	<0.01
Burmese (3)	3	0.01
Cambodian (1)	7	0.01
Chinese, ex. Taiwanese (130)	158	0.27
Filipino (81)	158	0.27
Hmong (1)	1	<0.01
Indian (233)	280	0.48
Indonesian (2)	5	0.01
Japanese (47)	82	0.14
Korean (139)	179	0.31
Laotian (3)	3	0.01
Malaysian (0)	0	<0.01
Nepalese (1)	1	<0.01
Pakistani (29)	30	0.05
Sri Lankan (4)	4	0.01
Taiwanese (5)	8	0.01
Thai (10)	18	0.03
Vietnamese (65)	72	0.12
Hawaii Native/Pacific Islander (54)	90	0.15
Not Hispanic (46)	70	0.12
Hispanic (8)	20	0.03
Fijian (0)	0	<0.01
Guamanian/Chamorro (16)	22	0.04
Marshallese (0)	0	<0.01
Native Hawaiian (7)	23	0.04
Samoan (5)	12	0.02
Tongan (0)	2	<0.01
White (37,356)	38,214	65.42
Not Hispanic (35,776)	36,450	62.40
Hispanic (1,580)	1,764	3.02

Notes: † The Census 2010 population figure is used to calculate the percentages in the Hispanic Origin and Race categories. Ancestry percentages are based on the 2006-2010 American Community Survey population (not shown); ‡ Numbers in parentheses indicate the number of people reporting a single ancestry; * Numbers in parentheses indicate the number of persons reporting this race alone, not in combination with any other race; Please refer to the Explanation of Data for more information.

Mount Pleasant

Place Type: Town
County: Charleston
Population: 67,843

Ancestry	Population	%
Afghan (0)	0	<0.01
African, Sub-Saharan (108)	171	0.27
African (32)	47	0.07
Cape Verdean (0)	0	<0.01
Ethiopian (0)	0	<0.01
Ghanaian (0)	0	<0.01
Kenyan (0)	0	<0.01
Liberian (0)	0	<0.01
Nigerian (0)	0	<0.01
Senegalese (0)	0	<0.01
Sierra Leonean (0)	0	<0.01
Somalian (0)	0	<0.01
South African (60)	108	0.17
Sudanese (0)	0	<0.01
Ugandan (0)	0	<0.01
Zimbabwean (0)	0	<0.01
Other Sub-Saharan African (16)	16	0.02
Albanian (0)	0	<0.01
Alsatian (0)	0	<0.01
American (7,092)	7,092	11.05
Arab (115)	299	0.47
Arab (0)	0	<0.01
Egyptian (0)	12	0.02
Iraqi (0)	0	<0.01
Jordanian (0)	0	<0.01
Lebanese (115)	287	0.45
Moroccan (0)	0	<0.01
Palestinian (0)	0	<0.01
Syrian (0)	0	<0.01
Other Arab (0)	0	<0.01
Armenian (21)	49	0.08
Assyrian/Chaldean/Syriac (0)	0	<0.01
Australian (0)	0	<0.01
Austrian (77)	215	0.33
Basque (0)	0	<0.01
Belgian (15)	36	0.06
Brazilian (0)	0	<0.01
British (203)	424	0.66
Bulgarian (29)	29	0.05
Cajun (0)	0	<0.01
Canadian (63)	75	0.12
Carpatho Rusyn (0)	0	<0.01
Celtic (17)	34	0.05
Croatian (4)	63	0.10
Cypriot (0)	0	<0.01
Czech (55)	295	0.46
Czechoslovakian (26)	71	0.11
Danish (30)	125	0.19
Dutch (310)	986	1.54
Eastern European (36)	56	0.09
English (4,029)	10,047	15.65
Estonian (0)	0	<0.01
European (1,229)	1,383	2.15
Finnish (28)	112	0.17
French, ex. Basque (683)	2,855	4.45
French Canadian (115)	158	0.25
German (3,416)	11,137	17.35
German Russian (0)	0	<0.01
Greek (231)	378	0.59
Guyanese (0)	0	<0.01
Hungarian (144)	422	0.66
Icelander (0)	0	<0.01
Iranian (0)	0	<0.01
Irish (4,437)	11,021	17.16
Israeli (10)	10	0.02
Italian (1,654)	4,378	6.82
Latvian (0)	0	<0.01
Lithuanian (92)	175	0.27
Luxemburger (0)	0	<0.01
Macedonian (0)	0	<0.01
Maltese (0)	0	<0.01
New Zealander (0)	0	<0.01
Northern European (136)	136	0.21

Ancestry (cont.)	Population	%
Norwegian (117)	448	0.70
Pennsylvania German (0)	13	0.02
Polish (438)	1,755	2.73
Portuguese (55)	193	0.30
Romanian (54)	85	0.13
Russian (325)	704	1.10
Scandinavian (82)	219	0.34
Scotch-Irish (1,682)	2,909	4.53
Scottish (1,274)	3,089	4.81
Serbian (0)	55	0.09
Slavic (0)	31	0.05
Slovak (63)	146	0.23
Slovene (22)	22	0.03
Soviet Union (0)	14	0.02
Swedish (200)	951	1.48
Swiss (94)	254	0.40
Turkish (14)	14	0.02
Ukrainian (63)	240	0.37
Welsh (131)	560	0.87
West Indian, ex. Hispanic (0)	0	<0.01
Bahamian (0)	0	<0.01
Barbadian (0)	0	<0.01
Belizean (0)	0	<0.01
Bermudan (0)	0	<0.01
British West Indian (0)	0	<0.01
Dutch West Indian (0)	0	<0.01
Haitian (0)	0	<0.01
Jamaican (0)	0	<0.01
Trinidadian/Tobagonian (0)	0	<0.01
U.S. Virgin Islander (0)	0	<0.01
West Indian (0)	0	<0.01
Other West Indian (0)	0	<0.01
Yugoslavian (0)	33	0.05

Hispanic Origin	Population	%
Hispanic or Latino (of any race)	1,850	2.73
Central American, ex. Mexican	138	0.20
Costa Rican	20	0.03
Guatemalan	53	0.08
Honduran	16	0.02
Nicaraguan	15	0.02
Panamanian	16	0.02
Salvadoran	18	0.03
Other Central American	0	<0.01
Cuban	124	0.18
Dominican Republic	31	0.05
Mexican	734	1.08
Puerto Rican	254	0.37
South American	356	0.52
Argentinean	41	0.06
Bolivian	6	0.01
Chilean	36	0.05
Colombian	111	0.16
Ecuadorian	47	0.07
Paraguayan	8	0.01
Peruvian	59	0.09
Uruguayan	10	0.01
Venezuelan	36	0.05
Other South American	2	<0.01
Other Hispanic or Latino	213	0.31

Race*	Population	%
African-American/Black (3,439)	3,701	5.46
Not Hispanic (3,403)	3,636	5.36
Hispanic (36)	65	0.10
American Indian/Alaska Native (166)	346	0.51
Not Hispanic (131)	288	0.42
Hispanic (35)	58	0.09
Alaska Athabascan (Ala. Nat.) (0)	0	<0.01
Aleut (Alaska Native) (0)	0	<0.01
Apache (0)	0	<0.01
Arapaho (0)	0	<0.01
Blackfeet (2)	5	0.01
Canadian/French Am. Ind. (0)	2	<0.01
Central American Ind. (1)	1	<0.01
Cherokee (32)	93	0.14
Cheyenne (0)	0	<0.01
Chickasaw (0)	2	<0.01
Chippewa (9)	9	0.01

Race* (cont.)	Population	%
Choctaw (4)	10	0.01
Colville (0)	0	<0.01
Comanche (3)	3	<0.01
Cree (0)	0	<0.01
Creek (2)	6	0.01
Crow (0)	0	<0.01
Delaware (2)	2	<0.01
Hopi (0)	0	<0.01
Houma (0)	0	<0.01
Inupiat (Alaska Native) (0)	0	<0.01
Iroquois (6)	7	0.01
Kiowa (0)	0	<0.01
Lumbee (9)	14	0.02
Menominee (0)	0	<0.01
Mexican American Ind. (18)	19	0.03
Navajo (1)	8	0.01
Osage (2)	2	<0.01
Ottawa (0)	0	<0.01
Paiute (0)	0	<0.01
Pima (0)	0	<0.01
Potawatomi (0)	1	<0.01
Pueblo (0)	0	<0.01
Puget Sound Salish (0)	0	<0.01
Seminole (0)	0	<0.01
Shoshone (0)	1	<0.01
Sioux (0)	2	<0.01
South American Ind. (1)	1	<0.01
Spanish American Ind. (1)	1	<0.01
Tlingit-Haida (Alaska Native) (1)	1	<0.01
Tohono O'Odham (0)	0	<0.01
Tsimshian (Alaska Native) (2)	2	<0.01
Ute (0)	0	<0.01
Yakama (0)	0	<0.01
Yaqui (0)	0	<0.01
Yuman (0)	0	<0.01
Yup'ik (Alaska Native) (0)	0	<0.01
Asian (1,115)	1,418	2.09
Not Hispanic (1,103)	1,381	2.04
Hispanic (12)	37	0.05
Bangladeshi (0)	0	<0.01
Bhutanese (0)	0	<0.01
Burmese (11)	11	0.02
Cambodian (15)	16	0.02
Chinese, ex. Taiwanese (296)	335	0.49
Filipino (120)	217	0.32
Hmong (1)	1	<0.01
Indian (282)	327	0.48
Indonesian (7)	13	0.02
Japanese (53)	88	0.13
Korean (109)	145	0.21
Laotian (6)	6	0.01
Malaysian (1)	5	0.01
Nepalese (6)	6	0.01
Pakistani (28)	29	0.04
Sri Lankan (5)	11	0.02
Taiwanese (14)	17	0.03
Thai (8)	12	0.02
Vietnamese (112)	134	0.20
Hawaii Native/Pacific Islander (25)	52	0.08
Not Hispanic (20)	44	0.06
Hispanic (5)	8	0.01
Fijian (0)	0	<0.01
Guamanian/Chamorro (19)	29	0.04
Marshallese (0)	0	<0.01
Native Hawaiian (4)	10	0.01
Samoan (1)	9	0.01
Tongan (0)	1	<0.01
White (61,938)	62,618	92.30
Not Hispanic (60,653)	61,219	90.24
Hispanic (1,285)	1,399	2.06

Notes: † The Census 2010 population figure is used to calculate the percentages in the Hispanic Origin and Race categories. Ancestry percentages are based on the 2006-2010 American Community Survey population (not shown); ‡ Numbers in parentheses indicate the number of people reporting a single ancestry; * Numbers in parentheses indicate the number of persons reporting this race alone, not in combination with any other race; Please refer to the Explanation of Data for more information.

North Charleston

Place Type: City
County: Charleston
Population: 97,471

Ancestry	Population	%
Afghan (0)	0	<0.01
African, Sub-Saharan (632)	1,027	1.09
African (580)	951	1.01
Cape Verdean (7)	7	0.01
Ethiopian (21)	21	0.02
Ghanaian (0)	0	<0.01
Kenyan (0)	0	<0.01
Liberian (0)	0	<0.01
Nigerian (0)	0	<0.01
Senegalese (0)	0	<0.01
Sierra Leonean (0)	0	<0.01
Somalian (0)	0	<0.01
South African (0)	24	0.03
Sudanese (9)	9	0.01
Ugandan (0)	0	<0.01
Zimbabwean (0)	0	<0.01
Other Sub-Saharan African (15)	15	0.02
Albanian (14)	22	0.02
Alsatian (0)	0	<0.01
American (6,527)	6,527	6.91
Arab (30)	71	0.08
Arab (17)	33	0.03
Egyptian (0)	0	<0.01
Iraqi (0)	0	<0.01
Jordanian (0)	0	<0.01
Lebanese (0)	0	<0.01
Moroccan (0)	9	0.01
Palestinian (0)	0	<0.01
Syrian (0)	16	0.02
Other Arab (13)	13	0.01
Armenian (0)	20	0.02
Assyrian/Chaldean/Syriac (0)	0	<0.01
Australian (40)	40	0.04
Austrian (46)	184	0.19
Basque (0)	0	<0.01
Belgian (22)	53	0.06
Brazilian (73)	73	0.08
British (57)	140	0.15
Bulgarian (0)	0	<0.01
Cajun (0)	0	<0.01
Canadian (100)	186	0.20
Carpatho Rusyn (0)	0	<0.01
Celtic (0)	0	<0.01
Croatian (0)	42	0.04
Cypriot (0)	0	<0.01
Czech (28)	120	0.13
Czechoslovakian (46)	46	0.05
Danish (20)	98	0.10
Dutch (66)	519	0.55
Eastern European (24)	24	0.03
English (2,397)	5,132	5.43
Estonian (0)	0	<0.01
European (594)	792	0.84
Finnish (0)	22	0.02
French, ex. Basque (534)	1,585	1.68
French Canadian (231)	423	0.45
German (3,039)	7,850	8.30
German Russian (0)	0	<0.01
Greek (55)	233	0.25
Guyanese (26)	32	0.03
Hungarian (54)	154	0.16
Icelander (0)	0	<0.01
Iranian (0)	0	<0.01
Irish (1,806)	5,476	5.79
Israeli (0)	0	<0.01
Italian (693)	1,869	1.98
Latvian (0)	47	0.05
Lithuanian (0)	0	<0.01
Luxemburger (0)	0	<0.01
Macedonian (12)	12	0.01
Maltese (0)	0	<0.01
New Zealander (18)	18	0.02
Northern European (48)	48	0.05

Ancestry	Population	%
Norwegian (121)	321	0.34
Pennsylvania German (13)	41	0.04
Polish (364)	1,154	1.22
Portuguese (151)	242	0.26
Romanian (10)	65	0.07
Russian (124)	248	0.26
Scandinavian (79)	229	0.24
Scotch-Irish (635)	1,346	1.42
Scottish (383)	1,098	1.16
Serbian (0)	0	<0.01
Slavic (11)	11	0.01
Slovak (34)	46	0.05
Slovene (0)	17	0.02
Soviet Union (0)	0	<0.01
Swedish (109)	328	0.35
Swiss (0)	57	0.06
Turkish (101)	101	0.11
Ukrainian (36)	228	0.24
Welsh (66)	325	0.34
West Indian, ex. Hispanic (368)	504	0.53
Bahamian (0)	0	<0.01
Barbadian (0)	0	<0.01
Belizean (0)	0	<0.01
Bermudan (0)	0	<0.01
British West Indian (37)	37	0.04
Dutch West Indian (46)	46	0.05
Haitian (27)	27	0.03
Jamaican (82)	136	0.14
Trinidadian/Tobagonian (101)	111	0.12
U.S. Virgin Islander (0)	0	<0.01
West Indian (75)	147	0.16
Other West Indian (0)	0	<0.01
Yugoslavian (15)	43	0.05

Hispanic Origin	Population	%
Hispanic or Latino (of any race)	10,617	10.89
Central American, ex. Mexican	1,142	1.17
Costa Rican	24	0.02
Guatemalan	558	0.57
Honduran	264	0.27
Nicaraguan	59	0.06
Panamanian	84	0.09
Salvadoran	147	0.15
Other Central American	6	0.01
Cuban	151	0.15
Dominican Republic	95	0.10
Mexican	7,157	7.34
Puerto Rican	831	0.85
South American	433	0.44
Argentinean	58	0.06
Bolivian	38	0.04
Chilean	15	0.02
Colombian	143	0.15
Ecuadorian	41	0.04
Paraguayan	1	<0.01
Peruvian	82	0.08
Uruguayan	11	0.01
Venezuelan	41	0.04
Other South American	3	<0.01
Other Hispanic or Latino	808	0.83

Race*	Population	%
African-American/Black (45,964)	47,316	48.54
Not Hispanic (45,507)	46,648	47.86
Hispanic (457)	668	0.69
American Indian/Alaska Native (453)	1,029	1.06
Not Hispanic (333)	818	0.84
Hispanic (120)	211	0.22
Alaska Athabascan (Ala. Nat.) (2)	2	<0.01
Aleut (Alaska Native) (0)	0	<0.01
Apache (4)	7	0.01
Arapaho (0)	0	<0.01
Blackfeet (2)	30	0.03
Canadian/French Am. Ind. (0)	0	<0.01
Central American Ind. (2)	3	<0.01
Cherokee (56)	246	0.25
Cheyenne (0)	0	<0.01
Chickasaw (0)	0	<0.01
Chippewa (2)	4	<0.01

Race* (cont.)	Population	%
Choctaw (3)	3	<0.01
Colville (0)	0	<0.01
Comanche (0)	7	0.01
Cree (2)	2	<0.01
Creek (3)	19	0.02
Crow (0)	5	0.01
Delaware (0)	0	<0.01
Hopi (0)	1	<0.01
Houma (1)	1	<0.01
Inupiat (Alaska Native) (1)	3	<0.01
Iroquois (0)	14	0.01
Kiowa (0)	0	<0.01
Lumbee (33)	38	0.04
Menominee (1)	1	<0.01
Mexican American Ind. (50)	54	0.06
Navajo (4)	5	0.01
Osage (0)	2	<0.01
Ottawa (0)	0	<0.01
Paiute (0)	0	<0.01
Pima (0)	0	<0.01
Potawatomi (1)	3	<0.01
Pueblo (0)	0	<0.01
Puget Sound Salish (0)	0	<0.01
Seminole (0)	5	0.01
Shoshone (0)	0	<0.01
Sioux (15)	34	0.03
South American Ind. (1)	1	<0.01
Spanish American Ind. (1)	3	<0.01
Tlingit-Haida (Alaska Native) (1)	1	<0.01
Tohono O'Odham (0)	0	<0.01
Tsimshian (Alaska Native) (1)	1	<0.01
Ute (0)	0	<0.01
Yakama (0)	0	<0.01
Yaqui (1)	2	<0.01
Yuman (0)	1	<0.01
Yup'ik (Alaska Native) (0)	0	<0.01
Asian (1,897)	2,485	2.55
Not Hispanic (1,871)	2,405	2.47
Hispanic (26)	80	0.08
Bangladeshi (9)	9	0.01
Bhutanese (0)	0	<0.01
Burmese (11)	11	0.01
Cambodian (5)	6	0.01
Chinese, ex. Taiwanese (284)	364	0.37
Filipino (699)	969	0.99
Hmong (2)	2	<0.01
Indian (264)	306	0.31
Indonesian (5)	7	0.01
Japanese (71)	170	0.17
Korean (122)	207	0.21
Laotian (6)	11	0.01
Malaysian (1)	7	0.01
Nepalese (1)	1	<0.01
Pakistani (13)	14	0.01
Sri Lankan (0)	0	<0.01
Taiwanese (4)	8	0.01
Thai (26)	53	0.05
Vietnamese (286)	317	0.33
Hawaii Native/Pacific Islander (157)	288	0.30
Not Hispanic (119)	228	0.23
Hispanic (38)	60	0.06
Fijian (0)	0	<0.01
Guamanian/Chamorro (76)	106	0.11
Marshallese (1)	1	<0.01
Native Hawaiian (29)	71	0.07
Samoan (12)	20	0.02
Tongan (0)	0	<0.01
White (40,514)	42,441	43.54
Not Hispanic (36,945)	38,468	39.47
Hispanic (3,569)	3,973	4.08

*Notes: † The Census 2010 population figure is used to calculate the percentages in the Hispanic Origin and Race categories. Ancestry percentages are based on the 2006-2010 American Community Survey population (not shown); ‡ Numbers in parentheses indicate the number of people reporting a single ancestry; * Numbers in parentheses indicate the number of persons reporting this race alone, not in combination with any other race; Please refer to the Explanation of Data for more information.*

Rock Hill

Place Type: City
County: York
Population: 66,154

Ancestry	Population	%
Afghan (0)	0	<0.01
African, Sub-Saharan (491)	550	0.87
African (408)	467	0.74
Cape Verdean (65)	65	0.10
Ethiopian (0)	0	<0.01
Ghanaian (0)	0	<0.01
Kenyan (0)	0	<0.01
Liberian (0)	0	<0.01
Nigerian (0)	0	<0.01
Senegalese (0)	0	<0.01
Sierra Leonean (0)	0	<0.01
Somalian (0)	0	<0.01
South African (0)	0	<0.01
Sudanese (0)	0	<0.01
Ugandan (0)	0	<0.01
Zimbabwean (0)	0	<0.01
Other Sub-Saharan African (18)	18	0.03
Albanian (0)	0	<0.01
Alsatian (0)	0	<0.01
American (3,840)	3,840	6.08
Arab (66)	81	0.13
Arab (0)	0	<0.01
Egyptian (0)	0	<0.01
Iraqi (0)	0	<0.01
Jordanian (0)	0	<0.01
Lebanese (29)	29	0.05
Moroccan (0)	0	<0.01
Palestinian (0)	0	<0.01
Syrian (24)	39	0.06
Other Arab (13)	13	0.02
Armenian (11)	11	0.02
Assyrian/Chaldean/Syriac (0)	0	<0.01
Australian (0)	0	<0.01
Austrian (25)	108	0.17
Basque (0)	0	<0.01
Belgian (0)	10	0.02
Brazilian (26)	26	0.04
British (151)	291	0.46
Bulgarian (0)	0	<0.01
Cajun (0)	11	0.02
Canadian (25)	49	0.08
Carpatho Rusyn (0)	0	<0.01
Celtic (0)	0	<0.01
Croatian (0)	9	0.01
Cypriot (0)	0	<0.01
Czech (64)	108	0.17
Czechoslovakian (0)	37	0.06
Danish (15)	109	0.17
Dutch (193)	730	1.16
Eastern European (15)	15	0.02
English (2,687)	5,454	8.64
Estonian (0)	0	<0.01
European (580)	662	1.05
Finnish (46)	69	0.11
French, ex. Basque (214)	1,391	2.20
French Canadian (48)	104	0.16
German (2,423)	7,124	11.29
German Russian (0)	0	<0.01
Greek (27)	93	0.15
Guyanese (8)	8	0.01
Hungarian (38)	72	0.11
Icelander (10)	24	0.04
Iranian (0)	0	<0.01
Irish (1,873)	6,334	10.04
Israeli (0)	0	<0.01
Italian (497)	1,636	2.59
Latvian (0)	0	<0.01
Lithuanian (0)	39	0.06
Luxemburger (0)	0	<0.01
Macedonian (0)	0	<0.01
Maltese (0)	0	<0.01
New Zealander (0)	0	<0.01
Northern European (0)	0	<0.01

Ancestry	Population	%
Norwegian (42)	199	0.32
Pennsylvania German (9)	9	0.01
Polish (164)	525	0.83
Portuguese (45)	54	0.09
Romanian (0)	0	<0.01
Russian (15)	24	0.04
Scandinavian (36)	36	0.06
Scotch-Irish (2,145)	3,164	5.01
Scottish (547)	1,401	2.22
Serbian (0)	0	<0.01
Slavic (12)	12	0.02
Slovak (13)	46	0.07
Slovene (0)	0	<0.01
Soviet Union (0)	0	<0.01
Swedish (36)	222	0.35
Swiss (0)	93	0.15
Turkish (0)	0	<0.01
Ukrainian (22)	81	0.13
Welsh (46)	376	0.60
West Indian, ex. Hispanic (0)	82	0.13
Bahamian (0)	0	<0.01
Barbadian (0)	0	<0.01
Belizean (0)	0	<0.01
Bermudan (0)	0	<0.01
British West Indian (0)	0	<0.01
Dutch West Indian (0)	0	<0.01
Haitian (0)	0	<0.01
Jamaican (0)	52	0.08
Trinidadian/Tobagonian (0)	0	<0.01
U.S. Virgin Islander (0)	0	<0.01
West Indian (0)	30	0.05
Other West Indian (0)	0	<0.01
Yugoslavian (17)	17	0.03

Hispanic Origin	Population	%
Hispanic or Latino (of any race)	3,761	5.69
Central American, ex. Mexican	421	0.64
Costa Rican	24	0.04
Guatemalan	63	0.10
Honduran	178	0.27
Nicaraguan	22	0.03
Panamanian	30	0.05
Salvadoran	100	0.15
Other Central American	4	0.01
Cuban	81	0.12
Dominican Republic	106	0.16
Mexican	2,002	3.03
Puerto Rican	465	0.70
South American	460	0.70
Argentinean	15	0.02
Bolivian	11	0.02
Chilean	18	0.03
Colombian	216	0.33
Ecuadorian	59	0.09
Paraguayan	1	<0.01
Peruvian	53	0.08
Uruguayan	69	0.10
Venezuelan	17	0.03
Other South American	1	<0.01
Other Hispanic or Latino	226	0.34

Race*	Population	%
African-American/Black (25,348)	26,236	39.66
Not Hispanic (25,148)	25,932	39.20
Hispanic (200)	304	0.46
American Indian/Alaska Native (322)	653	0.99
Not Hispanic (282)	595	0.90
Hispanic (40)	58	0.09
Alaska Athabascan (Ala. Nat.) (0)	1	<0.01
Aleut (Alaska Native) (0)	0	<0.01
Apache (1)	2	<0.01
Arapaho (0)	1	<0.01
Blackfeet (1)	18	0.03
Canadian/French Am. Ind. (0)	0	<0.01
Central American Ind. (2)	2	<0.01
Cherokee (38)	117	0.18
Cheyenne (0)	1	<0.01
Chickasaw (0)	0	<0.01
Chippewa (0)	1	<0.01

Race*	Population	%
Choctaw (4)	7	0.01
Colville (0)	0	<0.01
Comanche (1)	1	<0.01
Cree (0)	0	<0.01
Creek (5)	14	0.02
Crow (0)	0	<0.01
Delaware (0)	0	<0.01
Hopi (0)	0	<0.01
Houma (0)	0	<0.01
Inupiat (Alaska Native) (1)	1	<0.01
Iroquois (4)	8	0.01
Kiowa (0)	0	<0.01
Lumbee (13)	17	0.03
Menominee (0)	0	<0.01
Mexican American Ind. (10)	15	0.02
Navajo (0)	2	<0.01
Osage (4)	4	0.01
Ottawa (0)	0	<0.01
Paiute (0)	0	<0.01
Pima (0)	0	<0.01
Potawatomi (0)	0	<0.01
Pueblo (0)	0	<0.01
Puget Sound Salish (1)	1	<0.01
Seminole (1)	7	0.01
Shoshone (1)	1	<0.01
Sioux (1)	4	0.01
South American Ind. (0)	1	<0.01
Spanish American Ind. (0)	0	<0.01
Tlingit-Haida (Alaska Native) (5)	5	0.01
Tohono O'Odham (5)	5	0.01
Tsimshian (Alaska Native) (0)	0	<0.01
Ute (0)	0	<0.01
Yakama (0)	0	<0.01
Yaqui (0)	0	<0.01
Yuman (0)	0	<0.01
Yup'ik (Alaska Native) (1)	1	<0.01
Asian (1,118)	1,372	2.07
Not Hispanic (1,113)	1,348	2.04
Hispanic (5)	24	0.04
Bangladeshi (3)	3	<0.01
Bhutanese (0)	0	<0.01
Burmese (1)	1	<0.01
Cambodian (42)	55	0.08
Chinese, ex. Taiwanese (123)	170	0.26
Filipino (162)	213	0.32
Hmong (36)	37	0.06
Indian (222)	260	0.39
Indonesian (4)	5	0.01
Japanese (13)	43	0.06
Korean (64)	96	0.15
Laotian (19)	20	0.03
Malaysian (2)	4	0.01
Nepalese (0)	0	<0.01
Pakistani (16)	22	0.03
Sri Lankan (2)	2	<0.01
Taiwanese (4)	5	0.01
Thai (3)	17	0.03
Vietnamese (346)	384	0.58
Hawaii Native/Pacific Islander (69)	96	0.15
Not Hispanic (21)	42	0.06
Hispanic (48)	54	0.08
Fijian (0)	2	<0.01
Guamanian/Chamorro (57)	60	0.09
Marshallese (0)	0	<0.01
Native Hawaiian (2)	11	0.02
Samoan (4)	7	0.01
Tongan (3)	5	0.01
White (36,147)	37,269	56.34
Not Hispanic (34,594)	35,555	53.75
Hispanic (1,553)	1,714	2.59

Notes: † The Census 2010 population figure is used to calculate the percentages in the Hispanic Origin and Race categories. Ancestry percentages are based on the 2006-2010 American Community Survey population (not shown); ‡ Numbers in parentheses indicate the number of people reporting a single ancestry; * Numbers in parentheses indicate the number of persons reporting this race alone, not in combination with any other race; Please refer to the Explanation of Data for more information.

Ancestry Group Rankings

Afghan

Top 10 Places Sorted by Population
Based on all places, regardless of total population

Place	Population	%
Abbeville (city) Abbeville County	0	0.00
Aiken (city) Aiken County	0	0.00
Alcolu (cdp) Clarendon County	0	0.00
Allendale (town) Allendale County	0	0.00
Anderson (city) Anderson County	0	0.00
Andrews (town) Georgetown County	0	0.00
Antreville (cdp) Abbeville County	0	0.00
Arcadia (cdp) Spartanburg County	0	0.00
Arcadia Lakes (town) Richland County	0	0.00
Arial (cdp) Pickens County	0	0.00

Top 10 Places Sorted by Percent of Total Population
Based on all places, regardless of total population

Place	Population	%
Abbeville (city) Abbeville County	0	0.00
Aiken (city) Aiken County	0	0.00
Alcolu (cdp) Clarendon County	0	0.00
Allendale (town) Allendale County	0	0.00
Anderson (city) Anderson County	0	0.00
Andrews (town) Georgetown County	0	0.00
Antreville (cdp) Abbeville County	0	0.00
Arcadia (cdp) Spartanburg County	0	0.00
Arcadia Lakes (town) Richland County	0	0.00
Arial (cdp) Pickens County	0	0.00

Top 10 Places Sorted by Percent of Total Population
Based on places with total population of 50,000 or more

Place	Population	%
Charleston (city) Charleston County	0	0.00
Columbia (city) Richland County	0	0.00
Greenville (city) Greenville County	0	0.00
Mount Pleasant (town) Charleston County	0	0.00
North Charleston (city) Charleston County	0	0.00
Rock Hill (city) York County	0	0.00

African, Sub-Saharan

Top 10 Places Sorted by Population
Based on all places, regardless of total population

Place	Population	%
Sumter (city) Sumter County	3,075	7.62
Columbia (city) Richland County	2,206	1.73
North Charleston (city) Charleston County	1,027	1.09
Charleston (city) Charleston County	754	0.65
Gadsden (cdp) Richland County	593	28.52
West Columbia (city) Lexington County	560	3.82
Rock Hill (city) York County	550	0.87
Dentsville (cdp) Richland County	528	3.92
Dalzell (cdp) Sumter County	496	15.38
Burton (cdp) Beaufort County	454	6.35

Top 10 Places Sorted by Percent of Total Population
Based on all places, regardless of total population

Place	Population	%
Mulberry (cdp) Sumter County	104	31.52
Gadsden (cdp) Richland County	593	28.52
Oakland (cdp) Sumter County	273	20.06
Eastover (town) Richland County	118	18.73
South Sumter (cdp) Sumter County	403	16.69
Ridgeway (town) Fairfield County	86	16.54
Dalzell (cdp) Sumter County	496	15.38
Promised Land (cdp) Greenwood County	69	14.47
Wallace (cdp) Marlboro County	122	13.90
Swansea (town) Lexington County	78	9.67

Top 10 Places Sorted by Percent of Total Population
Based on places with total population of 50,000 or more

Place	Population	%
Columbia (city) Richland County	2,206	1.73
North Charleston (city) Charleston County	1,027	1.09
Rock Hill (city) York County	550	0.87
Charleston (city) Charleston County	754	0.65
Greenville (city) Greenville County	331	0.57
Mount Pleasant (town) Charleston County	171	0.27

African, Sub-Saharan: African

Top 10 Places Sorted by Population
Based on all places, regardless of total population

Place	Population	%
Sumter (city) Sumter County	3,059	7.58
Columbia (city) Richland County	1,837	1.44
North Charleston (city) Charleston County	951	1.01
Gadsden (cdp) Richland County	593	28.52
Charleston (city) Charleston County	577	0.50
Dentsville (cdp) Richland County	528	3.92
West Columbia (city) Lexington County	521	3.55
Dalzell (cdp) Sumter County	496	15.38
Rock Hill (city) York County	467	0.74
Burton (cdp) Beaufort County	454	6.35

Top 10 Places Sorted by Percent of Total Population
Based on all places, regardless of total population

Place	Population	%
Mulberry (cdp) Sumter County	104	31.52
Gadsden (cdp) Richland County	593	28.52
Oakland (cdp) Sumter County	273	20.06
Eastover (town) Richland County	118	18.73
South Sumter (cdp) Sumter County	403	16.69
Ridgeway (town) Fairfield County	86	16.54
Dalzell (cdp) Sumter County	496	15.38
Promised Land (cdp) Greenwood County	69	14.47
Wallace (cdp) Marlboro County	122	13.90
Swansea (town) Lexington County	78	9.67

Top 10 Places Sorted by Percent of Total Population
Based on places with total population of 50,000 or more

Place	Population	%
Columbia (city) Richland County	1,837	1.44
North Charleston (city) Charleston County	951	1.01
Rock Hill (city) York County	467	0.74
Charleston (city) Charleston County	577	0.50
Greenville (city) Greenville County	228	0.39
Mount Pleasant (town) Charleston County	47	0.07

African, Sub-Saharan: Cape Verdean

Top 10 Places Sorted by Population
Based on all places, regardless of total population

Place	Population	%
Hilton Head Island (town) Beaufort County	149	0.41
Rock Hill (city) York County	65	0.10
Greenville (city) Greenville County	30	0.05
Columbia (city) Richland County	9	0.01
North Charleston (city) Charleston County	7	0.01
Abbeville (city) Abbeville County	0	0.00
Aiken (city) Aiken County	0	0.00
Alcolu (cdp) Clarendon County	0	0.00
Allendale (town) Allendale County	0	0.00
Anderson (city) Anderson County	0	0.00

Top 10 Places Sorted by Percent of Total Population
Based on all places, regardless of total population

Place	Population	%
Hilton Head Island (town) Beaufort County	149	0.41
Rock Hill (city) York County	65	0.10
Greenville (city) Greenville County	30	0.05
Columbia (city) Richland County	9	0.01
North Charleston (city) Charleston County	7	0.01
Abbeville (city) Abbeville County	0	0.00
Aiken (city) Aiken County	0	0.00
Alcolu (cdp) Clarendon County	0	0.00
Allendale (town) Allendale County	0	0.00
Anderson (city) Anderson County	0	0.00

Top 10 Places Sorted by Percent of Total Population
Based on places with total population of 50,000 or more

Place	Population	%
Rock Hill (city) York County	65	0.10

(continued)

Place	Population	%
Greenville (city) Greenville County	30	0.05
Columbia (city) Richland County	9	0.01
North Charleston (city) Charleston County	7	0.01
Charleston (city) Charleston County	0	0.00
Mount Pleasant (town) Charleston County	0	0.00

African, Sub-Saharan: Ethiopian

Top 10 Places Sorted by Population
Based on all places, regardless of total population

Place	Population	%
Five Forks (cdp) Greenville County	217	1.65
Columbia (city) Richland County	64	0.05
Woodfield (cdp) Richland County	33	0.33
North Charleston (city) Charleston County	21	0.02
Anderson (city) Anderson County	13	0.05
Charleston (city) Charleston County	11	0.01
Sumter (city) Sumter County	5	0.01
Abbeville (city) Abbeville County	0	0.00
Aiken (city) Aiken County	0	0.00
Alcolu (cdp) Clarendon County	0	0.00

Top 10 Places Sorted by Percent of Total Population
Based on all places, regardless of total population

Place	Population	%
Five Forks (cdp) Greenville County	217	1.65
Woodfield (cdp) Richland County	33	0.33
Columbia (city) Richland County	64	0.05
Anderson (city) Anderson County	13	0.05
North Charleston (city) Charleston County	21	0.02
Charleston (city) Charleston County	11	0.01
Sumter (city) Sumter County	5	0.01
Abbeville (city) Abbeville County	0	0.00
Aiken (city) Aiken County	0	0.00
Alcolu (cdp) Clarendon County	0	0.00

Top 10 Places Sorted by Percent of Total Population
Based on places with total population of 50,000 or more

Place	Population	%
Columbia (city) Richland County	64	0.05
North Charleston (city) Charleston County	21	0.02
Charleston (city) Charleston County	11	0.01
Greenville (city) Greenville County	0	0.00
Mount Pleasant (town) Charleston County	0	0.00
Rock Hill (city) York County	0	0.00

African, Sub-Saharan: Ghanaian

Top 10 Places Sorted by Population
Based on all places, regardless of total population

Place	Population	%
Clemson (city) Pickens County	44	0.32
Central (town) Pickens County	40	0.82
Cayce (city) Lexington County	17	0.14
Newberry (city) Newberry County	15	0.15
Lexington (town) Lexington County	8	0.05
Columbia (city) Richland County	5	<0.01
Abbeville (city) Abbeville County	0	0.00
Aiken (city) Aiken County	0	0.00
Alcolu (cdp) Clarendon County	0	0.00
Allendale (town) Allendale County	0	0.00

Top 10 Places Sorted by Percent of Total Population
Based on all places, regardless of total population

Place	Population	%
Central (town) Pickens County	40	0.82
Clemson (city) Pickens County	44	0.32
Newberry (city) Newberry County	15	0.15
Cayce (city) Lexington County	17	0.14
Lexington (town) Lexington County	8	0.05
Columbia (city) Richland County	5	<0.01
Abbeville (city) Abbeville County	0	0.00
Aiken (city) Aiken County	0	0.00
Alcolu (cdp) Clarendon County	0	0.00
Allendale (town) Allendale County	0	0.00

Top 10 Places Sorted by Percent of Total Population
Based on places with total population of 50,000 or more

Place	Population	%
Columbia (city) Richland County	5	<0.01
Charleston (city) Charleston County	0	0.00
Greenville (city) Greenville County	0	0.00
Mount Pleasant (town) Charleston County	0	0.00
North Charleston (city) Charleston County	0	0.00
Rock Hill (city) York County	0	0.00

African, Sub-Saharan: Kenyan

Top 10 Places Sorted by Population
Based on all places, regardless of total population

Place	Population	%
Columbia (city) Richland County	72	0.06
Abbeville (city) Abbeville County	64	1.19
Greer (city) Greenville County	46	0.19
Spartanburg (city) Spartanburg County	36	0.10
Irmo (town) Richland County	14	0.13
Port Royal (town) Beaufort County	11	0.11
Bluffton (town) Beaufort County	9	0.08
Aiken (city) Aiken County	0	0.00
Alcolu (cdp) Clarendon County	0	0.00
Allendale (town) Allendale County	0	0.00

Top 10 Places Sorted by Percent of Total Population
Based on all places, regardless of total population

Place	Population	%
Abbeville (city) Abbeville County	64	1.19
Greer (city) Greenville County	46	0.19
Irmo (town) Richland County	14	0.13
Port Royal (town) Beaufort County	11	0.11
Spartanburg (city) Spartanburg County	36	0.10
Bluffton (town) Beaufort County	9	0.08
Columbia (city) Richland County	72	0.06
Aiken (city) Aiken County	0	0.00
Alcolu (cdp) Clarendon County	0	0.00
Allendale (town) Allendale County	0	0.00

Top 10 Places Sorted by Percent of Total Population
Based on places with total population of 50,000 or more

Place	Population	%
Columbia (city) Richland County	72	0.06
Charleston (city) Charleston County	0	0.00
Greenville (city) Greenville County	0	0.00
Mount Pleasant (town) Charleston County	0	0.00
North Charleston (city) Charleston County	0	0.00
Rock Hill (city) York County	0	0.00

African, Sub-Saharan: Liberian

Top 10 Places Sorted by Population
Based on all places, regardless of total population

Place	Population	%
Lancaster (city) Lancaster County	82	0.99
Columbia (city) Richland County	51	0.04
Abbeville (city) Abbeville County	0	0.00
Aiken (city) Aiken County	0	0.00
Alcolu (cdp) Clarendon County	0	0.00
Allendale (town) Allendale County	0	0.00
Anderson (city) Anderson County	0	0.00
Andrews (town) Georgetown County	0	0.00
Antreville (cdp) Abbeville County	0	0.00
Arcadia (cdp) Spartanburg County	0	0.00

Top 10 Places Sorted by Percent of Total Population
Based on all places, regardless of total population

Place	Population	%
Lancaster (city) Lancaster County	82	0.99
Columbia (city) Richland County	51	0.04
Abbeville (city) Abbeville County	0	0.00
Aiken (city) Aiken County	0	0.00
Alcolu (cdp) Clarendon County	0	0.00
Allendale (town) Allendale County	0	0.00
Anderson (city) Anderson County	0	0.00
Andrews (town) Georgetown County	0	0.00
Antreville (cdp) Abbeville County	0	0.00
Arcadia (cdp) Spartanburg County	0	0.00

Top 10 Places Sorted by Percent of Total Population
Based on places with total population of 50,000 or more

Place	Population	%
Columbia (city) Richland County	51	0.04
Charleston (city) Charleston County	0	0.00
Greenville (city) Greenville County	0	0.00
Mount Pleasant (town) Charleston County	0	0.00
North Charleston (city) Charleston County	0	0.00
Rock Hill (city) York County	0	0.00

African, Sub-Saharan: Nigerian

Top 10 Places Sorted by Population
Based on all places, regardless of total population

Place	Population	%
Charleston (city) Charleston County	94	0.08
Greenville (city) Greenville County	53	0.09
Summerville (town) Dorchester County	44	0.11
Columbia (city) Richland County	39	0.03
Simpsonville (city) Greenville County	23	0.13
Wade Hampton (cdp) Greenville County	23	0.11
Orangeburg (city) Orangeburg County	13	0.09
Sumter (city) Sumter County	11	0.03
Wellford (city) Spartanburg County	10	0.55
Central (town) Pickens County	9	0.18

Top 10 Places Sorted by Percent of Total Population
Based on all places, regardless of total population

Place	Population	%
Wellford (city) Spartanburg County	10	0.55
Central (town) Pickens County	9	0.18
Simpsonville (city) Greenville County	23	0.13
Summerville (town) Dorchester County	44	0.11
Wade Hampton (cdp) Greenville County	23	0.11
Greenville (city) Greenville County	53	0.09
Orangeburg (city) Orangeburg County	13	0.09
Charleston (city) Charleston County	94	0.08
Greer (city) Greenville County	9	0.04
Columbia (city) Richland County	39	0.03

Top 10 Places Sorted by Percent of Total Population
Based on places with total population of 50,000 or more

Place	Population	%
Greenville (city) Greenville County	53	0.09
Charleston (city) Charleston County	94	0.08
Columbia (city) Richland County	39	0.03
Mount Pleasant (town) Charleston County	0	0.00
North Charleston (city) Charleston County	0	0.00
Rock Hill (city) York County	0	0.00

African, Sub-Saharan: Senegalese

Top 10 Places Sorted by Population
Based on all places, regardless of total population

Place	Population	%
Orangeburg (city) Orangeburg County	40	0.29
Abbeville (city) Abbeville County	0	0.00
Aiken (city) Aiken County	0	0.00
Alcolu (cdp) Clarendon County	0	0.00
Allendale (town) Allendale County	0	0.00
Anderson (city) Anderson County	0	0.00
Andrews (town) Georgetown County	0	0.00
Antreville (cdp) Abbeville County	0	0.00
Arcadia (cdp) Spartanburg County	0	0.00
Arcadia Lakes (town) Richland County	0	0.00

Top 10 Places Sorted by Percent of Total Population
Based on all places, regardless of total population

Place	Population	%
Orangeburg (city) Orangeburg County	40	0.29
Abbeville (city) Abbeville County	0	0.00
Aiken (city) Aiken County	0	0.00
Alcolu (cdp) Clarendon County	0	0.00
Allendale (town) Allendale County	0	0.00
Anderson (city) Anderson County	0	0.00
Andrews (town) Georgetown County	0	0.00
Antreville (cdp) Abbeville County	0	0.00
Arcadia (cdp) Spartanburg County	0	0.00
Arcadia Lakes (town) Richland County	0	0.00

Top 10 Places Sorted by Percent of Total Population
Based on places with total population of 50,000 or more

Place	Population	%
Charleston (city) Charleston County	0	0.00
Columbia (city) Richland County	0	0.00
Greenville (city) Greenville County	0	0.00
Mount Pleasant (town) Charleston County	0	0.00
North Charleston (city) Charleston County	0	0.00
Rock Hill (city) York County	0	0.00

African, Sub-Saharan: Sierra Leonean

Top 10 Places Sorted by Population
Based on all places, regardless of total population

Place	Population	%
Edgefield (town) Edgefield County	8	0.17
Abbeville (city) Abbeville County	0	0.00
Aiken (city) Aiken County	0	0.00
Alcolu (cdp) Clarendon County	0	0.00
Allendale (town) Allendale County	0	0.00
Anderson (city) Anderson County	0	0.00
Andrews (town) Georgetown County	0	0.00
Antreville (cdp) Abbeville County	0	0.00
Arcadia (cdp) Spartanburg County	0	0.00
Arcadia Lakes (town) Richland County	0	0.00

Top 10 Places Sorted by Percent of Total Population
Based on all places, regardless of total population

Place	Population	%
Edgefield (town) Edgefield County	8	0.17
Abbeville (city) Abbeville County	0	0.00
Aiken (city) Aiken County	0	0.00
Alcolu (cdp) Clarendon County	0	0.00
Allendale (town) Allendale County	0	0.00
Anderson (city) Anderson County	0	0.00
Andrews (town) Georgetown County	0	0.00
Antreville (cdp) Abbeville County	0	0.00
Arcadia (cdp) Spartanburg County	0	0.00
Arcadia Lakes (town) Richland County	0	0.00

Top 10 Places Sorted by Percent of Total Population
Based on places with total population of 50,000 or more

Place	Population	%
Charleston (city) Charleston County	0	0.00
Columbia (city) Richland County	0	0.00
Greenville (city) Greenville County	0	0.00
Mount Pleasant (town) Charleston County	0	0.00
North Charleston (city) Charleston County	0	0.00
Rock Hill (city) York County	0	0.00

African, Sub-Saharan: Somalian

Top 10 Places Sorted by Population
Based on all places, regardless of total population

Place	Population	%
Taylors (cdp) Greenville County	149	0.69
Abbeville (city) Abbeville County	0	0.00
Aiken (city) Aiken County	0	0.00
Alcolu (cdp) Clarendon County	0	0.00
Allendale (town) Allendale County	0	0.00
Anderson (city) Anderson County	0	0.00
Andrews (town) Georgetown County	0	0.00
Antreville (cdp) Abbeville County	0	0.00
Arcadia (cdp) Spartanburg County	0	0.00
Arcadia Lakes (town) Richland County	0	0.00

Top 10 Places Sorted by Percent of Total Population
Based on all places, regardless of total population

Place	Population	%
Taylors (cdp) Greenville County	149	0.69
Abbeville (city) Abbeville County	0	0.00
Aiken (city) Aiken County	0	0.00
Alcolu (cdp) Clarendon County	0	0.00
Allendale (town) Allendale County	0	0.00
Anderson (city) Anderson County	0	0.00
Andrews (town) Georgetown County	0	0.00
Antreville (cdp) Abbeville County	0	0.00
Arcadia (cdp) Spartanburg County	0	0.00
Arcadia Lakes (town) Richland County	0	0.00

Top 10 Places Sorted by Percent of Total Population
Based on places with total population of 50,000 or more

Place	Population	%
Charleston (city) Charleston County	0	0.00
Columbia (city) Richland County	0	0.00
Greenville (city) Greenville County	0	0.00
Mount Pleasant (town) Charleston County	0	0.00
North Charleston (city) Charleston County	0	0.00
Rock Hill (city) York County	0	0.00

African, Sub-Saharan: South African

Top 10 Places Sorted by Population
Based on all places, regardless of total population

Place	Population	%
Mount Pleasant (town) Charleston County	108	0.17
Easley (city) Pickens County	60	0.30
Charleston (city) Charleston County	49	0.04
Summerville (town) Dorchester County	47	0.12
North Charleston (city) Charleston County	24	0.03
Bamberg (town) Bamberg County	20	0.55
Greenville (city) Greenville County	20	0.03
Beaufort (city) Beaufort County	15	0.12
Fort Mill (town) York County	12	0.12
Moncks Corner (town) Berkeley County	9	0.12

Top 10 Places Sorted by Percent of Total Population
Based on all places, regardless of total population

Place	Population	%
Bamberg (town) Bamberg County	20	0.55
Easley (city) Pickens County	60	0.30
Mount Pleasant (town) Charleston County	108	0.17
Edgefield (town) Edgefield County	8	0.17
Summerville (town) Dorchester County	47	0.12
Beaufort (city) Beaufort County	15	0.12
Fort Mill (town) York County	12	0.12
Moncks Corner (town) Berkeley County	9	0.12
Charleston (city) Charleston County	49	0.04
North Charleston (city) Charleston County	24	0.03

Top 10 Places Sorted by Percent of Total Population
Based on places with total population of 50,000 or more

Place	Population	%
Mount Pleasant (town) Charleston County	108	0.17
Charleston (city) Charleston County	49	0.04
North Charleston (city) Charleston County	24	0.03
Greenville (city) Greenville County	20	0.03
Columbia (city) Richland County	0	0.00
Rock Hill (city) York County	0	0.00

African, Sub-Saharan: Sudanese

Top 10 Places Sorted by Population
Based on all places, regardless of total population

Place	Population	%
Columbia (city) Richland County	47	0.04
West Columbia (city) Lexington County	39	0.27
Edgefield (town) Edgefield County	9	0.19
North Charleston (city) Charleston County	9	0.01
New Ellenton (town) Aiken County	6	0.28
Abbeville (city) Abbeville County	0	0.00
Aiken (city) Aiken County	0	0.00
Alcolu (cdp) Clarendon County	0	0.00
Allendale (town) Allendale County	0	0.00
Anderson (city) Anderson County	0	0.00

Top 10 Places Sorted by Percent of Total Population
Based on all places, regardless of total population

Place	Population	%
New Ellenton (town) Aiken County	6	0.28
West Columbia (city) Lexington County	39	0.27
Edgefield (town) Edgefield County	9	0.19
Columbia (city) Richland County	47	0.04
North Charleston (city) Charleston County	9	0.01
Abbeville (city) Abbeville County	0	0.00
Aiken (city) Aiken County	0	0.00
Alcolu (cdp) Clarendon County	0	0.00
Allendale (town) Allendale County	0	0.00
Anderson (city) Anderson County	0	0.00

Top 10 Places Sorted by Percent of Total Population
Based on places with total population of 50,000 or more

Place	Population	%
Columbia (city) Richland County	47	0.04
North Charleston (city) Charleston County	9	0.01
Charleston (city) Charleston County	0	0.00
Greenville (city) Greenville County	0	0.00
Mount Pleasant (town) Charleston County	0	0.00
Rock Hill (city) York County	0	0.00

African, Sub-Saharan: Ugandan

Top 10 Places Sorted by Population
Based on all places, regardless of total population

Place	Population	%
Wilkinson Heights (cdp) Orangeburg County	28	1.23
Abbeville (city) Abbeville County	0	0.00
Aiken (city) Aiken County	0	0.00
Alcolu (cdp) Clarendon County	0	0.00
Allendale (town) Allendale County	0	0.00
Anderson (city) Anderson County	0	0.00
Andrews (town) Georgetown County	0	0.00
Antreville (cdp) Abbeville County	0	0.00
Arcadia (cdp) Spartanburg County	0	0.00
Arcadia Lakes (town) Richland County	0	0.00

Top 10 Places Sorted by Percent of Total Population
Based on all places, regardless of total population

Place	Population	%
Wilkinson Heights (cdp) Orangeburg County	28	1.23
Abbeville (city) Abbeville County	0	0.00
Aiken (city) Aiken County	0	0.00
Alcolu (cdp) Clarendon County	0	0.00
Allendale (town) Allendale County	0	0.00
Anderson (city) Anderson County	0	0.00
Andrews (town) Georgetown County	0	0.00
Antreville (cdp) Abbeville County	0	0.00
Arcadia (cdp) Spartanburg County	0	0.00
Arcadia Lakes (town) Richland County	0	0.00

Top 10 Places Sorted by Percent of Total Population
Based on places with total population of 50,000 or more

Place	Population	%
Charleston (city) Charleston County	0	0.00
Columbia (city) Richland County	0	0.00
Greenville (city) Greenville County	0	0.00
Mount Pleasant (town) Charleston County	0	0.00
North Charleston (city) Charleston County	0	0.00
Rock Hill (city) York County	0	0.00

African, Sub-Saharan: Zimbabwean

Top 10 Places Sorted by Population
Based on all places, regardless of total population

Place	Population	%
Charleston (city) Charleston County	12	0.01
Abbeville (city) Abbeville County	0	0.00
Aiken (city) Aiken County	0	0.00
Alcolu (cdp) Clarendon County	0	0.00
Allendale (town) Allendale County	0	0.00
Anderson (city) Anderson County	0	0.00
Andrews (town) Georgetown County	0	0.00
Antreville (cdp) Abbeville County	0	0.00
Arcadia (cdp) Spartanburg County	0	0.00
Arcadia Lakes (town) Richland County	0	0.00

Top 10 Places Sorted by Percent of Total Population
Based on all places, regardless of total population

Place	Population	%
Charleston (city) Charleston County	12	0.01
Abbeville (city) Abbeville County	0	0.00
Aiken (city) Aiken County	0	0.00
Alcolu (cdp) Clarendon County	0	0.00
Allendale (town) Allendale County	0	0.00
Anderson (city) Anderson County	0	0.00
Andrews (town) Georgetown County	0	0.00
Antreville (cdp) Abbeville County	0	0.00
Arcadia (cdp) Spartanburg County	0	0.00
Arcadia Lakes (town) Richland County	0	0.00

Top 10 Places Sorted by Percent of Total Population
Based on places with total population of 50,000 or more

Place	Population	%
Charleston (city) Charleston County	12	0.01
Columbia (city) Richland County	0	0.00
Greenville (city) Greenville County	0	0.00
Mount Pleasant (town) Charleston County	0	0.00
North Charleston (city) Charleston County	0	0.00
Rock Hill (city) York County	0	0.00

African, Sub-Saharan: Other

Top 10 Places Sorted by Population
Based on all places, regardless of total population

Place	Population	%
St. Andrews (cdp) Richland County	117	0.56
Columbia (city) Richland County	82	0.06
Orangeburg (city) Orangeburg County	54	0.39
Spartanburg (city) Spartanburg County	23	0.06
Gantt (cdp) Greenville County	20	0.14
Rock Hill (city) York County	18	0.03
Mount Pleasant (town) Charleston County	16	0.02
North Charleston (city) Charleston County	15	0.02
Charleston (city) Charleston County	11	0.01
Edgefield (town) Edgefield County	9	0.19

Top 10 Places Sorted by Percent of Total Population
Based on all places, regardless of total population

Place	Population	%
St. Andrews (cdp) Richland County	117	0.56
Orangeburg (city) Orangeburg County	54	0.39
Edgefield (town) Edgefield County	9	0.19
Gantt (cdp) Greenville County	20	0.14
Port Royal (town) Beaufort County	8	0.08
Sangaree (cdp) Berkeley County	6	0.07
Columbia (city) Richland County	82	0.06
Spartanburg (city) Spartanburg County	23	0.06
Cayce (city) Lexington County	7	0.06
Rock Hill (city) York County	18	0.03

Top 10 Places Sorted by Percent of Total Population
Based on places with total population of 50,000 or more

Place	Population	%
Columbia (city) Richland County	82	0.06
Rock Hill (city) York County	18	0.03
Mount Pleasant (town) Charleston County	16	0.02
North Charleston (city) Charleston County	15	0.02
Charleston (city) Charleston County	11	0.01
Greenville (city) Greenville County	0	0.00

Albanian

Top 10 Places Sorted by Population
Based on all places, regardless of total population

Place	Population	%
Myrtle Beach (city) Horry County	243	0.91
Summerville (town) Dorchester County	52	0.13
Socastee (cdp) Horry County	43	0.25
Aiken (city) Aiken County	39	0.14
North Charleston (city) Charleston County	22	0.02
Wade Hampton (cdp) Greenville County	20	0.10
Port Royal (town) Beaufort County	15	0.14
Charleston (city) Charleston County	14	0.01
Easley (city) Pickens County	13	0.07
Abbeville (city) Abbeville County	0	0.00

Top 10 Places Sorted by Percent of Total Population
Based on all places, regardless of total population

Place	Population	%
Myrtle Beach (city) Horry County	243	0.91
Socastee (cdp) Horry County	43	0.25
Aiken (city) Aiken County	39	0.14
Port Royal (town) Beaufort County	15	0.14
Summerville (town) Dorchester County	52	0.13
Wade Hampton (cdp) Greenville County	20	0.10
Easley (city) Pickens County	13	0.07
North Charleston (city) Charleston County	22	0.02
Charleston (city) Charleston County	14	0.01
Abbeville (city) Abbeville County	0	0.00

Top 10 Places Sorted by Percent of Total Population
Based on places with total population of 50,000 or more

Place	Population	%
North Charleston (city) Charleston County	22	0.02
Charleston (city) Charleston County	14	0.01
Columbia (city) Richland County	0	0.00
Greenville (city) Greenville County	0	0.00
Mount Pleasant (town) Charleston County	0	0.00
Rock Hill (city) York County	0	0.00

Alsatian

Top 10 Places Sorted by Population
Based on all places, regardless of total population

Place	Population	%
Honea Path (town) Anderson County	27	0.71
North Myrtle Beach (city) Horry County	14	0.10
Hilton Head Island (town) Beaufort County	13	0.04
Myrtle Beach (city) Horry County	11	0.04
Abbeville (city) Abbeville County	0	0.00
Aiken (city) Aiken County	0	0.00
Alcolu (cdp) Clarendon County	0	0.00
Allendale (town) Allendale County	0	0.00
Anderson (city) Anderson County	0	0.00
Andrews (town) Georgetown County	0	0.00

Top 10 Places Sorted by Percent of Total Population
Based on all places, regardless of total population

Place	Population	%
Honea Path (town) Anderson County	27	0.71
North Myrtle Beach (city) Horry County	14	0.10
Hilton Head Island (town) Beaufort County	13	0.04
Myrtle Beach (city) Horry County	11	0.04
Abbeville (city) Abbeville County	0	0.00
Aiken (city) Aiken County	0	0.00
Alcolu (cdp) Clarendon County	0	0.00
Allendale (town) Allendale County	0	0.00
Anderson (city) Anderson County	0	0.00
Andrews (town) Georgetown County	0	0.00

Top 10 Places Sorted by Percent of Total Population
Based on places with total population of 50,000 or more

Place	Population	%
Charleston (city) Charleston County	0	0.00
Columbia (city) Richland County	0	0.00
Greenville (city) Greenville County	0	0.00
Mount Pleasant (town) Charleston County	0	0.00
North Charleston (city) Charleston County	0	0.00
Rock Hill (city) York County	0	0.00

American

Top 10 Places Sorted by Population
Based on all places, regardless of total population

Place	Population	%
Charleston (city) Charleston County	12,018	10.33
Columbia (city) Richland County	7,637	5.98
Mount Pleasant (town) Charleston County	7,092	11.05
North Charleston (city) Charleston County	6,527	6.91
Greenville (city) Greenville County	6,496	11.23
Summerville (town) Dorchester County	5,167	12.79
Rock Hill (city) York County	3,840	6.08
Greer (city) Greenville County	3,533	14.78
Goose Creek (city) Berkeley County	3,513	10.10
Easley (city) Pickens County	3,486	17.68

Top 10 Places Sorted by Percent of Total Population
Based on all places, regardless of total population

Place	Population	%
Islandton (cdp) Colleton County	19	100.00
Windsor (town) Aiken County	116	83.45
Coronaca (cdp) Greenwood County	277	70.13
Cottageville (town) Colleton County	495	49.70
Peak (town) Newberry County	20	47.62
Langley (cdp) Aiken County	647	44.93
Clearwater (cdp) Aiken County	1,820	42.94
Gloverville (cdp) Aiken County	1,396	42.68
Elgin (town) Kershaw County	658	41.46
Smyrna (town) York County	19	41.30

Top 10 Places Sorted by Percent of Total Population
Based on places with total population of 50,000 or more

Place	Population	%
Greenville (city) Greenville County	6,496	11.23
Mount Pleasant (town) Charleston County	7,092	11.05
Charleston (city) Charleston County	12,018	10.33
North Charleston (city) Charleston County	6,527	6.91
Rock Hill (city) York County	3,840	6.08
Columbia (city) Richland County	7,637	5.98

Arab: Total

Top 10 Places Sorted by Population
Based on all places, regardless of total population

Place	Population	%
Charleston (city) Charleston County	878	0.75
Columbia (city) Richland County	547	0.43
Greenville (city) Greenville County	420	0.73
Wade Hampton (cdp) Greenville County	418	2.06
Clemson (city) Pickens County	332	2.44
Simpsonville (city) Greenville County	324	1.85
Hanahan (city) Berkeley County	318	1.88
Mount Pleasant (town) Charleston County	299	0.47
Myrtle Beach (city) Horry County	163	0.61
Anderson (city) Anderson County	162	0.61

Top 10 Places Sorted by Percent of Total Population
Based on all places, regardless of total population

Place	Population	%
Atlantic Beach (town) Horry County	53	19.00
Pawleys Island (town) Georgetown County	4	4.00
Westminster (city) Oconee County	70	2.95
Honea Path (town) Anderson County	105	2.78
Clemson (city) Pickens County	332	2.44
Arcadia Lakes (town) Richland County	21	2.27
Pickens (city) Pickens County	70	2.23
Wade Hampton (cdp) Greenville County	418	2.06
Hanahan (city) Berkeley County	318	1.88
Simpsonville (city) Greenville County	324	1.85

Top 10 Places Sorted by Percent of Total Population
Based on places with total population of 50,000 or more

Place	Population	%
Charleston (city) Charleston County	878	0.75
Greenville (city) Greenville County	420	0.73
Mount Pleasant (town) Charleston County	299	0.47
Columbia (city) Richland County	547	0.43
Rock Hill (city) York County	81	0.13
North Charleston (city) Charleston County	71	0.08

Arab: Arab

Top 10 Places Sorted by Population
Based on all places, regardless of total population

Place	Population	%
Berea (cdp) Greenville County	111	0.86
Greenville (city) Greenville County	95	0.16
Westminster (city) Oconee County	70	2.95
Honea Path (town) Anderson County	44	1.16
Anderson (city) Anderson County	41	0.15
Clemson (city) Pickens County	39	0.29
Columbia (city) Richland County	38	0.03
Charleston (city) Charleston County	37	0.03
North Charleston (city) Charleston County	33	0.03
Easley (city) Pickens County	27	0.14

Top 10 Places Sorted by Percent of Total Population
Based on all places, regardless of total population

Place	Population	%
Westminster (city) Oconee County	70	2.95
Honea Path (town) Anderson County	44	1.16
Berea (cdp) Greenville County	111	0.86
Seabrook Island (town) Charleston County	9	0.50
St. Matthews (town) Calhoun County	8	0.39
Clemson (city) Pickens County	39	0.29
Piedmont (cdp) Anderson County	11	0.22
Greenville (city) Greenville County	95	0.16
Conway (city) Horry County	26	0.16
Anderson (city) Anderson County	41	0.15

Top 10 Places Sorted by Percent of Total Population
Based on places with total population of 50,000 or more

Place	Population	%
Greenville (city) Greenville County	95	0.16
Columbia (city) Richland County	38	0.03
Charleston (city) Charleston County	37	0.03
North Charleston (city) Charleston County	33	0.03
Mount Pleasant (town) Charleston County	0	0.00
Rock Hill (city) York County	0	0.00

Arab: Egyptian

Top 10 Places Sorted by Population
Based on all places, regardless of total population

Place	Population	%
Hanahan (city) Berkeley County	274	1.62
Simpsonville (city) Greenville County	224	1.28
Charleston (city) Charleston County	134	0.12
Columbia (city) Richland County	107	0.08
Lake Wylie (cdp) York County	75	0.90
Clemson (city) Pickens County	62	0.46
Fort Mill (town) York County	46	0.45
Wade Hampton (cdp) Greenville County	41	0.20
Aiken (city) Aiken County	38	0.13
Seven Oaks (cdp) Lexington County	34	0.21

Top 10 Places Sorted by Percent of Total Population
Based on all places, regardless of total population

Place	Population	%
Hanahan (city) Berkeley County	274	1.62
Simpsonville (city) Greenville County	224	1.28
Lake Wylie (cdp) York County	75	0.90
Clemson (city) Pickens County	62	0.46
Fort Mill (town) York County	46	0.45
Seven Oaks (cdp) Lexington County	34	0.21
Wade Hampton (cdp) Greenville County	41	0.20
West Columbia (city) Lexington County	24	0.16
Five Forks (cdp) Greenville County	18	0.14
Aiken (city) Aiken County	38	0.13

Top 10 Places Sorted by Percent of Total Population
Based on places with total population of 50,000 or more

Place	Population	%
Charleston (city) Charleston County	134	0.12
Columbia (city) Richland County	107	0.08
Mount Pleasant (town) Charleston County	12	0.02
Greenville (city) Greenville County	5	0.01
North Charleston (city) Charleston County	0	0.00
Rock Hill (city) York County	0	0.00

Arab: Iraqi

Top 10 Places Sorted by Population
Based on all places, regardless of total population

Place	Population	%
Charleston (city) Charleston County	21	0.02
Bluffton (town) Beaufort County	12	0.11
Columbia (city) Richland County	12	0.01
Abbeville (city) Abbeville County	0	0.00
Aiken (city) Aiken County	0	0.00
Alcolu (cdp) Clarendon County	0	0.00
Allendale (town) Allendale County	0	0.00
Anderson (city) Anderson County	0	0.00
Andrews (town) Georgetown County	0	0.00
Antreville (cdp) Abbeville County	0	0.00

Top 10 Places Sorted by Percent of Total Population
Based on all places, regardless of total population

Place	Population	%
Bluffton (town) Beaufort County	12	0.11
Charleston (city) Charleston County	21	0.02
Columbia (city) Richland County	12	0.01
Abbeville (city) Abbeville County	0	0.00
Aiken (city) Aiken County	0	0.00
Alcolu (cdp) Clarendon County	0	0.00
Allendale (town) Allendale County	0	0.00
Anderson (city) Anderson County	0	0.00
Andrews (town) Georgetown County	0	0.00
Antreville (cdp) Abbeville County	0	0.00

Top 10 Places Sorted by Percent of Total Population
Based on places with total population of 50,000 or more

Place	Population	%
Charleston (city) Charleston County	21	0.02
Columbia (city) Richland County	12	0.01
Greenville (city) Greenville County	0	0.00
Mount Pleasant (town) Charleston County	0	0.00
North Charleston (city) Charleston County	0	0.00
Rock Hill (city) York County	0	0.00

Arab: Jordanian

Top 10 Places Sorted by Population
Based on all places, regardless of total population

Place	Population	%
Wade Hampton (cdp) Greenville County	153	0.75
Charleston (city) Charleston County	140	0.12
Greenville (city) Greenville County	98	0.17
Mauldin (city) Greenville County	70	0.32
Newport (cdp) York County	24	0.61
Abbeville (city) Abbeville County	0	0.00
Aiken (city) Aiken County	0	0.00
Alcolu (cdp) Clarendon County	0	0.00
Allendale (town) Allendale County	0	0.00
Anderson (city) Anderson County	0	0.00

Top 10 Places Sorted by Percent of Total Population
Based on all places, regardless of total population

Place	Population	%
Wade Hampton (cdp) Greenville County	153	0.75
Newport (cdp) York County	24	0.61
Mauldin (city) Greenville County	70	0.32
Greenville (city) Greenville County	98	0.17
Charleston (city) Charleston County	140	0.12
Abbeville (city) Abbeville County	0	0.00
Aiken (city) Aiken County	0	0.00
Alcolu (cdp) Clarendon County	0	0.00
Allendale (town) Allendale County	0	0.00
Anderson (city) Anderson County	0	0.00

Top 10 Places Sorted by Percent of Total Population
Based on places with total population of 50,000 or more

Place	Population	%
Greenville (city) Greenville County	98	0.17
Charleston (city) Charleston County	140	0.12
Columbia (city) Richland County	0	0.00
Mount Pleasant (town) Charleston County	0	0.00
North Charleston (city) Charleston County	0	0.00
Rock Hill (city) York County	0	0.00

Arab: Lebanese

Top 10 Places Sorted by Population
Based on all places, regardless of total population

Place	Population	%
Charleston (city) Charleston County	312	0.27
Mount Pleasant (town) Charleston County	287	0.45
Greenville (city) Greenville County	222	0.38
Columbia (city) Richland County	208	0.16
Wade Hampton (cdp) Greenville County	168	0.83
Spartanburg (city) Spartanburg County	90	0.24
Myrtle Beach (city) Horry County	83	0.31
Little River (cdp) Horry County	75	0.86
Sumter (city) Sumter County	70	0.17
Anderson (city) Anderson County	60	0.23

Top 10 Places Sorted by Percent of Total Population
Based on all places, regardless of total population

Place	Population	%
Pawleys Island (town) Georgetown County	4	4.00
Arcadia Lakes (town) Richland County	21	2.27
Summerton (town) Clarendon County	18	1.75
Gilbert (town) Lexington County	8	1.64
Andrews (town) Georgetown County	41	1.39
Arcadia (cdp) Spartanburg County	15	0.99
Little River (cdp) Horry County	75	0.86
Wade Hampton (cdp) Greenville County	168	0.83
Folly Beach (city) Charleston County	20	0.79
Travelers Rest (city) Greenville County	29	0.65

Top 10 Places Sorted by Percent of Total Population
Based on places with total population of 50,000 or more

Place	Population	%
Mount Pleasant (town) Charleston County	287	0.45
Greenville (city) Greenville County	222	0.38
Charleston (city) Charleston County	312	0.27
Columbia (city) Richland County	208	0.16
Rock Hill (city) York County	29	0.05
North Charleston (city) Charleston County	0	0.00

Arab: Moroccan

Top 10 Places Sorted by Population
Based on all places, regardless of total population

Place	Population	%
Myrtle Beach (city) Horry County	58	0.22
Atlantic Beach (town) Horry County	53	19.00
Charleston (city) Charleston County	53	0.05
Cheraw (town) Chesterfield County	31	0.53
Edgefield (town) Edgefield County	18	0.38
Honea Path (town) Anderson County	17	0.45
Hanahan (city) Berkeley County	15	0.09
Lancaster (city) Lancaster County	13	0.16
Columbia (city) Richland County	12	0.01
North Charleston (city) Charleston County	9	0.01

Top 10 Places Sorted by Percent of Total Population
Based on all places, regardless of total population

Place	Population	%
Atlantic Beach (town) Horry County	53	19.00
Cheraw (town) Chesterfield County	31	0.53
Honea Path (town) Anderson County	17	0.45
Edgefield (town) Edgefield County	18	0.38
Myrtle Beach (city) Horry County	58	0.22
Lancaster (city) Lancaster County	13	0.16
Hanahan (city) Berkeley County	15	0.09
Charleston (city) Charleston County	53	0.05
Anderson (city) Anderson County	8	0.03
Columbia (city) Richland County	12	0.01

Top 10 Places Sorted by Percent of Total Population
Based on places with total population of 50,000 or more

Place	Population	%
Charleston (city) Charleston County	53	0.05
Columbia (city) Richland County	12	0.01
North Charleston (city) Charleston County	9	0.01
Greenville (city) Greenville County	0	0.00
Mount Pleasant (town) Charleston County	0	0.00
Rock Hill (city) York County	0	0.00

Arab: Palestinian

Top 10 Places Sorted by Population
Based on all places, regardless of total population

Place	Population	%
Seneca (city) Oconee County	78	0.97
Wade Hampton (cdp) Greenville County	39	0.19
Northlake (cdp) Anderson County	20	0.56
Port Royal (town) Beaufort County	18	0.17
Spartanburg (city) Spartanburg County	10	0.03
Greer (city) Greenville County	3	0.01
Abbeville (city) Abbeville County	0	0.00
Aiken (city) Aiken County	0	0.00
Alcolu (cdp) Clarendon County	0	0.00
Allendale (town) Allendale County	0	0.00

Top 10 Places Sorted by Percent of Total Population
Based on all places, regardless of total population

Place	Population	%
Seneca (city) Oconee County	78	0.97
Northlake (cdp) Anderson County	20	0.56
Wade Hampton (cdp) Greenville County	39	0.19
Port Royal (town) Beaufort County	18	0.17
Spartanburg (city) Spartanburg County	10	0.03
Greer (city) Greenville County	3	0.01
Abbeville (city) Abbeville County	0	0.00
Aiken (city) Aiken County	0	0.00
Alcolu (cdp) Clarendon County	0	0.00
Allendale (town) Allendale County	0	0.00

Top 10 Places Sorted by Percent of Total Population
Based on places with total population of 50,000 or more

Place	Population	%
Charleston (city) Charleston County	0	0.00
Columbia (city) Richland County	0	0.00
Greenville (city) Greenville County	0	0.00
Mount Pleasant (town) Charleston County	0	0.00
North Charleston (city) Charleston County	0	0.00
Rock Hill (city) York County	0	0.00

Arab: Syrian

Top 10 Places Sorted by Population
Based on all places, regardless of total population

Place	Population	%
Charleston (city) Charleston County	146	0.13
Pickens (city) Pickens County	70	2.23
Florence (city) Florence County	56	0.16
Lake Wylie (cdp) York County	43	0.51
Rock Hill (city) York County	39	0.06
Columbia (city) Richland County	36	0.03
Forest Acres (city) Richland County	34	0.33
Hanahan (city) Berkeley County	29	0.17
Irmo (town) Richland County	25	0.23
Conway (city) Horry County	18	0.11

Top 10 Places Sorted by Percent of Total Population
Based on all places, regardless of total population

Place	Population	%
Pickens (city) Pickens County	70	2.23
Richburg (town) Chester County	2	0.56
Lake Wylie (cdp) York County	43	0.51
Forest Acres (city) Richland County	34	0.33
Piedmont (cdp) Anderson County	14	0.28
Latta (town) Dillon County	4	0.24
Irmo (town) Richland County	25	0.23
Hanahan (city) Berkeley County	29	0.17
Seabrook Island (town) Charleston County	3	0.17
Florence (city) Florence County	56	0.16

Top 10 Places Sorted by Percent of Total Population
Based on places with total population of 50,000 or more

Place	Population	%
Charleston (city) Charleston County	146	0.13
Rock Hill (city) York County	39	0.06
Columbia (city) Richland County	36	0.03
North Charleston (city) Charleston County	16	0.02
Greenville (city) Greenville County	0	0.00
Mount Pleasant (town) Charleston County	0	0.00

Arab: Other

Top 10 Places Sorted by Population
Based on all places, regardless of total population

Place	Population	%
Clemson (city) Pickens County	218	1.60
Columbia (city) Richland County	134	0.11
Simpsonville (city) Greenville County	81	0.46
Goose Creek (city) Berkeley County	65	0.19
Anderson (city) Anderson County	53	0.20
Honea Path (town) Anderson County	44	1.16
Forest Acres (city) Richland County	44	0.42
Charleston (city) Charleston County	35	0.03
Myrtle Beach (city) Horry County	22	0.08
Taylors (cdp) Greenville County	15	0.07

Top 10 Places Sorted by Percent of Total Population
Based on all places, regardless of total population

Place	Population	%
Clemson (city) Pickens County	218	1.60
Honea Path (town) Anderson County	44	1.16
Simpsonville (city) Greenville County	81	0.46
Forest Acres (city) Richland County	44	0.42
Anderson (city) Anderson County	53	0.20
Goose Creek (city) Berkeley County	65	0.19
Columbia (city) Richland County	134	0.11
Myrtle Beach (city) Horry County	22	0.08
Taylors (cdp) Greenville County	15	0.07
Port Royal (town) Beaufort County	5	0.05

Top 10 Places Sorted by Percent of Total Population
Based on places with total population of 50,000 or more

Place	Population	%
Columbia (city) Richland County	134	0.11
Charleston (city) Charleston County	35	0.03
Rock Hill (city) York County	13	0.02
North Charleston (city) Charleston County	13	0.01
Greenville (city) Greenville County	0	0.00
Mount Pleasant (town) Charleston County	0	0.00

Armenian

Top 10 Places Sorted by Population
Based on all places, regardless of total population

Place	Population	%
Hilton Head Island (town) Beaufort County	119	0.32
Little River (cdp) Horry County	66	0.76
Charleston (city) Charleston County	61	0.05
Aiken (city) Aiken County	55	0.19
Mount Pleasant (town) Charleston County	49	0.08
Lexington (town) Lexington County	33	0.20
Columbia (city) Richland County	25	0.02
Surfside Beach (town) Horry County	20	0.50
North Charleston (city) Charleston County	20	0.02
Taylors (cdp) Greenville County	19	0.09

Top 10 Places Sorted by Percent of Total Population
Based on all places, regardless of total population

Place	Population	%
Lincolnville (town) Charleston County	12	0.81
Little River (cdp) Horry County	66	0.76
Surfside Beach (town) Horry County	20	0.50
South Congaree (town) Lexington County	11	0.46
Hilton Head Island (town) Beaufort County	119	0.32
Walterboro (city) Colleton County	15	0.28
Isle of Palms (city) Charleston County	9	0.21
Lexington (town) Lexington County	33	0.20
Aiken (city) Aiken County	55	0.19
Bennettsville (city) Marlboro County	17	0.18

Top 10 Places Sorted by Percent of Total Population
Based on places with total population of 50,000 or more

Place	Population	%
Mount Pleasant (town) Charleston County	49	0.08
Charleston (city) Charleston County	61	0.05
Columbia (city) Richland County	25	0.02
North Charleston (city) Charleston County	20	0.02
Rock Hill (city) York County	11	0.02
Greenville (city) Greenville County	0	0.00

Assyrian/Chaldean/Syriac

Top 10 Places Sorted by Population
Based on all places, regardless of total population

Place	Population	%
Columbia (city) Richland County	31	0.02
Garden City (cdp) Horry County	9	0.10
Abbeville (city) Abbeville County	0	0.00
Aiken (city) Aiken County	0	0.00
Alcolu (cdp) Clarendon County	0	0.00
Allendale (town) Allendale County	0	0.00
Anderson (city) Anderson County	0	0.00
Andrews (town) Georgetown County	0	0.00
Antreville (cdp) Abbeville County	0	0.00
Arcadia (cdp) Spartanburg County	0	0.00

Top 10 Places Sorted by Percent of Total Population
Based on all places, regardless of total population

Place	Population	%
Garden City (cdp) Horry County	9	0.10
Columbia (city) Richland County	31	0.02
Abbeville (city) Abbeville County	0	0.00
Aiken (city) Aiken County	0	0.00
Alcolu (cdp) Clarendon County	0	0.00
Allendale (town) Allendale County	0	0.00
Anderson (city) Anderson County	0	0.00
Andrews (town) Georgetown County	0	0.00
Antreville (cdp) Abbeville County	0	0.00
Arcadia (cdp) Spartanburg County	0	0.00

Top 10 Places Sorted by Percent of Total Population
Based on places with total population of 50,000 or more

Place	Population	%
Columbia (city) Richland County	31	0.02
Charleston (city) Charleston County	0	0.00
Greenville (city) Greenville County	0	0.00
Mount Pleasant (town) Charleston County	0	0.00
North Charleston (city) Charleston County	0	0.00
Rock Hill (city) York County	0	0.00

Australian

Top 10 Places Sorted by Population
Based on all places, regardless of total population

Place	Population	%
North Myrtle Beach (city) Horry County	155	1.16
Hilton Head Island (town) Beaufort County	113	0.31
North Charleston (city) Charleston County	40	0.04
Newport (cdp) York County	30	0.77
Columbia (city) Richland County	30	0.02
Beaufort (city) Beaufort County	23	0.18
Bamberg (town) Bamberg County	20	0.55
Manning (city) Clarendon County	19	0.45
Slater-Marietta (cdp) Greenville County	17	0.74
Port Royal (town) Beaufort County	17	0.16

Top 10 Places Sorted by Percent of Total Population
Based on all places, regardless of total population

Place	Population	%
North Myrtle Beach (city) Horry County	155	1.16
Newport (cdp) York County	30	0.77
Slater-Marietta (cdp) Greenville County	17	0.74
Bamberg (town) Bamberg County	20	0.55
Manning (city) Clarendon County	19	0.45
Hilton Head Island (town) Beaufort County	113	0.31
Latta (town) Dillon County	4	0.24
Clinton (city) Laurens County	16	0.19
Beaufort (city) Beaufort County	23	0.18
Port Royal (town) Beaufort County	17	0.16

Top 10 Places Sorted by Percent of Total Population
Based on places with total population of 50,000 or more

Place	Population	%
North Charleston (city) Charleston County	40	0.04
Columbia (city) Richland County	30	0.02
Charleston (city) Charleston County	15	0.01
Greenville (city) Greenville County	0	0.00
Mount Pleasant (town) Charleston County	0	0.00
Rock Hill (city) York County	0	0.00

Austrian

Top 10 Places Sorted by Population
Based on all places, regardless of total population

Place	Population	%
Mount Pleasant (town) Charleston County	215	0.33
North Charleston (city) Charleston County	184	0.19
Charleston (city) Charleston County	182	0.16
Hilton Head Island (town) Beaufort County	171	0.47
Columbia (city) Richland County	154	0.12
Clemson (city) Pickens County	117	0.86
Rock Hill (city) York County	108	0.17
Westminster (city) Oconee County	98	4.14
Aiken (city) Aiken County	89	0.31
Taylors (cdp) Greenville County	81	0.37

Top 10 Places Sorted by Percent of Total Population
Based on all places, regardless of total population

Place	Population	%
Westminster (city) Oconee County	98	4.14
Pawleys Island (town) Georgetown County	2	2.00
Central (town) Pickens County	72	1.48
Laurel Bay (cdp) Beaufort County	76	1.36
Dalzell (cdp) Sumter County	40	1.24
Murphys Estates (cdp) Edgefield County	26	1.15
Lesslie (cdp) York County	28	0.92
Seabrook Island (town) Charleston County	16	0.88
Clemson (city) Pickens County	117	0.86
Tega Cay (city) York County	59	0.84

Top 10 Places Sorted by Percent of Total Population
Based on places with total population of 50,000 or more

Place	Population	%
Mount Pleasant (town) Charleston County	215	0.33
North Charleston (city) Charleston County	184	0.19
Rock Hill (city) York County	108	0.17
Charleston (city) Charleston County	182	0.16
Columbia (city) Richland County	154	0.12
Greenville (city) Greenville County	64	0.11

Basque

Top 10 Places Sorted by Population
Based on all places, regardless of total population

Place	Population	%
Beaufort (city) Beaufort County	58	0.46
Greenville (city) Greenville County	15	0.03
Blacksburg (town) Cherokee County	13	0.65
Mauldin (city) Greenville County	10	0.05
Abbeville (city) Abbeville County	0	0.00
Aiken (city) Aiken County	0	0.00
Alcolu (cdp) Clarendon County	0	0.00
Allendale (town) Allendale County	0	0.00
Anderson (city) Anderson County	0	0.00
Andrews (town) Georgetown County	0	0.00

Top 10 Places Sorted by Percent of Total Population
Based on all places, regardless of total population

Place	Population	%
Blacksburg (town) Cherokee County	13	0.65
Beaufort (city) Beaufort County	58	0.46
Mauldin (city) Greenville County	10	0.05
Greenville (city) Greenville County	15	0.03
Abbeville (city) Abbeville County	0	0.00
Aiken (city) Aiken County	0	0.00
Alcolu (cdp) Clarendon County	0	0.00
Allendale (town) Allendale County	0	0.00
Anderson (city) Anderson County	0	0.00
Andrews (town) Georgetown County	0	0.00

Top 10 Places Sorted by Percent of Total Population
Based on places with total population of 50,000 or more

Place	Population	%
Greenville (city) Greenville County	15	0.03
Charleston (city) Charleston County	0	0.00
Columbia (city) Richland County	0	0.00
Mount Pleasant (town) Charleston County	0	0.00
North Charleston (city) Charleston County	0	0.00
Rock Hill (city) York County	0	0.00

Belgian

Top 10 Places Sorted by Population
Based on all places, regardless of total population

Place	Population	%
Summerville (town) Dorchester County	275	0.68
Walhalla (city) Oconee County	82	1.95
Hilton Head Island (town) Beaufort County	78	0.21
Surfside Beach (town) Horry County	72	1.82
Irmo (town) Richland County	63	0.57
Columbia (city) Richland County	60	0.05
Charleston (city) Charleston County	57	0.05
North Charleston (city) Charleston County	53	0.06
Five Forks (cdp) Greenville County	52	0.40
Lugoff (cdp) Kershaw County	48	0.68

Top 10 Places Sorted by Percent of Total Population
Based on all places, regardless of total population

Place	Population	%
Walhalla (city) Oconee County	82	1.95
Surfside Beach (town) Horry County	72	1.82
Kiawah Island (town) Charleston County	24	1.47
Summerville (town) Dorchester County	275	0.68
Lugoff (cdp) Kershaw County	48	0.68
Irmo (town) Richland County	63	0.57
Five Forks (cdp) Greenville County	52	0.40
Moncks Corner (town) Berkeley County	26	0.35
India Hook (cdp) York County	10	0.29
Lake Wylie (cdp) York County	23	0.28

Top 10 Places Sorted by Percent of Total Population
Based on places with total population of 50,000 or more

Place	Population	%
North Charleston (city) Charleston County	53	0.06
Mount Pleasant (town) Charleston County	36	0.06
Columbia (city) Richland County	60	0.05
Charleston (city) Charleston County	57	0.05
Rock Hill (city) York County	10	0.02
Greenville (city) Greenville County	0	0.00

Brazilian

Top 10 Places Sorted by Population
Based on all places, regardless of total population

Place	Population	%
Goose Creek (city) Berkeley County	278	0.80
Hanahan (city) Berkeley County	189	1.12
Easley (city) Pickens County	170	0.86
Wade Hampton (cdp) Greenville County	149	0.73
North Charleston (city) Charleston County	73	0.08
Boiling Springs (cdp) Spartanburg County	63	0.76
Oak Grove (cdp) Lexington County	58	0.55
Taylors (cdp) Greenville County	53	0.24
Slater-Marietta (cdp) Greenville County	45	1.96
Ladson (cdp) Berkeley County	42	0.30

Top 10 Places Sorted by Percent of Total Population
Based on all places, regardless of total population

Place	Population	%
Slater-Marietta (cdp) Greenville County	45	1.96
Jackson (town) Aiken County	23	1.43
Edisto Beach (town) Colleton County	8	1.38
Hanahan (city) Berkeley County	189	1.12
Easley (city) Pickens County	170	0.86
Goose Creek (city) Berkeley County	278	0.80
Boiling Springs (cdp) Spartanburg County	63	0.76
Wade Hampton (cdp) Greenville County	149	0.73
Oak Grove (cdp) Lexington County	58	0.55
Reidville (town) Spartanburg County	3	0.55

Top 10 Places Sorted by Percent of Total Population
Based on places with total population of 50,000 or more

Place	Population	%
North Charleston (city) Charleston County	73	0.08
Greenville (city) Greenville County	31	0.05
Charleston (city) Charleston County	42	0.04
Rock Hill (city) York County	26	0.04
Columbia (city) Richland County	33	0.03
Mount Pleasant (town) Charleston County	0	0.00

British

Top 10 Places Sorted by Population
Based on all places, regardless of total population

Place	Population	%
Charleston (city) Charleston County	801	0.69
Columbia (city) Richland County	762	0.60
Mount Pleasant (town) Charleston County	424	0.66
Hilton Head Island (town) Beaufort County	355	0.97
Greenville (city) Greenville County	337	0.58
Rock Hill (city) York County	291	0.46
Spartanburg (city) Spartanburg County	285	0.76
Clemson (city) Pickens County	262	1.93
Summerville (town) Dorchester County	253	0.63
Aiken (city) Aiken County	251	0.87

Top 10 Places Sorted by Percent of Total Population
Based on all places, regardless of total population

Place	Population	%
Oswego (cdp) Sumter County	9	20.00
Rockville (town) Charleston County	19	11.95
Pawleys Island (town) Georgetown County	6	6.00
Ward (town) Saluda County	4	4.49
Mayo (cdp) Spartanburg County	64	4.25
Mount Croghan (town) Chesterfield County	7	3.83
Sullivan's Island (town) Charleston County	70	3.42
Travelers Rest (city) Greenville County	140	3.13
Isle of Palms (city) Charleston County	112	2.67
Snelling (town) Barnwell County	6	2.07

Top 10 Places Sorted by Percent of Total Population
Based on places with total population of 50,000 or more

Place	Population	%
Charleston (city) Charleston County	801	0.69
Mount Pleasant (town) Charleston County	424	0.66
Columbia (city) Richland County	762	0.60
Greenville (city) Greenville County	337	0.58
Rock Hill (city) York County	291	0.46
North Charleston (city) Charleston County	140	0.15

Bulgarian

Top 10 Places Sorted by Population
Based on all places, regardless of total population

Place	Population	%
Lexington (town) Lexington County	102	0.62
Hilton Head Island (town) Beaufort County	98	0.27
Columbia (city) Richland County	57	0.04
Charleston (city) Charleston County	40	0.03
West Columbia (city) Lexington County	32	0.22
Myrtle Beach (city) Horry County	30	0.11
Mount Pleasant (town) Charleston County	29	0.05
Seven Oaks (cdp) Lexington County	21	0.13
Greer (city) Greenville County	13	0.05
Spartanburg (city) Spartanburg County	13	0.03

Top 10 Places Sorted by Percent of Total Population
Based on all places, regardless of total population

Place	Population	%
Jackson (town) Aiken County	12	0.74
Lexington (town) Lexington County	102	0.62
City View (cdp) Greenville County	6	0.42
Hilton Head Island (town) Beaufort County	98	0.27
West Columbia (city) Lexington County	32	0.22
Seven Oaks (cdp) Lexington County	21	0.13
Myrtle Beach (city) Horry County	30	0.11
Socastee (cdp) Horry County	11	0.06
Mount Pleasant (town) Charleston County	29	0.05
Greer (city) Greenville County	13	0.05

Top 10 Places Sorted by Percent of Total Population
Based on places with total population of 50,000 or more

Place	Population	%
Mount Pleasant (town) Charleston County	29	0.05
Columbia (city) Richland County	57	0.04
Charleston (city) Charleston County	40	0.03
Greenville (city) Greenville County	6	0.01
North Charleston (city) Charleston County	0	0.00
Rock Hill (city) York County	0	0.00

Cajun

Top 10 Places Sorted by Population
Based on all places, regardless of total population

Place	Population	%
Columbia (city) Richland County	130	0.10
Sumter (city) Sumter County	46	0.11
Charleston (city) Charleston County	45	0.04
Fort Mill (town) York County	25	0.24
Hilton Head Island (town) Beaufort County	25	0.07
Spartanburg (city) Spartanburg County	24	0.06
Taylors (cdp) Greenville County	21	0.10
Fairforest (cdp) Spartanburg County	18	0.95
Burton (cdp) Beaufort County	16	0.22
Rock Hill (city) York County	11	0.02

Top 10 Places Sorted by Percent of Total Population
Based on all places, regardless of total population

Place	Population	%
Fairforest (cdp) Spartanburg County	18	0.95
Holly Hill (town) Orangeburg County	9	0.82
Blacksburg (town) Cherokee County	10	0.50
Wellford (city) Spartanburg County	9	0.49
Sullivan's Island (town) Charleston County	7	0.34
Fort Mill (town) York County	25	0.24
Burton (cdp) Beaufort County	16	0.22
Sumter (city) Sumter County	46	0.11
Columbia (city) Richland County	130	0.10
Taylors (cdp) Greenville County	21	0.10

Top 10 Places Sorted by Percent of Total Population
Based on places with total population of 50,000 or more

Place	Population	%
Columbia (city) Richland County	130	0.10
Charleston (city) Charleston County	45	0.04
Rock Hill (city) York County	11	0.02
Greenville (city) Greenville County	0	0.00
Mount Pleasant (town) Charleston County	0	0.00
North Charleston (city) Charleston County	0	0.00

Canadian

Top 10 Places Sorted by Population
Based on all places, regardless of total population

Place	Population	%
Columbia (city) Richland County	214	0.17
Aiken (city) Aiken County	206	0.72
Charleston (city) Charleston County	194	0.17
North Charleston (city) Charleston County	186	0.20
Greenville (city) Greenville County	132	0.23
Mayo (cdp) Spartanburg County	127	8.43
Hilton Head Island (town) Beaufort County	125	0.34
Five Forks (cdp) Greenville County	123	0.94
Summerville (town) Dorchester County	107	0.26
Lexington (town) Lexington County	78	0.48

Top 10 Places Sorted by Percent of Total Population
Based on all places, regardless of total population

Place	Population	%
Mayo (cdp) Spartanburg County	127	8.43
Slater-Marietta (cdp) Greenville County	64	2.79
Burton (cdp) Beaufort County	69	0.97
Five Forks (cdp) Greenville County	123	0.94
Prosperity (town) Newberry County	9	0.93
Aiken (city) Aiken County	206	0.72
Port Royal (town) Beaufort County	55	0.53
Garden City (cdp) Horry County	46	0.52
Edisto Beach (town) Colleton County	3	0.52
North Hartsville (cdp) Darlington County	16	0.49

Top 10 Places Sorted by Percent of Total Population
Based on places with total population of 50,000 or more

Place	Population	%
Greenville (city) Greenville County	132	0.23
North Charleston (city) Charleston County	186	0.20
Columbia (city) Richland County	214	0.17
Charleston (city) Charleston County	194	0.17
Mount Pleasant (town) Charleston County	75	0.12
Rock Hill (city) York County	49	0.08

Carpatho Rusyn

Top 10 Places Sorted by Population
Based on all places, regardless of total population

Place	Population	%
Clemson (city) Pickens County	13	0.10
Abbeville (city) Abbeville County	0	0.00
Aiken (city) Aiken County	0	0.00
Alcolu (cdp) Clarendon County	0	0.00
Allendale (town) Allendale County	0	0.00
Anderson (city) Anderson County	0	0.00
Andrews (town) Georgetown County	0	0.00
Antreville (cdp) Abbeville County	0	0.00
Arcadia (cdp) Spartanburg County	0	0.00
Arcadia Lakes (town) Richland County	0	0.00

Top 10 Places Sorted by Percent of Total Population
Based on all places, regardless of total population

Place	Population	%
Clemson (city) Pickens County	13	0.10
Abbeville (city) Abbeville County	0	0.00
Aiken (city) Aiken County	0	0.00
Alcolu (cdp) Clarendon County	0	0.00
Allendale (town) Allendale County	0	0.00
Anderson (city) Anderson County	0	0.00
Andrews (town) Georgetown County	0	0.00
Antreville (cdp) Abbeville County	0	0.00
Arcadia (cdp) Spartanburg County	0	0.00
Arcadia Lakes (town) Richland County	0	0.00

Top 10 Places Sorted by Percent of Total Population
Based on places with total population of 50,000 or more

Place	Population	%
Charleston (city) Charleston County	0	0.00
Columbia (city) Richland County	0	0.00
Greenville (city) Greenville County	0	0.00
Mount Pleasant (town) Charleston County	0	0.00
North Charleston (city) Charleston County	0	0.00
Rock Hill (city) York County	0	0.00

Celtic

Top 10 Places Sorted by Population
Based on all places, regardless of total population

Place	Population	%
Oak Grove (cdp) Lexington County	61	0.58
Forestbrook (cdp) Horry County	40	0.95
Columbia (city) Richland County	39	0.03
Mount Pleasant (town) Charleston County	34	0.05
Greenville (city) Greenville County	29	0.05
Aiken (city) Aiken County	20	0.07
Greenwood (city) Greenwood County	16	0.07
Darlington (city) Darlington County	15	0.24
Forest Acres (city) Richland County	13	0.12
Lexington (town) Lexington County	12	0.07

Top 10 Places Sorted by Percent of Total Population
Based on all places, regardless of total population

Place	Population	%
Sycamore (town) Allendale County	4	2.80
Silverstreet (town) Newberry County	3	1.35
Forestbrook (cdp) Horry County	40	0.95
Oak Grove (cdp) Lexington County	61	0.58
Darlington (city) Darlington County	15	0.24
Forest Acres (city) Richland County	13	0.12
Aiken (city) Aiken County	20	0.07
Greenwood (city) Greenwood County	16	0.07
Lexington (town) Lexington County	12	0.07
Ladson (cdp) Berkeley County	9	0.06

Top 10 Places Sorted by Percent of Total Population
Based on places with total population of 50,000 or more

Place	Population	%
Mount Pleasant (town) Charleston County	34	0.05
Greenville (city) Greenville County	29	0.05
Columbia (city) Richland County	39	0.03
Charleston (city) Charleston County	0	0.00
North Charleston (city) Charleston County	0	0.00
Rock Hill (city) York County	0	0.00

Croatian

Top 10 Places Sorted by Population
Based on all places, regardless of total population

Place	Population	%
Florence (city) Florence County	85	0.24
Lake Wylie (cdp) York County	83	0.99
Aiken (city) Aiken County	81	0.28
Spartanburg (city) Spartanburg County	65	0.17
Mount Pleasant (town) Charleston County	63	0.10
Columbia (city) Richland County	55	0.04
Tega Cay (city) York County	51	0.73
North Myrtle Beach (city) Horry County	45	0.34
Myrtle Beach (city) Horry County	43	0.16
North Charleston (city) Charleston County	42	0.04

Top 10 Places Sorted by Percent of Total Population
Based on all places, regardless of total population

Place	Population	%
Lake Wylie (cdp) York County	83	0.99
Tega Cay (city) York County	51	0.73
Piedmont (cdp) Anderson County	20	0.40
North Myrtle Beach (city) Horry County	45	0.34
Aiken (city) Aiken County	81	0.28
Seabrook Island (town) Charleston County	5	0.28
Dentsville (cdp) Richland County	35	0.26
Lakewood (cdp) Sumter County	7	0.26
Valley Falls (cdp) Spartanburg County	14	0.25
Florence (city) Florence County	85	0.24

Top 10 Places Sorted by Percent of Total Population
Based on places with total population of 50,000 or more

Place	Population	%
Mount Pleasant (town) Charleston County	63	0.10
Columbia (city) Richland County	55	0.04
North Charleston (city) Charleston County	42	0.04
Greenville (city) Greenville County	13	0.02
Charleston (city) Charleston County	12	0.01
Rock Hill (city) York County	9	0.01

Cypriot

Top 10 Places Sorted by Population
Based on all places, regardless of total population

Place	Population	%
Five Forks (cdp) Greenville County	14	0.11
Columbia (city) Richland County	11	0.01
Abbeville (city) Abbeville County	0	0.00
Aiken (city) Aiken County	0	0.00
Alcolu (cdp) Clarendon County	0	0.00
Allendale (town) Allendale County	0	0.00
Anderson (city) Anderson County	0	0.00
Andrews (town) Georgetown County	0	0.00
Antreville (cdp) Abbeville County	0	0.00
Arcadia (cdp) Spartanburg County	0	0.00

Top 10 Places Sorted by Percent of Total Population
Based on all places, regardless of total population

Place	Population	%
Five Forks (cdp) Greenville County	14	0.11
Columbia (city) Richland County	11	0.01
Abbeville (city) Abbeville County	0	0.00
Aiken (city) Aiken County	0	0.00
Alcolu (cdp) Clarendon County	0	0.00
Allendale (town) Allendale County	0	0.00
Anderson (city) Anderson County	0	0.00
Andrews (town) Georgetown County	0	0.00
Antreville (cdp) Abbeville County	0	0.00
Arcadia (cdp) Spartanburg County	0	0.00

Top 10 Places Sorted by Percent of Total Population
Based on places with total population of 50,000 or more

Place	Population	%
Columbia (city) Richland County	11	0.01
Charleston (city) Charleston County	0	0.00
Greenville (city) Greenville County	0	0.00
Mount Pleasant (town) Charleston County	0	0.00
North Charleston (city) Charleston County	0	0.00
Rock Hill (city) York County	0	0.00

Czech

Top 10 Places Sorted by Population
Based on all places, regardless of total population

Place	Population	%
Charleston (city) Charleston County	393	0.34
Mount Pleasant (town) Charleston County	295	0.46
Goose Creek (city) Berkeley County	250	0.72
Columbia (city) Richland County	246	0.19
Hilton Head Island (town) Beaufort County	207	0.56
Bluffton (town) Beaufort County	133	1.24
North Charleston (city) Charleston County	120	0.13
Greenville (city) Greenville County	114	0.20
Florence (city) Florence County	113	0.31
Summerville (town) Dorchester County	110	0.27

Top 10 Places Sorted by Percent of Total Population
Based on all places, regardless of total population

Place	Population	%
Startex (cdp) Spartanburg County	17	2.30
St. George (town) Dorchester County	40	2.01
Seabrook Island (town) Charleston County	27	1.49
New Ellenton (town) Aiken County	29	1.33
Dunean (cdp) Greenville County	45	1.25
Bluffton (town) Beaufort County	133	1.24
Chapin (town) Lexington County	15	1.20
Starr (town) Anderson County	2	1.03
Aynor (town) Horry County	6	0.75
Goose Creek (city) Berkeley County	250	0.72

Top 10 Places Sorted by Percent of Total Population
Based on places with total population of 50,000 or more

Place	Population	%
Mount Pleasant (town) Charleston County	295	0.46
Charleston (city) Charleston County	393	0.34
Greenville (city) Greenville County	114	0.20
Columbia (city) Richland County	246	0.19
Rock Hill (city) York County	108	0.17
North Charleston (city) Charleston County	120	0.13

Czechoslovakian

Top 10 Places Sorted by Population
Based on all places, regardless of total population

Place	Population	%
Charleston (city) Charleston County	148	0.13
Socastee (cdp) Horry County	115	0.67
Columbia (city) Richland County	107	0.08
Summerville (town) Dorchester County	80	0.20
Mount Pleasant (town) Charleston County	71	0.11
North Charleston (city) Charleston County	46	0.05
Conway (city) Horry County	39	0.24
Rock Hill (city) York County	37	0.06
Hilton Head Island (town) Beaufort County	36	0.10
Red Hill (cdp) Horry County	32	0.23

Top 10 Places Sorted by Percent of Total Population
Based on all places, regardless of total population

Place	Population	%
Wedgefield (cdp) Sumter County	10	0.72
Socastee (cdp) Horry County	115	0.67
Ninety Six (town) Greenwood County	12	0.66
Arcadia Lakes (town) Richland County	5	0.54
Central (town) Pickens County	20	0.41
Little River (cdp) Horry County	25	0.29
Woodruff (city) Spartanburg County	12	0.29
Conway (city) Horry County	39	0.24
Awendaw (town) Charleston County	3	0.24
Red Hill (cdp) Horry County	32	0.23

Top 10 Places Sorted by Percent of Total Population
Based on places with total population of 50,000 or more

Place	Population	%
Charleston (city) Charleston County	148	0.13
Mount Pleasant (town) Charleston County	71	0.11
Columbia (city) Richland County	107	0.08
Rock Hill (city) York County	37	0.06
North Charleston (city) Charleston County	46	0.05
Greenville (city) Greenville County	0	0.00

Danish

Top 10 Places Sorted by Population
Based on all places, regardless of total population

Place	Population	%
Charleston (city) Charleston County	204	0.18
Columbia (city) Richland County	201	0.16
Summerville (town) Dorchester County	173	0.43
Seven Oaks (cdp) Lexington County	153	0.94
Mount Pleasant (town) Charleston County	125	0.19
Rock Hill (city) York County	109	0.17
Dentsville (cdp) Richland County	99	0.73
North Charleston (city) Charleston County	98	0.10
Greenville (city) Greenville County	92	0.16
Clearwater (cdp) Aiken County	87	2.05

Top 10 Places Sorted by Percent of Total Population
Based on all places, regardless of total population

Place	Population	%
Lodge (town) Colleton County	6	7.06
Starr (town) Anderson County	7	3.61
Clearwater (cdp) Aiken County	87	2.05
India Hook (cdp) York County	55	1.61
Kiawah Island (town) Charleston County	25	1.53
Ravenel (town) Charleston County	30	1.37
Travelers Rest (city) Greenville County	44	0.99
Seven Oaks (cdp) Lexington County	153	0.94
Prosperity (town) Newberry County	9	0.93
Burton (cdp) Beaufort County	65	0.91

Top 10 Places Sorted by Percent of Total Population
Based on places with total population of 50,000 or more

Place	Population	%
Mount Pleasant (town) Charleston County	125	0.19
Charleston (city) Charleston County	204	0.18
Rock Hill (city) York County	109	0.17
Columbia (city) Richland County	201	0.16
Greenville (city) Greenville County	92	0.16
North Charleston (city) Charleston County	98	0.10

Top 10 Places Sorted by Percent of Total Population
Based on places with total population of 50,000 or more

Place	Population	%
Mount Pleasant (town) Charleston County	56	0.09
Columbia (city) Richland County	76	0.06
Charleston (city) Charleston County	42	0.04
North Charleston (city) Charleston County	24	0.03
Rock Hill (city) York County	15	0.02
Greenville (city) Greenville County	11	0.02

Top 10 Places Sorted by Percent of Total Population
Based on places with total population of 50,000 or more

Place	Population	%
Charleston (city) Charleston County	26	0.02
Columbia (city) Richland County	9	0.01
Greenville (city) Greenville County	6	0.01
Mount Pleasant (town) Charleston County	0	0.00
North Charleston (city) Charleston County	0	0.00
Rock Hill (city) York County	0	0.00

Dutch

Top 10 Places Sorted by Population
Based on all places, regardless of total population

Place	Population	%
Charleston (city) Charleston County	1,301	1.12
Columbia (city) Richland County	1,053	0.83
Mount Pleasant (town) Charleston County	986	1.54
Greenville (city) Greenville County	813	1.41
Rock Hill (city) York County	730	1.16
Summerville (town) Dorchester County	652	1.61
Hilton Head Island (town) Beaufort County	638	1.74
North Charleston (city) Charleston County	519	0.55
Myrtle Beach (city) Horry County	401	1.50
Socastee (cdp) Horry County	338	1.98

Top 10 Places Sorted by Percent of Total Population
Based on all places, regardless of total population

Place	Population	%
Oswego (cdp) Sumter County	9	20.00
Lockhart (town) Union County	101	16.92
Hilda (town) Barnwell County	80	12.97
Pinopolis (cdp) Berkeley County	151	11.49
Reidville (town) Spartanburg County	44	8.06
Smoaks (town) Colleton County	8	7.08
Clover (town) York County	335	6.81
Waterloo (town) Laurens County	6	5.50
Inman (city) Spartanburg County	114	5.22
Lowndesville (town) Abbeville County	8	5.13

Top 10 Places Sorted by Percent of Total Population
Based on places with total population of 50,000 or more

Place	Population	%
Mount Pleasant (town) Charleston County	986	1.54
Greenville (city) Greenville County	813	1.41
Rock Hill (city) York County	730	1.16
Charleston (city) Charleston County	1,301	1.12
Columbia (city) Richland County	1,053	0.83
North Charleston (city) Charleston County	519	0.55

English

Top 10 Places Sorted by Population
Based on all places, regardless of total population

Place	Population	%
Charleston (city) Charleston County	14,530	12.49
Columbia (city) Richland County	12,269	9.61
Mount Pleasant (town) Charleston County	10,047	15.65
Greenville (city) Greenville County	7,396	12.79
Hilton Head Island (town) Beaufort County	5,758	15.68
Rock Hill (city) York County	5,454	8.64
North Charleston (city) Charleston County	5,132	5.43
Summerville (town) Dorchester County	4,341	10.74
Aiken (city) Aiken County	4,312	14.97
Spartanburg (city) Spartanburg County	3,823	10.20

Top 10 Places Sorted by Percent of Total Population
Based on all places, regardless of total population

Place	Population	%
Princeton (cdp) Laurens County	20	58.82
Glendale (cdp) Spartanburg County	141	40.99
Pawleys Island (town) Georgetown County	39	39.00
Clifton (cdp) Spartanburg County	276	38.02
Modoc (cdp) McCormick County	105	31.25
Tatum (town) Marlboro County	20	31.25
Plum Branch (town) McCormick County	17	30.91
Seabrook Island (town) Charleston County	546	30.07
Reevesville (town) Dorchester County	56	26.79
Pinopolis (cdp) Berkeley County	346	26.33

Top 10 Places Sorted by Percent of Total Population
Based on places with total population of 50,000 or more

Place	Population	%
Mount Pleasant (town) Charleston County	10,047	15.65
Greenville (city) Greenville County	7,396	12.79
Charleston (city) Charleston County	14,530	12.49
Columbia (city) Richland County	12,269	9.61
Rock Hill (city) York County	5,454	8.64
North Charleston (city) Charleston County	5,132	5.43

European

Top 10 Places Sorted by Population
Based on all places, regardless of total population

Place	Population	%
Charleston (city) Charleston County	1,434	1.23
Columbia (city) Richland County	1,415	1.11
Mount Pleasant (town) Charleston County	1,383	2.15
North Charleston (city) Charleston County	792	0.84
Rock Hill (city) York County	662	1.05
Greenville (city) Greenville County	601	1.04
Goose Creek (city) Berkeley County	477	1.37
Spartanburg (city) Spartanburg County	470	1.25
Aiken (city) Aiken County	443	1.54
Myrtle Beach (city) Horry County	410	1.54

Top 10 Places Sorted by Percent of Total Population
Based on all places, regardless of total population

Place	Population	%
Parksville (town) McCormick County	30	29.70
Pinopolis (cdp) Berkeley County	217	16.51
Rowesville (town) Orangeburg County	32	7.82
Westminster (city) Oconee County	138	5.82
Trenton (town) Edgefield County	9	5.73
Swansea (town) Lexington County	46	5.70
Seabrook Island (town) Charleston County	103	5.67
Briarcliffe Acres (town) Horry County	22	5.46
Joanna (cdp) Laurens County	78	5.41
Pine Ridge (town) Lexington County	98	4.45

Top 10 Places Sorted by Percent of Total Population
Based on places with total population of 50,000 or more

Place	Population	%
Mount Pleasant (town) Charleston County	1,383	2.15
Charleston (city) Charleston County	1,434	1.23
Columbia (city) Richland County	1,415	1.11
Rock Hill (city) York County	662	1.05
Greenville (city) Greenville County	601	1.04
North Charleston (city) Charleston County	792	0.84

Eastern European

Top 10 Places Sorted by Population
Based on all places, regardless of total population

Place	Population	%
Columbia (city) Richland County	76	0.06
Five Forks (cdp) Greenville County	72	0.55
Mount Pleasant (town) Charleston County	56	0.09
Hilton Head Island (town) Beaufort County	44	0.12
Charleston (city) Charleston County	42	0.04
North Myrtle Beach (city) Horry County	36	0.27
Roebuck (cdp) Spartanburg County	33	2.02
Sumter (city) Sumter County	30	0.07
Red Hill (cdp) Horry County	25	0.18
North Charleston (city) Charleston County	24	0.03

Top 10 Places Sorted by Percent of Total Population
Based on all places, regardless of total population

Place	Population	%
James (town) Berkeley County	2	3.77
Roebuck (cdp) Spartanburg County	33	2.02
Kiawah Island (town) Charleston County	20	1.22
Sullivan's Island (town) Charleston County	13	0.63
Five Forks (cdp) Greenville County	72	0.55
Lakewood (cdp) Sumter County	11	0.41
Lamar (town) Darlington County	3	0.39
Estill (town) Hampton County	9	0.37
Seabrook Island (town) Charleston County	6	0.33
Isle of Palms (city) Charleston County	12	0.29

Estonian

Top 10 Places Sorted by Population
Based on all places, regardless of total population

Place	Population	%
Charleston (city) Charleston County	26	0.02
Hilton Head Island (town) Beaufort County	22	0.06
Columbia (city) Richland County	9	0.01
Aiken (city) Aiken County	7	0.02
Greenville (city) Greenville County	6	0.01
Abbeville (city) Abbeville County	0	0.00
Alcolu (cdp) Clarendon County	0	0.00
Allendale (town) Allendale County	0	0.00
Anderson (city) Anderson County	0	0.00
Andrews (town) Georgetown County	0	0.00

Top 10 Places Sorted by Percent of Total Population
Based on all places, regardless of total population

Place	Population	%
Hilton Head Island (town) Beaufort County	22	0.06
Charleston (city) Charleston County	26	0.02
Aiken (city) Aiken County	7	0.02
Columbia (city) Richland County	9	0.01
Greenville (city) Greenville County	6	0.01
Abbeville (city) Abbeville County	0	0.00
Alcolu (cdp) Clarendon County	0	0.00
Allendale (town) Allendale County	0	0.00
Anderson (city) Anderson County	0	0.00
Andrews (town) Georgetown County	0	0.00

Finnish

Top 10 Places Sorted by Population
Based on all places, regardless of total population

Place	Population	%
Columbia (city) Richland County	149	0.12
Mount Pleasant (town) Charleston County	112	0.17
Five Forks (cdp) Greenville County	93	0.71
Bluffton (town) Beaufort County	76	0.71
Greer (city) Greenville County	76	0.32
Rock Hill (city) York County	69	0.11
Hilton Head Island (town) Beaufort County	64	0.17
Easley (city) Pickens County	63	0.32
Goose Creek (city) Berkeley County	54	0.16
Golden Grove (cdp) Greenville County	48	1.58

Top 10 Places Sorted by Percent of Total Population
Based on all places, regardless of total population

Place	Population	%
Golden Grove (cdp) Greenville County	48	1.58
Yemassee (town) Hampton County	13	1.21
Lyman (town) Spartanburg County	24	0.77
Five Forks (cdp) Greenville County	93	0.71
Bluffton (town) Beaufort County	76	0.71
Whitmire (town) Newberry County	11	0.70
Dalzell (cdp) Sumter County	20	0.62
Batesburg-Leesville (town) Lexington County	31	0.59
Laurel Bay (cdp) Beaufort County	31	0.55
Gaston (town) Lexington County	6	0.49

(French, except Basque — continued)

Top 10 Places Sorted by Percent of Total Population
Based on places with total population of 50,000 or more

Place	Population	%
Mount Pleasant (town) Charleston County	112	0.17
Columbia (city) Richland County	149	0.12
Rock Hill (city) York County	69	0.11
Charleston (city) Charleston County	44	0.04
North Charleston (city) Charleston County	22	0.02
Greenville (city) Greenville County	0	0.00

French, except Basque

Top 10 Places Sorted by Population
Based on all places, regardless of total population

Place	Population	%
Charleston (city) Charleston County	3,182	2.73
Mount Pleasant (town) Charleston County	2,855	4.45
Columbia (city) Richland County	2,527	1.98
North Charleston (city) Charleston County	1,585	1.68
Rock Hill (city) York County	1,391	2.20
Summerville (town) Dorchester County	1,381	3.42
Greenville (city) Greenville County	1,290	2.23
Hilton Head Island (town) Beaufort County	1,259	3.43
Hanahan (city) Berkeley County	829	4.89
Goose Creek (city) Berkeley County	827	2.38

Top 10 Places Sorted by Percent of Total Population
Based on all places, regardless of total population

Place	Population	%
McClellanville (town) Charleston County	40	11.83
Surfside Beach (town) Horry County	274	6.91
Startex (cdp) Spartanburg County	49	6.64
Fair Play (cdp) Oconee County	30	6.56
Pawleys Island (town) Georgetown County	6	6.00
India Hook (cdp) York County	203	5.94
Donalds (town) Abbeville County	21	5.90
Livingston (town) Orangeburg County	7	5.79
Sullivan's Island (town) Charleston County	114	5.57
Lake Murray of Richland (cdp) Richland County	262	5.40

Top 10 Places Sorted by Percent of Total Population
Based on places with total population of 50,000 or more

Place	Population	%
Mount Pleasant (town) Charleston County	2,855	4.45
Charleston (city) Charleston County	3,182	2.73
Greenville (city) Greenville County	1,290	2.23
Rock Hill (city) York County	1,391	2.20
Columbia (city) Richland County	2,527	1.98
North Charleston (city) Charleston County	1,585	1.68

French Canadian

Top 10 Places Sorted by Population
Based on all places, regardless of total population

Place	Population	%
Columbia (city) Richland County	442	0.35
North Charleston (city) Charleston County	423	0.45
Charleston (city) Charleston County	397	0.34
Five Forks (cdp) Greenville County	302	2.30
Greenville (city) Greenville County	290	0.50
Hilton Head Island (town) Beaufort County	261	0.71
Port Royal (town) Beaufort County	209	2.00
Summerville (town) Dorchester County	188	0.47
Lexington (town) Lexington County	158	0.96
Goose Creek (city) Berkeley County	158	0.45

Top 10 Places Sorted by Percent of Total Population
Based on all places, regardless of total population

Place	Population	%
Lydia (cdp) Darlington County	50	7.50
Cane Savannah (cdp) Sumter County	58	4.14
Westminster (city) Oconee County	84	3.54
Dalzell (cdp) Sumter County	97	3.01
Summit (town) Lexington County	13	2.90
Pelion (town) Lexington County	21	2.74
Five Forks (cdp) Greenville County	302	2.30
Port Royal (town) Beaufort County	209	2.00
Mount Croghan (town) Chesterfield County	3	1.64
Tigerville (cdp) Greenville County	15	1.63

(German — continued)

Top 10 Places Sorted by Percent of Total Population
Based on places with total population of 50,000 or more

Place	Population	%
Greenville (city) Greenville County	290	0.50
North Charleston (city) Charleston County	423	0.45
Columbia (city) Richland County	442	0.35
Charleston (city) Charleston County	397	0.34
Mount Pleasant (town) Charleston County	158	0.25
Rock Hill (city) York County	104	0.16

German

Top 10 Places Sorted by Population
Based on all places, regardless of total population

Place	Population	%
Charleston (city) Charleston County	14,321	12.31
Columbia (city) Richland County	12,047	9.44
Mount Pleasant (town) Charleston County	11,137	17.35
North Charleston (city) Charleston County	7,850	8.30
Rock Hill (city) York County	7,124	11.29
Greenville (city) Greenville County	6,981	12.07
Hilton Head Island (town) Beaufort County	6,412	17.46
Summerville (town) Dorchester County	6,379	15.79
Goose Creek (city) Berkeley County	5,005	14.40
Aiken (city) Aiken County	3,803	13.20

Top 10 Places Sorted by Percent of Total Population
Based on all places, regardless of total population

Place	Population	%
Riverview (cdp) York County	205	53.11
Newry (cdp) Oconee County	36	40.45
Plum Branch (town) McCormick County	21	38.18
Smyrna (town) York County	16	34.78
Modoc (cdp) McCormick County	116	34.52
Pelzer (town) Anderson County	30	34.48
Pomaria (town) Newberry County	51	34.23
Pinopolis (cdp) Berkeley County	449	34.17
Tatum (town) Marlboro County	20	31.25
Cokesbury (cdp) Greenwood County	32	30.77

Top 10 Places Sorted by Percent of Total Population
Based on places with total population of 50,000 or more

Place	Population	%
Mount Pleasant (town) Charleston County	11,137	17.35
Charleston (city) Charleston County	14,321	12.31
Greenville (city) Greenville County	6,981	12.07
Rock Hill (city) York County	7,124	11.29
Columbia (city) Richland County	12,047	9.44
North Charleston (city) Charleston County	7,850	8.30

German Russian

Top 10 Places Sorted by Population
Based on all places, regardless of total population

Place	Population	%
Spartanburg (city) Spartanburg County	29	0.08
North Augusta (city) Aiken County	17	0.08
Orangeburg (city) Orangeburg County	15	0.11
Abbeville (city) Abbeville County	0	0.00
Aiken (city) Aiken County	0	0.00
Alcolu (cdp) Clarendon County	0	0.00
Allendale (town) Allendale County	0	0.00
Anderson (city) Anderson County	0	0.00
Andrews (town) Georgetown County	0	0.00
Antreville (cdp) Abbeville County	0	0.00

Top 10 Places Sorted by Percent of Total Population
Based on all places, regardless of total population

Place	Population	%
Orangeburg (city) Orangeburg County	15	0.11
Spartanburg (city) Spartanburg County	29	0.08
North Augusta (city) Aiken County	17	0.08
Abbeville (city) Abbeville County	0	0.00
Aiken (city) Aiken County	0	0.00
Alcolu (cdp) Clarendon County	0	0.00
Allendale (town) Allendale County	0	0.00
Anderson (city) Anderson County	0	0.00
Andrews (town) Georgetown County	0	0.00
Antreville (cdp) Abbeville County	0	0.00

(Greek — continued)

Top 10 Places Sorted by Percent of Total Population
Based on places with total population of 50,000 or more

Place	Population	%
Charleston (city) Charleston County	0	0.00
Columbia (city) Richland County	0	0.00
Greenville (city) Greenville County	0	0.00
Mount Pleasant (town) Charleston County	0	0.00
North Charleston (city) Charleston County	0	0.00
Rock Hill (city) York County	0	0.00

Greek

Top 10 Places Sorted by Population
Based on all places, regardless of total population

Place	Population	%
Charleston (city) Charleston County	882	0.76
Columbia (city) Richland County	603	0.47
Wade Hampton (cdp) Greenville County	524	2.58
Mount Pleasant (town) Charleston County	378	0.59
Summerville (town) Dorchester County	283	0.70
North Charleston (city) Charleston County	233	0.25
Florence (city) Florence County	225	0.62
Aiken (city) Aiken County	203	0.70
Greenville (city) Greenville County	201	0.35
St. Andrews (cdp) Richland County	177	0.85

Top 10 Places Sorted by Percent of Total Population
Based on all places, regardless of total population

Place	Population	%
Rockville (town) Charleston County	10	6.29
Folly Beach (city) Charleston County	113	4.48
Aynor (town) Horry County	28	3.52
Wade Hampton (cdp) Greenville County	524	2.58
Reidville (town) Spartanburg County	12	2.20
Sullivan's Island (town) Charleston County	44	2.15
Hopkins (cdp) Richland County	65	2.12
Swansea (town) Lexington County	17	2.11
Arcadia Lakes (town) Richland County	19	2.05
Pelion (town) Lexington County	12	1.57

Top 10 Places Sorted by Percent of Total Population
Based on places with total population of 50,000 or more

Place	Population	%
Charleston (city) Charleston County	882	0.76
Mount Pleasant (town) Charleston County	378	0.59
Columbia (city) Richland County	603	0.47
Greenville (city) Greenville County	201	0.35
North Charleston (city) Charleston County	233	0.25
Rock Hill (city) York County	93	0.15

Guyanese

Top 10 Places Sorted by Population
Based on all places, regardless of total population

Place	Population	%
Dentsville (cdp) Richland County	45	0.33
North Charleston (city) Charleston County	32	0.03
Taylors (cdp) Greenville County	26	0.12
Port Royal (town) Beaufort County	18	0.17
St. Andrews (cdp) Richland County	14	0.07
North Augusta (city) Aiken County	9	0.04
Rock Hill (city) York County	8	0.01
Chesnee (city) Spartanburg County	7	0.94
Hilton Head Island (town) Beaufort County	7	0.02
Eutawville (town) Orangeburg County	2	0.37

Top 10 Places Sorted by Percent of Total Population
Based on all places, regardless of total population

Place	Population	%
Chesnee (city) Spartanburg County	7	0.94
Eutawville (town) Orangeburg County	2	0.37
Dentsville (cdp) Richland County	45	0.33
Port Royal (town) Beaufort County	18	0.17
Taylors (cdp) Greenville County	26	0.12
St. Andrews (cdp) Richland County	14	0.07
North Augusta (city) Aiken County	9	0.04
North Charleston (city) Charleston County	32	0.03
Hilton Head Island (town) Beaufort County	7	0.02
Rock Hill (city) York County	8	0.01

Top 10 Places Sorted by Percent of Total Population
Based on places with total population of 50,000 or more

Place	Population	%
North Charleston (city) Charleston County	32	0.03
Rock Hill (city) York County	8	0.01
Charleston (city) Charleston County	0	0.00
Columbia (city) Richland County	0	0.00
Greenville (city) Greenville County	0	0.00
Mount Pleasant (town) Charleston County	0	0.00

Hungarian

Top 10 Places Sorted by Population
Based on all places, regardless of total population

Place	Population	%
Mount Pleasant (town) Charleston County	422	0.66
Hilton Head Island (town) Beaufort County	402	1.09
Charleston (city) Charleston County	327	0.28
Columbia (city) Richland County	311	0.24
Anderson (city) Anderson County	160	0.60
North Charleston (city) Charleston County	154	0.16
Aiken (city) Aiken County	143	0.50
Greenville (city) Greenville County	117	0.20
North Myrtle Beach (city) Horry County	115	0.86
Ladson (cdp) Berkeley County	106	0.75

Top 10 Places Sorted by Percent of Total Population
Based on all places, regardless of total population

Place	Population	%
James (town) Berkeley County	6	11.32
Watts Mills (cdp) Laurens County	62	3.56
Aynor (town) Horry County	23	2.89
Iva (town) Anderson County	26	2.30
Kiawah Island (town) Charleston County	36	2.20
Loris (city) Horry County	40	1.65
Reidville (town) Spartanburg County	8	1.47
Rowesville (town) Orangeburg County	6	1.47
Holly Hill (town) Orangeburg County	15	1.36
Garden City (cdp) Horry County	105	1.18

Top 10 Places Sorted by Percent of Total Population
Based on places with total population of 50,000 or more

Place	Population	%
Mount Pleasant (town) Charleston County	422	0.66
Charleston (city) Charleston County	327	0.28
Columbia (city) Richland County	311	0.24
Greenville (city) Greenville County	117	0.20
North Charleston (city) Charleston County	154	0.16
Rock Hill (city) York County	72	0.11

Icelander

Top 10 Places Sorted by Population
Based on all places, regardless of total population

Place	Population	%
Red Hill (cdp) Horry County	78	0.56
Rock Hill (city) York County	24	0.04
Tega Cay (city) York County	22	0.31
Five Forks (cdp) Greenville County	14	0.11
Goose Creek (city) Berkeley County	13	0.04
Duncan (town) Spartanburg County	12	0.39
Greenville (city) Greenville County	12	0.02
Hilton Head Island (town) Beaufort County	9	0.02
North Myrtle Beach (city) Horry County	7	0.05
Sans Souci (cdp) Greenville County	5	0.06

Top 10 Places Sorted by Percent of Total Population
Based on all places, regardless of total population

Place	Population	%
Red Hill (cdp) Horry County	78	0.56
Duncan (town) Spartanburg County	12	0.39
Eutawville (town) Orangeburg County	2	0.37
Tega Cay (city) York County	22	0.31
Five Forks (cdp) Greenville County	14	0.11
Sans Souci (cdp) Greenville County	5	0.06
North Myrtle Beach (city) Horry County	7	0.05
Rock Hill (city) York County	24	0.04
Goose Creek (city) Berkeley County	13	0.04
Greenville (city) Greenville County	12	0.02

Top 10 Places Sorted by Percent of Total Population
Based on places with total population of 50,000 or more

Place	Population	%
Rock Hill (city) York County	24	0.04
Greenville (city) Greenville County	12	0.02
Charleston (city) Charleston County	0	0.00
Columbia (city) Richland County	0	0.00
Mount Pleasant (town) Charleston County	0	0.00
North Charleston (city) Charleston County	0	0.00

Iranian

Top 10 Places Sorted by Population
Based on all places, regardless of total population

Place	Population	%
Charleston (city) Charleston County	105	0.09
Pendleton (town) Anderson County	100	3.38
Columbia (city) Richland County	81	0.06
Taylors (cdp) Greenville County	55	0.25
Greenville (city) Greenville County	51	0.09
Isle of Palms (city) Charleston County	38	0.90
Florence (city) Florence County	34	0.09
West Columbia (city) Lexington County	27	0.18
Greer (city) Greenville County	27	0.11
Anderson (city) Anderson County	19	0.07

Top 10 Places Sorted by Percent of Total Population
Based on all places, regardless of total population

Place	Population	%
Pendleton (town) Anderson County	100	3.38
Isle of Palms (city) Charleston County	38	0.90
Blythewood (town) Richland County	6	0.41
Taylors (cdp) Greenville County	55	0.25
Central (town) Pickens County	10	0.21
West Columbia (city) Lexington County	27	0.18
Greer (city) Greenville County	27	0.11
Charleston (city) Charleston County	105	0.09
Greenville (city) Greenville County	51	0.09
Florence (city) Florence County	34	0.09

Top 10 Places Sorted by Percent of Total Population
Based on places with total population of 50,000 or more

Place	Population	%
Charleston (city) Charleston County	105	0.09
Greenville (city) Greenville County	51	0.09
Columbia (city) Richland County	81	0.06
Mount Pleasant (town) Charleston County	0	0.00
North Charleston (city) Charleston County	0	0.00
Rock Hill (city) York County	0	0.00

Irish

Top 10 Places Sorted by Population
Based on all places, regardless of total population

Place	Population	%
Charleston (city) Charleston County	12,396	10.65
Mount Pleasant (town) Charleston County	11,021	17.16
Columbia (city) Richland County	10,384	8.14
Rock Hill (city) York County	6,334	10.04
North Charleston (city) Charleston County	5,476	5.79
Hilton Head Island (town) Beaufort County	5,247	14.29
Summerville (town) Dorchester County	5,209	12.89
Greenville (city) Greenville County	4,691	8.11
Goose Creek (city) Berkeley County	3,872	11.14
Aiken (city) Aiken County	3,128	10.86

Top 10 Places Sorted by Percent of Total Population
Based on all places, regardless of total population

Place	Population	%
Newry (cdp) Oconee County	46	51.69
Riverview (cdp) York County	182	47.15
Antreville (cdp) Abbeville County	35	44.30
Mountville (cdp) Laurens County	53	39.55
Troy (town) Greenwood County	30	35.71
Smyrna (town) York County	16	34.78
Plum Branch (town) McCormick County	17	30.91
Lockhart (town) Union County	161	26.97
Pinopolis (cdp) Berkeley County	340	25.88
Lowndesville (town) Abbeville County	40	25.64

Top 10 Places Sorted by Percent of Total Population
Based on places with total population of 50,000 or more

Place	Population	%
Mount Pleasant (town) Charleston County	11,021	17.16
Charleston (city) Charleston County	12,396	10.65
Rock Hill (city) York County	6,334	10.04
Columbia (city) Richland County	10,384	8.14
Greenville (city) Greenville County	4,691	8.11
North Charleston (city) Charleston County	5,476	5.79

Israeli

Top 10 Places Sorted by Population
Based on all places, regardless of total population

Place	Population	%
Lexington (town) Lexington County	110	0.67
Myrtle Beach (city) Horry County	59	0.22
Socastee (cdp) Horry County	53	0.31
Hilton Head Island (town) Beaufort County	51	0.14
Travelers Rest (city) Greenville County	35	0.78
Sans Souci (cdp) Greenville County	28	0.34
Summerville (town) Dorchester County	23	0.06
Charleston (city) Charleston County	16	0.01
Bluffton (town) Beaufort County	12	0.11
Columbia (city) Richland County	12	0.01

Top 10 Places Sorted by Percent of Total Population
Based on all places, regardless of total population

Place	Population	%
Travelers Rest (city) Greenville County	35	0.78
Lexington (town) Lexington County	110	0.67
Sans Souci (cdp) Greenville County	28	0.34
Socastee (cdp) Horry County	53	0.31
Myrtle Beach (city) Horry County	59	0.22
Hilton Head Island (town) Beaufort County	51	0.14
St. Stephen (town) Berkeley County	3	0.14
Bluffton (town) Beaufort County	12	0.11
Summerville (town) Dorchester County	23	0.06
Mauldin (city) Greenville County	10	0.05

Top 10 Places Sorted by Percent of Total Population
Based on places with total population of 50,000 or more

Place	Population	%
Mount Pleasant (town) Charleston County	10	0.02
Charleston (city) Charleston County	16	0.01
Columbia (city) Richland County	12	0.01
Greenville (city) Greenville County	0	0.00
North Charleston (city) Charleston County	0	0.00
Rock Hill (city) York County	0	0.00

Italian

Top 10 Places Sorted by Population
Based on all places, regardless of total population

Place	Population	%
Charleston (city) Charleston County	4,553	3.91
Mount Pleasant (town) Charleston County	4,378	6.82
Columbia (city) Richland County	2,784	2.18
Hilton Head Island (town) Beaufort County	2,528	6.89
Summerville (town) Dorchester County	2,309	5.71
North Charleston (city) Charleston County	1,869	1.98
Myrtle Beach (city) Horry County	1,796	6.73
Rock Hill (city) York County	1,636	2.59
Goose Creek (city) Berkeley County	1,471	4.23
Greenville (city) Greenville County	1,445	2.50

Top 10 Places Sorted by Percent of Total Population
Based on all places, regardless of total population

Place	Population	%
Oswego (cdp) Sumter County	9	20.00
Reidville (town) Spartanburg County	75	13.74
Lesslie (cdp) York County	355	11.64
Forestbrook (cdp) Horry County	452	10.68
Five Forks (cdp) Greenville County	1,335	10.16
Tega Cay (city) York County	709	10.11
Briarcliffe Acres (town) Horry County	37	9.18
Bluffton (town) Beaufort County	890	8.28
Bradley (cdp) Greenwood County	13	8.28
Lake Wylie (cdp) York County	674	8.06

Please refer to the Explanation of Data in the front of the book for more detailed information.

Top 10 Places Sorted by Percent of Total Population
Based on places with total population of 50,000 or more

Place	Population	%
Mount Pleasant (town) Charleston County	4,378	6.82
Charleston (city) Charleston County	4,553	3.91
Rock Hill (city) York County	1,636	2.59
Greenville (city) Greenville County	1,445	2.50
Columbia (city) Richland County	2,784	2.18
North Charleston (city) Charleston County	1,869	1.98

Latvian

Top 10 Places Sorted by Population
Based on all places, regardless of total population

Place	Population	%
Beaufort (city) Beaufort County	78	0.62
North Charleston (city) Charleston County	47	0.05
Red Hill (cdp) Horry County	27	0.20
Columbia (city) Richland County	27	0.02
Hilton Head Island (town) Beaufort County	26	0.07
Cayce (city) Lexington County	25	0.20
Greenville (city) Greenville County	22	0.04
Marion (city) Marion County	16	0.23
Lake Wylie (cdp) York County	15	0.18
Clover (town) York County	13	0.26

Top 10 Places Sorted by Percent of Total Population
Based on all places, regardless of total population

Place	Population	%
Beaufort (city) Beaufort County	78	0.62
Edisto Beach (town) Colleton County	3	0.52
Clover (town) York County	13	0.26
Marion (city) Marion County	16	0.23
Red Hill (cdp) Horry County	27	0.20
Cayce (city) Lexington County	25	0.20
Lake Wylie (cdp) York County	15	0.18
Port Royal (town) Beaufort County	10	0.10
Hilton Head Island (town) Beaufort County	26	0.07
North Augusta (city) Aiken County	13	0.06

Top 10 Places Sorted by Percent of Total Population
Based on places with total population of 50,000 or more

Place	Population	%
North Charleston (city) Charleston County	47	0.05
Greenville (city) Greenville County	22	0.04
Columbia (city) Richland County	27	0.02
Charleston (city) Charleston County	7	0.01
Mount Pleasant (town) Charleston County	0	0.00
Rock Hill (city) York County	0	0.00

Lithuanian

Top 10 Places Sorted by Population
Based on all places, regardless of total population

Place	Population	%
Charleston (city) Charleston County	214	0.18
Mount Pleasant (town) Charleston County	175	0.27
Columbia (city) Richland County	113	0.09
Fort Mill (town) York County	83	0.81
Hilton Head Island (town) Beaufort County	82	0.22
Mauldin (city) Greenville County	70	0.32
Summerville (town) Dorchester County	69	0.17
North Myrtle Beach (city) Horry County	66	0.49
Clemson (city) Pickens County	64	0.47
Anderson (city) Anderson County	63	0.24

Top 10 Places Sorted by Percent of Total Population
Based on all places, regardless of total population

Place	Population	%
Briarcliffe Acres (town) Horry County	9	2.23
Chapin (town) Lexington County	14	1.12
Fort Mill (town) York County	83	0.81
Seabrook Island (town) Charleston County	14	0.77
Murphys Estates (cdp) Edgefield County	16	0.71
Clover (town) York County	34	0.69
Ninety Six (town) Greenwood County	12	0.66
Isle of Palms (city) Charleston County	27	0.64
Newport (cdp) York County	21	0.54
North Myrtle Beach (city) Horry County	66	0.49

Top 10 Places Sorted by Percent of Total Population
Based on places with total population of 50,000 or more

Place	Population	%
Mount Pleasant (town) Charleston County	175	0.27
Charleston (city) Charleston County	214	0.18
Columbia (city) Richland County	113	0.09
Rock Hill (city) York County	39	0.06
Greenville (city) Greenville County	12	0.02
North Charleston (city) Charleston County	0	0.00

Luxemburger

Top 10 Places Sorted by Population
Based on all places, regardless of total population

Place	Population	%
Columbia (city) Richland County	51	0.04
Abbeville (city) Abbeville County	0	0.00
Aiken (city) Aiken County	0	0.00
Alcolu (cdp) Clarendon County	0	0.00
Allendale (town) Allendale County	0	0.00
Anderson (city) Anderson County	0	0.00
Andrews (town) Georgetown County	0	0.00
Antreville (cdp) Abbeville County	0	0.00
Arcadia (cdp) Spartanburg County	0	0.00
Arcadia Lakes (town) Richland County	0	0.00

Top 10 Places Sorted by Percent of Total Population
Based on all places, regardless of total population

Place	Population	%
Columbia (city) Richland County	51	0.04
Abbeville (city) Abbeville County	0	0.00
Aiken (city) Aiken County	0	0.00
Alcolu (cdp) Clarendon County	0	0.00
Allendale (town) Allendale County	0	0.00
Anderson (city) Anderson County	0	0.00
Andrews (town) Georgetown County	0	0.00
Antreville (cdp) Abbeville County	0	0.00
Arcadia (cdp) Spartanburg County	0	0.00
Arcadia Lakes (town) Richland County	0	0.00

Top 10 Places Sorted by Percent of Total Population
Based on places with total population of 50,000 or more

Place	Population	%
Columbia (city) Richland County	51	0.04
Charleston (city) Charleston County	0	0.00
Greenville (city) Greenville County	0	0.00
Mount Pleasant (town) Charleston County	0	0.00
North Charleston (city) Charleston County	0	0.00
Rock Hill (city) York County	0	0.00

Macedonian

Top 10 Places Sorted by Population
Based on all places, regardless of total population

Place	Population	%
Greer (city) Greenville County	48	0.20
Charleston (city) Charleston County	14	0.01
North Charleston (city) Charleston County	12	0.01
Five Forks (cdp) Greenville County	10	0.08
Beaufort (city) Beaufort County	7	0.06
Greenville (city) Greenville County	6	0.01
Abbeville (city) Abbeville County	0	0.00
Aiken (city) Aiken County	0	0.00
Alcolu (cdp) Clarendon County	0	0.00
Allendale (town) Allendale County	0	0.00

Top 10 Places Sorted by Percent of Total Population
Based on all places, regardless of total population

Place	Population	%
Greer (city) Greenville County	48	0.20
Five Forks (cdp) Greenville County	10	0.08
Beaufort (city) Beaufort County	7	0.06
Charleston (city) Charleston County	14	0.01
North Charleston (city) Charleston County	12	0.01
Greenville (city) Greenville County	6	0.01
Abbeville (city) Abbeville County	0	0.00
Aiken (city) Aiken County	0	0.00
Alcolu (cdp) Clarendon County	0	0.00
Allendale (town) Allendale County	0	0.00

Top 10 Places Sorted by Percent of Total Population
Based on places with total population of 50,000 or more

Place	Population	%
Charleston (city) Charleston County	14	0.01
North Charleston (city) Charleston County	12	0.01
Greenville (city) Greenville County	6	0.01
Columbia (city) Richland County	0	0.00
Mount Pleasant (town) Charleston County	0	0.00
Rock Hill (city) York County	0	0.00

Top 10 Places Sorted by Percent of Total Population
Based on places with total population of 50,000 or more

Place	Population	%
Charleston (city) Charleston County	14	0.01
North Charleston (city) Charleston County	12	0.01
Greenville (city) Greenville County	6	0.01
Columbia (city) Richland County	0	0.00
Mount Pleasant (town) Charleston County	0	0.00
Rock Hill (city) York County	0	0.00

Maltese

Top 10 Places Sorted by Population
Based on all places, regardless of total population

Place	Population	%
Murphys Estates (cdp) Edgefield County	26	1.15
Greenville (city) Greenville County	14	0.02
Summerville (town) Dorchester County	11	0.03
Sumter (city) Sumter County	9	0.02
Port Royal (town) Beaufort County	3	0.03
Abbeville (city) Abbeville County	0	0.00
Aiken (city) Aiken County	0	0.00
Alcolu (cdp) Clarendon County	0	0.00
Allendale (town) Allendale County	0	0.00
Anderson (city) Anderson County	0	0.00

Top 10 Places Sorted by Percent of Total Population
Based on all places, regardless of total population

Place	Population	%
Murphys Estates (cdp) Edgefield County	26	1.15
Summerville (town) Dorchester County	11	0.03
Port Royal (town) Beaufort County	3	0.03
Greenville (city) Greenville County	14	0.02
Sumter (city) Sumter County	9	0.02
Abbeville (city) Abbeville County	0	0.00
Aiken (city) Aiken County	0	0.00
Alcolu (cdp) Clarendon County	0	0.00
Allendale (town) Allendale County	0	0.00
Anderson (city) Anderson County	0	0.00

Top 10 Places Sorted by Percent of Total Population
Based on places with total population of 50,000 or more

Place	Population	%
Greenville (city) Greenville County	14	0.02
Charleston (city) Charleston County	0	0.00
Columbia (city) Richland County	0	0.00
Mount Pleasant (town) Charleston County	0	0.00
North Charleston (city) Charleston County	0	0.00
Rock Hill (city) York County	0	0.00

New Zealander

Top 10 Places Sorted by Population
Based on all places, regardless of total population

Place	Population	%
Tega Cay (city) York County	24	0.34
North Charleston (city) Charleston County	18	0.02
Myrtle Beach (city) Horry County	17	0.06
Charleston (city) Charleston County	15	0.01
Columbia (city) Richland County	13	0.01
Abbeville (city) Abbeville County	0	0.00
Aiken (city) Aiken County	0	0.00
Alcolu (cdp) Clarendon County	0	0.00
Allendale (town) Allendale County	0	0.00
Anderson (city) Anderson County	0	0.00

Top 10 Places Sorted by Percent of Total Population
Based on all places, regardless of total population

Place	Population	%
Tega Cay (city) York County	24	0.34
Myrtle Beach (city) Horry County	17	0.06
North Charleston (city) Charleston County	18	0.02
Charleston (city) Charleston County	15	0.01
Columbia (city) Richland County	13	0.01
Abbeville (city) Abbeville County	0	0.00
Aiken (city) Aiken County	0	0.00
Alcolu (cdp) Clarendon County	0	0.00
Allendale (town) Allendale County	0	0.00
Anderson (city) Anderson County	0	0.00

Top 10 Places Sorted by Percent of Total Population
Based on places with total population of 50,000 or more

Place	Population	%
North Charleston (city) Charleston County	18	0.02
Charleston (city) Charleston County	15	0.01
Columbia (city) Richland County	13	0.01
Greenville (city) Greenville County	0	0.00
Mount Pleasant (town) Charleston County	0	0.00
Rock Hill (city) York County	0	0.00

Northern European

Top 10 Places Sorted by Population
Based on all places, regardless of total population

Place	Population	%
Columbia (city) Richland County	147	0.12
Mount Pleasant (town) Charleston County	136	0.21
Charleston (city) Charleston County	132	0.11
Five Forks (cdp) Greenville County	59	0.45
North Charleston (city) Charleston County	48	0.05
Simpsonville (city) Greenville County	29	0.17
Isle of Palms (city) Charleston County	27	0.64
Conway (city) Horry County	26	0.16
Mauldin (city) Greenville County	25	0.12
Greenville (city) Greenville County	24	0.04

Top 10 Places Sorted by Percent of Total Population
Based on all places, regardless of total population

Place	Population	%
Edisto Beach (town) Colleton County	10	1.73
Little Mountain (town) Newberry County	4	1.39
Jackson (town) Aiken County	16	0.99
Springdale (town) Lexington County	22	0.84
Isle of Palms (city) Charleston County	27	0.64
India Hook (cdp) York County	19	0.56
Five Forks (cdp) Greenville County	59	0.45
Surfside Beach (town) Horry County	17	0.43
Inman (city) Spartanburg County	6	0.27
Camden (city) Kershaw County	17	0.25

Top 10 Places Sorted by Percent of Total Population
Based on places with total population of 50,000 or more

Place	Population	%
Mount Pleasant (town) Charleston County	136	0.21
Columbia (city) Richland County	147	0.12
Charleston (city) Charleston County	132	0.11
North Charleston (city) Charleston County	48	0.05
Greenville (city) Greenville County	24	0.04
Rock Hill (city) York County	0	0.00

Norwegian

Top 10 Places Sorted by Population
Based on all places, regardless of total population

Place	Population	%
Columbia (city) Richland County	742	0.58
Charleston (city) Charleston County	734	0.63
Greenville (city) Greenville County	494	0.85
Mount Pleasant (town) Charleston County	448	0.70
Hilton Head Island (town) Beaufort County	339	0.92
North Charleston (city) Charleston County	321	0.34
Summerville (town) Dorchester County	266	0.66
Five Forks (cdp) Greenville County	248	1.89
Goose Creek (city) Berkeley County	236	0.68
Rock Hill (city) York County	199	0.32

Top 10 Places Sorted by Percent of Total Population
Based on all places, regardless of total population

Place	Population	%
Starr (town) Anderson County	14	7.22
Fair Play (cdp) Oconee County	29	6.35
Cowpens (town) Spartanburg County	61	3.56
Shell Point (cdp) Beaufort County	108	3.51
Pelzer (town) Anderson County	3	3.45
West Union (town) Oconee County	9	3.15
Laurel Bay (cdp) Beaufort County	173	3.09
Five Forks (cdp) Greenville County	248	1.89
Union (city) Union County	153	1.80
Port Royal (town) Beaufort County	161	1.54

Top 10 Places Sorted by Percent of Total Population
Based on places with total population of 50,000 or more

Place	Population	%
Greenville (city) Greenville County	494	0.85
Mount Pleasant (town) Charleston County	448	0.70
Charleston (city) Charleston County	734	0.63
Columbia (city) Richland County	742	0.58
North Charleston (city) Charleston County	321	0.34
Rock Hill (city) York County	199	0.32

Pennsylvania German

Top 10 Places Sorted by Population
Based on all places, regardless of total population

Place	Population	%
Berea (cdp) Greenville County	51	0.39
Liberty (city) Pickens County	50	1.54
Graniteville (cdp) Aiken County	44	1.55
St. Andrews (cdp) Richland County	44	0.21
North Charleston (city) Charleston County	41	0.04
Fort Mill (town) York County	40	0.39
Arcadia (cdp) Spartanburg County	29	1.92
Easley (city) Pickens County	28	0.14
Greer (city) Greenville County	26	0.11
Hilton Head Island (town) Beaufort County	25	0.07

Top 10 Places Sorted by Percent of Total Population
Based on all places, regardless of total population

Place	Population	%
Arcadia (cdp) Spartanburg County	29	1.92
Graniteville (cdp) Aiken County	44	1.55
Liberty (city) Pickens County	50	1.54
Springdale (cdp) Lancaster County	13	0.55
Berea (cdp) Greenville County	51	0.39
Fort Mill (town) York County	40	0.39
Clover (town) York County	18	0.37
Forestbrook (cdp) Horry County	15	0.35
Sullivan's Island (town) Charleston County	5	0.24
St. Andrews (cdp) Richland County	44	0.21

Top 10 Places Sorted by Percent of Total Population
Based on places with total population of 50,000 or more

Place	Population	%
North Charleston (city) Charleston County	41	0.04
Greenville (city) Greenville County	17	0.03
Charleston (city) Charleston County	19	0.02
Mount Pleasant (town) Charleston County	13	0.02
Rock Hill (city) York County	9	0.01
Columbia (city) Richland County	0	0.00

Polish

Top 10 Places Sorted by Population
Based on all places, regardless of total population

Place	Population	%
Charleston (city) Charleston County	2,127	1.83
Columbia (city) Richland County	1,762	1.38
Mount Pleasant (town) Charleston County	1,755	2.73
Hilton Head Island (town) Beaufort County	1,667	4.54
North Charleston (city) Charleston County	1,154	1.22
Summerville (town) Dorchester County	941	2.33
Greenville (city) Greenville County	862	1.49
Myrtle Beach (city) Horry County	778	2.91
Goose Creek (city) Berkeley County	681	1.96
Ladson (cdp) Berkeley County	547	3.86

Top 10 Places Sorted by Percent of Total Population
Based on all places, regardless of total population

Place	Population	%
Mount Croghan (town) Chesterfield County	16	8.74
Smyrna (town) York County	4	8.70
Warrenville (cdp) Aiken County	85	7.58
Converse (cdp) Spartanburg County	35	5.83
Murrells Inlet (cdp) Georgetown County	400	5.46
Folly Beach (city) Charleston County	133	5.27
Forestbrook (cdp) Horry County	209	4.94
Fort Mill (town) York County	485	4.72
Hilton Head Island (town) Beaufort County	1,667	4.54
Gilbert (town) Lexington County	22	4.52

Top 10 Places Sorted by Percent of Total Population
Based on places with total population of 50,000 or more

Place	Population	%
Mount Pleasant (town) Charleston County	1,755	2.73
Charleston (city) Charleston County	2,127	1.83
Greenville (city) Greenville County	862	1.49
Columbia (city) Richland County	1,762	1.38
North Charleston (city) Charleston County	1,154	1.22
Rock Hill (city) York County	525	0.83

Portuguese

Top 10 Places Sorted by Population
Based on all places, regardless of total population

Place	Population	%
Myrtle Beach (city) Horry County	357	1.34
North Charleston (city) Charleston County	242	0.26
Mount Pleasant (town) Charleston County	193	0.30
Summerville (town) Dorchester County	154	0.38
Hanahan (city) Berkeley County	138	0.81
Columbia (city) Richland County	113	0.09
Charleston (city) Charleston County	109	0.09
Hilton Head Island (town) Beaufort County	106	0.29
Conway (city) Horry County	84	0.51
Mauldin (city) Greenville County	81	0.37

Top 10 Places Sorted by Percent of Total Population
Based on all places, regardless of total population

Place	Population	%
Lincolnville (town) Charleston County	79	5.34
Myrtle Beach (city) Horry County	357	1.34
Pine Ridge (town) Lexington County	22	1.00
Golden Grove (cdp) Greenville County	28	0.92
Summerton (town) Clarendon County	9	0.87
India Hook (cdp) York County	29	0.85
Hanahan (city) Berkeley County	138	0.81
Hopkins (cdp) Richland County	23	0.75
Lakewood (cdp) Sumter County	19	0.70
Conway (city) Horry County	84	0.51

Top 10 Places Sorted by Percent of Total Population
Based on places with total population of 50,000 or more

Place	Population	%
Mount Pleasant (town) Charleston County	193	0.30
North Charleston (city) Charleston County	242	0.26
Columbia (city) Richland County	113	0.09
Charleston (city) Charleston County	109	0.09
Rock Hill (city) York County	54	0.09
Greenville (city) Greenville County	22	0.04

Romanian

Top 10 Places Sorted by Population
Based on all places, regardless of total population

Place	Population	%
Irmo (town) Richland County	167	1.51
Myrtle Beach (city) Horry County	116	0.43
Charleston (city) Charleston County	94	0.08
Mount Pleasant (town) Charleston County	85	0.13
Columbia (city) Richland County	82	0.06
Florence (city) Florence County	80	0.22
Greenville (city) Greenville County	79	0.14
Easley (city) Pickens County	72	0.37
Aiken (city) Aiken County	69	0.24
North Charleston (city) Charleston County	65	0.07

Top 10 Places Sorted by Percent of Total Population
Based on all places, regardless of total population

Place	Population	%
Cameron (town) Calhoun County	21	4.61
Holly Hill (town) Orangeburg County	18	1.63
Irmo (town) Richland County	167	1.51
Little Mountain (town) Newberry County	3	1.04
Kiawah Island (town) Charleston County	11	0.67
Cheraw (town) Chesterfield County	38	0.65
Centerville (cdp) Anderson County	41	0.64
Isle of Palms (city) Charleston County	27	0.64
Ravenel (town) Charleston County	11	0.50
Myrtle Beach (city) Horry County	116	0.43

Top 10 Places Sorted by Percent of Total Population
Based on places with total population of 50,000 or more

Place	Population	%
Greenville (city) Greenville County	79	0.14
Mount Pleasant (town) Charleston County	85	0.13
Charleston (city) Charleston County	94	0.08
North Charleston (city) Charleston County	65	0.07
Columbia (city) Richland County	82	0.06
Rock Hill (city) York County	0	0.00

Russian

Top 10 Places Sorted by Population
Based on all places, regardless of total population

Place	Population	%
Charleston (city) Charleston County	1,267	1.09
Mount Pleasant (town) Charleston County	704	1.10
Columbia (city) Richland County	602	0.47
Hilton Head Island (town) Beaufort County	557	1.52
North Charleston (city) Charleston County	248	0.26
Greenville (city) Greenville County	205	0.35
Summerville (town) Dorchester County	153	0.38
Red Hill (cdp) Horry County	145	1.05
Greer (city) Greenville County	129	0.54
Aiken (city) Aiken County	125	0.43

Top 10 Places Sorted by Percent of Total Population
Based on all places, regardless of total population

Place	Population	%
Modoc (cdp) McCormick County	16	4.76
Sullivan's Island (town) Charleston County	90	4.39
Langley (cdp) Aiken County	57	3.96
Pinopolis (cdp) Berkeley County	37	2.82
Inman Mills (cdp) Spartanburg County	35	2.40
Northlake (cdp) Anderson County	77	2.14
Saluda (town) Saluda County	63	1.83
Patrick (town) Chesterfield County	4	1.71
Tega Cay (city) York County	114	1.63
Seabrook Island (town) Charleston County	28	1.54

Top 10 Places Sorted by Percent of Total Population
Based on places with total population of 50,000 or more

Place	Population	%
Mount Pleasant (town) Charleston County	704	1.10
Charleston (city) Charleston County	1,267	1.09
Columbia (city) Richland County	602	0.47
Greenville (city) Greenville County	205	0.35
North Charleston (city) Charleston County	248	0.26
Rock Hill (city) York County	24	0.04

Scandinavian

Top 10 Places Sorted by Population
Based on all places, regardless of total population

Place	Population	%
Charleston (city) Charleston County	239	0.21
North Charleston (city) Charleston County	229	0.24
Mount Pleasant (town) Charleston County	219	0.34
Columbia (city) Richland County	102	0.08
Greenville (city) Greenville County	95	0.16
Lexington (town) Lexington County	89	0.54
Ladson (cdp) Berkeley County	69	0.49
Aiken (city) Aiken County	58	0.20
Sumter (city) Sumter County	54	0.13
Hilton Head Island (town) Beaufort County	52	0.14

Top 10 Places Sorted by Percent of Total Population
Based on all places, regardless of total population

Place	Population	%
Briarcliffe Acres (town) Horry County	7	1.74
Ware Shoals (town) Greenwood County	34	1.28
South Congaree (town) Lexington County	24	1.01
Lake Murray of Richland (cdp) Richland County	47	0.97
Central (town) Pickens County	36	0.74
Seabrook Island (town) Charleston County	13	0.72
St. Matthews (town) Calhoun County	13	0.63
Pacolet (town) Spartanburg County	11	0.55
Lexington (town) Lexington County	89	0.54
Ladson (cdp) Berkeley County	69	0.49

Top 10 Places Sorted by Percent of Total Population
Based on places with total population of 50,000 or more

Place	Population	%
Mount Pleasant (town) Charleston County	219	0.34
North Charleston (city) Charleston County	229	0.24
Charleston (city) Charleston County	239	0.21
Greenville (city) Greenville County	95	0.16
Columbia (city) Richland County	102	0.08
Rock Hill (city) York County	36	0.06

Scotch-Irish

Top 10 Places Sorted by Population
Based on all places, regardless of total population

Place	Population	%
Columbia (city) Richland County	4,743	3.72
Charleston (city) Charleston County	4,145	3.56
Rock Hill (city) York County	3,164	5.01
Mount Pleasant (town) Charleston County	2,909	4.53
Greenville (city) Greenville County	2,731	4.72
Florence (city) Florence County	2,209	6.13
Spartanburg (city) Spartanburg County	1,602	4.27
Summerville (town) Dorchester County	1,594	3.94
North Charleston (city) Charleston County	1,346	1.42
Anderson (city) Anderson County	1,231	4.63

Top 10 Places Sorted by Percent of Total Population
Based on all places, regardless of total population

Place	Population	%
Tatum (town) Marlboro County	27	42.19
Hodges (town) Greenwood County	36	22.22
Bradley (cdp) Greenwood County	33	21.02
Mount Croghan (town) Chesterfield County	37	20.22
Parksville (town) McCormick County	18	17.82
Pawleys Island (town) Georgetown County	17	17.00
Converse (cdp) Spartanburg County	99	16.50
Arcadia Lakes (town) Richland County	148	15.97
Riverview (cdp) York County	59	15.28
Pelzer (town) Anderson County	13	14.94

Top 10 Places Sorted by Percent of Total Population
Based on places with total population of 50,000 or more

Place	Population	%
Rock Hill (city) York County	3,164	5.01
Greenville (city) Greenville County	2,731	4.72
Mount Pleasant (town) Charleston County	2,909	4.53
Columbia (city) Richland County	4,743	3.72
Charleston (city) Charleston County	4,145	3.56
North Charleston (city) Charleston County	1,346	1.42

Scottish

Top 10 Places Sorted by Population
Based on all places, regardless of total population

Place	Population	%
Charleston (city) Charleston County	4,177	3.59
Columbia (city) Richland County	3,524	2.76
Mount Pleasant (town) Charleston County	3,089	4.81
Greenville (city) Greenville County	1,782	3.08
Rock Hill (city) York County	1,401	2.22
Goose Creek (city) Berkeley County	1,333	3.83
North Charleston (city) Charleston County	1,098	1.16
Spartanburg (city) Spartanburg County	1,087	2.90
Summerville (town) Dorchester County	1,027	2.54
Hilton Head Island (town) Beaufort County	888	2.42

Top 10 Places Sorted by Percent of Total Population
Based on all places, regardless of total population

Place	Population	%
Oswego (cdp) Sumter County	9	20.00
McClellanville (town) Charleston County	61	18.05
Pawleys Island (town) Georgetown County	11	11.00
Catawba (cdp) York County	171	9.95
Glendale (cdp) Spartanburg County	32	9.30
Fairforest (cdp) Spartanburg County	175	9.28
Seabrook Island (town) Charleston County	159	8.76
Cameron (town) Calhoun County	38	8.33
Troy (town) Greenwood County	7	8.33
Tatum (town) Marlboro County	5	7.81

Serbian

Top 10 Places Sorted by Population
Based on all places, regardless of total population

Place	Population	%
Dalzell (cdp) Sumter County	187	5.80
Columbia (city) Richland County	83	0.07
Mount Pleasant (town) Charleston County	55	0.07
Greenville (city) Greenville County	42	0.07
Seven Oaks (cdp) Lexington County	41	0.25
Ladson (cdp) Berkeley County	38	0.27
Greer (city) Greenville County	27	0.11
Florence (city) Florence County	27	0.07
Charleston (city) Charleston County	26	0.02
Aiken (city) Aiken County	20	0.07

Top 10 Places Sorted by Percent of Total Population
Based on all places, regardless of total population

Place	Population	%
Dalzell (cdp) Sumter County	187	5.80
Ridgeville (town) Dorchester County	8	0.46
Pacolet (town) Spartanburg County	8	0.40
Ladson (cdp) Berkeley County	38	0.27
Seven Oaks (cdp) Lexington County	41	0.25
Seabrook Island (town) Charleston County	3	0.17
Burton (cdp) Beaufort County	10	0.14
Greer (city) Greenville County	27	0.11
North Myrtle Beach (city) Horry County	13	0.10
Surfside Beach (town) Horry County	4	0.10

Top 10 Places Sorted by Percent of Total Population
Based on places with total population of 50,000 or more

Place	Population	%
Mount Pleasant (town) Charleston County	55	0.09
Columbia (city) Richland County	83	0.07
Greenville (city) Greenville County	42	0.07
Charleston (city) Charleston County	26	0.02
North Charleston (city) Charleston County	0	0.00
Rock Hill (city) York County	0	0.00

Slavic

Top 10 Places Sorted by Population
Based on all places, regardless of total population

Place	Population	%
Columbia (city) Richland County	119	0.09
Summerville (town) Dorchester County	116	0.29
Conway (city) Horry County	91	0.55
Goose Creek (city) Berkeley County	91	0.26
Greenville (city) Greenville County	41	0.07
Saluda (town) Saluda County	35	1.01
Port Royal (town) Beaufort County	32	0.31
Mount Pleasant (town) Charleston County	31	0.05
Charleston (city) Charleston County	30	0.03
Greer (city) Greenville County	28	0.12

Top 10 Places Sorted by Percent of Total Population
Based on all places, regardless of total population

Place	Population	%
Saluda (town) Saluda County	35	1.01
McClellanville (town) Charleston County	2	0.59
Conway (city) Horry County	91	0.55
Santee (town) Orangeburg County	4	0.44
Laurel Bay (cdp) Beaufort County	23	0.41
Port Royal (town) Beaufort County	32	0.31
Jefferson (town) Chesterfield County	3	0.30
Summerville (town) Dorchester County	116	0.29
Goose Creek (city) Berkeley County	91	0.26
Central (town) Pickens County	10	0.21

Top 10 Places Sorted by Percent of Total Population
Based on places with total population of 50,000 or more

Place	Population	%
Columbia (city) Richland County	119	0.09
Greenville (city) Greenville County	41	0.07
Mount Pleasant (town) Charleston County	31	0.05
Charleston (city) Charleston County	30	0.03
Rock Hill (city) York County	12	0.02
North Charleston (city) Charleston County	11	0.01

Slovak

Top 10 Places Sorted by Population
Based on all places, regardless of total population

Place	Population	%
Charleston (city) Charleston County	193	0.17
Hilton Head Island (town) Beaufort County	168	0.46
Mount Pleasant (town) Charleston County	146	0.23
Five Forks (cdp) Greenville County	99	0.75
Mauldin (city) Greenville County	99	0.46
Wade Hampton (cdp) Greenville County	90	0.44
North Myrtle Beach (city) Horry County	85	0.63
Columbia (city) Richland County	79	0.06
Newport (cdp) York County	73	1.86
Taylors (cdp) Greenville County	64	0.30

Top 10 Places Sorted by Percent of Total Population
Based on all places, regardless of total population

Place	Population	%
Perry (town) Aiken County	4	2.90
Newport (cdp) York County	73	1.86
Patrick (town) Chesterfield County	3	1.28
Pinopolis (cdp) Berkeley County	11	0.84
Five Forks (cdp) Greenville County	99	0.75
North Myrtle Beach (city) Horry County	85	0.63
York (city) York County	46	0.60
Awendaw (town) Charleston County	7	0.56
Sangaree (cdp) Berkeley County	49	0.54
Surfside Beach (town) Horry County	19	0.48

Top 10 Places Sorted by Percent of Total Population
Based on places with total population of 50,000 or more

Place	Population	%
Mount Pleasant (town) Charleston County	146	0.23
Charleston (city) Charleston County	193	0.17
Rock Hill (city) York County	46	0.07
Columbia (city) Richland County	79	0.06
North Charleston (city) Charleston County	46	0.05
Greenville (city) Greenville County	19	0.03

Slovene

Top 10 Places Sorted by Population
Based on all places, regardless of total population

Place	Population	%
Mauldin (city) Greenville County	90	0.42
Columbia (city) Richland County	64	0.05
Summerville (town) Dorchester County	49	0.12
Charleston (city) Charleston County	35	0.03
Hilton Head Island (town) Beaufort County	32	0.09
Mount Pleasant (town) Charleston County	22	0.03
Central (town) Pickens County	19	0.39
Myrtle Beach (city) Horry County	19	0.07
North Charleston (city) Charleston County	17	0.02
Simpsonville (city) Greenville County	15	0.09

Top 10 Places Sorted by Percent of Total Population
Based on all places, regardless of total population

Place	Population	%
Utica (cdp) Oconee County	14	0.85
Mauldin (city) Greenville County	90	0.42
Central (town) Pickens County	19	0.39
Piedmont (cdp) Anderson County	9	0.18
Little River (cdp) Horry County	13	0.15
Fort Mill (town) York County	14	0.14
Summerville (town) Dorchester County	49	0.12
Hilton Head Island (town) Beaufort County	32	0.09
Simpsonville (city) Greenville County	15	0.09
Red Hill (cdp) Horry County	11	0.08

Top 10 Places Sorted by Percent of Total Population
Based on places with total population of 50,000 or more

Place	Population	%
Columbia (city) Richland County	64	0.05
Charleston (city) Charleston County	35	0.03
Mount Pleasant (town) Charleston County	22	0.03
North Charleston (city) Charleston County	17	0.02
Greenville (city) Greenville County	7	0.01
Rock Hill (city) York County	0	0.00

Soviet Union

Top 10 Places Sorted by Population
Based on all places, regardless of total population

Place	Population	%
Mount Pleasant (town) Charleston County	14	0.02
Socastee (cdp) Horry County	12	0.07
Abbeville (city) Abbeville County	0	0.00
Aiken (city) Aiken County	0	0.00
Alcolu (cdp) Clarendon County	0	0.00
Allendale (town) Allendale County	0	0.00
Anderson (city) Anderson County	0	0.00
Andrews (town) Georgetown County	0	0.00
Antreville (cdp) Abbeville County	0	0.00
Arcadia (cdp) Spartanburg County	0	0.00

Top 10 Places Sorted by Percent of Total Population
Based on all places, regardless of total population

Place	Population	%
Socastee (cdp) Horry County	12	0.07
Mount Pleasant (town) Charleston County	14	0.02
Abbeville (city) Abbeville County	0	0.00
Aiken (city) Aiken County	0	0.00
Alcolu (cdp) Clarendon County	0	0.00
Allendale (town) Allendale County	0	0.00
Anderson (city) Anderson County	0	0.00
Andrews (town) Georgetown County	0	0.00
Antreville (cdp) Abbeville County	0	0.00
Arcadia (cdp) Spartanburg County	0	0.00

Top 10 Places Sorted by Percent of Total Population
Based on places with total population of 50,000 or more

Place	Population	%
Mount Pleasant (town) Charleston County	14	0.02
Charleston (city) Charleston County	0	0.00
Columbia (city) Richland County	0	0.00
Greenville (city) Greenville County	0	0.00
North Charleston (city) Charleston County	0	0.00
Rock Hill (city) York County	0	0.00

Swedish

Top 10 Places Sorted by Population
Based on all places, regardless of total population

Place	Population	%
Charleston (city) Charleston County	993	0.85
Mount Pleasant (town) Charleston County	951	1.48
Hilton Head Island (town) Beaufort County	655	1.78
Columbia (city) Richland County	504	0.39
Greenville (city) Greenville County	449	0.78
Summerville (town) Dorchester County	384	0.95
North Charleston (city) Charleston County	328	0.35
Goose Creek (city) Berkeley County	288	0.83
Spartanburg (city) Spartanburg County	260	0.69
Taylors (cdp) Greenville County	225	1.04

Top 10 Places Sorted by Percent of Total Population
Based on all places, regardless of total population

Place	Population	%
Cordova (town) Orangeburg County	7	5.38
Scotia (town) Hampton County	7	3.37
Mulberry (cdp) Sumter County	11	3.33
Cross Hill (town) Laurens County	11	3.06
Oakland (cdp) Sumter County	39	2.87
Pelion (town) Lexington County	22	2.87
Richburg (town) Chester County	10	2.78
Tega Cay (city) York County	175	2.50
Livingston (town) Orangeburg County	3	2.48
Stateburg (cdp) Sumter County	32	2.15

Top 10 Places Sorted by Percent of Total Population
Based on places with total population of 50,000 or more

Place	Population	%
Mount Pleasant (town) Charleston County	951	1.48
Charleston (city) Charleston County	993	0.85
Greenville (city) Greenville County	449	0.78
Columbia (city) Richland County	504	0.39
North Charleston (city) Charleston County	328	0.35
Rock Hill (city) York County	222	0.35

Swiss

Top 10 Places Sorted by Population
Based on all places, regardless of total population

Place	Population	%
Columbia (city) Richland County	308	0.24
Charleston (city) Charleston County	297	0.26
Greenville (city) Greenville County	262	0.45
Mount Pleasant (town) Charleston County	254	0.40
Hilton Head Island (town) Beaufort County	137	0.37
Anderson (city) Anderson County	126	0.47
Spartanburg (city) Spartanburg County	125	0.33
Tega Cay (city) York County	122	1.74
Aiken (city) Aiken County	107	0.37
Oak Grove (cdp) Lexington County	94	0.90

Top 10 Places Sorted by Percent of Total Population
Based on all places, regardless of total population

Place	Population	%
Plum Branch (town) McCormick County	6	10.91
Reevesville (town) Dorchester County	10	4.78
Elloree (town) Orangeburg County	17	2.66
Meggett (town) Charleston County	26	2.34
Cordova (town) Orangeburg County	3	2.31
Vance (town) Orangeburg County	5	2.25
McClellanville (town) Charleston County	7	2.07
Ravenel (town) Charleston County	41	1.87
Tega Cay (city) York County	122	1.74
Perry (town) Aiken County	2	1.45

Top 10 Places Sorted by Percent of Total Population
Based on places with total population of 50,000 or more

Place	Population	%
Greenville (city) Greenville County	262	0.45
Mount Pleasant (town) Charleston County	254	0.40
Charleston (city) Charleston County	297	0.26
Columbia (city) Richland County	308	0.24
Rock Hill (city) York County	93	0.15
North Charleston (city) Charleston County	57	0.06

Turkish

Top 10 Places Sorted by Population
Based on all places, regardless of total population

Place	Population	%
Greenville (city) Greenville County	125	0.22
North Charleston (city) Charleston County	101	0.11
Clemson (city) Pickens County	91	0.67
Five Forks (cdp) Greenville County	63	0.48
Wedgefield (cdp) Sumter County	61	4.39
Hilton Head Island (town) Beaufort County	60	0.16
Wade Hampton (cdp) Greenville County	57	0.28
Taylors (cdp) Greenville County	43	0.20
Sumter (city) Sumter County	41	0.10
Bennettsville (city) Marlboro County	39	0.42

Top 10 Places Sorted by Percent of Total Population
Based on all places, regardless of total population

Place	Population	%
Wedgefield (cdp) Sumter County	61	4.39
Neeses (town) Orangeburg County	5	1.89
Lincolnville (town) Charleston County	24	1.62
Westminster (city) Oconee County	28	1.18
Donalds (town) Abbeville County	3	0.84
Clemson (city) Pickens County	91	0.67
Five Forks (cdp) Greenville County	63	0.48
Bennettsville (city) Marlboro County	39	0.42
Gaston (town) Lexington County	5	0.41
Wade Hampton (cdp) Greenville County	57	0.28

Please refer to the Explanation of Data in the front of the book for more detailed information.

Column 1

Top 10 Places Sorted by Percent of Total Population
Based on places with total population of 50,000 or more

Place	Population	%
Greenville (city) Greenville County	125	0.22
North Charleston (city) Charleston County	101	0.11
Charleston (city) Charleston County	39	0.03
Columbia (city) Richland County	34	0.03
Mount Pleasant (town) Charleston County	14	0.02
Rock Hill (city) York County	0	0.00

Ukrainian

Top 10 Places Sorted by Population
Based on all places, regardless of total population

Place	Population	%
Boiling Springs (cdp) Spartanburg County	510	6.18
Charleston (city) Charleston County	408	0.35
Mount Pleasant (town) Charleston County	240	0.37
North Charleston (city) Charleston County	228	0.24
Spartanburg (city) Spartanburg County	157	0.42
Garden City (cdp) Horry County	145	1.64
Columbia (city) Richland County	142	0.11
Forest Acres (city) Richland County	121	1.16
Summerville (town) Dorchester County	114	0.28
Hilton Head Island (town) Beaufort County	112	0.31

Top 10 Places Sorted by Percent of Total Population
Based on all places, regardless of total population

Place	Population	%
Clifton (cdp) Spartanburg County	101	13.91
Boiling Springs (cdp) Spartanburg County	510	6.18
Garden City (cdp) Horry County	145	1.64
Duncan (town) Spartanburg County	47	1.52
Central (town) Pickens County	67	1.38
Forest Acres (city) Richland County	121	1.16
Pickens (city) Pickens County	36	1.15
Valley Falls (cdp) Spartanburg County	60	1.09
Seabrook Island (town) Charleston County	16	0.88
Bluffton (town) Beaufort County	86	0.80

Top 10 Places Sorted by Percent of Total Population
Based on places with total population of 50,000 or more

Place	Population	%
Mount Pleasant (town) Charleston County	240	0.37
Charleston (city) Charleston County	408	0.35
North Charleston (city) Charleston County	228	0.24
Greenville (city) Greenville County	89	0.15
Rock Hill (city) York County	81	0.13
Columbia (city) Richland County	142	0.11

Welsh

Top 10 Places Sorted by Population
Based on all places, regardless of total population

Place	Population	%
Charleston (city) Charleston County	909	0.78
Columbia (city) Richland County	697	0.55
Mount Pleasant (town) Charleston County	560	0.87
Greenville (city) Greenville County	417	0.72
Rock Hill (city) York County	376	0.60
Myrtle Beach (city) Horry County	350	1.31
Hilton Head Island (town) Beaufort County	335	0.91
Goose Creek (city) Berkeley County	330	0.95
North Charleston (city) Charleston County	325	0.34
Summerville (town) Dorchester County	322	0.80

Top 10 Places Sorted by Percent of Total Population
Based on all places, regardless of total population

Place	Population	%
Tatum (town) Marlboro County	5	7.81
Cameron (town) Calhoun County	35	7.68
Blacksburg (town) Cherokee County	78	3.89
Aynor (town) Horry County	29	3.65
Briarcliffe Acres (town) Horry County	13	3.23
Donalds (town) Abbeville County	11	3.09
Arcadia Lakes (town) Richland County	28	3.02
Gray Court (town) Laurens County	22	3.01
Springfield (town) Orangeburg County	14	2.83
Smoaks (town) Colleton County	3	2.65

Column 2

Top 10 Places Sorted by Percent of Total Population
Based on places with total population of 50,000 or more

Place	Population	%
Mount Pleasant (town) Charleston County	560	0.87
Charleston (city) Charleston County	909	0.78
Greenville (city) Greenville County	417	0.72
Rock Hill (city) York County	376	0.60
Columbia (city) Richland County	697	0.55
North Charleston (city) Charleston County	325	0.34

West Indian, excluding Hispanic

Top 10 Places Sorted by Population
Based on all places, regardless of total population

Place	Population	%
Columbia (city) Richland County	643	0.50
North Charleston (city) Charleston County	504	0.53
Seven Oaks (cdp) Lexington County	340	2.08
Anderson (city) Anderson County	280	1.05
Sangaree (cdp) Berkeley County	221	2.45
Charleston (city) Charleston County	199	0.17
Sumter (city) Sumter County	187	0.46
St. Andrews (cdp) Richland County	183	0.88
Greenville (city) Greenville County	182	0.31
Orangeburg (city) Orangeburg County	154	1.11

Top 10 Places Sorted by Percent of Total Population
Based on all places, regardless of total population

Place	Population	%
Quinby (town) Florence County	59	5.08
Wallace (cdp) Marlboro County	36	4.10
Heath Springs (town) Lancaster County	22	2.99
Cope (town) Orangeburg County	4	2.74
Sangaree (cdp) Berkeley County	221	2.45
Seven Oaks (cdp) Lexington County	340	2.08
Walhalla (city) Oconee County	68	1.62
Marion (city) Marion County	97	1.39
Wilkinson Heights (cdp) Orangeburg County	31	1.36
Port Royal (town) Beaufort County	138	1.32

Top 10 Places Sorted by Percent of Total Population
Based on places with total population of 50,000 or more

Place	Population	%
North Charleston (city) Charleston County	504	0.53
Columbia (city) Richland County	643	0.50
Greenville (city) Greenville County	182	0.31
Charleston (city) Charleston County	199	0.17
Rock Hill (city) York County	82	0.13
Mount Pleasant (town) Charleston County	0	0.00

West Indian: Bahamian, excluding Hispanic

Top 10 Places Sorted by Population
Based on all places, regardless of total population

Place	Population	%
Columbia (city) Richland County	97	0.08
Anderson (city) Anderson County	59	0.22
Seven Oaks (cdp) Lexington County	47	0.29
Beaufort (city) Beaufort County	46	0.37
St. Andrews (cdp) Richland County	24	0.12
Orangeburg (city) Orangeburg County	15	0.11
Florence (city) Florence County	15	0.04
Charleston (city) Charleston County	15	0.01
Denmark (city) Bamberg County	13	0.36
Clio (town) Marlboro County	6	0.70

Top 10 Places Sorted by Percent of Total Population
Based on all places, regardless of total population

Place	Population	%
Clio (town) Marlboro County	6	0.70
Beaufort (city) Beaufort County	46	0.37
Denmark (city) Bamberg County	13	0.36
Seven Oaks (cdp) Lexington County	47	0.29
Anderson (city) Anderson County	59	0.22
St. Andrews (cdp) Richland County	24	0.12
Orangeburg (city) Orangeburg County	15	0.11
Columbia (city) Richland County	97	0.08
Florence (city) Florence County	15	0.04
Charleston (city) Charleston County	15	0.01

Column 3

Top 10 Places Sorted by Percent of Total Population
Based on places with total population of 50,000 or more

Place	Population	%
Columbia (city) Richland County	97	0.08
Charleston (city) Charleston County	15	0.01
Greenville (city) Greenville County	2	<0.01
Mount Pleasant (town) Charleston County	0	0.00
North Charleston (city) Charleston County	0	0.00
Rock Hill (city) York County	0	0.00

West Indian: Barbadian, excluding Hispanic

Top 10 Places Sorted by Population
Based on all places, regardless of total population

Place	Population	%
Spartanburg (city) Spartanburg County	58	0.15
Wallace (cdp) Marlboro County	36	4.10
Port Royal (town) Beaufort County	33	0.32
North Augusta (city) Aiken County	26	0.13
Bennettsville (city) Marlboro County	14	0.15
Hollywood (town) Charleston County	13	0.28
Hilton Head Island (town) Beaufort County	10	0.03
Abbeville (city) Abbeville County	0	0.00
Aiken (city) Aiken County	0	0.00
Alcolu (cdp) Clarendon County	0	0.00

Top 10 Places Sorted by Percent of Total Population
Based on all places, regardless of total population

Place	Population	%
Wallace (cdp) Marlboro County	36	4.10
Port Royal (town) Beaufort County	33	0.32
Hollywood (town) Charleston County	13	0.28
Spartanburg (city) Spartanburg County	58	0.15
Bennettsville (city) Marlboro County	14	0.15
North Augusta (city) Aiken County	26	0.13
Hilton Head Island (town) Beaufort County	10	0.03
Abbeville (city) Abbeville County	0	0.00
Aiken (city) Aiken County	0	0.00
Alcolu (cdp) Clarendon County	0	0.00

Top 10 Places Sorted by Percent of Total Population
Based on places with total population of 50,000 or more

Place	Population	%
Charleston (city) Charleston County	0	0.00
Columbia (city) Richland County	0	0.00
Greenville (city) Greenville County	0	0.00
Mount Pleasant (town) Charleston County	0	0.00
North Charleston (city) Charleston County	0	0.00
Rock Hill (city) York County	0	0.00

West Indian: Belizean, excluding Hispanic

Top 10 Places Sorted by Population
Based on all places, regardless of total population

Place	Population	%
Summerville (town) Dorchester County	34	0.08
North Augusta (city) Aiken County	30	0.15
West Columbia (city) Lexington County	26	0.18
Beaufort (city) Beaufort County	10	0.08
Goose Creek (city) Berkeley County	10	0.03
Columbia (city) Richland County	10	0.01
Abbeville (city) Abbeville County	0	0.00
Aiken (city) Aiken County	0	0.00
Alcolu (cdp) Clarendon County	0	0.00
Allendale (town) Allendale County	0	0.00

Top 10 Places Sorted by Percent of Total Population
Based on all places, regardless of total population

Place	Population	%
West Columbia (city) Lexington County	26	0.18
North Augusta (city) Aiken County	30	0.15
Summerville (town) Dorchester County	34	0.08
Beaufort (city) Beaufort County	10	0.08
Goose Creek (city) Berkeley County	10	0.03
Columbia (city) Richland County	10	0.01
Abbeville (city) Abbeville County	0	0.00
Aiken (city) Aiken County	0	0.00
Alcolu (cdp) Clarendon County	0	0.00
Allendale (town) Allendale County	0	0.00

Please refer to the Explanation of Data in the front of the book for more detailed information.

Top 10 Places Sorted by Percent of Total Population
Based on places with total population of 50,000 or more

Place	Population	%
Columbia (city) Richland County	10	0.01
Charleston (city) Charleston County	0	0.00
Greenville (city) Greenville County	0	0.00
Mount Pleasant (town) Charleston County	0	0.00
North Charleston (city) Charleston County	0	0.00
Rock Hill (city) York County	0	0.00

West Indian: Bermudan, excluding Hispanic

Top 10 Places Sorted by Population
Based on all places, regardless of total population

Place	Population	%
Socastee (cdp) Horry County	57	0.33
Chester (city) Chester County	26	0.45
Cayce (city) Lexington County	20	0.16
Hilton Head Island (town) Beaufort County	16	0.04
Abbeville (city) Abbeville County	0	0.00
Aiken (city) Aiken County	0	0.00
Alcolu (cdp) Clarendon County	0	0.00
Allendale (town) Allendale County	0	0.00
Anderson (city) Anderson County	0	0.00
Andrews (town) Georgetown County	0	0.00

Top 10 Places Sorted by Percent of Total Population
Based on all places, regardless of total population

Place	Population	%
Chester (city) Chester County	26	0.45
Socastee (cdp) Horry County	57	0.33
Cayce (city) Lexington County	20	0.16
Hilton Head Island (town) Beaufort County	16	0.04
Abbeville (city) Abbeville County	0	0.00
Aiken (city) Aiken County	0	0.00
Alcolu (cdp) Clarendon County	0	0.00
Allendale (town) Allendale County	0	0.00
Anderson (city) Anderson County	0	0.00
Andrews (town) Georgetown County	0	0.00

Top 10 Places Sorted by Percent of Total Population
Based on places with total population of 50,000 or more

Place	Population	%
Charleston (city) Charleston County	0	0.00
Columbia (city) Richland County	0	0.00
Greenville (city) Greenville County	0	0.00
Mount Pleasant (town) Charleston County	0	0.00
North Charleston (city) Charleston County	0	0.00
Rock Hill (city) York County	0	0.00

West Indian: British West Indian, excluding Hispanic

Top 10 Places Sorted by Population
Based on all places, regardless of total population

Place	Population	%
Laurens (city) Laurens County	59	0.64
North Charleston (city) Charleston County	37	0.04
Golden Grove (cdp) Greenville County	21	0.69
Anderson (city) Anderson County	14	0.05
Ridgeland (town) Jasper County	9	0.22
Abbeville (city) Abbeville County	0	0.00
Aiken (city) Aiken County	0	0.00
Alcolu (cdp) Clarendon County	0	0.00
Allendale (town) Allendale County	0	0.00
Andrews (town) Georgetown County	0	0.00

Top 10 Places Sorted by Percent of Total Population
Based on all places, regardless of total population

Place	Population	%
Golden Grove (cdp) Greenville County	21	0.69
Laurens (city) Laurens County	59	0.64
Ridgeland (town) Jasper County	9	0.22
Anderson (city) Anderson County	14	0.05
North Charleston (city) Charleston County	37	0.04
Abbeville (city) Abbeville County	0	0.00
Aiken (city) Aiken County	0	0.00
Alcolu (cdp) Clarendon County	0	0.00
Allendale (town) Allendale County	0	0.00

	Population	%
Andrews (town) Georgetown County	0	0.00

Top 10 Places Sorted by Percent of Total Population
Based on places with total population of 50,000 or more

Place	Population	%
North Charleston (city) Charleston County	37	0.04
Charleston (city) Charleston County	0	0.00
Columbia (city) Richland County	0	0.00
Greenville (city) Greenville County	0	0.00
Mount Pleasant (town) Charleston County	0	0.00
Rock Hill (city) York County	0	0.00

West Indian: Dutch West Indian, excluding Hispanic

Top 10 Places Sorted by Population
Based on all places, regardless of total population

Place	Population	%
North Charleston (city) Charleston County	46	0.05
Laurel Bay (cdp) Beaufort County	20	0.36
Parker (cdp) Greenville County	19	0.18
Florence (city) Florence County	14	0.04
Taylors (cdp) Greenville County	13	0.06
Southern Shops (cdp) Spartanburg County	10	0.22
Dunean (cdp) Greenville County	6	0.17
West Union (town) Oconee County	3	1.05
Abbeville (city) Abbeville County	0	0.00
Aiken (city) Aiken County	0	0.00

Top 10 Places Sorted by Percent of Total Population
Based on all places, regardless of total population

Place	Population	%
West Union (town) Oconee County	3	1.05
Laurel Bay (cdp) Beaufort County	20	0.36
Southern Shops (cdp) Spartanburg County	10	0.22
Parker (cdp) Greenville County	19	0.18
Dunean (cdp) Greenville County	6	0.17
Taylors (cdp) Greenville County	13	0.06
North Charleston (city) Charleston County	46	0.05
Florence (city) Florence County	14	0.04
Abbeville (city) Abbeville County	0	0.00
Aiken (city) Aiken County	0	0.00

Top 10 Places Sorted by Percent of Total Population
Based on places with total population of 50,000 or more

Place	Population	%
North Charleston (city) Charleston County	46	0.05
Charleston (city) Charleston County	0	0.00
Columbia (city) Richland County	0	0.00
Greenville (city) Greenville County	0	0.00
Mount Pleasant (town) Charleston County	0	0.00
Rock Hill (city) York County	0	0.00

West Indian: Haitian, excluding Hispanic

Top 10 Places Sorted by Population
Based on all places, regardless of total population

Place	Population	%
Anderson (city) Anderson County	207	0.78
Dentsville (cdp) Richland County	73	0.54
Walhalla (city) Oconee County	68	1.62
Port Royal (town) Beaufort County	57	0.55
Columbia (city) Richland County	53	0.04
St. Andrews (cdp) Richland County	41	0.20
Marion (city) Marion County	33	0.47
Taylors (cdp) Greenville County	33	0.15
Goose Creek (city) Berkeley County	27	0.08
North Charleston (city) Charleston County	27	0.03

Top 10 Places Sorted by Percent of Total Population
Based on all places, regardless of total population

Place	Population	%
Walhalla (city) Oconee County	68	1.62
Heath Springs (town) Lancaster County	11	1.49
Quinby (town) Florence County	14	1.21
Anderson (city) Anderson County	207	0.78
Neeses (town) Orangeburg County	2	0.76
Port Royal (town) Beaufort County	57	0.55
Dentsville (cdp) Richland County	73	0.54
Marion (city) Marion County	33	0.47

Place	Population	%
Denmark (city) Bamberg County	14	0.39
Holly Hill (town) Orangeburg County	4	0.36

Top 10 Places Sorted by Percent of Total Population
Based on places with total population of 50,000 or more

Place	Population	%
Columbia (city) Richland County	53	0.04
Greenville (city) Greenville County	24	0.04
North Charleston (city) Charleston County	27	0.03
Charleston (city) Charleston County	0	0.00
Mount Pleasant (town) Charleston County	0	0.00
Rock Hill (city) York County	0	0.00

West Indian: Jamaican, excluding Hispanic

Top 10 Places Sorted by Population
Based on all places, regardless of total population

Place	Population	%
Columbia (city) Richland County	227	0.18
Sangaree (cdp) Berkeley County	221	2.45
Seven Oaks (cdp) Lexington County	155	0.95
Sumter (city) Sumter County	149	0.37
North Charleston (city) Charleston County	136	0.14
Charleston (city) Charleston County	132	0.11
Myrtle Beach (city) Horry County	105	0.39
Greenville (city) Greenville County	93	0.16
Marion (city) Marion County	64	0.92
Orangeburg (city) Orangeburg County	57	0.41

Top 10 Places Sorted by Percent of Total Population
Based on all places, regardless of total population

Place	Population	%
Quinby (town) Florence County	45	3.88
Cope (town) Orangeburg County	4	2.74
Sangaree (cdp) Berkeley County	221	2.45
Heath Springs (town) Lancaster County	11	1.49
Wilkinson Heights (cdp) Orangeburg County	31	1.36
Varnville (town) Hampton County	20	1.09
Seven Oaks (cdp) Lexington County	155	0.95
Marion (city) Marion County	64	0.92
Timmonsville (town) Florence County	20	0.76
Woodfield (cdp) Richland County	56	0.56

Top 10 Places Sorted by Percent of Total Population
Based on places with total population of 50,000 or more

Place	Population	%
Columbia (city) Richland County	227	0.18
Greenville (city) Greenville County	93	0.16
North Charleston (city) Charleston County	136	0.14
Charleston (city) Charleston County	132	0.11
Rock Hill (city) York County	52	0.08
Mount Pleasant (town) Charleston County	0	0.00

West Indian: Trinidadian and Tobagonian, excluding Hispanic

Top 10 Places Sorted by Population
Based on all places, regardless of total population

Place	Population	%
North Charleston (city) Charleston County	111	0.12
Columbia (city) Richland County	98	0.08
Bluffton (town) Beaufort County	79	0.74
Mauldin (city) Greenville County	66	0.30
Summerville (town) Dorchester County	52	0.13
Red Bank (cdp) Lexington County	42	0.42
Orangeburg (city) Orangeburg County	42	0.30
Bamberg (town) Bamberg County	32	0.88
Woodfield (cdp) Richland County	27	0.27
North Myrtle Beach (city) Horry County	25	0.19

Top 10 Places Sorted by Percent of Total Population
Based on all places, regardless of total population

Place	Population	%
Bamberg (town) Bamberg County	32	0.88
Bluffton (town) Beaufort County	79	0.74
Red Bank (cdp) Lexington County	42	0.42
Mauldin (city) Greenville County	66	0.30
Orangeburg (city) Orangeburg County	42	0.30
Woodfield (cdp) Richland County	27	0.27

North Myrtle Beach (city) Horry County — 25 — 0.19
Summerville (town) Dorchester County — 52 — 0.13
North Charleston (city) Charleston County — 111 — 0.12
Bennettsville (city) Marlboro County — 10 — 0.11

Top 10 Places Sorted by Percent of Total Population
Based on places with total population of 50,000 or more

Place	Population	%
North Charleston (city) Charleston County	111	0.12
Columbia (city) Richland County	98	0.08
Greenville (city) Greenville County	18	0.03
Charleston (city) Charleston County	14	0.01
Mount Pleasant (town) Charleston County	0	0.00
Rock Hill (city) York County	0	0.00

West Indian: U.S. Virgin Islander, excluding Hispanic

Top 10 Places Sorted by Population
Based on all places, regardless of total population

Place	Population	%
Port Royal (town) Beaufort County	10	0.10
Columbia (city) Richland County	9	0.01
Jackson (town) Aiken County	3	0.19
Abbeville (city) Abbeville County	0	0.00
Aiken (city) Aiken County	0	0.00
Alcolu (cdp) Clarendon County	0	0.00
Allendale (town) Allendale County	0	0.00
Anderson (city) Anderson County	0	0.00
Andrews (town) Georgetown County	0	0.00
Antreville (cdp) Abbeville County	0	0.00

Top 10 Places Sorted by Percent of Total Population
Based on all places, regardless of total population

Place	Population	%
Jackson (town) Aiken County	3	0.19
Port Royal (town) Beaufort County	10	0.10
Columbia (city) Richland County	9	0.01
Abbeville (city) Abbeville County	0	0.00
Aiken (city) Aiken County	0	0.00
Alcolu (cdp) Clarendon County	0	0.00
Allendale (town) Allendale County	0	0.00
Anderson (city) Anderson County	0	0.00
Andrews (town) Georgetown County	0	0.00
Antreville (cdp) Abbeville County	0	0.00

Top 10 Places Sorted by Percent of Total Population
Based on places with total population of 50,000 or more

Place	Population	%
Columbia (city) Richland County	9	0.01
Charleston (city) Charleston County	0	0.00
Greenville (city) Greenville County	0	0.00
Mount Pleasant (town) Charleston County	0	0.00
North Charleston (city) Charleston County	0	0.00
Rock Hill (city) York County	0	0.00

West Indian: West Indian, excluding Hispanic

Top 10 Places Sorted by Population
Based on all places, regardless of total population

Place	Population	%
North Charleston (city) Charleston County	147	0.16
Seven Oaks (cdp) Lexington County	138	0.84
Columbia (city) Richland County	134	0.11
St. Andrews (cdp) Richland County	118	0.57
Orangeburg (city) Orangeburg County	40	0.29
Charleston (city) Charleston County	38	0.03
Gaffney (city) Cherokee County	36	0.29
Gantt (cdp) Greenville County	36	0.26
Greenville (city) Greenville County	35	0.06
North Augusta (city) Aiken County	32	0.16

Top 10 Places Sorted by Percent of Total Population
Based on all places, regardless of total population

Place	Population	%
Mayesville (town) Sumter County	8	1.30
Elloree (town) Orangeburg County	8	1.25
Seven Oaks (cdp) Lexington County	138	0.84
Cottageville (town) Colleton County	7	0.70

Cherryvale (cdp) Sumter County — 19 — 0.62
St. Andrews (cdp) Richland County — 118 — 0.57
Ridgeland (town) Jasper County — 20 — 0.48
Mullins (city) Marion County — 18 — 0.38
Pickens (city) Pickens County — 12 — 0.38
Eutawville (town) Orangeburg County — 2 — 0.37

Top 10 Places Sorted by Percent of Total Population
Based on places with total population of 50,000 or more

Place	Population	%
North Charleston (city) Charleston County	147	0.16
Columbia (city) Richland County	134	0.11
Greenville (city) Greenville County	35	0.06
Rock Hill (city) York County	30	0.05
Charleston (city) Charleston County	38	0.03
Mount Pleasant (town) Charleston County	0	0.00

West Indian: Other, excluding Hispanic

Top 10 Places Sorted by Population
Based on all places, regardless of total population

Place	Population	%
Columbia (city) Richland County	15	0.01
Greenville (city) Greenville County	10	0.02
Abbeville (city) Abbeville County	0	0.00
Aiken (city) Aiken County	0	0.00
Alcolu (cdp) Clarendon County	0	0.00
Allendale (town) Allendale County	0	0.00
Anderson (city) Anderson County	0	0.00
Andrews (town) Georgetown County	0	0.00
Antreville (cdp) Abbeville County	0	0.00
Arcadia (cdp) Spartanburg County	0	0.00

Top 10 Places Sorted by Percent of Total Population
Based on all places, regardless of total population

Place	Population	%
Greenville (city) Greenville County	10	0.02
Columbia (city) Richland County	15	0.01
Abbeville (city) Abbeville County	0	0.00
Aiken (city) Aiken County	0	0.00
Alcolu (cdp) Clarendon County	0	0.00
Allendale (town) Allendale County	0	0.00
Anderson (city) Anderson County	0	0.00
Andrews (town) Georgetown County	0	0.00
Antreville (cdp) Abbeville County	0	0.00
Arcadia (cdp) Spartanburg County	0	0.00

Top 10 Places Sorted by Percent of Total Population
Based on places with total population of 50,000 or more

Place	Population	%
Greenville (city) Greenville County	10	0.02
Columbia (city) Richland County	15	0.01
Charleston (city) Charleston County	0	0.00
Mount Pleasant (town) Charleston County	0	0.00
North Charleston (city) Charleston County	0	0.00
Rock Hill (city) York County	0	0.00

Yugoslavian

Top 10 Places Sorted by Population
Based on all places, regardless of total population

Place	Population	%
Columbia (city) Richland County	74	0.06
Boiling Springs (cdp) Spartanburg County	52	0.63
North Charleston (city) Charleston County	43	0.05
Charleston (city) Charleston County	43	0.04
St. Andrews (cdp) Richland County	35	0.17
Berea (cdp) Greenville County	34	0.26
Mount Pleasant (town) Charleston County	33	0.05
Mauldin (city) Greenville County	30	0.14
Wade Hampton (cdp) Greenville County	29	0.14
Bluffton (town) Beaufort County	28	0.26

Top 10 Places Sorted by Percent of Total Population
Based on all places, regardless of total population

Place	Population	%
Pawleys Island (town) Georgetown County	2	2.00
Boiling Springs (cdp) Spartanburg County	52	0.63
Garden City (cdp) Horry County	25	0.28
Berea (cdp) Greenville County	34	0.26

Bluffton (town) Beaufort County — 28 — 0.26
Irmo (town) Richland County — 24 — 0.22
St. Andrews (cdp) Richland County — 35 — 0.17
Mauldin (city) Greenville County — 30 — 0.14
Wade Hampton (cdp) Greenville County — 29 — 0.14
Murrells Inlet (cdp) Georgetown County — 9 — 0.12

Top 10 Places Sorted by Percent of Total Population
Based on places with total population of 50,000 or more

Place	Population	%
Columbia (city) Richland County	74	0.06
North Charleston (city) Charleston County	43	0.05
Mount Pleasant (town) Charleston County	33	0.05
Charleston (city) Charleston County	43	0.04
Greenville (city) Greenville County	18	0.03
Rock Hill (city) York County	17	0.03

Hispanic Origin Rankings

Hispanic or Latino (of any race)

Top 10 Places Sorted by Population
Based on all places, regardless of total population

Place	Population	%
North Charleston (city) Charleston County	10,617	10.89
Hilton Head Island (town) Beaufort County	5,861	15.80
Columbia (city) Richland County	5,622	4.35
Rock Hill (city) York County	3,761	5.69
Myrtle Beach (city) Horry County	3,708	13.68
Greer (city) Greenville County	3,687	14.45
Berea (cdp) Greenville County	3,630	25.39
Charleston (city) Charleston County	3,451	2.87
Greenville (city) Greenville County	3,443	5.89
Greenwood (city) Greenwood County	2,550	10.98

Top 10 Places Sorted by Percent of Total Population
Based on all places, regardless of total population

Place	Population	%
Southern Shops (cdp) Spartanburg County	1,533	40.70
Fairforest (cdp) Spartanburg County	599	35.38
Arcadia (cdp) Spartanburg County	910	34.55
Saluda (town) Saluda County	1,208	33.88
City View (cdp) Greenville County	449	33.38
Watts Mills (cdp) Laurens County	479	29.30
Hardeeville (city) Jasper County	839	28.42
Berea (cdp) Greenville County	3,630	25.39
Walhalla (city) Oconee County	961	22.54
Saxon (cdp) Spartanburg County	768	22.43

Top 10 Places Sorted by Percent of Total Population
Based on places with total population of 50,000 or more

Place	Population	%
North Charleston (city) Charleston County	10,617	10.89
Greenville (city) Greenville County	3,443	5.89
Rock Hill (city) York County	3,761	5.69
Columbia (city) Richland County	5,622	4.35
Charleston (city) Charleston County	3,451	2.87
Mount Pleasant (town) Charleston County	1,850	2.73

Central American, excluding Mexican

Top 10 Places Sorted by Population
Based on all places, regardless of total population

Place	Population	%
North Charleston (city) Charleston County	1,142	1.17
Berea (cdp) Greenville County	954	6.67
Hilton Head Island (town) Beaufort County	729	1.97
Myrtle Beach (city) Horry County	628	2.32
Sans Souci (cdp) Greenville County	512	6.51
Saluda (town) Saluda County	498	13.97
Columbia (city) Richland County	473	0.37
Parker (cdp) Greenville County	436	3.81
Rock Hill (city) York County	421	0.64
Bluffton (town) Beaufort County	404	3.22

Top 10 Places Sorted by Percent of Total Population
Based on all places, regardless of total population

Place	Population	%
Saluda (town) Saluda County	498	13.97
City View (cdp) Greenville County	111	8.25
Berea (cdp) Greenville County	954	6.67
Sans Souci (cdp) Greenville County	512	6.51
Gray Court (town) Laurens County	50	6.29
Atlantic Beach (town) Horry County	20	5.99
Watts Mills (cdp) Laurens County	82	5.02
Windsor (town) Aiken County	5	4.13
Parker (cdp) Greenville County	436	3.81
Hardeeville (city) Jasper County	108	3.66

Top 10 Places Sorted by Percent of Total Population
Based on places with total population of 50,000 or more

Place	Population	%
North Charleston (city) Charleston County	1,142	1.17
Greenville (city) Greenville County	394	0.67
Rock Hill (city) York County	421	0.64
Columbia (city) Richland County	473	0.37

| Charleston (city) Charleston County | 296 | 0.25 |
| Mount Pleasant (town) Charleston County | 138 | 0.20 |

Central American: Costa Rican

Top 10 Places Sorted by Population
Based on all places, regardless of total population

Place	Population	%
Berea (cdp) Greenville County	119	0.83
Hilton Head Island (town) Beaufort County	108	0.29
Bluffton (town) Beaufort County	77	0.61
North Augusta (city) Aiken County	61	0.29
Sans Souci (cdp) Greenville County	58	0.74
Greenville (city) Greenville County	42	0.07
Parker (cdp) Greenville County	40	0.35
Wade Hampton (cdp) Greenville County	34	0.16
Greer (city) Greenville County	28	0.11
Charleston (city) Charleston County	26	0.02

Top 10 Places Sorted by Percent of Total Population
Based on all places, regardless of total population

Place	Population	%
Berea (cdp) Greenville County	119	0.83
West Pelzer (town) Anderson County	7	0.80
Sans Souci (cdp) Greenville County	58	0.74
Jonesville (town) Union County	6	0.66
Bluffton (town) Beaufort County	77	0.61
Burnet (town) Aiken County	11	0.41
Parker (cdp) Greenville County	40	0.35
Travelers Rest (city) Greenville County	14	0.31
Arcadia (cdp) Spartanburg County	8	0.30
Hilton Head Island (town) Beaufort County	108	0.29

Top 10 Places Sorted by Percent of Total Population
Based on places with total population of 50,000 or more

Place	Population	%
Greenville (city) Greenville County	42	0.07
Rock Hill (city) York County	24	0.04
Mount Pleasant (town) Charleston County	20	0.03
Charleston (city) Charleston County	26	0.02
North Charleston (city) Charleston County	24	0.02
Columbia (city) Richland County	17	0.01

Central American: Guatemalan

Top 10 Places Sorted by Population
Based on all places, regardless of total population

Place	Population	%
North Charleston (city) Charleston County	558	0.57
Saluda (town) Saluda County	490	13.74
Myrtle Beach (city) Horry County	384	1.42
Sans Souci (cdp) Greenville County	328	4.17
West Columbia (city) Lexington County	263	1.75
Berea (cdp) Greenville County	248	1.73
Parker (cdp) Greenville County	245	2.14
North Myrtle Beach (city) Horry County	202	1.47
Greenville (city) Greenville County	199	0.34
Wade Hampton (cdp) Greenville County	168	0.81

Top 10 Places Sorted by Percent of Total Population
Based on all places, regardless of total population

Place	Population	%
Saluda (town) Saluda County	490	13.74
Atlantic Beach (town) Horry County	16	4.79
Watts Mills (cdp) Laurens County	74	4.53
City View (cdp) Greenville County	57	4.24
Sans Souci (cdp) Greenville County	328	4.17
Windsor (town) Aiken County	5	4.13
Pelion (town) Lexington County	17	2.52
Parker (cdp) Greenville County	245	2.14
East Sumter (cdp) Sumter County	26	1.94
West Columbia (city) Lexington County	263	1.75

Top 10 Places Sorted by Percent of Total Population
Based on places with total population of 50,000 or more

Place	Population	%
North Charleston (city) Charleston County	558	0.57

Greenville (city) Greenville County	199	0.34
Columbia (city) Richland County	136	0.11
Rock Hill (city) York County	63	0.10
Charleston (city) Charleston County	93	0.08
Mount Pleasant (town) Charleston County	53	0.08

Central American: Honduran

Top 10 Places Sorted by Population
Based on all places, regardless of total population

Place	Population	%
Berea (cdp) Greenville County	455	3.18
Hilton Head Island (town) Beaufort County	311	0.84
North Charleston (city) Charleston County	264	0.27
Bluffton (town) Beaufort County	210	1.68
Greer (city) Greenville County	191	0.75
Rock Hill (city) York County	178	0.27
Myrtle Beach (city) Horry County	177	0.65
Woodfield (cdp) Richland County	111	1.19
Parker (cdp) Greenville County	101	0.88
Columbia (city) Richland County	99	0.08

Top 10 Places Sorted by Percent of Total Population
Based on all places, regardless of total population

Place	Population	%
Gray Court (town) Laurens County	29	3.65
Berea (cdp) Greenville County	455	3.18
City View (cdp) Greenville County	34	2.53
Troy (town) Greenwood County	2	2.15
Bluffton (town) Beaufort County	210	1.68
Hardeeville (city) Jasper County	47	1.59
Winnsboro Mills (cdp) Fairfield County	30	1.58
Springdale (cdp) Lancaster County	39	1.52
Shell Point (cdp) Beaufort County	34	1.46
Welcome (cdp) Greenville County	94	1.41

Top 10 Places Sorted by Percent of Total Population
Based on places with total population of 50,000 or more

Place	Population	%
North Charleston (city) Charleston County	264	0.27
Rock Hill (city) York County	178	0.27
Greenville (city) Greenville County	80	0.14
Columbia (city) Richland County	99	0.08
Charleston (city) Charleston County	57	0.05
Mount Pleasant (town) Charleston County	16	0.02

Central American: Nicaraguan

Top 10 Places Sorted by Population
Based on all places, regardless of total population

Place	Population	%
Hilton Head Island (town) Beaufort County	90	0.24
North Charleston (city) Charleston County	59	0.06
Bluffton (town) Beaufort County	38	0.30
Summerville (town) Dorchester County	33	0.08
Mauldin (city) Greenville County	27	0.12
Newberry (city) Newberry County	24	0.23
Rock Hill (city) York County	22	0.03
Goose Creek (city) Berkeley County	20	0.06
Charleston (city) Charleston County	20	0.02
Port Royal (town) Beaufort County	18	0.17

Top 10 Places Sorted by Percent of Total Population
Based on all places, regardless of total population

Place	Population	%
City View (cdp) Greenville County	9	0.67
Bluffton (town) Beaufort County	38	0.30
Southern Shops (cdp) Spartanburg County	10	0.27
South Congaree (town) Lexington County	6	0.26
Hilton Head Island (town) Beaufort County	90	0.24
Newberry (city) Newberry County	24	0.23
Arcadia (cdp) Spartanburg County	6	0.23
Pickens (city) Pickens County	7	0.22
Fort Lawn (town) Chester County	2	0.22
Port Royal (town) Beaufort County	18	0.17

Please refer to the Explanation of Data in the front of the book for more detailed information.

Top 10 Places Sorted by Percent of Total Population
Based on places with total population of 50,000 or more

Place	Population	%
North Charleston (city) Charleston County	59	0.06
Rock Hill (city) York County	22	0.03
Greenville (city) Greenville County	15	0.03
Charleston (city) Charleston County	20	0.02
Mount Pleasant (town) Charleston County	15	0.02
Columbia (city) Richland County	17	0.01

Central American: Panamanian

Top 10 Places Sorted by Population
Based on all places, regardless of total population

Place	Population	%
Columbia (city) Richland County	132	0.10
North Charleston (city) Charleston County	84	0.09
Charleston (city) Charleston County	72	0.06
Woodfield (cdp) Richland County	54	0.58
Dentsville (cdp) Richland County	41	0.29
Summerville (town) Dorchester County	34	0.08
Goose Creek (city) Berkeley County	31	0.09
Sumter (city) Sumter County	31	0.08
Rock Hill (city) York County	30	0.05
Forest Acres (city) Richland County	20	0.19

Top 10 Places Sorted by Percent of Total Population
Based on all places, regardless of total population

Place	Population	%
Woodfield (cdp) Richland County	54	0.58
Shell Point (cdp) Beaufort County	10	0.43
Springdale (cdp) Lancaster County	9	0.35
Rowesville (town) Orangeburg County	1	0.33
Oakland (cdp) Sumter County	4	0.32
Ridgeway (town) Fairfield County	1	0.31
Dentsville (cdp) Richland County	41	0.29
Ridge Spring (town) Saluda County	2	0.27
Blacksburg (town) Cherokee County	4	0.22
Edisto (cdp) Orangeburg County	5	0.20

Top 10 Places Sorted by Percent of Total Population
Based on places with total population of 50,000 or more

Place	Population	%
Columbia (city) Richland County	132	0.10
North Charleston (city) Charleston County	84	0.09
Charleston (city) Charleston County	72	0.06
Rock Hill (city) York County	30	0.05
Mount Pleasant (town) Charleston County	16	0.02
Greenville (city) Greenville County	7	0.01

Central American: Salvadoran

Top 10 Places Sorted by Population
Based on all places, regardless of total population

Place	Population	%
North Charleston (city) Charleston County	147	0.15
Berea (cdp) Greenville County	116	0.81
Rock Hill (city) York County	100	0.15
Greer (city) Greenville County	94	0.37
Hilton Head Island (town) Beaufort County	82	0.22
Taylors (cdp) Greenville County	79	0.37
Summerville (town) Dorchester County	75	0.17
North Myrtle Beach (city) Horry County	72	0.52
Columbia (city) Richland County	72	0.06
Wade Hampton (cdp) Greenville County	68	0.33

Top 10 Places Sorted by Percent of Total Population
Based on all places, regardless of total population

Place	Population	%
Gray Court (town) Laurens County	13	1.64
Walhalla (city) Oconee County	44	1.03
City View (cdp) Greenville County	11	0.82
Berea (cdp) Greenville County	116	0.81
West Pelzer (town) Anderson County	6	0.68
Arcadia (cdp) Spartanburg County	17	0.65
Westminster (city) Oconee County	13	0.54
Utica (cdp) Oconee County	8	0.54
North Myrtle Beach (city) Horry County	72	0.52
Startex (cdp) Spartanburg County	4	0.47

Top 10 Places Sorted by Percent of Total Population
Based on places with total population of 50,000 or more

Place	Population	%
North Charleston (city) Charleston County	147	0.15
Rock Hill (city) York County	100	0.15
Greenville (city) Greenville County	49	0.08
Columbia (city) Richland County	72	0.06
Mount Pleasant (town) Charleston County	18	0.03
Charleston (city) Charleston County	25	0.02

Central American: Other Central American

Top 10 Places Sorted by Population
Based on all places, regardless of total population

Place	Population	%
Spartanburg (city) Spartanburg County	10	0.03
Burton (cdp) Beaufort County	7	0.10
Easley (city) Pickens County	7	0.04
North Charleston (city) Charleston County	6	0.01
Summerville (town) Dorchester County	5	0.01
Rock Hill (city) York County	4	0.01
Sans Souci (cdp) Greenville County	3	0.04
Red Hill (cdp) Horry County	3	0.02
Charleston (city) Charleston County	3	<0.01
Edisto (cdp) Orangeburg County	2	0.08

Top 10 Places Sorted by Percent of Total Population
Based on all places, regardless of total population

Place	Population	%
Burton (cdp) Beaufort County	7	0.10
Edisto (cdp) Orangeburg County	2	0.08
Honea Path (town) Anderson County	2	0.06
Easley (city) Pickens County	7	0.04
Sans Souci (cdp) Greenville County	3	0.04
Spartanburg (city) Spartanburg County	10	0.03
Valley Falls (cdp) Spartanburg County	2	0.03
Bamberg (town) Bamberg County	1	0.03
Hardeeville (city) Jasper County	1	0.03
Saluda (town) Saluda County	1	0.03

Top 10 Places Sorted by Percent of Total Population
Based on places with total population of 50,000 or more

Place	Population	%
North Charleston (city) Charleston County	6	0.01
Rock Hill (city) York County	4	0.01
Charleston (city) Charleston County	3	<0.01
Greenville (city) Greenville County	2	<0.01
Columbia (city) Richland County	0	0.00
Mount Pleasant (town) Charleston County	0	0.00

Cuban

Top 10 Places Sorted by Population
Based on all places, regardless of total population

Place	Population	%
Columbia (city) Richland County	208	0.16
North Charleston (city) Charleston County	151	0.15
Charleston (city) Charleston County	150	0.12
Mount Pleasant (town) Charleston County	124	0.18
Simpsonville (city) Greenville County	85	0.47
Summerville (town) Dorchester County	83	0.19
Rock Hill (city) York County	81	0.12
Goose Creek (city) Berkeley County	78	0.22
Greenville (city) Greenville County	75	0.13
Mauldin (city) Greenville County	73	0.32

Top 10 Places Sorted by Percent of Total Population
Based on all places, regardless of total population

Place	Population	%
Ulmer (town) Allendale County	2	2.27
Pelzer (town) Anderson County	2	2.25
Edgefield (town) Edgefield County	50	1.05
Modoc (cdp) McCormick County	2	0.92
Ware Place (cdp) Greenville County	2	0.88
Rockville (town) Charleston County	1	0.75
Hardeeville (city) Jasper County	21	0.71
Eutawville (town) Orangeburg County	2	0.63
Springdale (town) Lexington County	14	0.53
Simpsonville (city) Greenville County	85	0.47

Top 10 Places Sorted by Percent of Total Population
Based on places with total population of 50,000 or more

Place	Population	%
Mount Pleasant (town) Charleston County	124	0.18
Columbia (city) Richland County	208	0.16
North Charleston (city) Charleston County	151	0.15
Greenville (city) Greenville County	75	0.13
Charleston (city) Charleston County	150	0.12
Rock Hill (city) York County	81	0.12

Dominican Republic

Top 10 Places Sorted by Population
Based on all places, regardless of total population

Place	Population	%
Columbia (city) Richland County	154	0.12
Rock Hill (city) York County	106	0.16
North Charleston (city) Charleston County	95	0.10
Greenville (city) Greenville County	84	0.14
Port Royal (town) Beaufort County	75	0.70
Goose Creek (city) Berkeley County	75	0.21
Greer (city) Greenville County	73	0.29
Summerville (town) Dorchester County	59	0.14
Charleston (city) Charleston County	55	0.05
Wade Hampton (cdp) Greenville County	53	0.26

Top 10 Places Sorted by Percent of Total Population
Based on all places, regardless of total population

Place	Population	%
Cross Anchor (cdp) Spartanburg County	5	3.97
Port Royal (town) Beaufort County	75	0.70
Greer (city) Greenville County	73	0.29
Clio (town) Marlboro County	2	0.28
Lake Wylie (cdp) York County	24	0.27
Burton (cdp) Beaufort County	19	0.27
Wade Hampton (cdp) Greenville County	53	0.26
Simpsonville (city) Greenville County	47	0.26
Dentsville (cdp) Richland County	37	0.26
Ladson (cdp) Berkeley County	36	0.26

Top 10 Places Sorted by Percent of Total Population
Based on places with total population of 50,000 or more

Place	Population	%
Rock Hill (city) York County	106	0.16
Greenville (city) Greenville County	84	0.14
Columbia (city) Richland County	154	0.12
North Charleston (city) Charleston County	95	0.10
Charleston (city) Charleston County	55	0.05
Mount Pleasant (town) Charleston County	31	0.05

Mexican

Top 10 Places Sorted by Population
Based on all places, regardless of total population

Place	Population	%
North Charleston (city) Charleston County	7,157	7.34
Hilton Head Island (town) Beaufort County	4,034	10.87
Columbia (city) Richland County	2,423	1.87
Myrtle Beach (city) Horry County	2,412	8.90
Greenwood (city) Greenwood County	2,035	8.76
Berea (cdp) Greenville County	2,021	14.14
Rock Hill (city) York County	2,002	3.03
Greer (city) Greenville County	1,906	7.47
Greenville (city) Greenville County	1,692	2.90
Gantt (cdp) Greenville County	1,610	11.31

Top 10 Places Sorted by Percent of Total Population
Based on all places, regardless of total population

Place	Population	%
Southern Shops (cdp) Spartanburg County	1,369	36.34
Fairforest (cdp) Spartanburg County	531	31.36
Arcadia (cdp) Spartanburg County	763	28.97
Watts Mills (cdp) Laurens County	370	22.63
Hardeeville (city) Jasper County	657	22.26
City View (cdp) Greenville County	299	22.23
Luray (town) Hampton County	27	21.26
Saxon (cdp) Spartanburg County	689	20.12
Saluda (town) Saluda County	681	19.10
Walhalla (city) Oconee County	795	18.65

Top 10 Places Sorted by Percent of Total Population
Based on places with total population of 50,000 or more

Place	Population	%
North Charleston (city) Charleston County	7,157	7.34
Rock Hill (city) York County	2,002	3.03
Greenville (city) Greenville County	1,692	2.90
Columbia (city) Richland County	2,423	1.87
Charleston (city) Charleston County	1,590	1.32
Mount Pleasant (town) Charleston County	734	1.08

Puerto Rican

Top 10 Places Sorted by Population
Based on all places, regardless of total population

Place	Population	%
Columbia (city) Richland County	1,337	1.03
North Charleston (city) Charleston County	831	0.85
Summerville (town) Dorchester County	529	1.22
Charleston (city) Charleston County	528	0.44
Rock Hill (city) York County	465	0.70
Goose Creek (city) Berkeley County	448	1.25
Greenville (city) Greenville County	337	0.58
Sumter (city) Sumter County	317	0.78
Port Royal (town) Beaufort County	309	2.89
Woodfield (cdp) Richland County	267	2.87

Top 10 Places Sorted by Percent of Total Population
Based on all places, regardless of total population

Place	Population	%
Laurel Bay (cdp) Beaufort County	173	2.94
Port Royal (town) Beaufort County	309	2.89
Woodfield (cdp) Richland County	267	2.87
Atlantic Beach (town) Horry County	8	2.40
Oakland (cdp) Sumter County	27	2.19
Coronaca (cdp) Greenwood County	4	2.09
Starr (town) Anderson County	3	1.73
Blythewood (town) Richland County	35	1.72
Paxville (town) Clarendon County	3	1.62
Woodford (town) Orangeburg County	3	1.62

Top 10 Places Sorted by Percent of Total Population
Based on places with total population of 50,000 or more

Place	Population	%
Columbia (city) Richland County	1,337	1.03
North Charleston (city) Charleston County	831	0.85
Rock Hill (city) York County	465	0.70
Greenville (city) Greenville County	337	0.58
Charleston (city) Charleston County	528	0.44
Mount Pleasant (town) Charleston County	254	0.37

South American

Top 10 Places Sorted by Population
Based on all places, regardless of total population

Place	Population	%
Greer (city) Greenville County	836	3.28
Hilton Head Island (town) Beaufort County	665	1.79
Mauldin (city) Greenville County	659	2.88
Greenville (city) Greenville County	600	1.03
Charleston (city) Charleston County	477	0.40
Rock Hill (city) York County	460	0.70
North Charleston (city) Charleston County	433	0.44
Columbia (city) Richland County	428	0.33
Taylors (cdp) Greenville County	393	1.82
Wade Hampton (cdp) Greenville County	374	1.81

Top 10 Places Sorted by Percent of Total Population
Based on all places, regardless of total population

Place	Population	%
Boykin (cdp) Kershaw County	4	4.00
Greer (city) Greenville County	836	3.28
Lowndesville (town) Abbeville County	4	3.13
Mauldin (city) Greenville County	659	2.88
Bluffton (town) Beaufort County	345	2.75
Berea (cdp) Greenville County	359	2.51
Simpsonville (city) Greenville County	345	1.89
Taylors (cdp) Greenville County	393	1.82
Wade Hampton (cdp) Greenville County	374	1.81
Hilton Head Island (town) Beaufort County	665	1.79

Top 10 Places Sorted by Percent of Total Population
Based on places with total population of 50,000 or more

Place	Population	%
Greenville (city) Greenville County	600	1.03
Rock Hill (city) York County	460	0.70
Mount Pleasant (town) Charleston County	356	0.52
North Charleston (city) Charleston County	433	0.44
Charleston (city) Charleston County	477	0.40
Columbia (city) Richland County	428	0.33

South American: Argentinean

Top 10 Places Sorted by Population
Based on all places, regardless of total population

Place	Population	%
Hilton Head Island (town) Beaufort County	221	0.60
Charleston (city) Charleston County	83	0.07
Bluffton (town) Beaufort County	64	0.51
North Charleston (city) Charleston County	58	0.06
Mount Pleasant (town) Charleston County	41	0.06
Columbia (city) Richland County	41	0.03
Goose Creek (city) Berkeley County	33	0.09
Greenville (city) Greenville County	33	0.06
Summerville (town) Dorchester County	20	0.05
Rock Hill (city) York County	15	0.02

Top 10 Places Sorted by Percent of Total Population
Based on all places, regardless of total population

Place	Population	%
Hilton Head Island (town) Beaufort County	221	0.60
Bluffton (town) Beaufort County	64	0.51
Arcadia Lakes (town) Richland County	3	0.35
Irwin (cdp) Lancaster County	4	0.28
Springdale (town) Lexington County	4	0.15
Forestbrook (cdp) Horry County	6	0.13
Utica (cdp) Oconee County	2	0.13
Gray Court (town) Laurens County	1	0.13
Oak Grove (cdp) Lexington County	11	0.11
Red Hill (cdp) Horry County	13	0.10

Top 10 Places Sorted by Percent of Total Population
Based on places with total population of 50,000 or more

Place	Population	%
Charleston (city) Charleston County	83	0.07
North Charleston (city) Charleston County	58	0.06
Mount Pleasant (town) Charleston County	41	0.06
Greenville (city) Greenville County	33	0.06
Columbia (city) Richland County	41	0.03
Rock Hill (city) York County	15	0.02

South American: Bolivian

Top 10 Places Sorted by Population
Based on all places, regardless of total population

Place	Population	%
Charleston (city) Charleston County	62	0.05
Bluffton (town) Beaufort County	55	0.44
North Charleston (city) Charleston County	38	0.04
Hilton Head Island (town) Beaufort County	29	0.08
Rock Hill (city) York County	11	0.02
Columbia (city) Richland County	10	0.01
Lake Murray of Richland (cdp) Richland County	8	0.15
Five Forks (cdp) Greenville County	8	0.06
Greer (city) Greenville County	8	0.03
Summerville (town) Dorchester County	7	0.02

Top 10 Places Sorted by Percent of Total Population
Based on all places, regardless of total population

Place	Population	%
Bluffton (town) Beaufort County	55	0.44
Clifton (cdp) Spartanburg County	2	0.37
Mayo (cdp) Spartanburg County	3	0.19
Lake Murray of Richland (cdp) Richland County	8	0.15
Williston (town) Barnwell County	3	0.10
Hilton Head Island (town) Beaufort County	29	0.08
Five Forks (cdp) Greenville County	8	0.06
Sullivan's Island (town) Charleston County	1	0.06
Charleston (city) Charleston County	62	0.05
Sangaree (cdp) Berkeley County	4	0.05

Top 10 Places Sorted by Percent of Total Population
Based on places with total population of 50,000 or more

Place	Population	%
Charleston (city) Charleston County	62	0.05
North Charleston (city) Charleston County	38	0.04
Rock Hill (city) York County	11	0.02
Columbia (city) Richland County	10	0.01
Mount Pleasant (town) Charleston County	6	0.01
Greenville (city) Greenville County	2	<0.01

South American: Chilean

Top 10 Places Sorted by Population
Based on all places, regardless of total population

Place	Population	%
Mount Pleasant (town) Charleston County	36	0.05
Charleston (city) Charleston County	27	0.02
Greenville (city) Greenville County	18	0.03
Rock Hill (city) York County	18	0.03
North Charleston (city) Charleston County	15	0.02
Columbia (city) Richland County	15	0.01
Mauldin (city) Greenville County	13	0.06
Lake Wylie (cdp) York County	11	0.12
Five Forks (cdp) Greenville County	9	0.06
Hilton Head Island (town) Beaufort County	9	0.02

Top 10 Places Sorted by Percent of Total Population
Based on all places, regardless of total population

Place	Population	%
Boykin (cdp) Kershaw County	4	4.00
Lowndesville (town) Abbeville County	4	3.13
Fairforest (cdp) Spartanburg County	3	0.18
Shell Point (cdp) Beaufort County	3	0.13
Lake Wylie (cdp) York County	11	0.12
Tega Cay (city) York County	8	0.10
Graniteville (cdp) Aiken County	2	0.08
Meggett (town) Charleston County	1	0.08
Mauldin (city) Greenville County	13	0.06
Five Forks (cdp) Greenville County	9	0.06

Top 10 Places Sorted by Percent of Total Population
Based on places with total population of 50,000 or more

Place	Population	%
Mount Pleasant (town) Charleston County	36	0.05
Greenville (city) Greenville County	18	0.03
Rock Hill (city) York County	18	0.03
Charleston (city) Charleston County	27	0.02
North Charleston (city) Charleston County	15	0.02
Columbia (city) Richland County	15	0.01

South American: Colombian

Top 10 Places Sorted by Population
Based on all places, regardless of total population

Place	Population	%
Greer (city) Greenville County	695	2.72
Mauldin (city) Greenville County	531	2.32
Greenville (city) Greenville County	427	0.73
Wade Hampton (cdp) Greenville County	341	1.65
Taylors (cdp) Greenville County	329	1.52
Berea (cdp) Greenville County	317	2.22
Simpsonville (city) Greenville County	268	1.47
Rock Hill (city) York County	216	0.33
Columbia (city) Richland County	188	0.15
Parker (cdp) Greenville County	143	1.25

Top 10 Places Sorted by Percent of Total Population
Based on all places, regardless of total population

Place	Population	%
Greer (city) Greenville County	695	2.72
Mauldin (city) Greenville County	531	2.32
Berea (cdp) Greenville County	317	2.22
Wade Hampton (cdp) Greenville County	341	1.65
Taylors (cdp) Greenville County	329	1.52
Simpsonville (city) Greenville County	268	1.47
Parker (cdp) Greenville County	143	1.25
Fountain Inn (city) Greenville County	72	0.92
Five Forks (cdp) Greenville County	125	0.88
Welcome (cdp) Greenville County	58	0.87

Please refer to the Explanation of Data in the front of the book for more detailed information.

Top 10 Places Sorted by Percent of Total Population
Based on places with total population of 50,000 or more

Place	Population	%
Greenville (city) Greenville County	427	0.73
Rock Hill (city) York County	216	0.33
Mount Pleasant (town) Charleston County	111	0.16
Columbia (city) Richland County	188	0.15
North Charleston (city) Charleston County	143	0.15
Charleston (city) Charleston County	126	0.10

South American: Ecuadorian

Top 10 Places Sorted by Population
Based on all places, regardless of total population

Place	Population	%
Charleston (city) Charleston County	83	0.07
Rock Hill (city) York County	59	0.09
Columbia (city) Richland County	50	0.04
Mount Pleasant (town) Charleston County	47	0.07
Goose Creek (city) Berkeley County	42	0.12
North Charleston (city) Charleston County	41	0.04
Summerville (town) Dorchester County	38	0.09
Fountain Inn (city) Greenville County	32	0.41
North Myrtle Beach (city) Horry County	31	0.23
Spartanburg (city) Spartanburg County	31	0.08

Top 10 Places Sorted by Percent of Total Population
Based on all places, regardless of total population

Place	Population	%
Fountain Inn (city) Greenville County	32	0.41
West Union (town) Oconee County	1	0.34
Westminster (city) Oconee County	7	0.29
Ridge Spring (town) Saluda County	2	0.27
Port Royal (town) Beaufort County	26	0.24
North Myrtle Beach (city) Horry County	31	0.23
Saxon (cdp) Spartanburg County	6	0.18
Travelers Rest (city) Greenville County	8	0.17
Elgin (town) Kershaw County	2	0.15
Lake Wylie (cdp) York County	12	0.14

Top 10 Places Sorted by Percent of Total Population
Based on places with total population of 50,000 or more

Place	Population	%
Rock Hill (city) York County	59	0.09
Charleston (city) Charleston County	83	0.07
Mount Pleasant (town) Charleston County	47	0.07
Columbia (city) Richland County	50	0.04
North Charleston (city) Charleston County	41	0.04
Greenville (city) Greenville County	18	0.03

South American: Paraguayan

Top 10 Places Sorted by Population
Based on all places, regardless of total population

Place	Population	%
Taylors (cdp) Greenville County	10	0.05
Mount Pleasant (town) Charleston County	8	0.01
Greenville (city) Greenville County	6	0.01
Seneca (city) Oconee County	5	0.06
Greenwood (city) Greenwood County	4	0.02
Charleston (city) Charleston County	4	<0.01
Columbia (city) Richland County	4	<0.01
Hilton Head Island (town) Beaufort County	3	0.01
Lake Wylie (cdp) York County	2	0.02
Port Royal (town) Beaufort County	2	0.02

Top 10 Places Sorted by Percent of Total Population
Based on all places, regardless of total population

Place	Population	%
West Union (town) Oconee County	1	0.34
Seneca (city) Oconee County	5	0.06
Taylors (cdp) Greenville County	10	0.05
Greenwood (city) Greenwood County	4	0.02
Lake Wylie (cdp) York County	2	0.02
Port Royal (town) Beaufort County	2	0.02
Mount Pleasant (town) Charleston County	8	0.01
Greenville (city) Greenville County	6	0.01
Hilton Head Island (town) Beaufort County	3	0.01
Anderson (city) Anderson County	2	0.01

Top 10 Places Sorted by Percent of Total Population
Based on places with total population of 50,000 or more

Place	Population	%
Mount Pleasant (town) Charleston County	8	0.01
Greenville (city) Greenville County	6	0.01
Charleston (city) Charleston County	4	<0.01
Columbia (city) Richland County	4	<0.01
North Charleston (city) Charleston County	1	<0.01
Rock Hill (city) York County	1	<0.01

South American: Peruvian

Top 10 Places Sorted by Population
Based on all places, regardless of total population

Place	Population	%
North Charleston (city) Charleston County	82	0.08
Columbia (city) Richland County	60	0.05
Mount Pleasant (town) Charleston County	59	0.09
Rock Hill (city) York County	53	0.08
Greer (city) Greenville County	52	0.20
Charleston (city) Charleston County	51	0.04
Greenville (city) Greenville County	45	0.08
Summerville (town) Dorchester County	43	0.10
Mauldin (city) Greenville County	37	0.16
Hilton Head Island (town) Beaufort County	26	0.07

Top 10 Places Sorted by Percent of Total Population
Based on all places, regardless of total population

Place	Population	%
India Hook (cdp) York County	13	0.39
Southern Shops (cdp) Spartanburg County	11	0.29
Ridgeland (town) Jasper County	11	0.27
City View (cdp) Greenville County	3	0.22
Greer (city) Greenville County	52	0.20
Port Royal (town) Beaufort County	21	0.20
Bluffton (town) Beaufort County	21	0.17
Laurel Bay (cdp) Beaufort County	10	0.17
Mauldin (city) Greenville County	37	0.16
Ladson (cdp) Berkeley County	20	0.15

Top 10 Places Sorted by Percent of Total Population
Based on places with total population of 50,000 or more

Place	Population	%
Mount Pleasant (town) Charleston County	59	0.09
North Charleston (city) Charleston County	82	0.08
Rock Hill (city) York County	53	0.08
Greenville (city) Greenville County	45	0.08
Columbia (city) Richland County	60	0.05
Charleston (city) Charleston County	51	0.04

South American: Uruguayan

Top 10 Places Sorted by Population
Based on all places, regardless of total population

Place	Population	%
Hilton Head Island (town) Beaufort County	189	0.51
Bluffton (town) Beaufort County	98	0.78
Rock Hill (city) York County	69	0.10
Greer (city) Greenville County	24	0.09
Greenville (city) Greenville County	15	0.03
Ladson (cdp) Berkeley County	12	0.09
North Charleston (city) Charleston County	11	0.01
Mauldin (city) Greenville County	10	0.04
Mount Pleasant (town) Charleston County	10	0.01
Simpsonville (city) Greenville County	9	0.05

Top 10 Places Sorted by Percent of Total Population
Based on all places, regardless of total population

Place	Population	%
Bluffton (town) Beaufort County	98	0.78
Hilton Head Island (town) Beaufort County	189	0.51
Catawba (cdp) York County	3	0.22
Rock Hill (city) York County	69	0.10
Andrews (town) Georgetown County	3	0.10
Greer (city) Greenville County	24	0.09
Ladson (cdp) Berkeley County	12	0.09
Roebuck (cdp) Spartanburg County	2	0.09
Winnsboro (town) Fairfield County	2	0.06
Kiawah Island (town) Charleston County	1	0.06

Top 10 Places Sorted by Percent of Total Population
Based on places with total population of 50,000 or more

Place	Population	%
Rock Hill (city) York County	69	0.10
Greenville (city) Greenville County	15	0.03
North Charleston (city) Charleston County	11	0.01
Mount Pleasant (town) Charleston County	10	0.01
Charleston (city) Charleston County	8	0.01
Columbia (city) Richland County	5	<0.01

South American: Venezuelan

Top 10 Places Sorted by Population
Based on all places, regardless of total population

Place	Population	%
Hilton Head Island (town) Beaufort County	53	0.14
Columbia (city) Richland County	53	0.04
North Charleston (city) Charleston County	41	0.04
Bluffton (town) Beaufort County	37	0.30
Greenville (city) Greenville County	36	0.06
Mount Pleasant (town) Charleston County	36	0.05
Charleston (city) Charleston County	30	0.02
Myrtle Beach (city) Horry County	22	0.08
Port Royal (town) Beaufort County	21	0.20
Mauldin (city) Greenville County	20	0.09

Top 10 Places Sorted by Percent of Total Population
Based on all places, regardless of total population

Place	Population	%
Slater-Marietta (cdp) Greenville County	7	0.32
Bluffton (town) Beaufort County	37	0.30
Edisto Beach (town) Colleton County	1	0.24
Port Royal (town) Beaufort County	21	0.20
Duncan (town) Spartanburg County	5	0.16
Elgin (town) Kershaw County	2	0.15
Pelion (town) Lexington County	1	0.15
Hilton Head Island (town) Beaufort County	53	0.14
Woodfield (cdp) Richland County	13	0.14
Hardeeville (city) Jasper County	4	0.14

Top 10 Places Sorted by Percent of Total Population
Based on places with total population of 50,000 or more

Place	Population	%
Greenville (city) Greenville County	36	0.06
Mount Pleasant (town) Charleston County	36	0.05
Columbia (city) Richland County	53	0.04
North Charleston (city) Charleston County	41	0.04
Rock Hill (city) York County	17	0.03
Charleston (city) Charleston County	30	0.02

South American: Other South American

Top 10 Places Sorted by Population
Based on all places, regardless of total population

Place	Population	%
Murrells Inlet (cdp) Georgetown County	8	0.11
Summerville (town) Dorchester County	6	0.01
Branchville (town) Orangeburg County	4	0.39
Woodfield (cdp) Richland County	4	0.04
Mauldin (city) Greenville County	4	0.02
Hilton Head Island (town) Beaufort County	4	0.01
Forest Acres (city) Richland County	3	0.03
Charleston (city) Charleston County	3	<0.01
North Charleston (city) Charleston County	3	<0.01
India Hook (cdp) York County	2	0.06

Top 10 Places Sorted by Percent of Total Population
Based on all places, regardless of total population

Place	Population	%
Branchville (town) Orangeburg County	4	0.39
Murrells Inlet (cdp) Georgetown County	8	0.11
City View (cdp) Greenville County	1	0.07
India Hook (cdp) York County	2	0.06
Clearwater (cdp) Aiken County	2	0.05
Blacksburg (town) Cherokee County	1	0.05
Woodfield (cdp) Richland County	4	0.04
Forest Acres (city) Richland County	3	0.03
Hartsville (city) Darlington County	2	0.03
Homeland Park (cdp) Anderson County	2	0.03

Top 10 Places Sorted by Percent of Total Population
Based on places with total population of 50,000 or more

Place	Population	%
Charleston (city) Charleston County	3	<0.01
North Charleston (city) Charleston County	3	<0.01
Columbia (city) Richland County	2	<0.01
Mount Pleasant (town) Charleston County	2	<0.01
Rock Hill (city) York County	1	<0.01
Greenville (city) Greenville County	0	0.00

Other Hispanic or Latino

Top 10 Places Sorted by Population
Based on all places, regardless of total population

Place	Population	%
North Charleston (city) Charleston County	808	0.83
Columbia (city) Richland County	599	0.46
Charleston (city) Charleston County	355	0.30
Hilton Head Island (town) Beaufort County	298	0.80
Myrtle Beach (city) Horry County	292	1.08
Goose Creek (city) Berkeley County	273	0.76
Greenville (city) Greenville County	261	0.45
Rock Hill (city) York County	226	0.34
Mount Pleasant (town) Charleston County	213	0.31
Socastee (cdp) Horry County	202	1.01

Top 10 Places Sorted by Percent of Total Population
Based on all places, regardless of total population

Place	Population	%
Boykin (cdp) Kershaw County	3	3.00
Glendale (cdp) Spartanburg County	9	2.93
Oswego (cdp) Sumter County	2	2.38
Shiloh (cdp) Sumter County	5	2.34
Fairforest (cdp) Spartanburg County	34	2.01
Walhalla (city) Oconee County	84	1.97
West Union (town) Oconee County	5	1.72
Southern Shops (cdp) Spartanburg County	64	1.70
Ehrhardt (town) Bamberg County	9	1.65
Arcadia (cdp) Spartanburg County	41	1.56

Top 10 Places Sorted by Percent of Total Population
Based on places with total population of 50,000 or more

Place	Population	%
North Charleston (city) Charleston County	808	0.83
Columbia (city) Richland County	599	0.46
Greenville (city) Greenville County	261	0.45
Rock Hill (city) York County	226	0.34
Mount Pleasant (town) Charleston County	213	0.31
Charleston (city) Charleston County	355	0.30

Racial Group Rankings

African-American/Black

Top 10 Places Sorted by Population
Based on all places, regardless of total population

Place	Population	%
Columbia (city) Richland County	55,929	43.26
North Charleston (city) Charleston County	47,316	48.54
Charleston (city) Charleston County	31,268	26.04
Rock Hill (city) York County	26,236	39.66
Sumter (city) Sumter County	20,346	50.21
Spartanburg (city) Spartanburg County	18,691	50.50
Greenville (city) Greenville County	18,069	30.94
Florence (city) Florence County	17,351	46.82
St. Andrews (cdp) Richland County	13,821	67.44
Orangeburg (city) Orangeburg County	10,590	75.84

Top 10 Places Sorted by Percent of Total Population
Based on all places, regardless of total population

Place	Population	%
Jenkinsville (town) Fairfield County	46	100.00
Brookdale (cdp) Orangeburg County	4,812	98.75
Gifford (town) Hampton County	275	95.49
Gadsden (cdp) Richland County	1,555	95.28
Eastover (town) Richland County	769	94.59
Promised Land (cdp) Greenwood County	481	94.13
Wilkinson Heights (cdp) Orangeburg County	2,328	93.38
Lane (town) Williamsburg County	464	91.34
Bucksport (cdp) Horry County	799	91.21
Carlisle (town) Union County	395	90.60

Top 10 Places Sorted by Percent of Total Population
Based on places with total population of 50,000 or more

Place	Population	%
North Charleston (city) Charleston County	47,316	48.54
Columbia (city) Richland County	55,929	43.26
Rock Hill (city) York County	26,236	39.66
Greenville (city) Greenville County	18,069	30.94
Charleston (city) Charleston County	31,268	26.04
Mount Pleasant (town) Charleston County	3,701	5.46

African-American/Black: Not Hispanic

Top 10 Places Sorted by Population
Based on all places, regardless of total population

Place	Population	%
Columbia (city) Richland County	55,158	42.67
North Charleston (city) Charleston County	46,648	47.86
Charleston (city) Charleston County	30,973	25.79
Rock Hill (city) York County	25,932	39.20
Sumter (city) Sumter County	20,156	49.74
Spartanburg (city) Spartanburg County	18,535	50.08
Greenville (city) Greenville County	17,855	30.57
Florence (city) Florence County	17,261	46.58
St. Andrews (cdp) Richland County	13,649	66.60
Orangeburg (city) Orangeburg County	10,504	75.22

Top 10 Places Sorted by Percent of Total Population
Based on all places, regardless of total population

Place	Population	%
Jenkinsville (town) Fairfield County	46	100.00
Brookdale (cdp) Orangeburg County	4,782	98.13
Gifford (town) Hampton County	275	95.49
Gadsden (cdp) Richland County	1,540	94.36
Promised Land (cdp) Greenwood County	481	94.13
Eastover (town) Richland County	761	93.60
Wilkinson Heights (cdp) Orangeburg County	2,313	92.78
Lane (town) Williamsburg County	463	91.14
Carlisle (town) Union County	395	90.60
Bucksport (cdp) Horry County	793	90.53

Top 10 Places Sorted by Percent of Total Population
Based on places with total population of 50,000 or more

Place	Population	%
North Charleston (city) Charleston County	46,648	47.86
Columbia (city) Richland County	55,158	42.67
Rock Hill (city) York County	25,932	39.20
Greenville (city) Greenville County	17,855	30.57

| Charleston (city) Charleston County | 30,973 | 25.79 |
| Mount Pleasant (town) Charleston County | 3,636 | 5.36 |

African-American/Black: Hispanic

Top 10 Places Sorted by Population
Based on all places, regardless of total population

Place	Population	%
Columbia (city) Richland County	771	0.60
North Charleston (city) Charleston County	668	0.69
Rock Hill (city) York County	304	0.46
Charleston (city) Charleston County	295	0.25
Summerville (town) Dorchester County	222	0.51
Greenville (city) Greenville County	214	0.37
Sumter (city) Sumter County	190	0.47
Dentsville (cdp) Richland County	173	1.23
St. Andrews (cdp) Richland County	172	0.84
Goose Creek (city) Berkeley County	163	0.45

Top 10 Places Sorted by Percent of Total Population
Based on all places, regardless of total population

Place	Population	%
Coronaca (cdp) Greenwood County	4	2.09
Greeleyville (town) Williamsburg County	8	1.83
Hemingway (town) Williamsburg County	8	1.74
Paxville (town) Clarendon County	3	1.62
Luray (town) Hampton County	2	1.57
Woodfield (cdp) Richland County	141	1.52
Shiloh (cdp) Sumter County	3	1.40
Edgefield (town) Edgefield County	62	1.31
Port Royal (town) Beaufort County	135	1.26
Dentsville (cdp) Richland County	173	1.23

Top 10 Places Sorted by Percent of Total Population
Based on places with total population of 50,000 or more

Place	Population	%
North Charleston (city) Charleston County	668	0.69
Columbia (city) Richland County	771	0.60
Rock Hill (city) York County	304	0.46
Greenville (city) Greenville County	214	0.37
Charleston (city) Charleston County	295	0.25
Mount Pleasant (town) Charleston County	65	0.10

American Indian/Alaska Native

Top 10 Places Sorted by Population
Based on all places, regardless of total population

Place	Population	%
Columbia (city) Richland County	1,141	0.88
North Charleston (city) Charleston County	1,029	1.06
Charleston (city) Charleston County	753	0.63
Rock Hill (city) York County	653	0.99
Summerville (town) Dorchester County	492	1.13
Goose Creek (city) Berkeley County	456	1.27
Greenville (city) Greenville County	425	0.73
McColl (town) Marlboro County	409	18.81
Myrtle Beach (city) Horry County	352	1.30
Mount Pleasant (town) Charleston County	346	0.51

Top 10 Places Sorted by Percent of Total Population
Based on all places, regardless of total population

Place	Population	%
McColl (town) Marlboro County	409	18.81
Tatum (town) Marlboro County	7	9.33
Clio (town) Marlboro County	61	8.40
Blenheim (town) Marlboro County	9	5.84
Wallace (cdp) Marlboro County	40	4.48
Williams (town) Colleton County	5	4.27
Plum Branch (town) McCormick County	3	3.66
Vance (town) Orangeburg County	6	3.53
West Union (town) Oconee County	10	3.44
Rembert (cdp) Sumter County	10	3.27

Top 10 Places Sorted by Percent of Total Population
Based on places with total population of 50,000 or more

Place	Population	%
North Charleston (city) Charleston County	1,029	1.06

Rock Hill (city) York County	653	0.99
Columbia (city) Richland County	1,141	0.88
Greenville (city) Greenville County	425	0.73
Charleston (city) Charleston County	753	0.63
Mount Pleasant (town) Charleston County	346	0.51

American Indian/Alaska Native: Not Hispanic

Top 10 Places Sorted by Population
Based on all places, regardless of total population

Place	Population	%
Columbia (city) Richland County	962	0.74
North Charleston (city) Charleston County	818	0.84
Charleston (city) Charleston County	665	0.55
Rock Hill (city) York County	595	0.90
Summerville (town) Dorchester County	441	1.02
Goose Creek (city) Berkeley County	412	1.15
McColl (town) Marlboro County	393	18.08
Greenville (city) Greenville County	334	0.57
Mount Pleasant (town) Charleston County	288	0.42
Sumter (city) Sumter County	280	0.69

Top 10 Places Sorted by Percent of Total Population
Based on all places, regardless of total population

Place	Population	%
McColl (town) Marlboro County	393	18.08
Tatum (town) Marlboro County	7	9.33
Clio (town) Marlboro County	59	8.13
Blenheim (town) Marlboro County	9	5.84
Wallace (cdp) Marlboro County	38	4.26
Plum Branch (town) McCormick County	3	3.66
Vance (town) Orangeburg County	6	3.53
Williams (town) Colleton County	4	3.42
Princeton (cdp) Laurens County	2	3.23
North (town) Orangeburg County	23	3.05

Top 10 Places Sorted by Percent of Total Population
Based on places with total population of 50,000 or more

Place	Population	%
Rock Hill (city) York County	595	0.90
North Charleston (city) Charleston County	818	0.84
Columbia (city) Richland County	962	0.74
Greenville (city) Greenville County	334	0.57
Charleston (city) Charleston County	665	0.55
Mount Pleasant (town) Charleston County	288	0.42

American Indian/Alaska Native: Hispanic

Top 10 Places Sorted by Population
Based on all places, regardless of total population

Place	Population	%
North Charleston (city) Charleston County	211	0.22
Columbia (city) Richland County	179	0.14
Sans Souci (cdp) Greenville County	109	1.39
West Columbia (city) Lexington County	94	0.63
Greenville (city) Greenville County	91	0.16
Charleston (city) Charleston County	88	0.07
Myrtle Beach (city) Horry County	79	0.29
Berea (cdp) Greenville County	70	0.49
Sumter (city) Sumter County	61	0.15
Mount Pleasant (town) Charleston County	58	0.09

Top 10 Places Sorted by Percent of Total Population
Based on all places, regardless of total population

Place	Population	%
Saxon (cdp) Spartanburg County	48	1.40
Sans Souci (cdp) Greenville County	109	1.39
West Union (town) Oconee County	4	1.37
Pelzer (town) Anderson County	1	1.12
Ridgeland (town) Jasper County	41	1.02
Arcadia (cdp) Spartanburg County	26	0.90
Southern Shops (cdp) Spartanburg County	34	0.90
Williams (town) Colleton County	1	0.85
Luray (town) Hampton County	1	0.79
Mulberry (cdp) Sumter County	4	0.76

Please refer to the Explanation of Data in the front of the book for more detailed information.

Top 10 Places Sorted by Percent of Total Population
Based on places with total population of 50,000 or more

Place	Population	%
North Charleston (city) Charleston County	211	0.22
Greenville (city) Greenville County	91	0.16
Columbia (city) Richland County	179	0.14
Mount Pleasant (town) Charleston County	58	0.09
Rock Hill (city) York County	58	0.09
Charleston (city) Charleston County	88	0.07

Top 10 Places Sorted by Percent of Total Population
Based on places with total population of 50,000 or more

Place	Population	%
Charleston (city) Charleston County	1	<0.01
Columbia (city) Richland County	1	<0.01
Greenville (city) Greenville County	0	0.00
Mount Pleasant (town) Charleston County	0	0.00
North Charleston (city) Charleston County	0	0.00
Rock Hill (city) York County	0	0.00

Top 10 Places Sorted by Percent of Total Population
Based on places with total population of 50,000 or more

Place	Population	%
Columbia (city) Richland County	1	<0.01
Rock Hill (city) York County	1	<0.01
Charleston (city) Charleston County	0	0.00
Greenville (city) Greenville County	0	0.00
Mount Pleasant (town) Charleston County	0	0.00
North Charleston (city) Charleston County	0	0.00

Alaska Native: Alaska Athabascan

Top 10 Places Sorted by Population
Based on all places, regardless of total population

Place	Population	%
Clemson (city) Pickens County	4	0.03
Summerville (town) Dorchester County	3	0.01
Ladson (cdp) Berkeley County	2	0.01
North Charleston (city) Charleston County	2	<0.01
Mayo (cdp) Spartanburg County	1	0.06
Abbeville (city) Abbeville County	1	0.02
Tega Cay (city) York County	1	0.01
Charleston (city) Charleston County	1	<0.01
Rock Hill (city) York County	1	<0.01
Aiken (city) Aiken County	0	0.00

Top 10 Places Sorted by Percent of Total Population
Based on all places, regardless of total population

Place	Population	%
Mayo (cdp) Spartanburg County	1	0.06
Clemson (city) Pickens County	4	0.03
Abbeville (city) Abbeville County	1	0.02
Summerville (town) Dorchester County	3	0.01
Ladson (cdp) Berkeley County	2	0.01
Tega Cay (city) York County	1	0.01
North Charleston (city) Charleston County	2	<0.01
Charleston (city) Charleston County	1	<0.01
Rock Hill (city) York County	1	<0.01
Aiken (city) Aiken County	0	0.00

Top 10 Places Sorted by Percent of Total Population
Based on places with total population of 50,000 or more

Place	Population	%
North Charleston (city) Charleston County	2	<0.01
Charleston (city) Charleston County	1	<0.01
Rock Hill (city) York County	1	<0.01
Columbia (city) Richland County	0	0.00
Greenville (city) Greenville County	0	0.00
Mount Pleasant (town) Charleston County	0	0.00

American Indian: Apache

Top 10 Places Sorted by Population
Based on all places, regardless of total population

Place	Population	%
Columbia (city) Richland County	19	0.01
North Charleston (city) Charleston County	7	0.01
Wade Hampton (cdp) Greenville County	6	0.03
Myrtle Beach (city) Horry County	6	0.02
Greenville (city) Greenville County	6	0.01
Summerville (town) Dorchester County	6	0.01
Charleston (city) Charleston County	6	<0.01
Hanahan (city) Berkeley County	5	0.03
Socastee (cdp) Horry County	5	0.03
Greer (city) Greenville County	5	0.02

Top 10 Places Sorted by Percent of Total Population
Based on all places, regardless of total population

Place	Population	%
Coronaca (cdp) Greenwood County	1	0.52
Catawba (cdp) York County	2	0.15
Gloverville (cdp) Aiken County	4	0.14
Elloree (town) Orangeburg County	1	0.14
Summerton (town) Clarendon County	1	0.10
Ware Shoals (town) Greenwood County	2	0.09
Elgin (town) Kershaw County	1	0.08
Oakland (cdp) Sumter County	1	0.08
Warrenville (cdp) Aiken County	1	0.08
Ridgeland (town) Jasper County	3	0.07

Top 10 Places Sorted by Percent of Total Population
Based on places with total population of 50,000 or more

Place	Population	%
Columbia (city) Richland County	19	0.01
North Charleston (city) Charleston County	7	0.01
Greenville (city) Greenville County	6	0.01
Charleston (city) Charleston County	6	<0.01
Rock Hill (city) York County	2	<0.01
Mount Pleasant (town) Charleston County	0	0.00

American Indian: Blackfeet

Top 10 Places Sorted by Population
Based on all places, regardless of total population

Place	Population	%
Columbia (city) Richland County	39	0.03
North Charleston (city) Charleston County	30	0.03
Summerville (town) Dorchester County	27	0.06
Charleston (city) Charleston County	24	0.02
Rock Hill (city) York County	18	0.03
Myrtle Beach (city) Horry County	17	0.06
Goose Creek (city) Berkeley County	17	0.05
Ladson (cdp) Berkeley County	16	0.12
Spartanburg (city) Spartanburg County	13	0.04
St. Andrews (cdp) Richland County	10	0.05

Top 10 Places Sorted by Percent of Total Population
Based on all places, regardless of total population

Place	Population	%
Reevesville (town) Dorchester County	4	2.04
Blenheim (town) Marlboro County	3	1.95
Windsor (town) Aiken County	1	0.83
Lowndesville (town) Abbeville County	1	0.78
Clio (town) Marlboro County	3	0.41
Atlantic Beach (town) Horry County	1	0.30
Startex (cdp) Spartanburg County	2	0.23
Graniteville (cdp) Aiken County	5	0.19
Varnville (town) Hampton County	4	0.19
Gloverville (cdp) Aiken County	5	0.18

Top 10 Places Sorted by Percent of Total Population
Based on places with total population of 50,000 or more

Place	Population	%
Columbia (city) Richland County	39	0.03
North Charleston (city) Charleston County	30	0.03
Rock Hill (city) York County	18	0.03
Charleston (city) Charleston County	24	0.02
Greenville (city) Greenville County	10	0.02
Mount Pleasant (town) Charleston County	5	0.01

Alaska Native: Aleut

Top 10 Places Sorted by Population
Based on all places, regardless of total population

Place	Population	%
Goose Creek (city) Berkeley County	5	0.01
Hilton Head Island (town) Beaufort County	4	0.01
Anderson (city) Anderson County	3	0.01
Ladson (cdp) Berkeley County	2	0.01
Catawba (cdp) York County	1	0.07
Ninety Six (town) Greenwood County	1	0.05
Bishopville (city) Lee County	1	0.03
Hopkins (cdp) Richland County	1	0.03
Bluffton (town) Beaufort County	1	0.01
Easley (city) Pickens County	1	0.01

Top 10 Places Sorted by Percent of Total Population
Based on all places, regardless of total population

Place	Population	%
Catawba (cdp) York County	1	0.07
Ninety Six (town) Greenwood County	1	0.05
Bishopville (city) Lee County	1	0.03
Hopkins (cdp) Richland County	1	0.03
Goose Creek (city) Berkeley County	5	0.01
Hilton Head Island (town) Beaufort County	4	0.01
Anderson (city) Anderson County	3	0.01
Ladson (cdp) Berkeley County	2	0.01
Bluffton (town) Beaufort County	1	0.01
Easley (city) Pickens County	1	0.01

American Indian: Arapaho

Top 10 Places Sorted by Population
Based on all places, regardless of total population

Place	Population	%
Privateer (cdp) Sumter County	1	0.04
Piedmont (cdp) Anderson County	1	0.02
Columbia (city) Richland County	1	<0.01
Rock Hill (city) York County	1	<0.01
Abbeville (city) Abbeville County	0	0.00
Aiken (city) Aiken County	0	0.00
Alcolu (cdp) Clarendon County	0	0.00
Allendale (town) Allendale County	0	0.00
Anderson (city) Anderson County	0	0.00
Andrews (town) Georgetown County	0	0.00

Top 10 Places Sorted by Percent of Total Population
Based on all places, regardless of total population

Place	Population	%
Privateer (cdp) Sumter County	1	0.04
Piedmont (cdp) Anderson County	1	0.02
Columbia (city) Richland County	1	<0.01
Rock Hill (city) York County	1	<0.01
Abbeville (city) Abbeville County	0	0.00
Aiken (city) Aiken County	0	0.00
Alcolu (cdp) Clarendon County	0	0.00
Allendale (town) Allendale County	0	0.00
Anderson (city) Anderson County	0	0.00
Andrews (town) Georgetown County	0	0.00

American Indian: Canadian/French American Indian

Top 10 Places Sorted by Population
Based on all places, regardless of total population

Place	Population	%
Forestbrook (cdp) Horry County	4	0.09
Fountain Inn (city) Greenville County	4	0.05
Summerville (town) Dorchester County	4	0.01
Charleston (city) Charleston County	4	<0.01
Wellford (city) Spartanburg County	3	0.13
Goose Creek (city) Berkeley County	3	0.01
Mauldin (city) Greenville County	3	0.01
Anderson (city) Anderson County	2	0.01
Socastee (cdp) Horry County	2	0.01
Mount Pleasant (town) Charleston County	2	<0.01

Top 10 Places Sorted by Percent of Total Population
Based on all places, regardless of total population

Place	Population	%
Clarks Hill (cdp) McCormick County	1	0.26
Wellford (city) Spartanburg County	3	0.13
Forestbrook (cdp) Horry County	4	0.09
Fountain Inn (city) Greenville County	4	0.05
Pageland (town) Chesterfield County	1	0.04
Hardeeville (city) Jasper County	1	0.03
Lakewood (cdp) Sumter County	1	0.03
Surfside Beach (town) Horry County	1	0.03
Piedmont (cdp) Anderson County	1	0.02
Walhalla (city) Oconee County	1	0.02

Top 10 Places Sorted by Percent of Total Population
Based on places with total population of 50,000 or more

Place	Population	%
Charleston (city) Charleston County	4	<0.01
Mount Pleasant (town) Charleston County	2	<0.01
Columbia (city) Richland County	1	<0.01
Greenville (city) Greenville County	0	0.00
North Charleston (city) Charleston County	0	0.00
Rock Hill (city) York County	0	0.00

American Indian: Central American Indian

Top 10 Places Sorted by Population
Based on all places, regardless of total population

Place	Population	%
Hardeeville (city) Jasper County	11	0.37
Sans Souci (cdp) Greenville County	11	0.14
Columbia (city) Richland County	8	0.01
Berea (cdp) Greenville County	7	0.05
Charleston (city) Charleston County	7	0.01
Goose Creek (city) Berkeley County	6	0.02
Sumter (city) Sumter County	6	0.01
Laurel Bay (cdp) Beaufort County	4	0.07
Parker (cdp) Greenville County	4	0.03
Myrtle Beach (city) Horry County	4	0.01

Top 10 Places Sorted by Percent of Total Population
Based on all places, regardless of total population

Place	Population	%
Smoaks (town) Colleton County	1	0.79
Hardeeville (city) Jasper County	11	0.37
Sans Souci (cdp) Greenville County	11	0.14
Laurel Bay (cdp) Beaufort County	4	0.07
City View (cdp) Greenville County	1	0.07
Berea (cdp) Greenville County	7	0.05
Blythewood (town) Richland County	1	0.05
Parker (cdp) Greenville County	4	0.03
Woodfield (cdp) Richland County	3	0.03
Bamberg (town) Bamberg County	1	0.03

Top 10 Places Sorted by Percent of Total Population
Based on places with total population of 50,000 or more

Place	Population	%
Columbia (city) Richland County	8	0.01
Charleston (city) Charleston County	7	0.01
North Charleston (city) Charleston County	3	<0.01
Rock Hill (city) York County	2	<0.01
Mount Pleasant (town) Charleston County	1	<0.01
Greenville (city) Greenville County	0	0.00

American Indian: Cherokee

Top 10 Places Sorted by Population
Based on all places, regardless of total population

Place	Population	%
Columbia (city) Richland County	256	0.20
North Charleston (city) Charleston County	246	0.25
Charleston (city) Charleston County	199	0.17
Goose Creek (city) Berkeley County	126	0.35
Summerville (town) Dorchester County	121	0.28
Rock Hill (city) York County	117	0.18
Greenville (city) Greenville County	113	0.19
Myrtle Beach (city) Horry County	105	0.39
Mount Pleasant (town) Charleston County	93	0.14
Spartanburg (city) Spartanburg County	75	0.20

Top 10 Places Sorted by Percent of Total Population
Based on all places, regardless of total population

Place	Population	%
Plum Branch (town) McCormick County	3	3.66
Boykin (cdp) Kershaw County	3	3.00
McColl (town) Marlboro County	59	2.71
Tatum (town) Marlboro County	2	2.67
Blenheim (town) Marlboro County	4	2.60
Cope (town) Orangeburg County	2	2.60
Mount Croghan (town) Chesterfield County	5	2.56
Rembert (cdp) Sumter County	5	1.63
Princeton (cdp) Laurens County	1	1.61
Olar (town) Bamberg County	4	1.56

Top 10 Places Sorted by Percent of Total Population
Based on places with total population of 50,000 or more

Place	Population	%
North Charleston (city) Charleston County	246	0.25
Columbia (city) Richland County	256	0.20
Greenville (city) Greenville County	113	0.19
Rock Hill (city) York County	117	0.18
Charleston (city) Charleston County	199	0.17
Mount Pleasant (town) Charleston County	93	0.14

American Indian: Cheyenne

Top 10 Places Sorted by Population
Based on all places, regardless of total population

Place	Population	%
Columbia (city) Richland County	5	<0.01
Judson (cdp) Greenville County	4	0.20
Saxon (cdp) Spartanburg County	2	0.06
Seven Oaks (cdp) Lexington County	2	0.01
Langley (cdp) Aiken County	1	0.07
McColl (town) Marlboro County	1	0.05
Darlington (city) Darlington County	1	0.02
Conway (city) Horry County	1	0.01
Easley (city) Pickens County	1	0.01
Five Forks (cdp) Greenville County	1	0.01

Top 10 Places Sorted by Percent of Total Population
Based on all places, regardless of total population

Place	Population	%
Judson (cdp) Greenville County	4	0.20
Langley (cdp) Aiken County	1	0.07
Saxon (cdp) Spartanburg County	2	0.06
McColl (town) Marlboro County	1	0.05
Darlington (city) Darlington County	1	0.02
Seven Oaks (cdp) Lexington County	2	0.01
Conway (city) Horry County	1	0.01
Easley (city) Pickens County	1	0.01
Five Forks (cdp) Greenville County	1	0.01
Gaffney (city) Cherokee County	1	0.01

Top 10 Places Sorted by Percent of Total Population
Based on places with total population of 50,000 or more

Place	Population	%
Columbia (city) Richland County	5	<0.01
Charleston (city) Charleston County	1	<0.01
Rock Hill (city) York County	1	<0.01
Greenville (city) Greenville County	0	0.00
Mount Pleasant (town) Charleston County	0	0.00
North Charleston (city) Charleston County	0	0.00

American Indian: Chickasaw

Top 10 Places Sorted by Population
Based on all places, regardless of total population

Place	Population	%
Orangeburg (city) Orangeburg County	5	0.04
Charleston (city) Charleston County	5	<0.01
North Augusta (city) Aiken County	4	0.02
Simpsonville (city) Greenville County	4	0.02
Summerville (town) Dorchester County	4	0.01
Columbia (city) Richland County	4	<0.01
Lake City (city) Florence County	3	0.04
Ladson (cdp) Berkeley County	3	0.02
Red Hill (cdp) Horry County	3	0.02
Spartanburg (city) Spartanburg County	3	0.01

Top 10 Places Sorted by Percent of Total Population
Based on all places, regardless of total population

Place	Population	%
Pinopolis (cdp) Berkeley County	2	0.21
Clio (town) Marlboro County	1	0.14
Graniteville (cdp) Aiken County	2	0.08
Gloverville (cdp) Aiken County	2	0.07
Johnsonville (city) Florence County	1	0.07
Mayo (cdp) Spartanburg County	1	0.06
Bonneau Beach (cdp) Berkeley County	1	0.05
Slater-Marietta (cdp) Greenville County	1	0.05
Orangeburg (city) Orangeburg County	5	0.04
Lake City (city) Florence County	3	0.04

Top 10 Places Sorted by Percent of Total Population
Based on places with total population of 50,000 or more

Place	Population	%
Charleston (city) Charleston County	5	<0.01
Columbia (city) Richland County	4	<0.01
Greenville (city) Greenville County	2	<0.01
Mount Pleasant (town) Charleston County	2	<0.01
North Charleston (city) Charleston County	0	0.00
Rock Hill (city) York County	0	0.00

American Indian: Chippewa

Top 10 Places Sorted by Population
Based on all places, regardless of total population

Place	Population	%
Columbia (city) Richland County	10	0.01
Walterboro (city) Colleton County	9	0.17
Mount Pleasant (town) Charleston County	9	0.01
Aiken (city) Aiken County	8	0.03
Florence (city) Florence County	7	0.02
Anderson (city) Anderson County	6	0.02
Charleston (city) Charleston County	6	<0.01
Goose Creek (city) Berkeley County	5	0.01
Clover (town) York County	4	0.08
Centerville (cdp) Anderson County	4	0.06

Top 10 Places Sorted by Percent of Total Population
Based on all places, regardless of total population

Place	Population	%
Luray (town) Hampton County	1	0.79
Gilbert (town) Lexington County	2	0.35
Rowesville (town) Orangeburg County	1	0.33
Lake Secession (cdp) Abbeville County	3	0.28
Walterboro (city) Colleton County	9	0.17
Cottageville (town) Colleton County	1	0.13
India Hook (cdp) York County	3	0.09
McColl (town) Marlboro County	2	0.09
Shell Point (cdp) Beaufort County	2	0.09
Clover (town) York County	4	0.08

Top 10 Places Sorted by Percent of Total Population
Based on places with total population of 50,000 or more

Place	Population	%
Columbia (city) Richland County	10	0.01
Mount Pleasant (town) Charleston County	9	0.01
Charleston (city) Charleston County	6	<0.01
North Charleston (city) Charleston County	4	<0.01
Greenville (city) Greenville County	1	<0.01
Rock Hill (city) York County	1	<0.01

American Indian: Choctaw

Top 10 Places Sorted by Population
Based on all places, regardless of total population

Place	Population	%
Columbia (city) Richland County	34	0.03
Summerville (town) Dorchester County	12	0.03
Charleston (city) Charleston County	12	0.01
Greenville (city) Greenville County	11	0.02
Mount Pleasant (town) Charleston County	10	0.01
Fort Mill (town) York County	9	0.08
Goose Creek (city) Berkeley County	9	0.03
Homeland Park (cdp) Anderson County	8	0.13
Socastee (cdp) Horry County	8	0.04
Rock Hill (city) York County	7	0.01

Top 10 Places Sorted by Percent of Total Population
Based on all places, regardless of total population

Place	Population	%
Warrenville (cdp) Aiken County	6	0.49
Neeses (town) Orangeburg County	1	0.27
South Congaree (town) Lexington County	6	0.26
Aynor (town) Horry County	1	0.18
Ehrhardt (town) Bamberg County	1	0.18
Kershaw (town) Lancaster County	3	0.18
Golden Grove (cdp) Greenville County	4	0.16
Harleyville (town) Dorchester County	1	0.15
Homeland Park (cdp) Anderson County	8	0.13
Duncan (town) Spartanburg County	4	0.13

Top 10 Places Sorted by Percent of Total Population
Based on places with total population of 50,000 or more

Place	Population	%
Columbia (city) Richland County	34	0.03
Greenville (city) Greenville County	11	0.02
Charleston (city) Charleston County	12	0.01
Mount Pleasant (town) Charleston County	10	0.01
Rock Hill (city) York County	7	0.01
North Charleston (city) Charleston County	3	<0.01

American Indian: Colville

Top 10 Places Sorted by Population
Based on all places, regardless of total population

Place	Population	%
Bluffton (town) Beaufort County	1	0.01
Abbeville (city) Abbeville County	0	0.00
Aiken (city) Aiken County	0	0.00
Alcolu (cdp) Clarendon County	0	0.00
Allendale (town) Allendale County	0	0.00
Anderson (city) Anderson County	0	0.00
Andrews (town) Georgetown County	0	0.00
Antreville (cdp) Abbeville County	0	0.00
Arcadia (cdp) Spartanburg County	0	0.00
Arcadia Lakes (town) Richland County	0	0.00

Top 10 Places Sorted by Percent of Total Population
Based on all places, regardless of total population

Place	Population	%
Bluffton (town) Beaufort County	1	0.01
Abbeville (city) Abbeville County	0	0.00
Aiken (city) Aiken County	0	0.00
Alcolu (cdp) Clarendon County	0	0.00
Allendale (town) Allendale County	0	0.00
Anderson (city) Anderson County	0	0.00
Andrews (town) Georgetown County	0	0.00
Antreville (cdp) Abbeville County	0	0.00
Arcadia (cdp) Spartanburg County	0	0.00
Arcadia Lakes (town) Richland County	0	0.00

Top 10 Places Sorted by Percent of Total Population
Based on places with total population of 50,000 or more

Place	Population	%
Charleston (city) Charleston County	0	0.00
Columbia (city) Richland County	0	0.00
Greenville (city) Greenville County	0	0.00
Mount Pleasant (town) Charleston County	0	0.00
North Charleston (city) Charleston County	0	0.00
Rock Hill (city) York County	0	0.00

American Indian: Comanche

Top 10 Places Sorted by Population
Based on all places, regardless of total population

Place	Population	%
North Charleston (city) Charleston County	7	0.01
Summerville (town) Dorchester County	6	0.01
Goose Creek (city) Berkeley County	5	0.01
Port Royal (town) Beaufort County	3	0.03
Anderson (city) Anderson County	3	0.01
Hilton Head Island (town) Beaufort County	3	0.01
Mount Pleasant (town) Charleston County	3	<0.01
New Ellenton (town) Aiken County	2	0.10
Greer (city) Greenville County	2	0.01
North Augusta (city) Aiken County	2	0.01

Top 10 Places Sorted by Percent of Total Population
Based on all places, regardless of total population

Place	Population	%
Pelzer (town) Anderson County	1	1.12
Cottageville (town) Colleton County	1	0.13
Pinopolis (cdp) Berkeley County	1	0.11
New Ellenton (town) Aiken County	2	0.10
Port Royal (town) Beaufort County	3	0.03
Dunean (cdp) Greenville County	1	0.03
Southern Shops (cdp) Spartanburg County	1	0.03
Williamston (town) Anderson County	1	0.03
Clover (town) York County	1	0.02
North Charleston (city) Charleston County	7	0.01

Top 10 Places Sorted by Percent of Total Population
Based on places with total population of 50,000 or more

Place	Population	%
North Charleston (city) Charleston County	7	0.01
Mount Pleasant (town) Charleston County	3	<0.01
Greenville (city) Greenville County	1	<0.01
Rock Hill (city) York County	1	<0.01
Charleston (city) Charleston County	0	0.00
Columbia (city) Richland County	0	0.00

American Indian: Cree

Top 10 Places Sorted by Population
Based on all places, regardless of total population

Place	Population	%
Shell Point (cdp) Beaufort County	4	0.17
Little River (cdp) Horry County	3	0.03
Hanahan (city) Berkeley County	3	0.02
Charleston (city) Charleston County	3	<0.01
North Charleston (city) Charleston County	2	<0.01
Pinopolis (cdp) Berkeley County	1	0.11
Stateburg (cdp) Sumter County	1	0.07
Utica (cdp) Oconee County	1	0.07
Wellford (city) Spartanburg County	1	0.04
Forestbrook (cdp) Horry County	1	0.02

Top 10 Places Sorted by Percent of Total Population
Based on all places, regardless of total population

Place	Population	%
Shell Point (cdp) Beaufort County	4	0.17
Pinopolis (cdp) Berkeley County	1	0.11
Stateburg (cdp) Sumter County	1	0.07
Utica (cdp) Oconee County	1	0.07
Wellford (city) Spartanburg County	1	0.04
Little River (cdp) Horry County	3	0.03
Hanahan (city) Berkeley County	3	0.02
Forestbrook (cdp) Horry County	1	0.02
Bluffton (town) Beaufort County	1	0.01
Lancaster (city) Lancaster County	1	0.01

Top 10 Places Sorted by Percent of Total Population
Based on places with total population of 50,000 or more

Place	Population	%
Charleston (city) Charleston County	3	<0.01
North Charleston (city) Charleston County	2	<0.01
Greenville (city) Greenville County	1	<0.01
Columbia (city) Richland County	0	0.00
Mount Pleasant (town) Charleston County	0	0.00
Rock Hill (city) York County	0	0.00

American Indian: Creek

Top 10 Places Sorted by Population
Based on all places, regardless of total population

Place	Population	%
North Charleston (city) Charleston County	19	0.02
Rock Hill (city) York County	14	0.02
Charleston (city) Charleston County	11	0.01
North Augusta (city) Aiken County	9	0.04
Goose Creek (city) Berkeley County	7	0.02
Branchville (town) Orangeburg County	6	0.59
Forestbrook (cdp) Horry County	6	0.13
Powdersville (cdp) Anderson County	6	0.08
Anderson (city) Anderson County	6	0.02
Mount Pleasant (town) Charleston County	6	0.01

Top 10 Places Sorted by Percent of Total Population
Based on all places, regardless of total population

Place	Population	%
Branchville (town) Orangeburg County	6	0.59
Chesnee (city) Spartanburg County	3	0.35
Scranton (town) Florence County	3	0.32
Wedgefield (cdp) Sumter County	3	0.19
McColl (town) Marlboro County	4	0.18
Holly Hill (town) Orangeburg County	2	0.16
Forestbrook (cdp) Horry County	6	0.13
Walhalla (city) Oconee County	5	0.12
Northlake (cdp) Anderson County	4	0.11
Burnet (town) Aiken County	3	0.11

Top 10 Places Sorted by Percent of Total Population
Based on places with total population of 50,000 or more

Place	Population	%
North Charleston (city) Charleston County	19	0.02
Rock Hill (city) York County	14	0.02
Charleston (city) Charleston County	11	0.01
Mount Pleasant (town) Charleston County	6	0.01
Columbia (city) Richland County	3	<0.01
Greenville (city) Greenville County	1	<0.01

American Indian: Crow

Top 10 Places Sorted by Population
Based on all places, regardless of total population

Place	Population	%
North Charleston (city) Charleston County	5	0.01
Columbia (city) Richland County	5	<0.01
Wellford (city) Spartanburg County	3	0.13
Myrtle Beach (city) Horry County	3	0.01
Kershaw (town) Lancaster County	2	0.11
Privateer (cdp) Sumter County	2	0.09
Clover (town) York County	2	0.04
Charleston (city) Charleston County	2	<0.01
Joanna (cdp) Laurens County	1	0.06
Pageland (town) Chesterfield County	1	0.04

Top 10 Places Sorted by Percent of Total Population
Based on all places, regardless of total population

Place	Population	%
Wellford (city) Spartanburg County	3	0.13
Kershaw (town) Lancaster County	2	0.11
Privateer (cdp) Sumter County	2	0.09
Joanna (cdp) Laurens County	1	0.06
Clover (town) York County	2	0.04
Pageland (town) Chesterfield County	1	0.04
North Charleston (city) Charleston County	5	0.01
Myrtle Beach (city) Horry County	3	0.01
Cayce (city) Lexington County	1	0.01
Clinton (city) Laurens County	1	0.01

Top 10 Places Sorted by Percent of Total Population
Based on places with total population of 50,000 or more

Place	Population	%
North Charleston (city) Charleston County	5	0.01
Columbia (city) Richland County	5	<0.01
Charleston (city) Charleston County	2	<0.01
Greenville (city) Greenville County	0	0.00
Mount Pleasant (town) Charleston County	0	0.00
Rock Hill (city) York County	0	0.00

American Indian: Delaware

Top 10 Places Sorted by Population
Based on all places, regardless of total population

Place	Population	%
Arcadia (cdp) Spartanburg County	4	0.15
Simpsonville (city) Greenville County	4	0.02
Goose Creek (city) Berkeley County	4	0.01
Florence (city) Florence County	3	0.01
Summerville (town) Dorchester County	3	0.01
Port Royal (town) Beaufort County	2	0.02
Ladson (cdp) Berkeley County	2	0.01
Seven Oaks (cdp) Lexington County	2	0.01
Columbia (city) Richland County	2	<0.01
Mount Pleasant (town) Charleston County	2	<0.01

Top 10 Places Sorted by Percent of Total Population
Based on all places, regardless of total population

Place	Population	%
Aynor (town) Horry County	1	0.18
Arcadia (cdp) Spartanburg County	4	0.15
Calhoun Falls (town) Abbeville County	1	0.05
Bishopville (city) Lee County	1	0.03
Simpsonville (city) Greenville County	4	0.02
Port Royal (town) Beaufort County	2	0.02
Homeland Park (cdp) Anderson County	1	0.02
Piedmont (cdp) Anderson County	1	0.02
Goose Creek (city) Berkeley County	4	0.01
Florence (city) Florence County	3	0.01

Top 10 Places Sorted by Percent of Total Population
Based on places with total population of 50,000 or more

Place	Population	%
Columbia (city) Richland County	2	<0.01
Mount Pleasant (town) Charleston County	2	<0.01
Greenville (city) Greenville County	1	<0.01
Charleston (city) Charleston County	0	0.00
North Charleston (city) Charleston County	0	0.00
Rock Hill (city) York County	0	0.00

American Indian: Hopi

Top 10 Places Sorted by Population
Based on all places, regardless of total population

Place	Population	%
Laurel Bay (cdp) Beaufort County	2	0.03
Williston (town) Barnwell County	1	0.03
Boiling Springs (cdp) Spartanburg County	1	0.01
Lancaster (city) Lancaster County	1	0.01
Columbia (city) Richland County	1	<0.01
Mauldin (city) Greenville County	1	<0.01
North Charleston (city) Charleston County	1	<0.01
Abbeville (city) Abbeville County	0	0.00
Aiken (city) Aiken County	0	0.00
Alcolu (cdp) Clarendon County	0	0.00

Top 10 Places Sorted by Percent of Total Population
Based on all places, regardless of total population

Place	Population	%
Laurel Bay (cdp) Beaufort County	2	0.03
Williston (town) Barnwell County	1	0.03
Boiling Springs (cdp) Spartanburg County	1	0.01
Lancaster (city) Lancaster County	1	0.01
Columbia (city) Richland County	1	<0.01
Mauldin (city) Greenville County	1	<0.01
North Charleston (city) Charleston County	1	<0.01
Abbeville (city) Abbeville County	0	0.00
Aiken (city) Aiken County	0	0.00
Alcolu (cdp) Clarendon County	0	0.00

Top 10 Places Sorted by Percent of Total Population
Based on places with total population of 50,000 or more

Place	Population	%
Columbia (city) Richland County	1	<0.01
North Charleston (city) Charleston County	1	<0.01
Charleston (city) Charleston County	0	0.00
Greenville (city) Greenville County	0	0.00
Mount Pleasant (town) Charleston County	0	0.00
Rock Hill (city) York County	0	0.00

American Indian: Houma

Top 10 Places Sorted by Population
Based on all places, regardless of total population

Place	Population	%
Goose Creek (city) Berkeley County	3	0.01
Summerville (town) Dorchester County	2	<0.01
Port Royal (town) Beaufort County	1	0.01
Sangaree (cdp) Berkeley County	1	0.01
Columbia (city) Richland County	1	<0.01
North Charleston (city) Charleston County	1	<0.01
Abbeville (city) Abbeville County	0	0.00
Aiken (city) Aiken County	0	0.00
Alcolu (cdp) Clarendon County	0	0.00
Allendale (town) Allendale County	0	0.00

Top 10 Places Sorted by Percent of Total Population
Based on all places, regardless of total population

Place	Population	%
Goose Creek (city) Berkeley County	3	0.01
Port Royal (town) Beaufort County	1	0.01
Sangaree (cdp) Berkeley County	1	0.01
Summerville (town) Dorchester County	2	<0.01
Columbia (city) Richland County	1	<0.01
North Charleston (city) Charleston County	1	<0.01
Abbeville (city) Abbeville County	0	0.00
Aiken (city) Aiken County	0	0.00
Alcolu (cdp) Clarendon County	0	0.00
Allendale (town) Allendale County	0	0.00

Alaska Native: Inupiat (Eskimo)

Top 10 Places Sorted by Population
Based on all places, regardless of total population

Place	Population	%
Charleston (city) Charleston County	7	0.01
Columbia (city) Richland County	5	<0.01
Lake Wylie (cdp) York County	4	0.05
Williston (town) Barnwell County	3	0.10
North Charleston (city) Charleston County	3	<0.01
Gaffney (city) Cherokee County	2	0.02
Lexington (town) Lexington County	2	0.01
Langley (cdp) Aiken County	1	0.07
Joanna (cdp) Laurens County	1	0.06
Dunean (cdp) Greenville County	1	0.03

Top 10 Places Sorted by Percent of Total Population
Based on all places, regardless of total population

Place	Population	%
Williston (town) Barnwell County	3	0.10
Langley (cdp) Aiken County	1	0.07
Joanna (cdp) Laurens County	1	0.06
Lake Wylie (cdp) York County	4	0.05
Dunean (cdp) Greenville County	1	0.03
Gaffney (city) Cherokee County	2	0.02
Charleston (city) Charleston County	7	0.01
Lexington (town) Lexington County	2	0.01
Little River (cdp) Horry County	1	0.01
Parker (cdp) Greenville County	1	0.01

Top 10 Places Sorted by Percent of Total Population
Based on places with total population of 50,000 or more

Place	Population	%
Charleston (city) Charleston County	7	0.01
Columbia (city) Richland County	5	<0.01
North Charleston (city) Charleston County	3	<0.01
Rock Hill (city) York County	1	<0.01
Greenville (city) Greenville County	0	0.00
Mount Pleasant (town) Charleston County	0	0.00

American Indian: Iroquois

Top 10 Places Sorted by Population
Based on all places, regardless of total population

Place	Population	%
Myrtle Beach (city) Horry County	23	0.08
Summerville (town) Dorchester County	14	0.03
North Charleston (city) Charleston County	14	0.01
Columbia (city) Richland County	11	0.01
North Myrtle Beach (city) Horry County	10	0.07
Goose Creek (city) Berkeley County	10	0.03
Charleston (city) Charleston County	10	0.01
Rock Hill (city) York County	8	0.01
Bluffton (town) Beaufort County	7	0.06
Ladson (cdp) Berkeley County	7	0.05

Top 10 Places Sorted by Percent of Total Population
Based on all places, regardless of total population

Place	Population	%
Pawleys Island (town) Georgetown County	1	0.97
Clio (town) Marlboro County	2	0.28
Elgin (town) Kershaw County	3	0.23
McClellanville (town) Charleston County	1	0.20
Johnsonville (city) Florence County	2	0.14
Mullins (city) Marion County	6	0.13
North (town) Orangeburg County	1	0.13
Blacksburg (town) Cherokee County	2	0.11
Lesslie (cdp) York County	3	0.10
Burton (cdp) Beaufort County	6	0.09

Top 10 Places Sorted by Percent of Total Population
Based on places with total population of 50,000 or more

Place	Population	%
North Charleston (city) Charleston County	14	0.01
Columbia (city) Richland County	11	0.01
Charleston (city) Charleston County	10	0.01
Rock Hill (city) York County	8	0.01
Mount Pleasant (town) Charleston County	7	0.01
Greenville (city) Greenville County	4	0.01

American Indian: Kiowa

Top 10 Places Sorted by Population
Based on all places, regardless of total population

Place	Population	%
Charleston (city) Charleston County	4	<0.01
Ninety Six (town) Greenwood County	3	0.15
Slater-Marietta (cdp) Greenville County	1	0.05
Walterboro (city) Colleton County	1	0.02
Hanahan (city) Berkeley County	1	0.01
Lake Wylie (cdp) York County	1	0.01
Port Royal (town) Beaufort County	1	0.01
Goose Creek (city) Berkeley County	1	<0.01
Greenville (city) Greenville County	1	<0.01
Hilton Head Island (town) Beaufort County	1	<0.01

Top 10 Places Sorted by Percent of Total Population
Based on all places, regardless of total population

Place	Population	%
Ninety Six (town) Greenwood County	3	0.15
Slater-Marietta (cdp) Greenville County	1	0.05
Walterboro (city) Colleton County	1	0.02
Hanahan (city) Berkeley County	1	0.01
Lake Wylie (cdp) York County	1	0.01
Port Royal (town) Beaufort County	1	0.01
Charleston (city) Charleston County	4	<0.01
Goose Creek (city) Berkeley County	1	<0.01
Greenville (city) Greenville County	1	<0.01
Hilton Head Island (town) Beaufort County	1	<0.01

Top 10 Places Sorted by Percent of Total Population
Based on places with total population of 50,000 or more

Place	Population	%
Charleston (city) Charleston County	4	<0.01
Greenville (city) Greenville County	1	<0.01
Columbia (city) Richland County	0	0.00
Mount Pleasant (town) Charleston County	0	0.00
North Charleston (city) Charleston County	0	0.00
Rock Hill (city) York County	0	0.00

American Indian: Lumbee

Top 10 Places Sorted by Population
Based on all places, regardless of total population

Place	Population	%
McColl (town) Marlboro County	56	2.58
North Charleston (city) Charleston County	38	0.04
Dillon (city) Dillon County	30	0.44
Florence (city) Florence County	29	0.08
Sumter (city) Sumter County	28	0.07
Columbia (city) Richland County	26	0.02
Clio (town) Marlboro County	25	3.44
Bennettsville (city) Marlboro County	24	0.26
Red Hill (cdp) Horry County	22	0.17
Goose Creek (city) Berkeley County	19	0.05

Top 10 Places Sorted by Percent of Total Population
Based on all places, regardless of total population

Place	Population	%
Clio (town) Marlboro County	25	3.44
McColl (town) Marlboro County	56	2.58
Tatum (town) Marlboro County	1	1.33
Patrick (town) Chesterfield County	4	1.14
Wallace (cdp) Marlboro County	8	0.90
Bethune (town) Kershaw County	3	0.90
Hemingway (town) Williamsburg County	4	0.87
Blenheim (town) Marlboro County	1	0.65
Wagener (town) Aiken County	4	0.50
Dillon (city) Dillon County	30	0.44

Top 10 Places Sorted by Percent of Total Population
Based on places with total population of 50,000 or more

Place	Population	%
North Charleston (city) Charleston County	38	0.04
Rock Hill (city) York County	17	0.03
Columbia (city) Richland County	26	0.02
Charleston (city) Charleston County	19	0.02
Mount Pleasant (town) Charleston County	14	0.02
Greenville (city) Greenville County	5	0.01

American Indian: Menominee

Top 10 Places Sorted by Population
Based on all places, regardless of total population

Place	Population	%
Port Royal (town) Beaufort County	2	0.02
Red Hill (cdp) Horry County	2	0.02
Warrenville (cdp) Aiken County	1	0.08
Duncan (town) Spartanburg County	1	0.03
Lakewood (cdp) Sumter County	1	0.03
North Charleston (city) Charleston County	1	<0.01
Abbeville (city) Abbeville County	0	0.00
Aiken (city) Aiken County	0	0.00
Alcolu (cdp) Clarendon County	0	0.00
Allendale (town) Allendale County	0	0.00

Top 10 Places Sorted by Percent of Total Population
Based on all places, regardless of total population

Place	Population	%
Warrenville (cdp) Aiken County	1	0.08
Duncan (town) Spartanburg County	1	0.03
Lakewood (cdp) Sumter County	1	0.03
Port Royal (town) Beaufort County	2	0.02
Red Hill (cdp) Horry County	2	0.02
North Charleston (city) Charleston County	1	<0.01
Abbeville (city) Abbeville County	0	0.00
Aiken (city) Aiken County	0	0.00
Alcolu (cdp) Clarendon County	0	0.00
Allendale (town) Allendale County	0	0.00

Top 10 Places Sorted by Percent of Total Population
Based on places with total population of 50,000 or more

Place	Population	%
North Charleston (city) Charleston County	1	<0.01
Charleston (city) Charleston County	0	0.00
Columbia (city) Richland County	0	0.00
Greenville (city) Greenville County	0	0.00
Mount Pleasant (town) Charleston County	0	0.00
Rock Hill (city) York County	0	0.00

American Indian: Mexican American Indian

Top 10 Places Sorted by Population
Based on all places, regardless of total population

Place	Population	%
Sans Souci (cdp) Greenville County	102	1.30
North Charleston (city) Charleston County	54	0.06
West Columbia (city) Lexington County	49	0.33
Greenville (city) Greenville County	47	0.08
Saxon (cdp) Spartanburg County	36	1.05
Ridgeland (town) Jasper County	34	0.84
Gantt (cdp) Greenville County	29	0.20
Columbia (city) Richland County	25	0.02
Greenwood (city) Greenwood County	21	0.09
Arcadia (cdp) Spartanburg County	20	0.76

Top 10 Places Sorted by Percent of Total Population
Based on all places, regardless of total population

Place	Population	%
Princeton (cdp) Laurens County	1	1.61
Sans Souci (cdp) Greenville County	102	1.30
Saxon (cdp) Spartanburg County	36	1.05
Ridgeland (town) Jasper County	34	0.84
Arcadia (cdp) Spartanburg County	20	0.76
Mulberry (cdp) Sumter County	4	0.76
City View (cdp) Greenville County	7	0.52
Southern Shops (cdp) Spartanburg County	19	0.50
West Columbia (city) Lexington County	49	0.33
Welcome (cdp) Greenville County	20	0.30

Top 10 Places Sorted by Percent of Total Population
Based on places with total population of 50,000 or more

Place	Population	%
Greenville (city) Greenville County	47	0.08
North Charleston (city) Charleston County	54	0.06
Mount Pleasant (town) Charleston County	19	0.03
Columbia (city) Richland County	25	0.02
Rock Hill (city) York County	15	0.02
Charleston (city) Charleston County	14	0.01

American Indian: Navajo

Top 10 Places Sorted by Population
Based on all places, regardless of total population

Place	Population	%
Columbia (city) Richland County	20	0.02
Port Royal (town) Beaufort County	11	0.10
Mount Pleasant (town) Charleston County	8	0.01
Fountain Inn (city) Greenville County	7	0.09
Summerville (town) Dorchester County	6	0.01
Berea (cdp) Greenville County	5	0.03
North Charleston (city) Charleston County	5	0.01
Arial (cdp) Pickens County	4	0.16
Fort Mill (town) York County	4	0.04
St. Andrews (cdp) Richland County	4	0.02

Top 10 Places Sorted by Percent of Total Population
Based on all places, regardless of total population

Place	Population	%
Salley (town) Aiken County	1	0.25
Arial (cdp) Pickens County	4	0.16
Lake View (town) Dillon County	1	0.12
Norris (town) Pickens County	1	0.12
Burnet (town) Aiken County	3	0.11
Port Royal (town) Beaufort County	11	0.10
Fountain Inn (city) Greenville County	7	0.09
McColl (town) Marlboro County	2	0.09
Edisto (cdp) Orangeburg County	2	0.08
Clearwater (cdp) Aiken County	3	0.07

Top 10 Places Sorted by Percent of Total Population
Based on places with total population of 50,000 or more

Place	Population	%
Columbia (city) Richland County	20	0.02
Mount Pleasant (town) Charleston County	8	0.01
North Charleston (city) Charleston County	5	0.01
Charleston (city) Charleston County	2	<0.01
Greenville (city) Greenville County	2	<0.01
Rock Hill (city) York County	2	<0.01

American Indian: Osage

Top 10 Places Sorted by Population
Based on all places, regardless of total population

Place	Population	%
Hanahan (city) Berkeley County	4	0.02
Rock Hill (city) York County	4	0.01
Sangaree (cdp) Berkeley County	3	0.04
Columbia (city) Richland County	3	<0.01
Goose Creek (city) Berkeley County	2	0.01
Mount Pleasant (town) Charleston County	2	<0.01
North Charleston (city) Charleston County	2	<0.01
Salley (town) Aiken County	1	0.25
Bluffton (town) Beaufort County	1	0.01
Ladson (cdp) Berkeley County	1	0.01

Top 10 Places Sorted by Percent of Total Population
Based on all places, regardless of total population

Place	Population	%
Salley (town) Aiken County	1	0.25
Sangaree (cdp) Berkeley County	3	0.04
Hanahan (city) Berkeley County	4	0.02
Rock Hill (city) York County	4	0.01
Goose Creek (city) Berkeley County	2	0.01
Bluffton (town) Beaufort County	1	0.01
Ladson (cdp) Berkeley County	1	0.01
North Myrtle Beach (city) Horry County	1	0.01
Columbia (city) Richland County	3	<0.01
Mount Pleasant (town) Charleston County	2	<0.01

Top 10 Places Sorted by Percent of Total Population
Based on places with total population of 50,000 or more

Place	Population	%
Rock Hill (city) York County	4	0.01
Columbia (city) Richland County	3	<0.01
Mount Pleasant (town) Charleston County	2	<0.01
North Charleston (city) Charleston County	2	<0.01
Charleston (city) Charleston County	1	<0.01
Greenville (city) Greenville County	0	0.00

American Indian: Ottawa

Top 10 Places Sorted by Population
Based on all places, regardless of total population

Place	Population	%
Bluffton (town) Beaufort County	4	0.03
Lyman (town) Spartanburg County	1	0.03
Five Forks (cdp) Greenville County	1	0.01
Anderson (city) Anderson County	1	<0.01
Columbia (city) Richland County	1	<0.01
Summerville (town) Dorchester County	1	<0.01
Abbeville (city) Abbeville County	0	0.00
Aiken (city) Aiken County	0	0.00
Alcolu (cdp) Clarendon County	0	0.00
Allendale (town) Allendale County	0	0.00

Top 10 Places Sorted by Percent of Total Population
Based on all places, regardless of total population

Place	Population	%
Bluffton (town) Beaufort County	4	0.03
Lyman (town) Spartanburg County	1	0.03
Five Forks (cdp) Greenville County	1	0.01
Anderson (city) Anderson County	1	<0.01
Columbia (city) Richland County	1	<0.01
Summerville (town) Dorchester County	1	<0.01
Abbeville (city) Abbeville County	0	0.00
Aiken (city) Aiken County	0	0.00
Alcolu (cdp) Clarendon County	0	0.00
Allendale (town) Allendale County	0	0.00

Top 10 Places Sorted by Percent of Total Population
Based on places with total population of 50,000 or more

Place	Population	%
Columbia (city) Richland County	1	<0.01
Charleston (city) Charleston County	0	0.00
Greenville (city) Greenville County	0	0.00
Mount Pleasant (town) Charleston County	0	0.00
North Charleston (city) Charleston County	0	0.00
Rock Hill (city) York County	0	0.00

American Indian: Paiute

Top 10 Places Sorted by Population
Based on all places, regardless of total population

Place	Population	%
Columbia (city) Richland County	1	<0.01
Abbeville (city) Abbeville County	0	0.00
Aiken (city) Aiken County	0	0.00
Alcolu (cdp) Clarendon County	0	0.00
Allendale (town) Allendale County	0	0.00
Anderson (city) Anderson County	0	0.00
Andrews (town) Georgetown County	0	0.00
Antreville (cdp) Abbeville County	0	0.00
Arcadia (cdp) Spartanburg County	0	0.00
Arcadia Lakes (town) Richland County	0	0.00

Top 10 Places Sorted by Percent of Total Population
Based on all places, regardless of total population

Place	Population	%
Columbia (city) Richland County	1	<0.01
Abbeville (city) Abbeville County	0	0.00
Aiken (city) Aiken County	0	0.00
Alcolu (cdp) Clarendon County	0	0.00
Allendale (town) Allendale County	0	0.00
Anderson (city) Anderson County	0	0.00
Andrews (town) Georgetown County	0	0.00
Antreville (cdp) Abbeville County	0	0.00
Arcadia (cdp) Spartanburg County	0	0.00
Arcadia Lakes (town) Richland County	0	0.00

Top 10 Places Sorted by Percent of Total Population
Based on places with total population of 50,000 or more

Place	Population	%
Columbia (city) Richland County	1	<0.01
Charleston (city) Charleston County	0	0.00
Greenville (city) Greenville County	0	0.00
Mount Pleasant (town) Charleston County	0	0.00
North Charleston (city) Charleston County	0	0.00
Rock Hill (city) York County	0	0.00

American Indian: Pima

Top 10 Places Sorted by Population
Based on all places, regardless of total population

Place	Population	%
Prosperity (town) Newberry County	1	0.08
Bamberg (town) Bamberg County	1	0.03
Newberry (city) Newberry County	1	0.01
Summerville (town) Dorchester County	1	<0.01
Wade Hampton (cdp) Greenville County	1	<0.01
Abbeville (city) Abbeville County	0	0.00
Aiken (city) Aiken County	0	0.00
Alcolu (cdp) Clarendon County	0	0.00
Allendale (town) Allendale County	0	0.00
Anderson (city) Anderson County	0	0.00

Top 10 Places Sorted by Percent of Total Population
Based on all places, regardless of total population

Place	Population	%
Prosperity (town) Newberry County	1	0.08
Bamberg (town) Bamberg County	1	0.03
Newberry (city) Newberry County	1	0.01
Summerville (town) Dorchester County	1	<0.01
Wade Hampton (cdp) Greenville County	1	<0.01
Abbeville (city) Abbeville County	0	0.00
Aiken (city) Aiken County	0	0.00
Alcolu (cdp) Clarendon County	0	0.00
Allendale (town) Allendale County	0	0.00
Anderson (city) Anderson County	0	0.00

Top 10 Places Sorted by Percent of Total Population
Based on places with total population of 50,000 or more

Place	Population	%
Charleston (city) Charleston County	0	0.00
Columbia (city) Richland County	0	0.00
Greenville (city) Greenville County	0	0.00
Mount Pleasant (town) Charleston County	0	0.00
North Charleston (city) Charleston County	0	0.00
Rock Hill (city) York County	0	0.00

American Indian: Potawatomi

Top 10 Places Sorted by Population
Based on all places, regardless of total population

Place	Population	%
Lake Murray of Richland (cdp) Richland County	5	0.09
Charleston (city) Charleston County	5	<0.01
Easley (city) Pickens County	3	0.02
North Charleston (city) Charleston County	3	<0.01
Honea Path (town) Anderson County	2	0.06
Surfside Beach (town) Horry County	2	0.05
Conway (city) Horry County	2	0.01
Goose Creek (city) Berkeley County	2	0.01
Mauldin (city) Greenville County	2	0.01
Columbia (city) Richland County	2	<0.01

Top 10 Places Sorted by Percent of Total Population
Based on all places, regardless of total population

Place	Population	%
Enoree (cdp) Spartanburg County	1	0.15
Lake Murray of Richland (cdp) Richland County	5	0.09
Honea Path (town) Anderson County	2	0.06
Surfside Beach (town) Horry County	2	0.05
Easley (city) Pickens County	3	0.02
Centerville (cdp) Anderson County	1	0.02
Conway (city) Horry County	2	0.01
Goose Creek (city) Berkeley County	2	0.01
Mauldin (city) Greenville County	2	0.01
Five Forks (cdp) Greenville County	1	0.01

Top 10 Places Sorted by Percent of Total Population
Based on places with total population of 50,000 or more

Place	Population	%
Charleston (city) Charleston County	5	<0.01
North Charleston (city) Charleston County	3	<0.01
Columbia (city) Richland County	2	<0.01
Mount Pleasant (town) Charleston County	1	<0.01
Greenville (city) Greenville County	0	0.00
Rock Hill (city) York County	0	0.00

American Indian: Pueblo

Top 10 Places Sorted by Population
Based on all places, regardless of total population

Place	Population	%
Seven Oaks (cdp) Lexington County	5	0.03
Woodfield (cdp) Richland County	4	0.04
Gaffney (city) Cherokee County	4	0.03
Hanahan (city) Berkeley County	4	0.02
Columbia (city) Richland County	4	<0.01
Dentsville (cdp) Richland County	3	0.02
West Columbia (city) Lexington County	3	0.02
North Augusta (city) Aiken County	3	0.01
Dillon (city) Dillon County	2	0.03
Converse (cdp) Spartanburg County	1	0.16

Top 10 Places Sorted by Percent of Total Population
Based on all places, regardless of total population

Place	Population	%
Converse (cdp) Spartanburg County	1	0.16
Woodfield (cdp) Richland County	4	0.04
Seven Oaks (cdp) Lexington County	5	0.03
Gaffney (city) Cherokee County	4	0.03
Dillon (city) Dillon County	2	0.03
Dalzell (cdp) Sumter County	1	0.03
Duncan (town) Spartanburg County	1	0.03
Hanahan (city) Berkeley County	4	0.02
Dentsville (cdp) Richland County	3	0.02
West Columbia (city) Lexington County	3	0.02

Top 10 Places Sorted by Percent of Total Population
Based on places with total population of 50,000 or more

Place	Population	%
Columbia (city) Richland County	4	<0.01
Charleston (city) Charleston County	1	<0.01
Greenville (city) Greenville County	0	0.00
Mount Pleasant (town) Charleston County	0	0.00
North Charleston (city) Charleston County	0	0.00
Rock Hill (city) York County	0	0.00

American Indian: Puget Sound Salish

Top 10 Places Sorted by Population
Based on all places, regardless of total population

Place	Population	%
Charleston (city) Charleston County	3	<0.01
Newberry (city) Newberry County	2	0.02
Hanahan (city) Berkeley County	2	0.01
Beaufort (city) Beaufort County	1	0.01
Rock Hill (city) York County	1	<0.01
Abbeville (city) Abbeville County	0	0.00
Aiken (city) Aiken County	0	0.00
Alcolu (cdp) Clarendon County	0	0.00
Allendale (town) Allendale County	0	0.00
Anderson (city) Anderson County	0	0.00

Top 10 Places Sorted by Percent of Total Population
Based on all places, regardless of total population

Place	Population	%
Newberry (city) Newberry County	2	0.02
Hanahan (city) Berkeley County	2	0.01
Beaufort (city) Beaufort County	1	0.01
Charleston (city) Charleston County	3	<0.01
Rock Hill (city) York County	1	<0.01
Abbeville (city) Abbeville County	0	0.00
Aiken (city) Aiken County	0	0.00
Alcolu (cdp) Clarendon County	0	0.00
Allendale (town) Allendale County	0	0.00
Anderson (city) Anderson County	0	0.00

Top 10 Places Sorted by Percent of Total Population
Based on places with total population of 50,000 or more

Place	Population	%
Charleston (city) Charleston County	3	<0.01
Rock Hill (city) York County	1	<0.01
Columbia (city) Richland County	0	0.00
Greenville (city) Greenville County	0	0.00
Mount Pleasant (town) Charleston County	0	0.00
North Charleston (city) Charleston County	0	0.00

American Indian: Seminole

Top 10 Places Sorted by Population
Based on all places, regardless of total population

Place	Population	%
Columbia (city) Richland County	11	0.01
Rock Hill (city) York County	7	0.01
Greenville (city) Greenville County	6	0.01
Oak Grove (cdp) Lexington County	5	0.05
Ladson (cdp) Berkeley County	5	0.04
North Charleston (city) Charleston County	5	0.01
Summerville (town) Dorchester County	5	0.01
Charleston (city) Charleston County	5	<0.01
Liberty (city) Pickens County	4	0.12
Goose Creek (city) Berkeley County	4	0.01

Top 10 Places Sorted by Percent of Total Population
Based on all places, regardless of total population

Place	Population	%
Williams (town) Colleton County	1	0.85
Liberty (city) Pickens County	4	0.12
Elgin (town) Kershaw County	1	0.08
Murphys Estates (cdp) Edgefield County	1	0.07
Oak Grove (cdp) Lexington County	5	0.05
Laurel Bay (cdp) Beaufort County	3	0.05
Clearwater (cdp) Aiken County	2	0.05
St. George (town) Dorchester County	1	0.05
Ware Shoals (town) Greenwood County	1	0.05
Ladson (cdp) Berkeley County	5	0.04

Top 10 Places Sorted by Percent of Total Population
Based on places with total population of 50,000 or more

Place	Population	%
Columbia (city) Richland County	11	0.01
Rock Hill (city) York County	7	0.01
Greenville (city) Greenville County	6	0.01
North Charleston (city) Charleston County	5	0.01
Charleston (city) Charleston County	5	<0.01
Mount Pleasant (town) Charleston County	0	0.00

American Indian: Shoshone

Top 10 Places Sorted by Population
Based on all places, regardless of total population

Place	Population	%
Charleston (city) Charleston County	4	<0.01
Utica (cdp) Oconee County	1	0.07
Beaufort (city) Beaufort County	1	0.01
Columbia (city) Richland County	1	<0.01
Mount Pleasant (town) Charleston County	1	<0.01
North Augusta (city) Aiken County	1	<0.01
Rock Hill (city) York County	1	<0.01
St. Andrews (cdp) Richland County	1	<0.01
Sumter (city) Sumter County	1	<0.01
Abbeville (city) Abbeville County	0	0.00

Top 10 Places Sorted by Percent of Total Population
Based on all places, regardless of total population

Place	Population	%
Utica (cdp) Oconee County	1	0.07
Beaufort (city) Beaufort County	1	0.01
Charleston (city) Charleston County	4	<0.01
Columbia (city) Richland County	1	<0.01
Mount Pleasant (town) Charleston County	1	<0.01
North Augusta (city) Aiken County	1	<0.01
Rock Hill (city) York County	1	<0.01
St. Andrews (cdp) Richland County	1	<0.01
Sumter (city) Sumter County	1	<0.01
Abbeville (city) Abbeville County	0	0.00

Top 10 Places Sorted by Percent of Total Population
Based on places with total population of 50,000 or more

Place	Population	%
Charleston (city) Charleston County	4	<0.01
Columbia (city) Richland County	1	<0.01
Mount Pleasant (town) Charleston County	1	<0.01
Rock Hill (city) York County	1	<0.01
Greenville (city) Greenville County	0	0.00
North Charleston (city) Charleston County	0	0.00

American Indian: Sioux

Top 10 Places Sorted by Population
Based on all places, regardless of total population

Place	Population	%
North Charleston (city) Charleston County	34	0.03
Columbia (city) Richland County	26	0.02
Summerville (town) Dorchester County	18	0.04
Ladson (cdp) Berkeley County	16	0.12
Socastee (cdp) Horry County	13	0.07
Greenville (city) Greenville County	12	0.02
Myrtle Beach (city) Horry County	11	0.04
Charleston (city) Charleston County	9	0.01
North Augusta (city) Aiken County	7	0.03
Valley Falls (cdp) Spartanburg County	6	0.10

Top 10 Places Sorted by Percent of Total Population
Based on all places, regardless of total population

Place	Population	%
Gramling (cdp) Spartanburg County	1	1.16
Monetta (town) Aiken County	1	0.42
Ehrhardt (town) Bamberg County	2	0.37
Aynor (town) Horry County	2	0.36
Rembert (cdp) Sumter County	1	0.33
Springfield (town) Orangeburg County	1	0.19
Warrenville (cdp) Aiken County	2	0.16
Pine Ridge (town) Lexington County	3	0.15
McColl (town) Marlboro County	3	0.14
Ladson (cdp) Berkeley County	16	0.12

Top 10 Places Sorted by Percent of Total Population
Based on places with total population of 50,000 or more

Place	Population	%
North Charleston (city) Charleston County	34	0.03
Columbia (city) Richland County	26	0.02
Greenville (city) Greenville County	12	0.02
Charleston (city) Charleston County	9	0.01
Rock Hill (city) York County	4	0.01
Mount Pleasant (town) Charleston County	2	<0.01

American Indian: South American Indian

Top 10 Places Sorted by Population
Based on all places, regardless of total population

Place	Population	%
Columbia (city) Richland County	9	0.01
Southern Shops (cdp) Spartanburg County	7	0.19
Charleston (city) Charleston County	6	<0.01
Goose Creek (city) Berkeley County	5	0.01
Blythewood (town) Richland County	4	0.20
Greenville (city) Greenville County	4	0.01
Pickens (city) Pickens County	3	0.10
Port Royal (town) Beaufort County	3	0.03
Hartsville (city) Darlington County	2	0.03
Red Hill (cdp) Horry County	2	0.02

Top 10 Places Sorted by Percent of Total Population
Based on all places, regardless of total population

Place	Population	%
Blythewood (town) Richland County	4	0.20
Southern Shops (cdp) Spartanburg County	7	0.19
Pickens (city) Pickens County	3	0.10
Cherryvale (cdp) Sumter County	1	0.04
Graniteville (cdp) Aiken County	1	0.04
Loris (city) Horry County	1	0.04
Port Royal (town) Beaufort County	3	0.03
Hartsville (city) Darlington County	2	0.03
Dalzell (cdp) Sumter County	1	0.03
Red Hill (cdp) Horry County	2	0.02

Top 10 Places Sorted by Percent of Total Population
Based on places with total population of 50,000 or more

Place	Population	%
Columbia (city) Richland County	9	0.01
Greenville (city) Greenville County	4	0.01
Charleston (city) Charleston County	6	<0.01
Mount Pleasant (town) Charleston County	1	<0.01
North Charleston (city) Charleston County	1	<0.01
Rock Hill (city) York County	1	<0.01

American Indian: Spanish American Indian

Top 10 Places Sorted by Population
Based on all places, regardless of total population

Place	Population	%
Dentsville (cdp) Richland County	8	0.06
Judson (cdp) Greenville County	5	0.24
Port Royal (town) Beaufort County	5	0.05
Moncks Corner (town) Berkeley County	4	0.05
Goose Creek (city) Berkeley County	4	0.01
West Union (town) Oconee County	3	1.03
Burton (cdp) Beaufort County	3	0.04
Easley (city) Pickens County	3	0.02
Columbia (city) Richland County	3	<0.01
North Charleston (city) Charleston County	3	<0.01

Top 10 Places Sorted by Percent of Total Population
Based on all places, regardless of total population

Place	Population	%
West Union (town) Oconee County	3	1.03
Judson (cdp) Greenville County	5	0.24
Arcadia (cdp) Spartanburg County	2	0.08
Dentsville (cdp) Richland County	8	0.06
Port Royal (town) Beaufort County	5	0.05
Moncks Corner (town) Berkeley County	4	0.05
Burton (cdp) Beaufort County	3	0.04
Easley (city) Pickens County	3	0.02
Bluffton (town) Beaufort County	2	0.02
Travelers Rest (city) Greenville County	1	0.02

Top 10 Places Sorted by Percent of Total Population
Based on places with total population of 50,000 or more

Place	Population	%
Columbia (city) Richland County	3	<0.01
North Charleston (city) Charleston County	3	<0.01
Greenville (city) Greenville County	2	<0.01
Mount Pleasant (town) Charleston County	1	<0.01
Charleston (city) Charleston County	0	0.00
Rock Hill (city) York County	0	0.00

Alaska Native: Tlingit-Haida

Top 10 Places Sorted by Population
Based on all places, regardless of total population

Place	Population	%
Rock Hill (city) York County	5	0.01
Dillon (city) Dillon County	3	0.04
Spartanburg (city) Spartanburg County	3	0.01
Sumter (city) Sumter County	3	0.01
Norway (town) Orangeburg County	2	0.59
Aiken (city) Aiken County	2	0.01
Greenwood (city) Greenwood County	2	0.01
Pawleys Island (town) Georgetown County	1	0.97
Stateburg (cdp) Sumter County	1	0.07
Beaufort (city) Beaufort County	1	0.01

Top 10 Places Sorted by Percent of Total Population
Based on all places, regardless of total population

Place	Population	%
Pawleys Island (town) Georgetown County	1	0.97
Norway (town) Orangeburg County	2	0.59
Stateburg (cdp) Sumter County	1	0.07
Dillon (city) Dillon County	3	0.04
Rock Hill (city) York County	5	0.01
Spartanburg (city) Spartanburg County	3	0.01
Sumter (city) Sumter County	3	0.01
Aiken (city) Aiken County	2	0.01
Greenwood (city) Greenwood County	2	0.01
Beaufort (city) Beaufort County	1	0.01

Top 10 Places Sorted by Percent of Total Population
Based on places with total population of 50,000 or more

Place	Population	%
Rock Hill (city) York County	5	0.01
Columbia (city) Richland County	1	<0.01
Mount Pleasant (town) Charleston County	1	<0.01
North Charleston (city) Charleston County	1	<0.01
Charleston (city) Charleston County	0	0.00
Greenville (city) Greenville County	0	0.00

American Indian: Tohono O'Odham

Top 10 Places Sorted by Population
Based on all places, regardless of total population

Place	Population	%
Rock Hill (city) York County	5	0.01
Forest Acres (city) Richland County	4	0.04
McColl (town) Marlboro County	3	0.14
Newberry (city) Newberry County	1	0.01
Abbeville (city) Abbeville County	0	0.00
Aiken (city) Aiken County	0	0.00
Alcolu (cdp) Clarendon County	0	0.00
Allendale (town) Allendale County	0	0.00
Anderson (city) Anderson County	0	0.00
Andrews (town) Georgetown County	0	0.00

Top 10 Places Sorted by Percent of Total Population
Based on all places, regardless of total population

Place	Population	%
McColl (town) Marlboro County	3	0.14
Forest Acres (city) Richland County	4	0.04
Rock Hill (city) York County	5	0.01
Newberry (city) Newberry County	1	0.01
Abbeville (city) Abbeville County	0	0.00
Aiken (city) Aiken County	0	0.00
Alcolu (cdp) Clarendon County	0	0.00
Allendale (town) Allendale County	0	0.00
Anderson (city) Anderson County	0	0.00
Andrews (town) Georgetown County	0	0.00

Top 10 Places Sorted by Percent of Total Population
Based on places with total population of 50,000 or more

Place	Population	%
Rock Hill (city) York County	5	0.01
Charleston (city) Charleston County	0	0.00
Columbia (city) Richland County	0	0.00
Greenville (city) Greenville County	0	0.00
Mount Pleasant (town) Charleston County	0	0.00
North Charleston (city) Charleston County	0	0.00

Alaska Native: Tsimshian

Top 10 Places Sorted by Population
Based on all places, regardless of total population

Place	Population	%
Laurens (city) Laurens County	2	0.02
Mount Pleasant (town) Charleston County	2	<0.01
Anderson (city) Anderson County	1	<0.01
North Charleston (city) Charleston County	1	<0.01
Abbeville (city) Abbeville County	0	0.00
Aiken (city) Aiken County	0	0.00
Alcolu (cdp) Clarendon County	0	0.00
Allendale (town) Allendale County	0	0.00
Andrews (town) Georgetown County	0	0.00
Antreville (cdp) Abbeville County	0	0.00

Top 10 Places Sorted by Percent of Total Population
Based on all places, regardless of total population

Place	Population	%
Laurens (city) Laurens County	2	0.02
Mount Pleasant (town) Charleston County	2	<0.01
Anderson (city) Anderson County	1	<0.01
North Charleston (city) Charleston County	1	<0.01
Abbeville (city) Abbeville County	0	0.00
Aiken (city) Aiken County	0	0.00
Alcolu (cdp) Clarendon County	0	0.00
Allendale (town) Allendale County	0	0.00
Andrews (town) Georgetown County	0	0.00
Antreville (cdp) Abbeville County	0	0.00

Top 10 Places Sorted by Percent of Total Population
Based on places with total population of 50,000 or more

Place	Population	%
Mount Pleasant (town) Charleston County	2	<0.01
North Charleston (city) Charleston County	1	<0.01
Charleston (city) Charleston County	0	0.00
Columbia (city) Richland County	0	0.00
Greenville (city) Greenville County	0	0.00
Rock Hill (city) York County	0	0.00

American Indian: Ute

Top 10 Places Sorted by Population
Based on all places, regardless of total population

Place	Population	%
Charleston (city) Charleston County	2	<0.01
Belvedere (cdp) Aiken County	1	0.02
Taylors (cdp) Greenville County	1	<0.01
Abbeville (city) Abbeville County	0	0.00
Aiken (city) Aiken County	0	0.00
Alcolu (cdp) Clarendon County	0	0.00
Allendale (town) Allendale County	0	0.00
Anderson (city) Anderson County	0	0.00
Andrews (town) Georgetown County	0	0.00
Antreville (cdp) Abbeville County	0	0.00

Top 10 Places Sorted by Percent of Total Population
Based on all places, regardless of total population

Place	Population	%
Belvedere (cdp) Aiken County	1	0.02
Charleston (city) Charleston County	2	<0.01
Taylors (cdp) Greenville County	1	<0.01
Abbeville (city) Abbeville County	0	0.00
Aiken (city) Aiken County	0	0.00
Alcolu (cdp) Clarendon County	0	0.00
Allendale (town) Allendale County	0	0.00
Anderson (city) Anderson County	0	0.00
Andrews (town) Georgetown County	0	0.00
Antreville (cdp) Abbeville County	0	0.00

Top 10 Places Sorted by Percent of Total Population
Based on places with total population of 50,000 or more

Place	Population	%
Charleston (city) Charleston County	2	<0.01
Columbia (city) Richland County	0	0.00
Greenville (city) Greenville County	0	0.00
Mount Pleasant (town) Charleston County	0	0.00
North Charleston (city) Charleston County	0	0.00
Rock Hill (city) York County	0	0.00

American Indian: Yakama

Top 10 Places Sorted by Population
Based on all places, regardless of total population

Place	Population	%
Sumter (city) Sumter County	4	0.01
Greenville (city) Greenville County	1	<0.01
North Augusta (city) Aiken County	1	<0.01
Wade Hampton (cdp) Greenville County	1	<0.01
Abbeville (city) Abbeville County	0	0.00
Aiken (city) Aiken County	0	0.00
Alcolu (cdp) Clarendon County	0	0.00
Allendale (town) Allendale County	0	0.00
Anderson (city) Anderson County	0	0.00
Andrews (town) Georgetown County	0	0.00

Top 10 Places Sorted by Percent of Total Population
Based on all places, regardless of total population

Place	Population	%
Sumter (city) Sumter County	4	0.01
Greenville (city) Greenville County	1	<0.01
North Augusta (city) Aiken County	1	<0.01
Wade Hampton (cdp) Greenville County	1	<0.01
Abbeville (city) Abbeville County	0	0.00
Aiken (city) Aiken County	0	0.00
Alcolu (cdp) Clarendon County	0	0.00
Allendale (town) Allendale County	0	0.00
Anderson (city) Anderson County	0	0.00
Andrews (town) Georgetown County	0	0.00

Top 10 Places Sorted by Percent of Total Population
Based on places with total population of 50,000 or more

Place	Population	%
Greenville (city) Greenville County	1	<0.01
Charleston (city) Charleston County	0	0.00
Columbia (city) Richland County	0	0.00
Mount Pleasant (town) Charleston County	0	0.00
North Charleston (city) Charleston County	0	0.00
Rock Hill (city) York County	0	0.00

American Indian: Yaqui

Top 10 Places Sorted by Population
Based on all places, regardless of total population

Place	Population	%
Saxon (cdp) Spartanburg County	4	0.12
Boiling Springs (cdp) Spartanburg County	3	0.04
Greenville (city) Greenville County	2	<0.01
North Charleston (city) Charleston County	2	<0.01
Rembert (cdp) Sumter County	1	0.33
Golden Grove (cdp) Greenville County	1	0.04
Port Royal (town) Beaufort County	1	0.01
Columbia (city) Richland County	1	<0.01
Greer (city) Greenville County	1	<0.01
Hilton Head Island (town) Beaufort County	1	<0.01

Top 10 Places Sorted by Percent of Total Population
Based on all places, regardless of total population

Place	Population	%
Rembert (cdp) Sumter County	1	0.33
Saxon (cdp) Spartanburg County	4	0.12
Boiling Springs (cdp) Spartanburg County	3	0.04
Golden Grove (cdp) Greenville County	1	0.04
Port Royal (town) Beaufort County	1	0.01
Greenville (city) Greenville County	2	<0.01
North Charleston (city) Charleston County	2	<0.01
Columbia (city) Richland County	1	<0.01
Greer (city) Greenville County	1	<0.01
Hilton Head Island (town) Beaufort County	1	<0.01

Top 10 Places Sorted by Percent of Total Population
Based on places with total population of 50,000 or more

Place	Population	%
Greenville (city) Greenville County	2	<0.01
North Charleston (city) Charleston County	2	<0.01
Columbia (city) Richland County	1	<0.01
Charleston (city) Charleston County	0	0.00
Mount Pleasant (town) Charleston County	0	0.00
Rock Hill (city) York County	0	0.00

American Indian: Yuman

Top 10 Places Sorted by Population
Based on all places, regardless of total population

Place	Population	%
Varnville (town) Hampton County	3	0.14
Belton (city) Anderson County	1	0.02
Beaufort (city) Beaufort County	1	0.01
Hilton Head Island (town) Beaufort County	1	<0.01
North Charleston (city) Charleston County	1	<0.01
Abbeville (city) Abbeville County	0	0.00
Aiken (city) Aiken County	0	0.00
Alcolu (cdp) Clarendon County	0	0.00
Allendale (town) Allendale County	0	0.00
Anderson (city) Anderson County	0	0.00

Top 10 Places Sorted by Percent of Total Population
Based on all places, regardless of total population

Place	Population	%
Varnville (town) Hampton County	3	0.14
Belton (city) Anderson County	1	0.02
Beaufort (city) Beaufort County	1	0.01
Hilton Head Island (town) Beaufort County	1	<0.01
North Charleston (city) Charleston County	1	<0.01
Abbeville (city) Abbeville County	0	0.00
Aiken (city) Aiken County	0	0.00
Alcolu (cdp) Clarendon County	0	0.00
Allendale (town) Allendale County	0	0.00
Anderson (city) Anderson County	0	0.00

Top 10 Places Sorted by Percent of Total Population
Based on places with total population of 50,000 or more

Place	Population	%
North Charleston (city) Charleston County	1	<0.01
Charleston (city) Charleston County	0	0.00
Columbia (city) Richland County	0	0.00
Greenville (city) Greenville County	0	0.00
Mount Pleasant (town) Charleston County	0	0.00
Rock Hill (city) York County	0	0.00

Alaska Native: Yup'ik

Top 10 Places Sorted by Population
Based on all places, regardless of total population

Place	Population	%
Columbia (city) Richland County	2	<0.01
Beaufort (city) Beaufort County	1	0.01
Hanahan (city) Berkeley County	1	0.01
Lexington (town) Lexington County	1	0.01
Rock Hill (city) York County	1	<0.01
Abbeville (city) Abbeville County	0	0.00
Aiken (city) Aiken County	0	0.00
Alcolu (cdp) Clarendon County	0	0.00
Allendale (town) Allendale County	0	0.00
Anderson (city) Anderson County	0	0.00

Top 10 Places Sorted by Percent of Total Population
Based on all places, regardless of total population

Place	Population	%
Beaufort (city) Beaufort County	1	0.01
Hanahan (city) Berkeley County	1	0.01
Lexington (town) Lexington County	1	0.01
Columbia (city) Richland County	2	<0.01
Rock Hill (city) York County	1	<0.01
Abbeville (city) Abbeville County	0	0.00
Aiken (city) Aiken County	0	0.00
Alcolu (cdp) Clarendon County	0	0.00
Allendale (town) Allendale County	0	0.00
Anderson (city) Anderson County	0	0.00

Top 10 Places Sorted by Percent of Total Population
Based on places with total population of 50,000 or more

Place	Population	%
Columbia (city) Richland County	2	<0.01
Rock Hill (city) York County	1	<0.01
Charleston (city) Charleston County	0	0.00
Greenville (city) Greenville County	0	0.00
Mount Pleasant (town) Charleston County	0	0.00
North Charleston (city) Charleston County	0	0.00

Asian

Top 10 Places Sorted by Population
Based on all places, regardless of total population

Place	Population	%
Columbia (city) Richland County	3,707	2.87
Charleston (city) Charleston County	2,557	2.13
North Charleston (city) Charleston County	2,485	2.55
Goose Creek (city) Berkeley County	1,848	5.14
Mount Pleasant (town) Charleston County	1,418	2.09
Rock Hill (city) York County	1,372	2.07
Clemson (city) Pickens County	1,220	8.77
Greenville (city) Greenville County	1,045	1.79
Summerville (town) Dorchester County	995	2.29
Mauldin (city) Greenville County	954	4.17

Top 10 Places Sorted by Percent of Total Population
Based on all places, regardless of total population

Place	Population	%
Clemson (city) Pickens County	1,220	8.77
Vance (town) Orangeburg County	11	6.47
Fairforest (cdp) Spartanburg County	104	6.14
Five Forks (cdp) Greenville County	734	5.19
Goose Creek (city) Berkeley County	1,848	5.14
Hanahan (city) Berkeley County	796	4.42
Lexington (town) Lexington County	756	4.23
Mauldin (city) Greenville County	954	4.17
Woodfield (cdp) Richland County	386	4.15
Boiling Springs (cdp) Spartanburg County	341	4.15

Top 10 Places Sorted by Percent of Total Population
Based on places with total population of 50,000 or more

Place	Population	%
Columbia (city) Richland County	3,707	2.87
North Charleston (city) Charleston County	2,485	2.55
Charleston (city) Charleston County	2,557	2.13
Mount Pleasant (town) Charleston County	1,418	2.09
Rock Hill (city) York County	1,372	2.07
Greenville (city) Greenville County	1,045	1.79

Asian: Not Hispanic

Top 10 Places Sorted by Population
Based on all places, regardless of total population

Place	Population	%
Columbia (city) Richland County	3,610	2.79
Charleston (city) Charleston County	2,491	2.07
North Charleston (city) Charleston County	2,405	2.47
Goose Creek (city) Berkeley County	1,795	4.99
Mount Pleasant (town) Charleston County	1,381	2.04
Rock Hill (city) York County	1,348	2.04
Clemson (city) Pickens County	1,209	8.69
Greenville (city) Greenville County	1,006	1.72
Summerville (town) Dorchester County	954	2.20
Mauldin (city) Greenville County	935	4.08

Top 10 Places Sorted by Percent of Total Population
Based on all places, regardless of total population

Place	Population	%
Clemson (city) Pickens County	1,209	8.69
Vance (town) Orangeburg County	11	6.47
Five Forks (cdp) Greenville County	724	5.12
Goose Creek (city) Berkeley County	1,795	4.99
Fairforest (cdp) Spartanburg County	84	4.96
Hanahan (city) Berkeley County	775	4.31
Lexington (town) Lexington County	750	4.20
Mauldin (city) Greenville County	935	4.08
Boiling Springs (cdp) Spartanburg County	335	4.08
Woodfield (cdp) Richland County	364	3.91

Top 10 Places Sorted by Percent of Total Population
Based on places with total population of 50,000 or more

Place	Population	%
Columbia (city) Richland County	3,610	2.79
North Charleston (city) Charleston County	2,405	2.47
Charleston (city) Charleston County	2,491	2.07
Mount Pleasant (town) Charleston County	1,381	2.04
Rock Hill (city) York County	1,348	2.04
Greenville (city) Greenville County	1,006	1.72

Asian: Hispanic

Top 10 Places Sorted by Population
Based on all places, regardless of total population

Place	Population	%
Columbia (city) Richland County	97	0.08
North Charleston (city) Charleston County	80	0.08
Charleston (city) Charleston County	66	0.05
Goose Creek (city) Berkeley County	53	0.15
Summerville (town) Dorchester County	41	0.09
Greenville (city) Greenville County	39	0.07
Mount Pleasant (town) Charleston County	37	0.05
Port Royal (town) Beaufort County	32	0.30
Sumter (city) Sumter County	30	0.07
Hilton Head Island (town) Beaufort County	26	0.07

Top 10 Places Sorted by Percent of Total Population
Based on all places, regardless of total population

Place	Population	%
Fairforest (cdp) Spartanburg County	20	1.18
Parksville (town) McCormick County	1	0.85
Enoree (cdp) Spartanburg County	4	0.60
Atlantic Beach (town) Horry County	2	0.60
Arcadia Lakes (town) Richland County	4	0.46
East Sumter (cdp) Sumter County	6	0.45
Pelion (town) Lexington County	3	0.45
Loris (city) Horry County	10	0.42
Monetta (town) Aiken County	1	0.42
Laurel Bay (cdp) Beaufort County	24	0.41

Top 10 Places Sorted by Percent of Total Population
Based on places with total population of 50,000 or more

Place	Population	%
Columbia (city) Richland County	97	0.08
North Charleston (city) Charleston County	80	0.08
Greenville (city) Greenville County	39	0.07
Charleston (city) Charleston County	66	0.05
Mount Pleasant (town) Charleston County	37	0.05
Rock Hill (city) York County	24	0.04

Asian: Bangladeshi

Top 10 Places Sorted by Population
Based on all places, regardless of total population

Place	Population	%
West Columbia (city) Lexington County	22	0.15
Columbia (city) Richland County	21	0.02
Dentsville (cdp) Richland County	9	0.06
North Charleston (city) Charleston County	9	0.01
Charleston (city) Charleston County	7	0.01
Clemson (city) Pickens County	6	0.04
Orangeburg (city) Orangeburg County	6	0.04
Seven Oaks (cdp) Lexington County	6	0.04
Five Forks (cdp) Greenville County	5	0.04
Greenville (city) Greenville County	5	0.01

Top 10 Places Sorted by Percent of Total Population
Based on all places, regardless of total population

Place	Population	%
West Columbia (city) Lexington County	22	0.15
Woodruff (city) Spartanburg County	4	0.10
Dentsville (cdp) Richland County	9	0.06
Clemson (city) Pickens County	6	0.04
Orangeburg (city) Orangeburg County	6	0.04
Seven Oaks (cdp) Lexington County	6	0.04
Five Forks (cdp) Greenville County	5	0.04
Oak Grove (cdp) Lexington County	4	0.04
Woodfield (cdp) Richland County	3	0.03
Moncks Corner (town) Berkeley County	2	0.03

Top 10 Places Sorted by Percent of Total Population
Based on places with total population of 50,000 or more

Place	Population	%
Columbia (city) Richland County	21	0.02
North Charleston (city) Charleston County	9	0.01
Charleston (city) Charleston County	7	0.01
Greenville (city) Greenville County	5	0.01
Rock Hill (city) York County	3	<0.01
Mount Pleasant (town) Charleston County	0	0.00

Asian: Bhutanese

Top 10 Places Sorted by Population
Based on all places, regardless of total population

Place	Population	%
St. Andrews (cdp) Richland County	4	0.02
Charleston (city) Charleston County	1	<0.01
Abbeville (city) Abbeville County	0	0.00
Aiken (city) Aiken County	0	0.00
Alcolu (cdp) Clarendon County	0	0.00
Allendale (town) Allendale County	0	0.00
Anderson (city) Anderson County	0	0.00
Andrews (town) Georgetown County	0	0.00
Antreville (cdp) Abbeville County	0	0.00
Arcadia (cdp) Spartanburg County	0	0.00

Top 10 Places Sorted by Percent of Total Population
Based on all places, regardless of total population

Place	Population	%
St. Andrews (cdp) Richland County	4	0.02
Charleston (city) Charleston County	1	<0.01
Abbeville (city) Abbeville County	0	0.00
Aiken (city) Aiken County	0	0.00
Alcolu (cdp) Clarendon County	0	0.00
Allendale (town) Allendale County	0	0.00
Anderson (city) Anderson County	0	0.00
Andrews (town) Georgetown County	0	0.00
Antreville (cdp) Abbeville County	0	0.00
Arcadia (cdp) Spartanburg County	0	0.00

Asian: Burmese

Top 10 Places Sorted by Population
Based on all places, regardless of total population

Place	Population	%
St. Andrews (cdp) Richland County	141	0.69
Taylors (cdp) Greenville County	63	0.29
Cayce (city) Lexington County	22	0.18
Charleston (city) Charleston County	16	0.01
Greer (city) Greenville County	11	0.04
Mount Pleasant (town) Charleston County	11	0.02
Columbia (city) Richland County	11	0.01
North Charleston (city) Charleston County	11	0.01
Arcadia Lakes (town) Richland County	8	0.93
Forest Acres (city) Richland County	7	0.07

Top 10 Places Sorted by Percent of Total Population
Based on all places, regardless of total population

Place	Population	%
Arcadia Lakes (town) Richland County	8	0.93
St. Andrews (cdp) Richland County	141	0.69
Taylors (cdp) Greenville County	63	0.29
Cayce (city) Lexington County	22	0.18
Loris (city) Horry County	3	0.13
Forest Acres (city) Richland County	7	0.07
Dillon (city) Dillon County	4	0.06
Greer (city) Greenville County	11	0.04
West Columbia (city) Lexington County	4	0.03
Mount Pleasant (town) Charleston County	11	0.02

Top 10 Places Sorted by Percent of Total Population
Based on places with total population of 50,000 or more

Place	Population	%
Mount Pleasant (town) Charleston County	11	0.02
Charleston (city) Charleston County	16	0.01
Columbia (city) Richland County	11	0.01
North Charleston (city) Charleston County	11	0.01
Greenville (city) Greenville County	3	0.01
Rock Hill (city) York County	1	<0.01

Asian: Cambodian

Top 10 Places Sorted by Population
Based on all places, regardless of total population

Place	Population	%
Spartanburg (city) Spartanburg County	71	0.19
Rock Hill (city) York County	55	0.08
Boiling Springs (cdp) Spartanburg County	37	0.45
Inman (city) Spartanburg County	36	1.55
Fairforest (cdp) Spartanburg County	33	1.95
Columbia (city) Richland County	27	0.02
Southern Shops (cdp) Spartanburg County	21	0.56
Hanahan (city) Berkeley County	17	0.09
Mount Pleasant (town) Charleston County	16	0.02
Landrum (city) Spartanburg County	13	0.55

Top 10 Places Sorted by Percent of Total Population
Based on all places, regardless of total population

Place	Population	%
Campobello (town) Spartanburg County	11	2.19
Fairforest (cdp) Spartanburg County	33	1.95
Inman (city) Spartanburg County	36	1.55
Inman Mills (cdp) Spartanburg County	7	0.67
Southern Shops (cdp) Spartanburg County	21	0.56
Landrum (city) Spartanburg County	13	0.55
Boiling Springs (cdp) Spartanburg County	37	0.45
Clifton (cdp) Spartanburg County	2	0.37
Saxon (cdp) Spartanburg County	12	0.35
Wellford (city) Spartanburg County	5	0.21

Top 10 Places Sorted by Percent of Total Population
Based on places with total population of 50,000 or more

Place	Population	%
Rock Hill (city) York County	55	0.08
Columbia (city) Richland County	27	0.02
Mount Pleasant (town) Charleston County	16	0.02
Charleston (city) Charleston County	10	0.01
Greenville (city) Greenville County	7	0.01
North Charleston (city) Charleston County	6	0.01

Asian: Chinese, except Taiwanese

Top 10 Places Sorted by Population
Based on all places, regardless of total population

Place	Population	%
Columbia (city) Richland County	800	0.62
Charleston (city) Charleston County	484	0.40
Clemson (city) Pickens County	464	3.34
North Charleston (city) Charleston County	364	0.37
Mount Pleasant (town) Charleston County	335	0.49
Goose Creek (city) Berkeley County	188	0.52
Florence (city) Florence County	173	0.47
Rock Hill (city) York County	170	0.26
Five Forks (cdp) Greenville County	169	1.20
Lexington (town) Lexington County	165	0.92

Top 10 Places Sorted by Percent of Total Population
Based on all places, regardless of total population

Place	Population	%
Clemson (city) Pickens County	464	3.34
Arcadia Lakes (town) Richland County	13	1.51
Mount Carmel (cdp) McCormick County	3	1.39
Five Forks (cdp) Greenville County	169	1.20
Johnsonville (city) Florence County	16	1.08
Lexington (town) Lexington County	165	0.92
Central (town) Pickens County	42	0.81
Harleyville (town) Dorchester County	5	0.74
Ehrhardt (town) Bamberg County	4	0.73
Burnet (town) Aiken County	19	0.71

Top 10 Places Sorted by Percent of Total Population
Based on places with total population of 50,000 or more

Place	Population	%
Columbia (city) Richland County	800	0.62
Mount Pleasant (town) Charleston County	335	0.49
Charleston (city) Charleston County	484	0.40
North Charleston (city) Charleston County	364	0.37
Greenville (city) Greenville County	158	0.27
Rock Hill (city) York County	170	0.26

Asian: Filipino

Top 10 Places Sorted by Population
Based on all places, regardless of total population

Place	Population	%
Goose Creek (city) Berkeley County	1,210	3.37
North Charleston (city) Charleston County	969	0.99
Charleston (city) Charleston County	522	0.43
Columbia (city) Richland County	519	0.40
Summerville (town) Dorchester County	407	0.94
Hanahan (city) Berkeley County	315	1.75
Ladson (cdp) Berkeley County	283	2.05
Sumter (city) Sumter County	283	0.70
Mount Pleasant (town) Charleston County	217	0.32
Rock Hill (city) York County	213	0.32

Top 10 Places Sorted by Percent of Total Population
Based on all places, regardless of total population

Place	Population	%
Goose Creek (city) Berkeley County	1,210	3.37
Ladson (cdp) Berkeley County	283	2.05
Hanahan (city) Berkeley County	315	1.75
Stateburg (cdp) Sumter County	22	1.59
Monetta (town) Aiken County	3	1.27
Oakland (cdp) Sumter County	15	1.22
Port Royal (town) Beaufort County	129	1.21
Shell Point (cdp) Beaufort County	28	1.20
Loris (city) Horry County	28	1.17
Laurel Bay (cdp) Beaufort County	67	1.14

Top 10 Places Sorted by Percent of Total Population
Based on places with total population of 50,000 or more

Place	Population	%
North Charleston (city) Charleston County	969	0.99
Charleston (city) Charleston County	522	0.43
Columbia (city) Richland County	519	0.40
Mount Pleasant (town) Charleston County	217	0.32
Rock Hill (city) York County	213	0.32
Greenville (city) Greenville County	158	0.27

Asian: Hmong

Top 10 Places Sorted by Population
Based on all places, regardless of total population

Place	Population	%
Spartanburg (city) Spartanburg County	61	0.16
Fairforest (cdp) Spartanburg County	54	3.19
Rock Hill (city) York County	37	0.06
Irmo (town) Richland County	21	0.19
Columbia (city) Richland County	20	0.02
Roebuck (cdp) Spartanburg County	17	0.77
Wellford (city) Spartanburg County	15	0.63
Boiling Springs (cdp) Spartanburg County	14	0.17
Pacolet (town) Spartanburg County	13	0.58
Saxon (cdp) Spartanburg County	12	0.35

Top 10 Places Sorted by Percent of Total Population
Based on all places, regardless of total population

Place	Population	%
Fairforest (cdp) Spartanburg County	54	3.19
Reidville (town) Spartanburg County	6	1.00
Roebuck (cdp) Spartanburg County	17	0.77
Wellford (city) Spartanburg County	15	0.63
Pacolet (town) Spartanburg County	13	0.58
Saxon (cdp) Spartanburg County	12	0.35
Newport (cdp) York County	12	0.29
Lyman (town) Spartanburg County	8	0.25
Arcadia (cdp) Spartanburg County	6	0.23
Southern Shops (cdp) Spartanburg County	8	0.21

Top 10 Places Sorted by Percent of Total Population
Based on places with total population of 50,000 or more

Place	Population	%
Rock Hill (city) York County	37	0.06
Columbia (city) Richland County	20	0.02
North Charleston (city) Charleston County	2	<0.01
Charleston (city) Charleston County	1	<0.01
Greenville (city) Greenville County	1	<0.01
Mount Pleasant (town) Charleston County	1	<0.01

Asian: Indian

Top 10 Places Sorted by Population
Based on all places, regardless of total population

Place	Population	%
Columbia (city) Richland County	953	0.74
Charleston (city) Charleston County	637	0.53
Clemson (city) Pickens County	483	3.47
Lexington (town) Lexington County	380	2.13
Mauldin (city) Greenville County	353	1.54
Mount Pleasant (town) Charleston County	327	0.48
North Charleston (city) Charleston County	306	0.31
Greenville (city) Greenville County	280	0.48
Rock Hill (city) York County	260	0.39
Five Forks (cdp) Greenville County	254	1.80

Top 10 Places Sorted by Percent of Total Population
Based on all places, regardless of total population

Place	Population	%
Vance (town) Orangeburg County	10	5.88
Clemson (city) Pickens County	483	3.47
Santee (town) Orangeburg County	21	2.19
Lexington (town) Lexington County	380	2.13
Arcadia (cdp) Spartanburg County	51	1.94
Five Forks (cdp) Greenville County	254	1.80
Kingstree (town) Williamsburg County	60	1.80
Hemingway (town) Williamsburg County	8	1.74
Manning (city) Clarendon County	68	1.66
Jefferson (town) Chesterfield County	12	1.59

Top 10 Places Sorted by Percent of Total Population
Based on places with total population of 50,000 or more

Place	Population	%
Columbia (city) Richland County	953	0.74
Charleston (city) Charleston County	637	0.53
Mount Pleasant (town) Charleston County	327	0.48
Greenville (city) Greenville County	280	0.48
Rock Hill (city) York County	260	0.39
North Charleston (city) Charleston County	306	0.31

Asian: Indonesian

Top 10 Places Sorted by Population
Based on all places, regardless of total population

Place	Population	%
Columbia (city) Richland County	20	0.02
Mount Pleasant (town) Charleston County	13	0.02
Anderson (city) Anderson County	12	0.04
Orangeburg (city) Orangeburg County	9	0.06
Charleston (city) Charleston County	7	0.01
North Charleston (city) Charleston County	7	0.01
Sumter (city) Sumter County	6	0.01
Little River (cdp) Horry County	5	0.06
Greenville (city) Greenville County	5	0.01
Hilton Head Island (town) Beaufort County	5	0.01

Top 10 Places Sorted by Percent of Total Population
Based on all places, regardless of total population

Place	Population	%
Dunean (cdp) Greenville County	4	0.11
Surfside Beach (town) Horry County	4	0.10
Orangeburg (city) Orangeburg County	9	0.06
Little River (cdp) Horry County	5	0.06
Boiling Springs (cdp) Spartanburg County	4	0.05
Anderson (city) Anderson County	12	0.04
Golden Grove (cdp) Greenville County	1	0.04
Landrum (city) Spartanburg County	1	0.04
Northlake (cdp) Anderson County	1	0.03
Williamston (town) Anderson County	1	0.03

Top 10 Places Sorted by Percent of Total Population
Based on places with total population of 50,000 or more

Place	Population	%
Columbia (city) Richland County	20	0.02
Mount Pleasant (town) Charleston County	13	0.02
Charleston (city) Charleston County	7	0.01
North Charleston (city) Charleston County	7	0.01
Greenville (city) Greenville County	5	0.01
Rock Hill (city) York County	5	0.01

Asian: Japanese

Top 10 Places Sorted by Population
Based on all places, regardless of total population

Place	Population	%
Columbia (city) Richland County	231	0.18
North Charleston (city) Charleston County	170	0.17
Charleston (city) Charleston County	158	0.13
Goose Creek (city) Berkeley County	126	0.35
Summerville (town) Dorchester County	96	0.22
Mount Pleasant (town) Charleston County	88	0.13
Greenville (city) Greenville County	82	0.14
Sumter (city) Sumter County	79	0.19
Aiken (city) Aiken County	74	0.25
Port Royal (town) Beaufort County	61	0.57

Top 10 Places Sorted by Percent of Total Population
Based on all places, regardless of total population

Place	Population	%
Donalds (town) Abbeville County	3	0.86
Parksville (town) McCormick County	1	0.85
Windsor (town) Aiken County	1	0.83
Oakland (cdp) Sumter County	10	0.81
Laurel Bay (cdp) Beaufort County	44	0.75
Port Royal (town) Beaufort County	61	0.57
Shell Point (cdp) Beaufort County	13	0.56
Woodfield (cdp) Richland County	50	0.54
Mount Carmel (cdp) McCormick County	1	0.46
Elloree (town) Orangeburg County	3	0.43

Top 10 Places Sorted by Percent of Total Population
Based on places with total population of 50,000 or more

Place	Population	%
Columbia (city) Richland County	231	0.18
North Charleston (city) Charleston County	170	0.17
Greenville (city) Greenville County	82	0.14
Charleston (city) Charleston County	158	0.13
Mount Pleasant (town) Charleston County	88	0.13
Rock Hill (city) York County	43	0.06

Asian: Korean

Top 10 Places Sorted by Population
Based on all places, regardless of total population

Place	Population	%
Columbia (city) Richland County	536	0.41
Charleston (city) Charleston County	244	0.20
North Charleston (city) Charleston County	207	0.21
Greenville (city) Greenville County	179	0.31
Mount Pleasant (town) Charleston County	145	0.21
Woodfield (cdp) Richland County	108	1.16
Sumter (city) Sumter County	100	0.25
Rock Hill (city) York County	96	0.15
Greer (city) Greenville County	93	0.36
Mauldin (city) Greenville County	84	0.37

Top 10 Places Sorted by Percent of Total Population
Based on all places, regardless of total population

Place	Population	%
Parksville (town) McCormick County	2	1.71
Woodfield (cdp) Richland County	108	1.16
Pelzer (town) Anderson County	1	1.12
Oakland (cdp) Sumter County	11	0.89
Central (town) Pickens County	44	0.85
Furman (town) Hampton County	2	0.84
Arcadia Lakes (town) Richland County	7	0.81
Neeses (town) Orangeburg County	3	0.80
Riverview (cdp) York County	5	0.73
Newry (cdp) Oconee County	1	0.58

Top 10 Places Sorted by Percent of Total Population
Based on places with total population of 50,000 or more

Place	Population	%
Columbia (city) Richland County	536	0.41
Greenville (city) Greenville County	179	0.31
North Charleston (city) Charleston County	207	0.21
Mount Pleasant (town) Charleston County	145	0.21
Charleston (city) Charleston County	244	0.20
Rock Hill (city) York County	96	0.15

Asian: Laotian

Top 10 Places Sorted by Population
Based on all places, regardless of total population

Place	Population	%
Spartanburg (city) Spartanburg County	112	0.30
Boiling Springs (cdp) Spartanburg County	33	0.40
Columbia (city) Richland County	21	0.02
Rock Hill (city) York County	20	0.03
Roebuck (cdp) Spartanburg County	19	0.86
Inman (city) Spartanburg County	18	0.78
Valley Falls (cdp) Spartanburg County	13	0.21
Irmo (town) Richland County	12	0.11
Arcadia (cdp) Spartanburg County	11	0.42
West Columbia (city) Lexington County	11	0.07

Top 10 Places Sorted by Percent of Total Population
Based on all places, regardless of total population

Place	Population	%
Central Pacolet (town) Spartanburg County	4	1.85
Roebuck (cdp) Spartanburg County	19	0.86
Inman (city) Spartanburg County	18	0.78
Clifton (cdp) Spartanburg County	4	0.74
Arcadia (cdp) Spartanburg County	11	0.42
Boiling Springs (cdp) Spartanburg County	33	0.40
Wellford (city) Spartanburg County	9	0.38
Lesslie (cdp) York County	10	0.32
Spartanburg (city) Spartanburg County	112	0.30
Duncan (town) Spartanburg County	8	0.25

Asian: Malaysian

Top 10 Places Sorted by Population
Based on all places, regardless of total population

Place	Population	%
Hilton Head Island (town) Beaufort County	7	0.02
North Charleston (city) Charleston County	7	0.01
Tega Cay (city) York County	6	0.08
Mount Pleasant (town) Charleston County	5	0.01
Rock Hill (city) York County	4	0.01
Charleston (city) Charleston County	4	<0.01
Columbia (city) Richland County	4	<0.01
Inman Mills (cdp) Spartanburg County	3	0.29
Sans Souci (cdp) Greenville County	3	0.04
Anderson (city) Anderson County	3	0.01

Top 10 Places Sorted by Percent of Total Population
Based on all places, regardless of total population

Place	Population	%
Inman Mills (cdp) Spartanburg County	3	0.29
Riverview (cdp) York County	1	0.15
Tega Cay (city) York County	6	0.08
Sans Souci (cdp) Greenville County	3	0.04
Hilton Head Island (town) Beaufort County	7	0.02
Port Royal (town) Beaufort County	2	0.02
Central (town) Pickens County	1	0.02
Chester (city) Chester County	1	0.02
North Charleston (city) Charleston County	7	0.01
Mount Pleasant (town) Charleston County	5	0.01

Top 10 Places Sorted by Percent of Total Population
Based on places with total population of 50,000 or more

Place	Population	%
North Charleston (city) Charleston County	7	0.01
Mount Pleasant (town) Charleston County	5	0.01
Rock Hill (city) York County	4	0.01
Charleston (city) Charleston County	4	<0.01
Columbia (city) Richland County	4	<0.01
Greenville (city) Greenville County	0	0.00

Asian: Nepalese

Top 10 Places Sorted by Population
Based on all places, regardless of total population

Place	Population	%
Columbia (city) Richland County	24	0.02
Simpsonville (city) Greenville County	12	0.07
Aiken (city) Aiken County	12	0.04
Spartanburg (city) Spartanburg County	10	0.03
Central (town) Pickens County	8	0.16
Florence (city) Florence County	8	0.02
Mount Pleasant (town) Charleston County	6	0.01
Charleston (city) Charleston County	5	<0.01
Clemson (city) Pickens County	4	0.03
Greer (city) Greenville County	4	0.02

Top 10 Places Sorted by Percent of Total Population
Based on all places, regardless of total population

Place	Population	%
Central (town) Pickens County	8	0.16
Simpsonville (city) Greenville County	12	0.07
Aiken (city) Aiken County	12	0.04
Golden Grove (cdp) Greenville County	1	0.04
Spartanburg (city) Spartanburg County	10	0.03
Clemson (city) Pickens County	4	0.03
Hardeeville (city) Jasper County	1	0.03
Columbia (city) Richland County	24	0.02
Florence (city) Florence County	8	0.02
Greer (city) Greenville County	4	0.02

Top 10 Places Sorted by Percent of Total Population
Based on places with total population of 50,000 or more

Place	Population	%
Columbia (city) Richland County	24	0.02
Mount Pleasant (town) Charleston County	6	0.01
Charleston (city) Charleston County	5	<0.01
Greenville (city) Greenville County	1	<0.01
North Charleston (city) Charleston County	1	<0.01
Rock Hill (city) York County	0	0.00

Asian: Pakistani

Top 10 Places Sorted by Population
Based on all places, regardless of total population

Place	Population	%
Columbia (city) Richland County	44	0.03
Dentsville (cdp) Richland County	42	0.30
Greenville (city) Greenville County	30	0.05
Mount Pleasant (town) Charleston County	29	0.04
Wade Hampton (cdp) Greenville County	28	0.14
Mauldin (city) Greenville County	24	0.10
Spartanburg (city) Spartanburg County	24	0.06
Rock Hill (city) York County	22	0.03
Charleston (city) Charleston County	20	0.02
Taylors (cdp) Greenville County	19	0.09

Top 10 Places Sorted by Percent of Total Population
Based on all places, regardless of total population

Place	Population	%
Cross Anchor (cdp) Spartanburg County	1	0.79
Dentsville (cdp) Richland County	42	0.30
Fairforest (cdp) Spartanburg County	5	0.30
Buffalo (cdp) Union County	3	0.24
Wade Hampton (cdp) Greenville County	28	0.14
Bishopville (city) Lee County	5	0.14
Barnwell (city) Barnwell County	6	0.13
Clemson (city) Pickens County	17	0.12
Five Forks (cdp) Greenville County	17	0.12
Hartsville (city) Darlington County	9	0.12

Top 10 Places Sorted by Percent of Total Population
Based on places with total population of 50,000 or more

Place	Population	%
Greenville (city) Greenville County	30	0.05
Mount Pleasant (town) Charleston County	29	0.04
Columbia (city) Richland County	44	0.03
Rock Hill (city) York County	22	0.03
Charleston (city) Charleston County	20	0.02
North Charleston (city) Charleston County	14	0.01

Asian: Sri Lankan

Top 10 Places Sorted by Population
Based on all places, regardless of total population

Place	Population	%
Clemson (city) Pickens County	31	0.22
Charleston (city) Charleston County	22	0.02
Columbia (city) Richland County	14	0.01
Mount Pleasant (town) Charleston County	11	0.02
Mauldin (city) Greenville County	7	0.03
Duncan (town) Spartanburg County	6	0.19
Anderson (city) Anderson County	6	0.02
Greer (city) Greenville County	5	0.02
Berea (cdp) Greenville County	4	0.03
Goose Creek (city) Berkeley County	4	0.01

Top 10 Places Sorted by Percent of Total Population
Based on all places, regardless of total population

Place	Population	%
Clemson (city) Pickens County	31	0.22
Duncan (town) Spartanburg County	6	0.19
Due West (town) Abbeville County	2	0.16
Riverview (cdp) York County	1	0.15
Awendaw (town) Charleston County	1	0.08
Brookdale (cdp) Orangeburg County	2	0.04
Folly Beach (city) Charleston County	1	0.04
Mauldin (city) Greenville County	7	0.03
Berea (cdp) Greenville County	4	0.03
Hardeeville (city) Jasper County	1	0.03

Please refer to the Explanation of Data in the front of the book for more detailed information.

Top 10 Places Sorted by Percent of Total Population
Based on places with total population of 50,000 or more

Place	Population	%
Charleston (city) Charleston County	22	0.02
Mount Pleasant (town) Charleston County	11	0.02
Columbia (city) Richland County	14	0.01
Greenville (city) Greenville County	4	0.01
Rock Hill (city) York County	2	<0.01
North Charleston (city) Charleston County	0	0.00

Asian: Taiwanese

Top 10 Places Sorted by Population
Based on all places, regardless of total population

Place	Population	%
Charleston (city) Charleston County	39	0.03
Columbia (city) Richland County	33	0.03
Florence (city) Florence County	29	0.08
Mount Pleasant (town) Charleston County	17	0.03
Clemson (city) Pickens County	14	0.10
Central (town) Pickens County	11	0.21
Hanahan (city) Berkeley County	10	0.06
Sumter (city) Sumter County	9	0.02
Greenville (city) Greenville County	8	0.01
North Charleston (city) Charleston County	8	0.01

Top 10 Places Sorted by Percent of Total Population
Based on all places, regardless of total population

Place	Population	%
Central (town) Pickens County	11	0.21
Clemson (city) Pickens County	14	0.10
Boiling Springs (cdp) Spartanburg County	7	0.09
Florence (city) Florence County	29	0.08
Stateburg (cdp) Sumter County	1	0.07
Hanahan (city) Berkeley County	10	0.06
Clover (town) York County	3	0.06
Tega Cay (city) York County	4	0.05
Cheraw (town) Chesterfield County	3	0.05
Cayce (city) Lexington County	5	0.04

Top 10 Places Sorted by Percent of Total Population
Based on places with total population of 50,000 or more

Place	Population	%
Charleston (city) Charleston County	39	0.03
Columbia (city) Richland County	33	0.03
Mount Pleasant (town) Charleston County	17	0.03
Greenville (city) Greenville County	8	0.01
North Charleston (city) Charleston County	8	0.01
Rock Hill (city) York County	5	0.01

Asian: Thai

Top 10 Places Sorted by Population
Based on all places, regardless of total population

Place	Population	%
Columbia (city) Richland County	70	0.05
North Charleston (city) Charleston County	53	0.05
Charleston (city) Charleston County	49	0.04
Sumter (city) Sumter County	48	0.12
Socastee (cdp) Horry County	46	0.23
Myrtle Beach (city) Horry County	36	0.13
Summerville (town) Dorchester County	35	0.08
Goose Creek (city) Berkeley County	26	0.07
North Myrtle Beach (city) Horry County	23	0.17
Clemson (city) Pickens County	22	0.16

Top 10 Places Sorted by Percent of Total Population
Based on all places, regardless of total population

Place	Population	%
Cherryvale (cdp) Sumter County	12	0.48
Inman (city) Spartanburg County	9	0.39
Dalzell (cdp) Sumter County	11	0.36
Cameron (town) Calhoun County	1	0.24
Socastee (cdp) Horry County	46	0.23
Hardeeville (city) Jasper County	6	0.20
Johnsonville (city) Florence County	3	0.20
Campobello (town) Spartanburg County	1	0.20
Laurel Bay (cdp) Beaufort County	11	0.19
Wedgefield (cdp) Sumter County	3	0.19

Top 10 Places Sorted by Percent of Total Population
Based on places with total population of 50,000 or more

Place	Population	%
Columbia (city) Richland County	70	0.05
North Charleston (city) Charleston County	53	0.05
Charleston (city) Charleston County	49	0.04
Greenville (city) Greenville County	18	0.03
Rock Hill (city) York County	17	0.03
Mount Pleasant (town) Charleston County	12	0.02

Asian: Vietnamese

Top 10 Places Sorted by Population
Based on all places, regardless of total population

Place	Population	%
Rock Hill (city) York County	384	0.58
Wade Hampton (cdp) Greenville County	369	1.79
Taylors (cdp) Greenville County	334	1.55
North Charleston (city) Charleston County	317	0.33
Charleston (city) Charleston County	243	0.20
Columbia (city) Richland County	196	0.15
Hanahan (city) Berkeley County	185	1.03
Socastee (cdp) Horry County	143	0.72
Mauldin (city) Greenville County	142	0.62
Mount Pleasant (town) Charleston County	134	0.20

Top 10 Places Sorted by Percent of Total Population
Based on all places, regardless of total population

Place	Population	%
Wade Hampton (cdp) Greenville County	369	1.79
Taylors (cdp) Greenville County	334	1.55
Hanahan (city) Berkeley County	185	1.03
Lowrys (town) Chester County	2	1.00
Berea (cdp) Greenville County	130	0.91
Lesslie (cdp) York County	26	0.84
Pine Ridge (town) Lexington County	15	0.73
Socastee (cdp) Horry County	143	0.72
Blythewood (town) Richland County	14	0.69
Glendale (cdp) Spartanburg County	2	0.65

Top 10 Places Sorted by Percent of Total Population
Based on places with total population of 50,000 or more

Place	Population	%
Rock Hill (city) York County	384	0.58
North Charleston (city) Charleston County	317	0.33
Charleston (city) Charleston County	243	0.20
Mount Pleasant (town) Charleston County	134	0.20
Columbia (city) Richland County	196	0.15
Greenville (city) Greenville County	72	0.12

Hawaii Native/Pacific Islander

Top 10 Places Sorted by Population
Based on all places, regardless of total population

Place	Population	%
Columbia (city) Richland County	338	0.26
North Charleston (city) Charleston County	288	0.30
Charleston (city) Charleston County	213	0.18
Goose Creek (city) Berkeley County	135	0.38
Myrtle Beach (city) Horry County	99	0.37
Rock Hill (city) York County	96	0.15
Summerville (town) Dorchester County	94	0.22
Greenville (city) Greenville County	90	0.15
Sumter (city) Sumter County	89	0.22
Woodfield (cdp) Richland County	65	0.70

Top 10 Places Sorted by Percent of Total Population
Based on all places, regardless of total population

Place	Population	%
Princeton (cdp) Laurens County	1	1.61
Ridge Spring (town) Saluda County	8	1.09
Briarcliffe Acres (town) Horry County	5	1.09
Reidville (town) Spartanburg County	6	1.00
Saluda (town) Saluda County	32	0.90
Cane Savannah (cdp) Sumter County	10	0.90
Monetta (town) Aiken County	2	0.85
Parksville (town) McCormick County	1	0.85
Windsor (town) Aiken County	1	0.83
Lowndesville (town) Abbeville County	1	0.78

Top 10 Places Sorted by Percent of Total Population
Based on places with total population of 50,000 or more

Place	Population	%
North Charleston (city) Charleston County	288	0.30
Columbia (city) Richland County	338	0.26
Charleston (city) Charleston County	213	0.18
Rock Hill (city) York County	96	0.15
Greenville (city) Greenville County	90	0.15
Mount Pleasant (town) Charleston County	52	0.08

Hawaii Native/Pacific Islander: Not Hispanic

Top 10 Places Sorted by Population
Based on all places, regardless of total population

Place	Population	%
Columbia (city) Richland County	304	0.24
North Charleston (city) Charleston County	228	0.23
Charleston (city) Charleston County	192	0.16
Goose Creek (city) Berkeley County	123	0.34
Summerville (town) Dorchester County	84	0.19
Myrtle Beach (city) Horry County	80	0.30
Sumter (city) Sumter County	79	0.19
Greenville (city) Greenville County	70	0.12
Woodfield (cdp) Richland County	52	0.56
Seven Oaks (cdp) Lexington County	48	0.32

Top 10 Places Sorted by Percent of Total Population
Based on all places, regardless of total population

Place	Population	%
Princeton (cdp) Laurens County	1	1.61
Ridge Spring (town) Saluda County	8	1.09
Briarcliffe Acres (town) Horry County	5	1.09
Reidville (town) Spartanburg County	6	1.00
Cane Savannah (cdp) Sumter County	10	0.90
Parksville (town) McCormick County	1	0.85
Lowndesville (town) Abbeville County	1	0.78
Oakland (cdp) Sumter County	8	0.65
Atlantic Beach (town) Horry County	2	0.60
Starr (town) Anderson County	1	0.58

Top 10 Places Sorted by Percent of Total Population
Based on places with total population of 50,000 or more

Place	Population	%
Columbia (city) Richland County	304	0.24
North Charleston (city) Charleston County	228	0.23
Charleston (city) Charleston County	192	0.16
Greenville (city) Greenville County	70	0.12
Mount Pleasant (town) Charleston County	44	0.06
Rock Hill (city) York County	42	0.06

Hawaii Native/Pacific Islander: Hispanic

Top 10 Places Sorted by Population
Based on all places, regardless of total population

Place	Population	%
North Charleston (city) Charleston County	60	0.06
Rock Hill (city) York County	54	0.08
Columbia (city) Richland County	34	0.03
Saluda (town) Saluda County	31	0.87
Hilton Head Island (town) Beaufort County	22	0.06
Charleston (city) Charleston County	21	0.02
Greenville (city) Greenville County	20	0.03
Myrtle Beach (city) Horry County	19	0.07
Socastee (cdp) Horry County	18	0.09
Newberry (city) Newberry County	14	0.14

Top 10 Places Sorted by Percent of Total Population
Based on all places, regardless of total population

Place	Population	%
Saluda (town) Saluda County	31	0.87
Windsor (town) Aiken County	1	0.83
Pelion (town) Lexington County	4	0.59
Monetta (town) Aiken County	1	0.42
Gray Court (town) Laurens County	3	0.38
Mulberry (cdp) Sumter County	2	0.38
Shell Point (cdp) Beaufort County	5	0.21
Watts Mills (cdp) Laurens County	3	0.18
Marion (city) Marion County	11	0.16
Welcome (cdp) Greenville County	11	0.16

Please refer to the Explanation of Data in the front of the book for more detailed information.

Top 10 Places Sorted by Percent of Total Population
Based on places with total population of 50,000 or more

Place	Population	%
Rock Hill (city) York County	54	0.08
North Charleston (city) Charleston County	60	0.06
Columbia (city) Richland County	34	0.03
Greenville (city) Greenville County	20	0.03
Charleston (city) Charleston County	21	0.02
Mount Pleasant (town) Charleston County	8	0.01

Hawaii Native/Pacific Islander: Fijian

Top 10 Places Sorted by Population
Based on all places, regardless of total population

Place	Population	%
Columbia (city) Richland County	6	<0.01
Florence (city) Florence County	3	0.01
Hilton Head Island (town) Beaufort County	3	0.01
St. Andrews (cdp) Richland County	3	0.01
Rock Hill (city) York County	2	<0.01
Bishopville (city) Lee County	1	0.03
Burton (cdp) Beaufort County	1	0.01
Ladson (cdp) Berkeley County	1	0.01
Port Royal (town) Beaufort County	1	0.01
Union (city) Union County	1	0.01

Top 10 Places Sorted by Percent of Total Population
Based on all places, regardless of total population

Place	Population	%
Bishopville (city) Lee County	1	0.03
Florence (city) Florence County	3	0.01
Hilton Head Island (town) Beaufort County	3	0.01
St. Andrews (cdp) Richland County	3	0.01
Burton (cdp) Beaufort County	1	0.01
Ladson (cdp) Berkeley County	1	0.01
Port Royal (town) Beaufort County	1	0.01
Union (city) Union County	1	0.01
Columbia (city) Richland County	6	<0.01
Rock Hill (city) York County	2	<0.01

Top 10 Places Sorted by Percent of Total Population
Based on places with total population of 50,000 or more

Place	Population	%
Columbia (city) Richland County	6	<0.01
Rock Hill (city) York County	2	<0.01
Charleston (city) Charleston County	1	<0.01
Greenville (city) Greenville County	0	0.00
Mount Pleasant (town) Charleston County	0	0.00
North Charleston (city) Charleston County	0	0.00

Hawaii Native/Pacific Islander: Guamanian or Chamorro

Top 10 Places Sorted by Population
Based on all places, regardless of total population

Place	Population	%
North Charleston (city) Charleston County	106	0.11
Columbia (city) Richland County	71	0.05
Rock Hill (city) York County	60	0.09
Sumter (city) Sumter County	38	0.09
Goose Creek (city) Berkeley County	37	0.10
Saluda (town) Saluda County	32	0.90
Mount Pleasant (town) Charleston County	29	0.04
Charleston (city) Charleston County	28	0.02
Myrtle Beach (city) Horry County	27	0.10
Greenville (city) Greenville County	22	0.04

Top 10 Places Sorted by Percent of Total Population
Based on all places, regardless of total population

Place	Population	%
Saluda (town) Saluda County	32	0.90
Starr (town) Anderson County	1	0.58
City View (cdp) Greenville County	6	0.45
Bishopville (city) Lee County	11	0.32
Cane Savannah (cdp) Sumter County	3	0.27
Neeses (town) Orangeburg County	1	0.27
Woodfield (cdp) Richland County	21	0.23
Dalzell (cdp) Sumter County	7	0.23
Shell Point (cdp) Beaufort County	5	0.21
Sharon (town) York County	1	0.20

Top 10 Places Sorted by Percent of Total Population
Based on places with total population of 50,000 or more

Place	Population	%
North Charleston (city) Charleston County	106	0.11
Rock Hill (city) York County	60	0.09
Columbia (city) Richland County	71	0.05
Mount Pleasant (town) Charleston County	29	0.04
Greenville (city) Greenville County	22	0.04
Charleston (city) Charleston County	28	0.02

Hawaii Native/Pacific Islander: Marshallese

Top 10 Places Sorted by Population
Based on all places, regardless of total population

Place	Population	%
Chester (city) Chester County	3	0.05
Charleston (city) Charleston County	1	<0.01
Columbia (city) Richland County	1	<0.01
Hilton Head Island (town) Beaufort County	1	<0.01
North Charleston (city) Charleston County	1	<0.01
Abbeville (city) Abbeville County	0	0.00
Aiken (city) Aiken County	0	0.00
Alcolu (cdp) Clarendon County	0	0.00
Allendale (town) Allendale County	0	0.00
Anderson (city) Anderson County	0	0.00

Top 10 Places Sorted by Percent of Total Population
Based on all places, regardless of total population

Place	Population	%
Chester (city) Chester County	3	0.05
Charleston (city) Charleston County	1	<0.01
Columbia (city) Richland County	1	<0.01
Hilton Head Island (town) Beaufort County	1	<0.01
North Charleston (city) Charleston County	1	<0.01
Abbeville (city) Abbeville County	0	0.00
Aiken (city) Aiken County	0	0.00
Alcolu (cdp) Clarendon County	0	0.00
Allendale (town) Allendale County	0	0.00
Anderson (city) Anderson County	0	0.00

Top 10 Places Sorted by Percent of Total Population
Based on places with total population of 50,000 or more

Place	Population	%
Charleston (city) Charleston County	1	<0.01
Columbia (city) Richland County	1	<0.01
North Charleston (city) Charleston County	1	<0.01
Greenville (city) Greenville County	0	0.00
Mount Pleasant (town) Charleston County	0	0.00
Rock Hill (city) York County	0	0.00

Hawaii Native/Pacific Islander: Native Hawaiian

Top 10 Places Sorted by Population
Based on all places, regardless of total population

Place	Population	%
Columbia (city) Richland County	116	0.09
North Charleston (city) Charleston County	71	0.07
Charleston (city) Charleston County	44	0.04
Goose Creek (city) Berkeley County	41	0.11
Summerville (town) Dorchester County	37	0.09
Aiken (city) Aiken County	24	0.08
Sumter (city) Sumter County	24	0.06
Greenville (city) Greenville County	23	0.04
Port Royal (town) Beaufort County	19	0.18
Beaufort (city) Beaufort County	19	0.15

Top 10 Places Sorted by Percent of Total Population
Based on all places, regardless of total population

Place	Population	%
Monetta (town) Aiken County	2	0.85
Parksville (town) McCormick County	1	0.85
Lowndesville (town) Abbeville County	1	0.78
Gray Court (town) Laurens County	4	0.50
Quinby (town) Florence County	4	0.43
Ehrhardt (town) Bamberg County	2	0.37
Fair Play (cdp) Oconee County	2	0.29
Laurel Bay (cdp) Beaufort County	16	0.27
Cane Savannah (cdp) Sumter County	3	0.27

| Oakland (cdp) Sumter County | 3 | 0.24 |

Top 10 Places Sorted by Percent of Total Population
Based on places with total population of 50,000 or more

Place	Population	%
Columbia (city) Richland County	116	0.09
North Charleston (city) Charleston County	71	0.07
Charleston (city) Charleston County	44	0.04
Greenville (city) Greenville County	23	0.04
Rock Hill (city) York County	11	0.02
Mount Pleasant (town) Charleston County	10	0.01

Hawaii Native/Pacific Islander: Samoan

Top 10 Places Sorted by Population
Based on all places, regardless of total population

Place	Population	%
Columbia (city) Richland County	56	0.04
Goose Creek (city) Berkeley County	20	0.06
North Charleston (city) Charleston County	20	0.02
Charleston (city) Charleston County	14	0.01
Greenville (city) Greenville County	12	0.02
Bishopville (city) Lee County	10	0.29
Port Royal (town) Beaufort County	9	0.08
Sumter (city) Sumter County	9	0.02
Mount Pleasant (town) Charleston County	9	0.01
McCormick (town) McCormick County	8	0.29

Top 10 Places Sorted by Percent of Total Population
Based on all places, regardless of total population

Place	Population	%
Princeton (cdp) Laurens County	1	1.61
Cane Savannah (cdp) Sumter County	4	0.36
Bishopville (city) Lee County	10	0.29
McCormick (town) McCormick County	8	0.29
Johnsonville (city) Florence County	4	0.27
Fort Lawn (town) Chester County	2	0.22
St. Matthews (town) Calhoun County	2	0.10
Summerton (town) Clarendon County	1	0.10
Yemassee (town) Hampton County	1	0.10
Inman (city) Spartanburg County	2	0.09

Top 10 Places Sorted by Percent of Total Population
Based on places with total population of 50,000 or more

Place	Population	%
Columbia (city) Richland County	56	0.04
North Charleston (city) Charleston County	20	0.02
Greenville (city) Greenville County	12	0.02
Charleston (city) Charleston County	14	0.01
Mount Pleasant (town) Charleston County	9	0.01
Rock Hill (city) York County	7	0.01

Hawaii Native/Pacific Islander: Tongan

Top 10 Places Sorted by Population
Based on all places, regardless of total population

Place	Population	%
Rock Hill (city) York County	5	0.01
Columbia (city) Richland County	5	<0.01
Briarcliffe Acres (town) Horry County	4	0.88
Fountain Inn (city) Greenville County	3	0.04
Pickens (city) Pickens County	2	0.06
North Myrtle Beach (city) Horry County	2	0.01
Greenville (city) Greenville County	2	<0.01
Folly Beach (city) Charleston County	1	0.04
East Gaffney (cdp) Cherokee County	1	0.03
Simpsonville (city) Greenville County	1	0.01

Top 10 Places Sorted by Percent of Total Population
Based on all places, regardless of total population

Place	Population	%
Briarcliffe Acres (town) Horry County	4	0.88
Pickens (city) Pickens County	2	0.06
Fountain Inn (city) Greenville County	3	0.04
Folly Beach (city) Charleston County	1	0.04
East Gaffney (cdp) Cherokee County	1	0.03
Rock Hill (city) York County	5	0.01
North Myrtle Beach (city) Horry County	2	0.01
Simpsonville (city) Greenville County	1	0.01
Columbia (city) Richland County	5	<0.01

Please refer to the Explanation of Data in the front of the book for more detailed information.

Place	Population	%
Greenville (city) Greenville County	2	<0.01

Top 10 Places Sorted by Percent of Total Population
Based on places with total population of 50,000 or more

Place	Population	%
Rock Hill (city) York County	5	0.01
Columbia (city) Richland County	5	<0.01
Greenville (city) Greenville County	2	<0.01
Mount Pleasant (town) Charleston County	1	<0.01
Charleston (city) Charleston County	0	0.00
North Charleston (city) Charleston County	0	0.00

White

Top 10 Places Sorted by Population
Based on all places, regardless of total population

Place	Population	%
Charleston (city) Charleston County	85,755	71.41
Columbia (city) Richland County	68,681	53.13
Mount Pleasant (town) Charleston County	62,618	92.30
North Charleston (city) Charleston County	42,441	43.54
Greenville (city) Greenville County	38,214	65.42
Rock Hill (city) York County	37,269	56.34
Summerville (town) Dorchester County	32,369	74.60
Hilton Head Island (town) Beaufort County	31,150	83.96
Goose Creek (city) Berkeley County	26,717	74.34
Myrtle Beach (city) Horry County	20,254	74.71

Top 10 Places Sorted by Percent of Total Population
Based on all places, regardless of total population

Place	Population	%
Salem (town) Oconee County	135	100.00
Pawleys Island (town) Georgetown County	103	100.00
Smyrna (town) York County	45	100.00
Newry (cdp) Oconee County	171	99.42
Smoaks (town) Colleton County	125	99.21
Sullivan's Island (town) Charleston County	1,772	98.94
Edisto Beach (town) Colleton County	409	98.79
Isle of Palms (city) Charleston County	4,059	98.21
Six Mile (town) Pickens County	659	97.63
Seabrook Island (town) Charleston County	1,669	97.37

Top 10 Places Sorted by Percent of Total Population
Based on places with total population of 50,000 or more

Place	Population	%
Mount Pleasant (town) Charleston County	62,618	92.30
Charleston (city) Charleston County	85,755	71.41
Greenville (city) Greenville County	38,214	65.42
Rock Hill (city) York County	37,269	56.34
Columbia (city) Richland County	68,681	53.13
North Charleston (city) Charleston County	42,441	43.54

White: Not Hispanic

Top 10 Places Sorted by Population
Based on all places, regardless of total population

Place	Population	%
Charleston (city) Charleston County	83,699	69.70
Columbia (city) Richland County	65,644	50.78
Mount Pleasant (town) Charleston County	61,219	90.24
North Charleston (city) Charleston County	38,468	39.47
Greenville (city) Greenville County	36,450	62.40
Rock Hill (city) York County	35,555	53.75
Summerville (town) Dorchester County	31,037	71.53
Hilton Head Island (town) Beaufort County	28,108	75.76
Goose Creek (city) Berkeley County	25,443	70.80
Aiken (city) Aiken County	19,642	66.53

Top 10 Places Sorted by Percent of Total Population
Based on all places, regardless of total population

Place	Population	%
Salem (town) Oconee County	135	100.00
Pawleys Island (town) Georgetown County	103	100.00
Smyrna (town) York County	45	100.00
Smoaks (town) Colleton County	125	99.21
Newry (cdp) Oconee County	170	98.84
Edisto Beach (town) Colleton County	408	98.55
Sullivan's Island (town) Charleston County	1,753	97.88
Six Mile (town) Pickens County	658	97.48
Isle of Palms (city) Charleston County	4,017	97.19

Place	Population	%
Lake Secession (cdp) Abbeville County	1,046	96.58

Top 10 Places Sorted by Percent of Total Population
Based on places with total population of 50,000 or more

Place	Population	%
Mount Pleasant (town) Charleston County	61,219	90.24
Charleston (city) Charleston County	83,699	69.70
Greenville (city) Greenville County	36,450	62.40
Rock Hill (city) York County	35,555	53.75
Columbia (city) Richland County	65,644	50.78
North Charleston (city) Charleston County	38,468	39.47

White: Hispanic

Top 10 Places Sorted by Population
Based on all places, regardless of total population

Place	Population	%
North Charleston (city) Charleston County	3,973	4.08
Hilton Head Island (town) Beaufort County	3,042	8.20
Columbia (city) Richland County	3,037	2.35
Charleston (city) Charleston County	2,056	1.71
Greer (city) Greenville County	1,768	6.93
Greenville (city) Greenville County	1,764	3.02
Rock Hill (city) York County	1,714	2.59
Mount Pleasant (town) Charleston County	1,399	2.06
Bluffton (town) Beaufort County	1,374	10.97
Summerville (town) Dorchester County	1,332	3.07

Top 10 Places Sorted by Percent of Total Population
Based on all places, regardless of total population

Place	Population	%
Fairforest (cdp) Spartanburg County	361	21.32
Arcadia (cdp) Spartanburg County	363	13.78
Southern Shops (cdp) Spartanburg County	506	13.43
City View (cdp) Greenville County	161	11.97
Luray (town) Hampton County	15	11.81
Hardeeville (city) Jasper County	341	11.55
Bluffton (town) Beaufort County	1,374	10.97
Watts Mills (cdp) Laurens County	169	10.34
Gramling (cdp) Spartanburg County	8	9.30
Windsor (town) Aiken County	11	9.09

Top 10 Places Sorted by Percent of Total Population
Based on places with total population of 50,000 or more

Place	Population	%
North Charleston (city) Charleston County	3,973	4.08
Greenville (city) Greenville County	1,764	3.02
Rock Hill (city) York County	1,714	2.59
Columbia (city) Richland County	3,037	2.35
Mount Pleasant (town) Charleston County	1,399	2.06
Charleston (city) Charleston County	2,056	1.71

Please refer to the Explanation of Data in the front of the book for more detailed information.

Climate

South Carolina Physical Features and Climate Narrative

PHYSICAL FEATURES. South Carolina is located on the southeastern coast of the United States between the southern part of the Appalachian Mountains and the Atlantic Ocean. Its north-south extent is 220 miles, from 32° to 35.2° N. latitude. The mountains in the extreme northwestern part of the State are 240 miles from the coastline. The coastline is 185 miles long and oriented southwest to northeast.

South Carolina shares some common topographic features with several eastern seaboard states. All of these features have a southwest to northeast orientation and extend across the whole State. The Blue Ridge Range of the Appalachian Mountains lies in the extreme northwestern part of the State. Elevations range from 1,000 to 2,000 feet with several peaks going over 3,000 feet. Sassafras Mountain, at 3,554 feet elevation, is the highest point in the State. The Mountain Region covers less than 10 percent of the State's area and to its southeast lies the Piedmont Plateau. The Plateau extends nearly to the center of the State with elevations decreasing northwest to southeast from 1,000 to 500 feet. There is a narrow hilly region where the Plateau descends to the Coastal Plain. In South Carolina this "fall line" region is known as the "Sand Hills;" where elevations range from 500 to 200 feet. The width of the Sand Hills area is about 30 to 40 miles. Between the Sand Hills and the Atlantic Ocean lies the Coastal Plain. The Plain is broad and nearly level with elevations mostly between 50 and 200 feet. About 40 percent of the area of the State lies in the Coastal Plain.

All of the State's rivers drain southeast from the Mountain Region or Piedmont Plateau toward the ocean. There are three major and one minor river-basin systems. The Santee is the largest and drains the entire center portion of the State. The Savannah drains the western part of the State. The third major system is the Pee Dee, located in the northeastern section. The Edisto is a lesser river system lying between the Santee and Savannah.

There are many low sea islands separated from the mainland by shallow straits, sounds, and coastal streams. The Intracoastal Waterway can be found along much of the coastline.

GENERAL CLIMATE. Several major factors combine to give South Carolina a pleasant, mild, and humid climate. It is located at a relatively low latitude (32 to 35° N.) and most of the State is under 1,000 feet in elevation. It has a long coastline along which moves the warm Gulf Stream current. The mountains to the north and west block or delay many cold air masses approaching from those directions. Even the deep cold air masses which cross the mountains rapidly are warmed somewhat as the air is heated by compression when it descends on the southeastern side. This effect can be seen on the maps of minimum temperature in January and to a lesser degree in July, where a fairly large area of relatively higher temperature appears just southeast of the mountains.

It is convenient for climatic discussion to divide the State into areas coinciding closely with the topographic features already discussed. Six areas can be defined: (1) the Outer Coastal Plain; (2) the Inner Coastal Plain; (3) the Sand Hills; (4) the Lower Piedmont Plateau; (5) the Upper Piedmont Plateau; and (6) the Mountain Region.

TEMPERATURE. Lower temperatures can be expected in the Upper Piedmont and Mountain Region, where latitude, elevation and distance inland all have large values. Higher temperatures will result from smaller values of the three factors, as are found along the southern coast. There is a gradual decrease in annual average temperature northwestward from 68°F. at the coast to 58°F. at the edge of the mountains. Within the Mountain Region, variations in temperature are due almost entirely to elevation differences. The ocean waters have very small daily and annual changes in temperature when compared with the land surface. The air over the coastal water is cooler than the air over the land in summer and warmer than the air over land in winter, and this has a controlling effect on the temperatures of locations on and very near the coast. The highest temperatures are found in the central part of the State with the coast being four to five degrees cooler. Clouds and rainfall have a minor effect on temperature. Maximum temperatures in summer are reduced slightly in areas where afternoon cloudiness and rain are persistent. Such an area is found along the Outer Coastal Plain where sea breezes produce clouds and rain nearly every summer day and dissipate at night.

Summers are rather hot and air conditioning is desirable at elevations below 500 feet. Fall and spring are mild and winters are rather cool at elevations above 500 feet.

PRECIPITATION. Rainfall is adequate in all parts of the State. Annual rainfall averages up to 80 inches in the highest part of the Mountain Region and less than 42 inches in parts of the Inner Coastal Plain and the Sand Hills. The Mountain Region is wet with amounts of 56 inches or more, the Upper Piedmont is relatively wet with amounts of 48 to 55 inches, the Lower Piedmont is relatively dry with amounts of 43 to 47 inches, the Outer Coastal Plain is relatively wet with amounts of 48 to 53 inches, and the Inner Coastal Plain is relatively dry with amounts of 38 to 47 inches. The Sand Hills area is less clear cut but is in general a relatively wet strip with a small dry area imbedded in it a few miles south of Columbia. The immediate south coast is also on the dry side. The driest period is in October and November when there is little cyclonic storm activity. Rainfall increases gradually and reaches a peak in March when cyclone and cold front activity are at a maximum. There is a general decrease again to a dry period from late April through early June. From the latter part of June through early September is a wet period primarily due to thunderstorm and shower activity which reaches its peak in July, the wettest summer month. The summer maximum stretches a little into the fall along the coast due to occasional tropical storm activity.

Solid forms of precipitation include snow, sleet, and hail. Hail is not frequent but does occur with spring thunderstorms from March through early May. Snow and sleet may occur separately, combined or mixed with rain during the winter months of December through February. Snow may occur from one to three times in winter. Seldom do accumulations remain very long on the ground except in the mountains. Statewide snows of notable amounts can occur when a cyclonic storm moves northeastward along or just off the coast. Freezing rain also occurs from one to three times per winter in the northern half of the State. Severe drought occurs about once in 15 years with less severe and less widespread droughts about once in seven or eight years.

OTHER CLIMATIC ELEMENTS. The percent of possible sunshine received varies over the State, similar to the variation in cloudiness and precipitation. Values in winter range from 50 to 60 percent, in summer from 60 to 70, with the dry periods in spring and fall receiving 70 to 75 percent. The variation in relative humidity with time of day is considerably greater than day to day and month to month variations. Highest values of 80 to 90 percent or more are reached at about sunrise and the lowest values of 45 to 50 percent occur an hour or two after local noon. There is about a 10 percent difference between winter and summer, with summer being the higher of the two seasons. The prevailing surface winds tend to be either from northeast or southwest due to the presence and orientation of the Appalachian Mountains. Winds of all directions occur throughout the State during the year, but the prevailing directions by seasons are: spring—southwest; summer—south and southwest; autumn—northeast; and winter—northeast and southwest.

STORMS. Severe weather comes to South Carolina occasionally in the form of violent thunderstorms, tornadoes and hurricanes. Although thunderstorms are common in the summer months, the more violent ones generally accompany the squall lines and active cold fronts of spring. Generally, they bring high winds, hail, and considerable lightning, and sometimes spawn a tornado (average of seven or eight a year). Sixty percent of the tornadoes occur from March through June with April being the peak month with 25 percent. Tropical storms or hurricanes affect the State about one year out of two. Most of the occurrences are tropical storms which do little damage, frequently bringing rains at a time when they are needed. Most of the hurricanes affect only the Outer Coastal Plain. If they do come far inland, they decrease in intensity quite rapidly. Considerable flooding accompanies hurricanes which come very far inland and high tides occur along the coast to the north and east of the storm centers.

There is minor flooding somewhere in the State every year. It can occur on any of the many streams and rivers. There is a major flood about once every seven or eight years.

There have been many earth tremors in South Carolina over the years. The southern part of the Coastal Plain is indicated as earthquake prone.

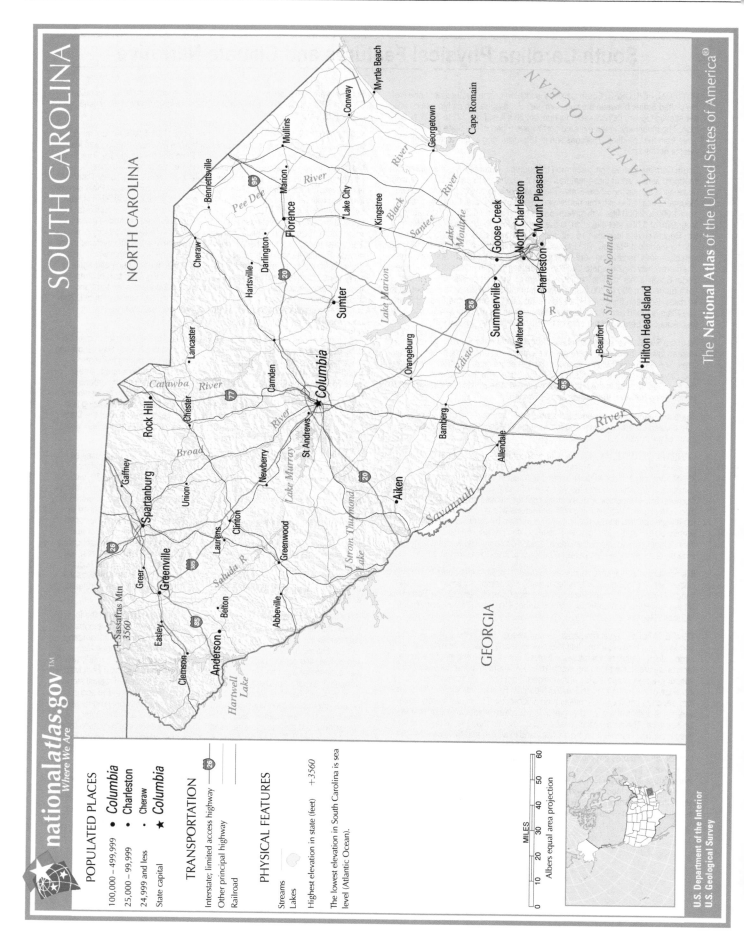

SOUTH CAROLINA

NORTH CAROLINA

GEORGIA

ATLANTIC OCEAN

The **National Atlas** of the United States of America®

nationalatlas.gov™
Where We Are

POPULATED PLACES

100,000 – 499,999   ● **Columbia**
25,000 – 99,999   ● Charleston
24,999 and less   • Cheraw
State capital   ★ *Columbia*

TRANSPORTATION

Interstate; limited access highway
Other principal highway
Railroad

PHYSICAL FEATURES

Streams
Lakes
Highest elevation in state (feet)   +3560

The lowest elevation in South Carolina is sea level (Atlantic Ocean).

MILES
0   10   20   30   40   50   60
Albers equal area projection

U.S. Department of the Interior
U.S. Geological Survey

Myrtle Beach
Conway
Georgetown
Cape Romain
Mullins
Bennettsville
Marion
Cheraw
Pee Dee
River
Lake City
Kingstree
Florence
Darlington
Hartsville
Black
Santee
River
Goose Creek
North Charleston
Mount Pleasant
Lake Moultrie
Sumter
Charleston
Lancaster
Lake Marion
Summerville
Orangeburg
Walterboro
St Helena Sound
Beaufort
Catawba River
Camden
Edisto
Hilton Head Island
Chester
Columbia
Rock Hill
St Andrews
Bamberg
Broad
Newberry
Lake Murray
River
Allendale
Gaffney
Union
Aiken
Spartanburg
Laurens
Clinton
J Strom Thurmond Lake
Savannah
River
Greenville
Greer
Greenwood
Saluda R
Abbeville
Belton
Sassafras Mtn 3560
Easley
Anderson
Clemson
Hartwell Lake

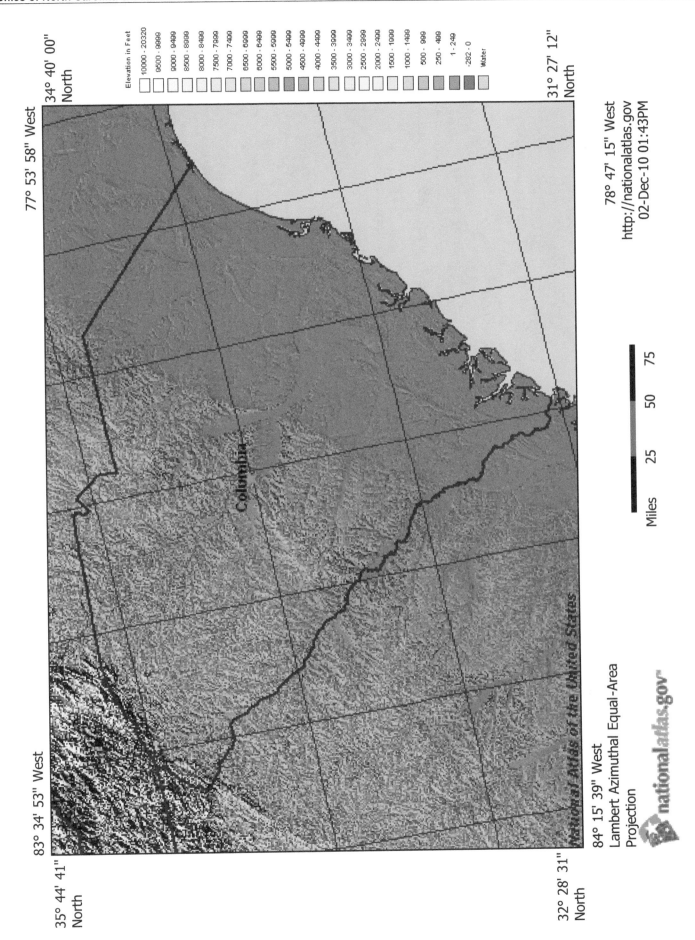

Elevation in Feet

10000 - 20320
9500 - 9999
9000 - 9499
8500 - 8999
8000 - 8499
7500 - 7999
7000 - 7499
6500 - 6999
6000 - 6499
5500 - 5999
5000 - 5499
4500 - 4999
4000 - 4499
3500 - 3999
3000 - 3499
2500 - 2999
2000 - 2499
1500 - 1999
1000 - 1499
500 - 999
250 - 499
1 - 249
-282 - 0
Water

34° 40' 00"
North

77° 53' 58" West

83° 34' 53" West

35° 44' 41"
North

Columbia

31° 27' 12"
North

78° 47' 15" West
http://nationalatlas.gov
02-Dec-10 01:43PM

32° 28' 31"
North

84° 15' 39" West
Lambert Azimuthal Equal-Area
Projection

National Atlas of the United States

Miles   25   50   75

nationalatlas.gov

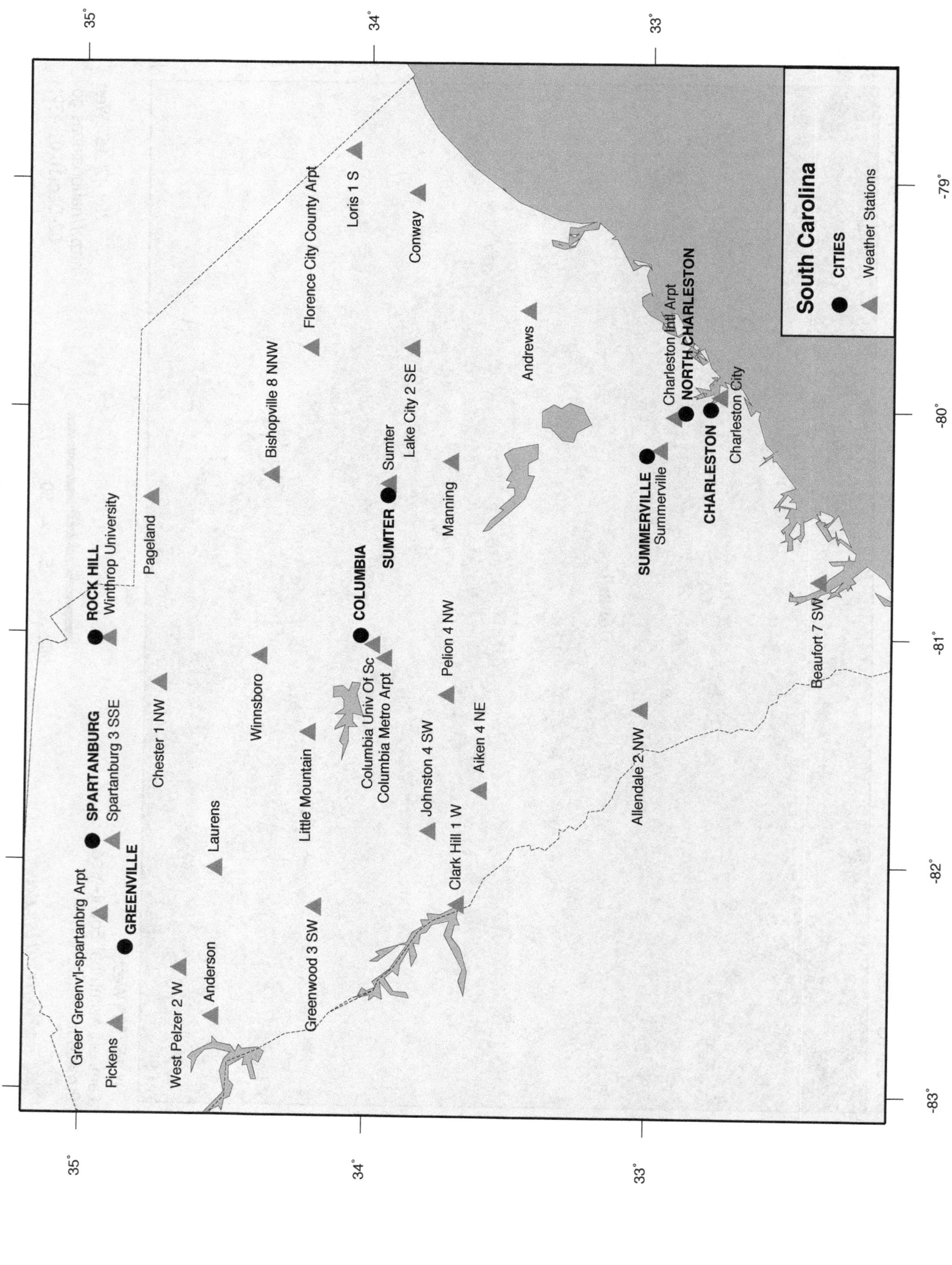

South Carolina

● CITIES

▲ Weather Stations

Loris 1 S

Florence City County Arpt

Conway

Bishopville 8 NNW

Andrews

Charleston Intl Arpt

NORTH CHARLESTON

Sumter

Lake City 2 SE

SUMTER

COLUMBIA

Manning

SUMMERVILLE

Summerville

CHARLESTON

Charleston City

ROCK HILL

Winthrop University

Pageland

Columbia Univ Of Sc

Columbia Metro Arpt

Pelion 4 NW

Chester 1 NW

Winnsboro

Johnston 4 SW

Aiken 4 NE

Beaufort 7 SW

SPARTANBURG

Spartanburg 3 SSE

Laurens

Little Mountain

Allendale 2 NW

GREENVILLE

Clark Hill 1 W

Greer Greenvl'-spartanbrg Arpt

Greenwood 3 SW

West Pelzer 2 W

Anderson

Pickens

South Carolina Weather Stations by County

County	Station Name
Aiken	Aiken 4 NE
Allendale	Allendale 2 NW
Anderson	Anderson West Pelzer 2 W
Beaufort	Beaufort 7 SW
Charleston	Charleston City Charleston Intl Arpt
Chester	Chester 1 NW
Chesterfield	Pageland
Clarendon	Manning
Dorchester	Summerville
Edgefield	Johnston 4 SW
Fairfield	Winnsboro
Florence	Florence City County Arpt Lake City 2 SE
Georgetown	Andrews
Greenwood	Greenwood 3 SW
Horry	Conway Loris 1 S
Laurens	Laurens
Lee	Bishopville 8 NNW
Lexington	Columbia Metro Arpt Pelion 4 NW
Mccormick	Clark Hill 1 W
Newberry	Little Mountain
Pickens	Pickens
Richland	Columbia Univ of SC
Spartanburg	Greer Greenville-Spartanbrg Arpt Spartanburg 3 SSE
Sumter	Sumter
York	Winthrop University

South Carolina Weather Stations by City

City	Station Name	Miles
Aiken	Augusta Bush Field, GA	18.4
	Aiken 4 NE	4.7
	Johnston 4 SW	18.2
Anderson	Hartwell, GA	20.0
	Anderson	1.6
	West Pelzer 2 W	13.1
Charleston	Charleston Intl Arpt	7.9
	Charleston City	3.1
	Summerville	17.5
Columbia	Columbia Metro Arpt	7.7
	Columbia Univ of SC	2.4
	Winnsboro	24.6
Easley	Anderson	20.6
	Greer Greenville-Spartanbrg Arpt	21.8
	Pickens	8.2
	West Pelzer 2 W	13.5
Florence	Florence City County Arpt	2.7
	Lake City 2 SE	23.1
Goose Creek	Charleston Intl Arpt	6.1
	Charleston City	14.1
	Summerville	11.1
Greenville	Greer Greenville-Spartanbrg Arpt	9.9
	Pickens	19.4
	West Pelzer 2 W	14.7
Greenwood	Greenwood 3 SW	3.2
	Laurens	23.4
Greer	Tryon, NC	18.5
	Greer Greenville-Spartanbrg Arpt	2.4
	Spartanburg 3 SSE	18.0
	West Pelzer 2 W	24.2
Hilton Head Island	Beaufort 7 SW	13.1
Mauldin	Greer Greenville-Spartanbrg Arpt	9.4
	Laurens	24.0
	Pickens	24.4
	Spartanburg 3 SSE	23.3
	West Pelzer 2 W	13.8
Mount Pleasant	Charleston Intl Arpt	11.9
	Charleston City	5.9
	Summerville	22.3
Myrtle Beach	Conway	13.3
	Loris 1 S	23.5
North Augusta	Appling 2 NW, GA	21.4
	Augusta Bush Field, GA	10.2
	Aiken 4 NE	17.3
	Clark Hill 1 W	16.3
	Johnston 4 SW	19.8
North Charleston	Charleston Intl Arpt	0.5
	Charleston City	9.4
	Summerville	10.8

City	Station Name	Miles
Rock Hill	Charlotte Douglas Intl Arpt, NC	19.6
	Gastonia, NC	23.3
	Chester 1 NW	18.9
	Winthrop University	0.7
Spartanburg	Forest City 6 SW, NC	22.3
	Tryon, NC	24.6
	Greer Greenville-Spartanbrg Arpt	16.5
	Spartanburg 3 SSE	3.2
St. Andrews	Columbia Metro Arpt	7.0
	Columbia Univ of SC	6.9
	Little Mountain	20.5
	Pelion 4 NW	24.9
	Winnsboro	21.8
Summerville	Charleston Intl Arpt	11.3
	Charleston City	21.0
	Summerville	1.2
Sumter	Manning	18.3
	Sumter	1.7
Taylors	Tryon, NC	20.4
	Greer Greenville-Spartanbrg Arpt	5.5
	Pickens	23.0
	Spartanburg 3 SSE	22.5
	West Pelzer 2 W	20.6
Wade Hampton	Tryon, NC	22.7
	Greer Greenville-Spartanbrg Arpt	6.7
	Pickens	21.7
	Spartanburg 3 SSE	23.6
	West Pelzer 2 W	18.1

Note: Miles is the distance between the geographic center of the city and the weather station.

South Carolina Weather Stations by Elevation

Feet	Station Name
1,162	Pickens
957	Greer Greenville-Spartanbrg Arpt
861	West Pelzer 2 W
799	Anderson
710	Little Mountain
689	Winthrop University
620	Johnston 4 SW
620	Pageland
615	Greenwood 3 SW
609	Spartanburg 3 SSE
588	Laurens
560	Winnsboro
520	Chester 1 NW
450	Pelion 4 NW
399	Aiken 4 NE
379	Clark Hill 1 W
249	Bishopville 8 NNW
242	Columbia Univ of SC
212	Columbia Metro Arpt
180	Allendale 2 NW
176	Sumter
146	Florence City County Arpt
100	Manning
89	Loris 1 S
75	Lake City 2 SE
40	Charleston Intl Arpt
35	Andrews
35	Summerville
20	Beaufort 7 SW
20	Conway
9	Charleston City

See User Guide for station inclusion criteria.

Charleston Int'l Airport

Charleston is a peninsula city bounded on the west and south by the Ashley River, on the east by the Cooper River, and on the southeast by a spacious harbor. Weather records for the airport are from a site some 10 miles inland. The terrain is generally level, ranging in elevation from sea level to 20 feet on the peninsula, with gradual increases in elevation toward inland areas.

The climate is temperate, modified considerably by the nearness to the ocean. The marine influence is noticeable during winter when the low temperatures are some-times 10-15 degrees higher on the peninsula than at the airport. By the same token, high temperatures are generally a few degrees lower on the peninsula. The pre-vailing winds are northerly in the fall and winter, southerly in the spring and summer.

Summer is warm and humid. Temperatures of 100 degrees or more are infrequent. High temperatures are generally several degrees lower along the coast than inland due to the cooling effect of the sea breeze. Summer is the rainiest season with 41 percent of the annual total. The rain, except during occasional tropical storms, gen-erally occurs as showers or thunderstorms.

The fall season passes through the warm Indian Summer period to the pre-winter cold spells which begin late in November. From late September to early November the weather is mostly sunny and temperature extremes are rare. Late summer and early fall is the period of maximum threat to the South Carolina coast from hurricanes.

The winter months, December through February, are mild with periods of rain. However, the winter rainfall is generally of a more uniform type. There is some chance of a snow flurry, with the best probability of its occurrence in January, but a significant amount is rarely measured. An average winter would experience less than one cold wave and severe freeze. Temperatures of 20 degrees or less on the peninsula and along the coast are very unusual.

The most spectacular time of the year, weatherwise, is spring with its rapid changes from windy and cold in March to warm and pleasant in May. Severe local storms are more likely to occur in spring than in summer.

The average occurrence of the first freeze in the fall is early December, and the average last freeze is late February, giving an average growing season of about 294 days.

Charleston Int'l Airport *Charleston County*　Elevation: 40 ft.　Latitude: 32° 54' N　Longitude: 80° 02' W

	JAN	FEB	MAR	APR	MAY	JUN	JUL	AUG	SEP	OCT	NOV	DEC	YEAR
Mean Maximum Temp. (°F)	59.1	62.8	69.5	76.4	83.1	88.3	91.2	89.6	84.9	77.0	69.7	61.7	76.1
Mean Temp. (°F)	48.7	52.0	58.4	65.1	72.7	79.2	82.4	81.2	76.4	67.1	58.8	51.3	66.1
Mean Minimum Temp. (°F)	38.3	41.2	47.2	53.8	62.2	70.0	73.6	72.8	67.9	57.2	48.0	40.8	56.1
Extreme Maximum Temp. (°F)	81	87	89	95	98	101	104	105	98	94	87	82	105
Extreme Minimum Temp. (°F)	6	16	15	30	42	53	62	57	46	34	24	11	6
Days Maximum Temp. ≥ 90°F	0	0	0	1	4	13	21	16	5	1	0	0	61
Days Maximum Temp. ≤ 32°F	0	0	0	0	0	0	0	0	0	0	0	0	0
Days Minimum Temp. ≤ 32°F	9	5	2	0	0	0	0	0	0	0	1	7	24
Days Minimum Temp. ≤ 0°F	0	0	0	0	0	0	0	0	0	0	0	0	0
Heating Degree Days (base 65°F)	501	368	228	83	9	0	0	0	2	62	212	426	1,891
Cooling Degree Days (base 65°F)	3	7	30	93	254	432	548	511	351	135	35	8	2,407
Mean Precipitation (in.)	3.63	2.92	3.83	3.00	3.09	5.48	6.43	6.84	5.56	3.77	2.49	3.07	50.11
Maximum Precipitation (in.)*	8.9	6.3	11.1	9.5	9.3	27.2	18.5	17.0	17.3	12.1	7.3	7.1	73.0
Minimum Precipitation (in.)*	0.6	0.3	0.7	trace	0.7	1.0	1.8	0.7	0.2	0.2	0.5	0.7	30.3
Extreme Maximum Daily Precip. (in.)	3.90	3.02	4.13	3.73	2.45	4.91	5.39	4.53	6.00	6.57	3.50	3.18	6.57
Days With ≥ 0.1" Precipitation	6	5	5	5	5	8	9	9	7	5	4	6	74
Days With ≥ 0.5" Precipitation	3	2	2	2	2	4	4	5	3	2	2	2	33
Days With ≥ 1.0" Precipitation	1	1	1	1	1	2	2	2	2	1	1	1	16
Mean Snowfall (in.)	0.0	trace	0.1	trace	trace	trace	trace	0.0	0.0	0.0	trace	0.5	0.6
Maximum Snowfall (in.)*	1	7	2	0	0	0	0	0	0	0	trace	8	9
Maximum 24-hr. Snowfall (in.)*	1	5	2	0	0	0	0	0	0	0	trace	8	9
Maximum Snow Depth (in.)	trace	1	1	trace	trace	trace	trace	0	0	0	trace	6	6
Days With ≥ 1.0" Snow Depth	0	0	0	0	0	0	0	0	0	0	0	8	8
Thunderstorm Days*	1	1	2	3	7	10	14	12	5	2	1	1	59
Foggy Days*	14	11	13	12	14	13	11	14	16	14	14	14	160
Predominant Sky Cover*	OVR	OVR	OVR	CLR	OVR	BRK	BRK	BRK	OVR	CLR	CLR	OVR	OVR
Mean Relative Humidity 7am (%)*	83	81	83	84	85	86	88	90	91	89	86	83	86
Mean Relative Humidity 4pm (%)*	55	52	51	51	56	62	66	66	65	58	56	55	58
Mean Dewpoint (°F)*	38	39	45	52	61	68	72	72	67	57	47	40	55
Prevailing Wind Direction*	NNE	SSW	SSW	SSW	S	S	SSW	S	NNE	NNE	NNE	NNE	NNE
Prevailing Wind Speed (mph)*	9	12	12	12	9	8	9	8	9	9	9	9	9
Maximum Wind Gust (mph)*	67	62	69	71	60	64	61	69	98	54	55	55	98

Note: (*) Period of record is 1945-1995

Columbia Metro Airport

Columbia is centrally located within the state of South Carolina and lies on the Congaree River near the confluence of the Broad and Saluda Rivers. The surrounding terrain is rolling, sloping from about 350 feet above sea level in northern Columbia to about 200 feet in the southeastern part of the city.

The climate in the Columbia area is relatively temperate. The Appalachian Mountain chain, some 150 miles to the northwest, frequently retards the approach of unseasonable cold weather in the winter. The terrain offers little moderating effect on the summer heat.

Long summers are prevalent with warm weather usually lasting from sometime in May into September. In summer the Bermuda high is the greatest single weather factor influencing the area. This permanent high more or less blocks the entry of cold fronts so that many stall before reaching central South Carolina. Also, the southwestern flow around the offshore Bermuda high pressure supplies moisture for the many summer thunderstorms. There are relatively few breaks in the heat during midsummer. The typical summer has about six days with 100 degrees or more. Thunderstorm activity usually shows a decided increase during June, decreasing about the first of September. About once or twice a year, passing tropical storms produce strong winds and heavy rains. The incidence of these storms is greatest in September, although they represent a possible threat from midsummer to late fall. Damage from tropical storms is usually minor in the Columbia area.

Fall is the most pleasant time of the year. Rainfall during the late fall is at an annual minimum, while the sunshine is at a relative maximum. Winters are mild with the cold weather usually lasting from late November to mid-March. The winter weather at Columbia is largely made up of polar air outbreaks that reach this area in a much modified form. On rare occasions in winter, Arctic air masses push southward as far as central South Carolina and cause some of the coldest temperatures. Disruption of activities from snowfall is unusual, in fact, more than three days of sustained snow cover is rare.

Spring is the most changeable season of the year. The temperature varies from an occasional cold snap in March to generally warm and pleasant in May. While tornadoes are infrequent, they occur most often in the spring. Hailstorms are not frequent, with the annual incidence at a maximum in spring and early summer. The average occurrence of the last spring freeze is very late March, and the first fall freeze is early November, for a growing period of about 218 days.

Columbia Metro Airport *Lexington County*   Elevation: 212 ft.   Latitude: 33° 57' N   Longitude: 81° 07' W

	JAN	FEB	MAR	APR	MAY	JUN	JUL	AUG	SEP	OCT	NOV	DEC	YEAR
Mean Maximum Temp. (°F)	56.0	60.4	68.1	76.1	83.7	89.7	92.6	90.8	85.1	75.9	67.2	58.4	75.3
Mean Temp. (°F)	44.8	48.5	55.4	63.1	71.4	78.7	82.0	80.7	74.6	63.8	54.6	46.8	63.7
Mean Minimum Temp. (°F)	33.6	36.5	42.6	50.0	59.0	67.7	71.3	70.5	64.0	51.7	42.0	35.2	52.0
Extreme Maximum Temp. (°F)	80	84	90	94	101	106	106	107	99	95	86	82	107
Extreme Minimum Temp. (°F)	-1	13	4	26	35	44	55	56	41	27	19	6	-1
Days Maximum Temp. ≥ 90°F	0	0	0	1	6	17	23	19	8	1	0	0	75
Days Maximum Temp. ≤ 32°F	0	0	0	0	0	0	0	0	0	0	0	0	0
Days Minimum Temp. ≤ 32°F	15	11	5	1	0	0	0	0	0	1	7	14	54
Days Minimum Temp. ≤ 0°F	0	0	0	0	0	0	0	0	0	0	0	0	0
Heating Degree Days (base 65°F)	619	464	309	123	18	1	0	0	8	114	319	560	2,535
Cooling Degree Days (base 65°F)	1	3	18	73	222	418	534	493	300	85	14	3	2,164
Mean Precipitation (in.)	3.62	3.57	4.00	2.65	3.05	4.63	5.25	5.18	3.71	3.16	2.75	3.21	44.78
Maximum Precipitation (in.)*	9.3	8.7	10.9	6.8	8.8	14.8	17.5	16.7	8.8	12.1	7.2	8.5	70.5
Minimum Precipitation (in.)*	0.8	0.3	0.6	0.3	0.3	0.7	0.6	1.0	0.1	trace	0.4	0.3	27.4
Extreme Maximum Daily Precip. (in.)	2.27	2.68	3.22	2.35	4.47	4.84	4.00	4.72	5.17	3.83	2.60	3.06	5.17
Days With ≥ 0.1" Precipitation	7	6	6	5	5	7	8	7	5	4	5	5	70
Days With ≥ 0.5" Precipitation	3	3	3	2	2	3	3	3	2	2	2	2	30
Days With ≥ 1.0" Precipitation	1	1	1	1	1	1	2	2	1	1	1	1	14
Mean Snowfall (in.)	0.6	0.4	0.2	trace	trace	trace	0.0	trace	0.0	0.0	trace	0.1	1.3
Maximum Snowfall (in.)*	4	16	4	0	0	0	0	0	0	0	trace	9	18
Maximum 24-hr. Snowfall (in.)*	4	12	4	0	0	0	0	0	0	0	trace	9	12
Maximum Snow Depth (in.)	4	4	4	trace	trace	trace	0	trace	0	0	trace	1	4
Days With ≥ 1.0" Snow Depth	0	0	0	0	0	0	0	0	0	0	0	0	0
Thunderstorm Days*	1	2	3	4	6	9	13	10	4	1	1	< 1	54
Foggy Days*	13	12	13	10	14	15	15	20	18	15	13	13	171
Predominant Sky Cover*	OVR	OVR	OVR	CLR	OVR	SCT	SCT	SCT	OVR	CLR	CLR	OVR	OVR
Mean Relative Humidity 7am (%)*	83	83	84	83	84	85	88	91	91	90	88	84	86
Mean Relative Humidity 4pm (%)*	51	47	44	41	46	50	54	56	54	49	48	51	49
Mean Dewpoint (°F)*	34	35	41	48	58	65	69	69	64	52	43	36	51
Prevailing Wind Direction*	WSW	WSW	SW	SW	SW	SW	SW	SW	NE	NE	SW	WSW	SW
Prevailing Wind Speed (mph)*	8	9	9	9	8	8	7	7	9	9	8	8	8
Maximum Wind Gust (mph)*	54	69	69	61	61	78	64	56	70	54	51	49	78

Note: (*) Period of record is 1948-1995

Greenville-Spartanbrg Airport

This station, three miles south of Greer, South Carolina, is located in the Piedmont section, on the eastern slope of the Southern Appalachian Mountains. It is rolling country with the first ridge of the mountains about 20 miles to the northwest and the main ridge about 55 miles to the northwest. These mountains usually protect this area from the full force of the cold air masses which move southeastward from central Canada during the winter months.

At present, the National Weather Service Office is located at the Greenville-Spartanburg Jet Age Airport, on a level with, or slightly higher than, most of the surrounding countryside. No bodies of water are nearby. Temperatures are quite consistent with those in Greer, Greenville, and Spartanburg.

The elevation of the area, ranging from 800 to 1,100 feet is conducive to cool nights, especially during the summer months. Winters are quite pleasant, with the temperature remaining below freezing throughout the daylight hours only a few times during a normal year. There are usually two freezing rainstorms each winter and two or three small snowstorms.

Rainfall in this section is usually abundant and spread quite evenly through the months. Droughts have been experienced, but are usually of short duration.

The mountain ridges, which lie in a northeast-southwest direction, appear to have a definite overall influence on the direction of the wind. The prevailing directions are northeast and southwest, divided almost evenly, with fall and winter favoring northeast and spring and summer favoring southwest. Destructive winds occur occasionally, while tornadoes are infrequent in this vicinity.

In the southern two-thirds of Greenville and Spartanburg Counties, including the cities of the same names, the average occurrence of the last temperature of 32 degrees in spring is late March and the average occurrence of the first in fall is early November, giving an average growing season of 225 days. In a normal year some flowering shrubs bloom through the winter. In the higher elevations in the northern thirds of these counties, the growing season begins about one month later and ends about one month earlier.

Greenville-Spartanbrg Airport *Spartanburg County*   Elevation: 957 ft.   Latitude: 34° 54' N   Longitude: 82° 13' W

	JAN	FEB	MAR	APR	MAY	JUN	JUL	AUG	SEP	OCT	NOV	DEC	YEAR
Mean Maximum Temp. (°F)	51.7	55.8	63.5	71.8	79.4	86.5	89.5	87.8	81.3	71.8	62.6	53.6	71.3
Mean Temp. (°F)	41.8	45.2	52.2	59.9	68.1	75.9	79.3	78.1	71.4	60.9	51.8	43.8	60.7
Mean Minimum Temp. (°F)	31.8	34.5	40.7	47.8	56.7	65.3	69.0	68.2	61.5	50.0	40.9	34.0	50.0
Extreme Maximum Temp. (°F)	78	81	89	93	94	100	104	105	96	92	83	79	105
Extreme Minimum Temp. (°F)	-4	8	11	24	31	47	56	53	39	26	19	5	-4
Days Maximum Temp. ≥ 90°F	0	0	0	0	2	10	16	12	3	0	0	0	43
Days Maximum Temp. ≤ 32°F	1	0	0	0	0	0	0	0	0	0	0	0	1
Days Minimum Temp. ≤ 32°F	17	12	6	1	0	0	0	0	0	1	6	15	58
Days Minimum Temp. ≤ 0°F	0	0	0	0	0	0	0	0	0	0	0	0	0
Heating Degree Days (base 65°F)	714	554	398	183	39	2	0	0	17	165	394	652	3,118
Cooling Degree Days (base 65°F)	0	0	7	36	141	336	450	412	216	45	4	1	1,648
Mean Precipitation (in.)	3.77	3.87	4.81	3.41	3.76	3.97	4.62	4.39	3.55	3.49	3.71	4.09	47.44
Maximum Precipitation (in.)*	7.2	7.4	11.4	11.3	8.9	10.1	13.6	17.4	11.6	10.2	7.8	8.4	70.4
Minimum Precipitation (in.)*	0.3	0.3	1.1	0.7	1.1	0.2	0.8	0.9	0.3	0.2	1.3	0.4	35.5
Extreme Maximum Daily Precip. (in.)	3.05	3.42	2.83	2.63	3.25	3.58	4.68	9.32	4.00	4.48	2.42	3.29	9.32
Days With ≥ 0.1" Precipitation	7	6	7	6	6	7	7	6	5	5	6	6	74
Days With ≥ 0.5" Precipitation	3	3	3	3	3	3	3	3	2	2	3	3	34
Days With ≥ 1.0" Precipitation	1	1	2	1	1	1	1	1	1	1	1	1	13
Mean Snowfall (in.)	2.4	1.2	1.0	trace	trace	trace	trace	trace	0.0	0.0	0.1	0.3	5.0
Maximum Snowfall (in.)*	12	12	10	trace	0	0	0	0	0	0	2	11	19
Maximum 24-hr. Snowfall (in.)*	12	8	9	trace	0	0	0	0	0	0	2	11	12
Maximum Snow Depth (in.)	12	6	5	trace	trace	trace	trace	trace	0	0	1	2	12
Days With ≥ 1.0" Snow Depth	2	0	0	0	0	0	0	0	0	0	0	0	2
Thunderstorm Days*	1	1	2	3	6	7	10	7	3	1	1	< 1	42
Foggy Days*	13	11	11	9	12	14	16	19	15	11	11	12	154
Predominant Sky Cover*	OVR	OVR	OVR	CLR	OVR	OVR	OVR	OVR	OVR	CLR	CLR	OVR	OVR
Mean Relative Humidity 7am (%)*	77	75	77	78	83	85	88	90	90	85	81	78	82
Mean Relative Humidity 4pm (%)*	52	47	46	44	51	54	57	58	57	51	51	53	52
Mean Dewpoint (°F)*	28	29	37	44	55	63	68	67	61	49	39	32	48
Prevailing Wind Direction*	SW	NE	SW	SW	SW	SW	SW	NNE	NE	NNE	NNE	SW	NE
Prevailing Wind Speed (mph)*	9	9	10	10	9	8	8	7	8	8	8	9	9
Maximum Wind Gust (mph)*	63	66	61	71	53	60	66	58	45	48	53	51	71

Note: (*) Period of record is 1962-1995

Aiken 4 NE *Aiken County*   Elevation: 399 ft.   Latitude: 33° 36' N   Longitude: 81° 41' W

	JAN	FEB	MAR	APR	MAY	JUN	JUL	AUG	SEP	OCT	NOV	DEC	YEAR
Mean Maximum Temp. (°F)	57.7	62.6	70.3	78.7	85.9	91.4	94.2	92.0	86.8	77.6	69.2	60.1	77.2
Mean Temp. (°F)	45.4	49.4	56.5	63.9	71.8	78.9	82.0	80.4	74.4	64.2	55.4	47.2	64.1
Mean Minimum Temp. (°F)	33.0	36.2	42.4	49.2	57.6	66.3	69.9	68.8	62.0	50.8	41.6	34.3	51.0
Extreme Maximum Temp. (°F)	82	88	89	99	101	107	108	109	100	97	85	82	109
Extreme Minimum Temp. (°F)	-4	9	13	21	34	42	51	52	37	25	16	4	-4
Days Maximum Temp. ≥ 90°F	0	0	0	2	9	20	26	21	10	1	0	0	89
Days Maximum Temp. ≤ 32°F	0	0	0	0	0	0	0	0	0	0	0	0	0
Days Minimum Temp. ≤ 32°F	16	11	6	2	0	0	0	0	0	1	7	14	57
Days Minimum Temp. ≤ 0°F	0	0	0	0	0	0	0	0	0	0	0	0	0
Heating Degree Days (base 65°F)	602	438	279	109	18	0	0	0	6	106	295	541	2,394
Cooling Degree Days (base 65°F)	1	4	22	82	235	422	535	485	295	89	15	2	2,187
Mean Precipitation (in.)	4.90	4.31	5.13	3.08	3.26	5.48	4.89	5.23	3.95	3.41	3.29	3.56	50.49
Extreme Maximum Daily Precip. (in.)	3.50	3.85	3.42	3.20	4.10	4.10	3.62	3.60	4.79	*4.00*	3.52	2.70	*4.79*
Days With ≥ 0.1" Precipitation	8	6	6	6	5	8	8	8	5	4	5	6	75
Days With ≥ 0.5" Precipitation	4	3	4	2	2	4	4	3	2	2	2	2	34
Days With ≥ 1.0" Precipitation	1	1	2	1	1	2	1	1	1	1	1	1	14
Mean Snowfall (in.)	0.4	trace	trace	0.0	0.0	0.0	0.0	0.0	0.0	0.0	trace	0.0	0.4
Maximum Snow Depth (in.)	3	trace	1	*0*	0	0	0	0	0	0	*0*	*trace*	3	*3*
Days With ≥ 1.0" Snow Depth	0	0	0	0	0	0	0	0	0	0	0	0	0

Allendale 2 NW *Allendale County*   Elevation: 180 ft.   Latitude: 33° 01' N   Longitude: 81° 19' W

	JAN	FEB	MAR	APR	MAY	JUN	JUL	AUG	SEP	OCT	NOV	DEC	YEAR
Mean Maximum Temp. (°F)	58.3	62.6	69.9	77.3	84.7	90.3	93.1	91.0	*86.2*	77.9	69.6	60.6	*76.8*
Mean Temp. (°F)	46.0	49.7	56.5	63.4	71.4	78.5	81.6	80.1	*74.7*	65.0	56.1	48.1	*64.2*
Mean Minimum Temp. (°F)	33.5	36.8	43.0	49.5	58.0	66.7	70.0	69.0	*63.1*	52.0	42.6	35.6	*51.7*
Extreme Maximum Temp. (°F)	82	87	88	97	100	106	106	106	*103*	96	88	83	*106*
Extreme Minimum Temp. (°F)	-2	13	16	25	38	46	56	53	*41*	28	17	5	*-2*
Days Maximum Temp. ≥ 90°F	0	0	0	2	8	18	24	20	*10*	1	0	0	*83*
Days Maximum Temp. ≤ 32°F	0	0	0	0	0	0	0	0	*0*	0	0	0	*0*
Days Minimum Temp. ≤ 32°F	15	10	5	1	0	0	0	0	*0*	1	6	13	*51*
Days Minimum Temp. ≤ 0°F	0	0	0	0	0	0	0	0	*0*	0	0	0	*0*
Heating Degree Days (base 65°F)	586	430	278	115	18	0	0	0	*5*	95	279	522	*2,328*
Cooling Degree Days (base 65°F)	2	5	22	74	222	413	520	474	*302*	100	19	5	*2,158*
Mean Precipitation (in.)	4.08	3.48	4.04	2.86	3.01	5.57	4.90	5.33	*3.56*	3.09	3.00	3.62	*46.54*
Extreme Maximum Daily Precip. (in.)	2.40	2.30	3.54	2.90	3.21	8.00	3.20	5.77	*4.35*	7.16	*4.20*	5.28	*8.00*
Days With ≥ 0.1" Precipitation	7	6	6	5	5	7	8	8	*5*	4	5	6	*72*
Days With ≥ 0.5" Precipitation	3	3	3	2	2	3	4	4	*2*	2	2	3	*32*
Days With ≥ 1.0" Precipitation	1	1	1	1	1	2	1	2	*1*	1	1	1	*14*
Mean Snowfall (in.)	trace	0.1	trace	0.0	0.0	0.0	0.0	0.0	*0.0*	0.0	trace	0.0	*0.1*
Maximum Snow Depth (in.)	trace	0	trace	0	0	0	0	0	*0*	0	*0*	0	*trace*
Days With ≥ 1.0" Snow Depth	0	0	0	0	0	0	0	0	*0*	0	0	0	*0*

Anderson *Anderson County*   Elevation: 799 ft.   Latitude: 34° 32' N   Longitude: 82° 40' W

	JAN	FEB	MAR	APR	MAY	JUN	JUL	AUG	SEP	OCT	NOV	DEC	YEAR
Mean Maximum Temp. (°F)	54.3	58.6	66.5	74.9	81.8	89.0	91.5	90.1	84.1	74.5	65.1	56.1	73.9
Mean Temp. (°F)	42.6	46.2	53.1	61.0	68.9	76.7	79.9	78.8	72.6	62.0	52.7	44.5	61.6
Mean Minimum Temp. (°F)	30.8	33.7	39.6	46.9	55.9	64.4	68.3	67.5	60.9	49.5	40.2	32.9	49.2
Extreme Maximum Temp. (°F)	80	80	88	94	100	102	106	104	100	91	85	80	106
Extreme Minimum Temp. (°F)	-5	10	5	24	33	42	53	52	40	28	14	4	-5
Days Maximum Temp. ≥ 90°F	0	0	0	0	2	14	21	18	6	0	0	0	61
Days Maximum Temp. ≤ 32°F	0	0	0	0	0	0	0	0	0	0	0	0	0
Days Minimum Temp. ≤ 32°F	18	13	7	1	0	0	0	0	0	1	7	16	63
Days Minimum Temp. ≤ 0°F	0	0	0	0	0	0	0	0	0	0	0	0	0
Heating Degree Days (base 65°F)	687	526	369	157	30	1	0	0	11	137	366	629	2,913
Cooling Degree Days (base 65°F)	0	0	6	43	157	360	469	435	245	53	5	1	1,774
Mean Precipitation (in.)	4.37	4.26	4.87	3.28	3.15	3.30	4.07	3.97	4.00	3.64	4.10	4.53	47.54
Extreme Maximum Daily Precip. (in.)	3.30	3.00	*3.20*	4.60	*4.05*	*2.70*	3.62	5.00	4.85	4.90	2.55	2.86	*5.00*
Days With ≥ 0.1" Precipitation	6	6	6	6	5	5	7	6	5	4	6	7	69
Days With ≥ 0.5" Precipitation	3	3	3	3	2	2	3	3	3	2	3	3	33
Days With ≥ 1.0" Precipitation	1	1	2	1	1	1	1	1	2	1	1	1	14
Mean Snowfall (in.)	0.6	0.7	0.4	0.0	0.0	0.0	0.0	0.0	0.0	0.0	0.0	0.1	1.8
Maximum Snow Depth (in.)	7	3	4	0	0	0	0	0	0	0	0	trace	7
Days With ≥ 1.0" Snow Depth	0	0	0	0	0	0	0	0	0	0	0	0	0

Andrews *Georgetown County*   Elevation: 35 ft.   Latitude: 33° 26' N   Longitude: 79° 34' W

	JAN	FEB	MAR	APR	MAY	JUN	JUL	AUG	SEP	OCT	NOV	DEC	YEAR
Mean Maximum Temp. (°F)	58.4	62.1	69.3	76.8	83.3	88.1	91.1	89.3	84.4	76.8	69.2	61.0	75.8
Mean Temp. (°F)	47.3	50.2	56.7	63.8	71.2	77.8	81.2	80.0	74.7	65.4	57.1	49.4	64.6
Mean Minimum Temp. (°F)	36.0	38.3	44.1	50.8	59.1	67.5	71.2	70.5	65.0	54.0	44.9	37.7	53.3
Extreme Maximum Temp. (°F)	82	85	90	95	99	105	103	105	97	95	89	85	105
Extreme Minimum Temp. (°F)	2	14	15	28	36	46	54	56	40	30	22	9	2
Days Maximum Temp. ≥ 90°F	0	0	0	1	5	13	20	15	5	1	0	0	60
Days Maximum Temp. ≤ 32°F	0	0	0	0	0	0	0	0	0	0	0	0	0
Days Minimum Temp. ≤ 32°F	12	8	4	0	0	0	0	0	0	0	4	11	39
Days Minimum Temp. ≤ 0°F	0	0	0	0	0	0	0	0	0	0	0	0	0
Heating Degree Days (base 65°F)	543	416	271	103	16	1	0	0	4	81	255	482	2,172
Cooling Degree Days (base 65°F)	2	5	21	74	215	392	509	471	302	102	24	6	49.84
Mean Precipitation (in.)	4.10	3.31	3.60	3.05	3.67	4.97	5.69	6.08	5.24	3.88	3.02	3.23	49.84
Extreme Maximum Daily Precip. (in.)	3.80	2.60	3.35	4.15	2.75	2.85	3.30	*5.30*	*6.20*	5.30	4.30	2.50	*6.20*
Days With ≥ 0.1" Precipitation	7	6	5	4	5	7	8	8	5	4	4	5	68
Days With ≥ 0.5" Precipitation	3	3	3	2	3	4	4	4	3	2	2	2	35
Days With ≥ 1.0" Precipitation	1	1	1	1	1	2	2	2	2	1	1	1	16
Mean Snowfall (in.)	0.2	trace	0.1	0.0	0.0	0.0	0.0	0.0	0.0	0.0	0.0	0.4	0.7
Maximum Snow Depth (in.)	0	0	0	0	0	0	0	0	0	0	0	8	8
Days With ≥ 1.0" Snow Depth	0	0	0	0	0	0	0	0	0	0	0	0	0

The period of record for all cooperative weather station data is 1980 – 2009. See User Guide for detailed explanation of data.

Beaufort 7 SW *Beaufort County* Elevation: 20 ft. Latitude: 32° 23' N Longitude: 80° 46' W

	JAN	FEB	MAR	APR	MAY	JUN	JUL	AUG	SEP	OCT	NOV	DEC	YEAR
Mean Maximum Temp. (°F)	59.6	62.8	69.5	76.4	82.9	87.9	90.8	89.2	84.8	77.1	69.5	61.3	76.0
Mean Temp. (°F)	50.1	53.0	59.3	66.1	73.5	79.6	82.7	81.5	77.0	68.5	60.3	52.1	67.0
Mean Minimum Temp. (°F)	40.5	43.2	49.0	55.8	64.0	71.3	74.6	73.7	69.1	59.8	51.1	42.9	57.9
Extreme Maximum Temp. (°F)	80	83	87	90	96	101	103	104	99	92	86	85	104
Extreme Minimum Temp. (°F)	5	19	21	33	46	53	66	56	52	39	31	10	5
Days Maximum Temp. ≥ 90°F	0	0	0	0	3	11	21	15	6	0	0	0	56
Days Maximum Temp. ≤ 32°F	0	0	0	0	0	0	0	0	0	0	0	0	0
Days Minimum Temp. ≤ 32°F	6	4	1	0	0	0	0	0	0	0	0	4	15
Days Minimum Temp. ≤ 0°F	0	0	0	0	0	0	0	0	0	0	0	0	0
Heating Degree Days (base 65°F)	458	338	199	62	6	0	0	0	1	44	175	401	1,684
Cooling Degree Days (base 65°F)	3	6	29	102	274	445	557	519	367	158	41	9	2,510
Mean Precipitation (in.)	4.00	3.31	3.80	3.16	2.66	6.11	5.41	6.89	4.86	3.85	2.84	2.84	49.73
Extreme Maximum Daily Precip. (in.)	3.08	5.10	3.12	4.06	1.98	7.65	5.55	5.69	na	6.59	3.40	2.45	na
Days With ≥ 0.1" Precipitation	7	6	6	5	5	8	7	9	6	5	5	5	74
Days With ≥ 0.5" Precipitation	3	2	2	2	2	4	3	4	3	2	2	2	31
Days With ≥ 1.0" Precipitation	1	1	1	1	1	2	1	2	1	1	1	1	14
Mean Snowfall (in.)	trace	trace	trace	0.0	0.0	0.0	0.0	0.0	0.0	0.0	0.0	0.2	0.2
Maximum Snow Depth (in.)	trace	trace	trace	0	0	na	0	0	na	na	0	5	na
Days With ≥ 1.0" Snow Depth	0	0	0	0	0	0	0	0	na	na	0	0	na

Bishopville 8 NNW *Lee County* Elevation: 249 ft. Latitude: 34° 20' N Longitude: 80° 18' W

	JAN	FEB	MAR	APR	MAY	JUN	JUL	AUG	SEP	OCT	NOV	DEC	YEAR
Mean Maximum Temp. (°F)	54.0	58.7	66.4	74.8	82.2	88.6	91.1	89.7	83.8	75.0	66.5	57.8	74.1
Mean Temp. (°F)	42.7	46.5	53.4	61.5	69.7	77.4	80.2	79.0	73.0	62.9	53.6	46.0	62.2
Mean Minimum Temp. (°F)	31.4	34.2	40.5	48.1	57.2	66.1	69.2	68.3	62.1	50.6	40.7	34.1	50.2
Extreme Maximum Temp. (°F)	82	85	88	93	100	104	105	106	98	96	87	83	106
Extreme Minimum Temp. (°F)	-2	11	8	24	31	48	54	55	41	28	18	5	-2
Days Maximum Temp. ≥ 90°F	0	0	0	1	4	14	20	16	6	0	0	0	61
Days Maximum Temp. ≤ 32°F	1	0	0	0	0	0	0	0	0	0	0	0	1
Days Minimum Temp. ≤ 32°F	18	13	7	1	0	0	0	0	0	1	7	15	62
Days Minimum Temp. ≤ 0°F	0	0	0	0	0	0	0	0	0	0	0	0	0
Heating Degree Days (base 65°F)	685	520	363	153	31	1	0	0	10	129	346	586	2,824
Cooling Degree Days (base 65°F)	1	2	12	55	185	379	479	442	257	71	11	2	1,896
Mean Precipitation (in.)	3.71	3.36	3.85	2.80	3.17	4.19	4.41	5.02	3.78	3.29	3.01	3.15	43.74
Extreme Maximum Daily Precip. (in.)	2.50	3.01	3.15	2.70	2.70	2.73	2.70	6.05	3.48	7.10	2.90	6.07	7.10
Days With ≥ 0.1" Precipitation	7	6	6	5	5	7	7	7	5	5	5	5	70
Days With ≥ 0.5" Precipitation	2	2	3	2	2	3	3	3	2	2	2	2	28
Days With ≥ 1.0" Precipitation	1	1	1	1	1	1	1	1	1	1	1	1	12
Mean Snowfall (in.)	0.2	0.2	0.2	0.0	0.0	0.0	0.0	0.0	0.0	0.0	0.0	0.1	0.7
Maximum Snow Depth (in.)	3	2	3	0	0	0	0	0	0	0	0	0	3
Days With ≥ 1.0" Snow Depth	0	0	0	0	0	0	0	0	0	0	0	0	0

Charleston City *Charleston County* Elevation: 9 ft. Latitude: 32° 47' N Longitude: 79° 56' W

	JAN	FEB	MAR	APR	MAY	JUN	JUL	AUG	SEP	OCT	NOV	DEC	YEAR
Mean Maximum Temp. (°F)	57.3	60.1	65.6	72.5	79.3	84.8	88.1	86.8	82.6	75.1	67.6	60.2	73.3
Mean Temp. (°F)	50.1	52.8	58.6	65.6	73.1	79.3	82.5	81.4	77.1	68.7	60.6	53.0	66.9
Mean Minimum Temp. (°F)	42.8	45.5	51.5	58.6	67.0	73.8	76.8	76.0	71.7	62.3	53.4	45.7	60.4
Extreme Maximum Temp. (°F)	78	82	87	94	96	104	101	103	98	93	84	81	104
Extreme Minimum Temp. (°F)	10	19	22	36	49	58	65	59	55	40	32	18	10
Days Maximum Temp. ≥ 90°F	0	0	0	0	1	5	11	8	3	0	0	0	28
Days Maximum Temp. ≤ 32°F	0	0	0	0	0	0	0	0	0	0	0	0	0
Days Minimum Temp. ≤ 32°F	3	1	0	0	0	0	0	0	0	0	0	2	6
Days Minimum Temp. ≤ 0°F	0	0	0	0	0	0	0	0	0	0	0	0	0
Heating Degree Days (base 65°F)	457	342	212	66	6	0	0	0	1	37	163	373	1,657
Cooling Degree Days (base 65°F)	1	4	21	90	266	437	549	516	371	160	38	8	2,461
Mean Precipitation (in.)	2.94	2.44	3.44	2.64	2.26	4.62	5.40	6.31	5.66	3.68	2.10	2.60	44.09
Extreme Maximum Daily Precip. (in.)	2.40	2.56	3.45	3.67	2.23	7.38	4.05	5.39	8.50	5.46	3.57	3.82	8.50
Days With ≥ 0.1" Precipitation	6	5	5	5	4	6	7	8	6	5	4	5	66
Days With ≥ 0.5" Precipitation	2	2	2	2	1	3	4	4	3	2	1	2	28
Days With ≥ 1.0" Precipitation	1	1	1	1	1	1	2	2	1	1	1	1	14
Mean Snowfall (in.)	na	na	na	na	na	na	na	na	na	na	na	na	na
Maximum Snow Depth (in.)	na	na	na	na	na	na	na	na	na	na	na	na	na
Days With ≥ 1.0" Snow Depth	na	na	na	na	na	na	na	na	na	na	na	na	na

Chester 1 NW *Chester County* Elevation: 520 ft. Latitude: 34° 43' N Longitude: 81° 13' W

	JAN	FEB	MAR	APR	MAY	JUN	JUL	AUG	SEP	OCT	NOV	DEC	YEAR
Mean Maximum Temp. (°F)	52.5	56.9	65.0	73.6	80.6	87.6	90.7	89.1	83.0	73.3	64.3	55.0	72.6
Mean Temp. (°F)	40.7	44.2	51.5	59.4	67.5	75.8	79.3	78.1	71.6	60.4	51.1	42.9	60.2
Mean Minimum Temp. (°F)	28.9	31.4	38.0	45.2	54.4	64.1	67.9	67.1	60.1	47.4	37.9	30.8	47.8
Extreme Maximum Temp. (°F)	80	83	88	92	96	101	105	106	98	93	84	79	106
Extreme Minimum Temp. (°F)	-3	5	4	21	31	43	53	50	37	22	14	4	-3
Days Maximum Temp. ≥ 90°F	0	0	0	1	2	12	19	15	5	0	0	0	54
Days Maximum Temp. ≤ 32°F	1	0	0	0	0	0	0	0	0	0	0	0	1
Days Minimum Temp. ≤ 32°F	20	17	10	3	0	0	0	0	0	3	11	19	83
Days Minimum Temp. ≤ 0°F	0	0	0	0	0	0	0	0	0	0	0	0	0
Heating Degree Days (base 65°F)	747	583	419	197	50	3	0	0	17	183	415	679	3,293
Cooling Degree Days (base 65°F)	0	0	7	37	136	335	451	414	221	46	6	1	1,654
Mean Precipitation (in.)	4.08	3.67	4.44	3.34	2.87	4.20	3.90	4.66	3.72	3.43	3.57	3.52	45.40
Extreme Maximum Daily Precip. (in.)	3.51	2.84	3.12	2.50	3.55	3.37	3.73	7.13	5.72	4.00	3.32	3.70	7.13
Days With ≥ 0.1" Precipitation	7	6	6	5	5	7	7	6	4	4	5	6	68
Days With ≥ 0.5" Precipitation	3	3	3	2	2	3	3	3	2	2	3	3	32
Days With ≥ 1.0" Precipitation	1	1	1	1	1	1	1	1	1	1	1	1	12
Mean Snowfall (in.)	1.0	0.5	0.5	0.0	0.0	0.0	0.0	0.0	0.0	0.0	0.0	0.1	2.1
Maximum Snow Depth (in.)	8	12	8	0	0	0	0	0	0	0	0	3	12
Days With ≥ 1.0" Snow Depth	1	0	0	0	0	0	0	0	0	0	0	0	1

The period of record for all cooperative weather station data is 1980 – 2009. See User Guide for detailed explanation of data.

Clark Hill 1 W *Mccormick County*   Elevation: 379 ft.   Latitude: 33° 40' N   Longitude: 82° 11' W

	JAN	FEB	MAR	APR	MAY	JUN	JUL	AUG	SEP	OCT	NOV	DEC	YEAR
Mean Maximum Temp. (°F)	55.5	60.1	68.1	76.4	84.2	90.3	93.6	92.3	86.6	76.9	67.6	57.6	75.8
Mean Temp. (°F)	42.9	46.7	53.8	61.5	69.7	77.0	80.7	79.4	73.4	62.7	53.7	45.1	62.2
Mean Minimum Temp. (°F)	30.3	33.4	39.5	46.5	55.1	63.7	67.7	66.5	60.2	48.5	39.8	32.7	48.7
Extreme Maximum Temp. (°F)	83	84	91	94	98	104	109	108	103	94	87	81	109
Extreme Minimum Temp. (°F)	-2	5	12	23	32	45	56	49	38	25	19	9	-2
Days Maximum Temp. ≥ 90°F	0	0	0	1	7	18	25	22	11	1	0	0	85
Days Maximum Temp. ≤ 32°F	0	0	0	0	0	0	0	0	0	0	0	0	0
Days Minimum Temp. ≤ 32°F	19	14	7	2	0	0	0	0	0	2	8	15	67
Days Minimum Temp. ≤ 0°F	0	0	0	0	0	0	0	0	0	0	0	0	0
Heating Degree Days (base 65°F)	677	511	349	151	28	1	0	0	10	132	340	608	2,807
Cooling Degree Days (base 65°F)	0	1	11	52	180	369	492	454	269	68	10	1	1,907
Mean Precipitation (in.)	4.16	4.10	4.69	2.75	2.79	4.40	4.17	4.16	3.45	3.84	3.13	3.43	45.07
Extreme Maximum Daily Precip. (in.)	2.25	3.10	3.90	3.22	2.90	3.90	5.27	3.41	7.10	9.40	5.55	2.13	9.40
Days With ≥ 0.1" Precipitation	6	6	7	5	5	7	7	6	5	4	5	5	68
Days With ≥ 0.5" Precipitation	3	3	3	2	2	3	3	2	2	2	2	2	29
Days With ≥ 1.0" Precipitation	1	1	2	1	1	1	1	1	1	1	1	1	13
Mean Snowfall (in.)	0.0	0.3	0.0	0.0	0.0	0.0	0.0	0.0	0.0	0.0	0.0	0.0	0.3
Maximum Snow Depth (in.)	0	8	0	0	0	0	0	0	0	0	0	0	8
Days With ≥ 1.0" Snow Depth	0	0	0	0	0	0	0	0	0	0	0	0	0

Columbia Univ of SC *Richland County*   Elevation: 242 ft.   Latitude: 33° 59' N   Longitude: 81° 01' W

	JAN	FEB	MAR	APR	MAY	JUN	JUL	AUG	SEP	OCT	NOV	DEC	YEAR
Mean Maximum Temp. (°F)	58.2	63.1	71.0	79.2	86.5	92.2	94.9	93.2	87.9	78.4	68.9	60.3	77.8
Mean Temp. (°F)	47.5	51.5	58.5	66.2	73.9	80.5	83.5	82.2	76.6	66.4	57.2	49.4	66.1
Mean Minimum Temp. (°F)	36.7	39.9	46.0	53.2	61.3	68.8	72.1	71.3	65.3	54.3	45.4	38.5	54.4
Extreme Maximum Temp. (°F)	83	86	92	97	102	109	109	109	102	96	88	84	109
Extreme Minimum Temp. (°F)	1	12	12	29	39	50	58	58	44	32	23	7	1
Days Maximum Temp. ≥ 90°F	0	0	0	3	10	21	27	24	13	1	0	0	99
Days Maximum Temp. ≤ 32°F	0	0	0	0	0	0	0	0	0	0	0	0	0
Days Minimum Temp. ≤ 32°F	12	7	3	0	0	0	0	0	0	0	3	10	35
Days Minimum Temp. ≤ 0°F	0	0	0	0	0	0	0	0	0	0	0	0	0
Heating Degree Days (base 65°F)	539	381	228	73	8	0	0	0	3	72	250	480	2,034
Cooling Degree Days (base 65°F)	2	6	35	117	290	472	580	542	359	122	23	5	2,553
Mean Precipitation (in.)	3.91	3.65	4.56	2.75	2.91	5.32	5.41	4.58	3.53	3.24	3.11	3.40	46.37
Extreme Maximum Daily Precip. (in.)	3.11	2.19	3.17	2.48	4.19	4.22	4.83	4.29	4.26	4.02	2.88	3.93	4.83
Days With ≥ 0.1" Precipitation	7	6	7	6	5	8	8	7	5	5	5	5	74
Days With ≥ 0.5" Precipitation	3	3	3	2	2	3	4	3	2	2	2	2	31
Days With ≥ 1.0" Precipitation	1	1	2	1	1	2	2	1	1	1	1	1	15
Mean Snowfall (in.)	0.4	0.3	0.1	0.0	0.0	0.0	0.0	0.0	0.0	0.0	0.0	trace	0.8
Maximum Snow Depth (in.)	4	2	trace	0	0	0	0	0	0	0	0	trace	4
Days With ≥ 1.0" Snow Depth	1	0	0	0	0	0	0	0	0	0	0	0	0

Conway *Horry County*   Elevation: 20 ft.   Latitude: 33° 50' N   Longitude: 79° 03' W

	JAN	FEB	MAR	APR	MAY	JUN	JUL	AUG	SEP	OCT	NOV	DEC	YEAR
Mean Maximum Temp. (°F)	57.6	61.0	67.8	75.5	82.5	88.1	91.2	89.6	84.8	76.8	69.2	60.3	75.4
Mean Temp. (°F)	46.0	49.1	55.7	63.3	71.2	78.2	81.6	80.4	75.0	65.4	57.0	48.7	64.3
Mean Minimum Temp. (°F)	34.6	37.1	43.5	51.1	59.7	68.3	72.0	71.0	65.2	54.0	44.8	37.2	53.2
Extreme Maximum Temp. (°F)	82	84	90	96	98	103	104	105	100	96	88	82	105
Extreme Minimum Temp. (°F)	4	12	12	22	41	42	56	55	45	30	24	8	4
Days Maximum Temp. ≥ 90°F	0	0	0	1	4	12	20	16	6	1	0	0	60
Days Maximum Temp. ≤ 32°F	0	0	0	0	0	0	0	0	0	0	0	0	0
Days Minimum Temp. ≤ 32°F	13	8	3	0	0	0	0	0	0	0	3	11	38
Days Minimum Temp. ≤ 0°F	0	0	0	0	0	0	0	0	0	0	0	0	0
Heating Degree Days (base 65°F)	583	448	300	115	18	1	0	0	3	86	255	506	2,315
Cooling Degree Days (base 65°F)	2	4	17	71	217	405	522	483	310	106	23	6	2,166
Mean Precipitation (in.)	4.07	3.42	4.08	3.08	3.55	4.94	6.92	7.32	5.35	3.30	2.77	3.45	52.25
Extreme Maximum Daily Precip. (in.)	3.45	4.00	4.07	3.10	2.90	3.08	6.55	5.07	11.35	4.82	3.20	6.60	11.35
Days With ≥ 0.1" Precipitation	7	6	6	5	5	7	9	8	6	5	4	6	74
Days With ≥ 0.5" Precipitation	3	2	3	2	2	3	4	5	3	2	2	2	33
Days With ≥ 1.0" Precipitation	1	1	2	1	1	1	2	2	2	1	1	1	16
Mean Snowfall (in.)	0.2	trace	0.0	0.0	0.0	0.0	0.0	0.0	0.0	0.0	0.0	0.5	0.7
Maximum Snow Depth (in.)	0	trace	6	0	0	0	0	0	0	0	0	13	13
Days With ≥ 1.0" Snow Depth	0	0	0	0	0	0	0	0	0	0	0	0	0

Florence City County Arpt *Florence County*   Elevation: 146 ft.   Latitude: 34° 12' N   Longitude: 79° 44' W

	JAN	FEB	MAR	APR	MAY	JUN	JUL	AUG	SEP	OCT	NOV	DEC	YEAR
Mean Maximum Temp. (°F)	55.7	59.9	67.8	76.0	82.9	88.6	91.4	89.8	84.5	75.7	67.3	58.3	74.8
Mean Temp. (°F)	45.4	48.8	55.8	63.4	71.2	78.3	81.5	80.2	74.5	64.5	55.6	47.6	63.9
Mean Minimum Temp. (°F)	34.9	37.7	43.8	50.8	59.4	67.9	71.5	70.5	64.5	53.2	43.8	36.8	52.9
Extreme Maximum Temp. (°F)	81	85	89	97	97	105	104	106	100	97	89	86	106
Extreme Minimum Temp. (°F)	0	11	11	26	36	49	57	55	43	30	20	8	0
Days Maximum Temp. ≥ 90°F	0	0	0	2	5	14	21	17	7	0	0	0	66
Days Maximum Temp. ≤ 32°F	0	0	0	0	0	0	0	0	0	0	0	0	0
Days Minimum Temp. ≤ 32°F	13	9	4	0	0	0	0	0	0	0	4	11	41
Days Minimum Temp. ≤ 0°F	0	0	0	0	0	0	0	0	0	0	0	0	0
Heating Degree Days (base 65°F)	605	456	297	118	20	1	0	0	7	103	293	538	2,438
Cooling Degree Days (base 65°F)	2	5	20	77	218	406	517	478	298	93	18	5	2,137
Mean Precipitation (in.)	3.25	2.81	3.53	2.66	3.24	4.37	5.12	5.25	3.51	3.08	2.66	3.03	42.51
Extreme Maximum Daily Precip. (in.)	2.10	2.07	3.81	2.62	2.42	3.67	3.47	4.22	3.72	4.35	2.35	4.09	4.35
Days With ≥ 0.1" Precipitation	6	6	6	5	6	7	8	7	6	4	5	6	72
Days With ≥ 0.5" Precipitation	2	2	2	2	2	3	4	3	2	2	2	2	28
Days With ≥ 1.0" Precipitation	1	1	1	1	1	1	1	2	1	1	1	1	13
Mean Snowfall (in.)	na	na	na	na	na	na	na	na	na	na	na	na	na
Maximum Snow Depth (in.)	na	na	na	na	na	na	na	na	na	na	na	na	na
Days With ≥ 1.0" Snow Depth	na	na	na	na	na	na	na	na	na	na	na	na	na

The period of record for all cooperative weather station data is 1980 – 2009. See User Guide for detailed explanation of data.

Greenwood 3 SW *Greenwood County*   Elevation: 615 ft.   Latitude: 34° 10' N   Longitude: 82° 12' W

	JAN	FEB	MAR	APR	MAY	JUN	JUL	AUG	SEP	OCT	NOV	DEC	YEAR
Mean Maximum Temp. (°F)	52.8	57.6	65.4	73.7	81.0	87.7	91.0	89.4	83.3	73.2	64.1	54.8	72.8
Mean Temp. (°F)	41.6	45.4	52.0	60.0	68.2	76.1	79.6	78.6	71.9	61.0	51.7	43.5	60.8
Mean Minimum Temp. (°F)	30.4	33.0	38.6	46.2	55.2	64.5	68.2	67.7	60.4	48.8	39.2	32.1	48.7
Extreme Maximum Temp. (°F)	77	80	89	92	95	102	106	105	97	92	82	78	106
Extreme Minimum Temp. (°F)	-2	8	3	24	32	41	53	52	36	25	17	5	-2
Days Maximum Temp. ≥ 90°F	0	0	0	0	2	12	19	15	5	0	0	0	53
Days Maximum Temp. ≤ 32°F	1	0	0	0	0	0	0	0	0	0	0	0	1
Days Minimum Temp. ≤ 32°F	19	14	9	2	0	0	0	0	0	1	8	16	69
Days Minimum Temp. ≤ 0°F	0	0	0	0	0	0	0	0	0	0	0	0	0
Heating Degree Days (base 65°F)	719	548	401	185	42	2	0	0	15	167	397	661	3,137
Cooling Degree Days (base 65°F)	0	0	6	40	148	343	461	428	228	50	5	1	1,710
Mean Precipitation (in.)	4.15	4.13	4.73	2.93	2.93	3.78	3.60	3.62	3.20	3.43	3.67	3.70	43.87
Extreme Maximum Daily Precip. (in.)	2.61	3.07	2.63	2.50	na	3.20	2.79	6.08	3.47	3.83	2.70	2.32	na
Days With ≥ 0.1" Precipitation	7	6	6	5	4	6	6	5	5	4	5	5	64
Days With ≥ 0.5" Precipitation	3	3	3	2	2	2	2	2	2	2	3	2	28
Days With ≥ 1.0" Precipitation	1	1	2	1	1	1	1	1	1	1	1	1	13
Mean Snowfall (in.)	1.1	0.5	0.4	0.0	0.0	0.0	0.0	0.0	0.0	0.0	0.0	0.2	2.2
Maximum Snow Depth (in.)	6	3	4	0	0	0	0	0	0	0	0	0	6
Days With ≥ 1.0" Snow Depth	0	0	0	0	0	0	0	0	0	0	0	0	0

Johnston 4 SW *Edgefield County*   Elevation: 620 ft.   Latitude: 33° 47' N   Longitude: 81° 51' W

	JAN	FEB	MAR	APR	MAY	JUN	JUL	AUG	SEP	OCT	NOV	DEC	YEAR
Mean Maximum Temp. (°F)	54.4	58.9	66.3	74.7	83.1	89.6	92.8	90.9	84.8	74.8	66.1	56.9	74.4
Mean Temp. (°F)	42.8	46.3	53.2	60.7	69.3	76.8	80.1	78.6	72.7	61.8	53.2	45.0	61.7
Mean Minimum Temp. (°F)	31.1	33.5	39.9	46.6	55.4	63.9	67.4	66.3	60.5	48.8	40.2	33.0	48.9
Extreme Maximum Temp. (°F)	81	83	89	94	100	105	107	110	105	93	88	81	110
Extreme Minimum Temp. (°F)	-2	9	1	19	34	46	52	47	41	24	18	5	-2
Days Maximum Temp. ≥ 90°F	0	0	0	1	6	17	24	19	9	0	0	0	76
Days Maximum Temp. ≤ 32°F	0	0	0	0	0	0	0	0	0	0	0	0	0
Days Minimum Temp. ≤ 32°F	18	14	7	2	0	0	0	0	0	1	7	17	66
Days Minimum Temp. ≤ 0°F	0	0	0	0	0	0	0	0	0	0	0	0	0
Heating Degree Days (base 65°F)	682	526	369	169	34	2	0	0	12	148	357	616	2,915
Cooling Degree Days (base 65°F)	0	2	8	46	172	361	476	430	250	56	9	1	1,811
Mean Precipitation (in.)	4.24	4.15	4.86	3.02	3.05	4.57	4.07	4.78	3.85	3.44	3.41	3.54	46.98
Extreme Maximum Daily Precip. (in.)	2.48	3.35	3.91	2.60	2.92	5.13	3.44	4.33	5.36	5.03	3.95	2.68	5.36
Days With ≥ 0.1" Precipitation	7	6	7	6	5	6	7	7	5	4	5	6	71
Days With ≥ 0.5" Precipitation	3	3	3	2	2	3	3	3	2	2	2	2	30
Days With ≥ 1.0" Precipitation	1	1	2	1	1	1	1	1	1	1	1	1	13
Mean Snowfall (in.)	0.8	0.5	0.2	0.0	0.0	0.0	0.0	0.0	0.0	0.0	0.0	0.1	1.6
Maximum Snow Depth (in.)	6	1	2	0	0	0	0	0	0	0	0	trace	6
Days With ≥ 1.0" Snow Depth	0	0	0	0	0	0	0	0	0	0	0	0	0

Lake City 2 SE *Florence County*   Elevation: 75 ft.   Latitude: 33° 51' N   Longitude: 79° 44' W

	JAN	FEB	MAR	APR	MAY	JUN	JUL	AUG	SEP	OCT	NOV	DEC	YEAR
Mean Maximum Temp. (°F)	56.6	60.3	67.8	75.8	*82.9*	88.7	91.7	90.2	84.9	76.4	68.5	59.2	*75.3*
Mean Temp. (°F)	44.9	48.0	54.8	62.2	*70.0*	77.6	81.0	79.8	73.9	63.8	55.1	46.9	*63.2*
Mean Minimum Temp. (°F)	33.1	35.5	41.7	48.4	*57.0*	66.2	70.2	69.4	62.8	51.2	41.6	34.7	*51.0*
Extreme Maximum Temp. (°F)	81	84	90	94	98	104	105	104	99	97	87	82	105
Extreme Minimum Temp. (°F)	2	14	10	26	35	46	53	55	42	27	20	6	2
Days Maximum Temp. ≥ 90°F	0	0	0	1	4	14	21	18	7	1	0	0	66
Days Maximum Temp. ≤ 32°F	0	0	0	0	0	0	0	0	0	0	0	0	0
Days Minimum Temp. ≤ 32°F	16	11	6	1	0	0	0	0	0	1	6	13	54
Days Minimum Temp. ≤ 0°F	0	0	0	0	0	0	0	0	0	0	0	0	0
Heating Degree Days (base 65°F)	617	473	326	137	*28*	*1*	0	0	6	112	309	555	*2,564*
Cooling Degree Days (base 65°F)	1	3	14	61	*190*	*385*	503	466	279	83	20	3	*2,008*
Mean Precipitation (in.)	3.76	3.27	4.27	2.84	2.92	4.36	5.15	5.93	4.41	3.11	2.70	3.40	46.12
Extreme Maximum Daily Precip. (in.)	3.60	3.68	*6.50*	*2.52*	2.43	*3.32*	3.02	5.38	4.20	7.30	*2.35*	*6.44*	*7.30*
Days With ≥ 0.1" Precipitation	6	5	5	4	4	6	6	7	5	4	4	5	61
Days With ≥ 0.5" Precipitation	2	2	3	2	2	3	3	4	3	2	2	2	30
Days With ≥ 1.0" Precipitation	1	1	1	1	1	1	2	2	2	1	1	1	15
Mean Snowfall (in.)	0.4	0.3	0.3	0.0	0.0	0.0	0.0	0.0	0.0	0.0	0.0	0.3	1.3
Maximum Snow Depth (in.)	7	5	2	0	0	0	0	0	0	0	*0*	8	*8*
Days With ≥ 1.0" Snow Depth	0	0	0	0	0	0	0	0	0	0	0	0	0

Laurens *Laurens County*   Elevation: 588 ft.   Latitude: 34° 31' N   Longitude: 82° 02' W

	JAN	FEB	MAR	APR	MAY	JUN	JUL	AUG	SEP	OCT	NOV	DEC	YEAR
Mean Maximum Temp. (°F)	53.4	57.5	65.5	73.9	81.7	88.6	91.6	90.3	84.0	74.2	65.1	55.9	73.5
Mean Temp. (°F)	40.8	44.1	51.6	59.5	68.2	76.1	79.5	78.2	71.5	60.2	51.0	43.0	60.3
Mean Minimum Temp. (°F)	28.2	30.6	37.6	45.1	54.6	63.6	67.4	66.1	58.8	46.2	36.9	30.1	47.1
Extreme Maximum Temp. (°F)	80	82	89	93	97	107	107	105	99	93	85	80	107
Extreme Minimum Temp. (°F)	-2	5	6	23	31	45	54	49	33	21	13	5	-2
Days Maximum Temp. ≥ 90°F	0	0	0	0	4	15	21	18	7	0	0	0	65
Days Maximum Temp. ≤ 32°F	1	0	0	0	0	0	0	0	0	0	0	0	1
Days Minimum Temp. ≤ 32°F	21	18	9	3	0	0	0	0	0	3	11	20	85
Days Minimum Temp. ≤ 0°F	0	0	0	0	0	0	0	0	0	0	0	0	0
Heating Degree Days (base 65°F)	744	586	415	194	42	2	0	0	18	181	418	676	3,276
Cooling Degree Days (base 65°F)	0	0	5	36	147	342	456	418	219	38	4	1	1,666
Mean Precipitation (in.)	4.16	3.98	4.91	3.28	3.12	4.02	3.55	3.65	3.50	3.64	3.63	3.94	45.38
Extreme Maximum Daily Precip. (in.)	2.68	2.27	3.00	3.05	2.95	4.18	4.68	5.11	4.27	5.35	4.25	2.85	5.35
Days With ≥ 0.1" Precipitation	7	7	7	6	5	7	6	5	5	4	5	6	70
Days With ≥ 0.5" Precipitation	3	3	3	2	2	3	2	2	2	2	3	3	30
Days With ≥ 1.0" Precipitation	1	1	1	1	1	1	1	1	1	1	1	1	12
Mean Snowfall (in.)	0.7	0.4	0.3	0.0	0.0	0.0	0.0	0.0	0.0	0.0	trace	0.1	1.5
Maximum Snow Depth (in.)	1	4	4	0	0	0	0	0	0	0	trace	3	4
Days With ≥ 1.0" Snow Depth	0	0	0	0	0	0	0	0	0	0	0	0	0

The period of record for all cooperative weather station data is 1980 – 2009. See User Guide for detailed explanation of data.

Little Mountain *Newberry County*   Elevation: 710 ft.   Latitude: 34° 12' N   Longitude: 81° 25' W

	JAN	FEB	MAR	APR	MAY	JUN	JUL	AUG	SEP	OCT	NOV	DEC	YEAR
Mean Maximum Temp. (°F)	53.6	58.3	65.8	73.7	80.7	87.0	89.9	88.2	82.6	73.3	64.5	55.8	72.8
Mean Temp. (°F)	44.1	47.7	54.5	62.0	69.6	76.6	79.7	78.4	72.5	62.6	54.1	46.1	62.3
Mean Minimum Temp. (°F)	34.5	37.2	43.2	50.3	58.5	66.2	69.3	68.5	62.4	52.0	43.6	36.3	51.8
Extreme Maximum Temp. (°F)	78	80	87	92	95	101	106	105	98	96	87	78	106
Extreme Minimum Temp. (°F)	-2	7	9	24	38	49	57	52	41	27	19	4	-2
Days Maximum Temp. ≥ 90°F	0	0	0	0	2	10	17	12	4	0	0	0	45
Days Maximum Temp. ≤ 32°F	1	0	0	0	0	0	0	0	0	0	0	0	1
Days Minimum Temp. ≤ 32°F	13	9	4	1	0	0	0	0	0	0	4	12	43
Days Minimum Temp. ≤ 0°F	0	0	0	0	0	0	0	0	0	0	0	0	0
Heating Degree Days (base 65°F)	642	483	331	139	29	1	0	0	13	132	331	582	2,683
Cooling Degree Days (base 65°F)	0	1	13	56	179	356	461	422	245	66	10	2	1,811
Mean Precipitation (in.)	4.14	3.93	4.54	2.97	2.78	4.16	4.59	4.59	3.85	3.50	3.32	3.62	45.99
Extreme Maximum Daily Precip. (in.)	2.18	2.60	2.92	2.23	2.53	4.18	5.22	6.46	3.99	3.41	3.84	2.89	6.46
Days With ≥ 0.1" Precipitation	7	6	7	6	5	6	7	7	5	5	5	6	72
Days With ≥ 0.5" Precipitation	3	3	3	2	2	3	3	3	2	2	3	2	31
Days With ≥ 1.0" Precipitation	1	1	2	1	1	1	1	2	1	1	1	1	14
Mean Snowfall (in.)	1.1	0.5	0.5	0.0	0.0	0.0	0.0	0.0	0.0	0.0	trace	0.2	2.3
Maximum Snow Depth (in.)	9	2	6	0	0	0	0	0	0	0	trace	1	9
Days With ≥ 1.0" Snow Depth	1	0	0	0	0	0	0	0	0	0	0	0	1

Loris 1 S *Horry County*   Elevation: 89 ft.   Latitude: 34° 03' N   Longitude: 78° 52' W

	JAN	FEB	MAR	APR	MAY	JUN	JUL	AUG	SEP	OCT	NOV	DEC	YEAR
Mean Maximum Temp. (°F)	56.0	60.0	66.8	74.5	81.7	86.9	90.4	89.0	84.2	76.1	68.0	58.4	74.3
Mean Temp. (°F)	44.3	47.5	53.4	61.2	69.0	76.0	80.1	78.8	73.3	63.4	54.7	46.1	62.3
Mean Minimum Temp. (°F)	32.7	35.0	40.1	47.6	56.2	65.1	69.6	68.5	62.4	50.6	41.4	33.9	50.3
Extreme Maximum Temp. (°F)	80	85	89	95	99	103	101	104	96	93	85	82	104
Extreme Minimum Temp. (°F)	2	11	12	21	35	47	53	50	43	27	20	9	2
Days Maximum Temp. ≥ 90°F	0	0	0	1	3	10	19	15	6	1	0	0	55
Days Maximum Temp. ≤ 32°F	0	0	0	0	0	0	0	0	0	0	0	0	0
Days Minimum Temp. ≤ 32°F	16	13	7	1	0	0	0	0	0	1	7	15	60
Days Minimum Temp. ≤ 0°F	0	0	0	0	0	0	0	0	0	0	0	0	0
Heating Degree Days (base 65°F)	635	492	364	159	36	2	0	0	9	123	316	582	2,718
Cooling Degree Days (base 65°F)	1	3	12	49	166	340	473	434	263	80	16	4	1,841
Mean Precipitation (in.)	4.01	3.58	4.09	3.06	3.73	5.31	6.12	6.88	5.84	3.03	2.71	2.93	51.29
Extreme Maximum Daily Precip. (in.)	2.50	3.99	4.52	2.99	3.08	3.32	3.40	5.78	10.02	4.11	2.26	2.43	10.02
Days With ≥ 0.1" Precipitation	7	6	6	5	6	7	8	9	6	4	4	5	73
Days With ≥ 0.5" Precipitation	3	2	3	2	2	4	4	4	3	1	2	2	32
Days With ≥ 1.0" Precipitation	1	1	1	1	1	2	2	2	2	1	1	1	16
Mean Snowfall (in.)	0.2	0.3	0.6	0.0	0.0	0.0	0.0	0.0	0.0	0.0	0.0	0.6	1.7
Maximum Snow Depth (in.)	3	3	7	0	0	0	0	0	0	0	0	14	14
Days With ≥ 1.0" Snow Depth	0	0	0	0	0	0	0	0	0	0	0	0	0

Manning *Clarendon County*   Elevation: 100 ft.   Latitude: 33° 42' N   Longitude: 80° 14' W

	JAN	FEB	MAR	APR	MAY	JUN	JUL	AUG	SEP	OCT	NOV	DEC	YEAR
Mean Maximum Temp. (°F)	56.9	61.3	69.2	77.8	85.2	90.8	93.4	92.2	86.1	76.9	68.7	59.6	76.5
Mean Temp. (°F)	45.3	48.7	55.7	63.5	71.4	78.4	81.4	80.4	74.3	64.2	55.7	47.6	63.9
Mean Minimum Temp. (°F)	33.7	36.0	42.1	49.3	57.5	65.9	69.3	68.7	62.5	51.4	42.7	35.5	51.2
Extreme Maximum Temp. (°F)	88	84	92	98	105	104	108	108	101	99	89	82	108
Extreme Minimum Temp. (°F)	0	12	7	24	34	40	48	49	37	24	20	7	0
Days Maximum Temp. ≥ 90°F	0	0	0	2	9	19	25	22	10	1	0	0	88
Days Maximum Temp. ≤ 32°F	0	0	0	0	0	0	0	0	0	0	0	0	0
Days Minimum Temp. ≤ 32°F	16	11	6	1	0	0	0	0	0	1	6	13	54
Days Minimum Temp. ≤ 0°F	0	0	0	0	0	0	0	0	0	0	0	0	0
Heating Degree Days (base 65°F)	605	459	301	114	20	1	0	0	7	108	290	538	2,443
Cooling Degree Days (base 65°F)	2	3	19	77	224	408	514	485	292	90	19	4	2,137
Mean Precipitation (in.)	4.16	3.69	4.03	3.32	3.78	5.25	5.47	5.78	4.37	3.45	2.91	3.57	49.78
Extreme Maximum Daily Precip. (in.)	3.50	2.72	3.08	2.50	2.33	2.80	3.62	3.80	2.80	2.80	2.80	2.49	3.80
Days With ≥ 0.1" Precipitation	8	7	6	6	7	9	8	8	6	6	5	6	82
Days With ≥ 0.5" Precipitation	3	2	3	2	2	4	4	4	3	2	2	2	33
Days With ≥ 1.0" Precipitation	1	1	1	1	1	1	1	2	1	1	1	1	13
Mean Snowfall (in.)	0.6	0.1	0.2	0.0	0.0	0.0	0.0	0.0	0.0	0.0	0.0	0.1	1.0
Maximum Snow Depth (in.)	5	6	4	0	0	0	0	0	0	0	0	1	6
Days With ≥ 1.0" Snow Depth	0	0	0	0	0	0	0	0	0	0	0	0	0

Pageland *Chesterfield County*   Elevation: 620 ft.   Latitude: 34° 46' N   Longitude: 80° 24' W

	JAN	FEB	MAR	APR	MAY	JUN	JUL	AUG	SEP	OCT	NOV	DEC	YEAR
Mean Maximum Temp. (°F)	54.7	59.4	66.9	75.1	81.9	88.4	91.1	89.6	83.9	74.7	66.0	57.3	74.1
Mean Temp. (°F)	44.0	47.7	54.2	62.3	69.7	77.1	80.4	79.1	73.2	62.9	54.2	46.6	62.6
Mean Minimum Temp. (°F)	33.2	35.9	41.5	49.4	57.6	65.7	69.6	68.5	62.5	51.0	42.3	35.9	51.1
Extreme Maximum Temp. (°F)	79	82	87	96	98	102	103	106	104	93	85	80	106
Extreme Minimum Temp. (°F)	3	5	6	23	32	46	54	54	40	28	19	4	3
Days Maximum Temp. ≥ 90°F	0	0	0	1	3	14	20	15	6	0	0	0	59
Days Maximum Temp. ≤ 32°F	0	0	0	0	0	0	0	0	0	0	0	0	0
Days Minimum Temp. ≤ 32°F	15	11	6	1	0	0	0	0	0	0	6	12	51
Days Minimum Temp. ≤ 0°F	0	0	0	0	0	0	0	0	0	0	0	0	0
Heating Degree Days (base 65°F)	646	486	341	141	29	2	0	0	10	129	328	566	2,678
Cooling Degree Days (base 65°F)	1	2	14	66	183	371	484	443	263	71	10	2	1,910
Mean Precipitation (in.)	4.12	3.58	4.21	3.09	2.73	3.94	4.88	4.74	3.58	3.88	3.43	3.44	45.62
Extreme Maximum Daily Precip. (in.)	3.70	2.32	2.83	2.60	2.50	4.70	4.90	4.76	4.30	11.00	5.40	2.03	11.00
Days With ≥ 0.1" Precipitation	7	6	7	6	6	6	7	7	5	5	5	6	73
Days With ≥ 0.5" Precipitation	3	3	3	2	2	3	3	3	2	2	2	2	30
Days With ≥ 1.0" Precipitation	1	1	1	1	1	1	1	2	2	1	1	1	14
Mean Snowfall (in.)	0.9	0.3	0.4	0.0	0.0	0.0	0.0	0.0	0.0	0.0	0.0	0.1	1.7
Maximum Snow Depth (in.)	9	3	trace	0	0	0	0	0	0	0	0	trace	9
Days With ≥ 1.0" Snow Depth	0	0	0	0	0	0	0	0	0	0	0	0	0

The period of record for all cooperative weather station data is 1980 – 2009. See User Guide for detailed explanation of data.

Pelion 4 NW *Lexington County*   Elevation: 450 ft.   Latitude: 33° 43' N   Longitude: 81° 16' W

	JAN	FEB	MAR	APR	MAY	JUN	JUL	AUG	SEP	OCT	NOV	DEC	YEAR
Mean Maximum Temp. (°F)	56.5	61.1	68.8	76.6	83.7	89.2	91.6	90.2	85.1	76.3	67.5	58.8	75.4
Mean Temp. (°F)	44.6	48.2	55.0	62.5	70.6	77.5	80.7	79.4	73.6	63.2	54.2	46.4	63.0
Mean Minimum Temp. (°F)	32.7	35.2	41.3	48.3	57.4	65.9	69.6	68.6	62.1	50.1	40.8	34.0	50.5
Extreme Maximum Temp. (°F)	83	84	89	94	98	103	107	107	99	98	85	83	107
Extreme Minimum Temp. (°F)	-2	10	-1	17	32	42	51	50	38	22	14	5	-2
Days Maximum Temp. ≥ 90°F	0	0	0	1	5	15	21	17	7	0	0	0	66
Days Maximum Temp. ≤ 32°F	0	0	0	0	0	0	0	0	0	0	0	0	0
Days Minimum Temp. ≤ 32°F	16	12	7	2	0	0	0	0	0	2	8	15	62
Days Minimum Temp. ≤ 0°F	0	0	0	0	0	0	0	0	0	0	0	0	0
Heating Degree Days (base 65°F)	625	472	317	132	21	1	0	0	8	122	331	572	2,601
Cooling Degree Days (base 65°F)	1	3	16	63	202	384	492	453	273	74	12	2	1,975
Mean Precipitation (in.)	4.36	4.13	4.58	3.03	3.00	5.29	5.60	5.37	4.17	3.47	3.35	3.75	50.10
Extreme Maximum Daily Precip. (in.)	3.65	3.20	3.23	3.05	2.65	5.11	4.36	5.30	7.10	3.82	3.02	2.80	7.10
Days With ≥ 0.1" Precipitation	8	7	7	6	5	8	9	8	6	5	5	6	80
Days With ≥ 0.5" Precipitation	3	3	3	2	2	3	4	4	3	2	2	2	33
Days With ≥ 1.0" Precipitation	1	1	2	1	1	2	2	2	1	1	1	1	16
Mean Snowfall (in.)	0.5	0.1	trace	0.0	0.0	0.0	0.0	0.0	0.0	0.0	0.0	trace	0.6
Maximum Snow Depth (in.)	3	trace	4	0	0	0	0	0	0	0	0	trace	4
Days With ≥ 1.0" Snow Depth	0	0	0	0	0	0	0	0	0	0	0	0	0

Pickens *Pickens County*   Elevation: 1,162 ft.   Latitude: 34° 53' N   Longitude: 82° 43' W

	JAN	FEB	MAR	APR	MAY	JUN	JUL	AUG	SEP	OCT	NOV	DEC	YEAR
Mean Maximum Temp. (°F)	52.1	56.3	64.7	73.0	79.9	86.6	89.3	88.2	82.0	72.5	63.2	53.8	71.8
Mean Temp. (°F)	41.2	44.8	52.3	60.0	67.7	75.2	78.4	77.6	71.3	61.0	51.4	43.2	60.3
Mean Minimum Temp. (°F)	30.3	33.3	39.9	47.1	55.6	63.7	67.5	66.9	60.5	49.4	39.6	32.5	48.8
Extreme Maximum Temp. (°F)	79	81	89	93	98	99	104	105	100	89	85	77	105
Extreme Minimum Temp. (°F)	-6	1	8	24	35	46	52	52	39	26	15	2	-6
Days Maximum Temp. ≥ 90°F	0	0	0	1	2	10	16	13	4	0	0	0	46
Days Maximum Temp. ≤ 32°F	1	0	0	0	0	0	0	0	0	0	0	0	1
Days Minimum Temp. ≤ 32°F	19	13	7	2	0	0	0	0	0	1	8	17	67
Days Minimum Temp. ≤ 0°F	0	0	0	0	0	0	0	0	0	0	0	0	0
Heating Degree Days (base 65°F)	730	565	391	180	42	2	0	0	14	163	403	670	3,160
Cooling Degree Days (base 65°F)	0	0	5	38	135	314	424	396	209	45	3	0	1,569
Mean Precipitation (in.)	4.85	4.49	5.05	3.76	4.00	4.30	4.80	5.03	4.41	3.97	4.18	4.93	53.77
Extreme Maximum Daily Precip. (in.)	5.25	3.69	4.85	2.40	2.92	5.56	3.40	5.18	8.02	3.16	3.58	3.60	8.02
Days With ≥ 0.1" Precipitation	7	7	7	7	6	7	7	7	6	5	6	7	79
Days With ≥ 0.5" Precipitation	3	3	3	3	3	3	3	3	3	2	3	4	36
Days With ≥ 1.0" Precipitation	1	1	2	1	1	1	1	2	1	1	1	2	15
Mean Snowfall (in.)	0.8	0.6	trace	trace	0.0	0.0	0.0	0.0	0.0	0.0	trace	0.1	1.5
Maximum Snow Depth (in.)	12	3	6	trace	0	0	0	0	0	0	trace	1	12
Days With ≥ 1.0" Snow Depth	0	0	0	0	0	0	0	0	0	0	0	0	0

Spartanburg 3 SSE *Spartanburg County*   Elevation: 609 ft.   Latitude: 34° 54' N   Longitude: 81° 55' W

	JAN	FEB	MAR	APR	MAY	JUN	JUL	AUG	SEP	OCT	NOV	DEC	YEAR
Mean Maximum Temp. (°F)	55.0	59.4	67.2	75.6	81.8	88.2	90.9	89.8	83.9	75.0	65.2	56.4	74.0
Mean Temp. (°F)	42.5	45.9	52.7	60.3	67.9	75.4	78.9	78.0	71.7	61.1	51.5	43.9	60.8
Mean Minimum Temp. (°F)	29.9	32.4	38.1	44.9	53.9	62.6	66.8	66.3	59.4	47.2	37.6	31.4	47.6
Extreme Maximum Temp. (°F)	79	82	90	94	96	101	106	106	98	94	84	80	106
Extreme Minimum Temp. (°F)	-5	6	12	22	29	37	51	46	35	23	13	0	-5
Days Maximum Temp. ≥ 90°F	0	0	0	1	3	13	19	15	5	0	0	0	56
Days Maximum Temp. ≤ 32°F	0	0	0	0	0	0	0	0	0	0	0	0	0
Days Minimum Temp. ≤ 32°F	19	15	10	3	0	0	0	0	0	3	11	18	79
Days Minimum Temp. ≤ 0°F	0	0	0	0	0	0	0	0	0	0	0	0	0
Heating Degree Days (base 65°F)	692	534	381	170	39	2	0	1	15	160	402	646	3,042
Cooling Degree Days (base 65°F)	0	0	6	36	136	322	438	411	222	48	2	0	1,621
Mean Precipitation (in.)	4.19	3.93	4.88	3.58	3.50	4.69	3.92	4.20	3.58	4.24	3.73	4.29	48.73
Extreme Maximum Daily Precip. (in.)	3.25	2.50	3.25	2.55	4.15	3.47	3.30	6.50	3.18	8.40	3.20	2.60	8.40
Days With ≥ 0.1" Precipitation	7	6	7	6	6	6	7	6	5	5	6	6	73
Days With ≥ 0.5" Precipitation	3	3	4	3	2	3	3	2	3	2	3	3	34
Days With ≥ 1.0" Precipitation	1	1	2	1	1	2	1	1	1	1	1	1	14
Mean Snowfall (in.)	0.9	0.1	0.2	0.0	0.0	0.0	0.0	0.0	0.0	0.0	0.0	0.1	1.3
Maximum Snow Depth (in.)	12	1	0	0	0	0	0	0	0	0	0	1	12
Days With ≥ 1.0" Snow Depth	1	0	0	0	0	0	0	0	0	0	0	0	1

Summerville *Dorchester County*   Elevation: 35 ft.   Latitude: 32° 59' N   Longitude: 80° 11' W

	JAN	FEB	MAR	APR	MAY	JUN	JUL	AUG	SEP	OCT	NOV	DEC	YEAR
Mean Maximum Temp. (°F)	58.6	62.3	69.6	76.0	83.5	88.4	91.4	89.9	85.3	76.7	69.0	61.4	76.0
Mean Temp. (°F)	46.8	49.8	56.5	62.4	71.2	77.9	81.2	80.1	75.0	65.1	56.3	49.1	64.3
Mean Minimum Temp. (°F)	34.9	37.3	43.3	48.9	58.9	67.3	71.0	70.4	64.7	53.4	43.6	36.8	52.5
Extreme Maximum Temp. (°F)	80	87	90	96	97	103	104	104	97	94	85	87	104
Extreme Minimum Temp. (°F)	5	15	19	27	38	49	56	55	43	31	23	9	5
Days Maximum Temp. ≥ 90°F	0	0	0	1	5	14	21	17	7	1	0	0	66
Days Maximum Temp. ≤ 32°F	0	0	0	0	0	0	0	0	0	0	0	0	0
Days Minimum Temp. ≤ 32°F	15	9	4	0	0	0	0	0	0	0	4	12	44
Days Minimum Temp. ≤ 0°F	0	0	0	0	0	0	0	0	0	0	0	0	0
Heating Degree Days (base 65°F)	562	428	277	129	17	1	0	0	4	94	274	490	2,276
Cooling Degree Days (base 65°F)	2	4	19	59	215	394	510	477	312	104	21	5	2,122
Mean Precipitation (in.)	4.34	3.23	4.03	3.43	3.37	5.72	5.96	6.60	5.52	3.92	3.29	3.29	52.70
Extreme Maximum Daily Precip. (in.)	3.60	3.30	4.45	3.33	3.56	4.30	3.92	4.20	na	5.52	3.37	na	na
Days With ≥ 0.1" Precipitation	7	5	5	5	5	7	8	9	6	5	6	6	74
Days With ≥ 0.5" Precipitation	3	2	3	2	2	3	4	4	3	2	2	2	32
Days With ≥ 1.0" Precipitation	1	1	1	1	1	2	2	2	2	1	1	1	16
Mean Snowfall (in.)	0.1	0.1	0.0	0.0	0.0	0.0	0.0	0.0	0.0	0.0	0.0	0.3	0.5
Maximum Snow Depth (in.)	1	2	1	0	0	0	0	0	0	0	0	5	5
Days With ≥ 1.0" Snow Depth	0	0	0	0	0	0	0	0	0	0	0	0	0

The period of record for all cooperative weather station data is 1980 – 2009. See User Guide for detailed explanation of data.

Sumter *Sumter County* Elevation: 176 ft. Latitude: 33° 56' N Longitude: 80° 21' W

	JAN	FEB	MAR	APR	MAY	JUN	JUL	AUG	SEP	OCT	NOV	DEC	YEAR
Mean Maximum Temp. (°F)	55.7	59.8	67.4	75.6	82.8	88.7	91.6	89.9	84.6	75.3	67.1	58.2	74.7
Mean Temp. (°F)	44.3	47.7	54.4	62.3	70.1	77.4	80.8	79.3	73.7	63.2	54.4	46.5	62.8
Mean Minimum Temp. (°F)	32.9	35.5	41.3	49.0	57.3	65.9	69.9	68.6	62.6	51.0	41.6	34.8	50.9
Extreme Maximum Temp. (°F)	81	85	90	93	100	103	105	105	99	96	86	83	105
Extreme Minimum Temp. (°F)	2	13	11	26	37	46	56	53	40	27	19	9	2
Days Maximum Temp. ≥ 90°F	0	0	0	1	5	14	22	17	6	0	0	0	65
Days Maximum Temp. ≤ 32°F	0	0	0	0	0	0	0	0	0	0	0	0	0
Days Minimum Temp. ≤ 32°F	16	12	6	1	0	0	0	0	0	1	6	14	56
Days Minimum Temp. ≤ 0°F	0	0	0	0	0	0	0	0	0	0	0	0	0
Heating Degree Days (base 65°F)	635	487	336	135	26	1	0	0	8	122	324	569	2,643
Cooling Degree Days (base 65°F)	1	3	14	62	190	380	496	449	275	73	13	3	1,959
Mean Precipitation (in.)	3.98	3.45	4.00	3.06	3.33	5.05	5.07	4.84	3.92	3.41	3.03	3.32	46.46
Extreme Maximum Daily Precip. (in.)	2.40	2.70	3.36	3.12	3.56	4.40	5.50	4.62	4.61	8.21	2.75	3.87	8.21
Days With ≥ 0.1" Precipitation	7	6	7	5	6	7	8	7	5	5	5	6	74
Days With ≥ 0.5" Precipitation	3	2	3	2	2	3	3	3	2	2	2	2	29
Days With ≥ 1.0" Precipitation	1	1	1	1	1	1	1	1	1	1	1	1	13
Mean Snowfall (in.)	0.1	0.2	trace	0.0	0.0	0.0	0.0	0.0	0.0	0.0	0.0	trace	0.3
Maximum Snow Depth (in.)	4	0	0	0	0	0	0	0	0	0	0	1	4
Days With ≥ 1.0" Snow Depth	0	0	0	0	0	0	0	0	0	0	0	0	0

West Pelzer 2 W *Anderson County* Elevation: 861 ft. Latitude: 34° 39' N Longitude: 82° 29' W

	JAN	FEB	MAR	APR	MAY	JUN	JUL	AUG	SEP	OCT	NOV	DEC	YEAR
Mean Maximum Temp. (°F)	52.4	56.5	64.5	72.9	80.2	86.9	90.6	88.8	82.3	72.7	63.9	54.6	72.2
Mean Temp. (°F)	41.4	44.9	52.1	60.1	68.1	75.8	79.5	78.3	71.6	60.8	51.9	43.6	60.7
Mean Minimum Temp. (°F)	30.5	33.2	39.6	47.2	55.9	64.6	68.5	67.7	60.7	48.8	39.8	32.5	49.1
Extreme Maximum Temp. (°F)	78	81	89	93	94	100	104	104	97	92	84	79	104
Extreme Minimum Temp. (°F)	-4	7	7	23	32	45	56	54	39	27	19	1	-4
Days Maximum Temp. ≥ 90°F	0	0	0	0	2	10	17	13	4	0	0	0	46
Days Maximum Temp. ≤ 32°F	1	0	0	0	0	0	0	0	0	0	0	0	1
Days Minimum Temp. ≤ 32°F	18	14	7	1	0	0	0	0	0	1	8	16	65
Days Minimum Temp. ≤ 0°F	0	0	0	0	0	0	0	0	0	0	0	0	0
Heating Degree Days (base 65°F)	724	562	400	179	40	2	0	0	16	166	391	659	3,139
Cooling Degree Days (base 65°F)	0	0	6	39	141	333	459	420	221	42	4	1	1,666
Mean Precipitation (in.)	4.20	4.01	4.51	2.95	3.01	3.23	3.32	3.49	3.60	3.34	3.71	4.00	43.37
Extreme Maximum Daily Precip. (in.)	3.24	3.35	2.44	**4.33**	2.75	2.49	3.95	12.81	4.06	2.43	3.84	3.97	**12.81**
Days With ≥ 0.1" Precipitation	6	6	6	5	5	5	5	5	4	4	5	6	62
Days With ≥ 0.5" Precipitation	3	3	3	2	2	2	2	2	2	2	3	3	29
Days With ≥ 1.0" Precipitation	1	1	2	1	1	1	1	1	1	1	1	1	13
Mean Snowfall (in.)	1.2	0.8	0.7	0.0	0.0	0.0	0.0	0.0	0.0	0.0	0.1	0.1	2.9
Maximum Snow Depth (in.)	11	3	5	0	0	0	0	0	0	0	1	trace	11
Days With ≥ 1.0" Snow Depth	1	0	0	0	0	0	0	0	0	0	0	0	1

Winnsboro *Fairfield County* Elevation: 560 ft. Latitude: 34° 22' N Longitude: 81° 06' W

	JAN	FEB	MAR	APR	MAY	JUN	JUL	AUG	SEP	OCT	NOV	DEC	YEAR
Mean Maximum Temp. (°F)	53.2	57.8	65.7	74.2	81.5	88.2	91.4	89.4	83.2	73.8	64.8	55.4	73.2
Mean Temp. (°F)	42.5	46.1	53.3	61.5	69.6	77.2	80.8	79.3	72.8	62.3	52.9	44.7	61.9
Mean Minimum Temp. (°F)	31.7	34.3	40.8	48.8	57.6	66.1	70.1	69.2	62.2	50.6	40.9	33.8	50.5
Extreme Maximum Temp. (°F)	79	82	87	92	97	102	106	106	98	93	84	79	106
Extreme Minimum Temp. (°F)	-1	8	5	26	36	42	58	56	41	30	19	7	-1
Days Maximum Temp. ≥ 90°F	0	0	0	1	3	14	21	16	6	0	0	0	61
Days Maximum Temp. ≤ 32°F	1	0	0	0	0	0	0	0	0	0	0	0	1
Days Minimum Temp. ≤ 32°F	17	13	7	1	0	0	0	0	0	0	6	15	59
Days Minimum Temp. ≤ 0°F	0	0	0	0	0	0	0	0	0	0	0	0	0
Heating Degree Days (base 65°F)	691	530	369	156	32	2	0	0	12	140	365	625	2,922
Cooling Degree Days (base 65°F)	0	2	12	57	181	375	497	451	252	62	9	1	1,899
Mean Precipitation (in.)	4.07	3.76	4.35	3.04	2.84	4.20	3.85	4.41	3.40	3.38	3.22	3.34	43.86
Extreme Maximum Daily Precip. (in.)	2.21	2.90	3.62	2.25	2.70	4.20	5.25	4.50	6.65	3.97	2.50	3.80	6.65
Days With ≥ 0.1" Precipitation	7	6	6	6	5	6	6	7	5	4	5	6	69
Days With ≥ 0.5" Precipitation	3	2	3	2	2	3	2	3	2	2	2	2	28
Days With ≥ 1.0" Precipitation	1	1	2	1	1	1	1	1	1	1	1	1	13
Mean Snowfall (in.)	0.4	0.1	0.1	0.0	0.0	0.0	0.0	0.0	0.0	0.0	0.0	0.0	0.6
Maximum Snow Depth (in.)	8	0	4	0	0	0	0	0	0	0	0	0	8
Days With ≥ 1.0" Snow Depth	0	0	0	0	0	0	0	0	0	0	0	0	0

Winthrop University *York County* Elevation: 689 ft. Latitude: 34° 56' N Longitude: 81° 02' W

	JAN	FEB	MAR	APR	MAY	JUN	JUL	AUG	SEP	OCT	NOV	DEC	YEAR
Mean Maximum Temp. (°F)	52.4	57.0	64.9	73.6	80.5	87.4	90.5	88.9	82.5	72.9	63.9	54.7	72.4
Mean Temp. (°F)	42.6	46.2	53.3	61.6	69.4	77.1	80.4	79.2	72.6	62.3	53.0	44.8	61.9
Mean Minimum Temp. (°F)	32.8	35.4	41.7	49.6	58.3	66.7	70.3	69.4	62.8	51.6	42.1	34.9	51.3
Extreme Maximum Temp. (°F)	80	83	87	93	95	101	104	106	96	92	84	80	106
Extreme Minimum Temp. (°F)	-4	7	4	22	37	46	56	54	41	26	17	3	-4
Days Maximum Temp. ≥ 90°F	0	0	0	0	2	12	18	14	4	0	0	0	50
Days Maximum Temp. ≤ 32°F	1	0	0	0	0	0	0	0	0	0	0	0	1
Days Minimum Temp. ≤ 32°F	15	11	6	1	0	0	0	0	0	0	6	13	52
Days Minimum Temp. ≤ 0°F	0	0	0	0	0	0	0	0	0	0	0	0	0
Heating Degree Days (base 65°F)	687	526	364	146	29	1	0	0	11	137	358	619	2,878
Cooling Degree Days (base 65°F)	1	1	9	50	172	370	485	445	248	59	6	1	1,847
Mean Precipitation (in.)	3.72	3.65	4.40	3.17	2.82	4.15	3.81	3.98	3.60	3.51	3.49	3.41	43.71
Extreme Maximum Daily Precip. (in.)	2.82	2.91	2.87	2.45	2.55	2.90	4.51	5.34	3.90	3.83	2.90	2.89	5.34
Days With ≥ 0.1" Precipitation	7	6	7	6	6	7	6	6	5	4	5	6	72
Days With ≥ 0.5" Precipitation	3	3	3	3	2	3	3	2	2	2	3	3	32
Days With ≥ 1.0" Precipitation	1	1	1	1	1	1	1	1	1	1	1	1	12
Mean Snowfall (in.)	1.8	1.4	0.5	trace	0.0	0.0	0.0	0.0	0.0	0.0	0.1	0.1	3.9
Maximum Snow Depth (in.)	12	17	10	trace	0	0	0	0	0	0	trace	3	17
Days With ≥ 1.0" Snow Depth	2	1	0	0	0	0	0	0	0	0	0	0	3

The period of record for all cooperative weather station data is 1980 – 2009. See User Guide for detailed explanation of data.

South Carolina Weather Station Rankings

Annual Extreme Maximum Temperature

	Highest			Lowest	
Rank	Station Name	°F	Rank	Station Name	°F
1	Johnston 4 SW	110	1	Beaufort 7 SW	**104**
2	Aiken 4 NE	109	1	Charleston City	104
2	Clark Hill 1 W	109	1	Loris 1 S	**104**
2	Columbia Univ of SC	109	1	Summerville	**104**
5	Manning	108	1	West Pelzer 2 W	104
6	Columbia Metro Arpt	107	6	Andrews	105
6	Laurens	107	6	Charleston Intl Arpt	105
6	Pelion 4 NW	107	6	Conway	105
9	Allendale 2 NW	**106**	6	Greer Greenville-Spartanbrg Arpt	105
9	Anderson	106	6	Lake City 2 SE	105
9	Bishopville 8 NNW	106	6	Pickens	105
9	Chester 1 NW	106	6	Sumter	105
9	Florence City County Arpt	106	13	Allendale 2 NW	**106**
9	Greenwood 3 SW	106	13	Anderson	106
9	Little Mountain	106	13	Bishopville 8 NNW	106
9	Pageland	106	13	Chester 1 NW	106
9	Spartanburg 3 SSE	106	13	Florence City County Arpt	106
9	Winnsboro	106	13	Greenwood 3 SW	106
9	Winthrop University	106	13	Little Mountain	106
20	Andrews	105	13	Pageland	106
20	Charleston Intl Arpt	105	13	Spartanburg 3 SSE	106
20	Conway	105	13	Winnsboro	106
20	Greer Greenville-Spartanbrg Arpt	105	13	Winthrop University	106
20	Lake City 2 SE	105	24	Columbia Metro Arpt	107
20	Pickens	105	24	Laurens	107

Annual Mean Maximum Temperature

	Highest			Lowest	
Rank	Station Name	°F	Rank	Station Name	°F
1	Columbia Univ of SC	77.8	1	Greer Greenville-Spartanbrg Arpt	71.3
2	Aiken 4 NE	77.2	2	Pickens	71.8
3	Allendale 2 NW	**76.8**	3	West Pelzer 2 W	72.2
4	Manning	76.5	4	Winthrop University	72.4
5	Charleston Intl Arpt	76.1	5	Chester 1 NW	72.6
6	Beaufort 7 SW	**76.0**	6	Greenwood 3 SW	72.8
6	Summerville	**76.0**	6	Little Mountain	72.8
8	Andrews	75.8	8	Winnsboro	73.2
8	Clark Hill 1 W	75.8	9	Charleston City	73.3
10	Conway	75.4	10	Laurens	73.5
10	Pelion 4 NW	75.4	11	Anderson	73.9
12	Columbia Metro Arpt	75.3	12	Spartanburg 3 SSE	74.0
12	Lake City 2 SE	**75.3**	13	Bishopville 8 NNW	74.1
14	Florence City County Arpt	74.8	13	Pageland	74.1
15	Sumter	74.7	15	Loris 1 S	**74.3**
16	Johnston 4 SW	74.5	16	Johnston 4 SW	74.5
17	Loris 1 S	**74.3**	17	Sumter	74.7
18	Bishopville 8 NNW	74.1	18	Florence City County Arpt	74.8
18	Pageland	74.1	19	Columbia Metro Arpt	75.3
20	Spartanburg 3 SSE	74.0	19	Lake City 2 SE	**75.3**
21	Anderson	73.9	21	Conway	75.4
22	Laurens	73.5	21	Pelion 4 NW	75.4
23	Charleston City	73.3	23	Andrews	75.8
24	Winnsboro	73.2	23	Clark Hill 1 W	75.8
25	Greenwood 3 SW	72.8	25	Beaufort 7 SW	**76.0**

Rankings include 25 highest/lowest stations. If state has less than 25 stations, all stations are included. The period of record is 1980–2009. See User Guide for detailed explanation of data.

Annual Mean Temperature

	Highest			Lowest	
Rank	Station Name	°F	Rank	Station Name	°F
1	Beaufort 7 SW	**67.0**	1	Chester 1 NW	60.2
2	Charleston City	66.9	2	Laurens	60.3
3	Charleston Intl Arpt	66.1	3	Pickens	60.4
3	Columbia Univ of SC	66.1	4	Greer Greenville-Spartanbrg Arpt	60.7
5	Andrews	64.6	4	West Pelzer 2 W	60.7
6	Allendale 2 NW	**64.3**	6	Greenwood 3 SW	60.8
6	Conway	64.3	6	Spartanburg 3 SSE	60.8
6	Summerville	**64.3**	8	Anderson	61.6
9	Aiken 4 NE	64.1	9	Johnston 4 SW	61.7
10	Florence City County Arpt	63.9	10	Winnsboro	61.9
10	Manning	63.9	10	Winthrop University	61.9
12	Columbia Metro Arpt	63.7	12	Bishopville 8 NNW	62.2
13	Lake City 2 SE	**63.2**	12	Clark Hill 1 W	62.2
14	Pelion 4 NW	63.0	14	Little Mountain	62.3
15	Sumter	62.8	14	Loris 1 S	**62.3**
16	Pageland	62.6	16	Pageland	62.6
17	Little Mountain	62.3	17	Sumter	62.8
17	Loris 1 S	**62.3**	18	Pelion 4 NW	63.0
19	Bishopville 8 NNW	62.2	19	Lake City 2 SE	**63.2**
19	Clark Hill 1 W	62.2	20	Columbia Metro Arpt	63.7
21	Winnsboro	61.9	21	Florence City County Arpt	63.9
21	Winthrop University	61.9	21	Manning	63.9
23	Johnston 4 SW	61.7	23	Aiken 4 NE	64.1
24	Anderson	61.6	24	Allendale 2 NW	**64.3**
25	Greenwood 3 SW	60.8	24	Conway	64.3

Annual Mean Minimum Temperature

	Highest			Lowest	
Rank	Station Name	°F	Rank	Station Name	°F
1	Charleston City	60.4	1	Laurens	47.1
2	Beaufort 7 SW	**57.9**	2	Spartanburg 3 SSE	47.6
3	Charleston Intl Arpt	56.1	3	Chester 1 NW	47.8
4	Columbia Univ of SC	54.4	4	Clark Hill 1 W	48.7
5	Andrews	53.3	4	Greenwood 3 SW	48.7
6	Conway	53.2	6	Johnston 4 SW	48.9
7	Florence City County Arpt	52.9	6	Pickens	48.9
8	Summerville	**52.5**	8	West Pelzer 2 W	49.1
9	Columbia Metro Arpt	52.0	9	Anderson	49.2
10	Little Mountain	51.8	10	Greer Greenville-Spartanbrg Arpt	50.0
11	Allendale 2 NW	**51.7**	11	Bishopville 8 NNW	50.2
12	Winthrop University	51.3	12	Loris 1 S	**50.3**
13	Manning	51.2	13	Pelion 4 NW	50.5
14	Pageland	51.1	13	Winnsboro	50.5
15	Aiken 4 NE	51.0	15	Sumter	50.9
15	Lake City 2 SE	**51.0**	16	Aiken 4 NE	51.0
17	Sumter	50.9	16	Lake City 2 SE	**51.0**
18	Pelion 4 NW	50.5	18	Pageland	51.1
18	Winnsboro	50.5	19	Manning	51.2
20	Loris 1 S	**50.3**	20	Winthrop University	51.3
21	Bishopville 8 NNW	50.2	21	Allendale 2 NW	**51.7**
22	Greer Greenville-Spartanbrg Arpt	50.0	22	Little Mountain	51.8
23	Anderson	49.2	23	Columbia Metro Arpt	52.0
24	West Pelzer 2 W	49.1	24	Summerville	**52.5**
25	Johnston 4 SW	48.9	25	Florence City County Arpt	52.9

Annual Extreme Minimum Temperature

	Highest			Lowest	
Rank	Station Name	°F	Rank	Station Name	°F
1	Charleston City	10	1	Pickens	-6
2	Charleston Intl Arpt	6	2	Anderson	-5
3	Beaufort 7 SW	5	2	Spartanburg 3 SSE	-5
3	Summerville	5	4	Aiken 4 NE	-4
5	Conway	4	4	Greer Greenville-Spartanbrg Arpt	-4
6	Pageland	3	4	West Pelzer 2 W	-4
7	Andrews	2	4	Winthrop University	-4
7	Lake City 2 SE	2	8	Chester 1 NW	-3
7	Loris 1 S	2	9	Allendale 2 NW	-2
7	Sumter	2	9	Bishopville 8 NNW	-2
11	Columbia Univ of SC	1	9	Clark Hill 1 W	-2
12	Florence City County Arpt	0	9	Greenwood 3 SW	-2
12	Manning	0	9	Johnston 4 SW	-2
14	Columbia Metro Arpt	-1	9	Laurens	-2
14	Winnsboro	-1	9	Little Mountain	-2
16	Allendale 2 NW	-2	9	Pelion 4 NW	-2
16	Bishopville 8 NNW	-2	17	Columbia Metro Arpt	-1
16	Clark Hill 1 W	-2	17	Winnsboro	-1
16	Greenwood 3 SW	-2	19	Florence City County Arpt	0
16	Johnston 4 SW	-2	19	Manning	0
16	Laurens	-2	21	Columbia Univ of SC	1
16	Little Mountain	-2	22	Andrews	2
16	Pelion 4 NW	-2	22	Lake City 2 SE	2
24	Chester 1 NW	-3	22	Loris 1 S	2
25	Aiken 4 NE	-4	22	Sumter	2

July Mean Maximum Temperature

	Highest			Lowest	
Rank	Station Name	°F	Rank	Station Name	°F
1	Columbia Univ of SC	94.9	1	Charleston City	88.1
2	Aiken 4 NE	94.2	2	Pickens	89.3
3	Clark Hill 1 W	93.6	3	Greer Greenville-Spartanbrg Arpt	89.5
4	Manning	93.4	4	Little Mountain	89.9
5	Allendale 2 NW	93.1	5	Loris 1 S	90.4
6	Johnston 4 SW	92.8	6	Winthrop University	90.5
7	Columbia Metro Arpt	92.6	7	West Pelzer 2 W	90.6
8	Lake City 2 SE	91.7	8	Chester 1 NW	90.7
9	Laurens	91.6	9	Beaufort 7 SW	90.8
9	Pelion 4 NW	91.6	10	Spartanburg 3 SSE	90.9
9	Sumter	91.6	11	Greenwood 3 SW	91.0
12	Anderson	91.5	12	Andrews	91.1
13	Florence City County Arpt	91.4	12	Bishopville 8 NNW	91.1
13	Summerville	91.4	12	Pageland	91.1
13	Winnsboro	91.4	15	Charleston Intl Arpt	91.2
16	Charleston Intl Arpt	91.2	15	Conway	91.2
16	Conway	91.2	17	Florence City County Arpt	91.4
18	Andrews	91.1	17	Summerville	91.4
18	Bishopville 8 NNW	91.1	17	Winnsboro	91.4
18	Pageland	91.1	20	Anderson	91.5
21	Greenwood 3 SW	91.0	21	Laurens	91.6
22	Spartanburg 3 SSE	90.9	21	Pelion 4 NW	91.6
23	Beaufort 7 SW	90.8	21	Sumter	91.6
24	Chester 1 NW	90.7	24	Lake City 2 SE	91.7
25	West Pelzer 2 W	90.6	25	Columbia Metro Arpt	92.6

Rankings include 25 highest/lowest stations. If state has less than 25 stations, all stations are included. The period of record is 1980–2009. See User Guide for detailed explanation of data.

January Mean Minimum Temperature

	Highest			Lowest	
Rank	Station Name	°F	Rank	Station Name	°F
1	Charleston City	42.8	1	Laurens	28.2
2	Beaufort 7 SW	40.5	2	Chester 1 NW	28.9
3	Charleston Intl Arpt	38.3	3	Spartanburg 3 SSE	29.9
4	Columbia Univ of SC	36.7	4	Clark Hill 1 W	30.3
5	Andrews	36.0	4	Pickens	30.3
6	Florence City County Arpt	34.9	6	Greenwood 3 SW	30.4
6	Summerville	34.9	7	West Pelzer 2 W	30.5
8	Conway	34.6	8	Anderson	30.8
9	Little Mountain	34.5	9	Johnston 4 SW	31.1
10	Manning	33.7	10	Bishopville 8 NNW	31.4
11	Columbia Metro Arpt	33.6	11	Winnsboro	31.7
12	Allendale 2 NW	33.5	12	Greer Greenville-Spartanbrg Arpt	31.8
13	Pageland	33.2	13	Loris 1 S	32.7
14	Lake City 2 SE	33.1	13	Pelion 4 NW	32.7
15	Aiken 4 NE	33.0	15	Winthrop University	32.8
16	Sumter	32.9	16	Sumter	32.9
17	Winthrop University	32.8	17	Aiken 4 NE	33.0
18	Loris 1 S	32.7	18	Lake City 2 SE	33.1
18	Pelion 4 NW	32.7	19	Pageland	33.2
20	Greer Greenville-Spartanbrg Arpt	31.8	20	Allendale 2 NW	33.5
21	Winnsboro	31.7	21	Columbia Metro Arpt	33.6
22	Bishopville 8 NNW	31.4	22	Manning	33.7
23	Johnston 4 SW	31.1	23	Little Mountain	34.5
24	Anderson	30.8	24	Conway	34.6
25	West Pelzer 2 W	30.5	25	Florence City County Arpt	34.9

Number of Days Annually Maximum Temperature ≥ 90°F

	Highest			Lowest	
Rank	Station Name	Days	Rank	Station Name	Days
1	Columbia Univ of SC	99	1	Charleston City	28
2	Aiken 4 NE	89	2	Greer Greenville-Spartanbrg Arpt	43
3	Manning	88	3	Little Mountain	45
4	Clark Hill 1 W	85	4	Pickens	46
5	Allendale 2 NW	83	4	West Pelzer 2 W	46
6	Johnston 4 SW	76	6	Winthrop University	50
7	Columbia Metro Arpt	75	7	Greenwood 3 SW	53
8	Florence City County Arpt	66	8	Chester 1 NW	54
8	Lake City 2 SE	66	9	Loris 1 S	55
8	Pelion 4 NW	66	10	Beaufort 7 SW	56
8	Summerville	66	10	Spartanburg 3 SSE	56
12	Laurens	65	12	Pageland	59
12	Sumter	65	13	Andrews	60
14	Anderson	61	13	Conway	60
14	Bishopville 8 NNW	61	15	Anderson	61
14	Charleston Intl Arpt	61	15	Bishopville 8 NNW	61
14	Winnsboro	61	15	Charleston Intl Arpt	61
18	Andrews	60	15	Winnsboro	61
18	Conway	60	19	Laurens	65
20	Pageland	59	19	Sumter	65
21	Beaufort 7 SW	56	21	Florence City County Arpt	66
21	Spartanburg 3 SSE	56	21	Lake City 2 SE	66
23	Loris 1 S	55	21	Pelion 4 NW	66
24	Chester 1 NW	54	21	Summerville	66
25	Greenwood 3 SW	53	25	Columbia Metro Arpt	75

Rankings include 25 highest/lowest stations. If state has less than 25 stations, all stations are included. The period of record is 1980–2009. See User Guide for detailed explanation of data.

Number of Days Annually Maximum Temperature ≤ 32°F

	Highest			Lowest	
Rank	Station Name	Days	Rank	Station Name	Days
1	Bishopville 8 NNW	1	1	Aiken 4 NE	0
1	Chester 1 NW	1	1	Allendale 2 NW	0
1	Greenwood 3 SW	1	1	Anderson	0
1	Greer Greenville-Spartanbrg Arpt	1	1	Andrews	0
1	Laurens	1	1	Beaufort 7 SW	0
1	Little Mountain	1	1	Charleston City	0
1	Pickens	1	1	Charleston Intl Arpt	0
1	West Pelzer 2 W	1	1	Clark Hill 1 W	0
1	Winnsboro	1	1	Columbia Metro Arpt	0
1	Winthrop University	1	1	Columbia Univ of SC	0
11	Aiken 4 NE	0	1	Conway	0
11	Allendale 2 NW	0	1	Florence City County Arpt	0
11	Anderson	0	1	Johnston 4 SW	0
11	Andrews	0	1	Lake City 2 SE	0
11	Beaufort 7 SW	0	1	Loris 1 S	0
11	Charleston City	0	1	Manning	0
11	Charleston Intl Arpt	0	1	Pageland	0
11	Clark Hill 1 W	0	1	Pelion 4 NW	0
11	Columbia Metro Arpt	0	1	Spartanburg 3 SSE	0
11	Columbia Univ of SC	0	1	Summerville	0
11	Conway	0	1	Sumter	0
11	Florence City County Arpt	0	22	Bishopville 8 NNW	1
11	Johnston 4 SW	0	22	Chester 1 NW	1
11	Lake City 2 SE	0	22	Greenwood 3 SW	1
11	Loris 1 S	0	22	Greer Greenville-Spartanbrg Arpt	1

Number of Days Annually Minimum Temperature ≤ 32°F

	Highest			Lowest	
Rank	Station Name	Days	Rank	Station Name	Days
1	Laurens	85	1	Charleston City	6
2	Chester 1 NW	83	2	Beaufort 7 SW	15
3	Spartanburg 3 SSE	79	3	Charleston Intl Arpt	24
4	Greenwood 3 SW	69	4	Columbia Univ of SC	35
5	Clark Hill 1 W	67	5	Conway	38
5	Pickens	67	6	Andrews	39
7	Johnston 4 SW	66	7	Florence City County Arpt	41
8	West Pelzer 2 W	65	8	Little Mountain	43
9	Anderson	63	9	Summerville	44
10	Bishopville 8 NNW	62	10	Allendale 2 NW	51
10	Pelion 4 NW	62	10	Pageland	51
12	Loris 1 S	60	12	Winthrop University	52
13	Winnsboro	59	13	Columbia Metro Arpt	54
14	Greer Greenville-Spartanbrg Arpt	58	13	Lake City 2 SE	54
15	Aiken 4 NE	57	13	Manning	54
16	Sumter	56	16	Sumter	56
17	Columbia Metro Arpt	54	17	Aiken 4 NE	57
17	Lake City 2 SE	54	18	Greer Greenville-Spartanbrg Arpt	58
17	Manning	54	19	Winnsboro	59
20	Winthrop University	52	20	Loris 1 S	60
21	Allendale 2 NW	51	21	Bishopville 8 NNW	62
21	Pageland	51	21	Pelion 4 NW	62
23	Summerville	44	23	Anderson	63
24	Little Mountain	43	24	West Pelzer 2 W	65
25	Florence City County Arpt	41	25	Johnston 4 SW	66

Rankings include 25 highest/lowest stations. If state has less than 25 stations, all stations are included. The period of record is 1980–2009. See User Guide for detailed explanation of data.

Number of Days Annually Minimum Temperature ≤ 0°F

	Highest			Lowest	
Rank	Station Name	Days	Rank	Station Name	Days
1	Aiken 4 NE	0	1	Aiken 4 NE	0
1	Allendale 2 NW	*0*	1	Allendale 2 NW	*0*
1	Anderson	0	1	Anderson	0
1	Andrews	0	1	Andrews	0
1	Beaufort 7 SW	*0*	1	Beaufort 7 SW	*0*
1	Bishopville 8 NNW	0	1	Bishopville 8 NNW	0
1	Charleston City	0	1	Charleston City	0
1	Charleston Intl Arpt	0	1	Charleston Intl Arpt	0
1	Chester 1 NW	0	1	Chester 1 NW	0
1	Clark Hill 1 W	0	1	Clark Hill 1 W	0
1	Columbia Metro Arpt	0	1	Columbia Metro Arpt	0
1	Columbia Univ of SC	0	1	Columbia Univ of SC	0
1	Conway	0	1	Conway	0
1	Florence City County Arpt	0	1	Florence City County Arpt	0
1	Greenwood 3 SW	0	1	Greenwood 3 SW	0
1	Greer Greenville-Spartanbrg Arpt	0	1	Greer Greenville-Spartanbrg Arpt	0
1	Johnston 4 SW	0	1	Johnston 4 SW	0
1	Lake City 2 SE	0	1	Lake City 2 SE	0
1	Laurens	0	1	Laurens	0
1	Little Mountain	0	1	Little Mountain	0
1	Loris 1 S	*0*	1	Loris 1 S	*0*
1	Manning	0	1	Manning	0
1	Pageland	0	1	Pageland	0
1	Pelion 4 NW	0	1	Pelion 4 NW	0
1	Pickens	0	1	Pickens	0

Number of Annual Heating Degree Days

	Highest			Lowest	
Rank	Station Name	Num.	Rank	Station Name	Num.
1	Chester 1 NW	3,293	1	Charleston City	1,657
2	Laurens	3,276	2	Beaufort 7 SW	*1,684*
3	Pickens	3,160	3	Charleston Intl Arpt	1,891
4	West Pelzer 2 W	3,139	4	Columbia Univ of SC	2,034
5	Greenwood 3 SW	3,137	5	Andrews	2,172
6	Greer Greenville-Spartanbrg Arpt	3,118	6	Summerville	*2,276*
7	Spartanburg 3 SSE	3,042	7	Conway	2,315
8	Winnsboro	2,922	8	Allendale 2 NW	*2,328*
9	Johnston 4 SW	2,915	9	Aiken 4 NE	2,394
10	Anderson	2,913	10	Florence City County Arpt	2,438
11	Winthrop University	2,878	11	Manning	2,443
12	Bishopville 8 NNW	2,824	12	Columbia Metro Arpt	2,535
13	Clark Hill 1 W	2,807	13	Lake City 2 SE	*2,564*
14	Loris 1 S	*2,718*	14	Pelion 4 NW	2,601
15	Little Mountain	2,683	15	Sumter	2,643
16	Pageland	2,678	16	Pageland	2,678
17	Sumter	2,643	17	Little Mountain	2,683
18	Pelion 4 NW	2,601	18	Loris 1 S	*2,718*
19	Lake City 2 SE	*2,564*	19	Clark Hill 1 W	2,807
20	Columbia Metro Arpt	2,535	20	Bishopville 8 NNW	2,824
21	Manning	2,443	21	Winthrop University	2,878
22	Florence City County Arpt	2,438	22	Anderson	2,913
23	Aiken 4 NE	2,394	23	Johnston 4 SW	2,915
24	Allendale 2 NW	*2,328*	24	Winnsboro	2,922
25	Conway	2,315	25	Spartanburg 3 SSE	3,042

Rankings include 25 highest/lowest stations. If state has less than 25 stations, all stations are included. The period of record is 1980–2009. See User Guide for detailed explanation of data.

Number of Annual Cooling Degree Days

	Highest			Lowest	
Rank	Station Name	Num.	Rank	Station Name	Num.
1	Columbia Univ of SC	2,553	1	Pickens	1,569
2	Beaufort 7 SW	*2,510*	2	Spartanburg 3 SSE	1,621
3	Charleston City	2,461	3	Greer Greenville-Spartanbrg Arpt	1,648
4	Charleston Intl Arpt	2,407	4	Chester 1 NW	1,654
5	Aiken 4 NE	2,187	5	Laurens	1,666
6	Conway	2,166	5	West Pelzer 2 W	1,666
7	Columbia Metro Arpt	2,164	7	Greenwood 3 SW	1,710
8	Allendale 2 NW	*2,158*	8	Anderson	1,774
9	Florence City County Arpt	2,137	9	Johnston 4 SW	1,811
9	Manning	2,137	9	Little Mountain	1,811
11	Andrews	2,123	11	Loris 1 S	*1,841*
12	Summerville	*2,122*	12	Winthrop University	1,847
13	Lake City 2 SE	*2,008*	13	Bishopville 8 NNW	1,896
14	Pelion 4 NW	1,975	14	Winnsboro	1,899
15	Sumter	1,959	15	Clark Hill 1 W	1,907
16	Pageland	1,910	16	Pageland	1,910
17	Clark Hill 1 W	1,907	17	Sumter	1,959
18	Winnsboro	1,899	18	Pelion 4 NW	1,975
19	Bishopville 8 NNW	1,896	19	Lake City 2 SE	*2,008*
20	Winthrop University	1,847	20	Summerville	*2,122*
21	Loris 1 S	*1,841*	21	Andrews	2,123
22	Johnston 4 SW	1,811	22	Florence City County Arpt	2,137
22	Little Mountain	1,811	22	Manning	2,137
24	Anderson	1,774	24	Allendale 2 NW	*2,158*
25	Greenwood 3 SW	1,710	25	Columbia Metro Arpt	2,164

Annual Precipitation

	Highest			Lowest	
Rank	Station Name	Inches	Rank	Station Name	Inches
1	Pickens	53.77	1	Florence City County Arpt	42.51
2	Summerville	*52.70*	2	West Pelzer 2 W	43.37
3	Conway	52.25	3	Winthrop University	43.71
4	Loris 1 S	*51.29*	4	Bishopville 8 NNW	43.74
5	Aiken 4 NE	50.49	5	Winnsboro	43.86
6	Charleston Intl Arpt	50.11	6	Greenwood 3 SW	43.87
7	Pelion 4 NW	50.10	7	Charleston City	44.09
8	Andrews	49.84	8	Columbia Metro Arpt	44.78
9	Manning	49.78	9	Clark Hill 1 W	45.07
10	Beaufort 7 SW	*49.73*	10	Laurens	45.38
11	Spartanburg 3 SSE	48.73	11	Chester 1 NW	45.40
12	Anderson	47.54	12	Pageland	45.62
13	Greer Greenville-Spartanbrg Arpt	47.44	13	Little Mountain	45.99
14	Johnston 4 SW	46.98	14	Lake City 2 SE	46.12
15	Allendale 2 NW	*46.54*	15	Columbia Univ of SC	46.37
16	Sumter	46.46	16	Sumter	46.46
17	Columbia Univ of SC	46.37	17	Allendale 2 NW	*46.54*
18	Lake City 2 SE	46.12	18	Johnston 4 SW	46.98
19	Little Mountain	45.99	19	Greer Greenville-Spartanbrg Arpt	47.44
20	Pageland	45.62	20	Anderson	47.54
21	Chester 1 NW	45.40	21	Spartanburg 3 SSE	48.73
22	Laurens	45.38	22	Beaufort 7 SW	*49.73*
23	Clark Hill 1 W	45.07	23	Manning	49.78
24	Columbia Metro Arpt	44.78	24	Andrews	49.84
25	Charleston City	44.09	25	Pelion 4 NW	50.10

Rankings include 25 highest/lowest stations. If state has less than 25 stations, all stations are included. The period of record is 1980–2009. See User Guide for detailed explanation of data.

Annual Extreme Maximum Daily Precipitation

	Highest			Lowest	
Rank	Station Name	Inches	Rank	Station Name	Inches
1	West Pelzer 2 W	12.81	1	Manning	3.80
2	Conway	11.35	2	Florence City County Arpt	4.35
3	Pageland	11.00	3	Aiken 4 NE	4.79
4	Loris 1 S	10.02	4	Columbia Univ of SC	4.83
5	Clark Hill 1 W	9.40	5	Anderson	5.00
6	Greer Greenville-Spartanbrg Arpt	9.32	6	Columbia Metro Arpt	5.17
7	Charleston City	8.50	7	Winthrop University	5.34
8	Spartanburg 3 SSE	8.40	8	Laurens	5.35
9	Sumter	8.21	9	Johnston 4 SW	5.36
10	Pickens	8.02	10	Andrews	6.20
11	Allendale 2 NW	8.00	11	Little Mountain	6.46
12	Lake City 2 SE	7.30	12	Charleston Intl Arpt	6.57
13	Chester 1 NW	7.13	13	Winnsboro	6.65
14	Bishopville 8 NNW	7.10	14	Bishopville 8 NNW	7.10
14	Pelion 4 NW	7.10	14	Pelion 4 NW	7.10
16	Winnsboro	6.65	16	Chester 1 NW	7.13
17	Charleston Intl Arpt	6.57	17	Lake City 2 SE	7.30
18	Little Mountain	6.46	18	Allendale 2 NW	8.00
19	Andrews	6.20	19	Pickens	8.02
20	Johnston 4 SW	5.36	20	Sumter	8.21
21	Laurens	5.35	21	Spartanburg 3 SSE	8.40
22	Winthrop University	5.34	22	Charleston City	8.50
23	Columbia Metro Arpt	5.17	23	Greer Greenville-Spartanbrg Arpt	9.32
24	Anderson	5.00	24	Clark Hill 1 W	9.40
25	Columbia Univ of SC	4.83	25	Loris 1 S	10.02

Number of Days Annually With ≥ 0.1 Inches of Precipitation

	Highest			Lowest	
Rank	Station Name	Days	Rank	Station Name	Days
1	Manning	82	1	Lake City 2 SE	61
2	Pelion 4 NW	80	2	West Pelzer 2 W	62
3	Pickens	79	3	Greenwood 3 SW	64
4	Aiken 4 NE	75	4	Charleston City	66
5	Beaufort 7 SW	74	5	Andrews	68
5	Charleston Intl Arpt	74	5	Chester 1 NW	68
5	Columbia Univ of SC	74	5	Clark Hill 1 W	68
5	Conway	74	8	Anderson	69
5	Greer Greenville-Spartanbrg Arpt	74	8	Winnsboro	69
5	Summerville	74	10	Bishopville 8 NNW	70
5	Sumter	74	10	Columbia Metro Arpt	70
12	Loris 1 S	73	10	Laurens	70
12	Pageland	73	13	Johnston 4 SW	71
12	Spartanburg 3 SSE	73	14	Allendale 2 NW	72
15	Allendale 2 NW	72	14	Florence City County Arpt	72
15	Florence City County Arpt	72	14	Little Mountain	72
15	Little Mountain	72	14	Winthrop University	72
15	Winthrop University	72	18	Loris 1 S	73
19	Johnston 4 SW	71	18	Pageland	73
20	Bishopville 8 NNW	70	18	Spartanburg 3 SSE	73
20	Columbia Metro Arpt	70	21	Beaufort 7 SW	74
20	Laurens	70	21	Charleston Intl Arpt	74
23	Anderson	69	21	Columbia Univ of SC	74
23	Winnsboro	69	21	Conway	74
25	Andrews	68	21	Greer Greenville-Spartanbrg Arpt	74

Rankings include 25 highest/lowest stations. If state has less than 25 stations, all stations are included. The period of record is 1980–2009. See User Guide for detailed explanation of data.

Number of Days Annually With ≥ 0.5 Inches of Precipitation

	Highest			Lowest	
Rank	Station Name	Days	Rank	Station Name	Days
1	Pickens	36	1	Bishopville 8 NNW	28
2	Andrews	35	1	Charleston City	28
3	Aiken 4 NE	34	1	Florence City County Arpt	28
3	Greer Greenville-Spartanbrg Arpt	34	1	Greenwood 3 SW	28
3	Spartanburg 3 SSE	34	1	Winnsboro	28
6	Anderson	33	6	Clark Hill 1 W	29
6	Charleston Intl Arpt	33	6	Sumter	29
6	Conway	33	6	West Pelzer 2 W	29
6	Manning	33	9	Columbia Metro Arpt	30
6	Pelion 4 NW	33	9	Johnston 4 SW	30
11	Allendale 2 NW	*32*	9	Lake City 2 SE	30
11	Chester 1 NW	32	9	Laurens	30
11	Loris 1 S	*32*	9	Pageland	30
11	Summerville	*32*	14	Beaufort 7 SW	*31*
11	Winthrop University	32	14	Columbia Univ of SC	31
16	Beaufort 7 SW	*31*	14	Little Mountain	31
16	Columbia Univ of SC	31	17	Allendale 2 NW	*32*
16	Little Mountain	31	17	Chester 1 NW	32
19	Columbia Metro Arpt	30	17	Loris 1 S	*32*
19	Johnston 4 SW	30	17	Summerville	*32*
19	Lake City 2 SE	30	17	Winthrop University	32
19	Laurens	30	22	Anderson	33
19	Pageland	30	22	Charleston Intl Arpt	33
24	Clark Hill 1 W	29	22	Conway	33
24	Sumter	29	22	Manning	33

Number of Days Annually With ≥ 1.0 Inches of Precipitation

	Highest			Lowest	
Rank	Station Name	Days	Rank	Station Name	Days
1	Andrews	16	1	Bishopville 8 NNW	12
1	Charleston Intl Arpt	16	1	Chester 1 NW	12
1	Conway	16	1	Laurens	12
1	Loris 1 S	*16*	1	Winthrop University	12
1	Pelion 4 NW	16	5	Clark Hill 1 W	13
1	Summerville	*16*	5	Florence City County Arpt	13
7	Columbia Univ of SC	15	5	Greenwood 3 SW	13
7	Lake City 2 SE	15	5	Greer Greenville-Spartanbrg Arpt	13
7	Pickens	15	5	Johnston 4 SW	13
10	Aiken 4 NE	14	5	Manning	13
10	Allendale 2 NW	*14*	5	Sumter	13
10	Anderson	14	5	West Pelzer 2 W	13
10	Beaufort 7 SW	*14*	5	Winnsboro	13
10	Charleston City	14	14	Aiken 4 NE	14
10	Columbia Metro Arpt	14	14	Allendale 2 NW	*14*
10	Little Mountain	14	14	Anderson	14
10	Pageland	14	14	Beaufort 7 SW	*14*
10	Spartanburg 3 SSE	14	14	Charleston City	14
19	Clark Hill 1 W	13	14	Columbia Metro Arpt	14
19	Florence City County Arpt	13	14	Little Mountain	14
19	Greenwood 3 SW	13	14	Pageland	14
19	Greer Greenville-Spartanbrg Arpt	13	14	Spartanburg 3 SSE	14
19	Johnston 4 SW	13	23	Columbia Univ of SC	15
19	Manning	13	23	Lake City 2 SE	15
19	Sumter	13	23	Pickens	15

Rankings include 25 highest/lowest stations. If state has less than 25 stations, all stations are included. The period of record is 1980–2009. See User Guide for detailed explanation of data.

Annual Snowfall

	Highest			Lowest	
Rank	Station Name	Inches	Rank	Station Name	Inches
1	Greer Greenville-Spartanbrg Arpt	5.0	1	Allendale 2 NW	*0.1*
2	Winthrop University	3.9	2	Beaufort 7 SW	*0.2*
3	West Pelzer 2 W	2.9	3	Clark Hill 1 W	0.3
4	Little Mountain	2.3	3	Sumter	0.3
5	Greenwood 3 SW	2.2	5	Aiken 4 NE	0.4
6	Chester 1 NW	2.1	6	Summerville	*0.5*
7	Anderson	1.8	7	Charleston Intl Arpt	*0.6*
8	Loris 1 S	*1.7*	7	Pelion 4 NW	0.6
8	Pageland	1.7	7	Winnsboro	0.6
10	Johnston 4 SW	1.6	10	Andrews	0.7
11	Laurens	1.5	10	Bishopville 8 NNW	0.7
11	Pickens	1.5	10	Conway	0.7
13	Columbia Metro Arpt	1.3	13	Columbia Univ of SC	0.8
13	Lake City 2 SE	1.3	14	Manning	1.0
13	Spartanburg 3 SSE	1.3	15	Columbia Metro Arpt	1.3
16	Manning	1.0	15	Lake City 2 SE	1.3
17	Columbia Univ of SC	0.8	15	Spartanburg 3 SSE	1.3
18	Andrews	0.7	18	Laurens	1.5
18	Bishopville 8 NNW	0.7	18	Pickens	1.5
18	Conway	0.7	20	Johnston 4 SW	1.6
21	Charleston Intl Arpt	*0.6*	21	Loris 1 S	*1.7*
21	Pelion 4 NW	0.6	21	Pageland	1.7
21	Winnsboro	0.6	23	Anderson	1.8
24	Summerville	*0.5*	24	Chester 1 NW	2.1
25	Aiken 4 NE	0.4	25	Greenwood 3 SW	2.2

Annual Maximum Snow Depth

	Highest			Lowest	
Rank	Station Name	Inches	Rank	Station Name	Inches
1	Winthrop University	17	1	Allendale 2 NW	Trace
2	Loris 1 S	*14*	2	Aiken 4 NE	*3*
3	Conway	13	2	Bishopville 8 NNW	3
4	Chester 1 NW	12	4	Columbia Metro Arpt	4
4	Greer Greenville-Spartanbrg Arpt	12	4	Columbia Univ of SC	4
4	Pickens	*12*	4	Laurens	4
4	Spartanburg 3 SSE	*12*	4	Pelion 4 NW	4
8	West Pelzer 2 W	11	4	Sumter	4
9	Little Mountain	9	9	Summerville	*5*
9	Pageland	9	10	Greenwood 3 SW	6
11	Andrews	8	10	Johnston 4 SW	6
11	Charleston Intl Arpt	*8*	10	Manning	6
11	Clark Hill 1 W	8	13	Anderson	7
11	Lake City 2 SE	*8*	14	Andrews	8
11	Winnsboro	8	14	Charleston Intl Arpt	*8*
16	Anderson	7	14	Clark Hill 1 W	8
17	Greenwood 3 SW	6	14	Lake City 2 SE	*8*
17	Johnston 4 SW	6	14	Winnsboro	8
17	Manning	6	19	Little Mountain	9
20	Summerville	*5*	19	Pageland	9
21	Columbia Metro Arpt	4	21	West Pelzer 2 W	11
21	Columbia Univ of SC	4	22	Chester 1 NW	12
21	Laurens	4	22	Greer Greenville-Spartanbrg Arpt	12
21	Pelion 4 NW	4	22	Pickens	*12*
21	Sumter	4	22	Spartanburg 3 SSE	*12*

Rankings include 25 highest/lowest stations. If state has less than 25 stations, all stations are included. The period of record is 1980–2009. See User Guide for detailed explanation of data.

Number of Days Annually With ≥ 1.0 Inch Snow Depth

	Highest			Lowest	
Rank	Station Name	Days	Rank	Station Name	Days
1	Winthrop University	3	1	Aiken 4 NE	0
2	Greer Greenville-Spartanbrg Arpt	2	1	Allendale 2 NW	*0*
3	Chester 1 NW	1	1	Anderson	0
3	Columbia Univ of SC	1	1	Andrews	0
3	Little Mountain	1	1	Bishopville 8 NNW	0
3	Spartanburg 3 SSE	*1*	1	Charleston Intl Arpt	*0*
3	West Pelzer 2 W	1	1	Clark Hill 1 W	0
8	Aiken 4 NE	0	1	Columbia Metro Arpt	0
8	Allendale 2 NW	*0*	1	Conway	0
8	Anderson	0	1	Greenwood 3 SW	0
8	Andrews	0	1	Johnston 4 SW	0
8	Bishopville 8 NNW	0	1	Lake City 2 SE	0
8	Charleston Intl Arpt	*0*	1	Laurens	0
8	Clark Hill 1 W	0	1	Loris 1 S	*0*
8	Columbia Metro Arpt	0	1	Manning	0
8	Conway	0	1	Pageland	0
8	Greenwood 3 SW	0	1	Pelion 4 NW	0
8	Johnston 4 SW	0	1	Pickens	*0*
8	Lake City 2 SE	0	1	Summerville	*0*
8	Laurens	0	1	Sumter	0
8	Loris 1 S	*0*	1	Winnsboro	0
8	Manning	0	22	Chester 1 NW	1
8	Pageland	0	22	Columbia Univ of SC	1
8	Pelion 4 NW	0	22	Little Mountain	1
8	Pickens	*0*	22	Spartanburg 3 SSE	*1*

Significant Storm Events in South Carolina: 2000 – 2009

Location or County	Date	Type	Mag.	Deaths	Injuries	Property Damage ($mil.)	Crop Damage ($mil.)
Florence	05/25/00	Hail	4.50 in.	0	2	30.0	0.0
Horry	07/13/00	Flood	na	0	0	2.0	0.0
Anderson	07/04/01	Thunderstorm Wind	58 mph	0	0	1.5	0.0
Horry	07/06/01	Tornado	F2	0	39	8.0	0.0
Horry County	11/27/01	Fog	na	1	10	0.0	0.0
Northwest South Carolina	12/04/02	Ice Storm	na	0	0	100.0	0.0
Darlington, Dillon, and Marlboro Counties	01/25/04	Ice Storm	na	0	0	3.0	0.0
Northeast South Carolina	01/26/04	Ice Storm	na	0	0	23.2	0.0
Northwest South Carolina	02/26/04	Heavy Snow	na	0	0	1.8	0.0
Greenville	07/29/04	Flash Flood	na	0	0	3.5	0.0
Georgetown and Horry Counties	08/14/04	Hurricane Charley	na	0	3	6.5	0.0
Berkeley, Charleston, and Dorchester Counties	08/29/04	Tropical Storm	na	0	0	16.6	0.0
Sumter	09/07/04	Tornado	F2	0	3	1.7	0.0
Fairfield	09/27/04	Tornado	F2	1	13	0.0	0.0
Laurens	01/13/05	Tornado	F2	0	1	2.0	0.0
Spartanburg	08/10/05	Flash Flood	na	0	0	1.5	0.0
Georgetown	10/06/05	Heavy Rain	na	0	0	1.5	0.0
Richland	06/12/06	Lightning	na	0	0	1.5	0.0
Spartanburg	06/14/07	Thunderstorm Wind	69 mph	0	0	8.0	0.0
Greenwood	03/15/08	Hail	1.75 in.	0	0	2.8	0.0
Aiken	04/10/09	Tornado	F3	0	14	5.0	0.0
Horry County	04/22/09	Wildfire	na	0	0	40.0	0.0

Note: Deaths, injuries, and damages are date and location specific.

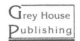

2015 Title List

Visit www.GreyHouse.com for Product Information, Table of Contents, and Sample Pages.

General Reference
An African Biographical Dictionary
America's College Museums
American Environmental Leaders: From Colonial Times to the Present
Encyclopedia of African-American Writing
Encyclopedia of Constitutional Amendments
Encyclopedia of Gun Control & Gun Rights
An Encyclopedia of Human Rights in the United States
Encyclopedia of Invasions & Conquests
Encyclopedia of Prisoners of War & Internment
Encyclopedia of Religion & Law in America
Encyclopedia of Rural America
Encyclopedia of the Continental Congress
Encyclopedia of the United States Cabinet, 1789-2010
Encyclopedia of War Journalism
Encyclopedia of Warrior Peoples & Fighting Groups
The Environmental Debate: A Documentary History
The Evolution Wars: A Guide to the Debates
From Suffrage to the Senate: America's Political Women
Global Terror & Political Risk Assessment
Media & Communications 1900-2020
Nations of the World
Political Corruption in America
Privacy Rights in the Digital Era
The Religious Right: A Reference Handbook
Speakers of the House of Representatives, 1789-2009
This is Who We Were: 1880-1900
This is Who We Were: A Companion to the 1940 Census
This is Who We Were: In the 1910s
This is Who We Were: In the 1920s
This is Who We Were: In the 1940s
This is Who We Were: In the 1950s
This is Who We Were: In the 1960s
This is Who We Were: In the 1970s
U.S. Land & Natural Resource Policy
The Value of a Dollar 1600-1865: Colonial Era to the Civil War
The Value of a Dollar: 1860-2014
Working Americans 1770-1869 Vol. IX: Revolutionary War to the Civil War
Working Americans 1880-1999 Vol. I: The Working Class
Working Americans 1880-1999 Vol. II: The Middle Class
Working Americans 1880-1999 Vol. III: The Upper Class
Working Americans 1880-1999 Vol. IV: Their Children
Working Americans 1880-2015 Vol. V: Americans At War
Working Americans 1880-2005 Vol. VI: Women at Work
Working Americans 1880-2006 Vol. VII: Social Movements
Working Americans 1880-2007 Vol. VIII: Immigrants
Working Americans 1880-2009 Vol. X: Sports & Recreation
Working Americans 1880-2010 Vol. XI: Inventors & Entrepreneurs
Working Americans 1880-2011 Vol. XII: Our History through Music
Working Americans 1880-2012 Vol. XIII: Education & Educators
World Cultural Leaders of the 20th & 21st Centuries

Education Information
Charter School Movement
Comparative Guide to American Elementary & Secondary Schools
Complete Learning Disabilities Directory
Educators Resource Directory
Special Education: A Reference Book for Policy and Curriculum
Development

Health Information
Comparative Guide to American Hospitals
Complete Directory for Pediatric Disorders
Complete Directory for People with Chronic Illness
Complete Directory for People with Disabilities
Complete Mental Health Directory
Diabetes in America: Analysis of an Epidemic
Directory of Drug & Alcohol Residential Rehab Facilities
Directory of Health Care Group Purchasing Organizations
Directory of Hospital Personnel
HMO/PPO Directory
Medical Device Register
Older Americans Information Directory

Business Information
Complete Television, Radio & Cable Industry Directory
Directory of Business Information Resources
Directory of Mail Order Catalogs
Directory of Venture Capital & Private Equity Firms
Environmental Resource Handbook
Food & Beverage Market Place
Grey House Homeland Security Directory
Grey House Performing Arts Directory
Grey House Safety & Security Directory
Grey House Transportation Security Directory
Hudson's Washington News Media Contacts Directory
New York State Directory
Rauch Market Research Guides
Sports Market Place Directory

Statistics & Demographics
American Tally
America's Top-Rated Cities
America's Top-Rated Smaller Cities
America's Top-Rated Small Towns & Cities
Ancestry & Ethnicity in America
The Asian Databook
Comparative Guide to American Suburbs
The Hispanic Databook
Profiles of America
"Profiles of" Series – State Handbooks
Weather America

Financial Ratings Series
TheStreet Ratings' Guide to Bond & Money Market Mutual Funds
TheStreet Ratings' Guide to Common Stocks
TheStreet Ratings' Guide to Exchange-Traded Funds
TheStreet Ratings' Guide to Stock Mutual Funds
TheStreet Ratings' Ultimate Guided Tour of Stock Investing
Weiss Ratings' Consumer Guides
Weiss Ratings' Guide to Banks
Weiss Ratings' Guide to Credit Unions
Weiss Ratings' Guide to Health Insurers
Weiss Ratings' Guide to Life & Annuity Insurers
Weiss Ratings' Guide to Property & Casualty Insurers

Bowker's Books In Print® Titles
American Book Publishing Record® Annual
American Book Publishing Record® Monthly
Books In Print®
Books In Print® Supplement
Books Out Loud™
Bowker's Complete Video Directory™
Children's Books In Print®
El-Hi Textbooks & Serials In Print®
Forthcoming Books®
Large Print Books & Serials™
Law Books & Serials In Print™
Medical & Health Care Books In Print™
Publishers, Distributors & Wholesalers of the US™
Subject Guide to Books In Print®
Subject Guide to Children's Books In Print®

Canadian General Reference
Associations Canada
Canadian Almanac & Directory
Canadian Environmental Resource Guide
Canadian Parliamentary Guide
Canadian Venture Capital & Private Equity Firms
Financial Services Canada
Governments Canada
Health Guide Canada
The History of Canada
Libraries Canada
Major Canadian Cities

2015 Title List

Visit www.SalemPress.com for Product Information, Table of Contents, and Sample Pages.

Science, Careers & Mathematics

Ancient Creatures: Unearthed
Applied Science
Applied Science: Engineering & Mathematics
Applied Science: Science & Medicine
Applied Science: Technology
Biomes and Ecosystems
Careers in Business
Careers in Chemistry
Careers in Communications & Media
Careers in Environment & Conservation
Careers in Healthcare
Careers in Hospitality & Tourism
Careers in Human Services
Careers in Law, Criminal Justice & Emergency Services
Careers in Physics
Careers in Technology Services & Repair
Computer Technology Innovators
Contemporary Biographies in Business
Contemporary Biographies in Chemistry
Contemporary Biographies in Communications & Media
Contemporary Biographies in Environment & Conservation
Contemporary Biographies in Healthcare
Contemporary Biographies in Hospitality & Tourism
Contemporary Biographies in Law & Criminal Justice
Contemporary Biographies in Physics
Earth Science
Earth Science: Earth Materials & Resources
Earth Science: Earth's Surface and History
Earth Science: Physics & Chemistry of the Earth
Earth Science: Weather, Water & Atmosphere
Encyclopedia of Energy
Encyclopedia of Environmental Issues
Encyclopedia of Environmental Issues: Atmosphere and Air Pollution
Encyclopedia of Environmental Issues: Ecology and Ecosystems
Encyclopedia of Environmental Issues: Energy and Energy Use
Encyclopedia of Environmental Issues: Policy and Activism
Encyclopedia of Environmental Issues: Preservation/Wilderness Issues
Encyclopedia of Environmental Issues: Water and Water Pollution
Encyclopedia of Global Resources
Encyclopedia of Global Warming
Encyclopedia of Mathematics & Society
Encyclopedia of Mathematics & Society: Engineering, Tech, Medicine
Encyclopedia of Mathematics & Society: Great Mathematicians
Encyclopedia of Mathematics & Society: Math & Social Sciences
Encyclopedia of Mathematics & Society: Math Development/Concepts
Encyclopedia of Mathematics & Society: Math in Culture & Society
Encyclopedia of Mathematics & Society: Space, Science, Environment
Encyclopedia of the Ancient World
Forensic Science
Geography Basics
Internet Innovators
Inventions and Inventors
Magill's Encyclopedia of Science: Animal Life
Magill's Encyclopedia of Science: Plant life
Notable Natural Disasters
Principles of Chemistry
Science and Scientists
Solar System
Solar System: Great Astronomers
Solar System: Study of the Universe
Solar System: The Inner Planets
Solar System: The Moon and Other Small Bodies
Solar System: The Outer Planets
Solar System: The Sun and Other Stars
World Geography

Literature

American Ethnic Writers
Classics of Science Fiction & Fantasy Literature
Critical Insights: Authors
Critical Insights: New Literary Collection Bundles
Critical Insights: Themes
Critical Insights: Works
Critical Survey of Drama
Critical Survey of Graphic Novels: Heroes & Super Heroes
Critical Survey of Graphic Novels: History, Theme & Technique
Critical Survey of Graphic Novels: Independents/Underground Classics
Critical Survey of Graphic Novels: Manga
Critical Survey of Long Fiction
Critical Survey of Mystery & Detective Fiction
Critical Survey of Mythology and Folklore: Heroes and Heroines
Critical Survey of Mythology and Folklore: Love, Sexuality & Desire
Critical Survey of Mythology and Folklore: World Mythology
Critical Survey of Poetry
Critical Survey of Poetry: American Poets
Critical Survey of Poetry: British, Irish & Commonwealth Poets
Critical Survey of Poetry: Cumulative Index
Critical Survey of Poetry: European Poets
Critical Survey of Poetry: Topical Essays
Critical Survey of Poetry: World Poets
Critical Survey of Shakespeare's Sonnets
Critical Survey of Short Fiction
Critical Survey of Short Fiction: American Writers
Critical Survey of Short Fiction: British, Irish, Commonwealth Writers
Critical Survey of Short Fiction: Cumulative Index
Critical Survey of Short Fiction: European Writers
Critical Survey of Short Fiction: Topical Essays
Critical Survey of Short Fiction: World Writers
Cyclopedia of Literary Characters
Holocaust Literature
Introduction to Literary Context: American Poetry of the 20th Century
Introduction to Literary Context: American Post-Modernist Novels
Introduction to Literary Context: American Short Fiction
Introduction to Literary Context: English Literature
Introduction to Literary Context: Plays
Introduction to Literary Context: World Literature
Magill's Literary Annual 2015
Magill's Survey of American Literature
Magill's Survey of World Literature
Masterplots
Masterplots II: African American Literature
Masterplots II: American Fiction Series
Masterplots II: British & Commonwealth Fiction Series
Masterplots II: Christian Literature
Masterplots II: Drama Series
Masterplots II: Juvenile & Young Adult Literature, Supplement
Masterplots II: Nonfiction Series
Masterplots II: Poetry Series
Masterplots II: Short Story Series
Masterplots II: Women's Literature Series
Notable African American Writers
Notable American Novelists
Notable Playwrights
Notable Poets
Recommended Reading: 500 Classics Reviewed
Short Story Writers

Grey House Publishing | Salem Press | H.W. Wilson | 4919 Route, 22 PO Box 56, Amenia NY 12501-0056

2015 Title List

Visit www.SalemPress.com for Product Information, Table of Contents, and Sample Pages.

History and Social Science

The 2000s in America
50 States
African American History
Agriculture in History
American First Ladies
American Heroes
American Indian Culture
American Indian History
American Indian Tribes
American Presidents
American Villains
America's Historic Sites
Ancient Greece
The Bill of Rights
The Civil Rights Movement
The Cold War
Countries, Peoples & Cultures
Countries, Peoples & Cultures: Central & South America
Countries, Peoples & Cultures: Central, South & Southeast Asia
Countries, Peoples & Cultures: East & South Africa
Countries, Peoples & Cultures: East Asia & the Pacific
Countries, Peoples & Cultures: Eastern Europe
Countries, Peoples & Cultures: Middle East & North Africa
Countries, Peoples & Cultures: North America & the Caribbean
Countries, Peoples & Cultures: West & Central Africa
Countries, Peoples & Cultures: Western Europe
Defining Documents: American Revolution (1754-1805)
Defining Documents: Civil War (1860-1865)
Defining Documents: Emergence of Modern America (1868-1918)
Defining Documents: Exploration & Colonial America (1492-1755)
Defining Documents: Manifest Destiny (1803-1860)
Defining Documents: Post-War 1940s (1945-1949)
Defining Documents: Reconstruction (1865-1880)
Defining Documents: The 1920s
Defining Documents: The 1930s
Defining Documents: The American West (1836-1900)
Defining Documents: The Ancient World (2700 B.C.E.-50 C.E.)
Defining Documents: The Middle Ages (524-1431)
Defining Documents: World War I
Defining Documents: World War II (1939-1946)
The Eighties in America
Encyclopedia of American Immigration
Encyclopedia of Flight
Encyclopedia of the Ancient World
The Fifties in America
The Forties in America
Great Athletes
Great Athletes: Baseball
Great Athletes: Basketball
Great Athletes: Boxing & Soccer
Great Athletes: Cumulative Index
Great Athletes: Football
Great Athletes: Golf & Tennis
Great Athletes: Olympics
Great Athletes: Racing & Individual Sports
Great Events from History: 17th Century
Great Events from History: 18th Century
Great Events from History: 19th Century
Great Events from History: 20th Century (1901-1940)
Great Events from History: 20th Century (1941-1970)
Great Events from History: 20th Century (1971-2000)
Great Events from History: Ancient World
Great Events from History: Cumulative Indexes
Great Events from History: Gay, Lesbian, Bisexual, Transgender Events
Great Events from History: Middle Ages
Great Events from History: Modern Scandals
Great Events from History: Renaissance & Early Modern Era

Great Lives from History: 17th Century
Great Lives from History: 18th Century
Great Lives from History: 19th Century
Great Lives from History: 20th Century
Great Lives from History: African Americans
Great Lives from History: Ancient World
Great Lives from History: Asian & Pacific Islander Americans
Great Lives from History: Cumulative Indexes
Great Lives from History: Incredibly Wealthy
Great Lives from History: Inventors & Inventions
Great Lives from History: Jewish Americans
Great Lives from History: Latinos
Great Lives from History: Middle Ages
Great Lives from History: Notorious Lives
Great Lives from History: Renaissance & Early Modern Era
Great Lives from History: Scientists & Science
Historical Encyclopedia of American Business
Immigration in U.S. History
Magill's Guide to Military History
Milestone Documents in African American History
Milestone Documents in American History
Milestone Documents in World History
Milestone Documents of American Leaders
Milestone Documents of World Religions
Musicians & Composers 20th Century
The Nineties in America
The Seventies in America
The Sixties in America
Survey of American Industry and Careers
The Thirties in America
The Twenties in America
United States at War
U.S.A. in Space
U.S. Court Cases
U.S. Government Leaders
U.S. Laws, Acts, and Treaties
U.S. Legal System
U.S. Supreme Court
Weapons and Warfare
World Conflicts: Asia and the Middle East

Health

Addictions & Substance Abuse
Adolescent Health
Cancer
Complementary & Alternative Medicine
Genetics & Inherited Conditions
Health Issues
Infectious Diseases & Conditions
Magill's Medical Guide
Psychology & Behavioral Health
Psychology Basics

Current Biography
Current Biography Cumulative Index 1946-2013
Current Biography Monthly Magazine
Current Biography Yearbook: 2003
Current Biography Yearbook: 2004
Current Biography Yearbook: 2005
Current Biography Yearbook: 2006
Current Biography Yearbook: 2007
Current Biography Yearbook: 2008
Current Biography Yearbook: 2009
Current Biography Yearbook: 2010
Current Biography Yearbook: 2011
Current Biography Yearbook: 2012
Current Biography Yearbook: 2013
Current Biography Yearbook: 2014
Current Biography Yearbook: 2015

Core Collections
Children's Core Collection
Fiction Core Collection
Middle & Junior High School Core
Public Library Core Collection: Nonfiction
Senior High Core Collection

The Reference Shelf
Aging in America
American Military Presence Overseas
The Arab Spring
The Brain
The Business of Food
Conspiracy Theories
The Digital Age
Dinosaurs
Embracing New Paradigms in Education
Faith & Science
Families: Traditional and New Structures
The Future of U.S. Economic Relations: Mexico, Cuba, and Venezuela
Global Climate Change
Graphic Novels and Comic Books
Immigration in the U.S.
Internet Safety
Marijuana Reform
The News and its Future
The Paranormal
Politics of the Ocean
Reality Television
Representative American Speeches: 2008-2009
Representative American Speeches: 2009-2010
Representative American Speeches: 2010-2011
Representative American Speeches: 2011-2012
Representative American Speeches: 2012-2013
Representative American Speeches: 2013-2014
Representative American Speeches: 2014-2015
Revisiting Gender
Robotics
Russia
Social Networking
Social Services for the Poor
Space Exploration & Development
Sports in America
The Supreme Court
The Transformation of American Cities
U.S. Infrastructure
U.S. National Debate Topic: Surveillance
U.S. National Debate Topic: The Ocean
U.S. National Debate Topic: Transportation Infrastructure
Whistleblowers

Readers' Guide
Abridged Readers' Guide to Periodical Literature
Readers' Guide to Periodical Literature

Indexes
Index to Legal Periodicals & Books
Short Story Index
Book Review Digest

Sears List
Sears List of Subject Headings
Sears: Lista de Encabezamientos de Materia

Facts About Series
Facts About American Immigration
Facts About China
Facts About the 20th Century
Facts About the Presidents
Facts About the World's Languages

Nobel Prize Winners
Nobel Prize Winners: 1901-1986
Nobel Prize Winners: 1987-1991
Nobel Prize Winners: 1992-1996
Nobel Prize Winners: 1997-2001

World Authors
World Authors: 1995-2000
World Authors: 2000-2005

Famous First Facts
Famous First Facts
Famous First Facts About American Politics
Famous First Facts About Sports
Famous First Facts About the Environment
Famous First Facts: International Edition

American Book of Days
The American Book of Days
The International Book of Days

Junior Authors & Illustrators
Tenth Book of Junior Authors & Illustrations

Monographs
The Barnhart Dictionary of Etymology
Celebrate the World
Guide to the Ancient World
Indexing from A to Z
The Poetry Break
Radical Change: Books for Youth in a Digital Age

Wilson Chronology
Wilson Chronology of Asia and the Pacific
Wilson Chronology of Human Rights
Wilson Chronology of Ideas
Wilson Chronology of the Arts
Wilson Chronology of the World's Religions
Wilson Chronology of Women's Achievements

Grey House Publishing | Salem Press | H.W. Wilson | 4919 Route, 22 PO Box 56, Amenia NY 12501-0056